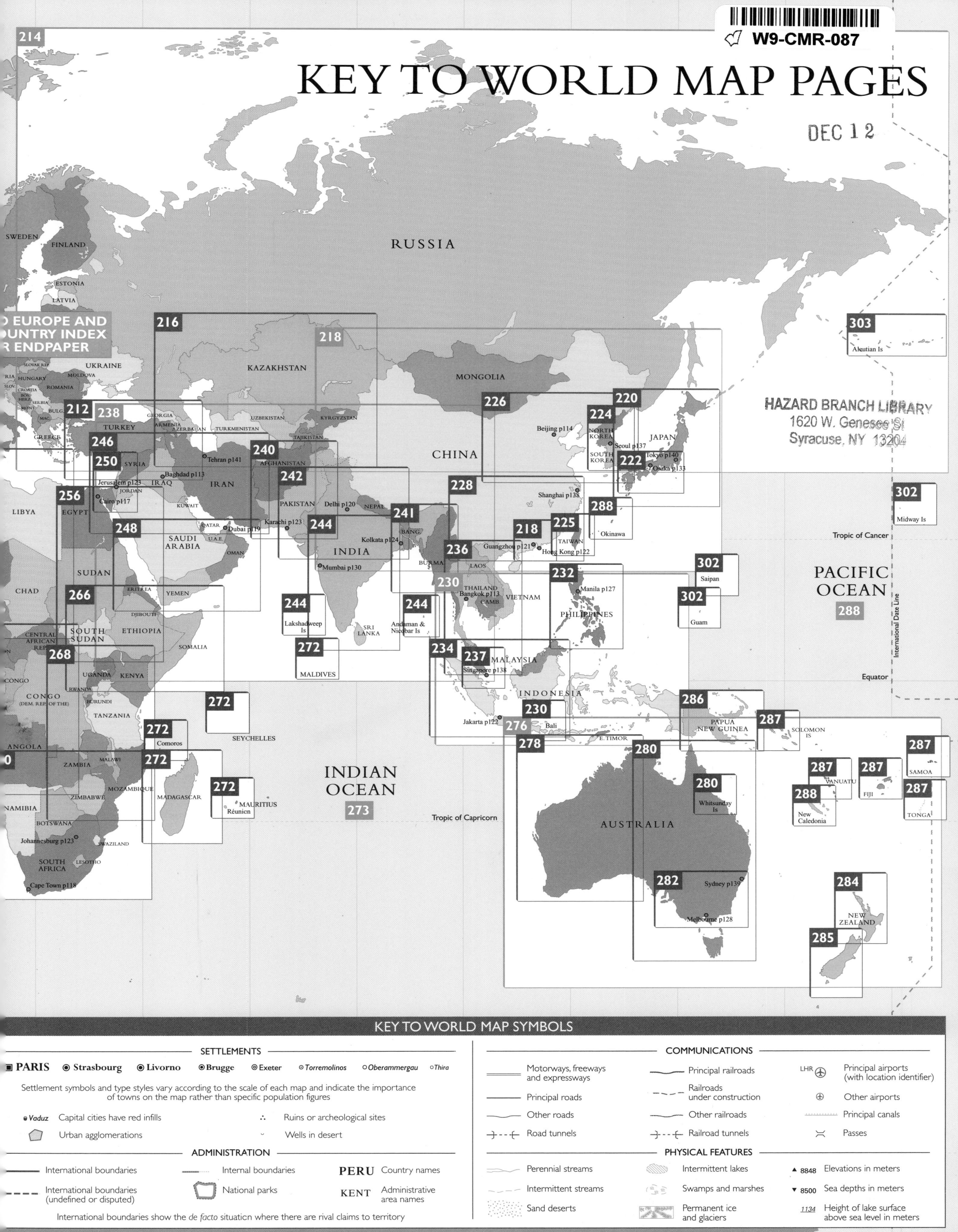

OXFORD
ATLAS
OF THE
WORLD

NINETEENTH EDITION

GAZETTEER OF NATIONS
TEXT Keith Lye

PHOTOGRAPHIC ACKNOWLEDGEMENTS
Alamy /*Peter Barritt* 10 (right),
/*Cultura* 13 (top),
/*David R. Frazier Photolibrary, Inc.* 12 (left);
Corbis /*William Caram* 103, /*P. Deliss* 10 (left),
/*Nigel J. Dennis*/*Gallo Images* 86, /*Jay Dickman* 109
(bottom left), /*Paulo Fridman* 8–9, /*Yang Liu* 91,
/*Gideon Mendel* 13 (centre), /*Radius Images* 11,
/*Royalty-Free* 97, /*Liba Taylor* 104, /*David Turnley* 109
(bottom right);
© Crown copyright 2007. Published by the Met Office,
UK 82;
Fugro NPA Ltd 14–31, 32–33, 84, 110–111, 144–145,
156–157, 208–209, 252–253, 274–275, 290–291,
324–325 /*Image provided by the USGS EROS Data
Center Satellite Systems Branch* 87;
Galaxy Picture Library /*Robin Scagell* 73;
iStockphoto.com 101;
Javier Méndez (ING)/Nik Szymanek (Univ. Herts) 68;
NASA/GSFC 83 (top and bottom), 98, /*Jacques
Descloitres, MODIS Rapid Response Team* 81;
Plantagon International 13 (bottom);
Science Photo Library /*Lawrence Migdale* 12 (right);
USGS/Landsat 66–67.

STAR CHARTS (PAGE 69)
Wil Tirion

CARTOGRAPHY BY PHILIP'S

WORLD CITIES
PAGE 120, DUBLIN: The town plan of Dublin is based on
Ordnance Survey Ireland by permission of the Government
Permit Number 8798. © Ordnance Survey Ireland and
Government of Ireland.

Ordnance Survey PAGE 121, EDINBURGH,
and PAGE 125, LONDON:
This product includes mapping data licensed from
Ordnance Survey® with the permission of the Controller
of Her Majesty's Stationery Office. © Crown copyright
2012. All rights reserved. Licence number 100011710.

FOREWORD

AN AUTHORITATIVE AND SERIOUS REFERENCE WORK, the Oxford *Atlas of the World* is one of the finest atlases available anywhere in the world. The atlas incorporates computer-derived maps that have been produced using the very latest in digital cartographic techniques. Country names are shown in conventional English form and are those that are in common usage. They are the forms used by publications such as *Newsweek* and *The Washington Post,* and by the BBC and the British Foreign Office. Alternative country names appear in parentheses on the maps where space permits – for example, Burma (Myanmar) – and are cross-referenced in the index, for example, Côte d'Ivoire = Ivory Coast.

HOW TO USE THE ATLAS
The atlas is divided into a number of sections which are explained below.

WORLD STATISTICS AND "WILL THE WORLD RUN OUT OF FOOD?"
World statistics on topics such as area and population for every country in the world. Also included in this section is a listing of the world's largest cities by population, arranged in country alphabetical order. This section is followed by the highly topical "Will the World Run Out of Food?" feature, which examines the issues and possible solutions to the world's most pressing problem.

IMAGES OF EARTH
A beautifully illustrated satellite imagery section showing 16 of the world's major cities in the Americas, Europe, Africa, Asia, and Australasia.

GAZETTEER OF NATIONS
A comprehensive A–Z reference providing concise profiles of every country's geography, climate, history, politics, and economy, together with ready-reference tables, and illustrated with flags and locator maps.

WORLD GEOGRAPHY
A richly informative section comprising 42 pages of maps, charts, graphs, and diagrams that explain key themes about the world in which we live. The topics covered include the Solar System, oceans, climate, the natural world, energy, and trade. Explanatory text on each spread describes the patterns shown by the data.

CITY MAPS
A detailed selection of maps for 70 urban areas around the world. These are useful for planning trips abroad as well as for comparative studies of cities worldwide.

WORLD MAPS
An outstanding collection of 179 pages of distinctive Philip's cartography. The highly acclaimed physical world maps combine relief shading with layer-colored contours to give a striking visual picture of the Earth's surface. Roads, railroads, canals, and airports are accurately depicted on the maps, and towns and cities are clearly marked. More information on the key features employed in the construction and presentation of the maps is given on the facing page.

GEOGRAPHICAL GLOSSARY AND INDEX
The 85,000-name index to the world maps includes geographical features as well as towns and cities, with both latitude/longitude and letter/figure grid references. Preceding the index is a list of geographical terms from various foreign languages that may be found in the place names on the maps and also in the index, together with their meanings.

SPECIALIST GEOGRAPHY CONSULTANTS

WILL THE WORLD RUN OUT OF FOOD?
The specialist consultant for the
"Will the World Run Out of Food?"
section is **Professor Keith W. T.
Goulding**, President of the
British Society of Soil Science
and Head: Department of
Sustainable and Grassland Systems,
Rothamsted Research, Harpenden, UK
(www.rothamsted.ac.uk).

Rothamsted Research
is an institute of the
Biotechnology and Biological
Sciences Research Council.

THE EDITORS are especially grateful to
Professor Goulding and **Dr Sharon Hall**
of Rothamsted Research for their invaluable
assistance in preparing this section.

THE EDITORS are grateful to the following
for their contributions to the *"World
Geography"* section in this atlas:

Dr Dibyesh Anand
John Burden
Peter Grego
Keith Lye
Garrett Nagle
Ross Reynolds
Robin Scagell
John Woodruff

THE EDITORS would also like to thank
Richard Chiles and the staff at
Fugro NPA Ltd, Edenbridge, Kent, UK
(www.fugro-npa.com) for sourcing and
processing the satellite imagery that appears
in the atlas.

USER GUIDE

The reference maps which form the main body of this atlas have been prepared in accordance with the highest standards of international cartography to provide an accurate and detailed representation of the Earth. The scales and projections used have been carefully chosen to give balanced coverage of the world, while emphasizing the most densely populated and economically significant regions. A hallmark of Philip's mapping is the use of hill shading and relief coloring to create a graphic impression of landforms: this makes the maps exceptionally easy to read. However, knowledge of the key features employed in the construction and presentation of the maps will enable the reader to derive the fullest benefit from the atlas.

MAP SEQUENCE

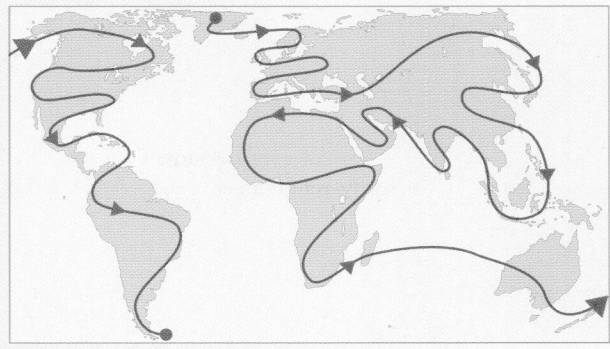

The atlas covers the Earth continent by continent: first Europe; then its land neighbor Asia (mapped north before south, in a clockwise sequence), then Africa, Australia and Oceania, North America, and South America. This is the classic arrangement adopted by most cartographers since the 16th century. For each continent, there are maps at a variety of scales. First, physical relief and political maps of the whole continent; then a series of larger-scale maps of the regions within the continent, each followed, where required, by still larger-scale maps of the most important or densely populated areas. The governing principle is that by turning the pages of the atlas, the reader moves steadily from north to south through each continent, with each map overlapping its neighbors.

MAP PRESENTATION

With very few exceptions (for example, for the Arctic and Antarctica), the maps are drawn with north at the top, regardless of whether they are presented upright or sideways on the page. In the borders will be found the map title; a locator diagram showing the area covered; continuation arrows showing the page numbers for maps of adjacent areas; the scale; the projection used; the degrees of latitude and longitude; and the letters and figures used in the index for locating place names and geographical features. Physical relief maps also have a height reference panel identifying the colors used for each layer of contouring.

MAP SYMBOLS

Each map contains a vast amount of detail which can only be conveyed clearly and accurately by the use of symbols. Points and circles of varying sizes locate and identify the relative importance of towns and cities; different styles of type are employed for administrative, geographical, and regional place names to aid identification. A variety of pictorial symbols denote landforms such as glaciers, marshes, and coral reefs, and man-made structures including roads, railroads, airports, and canals. International borders are shown by red lines. Where neighboring countries are in dispute, for example in parts of the Middle East, the maps show the *de facto* boundary between nations, regardless of the legal or historical situation.

The symbols are explained on the front endpapers of the atlas.

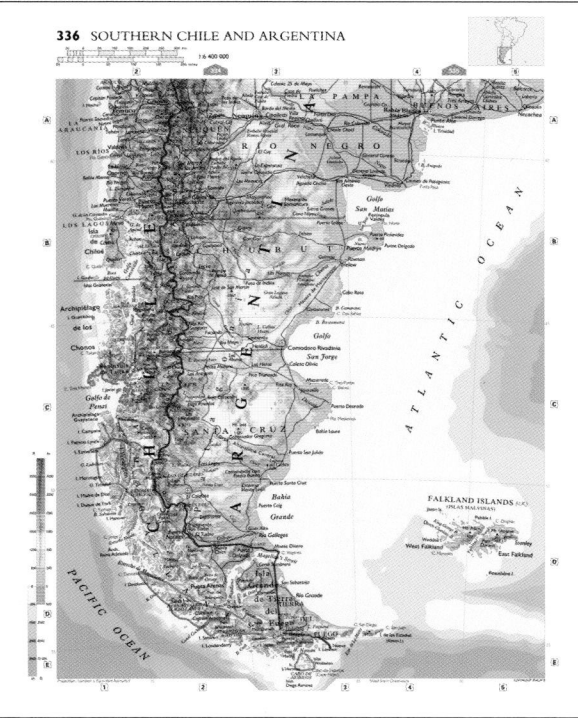

MAP SCALES

1:16 000 000
1 inch = 252 statute miles

The scale of each map is given in the numerical form known as the "representative fraction." The first figure is always one, signifying one unit of distance on the map; the second figure, usually in millions, is the number by which the map unit must be multiplied to give the equivalent distance on the Earth's surface. Calculations can easily be made in centimeters and kilometers, by dividing the Earth units figure by 100 000 (i.e. deleting the last five 0s). Thus 1:1 000 000 means 1 cm = 10 km. The calculation for inches and miles is more laborious, but 1 000 000 divided by 63 360 (the number of inches in a mile) shows that 1:1 000 000 means approximately 1 inch = 16 miles. The table below provides distance equivalents for scales down to 1:50 000 000.

LARGE SCALE		
1:1 000 000	1 cm = 10 km	1 inch = 16 miles
1:2 500 000	1 cm = 25 km	1 inch = 39.5 miles
1:5 000 000	1 cm = 50 km	1 inch = 79 miles
1:6 000 000	1 cm = 60 km	1 inch = 95 miles
1:8 000 000	1 cm = 80 km	1 inch = 126 miles
1:10 000 000	1 cm = 100 km	1 inch = 158 miles
1:15 000 000	1 cm = 150 km	1 inch = 237 miles
1:20 000 000	1 cm = 200 km	1 inch = 316 miles
1:50 000 000	1 cm = 500 km	1 inch = 790 miles
SMALL SCALE		

MEASURING DISTANCES

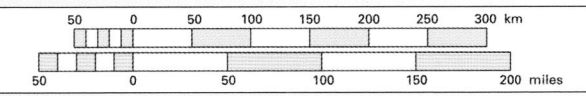

Although each map is accompanied by a scale bar, distances cannot always be measured with confidence because of the distortions involved in portraying the curved surface of the Earth on a flat page. As a general rule, the larger the map scale, the more accurate and reliable will be the distance measured. On small-scale maps such as those of the world and of entire continents, measurement may only be accurate along the "standard parallels," or central axes, and should not be attempted without considering the map projection.

MAP PROJECTIONS

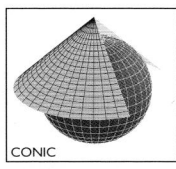
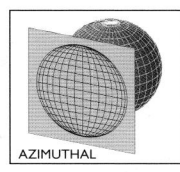
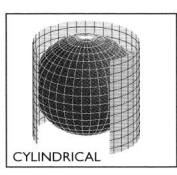

Unlike a globe, no flat map can give a true scale representation of the world in terms of area, shape, and position of every region. Each of the numerous systems that have been devised for projecting the curved surface of the Earth on to a flat page involves the sacrifice of accuracy in one or more of these elements. The variations in shape and position of land masses such as Alaska, Greenland, and Australia, for example, can be quite dramatic when different projections are compared.

For this atlas, the guiding principle has been to select projections that involve the least distortion of size and distance. The projection used for each map is noted in the border. Most fall into one of three categories – conic, azimuthal, or cylindrical – whose basic concepts are shown above. Each involves plotting the forms of the Earth's surface on a grid of latitude and longitude lines, which may be shown as parallels, curves, or radiating spokes.

LATITUDE AND LONGITUDE

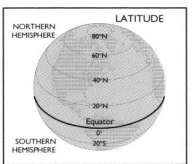
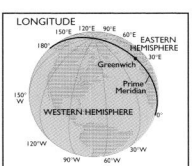
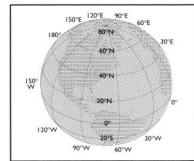

Accurate positioning of individual points on the Earth's surface is made possible by reference to the geometrical system of latitude and longitude. Latitude *parallels* are drawn west–east around the Earth and numbered by degrees north and south of the Equator, which is designated 0° of latitude. Longitude *meridians* are drawn north–south and numbered by degrees east and west of the *prime meridian*, 0° of longitude, which passes through Greenwich in England. By referring to these co-ordinates and their subdivisions of minutes (1/60th of a degree) and seconds (1/60th of a minute), any place on Earth can be located to within a few hundred meters. Latitude and longitude are indicated by blue lines on the maps; they are straight or curved according to the projection employed. Reference to these lines is the easiest way of determining the relative positions of places on different maps, and for plotting compass directions.

NAME FORMS

For ease of reference, both English and local name forms appear in the atlas. Oceans, seas, and countries are shown in English throughout the atlas; country names may be abbreviated to their commonly accepted form (for example, Germany, not The Federal Republic of Germany). Conventional English forms are also used for place names on the smaller-scale maps of the continents. However, local name forms are used on all large-scale and regional maps, with the English form given in brackets only for important cities – the large-scale map of Russia and Northern Asia thus shows Moskva (Moscow). For countries which do not use a Roman script, place names have been transcribed according to the systems adopted by the British and US Geographic Names Authorities. For China, the Pin Yin system has been used, with some more widely known forms appearing in brackets, as with Beijing (Peking). Both English and local names appear in the index, the English form being cross-referenced to the local form.

CONTENTS

WORLD STATISTICS

COUNTRIES 6
CITIES 7

WILL THE WORLD RUN OUT OF FOOD?

THE ISSUES 10–11
THE SOLUTIONS 12–13

IMAGES OF EARTH

LONDON, UK 16
ROME, ITALY 17
ISTANBUL, TURKEY 18
KABUL, AFGHANISTAN 19
MUMBAI, INDIA 20
SINGAPORE CITY, SINGAPORE 21
BRAZZAVILLE AND KINSHASA, AFRICA 22
JUBA, SOUTH SUDAN 23
CAPE TOWN, SOUTH AFRICA 24
SYDNEY, AUSTRALIA 25
AUCKLAND, NEW ZEALAND 26
QUÉBEC, CANADA 27
WASHINGTON, DC, USA 28
NEW YORK CITY, USA 29
CARACAS, VENEZUELA 30
BUENOS AIRES, ARGENTINA 31

GAZETTEER OF NATIONS

AN A–Z GAZETTEER OF COUNTRIES 34–65

WORLD GEOGRAPHY

THE UNIVERSE 68–69
THE SOLAR SYSTEM 70–71
SEASONS, TIME AND MOTION 72–73
GEOLOGY OF THE EARTH 74–75
OCEANS 76–77
THE ATMOSPHERE 78–79
CLIMATE 80–81
CLIMATE CHANGE AND GLOBAL WARMING 82–83
WATER AND VEGETATION 84–85
BIODIVERSITY AND THE NATURAL WORLD 86–87
POPULATION 88–89
CITIES 90–91
THE HUMAN FAMILY 92–93
CONFLICT AND COOPERATION 94–95
ENERGY 96–97
MINERALS 98–99
EMPLOYMENT AND INDUSTRY 100–101
TRADE 102–103
HEALTH 104–105
WEALTH 106–107
STANDARDS OF LIVING 108–109

WORLD CITIES

AMSTERDAM 112
ATHENS 112
ATLANTA 113
BAGHDAD 113
BANGKOK 113
BARCELONA 114
BEIJING 114
BERLIN 115
BOSTON 116
BRUSSELS 116
BUDAPEST 117
BUENOS AIRES 117
CAIRO 117
CAPE TOWN 118
COPENHAGEN 118
CHICAGO 119
DUBAI 119
DELHI 120
DUBLIN 120
EDINBURGH 121
GUANGZHOU (CANTON) 121
HELSINKI 121
HONG KONG 122
ISTANBUL 122
JAKARTA 122
JERUSALEM 123
JOHANNESBURG 123
KARACHI 123
KOLKATA (CALCUTTA) 124
LAGOS 124
LAS VEGAS 124
LIMA 124
LONDON 125
LISBON 126
LOS ANGELES 126
MADRID 127
MANILA 127
MELBOURNE 128
MEXICO CITY 128
MILAN 128
MIAMI 129
MOSCOW 129
MONTREAL 130
MUMBAI (BOMBAY) 130
MUNICH 131
NEW ORLEANS 131
NEW YORK 132
ORLANDO 133
OSAKA 133
OSLO 133
PARIS 134
PRAGUE 135
RIO DE JANEIRO 135
ROME 136
SAN FRANCISCO 136
ST PETERSBURG 137
SANTIAGO 137
SÃO PAULO 137
SEOUL 137
SHANGHAI 138
SINGAPORE 138
STOCKHOLM 139
SYDNEY 139
TOKYO 140
TEHRAN 141
TORONTO 141
VENICE 142
VIENNA 142
WARSAW 143
WASHINGTON 143

WORLD MAPS

THE WORLD

MAP SYMBOLS FRONT ENDPAPER

THE WORLD: PHYSICAL 146–147
1:76 000 000

THE WORLD: POLITICAL 148–149
1:76 000 000

ARCTIC OCEAN 150
1:28 000 000

ANTARCTICA 151
1:28 000 000

ATLANTIC OCEAN 152
1:41 000 000

ISLANDS OF THE ATLANTIC 153
BERMUDA 1:400 000
NEW PROVIDENCE ISLAND 1:400 000
MADEIRA 1:800 000
AZORES 1:1 600 000
CANARY ISLANDS 1:1 600 000
FALKLAND ISLANDS 1:6 400 000
ASCENSION ISLAND 1:400 000
ST HELENA 1:400 000
CAPE VERDE ISLANDS 1:8 000 000

GREENLAND 154
1:10 000 000

ICELAND 155
1:2 000 000

EUROPE

EUROPE: PHYSICAL 158
1:16 000 000

EUROPE: POLITICAL 159
1:16 000 000

SCANDINAVIA 160–161
1:4 800 000
ICELAND 1:4 800 000
FÆROE ISLANDS 1:4 800 000

DENMARK AND SOUTHERN SWEDEN 162–163
1:2 000 000

SOUTHERN NORWAY 164
1:2 000 000

BRITISH ISLES 165
1:4 000 000

IRELAND 166
1:1 600 000

SCOTLAND 167
1:1 600 000

ENGLAND AND WALES 168–169
1:1 600 000

NETHERLANDS, BELGIUM AND LUXEMBOURG 170
1:2 000 000

FRANCE 171
1:4 000 000

NORTHERN FRANCE 172–173
1:2 000 000

SOUTHERN FRANCE 174–175
1:2 000 000

CENTRAL EUROPE 176–177
1:4 000 000

GERMANY AND SWITZERLAND 178–179
1:2 000 000

AUSTRIA, CZECH REPUBLIC AND SLOVAK REPUBLIC 180–181
1:2 000 000

HUNGARY, ROMANIA AND THE LOWER DANUBE 182–183
1:2 000 000

POLAND AND THE SOUTHERN BALTIC 184–185
1:2 000 000

EASTERN EUROPE 186–187
1:8 000 000

BALTIC STATES, BELARUS AND UKRAINE 188–189
1:4 000 000

THE VOLGA BASIN AND THE CAUCASUS 190–191
1:4 000 000

SOUTHERN EUROPE 192–193
1:8 000 000

WESTERN SPAIN AND PORTUGAL 194–195
1:2 000 000

EASTERN SPAIN 196–197
1:2 000 000

NORTHERN ITALY, SLOVENIA AND CROATIA 198–199
1:2 000 000

SOUTHERN ITALY 200–201
1:2 000 000

THE BALKANS 202–203
1:2 000 000

SOUTHERN GREECE AND WESTERN TURKEY 204–205
1:2 000 000

MEDITERRANEAN ISLANDS 206–207
IBIZA, MAJORCA, MINORCA 1:800 000
MALTA 1:400 000
CORFU 1:800 000
RHODES 1:800 000
LEVKAS, ZANTE, CEPHALONIA 1:800 000
CRETE 1:1 000 000
CYPRUS 1:1 000 000

ASIA

ASIA: PHYSICAL 210
1:40 000 000

ASIA: POLITICAL 211
1:40 000 000

TURKEY AND TRANSCAUCASIA 212–213
1:4 000 000

CONTENTS

RUSSIA AND
NORTHERN ASIA 214–215
1:16 000 000

KAZAKHSTAN
AND CENTRAL ASIA 216–127
1:8 000 000

CHINA
AND THE FAR EAST 218–219
1:12 000 000

HONG KONG AND MACAU 1:800 000

JAPAN 220–221
1:4 000 000

RYUKYU ISLANDS 1:4 000 000

SOUTHERN JAPAN 222–223
1:2 000 000

KOREA 224
1:3 100 000

TAIWAN 225
1:1 400 000

NORTHERN CHINA
AND KOREA 226–227
1:4 800 000

SOUTHERN CHINA 228–229
1:4 800 000

SOUTHEAST ASIA 230–231
1:10 000 000

JAVA AND MADURA 1:6 000 000

BALI 1:1 600 000

PHILIPPINES 232–233
1:3 200 000

WESTERN INDONESIA
AND MALAYSIA 234–235
1:5 600 000

MAINLAND
SOUTHEAST ASIA 236–237
1:4 800 000

KO PHUKET 1:800 000

KO SAMUI 1:800 000

PINANG 1:800 000

SINGAPORE 1:800 000

SOUTHERN ASIA AND
THE MIDDLE EAST 238–239
1:14 000 000

AFGHANISTAN
AND PAKISTAN 240
1:5 600 000

BANGLADESH,
NORTHEASTERN INDIA
AND BURMA 241
1:4 800 000

NORTHERN INDIA,
PAKISTAN AND
NEPAL 242–243
1:4 800 000

SOUTHERN INDIA AND
SRI LANKA 244–245
1:4 800 000

LAKSHADWEEP ISLANDS 1:4 800 000

ANDAMAN AND
NICOBAR ISLANDS 1:4 800 000

THE MIDDLE EAST 246–247
1:5 600 000

SOUTHERN ARABIAN
PENINSULA 248–249
1:5 600 000

EASTERN
MEDITERRANEAN 250–251
1:2 000 000

AFRICA

AFRICA: PHYSICAL 254
1:33 600 000

AFRICA: POLITICAL 255
1:33 600 000

THE NILE VALLEY 256–257
1:6 400 000

THE NILE DELTA 1:3 200 000

CENTRAL NORTH
AFRICA 258–259
1:6 400 000

NORTHWEST AFRICA 260–261
1:6 400 000

WEST AFRICA 262–263
1:6 400 000

CENTRAL AFRICA 264–265
1:6 400 000

SÃO TOMÉ AND PRÍNCIPE 1:6 400 000

ETHIOPIA AND THE
HORN OF AFRICA 266–267
1:6 400 000

EAST AFRICA 268–269
1:6 400 000

SOUTHERN AFRICA 270–271
1:6 400 000

MADAGASCAR 272
1:6 400 000

COMOROS 1:2 000 000

MAYOTTE 1:800 000

SEYCHELLES 1:2 000 000

RÉUNION 1:800 000

MAURITIUS 1:800 000

MALDIVES 1:6 400 000

INDIAN OCEAN 273
1:40 000 000

AUSTRALIA AND OCEANIA

AUSTRALIA AND OCEANIA:
PHYSICAL
AND POLITICAL 276–277
1:16 000 000

WESTERN AUSTRALIA 278–279
1:6 400 000

EASTERN AUSTRALIA 280–281
1:6 400 000

WHITSUNDAY GROUP 1:2 000 000

TASMANIA 1:6 400 000

TORRES STRAIT 1:6 400 000

SOUTHEAST
AUSTRALIA 282–283
1:3 200 000

NEW ZEALAND –
NORTH ISLAND 284
1:2 800 000

NEW ZEALAND –
SOUTH ISLAND 285
1:2 800 000

CHATHAM ISLANDS 1:2 800 000

PAPUA NEW GUINEA 286
1:5 200 000

ISLANDS OF THE
SOUTHWEST PACIFIC 287
FIJI 1:4 000 000
VANUATU 1:4 000 000
SOLOMON ISLANDS 1:4 000 000
TONGA 1:4 000 000
YAP 1:830 000
CHUUK 1:830 000
SAMOAN ISLANDS 1:4 000 000

PACIFIC OCEAN 288–289
1:43 200 000
OKINAWA 1:1 550 000
IWO JIMA 1:200 000
PALAU 1:1 550 000
NEW CALEDONIA 1:5 750 000
TAHITI 1:1 150 000
FRENCH POLYNESIA 1:26 000 000
NIUE 1:830 000
RAROTONGA 1:415 000

NORTH AMERICA

NORTH AMERICA:
PHYSICAL 292
1:28 000 000

NORTH AMERICA:
POLITICAL 293
1:28 000 000

CANADA 294–295
1:12 000 000

WESTERN CANADA 296–297
1:5 600 000

EASTERN CANADA 298–299
1:5 600 000

UNITED STATES 300–301
1:12 000 000

ALASKA 1:12 000 000

HAWAI'I 1:12 000 000

HAWAI'I 302
1:2 500 000
HAWAIIAN ISLANDS 1:21 000 000
OAHU 1:500 000
NORTHERN MARIANAS 1:17 500 000
WAKE ISLAND 1:200 000
MIDWAY ISLANDS 1:200 000
GUAM 1:800 000
SAIPAN AND TINIAN 1:800 000
TUTUILA 1:640 000
MANUA ISLANDS 1:640 000

ALASKA 303
1:8 000 000

UNITED STATES –
WEST 304–305
1:5 360 000

CENTRAL AND SOUTHERN
CALIFORNIA AND WESTERN
WASHINGTON 306–307
1:2 000 000

UNITED STATES – MIDWEST
AND NORTHEAST 308–309
1:5 360 000

CHICAGO AND
THE MIDWEST 310–311
1:2 000 000

NORTHEASTERN
UNITED STATES 312–313
1:2 000 000

UNITED STATES –
SOUTH 314–315
1:5 360 000

SOUTHEASTERN
UNITED STATES 316–317
1:2 000 000

MEXICO 318–319
1:6 400 000

CENTRAL AMERICA AND
THE WEST INDIES 320–321
1:6 400 000

PUERTO RICO AND THE
VIRGIN ISLANDS 1:1 600 000

JAMAICA 1:1 600 000

PANAMA CANAL 1:800 000

LESSER ANTILLES 322–323
NORTHERN LEEWARDS 1:600 000
ANTIGUA AND BARBUDA 1:600 000
ST KITTS AND NEVIS 1:600 000
GUADELOUPE 1:600 000
ARUBA 1:600 000
BONAIRE AND CURAÇAO 1:600 000
MARTINIQUE 1:600 000
DOMINICA 1:600 000
ST LUCIA 1:600 000
ST VINCENT AND
THE GRENADINES 1:600 000
MONTSERRAT 1:600 000
GRENADA 1:600 000
BARBADOS 1:600 000
TRINIDAD AND TOBAGO 1:600 000

SOUTH AMERICA

SOUTH AMERICA:
PHYSICAL 326
1:28 000 000

SOUTH AMERICA:
POLITICAL 327
1:28 000 000

SOUTH AMERICA –
NORTHWEST 328–329
1:6 400 000

MARGARITA 1:600 000

SOUTH AMERICA –
WEST 330–331
1:6 400 000

GALAPAGOS ISLANDS 1:3 200 000

EASTER ISLAND 1:400 000

ROBINSON CRUSOE ISLAND 1:400 000

EASTERN BRAZIL 332–333
1:6 400 000

CENTRAL
SOUTH AMERICA 334–335
1:6 400 000

SOUTHERN CHILE AND
ARGENTINA 336
1:6 400 000

GEOGRAPHICAL
GLOSSARY 337–338

INDEX TO
WORLD MAPS 339–448

WORLD STATISTICS: COUNTRIES

This alphabetical list includes the principal countries and territories of the world. If a territory is not completely independent, the country it is associated with is named. The area figures give the total area of land, inland water, and ice. The population figures are 2011 estimates where available. The annual income is the Gross Domestic Product per capita in US dollars; the figures are the latest available, usually 2011 estimates.

Country/Territory	Area km^2 Thousands	Area miles^2 Thousands	Population Thousands	Capital	Annual Income US $
Afghanistan	652	252	29,835	Kabul	1,000
Albania	28.7	11.1	2,995	Tirana	7,800
Algeria	2,382	920	34,995	Algiers	7,200
American Samoa (US)	0.20	0.08	67	Pago Pago	8,000
Andorra	0.47	0.18	85	Andorra La Vella	37,200
Angola	1,247	481	13,339	Luanda	5,900
Anguilla (UK)	0.10	0.04	15	The Valley	12,200
Antigua & Barbuda	0.44	0.17	88	St John's	22,100
Argentina	2,780	1,074	41,770	Buenos Aires	17,400
Armenia	29.8	11.5	2,968	Yerevan	5,400
Aruba (Netherlands)	0.19	0.07	106	Oranjestad	21,800
Australia	7,741	2,989	21,767	Canberra	40,800
Austria	83.9	32.4	8,217	Vienna	41,700
Azerbaijan	86.6	33.4	8,372	Baku	10,200
Azores (Portugal)	2.2	0.86	236	Ponta Delgada	15,000
Bahamas	13.9	5.4	313	Nassau	30,900
Bahrain	0.69	0.27	1,215	Manama	27,300
Bangladesh	144	55.6	158,571	Dhaka	1,700
Barbados	0.43	0.17	287	Bridgetown	23,600
Belarus	208	80.2	9,578	Minsk	14,900
Belgium	30.5	11.8	10,431	Brussels	37,600
Belize	23.0	8.9	321	Belmopan	8,300
Benin	113	43.5	9,325	Porto-Novo	1,500
Bermuda (UK)	0.05	0.02	70	Hamilton	69,900
Bhutan	47.0	18.1	708	Thimphu	6,000
Bolivia	1,099	424	10,119	La Paz/Sucre	4,800
Bosnia-Herzegovina	51.2	19.8	4,622	Sarajevo	8,200
Botswana	582	225	2,065	Gaborone	16,300
Brazil	8,514	3,287	203,430	Brasília	11,600
Brunei	5.8	2.2	395	Bandar Seri Begawan	49,400
Bulgaria	111	42.8	7,149	Sofia	13,500
Burkina Faso	274	106	16,751	Ouagadougou	1,500
Burma (Myanmar)	677	261	53,414	Rangoon/Naypyidaw	1,300
Burundi	27.8	10.7	10,216	Bujumbura	400
Cambodia	181	69.9	14,702	Phnom Penh	2,300
Cameroon	475	184	19,711	Yaoundé	2,300
Canada	9,971	3,850	34,031	Ottawa	40,300
Canary Is. (Spain)	7.2	2.8	2,117	Las Palmas/Santa Cruz	19,900
Cape Verde Is.	4.0	1.6	516	Praia	4,000
Cayman Is. (UK)	0.26	0.10	51	George Town	43,800
Central African Republic	623	241	4,950	Bangui	800
Chad	1,284	496	10,759	Ndjaména	1,900
Chile	757	292	16,889	Santiago	16,100
China	9,597	3,705	1,336,718	Beijing	8,400
Colombia	1,139	440	44,726	Bogotá	10,100
Comoros	2.2	0.86	795	Moroni	1,200
Congo	342	132	4,244	Brazzaville	4,600
Congo (Dem. Rep. of the)	2,345	905	71,713	Kinshasa	300
Cook Is. (NZ)	0.24	0.09	11	Avarua	9,100
Costa Rica	51.1	19.7	4,577	San José	11,500
Croatia	56.5	21.8	4,484	Zagreb	18,300
Cuba	111	42.8	11,087	Havana	9,900
Curaçao (Netherlands)	0.44	0.17	142	Willemstad	15,000
Cyprus	9.3	3.6	1,120	Nicosia	29,100
Czech Republic	78.9	30.5	10,190	Prague	25,900
Denmark	43.1	16.6	5,530	Copenhagen	40,200
Djibouti	23.2	9.0	757	Djibouti	2,600
Dominica	0.75	0.29	73	Roseau	13,600
Dominican Republic	48.5	18.7	9,957	Santo Domingo	9,300
East Timor	14.9	5.7	1,178	Dili	3,100
Ecuador	284	109	15,007	Quito	8,300
Egypt	1,001	387	82,080	Cairo	6,500
El Salvador	21.0	8.1	6,072	San Salvador	7,600
Equatorial Guinea	28.1	10.8	668	Malabo	19,300
Eritrea	118	45.4	5,939	Asmara	700
Estonia	45.1	17.4	1,283	Tallinn	20,200
Ethiopia	1,104	426	90,874	Addis Ababa	1,100
Falkland Is. (UK)	12.2	4.7	3	Stanley	35,400
Faroe Is. (Denmark)	1.4	0.54	49	Tórshavn	30,500
Fiji	18.3	7.1	883	Suva	4,600
Finland	338	131	5,259	Helsinki	38,300
France	552	213	65,312	Paris	35,000
French Guiana (France)	90.0	34.7	229	Cayenne	8,300
French Polynesia (France)	4.0	1.5	295	Papeete	18,000
Gabon	268	103	1,577	Libreville	16,000
Gambia, The	11.3	4.4	1,798	Banjul	2,100
Gaza Strip (OPT)*	0.36	0.14	1,657	–	2,900
Georgia	69.7	26.9	4,586	Tbilisi	5,400
Germany	357	138	81,472	Berlin	37,900
Ghana	239	92.1	24,791	Accra	3,100
Gibraltar (UK)	0.006	0.002	29	Gibraltar Town	43,000
Greece	132	50.9	10,760	Athens	27,600
Greenland (Denmark)	2,176	840	58	Nuuk	37,400
Grenada	0.34	0.13	108	St George's	13,300
Guadeloupe (France)	1.7	0.66	452	Basse-Terre	7,900
Guam (US)	0.55	0.21	183	Agana	15,000
Guatemala	109	42.0	13,824	Guatemala City	5,000
Guinea	246	94.9	10,601	Conakry	1,100
Guinea-Bissau	36.1	13.9	1,597	Bissau	1,100
Guyana	215	83.0	775	Georgetown	7,500
Haiti	27.8	10.7	9,720	Port-au-Prince	1,200
Honduras	112	43.3	8,144	Tegucigalpa	4,300
Hungary	93.0	35.9	9,976	Budapest	19,600
Iceland	103	39.8	311	Reykjavik	38,000
India	3,287	1,269	1,189,173	New Delhi	3,700
Indonesia	1,905	735	245,613	Jakarta	4,700
Iran	1,648	636	77,891	Tehran	12,200
Iraq	438	169	30,400	Baghdad	3,900
Ireland	70.3	27.1	4,671	Dublin	39,500
Israel	20.6	8.0	7,473	Jerusalem	31,000
Italy	301	116	61,017	Rome	30,100
Ivory Coast (Côte d'Ivoire)	322	125	21,504	Yamoussoukro	1,600
Jamaica	11.0	4.2	2,868	Kingston	9,000
Japan	378	146	126,476	Tokyo	34,300
Jordan	89.3	34.5	6,508	Amman	5,900
Kazakhstan	2,725	1,052	15,522	Astana	13,000
Kenya	580	224	41,071	Nairobi	1,700
Kiribati	0.73	0.28	101	Tarawa	6,200
Korea, North	121	46.5	24,457	Pyŏngyang	1,800
Korea, South	99.3	38.3	48,755	Seoul	31,700
Kosovo	10.9	4.2	1,826	Pristina	6,500
Kuwait	17.8	6.9	2,596	Kuwait City	40,700
Kyrgyzstan	200	77.2	5,587	Bishkek	2,400
Laos	237	91.4	6,477	Vientiane	2,700

*OPT = Occupied Palestinian Territory

Country/Territory	Area km^2 Thousands	Area miles^2 Thousands	Population Thousands	Capital	Annual Income US $
Latvia	64.6	24.9	2,205	Riga	15,400
Lebanon	10.4	4.0	4,143	Beirut	15,600
Lesotho	30.4	11.7	1,925	Maseru	1,400
Liberia	111	43.0	3,787	Monrovia	400
Libya	1,760	679	6,598	Tripoli	14,100
Liechtenstein	0.16	0.06	35	Vaduz	141,100
Lithuania	65.2	25.2	3,536	Vilnius	18,700
Luxembourg	2.6	1.0	503	Luxembourg	84,700
Macedonia (FYROM)	25.7	9.9	2,077	Skopje	10,400
Madagascar	587	227	21,926	Antananarivo	900
Madeira (Portugal)	0.78	0.30	267	Funchal	22,700
Malawi	118	45.7	15,879	Lilongwe	900
Malaysia	330	127	28,729	Kuala Lumpur/Putrajaya	15,600
Maldives	0.30	0.12	395	Malé	8,400
Mali	1,240	479	14,160	Bamako	1,300
Malta	0.32	0.12	408	Valletta	25,700
Marshall Is.	0.18	0.07	67	Majuro	2,500
Martinique (France)	1.1	0.43	397	Fort-de-France	14,400
Mauritania	1,026	396	3,282	Nouakchott	2,200
Mauritius	2.0	0.79	1,304	Port Louis	15,000
Mayotte (France)	0.37	0.14	231	Mamoudzou	4,900
Mexico	1,958	756	113,714	Mexico City	15,100
Micronesia, Fed. States of	0.70	0.27	107	Palikir	2,200
Moldova	33.9	13.1	4,314	Kishinev	3,400
Monaco	0.001	0.0004	31	Monaco	63,400
Mongolia	1,567	605	3,133	Ulan Bator	4,500
Montenegro	14.0	5.4	662	Podgorica	11,200
Montserrat (UK)	0.10	0.39	5	Brades	3,400
Morocco	447	172	31,968	Rabat	5,100
Mozambique	802	309	22,949	Maputo	1,100
Namibia	824	318	2,148	Windhoek	7,300
Nauru	0.02	0.008	9	Yaren	5,000
Nepal	147	56.8	29,392	Katmandu	1,300
Netherlands	41.5	16.0	16,847	Amsterdam/The Hague	42,300
Netherlands Antilles (Neths)	0.8	0.31	229	Willemstad	1,600
New Caledonia (France)	18.6	7.2	256	Nouméa	15,000
New Zealand	271	104	4,290	Wellington	27,900
Nicaragua	130	50.2	5,666	Managua	3,200
Niger	1,267	489	16,469	Niamey	800
Nigeria	924	357	155,216	Abuja	2,600
Northern Mariana Is. (US)	0.46	0.18	46	Saipan	12,500
Norway	324	125	4,692	Oslo	53,300
Oman	310	119	3,028	Muscat	26,200
Pakistan	796	307	187,343	Islamabad	2,800
Palau	0.46	0.18	21	Melekeok	8,100
Panama	75.5	29.2	3,460	Panamá	13,600
Papua New Guinea	463	179	6,188	Port Moresby	2,500
Paraguay	407	157	6,459	Asunción	5,500
Peru	1,285	496	29,249	Lima	10,000
Philippines	300	116	101,834	Manila	4,100
Poland	323	125	38,442	Warsaw	20,100
Portugal	88.8	34.3	10,760	Lisbon	23,200
Puerto Rico (US)	8.9	3.4	3,989	San Juan	16,300
Qatar	11.0	4.2	848	Doha	102,700
Réunion (France)	2.5	0.97	839	St-Denis	6,200
Romania	238	92.0	21,905	Bucharest	12,300
Russia	17,075	6,593	138,740	Moscow	16,700
Rwanda	26.3	10.2	11,370	Kigali	1,300
St Kitts & Nevis	0.26	0.10	50	Basseterre	16,400
St Lucia	0.54	0.21	162	Castries	12,900
St Vincent & Grenadines	0.39	0.15	104	Kingstown	11,700
Samoa	2.8	1.1	193	Apia	6,000
San Marino	0.06	0.02	32	San Marino	36,200
São Tomé & Príncipe	0.96	0.37	180	São Tomé	2,000
Saudi Arabia	2,150	830	26,132	Riyadh	24,000
Senegal	197	76.0	12,644	Dakar	1,900
Serbia	77.5	29.9	7,311	Belgrade	10,700
Seychelles	0.46	0.18	89	Victoria	24,700
Sierra Leone	71.7	27.7	5,364	Freetown	800
Singapore	0.68	0.26	4,741	Singapore City	59,900
Slovak Republic	49.0	18.9	5,477	Bratislava	23,400
Slovenia	20.3	7.8	2,003	Ljubljana	29,100
Solomon Is.	28.9	11.2	572	Honiara	3,300
Somalia	638	246	9,926	Mogadishu	600
South Africa	1,221	471	49,004	Cape Town/Pretoria	11,000
Spain	498	192	46,755	Madrid	30,600
Sri Lanka	65.6	25.3	21,284	Colombo	5,600
Sudan	1,886	728	35,680	Khartoum	3,000
Sudan, South	620	239	8,260	Juba	1,546
Suriname	163	63.0	492	Paramaribo	9,500
Swaziland	17.4	6.7	1,370	Mbabane	5,200
Sweden	450	174	9,089	Stockholm	40,600
Switzerland	41.3	15.9	7,640	Bern	43,400
Syria	185	71.5	22,518	Damascus	5,100
Taiwan	36.0	13.9	23,072	Taipei	37,900
Tajikistan	143	55.3	7,627	Dushanbe	2,000
Tanzania	945	365	42,747	Dodoma	1,500
Thailand	513	198	66,720	Bangkok	9,700
Togo	56.8	21.9	6,772	Lomé	900
Tonga	0.65	0.25	106	Nuku'alofa	7,500
Trinidad & Tobago	5.1	2.0	1,228	Port of Spain	20,300
Tunisia	164	63.2	10,629	Tunis	9,500
Turkey	775	299	78,786	Ankara	14,600
Turkmenistan	488	188	4,998	Ashkhabad	7,500
Turks & Caicos Is. (UK)	0.43	0.17	45	Cockburn Town	11,500
Tuvalu	0.03	0.01	11	Fongafale	3,400
Uganda	241	93.l	34,612	Kampala	1,300
Ukraine	604	233	45,135	Kiev	7,200
United Arab Emirates	83.6	32.3	5,149	Abu Dhabi	48,500
United Kingdom	242	93.4	62,698	London	35,900
United States of America	9,629	3,718	313,232	Washington, DC	48,100
Uruguay	175	67.6	3,309	Montevideo	15,400
Uzbekistan	447	173	28,129	Tashkent	3,300
Vanuatu	12.2	4.7	225	Port-Vila	4,900
Venezuela	912	352	27,636	Caracas	12,400
Vietnam	332	128	90,549	Hanoi	3,300
Virgin Is. (UK)	0.15	0.06	25	Road Town	38,500
Virgin Is. (US)	0.35	0.13	110	Charlotte Amalie	14,500
Wallis & Futuna Is. (France)	0.20	0.08	15	Mata-Utu	3,800
West Bank (OPT)*	5.9	2.3	2,569	–	2,900
Western Sahara	266	103	507	El Aaiún	2,500
Yemen	528	204	24,133	Sana'	2,500
Zambia	753	291	13,881	Lusaka	1,600
Zimbabwe	391	151	12,084	Harare	500

This list shows the principal cities with more than 800,000 inhabitants. The figures are taken from the most recent census or estimate available, usually 2011, and as far as possible are the population of the metropolitan area or urban agglomeration. The list includes Metropolitan Statistical Areas from the United States 2010 Census. All the figures are in thousands. Local name forms have been used for the smaller cities (for example, Thessaloniki).

AFGHANISTAN
Kabul 3,895
ALGERIA
Algiers 3,260
ANGOLA
Luanda 4,965
Huambo 1,080
ARGENTINA
Buenos Aires 13,349
Córdoba 1,592
Rosario 1,312
Mendoza 1,072
San Miguel de Tucumán 837
ARMENIA
Yerevan 1,117
AUSTRALIA
Sydney 4,504
Melbourne 3,996
Brisbane 2,004
Perth 1,659
Adelaide 1,187
AUSTRIA
Vienna 1,698
AZERBAIJAN
Baku 2,052
BANGLADESH
Dhaka 14,825
Chittagong 5,015
Khulna 1,735
Rajshahi 870
BELARUS
Minsk 1,855
BELGIUM
Brussels 1,901
Antwerpen 960
BENIN
Cotonou 870
BOLIVIA
La Paz 1,703
Santa Cruz 1,682
BRAZIL
São Paulo 20,395
Rio de Janeiro 11,990
Belo Horizonte 5,910
Pôrto Alegre 4,115
Salvador 3,940
Recife 3,890
Fortaleza 3,740
Curitiba 3,490
Campinas 2,835
Brasília 2,330
Belém 2,205
Goiânia 2,155
Vitória 1,825
Santos 1,820
Manaus 1,802
Natal 1,315
São Luís 1,275
Guarulhos 1,222
Maceió 1,190
Joinville 1,065
Florianópolis 1,040
João Pessoa 1,010
Teresina 911
Londrina 800
BULGARIA
Sofia 1,175
BURKINA FASO
Ouagadougou 1,990
BURMA (MYANMAR)
Rangoon 4,440
Mandalay 1,050
Naypyidaw 1,025
CAMBODIA
Phnom Penh 1,610
CAMEROON
Douala 2,155
Yaoundé 1,795
CANADA
Toronto 5,741
Montréal 3,859
Vancouver 2,391
Calgary 1,243
Ottawa 1,239
Edmonton 1,176
CHAD
Ndjamena 865
CHILE
Santiago 6,045
Valparaiso 860
CHINA
Shanghai 16,575
Beijing 12,385
Chongqing 9,401
Shenzhen 9,005
Guangzhou, Guangdong 8,884
Tianjin 7,884
Wuhan 7,681
Hong Kong 7,069
Dongguan, Guangdong 5,347
Shenyang 5,166
Foshan 4,969
Chengdu 4,961
Xi'an, Shaanxi 4,747
Nanjing, Jiangsu 4,519
Harbin 4,251
Hangzhou 3,860
Changchun 3,597
Shantou 3,502
Guiyang 3,447
Qingdao 3,323
Dalian 3,306
Jinan, Shandong 3,237
Taiyuan, Shanxi 3,154
Kunming 3,116
Zibo 2,982
Zhengzhou 2,966
Fuzhou, Fujian 2,787
Nanchang 2,701
Wuxi, Jiangsu 2,682
Wenzhou 2,659
Shijiazhuang 2,487
Changsha 2,451
Lanzhou 2,411
Hefei 2,404
Suzhou, Jiangsu 2,398
Ürümqi (Wulumuchi) 2,398
Xiamen 2,371
Jinxi 2,268
Jilin 2,255
Ningbo 2,217
Zhongshan 2,211
Xuzhou 2,142
Nanning 2,096
Zaozhuang 2,096
Changzhou, Jiangsu 2,062
Nanchong 2,046
Linyi 2,035
Yantai 1,991
Wanxian 1,963
Baotou 1,920
Nanyang 1,830
Tangshan 1,825
Datong 1,763
Yancheng 1,678
Tianmen 1,676
Shangqiu 1,650
Lu'an 1,647
Luoyang 1,644
Hohhot 1,644
Anshan 1,611
Qiqihar 1,607
Tai'an 1,598
Daqing 1,594
Xinghua 1,587
Pingxiang 1,562
Handan 1,535
Xiantao 1,528
Zhanjiang 1,514
Weifang 1,498
Fushun 1,456
Xianyang 1,450
Luzhou 1,447
Neijiang 1,441
Changde 1,429
Huainan 1,420
Liuzhou 1,409
Suining, Sichuan 1,401
Quanzhou 1,377
Xintai 1,334
Mianyang 1,322
Heze 1,318
Yiyang 1,318
Yueyang 1,286
Suqian 1,258
Huai'an 1,243
Chifeng 1,238
Jingmen 1,228
Yuzhou 1,226
Zaoyang 1,210
Huzhou 1,203
Tianshui 1,199
Yongzhou 1,182
Mudanjiang 1,171
Liupanshui 1,149
Leshan 1,143
Jining, Shandong 1,143
Xiaoshan 1,130
Yixing 1,129
Zigong 1,087
Fuyu 1,068
Yulin 1,060
Baoding 1,042
Xinyi, Jiangsu 1,022
Zhuzhou 1,016
Jixi 1,012
Linqing 1,009
Jiamusi 1,006
Xiangfan 1,006
Zhangjiakou 1,001
Benxi 967
Xiangxiang 936
Zhangjiagang 936
Xinyu 932
Yichun, Heilongjiang 916
Yichun, Jiangxi 890
Jinzhou 888
Zhaotong 879
Yuyao 876
Anshun 864
Hengyang 853
Xuanzhou 851
Tongliao 847
Huaibei 830
Jiaxing 817
Kaifeng 810
Fuxin 807
COLOMBIA
Bogotá 7,594
Medellín 3,236
Cali 2,583
Barranquilla 1,918
Bucaramanga 1,069
Cartagena 1,002
Cúcuta 883
CONGO
Brazzaville 1,355
CONGO (DEM. REP. OF THE)
Kinshasa 9,070
Lubumbashi 1,610
Mbuji-Mayi 1,475
Kolwezi 1,207
Kananga 915
Kisangani 810
COSTA RICA
San José 1,485
CROATIA
Zagreb 1,067
CUBA
Havana 2,142
CZECH REPUBLIC
Prague 1,150
DENMARK
Copenhagen 1,180
DOMINICAN REPUBLIC
Santo Domingo 2,210
Santiago de los Caballeros 804
ECUADOR
Guayaquil 2,715
Quito 1,880
EGYPT
Cairo 11,146
Alexandria 3,760
Shubrâ el Kheima 937
EL SALVADOR
San Salvador 1,595
ETHIOPIA
Addis Ababa 3,040
FINLAND
Helsinki 1,125
FRANCE
Paris 10,485
Marseilles 1,475
Lyons 1,470
Lille 1,050
Nice 980
Toulouse 905
Bordeaux 845
GEORGIA
Tbilisi 1,120
GERMANY
Berlin 3,450
Hamburg 1,786
Munich 1,349
Cologne 1,001
GHANA
Accra 2,342
Kumasi 1,834
GREECE
Athens 3,265
Thessaloniki 840
GUATEMALA
Guatemala City 1,130
GUINEA
Conakry 1,710
HAITI
Port-au-Prince 2,160
HONDURAS
Tegucigalpa 1,050
HUNGARY
Budapest 1,706
INDIA
Delhi 22,630
Mumbai 21,290
Kolkata 15,835
Chennai 7,695
Bangalore 7,365
Hyderabad 6,885
Ahmedabad 5,835
Pune 5,105
Surat 4,265
Jaipur 4,245
Kanpur 3,430
Lucknow 2,930
Nagpur 2,665
Patna 2,370
Indore 2,220
Vadodara 1,910
Bhopal 1,880
Coimbatore 1,850
Ludhiana 1,800
Agra 1,740
Vishakhapatnam 1,655
Cochin 1,645
Nashik 1,625
Meerut 1,525
Varanasi 1,460
Asansol 1,423
Jamshedpur 1,420
Chandigarh 1,405
Jabalpur 1,400
Madurai 1,395
Rajkot 1,390
Dhanbad 1,360
Amritsar 1,330
Allahabad 1,310
Srinagar 1,245
Vijayawada 1,235
Aurangabad 1,230
Bhilainagar-Durg 1,195
Solapur 1,155
Ranchi 1,145
Jodhpur 1,085
Guwahati 1,075
Gwalior 1,065
Tiruchchirapalli 1,035
Trivandrum 1,010
Calicut 1,007
Hubli-Dharwad 970
Mysore 960
Raipur 960
Salem 950
Jalandhar 920
Bhubaneswar 910
Kota 905
Bareilly 890
Aligarh 880
Bhiwandi 859
Jammu 880
Moradabad 845
INDONESIA
Jakarta 13,215
Surabaya 2,765
Bandung 2,394
Medan 2,097
Semarang 1,556
Palembang 1,455
Ujung Pandang 1,338
Pekanbaru 898
Tegal 898
Bandar Lampung 882
Malang 820
IRAN
Tehran 7,315
Mashhad 2,695
Karaj 2,625
Esfahan 1,755
Tabriz 1,495
Shiraz 1,320
Ahvaz 1,065
Qom 1,040
Kermanshah 835
IRAQ
Baghdad 6,045
Mosul 1,490
Basra 1,187
Irbil 1,025
As'Sulaymaniyah 840
IRELAND
Dublin 1,115
ISRAEL
Tel Aviv-Yafo 3,305
Haifa 1,050
ITALY
Rome 4,184
Milan 3,760
Naples 3,020
Turin 1,315
Palermo 875
Genoa 803
IVORY COAST (CÔTE D'IVOIRE)
Abidjan 4,230
Yamoussoukro 885
JAMAICA
Kingston 875
JAPAN
Tokyo 12,064
Yokohama 6,427
Osaka 2,599
Nagoya 2,172
Sapporo 1,922
Kobe 1,493
Kyoto 1,468
Fukuoka 1,341
Kawasaki 1,250
Hiroshima 1,126
Kitakyushu 1,011
Sendai 1,008
Hamamatsu 1,000
Naha 970
Chiba 887
Niigata 800
JORDAN
Amman 1,292
KAZAKHSTAN
Almaty 1,390
KENYA
Nairobi 3,655
Mombasa 1,040
KOREA, NORTH
Pyöngyang 2,845
Namp'o 1,102
Hamhung 821
KOREA, SOUTH
Seoul 9,888
Busan 3,395
Incheon 2,884
Daegu 2,440
Daejeon 1,505
Gwangju 1,475
Seognam 1,353
Ulsan 1,340
Suwon 1,080
Ansan 984
Bucheon 900
KUWAIT
Kuwait City 2,345
KYRGYZSTAN
Bishkek 860
LAOS
Vientiane 830
LEBANON
Beirut 1,960
LIBERIA
Monrovia 827
LIBYA
Tripoli 2,098
Benghazi 1,114
MADAGASCAR
Antananarivo 1,940
MALAWI
Lilongwe 870
Blantyre 860
MALAYSIA
Kuala Lumpur 1,809
Johore Bharu 1,149
Klang 1,128
MALI
Bamako 1,775
MEXICO
Mexico City 19,565
Guadalajara 4,440
Monterrey 3,910
Puebla 2,325
Tijuana 1,680
Toluca 1,590
León 1,565
Ciudad Juárez 1,405
Torreón 1,190
San Luis Potosí 1,025
Querétaro 1,040
Mérida 1,010
Mexicali 940
Aguascalientes 940
Chihuahua 850
Culiacán 850
Saltillo 810
MONGOLIA
Ulan Bator 966
MOROCCO
Casablanca 3,315
Rabat 1,825
Fès 1,065
Marrakesh 940
MOZAMBIQUE
Maputo 2,505
NEPAL
Katmandu 1,085
NETHERLANDS
Amsterdam 1,053
Rotterdam 1,112
NEW ZEALAND
Auckland 1,404
NICARAGUA
Managua 1,165
NIGER
Niamey 1,095
NIGERIA
Lagos 10,855
Kano 3,490
Ibadan 2,915
Abuja 2,085
Kaduna 1,605
Benin City 1,340
Port Harcourt 1,130
Ogbomosho 1,032
Zaria 985
Maiduguri 975
Ilorin 865
Jos 802
NORWAY
Oslo 915
PAKISTAN
Karachi 14,818
Lahore 8,087
Faisalabad 2,849
Rawalpindi 2,026
Multan 1,705
Gujranwala 1,695
Hyderabad 1,635
Peshawar 1,460
Islamabad 856
Quetta 845
PANAMA
Panamá 1,405
PARAGUAY
Asunción 2,070
PERU
Lima 9,030
PHILIPPINES
Manila 11,628
Davao 1,535
Cebu 875
Zamboanga 854
POLAND
Warsaw 1,710
Lódz 910
PORTUGAL
Lisbon 3,035
Porto 1,475
PUERTO RICO
San Juan 2,690
ROMANIA
Bucharest 1,930
RUSSIA
Moscow 10,550
St Petersburg 4,555
Novosibirsk 1,400
Yekaterinburg 1,345
Nizhniy Novgorod 1,270
Kazan 1,140
Samara 1,120
Omsk 1,110
Chelyabinsk 1,090
Rostov 1,040
Ufa 1,020
Perm 975
Volgograd 970
Krasnoyarsk 960
Voronezh 830
Saratov 80
RWANDA
Kigali 975
SAUDI ARABIA
Riyadh 4,945
Jedda 3,290
Mecca 1,510
Medina 1,125
Dammam 920
SENEGAL
Dakar 2,940
SERBIA
Belgrade 1,095
SIERRA LEONE
Freetown 1,007
SINGAPORE
Singapore City 5,115
SOMALIA
Mogadishu 1,570
SOUTH AFRICA
Johannesburg 3,670
Cape Town 3,430
Durban 2,905
Pretoria 1,429
Vereeniging 1,140
Port Elizabeth 1,070
SPAIN
Madrid 5,851
Barcelona 5,083
Valencia 814
SRI LANKA
Colombo 2,115
SUDAN
Khartoum 5,320
SWEDEN
Stockholm 1,729
Gothenburg 829
SWITZERLAND
Zürich 1,150
SYRIA
Aleppo 3,155
Damascus 2,655
Homs 1,328
Hamah 897
TAIWAN
Taipei 2,633
Kaohsiung 1,611
T'aichung 1,251
TANZANIA
Dar es Salaam 3,475
THAILAND
Bangkok 7,065
TOGO
Lomé 1,730
TUNISIA
Tunis 2,385
TURKEY
Istanbul 13,275
Ankara 3,955
Izmir 2,755
Bursa 1,610
Adana 1,380
Gaziantep 1,125
Konya 995
Antalya 850
UGANDA
Kampala 1,675
UKRAINE
Kiev 2,815
Kharkov 1,450
Dnepropetrovsk 1,100
Odessa 1,010
Donetsk 970
UNITED ARAB EMIRATES
Dubai 1,567
Abu Dhabi 928
Sharjah 809
UNITED KINGDOM
London 8,631
Birmingham 2,302
Manchester 2,253
Liverpool 1,519
Glasgow 1,170
Newcastle-upon-Tyne 890
UNITED STATES OF AMERICA
New York 18,897
Los Angeles 12,829
Chicago 9,461
Dallas–Fort Worth 6,372
Philadelphia 5,965
Houston 5,947
Washington, DC 5,582
Miami 5,565
Atlanta 5,269
Boston 4,552
San Francisco 4,335
Detroit 4,296
Phoenix–Mesa 4,193
Seattle 3,440
Minneapolis–St Paul 3,280
San Diego 3,095
St Louis 2,813
Tampa–St Petersburg 2,783
Baltimore 2,710
Denver 2,543
Portland 2,356
Pittsburgh 2,356
Sacramento 2,149
San Antonio 2,143
Orlando 2,134
Cincinnati 2,130
Cleveland 2,077
Kansas City 2,035
Las Vegas 1,951
Columbus 1,837
San Jose 1,836
San Bernardino 1,807
Charlotte 1,758
Indianapolis 1,756
Austin 1,716
Norfolk–Virginia Beach 1,672
Providence 1,601
Nashville 1,590
Milwaukee 1,556
Jacksonville 1,346
Memphis 1,316
Louisville 1,284
Richmond 1,258
Oklahoma 1,253
Hartford 1,212
New Orleans 1,168
Buffalo 1,136
Raleigh 1,130
Birmingham 1,128
Salt Lake City 1,124
Rochester 1,054
Tucson 980
Honolulu 953
Tulsa 937
Fresno 930
Stamford 917
Albuquerque 887
Albany 870
Omaha 865
New Haven 862
Dayton 841
Bakersfield 839
Baton Rouge 802
El Paso 801
URUGUAY
Montevideo 1,640
UZBEKISTAN
Tashkent 2,245
VENEZUELA
Caracas 3,125
Maracaibo 2,220
Valencia 1,725
Barquisimeto 1,195
Maracay 1,075
Ciudad Guayana 966
VIETNAM
Ho Chi Minh City 6,167
Hanoi 2,814
Haiphong 1,970
Da Nang 840
YEMEN
Sana' 2,342
ZAMBIA
Lusaka 1,485
ZIMBABWE
Harare 1,665
Bulawayo 824

In many ways this image represents 21st-century world farming and how it may develop. It shows 25 combine harvesters on a huge farm in Mato Grosso state, western Brazil. They are harvesting soybeans (or soya beans), a crop where much of the world's production is from GM seed. Brazil is the second largest world producer and exporter after the US, followed by Argentina and Paraguay. This crop requires a hot summer to grow well and much land has been cleared in South America in order to grow it on a massive scale. Soybeans contain twice the protein of any other vegetable crop and there is a high demand from Asia as well as the food-processing industry, where it is used as a protein "extender" in pre-prepared meals. But is this type of large-scale farming desirable or sustainable?

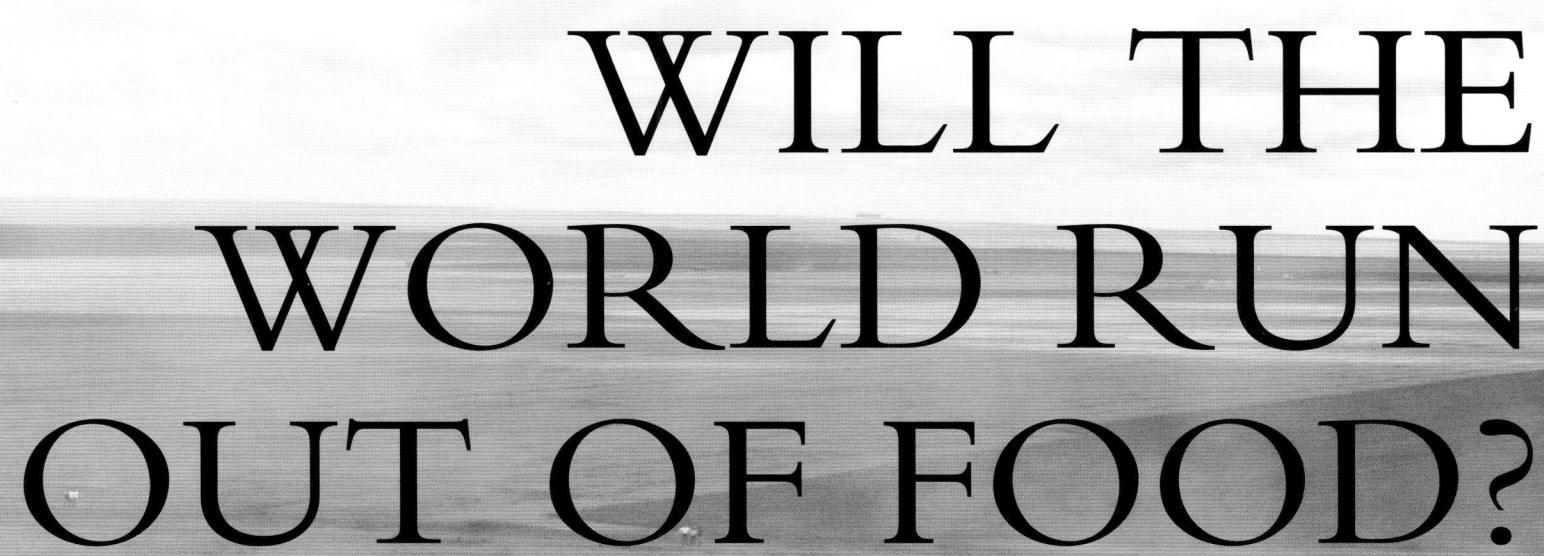

WILL THE WORLD RUN OUT OF FOOD?

For more information:

80 Temperature
   and precipitation

82 Climate change
   and global warming

84 Water
   distribution

88 Population

98 Minerals

▼ Supermarkets in the developed world carry a huge variety of fresh foods from all over the world, much of it out of season. A modern supermarket can often stock in excess of 130 varieties of vegetables and fruit for sale at any one time, much of it flown in chilled from abroad. As well as being extremely costly, these flights produce CO_2 emissions and, because of the high water content of fruit and vegetables, effectively export water and nutrients from countries that can often ill afford to do so. However, they do provide much needed income and employment for the producing country. By comparison, the market in the photograph (below right) only sells produce which can be grown locally and carried there, with no consequent CO_2 cost.

At current rates of growth, the world's population will increase to 9 billion people by 2050, from just over 6.5 billion today. To sustain this population there will have to be a 40% increase in food production which, as now, will have to be grown on the fertile soils irregularly distributed across just 11% of the Earth's surface. In addition, the fast growing and increasingly better-off economies of countries such as China and India are demanding a wider variety and better food in their diets, with many people eating more meat. However, the global trend in population is for people to move off the land toward the cities, resulting in fewer people to produce the food.

Similar conditions have been faced before: in 1898, the eminent Victorian scientist Sir William Crookes predicted that "England and all the civilized nations stand in deadly peril of not having enough to eat." But by 1909 the process to make synthetic nitrogen fertilizer from ammonia (the Haber-Bosch method) had been developed in Germany and Crookes' concerns were forgotten. Artificial nitrogen fixation has been a major factor in enabling the world's population to grow to today's levels. The process uses about 2% of the world's total energy demand to produce more than 100 million tonnes of nitrogen fertilizer, which helps feed about 30% of the world's population.

The issues in the developed world revolve around the quality and quantity of what we eat. The range of food available to consumers in a modern supermarket shows the extent to which food products are transported from around the world to satisfy the perceived need for such a wide variety of choice. There are also huge economic pressures from parts of the processed food industry to entice people in the developed world to eat more than is actually good for them. By comparison, in the developing world many struggle to achieve the minimum food intake to sustain life. Globally, about 1 billion people are malnourished and 1 billion are overweight. One of the biggest problems society faces is balancing this inequality of distribution, not only of food, but also of wealth.

Without the application of fertilizers, we would have been unable to sustain our historic growth rates of agricultural production. Yet the production of these is under pressure. The supply of phosphate rock, which occurs naturally and is currently the major source of phosphorus fertilizer (an essential plant nutrient), is predicted to peak in the 2030s and could be exhausted within 50 years or so, at the current rate of use. More phosphate rock is available but it would cost more to extract and contains cadmium and other contaminants, further increasing the cost of converting it into fertilizer. Nitrogen fertilizer currently uses expensive fossil fuels for its production, although an alternative production process using renewable hydroelectricity has been developed.

At the same time as the demand for food has increased, in recent years the demand for so-called "green" biofuels, derived from plant products, has also had an inflationary effect on prices by reducing the amount of land on which food can be grown.

In addition, because of the increase in the global demand for meat, more agricultural land is being used to grow crops to feed livestock, again pushing up the price of staple foods. This rise in prices disproportionately affects poorer developing economies, where a much higher proportion of family income is spent on food, perhaps as high as 50–70%.

SOIL FERTILITY

The map shows all soils, whether currently used for agriculture or covered by forest, grassland etc.

As much as 90% of all food is grown in soil, but fertile soil irregularly covers only 11% of the global land surface and is a non-renewable asset. Some soils are naturally fertile, such as the Black Earths of Russia and Ukraine. Natural soil fertility results from a combination of a temperate climate and nutrient-rich rocks that slowly weather. Those soils which are not naturally fertile, or which have been degraded by erosion or over-exploitation, require the incorporation of manures and fertilizers to improve soil fertility and maximize production.

This fragile asset is under threat from effects such as erosion and desertification, acidification, salinization, pollution and compaction (modern farm machinery gets heavier each year as its size increases).

Source: US Dept. of Agriculture Natural Resources Conservation Service – inherent land quality assessment map

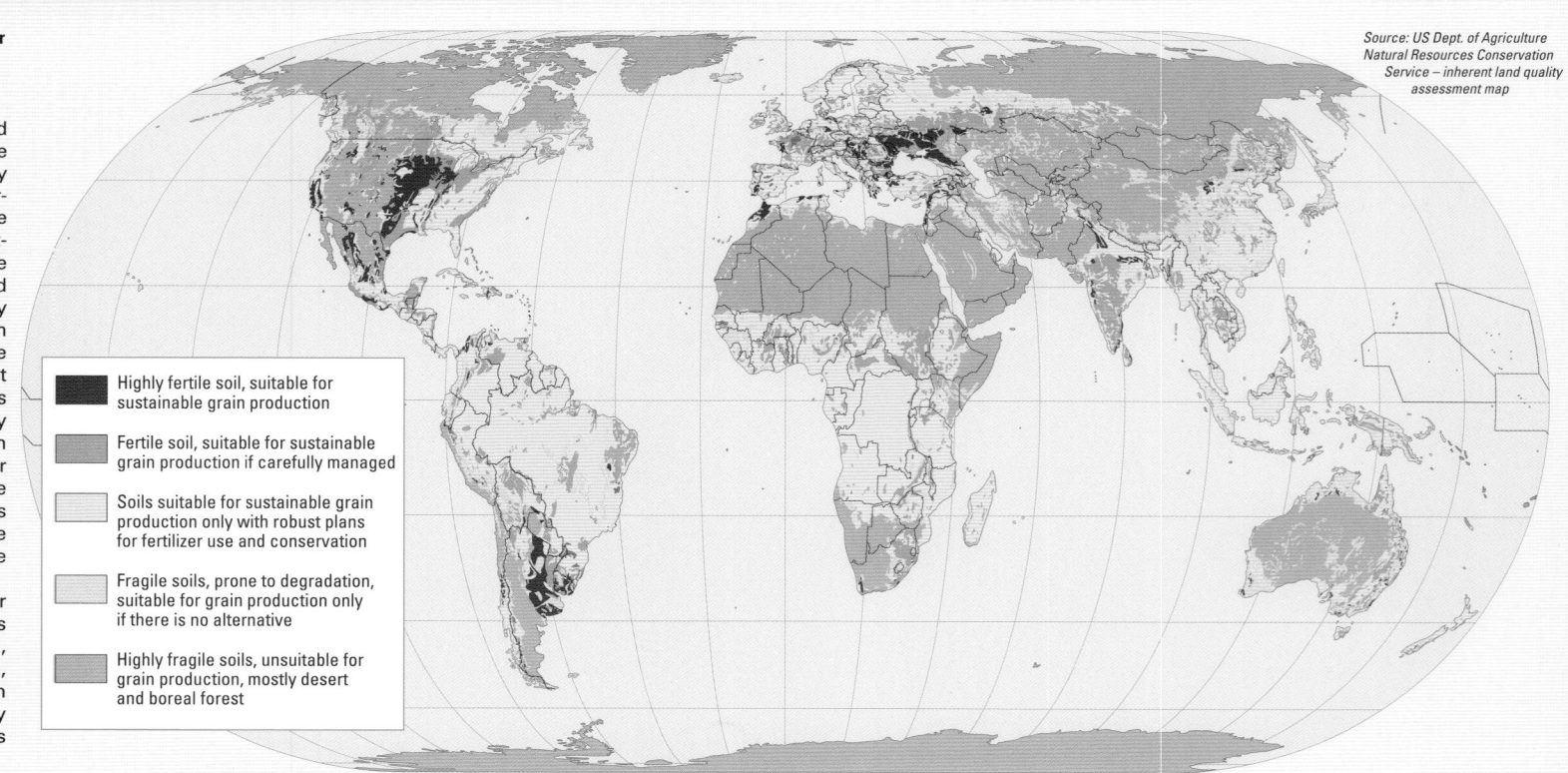

- Highly fertile soil, suitable for sustainable grain production
- Fertile soil, suitable for sustainable grain production if carefully managed
- Soils suitable for sustainable grain production only with robust plans for fertilizer use and conservation
- Fragile soils, prone to degradation, suitable for grain production only if there is no alternative
- Highly fragile soils, unsuitable for grain production, mostly desert and boreal forest

SOIL DEGRADATION

Areas of concern

- Areas of serious concern
- Areas of some concern
- Stable terrain
- Non-vegetated land

Causes of soil degradation (by region)

- Grazing practices
- Other agricultural practices
- Industrialization
- Deforestation
- Fuelwood collection

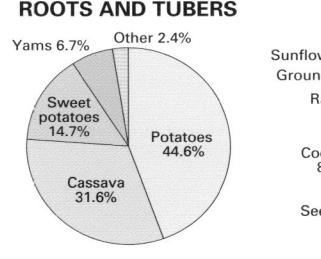

An estimated 75 billion tonnes of soil comprising 10 million hectares of potentially usable arable land are annually degraded or lost due to erosion. Current rates of loss in China are 57 times the rate of soil creation; in Europe the rate is 17 times and in the US 10 times. There have been frightening predictions of the loss of all fertile soil within 60 years.

COPYRIGHT PHILIP'S

WORLD CROP PRODUCTION

ROOTS AND TUBERS

- Yams 6.7%
- Other 2.4%
- Sweet potatoes 14.7%
- Potatoes 44.6%
- Cassava 31.6%

World total (2010): 727.3 million tonnes

OIL CROPS

- Olives 2.7%
- Other 2.3%
- Sunflower seeds 4.0%
- Groundnuts 4.9%
- Rapeseed 7.7%
- Coconuts 8.1%
- Seed cotton 8.9%
- Soybeans 34.0%
- Oil palm fruit 27.4%

World total (2010): 768.4 million tonnes

CEREALS

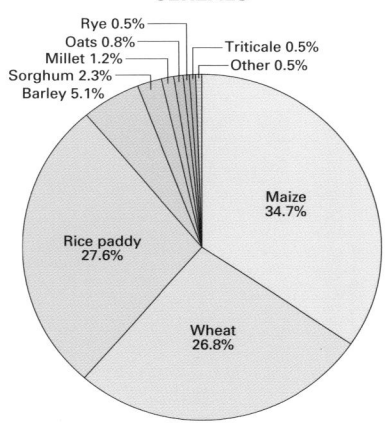

- Rye 0.5%
- Oats 0.8%
- Millet 1.2%
- Sorghum 2.3%
- Barley 5.1%
- Triticale 0.5%
- Other 0.5%
- Maize 34.7%
- Wheat 26.8%
- Rice paddy 27.6%

World total (2010): 2,432.2 million tonnes

BIOFUELS

Industrialized countries, looking to reduce their reliance on fossil fuels such as oil and gas, are setting targets for "bioenergy" production, i.e. energy from renewable sources such as maize, sugarcane, potatoes, or manioc. The EU has decided that 10% of its fuel for transport should be from these sources – mostly bioethanol – by 2020. This demand is resulting in both developed and developing countries converting food crops into bioethanol, jeopardizing food supplies. A major push by the US for bioethanol, coupled with poor harvests in Europe, Australia and the other grain-exporting countries, pushed grain prices up to unusually high levels in late 2007 and 2008; the poor suffered as a result.

This may be overcome as "first generation" biofuels – arable crops, which need fertilizers so the energy balance is not good – are replaced by "second generation" bioenergy crops such as willow and miscanthus grass, which need little if any fertilizer and can be grown on poorer soils not used for food crops.

GLOBAL LAND USAGE

Most suitable land for agriculture is already in use and much is lost to development and erosion each year. The amount of extra land for agriculture is very limited unless we cut down forests or plow up old grasslands, which results in the release of CO_2 into the atmosphere.

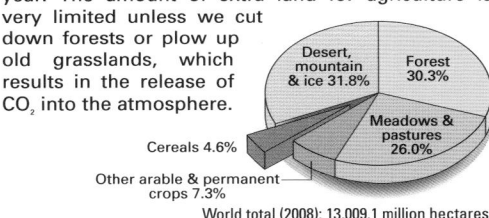

- Desert, mountain & ice 31.8%
- Forest 30.3%
- Cereals 4.6%
- Meadows & pastures 26.0%
- Other arable & permanent crops 7.3%

World total (2008): 13,009.1 million hectares

THE GREEN REVOLUTION

Fifty years ago there was a food crisis in the developing world, which was tackled by the so-called "Green Revolution." This combined the breeding of sturdy disease-resistant dwarf crop varieties with the use of irrigation, synthetic fertilizers, and chemical pesticides. Productivity per acre increased by up to 300%. Thus, countries that had only been able to grow enough for their own needs drove down the cost of food and became net exporters of food. Currently, 30–50% of crop yields can be attributed to fertilizer use.

Without fertilizer, under an ideal climate and with adequate pest and disease control, a wheat grain yield of 2–3 tonnes per hectare can be achieved; however, without good pest and disease control, 1 tonne per hectare is more likely. This can be compared with average wheat yields of about 8 tonnes per hectare in the UK, and the current (at the time of going to press) world record wheat yield in New Zealand of 15.6 tonnes per hectare.

The benefits of the Green Revolution plateaued out in the 1990s. There is now the need for a new phase to reinvigorate production to feed 9 billion people.

Using the latest technology to increase the worst yields to match the average, and the average to match the best, would transform food supplies.

YIELDS OF WHEAT GRAIN GROWN IN BROADBALK, ROTHAMSTED, FROM 1852 TO 2005

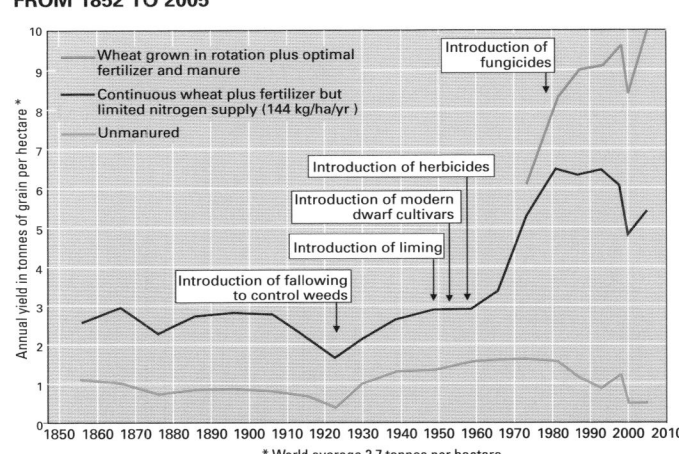

- Wheat grown in rotation plus optimal fertilizer and manure
- Continuous wheat plus fertilizer but limited nitrogen supply (144 kg/ha/yr)
- Unmanured

Introduction of fungicides
Introduction of herbicides
Introduction of modern dwarf cultivars
Introduction of liming
Introduction of fallowing to control weeds

Annual yield in tonnes of grain per hectare *

* World average 2.7 tonnes per hectare

LIVESTOCK

As can be seen on the graph below, world livestock production has increased dramatically over the last half century. Currently, over a third of the world's grain is fed to livestock for intensive stock raising, rising to 70% in developed countries where there is higher meat consumption per person.

Animals (and humans) are very inefficient in their utilization of nutrients – generally less than 20% of the nitrogen in their food is used; the rest is excreted, causing problems for recycling and the risk of environmental impact. Methane emissions from cattle are also a major contributor to greenhouse gases in the atmosphere. Additionally, meat is very expensive in terms of water consumption; for example, 1 lb [0.5 kg] of beef requires 1,857 gallons [8,442 liters] of water to produce it, taking account of the water used to grow feed, etc.

The adoption of vegetarianism has been suggested as a possible solution to some of these problems. However, even if this proved acceptable to the majority population, land in many parts of the world is suitable only for livestock production by extensive grazing. In any case, developing countries, which were previously predominantly vegetarian, are demanding more meat, regarded in some societies as a measurement of status. For example, Chinese meat consumption has risen from 9 lb [4 kg] per person in 1960 to 119 lb [54 kg] today. This compares with a figure of 176 lb [80 kg] in the UK and 254 lb [115 kg] in the United States.

WORLD LIVESTOCK PRODUCTION

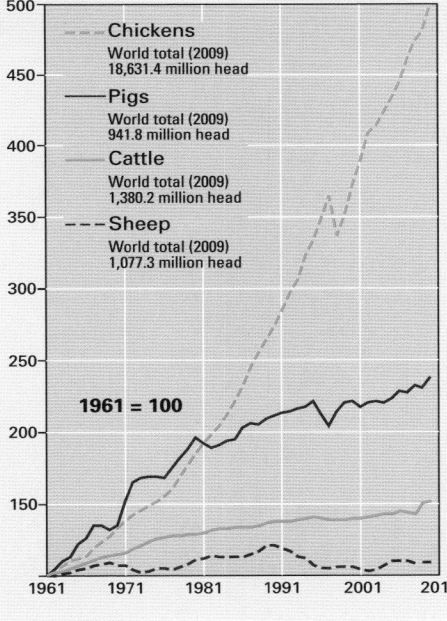

- **Chickens** World total (2009) 18,631.4 million head
- **Pigs** World total (2009) 941.8 million head
- **Cattle** World total (2009) 1,380.2 million head
- **Sheep** World total (2009) 1,077.3 million head

1961 = 100

◄ The top lines on the graph show the effects of fertilizers and other developments in agricultural practice on wheat production over time, in the longest running trial of this type. The Broadbalk Wheat Experiment at Rothamsted Research in the UK has been running on the same field since 1843. The lower line represents the same crop grown in the same conditions, but with none of these inputs applied – the equivalent of yields in many parts of the developing world.

FOOD & POPULATION

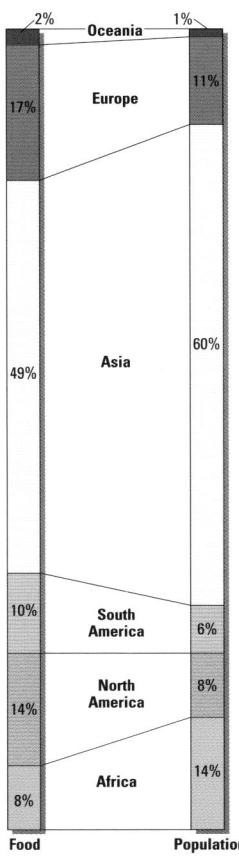

- Oceania 2% / 1%
- Europe 17% / 11%
- Asia 49% / 60%
- South America 10% / 6%
- North America 14% / 8%
- Africa 8% / 14%

Food   Population

Comparison of food production and population by continent
The left column indicates the proportion of world food production and the right shows population in proportion.

IRRIGATION

By 2030 there will be a 30% increase in water demand to support the world's population and its value will soar, so more efficient methods of collection and delivery will have to be developed.

China currently has 23% of the world's population, but only 11% of its water. The country is therefore building new reservoirs to catch runoff from Himalayan glaciers. Their efforts have, however, already resulted in a conference of the countries downstream on the Mekong River to discuss how to tackle the resultant reduced water flow.

Since over 71% of the Earth's surface is covered in water, it can hardly be said to be in short supply. However, less than 3% of this is fresh water and, of that, over two-thirds is frozen in ice caps and glaciers. The world, therefore, will never run out of water as such, but its over-exploitation in developed areas and availability in regions where it is scarce are major problems.

For more information:

84 Water
distribution

85 Natural
vegetation

86 Biodiversity and
the natural world

▼ If the ever-increasing world demand for food continues, it is likely that more intensive livestock production units will have to be adopted. Pictured below, this battery farm for chickens is in the US. In the past, these units have been synonymous in many people's minds with cruelty to the animals and issues associated with the spread of disease.

The growth of food crops in a protected environment without the use of soil as the growing medium will also become more widespread. In hydroponics the plants grow in nutrient-enriched water, as can be seen in the picture below right, taken at a research establishment in California.

How can we feed 9 billion people adequately and sustainably? There are some simple solutions that we should note before looking at more complicated and technological "fixes." Most agree that we should not be taking more land from forest and other uncropped areas into production because of the release of CO_2 that this would cause and the adverse impacts on predicted climate change and biodiversity. As already noted on page 11, enabling those producing the lowest yields to produce national average yields, and those producing average yields to equal the best, would transform food production. This is likely to involve better pest and disease control, and more widespread and effective use of fertilizers. The Alliance for the Green Revolution in Africa (AGRA), with initial support from the Rockefeller Foundation and the Bill and Melinda Gates Foundation, is looking to achieve this.

It is important to control pests and diseases in growing crops, but post-harvest crop losses from molds, insects, rodents, and birds are 10–40% of the total, according to the FAO. Again, the application of existing technologies could avoid these and make a significant impact on food supplies. Finally, the avoidance of waste would also make an important contribution in developed countries.

But if this is not sufficient, what then? The UK's Royal Society published a report in 2009 entitled "Reaping the benefits. Science and the sustainable intensification of global agriculture." It suggested that we will need to increase crop production but without cultivating more land, while sustaining the environment, preserving natural resources, and supporting farmers' livelihoods: that is, produce more using less and with less of an impact. The Royal Society saw good soil management, maintaining or enhancing crop genetic diversity, and introducing pest and disease resistance, as well as better nitrogen-use efficiency through GM technologies, as key to this.

Research is in progress now at such centers as the International Rice Research Institute in the Philippines and the John Innes Centre in the UK to develop cereals (rice and wheat, for example) that fix their own nitrogen and so do not need nitrogen fertilizer. Possible problems here are the carbon/energy cost to the plant of accommodating the nitrogen-fixing organisms or traits, and the consequent likely reductions in yield. In the longer-term, and even more aspirational, there is the idea of perennial cereals such as wheat, maize, and rice that would not need to be replanted each year, but would regrow and yield each year in the same way as a fruit tree.

However, some reject such technological approaches, saying that reliance on chemical fertilizers and pesticides is a threat to sustainability. They advocate extensive systems that could be viewed as "organic," "biodynamic" or "ecological." But these mostly involve mixed systems rather than the specialist crop or livestock production systems that dominate most developed countries, crop rotations to control pests and diseases, and legumes to supply nitrogen.

Finally, we must note the increasing interest in healthy eating and the efforts of many governments to promote this, mostly with a view to reducing obesity and other diet-induced health problems. This may well drive food production in a particular direction.

NITROGEN – THE KEY TO CROP GROWTH

In most countries, nitrogen is the main yield-determining plant nutrient; exceptions are areas where degraded soils are deficient in phosphorus, such as in parts of Africa and Australia. Adequate inputs of nitrogen are therefore essential for food security.

Total nitrogen fertilizer consumption in thousand tonnes (2009)

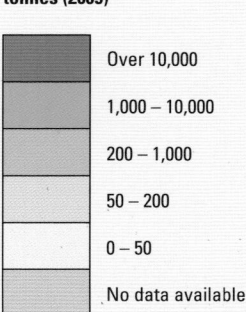

Over 10,000

1,000 – 10,000

200 – 1,000

50 – 200

0 – 50

No data available

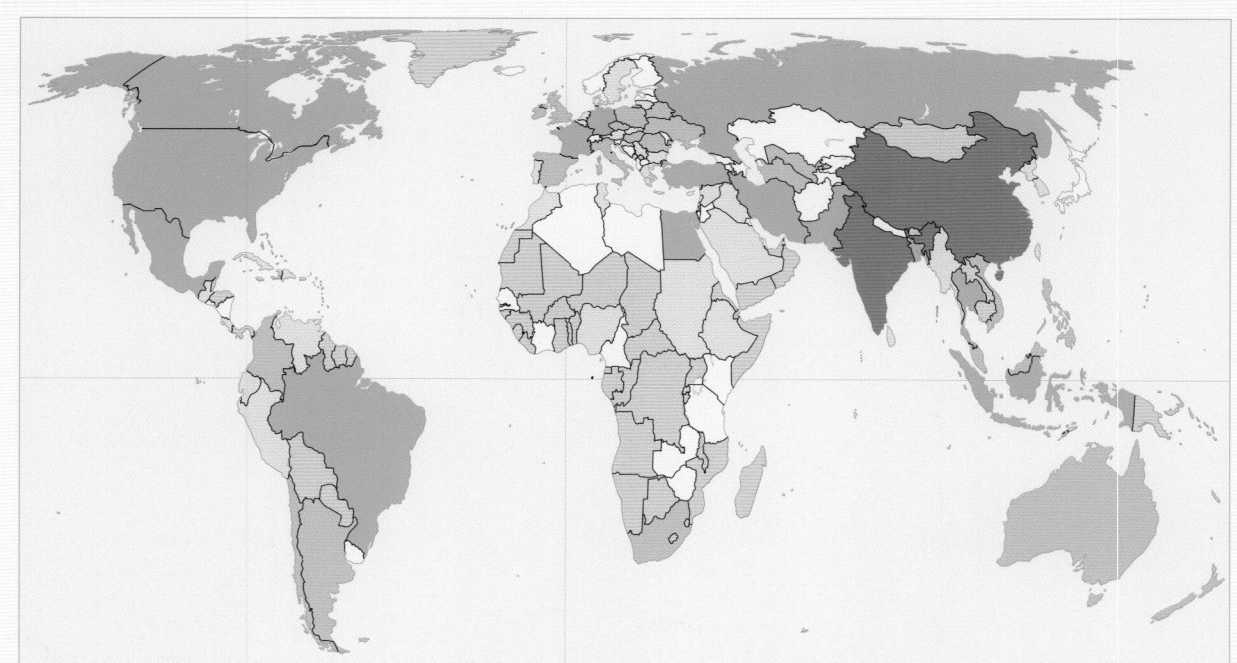

The map shows nitrogen fertilizer inputs across the world. This, in a very real sense, is an index of food production. However, producing nitrogen fertilizer requires energy, so many see a system in which the nitrogen is brought in (or fixed) by legumes such as clover and alfalfa (lucerne) as being more sustainable. However, the problem with such systems is that, in general, while the legume is being grown, a food crop is not being produced (apart from livestock that may graze the legume). In addition, pollution in the form of nitrogen losses to air and water from legume-based systems can be as large as those from fertilizers, and the energy needed to produce fertilizers could be obtained from renewable sources.

PESTS, DISEASES, AND WEEDS

Currently, 30% of the world's crop yield is lost because of the effects of pests, diseases, and weeds. Chemical controls (such as herbicides and fungicides) continue to be effective but are disliked by many.

REACH is a new EU regulation on chemicals and their safe use. It deals with the *R*egistration, *E*valuation, *A*uthorization and restriction of *CH*emical substances, and severely limits those chemicals that growers can use.

Because of this, research is focusing on isolating pest and disease resistance genes or traits using molecular methods. Breeding for resistance, transferring these identified traits into crop plants and animals, can be done using conventional plant breeding methods but is much quicker using GM methods (see below right).

Crop rotations can be used to control pests, diseases and weeds, as can mechanical methods, cultivations, and inter-cropping (that is, mixing crops) and trap crops (which protect the main crop from pests).

Although climate change is not accepted by some, whatever happens in the future, changing weather patterns have already caused the movement of pests and diseases around the world.

One example of this is "bluetongue," which has been monitored and action taken to prevent serious impact on food production in Europe. This disease, which affects livestock, has been spread by a species of tiny biting midge from sub-Saharan Africa into northwest Europe since 2006, before which it was never recorded in Europe.

A sustained research program, vector surveillance, restrictions on animal movements, and a vaccination program have helped limit the spread of the disease in the UK.

This map shows the spread of the disease between 2006 and 2009 in Europe as a whole.

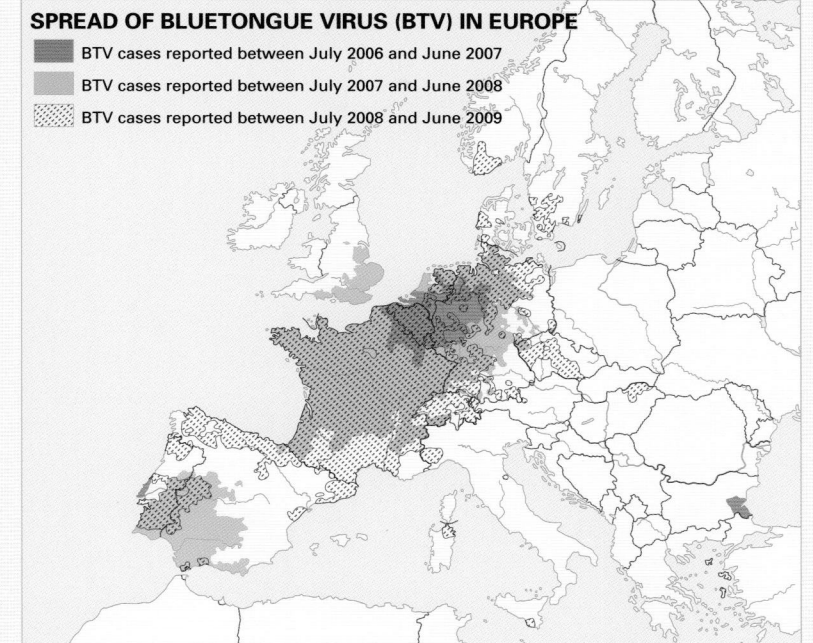

SPREAD OF BLUETONGUE VIRUS (BTV) IN EUROPE

- BTV cases reported between July 2006 and June 2007
- BTV cases reported between July 2007 and June 2008
- BTV cases reported between July 2008 and June 2009

AQUACULTURE

With a greater demand in some western countries for increased fish content in their diets, at the same time as fish stocks in the oceans are becoming depleted from overfishing, fish farming or "aquaculture" has become more important.

The term covers both salt and freshwater fish, and shellfish, but has the same inherent issues as livestock farming in relation to pollution and pest and disease problems. It contributes about a third of the total world fish catch, with carp, oysters, clams, salmon, mussels, and scallops forming some of the major varieties. China, India, and Southeast Asia, where it has always been important for local consumption, are the biggest producers.

It is estimated that 90% of the USA's consumption of shrimps are farmed and imported.

CUTTING BACK ON FOOD WASTE

Major retailers can be fussy because they know that their customers are fussy. Over 30 years ago, the singer Joni Mitchell wrote "Give me spots on my apples, but leave me the birds and bees," but not much has changed. The US Government has estimated that currently 60 million tonnes of food worth $5 billion is left in the fields because it is regarded as being of poor quality and unsaleable. More is left unsold in shops and discarded: in the UK it is estimated that 8.3 million tonnes of food worth £20 billion is sent to landfill each year, and some people now live on the food shops' throwaway ("Dumpster Diving" in the US; "Skipping" in the UK). A further fraction is bought but never consumed. It is estimated that food wasted by the US and Europe could feed the world three times over. Food waste now accounts for more than a quarter of the total freshwater consumption and 300 million barrels of oil per year. Clearly using this waste would make a big impact and must be part of sustainable food supply.

GENETIC MODIFICATION (GM)

Mankind has undertaken selective breeding of crops and livestock for thousands of years, to maintain and improve their most desirable characteristics. In the past 20–30 years, molecular genetics has increasingly been used to guide crop breeding. Biotechnological tools, such as molecular markers and genetic modification (GM), can complement conventional breeding processes to improve almost all important traits, including yield potential, plant structure, tolerance to abiotic stress (that is, salinity, cold, acidity), disease resistances, food and nutritional quality, and market preference.

GM critics suggest that there may be unforeseen effects on human health and the environment. However, in Europe and elsewhere, detailed risk analysis of potential effects of GM crops is made before licences to release the technology are granted. For example, UK Farm Scale Evaluations compared the effects on farmland biodiversity of growing conventional and GM (herbicide-resistant) sugar beet, maize, and oilseed rape. It was found that the species of crop grown (that is, beet, maize or rape) had a greater impact on biodiversity than whether the crop was GM or conventional.

Some would claim proven benefits and GM crops are currently grown in more than 23 countries, on over 114 million hectares worldwide, equivalent to about 5% of global cultivated land. These include eight EU states: Spain, France, Czech Republic, Portugal, Poland, Germany, Slovak Republic, and Romania. In addition, eight countries now grow more than 1 million hectares of GM crops: USA, Canada, China, India, South Africa, Paraguay, Argentina, and Brazil.

A major obstacle for GM acceptance is public perception of the technology. Biotechnology is only part of the solution; research in sustainable agriculture will provide new methods of crop and soil management, and support the development of improved varieties by both conventional breeding and GM.

IMPROVED LAND MANAGEMENT

Improved land management has a large part to play in improving food production. Many soils have been compacted through the use of heavy machinery or by regular plowing, which causes a "plow pan" (a thin compacted layer of soil) to develop just below the bottom of the plow. Other soils have been allowed to become acid or saline through acid rain, the inappropriate use of fertilizers or other amendments, or polluted by toxic metals such as cadmium, nickel, and copper, or by organic pollutants through the use of human and animal "wastes."

Conservation agriculture that includes "no-till" and "min-till" has many benefits in terms of allowing a stable and good soil structure to develop, retaining organic matter, nutrients and moisture. But perennial weeds can be a problem on "heavy" clay soils, requiring a greater use of herbicides.

Strip tillage (cultivating only a narrow strip in which the crop is planted) saves energy use, maintains a soil cover (preventing erosion), and generally carries the benefits of conservation tillage.

In the longer-term, "controlled traffic" in which tractors and other equipment travel along fixed paths, or in which equipment is run from gantries, all linked to GPS, are precision farming systems that would contribute to a high-tech solution to food security.

One matter still to be resolved is the importance of the biodiversity of soil organisms and micro-organisms (for example, earthworms, mycorrhizal fungi, bacteria) to soil fertility and thus sustainable food production. Plants can be grown in sand culture or hydroponics, suggesting that organisms, let alone biodiversity, are not essential. However, for many this is the key to a truly sustainable system based on soil.

THE FUTURE

If we adopt and develop appropriate techniques and practices, and modify our behavior, we stand a good chance of feeding the future, predominantly urban, world population. The image at bottom left shows one of several proposals for a new development currently under discussion: the "vertical farm," this from Plantagon International. Theoretically, this would consist of a giant self-contained production unit, enabling crop production to take place in a controlled environment, regardless of climatic variations, and situated within urban regions, the main areas of consumption.

Its proponents also claim that crops will be able to be grown throughout the year, making one acre in the controlled environment the equivalent of many times more acres grown outdoors. They also say that the units would grow the crops organically, would reduce runoff pollution, and would also ease the pressure on water demand by recycling the water used from evapotranspiration.

However, whether or not we can afford proposals such as these, it still seems likely that parts of the world will still be using subsistence agriculture to feed themselves (such as in the photograph at upper left, taken in southern Africa). Brazil, though, has developed from primarily subsistence agriculture to "modern" intensive methods, and China and India are currently undergoing a similar process. As people move away from the land to live in the growing urban centers, farm sizes can grow and opportunities, created by economies of scale, may evolve to improve the lifestyle of the subsistence farmer.

Whatever develops, it will be our choices that will influence it. What is your concept of a sustainable system of food supply that can feed 9 billion people and provide a livelihood for producers?

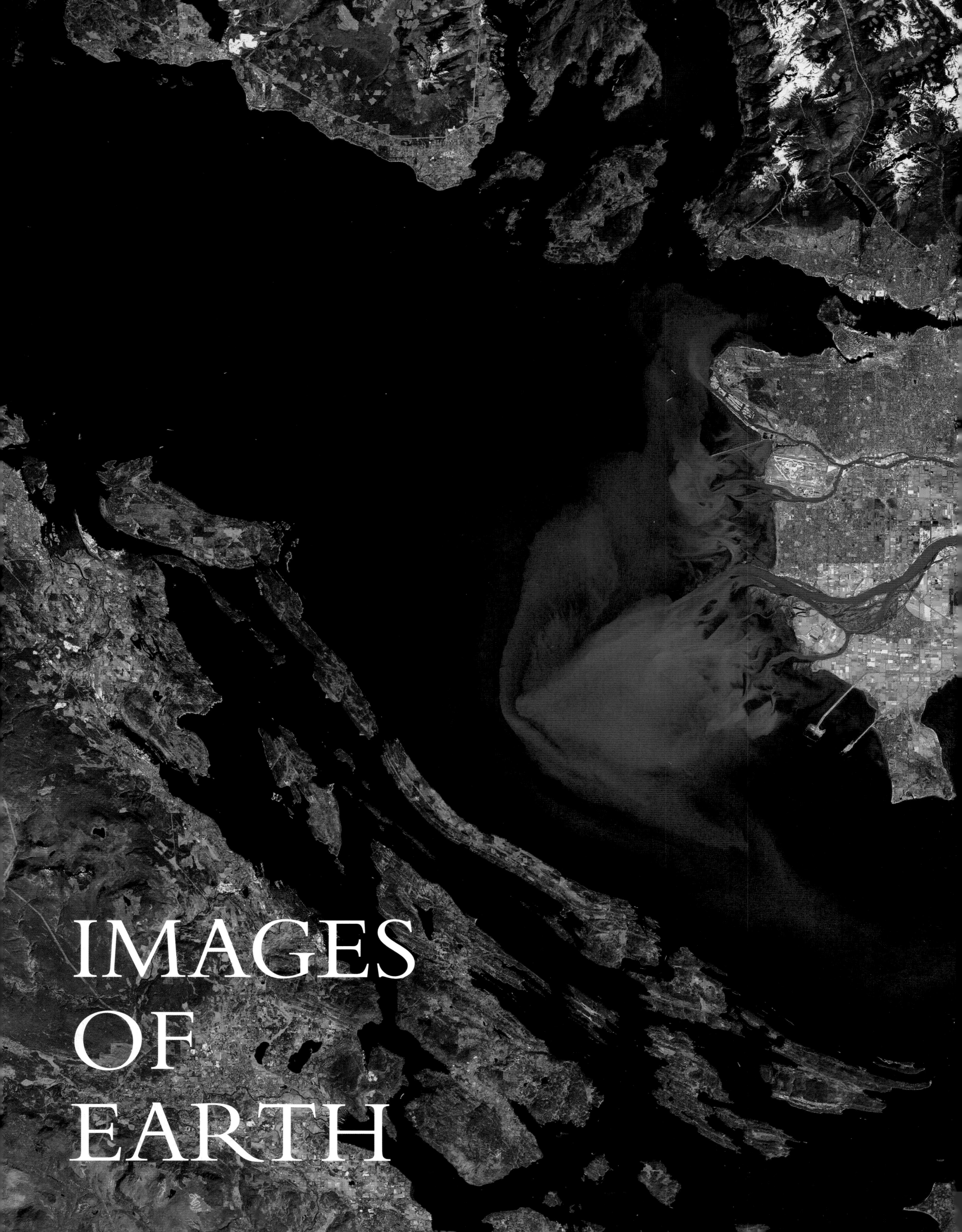

IMAGES

OF

EARTH

On the north side of the Fraser River delta, the city of Vancouver grew up around its fine, natural harbor, developing as the western railhead of the Canadian Pacific Railroad and terminus of the transcontinental highway. It is now the largest cargo port in Canada. Just clipping the southern tip of the delta runs the 49th parallel, the boundary between Canada and the USA. To the north of the city lie the Coast Mountains and on the left, across the Strait of Georgia, the outlying islands of Vancouver Island. [Map page 296]

© Fugro NPA/USGS Landsat

The River Thames snakes from Chelsea Bridge in the west to Tower Bridge in the east in this image covering both the West End and the City of London. Despite having a population in excess of 8 million people, there are still many parks and open spaces around the city center. St James's Park, Green Park, and part of Hyde Park, together with Buckingham Palace and its gardens, can be seen center left of the image, and farther north the eastern edge of Regent's Park can be seen. Just below the title, the newly developing area around St Pancras, the terminus of the direct high-speed rail link to Europe, can be seen. [Map page 125]
© Fugro NPA/Digital Globe

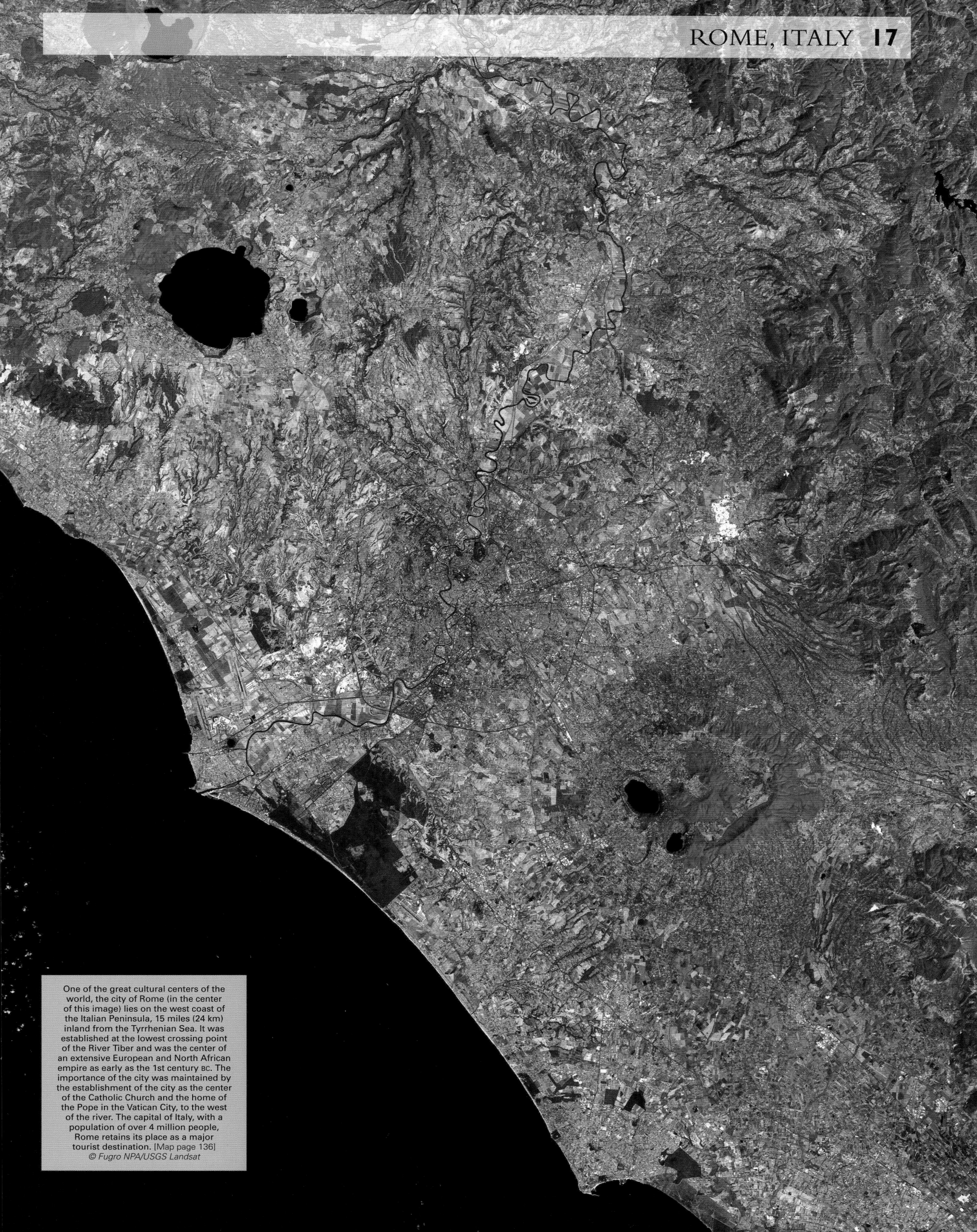

One of the great cultural centers of the world, the city of Rome (in the center of this image) lies on the west coast of the Italian Peninsula, 15 miles (24 km) inland from the Tyrrhenian Sea. It was established at the lowest crossing point of the River Tiber and was the center of an extensive European and North African empire as early as the 1st century BC. The importance of the city was maintained by the establishment of the city as the center of the Catholic Church and the home of the Pope in the Vatican City, to the west of the river. The capital of Italy, with a population of over 4 million people, Rome retains its place as a major tourist destination. [Map page 136]
© Fugro NPA/USGS Landsat

The city of Istanbul was formerly known as Constantinople and, before that, from the beginning in the 7th century BC, as Byzantium. It is split by the narrow stretch of water running from north to south called the Bosporus. This forms the continental boundary between Europe and Asia, connecting the Black Sea, to the north, to the Sea of Marmara, thence to the Mediterranean. It is because of this strategic position between the east–west (land) and north–south (sea) trade routes that the city has been important for such a long time. Under the Ottoman Empire it was the capital city of Turkey, but in 1923 this was moved to Ankara. Currently, over 13 million people live in Istanbul, the largest city in Turkey. [Map page 122]

© Fugro NPA/USGS Landsat

The ancient city of Kabul, believed to have been founded over 3,000 years ago, is situated at the head of the triangular-shaped valley seen just to the left of center of this image. At a height of 5,900 ft (1,800 m) above sea level, this capital city of over 3 million inhabitants sits on an upland plateau, south of the main Hindu Kush mountain range. The average summer high temperature is 90°F (32°C) and the winter low is 19°F (–7°C), with dry summers and rainfall concentrated between January and April. The runways of the international airport can clearly be seen to the northwest of the city in this image, but the US airbase at Bagram is 27 miles (47 km) north of Kabul, south of Charikar. [Map page 240]
© Fugro NPA/USGS Landsat

Also known as Bombay, Mumbai is the largest and most important commercial city in India, with a population of 21 million people. Its harbour is the best in the country, and the new port, built in 1989 and called Nhava Sheva (on the right-hand side of the image), handles 65% of the country's total container traffic. The growth of cotton weaving, and the opening of the Suez Canal in 1869, cemented its position as India's most important trading port. Diversifying into areas such as engineering and information technology, the city is also the center of the highly successful Hindi movie industry, or "Bollywood," which exports its products around the world.
[Map page 130] © *RapidEye AG/Fugro NPA*

Three separate countries can be seen in this image. At the top, partially covered by cloud, is the southern end of Malaysia; the large island just below is the independent country of Singapore; and the islands at the bottom of the image are part of Indonesia. Singapore has developed a fast-growing economy based on the trans-shipment of goods between the Far East and the West. As a result, it is one of the world's major ports and much new development, by reclaiming land from the sea, can be seen in the south, colored light brown in this image. The city state is one of the world's wealthiest countries, with a population of over 5 million people. [Map page 138]
© RapidEye AG/Fugro NPA

This image shows the Congo River where it splits to form Malebo Pool on its journey to the Atlantic Ocean, 314 miles (506 km) away. At the western end of the pool two capital cities face each other across the river – Brazzaville on the north bank, the capital city of the Republic of the Congo, and Kinshasa on the south bank, the capital of the Democratic Republic of the Congo. With the exception of Rome and the Vatican City, these are the two closest capital cities in the world – their combined total population is more than 10 million inhabitants. The Congo River stretches a further 3,826 miles (4,164 km) back to its source – it is also the world's deepest river with depths of over 750 ft (230 m) recorded. [Map pages 264–5]
© Fugro NPA/USGS Landsat

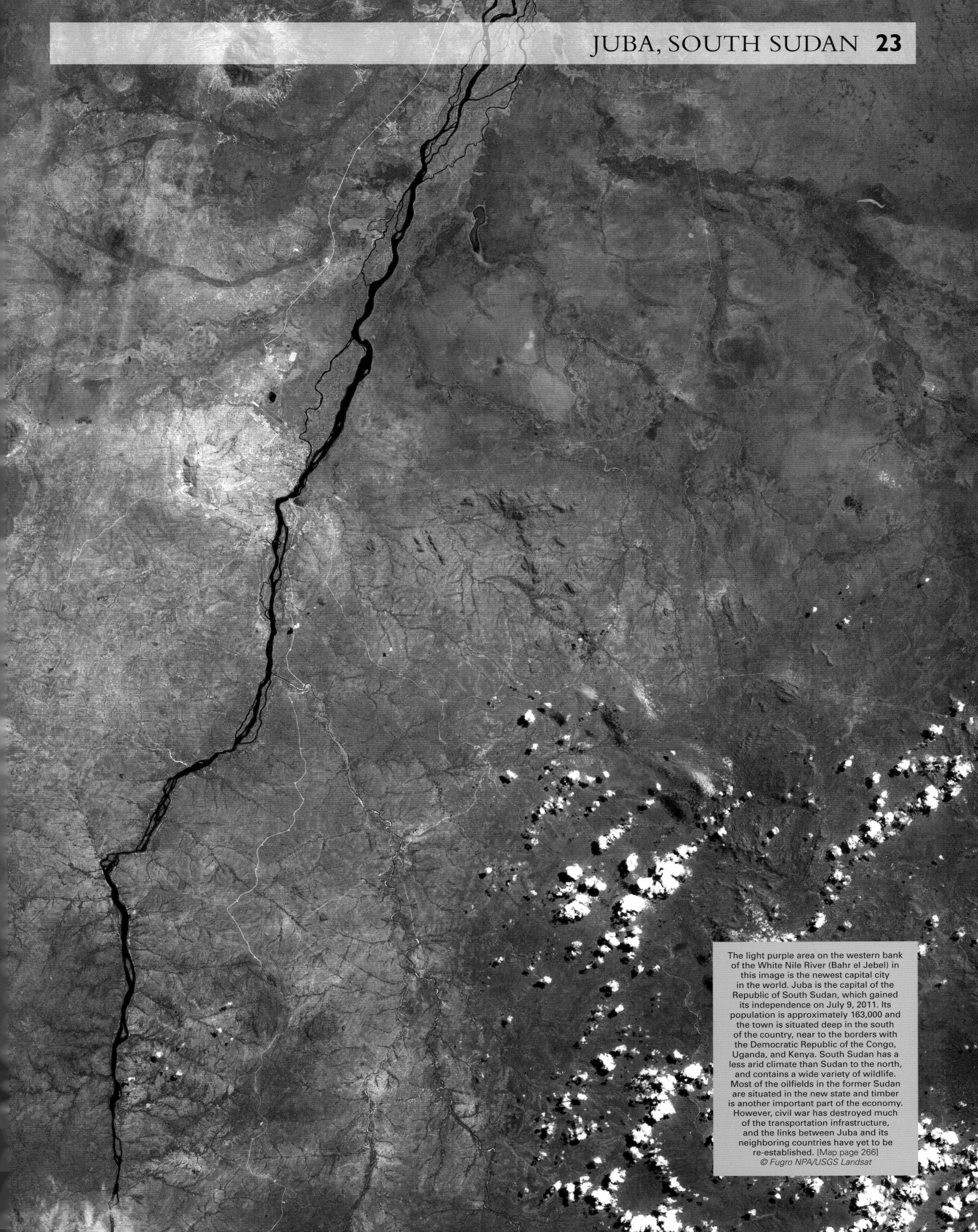

The light purple area on the western bank of the White Nile River (Bahr el Jebel) in this image is the newest capital city in the world. Juba is the capital of the Republic of South Sudan, which gained its independence on July 9, 2011. Its population is approximately 163,000 and the town is situated deep in the south of the country, near to the borders with the Democratic Republic of the Congo, Uganda, and Kenya. South Sudan has a less arid climate than Sudan to the north, and contains a wide variety of wildlife. Most of the oilfields in the former Sudan are situated in the new state and timber is another important part of the economy. However, civil war has destroyed much of the transportation infrastructure, and the links between Juba and its neighboring countries have yet to be re-established. [Map page 266]

© Fugro NPA/USGS Landsat

The city of Cape Town sits at the northern end of the Cape Peninsula beneath Table Mountain, its port facilities clearly visible in this image. It developed from the first settlement in the 17th century, by the Dutch East India Company, because of its safe harbor, which faces north, looking across Table Bay toward Robben Island. The urban area now spreads to the east of the peninsula down to False Bay. As well as being the second largest city in South Africa, after Johannesburg, it is also the seat of the National Parliament and is the legislative capital of the country. To the west of the port can be seen the oval shape of the Cape Town Stadium, which was built for the 2010 Soccer World Cup. [Map page 118]

© RapidEye AG/Fugro NPA

The largest city in Australia, Sydney was founded at the end of the 18th century on the north shore of Botany Bay. It has since spread inland along the valley of the Parramatta River, but is constrained by the Blue Mountains National Park in the west (the green area in this image). Within this area the reservoir Lake Burragong can be seen, which supplies 80% of the city's water. The runways of Australia's busiest airport are also visible, projecting from the north shore of Botany Bay. [Map page 139]
© Fugro NPA/USGS Landsat

Situated at the northern end of North Island, the city of Auckland was founded by the Maoris on the narrow isthmus at the top left of this image. It has since grown to become the largest settlement in the country. This is a landscape that has been shaped by volcanic forces – the dark circular shape to the east of the city is Rangitoto Island, the now-extinct remains of a volcano that erupted from the sea some 600 years ago. At the bottom of the image is the town of Hamilton. [Map page 284]
© Fugro NPA/USGS Landsat

Québec was founded as a trading post
in 1608, at the narrowest point of the
St Lawrence River, just to the southwest
of the Île d'Orléans, and is one of
the oldest cities in North America.
Strategically, the city controlled the
movement of shipping between the
Atlantic Ocean and the Great Lakes, and
consequently developed fortifications on
the cliffs of Cape Diamond, 320 ft (97 m)
above the river. The port is 850 miles
(1,370 km) from the Atlantic, 1,495 miles
(2,404 km) from Duluth, and 1,400 miles
(2,252 km) from Chicago. It has a
population of over 491,000 people and
is the capital city of the province of
the same name. [Map page 299]
© Fugro NPA/USGS Landsat

Washington is the capital of the United States and was created in 1790. It is named after George Washington and is in a unique federal district, the District of Columbia, so that it should not fall into any particular state. The city is in the center of this image, at the confluence of the Potomac and Anacostia rivers, just to the east of the original capital city, Georgetown. As well as being home to the President, in the White House, the majority of foreign embassies in the US are situated here, as are the headquarters of important global organizations such as the World Bank and the International Monetary Fund (IMF). To service the many branches of government and other institutions, over half a million people commute into the city every day.

[Map page 143] © RapidEye AG/Fugro NPA

This image covers parts of New York City (to the east) and Jersey City (to the west). Flowing from the north, the Hudson River divides them, and the elongated island of Manhattan with Central Park at its heart is clearly visible. This is one of the richest and most densely populated areas in the United States, with a population in excess of 1.5 million people. To the southeast is the end of Long Island on which the suburbs of Brooklyn and Queens are situated. Southwest of Manhattan are two small islands: the first is Ellis Island, where the early immigrants first disembarked, and beyond that is Liberty Island, where the famous Statue of Liberty is located.

[Map page 132] © *RapidEye AG/Fugro NPA*

The image shows how Caracas, the capital city of Venezuela, is situated inland at an altitude of about 3,000 ft (900 m) and runs east to west, confined in a valley in the Cordillera de la Costa. The altitude moderates the extremes of what would otherwise be a tropical climate. It was founded inland by the Spanish in 1567 to protect it from attack from the sea, and became the most important town in the region. On the narrow coastal plain, 19 miles (30 km) to the north, can be seen its port, La Guaira, which is reached by rail and highway across the mountainous El Ávila National Park. The oil boom experienced by the country in the early 20th century until the present time once again reinforced the city's importance. [Map page 328]

© Fugro NPA/USGS Landsat

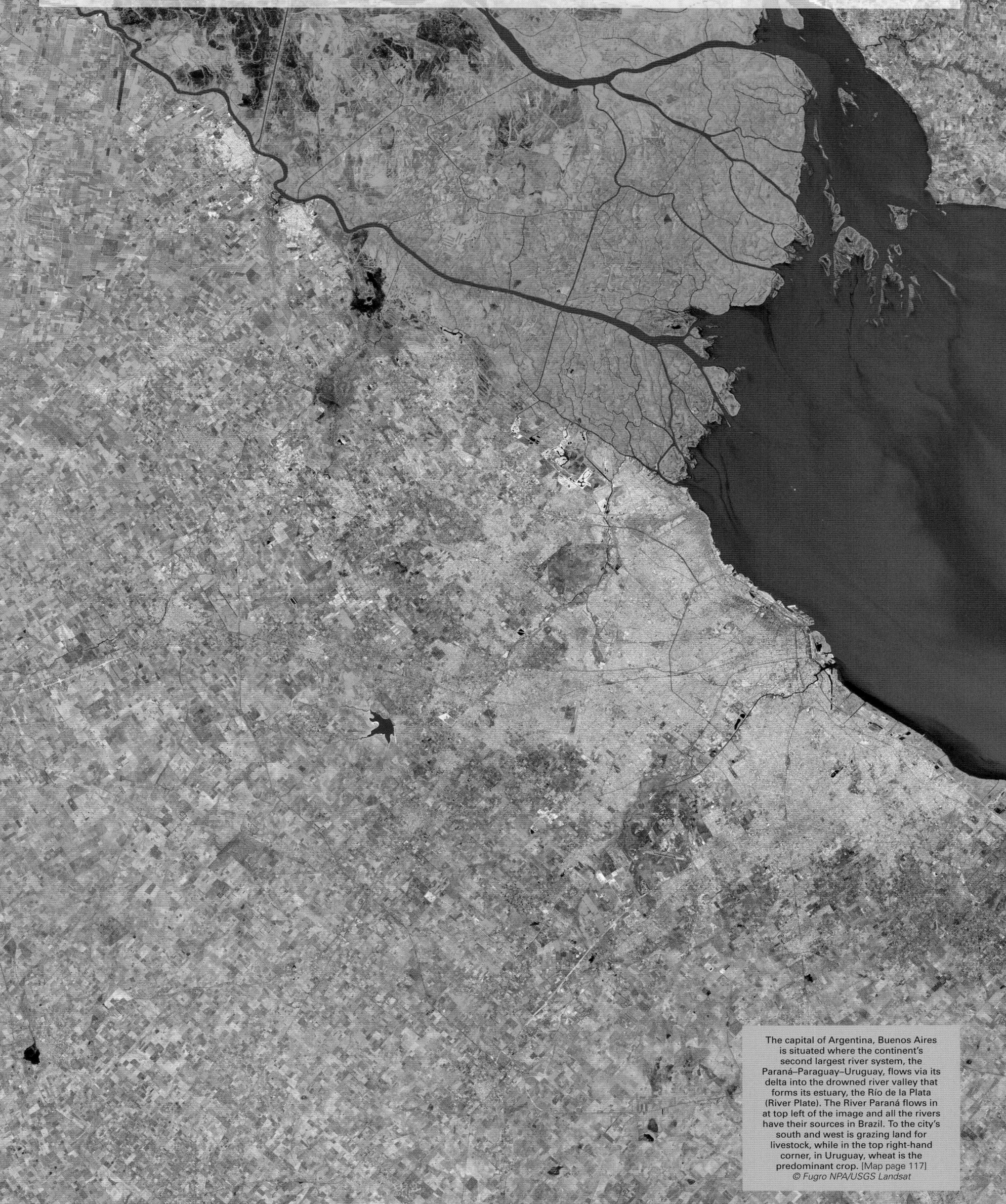

The capital of Argentina, Buenos Aires is situated where the continent's second largest river system, the Paraná–Paraguay–Uruguay, flows via its delta into the drowned river valley that forms its estuary, the Río de la Plata (River Plate). The River Paraná flows in at top left of the image and all the rivers have their sources in Brazil. To the city's south and west is grazing land for livestock, while in the top right-hand corner, in Uruguay, wheat is the predominant crop. [Map page 117]

© Fugro NPA/USGS Landsat

GAZETTEER
OF
NATIONS

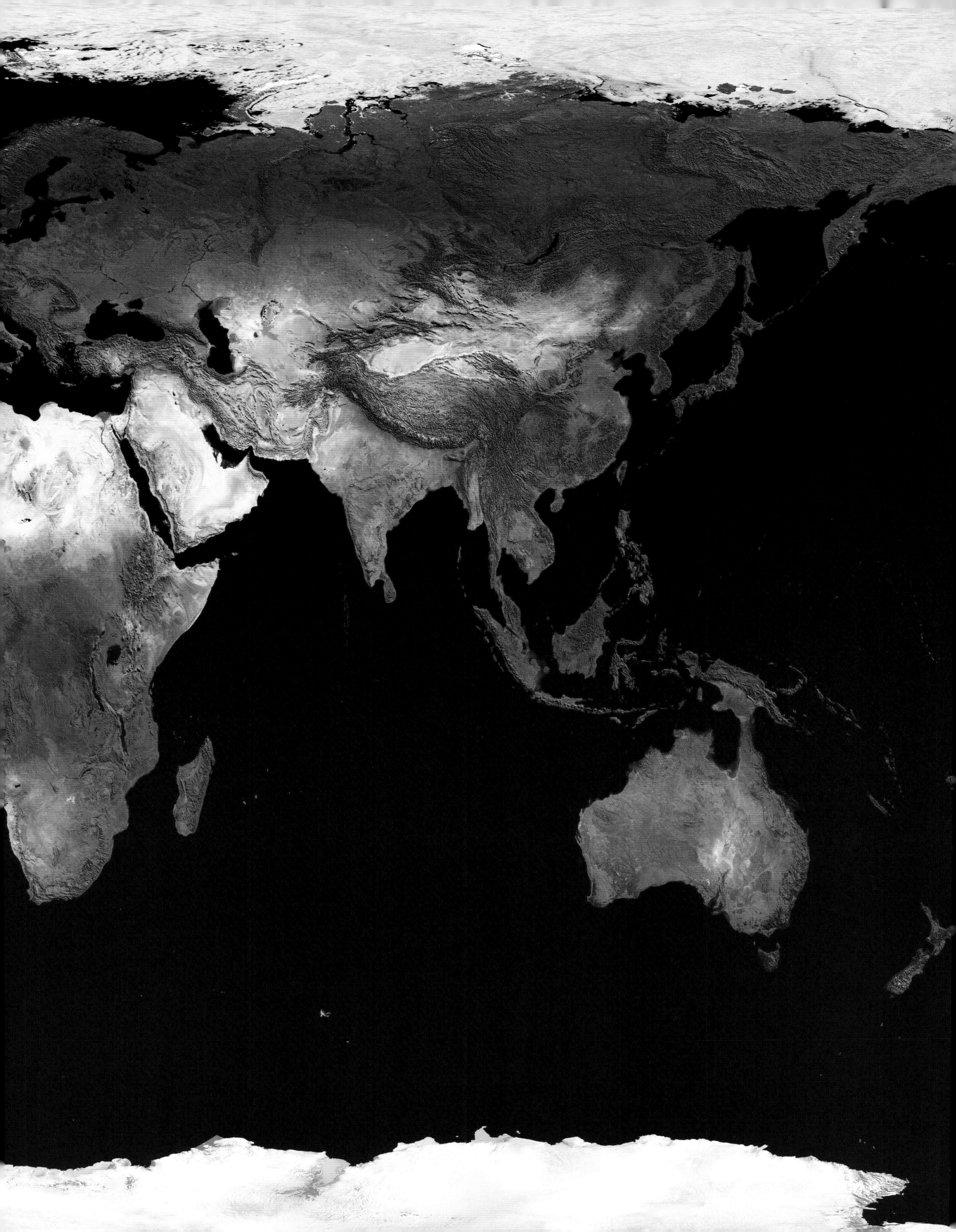

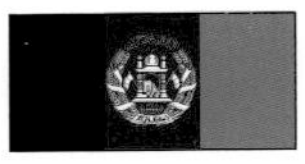
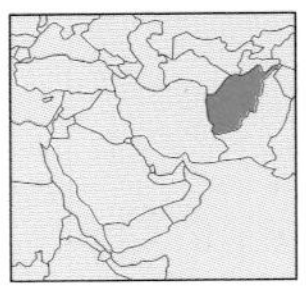

AFGHANISTAN

GEOGRAPHY The Republic of Afghanistan is a landlocked, mountainous country in southern Asia. The central highlands reach a height of more than 22,966 ft [7,000 m] in the east and make up nearly three-quarters of Afghanistan. The main range is the Hindu Kush. In winter, northerly winds bring cold, snowy weather to the mountains, but summers are hot and dry.

POLITICS & ECONOMY The modern history of Afghanistan began in 1747, when the various tribes in the area united for the first time. In the 19th century, Russia and Britain struggled for control of the country. Following Britain's withdrawal in 1919, Afghanistan became fully independent. Soviet troops invaded in 1979 to support a socialist regime in Kabul, but they withdrew in 1989. By 2001, a group called the Taliban ("Islamic students") controlled 90% of the country. In 2001, following the refusal of the Taliban to hand over the al Qaida terrorist leader Osama bin Laden, an international force invaded Afghanistan. In 2002, a coalition government was set up under Hamid Karzai. In late 2011, President Karzai stated that international support would still be needed after all foreign troops withdrew in 2014.

Afghanistan is a poor country and nearly 70% of its people are farmers or nomadic herders. Natural gas is produced, together with some coal, copper, gold, precious stones, and salt.

AREA 251,772 sq mi [652,090 sq km]
POPULATION 29,835,000 **CAPITAL** Kabul
GOVERNMENT Islamic Republic **ETHNIC GROUPS** Pashtun (Pathan) 44%, Tajik 25%, Hazara 10%, Uzbek 8%, others 13%
LANGUAGES Pashtu, Dari/Persian (both official), Uzbek
RELIGIONS Islam (Sunni Muslim 84%, Shi'ite Muslim 15%), others 1%
CURRENCY Afghani = 100 puls

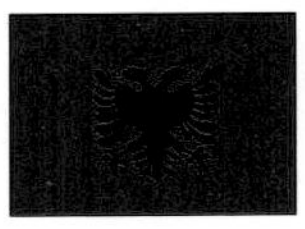
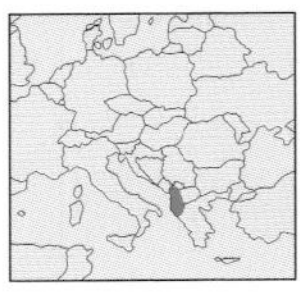

ALBANIA

GEOGRAPHY The Republic of Albania lies in the Balkan peninsula, facing the Adriatic Sea. About 70% of the land is mountainous, but most Albanians live in the west on the coastal lowlands.

The coastal areas of Albania experience a typical Mediterranean climate, with fairly dry, sunny summers and cool, moist winters. The mountains have a severe climate, with heavy winter snowfalls.

POLITICS & ECONOMY Albania is one of Europe's poorest nations. A former Communist country, Albania adopted a multiparty system in the early 1990s. The change proved difficult. But after elections in 1997, a socialist government committed to a market system took office. The transition to democracy has been challenging. Elections were held in 2005, and again in 2009 amid accusations of vote-rigging. Violent anti-government demonstrations occurred in January 2011.

In 2006, agriculture employed about 50% of the people. Since 1991, private ownership of land has been encouraged, replacing the former state farm and collective system. Albania has some minerals. Chromite, copper, and nickel are exported.

AREA 11,100 sq mi [28,748 sq km] **POPULATION** 2,995,000
CAPITAL Tirana **GOVERNMENT** Multiparty republic
ETHNIC GROUPS Albanian 95%, Greek 3%, Macedonian, Vlachs, Gypsy **LANGUAGES** Albanian (official) **RELIGIONS** Many people say they are non-believers; of the believers, 70% follow Islam and 30% follow Christianity (Orthodox 20%, Roman Catholic 10%)
CURRENCY Lek = 100 qindars

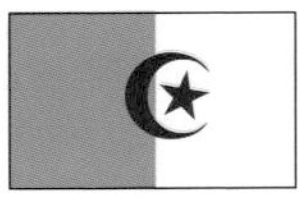
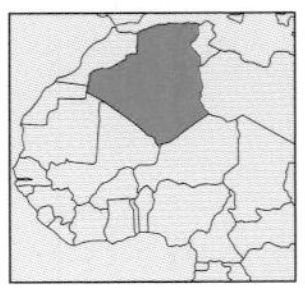

ALGERIA

GEOGRAPHY The People's Democratic Republic of Algeria is Africa's largest country. Most Algerians live in the north, on the fertile coastal plains and hill country bordering the Mediterranean Sea. Four-fifths of Algeria is in the Sahara, the world's largest desert. The coast has a Mediterranean climate but the arid Sahara is hot by day and cold at night.

POLITICS & ECONOMY France ruled Algeria from 1830 until 1962, when the socialist FLN (National Liberation Front) formed a one-party government. Following the recognition of opposition parties in 1989, a Muslim group, the FIS (Islamic Salvation Front), won an election in 1991. The FLN canceled the elections and civil conflict broke out. About 100,000 people were killed in the 1990s. Abdelaziz Bouteflika was elected president in 1999, 2004, and 2009. The scale of violence went down under his leadership. In 2011, protests broke out over food prices and unemployment, but the protests did not lead to the overthrow of the government as elsewhere in North Africa.

Algeria is a developing country, whose chief resources are oil and natural gas, which were discovered in the Sahara in 1956. The natural gas reserves are among the world's largest, and gas and oil account for more than 90% of the exports. Cement, iron and steel, textiles, and vehicles are manufactured. Barley, citrus fruits, dates, potatoes, and wheat are major crops.

AREA 919,590 sq mi [2,381,741 sq km]
POPULATION 34,995,000 **CAPITAL** Algiers
GOVERNMENT Socialist republic **ETHNIC GROUPS** Arab-Berber 99%
LANGUAGES Arabic and Berber (official), French **RELIGIONS** Sunni Muslim 99% **CURRENCY** Algerian dinar = 100 centimes

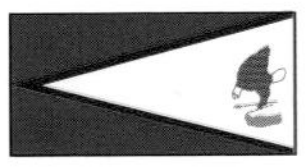
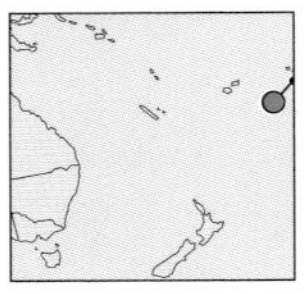

AMERICAN SAMOA

An "unincorporated territory" of the United States, American Samoa lies in the south-central Pacific Ocean.

AREA 77 sq mi [199 sq km]
POPULATION 67,000 **CAPITAL** Pago Pago

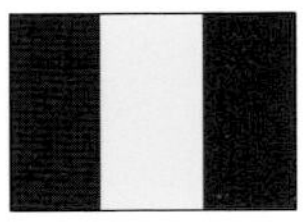
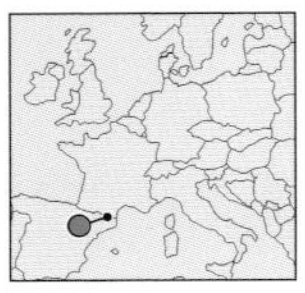

ANDORRA

A mini-state situated in the Pyrenees Mountains, Andorra is a coprincipality whose main activity is tourism. Most Andorrans live in the six valleys (the Valls) that drain into the River Valira.

AREA 181 sq mi [468 sq km]
POPULATION 85,000 **CAPITAL** Andorra La Vella

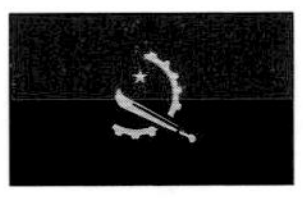
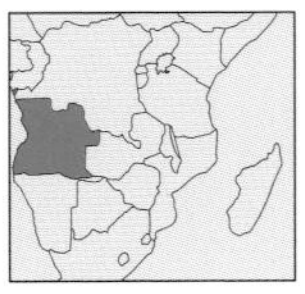

ANGOLA

GEOGRAPHY The Republic of Angola is a large country in southwestern Africa. Much of the country is part of the plateau that forms most of southern Africa, with a narrow coastal plain in the west.

Angola has a tropical climate, with temperatures of over 68°F [20°C] throughout the year, though the highest areas are cooler. The coast is dry, but the rainfall increases to the north and east.

POLITICS & ECONOMY Bantu-speaking people settled in Angola in the 13th century and later founded large kingdoms, such as the Kongo and Mbundu. Portugal controlled the coastal slave trade from the 17th century and extended its control inland in the 19th century. Angola became independent from Portugal in 1975, after which rival nationalist groups struggled for power. Despite a ceasefire in the mid-1990s, conflict finally ended only in 2002, when the rebel leader, Jonas Savimbi, was killed. Successful parliamentary elections were held in 2008.

Angola is a developing country, where 70% of the people are poor farmers. The main food crops are cassava and maize. Coffee is exported. Angola has important oil reserves and oil is exported. Angola also produces diamonds and has reserves of copper, manganese, and phosphates.

AREA 481,351 sq mi [1,246,700 sq km]
POPULATION 13,339,000 **CAPITAL** Luanda
GOVERNMENT Multiparty republic
ETHNIC GROUPS Ovimbundu 37%, Kimbundu 25%, Bakongo 13%, others 25% **LANGUAGES** Portuguese (official), many others
RELIGIONS Traditional beliefs 47%, Roman Catholic 38%, Protestant 15%
CURRENCY Kwanza = 100 lwei

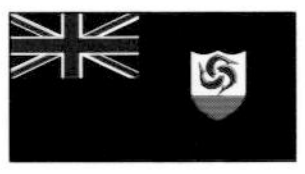
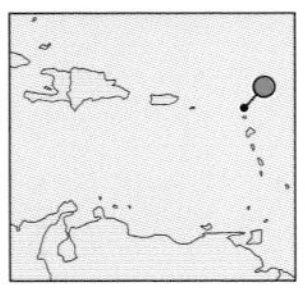

ANGUILLA

Formerly part of St Kitts and Nevis, Anguilla, the most northerly of the Leeward Islands, became a British dependency (now a British overseas territory) in 1980. The main source of revenue is now tourism, though lobster still accounts for half the island's exports.

AREA 37 sq mi [96 sq km]
POPULATION 15,000 **CAPITAL** The Valley

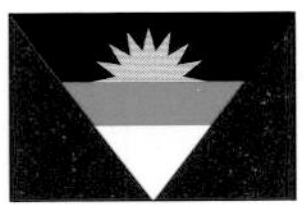
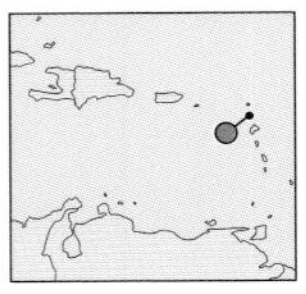

ANTIGUA & BARBUDA

A former British dependency in the Caribbean, Antigua and Barbuda became independent in 1981. Tourism is the main industry, though sugar is an important product.

AREA 171 sq mi [442 sq km]
POPULATION 88,000 **CAPITAL** St John's

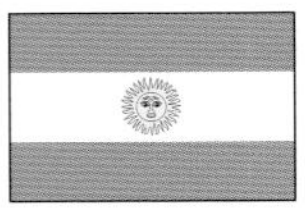
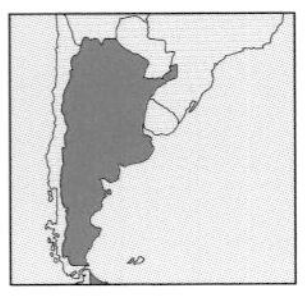

ARGENTINA

GEOGRAPHY The Argentine Republic is South America's second largest and the world's eighth largest country. The high Andes range in the west contains Mount Aconcagua, the highest peak in the Americas. In southern Argentina, the Andes Mountains overlook Patagonia, a plateau region. In east-central Argentina lies a fertile plain called the pampas.

The climate varies from subtropical in the north to temperate in the south. Rainfall is abundant in the northeast but lower to the west and south. Patagonia is largely desert.

POLITICS & ECONOMY The earliest people were American Indians, but 86% of the people are now of European ancestry. Spain took control in the 16th century and ruled until 1816. Argentina later suffered from instability and periods of military rule. In 1982, Argentina's military regime invaded the Falkland (Malvinas) Islands, but Britain regained the islands later that year. Argentina restored civilian rule in 1983. In 2007, Christina Fernández de Kirchner was elected president, succeeding her husband, Néstor Carlos Kirchner, who had served as president from 2003. She was the first woman to be Argentina's directly elected president. She was re-elected in 2011. The dispute with Britain resurfaced in 2012, the 30th anniversary of the Falklands war.

The World Bank classifies Argentina as an "upper-middle-income" developing country. About 92% of the people live in urban areas. Manufactures include food products, cars, electrical equipment, and textiles. Oil is the main resource and the chief farm products are beef, maize, and wheat. Exports include oil, meat, wheat, maize, vegetable oils, hides and skins, and wool. In 1991, Argentina, Brazil, Paraguay, and Uruguay set up an alliance, Mercosur, aimed at creating a common market.

AREA 1,073,512 sq mi [2,780,400 sq km]
POPULATION 41,770,000 **CAPITAL** Buenos Aires
GOVERNMENT Federal republic **ETHNIC GROUPS** European 97%, Mestizo, Amerindian **LANGUAGES** Spanish (official)
RELIGIONS Roman Catholic 92%, Protestant 2%, Jewish 2%, others **CURRENCY** Argentine peso = 10,000 australs

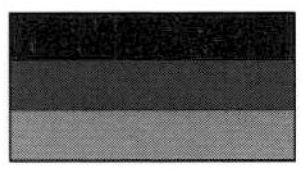
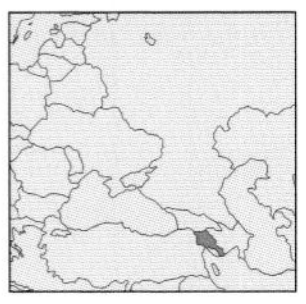

ARMENIA

GEOGRAPHY The Republic of Armenia is a landlocked country in southwestern Asia. Most of Armenia consists of a rugged plateau, crisscrossed by long faults (cracks). Movements along the faults cause earthquakes. The highest point is Mount Aragats, at 13,419 ft [4,090 m] above sea level.

The height of the land, which averages 4,920 ft [1,500 m] above sea level, gives rise to severe winters and cool summers. The highest peaks are snow-capped, but the total yearly rainfall is generally low.

POLITICS & ECONOMY In 1920, Armenia became a Communist republic and, in 1922, it became, with Azerbaijan and Georgia, part of the Transcaucasian Republic within the Soviet Union. But the three territories became separate Soviet Socialist Republics in 1936. After the breakup of the Soviet Union in 1991, Armenia became an independent republic. Fighting broke out over Nagorno-Karabakh, an area enclosed by Azerbaijan where most people are Armenians. In 1992, Armenia occupied the land between it and Nagorno-Karabakh. A ceasefire in 1994 left Armenia in control of about 20% of Azerbaijan's land area. In 2010, Armenia and Azerbaijan agreed to exchange prisoners taken during the Nagorno-Karabakh conflict.

Armenia's economy has suffered because of its former dependency on a centrally planned Soviet system.

AREA 11,506 sq mi [29,800 sq km]
POPULATION 2,968,000 **CAPITAL** Yerevan
GOVERNMENT Multiparty republic **ETHNIC GROUPS** Armenian 93%, Russian 2%, Azeri 1%, others (mostly Kurds) 4%
LANGUAGES Armenian (official) **RELIGIONS** Armenian Apostolic 94%
CURRENCY Dram = 100 couma

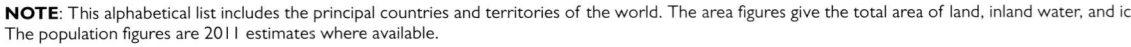

NOTE: This alphabetical list includes the principal countries and territories of the world. The area figures give the total area of land, inland water, and ice. The population figures are 2011 estimates where available.

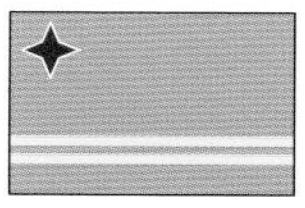
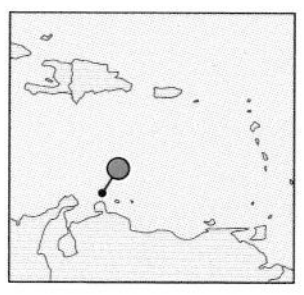

ARUBA

Formerly part of the Netherlands Antilles, Aruba (the most westerly of the Lesser Antilles) became a separate self-governing Dutch territory in 1986.

AREA 75 sq mi [193 sq km]
POPULATION 106,000 **CAPITAL** Oranjestad

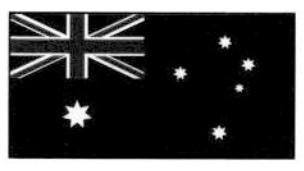
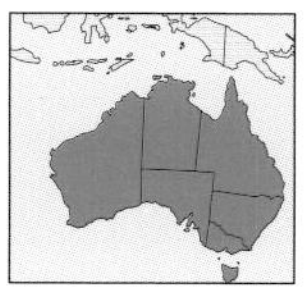

AUSTRALIA

GEOGRAPHY The Commonwealth of Australia, the world's sixth largest country, is also a continent. Australia is the flattest of the continents and the main highland area is in the east. Here the Great Dividing Range separates the eastern coastal plains from the Central Plains. This range extends from Cape York Peninsula to Victoria in the far south. The longest rivers, the Murray and Darling, drain the southeastern part of the Central Plains. The Western Plateau makes up two-thirds of Australia. A few mountain ranges break the monotony of the generally flat landscape. Only 10% of Australia, notably the tropical north, the northeast coast, and the southeast, has an average annual rainfall of more than 39 inches [1,000 mm]. But extreme weather events, including a prolonged drought in the Murray–Darling basin in the early 21st century and severe flooding in Queensland in 2010–12, cause periodic problems.

POLITICS & ECONOMY The Aboriginal people of Australia entered the continent from Southeast Asia more than 50,000 years ago. The first European explorers were Dutch in the 17th century, but they did not settle. In 1770, the British Captain Cook explored the east coast and, in 1788, the first British settlement was established for convicts on the site of what is now Sydney. Australia has strong ties with the British Isles. But in the last 50 years, people from other parts of Europe and, most recently, from Asia have settled in Australia. Ties with Britain were also weakened by Britain's membership of the European Union. Many Australians believe that they should become more involved with the nations of eastern Asia and the Americas rather than with Europe. In 1999, Australians voted to retain the country's status as a monarchy. In 2003, Australian troops joined in the invasion of Iraq. The Labor Party won the 2007 elections. The prime minister, Kevin Rudd, was succeeded in 2010 by Julia Gillard.

Australia is a prosperous country. Crops can be grown on only 6% of the land, but dry pasture covers another 58%. Yet the country remains a major producer and exporter of farm products, particularly cattle, wheat, and wool. Grapes grown for wine-making are also important. The country is a major producer of minerals, including bauxite, coal, copper, diamonds, gold, iron ore, manganese, nickel, silver, tin, tungsten, and zinc. Australia also produces oil and natural gas. Metals, minerals, and farm products account for the bulk of exports. Australia's imports are mostly manufactured goods, especially machinery, though industry is now important, especially the manufacture of consumer goods.

AREA 2,988,885 sq mi [7,741,220 sq km] **POPULATION** 21,767,000
CAPITAL Canberra **GOVERNMENT** Federal constitutional monarchy
ETHNIC GROUPS Caucasian 92%, Asian 7%, Aboriginal 1%
LANGUAGES English (official) **RELIGIONS** Roman Catholic 26%, Anglican 26%, other Christian 24%, non-Christian 24%
CURRENCY Australian dollar = 100 cents

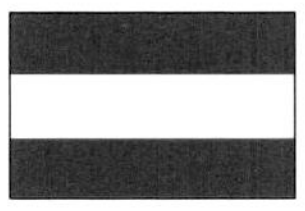
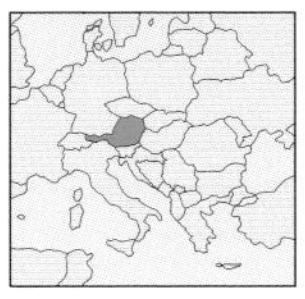

AUSTRIA

GEOGRAPHY Austria is a landlocked country in Europe. Northern Austria contains the valley of the River Danube, which flows from Germany to the Black Sea, and the Vienna basin. Southern Austria contains ranges of the Alps, their highest point at Grossglockner, 12,457 ft [3,797 m] above sea level.

The climate is temperate in the west and more continental in the east. Winters are cold and snowy. Summers are warm and dry in the east.

POLITICS & ECONOMY Formerly part of the monarchy of Austria–Hungary, which collapsed in 1918, Austria was annexed by Germany in 1938. After World War II, the Allies partitioned and occupied the country. In 1955, Austria became a neutral federal republic. It joined the European Union in 1995. In 2000, a coalition government was formed by the right-wing People's Party and the extreme right-wing Freedom Party, which lost much of its support in 2002. In 2008, the Social Democratic/People's Party coalition (formed in 2007) collapsed, but the same parties formed another government after elections, in which far-right parties won nearly 29% of the vote.

Austria has a highly developed economy, with plenty of hydroelectric power and some oil, gas, and coal reserves. The country's leading economic activity is manufacturing metals and metal products. Crops are grown on 18% of the land, and another 24% is pasture. Dairy and livestock farming are the leading activities. Major crops include barley, potatoes, rye, sugar beet, and wheat. Tourism is a major activity in this scenic country.

AREA 32,378 sq mi [83,859 sq km] **POPULATION** 8,217,000
CAPITAL Vienna **GOVERNMENT** Federal republic
ETHNIC GROUPS Austrian 90%, Croatian, Slovene, others
LANGUAGES German (official) **RELIGIONS** Roman Catholic 78%, Protestant 5%, Islam and others 17% **CURRENCY** Euro = 100 cents

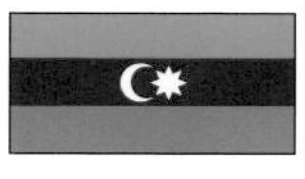
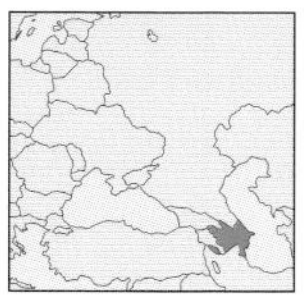

AZERBAIJAN

GEOGRAPHY The Azerbaijani Republic is a country in the southwest of Asia, facing the Caspian Sea to the east. It includes an area called the Naxçivan Autonomous Republic, which is completely cut off from the rest of Azerbaijan by Armenian territory. The Caucasus Mountains border Russia in the north.

Azerbaijan has hot summers and cool winters. The plains are fairly dry, but the mountains are rainy.

POLITICS & ECONOMY After the Russian Revolution of 1917, attempts were made to form a Transcaucasian Federation made up of Armenia, Azerbaijan, and Georgia. When this failed, Azerbaijanis set up an independent state. But Russian forces occupied the area in 1920. In 1922, the Communists set up a Transcaucasian Republic consisting of Armenia, Azerbaijan, and Georgia under Russian control. In 1936, the three areas became separate Soviet Socialist Republics within the Soviet Union. In 1991, following the breakup of the Soviet Union, Azerbaijan became an independent nation. After independence, Azerbaijan clashed with Armenia over the enclave of Nagorno-Karabakh, a region in Azerbaijan where the majority of the people are Armenian. A ceasefire in 1994 left Armenia in control of 20% of Azerbaijan's area, including Nagorno-Karabakh.

Azerbaijan has huge oil reserves. Oil extraction and manufacturing, including oil refining and the production of chemicals, machinery, and textiles are important.

AREA 33,436 sq mi [86,600 sq km] **POPULATION** 8,372,000
CAPITAL Baku **GOVERNMENT** Federal multiparty republic
ETHNIC GROUPS Azeri 90%, Dagestani 3%, Russian, Armenian, others **LANGUAGES** Azerbaijani (official), Russian, Armenian
RELIGIONS Islam 93%, Russian Orthodox 2%, Armenian Orthodox 2%
CURRENCY Azerbaijani manat = 100 gopik

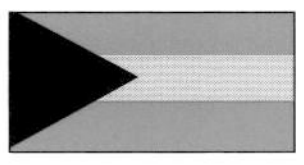
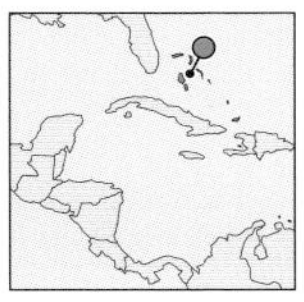

BAHAMAS

A coral-limestone archipelago off the coast of Florida, the Bahamas became independent from Britain in 1973, and has since developed strong ties with the United States. Tourism and banking are major activities.

AREA 5,358 sq mi [13,878 sq km]
POPULATION 313,000 **CAPITAL** Nassau

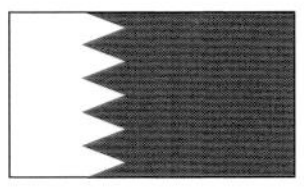
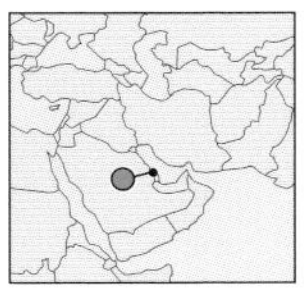

BAHRAIN

The Kingdom of Bahrain, an island nation in the Persian Gulf, became independent from the UK in 1971. Oil accounts for 80% of its exports.

In early 2011, demonstrators called for reform. Violence occurred, a state of emergency was declared, and troops from other Gulf states arrived to help control the situation. Demonstrations continued in 2012.

AREA 268 sq mi [694 sq km]
POPULATION 1,215,000 **CAPITAL** Manama

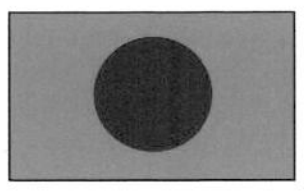
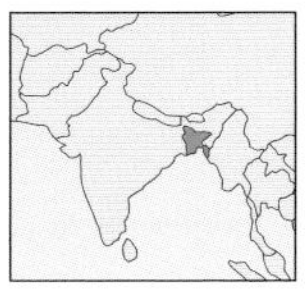

BANGLADESH

GEOGRAPHY The People's Republic of Bangladesh is one of the world's most densely populated countries. Apart from hilly regions in the far northeast and southeast, most of the land is flat and covered by fertile alluvium spread over the land by the Ganges, Brahmaputra, and Meghna rivers. These rivers overflow when they are swollen by the annual monsoon rains. Floods also occur along the coast, 357 mi [575 km] long, when cyclones (hurricanes) drive seawater inland. Bangladesh has a tropical monsoon climate. Dry northerly winds blow in winter, but moist southerly winds bring heavy rain in summer.

POLITICS & ECONOMY In 1947, British India was partitioned between the mainly Hindu India and the Muslim Pakistan. Pakistan consisted of two parts, West and East Pakistan, which were separated by about 1,000 mi [1,600 km] of Indian territory. Differences developed between West and East Pakistan. In 1971, the East Pakistanis rebeled. After a nine-month civil war, they declared East Pakistan to be a new nation named Bangladesh. A famine in 1974 and a coup in 1975 were followed by political upheavals. The army seized power in 2007, but elections in 2008 returned Sheikh Hasina's Awami League to power.

Bangladesh is one of the world's poorest countries. Its economy depends mainly on agriculture, which employs about 44% of the population. Bangladesh is the world's fourth largest producer of rice.

AREA 55,598 sq mi [143,998 sq km]
POPULATION 158,571,000 **CAPITAL** Dhaka
GOVERNMENT Multiparty republic **ETHNIC GROUPS** Bengali 98%, tribal groups **LANGUAGES** Bengali (official), English
RELIGIONS Islam 83%, Hinduism 16% **CURRENCY** Taka = 100 paisas

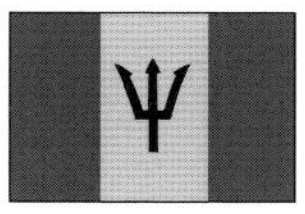
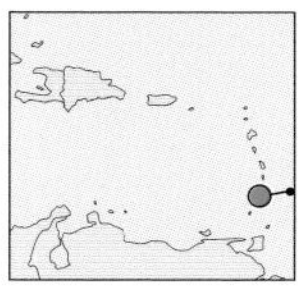

BARBADOS

The most easterly Caribbean country, Barbados became independent from the UK in 1960. A densely populated island, Barbados is prosperous by comparison with most Caribbean countries.

AREA 166 sq mi [430 sq km]
POPULATION 287,000 **CAPITAL** Bridgetown

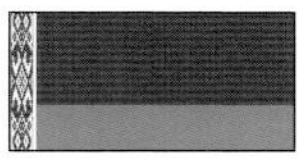
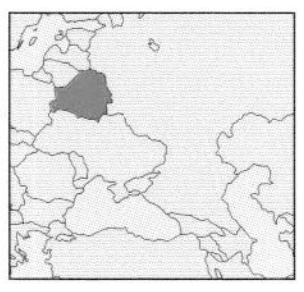

BELARUS

GEOGRAPHY The Republic of Belarus is a landlocked country in Eastern Europe. The land is low-lying and mostly flat. In the south, much of the land is marshy and this area contains Europe's largest marsh and peat bog, the Pripet Marshes. The climate is affected by both the moderating influence of the Baltic Sea and continental conditions to the east. The winters are cold and the summers warm.

POLITICS & ECONOMY In 1918, Belarus (White Russia) became an independent republic, but Russia invaded the country and, in 1919, a Communist state was set up. In 1922, Belarus became a founder republic of the Soviet Union. In 1991, Belarus again became an independent republic, and though Belarus continued to support reunification with Russia, any surrender of sovereignty was not expected. President Alexander Lukashenko, who was elected in flawed elections in 1994, 2001, 2006, and 2010, when he won nearly 80% of the vote amid opposition protests, has been criticized for his autocratic rule, his poor record on human rights, and his disregard for freedom of speech.

According to the World Bank, Belarus has an "upper-middle-income" economy. Most economic activities remain under government control and, from the 1990s, the economy has declined. Mining and manufacturing are the most valuable activities.

AREA 80,154 sq mi [207,600 sq km]
POPULATION 9,578,000 **CAPITAL** Minsk
GOVERNMENT Multiparty republic **ETHNIC GROUPS** Belarusian 81%, Russian 11%, Polish, Ukrainian, others **LANGUAGES** Belarusian, Russian (both official) **RELIGIONS** Eastern Orthodox 80%, others 20% **CURRENCY** Belarusian rouble = 100 kopecks

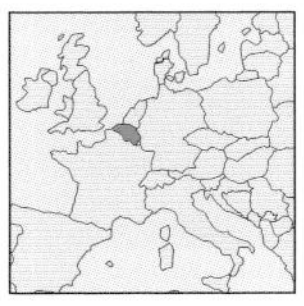

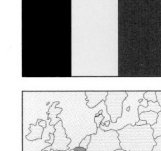

BELGIUM

GEOGRAPHY The Kingdom of Belgium is a densely populated country in western Europe. Behind the coastline on the North Sea, which is 39 mi [63 km] long, lie its coastal plains. Central Belgium consists of low plateaux and the only highland region is the Ardennes in the southeast.

Belgium has a cool, temperate climate. Moist winds from the Atlantic Ocean bring fairly heavy rain, especially in the Ardennes. In January and February much snow falls on the Ardennes.

POLITICS & ECONOMY In 1815, Belgium and the Netherlands united as the "low countries," but Belgium became independent in 1830. Belgium's economy was weakened by the two World

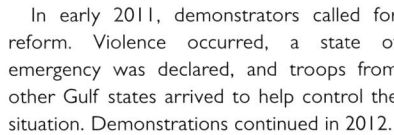

Wars, but, from 1945, the country recovered quickly, first through collaboration with the Netherlands and Luxembourg, which formed a customs union called Benelux, and later through its membership of the European Union.

A central political problem in Belgium has been the tension between the Dutch-speaking Flemings and the French-speaking Walloons. In the 1970s, the government divided the country into three economic regions: Dutch-speaking Flanders, French-speaking Wallonia, and bilingual Brussels. In 1993, Belgium adopted a federal constitution, giving each region its own parliament. In 2010, a coalition government set up in 2009 collapsed because of deep differences between the Flemish- and French-speaking parties. A prime minister was appointed in December 2011, following a world record of 541 days when Belgium had no government.

Belgium is a major trading nation, though most materials used in manufacturing are imported. Major products include chemicals, processed food, and steel. The textile industry has existed since medieval times in Flanders. Agriculture employs less than 2% of the people, but farmers produce most of the food the country needs. Barley and wheat are major crops, followed by flax, hops, potatoes, and sugar beet. But the most valuable agricultural activities are dairy farming and livestock rearing.

AREA 11,787 sq mi [30,528 sq km]
POPULATION 10,431,000
CAPITAL Brussels
GOVERNMENT Federal constitutional monarchy
ETHNIC GROUPS Belgian 89% (Fleming 58%, Walloon 31%), others 11% **LANGUAGES** Dutch, French, German (all official)
RELIGIONS Roman Catholic 75%, others 25%
CURRENCY Euro = 100 cents

BELIZE

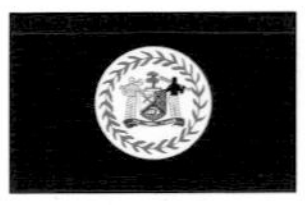

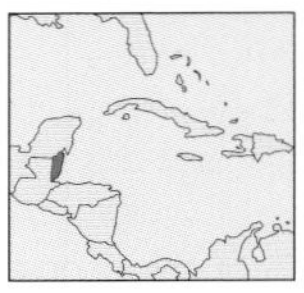

GEOGRAPHY Behind the southern coastal plain, the land rises to the Maya Mountains, which reach 3,674 ft [1,120 m] at Victoria Peak. The north is mostly low-lying and swampy. Temperatures are high all year round, while the average annual rainfall ranges from 51 inches [1,300 mm] in the north to over 150 inches [3,800 mm] in the south. Hurricanes caused much damage in the 1990s and 2000s, but tourist numbers have continued to increase.

POLITICS & ECONOMY From 1862, Belize (then called British Honduras) was a British colony. Full independence was achieved in 1981, but Guatemala, which had claimed the area since the early 19th century, opposed Belize's independence and British troops remained to prevent a possible invasion. Relations improved in the early 1990s, when Guatemala agreed to recognize Belize's independence and British troops withdrew. In 2011, the United States added Belize and El Salvador to its list of illegal drug producers or major transit routes into the US.

The World Bank classifies Belize as a "lower-middle-income" developing country. Its economy is based on agriculture and sugarcane is the chief commercial crop and export. Other crops include bananas, beans, citrus fruits, maize, and rice. Forestry, fishing, and tourism are other important activities.

AREA 8,867 sq mi [22,966 sq km]
POPULATION 321,000 **CAPITAL** Belmopan
GOVERNMENT Constitutional monarchy **ETHNIC GROUPS** Mestizo 49%, Creole 25%, Mayan Indian 11%, Garifuna 6%, others 9%
LANGUAGES English (official), Spanish, Creole
RELIGIONS Roman Catholic 50%, Protestant 27%, others
CURRENCY Belizean dollar = 100 cents

BENIN

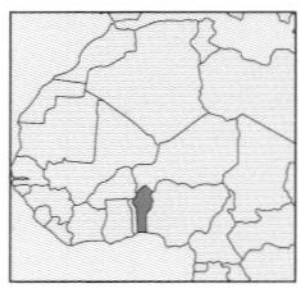

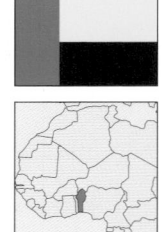

GEOGRAPHY The Republic of Benin is one of Africa's smallest countries. It extends north–south for about 390 mi [620 km]. Lagoons line the short coastline, and the country has no natural harbors.

Benin has a hot, wet climate. The average annual temperature on the coast is about 77°F [25°C], and the average rainfall is about 52 inches [1,330 mm]. The inland plains are wetter than the coast.

POLITICS & ECONOMY After slavery was ended in the 19th century, the French began to gain influence in the area. Benin became self-governing in 1958 and fully independent in 1960. After much instability and many changes of government, a military group took over in 1972. The country, renamed Benin in 1975, became a one-party socialist state. Socialism was abandoned in 1989. Former coup leader Mathieu Kérékou served as president until 2006, when a former banker, Yayi Boni, was elected president. He was re-elected in 2011.

Benin is a poor developing country. About half of the people live by farming, mainly at subsistence level. Exports include cotton, petroleum, and palm products. Cocoa, coffee, groundnuts (peanuts), tobacco, and shea nuts are also grown for export.

AREA 43,483 sq mi [112,622 sq km]
POPULATION 9,325,000 **CAPITAL** Porto-Novo
GOVERNMENT Multiparty republic **ETHNIC GROUPS** Fon, Adja, Bariba, Yoruba, Fulani **LANGUAGES** French (official), Fon, Adja, Yoruba
RELIGIONS Traditional beliefs 50%, Christianity 30%, Islam 20%
CURRENCY CFA franc = 100 centimes

BERMUDA

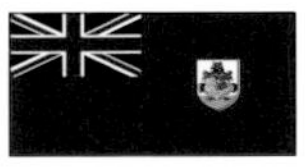

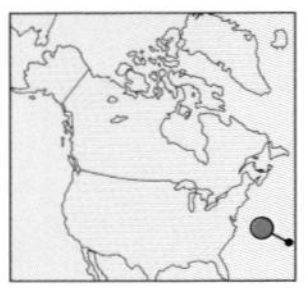

A group of about 150 small islands situated 570 mi [920 km] east of the USA. Bermuda remains Britain's oldest overseas territory, but it has a long tradition of self-government.

AREA 21 sq mi [53 sq km]
POPULATION 70,000 **CAPITAL** Hamilton

BHUTAN

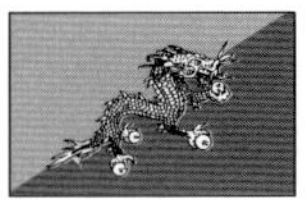

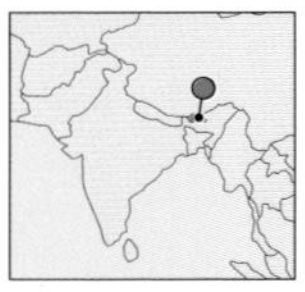

GEOGRAPHY A mountainous, isolated Himalayan country located between India and Tibet. The climate is similar to that of Nepal, being dependent on altitude and affected by monsoonal winds.

POLITICS & ECONOMY The monarch of Bhutan is head of both state and government, and this predominantly Buddhist country remains, even in the Asian context, both conservative and poor. In 2008, Bhutan held its first ever democratic elections, ending over a century of absolute royal rule and turning Bhutan into a constitutional monarchy.

AREA 18,147 sq mi [47,000 sq km] **POPULATION** 708,000
CAPITAL Thimphu **GOVERNMENT** Constitutional monarchy
ETHNIC GROUPS Bhutanese 50%, Nepalese 35%
LANGUAGES Dzongkha (official) **RELIGIONS** Buddhism 75%, Hinduism 25% **CURRENCY** Ngultrum = 100 chetrum

BOLIVIA

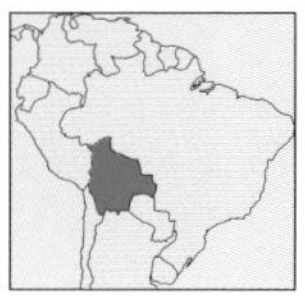

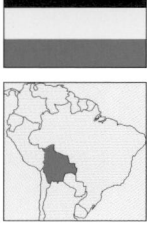

GEOGRAPHY The Plurinational State of Bolivia, as the country is officially called, is a landlocked South American country which straddles the Andes Mountains. The highest point is 21,391 ft [6,250 m] at Nevado Sajaama in the west. About 40% of Bolivians live on a high plateau called the Altiplano in the Andes. The sparsely populated east is a vast lowland plain.

The Bolivian climate is greatly affected by altitude, with the Andean peaks permanently snow-covered and the eastern plains remaining hot and humid.

POLITICS & ECONOMY American Indians have lived in Bolivia for at least 10,000 years. The main groups today are the Aymara and Quechua people.

In the last 50 years, Bolivia, an independent country since 1825, has been ruled by a succession of civilian and military governments, which violated human rights. Democracy was restored in 1982. Economic problems led a widening of the gap between rich and poor and, in 2005, Evo Morales, a left-wing Aymara farmer, was elected president. His policies of nationalization and redistributing wealth to peasants aroused opposition especially in the richer east. In 2009, Morales was re-elected president, but his popularity declined in 2010–11 because of food shortages and price rises.

Bolivia is one of South America's poorest countries. Resources include natural gas, silver, tin, and zinc, but the main activity is agriculture. Soybeans and soybean products are exported.

AREA 424,162 sq mi [1,098,581 sq km]
POPULATION 10,119,000 **CAPITAL** La Paz (seat of government); Sucre (legal capital/seat of judiciary)
GOVERNMENT Multiparty republic **ETHNIC GROUPS** Mestizo 30%, Quechua 30%, Aymara 25%, White 15% **LANGUAGES** Spanish, Aymara, Quechua (all official) **RELIGIONS** Roman Catholic 95%
CURRENCY Boliviano = 100 centavos

BOSNIA-HERZEGOVINA

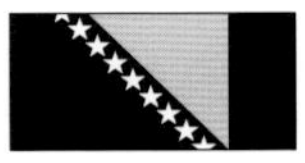

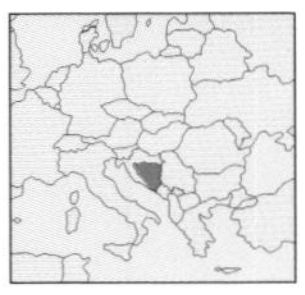

GEOGRAPHY The Republic of Bosnia-Herzegovina is one of the five republics to emerge from the former Federal People's Republic of Yugoslavia. Much of the country is mountainous or hilly, with an arid limestone plateau in the southwest. The River Sava, which forms most of the northern border with Croatia, is a tributary of the River Danube. Because of the country's odd shape, the coastline is limited to a short stretch of 13 mi [20 km] on the Adriatic coast.

A Mediterranean climate, with dry, sunny summers and moist, mild winters, prevails only near the coast. Inland, the weather is more severe, with hot, dry summers and bitterly cold, snowy winters.

POLITICS & ECONOMY In 1918, Bosnia-Herzegovina became part of the Kingdom of the Serbs, Croats, and Slovenes, which was renamed Yugoslavia in 1929. Germany occupied the area during World War II (1939–45). From 1945, Communist governments ruled Yugoslavia as a federation containing six republics, one of which was Bosnia-Herzegovina. In the 1980s, the country faced problems as Communist policies proved unsuccessful.

In 1990, free elections were held in Bosnia-Herzegovina and the non-Communists won a majority. A Muslim, Alija Izetbegovic, was elected president. In 1991, Croatia and Slovenia, other parts of the former Yugoslavia, declared themselves independent. In 1992, Bosnia-Herzegovina held a vote on independence. Most Bosnian Serbs boycotted the vote, while the Muslims and Bosnian Croats voted in favor. Many Bosnian Serbs, opposed to independence, started a war against the non-Serbs. They soon occupied more than two-thirds of the land. The Bosnian Serbs were accused of "ethnic cleansing" – that is, the killing or expulsion of other ethnic groups from Serb-occupied areas. The war was later extended when Croat forces seized other parts of the country.

In 1995, the country retained its boundaries, but it was divided into two self-governing provinces – one Bosnian Serb and the other Muslim Croat under a central government. Stability was restored with the help of NATO, but the country remained divided along ethnic lines, and in December 2011, Muslim Croat and Serb leaders agreed on the formation of a central government after 14 months of political crisis.

The economy of Bosnia-Herzegovina, the least developed of the six republics of the former Yugoslavia apart from Macedonia, was shattered by the war in the early 1990s. Before the war, manufactures were the main exports, including electrical, machinery and transport equipment, and textiles. Farm products include fruits, maize, tobacco, vegetables, and wheat, but food has to be imported.

AREA 19,767 sq mi [51,197 sq km]
POPULATION 4,622,000 **CAPITAL** Sarajevo
GOVERNMENT Federal republic **ETHNIC GROUPS** Bosnian 48%, Serb 37%, Croat 14% **LANGUAGES** Bosnian, Serbian, Croatian
RELIGIONS Islam 40%, Serbian Orthodox 31%, Roman Catholic 15%, others 14% **CURRENCY** Convertible marka = 100 convertible pfenniga

BOTSWANA

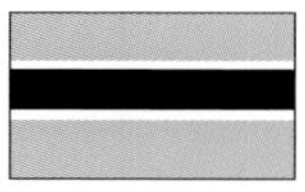

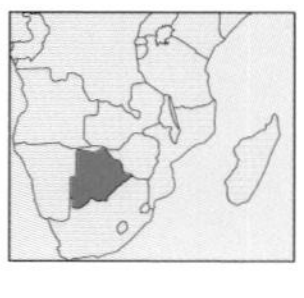

GEOGRAPHY The Republic of Botswana is a landlocked country in southern Africa. The Kalahari, a semidesert area covered mostly by grasses and thorn scrub, covers much of the country. Most of the south has no permanent streams. But large depressions in the north are inland drainage basins. In one of them, the Okavango River, which rises in Angola, forms a large, swampy delta.

Temperatures are high in the summer months (October to April), but the winter months are much cooler. In winter, night-time temperatures sometimes drop below freezing point. The average annual rainfall ranges from over 16 inches [400 mm] in the east to less than 8 inches [200 mm] in the southwest.

POLITICS & ECONOMY The earliest inhabitants of the region were the San, who are also called Bushmen. They had a nomadic way of life, hunting wild animals and collecting wild plant foods.

Britain ruled the area as the Bechuanaland Protectorate between 1885 and 1966. When the country became independent, it was renamed Botswana. Since then, the country has been a stable, multiparty democracy. However, a major setback occurred in the 21st century, when health officials announced that around 25% of the people were infected with HIV/AIDS.

In 1966, Botswana was extremely poor, depending on meat and live cattle for its exports. But the discovery of minerals, including coal, cobalt, copper, diamonds, and nickel, has boosted the economy. About 25% of the people now depend on agriculture, raising cattle, and growing crops. Industries include the processing of farm products.

AREA 224,606 sq mi [581,730 sq km]
POPULATION 2,065,000 **CAPITAL** Gaborone
GOVERNMENT Multiparty republic **ETHNIC GROUPS** Tswana (or Setswana) 79%, Kalanga 11%, Basarwa 3%, others
LANGUAGES English (official), Setswana **RELIGIONS** Traditional beliefs 85%, Christianity 15% **CURRENCY** Pula = 100 thebe

BRAZIL

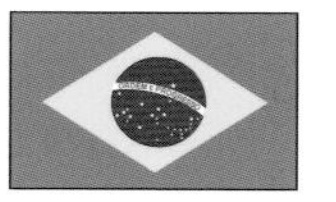

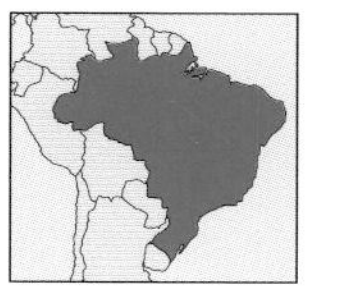

GEOGRAPHY The Federative Republic of Brazil is the world's fifth largest country. It contains three main regions. The Amazon basin in the north covers more than half of Brazil. The Amazon, the world's second longest river, has a far greater volume than any other river. The second region, the northeast, consists of a coastal plain and the *sertão*, which is the name for the inland plateaux and hill country. The main river in this region is the São Francisco.

The third region is made up of the plateaux in the southeast. This region, which covers about a quarter of the country, is the most developed and densely populated part of Brazil. Its main river is the Paraná, which flows south through Argentina.

Manaus has high temperatures all through the year. Rainfall is heavy, though the period from June to September is drier than the rest of the year. The capital, Brasília, and the city Rio de Janeiro also have tropical climates, with much more marked dry seasons than Manaus. The far south has a temperate climate. The northeastern interior is the driest region, with an average annual rainfall of only 10 inches [250 mm] in places. Rainfall is also unreliable and severe droughts are common in this region.

POLITICS & ECONOMY The Portuguese explorer Pedro Alvarez Cabral claimed Brazil for Portugal in 1500. With Spain occupied in western South America, the Portuguese began to develop their colony, which was more than 90 times as big as Portugal. To do this, they enslaved many local Amerindian people and introduced about 4 million African slaves. Brazil declared itself an independent empire in 1822 and a republic in 1889. From the 1930s, Brazil faced periods of military rule and widespread corruption. Civilian rule was restored in 1985. Brazil adopted a new constitution in 1988.

Brazil is described as a "Rapidly Industrializing Economy," and in 2012 the government announced that it was the world's sixth largest economy. But many people, including poor farmers and residents of the *favelas* (city slums), do not share in the country's fast economic growth. Poverty led to the election of President Luíz Inácio Lula da Silva (generally called "Lula") in 2002. His economic policies proved popular. In 2010, he was succeeded by Dilma Roussef, also of Lula's Workers Party. She became Brazil's first female president.

Industry is the most important economic sector. Brazil is among the world's top producers of bauxite, chrome, diamonds, gold, iron ore, manganese, and tin. It is also a major manufacturing country. Its products include aircraft, cars, chemicals, processed food, iron and steel, paper, and textiles. The discovery of a major offshore oilfield was announced in 2007. Brazil is a major farming nation and agriculture employs 17% of the people. Coffee is a leading export. Other products include bananas, citrus fruits, cocoa, maize, rice, soybeans, and sugarcane. Brazil is also South America's top producer of eggs, meat, and milk.

Forestry is a major industry, though many people fear that the destruction of the rain forests, which may accelerate global warming, is an impending disaster for the entire world.

AREA 3,287,338 sq mi [8,514,215 sq km]
POPULATION 203,430,000 **CAPITAL** Brasília
GOVERNMENT Federal republic
ETHNIC GROUPS White 48%, Mixed 43%, Black 8%, others 1%
LANGUAGES Portuguese (official)
RELIGIONS Roman Catholic 80%
CURRENCY Real = 100 centavos

BRUNEI

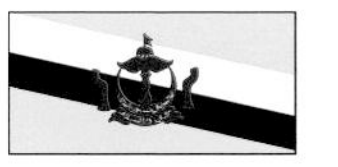

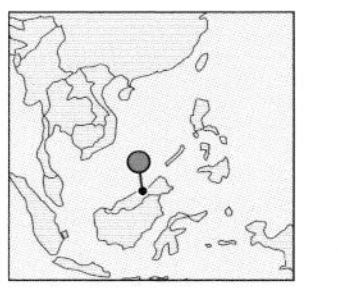

The Islamic Sultanate of Brunei, a British protectorate until 1984, lies on the north coast of Borneo. The climate is tropical and rain forests cover large areas. Brunei is a prosperous country because of its oil and natural gas production, and the Sultan is said to be among the world's richest men.

AREA 2,226 sq mi [5,765 sq km]
POPULATION 395,000 **CAPITAL** Bandar Seri Begawan

BULGARIA

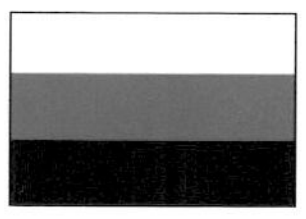

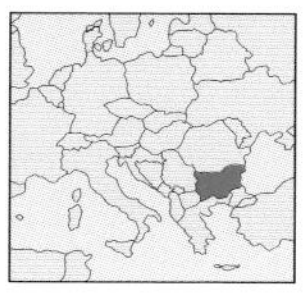

GEOGRAPHY The Republic of Bulgaria is a country in the Balkan peninsula, facing the Black Sea in the east. The heart of Bulgaria is mountainous. The main ranges are the Balkan Mountains in the center and the Rhodope (or Rhodopi) Mountains in the south.

Summers are hot and winters are cold, though seldom severe. The rainfall is moderate.

POLITICS & ECONOMY Ottoman Turks ruled Bulgaria from 1396 and ethnic Turks still form a sizable minority in the country. In 1879, Bulgaria became a monarchy, and in 1908 it became fully independent. Bulgaria was an ally of Germany in World War I (1914–18) and again in World War II (1939–45). In 1944, Soviet troops invaded Bulgaria and, after the war, the monarchy was abolished and the country became a Communist ally of the Soviet Union. Reforms in the Soviet Union in the late 1980s led Bulgaria's government to introduce a multi-party system in 1990. A non-Communist government was elected in 1991, in the first free elections in 44 years. Throughout the 1990s, Bulgaria faced many problems and it sought to become aligned to the West. Bulgaria became a member of NATO in 2004 and a member of the European Union in 2007. In 2009, the center-right GERB party, led by Boiko Borisov, who promised to tackle corruption and the economic crisis, won the parliamentary elections.

Bulgaria has a "lower-middle economy." It has some mineral deposits, including brown coal, manganese, and iron ore. But manufacturing is the leading activity, though, in the early 1990s, much of its industrial plant was out of date. Leading products include chemicals, processed foods, metal products, machinery, and textiles. Manufactures are the leading exports.

AREA 42,823 sq mi [110,912 sq km] **POPULATION** 7,149,000
CAPITAL Sofia **GOVERNMENT** Multiparty republic
ETHNIC GROUPS Bulgarian 84%, Turkish 9%, Gypsy 5%, Macedonian, Armenian, others **LANGUAGES** Bulgarian (official), Turkish **RELIGIONS** Bulgarian Orthodox 83%, Islam 12%, Roman Catholic 2%, others **CURRENCY** Lev = 100 stotinki

BURKINA FASO

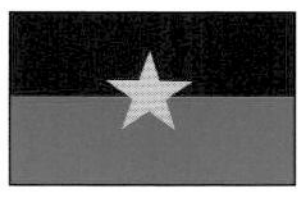

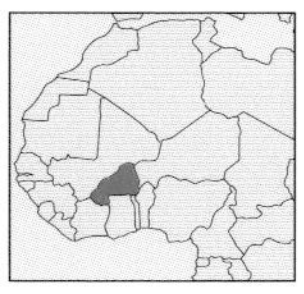

GEOGRAPHY The Democratic People's Republic of Burkina Faso is a landlocked country, a little larger than the United Kingdom, in West Africa. But Burkina Faso has only a quarter of the population of the UK. The country consists of a plateau, between about 650 ft and 2,300 ft [300 m to 700 m] above sea level. The plateau is cut by several rivers.

The capital city, Ouagadougou, in central Burkina Faso, has high temperatures throughout the year. Most of the rain falls between May and September, but the rainfall is erratic and droughts are common.

POLITICS & ECONOMY The people of Burkina Faso are divided into two main groups. The Voltaic group includes the Mossi, who form the largest single group, and the Bobo. The French conquered the Mossi capital of Ouagadougou in 1897 and they made the area a protectorate. In 1919, the area became a French colony called Upper Volta. After independence in 1960, Upper Volta became a one-party state. But it was unstable – military groups seized power several times and political killings took place. In 1984, the country's name was changed to Burkina Faso. In 1991, 1998, 2005, and 2010, the former coup leader, Captain Blaise Compaoré, was elected president.

Burkina Faso is one of the world's 20 poorest countries and has become very dependent on foreign aid. Most of Burkina Faso is dry with thin soils. The country's main food crops are beans, maize, millet, rice, and sorghum. Cotton, groundnuts (peanuts), and shea nuts, whose seeds produce a fat used to make cooking oil and soap, are grown for sale abroad. Livestock are also an important export.

The country has few resources and manufacturing is on a small scale. There are some deposits of manganese, zinc, lead, and nickel in the north of the country, but there is not yet a good enough transport system there. Many young men seek jobs abroad in Ghana and Ivory Coast. The money they send home to their families is important to the country's economy.

AREA 105,791 sq mi [274,000 sq km]
POPULATION 16,751,000 **CAPITAL** Ouagadougou
GOVERNMENT Multiparty republic **ETHNIC GROUPS** Mossi 40%, Gurunsi, Senufo, Lobi, Bobo, Mande, Fulani **LANGUAGES** French (official), Mossi, Fulani **RELIGIONS** Islam 50%, traditional beliefs 40%, Christianity 10% **CURRENCY** CFA franc = 100 centimes

BURMA (MYANMAR)

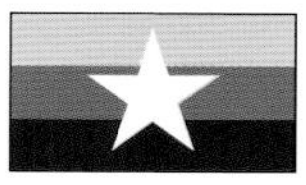

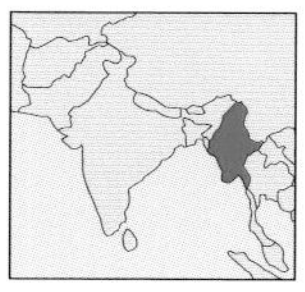

GEOGRAPHY The Union of Burma has been officially known as the Union of Myanmar since 1989. However, it is more usually referred to as Burma. Mountains border the country in the east and west, with the highest mountains in the north. Burma's highest mountain is Hkakabo Razi, which is 19,294 ft [5,881 m] high. Between these ranges is central Burma, which contains the fertile valleys of the Irrawaddy and Sittang rivers. The Irrawaddy delta is a leading rice-growing area.

Burma has a tropical monsoon climate with three seasons. The rainy season runs from late May to mid-October. A cool, dry season follows, between late October and the middle part of February. The hot season lasts from late February to mid-May. In May 2008, a typhoon devastated the south, including the Irrawaddy delta, killing more than 80,000 people.

POLITICS & ECONOMY Many groups settled in Burma in ancient times. Some, called the hill peoples, live in remote mountain areas where they have retained their own cultures. The ancestors of the country's main ethnic group today, the Burmese, arrived in the 9th century AD. Britain conquered Burma in the 19th century and made it a province of British India. But, in 1937, the British granted Burma limited self-government. Japan conquered Burma in 1942, but the Japanese were driven out in 1945. Burma became a fully independent country in 1948.

Revolts by Communists and various hill people led to instability in the 1950s. In 1962, Burma became a military dictatorship and, in 1974, a one-party state. Attempts to control minority liberation movements and the opium trade led to repressive rule. The National League for Democracy led by Aung San Suu Kyi won the elections in 1990, but the military continued their repressive rule.

In 2010, the military released Aung San Suu Kyi from house arrest, but she was not allowed to participate in elections. A military-backed party was victorious in elections in 2010, and in 2011 a civilian government backed by the military took power. In 2012, some political prisoners were released and Aung San Suu Kyi won a parliamentary seat in a by-election, while her party, the National League for Democracy, won 43 of the 44 contested seats. But the military and their allies held a large majority in parliament.

Agriculture is the main activity, employing 66% of the people. The chief crop is rice. Maize, pulses, oilseeds, and sugarcane are other major products. Forestry is important. Teak and rice together make up about two-thirds of the total value of exports. Burma has many mineral resources, though they are mostly undeveloped, but the country is famous for its precious stones, especially rubies. Manufacturing is mostly on a small scale.

AREA 261,227 sq mi [676,578 sq km] **POPULATION** 53,414,000
CAPITAL Rangoon (Yangon); Naypyidaw (administrative capital)
GOVERNMENT Military regime **ETHNIC GROUPS** Burman 68%, Shan 9%, Karen 7%, Rakhine 4%, Chinese, Indian, Mon
LANGUAGES Burmese (official); minority ethnic groups have their own languages **RELIGIONS** Buddhism 89%, Christianity, Islam
CURRENCY Kyat = 100 pyas

BURUNDI

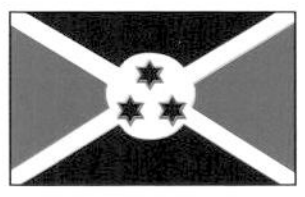

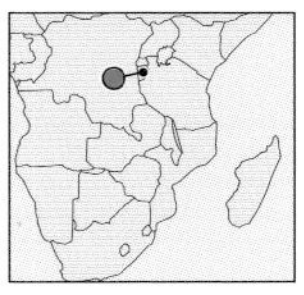

GEOGRAPHY The Republic of Burundi is the fifth smallest country in mainland Africa. It is also the second most densely populated after its northern neighbor, Rwanda. Part of the Great African Rift Valley, which runs throughout eastern Africa into southwestern Asia, lies in western Burundi. It includes part of Lake Tanganyika. Bujumbura, the capital city, lies on the shore of Lake Tanganyika and has a warm climate. A dry season occurs from June to September, but the other months are fairly rainy. The mountains and plateaux to the east are cooler and wetter, but the rainfall generally decreases to the east.

POLITICS & ECONOMY The Twa, a pygmy people, were the first known inhabitants of Burundi. About 1,000 years ago, the Hutu, a people who speak a Bantu language, gradually began to settle the area, pushing the Twa into remote areas.

From the 15th century, the Tutsi, a cattle-owning people from the northeast, gradually took over the country. The Hutu, though greatly outnumbering the Tutsi, were forced to serve the Tutsi overlords.

Germany conquered the area that is now Burundi and Rwanda in the late 1890s. The area, called Ruanda-Urundi, was taken by Belgium during World War I (1914–18). In 1961, the people of Urundi voted to become a monarchy, while the people of Ruanda voted to become a republic. The two territories became fully independent as Burundi and Rwanda in 1962. After 1962, the rivalries between the Hutu and Tutsi led to periodic outbreaks of

fighting. The Tutsi monarchy was ended in 1966 and Burundi became a republic. Instability continued with coups and massacres as Tutsis and Hutus fought against each other. A power-sharing agreement was reached in 2001. The government of President Pierre Nkurunziza, who was re-elected in 2010, faced many political and economic challenges.

Burundi is one of the world's poorest countries. About 93% of the people live by farming, mostly at subsistence level. Food crops include beans, cassava, maize, and sweet potatoes. Livestock are raised and fishing is important. But Burundi has to import food.

AREA 10,747 sq mi [27,834 sq km]
POPULATION 10,216,000 **CAPITAL** Bujumbura
GOVERNMENT Republic **ETHNIC GROUPS** Hutu 85%, Tutsi 14%, Twa (Pygmy) 1% **LANGUAGES** French and Kirundi (both official)
RELIGIONS Roman Catholic 62%, traditional beliefs 23%, Islam 10%, Protestant 5% **CURRENCY** Burundi franc = 100 centimes

CAMBODIA

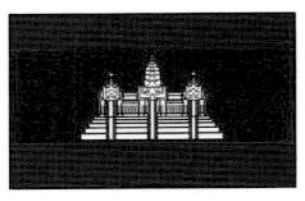

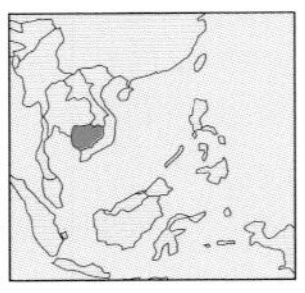

GEOGRAPHY The Kingdom of Cambodia is a country in Southeast Asia. Low mountains border the country except in the southeast. But most of Cambodia consists of plains drained by the River Mekong, which enters Cambodia from Laos in the north and exits through Vietnam in the southeast. The north-west contains Tonlé Sap (or Great Lake). In the dry season, this lake drains into the River Mekong. But in the wet season, the level of the Mekong rises and water flows in the opposite direction from the river into Tonlé Sap – the lake then becomes the largest freshwater lake in Asia.

Cambodia has a tropical monsoon climate, with high temperatures throughout the year. The dry season, when winds blow from the north or northeast, runs from November to April. During the rainy season (May to October), moist winds blow from the south or southeast. The high humidity and heat often make conditions unpleasant. Rainfall is heaviest near the coast, and rather lower inland.

POLITICS & ECONOMY From 802 to 1432, the Khmer people ruled a great empire, which reached its peak in the 12th century. The Khmer capital was at Angkor. The Hindu stone temples built there and at nearby Angkor Wat form the world's largest group of religious buildings. France ruled the country between 1863 and 1954, when the country became an independent monarchy. But the monarchy was abolished in 1970 and Cambodia became a republic.

In 1970, US and South Vietnamese troops entered Cambodia, but left after destroying North Vietnamese Communist camps in the east. The country became involved in the Vietnam War, and then in a civil war as Cambodian Communists of the Khmer Rouge organization fought for power. The Khmer Rouge took over Cambodia in 1975 and launched a reign of terror in which between 1 million and 2.5 million people were killed. In 1979, Vietnamese and Cambodian troops overthrew the Khmer Rouge government. But fighting continued between factions. Vietnam withdrew in 1989, and in 1991 Prince Sihanouk was recognized as head of state. Elections were held in May 1993, and in September 1993 the monarchy was restored. Elections were held in 1998, 2003, and 2008. In 2004, King Sihanouk abdicated because of ill health and his son, Prince Norodom Sihamoni, became king. Between 2008 and December 2011, Cambodian and Thai troops clashed periodically over a border dispute involving an area near the ancient Preah Vihear temple, a World Heritage Site.

Cambodia is a poor country whose economy has been wrecked by war. Farming is the main activity and rice, rubber, and maize are leading products. Manufacturing is on a small scale, but the discovery of oil reserves and an increase in tourism have recently boosted the economy.

AREA 69,898 sq mi [181,035 sq km] **POPULATION** 14,702,000
CAPITAL Phnom Penh **GOVERNMENT** Constitutional monarchy
ETHNIC GROUPS Khmer 90%, Vietnamese 5%, Chinese 1%, others
LANGUAGES Khmer (official), French, English
RELIGIONS Buddhism 95%, others 5% **CURRENCY** Riel = 100 sen

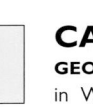

CAMEROON

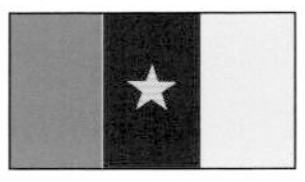

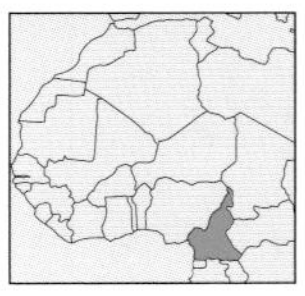

GEOGRAPHY The Republic of Cameroon in West Africa derived its name from the Portuguese word *camarões*, or prawns. This name was used by Portuguese explorers who fished for prawns along the coast. Behind the narrow coastal plains on the Gulf of Guinea, the land rises to a series of plateaux, with a mountainous region in the southwest where the volcano Mount Cameroun is situated. In the north, the land slopes down toward the Lake Chad basin.

The rainfall is heavy, especially in the highlands, but it becomes drier to the north. Temperatures are high on the coast, while the inland plateaux are cooler.

POLITICS & ECONOMY Germany lost Cameroon during World War I (1914–18). The country was then divided into two parts, one ruled by Britain and the other by France. In 1960, French Cameroon became the independent Cameroon Republic. In 1961, after a vote in British Cameroon, part of the territory joined the Cameroon Republic to become the Federal Republic of Cameroon – the other part joined Nigeria. In 1972, Cameroon became a unitary state called the United Republic of Cameroon. It adopted the name Republic of Cameroon in 1984, but the country had two official languages. In 1995, partly to placate the English-speaking people, Cameroon became the 52nd member of the Commonwealth. In 2008, parliament passed a controversial amendment enabling President Paul Biya, who had assumed office in 1982, to run for election for a third term, a contest which he won by a landslide.

Like most countries in tropical Africa, Cameroon's economy is based on agriculture, which employs 54% of the people. The chief food crops include cassava, maize, millet, sweet potatoes, and yams. Cocoa and coffee are exported, along with oil and bauxite. In 2002, Cameroon's claim over the disputed oil-rich Bakassi peninsula was upheld and the handover by Nigeria was finally completed in 2008. Cameroon has few manufacturing industries, but it is self-sufficient in food.

AREA 183,568 sq mi [475,442 sq km] **POPULATION** 19,711,000
CAPITAL Yaoundé **GOVERNMENT** Multiparty republic
ETHNIC GROUPS Cameroon Highlanders 31%, Bantu 27%, Kirdi 11%, Fulani 10%, others **LANGUAGES** French and English (both official)
RELIGIONS Christianity 40%, traditional beliefs 40%, Islam 20%
CURRENCY CFA franc = 100 centimes

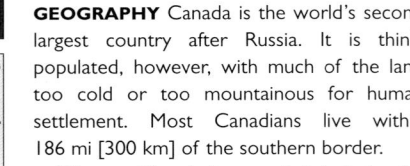

CANADA

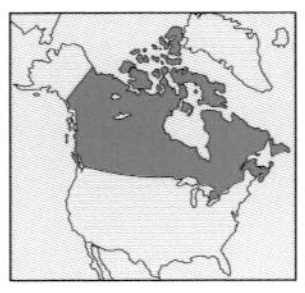

GEOGRAPHY Canada is the world's second largest country after Russia. It is thinly populated, however, with much of the land too cold or too mountainous for human settlement. Most Canadians live within 186 mi [300 km] of the southern border.

Western Canada is rugged. It includes the Pacific ranges and the mighty Rocky Mountains. East of the Rockies are the interior plains. In the north lie the bleak Arctic islands, while to the south lie the densely populated lowlands around lakes Erie and Ontario and in the St Lawrence River valley. The melting of Arctic ice, attributed to global warming, has led to concern about international rights over the Arctic waters off northern Canada.

Canada has a cold climate. In winter, temperatures fall below freezing point throughout most of Canada. But the southwestern coast has a relatively mild climate. Along the Arctic Circle, mean temperatures are below freezing for seven months a year. The west and southeast have high rainfall, but the prairies are dry with 10 inches to 20 inches [250 mm to 500 mm] of rain every year.

POLITICS & ECONOMY Canada's first people, the ancestors of the Native Americans, or Indians, arrived in North America from Asia around 40,000 years ago. The Inuit (Eskimos) were later arrivals from Asia. Europeans first reached Canada in 1497 and soon Britain and France began to compete for control.

France gained an initial advantage, and the French founded Québec in 1608. But the British later occupied eastern Canada. In 1867, Britain passed the British North America Act, which set up the Dominion of Canada, which was made up of Québec, Ontario, Nova Scotia, and New Brunswick. Other areas were added, the last being Newfoundland in 1949. Canada fought alongside Britain in both World Wars and many Canadians feel close ties with Britain. Canada is a constitutional monarchy, and the British monarch is Canada's head of state.

In 1995, the people of Québec voted narrowly against a move to make Québec a sovereign state. In 2006, the national parliament voted to recognize Québec as a nation within a united Canada – a symbolic act of reconciliation. Another major issue concerns the rights of Aboriginal minorities. In 1999, Canada created the territory of Nunavut for the Inuit population. Nunavut covers 64% of what was formerly the eastern part of the Northwest Territories. In 2006, the Conservative Party, led by Stephen Harper, was returned to power, ending 12 years of Liberal Party rule. Stephen Harper was re-elected in 2008 and 2011.

Canada is a highly developed and prosperous country. Although farmland covers only 8% of the country, Canadian farms are highly productive. Canada is one of the world's leading producers of barley, wheat, meat, and milk. Forestry and fishing are other important industries. It is rich in natural resources, especially oil and natural gas, and is a major exporter of minerals. The country also produces copper, gold, iron ore, uranium, and zinc. Manufacturing is important in the cities, where 80% of the people live. Manufactures include processed mineral and farm products, cars, chemicals, electronic goods, machinery, paper, and timber products.

AREA 3,849,653 sq mi [9,970,610 sq km]
POPULATION 34,031,000 **CAPITAL** Ottawa
GOVERNMENT Federal multiparty constitutional monarchy
ETHNIC GROUPS British origin 28%, French origin 23%, other European 15%, Amerindian/Inuit 2%, others
LANGUAGES English and French (both official)
RELIGIONS Roman Catholic 46%, Protestant 36%, Judaism, Islam, Hinduism **CURRENCY** Canadian dollar = 100 cents

CAPE VERDE

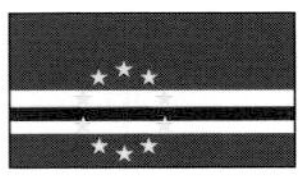

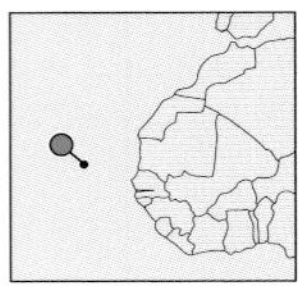

Cape Verde consists of ten large and five small islands, and is situated 350 mi [560 km] west of Dakar in Senegal. The islands have a tropical climate, with high temperatures all year round. Cape Verde became independent from Portugal in 1975 and is rated as a "low-income" developing country by the World Bank.

AREA 1,557 sq mi [4,033 sq km]
POPULATION 516,000 **CAPITAL** Praia

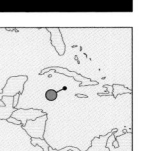

CAYMAN ISLANDS

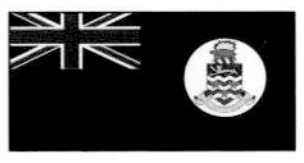

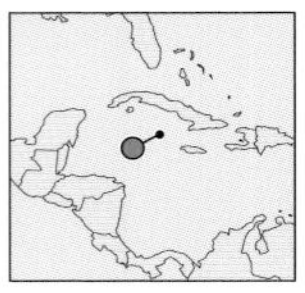

The Cayman Islands are an overseas territory of the UK, consisting of three low-lying islands. Financial services are the main economic activity and the islands offer a secret tax haven to many companies and banks.

AREA 102 sq mi [264 sq km]
POPULATION 51,000 **CAPITAL** George Town

CENTRAL AFRICAN REPUBLIC

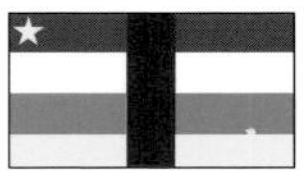

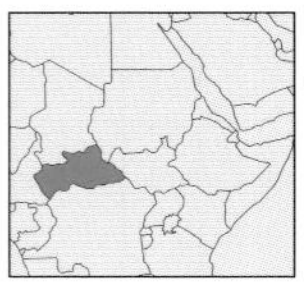

GEOGRAPHY The Central African Republic is a remote, landlocked country in the heart of Africa. It consists mostly of a plateau lying between 1,970 ft and 2,620 ft [600 m to 800 m] above sea level. The Ubangi drains the south, while the Chari (or Shari) River flows from the north to the Lake Chad basin. The climate is warm throughout the year, while the annual average rainfall in the capital Bangui totals 62 inches [1,574 mm]. The north is drier, with an average annual rainfall of about 31 inches [800 mm].

POLITICS & ECONOMY France set up an outpost at Bangui in 1889 and ruled the country as a colony from 1894. Known as Ubangi-Shari, the country was ruled by France as part of French Equatorial Africa until it gained independence in 1960.

Central African Republic became a one-party state in 1962, but army officers seized power in 1966. The head of the army, Jean-Bedel Bokassa, made himself emperor in 1976. The country was renamed the Central African Empire, but Bokassa was removed by a military coup in 1979. The country again became a republic.

The republic adopted a new multiparty constitution in 1991, and elections were held in 1993 and 1998. An army uprising in 2002 ended in the overthrow of the government in 2003. General François Bozize took power. He was elected president in 2005 and 2010. In 2006–7, rebel activities led thousands of refugees to flee into Chad and Cameroon, and in 2009 the US-based Fund for Peace classified the country as a "failed state."

The World Bank classifies Central African Republic as a "low-income" developing country. Over 80% of the people are farmers, and most of them produce little more than they need to feed their families. The main crops are bananas, maize, manioc, millet, and yams. Coffee, cotton, timber, and tobacco are produced for export. Development has been impeded by the country's remote position, its poor transport system, and its untrained work force. The country depends heavily on aid from France.

AREA 240,534 sq mi [622,984 sq km] **POPULATION** 4,950,000
CAPITAL Bangui **GOVERNMENT** Multiparty republic
ETHNIC GROUPS Baya 33%, Banda 27%, Mandjia 13%, Sara 10%, Mboum 7%, Mbaka 4%, others **LANGUAGES** French (official), Sangho
RELIGIONS Traditional beliefs 35%, Protestant 25%, Roman Catholic 25%, Islam 15% **CURRENCY** CFA franc = 100 centimes

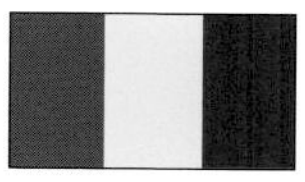

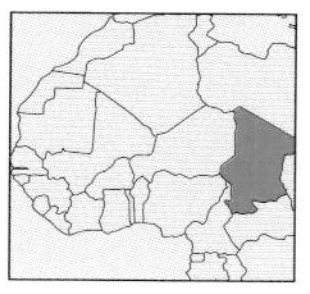

CHAD

GEOGRAPHY The Republic of Chad is a landlocked country in north-central Africa. It is Africa's fifth largest country and is over twice the size of France, the country which once ruled it as a colony.

Ndjamena in central Chad has a hot, tropical climate, with a marked dry season from November to April. The south of the country is wetter, with an average yearly rainfall of around 39 inches [1,000 mm]. The burning-hot desert in the north has an average yearly rainfall of less than 5 inches [130 mm].

POLITICS & ECONOMY Chad straddles two worlds. The north is populated by Muslim Arab and Berber peoples, while black Africans, who follow traditional beliefs or who have converted to Christianity, live in the south. French explorers were active in the area in the late 19th century. France made Chad a colony in 1902.

Chad became independent in 1960, but the 1970s were marked by ethnic conflict that led to civil wars, coups, and conflict with Libya, which supported rebel factions. Chad and Libya agreed a truce in 1987, and in 1994 the International Court of Justice ruled against Libya's claim on the Aozou Strip. From 2004, Chad forces clashed with pro-Sudanese militias as the conflict in Sudan's Darfur province spilled over the border. In 2010 a settlement was agreed with Sudan and Chad held elections in 2011.

Chad is one of the world's poorest countries. Farming and fishing employ 83% of the people. Food crops include groundnuts, millet, rice, and sorghum, but cotton is the chief export crop. Chad has few manufacturing industries, but its oil reserves hold out hope for development. Oil production began in 2003.

AREA 495,752 SQ MI [1,284,000 SQ KM]
POPULATION 10,759,000 **CAPITAL** NDJAMENA
GOVERNMENT MULTIPARTY REPUBLIC **ETHNIC GROUPS** 200 DISTINCT GROUPS: MOSTLY MUSLIM IN THE NORTH AND CENTER; MOSTLY CHRISTIAN OR ANIMIST IN THE SOUTH **LANGUAGES** FRENCH AND ARABIC (BOTH OFFICIAL), MANY OTHERS **RELIGIONS** ISLAM 51%, CHRISTIANITY 35%, ANIMIST 7%
CURRENCY CFA FRANC = 100 CENTIMES

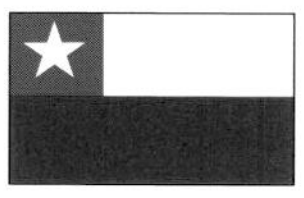

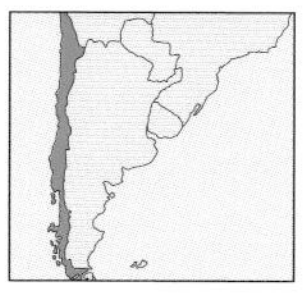

CHILE

GEOGRAPHY The Republic of Chile stretches about 2,650 mi [4,260 km] from north to south, although the maximum east–west distance is only about 267 mi [430 km]. The high Andes Mountains form Chile's eastern borders with Argentina and Bolivia. To the west are basins and valleys, with coastal uplands overlooking the shore. Most people live in the central valley, where Santiago is situated. Earthquakes are common. In February 2010, an earthquake with a magnitude of 8.8 (the biggest in 50 years) struck central Chile, killing more than 400 people.

Santiago has a Mediterranean climate with hot, dry summers and mild, moist winters. The Atacama Desert in the north is extremely arid, while the south is cold and stormy.

POLITICS & ECONOMY Amerindian people reached the southern tip of South America 8,000 years ago. In 1520, Portuguese navigator Ferdinand Magellan was the first European to sight Chile. The country became a Spanish colony in the 1540s. Chile became independent in 1818. During a war (1879–83), it gained mineral-rich areas from Peru and Bolivia.

In 1970, Salvador Allende became the first Communist leader to be elected democratically. He was overthrown in 1973 by army officers, who were supported by the CIA. General Augusto Pinochet then ruled as a dictator. A new constitution was introduced in 1981. Pinochet remained in power until 1989. In 2006, Michelle Bachelet, a center-left former torture victim under the Pinochet regime, became president. She was succeeded in 2010 by a right-winger, Sebastian Pinera.

According to the World Bank, Chile has a "lower-middle-income" economy. Mining, especially copper, is important and minerals dominate exports. But manufacturing is the most valuable activity. Products include processed foods, metals, iron and steel, transport equipment, and textiles. The chief crop is wheat, while beans, fruits, maize, and livestock products are also important. Chile's fishing industry is one of the world's largest.

AREA 292,133 SQ MI [756,626 SQ KM]
POPULATION 16,889,000 **CAPITAL** SANTIAGO
GOVERNMENT MULTIPARTY REPUBLIC **ETHNIC GROUPS** MESTIZO 95%, AMERINDIAN 3% **LANGUAGES** SPANISH (OFFICIAL)
RELIGIONS ROMAN CATHOLIC 89%, PROTESTANT 11%
CURRENCY CHILEAN PESO = 100 CENTAVOS

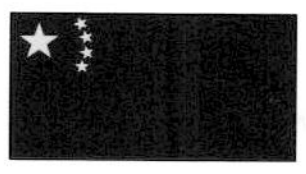

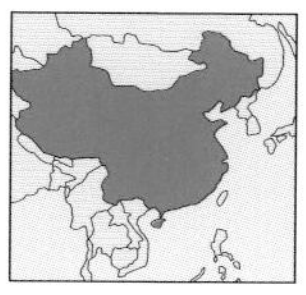

CHINA

GEOGRAPHY The People's Republic of China is the world's third largest country. Most people live in the east – on the coastal plains or in the fertile valleys of the Huang He (Hwang Ho or Yellow River), the Chang Jiang (Yangtze Kiang), which is Asia's longest river at 3,960 mi [6,380 km], and the Xi Jiang (Si Kiang). Western China is thinly populated. It includes the bleak Tibetan plateau, which is bounded by the Himalaya, the world's highest mountain range. Deserts include the Gobi Desert along the Mongolian border and the Taklamakan Desert in the far west. Earthquakes are common. In May 2008, a major earthquake in the southwest killed more than 69,000 people and made millions homeless.

Beijing has cold winters and warm summers with moderate rainfall. To the south, Shanghai has milder winters and more rain. The southeast has a wet, subtropical climate, but the west has a severe climate. Lhasa has very cold winters and a low rainfall.

POLITICS & ECONOMY China is one of the world's oldest civilizations, going back 3,500 years. Under the Han dynasty (202 BC to AD 220), the Chinese empire was as large as the Roman empire. Mongols conquered China in the 13th century, but Chinese rule was restored in 1368. The Manchu people of Mongolia ruled the country from 1644 to 1912, when the country became a republic.

War with Japan (1937–45) was followed by civil war between the nationalists and the Communists. The Communists triumphed in 1949, setting up the People's Republic of China. In the 1980s, following the death of the revolutionary leader Mao Zedong (Mao Tse-tung) in 1976, China encouraged formerly forbidden policies, namely private enterprise and foreign investment. But the Communist leaders have not permitted political freedom. Opponents are still harshly treated, while attempts to negotiate some degree of autonomy for Tibet have been rejected.

China's economy has expanded greatly since the 1970s and many new industries have been set up in the east. Between 1989 and 2008, the economy grew by around 9% per year. China has benefited from the return of Hong Kong in 1997 and its admission to the World Trade Organization in 2001. The global financial crisis in 2008 slowed the economic growth rate, though China's grew faster than any other major economy. In early 2011, China overtook Japan to become the world's second largest economy after the United States.

Despite its recent success, China remains a poor country. In 2009, agriculture employed 39% of the work force, although only 10% of the land is farmed. By 2010, the urban population had reached 53% of the total population. This was the first time that urban dwellers outnumbered the rural population.

Farm products include rice, sweet potatoes, tea, and wheat, and many fruits and vegetables. Livestock farming is important, and China has more than a third of the world's pigs. Resources include coal, iron ore, and other metals. Manufactures include cement, chemicals, fertilizers, machinery, telecommunications and recording equipment, and textiles. China is now a major producer of consumer goods, including cameras, computer products, refrigerators, and television sets.

AREA 3,705,387 SQ MI [9,596,961 SQ KM]
POPULATION 1,336,718,000 **CAPITAL** BEIJING
GOVERNMENT SINGLE-PARTY COMMUNIST REPUBLIC
ETHNIC GROUPS HAN CHINESE 92%, MANY OTHERS
LANGUAGES MANDARIN CHINESE (OFFICIAL) **RELIGIONS** ATHEIST (OFFICIAL)
CURRENCY RENMINBI YUAN = 10 JIAO = 100 FEN

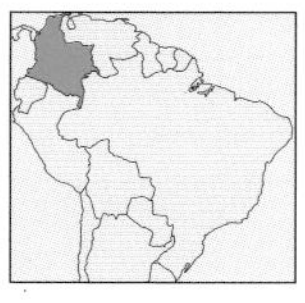

COLOMBIA

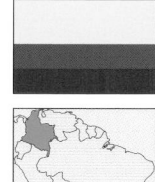

GEOGRAPHY The Republic of Colombia, in northeastern South America, is the only country in the continent to have coastlines on both the Pacific Ocean and the Caribbean Sea. Colombia also contains the northernmost ranges of the Andes Mountains.

There is a tropical climate in the lowlands, but the altitude greatly affects the climate in the Andes. The capital, Bogotá, which stands on a plateau in the eastern Andes at about 9,200 ft [2,800 m] above sea level, has mild temperatures throughout the year. Rainfall is heavy, especially on the Pacific coast.

POLITICS & ECONOMY Amerindian people have lived in Colombia for thousands of years. But today, only a small proportion of the people are of unmixed Amerindian ancestry. Mestizos (people of mixed white and Amerindian ancestry) form the largest group, followed by whites and mulattos (people of mixed European and African ancestry). Spaniards opened up the area in the early 16th century. They set up a territory known as the Viceroyalty of the New Kingdom of Granada, including Colombia, Ecuador, Panama, and Venezuela. In 1819, the area became independent, but Ecuador and Venezuela soon split away, followed by Panama in 1903.

Instability has marked its recent history. Colombia faces economic and security problems, notably combating left-wing guerrillas and right-wing paramilitaries, while controlling the illicit drugs industry. Andrés Pastrana, president in 1998–2002, tried to end the guerrilla war, but peace talks collapsed and conflict resumed. His successors, Alvaro Uribe and, from 2010, Juan Manuel Santos, pursued tough policies against the rebels.

Colombia has a "lower-middle-income" economy. It exports oil, coffee, and chemicals.

AREA 439,735 SQ MI [1,138,914 SQ KM] **POPULATION** 44,726,000
CAPITAL BOGOTÁ **GOVERNMENT** MULTIPARTY REPUBLIC
ETHNIC GROUPS MESTIZO 58%, WHITE 20%, MULATTO 14%, BLACK 4%
LANGUAGES SPANISH (OFFICIAL) **RELIGIONS** ROMAN CATHOLIC 90%
CURRENCY COLOMBIAN PESO = 100 CENTAVOS

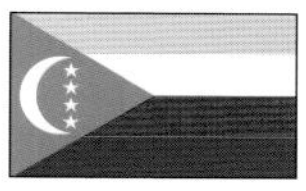

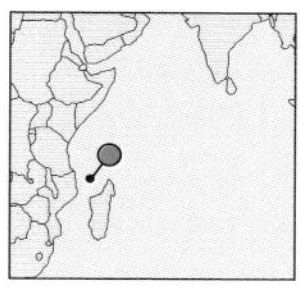

COMOROS

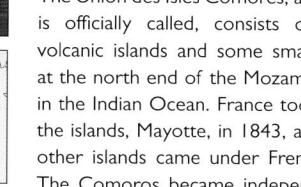

The Union des Isles Comores, as the Comoros is officially called, consists of three large volcanic islands and some smaller ones lying at the north end of the Mozambique Channel in the Indian Ocean. France took over one of the islands, Mayotte, in 1843, and in 1886 the other islands came under French protection. The Comoros became independent in 1974, but Mayotte remained French, becoming fully integrated with France in 2009. In the 1990s, the islands of Anjouan and Mohéli tried to secede, but, in 2004, the large islands were granted autonomy. In 2008, an illegal regime on Anjouan was overthrown. Exports include cloves, perfume oil, and vanilla.

AREA 863 SQ MI [2,235 SQ KM] **POPULATION** 795,000 **CAPITAL** MORONI

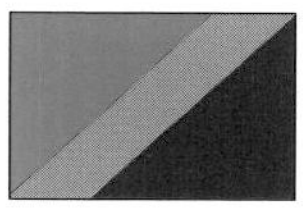

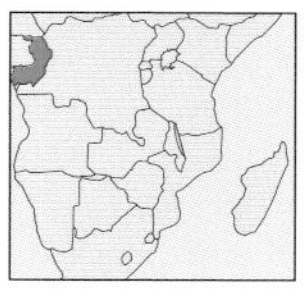

CONGO

GEOGRAPHY The Republic of the Congo is a country on the River Congo in west-central Africa. The equator runs through the center of the country. Congo has a narrow coastal plain on which its main port, Pointe Noire, stands. Behind the plain are uplands through which the River Niari has carved a fertile valley. Central Congo consists of high plains. The north contains large swampy areas in the valleys of the tributaries of the River Congo.

Congo has a hot, wet equatorial climate. Brazzaville has a dry season between June and September. The coast is drier and cooler than the rest of the Congo, because of the cold offshore Benguela ocean current.

POLITICS & ECONOMY Part of the huge Kongo kingdom between the 15th and 18th centuries, the coast of the Congo later became a center of the European slave trade. The area came under French protection in 1880. It was later governed as part of a larger region called French Equatorial Africa. The country remained under French control until 1960.

Congo became a one-party state in 1964 and a military group took over the government in 1968. In 1970, Congo declared itself a Communist country, though it continued to seek aid from Western countries. The government officially abandoned its Communist policies in 1990. Multiparty elections were held in 1992, but the elected president, Pascal Lissouba, was overthrown in 1997 by former president Denis Sassou-Nguesso. Civil war broke out in 1999 but peace was restored in 2002. Sassou-Nguesso was elected president. He was re-elected in 2009.

The World Bank classifies Congo as a "lower-middle-income" developing country. Agriculture is the most important activity, employing about 32% of the people. But many farmers produce little more than they need to feed their families. Major food crops include bananas, cassava, maize, and rice, while the leading cash crops are coffee and cocoa. Congo's main exports are oil (which makes up more than 90% of the total) and timber. Manufacturing is relatively unimportant at the moment, still hampered by poor transport links, but it is gradually being developed.

AREA 132,046 SQ MI [342,000 SQ KM]
POPULATION 4,244,000 **CAPITAL** BRAZZAVILLE
GOVERNMENT REPUBLIC **ETHNIC GROUPS** KONGO 48%, SANGHA 20%, TEKE 17%, M'BOCHI 12% **LANGUAGES** FRENCH (OFFICIAL), MANY OTHERS **RELIGIONS** CHRISTIANITY 50%, ANIMIST 48%, ISLAM 2%
CURRENCY CFA FRANC = 100 CENTIMES

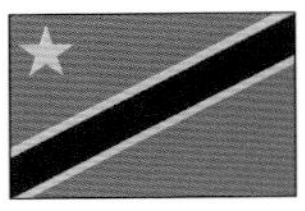
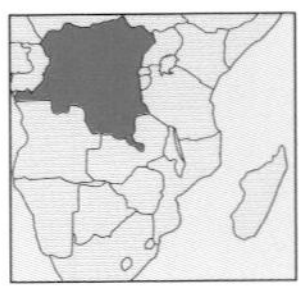

CONGO (DEMOCRATIC REPUBLIC OF THE)

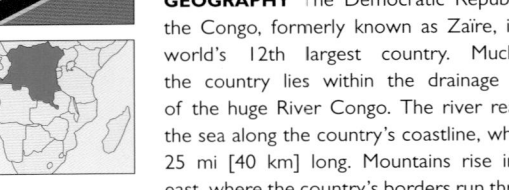

GEOGRAPHY The Democratic Republic of the Congo, formerly known as Zaïre, is the world's 12th largest country. Much of the country lies within the drainage basin of the huge River Congo. The river reaches the sea along the country's coastline, which is 25 mi [40 km] long. Mountains rise in the east, where the country's borders run through lakes Tanganyika, Kivu, Edward, and Albert. The equatorial region has high temperatures and heavy rainfall throughout the year.

POLITICS & ECONOMY Pygmies were the first inhabitants of the region, with Portuguese navigators not reaching the coast until 1482, but the interior was not explored until the late 19th century. In 1885, the country, called Congo Free State, became the personal property of King Léopold II of Belgium. In 1908, the country became a Belgian colony.

The Belgian Congo became independent in 1960 and was renamed Zaïre in 1971. Ethnic rivalries caused instability until 1965, when the country became a one-party state, ruled by President Mobutu. The government allowed the formation of political parties in 1990, but elections were repeatedly postponed. In 1996, fighting broke out in eastern Zaïre, as the Tutsi–Hutu conflict in Burundi and Rwanda spilled over. The rebel leader Laurent Kabila took power in 1997, ousting Mobutu and renaming the country. A rebellion against Kabila broke out in 1998. Rwanda and Uganda supported the rebels, while Angola, Chad, Namibia, and Zimbabwe assisted Kabila. A peace treaty was signed in 1999, but fighting continued. Kabila was assassinated in 2001. His son, Major-General Joseph Kabila, became president. But instability continued into 2011 as various militias, including Tutsi, Hutu, and Ugandan rebels clashed with government forces in the east.

The World Bank classifies the Democratic Republic of the Congo as a "low-income" developing country, despite its reserves of copper, the main export, and other minerals. Agriculture, mainly at subsistence level, employs 60% of the people.

AREA 905,350 sq mi [2,344,858 sq km]
POPULATION 71,713,000 **CAPITAL** Kinshasa
GOVERNMENT Single-party republic
ETHNIC GROUPS Over 200; the largest are Mongo, Luba, Kongo, Mangbetu-Azande
LANGUAGES French (official), tribal languages
RELIGIONS Roman Catholic 50%, Protestant 20%, Islam 10%, others
CURRENCY Congolese franc = 100 centimes

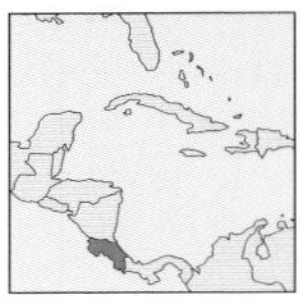

COSTA RICA

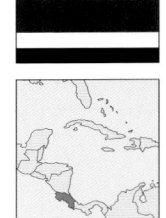

GEOGRAPHY The Republic of Costa Rica in Central America has coastlines on both the Pacific Ocean and the Caribbean Sea. Central Costa Rica consists of mountain ranges and plateaux with many volcanoes.

The coolest months of the year are December and January. The northeast trade winds bring heavy rain to the Caribbean coast, while there are lower amounts of rainfall in the highlands and on the Pacific coastlands.

POLITICS & ECONOMY Christopher Columbus reached the Caribbean coast in 1502 and rumors of treasure soon attracted many Spaniards to settle in the country. Spain ruled the country until 1821, when Spain's Central American colonies broke away to join Mexico in 1822. In 1823, the Central American states broke with Mexico and set up the Central American Federation. Later, this large union broke up and Costa Rica became fully independent in 1838.

From the late 19th century onward, Costa Rica experienced a number of revolutions, with periods of dictatorship alternating with spells of democracy. In 1948, following a revolt, the armed forces were completely abolished. Since that year, Costa Rica has enjoyed a long period of consistent stable democracy. In 2010, Costa Ricans elected their first woman president, Laura Chinchilla.

Costa Rica is classified by the World Bank as a "lower-middle-income" developing country and one of the most prosperous countries in Central America. There are high educational standards and a high average life expectancy (about 77 years for men and 81 years for women). Agriculture employs 12% of the people. Costa Rica's natural resources include its forests, but it lacks minerals apart from some bauxite and manganese. Manufacturing is increasing. The United States is Costa Rica's main trading partner. Tourism is a fast-growing industry.

AREA 19,730 sq mi [51,100 sq km] **POPULATION** 4,577,000
CAPITAL San José **GOVERNMENT** Multiparty republic
ETHNIC GROUPS White (including Mestizo) 94%, Black 3%, Amerindian 1%, Chinese 1%, others **LANGUAGES** Spanish (official), English **RELIGIONS** Roman Catholic 76%, Evangelical 14%
CURRENCY Costa Rican colón = 100 céntimos

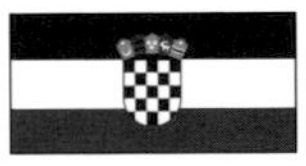
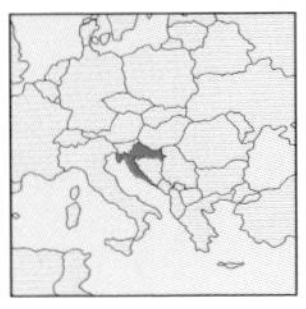

CROATIA

GEOGRAPHY The Republic of Croatia was one of the six republics that made up the former Communist country of Yugoslavia until it became independent in 1991. The region bordering the Adriatic Sea is called Dalmatia. It includes the coastal ranges, which contain large areas of bare limestone. Most of the rest of the country consists of the fertile Pannonian plains.

The coastal area has a typical Mediterranean climate, with hot, dry summers and mild, moist winters. Inland, the climate becomes more continental. Winters are cold, while temperatures often soar to 100°F [38°C] in the summer months.

POLITICS & ECONOMY Slav people settled in the area around 1,400 years ago. In 803, Croatia became part of the Holy Roman empire and the Croats soon adopted Christianity. Croatia was an independent kingdom in the 10th and 11th centuries. In 1102, the king of Hungary also became king of Croatia, creating a union that lasted 800 years. In 1526, part of Croatia came under the Turkish Ottoman empire, while the rest came under the Austrian Habsburgs.

After Austria–Hungary was defeated in World War I (1914–18), Croatia became part of the new Kingdom of the Serbs, Croats, and Slovenes. This kingdom was renamed Yugoslavia in 1929. Germany occupied Yugoslavia during World War II (1939–45). Croatia was proclaimed independent, but it was really ruled by the invaders.

After the war, Communists took power with Josip Broz Tito as the country's leader. Despite ethnic differences between the people, Tito held Yugoslavia together until his death in 1980. In the 1980s, economic and ethnic problems, including a deterioration in relations with Serbia, threatened stability. In the 1990s, Yugoslavia split into five nations, one of which was Croatia, which declared itself independent in 1991.

After Serbia supplied arms to Serbs living in Croatia, war broke out between the two republics, causing great damage. Croatia lost more than 30% of its territory. But in 1992, the United Nations sent a peacekeeping force to Croatia, which effectively ended the war with Serbia.

In 1992, when war broke out in Bosnia-Herzegovina, Bosnian Croats occupied parts of the country. But in 1994, Croatia helped to end Croat–Muslim conflict in Bosnia-Herzegovina and, in 1995, after retaking some areas occupied by Serbs, it helped to draw up the Dayton Peace Accord, ending the civil war. The conflict in the early 1990s disrupted the economy. Croatia's main exports are manufactures. In 2011, Croatia signed an accession treaty, paving the way for it to join the European Union in 2013. In 2012, the people voted in a referendum in favor of becoming an EU member.

AREA 21,829 sq mi [56,538 sq km] **POPULATION** 4,484,000
CAPITAL Zagreb **GOVERNMENT** Multiparty republic
ETHNIC GROUPS Croat 90%, Serb 5%, others
LANGUAGES Croatian 96% **RELIGIONS** Roman Catholic 88%, Orthodox 4%, Islam 1%, others **CURRENCY** Kuna = 100 lipas

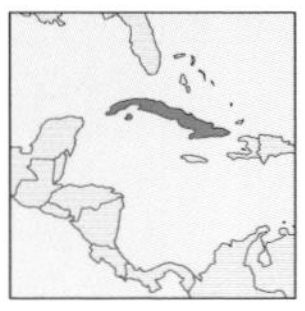

CUBA

GEOGRAPHY The Republic of Cuba is the largest island country in the Caribbean Sea. It consists of one large island, Cuba, the Isle of Youth (Isla de la Juventud), and about 1,600 small islets. Mountains and hills cover about a quarter of Cuba. The highest mountain range, the Sierra Maestra in the southeast, reaches 6,562 ft [2,000 m] above sea level. The rest of the land consists of gently rolling country or coastal plains, crossed by fertile valleys carved by the short, mostly shallow and narrow rivers.

Cuba lies in the tropics. But sea breezes moderate the temperature, warming the land in winter and cooling it in summer.

POLITICS & ECONOMY Christopher Columbus discovered the island in 1492 and Spaniards began to settle there from 1511. Spanish rule ended in 1898, when the United States defeated Spain in the Spanish–American War. American influence in Cuba remained strong until 1959, when revolutionary forces under the leadership of Fidel Castro overthrew the dictatorship of Fulgencio Batista.

The United States opposed Castro's policies, when he turned to the Soviet Union for assistance. In 1962, a world crisis occurred when, under intense US pressure, the Soviet Union withdrew missile sites that could have been used to launch nuclear strikes against the United States. The breakup of the Soviet Union in 1991 damaged Cuba's economy. Fidel Castro's brother, Raul, took over the leadership in 2008. He introduced reforms in 2009–12, including the overhaul of the state-run economy and the release of political prisoners. The government runs the Cuban economy, though, in 2011, a new law allowed people to buy and sell private property for the first time in 50 years. Nickel oxide is the main export. Other exports include sugar, cigars, medicines, citrus fruits, fish, and rum.

Before 1959, US companies owned most of Cuba's manufacturing industries. But under Fidel Castro, these became government property. After the collapse of Communist governments in the Soviet Union and its allies, Cuba worked to increase its trade with Latin America and China.

AREA 42,803 sq mi [110,861 sq km]
POPULATION 11,087,000 **CAPITAL** Havana
GOVERNMENT Socialist republic
ETHNIC GROUPS Mulatto 51%, White 37%, Black 11%
LANGUAGES Spanish (official) **RELIGIONS** Christianity
CURRENCY Cuban peso = 100 centavos

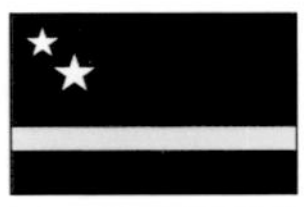
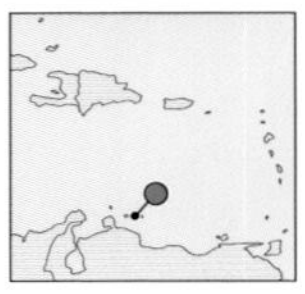

CURAÇAO

Part of the Netherlands Antilles until 2010, Curaçao is a self-governing territory within the Kingdom of the Netherlands. Oil refining, tourism, and trade are important.

AREA 171 sq mi [444 sq km]
POPULATION 142,000 **CAPITAL** Willemstad

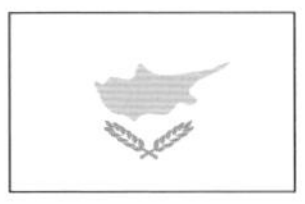
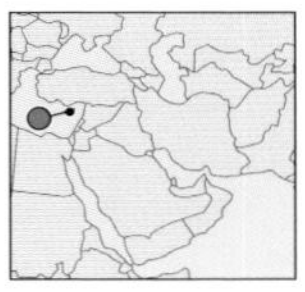

CYPRUS

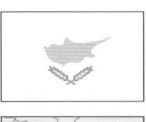

GEOGRAPHY The Republic of Cyprus is an island nation in the northeastern Mediterranean Sea. Geographers regard it as part of Asia, but it resembles southern Europe in many ways. Its scenic mountain ranges include the southern Troodos Mountains, which reach 6,401 ft [1,951 m] at Mount Olympus, and the Kyrenia range in the north. Between them lies the Mesaoria plain. The climate is Mediterranean, with hot, dry summers and mild, moist winters.

POLITICS & ECONOMY Greeks settled on Cyprus around 3,200 years ago. From AD 330, the island was part of the Byzantine empire. In the 1570s, Cyprus became part of the Turkish Ottoman empire. Turkish rule continued until 1878 when Cyprus was leased to Britain. Britain annexed the island in 1914 and proclaimed it a colony in 1925. In the 1950s, Greek Cypriots, who made up four-fifths of the population, began a campaign for *enosis* (union) with Greece. Their leader was the Greek Orthodox Archbishop Makarios. A secret guerrilla force called EOKA attacked the British, who exiled Makarios in 1956; he returned to Cyprus in 1959.

Cyprus became an independent country in 1960, although Britain retained two military bases. Independent Cyprus had a constitution which provided for power-sharing between the Greek and Turkish Cypriots. But the constitution proved unworkable and fighting broke out between the two communities. In 1964, the United Nations sent in a peacekeeping force, but communal clashes recurred in 1967.

In 1974, Makarios was overthrown by Greek officers and Turkey invaded northern Cyprus. In 1979, the north was proclaimed the Turkish Republic of Northern Cyprus. The only country to recognize this state was Turkey. In 2002, the European Union invited Cyprus to become a member in 2004. In 2004, the people voted on a UN plan to reunify Cyprus. The Turkish-Cypriots voted in favor, but the Greek-Cypriots voted against. As a result, only the south was admitted to EU membership on May 1, 2004. Talks on reunification began in 2008, but progress was slow.

Cyprus got its name from the Greek word *kypros*, meaning copper. But little copper remains and the chief minerals today are asbestos and chromium. However, the most valuable activity in Cyprus is tourism. Manufactures include cement, clothes, footwear, tiles, and wine.

In the early 1990s, the United Nations reclassified Cyprus as a developed rather than a developing country, reflecting the rapid economic progress in the south. But the north lagged far behind the prosperous Greek-Cypriot south.

AREA 3,572 sq mi [9,251 sq km]
POPULATION 1,120,000 **CAPITAL** Nicosia
GOVERNMENT Multiparty republic **ETHNIC GROUPS** Greek Cypriot 77%, Turkish Cypriot 18%, others **LANGUAGES** Greek and Turkish (both official), English **RELIGIONS** Greek Orthodox 78%, Islam 18%
CURRENCY Euro = 100 cents

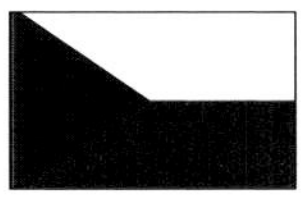
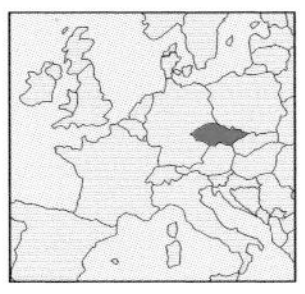

CZECH REPUBLIC

GEOGRAPHY The Czech Republic is the western three-fifths of the former country of Czechoslovakia. It contains two regions: Bohemia in the west and Moravia in the east. Mountains border much of the country in the west. The Bohemian basin in the north-center is a fertile lowland region, with Prague, the capital city, as its main center. Highlands cover much of the center of the country, with lowlands in the southeast.

The climate is influenced by the country's landlocked position in east-central Europe. Summers are warm and winters cold. Rainfall is moderate.

POLITICS & ECONOMY After World War I (1914–18), Czechoslovakia was created. Germany seized the country in World War II (1939–45). In 1948, Communist leaders took power and Czechoslovakia was allied to the Soviet Union. When democratic reforms were introduced in the Soviet Union in the late 1980s, the Czechs also demanded reforms. Free elections were held in 1990, but differences between the Czechs and Slovaks led to the partitioning of the country on January 1, 1993. The Czech Republic became a member of NATO in 1999 and a member of the European Union on May 1, 2004. Following elections in 2010, Petr Necas, leader of the conservative Civic Democratic Party, became prime minister.

Under Communist rule the Czech Republic became one of the most industrialized parts of Eastern Europe. The country has deposits of coal, uranium, iron ore, magnesite, tin, and zinc. Manufacturing employs about 27% of the Czech Republic's entire work force. Farming is also important. The main crops include barley, fruit, hops for beer-making, maize, potatoes, sugar beet, vegetables, and wheat.

AREA 30,450 sq mi [78,866 sq km]
POPULATION 10,190,000 **CAPITAL** Prague
GOVERNMENT Multiparty republic **ETHNIC GROUPS** Czech 81%, Moravian 13%, Slovak 3%, Polish, German, Silesian, Gypsy, Hungarian, Ukrainian **LANGUAGES** Czech (official) **RELIGIONS** Atheist 40%, Roman Catholic 39%, Protestant 4%, Orthodox 3%, others
CURRENCY Czech koruna = 100 haler

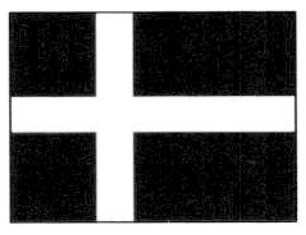
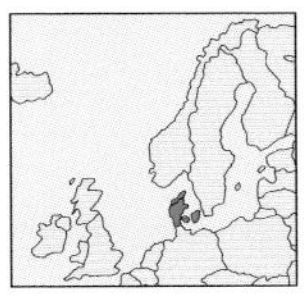

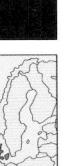

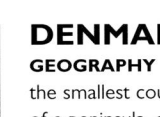

DENMARK

GEOGRAPHY The Kingdom of Denmark is the smallest country in Scandinavia. It consists of a peninsula, called Jutland (or Jylland), which is joined to Germany, and more than 400 islands, 89 of which are inhabited. The land is flat and mostly covered by rocks dropped there by huge ice sheets during the last Ice Age. The highest point in Denmark is on Jutland. It is only 568 ft [173 m] above sea level. Denmark has a mild, moist climate, except during cold spells in winter when the Sound (Øresund) between Sjælland and Sweden may freeze over.

POLITICS & ECONOMY Danish Vikings terrorized much of Western Europe for about 300 years after AD 800. In the late 14th century, Denmark formed a union with Norway and Sweden (which included Finland). Sweden broke away in 1523, while Denmark lost Norway to Sweden in 1814. After 1945, Denmark joined NATO and it became a member of the European Union in 1973. In 2010, Greenland, a former Danish territory, became a self-governing territory. In 2011, a center-left party won parliamentary elections in Denmark. Helle Thorning-Schmidt became the country's first female prime minister.

Denmark is a prosperous country. Reources include some oil and gas. Manufacturing employs 12% of the people. Products include furniture, processed food, machinery, television sets, and textiles. Farming employs 3% of the people, but it is highly scientific. Meat and dairy farming are the chief activities.

AREA 16,639 sq mi [43,094 sq km] **POPULATION** 5,530,000
CAPITAL Copenhagen **GOVERNMENT** Parliamentary monarchy
ETHNIC GROUPS Scandinavian, Inuit, Færoese **LANGUAGES** Danish (official), Greenlandic, English, Færoese **RELIGIONS** Evangelical Lutheran 95% **CURRENCY** Danish krone = 100 øre

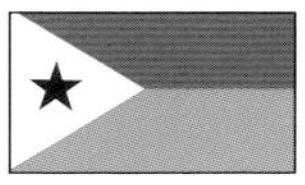
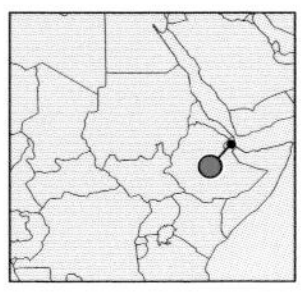

DJIBOUTI

GEOGRAPHY The Republic of Djibouti in eastern Africa occupies a strategic position where the Red Sea meets the Gulf of Aden. Djibouti has one of the world's hottest and driest climates.

POLITICS & ECONOMY France set up a territory called French Somaliland in 1888. Its capital, Djibouti, became important when a railroad was built to Addis Ababa and Djibouti became the main outlet for Ethiopian trade. In 1967, France renamed the dependency the French Territory of the Afars and Issas, but it was renamed Djibouti on independence in 1977. It became a one-party state in 1981, but a new constitution (1992) permitted four parties which had to maintain a balance between the country's ethnic groups. In 2008, a border dispute led to clashes between Djiboutian and Eritrean troops.

Djibouti is a poor country. Its economy is based largely on the revenue it gets from its port and the railroad to Addis Ababa.

AREA 8,958 sq mi [23,200 sq km] **POPULATION** 757,000
CAPITAL Djibouti **GOVERNMENT** Multiparty republic
ETHNIC GROUPS Somali 60%, Afar 35% **LANGUAGES** Arabic and French (both official) **RELIGIONS** Islam 94%, Christianity 6%
CURRENCY Djiboutian franc = 100 centimes

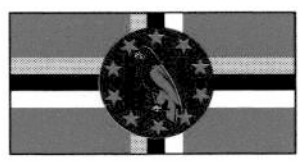
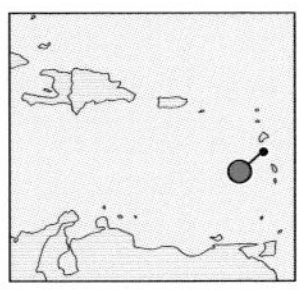

DOMINICA

The Commonwealth of Dominica, a former British colony, became independent in 1978. The island has a mountainous spine and less than 10% of the land is cultivated. But agriculture employs 18% of the people. The manufacture of coconut-based soap is important, while tourism and mining are other economic activities.

AREA 290 sq mi [751 sq km] **POPULATION** 73,000 **CAPITAL** Roseau

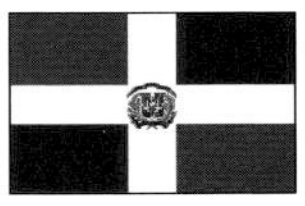
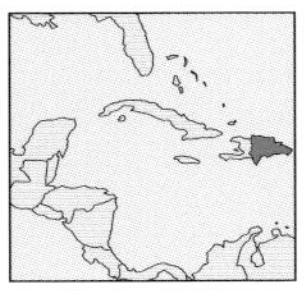

DOMINICAN REPUBLIC

GEOGRAPHY Second largest of the Caribbean nations in both area and population, the Dominican Republic shares the island of Hispaniola with Haiti, with the Dominican Republic occupying the eastern two-thirds. The country is mountainous, and the generally hot and humid climate eases with altitude.

POLITICS & ECONOMY In 1492, Christopher Columbus landed on Hispaniola and Spaniards soon settled the island, followed by the French, who occupied the western third of the island (which is now Haiti). The island was held by Haitians from 1822 until 1844, when the Dominican Republic was established. Civil war broke out in 1966 but US intervention ended the conflict. Since 1966, the young democracy has survived violent elections under the watchful eye of the United States.

The Dominican Republic is a developing country and agriculture is the chief activity. Sugarcane, rice, bananas, and cocoa are leading crops. Food processing is also important and some ferronickel is produced.

AREA 18,730 sq mi [48,511 sq km] **POPULATION** 9,957,000
CAPITAL Santo Domingo **GOVERNMENT** Multiparty republic
ETHNIC GROUPS Mulatto 73%, White 16%, Black 11%
LANGUAGES Spanish (official) **RELIGIONS** Roman Catholic 95%
CURRENCY Dominican peso = 100 centavos

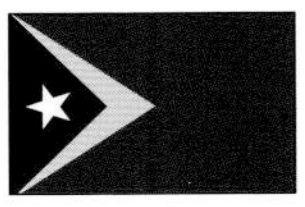
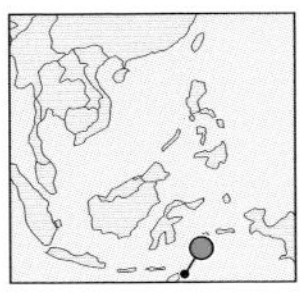

EAST TIMOR

The Republic of East Timor became fully independent on May 20, 2002. The land is mainly rugged. Temperatures are generally high and the rainfall is moderate. Portugal ruled the area from the late 19th century, when it was called Portuguese Timor. Portugal withdrew in 1975 and Indonesia seized the area. Guerrilla activity mounted under Indonesian rule and, in 1999, the people voted for independence. Agriculture is the main activity and East Timor is the poorest country in Southeast Asia. But, in 2006, East Timor and Australia signed a deal to share the revenue from the oil and natural gas deposits under the Timor Sea.

AREA 5,743 sq mi [14,874 sq km] **POPULATION** 1,178,000 **CAPITAL** Dili

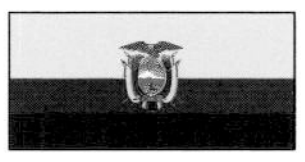
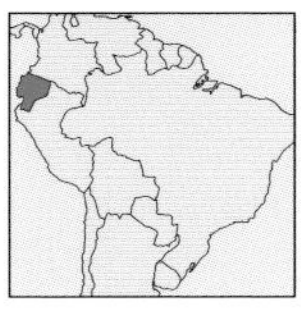

ECUADOR

GEOGRAPHY The Republic of Ecuador straddles the equator on the west coast of South America. Three ranges of the high Andes Mountains form the backbone of the country. Between the towering, snow-capped peaks of the mountains, some of which are volcanoes, lie a series of high plateaux, or basins. Nearly half of Ecuador's population lives on these plateaux. The coast has a warm tropical climate, despite the cold offshore Peruvian Current. Inland, the altitude gives the plateaux spring-like weather throughout the year.

POLITICS & ECONOMY The Inca people of Peru conquered much of what is now Ecuador in the late 15th century. They introduced their language, Quechua, which is widely spoken today. Spanish forces defeated the Incas in 1533 and took control of Ecuador. The country became independent in 1822, following the defeat of a Spanish force in a battle near Quito.

In the 19th and 20th centuries, Ecuador suffered from political instability, while successive governments failed to tackle the country's social and economic problems. A war with Peru in 1941 led to a loss of territory. Disputes continued until 1995, but a border agreement was signed in January 1998. Economic crises in the early 21st century led to the adoption of the US dollar as the official currency. Political instability marred progress. In 2006, the leftist Rafael Correa was elected president. In 2010, a state of emergency was declared following a coup attempt. In 2011, voters approved reforms in a referendum. Critics said the changes enhanced the president's powers even further.

The World Bank classifies Ecuador as a "lower-middle-income" developing country. Agriculture employs 8% of the people and bananas, cocoa, and coffee are all important crops. Fishing, forestry, mining, and manufacturing are other activities.

AREA 109,483 sq mi [283,561 sq km]
POPULATION 15,007,000 **CAPITAL** Quito
GOVERNMENT Multiparty republic
ETHNIC GROUPS Mestizo (mixed White/Amerindian) 65%, Amerindian 25%, White 7%, Black 3%
LANGUAGES Spanish (official), Quechua
RELIGIONS Roman Catholic 95%
CURRENCY US dollar = 100 cents

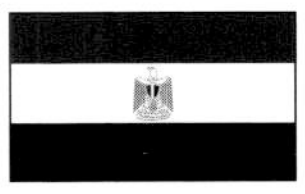
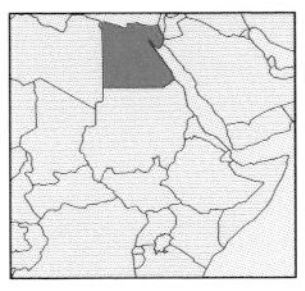

EGYPT

GEOGRAPHY The Arab Republic of Egypt is Africa's second largest country by population after Nigeria, though it ranks 13th in area. Most of Egypt is desert. Almost all the people live either in the Nile Valley and its fertile delta or along the Suez Canal, the artificial waterway between the Mediterranean and Red seas. This canal shortens the sea journey between the United Kingdom and India by 6,027 mi [9,700 km]. Recent attempts have been made to irrigate parts of the western desert and thus redistribute the rapidly growing Egyptian population into previously uninhabited regions.

Apart from the Nile Valley, Egypt has three other main regions. The Western and Eastern deserts are parts of the Sahara. The Sinai peninsula (Es Sina), to the east of the Suez Canal, is a mountainous desert region, geographically within Asia. It contains Egypt's highest peak, Gebel Katherina (8,650 ft [2,637 m]); few people live in this area.

Egypt is a dry country. The low rainfall occurs, if at all, in winter and the country is one of the sunniest places on Earth.

POLITICS & ECONOMY Ancient Egypt, which was founded about 5,000 years ago, was one of the great early civilizations. Throughout the country, pyramids, temples, and richly decorated tombs are memorials to its great achievements.

After Ancient Egypt declined, the country came under successive foreign rulers. Arabs occupied Egypt in AD 639–42. They introduced the Arabic language and Islam. Their influence was so great that most Egyptians now regard themselves as Arabs.

Egypt came under British rule in 1882, but it gained partial independence in 1922, becoming a monarchy. The monarchy was abolished in 1952, when Egypt became a republic. The creation of Israel in 1948 led Egypt into a series of wars in 1948–9, 1956, 1967, and 1973. Since the late 1970s, Egypt has sought for peace. In 1979, Egypt signed a peace treaty with Israel and regained the Sinai region which it had lost in a war in 1967. Extremists opposed contacts with Israel and, in 1981, President Sadat, who had signed the treaty, was assassinated.

While Egypt plays a major part in Arab affairs, most of its people are poor. In the 1990s, attacks on foreign visitors caused a decline in the valuable tourist industry. In February 2011, Hosni Mubarak,

Egypt's president since 1981, was forced out of office following huge popular demonstrations. A Supreme Military Council took power and organized elections in 2011–12. The leading parties were the political wing of the formerly banned Muslim Brotherhood and the more conservative Salafist Islamist Party. Mubarak was sentenced to life imprisonment in 2012 for failing to stop the killing of protesters in the 2011 uprising.

Egypt is Africa's second most industrialized country after South Africa, but most people are poor. Oil and textiles are the country's main exports. In 2007, the government announced plans to build several nuclear power stations to generate electricity.

AREA 386,659 sq mi [1,001,449 sq km] **POPULATION** 82,080,000
CAPITAL Cairo **GOVERNMENT** Republic
ETHNIC GROUPS Egyptians/Bedouins/Berbers 99%
LANGUAGES Arabic (official), French, English **RELIGIONS** Islam (mainly Sunni Muslim) 94%, Christianity (mainly Coptic Christian) and others 6% **CURRENCY** Egyptian pound = 100 piastres

EL SALVADOR

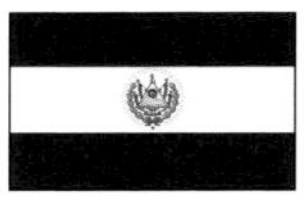

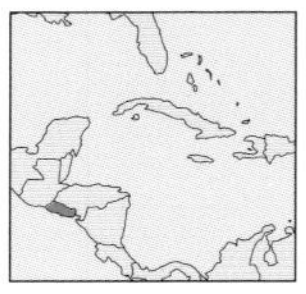

GEOGRAPHY The Republic of El Salvador is the only country in Central America not to have a coast on the Caribbean Sea. El Salvador has a narrow coastal plain along the Pacific Ocean. Behind the coastal plain, the coastal range is a zone of rugged mountains, including volcanoes, which overlooks a densely populated inland plateau. Beyond the plateau, the land rises to the sparsely populated interior highlands. The coast has a hot tropical climate, but inland this is moderated by the altitude. Rain is heavy between May and October. In October 2011, torrential rains caused flooding that killed several people in El Salvador.

POLITICS & ECONOMY Amerindians have lived in El Salvador for thousands of years. The ruins of Mayan pyramids built between AD 100 and 1000 are still found in the western part of the country. Spanish soldiers conquered the area in 1524 and 1525, and Spain ruled until 1821. In 1823, all the Central American countries, except for Panama, set up the Central American Federation. But El Salvador withdrew in 1840 and declared its independence in 1841. El Salvador suffered from instability throughout the 19th century. The 20th century saw more stable government, but from 1931 military dictatorships alternated with elected governments.

The country remained poor. In the 1970s, protesters demanded that the government introduce reforms to help the poor. Kidnappings and murders committed by left- and right-wing groups caused instability. A civil war broke out in 1979 between the US-backed government forces and left-wing guerrillas. A ceasefire was agreed in 1992. In 2011, the United States added El Salvador and Belize to its list of countries considered to be major producers or transit routes of illegal drugs.

The World Bank classifies El Salvador as a "lower-middle-income" economy. About three-quarters of the country is farmed. Coffee, grown in the highlands, is the main export, followed by sugar and cotton, which grow on the coastal lowlands. Fishing for lobsters and shrimps is important, but manufacturing is on a small scale.

AREA 8,124 sq mi [21,041 sq km]
POPULATION 6,072,000 **CAPITAL** San Salvador
GOVERNMENT Republic **ETHNIC GROUPS** Mestizo (mixed White and Amerindian) 90%, White 9%, Amerindian 1%
LANGUAGES Spanish (official) **RELIGIONS** Roman Catholic 83%
CURRENCY US dollar = 100 cents

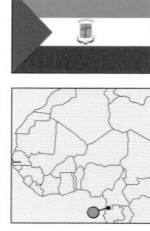

EQUATORIAL GUINEA

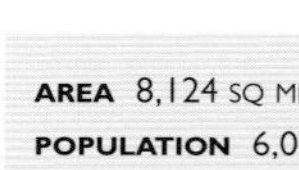

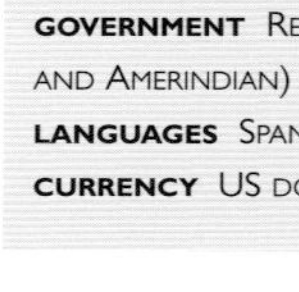

GEOGRAPHY The Republic of Equatorial Guinea is a small republic in west-central Africa. It consists of a mainland territory which makes up 90% of the land area, called Rio Muni, between Cameroon and Gabon, and five offshore islands in the Bight of Bonny, the largest of which is Bioko. The island of Annobon lies 350 mi [560 km] southwest of Rio Muni. Rio Muni consists mainly of hills and plateaux behind the coastal plains.

The climate is hot and humid. Bioko is mountainous, with the land rising to 9,869 ft [3,008 m], and hence it is particularly rainy. However, there is a marked dry season between the months of December and February. Mainland Rio Muni has a similar climate, though the rainfall diminishes inland.

POLITICS & ECONOMY Portuguese navigators reached the area in 1471. In 1778, Portugal granted Bioko, together with rights over Rio Muni, to Spain.

In 1959, Spain made Bioko and Rio Muni provinces of overseas Spain and, in 1963, it gave the provinces a degree of self-government. Equatorial Guinea became independent in 1968.

The first president of Equatorial Guinea, Francisco Macias Nguema, proved to be a tyrant. He was overthrown in 1979 and a group of officers, led by Lieutenant-Colonel Teodoro Obiang Nguema Mbasogo, set up a Supreme Military Council to rule the country. In 1991, a democratic system was restored, but alleged human rights abuses continued. In 2004, a coup attempt was foiled. In 2011, the corruption watchdog Transparency International placed the country in its list of the 12 most corrupt nations.

Agriculture employs two-thirds of the people. The most valuable crop is coffee. Oil, which has been produced since 1966, accounts for most of the export revenue.

AREA 10,830 sq mi [28,051 sq km] **POPULATION** 668,000
CAPITAL Malabo **GOVERNMENT** Multiparty republic (transitional)
ETHNIC GROUPS Bubi (on Bioko), Fang (in Rio Muni)
LANGUAGES Spanish and French (both official)
RELIGIONS Christianity **CURRENCY** CFA franc = 100 centimes

ERITREA

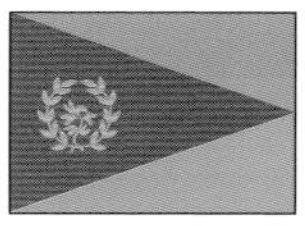

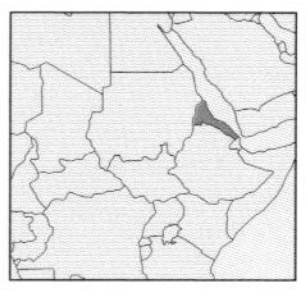

GEOGRAPHY The State of Eritrea consists of a hot, dry coastal plain facing the Red Sea, with a fairly mountainous area in the center. Most people live in the cooler highland area.

POLITICS & ECONOMY From the 1st century AD, Eritrea was part of the ancient Kingdom of Axum, which adopted Christianity in the 4th century AD. It began to decline in the 7th century. The Ottoman Turks took over the area in the 16th century and it became an Italian colony in the 1880s. The Italians were driven out in 1941 and, in 1952, it became part of Ethiopia. A guerrilla struggle launched in 1961 ended in 1993, when Eritrea became independent. Economic recovery was hampered by conflict with Yemen over three islands in the Red Sea. In 1988–9, clashes occurred along the border with Ethiopia. A peace agreement was signed in 2000, but problems continued. In 2011, the UN accused Eritrea of backing the Islamist al-Shabab in Eritrea. Tension between Eritrea and Ethiopia continued, and in 2012 Ethiopia attacked military bases in Eritrea where rebel groups were trained.

The main economic activities are farming and livestock rearing. The few manufacturing industries are based mainly in Asmara.

AREA 45,405 sq mi [117,600 sq km] **POPULATION** 5,939,000
CAPITAL Asmara **GOVERNMENT** Transitional government
ETHNIC GROUPS Tigrinya 50%, Tigre and Kunama 40%, Afar 4%, Saho 3%, others **LANGUAGES** Afar, Arabic, Tigre, Kunama, Tigrinya **RELIGIONS** Islam, Coptic Christian, Roman Catholic
CURRENCY Nakfa = 100 cents

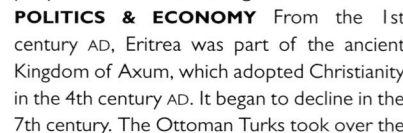

ESTONIA

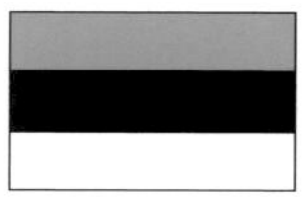

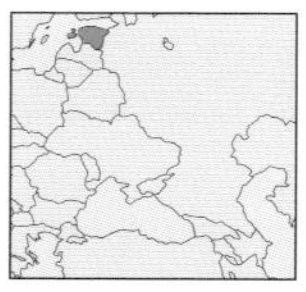

GEOGRAPHY The Republic of Estonia is the smallest of the three states on the Baltic Sea, which were formerly part of the Soviet Union, but became independent in the early 1990s. Estonia consists of a generally flat plain which was covered by ice sheets during the Ice Age. The land is strewn with moraine (rocks deposited by the ice).

The country is dotted with more than 1,500 small lakes. The large Lake Peipus (Chudskoye Ozero) and the River Narva together make up much of Estonia's eastern border with Russia. The largest of the islands is Saaremaa (Sarema). The climate is fairly mild because of the moderating effects of the sea.

POLITICS & ECONOMY The ancestors of the Estonians, who are related to the Finns, settled in the area several thousand years ago. German crusaders, known as the Teutonic Knights, introduced Christianity in the early 13th century. By the 16th century, German noblemen owned much of the land in Estonia. In 1561, Sweden took the northern part of the country and Poland the south. From 1625, Sweden controlled the entire country until Sweden handed it over to Russia in 1721.

Estonian nationalists campaigned for their independence from around the mid-19th century. Finally, Estonia was proclaimed independent in 1918. In 1919, the government began to break up the large estates and distribute land among the peasants.

In 1939, Germany and the Soviet Union agreed to take over parts of Eastern Europe. In 1940, Soviet forces occupied Estonia, but they were driven out by the Germans in 1941. Soviet troops returned in 1944 and Estonia became one of the 15 Soviet Socialist Republics of the Soviet Union. The Estonians strongly opposed Soviet rule. Many of them were deported to Siberia.

Political changes in the Soviet Union in the late 1980s led to renewed demands for freedom. In 1990, the Estonian government declared the country independent and, finally, the Soviet Union recognized this act in September 1991, shortly before the Soviet Union was dissolved. Estonia adopted a new constitution in 1992, and elections were held. In 1994, Russian troops withdrew, but anti-Russian sentiment continued. On January 1, 2011, Estonia became the 17th member of the eurozone.

Under Soviet rule, Estonia was the most prosperous of the three Baltic states. Since 1988, Estonia has worked to restructure its economy. Turning increasingly to the West, it became a member of both the North Atlantic Treaty Organization and the European Union in 2004. Estonia's resources include oil shale and its forests. Industries produce fertilizers, processed food, machinery, petrochemical products, wood products, and textiles. Agriculture and fishing are also important activities.

AREA 17,413 sq mi [45,100 sq km] **POPULATION** 1,283,000
CAPITAL Tallinn **GOVERNMENT** Multiparty republic
ETHNIC GROUPS Estonian 65%, Russian 28%, Ukrainian 3%, Belarusian 2%, Finnish 1% **LANGUAGES** Estonian (official), Russian
RELIGIONS Lutheran, Russian and Estonian Orthodox, Methodist, Baptist, Roman Catholic **CURRENCY** Euro = 100 cents

ETHIOPIA

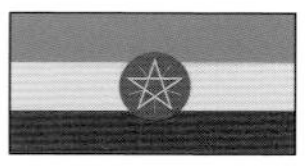

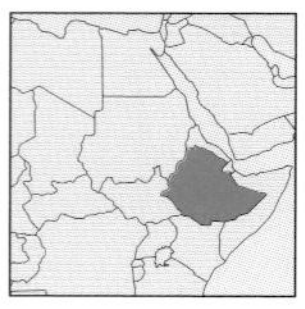

GEOGRAPHY Ethiopia is a landlocked country in northeastern Africa. The land is mainly mountainous, though there are extensive plains in the east, bordering southern Eritrea, and in the south, bordering Somalia. The highlands are divided into two blocks by an arm of the Great Rift Valley which runs throughout eastern Africa. North of the Rift Valley, the land is especially rugged, rising to 15,157 ft [4,620 m] at Ras Dashen. Southeast of Ras Dashen is Lake Tana, source of the River Abay (Blue Nile). The climate is affected by the altitude. The rainfall in the highlands is generally more than 39 inches [1,000 mm]. The lowlands are hot and arid.

POLITICS & ECONOMY Ethiopia was the home of an ancient monarchy, which became Christian in the 4th century. In the 7th century, Muslims gained control of the lowlands, but Christianity survived in the highlands. Ethiopia resisted attempts to colonize it, but Italy invaded the country in 1935. The Italians were driven out in 1941 during World War II.

In 1952, Eritrea, on the Red Sea coast, was federated with Ethiopia. But in 1961, Eritrean nationalists demanded their freedom and began a struggle that ended in their independence in 1993. In 1995, because of Ethiopia's great ethnic diversity, the country was divided into nine provinces, each with its own regional assembly. In 1998, boundary disputes with Eritrea led to conflict. A peace agreement was reached in 2001, but tensions mounted in 2005–6 when Ethiopia failed to accept an international ruling over Badme, a border settlement. In 2006, Ethiopian troops intervened in Somalia on behalf of its provisional government. Ethiopian troops defeated the Islamists, who had taken control of Mogadishu. Ethiopia withdrew its forces in 2009. In 2011, Ethiopian troops returned to Somalia in support of the African Union troops combating the Islamist al-Shabab forces.

Ethiopia is one of the world poorest countries. It is heavily dependent on aid. Agriculture is the main activity. Coffee and the drug khat are leading exports.

AREA 426,370 sq mi [1,104,300 sq km]
POPULATION 90,874,000 **CAPITAL** Addis Ababa
GOVERNMENT Federation of nine provinces
ETHNIC GROUPS Oromo 40%, Amhara and Tigre 32%, Sidamo 9%, Shankella 6%, Somali 6%, others **LANGUAGES** Amharic (official), many others **RELIGIONS** Islam 47%, Ethiopian Orthodox 40%, traditional beliefs 12% **CURRENCY** Birr = 100 cents

FALKLAND ISLANDS

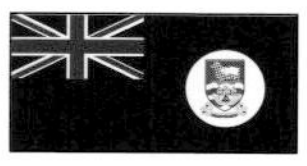

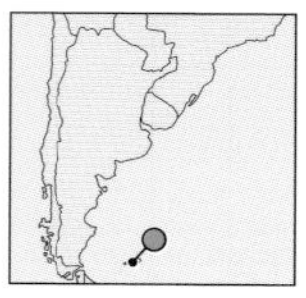

Comprising two main islands and over 200 small ones, the Falkland Islands (or the Islas Malvinas, as they are called in Argentina) lie 300 mi [480 km] from South America. Sheep farming is the main activity, though the search for oil and diamonds holds out hope for the future of this harsh and virtually treeless environment.

AREA 4,700 sq mi [12,173 sq km]
POPULATION 3,000 **CAPITAL** Stanley

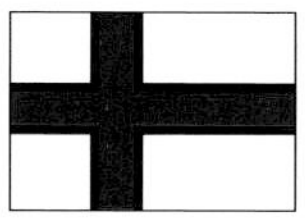

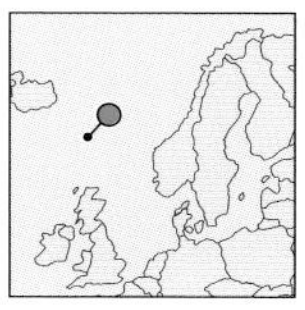

FÆROE ISLANDS

The Færoe Islands are a group of 18 volcanic islands and some reefs in the North Atlantic Ocean. The islands have been Danish since the 1380s, but they became largely self-governing in 1948. In 2001, a referendum on independence was called off after Denmark said that subsidies would end soon after independence.

AREA 540 sq mi [1,399 sq km]
POPULATION 49,000 **CAPITAL** Tórshavn

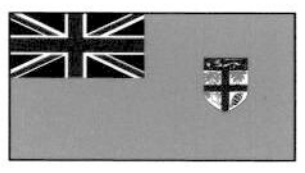

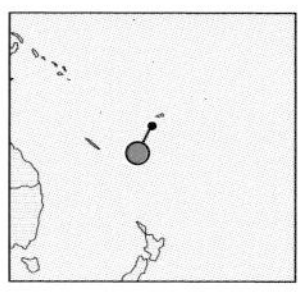

FIJI

The Republic of Fiji (the official name of Fiji since February 2011) consists of more than 800 Melanesian islands, the biggest being Viti Levu and Vanua Levu. The climate is tropical. A former British colony, Fiji became independent in 1970. Its recent history has been marred by efforts of ethnic Fijians to impose their rule, stopping members of the ethnic Indian community from holding senior cabinet posts. Coups have occurred in 1987, 2000, and 2006.

AREA 7,056 sq mi [18,274 sq km] **POPULATION** 883,000 **CAPITAL** Suva

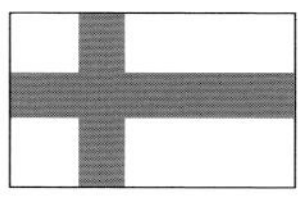

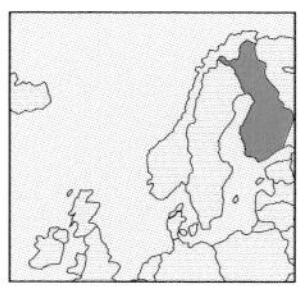

FINLAND

GEOGRAPHY The Republic of Finland is a beautiful country in northern Europe. In the south, behind the coastal lowlands where most Finns live, lies a region of sparkling lakes worn out by ice sheets in the Ice Age. The thinly populated northern uplands cover about two-fifths of the country.

Helsinki, the capital city, has warm summers, but the average temperatures between the months of December and March are below freezing point. Snow covers the land in winter. The north has less precipitation than the south, but it is much colder.

POLITICS & ECONOMY Between 1150 and 1809, Finland was under Swedish rule. The close links between the countries continue today. Swedish remains an official language in Finland and many towns have Swedish as well as Finnish names.

In 1809, Finland became a grand duchy of the Russian empire. It finally declared itself independent in 1917, after the Russian Revolution and the collapse of the Russian empire. But during World War II (1939–45), the Soviet Union declared war on Finland and took part of Finland's territory. Finland allied itself with Germany, but it lost more land to the Soviet Union at the end of the war.

After World War II, Finland became a neutral country and negotiated peace treaties with the Soviet Union. Finland also strengthened its relations with other northern European countries and became an associate member of the European Free Trade Association (EFTA) in 1961. Finland became a full member of EFTA in 1986, but then became a member of the European Union on January 1, 1995. It adopted the euro as its currency in 2002. In 2000 and 2006, the Social Democrat Tarja Halonen was elected Finland's first woman president, while in 2010, Mari Kiviniemi became its second woman prime minister.

Forests are the chief resource and wood, wood products, and paper once dominated the economy. They still make up about a quarter of exports, but, since World War II, Finland has set up many new industries, which employ around 17% of the work force. Major exports include telecommunications equipment, paper products, and iron and steel.

AREA 130,558 sq mi [338,145 sq km]
POPULATION 5,259,000 **CAPITAL** Helsinki
GOVERNMENT Multiparty republic **ETHNIC GROUPS** Finnish 93%, Swedish 6% **LANGUAGES** Finnish and Swedish (both official)
RELIGIONS Evangelical Lutheran 89% **CURRENCY** Euro = 100 cents

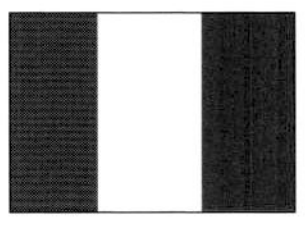

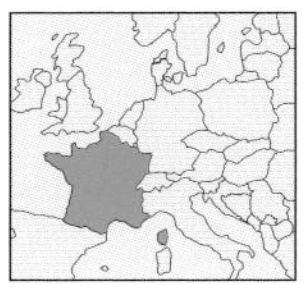

FRANCE

GEOGRAPHY The Republic of France is the largest country in Western Europe. The scenery is extremely varied. The Vosges Mountains overlook the Rhine valley in the northeast, the Jura Mountains and the Alps form the borders with Switzerland and Italy in the southeast, while the Pyrenees straddle France's border with Spain. The only large highland area entirely within France is the Massif Central between the Rhône-Saône valley and the basin of Aquitaine in southern France.

Brittany (Bretagne) and Normandy (Normande) form a scenic hill region. Fertile lowlands cover most of northern France, including the densely populated Paris basin. Another major lowland area, the Aquitanian basin, is in the southwest, while the Rhône-Saône valley and the Mediterranean lowlands are in the southeast.

The climate of France varies from west to east and from north to south. The west comes under the moderating influence of the Atlantic Ocean, giving generally mild weather. To the east, summers are warmer and winters colder. The climate also becomes warmer as one travels from north to south. The Mediterranean Sea coast has hot, dry summers and mild, moist winters. The Alps, Jura, and Pyrenees mountains have snowy winters. Winter sports centers are found in all three areas. Large glaciers occupy high valleys in the Alps.

POLITICS & ECONOMY The Romans conquered France (then called Gaul) in the 50s BC. Roman rule began to decline in the 5th century AD and, in 486, the Frankish realm (as France was called) became independent under a Christian king, Clovis. In 800, Charlemagne, who had been king since 768, became emperor of the Romans. He extended France's boundaries, but in 843 his empire was divided into three parts and the area of France contracted. After the Norman invasion of England in 1066, large areas of France came under English rule, but this was all but ended in 1453.

France later became a powerful monarchy. But the French Revolution (1789–99) ended absolute rule by French kings. In 1799, Napoleon Bonaparte took power and fought a series of brilliant military campaigns before his final defeat in 1815. The monarchy was restored until 1848, when the Second Republic was founded. In 1852, Napoleon's nephew became Napoleon III, but the Third Republic was established in 1875. France was the scene of much fighting during World War I (1914–18) and World War II (1939–45), causing great loss of life and much damage to the economy.

In 1946, France adopted a new constitution, establishing the Fourth Republic. But political instability and costly colonial wars slowed France's post-war recovery. In 1958, Charles de Gaulle was elected president and he introduced a new constitution, giving the president extra powers and inaugurating the Fifth Republic.

Since the 1960s, France has made rapid economic progress, becoming one of the most prosperous nations in the European Union. But France's government faced a number of problems, including unemployment, pollution, and the growing number of elderly people. In 2011–12, France faced economic difficulties linked to the problems of some eurozone member nations. A social issue concerns the large numbers of immigrants, including Muslims from North Africa.

In 2002, the euro became France's sole unit of currency, replacing the franc. In 2005, France was rocked by inter-ethnic violence and, in 2007, the right-wing Nicolas Sarkozy was elected president. In 2009, he announced that France would rejoin NATO, from which President de Gaulle had withdrawn in 1966. François Hollande, a socialist, was elected president in 2012.

France is one of the world's most developed countries. Its natural resources include its fertile soil, together with deposits of bauxite, coal, iron ore, oil and natural gas, and potash. France is also one of the world's top manufacturing nations, and it has often innovated in bold and imaginative ways. The TGV and hypermarkets are typical examples. Paris is a world center of fashion industries, but France has many other industrial towns and cities. Major manufactures include aircraft, cars, chemicals, electronic and metal products, machinery, processed food, steel, and textiles.

Agriculture employs about 3% of the people, but France is the largest producer of farm products in Western Europe, producing most of the food it needs. Wheat is the leading crop and livestock farming is of major importance. Fishing and forestry are leading industries, while tourism is a major activity.

AREA 212,934 sq mi [551,500 sq km] **POPULATION** 65,312,000
CAPITAL Paris **GOVERNMENT** Multiparty republic
ETHNIC GROUPS Celtic, Latin, Arab, Teutonic, Slavic
LANGUAGES French (official) **RELIGIONS** Roman Catholic 85%, Islam 8%, others **CURRENCY** Euro = 100 cents

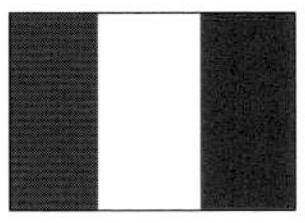

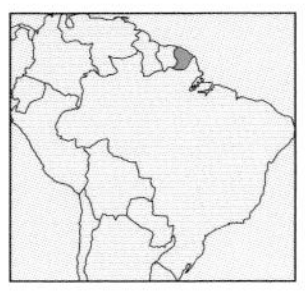

FRENCH GUIANA

GEOGRAPHY French Guiana is the smallest country in mainland South America. The coastal plain is swampy in places, but some dry areas are cultivated. Inland lies a plateau, with the low Tumachumac Mountains in the south. Most of the rivers run north toward the Atlantic Ocean.

French Guiana has a hot, equatorial climate, with high temperatures throughout the year. The rainfall is heavy, especially between December and June, but the climate is dry between August and October. The northeast trade winds blow constantly across the country.

POLITICS & ECONOMY The first people to live in what is now French Guiana were Amerindians. Today, only a few of them survive in the interior. The first Europeans to explore the coast arrived in 1500, and they were followed by adventurers seeking El Dorado, the mythical city of gold. Cayenne was founded in 1637 by a group of French merchants. The area became a French colony in the late 17th century.

France used the colony as a penal settlement for political prisoners from the times of the French Revolution in the 1790s. From the 1850s to 1945, the country became notorious as a place where prisoners were harshly treated. Many of them died, unable to survive in the tropical conditions.

In 1946, French Guiana became an overseas department of France, and in 1974 it also became an administrative region. An independence movement developed in the 1980s, but most people want to retain their links with France. In 2010, the people voted in a referendum to reject plans for increased autonomy.

Although it has rich forest and mineral resources, such as bauxite (aluminum ore), French Guiana is a developing country. It depends greatly on France for money to run its services and the government is the country's biggest employer. Since 1968, Kourou in French Guiana, the European Space Agency's rocket-launching site, has earned money for France by sending communications satellites into space.

AREA 34,749 sq mi [90,000 sq km]
POPULATION 229,000 **CAPITAL** Cayenne
GOVERNMENT Overseas department of France
ETHNIC GROUPS Black or Mulatto 66%, East Indian/Chinese and Amerindian 12%, White 12%, others 10% **LANGUAGES** French (official) **RELIGIONS** Roman Catholic **CURRENCY** Euro = 100 cents

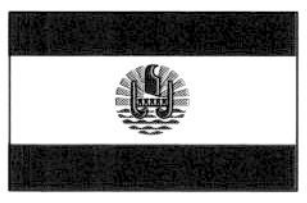

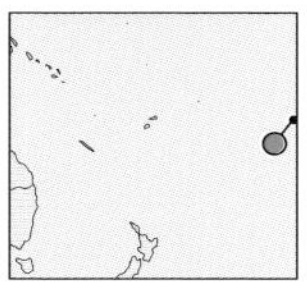

FRENCH POLYNESIA

French Polynesia consists of 130 islands, scattered over 1.5 million sq mi [4 million sq km] of the Pacific Ocean. Tribal chiefs in the area agreed to a French protectorate in 1843. They gained increased autonomy in 1984, but the links with France ensure a high standard of living.

AREA 1,544 sq mi [4,000 sq km]
POPULATION 295,000 **CAPITAL** Papeete

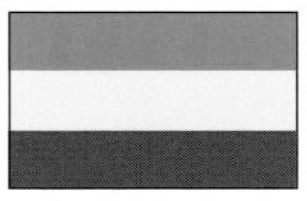

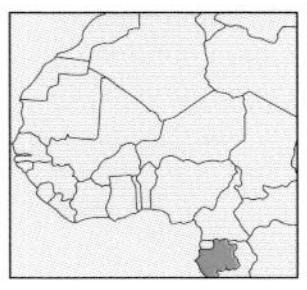

GABON

GEOGRAPHY The Gabonese Republic lies on the equator in west-central Africa. In area, it is a little larger than the United Kingdom, with a coastline 500 mi [800 km] long. Behind the narrow, partly lagoon-lined coastal plain, the land rises to hills, plateaux, and mountains divided by deep valleys carved by the River Ogooué and its tributaries.

Most of Gabon has an equatorial climate, with high temperatures and humidity throughout the year. Rainfall is heavy and the skies are often cloudy.

POLITICS & ECONOMY Gabon became a French colony in the 1880s, but it achieved full independence in 1960. In 1964, an attempted coup was put down when French troops intervened and crushed the revolt. In 1967, Bernard-Albert Bongo, who later renamed himself El Hadj Omar Bongo, became president. He declared Gabon a one-party state in 1968. Opposition parties were legalized in 1991, but Bongo was re-elected president in 1993. Following his death in 2008, he was succeeded by his son Ali Ben Bongo, who was elected in 2009.

Gabon's natural resources include its forests, oil and gas deposits, manganese, and uranium. Its mineral deposits make it one of Africa's better-off countries. But agriculture still employs about 30% of the people and many farmers produce little more than they need to support their families.

AREA 103,347 sq mi [267,668 sq km]
POPULATION 1,577,000 **CAPITAL** Libreville
GOVERNMENT Multiparty republic
ETHNIC GROUPS Four major Bantu tribes: Fang, Bapounou, Nzebi and Obamba **LANGUAGES** French (official), Fang, Myene, Nzebi, Bapounou/Eschira, Bandjabi
RELIGIONS Christianity 75%, animist, Islam
CURRENCY CFA franc = 100 centimes

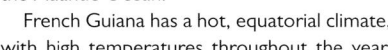

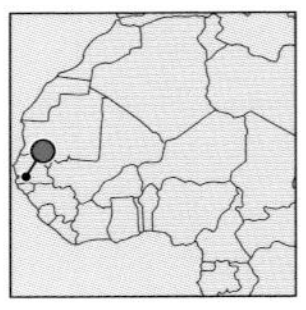

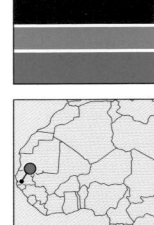

GAMBIA, THE

GEOGRAPHY The Republic of The Gambia is the smallest country in mainland Africa. It consists of a narrow strip of land bordering the River Gambia. The Gambia is almost entirely enclosed by Senegal, except along the short Atlantic coastline.

The Gambia has hot and humid summers, but winter temperatures (November to May) drop to around 61°F [16°C]. In the summer, moist southwesterlies bring rain, which is heaviest on the coast.

POLITICS & ECONOMY English traders bought rights to trade on the River Gambia in 1588, and in 1664 the English established a settlement on an island in the river estuary. In 1765, the British founded Senegambia, which included parts of The Gambia and Senegal. In 1783, Britain handed this colony over to France. In the 19th century, Britain and France discussed the exchange of The Gambia for some other French territory, but an agreement was reached and Britain made The Gambia a British colony in 1888.

The Gambia achieved independence in 1965 and it became a republic in 1970. In 1981, an attempted coup in The Gambia was put down with the help of Senegalese troops. In 1982, The Gambia and Senegal set up a defense alliance, called the Confederation of Senegambia. But this alliance was dissolved in 1989. In 1994, a military group led by Captain Yahya Jammeh overthrew the government of Sir Dawda Jawara. Jammeh became president and was re-elected in 1996, 2001, 2006, and 2011.

Agriculture is the chief activity. Food crops include cassava, millet, and sorghum, but groundnuts (peanuts) and groundnut products are the main exports. Tourism is growing and offshore oilfields were discovered in 2004. In the early 21st century, The Gambia became a transit point for drugs from Latin America.

AREA 4,361 SQ MI [11,295 SQ KM]
POPULATION 1,798,000 **CAPITAL** BANJUL
GOVERNMENT REPUBLIC
ETHNIC GROUPS MANDINKA 42%, FULA 18%, WOLOF 16%, JOLA 10%, SERAHULI 9%, OTHERS
LANGUAGES ENGLISH (OFFICIAL), MANDINKA, WOLOF, FULA
RELIGIONS ISLAM 90%, CHRISTIANITY 9%, TRADITIONAL BELIEFS 1%
CURRENCY DALASI = 100 BUTUT

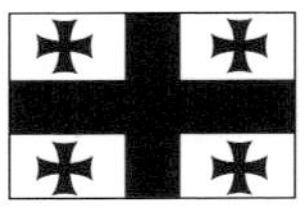

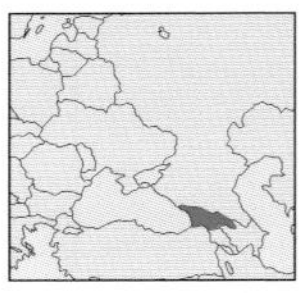

GEORGIA

GEOGRAPHY Georgia is a country on the borders of Europe and Asia, facing the Black Sea. The land is rugged with the Caucasus Mountains forming its northern border. The highest mountain in this range, Mount Elbrus (18,510 ft [5,642 m]), lies over the border in Russia. The Black Sea plains have hot summers and mild winters. The rainfall is heavy, though inland areas are drier.

POLITICS & ECONOMY The first Georgian state was set up nearly 2,500 years ago. But for much of its history, the area was ruled by various conquerors. Christianity was introduced in AD 330. Georgia freed itself of foreign rule in the 11th and 12th centuries, but Mongol armies attacked in the 13th century. From the 16th to the 18th centuries, Persia and the Turkish Ottoman empire struggled for control of the area, and in the late 18th century Georgia sought the protection of Russia. By the early 19th century, it was part of the Russian empire. After the Russian Revolution of 1917, Georgia declared its independence, but Russia invaded, making the country part of the Soviet regime. Georgia declared itself independent in 1991. It became a separate country when the Soviet Union was dissolved in December 1991.

Georgia contains three regions containing minority peoples: Abkhazia in the northwest, South Ossetia in north-central Georgia, and Adjaria (also spelled Adzharia) in the southwest. Civil war broke out in South Ossetia in the early 1990s, while fierce fighting continued in Abkhazia until the late 1990s. In 2000, Georgia agreed to recognize Adjaria's autonomy in the country's constitution. In 2003, the pro-Western Mikhail Saakashvili was elected president following the "Rose Revolution." Following Saakashvili's re-election in 2008, relations with Russia deteriorated. In August 2008, Georgia tried to retake South Ossetia by force. Russian troops counter-attacked and drove Georgian troops out of South Ossetia and Abkhazia. Despite Georgian and Western protests, Russia recognized both of these breakaway regions as independent nations.

Georgia is a developing country. Agriculture, food processing, and perfume-making are important activities. Products include barley, citrus fruits, grapes for wine-making, maize, tea, tobacco, and vegetables. Sheep and cattle are reared.

AREA 26,911 SQ MI [69,700 SQ KM]
POPULATION 4,586,000 **CAPITAL** TBILISI
GOVERNMENT MULTIPARTY REPUBLIC
ETHNIC GROUPS GEORGIAN 70%, ARMENIAN 8%, RUSSIAN 6%, AZERI 6%, OSSETIAN 3%, GREEK 2%, ABKHAZ 2%, OTHERS 3%
LANGUAGES GEORGIAN (OFFICIAL), RUSSIAN
RELIGIONS GEORGIAN ORTHODOX 65%, ISLAM 11%, RUSSIAN ORTHODOX 10%, ARMENIAN APOSTOLIC 8% **CURRENCY** LARI = 100 TETRI

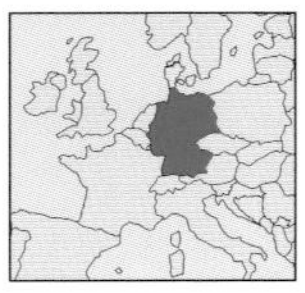

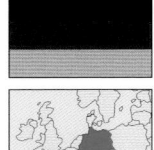

GERMANY

GEOGRAPHY The Federal Republic of Germany is the fourth largest country in Western Europe, after France, Spain, and Sweden. The North German Plain borders the North Sea in the northwest and the Baltic Sea in the northeast. Major rivers draining the plain include the Weser, Elbe, and Oder.

The central highlands include the Harz Mountains, the Thuringian Forest (Thüringer Wald), the Ore Mountains (Erzgebirge), and the Bohemian Forest (Böhmerwald) on the Czech border. The Bavarian Alps in the south contain Germany's highest peak, Zugspitze, at 9,718 ft [2,962 m] above sea level. The Black Forest (Schwarzwald) in the southwest overlooks the River Rhine. Northwestern Germany has a mild climate, but the Baltic coasts are cooler. To the south, the climate becomes more continental, especially in the highlands. Precipitation is greatest on the uplands, with snow in winter.

POLITICS & ECONOMY Germany and its allies were defeated in World War I (1914–18) and the country became a republic. Adolf Hitler came to power in 1933 and ruled as a dictator. His order to invade Poland led to the start of World War II (1939–45), which ended with Germany in ruins.

In 1945, Germany was divided into four military zones. In 1949, the American, British, and French zones were amalgamated to form the Federal Republic of Germany (West Germany), while the Soviet zone became the German Democratic Republic (East Germany), a Communist state. Berlin, which had also been partitioned, became a divided city. West Berlin was part of West Germany, while East Berlin became the capital of East Germany. Bonn was the capital of West Germany.

Tension between East and West mounted during the Cold War, but West Germany rebuilt its economy quickly. In East Germany, the recovery was less rapid. In the late 1980s, reforms in the Soviet Union led to unrest in East Germany. Free elections were held in East Germany in 1990 and, on October 3, 1990, Germany was reunited.

The united Germany adopted West Germany's official name, the Federal Republic of Germany. In the 1990s, the government faced many problems, especially those arising from reunification. In 1999, the parliament moved from Bonn to the reconstructed Reichstag building in Berlin. In 2005, Angela Merkel became Germany's first female Chancellor. She was swept back into power in elections in 2009.

West Germany's "economic miracle" after World War II was greatly helped by foreign aid. Today, Germany is one of the world's leading economic powers. It is a leading member of the European Union and the 17-member eurozone. In 2011–12, it helped to maintain the eurozone in supporting debt-ridden countries, such as Greece. The mainstay of its export-led economy is manufacturing. Exports include machinery, metals, chemicals, and vehicles. Germany has some coal, potash, and rock salt deposits, but it imports many industrial raw materials. Germany also imports food. Leading agricultural products include fruits, grapes for wine-making, potatoes, sugar beet, and vegetables. Livestock include beef and dairy cattle.

AREA 137,846 SQ MI [357,022 SQ KM]
POPULATION 81,472,000 **CAPITAL** BERLIN
GOVERNMENT FEDERAL MULTIPARTY REPUBLIC
ETHNIC GROUPS GERMAN 92%, TURKISH 3%, SERBO-CROATIAN, ITALIAN, GREEK, POLISH, SPANISH **LANGUAGES** GERMAN (OFFICIAL)
RELIGIONS PROTESTANT (MAINLY LUTHERAN) 34%, ROMAN CATHOLIC 34%, ISLAM 4%, OTHERS **CURRENCY** EURO = 100 CENTS

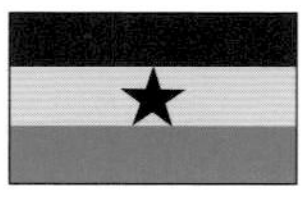

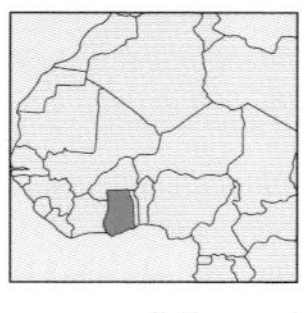

GHANA

GEOGRAPHY The Republic of Ghana faces the Gulf of Guinea in West Africa. This hot country, just north of the equator, was formerly called the Gold Coast. Behind the thickly populated southern coastal plains, which are lined with lagoons, lies a plateau region in the southwest.

Accra has a hot, tropical climate. Rain occurs all through the year, though Accra is drier than areas inland.

POLITICS & ECONOMY Portuguese explorers reached the area in 1471 and named it the Gold Coast. The area became a center of the slave trade in the 17th century. The slave trade was ended in the 1860s and, gradually, the British took control of the area. After independence in 1957, attempts were made to develop the economy by creating large state-owned manufacturing industries. But debt and corruption, together with falls in the price of cocoa, the chief export, caused economic problems. This led to instability and frequent coups. In 1981, power was invested in a Provisional National Defense Council, led by Flight-Lieutenant Jerry Rawlings.

The government steadied the economy and introduced reforms. In 1992, a new constitution allowing for multiparty elections was adopted. Rawlings was elected president in 1992 and 1996. He retired in 2002 and was succeeded as president by John Ageykum Kufuor. In 2008, opposition leader John Atta-Mills was narrowly elected president. The World Bank classifies Ghana as a "low-income" developing country. Most people are poor and farming employs 50% of the population.

AREA 92,098 SQ MI [238,533 SQ KM] **POPULATION** 24,791,000
CAPITAL ACCRA **GOVERNMENT** REPUBLIC
ETHNIC GROUPS AKAN 44%, MOSHI-DAGOMBA 16%, EWE 13%, GA 8%, GURMA 3%, YORUBA 1% **LANGUAGES** ENGLISH (OFFICIAL), AKAN, MOSHI-DAGOMBA, EWE, GA **RELIGIONS** CHRISTIANITY 63%, TRADITIONAL BELIEFS 21%, ISLAM 16% **CURRENCY** CEDI = 100 PESEWAS

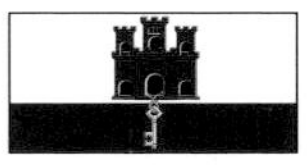

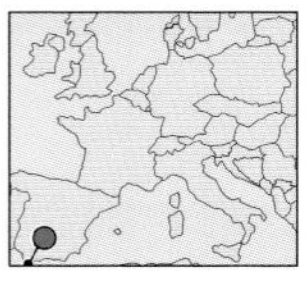

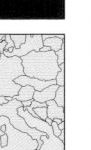

GIBRALTAR

Gibraltar occupies a strategic position on the south coast of Spain where the Mediterranean meets the Atlantic. It was recognized as a British possession in 1713 and, despite Spanish claims, its population has consistently voted to retain its contacts with Britain.

AREA 2.3 SQ MI [6 SQ KM]
POPULATION 29,000 **CAPITAL** GIBRALTAR TOWN

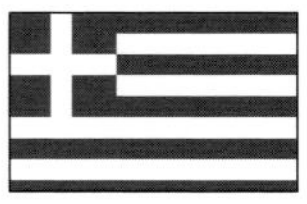

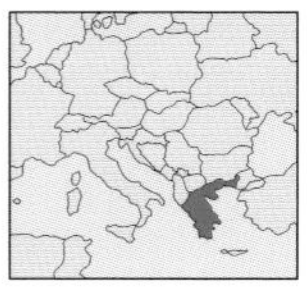

GREECE

GEOGRAPHY The Hellenic Republic, as Greece is officially called, is a rugged country situated at the southern end of the Balkan peninsula. Olympus, at 9,570 ft [2,917 m], is the highest peak. Islands make up about a fifth of the land area.

Low-lying areas in Greece have mild, moist winters and hot, dry summers. The east coast has more than 2,700 hours of sunshine a year and only about half of the rainfall of the west. The mountains have a much more severe climate, with snow on the higher slopes in winter.

POLITICS & ECONOMY Around 2,500 years ago, Greece became the birthplace of Western civilization, and Ancient Greek ruins and art still attract millions of tourists to the country. The first civilization, the Minoan, was centered on Crete. It flourished between about 3000 and 1400 BC. Following the end of the related Mycaenean period on the mainland (1580–1100 BC), a "dark age" lasted until about 800 BC. But from 750 BC, Greeks became rich traders and the city-state of Athens reached its peak in 461–431 BC. Greece became a Roman province in 146 BC and, in AD 365, it became part of the Byzantine empire.

The Byzantine empire fell to the Turks in 1453. But Greece became an independent monarchy in 1830. After World War II (1939–45), when Germany ruled Greece, a civil war broke out between Greek Communists and nationalists. It ended in 1949 and a military dictatorship seized power in 1967. The monarchy was abolished in 1973 and democracy was restored in 1974. Greece joined the European Community (now the European Union) in 1981 and, on January 1, 2002, the euro became the sole unit of currency in Greece. In 2010–12, its government faced a debt crisis and was forced to take drastic emergency measures.

Greece is one of the EU's less economically developed members. Manufactured products include processed food, cement, chemicals, metal products, textiles, and tobacco. Greece also mines lignite (brown coal), bauxite, and chromite. Farmland covers about a third of the country and pasture 40%. Crops include barley, grapes, dried fruits, olives, potatoes, sugar beet, and wheat. Livestock farming is important and tourism is a major industry.

AREA 50,949 SQ MI [131,957 SQ KM]
POPULATION 10,760,000 **CAPITAL** ATHENS
GOVERNMENT MULTIPARTY REPUBLIC **ETHNIC GROUPS** GREEK 98%
LANGUAGES GREEK (OFFICIAL) **RELIGIONS** GREEK ORTHODOX 98%
CURRENCY EURO = 100 CENTS

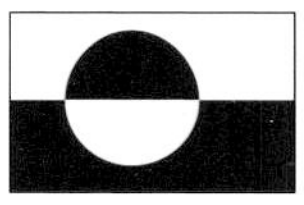
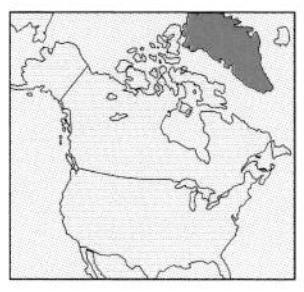

GREENLAND

Greenland is the world's largest island. Settlements are confined to the coast, because an ice sheet covers four-fifths of the land. Greenland became a Danish possession in 1380. Full internal self-government was granted in 1981 and, in 2009, Greenland became a self-governing territory, though it remains dependent on Danish subsidies.

AREA 838,999 SQ MI [2,175,600 SQ KM]
POPULATION 58,000 **CAPITAL** NUUK

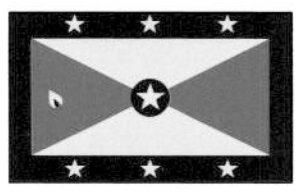
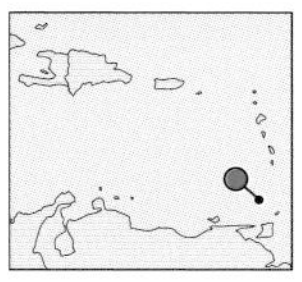

GRENADA

The most southerly of the Windward Islands in the Caribbean Sea, Grenada became independent from the UK in 1974. A military group seized power in 1983, when the prime minister was killed. US troops intervened and restored order and constitutional government.

AREA 133 SQ MI [344 SQ KM]
POPULATION 108,000 **CAPITAL** ST GEORGE'S

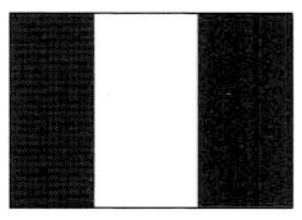
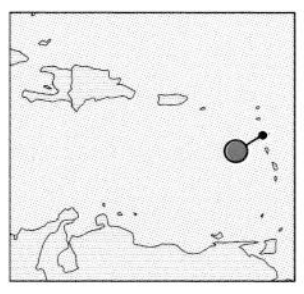

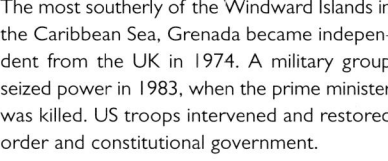

GUADELOUPE

Guadeloupe is a French overseas department which includes seven Caribbean islands, the largest of which is Basse-Terre. French aid has helped to maintain a reasonable standard of living for the people.

AREA 658 SQ MI [1,705 SQ KM]
POPULATION 452,000 **CAPITAL** BASSE-TERRE

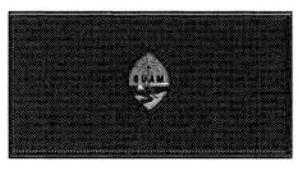
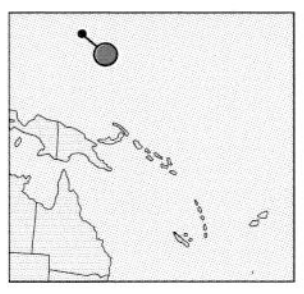

GUAM

Guam, a strategically important "unincorporated territory" of the USA, is the largest of the Mariana Islands in the Pacific Ocean. It is composed of a coralline limestone plateau.

AREA 212 SQ MI [549 SQ KM]
POPULATION 183,000 **CAPITAL** AGANA

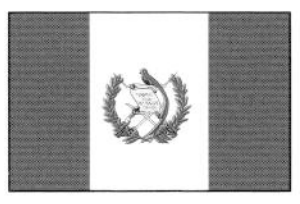
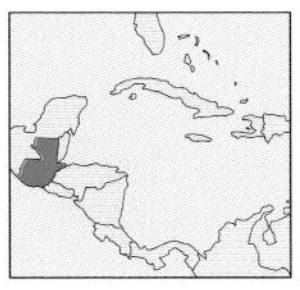

GUATEMALA

GEOGRAPHY The Republic of Guatemala in Central America contains a densely populated mountain region, with fertile soils. The mountains, which run in an east–west direction, contain many volcanoes, some of which are active. Volcanic eruptions and earthquakes are common in the highlands. South of the mountains lie the thinly populated Pacific coastlands, while a large inland plain occupies the north.

The lowlands of Guatemala are hot and rainy, but the central highlands are cooler and drier. Guatemala City has a pleasant, warm climate with a dry season between November and April.

POLITICS & ECONOMY Much of what is now Guatemala was part of the Maya empire which thrived between AD 300 and 900. Spain ruled the area from the 1520s until 1821. In 1823, Guatemala joined the Central American Federation. But it became fully independent in 1839. Instability and periodic violence have marred its progress. Guatemala has a long-standing claim over Belize, but this was reduced in 1983 to the southern fifth of the country. Between 1960 and 1996, civil war occurred between left-wing groups, including many Amerindians, and government forces. The war claimed perhaps 200,000 lives. In 2011, former army general Otto Perez Molina of the right-wing Patriotic Party was elected president.

Guatemala is ranked as a "lower-middle-income" economy. Agriculture employs 38% of the population. Coffee, sugar, bananas, and beef are exported, and the spice cardamom and cotton are also important. Maize is the main food crop.

AREA 42,042 SQ MI [108,889 SQ KM]
POPULATION 13,824,000 **CAPITAL** GUATEMALA CITY
GOVERNMENT REPUBLIC **ETHNIC GROUPS** LADINO (MIXED HISPANIC AND AMERINDIAN) 55%, AMERINDIAN 43%, OTHERS 2%
LANGUAGES SPANISH (OFFICIAL), AMERINDIAN LANGUAGES
RELIGIONS CHRISTIANITY, INDIGENOUS MAYAN BELIEFS
CURRENCY US DOLLAR; QUETZAL = 100 CENTAVOS

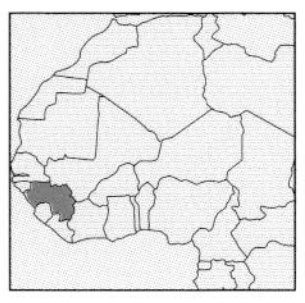

GUINEA

GEOGRAPHY The Republic of Guinea faces the Atlantic Ocean in West Africa. A flat, swampy plain borders the coast. Behind this plain, the land rises to a plateau region called Fouta Djalon. The Upper Niger Plains, named after one of Africa's longest rivers, the Niger, which rises there, are in the northeast.

Guinea has a tropical climate and Conakry has its rainy period between May and November, the coolest season. In the dry season, hot harmattan winds blow from the Sahara.

POLITICS & ECONOMY Guinea came under the influence of several medieval African states, including Ancient Ghana and Ancient Mali. France began to control the area in the late 19th century. Guinea became independent in 1958. Its leaders pursued socialist policies but resorted to repressive measures to hold on to power. A military regime under Lansana Conté took over in 1984, but a multiparty system was restored in 1992. Conté was elected president in 1993, 1998, and 2002. But following his death in 2008, an army group led by Captain Mousa Dadis Camara seized power. But in 2010, Alpha Condé was elected president in Guinea's first democratic election since independence.

Guinea is a "low-income" developing country. Its resources include bauxite (aluminum ore), diamonds, gold, iron ore, and uranium. Bauxite and alumina (processed bauxite) account for more than half of the country's exports. Agriculture employs more than 70% of the people, but most farmers are poor. Manufactures include alumina, processed food, and textiles.

AREA 94,925 SQ MI [245,857 SQ KM]
POPULATION 10,601,000 **CAPITAL** CONAKRY
GOVERNMENT MULTIPARTY REPUBLIC
ETHNIC GROUPS PEUHL 40%, MALINKE 30%, SOUSSOU 20%, OTHERS 10% **LANGUAGES** FRENCH (OFFICIAL)
RELIGIONS ISLAM 85%, CHRISTIANITY 8%, TRADITIONAL BELIEFS 7%
CURRENCY GUINEAN FRANC = 100 CAURIS

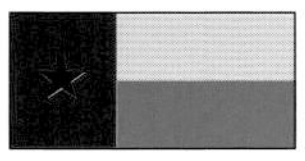
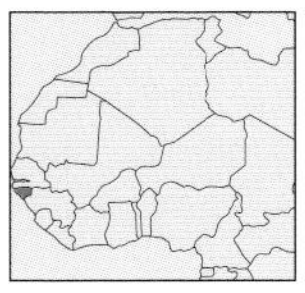

GUINEA-BISSAU

GEOGRAPHY The Republic of Guinea-Bissau, formerly known as Portuguese Guinea, is a small country in West Africa. The land is mostly low-lying, with a broad, swampy coastal plain and many flat offshore islands. The country has a tropical climate, with a dry season (December to May) and a wet season (June to November).

POLITICS & ECONOMY Portuguese explorers reached Guinea-Bissau in 1446 and the area became a center of the slave trade. From 1836, Portugal administered Guinea-Bissau with the Cape Verde Islands, but in 1879 the territories were separated. Guinea-Bissau became a separate colony called Portuguese Guinea. But economic development in the colony was slow.

In 1956, African nationalists in Portuguese Guinea and Cape Verde founded the African Party for the Independence of Guinea and Cape Verde (PAIGC). The PAIGC began a guerrilla war in 1963 and, by 1968, it held two-thirds of the country. In 1972, a rebel National Assembly, elected by the people in the PAIGC-controlled area, voted to make the country independent as Guinea-Bissau.

In 1974, newly independent Guinea-Bissau faced many problems arising from its underdeveloped economy and its lack of trained people to work in the administration. One objective of the leaders of Guinea-Bissau was to unite their country with Cape Verde. But, in 1980, army leaders overthrew Guinea-Bissau's government. The Revolutionary Council, which took over, opposed unification with Cape Verde. Guinea-Bissau ceased to be a one-party state in 1991 and multiparty elections were held in 1994. Civil war broke out in 1998 and a military coup occurred in 1999. Elections were held in 2000. Another coup occurred in 2003, but civilian government was restored in 2004. In 2005, a former military leader, Joao Bernardo Vieira, became president but he was assassinated in 2009. A former president, Malam Bacai Sanha, was elected president in July 2009, but he died in 2012.

Agriculture employs 79% of the people. Crops include coconuts, groundnuts (peanuts), maize, and rice. The country is a major hub for drug trafficking between Latin America and Europe.

AREA 13,948 SQ MI [36,125 SQ KM]
POPULATION 1,597,000 **CAPITAL** BISSAU
GOVERNMENT "INTERIM" GOVERNMENT
ETHNIC GROUPS BALANTA 30%, FULA 20%, MANJACA 14%, MANDINGA 13%, PAPEL 7% **LANGUAGES** PORTUGUESE (OFFICIAL), CRIOULO
RELIGIONS TRADITIONAL BELIEFS 50%, ISLAM 45%, CHRISTIANITY 5%
CURRENCY CFA FRANC = 100 CENTIMES

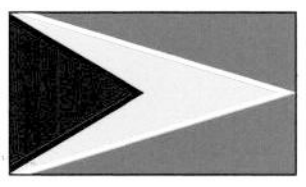
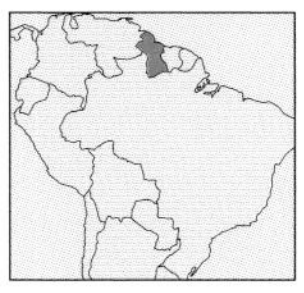

GUYANA

GEOGRAPHY The Cooperative Republic of Guyana is a country facing the Atlantic Ocean in northeastern South America. The coastal plain is flat and much of it is below sea level.

The climate is hot and humid, though the interior highlands are cooler than the coast. Rainfall is heavy, occurring on more than 200 days a year.

POLITICS & ECONOMY Britain gained control of the area in 1814 and ruled British Guiana until it became independent as Guyana in 1966. A black lawyer, Forbes Burnham, was the first prime minister. Under a new constitution adopted in 1980, the president's powers were increased. Burnham became president and served in this post until he died in 1985. He was succeeded by Hugh Desmond Hoyte, who was defeated in 1993 by an ethnic Indian, Cheddi Jagan. Jagan died in 1997 and was succeeded by his wife, Janet. In 1999, Bharrat Jagdeo was elected president. He was succeeded by Donald Ramotar in 2011.

Guyana is a poor country. Its resources include gold, bauxite (aluminum ore) and other minerals, forests, and fertile soils. Sugarcane and rice are leading crops. Guyana has potential for producing hydroelectricity from its many rivers.

AREA 83,000 SQ MI [214,969 SQ KM]
POPULATION 775,000 **CAPITAL** GEORGETOWN
GOVERNMENT MULTIPARTY REPUBLIC
ETHNIC GROUPS EAST INDIAN 50%, BLACK 36%, AMERINDIAN 7%, OTHERS 7% **LANGUAGES** ENGLISH (OFFICIAL), CREOLE, HINDI, URDU
RELIGIONS CHRISTIANITY 50%, HINDUISM 35%, ISLAM 10%, OTHERS 5%
CURRENCY GUYANESE DOLLAR = 100 CENTS

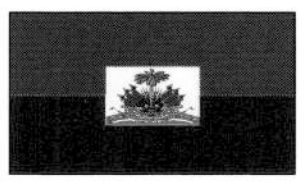
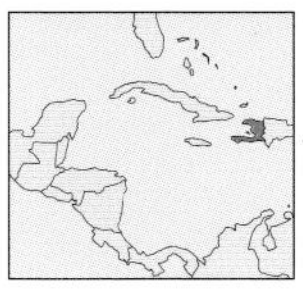

HAITI

GEOGRAPHY The Republic of Haiti occupies the western third of Hispaniola in the Caribbean. The land is mainly mountainous. The climate is hot and humid, though the northern highlands, with about 79 inches [200 mm], have more than twice as much rainfall as the southern coast.

POLITICS & ECONOMY Visited by Christopher Columbus in 1492, Haiti was later developed by the French. The African slaves revolted in 1791 and the country became independent in 1804. Haiti subsequently suffered from instability, violence, and dictatorial rule. Elections in 1990 returned Jean-Bertrand Aristide as president, but he was overthrown in 1991. In 1995, René Préval was elected president, but Aristide was again elected president in 2000. In 2004, rebel activity forced Aristide to flee the country.

In January 2010, an earthquake hit Port-au-Prince, killing up to 230,000 people and devastating the economy. Thousands were made homeless and cholera killed several thousand people.

AREA 10,714 SQ MI [27,750 SQ KM]
POPULATION 9,720,000 **CAPITAL** PORT-AU-PRINCE
GOVERNMENT MULTIPARTY REPUBLIC **ETHNIC GROUPS** BLACK 95%, MULATTO/WHITE 5% **LANGUAGES** FRENCH AND CREOLE (BOTH OFFICIAL)
RELIGIONS ROMAN CATHOLIC 80%, VOODOO
CURRENCY GOURDE = 100 CENTIMES

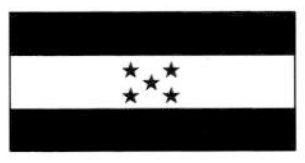
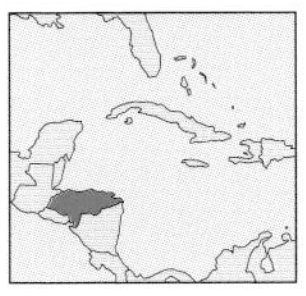

HONDURAS

GEOGRAPHY The Republic of Honduras is the second largest country in Central America. The northern coast, on the Caribbean Sea, extends more than 373 mi [600 km], but the Pacific coast in the southeast is only about 50 mi [80 km] long. Honduras has a tropical climate, but the highlands are cooler. The rainiest months are between May and November. Hurricanes often hit the north coast. Hurricane Mitch in 1998 caused the worst destruction in modern times.

POLITICS & ECONOMY Western Honduras was part of the Maya empire which flourished between AD 300 and 900. Christopher Columbus claimed the area for Spain in 1502 and Spain ruled from 1625 until 1821. Honduras became part of the Central American Federation but withdrew in 1838.

In the 1890s, American companies developed plantations to grow bananas and Honduras became known as a "banana state." But instability slowed economic progress. Since 1980, civilian governments friendly toward the United States have ruled Honduras, but in 2008 it joined the "Bolivarian Alternative to the Americas," a left-wing alliance headed by Venezuelan President Hugo Chavez. A military coup in 2009 removed

President Manuel Zelaya from office. In elections in November 2009, Porfiro Lobo was elected president.

Honduras is a developing country. Its few resources include silver, lead, and zinc. Agriculture is the main activity. Bananas and coffee are exported and maize is the chief food crop. Honduras is one of Central America's least industrialized countries. Products include processed food, textiles, and wood products.

AREA 43,277 SQ MI [112,088 SQ KM]
POPULATION 8,144,000 **CAPITAL** TEGUCIGALPA
GOVERNMENT REPUBLIC **ETHNIC GROUPS** MESTIZO 90%, AMERINDIAN 7%, BLACK (INCLUDING BLACK CARIB) 2%, WHITE 1% **LANGUAGES** SPANISH (OFFICIAL), AMERINDIAN DIALECTS **RELIGIONS** ROMAN CATHOLIC 97%
CURRENCY HONDURAN LEMPIRA = 100 CENTAVOS

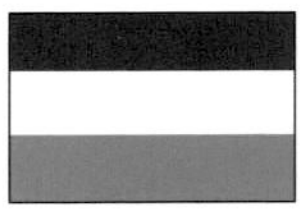

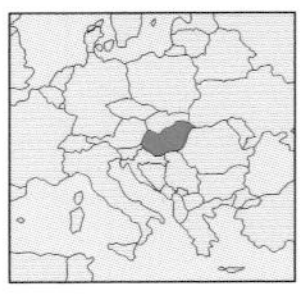

HUNGARY

GEOGRAPHY Hungary is a landlocked country in central Europe. The land is mostly low-lying and drained by the Danube (Duna) and its tributary, the Tisza. Most of the land east of the Danube belongs to a region called the Great Plain (Nagyalföld), which covers about half of Hungary.

Hungary lies far from the moderating influence of the sea. As a result, summers are warmer and sunnier, and the winters colder than in Western Europe.

POLITICS & ECONOMY Hungary entered World War II (1939–45) in 1941, as an ally of Germany, but the Germans occupied the country in 1944. The Soviet Union invaded Hungary in 1944 and, in 1946, the country became a republic. The Communists gradually took over the government, taking complete control in 1949. From this time, Hungary was an ally of the Soviet Union. In 1956, Soviet troops crushed an anti-Communist revolt. But in the 1980s, reforms in the Soviet Union led to the growth of anti-Communist groups in Hungary. In 1989, Hungary adopted a new constitution making it a multiparty state. Elections held in 1990 led to a victory for the non-Communist Democratic Forum. In 2002, the Hungarian Socialist Party, in alliance with the liberal Free Democrats, won a majority in parliament. In 2004, Hungary became a member of both the North Atlantic Treaty Organization and the European Union.

Before World War II, Hungary's economy was based mainly on agriculture. But the Communists set up many manufacturing industries. From the late 1980s, private ownership increased. This caused problems, including inflation and high rates of unemployment. Elections in 2010 resulted in victory for the center-right Fidezs Party led by Viktor Oban. In 2011–12, government austerity measures caused unrest.

Leading manufactures include aluminum, chemicals, electrical and electronic goods, and telecommunications equipment.

AREA 35,920 SQ MI [93,032 SQ KM]
POPULATION 9,976,000 **CAPITAL** BUDAPEST
GOVERNMENT MULTIPARTY REPUBLIC
ETHNIC GROUPS MAGYAR 90%, GYPSY, GERMAN, SERB, ROMANIAN, SLOVAK **LANGUAGES** HUNGARIAN (OFFICIAL)
RELIGIONS ROMAN CATHOLIC 68%, CALVINIST 20%, LUTHERAN 5%, OTHERS **CURRENCY** FORINT = 100 FILLÉR

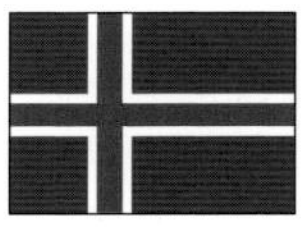

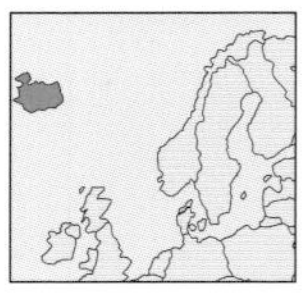

ICELAND

GEOGRAPHY The Republic of Iceland, in the North Atlantic Ocean, is closer to Greenland than Scotland. Iceland sits astride the Mid-Atlantic Ridge. It is slowly getting wider as the ocean is being stretched apart by continental drift.

Iceland has around 200 volcanoes, and eruptions are frequent. An eruption under the Vatnajökull ice cap in 1996 created a subglacial lake which subsequently burst, causing severe flooding. Geysers and hot springs are common, and in 2010 a volcanic eruption and its resulting ash cloud disrupted international air services. Ice caps and glaciers cover about an eighth of the land. The only habitable regions are the coastal lowlands. Despite its northerly position, Iceland's climate is moderated by the warm waters of the Gulf Stream. The port of Reykjavik is ice-free all year round.

POLITICS & ECONOMY Norwegian Vikings colonized Iceland in AD 874, and in 930 the settlers founded the world's oldest parliament, the Althing.

Iceland united with Norway in 1262. But when Norway united with Denmark in 1380, Iceland came under Danish rule. Iceland became a self-governing kingdom, united with Denmark, in 1918. It became a fully independent republic in 1944, following a referendum in which 97% of the people voted to break their country's ties with Denmark. Iceland has played a leading part in European affairs and is a member of the North Atlantic Treaty Organization. But it has been involved in fishing and whaling disputes. Iceland has few resources besides its fishing grounds, and fishing and fish processing dominate Iceland's overseas trade. Barely 1% of the land is used to grow crops, but 23% of the country can be used for grazing sheep and cattle. Vegetables and fruit are grown in greenhouses, heated by water from the hot springs. Iceland's economy was hit by the global financial crisis of 2008–9, causing the collapse of its currency and banking system. In 2009, Johanna Sigurdardottir became Iceland's first female prime minister and Iceland applied for membership of the European Union.

AREA 39,768 SQ MI [103,000 SQ KM]
POPULATION 311,000 **CAPITAL** REYKJAVIK
GOVERNMENT MULTIPARTY REPUBLIC
ETHNIC GROUPS ICELANDIC 97%, DANISH 1%
LANGUAGES ICELANDIC (OFFICIAL) **RELIGIONS** EVANGELICAL LUTHERAN 87%, OTHER PROTESTANT 4%, ROMAN CATHOLIC 2%, OTHERS
CURRENCY ICELANDIC KRÓNA = 100 AURAR

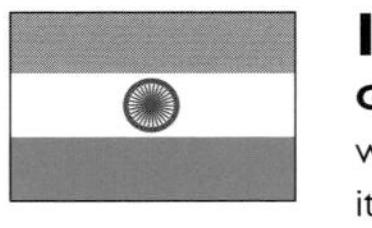

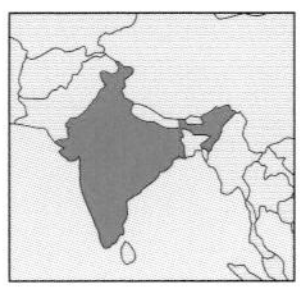

INDIA

GEOGRAPHY The Republic of India is the world's seventh largest country. In population, it ranks second only to China. The north is mountainous, with mountains and foothills of the Himalayan range. Rivers, such as the Brahmaputra and Ganges (Ganga), rise in the Himalaya and flow across the fertile northern plains. Southern India consists of a large plateau, called the Deccan. The Deccan is bordered by two mountain ranges, the Western Ghats and the Eastern Ghats.

India has three main seasons. The cool season runs from October to February. The hot season runs from March to June. The rainy monsoon season starts in the middle of June and continues into September. Delhi has moderate rainfall, with about 25 inches [640 mm] a year. The southwestern coast and the northeast have far more rain. Darjeeling in the northeast has an average annual rainfall of 120 inches [3,040 mm]. But parts of the Thar Desert in the northwest have only 2 inches [50 mm] of rain per year.

POLITICS & ECONOMY In southern India, most of the people are descendants of the dark-skinned Dravidians, who were among India's earliest people. Most northerners are descendants of lighter-skinned Aryans who arrived around 3,500 years ago.

India was the birthplace of several major religions, including Hinduism, Buddhism, and Sikhism. Islam was introduced from about AD 1000. The Muslim Mughal empire was founded in 1526. From the 17th century, Britain began to gain influence. From 1858 to 1947, India was ruled as part of the British empire. An independence movement began after the Sepoy Rebellion (1857–9), and in 1885 the Indian National Congress was formed. In 1920, Mohandas K. Gandhi became its leader and it soon became a mass movement. When independence was finally achieved in 1947, British India was divided into modern India and Muslim Pakistan. Partition was marred by mass slaughter as Hindus and Sikhs fled from Pakistan, and Indian Muslims poured into Pakistan. In the ensuing disputes, some 1 million people were killed.

India has 15 major languages and hundreds of minor ones, together with many religions. The country remains the world's largest democracy. It has faced many problems, especially with Pakistan, over the disputed territory of Jammu and Kashmir. Two wars in 1965 and 1972 failed to alter greatly the 1948 ceasefire lines. In the late 1980s, Kashmiri nationalists in the Indian-controlled area waged a campaign, demanding either integration into Pakistan or independence. India sent in troops and accused Pakistan of intervention. In the 1990s, Pakistani-backed guerrillas fought to break India's hold on the Srinagar valley, Kashmir's most populous region. Tension mounted following the testing of nuclear devices by both countries in 1998. Relations improved, but an attack on buildings in Mumbai in 2008, allegedly by Pakistanis, caused tension. In 2009–11, the dispute with Maoists in central and eastern India flared up again.

The World Bank classifies India as a developing country and a large number of people are poor. However, since 2004, under a government led by the United Progressive Alliance, led by Manmohan Singh, the national economy developed rapidly. By 2010–11, India's economy was the world's second fastest growing after China.

Agriculture employs 52% of the people. Crops include rice, wheat, millet, sorghum, peas, and beans. India has more cattle than any other country. Milk is produced, but Hindus do not eat beef. Resources include coal, iron ore, and oil. Manufacturing has expanded greatly since 1947. Iron and steel, machinery, refined petroleum, textiles, and transport equipment are major products.

AREA 1,269,212 SQ MI [3,287,263 SQ KM]
POPULATION 1,189,173,000 **CAPITAL** NEW DELHI
GOVERNMENT MULTIPARTY FEDERAL REPUBLIC
ETHNIC GROUPS INDO-ARYAN (CAUCASOID) 72%, DRAVIDIAN (ABORIGINAL) 25%, OTHERS (MAINLY MONGOLOID) 3%
LANGUAGES HINDI, ENGLISH, TELUGU, BENGALI, MARATHI, TAMIL, URDU, GUJARATI, MALAYALAM, KANNADA, ORIYA, PUNJABI, ASSAMESE, KASHMIRI, SINDHI, AND SANSKRIT ARE ALL OFFICIAL LANGUAGES
RELIGIONS HINDUISM 82%, ISLAM 12%, CHRISTIANITY 2%, SIKHISM 2%, BUDDHISM, AND OTHERS **CURRENCY** INDIAN RUPEE = 100 PAISA

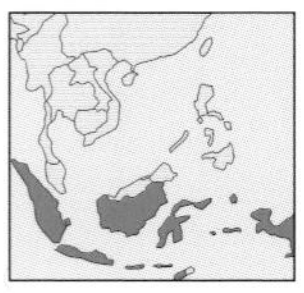

INDONESIA

GEOGRAPHY The Republic of Indonesia is an island nation in Southeast Asia. In all, Indonesia contains about 13,600 islands, fewer than 6,000 of which are inhabited. Three-quarters of the country is made up of five main areas: the islands of Sumatra, Java, and Sulawesi (Celebes), together with Kalimantan (southern Borneo) and Irian Jaya (western New Guinea). The islands are generally mountainous and volcanic. The larger islands have extensive coastal lowlands. The climate is hot and humid, with a high rainfall. Only Java and the Sunda Islands have relatively dry seasons.

POLITICS & ECONOMY Indonesia is the world's most populous Muslim nation, though Islam was introduced as recently as the 15th century. The Dutch became active in the area in the early 17th century and Indonesia became a Dutch colony in 1799. After a long struggle, the Netherlands recognized Indonesia's independence in 1949. The economy has expanded, but ethnic and religious conflict have slowed down economic progress.

In the early 21st century, Indonesia was facing many problems, arising from widespread corruption in the government and the army. Separatists were operating in Aceh province in northern Sumatra and in West Papua (formerly Irian Jaya), Christian-Muslim clashes led to loss of life in the Moluccas, and East (formerly Portuguese) Timor became an independent country. Terrorist incidents occurred in the early 21st century. In December 2004, a tsunami killed more than 100,000 people. Aceh province was granted autonomy in 2006.

In 2011, separatists in the Papua region demonstrated in favor of independence. Indonesia, a developing country, has a growing industrial sector. It exports oil and natural gas, and mines tin and other minerals. Timber, textiles, rubber, coffee, and tea are also exported. Rice is the main food crop.

AREA 735,354 SQ MI [1,904,569 SQ KM]
POPULATION 245,613,000 **CAPITAL** JAKARTA
GOVERNMENT MULTIPARTY REPUBLIC
ETHNIC GROUPS JAVANESE 45%, SUNDANESE 14%, MADURESE 7%, COASTAL MALAYS 7%, APPROXIMATELY 300 OTHERS
LANGUAGES BAHASA INDONESIAN (OFFICIAL), MANY OTHERS
RELIGIONS ISLAM 88%, ROMAN CATHOLIC 3%, HINDUISM 2%, BUDDHISM 1%
CURRENCY INDONESIAN RUPIAH = 100 SEN

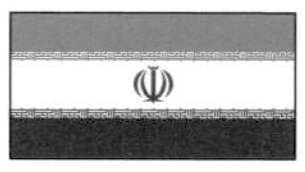

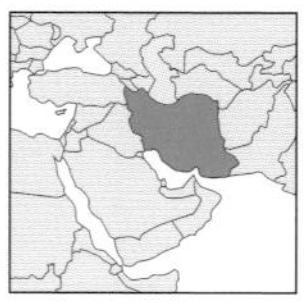

IRAN

GEOGRAPHY The Republic of Iran contains a barren central plateau which covers about half of the country. It includes the Dasht-e-Kavir (Great Salt Desert) and the Dasht-e-Lut (Great Sand Desert). The Elburz Mountains north of the plateau contain Iran's highest peak, Damavand, while narrow lowlands lie between the mountains and the Caspian Sea. West of the plateau are the Zagros Mountains, beyond which the land descends to the plains bordering the Persian Gulf.

Much of Iran has a severe, dry climate, with hot summers and cold winters. In Tehran, rain falls on only about 30 days in the year and the annual temperature range is more than 45°F [25°C]. The climate in the lowlands, however, is generally milder.

POLITICS & ECONOMY Iran was called Persia until 1935. The empire of Ancient Persia flourished between 550 and 350 BC, when it fell to Alexander the Great. Islam was introduced in AD 641.

Britain and Russia competed for influence in the area in the 19th century, and in the early 20th century the British began to develop the country's oil resources. In 1925, the Pahlavi family took power.

Reza Khan became shah (king) and worked to modernize the country. The Pahlavi dynasty was ended in 1979 when a religious leader, Ayatollah Ruhollah Khomeini, made Iran an Islamic republic. In 1980–8, Iran and Iraq fought a war over disputed borders. Khomeini died in 1989, but his fundamentalist views and anti-Western attitudes continued to dominate politics. In 2005, a hardliner, Mahmoud Ahmadinejad, was elected president. Iran's nuclear policies, which many in the West considered were to develop nuclear weapons, led to the application of international sanctions against Iran in 2009–12.

Iran's prosperity is based on its oil production and oil accounts for more than 80% of the country's exports. However, the economy was severely damaged by the Iran–Iraq war in the 1980s. Oil revenues have been used to develop a growing manufacturing sector. Agriculture is important even though farms cover only a tenth of the land. The main crops are wheat and barley. Livestock farming and fishing are other important activities, although Iran has to import much of the food it needs.

AREA 636,368 sq mi [1,648,195 sq km]
POPULATION 77,891,000 **CAPITAL** Tehran
GOVERNMENT Islamic republic **ETHNIC GROUPS** Persian 51%, Azeri 24%, Gilaki and Mazandarani 8%, Kurd 7%, Arab 3%, Lur 2%, Baluchi 2%, Turkmen 2% **LANGUAGES** Persian 58%, Turkic 26%, Kurdish **RELIGIONS** Islam (Shi'ite Muslim 89%)
CURRENCY Iranian rial = 100 dinars

IRAQ

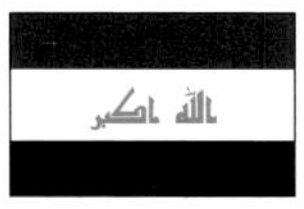

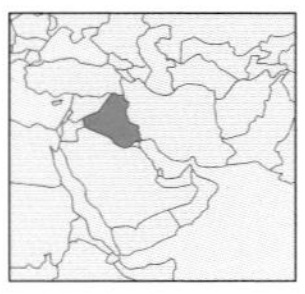

GEOGRAPHY The Republic of Iraq is a southwest Asian country at the head of the Persian Gulf. Rolling deserts cover western and southwestern Iraq, with part of the Zagros Mountains in the northeast, where farming can be practised without irrigation. The northern plains, across which flow the rivers Euphrates (Nahr al Furat) and Tigris (Nahr Dijlah), are dry. But the southern plains, including Mesopotamia and the delta of the Shatt al Arab, contain irrigated farmland, together with marshland.

The climate of Iraq ranges from temperate in the north to subtropical in the south. Baghdad, in central Iraq, has cool winters, with occasional frosts, and hot summers. The rainfall is generally low.

POLITICS & ECONOMY Mesopotamia was the home of several great civilizations, including Sumer, Babylon, and Assyria. It later became part of the Persian empire. Islam was introduced in AD 637 and Baghdad became the brilliant capital of the powerful Arab empire. But Mesopotamia declined after the Mongols invaded it in 1258. From 1534, Mesopotamia became part of the Turkish Ottoman empire. Britain invaded the area in 1916. In 1921, Britain renamed the country Iraq and set up an Arab monarchy. Iraq finally became independent in 1932.

By the 1950s, oil dominated Iraq's economy. In 1952, Iraq agreed to take 50% of the profits of the foreign oil companies. This revenue enabled the government to pay for welfare services and development projects. But many Iraqis felt that they should benefit more from their oil. Since 1958, when army officers killed the king and made Iraq a republic, Iraq has undergone turbulent times. In the 1960s, the Kurds, who live in northern Iraq and also in Iran, Turkey, Syria, and Armenia, asked for self-rule. The government rejected their demands and war broke out. A peace treaty was signed in 1975, but conflict has continued.

In 1979, Saddam Hussein became Iraq's president. Under his leadership, Iraq invaded Iran in 1980, starting an eight-year war. Iraqi Kurds supported Iran and the Iraqi government attacked Kurdish villages with poison gas. In 1990, Iraqi troops occupied Kuwait, but an international force drove them out in 1991. From 1991, Iraqi troops attacked Shi'ite Marsh Arabs and Kurds. In 1998, Iraq's failure to permit UN inspectors, charged with disposing of Iraq's deadliest weapons, access to suspect sites led to the Western bombardment of Iraqi military sites. Another major offensive occurred in 2001. In 2002–3, pressure mounted on Iraq to dispose of its alleged weapons of mass destruction. In March–April 2003, a coalition force headed by the United States invaded Iraq, overthrowing Saddam Hussein's regime. Despite ongoing violence, elections were held in 2005, and again in 2010. Following a period of deadlock, Nouri al-Maliki continued as prime minister. Political disputes and an upsurge of violence occurred in 2011–12.

Civil war, war damage, mismanagement, and UN sanctions have damaged the economy. Oil remains the main resource. Farmland, including pasture, covers about a fifth of the land. Products include barley, cotton, dates, fruit, livestock, wheat, and wool. But Iraq still has to import food. Manufactures include refined oil, petrochemicals, and consumer goods.

AREA 169,235 sq mi [438,317 sq km]
POPULATION 30,400,000 **CAPITAL** Baghdad
GOVERNMENT Parliamentary democracy **ETHNIC GROUPS** Arab 77%, Kurdish 19%, Assyrian, and others **LANGUAGES** Arabic (official), Kurdish (official in Kurdish areas), Assyrian, Armenian **RELIGIONS** Islam 97%, Christianity, and others **CURRENCY** New Iraqi dinar

IRELAND

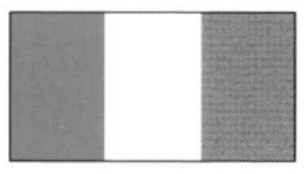

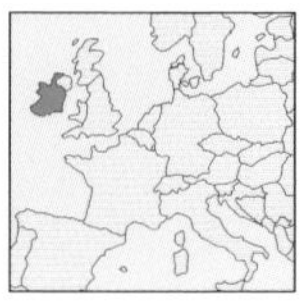

GEOGRAPHY Ireland occupies five-sixths of the island which is also called Ireland. The country consists of a large lowland region surrounded by a broken rim of low mountains. The uplands include the Mountains of Kerry where Carrauntoohill, Ireland's highest peak at 3,415 ft [1,041 m], is situated. The River Shannon is the longest in Ireland, flowing through three large lakes, loughs Allen, Ree, and Derg.

Ireland has a mild, rainy climate influenced by the warm Gulf Stream current, whose effects are greatest in the west. However, Dublin in the east is cooler than places on the west coast.

POLITICS & ECONOMY In 1801, the Act of Union created the United Kingdom of Great Britain and Ireland. But Irish discontent intensified in the 1840s when a potato blight caused a famine in which a million people died and nearly a million emigrated. Britain was blamed for not having done enough to help. In 1916, an uprising in Dublin was crushed, but between 1919 and 1922 civil war occurred. In 1922, the Irish Free State was created as a Dominion in the British Commonwealth. But Northern Ireland remained part of the UK.

Ireland became a republic in 1949. In 1973, it became a member of the European Community (now the European Union) and, until the global financial crisis of 2008–9, it prospered. In 1998, Ireland took part in the negotiations to produce a constitutional settlement in Northern Ireland. Ireland agreed to give up its claim on Northern Ireland and, in 2007, a power-sharing government was set up in the north.

Major farm products in Ireland include barley, cattle and dairy products, pigs, potatoes, poultry, sheep, sugar beet, and wheat, while fishing is also important. But manufacturing is the leading activity. In 2010, the economy worsened and Ireland sought assistance from the EU and the IMF. Following elections in 2011, a coalition government was set up by two opposition parties, Fine Gael and the center-left Labour Party.

AREA 27,132 sq mi [70,273 sq km]
POPULATION 4,671,000 **CAPITAL** Dublin
GOVERNMENT Multiparty republic **ETHNIC GROUPS** Irish 94%
LANGUAGES Irish (Gaelic) and English (both official)
RELIGIONS Roman Catholic 92%, Protestant 3%
CURRENCY Euro = 100 cents

ISRAEL

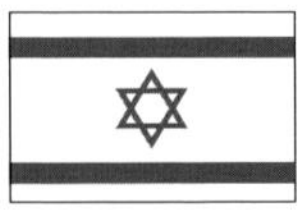

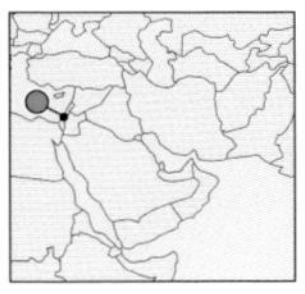

GEOGRAPHY The State of Israel is a small country in the eastern Mediterranean. It includes a fertile coastal plain, where Israel's main industrial cities, Haifa (Hefa) and Tel Aviv-Jaffa, are situated. Inland lie the Judaeo-Galilean highlands, which run from northern Israel to the northern tip of the Negev Desert. To the east lies part of the Great Rift Valley, which contains the River Jordan, the Sea of Galilee, and the Dead Sea. Summers are hot and dry. Winters on the coast are mild and moist, but rainfall decreases from west to east and from north to south.

POLITICS & ECONOMY Israel is part of a region called Palestine. Some Jews have always lived in the area, though most modern Israelis are descendants of immigrants who began to settle there from the 1880s. Britain ruled Palestine from 1917. Large numbers of Jews escaping Nazi persecution arrived in the 1930s, provoking an Arab uprising against British rule. In 1947, the UN agreed to partition Palestine into an Arab and a Jewish state. Fighting broke out after Arabs rejected the plan. The State of Israel came into being in May 1948, but fighting continued into 1949. Other Arab-Israeli wars in 1956, 1967, and 1973 led to land gains for Israel.

In 1978, Israel signed a treaty with Egypt which led to the return of the occupied Sinai peninsula to Egypt in 1979. But conflict continued between Israel and the PLO (Palestine Liberation Organization). In 1993, the PLO and Israel agreed to establish Palestinian self-rule in two areas: the occupied Gaza Strip, and in the town of Jericho in the occupied West Bank. The agreement was extended in 1995 to include more than 30% of the West Bank. Israel's prime minister, Yitzhak Rabin, was assassinated in 1995. In 1996, Benjamin Netanyahu was elected prime minister. The peace process stalled until Ehud Barak defeated Netanyahu in 1999. In 2001, Ariel Sharon became prime minister. In 2005, he handed over the Gaza Strip to the Palestinian Authority. Sharon formed a new political party, Kadima. After Sharon suffered a stroke, Ehud Olmert became prime minister. Israeli forces clashed with Palestinians in Gaza and southern Lebanon in 2005–9. In 2009, Benjamin Netanyahu became prime minister. In 2010, talks between Israel and the Palestinian Authority collapsed. Clashes between Israel and Gaza continued into 2012.

Manufacturing is the most valuable activity. Products include chemicals, electronic equipment, plastics, processed food, scientific instruments, and textiles. Fruit and vegetables are major exports.

AREA 7,954 sq mi [20,600 sq km] **POPULATION** 7,473,000
CAPITAL Jerusalem **GOVERNMENT** Multiparty republic
ETHNIC GROUPS Jewish 80%, Arab and others 20%
LANGUAGES Hebrew and Arabic (both official)
RELIGIONS Judaism 80%, Islam (mostly Sunni) 14%, Christianity 2%, Druze and others 2% **CURRENCY** New Israeli shekel = 100 agorat

ITALY

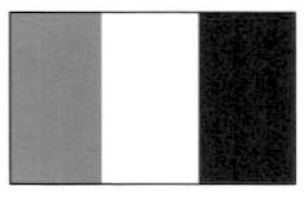

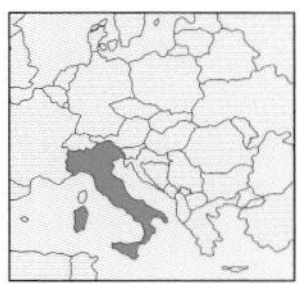

GEOGRAPHY The Republic of Italy is famous for its history and traditions, its art and culture, and its beautiful scenery. Northern Italy is bordered in the north by the high Alps, with their many climbing and skiing resorts. The Alps overlook the northern plains – Italy's most fertile and densely populated region – drained by the River Po. The rugged Apennines form the backbone of southern Italy. Bordering the range are scenic hilly areas and coastal plains. Southern Italy contains a string of volcanoes, stretching from Vesuvius, through the Lipari Islands, to Etna on Sicily, the largest Mediterranean island. Northern Italy has cold, often snowy, winters, but the summer months are warm and sunny, with brief summer thunderstorms. Rainfall is abundant. The south has mild, moist winters and warm, dry summers.

POLITICS & ECONOMY Magnificent ruins throughout Italy testify to the glories of the ancient Roman empire, which was founded, according to legend, in 753 BC. It reached its peak in the AD 100s. It finally collapsed in the 400s, although the Eastern Roman empire, also called the Byzantine empire, survived for another 1,000 years.

In the Middle Ages, Italy was split into many tiny states. These states made a great contribution to the revival of art and learning, called the Renaissance, in the 14th to 16th centuries. Beautiful cities, such as Florence (Firenze) and Venice (Venézia), testify to the artistic achievements of this period.

Italy finally became a united kingdom in 1861, although the Papal Territories (a large area ruled by the Roman Catholic Church) was not added until 1870. The Pope and his successors disputed the takeover of the Papal Territories. The dispute was finally resolved in 1929, when the Vatican City was set up in Rome as a fully independent state.

Italy fought in World War I (1914–18) alongside the Allies – Britain, France, and Russia. In 1922, the dictator Benito Mussolini, leader of the Fascist Party, took power. Under Mussolini, Italy conquered Ethiopia. During World War II (1939–45), Italy at first fought on Germany's side against the Allies. But in late 1943, Italy declared war on Germany. Italy became a republic in 1946. It has played an important part in European affairs. It was a founder member of the North Atlantic Treaty Organization (NATO) in 1949 and also, in 1958, of what has since become the European Union.

After the setting up of the European Union, Italy's economy developed quickly. But the country faced many problems. For example, much of the economic development was in the north. This forced many people to leave the poor south to find jobs in the north or abroad. Social problems, corruption at high levels of society, and a succession of weak coalition governments all contributed to instability. From 1998, power shifted between center-left coalitions led by Romano Prodi and center-right coalitions led by media tycoon Silvio Berlusconi. Berlusconi won elections in 2008. In 2011, faced with a major economic crisis, Berlusconi resigned and was succeeded by Mario Monti, a former European Union Commissioner.

Only 50 years ago, Italy was a mainly agricultural society. But today it is a leading industrial power. It lacks mineral resources, and imports most of the raw materials used in industry. Manufactures include textiles and clothing, processed food, machinery, cars, and chemicals. The chief industrial region is in the northwest.

Farmland covers around 42% of the land, pasture 17%, and forest and woodland 22%. Major crops include citrus fruits, grapes which are used to make wine, olive oil, sugar beet, and vegetables. Livestock farming is important, though meat is imported.

AREA 116,339 SQ MI [301,318 SQ KM]
POPULATION 61,017,000 **CAPITAL** ROME
GOVERNMENT MULTIPARTY REPUBLIC **ETHNIC GROUPS** ITALIAN 94%, GERMAN, FRENCH, ALBANIAN, SLOVENE, GREEK **LANGUAGES** ITALIAN (OFFICIAL), GERMAN, FRENCH, SLOVENE **RELIGIONS** PREDOMINANTLY ROMAN CATHOLIC **CURRENCY** EURO = 100 CENTS

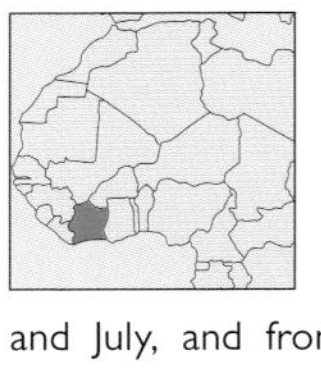

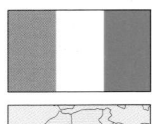

IVORY COAST

GEOGRAPHY The Republic of the Ivory Coast, in West Africa, is officially known as Côte d'Ivoire. The southeast coast is bordered by sand bars that enclose lagoons. The southwest coast is lined by rocky cliffs.

Ivory Coast has a hot and humid tropical climate, with high temperatures all year. The south has two rainy seasons: between May and July, and from October to November. Inland, the rainfall decreases and the north has one dry and one rainy season.

POLITICS & ECONOMY From 1895, Ivory Coast was governed as part of French West Africa, which also included what are now Benin, Burkina Faso, Guinea, Mali, Mauritania, Niger, and Senegal. In 1946, Ivory Coast became a territory in the French Union.

Ivory Coast became fully independent in 1960. Its first president, Félix Houphouët-Boigny, became the longest serving head of state in Africa with an uninterrupted period in office which ended with his death in 1993. Houphouët-Boigny, a pro-Western leader, made Ivory Coast a one-party state. In 1983, the National Assembly voted to make Yamoussoukro, the president's birthplace, the new capital. In 1999, a military coup occurred, but civilian rule was restored in 2000, when Laurent Gbagbo was elected president. An army rebellion began in 2002. By 2004, the government held the south, while mainly Muslim rebels held the north. A peace deal was agreed in 2007. Elections held in 2010 were won by opposition leader Alassane Ouattara, but President Laurent Gbagbo refused to stand down. After much fighting, Gbagbo was finally arrested in April 2011.

Agriculture employs 42% of the people. Cocoa beans, farm products, and petroleum products are exported.

AREA 124,503 SQ MI [322,463 SQ KM]
POPULATION 21,504,000 **CAPITAL** YAMOUSSOUKRO
GOVERNMENT MULTIPARTY REPUBLIC **ETHNIC GROUPS** AKAN 42%, VOLTAIQUES 18%, NORTHERN MANDES 16%, KROUS 11%, SOUTHERN MANDES 10% **LANGUAGES** FRENCH (OFFICIAL), MANY NATIVE DIALECTS
RELIGIONS ISLAM 40%, CHRISTIANITY 30%, TRADITIONAL BELIEFS 30%
CURRENCY CFA FRANC = 100 CENTIMES

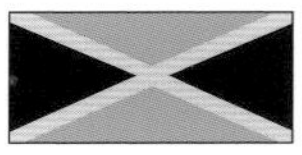

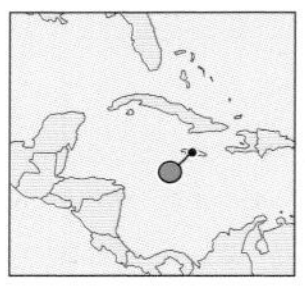

JAMAICA

GEOGRAPHY The third largest of the Caribbean islands, half of Jamaica lies above 1,000 ft [300 m] and moist southeast trade winds bring rain to the central mountain range.

The "cockpit country" in the northwest of the island is an inaccessible limestone area of steep broken ridges and isolated basins.

POLITICS & ECONOMY Britain took Jamaica from Spain in the 17th century, and the island did not gain its independence until 1962. Power has alternated between the People's National Party (PNP) and Jamaica Labor Party. In 2006, Portia Simpson Miller became prime minister. She was defeated in elections in 2007, but returned as prime minister in 2011. Tourism and sugarcane farming are important, but alumina and bauxite are the main exports.

AREA 4,244 SQ MI [10,991 SQ KM]
POPULATION 2,868,000 **CAPITAL** KINGSTON
GOVERNMENT CONSTITUTIONAL MONARCHY
ETHNIC GROUPS BLACK 91%, MIXED 7%, EAST INDIAN 1%
LANGUAGES ENGLISH (OFFICIAL), PATOIS ENGLISH
RELIGIONS PROTESTANT 61%, ROMAN CATHOLIC 4%
CURRENCY JAMAICAN DOLLAR = 100 CENTS

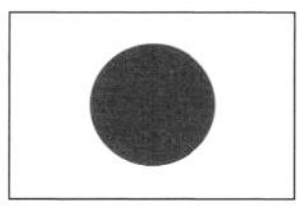

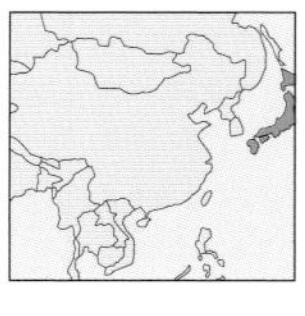

JAPAN

GEOGRAPHY Japan's four largest islands – Honshu, Hokkaido, Kyushu, and Shikoku – make up 98% of the country. But Japan contains thousands of small islands. The four largest islands are mainly mountainous, while many of the small islands are the tips of volcanoes. Japan has more than 150 volcanoes, about 60 of which are active. Volcanic eruptions, earthquakes, and tsunamis (powerful sea waves) are common. In March 2011, an earthquake. the most powerful recorded in Japan (magnitude 9.0) struck northeast Japan. The tremors and a tsunami caused great loss of life and severe damage to nuclear reactors at Fukushima.

The climate of Japan varies greatly from north to south. Hokkaido in the north has cold, snowy winters. At Sapporo, temperatures below 4°F [–20°C] have been recorded between December and March. But summers are warm, with temperatures sometimes exceeding 86°F [30°C]. Rain falls throughout the year, though Hokkaido is one of the driest parts of Japan. Tokyo has higher rainfall and temperatures, while the southern islands of Shikoku and Kyushu have warm temperate climates. Summers are long and hot; winters are cold.

POLITICS & ECONOMY In the late 19th century, Japan began a program of modernization. Under its new imperial leaders, it began to look for lands to conquer. In 1894–5, it fought a war with China and, in 1904–5, it defeated Russia. Soon its overseas empire included Korea and Taiwan. In 1930, Japan invaded Manchuria (northeast China), and in 1937 it began a war against China. In 1941, Japan launched an attack on the US base at Pearl Harbor in Hawai'i. This drew both Japan and the United States into World War II.

Japan surrendered in 1945 when the Americans dropped atomic bombs on two cities, Hiroshima and Nagasaki. The United States occupied Japan until 1952. During this period, Japan adopted a democratic constitution. The emperor, who had previously been regarded as a god, became a constitutional monarch. Power was vested in the prime minister and cabinet, who are chosen from the Diet (elected parliament).

From the 1960s, Japan experienced many changes as the country rapidly built up new industries. By the early 1990s, Japan had become the world's second richest economic power after the US. But economic success has brought problems. For example, the rapid growth of cities has led to housing shortages and pollution. Another problem is that the proportion of people over 65 years of age is steadily increasing.

In 2011, China overtook Japan as the world's second largest economy after the United States. Japan had held second place since 1968, and, although its economy grew by nearly 4% in 2010, it was insufficient to keep it in second place.

The leading activity is manufacturing. Japan imports most of the materials and fuels it needs, and its success has been based on its use of the latest technology, its skilled work force, its vigorous export policies, and the relatively low expenditure on defense. Exports include machinery, electrical and electronic equipment, iron and steel, chemicals, textiles, and ships. Japan's economy suffered a stagnation in the 1990s. Signs of recovery from 2005 were shattered by the global financial crisis in 2008–9, when exports greatly declined.

Japan is one of the world's top fishing nations and fish is an important source of protein. Because the land is so rugged, only 15% of the country can be farmed. Yet Japan produces about 70% of the food it needs. Rice is the chief crop, taking up about half of the total farmland. Other major products include fruits, sugar beet, tea, and vegetables. Livestock farming has increased since the 1950s.

AREA 145,880 SQ MI [377,829 SQ KM]
POPULATION 126,476,000 **CAPITAL** TOKYO
GOVERNMENT CONSTITUTIONAL MONARCHY
ETHNIC GROUPS JAPANESE 99%, CHINESE, KOREAN, BRAZILIAN, AND OTHERS
LANGUAGES JAPANESE (OFFICIAL) **RELIGIONS** SHINTOISM AND BUDDHISM 84% (MOST JAPANESE CONSIDER THEMSELVES TO BE BOTH SHINTO AND BUDDHIST), OTHERS **CURRENCY** YEN = 100 SEN

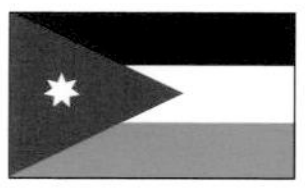

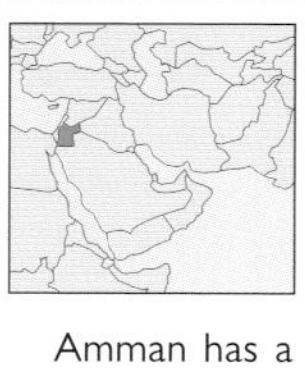

JORDAN

GEOGRAPHY The Hashemite Kingdom of Jordan is an Arab country in southwestern Asia. The Great Rift Valley in the west contains the River Jordan and the Dead Sea, which Jordan shares with Israel. East of the Rift Valley is the Transjordan plateau, where most Jordanians live. To the east and south lie vast areas of desert.

Amman has a much lower rainfall and longer dry season than the Mediterranean lands to the west. The Transjordan plateau, on which Amman stands, is a transition zone between the Mediterranean climate zone and the desert climate to the east.

POLITICS & ECONOMY In 1921, Britain created a territory called Transjordan east of the River Jordan. In 1923, Transjordan became self-governing, but Britain retained control of its defenses, finances, and foreign affairs. This territory became fully independent as Jordan in 1946. Jordan has suffered from instability arising from the Arab–Israeli conflict since the creation of the State of Israel in 1948. After the first Arab–Israeli War in 1948–9, Jordan acquired East Jerusalem and a fertile area called the West Bank. In 1967, Israel occupied this area. In Jordan, the presence of Palestinian refugees led to civil war in 1970–1.

In 1974, Arab leaders declared that the PLO (Palestine Liberation Organization) was the sole representative of the Palestinian people. In 1988, King Hussein of Jordan renounced Jordan's claims to the West Bank and passed responsibility for it to the PLO. Opposition parties were legalized in 1991 and elections were held in 1993. In October 1994, Jordan and Israel signed a peace treaty, ending a state of war that had lasted more than 40 years. Jordan's King Hussein commanded respect for his role in Middle Eastern affairs until his death in 1999. He was succeeded by his eldest son, who became Abdullah II. Jordan supported the US-led war on terrorism. In 2005, suicide bombings on hotels in Amman damaged Jordan's reputation as a stable country. In 2009, the king dissolved parliament. Elections were held in 2010, but anti-government protests occurred in early 2011.

Jordan has a "lower-middle-income" economy. It lacks natural resources, apart from phosphates and potash, and depends on substantial aid. Less than 6% of the land is farmed or used as pasture. Jordan has an oil refinery and manufactures include cement, pharmaceuticals, processed food, fertilizers, and textiles.

AREA 34,495 SQ MI [89,342 SQ KM]
POPULATION 6,508,000 **CAPITAL** AMMAN
GOVERNMENT CONSTITUTIONAL MONARCHY **ETHNIC GROUPS** ARAB 98%, OF WHICH PALESTINIANS MAKE UP ROUGHLY HALF **LANGUAGES** ARABIC (OFFICIAL) **RELIGIONS** ISLAM (MOSTLY SUNNI) 94%, CHRISTIANITY (MOSTLY GREEK ORTHODOX) 6% **CURRENCY** JORDANIAN DINAR = 1,000 FILS

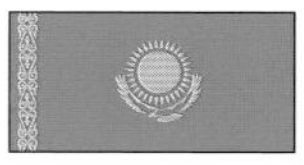

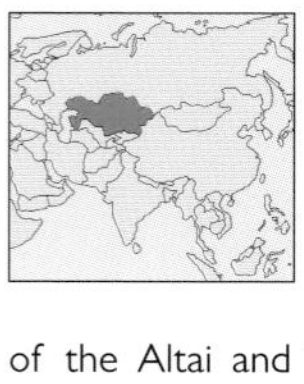

KAZAKHSTAN

GEOGRAPHY Kazakhstan is a large country in west-central Asia. In the west, the Caspian Sea lowlands include the Karagiye depression, which reaches 433 ft [132 m] below sea level. The lowlands extend eastward through the Aral Sea area. The north contains high plains, but the highest land is along the eastern and southern borders. These areas include parts of the Altai and Tian Shan mountain ranges. Eastern Kazakhstan contains several freshwater lakes, the largest of which is Lake Balkhash. The water in the rivers has been used for irrigation, causing ecological problems. For example, the Aral Sea, deprived of water, shrank from 25,830 sq mi [66,900 sq km] in 1960 to 12,989 sq mi [33,642 sq km] in 1993. Large areas are now barren desert.

Kazakhstan has an extreme climate. Winters are cold and snowy. The rainfall is generally low.

POLITICS & ECONOMY After the Russian Revolution of 1917, many Kazakhs wanted to make their country independent. But the Communists prevailed and in 1936 Kazakhstan became a republic of the Soviet Union, called the Kazakh Soviet Socialist Republic. During World War II and also after the war, the Soviet government moved many people from the west into Kazakhstan. From the 1950s, people were encouraged to work on a "Virgin Lands" project, which involved bringing large areas of grassland under cultivation.

Reforms in the Soviet Union in the 1980s led to its breakup in December 1991. Kazakhstan maintained contacts with Russia through the Commonwealth of Independent States (CIS). In 1997, the government moved its capital from Almaty to Aqmola (later renamed Astana), a town in the north. By the mid-2000s, the economy was in better shape than the other ex-Soviet republics in Central Asia. But President Nursultan Nazarbaev was criticized for his authoritarian rule. In 2007, constitutional changes enabled Nazarbaev to stand for the presidency as many times as he wished. In 2011, he was re-elected, despite opposition protests that he had given them no time to prepare.

The World Bank classifies Kazakhstan as a "lower-middle-income" developing country. Livestock farming, especially sheep and cattle, is an important activity, and major crops include barley, cotton, rice, and wheat. The country is rich in mineral resources, including coal and oil reserves, together with bauxite, copper, lead, tungsten, and zinc. Manufactures include chemicals, food products, machinery, and textiles. Oil is exported via a pipeline through Russia. However, to reduce the country's dependence on Russia, another pipeline to China was inaugurated in 2009. Other exports include metals, chemicals, grain, wool, and meat.

AREA 1,052,084 SQ MI [2,724,900 SQ KM] **POPULATION** 15,522,000
CAPITAL ASTANA **GOVERNMENT** MULTIPARTY REPUBLIC
ETHNIC GROUPS KAZAKH 53%, RUSSIAN 30%, UKRAINIAN 4%, GERMAN 2%, UZBEK 2% **LANGUAGES** KAZAKH (OFFICIAL); RUSSIAN, THE FORMER OFFICIAL LANGUAGE, IS WIDELY SPOKEN **RELIGIONS** ISLAM 47%, RUSSIAN ORTHODOX 44% **CURRENCY** TENGE = 100 TIYN

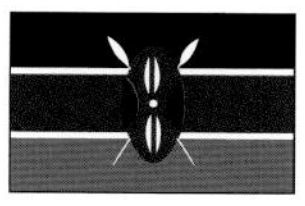
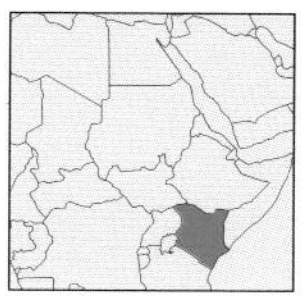

KENYA

GEOGRAPHY The Republic of Kenya is a country in East Africa which straddles the equator. Behind the narrow coastal plain on the Indian Ocean, the land rises to high plains and highlands, broken by volcanic mountains, including Mount Kenya, the country's highest peak at 17,057 ft [5,199 m]. Crossing the country is an arm of the Great Rift Valley, on the floor of which are several lakes, including Baringo, Magadi, Naivasha, Nakuru, and, on the northern frontier, Lake Turkana (formerly Lake Rudolf). Nairobi, in the southwestern highlands, has summer temperatures which are about 18°C [10°F] lower than humid Mombasa. Only about 15% of Kenya has a reliable annual rainfall of 31 inches [800 mm].

POLITICS & ECONOMY The Kenyan coast has been a trading center for more than 2,000 years. Britain took over the coast in 1895 and soon extended its influence inland. In the 1950s, a secret movement, called Mau Mau, launched an armed struggle against British rule. Although Mau Mau was eventually defeated, Kenya became independent in 1963.

Kenya was a one-party state for much of the time after 1963. Democracy was restored in 1992. Elections in 2007 led to inter-ethnic violence when the opposition refused to accept the declared results. A deal was agreed by President Mwai Kibaki and Raila Odinga, who became prime minister. Kenya adopted a new constitution in 2010. In 2011, Somali attacks and kidnappings in northern Kenya provoked Kenya to send forces into Somalia to combat the Islamist al-Shabab group.

Kenya remains a "low-income" developing country. Many Kenyans are subsistence farmers. The chief food crop is maize. The main cash crops and the leading exports are coffee and tea. Manufactures include chemicals, leather and footwear, processed food, petroleum products, and textiles.

AREA 224,080 sq mi [580,367 sq km]
POPULATION 41,071,000 **CAPITAL** Nairobi
GOVERNMENT Multiparty republic **ETHNIC GROUPS** Kikuyu 22%, Luhya 14%, Luo 13%, Kalenjin 12%, Kamba 11%, others
LANGUAGES Kiswahili and English (both official)
RELIGIONS Protestant 45%, Roman Catholic 33%, traditional beliefs 10%, Islam 10% **CURRENCY** Kenyan shilling = 100 cents

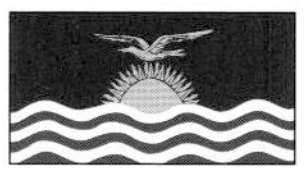
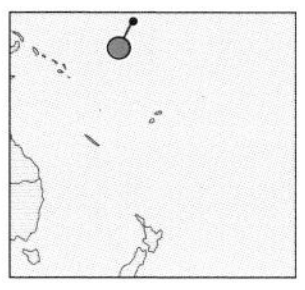

KIRIBATI

The Republic of Kiribati comprises three groups of coral atolls scattered over about 2 million sq mi [5 million sq km]. Kiribati straddles the equator and temperatures are high and the rainfall is abundant.

Formerly part of the British Gilbert and Ellice Islands, Kiribati became independent in 1979. The main export is copra and the country depends heavily on foreign aid.

AREA 280 sq mi [726 sq km] **POPULATION** 101,000 **CAPITAL** Tarawa

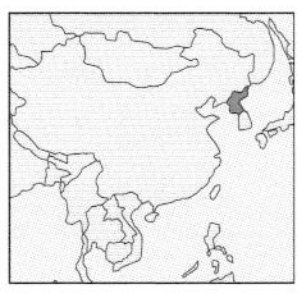

KOREA, NORTH

GEOGRAPHY The Democratic People's Republic of Korea occupies the northern part of the Korean peninsula, which extends south from northeastern China. Mountains form the heart of the country, with the highest peak, Paektu-san, reaching 9,003 ft [2,744 m] on the northern border.

North Korea has a fairly severe climate, with cold, snowy winters. In summer, moist winds from the oceans bring rain.

POLITICS & ECONOMY North Korea was created in 1945, when the peninsula, which had been a Japanese colony since 1910, was divided into two parts. Soviet forces occupied the north, with US forces in the south. Soviet occupation led to a Communist government being established in 1948 under the leadership of Kim Il Sung, who effectively became a dictator.

The Korean War began in June 1950 when North Korean troops invaded the south. North Korea, aided by China and the Soviet Union, fought with South Korea, which was supported by troops from the United States and other UN members. The war ended in July 1953. An armistice was signed but no permanent peace treaty was agreed. The end of the Cold War in the late 1990s eased the situation. North and South Korea joined the United Nations in 1991, though North Korea remained isolated from most other countries. In 1993, North Korea withdrew from the Nuclear Non-Proliferation Treaty, arousing suspicions that it was developing nuclear weapons. Kim Il Sung died in 1994 and was succeeded by his son, Kim Jong Il. From 2003, the United States accused North Korea of developing nuclear weapons, and in 2006 it conducted its first nuclear test. Kim Jong Il died in 2011. His son, Kim Jong-un, succeeded him.

North Korea's resources include coal, copper, iron ore, lead, tin, tungsten, and zinc. Under Communism, the country developed heavy, state-owned industries. Manufactures include chemicals, iron and steel, machinery, processed food, and textiles. Agriculture employs 27% of the people. Rice is the chief food crop, but food shortages have occurred in recent years.

AREA 46,540 sq mi [120,538 sq km]
POPULATION 24,457,000 **CAPITAL** Pyŏngyang
GOVERNMENT Single-party people's republic
ETHNIC GROUPS Korean 99%
LANGUAGES Korean (official)
RELIGIONS Buddhism and Confucianism
CURRENCY North Korean won = 100 chon

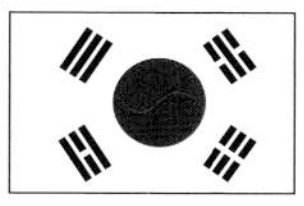
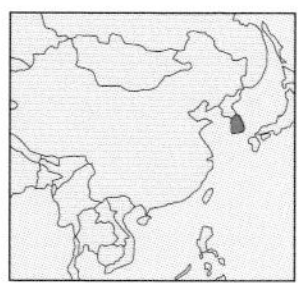

KOREA, SOUTH

GEOGRAPHY The Republic of Korea, as South Korea is officially known, occupies the southern part of the Korean peninsula. Mountains cover much of the country. The southern and western coasts are major farming regions. Many islands are found along the west and south coasts. The largest of these is Cheju-do, which contains South Korea's highest peak, Halla-San, which rises to 6,398 ft [1,950 m].

Like North Korea, South Korea is chilled in winter by cold, dry winds from central Asia. Summers are hot and wet, especially in July and August.

POLITICS & ECONOMY After Japan's defeat in World War II (1939–45), North Korea was occupied by troops from the Soviet Union, while South Korea was occupied by United States forces. A National Assembly elected in 1948 in South Korea created the Republic of Korea, while North Korea became a Communist state. North Korea invaded the South in June 1950, sparking off the Korean War (1950–3). Despite the destruction caused by the war, South Korea under a series of rather authoritarian governments began to industrialize the economy between the 1960s and 1980s. In 1987, a new constitution permitted the election of presidents every five years. In the 2000s, South Korea worked for closer contacts with the North, but tension continued into 2012.

Until the onset of the global financial crisis in 2008, South Korea had one of the world's fastest growing economies. Its main manufactures are processed food and textiles. Heavy industries produce chemicals, fertilizers, and iron and steel, together with a wide range of consumer products, such as computers, cars, and television sets.

Farming remains important in South Korea. Rice is the chief crop, together with fruits, grains, and vegetables, while fishing provides a major source of protein.

AREA 38,327 sq mi [99,268 sq km]
POPULATION 48,755,000 **CAPITAL** Seoul
GOVERNMENT Multiparty republic **ETHNIC GROUPS** Korean 99%
LANGUAGES Korean (official) **RELIGIONS** No affiliation 46%, Christianity 26%, Buddhism 26%, Confucianism 1%
CURRENCY South Korean won = 100 chon

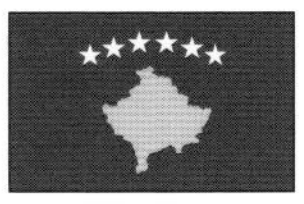
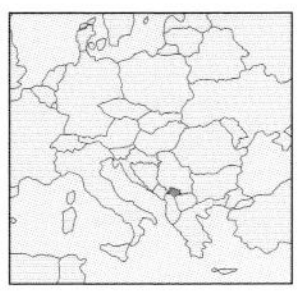

KOSOVO

GEOGRAPHY The Republic of Kosovo, formerly part of Serbia and, before 2003, part of Yugoslavia, declared its independence in February 2008. Its independence was recognized by the United States and major EU countries. But Serbia and its ally Russia refused recognition. It is a landlocked country, consisting of a river basin bounded by uplands in the north and southwest. It has cold, snowy winters and hot, dry summers.

POLITICS & ECONOMY Most people are Albanian-speakers who are Muslims, but there is an important Christian Serb minority. In the early 13th century, Kosovo was part of the Serbian empire but, after 1389, it came under Muslim Turkish Ottoman rule. Serbia regained control of Kosovo in 1912 and, in 1918, it became part of the Kingdom of Serbia. In 1946, it became part of the Socialist Federal Republic of Yugoslavia, becoming an autonomous province within the Republic of Serbia. In 1989, Serbia curtailed Kosovo's autonomy, while Albanian speakers declared their province independent. In 1995, the Albanian speakers set up the Kosovo Liberation Army, which launched an uprising against Serbia. In 1998, Serbia began repressive measures against Kosovo, resulting in massacres and ethnic cleansing of Albanian-speaking Kosovars. In 1999, NATO forces bombed Serbia and placed Kosovo under a temporary administration. Finally, the Kosovo Assembly declared its independence on February 17, 2008. In 2011, Kosovo and Serbia resolved a border dispute.

Kosovo is a poor country, with the lowest per capita income in Europe. Many people are subsistence farmers and its industries have declined because of lack of investment. The economy is highly dependent on international aid.

AREA 4,203 sq mi [10,887 sq km]
POPULATION 1,826,000 **CAPITAL** Pristina
GOVERNMENT Republic
ETHNIC GROUPS Albanian 88%, Serb 7%, others 5%
LANGUAGES Albanian and Serbian (both official), Turkish
RELIGIONS Islam, Serbian Orthodox, Roman Catholic
CURRENCY Euro = 100 cents

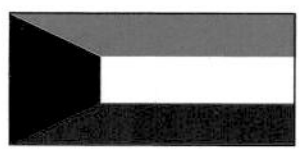
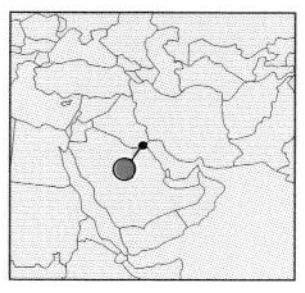

KUWAIT

GEOGRAPHY The State of Kuwait at the north end of the Persian Gulf is an emirate (ruled by an emir, or amir). The land is low-lying and largely desert in nature. Summer temperatures are high but winters are cooler. Rainfall is low.

POLITICS & ECONOMY British influence began in 1775 and, in 1899, the local ruler concluded a treaty with Britain, agreeing to support British interests in return for British protection. Kuwait became independent in 1961. Its revenue from its oil exports made it highly prosperous. Iraq invaded Kuwait in 1990, but it was liberated in 1991 by a coalition force. In 2004, the government announced legislation for women to vote and stand for parliament. Women stood in the 2008 elections, but none was elected.

AREA 6,880 sq mi [17,818 sq km]
POPULATION 2,596,000 **CAPITAL** Kuwait City

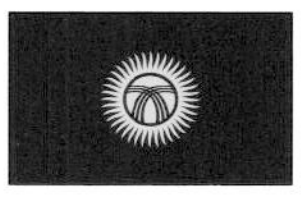
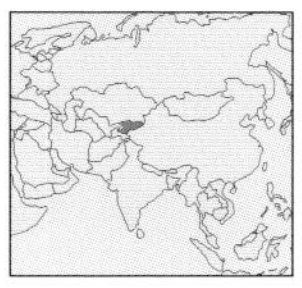

KYRGYZSTAN

GEOGRAPHY The Republic of Kyrgyzstan is a landlocked country between China, Tajikistan, Uzbekistan, and Kazakhstan. The country is mountainous, with spectacular scenery. The highest mountain, Pik Pobedy in the Tian Shan range, reaches 24,406 ft [7,439 m] in the east. The lowlands have warm summers and cold winters. But January temperatures in the mountains plummet to –18°F [–28°C]. Kyrgyzstan has a low annual rainfall.

POLITICS & ECONOMY In 1876, Kyrgyzstan became a province of Russia and Russian settlement in the area began. In 1916, Russia crushed a rebellion among the Kyrgyz, and many subsequently fled to China. In 1922, the area became an autonomous oblast (self-governing region) of the newly formed Soviet Union, but in 1936 it became one of the Soviet Socialist Republics. Under Communist rule, local customs and religious worship were suppressed, but education and health services were greatly improved.

In 1991, Kyrgyzstan became an independent country following the breakup of the Soviet Union. The Communist Party was dissolved, but the country maintained ties with Russia through an organization called the Commonwealth of Independent States. Elections were held under a new constitution adopted in 1994. Massive protests followed elections in 2005. President Askar Akayev fled the country. His successor, Kurmanbek Bakiyev, faced huge protests in 2010 and he also fled. In 2011, Almazbek Atambayev was elected president.

In the 1990s, Kyrgyzstan sought to reform its Soviet-style economy. Now classified as a "lower-middle income" developing country, agriculture is the main activity. Major products include cotton, eggs, fruits, grain, tobacco, vegetables, and wool. But food is imported. Most industries are concentrated around the capital Bishkek.

AREA 77,181 sq mi [199,900 sq km]
POPULATION 5,587,000 **CAPITAL** Bishkek
GOVERNMENT Multiparty republic
ETHNIC GROUPS Kyrgyz 65%, Russian 13%, Uzbek 13%
LANGUAGES Kyrgyz and Russian (both official)
RELIGIONS Islam 75%, Russian Orthodox 20%
CURRENCY Kyrgyzstani som = 100 tyiyn

LAOS

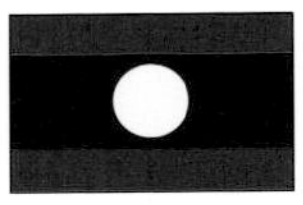

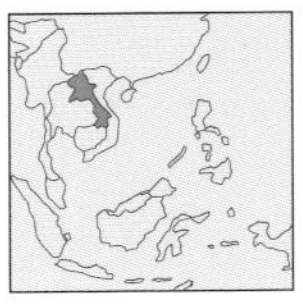

GEOGRAPHY The Lao People's Democratic Republic is a landlocked country in Southeast Asia. Mountains and plateaux cover much of the country. Most people live on the plains bordering the River Mekong and its tributaries. This river, one of Asia's longest, forms much of the country's northwestern and southwestern borders.

Laos has a tropical monsoon climate. Winters are dry and sunny with winds blowing from the northeast. From April, the monsoon season starts with the arrival of moist southwesterly winds.

POLITICS & ECONOMY France made Laos a protectorate in the late 19th century and ruled it, with Cambodia and Vietnam, as part of French Indochina. Laos became an independent kingdom in 1954. After independence, a power struggle between royalist government forces and a pro-Communist group called Pathet Lao caused instability. A civil war broke out and continued into the 1970s. The Pathet Lao took control in 1975 and the king abdicated. In the 1990s, Laos started to open to the world and began tentative reforms. In 2011, a stock exchange was opened in Vientiane, as part of a gradual move toward capitalism.

Laos is one of the world's poorest countries. Agriculture employs nearly 80% of the population and accounts for 31% of the gross domestic product. Rice is the main crop. Timber and coffee are exported. But the most valuable export is electricity, which is produced at hydroelectric power stations on the River Mekong and is exported to Thailand. Laos also produces opium.

AREA 91,428 sq mi [236,800 sq km]
POPULATION 6,477,000 **CAPITAL** Vientiane
GOVERNMENT Single-party republic
ETHNIC GROUPS Lao Loum 68%, Lao Theung 22%, Lao Soung 9%
LANGUAGES Lao (official), French, English **RELIGIONS** Buddhism 60%, traditional beliefs and others 40% **CURRENCY** Kip = 100 at

LATVIA

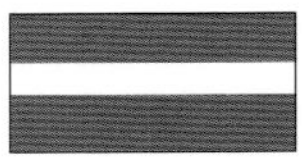

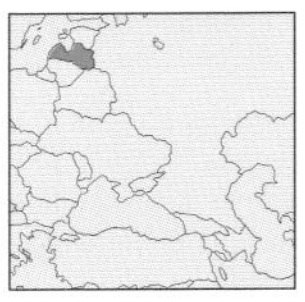

GEOGRAPHY The Republic of Latvia is one of three states on the southeastern corner of the Baltic Sea which were ruled as parts of the Soviet Union between 1940 and 1991. Latvia consists mainly of flat plains separated by low hills, composed of moraine (ice-worn rocks).

Riga has warm summers, but the winter months are subzero. The rainfall is moderate.

POLITICS & ECONOMY In 1800, Russia was in control of Latvia, but Latvians declared their independence after World War I. In 1940, under a German-Soviet pact, Soviet troops occupied Latvia, but they were driven out by the Germans in 1941. Soviet troops returned in 1944 and Latvia became part of the Soviet Union. Under Soviet rule, many Russian immigrants settled in Latvia and many Latvians feared that the Russians would become the dominant ethnic group.

In the late 1980s, when reforms were being introduced in the Soviet Union, Latvia's government ended absolute Communist rule and made Latvian the official language. In 1990, it declared the country to be independent, an act which was finally recognized by the Soviet Union in September 1991.

Latvia held the first free elections to its parliament (the Saeima) in 1993. Voting was limited only to citizens of Latvia on June 17, 1940, and their descendants. This meant that about 34% of Latvian residents were unable to vote. In 1994, Latvia restricted the naturalization of non-Latvians, including many Russian settlers, who were not allowed to vote or own land. However, in 1998, the government agreed that all children born since independence should have automatic citizenship. In 2004, Latvia became a member of the North Atlantic Treaty Organization and the European Union. Latvia was hit hard by the global financial crisis in 2009. In 2011, a new coalition government was formed, excluding a pro-Russian party that had won the most votes.

The World Bank classifies Latvia as a "lower-middle-income" country. Manufactures include electronic goods, farm machinery, fertilizers, processed food, plastics, radios, and vehicles. Latvia produces only about a tenth of the electricity it needs. It imports the rest from Belarus, Russia, and Ukraine.

AREA 24,942 sq mi [64,600 sq km]
POPULATION 2,205,000 **CAPITAL** Riga
GOVERNMENT Multiparty republic
ETHNIC GROUPS Latvian 58%, Russian 30%, Belarusian, Ukrainian, Polish, Lithuanian **LANGUAGES** Latvian (official), Lithuanian, Russian **RELIGIONS** Lutheran, Roman Catholic, Russian Orthodox
CURRENCY Latvian lats = 10 santimi

LEBANON

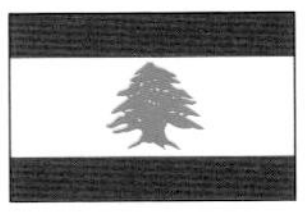

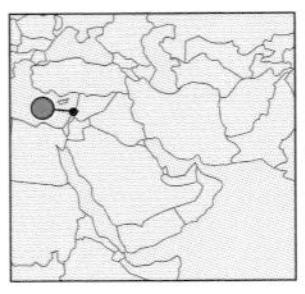

GEOGRAPHY The Republic of Lebanon is a country on the eastern shores of the Mediterranean Sea. Behind the coastal plain are the rugged Lebanon Mountains (Jabal Lubnan), which rise to 10,131 ft [3,088 m]. Another range, the Anti-Lebanon Mountains (Al Jabal Ash Sharqi), forms the eastern border with Syria. Between the two ranges is the Bekaa (Beqaa) Valley, a fertile farming region.

The coast has hot, dry summers and mild, wet winters. Heavy rain falls on the mountains, with snow at high altitudes.

POLITICS & ECONOMY Lebanon was ruled by Turkey from 1516 until World War I. France ruled the country from 1923, but Lebanon became independent in 1946. After independence, the Muslims and Christians agreed to share power, and Lebanon made rapid economic progress. But from the late 1950s, development was slowed by periodic conflict between Sunni and Shia Muslims, Druze, and Christians. The situation was further complicated by the presence of Palestinian refugees who used bases in Lebanon to attack Israel.

In 1975, civil war broke out as private armies representing the many factions struggled for power. This led to intervention by Israel in the south and Syria in the north. UN peacekeeping forces arrived in 1978, but violence continued in the 1980s. Peace was restored in the 1990s, but, in 2005, the assassination of Rafik Hariri, former prime minister, was blamed on Syria. Under pressure, Syria withdrew its forces from Lebanon. In 2006, a 34-day conflict between Israeli troops and Hezbollah guerrillas caused devastation in southern Lebanon. In 2008–9, relations with Syria improved. In 2011, a new cabinet was formed with the militant Hezbollah holding a majority of the seats.

Lebanon's civil war almost destroyed valuable trade and financial services that had been Lebanon's chief source of income, together with tourism. Manufacturing, formerly a major activity, was badly hit.

AREA 4,015 sq mi [10,400 sq km]
POPULATION 4,143,000 **CAPITAL** Beirut
GOVERNMENT Multiparty republic **ETHNIC GROUPS** Arab 95%, Armenian 4%, others **LANGUAGES** Arabic (official), French, English, Armenian **RELIGIONS** Islam 70%, Christianity 30%
CURRENCY Lebanese pound = 100 piastres

LESOTHO

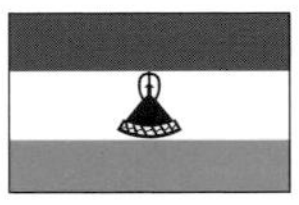

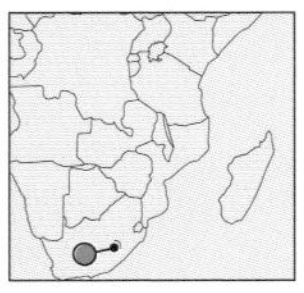

GEOGRAPHY The Kingdom of Lesotho is a landlocked country, completely enclosed by South Africa. The land is mountainous, rising to 11,424 ft [3,482 m] on the northeastern border. The Drakensberg range covers most of the country.

The climate of Lesotho is greatly affected by the altitude, because most of the country lies above 4,920 ft [1,500 m]. Summers are warm but winters are cold. The rainfall averages about 28 inches [700 mm].

POLITICS & ECONOMY The Basotho nation was founded in the 1820s by King Moshoeshoe I, who united various groups fleeing from tribal wars in southern Africa. Britain made the area a protectorate in 1868 and, in 1871, placed it under the British Cape Colony in South Africa. But in 1884, Basutoland, as the area was called, was reconstituted as a British protectorate, where whites were not allowed to own land.

The country finally became independent in 1966 as the Kingdom of Lesotho, with Moshoeshoe II, great-grandson of Moshoeshoe I, as its king. Since independence, Lesotho has suffered instability. The military seized power in 1986 and stripped Moshoeshoe II of his powers in 1990, installing his son, Letsie III, as monarch. After elections in 1993, Moshoeshoe II was restored to office in 1995. But after his death in a car crash in 1996, Letsie III again became king. In 1998, an army revolt, following an election in which the ruling party won 79 out of the 80 seats, caused much damage to the economy. Lesotho has faced many problems, including drought, while 24% of the people were reported in 2009 to be infected with the HIV virus.

Lesotho lacks natural resources, and the UN has stated that 40% of the people are "ultra-poor." Agriculture employs 18% of the people, mostly at subsistence level. Remittances sent home by Basotho working abroad are important to the economy.

AREA 11,720 sq mi [30,355 sq km]
POPULATION 1,925,000 **CAPITAL** Maseru
GOVERNMENT Constitutional monarchy
ETHNIC GROUPS Sotho 99% **LANGUAGES** Sesotho and English (both official) **RELIGIONS** Christianity 80%, traditional beliefs 20%
CURRENCY Loti = 100 lisente

LIBERIA

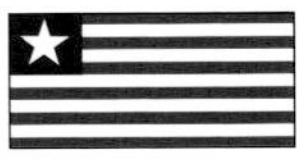

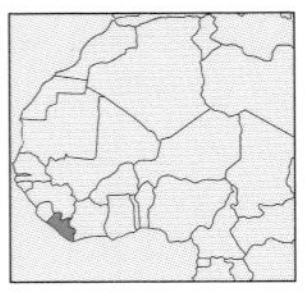

GEOGRAPHY The Republic of Liberia is a country in West Africa. Behind the coastline, 311 mi [500 km] long, lies a narrow coastal plain. Beyond, the land rises to a plateau region, with the highest land along the border with Guinea. Liberia has a tropical climate with high temperatures and high humidity all through the year. Rainfall is abundant all year round, but there is a particularly wet period from June to November. Rainfall generally increases from east to west.

POLITICS & ECONOMY In the late 18th century, some white Americans in the United States wanted to help freed black slaves to return to Africa. In 1816, they set up the American Colonization Society, which bought land in what is now Liberia.

In 1822, the Society landed former slaves at a settlement on the coast which they named Monrovia. In 1847, Liberia became a fully independent republic with a constitution much like that of the United States. For many years, Americo-Liberians controlled the country's government. US influence remained strong and the American Firestone Company, which ran the rubber plantations, was especially influential. Foreign companies were also involved in exploiting Liberia's mineral resources, including its huge iron-ore deposits.

In 1980, a military group composed of people from the local population killed the Americo-Liberian president, William R. Tolbert. An army sergeant, Samuel K. Doe, was made president of Liberia. Elections held in 1985 resulted in victory for Doe. From 1989, the country was plunged into civil war between various ethnic groups. Doe was assassinated in 1990 and the struggle with rebel groups continued. West African peacekeeping forces arrived in Liberia and, in 1995, a ceasefire was agreed. A council of state, composed of former warlords, was set up in 1997 and Charles Taylor became president. Taylor fled the country in 2003, and in 2006 he was extradited and faced war crimes charges, on several of which he was convicted in 2012. Following elections in 2005, Ellen Sirleaf-Johnson was elected president. She became Africa's first woman president. She was re-elected in 2011.

Liberia's economy was devastated by the civil war. Agriculture is important, but most farmers live at subsistence level. Food crops include cassava, rice, and sugarcane, while rubber, cocoa, and coffee are exported. The most valuable export is rubber.

Liberia also obtains revenue from its "flag of convenience," which is used by about one-sixth of the world's commercial shipping, exploiting low taxes.

AREA 43,000 sq mi [111,369 sq km]
POPULATION 3,787,000 **CAPITAL** Monrovia
GOVERNMENT Multiparty republic **ETHNIC GROUPS** Indigenous African tribes 95% (including Kpelle, Bassa, Grebo, Gio, Kru, Mano)
LANGUAGES English (official), ethnic languages
RELIGIONS Christianity 40%, Islam 20%, traditional beliefs and others 40% **CURRENCY** Liberian dollar = 100 cents

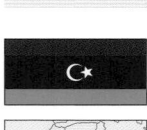

LIBYA

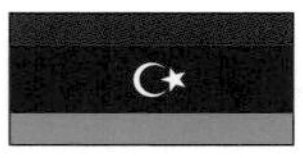

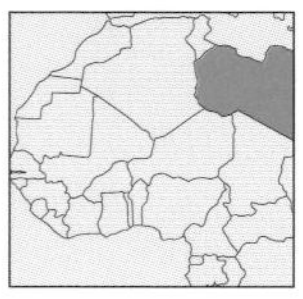

GEOGRAPHY The Socialist People's Libyan Arab Jamahiriya, as Libya is officially called, is a large country in North Africa. Most people live on the coastal plains in the northeast and northwest. The Sahara, the world's largest desert, which occupies 95% of Libya, reaches the Mediterranean coast along the Gulf of Sidra (Khalij Surt).

The coastal plains in the northeast and northwest have Mediterranean climates, with hot, dry summers and mild, sometimes wet winters. Hot desert conditions prevail inland.

POLITICS & ECONOMY Italy took over Libya in 1911, but lost it during World War II. Britain and France jointly ruled Libya until 1951, when the country became an independent kingdom.

In 1969, a military group headed by Colonel Muammar Gaddafi deposed the king and set up a military government. Under Gaddafi, the government took control of the economy and used money from oil exports to finance welfare services and development projects. Gaddafi was criticized for supporting terrorist groups around the world, and Libya became isolated from the mid-1980s.

From 2004, relations with the West improved and diplomatic relations were restored with many nations, including the United States. However, in February 2011, the arrest of a human rights campaigner sparked off protests in Benghazi. The protests rapidly spread to other cities. As the fighting intensified, the UN sanctioned Western governments to impose a no-fly zone over Libya to protect civilians. In October, Gaddafi was killed and a National Transition Council was set up as the *de facto* government. In 2012, clashes between former rebel groups indicated discontent with the pace and nature of change in Libya.

The discovery of oil and natural gas in 1959 led to a transformation of Libya's economy. This formerly poor country soon became Africa's richest in terms of its per capita income. But it remains a developing country, because oil accounts for nearly all its export revenues. Agriculture is important, although Libya imports food. Crops include barley, citrus fruits, dates, olives, potatoes, and wheat, while cattle, sheep, and poultry are raised. Libya has oil refineries and petrochemical plants. Other manufactures include cement and steel.

AREA 679,358 SQ MI [1,759,540 SQ KM] **POPULATION** 6,598,000
CAPITAL TRIPOLI **GOVERNMENT** SINGLE-PARTY SOCIALIST STATE
ETHNIC GROUPS LIBYAN ARAB AND BERBER 97%
LANGUAGES ARABIC (OFFICIAL), BERBER **RELIGIONS** ISLAM (SUNNI MUSLIM) 97% **CURRENCY** LIBYAN DINAR = 1,000 DIRHAMS

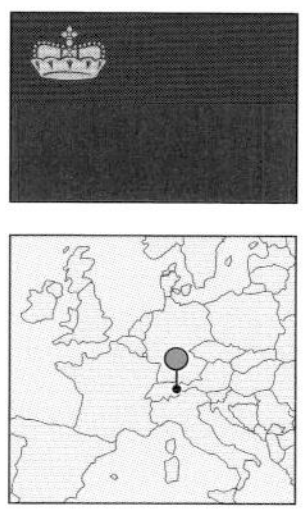

LIECHTENSTEIN

The tiny Principality of Liechtenstein is sandwiched between Switzerland and Austria. The River Rhine flows along its western border, while Alpine peaks rise in the east and south. The climate is relatively mild. Since 1924, Liechtenstein has been in a customs union with Switzerland. Taxation is low and the country is a haven for foreign companies. In 2004, the head of state Prince Hans-Adam II handed over the running of the country to his son, Prince Alois, though he remained titular head of state. In 2009, Liechtenstein agreed to share tax information with a number of countries, including Germany, the UK, and the US.

AREA 62 SQ MI [160 SQ KM] **POPULATION** 35,000 **CAPITAL** VADUZ

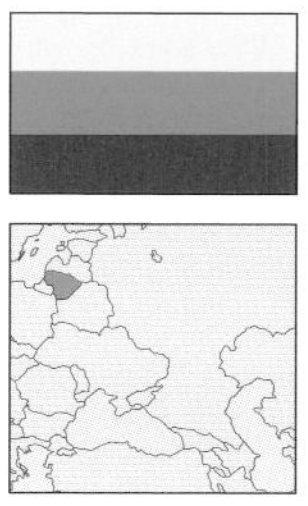

LITHUANIA

GEOGRAPHY The Republic of Lithuania is the southernmost of the three Baltic states which were ruled as part of the Soviet Union between 1940 and 1991. Much of the land is flat or gently rolling, with the highest land in the southeast.

Winters are cold and summers warm. The annual rainfall in the west is about 25 inches [630 mm]. Eastern areas are drier.

POLITICS & ECONOMY The Lithuanian people were united into a single nation in the 12th century, and later joined a union with Poland. In 1795, Lithuania came under Russian rule. After World War I (1914–18), Lithuania declared itself independent, and in 1920 it signed a peace treaty with the Russians, though Poland held Vilnius until 1939. In 1940, the Soviet Union occupied Lithuania, but the Germans invaded in 1941. Soviet forces returned in 1944, and Lithuania was integrated into the Soviet Union. In 1988, when the Soviet Union was introducing reforms, the Lithuanians demanded independence. Their language is one of the oldest in the world, and the country was always the most homogenous of the Baltic states, staunchly Catholic and resistant of attempts to suppress its culture. Pro-independence groups won the national elections in 1990 and, in 1991, the Soviet Union recognized Lithuania's independence.

Since 1991, Lithuania has sought to reform its economy and introduce a private enterprise system. Lithuania has also drawn closer to the West and, in 2004, it became a member of both the North Atlantic Treaty Organization and the European Union.

The World Bank classifies Lithuania as a "lower-middle-income" developing country. Lithuania lacks natural resources, but manufacturing, based on imported materials, is the most valuable activity.

AREA 25,174 SQ MI [65,200 SQ KM]
POPULATION 3,536,000 **CAPITAL** VILNIUS
GOVERNMENT MULTIPARTY REPUBLIC
ETHNIC GROUPS LITHUANIAN 80%, RUSSIAN 9%, POLISH 7%, BELARUSIAN 2% **LANGUAGES** LITHUANIAN (OFFICIAL), RUSSIAN, POLISH
RELIGIONS MAINLY ROMAN CATHOLIC **CURRENCY** LITAS = 100 CENTAI

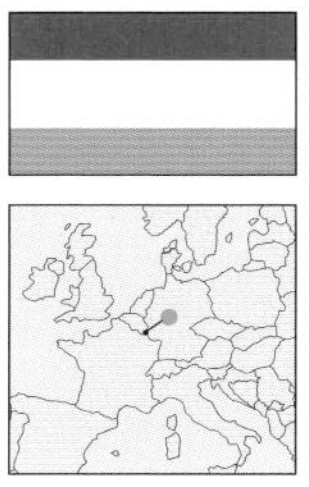

LUXEMBOURG

GEOGRAPHY The Grand Duchy of Luxembourg is one of the smallest and oldest countries in Europe. The north belongs to an upland region which includes the Ardenne in Belgium and Luxembourg, and the Eifel highlands in Germany.

Luxembourg has a temperate climate. The south has warm summers and falls, when grapes ripen in sheltered southeastern valleys. Winters are sometimes severe, especially in upland areas.

POLITICS & ECONOMY Germany occupied Luxembourg in World Wars I and II. In 1944–5, northern Luxembourg was the scene of the Battle of the Bulge. In 1948, Luxembourg joined Belgium and the Netherlands in a union called Benelux. In the 1950s, it was one of the six founders of what is now the European Union. Its capital is a major financial center and contains several international agencies. In 2008, parliament restricted the monarch to a ceremonial role following the grand duke's refusal to sign a law allowing euthanasia.

Luxembourg has iron-ore reserves and is a major steel producer. It also has many high-technology industries, producing electronic goods and computers. Steel and other manufactures, including chemicals, rubber products, glass, and aluminum, dominate the country's exports. Other major activities include tourism and financial services.

AREA 998 SQ MI [2,586 SQ KM]
POPULATION 503,000 **CAPITAL** LUXEMBOURG
GOVERNMENT CONSTITUTIONAL MONARCHY (GRAND DUCHY)
ETHNIC GROUPS LUXEMBOURGER 71%, PORTUGUESE, ITALIAN, FRENCH, BELGIAN, SLAVS **LANGUAGES** LUXEMBOURGISH (OFFICIAL), FRENCH, GERMAN **RELIGIONS** ROMAN CATHOLIC 87%, OTHERS 13%
CURRENCY EURO = 100 CENTS

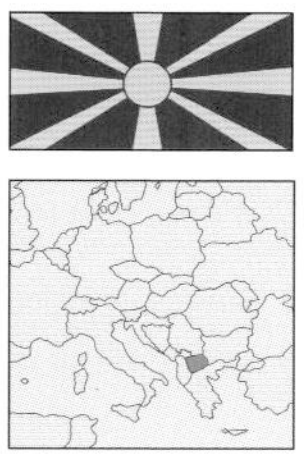

MACEDONIA (FYROM)

GEOGRAPHY The Republic of Macedonia is a country in southeastern Europe, which was once one of the six republics that made up the former Federal People's Republic of Yugoslavia. This landlocked country is largely mountainous or hilly. Macedonia has hot summers, though highland areas are cooler. Winters are cold and snowfalls are often heavy. The climate is fairly continental in character and rain occurs throughout the year.

POLITICS & ECONOMY Until the 20th century, Macedonia's history was closely tied to a larger area, also called Macedonia, which included parts of northern Greece and southwestern Bulgaria. This region reached its peak in power at the time of Philip II (382–336 BC) and his son Alexander the Great (336–323 BC). After Alexander's death, his empire was split up and it gradually declined. The area became a Roman province in the 140s BC and part of the Byzantine empire from AD 395. In the 6th century, Slavs from eastern Europe settled in the area, followed by Bulgars from central Asia in the 9th century. The Byzantine empire regained control in 1018, but Serbia took Macedonia in the early 14th century. In 1371, the Ottoman Turks conquered the area and ruled it for more than 500 years.

In 1913, at the end of the Balkan Wars, the area was divided between Serbia, Bulgaria, and Greece. At the end of World War I, Serbian Macedonia became part of the Kingdom of the Serbs, Croats, and Slovenes, which was renamed Yugoslavia in 1929. After World War II, Yugoslavia became a Communist country under ex-partisan leader Josip Broz Tito.

Tito died in 1980 and, in the early 1990s, the country broke up into five separate republics. Macedonia declared its independence in September 1991. Greece objected to this territory using the name Macedonia, which it considered to be a Greek name. It also objected to a symbol on Macedonia's flag and a reference in the constitution to the desire to reunite the three parts of the old Macedonia.

Macedonia adopted a new clause in its constitution rejecting any Macedonian claims on Greek territory and, in 1993, the United Nations accepted the new republic as a member under the name of the Former Yugoslav Republic of Macedonia (FYROM). By the end of 1993, all the countries of the EU, except Greece, were establishing diplomatic relations with the FYROM. In 1995, Greece lifted its trade ban when Macedonia agreed to redesign its flag, though the issue over its name remained unresolved. In 2001, fighting along the Kosovo border was attributed to people who wanted to create a Greater Albania. The uprising ended when Macedonia granted its Albanian-speakers increased rights. In 2011, the International Court of Justice ruled that Greece was wrong to block Macedonia's bid to join NATO in 2008 because of the dispute over its name.

The World Bank describes Macedonia as a "lower-middle-income" economy. Manufactures dominate the country's exports. Coal is mined, but oil and natural gas are imported. The country is self-sufficient in its basic food needs.

AREA 9,928 SQ MI [25,713 SQ KM] **POPULATION** 2,077,000
CAPITAL SKOPJE **GOVERNMENT** MULTIPARTY REPUBLIC
ETHNIC GROUPS MACEDONIAN 64%, ALBANIAN 25%, TURKISH 4%, ROMANIAN 3%, SERB 2% **LANGUAGES** MACEDONIAN AND ALBANIAN (OFFICIAL) **RELIGIONS** MACEDONIAN ORTHODOX 70%, ISLAM 29%
CURRENCY MACEDONIAN DENAR = 100 PARAS

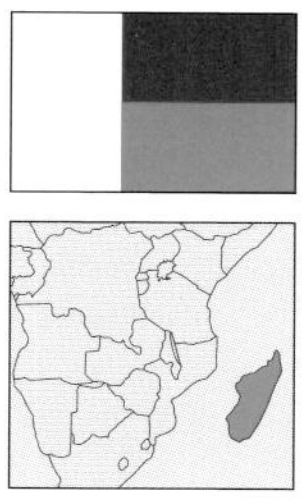

MADAGASCAR

GEOGRAPHY The Democratic Republic of Madagascar, in southeastern Africa, is an island nation, which has a larger area than France. Behind the narrow coastal plains in the east lies a highland zone, mostly between 2,000 ft and 4,000 ft [610 m to 1,220 m] above sea level. Broad plains border the Mozambique Channel in the west.

Temperatures in the highlands are moderated by the altitude. The winters (from April to September) are dry, but heavy rains occur in summer. The eastern coastlands are warm and humid. The west is drier, and the south and southwest are hot and dry.

POLITICS & ECONOMY People from Southeast Asia began to settle on Madagascar around 2,000 years ago. Subsequent influxes from Africa and Arabia added to the island's diverse heritage, culture, and language.

French troops defeated a Malagasy army in 1895 and Madagascar became a French colony. In 1960, it achieved full independence as the Malagasy Republic. In 1972, army officers seized control and, in 1975, under the leadership of Lieutenant-Commander Didier Ratsiraka, the country was renamed Madagascar. In 2002, the country came close to civil war when Ratsiraka and his opponent Marc Ravalomanana both claimed victory in presidential elections. Ravalomanana became president, but he was deposed in 2009 by Andry Rajoelina, who became *de facto* president. In 2010, a new constitution was adopted in a referendum, enabling Rajoelina to run for president.

Madagascar is a poor country. Poverty and population growth impose pressure on the dwindling forests and the unique wildlife, as well as causing severe soil erosion. Farming, fishing, and forestry employ about 80% of the people. Food crops include bananas, cassava, rice, and sweet potatoes. Coffee is exported.

AREA 226,657 SQ MI [587,041 SQ KM]
POPULATION 21,926,000 **CAPITAL** ANTANANARIVO
GOVERNMENT REPUBLIC **ETHNIC GROUPS** MERINA, BETSIMISARAKA, BETSILEO, TSIMIHETY, SAKALAVA, AND OTHERS
LANGUAGES MALAGASY AND FRENCH (BOTH OFFICIAL)
RELIGIONS TRADITIONAL BELIEFS 52%, CHRISTIANITY 41%, ISLAM 7%
CURRENCY MALAGASY FRANC = 100 CENTIMES

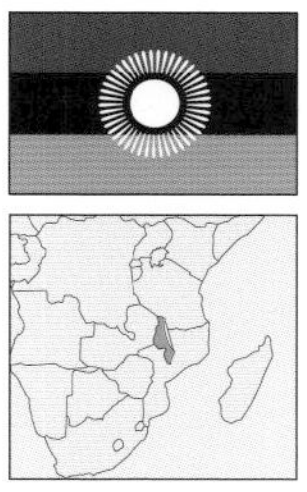

MALAWI

GEOGRAPHY The Republic of Malawi includes part of Lake Malawi, which is drained by the River Shire, a tributary of the River Zambezi. The land is mostly mountainous. The highest peak, Mulanje, reaches 9,843 ft [3,000 m] in the southeast.

While the low-lying areas of Malawi are hot and humid all year round, the uplands have a pleasant climate. Lilongwe has a warm and sunny climate. Frosts sometimes occur in July and August, in the middle of the long dry season.

POLITICS & ECONOMY Malawi, then called Nyasaland, became a British protectorate in 1891. In 1953, Britain established the Federation of Rhodesia and Nyasaland, which also included what are now Zambia and Zimbabwe. Black African opposition, led in Nyasaland by Dr Hastings Kamuzu Banda, led to the dissolution of the federation in 1963. In 1964, Nyasaland became independent as Malawi, with Banda as prime minister. Banda became president when the country became a republic in 1966, and in 1971 he was made president for life. Banda was an autocrat, ruling through the only party, the Malawi Congress Party. But a multiparty system was restored in 1993. Bakili Muluzi became president, and in 2004 he was succeeded by Bingu wa Mutharika, leader of the United Democratic Front (UDF). In 2005, he resigned from the UDF and set up the Democratic Progressive Party. Mutharika died in 2012 and was succeeded by Vice-President Joyce Banda.

Malawi is one of the world's poorest countries. More than 80% of the people are farmers, but many grow little more than they need to feed their families.

AREA 45,747 SQ MI [118,484 SQ KM]
POPULATION 15,879,000 **CAPITAL** LILONGWE
GOVERNMENT MULTIPARTY REPUBLIC
ETHNIC GROUPS CHEWA, NYANJA, TONGA, TUMBUKA, LOMWE, YAO, NGONI, AND OTHERS
LANGUAGES CHICHEWA AND ENGLISH (BOTH OFFICIAL)
RELIGIONS PROTESTANT 55%, ROMAN CATHOLIC 20%, ISLAM 20%
CURRENCY MALAWIAN KWACHA = 100 TAMBALA

MALAYSIA

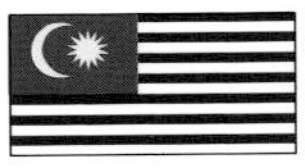

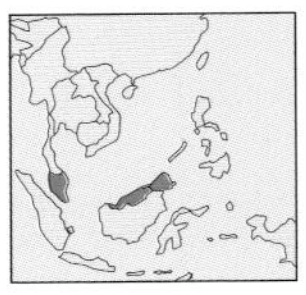

GEOGRAPHY The Federation of Malaysia consists of two main parts. Peninsular Malaysia, which is joined to mainland Asia, contains about 80% of the population. The other main regions, Sabah and Sarawak, are in northern Borneo, an island which Malaysia shares with Indonesia. Behind the coastal lowlands, the interior is mountainous.

Malaysia has a hot equatorial climate. The temperatures are high all through the year, though the mountains are much cooler than the lowland areas. Rainfall is heavy throughout the year.

POLITICS & ECONOMY Around 1,200 years ago, Indian traders introduced Hinduism and Buddhism into the Malay peninsula, while Arabs introduced Islam in the 15th century. Portuguese traders reached Melaka in 1509, but the Dutch took over in 1641. Britain became established in the area in 1786.

Japan occupied the area during World War II (1939–45), but the area reverted to British rule in 1945. In the 1940s and 1950s, Communist guerrillas battled unsuccessfully for power. Malaya (Peninsular Malaysia) became independent in 1957. Malaysia was created in 1963, when Malaya, Singapore, Sabah, and Sarawak agreed to unite, but Singapore withdrew in 1965.

From 1981, Malaysia achieved rapid economic progress, but it experienced an economic recession in 1997. The government took action to restore confidence. In 2003, Mahathir bin Mohamad was succeeded by Abdullah Ahmad Badawi, who stood down in 2009. His deputy, Najib Razak, took over as prime minister.

The World Bank classifies Malaysia as an "upper-middle-income" developing country. Palm oil, rubber, and tin are major products. Manufactures include cars, chemicals, a wide range of electronic goods, plastics, textiles, rubber, and wood products.

AREA 127,320 sq mi [329,758 sq km] **POPULATION** 28,729,000
CAPITAL Kuala Lumpur; Putrajaya (administrative capital awaiting completion)
GOVERNMENT Federal constitutional monarchy
ETHNIC GROUPS Malay and other indigenous groups 58%, Chinese 24%, Indian 8%, others **LANGUAGES** Malay (official), Chinese, English **RELIGIONS** Islam, Buddhism, Daoism, Hinduism, Christianity, Sikhism **CURRENCY** Ringgit = 100 cents

MALDIVES

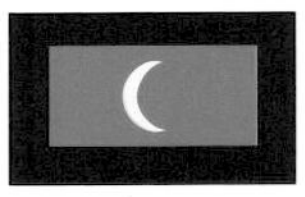

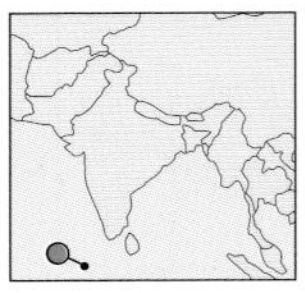

The Republic of the Maldives consists of about 1,200 low-lying coral islands, south of India. The highest point is 79 ft [24 m], but most of the land is only 6 ft [1.8 m] above sea level. The islands became a British territory in 1887 and independence was achieved in 1965. Tourism and fishing are the main industries.

AREA 115 sq mi [298 sq km] **POPULATION** 395,000 **CAPITAL** Malé

MALI

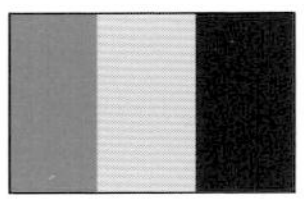

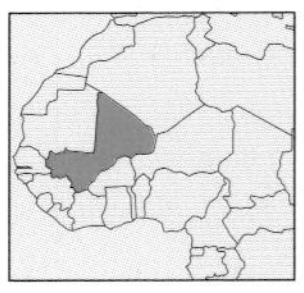

GEOGRAPHY The Republic of Mali is a landlocked country in northern Africa. The land is generally flat, with the highest land in the north. Northern Mali is hot and practically rainless. The south has enough rain for farming.

POLITICS & ECONOMY Between the 4th and 16th centuries, Mali was part of three African empires – Ancient Ghana, Ancient Mali, and Songhay. However, after 1591, when Songhay was defeated by Morocco, the area was divided into small kingdoms. France ruled the area, then known as French Sudan, from 1893 until the country became independent as Mali in 1960.

The first socialist government was overthrown in 1968 by an army group led by Moussa Traoré, but he was ousted in 1991. Multiparty democracy was restored in 1992 and Alpha Oumar Konaré was elected president. Konaré stood down in 2002 and Ahmadou Toure, who had restored democracy in 1992, was elected president. In 2012, an army coup overthrew Toure. The coup leaders said that the government was failing to give them enough arms to tackle a rebellion by ethnic Tuaregs in northern Mali, many of whom had returned from Libya. During the upheaval, the Tuaregs captured key cities in the north.

Mali is one of the world's poorest countries and 70% of the land is desert or semidesert. Only about 2% of the land is used for growing crops, while 25% is used for grazing animals. Agriculture employs more than one-third of the people, many of whom subsist by nomadic livestock rearing.

AREA 478,838 sq mi [1,240,192 sq km]
POPULATION 14,160,000 **CAPITAL** Bamako
GOVERNMENT Multiparty republic **ETHNIC GROUPS** Mande 50% (Bambara, Malinke, Soninke), Peul 17%, Voltaic 12%, Songhai 6%, Tuareg and Moor 10%, others **LANGUAGES** French (official), many African languages **RELIGIONS** Islam 90%, traditional beliefs 9%, Christianity 1% **CURRENCY** CFA franc = 100 centimes

MALTA

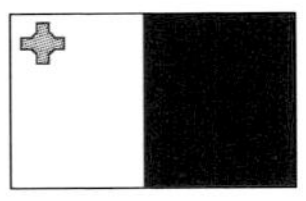

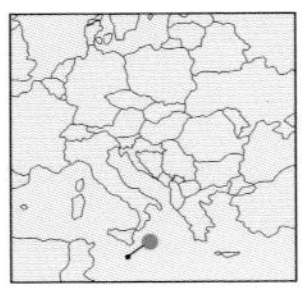

GEOGRAPHY The Republic of Malta consists of two main islands, Malta and Gozo, with a third, much smaller island called Comino lying between the two large islands and two islets. The climate is typically Mediterranean, with hot, dry summers and mild, moist winters.

POLITICS & ECONOMY Malta has fascinating Stone Age and Bronze Age remains. The islands later came under Phoenician, Greek, Carthaginian, Roman, and Arab rule. In about 1090, Malta came under the Norman kings of Sicily and, from 1530, the Knights Hospitallers (also called the Knights of St John of Jerusalem). France took the islands in 1798, but the British drove them out in 1800. British rule was officially recognized in 1815.

During World War I (1914–18), Malta was an important naval base. In World War II (1939–45), Italian and German aircraft bombed the islands. In recognition of the islanders' bravery, the British King George VI awarded the George Cross to Malta in 1942. In 1953, Malta became a base for NATO (North Atlantic Treaty Organization). Malta became independent in 1964 and a republic in 1974. In 1979, Malta ceased to be a British military base. Malta was declared a neutral country in the 1980s. It became a member of the European Union on May 1, 2004, and adopted the euro as its official currency in 2008.

The World Bank classifies Malta as an "upper-middle-income" developing country. It lacks natural resources, and most people work in the former naval dockyards, which are now used for commercial shipbuilding and repair, in manufacturing industries, and in the tourist industry.

Manufactures include processed food and chemicals. Farming is difficult, because of the rocky soils. Crops include barley, fruits, potatoes, and wheat. Malta also has a small fishing industry.

AREA 122 sq mi [316 sq km] **POPULATION** 408,000
CAPITAL Valletta **GOVERNMENT** Multiparty republic
ETHNIC GROUPS Maltese 96%, British 2% **LANGUAGES** Maltese and English (both official) **RELIGIONS** Roman Catholic 98%
CURRENCY Euro = 100 cents

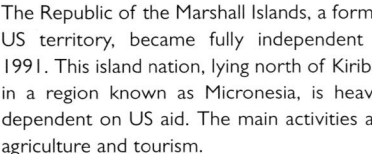

MARSHALL ISLANDS

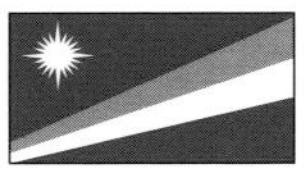

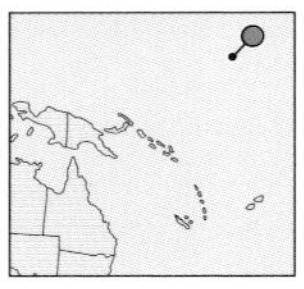

The Republic of the Marshall Islands, a former US territory, became fully independent in 1991. This island nation, lying north of Kiribati in a region known as Micronesia, is heavily dependent on US aid. The main activities are agriculture and tourism.

AREA 70 sq mi [181 sq km]
POPULATION 67,000 **CAPITAL** Majuro

MARTINIQUE

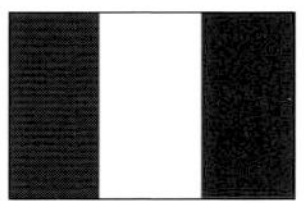

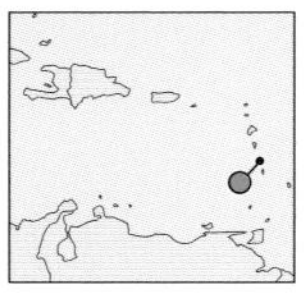

Martinique, a volcanic island nation in the Caribbean, was colonized by France in 1635. It became a French overseas department in 1946. Tourism and agriculture are major activities. About 70% of Martinique's gross domestic product is provided by the French government, allowing for a good standard of living.

AREA 425 sq mi [1,102 sq km]
POPULATION 397,000 **CAPITAL** Fort-de-France

MAURITANIA

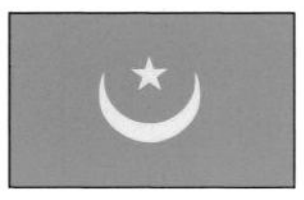

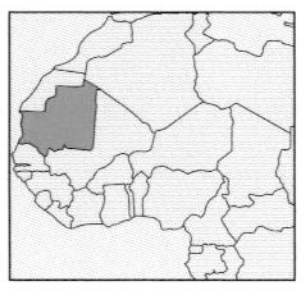

GEOGRAPHY The Islamic Republic of Mauritania in northwestern Africa is nearly twice the size of France. But France has almost 20 times as many people. Part of the world's largest desert, the Sahara, covers northern Mauritania and most Mauritanians live in the southwest. The amount of rainfall and the length of the rainy season increase from north to south. Much of the land is desert, but southwesterly winds bring summer rain to the south.

POLITICS & ECONOMY Originally part of the great African empires of Ghana and Mali, Mauritania became a French protectorate in 1903. In 1920, the country became a territory of French West Africa and a French colony. French West Africa included present-day Benin, Burkina Faso, Guinea, Ivory Coast, Mali, Niger, and Senegal, as well as Mauritania. Mauritania finally became independent in 1960.

In 1976, Spain withdrew from Spanish (now Western) Sahara, a territory bordering Mauritania to the north. Morocco occupied the northern two-thirds of this territory, while Mauritania took the rest. But Saharan guerrillas belonging to POLISARIO (the Popular Front for the Liberation of Saharan Territories) began an armed struggle for independence. In 1979, Mauritania withdrew from the southern part of Western Sahara, which was then occupied by Morocco. Democracy was restored after a new constitution was adopted in 1991. A military group seized power in 2005, but democratic elections were held in 2007. The military again seized control in 2008, and in 2009 its leader, Mohamad Ould Abdelaziz, was elected president. In 2010–11, al Qaida militants committed terrorist acts in Mauritania.

Mauritania is a "low-income" developing country. Nearly half of the people are engaged in agriculture. In 2006, Mauritania became Africa's newest oil producer, when an offshore platform came online for the first time.

AREA 395,953 sq mi [1,025,520 sq km]
POPULATION 3,282,000 **CAPITAL** Nouakchott
GOVERNMENT Multiparty Islamic republic
ETHNIC GROUPS Mixed Moor/Black 40%, Moor 30%, Black 30%
LANGUAGES Arabic and Wolof (both official), French
RELIGIONS Islam
CURRENCY Ouguiya = 5 khoums

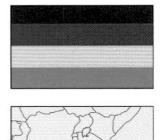

MAURITIUS

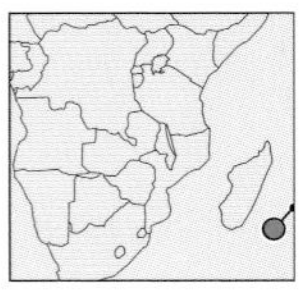

The Republic of Mauritius, an Indian Ocean nation lying east of Madagascar, was previously ruled by France and Britain until it achieved independence in 1968. It became a republic in 1992. Sugar production is in decline but tourism is vital to the economy.

AREA 788 sq mi [2,040 sq km]
POPULATION 1,304,000 **CAPITAL** Port Louis

MEXICO

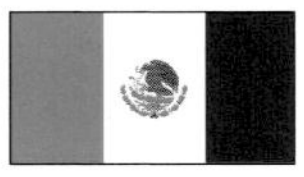

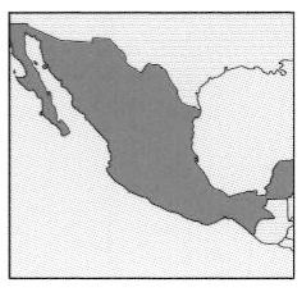

GEOGRAPHY The United Mexican States, as Mexico is officially named, is the world's most populous Spanish-speaking country. Much of the land is mountainous, although most people live on the central plateau. Mexico contains two large peninsulas: Lower (or Baja) California in the northwest, and the flat Yucatán peninsula in the southeast.

The climate varies according to the altitude. The resort of Acapulco on the southwest coast has a dry and sunny climate. Mexico City, at about 7,546 ft [2,300 m] above sea level, is much cooler. Most rain occurs between June and September. Rainfall decreases north of Mexico City and northern Mexico is mainly arid.

POLITICS & ECONOMY In the mid-19th century, Mexico lost land to the United States, and between 1910 and 1921 violent revolutions created chaos. Reforms were introduced in the 1920s and, in 1929, the Institutional Revolutionary Party (PRI) was formed. The PRI ruled Mexico effectively as a one-party state until it was finally defeated in 2001. The new president, Vicente Fox, faced many problems. He was succeeded by Felipe Calderón. In 2008–12, killings associated with the illegal drug traffic increased, spreading over the border into the United States.

The World Bank classifies Mexico as an "upper-middle-income" developing country. Agriculture is important. Food crops include beans, maize, rice, and wheat, while cash crops include coffee, cotton, fruits, and vegetables. Beef cattle, dairy cattle, and other livestock are raised, and fishing is also important.

But oil and oil products are the chief exports, while manufacturing is the most valuable activity. Mexico is the world's leading silver producer, and it also mines copper, gold, lead, zinc, and other minerals. Many factories near the northern border assemble goods, such as car parts and electrical products, for US companies.

Hopes for the future lie in increasing cooperation with the US and Canada. However, problems with the United States mounted

from 2008 as drug cartels carried out large numbers of killings, mostly along the US border.

AREA 756,061 sq mi [1,958,201 sq km]
POPULATION 113,714,000 **CAPITAL** Mexico City
GOVERNMENT Federal republic
ETHNIC GROUPS Mestizo 60%, Amerindian 30%, White 9%
LANGUAGES Spanish (official)
RELIGIONS Roman Catholic 90%, Protestant 6%
CURRENCY Mexican peso = 100 centavos

MICRONESIA

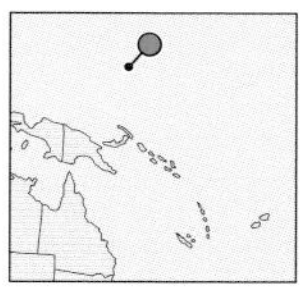

The Federated States of Micronesia, a former US territory covering a vast area in the western Pacific Ocean, became fully independent in 1991. The main export is copra. Fishing and tourism are also important.

AREA 271 sq mi [702 sq km]
POPULATION 107,000 **CAPITAL** Palikir

MOLDOVA

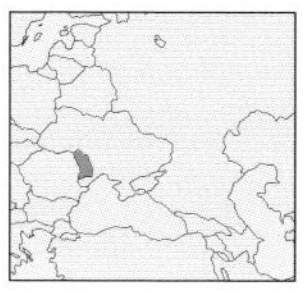

GEOGRAPHY The Republic of Moldova is a small country sandwiched between Ukraine and Romania. It was formerly one of the 15 republics that made up the Soviet Union. Much of the land is hilly and the highest areas are near the center of the country.

Moldova has a moderately continental climate, with warm summers and fairly cold winters when temperatures dip below freezing point. Most of the rain comes in the warmer months.

POLITICS & ECONOMY In the 14th century, the Moldavians formed a state called Moldavia. It included part of Romania and Bessarabia (now the modern country of Moldova). The Ottoman Turks took the area in the 16th century, but in 1812 Russia took over Bessarabia. In 1861, Moldavia and Walachia united to form Romania. Russia retook southern Bessarabia in 1878. After World War I (1914–18), all of Bessarabia was returned to Romania, but the Soviet Union did not recognize this act. From 1944, the Moldovan Soviet Socialist Republic was part of the Soviet Union.

In 1989, the Moldovans asserted their independence and ethnicity by making Romanian the official language and, at the end of 1991, Moldova became an independent nation. But Trans-Dniester, an area east of the River Dniester, has sought autonomy. In 2006, its people voted for independence and union with Russia. This vote was not recognized internationally.

In 2001, Moldovans returned the Communist Party to power in a general election. Under President Vladimir Voronin, Moldova enjoyed a period of economic growth. The Communist Party was re-elected in 2005 and 2009. Following allegations of fraud, further elections were held in 2010. In 2012, Nicolae Timoftu was elected president, after several inconclusive votes.

In terms of its GNP per capita, Moldova is one of Europe's poorest countries. Agriculture is the leading activity and products include fruits, maize, tobacco, and wine. Moldova has few natural resources and it imports materials and fuels for its industries. Light industries, such as food processing and factories making household appliances, are increasing.

AREA 13,070 sq mi [33,851 sq km]
POPULATION 4,314,000 **CAPITAL** Kishinev
GOVERNMENT Multiparty republic
ETHNIC GROUPS Moldovan/Romanian 65%, Ukrainian 14%, Russian 13%, others
LANGUAGES Moldovan/Romanian and Russian (official)
RELIGIONS Eastern Orthodox 98%
CURRENCY Moldovan leu = 100 bani

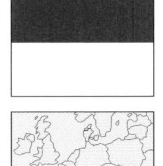

MONACO

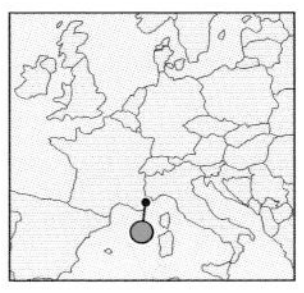

The tiny Principality of Monaco consists of a narrow strip of coastline and a rocky peninsula on the French Riviera. Its considerable wealth is derived largely from banking, finance, gambling, and tourism. Monaco's citizens do not pay any state tax. The reigning prince is Albert II. In 2008, plans to extend the area of Monaco by reclaiming land from under the sea were shelved.

AREA 0.4 sq mi [1 sq km] **POPULATION** 31,000 **CAPITAL** Monaco

MONGOLIA

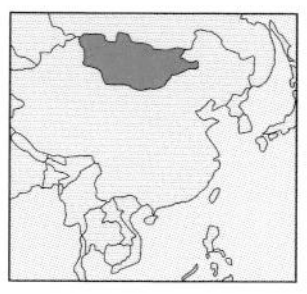

GEOGRAPHY The State of Mongolia is the world's largest landlocked country. It consists mainly of high plateaux, with the Gobi Desert in the southeast.

Ulan Bator lies on the northern edge of a desert plateau. It has bitterly cold winters. Summer temperatures are moderated by the altitude.

POLITICS & ECONOMY In the 13th century, Genghis Khan united the Mongolian peoples and built up a great empire. Under his grandson, Kublai Khan, the Mongol empire extended from Korea and China to eastern Europe and present-day Iraq.

The Mongol empire broke up in the late 14th century. In the early 17th century, Inner Mongolia came under Chinese control, and by the late 17th century Outer Mongolia had become a Chinese province. In 1911, the Mongolians drove the Chinese out of Outer Mongolia and made the area a Buddhist kingdom. But in 1924, under Russian influence, the Communist Mongolian People's Republic was set up. From the 1950s, Mongolia supported the Soviet Union in its disputes with China. In 1990, the people demonstrated for more freedom, and free elections in June 1990 were won by the Communist Mongolian People's Revolutionary Party (MPRP). The Democratic Union coalition won power in 1996, but the MPRP regained power in 2000. In 2004, after disputed elections, a coalition government was set up. In 2009, the Democratic Union candidate, Tsakhiagiin Elbegdorj, was elected president.

The World Bank classifies Mongolia as a "lower-middle-income" developing country. Most people were once nomads, who moved around with their herds of sheep, cattle, goats, and horses. Under Communist rule, most people were moved into permanent homes on government-owned farms. Livestock and animal products remain important, but minerals and fuels now account for more than three-fifths of Mongolia's exports.

AREA 604,826 sq mi [1,566,500 sq km]
POPULATION 3,133,000 **CAPITAL** Ulan Bator
GOVERNMENT Multiparty republic **ETHNIC GROUPS** Khalkha Mongol 85%, Kazakh 6% **LANGUAGES** Khalkha Mongolian (official), Turkic, Russian **RELIGIONS** Tibetan Buddhist Lamaism 96%
CURRENCY Tugrik = 100 möngös

MONTENEGRO

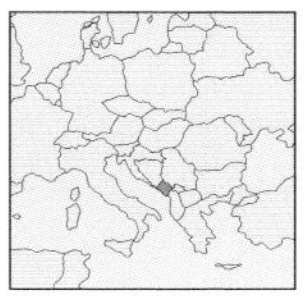

The Republic of Montenegro became a fully independent nation in 2006. It was formerly part of the Union of Serbia and Montenegro and, before 2003, part of Yugoslavia.

The coastal region has a Mediterranean climate. However, inland, the Dinaric Alps, which reach a height of 8,274 ft [2,522 m], have a more severe climate.

Serbia fell under Turkish rule in the 14th century, but Montenegro remained Christian. Montenegro was absorbed into Serbia in 1918. It became part of the Kingdom of the Serbs, Croats, and Slovenes, which was renamed Yugoslavia in 1929. After World War II, Montenegro was recognized as one of the six republics in the Federal Republic of Yugoslavia.

Elections were held in 2009, and in 2010 Igor Luksic became prime minister, following the retirement of Milo Djukanovic.

Manufacturing is the leading activity, and steel and aluminum are major products. But farming remains important. Forests cover more than half of the land.

AREA 5,415 sq mi [14,026 sq km]
POPULATION 662,000 **CAPITAL** Podgorica
GOVERNMENT Republic **ETHNIC GROUPS** Montenegrin 43%, Serb 32%, Bosnian 8%, Albanian 5%, others
LANGUAGES Serbian (official), Bosnian, Albanian, Croatian
RELIGIONS Orthodox, Islam, Roman Catholic
CURRENCY Euro = 100 cents

MONTSERRAT

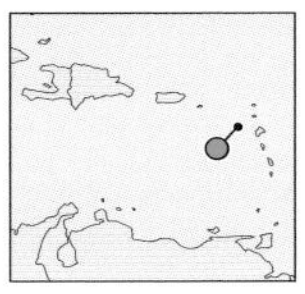

Montserrat is a British overseas territory in the Caribbean Sea. The climate is tropical and hurricanes often cause much damage. Intermittent eruptions of the Soufrière Hills volcano between 1995 and 1998, and again in 2003, led to the emigration of many people and the virtual destruction of Plymouth, the then capital. A new airport was opened in 2005.

AREA 39 sq mi [102 sq km] **POPULATION** 5,000 **CAPITAL** Brades

MOROCCO

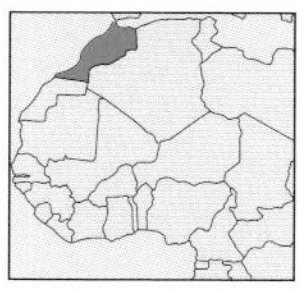

GEOGRAPHY The Kingdom of Morocco lies in northwestern Africa. Its name comes from the Arabic Maghreb-el-Aksa, meaning "the farthest west." Behind the western coastal plain the land rises to a broad plateau and ranges of the Atlas Mountains. The High (Haut) Atlas contains the highest peak, Djebel Toubkal, at 13,665 ft [4,165 m]. East of the mountains, the land descends to the Sahara. The Canaries Current cools the Atlantic coast. Inland, summers are hot and dry. Winters are mild, with moderate rainfall. Snow often falls on the High Atlas Mountains.

POLITICS & ECONOMY The original people of Morocco were the Berbers. But in the 680s, Arab invaders introduced Islam and the Arabic language. By the early 20th century, France and Spain controlled Morocco, which became an independent kingdom in 1956. Although Morocco is a constitutional monarchy, King Hassan II ruled the country in a generally authoritarian way from the time of his accession to the throne in 1961 to his death in 1999. His successor, Mohamed VI, faced several problems, including that of Western Sahara, which he claimed for Morocco, and the activities of Islamist extremists. In 2011, the people approved a new constitution, granting the prime minister more power.

Morocco is classified as a "lower-middle-income" developing country. It is the world's third largest producer of phosphate rock, which is used to make fertilizer. One of the reasons why Morocco wants to keep Western Sahara is that it, too, has large phosphate reserves. Farming employs about 39% of Moroccans. Chief crops include barley, beans, citrus fruits, maize, olives, sugar beet, and wheat. Processed phosphates are exported, but most of Morocco's manufactures are for home consumption. Fishing and tourism are also important.

AREA 172,413 sq mi [446,550 sq km]
POPULATION 31,968,000 **CAPITAL** Rabat
GOVERNMENT Constitutional monarchy
ETHNIC GROUPS Arab-Berber 99%
LANGUAGES Arabic (official), Berber dialects, French
RELIGIONS Islam 99% **CURRENCY** Moroccan dirham = 100 centimes

MOZAMBIQUE

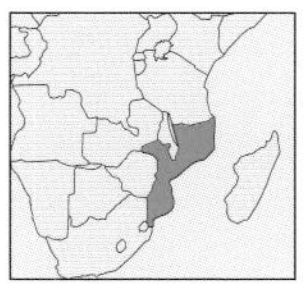

GEOGRAPHY The Republic of Mozambique borders the Indian Ocean in southeastern Africa. The coastal plains are narrow in the north but broaden in the south. Inland lie plateaux and hills, which make up another two-fifths of the country. Mozambique has a mostly tropical climate. The capital Maputo, which lies outside the tropics, has hot and humid summers, though the winters are mild and fairly dry.

POLITICS & ECONOMY In 1885, when the European powers divided Africa, Mozambique was recognized as a Portuguese colony. But black African opposition to European rule gradually increased. In 1961, the Front for the Liberation of Mozambique (FRELIMO) was founded to oppose Portuguese rule. In 1964, FRELIMO launched a guerrilla war, which continued for ten years. Mozambique became independent in 1975.

After independence, Mozambique became a one-party state. Its government aided African nationalists in Rhodesia (now Zimbabwe) and South Africa. But the white governments of these countries helped an opposition group, the Mozambique National Resistance Movement (RENAMO) to lead an armed struggle against Mozambique's government. Civil war, combined with droughts, caused much suffering in the 1980s. In 1989, FRELIMO ended one-party rule. The war ended in 1992 and multiparty elections were held in 1994. In 1995 Mozambique became the 53rd member of the Commonwealth. In 2004, and again in 2009, FRELIMO leader Antonio Guebuza was elected president.

In the early 1990s, the UN rated Mozambique as one of the world's poorest countries. The second half of the 1990s saw the start of renewed economic growth, but floods in 2000–1, 2007, and 2008, and prolonged droughts in the mid-2000s and 2008, were major setbacks. About 80% of the people are poor farmers. Crops include cassava, cotton, maize, rice, and tea.

AREA 309,494 sq mi [801,590 sq km]
POPULATION 22,949,000 **CAPITAL** Maputo
GOVERNMENT Multiparty republic **ETHNIC GROUPS** Indigenous tribal groups (Shangaan, Chokwe, Manyika, Sena, Makua, others) 99%
LANGUAGES Portuguese (official), many others
RELIGIONS Traditional beliefs 50%, Christianity 30%, Islam 20%
CURRENCY Metical = 100 centavos

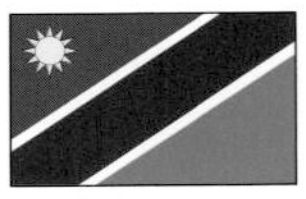
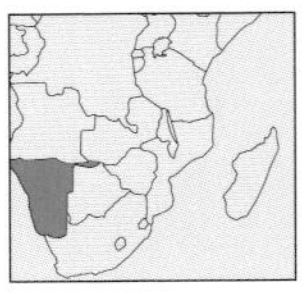

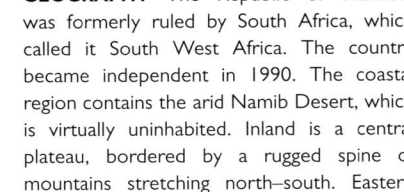

NAMIBIA

GEOGRAPHY The Republic of Namibia was formerly ruled by South Africa, which called it South West Africa. The country became independent in 1990. The coastal region contains the arid Namib Desert, which is virtually uninhabited. Inland is a central plateau, bordered by a rugged spine of mountains stretching north–south. Eastern Namibia contains part of the Kalahari Desert, a semidesert area extending into Botswana. Namibia has a warm and arid climate. Windhoek has an average annual rainfall of 15 inches [370 mm], which often occurs in thunderstorms during the hot summer.

POLITICS & ECONOMY During World War I, South African troops defeated the Germans who ruled what is now Namibia. After World War II, many people challenged South Africa's right to govern the territory, and a civil war began in the 1960s between African guerrillas and South African troops. A ceasefire was agreed in 1989 and Namibia became independent in 1990. In the 1990s, the government pursued a policy of "national reconciliation." An enclave on the coast, called Walvis Bay (Walvisbaai), remained part of South Africa until 1994, when it was transferred to Namibia. In 2004, the nationalist leader, Sam Nujoma, president since 1990, retired. He was succeeded by Hifikepunye Pohamba, who was re-elected in 2009.

Namibia has reserves of diamonds, uranium, zinc, and copper. Minerals make up the bulk of exports, though agriculture employs 20% of the people. Fishing is important. Namibia has few industries. Oil has been discovered and tourism is expanding.

AREA 318,259 sq mi [824,292 sq km]
POPULATION 2,148,000 **CAPITAL** Windhoek
GOVERNMENT Multiparty republic **ETHNIC GROUPS** Ovambo 50%, Kavango 9%, Herero 7%, Damara 7%, White 6%, Nama 5%
LANGUAGES English (official), Afrikaans, German, indigenous dialects **RELIGIONS** Christianity 90% (Lutheran 51%)
CURRENCY Namibian dollar = 100 cents

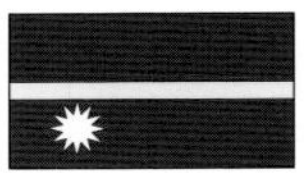
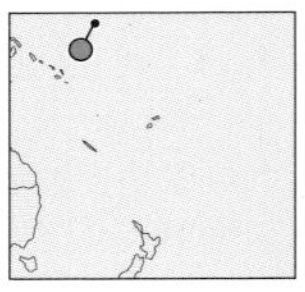

NAURU

Nauru is the world's smallest republic, located in the western Pacific Ocean, close to the equator. Independent since 1968, Nauru's prosperity is based on phosphate mining, but the reserves are running out.

AREA 8 sq mi [21 sq km]
POPULATION 9,000 **CAPITAL** Yaren

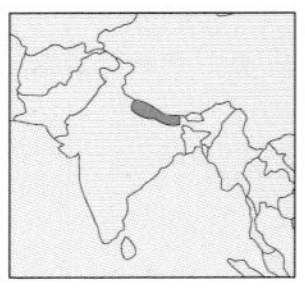

NEPAL

GEOGRAPHY Over three-quarters of Nepal lies in the Himalayan region, culminating in the world's highest peak (Mount Everest, or Chomolongma in Nepali) at 29,035 ft [8,850 m]. As a result, climatic conditions vary widely according to the altitude.

POLITICS & ECONOMY Nepal was united in the late 18th century, although its complex topography has ensured that it remains a diverse patchwork of peoples. From the mid-19th century to 1951, power was held by the royal Rana family. The first democratic elections in 32 years were held in 1991, but, by the early 21st century, Nepal faced many problems, including an uprising of Maoist guerrillas. In 2005, King Gyanendra seized power but failed to stop the conflict. In 2006, the Maoists joined a provisional coalition government. In elections in April 2008, the Maoists became the largest single party. In May, Nepal became a republic and the Maoist leader, named Prachanda, became prime minister in August. He resigned in 2009. In 2011, a Maoist, Baburam Bhattari, became prime minister.

Agriculture is the main activity in this overwhelmingly rural country, and Nepal is heavily dependent on aid. Tourism, based on the attractions of the high Himalaya, is growing in importance. There are also ambitious plans to exploit the hydroelectric potential offered by the ferocious Himalayan rivers.

AREA 56,827 sq mi [147,181 sq km] **POPULATION** 29,392,000
CAPITAL Katmandu **GOVERNMENT** Multiparty republic
ETHNIC GROUPS Brahman, Chetri, Newar, Gurung, Magar, Tamang, Sherpa, and others
LANGUAGES Nepali (official), local languages
RELIGIONS Hinduism 86%, Buddhism 8%, Islam 4%
CURRENCY Nepalese rupee = 100 paisa

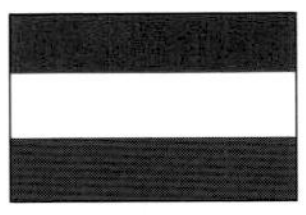
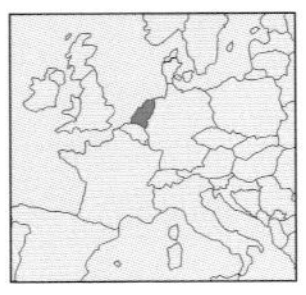

NETHERLANDS

GEOGRAPHY The Netherlands lies at the western end of the North European Plain, which extends to the Ural Mountains in Russia. Except for the far southeastern corner, the Netherlands is flat and about 40% lies below sea level at high tide. To prevent flooding, the Dutch have built dykes (sea walls) to hold back the waves. Large areas which were once under the sea, but which have been reclaimed, are called polders. Because of its position on the North Sea, the Netherlands has a temperate climate, with mild, rainy winters.

POLITICS & ECONOMY Before the 16th century, the area that is now the Netherlands was under a succession of foreign rulers, including the Romans, the Germanic Franks, the French, and the Spanish. The Dutch declared their independence from Spain in 1581 and their status was finally recognized by Spain in 1648. In the 17th century, the Dutch built up a great overseas empire, especially in Southeast Asia. But in the early 18th century, the Dutch lost control of the seas to England.

France controlled the Netherlands from 1795 to 1813. In 1815, the Netherlands, then containing Belgium and Luxembourg, became an independent kingdom. Belgium broke away in 1830 and Luxembourg followed in 1890.

The Netherlands was neutral in World War I (1914–18), but was occupied by Germany in World War II (1939–45). After the war, the Netherlands Indies became independent as Indonesia. The Netherlands became active in West European affairs. With Belgium and Luxembourg, it formed a customs union called Benelux in 1948. In 1949, it joined NATO (the North Atlantic Treaty Organization), and the European Coal and Steel Community (ECSC) in 1953. In 1957, it became a founder member of the European Economic Community (now the European Union), and in 2002 it adopted the euro as its sole unit of currency. Since 2002, five coalition governments have collapsed, the latest in early 2012 when the right-wing Freedom Party refused to back the coalition's austerity measures.

In 2010, the Netherlands Antilles, an island territory in the Caribbean, was dissolved. Curaçao and St Maarten became nations in the Kingdom of the Netherlands. The small islands of Bonaire, St Eustatius, and Saba became special municipalities of the Netherlands.

The Netherlands is a highly industrialized country, and industry and commerce are the most valuable activities. Its resources include natural gas, some oil, salt, and china clay. But the Netherlands imports many of the materials needed by its industries and it is, therefore, a major trading country. Industrial products are wide-ranging, including aircraft, chemicals, electronic equipment, machinery, textiles, and vehicles. Farming is scientific and yields are high. Dairy farming is the leading farming activity. Major products include barley, flowers and bulbs, potatoes, sugar beet, and wheat.

AREA 16,033 sq mi [41,526 sq km]
POPULATION 16,847,000
CAPITAL Amsterdam; The Hague (seat of government)
GOVERNMENT Constitutional monarchy
ETHNIC GROUPS Dutch 83%, Indonesian, Turkish, Moroccan, and others **LANGUAGES** Dutch (official), Frisian
RELIGIONS Roman Catholic 31%, Protestant 21%, Islam 4%, others
CURRENCY Euro = 100 cents

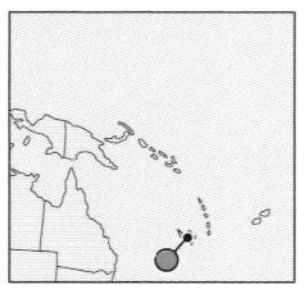

NEW CALEDONIA

New Caledonia is the most southerly of the Melanesian countries in the Pacific. It has been a French possession since 1853 and an Overseas Territory since 1958. In 1998, France announced an agreement with local Melanesians that a vote on independence would be postponed until 2014. The country is rich in mineral resources, especially nickel.

AREA 7,172 sq mi [18,575 sq km] **POPULATION** 256,000 **CAPITAL** Nouméa

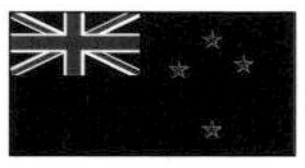
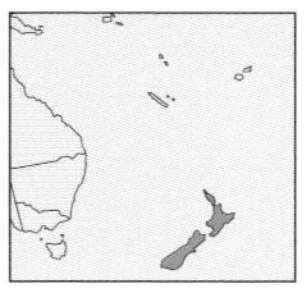

NEW ZEALAND

GEOGRAPHY New Zealand lies about 994 mi [1,600 km] southeast of Australia. It consists of two main islands and several other small ones. Much of North Island is volcanic. Active volcanoes include Ngauruhoe and Ruapehu. Hot springs and geysers are common, and steam from the ground is used to produce electricity. The Southern Alps, which contain the country's highest peak, Aoraki Mount Cook, at 12,313 ft [3,753 m], form the backbone of South Island. This island also has some large, fertile plains.

New Zealand lies on the geologically active "Pacific ring of fire." Most of the 14,000 earthquakes that occur every year have a magnitude of less than 5.0. But, in 2010 and 2011, two earthquakes, with magnitudes of 7.0 and 6.3 respectively, struck Christchurch on South Island, causing great damage. The 2011 earthquake resulted in a death toll of more than 180.

Auckland in the north has a warm, humid climate throughout the year. Wellington has cooler summers, while in Dunedin, in the southeast, temperatures sometimes dip below freezing in winter. The rainfall is heaviest on the western highlands.

POLITICS & ECONOMY Evidence suggests that early Maori settlers arrived in New Zealand more than 1,000 years ago. The Dutch navigator Abel Tasman reached New Zealand in 1642, but his discovery was not followed up. In 1769, the British Captain James Cook rediscovered the islands. In the early 19th century, British settlers arrived and, in 1840, under the Treaty of Waitangi, Britain took possession of the islands. From the 1870s, the Maoris were gradually integrated into colonial society.

In 1907, New Zealand became a self-governing dominion in the British Commonwealth. The country's economy developed quickly and the people became increasingly prosperous. However, after Britain joined the European Economic Community in 1973, New Zealand's exports to Britain shrank and the country had to reassess its economic and defense strategies and seek new markets. The world recession led the government to cut back on welfare spending in the 1990s. The preservation of Maori culture and Maori rights are major issues. The Maoris, a Polynesian people, make up about 13% of the population. Other mainly Polynesian Pacific people make up another 6%. Ties with Britain have been reduced. Helen Clark, leader of the Labor Party and prime minister from 1999–2008, has expressed the view that New Zealand will eventually abolish the monarchy and become a republic. In November 2008, the center-right National Party defeated the Labor Party in elections. John Key became prime minister and he was re-elected in 2011.

The economy once depended on agriculture, but manufacturing now employs twice as many people as farming. Meat and dairy products are leading commodities. Sheep rearing has declined as the area under cattle, deer, and vines has expanded. Crops include barley, fruits, potatoes and other vegetables, and wheat. In 2008–9, New Zealand's economy entered a period of recession. Full recovery was expected to be slow.

AREA 104,453 sq mi [270,534 sq km]
POPULATION 4,290,000 **CAPITAL** Wellington
GOVERNMENT Constitutional monarchy
ETHNIC GROUPS New Zealand European 74%, New Zealand Maori 13%, Polynesian 6% **LANGUAGES** English and Maori (both official) **RELIGIONS** Anglican 24%, Presbyterian 18%, Roman Catholic 15%, others
CURRENCY New Zealand dollar = 100 cents

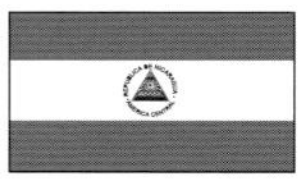
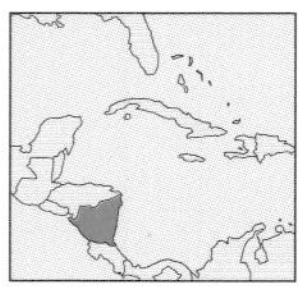

NICARAGUA

GEOGRAPHY The Republic of Nicaragua is a large country in Central America. In the east is a broad plain bordering the Caribbean Sea. The plain is drained by rivers that flow from the Central Highlands. The fertile western Pacific region contains about 40 volcanoes, many of which are active, and earthquakes are common.

Nicaragua has a tropical climate. Managua is hot throughout the year and there is a marked rainy season from May to October. In October 1998, Hurricane Mitch caused great devastation in Nicaragua. The Central Highlands and Caribbean region are cooler and wetter. The wettest region is the humid Caribbean plain.

POLITICS & ECONOMY In 1502, Christopher Columbus claimed the area for Spain, which ruled Nicaragua until 1821. By the early 20th century, the United States had considerable influence in the country and, in 1912, US forces entered Nicaragua to protect US interests. From 1927 to 1933, rebels under General Augusto César Sandino tried to drive US forces out of the country. In 1933, US marines set up a Nicaraguan army, the National Guard, to help to defeat the rebels. Its leader, Anastasio Somoza Garcia, had Sandino murdered in 1934, and from 1937 Somoza ruled as a dictator.

In the mid-1970s, many people began to protest against Somoza's rule. Many joined a guerrilla force, called the Sandinista National Liberation Front, named after General Sandino. The rebels defeated the Somoza regime in 1979. In the 1980s, US-supported forces, called the "Contras," launched a campaign

against the Sandinista government. The US government opposed the Sandinista regime, under Daniel José Ortega Saavedra, claiming that it was a Communist dictatorship. A coalition, the National Opposition Union, defeated the Sandinistas in 1990. In 2001, the Sandinista candidate, Ortega, was defeated in presidential elections, but he was re-elected in 2006. In 2009, he announced plans to change the constitution so that he could stand for another term. He was re-elected president in 2011.

In the early 1990s, Nicaragua faced many problems in rebuilding its shattered economy. Agriculture employs about 26% of the people. Coffee, cotton, sugar, and bananas are grown for export, while rice is the main food crop.

AREA 50,193 sq mi [130,000 sq km]
POPULATION 5,666,000 **CAPITAL** Managua
GOVERNMENT Multiparty republic
ETHNIC GROUPS Mestizo 69%, White 17%, Black 9%, Amerindian 5%
LANGUAGES Spanish (official)
RELIGIONS Roman Catholic 85%, Protestant
CURRENCY Córdoba oro (gold córdoba) = 100 centavos

NIGER

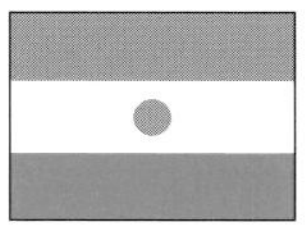

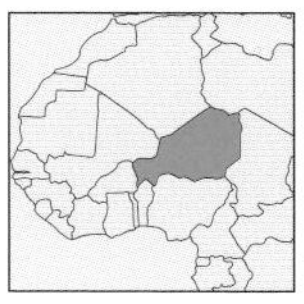

GEOGRAPHY The Republic of Niger is a landlocked nation in north-central Africa. The northern plateaux lie in the Sahara Desert, while Central Niger contains the rugged Aïr Mountains. The most fertile, densely populated region is the Niger valley in the southwest.

Niger has a tropical climate and the south has a rainy season between June and September. The north is practically rainless.

POLITICS & ECONOMY Since independence in 1960, Niger, a French territory from 1900, has suffered severe droughts. Food shortages and the collapse of the traditional nomadic way of life of some of Niger's people have caused political instability. After a period of military rule, a multiparty constitution was adopted in 1992, but the military again seized power in 1996. Later that year, the coup leader, Colonel Ibrahim Barre Mainassara, was elected president. He was assassinated in 1999, but parliamentary rule was restored and Mamadou Tandja was elected president. He was overthrown in a coup in 2010 and a military regime took power. But democratic elections took place in 2011.

Niger's chief resource is uranium and the country is the world's fifth largest producer. Some tin and tungsten are also mined, though other mineral reserves are largely untouched. Despite its considerable resources, Niger remains one of the world's poorest countries. Only 3% of the land can be used for growing crops.

AREA 489,189 sq mi [1,267,000 sq km]
POPULATION 16,469,000 **CAPITAL** Niamey
GOVERNMENT Multiparty republic **ETHNIC GROUPS** Hausa 56%, Djerma 22%, Tuareg 8%, Fula 8%, others **LANGUAGES** French (official), Hausa, Djerma **RELIGIONS** Islam 80%, indigenous beliefs, Christianity **CURRENCY** CFA franc = 100 centimes

NIGERIA

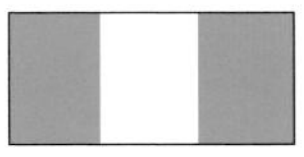

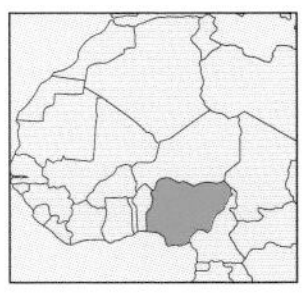

GEOGRAPHY The Federal Republic of Nigeria is the most populous nation in Africa. The country's main rivers are the Niger and Benue, which meet in central Nigeria. North of the two river valleys are high plains and plateaux. The Lake Chad basin is in the northeast, with the Sokoto plains in the northwest. The south contains hilly uplands and plains. The south has a hot, rainy climate. The north is drier and often hotter than the south.

POLITICS & ECONOMY Nigeria has a long artistic tradition. Major cultures include the Nok (500 BC to AD 200), the Ife, a major Yoruba culture which developed about 1,000 years ago, and the Benin (15th to 17th centuries). Britain gradually extended its influence over the area in the second half of the 19th century.

Nigeria became independent in 1960 and a federal republic in 1963. A federal constitution dividing the country into regions was necessary because Nigeria contains more than 250 ethnic and linguistic groups, as well as several religious ones. Local rivalries have long been a threat to national unity, and six new states were created in 1996 in an attempt to overcome this. Civil war occurred between 1967 and 1970, when the people of the southeast attempted unsuccessfully to secede during the Biafran War. Between 1960 and 1998, Nigeria had only nine years of civilian government.

In 1998–9, civilian rule was restored and Olusegun Obasanjo became president. Nigeria faced many problems, including violence in the Niger delta region and religious conflict. In 2011–12, northern Nigeria was hit by a series of violent attacks made by an Islamist organization called Boko Haram, a Hausa term meaning "Western education is a sin." In late 2011, Nigeria's President Goodluck Jonathan declared an emergency in some areas.

Nigeria is a developing country with great potential. Its chief natural resource is oil, which accounts for most of its exports. Agriculture employs 59% of the people and the country is a major producer of cocoa, palm oil and palm kernels, groundnuts (peanuts), and rubber. Industry is increasing and manufactures include cement, chemicals, fertilizers, textiles, and timber.

AREA 356,667 sq mi [923,768 sq km] **POPULATION** 155,216,000
CAPITAL Abuja **GOVERNMENT** Federal multiparty republic
ETHNIC GROUPS Hausa and Fulani 29%, Yoruba 21%, Ibo (or Igbo) 18%, Ijaw 10%, Kanuri 4%, many others
LANGUAGES English (official), Hausa, Yoruba, Ibo
RELIGIONS Islam 50%, Christianity 40%, traditional beliefs 10%
CURRENCY Naira = 100 kobo

NORTHERN MARIANA ISLANDS

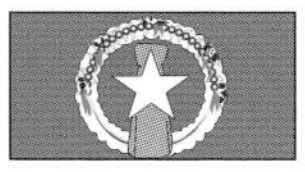

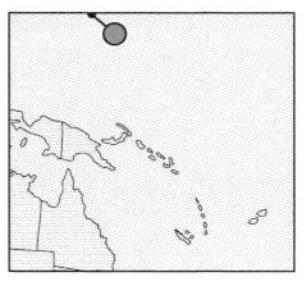

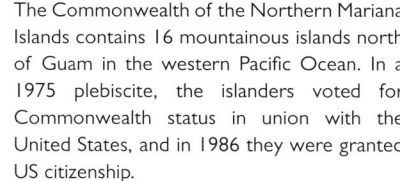

The Commonwealth of the Northern Mariana Islands contains 16 mountainous islands north of Guam in the western Pacific Ocean. In a 1975 plebiscite, the islanders voted for Commonwealth status in union with the United States, and in 1986 they were granted US citizenship.

AREA 179 sq mi [464 sq km] **POPULATION** 46,000 **CAPITAL** Saipan

NORWAY

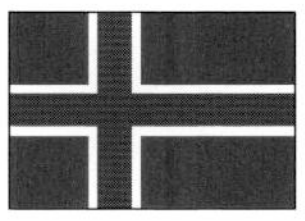

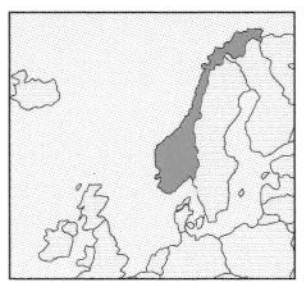

GEOGRAPHY The Kingdom of Norway forms the western part of the rugged Scandinavian peninsula. The deep inlets along the highly indented coastline were worn out by glaciers during the Ice Age. The warm North Atlantic Drift off the coast of Norway moderates the climate, with mild winters and cool summers. Nearly all the ports are ice-free throughout the year. Inland, winters are colder and snow cover lasts for at least three months a year.

POLITICS & ECONOMY Between about AD 800 and 1100, Norwegian Vikings ravaged western Europe. In 1380, Norway was united with Denmark. But in 1814, Denmark handed Norway over to Sweden, though it kept Norway's colonies – Greenland, Iceland, and the Færoe Islands. Norway briefly became independent, but Swedish forces defeated the Norwegians and Norway had to accept Sweden's king as its ruler. The union with Sweden ended in 1903. Germany occupied Norway during World War II (1939–45). Norway recovered quickly after the war and it now has one of the world's highest standards of living. In 1960, Norway and six other countries formed the European Free Trade Association (EFTA). But, in 1994, Norway voted against joining the European Union. In 2009, the center-left coalition led by Prime Minister Jens Stoltenberg was narrowly re-elected.

Norway's chief resources and exports are oil and natural gas which come from wells under the North Sea. Farmland covers only 3% of the land. Dairy farming and meat production are important, but Norway has to import food. Norway has many industries powered by cheap hydroelectricity.

AREA 125,049 sq mi [323,877 sq km]
POPULATION 4,692,000 **CAPITAL** Oslo
GOVERNMENT Constitutional monarchy
ETHNIC GROUPS Norwegian 97%
LANGUAGES Norwegian (official)
RELIGIONS Evangelical Lutheran 86%
CURRENCY Norwegian krone = 100 ore

OMAN

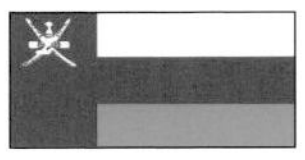

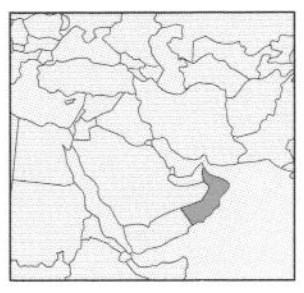

GEOGRAPHY The Sultanate of Oman occupies the southeastern corner of the Arabian peninsula. It also includes the tip of the Musandam peninsula, overlooking the strategic Strait of Hormuz.

Oman has a hot tropical climate. In Muscat, temperatures may reach 117°F [47°C] in the summer months.

POLITICS & ECONOMY British influence in Oman dates back to the end of the 18th century, but the country became fully independent in 1971. Since then, using revenue from oil, which was discovered in 1964, the absolute ruler, Qaboos ibn Said, and his government have sought to modernize Oman. In 2000, Oman held elections to its consultative parliament. In 2004, the Sultan appointed Oman's first woman minister without portfolio. In 2011, following anti-government demonstrations, Sultan Qaboos ibn Said promised jobs and benefits.

Oil and natural gas make up about 80% of Oman's exports. Agriculture and fishing remain important. Crops include alfalfa, bananas, coconuts, dates, limes, tobacco, vegetables, and wheat. However, Oman has to import food.

AREA 119,498 sq mi [309,500 sq km]
POPULATION 3,028,000 **CAPITAL** Muscat
GOVERNMENT Monarchy with consultative council
ETHNIC GROUPS Arab, Baluchi, Indian, Pakistani
LANGUAGES Arabic (official), Baluchi, English
RELIGIONS Islam (mainly Ibadhi), Hinduism
CURRENCY Omani rial = 1,000 baizas

PAKISTAN

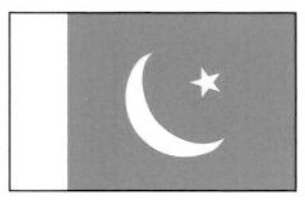

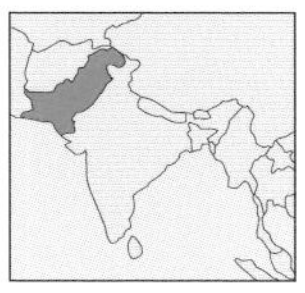

GEOGRAPHY The Islamic Republic of Pakistan contains high mountains, fertile plains, and rocky deserts. The Karakoram range, which contains K2, the world's second highest peak, lies in the northern part of Jammu and Kashmir, which is occupied by Pakistan but claimed by India. Other mountains rise in the west. Plains, drained by the River Indus and its tributaries, occupy much of eastern Pakistan. Arid areas include the Thar Desert and the Baluchistan plateau. Most of Pakistan has hot summers and mild winters, though the mountains have cold winters. The rainfall is generally sparse.

POLITICS & ECONOMY Pakistan was the site of the Indus Valley civilization which developed about 4,500 years ago. But Pakistan's modern history dates from 1947, when British India was divided into India and Pakistan. Muslim Pakistan was divided into two parts: East and West Pakistan, but East Pakistan broke away in 1971 to become Bangladesh. In 1948–9, 1965, and 1971, Pakistan and India clashed over Kashmir. In 1998, Pakistan responded in kind to India's nuclear weapons tests, but, in 2003–7, Pakistan and India launched a series of initiatives aimed at achieving peace.

Pakistan has been subject to several periods of military rule, but elections in 1988 led to Benazir Bhutto becoming prime minister. She was removed from office in 1990, but she returned as prime minister between 1993 and 1996. In 1997, Narwaz Sharif was elected prime minister, but a military coup in 1999 brought General Pervez Musharraf to power. The security situation deteriorated in 2006–7. In 2007, in the run-up to elections in February 2008, Benazir Bhutto was assassinated, but in the elections, the opposition parties heavily defeated Musharraf's supporters. Musharraf resigned in August 2008 and was succeeded as president by Benazir Bhutto's widower, Asif Ali Zardari. The security situation in the northwestern border regions worsened. In 2011, relations with the United States deteriorated after the US accused Pakistan's government of supporting militants.

According to the World Bank, Pakistan is a "low-income" developing country. The economy is based on farming and rearing goats and sheep. Agriculture employs 42% of the people. Major crops include cotton, fruits, rice, sugarcane, and wheat.

AREA 307,372 sq mi [796,095 sq km]
POPULATION 187,343,000 **CAPITAL** Islamabad
GOVERNMENT Military regime **ETHNIC GROUPS** Punjabi, Sindhi, Pashtun (Pathan), Baluchi, Muhajir
LANGUAGES Urdu (official), many others
RELIGIONS Islam 97%, Christianity, Hinduism
CURRENCY Pakistani rupee = 100 paisa

PALAU

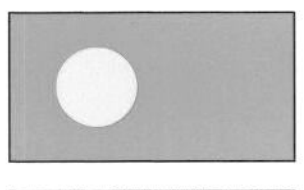

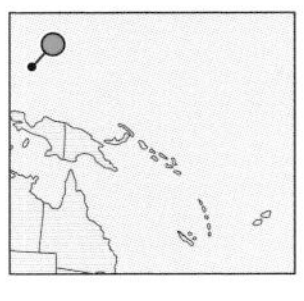

The Republic of Palau became fully independent in 1994, after the USA refused to accede to a 1979 referendum that declared this island nation a nuclear-free zone. In December 1994 Palau joined the United Nations. The economy relies heavily on US aid, tourism, fishing, and subsistence agriculture. The main crops include cassava, coconuts, and copra.

AREA 177 sq mi [459 sq km] **POPULATION** 21,000 **CAPITAL** Melekeok

PANAMA

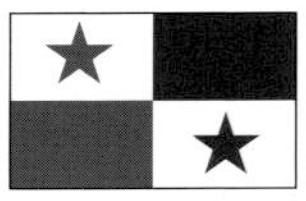

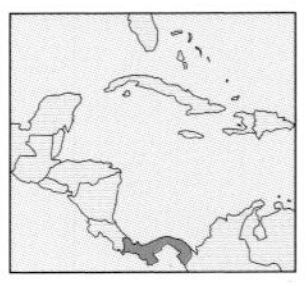

GEOGRAPHY The Republic of Panama forms an isthmus linking Central America to South America. The Panama Canal, which is 50.7 mi [81.6 km] long, cuts across the isthmus. It has made the country a major transport center.

Panama has a tropical climate. Temperatures are high, though the mountains are much cooler than the coastal plains. The main rainy season is between May and December.

POLITICS & ECONOMY Christopher Columbus landed in Panama in 1502 and Spain soon took the area. In 1821, Panama became independent from Spain and a province of Colombia.

In 1903, Colombia refused a request by the United States to build a canal. Panama then revolted against Colombia, and became independent. The United States then began to build the canal, which was opened in 1914. The United States administered the Panama Canal Zone, a strip of land along the canal. But many Panamanians resented US influence and, in 1979, the Canal Zone was returned to Panama. Control of the canal itself was handed over by the USA to Panama on December 31, 1999.

Panama's government has changed many times since independence, and there have been periods of military dictatorships, including that of General Manuel Antonio Noriega in the 1980s. He was finally convicted of drug offences in the United States in 1992. In May 2009, Ricardo Marinelli of the conservative Alliance for Change coalition was elected president. In 2011, the US Congress approved a long-stalled free-trade agreement with Panama.

The World Bank classifies Panama as a "lower-middle-income" developing country. The Panama Canal is an important source of revenue and, in 2006, work began on widening the canal to take giant container ships. Away from the canal, the main activity is agriculture, which employs 13% of the people.

AREA 29,157 sq mi [75,517 sq km] **POPULATION** 3,460,000
CAPITAL Panamá **GOVERNMENT** Multiparty republic
ETHNIC GROUPS Mestizo 70%, Black and Mulatto 14%, White 10%, Amerindian 6% **LANGUAGES** Spanish (official), English **RELIGIONS** Roman Catholic 85%, Protestant 15%
CURRENCY US dollar; Balboa = 100 centésimos

PAPUA NEW GUINEA

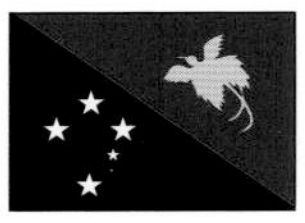

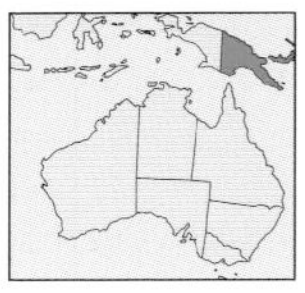

GEOGRAPHY Papua New Guinea is an independent country in the Pacific Ocean, north of Australia. It is part of a Pacific island region called Melanesia. Papua New Guinea includes the eastern part of New Guinea, the Bismarck Archipelago, the northern Solomon Islands, the D'Entrecasteaux Islands, and the Louisiade Archipelago. The land is largely mountainous.

Papua New Guinea has a tropical climate, with high temperatures. Most of the rain occurs during the monsoon season (December–April), when northwesterly winds blow. In the dry season, winds blow from the southeast.

POLITICS & ECONOMY The Dutch took western New Guinea (now part of Indonesia) in 1828, but it was not until 1884 that Germany took northeastern New Guinea and Britain took the southeast. In 1906, Britain handed the southeast over to Australia. It then became known as the Territory of Papua. When World War I broke out in 1914, Australia took German New Guinea, and in 1921 the League of Nations gave Australia a mandate to rule the area, which was named the Territory of New Guinea. Japan invaded New Guinea in 1942, but the Allies reconquered the area in 1944. In 1949, Papua and New Guinea were combined into the Territory of Papua and New Guinea. Papua New Guinea became fully independent in 1975.

Mining is important. An important mine was on Bougainville, where a secessionist group declared the island independent. Under a peace treaty in 2001, Bougainville became autonomous and held elections in 2005. A crisis occurred in 2011–12, when Prime Minister Michael Somare was replaced by Peter O'Neill, following Somare's absence abroad for medical treatment. When Somare returned, a stand-off developed between the two men.

The country has a "lower-middle-income" economy. Agriculture employs 70% of the people, mostly at subsistence level. Petroleum and minerals, notably copper, are major exports.

AREA 178,703 sq mi [462,840 sq km] **POPULATION** 6,188,000
CAPITAL Port Moresby **GOVERNMENT** Constitutional monarchy
ETHNIC GROUPS Papuan, Melanesian, Micronesian **LANGUAGES** English (official), Melanesian Pidgin; more than 700 indigenous languages **RELIGIONS** Traditional beliefs 34%, Roman Catholic 22%, Lutheran 16% **CURRENCY** Kina = 100 toea

PARAGUAY

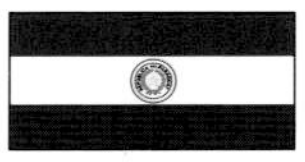

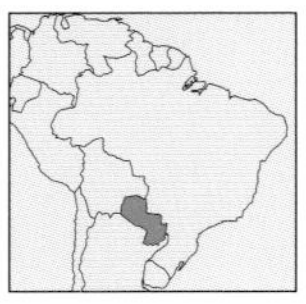

GEOGRAPHY The Republic of Paraguay is a landlocked country and rivers, notably the Paraná, Pilcomayo (Brazo Sur), and Paraguay, form most of its borders. A flat region called the Gran Chaco lies in the northwest, while the southeast contains plains, hills, and plateaux. Northern Paraguay lies in the tropics, while the south is subtropical. Most of the country has a warm, humid climate.

POLITICS & ECONOMY In 1776, Paraguay became part of a large colony called the Viceroyalty of La Plata, with Buenos Aires as the capital. Paraguayans opposed this move and the country declared its independence in 1811.

For many years, Paraguay was torn by internal strife and conflict with its neighbors. A war against Brazil, Argentina, and Uruguay (1865–70) led to the deaths of more than half of Paraguay's population, and a great loss of territory.

General Alfredo Stroessner took power in 1954 and ruled as a dictator. His government imprisoned many opponents. Stroessner was overthrown in 1989 (he died in exile in Brazil in 2006). However, the return of democracy in the years that followed often seemed precarious, because of rivalries between politicians and army leaders, together with economic problems arising partly from the severe problems experienced in neighboring Argentina and Brazil in 1999. In 2008, a former Roman Catholic bishop, Fernando Lugo, who was regarded as a champion of the poor, was elected president. His victory ended more than six decades of rule by the Colorado Party.

The World Bank classifies Paraguay as a "lower-middle-income" developing country. Agriculture and forestry, employing about a third of the population, are important. Paraguay produces hydroelectricity and exports power to its neighbors.

AREA 157,047 sq mi [406,752 sq km]
POPULATION 6,459,000 **CAPITAL** Asunción
GOVERNMENT Multiparty republic **ETHNIC GROUPS** Mestizo 95%
LANGUAGES Spanish and Guaraní (both official)
RELIGIONS Roman Catholic 90%, Protestant
CURRENCY Guaraní = 100 céntimos

PERU

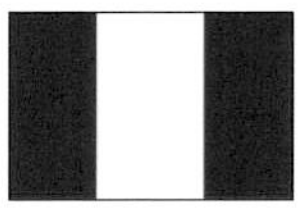

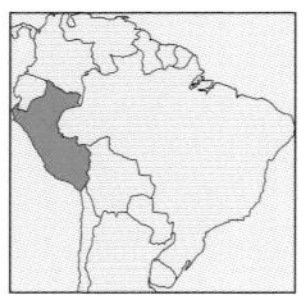

GEOGRAPHY The Republic of Peru lies in the tropics in western South America. A narrow coastal plain borders the Pacific Ocean in the west. Inland are ranges of the Andes Mountains, which rise to 22,205 ft [6,768 m] at Mount Huascarán, an extinct volcano. East of the Andes lies the Amazon basin.

Lima, on the coastal plain, has an arid climate. The coastal region is chilled by the cold, offshore Humboldt Current. Rainfall increases inland and many mountains in the high Andes are snow-capped.

POLITICS & ECONOMY Spanish *conquistadores* conquered Peru in the 1530s. In 1820, an Argentinian, José de San Martín, led an army into Peru and declared it independent. But Spain still held large areas. In 1823, the Venezuelan Simon Bolívar led another army into Peru and, in 1824, one of his generals defeated the Spaniards at Ayacucho. The Spaniards surrendered in 1826. Peru suffered much instability throughout the 19th century.

Instability continued in the 20th century. In 1980, when civilian rule was restored, a left-wing group called the Sendero Luminoso, or the "Shining Path," began guerrilla warfare against the government. In 1990, Alberto Fujimori, son of Japanese immigrants, became president. In 1992, he suspended the constitution and dismissed the legislature. The guerrilla leader, Abimael Guzmán, was arrested in 1992 and, in 2006, he was sentenced to life imprisonment. Fujimori left Peru but was later extradited, and in 2009 he was found guilty of ordering killings and kidnapping during the conflict and sentenced to 25 years in jail. In 2006, Alan Garcia was elected president. In 2011, Ollanta Humala won presidential elections in a run-off, defeating Keiko Fujimori.

The World Bank classifies Peru as a "lower-middle-income" developing country. Major food crops include beans, maize, potatoes, and rice. Fish products are exported, but the most valuable export is copper. Peru also produces lead, silver, zinc, and iron ore.

AREA 496,222 sq mi [1,285,216 sq km]
POPULATION 29,249,000 **CAPITAL** Lima
GOVERNMENT Constitutional republic **ETHNIC GROUPS** Amerindian 45%, Mestizo 37%, White 15% **LANGUAGES** Spanish and Quechua (both official), Aymara, other Amazonian languages **RELIGIONS** Roman Catholic 90% **CURRENCY** New sol = 100 centavos

PHILIPPINES

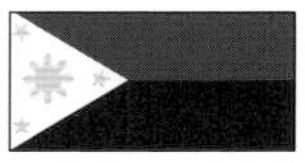

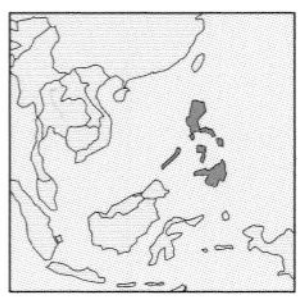

GEOGRAPHY The Republic of the Philippines is an island country in southeastern Asia. It includes about 7,100 islands, of which 2,770 are named and about 1,000 are inhabited. Luzon and Mindanao, the two largest islands, make up more than two-thirds of the country. The land is mainly mountainous.

The country has a hot tropical climate. The dry season runs from December to April. The rest of the year is wet. Much of the rainfall comes from the typhoons which periodically strike the east coast. In November 2006, a powerful typhoon struck Luzon in the Philippines. The typhoon triggered mudslides on the slopes of Mount Mayon, one of the country's many volcanoes. The mudslides destroyed several villages and killed around 1,000 people.

POLITICS & ECONOMY The first European to reach the Philippines was the Portuguese navigator Ferdinand Magellan in 1521. Spanish explorers claimed the region in 1565 when they established a settlement on Cebu. The Spaniards ruled the country until 1898, when the United States took over at the end of the Spanish–American War. Japan invaded the Philippines in 1941, but US forces returned in 1944. The country became fully independent as the Republic of the Philippines in 1946.

Since independence, the country's problems have included armed uprisings by left-wing guerrillas demanding land reform, Muslim separatist groups, crime, corruption, and unemployment. The dominant figure in recent times was Ferdinand Marcos, who ruled in a dictatorial manner from 1965 to 1986. His successors were Corazon Aquino (1986–92), Fidel Ramos (1992–8), and Joseph Estrada, who resigned following accusations of corruption. He was succeeded by Vice-President Gloria Arroyo, who was re-elected president in 2004. In 2010, Benigno Aquino was elected president. Fighting, killings, and kidnappings continued throughout the 2000s, while the government attempted to agree a peace settlement with rebel groups.

The Philippines is a developing country. Agriculture employs around 32% of the people. The main foods are rice and maize, while bananas, cocoa, coffee, sugarcane, and tobacco are grown commercially. Shellfish and sea fishing in coastal waters are also important, while manufacturing plays an increasingly significant part in the economy.

AREA 115,830 sq mi [300,000 sq km]
POPULATION 101,834,000 **CAPITAL** Manila
GOVERNMENT Multiparty republic
ETHNIC GROUPS Christian Malay 92%, Muslim Malay 4%, Chinese, and others **LANGUAGES** Filipino (Tagalog) and English (both official), Spanish, many others
RELIGIONS Roman Catholic 83%, Protestant 9%, Islam 5%
CURRENCY Philippine peso = 100 centavos

PITCAIRN

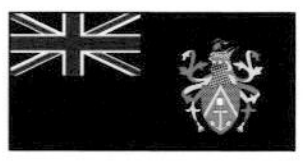

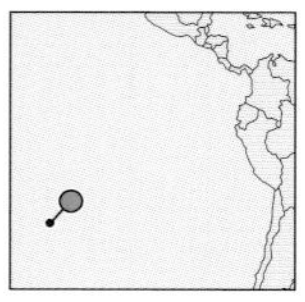

Pitcairn Island is a British overseas territory in the Pacific Ocean. Its inhabitants are descendants of the original settlers – nine mutineers from HMS *Bounty* and 18 Tahitians who arrived in 1790.

AREA 21 sq mi [55 sq km]
POPULATION 48 **CAPITAL** Adamstown

POLAND

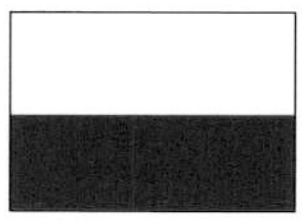

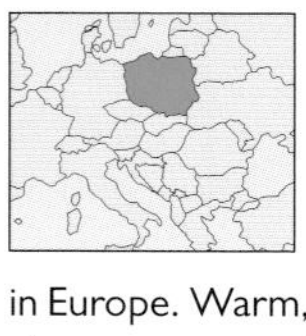

GEOGRAPHY The Republic of Poland faces the Baltic Sea and behind its lagoon-fringed coast lies a broad plain. A plateau lies in the southeast, while the Sudeten Highlands straddle part of the border with the Czech Republic. Part of the Carpathian Range (the Tatra) lies in the southeast.

Poland's climate is influenced by its position in Europe. Warm, moist air masses come from the west, while cold air masses come from the north and east. Summers are warm, but winters are cold and snowy.

POLITICS & ECONOMY Poland's boundaries have changed several times in the last 200 years, partly as a result of its geographical location between the powers of Germany and Russia. It disappeared from the map in the late 18th century, when a Polish state called the Grand Duchy of Warsaw was set up. But in 1815, the country was partitioned between Austria, Prussia, and Russia. Poland became independent in 1918, but in 1939 it was divided between Germany and the Soviet Union. The country again became independent in 1945, when it lost land to Russia

but gained some from Germany. Communists took power in 1948, but opposition mounted and eventually became focused through an organization called Solidarity.

Solidarity was led by a trade unionist, Lech Walesa. A coalition government was formed between Solidarity and the Communists in 1989. In 1990, the Communist Party was dissolved and Walesa became president. But he faced many problems in turning Poland toward a market economy, and was defeated in presidential elections in 1995. But his successor followed westward-looking policies. Poland joined NATO in 1999 and the European Union in 2004. In 2005, a nationalist, Lech Kaczynski, was elected president. But, along with other prominent Poles, he was killed in a plane crash in Russia in 2010. In 2011, Prime Minister Donald Tusk's center-right Civic Platform Party won parliamentary elections.

Poland has reserves of coal and various minerals which are used in its industries. Manufactures include chemicals, food, machinery, ships, steel, and textiles.

AREA 124,807 sq mi [323,250 sq km]
POPULATION 38,442,000 **CAPITAL** Warsaw
GOVERNMENT Multiparty republic
ETHNIC GROUPS Polish 97%, Belarusian, Ukrainian, German
LANGUAGES Polish (official) **RELIGIONS** Roman Catholic 95%, Eastern Orthodox **CURRENCY** Zloty = 100 groszy

PORTUGAL

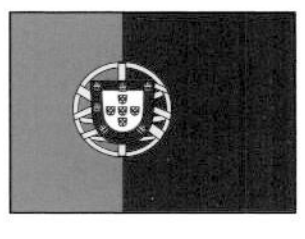
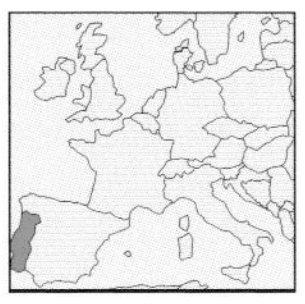

GEOGRAPHY The Republic of Portugal is the most westerly of Europe's mainland countries. The land rises from the coastal plains on the Atlantic Ocean to the western edge of the huge plateau, or Meseta, which occupies most of the Iberian peninsula. The climate is moderated by winds blowing from the Atlantic Ocean. Summers are cooler and winters are milder than in other Mediterranean lands. Portugal also contains two autonomous regions: the Azores and Madeira island groups.

POLITICS & ECONOMY Portugal became a separate country, independent of Spain, in 1143. In the 15th century, Portugal led the "Age of European Exploration." This led to the growth of a large Portuguese empire, with colonies in Africa, Asia, and, most valuable of all, Brazil in South America. Portuguese power began to decline in the 16th century and, between 1580 and 1640, Portugal was ruled by Spain. Portugal lost Brazil in 1822, and in 1910 Portugal became a republic. Instability hampered progress and army officers seized power in 1926. In 1928, they chose Antonio de Salazar to be minister of finance.

Salazar became prime minister in 1932 and ruled as a dictator from 1933 until 1968. In 1974, army officers mounted a coup. The new regime made most of Portugal's colonies independent and held free elections in 1978. Portugal joined the European Community (now the European Union) in 1986, and in 2002 the euro became the sole unit of currency. In 2011–12, Portugal experienced many problems when it sought to introduce austerity measures so that it could obtain a huge bail-out to help its weak economy. Public protests against the cuts increased.

Agriculture and fishing were the mainstays of the economy until the mid-20th century, when manufacturing became the most valuable activity.

AREA 34,285 sq mi [88,797 sq km]
POPULATION 10,760,000 **CAPITAL** Lisbon
GOVERNMENT Multiparty republic **ETHNIC GROUPS** Portuguese 99%
LANGUAGES Portuguese (official) **RELIGIONS** Roman Catholic 94%, Protestant **CURRENCY** Euro = 100 cents

PUERTO RICO

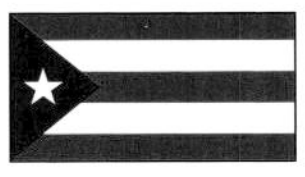
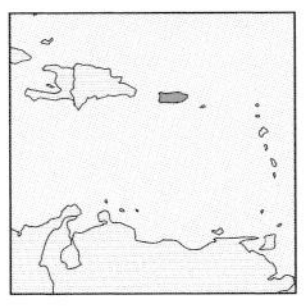

The Commonwealth of Puerto Rico, a mainly mountainous island, is the easternmost of the Greater Antilles chain. The climate is hot and wet. Puerto Rico is a dependent territory of the USA and the people are US citizens. In 1998, 50.2% of the population voted in a referendum on possible statehood to maintain the status quo.

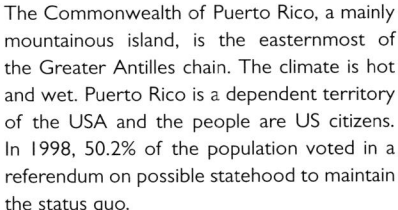

Puerto Rico is the most industrialized country in the Caribbean. Tax exemptions attract US companies to the island and manufacturing is expanding. The chief exports are chemicals and chemical products, machinery, and food.

AREA 3,427 sq mi [8,875 sq km]
POPULATION 3,989,000 **CAPITAL** San Juan

QATAR

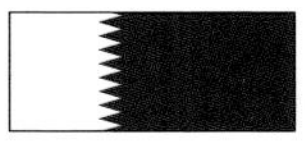
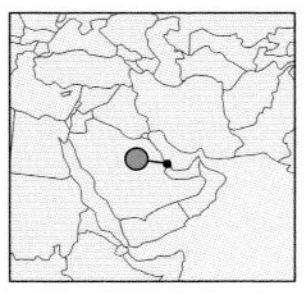

The State of Qatar occupies a low, barren peninsula that extends northward from the Arabian peninsula into the Persian Gulf. The climate is hot and dry. Qatar became a British protectorate in 1916, but it became fully independent in 1971. Oil, first discovered in 1939, is the mainstay of the economy of this prosperous nation.

AREA 4,247 sq mi [11,000 sq km] **POPULATION** 848,000 **CAPITAL** Doha

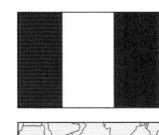

RÉUNION

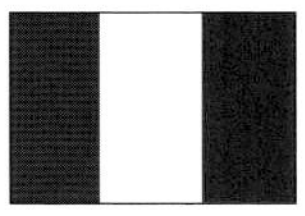
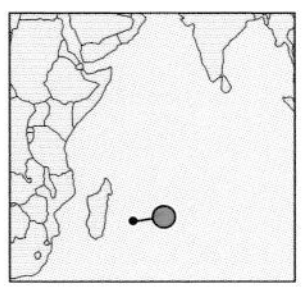

Réunion is a French overseas department in the Indian Ocean. The land is mainly mountainous, though the lowlands are intensely cultivated. Sugar and sugar products are the main exports, but French aid, given to the island in return for its use as a military base, is important to the economy.

AREA 969 sq mi [2,510 sq km]
POPULATION 839,000 **CAPITAL** St-Denis

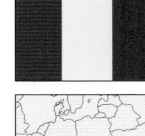

ROMANIA

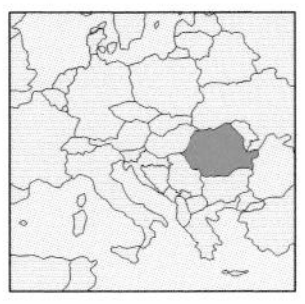

GEOGRAPHY Romania is a country on the Black Sea in eastern Europe. Eastern and southern Romania form part of the Danube river basin. The delta region, near the mouths of the Danube, where the river flows into the Black Sea, is one of Europe's finest wetlands. The southern part of the coast contains several resorts. The heart of the country is called Transylvania. It is ringed in the east, south, and west by scenic mountains which are part of the Carpathian mountain system. Romania has hot summers and cold winters. Rainfall is heaviest in spring and early summer.

POLITICS & ECONOMY From the late 18th century, the Turkish empire began to break up. The modern history of Romania began in 1861 when Walachia and Moldavia united. After World War I (1914–18), Romania, which had fought on the side of the victorious Allies, obtained large areas, including Transylvania, where most people were Romanians. This almost doubled the country's size and population. In 1939, Romania lost territory to Bulgaria, Hungary, and the Soviet Union. Romania fought alongside Germany in World War II, and Soviet troops occupied the country in 1944. Hungary returned northern Transylvania to Romania in 1945, but Bulgaria and the Soviet Union kept former Romanian territory. In 1947, Romania officially became a Communist country.

In 1990, Romania held its first free elections since the end of World War II. The National Salvation Front, led by Ion Iliescu and containing many former Communist leaders, won a large majority. A new constitution, approved in 1991, made the country a democratic republic. Elections held under this constitution in 1992 again resulted in victory for Ion Iliescu, whose party was renamed the Party of Social Democracy in 1993. Iliescu was defeated in 1996, but he served again as president in 2000–4. Romania joined NATO in 2004 and the European Union in 2007. In 2010, the European Union called on Romania to take urgent action to combat crime and corruption.

Romania has a "lower-middle-income" economy. Under Communist rule, industry, including mining and manufacturing, became more important than farming.

AREA 92,043 sq mi [238,391 sq km]
POPULATION 21,905,000 **CAPITAL** Bucharest
GOVERNMENT Multiparty republic
ETHNIC GROUPS Romanian 89%, Hungarian 7%, Roma 2%, Ukrainian **LANGUAGES** Romanian (official), Hungarian, German **RELIGIONS** Eastern Orthodox 87%, Protestant 7%, Roman Catholic 5% **CURRENCY** Leu = 100 bani

RUSSIA

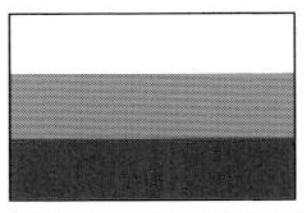
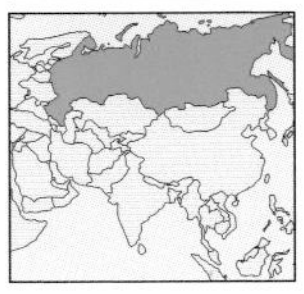

GEOGRAPHY Russia is the world's largest country. About 25% lies west of the Ural Mountains in European Russia, where 80% of the population lives. It is mostly flat or undulating, but the land rises to the Caucasus Mountains in the south, where Russia's highest peak, Elbrus, at 18,481 ft [5,633 m], is found. Asian Russia, or Siberia, contains vast plains and plateaus, with mountains in the east and south. The Kamchatka peninsula in the far east has many active volcanoes. Russia contains several of the world's longest rivers. It also includes part of the world's largest inland body of water, the Caspian Sea, and Lake Baikal, the world's deepest lake.

Moscow has a continental climate, with cold, snowy winters and hot summers. Siberia has a harsher, drier climate. In 2010, during a long heat wave, devastating wildfires swept over large areas.

POLITICS & ECONOMY In the 9th century AD, a state called Kievan Rus was formed by a group of people called the East Slavs. Kiev, now capital of Ukraine, became a major trading center, but, in 1237, Mongol armies conquered Russia and destroyed Kiev. Russia was part of the Mongol empire until the late 15th century. Under Mongol rule, Moscow became the leading Russian city.

In the 16th century, Moscow's grand prince was retitled "tsar." The first tsar, Ivan the Terrible, expanded Russian territory. In 1613, after a period of civil war, Michael Romanov became tsar, founding a dynasty which ruled until 1917. In the early 18th century, Tsar Peter the Great began to westernize Russia and, by 1812, when Napoleon failed to conquer the country, Russia was a major European power. But during the 19th century, many Russians demanded reforms and discontent was widespread.

In World War I (1914–18), the Russian people suffered great hardships and, in 1917, Tsar Nicholas II was forced to abdicate. In November 1917, the Bolsheviks seized power under Vladimir Lenin. The Bolsheviks set up the Union of Soviet Socialist Republics (also called the USSR or the Soviet Union).

From 1924, Joseph Stalin introduced a socialist economic program, suppressing all opposition. In 1939, the Soviet Union and Germany signed a non-aggression pact, but Germany invaded the Soviet Union in 1941. Soviet forces pushed the Germans back, occupying eastern Europe. They reached Berlin in May 1945. From the late 1940s, tension between the Soviet Union and its allies and Western nations developed into a "Cold War." This continued until 1991, when the Soviet Union was dissolved.

The Soviet Union collapsed because of the failure of its economic policies. From 1991, President Boris Yeltsin introduced democratic and economic reforms. Yeltsin retired in 1999 and, in 2000, was succeeded by Vladimir Putin. Putin, who was re-elected in 2004, sought to develop contacts with the West. He supported the US-declared "war on terrorism," though he opposed the invasion of Iraq in 2003. The secessionist conflict in Chechenia, including the occupation of a school by Muslim extremists in 2004, causing more than 330 deaths, provoked outrage. In 2005, violent incidents in the republics of Dagestan, Ingushetia, and Kabardino-Balkaria further confirmed that Russia's size and diversity make national unity hard to achieve. From 2006, relations with the West appeared to deteriorate, with Russia criticizing the expansion of NATO in Eastern Europe.

In 2008, Putin, having served two terms as president, was replaced by Dmitry Medvedev, but Putin was again re-elected to the presidency in 2012. In August 2008, Russia fought a short war against Georgia, which had attacked the secessionist region of South Ossetia. In 2010, Muslim militants from the troubled region of the North Caucasus were accused of bomb attacks on the Moscow Metro.

Russia's economy was thrown into disarray after the collapse of the Soviet Union, and in the early 1990s the World Bank described Russia as a "lower-middle-income" economy. Russia was admitted to the Council of Europe in 1997 and was also invited to attend the G7 summit in 1997, which then became known as the G8. Industry is Russia's leading economic activity. Resources include oil and natural gas, coal, timber, metal ores, and hydroelectric power.

Russia is a major producer of farm products, though it imports grains. Major crops include barley, flax, fruits, oats, rye, potatoes, sugar beet, sunflower seeds, vegetables, and wheat.

AREA 6,592,812 sq mi [17,075,400 sq km]
POPULATION 138,740,000 **CAPITAL** Moscow
GOVERNMENT Federal multiparty republic
ETHNIC GROUPS Russian 82%, Tatar 4%, Ukrainian 3%, Chuvash 1%, more than 100 others **LANGUAGES** Russian (official), many others
RELIGIONS Mainly Russian Orthodox, Islam, Judaism
CURRENCY Russian ruble = 100 kopeks

RWANDA

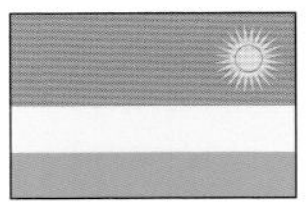
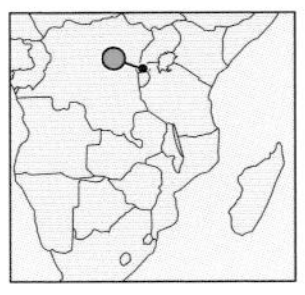

GEOGRAPHY The Republic of Rwanda is a small, landlocked country in east-central Africa. Lake Kivu and the River Ruzizi in the Great African Rift Valley form the country's western border.

Kigali stands on the central plateau of Rwanda. Here, temperatures are moderated by the altitude. Rainfall is abundant, but much

heavier rain falls on the western uplands, while the Rift Valley floor is drier and warmer than the rest of Rwanda.

POLITICS & ECONOMY Germany conquered the area, called Ruanda-Urundi, in the 1890s. However, Belgium occupied the region during World War I (1914–18) and ruled it until 1961, when the people of Ruanda voted for their country to become a republic, called Rwanda. This decision followed a rebellion by the majority Hutu people against the Tutsi monarchy. About 150,000 deaths resulted from this conflict. Many Tutsis fled to Uganda, where they formed a rebel army. Relations between Hutus and Tutsis deteriorated and, in 1994, between 500,000 and 800,000 people were massacred in Rwanda. After the Tutsis had restored order, Hutu rebels fled into the Democratic Republic of the Congo. Rwanda intervened in the Congo in 1996, 2002, and again in 2009. In 2009, Rwanda became the 54th member of the Commonwealth.

According to the World Bank, Rwanda is a "low-income" developing country. Most people are poor farmers. Food crops include bananas, beans, cassava, and sorghum. Some cattle are raised.

AREA 10,169 sq mi [26,338 sq km]
POPULATION 11,370,000 **CAPITAL** Kigali
GOVERNMENT Republic **ETHNIC GROUPS** Hutu 84%, Tutsi 15%, Twa 1% **LANGUAGES** French, English and Kinyarwanda (all official) **RELIGIONS** Roman Catholic 57%, Protestant 26%, Adventist 11%, Islam 5% **CURRENCY** Rwandan franc = 100 centimes

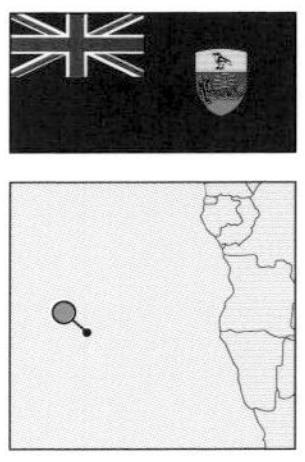

ST HELENA

St Helena, which became a British colony in 1834, is an isolated volcanic island in the South Atlantic Ocean. Now a British overseas territory, it is also the administrative center of Ascension and Tristan da Cunha.

AREA 47 sq mi [122 sq km]
POPULATION 4,000 **CAPITAL** Jamestown

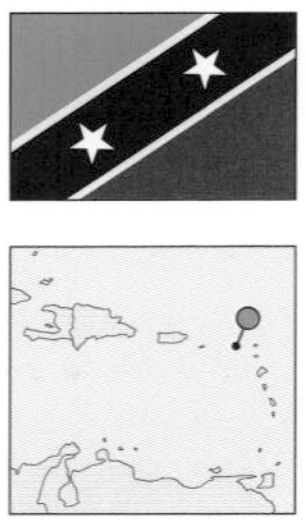

ST KITTS AND NEVIS

The Federation of St Kitts and Nevis comprises two well-watered volcanic islands, with mountains rising to around 3,300 ft [1,000 m]. The islands were the first in the Caribbean to be colonized by Britain (in 1623 and 1628), and they became an independent country in 1983. In 1998, a vote for the secession of Nevis fell short of the two-thirds majority required. Tourism has replaced sugar as the principal earner.

AREA 101 sq mi [261 sq km]
POPULATION 50,000 **CAPITAL** Basseterre

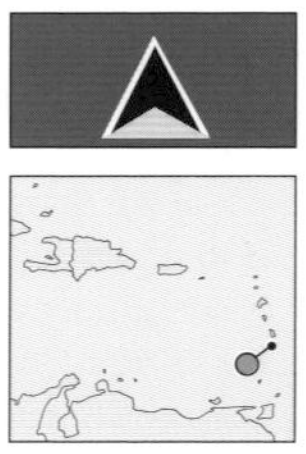

ST LUCIA

St Lucia, which became independent from Britain in 1979, is a mountainous, forested island of extinct volcanoes. It exports bananas and coconuts, and now attracts many tourists.

AREA 208 sq mi [539 sq km]
POPULATION 162,000 **CAPITAL** Castries

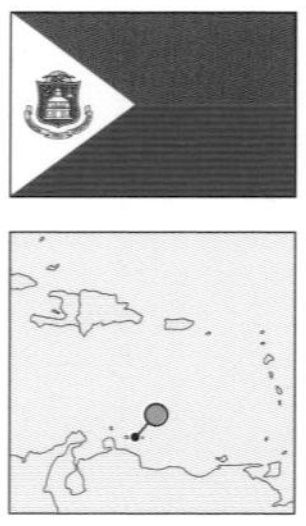

ST MAARTEN

Part of the Netherlands Antilles until 2010, the southern part of the island of St Maarten (called Sint Maarten in Dutch) is a self-governing territory within the Kingdom of the Netherlands.

AREA 13 sq mi [34 sq km]
POPULATION 37,000 **CAPITAL** Philipsburg

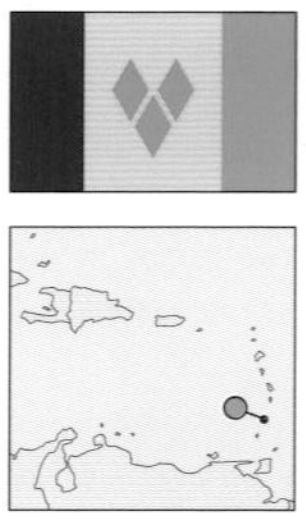

ST VINCENT AND THE GRENADINES

St Vincent and the Grenadines achieved its independence from Britain in 1979. Tourism is growing, but the territory is less prosperous than its neighbors.

AREA 150 sq mi [388 sq km]
POPULATION 104,000 **CAPITAL** Kingstown

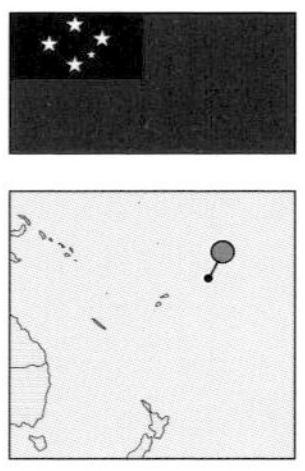

SAMOA

The Independent State of Samoa (formerly Western Samoa) comprises two islands in the south Pacific Ocean. Governed by New Zealand from 1920, the territory became independent in 1962. Exports include coconut cream and beer.

AREA 1,093 sq mi [2,831 sq km]
POPULATION 193,000 **CAPITAL** Apia

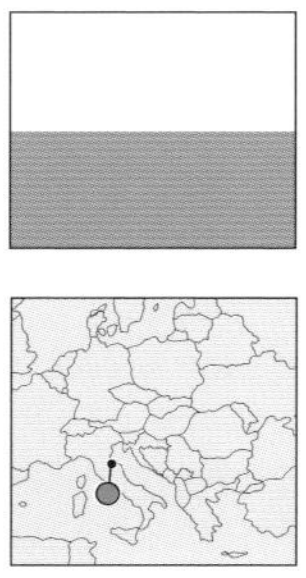

SAN MARINO

San Marino in northern Italy has been independent since 885 and a republic since the 14th century. It is the world's oldest republic. It has a friendship and cooperation treaty with Italy dating back to 1862. The state is governed by an elected council and has its own legal system. It has no armed forces and the police are "hired" from the Italian constabulary. The chief occupations are tourism, limestone quarrying, textiles, and wine-making.

AREA 24 sq mi [61 sq km] **POPULATION** 32,000 **CAPITAL** San Marino

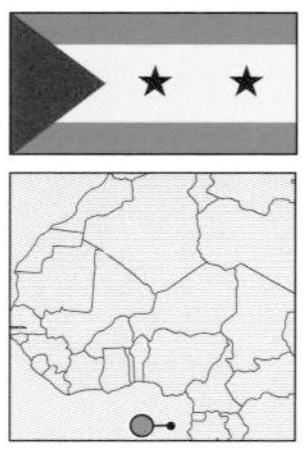

SÃO TOMÉ AND PRÍNCIPE

The Democratic Republic of São Tomé and Príncipe, a mountainous island territory west of Gabon, became a Portuguese colony in 1522. Following independence in 1975, the islands became a one-party Marxist state, but multiparty elections were held from 1991.

AREA 372 sq mi [964 sq km] **POPULATION** 180,000 **CAPITAL** São Tomé

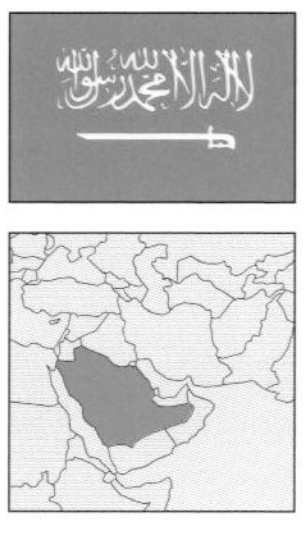

SAUDI ARABIA

GEOGRAPHY The Kingdom of Saudi Arabia occupies about three-quarters of the Arabian peninsula in southwest Asia. Deserts cover most of the land. Mountains border the Red Sea plains in the west. In the north is the sandy Nafud Desert (An Nafud). In the south is the Rub' al Khali (the "Empty Quarter"), one of the world's bleakest deserts. Saudi Arabia has a hot dry climate. Summer temperatures in Riyadh often exceed 104°F [40°C]. The nights are cool.

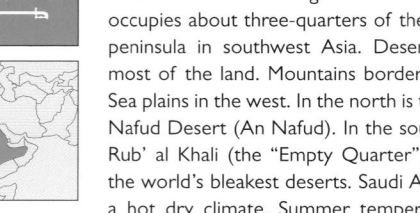

POLITICS & ECONOMY Saudi Arabia contains the two holiest places in Islam – Mecca (or Makka), the birthplace of the Prophet Muhammad in AD 570, and Medina (Al Madinah) where Muhammad went in 622. These places are visited by many pilgrims.

Since 1933, oil has been the mainstay of the economy. The monarch has supreme authority. Many of the terrorists involved in attacks on the US on September 11, 2001, were Saudi nationals. Saudi Arabia condemned the violence and, from 2003, Islamists launched attacks in Saudi Arabia. In 2011, King Abdullah announced more rights for women, including the rights to vote and to stand in municipal elections.

Saudi Arabia has about 25% of the world's known oil reserves and oil products make up about 90% of the exports. Irrigation and desalination projects have increased crop production.

AREA 829,995 sq mi [2,149,690 sq km]
POPULATION 26,132,000 **CAPITAL** Riyadh
GOVERNMENT Absolute monarchy with consultative assembly
ETHNIC GROUPS Arab 90%, Afro-Asian 10%
LANGUAGES Arabic (official)
RELIGIONS Islam 100%
CURRENCY Saudi riyal = 100 halalas

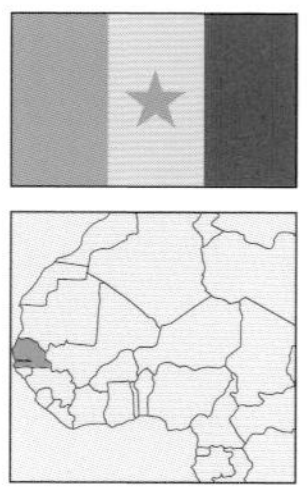

SENEGAL

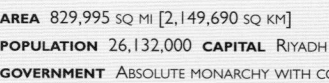

GEOGRAPHY The Republic of Senegal is on the northwest coast of Africa. The volcanic Cape Verde (Cap Vert), on which Dakar stands, is the most westerly point in Africa. Plains cover most of Senegal, though the land rises gently in the southeast.

Dakar has a tropical climate, with a short rainy season between July and October.

POLITICS & ECONOMY In 1882, Senegal became a French colony, and from 1895 it was ruled as part of French West Africa, the capital of which, Dakar, developed as a major port and city.

In 1959, Senegal joined French Sudan (now Mali) to form the Federation of Mali. But Senegal withdrew in 1960 and became the separate Republic of Senegal. Its first president, Léopold Sédar Senghor, served until 1981, when he was succeeded by Abdou Diouf. However, in 2000, Diouf was defeated in elections by Abdoulaye Wade. Wade served until 2012, when, controversially seeking a third term in office, he was defeated by a former prime minister, Macky Sall.

According to the World Bank, Senegal is a "lower-middle-income" developing country. It was badly hit in the 1960s and 1970s by droughts, which caused starvation. Agriculture still employs 30% of the population, though many farmers produce little more than they need to feed their families. Food crops include groundnuts (peanuts), millet, and rice. Phosphates are the country's chief resource, but Senegal also refines oil, which it imports from Gabon and Nigeria. Dakar is a busy port and has many industries.

AREA 75,954 sq mi [196,722 sq km]
POPULATION 12,644,000 **CAPITAL** Dakar
GOVERNMENT Multiparty republic
ETHNIC GROUPS Wolof 44%, Pular 24%, Serer 15%
LANGUAGES French (official), tribal languages
RELIGIONS Islam 94%, Christianity (mainly Roman Catholic) 5%, traditional beliefs 1%
CURRENCY CFA franc = 100 centimes

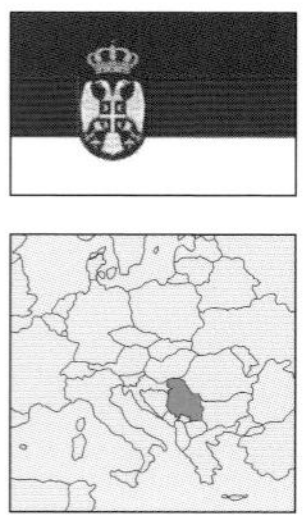

SERBIA

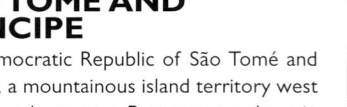

GEOGRAPHY The Republic of Serbia lies in the central Balkan peninsula. A landlocked country, it contains large, fertile lowlands drained by the River Danube and its tributaries, with uplands in the south. Most of Serbia has a continental climate, with cold, snowy winters and hot, dry summers. Heavy rains occur in the spring and the fall.

POLITICS & ECONOMY Around 1,500 years ago, South Slavs moved into the Balkan peninsula, and each group founded its own state. Serbia came under the Turkish Ottoman empire in the 15th century. In the 19th century, many Slavs worked for independence and Slavic unity. In 1914, Austria–Hungary declared war on Serbia, blaming it for the assassination of Archduke Franz Ferdinand of Austria–Hungary. In 1918, the South Slavs united in the Kingdom of the Serbs, Croats, and Slovenes, which was renamed Yugoslavia in 1929. Germany invaded in 1941, but Communist partisans, led by Josip Broz Tito, took power in 1945.

From 1945, the country became the Federal People's Republic of Yugoslavia. In 1991–2, the country split apart, with Bosnia-Herzegovina, Croatia, Macedonia, and Slovenia proclaiming their independence. The remaining republics, Serbia and Montenegro, retained the name Yugoslavia. In 2003, these two republics agreed to form the loose Union of Serbia and Montenegro. In 2006, the Montenegrins voted for full independence, and Serbia and Montenegro became separate republics. In 2008, the province of Kosovo declared itself independent. Serbia did not recognize this act. In 2011, the European Commission recommended Serbia for European Union candidate status, but said talks could start only after it normalized ties with Kosovo.

Serbia's resources include bauxite, coal, copper, and other metals, together with oil and natural gas. Manufactured products include aluminum, machinery, plastics, steel, textiles, and vehicles. Crops include fruits, maize, potatoes, tobacco, and wheat. Livestock include cattle, pigs, and sheep.

AREA 29,913 sq mi [77,474 sq km]
POPULATION 7,311,000 **CAPITAL** Belgrade
GOVERNMENT Republic
ETHNIC GROUPS Serb 83%, Hungarian 4%, others
LANGUAGES Serbian (official), Hungarian
RELIGIONS Serbian Orthodox, Roman Catholic, Islam, Protestant
CURRENCY New dinar = 100 paras

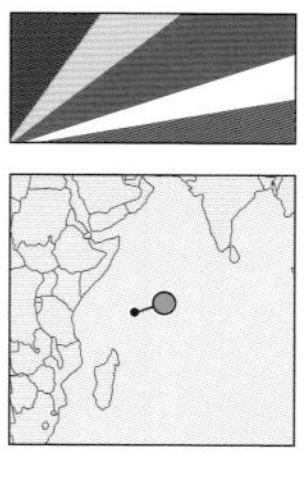

SEYCHELLES

The Republic of Seychelles in the western Indian Ocean achieved independence from Britain in 1976. Coconuts are the main cash crop, and fishing and tourism are important to the country's economy.

AREA 176 sq mi [455 sq km]
POPULATION 89,000 **CAPITAL** Victoria

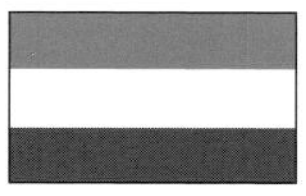
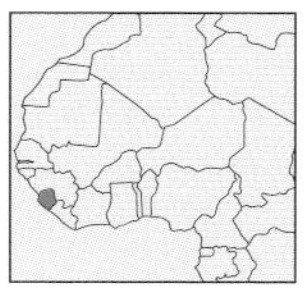

SIERRA LEONE

GEOGRAPHY The Republic of Sierra Leone in West Africa is about the same size as the country of Ireland. The coast contains several deep estuaries in the north, with lagoons in the south. The most prominent feature is the mountainous Freetown (or Sierra Leone) peninsula.

Sierra Leone has a tropical climate, with heavy rainfall between April and November.

POLITICS & ECONOMY A former British territory, Sierra Leone became independent in 1961 and a republic in 1971. It became a one-party state in 1978, but, in 1991, the people voted for the restoration of democracy. The military seized power in 1992 and a civil war caused much destruction in 1994–5. Elections in 1996 were followed by another military coup. In 1998, the West African Peace Force restored the deposed President Ahmed Tejan Kabbah. In 1999, a peace agreement followed further conflict. As part of this agreement, Foday Sankoh, one of the rebel leaders, became vice-president. However, he was arrested in 2000 and charged with war crimes. Another ceasefire was agreed in 2004. The last of the UN troops left the country in 2005, and national elections were held in 2007. In 2010, the UN Security Council lifted the last remaining sanctions against Sierra Leone.

Sierra Leone has a "low-income" economy. About 59% of the people live by farming, mainly at subsistence level. The leading exports are minerals, including diamonds, bauxite, and rutile (titanium ore). The country has few manufacturing industries.

AREA 27,699 sq mi [71,740 sq km]
POPULATION 5,364,000 **CAPITAL** Freetown
GOVERNMENT Single-party republic **ETHNIC GROUPS** Native African tribes 90% **LANGUAGES** English (official), Mende, Temne, Krio
RELIGIONS Islam 60%, traditional beliefs 30%, Christianity 10%
CURRENCY Leone = 100 cents

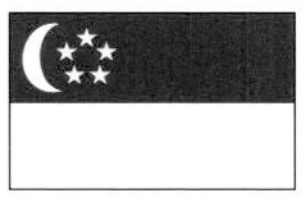
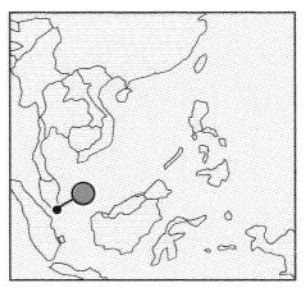

SINGAPORE

GEOGRAPHY The Republic of Singapore is an island country at the southern tip of the Malay peninsula. It consists of the large Singapore Island and 58 small islands, 20 of which are inhabited. The climate is hot and humid. Temperatures are high and rainfall is heavy throughout the year.

POLITICS & ECONOMY In 1819, Sir Thomas Stamford Raffles (1781–1826), agent of the British East India Company, made a treaty with the Sultan of Johor allowing the British to build a settlement on Singapore Island. Singapore soon became the leading British trading center in Southeast Asia and it later became a naval base. Japanese forces seized the island in 1942, but British rule was restored in 1945.

In 1963, Singapore became part of the Federation of Malaysia, which also included Malaya and the territories of Sabah and Sarawak on Borneo. In 1965, Singapore broke away and became independent.

The People's Action Party (PAP) has ruled Singapore since 1959. Its leader, Lee Kuan Yew, served as prime minister from 1959 until 1990, when he resigned and was succeeded by Goh Chok Tong. In 2004, Lee Hsien Loong, son of Lee Kuan Yew, became prime minister.

The World Bank classifies Singapore as a "high-income" economy, where a skilled work force has created a fast-growing economy. Trade and finance are major activities. The global financial crisis in 2008–9 caused great concern, but recovery was rapid. Manufactures include electronic products, machinery, scientific instruments, textiles, and ships. Petroleum products and manufactures are the main exports.

AREA 264 sq mi [683 sq km]
POPULATION 4,741,000 **CAPITAL** Singapore City
GOVERNMENT Multiparty republic
ETHNIC GROUPS Chinese 77%, Malay 14%, Indian 8%
LANGUAGES Chinese, Malay, Tamil and English (all official)
RELIGIONS Buddhism, Islam, Christianity, Hinduism
CURRENCY Singapore dollar = 100 cents

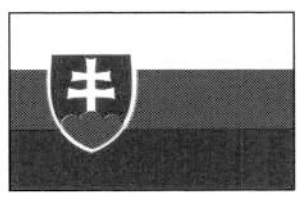
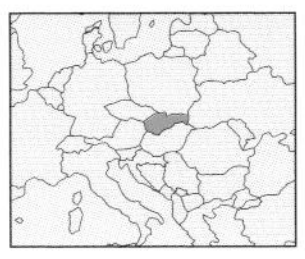

SLOVAK REPUBLIC

GEOGRAPHY The Slovak Republic is a predominantly mountainous country, consisting of part of the Carpathian range. The highest peak is Gerlachovsky in the Tatra Mountains, which reaches 8,711 ft [2.655 m]. The south is a fertile lowland. The Slovak Republic has cold winters and warm summers. Kosice, in the east, has average temperatures ranging from 27°F [–3°C] in January to 68°F [20°C] in July. The highland areas are much colder. Snow or rain falls throughout the year. Kosice has an average annual rainfall of 24 inches [600 mm], the wettest months being July and August.

POLITICS & ECONOMY Slavic peoples settled in the region in the 5th century AD. They were subsequently conquered by Hungary, beginning a millennium of Hungarian rule and suppression of Slovak culture.

In 1867, Hungary and Austria united to form Austria–Hungary, of which the present-day Slovak Republic was a part. Austria–Hungary collapsed at the end of World War I (1914–18). The Czech and Slovak people then united to form a new nation, Czechoslovakia. But Czech domination led to resentment by many Slovaks. In 1939, the Slovak Republic declared itself independent, but Germany occupied the country. At the end of World War II, the Slovak Republic again became part of Czechoslovakia.

The Communist Party took control in 1948. In the 1960s, many people sought reform, but they were crushed by the Russians. In the late 1980s, demands for democracy mounted and a non-Communist government took office in 1990. Elections in 1992 led to victory for the Movement for a Democratic Slovakia headed by a former Communist and nationalist, Vladimir Meciar, and the independent Slovak Republic came into existence on January 1, 1993.

Independence raised national aspirations among Slovakia's Magyar-speaking community, but relations with Hungary deteriorated when the Magyars felt that administrative changes under-represented them politically. The government also made Slovak the only official language. The Slovak Republic became a member of NATO and the European Union in 2004. On January 1, 2009, it became the 16th country to adopt the euro as its official currency. In 2012, the opposition party Smer, led by former Prime Minister Robert Fico, won a landslide victory in a general election, taking over half of the seats in parliament.

Before 1948, the Slovak Republic's economy was based on farming, but Communist governments developed manufacturing industries, producing such things as chemicals, machinery, steel, and weapons. Since the late 1980s, many state-run businesses have been handed over to private owners.

AREA 18,924 sq mi [49,012 sq km]
POPULATION 5,477,000 **CAPITAL** Bratislava
GOVERNMENT Multiparty republic
ETHNIC GROUPS Slovak 86%, Hungarian 11%
LANGUAGES Slovak (official), Hungarian
RELIGIONS Roman Catholic 60%, Protestant 8%, Orthodox 4%, others **CURRENCY** euro = 100 cents

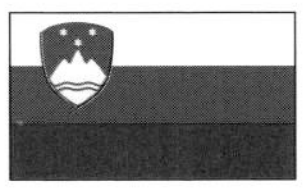
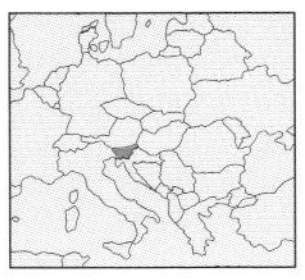

SLOVENIA

GEOGRAPHY The Republic of Slovenia was one of the six republics which made up the former Yugoslavia. Much of the land is mountainous, rising to 9,393 ft [2,863 m] at Mount Triglav in the Julian Alps (Julijske Alpe) in the northwest. Central Slovenia contains the limestone Karst region. The Postojna caves near Ljubljana are among the largest in Europe.

The coast has a mild Mediterranean climate, but inland the climate is more continental. The mountains are snow-capped in winter.

POLITICS & ECONOMY In the last 2,000 years, the Slovene people have been independent as a nation for less than 50 years. The Austrian Habsburgs ruled over the region from the 13th century until World War I. Slovenia became part of the Kingdom of the Serbs, Croats, and Slovenes (later called Yugoslavia) in 1918. During World War II, Slovenia was invaded and partitioned between Italy, Germany, and Hungary, but, after the war, Slovenia again became part of Yugoslavia.

From the late 1960s, some Slovenes demanded independence, but the central government opposed the breakup of the country. In 1990, when Communist governments had collapsed throughout Eastern Europe, elections were held and a non-Communist coalition government was set up. Slovenia then declared itself independent. This led to fighting between Slovenes and the federal army, but Slovenia did not become a battlefield. Slovenia's independence was recognized in 1992 and a coalition led by the Liberal Democrats was elected in 1992, 1996, and 2000. In 2004, Slovenia became a member of the North Atlantic Treaty Organization and the European Union. In 2009, Slovenia became the first former Communist country to assume the presidency of the European Union. In 2011, the newly formed Positive Slovenia Party scored a surprise win in parliamentary elections. The former ruling Social Democrats dropped to third place.

The reform of the formerly state-run economy caused problems for Slovenia. However, since 1993, the country has made considerable economic progress.

Manufacturing is the leading activity and manufactures are the main exports. Manufactures include chemicals, machinery and transport equipment, metal goods, and textiles. Slovenia mines some iron ore, lead, lignite, and mercury. Agriculture and forestry employ 9% of the people. Fruits, maize, potatoes, and wheat are major crops, and many farmers raise animals.

AREA 7,821 sq mi [20,256 sq km]
POPULATION 2,003,000 **CAPITAL** Ljubljana
GOVERNMENT Multiparty republic
ETHNIC GROUPS Slovene 92%, Croat 1%, Serb, Hungarian, Bosniak
LANGUAGES Slovenian (official), Serbo-Croatian
RELIGIONS Mainly Roman Catholic
CURRENCY Euro = 100 cents

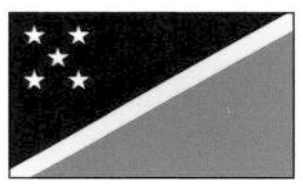
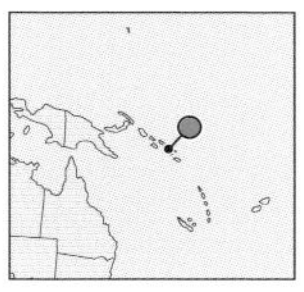

SOLOMON ISLANDS

The Solomon Islands, a chain of mainly volcanic islands in the Pacific Ocean, were a British territory between 1893 and 1978. The chain extends for some 1,400 mi [2,250 km]. They were the scene of fierce fighting during World War II. Most people are Melanesians, and the islands have a young population profile, with 40% of the people aged under 15. Fish, coconuts, and cocoa are leading products, though development is hampered by mountainous, forested terrain.

AREA 11,157 sq mi [28,896 sq km]
POPULATION 572,000 **CAPITAL** Honiara

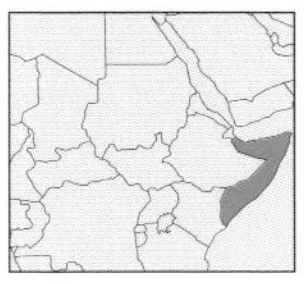

SOMALIA

GEOGRAPHY The Somali Democratic Republic, or Somalia, is in a region known as the "Horn of Africa." It is more than twice the size of Italy, the country which once ruled the southern part of Somalia. The most mountainous part of the country is in the north, behind the narrow coastal plains that border the Gulf of Aden. Rainfall is sparse, with the wettest regions in the south and northern mountains. Droughts are common and temperatures are generally high.

POLITICS & ECONOMY European powers became interested in the Horn of Africa in the 19th century. In 1884, Britain made the northern part of what is now Somalia a protectorate, while Italy took the south in 1905. The new boundaries divided the Somalis into five areas: the two Somalilands, Djibouti (which was taken by France in the 1880s), Ethiopia, and Kenya. Since then, many Somalis have wanted to create a Greater Somalia. Italy invaded British Somaliland in 1940, but was defeated in 1941. Britain ruled both Somalilands until 1950, when the United Nations asked Italy to take over the former Italian Somaliland for ten years. In 1960, the two Somalilands united to become Somalia.

Somalia has faced many problems. Economic difficulties led a military group to seize power in 1969. In the 1970s, Somalia supported an uprising of Somali-speaking people in the Ogaden region of Ethiopia. But, in 1988, Somalia and Ethiopia signed a peace treaty. In the 1990s, Somalia gradually broke apart. In 1991, the people in what was once British Somaliland set up the "Somaliland Republic," but it failed to get international recognition. The northeast, called Puntland, also seceded, while the south was riven by clan warfare. In 2004–5, a Somali parliament was set up in Kenya. In 2006, it moved to Baidoa, in Somalia (Mogadishu was regarded as unsafe). In 2006, Mogadishu was taken over by the Islamist Union of Islamic Courts, but government forces backed by Ethiopian troops defeated the Islamists. Ethiopia finally withdrew all its troops in January 2009. By 2011, the militant group al-Shabab controlled much of central and southern Somalia, while Somali pirates were a major threat to international shipping.

Somalia's economy has been shattered by war, droughts, and periodic floods. Many Somalis are nomads, who raise livestock. Live animals, meat, and hides and skins are exported. Crops include bananas, citrus fruits, cotton, maize, and sugarcane. Mining and manufacturing are relatively unimportant.

AREA 246,199 sq mi [637,657 sq km] **POPULATION** 9,926,000
CAPITAL Mogadishu **GOVERNMENT** Single-party republic, military dominated **ETHNIC GROUPS** Somali 85%, Bantu, Arab
LANGUAGES Somali (official), Arabic **RELIGIONS** Islam (Sunni Muslim)
CURRENCY Somali shilling = 100 cents

SOUTH AFRICA

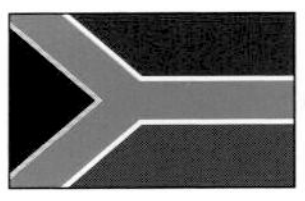

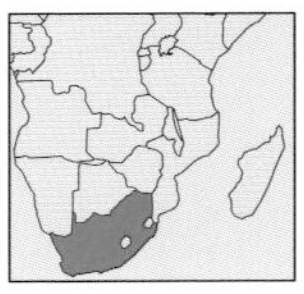

GEOGRAPHY The Republic of South Africa is made up largely of the southern part of the huge plateau which makes up most of southern Africa. The highest peaks are in the Drakensberg range. Part of the Namib Desert is in the northwest. The area around Cape Town has a sunny climate with mild, rainy winters. Inland, large areas of the plateau are arid.

POLITICS & ECONOMY Early inhabitants in South Africa were the Khoisan. In the last 2,000 years, Bantu-speaking people moved into the area. Their descendants include the Zulu, Xhosa, Sotho, and Tswana. The Dutch founded a settlement at the Cape in 1652, but Britain took over in the early 19th century, making the area a colony. The Dutch, called Boers or Afrikaners, resented British rule and moved inland. Rivalry between the groups led to Anglo–Boer Wars in 1880–1 and 1899–1902.

In 1910, the country was united as the Union of South Africa. In 1948, the National Party won power and introduced a policy known as apartheid, under which non-whites had no votes and their human rights were strictly limited. In 1990, Nelson Mandela, leader of the African National Congress (ANC), was released from prison. Multi-racial elections were held in 1994 and Mandela became president. After Mandela retired, the ANC won elections in 1999 and 2004, led by Thabo Mbeki, and in 2009 when Jacob Zuma became president. The government has faced many problems, including a health crisis – South Africa has more people infected with the HIV virus than any other country.

South Africa is Africa's most developed country. However, most of the black people are poor, with low standards of living. Natural resources include diamonds, gold, and many other metals. Mining and manufacturing are the most valuable activities.

AREA 471,442 sq mi [1,221,037 sq km] **POPULATION** 49,004,000
CAPITAL Cape Town (legislative); Pretoria/Tshwane (administrative); Bloemfontein (judiciary) **GOVERNMENT** Multiparty republic
ETHNIC GROUPS Black 76%, White 13%, Colored 9%, Asian 2%
LANGUAGES Afrikaans, English, Ndebele, Pedi, Sotho, Swazi, Tsonga, Tswana, Venda, Xhosa, and Zulu (all official)
RELIGIONS Christianity 68%, Islam 2%, Hinduism 1%
CURRENCY Rand = 100 cents

SPAIN

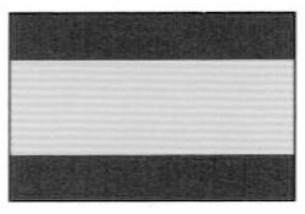

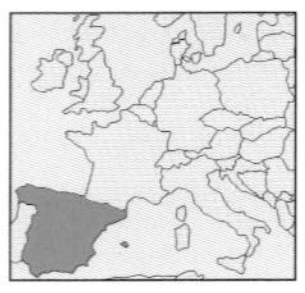

GEOGRAPHY The Kingdom of Spain is the second largest country in Western Europe after France. It shares the Iberian peninsula with Portugal. A large plateau, called the Meseta, covers most of Spain. Much of the Meseta is flat, but it is crossed by several mountain ranges, called sierras.

The northern highlands include the Cantabrian Mountains (Cordillera Cantabrica) and the high Pyrenees, which form Spain's border with France. But Mulhacén, the highest peak on the Spanish mainland, is in the Sierra Nevada in the southeast. Spain also contains fertile coastal plains. Other major lowlands are the Ebro river basin in the northeast and the Guadalquivir river basin in the southwest. Spain also includes the Balearic Islands in the Mediterranean Sea and the Canary Islands off the northwest coast of Africa.

The Meseta has a continental climate, with hot summers and cold winters, when temperatures often fall below freezing point. Snow frequently covers the mountain ranges on the Meseta. The Mediterranean coasts have hot, dry summers and mild winters.

POLITICS & ECONOMY In the 16th century, Spain became a world power. At its peak, it controlled much of Central and South America, parts of Africa, and the Philippines in Asia. Spain began to decline in the late 16th century. Its sea power was destroyed by a British fleet in the Battle of Trafalgar (1805). By the 20th century, it was a poor country.

Spain became a republic in 1931, but the republicans were defeated in the Spanish Civil War (1936–9). General Francisco Franco became the country's dictator, though technically Spain remained a monarchy. After Franco died in 1975, Prince Juan Carlos became king.

Spain has several groups with their own languages and cultures. Some of these people want to run their own regional affairs. In the northern Basque region, some nationalists have waged a terrorist campaign. A truce in 1998 was ended in 1999 when talks failed to produce results.

Since the 1970s, regional parliaments with a large degree of autonomy have been set up in the Basque Country, in Catalonia in the northeast, and in Galicia in the northwest. From the 1960s, ETA, a Basque terrorist group, waged a violent campaign for the secession of the Basque Country. In 2011, ETA declared an end to shootings and bombings.

In the last 50 years, Spain has changed from one of Europe's poorest countries into a prosperous nation and major holiday destination. Agriculture employs 4% of the people, as compared with 14% in mining and manufacturing. Farmland makes up two-thirds of Spain, with forests covering most of the rest. Crops include barley, citrus fruits, grapes for wine-making, olives, potatoes, and wheat. Spain lacks natural resources apart from some high-grade iron ore in the north. Manufactures include cars, chemicals, electronic goods, food, metal goods, and textiles.

AREA 192,103 sq mi [497,548 sq km] **POPULATION** 46,755,000
CAPITAL Madrid **GOVERNMENT** Constitutional monarchy
ETHNIC GROUPS Composite of Mediterranean and Nordic types
LANGUAGES Castilian Spanish (official) 74%, Catalan 17%, Galician 7%, Basque 2%
RELIGIONS Roman Catholic 94%, others
CURRENCY Euro = 100 cents

SRI LANKA

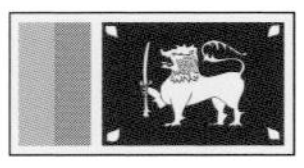

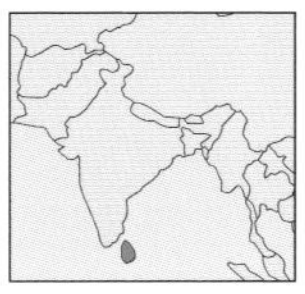

GEOGRAPHY The Democratic Socialist Republic of Sri Lanka is an island nation, separated from the southeast coast of India by the Palk Strait. The land is mostly low-lying, but a mountain region dominates the south-central part of the country.

The western part of Sri Lanka has a wet equatorial climate. Temperatures are high and the rainfall is heavy.

POLITICS & ECONOMY From the early 16th century, Ceylon (as Sri Lanka was then known) was ruled successively by the Portuguese, Dutch, and British. Independence was achieved in 1948 and the country was renamed Sri Lanka in 1972.

After independence, rivalries between the two main ethnic groups, the Sinhalese and Tamils, marred progress. In the 1950s, the government made Sinhala the official language. Following protests, the prime minister made provisions for Tamil to be used in some areas. In 1959, the prime minister was assassinated by a Sinhalese extremist and he was succeeded by Sirimavo Bandanaraike, the world's first woman prime minister.

Conflict between Tamils and Sinhalese continued in the 1970s and 1980s. In 1987, India helped to engineer a ceasefire. Indian troops arrived to enforce the agreement, but withdrew in 1990 after failing to subdue the main guerrilla group, the Tamil Tigers, who wanted to set up an independent Tamil homeland in northern Sri Lanka. The Tamil Tigers were finally defeated in May 2009 and, in 2010, Mahinda Rajapaksa was re-elected president of Sri Lanka.

In late 2004, a natural disaster occurred when a tsunami, caused by a sudden movement of the plates underlying the eastern Indian Ocean, struck parts of the coast of Sri Lanka. killing more than 30,000 people.

Sri Lanka is classed as a "low-income" economy. Agriculture employs about 30% of the people. Coconuts, rubber, and tea are exported, but rice is the main food crop. Factories process farm products and manufacture textiles.

AREA 25,332 sq mi [65,610 sq km]
POPULATION 21,284,000 **CAPITAL** Colombo
GOVERNMENT Multiparty republic
ETHNIC GROUPS Sinhalese 74%, Tamil 18%, Moor 7%
LANGUAGES Sinhala and Tamil (both official)
RELIGIONS Buddhism 70%, Hinduism 15%, Christianity 8%, Islam 7%
CURRENCY Sri Lankan rupee = 100 cents

SUDAN

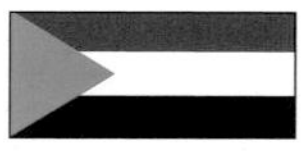

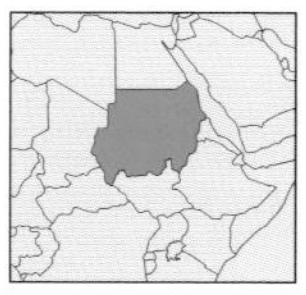

GEOGRAPHY The Republic of Sudan was Africa's largest country until 2011, when the people in the south voted to secede and set up a new nation called South Sudan. Sudan is mainly arid, with part of the vast Sahara in the north. The main feature is the fertile River Nile valley, where most people live.

POLITICS & ECONOMY In the 19th century, Egypt gradually took over Sudan. In 1881, a Muslim religious teacher, the Mahdi ("divinely appointed guide"), led an uprising. Britain and Egypt put the rebellion down in 1898. In 1899, they agreed to rule Sudan jointly as a condominium. After independence in 1952, the black Africans in the south, who were either Christians or followers of traditional religions, feared domination by the Muslim north. They objected to Arabic becoming the sole official language and, in 1964, civil war broke out. The war ended in 1972, when the south was granted regional self-government.

In 1983, the announcement that Islamic law would apply throughout Sudan sparked off further resistance from the rebel Sudan People's Liberation Army (SPLA) in the south. In 1998, Sudan's government announced that it accepted the idea of a referendum in the south. In 2005, a peace agreement was signed, bringing peace to the south. The referendum took place in January 2011, when around 99% of the people in the south voted to set up their own country, South Sudan.

Since 2003, another conflict has raged in the western province of Darfur, where government-backed militias battled with local rebel forces. In 2008, the International Criminal Court charged President al-Bashir with war crimes, but he was re-elected president in national elections in 2010.

Cotton is the chief crop in Sudan. Cotton, gum arabic, and sesame seeds are exported, but the most valuable exports are oil and oil products. More than 80% of the oil is produced in South Sudan, but Sudan has the infrastructure to exploit and export it.

AREA 728,222 sq mi [1,886,086 sq km] **POPULATION** 35,680,000
CAPITAL Khartoum **GOVERNMENT** Federal presidential democratic republic **ETHNIC GROUPS** Arab, Black, Beja, others
LANGUAGES Arabic, Nubian, Beja, English
RELIGIONS Islam, traditional beliefs
CURRENCY Sudanese pound

SUDAN, SOUTH

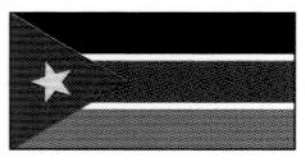

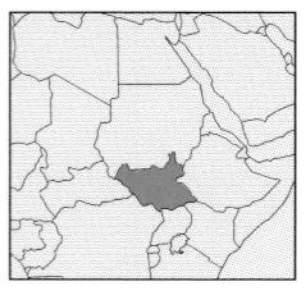

GEOGRAPHY The Republic of South Sudan is a landlocked country in northeastern Africa. Much of the land is low-lying and drained by the White Nile and its tributaries. Mountains lie in the far south. The country has a wet tropical climate. Forests, swamps, and grasslands cover large areas.

POLITICS & ECONOMY South Sudan has about 200 ethnic groups, including the Dinka and Nuer. Each group has its own traditional beliefs and languages. The South's deep cultural differences with the mainly Arab-Muslim north led to civil war (1964–1972 and 1983–2005). In January 2011, as part of the peace agreement, a referendum was held in which the vast majority of the people in the south voted for independence on July 9, 2011. After independence, South Sudan and Sudan clashed along disputed borders, while ethnic conflicts occurred in South Sudan.

Most people depend on agriculture and forestry, but South Sudan has many mineral resources, including oil.

AREA 239,285 sq mi [619,745 sq km] **POPULATION** 8,260,000
CAPITAL Juba **GOVERNMENT** Transitional
ETHNIC GROUPS Dinka, Nuer, others
LANGUAGES Local languages
RELIGIONS Traditional beliefs, Christianity
CURRENCY Sudanese pound

SURINAME

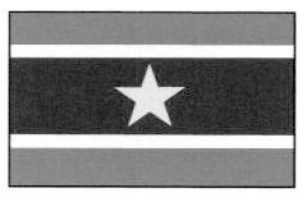

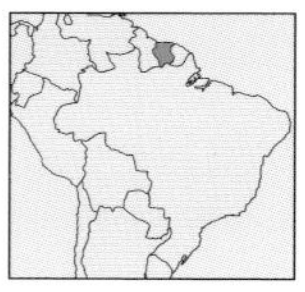

GEOGRAPHY The Republic of Suriname is sandwiched between French Guiana and Guyana in northeastern South America. The narrow coastal plain was once swampy, but it has been drained and now consists mainly of farmland. Inland lie hills and low mountains, which rise to 4,199 ft [1,280 m].

Suriname has a hot, wet and humid climate. Temperatures are high throughout the year.

POLITICS & ECONOMY In 1667, the British handed Suriname to the Dutch in return for New Amsterdam, an area that is now the state of New York. Slave revolts and Dutch neglect hampered development. In the early 19th century, Britain and the Netherlands disputed the ownership of the area. The British gave up their claims in 1813. Slavery was abolished in 1863 and, soon afterward, Indian and Indonesian laborers were introduced to work on the plantations.

Suriname became fully independent in 1975, but the economy was weakened when thousands of skilled people emigrated from Suriname to the Netherlands. Following a coup in 1980, Suriname was ruled by a military dictator, Dési Bouterse. The adoption of a new constitution led to the restoration of democracy in 1988, though another military coup occurred in 1990. Ronald Venetiaan was elected president in 2000, and his government replaced the guilder with the Surinamese dollar in 2004. In 2010, the Mega Combination coalition, led by Dési Bouterse, won parliamentary elections and Bouterse became president.

The World Bank classifies Suriname as an "upper-middle-income" developing country. Its economy is based on mining and metal processing. Suriname is a leading producer of bauxite, from which the metal aluminum is made.

AREA 63,037 sq mi [163,265 sq km]
POPULATION 492,000 **CAPITAL** Paramaribo
GOVERNMENT Multiparty republic
ETHNIC GROUPS Hindustani/East Indian 37%, Creole (mixed White and Black) 31%, Javanese 15%, Black 10%, Amerindian 2%, Chinese 2%, others **LANGUAGES** Dutch (official), Sranang Tonga
RELIGIONS Hinduism 27%, Protestant 25%, Roman Catholic 23%, Islam 20% **CURRENCY** Surinamese dollar= 100 cents

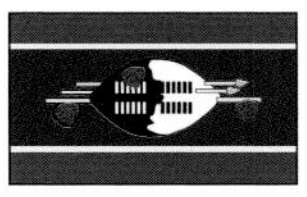

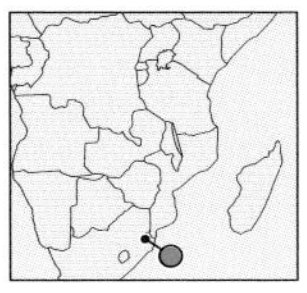

SWAZILAND

GEOGRAPHY The Kingdom of Swaziland is a small, landlocked country in southern Africa. The country has four regions which run north–south. In the west, the Highveld, with an average height of 3,950 ft [1,200 m], makes up 30% of Swaziland. The Middleveld, between 1,150 ft and 3,280 ft [350 m to 1,000 m], covers 28% of the country. The Lowveld, with an average height of 886 ft [270 m], covers another 33%. Finally, the Lebombo Mountains reach 2,600 ft [800 m] along the eastern border. The Lowveld is almost tropical, with average temperatures of 72°F [22°C] and low rainfall.

POLITICS & ECONOMY In 1894, Britain and the Boers of South Africa agreed to put Swaziland under the control of the South African Republic (the Transvaal). But at the end of the Anglo–Boer War (1899–1902), Britain took control of the country. In 1968, when Swaziland became fully independent as a constitutional monarchy, the head of state was King Sobhuza II. Sobhuza died in 1982 and was succeeded by his son, who, in 1986, became King Mswati III. Political parties were banned in elections in 1993 and 1998. Mswati ruled by decree. In 2005, Mswati signed a new constitution, but Swaziland remained an absolute monarchy.

Swaziland is a developing country. Farm products and processed food and drink, sugar, wood pulp, citrus fruits, and canned fruit are the leading exports. Many farmers live at subsistence level. Swaziland is heavily dependent on South Africa and it shares two problems with its large neighbor – widespread poverty and a high incidence of HIV/AIDS.

AREA 6,704 sq mi [17,364 sq km]
POPULATION 1,370,000 **CAPITAL** Mbabane
GOVERNMENT Monarchy **ETHNIC GROUPS** African 97%, European 3% **LANGUAGES** Siswati and English (both official)
RELIGIONS Zionist (a mix of Christianity and traditional beliefs) 40%, Roman Catholic 20%, Islam 10% **CURRENCY** Lilangeni = 100 cents

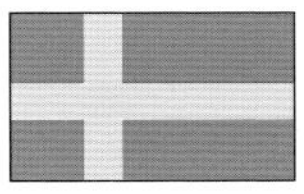

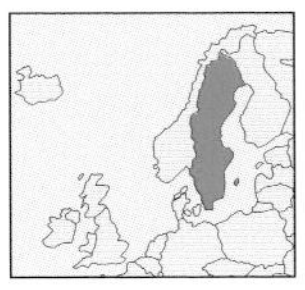

SWEDEN

GEOGRAPHY The Kingdom of Sweden is the largest of the countries of Scandinavia in both area and population. It shares the Scandinavian peninsula with Norway. The western part of the country, along the border with Norway, is mountainous. The highest point is Kebnekaise, which reaches 6,946 ft [2,117 m] in the northwest. The climate becomes increasingly severe from south to north.

POLITICS & ECONOMY Swedish Vikings plundered areas to the south and east between the 9th and 11th centuries. Sweden, Denmark, and Norway were united in 1397, but Sweden regained its independence in 1523. In 1809, Sweden lost Finland to Russia, but, in 1814, it gained Norway from Denmark. The union between Sweden and Norway was dissolved in 1905. Sweden was neutral in World Wars I and II. Since 1945, Sweden has become a prosperous country. In 1995, it joined the European Union. However, it did not adopt the euro in 1999.

Sweden has wide-ranging welfare services. But many people are concerned about the high cost of these services and the high taxes they must pay. In 2006, a center-right alliance defeated the Social Democrats, who had ruled Sweden for 65 of the previous 74 years. Fredrik Reinfeldt replaced Göran Persson as prime minister.

Sweden is a highly developed industrial country. Major products include steel and steel goods. Steel is used in the engineering industry to manufacture aircraft, cars, machinery, and ships. Sweden has some of the world's richest iron ore deposits. They are located near Kiruna in the far north. But most of this ore is exported, and Sweden imports most of the materials needed by its industries. Forestry is also important and hydroelectricity is a major source of energy. In 1996, Sweden announced the decommissioning of its nuclear power stations. The first reactor closed in 1999, followed by a second in 2005. But in 2009, the government, under pressure to diversify from fossil fuels, reversed this policy.

AREA 173,731 sq mi [449,964 sq km]
POPULATION 9,089,000 **CAPITAL** Stockholm
GOVERNMENT Constitutional monarchy **ETHNIC GROUPS** Swedish 91%, Finnish, Sami **LANGUAGES** Swedish (official), Finnish, Sami
RELIGIONS Lutheran 87%, Roman Catholic, Orthodox
CURRENCY Swedish krona = 100 öre

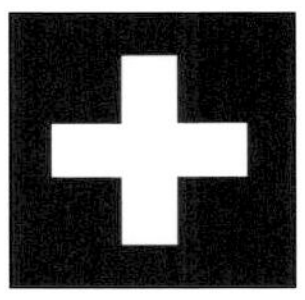

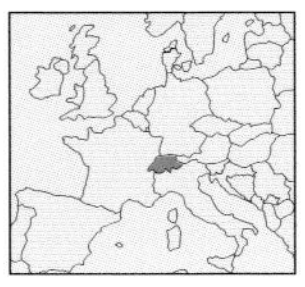

SWITZERLAND

GEOGRAPHY The Swiss Confederation is a landlocked country in Western Europe. Much of the land is mountainous. The Jura Mountains lie along Switzerland's western border with France, while the Swiss Alps make up about 60% of the country in the south and east. Four-fifths of the people of Switzerland live on the fertile Swiss plateau, which contains most of Switzerland's large cities.

The climate of Switzerland varies greatly according to the altitude. The plateau has warm summers and cold, snowy winters. Rain occurs throughout the year.

POLITICS & ECONOMY In 1291, three small cantons (states) united to defend their freedom against the Habsburg rulers of the Holy Roman empire. They were Schwyz, Uri, and Unterwalden, and they called the confederation they formed "Switzerland." Switzerland expanded and, in the 14th century, defeated Austria in three wars of independence. After a defeat by the French in 1515, the Swiss adopted a policy of neutrality, which they still follow. In 1815, the Congress of Vienna expanded Switzerland to 22 cantons and guaranteed its neutrality. Switzerland's 23rd canton, Jura, was created in 1979 from part of Bern.

Neutrality combined with the vigor and independence of its people have made Switzerland prosperous. In 2002, Switzerland became a member of the United Nations, though it still maintained its tradition of neutrality. In 2010, a fourth female minister was elected by the Federal Assembly to the seven-member Federal Council. For the first time, women were in the majority in the country's cabinet.

Although lacking in natural resources, Switzerland is a wealthy, industrialized country. Products include chemicals, electrical equipment, machinery and machine tools, precision instruments, processed food, watches, and textiles. Farmers produce about three-fifths of the country's food – the rest is imported. Crops include fruits, potatoes, and wheat. Tourism and banking are also important. Swiss banks attract investors from all over the world.

AREA 15,940 sq mi [41,284 sq km] **POPULATION** 7,640,000
CAPITAL Bern **GOVERNMENT** Federal republic
ETHNIC GROUPS German 65%, French 18%, Italian 10%, Romansch 1%, others **LANGUAGES** French, German, Italian, and Romansch (all official) **RELIGIONS** Roman Catholic 46%, Protestant 40% **CURRENCY** Swiss franc = 100 centimes

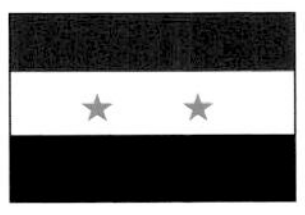

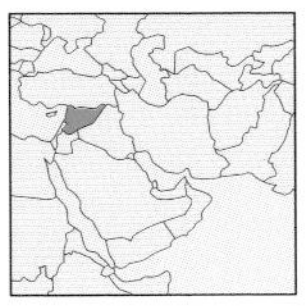

SYRIA

GEOGRAPHY The Syrian Arab Republic is a country in southwestern Asia. The narrow coastal plain is overlooked by a low mountain range which runs north–south. Another range, the Jabal ash Sharqi, runs along the border with Lebanon. South of this range is the Golan Heights, which Israel has occupied since 1967.

The coast has a Mediterranean climate, with dry, warm summers and wet, mild winters. The low mountains cut off Damascus from the sea. It has less rainfall than the coastal areas. To the east, the land becomes drier.

POLITICS & ECONOMY After the collapse of the Turkish Ottoman empire in World War I, Syria was ruled by France. Since independence in 1946, Syria has been involved in the Arab–Israeli wars, and in 1967 it lost a strategic border area, the Golan Heights, to Israel. In 1970, Lieutenant-General Hafez al-Assad took power, establishing a stable but repressive regime. Syria sent troops into Lebanon in 1976 in an effort to halt the civil war there, but, in 2005, following demonstrations, Syria withdrew its troops. Hafez al-Assad died in 2000 and was succeeded by his son, Bashar al-Assad. In 2011–12, government forces caused the deaths of thousands of anti-government demonstrators, while international efforts were made to achieve a ceasefire.

The World Bank classifies Syria as a "lower-middle-income" developing country. But it has great potential for development. Its main resources are oil, hydroelectricity from the dam at Lake Assad, and fertile land. Oil is the main export; farm products, textiles, and phosphates are also important. Agriculture employs about 17% of the work force.

AREA 71,498 sq mi [185,180 sq km]
POPULATION 22,518,000 **CAPITAL** Damascus
GOVERNMENT Multiparty republic **ETHNIC GROUPS** Arab 90%, Kurdish, Armenian, others **LANGUAGES** Arabic (official), Kurdish, Armenian **RELIGIONS** Sunni Muslim 74%, other Islam 16%
CURRENCY Syrian pound = 100 piastres

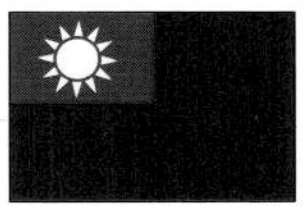

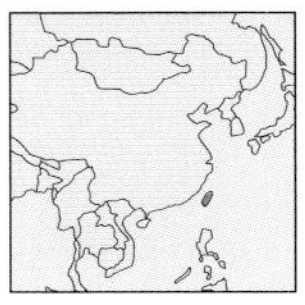

TAIWAN

GEOGRAPHY High mountain ranges run down the length of the island, with dense forest in many areas. The climate is warm, moist, and suitable for agriculture.

POLITICS & ECONOMY Chinese settlers occupied Taiwan from the 7th century. In 1895, Japan seized the territory from the Portuguese, who had named it Isla Formosa, or "beautiful island." China regained the island after World War II. In 1949, it became the refuge of the Nationalists who had been driven out of China by the Communists. They set up the Republic of China, which, with US help, began to expand its economy. Today, it produces a wide range of manufactured goods.

In the early 21st century, the Taiwanese declared full nationhood for Taiwan. But the government of mainland China threatened to attack the territory if it did not accept the fact that it was a self-governing province of China. However, in 2010, Taiwan and China signed a free-trade pact.

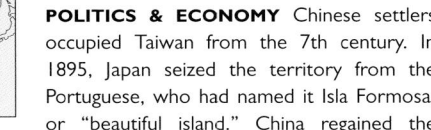

AREA 13,900 sq mi [36,000 sq km]
POPULATION 23,072,000 **CAPITAL** Taipei
GOVERNMENT Unitary multiparty republic
ETHNIC GROUPS Taiwanese 84%, mainland Chinese 14%
LANGUAGES Mandarin Chinese (official), Min, Hakka
RELIGIONS Buddhism, Taoism, Confucianism
CURRENCY New Taiwan dollar = 100 cents

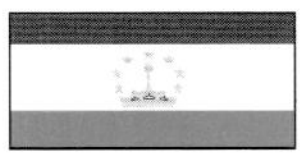

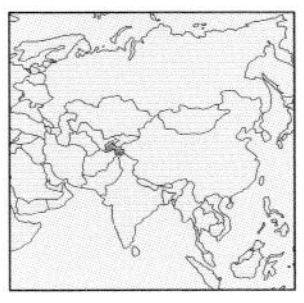

TAJIKISTAN

GEOGRAPHY The Republic of Tajikistan is one of the five central Asian republics that formed part of the former Soviet Union. Only 7% of the land is below 3,280 ft [1,000 m], while almost all of eastern Tajikistan is above 9,840 ft [3,000 m]. The highest point is Pik Imeni Ismail Samani (formerly known as Communism Peak or Pik Kommunizma), which reaches 24,590 ft [7,495 m]. The main ranges are the westward extension of the Tian Shan Range in the north and the snow-capped Pamirs in the southeast. Earthquakes are common throughout the country. The climate is continental, with hot, dry summers in the lower valleys and bitterly cold winters, especially in the mountains.

POLITICS & ECONOMY Russia conquered parts of Tajikistan in the late 19th century, and by 1920 Russia took complete control. In 1924, Tajikistan became part of the Uzbek Soviet Socialist Republic, but, in 1929, it was expanded, taking in some areas populated by Uzbeks, becoming the Tajik Soviet Socialist Republic.

While the Soviet Union began to introduce reforms during the 1980s, many Tajiks demanded freedom. In 1989, the Tajik government made Tajik the official language instead of Russian and, in 1990, it stated that its local laws overruled Soviet ones. Tajikistan became fully independent in 1991, following the breakup of the Soviet Union. In 1992, civil war broke out between the government, which was run by former Communists, and an alliance of democrats and Islamic forces. A ceasefire was agreed in 1996. In 2006, President Emomali Rahmon, president since 1994, was re-elected. In 2010, his party won parliamentary elections amid accusations of fraud.

The World Bank classifies Tajikistan as a "low-income" developing country and, in 2009, an international think tank warned that it risked becoming a failed state, with 70% of its people living in abject poverty. Agriculture, mainly on irrigated land, is the main activity and cotton is the chief product. Other crops include fruits, grains, and vegetables. The country has large hydroelectric resources and it produces aluminum.

AREA 55,521 sq mi [143,100 sq km]
POPULATION 7,627,000 **CAPITAL** Dushanbe
GOVERNMENT Transitional democracy
ETHNIC GROUPS Tajik 65%, Uzbek 25%, Russian
LANGUAGES Tajik (official), Russian
RELIGIONS Islam (Sunni Muslim 85%)
CURRENCY Somoni = 100 dirams

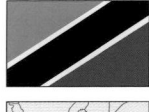

TANZANIA

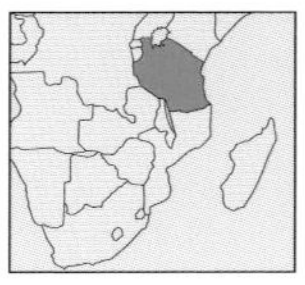

GEOGRAPHY The United Republic of Tanzania consists of the former mainland country of Tanganyika and the island nation of Zanzibar, which also includes the island of Pemba. Behind a narrow coastal plain, most of Tanzania is a plateau, which is broken by arms of the Great African Rift Valley. In the west, this valley contains lakes Nyasa and Tanganyika. The highest peak is Kilimanjaro, Africa's tallest mountain at 19,340 ft [5,895 m].

The coast has a hot and humid climate, with the greatest rainfall in April and May. The inland plateaux and mountains are cooler and less humid.

POLITICS & ECONOMY Mainland Tanganyika became a German territory in the 1880s, while Zanzibar and Pemba became a British protectorate in 1890. Following Germany's defeat in World War I, Britain took over Tanganyika, which remained a British territory until its independence in 1961. In 1964, Tanganyika and Zanzibar united to form the United Republic of Tanzania. The country's president, Julius Nyerere, pursued socialist policies of self-help (*ujamaa*) and egalitarianism. Many of its social reforms were successful, though the country failed to make economic progress. Nyerere resigned as president in 1985. His successors followed more liberal economic policies. In 2009, Tanzania joined with Burundi, Kenya, Rwanda, and Uganda in a common market agreement, allowing free movement of goods and people between them.

Tanzania is a poor country. Crops are grown on only 4% of the land, yet agriculture employs about 75% of the people. Food crops include bananas, cassava, maize, millet, and rice. Minerals, including gold, as well as cashews, tobacco, coffee, and tea are exported.

AREA 364,899 SQ MI [945,090 SQ KM]
POPULATION 42,747,000 **CAPITAL** DODOMA
GOVERNMENT MULTIPARTY REPUBLIC
ETHNIC GROUPS NATIVE AFRICAN 99% (OF WHICH 95% ARE BANTU CONSISTING OF MORE THAN 130 TRIBES)
LANGUAGES SWAHILI (KISWAHILI) AND ENGLISH (BOTH OFFICIAL)
RELIGIONS ISLAM 35% (99% IN ZANZIBAR), TRADITIONAL BELIEFS 35%, CHRISTIANITY 30% **CURRENCY** TANZANIAN SHILLING = 100 CENTS

THAILAND

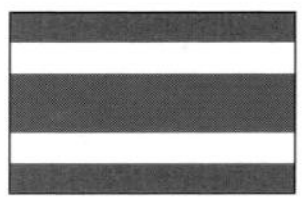

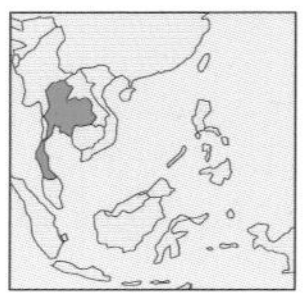

GEOGRAPHY The Kingdom of Thailand is one of the ten countries in Southeast Asia. The highest land is in the north, where Doi Inthanon, the highest peak, reaches 8,415 ft [2,565 m]. The Khorat plateau, in the northeast, makes up about 30% of the country and is the most heavily populated part of Thailand. In the south, Thailand shares the finger-like Malay peninsula with Burma and Malaysia.

Thailand has a tropical climate. Monsoon winds from the southwest bring heavy rains in May to October. Mountains shelter the central plains from the rain-bearing winds.

POLITICS & ECONOMY The first Thai state was set up in the 13th century. By 1350, it included most of what is now Thailand. European contact began in the early 16th century. But, in the late 17th century, the Thais, fearing interference in their affairs, forced all Europeans to leave. This policy continued for 150 years. In 1782, a Thai General, Chao Phraya Chakkri, became king, founding a dynasty which continues today. The country became known as Siam, and Bangkok became its capital. From the mid-19th century, contacts with the West were restored. In World War I, Siam supported the Allies against Germany and Austria–Hungary. But in 1941, the country was conquered by Japan and became its ally. After 1945, it became an ally of the United States.

After 1967, when Thailand became a member of ASEAN (Association of Southeast Asian Nations), its economy expanded rapidly, especially in manufacturing and service industries. In 1997, with other eastern Asian economies, it suffered an economic recession. Thailand has also faced conflict in southern Thailand, where the government has clashed with Muslim groups who feel that the government discriminates against them. In 2001, Thaksin Shinawatra, a businessman, became prime minister. In 2006, his party won a majority, the result of a boycott of opposition parties. Following mass protests, a military *junta* took power. Civilian rule was restored in 2007. In 2011, Thaksin's sister, Yingluck Shinawatra, was elected prime minister. She became the first Thai woman to be prime minister.

Agriculture employs 41% of the people and rice is the chief crop. Cassava, cotton, maize, rubber, sugarcane, and tobacco are also grown. Tin is mined, but the chief exports are manufactures and food products. Tourism is also important.

AREA 198,114 SQ MI [513,115 SQ KM]
POPULATION 66,720,000 **CAPITAL** BANGKOK
GOVERNMENT CONSTITUTIONAL MONARCHY
ETHNIC GROUPS THAI 75%, CHINESE 14%, OTHERS 11%
LANGUAGES THAI (OFFICIAL), ENGLISH, ETHNIC AND REGIONAL DIALECTS
RELIGIONS BUDDHISM 95%, ISLAM, CHRISTIANITY
CURRENCY BAHT = 100 SATANG

TOGO

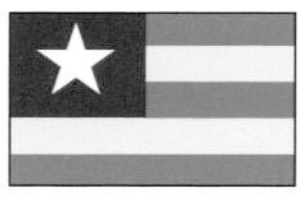

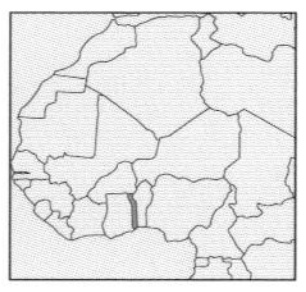

GEOGRAPHY The Republic of Togo is a long, narrow country in West Africa. From north to south, it extends about 311 mi [500 km]. Its coastline on the Gulf of Guinea is only 40 mi [64 km] long and it is only 90 mi [145 km] at its widest point.

Togo has high temperatures all through the year. The main wet season is from March to July, with a minor wet season in October and November.

POLITICS & ECONOMY Togo became a German protectorate in 1884, but, in 1919, Britain took over the western third of the territory, while France took over the eastern two-thirds. In 1956, the people of British Togoland voted to join Ghana, while French Togoland became an independent republic in 1960.

A military regime took power in 1963. In 1967, General Gnassingbé Eyadéma became head of state and suspended the constitution. Under a new constitution adopted in 1992, multiparty elections were held in 1994. However, in 1998, the count in the presidential elections was stopped when it became clear that Eyadéma had been defeated. The opposition boycotted subsequent elections. Eyadéma died in 2005. His son, Faure Gnassingbé, took over as president, but international pressure forced him to step down. However, he was elected president in 2005 and 2010.

Togo is a poor, developing country dependent on agriculture. Major food crops include cassava, maize, millet, and yams. Phosphate rock is the leading export.

AREA 21,925 SQ MI [56,785 SQ KM]
POPULATION 6,772,000 **CAPITAL** LOMÉ
GOVERNMENT MULTIPARTY REPUBLIC **ETHNIC GROUPS** NATIVE AFRICAN 99% (LARGEST TRIBES ARE EWE, MINA AND KABRE) **LANGUAGES** FRENCH (OFFICIAL), AFRICAN LANGUAGES **RELIGIONS** TRADITIONAL BELIEFS 51%, CHRISTIANITY 29%, ISLAM 20% **CURRENCY** CFA FRANC = 100 CENTIMES

TONGA

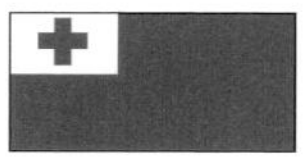

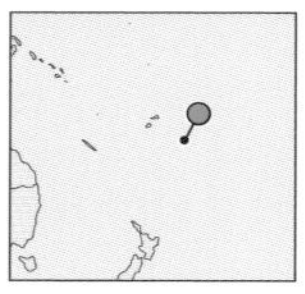

The Kingdom of Tonga, a former British protectorate, became independent in 1970. Situated in the south Pacific Ocean, it contains more than 170 islands, 36 of which are inhabited. In 2010, Tonga held its first election for a popularly elected parliament. Agriculture is the main activity.

AREA 251 SQ MI [650 SQ KM] **POPULATION** 106,000 **CAPITAL** NUKU'ALOFA

TRINIDAD AND TOBAGO

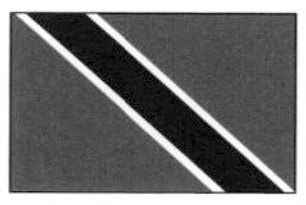

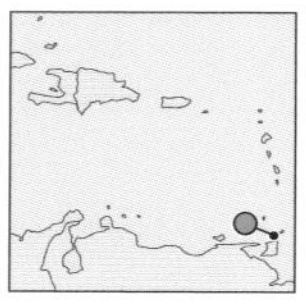

The Republic of Trinidad and Tobago became independent from Britain in 1962. These tropical islands, populated by people of African, Asian (mainly Indian), and European origin, are hilly and forested, though there are some fertile plains. Oil production is the mainstay of the economy.

AREA 1,981 SQ MI [5,130 SQ KM]
POPULATION 1,228,000 **CAPITAL** PORT OF SPAIN

TUNISIA

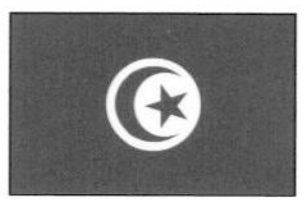

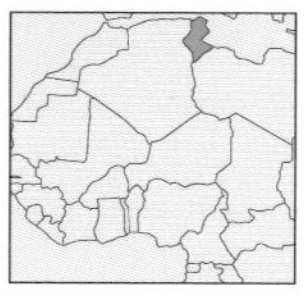

GEOGRAPHY The Republic of Tunisia is the smallest country in North Africa. The mountains in the north are an eastward and comparatively low extension of the Atlas Mountains. To the north and east of the mountains lie fertile plains, especially between Sfax, Tunis, and Bizerte. In the south, low-lying regions contain a vast salt pan, called the Chott Djerid, and part of the Sahara Desert.

Northern Tunisia has a Mediterranean climate, with dry, sunny summers, and mild winters with a moderate rainfall. The average yearly rainfall decreases toward the south.

POLITICS & ECONOMY In 1881, France established a protectorate over Tunisia and ruled the country until 1956. The new parliament abolished the monarchy and declared Tunisia to be a republic in 1957, with the nationalist leader, Habib Bourguiba, as president. His government introduced many reforms, including votes for women, but various problems arose, including unemployment among the middle class and fears that Western values introduced by tourists might undermine Muslim values. In 1987, the prime minister, Zine el Abidine Ben Ali, removed Bourguiba, and became president. He was re-elected to a fifth term in 2009. In 2011, anti-government demonstrations forced the president to flee the country. Elections were won by the moderate Islamist party Ennahda, though without an absolute majority.

The World Bank classifies Tunisia as a "middle-income" developing country. The main resources and chief exports are phosphates and oil. Most industries are concerned with food processing. Barley, dates, grapes, olives, and wheat are major crops. Fishing is important, as also is tourism.

AREA 63,170 SQ MI [163,610 SQ KM] **POPULATION** 10,629,000
CAPITAL TUNIS **GOVERNMENT** MULTIPARTY REPUBLIC
ETHNIC GROUPS ARAB 98%, EUROPEAN 1% **LANGUAGES** ARABIC (OFFICIAL), FRENCH **RELIGIONS** ISLAM 98%, CHRISTIANITY 1%, OTHERS
CURRENCY TUNISIAN DINAR = 1,000 MILLIMES

TURKEY

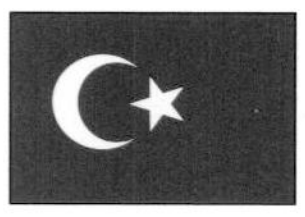

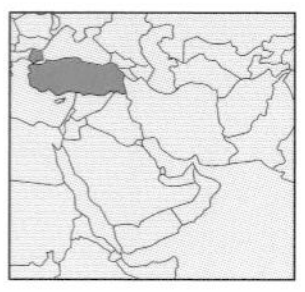

GEOGRAPHY The Republic of Turkey lies in two continents. European Turkey, also called Thrace, lies west of a waterway linking the Mediterranean and Black seas. Most of Asian Turkey consists of plateaux and mountains, which rise to 16,945 ft [5,165 m] at Mount Ararat (Agri Dagi) near the border with Armenia. Earthquakes are common. Central Turkey has a dry climate, with hot, sunny summers and cold winters. The west has a Mediterranean climate, but the Black Sea coast has cooler summers.

POLITICS & ECONOMY In AD 330, the Roman empire moved its capital to Byzantium, which it renamed Constantinople. Constantinople became capital of the East Roman (or Byzantine) empire in 395. Muslim Seljuk Turks from central Asia invaded Anatolia in the 11th century. In the 14th century, another group of Turks, the Ottomans, conquered the area. In 1453, the Ottoman Turks took Constantinople, which they called Istanbul. The Ottomans built up a vast empire which finally collapsed during World War I (1914–18). Turkey became a republic in 1923. Its leader, Mustafa Kemal, or Atatürk ("father of the Turks"), began to modernize and secularize the country.

Since the 1940s, Turkey has sought to strengthen its ties with Western powers. It joined NATO (North Atlantic Treaty Organization) in 1951 and it applied to join the European Economic Community in 1987. But Turkey's conflict with Greece, together with its invasion of northern Cyprus in 1974, have led many Europeans to treat Turkey's aspirations with caution. Political instability, military coups, conflict with Kurdish nationalists in eastern Turkey, and concern about the country's record on human rights are other problems.

Turkey has enjoyed democracy since 1983, though, in 1998, the government banned the Islamist Welfare Party, which it accused of violating secular principles. In 1999, the Muslim Virtue Party (successor to the Islamist Welfare Party) lost ground. The largest numbers of parliamentary seats were won by the ruling Democratic Left Party and the far-right National Action Party. However, in the elections in 2002, the moderate Islamic Justice and Development Party (AKP) won 362 of the 500 seats in parliament. Despite concerns about its Islamist roots, the AKP was re-elected in 2007. In 2007–8, the activities of the separatist Kurdish Workers Party (PKK) guerrillas provoked Turkey to bomb its bases in northern Iraq. In 2009–12, trials were held of secular military rulers, who were accused of undermining the government.

Turkey came close to economic collapse in 2002, but its recovery enabled it to withstand the global financial crisis in 2008, and its economy bounced back in 2010–11. Agriculture employs 21% of the people. Barley, cotton, fruits, maize, tobacco, and wheat are major crops. But manufactures, including textiles, cars, machinery, and paper products, are among the leading exports.

AREA 299,156 SQ MI [774,815 SQ KM]
POPULATION 78,786,000 **CAPITAL** ANKARA
GOVERNMENT MULTIPARTY REPUBLIC **ETHNIC GROUPS** TURKISH 80%, KURDISH 20% **LANGUAGES** TURKISH (OFFICIAL), KURDISH, ARABIC
RELIGIONS ISLAM (MAINLY SUNNI MUSLIM) 99%
CURRENCY NEW TURKISH LIRA = 100 KURUS

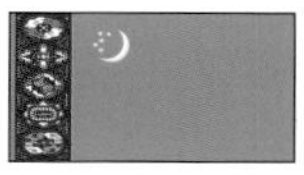

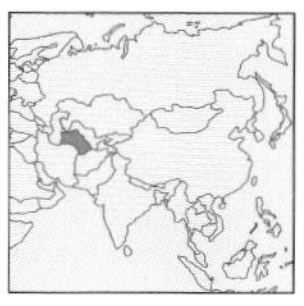

TURKMENISTAN

GEOGRAPHY The Republic of Turkmenistan is one of the five central Asian republics which once formed part of the former Soviet Union. Most of the land is low-lying, with mountains lying on the southern and southwestern borders. In the west lies the salty Caspian Sea. Most of Turkmenistan is arid and the Garagum, Asia's largest sand desert, covers about 80% of the country. Turkmenistan has a continental climate, with average annual rainfall varying from 3 inches [80 mm] in the desert to 12 inches [300 mm] in the mountains. Summer months are hot, but winter temperatures drop well below freezing point.

POLITICS & ECONOMY Just over 1,000 years ago, Turkic people settled in the lands east of the Caspian Sea and the name "Turkmen" comes from this time. Mongol armies conquered the area in the 13th century and Islam was introduced in the 14th century. Russia took over the area in the 1870s and 1880s. The area came under Communist rule in 1917 and, in 1924, it became the Turkmen Soviet Socialist Republic. The Communists controlled all aspects of life, but they raised living standards.

In the 1980s, when the Soviet Union began to introduce reforms, the Turkmen began to demand more freedom. In 1990, the Turkmen government stated that its laws overruled Soviet ones. In 1991, Turkmenistan became fully independent after the breakup of the Soviet Union. But the country kept ties with Russia through the Commonwealth of Independent States (CIS).

In 1992, Turkmenistan adopted a new constitution, allowing for the setting up of political parties, providing that they were not ethnic or religious in character. But, effectively, Turkmenistan remained a one-party state and, in 1992, Saparmurad Niyazov, the former Communist and at that time Democratic Party leader, was the only presidential candidate. In 1999, parliament declared Niyazov president for life. Niyazov died in 2006 and was succeeded by Gurbanguly Berdymukhamedov. In 2012, he was re-elected, winning more than 97% of the vote.

Faced with many economic problems, Turkmenistan began to look south rather than to the CIS for support. As part of this policy, it joined the Economic Cooperation Organization, which had been set up in 1985 by Iran, Pakistan, and Turkey. In 1996, the completion of a rail link from Turkmenistan to the Iranian coast was an important step in the development of Central Asia. Oil and natural gas are the chief resources, and gas pipelines to China and Iran were opened in 2009 and 2010. But agriculture is the main activity. Cotton is the main commercial crop. Manufactures include cement, glass, petrochemicals, and textiles.

AREA 188,455 sq mi [488,100 sq km] **POPULATION** 4,998,000
CAPITAL Ashkhabad **GOVERNMENT** Single-party republic
ETHNIC GROUPS Turkmen 85%, Uzbek 5%, Russian 4%
LANGUAGES Turkmen (official), Russian, Uzbek **RELIGIONS** Islam 89%, Eastern Orthodox 9% **CURRENCY** Turkmen manat = 100 tenesi

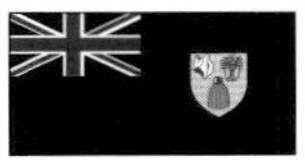

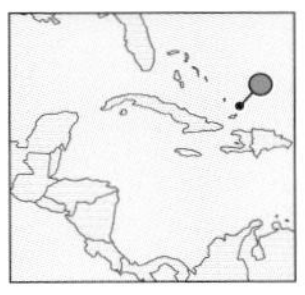

TURKS AND CAICOS ISLANDS

The Turks and Caicos Islands, a British territory in the Caribbean since 1776, are a group of about 30 islands. Fishing and tourism are major activities.

AREA 166 sq mi [430 sq km]
POPULATION 45,000 **CAPITAL** Cockburn Town

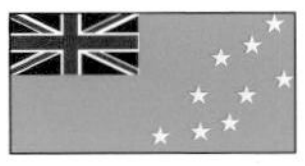

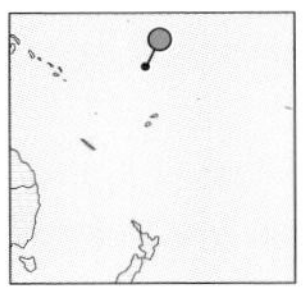

TUVALU

Tuvalu, formerly called the Ellice Islands, was a British territory from the 1890s until it became independent in 1978. It consists of nine low-lying coral atolls in the southern Pacific Ocean. Copra is the chief export.

AREA 10 sq mi [26 sq km]
POPULATION 11,000 **CAPITAL** Fongafale

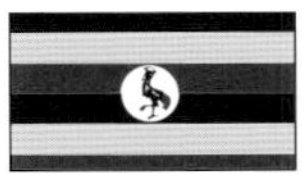

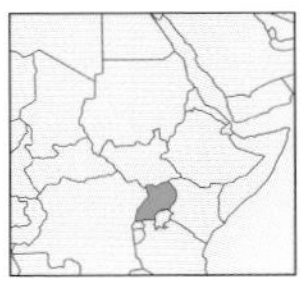

UGANDA

GEOGRAPHY The Republic of Uganda is a landlocked country on the East African plateau. It contains part of Lake Victoria, Africa's largest lake and a source of the River Nile, which occupies a shallow depression in the plateau.

The equator runs through Uganda and the country is warm throughout the year, though the high altitude moderates the temperature. The wettest regions are the lands to the north of Lake Victoria, where Kampala is situated, and the western mountains, especially the high Ruwenzori range.

POLITICS & ECONOMY Little is known of the early history of Uganda. When Europeans first reached the area in the 19th century, many of the people were organized in kingdoms, the most powerful of which was Buganda, the home of the Baganda people. Britain took over the country between 1894 and 1914, and ruled it until independence in 1962.

In 1967, Uganda became a republic and Buganda's Kabaka (king), Sir Edward Mutesa II, was made president. But tensions between the Kabaka and the prime minister, Apollo Milton Obote, led to the dismissal of the Kabaka in 1966. Obote also abolished the traditional kingdoms, including Buganda. Obote was overthrown in 1971 by an army group led by General Idi Amin Dada. Amin ruled as a dictator. He forced most of the Asians who lived in Uganda to leave the country and had many of his opponents killed.

In 1978, a border dispute between Uganda and Tanzania led Tanzanian troops to enter Uganda. With help from Ugandan opponents of Amin, they overthrew Amin's government. In 1980, Obote led his party to victory in national elections. But after charges of fraud, Obote's opponents began guerrilla warfare. A military group overthrew Obote in 1985, though strife continued until 1986, when Yoweri Museveni's National Resistance Movement seized power. In 1993, Museveni restored the traditional kingdoms. Elections were held in 1994, but political parties were forbidden. Museveni was elected in 1996, 2001, 2006, and 2011. In recent years, Uganda has faced the rebel Lord's Resistance Army (LRA) in the north. The LRA extended its activities into the Central African Republic, the Democratic Republic of the Congo, and Sudan. In 2010, two bombings in Kampala, killing 74 people, were carried out by a Somali Islamist group, al-Shabab, which said it was a response to Uganda's role in supplying troops to the African Union mission in Somalia.

Agriculture dominates the economy, employing 66% of the people. The chief export is coffee.

AREA 93,065 sq mi [241,038 sq km]
POPULATION 34,612,000 **CAPITAL** Kampala
GOVERNMENT Republic
ETHNIC GROUPS Baganda 17%, Ankole 8%, Basogo 8%, Iteso 8%, Bakiga 7%, Langi 6%, Rwanda 6%, Bagisu 5%, Acholi 4%, Lugbara 4%, and others
LANGUAGES English and Swahili (both official), Ganda
RELIGIONS Roman Catholic 33%, Protestant 33%, traditional beliefs 18%, Islam 16%
CURRENCY Ugandan shilling = 100 cents

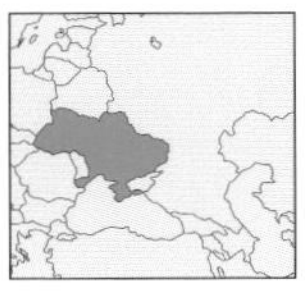

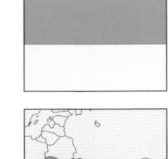

UKRAINE

GEOGRAPHY Ukraine is the second largest country in Europe after Russia. It was formerly part of the Soviet Union, which split apart in 1991. This mostly flat country faces the Black Sea in the south. The Crimean peninsula includes a highland region overlooking Yalta. Ukraine has warm summers, but the winters are cold, becoming more severe from west to east. In the summer, the east is often warmer than the west. Most rain comes in summer.

POLITICS & ECONOMY Kiev was the original capital of the early Slavic civilization known as Kievan Rus. In the 17th and 18th centuries, parts of Ukraine came under Polish and Russian rule. But Russia gained most of Ukraine in the late 18th century. In 1918, Ukraine became independent, but in 1922 it became part of the Soviet Union.

In the 1980s, Ukrainian people demanded more say over their affairs. The country became independent in 1991. Leonid Kuchma, who became president in 1994, came under fire in the early 2000s for maladministration and for his alleged involvement in the murder of a journalist. In 2005, the pro-Western leader Viktor Yushchenko was elected president. Economic problems and political infighting led to a Russian-leaning party, led by Viktor Yanukovych, winning most seats in parliament in 2006. Yanukovych became prime minister, but an election in 2007 resulted in a pro-Western coalition government led by a former prime minister, Yulia Tymoshenko. In 2010, the pro-Russian Viktor Yanukovych was declared winner of the presidential election. Tymoshenko was later accused of exceeding her powers when she signed a gas deal with Russia. She was sentenced to seven years in prison.

The World Bank classifies Ukraine as a "lower-middle-income" economy. Agriculture is important. Wheat and sugar are exported. Barley, maize, potatoes, sunflowers, and tobacco are also grown. Livestock rearing and fishing are also important.

Manufacturing is the chief economic activity. Major manufactures include iron and steel, machinery, and vehicles. Ukraine has large coalfields. The country imports oil and natural gas, but it has hydroelectric and nuclear power stations.

AREA 233,089 sq mi [603,700 sq km]
POPULATION 45,135,000 **CAPITAL** Kiev
GOVERNMENT Multiparty republic
ETHNIC GROUPS Ukrainian 78%, Russian 17%, Belarusian, Moldovan, Bulgarian, Hungarian, Polish
LANGUAGES Ukrainian (official), Russian
RELIGIONS Mostly Ukrainian Orthodox
CURRENCY Hryvnia = 100 kopiykas

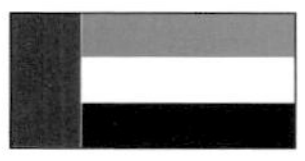

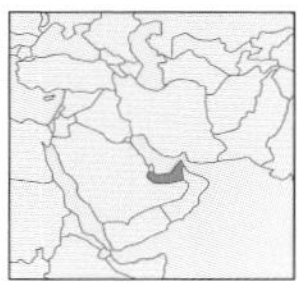

UNITED ARAB EMIRATES

The United Arab Emirates were formed in 1971 when the seven Trucial States of the Persian Gulf (Abu Dhabi, Dubai, Sharjah, Ajman, Umm al Qawayn, Ra's al Khaymah, and Al Fujayrah) opted to join together and form an independent country. The economy of this hot and dry country depends on oil production, and oil revenues give the United Arab Emirates one of the highest per capita GDPs in Asia.

AREA 32,278 sq mi [83,600 sq km]
POPULATION 5,149,000 **CAPITAL** Abu Dhabi

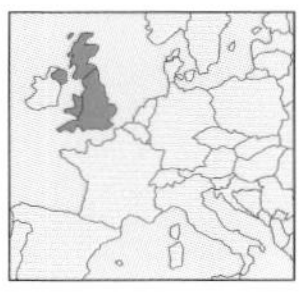

UNITED KINGDOM

GEOGRAPHY The United Kingdom (or UK) is a union of four countries. Three of them – England, Scotland, and Wales – make up Great Britain. The fourth country is Northern Ireland. The Isle of Man and the Channel Islands, including Jersey and Guernsey, are not part of the UK. They are self-governing British dependencies.

The land is highly varied. Much of Scotland and Wales is mountainous, and the highest peak is Scotland's Ben Nevis at 4,409 ft [1,344 m]. England has some highland areas, including the Cumbrian Mountains (or Lake District) and the Pennine range in the north. But England also has large areas of fertile lowland. Northern Ireland is also a mixture of lowlands and uplands. It contains the UK's largest lake, Lough Neagh.

The UK has a mild climate, influenced by the warm Gulf Stream which flows across the Atlantic from the Gulf of Mexico, then past the British Isles. Moist winds from the southwest bring rain, but the rainfall decreases from west to east. Winds from the east and north bring cold weather in winter.

POLITICS & ECONOMY In ancient times, Britain was invaded by many peoples, including Iberians, Celts, Romans, Angles, Saxons, Jutes, Norsemen, Danes, and the Normans, who arrived in 1066. The evolution of the United Kingdom spanned hundreds of years. The Normans finally overcame Welsh resistance in 1282, when King Edward I annexed Wales and united it with England. Union with Scotland was achieved by the Act of Union of 1707. This created a country known as the United Kingdom of Great Britain.

Ireland came under Norman rule in the 11th century, and much of its later history was concerned with a struggle against English domination. In 1801, Ireland became part of the United Kingdom of Great Britain and Ireland. But in 1921, southern Ireland broke away to become the Irish Free State. Most of the people in the Irish Free State were Roman Catholics. In Northern Ireland, where the majority of the people were Protestants, most people wanted to remain citizens of the United Kingdom. As a result, the country's official name changed to the United Kingdom of Great Britain and Northern Ireland.

The modern history of the UK began in the 18th century when the British empire began to develop, despite the loss in 1783 of its 13 North American colonies, which became the core of the modern United States. The other major event occurred in the late 18th century, when the UK became the first country to industrialize its economy.

The British empire broke up after World War II (1939–45), though the UK still administers many small, mainly island, territories around the world. The empire was transformed into the Commonwealth of Nations, a free association of independent countries which numbered 54 in 2011.

The UK has retained an important world role. For example, in 2001, it played a prominent role in creating a broad alliance to counter international terrorism following the attacks on the United

States. It was also a prominent member of the coalition force which invaded Iraq in 2003. However, the UK has recognized that its economic future lies within Europe. It became a member of the European Economic Community (now the European Union) in 1973. Membership of the EU has been important to the British economy, but some people fear a loss of British identity should the EU ever evolve into a political union. Another matter of public concern is large-scale immigration, both from the EU and outside.

The UK is a major industrial and trading nation. It lacks natural resources apart from coal, iron ore, oil, and natural gas, and has to import most of the materials it needs for its industries. The UK also has to import food, because it produces only about two-thirds of the food it needs. In the first half of the 20th century, Britain was a major exporter of cars, ships, steel, and textiles. But many industries have suffered from competition from other countries, with lower labor costs. From 2008, Britain's economy was hit by a global financial crisis, which led the country into recession. Severe austerity measures were introduced.

The UK is one of the world's most urbanized countries, and agriculture employs only 1% of the people. Production is high because of the use of scientific methods and modern machinery. However, in the early 21st century, especially following the outbreak of foot-and-mouth disease in 2001, questions were raised about the future of rural industries. Major crops include barley, potatoes, sugar beet, and wheat. Sheep are the leading livestock, but beef and dairy cattle, pigs, and poultry are also important. Fishing is another major activity and the UK is one of the largest fishing countries in the EU. Important catches include cod, haddock, plaice, and mackerel.

Service industries play a major part in the UK's economy. Financial and insurance services bring in much-needed foreign exchange, while tourism has become a major earner.

AREA 93,381 sq mi [241,857 sq km]
POPULATION 62,698,000 **CAPITAL** London
GOVERNMENT Constitutional monarchy
ETHNIC GROUPS English 82%, Scottish 10%, Irish 2%, Welsh 2%, Ulster 2%, West Indian, Indian, Pakistani, and others **LANGUAGES** English (official), Welsh, Gaelic
RELIGIONS Christianity (Anglican, Roman Catholic, Presbyterian, Methodist), Islam, Sikhism, Hinduism, Judaism
CURRENCY Pound sterling = 100 pence

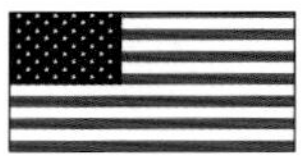

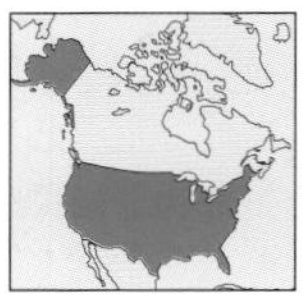

UNITED STATES OF AMERICA

GEOGRAPHY The United States of America is the world's fourth largest country in area and the third largest in population. It contains 50 states, 48 of which lie between Canada and Mexico, plus Alaska in northwestern North America, and Hawai'i, a group of volcanic islands in the north Pacific Ocean. Densely populated coastal plains lie to the east and south of the Appalachian Mountains. The central lowlands, drained by the Mississippi–Missouri rivers, stretch from the Appalachians to the Rocky Mountains in the west. The Pacific region contains fertile valleys, separated by mountain ranges.

The climate varies greatly, ranging from the Arctic cold of Alaska to the intense heat of Death Valley, a bleak desert in California. Of the 48 states between Canada and Mexico, winters are cold and snowy in the north, but mild in the south, a region which is often called the "Sun Belt."

POLITICS & ECONOMY The first people in North America, the ancestors of the Native Americans (or American Indians) arrived perhaps 40,000 years ago from Asia. Although Vikings probably reached North America 1,000 years ago, European exploration proper did not begin until the late 15th century.

The first Europeans to settle in large numbers were the British, who founded settlements on the eastern coast in the early 17th century. British rule ended in the War of Independence (1775–83). The country expanded in 1803 when a vast territory in the south and west was acquired through the Louisiana Purchase, while the border with Mexico was fixed in the mid-19th century. The Civil War (1861–5) ended slavery and the serious threat that the nation might split into two parts. In the late 19th century, the West was opened up, while immigrants flooded in from Europe and elsewhere.

During the late 19th and early 20th centuries, industrialization led to the United States becoming the world's leading economic superpower and a pioneer in science and technology. It took on the mantle of the champion of Western democracy and, following the breakup of the former Soviet Union, it became the world's only superpower. But the attacks on the country on September 11, 2001, revealed its vulnerability to terrorists and rogue states. The response was vigorous. In 2001, it attacked the Taliban government in Afghanistan, which was protecting al Qaida terrorists. Then, in 2003, it led a coalition force to invade Iraq and overthrow Saddam Hussein. President George W. Bush was re-elected in 2004, and the conflicts in Afghanistan and Iraq continued. In 2008, the Democratic Party candidate, Barack Obama, defeated the Republican John McCain in the presidential elections. Obama, the first black president in US history, faced many challenges, including those arising from the global financial crisis and the conflicts in southwestern Asia.

The United States has the world's largest economy in terms of the total value of its production. Although agriculture employs only about 1.4% of the people, farming is highly mechanized and scientific, and the United States leads the world in farm production. Major products include beef and dairy cattle, together with such crops as cotton, fruits, groundnuts (peanuts), maize, potatoes, soybeans, tobacco, and wheat.

Natural resources include oil, natural gas, coal, a wide range of metal ores, and timber, especially from the Pacific northwest. Manufacturing is the single most valuable activity, employing 10.3% of the people. Major products include vehicles, food products, chemicals, machinery, printed goods, metal products, and scientific instruments. California, with its high-tech electronics industries, is the top manufacturing state.

AREA 3,717,792 sq mi [9,629,091 sq km]
POPULATION 313,232,000 **CAPITAL** Washington, DC
GOVERNMENT Federal republic
ETHNIC GROUPS White 77%, African American 13%, Asian 4%, Amerindian 2%, others **LANGUAGES** English, Spanish, more than 30 others **RELIGIONS** Protestant 56%, Roman Catholic 28%, Islam 2%, Judaism 2%
CURRENCY US dollar = 100 cents

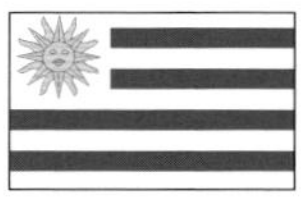

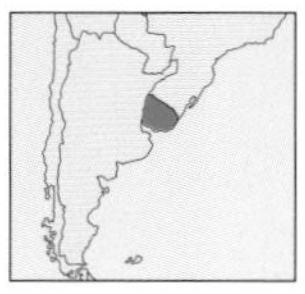

URUGUAY

GEOGRAPHY Uruguay is South America's second smallest independent country after Suriname. The land consists mainly of flat plains and hills. The River Uruguay, which forms the country's western border, flows into the Río de la Plata, a large estuary which leads into the South Atlantic Ocean.

Uruguay has a mild climate, with rain in every month, though droughts sometimes occur. Summers are pleasantly warm and winters relatively mild.

POLITICS & ECONOMY In 1726, Spanish settlers founded Montevideo in order to halt the Portuguese gaining influence in the area. By the late 18th century, Spaniards had settled in most of the country. Uruguay became part of a colony called the Viceroyalty of La Plata, which also included Argentina, Paraguay, and parts of Bolivia, Brazil, and Chile. In 1820 Brazil annexed Uruguay, ending Spanish rule. In 1825, Uruguayans, supported by Argentina, began a struggle for independence. Finally, in 1828, Brazil and Argentina recognized Uruguay as an independent republic. Social and economic developments were slow, but, from 1903, Uruguay became stable and democratic.

From the 1950s, economic problems caused unrest. Terrorist groups, notably the Tupumaros, carried out murders and kidnappings. The army crushed the Tupumaros in 1972, and took over the government in 1973. Military rule continued until 1984 when elections were held. In the early 21st century, Uruguay faced many economic problems, many of which were the result of the economic crisis in its neighbor, Argentina, and its imposition of banking controls. In 2009, the former left-wing rebel-turned-moderate Jose Mujica, of the governing Broad Front, was elected president.

The World Bank classifies Uruguay as an "upper-middle-income" developing country. Agriculture employs 10% of the people, but farm products, notably hides and leather goods, beef, and wool, are the main exports, while many manufacturing industries process farm products. Crops include maize, potatoes, wheat, and sugar beet. Uruguay depends largely on hydroelectric power for energy. In 2008, Uruguay announced the discovery of a natural gas field off the country's coast.

AREA 67,574 sq mi [175,016 sq km]
POPULATION 3,309,000 **CAPITAL** Montevideo
GOVERNMENT Multiparty republic
ETHNIC GROUPS White 88%, Mestizo 8%, Mulatto or Black 4%
LANGUAGES Spanish (official)
RELIGIONS Roman Catholic 66%, Protestant 2%, Judaism 1%
CURRENCY Uruguayan peso = 100 centésimos

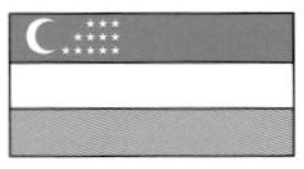

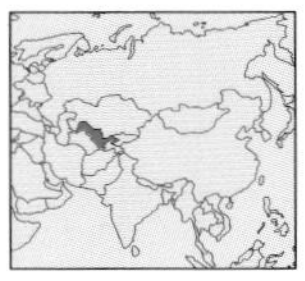

UZBEKISTAN

GEOGRAPHY The Republic of Uzbekistan is one of the five republics in Central Asia which were once part of the Soviet Union. Plains cover most of western Uzbekistan, with highlands in the east. The main rivers, the Amu (or Amu Darya) and Syr (or Syr Darya), drain into the Aral Sea. So much water has been taken from these rivers to irrigate the land that the Aral Sea has now shrunk to about a quarter of its size in 1960. The former lake area is now desert. Uzbekistan has cold winters and hot summers. The largely uninhabited Kyzyl Kum Desert lies in central Uzbekistan.

POLITICS & ECONOMY Russia took the area in the 19th century. After the Russian Revolution of 1917, the Communists took over and, in 1924, they set up the Uzbek Soviet Socialist Republic. Under Communism, all aspects of Uzbek life were controlled and religious worship was discouraged. But education, health, housing, and transport were improved. In the late 1980s, the people demanded more freedom, and in 1990 the government stated that its laws overruled those of the Soviet Union. Uzbekistan became independent in 1991 when the Soviet Union broke up, but it continued to retain links with Russia through the Commonwealth of Independent States.

Islam Karimov, leader of the People's Democratic Party (formerly the Communist Party), was elected president in December 1991. In 1992–3, many opposition leaders were arrested because the government said that they threatened national stability. In 1994–5, the PDP was victorious in national elections. Karimov was re-elected in 2001 and 2007. Initially, his government allowed the US to use bases in Uzbekistan for its military campaign in Afghanistan. It asked the US to remove its troops in 2005, but, in 2009, it allowed the US to transport supplies through Uzbekistan to its troops in Afghanistan. In 2010, the United Nations called on Uzbekistan to improve its human rights record.

The World Bank classifies Uzbekistan as a "lower-middle-income" developing country and the government still controls most economic activity. The country produces coal, copper, gold, oil, and natural gas.

AREA 172,741 sq mi [447,400 sq km
POPULATION 28,129,000 **CAPITAL** Tashkent
GOVERNMENT Socialist republic **ETHNIC GROUPS** Uzbek 80%, Russian 5%, Tajik 5%, Kazakh 3%, Tatar 2%, Kara-Kalpak 2%
LANGUAGES Uzbek (official), Russian **RELIGIONS** Islam 88%, Eastern Orthodox 9% **CURRENCY** Uzbekistani sum = 100 tyiyn

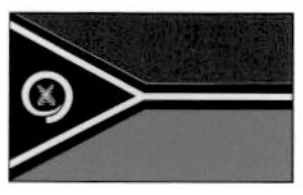

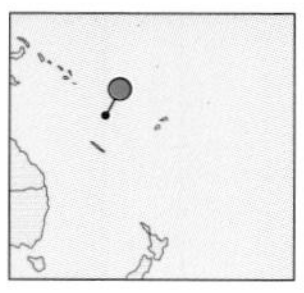

VANUATU

The Republic of Vanuatu, formerly the Anglo-French Condominium of the New Hebrides, became independent in 1980. It consists of a chain of 80 islands in the south Pacific Ocean. Its economy is based on agriculture, and it exports copra, beef and veal, timber, and cocoa.

AREA 4,706 sq mi [12,189 sq km]
POPULATION 225,000 **CAPITAL** Port-Vila

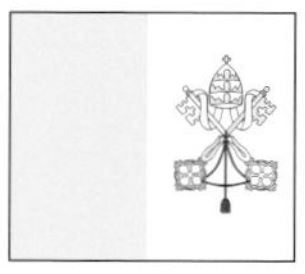

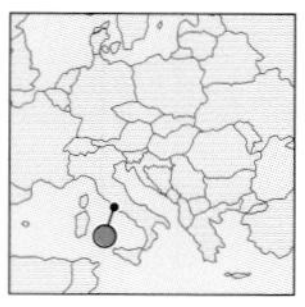

VATICAN CITY

Vatican City State, the world's smallest independent nation, is an enclave on the west bank of the River Tiber in Rome. It forms an independent base for the Holy See, the governing body of the Roman Catholic Church.

AREA 0.17 sq mi [0.44 sq km]
POPULATION 832

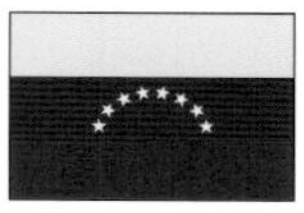

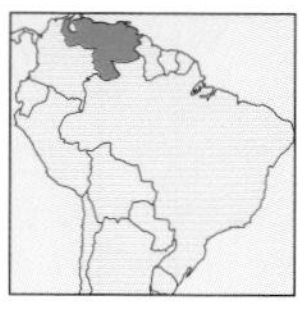

VENEZUELA

GEOGRAPHY The Bolivarian Republic of Venezuela, in northern South America, contains the Maracaibo lowlands around the oil-rich Lake Maracaibo in the west. Andean ranges enclose the lowlands and extend across most of the northern part of the country. The Orinoco river basin, containing tropical grasslands called *llanos*, lies between the northern highlands and the Guiana Highlands in the southeast. The Orinoco is Venezuela's longest river.

Venezuela has a tropical climate. Temperatures are high throughout the year on the lowlands, though the mountains are cooler. Rainfall is heaviest in the mountains. But much of the country has a dry season between December and April.

POLITICS & ECONOMY In the early 19th century, Venezuelans, such as Simón Bolívar and Francisco de Miranda, began a struggle against Spanish rule. Venezuela declared its independence in 1811. But it only became truly independent in 1821, when the Spanish were defeated in a battle near Valencia.

The development of Venezuela in the 19th and the first half of the 20th centuries was marred by instability, violence, and periods of harsh dictatorial rule. But Venezuela has had elected governments since 1958. The country has greatly benefited from its oil resources, which were first exploited in 1917. In 1960, Venezuela helped to form OPEC (the Organization of Petroleum Exporting Countries) and, in 1976, the government of Venezuela took control of the country's entire oil industry. In 1999, Hugo Chavez, who had staged an unsuccessful coup in 1992, was elected president. In 2004, he won a majority in a referendum that had been intended by the opposition to remove him from office. He was re-elected in 2006, and his left-wing policies continued to arouse US hostility. In 2010, the opposition made gains in parliamentary elections. In 2011–12, Hugo Chavez made several visits to Cuba for treatment for cancer.

With oil accounting for about 90% of its exports, Venezuela has an "upper-middle-income" economy. Other exports include bauxite and aluminum, iron ore, and farm products. Beef cattle, dairy cattle, and poultry are raised. Crops include bananas, cassava, citrus fruits, coffee, and rice. The main industry is petroleum refining. Cement, steel, and textiles are also produced.

AREA 352,143 sq mi [912,050 sq km] **POPULATION** 27,636,000
CAPITAL Caracas **GOVERNMENT** Federal republic
ETHNIC GROUPS Spanish, Italian, Portuguese, Arab, German, African, indigenous people **LANGUAGES** Spanish (official), indigenous dialects **RELIGIONS** Roman Catholic 96%
CURRENCY Bolívar = 100 céntimos

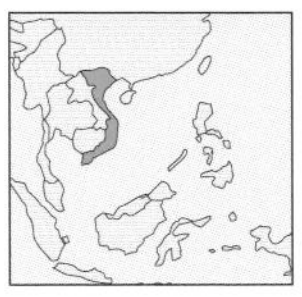

VIETNAM

GEOGRAPHY The Socialist Republic of Vietnam occupies an S-shaped strip of land facing the South China Sea in Southeast Asia. The coastal plains include two densely populated, fertile delta regions: the Red (Hong) delta facing the Gulf of Tonkin in the north and the Mekong delta in the south.

Vietnam has a tropical climate, though the driest months of January to March are a little cooler than the wet, hot summer months, when monsoon winds blow from the south-west. Typhoons (cyclones or hurricanes) sometimes hit the coast, causing extensive flooding and much damage.

POLITICS & ECONOMY China dominated Vietnam for a thousand years before AD 939, when a Vietnamese state was founded. The French took over the area between the 1850s and 1880s. They ruled Vietnam as part of French Indochina, which also included Cambodia and Laos.

Japan conquered Vietnam during World War II (1939–45). In 1946, war broke out between a nationalist group, called the Vietminh, and the French colonial government. France withdrew in 1954 and Vietnam was divided into a Communist North Vietnam, led by the Vietminh leader, Ho Chi Minh, and a non-Communist South.

A force called the Viet Cong rebeled against South Vietnam's government in 1957 and a war began, which gradually increased in intensity. The United States aided the South, but after it withdrew in 1975, South Vietnam surrendered. In 1976, the united Vietnam became a socialist republic. Vietnamese troops intervened in Cambodia in 1978 to defeat the Khmer Rouge government, but it withdrew its troops in 1989. Following reforms in Vietnam, the US opened an embassy in Hanoi in 1995, and, in 2002, trade relations with the US were normalized. In 2007, Vietnam became a member of the World Trade Organization. By 2011, economic reforms were continuing, but Vietnam resisted calls for increased human rights.

Agriculture remains the main activity and rice the main food crop. Vietnam produces chromium, tin, and phosphates.

AREA 128,065 sq mi [331,689 sq km]
POPULATION 90,549,000 **CAPITAL** Hanoi
GOVERNMENT Socialist republic
ETHNIC GROUPS Vietnamese 87%, Chinese, Hmong, Thai, Khmer, Cham, mountain groups **LANGUAGES** Vietnamese (official), English, Chinese **RELIGIONS** Buddhism, Christianity, indigenous beliefs
CURRENCY Dong = 10 hao = 100 xu

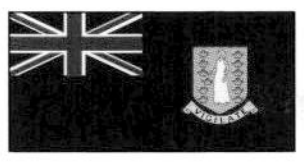

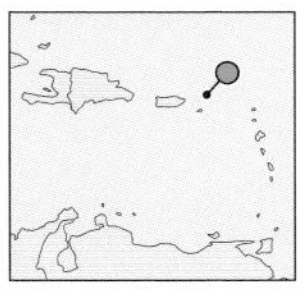

VIRGIN ISLANDS, BRITISH

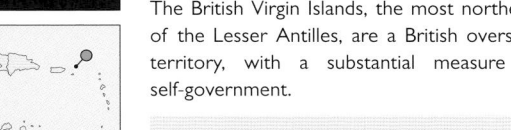

The British Virgin Islands, the most northerly of the Lesser Antilles, are a British overseas territory, with a substantial measure of self-government.

AREA 58 sq mi [151 sq km]
POPULATION 25,000 **CAPITAL** Road Town

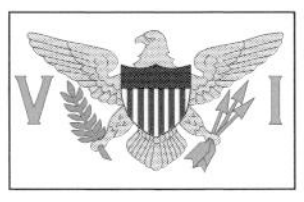

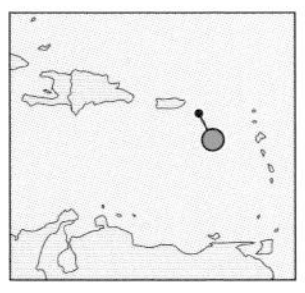

VIRGIN ISLANDS, US

The Virgin Islands of the United States, a group of three islands and 65 small islets, are a self-governing US territory, which was purchased from Denmark in 1917. Its residents are US citizens and they elect a non-voting delegate to the US House of Representatives.

AREA 134 sq mi [347 sq km]
POPULATION 110,000 **CAPITAL** Charlotte Amalie

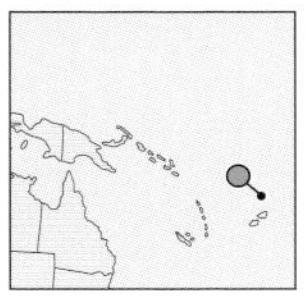

WALLIS AND FUTUNA

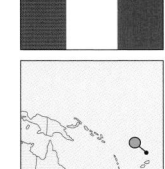

Wallis and Futuna, in the south Pacific Ocean, is the smallest and the poorest of France's overseas territories. French aid remains vital to an economy based on subsistence agriculture.

AREA 77 sq mi [200 sq km]
POPULATION 15,000 **CAPITAL** Mata-Utu

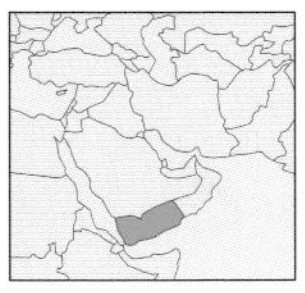

YEMEN

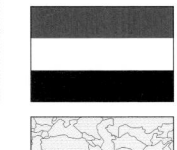

GEOGRAPHY The Republic of Yemen faces the Red Sea and the Gulf of Aden in the southwestern corner of the Arabian peninsula. Behind the narrow coastal plain along the Red Sea, the land rises to a mountain region called High Yemen. The climate ranges from hot and often humid conditions on the coast to the cooler highlands. Most of the country is arid. The south coasts are particularly hot and humid.

POLITICS & ECONOMY After World War I, northern Yemen, which had been ruled by Turkey, began to evolve into a separate state from the south, where Britain was in control. Britain withdrew in 1967 and a left-wing government took power in the south. In North Yemen, the monarchy was abolished in 1962 and the country became a republic.

Clashes occurred between the traditionalist Yemen Arab Republic in the north and the formerly British Marxist People's Democratic Republic of Yemen, but, in 1990, the two Yemens merged to form a single country. Further conflict occurred in 1994, when southern secessionists were defeated. However, in the 2000s, the government faced conflict with Shi'ite northern rebels, called Houthis, al Qaida supporters, and southern separatists. In 2011, protesters in the cities called on President Ali Abdullah Saleh to resign. He pledged not to run at the next election and to introduce constitutional reforms, including the introduction of a parliamentary system, but the violent protests continued. In 2012, Saleh left the country and the vice-president, Abdrabbuh Mansour Hadi, became president.

Yemen is a developing country and agriculture employs about half of the people. Sheep are reared and such crops as barley, fruits, wheat, and vegetables are grown in highland valleys and around oases. Cash crops include coffee and cotton. Since the 1980s, petroleum extraction has been important in the economy. Manufactures include handicrafts, leather goods, and textiles. Remittances from Yemenis abroad are a major source of revenue.

AREA 203,848 sq mi [527,968 sq km] **POPULATION** 24,133,000
CAPITAL Sana' **GOVERNMENT** Multiparty republic
ETHNIC GROUPS Predominantly Arab **LANGUAGES** Arabic (official)
RELIGIONS Islam **CURRENCY** Yemeni rial = 100 fils

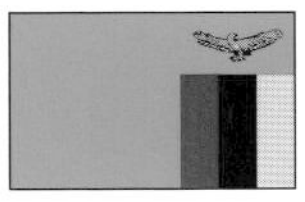

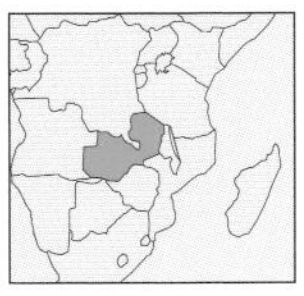

ZAMBIA

GEOGRAPHY The Republic of Zambia is a landlocked country in southern Africa. Zambia lies on the plateau that makes up most of southern Africa. Much of the land is between 2,950 ft and 4,920 ft [900 m to 1,500 m] above sea level. The Muchinga Mountains in the northeast rise above this flat land. Lakes include Bangweulu, which is entirely within Zambia, together with parts of lakes Mweru and Tanganyika in the north. Zambia lies in the tropics, but temperatures are moderated by the altitude.

POLITICS & ECONOMY European contact with Zambia began in the 19th century, when the explorer David Livingstone crossed the River Zambezi. In the 1890s, the British South Africa Company, set up by Cecil Rhodes (1853–1902), the British financier and statesman, made treaties with local chiefs and gradually took over the area. In 1911, the Company named the area Northern Rhodesia. In 1924, Britain took over the government of the country.

In 1953, Britain formed a federation of Northern Rhodesia, Southern Rhodesia (now Zimbabwe), and Nyasaland (now Malawi). Because of African opposition, the federation was dissolved in 1963 and Northern Rhodesia became independent as Zambia in 1964. Kenneth Kaunda became president and one-party rule was introduced in 1972. Under a new constitution, Frederick Chiluba was elected president in 1996. He stood down in 2001 and Levy Mwanawasa became president. In 2011, Michael Sata was elected president, defeating the incumbent Rupiah Banda.

Copper, the main resource, accounts for about 64% of the country's exports. Zambia also produces cobalt, lead, zinc, and gemstones. Agriculture employs about 60% of the people, as compared with less than 4% in industry and mining. Food crops include cassava, fruits and vegetables, maize, millet, and sorghum. Cash crops include coffee, sugarcane, and tobacco.

AREA 290,586 sq mi [752,618 sq km]
POPULATION 13,881,000 **CAPITAL** Lusaka
GOVERNMENT Multiparty republic **ETHNIC GROUPS** Native African (Bemba, Tonga, Maravi/Nyanja) **LANGUAGES** English (official), Bemba, Kaonda, Nyanja, and about 70 others **RELIGIONS** Christianity 70%, Islam, Hinduism **CURRENCY** Zambian kwacha = 100 ngwee

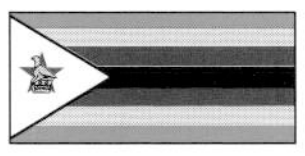

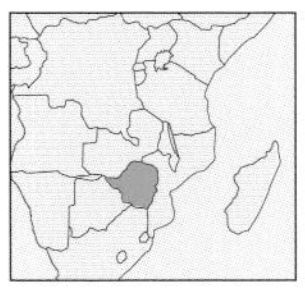

ZIMBABWE

GEOGRAPHY The Republic of Zimbabwe is a landlocked country in southern Africa. Most of the country lies on a high plateau between the Zambezi and Limpopo rivers, ranging from 2,950 ft to 4,920 ft [900 m to 1,500 m] above sea level. From October to March, the weather is hot and wet, but in the winter, daily temperatures can vary greatly.

POLITICS & ECONOMY The Shona people became dominant in the region about 1,000 years ago. The British South Africa Company, under the statesman Cecil Rhodes (1853–1902), occupied the area in the 1890s, after obtaining mineral rights from local chiefs. The area was named Rhodesia and later Southern Rhodesia. It became a self-governing British colony in 1923. Between 1953 and 1963, Southern and Northern Rhodesia (now Zambia) were joined to Nyasaland (Malawi) in the Central African Federation.

In 1965, the European government of Southern Rhodesia (then called Rhodesia) declared their country independent, but Britain refused to accept this. Finally, after a civil war, the country became legally independent in 1980, though rivalries between the Shona and Ndebele people threatened stability. Order was restored when the Shona prime minister, Robert Mugabe, brought his Ndebele rivals into his government. In 1987, Mugabe became the country's executive president, and in 1991 the government renounced its Marxist ideology. Mugabe was re-elected president in 1990 and 1996.

From the late 1990s, Mugabe's government seized white-owned farms and landless "war veterans" began to occupy them. In 2002, Mugabe was re-elected amid accusations of electoral irregularities. In elections in 2008, Mugabe's party was defeated and Mugabe lost to Morgan Tsvangirai in the presidential election. A presidential run-off was ordered, but intimidation of opposition supporters led Tsvangirai to withdraw. In September 2008, a power-sharing agreement was signed and a power-sharing government was set up, with Mugabe as president and Tsvangirai as prime minister. But relations between them proved difficult.

In the 2000s, the economy collapsed. Hyperinflation occurred and many people starved, while the breakdown of public services led to a cholera epidemic. Zimbabwe has valuable mineral reserves and minerals are important exports. Agriculture employs 56% of the people. Maize is the main food crop. Cash crops include cotton, sugar, and tobacco. Cattle ranching is also important.

AREA 150,871 sq mi [390,757 sq km]
POPULATION 12,084,000 **CAPITAL** Harare
GOVERNMENT Multiparty republic **ETHNIC GROUPS** Shona 82%, Ndebele 14%, other African groups 2%, mixed and Asian 1%
LANGUAGES English (official), Shona, Ndebele
RELIGIONS Christianity, traditional beliefs
CURRENCY Zimbabwean new dollar = 100 cents [suspended in 2009]

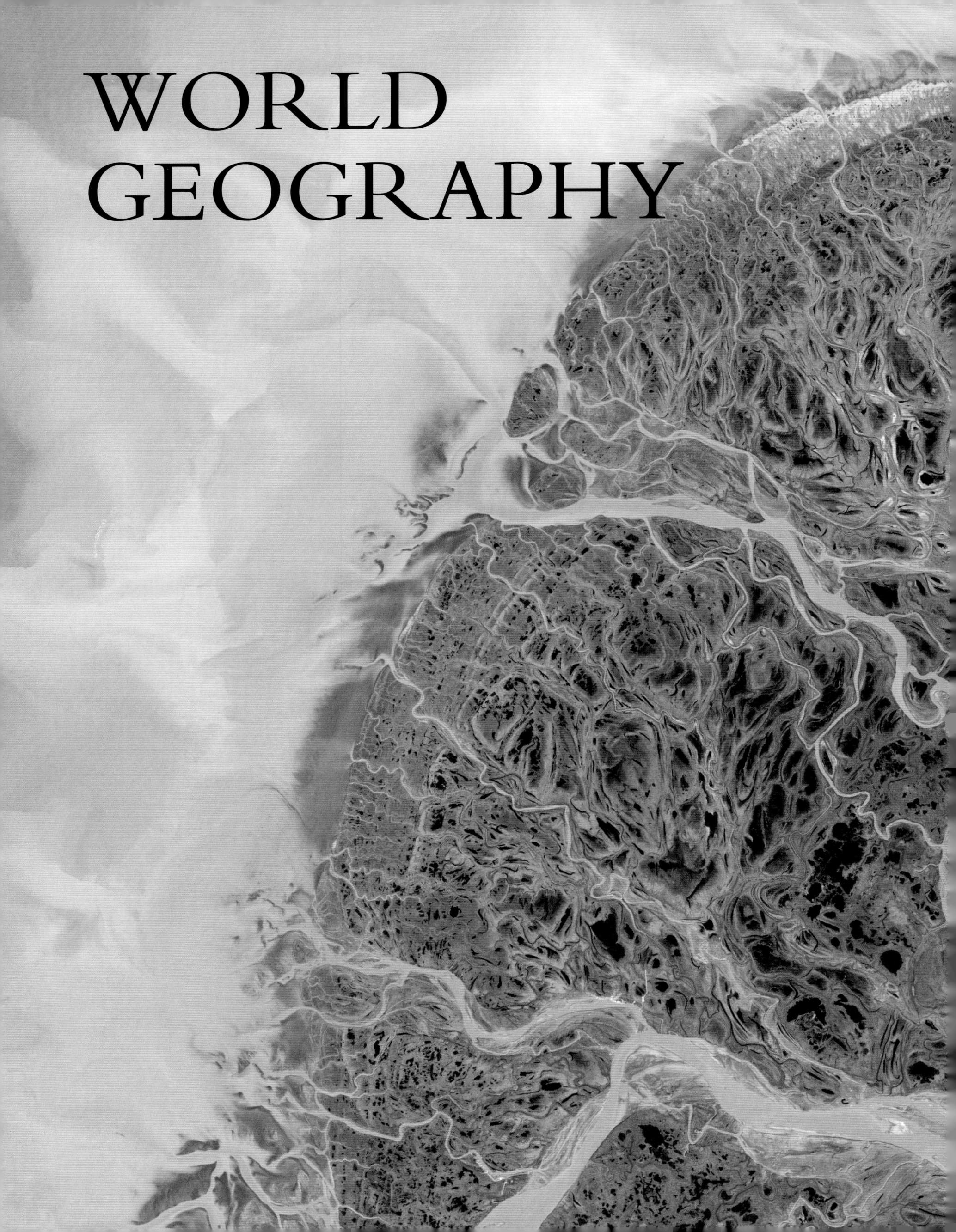

WORLD
GEOGRAPHY

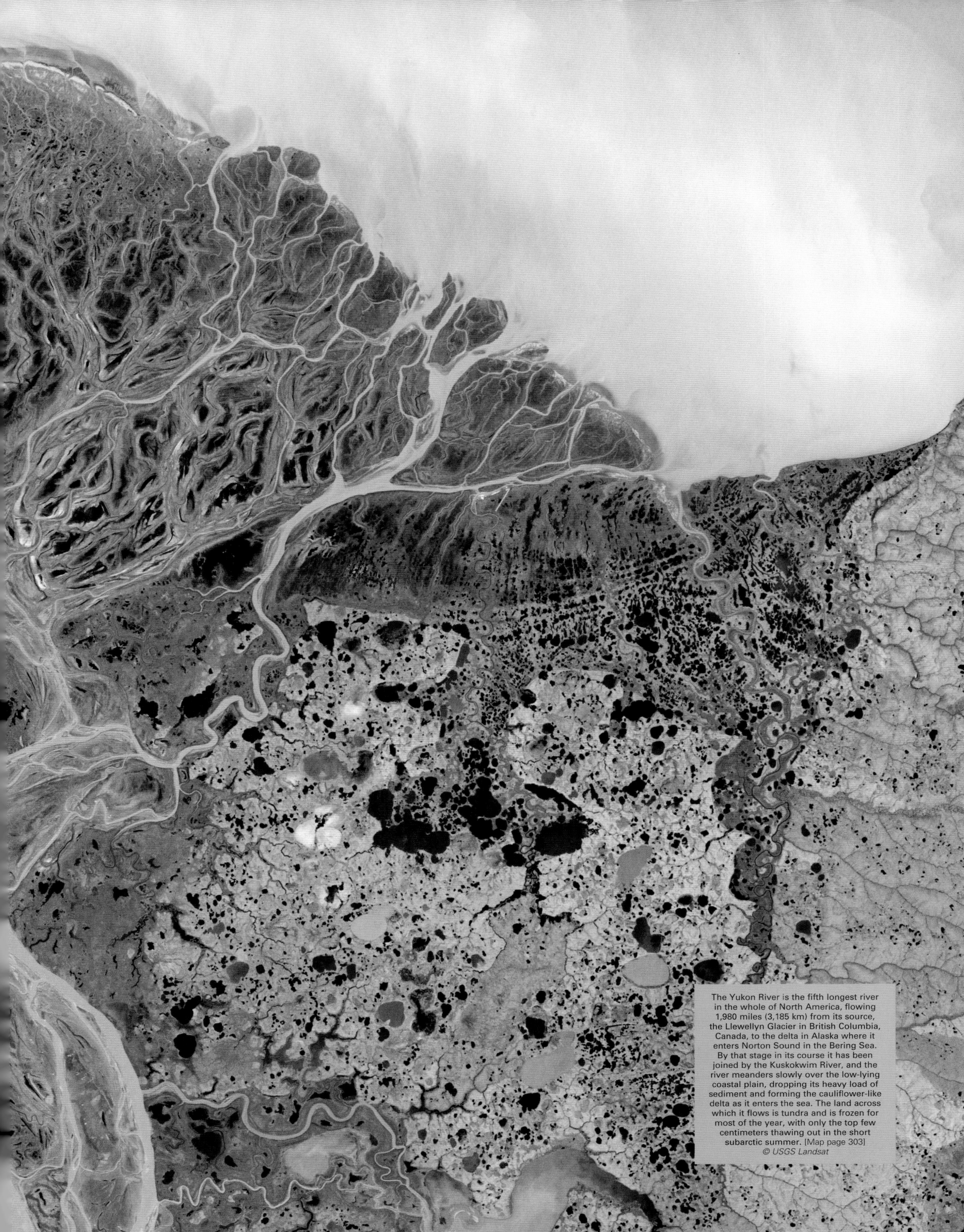

The Yukon River is the fifth longest river in the whole of North America, flowing 1,980 miles (3,185 km) from its source, the Llewellyn Glacier in British Columbia, Canada, to the delta in Alaska where it enters Norton Sound in the Bering Sea. By that stage in its course it has been joined by the Kuskokwim River, and the river meanders slowly over the low-lying coastal plain, dropping its heavy load of sediment and forming the cauliflower-like delta as it enters the sea. The land across which it flows is tundra and is frozen for most of the year, with only the top few centimeters thawing out in the short subarctic summer. [Map page 303]
© USGS Landsat

For more information:
70 Orbits of the planets
Planetary data

About 13.7 billion years ago, time and space began with the most colossal explosion in cosmic history: the so-called Big Bang that is believed to have initiated the Universe. According to current theory, in the first millionth of a second of its existence it expanded from a dimensionless point of infinite mass and density into a fireball about the size of our present Solar System – and it has been expanding ever since.

It took about 300,000 years for the primal fireball to cool enough for atoms to form. They were mostly hydrogen which is still the most abundant material in the Universe. The radiation from this era still pervades the Universe, though its subsequent expansion means that we see it at about 3° above

absolute zero instead of its original 3,000°C. Observations of this faint background glow reveal slight fluctuations. It is these which appear to have become, over the next billion years or so, the large-scale structures in the present Universe. As well as the matter which we can see, there is evidence of a much greater quantity of dark matter whose nature remains unknown. Within knots of this dark matter, the first stars and galaxies formed, probably within the first billion years of the life of the Universe. Our own Galaxy was among them.

There were several generations of stars, each feeding on the wreckage of its extinct predecessors as well as the original galactic gas swirls. With each new generation, pro-

gressively larger atoms were forged in stellar furnaces, and the Galaxy's range of elements, once restricted to hydrogen and helium, grew larger. About 9 billion years after the Big Bang, a star formed on the outskirts of our Galaxy with enough matter left over to create a retinue of planets. Nearly 5 billion years after that, human beings evolved.

The Sun is one of more than 100 billion stars in the Home Galaxy alone. Our Galaxy, in turn, forms part of a local group consisting of approximately 30 similar structures, mostly small "dwarf" galaxies but a few large ones, and one – the Andromeda Galaxy – larger than our own. There are at least 100 billion galaxies in the Universe, many of which are members of huge galaxy clusters.

LIFE OF A STAR

For most of its existence, a star produces energy by the nuclear fusion of hydrogen into helium at its core. The duration of this hydrogen-burning period – known as the *main sequence* – depends on the star's mass; the greater the mass, the higher the core temperatures and the sooner the star's supply of hydrogen is exhausted. Dim, dwarf stars consume their hydrogen slowly, eking it out over billions of years. The Sun, like other stars of its mass, should spend about 10 billion years on the main sequence; since it was formed less than 5 billion years ago, it still has half its life left.

Once all of a star's core hydrogen has been fused into helium, nuclear activity moves outward into layers of unconsumed hydrogen. For a time, energy production sharply increases: the star grows hotter and expands enormously, turning into a so-called red giant. Its energy output will increase a thousandfold, and it will swell to a hundred times its former diameter.

After a few hundred million years, helium in the core will become sufficiently compressed to initiate a new cycle of nuclear fusion: from helium to carbon. The star will contract somewhat, before beginning its last expansion, in the Sun's case engulfing the Earth and perhaps Mars. In this bloated condition, the Sun's outer layers will break off into space, leaving a tiny inner core, mainly of carbon, that shrinks progressively under its own gravity. The white dwarf star thus formed can attain a density more than 10,000 times that of normal matter, with crushing surface gravity to match. Gradually, the nuclear fires will die down, and the Sun will reach its terminal stage: a black dwarf, emitting insignificant amounts of energy.

Black holes
However, stars more massive than the Sun may undergo a different transformation. The additional mass allows gravitational collapse to continue indefinitely: eventually, all the star's remaining matter shrinks to a point, and its density approaches infinity – a state that will not permit even subatomic structures to survive.

The star has become a *black hole*: an anomalous "singularity" in the fabric of space and time. Although vast coruscations of radiation will be emitted by any matter falling into its grasp, the singularity itself has an escape velocity that exceeds the speed of light, and nothing can ever be released from it. Within the boundaries of the black hole, the laws of physics are suspended.

GALACTIC STRUCTURES

Many of the Universe's 100 billion galaxies show clear structural patterns, originally classified by the American astronomer Edwin Hubble in 1925. Spiral galaxies like our own have a central, almost spherical bulge and a surrounding disk composed of spiral arms. Barred spirals have a central bar of stars across the nucleus, with spiral arms trailing from the ends of the bar. Elliptical galaxies have a more uniform appearance, ranging from a flattened disk to a near sphere.

▲ M51, the Whirlpool Nebula, comprises the large spiral galaxy NGC 5194 and its smaller, barred companion NGC 5195. M51 was the first astronomical object in which a spiral structure was identified, in 1845. Although smaller and less massive than our own Galaxy, M51 is much brighter, due to recent star formation.

Most galaxies, however, have no obvious structure at all. Galaxies also vary enormously in size, from dwarf galaxies only 2,000 light-years across to great assemblies of stars 80 or more times larger.

THE HOME GALAXY

The Sun and its planets are located in one of the spiral arms of the Galaxy, about 26,000 light-years from the galactic center and orbiting around it in a period of about 220 million years. The center is invisible from the Earth, masked by vast, light-absorbing clouds of interstellar dust.

The Galaxy is probably around 12 billion years old and, like other spiral galaxies, has three distinct regions. The central bulge is about 30,000 light-years in diameter. The disk in which the Sun is located is not much more than 1,000 light-years thick, but approximately 100,000 light-years from end to end. Around the Galaxy is the halo, a spherical zone 300,000 light-years across, studded with globular star clusters and sprinkled with individual suns.

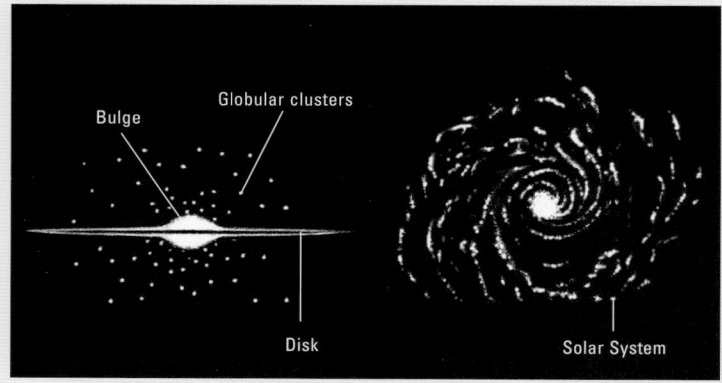

THE END OF THE UNIVERSE

The likely fate of the Universe is disputed. According to one theory (*top of diagram, below*), the expansion begun at the time of the Big Bang will continue "indefinitely," with aging galaxies moving further and further apart in an immense, dark graveyard.

Alternatively, gravity may overcome the expansion (*bottom of diagram*). Galaxies will fall back together until

everything is again concentrated at a single point, followed by a new Big Bang and a new expansion, in an endlessly repeated cycle.

The first theory is supported by the amount of visible matter in the Universe; the second theory assumes that there is enough dark material in the Universe to bring about the gravitational collapse.

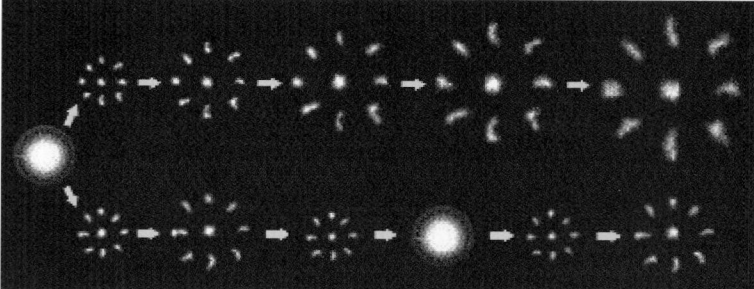

THE NEAREST STARS

The 22 nearest stars, excluding the Sun, with their distance from Earth in light-years*

Proxima Centauri	4.2	UV Ceti A	8.7	61 Cygni A	11.4
Alpha Centauri A	4.4	UV Ceti B	8.7	Procyon A	11.4
Alpha Centauri B	4.4	Ross 154	9.7	Procyon B	11.4
Barnard's Star	5.9	Ross 248	10.3	61 Cygni B	11.4
Wolf 359	7.8	Epsilon Eridani	10.5	HD 173740	11.5
Lalande 21185	8.3	HD 217987	10.7	HD 173739	11.7
Sirius A	8.6	Ross 128	10.9	* A light-year is about 5,900	
Sirius B	8.6	L789-6	11.2	billion miles [9,500 billion km]	

Many of the nearest stars, like Alpha Centauri A and B, are double stars, orbiting about their common center of gravity and to all intents and purposes equidistant from Earth. Many of them are dim objects, with no name other than the designation given to them by the astronomers who first investigated them.

However, they include Sirius, the brightest star in the sky, and Procyon, the seventh brightest. Both are larger than the Sun; of the nearest stars, only Epsilon Eridani is similar in size and luminosity. Most of the other bright stars in the sky are within 500 light-years of the Sun – a small fraction of the diameter of our Galaxy.

STAR CHARTS

NORTHERN HEMISPHERE SKY

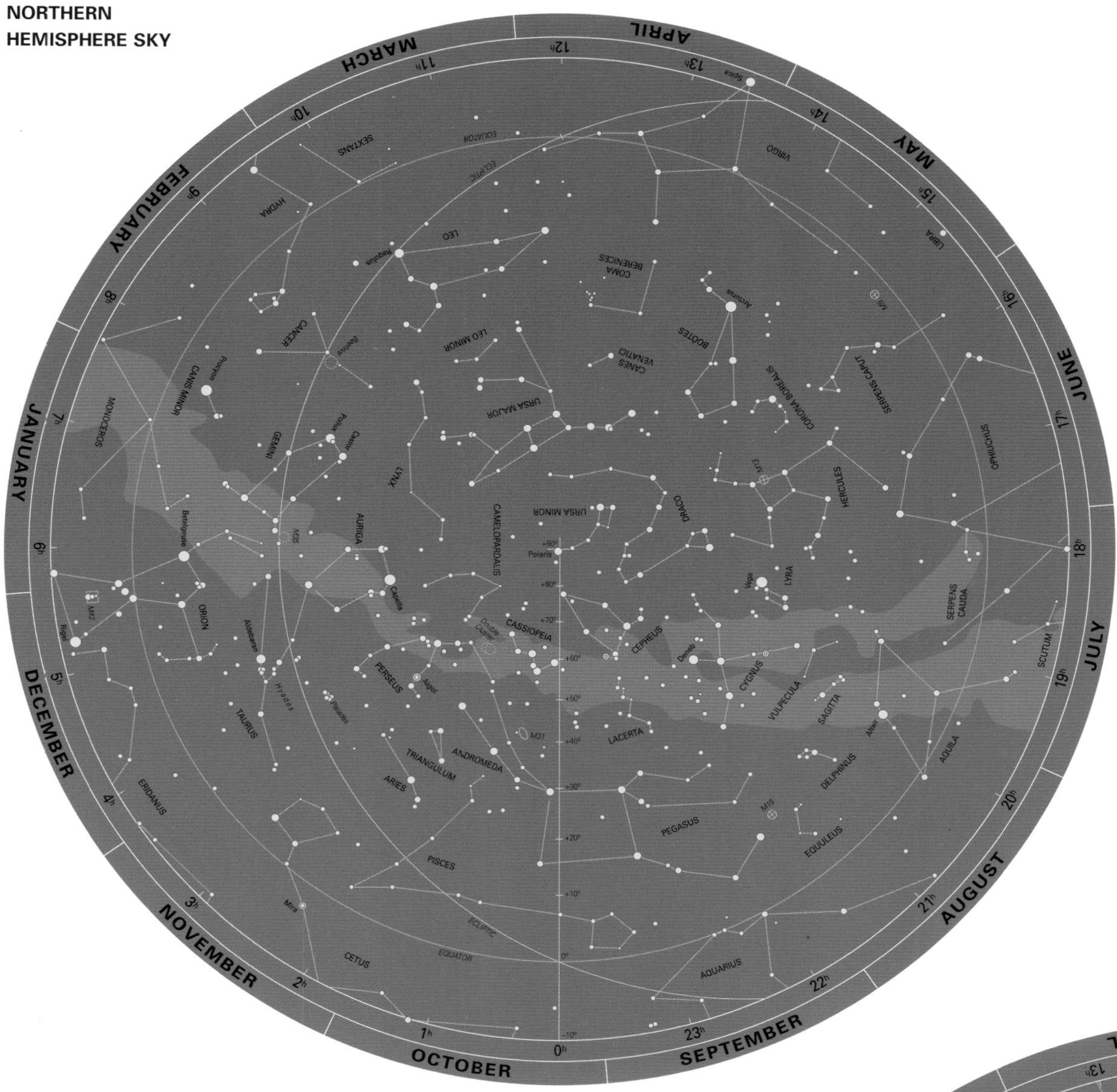

THE CONSTELLATIONS
The constellations and their English names

Andromeda	Andromeda	Lacerta	Lizard
Antlia	Air Pump	Leo	Lion
Apus	Bird of Paradise	Leo Minor	Little Lion
Aquarius	Water Carrier	Lepus	Hare
Aquila	Eagle	Libra	Scales
Ara	Altar	Lupus	Wolf
Aries	Ram	Lynx	Lynx
Auriga	Charioteer	Lyra	Lyre
Boötes	Herdsman	Mensa	Table Mountain
Caelum	Chisel	Microscopium	Microscope
Camelopardalis	Giraffe	Monoceros	Unicorn
Cancer	Crab	Musca	Fly
Canes Venatici	Hunting Dogs	Norma	Level
Canis Major	Great Dog	Octans	Octant
Canis Minor	Little Dog	Ophiuchus	Serpent Bearer
Capricornus	Sea Goat	Orion	Orion
Carina	Ship's Keel	Pavo	Peacock
Cassiopeia	Cassiopeia	Pegasus	Winged Horse
Centaurus	Centaur	Perseus	Perseus
Cepheus	Cepheus	Phoenix	Phoenix
Cetus	Whale	Pictor	Easel
Chamaeleon	Chamaeleon	Pisces	Fishes
Circinus	Compasses	Piscis Austrinus	Southern Fish
Columba	Dove	Puppis	Ship's Stern
Coma Berenices	Berenice's Hair	Pyxis	Mariner's Compass
Corona Australis	Southern Crown	Reticulum	Net
Corona Borealis	Northern Crown	Sagitta	Arrow
Corvus	Crow	Sagittarius	Archer
Crater	Cup	Scorpius	Scorpion
Crux	Southern Cross	Sculptor	Sculptor
Cygnus	Swan	Scutum	Shield
Delphinus	Dolphin	Serpens	Serpent
Dorado	Swordfish	Sextans	Sextant
Draco	Dragon	Taurus	Bull
Equuleus	Little Horse	Telescopium	Telescope
Eridanus	River Eridanus	Triangulum	Triangle
Fornax	Furnace	Triangulum Australe	Southern Triangle
Gemini	Twins	Tucana	Toucan
Grus	Crane	Ursa Major	Great Bear
Hercules	Hercules	Ursa Minor	Little Bear
Horologium	Clock	Vela	Ship's Sails
Hydra	Water Snake	Virgo	Virgin
Hydrus	Sea Serpent	Volans	Flying Fish
Indus	Indian	Vulpecula	Fox

SOUTHERN HEMISPHERE SKY

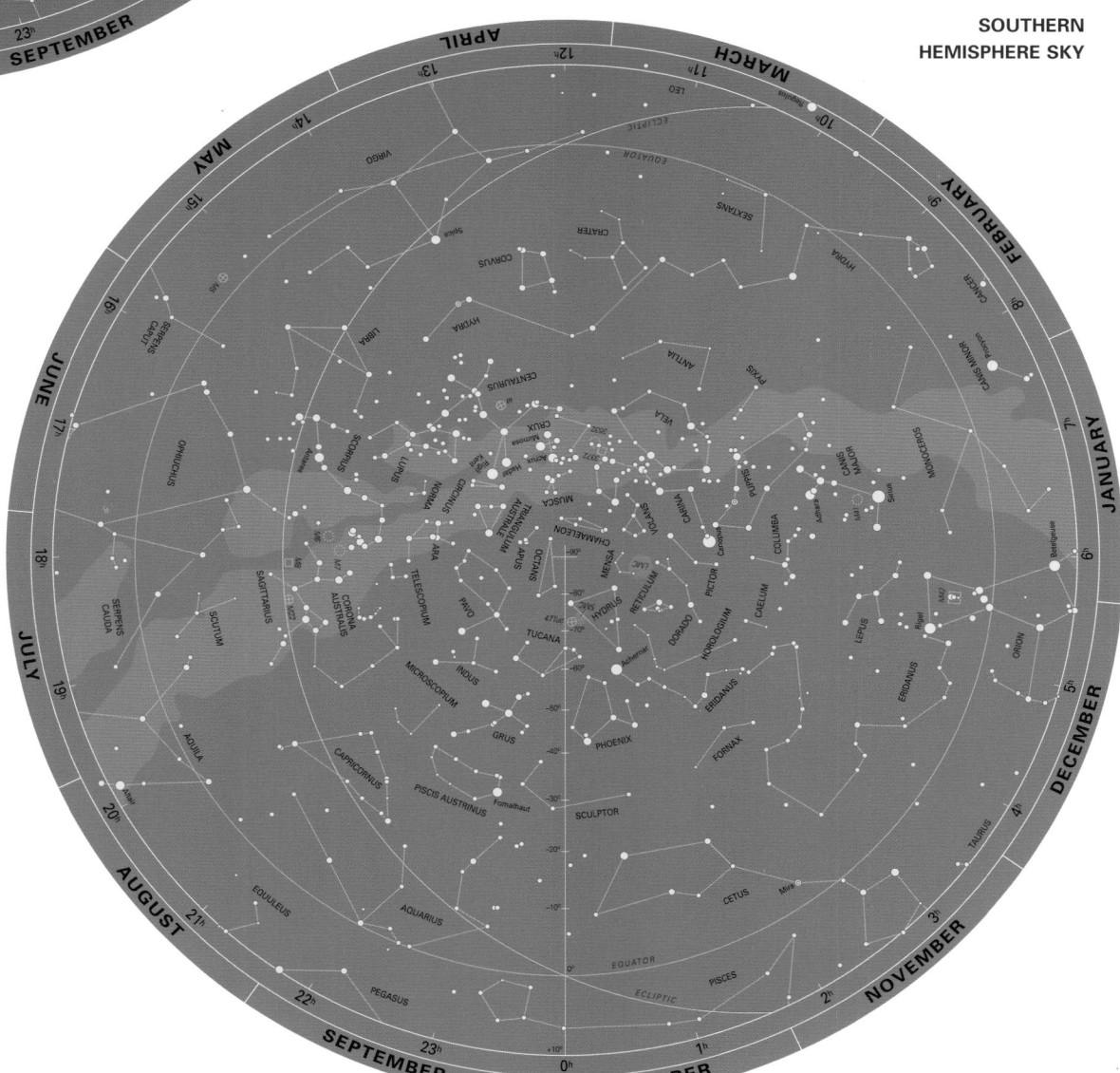

The charts on this page show the entire heavens divided into northern and southern hemispheres, with 10° of overlap between them around the perimeter of each one. However, the view from any particular location on Earth will be different, and will change both hourly as the Earth turns, and throughout the year as the Earth goes around the Sun.

The Sun's annual path through the heavens is known as the "ecliptic," and is shown here by an orange line. When the Sun is in the sky its light drowns out our view of the stars, so only that part of the heavens opposite the Sun is visible at a particular time. The sky's equivalent of longitude is known as "right ascension." As the stars appear to rotate around the Earth once every 24 hours, right ascension is measured eastward in hours and minutes, and is marked around the edge of the maps. The equivalent of latitude is "declination," measured in degrees north or south of the celestial equator, and shown by the vertical line on each chart.

Using the charts
At any place and time you can see half of the whole sky, assuming a flat horizon. If you were at one of the poles your view would be shown as a circle centered on the middle of the map for the appropriate hemisphere, with the horizon marked by the celestial equator. From all other locations the center of your view (your overhead point) will be at some other point on the map whose location changes with time. The closer you are to Earth's equator, the closer the center will be to the edge of the map and more stars in the opposite hemisphere will be visible.

So first choose the appropriate chart for your hemisphere and hold it with the month at the bottom. At 11 p.m., not allowing for Daylight Saving Time (Summer Time), your overhead point will be at the same declination as your geographical latitude and stars lower on the map will be due south (or north in the southern hemisphere). From latitude 50° in mid August, for example, your overhead point will be close to the star Deneb in the constellation of Cygnus. Stars on the opposite side of the map will be below your northern horizon, while stars below Deneb will be due south.

STAR MAGNITUDES
Apparent visual magnitudes

The magnitude scale of star brightnesses is developed from the system used by the Ancient Greeks in which the brightest stars were first magnitude and the faintest visible to the naked eye were sixth. Today the scale has a mathematical basis and extends, at the brightest end, through to negative magnitudes.

The Milky Way is shown in light blue on these charts.

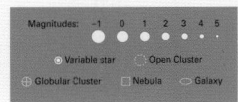

Magnitudes: -1 0 1 2 3 4 5
○ Variable star □ Open Cluster
⊕ Globular Cluster ▢ Nebula ▨ Galaxy

For more information:
68 The Home Galaxy
72 The seasons
    Day and night
73 The Moon

Lying about halfway from the center of one of billions of galaxies that populate the observable Universe, our Solar System contains eight planets and their moons, five dwarf planets, innumerable asteroids, comets and other icy bodies, and a miscellany of dust and gas, all tethered by the immense gravitational field of the Sun, the star whose thermonuclear furnaces provide them all with heat and light.

The Solar System was formed about 5 billion years ago, when a spinning cloud of gas, mostly hydrogen but seeded with other heavier elements, condensed enough to ignite a nuclear reaction and create a star. The Sun still accounts for almost 99.9% of the system's total mass.

By composition as well as distance, the planetary array divides quite neatly in two: an inner system of four small, solid planets, including the Earth, and an outer system, from Jupiter to Neptune, of four much larger planets composed of lighter materials, such as gas, liquid, and ice. Lying mostly between the two groups is a scattering of rocky asteroids, numbering perhaps a million or more. They may be debris left over from the formation of the inner Solar System. In 2006, Pluto was demoted from its former status as a planet and is now regarded as a member of the Kuiper Belt of icy bodies at the fringes of the Solar System.

Much of the early history of science is the story of people trying to make sense of the wandering points of light that were all they knew of the planets. Now, men have stood on the Earth's Moon, space probes have landed on Mars and Venus, and distant landscapes have been mapped with astonishing accuracy, transforming our knowledge of our celestial environment.

In the 1980s, the Voyager space probes skimmed all four major planets of the outer Solar System, bringing new revelations with each close approach. The Magellan (Venus), Galileo (Jupiter) and Cassini–Huygens (Saturn) missions have transformed our knowledge of those planets and the giants' moons, and a host of orbiters and landers have shown us Mars in a new light. A spacecraft is also on its way to visit Pluto.

Diagram not drawn to scale

ORBITS OF THE PLANETS

The diagram above shows the Solar System as it might appear to an observer a few light-hours away in the direction of the constellation Hercules. Seen from such a position, above the plane of the ecliptic, all the planets revolve about the Sun in a counterclockwise direction. The perspective view exaggerates the elliptical form of all the planetary orbits: only Mercury follows a path that deviates noticeably from circularity.

The diagram also shows the main swarm of asteroids between Mars and Jupiter, and the orbit of a comet. Comets reside in a vast spherical halo beyond the Solar System, and are occasionally diverted toward the Sun on highly elliptical orbits which may take many thousands of years to complete. Most, therefore, still await discovery, though there are a number of shorter-period comets which return regularly, such as Halley's Comet.

PLANETARY DATA

	Mean distance from Sun (million miles)	Mass (Earth = 1)	Period of orbit (Earth days/years)	Period of rotation (Earth days)	Equatorial diameter (miles)	Average density (water = 1)	Surface gravity (Earth = 1)	Number of known satellites*
Sun	–	332,946	–	25.38	865,000	1.41	27.9	–
Mercury	36.0	0.06	87.97d	58.65	3,032	5.43	0.38	0
Venus	67.2	0.82	224.7d	243.02	7,521	5.24	0.91	0
Earth	93.0	1.00	365.3d	1.00	7,926	5.52	1.00	1
Mars	141.6	0.11	687.0d	1.029	4,220	3.94	0.38	2
Jupiter	483.7	317.8	11.86y	0.411	88,848	1.33	2.36	67
Saturn	886.6	95.2	29.45y	0.428	74,900	0.69	0.91	62
Uranus	1,784.0	14.5	84.02y	0.720	31,764	1.27	0.89	27
Neptune	2,795.2	17.2	164.8y	0.673	30,776	1.64	1.13	13

Planetary days are given in sidereal days – that is, with respect to the stars rather than the Sun. The difference is caused by the movement of the planet in its orbit, so the interval between successive noons is slightly different from that between the rising of a particular star. The Earth's own sidereal day is 23h 56m in solar time. The equatorial diameters of most planets differ from their polar diameters as a consequence of their rotation, which is most marked in the case of Jupiter and Saturn, which are very noticeably flattened at the poles. Strictly speaking, the figures for surface gravity apply to the four inner planets only, as the outer planets have no solid surfaces. In their case, the figure is given for an arbitrary point in the atmosphere where the pressure is 1 bar.

* Number of known satellites at mid-2012

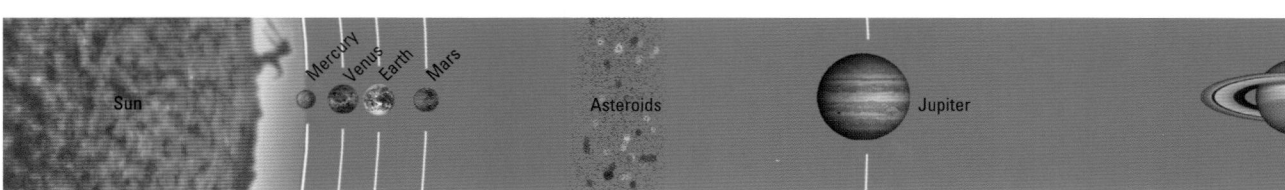

THE PLANETS

Mercury is the closest planet to the Sun and hence the fastest-moving. It is very hot, with a cratered, wrinkled surface very similar to that of Earth's Moon. It is small and has low gravity, so there is no significant atmosphere.

Venus has much the same physical dimensions as Earth. Its dense atmosphere is composed of 97% carbon dioxide resulting in a runaway greenhouse effect that makes the surface, at 890°F, the hottest of all the planets in the Solar System. Radar mapping revealed a terrain consisting of highland regions and vast, rolling plains crossed by volcanic flows and dotted with craters. Discharges from volcanic regions could explain the sulfuric-acid rain detected by spacecraft. Soft-landers last less than an hour in Venus's fierce climate.

Earth seen from space is easily the most beautiful of the inner planets; it is also, and more objectively, the largest, as well as the only known home of life. Living things are the main reason why the Earth is able to retain a substantial proportion of reactive oxygen in its atmosphere; the oxygen in turn supports the life that constantly regenerates it. The Earth's natural satellite, the Moon, is believed to have been created when an asteroid struck our planet in its infancy.

Mars, smaller and cooler than the Earth, is nevertheless the most likely planet other than Earth where life may have formed. The planet was until recently (in astronomical terms) a geologically active world with water on its surface: rivers, lakes, and even an ocean. Liquid water may well exist today, but trapped beneath its dusty, boulder-strewn surface. The Martian landscape features huge extinct volcanoes, a giant canyon system, craters, and sand dunes. Its thin atmosphere is mostly carbon dioxide, and its polar caps are of frozen carbon dioxide and water ice. It has two tiny moons, probably captured asteroids.

Jupiter has about three times the mass of all the other planets combined. The planet is mostly gas, under intense pressure in the lower atmosphere above a core of fiercely compressed hydrogen and helium. The upper layers form strikingly colored rotating belts, the outward sign of the intense storms created by Jupiter's rapid rotation. The Great Red Spot is a storm feature that has persisted for at least 170 years. Jupiter has at least 67 moons. Most are very small, but the four largest – Io, Europa, Ganymede, and Callisto – are fascinating worlds in their own right. Io is the most volcanically active world known, and Europa possesses an ocean deep below its icy surface. The planet also has a system of rings, though nowhere near as prominent as Saturn's.

Saturn is structurally similar to Jupiter, rotating fast enough to produce an obvious bulge at its equator. It is composed of 89% hydrogen and 11% helium, and has wind velocities in the outer atmosphere of 1,600 ft/sec. Ever since the invention of the telescope, Saturn's rings have been the feature that has most attracted observers. The rings consist of thousands of individual ringlets, composed of icy particles ranging in size from 30 feet down to microscopic. Titan, the largest of Saturn's 62 known moons, has a dense atmosphere.

Uranus was unknown to the ancients. Although it is faintly visible to the naked eye, it was not established as a planet until 1781. In its interior is probably a rocky core surrounded by frozen methane, water, and ammonia; the atmosphere is of hydrogen, helium, and some methane, which gives the planet its greenish-blue color. There is a system of thin, dark rings and a retinue of 27 moons, all but five of which are small.

Neptune is always more than 2.5 billion miles from Earth, and despite its diameter of over 31,000 miles, it can only be seen by telescope. Its discovery in 1846 was the result of mathematical predictions by astronomers seeking to explain irregularities in the orbit of Uranus. Like Uranus, it has a ring system; recent observations have revealed a total of 13 moons.

In 2006, following an increasing number of discoveries of objects orbiting the Sun of similar size to Pluto but at a greater distance, the International Astronomical Union issued for the first time a definition of a planet. A planet is defined as "a body orbiting the Sun, which is essentially round as a consequence of its gravity, and which does not share its orbital neighborhood with similar bodies." On this definition, Pluto is no longer classified as a planet, but is instead a member of a new category of "dwarf planet," which relaxes the last criterion but excludes bodies in orbit around another one.

Diagrams not drawn to scale

Mean distance from the Sun in millions of miles

Mercury	**36.0** Mercury
Venus	**67.2** Venus
Earth	**93.0** Earth
Mars	**141.6** Mars
Jupiter	**483.7** Jupiter
Saturn	**886.6** Saturn
Uranus	**1,784.0** Uranus
Neptune	**2,795.2** Neptune

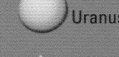 Uranus

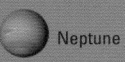 Neptune

For more information:

70 Orbits of the planets

77 Ocean currents

78 Circulation of the air

80 Climate

The basic units of time measurement are the day and the year. The day is one rotation of the Earth on its axis. Our present calendar is based on the solar year of 365.24 days, the time taken by the Earth to orbit the Sun. Calendars based on the movements of the Sun and Moon have been used since ancient times. The length of the year, reckoned by the Julian Calendar introduced by Julius Caesar, was about 11 minutes too long. The cumulative error was rectified in 1582 by the Gregorian Calendar, when Pope Gregory XIII decreed that the day following October 4 was October 15, and that century years did not count as leap years unless they were divisible by 400. England finally adopted the reformed calendar in 1752, when it was 11 days behind the European mainland.

The rotation of the Earth on its axis causes day and night. The Earth rotates through 360° every 24 hours, and the world is divided into 24 time zones centered on lines of longitude at 15° intervals.

The tilt of the Earth's axis, which is also called the "obliquity of the ecliptic," accounts for the seasons which are so familiar in the middle latitudes. However, geological evidence shows that, over long periods of time, climates change, and the advances and retreats of the ice during the Pleistocene Ice Age may have been caused by regular variations in the Earth's tilt, its orbit around the Sun, and changes in the season when it is closest to the Sun (perihelion).

THE SEASONS

Seasons occur because the Earth's axis is tilted at an angle of approximately 23½°. When the northern hemisphere is tilted to a maximum extent toward the Sun, on June 21, the Sun is overhead at the Tropic of Cancer (latitude 23½° North). This is midsummer, or the summer solstice, in the northern hemisphere.

On September 22 or 23, the Sun is overhead at the equator, and day and night are of equal length throughout the world. This is the autumnal equinox in the northern hemisphere.

On December 21 or 22, the Sun is overhead at the Tropic of Capricorn (23½° South), the winter solstice in the northern hemisphere. The overhead Sun then tracks north until, on March 21, it is overhead at the equator. This is the spring (vernal) equinox in the northern hemisphere.

In the southern hemisphere, the seasons are the reverse of those in the north.

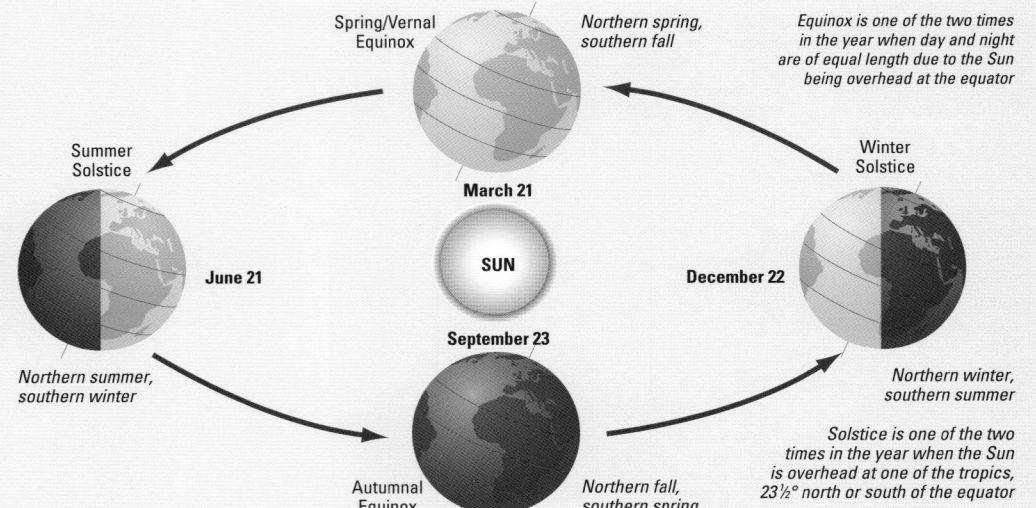

Equinox is one of the two times in the year when day and night are of equal length due to the Sun being overhead at the equator

Solstice is one of the two times in the year when the Sun is overhead at one of the tropics, 23½° north or south of the equator

DAY AND NIGHT

The Sun appears to rise in the east, reach its highest point at noon, and then set in the west, to be followed by night. In reality, it is not the Sun that is moving but the Earth rotating from west to east. The moment when the Sun's upper limb first appears above the horizon is termed sunrise; the moment when the Sun's upper limb disappears below the horizon is sunset.

At the summer solstice in the northern hemisphere (June 21), the Arctic has total daylight and the Antarctic total darkness. The opposite occurs at the winter solstice (December 21 or 22). At the equator, the length of day and night are almost equal all year.

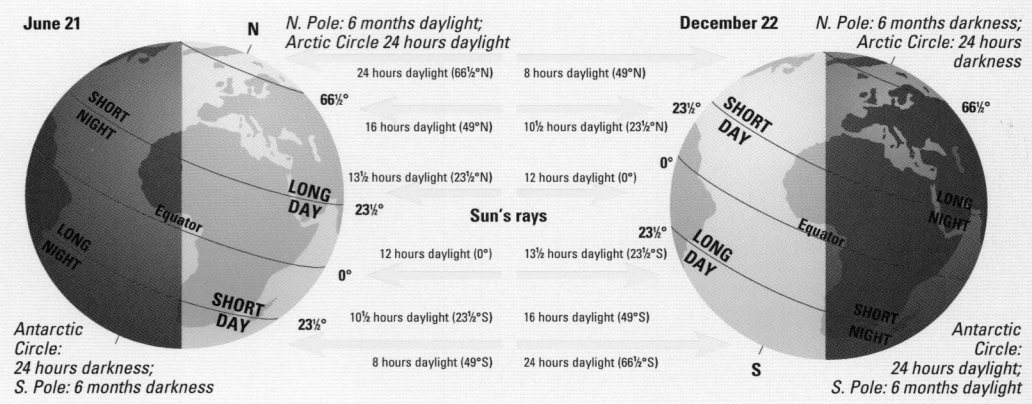

EARTH DATA

Aphelion (maximum distance from Sun):	94,508,166 miles	Length of year:	365 days, 5 hours, 48 minutes, 46 seconds of mean solar time	Polar circumference:	24,860 miles
Perihelion (minimum distance from Sun):	91,403,477 miles			Equatorial diameter:	7,926 miles
		Superficial area:	197,000,000 sq miles	Polar diameter:	7,900 miles
Angle of tilt (obliquity of the ecliptic):	23° 27′ 08″	Land surface:	57,500,000 sq miles (29.2%)	Equatorial radius:	3,963 miles
		Water surface:	139,500,000 sq miles (70.8%)	Polar radius:	3,950 miles
Length of year – solar tropical (equinox to equinox):	365.24 days			Volume of the Earth:	259,880 × 10⁶ cu miles
		Equatorial circumference:	24,901 miles	Mass of the Earth:	5.97 × 10²⁴ kg

SUNRISE AND SUNSET

The term "equinox" comes from the Latin for "equal night." At the spring and autumnal equinoxes, the Sun is vertically overhead at midday at the equator and all places on Earth have 12 hours of darkness and 12 hours of daylight. The graphs of sunrise and sunset show that these occasions occur on March 21 and on September 22 or 23. The graphs also show that, because the Sun remains high in the sky at the equator throughout the year, the length of day and night there remains roughly the same throughout the year, with sunrise around 6 a.m. and sunset around 6 p.m.

The further north or south one travels, the greater the difference between the number of hours of daylight and darkness. For example, the graph (*right*) shows that at latitude 60°N sunrise varies from just after 9 a.m. in midwinter (on December 22 or 23) to about 2.30 a.m. in midsummer (around the summer solstice on June 21). By contrast, the second graph (*far right*) shows that sunset at latitude 60°N occurs at about 2.45 p.m. in midwinter and 9.20 p.m. in midsummer.

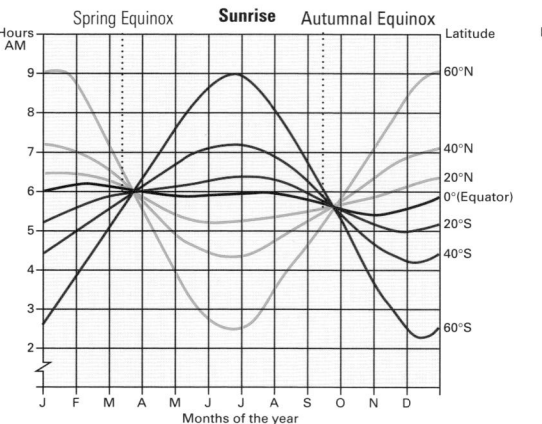

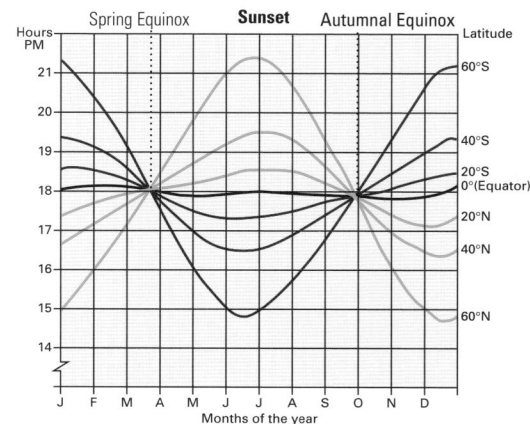

THE MOON

The Moon rotates more slowly than the Earth, taking just over 27 days to make one complete rotation on its axis. This corresponds to the Moon's orbital period around the Earth, and therefore the Moon always presents the same hemisphere toward us; some 41% of the Moon's far side is never visible from the Earth. The interval between one New Moon and the next is 29½ days – this is called a lunation, or lunar month. The Moon shines only by reflected sunlight, and emits no light of its own. During each lunation the Moon displays a complete cycle of phases, caused by the changing angle of illumination from the Sun.

PHASES OF THE MOON

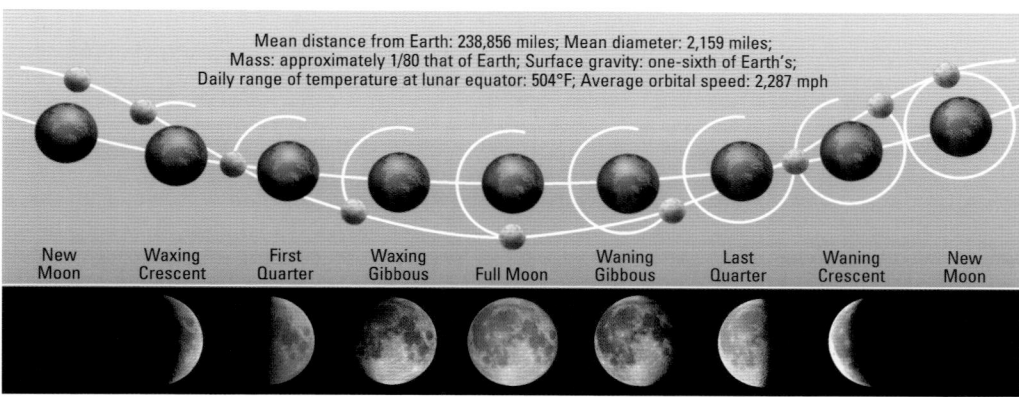

Mean distance from Earth: 238,856 miles; Mean diameter: 2,159 miles; Mass: approximately 1/80 that of Earth; Surface gravity: one-sixth of Earth's; Daily range of temperature at lunar equator: 504°F; Average orbital speed: 2,287 mph

| New Moon | Waxing Crescent | First Quarter | Waxing Gibbous | Full Moon | Waning Gibbous | Last Quarter | Waning Crescent | New Moon |

MOON DATA

Distance from Earth
The Moon orbits at a mean distance of 238,856 miles, at an average speed of 2,287 mph in relation to the Earth.

Size and mass
The average diameter of the Moon is 2,159 miles. It is 400 times smaller than the Sun but is about 400 times closer to the Earth, so we see them as the same size. The Moon has a mass of 7.35×10^{22} kg, with a density 3.344 times that of water.

Visibility
Only 59% of the Moon's surface is visible from the Earth over time. Sunlight reflected from the Moon takes 1.3 seconds to reach the Earth (the Sun itself is around 8½ light-minutes away).

Temperature
With the Sun overhead, the temperature on the lunar equator can reach 243°F [117°C]. At night it can sink to −261°F [−163°C].

ECLIPSES

When the Moon passes between the Sun and the Earth, the Sun becomes partially eclipsed (1). A partial eclipse becomes a total eclipse if the Moon proceeds to cover the Sun completely (2) and the dark central part of the lunar shadow touches the Earth. The broad geographical zone covered by the Moon's outer shadow (P) has only a very small central area (often less than 62 miles wide) that experiences totality. Totality can never last for more than 7½ minutes at maximum, but is usually much briefer than this. Lunar eclipses take place when the Moon moves through the shadow of the Earth, and can be partial or total. Any single location on Earth can experience a maximum of four solar and three lunar eclipses in any single year, while a total solar eclipse occurs an average of once every 360 years for any given location.

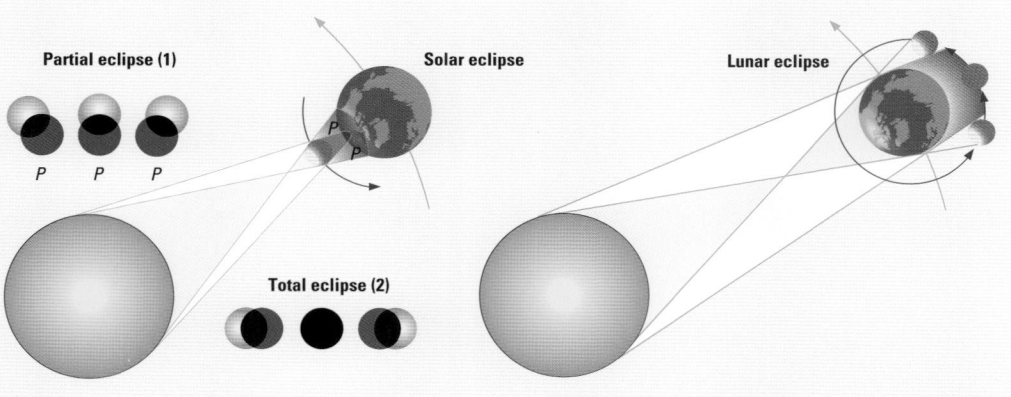

Partial eclipse (1)

Solar eclipse

Lunar eclipse

Total eclipse (2)

TIDES

The daily rise and fall of the ocean's tides are the result of the gravitational pull of the Moon and that of the Sun, though the effect of the latter is not as strong as that of the Moon. This effect is greatest on the hemisphere facing the Moon and causes a tidal "bulge." Spring tides occur when the Sun, Earth, and Moon are aligned; high tides are at their highest, and low tides fall to their lowest. When the Moon and Sun are furthest out of line (near the Moon's First and Last Quarters), neap tides occur, producing the smallest range between high and low tides.

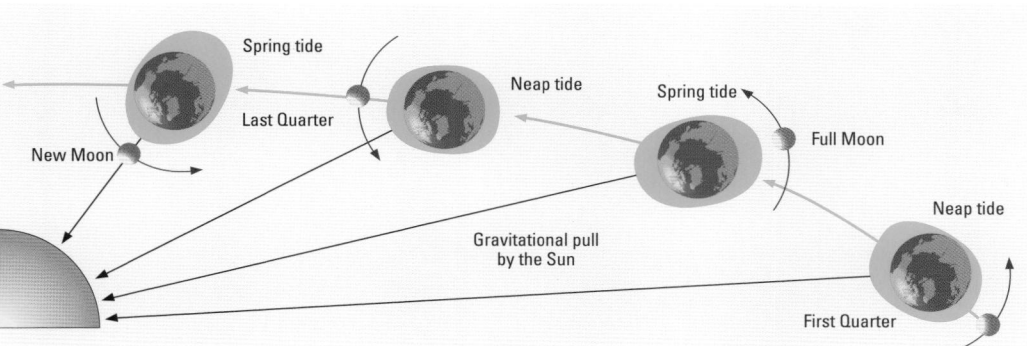

Spring tide

Neap tide

Spring tide

Last Quarter

New Moon

Full Moon

Neap tide

Gravitational pull by the Sun

First Quarter

TIME ZONES

The Earth rotates through 360° in 24 hours, and so moves 15° every hour. The world is divided into 24 standard time zones, each centered on lines of longitude at 15° intervals. At the center of the first zone is the prime meridian, or Greenwich meridian. All places to the west of Greenwich are one hour behind for every 15° of longitude; places to the east are ahead by one hour for every 15°.

International Date Line
When it is 12 noon on the Greenwich meridian, 180° east it is midnight of the same day – while 180° west the day is just beginning. To overcome this, the International Date Line was established, approximately following the 180° meridian. Thus, if you were to travel eastward from Japan (140°E) to Hawai'i (160°W), you would pass from Sunday night into Sunday morning.

10   Hours behind or ahead of UT or Coordinated Universal Time

Zones using UT (GMT)

Zones behind UT (GMT)

International boundaries

Zones ahead of UT (GMT)

Half-hour zones

Time-zone boundaries

International Date Line

Actual solar time when time at Greenwich is 12:00 (noon)

Note: Some of the above time zones are affected by the incidence of Daylight Saving Time in countries where it is adopted.

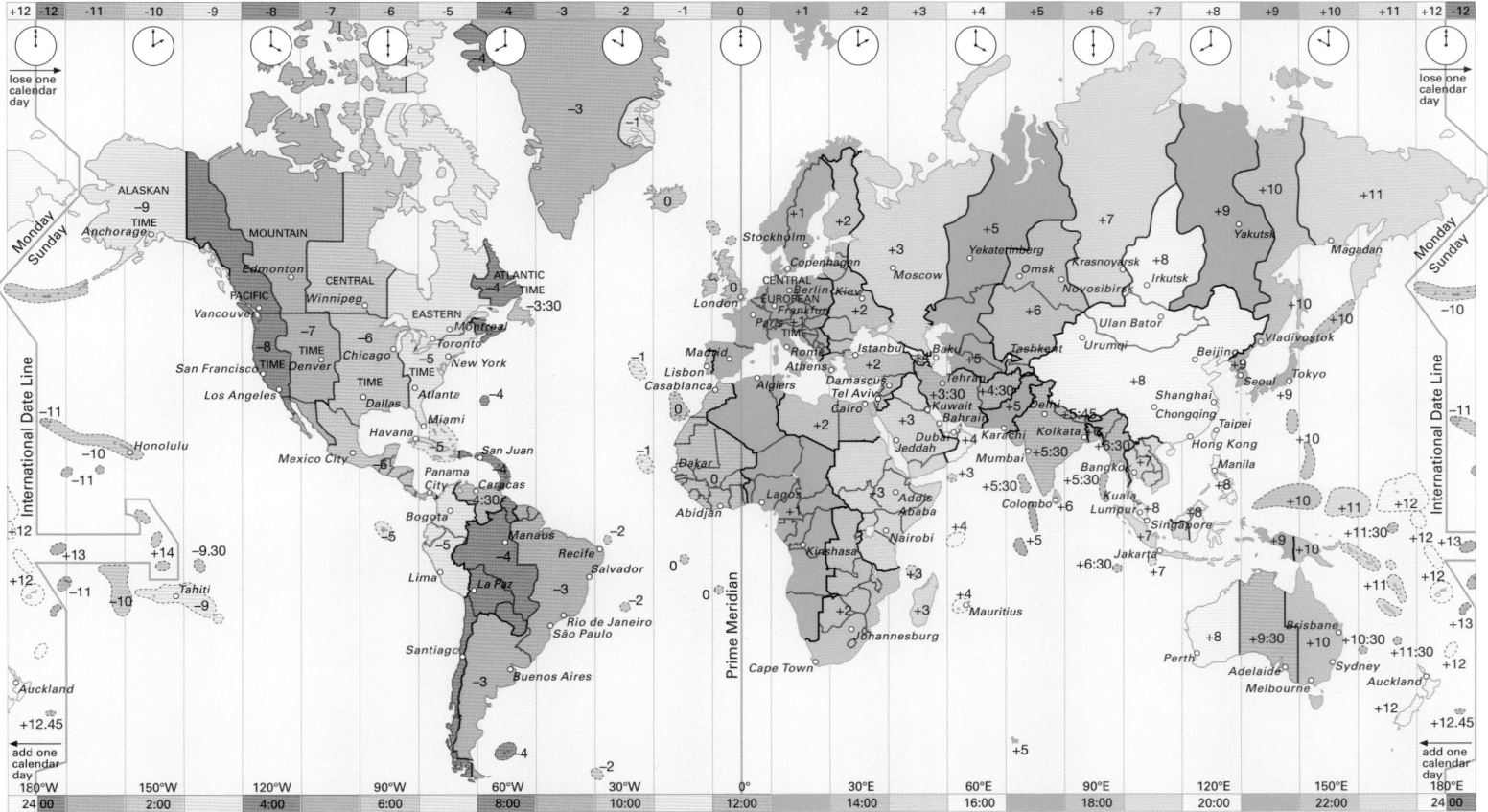

Projection: *Mercator*

COPYRIGHT PHILIP'S

For more information:
98 Minerals

Every year, earthquakes and volcanic eruptions cause much destruction throughout the world. Such phenomena were once thought to be unconnected, but since the late 1960s, scientists have understood that these events are surface manifestations of the tremendous forces operating in the Earth's interior that are slowly but constantly changing the face of our planet.

The Earth is divided into three zones. The crust, a brittle, low-density zone, overlies the dense mantle. Separating the crust from the mantle is a distinct boundary called the Mohorovičić (or Moho) discontinuity. Enclosed by the mantle is the Earth's core, which consists mainly of iron and nickel.

Temperatures inside the Earth range from about 1,600°F in the upper mantle to perhaps 9,000°F in the core. Heat creates convection currents in a semimolten part of the mantle called the asthenosphere. Above the asthenosphere is the lithosphere, a solid layer about 40 miles thick, consisting of the crust and part of the mantle. The lithosphere is divided into rigid plates, moved around by the currents in the asthenosphere, a process named plate tectonics.

The Earth was formed around 4.6 billion years ago. Lighter elements floated toward the surface, where they formed crustal rocks. The oldest rocks so far discovered are about 4 billion years old, while the oldest fossils occur in rocks formed around 3.5 billion years ago. An explosion of life occurred at the start of the Cambrian period, 570 million years ago. The fossil record since the start of the Cambrian has enabled scientists to piece together the story of life on Earth.

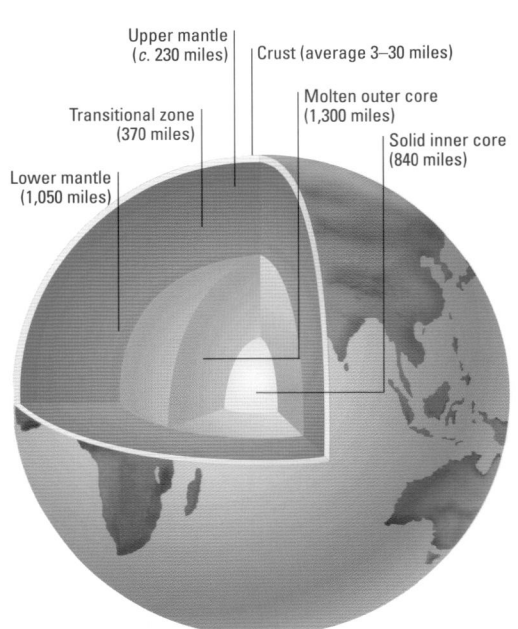

Upper mantle (c. 230 miles) | Crust (average 3–30 miles)
Transitional zone (370 miles)
Molten outer core (1,300 miles)
Lower mantle (1,050 miles)
Solid inner core (840 miles)

CONTINENTAL DRIFT

Trench
Rift
New ocean floor
Zones of slippage

In 1915, Alfred Wegener produced a series of world maps proposing that, around 200 million years ago, the continents had been joined together in a supercontinent that he called Pangaea. This land mass started to break up about 180 million years ago and the parts drifted to their present positions. In the 1950s and 1960s, evidence from studies of the ocean floor suggested that the low-density continents rest on huge slow-moving plates. The arrows on the present-day world map (*below*) show that the continents are still on the move.

180 million years ago

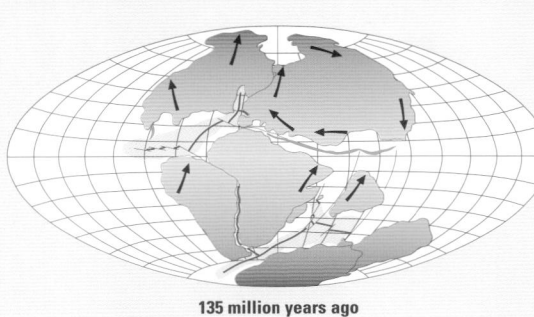

135 million years ago

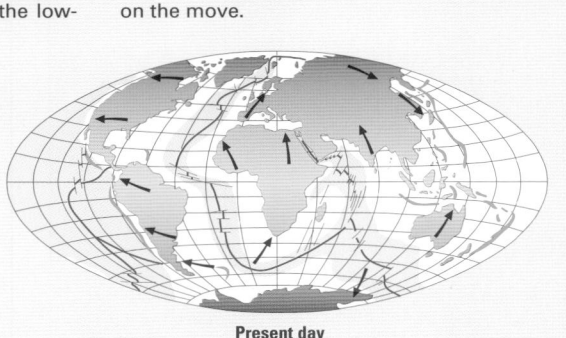

Present day

DISTRIBUTION OF VOLCANOES

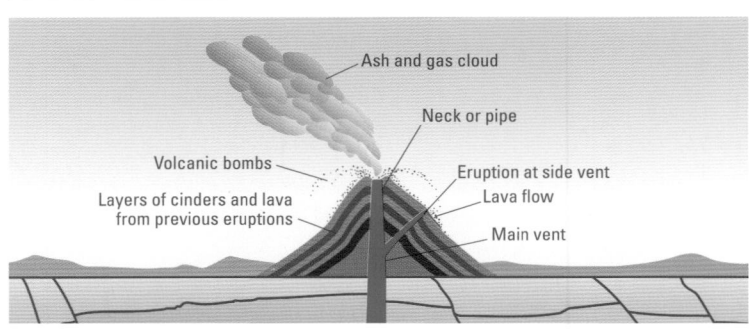

Ash and gas cloud
Neck or pipe
Volcanic bombs
Eruption at side vent
Layers of cinders and lava from previous eruptions
Lava flow
Main vent

Volcanoes occur when hot liquefied rock beneath the Earth's crust is pushed up by pressure to the surface as molten lava. There are some 550 known active volcanoes, around 20 of which are erupting at any one time.

○ Submarine volcanoes
▲ Land volcanoes active since 1700
— Boundaries of tectonic plates

PLATE TECTONICS

The huge ridges that run through the oceans represent boundaries between plates. Here plates are diverging and molten magma from the mantle rises along a central rift valley to form new crustal rock. These ocean ridges, which are active zones where earthquakes and volcanic eruptions are common, are called constructive plate margins. Destructive plate margins, which occur when two contrasting plates converge, are marked by deep-ocean trenches as one plate is forced under the other. The descending plate is melted to produce the magma that fuels volcanoes alongside the trenches. Movements of descending plates are often sudden, triggering earthquakes in overlying continental areas.

Sea-floor spreading in the Atlantic Ocean and plate collision

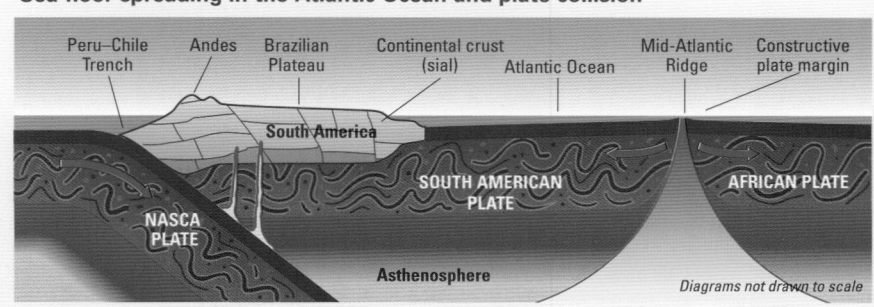

Peru–Chile Trench | Andes | Brazilian Plateau | Continental crust (sial) | Atlantic Ocean | Mid-Atlantic Ridge | Constructive plate margin
South America
SOUTH AMERICAN PLATE | AFRICAN PLATE
NASCA PLATE
Asthenosphere | Diagrams not drawn to scale

Sea-floor spreading in the Indian Ocean and continental plate collision

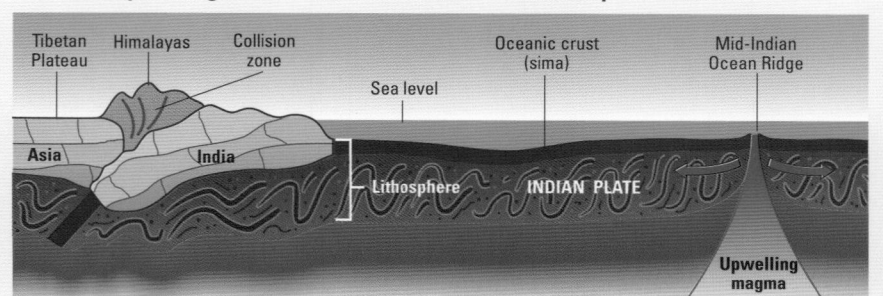

Tibetan Plateau | Himalayas | Collision zone | Oceanic crust (sima) | Mid-Indian Ocean Ridge
Sea level
Asia | India | Lithosphere | INDIAN PLATE
Upwelling magma

GEOLOGICAL TIME

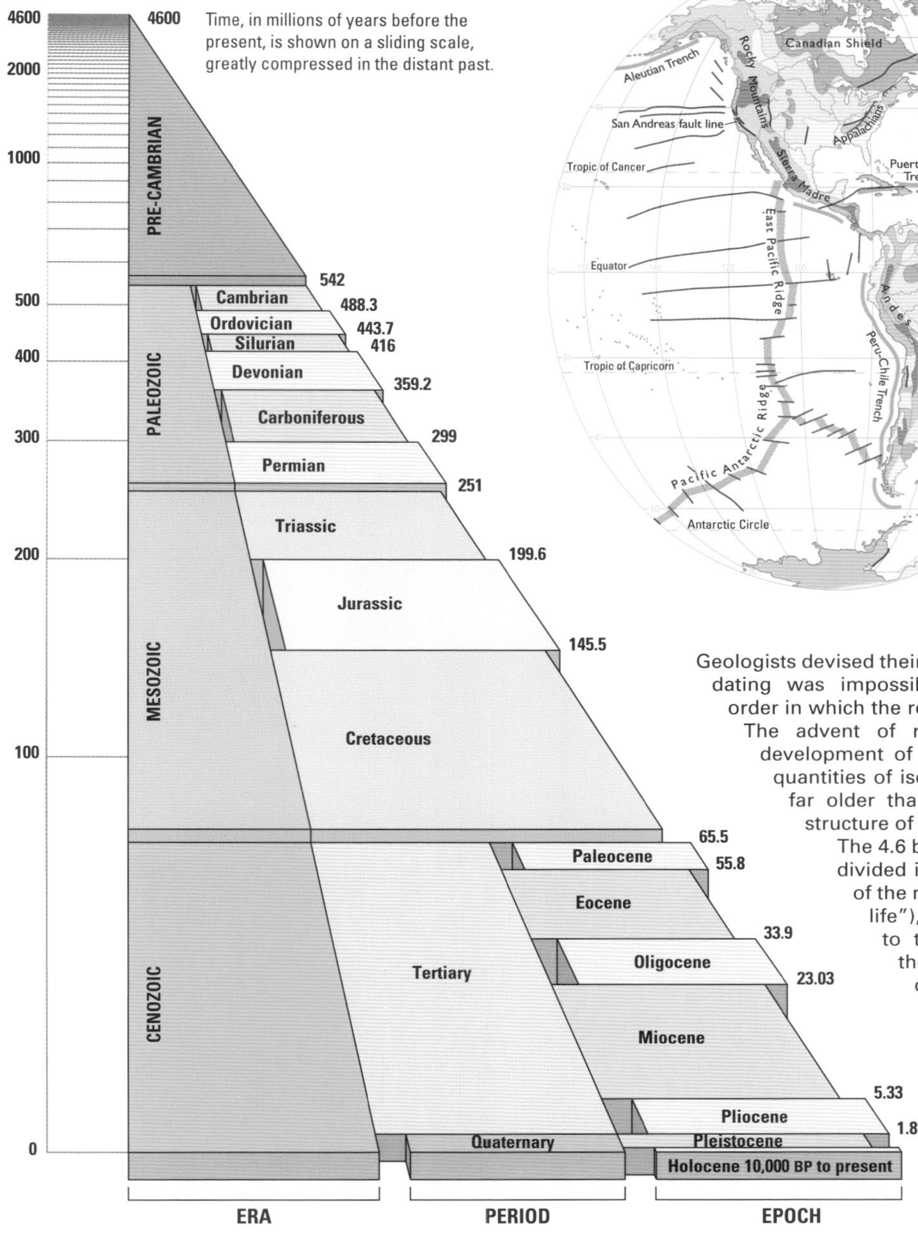

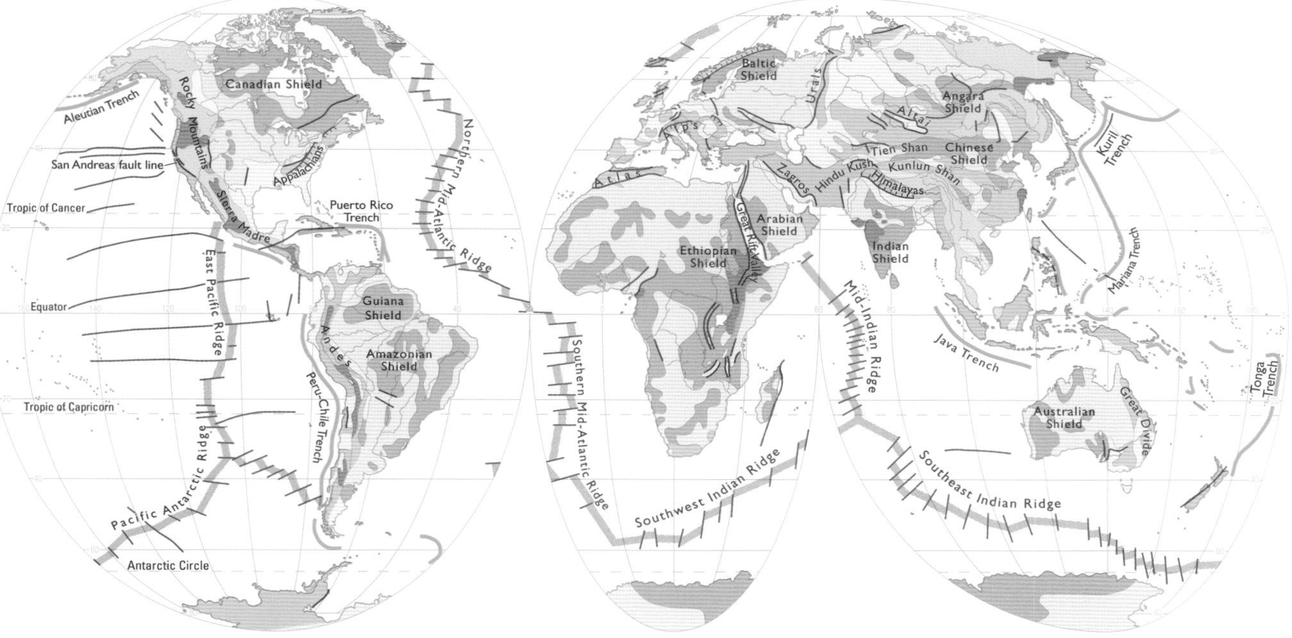

Time, in millions of years before the present, is shown on a sliding scale, greatly compressed in the distant past.

ERA	PERIOD	EPOCH
PRE-CAMBRIAN		
PALEOZOIC	Cambrian 542	
	Ordovician 488.3	
	Silurian 443.7	
	Devonian 416	
	Carboniferous 359.2	
	Permian 299	
MESOZOIC	Triassic 251	
	Jurassic 199.6	
	Cretaceous 145.5	
CENOZOIC	Tertiary	Paleocene 65.5
		Eocene 55.8
		Oligocene 33.9
		Miocene 23.03
		Pliocene 5.33
	Quaternary	Pleistocene 1.81
		Holocene 10,000 BP to present

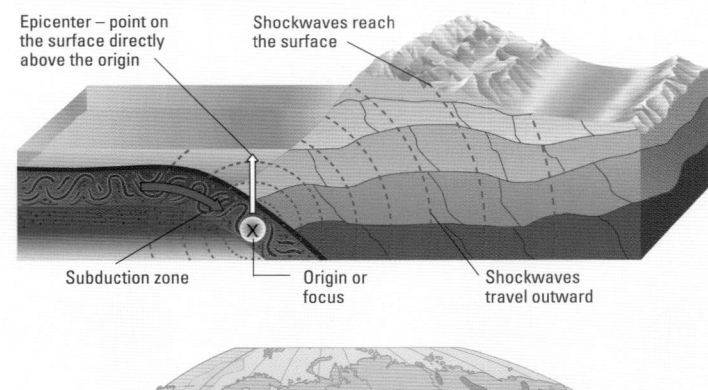

Geologists devised their timescale on the basis of relative, not calendar, ages. Accurate dating was impossible and estimates were often bitterly disputed, but the order in which the rocks were formed could be deduced from careful observation. The advent of radioactive dating – culminating in the 1950s with the development of a mass spectrometer capable of accurately measuring tiny quantities of isotopes – appears to have settled the arguments. The Earth is far older than geologists first imagined, but their painstakingly-created structure of geological time has withstood the advent of high technology.

The 4.6 billion (4,600 million) years since the formation of the Earth are divided into four great eras, further split into periods and, in the case of the most recent era, epochs. The present era is the Cenozoic ("new life"), extending backward through "middle life" and "ancient life" to the Pre-Cambrian, named after the Latin word for Wales, the location of some of the earliest known fossils. Most of the Earth's geological history is encompassed by the Pre-Cambrian: though traces of ancient life have since been found, it was largely the proliferation of fossils from the beginning of the Paleozoic era onward, some 570 million years ago, which first allowed precise subdivisions to be made.

Like the Cambrian, most are named after regions exemplifying a period's geology. Others – such as the Carboniferous ("coal-bearing") or the Cretaceous ("chalk-bearing") – are more directly descriptive.

- Pre-Cambrian shields
- Sedimentary cover on Pre-Cambrian shields
- Paleozoic (Caledonian and Hercynian) folding
- Sedimentary cover on Paleozoic folding
- Mesozoic folding
- Sedimentary cover on Mesozoic folding
- Cenozoic (Alpine) folding
- Sedimentary cover on Cenozoic folding
- Intensive Mesozoic and Cenozoic vulcanism
- Principal faults
- Oceanic marginal troughs
- Mid-oceanic ridges
- Overthrust faults

EARTHQUAKES

Earthquake magnitude is usually rated according to either the Richter scale or the Modified Mercalli scale, both devised by seismologists in the 1930s. The Richter scale measures absolute earthquake power with mathematical precision: each step upward represents a tenfold increase in the amplitude of the shockwave. Theoretically, there is no upper limit, but most of the largest earthquakes measured have been rated at between 8.8 and 8.9. The 12-point Mercalli scale, based on observed effects, is often more meaningful, ranging from I (earthquakes noticed only by seismographs) to XII (total destruction); intermediate points include V (people awakened at night; unstable objects overturned), VII (collapse of ordinary buildings; chimneys and monuments fall), and IX (conspicuous cracks in ground; serious damage to reservoirs).

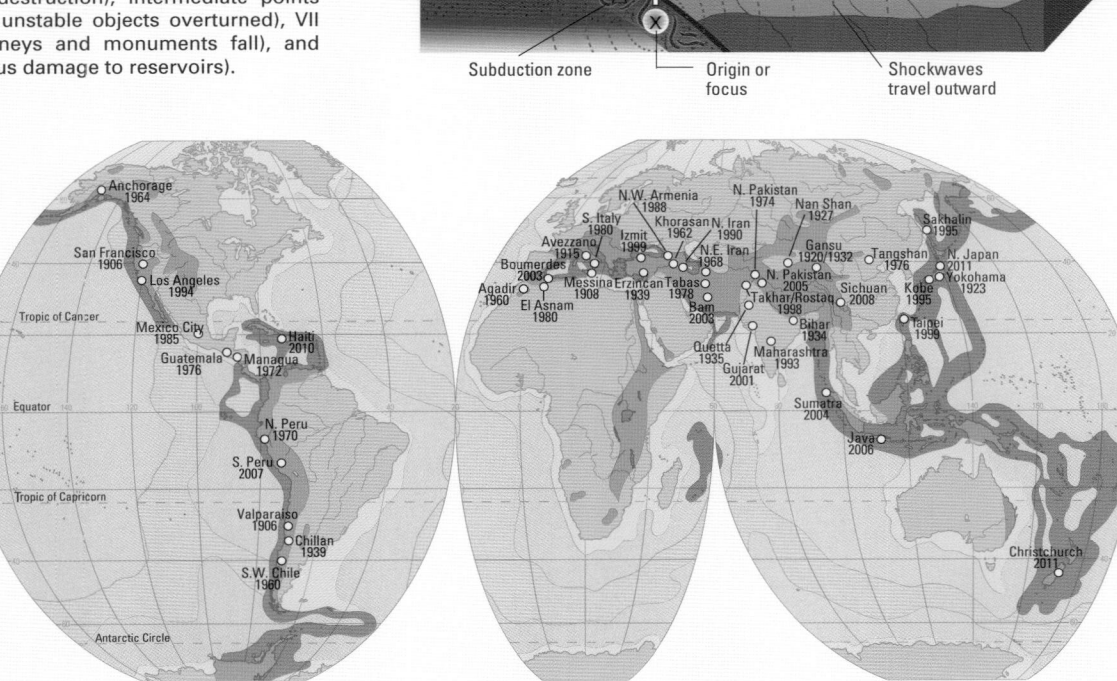

Epicenter – point on the surface directly above the origin

Shockwaves reach the surface

Subduction zone

Origin or focus

Shockwaves travel outward

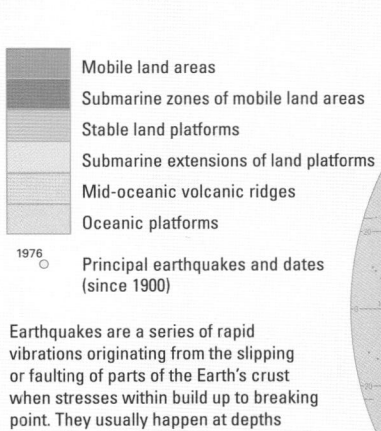

- Mobile land areas
- Submarine zones of mobile land areas
- Stable land platforms
- Submarine extensions of land platforms
- Mid-oceanic volcanic ridges
- Oceanic platforms

1976 ○ Principal earthquakes and dates (since 1900)

Earthquakes are a series of rapid vibrations originating from the slipping or faulting of parts of the Earth's crust when stresses within build up to breaking point. They usually happen at depths varying from 5 to 20 miles. Severe earthquakes cause extensive damage when they take place in populated areas, destroying structures and severing communications. Most initial loss of life occurs due to secondary causes such as falling masonry, fires, and flooding.

Notable Earthquakes Since 1900

Year	Location	Mag.	Deaths
1906	San Francisco, USA	8.3	3,000
1906	Valparaiso, Chile	8.6	22,000
1908	Messina, Italy	7.5	83,000
1915	Avezzano, Italy	7.5	30,000
1920	Gansu (Kansu), China	8.6	180,000
1923	Yokohama, Japan	8.3	143,000
1927	Nan Shan, China	8.3	200,000
1932	Gansu (Kansu), China	7.6	70,000
1933	Sanriku, Japan	8.9	2,990
1934	Bihar, India/Nepal	8.4	10,700
1935	Quetta, India*	7.5	60,000
1939	Chillan, Chile	8.3	28,000
1939	Erzincan, Turkey	7.9	30,000
1960	S. W. Chile	9.5	2,200
1960	Agadir, Morocco	5.8	12,000
1962	Khorasan, Iran	7.1	12,230
1964	Anchorage, USA	9.2	125
1968	N. E. Iran	7.4	12,000
1970	N. Peru	7.8	70,000
1972	Managua, Nicaragua	6.2	5,000
1974	N. Pakistan	6.3	5,200
1976	Guatemala	7.5	22,500
1976	Tangshan, China	8.2	255,000
1978	Tabas, Iran	7.7	25,000
1980	El Asnam, Algeria	7.3	20,000
1980	S. Italy	7.2	4,800
1985	Mexico City, Mexico	8.1	4,200
1988	N.W. Armenia	6.8	55,000
1990	N. Iran	7.7	36,000
1993	Maharashtra, India	6.4	30,000
1994	Los Angeles, USA	6.6	51
1995	Kobe, Japan	7.2	5,000
1995	Sakhalin, Russia	7.5	2,000
1998	Takhar, Afghanistan	6.1	4,200
1998	Rostaq, Afghanistan	7.0	5,000
1999	Izmit, Turkey	7.4	15,000
1999	Taipei, Taiwan	7.6	1,700
2001	Gujarat, India	7.7	14,000
2003	Boumerdes, Algeria	6.8	2,200
2003	Bam, Iran	6.6	30,000
2004	Sumatra, Indonesia	9.0	250,000
2005	N. Pakistan	7.6	74,000
2006	Java, Indonesia	6.4	6,200
2007	S. Peru	8.0	600
2008	Sichuan, China	7.9	70,000
2010	Haiti	7.0	230,000
2011	Christchurch, NZ	6.3	182
2011	N. Japan	9.0	20,000

* now Pakistan

For more information:
73 Tides
74 Plate tectonics
78 Atmosphere
84 Hydrological cycle
   Water distribution
85 Watersheds
103 World shipping

The last 50 years have been described as the "Space Age," but another exciting and perhaps even more important area of discovery, proceeding at the same time, has been the exploration of the oceans, which cover more than 70% of our planet. Studies of the ocean floor and oceanic islands have revealed features that help to explain how continents move, and how the movements are related to earthquakes and volcanic activity.

Manned submersibles have established that life exists even in the deepest trenches, where the pressure reaches 1,000 atmospheres, the equivalent of the force of 1 tonne bearing down on every square centimeter. Further exploration in the pitch-black environment of the ocean ridges has revealed strange forms of marine life around scalding hot vents. The creatures include giant tubeworms, blind shrimps, and bacteria, some of which are genetically very different from any other known life forms. In 1996, an analysis of one micro-organism revealed that at least half of its 1,700 or so genes were hitherto unknown. This environment, which is based on chemicals, not sunlight, may resemble the places where life on Earth first began.

Another vital area of contemporary research concerns the interactions between the oceans and the atmosphere, as exemplified in the El Niño–Southern Oscillation (ENSO) cycle, and the bearing that these have on climatic change (see below).

Most geographers divide the world's ocean waters into five areas: the Pacific, Atlantic, Indian, Southern, and Arctic oceans. The most active zone in the oceans is the sunlit upper layer, where the water is moved around by wind-blown currents. It is the home of most sea life and acts as a membrane through which the ocean breathes,

ATOLL BUILDING

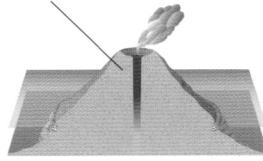
Volcano rises from ocean floor

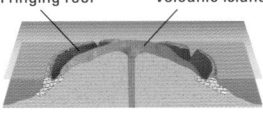
Fringing reef | Extinct, eroding volcanic island

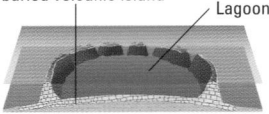
After subsidence, reef covers buried volcanic island | Lagoon

A coral atoll usually begins existence as a bare volcanic peak, thrusting above the surface of the ocean. A colony of coral – organisms with calcium carbonate skeletons – forms itself in the shallow water around the peak. The volcano is eroded and slowly sinks, leaving the coral forming a ring of hard limestone around its remnant. In time, the barrier reef of an atoll is all that remains.

LIFE IN THE OCEANS

An imaginary profile of the typical coastal and oceanic zones is shown, with a selection of the life forms that might occur in the waters off the Pacific Coast of Central America. The animals illustrated are not drawn to scale as the range of sizes is too great. Most marine life is confined to the first 650 feet, the upper sunlit (photic) zone, where sunlight can still penetrate. Plant and animal plankton, the basis of life in the oceans, occur in great quantities in all zones.

In the pelagic environment (open sea), vertical gradients, including those of light, temperature, and salinity, determine the distribution of organisms. From the tidal zone at the coastline, the continental shelf, geologically still part of the continental land mass, drops gently to about 650 feet – the sunlit zone. At the end of the shelf, the seabed falls away in the steeper angle of the continental slope. The subsequent descent to the deep-ocean floor, known as the "continental rise," is more gentle, with gradients between 1 in 100 and 1 in 700 until the abyssal plains and hills between 8,000 and 19,500 feet below the surface.

The deep-sea floor contains seamounts, some of which are capped by coral reefs, ocean ridges – the longest mountain chains on Earth – and deep-ocean trenches, especially in the Pacific Ocean where six trenches reach depths of more than 33,000 feet, including the Mariana Trench at 36,161 feet deep.

Each of these zones contains a distinctive community of species adapted to the different conditions of salinity, temperature, and light intensity. Indeed, a few organisms have been found even in the abyssal darkness of the great ocean trenches.

absorbing great quantities of carbon dioxide and partly exchanging it for oxygen.

As the depth increases, so light fades and temperatures fall until just before 3,000 feet where there is a marked temperature change at the thermocline, the boundary between the warm surface zone and the cold deep zone. Below the thermocline, slow currents are caused by density differences between bodies of water with varying temperatures and salinity.

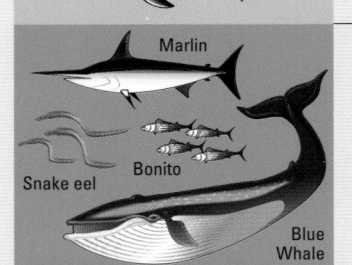
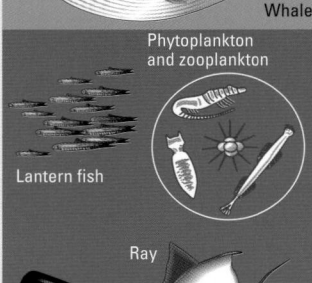

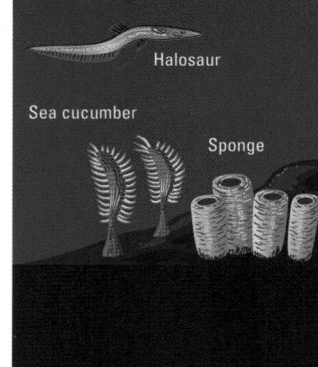

EL NIÑO PHENOMENON

Typical air and sea circulation pattern

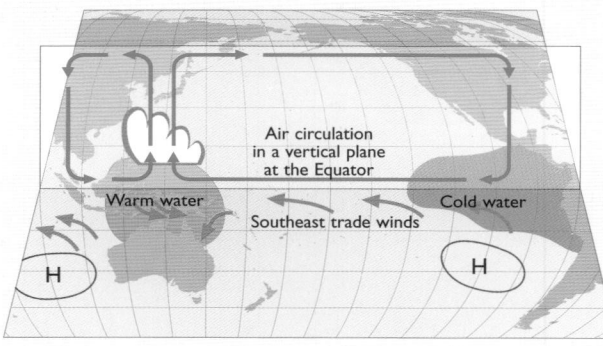

El Niño air and sea circulation pattern

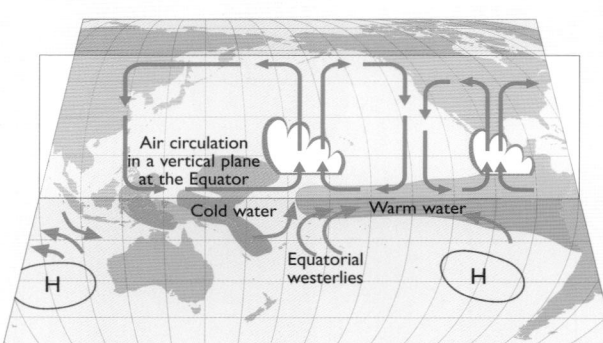

The importance of the ocean–atmosphere interaction is nowhere more dramatically demonstrated than in the El Niño phenomenon of the southern Pacific Ocean. Under normal conditions, called La Niña, cold, nutrient-rich water rises to the surface off South America and spreads westward. In the western Pacific, sea surface temperatures reach 82°F or more and warm air rises, creating a low-pressure air system and causing heavy rains. The rising air spreads out and some of it descends over South America and the eastern Pacific, creating a high-pressure air system from which winds blow westward.

An El Niño event is characterized by a reversal of currents. The upwelling of cold water is greatly reduced and surface water temperatures rise, causing a drastic reduction in fish life. The heaviest rainfall is over the eastern Pacific, while Southeast Asia is drier than usual. However, each El Niño event is unique in terms of its strength as well as its impact.

During an intense El Niño, the effects of the current and wind reversals affect the weather around the world. In the 1997 El Niño event there was a very suppressed hurricane season in the Caribbean but numerous super typhoons in the Pacific. Whilst South America and East Africa were much wetter than average, West Africa and parts of Indonesia were much drier than normal. Algal blooms occurred in Australia's drought-stricken rivers and there were numerous bush fires in Indonesia.

Scientists have found evidence that the frequency of the El Niño event, which normally occurs every three to seven years, and lasts between 12–18 months, may have increased in recent years.

We do not fully understand the causes of the El Niño event, though some researchers are currently investigating possible connections between major volcanic eruptions in the tropical Pacific region, the El Niño–Southern Oscillation (ENSO) cycle, and atmospheric circulation.

OCEAN CURRENTS

JANUARY CURRENTS
(Northern Hemisphere: winter)

Cold Warm Speed (knots)
- Less than 0.5
- 0.5 – 1.0
- Over 1.0

JULY CURRENTS
(Northern Hemisphere: summer)

Cold Warm Speed (knots)
- Less than 0.5
- 0.5 – 1.0
- Over 1.0

Moving immense quantities of energy as well as billions of tonnes of water every hour, the ocean currents are a vital part of the great heat engine that drives the Earth's climate. They themselves are produced by a twofold mechanism. At the surface, winds push huge masses of water before them; in the deep ocean below, an abrupt temperature gradient separates the churning surface waters from the still depths (see the ocean conveyor belt diagram, below left).

Coriolis effect
The pattern of circulation of the great surface currents is determined by the displacement known as the "Coriolis effect." As the Earth turns, the vast mass of ocean water is deflected to one side. The deflection is most obvious near the equator, where the Earth's surface is spinning eastward at 1,000 mph; currents moving poleward are curved clockwise in the northern hemisphere and counterclockwise in the southern hemisphere.

Ocean currents
The result is a system of spinning circles known as "gyres." Warm currents move constantly from the equator toward the poles, while cold water moves in the reverse direction. In this way, ocean currents act like a thermostat, helping to regulate temperatures around the world.

Depending on the annual movements of the prevailing wind belts, some currents on or near the equator may reverse their direction in the course of the year, a variation on which Asia's monsoon rains depend and whose occasional failure has brought disaster to millions of people.

THE OCEAN CONVEYOR BELT

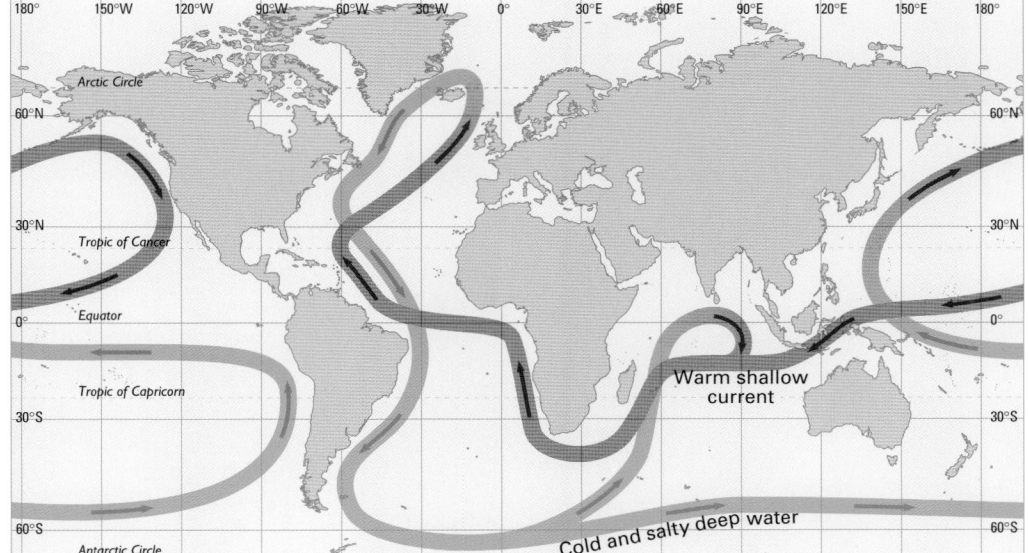

Thermohaline circulation, or the ocean conveyor belt, refers to the global, density-driven circulation of the oceans. The name comes from "thermo," for temperature, and "haline," for salt, which together determine the density of sea water.

The cycle starts near the equator in the Pacific Ocean, where surface currents drive the water westward. This water is warm and not very salty, making it lightweight, so it travels along the surface of the ocean. As the water progresses west it eventually works its way into the North Atlantic where it cools, increases in salinity and sinks. It slowly circulates southward then eastward toward the Antarctic, where it splits into two routes: one to the Indian Ocean and one into the Pacific.

As the water recycles, it once again becomes warmer, less salty, lighter, and upwells in the Pacific to start the cycle all over again.

WORLD FISH CATCH

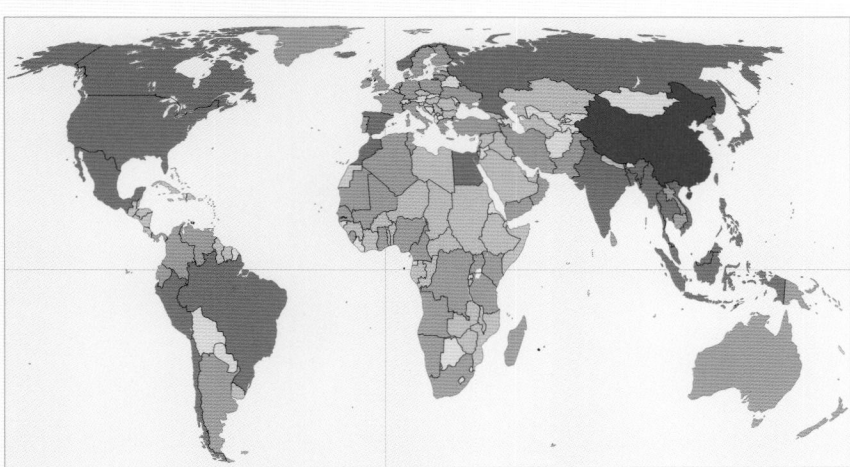

Total world fish catch in metric tonnes (2009)
(inland and marine fishing)

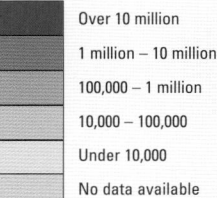

- Over 10 million
- 1 million – 10 million
- 100,000 – 1 million
- 10,000 – 100,000
- Under 10,000
- No data available

Leading fishing nations
(percentage of total world catch)

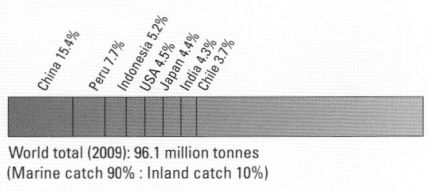

China 15.8% | Peru 7.7% | Indonesia 5.2% | USA 4.5% | Japan 4.4% | India 4.3% | Chile 3.7%

World total (2009): 96.1 million tonnes
(Marine catch 90% : Inland catch 10%)

With many marine stocks now fully exploited or over-exploited, future fish supplies are likely to be constrained by resource limits.

For more information:
76 El Niño phenomenon
77 Ocean currents
81 Beaufort wind scale
   Monsoon
82 Climate change
   Global warming

The atmosphere is a meteor shield, a radiation deflector, a thermal blanket, and a source of chemical energy for the Earth's diverse life forms. Five-sixths of its mass is in the lowest layer, the troposphere, which ranges in thickness from 11–6 miles between the equator and the poles. Powered by the Sun, the air is always on the move, flowing generally from high- to low-pressure areas. The troposphere is the layer where virtually all weather phenomena, including clouds, precipitation, and winds, occur. Above the troposphere is the stratosphere, which contains the important ozone layer and extends to about 30 miles above the Earth's surface. Beyond 60 miles, atmospheric density is lower than most laboratory vacuums.

STRUCTURE OF THE ATMOSPHERE

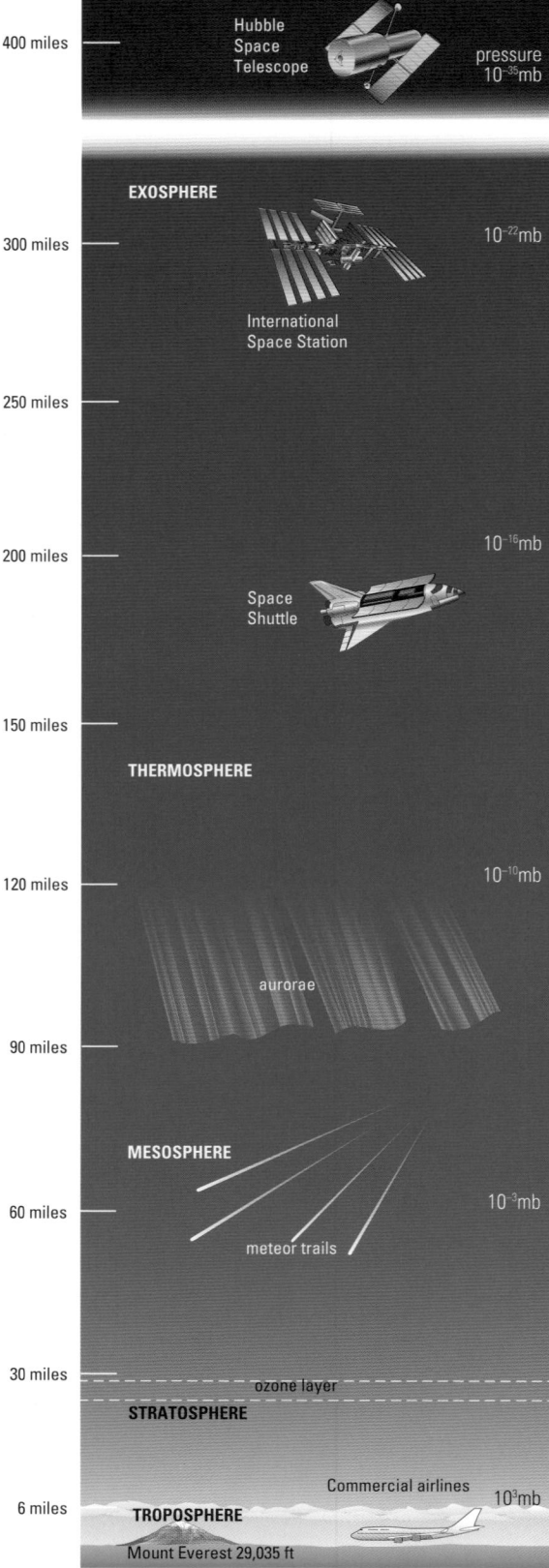

400 miles — Hubble Space Telescope   pressure 10⁻³⁵mb

EXOSPHERE

300 miles — 10⁻²²mb

International Space Station

250 miles —

200 miles — 10⁻¹⁶mb

Space Shuttle

150 miles —

THERMOSPHERE

120 miles — 10⁻¹⁰mb

aurorae

90 miles —

MESOSPHERE

60 miles — 10⁻³mb

meteor trails

30 miles — ozone layer

STRATOSPHERE

Commercial airlines   10³mb

6 miles — **TROPOSPHERE**

Mount Everest 29,035 ft

CIRCULATION OF THE AIR

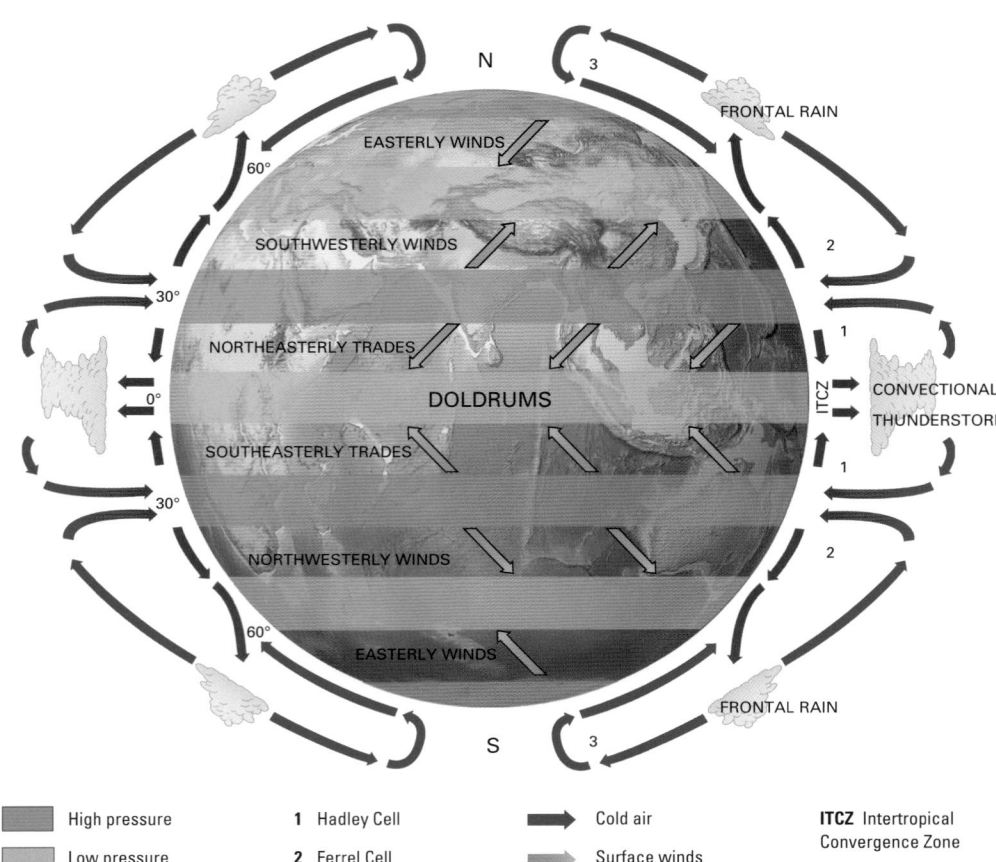

N   3

FRONTAL RAIN

EASTERLY WINDS

60°

SOUTHWESTERLY WINDS   2

30°   1

NORTHEASTERLY TRADES

0°   DOLDRUMS   ITCZ   CONVECTIONAL THUNDERSTORM

1

SOUTHEASTERLY TRADES

30°   2

NORTHWESTERLY WINDS

60°   EASTERLY WINDS

3

FRONTAL RAIN

S   3

�v High pressure	**1** Hadley Cell	➡ Cold air	**ITCZ** Intertropical Convergence Zone
Low pressure	**2** Ferrel Cell	➡ Surface winds	
➡ Warm air	**3** Polar Cell	Clouds	

FRONTAL SYSTEMS

Depressions, also known as cyclones or lows, form on the polar front where relatively cold and dry polar air flows alongside warmer, moister subtropical air. They occur when the flow high above the polar front generates a surface inward-swirling circulation that moves along the polar front as a wave.

The warm front is the leading edge of the subtropical air that glides up and over the cooler air ahead of it. This gently ascending flow produces a characteristic sequence of clouds ahead of the warm front and a band of precipitation a few hundred miles wide immediately in advance it. Conditions within the warm sector are often overcast with layer cloud and generally light rain or drizzle. The cloud sometimes breaks up downwind of hills.

Another band of precipitation often occurs just ahead of the cold front that is the leading edge of the cooler polar air. Cumulus clouds tend to occur in the air behind the cold front, producing scattered showers. The changes of temperature, wind direction, and cloud, etc, are illustrated by the diagram below.

CHEMICAL COMPOSITION

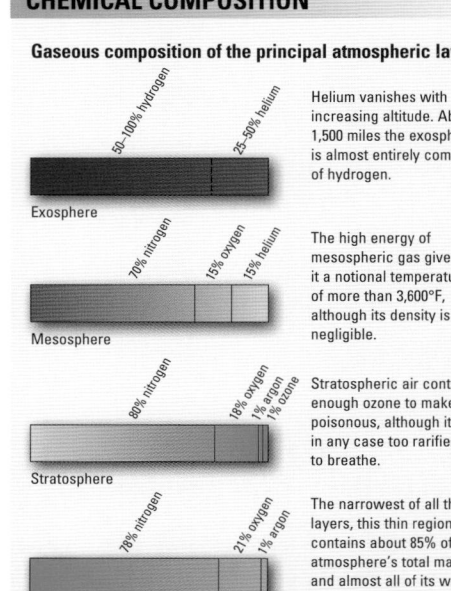

Gaseous composition of the principal atmospheric layers

50–100% hydrogen | 25–50% helium

Exosphere

70% nitrogen | 15% oxygen | 15% helium

Mesosphere

80% nitrogen | 19% oxygen | 1% argon 1% ozone

Stratosphere

78% nitrogen | 21% oxygen | 1% argon

Troposphere

Helium vanishes with increasing altitude. Above 1,500 miles the exosphere is almost entirely composed of hydrogen.

The high energy of mesospheric gas gives it a notional temperature of more than 3,600°F, although its density is negligible.

Stratospheric air contains enough ozone to make it poisonous, although it is in any case too rarified to breathe.

The narrowest of all the layers, this thin region contains about 85% of the atmosphere's total mass and almost all of its water vapor. It is also the realm of the Earth's weather.

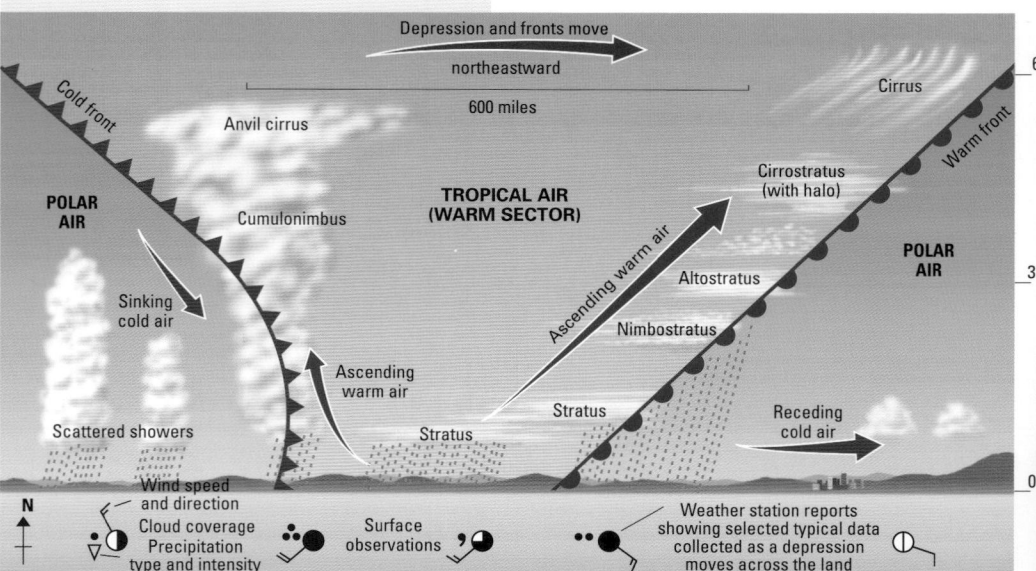

Depression and fronts move northeastward

600 miles   6

Cold front   Cirrus   Warm front

Anvil cirrus

POLAR AIR   Cirrostratus (with halo)

Cumulonimbus   **TROPICAL AIR (WARM SECTOR)**   Ascending warm air   3   **POLAR AIR**

Altostratus

Sinking cold air   Nimbostratus

Ascending warm air   Stratus   Receding cold air

Scattered showers   Stratus   0

N   Wind speed and direction   Cloud coverage   Surface observations   Weather station reports showing selected typical data collected as a depression moves across the land
Precipitation type and intensity

AIR MASSES

Air masses are extensive regions of air, typically a few thousand miles across, that have horizontally gently varying temperature and humidity characteristics produced by the underlying continental or maritime surfaces over which they occur. They can, for example, be warm and moist air or cold and dry air that spiral slowly out from their "source regions." These are the highs marked on the world maps below.

A particular location's weather associated with an air mass depends on the air's source region (for example, the North Atlantic sub-tropical high), the track it has taken (for example, long maritime or continental track), and the time of year (for example, across a cold or strongly heated continent). The polar front (and its frontal cyclones) is a gently sloping, troposphere-deep surface that separates two air masses – the North Atlantic subtropical high and the North American wintertime anticyclone. The warmer, damper subtropical air rides up and over the cooler, drier polar air to produce widespread frontal cloud and precipitation.

Air masses are classified as, amongst others, "polar continental," "polar maritime" or "tropical maritime." The massive Asian high in January is a source of polar continental, very cold, very dry air, while in contrast the extensive North Pacific and North Atlantic highs are sources of warm and very moist air throughout the year.

CLASSIFICATION OF CLOUDS

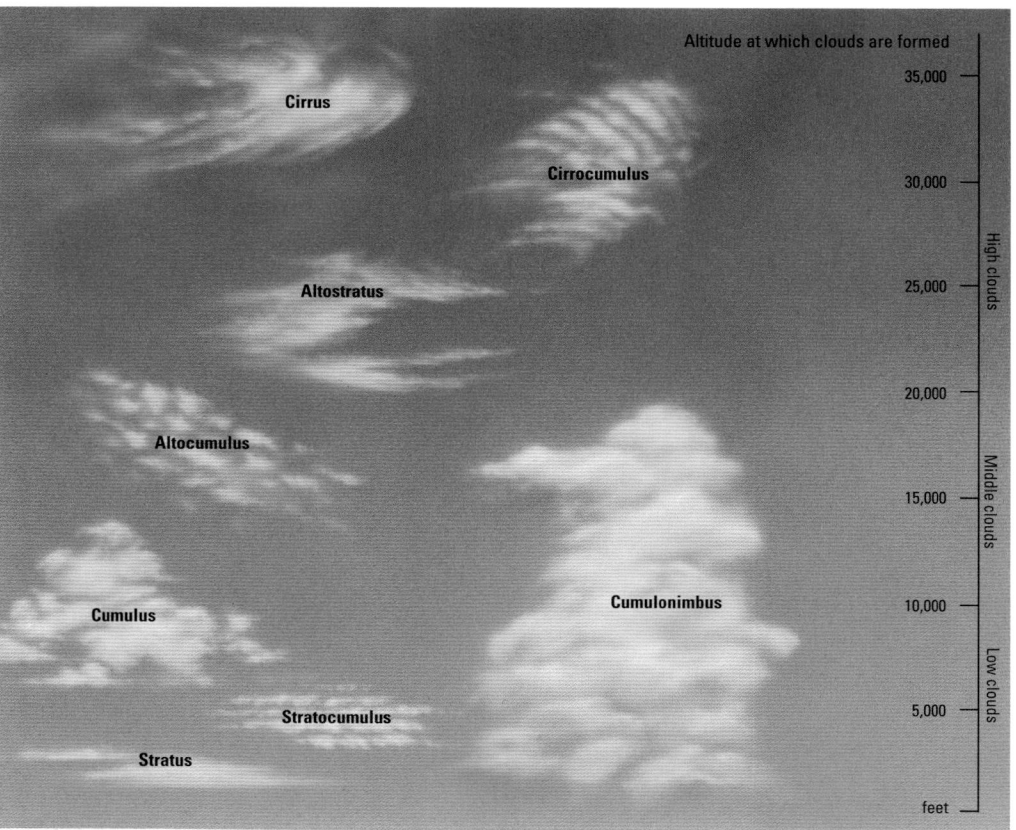

Clouds form when damp, usually rising, air is cooled. Thus they form when a wind rises to cross hills or mountains; when a mass of air rises over, or is pushed up by, another mass of denser air; or when local heating of the ground causes convection currents.

The first classification of clouds was developed by a London chemist, Luke Howard, in 1803, and it was later modified by the World Meteorological Organization. The types of clouds are classified according to altitude as high, middle, or low. The high ones, composed of ice crystals, are cirrus, cirrostratus, and cirrocumulus.

The middle clouds are altostratus – a gray or bluish striated, fibrous or uniform sheet producing light drizzle – and altocumulus, a thicker and fluffier version of cirrocumulus.

Low clouds include nimbostratus, a dark gray layer that brings rain or snow; cumulus, a detached heap, dark at the base; stratus, which forms dull, overcast skies at low levels; and stratocumulus, which consists of fluffy grayish-white layers.

Cumulonimbus, associated with storms and rains, heavy and dense with a flat base and a high, fluffy outline, can be tall enough to occupy middle as well as low altitudes.

PRESSURE AND SURFACE WINDS

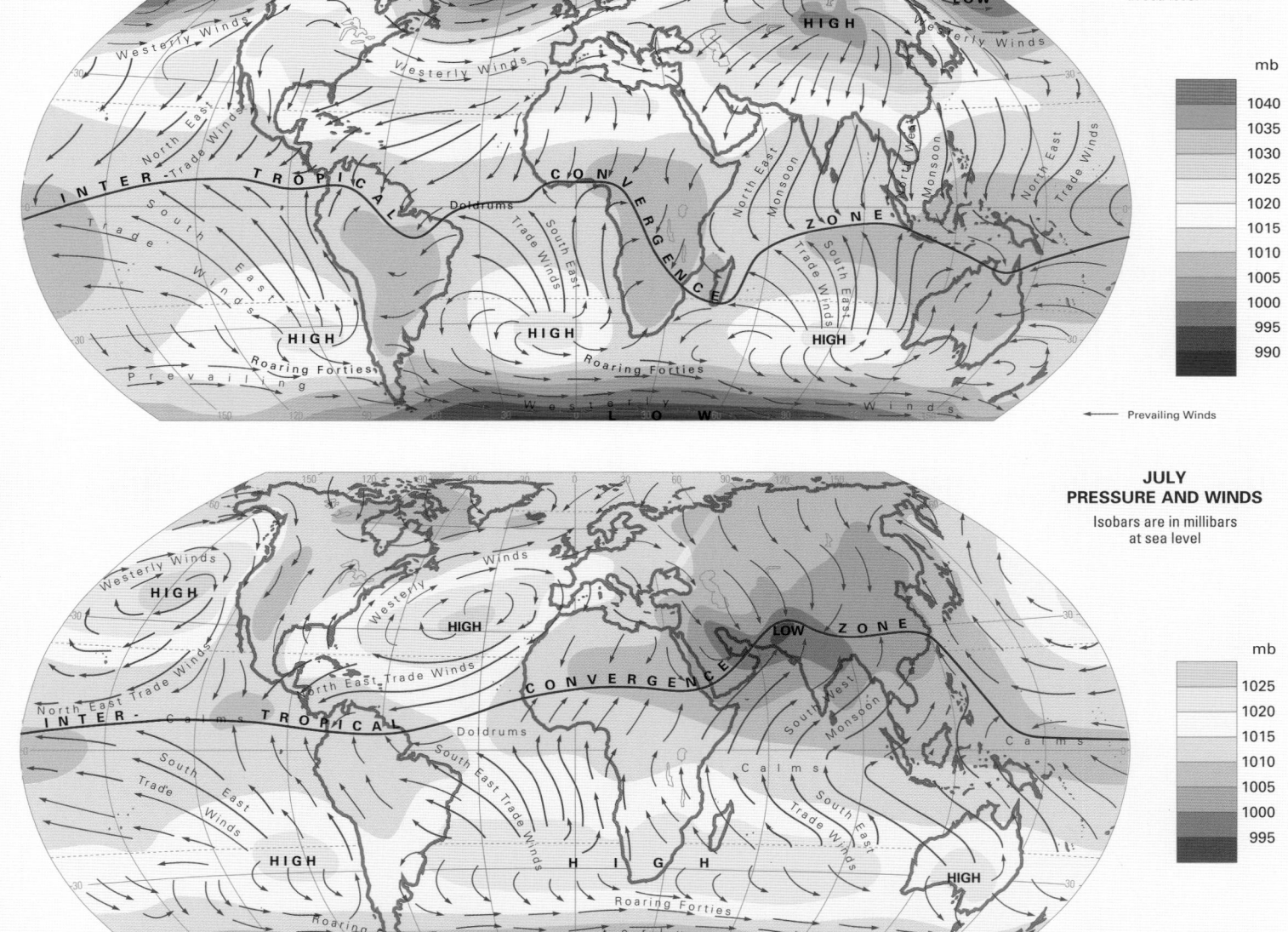

WEATHER RECORDS

Pressure and winds

Highest barometric pressure:
Agata, Siberia, 1,083.8 mb at altitude 862 ft [262 m], December 31, 1968.

Lowest barometric pressure:
Typhoon Tip, 300 mi [480 km] west of Guam, Pacific Ocean, 870 mb, October 12, 1979.

Highest recorded wind speed:
Bridge Creek, Oklahoma, USA, 318 mph [512 km/h], May 3, 1999. Measured by Doppler radar monitoring a tornado.

Windiest place:
Port Martin, Antarctica, where winds of more than 40 mph [64 km/h] occur for not less than 100 days a year.

Worst recorded storm:
Bangladesh (then East Pakistan) cyclone, November 13, 1970 – over 300,000 dead or missing. The 1991 cyclone, Bangladesh's and the world's second worst in terms of loss of life, killed an estimated 138,000 people.

Worst recorded tornado:
Tri-state tornado – Missouri/Illinois/Indiana, USA, March 18, 1925 – 695 deaths, lasted 3 hours with 219 mi [352 km] path length. A suspected tornado in Bangladesh on April 26, 1989, killed approximately 1,300 people.

For more information:

77 Ocean currents
78 Circulation of the air
79 Classification of clouds
     Pressure and winds
82 Climate change
     Global warming
84 Hydrological cycle
85 Natural vegetation

Weather is the day-to-day or hour-to-hour condition of the air, while climate is weather in the long term – the seasonal pattern of hot and cold, wet and dry, averaged over a long period.

Most classifications of climate are based on a system developed in the early 19th century by Vladimir Köppen, a Russian meteorologist. Using a code based on letters and a classification centered on two main features, temperature and precipitation, he identified five main climatic types: tropical (A), dry (B), warm temperate (C), cold temperate (D), and polar (E). A highland mountain climate (H) was added later to account for the variety of altitudinal climatic zones on high mountains. Each

of these main regions was then further subdivided.

Latitude is a major factor in determining climate, but other factors add to the complexity. These include the differential heating of land and sea, the distance from the sea, the effect of mountains on winds, and the influence of ocean currents. For example, New York City, Naples, and the Gobi Desert share almost the same latitude, but their climates are very different.

During the last Ice Age, the Earth underwent alternating cold periods, called glacials, separated by warm interglacials. The Milankovich theory suggests such cycles may be caused by variations in the Earth's path around the Sun, changing

from almost circular to elliptical every 95,000 years, and variations in the Earth's tilt from 21.5° to 24.5° every 42,000 years. Another factor is that the Earth is now closest to the Sun in the middle of winter in the northern hemisphere and furthest away in summer. But 12,000 years ago, at the height of the last glacial period, the northern winter fell with the Sun at its most distant.

Studies of these cycles suggest that we are now in an interglacial with a new glacial period on the way. However, scientists believe that global warming, largely a result of burning fossil fuels and deforestation, may be occurring much faster than the great, slow cycles of the Solar System.

Tropical rainy climates
All mean monthly temperatures above 64°F [18°C].

Af	Rain forest climate
Am	Monsoon climate
Aw	Savanna climate

Dry climates
Low rainfall combined with a wide range of temperatures.

| BS | Steppe climate |
| BW | Desert climate |

Warm temperate rainy climates
The mean temperature is below 64°F [18°C] but above 26°F [–3°C] and that of the warmest month is over 50°F [10°C].

Cw	Dry winter climate
Cs	Dry summer climate
Cf	Climate with no dry season

Cold temperate rainy climates
The mean temperature of the coldest month is below 26°F [–3°C] but that of the warmest month is still over 50°F [10°C].

| Dw | Dry winter climate |
| Df | Climate with no dry season |

Polar climates
The mean temperature of the warmest month is below 50°F [10°C], giving permanently frozen subsoil.

| ET | Tundra climate |

The mean temperature of the warmest month is below 32°F [0°C], giving permanent ice and snow.

| EF | Polar climate |

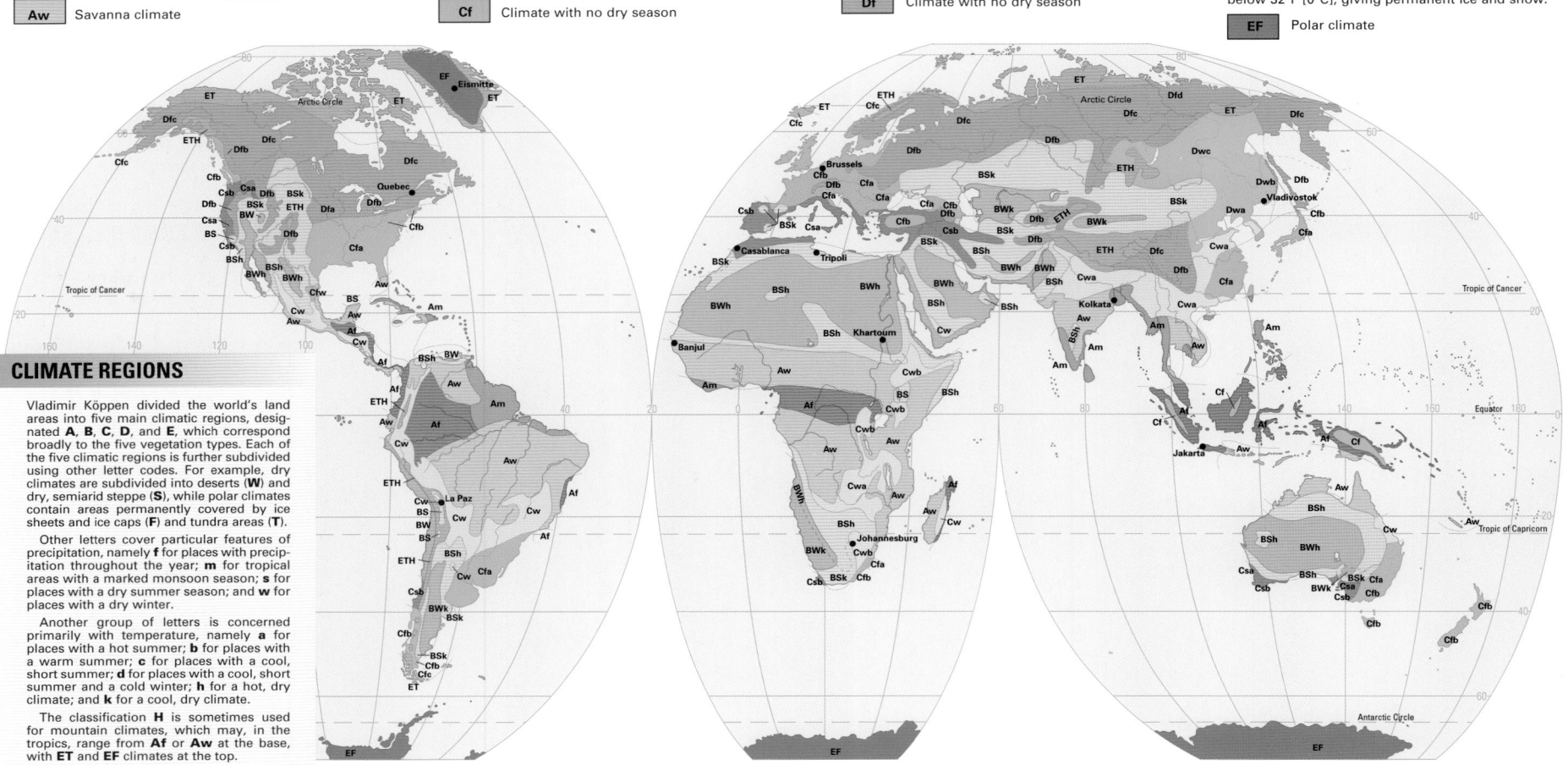

CLIMATE REGIONS

Vladimir Köppen divided the world's land areas into five main climatic regions, designated **A, B, C, D,** and **E,** which correspond broadly to the five vegetation types. Each of the five climatic regions is further subdivided using other letter codes. For example, dry climates are subdivided into deserts (**W**) and dry, semiarid steppe (**S**), while polar climates contain areas permanently covered by ice sheets and ice caps (**F**) and tundra areas (**T**).

Other letters cover particular features of precipitation, namely **f** for places with precipitation throughout the year; **m** for tropical areas with a marked monsoon season; **s** for places with a dry summer season; and **w** for places with a dry winter.

Another group of letters is concerned primarily with temperature, namely **a** for places with a hot summer; **b** for places with a warm summer; **c** for places with a cool, short summer; **d** for places with a cool, short summer and a cold winter; **h** for a hot, dry climate; and **k** for a cool, dry climate.

The classification **H** is sometimes used for mountain climates, which may, in the tropics, range from **Af** or **Aw** at the base, with **ET** and **EF** climates at the top.

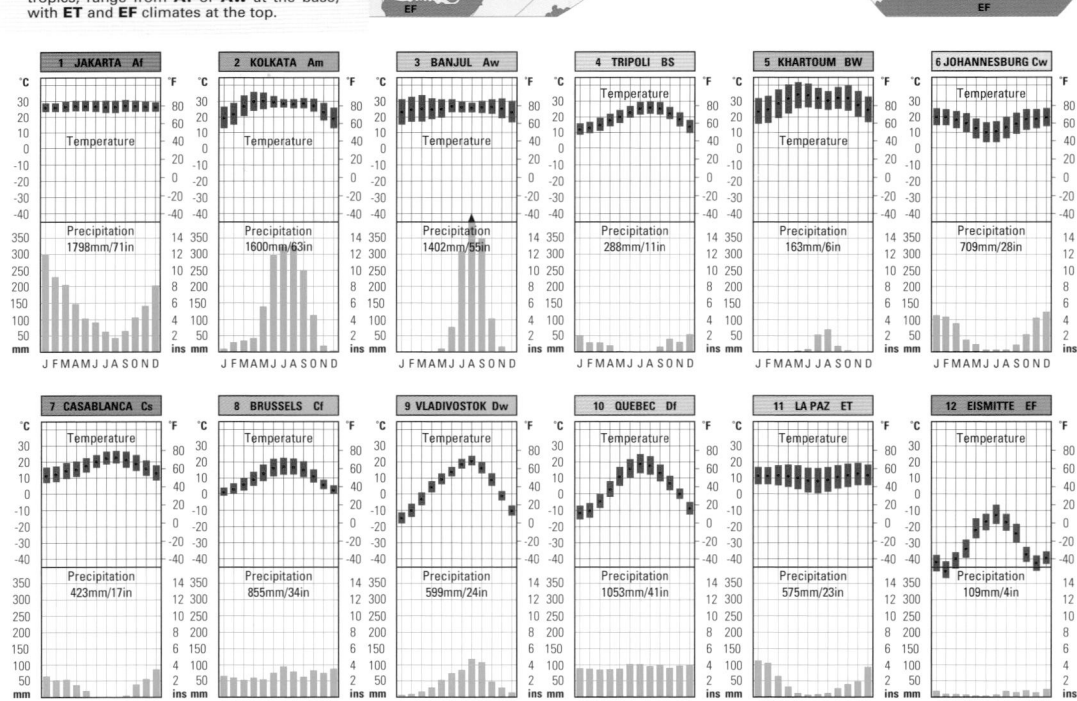

CLIMATE AND WEATHER TERMS

Anticyclone: area of high pressure with light winds and generally quiet weather.

Absolute humidity: mass of water vapor contained in a given volume of air.

Cloud cover: amount of cloud in the sky; measured in oktas (from 0–9), with 0 clear, and 9 "sky obscured."

Condensation: the conversion of water vapor into liquid.

Cyclone: violent storm resulting from counterclockwise rotation of winds in the northern hemisphere and clockwise in the southern: called hurricane in North America, typhoon in the Far East.

Depression: large area of low barometric pressure, a few thousand miles across.

Dew: deposition of small water droplets on the Earth's surface by direct condensation of water vapor.

Dew point: the temperature at which air becomes saturated by cooling at constant barometric pressure and absolute humidity

Drizzle: precipitation drops between 0.01–0.02 inches [0.2 and 0.5 mm] in diameter.

Evaporation: conversion of water from liquid into vapor or moisture in the air.

Front: the dividing line between two air masses.

Frost: the surface deposition of water vapor as minute ice crystals, when temperature reaches the frost point.

Hail: variably-sized pieces of ice that fall in downdrafts from cumulonimbus clouds.

Humidity: amount of water vapor in the air.

Isobar: line joining places with the same barometric pressure.

Isotherm: line connecting places of equal temperature.

Lightning: massive electrical discharge released in thunderstorm from cloud to cloud or cloud to ground, the result of the top becoming positively charged and the bottom negatively charged.

Precipitation: measurable rain, snow, sleet, or hail.

Prevailing wind: most common direction of wind at a given location.

Rain: precipitation of liquid particles with diameter larger than 0.02 inches [0.5 mm].

Relative humidity: observed quantity of water vapor in a mass of air over the saturation value at a given temperature (as a percentage).

Snow: flake-like coagulations of ice crystals that fall from clouds in subzero temperatures.

Thunder: sound produced by the rapid expansion of air heated by lightning.

Tornado: rapidly-rotating funnel-shaped cloud or debris column that must reach the surface and be attached to a parent cumulonimbus cloud.

BEAUFORT WIND SCALE

Named after Admiral Sir Francis Beaufort, the 19th-century British naval officer who devised it, the Beaufort Scale assesses wind speed according to its effects. It was originally designed as an aid for sailors, but has since been adapted for use on the land. It is used internationally.

Scale	Wind speed mph	km/h	Effect
0	0–1	0–1	**Calm**
			Smoke rises vertically
1	1–3	1–5	**Light air**
			Wind direction shown only by smoke drift
2	4–7	6–11	**Light breeze**
			Wind felt on face; leaves rustle; vanes moved by wind
3	8–12	12–19	**Gentle breeze**
			Leaves and small twigs in constant motion; wind extends small flag
4	13–18	20–28	**Moderate**
			Raises dust and loose paper; small branches move
5	19–24	29–38	**Fresh**
			Small trees in leaf sway; crested wavelets on inland waters
6	25–31	39–49	**Strong**
			Large branches move; difficult to use umbrellas; overhead wires whistle
7	32–38	50–61	**Near gale**
			Whole trees in motion; difficult to walk against wind
8	39–46	62–74	**Gale**
			Twigs break from trees; walking very difficult
9	47–54	75–88	**Strong gale**
			Slight structural damage
10	55–63	89–102	**Storm**
			Trees uprooted; serious structural damage
11	64–72	103–117	**Violent storm**
			Widespread damage
12	73+	118+	**Hurricane**

▲ On September 14, 2003, Hurricane Isabel was located over the Atlantic Ocean, 400 miles [640 km] north of Puerto Rico. It moved in a northwestward direction with maximum winds of 155 mph [250 km/h], making it a Category 5 hurricane.

THE MONSOON

Monsoon is the term given to the seasonal reversal of wind direction, most noticeably in Southeast Asia. It results from a combination of factors: the extreme heating and cooling of large land masses in relation to the less marked changes in temperature of the adjacent seas; the northward movement of the Intertropical Convergence Zone (ITCZ); and the effect of the Himalayas on the circulation of the air.

In March, winds blow outward from the mainland. But as the Sun and the ITCZ move northward, the land is intensely heated, and a low-pressure system develops. The southeast trade winds change direction and are sucked into the interior to become southwesterlies, bringing heavy rain. By November, the Sun and the ITCZ have again moved south and the wind directions are again reversed. Cool winds blow from the Asian interior to the sea, losing any moisture on the Himalayas before descending to the coast.

TEMPERATURE

Average temperature in January

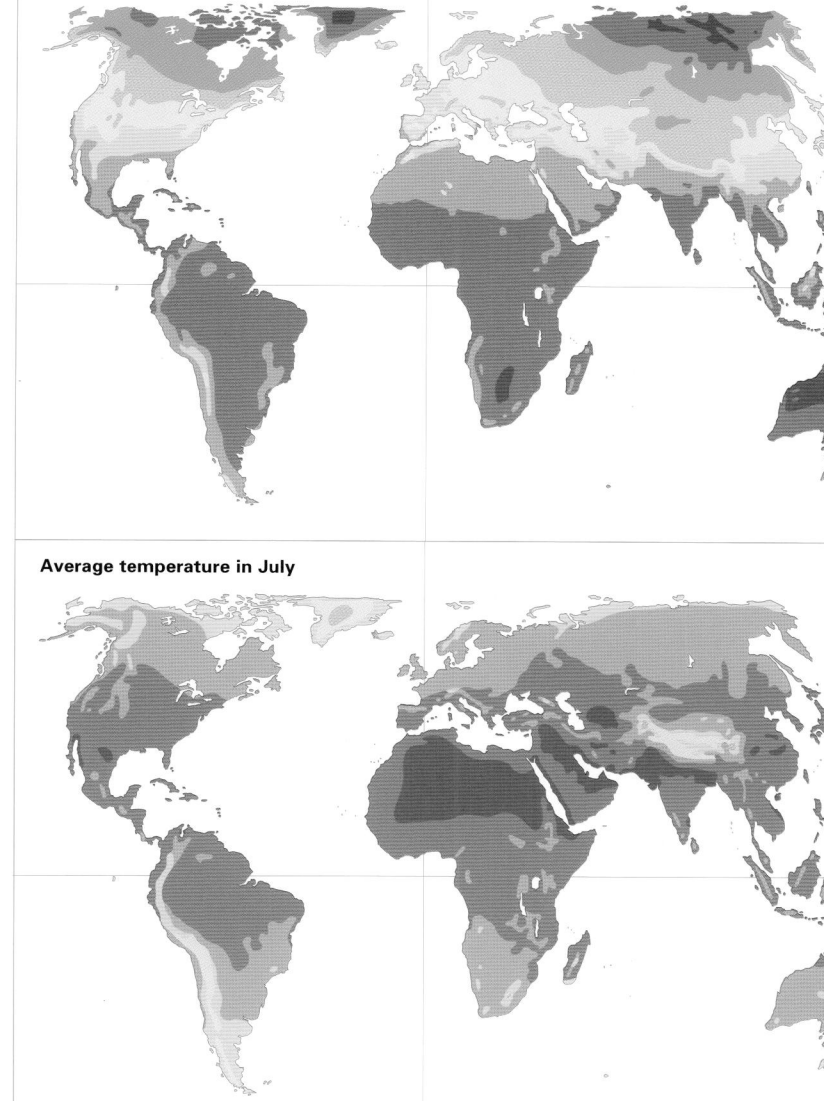

Average temperature

	86°F
	68°F
	50°F
	32°F
	14°F
	−4°F
	−22°F
	−40°F

Average temperature in July

Average temperature

	86°F
	68°F
	50°F
	32°F
	14°F

PRECIPITATION (RAINFALL AND SNOW)

Average annual precipitation

	120 inches
	80 inches
	40 inches
	20 inches
	10 inches

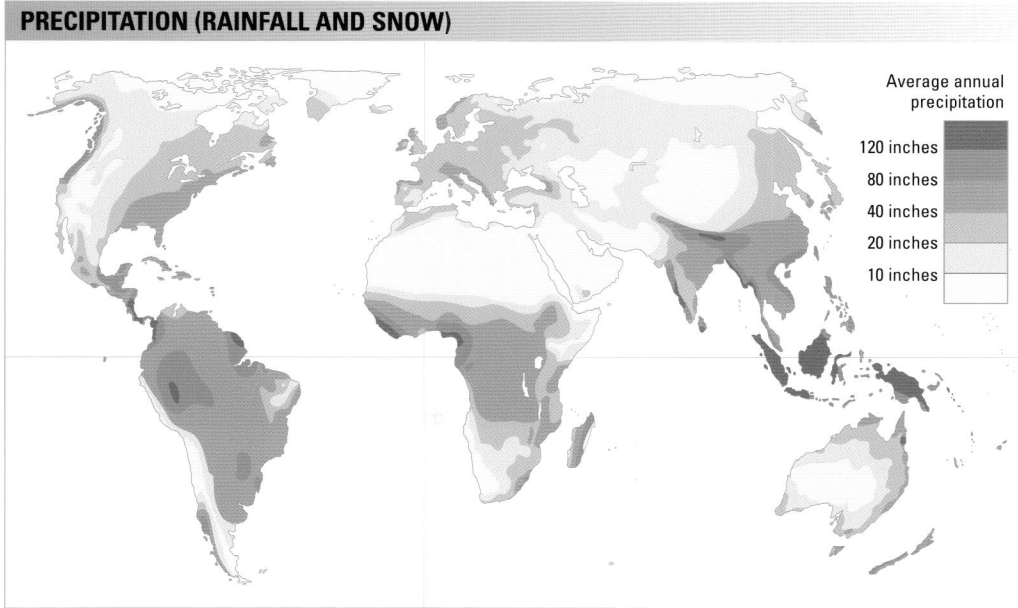

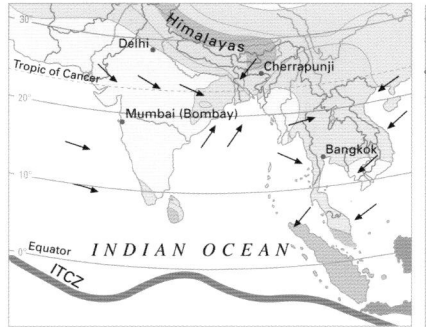

March – Start of the hot, dry season. The ITCZ is over the southern Indian Ocean.

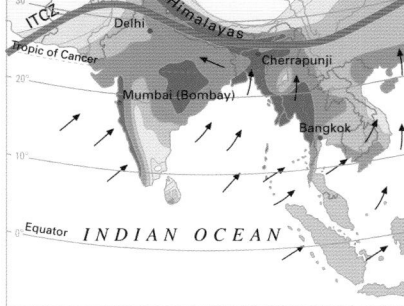

July – The rainy season. The ITCZ has migrated northward; winds blow onshore.

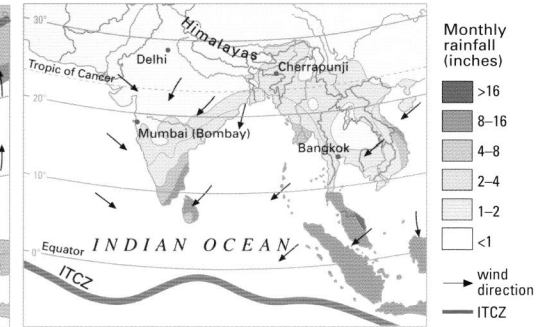

November – The ITCZ has returned south. The offshore winds are cool and dry.

Monthly rainfall (inches)

	>16
	8–16
	4–8
	2–4
	1–2
	<1

→ wind direction
— ITCZ

CLIMATE RECORDS

TEMPERATURE

Highest recorded temperature:
Al Aziziyah, Libya, 135.9°F [57.7°C], September 13, 1922.

Highest mean annual temperature:
Dallol, Ethiopia, 94°F [34.4°C], 1960–6.

Longest heatwave:
Marble Bar, W. Australia, 162 days over 100°F [38°C], October 23, 1923, to April 7, 1924.

Lowest recorded temperature (outside poles):
Verkhoyansk, Siberia, −93.6°F [−69.8°C], February 7, 1982. Verkhoyansk also registered the greatest annual range of temperature: −90°F to 98°F [−68°C to 37°C].

Lowest mean annual temperature:
Polus Nedostupnosti, Pole of Cold, Antarctica, −72°F [−57.8°C].

PRECIPITATION

Driest place:
Quillagua, N. Chile, mean annual rainfall 0.02 inches [0.5 mm], 1964–2001.

Wettest place (average):
Mt Wai'ale'ale, Hawai'i, USA, mean annual rainfall 459.8 inches [11,680 mm].

Wettest place (12 months):
Cherrapunji, Meghalaya, N.E. India, 1,042 inches [26,461 mm], August 1860 to August 1861. Cherrapunji also holds the record for rainfall in one month: 115 inches [2,930 mm], July 1861. (See Monsoon maps below.)

Wettest place (24 hours):
Fac Fac, Réunion, Indian Ocean, 71.9 inches [1,825 mm], March 15–16, 1952.

Heaviest hailstones:
Gopalganj, Bangladesh, up to 2.25 lb [1.02 kg], April 14, 1986 (killed 92 people).

Heaviest snowfall (continuous):
Bessans, Savoie, France, 68 inches [1,730 mm] in 19 hours, April 5–6, 1969.

Heaviest snowfall (season/year):
Mt Baker, Washington, USA, 1,140 inches [28,956 mm], June 1998 to June 1999.

For more information:

77 Ocean currents

78 Atmosphere

80 Climate

Ever since the Industrial Revolution began, the amount of carbon dioxide in the atmosphere has steadily increased. It is the result of burning fossil fuels (coal, oil, and natural gas), and also the destruction of forests which absorb carbon dioxide. In the late 18th century, carbon dioxide made up about 280 parts per million by volume (ppmv). Since 1958, regular measurements have been made at the Mauna Kea Observatory, Hawai'i, to avoid local pollution. It has since risen from 316 ppmv to 390 ppmv in 2010.

Carbon dioxide is one of the "greenhouse gases," which also include CFCs (which also cause ozone depletion in the upper atmosphere), methane, and nitrous oxides. Water vapor is another greenhouse gas. The volume of vapor in the atmosphere is not changing significantly, though it may increase if the atmosphere warms up, causing an increase in the evaporation of surface waters.

Greenhouse gases are so-called because they slow the escape of heat that is reradiated from the Earth's surface, in much the same way the glass walls and roof of a greenhouse block the escape of heat. The greenhouse effect is essential for life on Earth. Without it, our planet would be some 54°F [30°C] colder than it is. But the increase in the volume of carbon dioxide in particular has caused global temperatures to rise. These changes were detailed by the Intergovernmental Panel on Climate Change (IPCC) report in 2007. While computer projections are difficult to make, the IPCC report concluded that a rise in temperatures of 7°F [4°C] was likely by 2100. Global warming will almost certainly alter weather patterns, causing extreme food and water shortages in vulnerable parts of the world, massive floods, and a rise in sea levels of between 7 inches and 23 inches [18–59 cm].

While an international ban has been imposed on some greenhouse gases, their residence time in the atmosphere may have

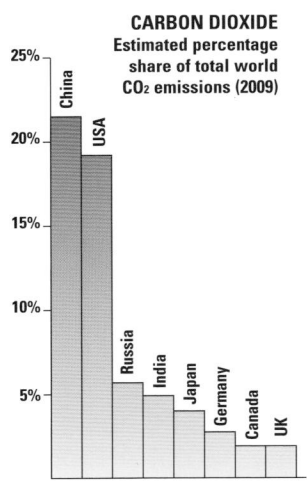

CARBON DIOXIDE
Estimated percentage share of total world CO_2 emissions (2009)

In 2007 it was estimated that China was building two coal-fired power stations every week to support its economic boom. It has since overtaken the USA to become the world's biggest producer of carbon dioxide.

GLOBAL WARMING

High atmospheric concentrations of heat-absorbing gases appear to be causing a rise in average temperatures worldwide – up by approximately 3°F [1.5°C] by the year 2020, according to some estimates. Global warming is also likely to bring about a rise in sea levels that may flood some of the world's densely populated coastal areas.

Evidence of global warming is attributed mainly to the "greenhouse effect," caused by the emission of certain gases, notably carbon dioxide, into the atmosphere. Despite international action to control emissions of some greenhouse gases, carbon dioxide levels are still rising.

Carbon dioxide emissions in tonnes per capita (2009)

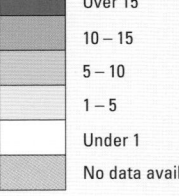

- Over 15
- 10 – 15
- 5 – 10
- 1 – 5
- Under 1
- No data available

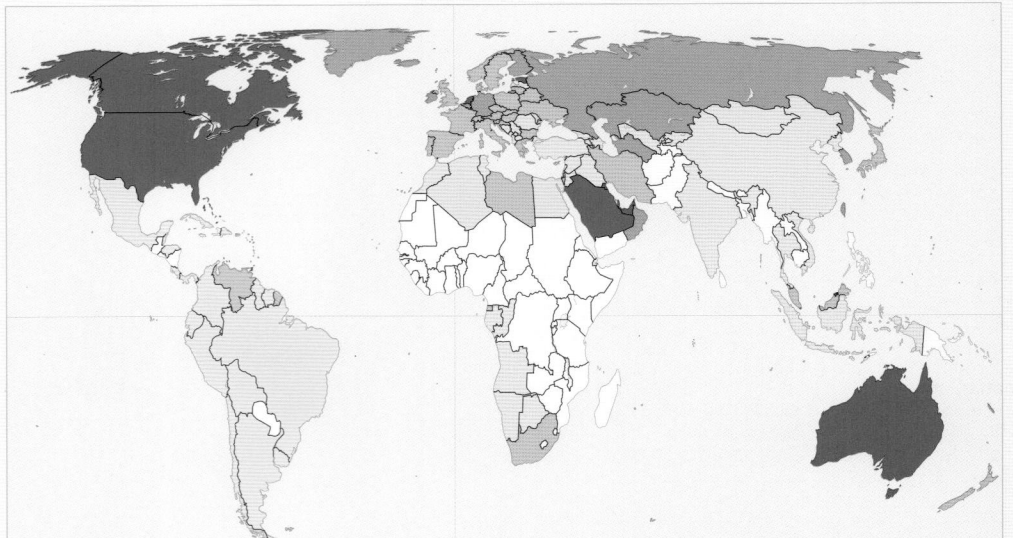

CLIMATE CHANGE

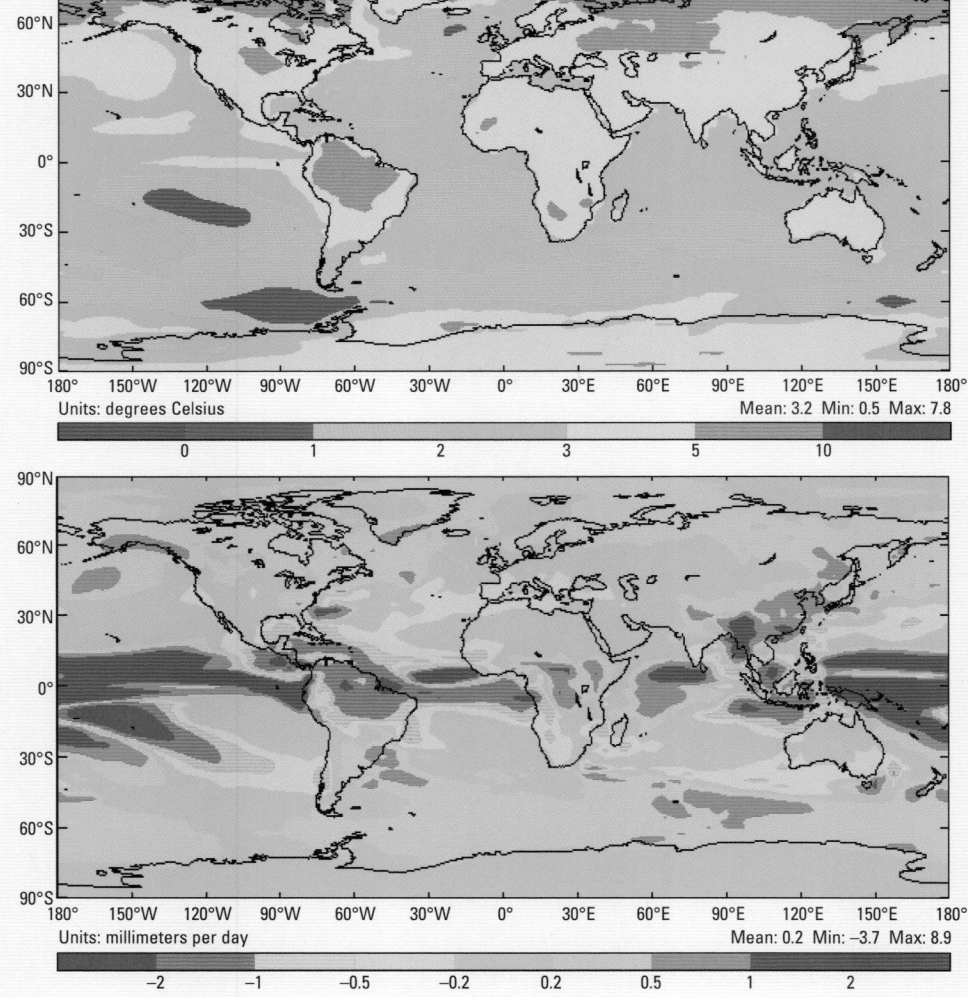

Units: degrees Celsius — Mean: 3.2 Min: 0.5 Max: 7.8

Units: millimeters per day — Mean: 0.2 Min: –3.7 Max: 8.9

Annual average surface air temperature

The map summarizes the change in long-term mean values between the predicted average for the period from 2070 to 2100, and the observed average for 1960 to 1990. The predictions are from a long-term "run" of a "coupled" atmosphere-ocean computer model that represents the complex processes in the Earth's climate system. It assumes that the atmospheric concentration of carbon dioxide will increase more than twofold during the 21st century, assuming "medium growth" of the global economy, and that no measures to combat the emission of greenhouse gases are taken. Note that the predicted increase in average surface temperature suggests a warming across Britain and Ireland of between 2°C [3.6°F] in the north and west to possibly 4°C [7.2°F] in the southeast. Very broadly, the oceans and some adjacent continental areas are likely to see the smaller increases.

Annual average precipitation

Predictions from climate models always involve some degree of uncertainty. This is because our understanding of the climate system and its complex workings are imperfect, as are the model representations of the physical system. Additionally, we are unsure quite how the world will evolve economically and politically over the coming decades – although different scenarios are used in this regard. The map of predicted precipitation change indicates broadly, for example, an increase across Britain and Ireland. The largest increases of some 0.01–0.02 inches [0.2–0.5 mm] a day are anticipated to be over northern and western areas. This equates to some 3–7 inches [75–180 mm] a year.

It should be noted that both these maps mask quite significant seasonal detail, which is also predicted by the models.

ANTARCTICA

▶ Between January and March 2002, the 1,255 sq mi [3,250 sq km] Larsen B ice shelf on the Antarctic Peninsula collapsed. The left-hand image shows its area (in blue) in December 2001 before the collapse, while the right-hand image shows the area fragmented in December 2002 after the collapse. The 656 ft [200 m] thick ice sheet had been retreating before this date, but over 500 billion tonnes of ice collapsed in under a month. This was due to rising temperatures of 0.9°F [0.5°C] per year in this part of Antarctica.

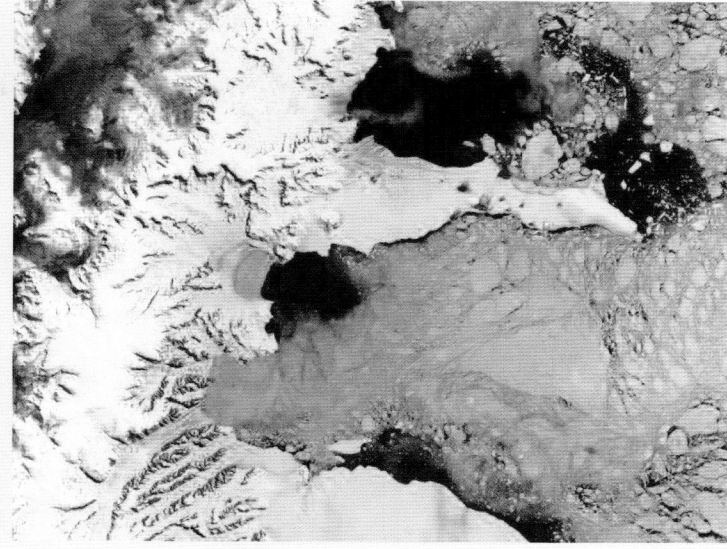

TEMPERATURE CHANGE

Climate modelers have produced simulations of global and continental surface temperature changes over the last century. This is done using only "natural forcing" by modeling the impact on atmospheric temperatures from known solar variability and volcanic eruptions. In addition, the same period of time is simulated by adding to natural forcing the impact of anthropogenic (human) influence due to measured changes in the concentration of greenhouse gases, particulate matter, etc.

The separate model "runs" are then compared with the observed temperature changes to illustrate which of the simulations matches the observations best.

This is a powerful means of verifying the relative roles of natural and human induced changes in atmospheric composition, and known solar output fluctuations on climate change.

▶ Climate model simulations for 1906 to 2005 using "natural forcings only" (blue bands) and "natural plus anthropogenic forcings" (pink bands). Regional decadal averages of observed temperature (black lines) are plotted as anomalies with respect to the 1901 to 1950 average. Blue and pink bands define the 5% to 95% range of possibilities for 19 runs produced by five models (natural forcing), and 58 simulations from 14 models (natural plus anthropogenic forcing).

Models using only natural forcings

Models using both natural and anthropogenic forcings

━━ Observations
(dashed when spatial coverage is less than 50%)

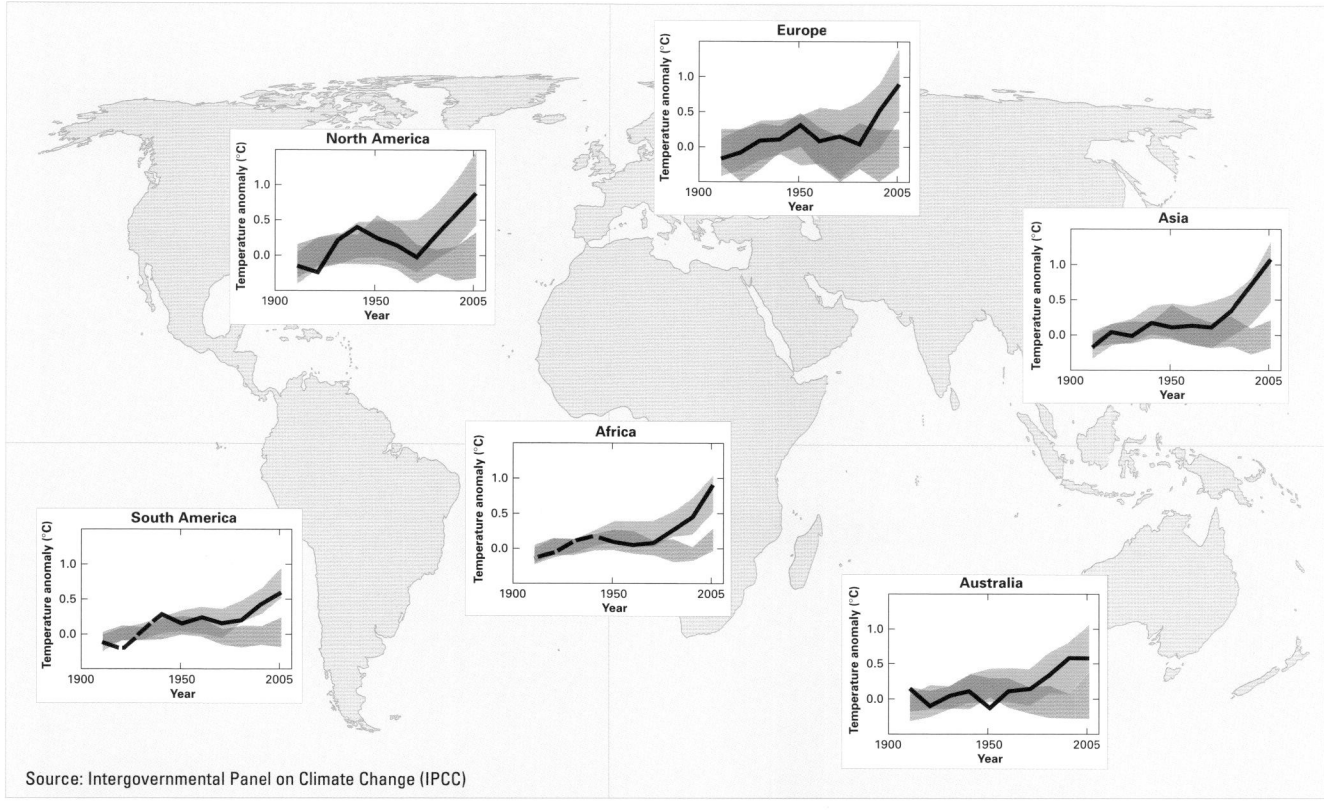

Source: Intergovernmental Panel on Climate Change (IPCC)

PROJECTED CHANGE IN GLOBAL WARMING

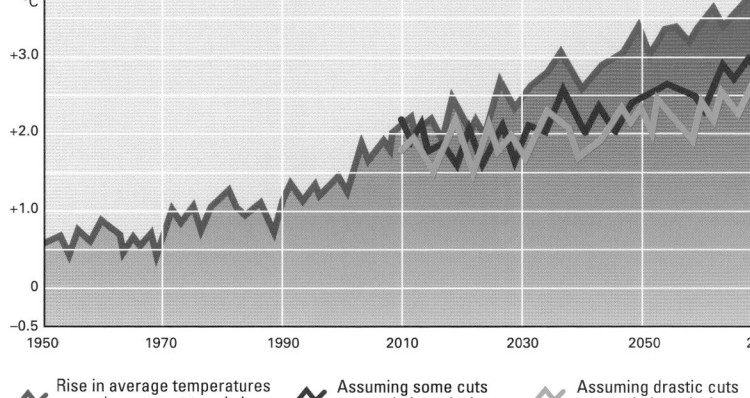

⋀ Rise in average temperatures assuming present trends in CO₂ emissions continue

⋀ Assuming some cuts are made in emissions

⋀ Assuming drastic cuts are made in emissions

Climate models are used to provide the best scientifically-based estimates of the future global climate. A typical method is to run the models for some decades ahead and then to compare the predicted average with a past 30-year period. A range of climate models are used, run with different scenarios that express the breadth of possibilities of, for example, industrial development, and the degree of atmospheric pollution "clean-up" by industrial nations.

The diagram above shows global observed and predicted surface mean temperature change from 1950 to 2070 with three prediction scenarios. The first (red) assumes rapid economic growth and continued population increases. The second (blue) assumes some attempts are made to cut greenhouse gas emissions, while the green line involves the greater use of cleaner technologies, with global population peaking mid-century then declining.

THE OZONE LAYER

Total atmospheric ozone concentration in the southern hemisphere (2010)

In 1985, scientists working in Antarctica discovered a thinning of the ozone layer, resulting in what is commonly known as the "ozone hole." This caused immediate alarm because the ozone layer absorbs most of the Sun's dangerous ultraviolet radiation, which is believed to cause an increase in skin cancer, cataracts, and damage to the immune system.

Between 1985 and 2001 the ozone depletion increased and, by 2002, the ozone hole over the South Pole was estimated to be three times as large as the USA. This false-color image shows the total atmospheric ozone concentration in the southern hemisphere in October 2010, with the ozone hole clearly identifiable in purple and blue at the center. The data is from NASA's Aura satellite, ESA's ERS-2 satellite, and the NOAA-16 weather-forecasting satellite. The colors represent the ozone concentration in Dobson Units (DU).

Scientists agree that ozone depletion is caused by CFCs, a group of manufactured chemicals that were used in refrigerators and air-conditioning systems. In the Montreal Protocol in 1987, industrial nations agreed to phase out CFCs, and a complete ban on most CFCs was agreed after the end of 1995.

Since 2001 the amount of ozone in the atmosphere has stabilized and so too has the hole. While scientists believe that the chemicals may remain in the atmosphere for 50 to 100 years, if current trends are maintained it is possible that ozone levels may recover by 2050.

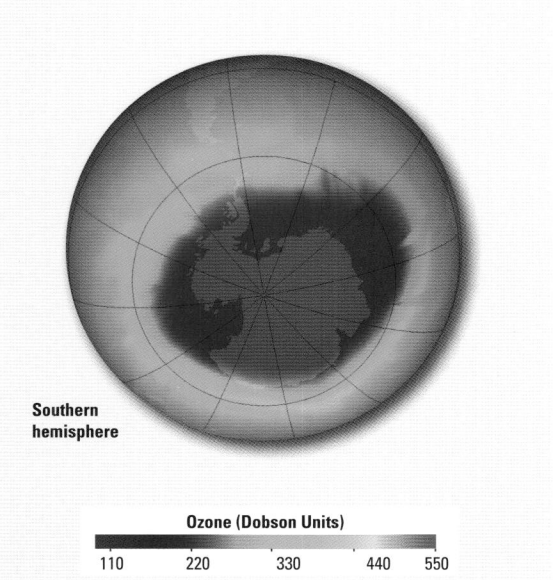

Southern hemisphere

Ozone (Dobson Units)

110   220   330   440   550

For more information:

80 Climate regions
81 Precipitation
86 Biodiversity

Without the hydrological cycle, by which water is constantly recycled between the oceans, the atmosphere and the land, the continents would be barren. Precipitation enables plants to grow and soils to form, creating the world's natural vegetation regions and the ecosystems that support animal life.

Running water also plays a major role in shaping landforms. Yet in many parts of the world, people do not have safe water to drink and suffer from diseases caused by water-borne organisms and pollution. It is estimated that 780 million people lacked access to safe water and more people had a mobile phone than a toilet.

Experts argue that world demand for water is increasing at about twice the rate of population growth. It is predicted that, by 2025, half the world's population will face water shortages. This could lead to conflict and even boundary wars – 300 major rivers cross national frontiers and access to their water is likely to be disputed.

THE HYDROLOGICAL CYCLE

The world's water balance is regulated by the constant recycling of water between the oceans, the atmosphere and the land. The movement of water between these three reservoirs is known as the "hydrological cycle." The oceans play a vital role in the hydrological cycle: 74% of the total precipitation falls over the oceans and 84% of the total evaporation comes from the oceans. Water vapor in the atmosphere circulates around the planet, transporting energy as well as the water itself. When the vapor cools, it falls as rain or snow. The whole cycle is driven by the Sun.

Transfer of water vapor
10% of the balance of precipitation/evaporation over oceans

Evaporation from oceans
84% of total evaporation

Evapotranspiration
16% of total evaporation

Precipitation
74% of total precipitation

Precipitation
26% of total precipitation

Runoff
10% of the balance of precipitation/evaporation over land

Surface runoff

Surface storage

Infiltration

Groundwater flow

WATER DISTRIBUTION

The distribution of planetary water is shown by percentage. Oceans and ice caps together account for more than 99% of the total; the breakdown of the remainder is estimated.

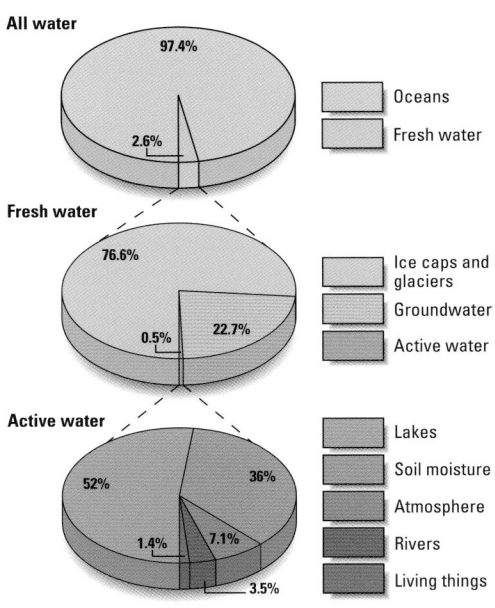

All water
97.4%
2.6%

Oceans
Fresh water

Fresh water
76.6%
0.5% 22.7%

Ice caps and glaciers
Groundwater
Active water

Active water
52% 36%
1.4% 7.1%
3.5%

Lakes
Soil moisture
Atmosphere
Rivers
Living things

Almost all the world's water is 3,000 million years old, and all of it cycles endlessly through the hydrosphere, though at different rates. Water vapor circulates over days, even hours; deep-ocean water circulates over millennia; and ice-cap water remains solid for millions of years.

ANNUAL SEDIMENT YIELD

Around 20% of all land-derived sediment is carried by three Asian rivers: the Brahmaputra, the Hwang Ho (Yellow River), and the Ganges. Together, these three rivers carry up to 3,206 million tonnes of sediment each year into the oceans. Sediment yield is affected by runoff and vegetation cover, and is steadily increasing due to large-scale deforestation, most notably in Southeast Asia and the Amazon basin. In these regions, deforesting the slopes allows the heavy tropical rains to wash away whatever thin and fragile soil there is, leading to severe erosion of the land.

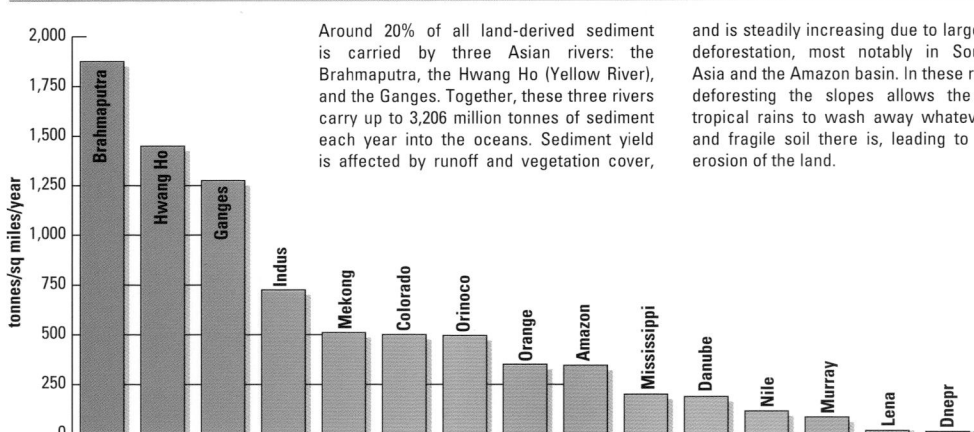

tonnes/sq miles/year

2,000
1,750
1,500
1,250
1,000
750
500
250
0

Brahmaputra
Hwang Ho
Ganges
Indus
Mekong
Colorado
Orinoco
Orange
Amazon
Mississippi
Danube
Nile
Murray
Lena
Dnepr

WATER RUNOFF

Annual fresh water runoff by continent in cubic miles

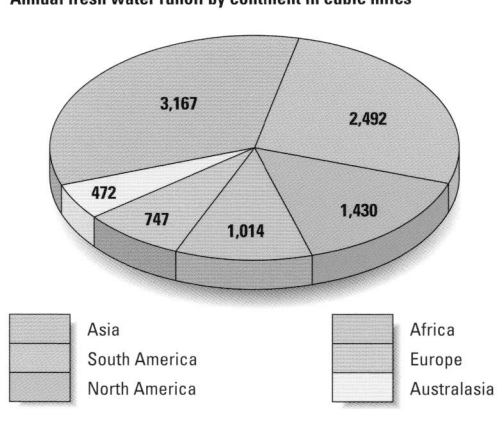

3,167
2,492
472
747
1,014
1,430

Asia
South America
North America
Africa
Europe
Australasia

► The River Amazon is the world's second-longest river (after the River Nile), draining the vast rain forest basin of northern South America. The Amazon carries by far the greatest volume of water of any river in the world: the average rate of discharge is approximately 3,355,000 cu ft [95,000 cu m] per second, nearly three times as much as its nearest rival, the Congo. The flow is so great that its silt discolors the water up to 125 miles [200 km] into the Atlantic. At approximately 2.7 million sq miles [7 million sq km], the Amazon basin comprises nearly 40% of the whole of South America. Nevertheless, in 2005 large parts of the Amazon rain forest were at their driest in living memory, partly related to the severe hurricane season off the US Gulf coast. Rainfall was significantly below average, causing water levels to drop to record lows. At Tabatinga, 600 miles [970 km] west of Manaus, rainfall was almost 70% down from 2004. Rivers and lakes began to dry up, revealing huge sandbanks and making navigation difficult for boats.

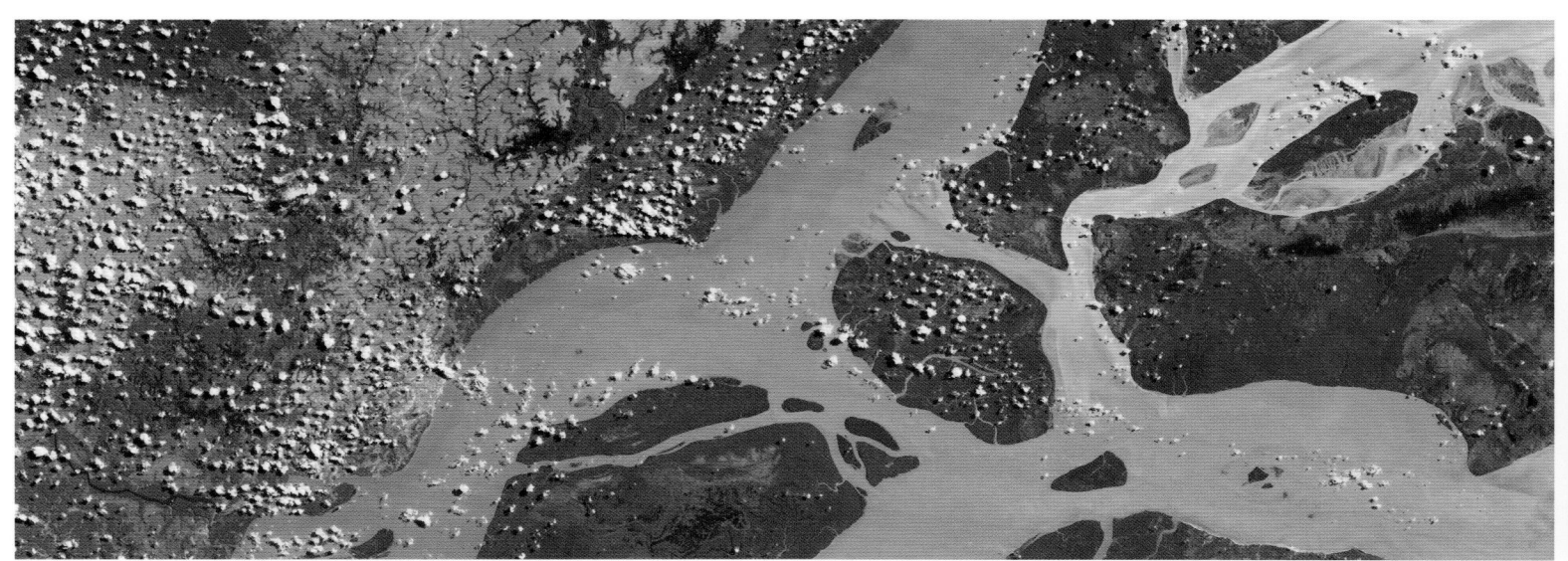

WATERSHEDS

The map below shows the world's major rivers, with the ranking of the 20 longest rivers shown in square brackets after their name, led by the Nile [1] and the Amazon [2].

The map shows the direction of freshwater flow on a continental scale, whereas the water runoff chart on the facing page indicates the quantities involved annually.

The rate of runoff varies seasonally and is affected by the surface vegetation and climate. Most of the world's major rivers discharge into the Atlantic Ocean.

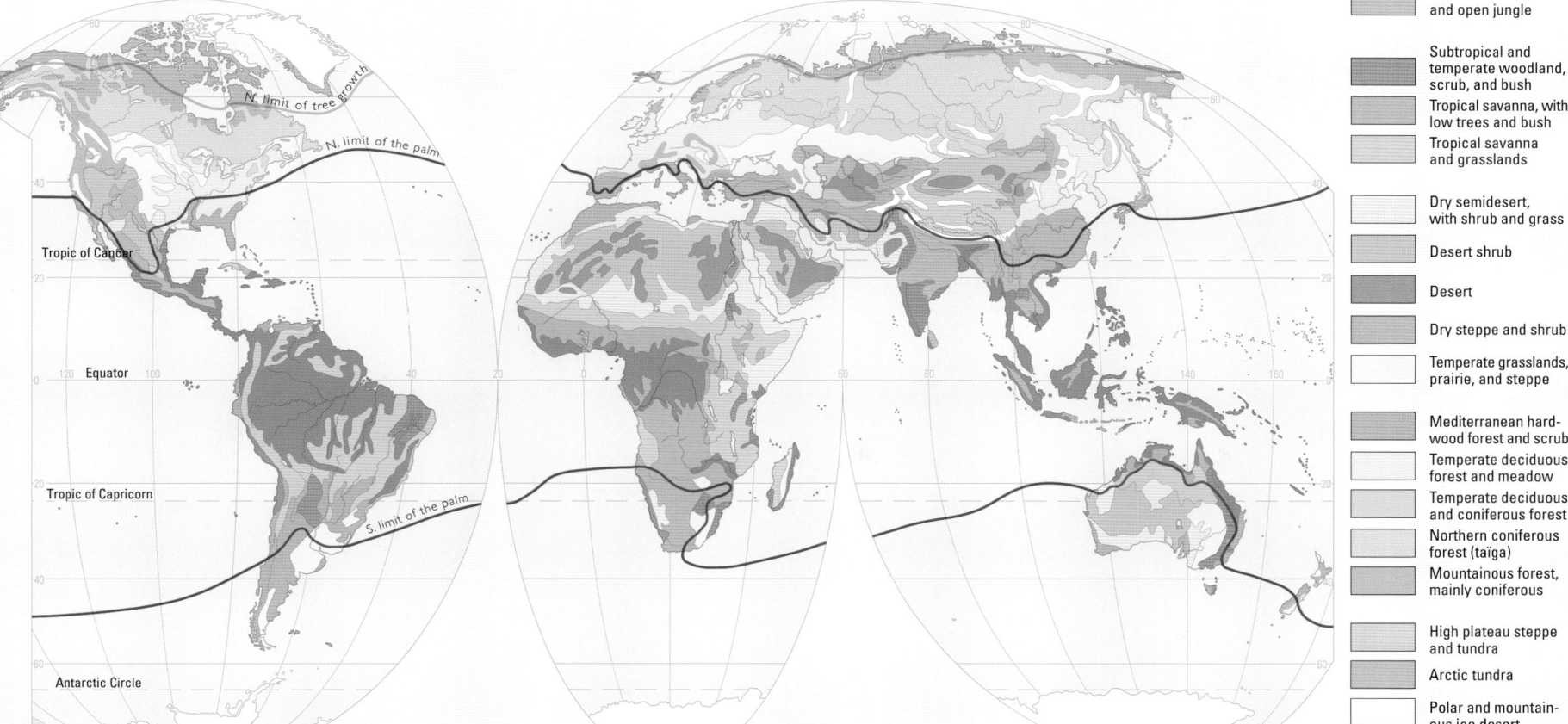

Where the rivers run

- Pacific Ocean
- Indian Ocean
- Arctic Ocean
- Atlantic Ocean
- Caribbean Sea– Gulf of Mexico
- Mediterranean Sea
- Inland basins, ice caps, and deserts

NATURAL VEGETATION

The map below illustrates the natural "climax vegetation" of a region, as dictated by its climate and topography. In most cases, human agricultural activity has drastically altered the pattern of the vegetation. The various vegetation regions support different kinds of animals and wildlife, and, in an undisturbed state, they are highly developed biological communities, or "biomes."

The blue line on the map represents the northern limit of tree growth, and the red lines indicate the northern and southern limits of palm growth. The majority of the numerous species are tropical or subtropical. Some, such as the coconut, date, sago, and oil palms, are important economically.

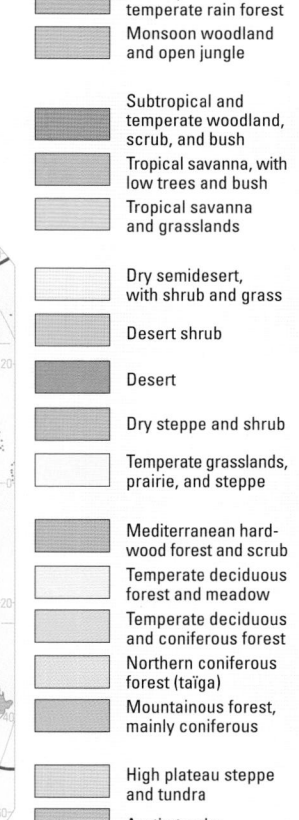

- Tropical rain forest
- Subtropical and temperate rain forest
- Monsoon woodland and open jungle
- Subtropical and temperate woodland, scrub, and bush
- Tropical savanna, with low trees and bush
- Tropical savanna and grasslands
- Dry semidesert, with shrub and grass
- Desert shrub
- Desert
- Dry steppe and shrub
- Temperate grasslands, prairie, and steppe
- Mediterranean hard-wood forest and scrub
- Temperate deciduous forest and meadow
- Temperate deciduous and coniferous forest
- Northern coniferous forest (taïga)
- Mountainous forest, mainly coniferous
- High plateau steppe and tundra
- Arctic tundra
- Polar and mountain-ous ice desert

COPYRIGHT PHILIP'S

For more information:
76 Life in the oceans
80 Climate
82 Climate change
   Global warming
85 Natural vegetation

Biodiversity refers to the variety of living material. It includes the variety of species, the variety within the same species, and the variety of ecosystems within which species operate. Estimates of the number of species in the world vary from between 7 million and 80 million. The currently accepted total is about 14 million, yet only 2 million species have been formally identified.

Biodiversity is vital for human survival. It remains the basis for our food and most of our medicine. In less economically developed countries (LEDCs), over 20% of the food consumed is gathered from natural sources. At a global level, over 15% of animal protein consumed is from sea fish caught in the wild. More than 60% of the world's population rely on traditional medicines for their health care. In Mexico, the Popoluca Indians "farm" over 250 species of plant. Many medicines come from natural sources. Aspirin, for example, comes from an acid taken from the bark of willow trees. The anti-cancer drug "taxol" originates from the wild Pacific yew tree. It is estimated that

the pharmaceuticals industry gains US $32 billion per year in profits from traditional remedies.

However, the loss of biodiversity is increasing at an accelerating rate. Up to 27,000 species a year may be lost, and the United Nations Environment Program (UNEP) suggests that the current rate of extinction is 50–100 times greater than "normal," and believes that up to 25% of all the world's species may be lost by 2025. The main reasons for the decline are the introduction of alien species and habitat destruction. Human impact on biodiversity has brought about more extinctions than any other single factor since the extinction of the dinosaurs (65 million years ago).

Since 1600, 39% of animal extinctions have been due to the introduction of alien species, 36% from habitat destruction, and 23% from hunting or deliberate extermination. The introduction of rats, cats, and other species has led to the extinction of many flightless birds in Polynesia. Plantation crops, such as rubber, often thrive best when taken away from their natural homes,

since in the new lands there may not be the pests to control them. One noted example of extinction was caused by the introduction of the Nile perch into Lake Victoria, East Africa: introduced in the 1960s, it led to the extinction of some 50 species of cichlid fish within 20 years.

In 2009, a report by the International Union for the Conservation of Nature listed 18,788 organisms facing extinction. Up to 46% of primates are said to be at risk of extinction. Overall, some 21% of mammals are endangered – including "charismatic" species such as the tiger and the panda, but equally less recognizable species of bats, rodents, and marsupials. Up to one-fifth of reptiles, one-third of amphibians, and one-third of bird species are at risk of extinction. The most threatened group are fish (one-third are at risk), largely as a result of overfishing. The World Conservation Union reported that 8% of mammals were threatened in the US, compared with 32% in the Philippines and 44% in Madagascar, two countries where habitat destruction has been proceeding on a large scale.

LEVELS OF ENDEMISM
Known endemic species per
100 sq miles, selected countries (2008)

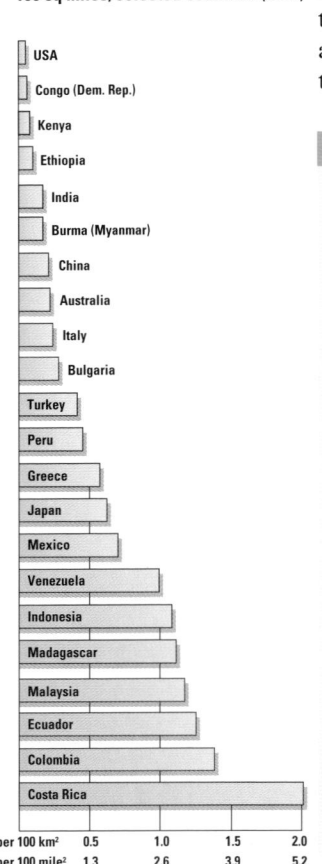

USA
Congo (Dem. Rep.)
Kenya
Ethiopia
India
Burma (Myanmar)
China
Australia
Italy
Bulgaria
Turkey
Peru
Greece
Japan
Mexico
Venezuela
Indonesia
Madagascar
Malaysia
Ecuador
Colombia
Costa Rica

| per 100 km² | 0.5 | 1.0 | 1.5 | 2.0 |
| per 100 mile² | 1.3 | 2.6 | 3.9 | 5.2 |

THREATENED MAMMAL SPECIES

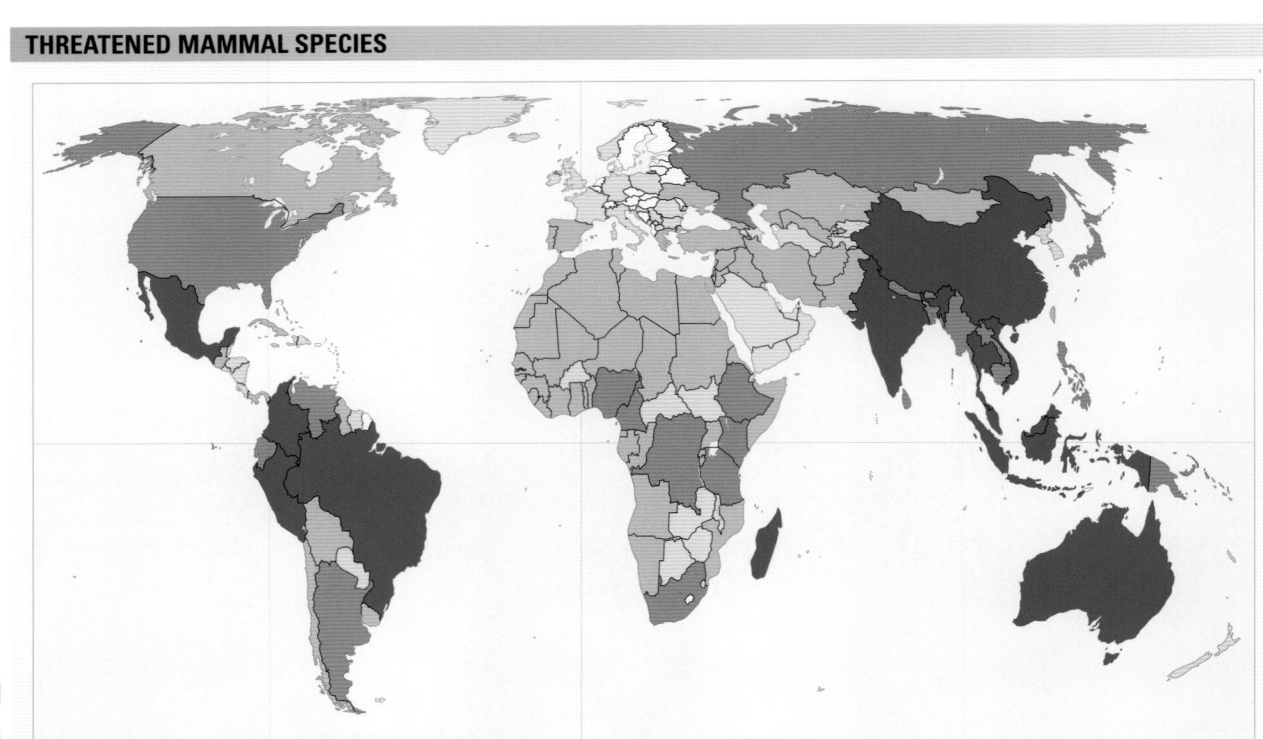

Mammal species threatened with extinction (2011)

	Over 50
	25 – 50
	10 – 25
	5 – 10
	0 – 5
	No data

Countries with the highest number of mammal species threatened with extinction (2011)

Indonesia	184
Mexico	100
India	94
Brazil	81
China	75
Malaysia	70
Madagascar	65
Thailand	57
Australia	55
Peru	54
Vietnam	54
Colombia	52

NATIVE ("ENDEMIC") SPECIES AS A PROPORTION OF TOTAL SPECIES (SELECTED COUNTRIES)

Country	Mammals (2008) Total endemic	Mammals (2008) Threatened endemic	Birds (2008) Total endemic	Birds (2008) Threatened endemic	Amphibians (2008) Total endemic	Amphibians (2008) Threatened endemic
Argentina	82	13	12	0	36	21
Australia	241	49	322	27	209	47
Bolivia	22	4	15	5	64	27
Brazil	185	54	203	71	529	26
China	82	17	59	17	169	74
Colombia	37	9	68	43	333	154
Congo (Dem. Rep.)	25	4	12	8	42	4
Cuba	21	12	22	8	59	49
Ecuador	30	12	34	19	156	98
Ethiopia	32	18	15	10	24	9
India	44	29	54	16	150	61
Indonesia	257	114	378	70	172	21
Japan	41	16	15	6	45	17
Kenya	12	7	8	6	14	4
Madagascar	186	58	107	28	242	67
Malaysia	19	3	7	0	45	22
Mexico	158	80	88	22	245	171
Panama	13	4	8	3	27	13
Papua New Guinea	69	20	84	16	174	9
Peru	55	19	106	36	223	70
Philippines	111	25	196	59	79	48
South Africa	31	11	16	4	42	16
Tanzania	22	18	24	15	72	48
USA	104	20	67	35	182	49
Venezuela	19	6	39	14	142	63

▲ Madagascar has developed in isolation since it split from Africa 150 million years ago. As a result of this isolation, a unique range of plants and animals has evolved, adapted to its own specific conditions. Over 95% of Madagascar's mammals, 90% of its reptiles, over 66% of its plants, and over 40% of its breeding birds do not exist anywhere else in the world.

Madagascar is home to all of the world's lemurs (all of which are endangered, such as the aye-aye pictured above) and two-thirds of the world's chameleons. Its plant species include pitcher plants, orchids, and the Madagascan rosy periwinkle (the most effective known treatment for childhood leukemia). However, large-scale deforestation since the 1970s has reduced Madagascar's cover of rain forest to less than 10% of the island's original forest cover.

ENVIRONMENTAL HOTSPOTS

Up to 75% of the world's most threatened mammals, birds and amphibians live in an area covering just 2.3% of the Earth's surface, and roughly half of all flowering plant species and 42% of land-based vertebrates exist in 34 biological hotspots.

Scientists argue that, with limited financial resources, governments and conservationists should prioritize by protecting the small total land areas that account for a very high percentage of global biodiversity. In 1999, scientists identified 25 such areas, mostly in the tropics, which were the center of global biodiversity.

The number of hotspots has risen to 34. These include the mountains of central Asia, the whole of Japan, the Horn of Africa including the Ethiopian highlands, and the Himalayas region. The hotspots once covered 15.7% of the Earth's surface, an area roughly the size of Russia and Australia combined – now they cover only 2.3% of the Earth's surface, an area slightly larger than India.

Over 70% of all mammals, 86% of all birds, and 92% of all amphibians are crammed into this small area of the world's total land mass. Madagascar and the Indian Ocean Islands hotspot was found to have very high concentrations of plant and vertebrate families that are found nowhere else on the globe.

Global warming could have a devastating effect on biodiversity hotspots such as the Amazonian and Indonesian rain forests. By 2100, between 12% and 39% of the land surface of the Earth will have a new climate. There are numerous species that will be unable to move in order to stay within their preferred climate range. These species will either have to evolve rapidly or die out.

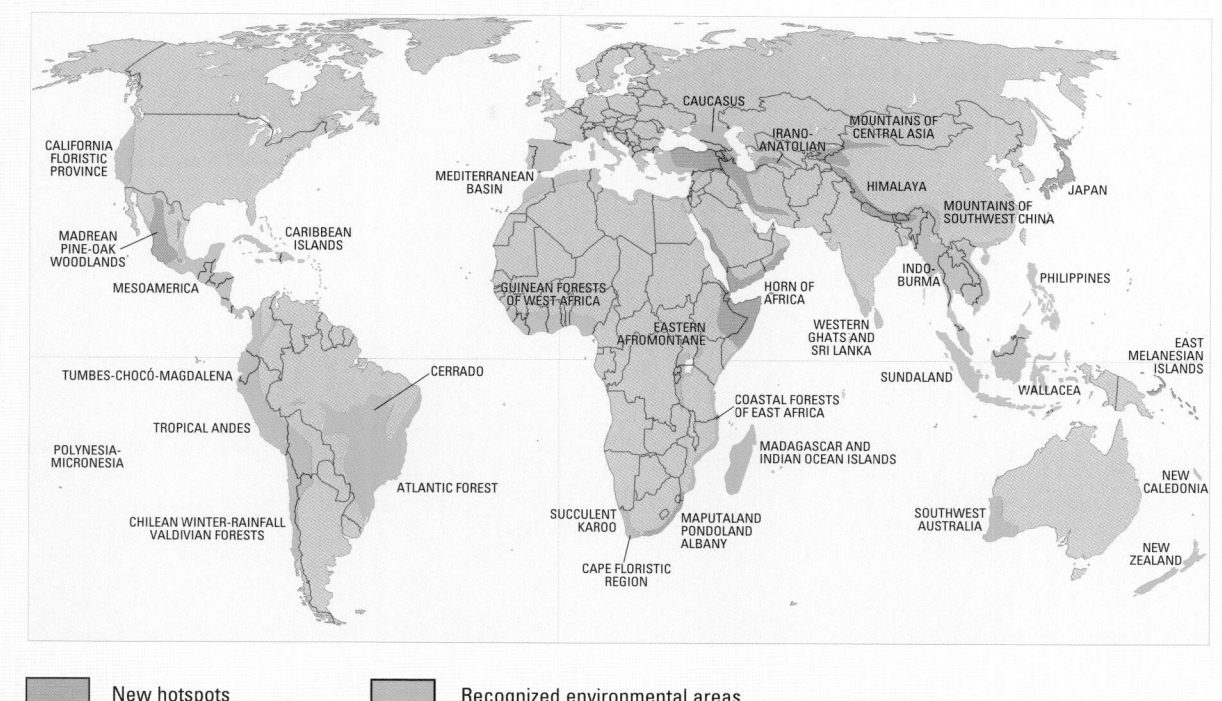

New hotspots | Recognized environmental areas

AUSTRALIA'S INTRODUCED SPECIES

Australia's native plants and animals adapted to life on an isolated continent over millions of years. Since European settlement in the 18th century they have had to compete with a range of species introduced by the settlers, which impact on the native species by predation, competition for food and shelter, destroying habitat, and by spreading diseases. Introduced species typically have few predators or fatal diseases, and some have very high reproductive rates.

Management and the prevention of the introduction of new invasive species are key environmental and agricultural policy issues for the Australian federal and state governments.

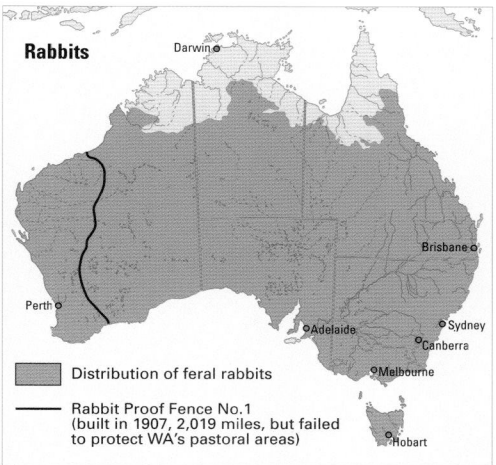

Rabbits

■ Distribution of feral rabbits
— Rabbit Proof Fence No.1 (built in 1907, 2,019 miles, but failed to protect WA's pastoral areas)

▲ Rabbits were introduced to Australia from England in 1859 for hunting, and quickly spread throughout the country. They are one of the most destructive introduced species in Australia, competing with native wildlife, damaging vegetation, and degrading the land.

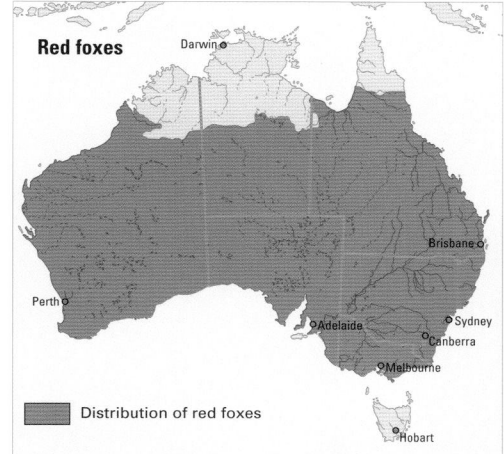

Red foxes

■ Distribution of red foxes

▲ The red fox was introduced from Europe for recreational hunting in 1855 and populations became established in the wild within 15 years. They prey on newborn lambs and have also been responsible for the decline of a number of native species.

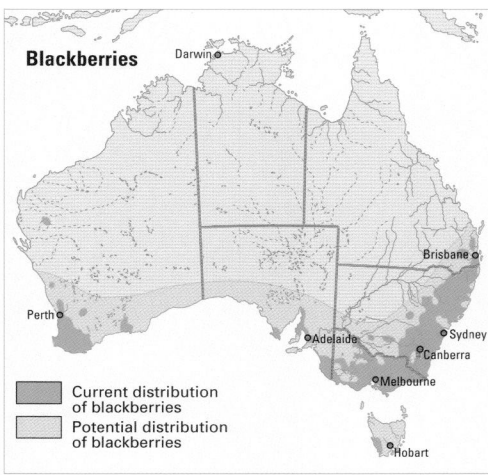

Blackberries

■ Current distribution of blackberries
■ Potential distribution of blackberries

▲ The blackberry was introduced from Europe as a source of fresh fruit. It is now regarded as one of the worst weeds in Australia because of its invasiveness, spreading through farmland, forests, and scrub. It out-competes many native plants, prevents light reaching the ground below, and provides food and shelter for pests.

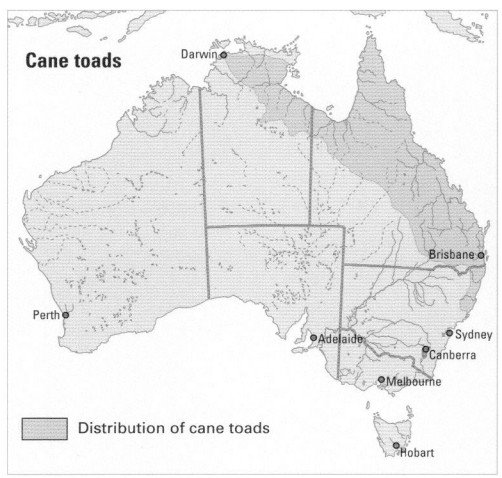

Cane toads

■ Distribution of cane toads

▲ Cane toads were introduced in 1935 to control beetles which were threatening the sugarcane industry. However, this was a failure and both the toad and the beetle are still thriving. They adapted well to the Australian environment and with no natural predators they quickly spread. They eat small native wildlife and poison any predators.

ESTIMATED VALUE OF WILD RESOURCES IN LESS ECONOMICALLY DEVELOPED COUNTRIES

Tropical non-coniferous forest product exports	US $11 billion per year
Fruit/latex harvesting, Peru	US $6,330 per hectare
Sustainable timber harvesting, Peru	US $490 per hectare
Buffalo range ranching, Zimbabwe	US $3.5–4.5 per hectare
Wetlands fish and fuelwood, Nigeria	US $38–59 per hectare
Viewing value of elephants, Kenya	US $25 million per year
Ecotourism, Costa Rica	US $1,250 per hectare
Tourism, Thailand	US $385,000–860,000 per year
Research/education, Thailand	US $38,000–77,000 per year
Tourism, Cameroon	US $10 per hectare
Genetic value, Cameroon	US $7 per hectare
Pharmaceutical prospecting, Costa Rica	US $4,981 million per product

▲ Bolivia has over 100,000 sq miles [250,000 sq km] of dry tropical forest, home to animals such as jaguars and ocelots. It is, however, being cleared at a rate of over 2% per annum. This false-color image shows an area that has been almost completely cleared. The darkest areas are remnants of the original forest, some of which have been retained as wind-breaks between newly created arable fields. The radial patterns are fields with new villages at their centers, part of a government resettlement scheme.

For more information:

11 Food and population

90 Urbanization of the Earth

Urban population

91 Largest cities

In 8000 BC, following the development of agriculture, the world had an estimated population of 8 million and by AD 1000 it was about 300 million. The onset of the Industrial Revolution in the late 18th century led to a population explosion. The 1,000 million mark was passed by 1850, it doubled by the 1920s, and doubled again to 4,000 million by 1975.

In the 1990s, demographers estimated that the world's population, which passed the 7 billion mark in 2012, would reach 9.3 billion by 2050 and only level out in 2200, at a peak of around 11 billion. However, in the early 21st century, after the rate of population growth had shown signs of decline, the Institute for Applied Systems Analysis suggested that the world's population might peak at about 9 billion in 2070. Whatever the global projections, everyone agreed that the greatest population growth would be in the developing countries.

The developing world includes what the World Bank (2010) describes as low-income economies (per capita GNI of US $995 or less), lower-middle-income economies (per capita GNI of US $996 to US $3,945), and upper-middle-income economies (per capita GNI of US $3,946 to US $12,195). Most developing countries are in Africa, Asia, and Latin America. The developed world, made up of high-income, industrialized economies (per capita GNI of US $12,196 or more), contains Australasia, most of Europe and North America, and Japan.

In developing countries, a high proportion of the population is young and so these countries face high expenditure on health and education. In developed countries, the population pyramids are becoming top-heavy, with increasingly aging populations.

LARGEST NATIONS

The world's most populous nations, in millions (2011)

1.	China	1,337
2.	India	1,189
3.	USA	313
4.	Indonesia	246
5.	Brazil	203
6.	Pakistan	187
7.	Bangladesh	159
8.	Nigeria	155
9.	Russia	139
10.	Japan	126
11.	Mexico	113
12.	Philippines	101
13.	Ethiopia	91
14.	Vietnam	91
15.	Egypt	82
16.	Germany	81
17.	Turkey	79
18.	Iran	78
19.	Congo (Dem. Rep.)	72
20.	Thailand	67
21.	France	65
22.	UK	63
23.	Italy	61
24.	Burma (Myanmar)	53
25.	Korea, South	49

MOST CROWDED NATIONS

Population per square mile (2011)

1.	Monaco	43,796
2.	Singapore	17,689
3.	Gaza Strip (OPT)	11,922
4.	Samoa	8,048
5.	Bahrain	4,726
6.	Maldives	3,405
7.	Malta	3,347
8.	Bangladesh	2,852
9.	Barbados	1,727
10.	Taiwan	1,661

LEAST CROWDED

Population per square mile (2011)

1.	Western Sahara	4.9
2.	Mongolia	5.2
3.	Namibia	6.7
4.	Australia	7.3
5.	Suriname	7.8
6.	Iceland	7.8
7.	Mauritania	8.2
8.	Canada	8.8
9.	Botswana	8.9
10.	Guyana	9.3

POPULATION DENSITY

The places marked on the map reflect the size of the urban agglomerations and conurbations, rather than the actual city limits. San Francisco itself, for example, has an official population of less than a million people.

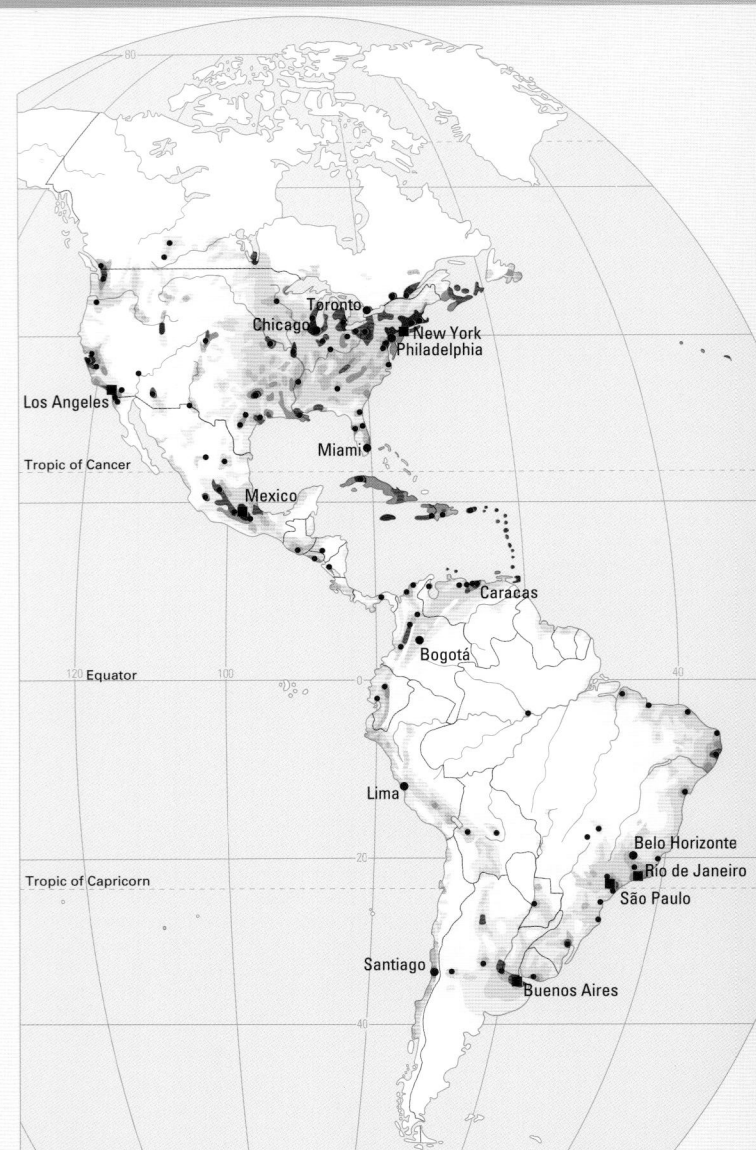

Inhabitants per square mile

- Over 500
- 250 – 500
- 125 – 250
- 65 – 125
- 15 – 65
- 8 – 15
- 3 – 8
- Under 3

Urban population

- ■ Over 10,000,000
- ● 5,000,000 – 10,000,000
- · 1,000,000 – 5,000,000

POPULATION CHANGE

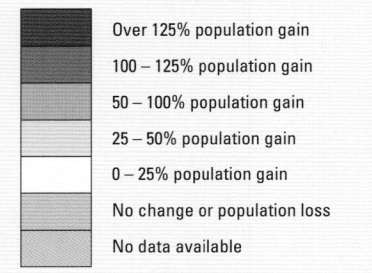

The projected population change for the years 2004–2050

- Over 125% population gain
- 100 – 125% population gain
- 50 – 100% population gain
- 25 – 50% population gain
- 0 – 25% population gain
- No change or population loss
- No data available

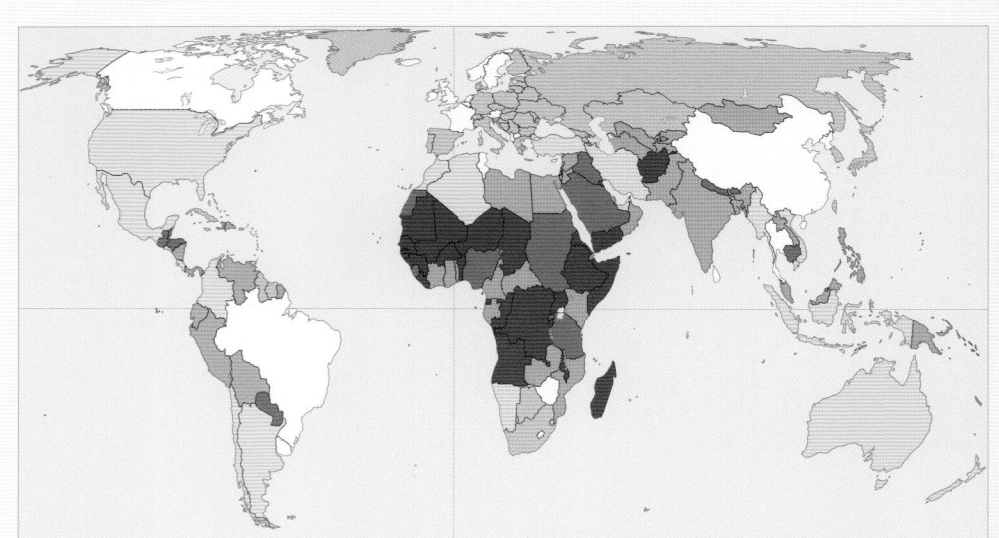

Based on estimates for the year 2050, below are listed the ten most populous nations in the world, in millions:

1.	India	1,628	6.	Pakistan	295
2.	China	1,437	7.	Bangladesh	280
3.	USA	420	8.	Brazil	221
4.	Indonesia	308	9.	Congo (Dem. Rep.)	181
5.	Nigeria	307	10.	Ethiopia	173

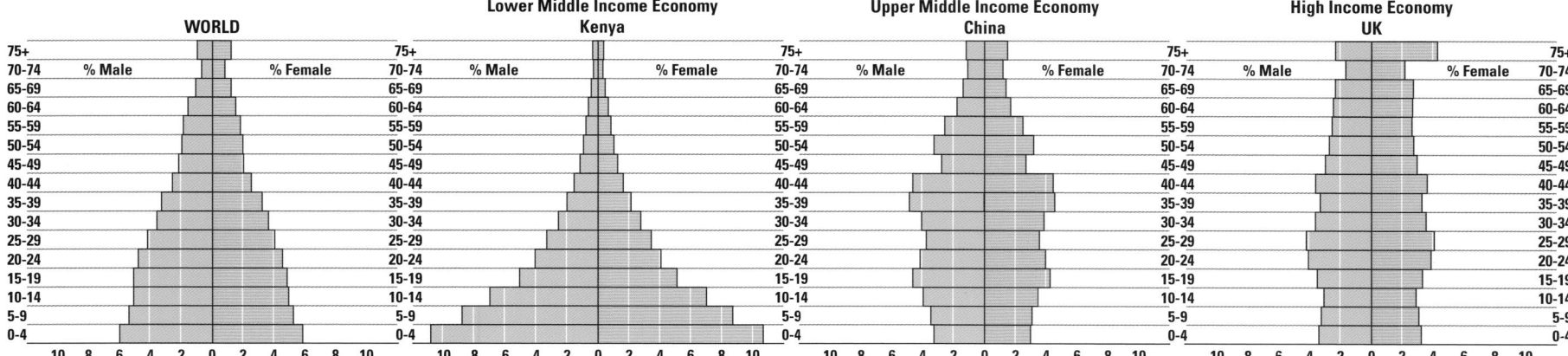

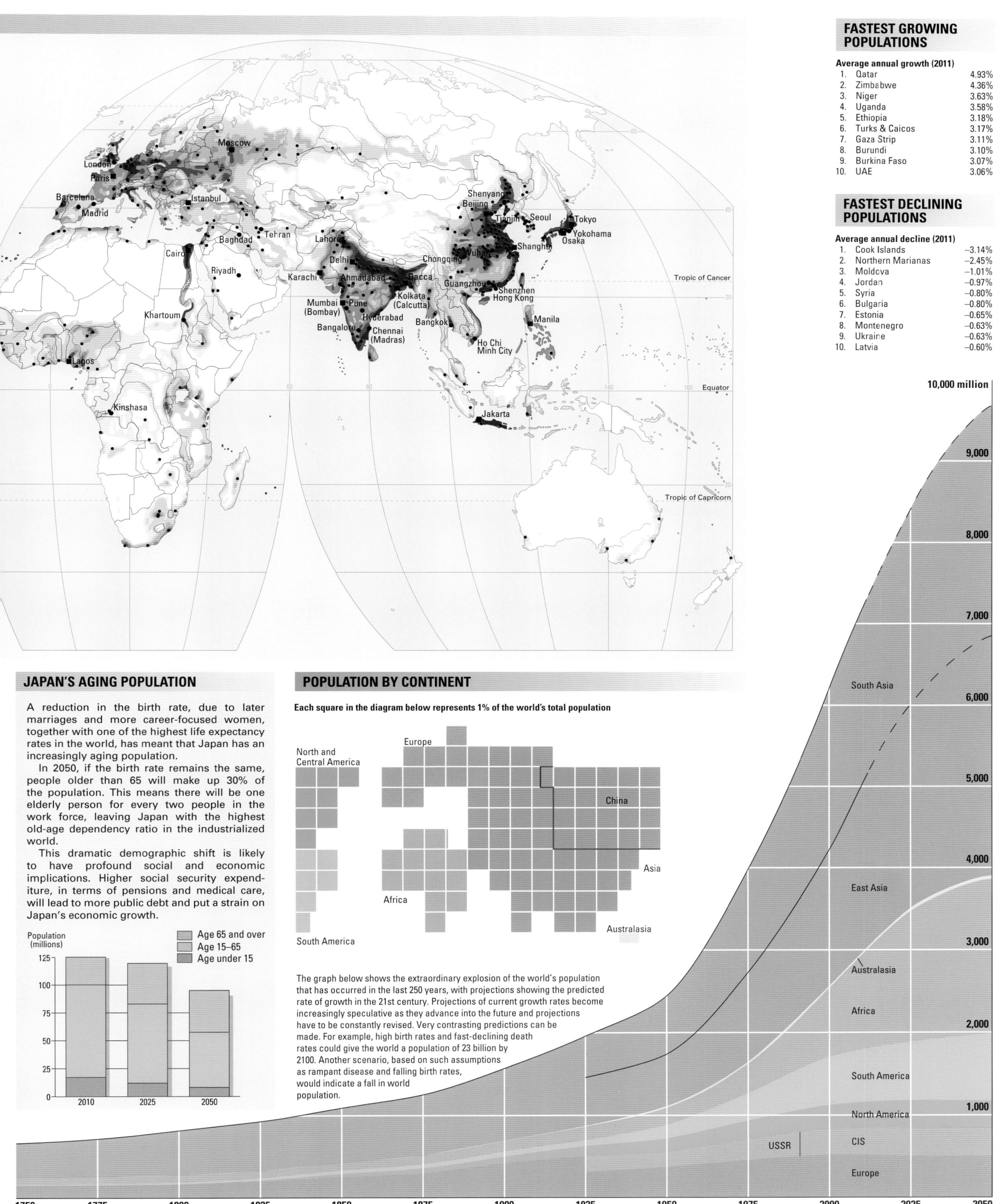

FASTEST GROWING POPULATIONS

Average annual growth (2011)

1.	Qatar	4.93%
2.	Zimbabwe	4.36%
3.	Niger	3.63%
4.	Uganda	3.58%
5.	Ethiopia	3.18%
6.	Turks & Caicos	3.17%
7.	Gaza Strip	3.11%
8.	Burundi	3.10%
9.	Burkina Faso	3.07%
10.	UAE	3.06%

FASTEST DECLINING POPULATIONS

Average annual decline (2011)

1.	Cook Islands	−3.14%
2.	Northern Marianas	−2.45%
3.	Moldova	−1.01%
4.	Jordan	−0.97%
5.	Syria	−0.80%
6.	Bulgaria	−0.80%
7.	Estonia	−0.65%
8.	Montenegro	−0.63%
9.	Ukraine	−0.63%
10.	Latvia	−0.60%

JAPAN'S AGING POPULATION

A reduction in the birth rate, due to later marriages and more career-focused women, together with one of the highest life expectancy rates in the world, has meant that Japan has an increasingly aging population.

In 2050, if the birth rate remains the same, people older than 65 will make up 30% of the population. This means there will be one elderly person for every two people in the work force, leaving Japan with the highest old-age dependency ratio in the industrialized world.

This dramatic demographic shift is likely to have profound social and economic implications. Higher social security expenditure, in terms of pensions and medical care, will lead to more public debt and put a strain on Japan's economic growth.

POPULATION BY CONTINENT

Each square in the diagram below represents 1% of the world's total population

The graph below shows the extraordinary explosion of the world's population that has occurred in the last 250 years, with projections showing the predicted rate of growth in the 21st century. Projections of current growth rates become increasingly speculative as they advance into the future and projections have to be constantly revised. Very contrasting predictions can be made. For example, high birth rates and fast-declining death rates could give the world a population of 23 billion by 2100. Another scenario, based on such assumptions as rampant disease and falling birth rates, would indicate a fall in world population.

For more information:
82 Greenhouse gases
84 Water distribution
88 Population density
102 World trade

Following the development of agriculture more than 10,000 years ago, people began to live in farming villages. Around 5,500 years ago, the world's first cities appeared in the lower Tigris and Euphrates valleys in Mesopotamia. Cities were founded in Ancient Egypt around 5,000 years ago and in China around 3,600 years ago. By contrast with the villages, most people in the early cities were not engaged in farming. Instead, they worked in craft industries, in government services, in religion, and in trade. The cities became centers of early civilizations and, through trade, their influence spread far and wide. However, they were dependent on the surrounding farming communities for their food and other materials.

In 1750, prior to the start of the Industrial Revolution, barely 3% of the world's population lived in urban areas. By 1850, London and Paris had more than a million people, and, by 1900, 14% of the world's population lived in cities. By 1950, the world had 83 cities with more than a million people, and

by 1996 there were 280; by 2015, experts predict there will be more than 500.

New York City was the only city with a population in excess of 10 million in 1950; by 2015, experts predict there will be 27 such cities worldwide, the majority located in the developing world. In addition, many of the world's largest cities are now merging to form "mega regions," such as Hong Kong-Shenzhen-Guangzhou in China, and these are becoming major economic drivers, on a world scale.

In 2008, for the first time in history, more than half of the world's population lived in urban areas. By 2050, it is thought that 5.3 billion people in the developing world will be living in an urban environment, with Asia having over 60% of the world's urban population and Africa almost 25%.

Urbanization is greatest in industrialized countries. For example, in 2010, 82% of the people in the US lived in urban areas; but in low-income countries, which had nearly 40% of the world's population in the early 21st century, only 31% lived in urban areas.

The rapid rate of urbanization has created many social problems, especially in cities that have been unable to provide enough jobs and services for the new arrivals. Many of the new city dwellers come from rural areas and take time to adjust to urban life and employment possibilities.

A typical city in a developing country contains millions of people living, often illegally, in shanty towns (or "informal settlements"), while thousands live on the streets. Yet many of these shanty towns are healthier than the industrial cities of 19th-century Europe and North America. Indeed, surveys have shown that migrants to cities in developing countries are less likely to face poverty than they are in rural areas, while benefiting from greater access to healthcare services and education.

Modern cities face many problems today, including pollution, unemployment, and crime. Yet, with competent government, they are capable of generating the wealth they need to solve them, as well as making a major contribution to the nation's economy.

URBAN POPULATION

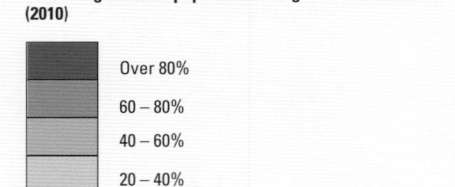

Percentage of total population living in towns and cities (2010)

- Over 80%
- 60 – 80%
- 40 – 60%
- 20 – 40%
- Under 20%
- No data available

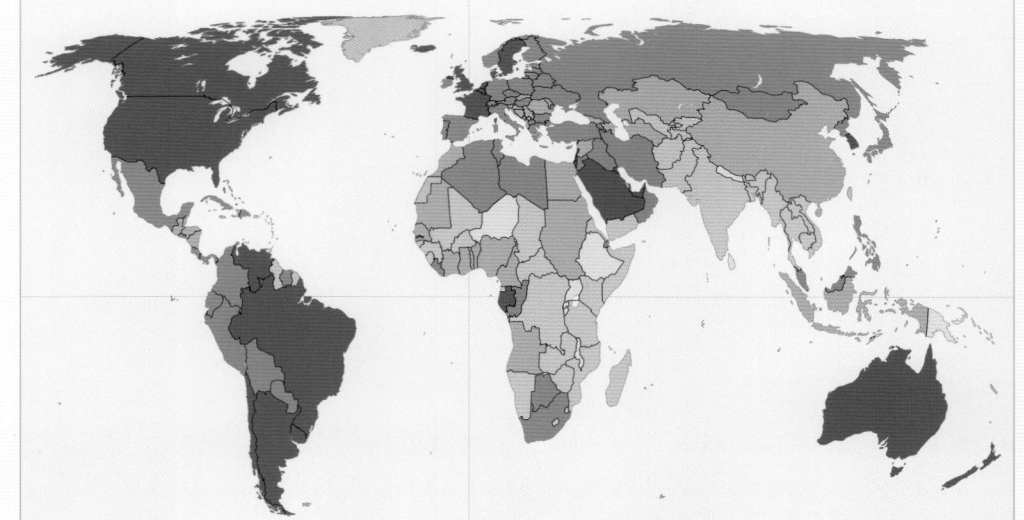

Most urbanized		Least urbanized	
Singapore	100%	Burundi	11%
Kuwait	98%	Papua New Guinea	13%
Belgium	97%	Uganda	13%
Qatar	96%	Trinidad & Tobago	14%
Malta	95%	Sri Lanka	15%

THE URBANIZATION OF THE EARTH

City-building, 1900–2005; each white spot represents a city of at least 1 million inhabitants

1900

1950

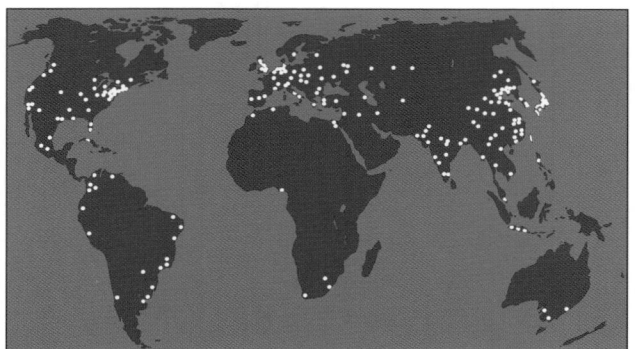

1975

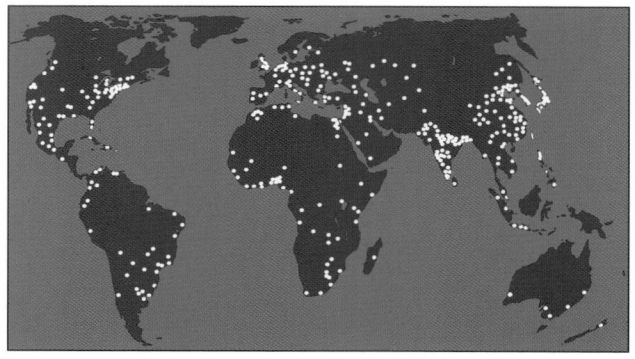

2005

URBANIZATION

The urban population of 3.5 billion people in 2010 was larger than the entire global population in 1947, 61 years earlier. Cities and urban areas are gaining an estimated 60 million people per year – over 1 million every week.

Urbanization rates vary across the world; the US and UK have far lower rates of urbanization compared to less developed countries. This is because a high proportion of their populations already live in cities. The largest percentage increases in the urban population in the next decade will be in Africa and Asia. For example, Lagos in Nigeria has increased from 675,000 inhabitants in 1960 to 10,855,000 in 2010.

Rapid urban growth reflects three factors:
1. Migration to cities from rural areas.
2. Natural population increases (births minus deaths).
3. Reclassification of previously rural areas as urban as they become built up and engulfed by urban sprawl.

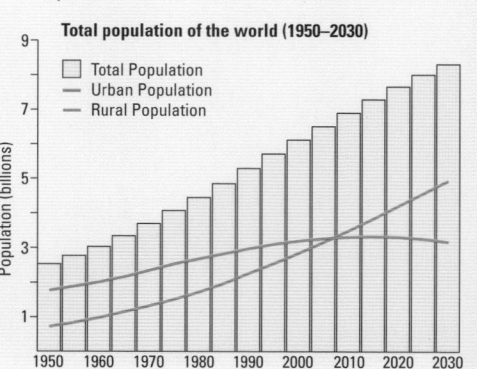

Total population of the world (1950–2030)

- Total Population
- Urban Population
- Rural Population

SLUM CITIES

The total number of slum dwellers in the world reached 1 billion in 2007, with one in every three city residents living in inadequate housing, with no or few basic services.

Urbanization in most developing countries has been proceeding so rapidly that local governments have been unable to provide the necessary services and housing to meet demand.

In some cities, many people make their homes in squatter settlements, or slums, which are frequently without basic services such as power, water, and sanitation. They are often on hazardous, dangerous or polluted land, and the building structures are inadequate and sometimes unsafe. Slum dwellers have limited access to credit and formal job markets due to stigmatization, discrimination, and geographical isolation.

Slums have a high concentration of poverty and social and economic deprivation, which may include broken families, unemployment, and economic, physical, and social exclusion. Yet these communities are often a dynamic part of the city's economy, keeping the wheels of the city turning in many different ways. Their inhabitants often take the initiative in setting up their own local government and self-help associations.

Some of the world's richest cities also have a homeless underclass, although calculating the numbers of people involved is problematic. Yet it is the case that homelessness and unemployment are currently affecting an increasing number of people in the developed world.

The locus of poverty is moving from the countryside to cities, in a process now recognized as the "urbanization of poverty."

Efforts to improve the living conditions of slum dwellers peaked during the 1980s. However, renewed concern about poverty has recently led governments to adopt specific targets on slums in the United Nations Millennium Declaration, which aims to improve the lives of at least 100 million slum dwellers by the year 2020.

CITIES IN DANGER

In mid-2002, a "brown haze," stretching 2 miles [3 km] high, covered much of southern Asia. Caused mainly by the burning of coal and biomass, it caused respiratory diseases and many deaths. Alarm concerning urban air pollution had been expressed much earlier, but controls since the 1980s had proved difficult to enforce and expensive to introduce.

Those cities taking part in the United Nation's Global Environment Monitoring System frequently show dangerous levels of pollutants, ranging from soot to sulfur dioxide and photochemical smog. Air in the majority of cities without such sampling equipment is likely to be at least as bad. Traffic, a major source of air pollution worldwide, loses Thailand's work force 44 working days each year. It was also a major cause for concern in the run-up to the 2008 Beijing Olympic Games.

SLUM FACTBOX

● 78% of the urban population in developing countries live in slums.

● The total number of slum dwellers in the world increased by about 36% during the 1990s.

● More than 41% of Kolkata's slum households have lived there for more than 30 years.

● In most African cities between 40% and 70% of the city's population live in slums or squatter settlements.

● Slum populations in some parts of the world (for example, Pune in India and Ibadan in Nigeria) quite often include university lecturers, students, civil servants, and formal private-sector employees.

● All slum households in Bangkok have a color television.

● Singapore is one of the few countries that successfully practises comprehensive public-sector housing development.

CITY GROWTH

The growth of some of the world's largest cities in millions, 1950–2015
Comparisons of city populations over time are problematic due to changes in the definition of the city limits. These figures attempt to take such changes into consideration.

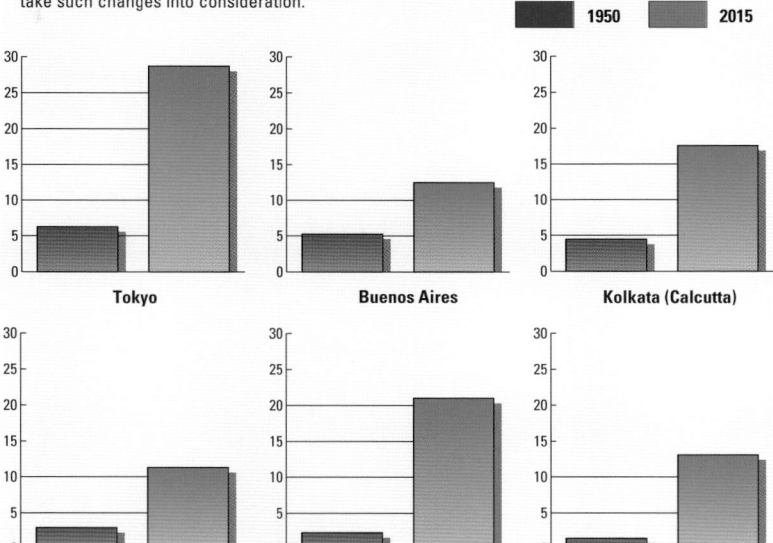

LARGEST CITIES

◄ Originally a fishing village, Shanghai's skyscrapers and modern lifestyle are often seen as representing China's recent economic development. It is now the sixth largest city in the world and home to many of Asia's tallest buildings, including the Jinmao Tower on the right of this image.

In 2008, for the first time in history, the majority of the world's population lived in cities. Below is a list of all the cities that are expected to have more than 10 million inhabitants by the year 2015, based on current estimates:

1.	Tokyo–Yokohama	28.7
2.	Mumbai (Bombay)	27.4
3.	Lagos	24.1
4.	Shanghai	23.2
5.	Jakarta	21.5
6.	São Paulo	21.0
7.	Karachi	20.6
8.	Beijing	19.6
9.	Dhaka	19.2
10.	Mexico City	19.1
11.	Kolkata (Calcutta)	17.6
12.	Delhi	17.5
13.	New York City	17.4
14.	Tianjin	17.1
15.	Manila	14.9
16.	Cairo	14.7
17.	Los Angeles	14.5
18.	Seoul	13.1
19.	Buenos Aires	12.5
20.	Istanbul	12.1
21.	Rio de Janeiro	11.3
22.	Lahore	10.9
23.	Hyderabad	10.6
24.	Bangkok	10.4
25.	Osaka	10.2
26.	Lima	10.1
27.	Tehran	10.0

The city populations above are based on urban agglomerations rather than legal city limits. In some cases, where two adjacent cities have merged into one concentration, such as Tokyo–Yokohama, they have been regarded as a single unit.

URBAN ADVANTAGES

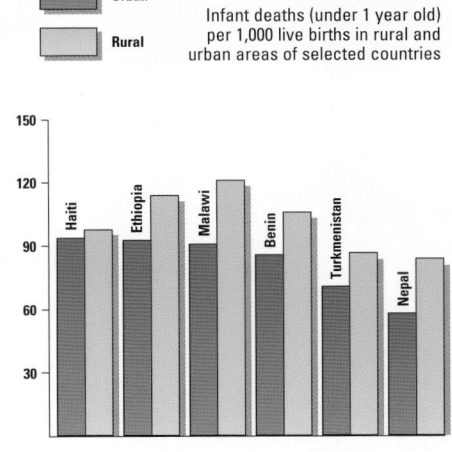

RELATIVE MORTALITY
Infant deaths (under 1 year old) per 1,000 live births in rural and urban areas of selected countries

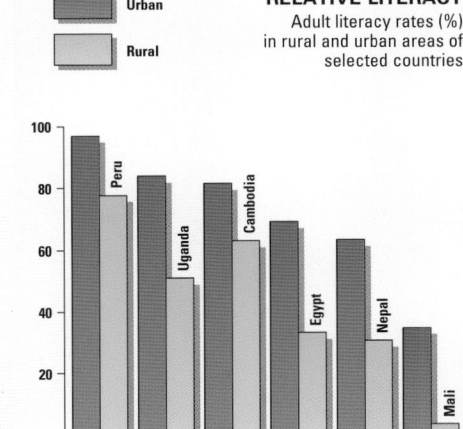

RELATIVE LITERACY
Adult literacy rates (%) in rural and urban areas of selected countries

Despite overcrowding and poor housing, living standards in the developing world's cities are almost invariably better than in the surrounding countryside. Resources – financial, material, and administrative – are concentrated in the towns, which are usually also the centers of political activity and pressure. Governments – frequently unstable, and rarely established on a solid democratic base – are usually more responsive to urban discontent than to rural misery.

In many developing countries, especially in Africa, food prices are kept artificially low, thus appeasing the underemployed urban masses at the expense of agricultural development.

This imbalance encourages further cityward migration, helping to account for the astonishing rate of post-1950 urbanization and putting great strain on the ability of many nations to provide even modest improvements for their people.

For more information:
88 Population density
94 The world's refugees
   War since 1945
95 United Nations
   International
   organizations

Racial, language, and religious differences have led to appalling acts of inhumanity throughout history. Yet, strictly speaking, all human beings belong to one species, *Homo sapiens*, which has no subspecies. The differences between the three racial types which most people identify – Caucasoid, Mongoloid, and Negroid – reflect not so much evolutionary differences as long periods of separation.

Migration has recently mingled the various groups to an unprecedented extent, and most nations now have some degree of racial mixing. For example, the USA has often been called a melting pot, because of the large numbers of people from various geographical locations that make up the population. The country has no official language but, until recently, English was spoken by the vast majority of the people. But in recent years, some of the immigrants from Mexico, Cuba, and other parts of Latin America have not learned English and speak only Spanish. This development disturbs those Americans who believe that the use of English binds the nation together, and several states have passed laws stating that English is their only official language.

Language is fundamental to human culture. Because definitions of languages vary, estimates of the total number range from 3,000 to 6,000, although most are spoken by only a few people. Chinese is spoken by more people as a first language than any other, while Spanish ranks second, but English is the leading international language, because so many people speak it as their second tongue.

Like language, religion encourages cohesion in single human groups and it satisfies a deep human need by assigning people a place in a divinely ordered world. Religion is a way in which a culture can express its individuality. For example, the rise of Islamic fundamentalism in the late 20th century was partly an expression of resentment that secular Western values were being imposed on Muslims.

WORLD MIGRATION

The greatest voluntary migration was the colonization of North America by 30–35 million European settlers during the 19th century. The greatest forced migration involved 9–11 million Africans taken as slaves to America between 1550 and 1860. The migrations shown on the map below are mostly international, as population movements within borders are not usually recorded. Many of the statistics are necessarily estimates as so many refugees and migrant workers enter countries illegally and unrecorded. Emigrants may have a variety of motives for leaving, thus making it difficult to distinguish between voluntary and involuntary migrations.

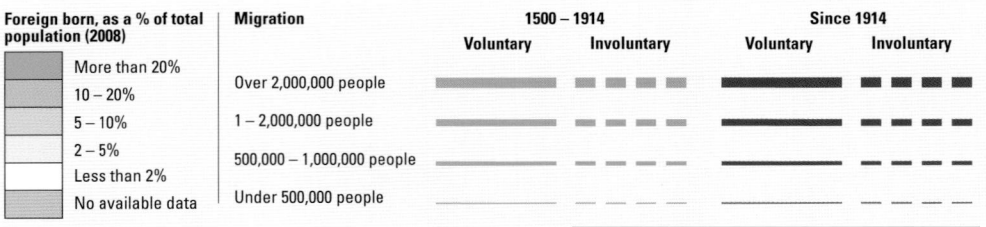

Foreign born, as a % of total population (2008)
- More than 20%
- 10 – 20%
- 5 – 10%
- 2 – 5%
- Less than 2%
- No available data

Migration
- Over 2,000,000 people
- 1 – 2,000,000 people
- 500,000 – 1,000,000 people
- Under 500,000 people

	1500 – 1914		Since 1914	
	Voluntary	Involuntary	Voluntary	Involuntary

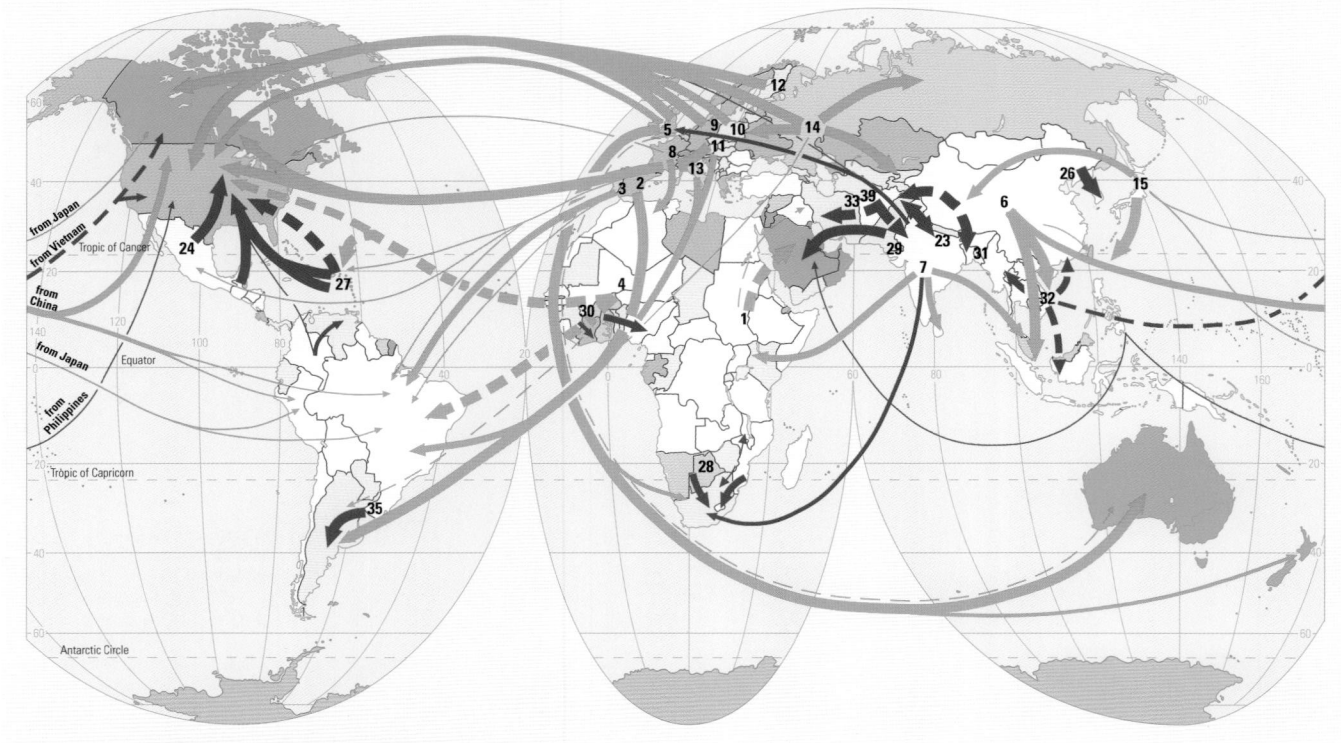

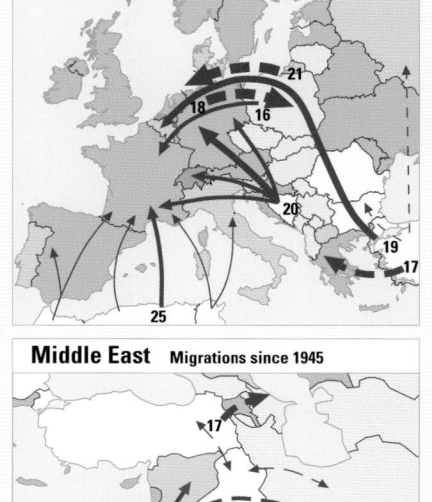

Europe Migrations since 1914

Middle East Migrations since 1945

Major world migrations since 1500 (over 1 million people)

1. North and East African slaves to Arabia (4.3m) 1500–1900
2. Spanish to South and Central America (2.3m) 1530–1914
3. Portuguese to Brazil (1.4m) 1530–1914
4. West African slaves to South America (4.6m) 1550–1860
   to Caribbean (4m) 1580–1860
   to North/Central America (1m) 1650–1820
5. British and Irish to North America (13.5m) 1620–1914
   to Australasia and South Africa (3m) 1790–1914
6. Chinese to Southeast Asia (22m) 1820–1914
   to North America (1m) 1880–1914
7. Indian migrant workers (3m) 1850–1914
8. French to North Africa (1.5m) 1850–1914
9. Germans to North America (5m) 1850–1914
10. Poles to North America (3.6m) 1850–1914
11. Austro-Hungarians to North America (3.2m) 1850–1914
   to Western Europe (3.4m) 1850–1914
   to South America (1.8m) 1850–1914

12. Scandinavians to North America (2.7m) 1850–1914
13. Italians to North America (5m) 1860–1914
   to South America (3.7m) 1860–1914
14. Russians to North America (2.2m) 1880–1914
   to Western Europe (2.2m) 1880–1914
   to Siberia (6m) 1880–1914
   to Central Asia (4m) 1880–1914
15. Japanese to Eastern Asia, Southeast Asia and America (8m) 1900–1914
16. Poles to Western Europe (1m) 1920–1940
17. Greeks and Armenians from Turkey (1.6m) 1922–1923
18. European Jews to extermination camps (5m) 1940–1944
19. Turks to Western Europe (1.9m) 1940–
20. Yugoslavs to Western Europe (2m) 1940–
21. Germans to Western Europe (9.8m) 1945–1947
22. Palestinian refugees (2m) 1947–
23. Indian and Pakistani refugees (15m) 1947
24. Mexicans to North America (9m) 1950–

25. North Africans to Western Europe (1.1m) 1950–
26. Korean refugees (5m) 1950–1954
27. Latin Americans and West Indians to North America (4.7m) 1960–
28. Migrant workers to South Africa (1.5m) 1960–
29. Indians and Pakistanis to the Persian Gulf (2.4m) 1970–
30. Migrant workers to Nigeria and Ivory Coast (3m) 1970–
31. Bangladeshi and Pakistani refugees (2m) 1972
32. Vietnamese and Cambodian refugees (1.5m) 1975–
33. Afghan refugees (6.1m) 1979–
34. Egyptians to the Persian Gulf and Libya (2.9m) 1980–
35. Migrant workers to Argentina (2m) 1980–
36. Mozambique refugees (1.7m) 1985–
37. Yugoslav/Balkan refugees (1.7m) 1992–
38. Rwanda/Burundi refugees (2.6m) 1994–
39. Afghan refugees (2.1m) 2001–

BUILDING THE USA

US Immigration, 1920 and 2011

For decades the USA was the magnet that attracted millions of immigrants, notably from Central and Eastern Europe, the flow peaking in the early years of the 20th century. By the mid-1990s the proportion of immigrants had increased again to pre-World War II rates, reaching 12.9% by 2011. However, the balance of origin had swung from Europe to Latin America and Asia, as the graphs indicate.

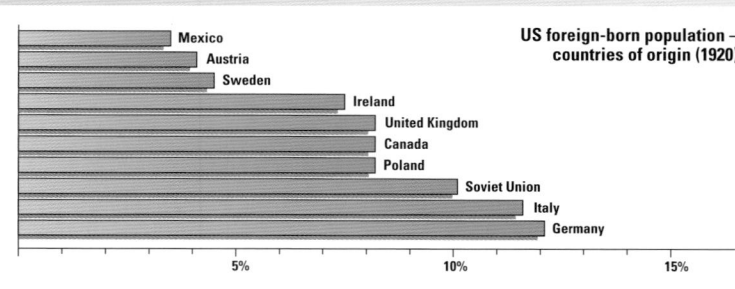

US foreign-born population – countries of origin (1920)

Mexico, Austria, Sweden, Ireland, United Kingdom, Canada, Poland, Soviet Union, Italy, Germany

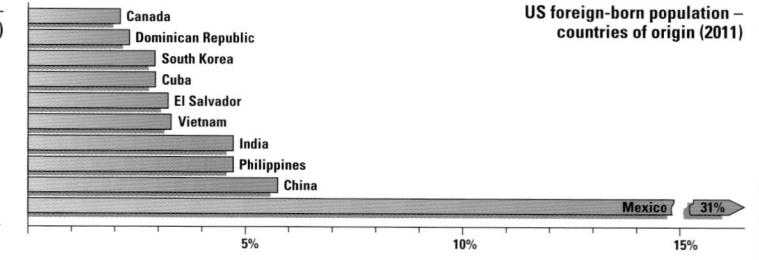

US foreign-born population – countries of origin (2011)

Canada, Dominican Republic, South Korea, Cuba, El Salvador, Vietnam, India, Philippines, China, Mexico 31%

PREDOMINANT LANGUAGES

INDO-EUROPEAN FAMILY

1	Balto-Slavic group (incl. Russian, Ukrainian)
2	Germanic group (incl. English, German)
3	Celtic group
4	Greek
5	Albanian
6	Iranian group
7	Armenian
8	Romance group (incl. Spanish, Portuguese, French, Italian)
9	Indo-Aryan group (incl. Hindi, Bengali, Urdu, Punjabi, Marathi)
10	**CAUCASIAN FAMILY**

AFRO-ASIATIC FAMILY

11	Semitic group (incl. Arabic)
12	Kushitic group
13	Berber group
14	**KHOISAN FAMILY**
15	**NIGER-CONGO FAMILY**
16	**NILO-SAHARAN FAMILY**
17	**URALIC FAMILY**

ALTAIC FAMILY

18	Turkic group (incl. Turkish)
19	Mongolian group
20	Tungus-Manchu group
21	Japanese and Korean

SINO-TIBETAN FAMILY

22	Sinitic (Chinese) languages (incl. Mandarin, Wu, Yue)
23	Tibetic-Burmic languages
24	**TAI FAMILY**

AUSTRO-ASIATIC FAMILY

25	Mon-Khmer group
26	Munda group
27	Vietnamese
28	**DRAVIDIAN FAMILY** (incl. Telugu, Tamil)
29	**AUSTRONESIAN FAMILY** (incl. Malay-Indonesian, Javanese)
30	**OTHER LANGUAGES**

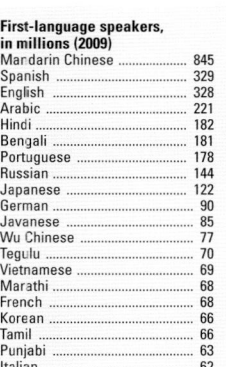

First-language speakers, in millions (2009)

Mandarin Chinese	845
Spanish	329
English	328
Arabic	221
Hindi	182
Bengali	181
Portuguese	178
Russian	144
Japanese	122
German	90
Javanese	85
Wu Chinese	77
Tegulu	70
Vietnamese	69
Marathi	68
French	68
Korean	66
Tamil	66
Punjabi	63
Italian	62

Languages form a kind of tree of development, splitting from a few ancient proto-tongues into branches that have grown apart and further divided with the passage of time. English and Hindi, for example, both belong to the great Indo-European family, although the relationship is only apparent after much analysis and comparison with non-Indo-European languages such as Chinese or Arabic. Hindi is part of the Indo-Aryan subgroup, whereas English is a member of Indo-European's Germanic branch. French, another Indo-European tongue, traces its descent through the Latin, or Romance, branch. A few languages – Basque is one example – have no apparent links with any other, living or dead. Most modern languages, of course, have acquired enormous quantities of vocabulary from each other.

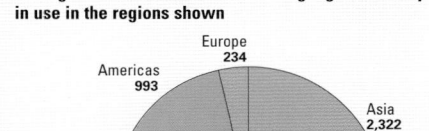

DISTRIBUTION OF LIVING LANGUAGES

The figures refer to the number of languages currently in use in the regions shown

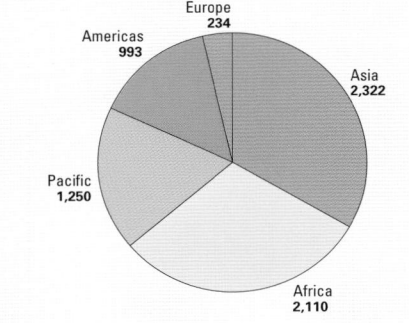

Europe	234
Americas	993
Asia	2,322
Pacific	1,250
Africa	2,110

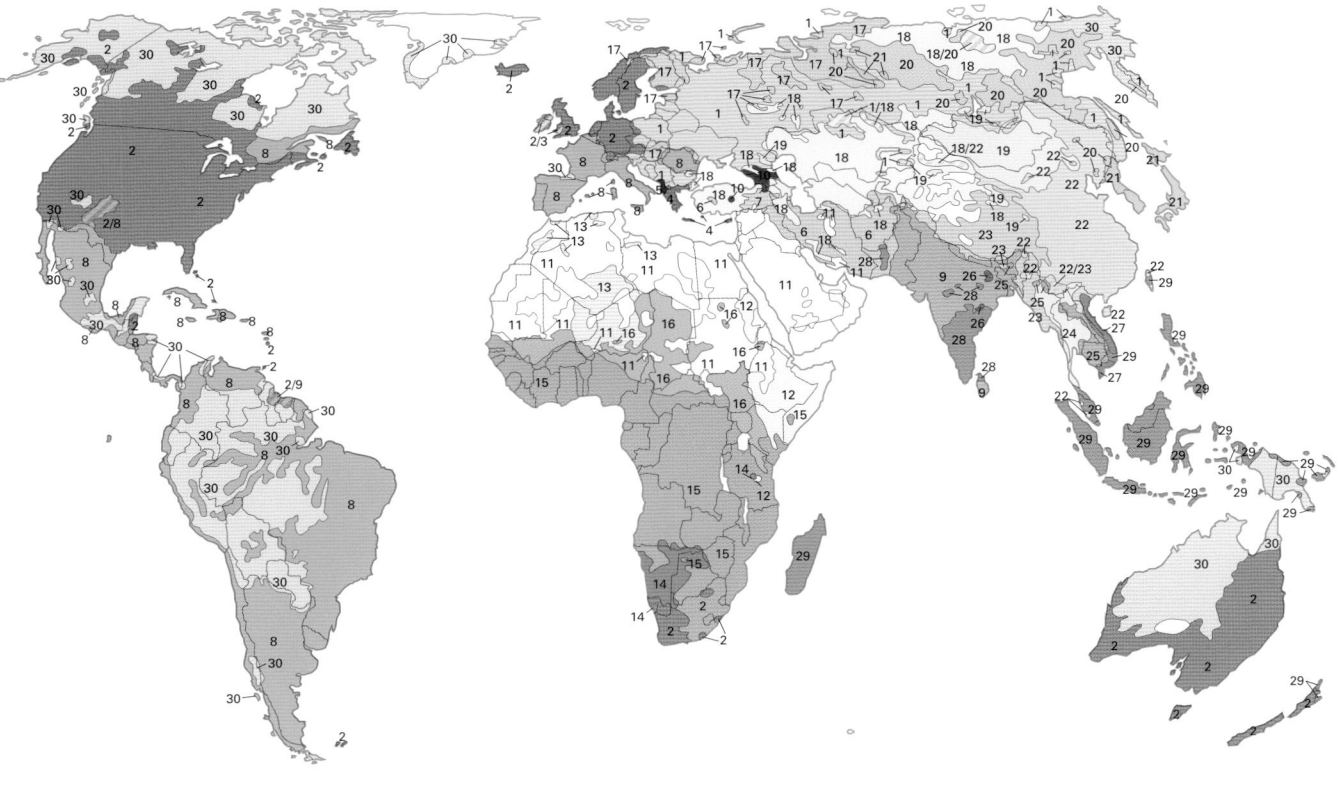

PREDOMINANT RELIGIONS

- ▲ Roman Catholicism
- Orthodox and other Eastern Churches
- ● Protestantism
- Sunni Islam
- Shia Islam
- Buddhism
- Hinduism
- Confucianism
- ● Judaism
- Shintoism
- Tribal Religions

Religions are not as easily mapped as the physical contours of the land. Divisions are often blurred and frequently overlapping: most nations include people of many different faiths – or no faith at all. Some religions, like Islam and Christianity, have proselytes worldwide; others, like Hinduism and Confucianism, are restricted to a particular area, though modern migrations have taken some Indians and Chinese very far from their cultural origins. It is also difficult to show the degree to which religion controls daily life: Christian Western Europe, for example, is now far less dominated by its religion than are the Islamic nations of the Middle East. Similarly, figures for the major faiths' adherents make no distinction between nominal believers enrolled at birth and those for whom religion is a vital part of their existence.

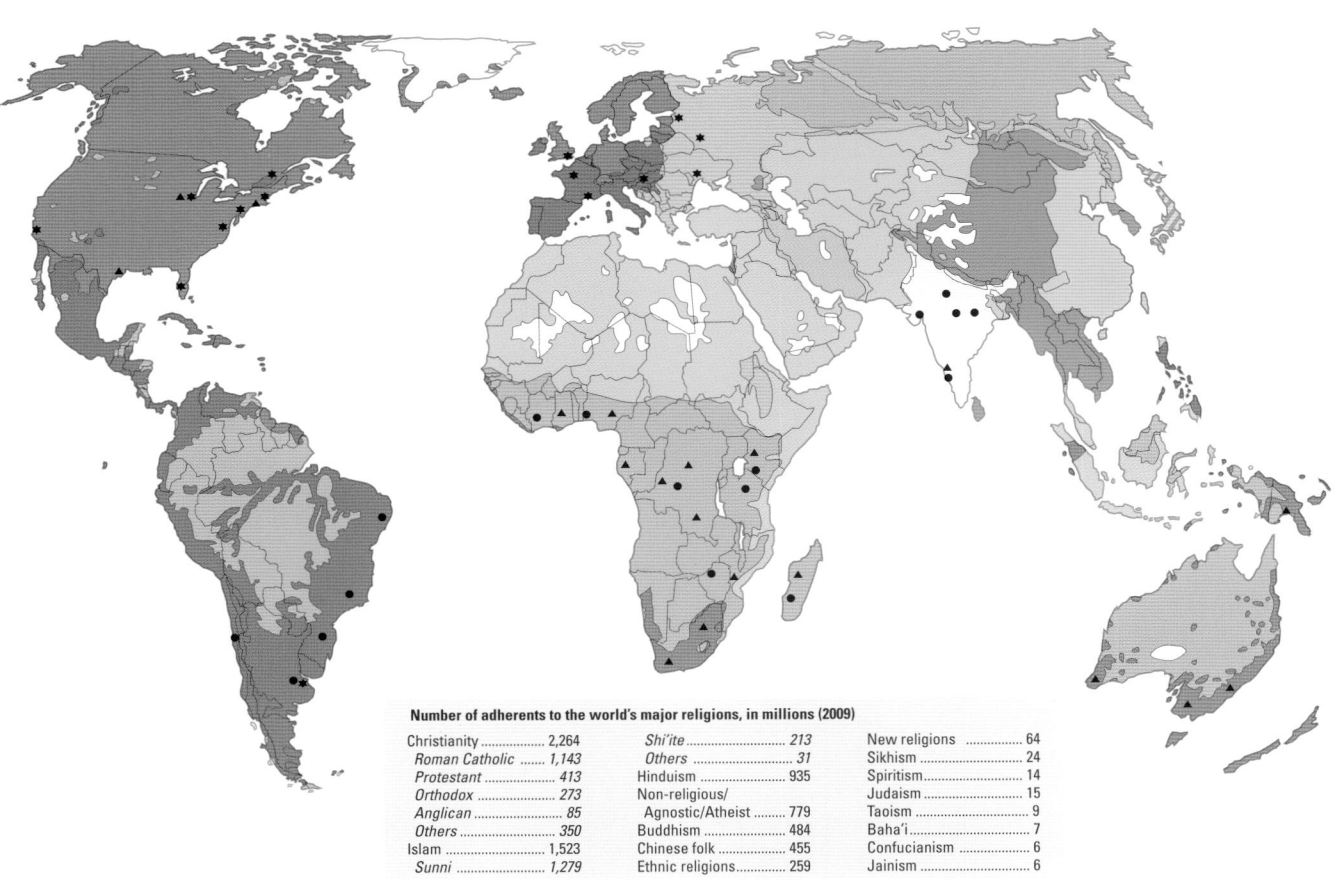

Number of adherents to the world's major religions, in millions (2009)

Christianity	2,264	Shi'ite	213	New religions	64
Roman Catholic	*1,143*	*Others*	*31*	Sikhism	24
Protestant	*413*	Hinduism	935	Spiritism	14
Orthodox	*273*	Non-religious/		Judaism	15
Anglican	*85*	Agnostic/Atheist	779	Baha'i	7
Others	*350*	Buddhism	484	Taoism	9
Islam	1,523	Chinese folk	455	Confucianism	6
Sunni	*1,279*	Ethnic religions	259	Jainism	6

For more information:

92 Migration

93 Religion

The 20th century witnessed two world wars, followed by a Cold War which several times threatened to erupt into a third world war, fought with nuclear weapons. The Cold War was marked by a great number of conflicts. Some were colonial wars, as the empires of the first half of the century fell apart, some were border wars, and some were civil wars. All the wars have caused great suffering among civilians, many of whom were forced to join the ranks of the world's refugees.

In the late 1980s, many people hoped that the end of the Cold War, following the collapse of Communist regimes in the former Soviet Union and Eastern Europe, would herald a new era of international stability. Instead, old ethnic and religious antagonisms surfaced in many areas, leading to civil war in such places as Chechenia, in Russia, and the former Yugoslavia. Nationalist rivalries, suppressed under Communist rule, replaced ideological factors as the major cause of conflict.

War is a very human activity, with no real equivalent in any other species. Yet humans also function well when they cooperate – evolution has made this so. Hunter-gatherers in cooperative bands were far more effective than animals that prowled. Agriculture, urbanization, and industrialization all depend on the ability of humans to cooperate.

The creation of the United Nations in 1945 held out hope that the world's nations, tired of war, would have the means to control humanity's aggressive instincts. Although the UN lacks the power to halt conflicts, it has often helped to achieve negotiation. Economic pressures have led to another kind of cooperation, resulting in the creation of common markets and economic unions, such as ASEAN in Southeast Asia, the European Union, and NAFTA in North America.

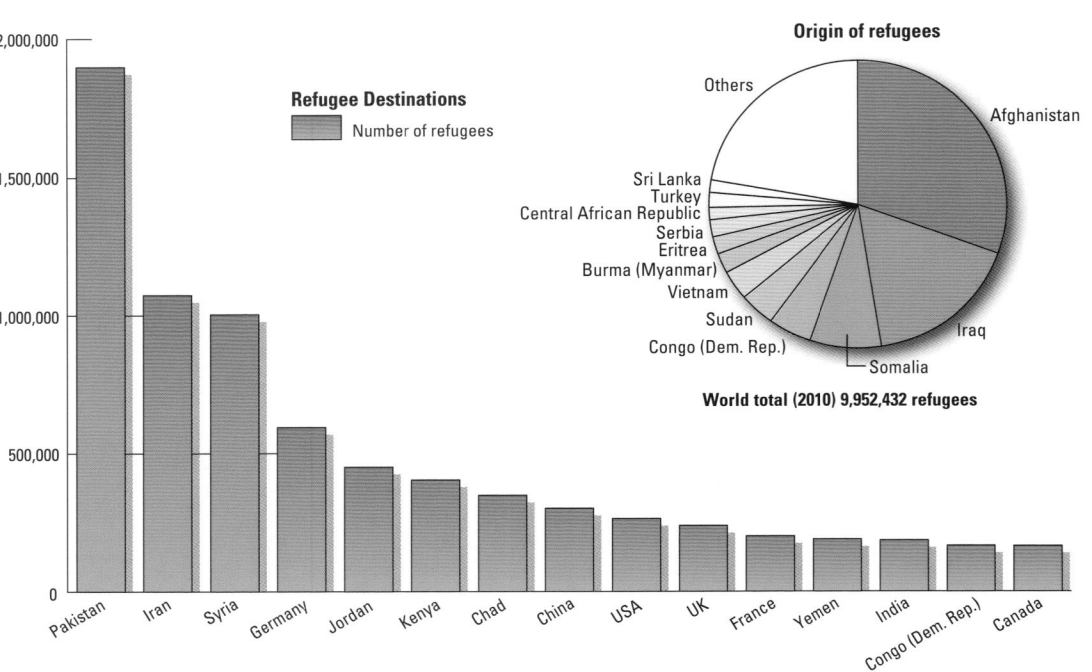

Origin of refugees

World total (2010) 9,952,432 refugees

THE WORLD'S REFUGEES

Refugees by host nation (bar-chart, left) and by nation of origin (pie-chart, left) (2010). The source is the United Nations High Commission for Refugees (UNHCR).

The pie-chart shows the origins of the world's refugees, while the bar-chart below shows their destinations. According to the United Nations High Commission for Refugees (UNHCR) in 2010 there were 9.9 million refugees. However, the UNHCR definition of a refugee, "a person who has left or remains outside their own country because they have a well-founded fear of persecution, or because their safety is threatened by events seriously disturbing public order," does not include people who are in a refugee-like situation but who have not been formally recognized. In 2010, there were a further 14.7 million people who were internally displaced, and a total "population of concern" of 33.9 million people, worldwide.

All but a few who cross international boundaries seek asylum in neighboring countries, which are often the least equipped to deal with them. Lacking any rights or power, they frequently become an unwelcome burden to their hosts. Usually, the best any refugee can hope for is rudimentary food and shelter in temporary camps. Many Palestinians have been forced to live in camps since 1948.

WAR SINCE 1994

Countries in the top half of the Human Development Index (HDI)

Countries in the bottom half of the HDI

☆ Countries with at least one armed conflict between 1994 and 2010

UNITED NATIONS

The United Nations Organization was born as World War II drew to its conclusion. Six years of strife had strengthened the world's desire for peace, but an effective international organization was needed to help achieve it. That body would replace the League of Nations which, since its inception in 1920, had failed to curb the aggression of at least some of its member nations. At the United Nations Conference on International Organization held in San Francisco, the United Nations Charter was drawn up. Ratified by the Security Council and signed by the 51 original members, it came into effect on October 24, 1945.

The Charter set out the aims of the organization: to maintain peace and security, and to develop friendly relations between nations; to achieve international cooperation in solving economic, social, cultural, and humanitarian problems; to promote respect for human rights and fundamental freedoms; and to harmonize the activities of nations in order to achieve these common goals.

Membership From the original 51, membership of the UN has now grown to 193. Recent additions include East Timor, Switzerland, Montenegro and South Sudan. There are only two independent states which are not members – Taiwan and the Vatican City. Official languages are Chinese, English, French, Russian, Spanish, and Arabic.

Funding The UN budget for 2012 was US $5.2 billion. Contributions are assessed by the members' ability to pay, with the maximum 22% of the total (the USA's share), and the minimum 0.019%. The 27-member EU pays 40% of the budget.

Peacekeeping The UN has been involved in 64 peacekeeping operations worldwide since 1948.

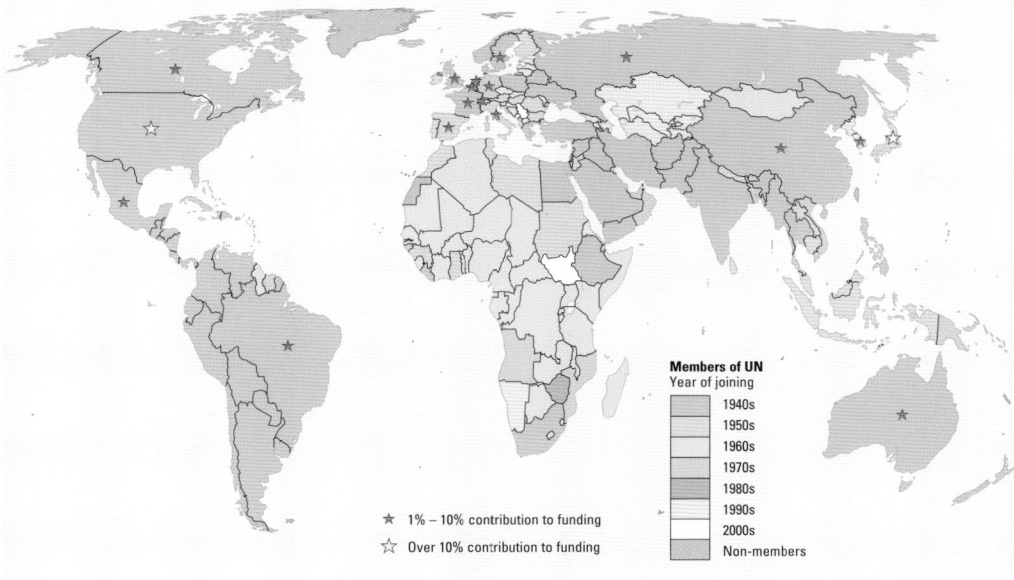

Members of UN
Year of joining

- 1940s
- 1950s
- 1960s
- 1970s
- 1980s
- 1990s
- 2000s
- Non-members

★ 1% – 10% contribution to funding
☆ Over 10% contribution to funding

OCEAN PIRACY

Piracy, or the robbing or hijacking of ships, their crews, and their cargoes, has been increasing steadily in certain parts of the world over recent years. In 2011, the International Maritime Bureau recorded 439 attacks on vessels worldwide, compared with 239 attacks in 2006. The most high-profile acts of piracy were off the coasts of Nigeria and Indonesia, and, most particularly, off the Somali coast in the Gulf of Aden (see map right).

Some of the ships involved have been large ocean-going tankers, bulk carriers, and container vessels, and the pirates have proved that they can sail these without the crew. Attacks have taken place up to 1,150 miles [1,852 km] off the Somali coast when larger "mother ships" are used, from which smaller vessels operate. Firearms and rocket-propelled grenades have been used by the hijackers and many millions of pounds paid in ransom by the ships' owners to release their vessels, much of which goes to support terrorist groups.

To counter this very real threat, both the United States and the European Union have introduced naval operations in the area to try to protect their shipping interests, with some success. However, with such a large area of ocean to cover, it is very difficult to police.

As a result of the pirate activity, insurance premiums have risen and, should this continue, shipping will start to avoid the Suez Canal and take the longer and more expensive route around the Cape of Good Hope.

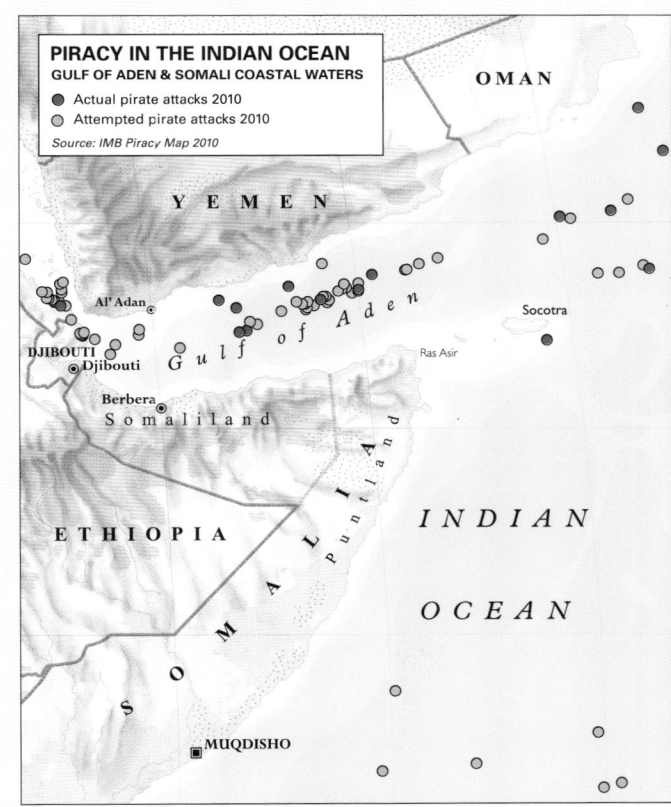

PIRACY IN THE INDIAN OCEAN
GULF OF ADEN & SOMALI COASTAL WATERS
- ● Actual pirate attacks 2010
- ● Attempted pirate attacks 2010
Source: IMB Piracy Map 2010

INTERNATIONAL ORGANIZATIONS

OAS Organization of American States (formed in 1948). It aims to promote social and economic cooperation between countries in the developed North America and developing Latin America.
EU European Union (evolved from the European Community in 1993). Cyprus, the Czech Republic, Estonia, Hungary, Latvia, Lithuania, Malta, Poland, the Slovak Republic, and Slovenia joined the EU in May 2004; Bulgaria and Romania joined in 2007. The other 15 members of the EU are Austria, Belgium, Denmark, Finland, France, Germany, Greece, Ireland, Italy, Luxembourg, Netherlands, Portugal, Spain, Sweden, and the UK. Together, the 27 members aim to integrate economies, coordinate social developments, and bring about political union.
AU The African Union was set up in 2002, taking over from the Organization of African Unity (1963). It has 53 members. Working languages are Arabic, English, French, and Portuguese.
COLOMBO PLAN (formed in 1951) Its 25 members aim to promote economic and social development in Asia and the Pacific.

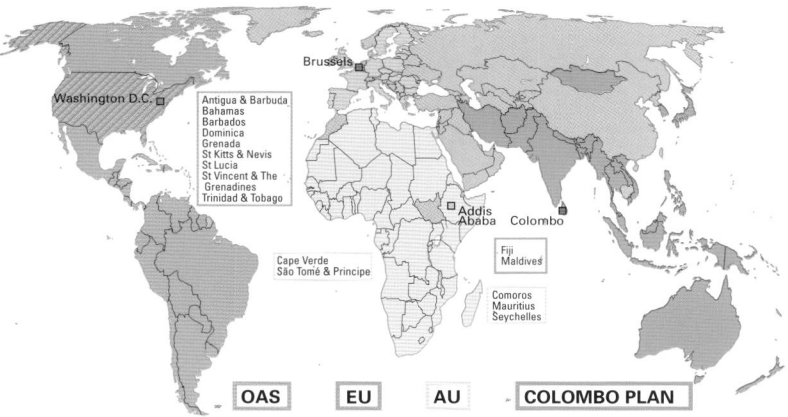

OAS | EU | AU | COLOMBO PLAN

G8 Group of eight leading industrialized nations, comprising Canada, France, Germany, Italy, Japan, Russia, the UK, and the USA. Periodic meetings are held to discuss major world issues, such as world recessions.
OECD Organization for Economic Cooperation and Development (formed in 1961). It comprises 34 major free-market economies. The "G8" is its "inner group" of leading industrial nations, comprising Canada, France, Germany, Italy, Japan, Russia, the UK, and the USA.
ACP African-Caribbean-Pacific (formed in 1963). Members enjoy economic ties with the EU.
OPEC Organization of Petroleum Exporting Countries (formed in 1960). It controls about three-quarters of the world's oil supply. Gabon formally withdrew from OPEC in August 1996.
APEC Asia-Pacific Economic Cooperation (formed in 1989). It aims to enhance economic growth and prosperity for the region and to strengthen the Asia-Pacific community. APEC is the only intergovernmental grouping in the world operating on the basis of non-binding commitments, open dialogue, and equal respect for the views of all participants. There are 21 member economies.

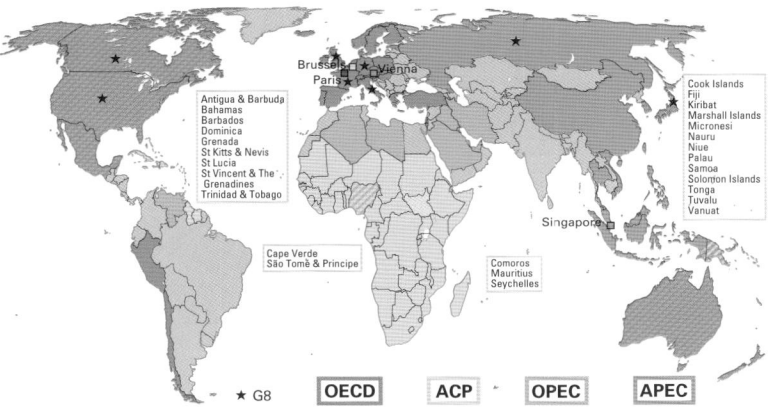

★ G8 | OECD | ACP | OPEC | APEC

NATO North Atlantic Treaty Organization (formed in 1949). It continues despite the winding-up of the Warsaw Pact in 1991. Bulgaria, Estonia, Latvia, Lithuania, Romania, the Slovak Republic, and Slovenia became members in 2004 and Albania and Croatia in 2009.
LAIA The Latin American Integration Association (formed in 1980) superceded the Latin American Free Trade Association formed in 1961. Its aim is to promote freer regional trade.
ARAB LEAGUE (1945) Aims to promote economic, social, political, and military cooperation. There are 22 member nations.
COMMONWEALTH The Commonwealth of Nations evolved from the British Empire. Pakistan was suspended in 1999, but reinstated in 2004. Zimbabwe was suspended in 2002 and, in response to its continued suspension, Zimbabwe left the Commonwealth in 2003. Fiji was suspended in 2006 following a military coup. Rwanda joined the Commonwealth in 2009, as the 54th member state, becoming only the second country which was not formerly a British colony to be admitted to the group.
ASEAN Association of Southeast Asian Nations (formed in 1967). Cambodia joined in 1999.

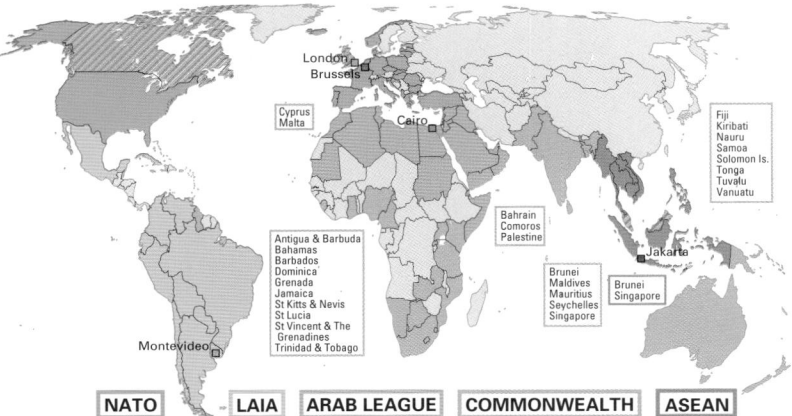

NATO | LAIA | ARAB LEAGUE | COMMONWEALTH | ASEAN

For more information:
82 Global warming
    Carbon dioxide
98 Minerals
103 World shipping

Every year, the world's energy consumption is about the equivalent of what would come from burning 10,000 million tonnes of oil (10,000 MtOe) – a 20-fold increase since 1850. Two-fifths of this total actually comes from burning oil and most of the rest comes from coal and natural gas.

The oil crises in the 1970s precipitated concern over dependence on finite fossil fuels as the primary source of energy, and growing environmental awareness has added impetus to the search for alternative energy resources. Fossil fuel combustion damages the environment through the release of gases and particulate matter, but two other major sources of energy, hydroelectricity and nuclear power, are also controversial. Hydro-electricity production involves flooding large areas to create reservoirs, while nuclear power stations generate dangerous radioactive wastes and can cause major disasters. Nuclear power has been a growing source of energy, but the 2011 Japanese earthquake, with the consequent serious damage to the Fukushima nuclear power station, has caused many countries to rethink their energy strategies.

Alternative energy resources may soon provide a much larger proportion of the world's energy consumption. Solar and wind energy may become important in such countries as China and India, while tidal, wave, and geothermal energy all have potential in appropriate areas. Experts calculate that solar power could, in theory, supply between five and ten times the present electricity supply of developing countries.

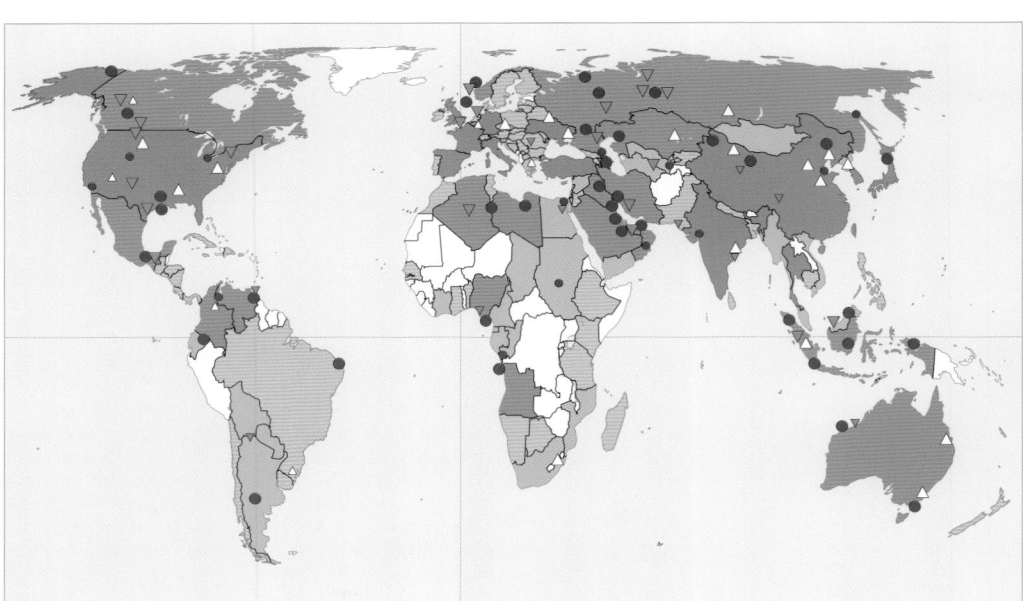

ENERGY BALANCE

Difference between energy production and consumption in millions of tonnes of oil equivalent (MtOe) (2009)

- Over 35 MtOe surplus
- 1 – 35 MtOe surplus
- Between 1 deficit – 1 surplus (approx. balance)
- 1 – 35 MtOe deficit
- Over 35 MtOe deficit
- No data

- ● Principal oilfields
- • Secondary oilfields
- ▼ Principal gasfields
- ▽ Secondary gasfields
- △ Principal coalfields
- △ Secondary coalfields

ENERGY CONSUMPTION

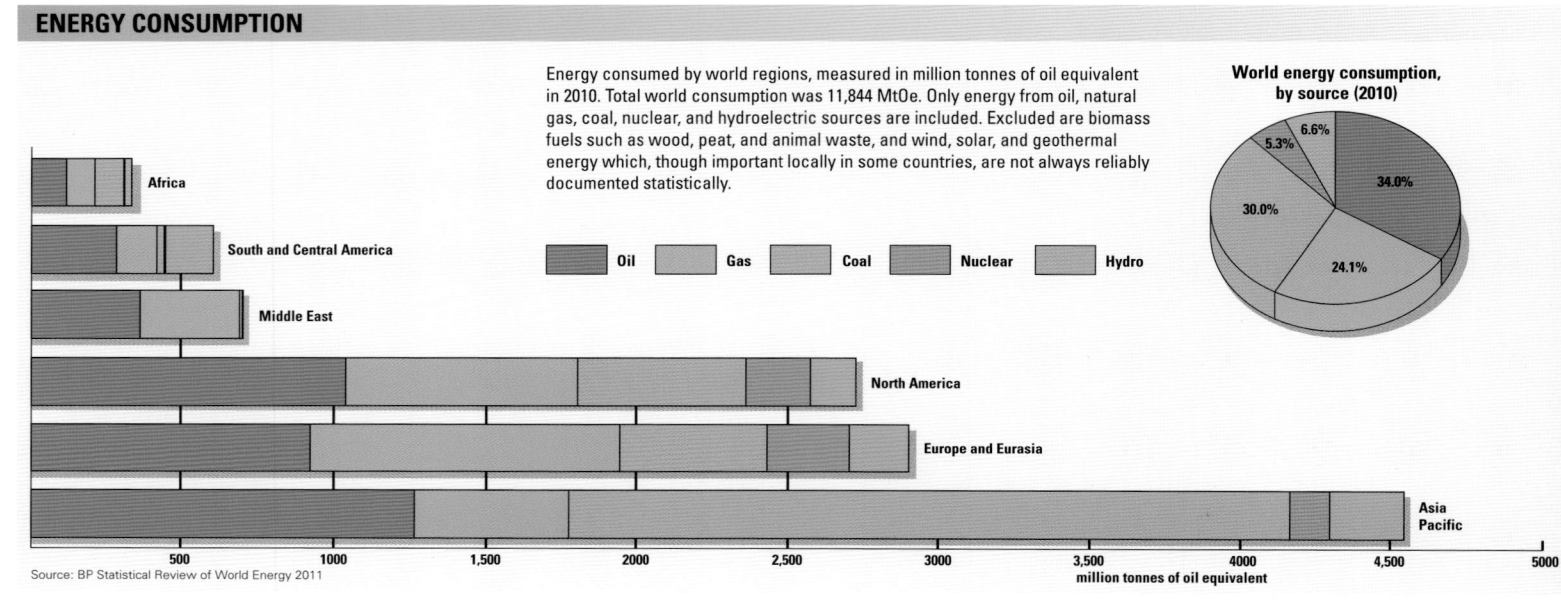

Energy consumed by world regions, measured in million tonnes of oil equivalent in 2010. Total world consumption was 11,844 MtOe. Only energy from oil, natural gas, coal, nuclear, and hydroelectric sources are included. Excluded are biomass fuels such as wood, peat, and animal waste, and wind, solar, and geothermal energy which, though important locally in some countries, are not always reliably documented statistically.

Oil   Gas   Coal   Nuclear   Hydro

World energy consumption, by source (2010)

34.0%
24.1%
30.0%
5.3%
6.6%

Africa
South and Central America
Middle East
North America
Europe and Eurasia
Asia Pacific

500 1000 1,500 2000 2,500 3000 3,500 4000 4,500 5000
million tonnes of oil equivalent

Source: BP Statistical Review of World Energy 2011

ENERGY PRODUCTION

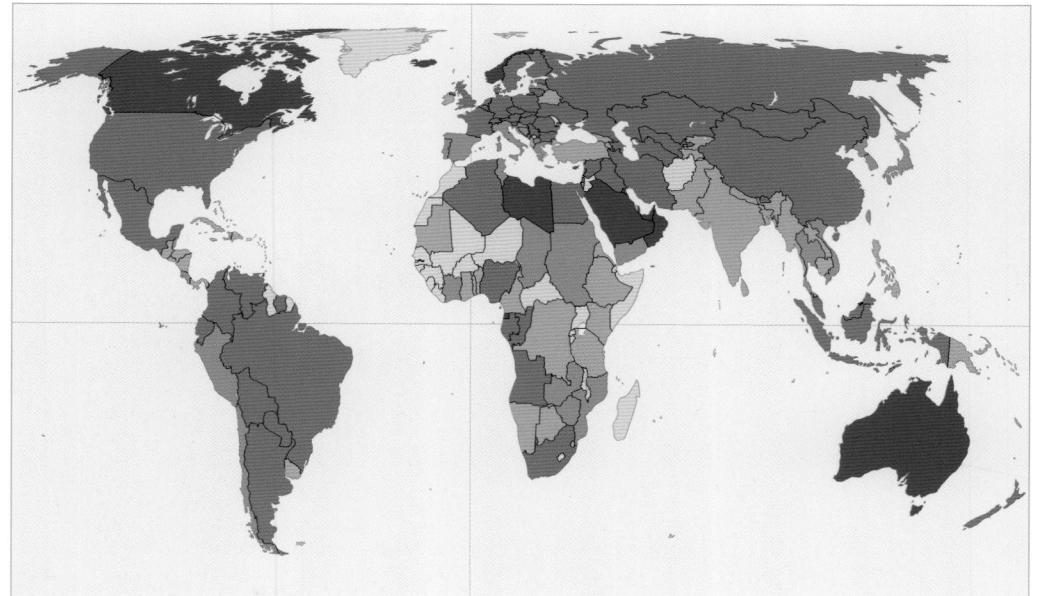

Energy production in tonnes of oil equivalent per capita (2009)

- Over 10
- 1 – 10
- 0.5 – 1
- 0.1 – 0.5
- Under 0.1
- No data available

Highest energy producers, tonnes of oil equivalent per capita (2009)

Qatar	167.9
Brunei	48.8
Kuwait	48.4
Norway	44.0
Equatorial Guinea	36.6

OIL MOVEMENTS

Major world movements of oil in millions of tonnes (2010)

1.	Former Soviet Union to Europe	295.2
2.	Middle East to Asia (not China or Japan)	227.1
3.	Middle East to Japan	179.9
4.	Canada to USA	125.0
5.	Middle East to China	118.4
6.	Middle East to Europe	116.7
7.	South and Central America to USA	109.3
8.	Middle East to USA	86.0
9.	West Africa to USA	83.8
10.	North Africa to Europe	83.0
11.	Mexico to USA	63.5

Total world imports 2,633.5 million tonnes

In 1990, China consumed 120 million tonnes of oil, leaving a surplus for export. In 2010 it consumed 447 million tonnes, of which it had to import around half. It is predicted that by 2030 China will be consuming over 800 million tonnes of oil, importing around three-quarters.

The majority of China's imported oil comes from the Middle East and Africa and has to pass through the narrow and crowded Singapore Strait. The Chinese government is pushing for alternative routes, such as a pipeline from Kazakhstan and a transit route from the Indian Ocean through Burma (Myanmar) to southern China.

◄ With many of the world's onshore oilfields reaching their maturity, exploration and production in ever-deeper ocean waters is taking place to try to satisfy demand. The "Deepwater Horizon" rig in the Gulf of Mexico drilled one of the world's deepest oil wells with a depth of 35,055 ft [10,685 m] before an explosion in April 2010 resulted in a major oil spill.

ENERGY RESERVES

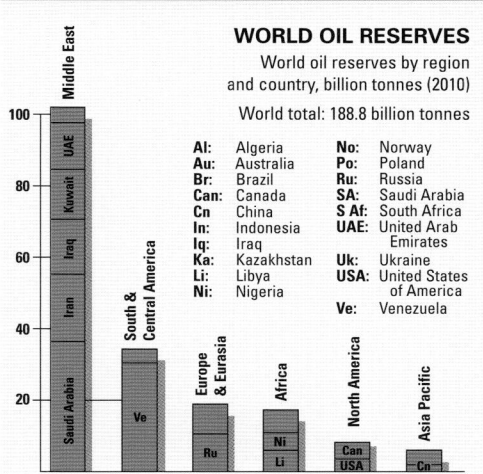

WORLD OIL RESERVES
World oil reserves by region and country, billion tonnes (2010)
World total: 188.8 billion tonnes

Al:	Algeria	No:	Norway
Au:	Australia	Po:	Poland
Br:	Brazil	Ru:	Russia
Can:	Canada	SA:	Saudi Arabia
Cn:	China	S Af:	South Africa
In:	Indonesia	UAE:	United Arab Emirates
Iq:	Iraq		
Ka:	Kazakhstan	Uk:	Ukraine
Li:	Libya	USA:	United States of America
Ni:	Nigeria		
		Ve:	Venezuela

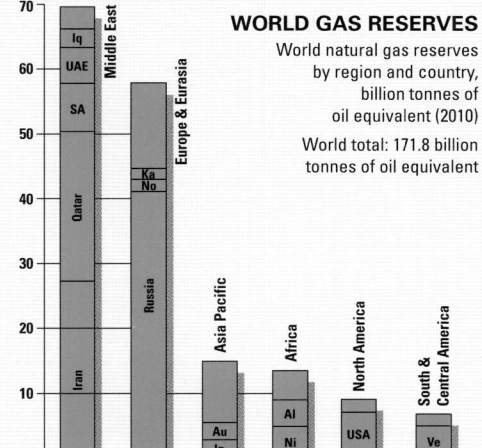

WORLD GAS RESERVES
World natural gas reserves by region and country, billion tonnes of oil equivalent (2010)
World total: 171.8 billion tonnes of oil equivalent

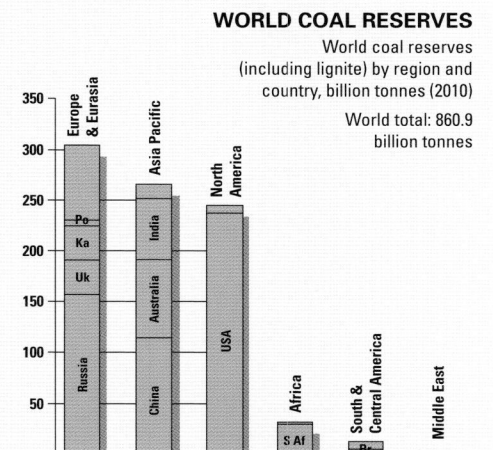

WORLD COAL RESERVES
World coal reserves (including lignite) by region and country, billion tonnes (2010)
World total: 860.9 billion tonnes

NUCLEAR POWER

Major producers by percentage of world total and by percentage of domestic electricity generation (2010)

Country	% of world total production	Country	% of nuclear as proportion of domestic electricity
1. United States	30.7	1. France	74.7
2. France	15.5	2. Slovak Rep.	53.1
3. Japan	10.6	3. Belgium	49.2
4. Russia	6.2	4. Ukraine	47.4
5. Korea, South	5.3	5. Hungary	42.1
6. Germany	5.1	6. Sweden	37.7
7. Canada	3.2	7. Switzerland	37.3
8. Ukraine	3.2	8. Bulgaria	33.1
9. China	2.7	9. Czech Republic	32.6
10. UK	2.2	10. Korea, South	29.7

Although the 1980s were a bad time for the nuclear power industry (fears of long-term environmental damage were heavily reinforced by the 1986 disaster at Chernobyl), the industry picked up in the early 1990s. Despite this, growth has recently been curtailed whilst countries review their energy mix, in light of the March 2011 Japanese earthquake and tsunami which seriously damaged the Fukushima nuclear power station.

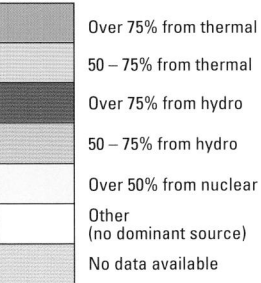

ELECTRICITY PRODUCTION

Percentage of electricity generated by source (2010)

- Over 75% from thermal
- 50 – 75% from thermal
- Over 75% from hydro
- 50 – 75% from hydro
- Over 50% from nuclear
- Other (no dominant source)
- No data available
- ● Selected geothermal plants
- ◆ Selected hydroelectric plants

HYDROELECTRICITY

Major producers by percentage of world total and by percentage of domestic electricity generation (2010)

Country	% of world total production	Country	% of hydroelectric as proportion of domestic electricity
1. China	21.0	1. Norway	94.8
2. Brazil	11.6	2. Brazil	81.7
3. Canada	10.7	3. Colombia	70.7
4. United States	7.6	4. Venezuela	65.8
5. Russia	4.9	5. Canada	58.1
6. Norway	3.4	6. New Zealand	56.4
7. India	3.2	7. Peru	56.0
8. Japan	2.5	8. Switzerland	50.6
9. Venezuela	2.2	9. Austria	48.9
10. Sweden	2.0	10. Ecuador	44.3

Countries heavily reliant on hydroelectricity are usually small and non-industrial: a high proportion of hydroelectric power more often reflects a modest energy budget than vast hydroelectric resources. The USA, for instance, produces only 6% of its domestic power requirements from hydroelectricity; yet that 6% amounts to almost half the hydropower generated by the whole of Africa.

ALTERNATIVE ENERGY RESOURCES

Solar: Each year the Sun bestows upon the Earth almost a million times as much energy as is locked up in all the planet's oil reserves, but only an insignificant fraction is trapped and used commercially. In a few installations around the world, mirrors focus the Sun's rays on to boilers, whose steam generates electricity by spinning turbines.

Wind: Caused by uneven heating of the Earth, winds are themselves a form of solar energy. Windmills have been long used for wind power; recent models, often arranged in banks on wind-swept high ground or off coastlines, usually generate electricity. Wind-power figures are given in the table (*right*). Although it currently produces less than 1% of the world's electricity, wind power contributes 19% of all electricity generated in Denmark.

Tidal: The energy from tides is potentially enormous, although only a few installations have so far been built to exploit it. In theory, at least, waves and currents could also provide almost unimaginable power, and the thermal differences in the ocean depths are another huge well

of potential energy. But work on extracting it is still at the experimental stage.

Geothermal: The Earth's temperature rises by 1°F for every 50 feet descent, with much steeper temperature gradients in geologically active areas. El Salvador, for example, produces 25% of its electricity from geothermal power stations, whilst the USA is the world's leading producer. Some of the oldest and most successful applications are in Iceland, where 86% of all households are heated by geothermal energy.

Biomass: The oldest of human fuels ranges from animal dung, still burned in cooking fires in much of North Africa and elsewhere, to sugarcane plantations feeding high-technology distilleries to produce ethanol for motor-vehicle engines. In Brazil and South Africa, plant ethanol provides up to 25% of motor fuel. Throughout the developing world, most biomass energy comes from firewood: although accurate figures are impossible to obtain, it may yield as much as 10% of the world's total energy consumption.

WIND POWER

World wind energy generating capacity, in megawatts

1984	600
1986	1,270
1988	1,580
1990	1,930
1992	2,510
1994	3,710
1996	6,115
1998	9,600
2000	17,800
2002	31,000
2003	39,300
2004	47,671
2005	58,982
2006	74,151
2007	93,927
2008	121,188
2009	157,899
2010	196,653
2011	239,000

For more information:

74 Geology

101 Patterns of production

103 World shipping

The use of metals played a vital part in the evolving technologies of early peoples. Copper first came into use around 10,000 years ago, bronze about 5,000 years ago, and iron 3,300 years ago. In the early stages of the Industrial Revolution, the location of coal, iron ore, and water power usually determined the location of new industries. But due to continuing improvements in transport, including oil pipelines, industries can now be located almost anywhere.

Minerals are distributed unevenly and some industrial countries, lacking their own mineral resources, import most of the raw materials they need. Some imports come from mineral-rich countries, such as Australia, but others come from developing countries, especially in Africa and South America. Most developing countries export unprocessed ores, losing out on the higher revenues gained from exporting metals.

Most minerals come from land deposits, because undersea deposits, with the exception of oil reserves under the continental shelves, have been inaccessible. But shortages of terrestrial minerals may one day encourage exploitation of the ocean floor.

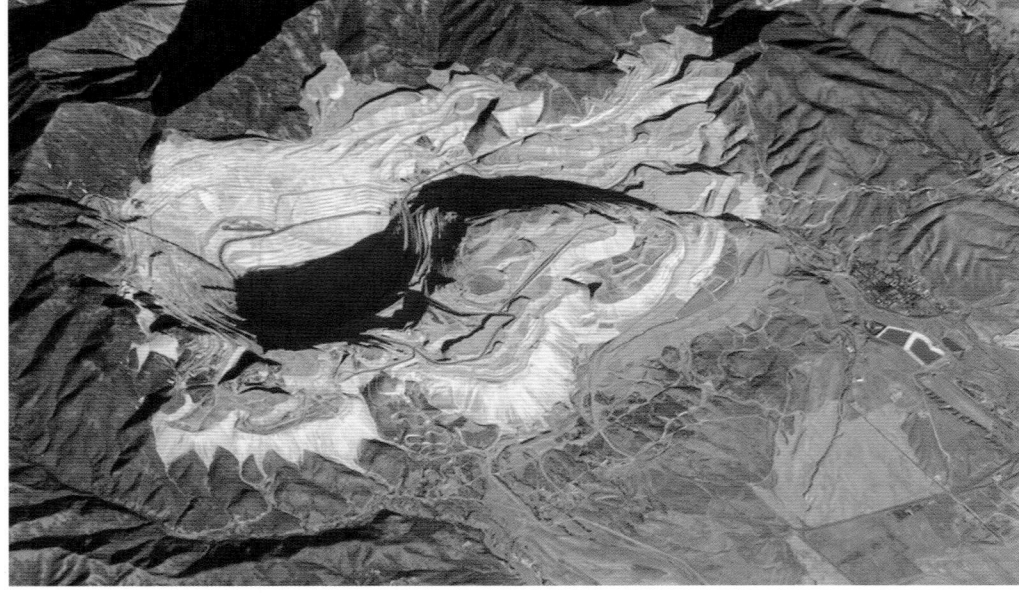

▶ Bingham Canyon Mine in Utah, USA, is one of the largest open-pit mines in the world. It measures over 2.5 miles [4 km] wide and 3,900 ft [1,200 m] deep. Copper-containing rocks are excavated from the surface downward in terraces. These terraces are 50–80 ft [15–25 m] high and provide access for equipment to work the rock face whilst maintaining stability of the sloping pit walls.

Today's copper market is booming due to global demands from construction, telecommunications, and electronics companies. Over 17 million tonnes of copper have been mined from Bingham Canyon Mine to date.

URANIUM

Uranium was first discovered by the German chemist Martin Klaproth in 1789. In its pure state, uranium is an immensely heavy, white metal. Its main use is as a fuel in nuclear reactors and in nuclear weaponry, although depleted uranium is employed as a projectile in anti-missile cannons, where its mass ensures a lethal punch.

Uranium is very scarce: the main source is the rare ore pitchblende, which itself contains only 0.2% uranium oxide. This blackish, lustrous ore occurs in quartz veins. Only a minute fraction of that is the radioactive U^{235} isotope, though so-called breeder reactors can transmute the more common U^{238} into highly radioactive plutonium.

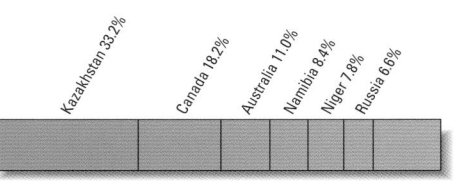

World total (2010): 53,700 tonnes

DIAMOND

Most of the world's diamond is found in kimberlite, or "blue ground," a basic peridotite rock; erosion may wash the diamond from its kimberlite matrix and deposit it with sand or gravel on river beds. Only a small proportion of the world's diamond, the most flawless, is cut into gemstones – "diamonds"; most are used in industry, where the material's remarkable hardness and abrasion resistance finds a use in cutting tools, drills, and dies. In 2009, the world's major producers are the Democratic Republic of the Congo (27.1%), Australia (19.3%), Russia (18.8%), Botswana (10.0%) and South Africa (9.6%),. Natural diamonds now account for less than 10% of all industrial diamond output. Synthetic diamond production in centers such as Ireland, Japan, Russia, and the USA far exceeds it.

METALS

Figures refer to ore production unless otherwise specified after the world total figure.

The world's leading producers of aluminum ore (bauxite) in 2010 were as follows:

1. Australia 32.7%
2. China................................ 21.1%
3. Brazil 13.4%
4. India 8.6%
5. Guinea 8.3%
6. Jamaica 4.1%
7. Russia 2.6%
8. Kazakhstan 2.4%
9. Suriname 1.9%
10. Venezuela 1.2%

The figures shown above are in stark contrast to the figures showing aluminum production (see above right). Australia, for example, produces 32.7% of the world's bauxite but only 4.7% of aluminum. Guinea and Jamaica account for almost 12.5% of the bauxite mined but have no smelters and export virtually all of it to countries like the USA and Canada.

Aluminum: Produced mainly from its oxide, bauxite, which yields 25% of its weight in aluminum. The cost of refining and production is often too high for producer-countries to bear, so bauxite is largely exported. Lightweight and corrosion resistant, aluminum alloys are widely used in aircraft, vehicles, cans, and packaging.

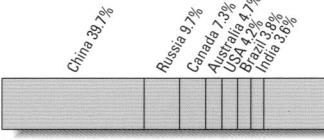

World total (2010): 40,800,000 tonnes

Lead: A soft metal, obtained mainly from galena (lead sulfide), which occurs in veins associated with iron, zinc, and silver sulfides. Its use in vehicle batteries accounts for the USA's prime consumer status; lead is also made into sheeting and piping. Its use as an additive to paints and petrol is decreasing.

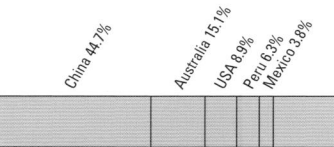

World total (2010): 4,140,000 tonnes

Tin: Soft, pliable and non-toxic, used to coat "tin" (tin-plated steel) cans, in the manufacture of foils and in alloys. The principal tin-bearing mineral is cassiterite (SnO_2), found in ore formed from molten rock.

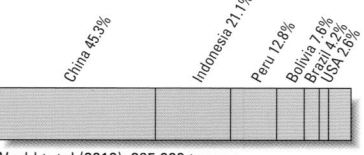

World total (2010): 265,000 tonnes

Gold: Regarded for centuries as the most valuable metal in the world and used to make coins, gold is still recognized as the monetary standard. A soft metal, it is alloyed to make jewelry; the electronics industry values its corrosion resistance and conductivity.

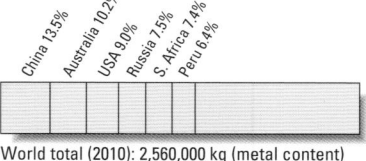

World total (2010): 2,560,000 kg (metal content)

Copper: Derived from low-yielding sulfide ores, copper is an important export for several developing countries. An excellent conductor of heat and electricity, it forms part of most electrical items, and is used in the manufacture of brass and bronze. Major importers include Japan and Germany.

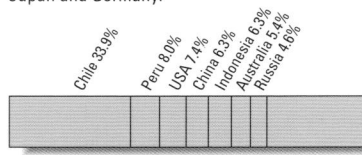

World total (2010): 15,900,000 tonnes

Mercury: The only metal that is liquid at normal temperatures, most is derived from its sulfide, cinnabar, found only in small quantities in volcanic areas. Apart from its value in thermometers and other instruments, most mercury production is used in anti-fungal and anti-fouling preparations, and to make detonators.

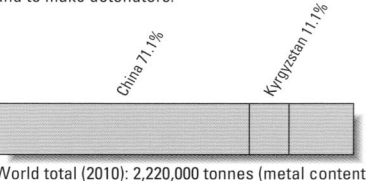

World total (2010): 2,220,000 tonnes (metal content)

Zinc: Often found in association with lead ores, zinc is highly resistant to corrosion, and about 40% of the refined metal is used to plate sheet steel, particularly vehicle bodies – a process known as galvanizing. Zinc is also used in dry batteries, paints, and dyes.

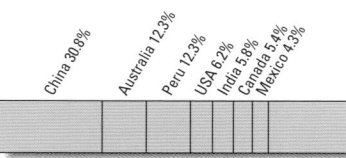

World total (2010): 12,000,000 tonnes

Silver: Most silver comes from ores mined and processed for other metals (including lead and copper). Pure or alloyed with harder metals, it is used for jewelry and ornaments. Industrial use includes dentistry, electronics, photography, and as a chemical catalyst.

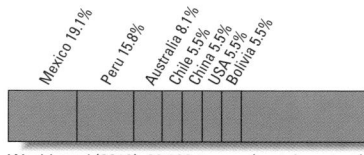

World total (2010): 23,100 tonnes (metal content)

DISTRIBUTION OF MINERALS

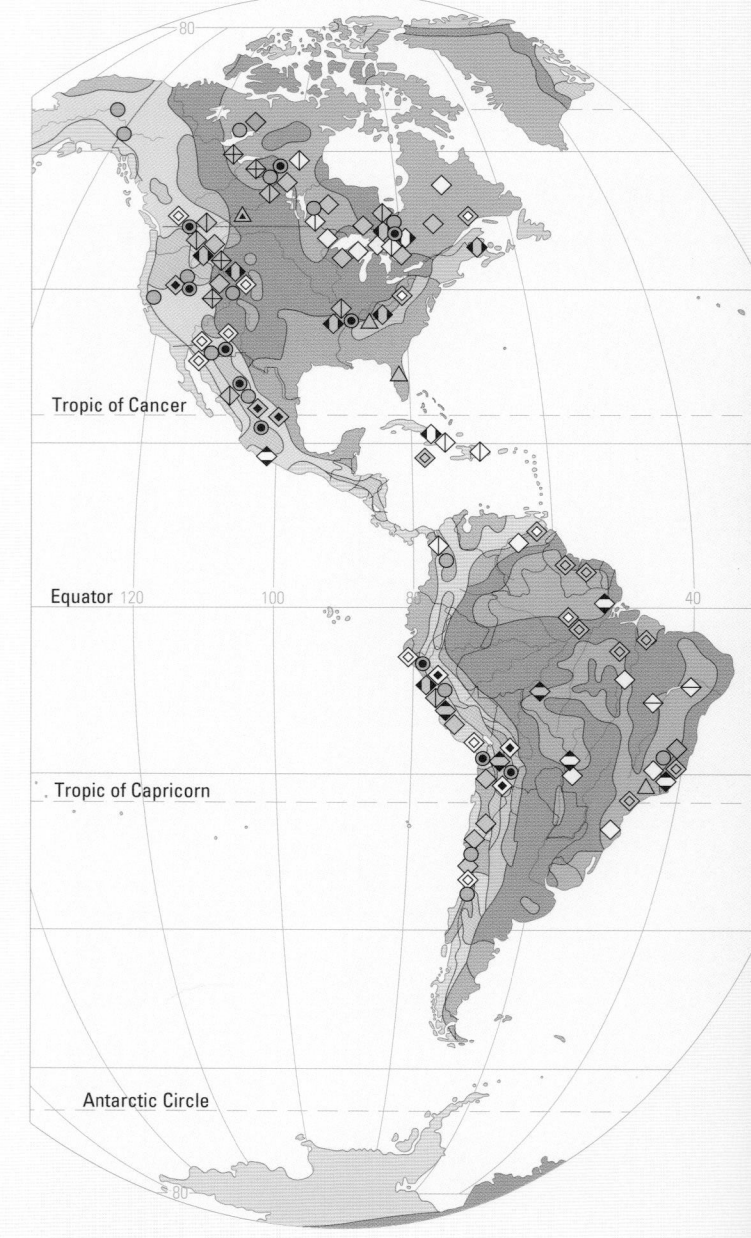

IRON ORE

Ever since the art of high-temperature smelting was discovered, some time in the second millennium BC, iron has been by far the most important metal known to man. The earliest iron plows transformed primitive agriculture and led to the first human population explosion, while iron weapons – or the lack of them – ensured the rise or fall of entire cultures.

Widely distributed around the world, iron ores usually contain 25–60% iron; blast furnaces process the raw product into pig-iron, which is then alloyed with carbon and other minerals to produce steels of various qualities. From the time of the Industrial Revolution, steel has been almost literally the backbone of modern civilization, the prime structural material on which all else is built.

Iron smelting usually developed close to the sources of ore and, later, to the coalfields that fueled the furnaces. Today, most ore comes from a few richly-endowed locations where large-scale mining is possible.

Iron and steel plants are generally built at coastal sites so that giant ore carriers, which account for a sizable proportion of the world's merchant fleet, can easily discharge their cargoes.

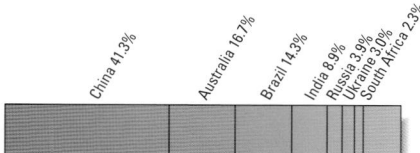

World total (2010): 2,590,000,000 tonnes

World production of pig-iron (2010)

Total world production: 1,030,000,000 tonnes

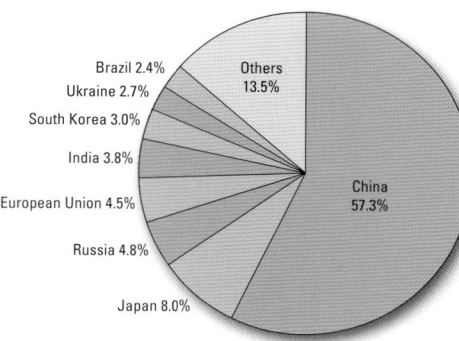

Manganese: In its pure state, manganese is a hard, brittle metal. Alloyed with chromium, iron and nickel, it produces abrasion-resistant steels; manganese-aluminum alloys are light but tough. Found in batteries and inks, manganese is also used in glass production. Manganese ores are frequently found in the same location as sedimentary iron ores. Pyrolusite (MnO₂) and psilomelane are the main economically-exploitable sources.

World total (2010): 13,900,000 tonnes

Chromium: Most of the world's chromium product on is alloyed with iron and other metals to produce steels with various different properties. Combined with iron, nickel, cobalt, and tungsten, chromium produces an exceptionally hard steel, which is resistant to heat; chrome steels are used for many household items where utility must be matched with appearance – cutlery, for example. Chromium is also used in the production of refractory bricks, and its salts for tanning and dyeing leather and cloth.

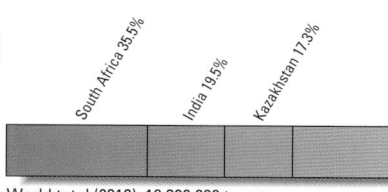

World total (2010): 19,300,000 tonnes

Nickel: Combined with chromium and iron, nickel produces stainless and high-strength steels; similar alloys go to make magnets and electrical heating elements. Nickel combined with copper is widely used to make coins; cupro-nickel alloy is very resistant to corrosion. Its ores yield only modest quantities of nickel – 0.5% to 3% – but also contain copper, iron, and small amounts of precious metals. Japan, USA, UK, Germany, and France are the principal importers.

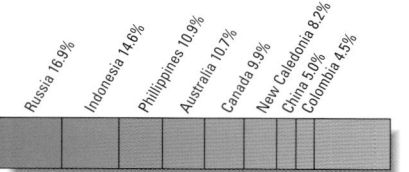

World total (2010): 1,590,000 tonnes

SCRAP METAL

Scrap metal has been an important source material for the manufacturing industry in domestic markets for decades, its value fluctuating according to the state of the local economy. Recently, however, with growing concern for the global environment and the rapid development of the economies in the Far East, the industry has become far more globalized. Container loads of processed-metal scrap from time-expired machinery in the Western world are now being exported to the Far East to be recycled. Processed-steel scrap accounts for almost half of the requirements for "furnace feed" for the world's steelmakers, and 40% of the world's copper requirements are derived from scrap.

Two major advantages of using scrap rather than refining mined ore are the energy and raw material savings that can be made. If 1 tonne of steel scrap is recycled, it saves 120 lb [54 kg] of limestone, 2,500 lb [1,130 kg] of iron ore and 1,400 lb [635 kg] of coal, with a consequent 86% reduction in air pollution, 40% saving in water use, and 76% reduction in water pollution. Huge energy savings, with consequent cuts in greenhouse-gas emissions, can also be made by using scrap.

As well as bulk minerals, such as those quoted above, alloys using nickel, chromium, tungsten, molybdenum, cobalt, and titanium, which are often only available in limited supplies and are expensive to produce, can also be recycled. The techniques involved to do this work are often very sophisticated, involving X-ray spectrometry and other computer-controlled methods, in order to recover high-value but low-volume metals from devices such as computers and televisions.

With companies having to take increased responsibility for their products, from manufacturing to sale and thence to their ultimate disposal at the end of their useful life, recycling scrap metals will become a much more important method of conserving the world's raw materials and preserving the environment in the future.

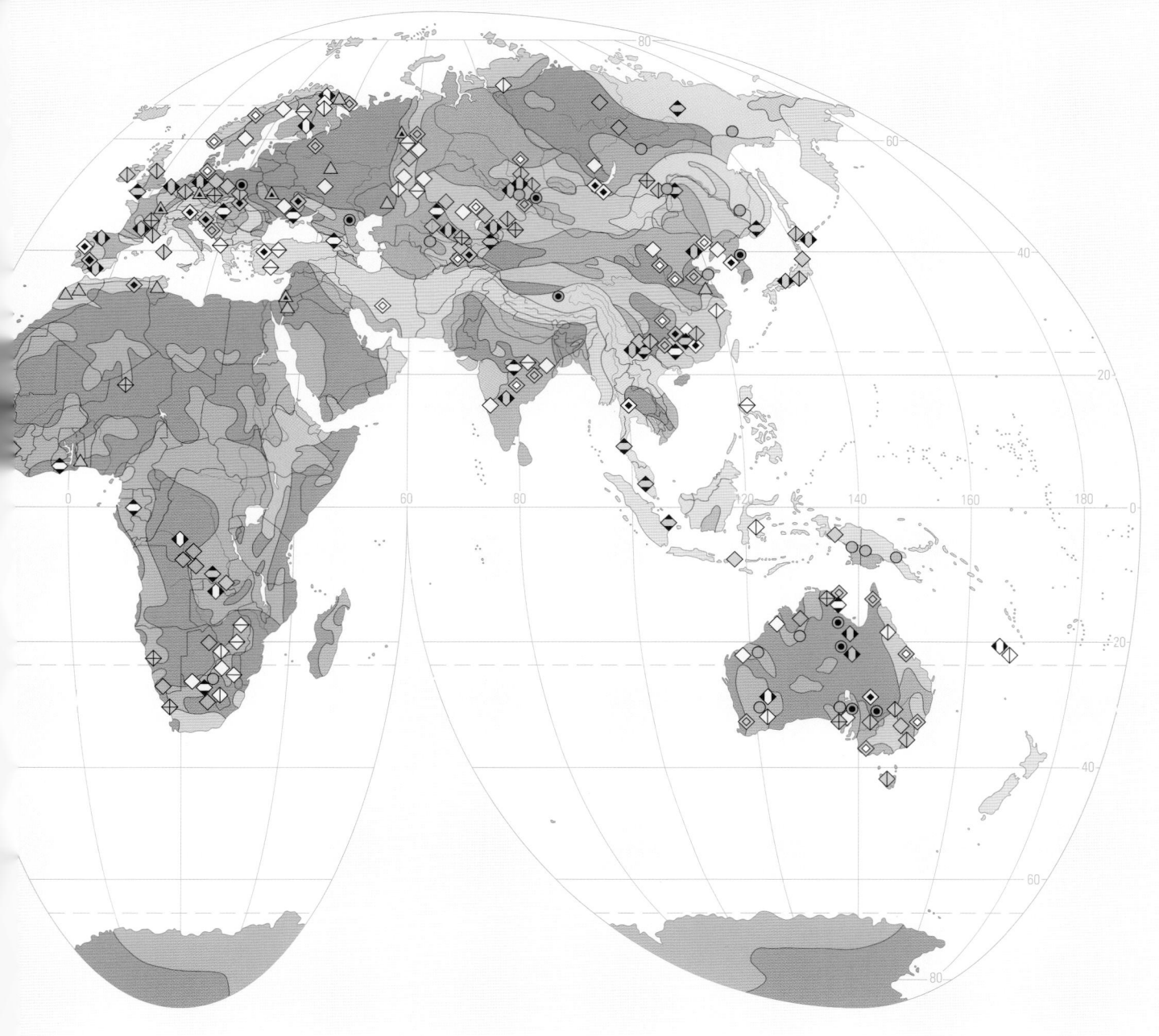

STRUCTURAL REGIONS

Pre-Cambrian shields
Sedimentary cover on Pre-Cambrian shields
Paleozoic (Caledonian and Hercynian) folding
Sedimentary cover on Paleozoic folding
Mesozoic folding
Sedimentary cover on Mesozoic folding
Cenozoic (Alpine) folding
Sedimentary cover on Cenozoic folding
Intensive Mesozoic and Cenozoic vulcanism

DISTRIBUTION
Iron and ferro-alloys
Chromium
Cobalt
Iron ore
Manganese
Molybdenum
Nickel ore
Tungsten

Non-ferrous metals
Bauxite (Aluminum)
Copper
Lead
Mercury
Tin
Zinc
Uranium

Precious metals and stones
Diamonds
Gold
Silver

Fertilizers
Phosphates
Potash

For more information:

84 Water distribution
98 Minerals
99 Iron and ferro-alloys
102 Major exports
      Traded products

The Industrial Revolution, which began in Britain in the late 18th century, represented a major technological advance in the evolution of human society. It enabled a group of countries to become prosperous by replacing expensive human labor with increasingly sophisticated machinery. In economic terms, manufacturing is the transformation of raw materials, energy, labor, and machines into finished goods, which have a higher value than the various elements used in production.

The economies of countries can be compared by reference to their per capita Gross Domestic Products (GDPs), namely, the total value of goods and services produced within a country in a year, divided by the population. The industrialized, or developed, countries accounted for 19% of the world's population in 2010 with an average per capita GDP of more than US $40,000. On the other hand, low-income developing countries, with small industrial sectors, accounted for 38% of the world's population. Their per capita GDPs are less than $1,200, with some as low as $300.

Kenya, with its low-income economy, had a per capita GDP in 2010 of US $1,600. Agriculture employs 75% of the people, while industry together with services employs 25%. The main industries are the processing of agricultural imports and import substitution (making such necessities as cement, footwear, and textiles). Heavy industry plays only a small part. By contrast, Germany had a per capita GDP in 2010 of $34,100. Agriculture employs only 2% of the population, with 30% in industry and 68% in services. Germany's industrial sector differs greatly from Kenya's, with its emphasis on vehicles, machinery, chemicals, and electronics.

Since the 1970s, some former developing countries in eastern Asia achieved rapid economic growth through industrialization. Despite setbacks in the late 1990s, they demonstrated that a developing industrial sector can transform an economy, which starts off with certain advantages, such as low labor costs. But economic success also depends on such factors as education to provide skills, and regulations that attract foreign investors. China, whose economy grew by more than 9% per year between 2001 and 2010, satisfies many of these criteria, though its record on human rights leaves much to be desired.

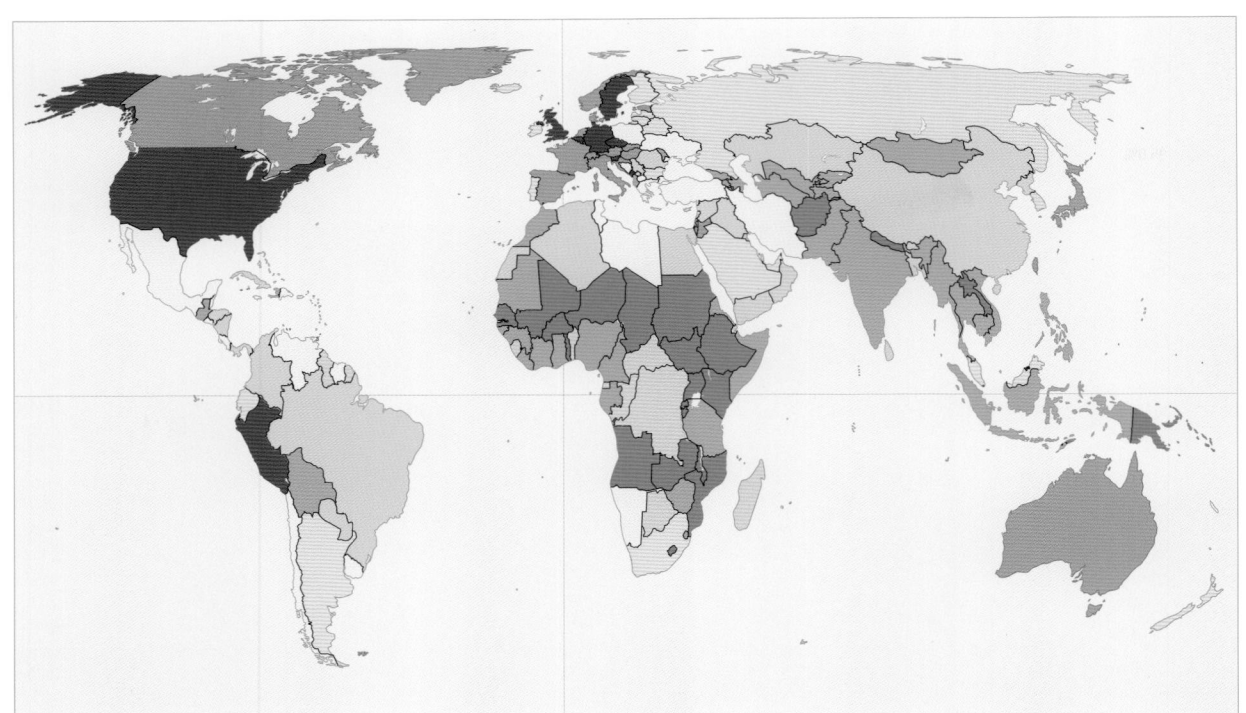

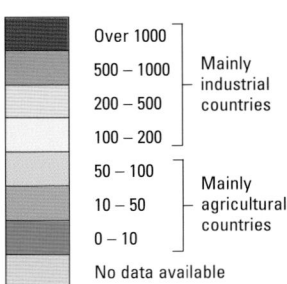

EMPLOYMENT

The number of workers employed in manufacturing for every 100 workers engaged in agriculture (2010)

Over 1000	Mainly industrial countries
500 – 1000	
200 – 500	
100 – 200	
50 – 100	Mainly agricultural countries
10 – 50	
0 – 10	
No data available	

Countries with the highest number of workers employed in manufacturing per 100 workers in agriculture (2010)

Singapore	30,200
San Marino	18,150
Bahrain	7,900
Micronesia, Fed. States of	3,820
Peru	3,400
USA	2,900
Sweden	2,560
Liechtenstein	2,540
Malta	1,910
Slovenia	1,590

DIVISION OF EMPLOYMENT

Distribution of workers between agriculture, industry and services, selected countries (2010)

The six countries selected illustrate the usual stages of economic development, from dependence on agriculture through industrial growth to the expansion of the service sector.

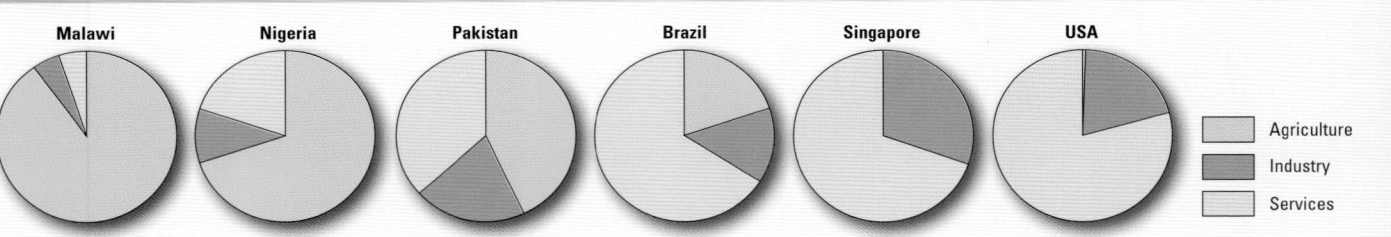

Malawi   Nigeria   Pakistan   Brazil   Singapore   USA

Agriculture
Industry
Services

THE WORK FORCE

Percentages of men and women between 15 and 64 in employment (selected countries)

The figures include employees and the self-employed, who in developing countries are often subsistence farmers. People in full-time education are excluded. Because of the population age structure in developing countries, the employed population has to support a far larger number of non-workers than its industrial equivalent. For example, more than 52% of Kenya's people are under 15, an age group that makes up less than a tenth of the UK population.

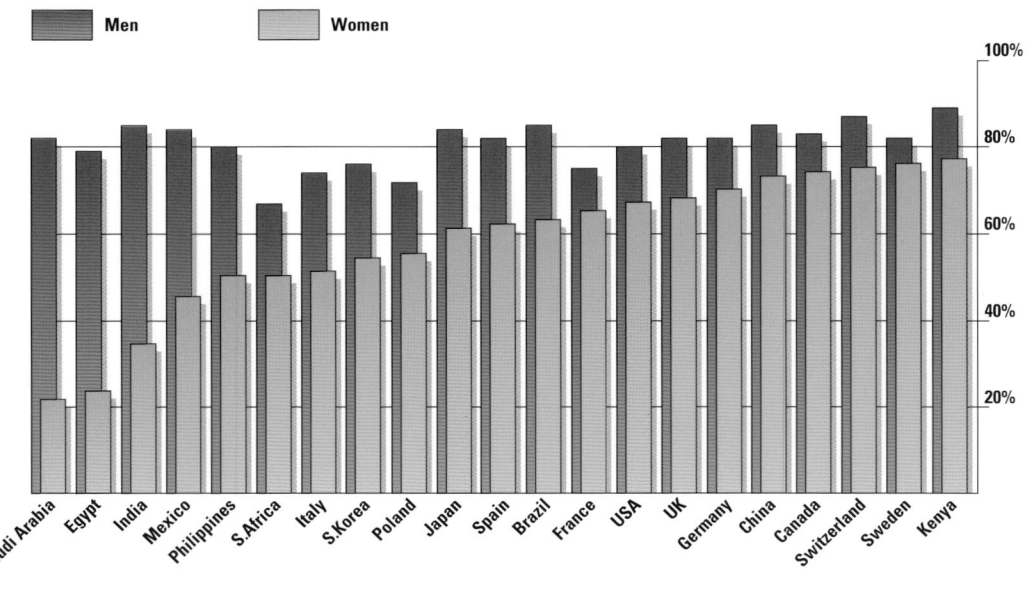

Men   Women

Saudi Arabia, Egypt, India, Mexico, Philippines, S.Africa, Italy, S.Korea, Poland, Japan, Spain, Brazil, France, USA, UK, Germany, China, Canada, Switzerland, Sweden, Kenya

WEALTH CREATION

The Gross National Income (GNI) of the world's largest economies, US $ million (2010)

1.	USA	14,645,629	21.	Belgium	499,506
2.	China	5,720,811	22.	Poland	474,891
3.	Japan	5,334,370	23.	Sweden	469,954
4.	Germany	3,521,983	24.	Saudi Arabia	439,021
5.	France	2,749,821	25.	Norway	411,776
6.	UK	2,387,064	26.	Austria	394,575
7.	Italy	2,125,845	27.	Argentina	348,387
8.	Brazil	1,830,384	28.	Venezuela	334,055
9.	India	1,553,937	29.	Iran	330,619
10.	Canada	1,475,865	30.	Denmark	327,369
11.	Spain	1,462,894	31.	Greece	304,963
12.	Russia	1,403,847	32.	South Africa	304,591
13.	Taiwan	1,016,390	33.	Thailand	286,553
14.	Mexico	1,008,003	34.	Finland	255,978
15.	South Korea	972,299	35.	Colombia	255,271
16.	Australia	957,529	36.	Portugal	232,908
17.	Netherlands	814,762	37.	Hong Kong (China)	231,658
18.	Turkey	719,878	38.	Malaysia	220,362
19.	Indonesia	599,157	39.	Israel	207,195
20.	Switzerland	559,735	40.	North Korea	205,000

INDUSTRIAL OUTPUT

Largest industrial output (mining, manufacturing, construction and energy), US $ billion (2011)

1.	China	3,416	22.	Norway	185
2.	USA	3,336	23.	Switzerland	175
3.	Japan	1,409	24.	Poland	173
4.	Germany	1,005	25.	Taiwan	149
5.	Russia	685	26.	Sweden	145
6.	Brazil	671	27.	Argentina	137
7.	Italy	554	28.	South Africa	129
8.	UK	522	29.	Colombia	125
9.	France	514	30.	Austria	124
10.	Canada	477	31.	Thailand	118
11.	India	441	32.	Algeria	117
12.	South Korea	438	33.	Belgium	111
13.	Saudi Arabia	390	34.	Malaysia	111
14.	Indonesia	389	35.	Venezuela	110
15.	Spain	387	36.	Chile	104
16.	Australia	381	37.	Egypt	93
17.	Mexico	379	38.	Czech Rep.	83
18.	UAE	214	39.	Finland	78
19.	Turkey	209	40.	Israel	76
20.	Netherlands	203	41.	Philippines	71
21.	Iran	196	42.	Singapore	69

INDUSTRY AND TRADE

Manufactured goods (including machinery and transport) as a percentage of total exports (2010)

- Over 75%
- 50 – 75%
- 25 – 50%
- 10 – 25%
- Under 10%
- No data available

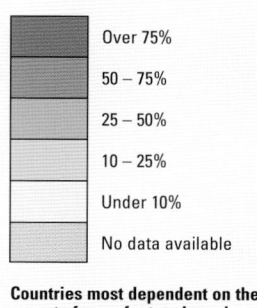

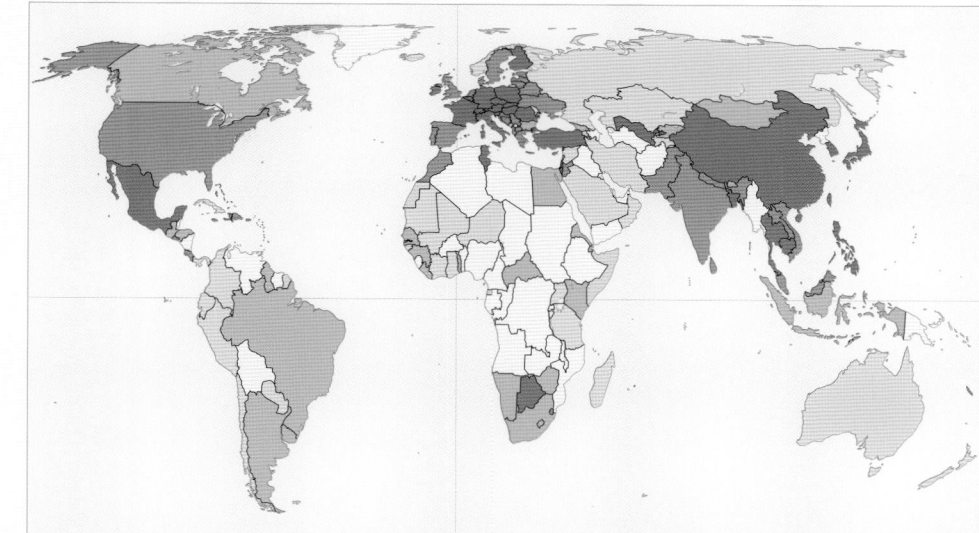

Countries most dependent on the export of manufactured goods

Cambodia	96%
China	94%
Israel	93%
Japan	89%
South Korea	89%
Switzerland	89%

UNEMPLOYMENT

Highest rates of unemployment, percentage of the labor force (2010)

1.	Zimbabwe	95.0%
2.	Burkina Faso	77.0%
3.	Turkmenistan	60.0%
4.	Djibouti	59.0%
5.	Namibia	51.2%
6.	Senegal	48.0%
7.	Nepal	46.0%
8.	Kosovo	45.3%
9.	Lesotho	45.0%
10.	Bosnia & Herzegovina	43.5%
11.	Haiti	40.6%
12.	Swaziland	40.0%
13.	Gaza Strip	40.0%
14.	Kenya	40.0%
15.	Afghanistan	35.0%
16.	Yemen	35.0%
17.	Cameroon	30.0%
18.	Libya	30.0%
19.	Mali	30.0%
20.	Mauritania	30.0%

IMPORTANCE OF SERVICE SECTOR

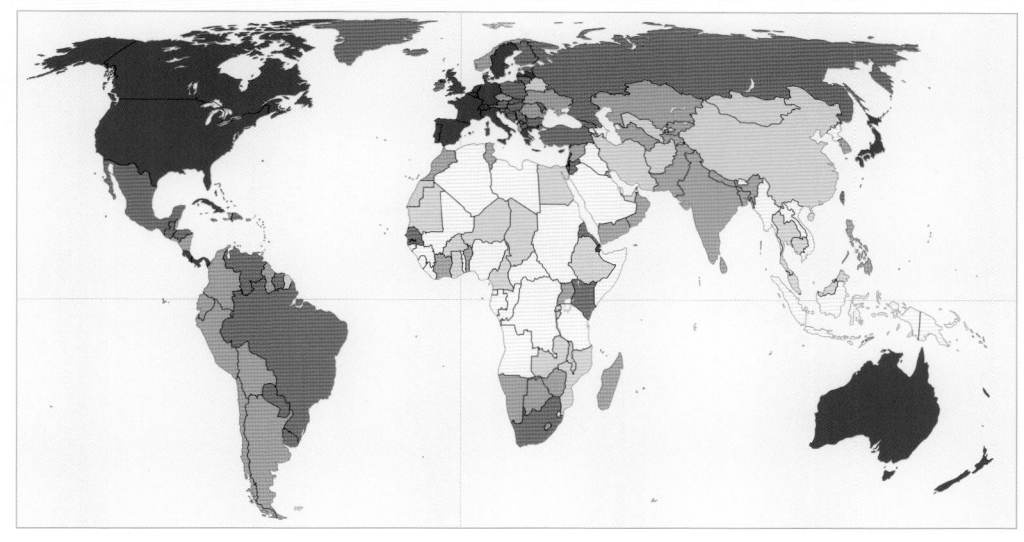

Percentage of total GDP from service sector (2010)

- Over 70%
- 60 – 70%
- 50 – 60%
- 40 – 50%
- Under 40%
- No data available

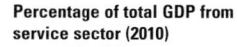
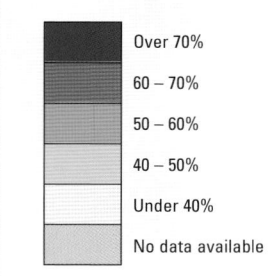

Countries most dependent on the service sector

Monaco	95%
Luxembourg	86%
Bahamas	84%
Djibouti	82%
Palau	82%

Leather Footwear
Production in thousands of pairs (2008)

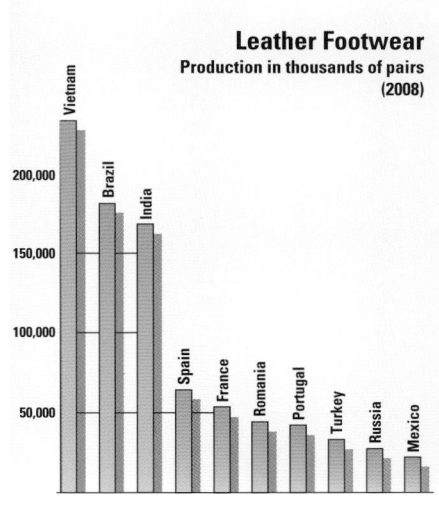

◀ This photograph shows a cement-manufacturing plant in Vác, Hungary. Cement production figures are often an indicator of the relative prosperity of a country, since they show the construction of roads, dams, and other infrastructure projects (*see the graph below*). However, cement manufacture emits high levels of carbon dioxide into the atmosphere.

Steel Production
Steel output in thousand tonnes (2011)

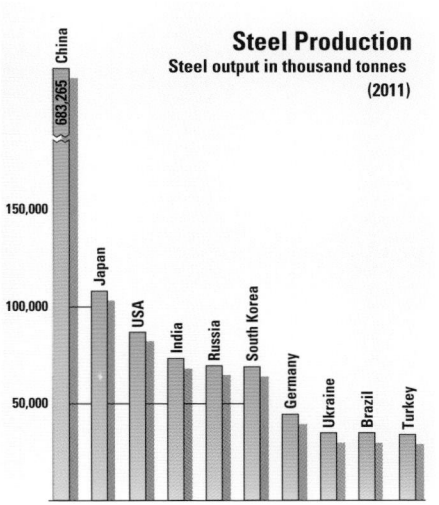

Cement Production
Cement production in thousand tonnes (2011)

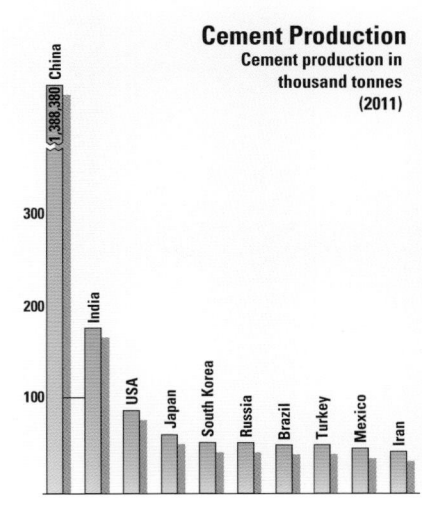

Paper and Cardboard
Paper and cardboard production (2011)

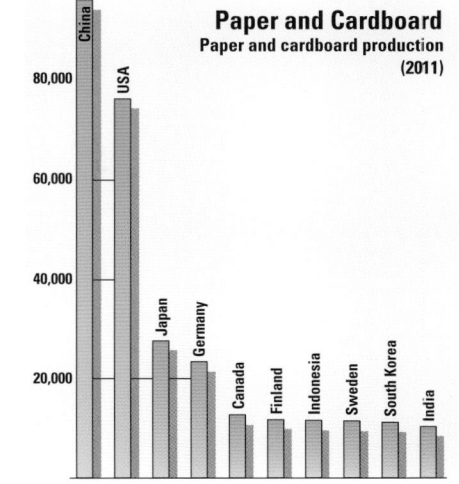

Automobiles
Production of passenger cars in thousands, (2010)

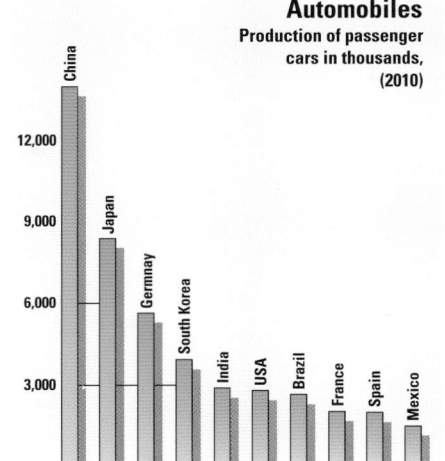

For more information:

95 International organizations

97 Movements of oil

98 Minerals

100 Wealth creation

101 Industry and trade

107 Air travel and tourism

Inflation

Trade played a vital role in the growth of early civilizations and it was later a spur to European exploration and colonization. The colonial powers grew rich by exporting cheap manufactures, such as clothing and footwear, while obtaining primary products from their colonies.

From the late 19th century to the early 1950s, as transport technology improved, primary products, especially oil in the later stages of this period, dominated world trade. However, since that time, manufactures have become the chief commodities in world trade, which is dominated by the industrialized countries. Nearly half of all world trade flows between the developed market economies of the European Union, the United States, and Japan, although a number of Asian economies, notably China, India, Malaysia, Singapore, South Korea, Taiwan, and Thailand, have dramatically increased their share since the 1990s.

China's remarkable growth means that it has rapidly overtaken countries such as Japan, Mexico, and Germany, to become the second biggest exporter to the United States. China's low production costs, especially its cheap labor, were estimated to be one-twentieth of those of Japan, making its high-quality exports highly competitive in price. Growth in world trade is regarded as a sign of economic health, as is a favorable balance of trade (or trade surplus) in any country.

WORLD TRADE

Percentage share of total world exports by value (2011)

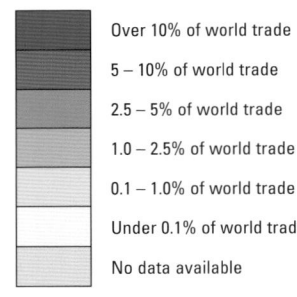

- Over 10% of world trade
- 5 – 10% of world trade
- 2.5 – 5% of world trade
- 1.0 – 2.5% of world trade
- 0.1 – 1.0% of world trade
- Under 0.1% of world trade
- No data available

○ Top ten container ports
(see graph on opposite page)

International trade is dominated by a handful of powerful maritime nations: the members of "G8" (Canada, France, Germany, Italy, Japan, Russia, UK and USA) and the "BRIC" nations (Brazil, Russia, India and China).

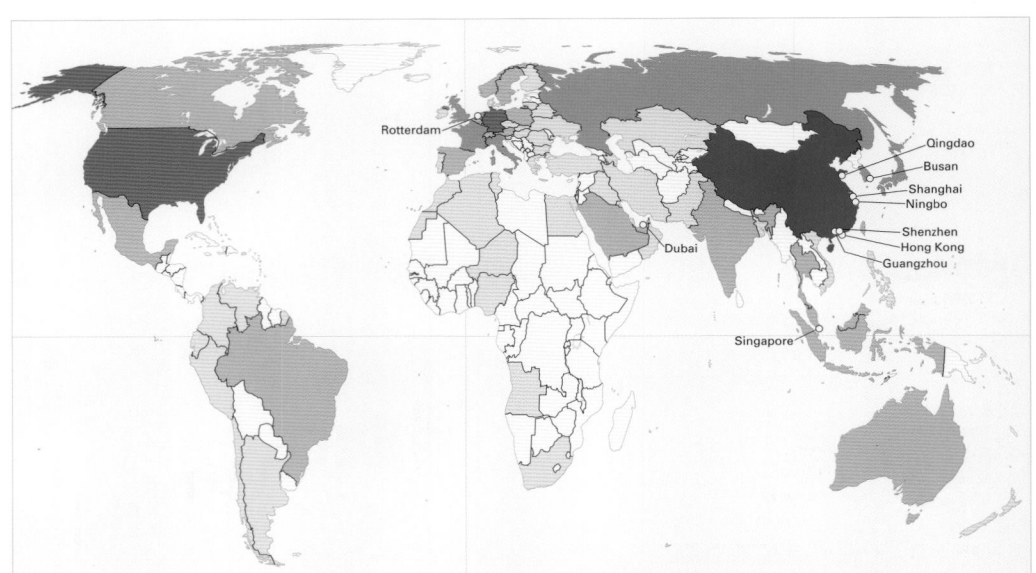

DEPENDENCE ON TRADE

Exports as a percentage of GDP (2011)

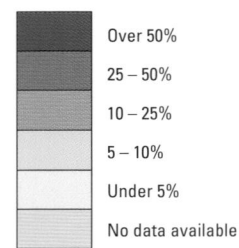

- Over 50%
- 25 – 50%
- 10 – 25%
- 5 – 10%
- Under 5%
- No data available

The character of world trade has changed a great deal in the last 60 years or so. While many developing countries still remain heavily dependent on exporting mineral ores, fossil fuels or farm products, such as coffee or cocoa, world trade is now dominated by manufactured goods. Since the 1980s, high-tech products, such as computer equipment, telecommunications gear, and transistors, have become increasingly important.

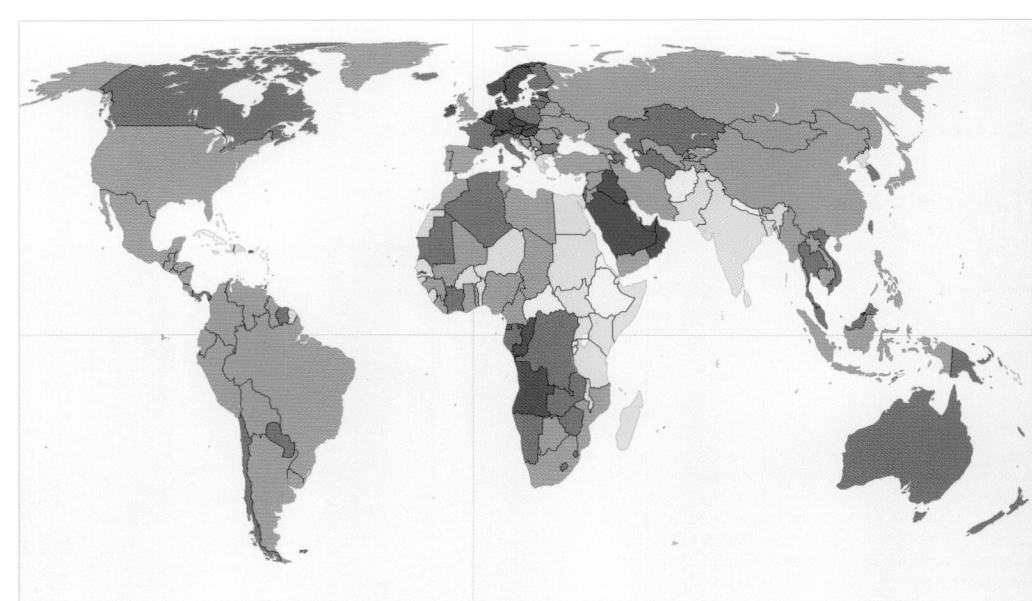

TRADED PRODUCTS

World merchandise exports by product, percentage of total value (2010)

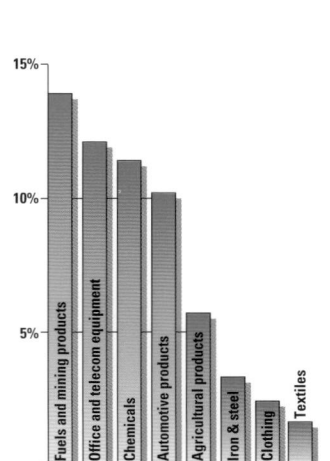

MAJOR EXPORTS

Leading manufactured items and their exporters

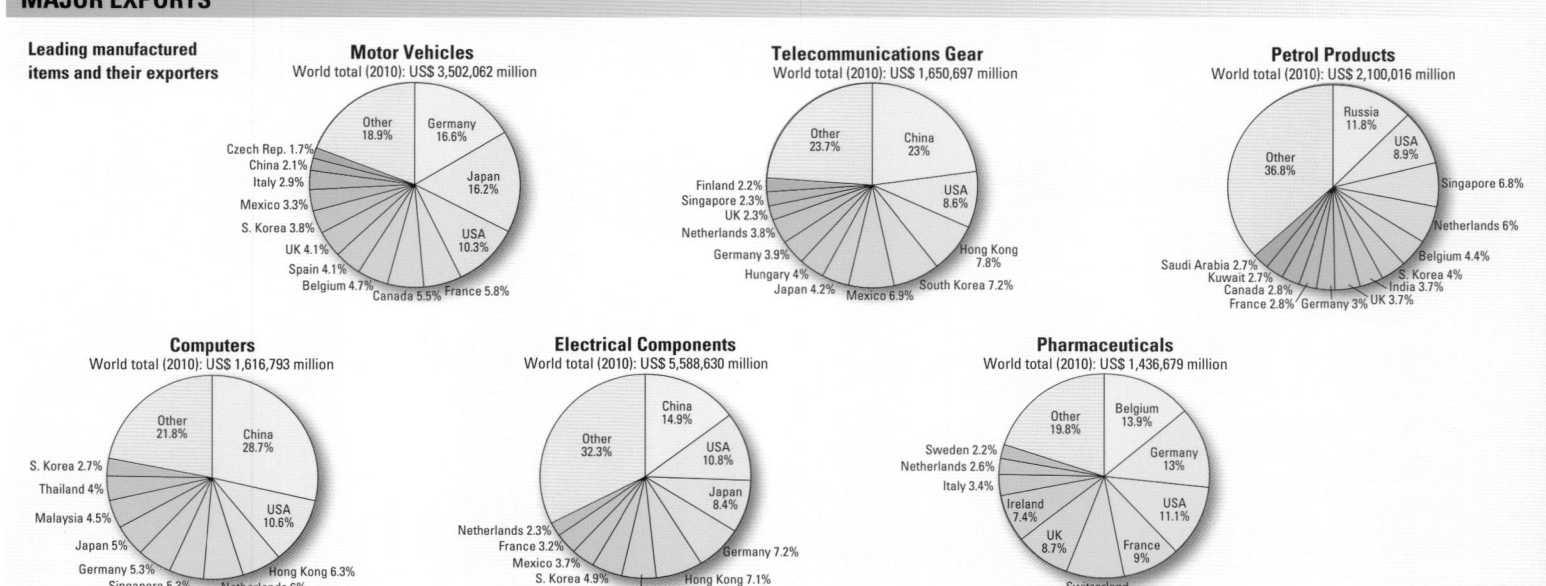

Motor Vehicles
World total (2010): US$ 3,502,062 million
- Germany 16.6%
- Japan 16.2%
- USA 10.3%
- France 5.8%
- Canada 5.5%
- Belgium 4.7%
- Spain 4.1%
- UK 4.1%
- S. Korea 3.8%
- Mexico 3.3%
- Italy 2.9%
- China 2.1%
- Czech Rep. 1.7%
- Other 18.9%

Telecommunications Gear
World total (2010): US$ 1,650,697 million
- China 23%
- USA 8.6%
- Hong Kong 7.8%
- South Korea 7.2%
- Mexico 6.9%
- Japan 4.2%
- Hungary 4%
- Germany 3.9%
- Netherlands 3.8%
- UK 2.3%
- Singapore 2.3%
- Finland 2.2%
- Other 23.7%

Petrol Products
World total (2010): US$ 2,100,016 million
- Russia 11.8%
- USA 8.9%
- Singapore 6.8%
- Netherlands 6%
- Belgium 4.4%
- S. Korea 4%
- India 3.7%
- UK 3.7%
- Germany 3%
- France 2.8%
- Canada 2.8%
- Kuwait 2.7%
- Saudi Arabia 2.7%
- Other 36.8%

Computers
World total (2010): US$ 1,616,793 million
- China 28.7%
- USA 10.6%
- Hong Kong 6.3%
- Netherlands 6%
- Singapore 5.3%
- Germany 5.3%
- Japan 5%
- Malaysia 4.5%
- Thailand 4%
- S. Korea 2.7%
- Other 21.8%

Electrical Components
World total (2010): US$ 5,588,630 million
- China 14.9%
- USA 10.8%
- Japan 8.4%
- Germany 7.2%
- Hong Kong 7.1%
- Singapore 5.2%
- S. Korea 4.9%
- Mexico 3.7%
- France 3.2%
- Netherlands 2.3%
- Other 32.3%

Pharmaceuticals
World total (2010): US$ 1,436,679 million
- Belgium 13.9%
- Germany 13%
- USA 11.1%
- France 9%
- Switzerland 8.8%
- UK 8.7%
- Ireland 7.4%
- Italy 3.4%
- Netherlands 2.6%
- Sweden 2.2%
- Other 19.8%

WORLD SHIPPING

While ocean passenger traffic is relatively modest nowadays, sea transport still carries most of the world's trade. Oil and bulk carriers make up the majority of the world fleet, although the general cargo category is the fastest growing. Two innovations have revolutionized sea transport. The first is the development of the roll-on/roll-off (Ro-Ro) method where trucks or even trains loaded with freight are driven straight on to the ship, thus saving time. The second is containerization in which goods are packed into containers (the dimensions of which are fixed) at the factory, driven to the port, and loaded on board by specialist machinery.

Over 40% of world shipping today sails under a "flag of convenience," whereby owners take advantage of low taxes by registering their vessels in a foreign country the ships will never see, notably Panama and Liberia.

TYPES OF VESSELS
World merchant fleet by type of vessel (2010)

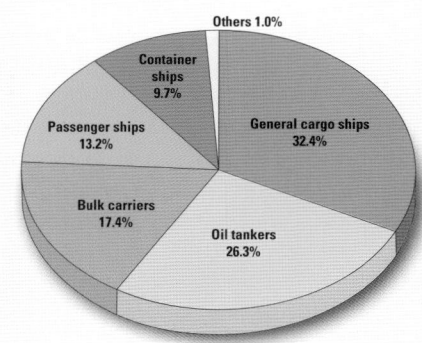

- Others 1.0%
- Container ships 9.7%
- Passenger ships 13.2%
- General cargo ships 32.4%
- Bulk carriers 17.4%
- Oil tankers 26.3%

MERCHANT FLEETS
Merchant fleets in thousand gross registered tonnage (2010).

Although a large number of vessels are registered in Liberia and Panama, they are not part of the national fleet.

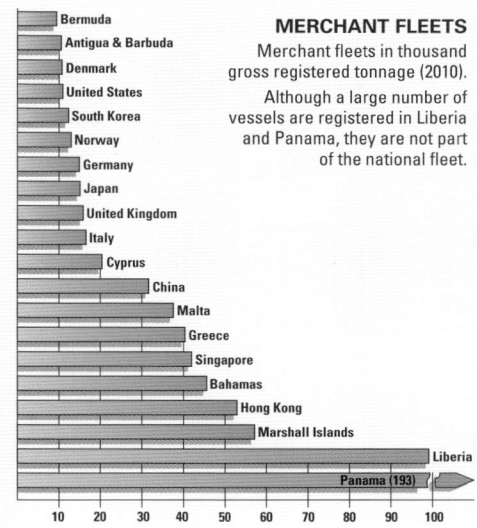

Bermuda, Antigua & Barbuda, Denmark, United States, South Korea, Norway, Germany, Japan, United Kingdom, Italy, Cyprus, China, Malta, Greece, Singapore, Bahamas, Hong Kong, Marshall Islands, Liberia, Panama (193)

TOP TEN PORTS
Total container traffic, in million TEU (2010)

("TEU" stands for Twenty-foot Equivalent Unit, the equivalent of a standard container)

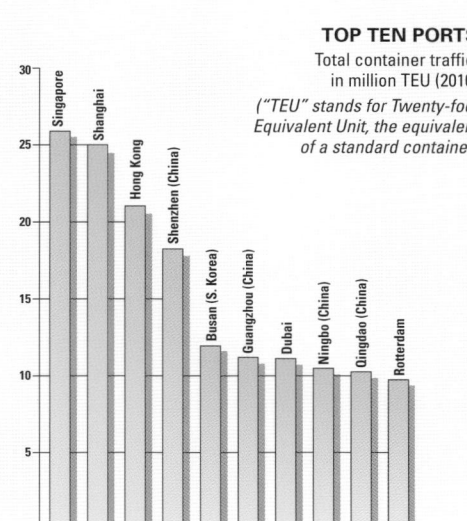

Singapore, Shanghai, Hong Kong, Shenzhen (China), Busan (S. Korea), Guangzhou (China), Dubai, Ningbo (China), Qingdao (China), Rotterdam

▲ A container ship being unloaded in the port of Melbourne, Australia. World trade depends on transport. Containerization, introduced in the 1950s, reduced the risk of damage to cargo and cut the time and cost of loading and unloading.

TRADE IN PRIMARY EXPORTS

Primary exports as a percentage of total export value (2008)

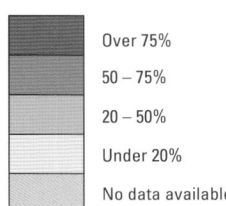

- Over 75%
- 50 – 75%
- 20 – 50%
- Under 20%
- No data available

Primary exports are raw materials or partly processed products that form the basis for manufacturing. They are the necessary requirements of industries and include agricultural products, minerals, fuels, and timber, as well as many semimanufactured goods such as cotton, which has been spun but not woven, wood pulp, or flour. Many developed countries have few natural resources and rely on imports for the majority of their primary products. The countries of Southeast Asia export hardwoods to the rest of the world, while many South American countries are heavily dependent on coffee exports.

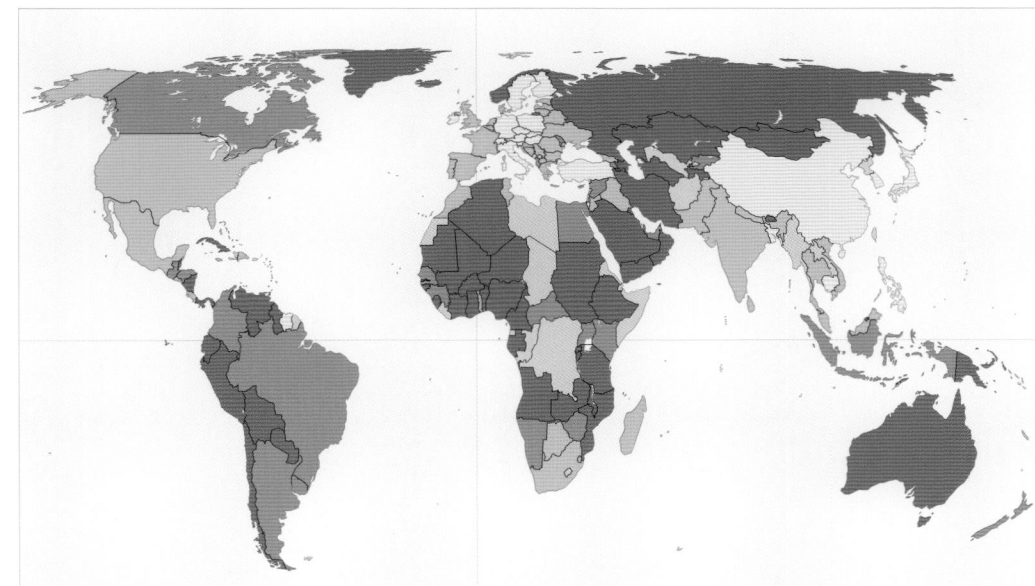

BALANCE OF TRADE

Value of exports in proportion to the value of imports (2011)

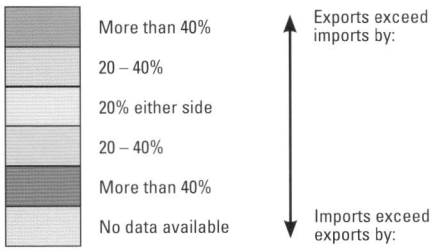

- More than 40% } Exports exceed imports by:
- 20 – 40%
- 20% either side
- 20 – 40%
- More than 40% } Imports exceed exports by:
- No data available

The total world trade balance should amount to zero, since exports must equal imports on a global scale. In practice, though, at least US $100 billion in exports go unrecorded, leaving the world with an apparent deficit and many countries in a better position than public accounting reveals. However, a favorable trade balance is not necessarily a sign of prosperity: many poorer countries must maintain a high surplus in order to service debts, and do so by restricting imports below the levels needed to sustain successful economies.

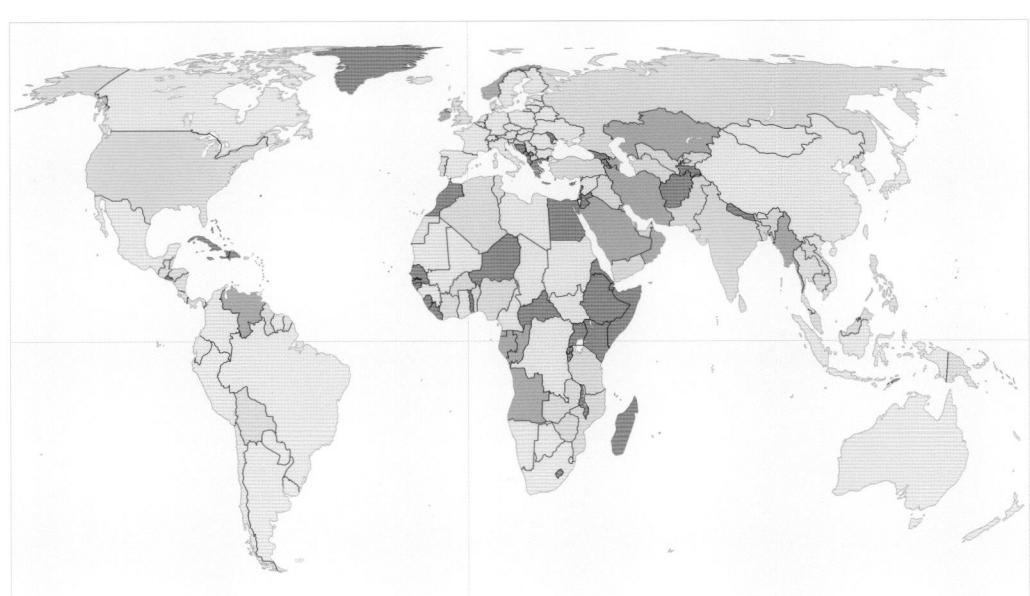

For more information:
84 Water distribution
91 Urban pollution
   Urban advantages
109 Distribution of
   spending

Until the late 1990s, when the full extent of the AIDS crisis emerged, average life expectancies at birth were rising almost everywhere. By 2010, they ranged from 80 years in high-income economies to 54 in sub-Saharan Africa. These figures represented an enormous advance on the situation in 1880, when citizens of Berlin had an estimated life expectancy of 30 years.

The ravages of AIDS have been greatest in southern Africa. One of the worst affected countries is Swaziland, where over 25% of the adult population were thought to be infected in 2009. Life expectancy has fallen from 61 years in 2000, to 32 years in 2009 and 7,000 people died from AIDS in 2009. However, in much of the world, average life expectancies are still increasing. The rises are attributed to improvements in agriculture and, hence, nutrition, as well as health education, improved sanitation and the quality of drinking water, together with advances in medicine.

Besides AIDS, the people of the developing world are subject to another affliction – malnutrition. The map below shows that in most of Africa, Asia, and Latin America, the average daily calorie supply per person is so low as to cause malnutrition. Malnutrition is a serious condition – among pregnant women it causes high rates of child mortality.

Deficiency diseases occur when people do not have a balanced diet. Protein deficiency causes stunting and kwashiorkor, which can be fatal, especially among young children, while vitamin deficiencies cause such illnesses as beri beri, pellagra, scurvy, and rickets. Iron deficiency causes anemia, while a lack of iodine causes mental retardation.

Infectious diseases, in association with deficient diets, continue to affect people in developing countries. Around the turn of the century, a WHO report stated that infectious diseases cause over 16 million deaths a year. Most of the victims are young and otherwise fit people in developing countries. The major killers are AIDS, cholera, dysentery, malaria, measles, pneumonia, respiratory infections, tuberculosis, and typhoid.

Infectious diseases are much less important as causes of death in developed countries, where cancer and circulatory diseases, such as atherosclerosis and hypertension, which cause strokes and heart attacks, are the most common causes of fatality. Because these diseases tend to kill older people, they are relatively less important in the developing countries where people have shorter lifespans.

Harmful habits are also generally practiced more by the rich than the poor. For example, smoking is an important cause of death in developed countries, while poor diet and high alcohol consumption can badly affect health.

▲ Almost 25% of the world's population does not have access to safe water (the diagram at the bottom left-hand corner of this page shows how this breaks down by region). This places a huge strain on the millions of mainly women and children who have to walk, collect, and carry drinkable water in order to survive. UNICEF is dedicated to help improve this situation and to react swiftly in the case of emergencies such as civil war, as with the case of this man in Liberia.

FOOD CONSUMPTION

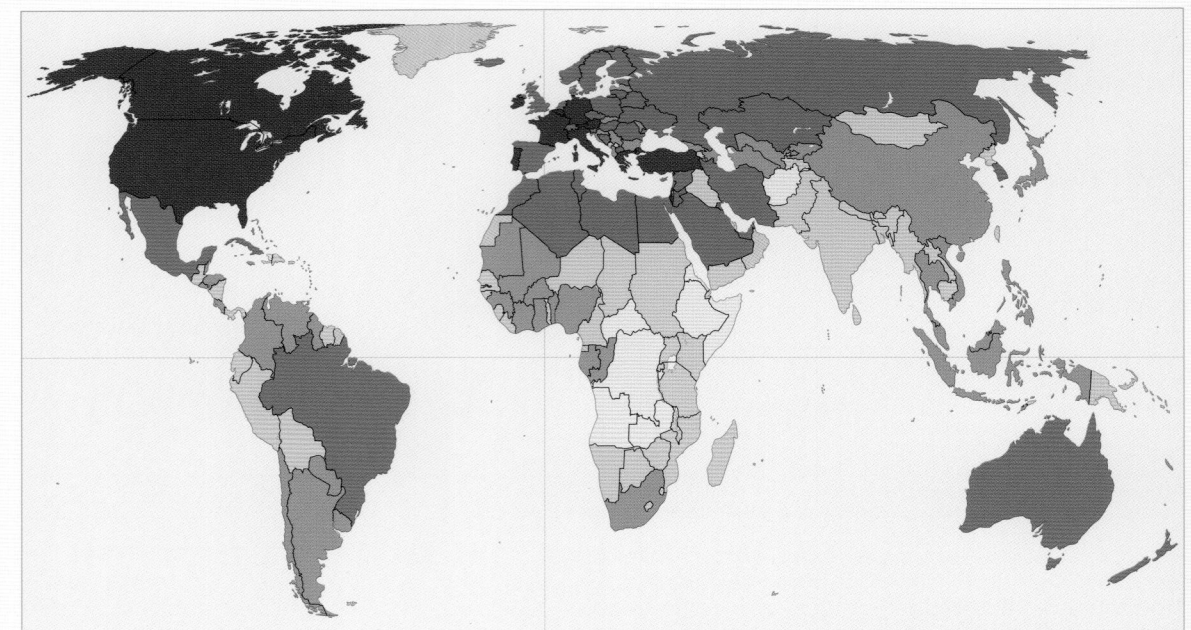

Average daily food intake in calories per person (2007)

- Over 3,500 calories
- 3,000 – 3,500 calories
- 2,500 – 3,000 calories
- 2,000 – 2,500 calories
- Under 2,000 calories
- No data available

The daily food intake rated adequate by the World Health Organization is between 2,300 and 2,500 calories per day. Approximately 6 million children under the age of 5 years die of starvation each year, the vast majority in Africa. In 2010, the FAO estimated that 925 million people were undernourished, contrasting sharply with the overconsumption of food in some Western cultures.

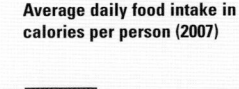

ACCESS TO SAFE WATER
Proportion of urban and rural population with access to safe water, by region (2008)

- Urban (World 95.7%)
- Rural (World 77.8%)

Regions: North America; Latin America & Caribbean; Middle East & North Africa; Sub-Saharan Africa; Europe & Central Asia; East Asia & Pacific; South Asia

TOBACCO

Up to 1.3 billion people smoke worldwide (1 billion men and 0.3 billion women). According to the World Health Organization, tobacco claims 4.9 million lives each year. At the end of 2009, 90 countries had introduced smoking bans in public places.

Percentage of population who smoke (2009)

	Men	Women
Africa	19%	3%
North and South America	25%	12%
Eastern Mediterranean	34%	5%
Europe	40%	21%
Southeast Asia	41%	8%
Western Pacific	43%	14%

Countries with the highest annual consumption of cigarettes per person (2009)

1. Greece	3,017	5. Czech Republic	2,368
2. Slovenia	2,537	6. Macedonia	2,336
3. Ukraine	2,526	7. Russia	2,319
4. Bulgaria	2,437	8. Moldova	2,239

ALCOHOL

The average Western European and North American drinks over a third more alcohol than the average person living in any other region. Globally, alcohol consumption has increased in recent decades, with all of that increase being found in developing countries. Alcohol consumption has health and social consequences, and is responsible for 1.8 millions deaths per year.

Liters of alcohol consumed per person per year

	1980	1990	2000	2009
Developed countries	11.1	9.5	8.9	8.8
Developing countries	2.0	2.4	2.9	3.0

Countries with the highest annual consumption of alcohol per person in liters (2009)

1. Moldova	12.8	6. Denmark	10.9
2. Czech Republic	12.1	7. UK	10.2
3. Luxembourg	11.8	8. Croatia	10.1
4. Hungary	11.8	9. Spain	10.0
5. Ireland	11.3	10. Germany	9.9

INFANT MORTALITY

Number of babies who died under the age of one, per 1,000 live births (2011)

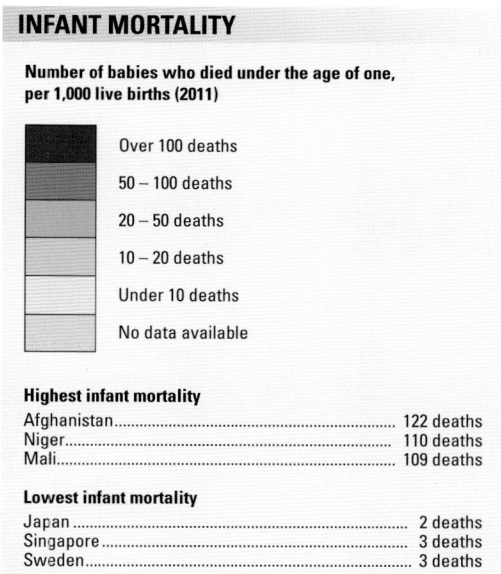

	Over 100 deaths
	50 – 100 deaths
	20 – 50 deaths
	10 – 20 deaths
	Under 10 deaths
	No data available

Highest infant mortality

Afghanistan	122 deaths
Niger	110 deaths
Mali	109 deaths

Lowest infant mortality

Japan	2 deaths
Singapore	3 deaths
Sweden	3 deaths

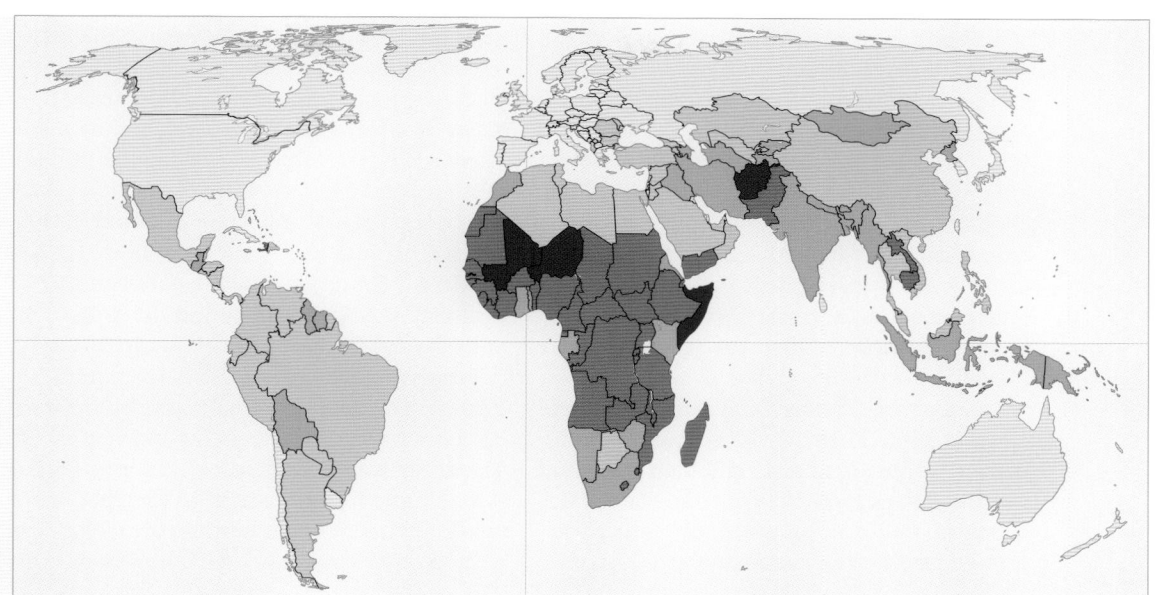

THE AIDS CRISIS

Number of children orphaned due to AIDS (2009)

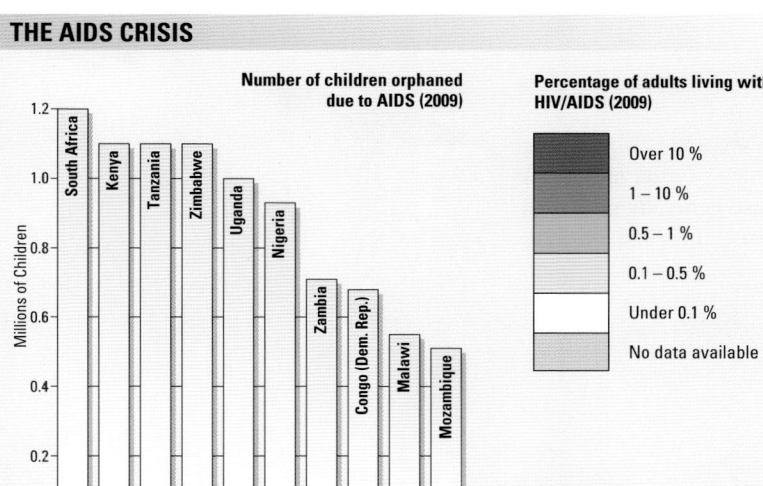

Millions of Children

South Africa, Kenya, Tanzania, Zimbabwe, Uganda, Nigeria, Zambia, Congo (Dem. Rep.), Malawi, Mozambique

Percentage of adults living with HIV/AIDS (2009)

	Over 10 %
	1 – 10 %
	0.5 – 1 %
	0.1 – 0.5 %
	Under 0.1 %
	No data available

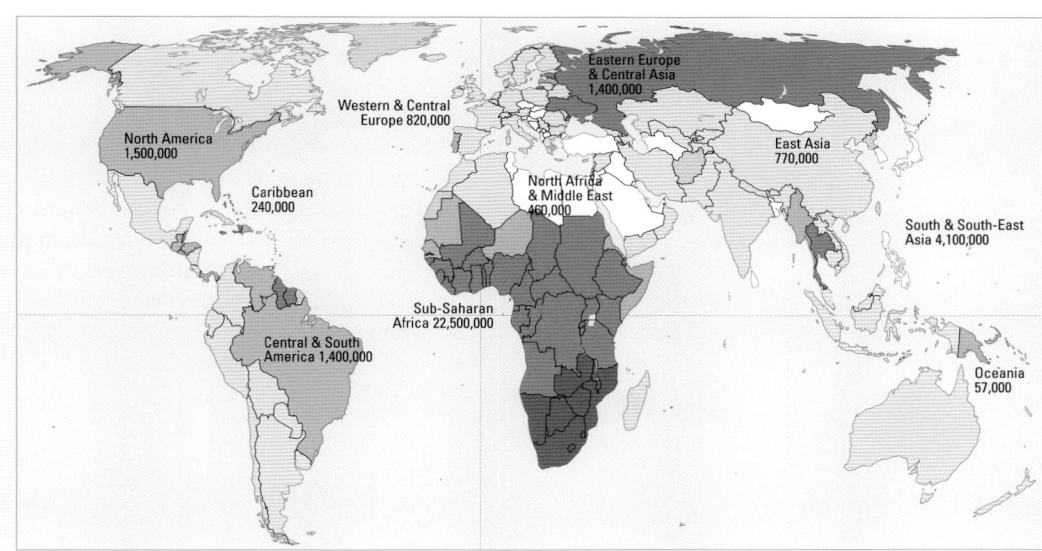

North America 1,500,000
Caribbean 240,000
Central & South America 1,400,000
Western & Central Europe 820,000
Eastern Europe & Central Asia 1,400,000
North Africa & Middle East 460,000
Sub-Saharan Africa 22,500,000
East Asia 770,000
South & South-East Asia 4,100,000
Oceania 57,000

EXPENDITURE ON HEALTH

Public health expenditure per capita, in US $ (2009)

Countries with the highest spending		Countries with the lowest spending	
Luxembourg	$8,183	Eritrea	$10
Norway	$7,662	Burma (Myanmar)	$12
USA	$7,410	Ethiopia	$15
Switzerland	$7,141	Congo (Democratic Republic)	$16
Monaco	$7,137	Madagascar	$18
Denmark	$6,273	Guinea-Bissau	$18
Netherlands	$5,164	Bangladesh	$18
Belgium	$5,104	Guinea	$19
Austria	$5,037	Malawi	$19
Ireland	$4,952	Central African Republic	$19

The allocation of limited funds for health care in developing countries is rarely evenly spread – for example, the quality of treatment can vary enormously from place to place within the same country. Urban dwellers tend to have much better access to health provisions than those living in rural areas.

CAUSES OF DEATH

Accidents, poisoning, and violence	Metabolic disorders
Respiratory and digestive diseases	Cancers
Nervous and circulatory diseases	Infectious and parasitic diseases

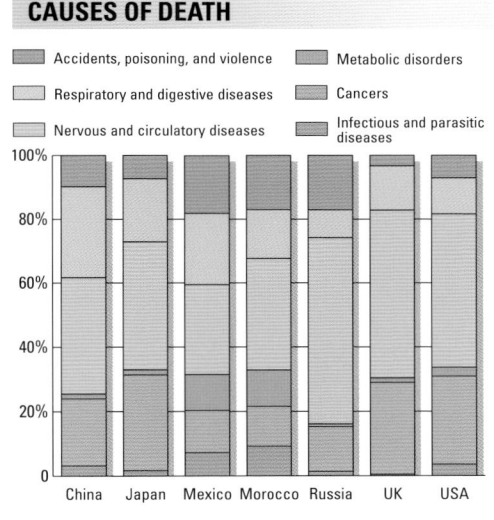

China, Japan, Mexico, Morocco, Russia, UK, USA

MEDICAL PROVISION

Doctors per 100,000 population, selected countries (2009)

Although the ratio of people to doctors gives a good approximation of a country's health provision, it is not an absolute indicator. Raw numbers may mask inefficiency and other weaknesses. The definition of a doctor also varies from nation to nation.

Eritrea	5
Kenya	14
India	60
Turkey	145
USA	267
United Kingdom	274
France	274
Egypt	283
Australia	299
Hungary	310
Armenia	370
Italy	424

OBESITY IN EUROPE

The percentage of adults who are obese (2008)

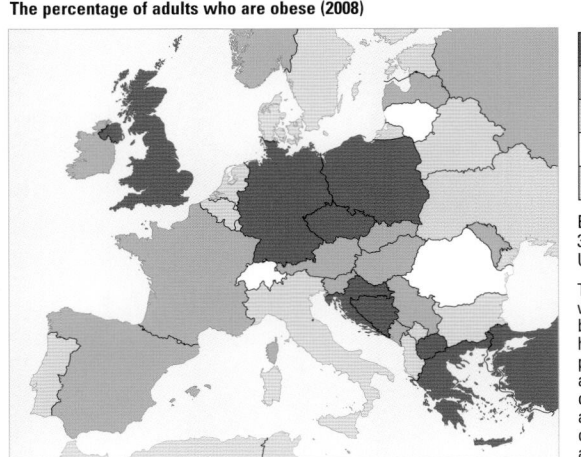

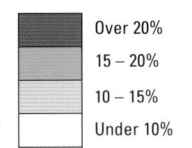

	Over 20%
	15 – 20%
	10 – 15%
	Under 10%
	No data available

By comparison, over 35% of people in the USA are obese.

The global epidemic of overweight and obesity is rapidly becoming a major public health problem in many parts of the world. It is associated with diet-related chronic diseases such as diabetes, strokes, cardiovascular disease, and certain cancers.

SANITATION

Percentage of population with access to sanitation services, selected countries (2008)

	Urban
	Rural

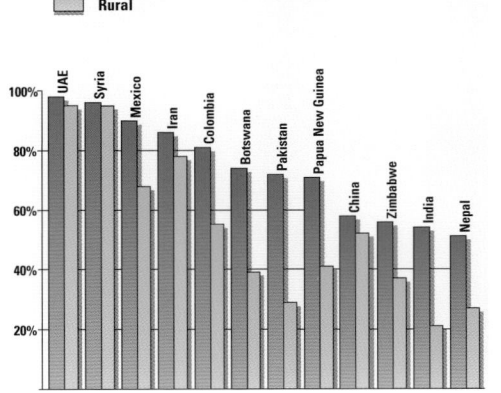

UAE, Syria, Mexico, Iran, Colombia, Botswana, Pakistan, Papua New Guinea, China, Zimbabwe, India, Nepal

MALARIA

Cases of malaria per 100,000 people exposed to malaria-infected environments (2009)

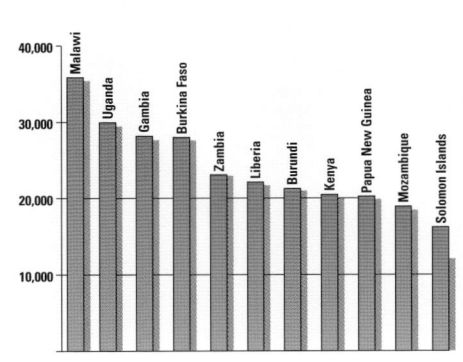

Malawi, Uganda, Gambia, Burkina Faso, Zambia, Liberia, Burundi, Kenya, Papua New Guinea, Mozambique, Solomon Islands

For more information:

100 Wealth creation
101 Industrial output
102 World trade
    Major exports
103 Balance of trade
109 Distribution of
    spending

Perhaps the most glaring differences in the world today are those between the rich and the poor. The World Bank divides countries into three main groups based on average economic production expressed in terms of per capita GNI (Gross National Income). They are the low-income economies (most African countries and much of Asia), the middle-income economies (most of Latin America and most of the former USSR), and the high-income economies of Canada, the United States, Western Europe, Japan, and Australia.

Per capita GNIs are a measure of the total goods and services produced by a country divided by the population, and then converted into US dollars at official exchange rates. They are useful indicators of a country's prosperity, though, like all statistics, they must be treated with care. For example, the prices for goods and services in China are far cheaper than they are in the United States. China's per capita GNI in 2010 was $4,270 (as compared with $47,390 in the US), but the PPP (Purchasing Power Parity, which adjusts the figure for cost-of-living differences) estimate of China's per capita GNI was considerably higher at $7,640. Another problem with per capita GNIs is that they are averages, which often conceal wide internal variations.

The pattern of poverty varies from region to region. In Latin America, much progress

has been made through industrialization, though startling inequalities still exist between rich and poor. China and other countries in eastern Asia, including South Korea and Taiwan, have followed Japan's example in pursuing export-led industrial policies. The success of China's Special Economic Zones, where foreign investment is encouraged, has led to a huge rise in China's per capita GNI.

In contrast to the dynamism of Asia, Africa lags behind as an impoverished continent. Corrupt governments, wasteful expenditures, civil wars, natural disasters, faulty national and international policy environments, high population growth, and the failure to break away from the neo-colonial trading patterns – all these contribute to keeping the majority of Africans impoverished. An initiative in some African countries has been to improve the infrastructure and develop tourism, creating employment and providing much-needed foreign currency. But the social and environmental cost of mass tourism needs to be taken seriously too.

The International Monetary Fund and the World Bank argue that real economic progress in Africa will be achieved only when African countries create market-friendly economies that encourage trade through export-led manufacturing, while at the same time strictly controlling public spending.

CONTINENTAL SHARES

Shares of population and of wealth (GNI) by continent

These generalized continental figures show the startling difference between rich and poor, but mask the successes or failures of individual countries. (Japan, for example, with less than 4% of Asia's population, produces almost 13% of the continent's output.) Within countries, the difference between rich and poor can also be startling. In Brazil, for example, the richest 20% of the population own 60% of the wealth.

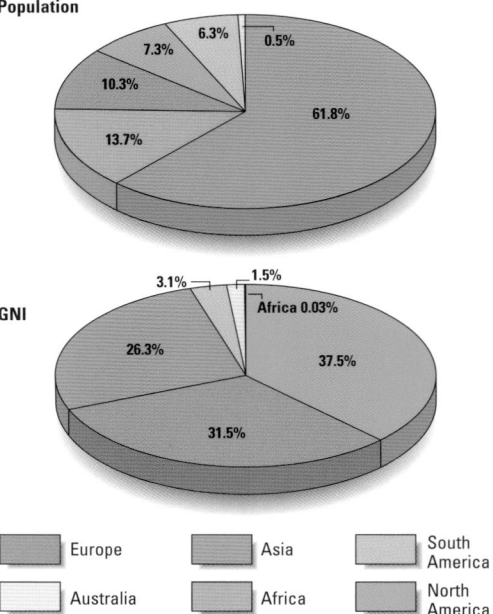

Population

GNI

Europe | Asia | South America
Australia | Africa | North America

LEVELS OF INCOME

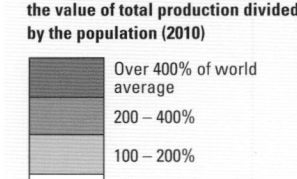

Gross National Income per capita: the value of total production divided by the population (2010)

Over 400% of world average
200 – 400%
100 – 200%
50 – 100%
25 – 50%
10 – 25%
Under 10%
No data available

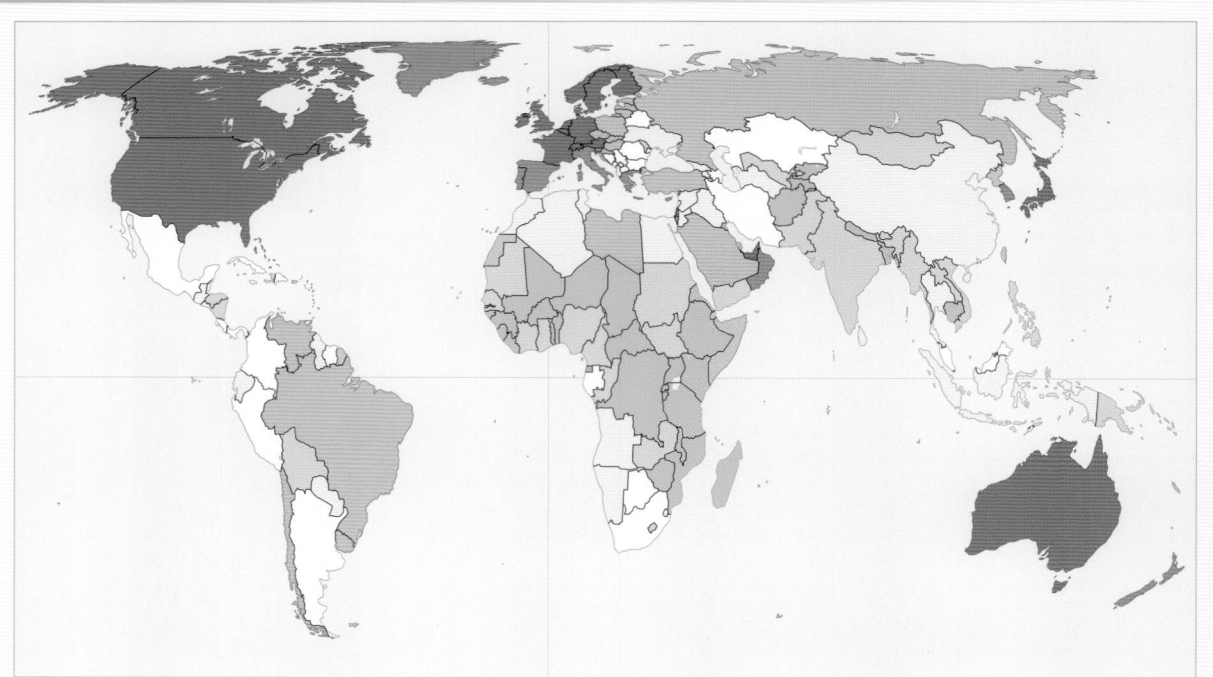

Richest countries (GNI per capita)
Monaco .... US $183,150
Leichtenstein .... US $137,070
Norway .... US $87,350
Luxembourg .... US $76,980
Switzerland .... US $71,520

Poorest countries (GNI per capita)
Burundi .... US $170
Congo (Dem. Rep.) .... US $180
Liberia .... US $200
Malawi .... US $330
Sierra Leone .... US $340

INDICATORS

The gap between the world's rich and poor is now so great that it is difficult to illustrate on a single graph. Within each income group (as defined by the World Bank), however, comparisons have some meaning. The wealth gap in many developing countries, though, is wide, with a small, rich class and a large, impoverished majority, while many high-income countries contain an underclass of unemployed and homeless people.

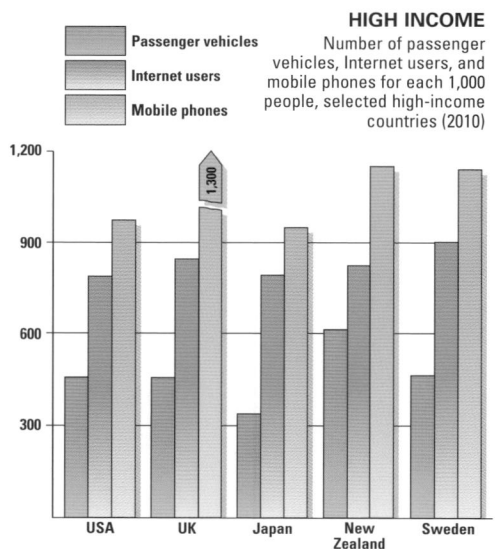

HIGH INCOME

Passenger vehicles
Internet users
Mobile phones

Number of passenger vehicles, Internet users, and mobile phones for each 1,000 people, selected high-income countries (2010)

USA | UK | Japan | New Zealand | Sweden

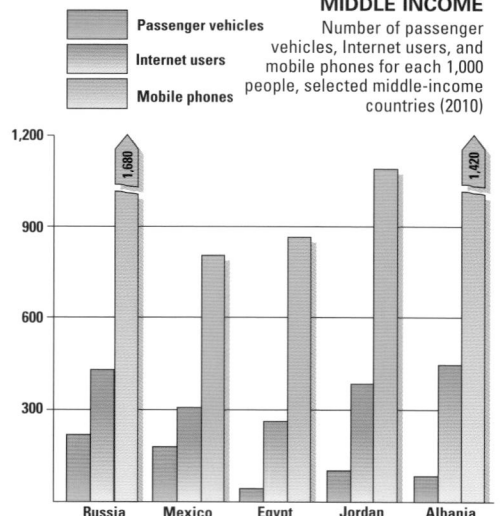

MIDDLE INCOME

Passenger vehicles
Internet users
Mobile phones

Number of passenger vehicles, Internet users, and mobile phones for each 1,000 people, selected middle-income countries (2010)

Russia | Mexico | Egypt | Jordan | Albania

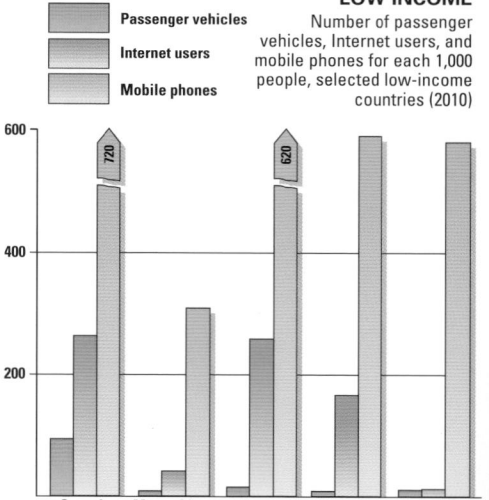

LOW INCOME

Passenger vehicles
Internet users
Mobile phones

Number of passenger vehicles, Internet users, and mobile phones for each 1,000 people, selected low-income countries (2010)

Georgia | Mozambique | Kenya | Pakistan | Cambodia

STATE FINANCE

Inflation rates (*shown on the map, right*) are an indication of a country's financial stability and, usually, of its prosperity. Annual inflation rates above 20% are usually marked by slow or even negative growth of the GNI. Above 50%, it becomes hyperinflation and an economy is left reeling.

In the late 1980s and early 1990s, many high-income countries had to contend with annual inflation rates of 10% or more, while Japan, the growth leader, had an average inflation rate of just 1.3% between 1985 and 1994.

Market-friendly policies, including low taxes and state spending, liberal trade policies, and a warm welcome for foreign investors, are major factors in countries that have enjoyed rapid economic growth in the decades since 1980. For example, the setting-up of Special Economic Zones in eastern China has led to a spectacular rise in that country's per capita GNI. However, an effective state remains a crucial factor in economic growth in most countries.

Other successful countries include South Korea and Singapore, although an Asian market crash in 1997 temporarily halted the dramatic economic expansion of these countries.

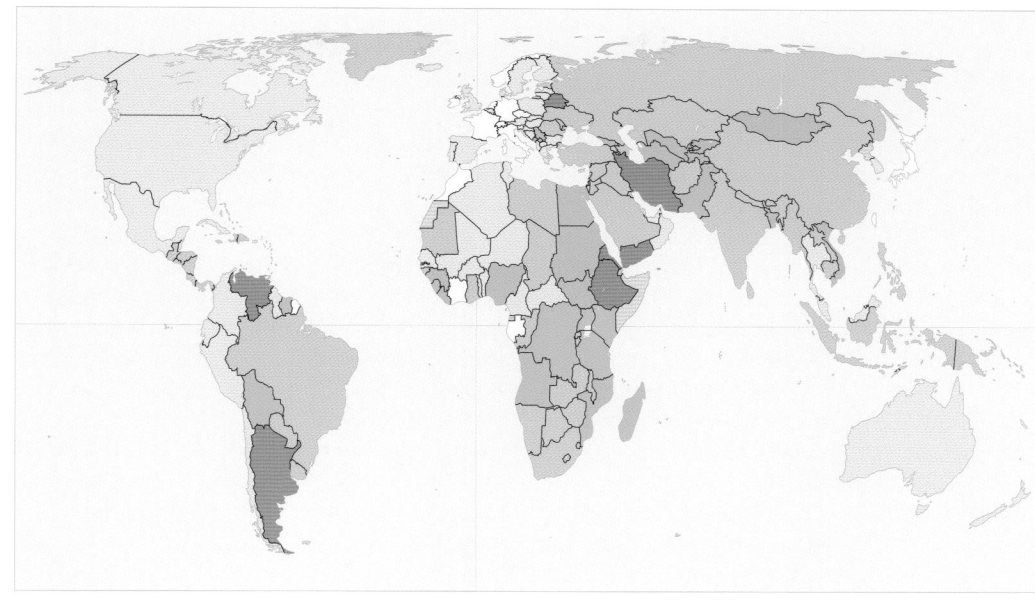

INFLATION

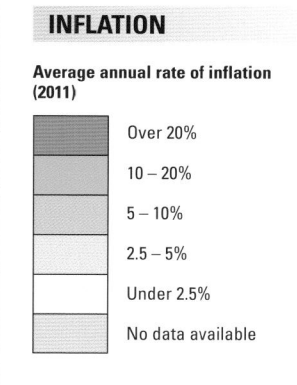

Average annual rate of inflation (2011)

	Over 20%
	10 – 20%
	5 – 10%
	2.5 – 5%
	Under 2.5%
	No data available

Highest average inflation

Belarus	41%
Venezuela	29%
Ethiopia	29%

Lowest average inflation

Bahrain	0.3%
Switzerland	0.4%
Japan	0.4%

GROWTH IN GNI

GNI average annual change (1999–2010)

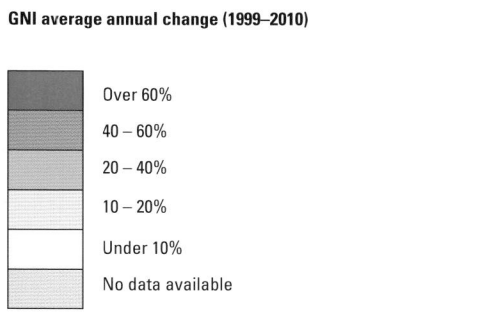

	Over 60%
	40 – 60%
	20 – 40%
	10 – 20%
	Under 10%
	No data available

Countries with the highest rate of change

Equatorial Guinea	167%
Azerbaijan	84%
Angola	82%
Turkmenistan	52%
Kazakhstan	49%

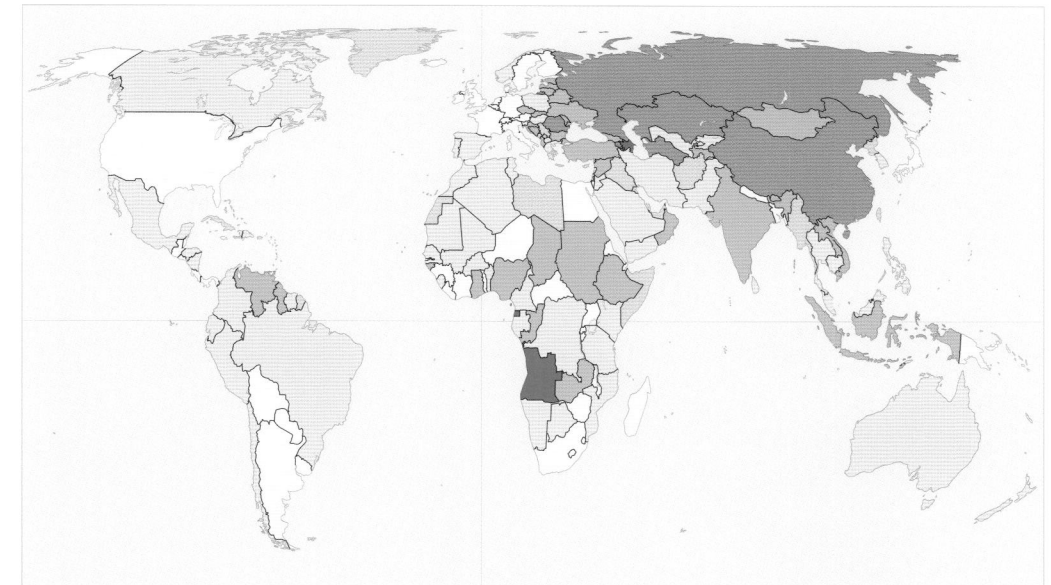

WORLD AIR TRAVEL

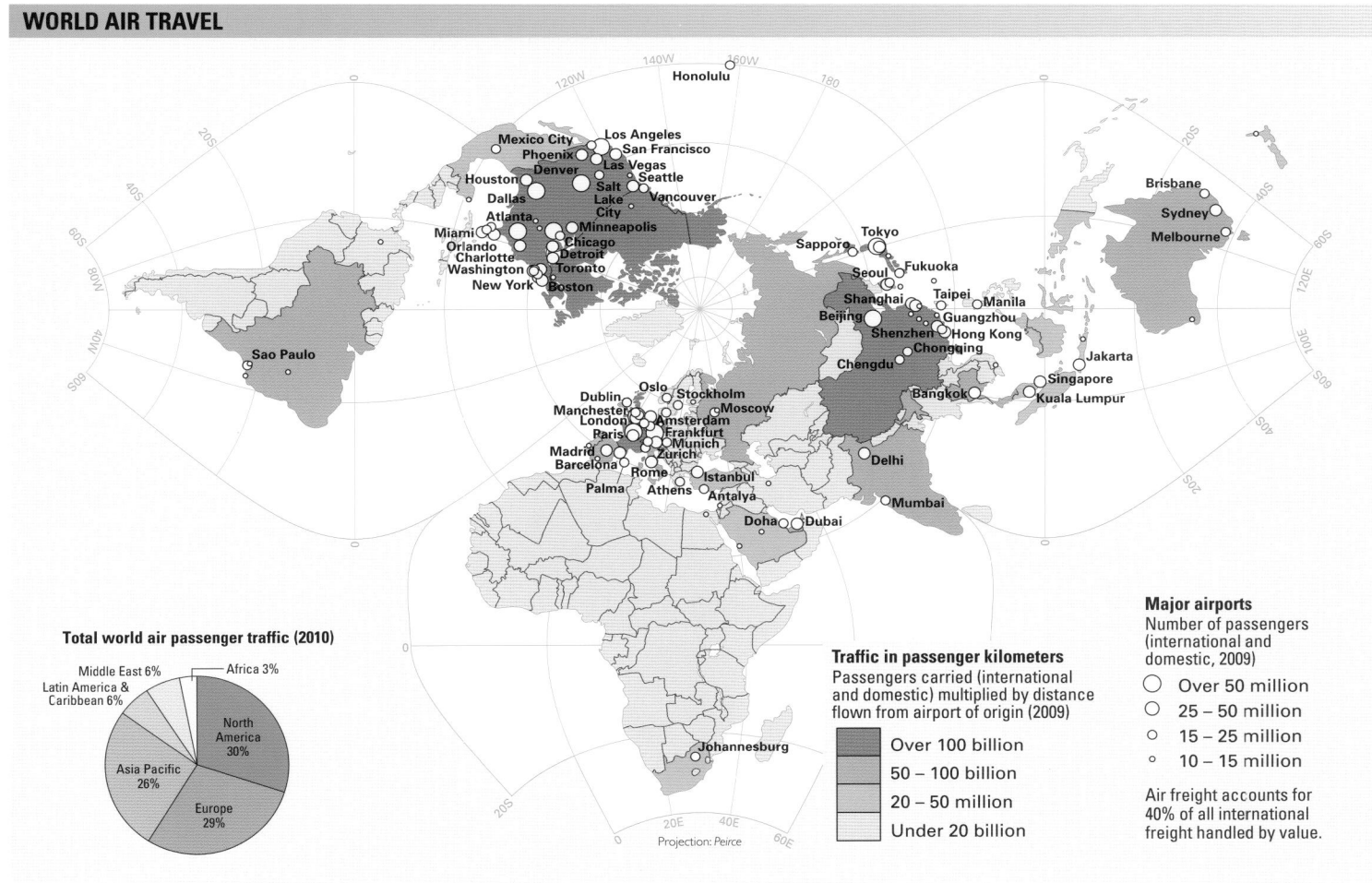

Leisure and tourism is the world's second largest industry in terms of revenue generated. Small economies in attractive areas are often completely dominated by tourism: in some Caribbean islands, for example, tourist spending provides over 90% of the total income and is the biggest foreign-exchange earner.

In cash terms, the United States is the world leader: its 2009 earnings exceeded US $94 billion, although that sum amounted to approximately 0.6% of its total GNI. Of the 56 million visitors to the US, 29% came from Canada and 20% came from Mexico. Germany spends the most on overseas tourism; this amounts to nearly US $81 billion. The next biggest spenders are the US, the UK, and China.

The world's travel and tourist industry was predicted to generate 100 million jobs by the end of 2012. If the broader travel and tourist economy is considered, this total would increase to 260 million.

Total world air passenger traffic (2010)

Middle East 6%
Africa 3%
Latin America & Caribbean 6%
North America 30%
Asia Pacific 26%
Europe 29%

Traffic in passenger kilometers
Passengers carried (international and domestic) multiplied by distance flown from airport of origin (2009)

	Over 100 billion
	50 – 100 million
	20 – 50 million
	Under 20 billion

Major airports
Number of passengers (international and domestic, 2009)

	Over 50 million
	25 – 50 million
	15 – 25 million
	10 – 15 million

Air freight accounts for 40% of all international freight handled by value.

Projection: Peirce

WORLD'S BUSIEST AIRPORTS
Total passengers in millions (2011)

1.	Atlanta Hartsfield Intl. (ATL)	92.4
2.	Beijing Capital Intl. (PEK)	77.4
3.	London Heathrow (LHR)	69.4
4.	Chicago O'Hare Intl. (ORD)	66.5
5.	Tokyo Haneda (HND)	62.2
6.	Los Angeles Intl. (LAX)	61.8
7.	Paris Charles de Gaulle (CDG)	60.9
8.	Dallas Fort Worth Intl. (DFW)	57.8
9.	Frankfurt Intl. (FRA)	56.4
10.	Hong Kong Intl. (HKG)	53.3

For more information:

84   Water supply
88   Population density
90   Urban population
91   Urban advantages
94   World's refugees
     War since 1945
100 Employment
     The work force
105 Infant mortality
106 Wealth

Wealth is a basic factor in determining standards of living. Everywhere, the rich have more of everything, including higher average life expectancies, while the poor have to spend most of their income on basic human needs, such as food and clothing. Yet poverty and wealth are relative terms: slum dwellers living on social security in an industrial society feel their poverty acutely, but have far more resources than an average African living in a rural area.

In 1990 the United Nations Development Program published its first Human Development Index (HDI), an attempt to construct a comparative scale by which a simplified form of well-being might be measured. The HDI, expressed as a value between 0 and 0.999, combines figures for life expectancy and literacy with a wealth scale, based on Purchasing Power Parity.

The world's countries are divided into three groups: those with a high HDI (0.8 and above); those with a medium HDI (0.5 to 0.799); and those with a low HDI (below 0.5). In 2011, Norway and Australia were top in the world rankings and Congo DR was bottom. In fact, 29 of the 32 countries with a low HDI were from Africa. Besides having low per capita GNIs, the average life expectancy in these

countries was 58 years, while the adult literacy rate was 36%. By comparison, the average life expectancy at birth in countries in the high HDI group was 72 years, while the literacy rate was 94%.

Comparisons between countries with similar per capita GNIs reveal the effects of government actions. For example, the World Bank classifies both India and China as low-income economies, but India's HDI at 0.547 is much lower than that of China, at 0.687. This reflects not only China's economic progress in the 1980s and 1990s, but also differences in average life expectancies (67 years in India and 75 years in China), and adult literacy rates (66% in India and 93% in China).

Disparities in standards of living exist not only between countries but also between individuals, groups, and regions within countries. For example, income distribution figures show that, in the United States, the poorest 10% of households received less than 2% of the income.

Other contrasts exist in developing countries between rural communities, where incomes are low and basic services are often in short supply, and urban areas, where even those living in slums are

generally better off than their rural neighbors. Other striking differences exist between men and women. For example, while adult literacy rates for men and women living in developed countries are more or less the same, large differences exist in many developing countries. In countries in the lowest HDI category, only 36% of women were literate, as compared with 58% of men.

Female education is a factor in population control, especially as women's fertility rates appear to fall in direct proportion to the amount of secondary education they receive. This point was acknowledged in 2004 by the UN Population Fund, which defined four main objectives relating to women and population control: the reduction of maternal, infant, and child mortality; better education, especially for girls; universal access to reproductive health services; and gender equality.

Statistical analysis presents many problems of interpretation, especially when trying to define such intangible factors as a sense of well-being. For example, education helps create wealth; but are rich countries wealthy because their people are well educated, or are they well educated because they are rich?

HUMAN DEVELOPMENT INDEX

The Human Development Index (HDI), calculated by the UN Development Program (UNDP), gives a value to countries using indicators of life expectancy, education, and standards of living (2011). Higher values show more developed countries.

■	Over 0.9
■	0.8 – 0.9
■	0.7 – 0.8
■	0.6 – 0.7
■	0.5 – 0.6
□	Under 0.5
■	No data available

Highest values
Norway 0.943
Australia 0.929
Netherlands 0.910
USA 0.910
Canada 0.908

Lowest values
Congo (Dem. Rep) 0.286
Niger 0.295
Burundi 0.316
Mozambique 0.322
Chad 0.328

EDUCATION

The developing countries made great efforts in the 1970s and 1980s to bring at least a basic education to their people. In all but the poorest nations, primary school enrolments rose above 60%. However, figures often include teenagers or young adults, and there are still 300 million children worldwide who receive no schooling at all. A lack of resources has restricted the development of secondary and higher education. Most primary school education is free in the poorer countries, but fees are often paid for secondary and higher education, thus heightening the differences between rich and poor.

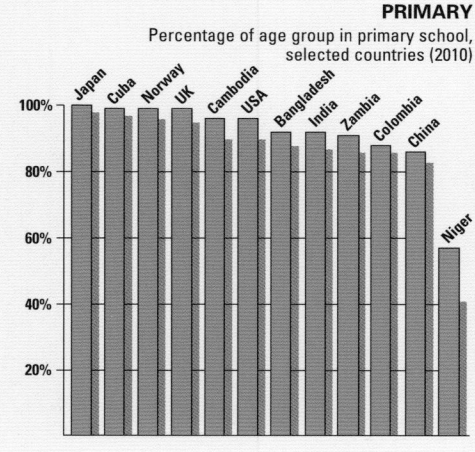

PRIMARY
Percentage of age group in primary school, selected countries (2010)

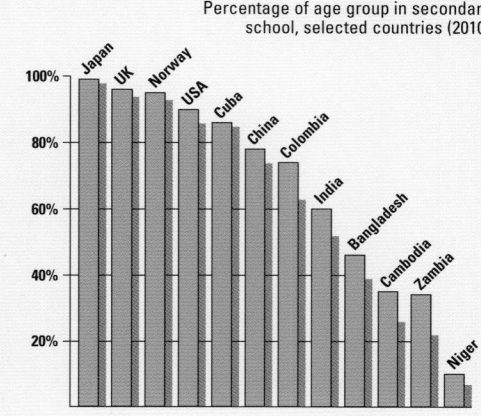

SECONDARY
Percentage of age group in secondary school, selected countries (2010)

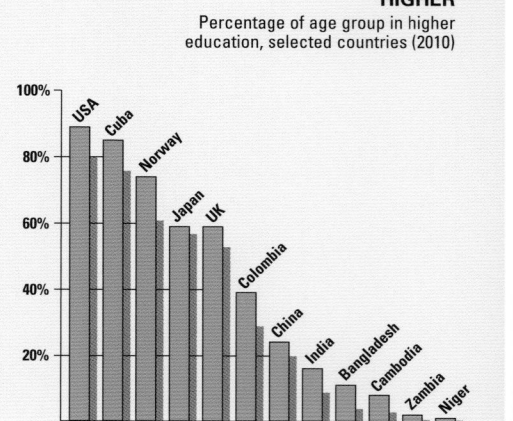

HIGHER
Percentage of age group in higher education, selected countries (2010)

DISTRIBUTION OF SPENDING

Percentage share of household spending

A high proportion of the average income of households in developing nations is spent on basic needs such as food and clothing. In most Western countries food and clothing account for less than 25% of expenditure.

Legend:
- Food
- Clothing
- Energy & Housing
- Medicine & Education
- Transport
- Other

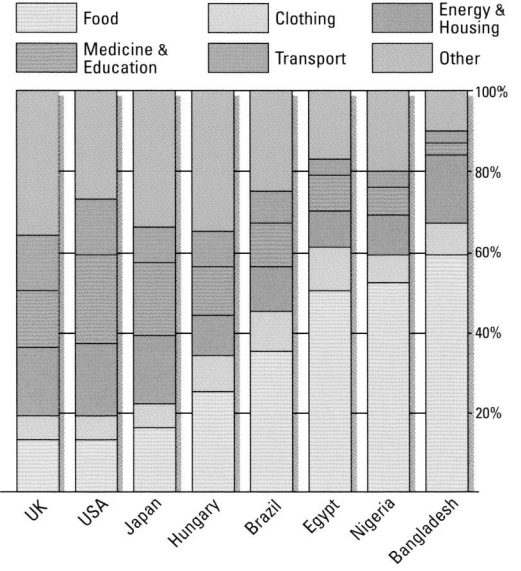

STANDARDS OF LIVING IN THE USA BY RACE, AGE AND REGION

A comparison of measures of income and education, by selected characteristics (2009)

Median income per household (US $), by age and region

15–24 years	26,365
25–44 years	56,832
45–64 years	63,121
65 years and over	32,753
Northeast	57,208
Midwest	49,932
South	47,024
West	56,171

Per capita income (US $), by race and Hispanic origin of householder (2009)

ALL RACES	27,041
White	29,818
Black	17,887
Asian and Pacific Is.	29,679
Hispanic (any race)	15,505

The poorest 20% of households received just 2.4% of the income, whereas the richest 20% received 55.4%.

Percentage of persons aged 25 and over who have completed High School, by race or origin

ALL RACES	1975	62.5
	2008	84.5
White	1975	64.5
	2008	86.9
Black	1975	42.5
	2008	80.0
Hispanic	1975	37.9
	2008	60.5

FERTILITY AND EDUCATION

Fertility rates compared with female education, selected countries (2009)

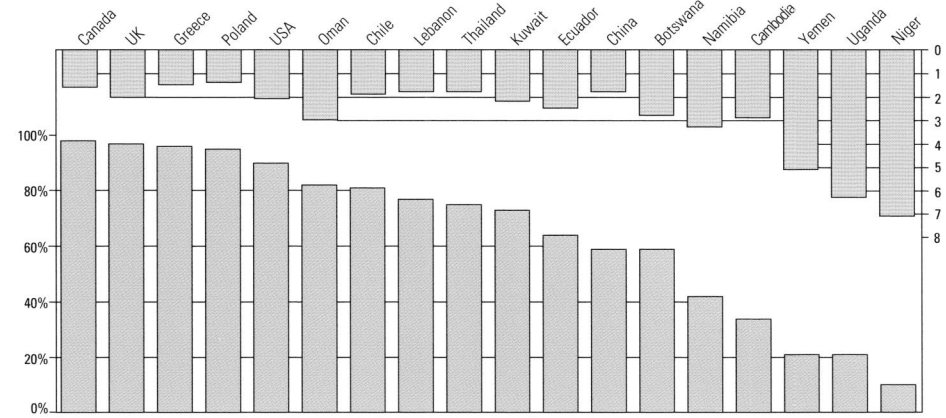
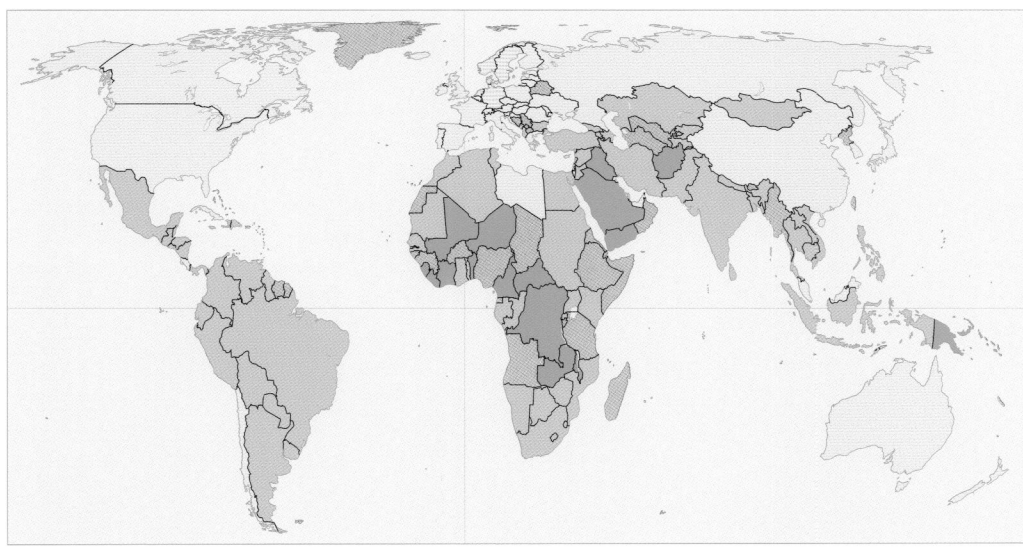
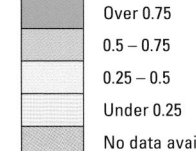

There seems to be a strong link between access to secondary education and the fertility rate. In developed countries, young girls have a high access to education and a low fertility rate. In contrast, in many developing countries women have a high fertility rate but lack access to education. This can be for a complex mix of social, economic, and cultural reasons. Despite a few high-profile examples of female politicians in different parts of the world, all evidence points to the continuing marginalization of women from the political and economic processes of decision-making. Female wages are, on average, only two-thirds of those of men.

- Fertility rate: average number of children borne per woman
- Percentage of females aged 12–17 in secondary education

GENDER INEQUALITY INDEX

The Gender Inequality Index is a composite measure reflecting inequality in achievements between women and men in three categories: reproductive health, empowerment, and the labor market. It varies between 0, when women and men fare equally, and 1, when women or men fare poorly compared to the other in all categories (2009)

- Over 0.75
- 0.5 – 0.75
- 0.25 – 0.5
- Under 0.25
- No data available

Most equal

Netherlands	0.174
Denmark	0.209
Sweden	0.212

Least equal

Yemen	0.853
Congo (Dem. Rep.)	0.814
Niger	0.807

REGIONAL INEQUALITY IN ITALY

The southern part of Italy, known as the *Mezzogiorno*, has been described as one of the poorest parts of the European Union. It is identifiable on the map (*right*) as all the regions with a GDP per capita of less than US $30,000 (including the two islands of Sicily and Sardinia).

The *Mezzogiorno* region suffers from a lack of energy resources, minerals, industry, commerce, services, and skilled labor. As a result, standards of living in the region are well below the rest of Italy. Employment is predominantly agricultural and small-scale.

The north of Italy accounts for 60% of the population but 80% of the GDP, whereas the *Mezzogiorno* accounts for 40% of the population and only 20% of the GDP. Manpower surpluses in the south led to emigration to other parts of Europe and the Americas.

It has also led, especially in the last 50 years, to inter-regional migration from the islands and the southern mainland to the north. The main regions attracting migrants are the northwest (the prosperous Liguria–Piedmont–Lombardy triangle, with its great industrial cities of Genoa, Milan and Turin) and the Venetia region in the northeast.

As a result, the north has experienced much higher population growth rates than the rest of Italy.

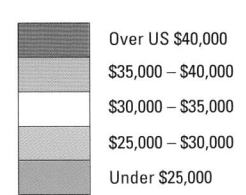

Gross Domestic Product (GDP) per capita in Italy, by region (2010)

- Over US $40,000
- $35,000 – $40,000
- $30,000 – $35,000
- $25,000 – $30,000
- Under $25,000

The average GDP per capita for Italy is US $30,100. By comparison, the GDP for the UK is $35,900; for the USA $48,100; and for the EU $33,500.

The number of inhabitants per doctor, another social indicator, varies from less than 600 in the northwest of Italy to nearly 800 in the far south (the *Mezzogiorno*), with a national average of 628.

◄ These two images illustrate the reality of suburban life for people at either end of the economic scale. On the far left is part of a huge area of "tract housing" in California, where large houses of a similar design are laid out by a developer, complete with gardens, drives, and swimming pools. On the right is a much more haphazard arrangement of home-built, rudimentary shelters, many without sanitation and most with no electricity, in Crossroads Township, outside Cape Town in South Africa.

WORLD CITIES

This image covers one of the most
dynamic areas in the world, Hong Kong,
with Shenzhen to its north. Hong Kong
became a major port and international
financial center during the period of
British rule up to 1997, when sovereignty
was handed back to China. Despite this,
Hong Kong retains a special status as
a Special Administrative Region (SAR)
and has a high degree of economic
autonomy, including the retention of the
Hong Kong dollar. To its north Shenzhen,
on the east side of the Pearl River delta,
was established by China as a Special
Economic Zone (SEZ) in 1979, to attract
foreign industry and investment.
This has proved very successful and
communications between the two have
also improved, as can be seen by the
sinuous Shenzhen Bay Bridge in
the middle of the left-hand page.

[Map page 122] © *RapidEye AG/Fugro NPA*

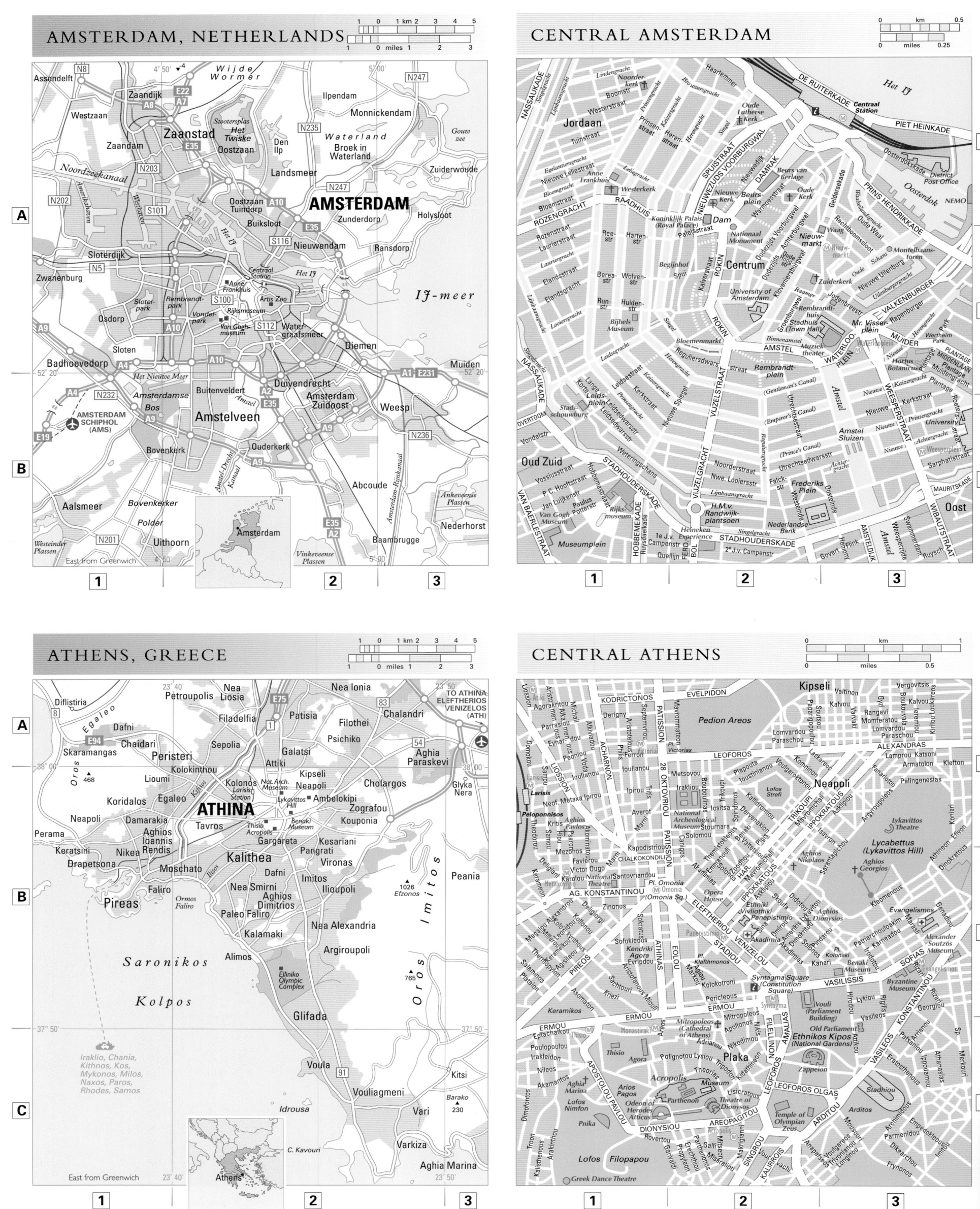

ATLANTA, GEORGIA

Interstate route numbers   U.S. route numbers   State route numbers

BAGHDAD, IRAQ

International Zone (Green Zone)

BANGKOK, THAILAND

CENTRAL BANGKOK

Skytrain   Shrine   Temple

COPYRIGHT PHILIP'S

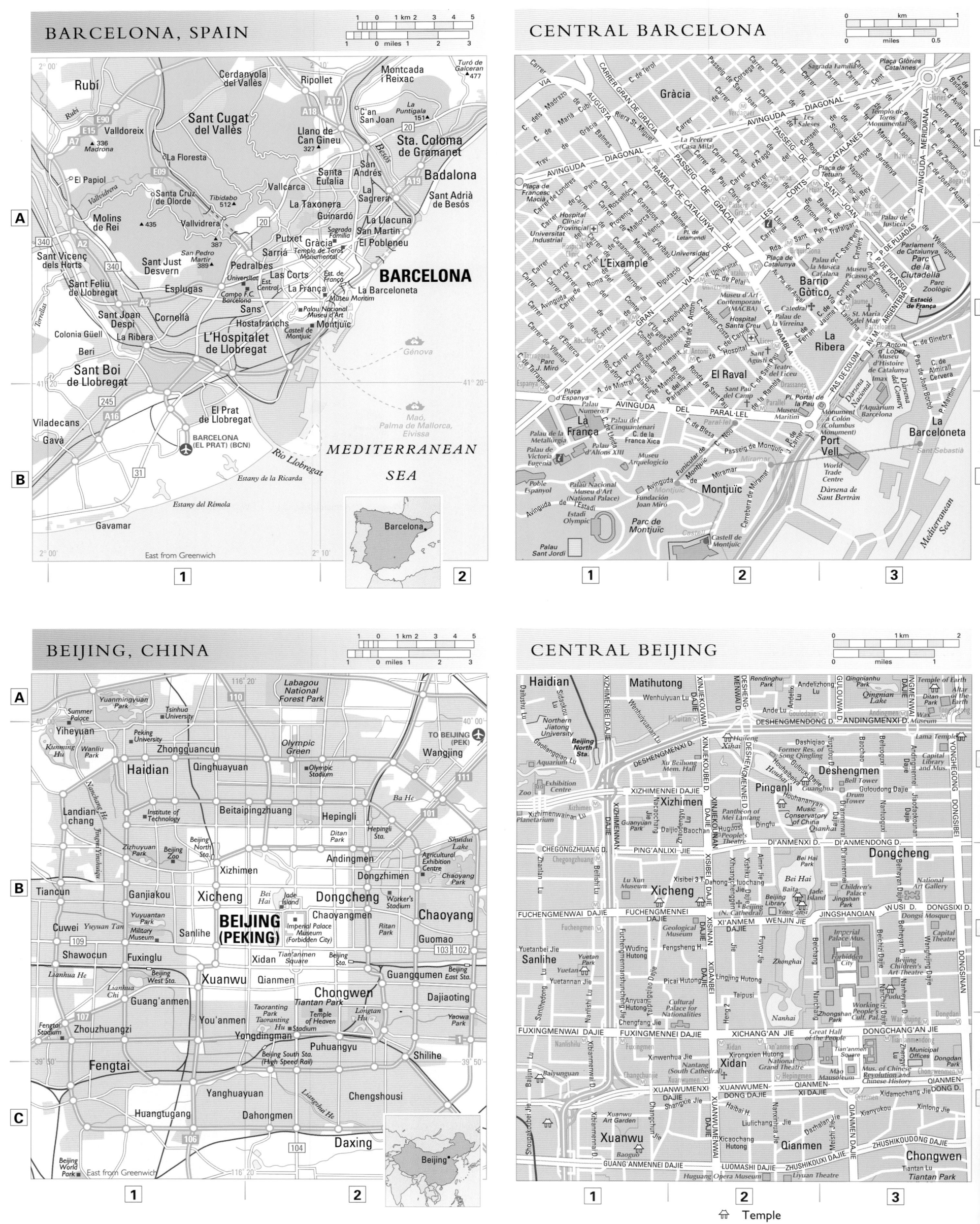

BARCELONA, SPAIN

Rubí
Cerdanyola del Vallès
Ripollet
Montcada i Reixac
Turó de Galceran ▲477

Valldoreix
E90
E15
A7
▲336 Madrona
Sant Cugat del Vallès 327▲
Llano de Can Gineu
C'an San Joan
La Puntigala 151▲
20
A17
A18
E09
La Floresta
Santa Eulàlia
San Andrés
La Sagrera
Sta. Coloma de Gramanet
Badalona
A19
Sant Adrià de Besós
Vallcarca
La Taxonera
Guinardó
La Llacuna
San Martin
El Poblenou
A
Molins de Rei
○Santa Cruz de Olorde
Tibidabo 512▲
Vallvidrera
20
▲435
387
Gràcia
Sagrada Familia
Templo de Toros Monumental
Sant Vicenç dels Horts
340
A2
Sant Just Desvern 389▲
San Pedro Martir
Pedralbes
Sarrià
Las Corts
La Franca
BARCELONA
La Barceloneta
Sant Feliu de Llobregat
Esplugas
A2
Universitat Est. Central
Campo F.C. Barcelona
Est. de Franco
Museu Maritim
Colonia Güell
Cornellà
Sans
Hostafranchs
41°20'
41°20'
Beri
La Ribera
Sant Joan Despi
L'Hospitalet de Llobregat
Castell de Montjuic
Montjuic
Génova
Sant Boi de Llobregat
245
A16
Viladecans
31
El Prat de Llobregat
Maó, Palma de Mallorca, Eivissa
B
Gavà
BARCELONA (EL PRAT) (BCN)
Rio Llobregat
MEDITERRANEAN SEA
Estany de la Ricarda
Gavamar
Estany del Rémola
East from Greenwich
2°00'
2°10'

Barcelona

1 **2**

CENTRAL BARCELONA

Gràcia
Sagrada Familia
Plaça Glòries Catalanes
a
La Pedrera (Casa Mila)
L'Eixample
b
Barrio Gòtic
La Ribera
Estació de França
El Raval
Plaça d'Espanya
Palau
La Franca
Montjuic
Parc de Montjuic
La Barceloneta
Port Vell
Palau Nacional Museu d'Art (National Palace)
Estadi Olympic
Palau Sant Jordi
Castell de Montjuic
Mediterranean Sea
c

1 **2** **3**

BEIJING, CHINA

Labagou National Forest Park
110
A
Summer Palace
Yuanmingyuan Park
Tsinhua University
TO BEIJING (PEK)
40°00'
Yiheyuan
Peking University
Zhongguancun
Olympic Green
Wangjing
Kunming Hu
Wanliu Park
Haidian
Qinghuayuan
Olympic Stadium
111
Landian chang
Institute of Technology
Beitaipingzhuang
Hepingli
101
Ba He
Zizhuyuan Park
Beijing Zoo
Beijing North Sta.
Ditan Park
Shudui Lake
B
Tiancun
Ganjiakou
Xicheng
Bei Hai
Jade Island
Dongcheng
Xizhimen
Andingmen
Dongzhimen
Agricultural Exhibition Centre
Chaoyang Park
Cuwei
Yuyuantan Park
Military Museum
BEIJING (PEKING)
Imperial Palace Museum (Forbidden City)
Chaoyangmen
Worker's Stadium
Chaoyang
Shawocun
Fuxinglu
Sanlihe
Xidan
Tian'anmen Square
Beijing Sta.
Ritan Park
Guomao
103 102
Lianhua He
Beijing West Sta.
Xuanwu
Qianmen
Guangqumen
Beijing East Sta.
Dajiaoting
109
Guang'anmen
You'anmen
Taoranting Park
Chongwen
Tiantan Park
Temple of Heaven
Longtan Hu
Yaowa Park
Fengtai Stadium
107
Zhouzhuangzi
Yongdingman
Puhuangyu
Shilihe
Fengtai
Yanghuayuan
Beijing South Sta. (High Speed Rail)
Liangshui He
Chengshousi
C
Huangtugang
Dahongmen
106
104
Daxing
Beijing World Park
East from Greenwich
116°20'

Beijing

1 **2**

CENTRAL BEIJING

Haidian
Matihutong
XIZHIKOUWAI DESHENGMENWAI D.
Rendingho Park
Andelizhong Lu
Temple of Earth
a
Northern Jiatong University
Xizhimen
Deshengmen
Pingali
Lama Temple
YONGHEGONG
Zoo
Exhibition Centre
Xicheng
Bei Hai
Jade Island
Dongcheng
National Art Gallery
Sanlihe
Xidan
Forbidden City
Working People's Cult. Pal.
DONGDAN
Xuanwu
Qianmen
Chongwen
Tiantan Park

1 **2** **3**

⚐ Temple

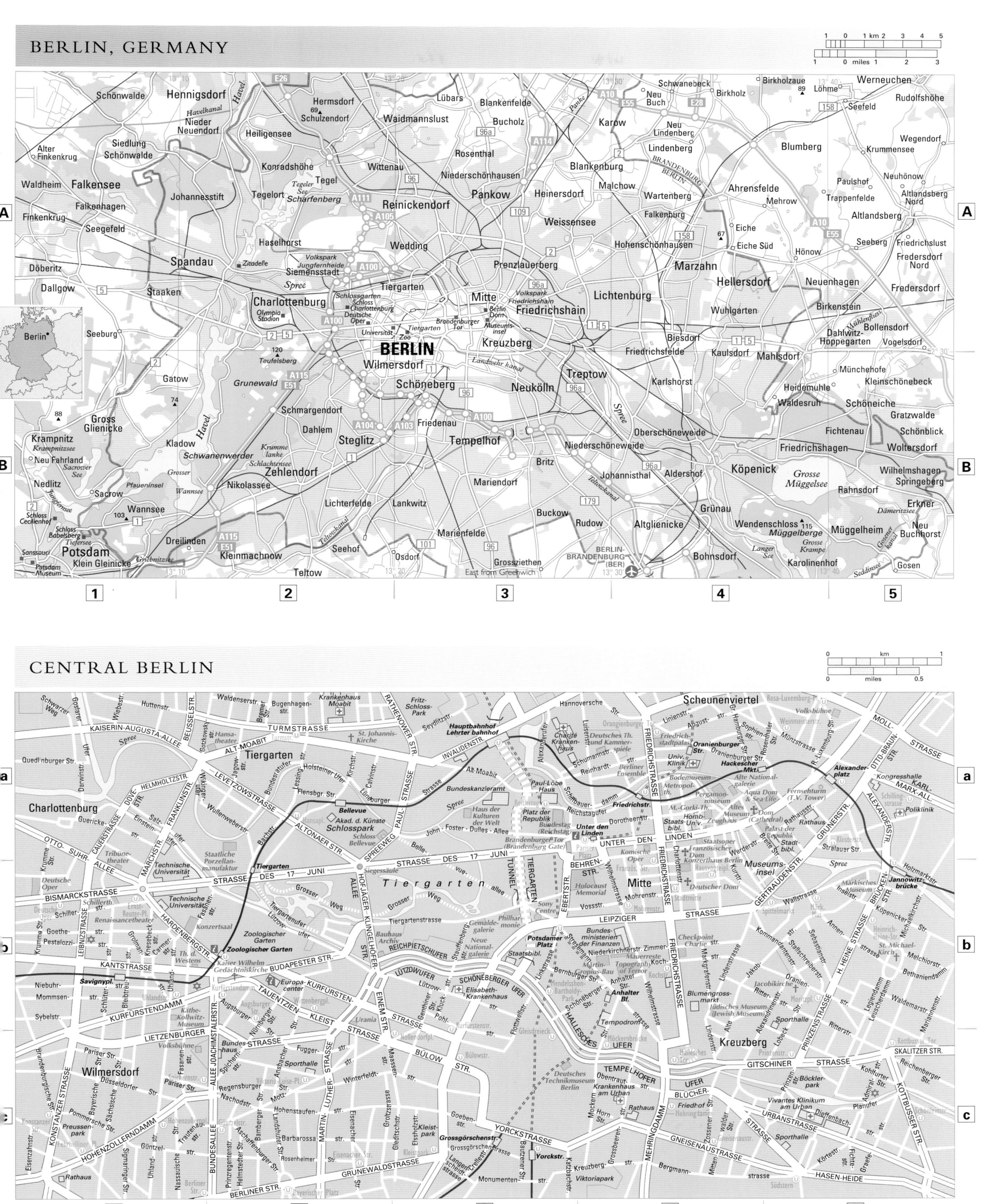

BERLIN, GERMANY

Schönwalde
Hennigsdorf
Hermsdorf
Lübars
Blankenfelde
Schwanebeck
Birkholzaue
Birkholz
Löhme
Werneuchen
Nieder Neuendorf
Schulzendorf
Waidmannslust
Bucholz
Karow
Neu Buch
Neu Lindenberg
Seefeld
Rudolfshöhe
Alter Finkenkrug
Siedlung Schönwalde
Heiligensee
Konradshöhe
Tegel
Rosenthal
Niederschönhausen
Lindenberg
Blumberg
Wegendorf
Krummensee
Neuhönow
Waldheim
Falkensee
Johannesstift
Tegelort
Scharfenberg
Wittenau
Pankow
Heinersdorf
Malchow
Wartenberg
Ahrensfelde
Mehrow
Trappenfelde
Altlandsberg Nord
Finkenkrug
Falkenhagen
Haselhorst
Reinickendorf
Weissensee
Falkenburg
Hohenschönhausen
Eiche
Eiche Süd
Hönow
Seeberg
Friedrichslust
Fredersdorf Nord
Döberitz
Spandau
Wedding
Prenzlauerberg
Marzahn
Seegefeld
Siemensstadt
Tiergarten
Mitte
Hellersdorf
Neuenhagen
Fredersdorf
Dallgow
Staaken
Charlottenburg
Friedrichshain
Lichtenburg
Wuhlgarten
Birkenstein
Olympia Stadion
BERLIN
Kreuzberg
Berlin Dom
Biesdorf
Friedrichsfelde
Dahlwitz-Hoppegarten
Bollersdorf
Gatow
Teufelsberg
Wilmersdorf
Schöneberg
Kaulsdorf
Mahlsdorf
Vogelsdorf
Grunewald
Schmargendorf
Neukölln
Treptow
Karlshorst
Münchehofe
Kleinschönebeck
Gross Glienicke
Kladow
Dahlem
Steglitz
Friedenau
Tempelhof
Oberschöneweide
Heidemühle
Schöneiche
Krampnitz
Schwanenwerder
Zehlendorf
Britz
Niederschöneweide
Aldershof
Köpenick
Gratzwalde
Fichtenau
Schönblick
Neu Fahrland
Nikolassee
Mariendorf
Johannisthal
Grosse Müggelsee
Friedrichshagen
Woltersdorf
Nedlitz
Sacrow
Wannsee
Lichterfelde
Lankwitz
Grünau
Rahnsdorf
Wilhelmshagen
Springeberg
Schloss Cecilienhof
Schloss Babelsberg
Dreilinden
Kleinmachnow
Marienfelde
Buckow
Rudow
Altglienicke
Wendenschloss
Müggelberge
Müggelheim
Neu Buchhorst
Erkner
Potsdam
Klein Gleinicke
Teltow
Seehof
Osdorf
Grossziethen
BERLIN-BRANDENBURG (BER)
Bohnsdorf
Karolinenhof
Gosen
Sanssouci
Potsdam Museum
East from Greenwich

CENTRAL BERLIN

Charlottenburg
Tiergarten
Scheunenviertel
Hauptbahnhof Lehrter bahnhof
Bellevue
Schlosspark
Schloss Bellevue
Tiergarten
Zoologischer Garten
Savignypl.
Kurfürstendamm
Wilmersdorf
Potsdamer Platz
Mitte
Museuminsel
Jannowitz brücke
Kreuzberg
Yorckstrasse

COPYRIGHT PHILIP'S

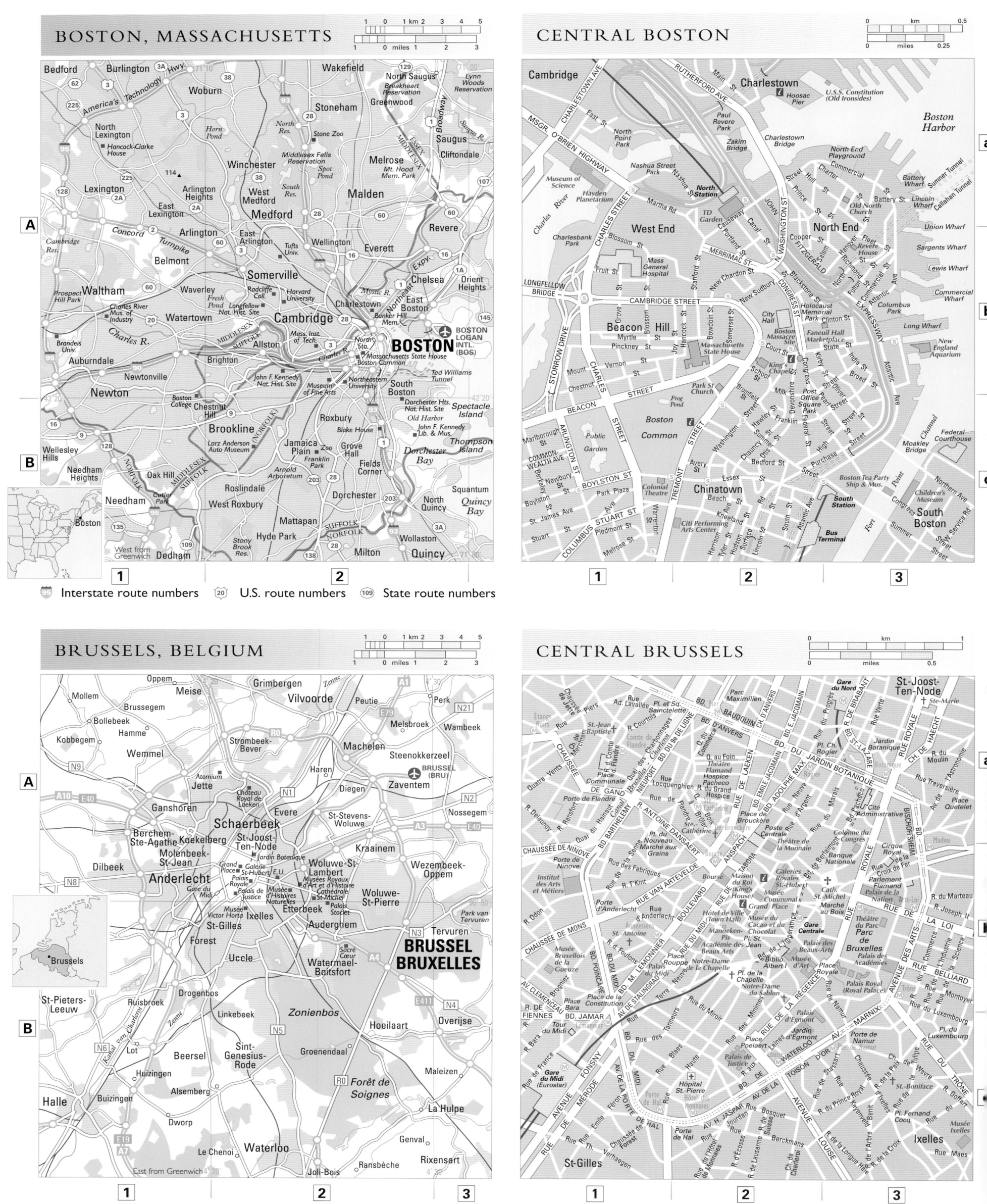

BOSTON, MASSACHUSETTS

CENTRAL BOSTON

BRUSSELS, BELGIUM

CENTRAL BRUSSELS

Interstate route numbers U.S. route numbers State route numbers

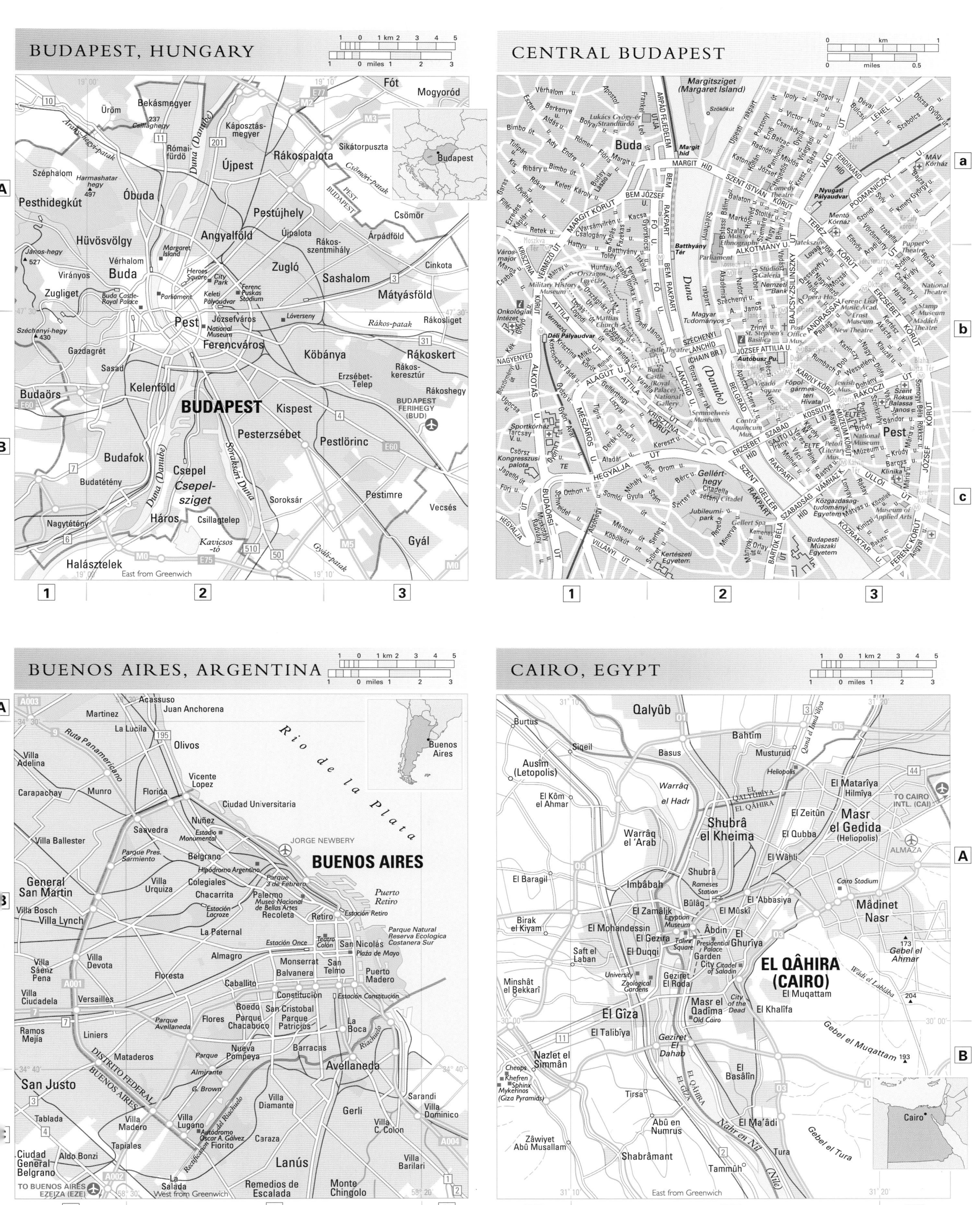

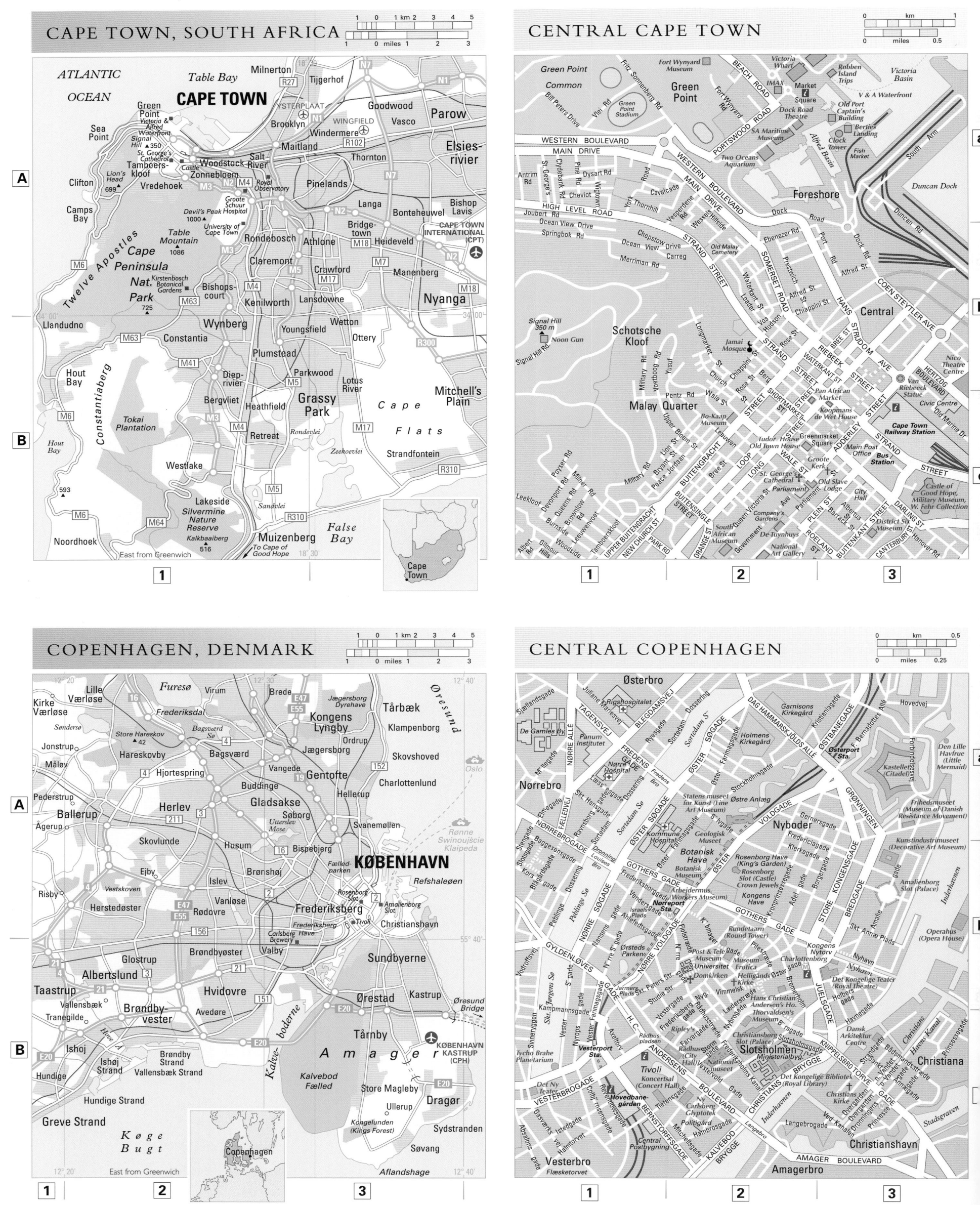

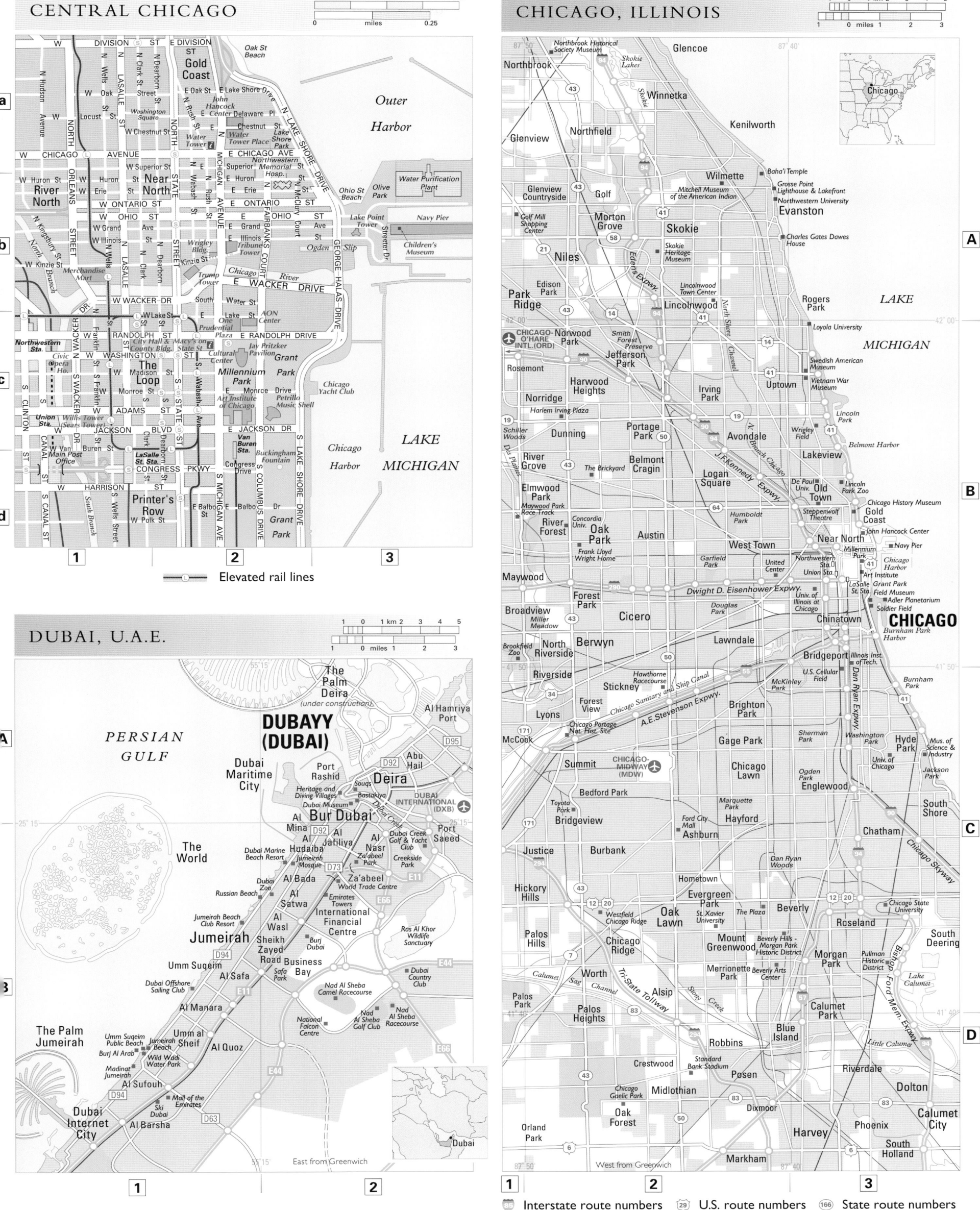

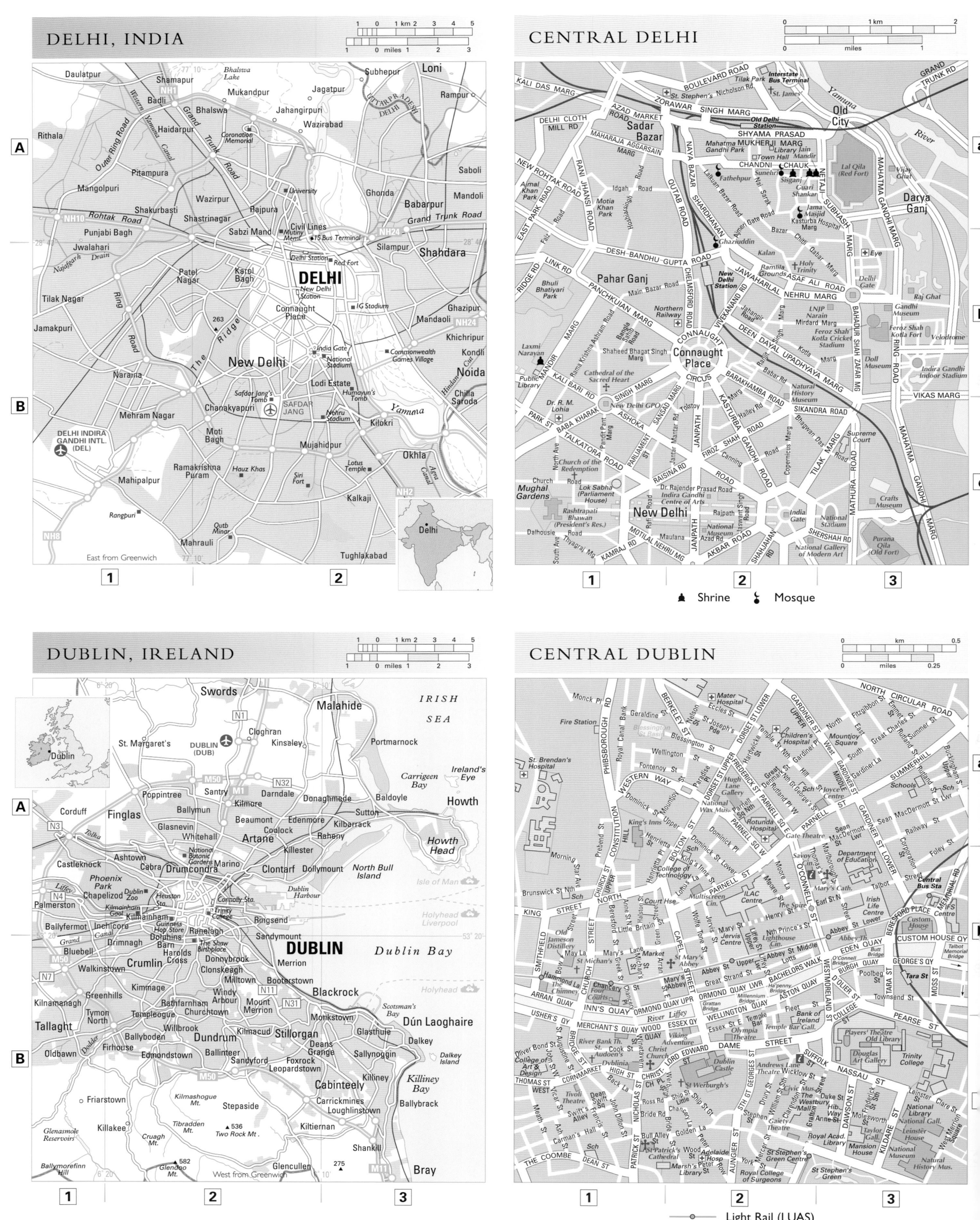

DELHI, INDIA

CENTRAL DELHI

♠ Shrine   ♟ Mosque

DUBLIN, IRELAND

CENTRAL DUBLIN

Light Rail (LUAS)

EDINBURGH, U.K.

CENTRAL EDINBURGH

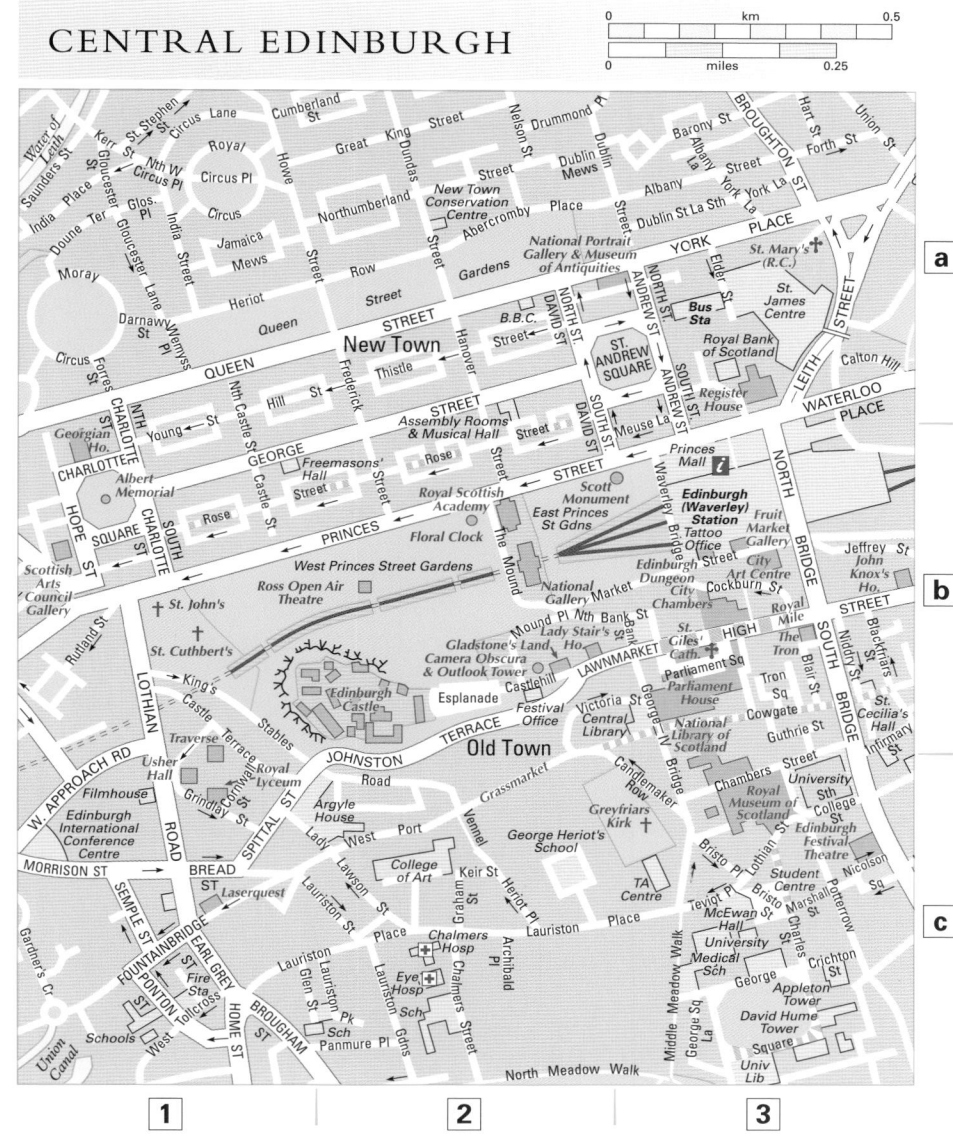

GUANGZHOU, CHINA

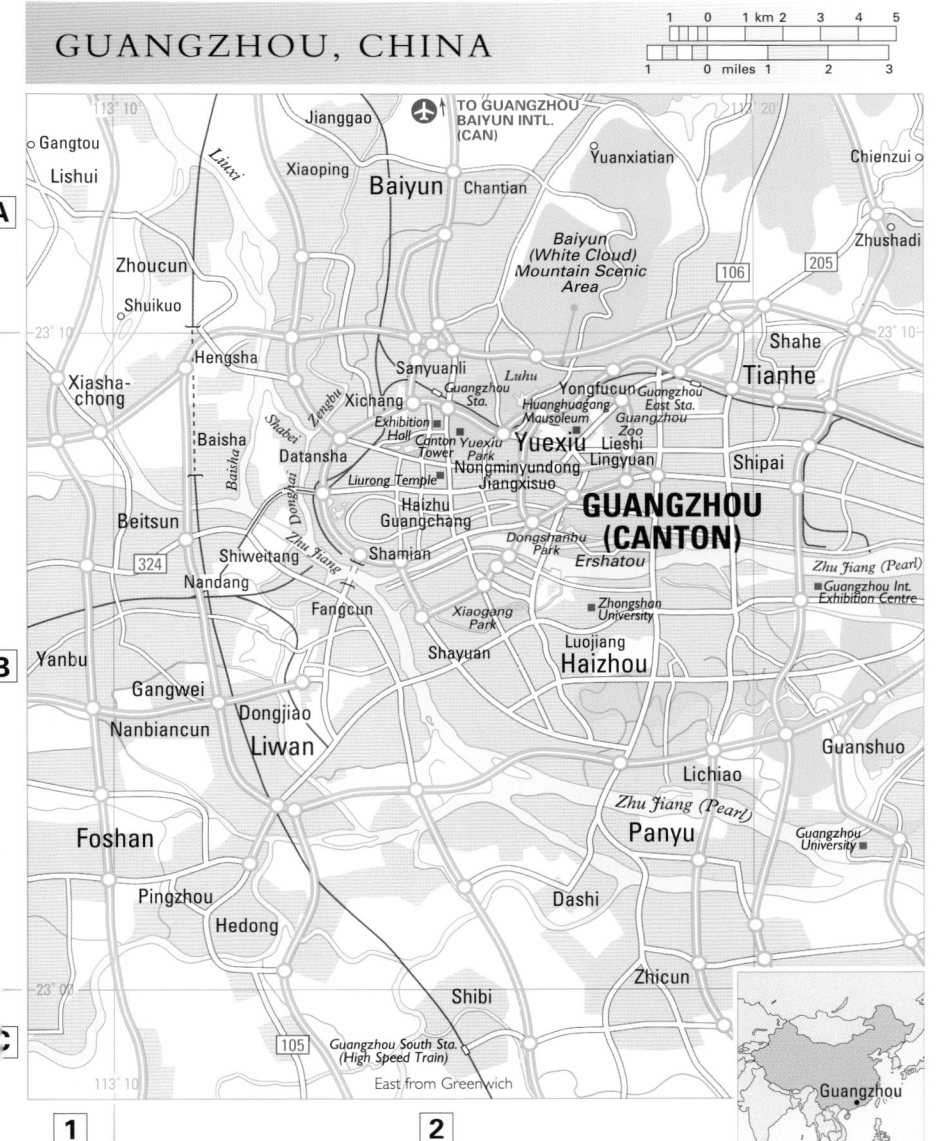

HELSINKI, FINLAND

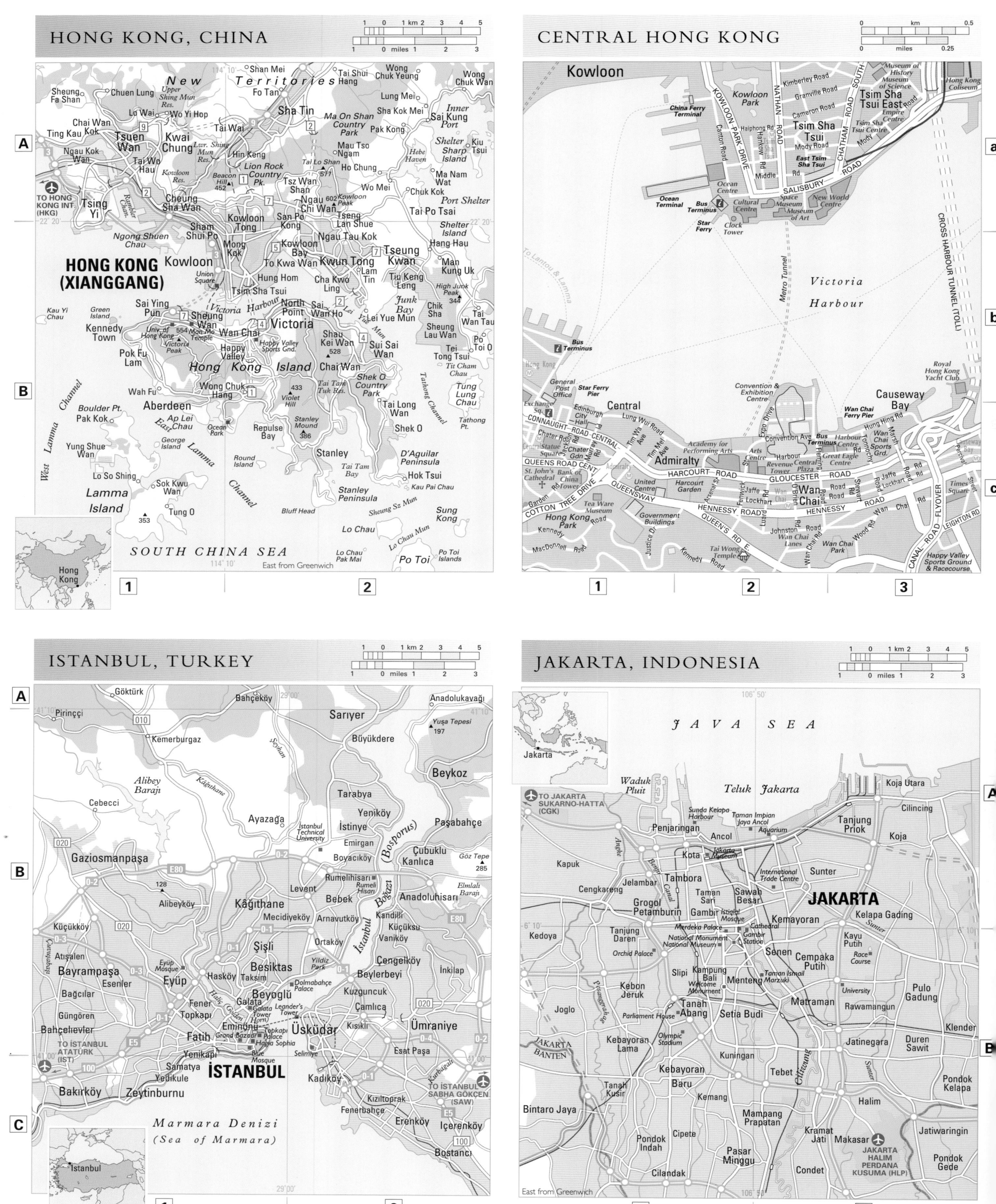

JERUSALEM, ISRAEL / W. BANK

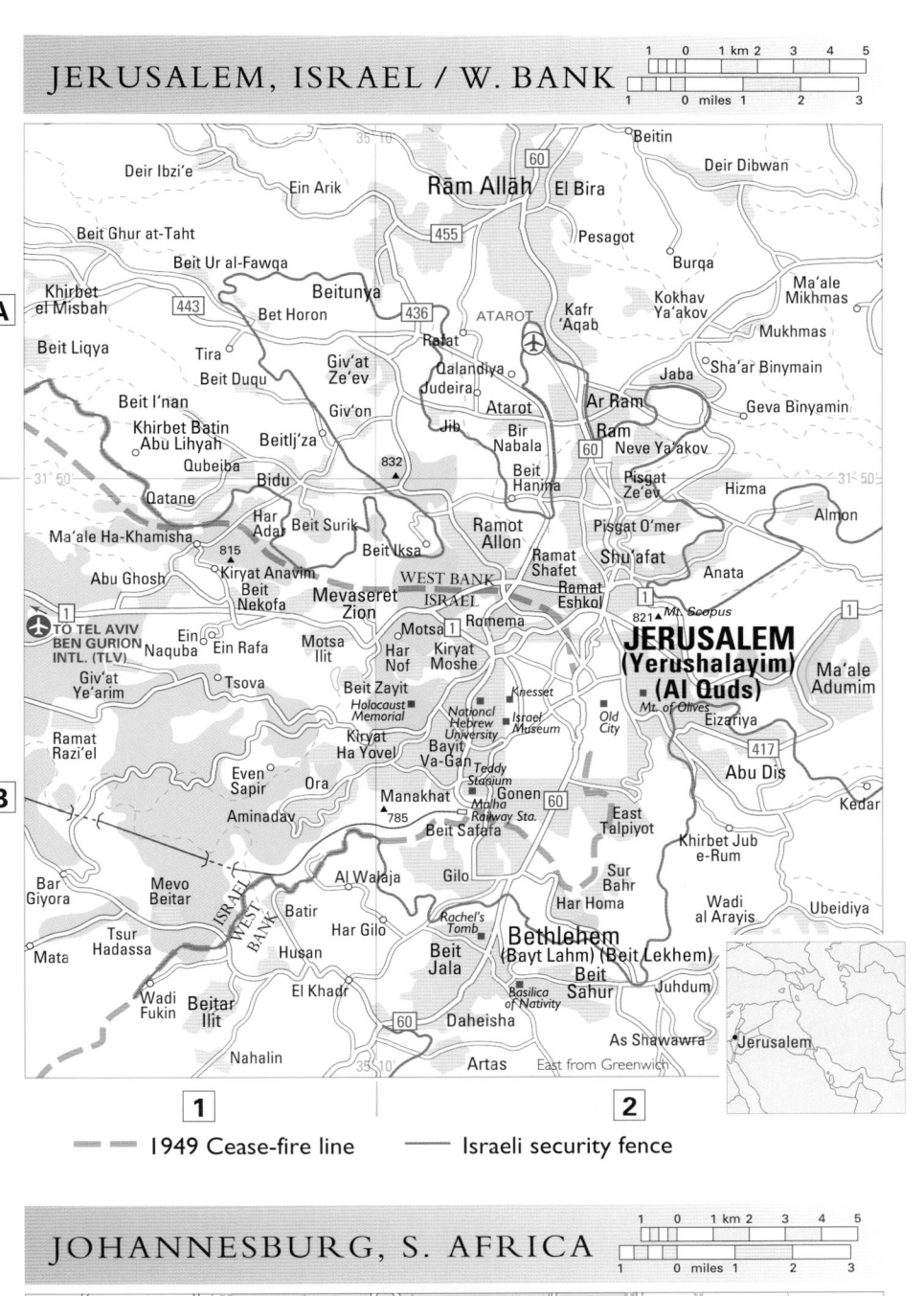

CENTRAL JERUSALEM

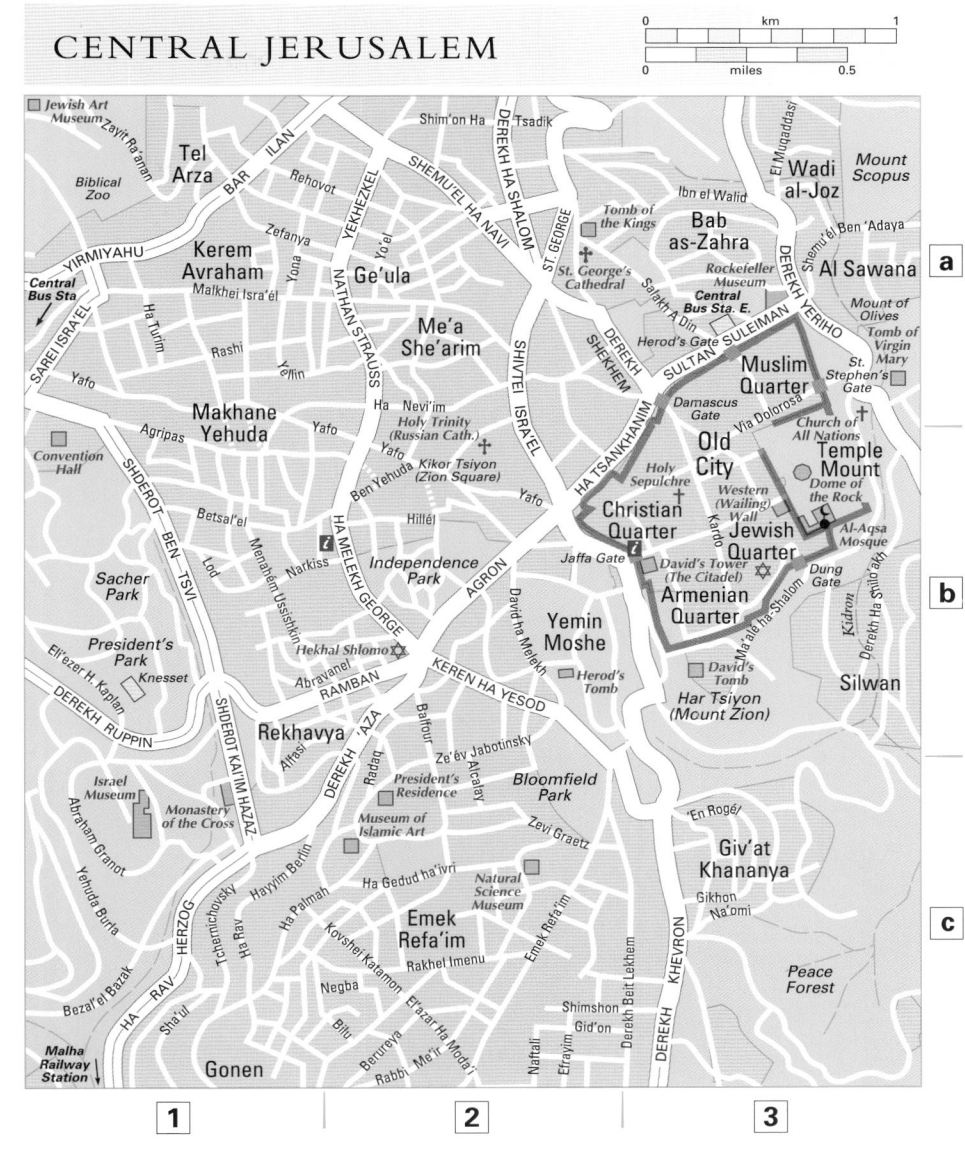

- - - 1949 Cease-fire line   —— Israeli security fence

JOHANNESBURG, S. AFRICA

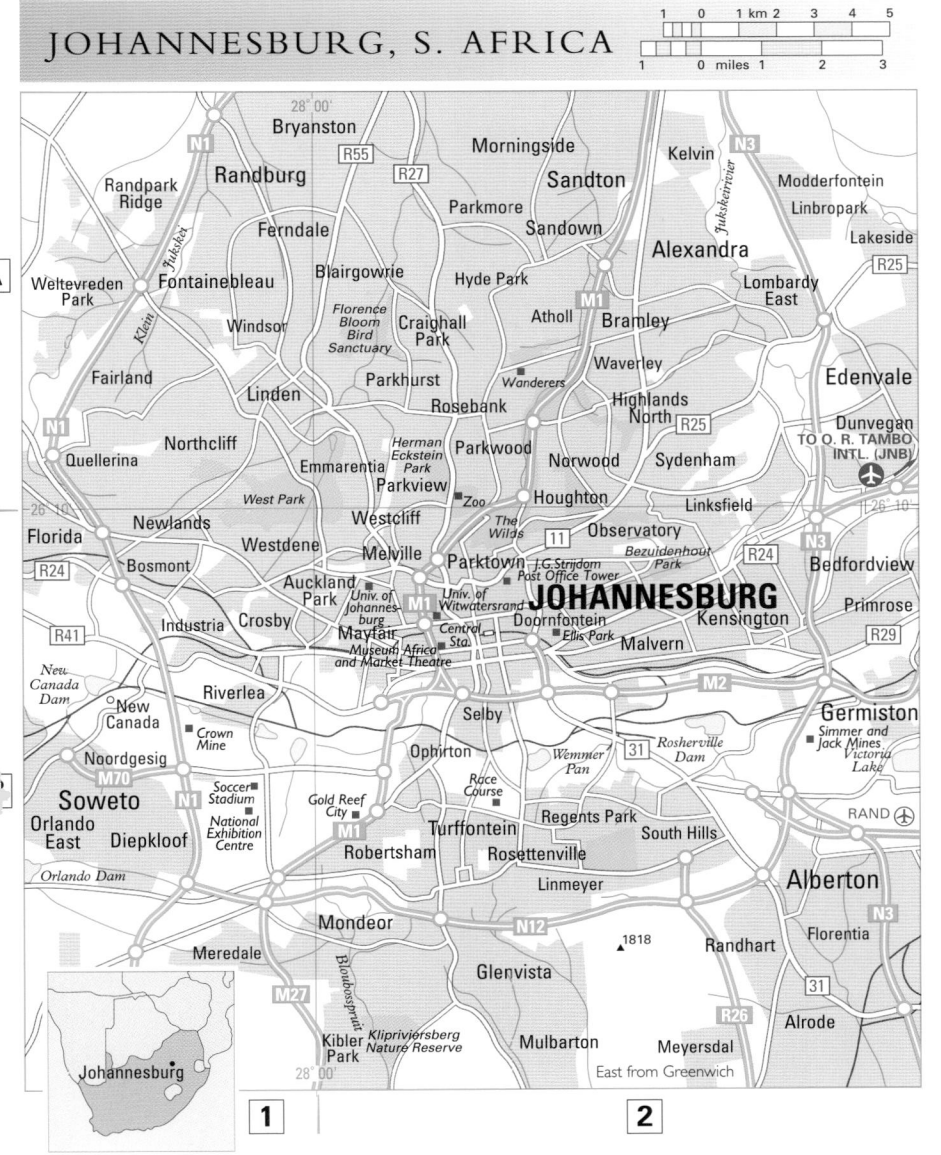

KARACHI, PAKISTAN

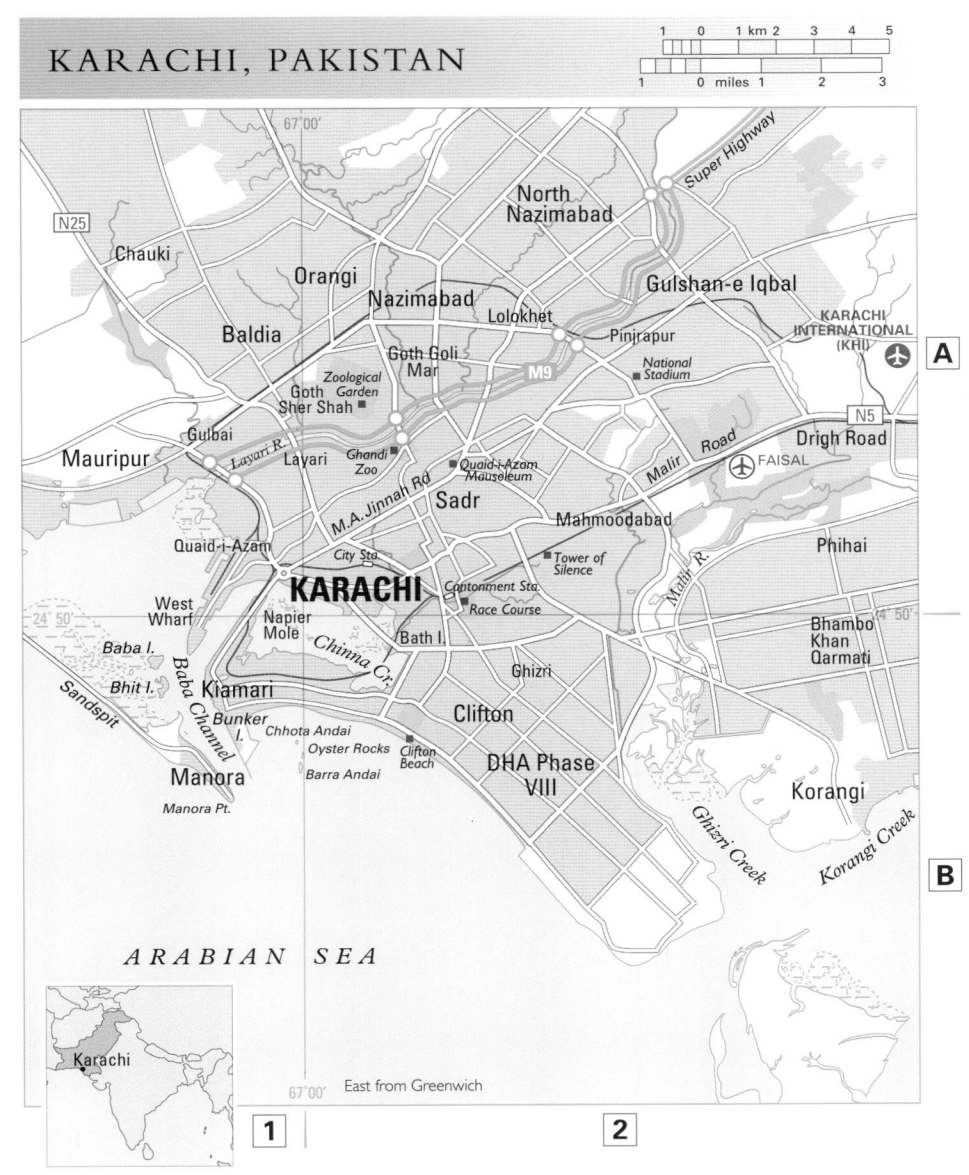

KOLKATA, INDIA

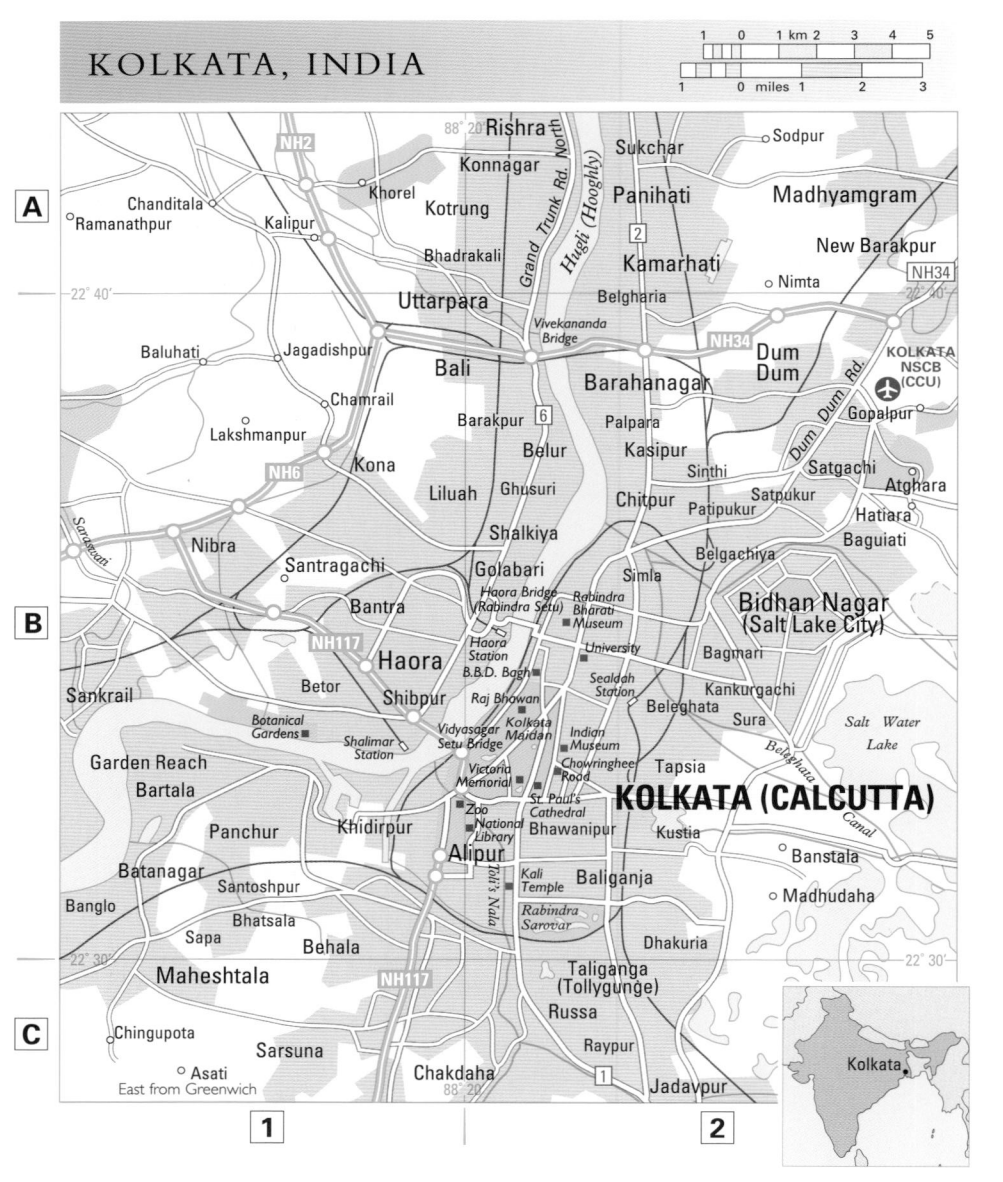

LAGOS, NIGERIA

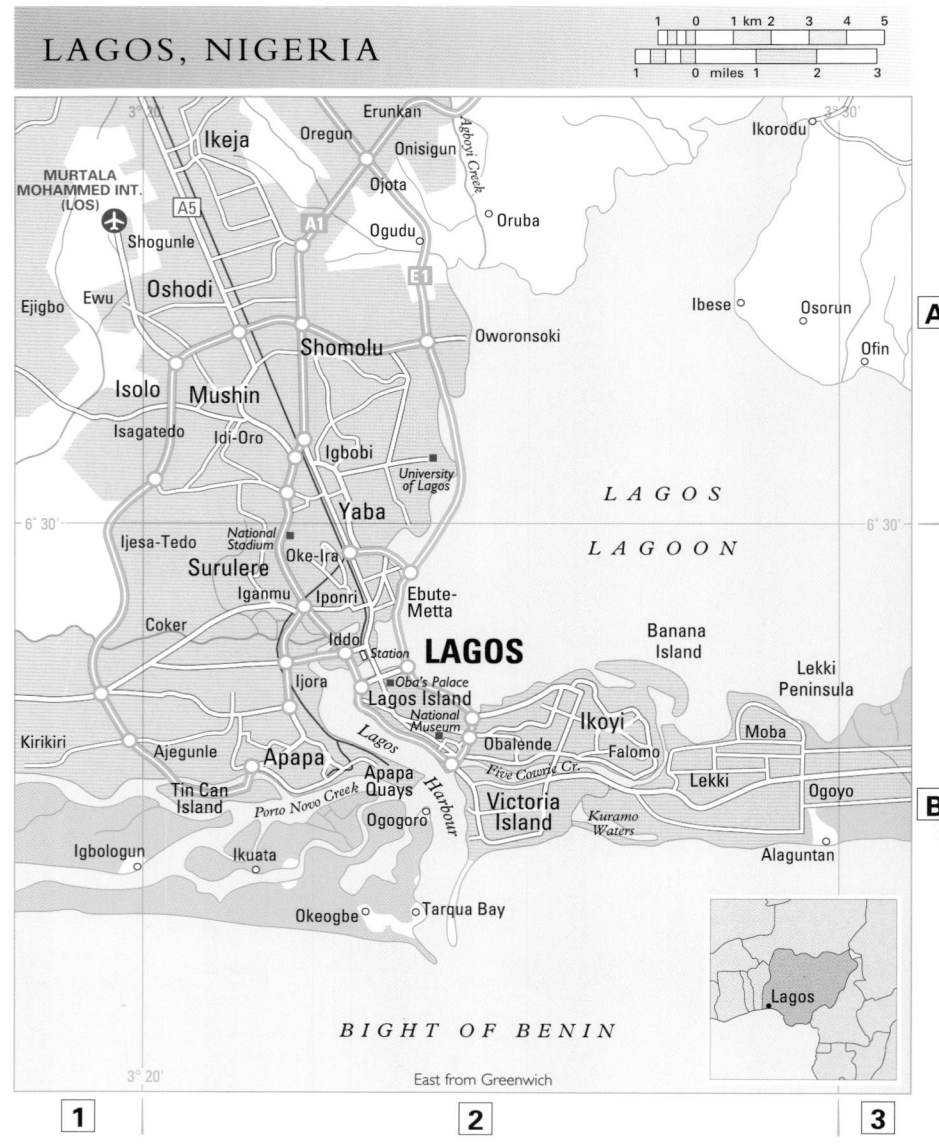

LAS VEGAS, NEVADA

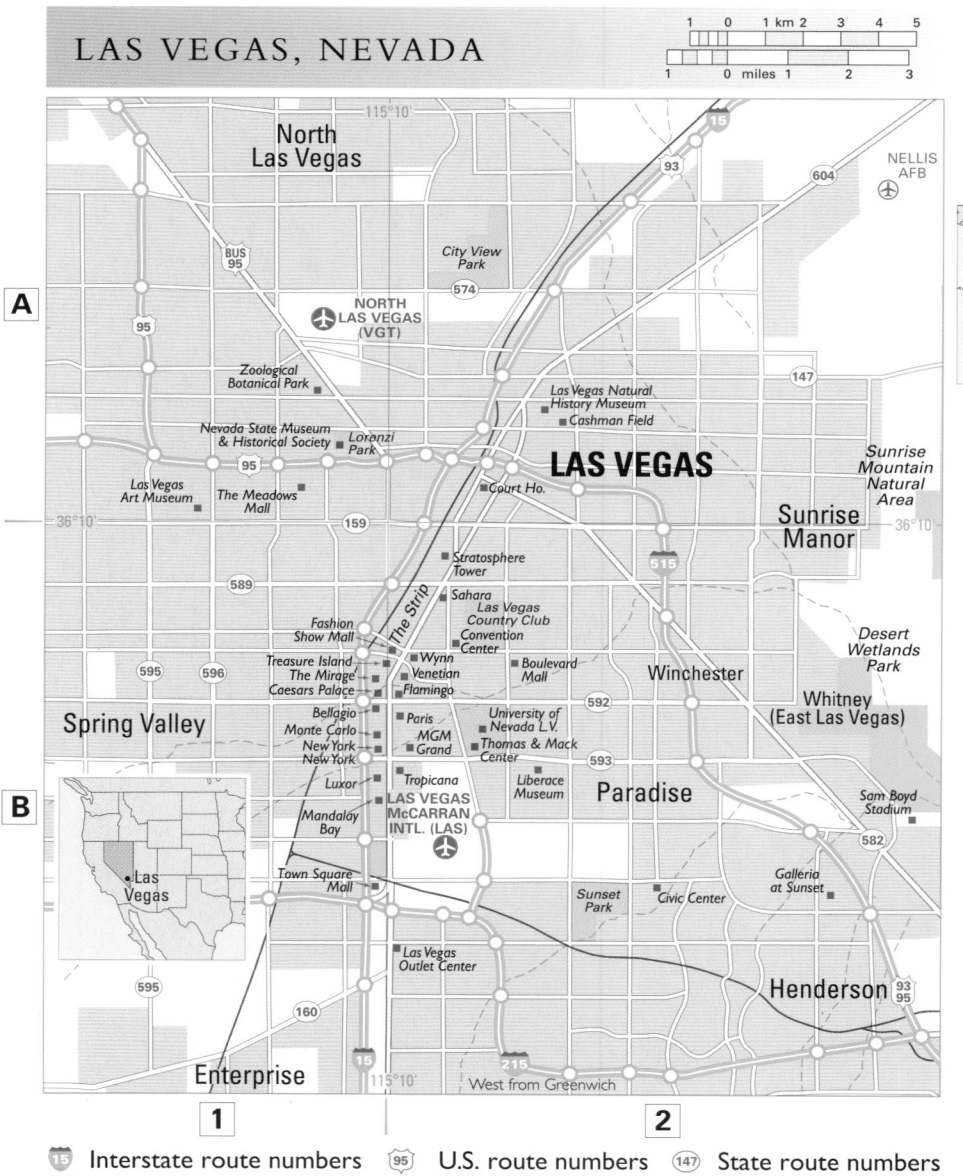

LIMA, PERU

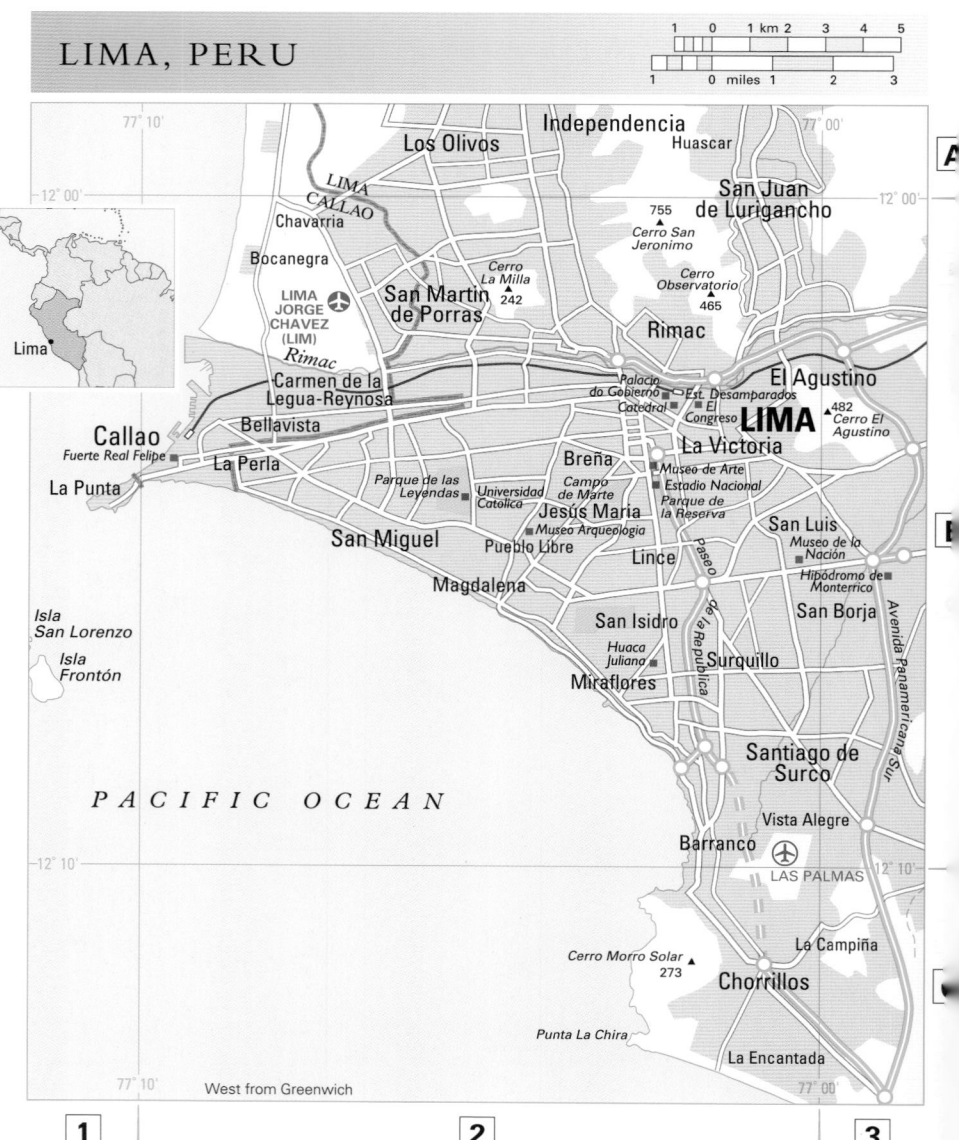

Interstate route numbers   U.S. route numbers   State route numbers

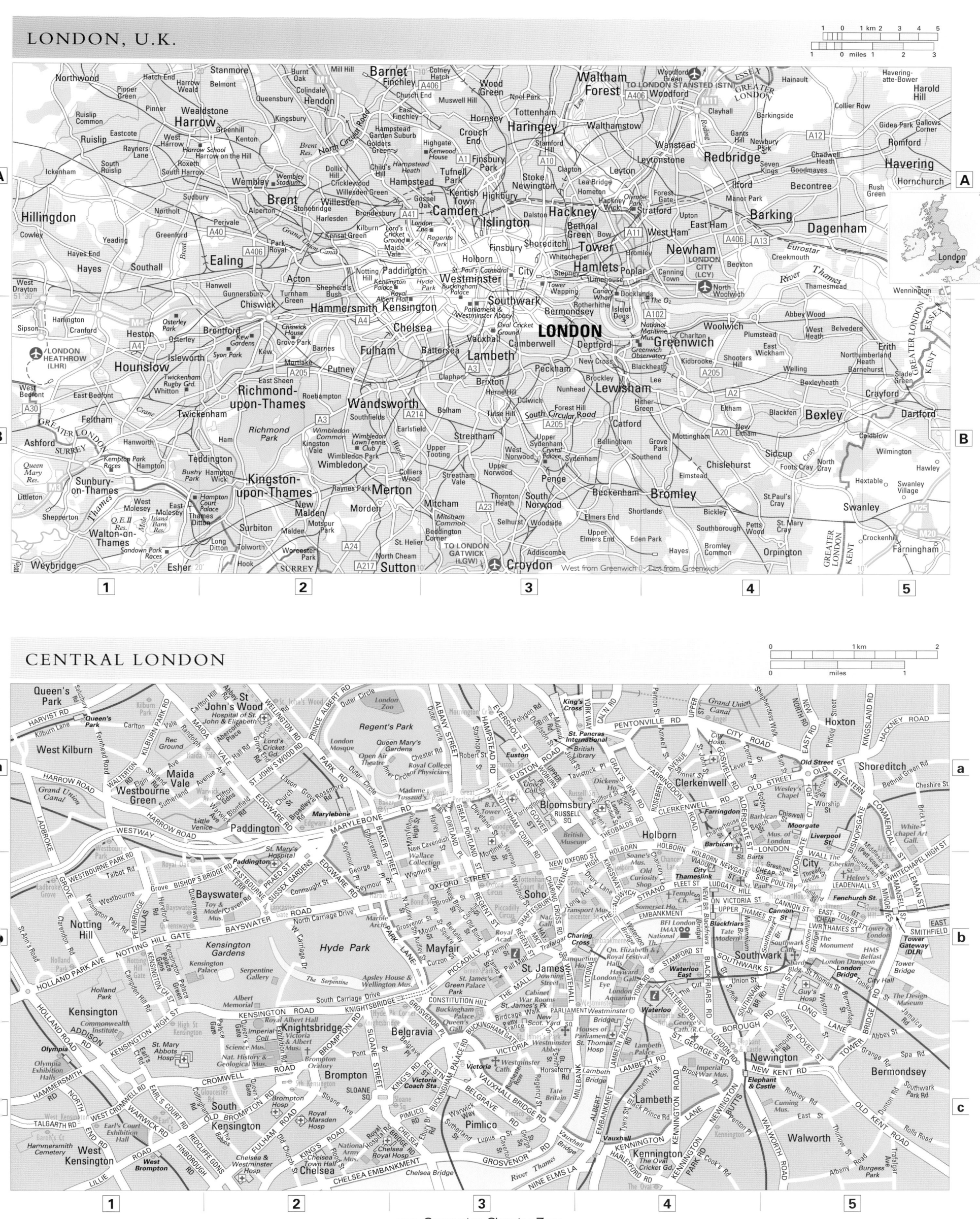

LONDON, U.K.

Congestion Charging Zone

COPYRIGHT PHILIP'S

LISBON, PORTUGAL

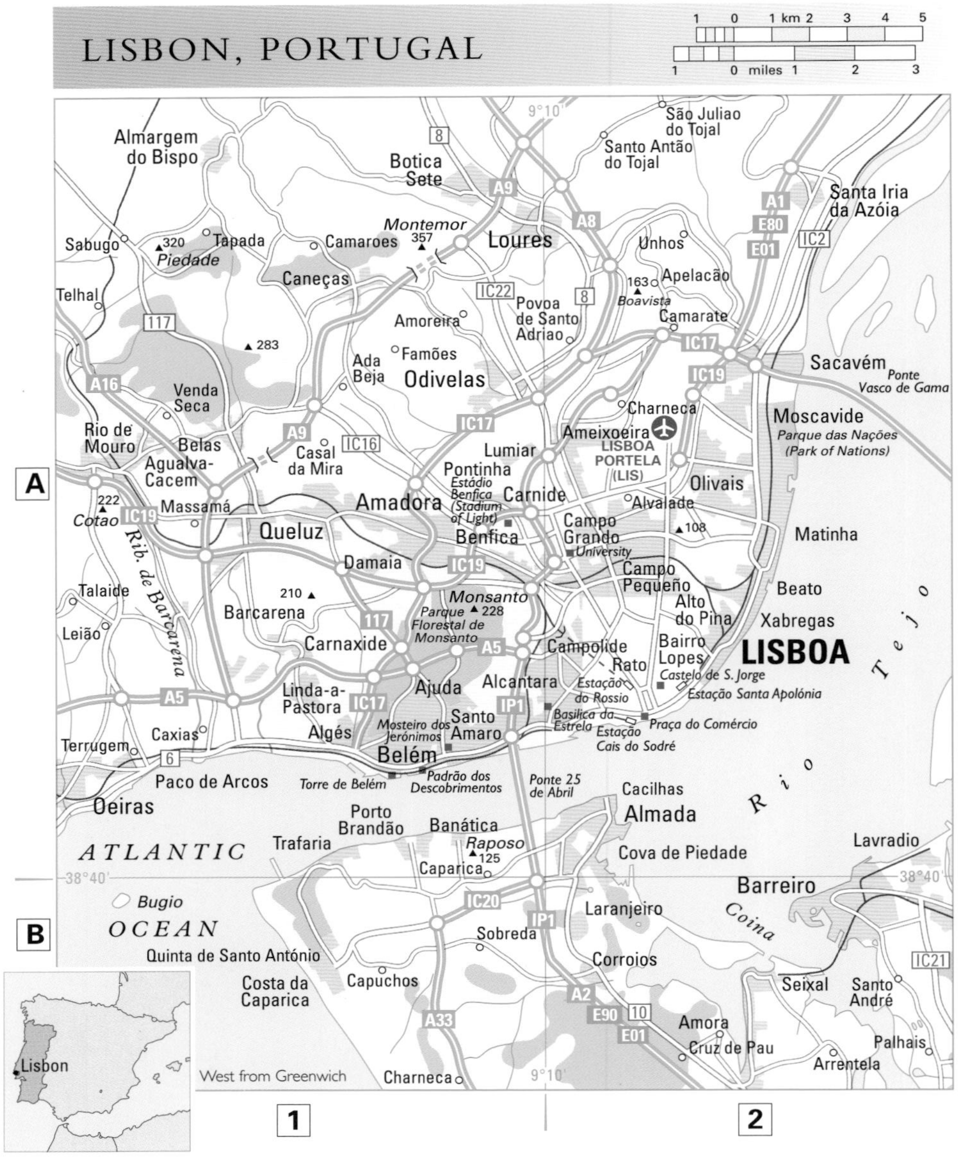

1 0 1 km 2 3 4 5
1 0 miles 1 2 3

Almargem do Bispo
Botica Sete
Santo Antão do Tojal
São Julião do Tojal
8
Tapada
320 Piedade
Sabugo
Telhal
Montemor
357
Camaroes
Loures
Caneças
A8
Santo Antão do Tojal
A9
Unhos
Apelação
Santa Iria da Azóia
Santa Iria da Azóia
IC2
E80
E01
A1
Venda Seca
Rio de Mouro
Belas
Aguava-Cacem
222
Cotão
A16
A9
Casal da Mira
IC16
Amoreira
Povoa de Santo Adriao
Boavista
163
Camarate
Sacavém
IC22
283
Ada Beja
Famões
Odivelas
IC19
Ponte Vasco da Gama
IC17
Massamá
Queluz
Lumiar
Pontinha
Estádio Benfica (Stadium of Light)
Carnide
Ameixoeira
LISBOA PORTELA (LIS)
Olivais
Moscavide
Parque das Nações (Park of Nations)
Damaia
Amadora
Benfica
Campo Grande University
Alvalade
Matinha
A5
IC19
210
Monsanto
228
Campo Pequeno
108
Beato
Talaide
Barcarena
Parque Florestal de Monsanto
Alto do Pina
Xabregas
Leião
Carnaxide
117
Campolide
Bairro Lopes
LISBOA
Linda-a-Pastora
Ajuda
Alcântara
Rato
Castelo de S. Jorge
Caxias
Algés
Estação do Rossio
Estação Santa Apolónia
Terrugem
Mosteiro dos Jerónimos
Santo Amaro
IP1
Estação Cais do Sodré
Praça do Comércio
Oeiras
Paço de Arcos
Torre de Belém
Belém
Padrão dos Descobrimentos
Basílica da Estrela
Ponte 25 de Abril
Cacilhas
Rio Tejo
ATLANTIC
Trafaria
Porto Brandão
Banática
Raposo
125
Almada
Cova de Piedade
Lavradio
Bugio
OCEAN
Quinta de Santo António
Caparica
Sobreda
Barreiro
IC20
Laranjeiro
Coina
38°40'
Costa da Caparica
Capuchos
Corroios
IP1
Seixal
Santo André
A2
A33
Amora
Cruz de Pau
E90
E01
10
Palhais
Arrentela
Charneca
West from Greenwich
9°10'
IC21

Lisbon

1   2

CENTRAL LISBON

km
0   0.5
miles

Palacio de Penitenciária
Palacio de Justiça
Hosp. Infantil
Maternidade
Instituto Superior Técnico
Praça Duque Saldanha
Estefânia
Penha França
Amoreiros
Rato
Anjos
Hospital M. Bombarda
Hospital de Santa Marta
Bairro Lopes
Jardim Botânico
Graça
Instituto de Medicina Legal
Palácio de Assembleia Nacional
Bairro Alto
Elevador de santa justa
Castelo de São Jorge (St. George's Castle)
Museu do Arqueologia
Estação do Rossio
Praça Rossio
Museu de Arte Decorativas
Alfama
Estação Santa Apolónia
Museu do Chiado
Sé Catedral
Baixa
Praça do Comércio
Dom José I
Estação Cais do Sodré
AV. VINTE E QUATRO DE JULHO
AV. RIBEIRA DAS NAUS
Estação Fluvial
AVENIDA INFANTE DOM HENRIQUE
Rio Tejo (Tagus)

a

b

c

1   2   3

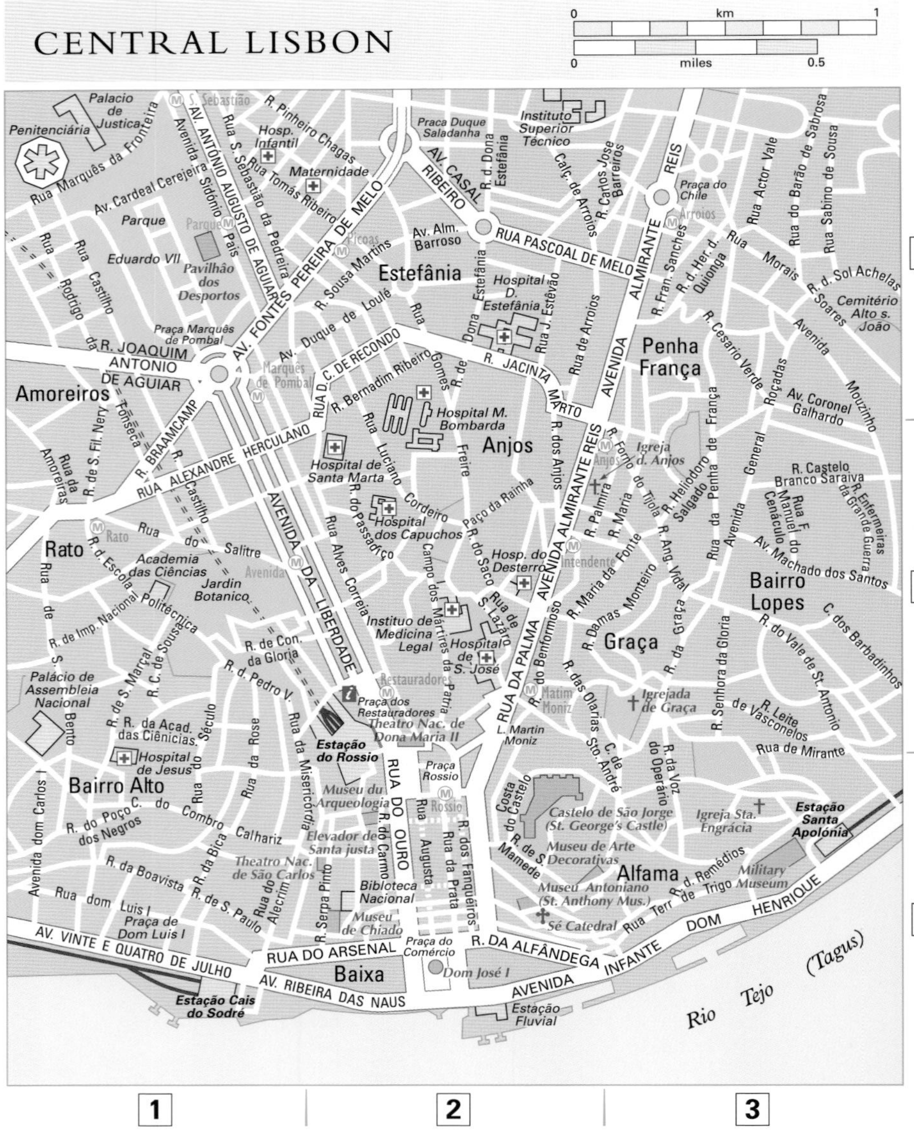

LOS ANGELES, CALIFORNIA

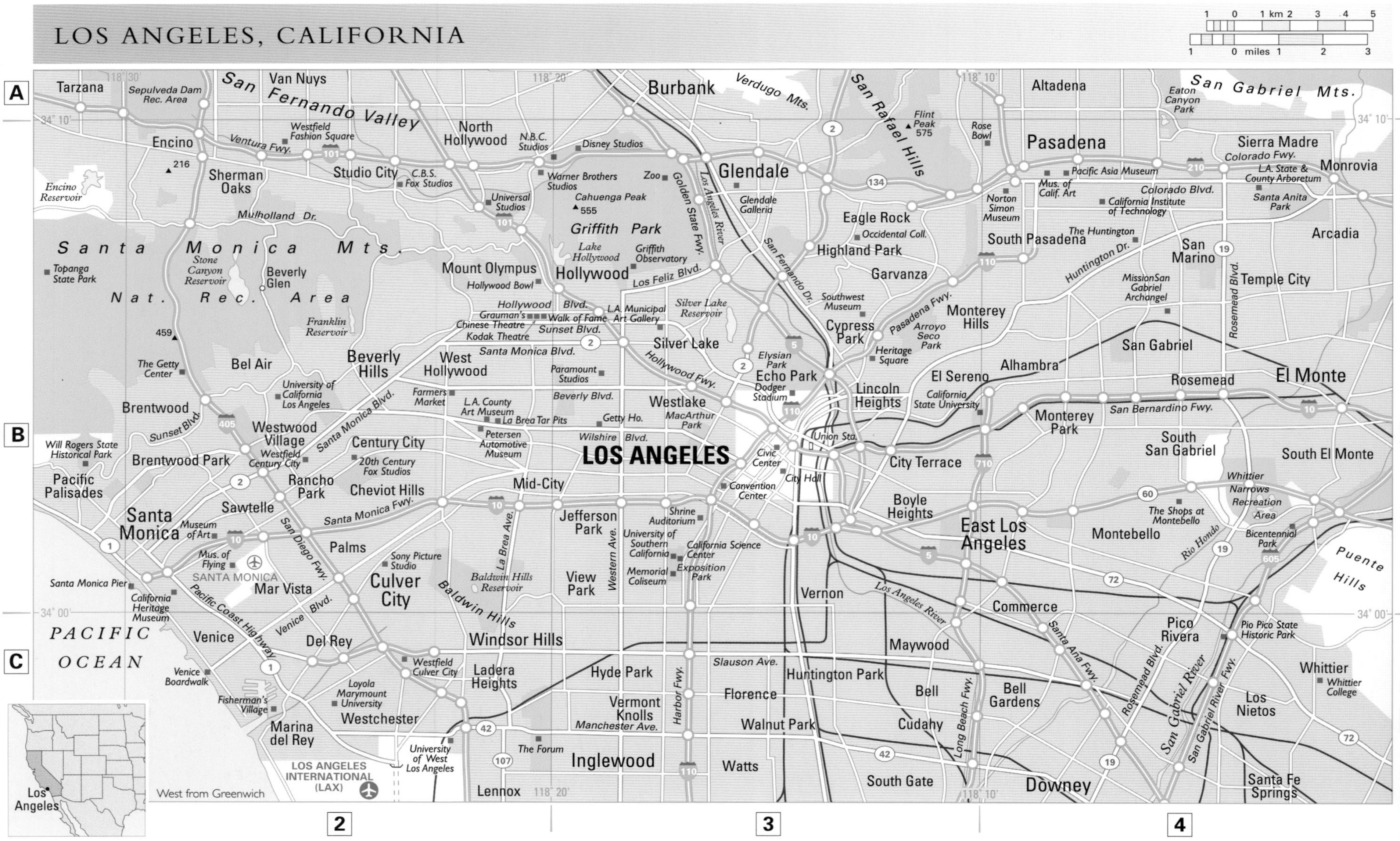

1 0 1 km 2 3 4 5
1 0 miles 1 2 3

Tarzana
Sepulveda Dam Rec. Area
Van Nuys
San Fernando Valley
Burbank
Verdugo Mts.
San Rafael Hills
Altadena
Eaton Canyon Park
San Gabriel Mts.
34°10'
Encino
Ventura Fwy.
Westfield Fashion Square
North Hollywood
N.B.C. Studios
Disney Studios
Flint Peak 575
Rose Bowl
Pasadena
Sierra Madre
Colorado Fwy.
Monrovia
216
Sherman Oaks
Studio City
C.B.S.
Fox Studios
Warner Brothers Studios
Zoo
Glendale
Glendale Galleria
Norton Simon Museum
Pacific Asia Museum
Mus. of Calif. Art
Colorado Blvd.
California Institute of Technology
Santa Anita Park
Arcadia
Encino Reservoir
Cahuenga Peak 555
Griffith Park
Eagle Rock
Occidental Coll.
Southwest Museum
South Pasadena
The Huntington
San Marino
Santa Monica Mts.
Mulholland Dr.
Mount Olympus
Lake Hollywood
Hollywood
Griffith Observatory
Highland Park
Garvanza
Huntington Dr.
Mission San Gabriel Archangel
Temple City
Topanga State Park
Stone Canyon Reservoir
Beverly Glen
Hollywood Bowl
Los Feliz Blvd.
Silver Lake Reservoir
Monterey Hills
19
459
Nat. Rec. Area
Franklin Reservoir
Grauman's Chinese Theatre
Kodak Theatre
Hollywood Blvd.
Walk of Fame
Sunset Blvd.
LA Municipal Art Gallery
Silver Lake
Arroyo Seco Park
Heritage Square
Alhambra
San Gabriel
The Getty Center
Bel Air
Beverly Hills
West Hollywood
Santa Monica Blvd.
Paramount Studios
Hollywood Fwy.
Elysian Park
Pasadena Fwy.
Cypress Park
El Sereno
Rosemead
El Monte
Brentwood
University of California Los Angeles
Farmers Market
Beverly Blvd.
Getty Ho.
Echo Park
Dodger Stadium
Lincoln Heights
California State University
Monterey Park
Will Rogers State Historical Park
Westwood Village
Westfield Century City
L.A. County Art Museum
La Brea Tar Pits
Wilshire Blvd.
Westlake
MacArthur Park
Union Sta.
City Terrace
South San Gabriel
South El Monte
Brentwood Park
Century City
Petersen Automotive Museum
LOS ANGELES
Civic Center
City Hall
Boyle Heights
Whittier Narrows Recreation Area
Pacific Palisades
20th Century Fox Studios
Rancho Park
Cheviot Hills
Mid-City
Jefferson Park
Shrine Auditorium
Convention Center
East Los Angeles
Montebello
60
Santa Monica
Museum of Art
Sawtelle
Palms
Santa Monica Fwy.
University of Southern California
California Science Center
Exposition Park
Bicentennial Park
Pio Pico State Historic Park
Mus. of Flying
Sony Picture Studio
Culver City
Baldwin Hills Reservoir
View Park
Memorial Coliseum
Vernon
Commerce
Pico Rivera
Puente Hills
34°00'
California Heritage Museum
Mar Vista
Venice Blvd.
Baldwin Hills
Los Angeles River
Santa Ana Fwy.
PACIFIC
Santa Monica Pier
Venice
Del Rey
Windsor Hills
Hyde Park
Slauson Ave.
Huntington Park
Maywood
Bell
Bell Gardens
Whittier
OCEAN
Venice Boardwalk
Westfield Culver City
Ladera Heights
Vermont Knolls
Manchester Ave.
Florence
Cudahy
Rosemead Blvd.
Los Nietos
Whittier College
Fisherman's Village
Loyola Marymount University
Westchester
42
Harbor Fwy.
Walnut Park
72
Marina del Rey
107
The Forum
Inglewood
Watts
South Gate
Downey
19
Santa Fe Springs
LOS ANGELES INTERNATIONAL (LAX)
University of West Los Angeles
Lennox
118°20'
110
118°10'
West from Greenwich

Los Angeles

85 Interstate route numbers   166 State route numbers

A

B

C

2   3   4

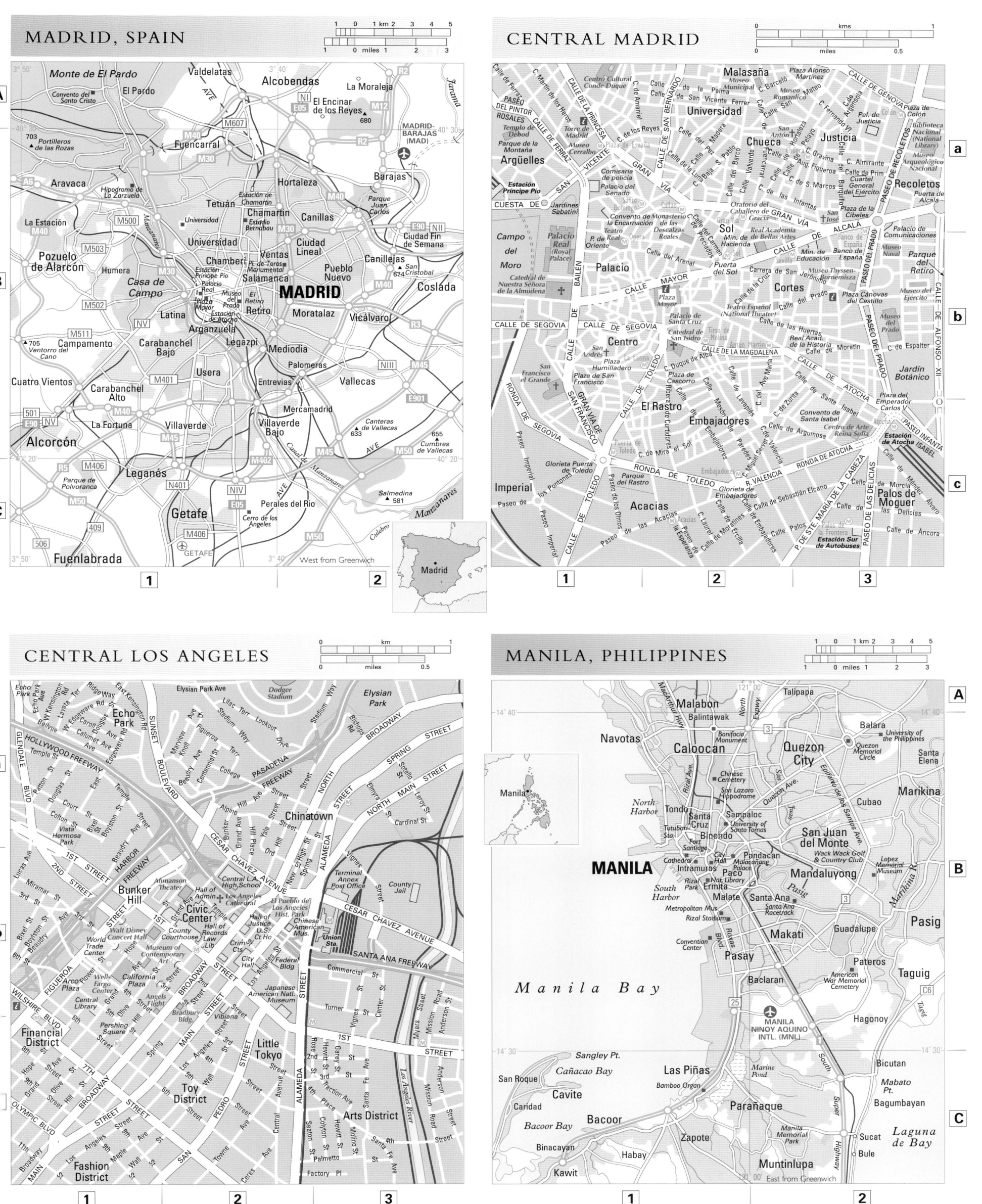

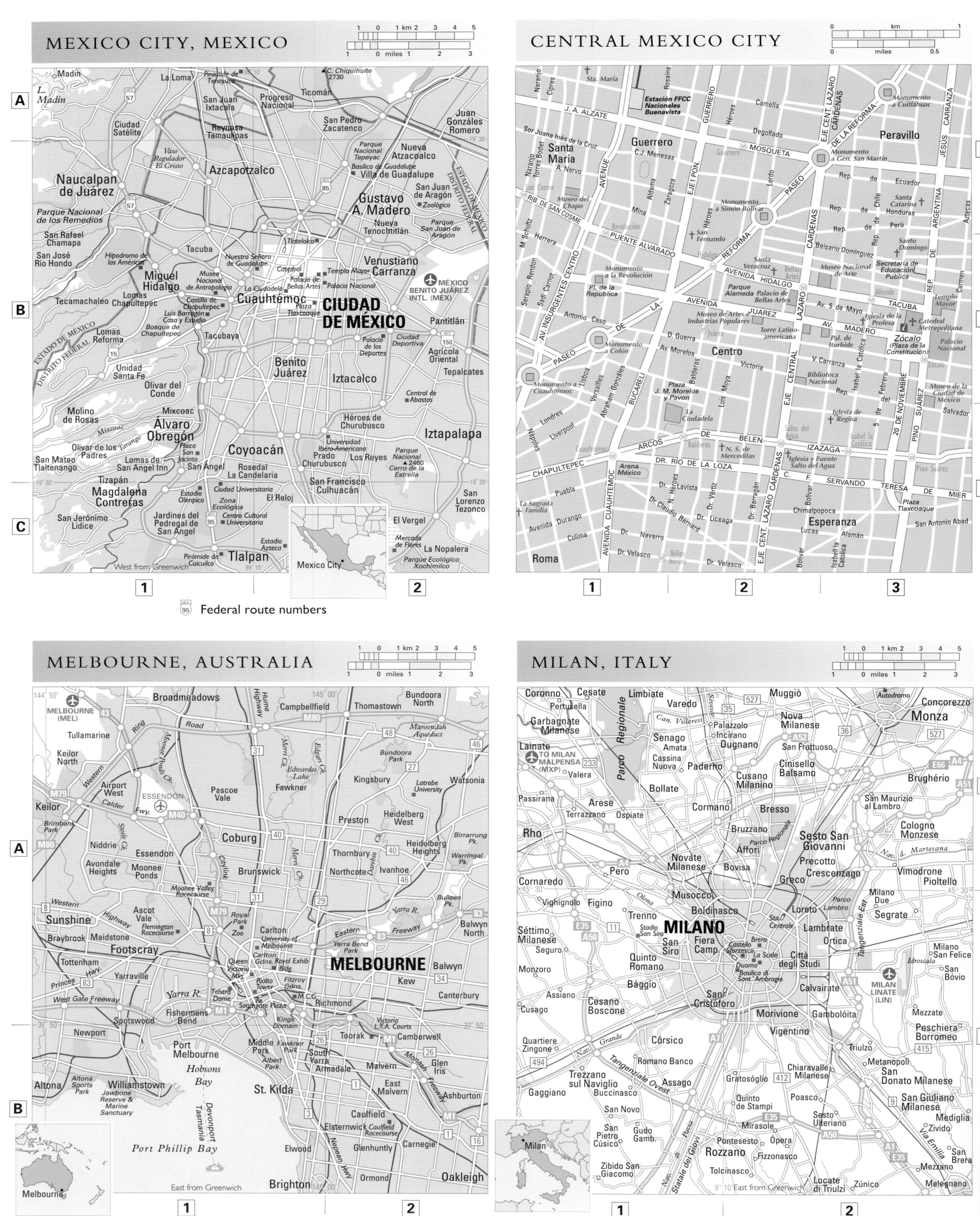

MEXICO CITY, MEXICO

1 0 1 km 2 3 4 5
1 0 miles 1 2 3

Madín
L. Madín
La Loma
Pirámide de Tenayuca
Progreso Nacional
Ticomán
C. Chiquihuite 2730

San Juan Ixtacala
San Pedro Zacatenco
Juan Gonzáles Romero

Ciudad Satélite
Reynosa Tamaulipas
Parque Nacional Tepeyac
Nueva Atzacoalco

Vaso Regulador El Cristo
Azcapotzalco
Basílica de Guadalupe
Villa de Guadalupe

Naucalpan de Juárez
Gustavo A. Madero
San Juan de Aragón
Zoológico
Estado de México Distrito Federal

Parque Nacional de los Remedios
Nueva Tenochtitlán
Parque San Juan de Aragón

San Rafael Chamapa
Tacuba
Tlatelolco
Venustiano Carranza

San José Río Hondo
Hipódromo de las Américas
Nuestra Señora de Guadalupe
Catedral
Templo Mayor
MÉXICO BENITO JUÁREZ INTL. (MEX)

Tecamachalco
Miguel Hidalgo
Museo Nacional de Antropología
Palacio de Bellas Artes
Palacio Nacional
CIUDAD DE MÉXICO

Lomas Chapultepec
Castillo de Chapultepec
La Ciudadela
Tlaxcoaque
Pantitlán

Luis Barragán Casa y Estudio
Cuauhtémoc

Lomas Reforma
Bosque de Chapultepec
Tacubaya

Estado de México Distrito Federal
Palacio de los Deportes
Ciudad Deportiva
Agrícola Oriental
150

Unidad Santa Fe
Benito Juárez
Iztacalco
Tepalcates

Olivar del Conde
Mixcoac
Central de Abastos

Molino de Rosas
Álvaro Obregón
Universidad Ibero-Americana
Héroes de Churubusco
Iztapalapa

Olivar de los Padres
Plaza San Jacinto
Coyoacán
Prado Churubusco
Los Reyes

San Mateo Tlaltenango
San Angel
Rosedal La Candelaria
Parque Nacional Cerro de la Estrella
2460

Lomas de San Angel Inn
San Francisco Culhuacán

Tizapán
Ciudad Universitaria
El Reloj
San Lorenzo Tezonco

Magdalena Contreras
Estadio Olímpico
Zona Ecológica

San Jerónimo Lídice
Jardines del Pedregal de San Angel
Centro Cultural Universitario
El Vergel
95

Pirámide de Cuicuilco
Tlalpan
Estadio Azteca
Mercado de Flores
La Nopalera

West from Greenwich
99 10
Parque Ecológico Xochimilco

Mexico City

CENTRAL MEXICO CITY

0 km 1
0 miles 0.5

Sta. María
Estación FFCC Nacionales Buenavista
Monumento a Cuitláhuac

J. A. ALZATE
Guerrero
Degollado
Peravillo

Santa María
Monumento a Gen. San Martín

Museo del Chapo
Monumento a Simón Bolívar
Rep.
Ecuador
Santa Catarina

PUENTE ALVARADO
Monumento a San Fernando
REFORMA
Rep.
de
Chile
Honduras
Perú

AVENIDA HIDALGO
Santo Domingo
Secretaría de Educación Pública

Monumento a la Revolución
Pl. de la República
Museo de Artes e Industrias Populares
Palacio de Bellas Artes
Av. 5 de Mayo
TACUBA
Iglesia de la Profesa
Catedral Metropolitana

Monumento a Colón
Torre Latino-americana
AV. MADERO
Zócalo (Plaza de la Constitución)
Palacio Nacional

Centro
V. Carranza
Iglesia de Regina
Museo de la Ciudad de México

Monumento a Cuauhtémoc
La Ciudadela
Biblioteca Nacional
Salvador

ARCOS
DE BELEN
IZAZAGA
20 DE NOVIEMBRE
PINO SUAREZ

CHAPULTEPEC
N. S. de Mercaditas
Iglesia y Fuente Salto del Agua

Arena México
DR. RÍO DE LA LOZA
C. F. SERVANDO TERESA DE MIER

La Sagrada Familia
Esperanza
Plaza Tlaxcoaque

Roma
San Antonio Abad

MELBOURNE, AUSTRALIA

1 0 1 km 2 3 4 5
1 0 miles 1 2 3

144 50'
Broadmeadows
145 00'
Bundoora North

MELBOURNE (MEL)
Campbellfield
Thomastown

Tullamarine
Hume Highway
M80

Keilor North
48
Maroondah Aqueduct
46

Airport West
31
Bundoora Park
27

Keilor
M79
Calder Fwy.
ESSENDON
Pascoe Vale
Kingsbury
Latrobe University
Watsonia

Brimbank Park
M80
Niddrie
Essendon
Preston
Heidelberg West

Sunshine
Avondale Heights
Moonee Ponds
Coburg
40
Thornbury
Heidelberg Heights

Ascot Vale
Brunswick
Northcote
Ivanhoe
46

Braybrook
Maidstone
Moonee Valley Racecourse
31
Eastern Yarra Bend Park
83
Freeway

Footscray
Flemington Racecourse
M79
Royal Park Zoo
29
Yarra R.
Bulleen Pk.
83
Balwyn North

Tottenham
8
Carlton University of Melbourne
Fitzroy Gdns.
Kew
34
Canterbury

Yarraville
Princes Hwy
83
Queen Victoria Mkt.
Royal Exhib. Bldg.
MELBOURNE
Balwyn

West Gate Freeway
Telstra Dome
Rialto Tower
M.C.G.
Richmond

Spotswood
Southgate Plaza
M1
Kings Domain
Camberwell

Newport
Fishermans Bend
Victoria L.T.A. Courts
M1

Altona
Altona Sports Park
Williamstown
Port Melbourne
Middle Park
Fawkner Park
Toorak
Glen Iris
Ashburton

Jawbone Reserve & Marine Sanctuary
Hobsons Bay
South Yarra
Albert Park
Armadale
Malvern

Devonport Tasmania
St. Kilda
26
East Malvern
M1

Port Phillip Bay
Caulfield
16

Melbourne
Elsternwick
Caulfield Racecourse

East from Greenwich
Elwood
Glenhuntly
Carnegie

Brighton
Ormond
Oakleigh

MILAN, ITALY

1 0 1 km 2 3 4 5
1 0 miles 1 2 3

Coronno
Cesate
Limbiate
Varedo
Muggiò
Autodromo
Concorezzo

Pertusella
Garbagnate Milanese
527
Nova Milanese
36
Monza

Lainate
Palazzolo
Incirano
Dugnano
San Fruttuoso
527

TO MILAN MALPENSA (MXP)
233
Senago
Amata
Cassina Nuova
Paderno
Cinisello Balsamo
E66
A4

Valera
Arese
Ospiate
Cusano Milanino
Brughério

Passirana
Terrazzano
Bollate
San Maurizio al Lambro
Cologno Monzese

Rho
Cormano
Bresso
A51

Novate Milanese
Bruzzano
Affori
Parco Regionale
Sesto San Giovanni
Vimodrone

Cornaredo
Pero
Musocco
Greco
Precotto
Pioltello

Vighignolo
Figino
Boldinasco
Crescenzago
Milano Due
Segrate

Séttimo Milanese
Trenno
Stadio San Siro
Staz. Centrale
Loreto
Parco Lambro
Martesana

Rho
San Siro
Fiera Camp.
Brera
La Scala
Lambrate
Ortica
Milano San Felice

Monzoro
Quinto Romano
Castello Sforzesco
Duomo
Città degli Studi
Idroscalo

Cesano Boscone
Baggio
Basilica di Sant'Ambrogio
Calvairate
MILAN LINATE (LIN)
San Bóvio

Assiano
Cusago
Moriviole
San Cristóforo
Gamboléita
Mezzate

Quartiere Zingone
Vigentino
A7
Peschiera Borromeo

Córsico
Romano Banco
Triulzo
Metanópoli
San Donato Milanese

Trezzano sul Naviglio
Assago
Chiaravalle Milanese
Gratosóglio
412
San Giuliano Milanese

Gaggiano
Quinto de Stampi
Poasco
Sesto Ulteriano
Mediglia

San Novo
Mirasole
Zivido
9

San Pietro Cúsico
Gudo Gamb.
Pontesesto
Ópera
San Brera

Zibido San Giacomo
Tolcinasco
Rozzano
Fizzonasco
Locate di Triulzi
Zúnico
A1
E35
Mezzano
Melegnano

9 10' East from Greenwich

95 Federal route numbers

COPYRIGHT PHILIP'S

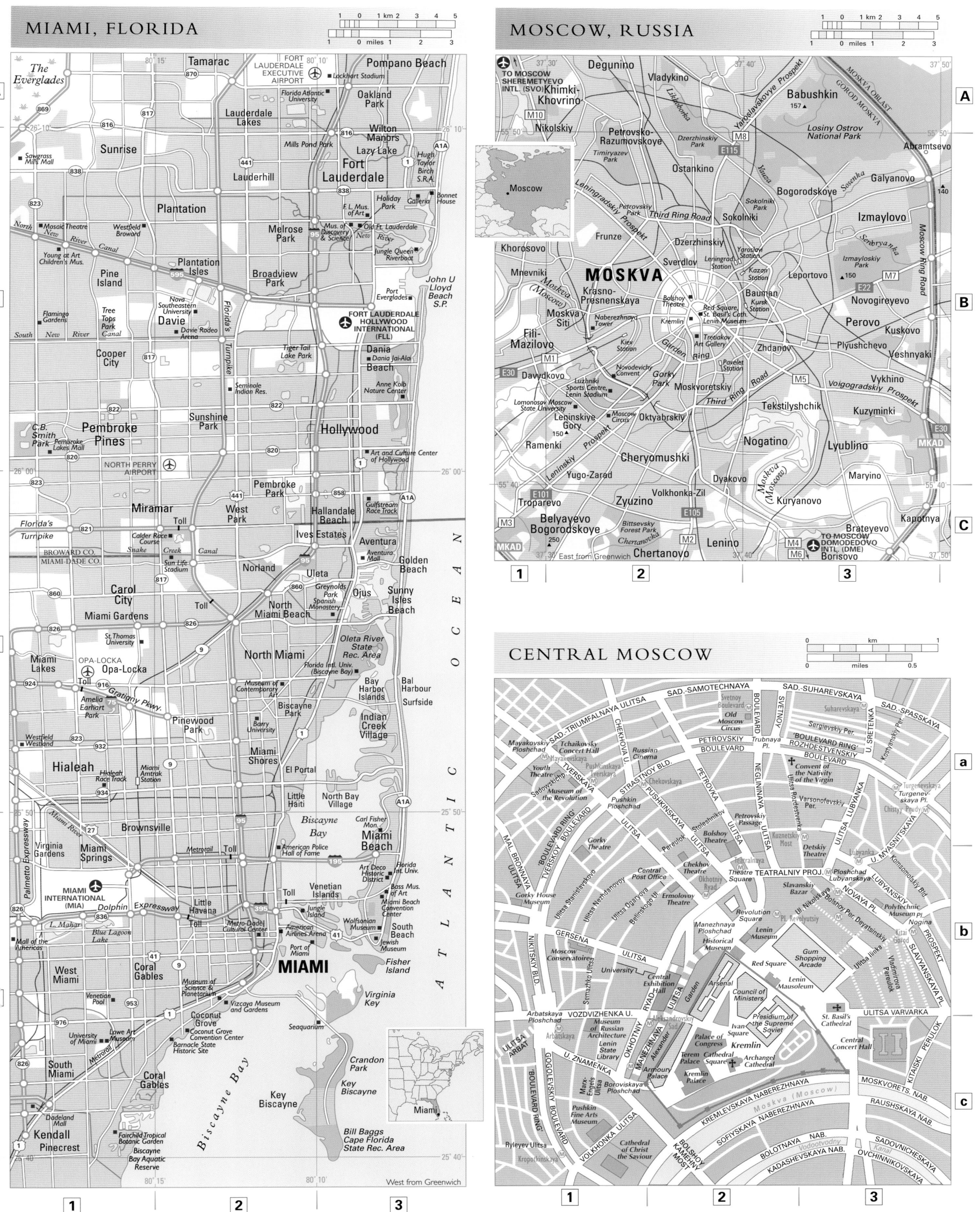

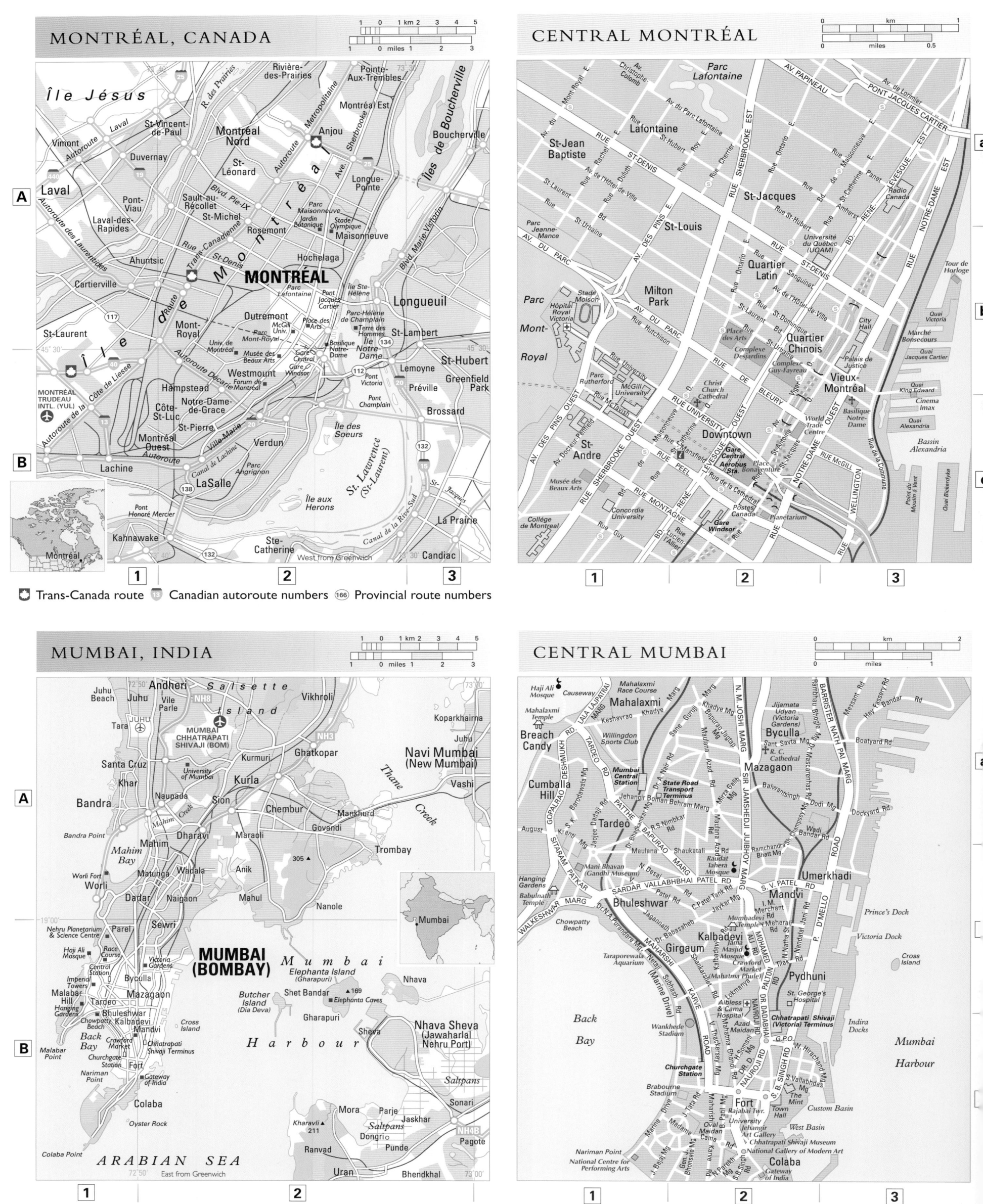

MUNICH, GERMANY

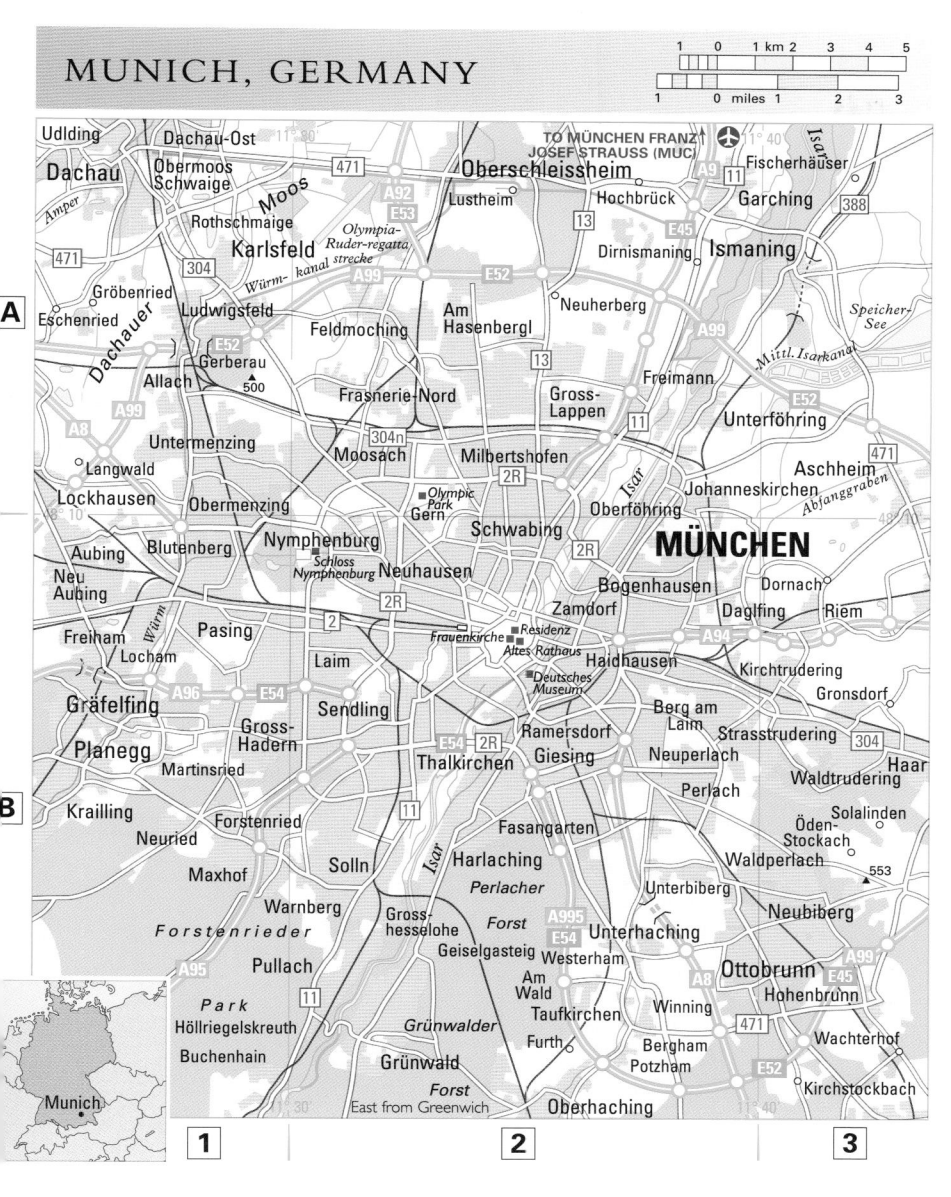

CENTRAL MUNICH

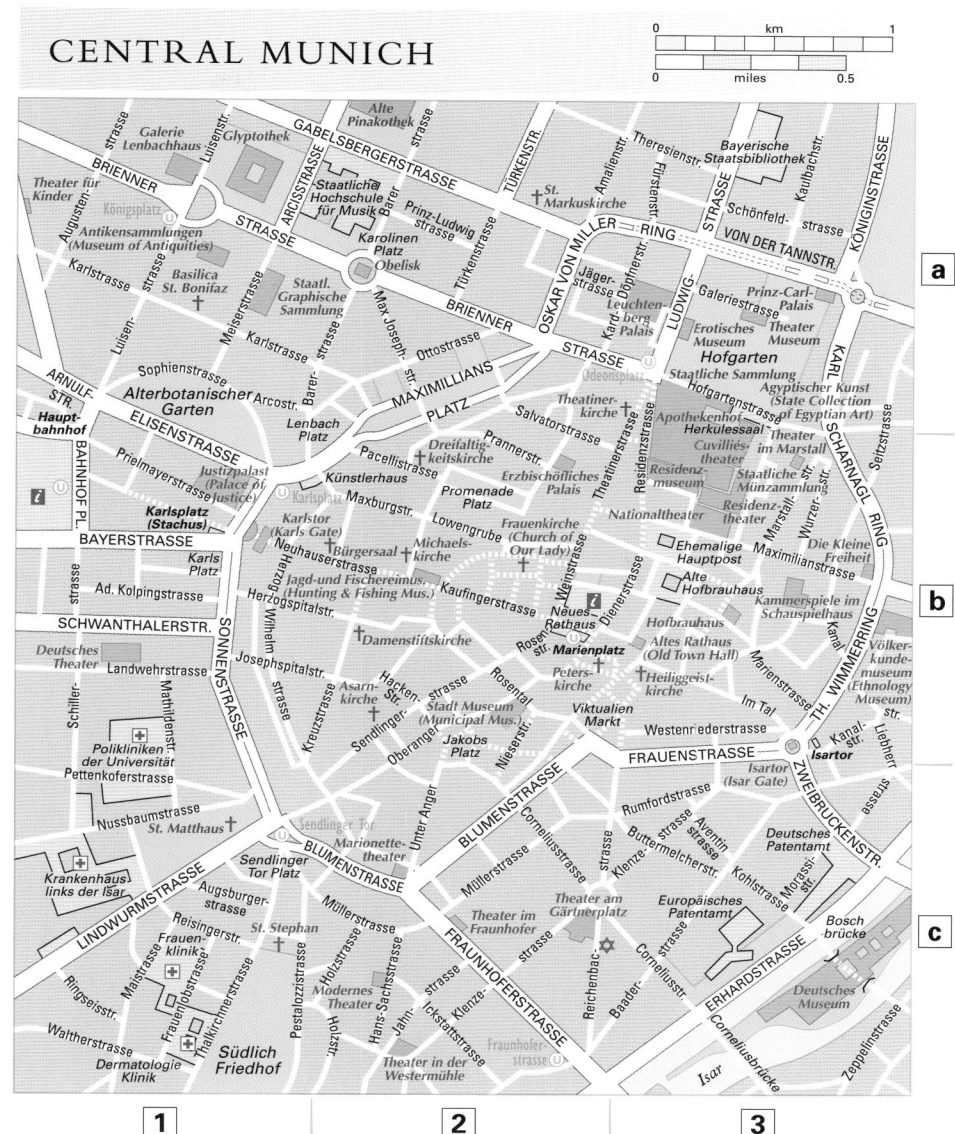

NEW ORLEANS, LOUISIANA

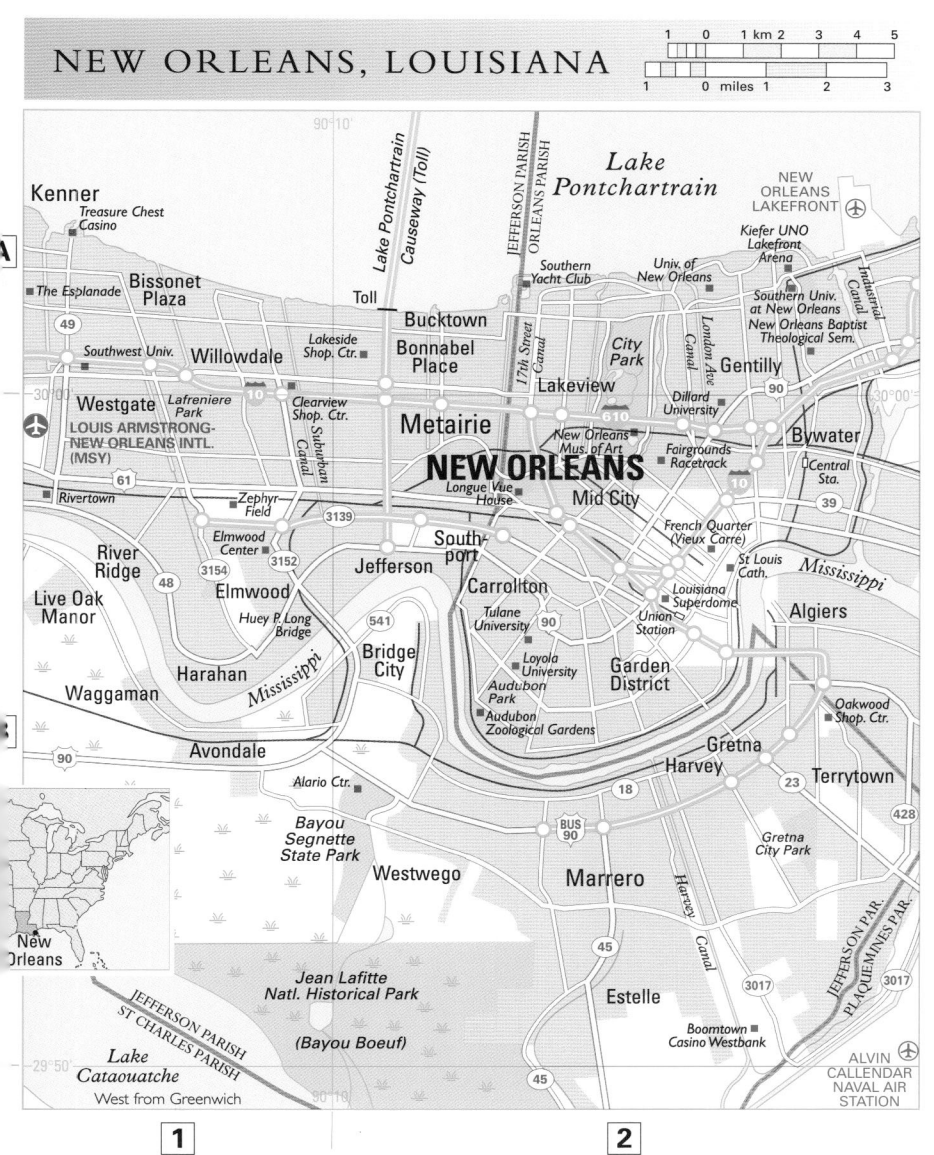

CENTRAL NEW ORLEANS

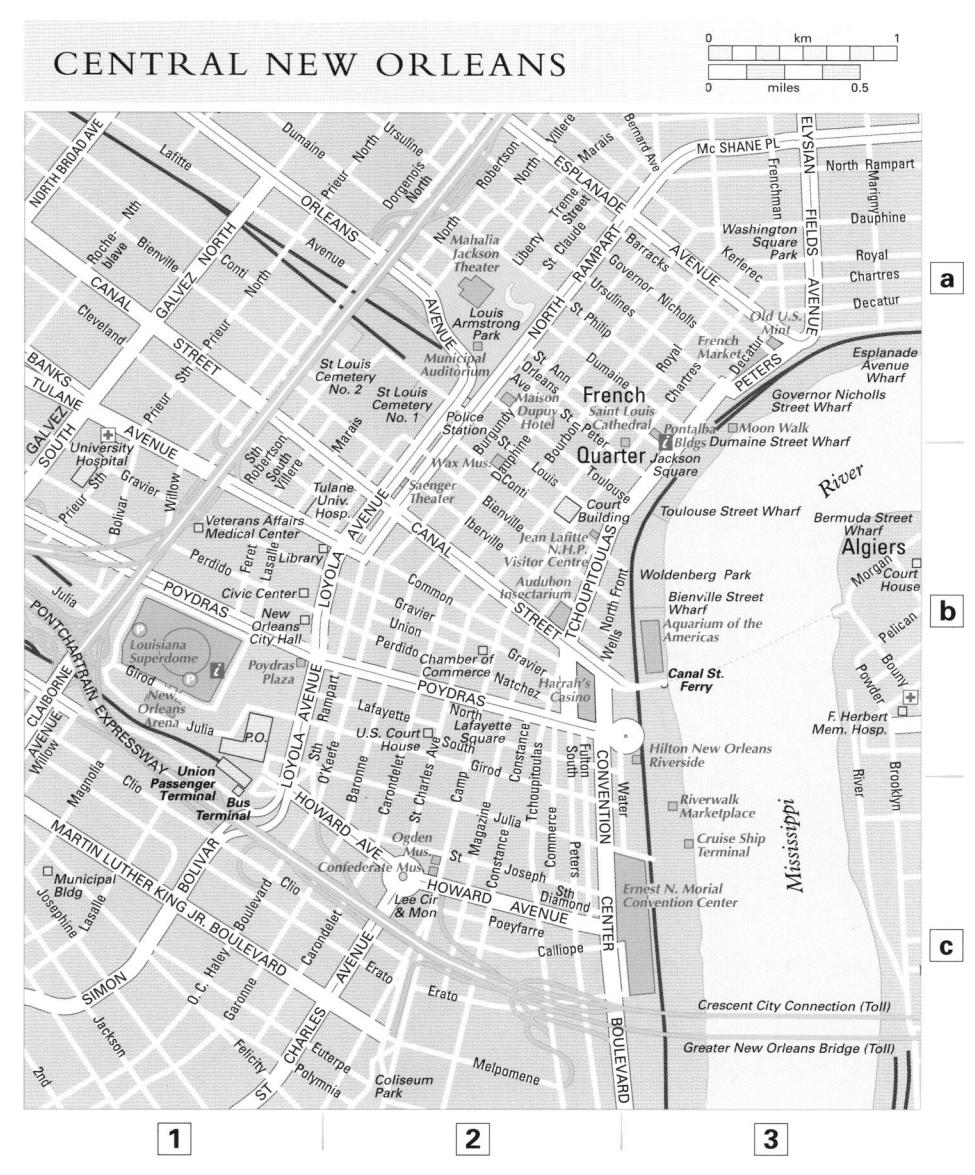

4 Interstate route numbers   17 U.S. route numbers   417 State route numbers

NEW YORK, NEW YORK

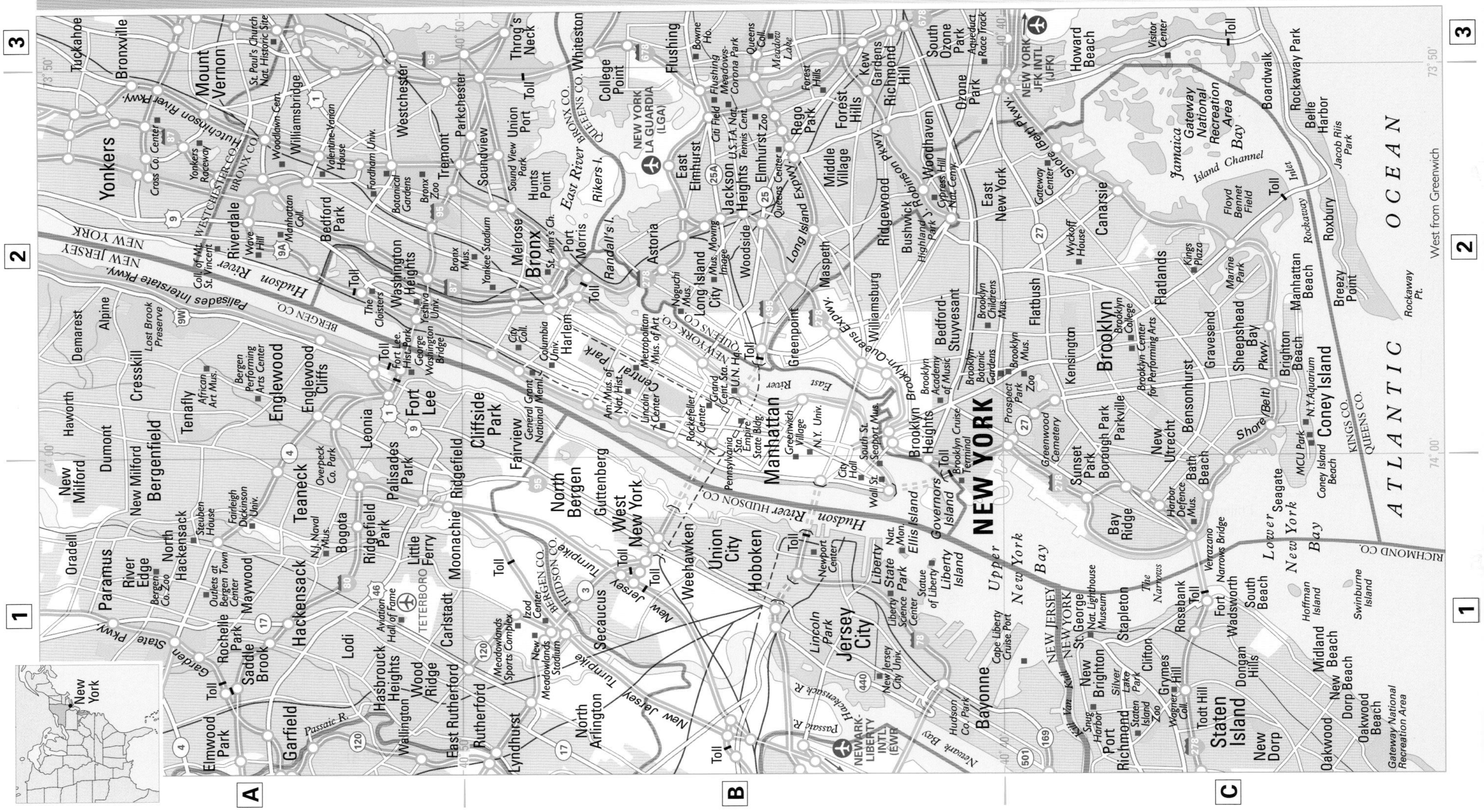

1 0 1 km 2 3 4 5
1 0 miles 1 2 3

3 | 2 | 1

A | B | C

ATLANTIC OCEAN

NEW YORK

Yonkers, Mount Vernon, Bronxville, Tuckahoe, Westchester, Parkchester, Throg's Neck, Whitestone, College Point, Flushing, Bronx, Queens, Long Island City, Astoria, Woodside, Elmhurst, Jackson Heights, Rego Park, Forest Hills, Kew Gardens, Richmond Hill, South Ozone Park, Howard Beach, Rockaway Park, Belle Harbor, Breezy Point

Englewood, Englewood Cliffs, Fort Lee, Leonia, Palisades Park, Fairview, Cliffside Park, Ridgefield, North Bergen, West New York, Guttenberg, Weehawken, Union City, Hoboken, Jersey City, Bayonne

Washington Heights, Harlem, Central Park, Manhattan, Brooklyn Heights, Greenpoint, Williamsburg, Bushwick, Bedford-Stuyvesant, Brooklyn, Flatbush, Flatlands, Canarsie, Bensonhurst, Gravesend, Sheepshead Bay, Brighton Beach, Coney Island, Manhattan Beach

Paramus, Hackensack, Teaneck, Bergenfield, Tenafly, New Milford, Oradell, Elmwood Park, Garfield, Lodi, Lyndhurst, Rutherford, Secaucus, Kearny, Newark

Staten Island, New Brighton, Port Richmond, New Dorp, Oakwood, Midland Beach, Tottenville

NEWARK LIBERTY INTL (EWR), NEW YORK JFK INTL (JFK), NEW YORK LA GUARDIA (LGA)

West from Greenwich 74°00' 73°50'

CENTRAL NEW YORK

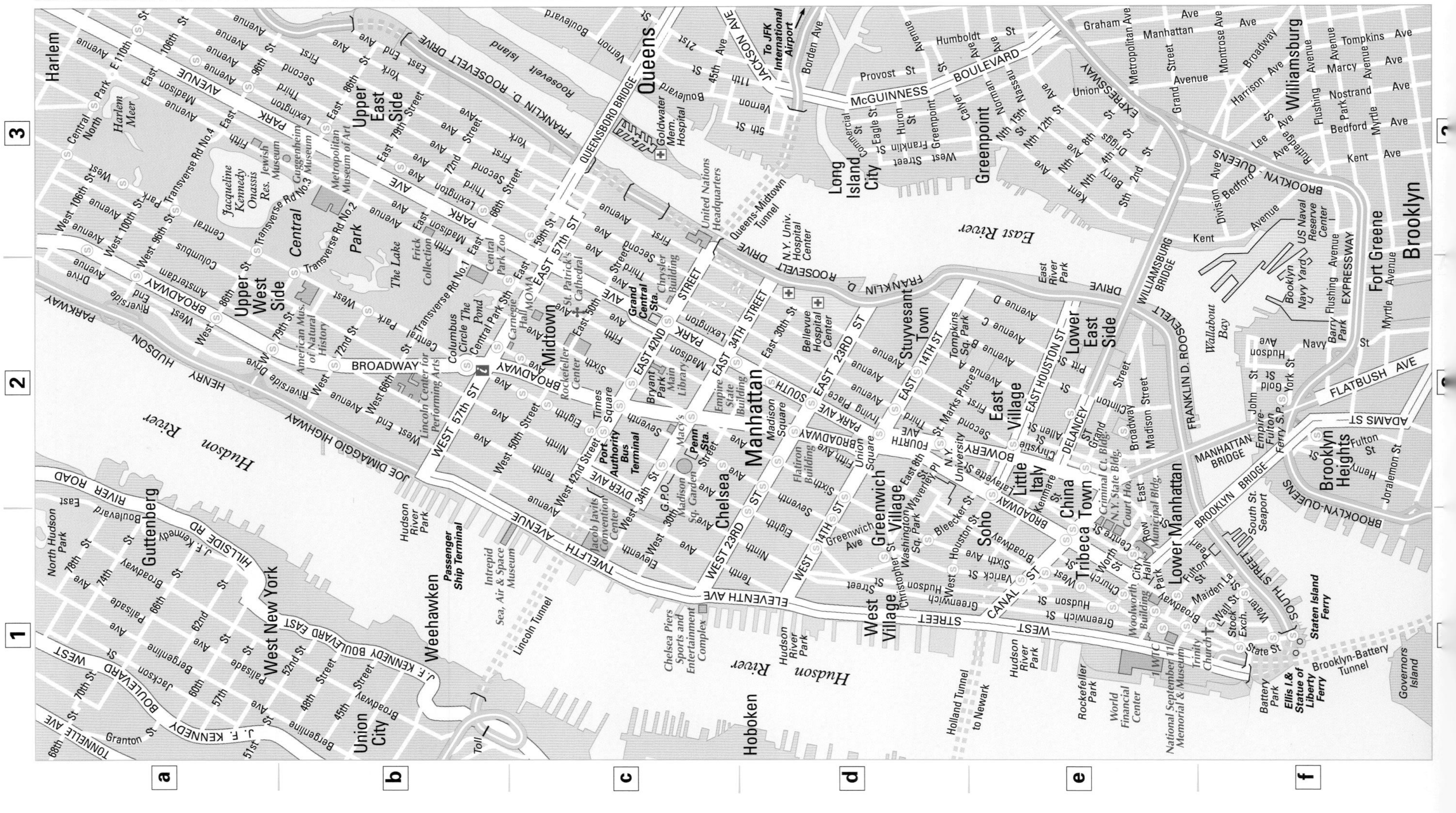

0 1 km 2
0 miles 1

3 | 2 | 1

a | b | c | d | e | f

Harlem, Upper East Side, Upper West Side, Central Park, Midtown, Manhattan, Chelsea, Greenwich Village, West Village, East Village, Lower East Side, Stuyvesant Town, Little Italy, Chinatown, Soho, Tribeca, Lower Manhattan

Queens, Long Island City, Greenpoint, Williamsburg, Brooklyn, Fort Greene, Brooklyn Heights

Hudson River, East River, Hoboken, Weehawken, West New York, Union City, North Hudson Park, Guttenberg

Lincoln Center for the Performing Arts, Columbus Circle, Carnegie Hall, MoMA, Rockefeller Center, St Patrick's Cathedral, Grand Central Sta., Chrysler Building, United Nations Headquarters, New York Public Library, Bryant Park, Times Square, Empire State Building, Madison Square Garden, Penn Sta., Port Authority Bus Terminal, Jacob Javits Convention Center, Chelsea Piers, Flatiron Building, Union Square, Washington Square, Bowery, Cooper Union, Battery Park, World Financial Center, National September 11 Memorial & Museum, Trinity Church, Stock Exchange, South St. Seaport, Staten Island Ferry, Ellis I. & Statue of Liberty Ferry, Brooklyn-Battery Tunnel, Holland Tunnel, Lincoln Tunnel, Queens-Midtown Tunnel, Brooklyn Bridge, Manhattan Bridge, Williamsburg Bridge, Queensboro Bridge

ORLANDO, FLORIDA

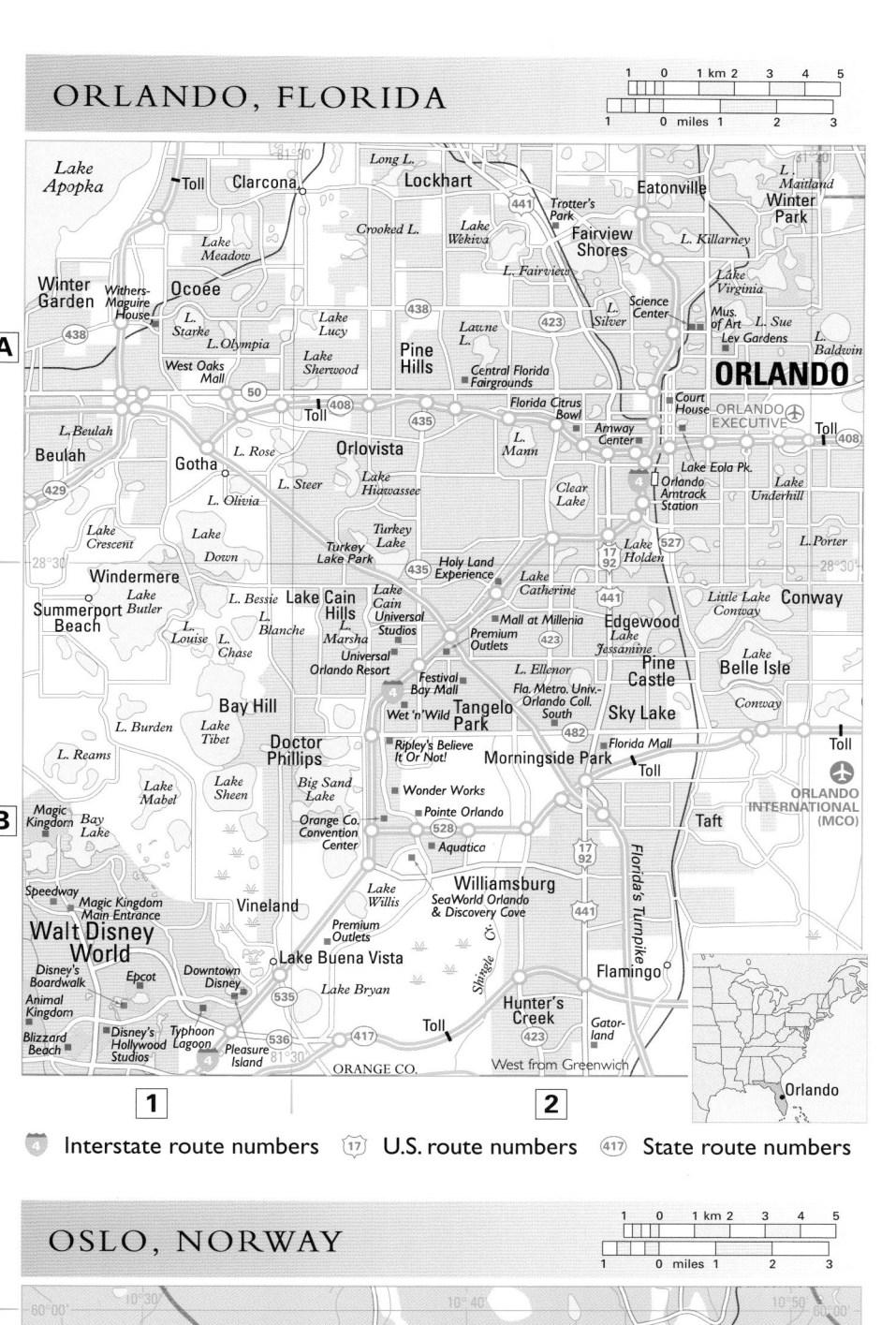

OSAKA, JAPAN

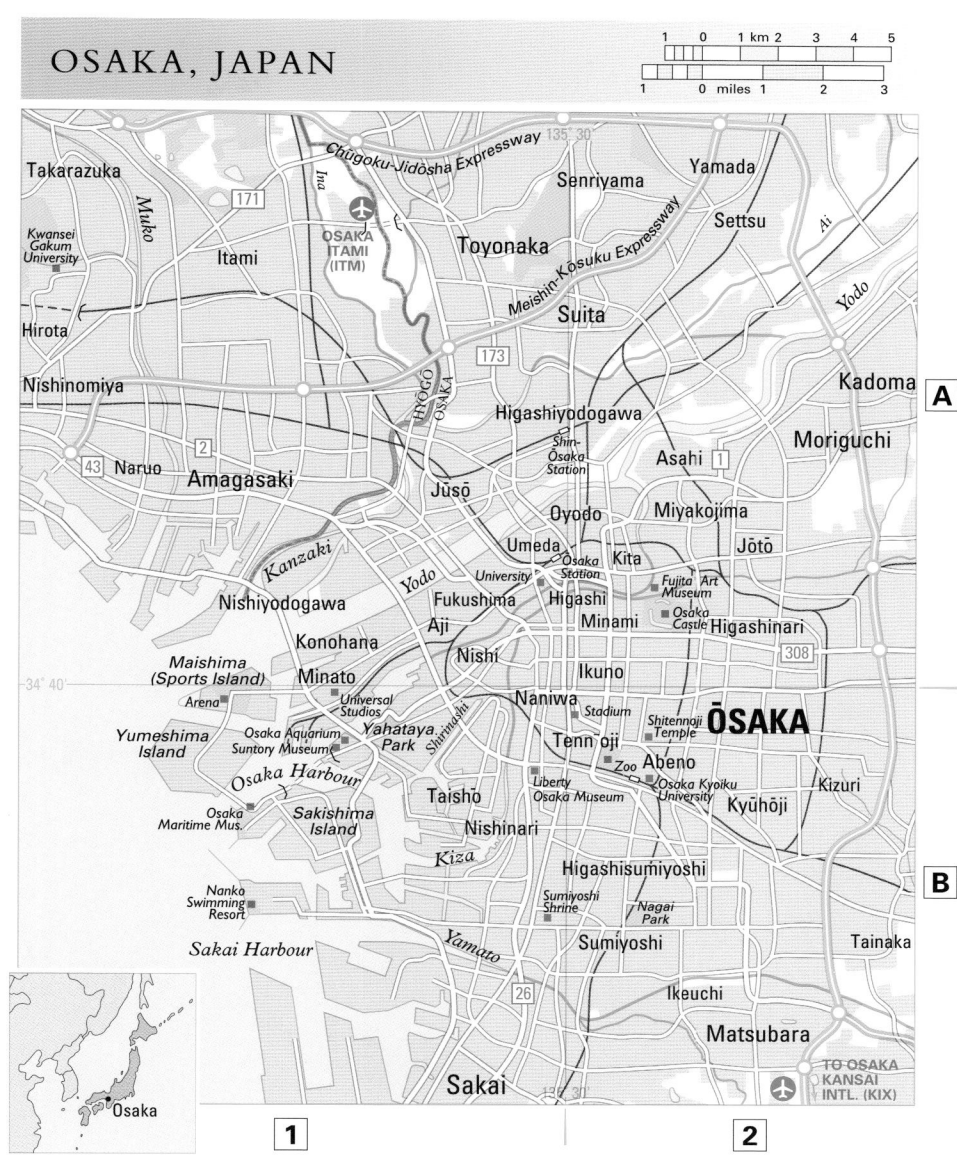

OSLO, NORWAY

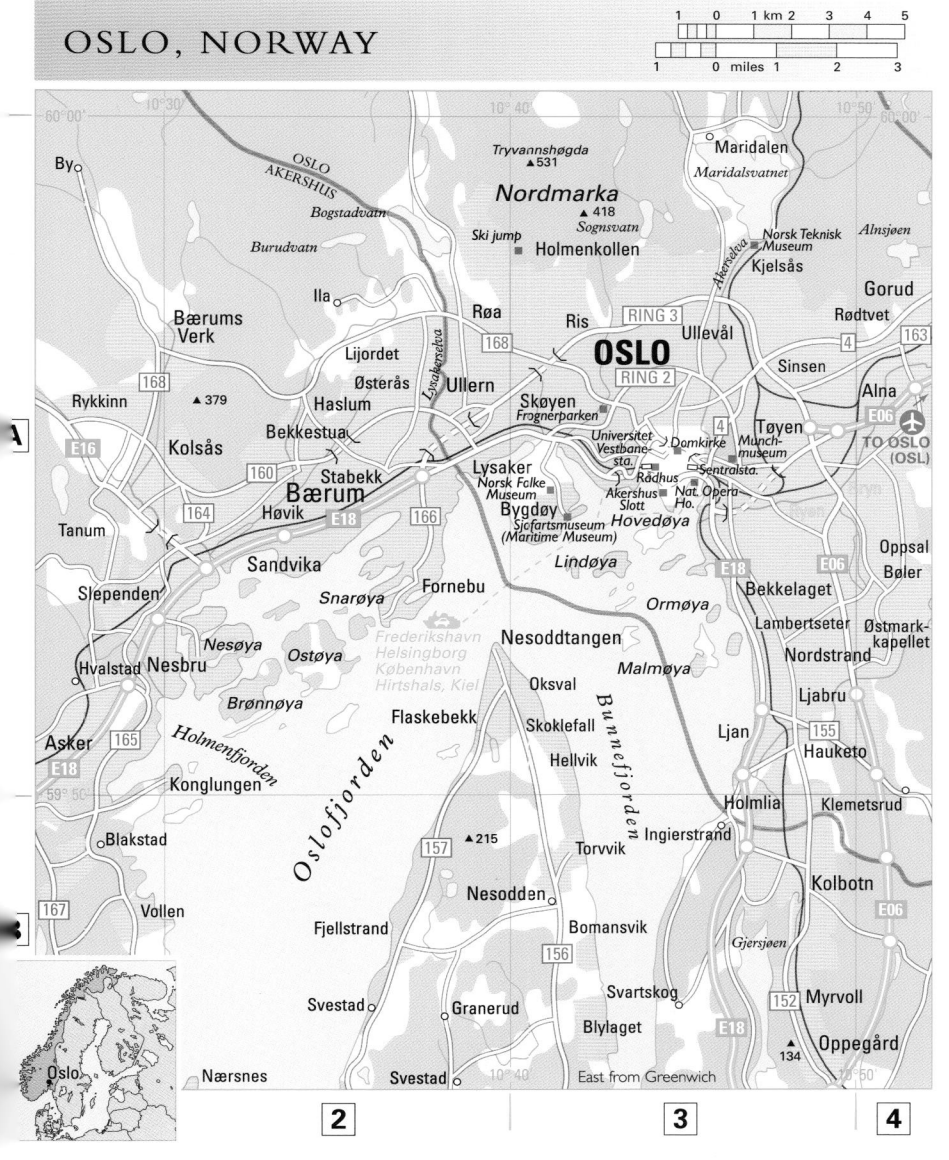

CENTRAL OSLO

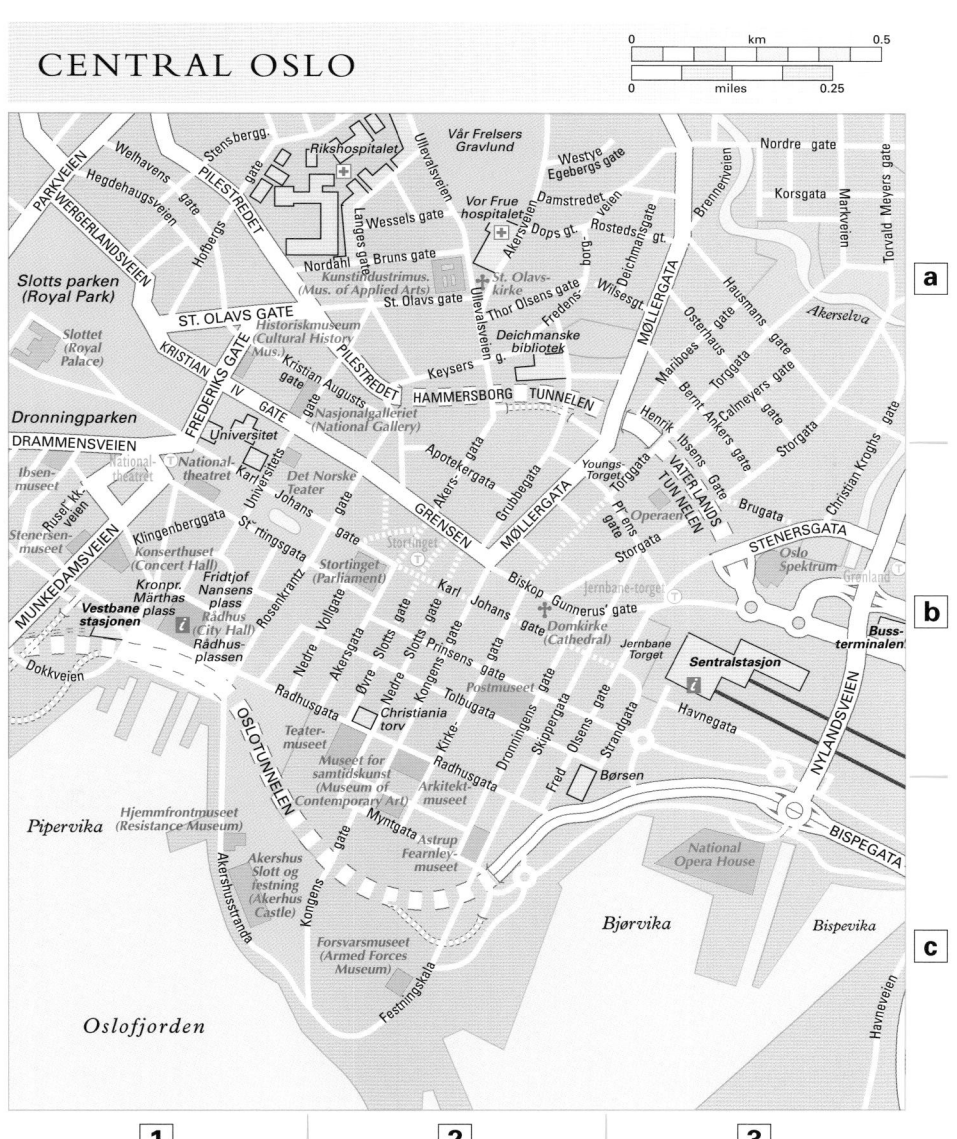

PARIS, FRANCE

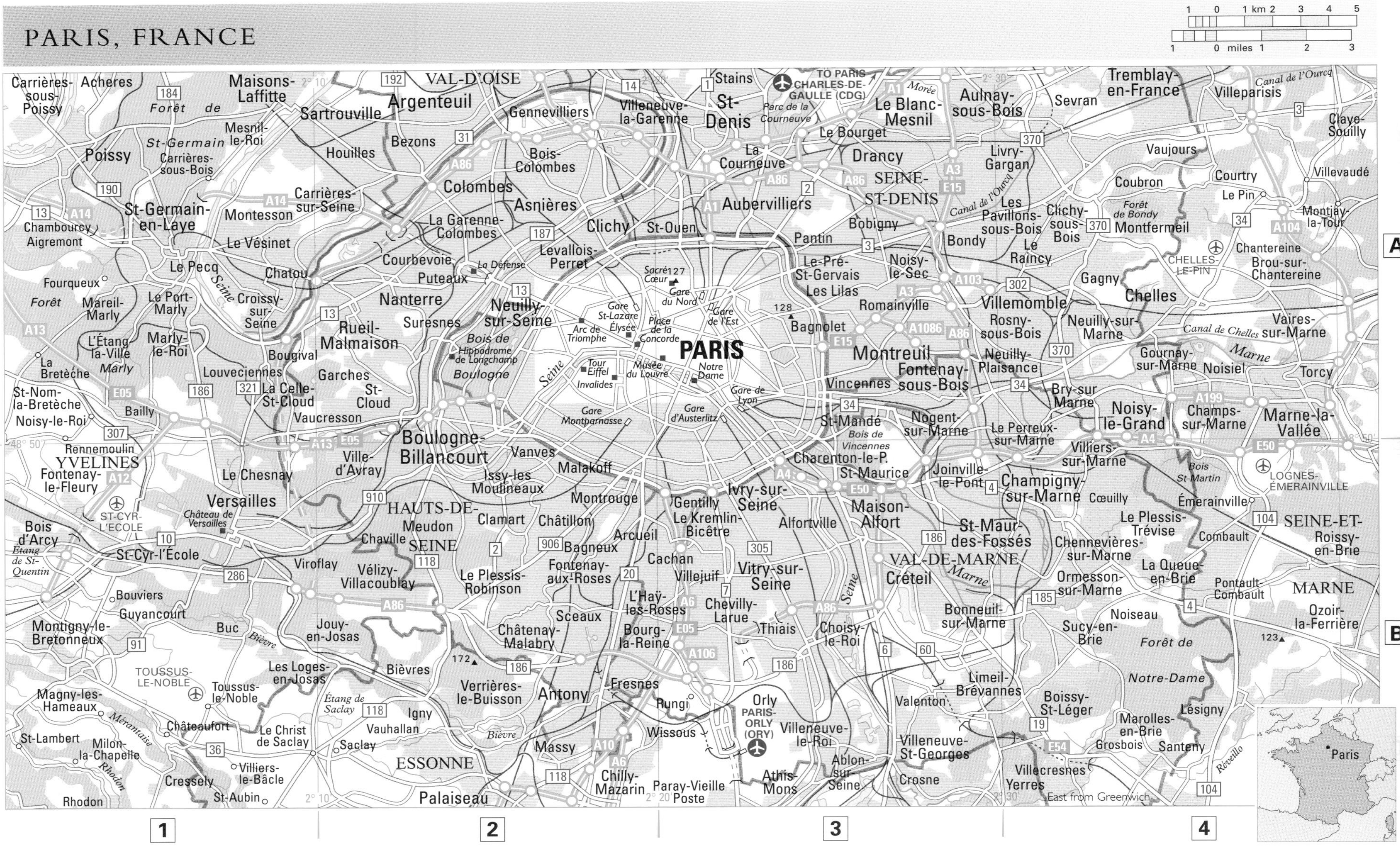

CENTRAL PARIS

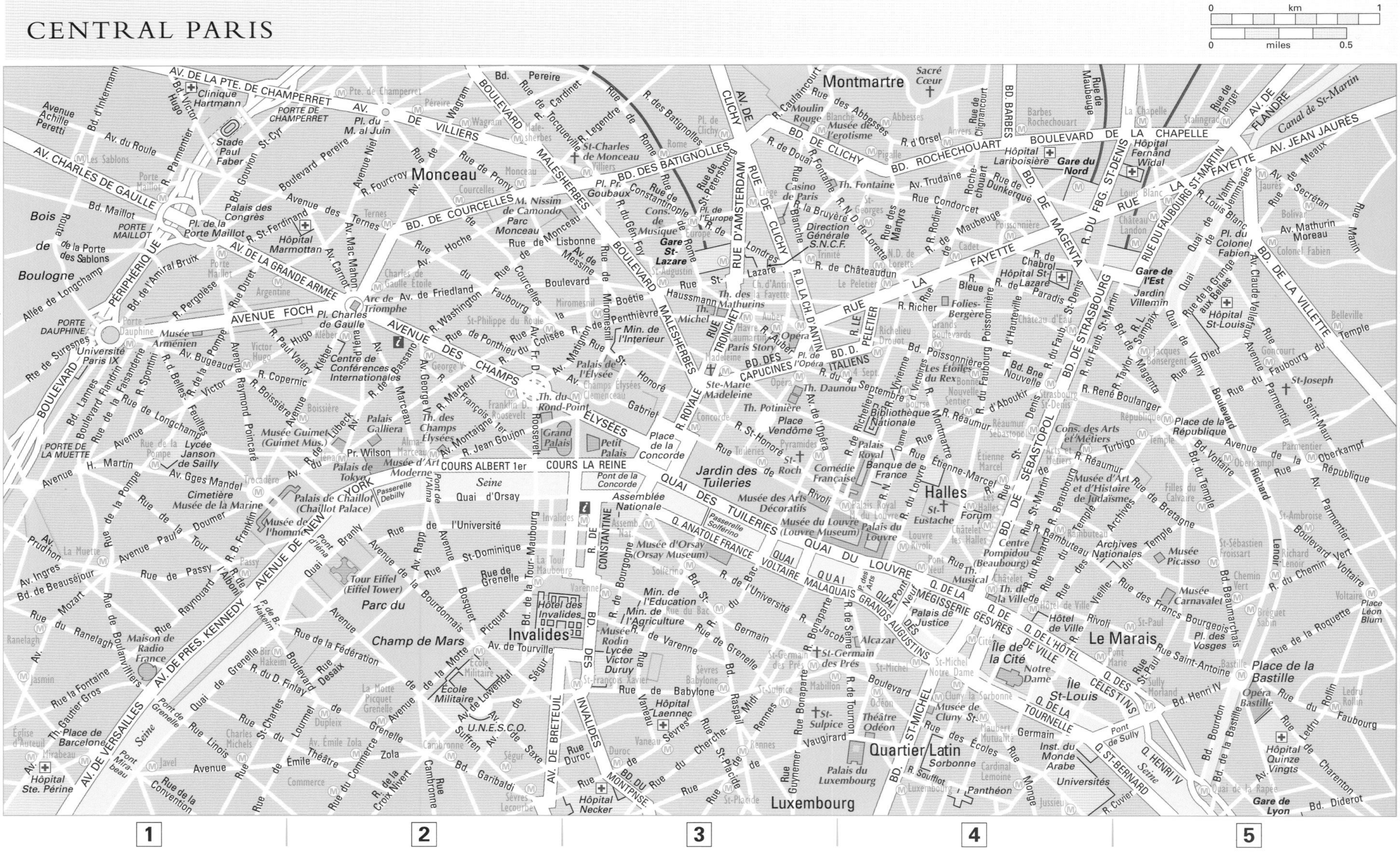

PRAGUE, CZECH REPUBLIC

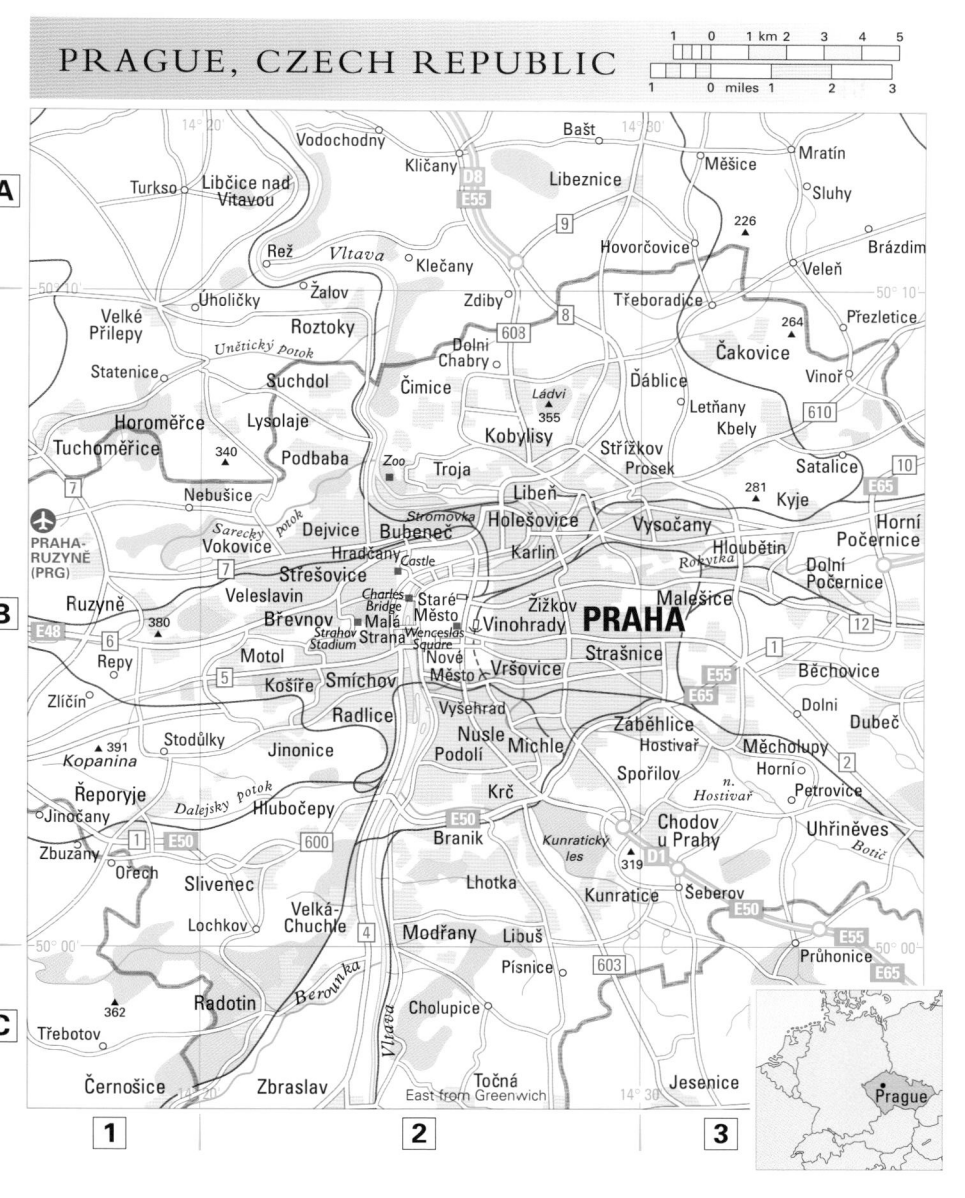

CENTRAL PRAGUE

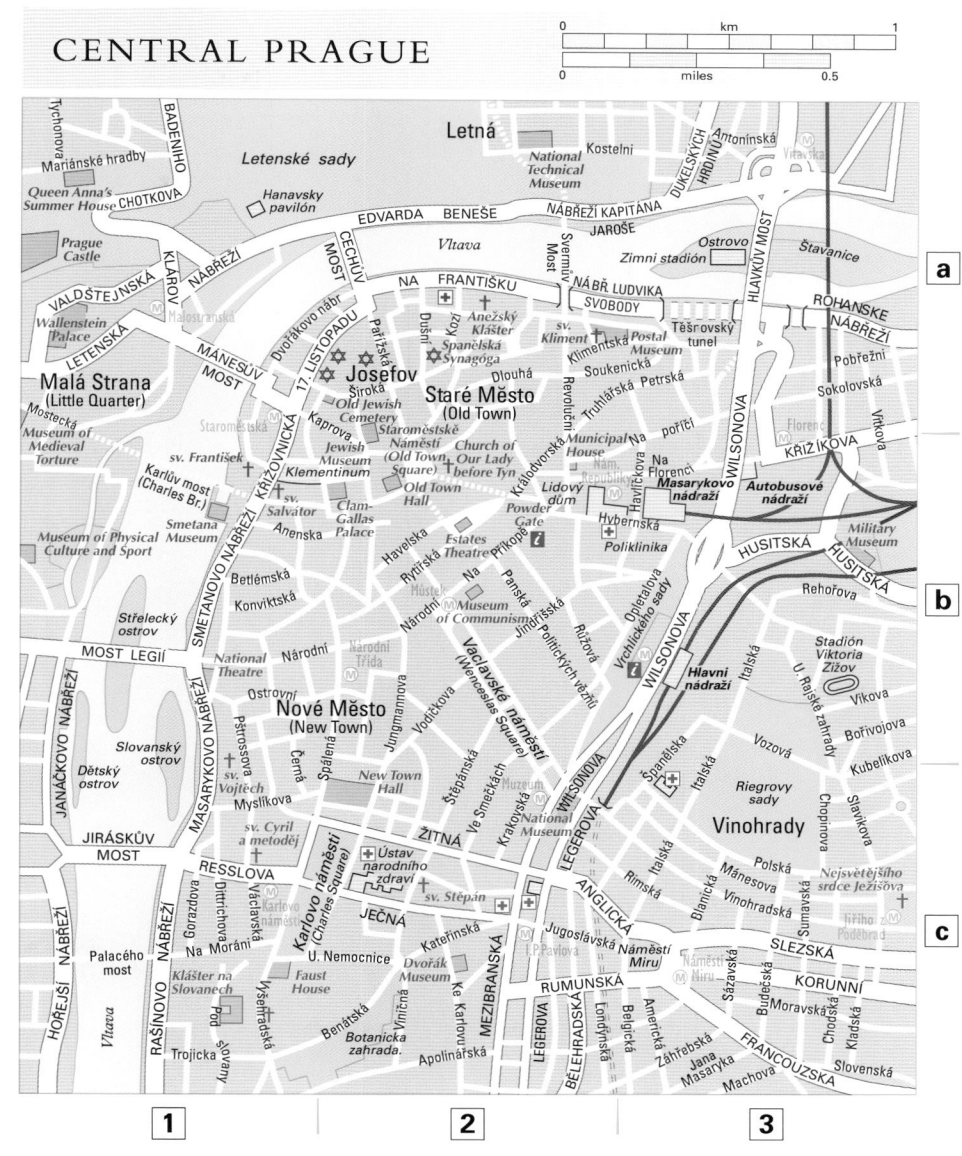

RIO DE JANEIRO, BRAZIL

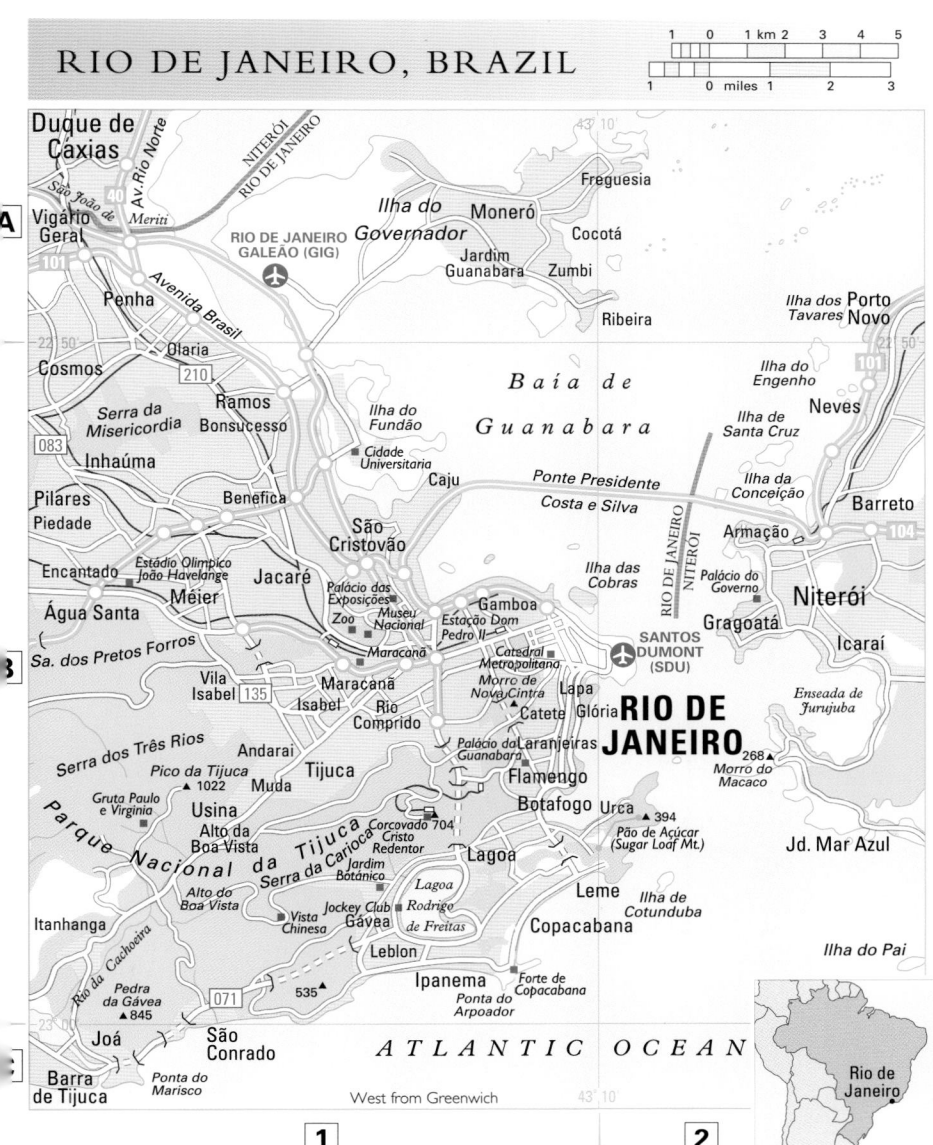

CENTRAL RIO DE JANEIRO

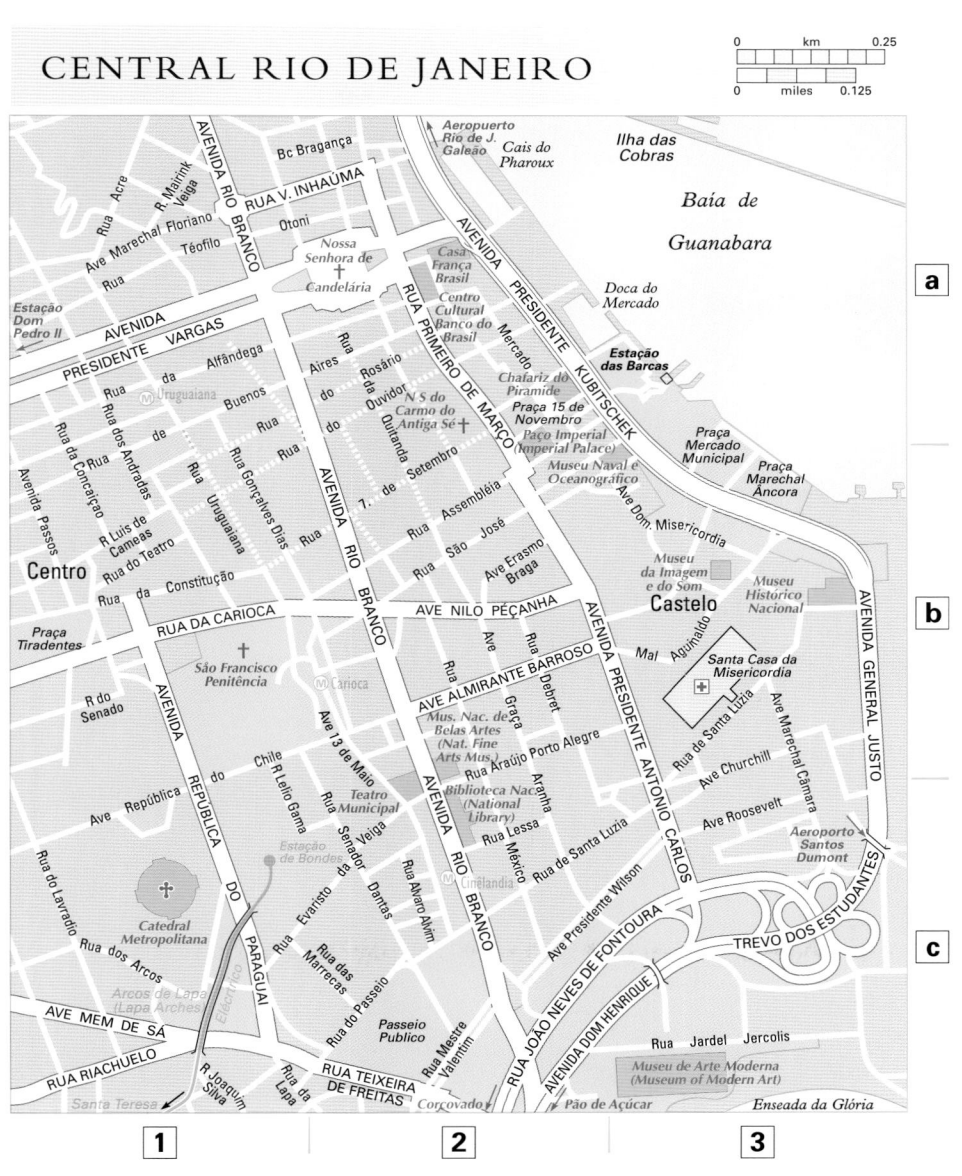

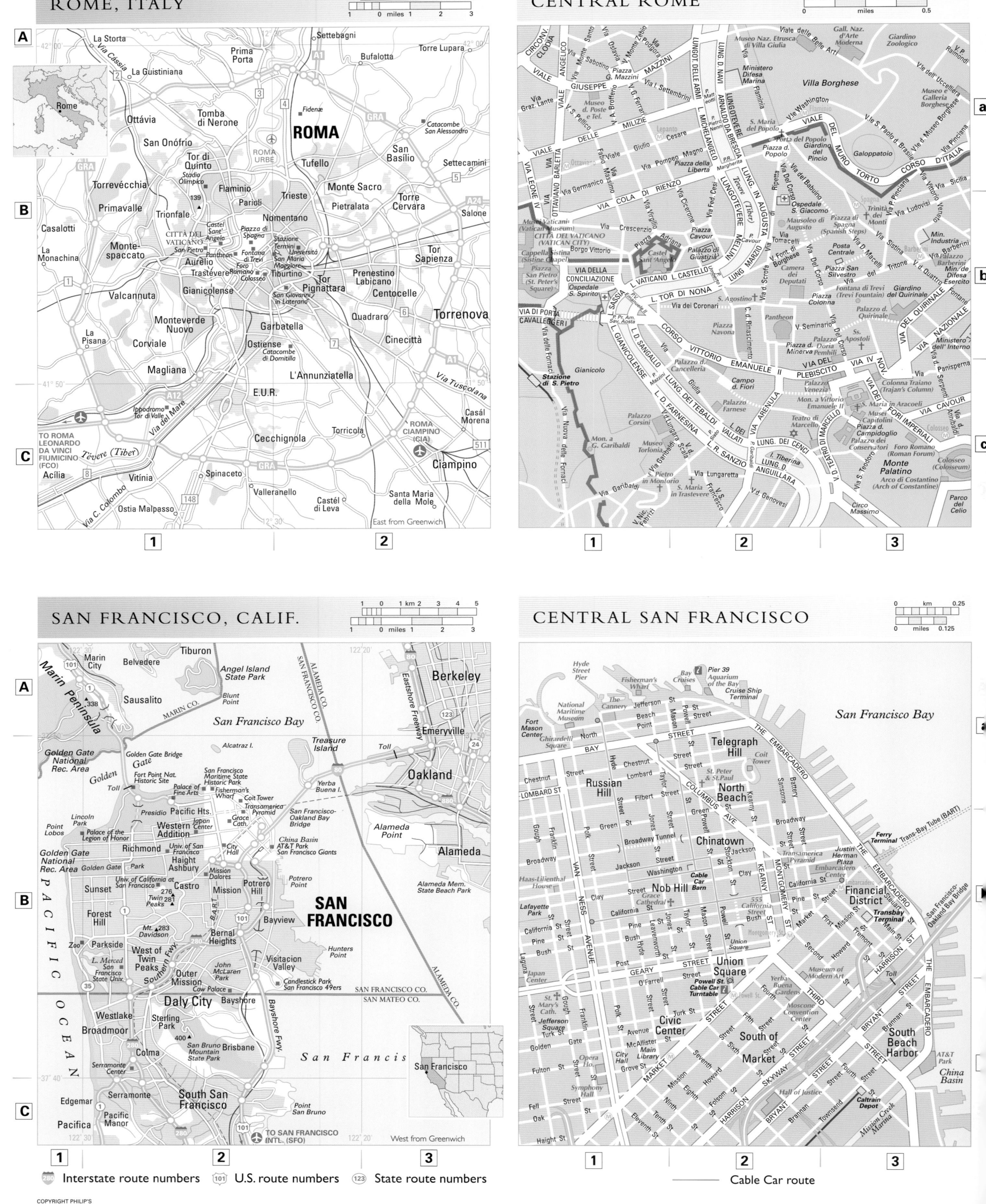

ROME, ITALY

CENTRAL ROME

SAN FRANCISCO, CALIF.

CENTRAL SAN FRANCISCO

▬▬ Interstate route numbers   ▬▬ U.S. route numbers   ▬▬ State route numbers

—— Cable Car route

COPYRIGHT PHILIP'S

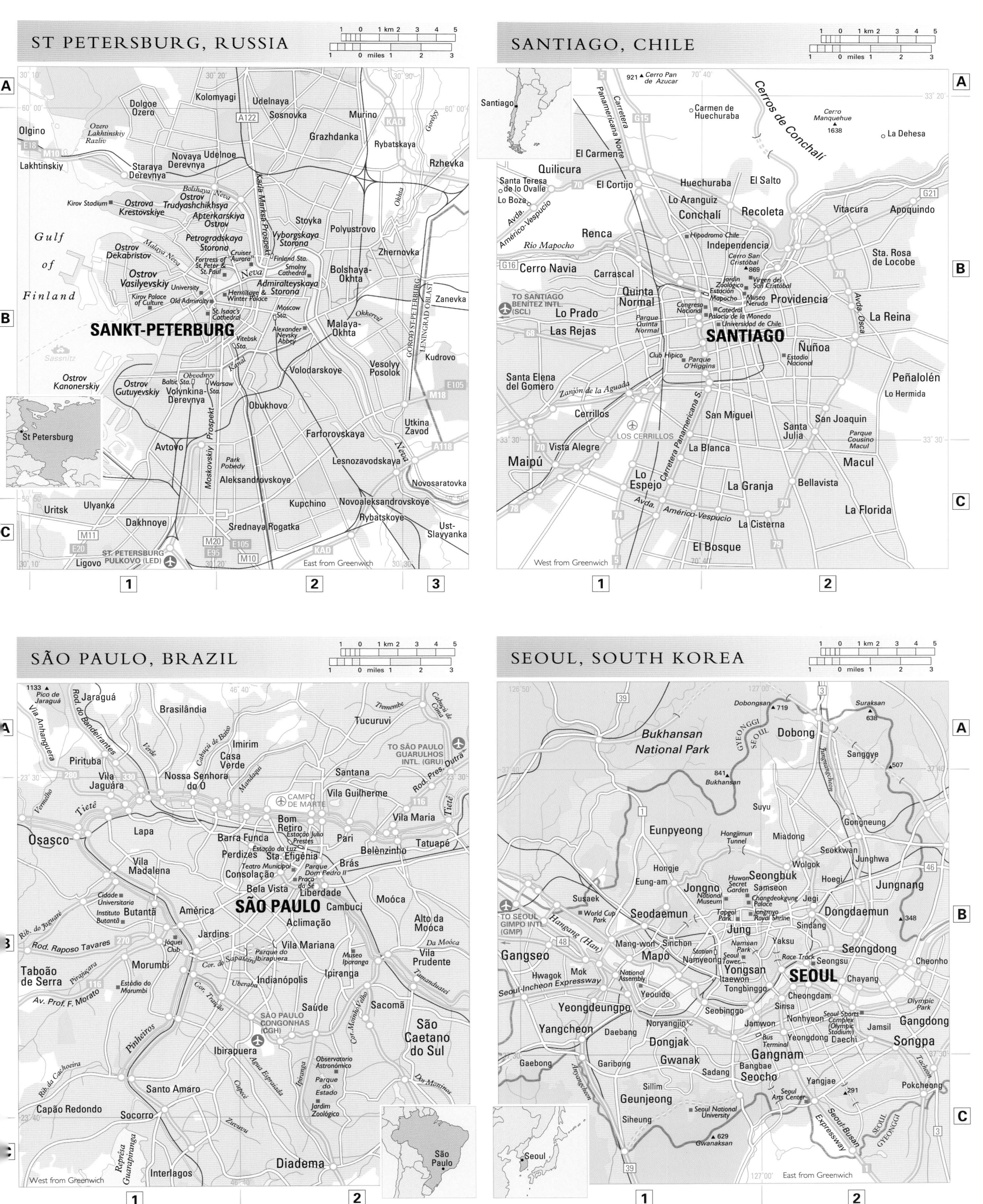

ST PETERSBURG, RUSSIA

SANTIAGO, CHILE

SÃO PAULO, BRAZIL

SEOUL, SOUTH KOREA

COPYRIGHT PHILIP'S

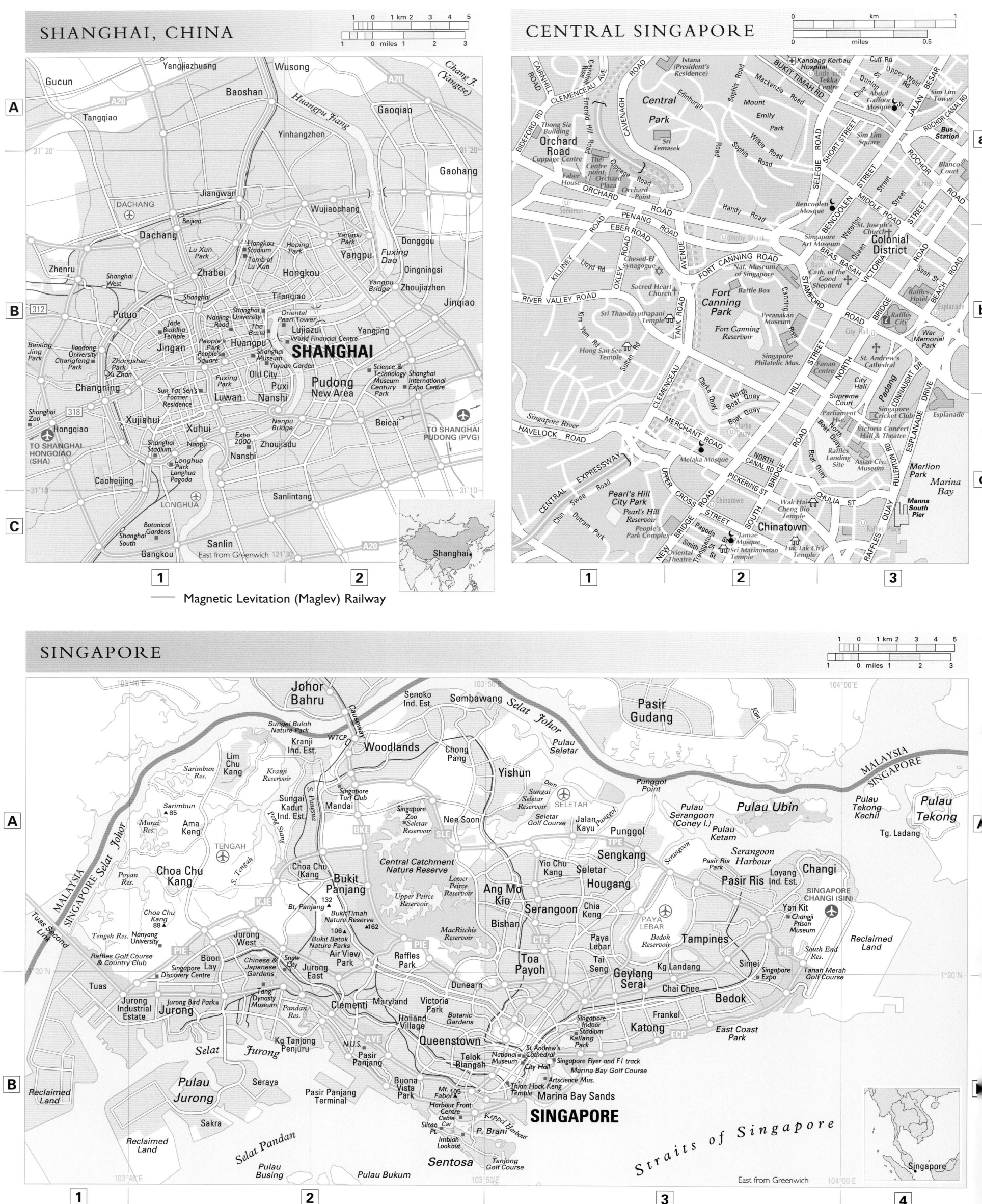

STOCKHOLM, SWEDEN

CENTRAL STOCKHOLM

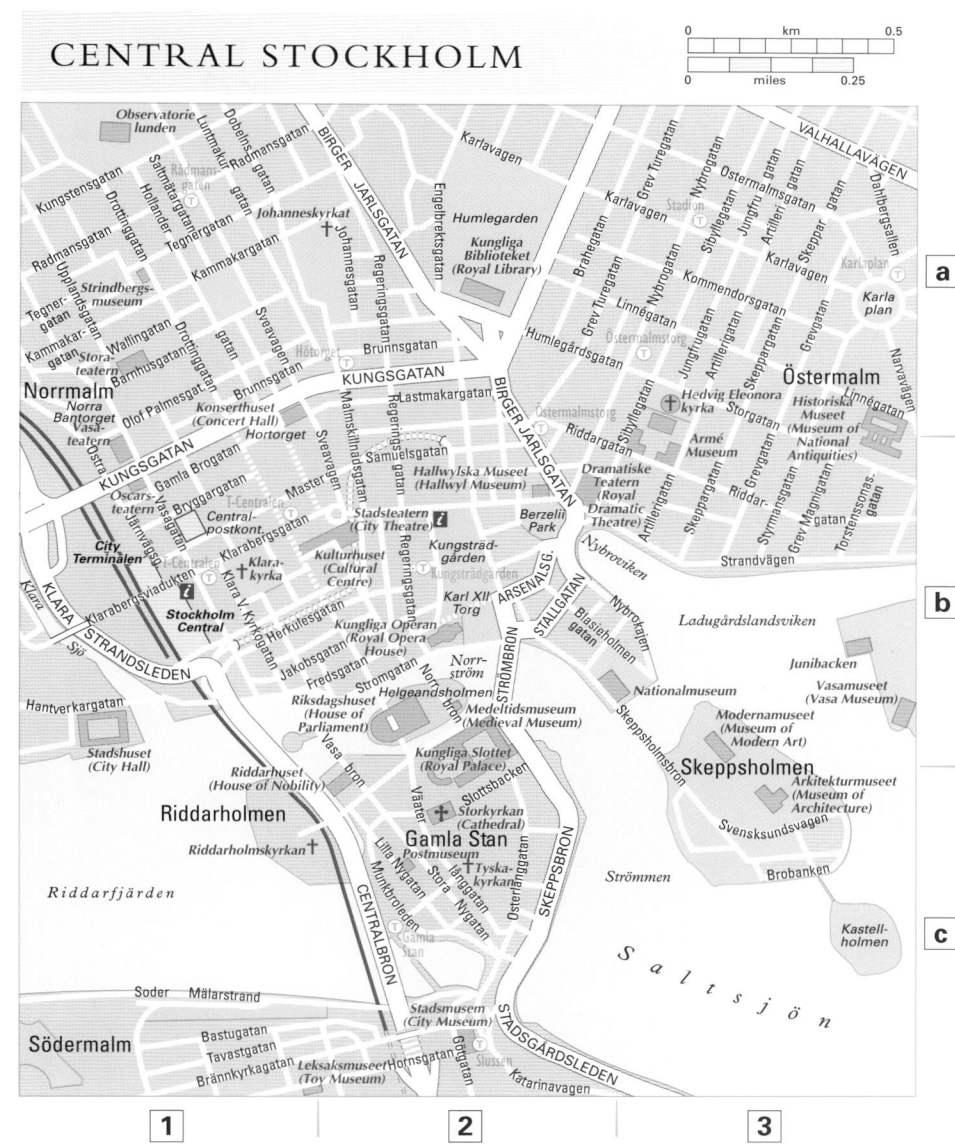

SYDNEY, AUSTRALIA

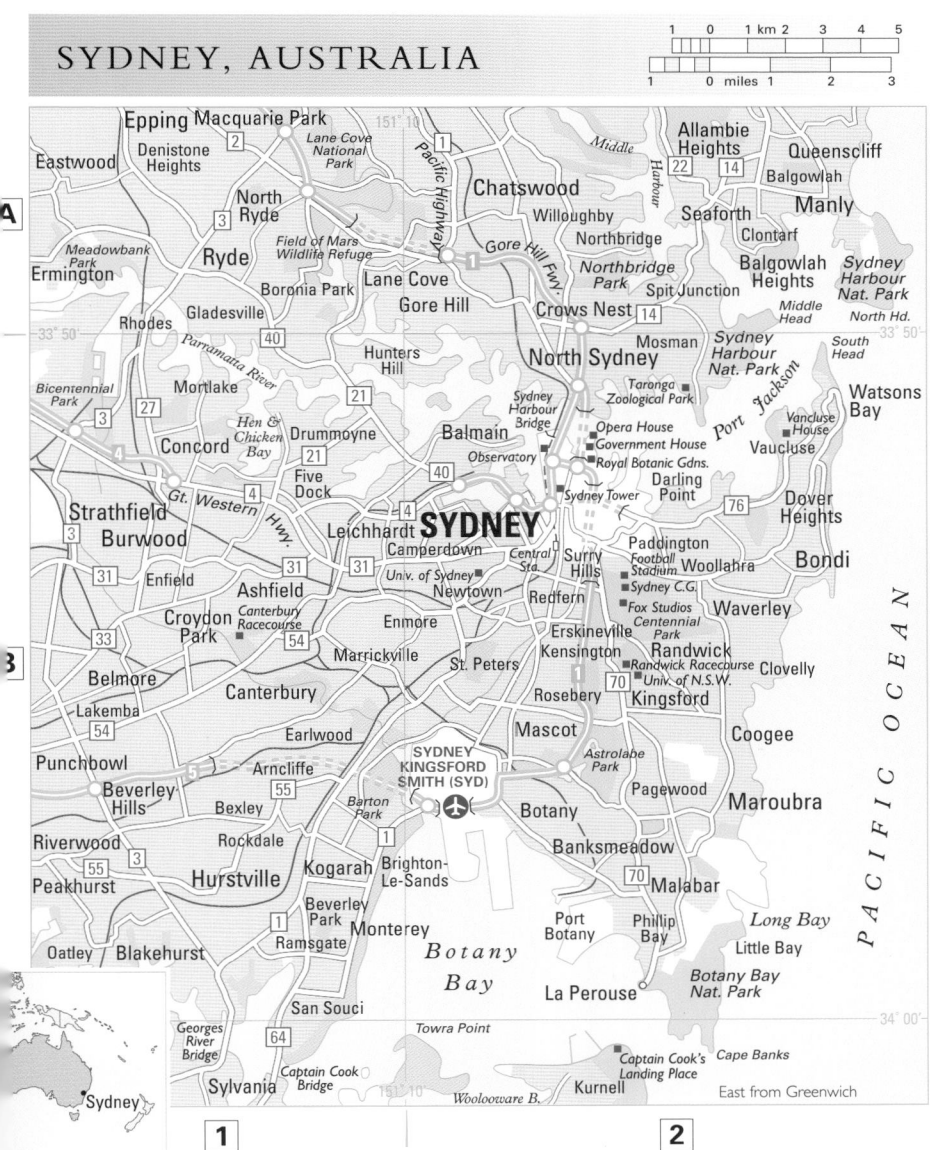

CENTRAL SYDNEY

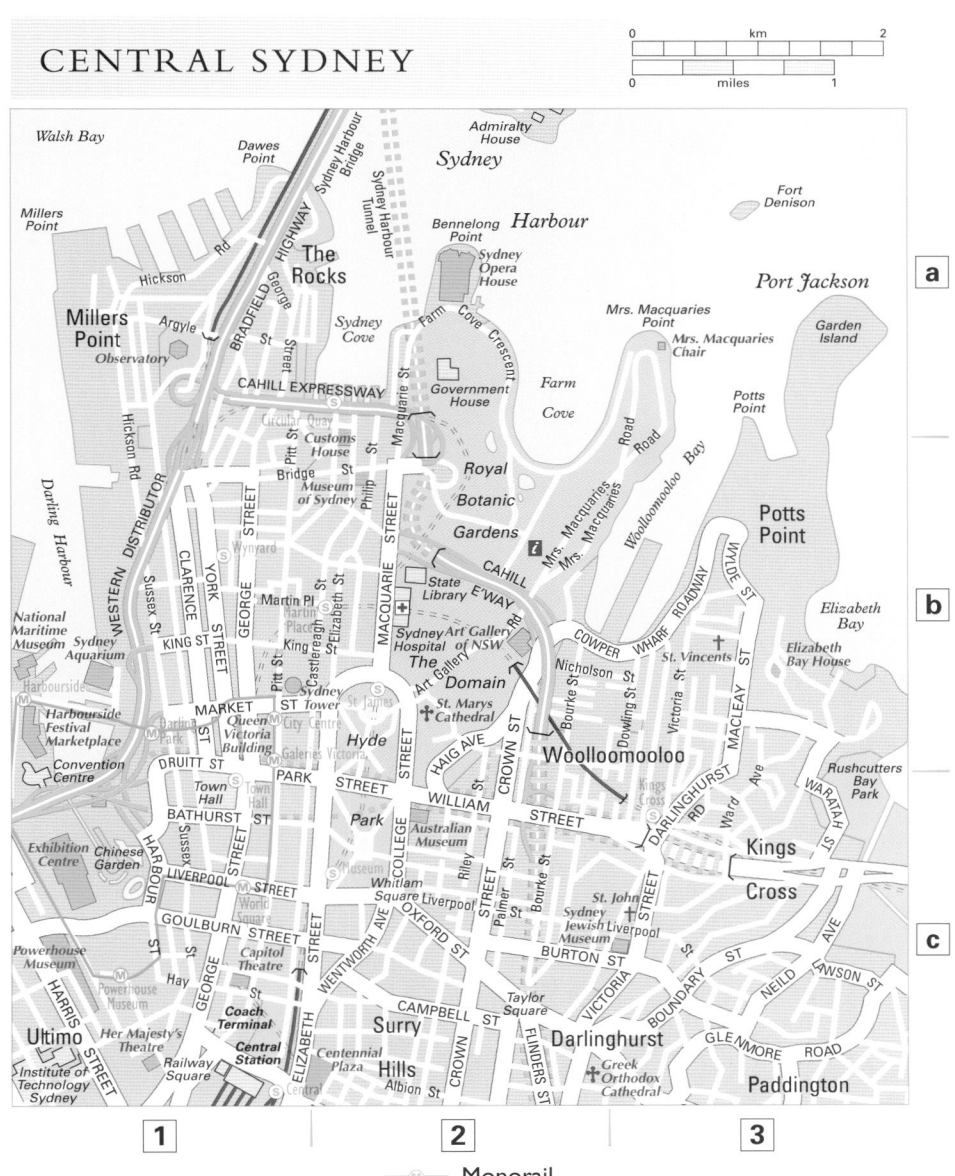

—M— Monorail

TOKYO, JAPAN

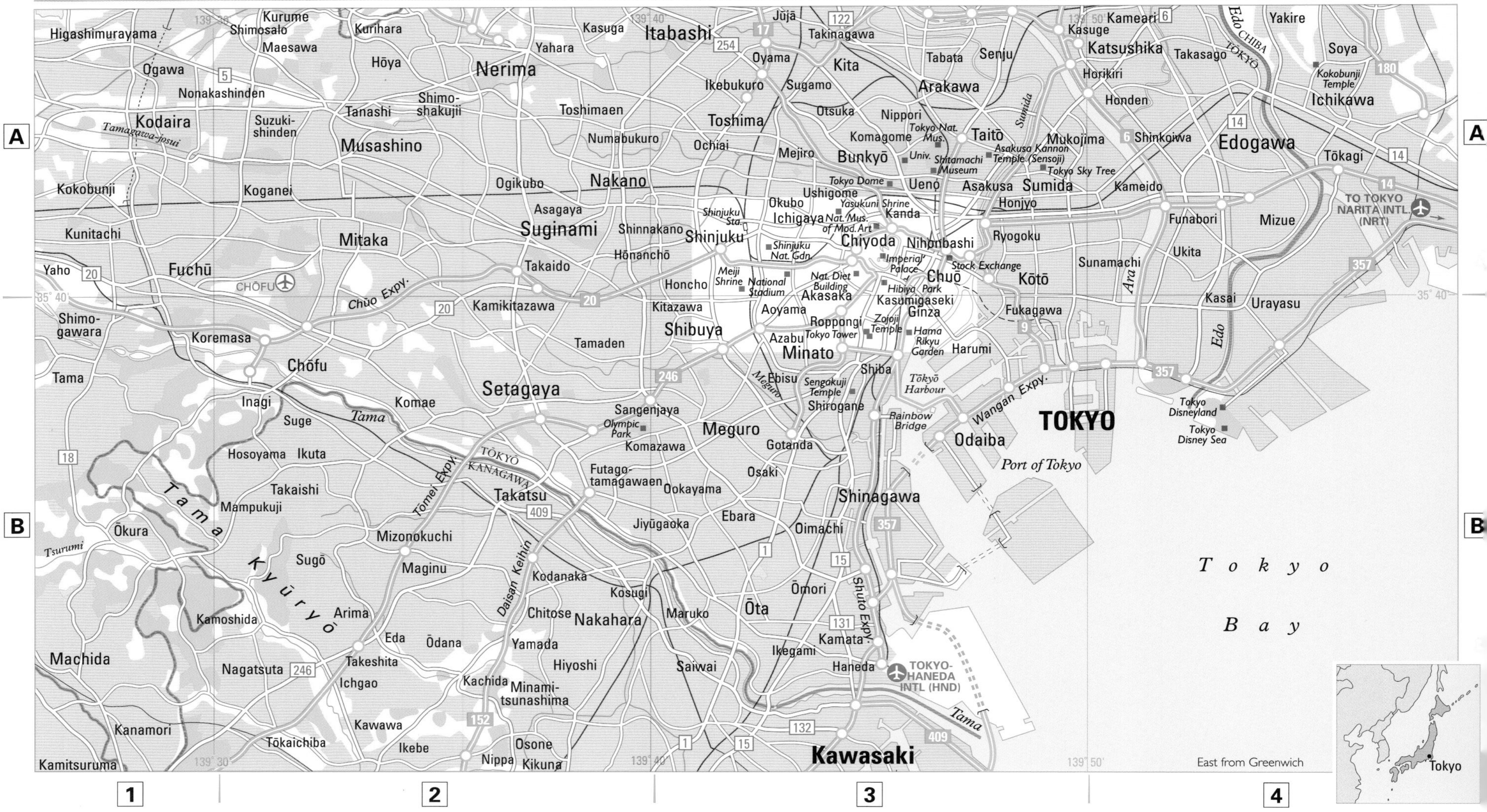

Higashimurayama · Kurume · Shimosalo · Kurihara · Kasuga · Itabashi · Jūjō · Takinagawa · Kameari · Yakire · Soya

Ogawa · Shimoshakuji · Yahara · Oyama · Kita · Tabata · Senju · Katsushika · Takasago · Kokubunji Temple · Ichikawa

Kodaira · Nonakashinden · Hōya · Tanashi · Toshimaen · Ikebukuro · Sugamo · Otsuka · Nippori · Tokyo Nat. Mus. · Mukojima · Shinkoiwa · Edogawa

Suzuki-shinden · Numabukuro · Ochiai · Mejiro · Komagome · Taitō · Asakusa Kannon Temple (Sensoji) · Tōkagi

Kokobunji · Koganei · Ogikubo · Nakano · Univ. · Shitamachi · Ushigome · Asakusa Sumida · Tokyo Sky Tree

Kunitachi · Mitaka · Asagaya · Suginami · Shinnakano · Shinjuku Sta. · Ichigaya Nat. Mus. of Mod. Art · Ueno · Honjyo · Kameido · Mizue

Yaho · Fuchū · Takaido · Honchō · Shinjuku · Nat. Mus. of Mod. Art · Kanda · Nihonbashi · Ryogoku · Funabori

CHŌFU · Kamikitazawa · Meiji Shrine · National Stadium · Imperial Palace · Chūo · Stock Exchange · Kōtō · Sunamachi · Ukita · Kasai

Shimogawara · Koremasa · Kitazawa · Aoyama · Akasaka · Hibiya Park · Ginza · Fukagawa · Urayasu

Tama · Chōfu · Komae · Setagaya · Tamaden · Shibuya · Roppongi · Kasumigaseki · Hama Rikyū Garden · Harumi

Inagi · Suge · Tama · Sangenjaya · Meguro · Minato · Azabu · Tokyo Tower · Zojoji Temple · Shiba · Tōkyō Harbour

Hosoyama · Ikuta · Olympic Park · Komazawa · Ebisu · Sengokuji Temple · Shirogane · Rainbow Bridge · Odaiba · Tokyo Disneyland

Takaishi · Mampukuji · Mizonokuchi · Futago-tamagawaen · Jiyūgaoka · Gotanda · Shirokane · Wangan Expy. · Port of Tokyo · Tokyo Disney Sea

Ōkura · Sugō · Takatsu · Ookayama · Osaki · Shinagawa · TOKYO

Kamoshida · Arima · Daisen Keihin · Kodanaka · Ebara · Ōimachi

Machida · Eda · Ōdana · Chitose · Nakahara · Maruko · Ōmori · Kamata · Tokyo · Bay

Nagatsuta · Takeshita · Yamada · Saiwai · Ikegami · Haneda · TOKYO-HANEDA INTL (HND)

Kanamori · Ichgao · Hiyoshi · Minami-tsunashima · Kawawa · Kachida · Tama

Kamitsuruma · Tōkaichiba · Ikebe · Osone · Nippa · Kikuna · Kawasaki

Tokyo Bay · East from Greenwich

CENTRAL TOKYO

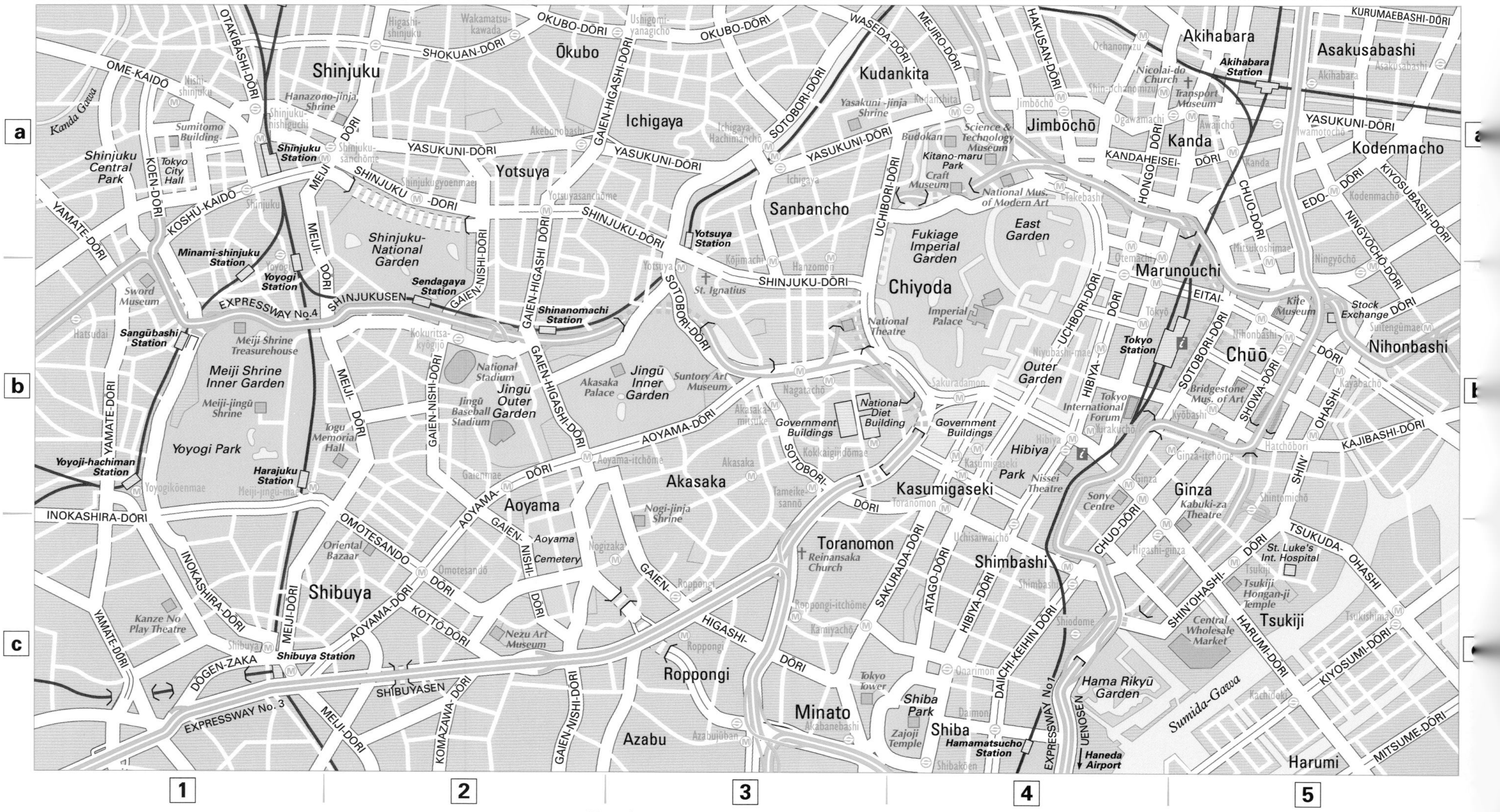

Toei Subway · Tokyo Metro

TEHRAN, IRAN

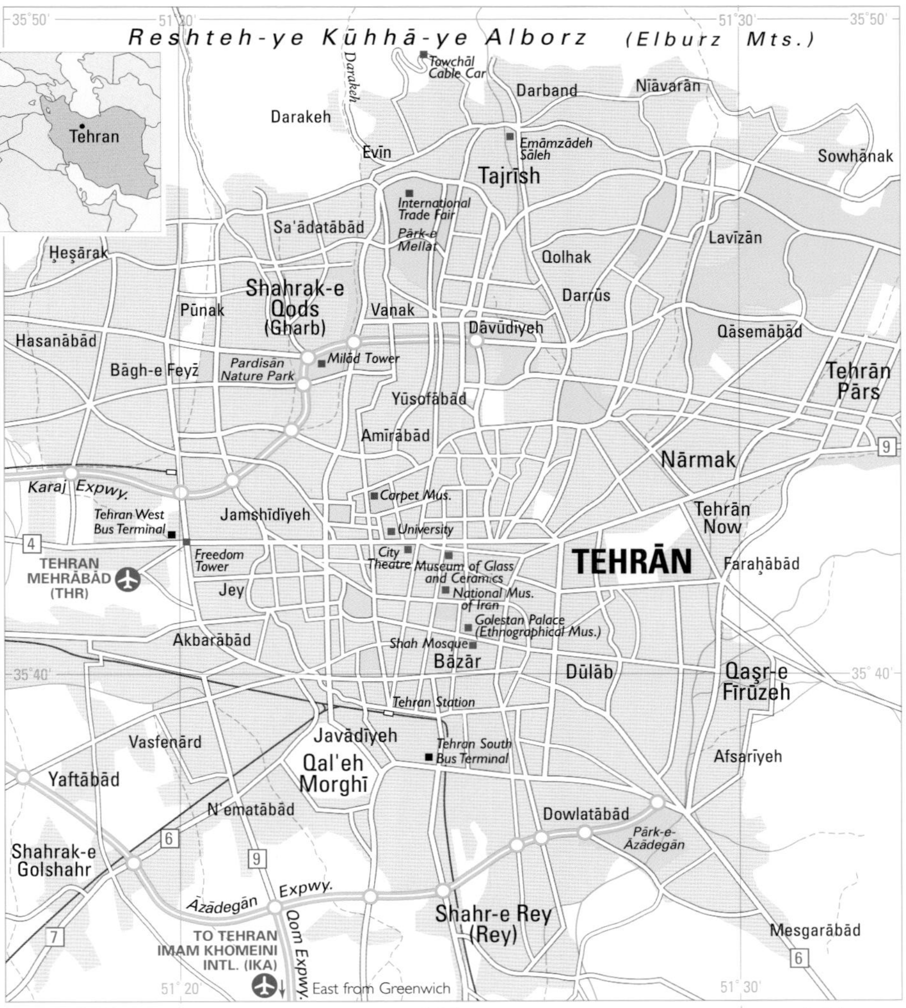

Reshteh-ye Kūhhā-ye Alborz (Elburz Mts.)

Tehran

Darakeh
Darband
Niāvarān
Evin
Emāmzādeh Sāleh
Sowhānak
Towchāl Cable Car
Sa'ādatābād
Tajrīsh
International Trade Fair
Pārk-e Mellat
Lavīzān
Shahrak-e Qods (Gharb)
Pūnak
Vanak
Qolhak
Darrūs
Qāsemābād
Bāgh-e Feyż
Pardisān Nature Park
Dāvūdiyeh
Tehrān Pārs
Hasanābād
Mīlād Tower
Amīrābād
Yūsofābād
Karaj Expwy
Nārmak
Carpet Mus.
Tehran West Bus Terminal
Jamshīdīyeh
University
Tehrān Now
TEHRAN
Freedom Tower
City Theatre
Museum of Glass and Ceramics
Farahābād
TEHRAN MEHRĀBĀD (THR)
Jey
National Mus. of Iran
Akbarābād
Shah Mosque
Golestan Palace (Ethnographical Mus.)
Bāzār
Dūlāb
Qaṣr-e Fīrūzeh
Tehran Station
Vasfenārd
Javādīyeh
Qal'eh Morghī
Tehran South Bus Terminal
Afsarīyeh
Yaftābād
N'ematābād
Dowlatābād
Pārk-e Āzādegān
Shahrak-e Golshahr
Āzādegān Expwy.
Qom Expwy
Shahr-e Rey (Rey)
Mesgarābād
TO TEHRAN IMAM KHOMEINI INTL. (IKA)
East from Greenwich

CENTRAL TORONTO

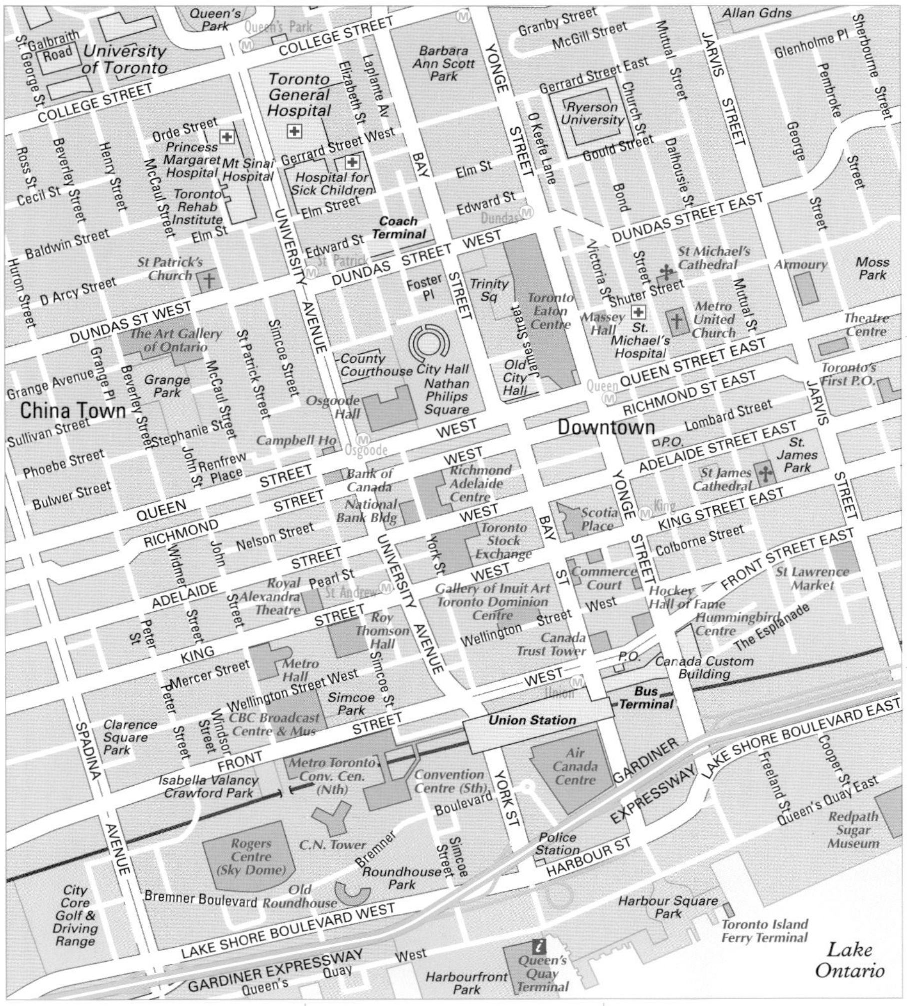

Queen's Park
University of Toronto
COLLEGE STREET
Galbraith Road
St George St
Toronto General Hospital
Orde Street
Princess Margaret Hospital
Mt Sinai Hospital
Hospital for Sick Children
Barbara Ann Scott Park
Granby Street
McGill Street
Gerrard Street East
Ryerson University
Ross St
Beverley Street
Henry Street
McCaul Street
Gerrard Street West
Toronto Rehab Institute
Elm St
Edward St
Dundas St
Coach Terminal
DUNDAS STREET EAST
St Michael's Cathedral
Moss Park
Baldwin Street
D Arcy Street
St Patrick's Church
Foster Pl
Trinity Sq
Toronto Eaton Centre
Massey Hall
St Michael's Hospital
Metro United Church
Armoury
Theatre Centre
China Town
Grange Avenue
Grange Park
County Courthouse
City Hall
Nathan Phillips Square
Old City Hall
Downtown
QUEEN STREET EAST
Toronto's First P.O.
Sullivan Street
Osgoode Hall
Lombard Street
Phoebe Street
Campbell Ho
Osgoode
RICHMOND STREET EAST
ADELAIDE STREET EAST
St James Park
Bulwer Street
Bank of Canada
National Bank Bldg
Richmond Adelaide Centre
Scotia Plaza
St James Cathedral
QUEEN
RICHMOND
Nelson Street
WEST
Toronto Stock Exchange
Colborne Street
ADELAIDE
John
Pearl St
Royal
Gallery of Inuit Art
Toronto Dominion Centre
Commerce Court
Hockey Hall of Fame
FRONT STREET EAST
Peter St
Mercer Street
St Andrew
Roy Thomson Hall
Canada Trust Tower
Hummingbird Centre
St Lawrence Market
KING
Wellington
P.O.
The Esplanade
Clarence Square Park
Wellington Street West
Simcoe Park
Canada Custom Building
CBC Broadcast Centre & Mus
FRONT
Union Station
Bus Terminal
Isabella Valancy Crawford Park
Metro Toronto Conv. Cen. (Nth)
Convention Centre (Sth)
Air Canada Centre
LAKE SHORE BOULEVARD EAST
Queen's Quay East
Rogers Centre (Sky Dome)
C.N. Tower
Bremner
Simcoe Park
Police Station
HARBOUR ST
Redpath Sugar Museum
City Core Golf & Driving Range
Bremner Boulevard
Roundhouse
Roundhouse Park
GARDINER
Harbour Square Park
Toronto Island Ferry Terminal
LAKE SHORE BOULEVARD WEST
GARDINER EXPRESSWAY
West
Harbourfront Park
Queen's Quay Terminal
Queen's Quay
Lake Ontario

TORONTO, CANADA

Boyd Conservation Area
East Don
Toronto Zoo
Fairport
Vaughan
Thornhill
The Promenade
Markham
Brown
Rouge
Little Rouge
West Rouge
Rouge Hill
Woodbridge
Pine Grove
Edgeley
Concord
Newtonbrook
Agincourt
Malvern
Glen Rouge Park
Port Union
Fisherville
G. Ross Lord Park
Willowdale
York University
East Don Parkland
Fairview Mall
Scarborough Town Centre
Highland Creek
Humber Summit
Black Creek Pioneer Village
York University
North York
Northmount
Lansing
Macdonald-Cartier Frwy.
Morningside Park
Woburn
Beaumonte Heights
Northwood Park
Black Creek
Downsview Park
Armour Heights
York Mills
Wexford
Bendale
West Hill
Thistletown
Don Mills
Scarborough
Highland
Creek
Hague Park
Eastpoint Park
Clairville Reservoir
Humberwood Park
Woodbine Centre
Kipling Heights
Downsview
Lawrence Heights
York Univ.
Sunnybrook Health Science Centre
Ontario Science Centre
Cliffside
Danforth
Malton
Rexdale
Humberlea
Weston
Yorkdale Shopping Centre
Forest Hill
Thorncliffe
Bluffers Park
Woodbine Race Track
Cedarvale Park
York
Casa Loma
East York
Dentonia Park
Scarborough Bluffs
TORONTO LESTER B. PEARSON INTL. (YYZ)
Humber Valley Village
Mount Dennis
Royal Ontario Museum
Riverdale Park
Birch Cliff
Kew Gardens
Hanlon
Lambton Mills
Swansea
University of Toronto
Parliament Buildings
Ashbridge's Bay Park
Etobicoke
Islington
Kingsway
High Park
Old City Hall
C.N. Tower & Rogers Centre
Union Sta.
Gardiner Expy.
TORONTO
Markland Wood
Humber Bay
Parkdale
Old Fort York
Exhibition Place
Ontario Place
Toronto City (Island)
Toronto Harbour
Tommy Thompson Park
Burnhamthorpe
Summerville
Humber Bay Park
New Toronto
Toronto Islands
Island Park
Gibraltar Point
LAKE ONTARIO
Mimico
Dixie Mall
Square One
Humber College
Samuel Smith Park
Cooksville
Mississauga
Long Branch
West from Greenwich
Toronto

427 Provincial route numbers

COPYRIGHT PHILIP'S

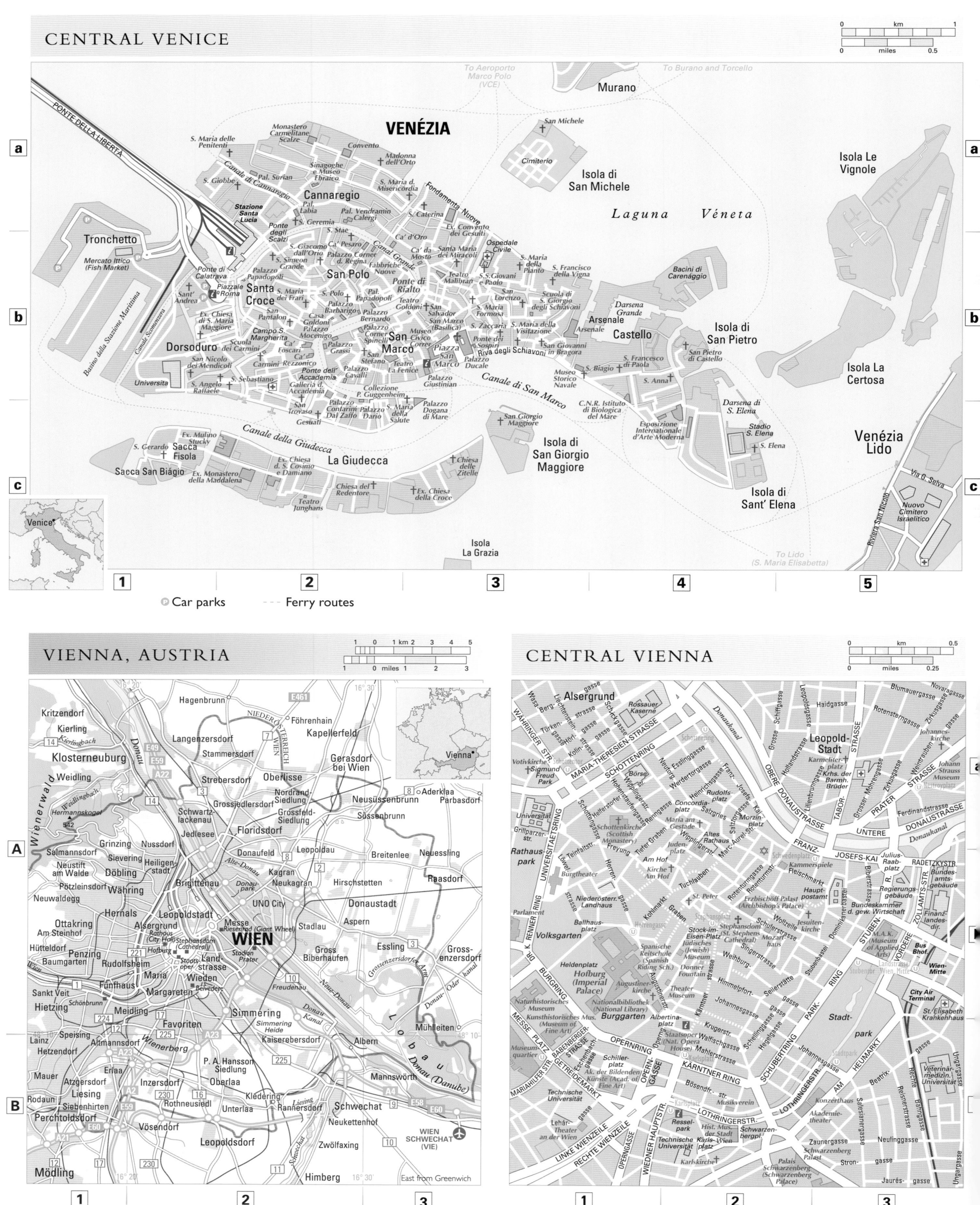

CENTRAL VENICE

0 km 1

0 miles 0.5

To Aeroporto Marco Polo (VCE)

To Burano and Torcello

Murano

VENÉZIA

San Michele

Cimitero

Isola di San Michele

Laguna   Véneta

Isola Le Vignole

S. Maria delle Penitenti

Monastero Carmelitane Scalze

Convento

Madonna dell'Orto

Sinagoghe e Museo Ebraico

Pal. Surian

S. Maria d. Misericordia

S. Giobbe

Canale di Cannaregio

Cannaregio

Fondamenta Nuove

S. Caterina

Pal. Labia

Pal. Vendramin Calergi

Stazione Santa Lucia

Ponte degli Scalzi

S. Geremia

Ex. Convento dei Gesuiti

Ospedale Civile

S. Maria dei Miracoli

S. Maria della Pianto

S. Francisco della Vigna

Bacini di Carenaggio

Tronchetto

Mercato Ittico (Fish Market)

S. Simeon Grande

S. Marcuola

S. Stae

Ca' Pesaro

Ca' d'Oro

Ca' da Mosto

Canal Grande

Teatro Malibran

S.S. Giovani e Paolo

Darsena Grande

Ponte di Calatrava

Palazzo Papadopoli

Sant' Andrea

Piazzale Roma

Santa Croce

S. Giacomo dall'Orio

Palazzo Corner d. Regina

Fabbriche Nuove

San Polo

Ponte di Rialto

Palazzo Corner

S. Polo

S. Lorenzo

Scuola di San Giorgio degli Schiavoni

Arsenale

Darsena Arsenale

Isola di San Pietro

S. Maria d. di S. Maria Maggiore

Campo S. Margherita

S. Maria dei Frari

Palazzo Barbarigo

Pal. Papadopoli

Teatro Goldoni

S. Salvador

S. Maria Formosa

S. Zaccaria

S. Giovanni in Bragora

Castello

S. Francesco di Paola

S. Pietro di Castello

Dorsoduro

Scuola dei Carmini

Palazzo Mocenigo

Casa Goldoni

Palazzo Bernardo

Museo Correr

San Marcó

Ponte dei Sospiri

Palazzo Ducale

S. Biagio

S. Anna

Darsena di S. Elena

Isola di San Pietro

Carmini

Ca' Foscari

Palazzo Grassi

Campo S. Stefano

San Marcó

Piazza San Marcó

Palazzo Giustinian

Museo Storico Navale

Isola La Certosa

S. Nicolo dei Mendicoli

Ponte dell' Accademia

Palazzo Cavalli

Teatro La Fenice

Palazzo Dogana di Mare

S. Angelo Raffaele

Galleria d. Accademia

S. Sebastiano

Palazzo Contarini Dal Zaffo

Collezione P. Guggenheim

S. Maria della Salute

C.N.R. Istituto di Biologica del Mare

Esposizione Internazionale d'Arte Moderna

Stádio S. Elena

Universita

S. Trovaso

Palazzo Dario

S. Giorgio Maggiore

S. Elena

Venézia Lido

Canale della Giudecca

Canale di San Marco

Ex. Mulino Stucky

S. Gerardo

Sacca Fisola

Ex. Chiesa d. S. Cosimo e Damiano

La Giudecca

Chiesa delle Zitelle

Isola di San Giorgio Maggiore

Via G. Selva

Sacca San Biágio

Ex. Monastero della Maddalena

Chiesa del Redentore

Ex. Chiesa della Croce

Nuovo Cimitero Israelitico

Riviera S. Nicolò

Teatro Junghans

Isola di Sant' Elena

Isola La Grazia

To Lido (S. Maria Elisabetta)

a **b** **c**

1 **2** **3** **4** **5**

Venice

ⓅCar parks   - - - Ferry routes

VIENNA, AUSTRIA

1 0 1 km 2 3 4 5
1 0 miles 1 2 3

Vienna•

Kritzendorf

Kierling

Hagenbrunn

Föhrenhain

Kapellerfeld

NIEDER OSTERREICH WIEN

Klosterneuburg

Weidling

Kierlingbach

Langenzersdorf

Stammersdorf

Gerasdorf bei Wien

Wienerwald

Weidling

Streberdorf

Oberlisse

Aderklaa

Parbasdorf

Hermannskogel

Schwartz-lackenau

Grossjedlersdorf

Nordrand-Siedlung

Neusüssenbrunn

Sössenbrunn

Sälmannsdorf

Grinzing

Nussdorf

Floridsdorf

Grossfeld-Siedlung

Neüstift am Walde

Sievering

Heiligen-stadt

Donaufeld

Leopoldau

Breitenlee

Neuessling

Pötzleinsdorf

Döbling

Kagran

Hirschstetten

Raasdorf

Neuwaldegg

Währing

Brigittenau

Donau-park

Neukagran

Hernals

Leopoldstadt

UNO City

Donaustadt

Ottakring Am Steinhof

Alsergrund

Messe Riesenrad (Giant Wheel)

Stadlau

Aspern

Hütteldorf

Penzing Baumgarten

Rathaus (City Hall)

WIEN

Stadion Prater

Gross Biberhaufen

Essling

Gross-enzersdorf

Rudolfsheim

Hofburg

Staats-oper (Cathedral)

Land-strasse

Wieden

Belvedere

Sankt Veit

Fünfhaus

Maria

Margareten

Freudenau

Mühlleiten

Lainz

Hietzing

Schönbrunn

Meidling

Favoriten

Simmering

Simmering Heide

Albern

Speising

Altmannsdorf

Wienerberg

Kaisereberdsorf

Mauer

Atzgersdorf

Inzersdorf

Oberlaa

Kledering

Mannswörth

Rodaun

Liesing

Siebenhirten

Rothneusiedl

Unterlaa

Schwechat

Neukettenhof

Perchtoldsdorf

Vösendorf

Leopoldsdorf

Zwölfaxing

WIEN SCHWECHAT (VIE)

Mödling

Himberg

East from Greenwich

A **B**

1 **2** **3**

CENTRAL VIENNA

0 km 0.5

0 miles 0.25

Alsergrund

Rossauer Kaserne

Leopold-Stadt

Johann Strauss Museum

Votivkirche

Sigmund Freud Park

MARIA-THERESIEN-STRASSE

SCHOTTENRING

Börse

Karmeliter platz

Krhs. der Barmh. Brüder

Universität

Schottenkirche (Scottish Monastery)

Concordia-platz

PRATER

Rathaus-park

Tiefer Graben

Juden-platz

Altes Rathaus

UNIVERSITAETSRING

Grillparzer-str.

Burgtheater

Am Hof

Kirche Am Hof

Parlament

Niederöster. Landhaus

St. Peter

Graben

Erzbischöfl. Palast (Archbishop's Palace)

FRANZ-JOSEFS-KAI

Julius-Raab-platz

RADETZKYSTR.

Volksgarten

Stephansdom (St. Stephens Cathedral)

Bundeskammer d. gew. Wirtschaft

Finanz-landes-dir.

Ballhaus-platz

Mozart-haus

Jüdisches Museum

Spanische Reitschule (Spanish Riding Sch.)

Donner Fountain

M.A.K. (Museum of Applied Arts)

Bus Bhof.

Heldenplatz

Hofburg (Imperial Palace)

Augustiner-kirche

Theater Museum

Wien-Mitte

Naturhistorisches Museum

Nationalbibliothek (National Library)

Albertina-platz

Stadt-park

City Air Terminal

Kunsthistorisches Mus. (Museum of Fine Art)

Burggarten

Staatsoper (Nat. Opera House)

St. Elisabeth Krankenhaus

Museumsquartier

OPERNRING

Ak. der Bildenden Künste (Acad. of Fine Art)

Technische Universität

Schiller-platz

KÄRNTNER RING

SCHUBERTRING

Veterinär-medizin. Universität

Lehár-Theater an der Wien

LOTHRINGERSTR.

Konzerthaus

Musikverein

Hist. Mus. der Stadt Wien

Karls-platz

Schwarzenbergpl.

Ressel-park

Technische Universität

Karlskirche

Zaunergasse

Palais Schwarzenberg (Schwarzenberg Palace)

a **b**

1 **2** **3**

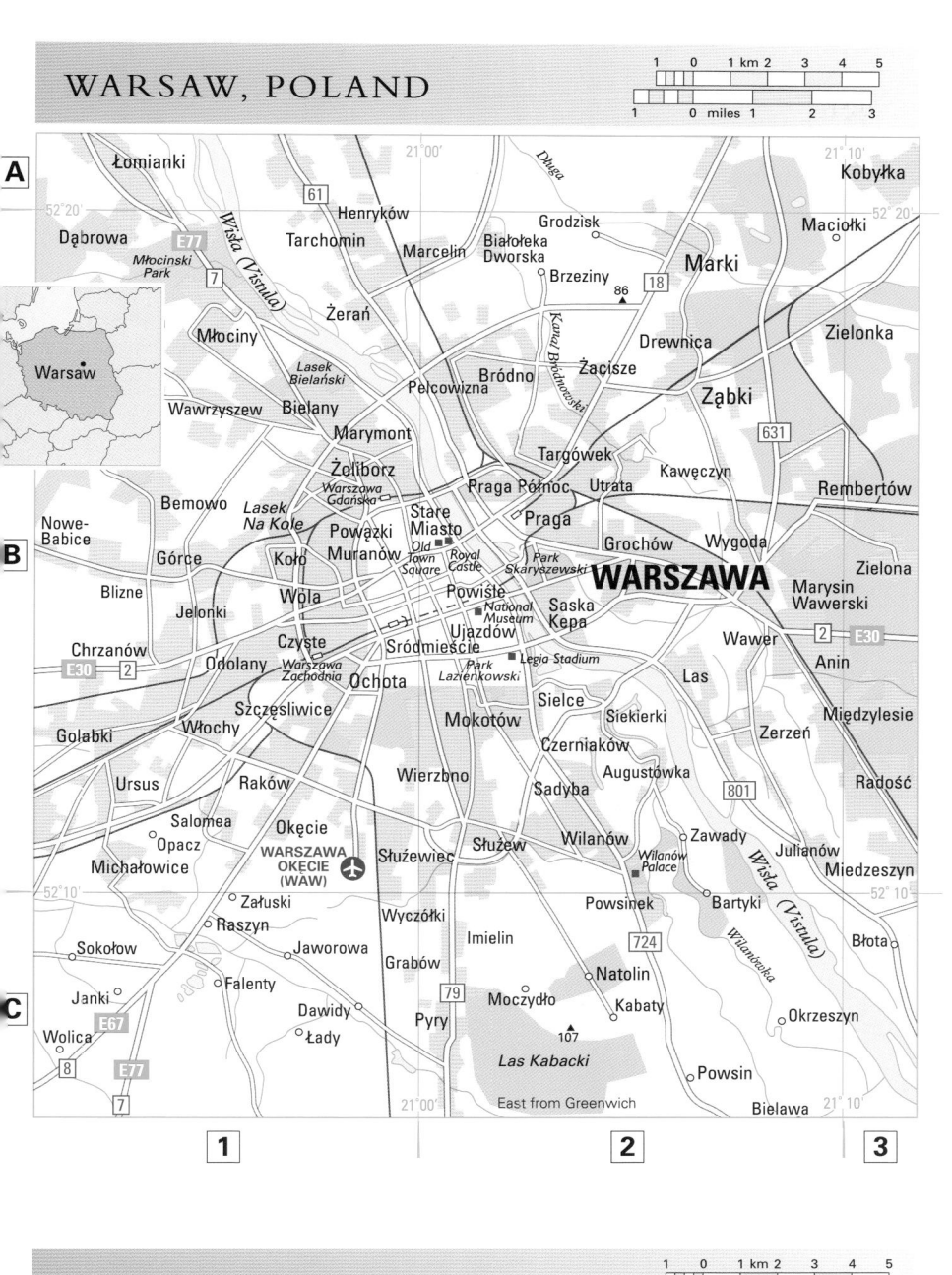

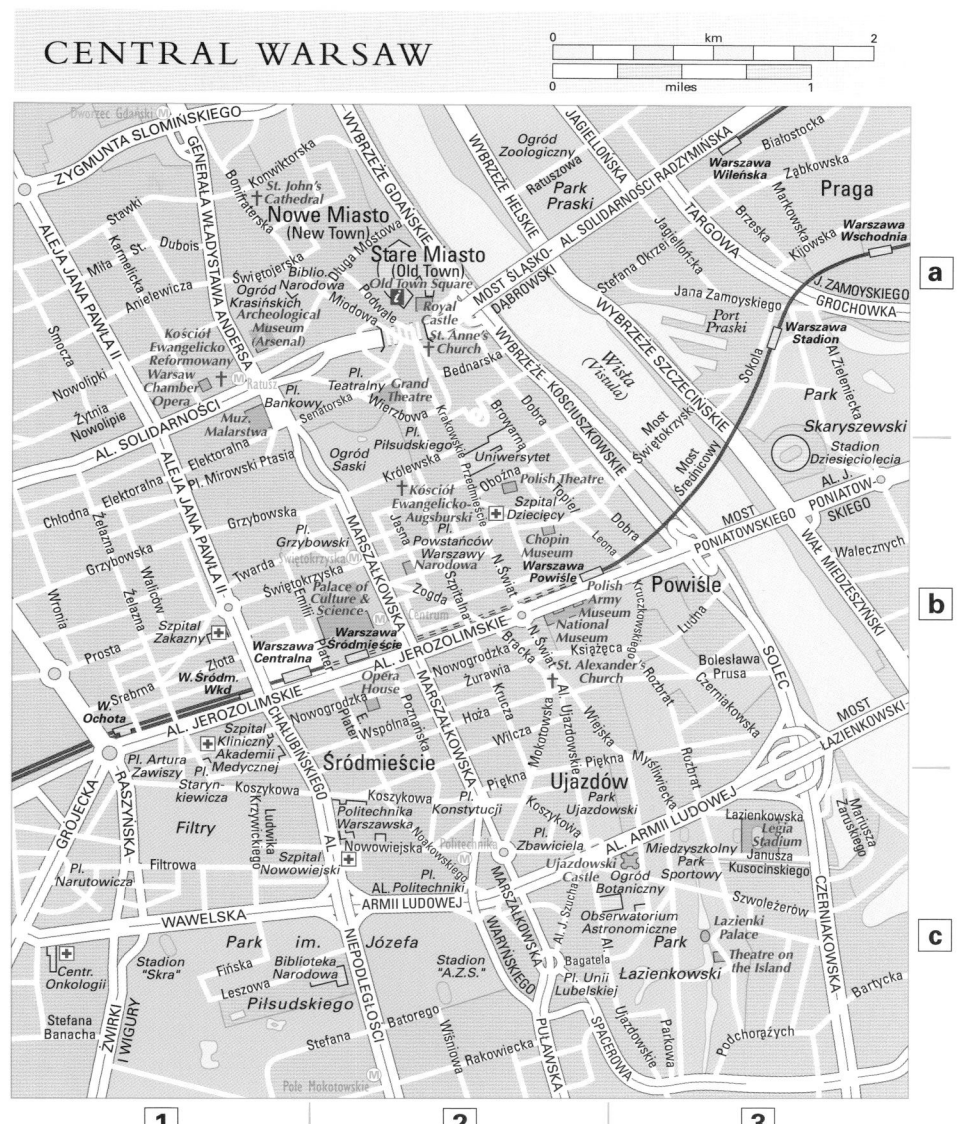

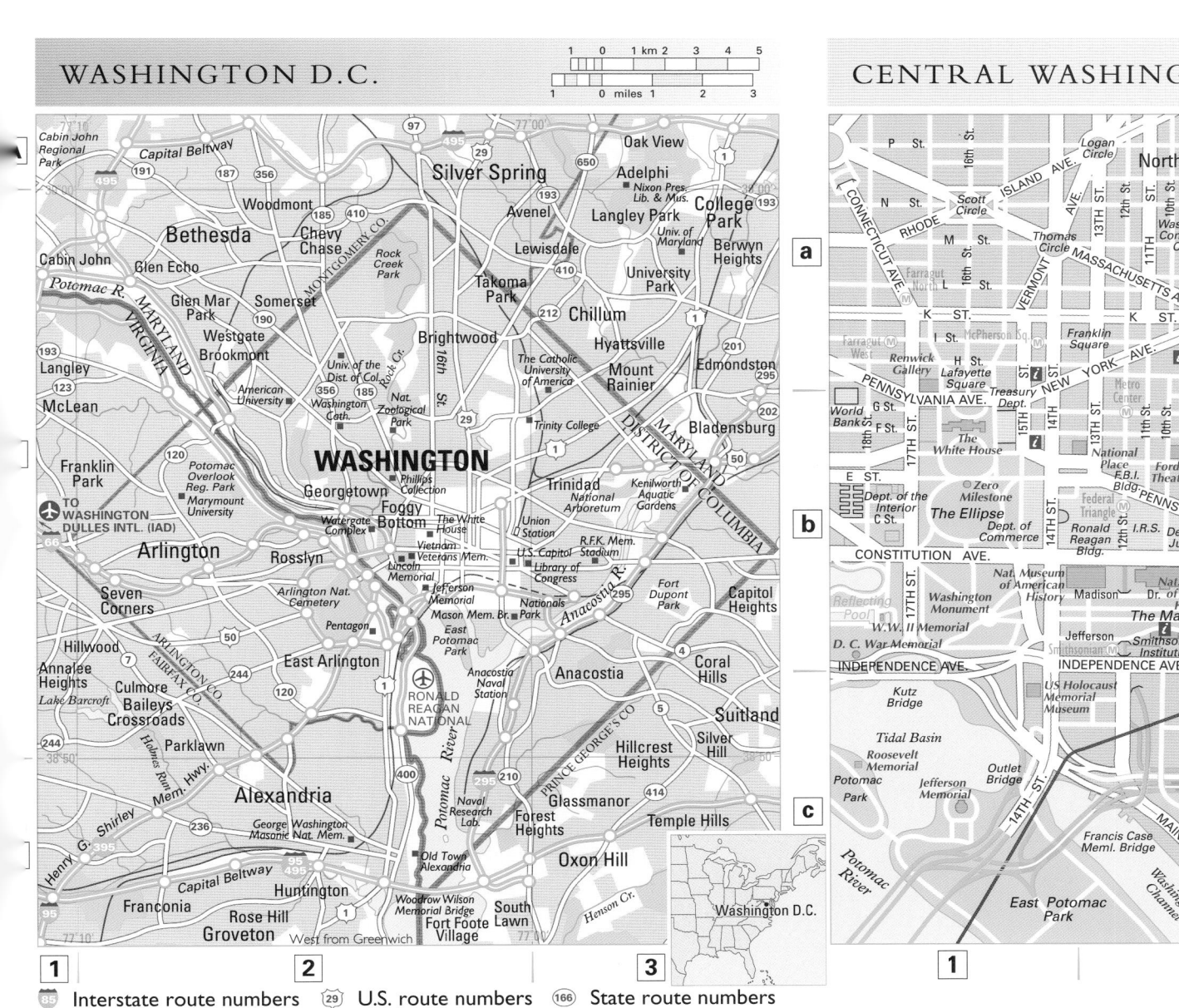

85 Interstate route numbers   29 U.S. route numbers   166 State route numbers

A B C D E F G H

1 2 3 4 5 6 7 8 9

Pt. Barrow
Beaufort Sea
Banks I.
Parry Is.
Queen Elizabeth Islands
North Magnetic Pole
Devon I.
Ellesmere I.
Greenland
Greenland Sea
Jan Mayen
Norwegia Sea
Bering Str.
Alaska
Mt. McKinley 6194 (Denali)
Victoria I.
Gr. Bear L.
Baffin Island
Arctic Circle
3360
Denmark Str.
2118
Iceland
Faroe Is.
Bering Sea
Gulf of Alaska
Kodiak I.
Haida Gwaii (Queen Charlotte Is.)
Aleutian Is.
Gr. Slave L.
Peace
Hudson Str.
Labrador Sea
C. Farewell
British Isles
3342
North Sea
Vancouver I.
Nelson
Hudson Bay
Labrador
Newfoundland
C. Race
B. of Biscay
Pic d'Aneto 3404
Iberian Pen.
North America
L. Winnipeg
Great Lakes
Laurentian Plateau
Gf. of St. Lawrence
Nova Scotia
Azores
Str. of Gibraltar
Maghreb
A 40
C. Mendocino
Great Basin
Rocky Mountains
Great Plains
Missouri
Ohio
C. Cod
Madeira
Mt. Elbert 4399
Arkansas
Mt. Whitney 4418
Death Valley
Colorado
Sierra Nevada
Mississippi
Mt. Mitchell 2037
Appalachian Mts.
C. Hatteras
Bermuda
ATLANTIC
Canary Is. 3718
Tropic of Cancer
Lower California
Gf. of California
Rio Grande
Florida
Sargasso Sea
OCEAN
Hawaiian Is.
Mauna Kea 4205
C. San Lucas
Gulf of Mexico
Florida Str.
Bahamas
Cuba
Hispaniola
Revilla Gigedo Is.
Popocatepetl 5452
Pico de Orizaba 5610
Yucatan
Greater Antilles
Jamaica
3175
Milwaukee Deep 8605
Puerto Rico
Lesser Antilles
C. Verde Is.
C. Verde
Af
Sa
PACIFIC
4093
Central America
Caribbean Sea
Trinidad
5776
Orinoco
Sahara
Guinea
Line Is.
Kiritimati
Isthmus of Panama
Llanos
Guiana Highlands
Mt. Roraima 2810
Negro
2964
Equator
C. Palmas
Gulf of Guinea
Galapagos Is.
Chimborazo 6310
Japurá
South America
Amazon
Ascension
Marañon
6768
Purus
Selvas
Madeira
Tapajos
Xingu
Tocantins
São Francisco
Marquesas Is.
OCEAN
8425
L. Titicaca
Bolivian Plateau
Plateau of Mato Grosso
Brazilian Highlands
St. Helena
Society Is.
Tahiti
Tuamotu Is.
Polynesia
2890
C. Frio
Trindade
Tropic of Capricorn
Cook Is.
20
Chile Trench 8050
Gran Chaco
Paraná
ATLANTIC
Tubuai Is.
Pitcairn I.
Easter I.
Cerro Ojos del Salado 6863
Arch. de Juan Fernández
Cerro Aconcagua 6960
Pampas
R. de la Plata
Tristan da Cunha
OCEAN
Negro
40
Patagonia
4058
105
Falkland Is.
2937
S. Georgia
South Sandwich Is.
Magellan's Str.
Tierra del Fuego
C. Horn
Scotia Sea
Drake Passage
South Shetland Is.
South Orkney Is.
Antarctic Circle
Bellingshausen Sea
Antarctic Peninsula
Weddell Sea
Amundsen Sea
Thurston I.
Alexander I.
Palmer Land
Caird Coast
Roosevelt I.
Marie Byrd Land
Ellsworth Land
Vinson Massif 4897
Ronne Ice Shelf
Berkner I.
Coats Land
Ross Sea

Projection: Winkel III

West from Greenwich

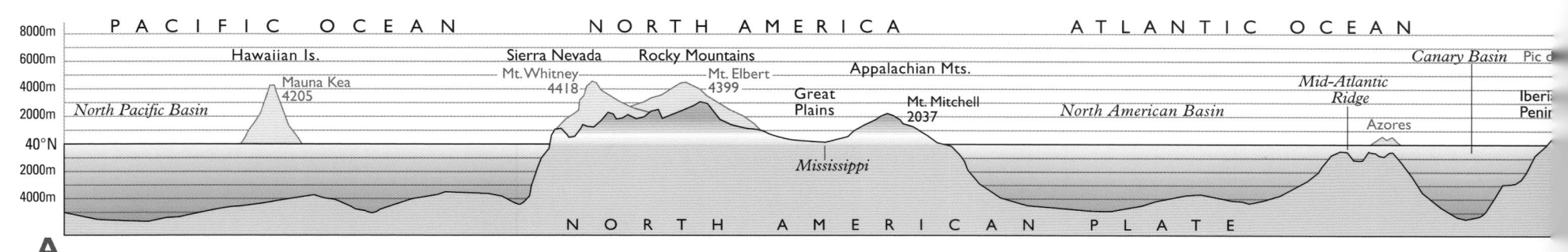

8000m 6000m 4000m 2000m 40°N 2000m 4000m

PACIFIC OCEAN   NORTH AMERICA   ATLANTIC OCEAN
Hawaiian Is.   Sierra Nevada   Rocky Mountains   Appalachian Mts.   Canary Basin   Pic d
Mauna Kea 4205   Mt. Whitney 4418   Mt. Elbert 4399   Mid-Atlantic Ridge   Iberi
North Pacific Basin   Great Plains   Mt. Mitchell 2037   North American Basin   Azores   Peni
Mississippi
NORTH AMERICAN PLATE

A

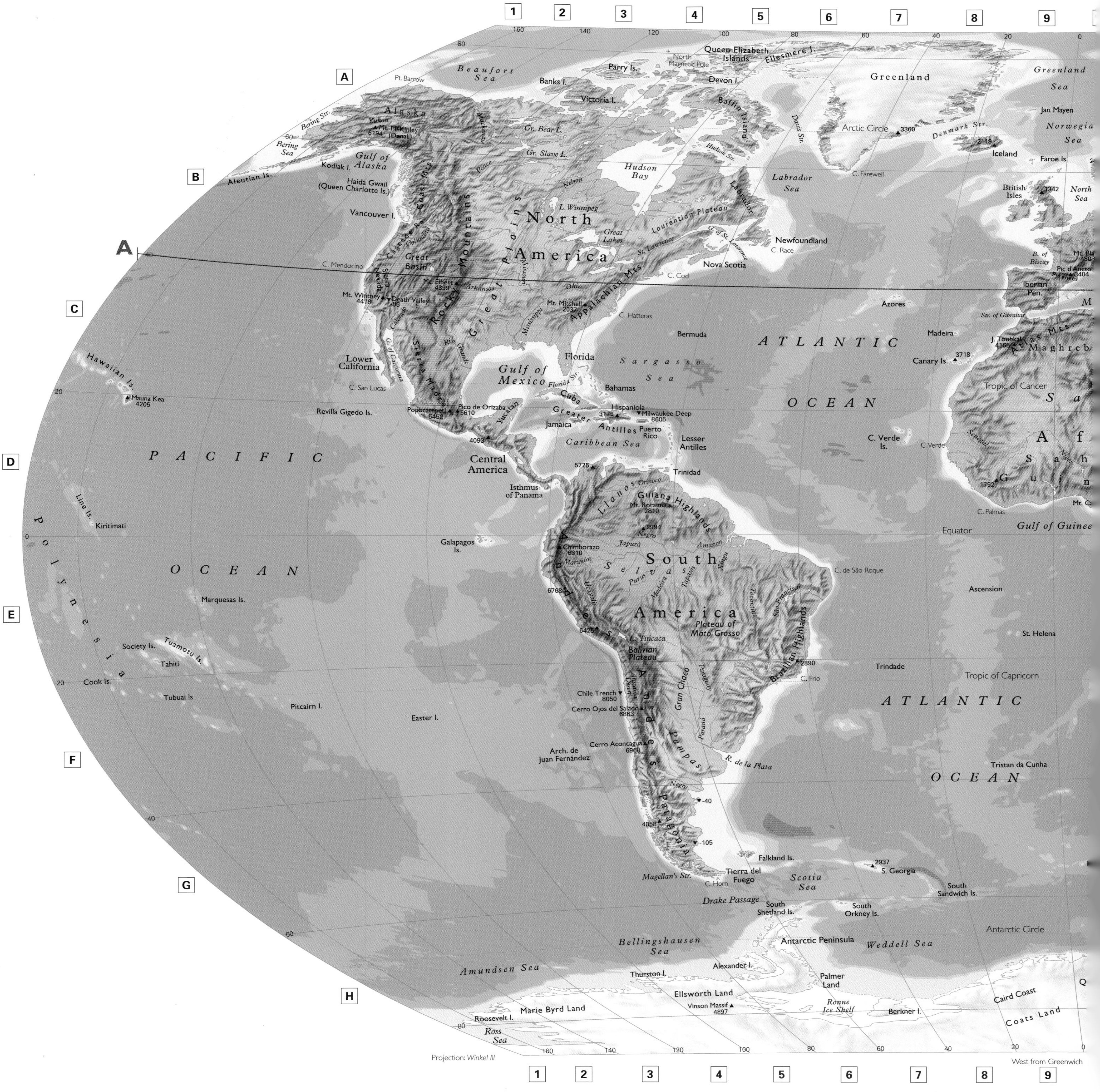

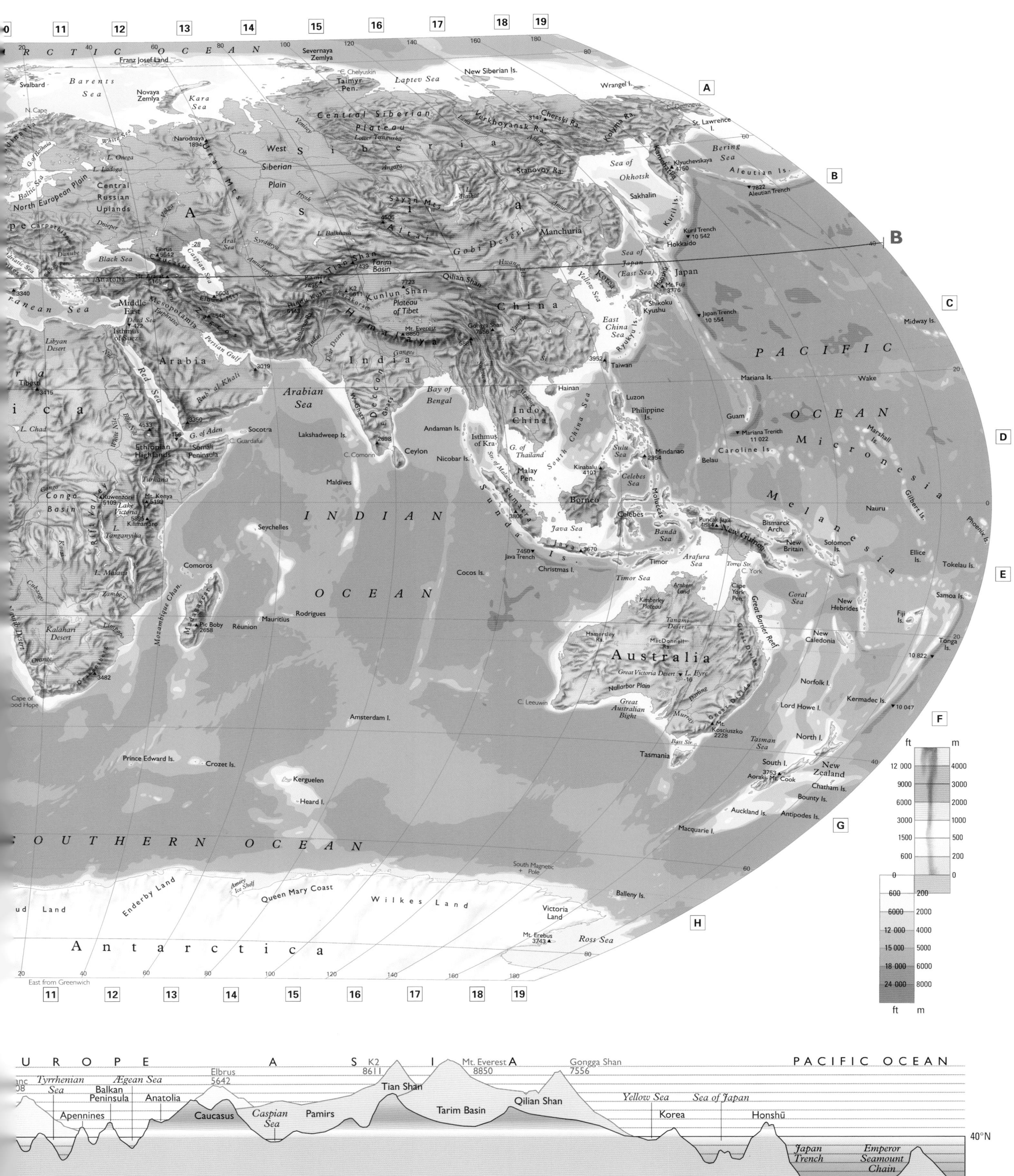

Equatorial Scale 1·76 000 000

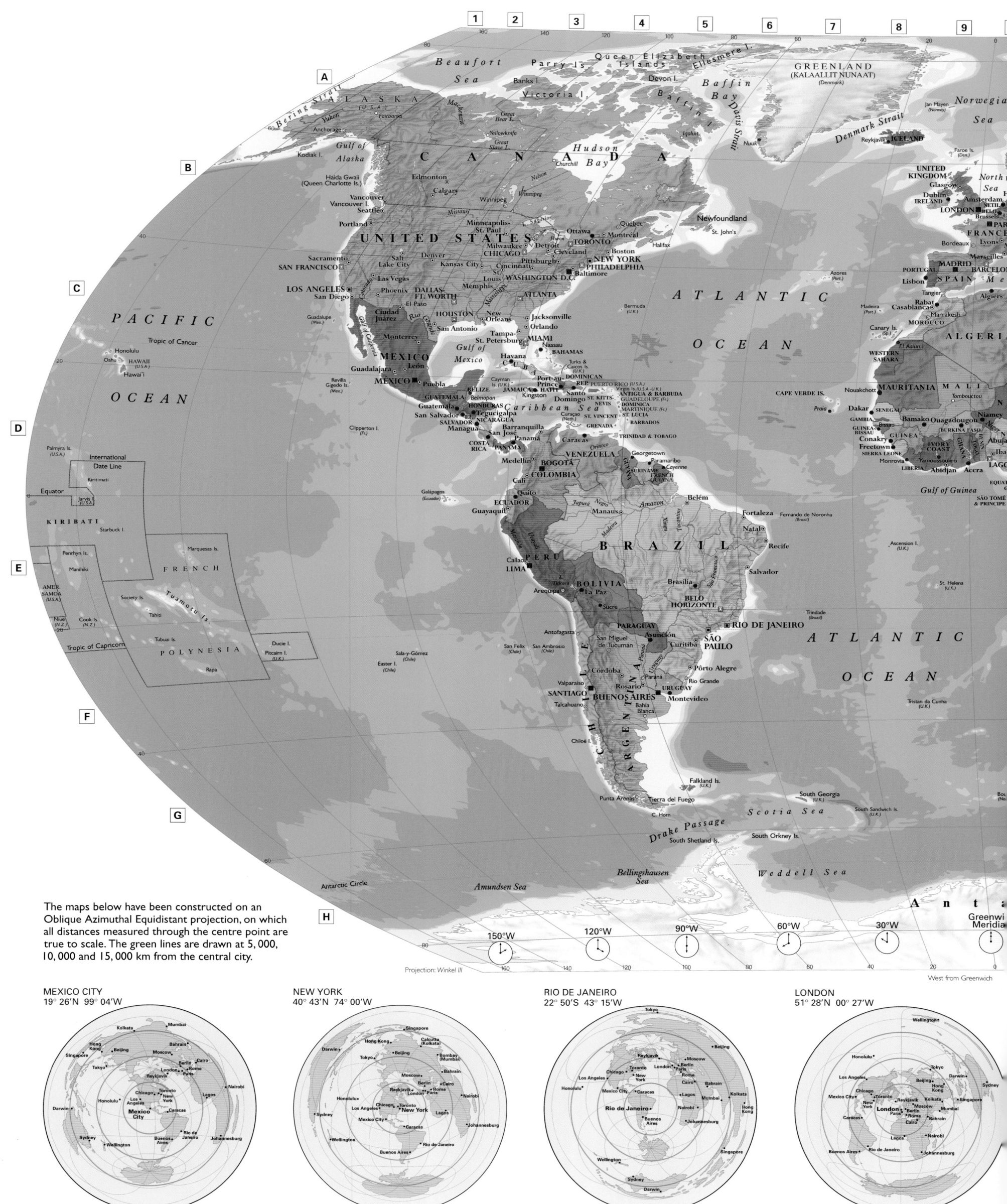

The maps below have been constructed on an Oblique Azimuthal Equidistant projection, on which all distances measured through the centre point are true to scale. The green lines are drawn at 5,000, 10,000 and 15,000 km from the central city.

Projection: Winkel III

West from Greenwich

MEXICO CITY
19° 26'N 99° 04'W

NEW YORK
40° 43'N 74° 00'W

RIO DE JANEIRO
22° 50'S 43° 15'W

LONDON
51° 28'N 00° 27'W

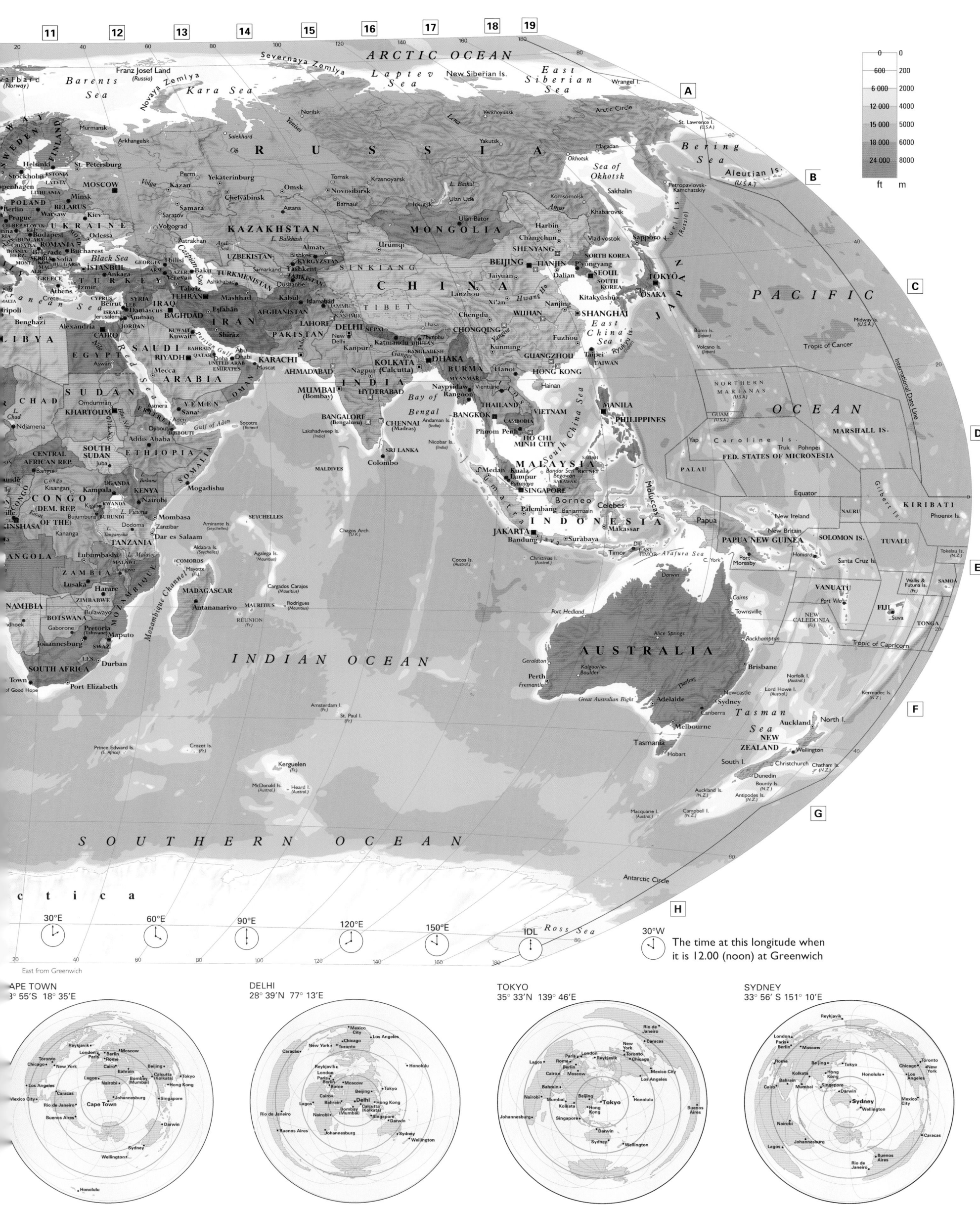

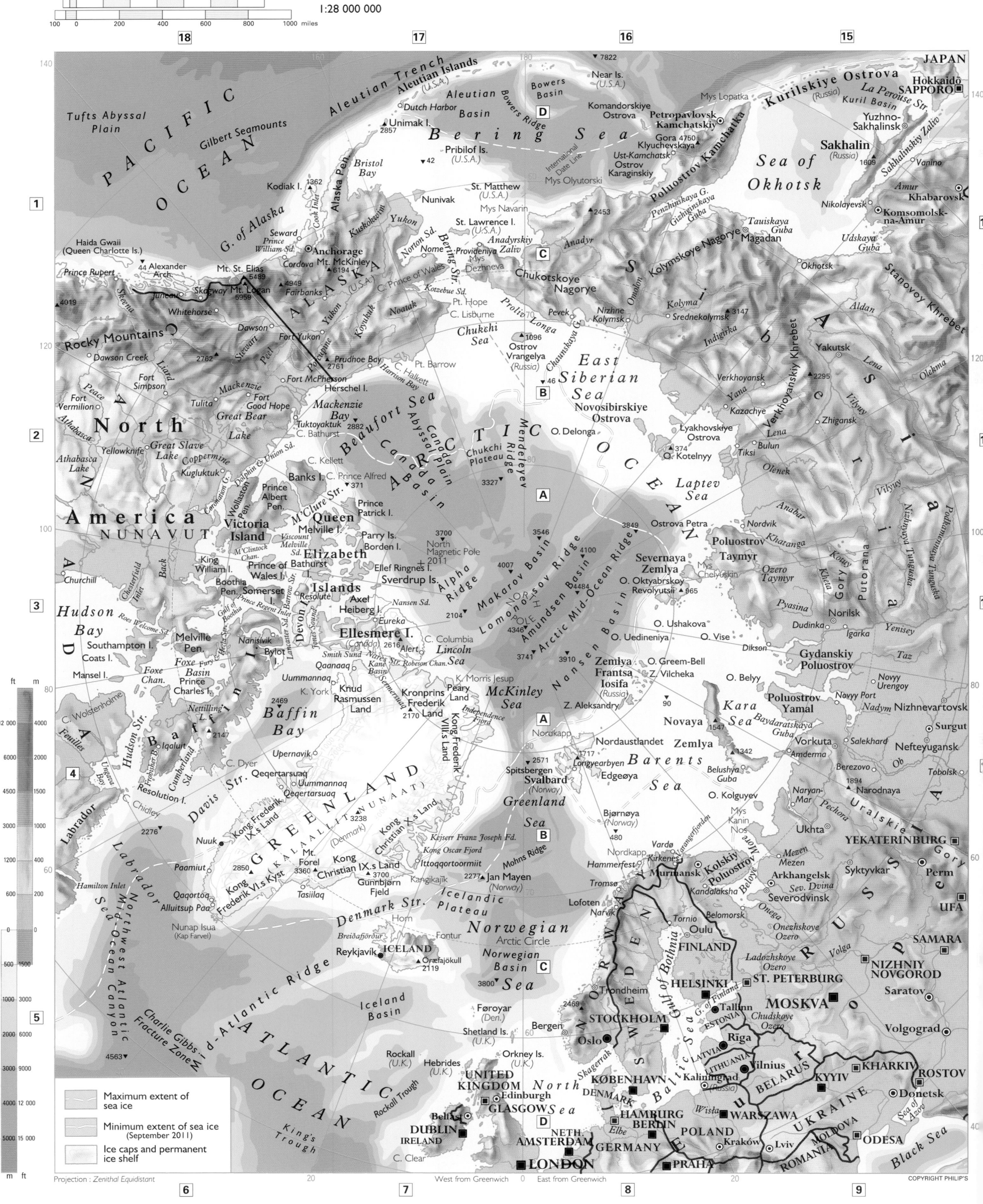

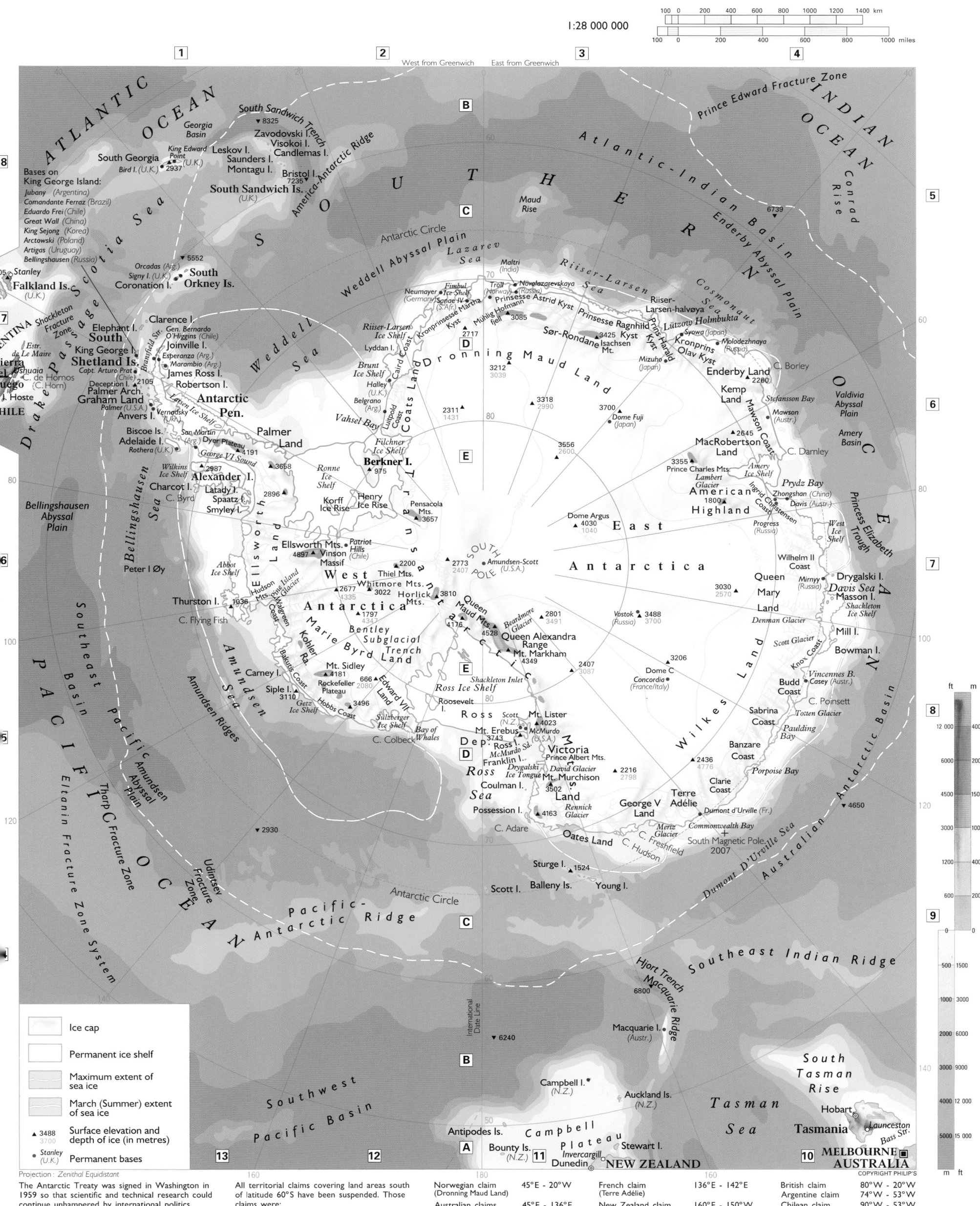

ANTARCTICA 151

1:28 000 000

100 0 200 400 600 800 1000 1200 1400 km

100 0 200 400 600 800 1000 miles

West from Greenwich | East from Greenwich

Projection: *Zenithal Equidistant*

160 COPYRIGHT PHILIP'S

The Antarctic Treaty was signed in Washington in 1959 so that scientific and technical research could continue unhampered by international politics.

All territorial claims covering land areas south of latitude 60°S have been suspended. Those claims were:

Norwegian claim (Dronning Maud Land)	45°E – 20°W	French claim (Terre Adélie)	136°E – 142°E	British claim	80°W – 20°W
Australian claims	45°E – 136°E 142°E – 160°E	New Zealand claim (Ross Dependency)	160°E – 150°W	Argentine claim	74°W – 53°W
				Chilean claim	90°W – 53°W

Bases on King George Island:
Jubany (Argentina)
Comandante Ferraz (Brazil)
Eduardo Frei (Chile)
Great Wall (China)
King Sejong (Korea)
Arctowski (Poland)
Artigas (Uruguay)
Bellingshausen (Russia)

Legend:
- Ice cap
- Permanent ice shelf
- Maximum extent of sea ice
- March (Summer) extent of sea ice
- ▲ 3488 / 3700 Surface elevation and depth of ice (in metres)
- • Stanley (U.K.) Permanent bases

Equatorial Scale 1:41 000 000

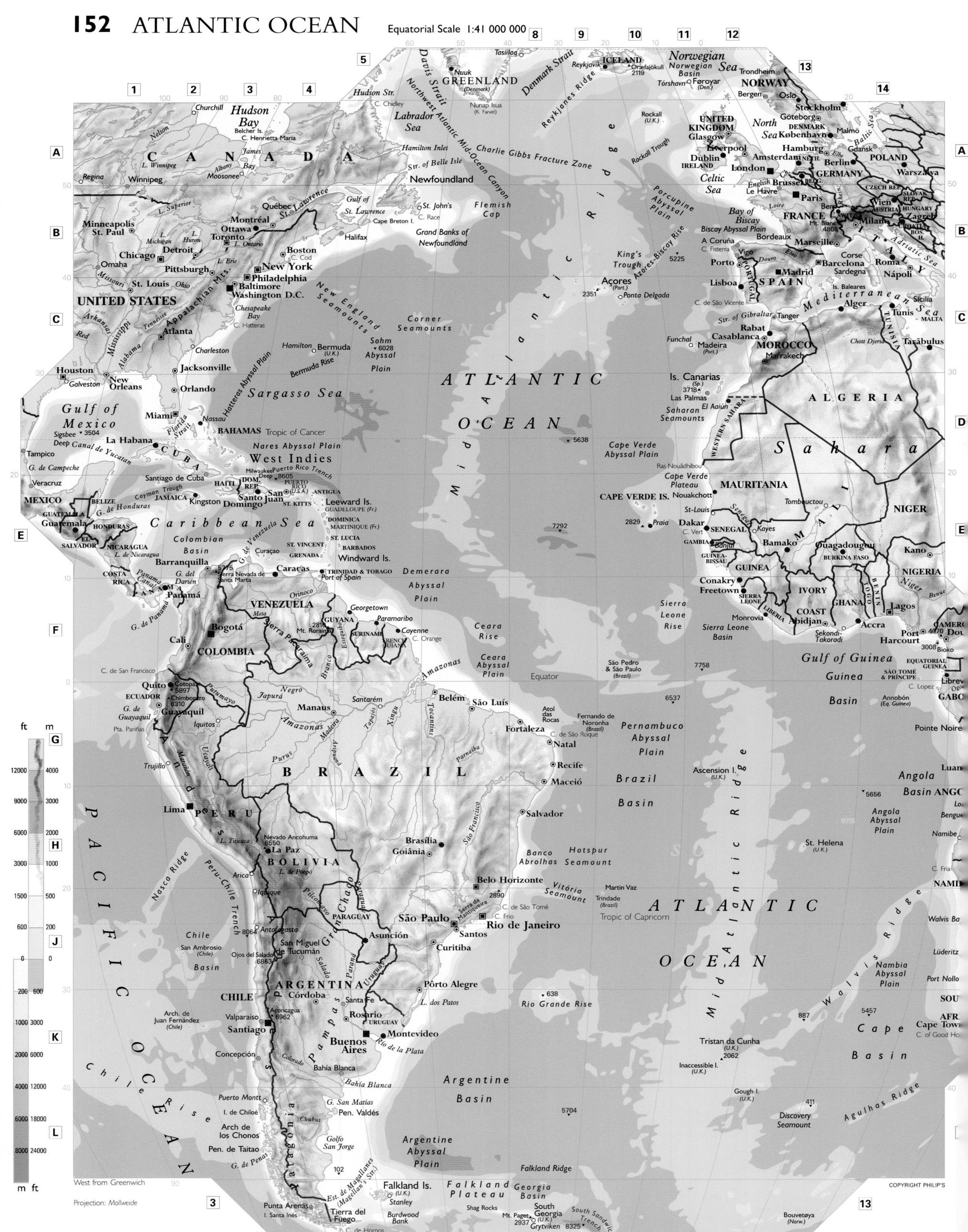

West from Greenwich

Projection: Mollweide

COPYRIGHT PHILIP'S

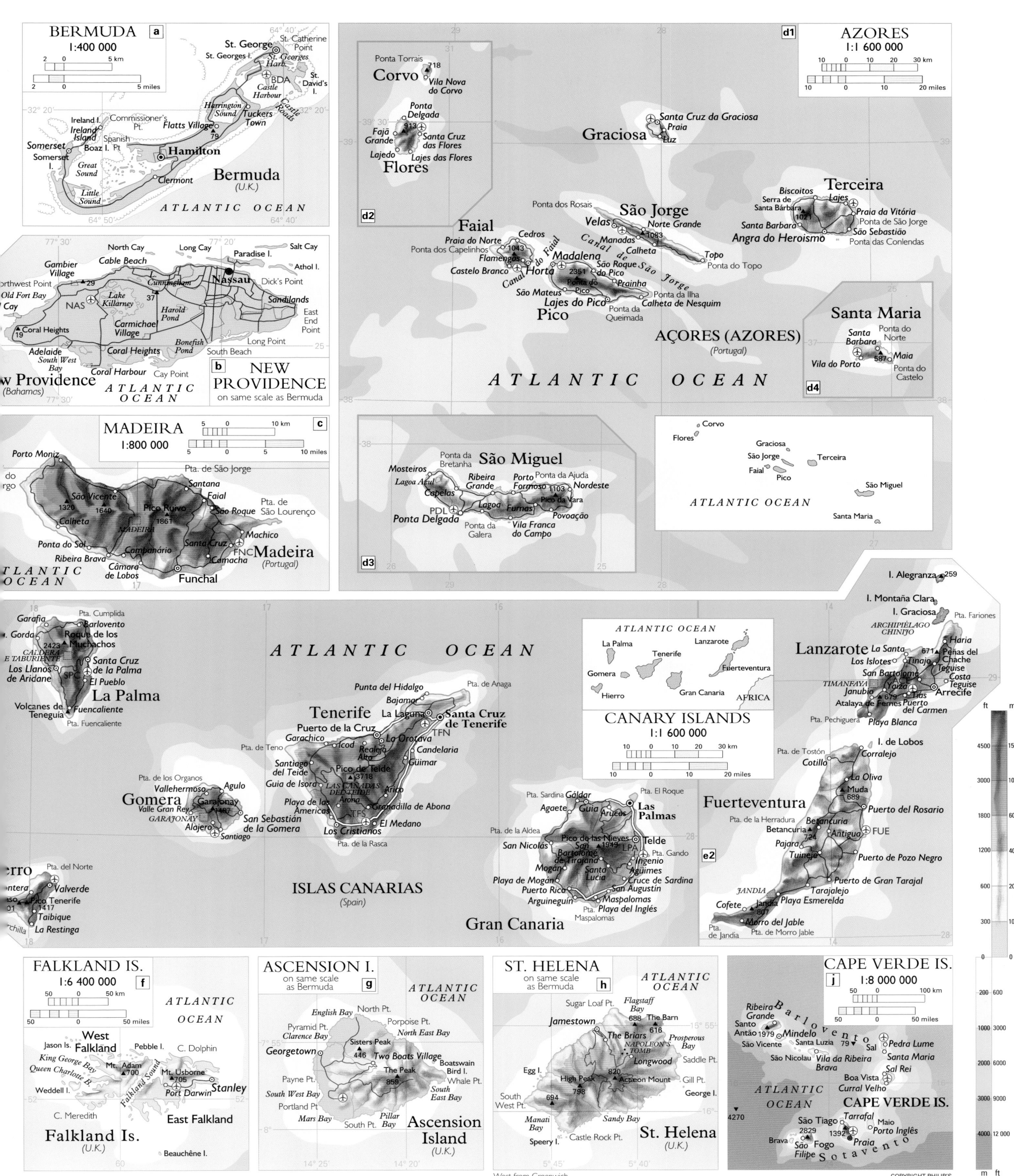

BERMUDA
1:400 000 **a**

2 0 5 km
2 0 5 miles

St. George
St. Georges I.
St. Catherine Point
St. George's Harb.
St. David's I.
Commissioner's Pt.
Harrington Sound
Tuckers Town
79
BDA
Castle Harbour
Castle Roads
Spanish
Ireland I.
Ireland Island
Somerset
Boaz I.
Somerset I.
Pt.
Flatts Village
Hamilton
Great Sound
Little Sound
Clermont
Bermuda (U.K.)

ATLANTIC OCEAN

NEW PROVIDENCE **b**
on same scale as Bermuda

North Cay
Long Cay
Paradise I.
Salt Cay
Gambier Village
Cable Beach
Cunningham
Nassau
Dick's Point
Athol I.
Old Fort Bay
Cay
29
NAS
Lake Killarney
37
Harold Pond
Sandilands
East End Point
Coral Heights
19
Carmichael Village
Bonefish Pond
Adelaide
South West Bay
Coral Heights
Coral Harbour
Cay Point
Long Point
South Beach
New Providence (Bahamas)

ATLANTIC OCEAN

MADEIRA
1:800 000 **c**

5 0 10 km
5 0 10 miles

Porto Moniz
Pta. de São Jorge
do rgo
São Vicente
Santana
Faial
1320
1640
Pico Ruivo
São Roque
Pta. de São Lourenço
Calheta
MADEIRA
1861
Ponta do Sol
Campanário
Santa Cruz
Machico
Ribeira Brava
Câmara de Lobos
Camacha
Funchal
FNC Madeira (Portugal)

ATLANTIC OCEAN

AZORES
1:1 600 000 **d1**

10 0 10 20 30 km
10 0 10 20 miles

Ponta Torrais
718
Corvo
Vila Nova do Corvo **d2**
Ponta Delgada
913
Fajã Grande
Santa Cruz das Flores
Lajedo
Flores
Lajes das Flores

Santa Cruz da Graciosa
Praia
Graciosa
Luz

Ponta dos Rosais
São Jorge
Velas
Norte Grande
1083
Manadas
Calheta
Topo
Ponta do Topo

Biscoitos
Terceira
Serra de Santa Bárbara
Lajes
1021
Praia da Vitória
Santa Bárbara
Ponta de São Jorge
Angra do Heroismo
São Sebastião
Ponta das Conlendas

Faial
Praia do Norte
Cedros
Ponta dos Capelinhos
1043
Flamengos
Madalena
Horta
Castelo Branco
2351
São Roque do Pico
Prainha
São Mateus
Ponta do Pico
Lajes do Pico
Calheta de Nesquim
Pico
Ponta da Ilha
Ponta da Queimada

ACÒRES (AZORES) (Portugal)

Santa Maria **d4**
Santa Bárbara
587
Maia
Vila do Porto
Ponta do Castelo

ATLANTIC OCEAN

São Miguel **d3**

Mosteiros
Ponta da Bretanha
São Miguel
Ribeira Grande
Porto
Ponta da Ajuda
Lagoa Azul
Capelas
Formoso
1103
Nordeste
Lagoa
Furnas
Pico da Vara
PDL
Ponta Delgada
Vila Franca do Campo
Povoação
Ponta da Galera

Corvo
Flores
Graciosa
São Jorge
Terceira
Faial
Pico
São Miguel
Santa Maria

ATLANTIC OCEAN

ISLAS CANARIAS (Spain)

ATLANTIC OCEAN

I. Alegranza
259
I. Montaña Clara
I. Graciosa
Pta. Fariones
ARCHIPIÉLAGO CHINIJO
Haria
671
Peñas del Chache
Lanzarote
La Santa
Los Islotes
Tinajo
Teguise
San Bartolomé
Costa Teguise
TIMANFAYA
679
Tías
Arrecife
Janubio
Yaiza
Atalaya de Femes
Puerto del Carmen
Pta. Pechiguera
Playa Blanca

Garafía
Pta. Cumplida
Barlovento
Gorda
Roque de los Muchachos
2423
La Santa
CALDERA
E TABURIENTE
Santa Cruz de la Palma
Los Llanos de Aridane
El Pueblo
SPC
La Palma
Fuencaliente
Volcanes de Teneguía
Pta. Fuencaliente

Punta del Hidalgo
Pta. de Anaga
Bajamar
Tenerife
La Laguna
Santa Cruz de Tenerife
Puerto de la Cruz
La Orotava
TFN
Garachico
Icod
Realejo Alto
Candelaria
Santiago del Teide
Pico de Teide
Güimar
Guía de Isora
3718
LAS CAÑADAS DEL TEIDE
Arico
Playa de las Américas
Granadilla de Abona
TFS
El Medano
Los Cristianos
Pta. de la Rasca

Pta. de los Organos
Vallehermoso
Agulo
Gomera
Valle Gran Rey
Garajonay
San Sebastián de la Gomera
GARAJONAY
1484
Alajeró
Santiago

Pta. del Norte
erro
ontera
Valverde
Pico Teneríte
1417
Taibique
La Restinga

Pta. de Teno

Pta. Sardina
Gáldar
Pta. El Roque
Agaete
Guía
Las Palmas
Arucas
San Nicolás
Pta. de la Aldea
Pico de las Nieves
Telde
San Bartolomé de Tirajana
1949
LPA
Mogán
Santa Lucía
Ingenio
Agüimes
Playa de Mogán
Cruce de Sardina
Puerto Rico
San Augustín
Arguineguín
Maspalomas
Pta. Playa del Inglés
Maspalomas
Gran Canaria

Fuerteventura **e2**
I. de Lobos
Corralejo
Cotillo
La Oliva
Pta. de Tostón
Muda
689
Puerto del Rosario
FUE
Betancuria
Betancuria
724
Antigua
Pajara
Tuineje
Puerto de Pozo Negro
JANDIA
Tarajalejo
Cofete
Jandía
Playa Esmerelda
807
Morro del Jable
Pta. de Jandia
Pta. de Morro Jable

CANARY ISLANDS
1:1 600 000

ATLANTIC OCEAN
La Palma
Lanzarote
Tenerife
Gomera
Fuerteventura
Hierro
Gran Canaria
AFRICA

10 0 10 20 30 km
10 0 10 20 miles

FALKLAND IS.
1:6 400 000 **f**

50 0 50 km
50 0 50 miles

ATLANTIC OCEAN
West Falkland
Jason Is.
Pebble I.
C. Dolphin
King George Bay
Queen Charlotte B.
Mt. Adam
700
Mt. Usborne
705
Stanley
Weddell I.
Falkland Sound
Port Darwin
East Falkland
C. Meredith
Falkland Is. (U.K.)
Beauchêne I.

ASCENSION I. **g**
on same scale as Bermuda

English Bay
North Pt.
Pyramid Pt.
Porpoise Pt.
Clarence Pt.
North East Bay
Georgetown
Sisters Peak
446
Two Boats Village
Boatswain Bird I.
Payne Pt.
The Peak
859
Whale Pt.
South East Bay
Portland Pt.
South West Bay
Mars Bay
Pillar Bay
South Pt.
Ascension Island (U.K.)

ATLANTIC OCEAN

ST. HELENA **h**
on same scale as Bermuda

Sugar Loaf Pt.
Flagstaff Bay
Jamestown
The Barn
688
616
The Briars
Prosperous Bay
NAPOLEON'S TOMB
Longwood
Saddle Pt.
Egg I.
High Peak
820
Acteon Mount
Gill Pt.
694
798
George I.
South West Pt.
Manati Bay
Sandy Bay
St. Helena (U.K.)
Speery I.
Castle Rock Pt.

ATLANTIC OCEAN

CAPE VERDE IS.
1:8 000 000 **j**

50 0 100 km
50 0 50 miles

Ribeira Grande
Barlovento
Santo Antão
1979
Mindelo
São Vicente
Santa Luzia
79
Sal
Pedra Lume
São Nicolau
Vila da Ribeira Brava
Santa Maria
Boa Vista
Sal Rei
Curral Velho
CAPE VERDE IS.

ATLANTIC OCEAN
4270
São Tiago
Tarrafal
Maio
2829
1392
Porto Inglês
Brava
Praia
São Filipe
Fogo
Sotavento

ft m
4500 1500
3000 1000
1800 600
1200 400
600 200
300 100
0 0
200 600
1000 3000
2000 6000
3000 9000
4000 12 000
m ft

West from Greenwich

COPYRIGHT PHILIP'S

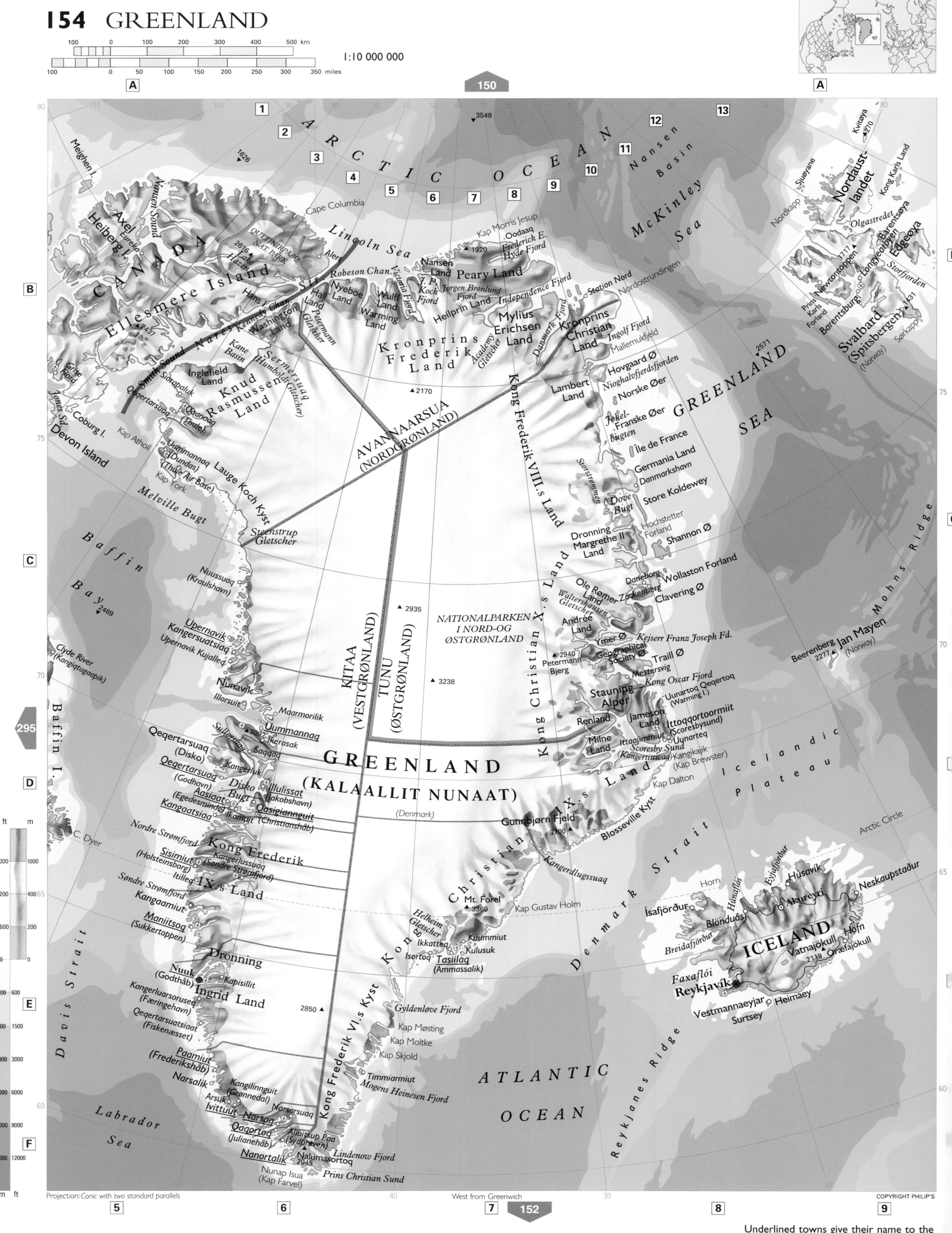

1:10 000 000

Projection: Conic with two standard parallels

West from Greenwich

COPYRIGHT PHILIP'S

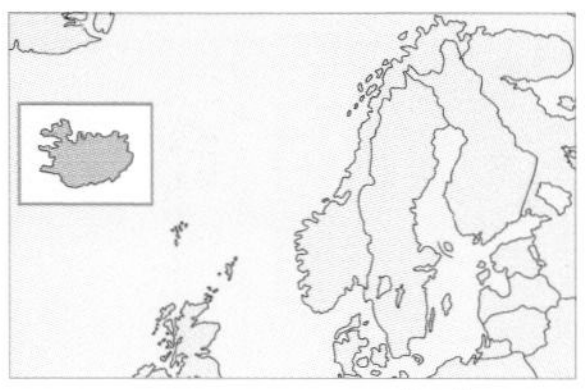

1:2 000 000

| 10 | 0 | 10 | 20 | 30 | 40 | 50 | 60 | 70 | 80 | 100 km |
| 10 | 0 | 10 | 20 | 30 | 40 | 50 | 60 miles |

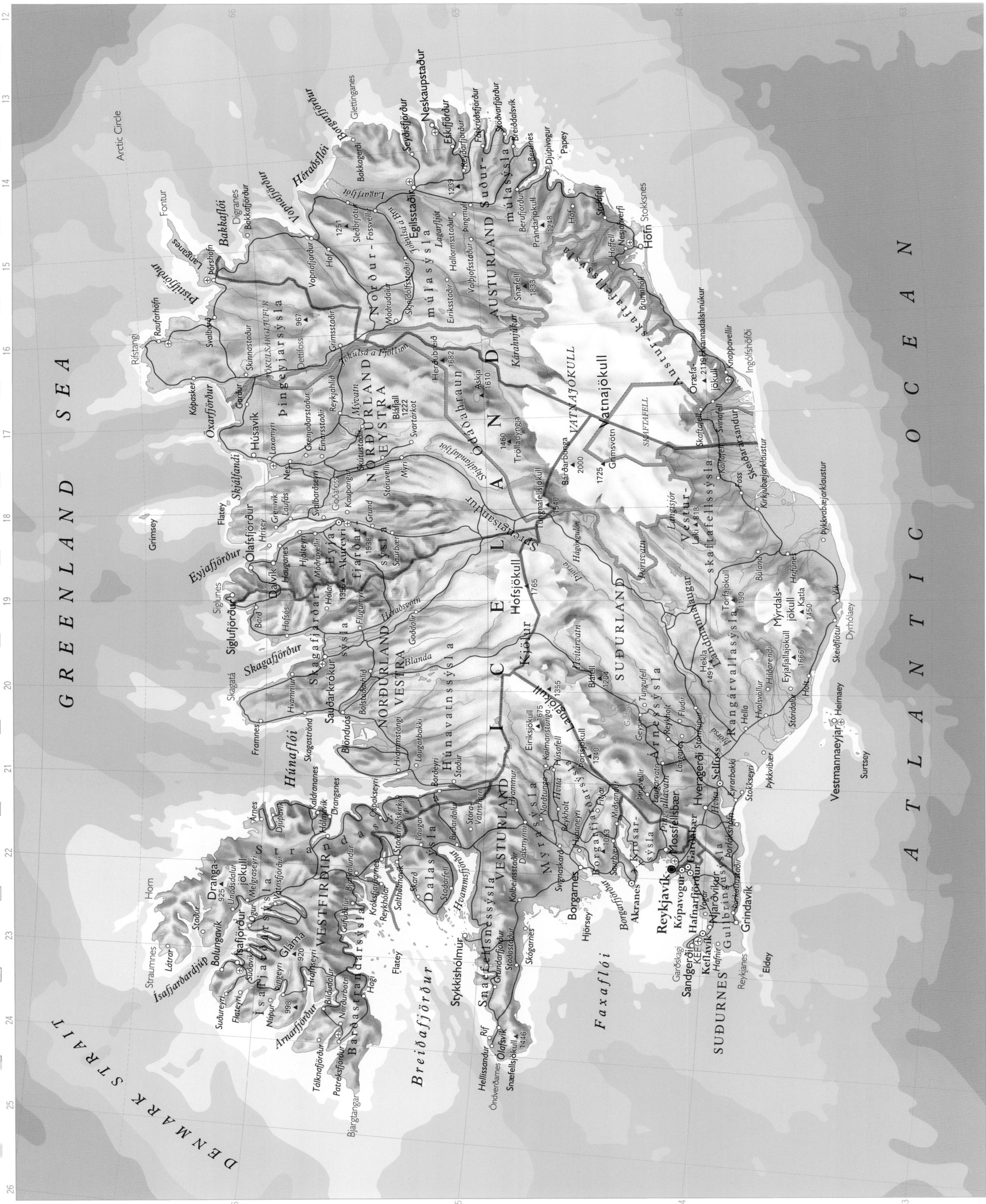

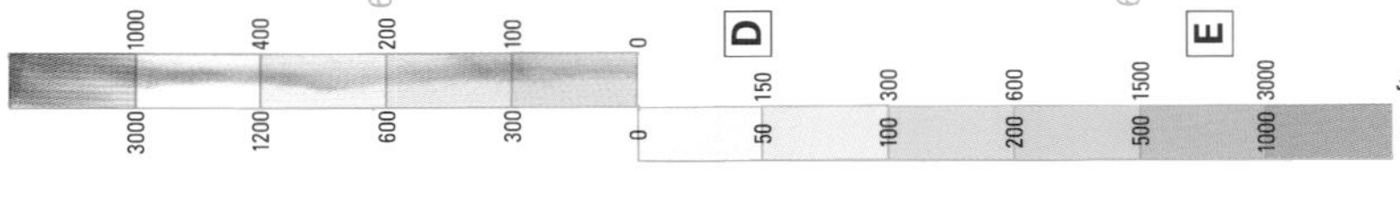

Projection: Polyconic

GREENLAND SEA

DENMARK STRAIT

ATLANTIC OCEAN

ICELAND

Arctic Circle

West from Greenwich

Regions/Sýsla:
NORÐURLAND EYSTRA
NORÐURLAND VESTRA
AUSTURLAND
SUÐURLAND
VESTURLAND
VESTFIRÐIR
SUÐURNES
Múlasýsla
Þingeyjarsýsla
Skagafjarðar sýsla
Húnavatnssýsla
Eyjafjarðar sýsla
Snæfellsnessýsla
Dalasýsla
Mýrasýsla
Borgarfjarðarsýsla
Árnessýsla
Rangárvallasýsla
Skaftafellssýsla
Strandasýsla
Barðastrandarsýsla
Ísafjarðarsýsla
Gullbringu sýsla
Austur-
Vestur-
Suður-
Norður-

Cities and towns:
Reykjavík, Kópavogur, Hafnarfjörður, Garðabær, Njarðvík, Keflavík, Grindavík, Sandgerði, Garðskagi, Akranes, Borgarnes, Stykkishólmur, Ísafjörður, Bolungarvík, Súðavík, Patreksfjörður, Sauðárkrókur, Blönduós, Siglufjörður, Ólafsfjörður, Dalvík, Akureyri, Húsavík, Kópasker, Raufarhöfn, Þórshöfn, Vopnafjörður, Egilsstaðir, Seyðisfjörður, Neskaupstaður, Eskifjörður, Reyðarfjörður, Fáskrúðsfjörður, Stöðvarfjörður, Breiðdalsvík, Djúpivogur, Höfn, Stokksnes, Kirkjubæjarklaustur, Vík, Hvolsvöllur, Hella, Selfoss, Hveragerði, Þorlákshöfn, Eyrarbakki, Stokkseyri, Vestmannaeyjar, Heimaey

Physical features:
VATNAJÖKULL, Hofsjökull, Langjökull, Mýrdalsjökull, Eyjafjallajökull, Drangajökull, Snæfellsjökull, Tungnafellsjökull, Skaftafell, Bárðarbunga 2000, Grímsvötn 1725, Hvannadalshnúkur 2119, Hekla 1491, Katla 1450, Öræfajökull

Faxaflói, Breiðafjörður, Húnaflói, Skagafjörður, Eyjafjörður, Þistilfjörður, Héraðsflói, Borgarfjörður, Berufjörður, Ísafjarðardjúp, Arnarfjörður

Surtsey, Grímsey, Papey, Eldey, Flatey

Langanes, Fontur, Horn, Straumnes, Látrar, Bjargtangar, Reykjanes, Dyrhólaey

Jökulsá á Fjöllum, Dettifoss, Mývatn, Askja 1510, Herðubreið 1682, Þjórsá, Hvítá, Ölfusá, Lagarfljót

1:16 000 000

COPYRIGHT PHILIP'S

Projection: Bonne

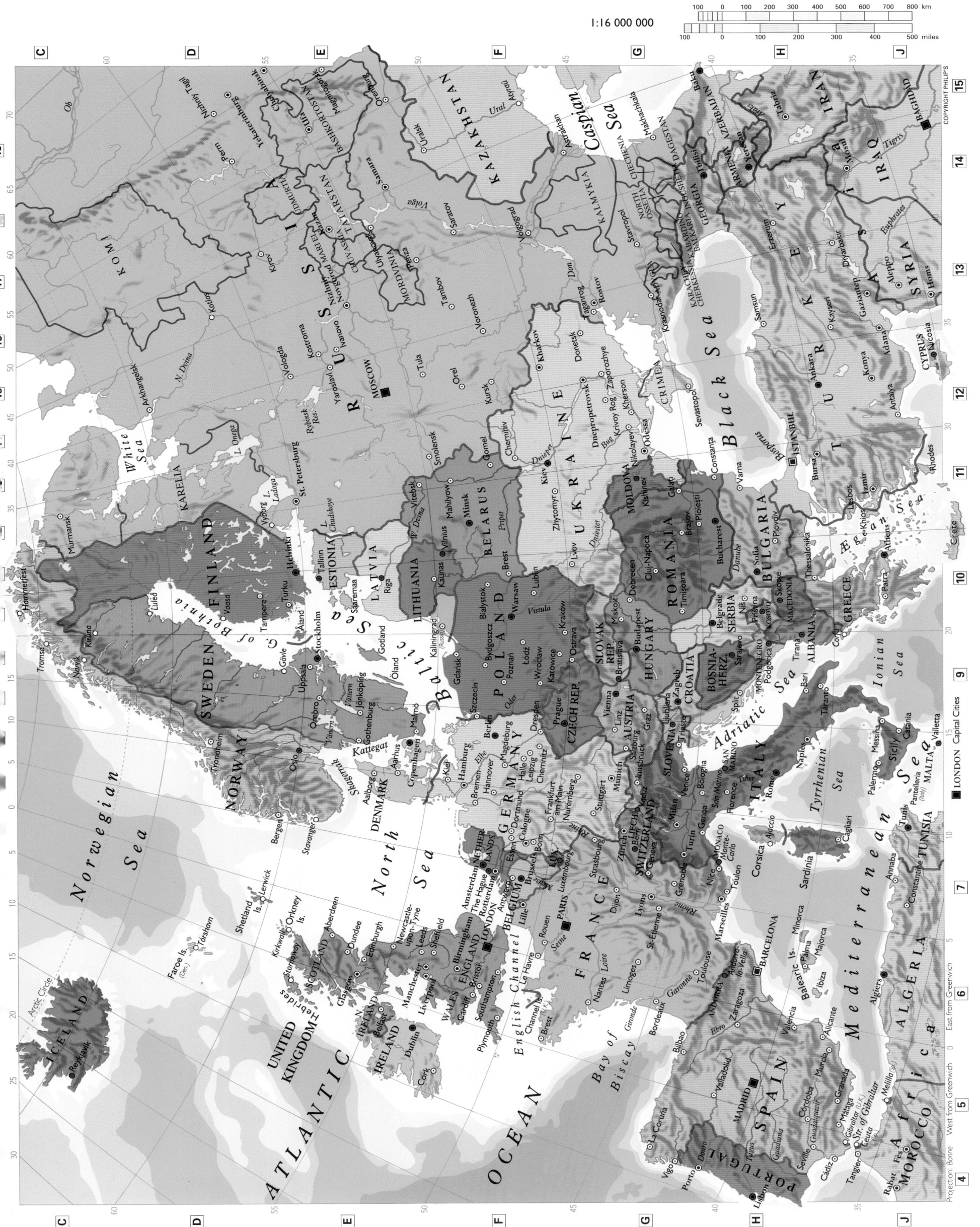

1:16 000 000

100 0 100 200 300 400 500 600 700 800 km
100 0 100 200 300 400 500 miles

Projection: Bonne   West from Greenwich   East from Greenwich   COPYRIGHT PHILIPS

1:4 800 000

50 0 25 50 75 100 125 150 175 km

50 0 25 50 75 100 125 miles

ICELAND
on same scale

FAEROE ISLANDS
on same scale

BARENTS SEA

R U S S I A

KARELIA

F I N L A N D

Lapland

N O R W A Y

S W E D E N

Gulf of Bothnia

ATLANTIC OCEAN

NORWEGIAN SEA

ICELAND

FÆROE ISLANDS
(Faeroe Is.)
(Den.)

Reykjavik

Murmansk

Oulu

Tampere

Trondheim

Östersund

Arctic Circle

West from Greenwich

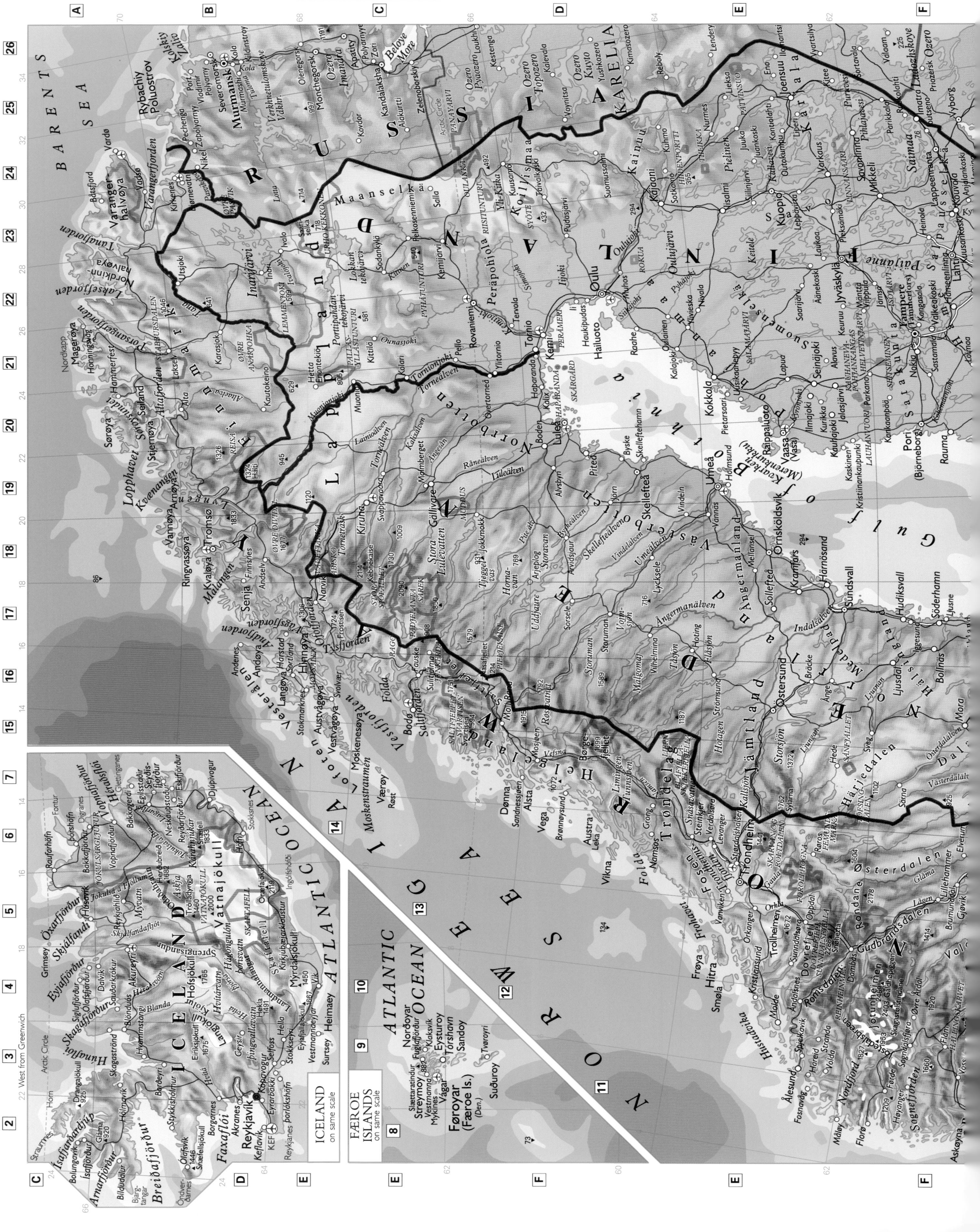

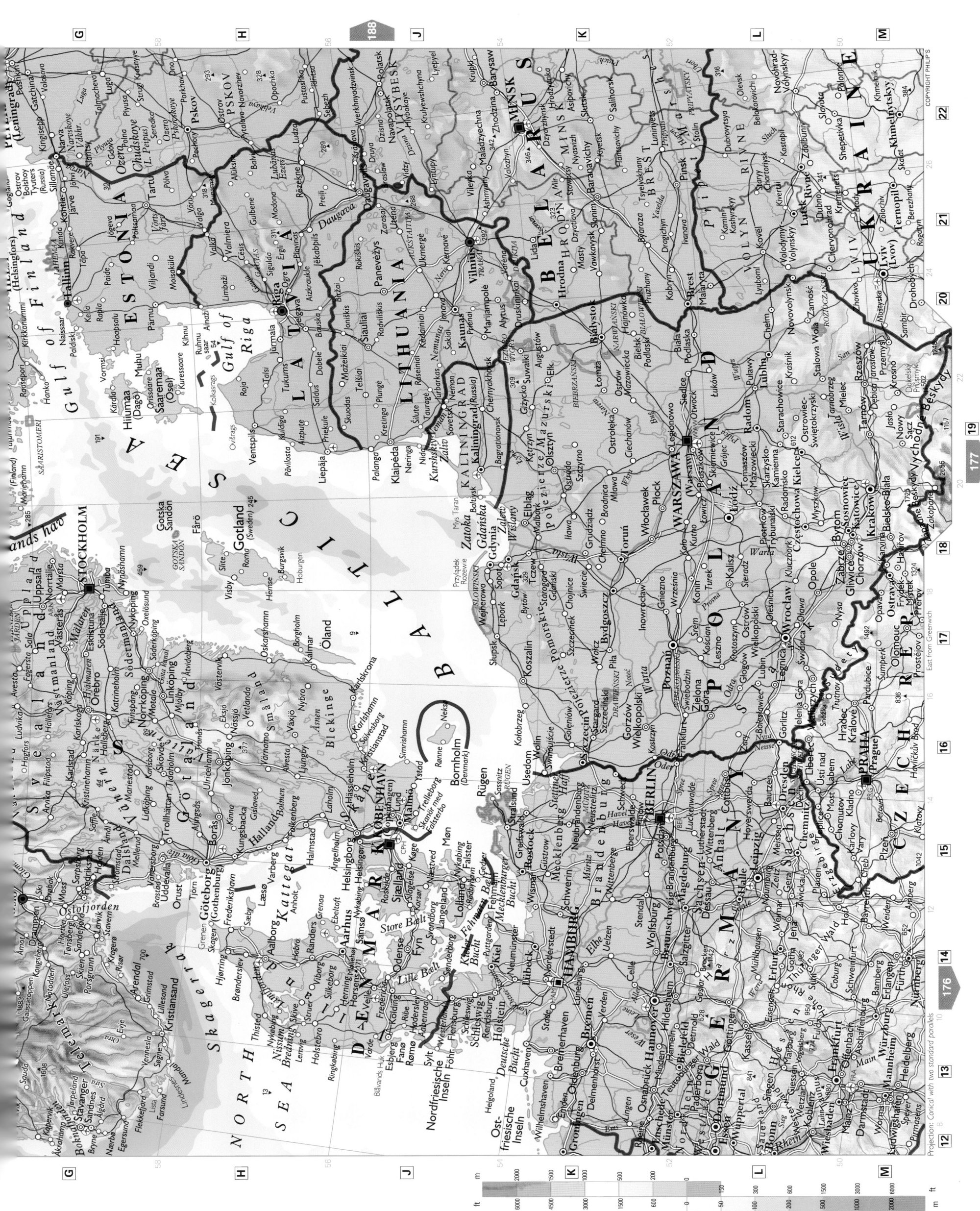

Projection: Lambert's Conformal Conic

East from Greenwich

1:2 000 000

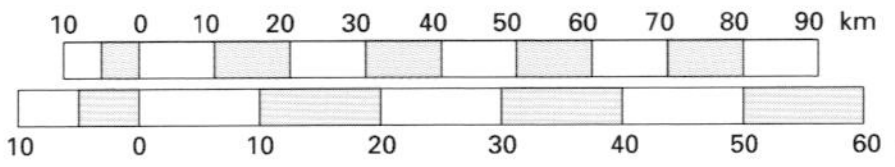

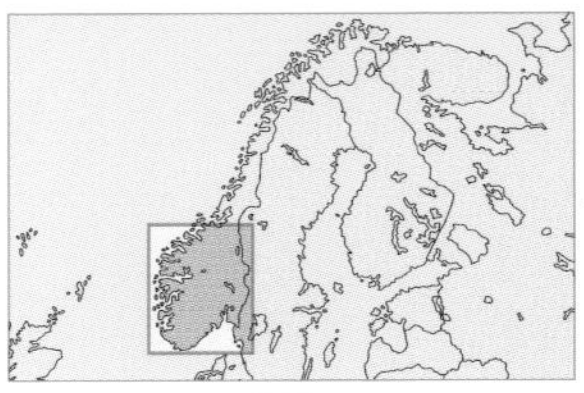

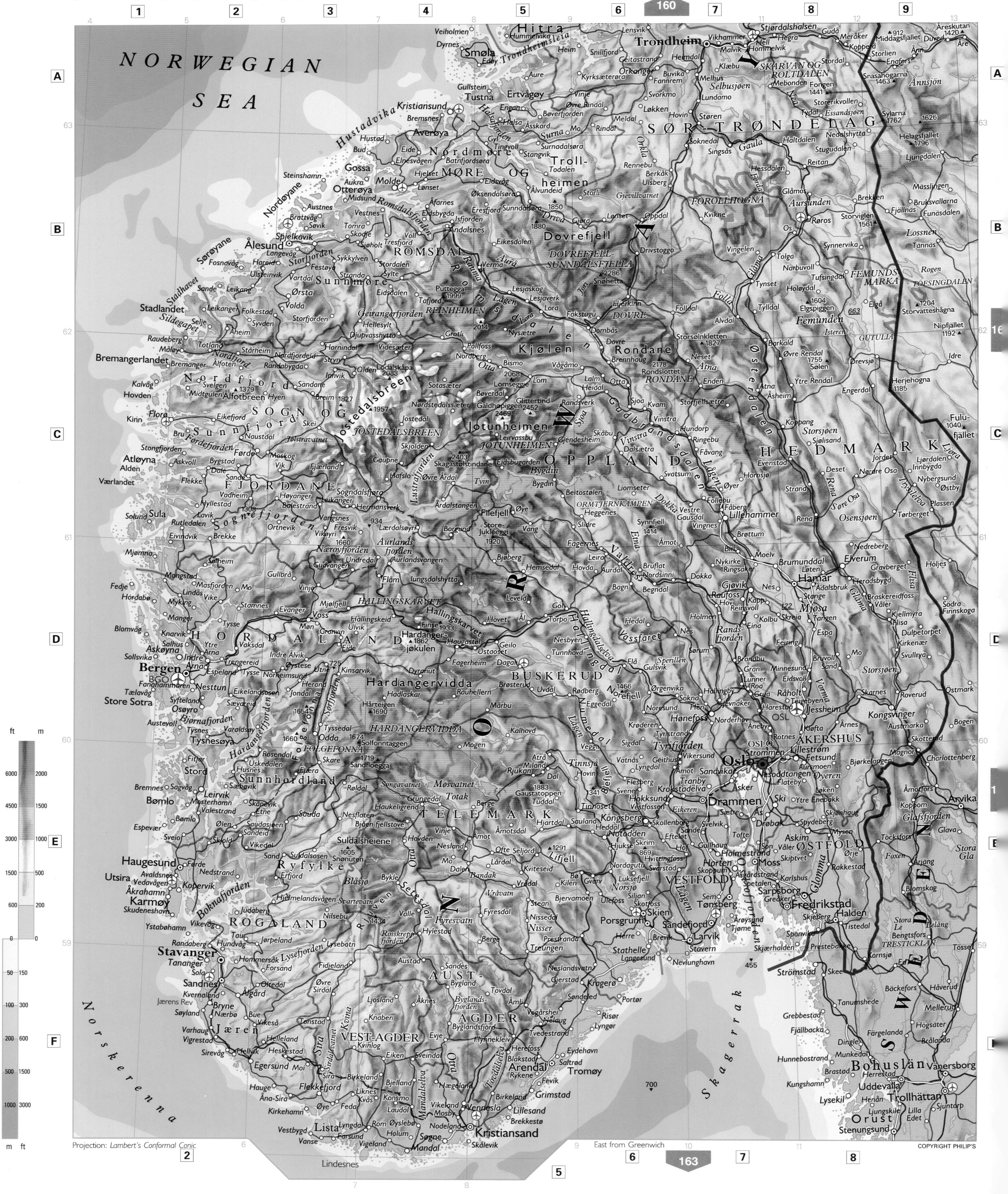

Projection: Lambert's Conformal Conic

East from Greenwich

1:4 000 000

Projection: Conical with two standard parallels

West from Greenwich

East from Greenwich
COPYRIGHT PHILIP'S

NORWAY

NETHERLANDS

BELGIUM

FRANCE

A T L A N T I C   O C E A N

N O R T H   S E A

I R I S H   S E A

C E L T I C   S E A

English Channel

Bergen
Askøyna
Osøyro
Stord
Bømlo
Leirvik
Haugesund
Kopervik
Åkrahamn
Stavanger
Sandnes
Bryne
Nærbø
Boknafjorden

Shetland Is.
(U.K.)
Yell
Unst
Fetlar
453
Foula
Mainland
Lerwick

Fair Isle

Orkney Is.
Westray
Sanday
Stronsay
Mainland
Kirkwall
Hoy
481
South
Ronaldsay

Pentland Firth

C. Wrath
Thurso
Wick
Helmsdale
Golspie
Lairg
Tain
Invergordon
Dingwall
Inverness
Nairn
Elgin
Buckie
Banff
Fraserburgh
Huntly
Peterhead
Inverurie
Aberdeen

Lewis
Stornoway
Harris
North
Uist
Benbecula
South Uist
Barra
Skye
Portree
Mallaig
Eigg
Rum
Coll
Tiree
Mull
Iona
Colonsay
Tobermory
Oban

St. Kilda
(U.K.)

Outer Hebrides
Inner Hebrides
North Minch
Sea of the Hebrides
North West Highlands

SCOTLAND
Grampian Mts.
CAIRNGORMS Mts.
Glen Mor
L. Ness
Aviemore
Ben Nevis
1344
Fort William
Glen
Dee
Ballater
Stonehaven
Montrose
Forfar
Arbroath
Dundee
St. Andrews
Perth
Stirling
Glenrothes
Kirkcaldy
Dunfermline
Dunbar

L. LOMOND
& TROSSACHS
L. Lomond
L. Awe
L. Fyne
Jura
Islay
Arran
Campbeltown

GLASGOW
Paisley
Greenock
Dumbarton
Motherwell
Hamilton
East Kilbride
Kilmarnock
Irvine
Ayr
Edinburgh
Galashiels
Jedburgh
Hawick
Berwick-upon-Tweed

Southern Uplands
Cheviot Hills
816
Alnwick

Malin Hd.
Girvan
Stranraer
Kirkcudbright
Dumfries
Carlisle
Annan
Hexham
NORTHUMBERLAND
Newcastle-upon-Tyne
South Shields
Sunderland
Gateshead
Durham
Hartlepool
Redcar
Darlington
Middlesbrough
Stockton-
on-Tees
N. YORK MOORS
Scarborough

North Channel
Firth of Clyde

Buncrana
Arranmore
Letterkenny
Coleraine
Derry/Londonderry
Ballymena
Larne
Donegal
Lifford
Antrim
Bangor
Omagh
Lurgan
Belfast
Lisburn
NORTHERN IRELAND
Ulster
Lough
Neagh
Armagh
Portadown
Newry
GLENVEAGH

Bundoran
Ballina
Enniskillen
Clones
Castlebar
Sligo
Lower L.
Erne
Leitrim
Cavan
Castleblaney
620
Mull of
Galloway
I. of Man
Douglas
852

Workington
Whitehaven
Cumbrian
Mts.
978
LAKE
DISTRICT
Barrow-
in-Furness
Lancaster
Pennines
893
YORKSHIRE
DALES

UNITED

KINGDOM

Achill I.
Westport
Lough
Mask
Connemara
Galway B.
Aran Is.
Galway
BURREN
Lough
Corrib
Roscommon
Longford
Athlone
Lough
Ree
Mullingar
Ennis
Kilrush
Nenagh
Limerick
Thurles
Tipperary
Clonmel
920
Mallow
Tralee
Listowel
Dingle
Killarney
926
Macgillycuddy's Reeks
1041
Carrauntoohill
Kenmare
Bandon
Cork
Cóbh
Kinsale
Bantry
C. Clear

IRELAND
Shannon
Lough
Derg
Roscrea
Portlaoise
Carlow
Kilkenny
Carrick-on-Suir
Waterford
Dungarvan
Youghal
Wexford
Rosslare

DUBLIN
Dun Laoghaire
Bray
Arklow
Wicklow
Wicklow Mts.
Athy
Kildare
Kells
Boyne
Drogheda
Dundalk
Liffey
Tullamore
Ballinasloe
Blackwater
Barrow

Holyhead
Anglesey
Bangor
Colwyn Bay
Conway
Llandudno
Rhyl
Wrexham
Chester
Crewe
1085
Snowdon
SNOWDONIA
Pwllheli
Cardigan
Bay
Aberystwyth
Welshpool
Shrewsbury
Cambrian Mts.
886
WALES
Brecon
BRECON
BEACONS
Carmarthen
Merthyr Tydfil
Neath
Llanelli
Swansea
Port Talbot
Rhondda
Cwmbran
Pontypridd
Newport
Cardiff
Barry
PEMBROKESHIRE
COAST
Milford Haven
Haverfordwest
Pembroke
Fishguard

Blackpool
Preston
Blackburn
Burnley
Keighley
Bradford
Leeds
Bolton
Oldham
636
Huddersfield
Halifax
Barnsley
MANCHESTER
Stockport
Warrington
LIVERPOOL
Crewe
Stoke-
on-Trent
Sheffield
Rotherham
Chesterfield
Mansfield
PEAK
DISTRICT
Derby
Nottingham
Stafford
Telford
Wolverhampton
BIRMINGHAM
Redditch
Nuneaton
Coventry
Royal
Leamington Spa
Worcester
Hereford
Cheltenham
Gloucester
ENGLAND
Cotswold Hills
Stratford
Rugby
Leicester
Corby
Northampton
Milton Keynes
Bedford
Cambridge

York
Beverley
Kingston upon Hull
Humber
Goole
Scunthorpe
Grimsby
Lincoln
Louth
Skegness
The Wash
Boston
Grantham
Trent
Nene
King's Lynn
THE
BROADS
Norwich
Great Yarmouth
Lowestoft
Cromer
Ely
Thetford
Bury St. Edmunds
Peterborough
Harrogate
Bridlington

Texel
Den Helder
Alkmaar
Haarlem
's-Gravenhage
(Den Haag)
Hoek van Holland
ROTTERDAM
Dordrecht
Vlissingen
Zeebrugge
Oostende
Brugge
Gent
Antwerpen
Mechelen
BRUSSEL
(Bruxelles)
Tournai
LILLE
Roubaix
Tourcoing
Villeneuve
d'Ascq

IRELAND
St. George's Channel

Cardigan
Bay

Bristol Channel
Exmoor
EXMOOR
Barnstaple
Bude
Newquay
Truro
Penzance
Land's End
Isles of Scilly
Falmouth
St. Austell
Plymouth
DARTMOOR
618
Exeter
Exmouth
Torbay
Taunton
Yeovil
Weston-super-
Mare
Bath
Bristol
Newbury
Swindon
Reading
Basingstoke
Salisbury
NEW
FOREST
Southampton
Bournemouth
Poole
Newport
Isle of
Wight
Weymouth
Portsmouth
Fareham
Havant
Winchester
Guildford
LONDON
Slough
High Wycombe
Oxford
Hemel
Hempstead
Watford
Luton
Stevenage
Harlow
Chelmsford
Basildon
Southend-on-Sea
Chatham
Maidstone
Royal
Tunbridge Wells
Crawley
Brighton
Worthing
Eastbourne
Hastings
Folkestone
Dover
Canterbury
Margate
Ashford
Reigate
SOUTH
DOWNS
Thames
LGW
LHR

Str. of Dover
C.
Gris-
Nez
Calais
Dunkerque
Boulogne-
sur-Mer
Le Touquet-
Paris-Plage
33
St-Omer
Béthune
Bruay-la-
Buissière
Lens
Valenciennes
Cambrai
BELGIUM
FRANCE
Picardie
Abbeville
Le Tréport
Dieppe
Fécamp
Pays de
Caux
Amiens
St.
Quentin
Laon
Le Havre
Rouen
Bolbec
Elbeuf
Seine
Lisieux
Caen
Bayeux
Trouville-
sur-Mer
Cherbourg
Valognes
Pte. de
Barfleur
C. de la
Hague
Alderney
Guernsey
St. Peter
Port
Sark
Jersey
St. Helier
Channel Is.
(U.K.)
Cotentin

161
176
171

ft   m
3000   1000
1500   500
600   200
0   0
50   150
100   300
200   500
500   1500
1000   3000
2000   6000
m   ft

1:1 600 000

10 0 10 20 30 40 50 60 70 80 km
10 0 10 20 30 40 50 miles

SCOTLAND
Kintyre
Brodick
Arran
Mull of Oa
Campbeltown
Mull of Kintyre
Ailsa Craig
Firth of Clyde
L. Ryan
Cairnryan
Stranraer
Portpatrick

Malin Hd.
Inishtrahull
Trawbreaga B.
Fanad Hd.
Malin Pen.
Mulroy B.
Carndonagh
Giants Causeway
Rathlin I.
Fair Hd.
Ballycastle
Sheep Haven
Lough Swilly
Inishowen Pen.
Moville
Portstewart
Portrush
Coleraine
Cushendall
Garron Pt.
Horn Hd.
Tory I.
Dunfanaghy
Buncrana
Limavady
Ballymoney
Trostan 554
Carncastle
Larne
Bloody Foreland
Cloghaneely
L. Foyle
Londonderry (Derry)
Dungiven
Ballymena
Randalstown
Carrickfergus
Arranmore
The Rosses
Errigal 752
Dunglow
Letterkenny
Rathmelton
Strabane
Sawel Mt. 683
Maghera
ANTRIM
Belfast L.
Bangor
Mts. of Antrim
Crohy Hd.
Gweebarra B.
883
Lifford
Sion Mills
Newtownstewart
Magherafelt
Moneymore
Antrim
Newtownabbey
Holywood
Donaghadee
Newtownards
Dawros Hd.
Glenveagh
DONEGAL
LONDONDERRY
Sperrin Mts.
Cookstown
Lough Neagh
Belfast
Lisburn
Comber
Ards Pen.
Rossan Pt.
Glencolumbkille
601 Slieve League
Killybegs
Donegal
Castlederg
TYRONE
Omagh
Coalisland
Dungannon
NORTHERN
Lurgan
Craigavon
Portadown
Lagan
Ballynahinch
Portaferry
St. John's Pt.
Donegal Bay
Ballyshannon
Bundoran
Lough Erne
Dromore
Irvinestown
Ballygawley
Clogher
IRELAND
Armagh
Banbridge
Dromore
Ballyquintin Pt.
Inishmurray
Lower L. Erne
Enniskillen
Monaghan
Middletown
Keady
DOWN
Dundrum B.
Lough Melvin
Manorhamilton
Belturbet
Clones
MONAGHAN
Castleblaney
Cootehill
Newry
Mourne Mts.
Slieve Donard 852
Newcastle
Ardglass
St. John's Pt.
Drumcliff
Sligo
Lackagh Hills
Upper L. Erne
Annalee
577 Slieve Gullion
Warrenpoint
Kilkeel
Sligo Bay
L. Arrow
FERMANAGH
Carrickmacross
Dundalk (Dún Dealgan)
Greenore
Downpatrick
Broad Haven
Portacloy
Downpatrick Hd.
Lenadoon Pt.
Killala B.
Dromore West
L. Allen
LEITRIM
Ballyconnell
Carrickmacross
LOUTH
Carlingford L.
Erris Hd.
Belmullet
380
Killala
Leitrim
L. Oughter
Cavan
Baileborough
Kingscourt
Ardee
Dunleer
Clogher Hd.
Mullet Pen.
Crossmolina
Ballina
Tobercurry
Boyle
Carrick-on-Shannon
CAVAN
L. Gowna
L. Sheelin
Kells (Ceanannus Mor)
Blackwater
Drogheda (Droichead Átha)
Inishkea North
BALLYCROY
L. Conn
Foxford
544
SLIGO
Ballymote
L. Key
Granard
Oldcastle
BEND OF THE BOYNE
Inishkea South
Blacksod Bay
Slieve Gamph
Charlestown
L. Gara
Ballaghaderreen
Strokestown
LONGFORD
Castlepollard
Balbriggan
Achill Hd.
672
Nephin Beg Range
806
Nephin
Swinford
Knock
ROSCOMMON
Castlerea
Longford
Roscommon
MEATH
Navan (An Uaimh)
Skerries
Ballyboghil
Rush
Achill I.
461
Clare I.
Clew Bay
Westport
Castlebar
MAYO
Ballyhaunis
Castlerea
Athboy
Trim
Dunshaughlin
Swords
Malahide
Inishturk
765
Croagh Patrick
Louisburgh
Newport
Claremorris
IRELAND
Royal Canal
Maynooth
Lambay I.
Inishbofin
Mweelrea 819
683
Partry Mts.
L. Carra
Ballinrobe
Glennamaddy
Leinster
Mullingar
WESTMEATH
Moate
Kilbeggan
Edenderry
Celbridge
Lucan
DUBLIN (Baile Átha Cliath)
Howth
Inishshark
Killary Harbour
Lough Mask
Tuam
Mount Bellew Bridge
Lough Ree
Athlone
Clara
Ferbane
Tullamore
Daingean
Rathangan
KILDARE
Newbridge
Naas
Dún Laoghaire
Dalkey
Killiney
Connemara
CONNEMARA
Lough Corrib
Oughterard
GALWAY
Athenry
Ballinasloe
Shannonbridge
Banagher
OFFALY
Bog of Allen
Kildare
Monasterevin
Bray
Greystones
Clifden
Slyne Hd.
Roundstone
Spiddle
Galway (Gaillimh)
Loughrea
Aughrim
Portumna
Birr
Portarlington
Mountmellick
Portlaoise
Athy
Kippure 752
WICKLOW
WICKLOW MTS.
Wicklow
Bertraghboy B.
Kilkieran B.
Galway Bay
Black Hd.
Burren
Kinvarra
Slieve Aughty
368
Gort
Portumna
Borrisokane
Roscrea
Slieve Bloom
528 Arderin
LAOIS
Abbeyleix
Durrow
Castlecomer
Poulaphouca Res.
Lugnaquilla 926
Wicklow Hd.
Inishmore
Aran Is.
Inishmaan
Inisheer
345
Lisdoonvarna
BURREN
Crusheen
Feakle
Tulla
Nenagh
Donaghmore
Mountrath
CARLOW
Carlow
Tullow
Arklow
Cliffs of Moher
Hags Hd.
Liscannor Bay
Ennistimon
Lough Derg
Killaloe
Silvermine Mts.
694 Keeper Hill
Templemore
Johnstown
Kilkenny
Bagenalstown (Muine Bheag)
Bunclody
Gorey
Mal Bay
Mutton I.
Milltown Malbay
CLARE
Ennis
Sixmilebridge
Thurles
KILKENNY
Callan
796 Mt. Leinster
Shillelagh
Ballycanew
Loop Hd.
Kilkee
Shannon
Limerick (Luimneach)
TIPPERARY
Golden Vale
Tipperary
Cashel
754
Thomastown
Blackstairs Mt.
Enniscorthy
Cahore Pt.
Kilrush
Tarbert
Foynes
Glin
Adare
Rathkeale
Johnstown
Clonmel
Carrick-on-Suir
WEXFORD
Mouth of the Shannon
Ballybunion
Newcastle West
LIMERICK
Kilfinnane
Galtymore 920
Galty Mts.
Caher
Slievenamon 722
New Ross
Wexford
Kerry Hd.
Listowel
Feale
Abbeyfeale
Charleville (Rath Luirc)
519
Mitchelstown
Ballyporeen
Comeragh Mts. 792
Knockmealdown Mts. 795
Waterford (Port Láirge)
Passage East
Rosslare Harbour
Rosslare (Europort)
Smerwick Harbour
Brandon B.
Tralee B.
Ardfert
Ballyheige
Newmarket
Buttevant
Fermoy
Lismore
Dungarvan
Dunmore East
Hook Hd.
Kilmore Quay
Carnsore Pt.
Great Blasket I.
Dingle Pen.
953
Brandon Mt.
Slieve Mish 863
Castleisland
KERRY
Maine
Kanturk
Mallow
Nagles Mts.
429
Blackwater
Dungarvan Harbour
Tramore
Waterford Harbour
Saltee Is.
Dingle
Castlemaine
Laune
Killarney
Milstreet
WATERFORD
Tramore B.
Slea Hd.
Inishvickillane
Dingle Bay
Glenbeigh
Killorglin
L. Leane
775
Macgillycuddy's Reeks
Carrauntoohil 1041
KILLARNEY
Boggeragh Mts.
646
CORK
Cork (Corcaigh)
Youghal
Youghal B.
Valencia I.
Puffin I.
Cahirciveen
Iveragh Pen.
Kilgarvan
707
Macroom
Blarney
Midleton
Cobh
St. David's Hd.
St. David's
Great Skellig
Ballinskelligs B.
Sneem
Kenmare River
Caha Mts. 686
Glengarriff
Ballincollig
Passage West
Crosshaven
St. Brides Bay
Scariff I.
L. Currane
Kenmare
Dunmanway
Bandon
Carrigaline
Cork Harbour
WALES
Dursey I.
Castletown Bearhaven
Bear I.
Whiddy I.
Bantry
Timoleague
Kinsale
Old Head of Kinsale
Crow Hd.
Bantry Bay
Ballydehob
Clonakilty
Clonakilty B.
Galley Hd.
Dunmanus B.
Skull
Long I.
Baltimore
Sherkin I.
Mizen Hd.
C. Clear
Clear I.
Fastnet Rock

ATLANTIC OCEAN
NORTH CHANNEL
IRISH SEA
** St. George's Channel**
CELTIC SEA

Ulster
Connaught
Leinster
Munster

West from Greenwich

Projection: Lambert's Conformal Conic

COPYRIGHT PHILIP'S

1:1 600 000

Key to Scottish unitary
authorities on map
1 CITY OF ABERDEEN 8 EAST RENFREWSHIRE
2 DUNDEE CITY 9 NORTH LANARKSHIRE
3 WEST DUNBARTONSHIRE 10 FALKIRK
4 EAST DUNBARTONSHIRE 11 CLACKMANNANSHIRE
5 CITY OF GLASGOW 12 WEST LOTHIAN
6 INVERCLYDE 13 CITY OF EDINBURGH
7 RENFREWSHIRE 14 MIDLOTHIAN

ORKNEY IS.
on same scale

ORKNEY

SHETLAND IS.
on same scale

SHETLAND

Projection : Lambert's Conformal Conic

West from Greenwich

COPYRIGHT PHILIP'S

ATLANTIC OCEAN

SCOTLAND

NORTH SEA

ENGLAND

NORTHERN IRELAND

North Channel

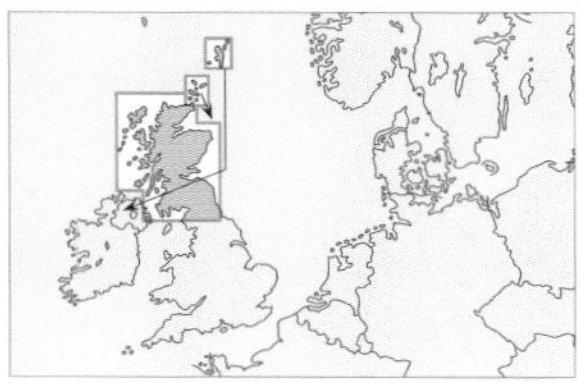

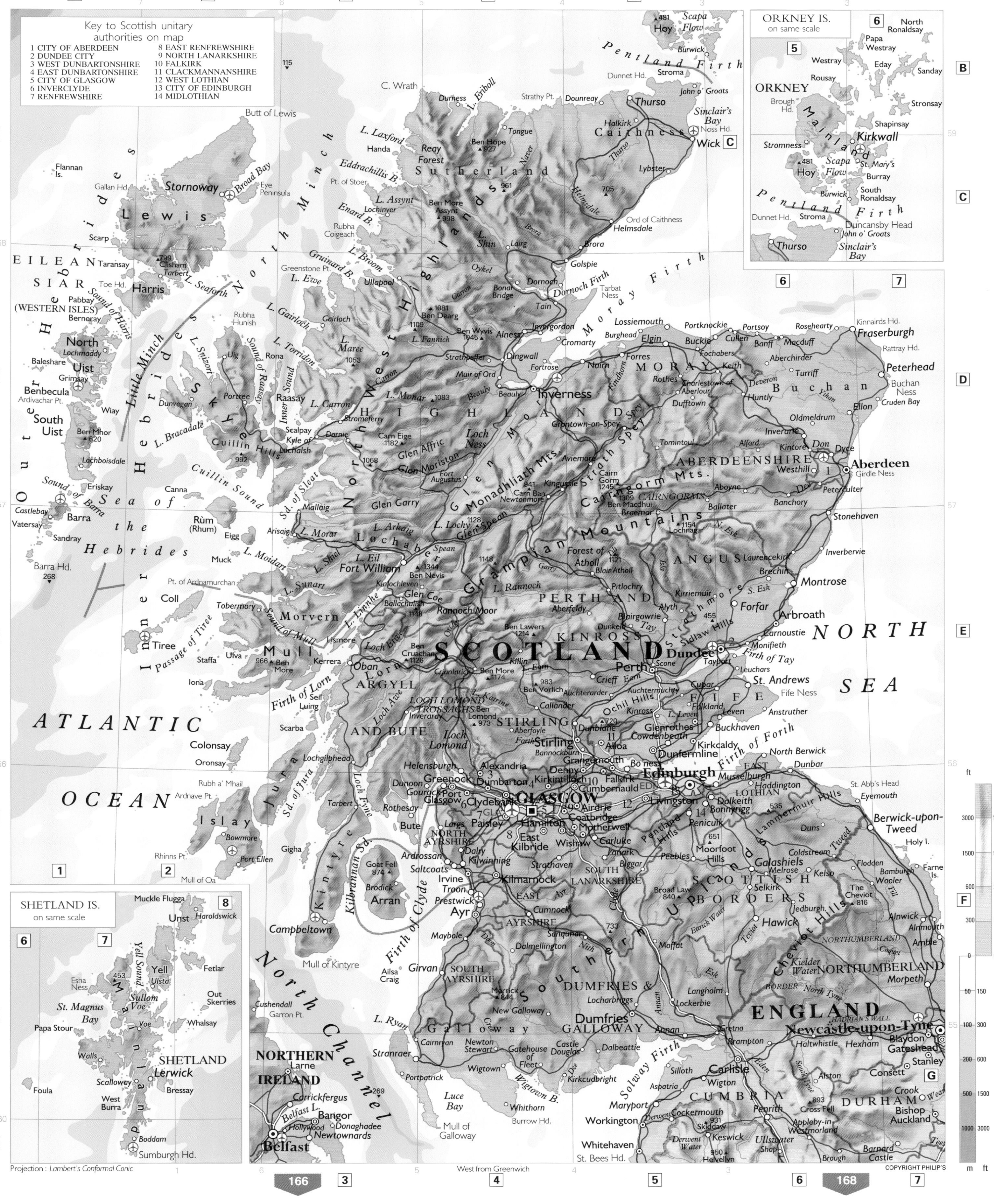

10 10 20 30 40 50 60 70 80 km

1:1 600 000

10 0 10 20 30 40 50 miles

167
166

Key to English unitary
authorities on map

25 HARTLEPOOL
26 DARLINGTON
27 STOCKTON-ON-TEES
28 MIDDLESBROUGH
29 REDCAR AND CLEVELAND
30 BLACKPOOL
31 BLACKBURN WITH DARWEN
32 HALTON
33 WARRINGTON
34 KINGSTON UPON HULL
35 NORTH EAST LINCOLNSHIRE
36 STOKE-ON-TRENT
37 TELFORD AND WREKIN
38 DERBY CITY
39 CITY OF NOTTINGHAM
40 LEICESTER CITY
41 RUTLAND
42 PETERBOROUGH
43 MILTON KEYNES
44 LUTON
45 NORTH SOMERSET
46 CITY OF BRISTOL
47 BATH AND NORTH EAST SOMERSET
48 SWINDON
49 READING
50 WOKINGHAM
51 WINDSOR AND MAIDENHEAD
52 SLOUGH
53 BRACKNELL FOREST
54 THURROCK
55 SOUTHEND-ON-SEA
56 MEDWAY
57 PLYMOUTH
58 TORBAY
59 POOLE
60 BOURNEMOUTH
61 SOUTHAMPTON
62 PORTSMOUTH
63 BRIGHTON AND HOVE
64 BEDFORD
65 CENTRAL BEDFORDSHIRE
66 CHESHIRE WEST AND CHESTER
67 CHESHIRE EAST

Key to Welsh unitary
authorities on map

15 SWANSEA
16 NEATH PORT TALBOT
17 BRIDGEND
18 RHONDDA CYNON TAFF
19 MERTHYR TYDFIL
20 CAERPHILLY
21 BLAENAU GWENT
22 TORFAEN
23 CARDIFF
24 NEWPORT

N O R T H   S E A

I R I S H   S E A

North Channel

S C O T L A N D

NORTHERN IRELAND

NORTHUMBERLAND

CUMBRIA

LANCASHIRE

YORKSHIRE

LINCOLNSHIRE

ISLE OF MAN

Edinburgh · Glasgow · Newcastle-upon-Tyne · Sunderland · Middlesbrough · Kingston upon Hull · Sheffield · Manchester · Liverpool · Leeds · Bradford · Derby · Stoke-on-Trent · Chester · Belfast

The Wash

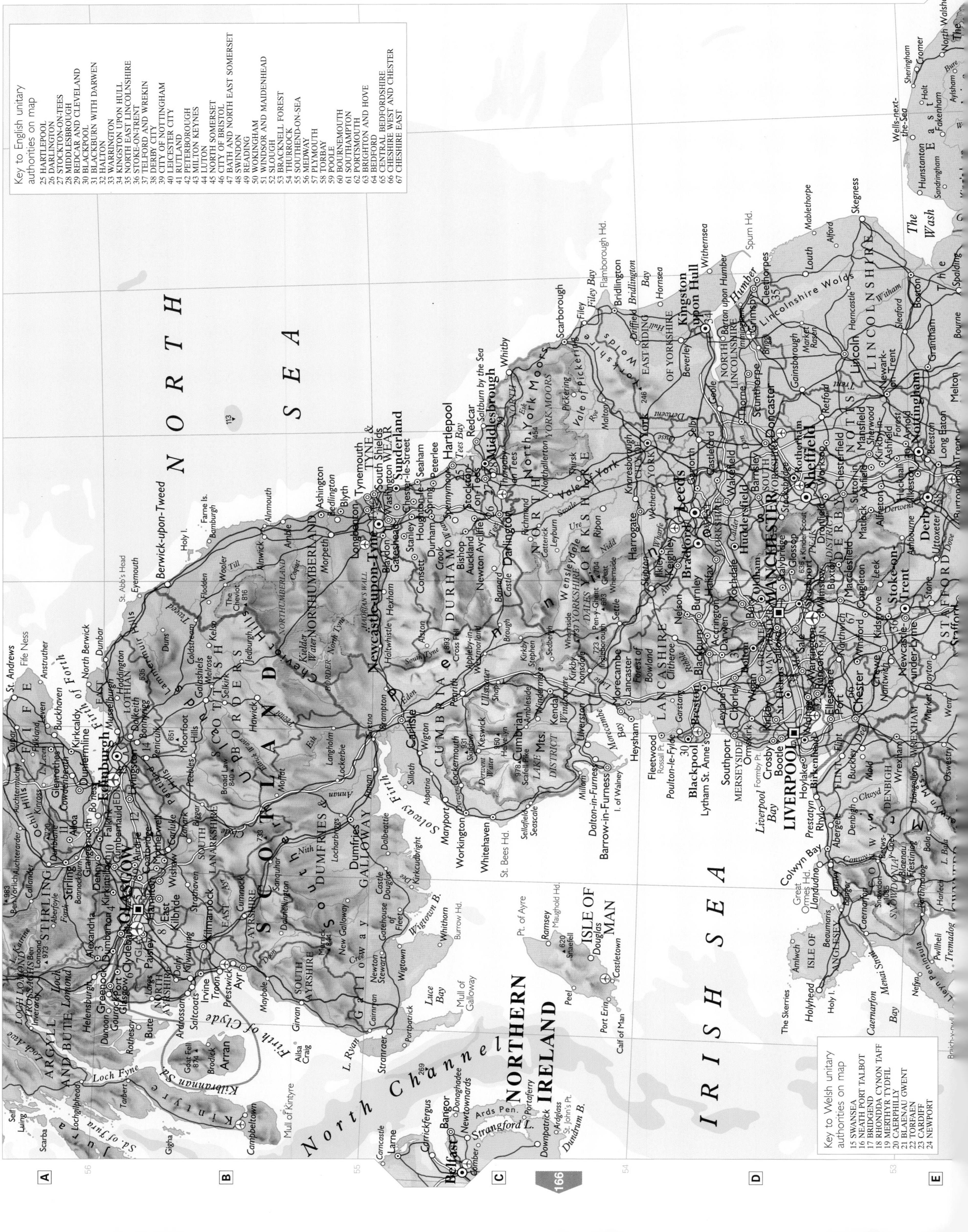

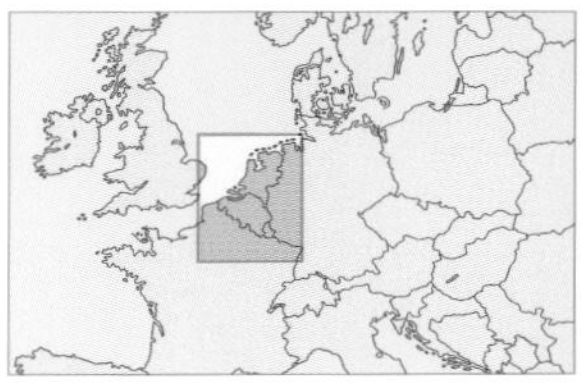

1:2 000 000

10 0 10 20 30 40 50 60 70 80 90 km
10 0 10 20 30 40 50 60 miles

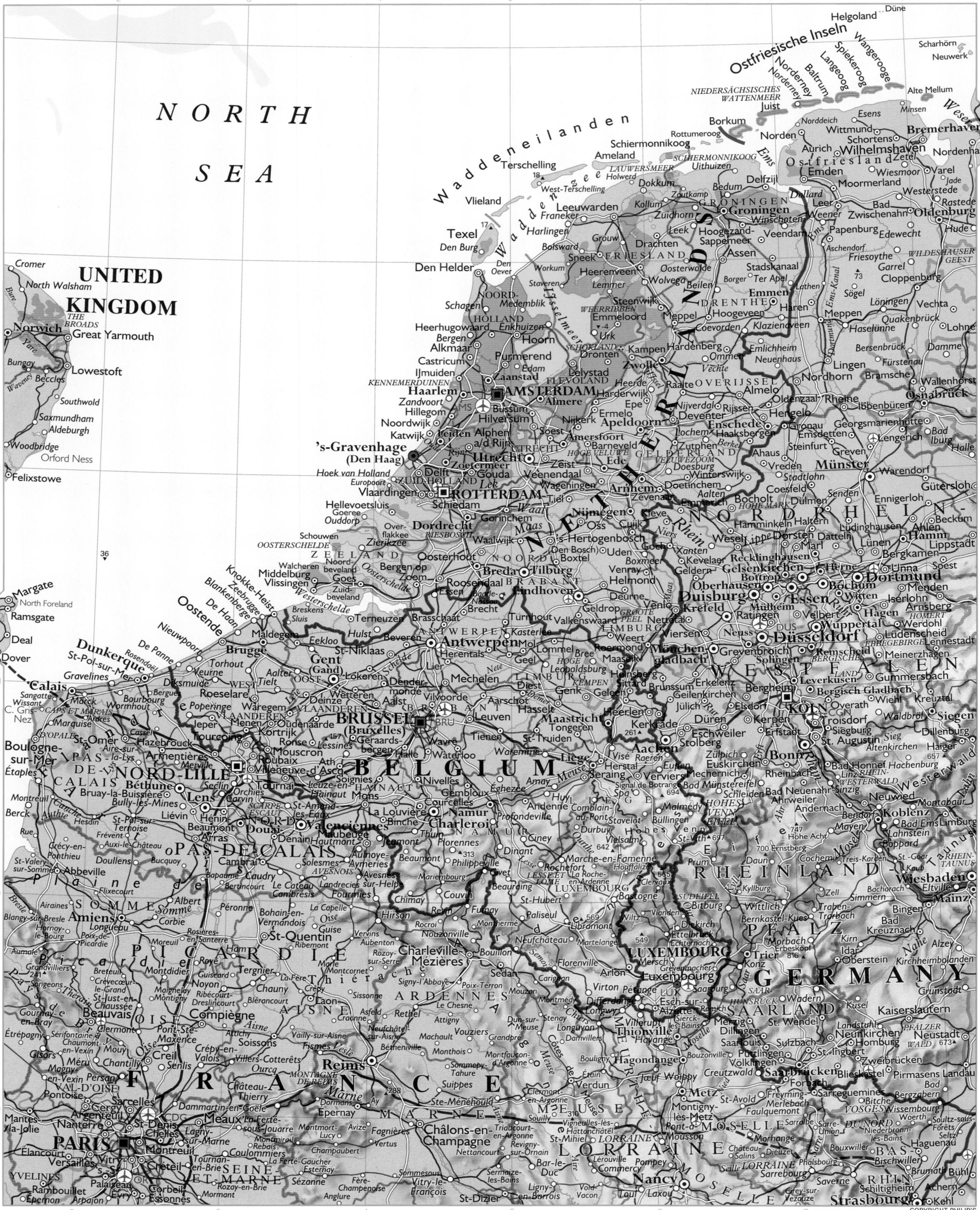

NORTH SEA

UNITED KINGDOM

NETHERLANDS

BELGIUM

LUXEMBOURG

GERMANY

FRANCE

AMSTERDAM
's-Gravenhage (Den Haag)
ROTTERDAM
Utrecht
BRUSSEL (Bruxelles)
Antwerpen
Gent (Gand)
PARIS
Reims
Nancy
Strasbourg
Luxembourg

Cromer · North Walsham · Norwich · Great Yarmouth · Lowestoft · Southwold · Aldeburgh · Woodbridge · Orford Ness · Felixstowe · Margate · North Foreland · Ramsgate · Deal · Dover · Calais

Groningen · Leeuwarden · Assen · Zwolle · Emmen · Haarlem · Alkmaar · Hoorn · Almere · Apeldoorn · Enschede · Arnhem · Nijmegen · Eindhoven · Tilburg · Breda · Venlo · Maastricht · Heerlen

Bremerhaven · Wilhelmshaven · Oldenburg · Emden · Osnabrück · Münster · Dortmund · Bochum · Essen · Duisburg · Düsseldorf · Mönchengladbach · Köln · Bonn · Aachen · Koblenz · Wiesbaden · Mainz · Saarbrücken · Kaiserslautern

Oostende · Brugge · Antwerpen · Mechelen · Leuven · Namur · Charleroi · Liège · Verviers · Mons · Tournai · Arlon · Bastogne

Dunkerque · Lille · Valenciennes · Amiens · St-Quentin · Laon · Reims · Charleville-Mézières · Sedan · Verdun · Metz · Thionville

— High-speed rail routes

Underlined towns give their name to the administrative area in which they stand.

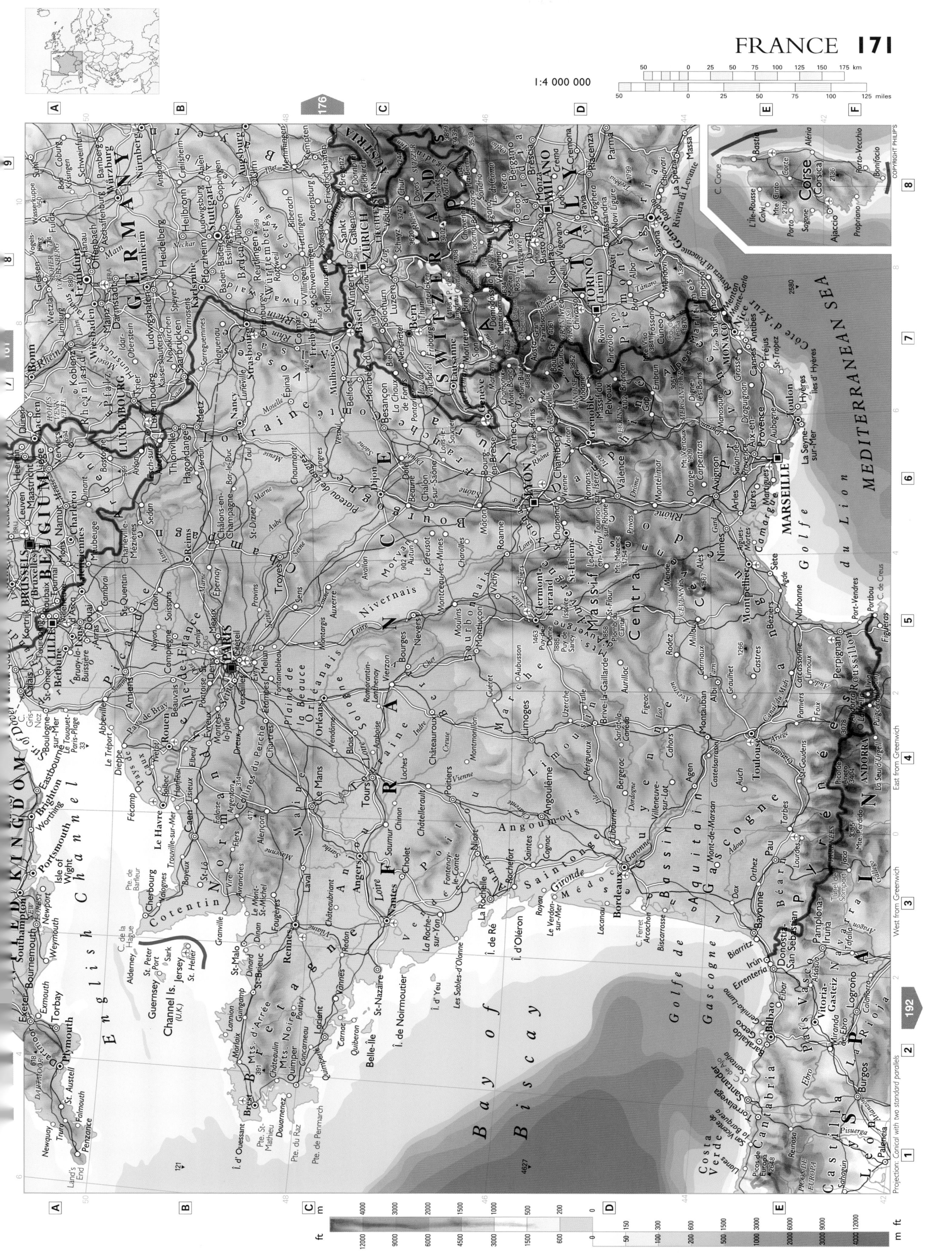

1:4 000 000

50 0 25 50 75 100 125 150 175 km

50 0 25 50 75 100 125 miles

Corse (Corsica)

MEDITERRANEAN SEA

Projection: Conical with two standard parallels

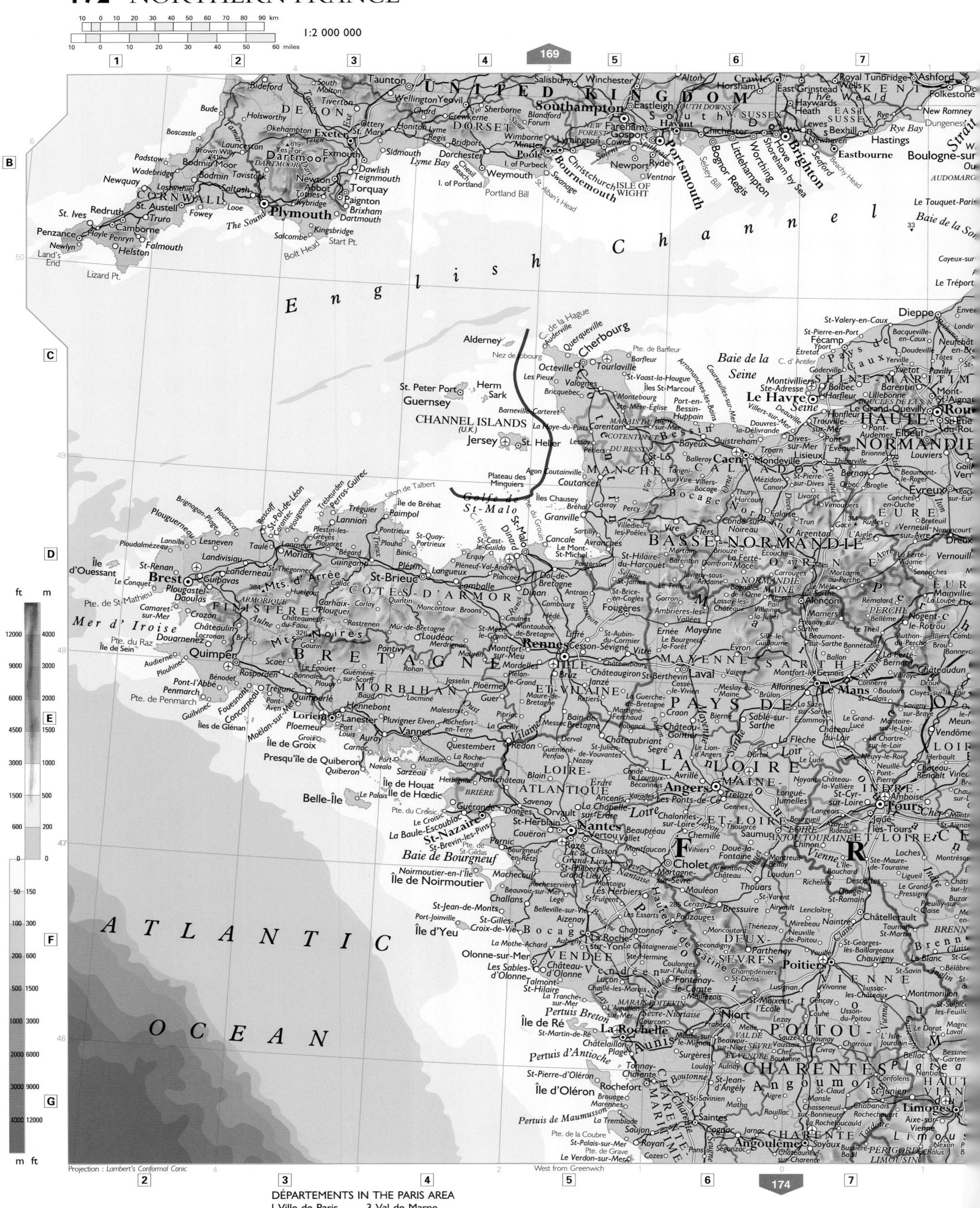

1:2 000 000

10 0 10 20 30 40 50 60 70 80 90 km

10 0 10 20 30 40 50 60 miles

ft m

12000 4000

9000 3000

6000 2000

4500 1500

3000 1000

1500 500

600 200

0 0

50 150

100 300

200 600

500 1500

2000 6000

3000 9000

4000 12000

m ft

Projection : Lambert's Conformal Conic

West from Greenwich

DÉPARTEMENTS IN THE PARIS AREA
1 Ville de Paris   3 Val-de-Marne
2 Seine-St-Denis   4 Hauts-de-Seine

Underlined towns give their name to the
administrative area in which they stand.

East from Greenwich

COPYRIGHT PHILIP'S

———— TGV (Train à Grande Vitesse)

TGV (Train à Grande Vitesse)

50 25 0 25 50 75 100 125 150 175 km
50 25 0 25 50 75 100 125 miles

1:4 000 000

Projection: Conical with two standard parallels

NORTH SEA

BALTIC SEA

ADRIATIC SEA

UNITED KINGDOM

Norwich · Great Yarmouth · Lowestoft · Ipswich · Felixstowe · Harwich · Margate · Dover · Calais · Dunkerque · Boulogne-sur-Mer · Cromer

NETHERLANDS
AMSTERDAM · Haarlem · 's-Gravenhage (Den Haag) · Leiden · Gouda · ROTTERDAM · Dordrecht · Utrecht · Hilversum · Almere · Den Helder · Alkmaar · Hoorn · Groningen · Leeuwarden · Assen · Emmen · Zwolle · Deventer · Apeldoorn · Arnhem · Nijmegen · Breda · Tilburg · 's-Hertogenbosch · Eindhoven · Texel · Terschelling · Ameland

BELGIUM
BRUSSELS (Bruxelles) · Antwerpen · Gent · Brugge · Oostende · Mechelen · Leuven · Namur · Charleroi · Liège · Mons · Tournai · Kortrijk · Hasselt · Maastricht · Aachen

LUXEMBOURG
Luxembourg · Esch-sur-Alzette · Arlon

FRANCE
PARIS · Lille · Roubaix · Valenciennes · Douai · Arras · Amiens · Abbeville · Beauvais · Compiègne · Laon · St-Quentin · Cambrai · Reims · Châlons-en-Champagne · Épernay · Meaux · Melun · Troyes · Sens · Auxerre · Dijon · Chaumont · Nancy · Metz · Verdun · Thionville · Épinal · Mulhouse · Belfort · Besançon · Lons-le-Saunier · Mâcon · Bourg-en-Bresse · LYON · St-Étienne · Vienne · Chambéry · Grenoble · Annecy · Valence · Montélimar · Avignon · Nîmes · Arles · Aix-en-Provence · MARSEILLE · Toulon · Hyères · Nice · Cannes · Antibes · Monaco · Menton · Strasbourg · Colmar · Freiburg · Mont Blanc 4808 · Massif Central

GERMANY
BERLIN · HAMBURG · Hannover · Bremen · Bremerhaven · Kiel · Lübeck · Rostock · Schwerin · Wismar · Flensburg · Neumünster · Oldenburg · Wilhelmshaven · Emden · Osnabrück · Münster · Bielefeld · Dortmund · Essen · Duisburg · Düsseldorf · KÖLN (Cologne) · Bonn · Wuppertal · Bochum · Gelsenkirchen · Krefeld · Mönchengladbach · Aachen · Kassel · Göttingen · Braunschweig · Wolfsburg · Magdeburg · Potsdam · Frankfurt · Wiesbaden · Mainz · Darmstadt · Mannheim · Heidelberg · Karlsruhe · Pforzheim · Stuttgart · Ulm · Augsburg · MÜNCHEN (Munich) · Nürnberg · Fürth · Regensburg · Ingolstadt · Würzburg · Erlangen · Bamberg · Bayreuth · Hof · Leipzig · Halle · Dresden · Chemnitz · Zwickau · Erfurt · Weimar · Jena · Gera · Gotha · Eisenach · Fulda · Gießen · Koblenz · Trier · Saarbrücken · Kaiserslautern · Freising · Landshut · Passau · Rosenheim · Kempten · Memmingen · Garmisch-Partenkirchen · Zugspitze 2962

DENMARK
Sylt · Flensburg · Sønderborg · Svendborg · Nakskov · Rødby · Nykøbing · Møn · Rügen

POLAND
Szczecin · Gorzów Wielkopolski · Zielona Góra · Cottbus · Legnica · Wałbrzych · Jelenia Góra · Kołobrzeg · Koszalin · Świnoujście · Police · Goleniów · Stargard Szczeciński

CZECH
PRAHA (Prague) · Plzeň · Karlovy Vary · Kladno · Most · Teplice · Liberec · Ústí nad Labem · Děčín · Hradec Králové · České Budějovice · Tábor · Písek · Klatovy · Jihlava · Třebíč · Jindřichův Hradec

SWITZERLAND
ZÜRICH · Bern · Basel · Genève · Lausanne · Luzern · Winterthur · St. Gallen · Montreux · Sion · Chur · Davos · Interlaken · Thun · Neuchâtel · Biel · Solothurn · Zug · Schwyz · Jungfrau · Matterhorn 4478

LIECHTENSTEIN · Vaduz

AUSTRIA
Wien · Innsbruck · Salzburg · Linz · Graz · Klagenfurt · Villach · Bregenz · Feldkirch · Steyr · Wels · Krems · Melk · Amstetten · Grossglockner · Bad Ischl

ITALY
MILANO · TORINO (Turin) · Genova · Bergamo · Brescia · Verona · Padova · Venezia (Venice) · Trieste · Bolzano · Trento · Belluno · Udine · Pordenone · Como · Lecco · Varese · Novara · Vercelli · Biella · Asti · Alessandria · Cuneo · San Remo · Imperia · Savona · La Spezia · Parma · Modena · Bologna · Ferrara · Ravenna · Rimini · Piacenza · Cremona · Mantova · Pavia · Vicenza · Treviso · Rovigo · Forlì · Cesena · Faenza · Imola · Carrara · Massa · Lucca · Pisa · Firenze (Florence) · Prato · SAN MARINO · Pesaro · Fano

SLOVENIA
Ljubljana · Maribor · Celje · Kranj · Koper · Nova Gorica

ZAGREB · Rijeka · Karlovac · Pula

Golfo di Genova · Golfo di Venezia

East from Greenwich

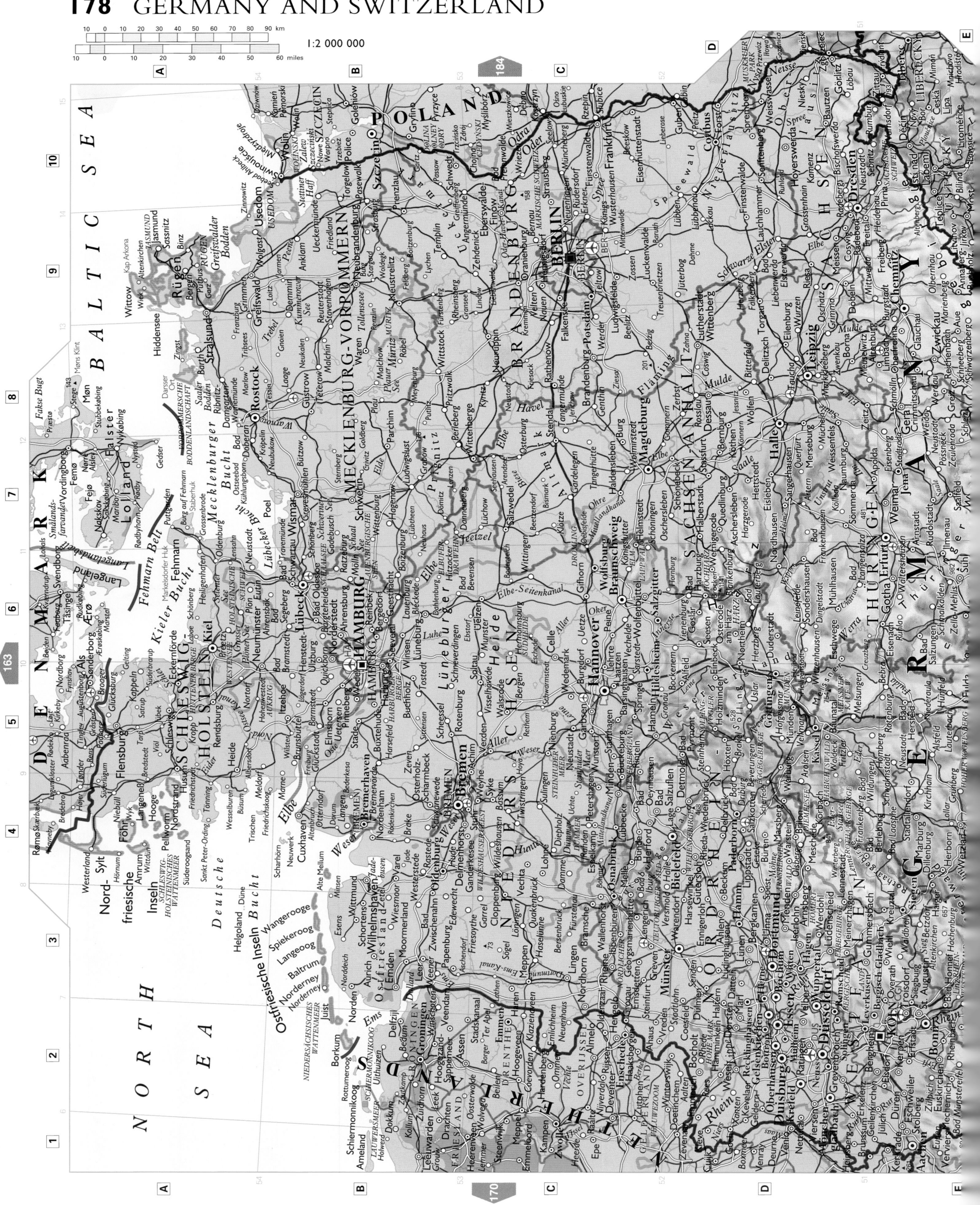

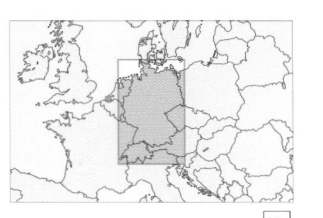

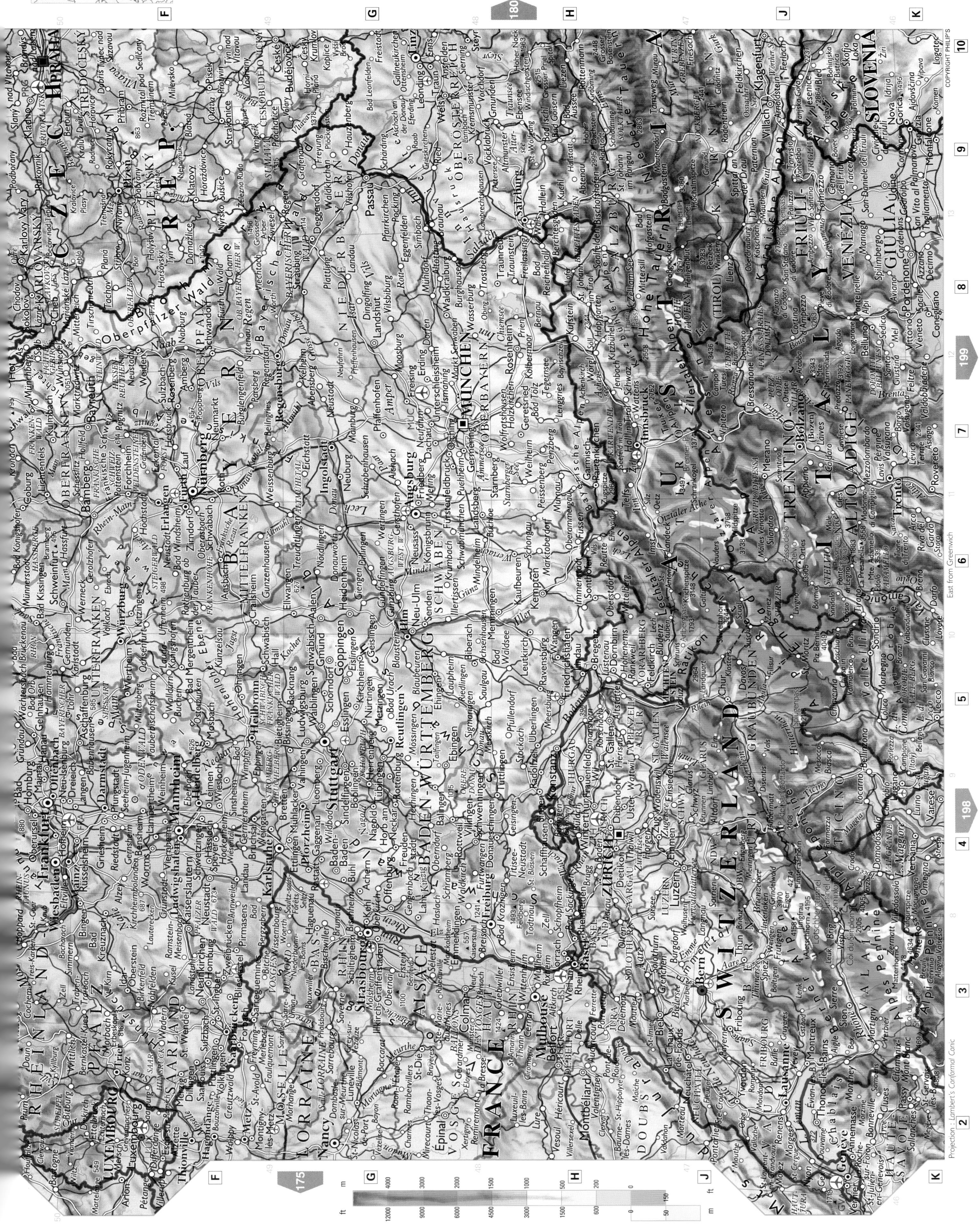

Underlined towns give their name to the administrative area in which they stand.

——— High-speed rail routes

East from Greenwich

Projection : Lambert's Conformal Conic

COPYRIGHT PHILIP'S

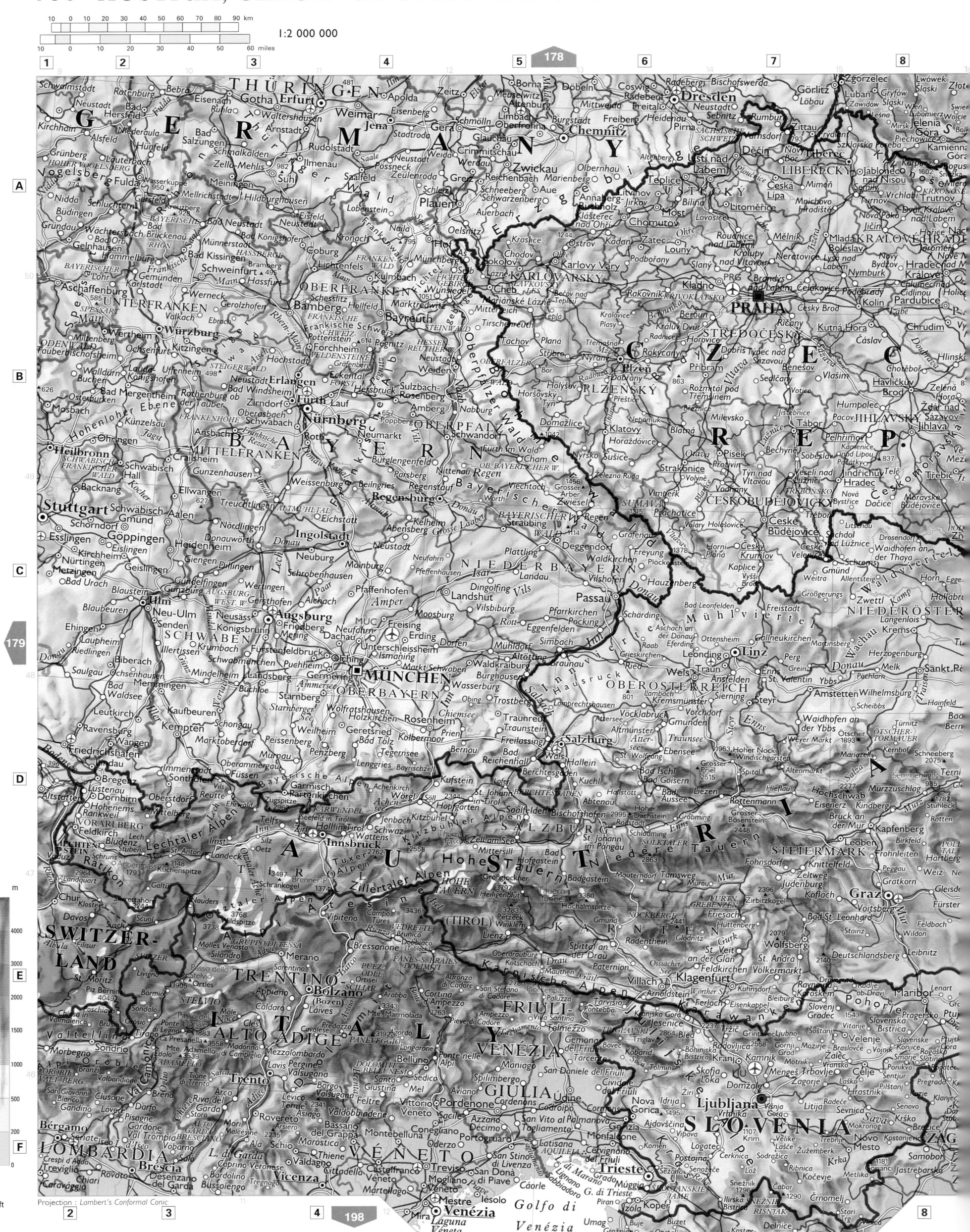

East from Greenwich

COPYRIGHT PHILIP'S

Underlined towns give their name to the
administrative area in which they stand.

1:2 000 000

Administrative divisions in Croatia:
1 Brodsko-Posavska   5 Osječko-Baranjska   9 Vukovarsko-Srijemska
2 Koprivničko-Križevačka   6 Požeško-Slavonska
4 Medimurska   8 Virovitičko-Podravska

Underlined towns give their name to the
administrative area in which they stand.

COPYRIGHT PHILIP'S

10 0 10 20 30 40 50 60 70 80 90 km

1:2 000 000

10 0 10 20 30 40 50 60 miles

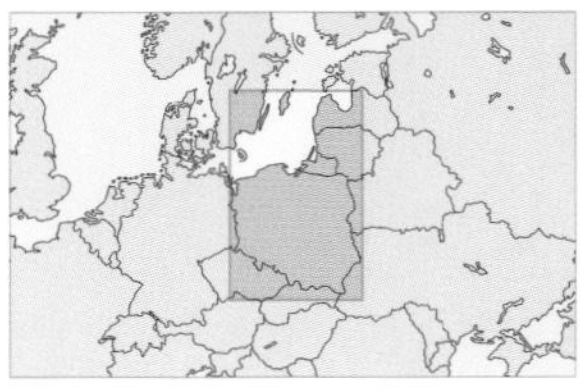

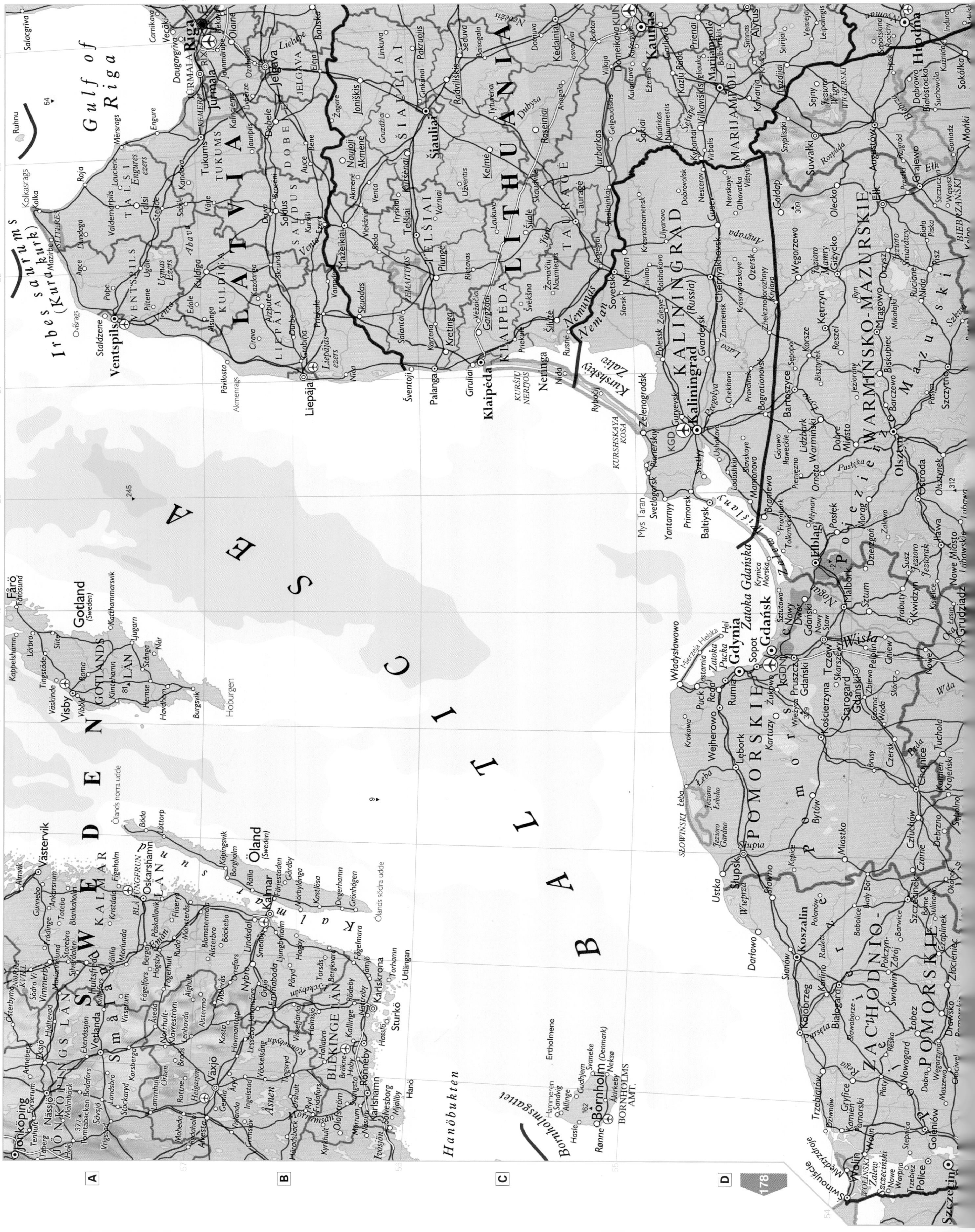

Gulf of Riga

LATVIA

LITHUANIA

KALININGRAD (Russia)

SWEDEN

Gotland (Sweden)

Öland (Sweden)

Bornholm (Denmark)

BALTIC SEA

POMORSKIE

WARMIŃSKO-MAZURSKIE

ZACHODNIO-POMORSKIE

Gdańsk

Gdynia

Kaliningrad

Klaipėda

Šiauliai

Kaunas

Ventspils

Liepāja

Rīga

Jūrmala

Underlined towns give their name to the administrative area in which they stand.

COPYRIGHT PHILIP'S

East from Greenwich

Projection : Lambert's Conformal Conic

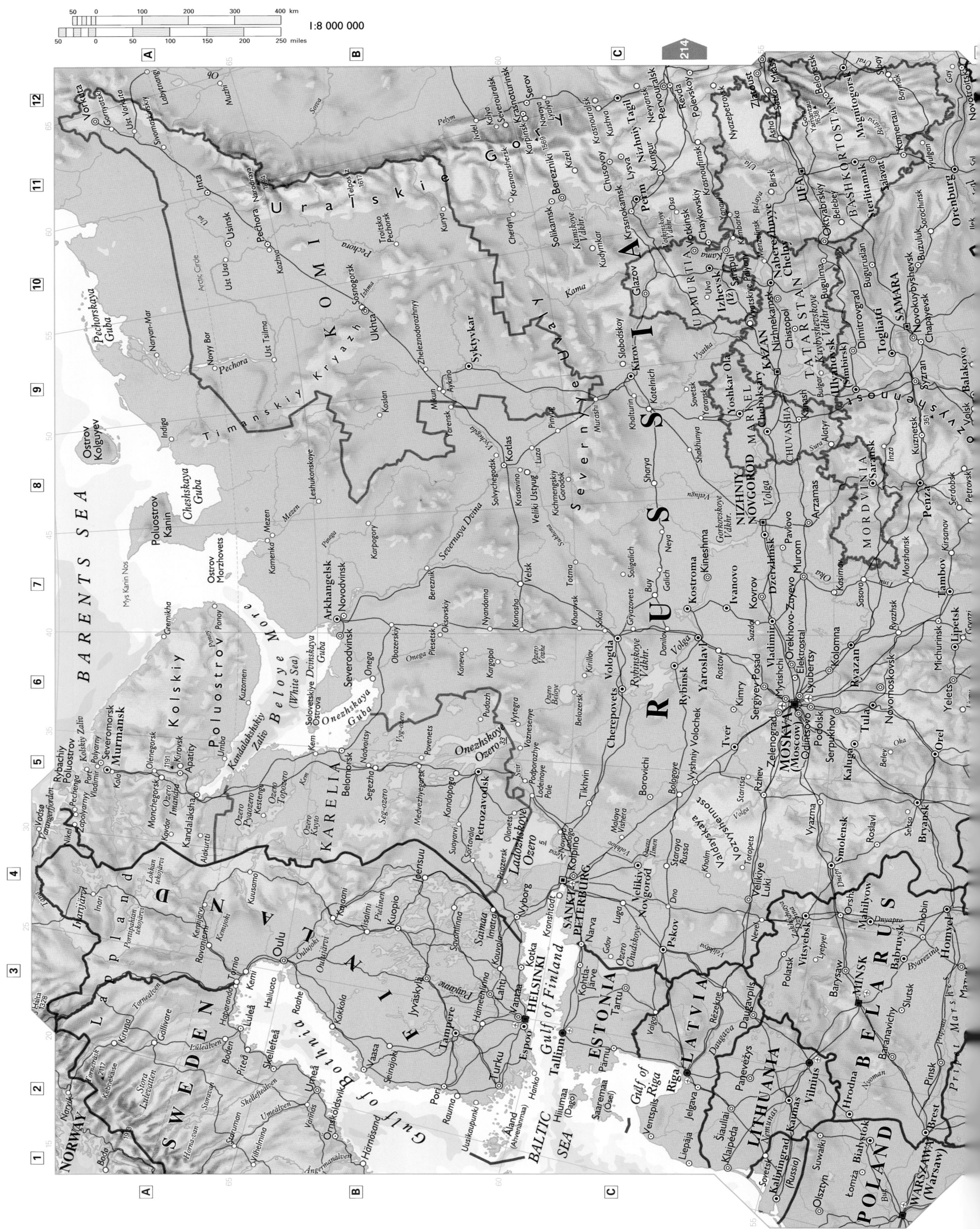

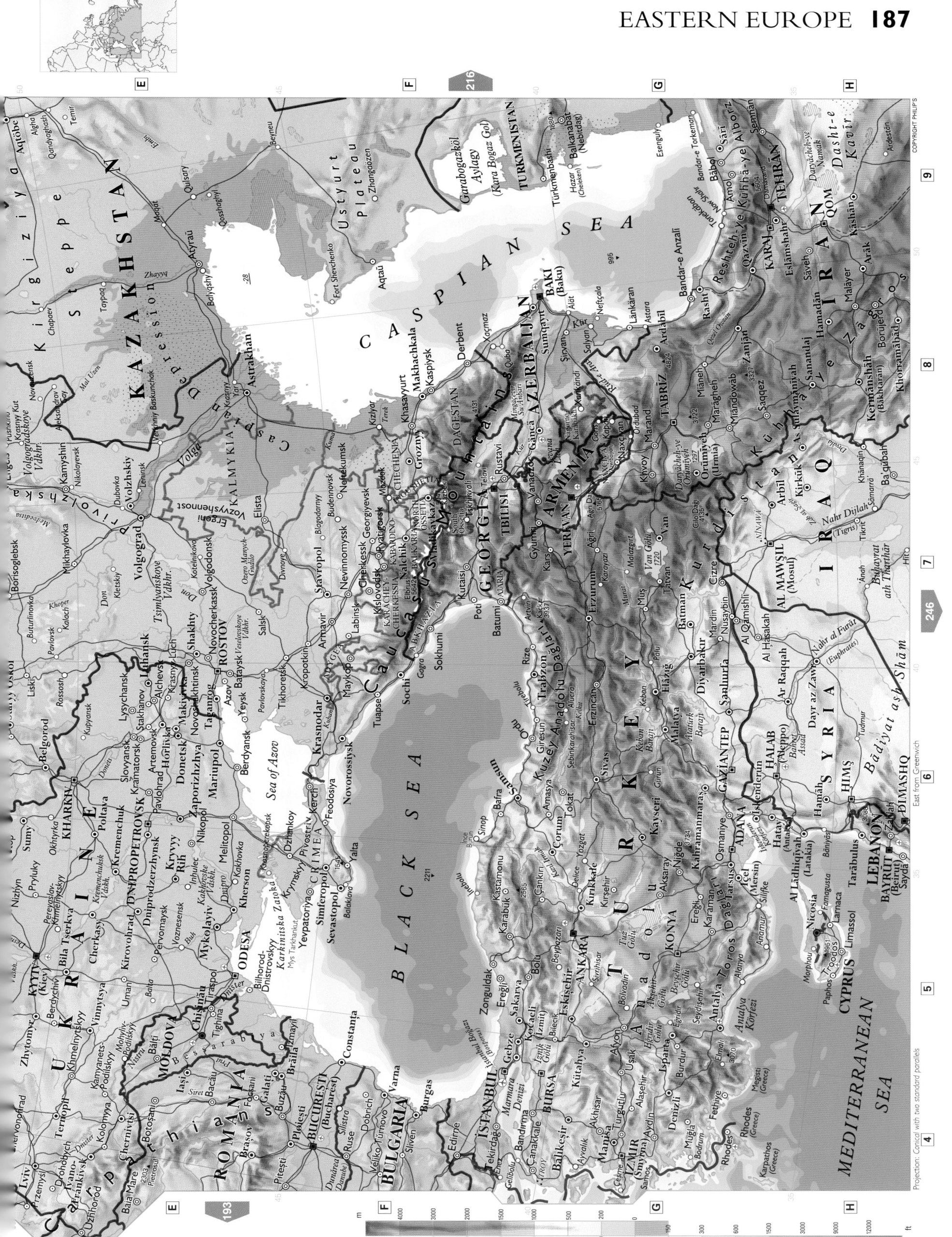

Projection: Conical with two standard parallels

East from Greenwich

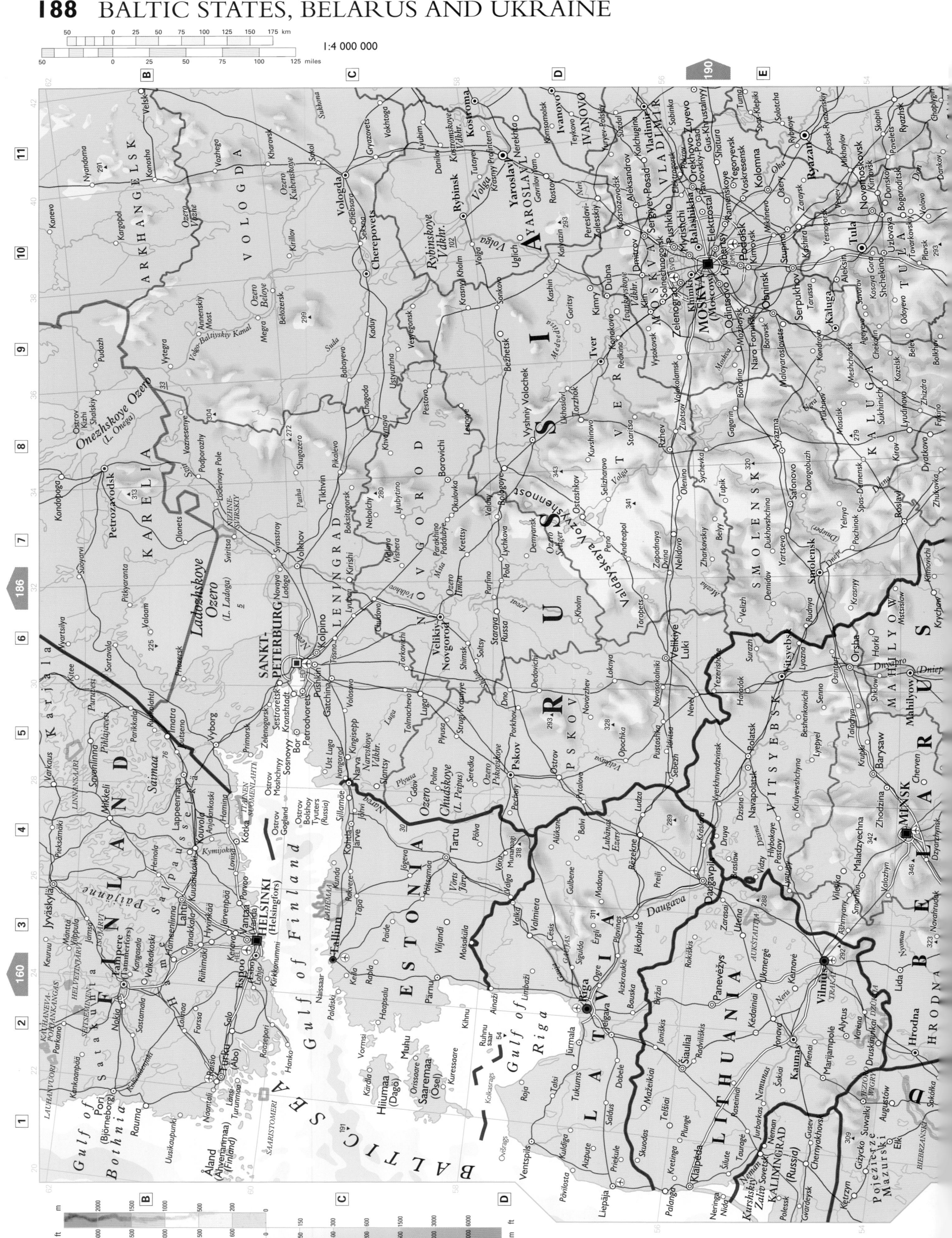

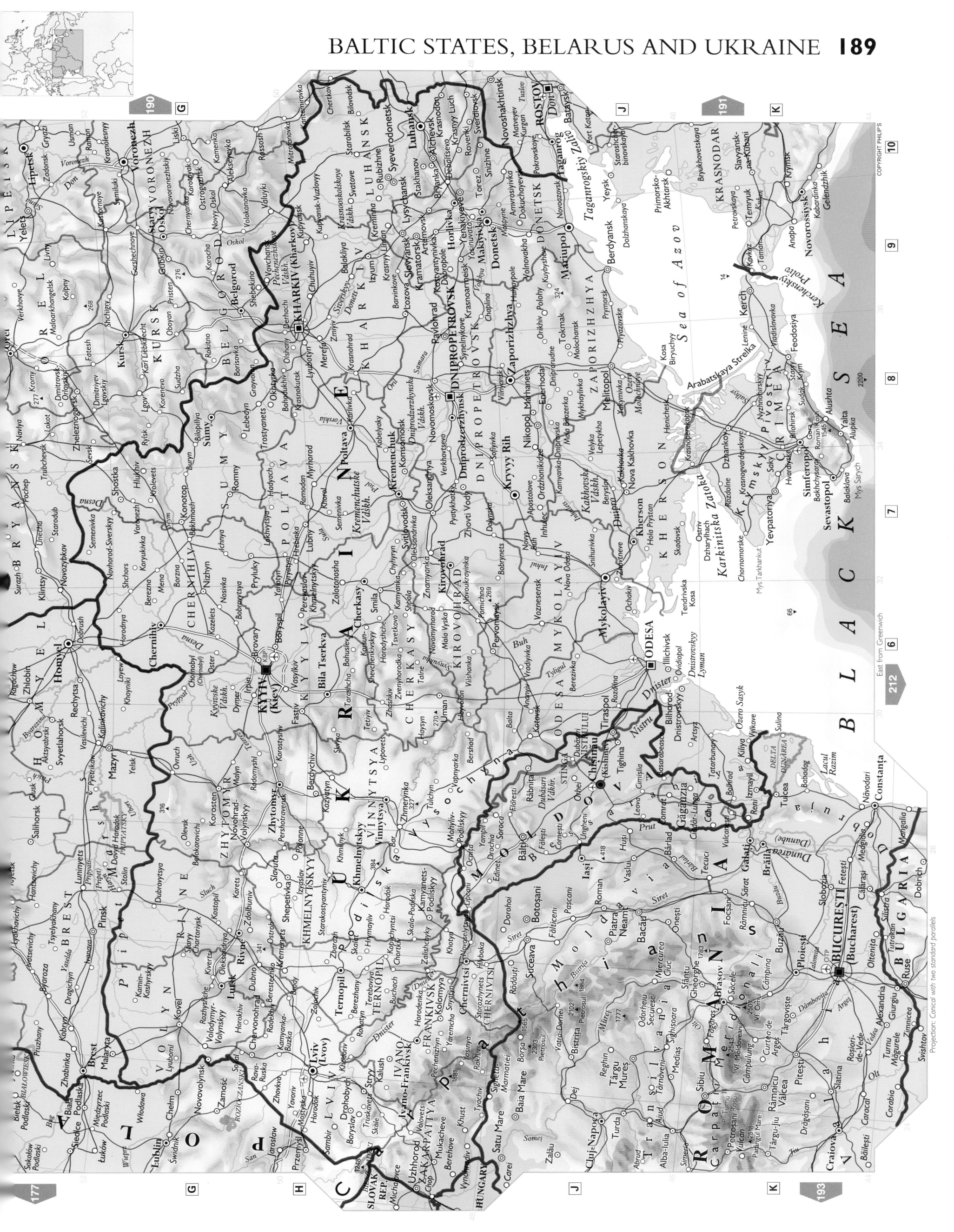

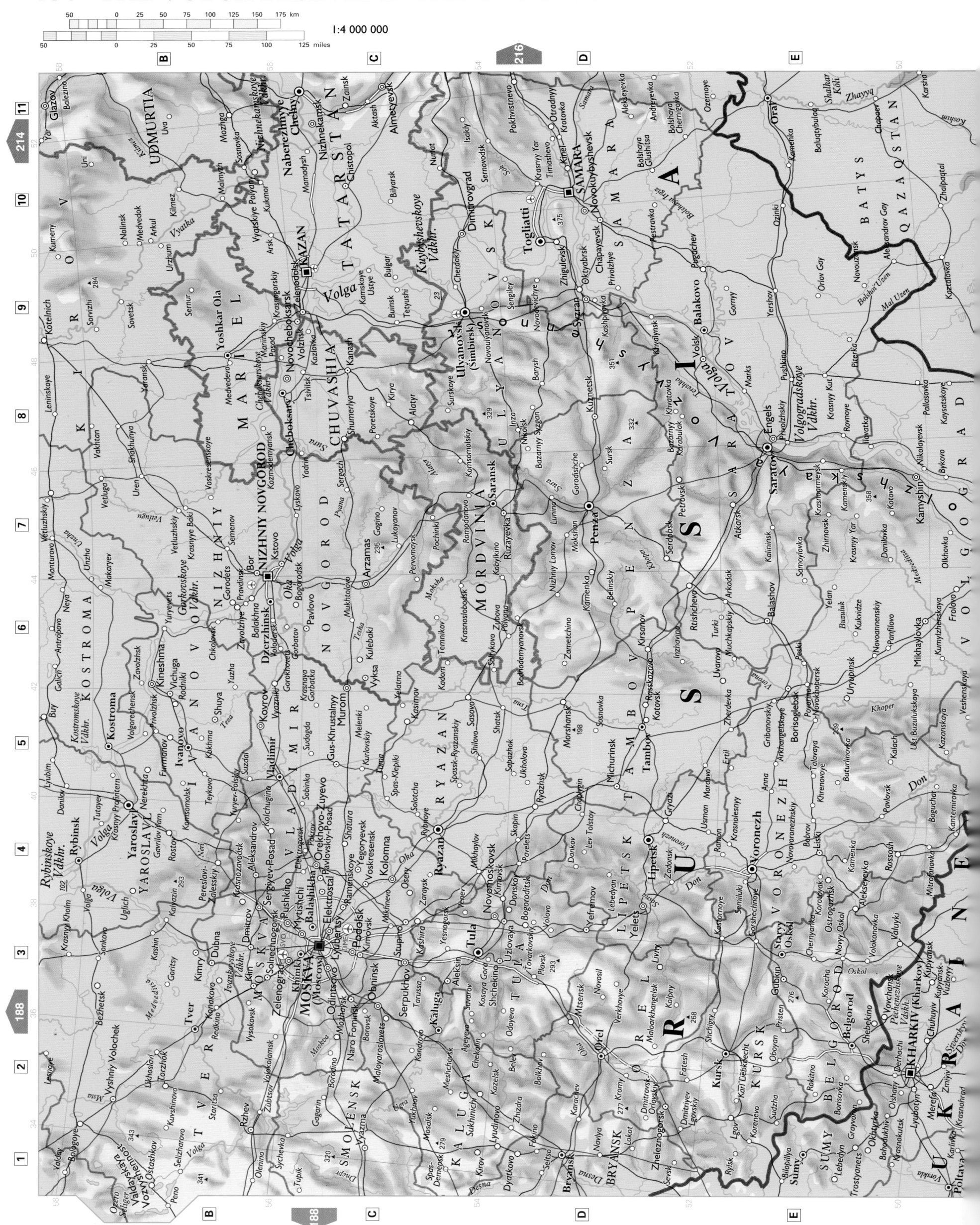

CASPIAN SEA
BLACK SEA
Sea of Azov
KAZAKHSTAN
KALMYKIA
ASTRAKHAN
DAGESTAN
CHECHENIA
INGUSHETIA
NORTH OSSETIA
KABARDINO-BALKARIA
KARACHAY-CHERKESSIA
STAVROPOL
KRASNODAR
ADYGEA
ABKHAZIA
GEORGIA
ARMENIA
AZERBAIJAN
TURKEY
ROSTOV
DONETSK
ZAPORIZHZHYA
DNIPROPETROVSK
Astrakhan
Volgograd
Elista
Stavropol
Krasnodar
Makhachkala
Grozny
Vladikavkaz
Nalchik
TBILISI
YEREVAN
BAKI (Baku)
Sochi
Novorossiysk
Taganrog
Donetsk
Luhansk
Mariupol
Zaporizhzhya
Kerch
Batumi
Trabzon
Samsun
Chernyye Zemli
Kuzey Anadolu Dağlari
Taganrogskiy Zaliv
Tsimlyanskoye Vdkhr.
Projection: Conical with two standard parallels
East from Greenwich
COPYRIGHT PHILIP'S
216
213
189

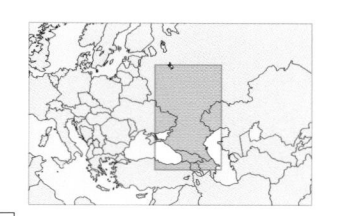

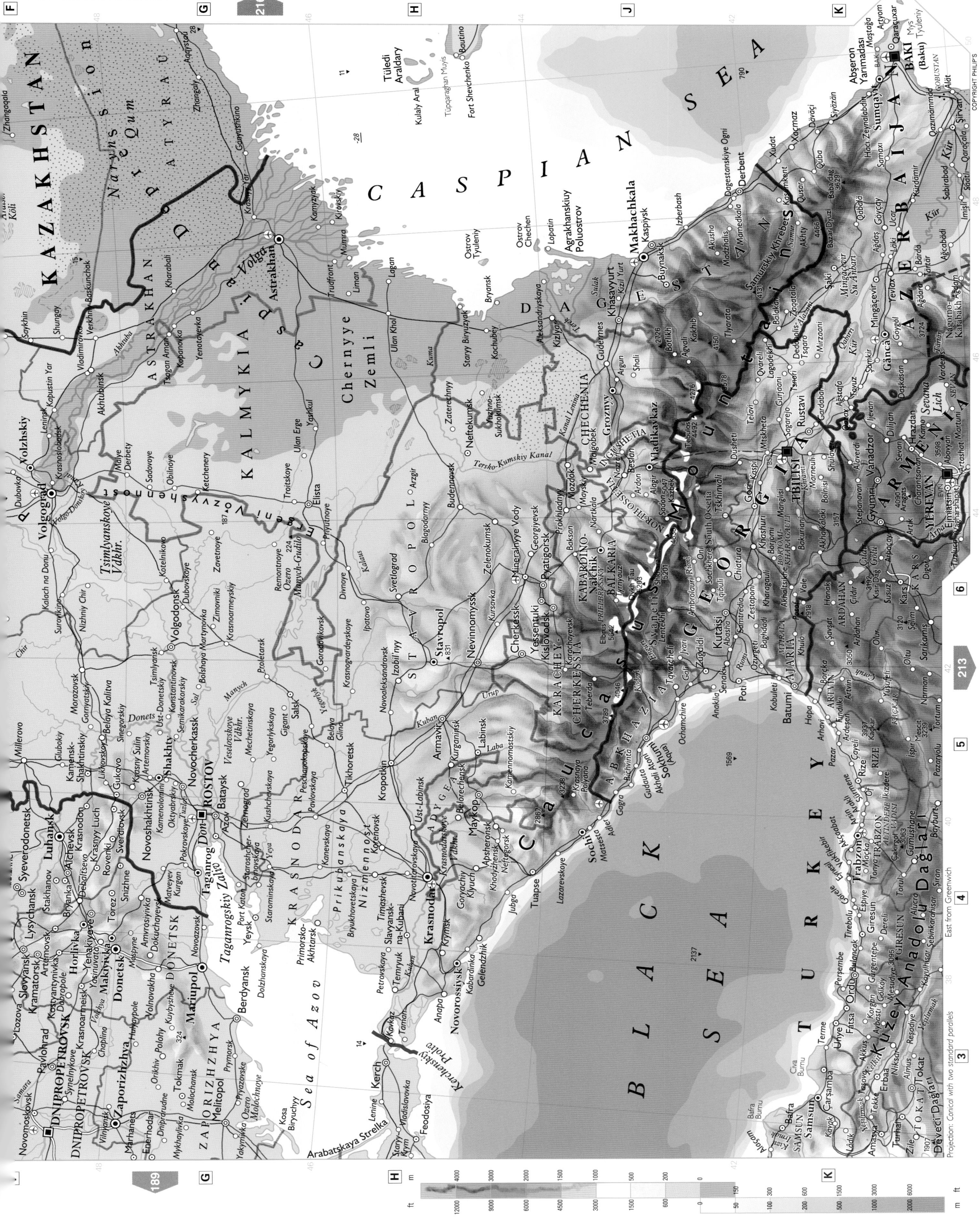

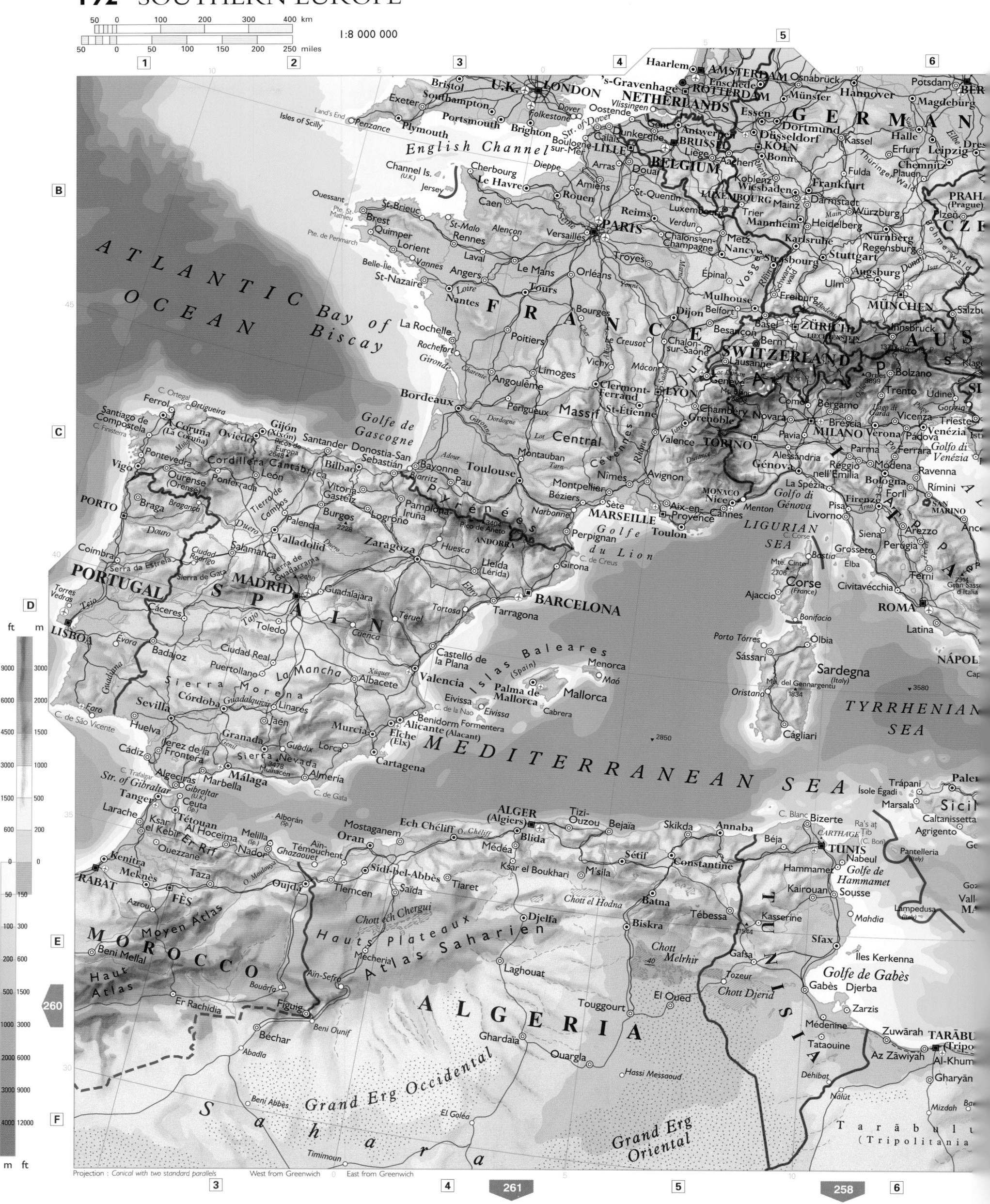

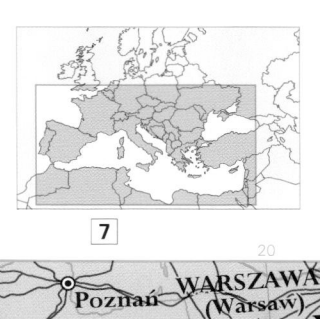

7   8   9   10   11   12

POLAND

WARSZAWA (Warsaw)
Poznań
Kalisz
Łódź
Legnica
Wrocław
Opole
Walbrzych
Chorzów
Tychy
Katowice
Kraków
Częstochowa
Radom
Kielce
Lublin
Brest
Pinsk

Pripet Marshes

Kovel
Rivne
Lutsk
Chervonohrad
Lviv
Przemyśl
Tarnów
Rzeszów
Drohobych
Ivano-Frankivsk

Korosten
Zhytomyr
KYYIV (Kiev)
Bila Tserkva
Berdychiv
Vinnytsya

Nizhyn
Pryluky
Sumy
Okhtyrka

Belgorod
KHARKIV
RUSSIA

UKRAINE

Khmelnytskyy
Kamyanets-Podilskyy
Mohyliv-Podilskyy
Cherkasy
Kirovohrad
Uman
Pervomaysk
Voznesensk

Kremenchuk
Poltava
Dniprodzerzhynsk
DNIPROPETROVSK
Kryvyy Rih
Nikopol

Lysychansk
Stakhanov
Slovyansk
Kramatorsk
Artemovsk
Horlivka
Donetsk
Makiyivka
Zaporizhzhya
Mariupol

Luhansk
Alchevsk
Krasny Luch
Shakhty
Novoshakhtinsk
Taganrog
ROSTOV
Novocherkassk
Azov
Yeysk

HUNGARY
BUDAPEST
Győr
Kecskemét
Hódmezővásárhely
Szeged
Miskolc
Debrecen

SLOVAK REP.
Bratislava
Košice
Uzhhorod

ROMANIA
Cluj-Napoca
Baia Mare
Satu Mare
Oradea
Arad
Timişoara
Sibiu
Braşov
Ploieşti
BUCUREŞTI (Bucharest)
Craiova
Piteşti
Râmnicu Vâlcea
Drobeta-Turnu Severin

MOLDOVA
Iaşi
Bacău
Focşani
Galaţi
Brăila
Buzău
Botoşani
Chişinău
Tiraspol
Tighina

ODESA
Izmayil
Bilhorod-Dnistrovskyy

BLACK SEA

CROATIA
ZAGREB

SERBIA
BEOGRAD
Novi Sad
Subotica
Sombor

BOSNIA-HERZEGOVINA
Sarajevo
Banja Luka
Tuzla
Mostar

MONTENEGRO
Podgorica

KOSOVO
Priština

MACEDONIA
Skopje
Bitola

ALBANIA
Tiranë
Durrës
Elbasan
Vlorë

BULGARIA
SOFIYA
Plovdiv
Khaskovo
Burgas
Varna
Ruse
Pleven
Véliko Túrnovo
Dobrich
Silistra
Vidin

GREECE
Thessaloníka
Serres
Kavala
Alexandroúpoli
Lárisa
Volos
Lamía
Ioánnina
Pátra
ATHINA (Athens)
Pireás
Kórinthos
Kalamáta
Spárti

TURKEY
İSTANBUL
ANKARA
BURSA
İZMIR (Smyrna)
Kocaeli (İzmit)
Balıkesir
Manisa
Aydın
Denizli
Muğla
KONYA
ADANA
GAZİANTEP
Kayseri
Sivas
Kahramanmaraş

Kuzey Andolu Daglari

MEDITERRANEAN SEA

CYPRUS
Nicosia
Limassol
Paphos
Larnaca

SYRIA
HALAB (Aleppo)
Hamah
HIMS

LEBANON
BAYRÛT (Beirut)

ISRAEL
TEL AVIV-YAFO
Jerusalem
GAZA STRIP

LIBYA
BANGHÂZÎ
Darnah
Al Bayḍā
Tubruq
Bardiyah

Khalij Surt (Gulf of Sidra)
Surt
Ajdābiyā
Barqah (Cyrenaica)

EGYPT
EL ISKANDARÎYA (Alexandria)
Dumyât
Bûr Sa'îd (Port Said)
EL QÂHIRA (Cairo)
EL GÎZA
El Faiyûm
Beni Suef
Ismâ'îliya
El Suweis (Suez)

Marsá Matrûh
El Alamein

7   8   9   10

1:2 000 000

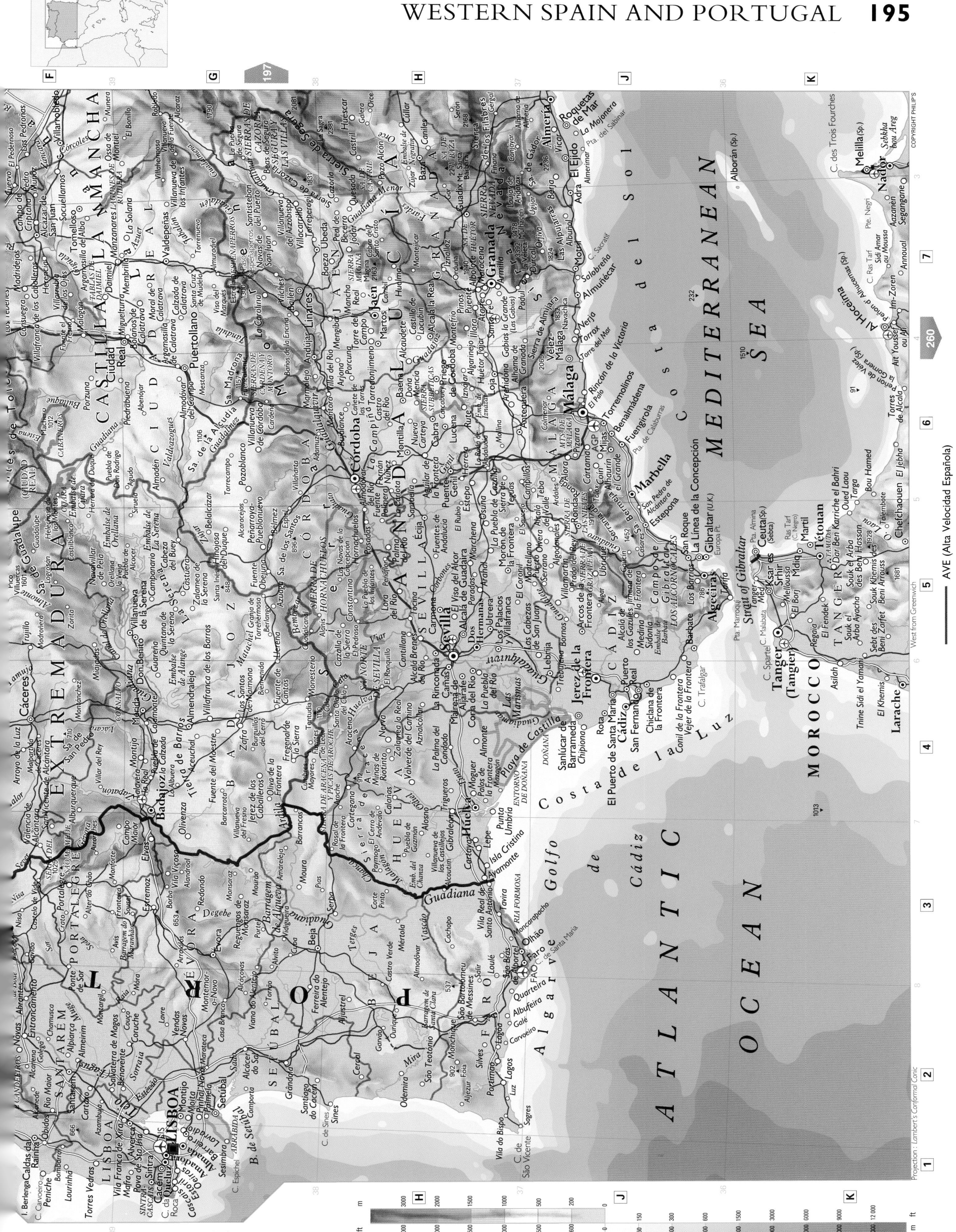

MEDITERRANEAN SEA

ATLANTIC OCEAN

MOROCCO

Costa de la Luz

Golfo de Cádiz

Algarve

Projection : Lambert's Conformal Conic

AVE (Alta Velocidad Española)

West from Greenwich

Projection: Lambert's Conformal Conic

nistrative divisions in Croatia:
- dsko-Posavska
- rivničko-Križevačka
- pinsko-Zagorska

4 Medimurska
6 Požeško-Slavonska
7 Varaždinska

8 Virovitičko-Podravska
10 Zagreba čka

—— TAV (Treno Alta Velocità)

COPYRIGHT PHILIP'S

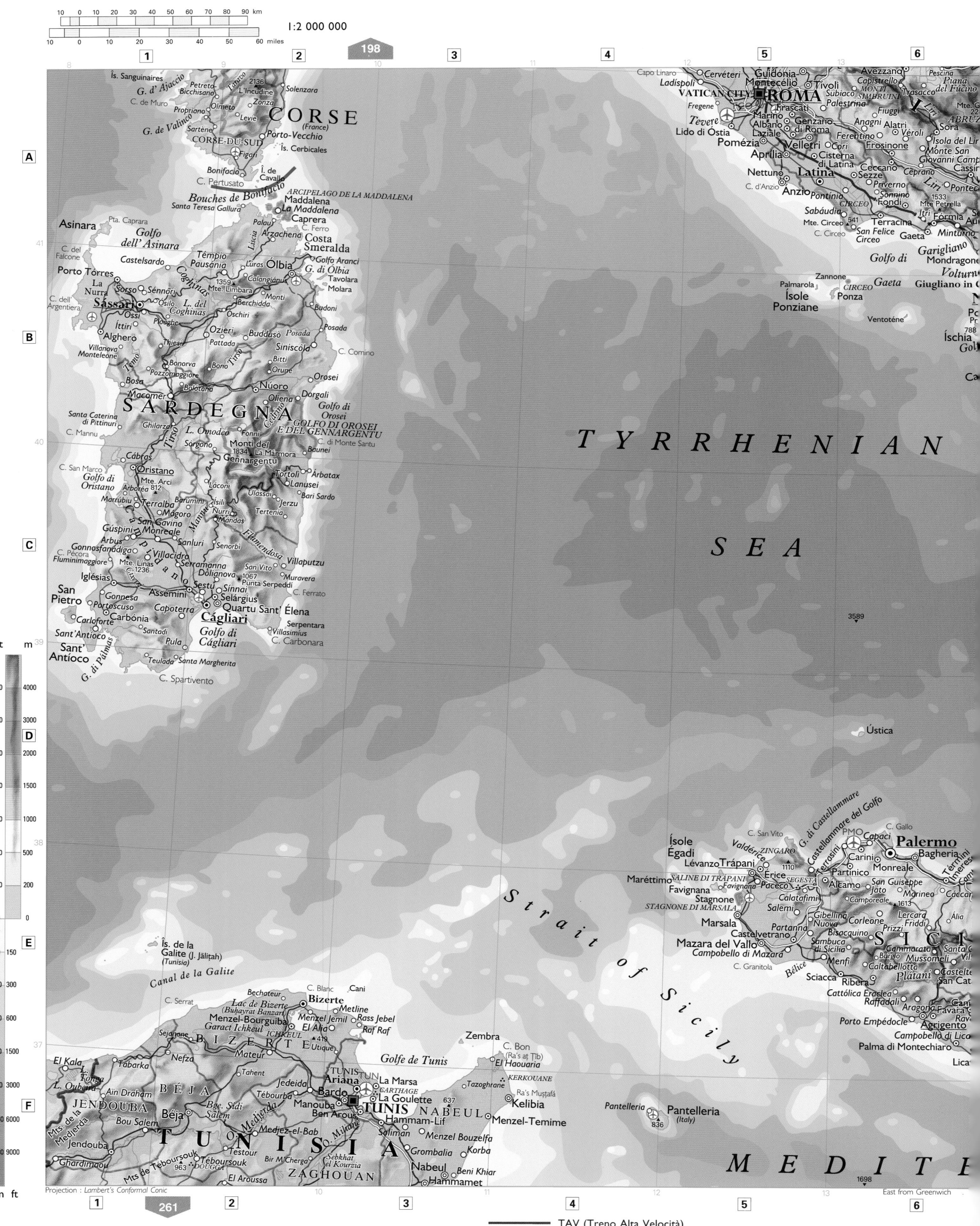

1:2 000 000

TYRRHENIAN

SEA

CORSE
(France)

SARDEGNA

Strait of Sicily

TUNISIA

MEDITE

Projection : Lambert's Conformal Conic

TAV (Treno Alta Velocità)

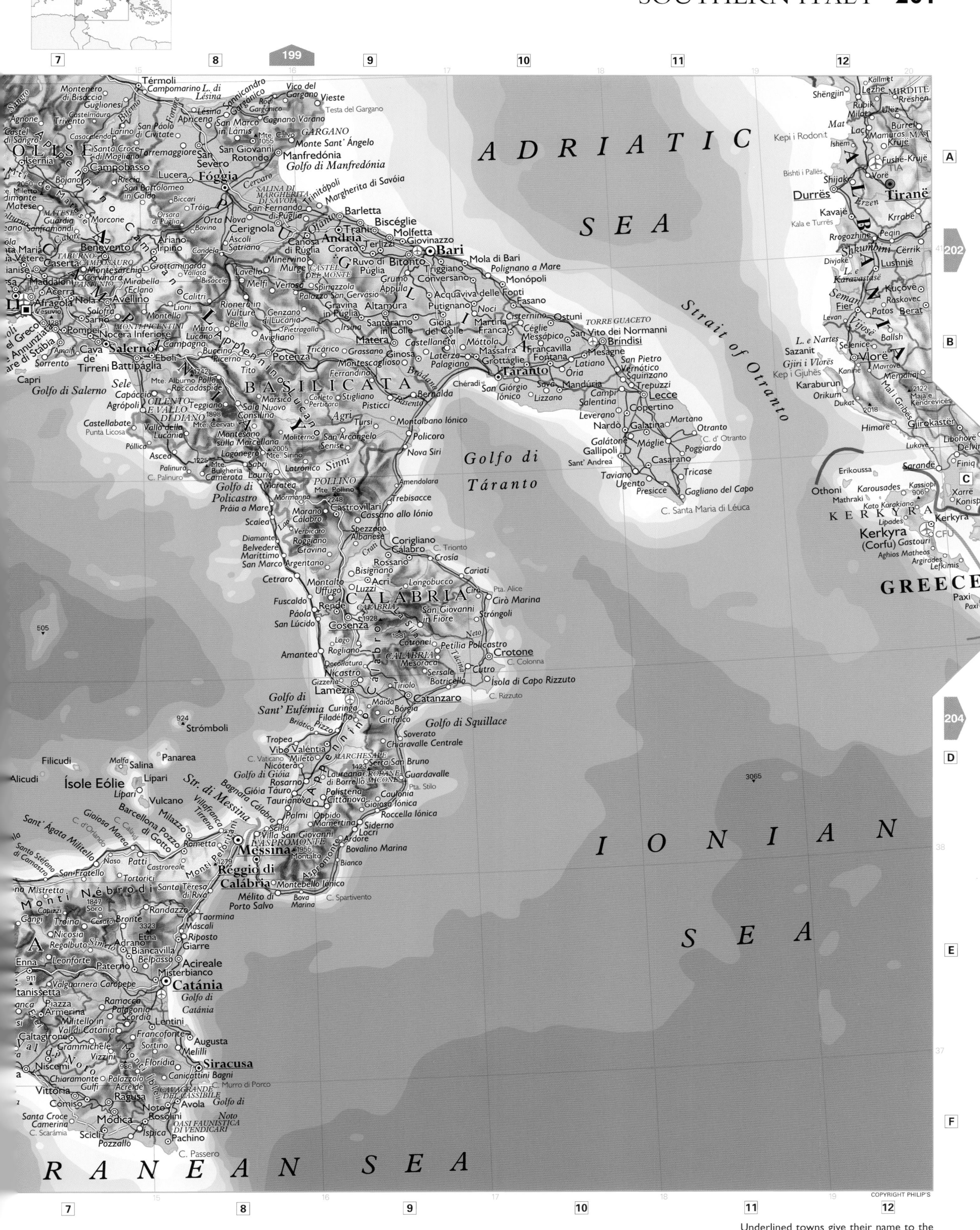

Underlined towns give their name to the
administrative area in which they stand.

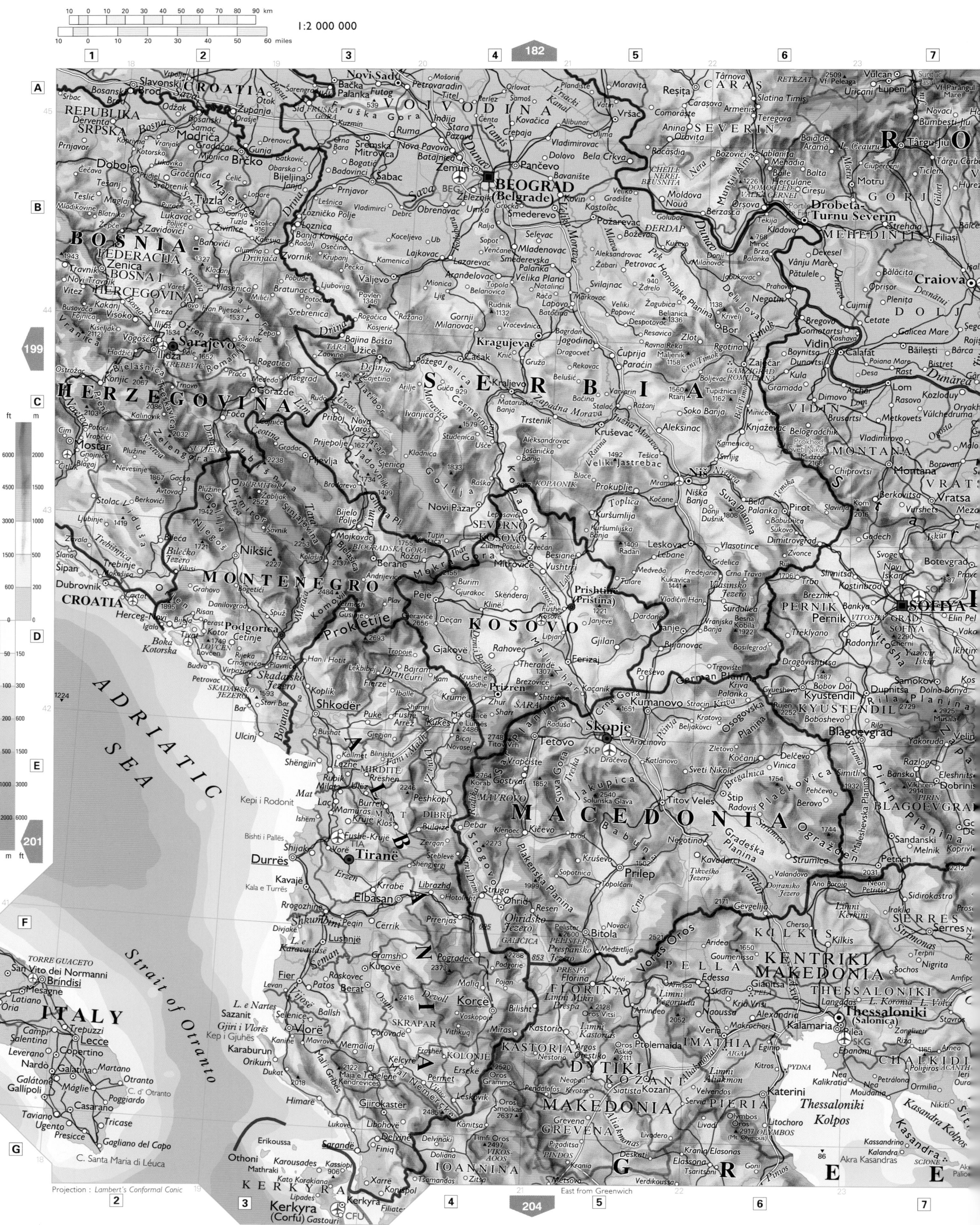

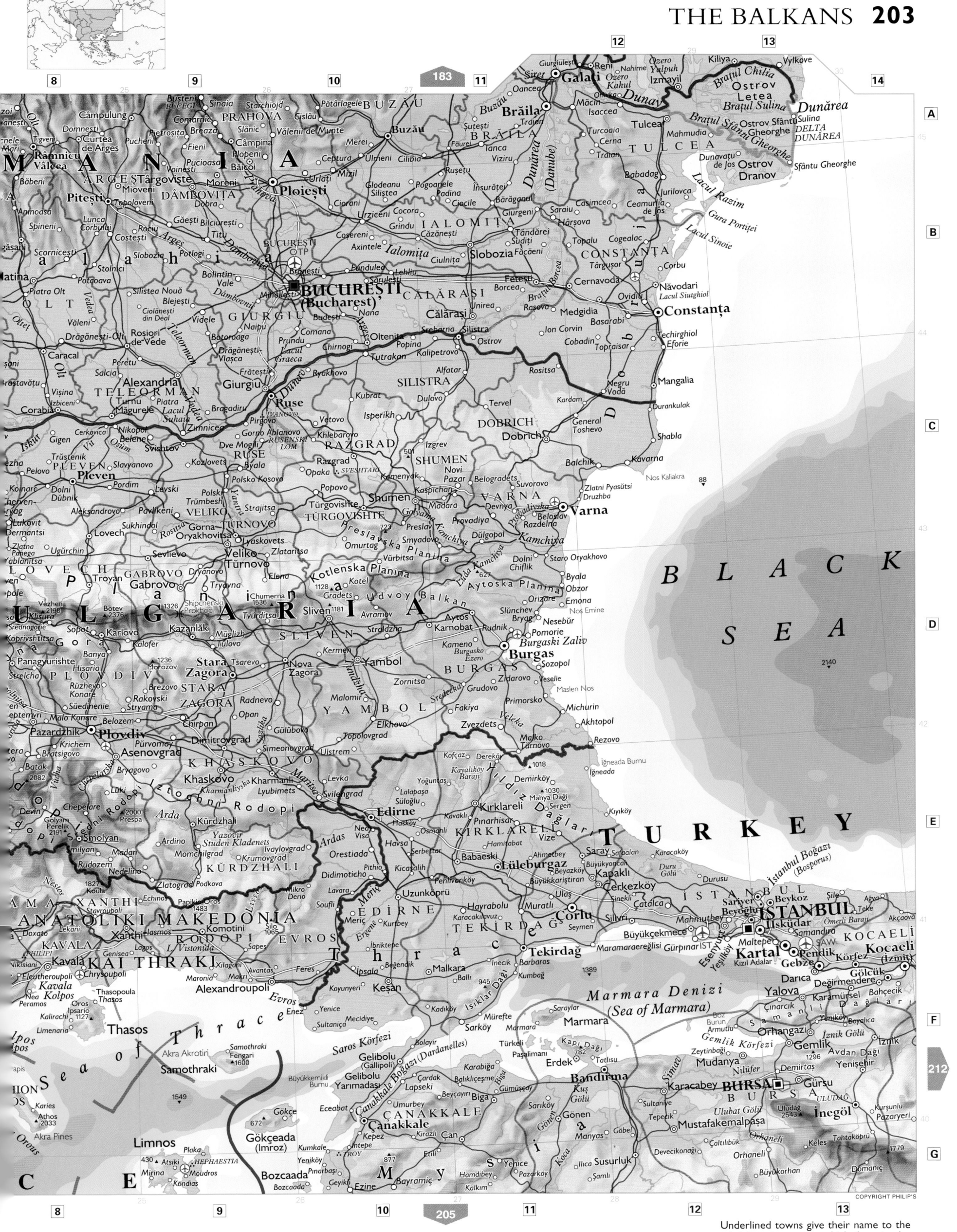

Underlined towns give their name to the
administrative area in which they stand.

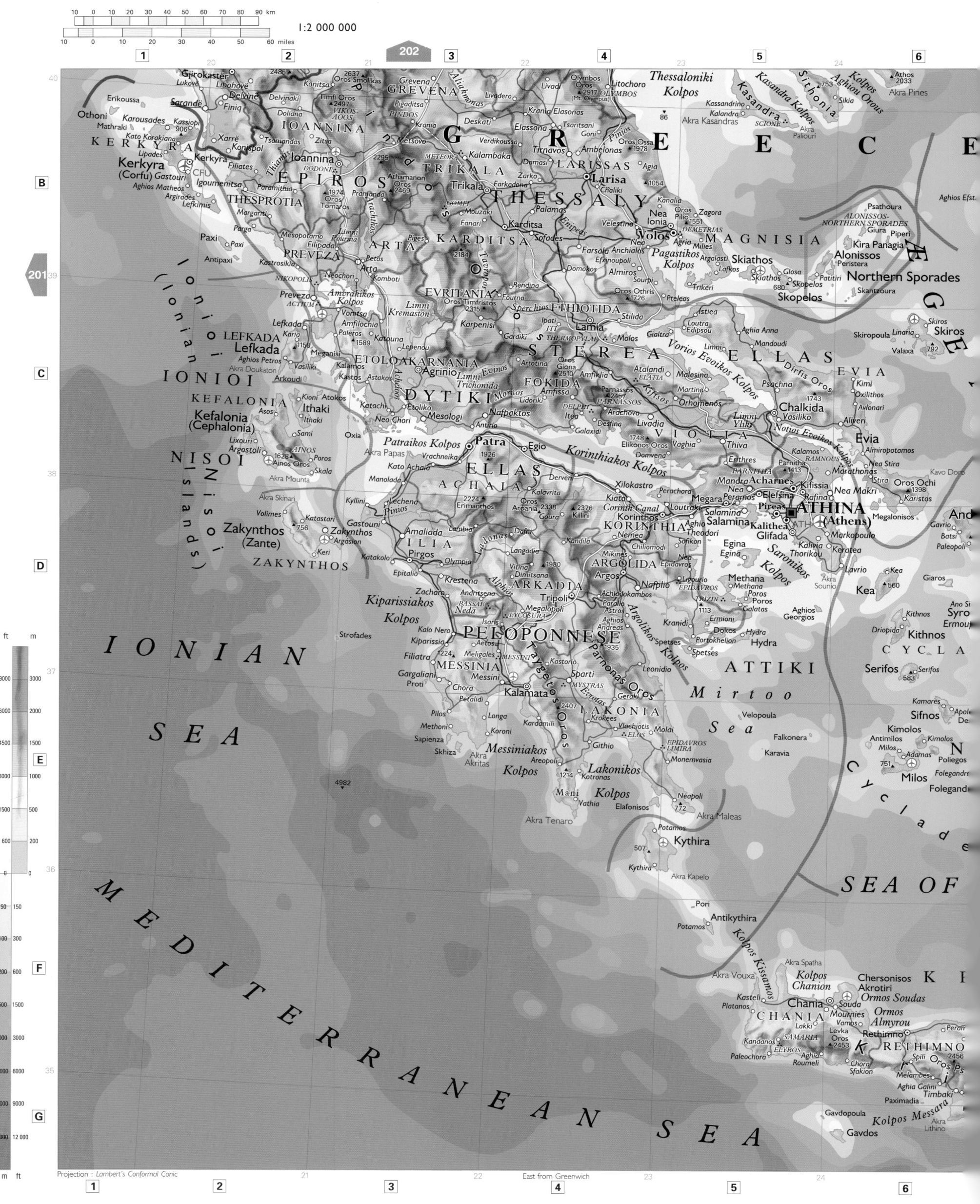

1:2 000 000

Projection : Lambert's Conformal Conic

East from Greenwich

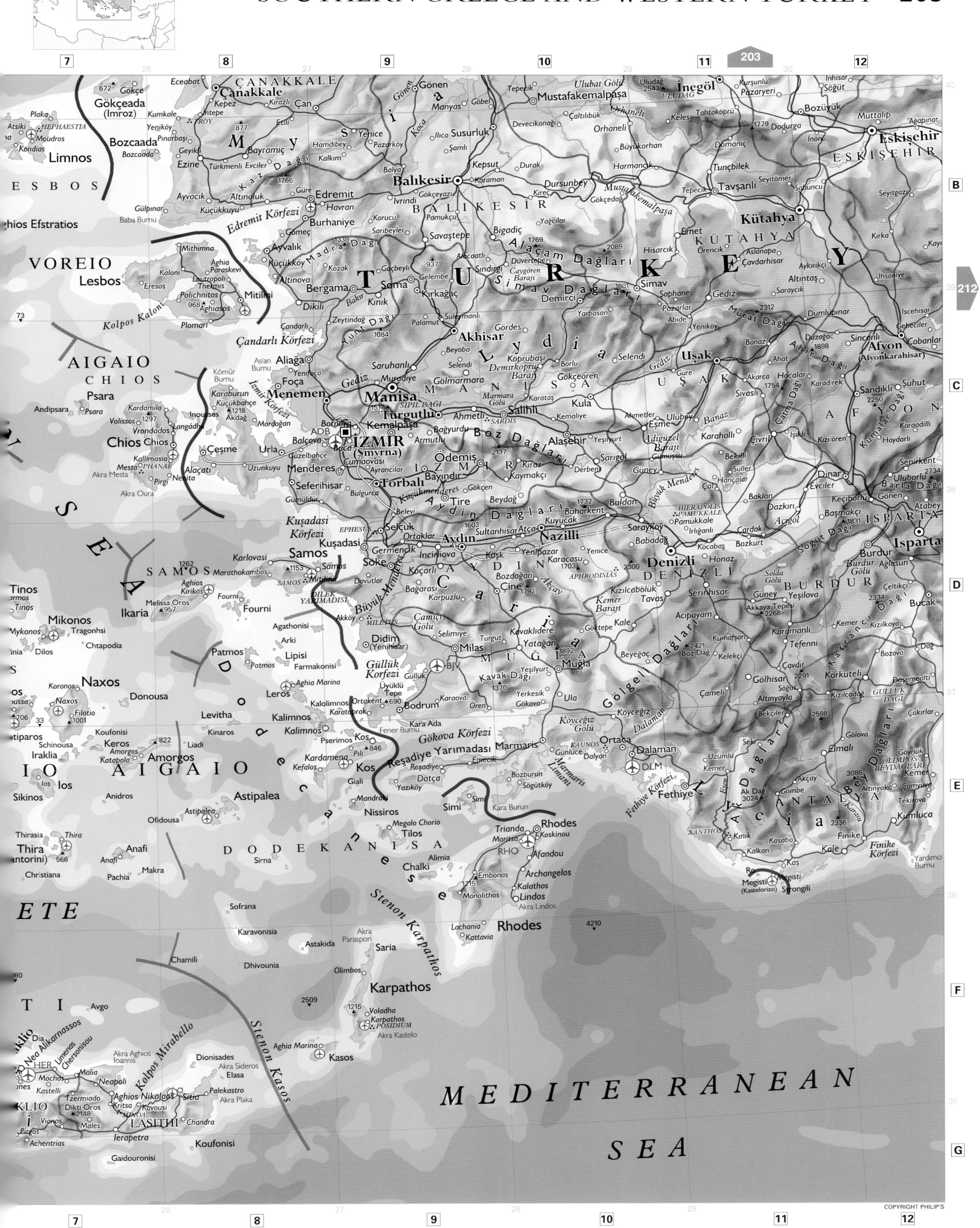

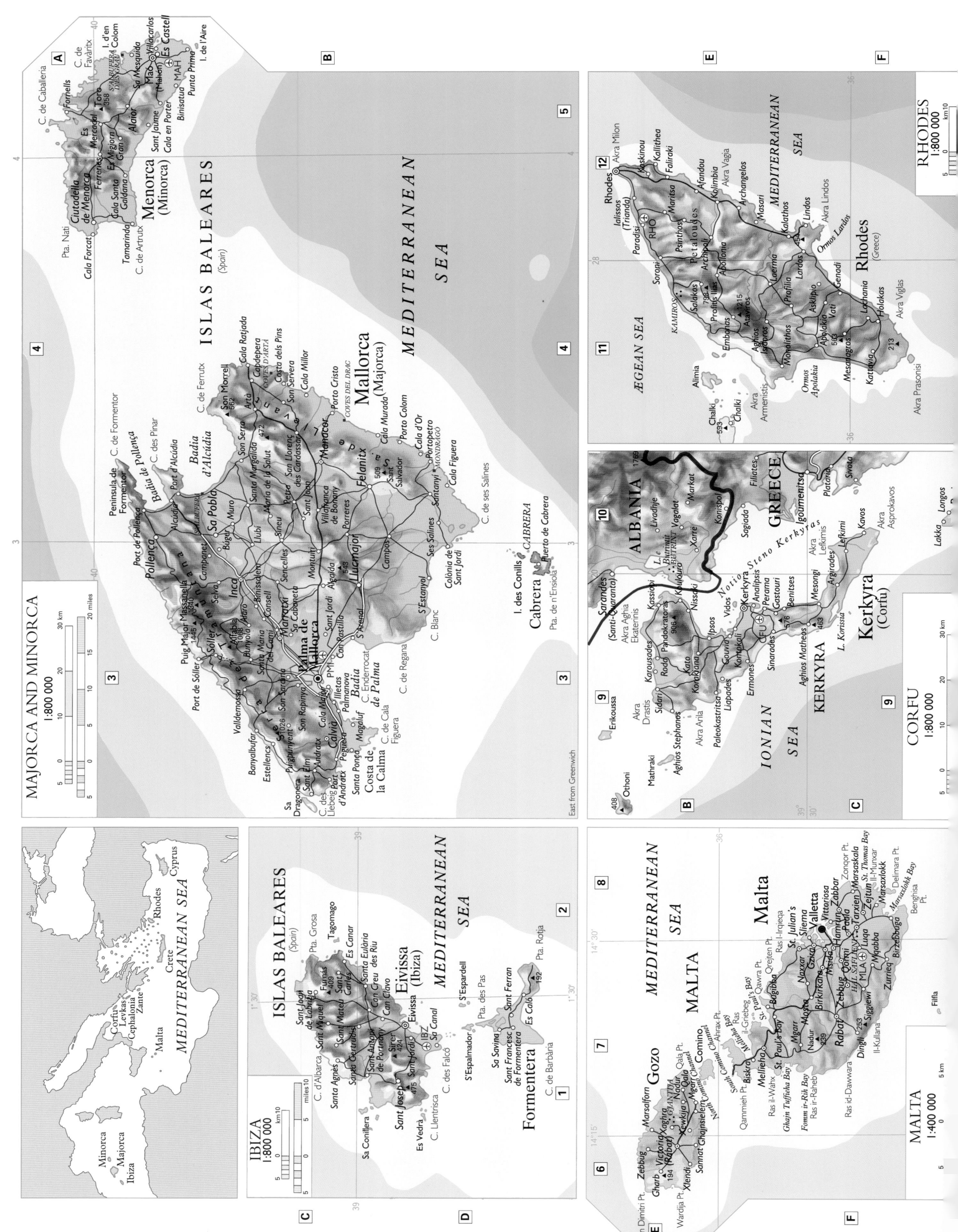

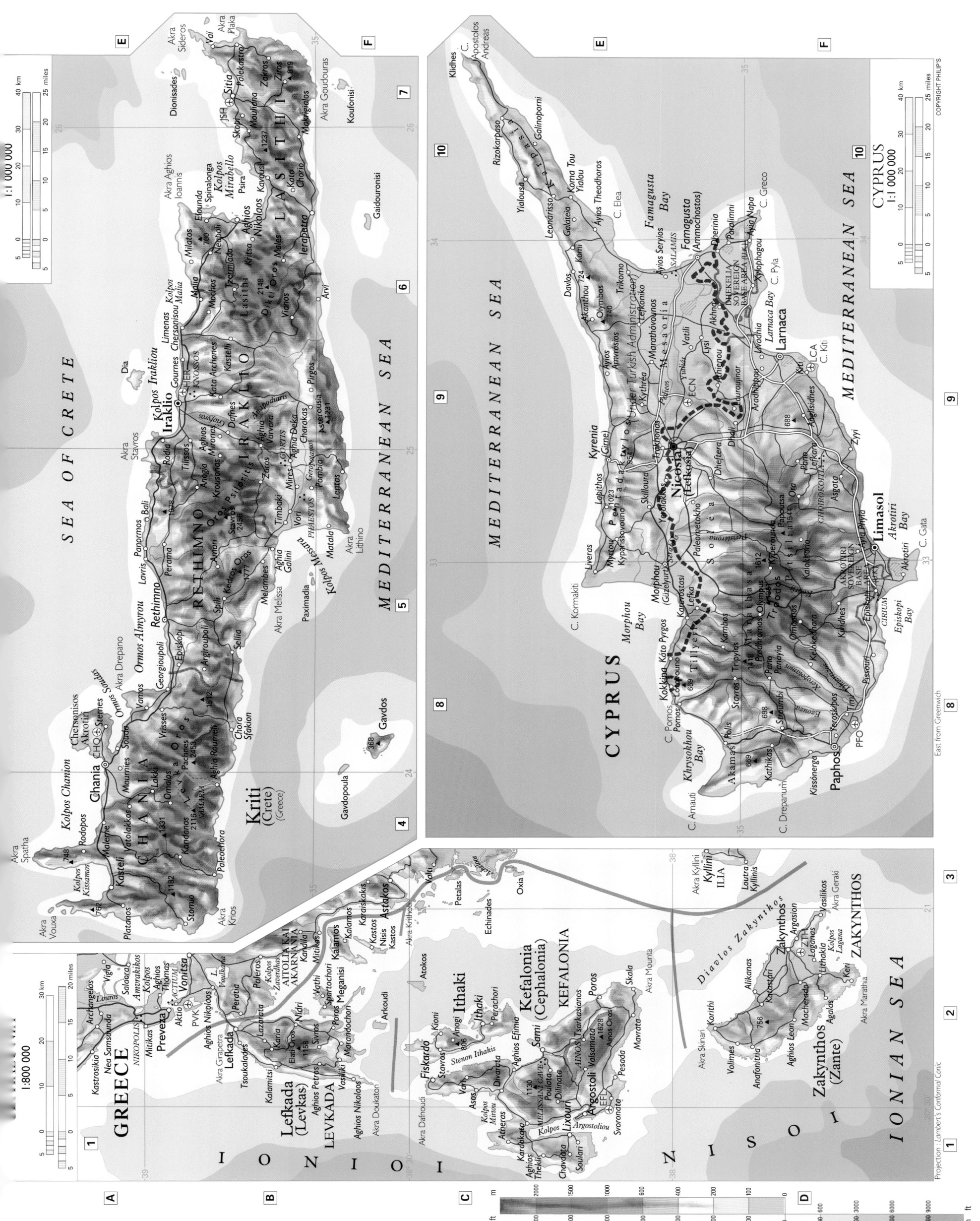

1:1 000 000

SEA OF CRETE

MEDITERRANEAN SEA

Kriti
(Crete)
(Greece)

Iraklion

HANIA

RETHIMNO

IRAKLIO

LASITHI

Ghania

Rethimno

Gavdos

GREECE

1:800 000

IONIOI NISOI

Preveza

Lefkada
(Levkas)

LEVKADA

Ithaki

Kefalonia
(Cephalonia)

KEFALONIA

Zakynthos
(Zante)

ZAKYNTHOS

IONIAN SEA

AITOLIA KAI
AKARNANIA

IONION

MEDITERRANEAN SEA

MEDITERRANEAN SEA

CYPRUS

CYPRUS
1:1 000 000

Nicosia
(Lefkosia)

Famagusta
(Ammochostos)

Famagusta
Bay

Kyrenia
(Girne)

Morphou
Bay

Larnaca

Limasol

Paphos

Akrotiri
Bay

Episkopi
Bay

Mesaoria

TROODOS

Projection : Lambert's Conformal Conic

East from Greenwich

ASIA

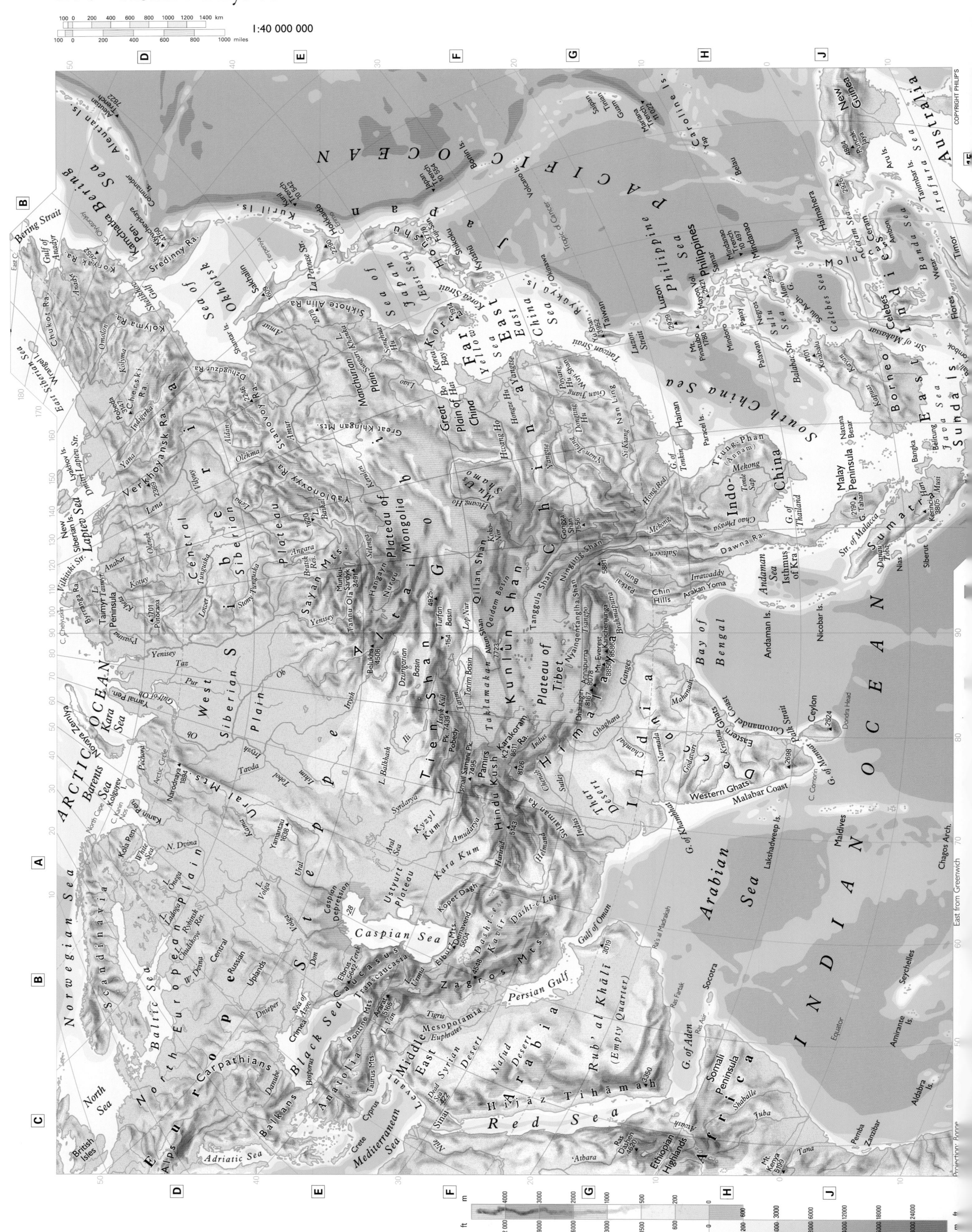

1:40 000 000

COPYRIGHT PHILIPS

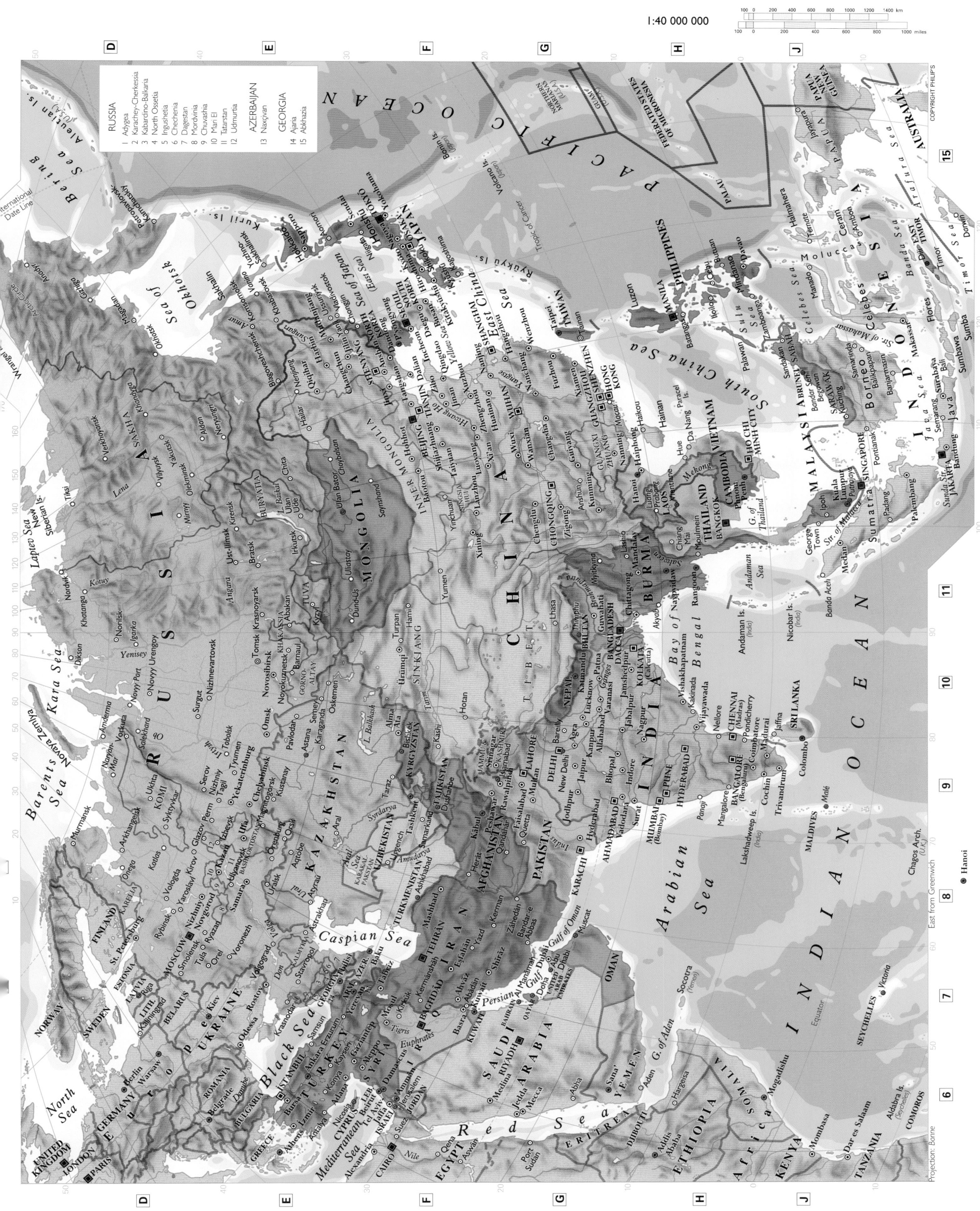

1:40 000 000

1 : 4 000 000

50 0 25 50 75 100 125 150 175 km
50 0 25 50 75 100 125 miles

BULGARIA

B L A C K   S E A

Stara Zagora · Yambol · Aytos · Burgas · Nos Emine
Elkhovo · Michurin
Kırklareli · Edirne · Pınarhisar · İğneada · İğneada Burnu
Orestiada · Babaeski · Vize · Demirköy
Uzunköprü · Hayrabolu · Lüleburgaz · Çerkezköy
Keşan · Malkara · Silivri · İSTANBUL
Tekirdağ · Büyükçekmece · Kartal · Kocaeli (İzmit) Sakarya (Adapazarı)
İstanbul Boğazı (Bosporus)
Çorlu · Çatalca · Gebze · Darıca
Marmara Denizi (Sea of Marmara)
Gelibolu · Bandırma · Mudanya · Yalova · Gölcük
Çanakkale (Dardanelles) · BURSA · İznik · İnegöl
TROY · Biga · Gönen · Yenişehir · Bilecik · Söğüt
Edremit · Balıkesir · Dursunbey · Bozüyük · Eskişehir
KÜTAHYA · Kütahya · Seyitgazi
MANISA · Akhisar · Uşak · Afyon (Afyonkarahisar)
İZMİR (Smyrna) · Turgutlu · Salihli · Sandıklı
EPHESUS · Aydın · Nazilli · DENİZLİ · Denizli
HIERAPOLIS PAMUKKALE · Burdur · Isparta

Lesbos · **Chios** · **Samos**

GREECE · Rhodes

ANKARA · Kırıkkale · YOZGAT · Kırşehir · NEVŞEHİR · KAYSERİ
Aksaray · KONYA · Konya · NIĞDE · Niğde
ADANA · Adana · KAHRAMANMARAŞ · Kahramanmaraş
GAZİANTEP · Gaziantep (Antep)
İskenderun · HATAY · Antakya

SAMSUN · Samsun · ÇANKIRI · ÇORUM · Çorum · TOKAT · Tokat · SİVAS · Sivas
Kastamonu · SİNOP · Sinop · Amasya · Merzifon

A n a t o l i a · **T U R K E Y**

Toros Dağları

CYPRUS (Under Turkish Administration)
Morphou · Kyrenia · Nicosia · Famagusta
Troodos · Olympus 1951 · Larnaca · Limassol
Paphos · Episkopi · Akrotiri

Al Lādhiqīyah (Latakia) · Hamāh · HAMĀH
HIMŞ (Homs) · Tarābulus (Tripoli) Al Batrūn
LEBANON · BAYRŪT (Beirut) · Saydā
DIMASHQ (Damascus) · Jaramānah

S Y R I A

HEFA (Haifa) · Nazerat
ISRAEL · Hadera · Netanya
TEL AVIV-YAFO · **WEST BANK** · Nābulus
Ashdod · Ashqelon · Jerusalem · **AMMĀN**

J O R D

M E D I T E R R A N E A N   S E A

Projection: Conical with two standard parallels

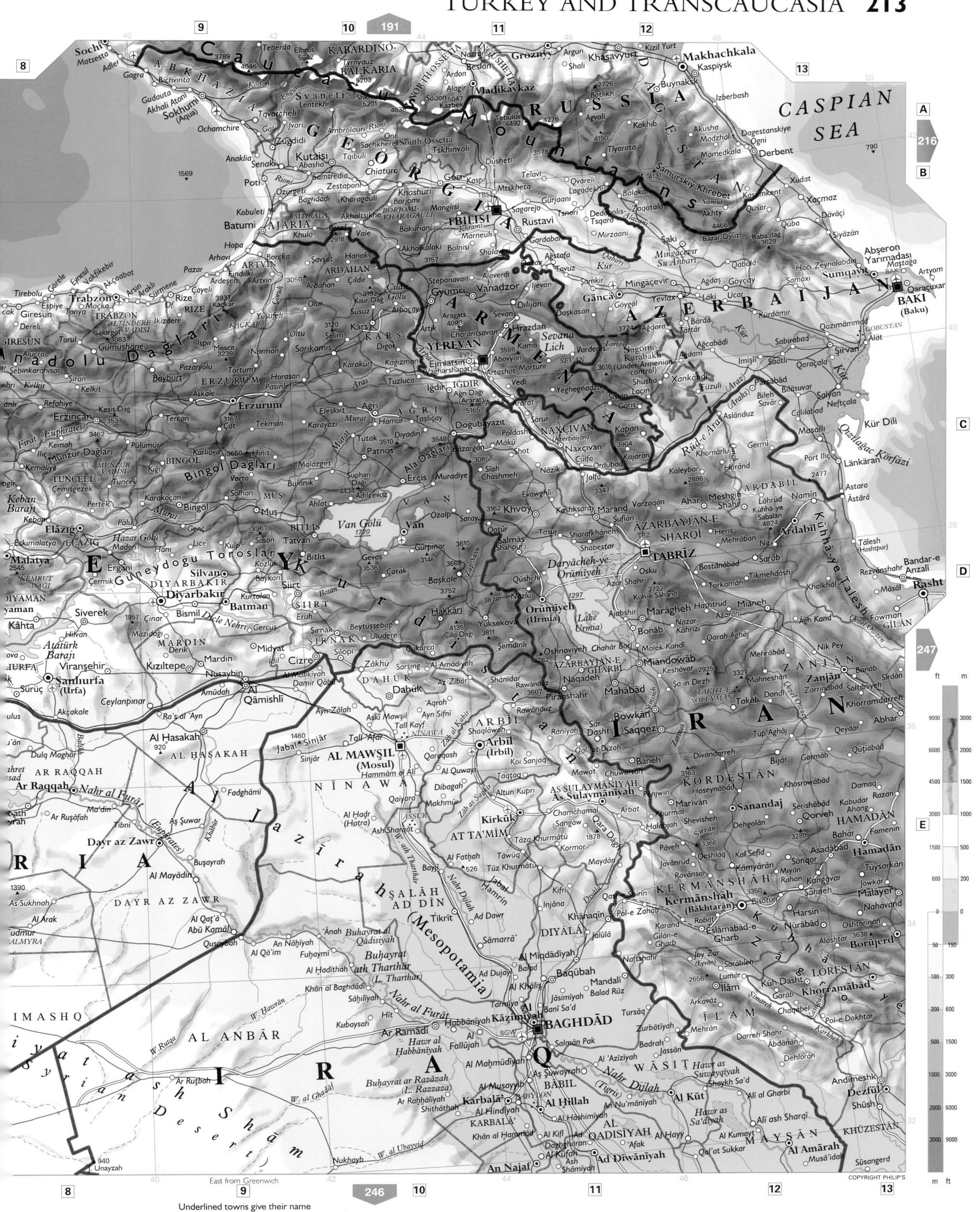

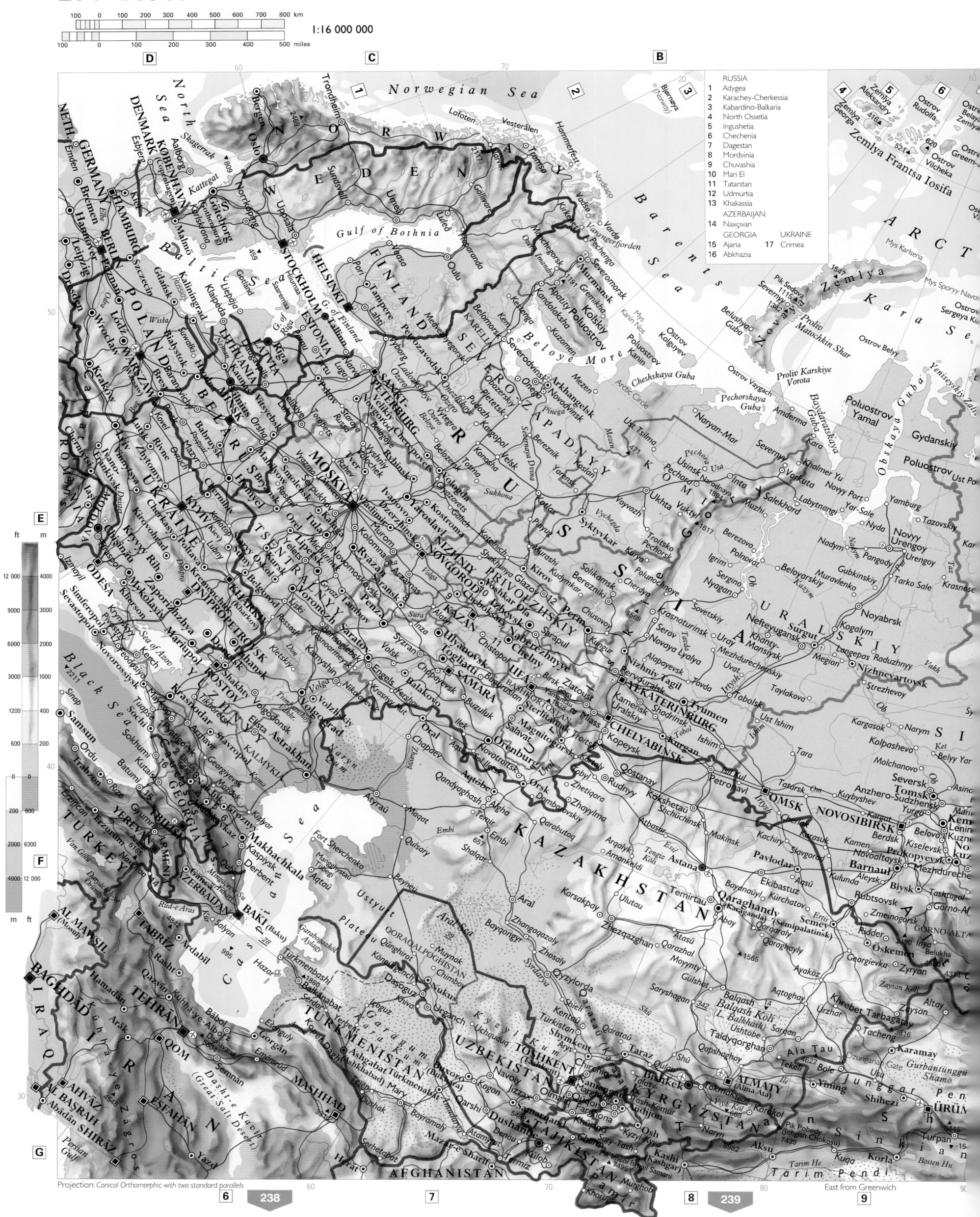

1:16 000 000

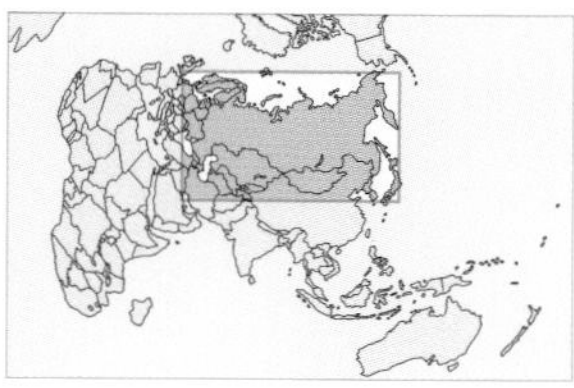

OCEAN

East Siberian Sea

Laptev Sea

Bering Sea

Sea of Okhotsk

Sea of Japan (East Sea)

Severnaya Zemlya

Ostrov Shmidta
Mys Arkticheskiy
Ostrov Ishakova
Ostrov Komsomolets
Ostrov Pioner
Ostrov Oktyabrskoy Revolyutsii
Ostrov Bolshevik
Ostrov Malyy Taymyr

Mys Dezhneva (East C.)
Chukchi Sea
Bering Str.
St. Lawrence I. (U.S.A.)
International Date Line
Mys Navarin

Poluostrov Taymyr
Gory Byrranga
Oz. Taymyr
Nordvik

Novaya Sibir
Ostrova Novosibirskiye Ostrova
Ostrov Kotelnyy
Ostrov Belkovskiy
Ostrov Stolbovoy
Lyakhovskiye Ostrova

Ostrov Vrangelya
Ostrova Medvezhi

Chaunskaya Guba
Pevek
Chukotskoye Nagorye
Anadyr
Anadyrskiy Zaliv
Providemya
Uelen

Kolymskoye Nagorye
Koryakskoye Nagorye
Sredinnyy Khrebet
Poluostrov Kamchatka
Petropavlovsk-Kamchatskiy

K H R E B E T   C H E R S K O G O
V e r k h o y a n s k i y   K h r e b e t
S A K H A
D A L N E V O S T O C H N Y Y

Verkhoyansk
Batagay
Zhigansk
Sangar
Yakutsk
Pokrovsk
Olekminsk
Aldan
Tommot
Neryungri

Mirnyy
Lensk
Vitim
Yenyuka
Nagornyy

Stanovoy Khrebet
Yablonovyy Khrebet
Khrebet Dzhugdzur

Sea of Okhotsk
Okhotsk
Magadan
Ust-Omchug

Sakhalin
Yuzhno-Sakhalinsk
Kholmsk
Korsakov
Tatarskiy Proliv

Kurilskiye Ostrova
Hokkaido
SAPPORO
Hakodate

Bratsk
Bratskoye Vdkhr.
Ust-Ilimsk
Kirensk
Magistralnyy
Severobaykalsk

Krasnoyarsk
Angarsk
Irkutsk
Ulan Ude
Chita
Ozero Baykal (L. Baikal)

Kyzyl
Sayan

MONGOLIA
Ulaanbaatar
Hangayn Nuruu
Hentiyn Nuruu
Erdenet
Mörön
Choybalsan
Tamsagbulag
Baruun-Urt
Öndörhaan

Gobi
Aerhtai Shan (Altay)
Dalandzadgad
Buyant-Uhaa

C H I N A
BAOTOU
HOHHOT
ZHANGJIAKOU
BEIJING
TANGSHAN
DALIAN
SHENYANG
ANSHAN
FUSHUN
CHANGCHUN
JILIN
HARBIN
QIQIHAR
DAQING
JIAMUSI
JIXI
MUDANJIANG
Manchuria (Dong bei)

Vladivostok
Khabarovsk
Komsomolsk-na-Amur
Birobidzhan
Blagoveshchensk
Heihe
Amur

NORTH KOREA
PYONGYANG
NAMPO
Hamhung
Wonsan
Ch'ongjin

SOUTH KOREA
SEOUL
INCHEON
DAEJEON
DAEGU
BUSAN
GWANGJU

JAPAN
Honshu
KYOTO
KOBE
OSAKA

COPYRIGHT PHILIP'S

Petukhovo · Bulavo · Om · Tatarsk · **NOVOSIBIRSK** · Berdsk · Leninsk-Kuznetskiy · Belovo · Chernogorsk · Minusinsk · Toora-Khem
Mamlyutka · Isil Kul · Kalachinsk · Novosibirskoye Vdkhr. · Iskitim · Prokopyevsk · Kiselevsk · Abakan · Shushenskoye · Turan · Kyzyl
Petropavl · **OMSK** · Cherlak · Karasuk · Kamen · Suzun · Novokuznetsk · Zarinsk · Mezhdurechensk · Krasnoyarsk · Khrebet Akademika Obrucheva

SOLTÜSTIK · QAZAQSTAN · Tayynsha · Kishkeneköl · Ozero Chany · Novoaltaysk · Temirtag · Tashtagol · **TUVA** · Ak-Dovurak · Erzin · Dzur
Saümalköl · Kökshetaü · Shchüchinsk · Ertis · Slavgorod · **Barnaul** · Biysk · Gorno-Altaysk · Belukha 4506 · Uvs Nuur

PAVLODAR · **Pavlodar** · Kulunda · Rubtsovsk · Zmeinogorsk · Ridder · GORNO-ALTAY · Ulaangom · **MONGOLIA**
Esil · Atbasar · Ekibastuz · Mayqayyng · Kürchatov · Shemonaïkha · Pervomayskiy · ALTAI · Ölgiy · Tolbo

Astana · AQMOLA · Osakarovka · Bayanaül · Semey (Semipalatinsk) · Glüboke · Belousovka · Zyryan · Qotanqaraghay · Altai · Burqin
Derzhavinsk · Qorghalzhyn · Temirtaü · Öskemen · Serebryansk · Georgievka · Tarbagatay · Fuyun · Qinghe

QAZAQSTAN · **Qaraghandy (Karaganda)** · Abay · Qaraghayly · SHYGHYS · QAZAQSTAN · Kürshim · Zaysan Köli (Oz. Zaysan) · HOVD
Sätbaev · Zhezqazghan · Qarazhal · Aqshataü · Ayaköz · Ürzhar · Khrebet Tarbagatay · Emin · Gurbantünggüt Shamo

KAZAKHSTAN · Betpaqdala · Moyynty · Balqash · ALMATY · Qabanbay · Karamay · Junggar Pendi · **ÜRÜMQI**
Balqash Köli (L. Balkhash) · Saryshaghan · Ushtöbe · Sarqan · Ala Tau · Bole (Bortala) · Changji · Bogda Shan

ONGTÜSTIK · QAZAQSTAN · Ülken · Taldyqorghan · Molaly · Tekeli · Yining (Gulja) · Shihezi · Miquan · Turpan · Turpan Pendi
Shyghanaq · Bürylbaytal · Balpyq Bi · Zharkent · Köktal · Huocheng · Borohoro Shan · Erbeng Shan · Hoxud

ZHAMBYL · Moyynqum · Shü · Qapshaghay · Shelek · Shonzhy · Gongliu · Qapqal · Hejing · Korla (Lop Nur) · Kuruktag
Sozaq · Zhangatas · Moyynqum · **ALMATY (Alma Ata)** · Talghar · Ala Too · Tüp · Karakol · Baicheng · Yuli · Lop Nur

Kentaü · Qaratau · Taraz (Zhambyl) · Kant · **Bishkek** · Tokmok · Cholpon-Ata · Ysyk-Köl · Yarkand · Aksu · Tarim He
Türkistan · Shymkent (Chimkent) · Lennger · Kochkor · Naryn · Jengish Chokusu · Wensu · Tarim Pendi

TOSHKENT (Tashkent) · Angren · Namangan · Andijon · Osh · At-Bashy · Wushi · Aksu He · Taklamakan · **XINJIANG UYGUR ZIZHIQU (SINKIANG)**
Shardara · Yangiyul · Qüqan (Kokand) · Farghona · Jalal-Abad · Toshkent · Kara-Köl · Kashi (Kashgar) · Shule · Markit · Shamo

SIRDARYO · Bekabad · Khujand · Istaravshan · Batken · Uluqqat · Wuqia · Yengisar · Shache (Yarkand) · Akto · Altun Shan
Jizzax · Samarqand · **TAJIKISTAN** · Gharm · Murghob · Taxkorgan · Zepu · Yecheng · Pishan · Minfeng

SURXON-DARYO · Tursunzoda · **Dushanbe** · Vahdat · KÜHISTON BADAKHSHON (GORNO-BADAKHSHON) · Pamir · Hotan · Moyu · Qira
Denov · Kulob · Khorugh · Feyzabad · Pamir · Kokyar · Lop · **CHINA**

Termiz · Qürghonteppa · Dusti · Ishkoshim · Karakoram Range · Mazar · Xaidulla · Aksai Chin · KUNLUN SHAN
BALKH · Mazar-e Sharif · Baghlan · Talogan · Gilgit-Baltistan · Nanga Parbat · Karakoram Pass · Sumdo · XIZANG ZIZHIQU (TIBET)

KABUL · Charikar · Jalalabad · HINDU KUSH · KHYBER PAKHTUNKHWA · **PAKISTAN** · JAMMU & KASHMIR · **SRINAGAR** · **INDIA** · Leh

Underlined towns give their name to the administrative area in which they stand.

COPYRIGHT PHILIP'S

1:12 000 000

100   0   100   200   300   400   500   600 km
100   0   100   200   300   400 miles

Projection: Bonne

East from
Greenwich

COPYRIGHT PHILIP'S

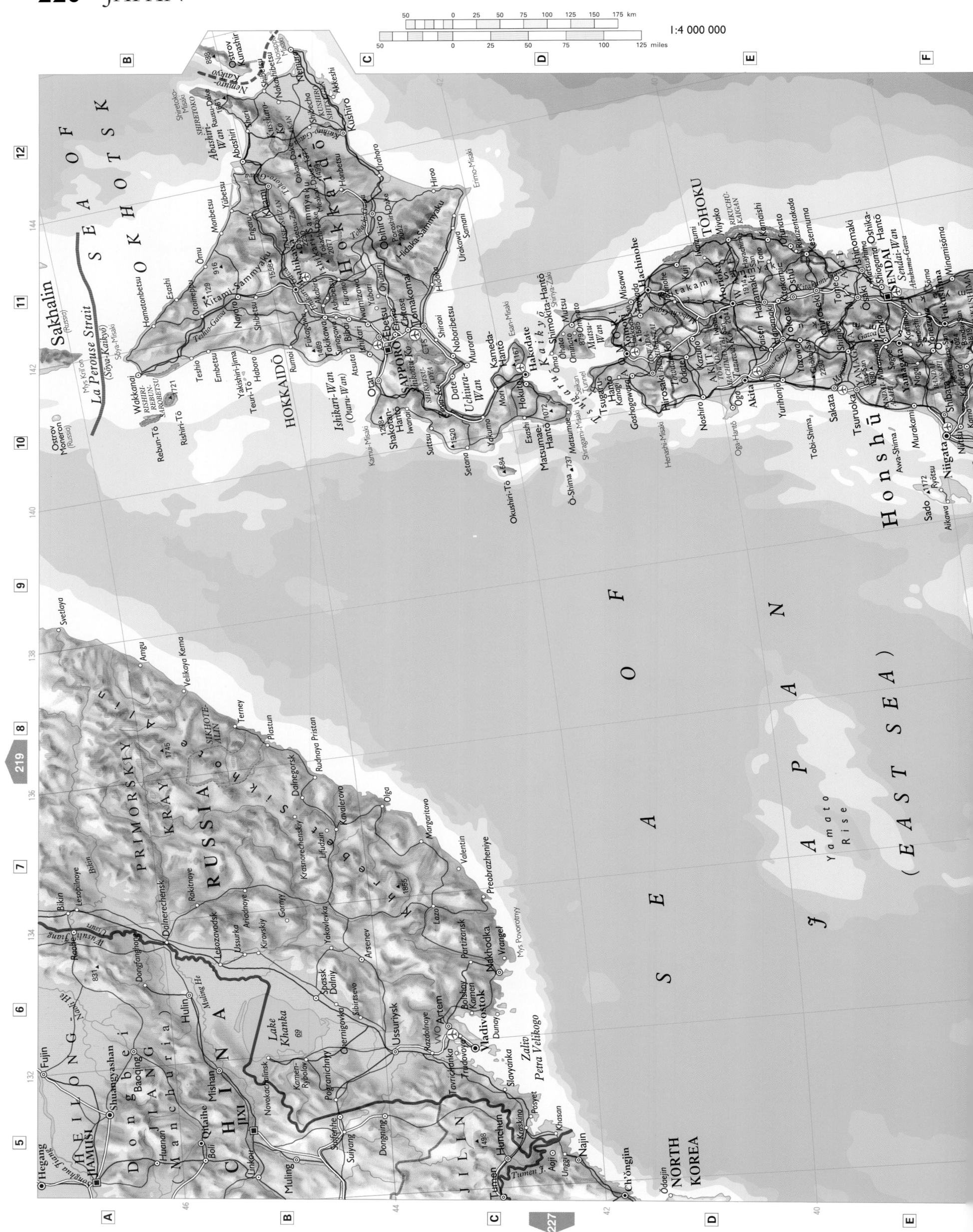

1:4 000 000

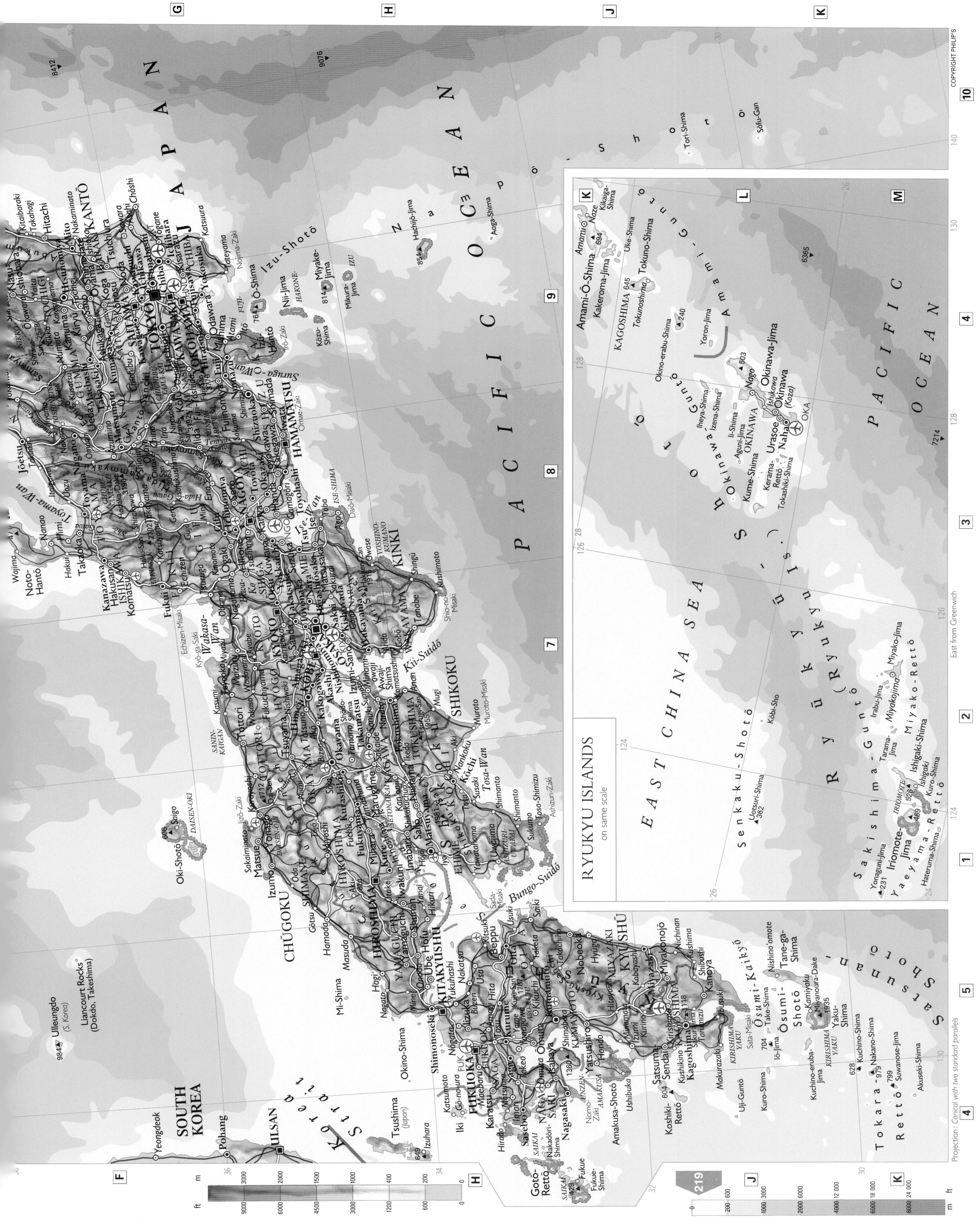

G H J K

10

8412 ▲

9076 ▼

J A P A N

Kitaibaraki
Takahagi
Hitachi

KANTŌ
Kitaminato
Nakaminato
Mito
Tsuchiura
Tsukuba
Ishioka
Narita
Yachiyo
Kashiwa
Katsuura
Kisarazu
Chōshi
Togane
Nojima-Zaki
Tateyama

Izu-Shotō

Hachijō-Jima

Aoga-Shima

Ō-Shima
Nii-Jima
Miyake-Jima
Mikura-Jima
Kōzu-Shima

854 ▲
811 ▲
IZU
HAKONE
766 ▲

P A C I F I C   O C E A N

Tori-Shima
Sōfu-Gan

K L M

26

6365 ▼

RYUKYU ISLANDS
on same scale

Amami
Naze
Kikaiga-Shima
Amami-Ō-Shima
Kakeroma-Jima
Uke-Shima
Tokuno-Shima
KAGOSHIMA
Tokunoshima
694 ▲
645 ▲
240 ▲
Yoron-Jima

Okino-erabu-Shima

Iheya-Shima
Ii-Shima
Izena-Shima
Aguni-Jima
OKINAWA
Nago
Okinawa-Jima
Ishikawa
Urasoe
Kerama-Rettō
Nahá
Okinawa (Koza)
Kume-Shima
Tokashiki-Shima

503 ▲

OKA

7214 ▼

P A C I F I C   O C E A N

130
128

4

3

E A S T   C H I N A   S E A

124
126
126

Senkaku-Shotō
Uotsuri-Shima
Kōbi-Sho
362 ▲

R y ū   (R y u k y u)

Sakishima-Guntō
Tarama-Jima
Irabu-Jima
Miyako-Jima
Miyako-Rettō
Miyakojima
Ishigaki-Shima
Ishigaki
Kuro-Shima
Yonaguni-Jima
231 ▲
IRIOMOTE
Iriomote-Jima
524 ▲
469 ▲
Yaeyama-Shima
Hateruma-Shima
Yaeyama-Rettō

2

1

24

P A C I F I C   O C E A N

9

8

7

Miyako
Chiba
TŌKYŌ
YOKOHAMA
KAWASAKI
Odawara
Itami

CHŪBU
FUJI
Hamamatsu
Shizuoka
Suruga-Wan

NAGOYA
NAGANO
GIFU
AICHI
MIE
Ise-Wan
Tsu
ISE-SHIMA
Daiō-Misaki

KINKI
Shingū
YOSHINO-KUMANO
Owase
KYŌTO
ŌSAKA
KŌBE
NARA
WAKAYAMA
Kii-Suidō
Shio-no-Misaki

SETO NAIKAI

OKAYAMA
HIROSHIMA
TOKUSHIMA
SHIKOKU
KŌCHI
Tosa-Wan
Muroto
Muroto-Misaki
Ashizuri-Zaki
Tosa-Shimizu
Shimanto

TOTTORI
SAN'IN-KAIGAN
Tottori
SHIMANE
Matsue
Izumo
CHŪGOKU
Gōtsu
Hamada
Masuda

Oki-Shotō

Dōgo
Dōzen
DAISEN-OKI

Oi

Mi-Shima

 Creating Shimonoseki
KITAKYŪSHŪ
YAMAGUCHI
FUKUOKA
Ōita
Beppu
KYŪSHŪ
KUMAMOTO
Miyazaki
NAGASAKI
SAGA

Tsushima (Japan)
Izuhara

Iki
Gotō-Rettō
Fukue-Shima
Fukue
429 ▲
Amakusa-Shotō

6
5
4

SOUTH KOREA
Yeongdeok
Pohang
ULSAN

Liancourt Rocks
(Dokdo, Takeshima)

Ulleungdo
(S. Korea)
984 ▲

Korea Strait

34
36

S A T S U N A N   S H O T Ō

KAGOSHIMA
Kirishima
Ōsumi-Kaikyō
Sata-Misaki
Ōsumi-Shotō
Tane-ga-Shima
Yaku-Shima
Nishino'omote
Kuchino-erabu-Jima

KIRISHIMA-YAKU
704 ▲
1935 ▲

Tokara-Rettō
Kuchino-Shima
Nakano-Shima
979 ▲
799 ▲
Suwanose-Jima
Akuseki-Shima
628 ▲

130

5

4

Projection: Conical with two standard parallels

East from Greenwich

m / ft scale bars

F H J K

10 0 10 20 30 40 50 60 70 80 90 km

1:2 000 000

10 0 10 20 30 40 50 60 miles

SEA OF JAPAN

(EAST SEA)

Yeongdeok

224

Heunghae

Pohang

SOUTH KOREA

Oki-Shotō

Daimanji-San
Dōgo▲608
Saigō

Dōzen

DAISEN-OKI

H o n s

SANIN-KAIGAN

DAISEN-OKI Shimane-Hantō Jizō-Zaki Iwami Kasumi
Hi-no-Misaki Hirata Shinji- Matsue Sakaiminato Yonago **TOTTORI** Tottori Toyooka
Taisha Kō Dai-Sen Kurayoshi Hidaka Suga-no-Sen Wadayama
CHŪGOKU-DISTRICT Izumo Yasugi ▲1729 Chizu 1510 **HYŌG**

H

Shinji Kisuki Daitō Nishiv

Oda Sanbe-San Dōgo-San Katsuyama Tsuyama Yamasaki Nishiv
IWAMI GINZAN 1126 ▲1269 Ochiai Yinahara Sayo Kasai
Yunotsu Gō-Gawa Shōbara Bingo Ochiai Tōjō **OKAYAMA** Takahashi Tatsuno Aigi **Himeji**
Gōtsu Miyoshi Yakage Sōja Bizen Takasago

Hamada **SHIMANE** Yoshida **HIROSHIMA** Fuchū Ibara **Okayama** Wake Kakoga

Masuda Akiota Kannon-Yama Higashi- Mihara Onomichi Kurashiki Saidaiji Ieshima Kas

Ōmi-Shima Hagi Aono-Yama 1339 Hiroshima Fukuyama Kasaoka Shōdo- Shōtō Harima-
Tsuno-Shima Nagato ▲808 Atō **HIROSHIMA** Kaita Takehara In'noshima Tamano Shima Tonoshō Nada Kas

Mi-Shima **YAMAGUCHI** Matsunaichi Kure Konkō

Tsushima Toyoura Yamaguchi Itsukinichi Ōtake Ondo Ōmi- Sakaide **Takamatsu** Awaji-Shima
Hōfu Kurahashi- Shima Marugame **KAGAWA** Sumoto
Kamiagata Kara-Saki Mine Ogōri San'yō Iwakuni Jima Aki-Nada Tadotsu Miki Naruto

Kamitsushima Hibiki- Nagato Shin-Nan'yō Hiuchi- Kan'oji Zentsuji kagawa Minan

Mitsushima Nada San'yō Shunan Yashiro- Nada Onohara Kotohira Sanuki- Itano awa
Izuhara Toyoura Onoda Ube Kudamatsu Jima Niihama Shikokuchūō Mima Yoshino- Tokushi
649 Hikari Yanai Iwai-Jima Imabari gawa

Kō-Saki Higashi-Suidō Shimonoseki Naga-Shima Matsuyama Tōyo Ikeda **TOKUSHIMA**

Genkai- Ō-Shima Heigun-Tō **EHIME** Iyo- Saijō Ishizuchi-Yama Tsurugi-San Anan
Katsumoto Nada Munakata Nakama Iyo-Nada Mishima ▲1981 ▲1955
Iki **KITAKYŪSHŪ** Suō-Nada Matsuyama Kuma Nankoku Kami Gam
Gō-no-ura Nōgata Ōzu 1562 Ino Noichi Saki

Ikitsuki- Yobuko Fukuma Yukuhashi Nagahama Uchiko Sakawa **Kōchi** Aki
Shima Iki-Kaikyō Koga Miyata Buzen Yawatahama Tosa Tōyō
FUKUOKA Iizuka Tagawa Usa Mie Uwa Susaki Muroto

Ō-Shima Maebaru Dazaifu Kama Bungotakada Ōzu Kihoku Muroto-Misaki
Hirado- Hirado Matsuura Kasuga Chikushino 1200 Kitsuki Sada-Misaki-Hantō Uwajima Nishi-Tosa Shimanto
Shima Karatsu FUK Sefuri- Amagi Hita Hiji Sada-Misaki Tsushima Saga

SAIKAI Imari Yobuko Sanchi 1055 Ogōri Yufu-Dake **Beppu-Wan** Misho Sukumo
574 Saza Ogi Tosu 1584 Saiki Oki-no-Shima Tosa-Shimizu Tosa-Wan
Takeo Taku Saga Kurume Kusu **Beppu** Ashizuri- 865 Tōsa-Shimizu
NAGASAKI Arita Okawa Yame **Ōita** Saganoseki Uwakai Ashizuri-Zaki
Yanagawa Chikugo Ogani Usuki Tsurumi-Saki

Nishi-Sonogi-Hantō Ōmura- Ureshino Kurogi 1787 Kujū-San **OITA** Tsukumi Ashizuri-Uwakai
Ōmura Wan Isahaya Tara-Dake Yamaga Aso Kae Kamae
Nagayo Omuta Arao Kikuchi **ASO-** Oguni Ichinomiya Taketa Saiki

Nagasaki Unzen- Tamana **KUJŪ** Kōshi 1592 **Takachiho** Nobeoka
Shimabara Dake Ōzu Aso-Zan Sōbo-Yama

Nomo-Zaki 1360 **Kumamoto** Mashiki 1758 Hinokage
Obama **UNZEN AMAKUSA** Uto **KUMAMOTO** Takachiho

Amakusa- Kuchinotsu Matsubase Shiba **Hyūga**
Amakusa- Hondo Matsushima Misumi Kunimi-Dake Hyūga
Shotō Shimo- Kami- 1739

Ushibuka Unzen-Jima **Yatsushiro** Itsuki Taragi **MIYAZAKI**
Nada AMAKUSA Jima Yatsushiro-Kai Shiiba

Naga-Shima Minamata Hitoyoshi Saito Takanabe
Izumi Taragi

Kami-Koshiki- Akune Ōkuchi Ebino Kobayashi **Kyūshū**
Jima Yoshimatsu 1700 Sadowara **KYŪSHŪ-DISTRICT**

Koshiki- Miyanojō Kurino Kirishima-Yama **Miyazaki**
Rettō 604 Satsuma- Kushikino 1118 Soo Nichinan
Sendai Aira **KIRISHIMA** Miyakonojō Aburatsu
Shimo-Koshiki- On-Take YAKI
Jima **Kagoshima** Hayato Kirishima
Ijūin Sakurajima **Kyūshū Trenc**
KAGOSHIMA 1118

Fukiage Tarumizu Shibushi
Noma-Saki Kaseda Fukiage **KAGOSHIMA** Kanoya Kushima
Koshiki- Kiire Osaki Kōyama ▼5737
Kaikyo Kawanabe 968 Shibushi-Wan

Makurazaki Bō-no-Misaki
Kaimon-Dake Yamagawa
924 Ibusuki
KIRISHIMA Sata-Misaki
YAKU

Korea Strait

Higashi-Suidō

Shikoku
SHIKOKU-DISTRICT

Kyūshū
KYŪSHŪ-DISTRICT

CHŪGOKU-DISTRICT

Projection:
Lambert's Conformal
Conic

Shinkansen lines

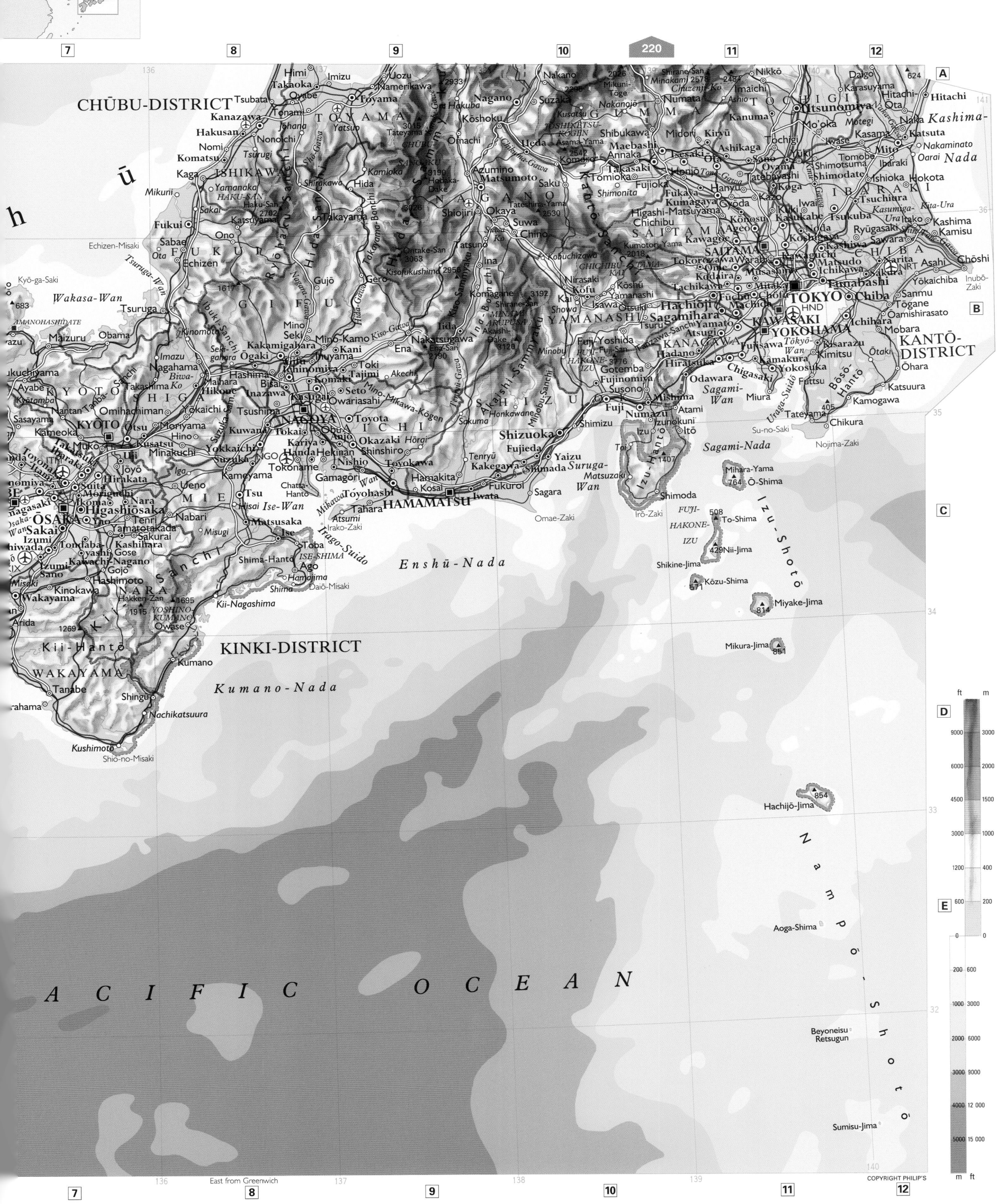

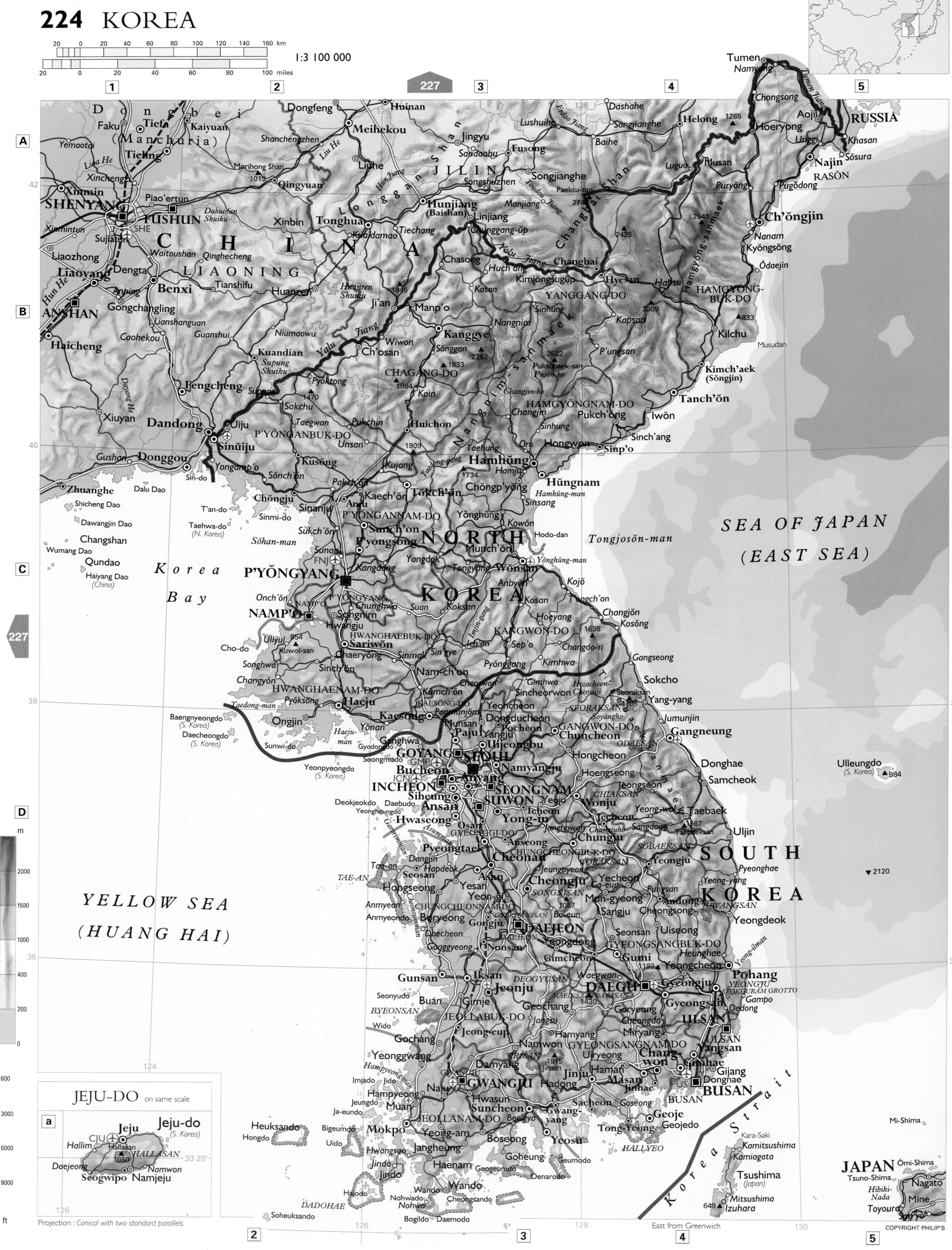

1:3 100 000

SEA OF JAPAN
(EAST SEA)

YELLOW SEA
(HUANG HAI)

Korea
Bay

CHINA

RUSSIA

NORTH
KOREA

SOUTH
KOREA

JAPAN

JEJU-DO on same scale

Jeju-do
(S. Korea)

Projection : Conical with two standard parallels

COPYRIGHT PHILIP'S

Korea Train eXpress (KTX)

1:1 400 000

5 0 10 20 30 40 50 60 70 km
5 0 10 20 30 40 50 miles

CHINA FUJIAN
Jimei Shijing Jinjing
Xinglin XMN Kaohao
Xiamen Chinmen (Quemoy)
Hsiao-chinmen Tao Chinmen Tao
Zhenhai *Taiwan Strait*

CHINMEN on same scale a

CHINA FUJIAN
Huangqi Liang Tao Tungyin Tao
Lianjiang Peikant'ang Tao Tongsha Tao
Langqi Min Jiang Matsu Tao *(Taiwan)*
Changle Paichuan Liehtao *Taiwan Strait*
FOC

MATSU on same scale b

229

T A I W A N   S T R A I T

P A C I F I C   O C E A N

B a s h i   C h a n n e l

Projection: Lambert Conformal Conic

East from Greenwich

COPYRIGHT PHILIP'S

232

—— Taiwan High Speed Rail (THSR)

Fukuei Chiao Shihmen
Tanshui Chinshan
T'AIPEI YANGMINGSHAN 1103 Chilung (Keelung)
Peitou Wanli Pitou Chiao
Kuanyin Sanchung Nankang Kungliao
TAOYUAN Panch'iao **TAIPEI** Maoao Santiao Chiao
Chungli Taoyuan Chingho Pinglin Talichien
Pate Hsintien Waiao Kueishan Tao
Hsinfeng Tach'i Wulai T'ouch'eng
Nanliao Huk'ou Kuanhsi Fuhsing Chiaohsi
Hsinchu Chupei Chutung Ilan Chuangwei Wuchieh
Hsiangshan Neiwan Sanhsing Lotung
Chunan Toufen HSINCHU Suao
Houlung Miaoli Shihtan Yuanshan Tungshan
Kungssuliao Tsaochiao Nanao
MIAOLI Shihiu 2573 Tungao
Chungtungwan Kungkuan ILAN Kuanyin
T'unghsiao Tunglo Tachoshui
Yüanli Sani Tahu SHEI PA 3740 2646
Taan Hsüeh Shan Chingshui
Tachia 3886 3605
Ch'ingshui T'engyüan Shei Shan TAROKO T'ailuko
Wuch'i Lungching Tungshih Hoping Hsinch'eng
Shalu T'antzu Peitun Hsinche
Shenkang Taping HUALIEN
Homei **T'AICHUNG** Kuohsing Hualien
Changhua Wujih Wufeng Jenai Jenho
Lukang Hsiushui Shihkangkeng 3349
Fuhsing CHANGHUA Fenyuan Chian
Wangkung Chihu Yünlin NANTOU Puli Shoufeng
Fangyüan Pitou Nant'ou Yüchih Fenglin
Emlin T'enchang Shetou Chichi 3344 Chichi
Tacheng Hsilo Chilei'ou Chushan Wulicheng Kuangfu
Maliao Lunpei Tzutung Tingkan Wanjung Tafu
Taihsi YÜNLIN Linnei Luku Hsini Fengpin
Santiaolun Huwei Touliu Alishan 2480 Luyeh
K'ouhu Ssuhu Talin Meishan 3833 Takangkou
Peikang Tuku Touhan Fenchih Chingpu
Kanghsi Minhsiung 3952 YÜ SHAN Changyuan
Putai Chuchi Chungpu Sanhsien
Chiai Fanlu Leyeh Choch'i Ch'angpin
CHIAI Shuishang 1331
Ichu Houpi Paiho Yüli
Peimen Yenshui Tapu Kuan Shan Antung
Hsüehchia Liuying Shanhua Fuhsing Wulu Sanhsien
Chiali Matou Hsinying Meinong Chihshang 1682 Hoping
Chiku Shanhua Tsengwen Taoyuan Ch'engkung
Hsikang Shanshang Yuching Peiranchu Shan
Chengnan Hsinhua Chiahsien Kuanshan
T'AINAN Yungk'ang Shanlin T'AITUNG Tungho
Jente Luikuei Peinan Tulan
Chiehting Ch'ishan Lichia Chialulantsun
Luchu Alien Meinung Lichia T'aitung
Yungan Kaoshu Peinan
Kangshan Yenchiao Chianapu Lü Tao (Green I.)
Tzukuan Likang Yenpu Lütao
Chiaot'ou Santi P'ING T'aimali
KAOHSIUNG Jenwu Chuju Changchih
Tsoying Kangshan Fengshan Peitawu Shan 3090 Ch'inlun
Chienchen Talias Wantan Hsiatahsi
Hsiaokang Neipu Ch'aochou Tawu
Hsinchuang Hsinyuan TUNG Tajen
Linyuan Limpien Shouchia
Tungkang Shuitiliao Taniao
Chiatung Hsinpi Taniao
Liuch'iu Yü Fangliao Tawu
Liuch'iu Fangshan Fengkang
Ch'ulin Tanlu Hsühaitsun
Mutanshe
Ch'ech'eng Kangtzu
Hengch'un Manchou 548 Lan Yü (Orchid I.)
Maopi T'ou Nanwan Lanyu Hsiaohungt'ou Hsü
Oluan Pi Oluanpi

T A I W A N

P'enghu
Yüweng Tao Paisha
Hsiyu Huhsi
Makung P'enghu Tao
P'ENGHU Ch'üntou (Pescadores)
Hua Yü Waisanting
Wangan Pachao Yü
Ch'imei Yü Ch'imei
Tungchi Yü

Chipei Tao

Tropic of Cancer

5391

ft   m
9000 3000
6000 2000
4500 1500
3000 1000
1200   400
 600   200
   0   0
 200   600
1000 3000
2000 6000
3000 9000
4000 12 000
5000 15 000
m   ft

A
B
C
D

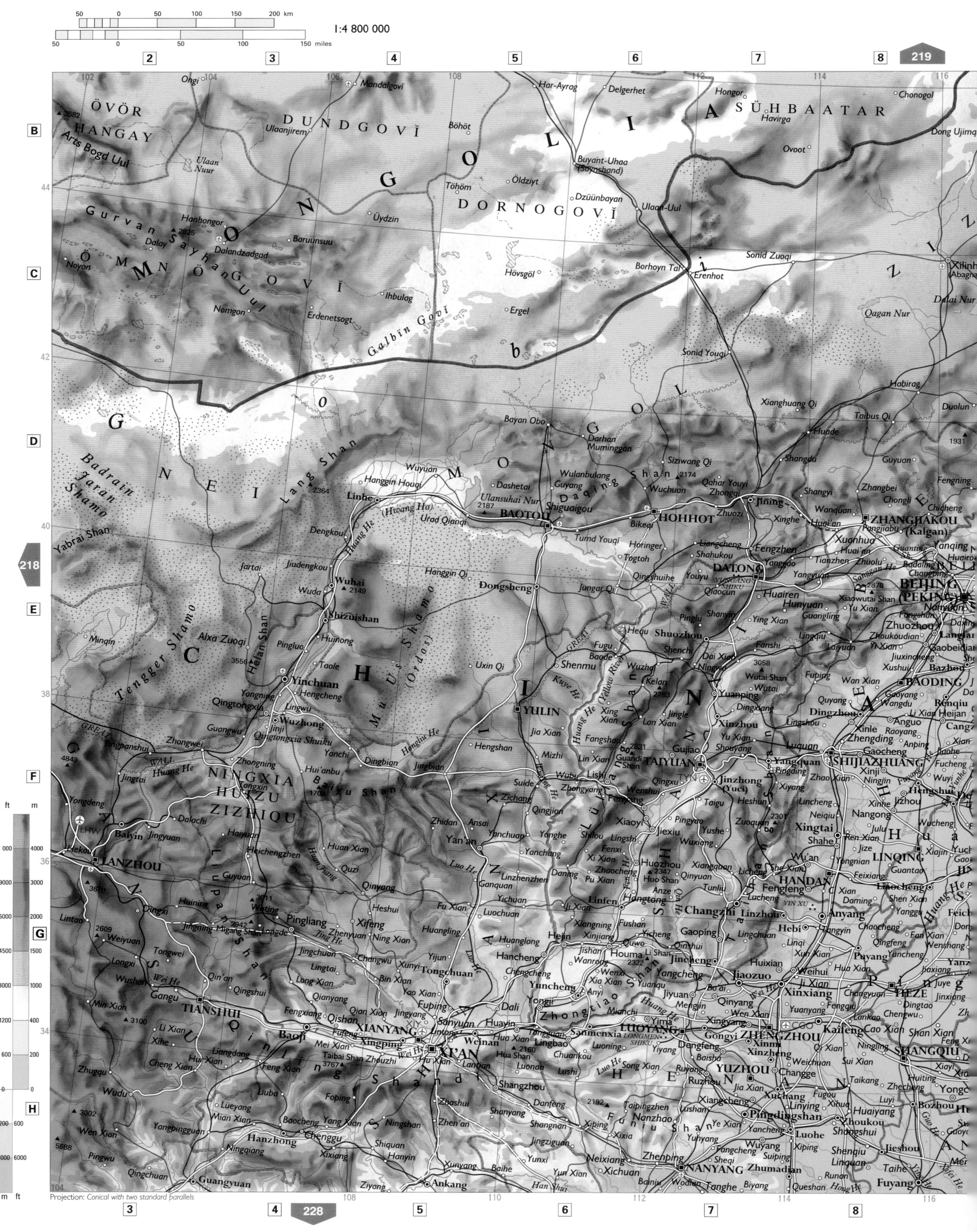

Projection: Conical with two standard parallels

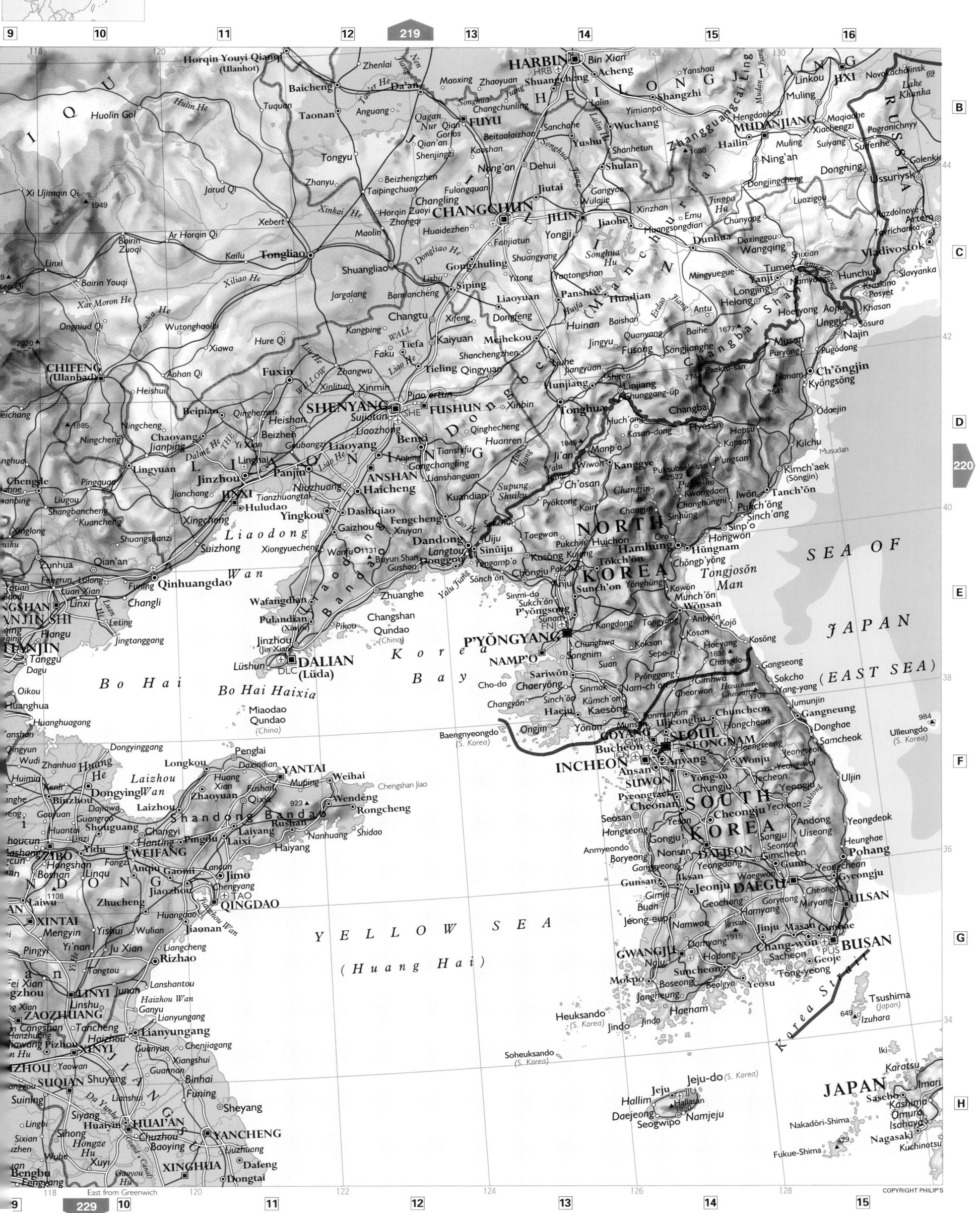

East from Greenwich

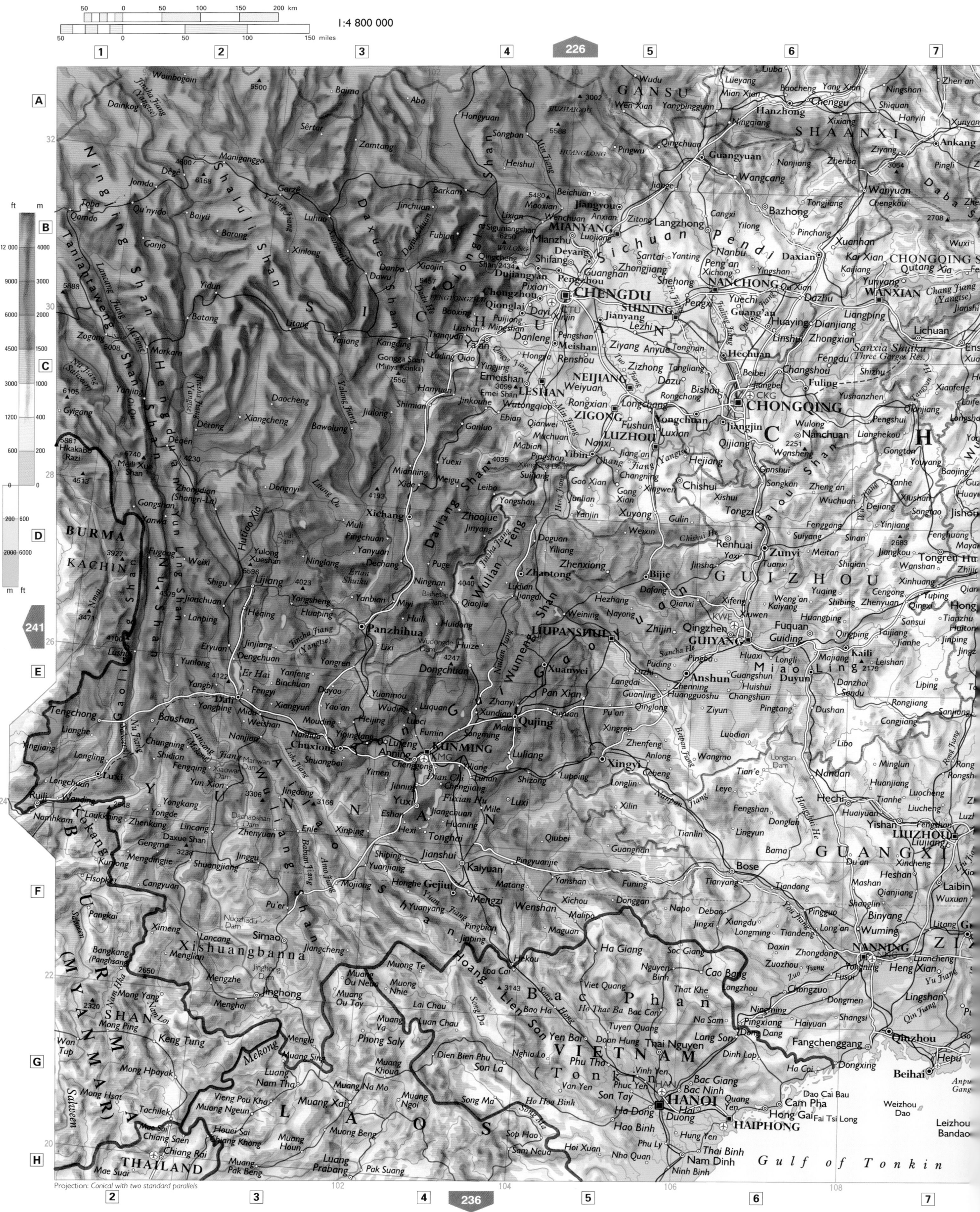

1:4 800 000

Projection: Conical with two standard parallels

East from Greenwich

COPYRIGHT PHILIP'S

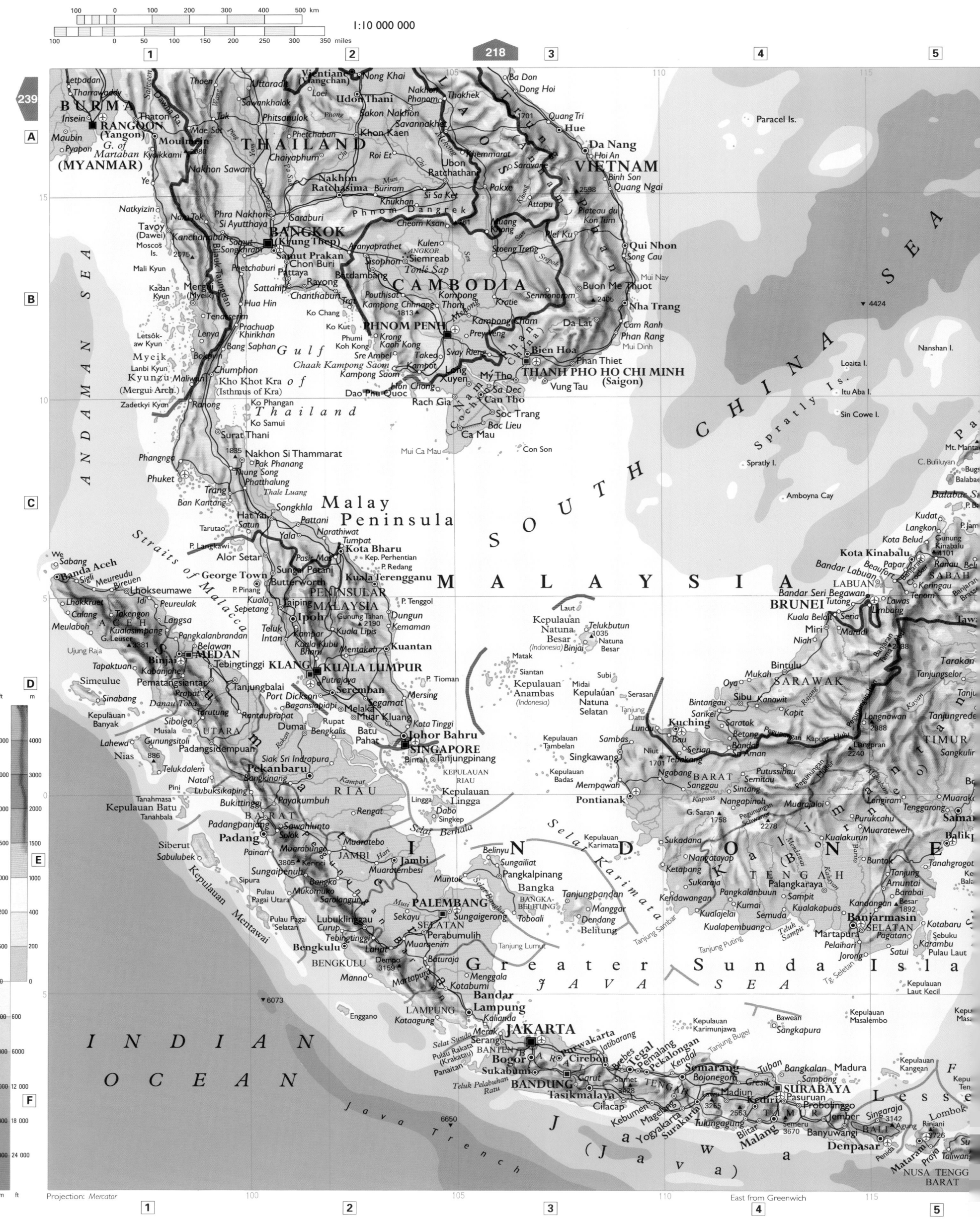

100 0 100 200 300 400 500 km

100 0 50 100 150 200 250 300 350 miles

218

BURMA
(MYANMAR)

THAILAND

VIETNAM

CAMBODIA

PHNOM PENH

THANH PHO HO CHI MINH
(Saigon)

ANDAMAN SEA

Gulf

of

Thailand

Malay

Peninsula

S O U T H   C H I N A   S E A

M A L A Y S I A

BRUNEI

PENINSULAR
MALAYSIA

Kota Kinabalu

SABAH

SARAWAK

Kuching

MEDAN

KUALA LUMPUR
KLANG

Johor Bahru
SINGAPORE

Straits of Malacca

I N D O N E S I A

(B o r n e o)

Pontianak

Banjarmasin

PALEMBANG

Greater   Sunda   Isla

J A V A   S E A

BENGKULU

BANDAR
LAMPUNG

I N D I A N

O C E A N

JAKARTA

BANDUNG

SEMARANG

SURABAYA

Denpasar

J   a   v   a

(J a v a)

NUSA TENGG
BARAT

Java Trench

Projection: Mercator

East from Greenwich

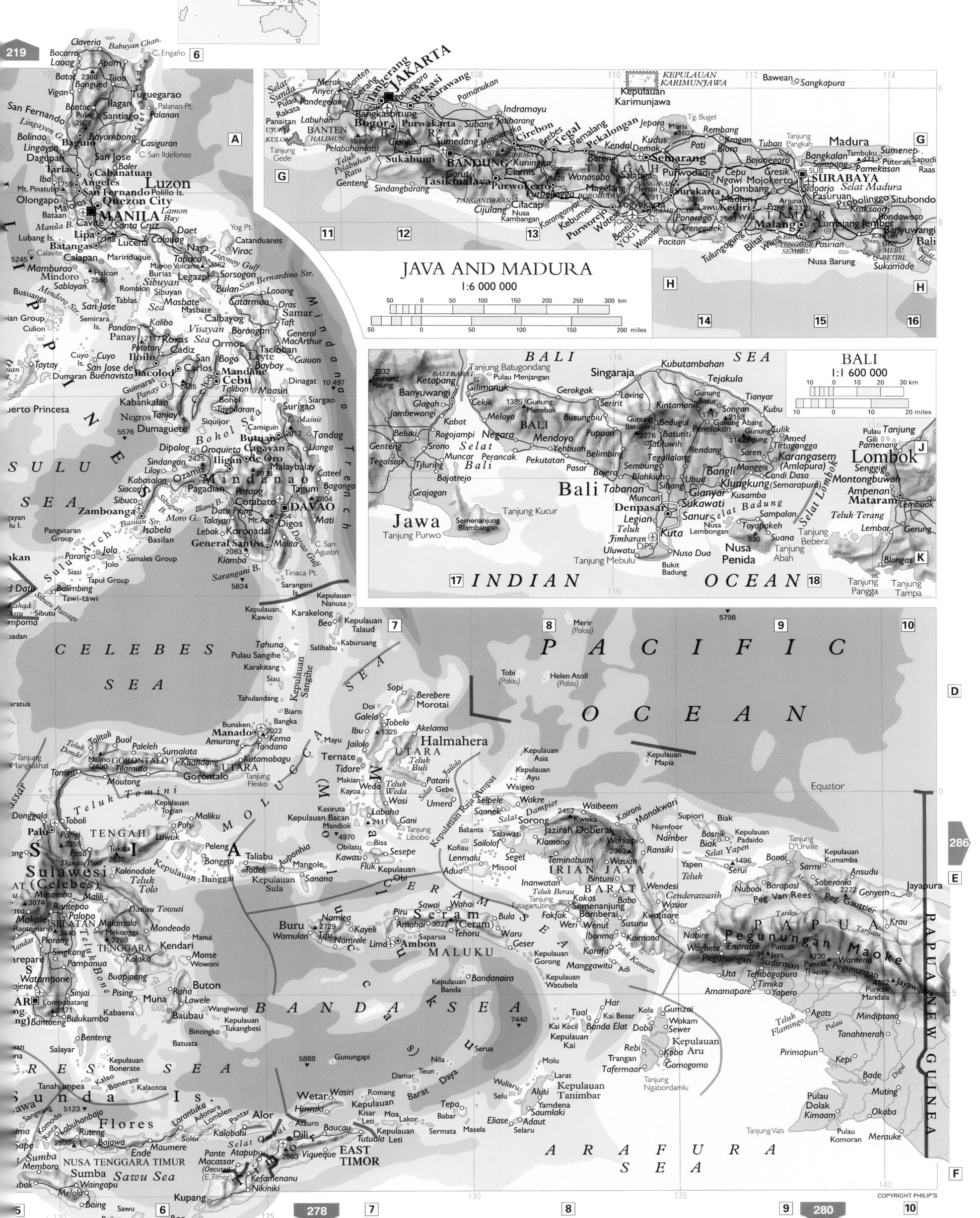

JAVA AND MADURA
1:6 000 000

50   0   50   100 150 200 250 300 km
50   0   50   100   150   200 miles

BALI
1:1 600 000

10   0   10   20   30 km
10   0   10   20 miles

219

286

278   280

COPYRIGHT PHILIP'S

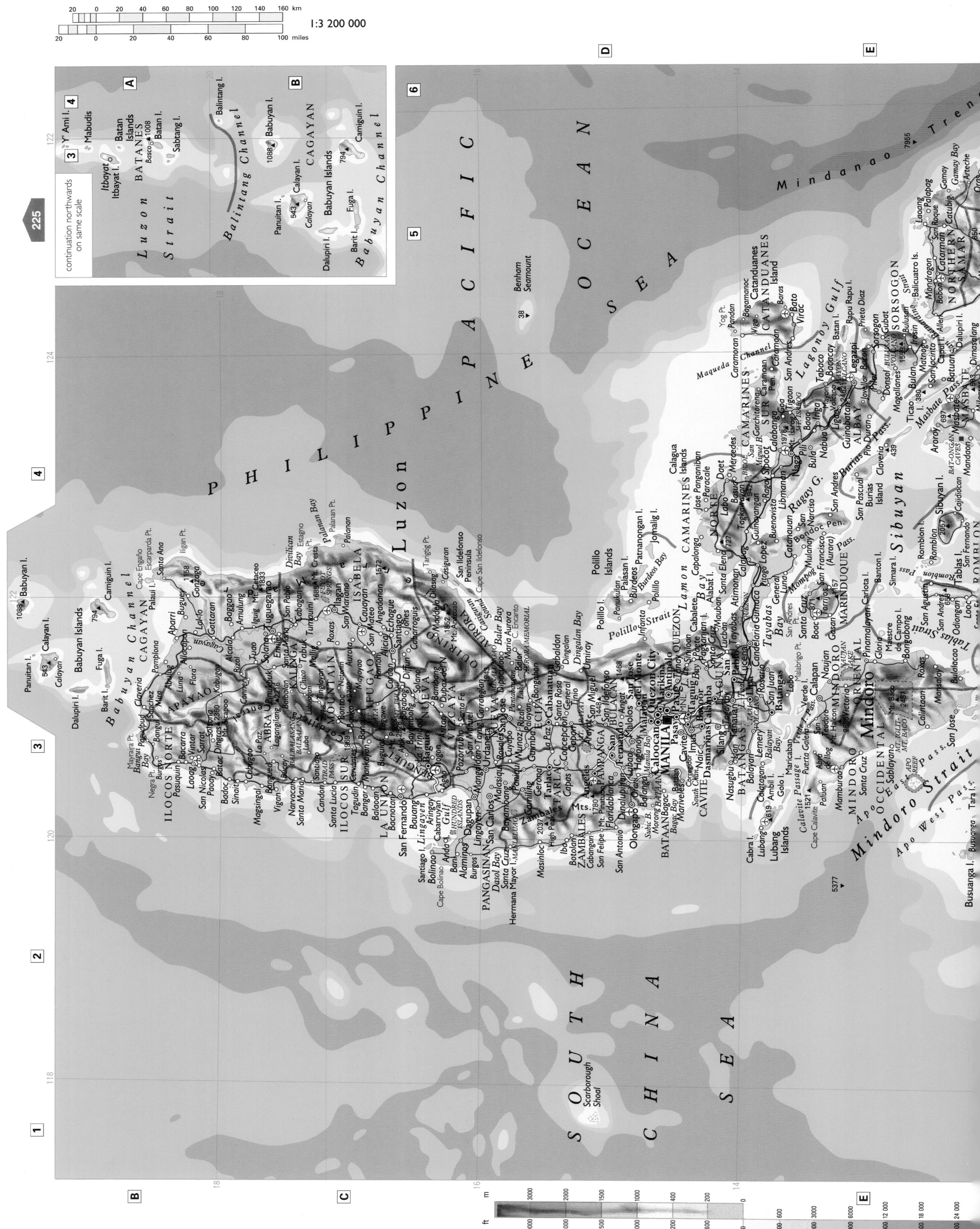

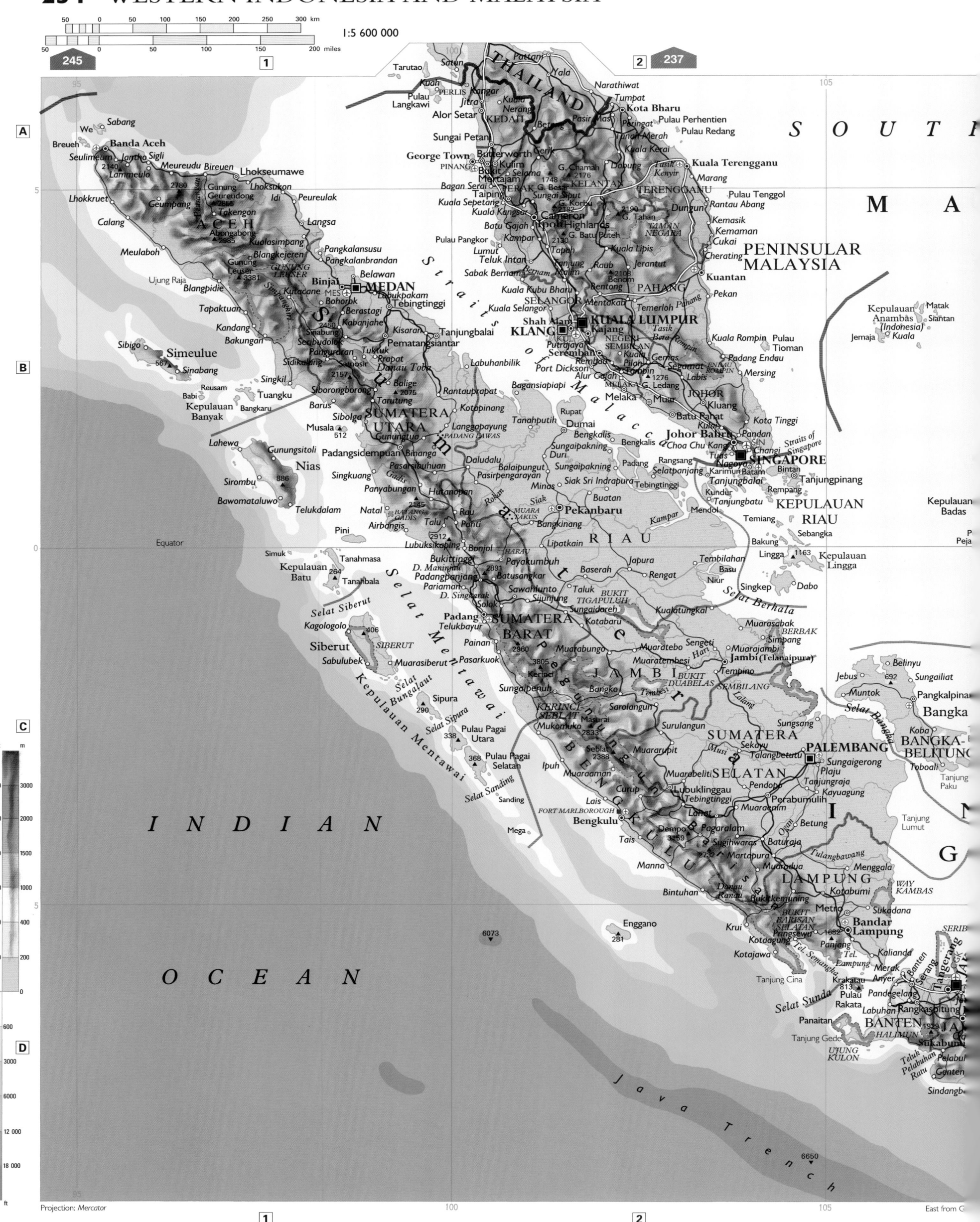

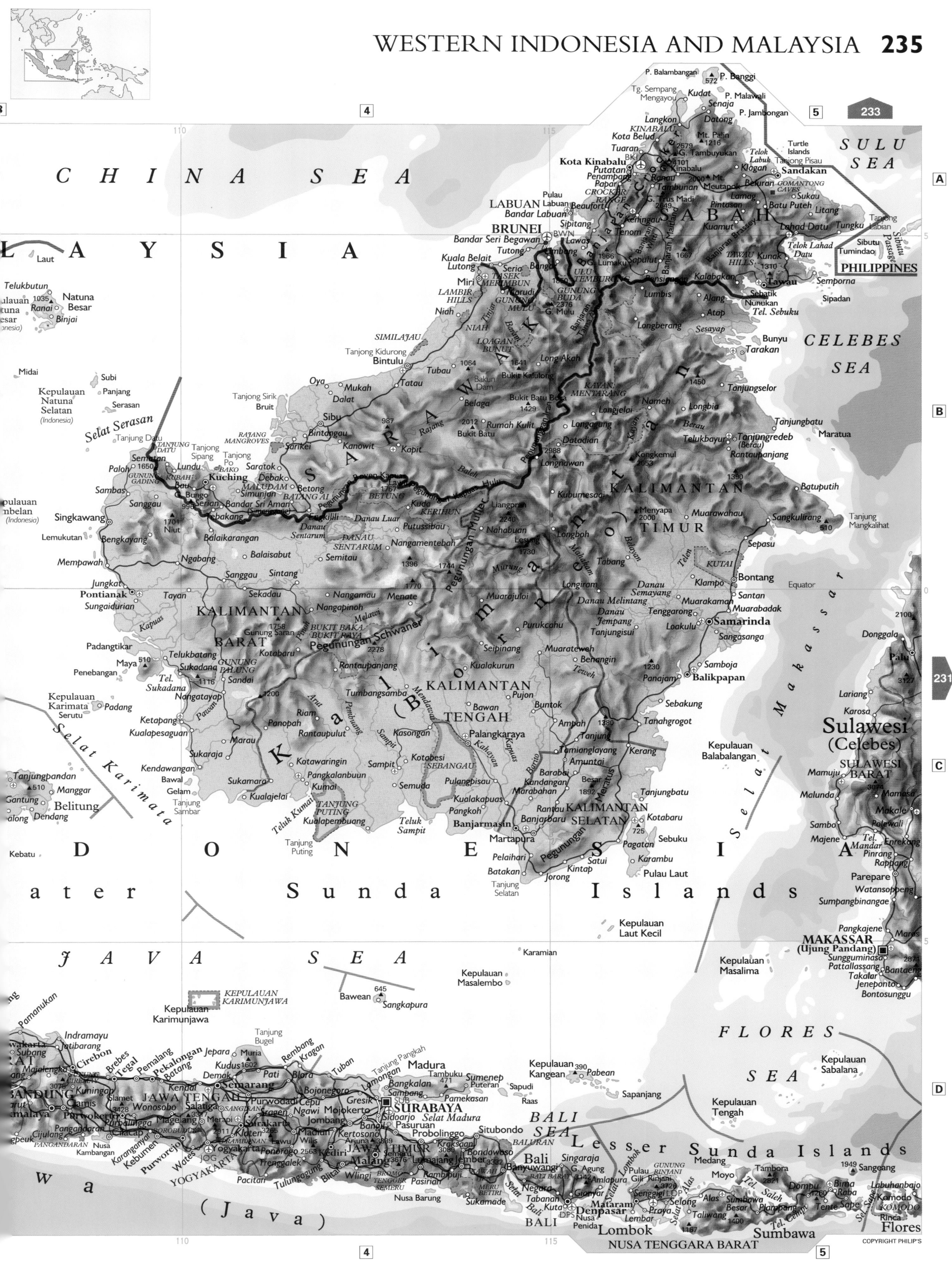

231

SULU SEA

CHINA SEA

MALAYSIA

CELEBES SEA

LABUAN
BRUNEI
Bandar Seri Begawan
PHILIPPINES

Kota Kinabalu
Sandakan

SABAH

SARAWAK

KALIMANTAN TIMUR

KALIMANTAN BARAT

KALIMANTAN TENGAH

KALIMANTAN SELATAN

Pontianak

Samarinda
Balikpapan

Banjarmasin

Sulawesi (Celebes)

SULAWESI BARAT

Makassar
(Ujung Pandang)

Kuching

I N D O N E S I A

Greater Sunda Islands

JAVA SEA

FLORES SEA

BALI SEA

Surabaya

J A W A T E N G A H

JAWA TIMUR

YOGYAKARTA

Bandung

Denpasar
Mataram

BALI

Lombok

Sumbawa

Flores

Lesser Sunda Islands

NUSA TENGGARA BARAT

(Java)

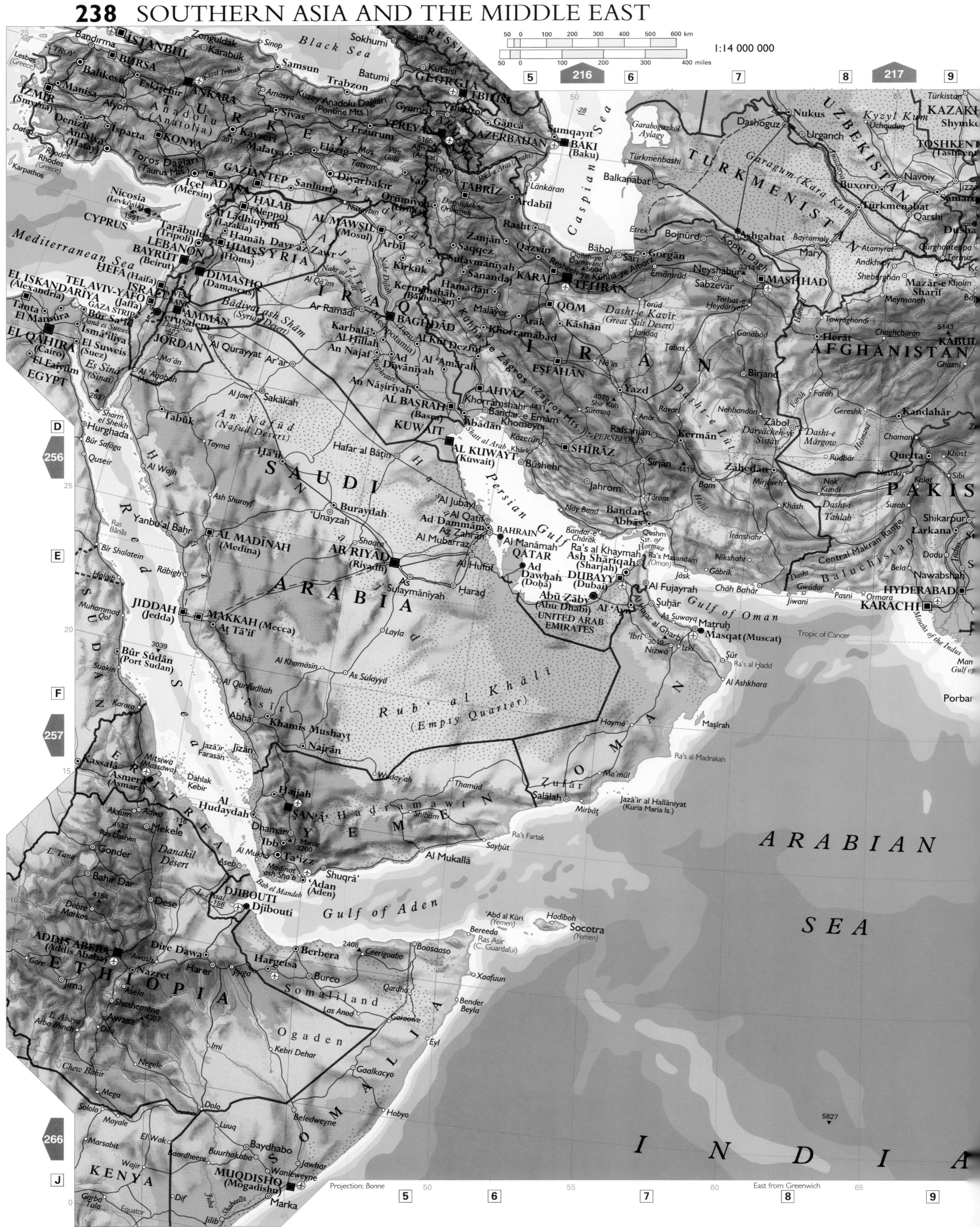

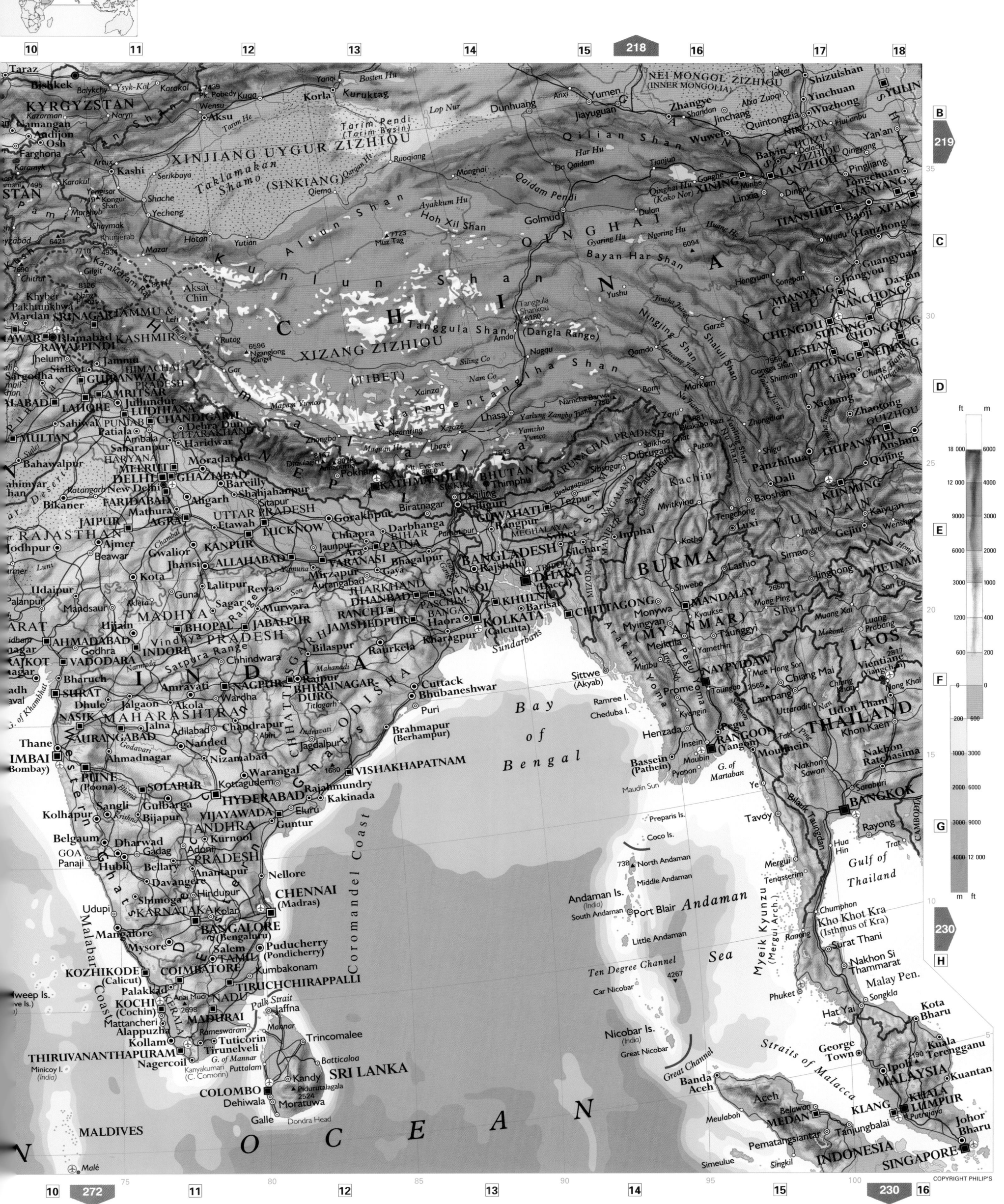

1:5 600 000

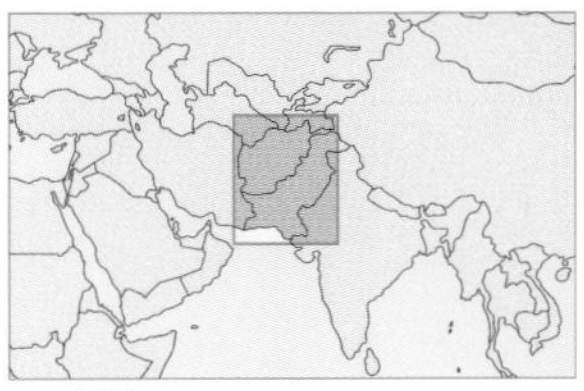

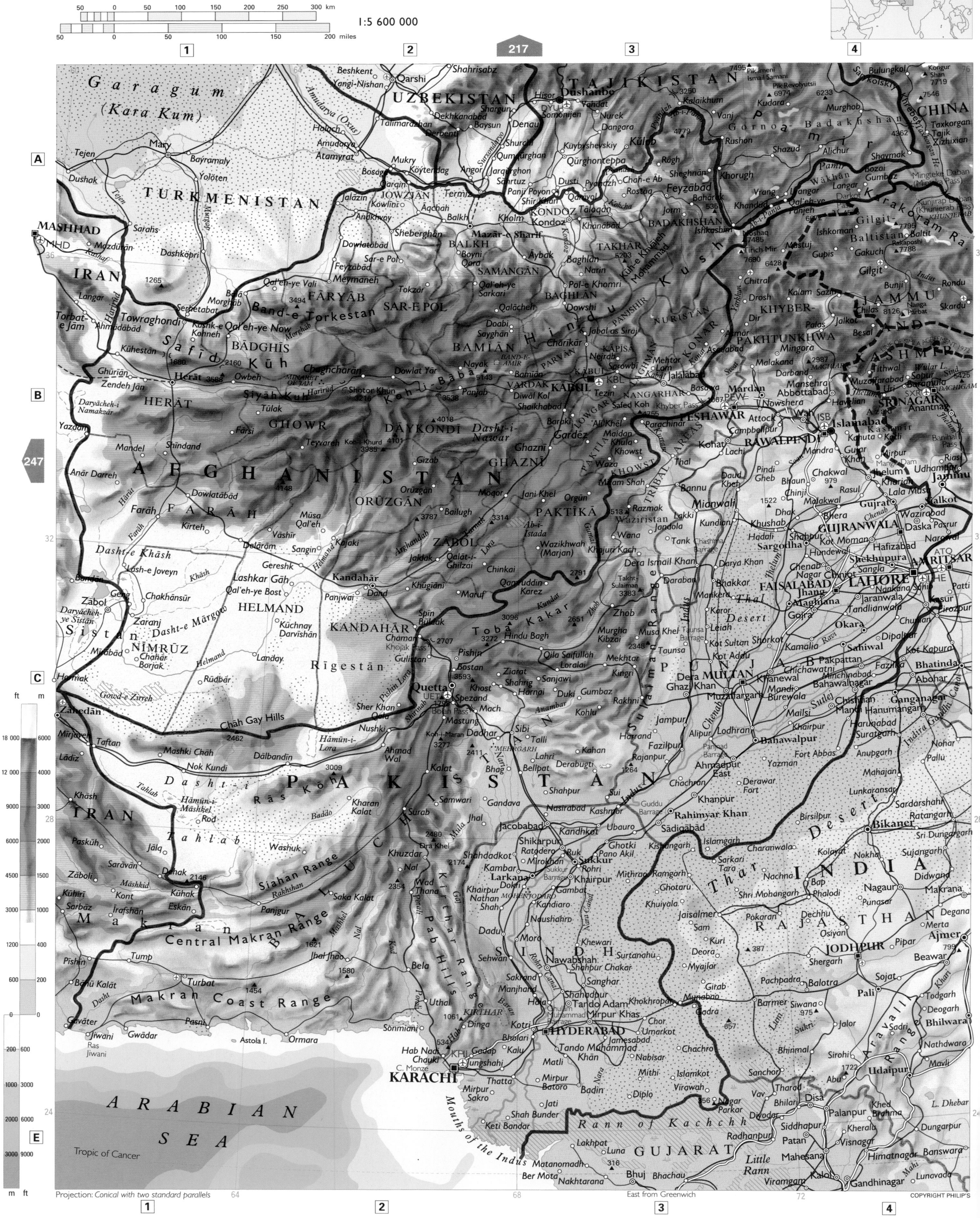

50 0 50 100 150 200 250 300 km
50 0 50 100 150 200 miles

Projection: Conical with two standard parallels

COPYRIGHT PHILIP'S

TURKMENISTAN
UZBEKISTAN
TAJIKISTAN
CHINA
IRAN
AFGHANISTAN
PAKISTAN
INDIA

Garagum (Kara Kum)

Hindu Kush

Makran Coast Range

ARABIAN SEA

Tropic of Cancer

Mouths of the Indus

Rann of Kachchh

GUJARAT
RAJASTHAN
SIND
PUNJAB
BALUCHISTAN
HELMAND
FARAH
HERAT
GHOWR
GHAZNI
ZABOL
NIMRUZ

MASHHAD
KABUL
PESHAWAR
RAWALPINDI
Islamabad
LAHORE
AMRITSAR
GUJRANWALA
FAISALABAD
MULTAN
HYDERABAD
KARACHI
Quetta
Kandahar
Herat
JODHPUR
BIKANER
Dushanbe

East from Greenwich

1:4 800 000

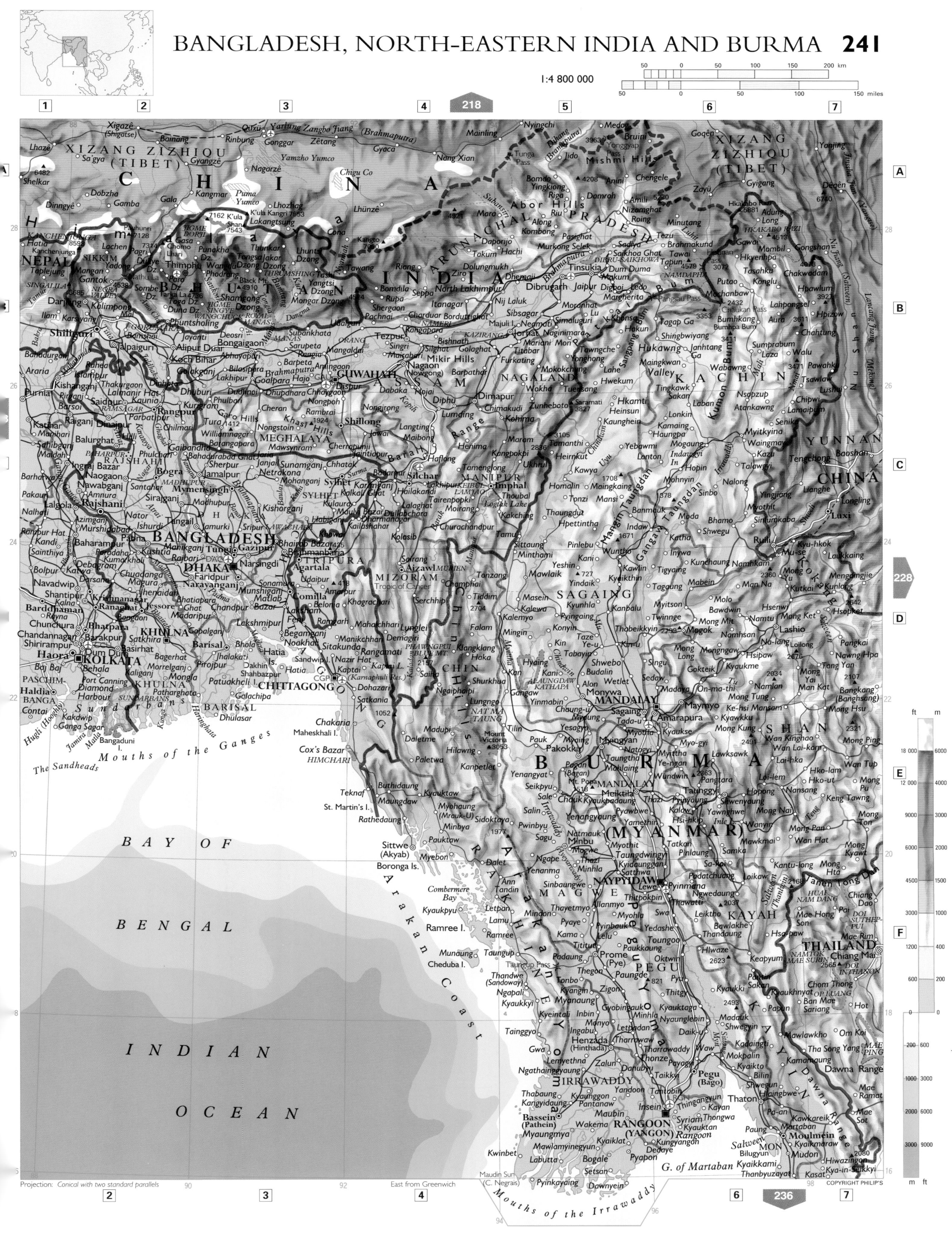

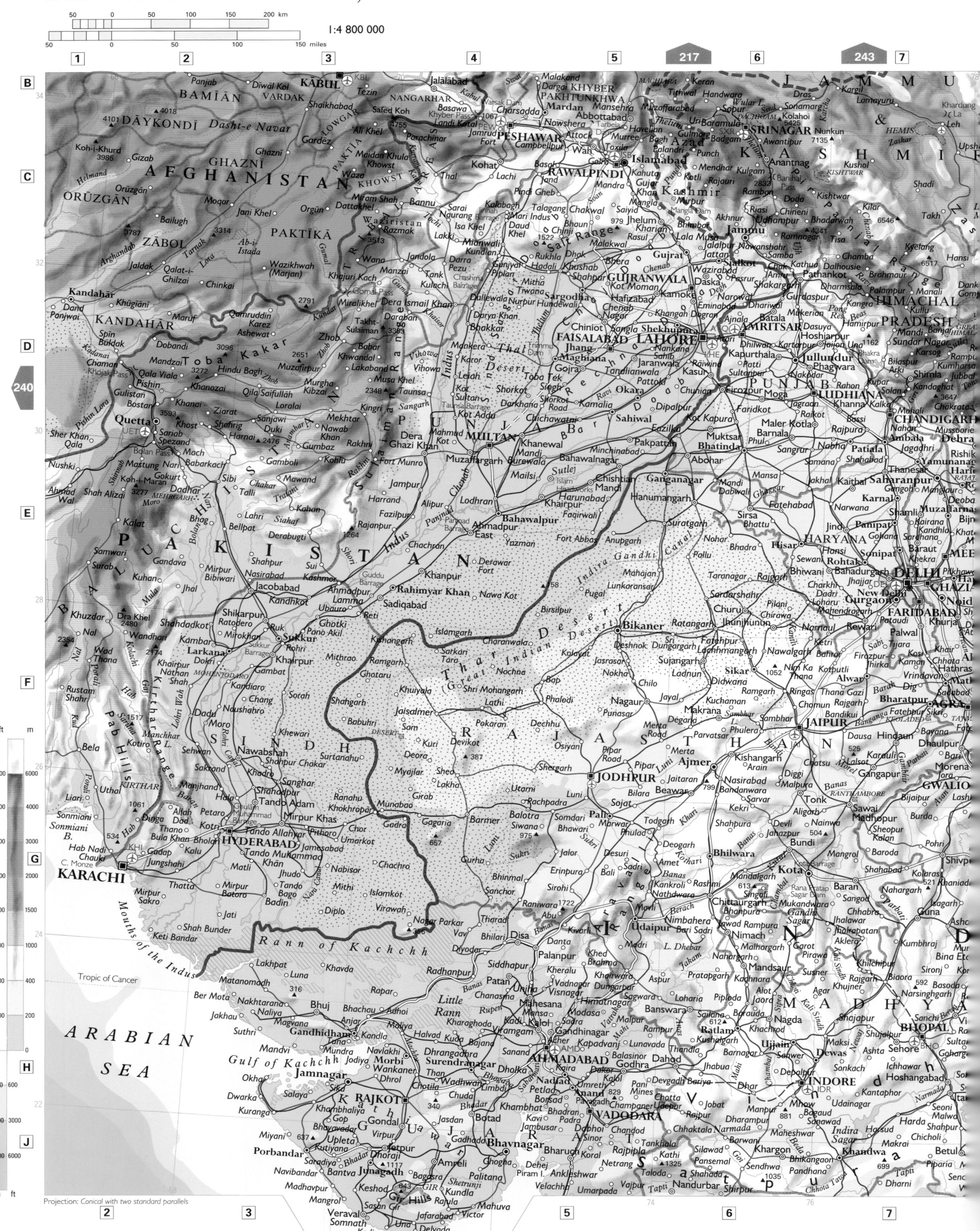

1:4 800 000

Projection: Conical with two standard parallels

JAMMU AND KASHMIR
on same scale

1:4 800 000

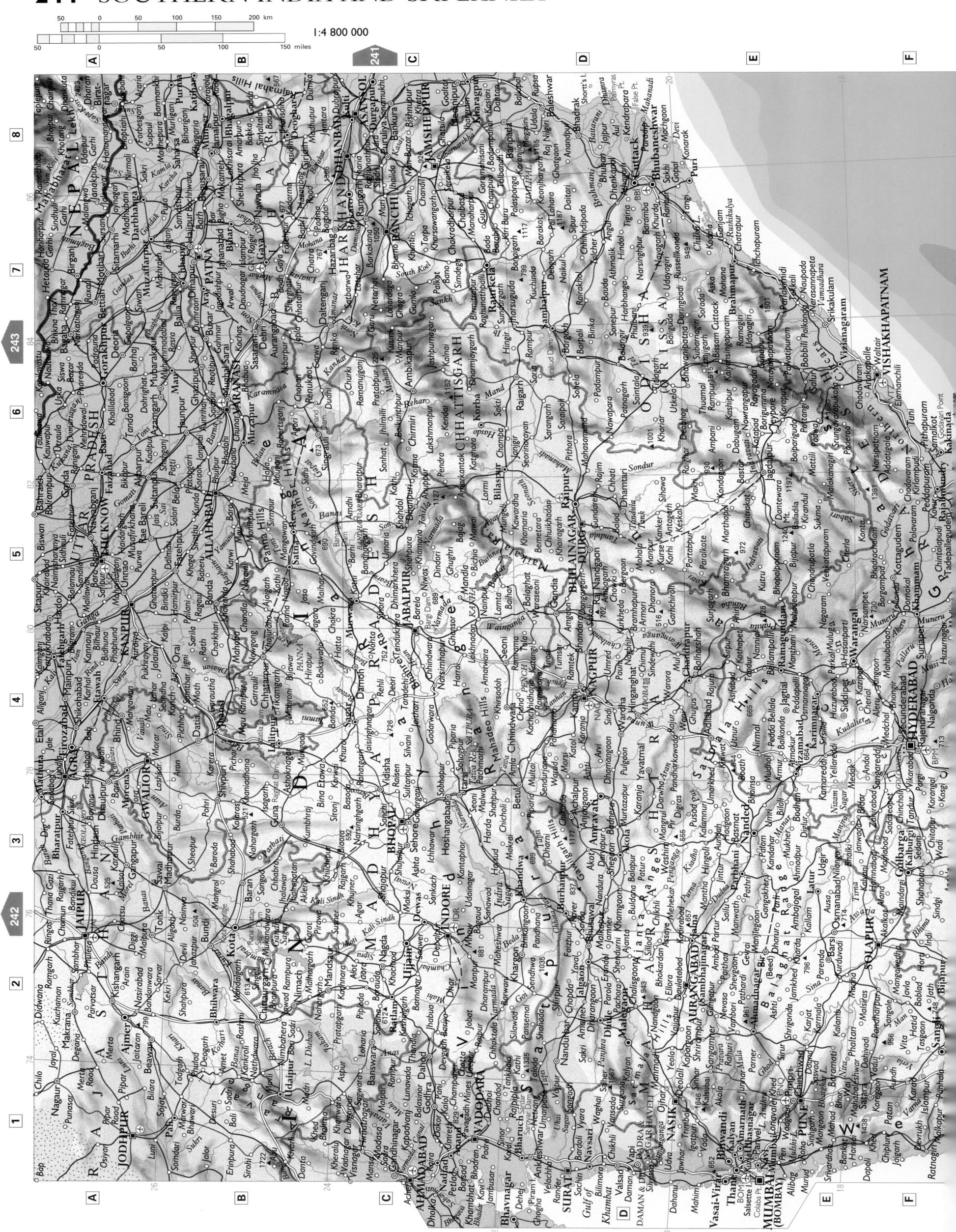

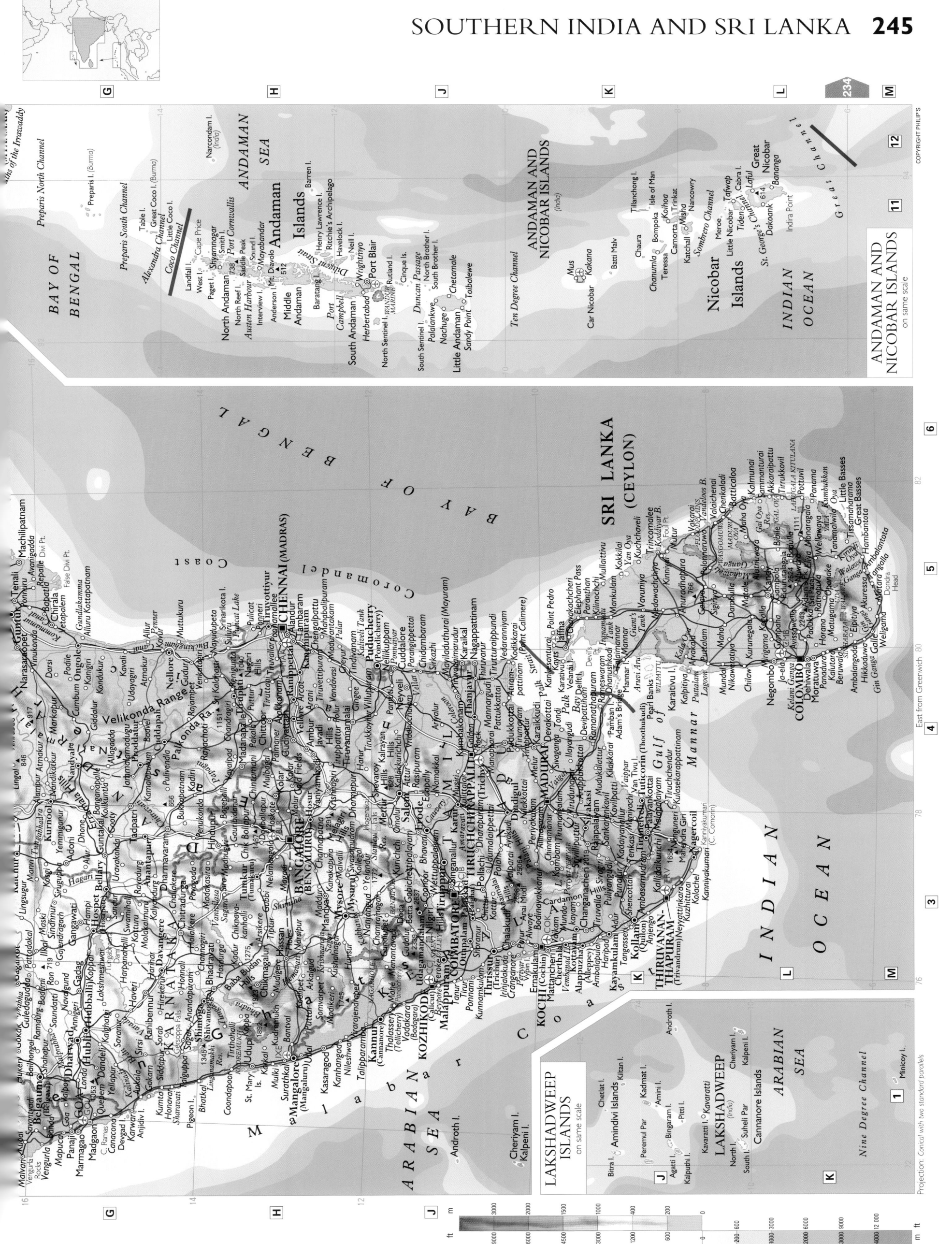

ANDAMAN AND
NICOBAR ISLANDS
on same scale

LAKSHADWEEP
ISLANDS
on same scale

Projection: Conical with two standard parallels

50   0   50   100   150   200   250   300 km
1:5 600 000
50   0   50   100   150   200 miles

Projection: Conical with two standard parallels

Underlined towns in Iraq give their name
to the administrative area in which they stand

∨∨∨∨∨
∨∨∨∨∨ Lava fields
∨∨∨∨∨

TURKMENISTAN
Garagum (Kara Kum)
Kopet Dagh
CASPIAN SEA
IRAN
AFGHANISTAN
PAKISTAN
KUWAYT (Kuwait)
KUWAIT
BAHRAIN
QATAR
UNITED ARAB EMIRATES
OMAN
PERSIAN GULF
Gulf of Oman
Str. of Hormuz
Dasht-e Kavīr (Great Salt Desert)
Dasht-e Lūt
Reshteh-ye Kūhhā-ye Alborz (Elburz Mts.)
Kūh-e Dīnār
Kūhhā-ye Bashākerd
Makran
Safīd Kūh
Dasht-e Khāsh
Dasht-e Mārgow
Sīstān
Daryācheh-ye Namak
Daryācheh-ye Bakhtegān
Türkmenbashi
Balkanabat (Nebitdag)
Ashgabat
Mary
Türkmenabat (Chardzhou)
BAKI (Baku)
Länkäran
Astara
Ardabīl
Rasht
Qazvīn
Karaj
TEHRĀN
Sārī
Gorgān
Semnān
Bojnūrd
MASHHAD
Neyshābūr
Sabzevār
Torbat-e Heydarīyeh
Qom
Kāshān
Arāk
Hamadān
Malāyer
Borūjerd
Khorramābād
Dezfūl
AHVĀZ
Ābādān
Khorramshahr
Bandar-e Emām Khomeynī
Esfahan
Najafābād
Shahr-e Kord
Yazd
Tabas
Ferdows
Bīrjand
Zābol
Zāhedān
Kermān
Rafsanjān
Sīrjān
Bam
Jīroft
Shīrāz
Būshehr
Kāzerūn
Bandar-e Abbās
Khāsh
Īrānshahr
Chāh Bahār
Herāt
Farāh
Ad Dammām
Al Manāmah
Ad Dawhah (Doha)
Dubayy (Dubai)
Ash Shāriqah (Sharjah)
Abū Ẓaby (Abu Dhabi)
Al Fujayrah
Ra's al Khaymah
Al 'Ayn
Al Hufūf
Al Jubayl
East from Greenwich

216 240 249

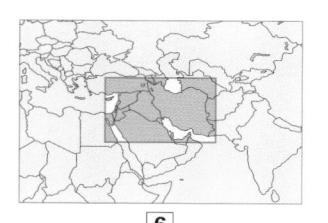

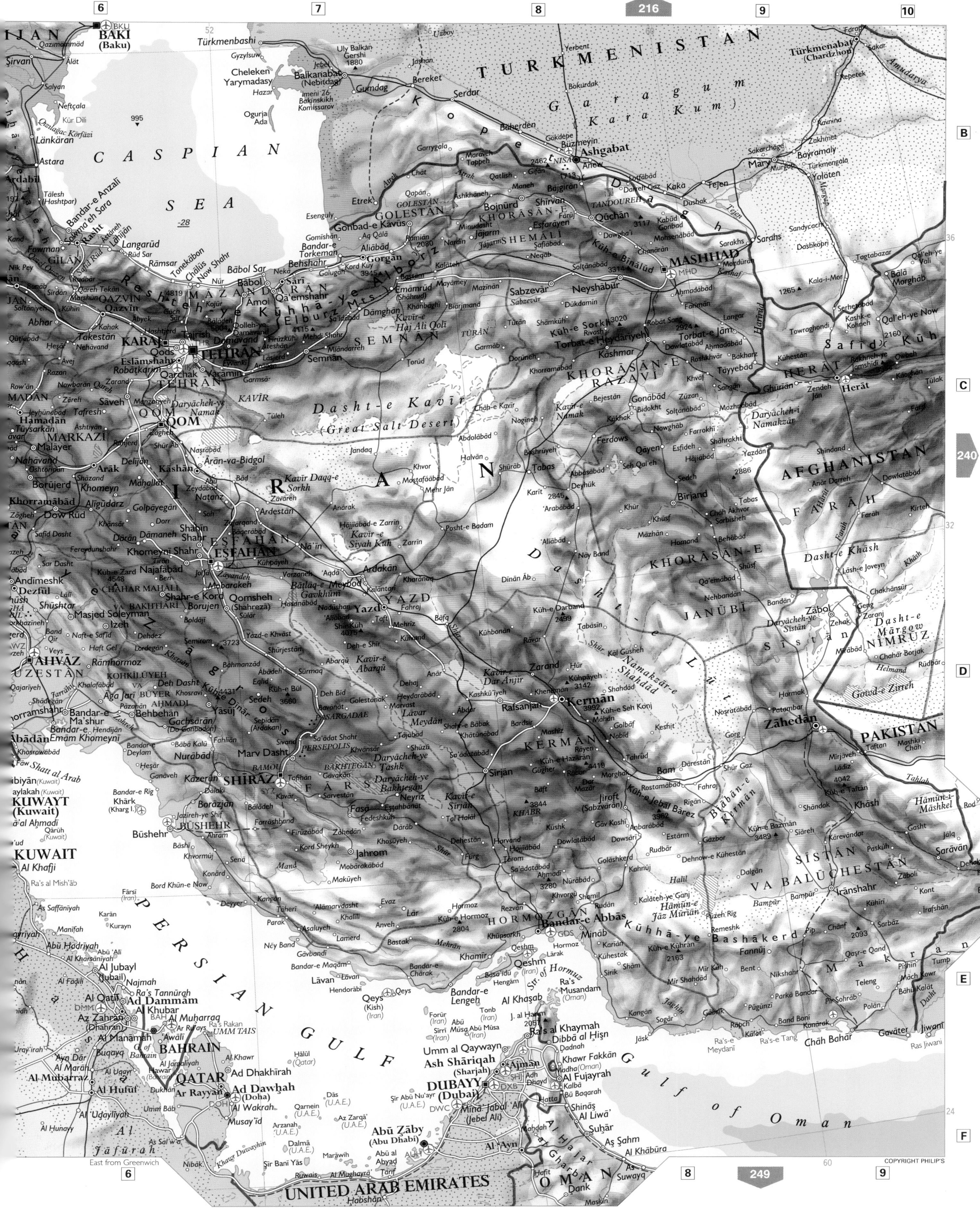

1:5 600 000

50 0 50 100 150 200 250 300 km
50 0 50 100 150 200 miles

246

257

267

Projection: Conical with two standard parallels

Lava fields

ft m
12 000 4000
9000 3000
6000 2000
4500 1500
3000 1000
1200 400
600 200
0 0
200 600
1000 3000
2000 6000
3000 9000
4000 12 000
m ft

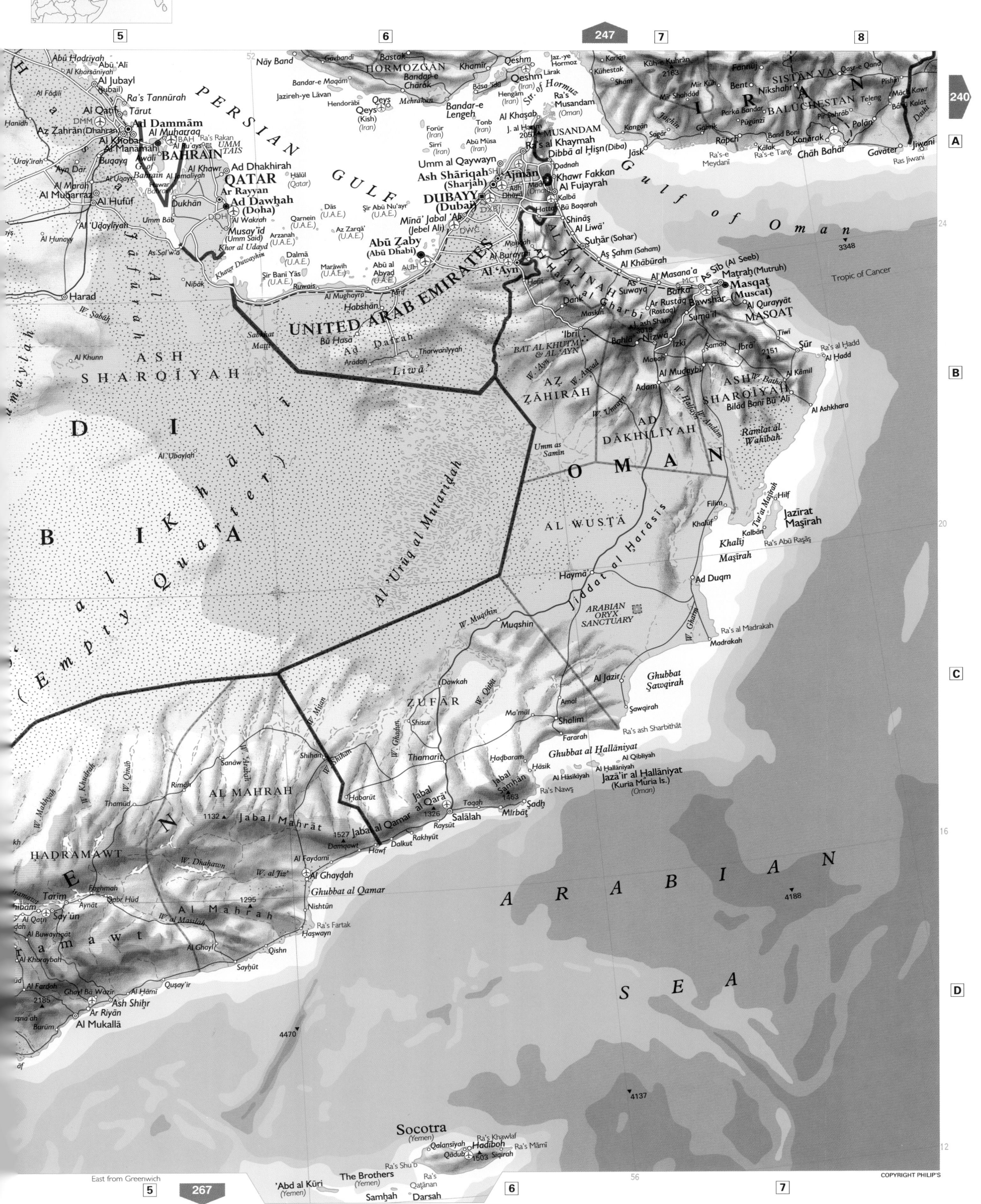

COPYRIGHT PHILIP'S

1:2 000 000

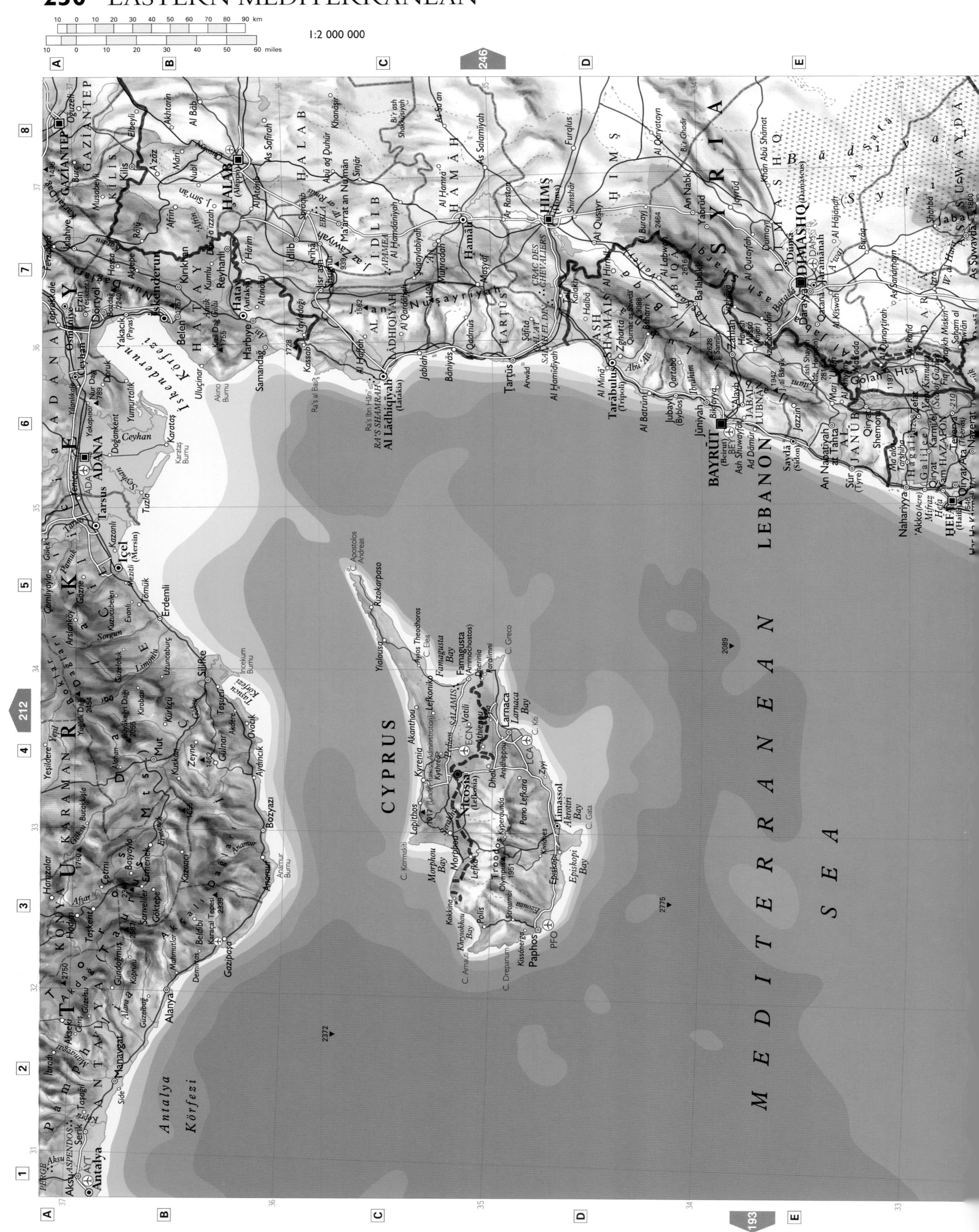

212

193

Lava fields

1974 Cease Fire Lines

Projection : Polyconic

East from Greenwich

m												ft
	3000		2000		1500		1000		600		300	

ft 9000 6000 4500 3000 1200 600 0

m 2400 1800 1500 1200 600 200 0 100 - 300 500 1500 1000 3000 6000

AFRICA

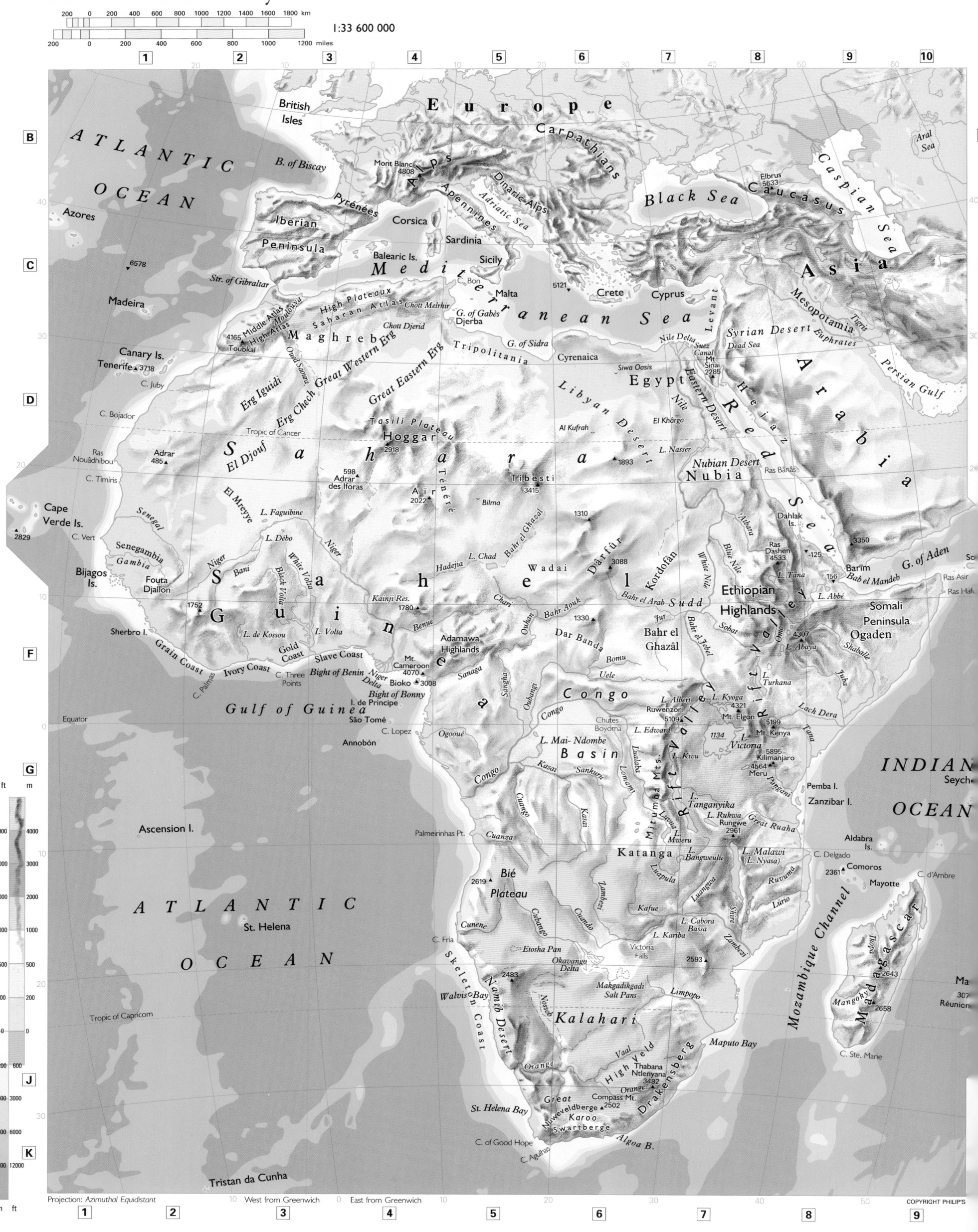

1:33 600 000

Projection: Azimuthal Equidistant   West from Greenwich   East from Greenwich   COPYRIGHT PHILIP'S

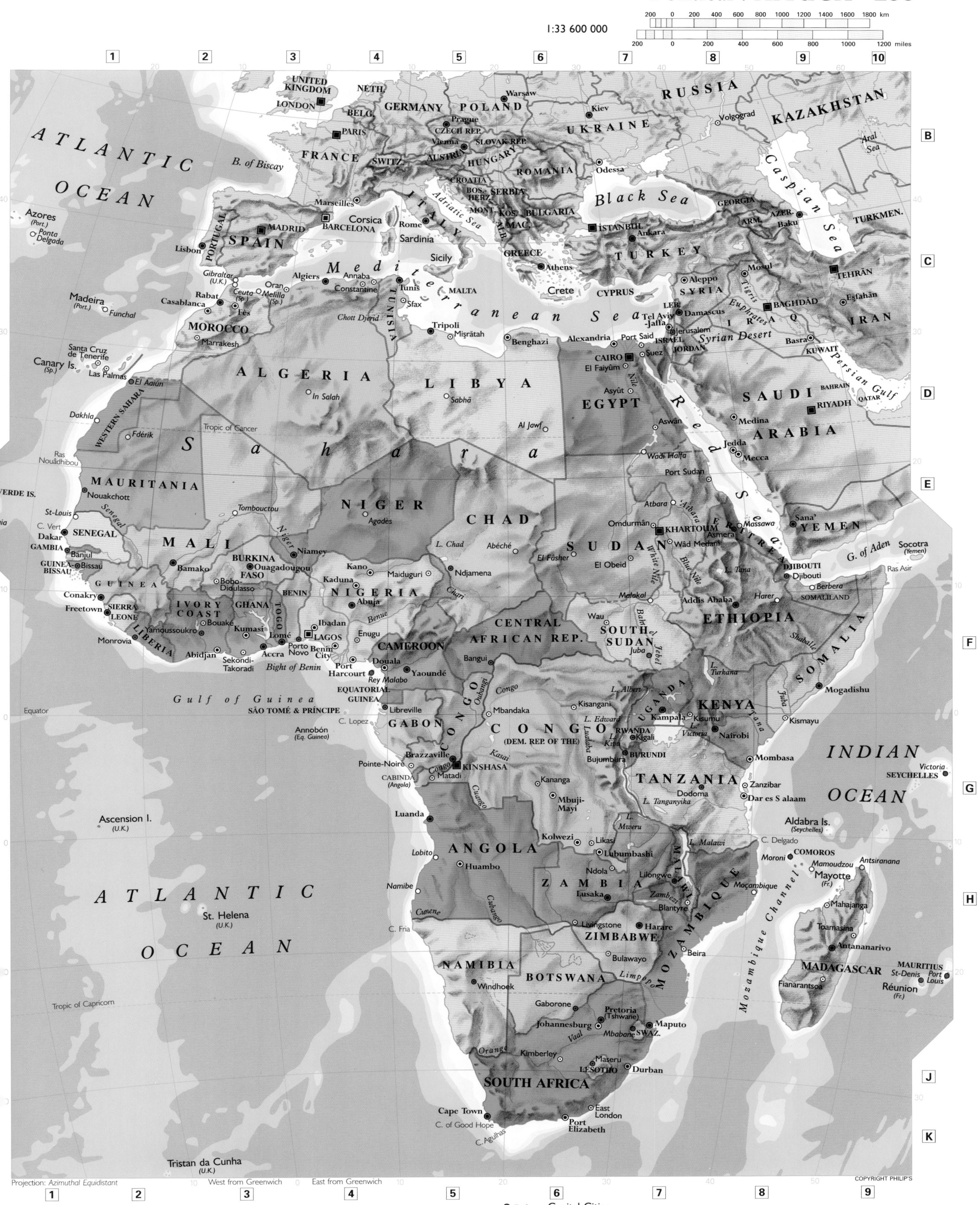

1:33 600 000

200 0 200 400 600 800 1000 1200 1400 1600 1800 km

200 0 200 400 600 800 1000 1200 miles

● Dakar Capital Cities

Projection: Azimuthal Equidistant

West from Greenwich   East from Greenwich

COPYRIGHT PHILIP'S

1:6 400 000

THE NILE DELTA
1:3 200 000

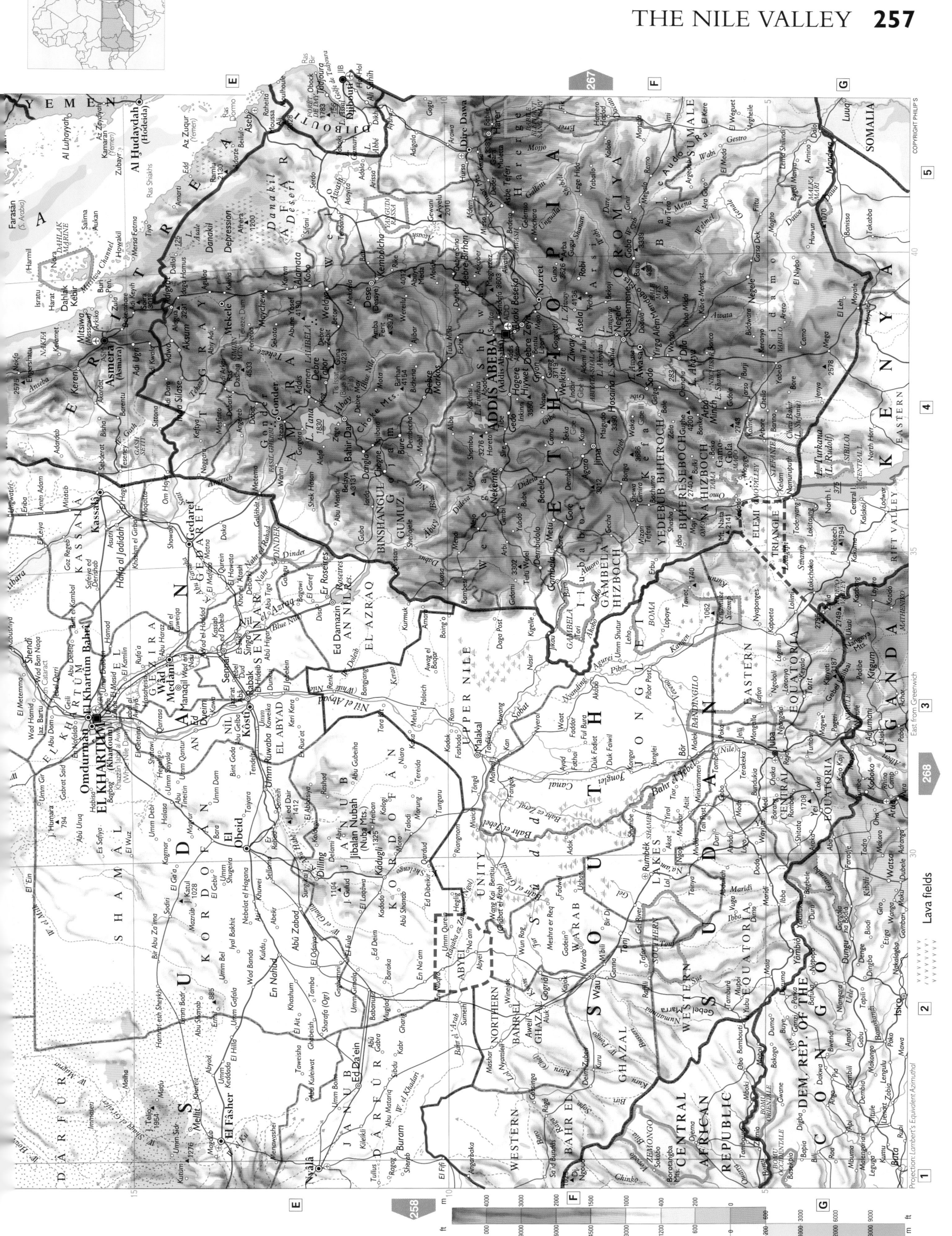

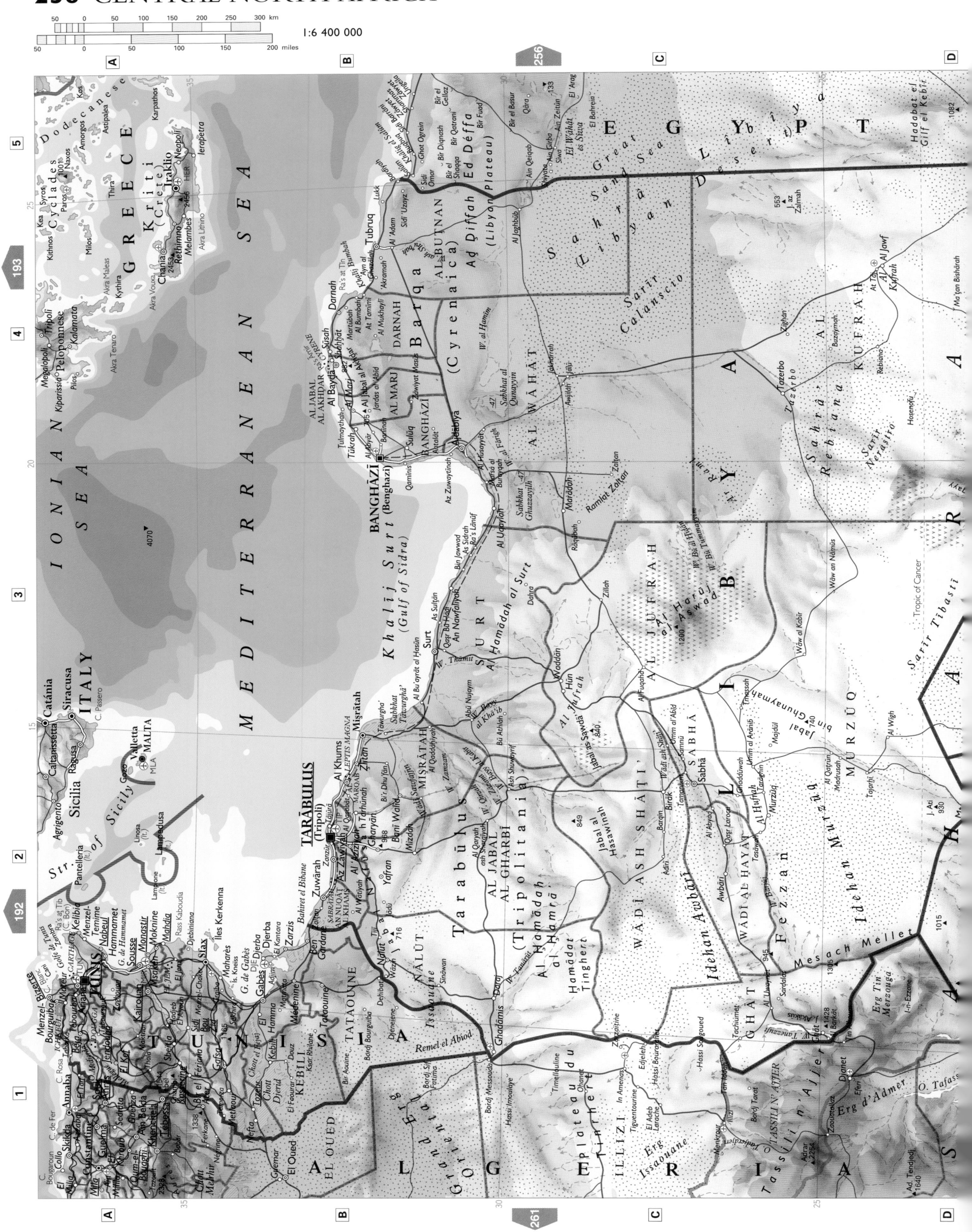

1:6 400 000

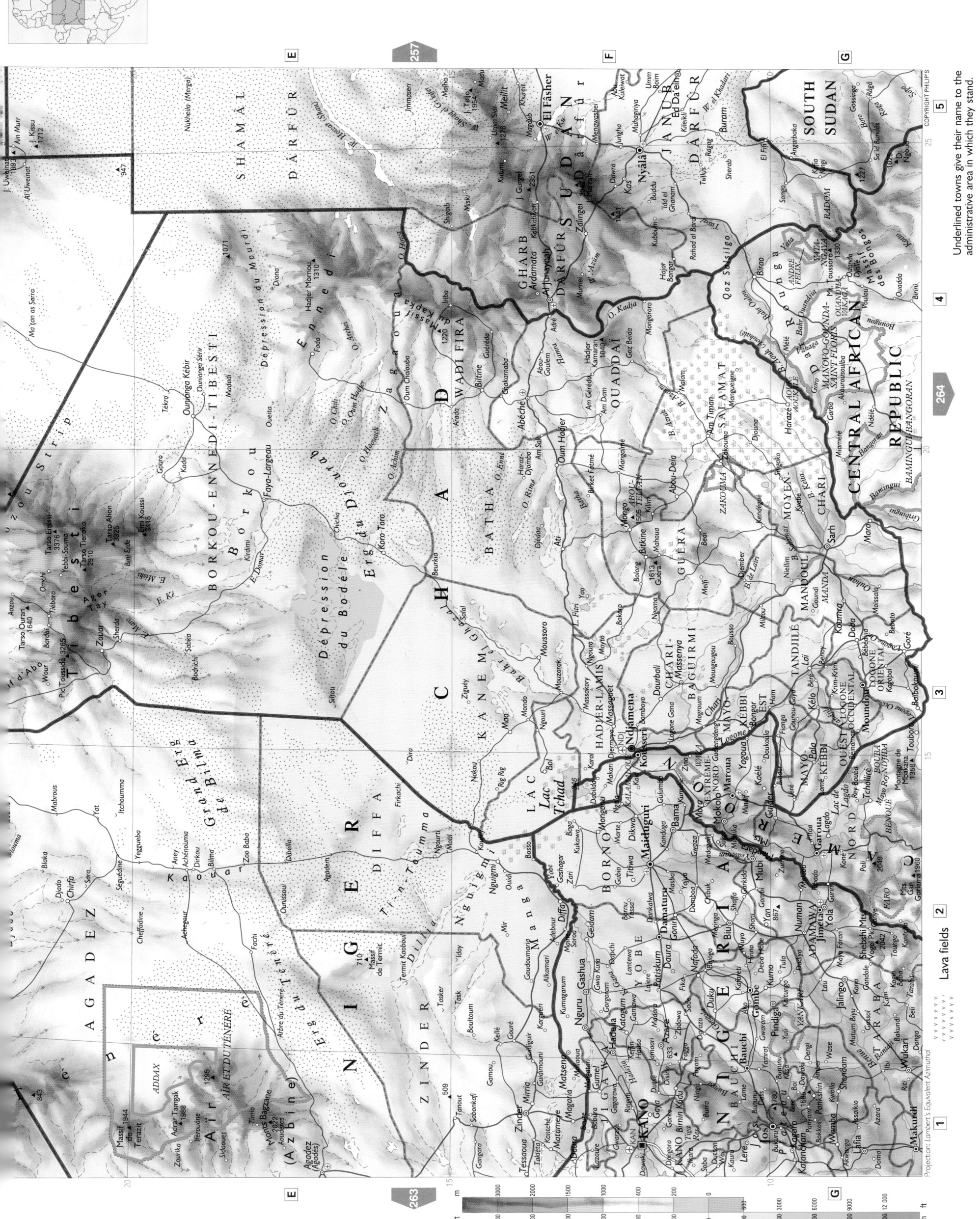

263
264

Underlined towns give their name to the
administrative area in which they stand.

Lava fields

Projection: Lambert's Equivalent Azimuthal

COPYRIGHT PHILIP'S

50 0 50 100 150 200 250 300 km
1:6 400 000
50 0 50 100 150 200 miles

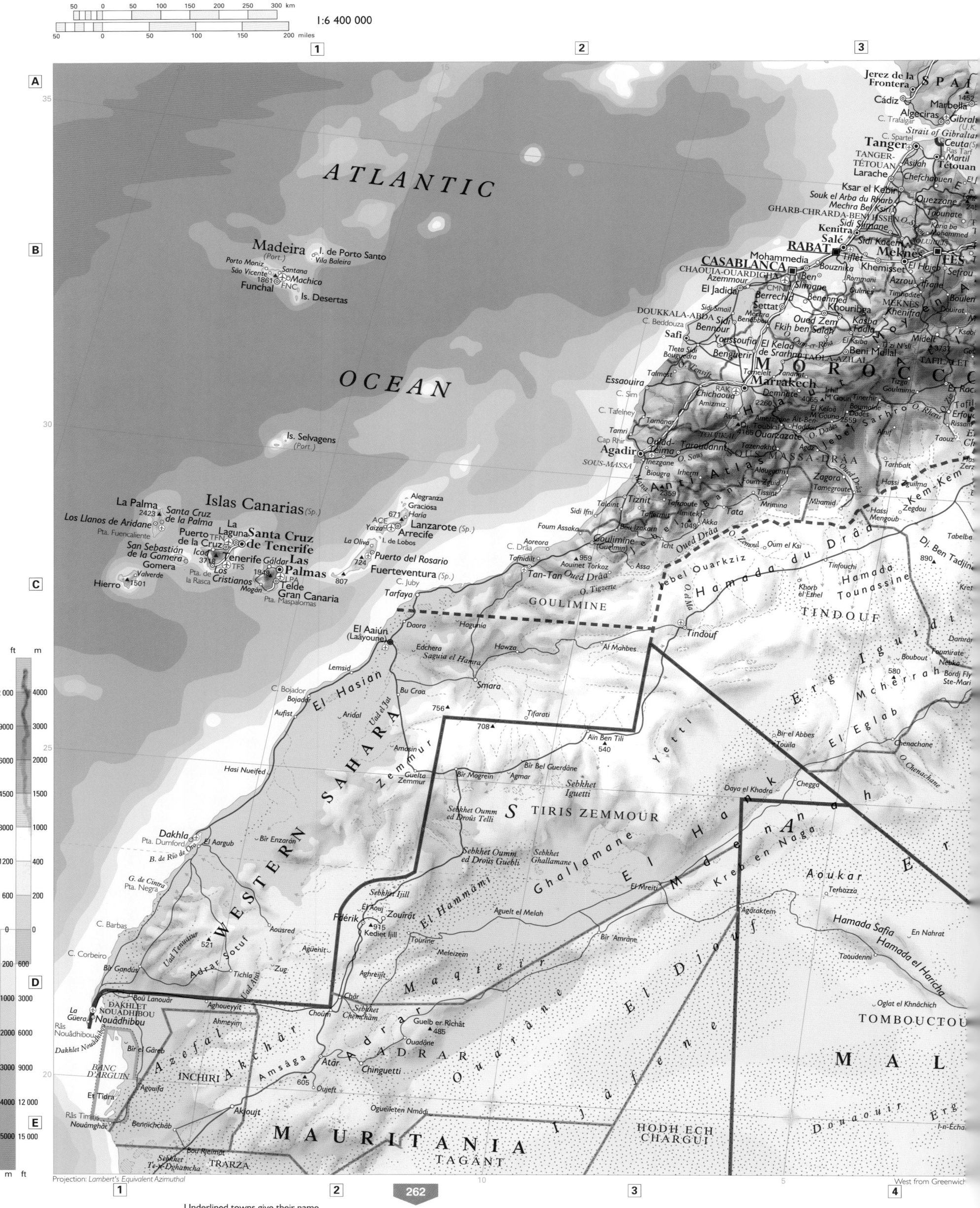

ATLANTIC

OCEAN

Jerez de la Frontera
Cádiz
Marbella
Algeciras
C. Trafalgar
C. Spartel
Strait of Gibraltar
Ras Tarf
Martil
Ceuta
Tanger
TANGER-TÉTOUAN
Asilah
Chefchaouen
Larache
Ksar el Kebir
Souk el Arba du Rharb
Quezzane
Taounate
Mechra Bel Ksiri
GHARB-CHRARDA-BENI-HSSEN
Sidi Slimane
Kenitra
Salé
RABAT
Mohammedia
CASABLANCA
CHAOUIA-OUARDIGHA
Azemmour
El Jadida
Berrechid
DOUKKALA-ABDA
C. Beddouza
Safi
Youssoufia
Bennour
El Kelaa de Srarhna
Benguerir
Essaouira
C. Sim
Chichaoua
Marrakech
C. Rhir
Agadir
Oulad-Teima
SOUS-MASSA-DRÂA
Inezgane
Biougra
Tiznit
Sidi Ifni
Foum Assaka
Goulimine (Guelm.)
GOULIMINE
Tan-Tan
Tarfaya

Madeira (Port.)
I. de Porto Santo
Vila Baleira
Porto Moniz
Santana
São Vicente
Machico
Funchal
Is. Desertas

Is. Selvagens (Port.)

Islas Canarias (Sp.)
Alegranza
Graciosa
Haria
La Palma
Santa Cruz de la Palma
Lanzarote (Sp.)
Los Llanos de Aridane
Yaiza
Arrecife
La Laguna
Santa Cruz de Tenerife
La Oliva
I. de Lobos
San Sebastián de la Gomera
Icod
Tenerife
Gáldar
Las Palmas
Puerto del Rosario
Gomera
Los Cristianos
Mogán
Telde
Fuerteventura (Sp.)
Hierro
Gran Canaria
Pta. Maspalomas
C. Juby

MOROCCO

El Aaiún (Laâyoune)
Daora
Hagunia
Edchera
Saguia el Hamra
Lemsid
C. Bojador
Bojador
Bu Craa
Smara
Aridal
Tifariti
WESTERN SAHARA
Amosin
Zemmour
TIRIS ZEMMOUR
Ain Ben Tili
Bîr Mogrein
Sebkhet Iguetti
Dakhla
Bîr Enzarán
El Aargub
Sebkhet Oumm ed Droûs Telli
Sebkhet Oumm ed Droûs Guebli
Sebkhet Ghallamane
Ghallamane
El Mreiti
Fdérik
Sebkhet Ijill
Zouîrât
El Hammâmi
Kediet Ijill
Tourine
Aguelt el Melah
Bîr 'Amrâne
Aousred
Agüenit
Aghrèijît
Maqteïr
ADRAR
Char
Sebkhet Chemchâm
Guelb er Richât
Ouarâne
El Djouf
Chinguetti
Atâr
Oujeft
Akjoujt
TOMBOUCTOU
MALI

NOUADHIBOU
Nouâdhibou
Ras Nouâdhibou
INCHIRI
Akchâr
Amsâga
Zug
Oued Drâa
Adrar Akchâr
MAURITANIA
TAGANT
TRARZA
HODH ECH CHARGUI

TINDOUF
Tindouf
Al Mahbes
Erg Iguidi
Hamada du Drâa
Hamada Tounassine
Erg Chech
Aoukar
Hamada Safi
Hamada el Haricha
Taoudenni

Projection: Lambert's Equivalent Azimuthal

Underlined towns give their name
to the administrative area in which they stand

West from Greenwich

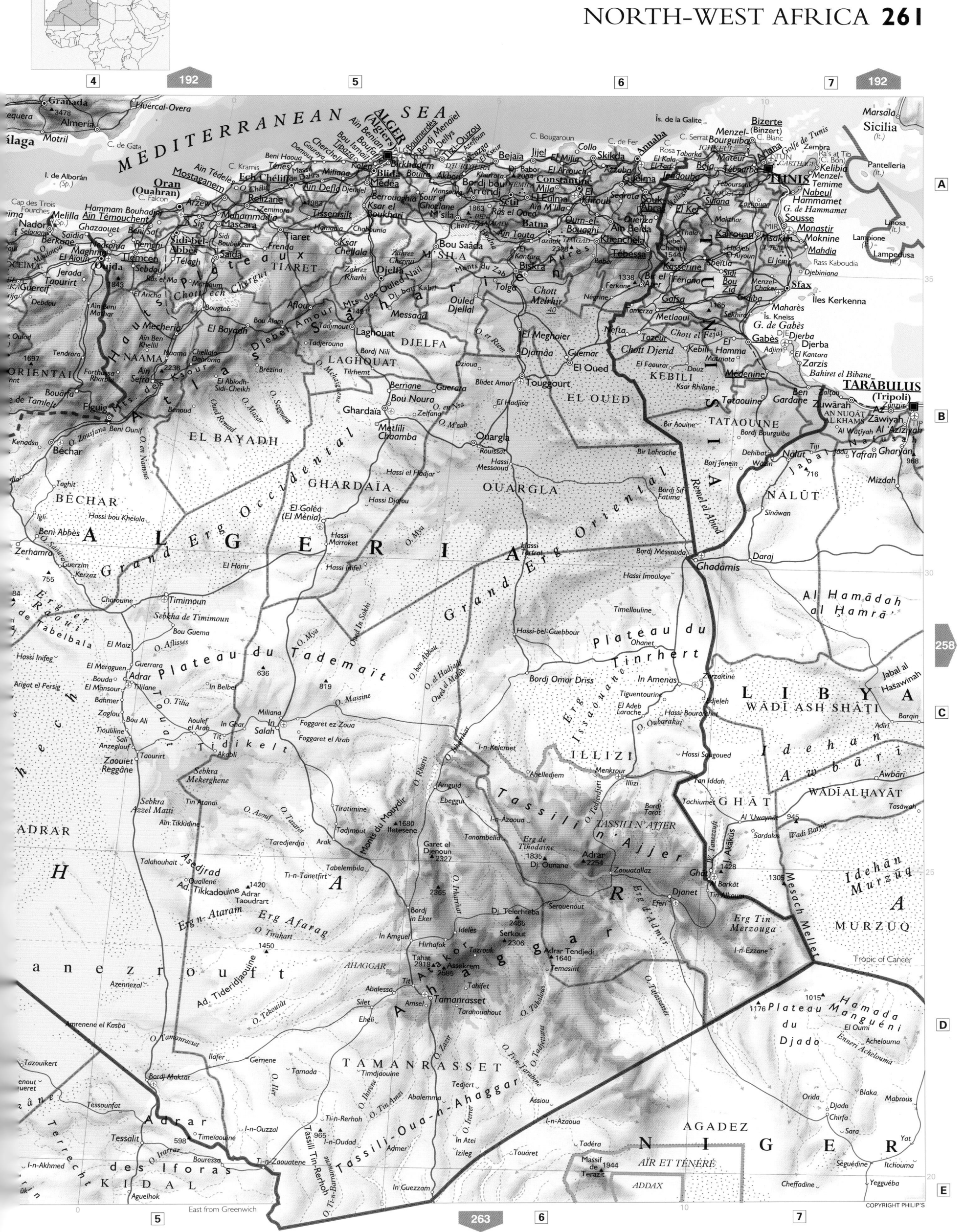

MEDITERRANEAN SEA

Granada
Almería
Motril
Huércal-Overa
C. de Gata
Marsala
Sicilia
(It.)

ALGER
(ALGIERS)
Oran
(Ouahran)
Mostaganem
Arzew
Melilla
Nador

A

MÉDITERRANEAN

Béchar

ALGERIA
Grand Erg Occidental

Grand Erg Oriental

B

EL BAYADH
GHARDAÏA
OUARGLA

Ghadâmis

LIBYA

C

Plateau du Tademaït
Plateau du Tinrhert

ADRAR
ILLIZI
GHAT
WĀDĪ AL ḤAYĀT

H
A
Tassili-n-Ajjer
R

AHAGGAR
Tamanrasset

Idehân
Murzūq

MURZŪQ

D

TAMANRASSET
Tropic of Cancer

Plateau du Djado
Hamada Manguéni

E

Adrar
des Iforas
KIDAL

NIGER
AGADEZ

AÏR ET TÉNÉRÉ
ADDAX

East from Greenwich

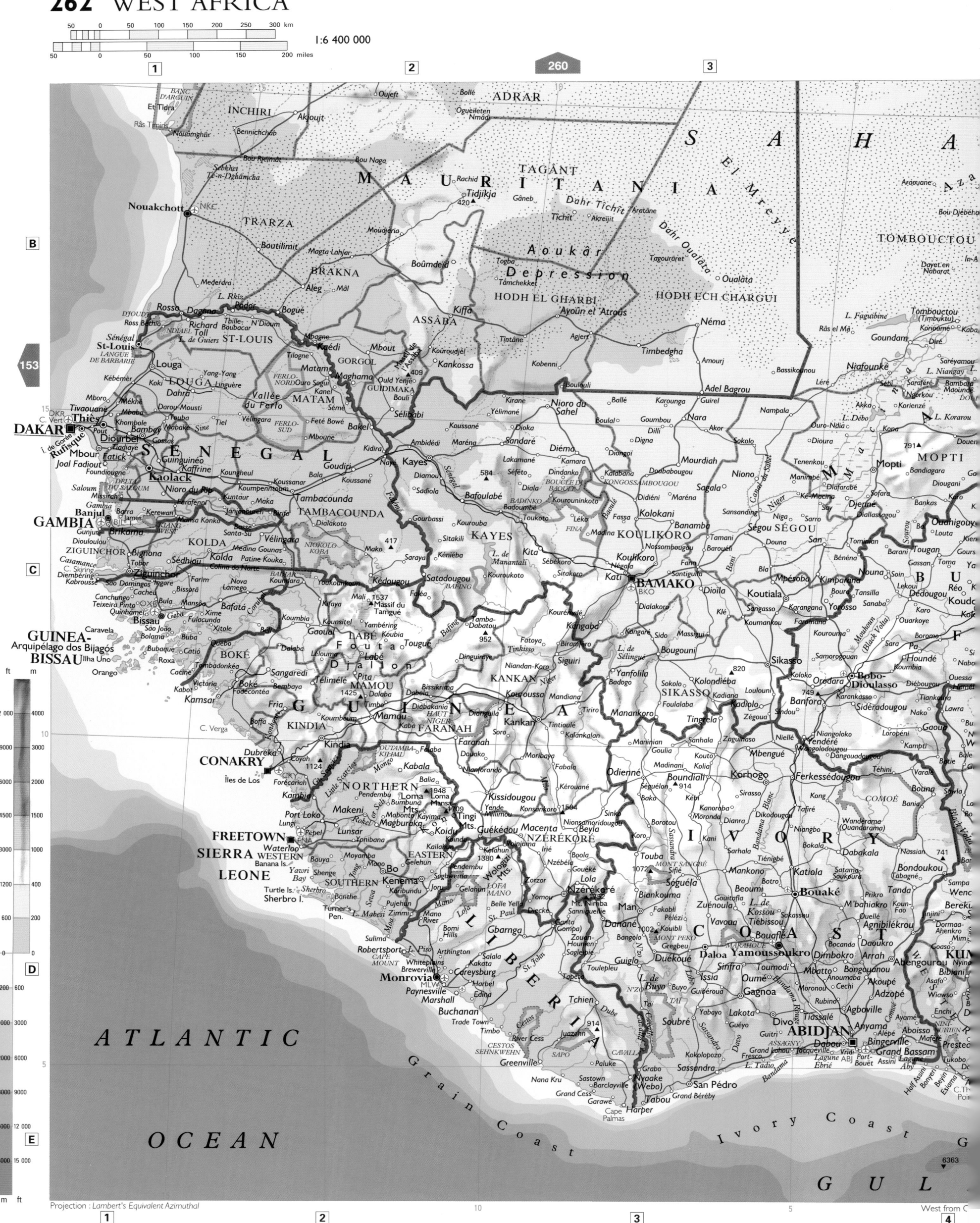

260

1:6 400 000

Projection : Lambert's Equivalent Azimuthal

Underlined towns give their name to the
administrative area in which they stand.

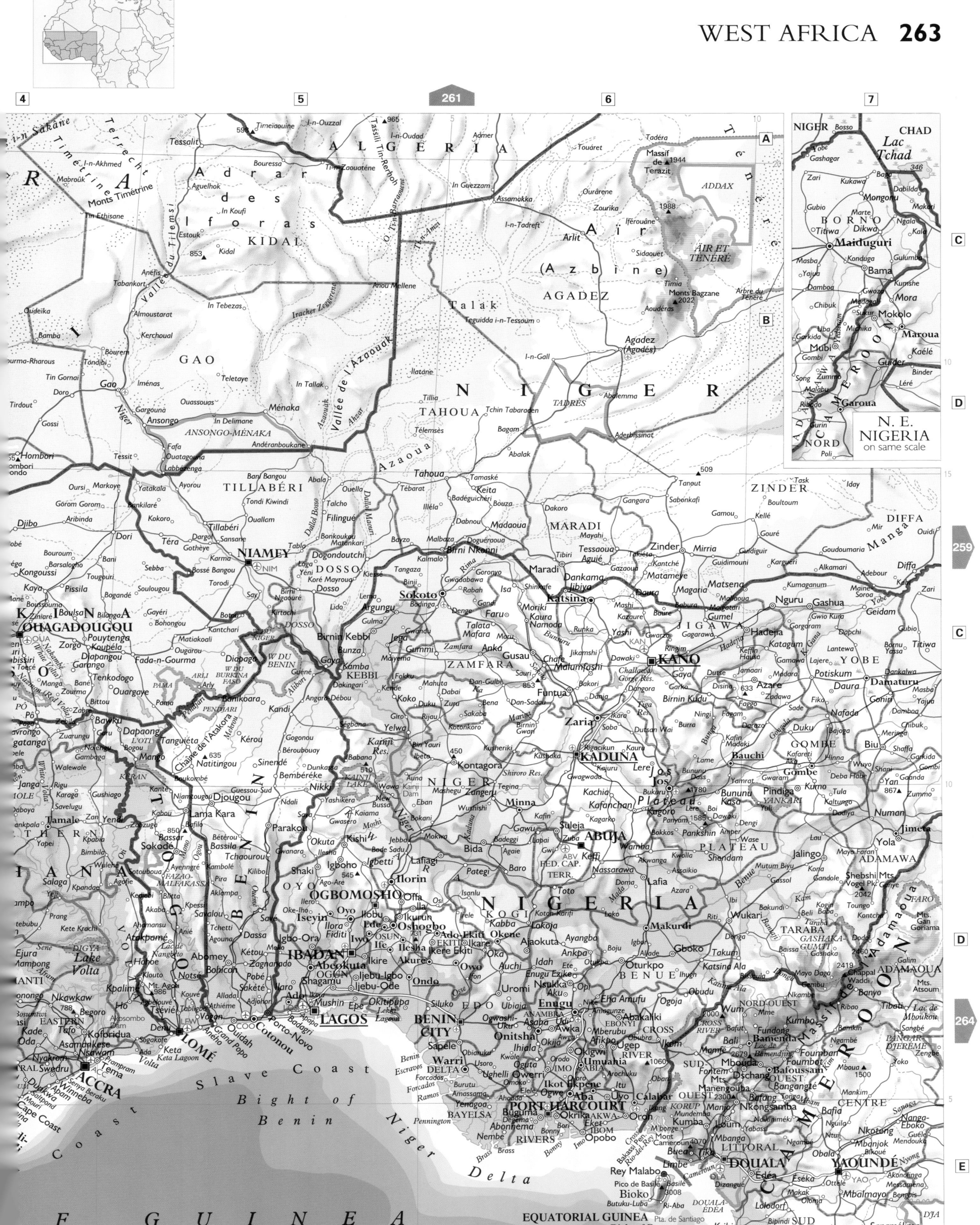

261
259
264

N. E.
NIGERIA
on same scale

COPYRIGHT PHILIP'S

East from Greenwich

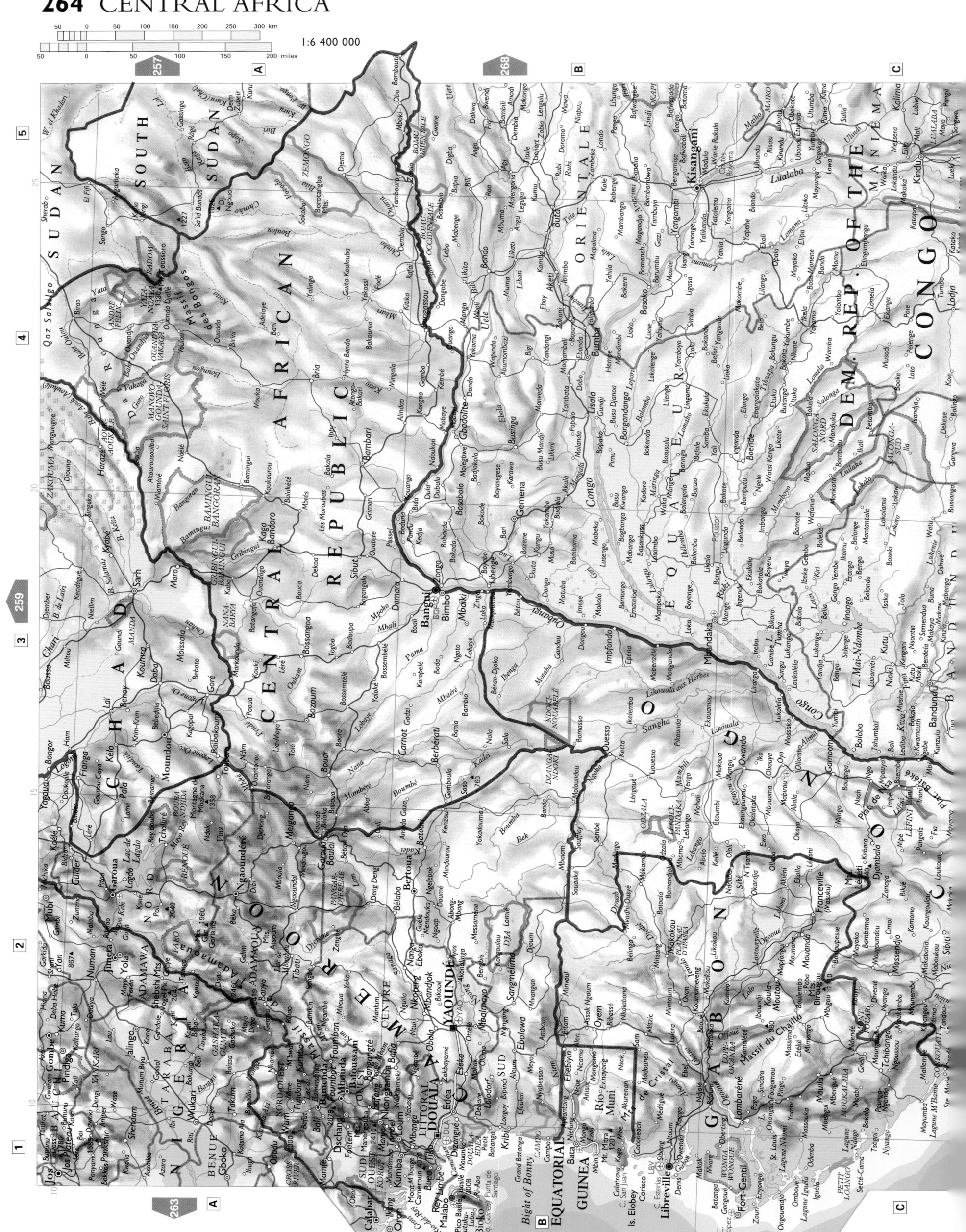

ATLANTIC
OCEAN
A N G O L A
Z A M B I A
N A M I B I A
B O T S W A N A
LUANDA
HUAMBO
LUBUMBASHI
KOLWEZI
Benguela
Lobito
Namibe
Lubango
Livingstone
SÃO TOMÉ AND PRÍNCIPE
on same scale
ATLANTIC
OCEAN
Príncipe
São Tomé
East from Greenwich
Projection: Lambert's Equivalent Azimuthal
COPYRIGHT PHILIP'S

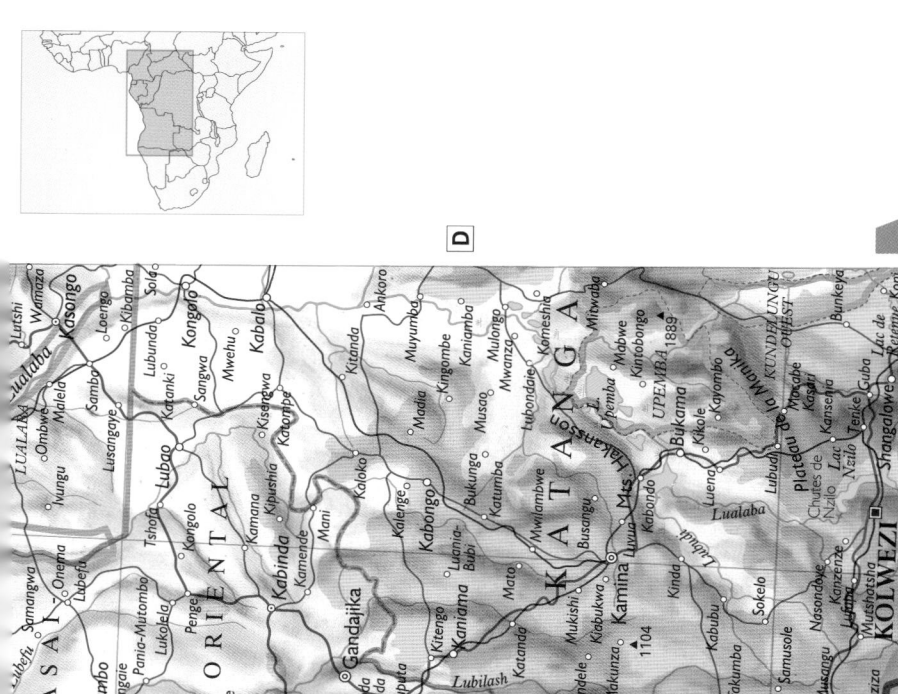

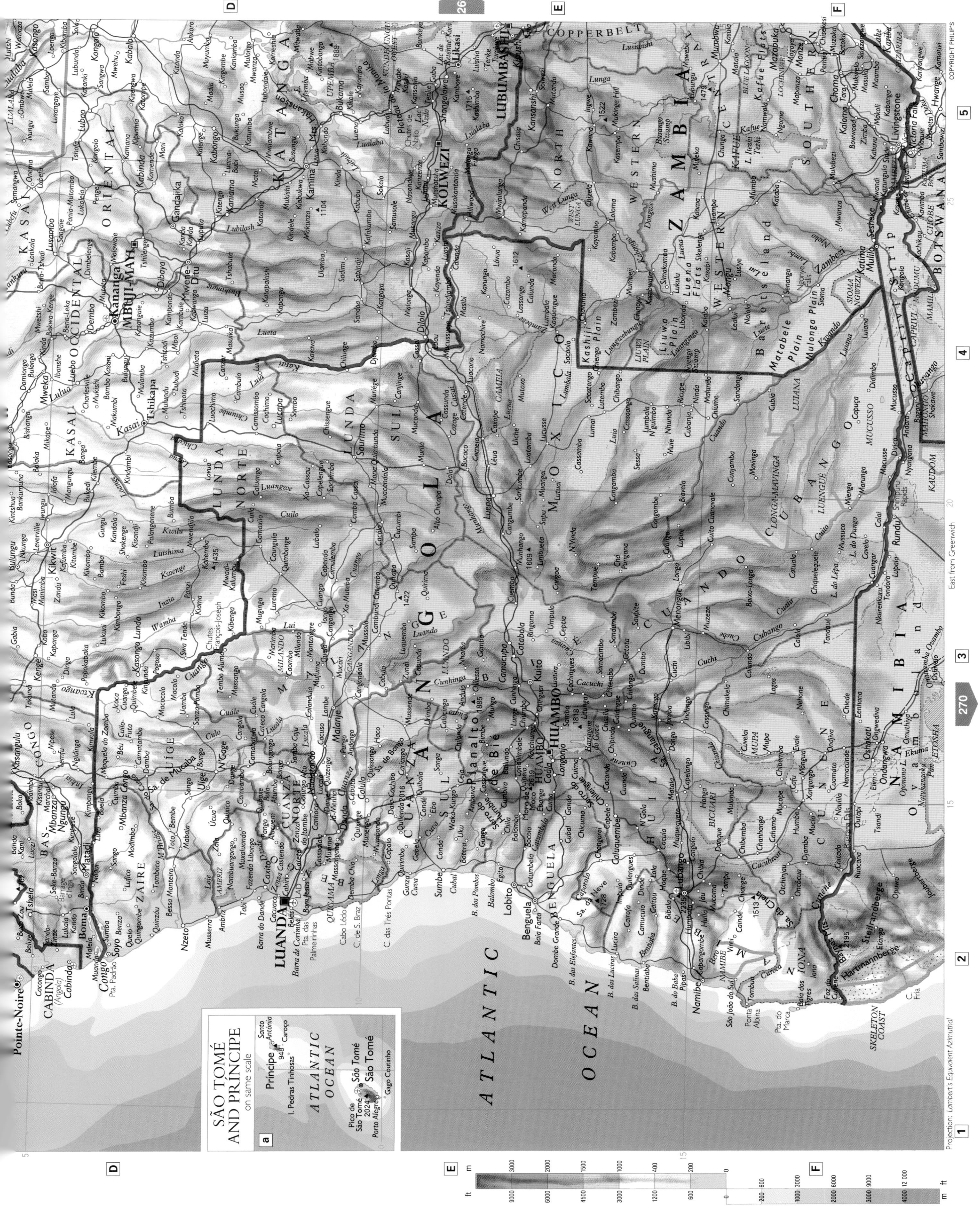

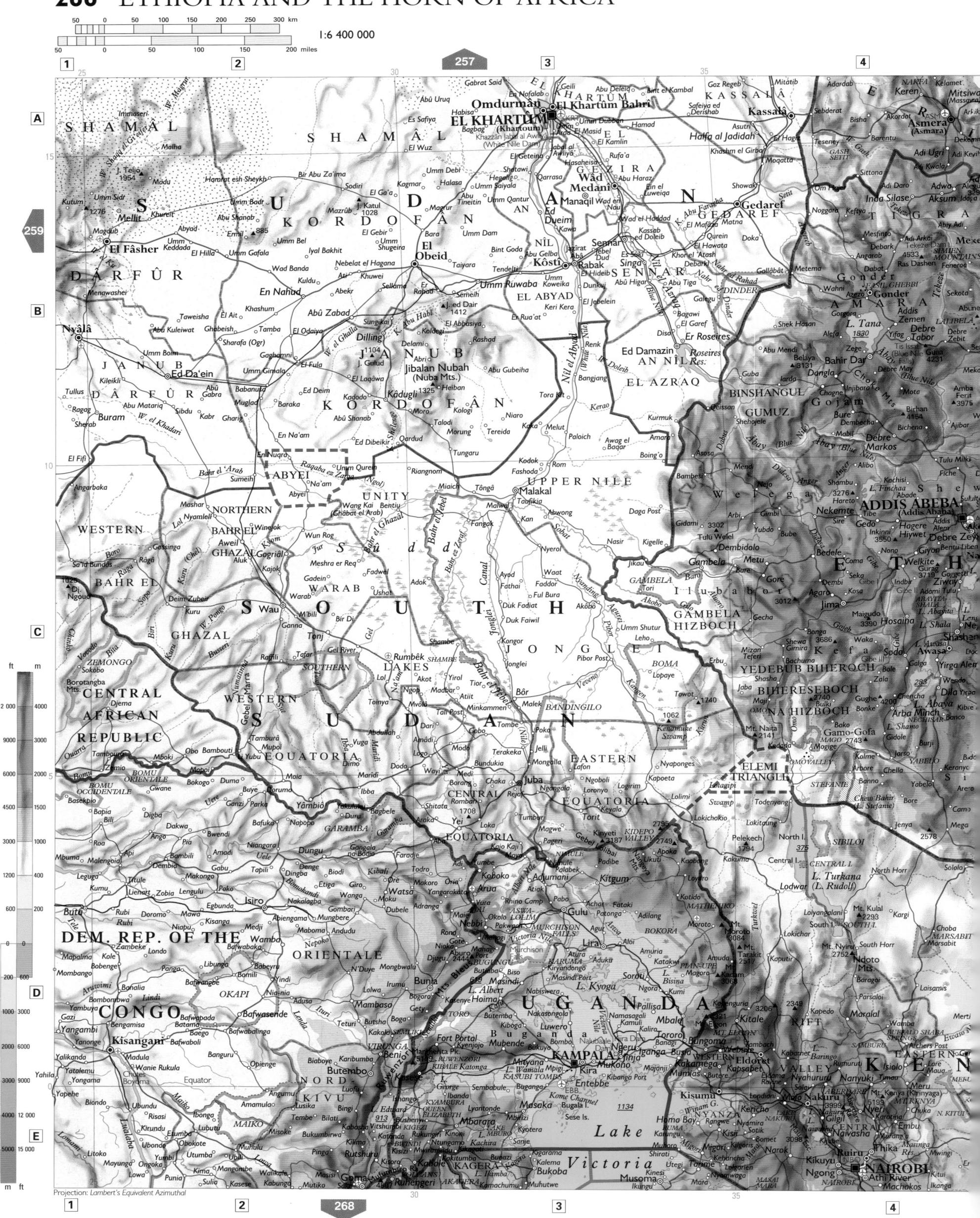

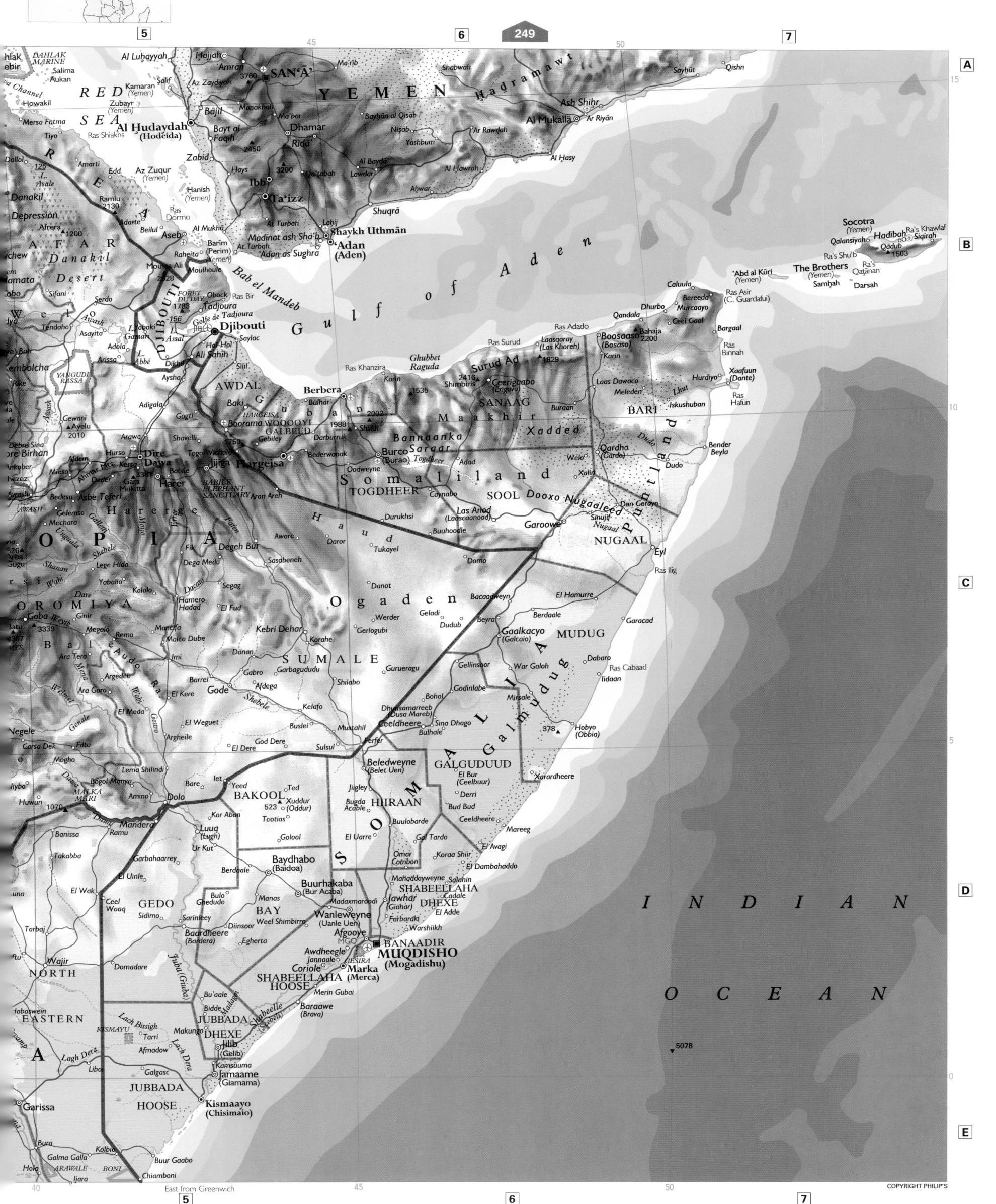

DAHLAK MARINE

hlak
ebir

Al Luhayyah
Hajjah
'Amrān
SAN'Ā'
Ma'rib
Shabwah
Hadramawt
Sayhūt
Qishn

RED
Kamaran (Yemen)
Salif
Az Zaydīyah
3760
Ash Shir
Al Mukallā
Ar Riyān

Aukan
Zubayr (Yemen)
Bājil
Manākhah
Ma'bar
Bayhān al Qisab
Ar Rawdah
Al Hasy

SEA
Al Hudaydah (Hodeida)
Bayt al Faqih
Dhamar
Rida'
Yashbum
Ahwar
Shuqrā

Mersa Fatma
Ras Shiakhs
Zabid
3200
Al Baydā
Lawdar

Edd
Az Zuqur (Yemen)
Hays
Ibb
Qa'tabah

Danakil
Ramlu 2130
Hanish (Yemen)
Ta'izz
At Turbah
Lahij
Shuqrā

Socotra (Yemen)
Qalansiyah
Hadibo
Siqirah
Qādub 1503

Ramlu
Ras Dormo
Al Mukha
Mādīnat ash Sha'b
Shaykh Uthmān
Ra's Shu'b

Afrera 1200
Adarte
Beilul
Shaykh Uthmān
Adan (Aden)
The Brothers (Yemen)
Samhah
Darsah

Sifani
Moussa Ali 2828
Bab el Mandeb
'Abd al Kūri (Yemen)

RED
Moulhoule
FORET DU'DAY
Obock
Ras Bir
Caluula
Ras Asir (C. Guardafui)

Serdo
Tadjoura 1783
Bosaso
Bereeda
Murcaayo
Ras Binnah

Asayita
DJIBOUTI
Djibouti
Qandala
Ceel Gaal

Adola
Ali Sabih
Ras Surud
Ghubbet Raguda
Laasgoray (Las Khoreh)
Boosaaso (Bosaso) 2200

G u l f   o f   A d e n

SANAAG
BARI

Berbera
Karin
Surud Ad
Shimbiris 2416
Ceerigaabo (Erigavo)
Laas Dawaco
Hurdiyo
Xaafuun (Dante)

AWDAL
Bulhar
Malaakh
Xadded
Buraan
Ras Hafun

Baki
WOQOOYI GALBEED
1988
Bannaanka Saraar
Qardho (Gardo)
Dudo
Bender Beyla

Boorama
HARGEISA
Gebiley
Darbutruk
Burco (Burao)
Welo
Xalin

Hargeisa
Togdheer
Somaliland
Dan Gorayo
Sinujiif
Nugaal

OROMIYA
Durukhsi
Las Anod (Loascaanood)
Dooxo Nugaaleed
Garoowe
Eyl

Dire Dawa
Harer
TOGDHEER
Caynabo
SOOL
Ras Ilig

OPIA
Hareige
Fafan
Degeh Bur
Aware
Buuhoodle
Domo
NUGAAL

Kolalo
Haud
Daror
Tukayel

Ogaden
Danot
Bacaadweyn
El Hamurre
Garacad
Ras Cabaad

Megalo
Kebri Dehar
Werder
Gerlogubi
Berdaale
MUDUG

Bale
Imi
Korahe
Geladi
Dudub
Gaalkacyo (Galcaio)
War Galoh

SUMALE
Gabro
Garbagududu
Shilabo
Gellinsoor
Dabaro
Iidaan

Gode
Afdega
Kelafo
Godinlabe

El Kere
Shebele
Buslei
Mustahil
Ceeldheere
Mirsale
378
Hobyo (Obbia)

Argheile
God Dere
Sulsul
Ferfer
Dhuusamarreeb (Dusa Mareb)
Bulhale
Sina Dhago

Beledweyne (Belet Uen)
GALGUDUUD
El Bur (Ceelbuur)
Xarardheere

Yeed
Ted
Jiigley
Derri

BAKOOL
Xuddur (Oddur) 523
Bugda Acable
HIIRAAN
Bud Bud
Ceeldheere

Tootias
El Uarre
Buulobarde
Mareeg

Luuq (Lugh)
Golool
Gal Tardo
El'Avagi

Ur Kut
Omar Cotnbon
Koraa Shiir
El Dambahaddo

Baydhabo (Baidoa)
Matiqaddweyne
Salahin

GEDO
Buurhakaba (Bur Acaba)
SHABEELLAHA DHEXE
Cadale

Ceel Waaq
Manas
Jawhar (Giohar)
El Adde

Sarinleey
Weel Shimbirro
Madaxmaroodi
Fairbardki

Diinsoor
BAY
Wanleweyne (Uanle Uen)
Warshiikh

Baardheere (Bardera)
Egherta
Afgooye
BANAADIR

NORTH
Domadare
Awdheegle
Jannaale
MUQDISHO (Mogadishu)

Bu'ale
Coriole
GESIRA
Marka (Merca)

Wajir
JUBBADA
SHABEELLAHA HOOSE
Merin Gubai

EASTERN
Bidde
Baraawe (Brava)

JUBBADA DHEXE
Jilib (Gelib)

Afmadow
Kamsuuma
INDIAN

A
JUBBADA HOOSE
Jamaame (Giamama)
5078

Garissa
Kismaayo (Chisimaio)
OCEAN

Bura
Galma Galla
BONI
Buur Gaabo
Chiamboni

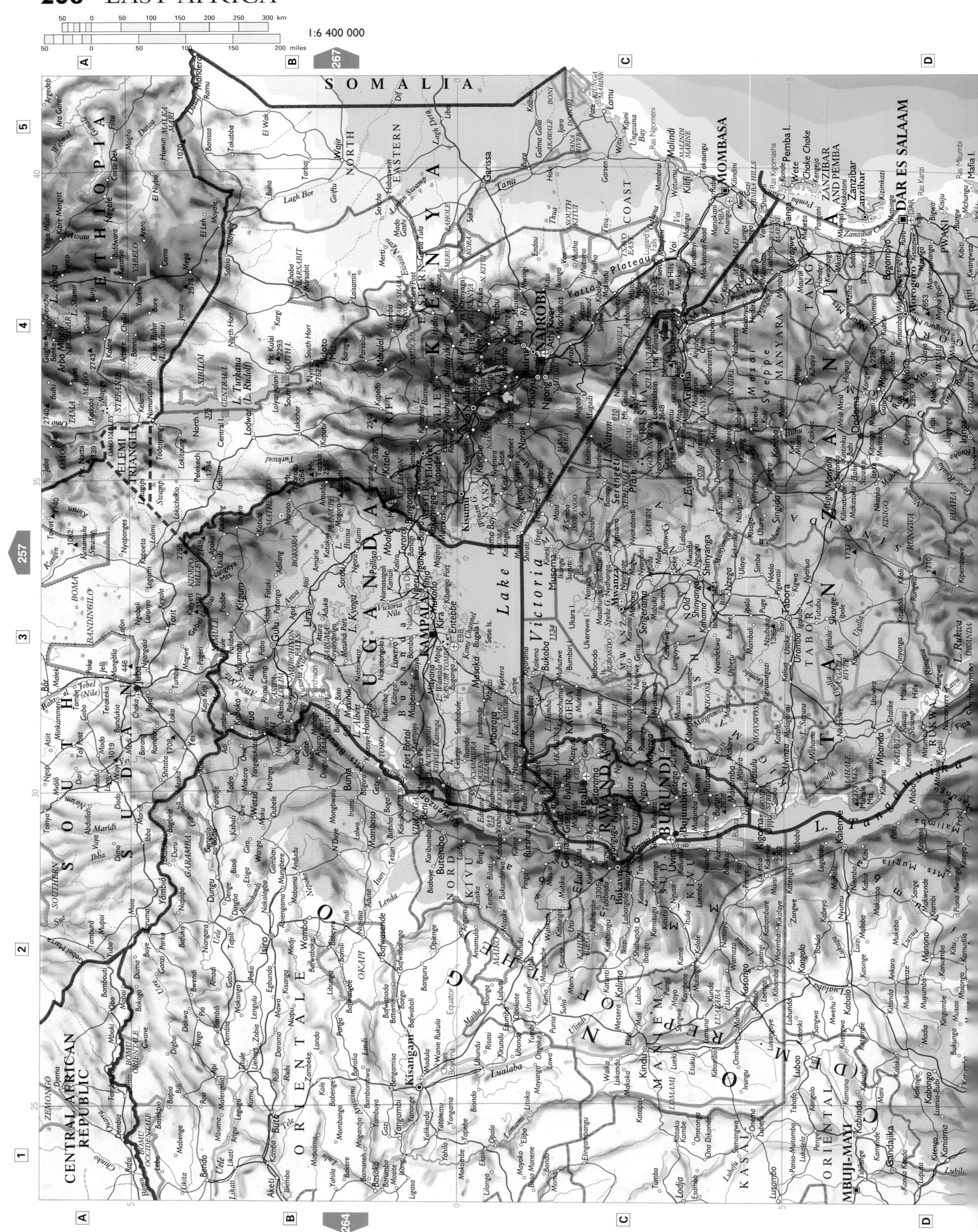

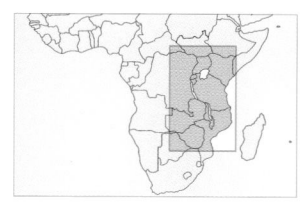

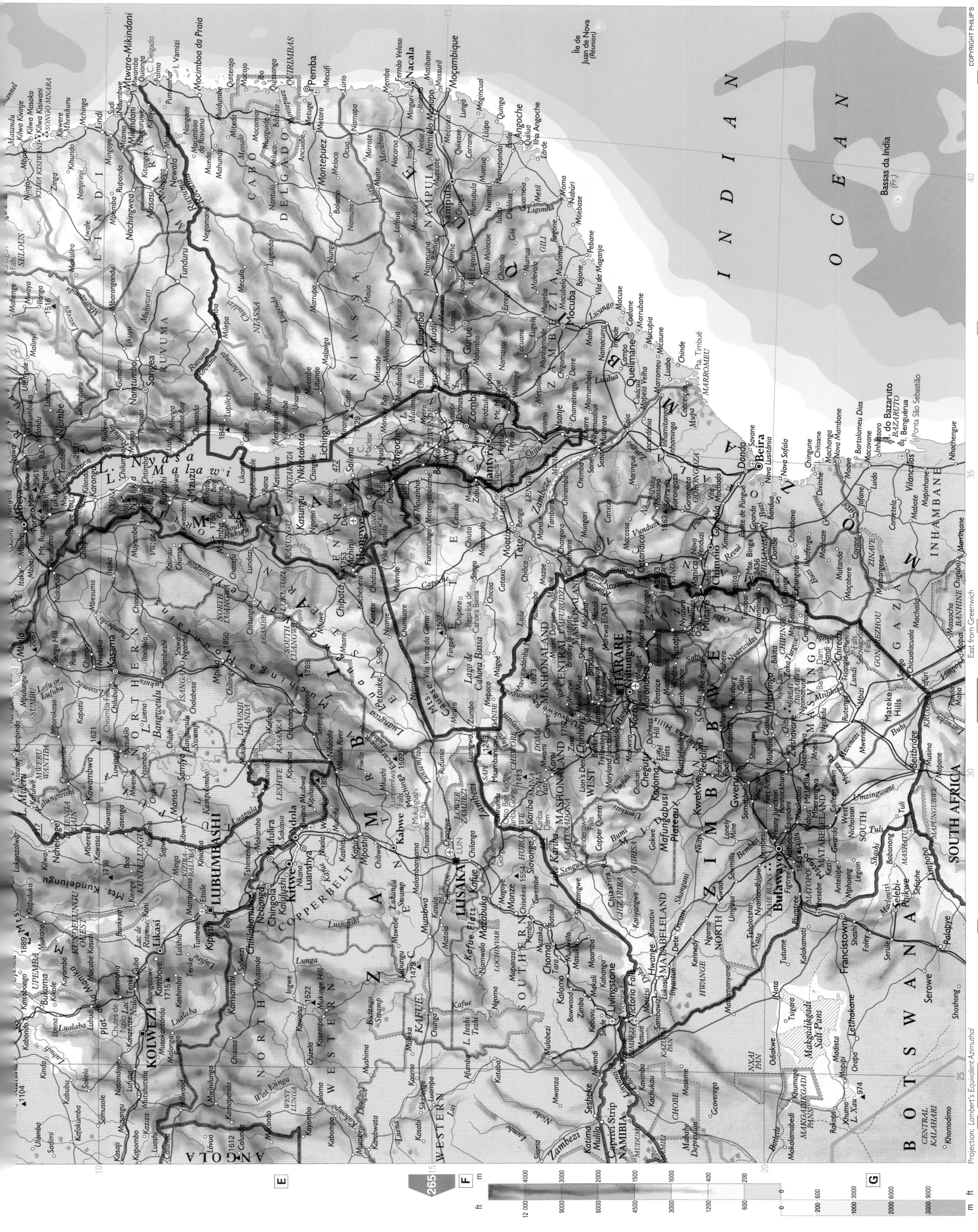

I N D I A N

O C E A N

Bassas da India
(Fr.)

Île de Nova
(Réunion)

MOÇAMBIQUE

QUIRIMBAS

DELGADO

NIASSA

NAMPULA

ZAMBÉZIA

MALAWI

L. Nyasa
or Malawi

ZAMBIA

NORTHERN

MUCHINGA MTS

COPPERBELT

SOUTHERN

WESTERN

KOLWEZI

LUBUMBASHI

A N G O L A

N A M I B I A

B O T S W A N A

Caprivi Strip

CENTRAL
KALAHARI

MAKGADIKGADI
PANS

NXAI
PAN

MOZAMBIQUE

INHAMBANE

GAZA

MANICA

SOFALA

TETE

Beira

Dondo

Quelimane

Mocuba

Nacala
Pemba

MASHONALAND

MATABELELAND

Z I M B A B W E

Harare

Bulawayo

Gwezu

Mutare

Chimoio

MASVINGO

MANICALAND

S O U T H   A F R I C A

Francistown

Serowe

Victoria Falls

Livingstone

LUSAKA

Kitwe

Lilongwe

Blantyre

Projection: Lambert's Equivalent Azimuthal

East from Greenwich

m
ft
4000 12 000
3000 9000
2000 6000
1500 4500
1000 3000
400 1200
200 600
0 0

ft m
12 000 4000
9000 3000
6000 2000
4500 1500
3000 1000
1200 400
600 200
0 0

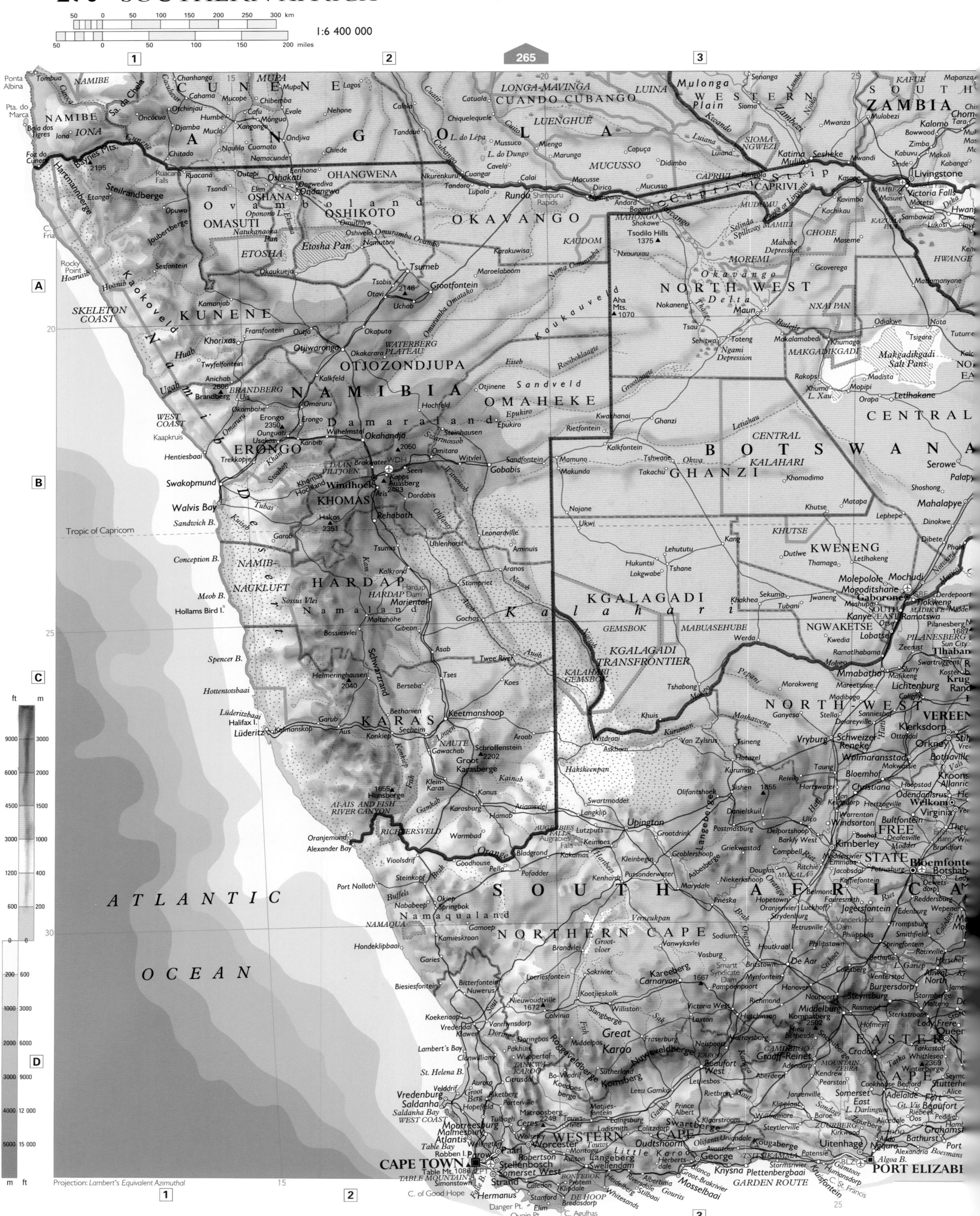

1:6 400 000

Projection: Lambert's Equivalent Azimuthal

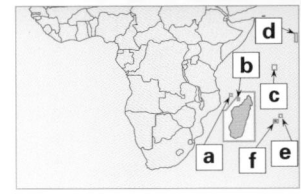

COMOROS
1:2 000 000
10 0 10 20 30 40 50 km
10 0 10 20 30 miles

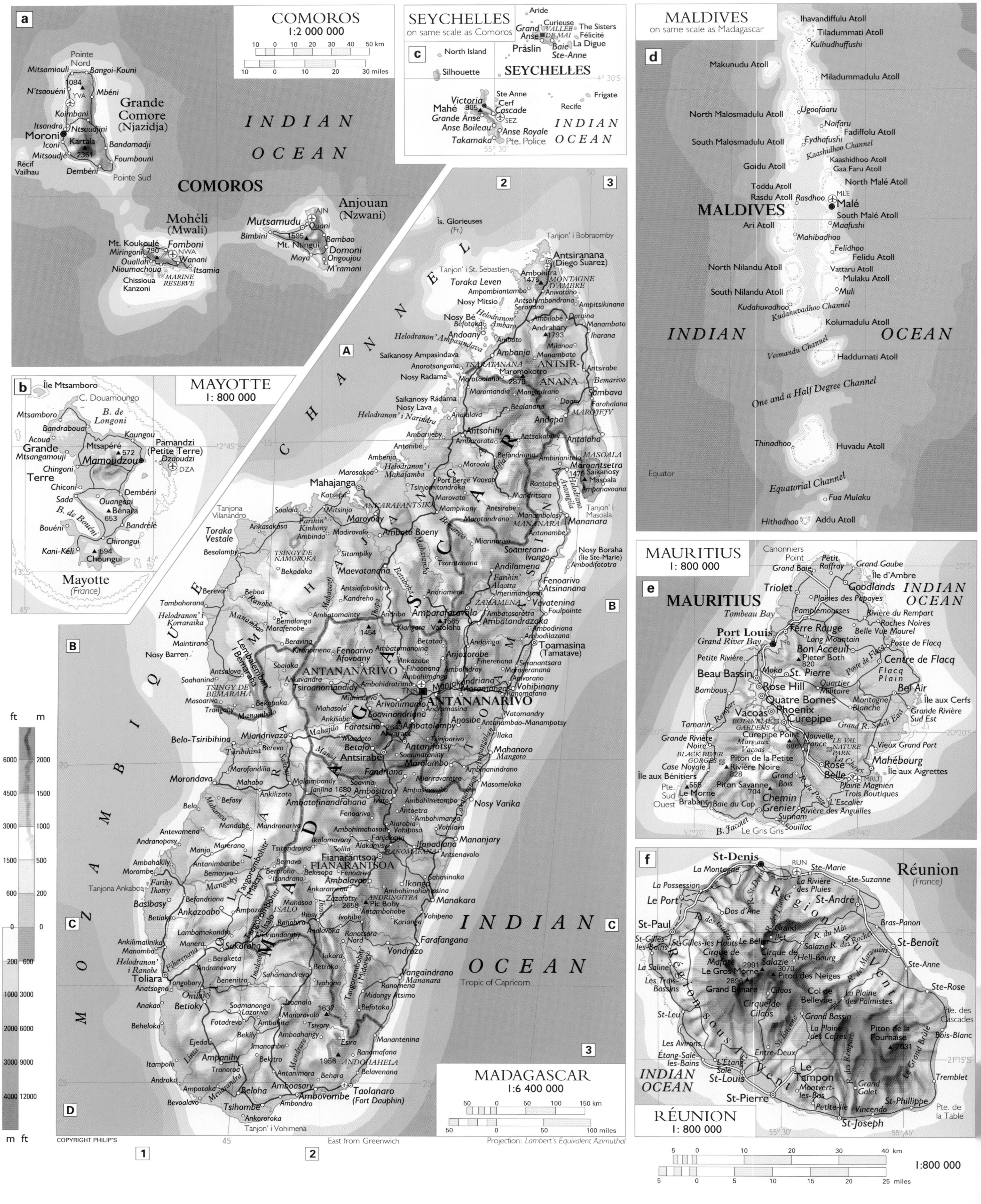

SEYCHELLES
on same scale as Comoros

SEYCHELLES

MALDIVES
on same scale as Madagascar

MAYOTTE
1:800 000

Mayotte
(France)

MAURITIUS
1:800 000

MAURITIUS

RÉUNION
1:800 000

Réunion
(France)

MADAGASCAR
1:6 400 000
50 0 50 100 150 km
50 0 50 100 miles

INDIAN OCEAN

MOZAMBIQUE CHANNEL

COMOROS

MALDIVES

MADAGASCAR

COPYRIGHT PHILIP'S

East from Greenwich

Projection: Lambert's Equivalent Azimuthal

1:800 000
5 0 10 20 30 40 km
5 0 5 10 15 20 25 miles

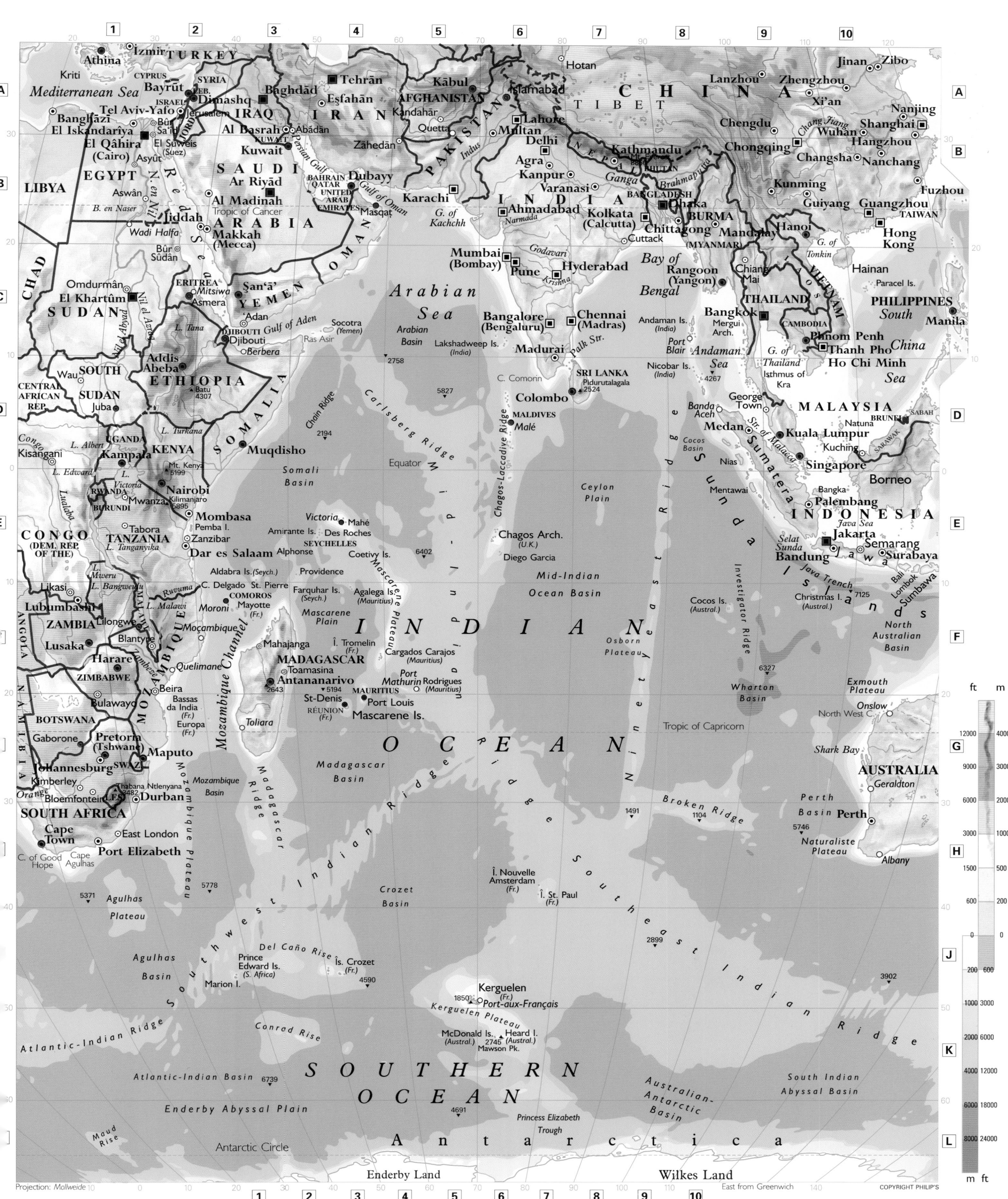

Athina İzmir TURKEY
Kriti CYPRUS Jinan Zibo
Mediterranean Sea Bayrut SYRIA Tehrān Kābul Islamabad Lanzhou Zhengzhou
Banghāzi Tel Aviv-Yafo Dimashq Baghdād Eşfahān AFGHANISTAN CHINA Xi'an
El Iskandariya Jerusalem IRAQ IRAN Kandahār Lahore Chengdu Nanjing
El Qāhira Būr Al Başrah Ābādān Quetta Multan TIBET Chongqing Shanghai
(Cairo) Sa'id Kuwait Zāhedān Delhi NEPAL Kathmandu Changsha Nanchang
LIBYA El Suweis (Suez) SAUDI Karachi Agra Kanpur Ganga Brahmaputra Kunming Guiyang Guangzhou
EGYPT Aswân Ar Riyād BAHRAIN Dubayy INDIA Varanasi BANGLADESH BURMA Fuzhou
CHAD B. en Naser Al Madinah QATAR Masqat Ahmadabad Kolkata Dhaka Mandalay TAIWAN
Wadi Halfa Tropic of Cancer UNITED ARAB EMIRATES G. of Kachchh (Calcutta) Chittagong (MYANMAR) Hong Kong
Omdurmân Bûr Sûdân Jiddah Makkah (Mecca) Narmada Mumbai (Bombay) Godavari Hyderabad Chiang Mai Hanoi G. of Tonkin
El Khartûm Nîl el Azraq ARABIA OMAN Pune Krishna Bay of Bengal Rangoon (Yangon) THAILAND Hainan
SUDAN ERITREA Şan'a' Arabian Sea Bangalore (Bengaluru) Chennai (Madras) Bangkok Paracel Is.
SOUTH SUDAN Mitsiwa YEMEN Gulf of Aden Socotra (Yemen) Arabian Basin Lakshadweep Is. (India) Andaman Is. (India) Mergui Arch. CAMBODIA PHILIPPINES
CENTRAL AFRICAN REP. Asmera 'Adan Ras Asir Madurai Port Blair Phnom Penh South China
Wau Addis Abeba DJIBOUTI Berbera 2758 C. Comorin SRI LANKA Andaman Sea Thanh Pho Manila
ETHIOPIA Batu 4307 5827 Pidurutalagala 2524 Nicobar Is. (India) Isthmus of Kra Ho Chi Minh Sea
Juba Colombo 4267 George Town MALAYSIA
SOMALIA Chain Ridge MALDIVES Banda Aceh SABAH
UGANDA KENYA 2194 Malé Medan Kuala Lumpur BRUNEI
Kisangani L. Albert Muqdisho Carlsberg Ridge Chagos-Laccadive Ridge Ceylon Plain Nias Kuching SARAWAK
Kampala L. Turkana Equator Cocos Basin Mentawai Singapore Borneo
Mt. Kenya 5199 Somali Basin INDONESIA
Nairobi Kilimanjaro 5895 Victoria Mahé Chagos Arch. (U.K.) Palembang Java Sea
RWANDA L. Victoria Amirante Is. Des Roches Diego Garcia Cocos Is. (Austral.) Jakarta
BURUNDI Mwanza SEYCHELLES Mid-Indian Bangka Semarang
CONGO (DEM. REP. OF THE) Mombasa Pemba I. Alphonse Coetivy Is. 6402 Ocean Basin Selat Sunda Bandung Surabaya
TANZANIA Zanzibar Aldabra Is. (Seych.) Providence Christmas I. (Austral.) 7125 Bali Lombok
Tabora L. Tanganyika Dar es Salaam C. Delgado St. Pierre Farquhar Is. (Seych.) Agalega Is. (Mauritius) North Australian Basin
Lubumbashi L. Mweru COMOROS Mayotte (Fr.) Mascarene Plain Osborn Plateau Sūmbawa
ZAMBIA L. Bangweulu Moroni Moçambique Î. Tromelin (Fr.) Cargados Carajos (Mauritius) INDIAN Cocos Is. (Austral.) 6327 Exmouth Plateau
Lusaka L. Malawi Mahajanga Wharton Basin North West C.
Likasi Lilongwe Blantyre MADAGASCAR Toamasina Port Mathurin Rodrigues (Mauritius) OCEAN Onslow AUSTRALIA
Harare ZIMBABWE Quelimane Antananarivo 5194 MAURITIUS Geraldton
ANGOLA Beira 2643 St-Denis Port Louis Tropic of Capricorn Shark Bay
MOZAMBIQUE Madagascar Basin RÉUNION (Fr.) Mascarene Is. Perth Basin
NAMIBIA Bulawayo Bassas da India (Fr.) Toliara Perth
BOTSWANA Gaborone Pretoria (Tshwane) Europa (Fr.) Madagascar Basin Ninetyeast Ridge Broken Ridge 1104 Naturaliste Plateau
Johannesburg SWAZI Maputo 1491 5746 Albany
Kimberley Thabana Ntlenyana 3482 LESOTHO Durban Mozambique Plateau
Orange Bloemfontein SOUTH AFRICA 5778 Crozet Basin Î. Nouvelle Amsterdam (Fr.) 2899
Cape Town East London Î. St. Paul (Fr.) 3902
C. of Good Hope Cape Agulhas Port Elizabeth Agulhas Plateau Del Caño Rise Îs. Crozet Kerguelen (Fr.)
5371 Agulhas Basin Prince Edward Is. (S. Africa) 4590 Port-aux-Français
Atlantic-Indian Ridge Marion I. Conrad Rise 1850 Kerguelen Plateau
Atlantic-Indian Basin 6739 McDonald Is. (Austral.) Heard I. (Austral.) South Indian Abyssal Basin
SOUTHERN 2745 Mawson Pk. Australian-Antarctic Basin
Enderby Abyssal Plain OCEAN 4691 Princess Elizabeth Trough
Maud Rise Antarctic Circle Antarctica
Projection: Mollweide Enderby Land Wilkes Land East from Greenwich COPYRIGHT PHILIP'S

ft m
12000 4000
9000 3000
6000 2000
3000 1000
0 0
200 600
1000 3000
2000 6000
4000 12000
6000 18000
8000 24000
m ft

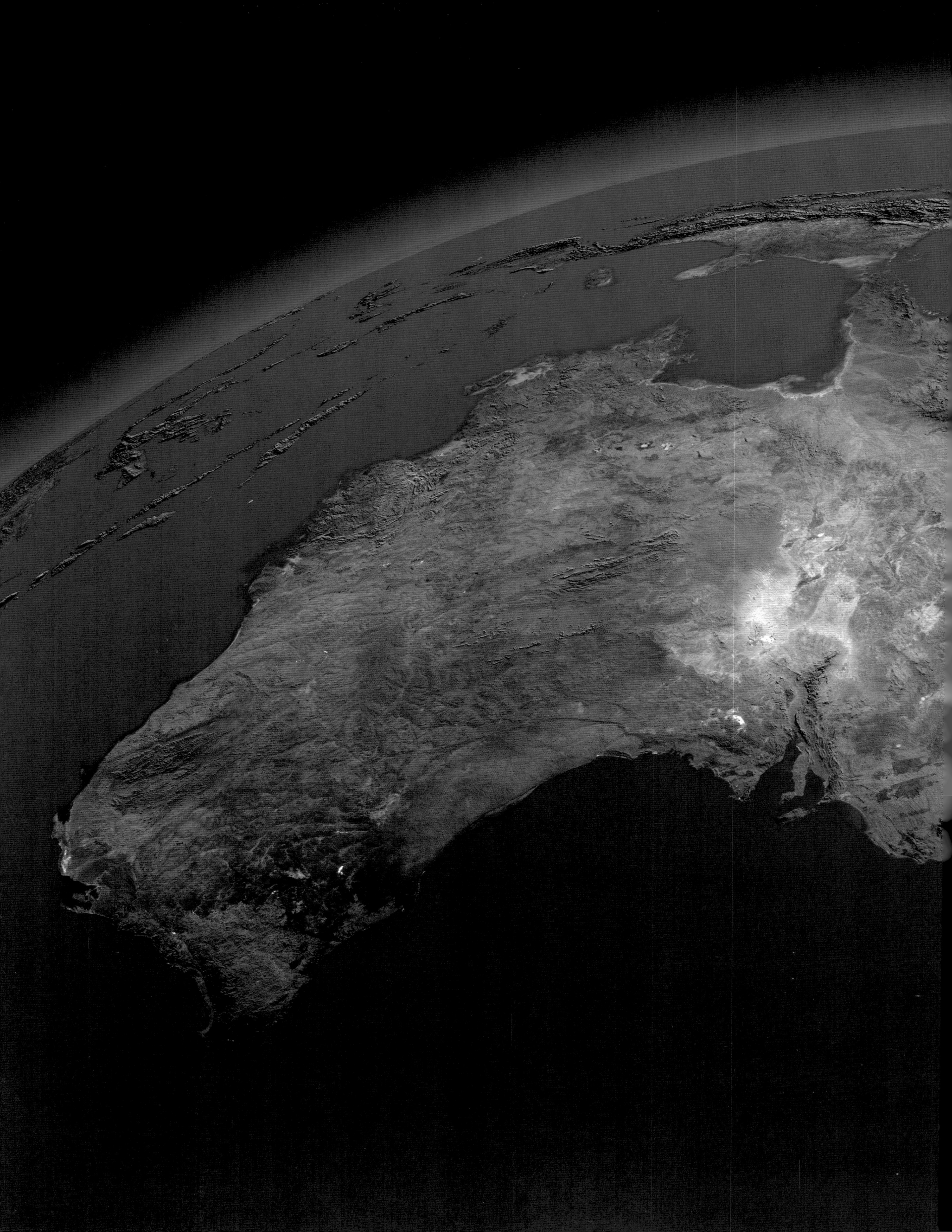

AUSTRALIA
AND
OCEANIA

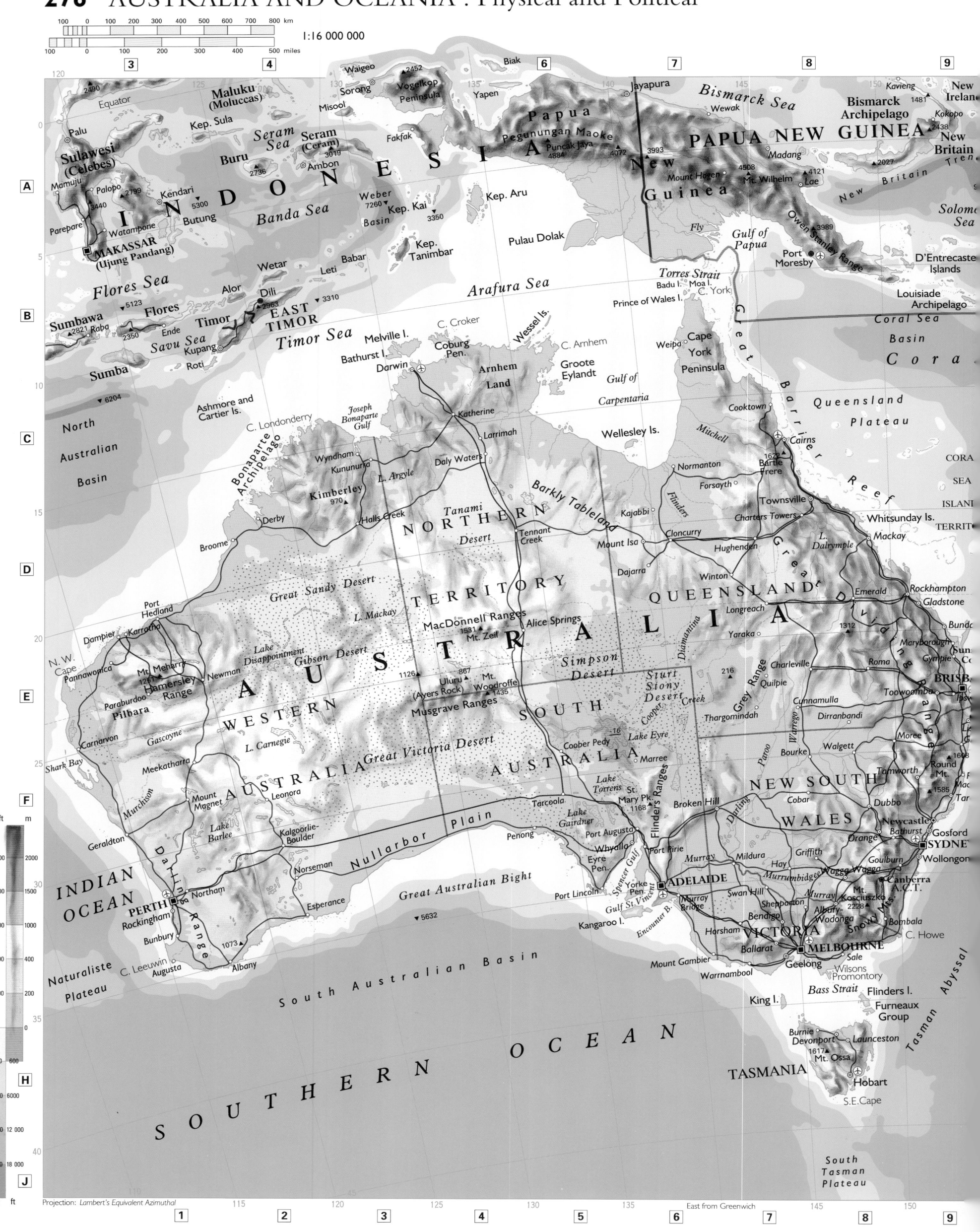

10 **11** **12** **13** **14** **15** **16**

Ontong
M *Java*
Plateau

Solomon Rise

Tabiteuea Beru Nikunau
Onotoa Tamana
Gilbert Tamana
Is. Arorae

K

e

Baker I.
(U.S.A.)

Equator

Winslow
Reef

▼ 6195

R

3 **Bougainville**
. Balbi
rtland
Is.
a Lavella
1067
SOLOMON
Santa Isabel
ISLANDS
New
Georgia Is.
Vangunu
Russell Is.
Honiara ▲2439
1250
Guadalcanal
Bellona
Rennell

1219
Florida
Is.
1432
Makira
(San Cristóbal)

M

e

l

South Solomon Trench
7223
9165

Reef Is.
Duff Is.
Nendo
Santa Cruz
Is.
Vanikoro
Fataka

Vitiaz Trench

Tikopia

n

e

s

Namumea
Nanumanga

Niutao

Namumea

Nui Vaitupu

TUVALU
(Ellice Is.) Funafuti ● Fongafale

Nukulaelae

i

Niulakita

a

McKean

Abariringa
Birnie
Nikumaroro Orona
Carondelet
Reef

Atafu
Nukunonu
Fakaofo

Enderbury
Phoenix Is.
Rawaki
Manra

Tokelau Is.
(N.Z.)
International Date Line

A

5

B

ea

Is. Torres
Vanua Lava Is. Banks
Gaua

Espíritu Santo ⊕1879
VANUATU
Malakula ▲863 **(New Hebrides)**
Epi
Shepherd Is.
Port Vila ⊕ Efate
Erromango
1084 ● Tanna
7569
Aneityum

Rotuma

Wallis & Futuna
Mata-Utu ⊕ Uvea
Horn (Fr.)
Alofi

SAMOA
Savai'i 1858 ⊕ Apia
'Upolu ● Pago
Pago
Tutuila

American
Samoa
(U.S.A.)

C

Vanua Levu
1031
Taveuni

Niuafo'ou

Niua
Group Niuatoputapu

15

Îles D'Entrecasteaux
Îles Chesterfield
Îles
Bélep
3628
Î.Lifou
New
Caledonia Î. Maré
(Fr.) La Foa
Nouméa ⊕ Yaté
Î. des Pins

West

Fiji

Basin

Viti Levu
1323
Suva
Kadavu

FIJI

Lau Group

Vava'u Group
Lau Late
Ha'apai Group
Basin
Nuku'alofa ● Eua
Tongatapu
Group
Ata

TONGA

Alofi ● **Niue**
(N.Z.)

D

South New Hebrides Trench
Îles Loyauté
Î. Matthew

Ceve-i-Ra

Lau Ridge

Tonga Trench

10 882

20

P **A** **C** **I** **F** **I** **C**

Lord Howe Seamount Chain
New
Caledonia
Ridge
Norfolk
Ridge

5303

South

Fiji

Basin

O **C** **E** **A** **N**

Tropic of Capricorn

E

25

Norfolk I.
(Austral.)

Norfolk
Basin

Lord Howe I.
(Austral.)
▼734

Lord
Howe
Lord Howe Trough

Rise

Kermadec Is.
(N.Z.)

Raoul I.

Macauley I.
Curtis I.
10 047

Kermadec Trench

Colville Ridge

Southwest

Pacific

Basin

F

30

asman Sea

North C.
Kaitaia
Whangarei

AUCKLAND ■
Hamilton

▼5267

NEW
ZEALAND

North Island
Bay of
Plenty
Tauranga
Challenger Rotorua
Plateau New Plymouth Ruapehu
▲4797
Wanganui Napier
Palmerston
North
Nelson Masterton
Blenheim Wellington
Greymouth Cook Strait

Gisborne

International Date Line

Southwest
Pacific
Basin

G

35

South Island
Aoraki Mt. Cook
▲3753
Queenstown Timaru
Invercargill Dunedin
Stewart I.

Southern Alps
Christchurch Chatham

Rise
Chatham I.
Pitt I.
Chatham Is.
(N.Z.)

H

J

10 **11** **12** **13** **14** **15** **16** **17** **18**

160 165 170 175 West from Greenwich 170 165 160 COPYRIGHT PHILIP'S

1:6 400 000

WESTERN AUSTRALIA

INDIAN OCEAN

SOUTHERN OCEAN

SOUTH AUSTRALIA

Great Australian Bight

Nullarbor Plain

Hampton Tableland

NULLARBOR

Great Victoria Desert

SPINIFEX

CENTRAL DESERT

Petermann Ranges

Musgrave Ranges

ANANGU PITJANTJATJARA

MARALINGA TJARUTJA

PERTH

Kalgoorlie-Boulder

Geraldton

Esperance

Albany

Bunbury

Mandurah

Fremantle

Rockingham

Wanneroo

Carnarvon

COPYRIGHT PHILIP'S

East from Greenwich

Aboriginal lands

1. NGALIWURRU/NUNGALI
2. WINIMIYN
3. WAMBARDI
4. LHALALTUMA
5. RODNA
6. NTARIA
7. ROULPMAULPMA
8. URUNA

m ft
3000
1200
600
0

ft m
18 000 6000
12 000 4000
6000 2000
3000 1000
2000 600
1000 400
600 200
0 0

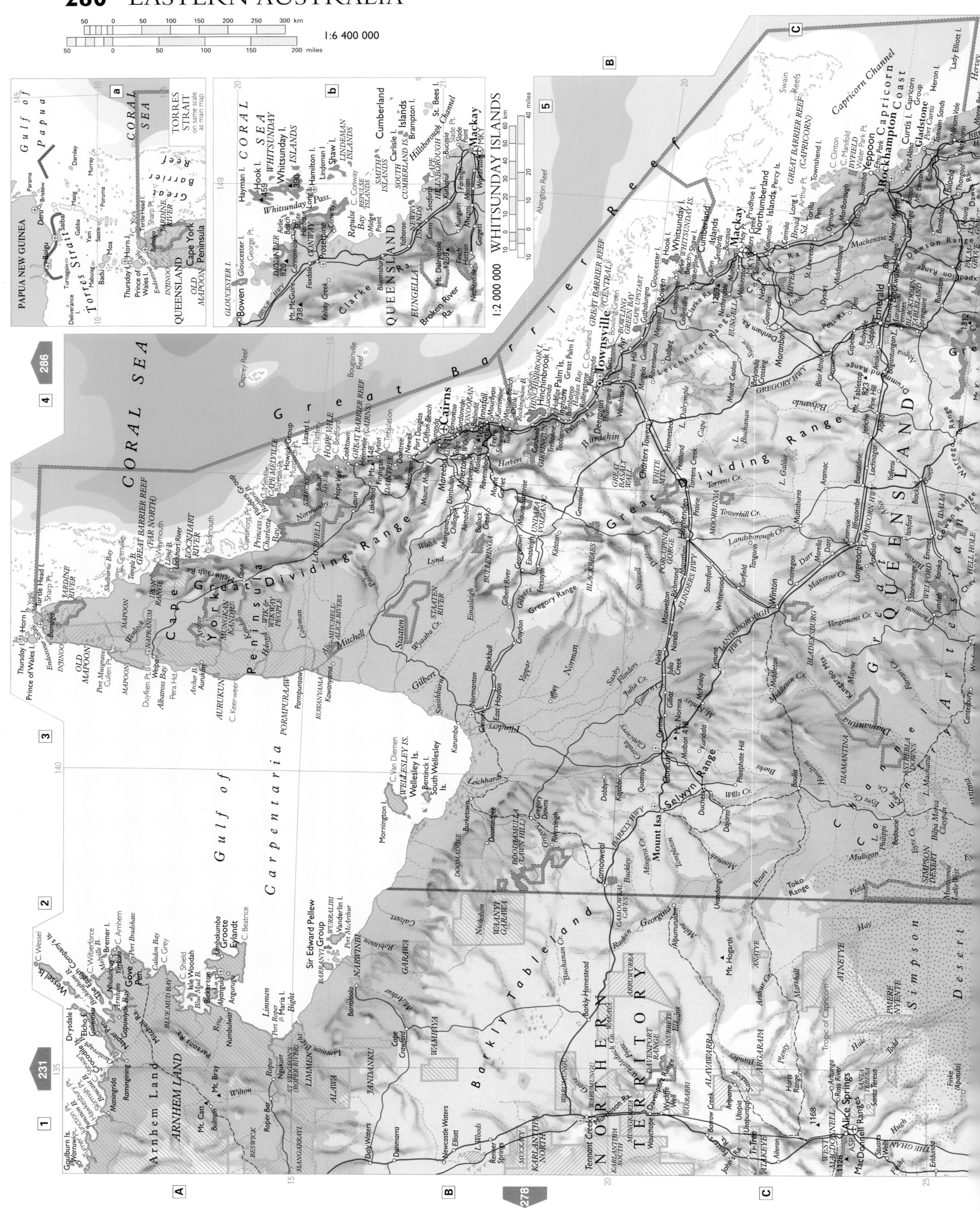

TASMAN SEA

NEW SOUTH WALES

SOUTH AUSTRALIA

BRISBANE

SYDNEY

MELBOURNE

ADELAIDE

Canberra

Newcastle

Wollongong

Gold Coast

Sunshine Coast

Hervey Bay

Toowoomba

Roma

Charleville

Broken Hill

Port Augusta

Port Pirie

Whyalla

Port Lincoln

Mildura

Wagga Wagga

Albury

Bendigo

Ballarat

Geelong

Warrnambool

Mount Gambier

Bass Strait

King Island (Tasmania)

Flinders Island

Furneaux Group

Cape Barren I.

TASMANIA

Hobart

Launceston

Devonport

Sturt Stony Desert

Strzelecki Desert

Simpson Desert

Tirari Desert

Lake Eyre (North)

Lake Eyre (South)

Lake Torrens

Lake Gairdner

Lake Frome

Lake Blanche

Flinders Ranges

Gammon Ranges

Barrier Range

Grey Range

Great Dividing Range

Darling Range

Darling Downs

Eyre Peninsula

Yorke Peninsula

Kangaroo I.

Spencer Gulf

Gulf St. Vincent

Murray

Darling

Cooper Cr.

Barcoo

Warrego

Stuart Hwy.

Eyre Hwy.

Barrier Hwy.

on same scale

East from Greenwich

Projection: Bonne

COPYRIGHT PHILIP'S

Aboriginal lands

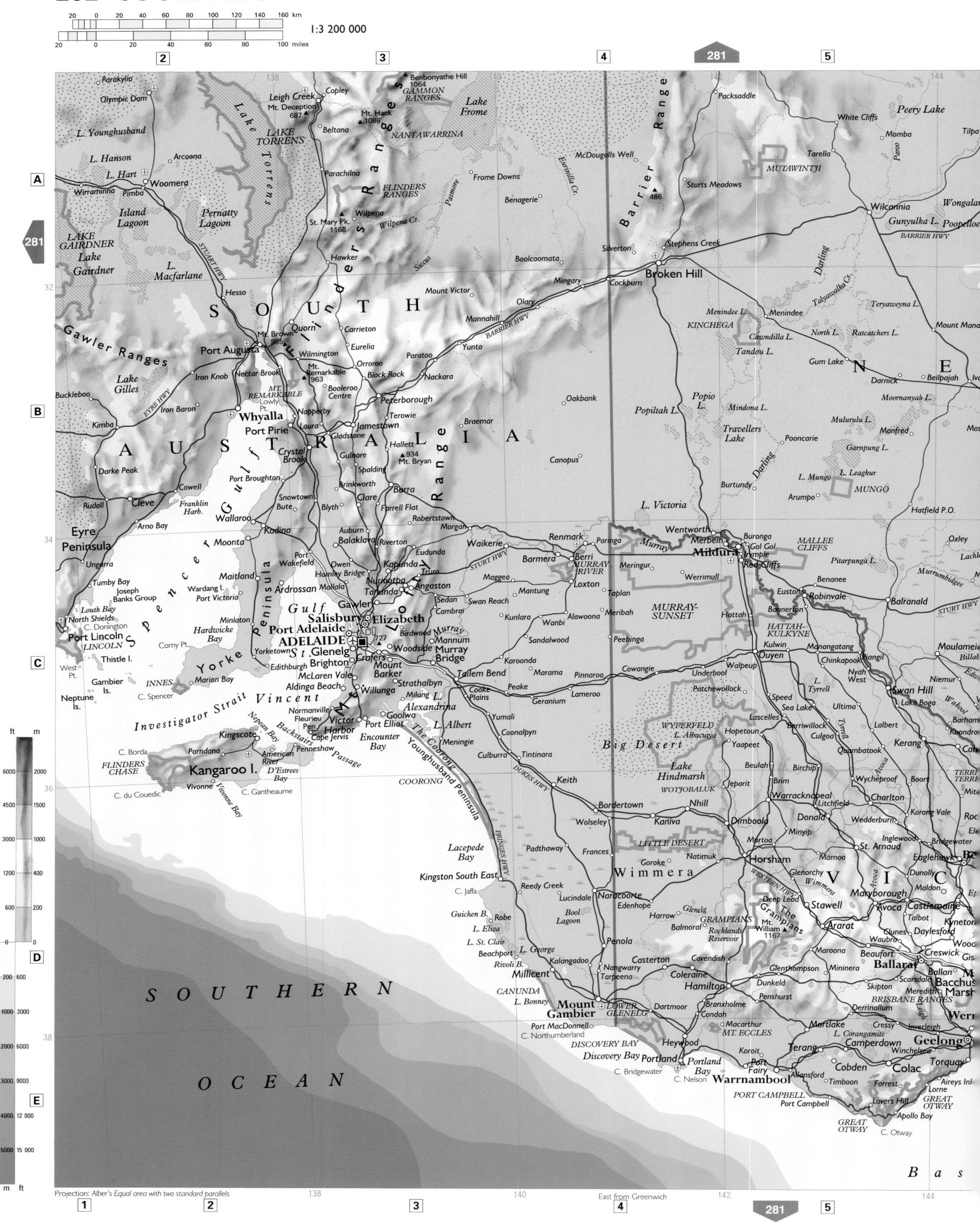

1:3 200 000

Projection: Alber's Equal area with two standard parallels

East from Greenwich

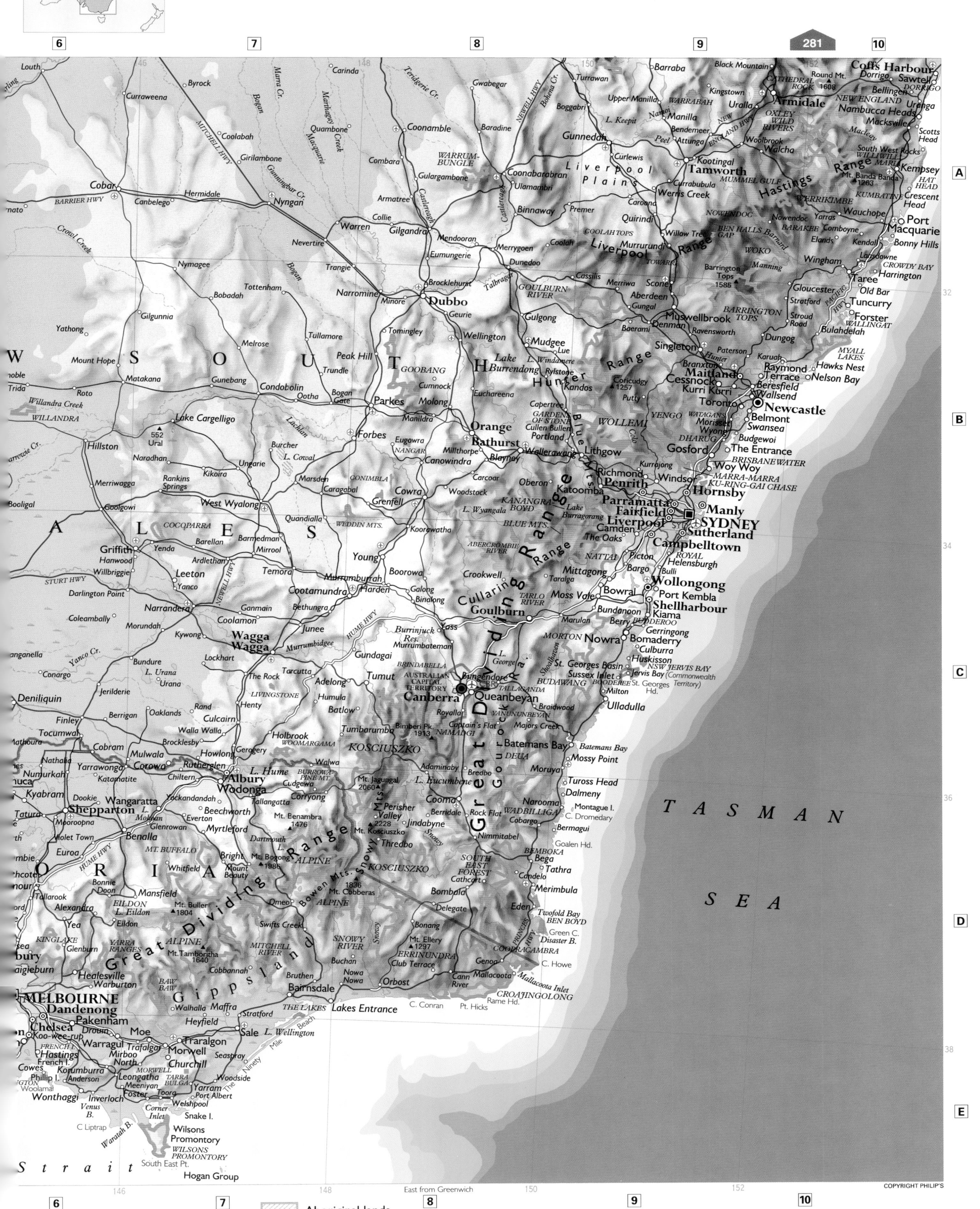

Aboriginal lands

COPYRIGHT PHILIP'S

East from Greenwich

10 0 20 40 60 80 100 120 140 km
10 0 20 40 60 80 100 miles

1:2 800 000

| 1 | 2 | 3 | 4 | 5 | 6 | 7 | 8 |

P A C I F I C

O C E A N

1320

NORTHLAND

C. Reinga
Waitiki Landing
North C.
C. Maria van Diemen
Parengarenga Harbour
Houhora Heads
Ninety Mile Beach
Rangaunu B.
Awanui
Mongonui
C. Karikari
Doubtless B.
Cavalli Is.
Whangaroa Harb.
Ahipara B.
Kaitaia
Kaeo
Waitangi
B. of Islands
C. Brett
Herekino
Kerikeri
Russell
Okaihau
Paihia
Opua
Poor Knights Is.
Kohukohu
Kaikohe
Kawakawa
Whangaruru Harb.
Rawene
Moerewa
781
Hokianga Harbour
Omapere
Hikurangi
Waipoua Forest
Donnelly's Crossing
Wairoa
Kamo
Whangarei
Aranga
Kirikopuni
Onerahi
Whangarei Harb.
Bream Hd.
Dargaville
Marsden Point
Bream B.
Hen & Chickens Is.
Te Kopuru
Waipu
Bream Tail
Waikiekie
Paparoa
Maungaturoto
Needles Pt.
Ruawai
Wellsford
Little Barrier I.
Port Fitzroy
Great Barrier I.
Matakana
C. Rodney
722
627
Tryphena
Kaipara Harbour
Warkworth
Kawau I.
Coromandel Chan.
Colville Chan.
C. Barrier
Helensville
Snells Beach
C. Colville
892
Port Charles
Hauraki G.
Cuvier I.
AUCKLAND
Whangaparaoa Pen.
Coromandel
Mercury Is.
Ostend
AUCKLAND
Takapuna
Waiheke I.
Mercury B.
Muriwai Beach
Mt. Wellington
Whitianga
Piha
AKL
Howick
Coromandel Pen.
Onehunga
Otahuhu
Tairua
Papatoetoe
Pauanui
Manukau
Papakura
846
Thames
Manukau Harbour
Whangamata
Waiuku
Pukekohe
Tuakau
Mercer
Tairua
Mayor I.
WAIKATO
Te Kauwhata
L. Waikare
Waihi
Waihi Beach
Waikato
Paeroa
Katikati
BAY OF PLENTY
Huntly
Te Aroha
Tauranga Harb.
Whakaari (White I.)
Glen Afton
Waitoa
Matakana I.
Glen Massey
Ngaruawahia
Morrinsville
Motiti I.
C. Runaway
Hicks Bay
Hamilton
Tauranga
Mount Maunganui
Te Kaha
Raglan Harbour
Waharoa
Matamata
Te Puke
Bay of Plenty
Te Araroa
East C.
Raglan
Cambridge
Te Kaha
1067
Aotea Harbour
Karapiro
Paengaroa
Matata
Edgecumbe
1753
Ruatoria
Te Awamutu
Leamington
Tirau
L. Rotorua
Whakatane
Hikurangi
Kawhia Harbour
Kihikihi
Putaruru
Kawerau
Ohiwa Harbour
Opotiki
Waipiro Bay
Albatross Pt.
Arapuni
Tokomaru Bay
Kawhia
Ngongotaha
Te Teko
Tangatu
Otorohanga
Waitomo Caves
Tokoroa
Rotorua
Tolaga Bay
Te Kuiti
Kinleith
Mt. Tarawera
GISBORNE
1111
Matawai
Puha
Mangakino
Te Karaka
Herangi Ra.
Waiotapu
Ormond
Aria
Atiamuri
UREWERA
Ngatapa
1185
Whakamaru
Mokai
Galatea
Murupara
Gisborne
Mokau
Ongarue
Wairakei
Manuoha
Pututahi
1392
Waikaremoana
Poverty B.
North Taranaki Bight
Pukearuhe
Ohakune
Taupo
369
L. Taupo
1383
Tuai
Tuaheni Pt.
Waitara
Taumarunui
Turangi
Ahimanawa Mts.
Fraserton
New Plymouth
Tahora
Tokaanu
Rangitaiki
Tarawera
Nuhaka
Okato
Inglewood
L. Rotoaira
Mohaka
Waikokopu
Whangamomona
Mt. Tongariro
1728
Table C.
TARANAKI
Huiroa
1965
403
Mahia Pen.
C. Egmont
Mt. Taranaki or Mt. Egmont
Mt. Ngauruhoe 2287
TONGARIRO
Kaweka Ra.
Rahotu
2518
Midhirst
746
Ruapehu
Putorino
EGMONT
Kaponga
Stratford
Ohakune
2797
Wairoa
Opunake
Kapuni
Eltham
Rangataua
Bay View
Manaia
Normanby
Pipiriki
Raetihi
Waiouru
Taradale
Napier
Hawera
Raetihi
Clive
South Taranaki Bight
Patea
Waverley
Maxwell
Taihape
Hastings
C. Kidnappers
Waitotara
Hunterville
Mangaweka
Opapa
Havelock North
Wanganui
Castlecliff
Mangaweka
Apiti
1733
Otane
Hawke Bay
Turakina
Marton
Halcombe
Norsewood
Waipawa
MANAWATU-WANGANUI
Bulls
Feilding
Ormondville
Takapau
Waipukurau
Rangitikei
Bunnythorpe
Danevirke
Porangahau
Palmerston North
Rongotea
Ashhurst
Pahiatua
803
Foxton
Woodville
Weber
112
Manawatu
Longburn
C. Turnagain
Herbertville
Levin
Shannon
Pahiatua
Golden Bay
C. Farewell
Farewell Spit
Otaki
Eketahuna
Alfredton
Collingwood
C. Stephens
Stephens I.
1571
Mauriceville
Takaka
Rangitoto ke te tonga (D'Urville I.)
Kapiti I.
Mt. Mere
Tinui
Castlepoint
Kahurangi Pt.
French Pass
Paraparaumu
ABEL TASMAN N.P.
Paekakariki
Carterton
Devil River Pk.
Tasman
Masterton
1780
Riwaka
Tasman Bay
Paraparaumu
Upper Hutt
Greytown
KAHURANGI MTS.
Motueka
1203
Porirua
Featherston
WELLINGTON
Karamea
NELSON
Pelorus
Johnsonville
Wairarapa
Mt. Owen
Brightwater
Queen Charlotte
Lower Hutt
L. Onoke
Flat Pt.
Karamea
Nelson
Stoke
Havelock
Arapawa
Petone
665
Wakefield
Richmond
Picton
WLG
Wainuiomata
Tadmor
Mt. Owen 1756
Tuamarina
Wellington
Belgrove
Richmond Ra.
Cloudy B.
Port Nicholson
Eastbourne
Mokihinui
Renwick
Wairau
Turakirae Hd.
Palliser B.
Aorangi Mts.
981
Lyell
Glenhope
Blenheim
Ruamahanga
C. Palliser
3122
TASMAN
1875
2120
Seddon
Murchison
L. Rototti
1780
Ward
Awatere
C. Campbell

T A S M A N

S E A

Cook Strait

Projection: Conical with two standard parallels

East from Greenwich

COPYRIGHT PHILIP'S

ft m
9000 3000
6000 2000
3000 1000
600 200
0 0
200 600
1000 3000
1500 4500
3000 9000
m ft

1:2 800 000

10 0 20 40 60 80 100 120 140 km
10 0 20 40 60 80 100 miles

284

Projection: Conical with two standard parallels

TASMAN SEA

PACIFIC OCEAN

CHATHAM ISLANDS
on same scale

PACIFIC OCEAN

Chatham Islands (Wharekauri)

C. Young
Munning Pt.
Western Reef
Te One
Waitangi
Owenga
C. Fournier
The Horns
Pitt Strait
Mangere I.
Pitt I.
Rangatira I.
The Pyramid
The Sisters
Chatham I. (Rekohu)
The Forty Fours
Star Keys

West from Greenwich

COPYRIGHT PHILIP'S

Selected place names

C. Farewell
Farewell Spit
Collingwood
Golden Bay
Takaka
C. Stephens
Stephens I.
Rangitoto ke te tonga (D'Urville I.)
French Pass
Kahurangi Pt.
Separation Pt.
ABEL TASMAN
Tasman
Devil River Pk.
1780
Riwaka
Motueka
Tasman Bay
Forsyth I.
C. Jackson
Pelorus Sd.
Queen Charlotte Sd.
Arapawa I.
KAHURANGI
Karamea
Karamea Bight
Brightwater
Wakefield
Tadmor
NELSON
Stoke
Havelock
Picton
Tuamarina
Cloudy B.
Waimarie
Seddonville
Mokihinua
Mt. Owen
1875
Glenhope
Mt. Richmond
Belgrove
1756
Richmond
Richmond Ra.
Blenheim
Renwick
Wairau
Granity
Millerton
Matiri Ra.
Seddon
C. Campbell
Westport
Lyell
Buller Gorge
Murchison
TASMAN
Spenser Mts.
St Arnaud Ra.
MARLBOROUGH
Ward
C. Foulwind
Inangahua
2120
1780
Mt. Travers
2337
NELSON LAKES
Inland Kaikoura Ra.
Wharanui
PAPAROA
Reefton
Mt. Franklin
2340
2885
Tapuae-o-Uenuku
Punakaiki
Paparoa Ra.
Ikamatua
Grey
Maruia
Molesworth
Seaward Kaikoura Ra.
Manakau
2608
Blackball
Runanga
Maruia Springs
Lewis Pass
Hanmer Springs
1747
Kaikoura
Greymouth
Taramakau
L. Kaimata
L. Brunner
Mt. Ajax
1834
1615
Waiau
Parnassus
Kaikoura Pen.
Hokitika
Kumara
ARTHUR'S PASS
Otira
Mt. Crossley
1980
Culverden
Waikari
Domett
Sedgill
Ross
Jacksons
Arthur's Pass
926
Pulteteraki
Waipara
Amberley
Pegasus Bay
Wanganui
Abut Hd.
Harihari
2650
Mt. Murchison
2405
Whitcombe Pass
Lake Coleridge
Springfield
Oxford
Rangiora
Sefton
Whataroa
Okarito
Mt. Taylor
2333
Sheffield
Kaiapoi
Belfast
Gillespies Pt.
Arrowsmith
2781
Col_eridge
Whitecliffs
Darfield
CHCH
Christchurch
New Brighton
Franz Josef Glacier
MT. COOK
Mt. Taylor
South Branch
Highbank
Rolleston
Hornby
Sumner
Bruce B.
Fox Glacier
Mt. Tasman
3753
Aoraki Mount Cook
Mount Cook
Methven
Lincoln
Leeston
Banks Pen.
Tititira Hd.
Tasman Gl.
2251
Mount Somers
919
Little River
Akaroa
Haast
Glenmary
Ben Ohau Ra.
L. Tekapo
Geraldine
Ashburton
Tinwald
L. Ellesmere
Southbridge
Jackson Hd.
Okuru
Haast
2590
L. Pukaki
Mackenzie Plains
Fairlie
Hinds
Akaroa Harbour
Cascade Pt.
Waitaki Plains
1894
Winchester
Temuka
Ashburton
Canterbury Bight
L. Ohau
Lake Pukaki
Benmore Pk.
The Hunter Hills
Pleasant Point
Timaru
Awarua Pt.
Awarua B.
Mt. Aspiring
MOUNT ASPIRING
Hawea
Hawea Flat
L. Aviemore
Kirkliston Ra.
St. Andrews
Yates Pt.
Milford Sd.
Mt. McKerrow
2723
Barrier Ra.
3033
L. Wanaka
Kurow
Studholme
Hunter
Mitre Peak
1683
Mt. Earnslaw
2819
Wanaka
Mt. St. Bathan's
2087
Hakataramea
Waimate
Bligh Sound
Milford Sound
1936
Dunstan Mts.
St. Bathans
Duntroon
Waihao
Morven
George Sound
Glenorchy
Hawkdun Ra.
Tokarahi
Ngapara
Glenavy
Caswell Sound
Harris Mts.
Arrowtown
Naseby
Kakanui Mts.
Windsor
Maheno
Charles Sound
1610
Cromwell
Clyde
Ranfurly
Pukeuri
Oamaru
Thompson Sd.
Murchison Mts.
L. Te Anau
Queenstown
The Remarkables
2315
Alexandra
Rough Ridge
Hyde
Hampden
Secretary I.
Mt. Lyall
1892
Double Cone
Roxburgh
Middlemarch
Dunback
Palmerston
Doubtful Sd.
Kepler Mts.
Garvies Mts.
Kingston
Sutton
Waikouaiti Downs
Shag Pt.
Dagg Sd.
L. Manapouri
Te Anau
Athol
Miller's Flat
Waikouaiti
Dusky Sd.
FIORDLAND
Manapouri
Umbrella Mts.
Edievale
Beaumont
Port Chalmers
Otago Harbour
Breaksea Sd.
OTAGO
Waikaia
Waipahi
Lawrence
Warrington
Otago Pen.
Resolution I.
Mossburn
Lumsden
Waikaka
SOUTHLAND
Clinton
Dunedin
C. Saunders
Chalky Inlet
Cameron Mts.
Dipton
Waimea Plain
Mataura
Clinton
Mosgiel
St. Kilda
Preservation Inlet
1704
Monowai
Birchwood
Ohai
Nightcaps
Riversdale
Tapanui
Kelso
Balclutha
Taieri
Puysegur Pt.
L. Hauroko
Otautau
Winton
Hedgehope
Mataura
Waipahi
Stirling
Kaitangata
Te Waewae
Orawia
Tuatapere
Orepuki
Thornbury
Makarewa
Gore
Edendale
Wyndham
Owaka
Pahia Pt.
Riverton
Wallacetown
Invercargill
Glenham
Tahakopa
Nugget Pt.
Centre I.
South Invercargill
Fortrose
Toetoes
Tokanui
Long Pt.
Bluff
Bluff Harbour
Waipapa Pt.
Chaslands Mistake
Solander I.
Mt. Anglem
980
Codfish I.
Paterson Inlet
Stewart I. (Rakiura)
RAKIURA
Mason B.
Halfmoon Bay
Doughboy B.
Port Pegasus
Ruapuke I.
Foveaux Str.
South West C.

ft m
9000 3000
6000 2000
3000 1000
1200 400
600 200
0 0
200 600
1000 3000
1500 4500
3000 9000
4000 12 000
m ft

East from Greenwich

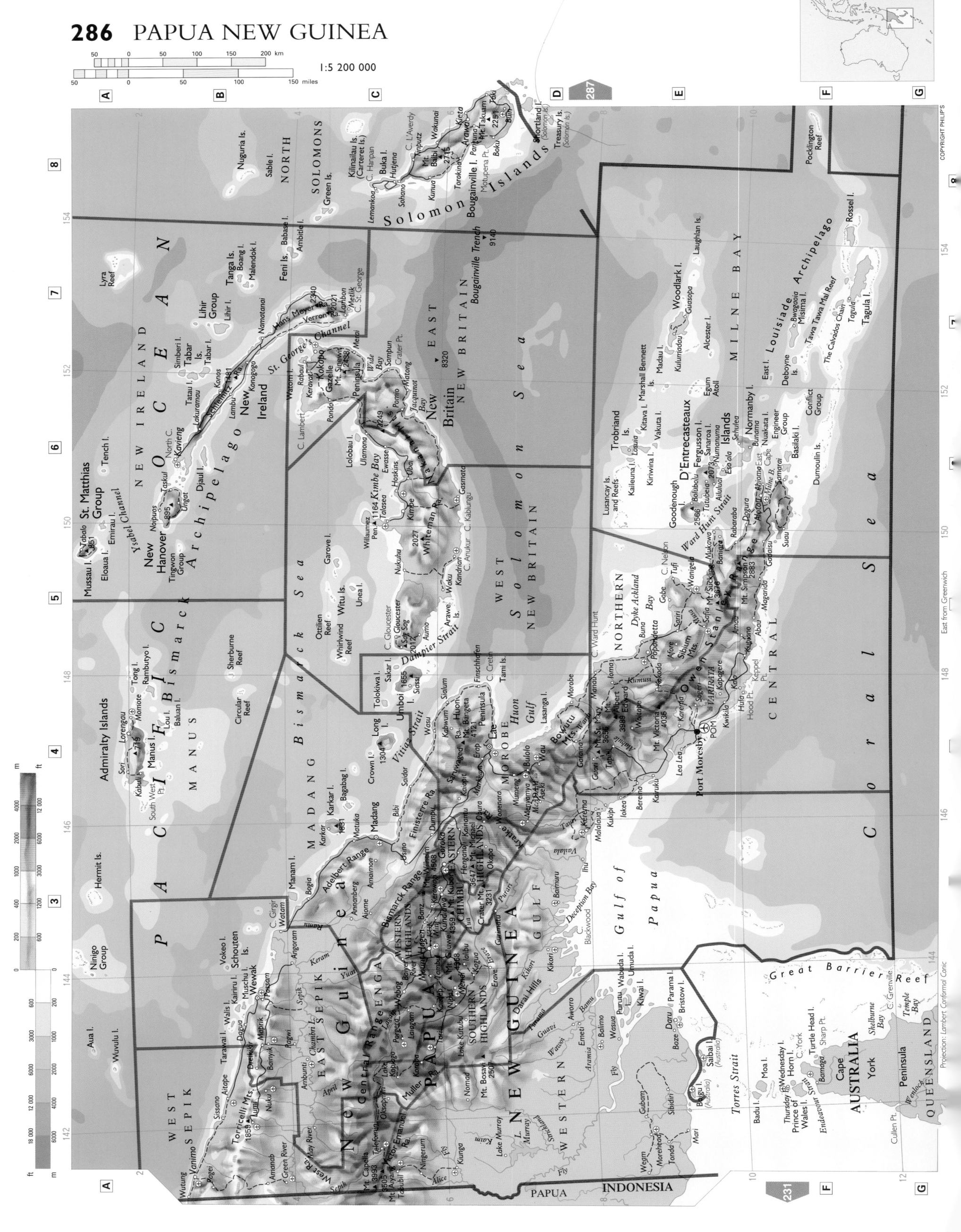

1:5 200 000

50   0   50   100   150   200 km
50   0   50   100   150 miles

COPYRIGHT PHILIP'S

East from Greenwich

Projection: Lambert Conformal Conic

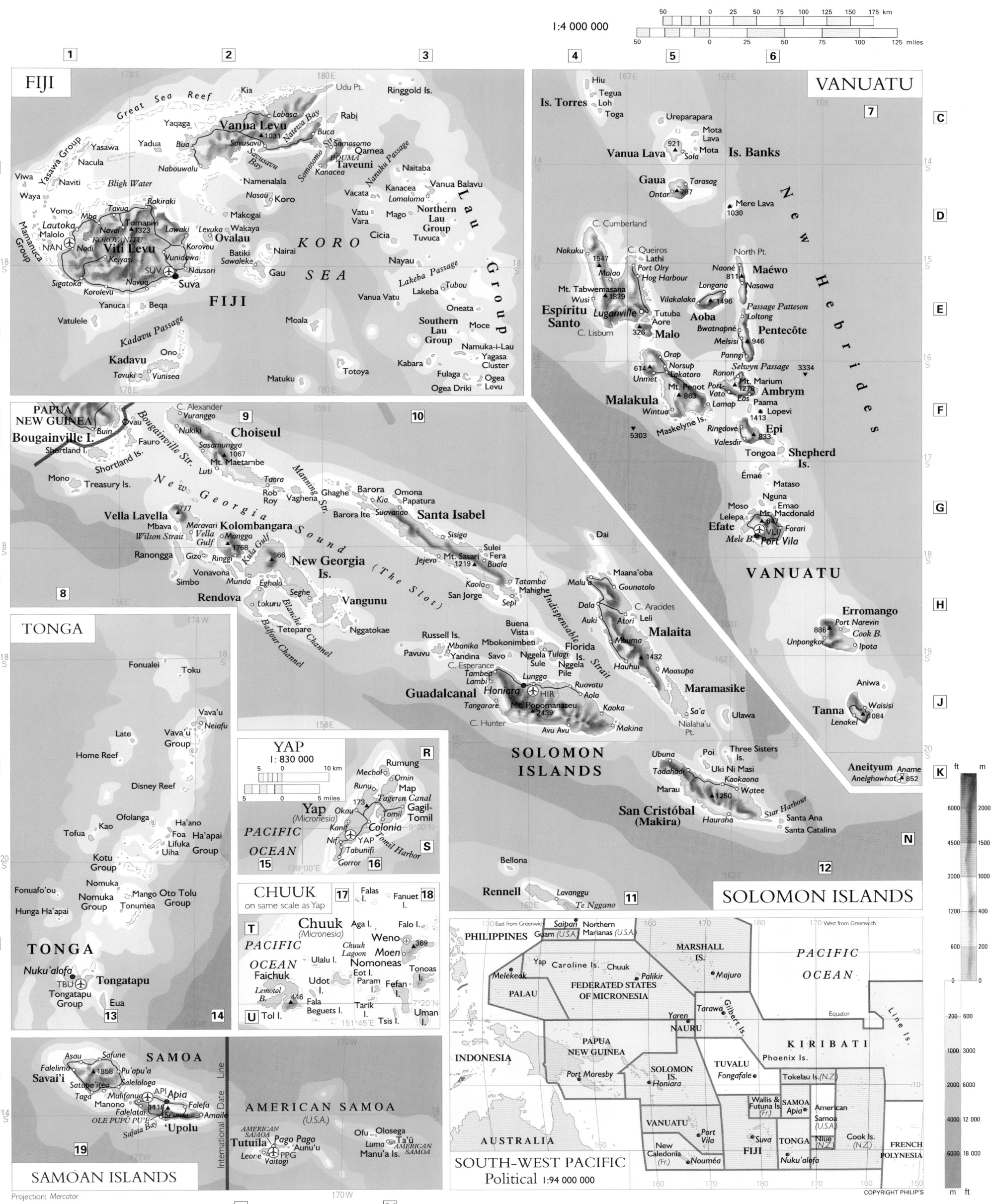

1:4 000 000

50 0 25 50 75 100 125 150 175 km

50 0 25 50 75 100 125 miles

FIJI

Great Sea Reef

Kia
Udu Pt.
Ringgold Is.

Yaqaga
Labasa Natewa Bay
Vanua Levu △1031 Buca Rabi
Savusavu Somosomo Str.
Yadua Bua Nabouwalu BOUMA Qamea
Yasawa Seqaqa Bay Taveuni
Nacula Namenalala Naitaba
Nasau Koro Kanacea Vanua Balavu
Vacata Lomaloma
Rakiraki Makogai Mago Northern Lau Group
Waya Tavua Levuka Wakaya Cicia Tuvuca
Vomo Tomaniivi Ovalau Nairai Nayau
Lautoka △1323 Korovou Batiki Sawaleke
Malolo NADI KOROYANITU Vunidawa Gau Lakeba Passage Tubou
Nadi Viti Levu Keiyasi Nausori Lakeba Oneata
SUV Suva Vanua Vatu
Sigatoka Korolevu Navua Moala Moce
Yanuca Beqa KORO SEA FIJI Totoya Fulaga
Vatulele Southern Lau Group Namuka-i-Lau Yagasa Cluster
Kadavu Passage Ono Kabara Ogea Levu
Kadavu Tavuki Vunisea Matuku Ogea Driki

VANUATU

Hiu Is. Torres Tegua Loh Toga
Ureparapara Mota Lava Is. Banks
Vanua Lava △921 Sola Mota
Gaua Tarasag Mere Lava △1030
Ontar △787
C. Cumberland
Nokuku △1547 C. Queiros North Pt. New Hebrides
Malao Lathi Naoné Maéwo △811
Mt. Tabwemasana Port Olry Hog Harbour Longana Nasawa
Wusi △1879 Tutuba Vilakalaka Aoba △1496 Passage Patteson
Espíritu Santo Luganville Aore 326 Loltong Pentecôte
C. Lisburn Malo Bwatnapné Melsisi △946 Panngi
Orap Selwyn Passage
Norsup Lakatoro Ranon △3334
614 Unmet Mt. Penot Port Mt. Marium Ambrym
Mt. Penot Vato △1278 Paama
△863 Lamap Eas Lopevi
Malakula Wintua △1413
Maskelyne Is. Ringdove Epi △833
△5303 Valesdir Tongoa Shepherd Is.
Émaé
Mataso
Nguna
Moso Emao
Lelepa Mt. Macdonald
Efate △647 Forari
Mele B. VLI Port Vila

VANUATU

Erromango
886 Port Narevin Cook B.
Unpongkor Ipota
Aniwa
Tanna Waisisi △1084
Lenakel
Aneityum Aname △852
Anelghowhat

PAPUA NEW GUINEA
Bougainville I.
△ Buin C. Alexander Vuranggo
Ovau Nukiki Choiseul
Buka Fauro Sasamungga △1067
Shortland I. Shortland Is. Mt. Maetambe
Mono Luti
Treasury Is. Taora
Rob Ghaghe Barora Omona Papatura
Vella Lavella △777 Vaghena Kia Papatura Ite
Mbava Maravari Barora Ite Suavanao Santa Isabel
Kolombangara Mongga △1768 Sisiga
Ranongga Vella Gulf △666 Jejevo Sulei
Gizo Ringgi Kula Gulf New Georgia Is. Mt. Sasari Fera
Vonavona Munda △1219 Buala
Simbo Egholo Kaolo Tatamba Mahighe
Rendova Seghe San Jorge Sepi
Lokuru Vangunu Russell Is. Buena
Tetepare Nggatokae Mbanika Vista
Mbokonimbeti
Balfour Channel Pavuvu Yandina Savo Nggela Tulagi Malu'a
Blanche Channel C. Esperance Sule Nggela Maana'oba
Tambea Lambi Ruavatu Pile Gounatolo
Guadalcanal Honiara Lungga Aola Dala C. Aracides
Tangarare HIR Mt. Popomanaseu Auki Atori Leli
C. Hunter △2439 Avu Avu Hauhui Malaita △1432
SOLOMON Makina Sa'a Maasupa
ISLANDS Maramasike
Nialaha'u Pt. Ulawa
Three Sisters Is.
San Cristóbal Ubuna Poi Uki Ni Masi
(Makira) Tadahadi Kaokaona Watee
Marau △1250 Star Harbour Santa Ana
Haraha Santa Catalina

Bellona Lavanggu
Rennell Te Nggano

TONGA

Fonualei Toku
Vava'u Neiafu
Late Vava'u Group
Home Reef
Disney Reef
Ofolanga Ha'ano
Tofua Kao Foa Ha'apai
Lifuka Ha'apai Group
Uiha
Kotu Group Mango Oto Tolu Group
Fonuafo'ou Nomuka Tonumea
Hunga Ha'apai Nomuka Group

TONGA

Nuku'alofa Tongatapu
TBU Eua
Tongatapu Group

YAP
1: 830 000
0 10 km
5 0 5 miles
R
Rumung
Mechol Omin
Runu Map
Tageren Canal
Okau 173 Tomil Gagil-Tomil
PACIFIC Yap Kanif Colonia
OCEAN (Micronesia) YAP
Nif Tabunifi Tomil Harbor
Gorror S

CHUUK
on same scale as Yap
Falas I. Fanuet I.
17 18
Aga I. Falo I.
Chuuk Weno △369
T (Micronesia)
PACIFIC Chuuk Moen
OCEAN Ulalu I. Lagoon Nomoneas Tonoas
Faichuk Eot I. Fefan I.
Udot I. Param I.
Lemotol B. 446 Tarik I.
Fala I. Uman I.
U Tol I. Beguets I. Tsis I.

SAMOA
Asau Safune
Falelima △1858 Pu'apu'a
Savai'i Salelologa
Sataua Satupa'itea Taga Mulifanua API Apia
Manono △1116 Siumu Falefa
Falelatai Apolima Lefaga Amaile
OLE PUPU PU'E 'Upolu
Safata Bay

AMERICAN SAMOA
(U.S.A.)
AMERICAN SAMOA Ofu Olosega
Tutuila Pago Pago Aunu'u Ta'ū
Leone PPG Luma Manu'a Is.
Vaitogi AMERICAN SAMOA

SAMOAN ISLANDS

Projection: Mercator

SOUTH-WEST PACIFIC
Political 1:94 000 000

130 East from Greenwich Saipan Northern 170 West from Greenwich
PHILIPPINES Guam (U.S.A.) Marianas (U.S.A.) MARSHALL IS. PACIFIC
Yap Caroline Is. Chuuk Palikir Majuro OCEAN
Melekeok FEDERATED STATES Pohnpei
PALAU OF MICRONESIA Tarawa Gilbert Is.
Yaren NAURU KIRIBATI
INDONESIA Equator Line Is.
PAPUA Port Moresby NEW GUINEA Phoenix Is.
SOLOMON TUVALU Tokelau Is. (N.Z.)
IS. Honiara Fongafale SAMOA
AUSTRALIA VANUATU Wallis & Futuna (Fr.) Apia American Samoa (U.S.A.)
Port Vila Suva Niue (N.Z.) Cook Is. (N.Z.)
New Caledonia (Fr.) FIJI TONGA FRENCH
Nouméa Nuku'alofa POLYNESIA

SOLOMON ISLANDS

COPYRIGHT PHILIP'S

ft m
6000 2000
4500 1500
3000 1000
1200 400
600 200
0 0
200 600
1000 3000
2000 6000
4000 12 000
6000 18 000
m ft

Equatorial Scale 1:43 200 000

OKINAWA
on same scale as Palau
a

Hedo-misaki Hedo
Kunigami
Ie-shima Kourishima Yagaji-shima 503 Yonaha-Dake
Seseko-shima Nakijin
Minna-shima Motobu
Nago-wan Nago Arume-wan Banno-saki

Okinawa (Japan)

EAST CHINA SEA

Onna Ishikawa Kin-wan Ikei-shima
Kadena Uruma
Kadena Henna
Ginowan Heanza-shima
Tsuken-jima
Naha Nakagusuku-wan Kudaka-shima
OKA Shuri Takabanare-shima
Urasoe Gushikami
Rukan-sho
Kyan-zaki Itoman

PACIFIC OCEAN

128° E

IWO-JIMA
b
Kangoku Kitano Hana
Iwa
Iwo-Jima (Japan) Hanare Iwa
Kama 108
Iwa IWO JIMA AIRFIELD
Suribachi COAST GUARD STATION
Yama 167 Fatatsu Ne
Tobiishi Hana

PACIFIC OCEAN

141° 20' E

IWO-JIMA
1: 200 000
1 0 1 2 3 km
1 0 1 2 m

PALAU
c
Ngaregur
Konrei
Ngardmau Bay
Ngardmau 218
Babelthuap I. Namai Bay
Melekeok
Komebail Koror
Lagoon ROR
Malakal Harbor Garusuun
Aulong Garreru
Apurashokoru Koror I.
Ngobasango
Orukuizul Sar Passage
Shonian Harbor Eil Malk I.
Barnum Bay Ngeregong
Ngergoi
Ngesebus Kongauru I.
Ngardololok
Peleliu I.

PACIFIC OCEAN

Angaur I.

7° N

1:1 550 000
10 0 10 20 30 km
10 0 10 20 miles

NEW CALEDONIA
d
1:5 750 000
50 0 50 100 km
50 0 50 miles

Îles Belep
Récif de Cook
Île Art
Récif de l'Astrolabe
Poum
Nouvelle-Calédonie (France)
Ouégoa Pouébo
Île Balabio
Koumac Mt. Panié 1628
Hienghène
Kaala-Gomén
Voh Poindimié
Koné Ponérihouen
Poya Houaïlou
3566 Canala Île Ouvéa
Fayaoué
C. Escarpé 7570
Wé Île Lifou
La Foa Mou
Bouraïl C. de
Boulouparis 1818 Flotte
Mt. Humbolt La Roche
Paita Thio Île Tiga
NOU Drambéa Yaté
2212 Île Maré
Nouméa Mont Dore
Ndoua Île des Pins
Grand Récif Sud

165° E 166° E

CORAL SEA

RUSSIA

Okhotsk
Irkutsk Lena Chita
Oz. Baykal Blagoveshchensk
Ulaanbaatar Khabarovsk
Amur

Sea of Okhotsk

Sakhalin
Poluostrov Kamchatka
Petropavlovsk-Kamchatskiy

Kuril'skiye Ostrova (Russia)
La Pérouse Str.
Kuril-Kamchatka Trench
10,542

Near Is.
Komandorskiye Ostrova (Russia)
Aleutian Basin
Andreano
Shirshov Ridge
7822
Aleutian Trench

MONGOLIA

Ürümqi
Changchun
Harbin
Sapporo
Hokkaidō
Hakodate

CHINA

Shenyang
Beijing NORTH KOREA
Tianjin Dalian Seoul
Taiyuan SOUTH KOREA Nagoya
Lanzhou Qingdao Kyōto
Huang He Sendai
Xi'an Yellow Sea Kitakyūshū Osaka JAPAN
Nanjing Shikoku
Chengdu Wuhan Shanghai Kyūshū
Chongqing Hangzhou East China Sea
Chang J. Changsha Fuzhou
Kunming Taipei
Guangzhou TAIWAN
Macau Hong Kong

Vladivostok
Sea of Japan
Honshū
Fuji-San Tōkyō
3776 Yokohama

Pacific

Shatsky Rise
Northwest

Emperor Seamount Chain

Midway Is. (U.S.A.)

Lisianski I. (U.S.A.)

Iwo-Jima (Japan)
Ogasawara Gunto (Japan)
Kazan-Rettō (Japan)
Minami-Tori-Shima (Japan)
Wake I. (U.S.A.)

Basin

XIZANG
Kunlun Shan
Lhasa
Brahmaputra
Dhaka
Mandalay
BURMA
Irrawaddy
LAOS
Hanoi
Rangoon
THAILAND
Bangkok CAMBODIA
Phnom Penh
Mekong Thanh Pho Ho Chi Minh
G. of Thailand

SRI LANKA
Colombo
Nicobar Is. (India)

MALAYSIA 4101
Kuala Lumpur PEN. MALAYSIA
Singapore
SARAWAK SABAH
BRUNEI

Sumatra
Palembang Java Sea
Jakarta
Surabaya
Sunda Trench (Java Trench)

INDONESIA

INDIAN OCEAN

Cocos Is. (Austral.)
Christmas I. (Austral.)

Ninetyeast Ridge
Wharton Basin
Broken Ridge

South China Sea
Hainan
Luzon
Paracel Is.
Manila
PHILIPPINES
Mindoro
Palawan Samar
Sulu Sea Mindanao
Davao
Celebes Sea
Philippine Trench

Philippine Sea
C. Engano
West Mariana Basin
NORTHERN MARIANAS (U.S.A.)
Tinian Saipan
GUAM (U.S.A.)
Challenger Deep 11,022
Mariana Trench

East Mariana Basin

MARSHALL IS.
Bikini Ratak Chain
Enewetak Atoll
Kwajalein
Majuro
Jaluit I.

Micronesia
Yap Caroline Is. Chuuk
FED. STATES OF MICRONESIA
Melekeok Pohnpei
PALAU Palikir
West Caroline Basin East Caroline Basin
Eauripik Rise

Melanesia
Solomon Rise
Melanesian Basin
Butaritari
Tarawa
Nauru
NAURU
Banaba
Gilbert Is.

Howland I.
Baker I.
Phoenix Is.
Abariringa
Enderbury

Pacific

International Date Line

Halmahera
Seram
Buru
Banda Sea
Flores Sea
Bali Flores
Sumbawa Sumba
Dili EAST TIMOR
Arafura Sea
Torres Strait
C. York

Sulawesi
Makassar
Maluku

New Guinea
Admiralty Is. New Ireland
Bismarck Arch.
PAPUA NEW GUINEA
Puncak Jaya 4884 PAPUA
Lae New Britain
Kokopo Bougainville
Port Moresby
Louisiade Arch.
Honiara
Guadalcanal
SOLOMON IS.
Santa Cruz Is. 9165

Yaren
Fongafale
TUVALU
Tokelau (N.Z.)
Rotuma
Is. Wallis & Futuna (Fr.)
VANUATU
Espiritu Santo
Port Vila
Îs. Chesterfield
7570
West Fiji Basin
Vanua Levu
Viti Levu
FIJI
Suva
Nuku'alofa
Tonga Trench

AUSTRALIA
Darwin
C. Arnhem
Gulf of Carpentaria
North Australian Basin
Cairns
Townsville
Mount Isa
Alice Springs
Broome
L. Eyre
Great Dividing Ra.
Exmouth Plateau
North West C.
Rockhampton
Brisbane
Geraldton
Perth Basin
Perth Naturaliste Plateau
Albany
Great Australian Bight
Adelaide
Murray
Canberra
Sydney
Mt. Kosciuszko 2228
Melbourne
Bass Str.
Tasmania
Hobart
South Australian Basin
South Tasman Rise

Coral Sea
Great Barrier Reef
Coral Sea Basin
NEW CALEDONIA (Fr.)
Nouméa
Is. Loyauté
Middleton Basin
Norfolk I. (Austral.)
Lord Howe I. (Austral.)
Lord Howe Rise
New Caledonia Trough
Norfolk Ridge
South Fiji Basin
Kermadec Is. (N.Z.)
Kermadec Trench
10,822
10,047

Tasman Sea
East Tasman Plateau
Tasman Basin

NEW ZEALAND
Auckland
Cook Strait
Wellington
Aoraki Mt. Cook 3753
Christchurch
Chatham Rise
Dunedin
Invercargill
Bounty Trough
Bounty Is. (N.Z.)
Antipodes Is. (N.Z.)
Auckland Is. (N.Z.)
Campbell Plateau
Campbell I.
Macquarie I. (Austral.)

SOUTHERN OCEAN

Projection: Mollweide's Homolographic
East from Greenwich

Main Map

Arctic Circle
ALASKA (U.S.A.)
Anchorage
Bristol Bay
Gulf of Alaska
CANADA
Juneau
Prince of Wales I. (U.S.A.)
Haida Gwaii (Queen Charlotte Is.) (Canada)
Edmonton
Calgary
Vancouver
Vancouver I.
Victoria
Seattle
Portland
Boise
Salt Lake City
Denver
Tufts Abyssal Plain
Northeast
Mendocino Fracture Zone
C. Mendocino
Sacramento
San Francisco
Murray Fracture Zone
Pacific
Los Angeles
San Diego
Phoenix
UNITED STATES
Oklahoma City
Dallas
Memphis
Atlanta
Houston
San Antonio
Jacksonville
New Orleans
Ciudad Juárez
Gulf of Mexico
Miami
BAHAMAS
Monterrey
Guadalupe (Mex.)
Tropic of Cancer
Basin
Molokai Fracture Zone
Baja California
Golfo de California
La Habana
CUBA
Honolulu
O'ahu
HAWAI'I (U.S.A.)
Hawai'i
Guadalajara
Mexico
Puebla
Mérida
HAITI
Kingston
JAMAICA
Acapulco
Clarion Fracture Zone
Is. de Revillagigedo (Mex.)
BELIZE
GUATEMALA
Caribbean Sea
Middle America Trench
San Salvador
EL SALVADOR
HONDURAS
Managua
NICARAGUA
Barranquilla
San José
COSTA RICA
Colón
Panamá
PANAMA
Medellín
Cali
COLOMBIA
I. del Coco (Costa Rica)
I. de Malpelo (Colombia)
Î. Clipperton (Fr.)
Clipperton Fracture Zone
Guatemala Basin
Cocos Ridge
Panama Basin
Palmyra Is. (U.S.A.)
Teraina
Tabuaeran
Kiritimati
Jarvis I. (U.S.A.)
Cooper Ridge
Equator
Galapagos Fracture Zone
Galápagos (Ecuador)
Carnegie Ridge
Quito
ECUADOR
Guayaquil
C. Pariñas
KIRIBATI
Malden I.
Starbuck I.
Caroline I. (Millennium I.)
Vostok I.
Flint I.
Nuku Hiva
Îs. Marquises
Hiva Oa
Marquesas Fracture Zone
Yupanqui Basin
Mendaña Fracture Zone
Peru Basin
Trujillo
PERU
Lima
Cusco
L. Titicaca
Arequipa
Nevado Ancohuma
La Paz
BOLIVIA
Arica
Iquique
Chile Basin
Antofagasta
CHILE
Penrhyn (Tongareva)
Manihiki
Pukapuka
Suwarrow Is.
Cook Is. (N.Z.)
Aitutaki
Atiu
Rarotonga
Mangaia
Îs. de la Société
Bora Bora
Huahine
Raiatéa
Papeete
Tahiti
FRENCH POLYNESIA
Îs. Tuamotu
Rangiroa
Îs. Gambier
Mururoa
Îs. Tubuaï
Tropic of Capricorn
Oeno I.
Henderson I.
Ducie I.
Pitcairn I. (U.K.)
Rapa
Easter Fracture Zone
Sala-y-Gómez (Chile)
I. de Pascua (Chile)
Sala y Gómez Ridge
Nasca Ridge
San Félix (Chile)
San Ambrosio (Chile)
PARAGUAY
Asunción
San Miguel de Tucumán
Pôrto Alegre
Roggeveen Basin
Arch. de Juan Fernández (Chile)
Valparaíso
Aconcagua
Santiago
Córdoba
Rosario
Buenos Aires
URUGUAY
Montevideo
Río de la Plata
Concepción
ARGENTINA
Southwest Pacific Basin
Challenger Fracture Zone
Chile Rise
Menard Fracture Zone
Nemo Point
Pacific-Antarctic Ridge
Southeast Pacific Basin
Punta Arenas
Est. de Magallanes
Tierra del Fuego
C. de Hornos
Drake Passage
ATLANTIC OCEAN
Falkland Is. (U.K.)
Falkland Plateau
Argentine Basin
Georgia Basin
South Georgia (U.K.)
South Georgia Ridge
West from Greenwich
COPYRIGHT PHILIP'S

Inset: TAHITI (1:1 150 000)

Papeete
Moorea
Mt. Aorai
Mt. Orohena 2241
Tahiti (France)
Faaa
Pirae
Punaauia
Presqu'île de Taiarapu

Inset: FRENCH POLYNESIA (1:26 000 000)

Îles Marquises
Nuku Hiva
Ua Huka
Ua Pu
Hiva Oa
Tahuata
Îles du Roi-Georges
Îles Tuamotu
Îles de la Société
Tahiti
Îles Tubuaï (Îles Australes)
Îles Gambier

Inset: NIUE (1:830 000)

Niue (N.Z.)
Alofi
PACIFIC OCEAN

Inset: RAROTONGA (1:415 000)

Rarotonga (N.Z.)
Avarua
Avatiu Harbour
PACIFIC OCEAN

NORTH AMERICA

1:28 000 000

Projection: Bonne

West from Greenwich

COPYRIGHT PHILIP'S

1:28 000 000

100 0 200 400 600 800 1000 1200 1400 km
100 0 200 400 600 800 1000 miles

Projection: *Bonne*

7 ■ MÉXICO Capital Cities 8   9   West from Greenwich   10   11   12

COPYRIGHT PHILIP'S

1:12 000 000

Projection: Bonne

West from Greenwich

NORTHERN CANADA
continuation northwards on same scale as main map

COPYRIGHT PHILIP'S

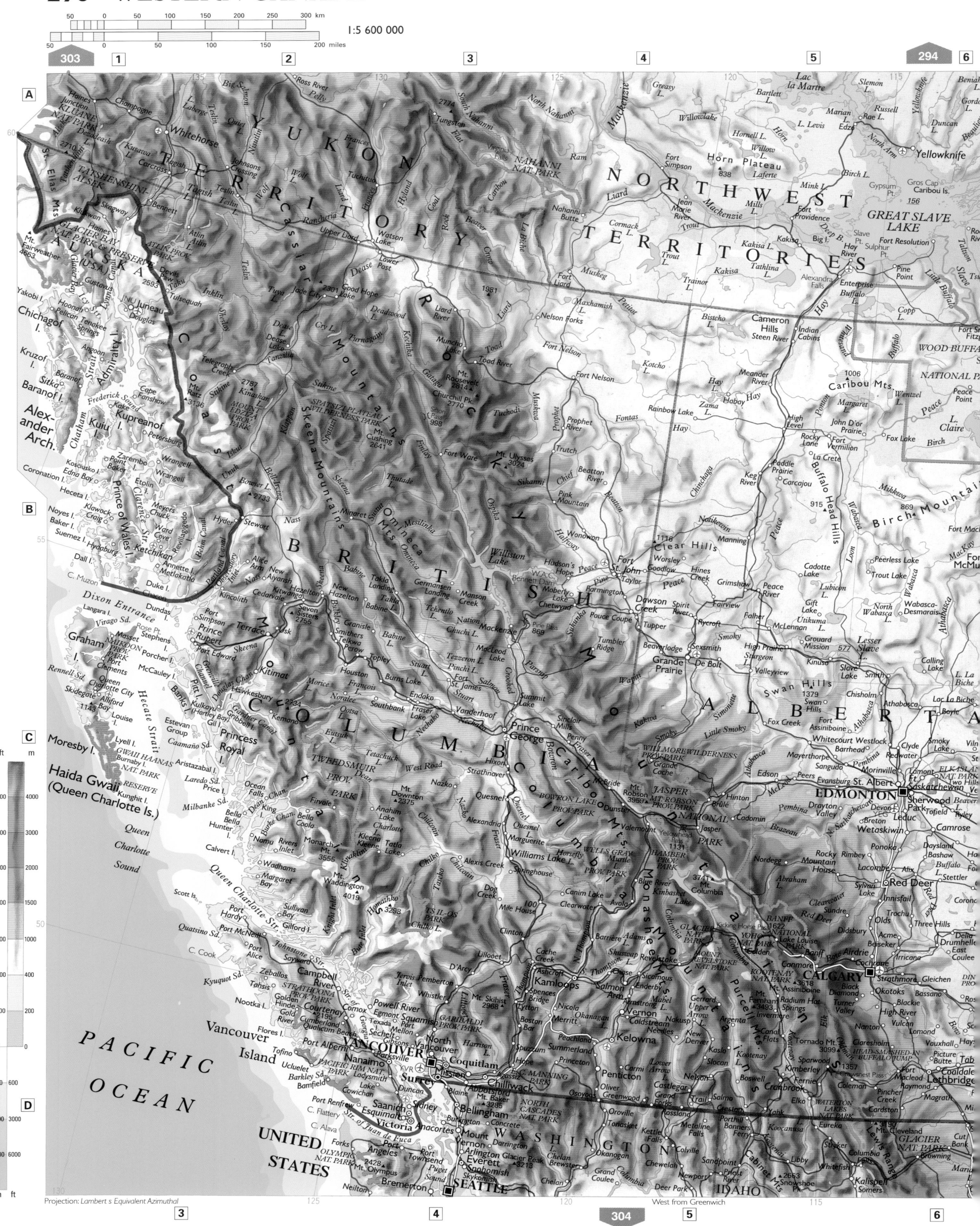

1:5 600 000

50   0   50   100   150   200   250   300 km

50   0   50   100   150   200 miles

Projection: Lambert's Equivalent Azimuthal

West from Greenwich

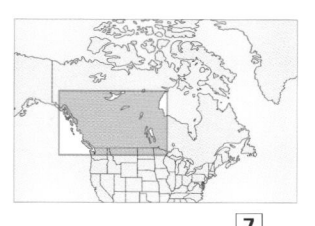

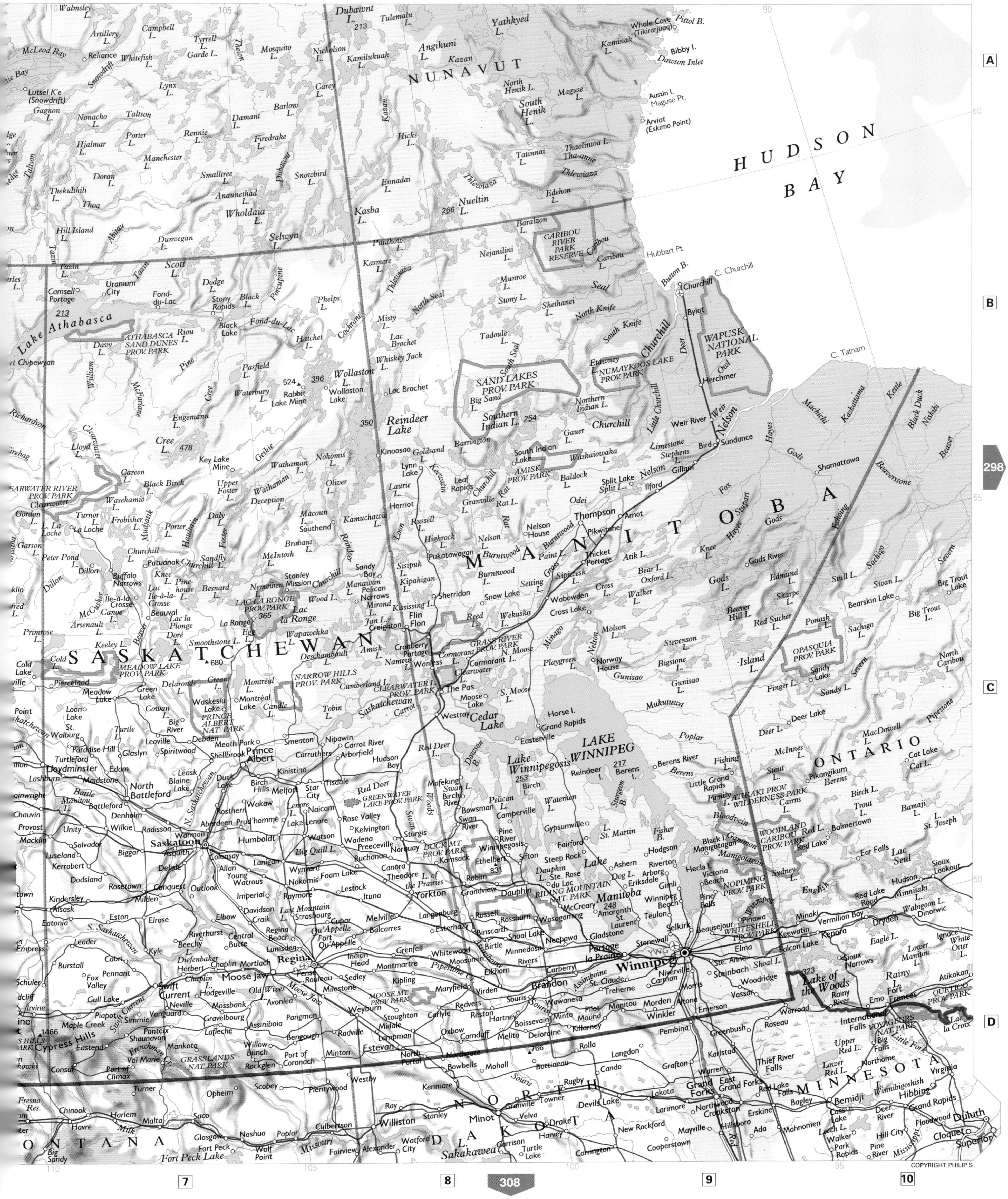
7
8
9
10
11
A
B
C
D
298
308
NUNAVUT
HUDSON
BAY
MANITOBA
SASKATCHEWAN
ONTARIO
MINNESOTA
NORTH DAKOTA
MONTANA
Lake Athabasca
Reindeer Lake
LAKE WINNIPEG
Lake Winnipegosis
Lake Manitoba
Cedar Lake
Lake of the Woods
Dubawnt L.
Yathkyed L.
Nueltin L.
Kasba L.
Wollaston L.
Southern Indian L.
Churchill
C. Churchill
C. Tatnam
Hubbart Pt.
Whale Cove (Tikirarjuaq)
Arviat (Eskimo Point)
WAPUSK NATIONAL PARK
SAND LAKES PROV. PARK
CARIBOU RIVER PARK RESERVE
NUMAYKOOS LAKE PROV. PARK
ATHABASCA SAND DUNES PROV. PARK
PRINCE ALBERT NAT. PARK
RIDING MOUNTAIN NAT. PARK
GRASSLANDS NAT. PARK
VOYAGEURS NAT. PARK
QUETICO PROV. PARK
Uranium City
Fond-du-Lac
Lynn Lake
Thompson
Gillam
Flin Flon
The Pas
La Ronge
Prince Albert
North Battleford
Lloydminster
Saskatoon
Regina
Moose Jaw
Swift Current
Yorkton
Brandon
Portage la Prairie
Winnipeg
Selkirk
Dauphin
Kenora
Dryden
Fort Frances
Estevan
Weyburn
Minot
Williston
Grand Forks
Devils Lake
Bemidji
Duluth
Cypress Hills
COPYRIGHT PHILIP'S

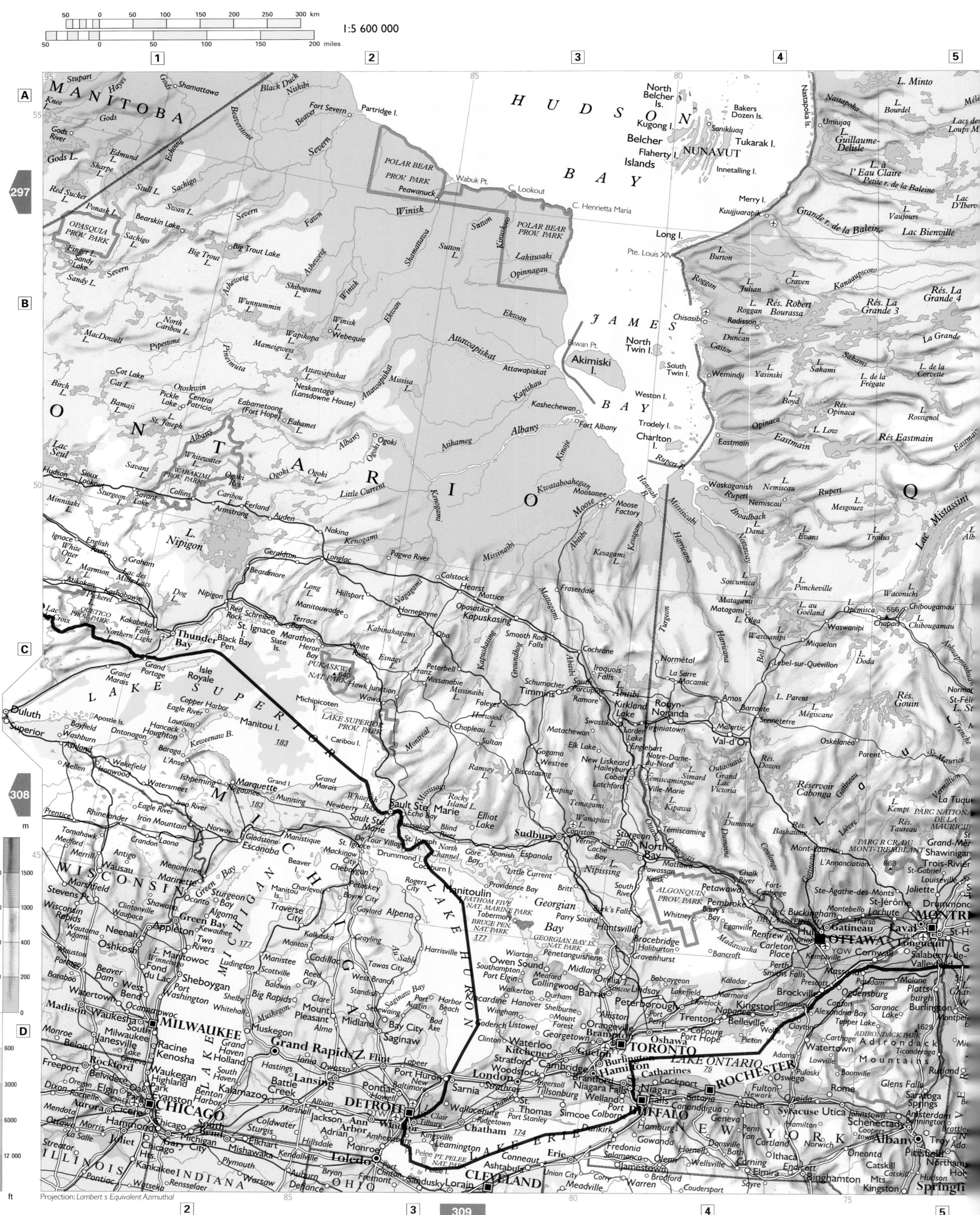

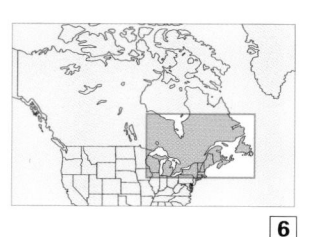

LABRADOR SEA

NEWFOUNDLAND & LABRADOR

QUÉBEC

Labrador

GULF OF ST. LAWRENCE

ATLANTIC OCEAN

NEW BRUNSWICK

PRINCE EDWARD ISLAND

NOVA SCOTIA

MAINE

UNITED STATES

BOSTON

Cabot Strait

ST-PIERRE-ET-MIQUELON (France)

Halifax

St. John's

Corner Brook

Gander

Sept-Îles

Labrador City

Happy Valley-Goose Bay

Churchill Falls

Smallwood Reservoir

Île d'Anticosti

Pén. de la Gaspésie

Cape Breton Island

West from Greenwich

COPYRIGHT PHILIP'S

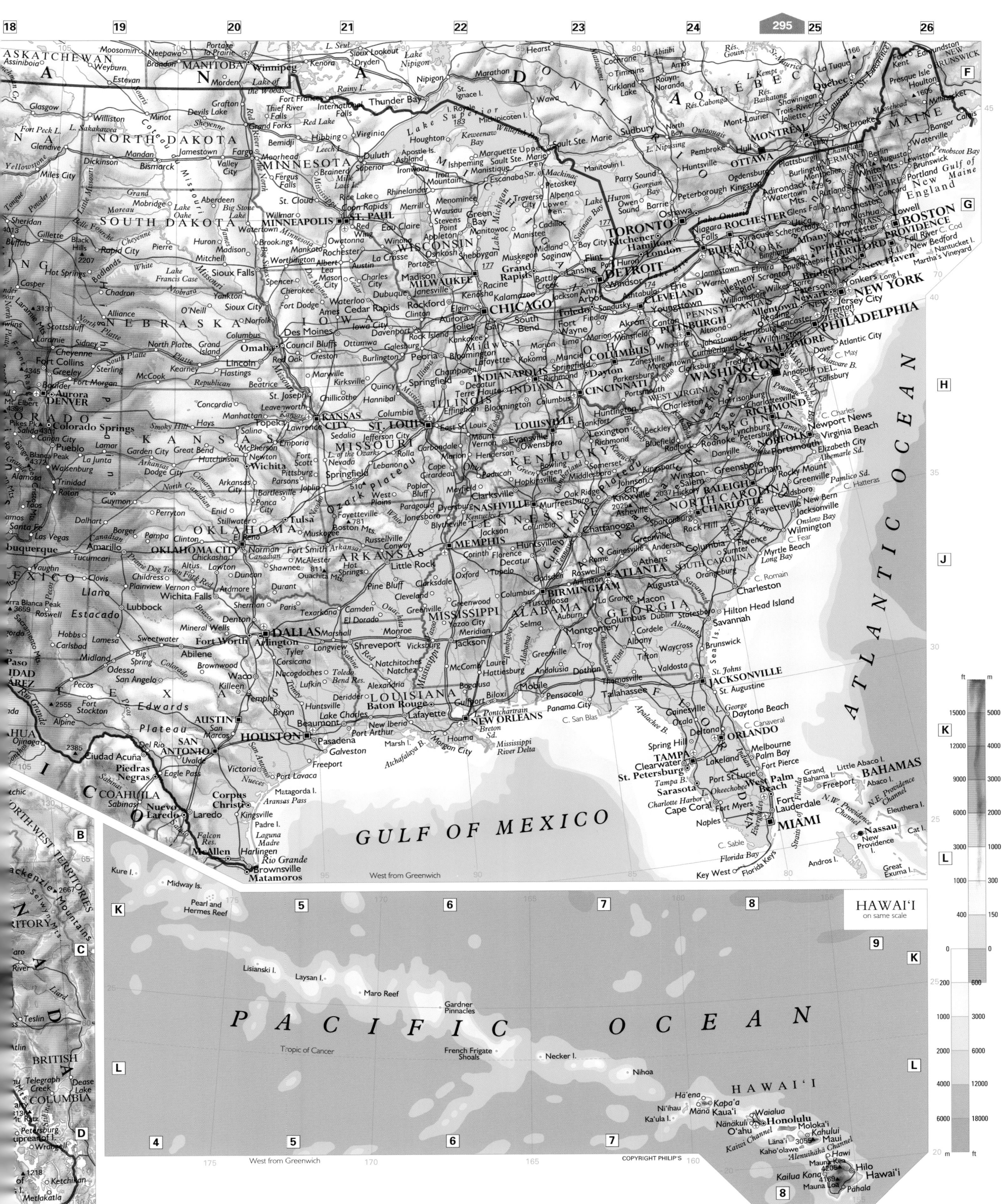

Midway Is.
Northern Marianas
Saipan
Tinian
Guam
Wake I.
Hawaiʻi
American Samoa

HAWAIʻI
1: 2 500 000
Projection: Lambert's Conformal Conic
KAUAI COUNTY
Kauaʻi
Niʻihau
Lehua I.
Pāniʻau
Puʻuwai
Kawaihoa Pt.
Nāpali Coast
Princeville
Kīlauea
Anahola
Kapaʻa
Wailua
Hanamaulu
Līhuʻe
LIH
Waimea
Kekaha
Hanapēpē
Kalaheo
Kawaikini
Waiʻaleʻale
Kaulakahi Channel
Kauai Channel
PACIFIC OCEAN
Oʻahu
Kahuku Pt.
Lāʻie
HONOLULU COUNTY
Kaʻena Pt.
Waialua
Wahiawā
Kāneʻohe
Kailua
Waiʻanae
Nānākuli
Barbers Pt.
HNL
Honolulu
Makapuʻu Pt.
Pearl Hbr.
Kaiwi Channel
Molokaʻi
KALAWAO COUNTY
KALAUPAPA NAT. HIST. PARK
Kalaupapa
Hoʻolehua
Maunaloa
Kaunakakai
Kamalō
Kualapuʻu
Lāʻau Pt.
ʻĪlio Pt.
C. Hālawa
Pailolo Channel
Kalohi Channel
Lānaʻi
Lānaʻi City
Lānaʻihale
Palaoa Pt.
Nakalele Pt.
Kapalua
Napili-Honokowai
Lahaina
Wailuku
Kahului
OGG
Paia
Haiku-Pauwela
Maui
Pukalani
Makawao
Kīhei
Wailea-Makena
Molokini I.
Haleakalā
ROAD TO HĀNA
Hāna
HALEAKALĀ NAT. PARK
Puʻuʻulaʻula
Ulupalakua
Kealaikahiki Channel
Lua Makiki
MAUI COUNTY
Kahoʻolawe
Lae ʻo Kealaikahiki
Alalākeiki Channel
ʻAlenuihāhā Channel
Upolu Pt.
Hawi
Hawaiʻi
Kohala Mts.
Kukuihaele
Honokaʻa
Paʻauilo
Kawaihae Bay
PUʻUKOHOLĀ HEIAU NAT. HISTORIC SITE
Waimea (Kamuela)
Waikoloa Village
Kīholo Bay
Mauna Kea
Hilo Bay
Hilo
ITO
KOA
Keahole Pt.
Kalaoa
Hualālai
KALOKO-HONOKŌHAU NAT. HISTORICAL PARK
Kailua Kona
Holualoa
Honomu
Pepeekeo
Pāpaʻikou
Keaʻau
Mountain View
Kurtistown
Cape Kumukahi
Pāhoa
Kapoho
Opihikao
Kehena
Kalapana
Captain Cook
Hōnaunau
Kealakekua
Mauna Loa
Volcano
Kīlauea Caldera
PUʻUHONUA O HŌNAUNAU NAT. HISTORIC PARK
HAWAIʻI VOLCANOES NATIONAL PARK
Kaʻū Desert
Pāpā
Miloliʻi
Puʻuʻōkeʻokeʻo
Pāhala
Nāʻālehu
Kaunā Pt.
Pōhue Bay
Kalae
HAWAIʻI COUNTY
Projection: Albers Equal Area
West from Greenwich
HAWAIIAN ISLANDS
1:21 000 000
Kure I.
Midway Is.
HONOLULU COUNTY
Pearl and Hermes Reef
Lisianski I.
Laysan I.
Maro Reef
Gardner Pinnacles
French Frigate Shoals
Necker I.
Nihoa
Hawaiian Islands
PAPAHĀNAUMOKUĀKEA MARINE NAT. MONUMENT
Tropic of Cancer
OʻAHU
1: 500 000
Kahuku Pt.
Kawela
Waialeʻe
Kahuku
Sunset Beach
Pūpūkea
Waimea
Waimea Bay
Kawailoa Beach
KOʻOLAULOA
Lāʻie
POLYNESIAN CULTURAL CENTER
Hauʻula
Punaluʻu
Kahana Bay
Kaʻaʻawa
KAHANA VALLEY STATE PARK
North Shore
Kauai Channel
Puaʻena Pt.
Waialua Bay
Mokulēʻia
Haleʻiwa
Waialua
WAIALUA
Kaʻena
Kaʻena Pt.
Makua
MT. KAʻALA NAT. AREA RESERVE
PAHOLE NAT. AREA RESERVE
Kaʻala
Schofield Barracks
Whitmore Village
Wahiawā
WAHIAWA
Koʻolau Range
Waiʻanae Range
Kepuhi Pt.
Mākaha
Lahilahi Pt.
Pōkaʻī Bay
Kaneilio Pt.
Waiʻanae
Māʻili
Māʻili Pt.
WAIʻANAE
Mililani Town
Waipiʻo Acres
ʻEWA
Waipio
Pacific Palisades
Pearl City
Waipahu
Waimalu
Hālawa Heights
ʻAiea
Pearl Harbor
U.S.S. ARIZONA MEMORIAL
Ford I.
Salt Lake
Nānākuli
Palikea
Makakilo City
Kapolei
Honokai Hale
Kō ʻOlina
ʻEwa Villages
ʻEwa Beach
Barbers Pt.
Iroquois Point
Hickam Housing
HNL
Keʻehi Lagoon
Honolulu
HONOLULU
IOLANI PALACE
Sand I.
Waikīkī
Kapahulu
Diamond Head
Māmala Bay
Kāneʻohe
Kaneohe Station
Heʻeia
Kahaluʻu
Kualoa Pt.
Mokoliʻi I.
Kāneʻohe Bay
Kapapa I.
Mokumanu
Mōkapu Pt.
Mōkapu Peninsula
Kailua
Kailua Bay
Lanikai
Mokulua Is.
KOʻOLAUPOKO
Maunawili
Waimānalo
Waimānalo Bay
Waimānalo Beach
Mānana I.
Makapuʻu Pt.
Kuapā Pond
Hawaiʻi Kai
Hanauma Bay
Koko Head
Maunalua Bay
Kūpikipikiʻō Pt.
Niu Valley
Kaiwi Channel
HONOLULU COUNTY
PACIFIC OCEAN
Waiʻanae Coast
West from Greenwich
NORTHERN MARIANAS
1: 17 500 000
Farallon de Pajaros
Maug Is.
Asuncion
Agrihan
Pagan
Alamagan
Guguan
Sarigan
Anatahan
Farallon de Medinilla
Saipan
Tinian
Rota
Mariana Islands
Mariana Trench
Northern Marianas (U.S.A.)
Guam (U.S.A.)
Agana
PACIFIC OCEAN
WAKE I.
1:200 000
Toki Point
Peale Island
Kuku Point
Flipper Pt.
Heel Point
Lagoon
Boat Basin
Settlement
Wilkes Island
Wake I. (U.S.A.)
WAKE AIRFIELD
Peacock Point
PACIFIC OCEAN
MIDWAY IS.
1:200 000
Sand Islet
Middle Ground
North Breakers
Midway Islands (U.S.A.)
Seaward Roads
Anchorage
Sand Island
Welles Harbor
Eastern Island
MIDWAY AIRFIELD
Channel
PACIFIC OCEAN
GUAM
1: 800 000
Ritidian Pt.
Pati Pt.
Santa Ana
UAM
Mt. Santa Rosa
Yigo
Dededo
Tumon Bay
Tamuning
Agana Bay
GUM
Mongmong
Cabras I.
Apra Harbor
Piti
Agana (Hagåtña)
Barrigada
Guam (Guahan) (U.S.A.)
Orote Peninsula
WAR IN THE PACIFIC N.H.P.
Yona
Pago Bay
Agat
Santa Rita
Talofofo
Mt. Lamlam
Umatac
Merizo
Inarajan
Jalaihai Pt.
Cocos I.
Aga Pt.
PACIFIC OCEAN
SAIPAN & TINIAN
1: 800 000
Sabaneta Pt.
Tanapag
San Roque
Garapan
Capitol Hill
Mt. Tapochau
San Jose
San Vicente
Chalan Kanoa
Laulau B.
San Antonio
Saipan (U.S.A.)
SPN
Naftan Pt.
Tahgong Pt.
Saipan Channel
Tinian (U.S.A.)
Lananibot Pt.
Masalog Pt.
Diablo Pt.
San Jose
Tinian Channel
Carolinas Pt.
PACIFIC OCEAN
TUTUILA (AMER. SAMOA)
1: 640 000
Pola I.
Afono B.
Masefau B.
Cape Matatula
AMERICAN SAMOA
Vatia
Pago Pago
Aua
Tula
Fagasa
Fagatogo
Alofau
Aunuu
Fagamalo
Mt. Matafao
Amanave
Faleniu
Nuʻuuli
Leone
Vailoatai
Futiga
PPG
Taputimu
Vaitogi
Pago Pago Harbor
C. Taputapu
Steps Pt.
Tutuila (U.S.A.)
PACIFIC OCEAN
MANUA IS. (AMER. SAMOA)
1: 640 000
Asaga Str.
Olosega (U.S.A.)
Ofu
Piumafua Mt.
Olosega
Ofu (U.S.A.)
Siulagi Pt.
Luma
Maia
Leusoalii
Lata Mt.
AMERICAN SAMOA
Tau
Tau (U.S.A.)
Tufu Pt.
Siufaalele Pt.
PACIFIC OCEAN
1: 17 500 000
1:800 000
1: 200 000
1: 640 000
COPYRIGHT PHILIP'S

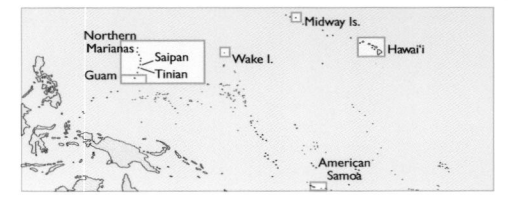

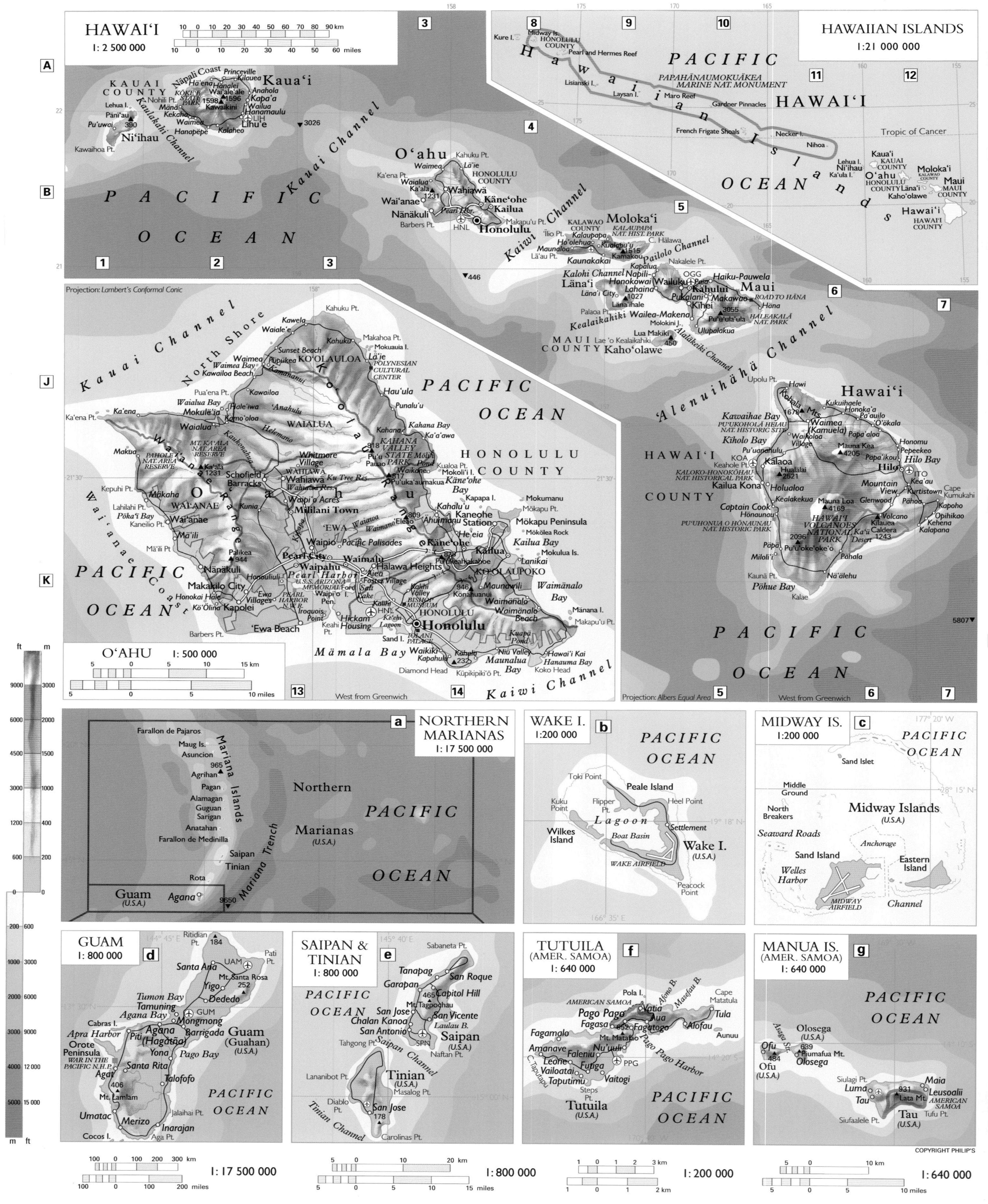

1:8 000 000

50 0 50 100 200 300 400 km
50 0 50 100 150 200 250 miles

continuation westwards
on same scale

RUSSIA

ARCTIC OCEAN

CHUKCHI SEA

BEAUFORT SEA

NORTH WEST TERRITORIES

CANADA

YUKON TERRITORY

BRITISH COLUMBIA

BERING SEA

Gulf of Alaska

PACIFIC OCEAN

Aleutian Islands

Alexander Archipelago

Kodiak I.

Alaska Peninsula

Seward Peninsula

Brooks Range

Mackenzie Mts.

1 ANCHORAGE
2 BRISTOL BAY
3 HAINES
4 SKAGWAY-HOONAH-ANGOON
5 KETCHIKAN GATEWAY

Projection : Bipolar oblique conic conformal

West from Greenwich

East from Greenwich

m ft

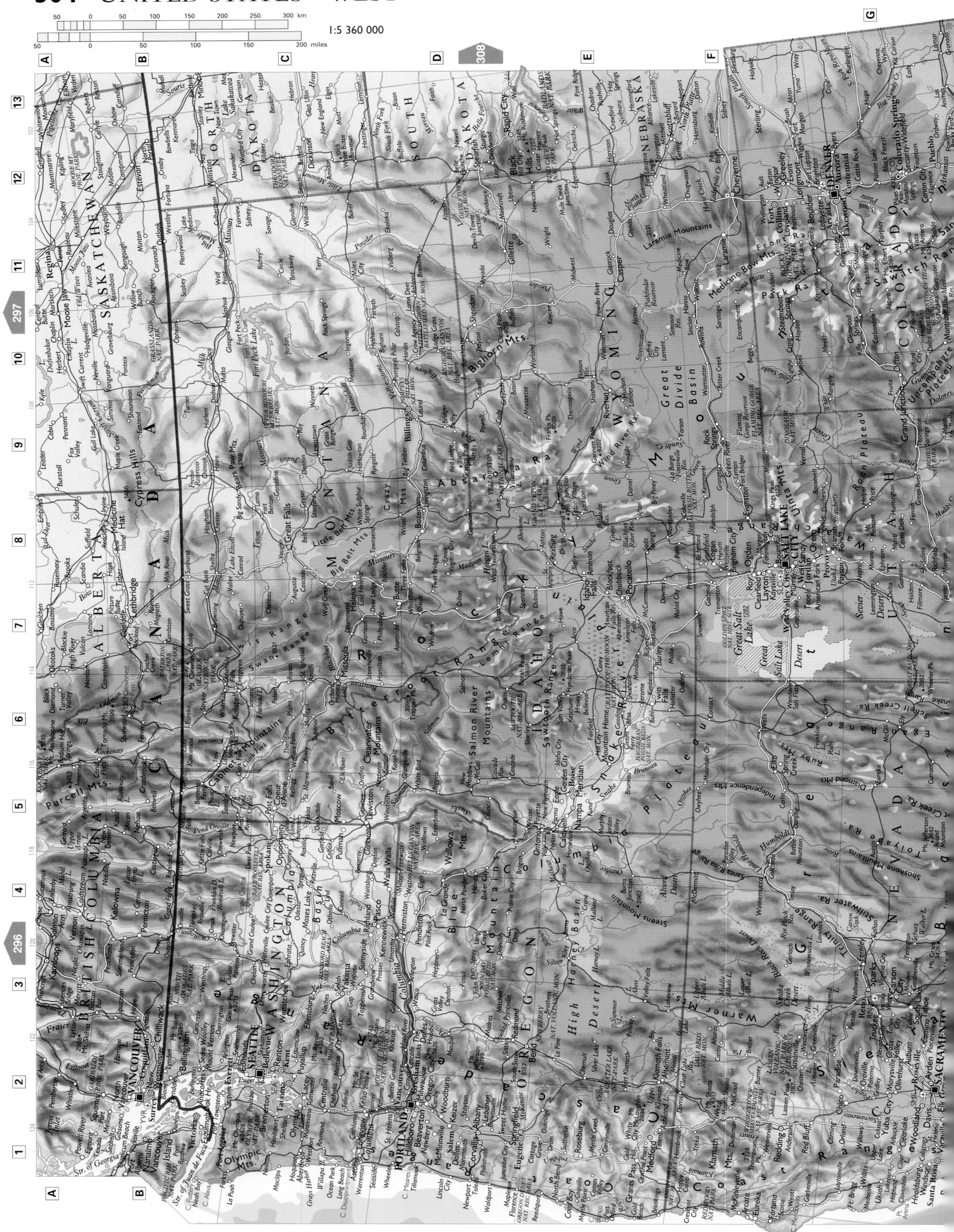

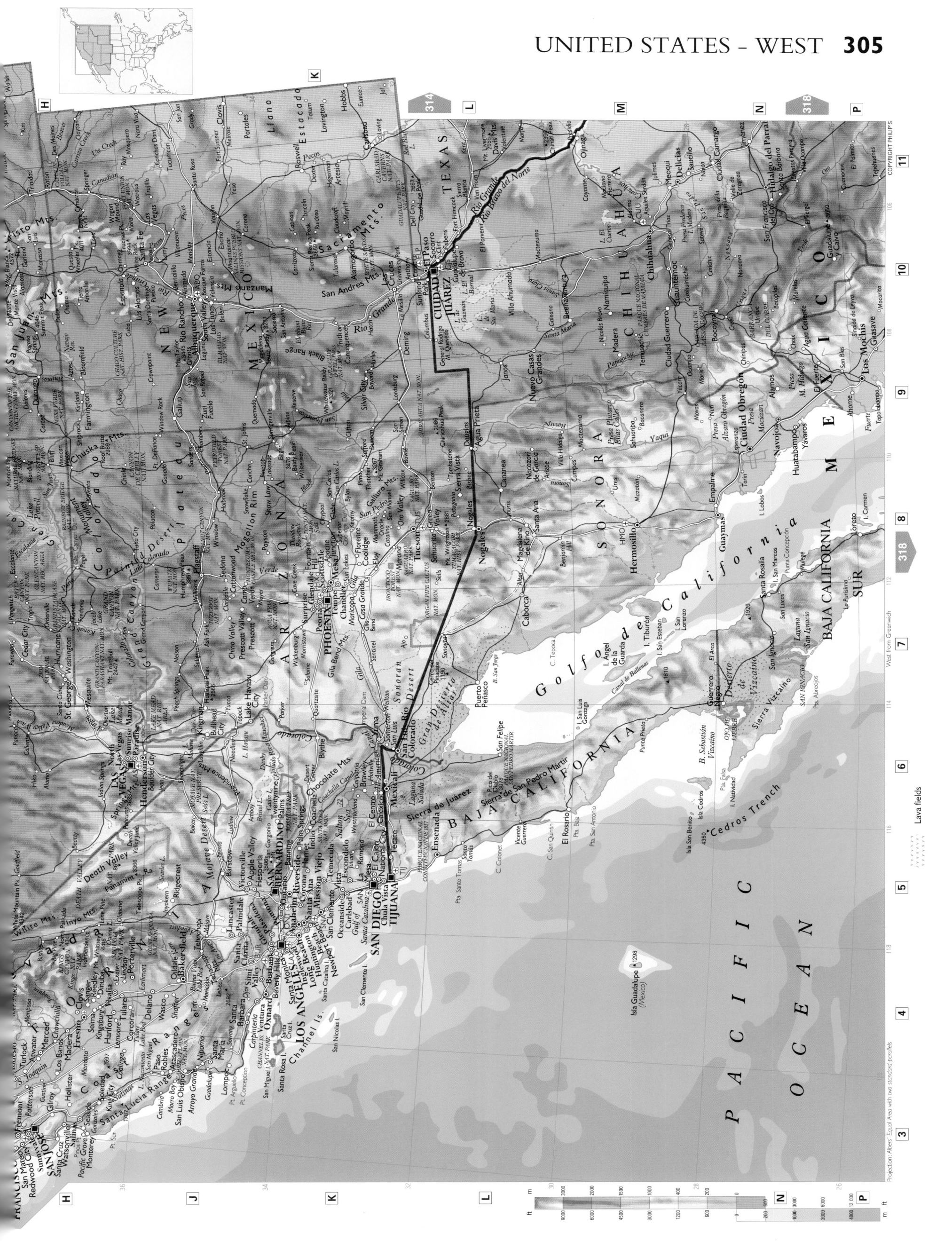

Lava fields

Projection: Albert Equal Area with two standard parallels

COPYRIGHT PHILIP'S

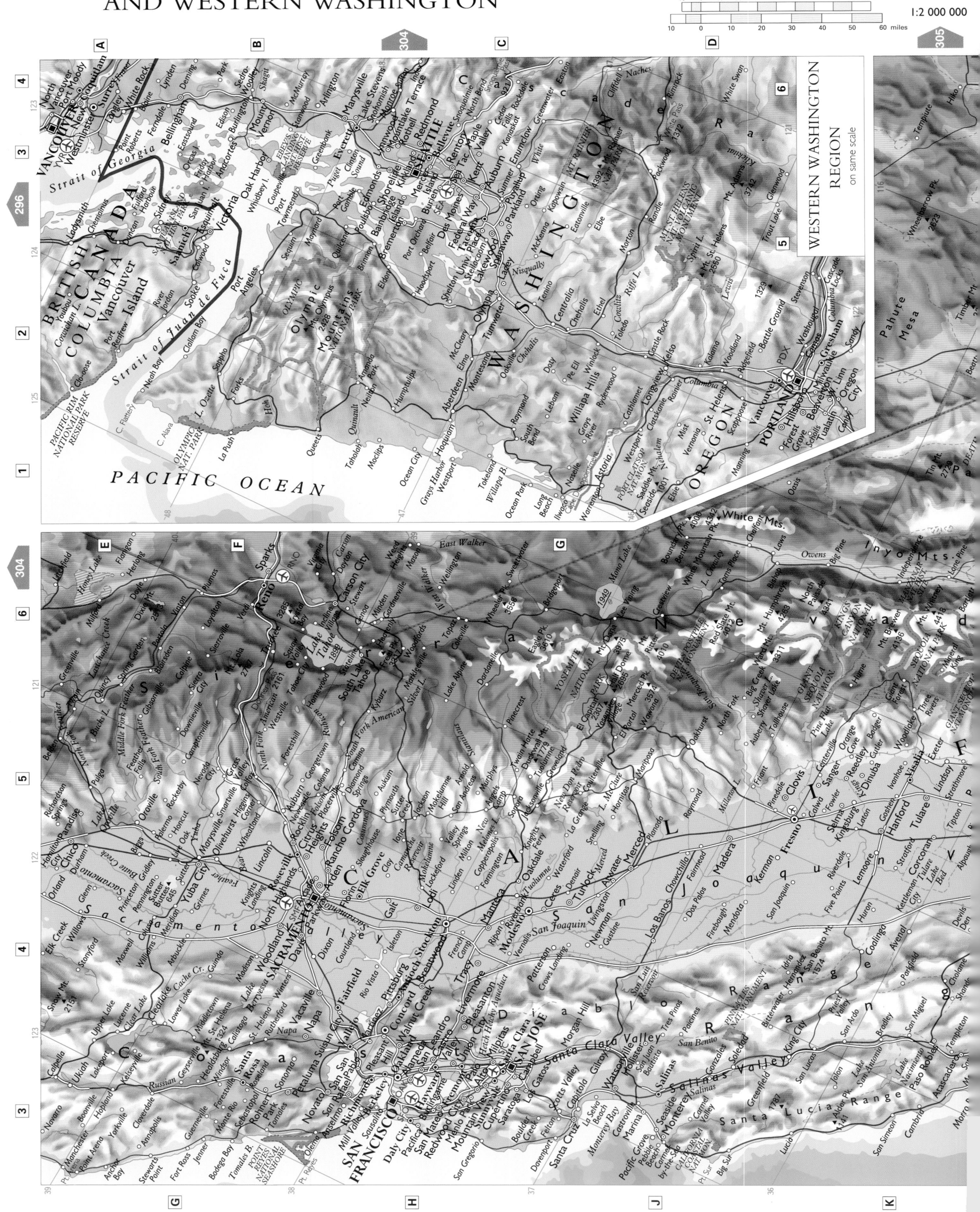

WESTERN WASHINGTON
REGION
on same scale

1:2 000 000

Lava fields

West from Greenwich

Projection: Bonne

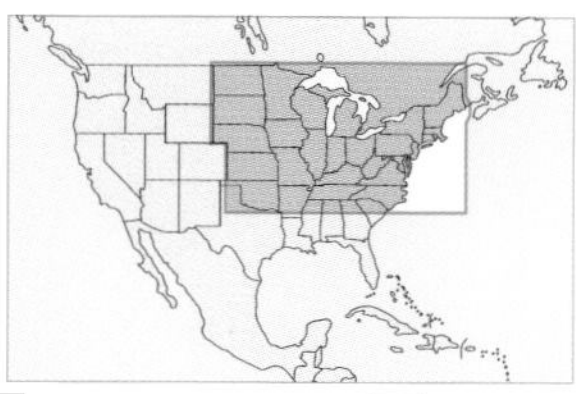

C A N A D A

O N T A R I O

Q U É B E C

MAINE

NEW HAMPSHIRE

VERMONT

NEW YORK

PENNSYLVANIA

OHIO

WEST VIRGINIA

VIRGINIA

MARYLAND

NEW JERSEY

NORTH CAROLINA

SOUTH CAROLINA

GEORGIA

LAKE HURON

LAKE ONTARIO

LAKE ERIE

LAKE SUPERIOR PROV. PARK

ALGONQUIN PROV. PARK

ADIRONDACK PARK

Gulf of Maine

A T L A N T I C   O C E A N

Chesapeake Bay

Delaware Bay

Major cities: Montreal, Ottawa, Toronto, Buffalo, Rochester, Detroit, Cleveland, Pittsburgh, Columbus, Cincinnati, Philadelphia, NEW YORK, Boston, Providence, Hartford, Baltimore, WASHINGTON D.C., Richmond, Norfolk, Raleigh, Charlotte, Atlanta, Québec, Sherbrooke, Syracuse, Albany, Springfield, Toledo, Columbia

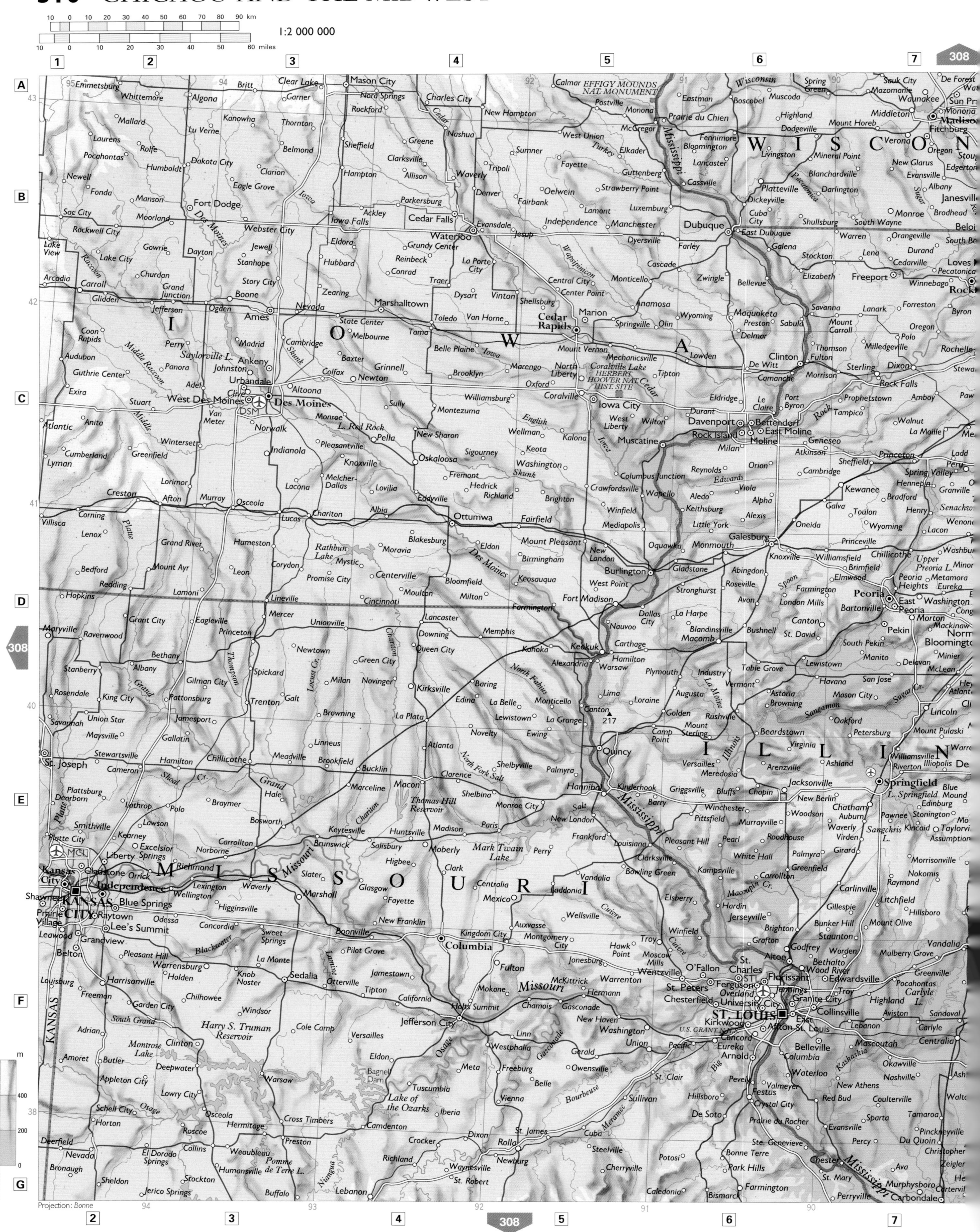

308

10 0 10 20 30 40 50 60 70 80 90 km
1:2 000 000
10 0 10 20 30 40 50 60 miles

Projection: Bonne

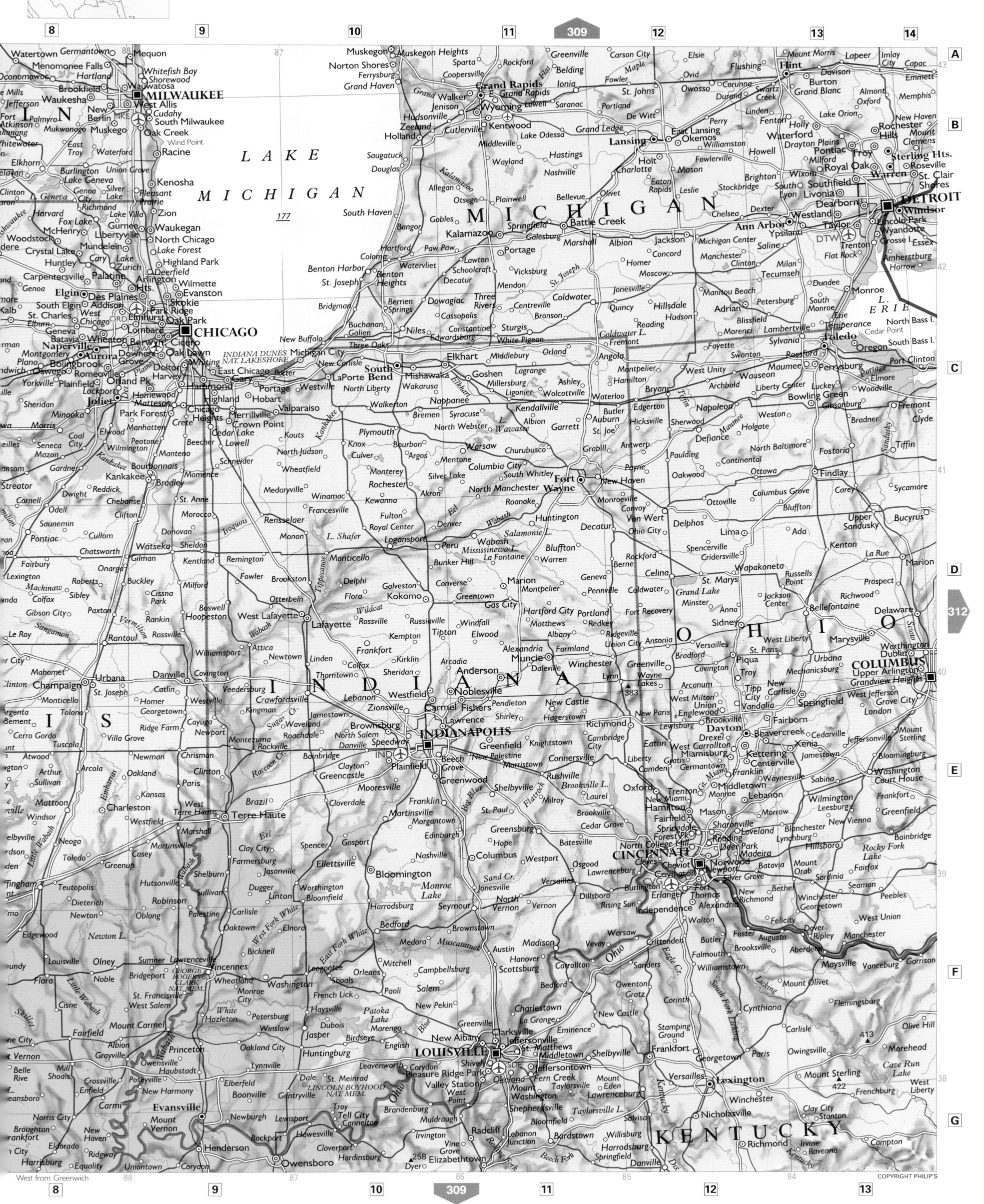

1:2 000 000

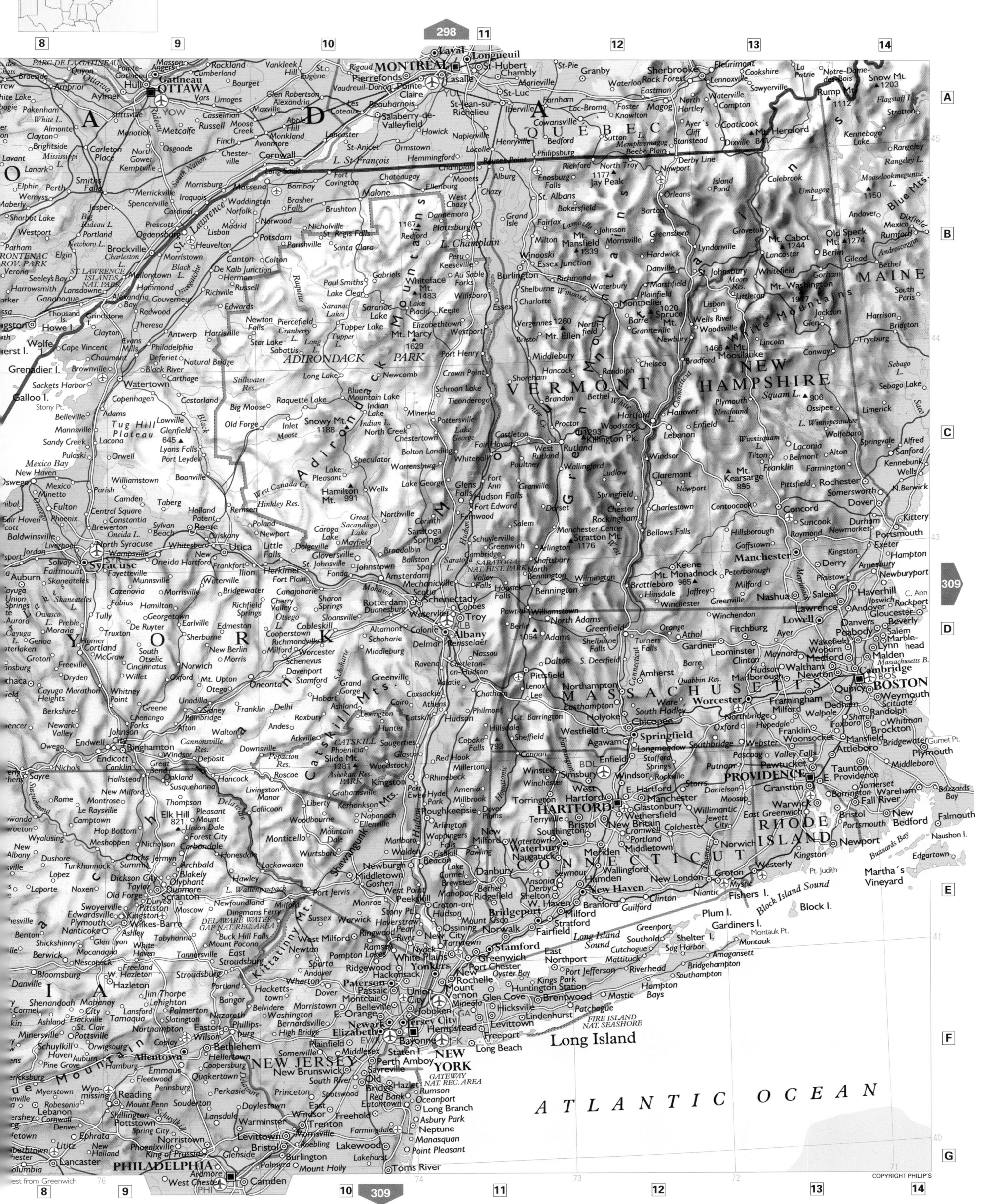

1:2 000 000

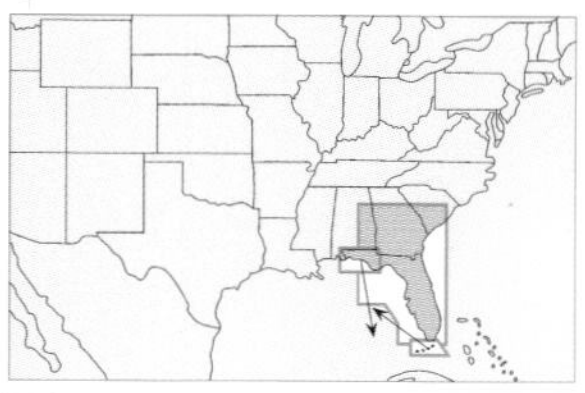

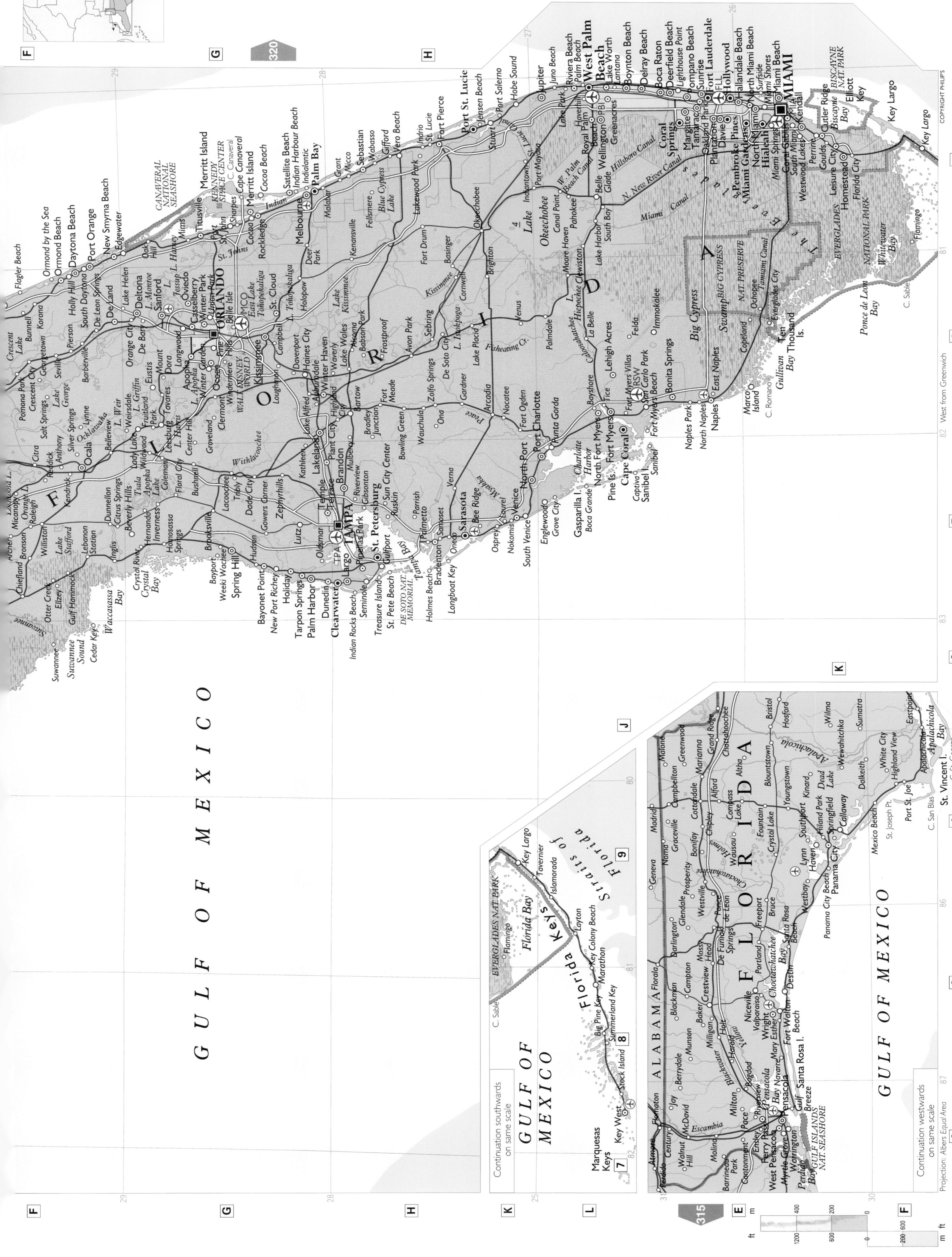

COPYRIGHT PHILIPS

GULF OF MEXICO

F L O R I D A

CANAVERAL NATIONAL SEASHORE

KENNEDY SPACE CENTER

WALT DISNEY WORLD

ORLANDO

TAMPA

St. Petersburg

Clearwater

MIAMI

West Palm Beach

Fort Lauderdale

Kissimmee

EVERGLADES NATIONAL PARK

BIG CYPRESS NAT. PRESERVE

BISCAYNE NAT. PARK

DE SOTO NAT. MEMORIAL

Continuation southwards on same scale

GULF OF MEXICO

Florida Keys

Florida Bay

Straits of Florida

Key West

Key Largo

Marathon

Islamorada

Tavernier

Marquesas Keys

Continuation westwards on same scale

F L O R I D A

A L A B A M A

GULF OF MEXICO

Apalachicola

Panama City

Pensacola

GULF ISLANDS NAT. SEASHORE

Projection: Albers Equal Area

315

320

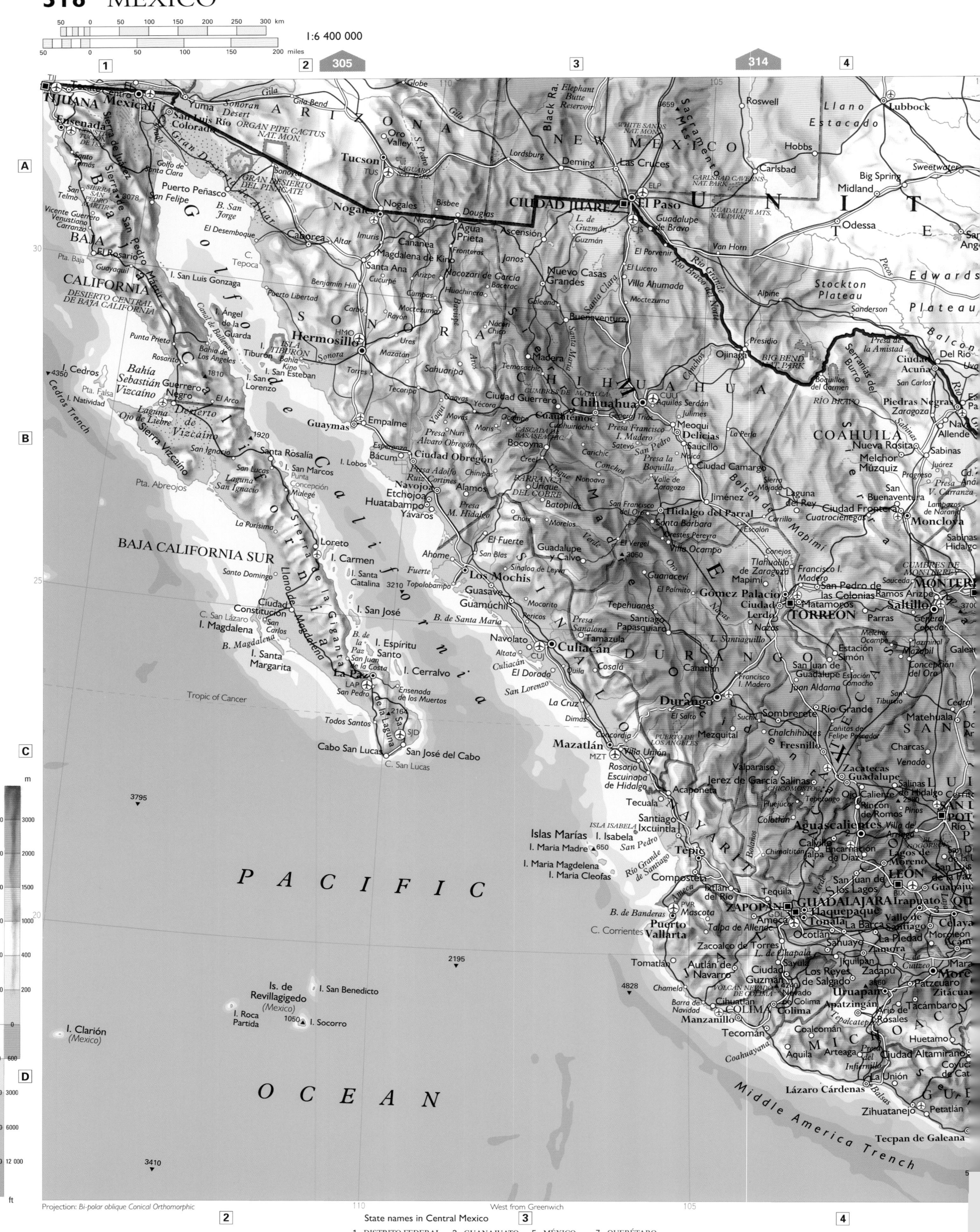

1:6 400 000

Projection: Bi-polar oblique Conical Orthomorphic

West from Greenwich

State names in Central Mexico

1 DISTRITO FEDERAL   3 GUANAJUATO   5 MÉXICO   7 QUERÉTARO
2 AGUASCALIENTES   4 HIDALGO   6 MORELOS   8 TLAXCALA

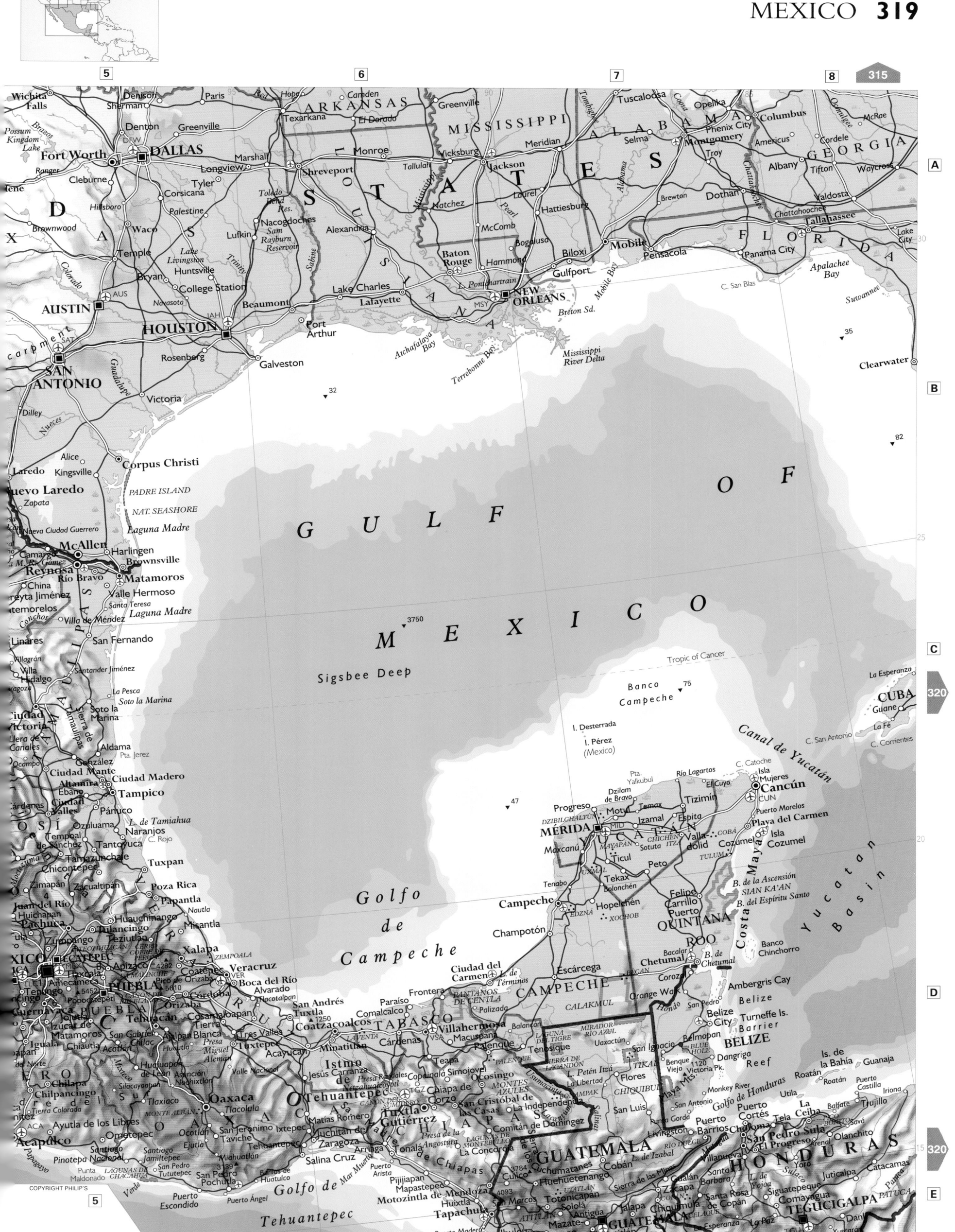

5   **6**   **7**   **8**

A

B

320

C

D

E

320

COPYRIGHT PHILIP'S

PUERTO RICO AND THE VIRGIN IS.
b 1:1 600 000

10 0 10 20 30 40 50 60 70 km
10 0 10 20 30 40 50 miles

ATLANTIC OCEAN

The Settlement
Ruffling Pt.
Anegada
East Pt.

VIRGIN ISLANDS (U.K.)

Jost Van Dyke I. Guana I. Great Camanoe
Hans Lollik I. Tortola Road Town Beef I. Virgin Gorda
STT Road Town Spanish Town
Charlotte Amalie St. Thomas I. Cruz Bay VIRGIN IS. NAT. PARK Peter I.
St. John I. VIRGIN ISLANDS (U.S.A.)

Aguadilla Pta. Aguijereada Quebradillas Hatillo Arecibo Barceloneta Vega Baja Levittown SAN JUAN SJU Carolina
Isabela Moca PARQUE DE LAS CAVERNAS DEL RIO CAMUY OBSERVATORIO DE ARECIBO Vega Alta Manatí Río Grande Trujillo Alto Luquillo
Pta. Higuero Aguada San Sebastián Florida Ciales Bayamón Guaynabo Sierra de Luquillo Fajardo Ceiba
Rincón Lares Comerío Gurabo EL YUNQUE Naguabo Pta. Puerca
Añasco Maricao PUERTO RICO (U.S.A.) Caguas Juncos Las Piedras Humacao
Mayagüez Hormigueros Adjuntas 1338 Cayey Cidra Dewey I. Culebra Isabel Segunda
San Germán Sabana Grande Cordillera Central Mts. de Uroyan Cerro de Punta Villalba Barranquitas Aibonito Pta. Arenas
Cabo Rojo Yauco Juana Díaz Coamo Cayey Patillas Yabucoa Esperanza Vieques
Parguera Sabana Grande Guayanilla Ponce Salinas Guayama Maunabo
Pta. Aguila Guánica Santa Isabel I. Caja de Muertos

CARIBBEAN SEA

353 Mt. Eagle Christiansted East Pt.
Frederiksted St. Croix I. (U.S.A.)
Southwest Pt.

West from Greenwich

MAS

ur's Town
New Bight
Cat I.
an Salvador I.
Conception I.
Rum Cay
Tropic of Cancer
Long I.
Clarence Town
Samana Cay
Crooked I.
Plana Cays
Albert Town Snug Corner
Acklins I.
Mira por vos Cay
Cay Verde
Hogsty Reef
Little Inagua I.
INAGUA
Lake Rose
Matthew Town
Great Inagua I.
Mayaguana I.
Caicos Passage
Turks & Caicos Is. (U.K.)
PLS Caicos Is.
Cockburn Town Turks Is.
Turks Island Passage

5560

Mouchoir Bank Silver Bank

Santa omingo
Lucrecia
Moa
ALEJANDRO DE HUMBOLDT
Baracoa
Pta. de Maisí
Maisí
antánamo
ANTANAMO (U.S.A.)
Paso de los Vientos (Windward Passage)

Navidad Bank

Puerto Rico Trench

Î. de la Tortue Monte Cristi LA ISABELA Santiago de los Caballeros
Cap-Haïtien Puerto Plata San Francisco de Macorís
Jean Rabel Port-de-Paix Fort Liberté La Vega Nagua Samana
Cap-à-Foux Gonaïves Hinche Central Pico Duarte 3175 Sánchez Sabana de la Mar
G. de la Gonâve St-Marc ARMANDO BERMÚDEZ HAITISES Hato Mayor C. Engaño
Jérémie HAITI DOMINICAN REP. San Pedro de Macorís Higüey PUJ
Î. de la Gonâve PORT-AU-PRINCE San Juan L. Enriquillo Azua de Compostela La Romana
ssa Dame Massif de la Hotte Petit Goâve 2680 SIERRA DE BAHORUCO ESTE B. de Yuma
Marie Les Cayes Aquín Jacmel Barahona San Cristóbal SANTO DOMINGO I. Saona
Pointe-à-Gravois Î. à Vache Pedernales I. Beata C. Beata

Hispaniola Antilles

Bayamón SAN JUAN Carolina
Aguadilla Arecibo St. Thomas Virgin Gorda Anegada Virgin Is. (U.K.) Sombrero (U.K.)
Tortola Road Town Anguilla (U.K.)
Virgin Is. (U.S.A.) Charlotte Amalie Anegada Passage St-Martin (Fr.)
Mayagüez Ponce Caguas Culebra SXM St. Maarten (Neth.) St-Barthélemy (Fr.)
Vieques Virgin Is. (U.S.A.) Saba (Neth.) Barbuda
PUERTO RICO (U.S.A.) Guayama Christiansted St. Croix St. Eustatius (Neth.) 1156 Mt. Liamuiga ANTIGUA & BARBUDA
Frederiksted ST. KITTS & NEVIS SKB St. John's
Nevis ANU Antigua
Redonda Soufrière Hills 914 Guadeloupe Passage
Montserrat (U.K.) PTP Le Moule
Ste-Rose La Désirade
GUADELOUPE (Fr.) 1467 Pointe-à-Pitre
Basse-Terre Marie-Galante (Fr.) Grand-Bourg
I. des Saintes Dominica Passage
Portsmouth Morne DOMINICA DOM
Diablotin Roseau TROIS PITONS
Martinique Passage
Mt. Pelée 1397 Ste-Marie
Fort-de-France FDF Le Robert Rivière-Pilote MARTINIQUE (Fr.)
St. Lucia Channel
Castries 350 ST. LUCIA
Soufrière UVF
St. Vincent Passage
Soufrière 1234 St. Vincent Speightstown BGI
Kingstown SVD Bridgetown BARBADOS
Bequia Tobago ST. VINCENT & THE GRENADINES
Canouan Basin
Carriacou 840
St. George's GND GRENADA

Venezuelan Sea Basin

I. de Aves (Venezuela)

Aves Ridge

Beata Ridge

Leeward Islands Lesser Antilles

Windward Islands Grenada

The Grenadines

BEAN SEA BASIN

5500 Muertas Trough
4530
5420

omian asin

ABC Lesser Antilles Islands
Oranjestad Aruba (Neth.) AUA Curaçao Bonaire
Willemstad CUR

I. Orchila (Ven.)
ARC. LOS ROQUES
I. Las Aves (Ven.) Is. Los Roques (Ven.)
I. Blanquilla (Ven.) Is. Los Hermanos (Ven.)
NUEVA ESPARTA Is. Los Testigos (Ven.)
I. de Margarita (Ven.) Tobago Scarborough
Cerro El Copey 920 La Asunción Port of Spain Galera Pt.
Porlamar Trinidad Arima POS
PMV Rio Claro
TRINIDAD & TOBAGO
Serpent's Mouth

COLOMBIA
GUAJIRA
Pta. Gallinas
MACUIRA
C. San Román
Pen. de la Guajira Pta. Espada Pen. de Paraguaná
Riohacha Uribia Golfo de Venezuela Punta Cardón Punto Fijo
Maicao Coro La Vela MÉDANOS DE CORO Puerto Cumarebo
San Rafael Altagracia Mene de Mauroa CUEVA DE LA QUEBRADA EL TORO
Santa Marta ISLA DE STA. MARTA SA. NEVADA DE STA. MARTA 5775 FALCÓN
TAYRONA Ciénaga Santa Marta San Carlos del Zulia Tucacas
MAIQUETÍA CARACAS Vargas Cumaná Río Caribe Pen. de Paria Güiria
Maiquetía La Guaira Caripe Carúpano San Fernando
BARRAN-ILLA Soledad MARACAIBO LARA Puerto Cabello HENRI PITTIER MIRANDA Higuerote SUCRE
Santa Marta Cabimas Barquisimeto San Felipe 2640 Cariaco TORTUGUERO GUACHARO El Guacharo
Fundación La Concepción Santa Rita Baragua CERRO SAROCHE Los Teques Ocumare del Tuy Barcelona
Calamar Villa del Rosario Ciudad Ojeda Machiques YARACUY VALENCIA Villa de Cura Río Chico Puerto La Cruz Maturín
Plato Agustín Codazzi ZULIA Lago de Maracaibo Mene Grande CARABOBO Yaritagua San Juan de los Morros Aragua de Barcelona Anaco Cantaura MONAGAS
MAGDALENA CÉSAR PERIJÁ Trujillo ARAGUA Acarigua COJEDES San Carlos El Sombrero DELTA
Zambrano El Banco CIÉNAGAS DEL CATATUMBO Betijoque GUÁRICO Valle de la Pascua El Tigre MARIUSA
Mompós SANTANDER San Carlos del Zulia Valera PORTUGUESA EL GUACHE Calabozo AMACURO
Magangué Encontrados BARINAS Guanare Portuguesa Santa María de Ipire Los Barrancos
Barancas NORTE DE SANTANDER Barinas El Baúl ANZOÁTEGUI Soledad Ciudad Guayana
Corozal Mérida Libertad GUÁRICO El Pao Sierra Imataca
ahán Pamplona CATATUMBO-BARI SA. DE LA CULATA San Fernando Upata
arcos Ocaña SA. NEVADA 5981 Ciudad Bolivia Pariaguán Ciudad Bolívar
BOLÍVAR MÉRIDA Pico Bolívar de Nutrias AGUARO-GUARIQUITO El Callao Tumeremo
eo Simití TÁCHIRA PÁRAMO DEL BATALLÓN TAPO-CAPARO San Fernando de Apure Guasdualito
Caucasia Cúcuta San Cristóbal Santa Bárbara BARINAS Bruzual Apure Cabruta Orinoco Embalse de Guri Guasipati
VENEZUELA Achaguas Caicara

West from Greenwich

COPYRIGHT PHILIP'S

4000 3000 2000 1000 600 0
12 000 9000 6000 4500 3000 1500 600 0
600 3000 6000 12 000 18 000 24 000 ft
200 1000 2000 4000 6000 8000 m

5 0 5 10 15 20 25 30 km
1:600 000
5 0 5 10 15
20 miles

a

Prickly Pear Cays
Snake Pt.
Grafton's Pt.
Seal I.
Island Harbour
Scrub I.
Crocus Bay
Sandy I.
The Quarter
59
Anguilla (U.K.)
The Valley
Sandy Ground Village
South Hill Village
Sandy Hill Bay
West End Village
Blowing Point Village
Anguillita I.
Blowing Rock
Île Tintamarre
Anguilla Channel
Pte. du Canonnier
Grand Case
Cul de Sac
Île
Marigot
Quartier
424
D'Orléans
Colombier
Simpson Bay Lagoon
Mulletbaai
241
Cul de Sac
SXM
Sentry Hill
Simsonbaai
Philipsburg
St. Maarten (Netherlands)
Pte. Blanche
Amegada Passage

Saint Martin (France)

b
ANTIGUA AND BARBUDA
ATLANTIC OCEAN
Dickinson Bay
Boon Pt.
Beggars Pt.
Long I.
Runaway Bay
St. Johnston
Crabs
Guiana I.
Village
Pen.
ANU
Antigua
St. John's
Potters
Willikies
Village
Indian
Five I. Harbour
Pt.
DEVIL'S
BRIDGE
Mt. Obama
English
Nonsuch Bay
395
Harbour
Green I.
Johnsons
Town
Freetown
York I.
Pt.
368
Soldier Pt.
Old Road
Willoughby
Bluff
NELSON'S
Bay
DOCKYARD
Nanton Pt.
West from Greenwich

c
Goat Pt.
Billy Pt.
Goat I.
Kid I.
Hog I.
Cedar
Tree Pt.
39
Low
The Highlands
Bay
Codrington
Dulcina
Palmetto Pt.
Barbuda
Cocoa Point
Spanish Pt.
West from Greenwich

ST. KITTS AND NEVIS / d
Helden's Pt.
Dieppe Bay Town
Sadlers
Sandy Point
Tabernacle
Town
1156
Cayon
BRIMSTONE
847
HILL FORT
Old Road Town
St. Kitts
Middle
Island
SKB
Palmetto Pt.
Basseterre
Frigate Bay
Friar's Bay
Sand Bank Bay
Gt. Salt Pond
319
CARIBBEAN
SEA
Nags Head
The Narrows
309
Round Hill
Cotton Ground
Nevis
Nevis Peak
873
Charlestown
Fig Tree
Bath
381
Saddle

St. Kitts & Nevis
Barbuda
Antigua
West from Greenwich

Northern Leewards

e
Guadeloupe Passage
Anse-Bertrand
Pte. de la Grande Vigie
Pte. du Piton
Haut de la Montagne
Campêche
Port-Louis
Beauport
Gros Cap
ATLANTIC OCEAN
Pte. d'Antigues
Les Mangles
Ste-Marguerite
Petit-Canal
Îlet à Fajou
Pte. Macou
Îlet à Kahouanne
Pointe Allègre
Grand Cul-de-Sac Marin
Morne-à-l'Eau
Vieux Bourg
Bazin
Château Gaillard
Le Moule
La Désirade
Grande Anse
Duzer
Ste-Rose
611
Deshaies
Sofaia
Goyaves
MUSÉE DU RHUM
Pte. de la
Grde. Riv.
L'Autre Bord
Zévallos
MAISON COLONIALE
Le Souffleur
Lamentin
Grande-Terre
Les Abymes
Les Grands Fonds
Douville
Plaine de la Simonière
Pte. des Colibris
Beauséjo
Baille-Argent
715
Castel
PTP
Baie Mahault
Bas du Fort
Pointe-à-Pitre
Ste-Marthe
Kahouanne
St-François
Pointe des Châteaux
Morne-à-Pitre
Morne-Noire
744 Ravine Chaude
Morne Jeanneton
Petit-Bourg
Le Gosier
Ste-Anne
Îles de la Petite Terre
Mahaut
631
Vernou
Petit Cul-de-Sac Marin
Terre de Bas
Pigeon
Pitons (ou Sauts) de Bouillante
Montebello
1088
PARC
Morne Moustique
Goyave
Bouillante
1150 ou Joffre
Pte. de la Rivière à Goyave
Guadeloupe (France)
Marigot
NATIONAL
1354
Grde. Riv. de la Capesterre
Ste-Marie
Vieux-Habitants
DE LA
1263
Capesterre
Matouba
GUADELOUPE
1467 CHUTES DU
Capesterre-Belle-Eau
Baillif
St-Claude
Soufrière
CARBET
St-Louis
Grosse Pointe
Vieux Fort
Basse-Terre
Gourbeyre
Bananier
Pte. du Vieux Fort
Monts
Grande Pte.
LE TROU À DIABLE
Caraïbes
Trois-Rivières
Canal de Marie-Galante
204
Vieux-Fort
Marie-Galante
Pte. du Vieux Fort
Canal des Saintes
Pte. de Folle Anse
Grand-Bourg
Capesterre-de-Marie-Galante
Îles des Saintes
FORT NAPOLÉON
CHÂTEAU MURAT
Pte. des Basses
Terre-de-Bas
309
Terre-de-Haute
Petites-Anses
Le Chameau
Grand Îlet
West from Greenwich
Dominica Passage
Guadeloupe
Martinique

GUADELOU
MARTINIQ

f
Kudarebe
CARIBBEAN SEA
Malmok
Palm Beach
Noord
Eagle Beach
Bushiribana
BUBALI BIRD
Noordkaap
SANCTUARY
Oranjestad
165
Paradera
AUA
Santa Cruz
ARIKOK
188
Spaans Lagoen
Pos Chiquito
Savaneta
Aruba (Netherlands)
Sint Nicolaas
Seroe Colorado
Punta Basora
West from Greenwich

Aruba
Curaçao
Bonaire

h
CARIBBEAN SEA
Noordpunt
Boca Slagbaai
240
Washington
Brandaris
Onima
Bonaire (Netherlands)
Gotomeer
WASHINGTON
Rincon
SLAGBAAI
Wekoewa Pt.
Noord Saliña
Hato
115
Klein
Antriol
Bonaire
Nikiboko
Tera Kora
Kralendijk
Punto Blanco
Bachelor's Beach
Wanapa
Vierkant Pt.
Lac Bay
Hoop
Pink Beach
Witte Pan (Salt Flats)
Lacre Punt
West from Greenwich

ABC ISLANDS

g
Noordpunt
BOKA TABLA
Westpunt
Savonet
CHRISTOFFEL
375
St. Christoffelberg
Lagún
Bartolbaai
B. Santa Cruz
Santa Cruz
Soto
Barber
St. Nicolaas
St. Marthabaai
San
Juan
Siberie
St. Willibrordus
St. Michiel
K. St. Marie
CUR
Bullenbaai
Hato
HATO CAPES
Stenen Koraal
Julianadorp
Brievengat
Gasparito
Buena Vista
St. Jorisbaai
Emmastad
Santa Rosa
Otrobanda
Schottegat
Punda
Santa
Willemstad
St. Annabaai
Bottelier
Barbara
SEAQUARIUM
Tafelberg
CARIBBEAN SEA
193
Curaçao (Netherlands)
Spaanse Water
Lagún Blanku
West from Greenwich
Nieuwpoort

Projection: Conical with two standard parallels

NORTHERN LEEWARDS
Mt. Scenery
871
Saba (Netherlands)
The Bottom
Hells Gate
Fort Bay
Windward Side
CARIBBEAN
SEA
Zeelandia
St. Eustatius (Statia) (Netherlands)
Oranjestad
604
The Quill
West from Greenwich

Île Fourchue
Île Chevreau
Flamands
St-Jean
Lorient
Corossol
Toiny
Gustavia
281
Grand
Fond
Saint Barthélemy (St. Barts) (France)

j
Martinique Passage
Grand' Rivière
Macouba
Basse-Pointe
Cap St-Martin
GORGES DE LA FALAISE
ATLANTIC OCEAN
1397
Le Prêcheur
Montagne Pelée
Le Lorrain
Le Marigot
Ste-Marie
Pte. Lamare
Le Morne Rouge
884
CHÂTEAU DUBUC
Presqu'île de la Caravelle
St-Pierre
Fonds-St-Denis
Morne des Esses
Tartane
Pte. Caracoli
Rade de St-Pierre
Beauséjour
La Trinité
Le Carbet
Le Morne-Vert
1109
Gros-Morne
Baie du Galion
Bellefontaine
Pitons du Carbet
JARDIN DE BALATA
Îlet Chancel ou Ramville
Case-Pilote
St-Joseph
Le Robert
Havre du Robert
Fond Rousseau
334
Pte. Larose
Schoelcher
FDE
Le Lamentin
Îlet Long
Fort-de-France
Ducos
Le François
Pte. des Nègres
Montagne du Vauclin
Baie de Fort-de-France
L'Anse Mitan
B. de
504
Pte. de Vauclin
Pte. du Bout
Génipa
Le St-Esprit
L'Anse à l'Âne
Les Trois-Îlets
Le Vauclin
LA PAGERIE
Rivière-Salée
Pte. Ducassou
Cap Salomon
Grande Anse
460
Martinique (France)
Les Anses-d'Arlet
Le Diamant
359
Rivière-Pilote
Le Marin
Petite Anse
Trois Rivières
Barrière-la-Croix
Ste-Luce
Cap Ferré
Rocher du Diamant
Pte. du Diamant
Pte. Borgnesse
Ste-Anne
Îlet Chevalier
CARIBBEAN SEA
Étang des Salines
Pte. Baham
Pte. des Salines
Pte. d'Enfer
Îlet Cabrits
St. Lucia Channel

ft m
3000 1000
1200 400
600 200
0 0
100 300
200 600
500 1500
1000 3000
2000 6000
m ft

■ Place of interest
Mangrov

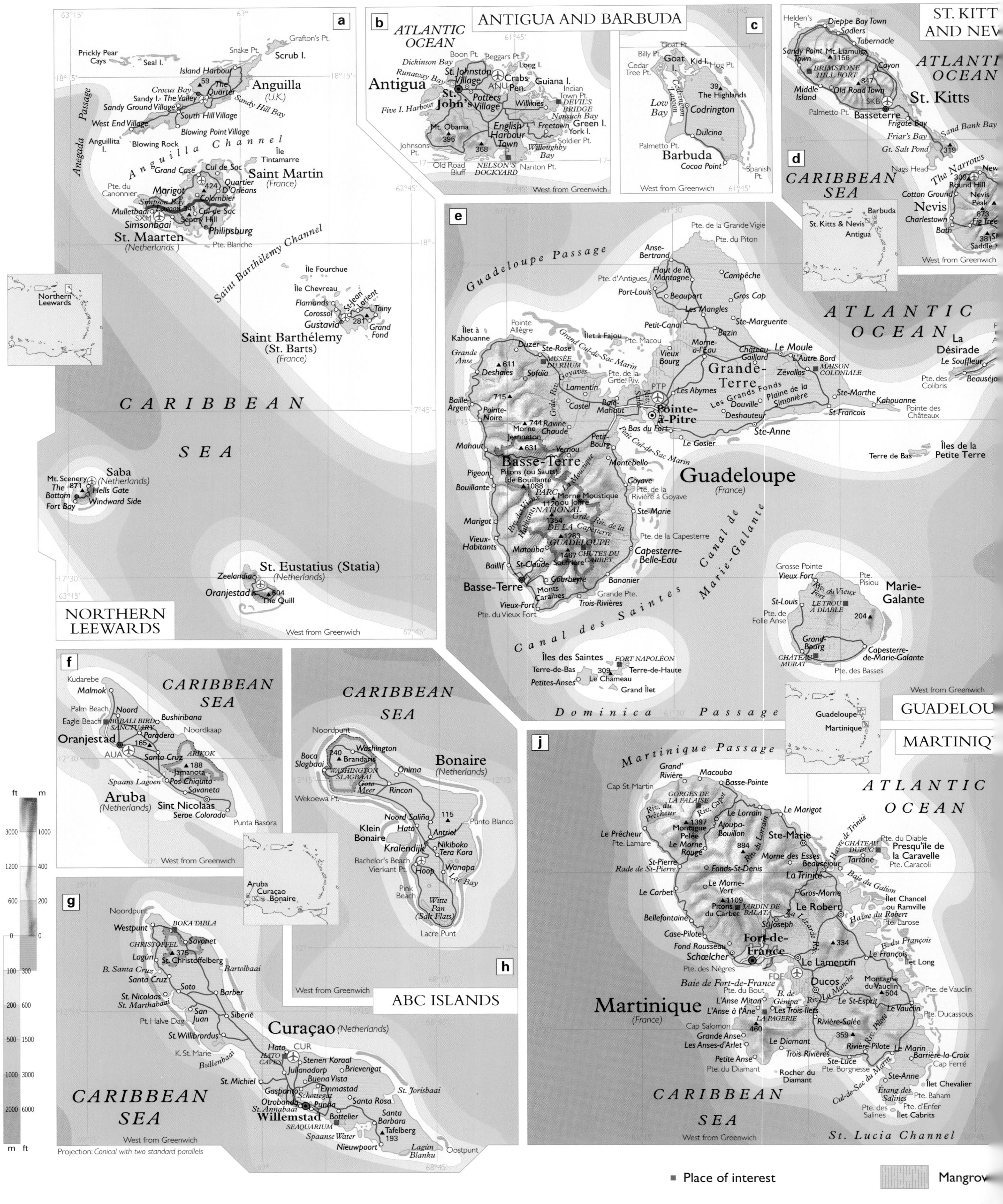

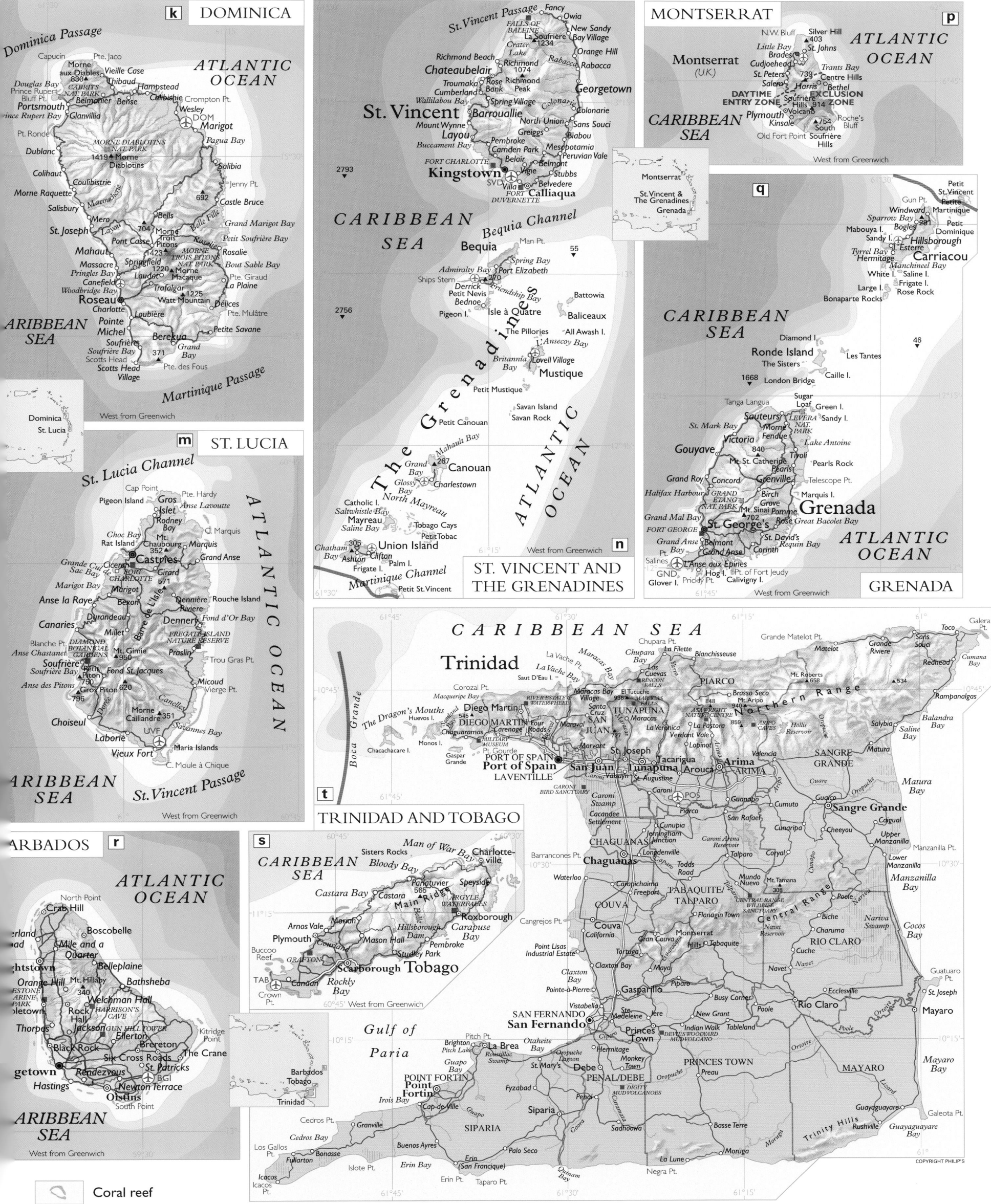

DOMINICA

Dominica Passage

ATLANTIC OCEAN

Capucin · Pte. Jaco
Morne aux Diables 830▲
Vieille Case
Douglas Bay · Thibaud · Hampstead
Prince Rupert Bluff Pt. · CABRITS NAT. PARK
Portsmouth · Belmanier · Bense · Callibishie · Crompton Pt.
Prince Rupert Bay · Glanvillia · Wesley
DOM
Pt. Ronde · Marigot
Pagua Bay

Dublanc
MORNE DIABLOTINS NAT. PARK
692
Colihaut · 1419▲ Morne Diablotins
Morne Raquette · Salibia
Jenny Pt.
Salisbury · Macoucherie · Castle Bruce
Mero · 704 · Grand Marigot Bay
St. Joseph · Pont Casse · 571 Morne Trois Pitons · Rosalie
Mahaut · 1423▲ · Petit Soufrière Bay
Massacre · Springfield · 1220 MORNE TROIS PITONS NAT. PARK · Bout Sable Bay
Canefield · Loudat · Morne Macaque · Pte. Giraud
Woodbridge Bay · Trafalgar · 1225 · La Plaine
Roseau · Watt Mountain · Délices
Charlotte · Loubière · Pte. Mulâtre
CARIBBEAN SEA
Pointe Michel · Berekua · Petite Savane
Soufrière · 371 · Grand Bay
Soufrière Bay · Pte. des Fous
Scotts Head · Scotts Head Village

Martinique Passage

Dominica St. Lucia

West from Greenwich

ST. LUCIA

St. Lucia Channel

Cap Point
Pigeon Island · Pte. Hardy
Gros Islet · Anse Lavoutte
Choc Bay · Rodney Bay
Rat Island · Mt. Chaubourg · Marquis · C. Marquis
Grande Cul · 352▲ · Grand Anse
Sac Bay · FORT CHARLOTTE · Castries
Marigot Bay · Girard
Anse la Raye · Bexon · Dennière Riviere · Rouche Island
Durandeau · Fond d'Or Bay
Canaries · Millet · Praslin
Blanche Pt. · DIAMOND BOTANICAL GARDENS · Mt. Gimie 950▲ · Trou Gras Pt.
Anse Chastanet · Soufrière · FREGATE ISLAND NATURE RESERVE
Soufrière Bay · Petit Piton 743 · Fond St. Jacques
Anse des Pitons · Gros Piton 620 · Micoud · Vierge Pt.
796 · Canelles
Choiseul · Morne Caillandre 351▲
Laborie · Savannes Bay
UVF
Vieux Fort
Maria Islands
CARIBBEAN SEA
C. Moule à Chique
St. Vincent Passage

West from Greenwich

ATLANTIC OCEAN

ST. VINCENT AND THE GRENADINES

St. Vincent Passage · Fancy · Owia
FALLS OF BALEINE · New Sandy Bay Village
La Soufrière 1234▲ · Orange Hill
Richmond Beach · Crater Lake · Rabacca
Chateaubelair · Richmond 1074 · Georgetown
Troumaka · Rose Richmond Peak · Rabacca
Cumberland · Spring Village · Colonarie
Wallilabou Bay · North Union · Sans Souci
Barrouallie · Greiggs · Colonie
Mount Wynne · Biabou
Layou · Pembroke · Mesopotamia
Buccament Bay · Camden Park · Peruvian Vale
FORT CHARLOTTE · Belair · Belmont
2793 · Villa · Vigie · Stubbs
Kingstown · SVD · Belvedere
FORT DUVERNETTE · Calliaqua

CARIBBEAN SEA

Bequia Channel
2756
Bequia · Man Pt. · 55
Spring Bay
Admiralty Bay · Port Elizabeth
Ships Stern · 270 · Friendship Bay
Derrick · Battowia
Petit Nevis · Isle à Quatre
Bednoe · Baliceaux
Pigeon I.
The Pillories · All Awash I.
L'Ansecoy Bay
Britannia Bay · Lovell Village
Mustique
Petit Mustique
Savan Island
Petit Canouan · Savan Rock

The Grenadines

Grand Bay · 267 · Canouan
Glossy Bay · Charlestown
Catholic I.
Saltwhistle Bay · Mahault Bay
Mayreau · North Mayreau
Saline Bay · Tobago Cays
Chatham Bay · 305 · Petit Tobac
Ashton · Clifton · Palm I.
Frigate I.
Union Island
Martinique Channel
Petit St. Vincent

West from Greenwich

ATLANTIC OCEAN

MONTSERRAT

N.W. Bluff · Silver Hill
Little Bay · 403▲ · St. Johns
Cudjoehead · Trants Bay
Montserrat (U.K.) · St. Peters · 739▲ · Centre Hills
Salem · Harris · Bethel
DAYTIME ENTRY ZONE · EXCLUSION ZONE
Plymouth · Soufrière Hills 914▲ · Volcano
Kinsale · 754▲ South · Roche's Bluff
Old Fort Point · Soufrière Hills

CARIBBEAN SEA

ATLANTIC OCEAN

West from Greenwich

Montserrat
St. Vincent & The Grenadines
Grenada

GRENADA

Petit St. Vincent
Gun Pt. · Petite Martinique
Windward · 281
Mabouya I. · Bogles · Petit Dominique
Sandy I. · Hillsborough
Tyrrel Bay · Esterre · Carriacou
Hermitage · Manchineel Bay
White I. · Saline I.
Large I. · Frigate I.
Bonaparte Rocks · Rose Rock

CARIBBEAN SEA

Diamond I.
Ronde Island · Les Tantes
The Sisters · Caille I.
1668 · London Bridge
Tanga Langua · Sugar Loaf · 46
Green I.
St. Mark Bay · Sauteurs · LEVERA NAT. PARK · Sandy I.
Morne Fendue · Green I.
Gouyave · Victoria · 840 · Tivoli · Lake Antoine
Mt. St. Catherine · Pearls
Grand Roy · Concord · Pearls Rock
Halifax Harbour · GRAND ETANG NAT. PARK · Grenville · Telescope Pt.
Grand Mal Bay · Birch Grove
Mt. Sinai Pomme · Marquis I.
St. George's · 702▲ · Rose · Great Bacolet Bay
FORT GEORGE · Grand Anse
Grand Anse · Belmont · St. David's · Requin Bay
Salines · Corinth
GND · L'Anse aux Épines · Pt. of Fort Jeudy
Glover I. · Hog I. · Calivigny I.
Prickly Pt.

West from Greenwich

CARIBBEAN SEA · ATLANTIC OCEAN

TRINIDAD AND TOBAGO

CARIBBEAN SEA

Chupara Pt. · Grande Matelot Pt. · Matelot · Grande Riviere · Sans Souci · Galera Pt.
La Filette · Blanchisseuse
Trinidad · Las Cuevas · Toco
La Vache Bay · Chupara Bay · Mt. Roberts 658▲ · Rampanalgas
Maracas Bay · RINCON FALLS · 534▲
Corozal Pt. · Saut D'Eau Pt. · Brasso Seco
Maracas Bay · ARIMA RIGHT NAT. CENTRE · 859▲ · Balandra Bay
Macqueripe Bay · Maraval · Northern Range · Saline Bay
RIVER ESTATE WATERWHEEL · ASA WRIGHT NAT. CENTRE · ARIPO CAVES
Diego Martin · 988▲ · Mt. Aripo 940 · Matura Bay
The Dragon's Mouths · Carenage · 848 · La Pastora
Huevos I. · DIEGO MARTIN · Four Roads · La Veronica · Verdant Vale
Chaguaramas · St. Ann's · Maracas · Lopinot · Valencia
Monos I. · San Juan · Tunapuna · Arouca · ARIMA · SANGRE GRANDE
Gaspar Grande · Morvant · St. Joseph · Tacarigua · Cuare · Matura
Chacachacare I. · MILITARY MUSEUM · PORT OF SPAIN · San Juan · Arima · Guanapo · Cumuto · Cunaripa · Cheeyou
Pt. Gourde · LAVENTILLE · St. Augustine · Guanapo · San Rafael · Upper Manzanilla
PORT OF SPAIN · CARONI BIRD SANCTUARY · POS · Valsayn · Piarco · Coryal · Lower Manzanilla
Caroni Swamp · Caroni · Cunupia · Jerningham Junction · Talparo · Manzanilla Pt.
CHAGUANAS · Longdenville · Caroni Arena Reservoir · Biche · Manzanilla Bay
Barrancones Pt. · Chaguanas · Todds Road · Flanagin Town · CENTRAL RANGE WILDLIFE SANCTUARY · Caigual
Waterloo · Carapichaima · Freeport · Mundo Nuevo · Central Range · Cocos Bay
TABAQUITE/TALPARO · Mt. Tamana 308▲ · Charuma
COUVA · Montserrat · Tabaquite · Poole · Nariva Swamp
Point Lisas Industrial Estate · Gran Couva · RIO CLARO · Navet
Claxton Bay · Couva · California · Cuche · Navet Reservoir · Guatuaro Pt.
Tortuga · Claxton Bay · Mayo · Cunapo · Rio Claro · Mayaro
Pointe-à-Pierre · Ste. Madeleine · New Grant · Poole · St. Joseph
SAN FERNANDO · Jere · Indian Walk · Tableland · MAYARO
San Fernando · PRINCES TOWN · Mayaro Bay
Pitch Lake · Otaheite Bay · Princes Town · Preau
La Brea · Brighton · Oropuche Lagoon · PENAL/DEBE · Trinity Hills · Rushville
Guapo Bay · Pitch Lake · St. Mary's · Monkey Town · Guayaguayare
POINT FORTIN · Guapo · Debe · Ortoire · Guayaguayare Bay
Point Fortin · Fyzabad · Penal · DEVIL'S WOODFORD MUD VOLCANOES · Galeota Pt.
Irois Bay · Cap-de-Ville · Siparia · Basse Terre
Cedros Pt. · Granville · Erin · Palo Seco · Moruga
Buenos Ayres · Coora · Sadhoowa · La Lune
SIPARIA · Fyzabad · Negra Pt.
Los Gallos Pt. · Bonasse · Erin Bay · (San Francique)
Icacos Pt. · Icacos · Fullarton · Erin Pt. · Taparo Pt.
Cedros Bay

Barbados Tobago Trinidad

COPYRIGHT PHILIP'S

BARBADOS

ATLANTIC OCEAN
North Point
Crab Hill · Boscobelle
Mile and a Quarter
Cumberland · Belleplaine
Road · Mt. Hillaby 340 · Bathsheba
Orange Hill · Welchman Hall
LIMESTONE CAVE MARINE PARK · HARRISON'S CAVE · Rock Hall
Thorpes · GUN HILL TOWER
Jackson · Ellerton
Black Rock · Brereton · The Crane
Bridgetown · Six Cross Roads · Kitridge Pt.
St. Patricks · Newton Terrace
BGI
Rendezvous
Hastings · Oistins
CARIBBEAN SEA · South Point

TOBAGO

Man of War Bay
Sisters Rocks · Charlotteville
CARIBBEAN SEA
Bloody Bay · Speyside
Castara Bay · Parlatuvier · 565 · Main Ridge
Castara · ARGYLE WATERFALLS
Arnos Vale · Moriah · Roxborough
Plymouth · Hillsborough Dam · Carapuse Bay
Courland · Mason Hall · Pembroke
Buccoo Reef · GRAFTON · Studley Park
TAB · Scarborough · Tobago
Canaan · Rockly Bay
Crown Pt.

West from Greenwich

⬦ Coral reef

SOUTH AMERICA

1:28 000 000

PACIFIC OCEAN

ATLANTIC OCEAN

Caribbean Sea

West Indies

Greater Antilles

Lesser Antilles

Central America

Amazon Basin

Selva

Guiana Highlands

Brazilian Highlands

Andes

Pampas

Patagonia

Tierra del Fuego

Tropic of Cancer

Equator

Tropic of Capricorn

Projection: Lambert's Azimuthal Equal Area

COPYRIGHT PHILIP'S

1:28 000 000

1 **2** **3** **4** **5** **6** **7**

A

Tropic of Cancer

Havana
CUBA
BAHAMAS
Turks & Caicos Is.
(U.K.)

A

Cayman Is.
(U.K.)

HAITI
DOMINICAN
REP.
San Juan
Virgin Is. (U.S.A. - U.K.)
Anguilla (U.K.)
St. Martin (Fr. - Neth.)

MEXICO
BELIZE
JAMAICA
Kingston
Port-au-
Prince
Santo
Domingo
PUERTO
RICO
(U.S.A.)
ST. KITTS
& NEVIS
ANTIGUA &
BARBUDA
Basse-Terre
GUADELOUPE
(Fr.)

GUATEMALA
HONDURAS
Tegucigalpa
Caribbean Sea
DOMINICA
Fort-de-France
MARTINIQUE
(Fr.)

Guatemala
San Salvador
EL SALVADOR
NICARAGUA
Managua
Castries
ST. LUCIA
ST. VINCENT
Kingstown
BARBADOS
Bridgetown

COSTA
RICA
San José
Panamá
PANAMA
G. of
Darién
Barranquilla
Cartagena
Maracaibo
Caracas
ARUBA
(Neth.)
Oranjestad
Willemstad
CURAÇAO
(Neth.)
GRENADA
St. George's
Port of
Spain
TRINIDAD &
TOBAGO

B

I. del Coco
(Costa Rica)
Gulf of Panama
Cúcuta
San Cristóbal
Barquísimeto
Valencia
Orinoco
Ciudad Guayana

I. de Malpelo
(Colombia)
Medellín
VENEZUELA
Bucaramanga
GUYANA
Georgetown
Paramaribo
SURINAME
Cayenne
C. Orange
FRENCH
GUIANA

C

Cali
BOGOTÁ
COLOMBIA
Boa Vista
RORAIMA
AMAPÁ
Macapá
Equator

Galapagos Is.
(Ecuador)
Quito
ECUADOR
Guayaquil
G. of Guayaquil
Napo
Putumayo
Japurá
Amazon
Manaus
Santarém
Marajó
I.
Belém
São Luís
Fortaleza

PACIFIC
Iquitos
Marañón
AMAZONAS
Juruá
Purus
Madeira
Tapajós
Xingu
PARÁ
MARANHÃO
Teresina
CEARÁ
RIO G.
DO NORTE
Natal

Chiclayo
Trujillo
Chimbote
ACRE
Rio Branco
Pôrto Velho
RONDÔNIA
Imperatriz
PIAUÍ
PERNAMBUCO
Campina Grande
PARAÍBA
João
Pessoa
Recife

D

PERU
Callao
LIMA
Madre de Dios
BRAZIL
MATO GROSSO
Cuiabá
Palmas
TOCANTINS
GOIÁS
BAHIA
São Francisco
ALAGOAS
SERGIPE
Maceió
Aracaju
Salvador

Cusco
Titicaca
BOLIVIA
La Paz
Cochabamba
Santa Cruz
Sucre
DIS. FED.
Brasília
Goiânia

Arequipa
Iquique
MATO GROSSO
DO SUL
Campo
Grande
Ribeirão
Prêto
MINAS GERAIS
BELO
HORIZONTE
ESPÍRITO
SANTO

E

Antofagasta
Salta
PARAGUAY
Paraná
Pilcomayo
SÃO PAULO
Campinas
Juiz
de Fora
Vitória
Campos

San Félix
(Chile)
San Ambrosio
(Chile)
Tropic of Capricorn
San Miguel
de Tucumán
Asunción
PARANÁ
SÃO
PAULO
Santos
RIO DE
JANEIRO
Niterói
R. DE J.

F

Arch. de Juan Fernández
(Chile)
Resistencia
Corrientes
Curitiba
SANTA CATARINA
Florianópolis

OCEAN
Córdoba
San Juan
Santa Fé
Paraná
RIO GRANDE
DO SUL
Pôrto Alegre
Uruguay
Pelotas

Robinson
Crusoe
Viña del Mar
Valparaíso
SANTIAGO
Mendoza
Rosario
URUGUAY

G

Talca
BUENOS AIRES
La Plata
Montevideo
Mar del Plata
Río de la Plata

Concepción
ARGENTINA
Bahía
Blanca
Colorado

Valdivia
Neuquén
Negro
Viedma

Puerto Montt
ATLANTIC
OCEAN

H

Gulf of Penas
Comodoro Rivadavia
Gulf of San Jorge

CHILE
Chubut

Punta Arenas
Magellan's Str.
Tierra del Fuego
West Falkland
FALKLAND IS.
(U.K.)
Stanley
East Falkland

C. Horn
South Georgia
(U.K.)

Projection: Lambert's Azimuthal Equal Area

■ LIMA Capital Cities

COPYRIGHT PHILIP'S

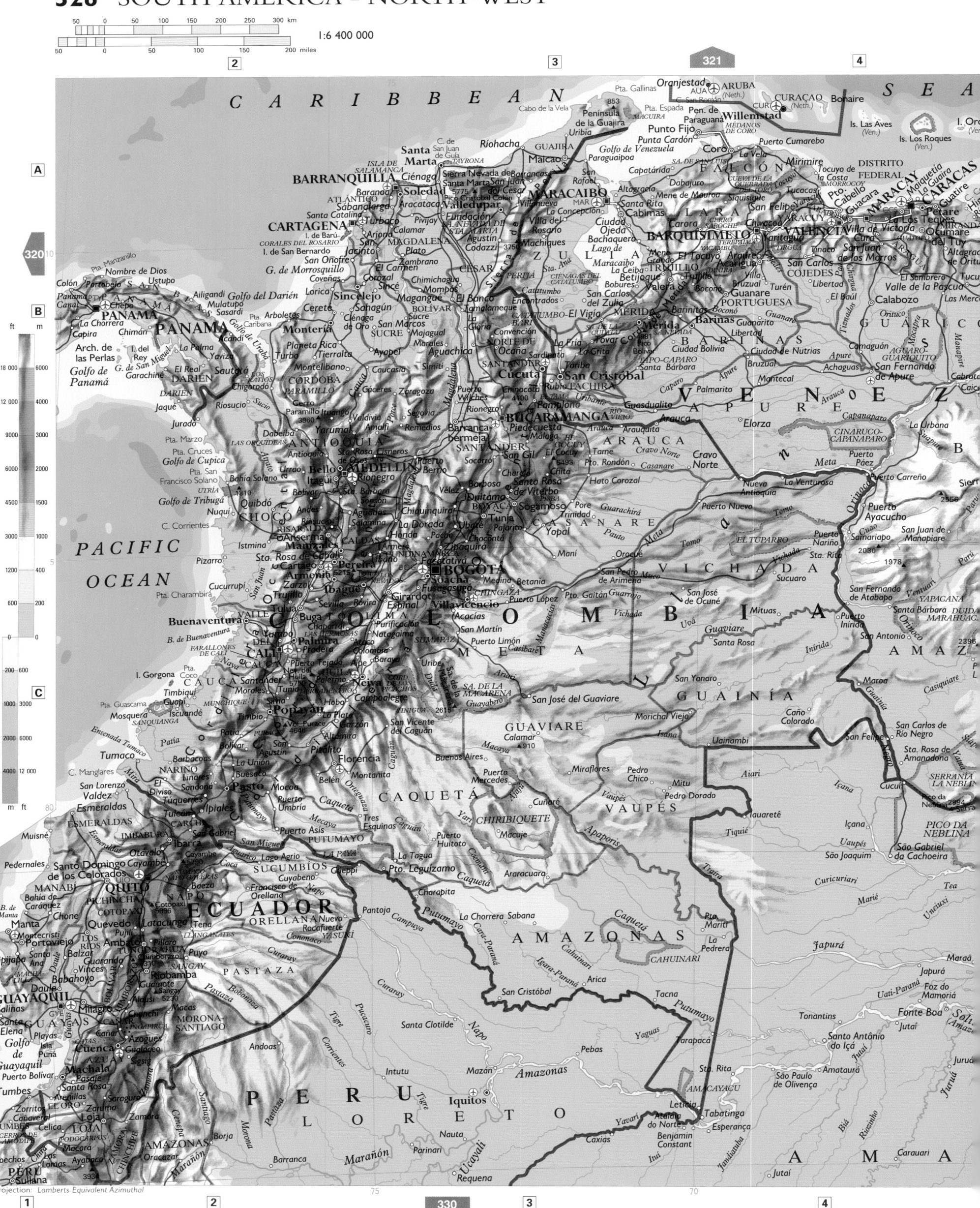

Projection: Lamberts Equivalent Azimuthal

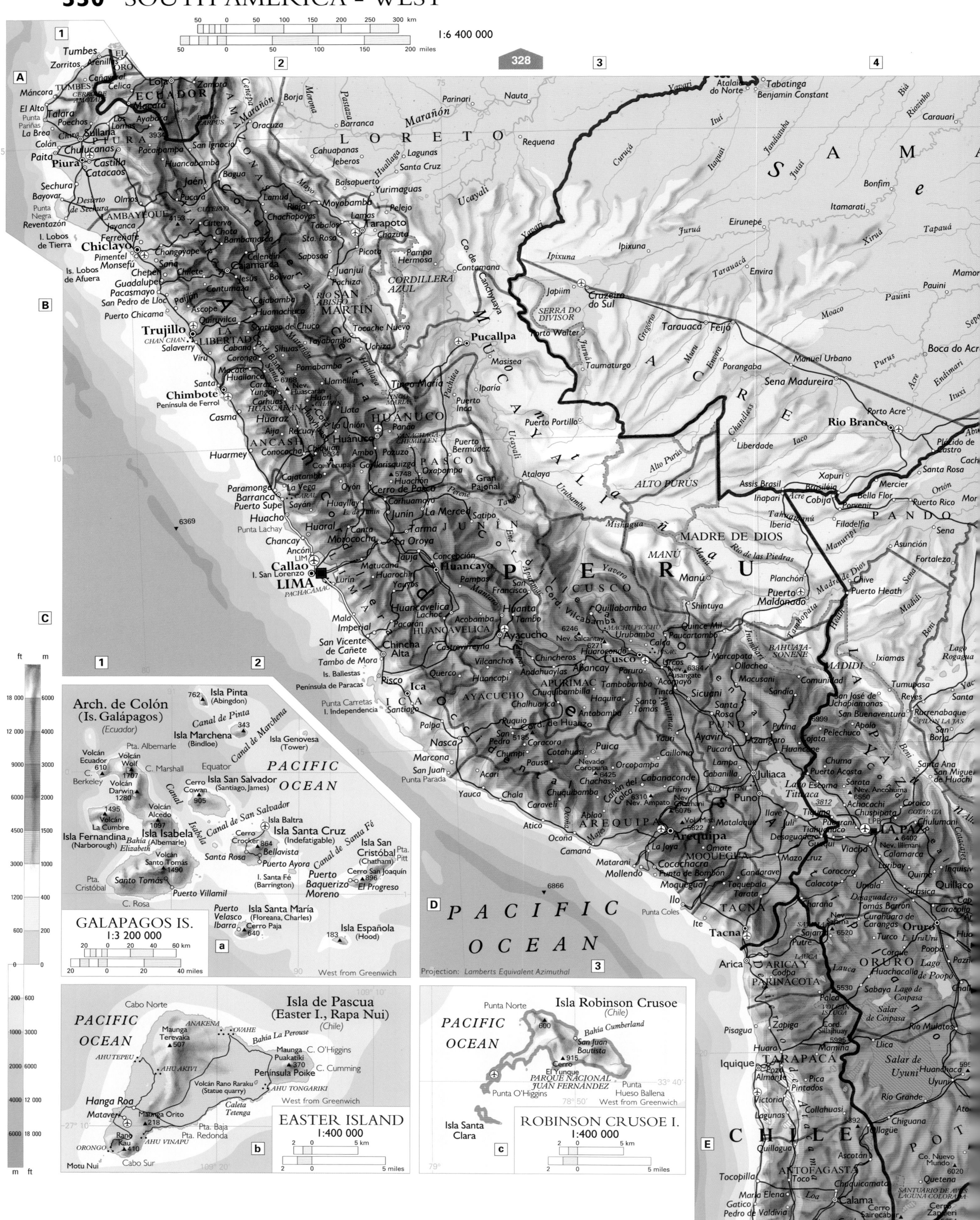

a
b
c

5
329
6
7
A
B
C
D
E
332
333
L. de Coari
Coari
Lima
Andrade
Paricatuba
Itanhauã
Purus
Arumã
Canumã
Borba
Itaituba
AMAZÔNIA
Rurópolis
Iriri
Bacajá
São Luís do Tapajós
Tapajós
Maués
Abacaxis
Madeira
Preto do Igapó-Açu
Novo Aripuanã
Hevelândia
Tefé
Coari
Jaburu
Tapauá
Democracia
Manicoré
Capoeira
Tucunaré
Entre Rios
Itatuba
Tapauá
Santa Maria dos Marmelos
Aripuanã
Canumã
Miriti
Sai-Cinza
Canutama
Pinhuá
Caranapatuba
Três Casas
Crepori
Jamanxim
Curuá
Iriri
São Félix do Xingu
Purus
Lábrea
Ipixuna
Mucuim
Maici
Marmelos
Sucunduri
Prainha Nova
Barra de São Manuel
Humaitá
Inuxi
Samaúma
Juruena
Teles Pires
Cururu
Serra do Cachimbo
Curuá
Curuaés
Xingu
Riosinho
Calama
Madeira
Aripuanã
Porto Velho
Jiparaná
Tabajara
404
Bom Comércio
Manoa
Jaci-Paraná
Caritianas
Candeias
Jamari
Ariquemes
Abunã
Roosevelt
S. Benedito
Serra dos Apiacás
Cachimbo
Alto Iriri
Iriri Novo
Alta Floresta
Guarantã do Norte
Villa Bella
Nova Vida
Jaru
Jaru
Sa. dos Pacaás Novos
Guajará-Mirim
Guayaramerín
Ouro Preto do Oeste
Ji-Paraná
Jiparaná
Aripuanã
Moreru
Serra do Norte
Peixoto de Azevedo
Peixoto Azevedo
São José do Xingu
Liberdade
PACAÁS NOVOS
Mamoré
RONDÔNIA
Presidente Médici
Cacoal
Pimenta Bueno
Serra
Apidiá
Marco Rondon
Tenente Marques
Juína
Sangue
Juara
Porto dos Gaúchos
Serra do Tombador
Serra dos Caiabis
Serra Formosa
Colíder
Manitsauá-Missu
Sinop
Suiá Missu
Liquilândia
Arinos
Arraias
Xingu
Serra do Roncador
Yata
Príncipe da Beira
663
Vilhena
Camararé
Saturnina
Nhambiquara
Juruena
Utiariti
Sorriso
Teles Pires
Romuro
Culuene
Culiseu
Puerto Siles
San Joaquín
Lago Rogoaguado
Versalles
Mategua
Pedras Negras
Guaporé
Magdalena
San Ramón
Baures
Pimenteiras
Puerto Villazón
Lago de San Luis
El Carmen
Mamoré
San Joaquín
San Martín
NOEL KEMPFF MERCADO
Paraguá
Serranía de Huanchaca
Juruena
São José do Rio Claro
Sangue
Verde
Nova Mutum
Planalto
MATO
GROSSO
Apere
San Javier
Trinidad
San Ignacio
Llanos de Mojos
San Francisco
Loreto
San Lorenzo
Perseverancia
Blanco
San Miguel
Parecis
669
Vila Bela da Santíssima Trindade
1995
Guaporé
Pontes e Lacerda
Nortelândia
Arenápolis
Tangará da Serra
Rosário Oeste
Barra do Bugres
Diamantino
Alto Paraguai
Cuiabá
Paranatinga
do
Serra Azul
Mato Grosso
915
Nova Xavantina
Aruanã
Britânia
Araguaia
Negro
Añez
Santa Rosa de la Roca
Grande
BOLIVIA
Concepción
San Javier
San Ignacio
Aguapeí
Porto Esperidião
Jauru
Acorizal
CHAPADA DOS GUIMARÃES
Chapada dos Guimarães
Várzea Grande
Cuiabá
Nossa Senhora do Livramento
CGB
Cáceres
Santo Antônio do Leverger
Coronel Ponce
Mortes
Barra do Garças
Araguaiana
Aragarça
Poxoréo
Tesouro
Rio das Garças
Jaciara
Barão de Melgaço
Poconé
San Matías
Chaparé
Ichilo
Piray
Santa Rosa del Palmar
San Miguel
San Rafael
Guiratinga
Baliza
Iporã
Ivolândia
Rondonópolis
Ponte Branca
São Lourenço
Cuiabá
CARRASCO
Santa Rosa
SANTA CRUZ
Cochabamba
Portachuelo
Montero
Warnes
El Cerro
Laguna Concepción
Lagoa Uberaba
Itiquira
Alto Garças
Alto Araguaia
Caiapônia
Santa Rita do Araguaia
Sa. das Divisões
San Carlos
Buena Vista
AMBORÓ
Cotoca
SANTA CRUZ
VVI
PANTANAL MATOGROSSENSE
Porto Jofre
Itiquira
Araguaia
Caiapó
GOIÁS
Totora
Comarapa
Aiquile
Pampa Grande
El Palmar
Llanos de Chiquitos
San José de Chiquitos
Santo Corazón
Pantanal do São Lourenço
Correntes
Serra do Caiapó
Mineiro
Rio Verde
Pasorapa
Samaipata
Vallegrande
Grande o Guapay
1485
Serra Santiago de Chiquitos
Roboré
Serra de Santiago
La Cal
Lagoa Mandioré
Taquari
Verde
Jataí
EMAS
Presto
Pucará
Bañados de Izozog
Abapó
Paraguai
Taquari
Coxim
MATO GROSSO
Serranópolis
Claro
Sucre
Tarabuco
Zudáñez
Parapetí
KAA-IYA
Santa Ana
Puerto Suárez
Corumbá
Ladário
Pantanal do Rio Negro
Nhecolândia
Rio Verde de Mato Grosso
Baús
Itarumã
Cachoeira Alta
Yotala
Padilla
Gutiérrez
CERRO CHOVORECA
OTUQUIS
DO SUL
Aporé
Cassilândia
Betanzos
Sopachuy
Lagunillas
Fortín General Pando
Albuquerque
Paraíso
Puna
Monteagudo
Charagua
Mayor Pablo Lagerenza
Porto Esperança
Negro
Alto Sucuriú
Coxim
Azurduy
Camiri
Coimbra
Corguinho
Camapuã
Inocência
Paranaíba
Pto. Alencastro
San Lucas
Cuevo
Chaco Boreal
Bahía Negra
Miranda
Rochedo
Jaraguari
Verde
Sucuriú
Aparecida do Taboado
CHUQUISACA
Camargo
Boyuibe
General Eugenio A. Garay
DEFENSORES DEL CHACO
Paraguai
Miranda
Aquidauana
Terenos
Campo Grande
Ribas do Rio Pardo
Água Clara
Rubinéia
Pilcomayo
Carandaiti
Huacaya
Fortín Madrejón
ALTO
Sa. da Bodoquena
Aquidauana
Pardo
Garcias
Pereira Barreto
Cotagaita
Villa Abecia
Pilaya
Villa Montes
PARAGUAY
Fuerte Olimpo
Bonito
Nioaque
Serra de Maracaju
Sidrolândia
Xavantina
Três Lagoas
Andradina
San Lorenzo
Entre Ríos
Fortín Teniente Primero Ramiro Espínola
TTE. AGRIPINO ENCISO
Puerto Guaraní
Jardim
Nova Alvorada do Sul
Mirandópolis
Tarija
Iscayachi
Uriondo
TARIJA
Sanandita
BOQUERÓN
PARAGUAY
Porto Murtinho
Guia Lopes da Laguna
Maracaju
Anhanduí
Panorama
Aguapeí
Cuevas
5603
Padcaya
Yacuiba
Abra Pampa
Tartagal
Itiyuro
Dr. Pedro P. Peña
SALTA
60
West from Greenwich
55
65
10
15
20
5
334
6
335
7
COPYRIGHT PHILIP'S

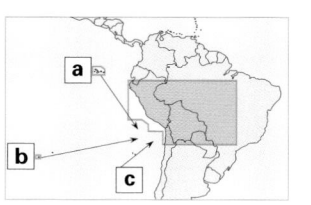

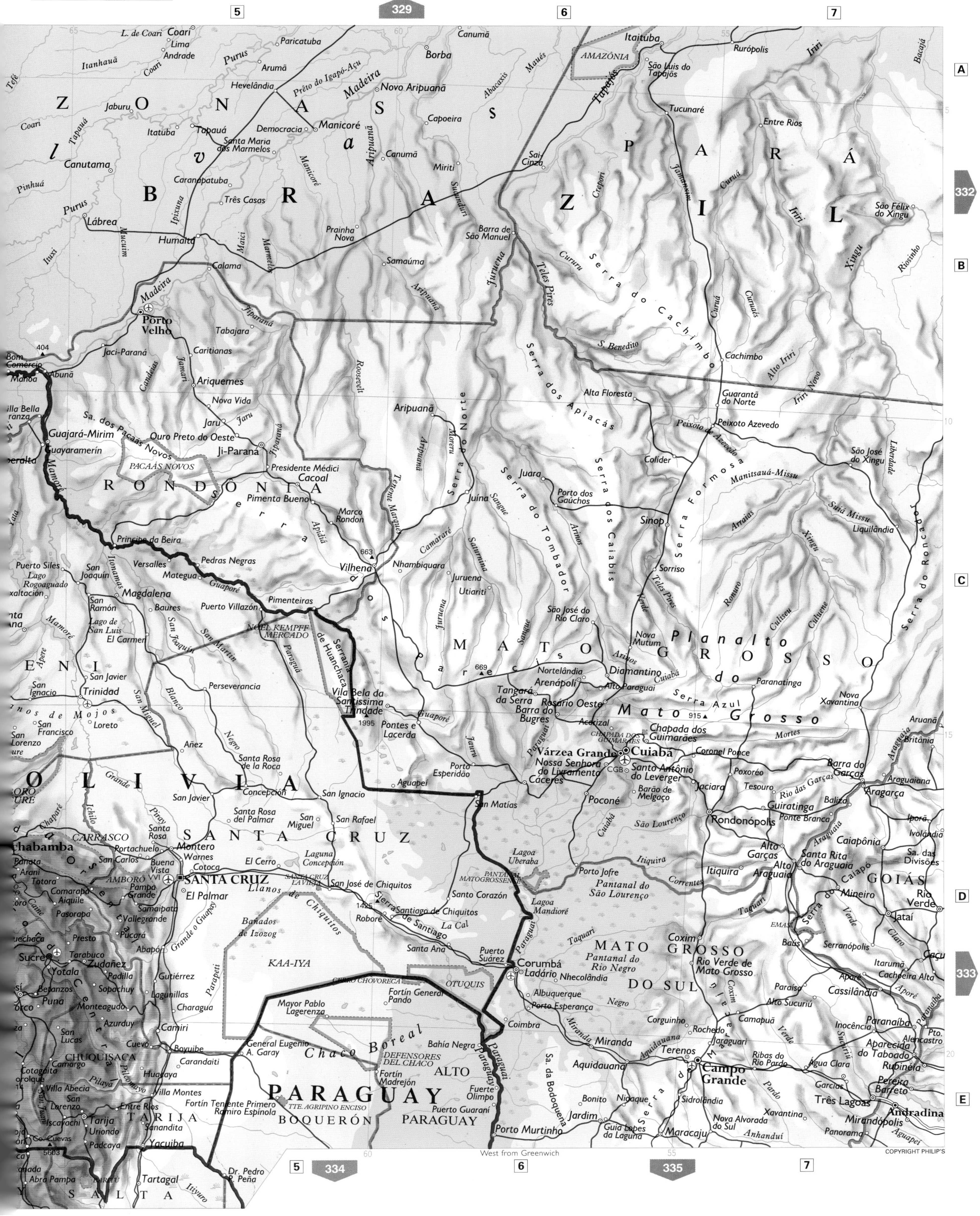

1:6 400 000

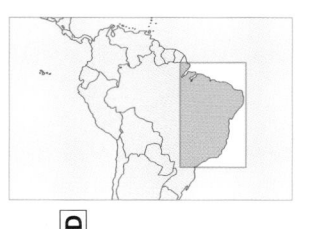

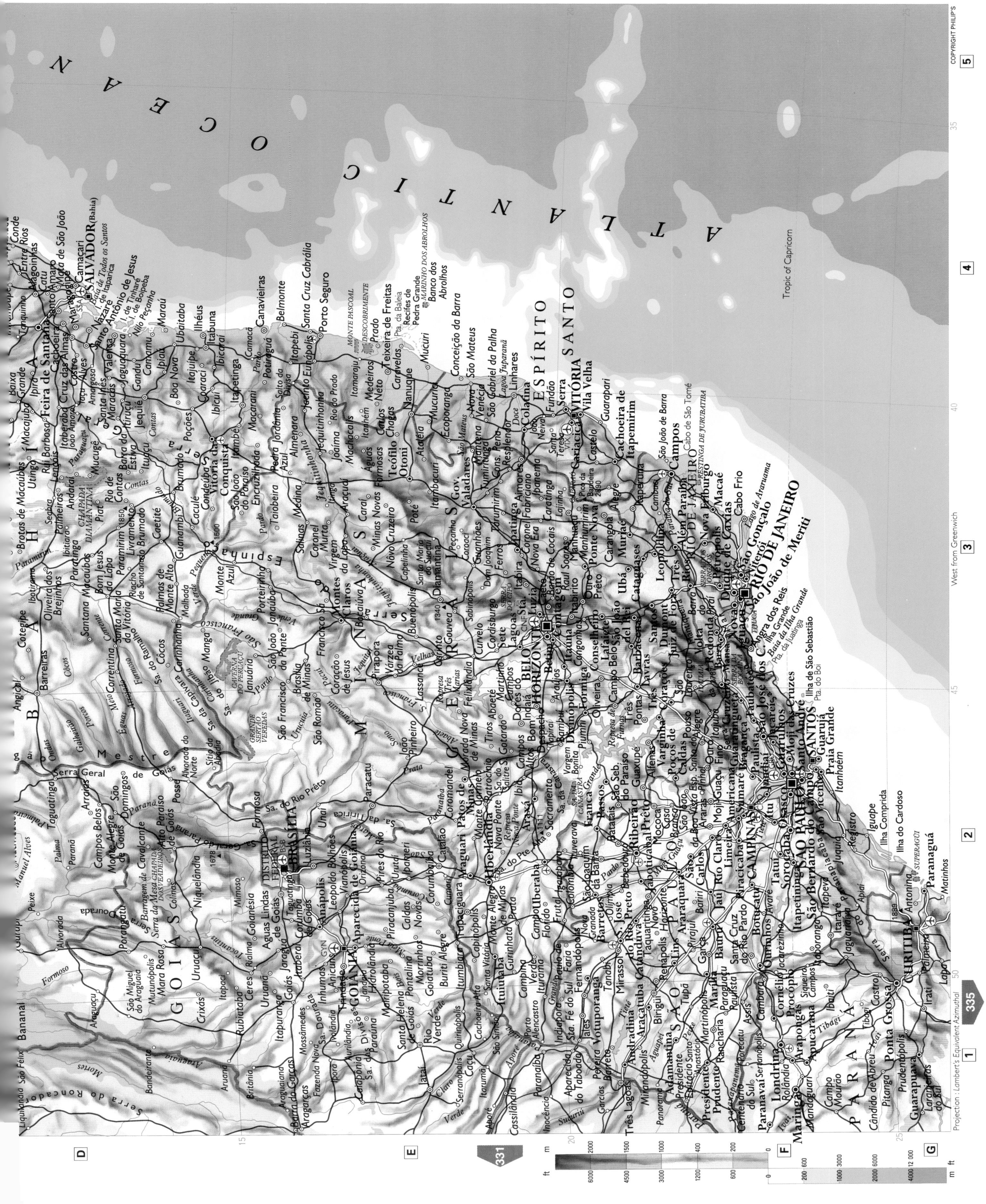
ATLANTIC OCEAN
BAHIA
MINAS GERAIS
ESPÍRITO SANTO
GOIÁS
SÃO PAULO
PARANÁ
RIO DE JANEIRO
SALVADOR (Bahia)
BRASÍLIA
BELO HORIZONTE
VITÓRIA
GOIÂNIA
CAMPINAS
SANTOS
CURITIBA
Tropic of Capricorn
West from Greenwich
COPYRIGHT PHILIP'S
Projection : Lambert's Equivalent Azimuthal
331
335

50 0 50 100 150 200 250 300 km

1:6 400 000

50 0 50 100 150 200 miles

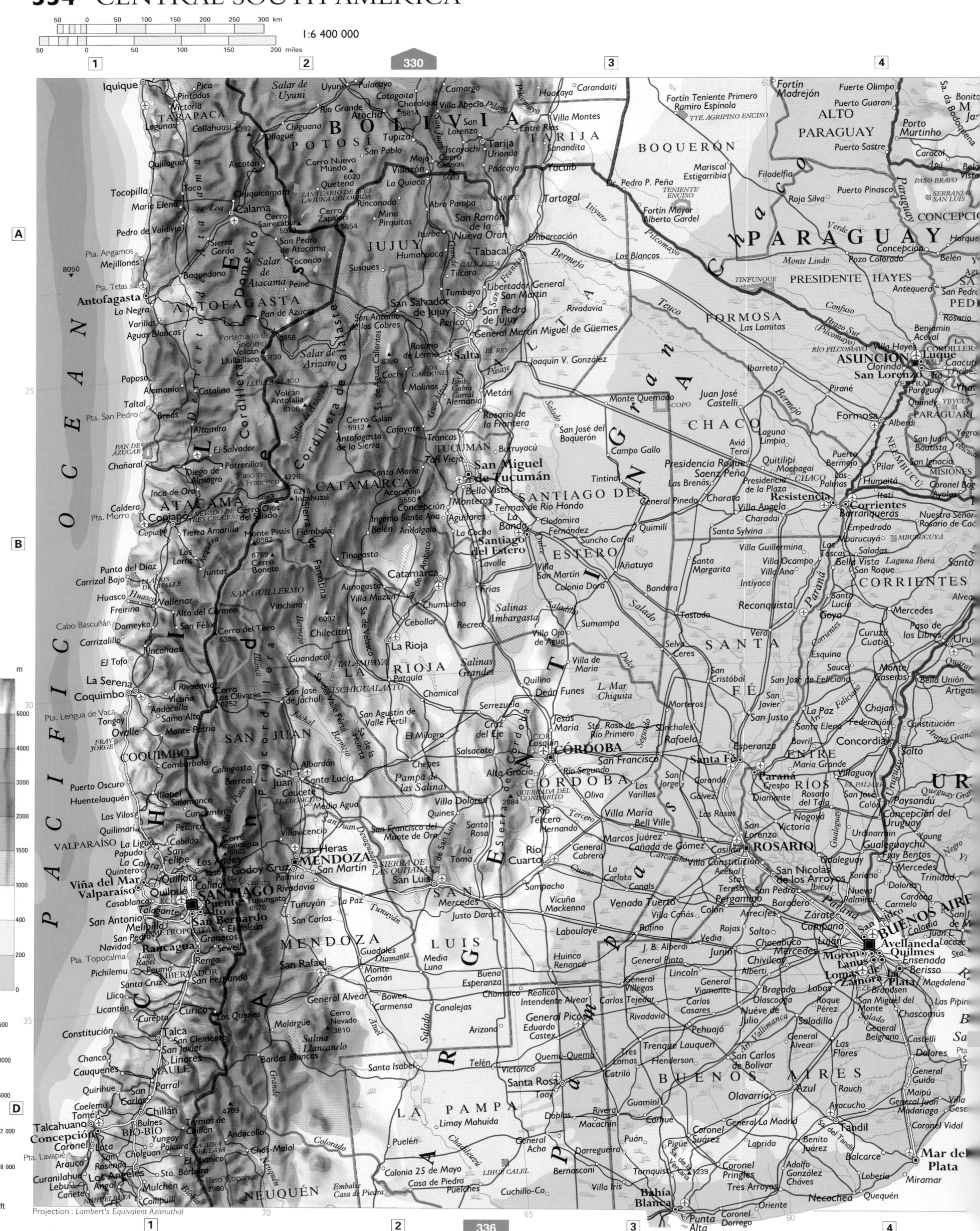

ft   m

18 000   6000
12 000   4000
9000   3000
6000   2000
4500   1500
3000   1000
1200   400
600   200
0   0
200   600
1000   3000
2000   6000
4000   12 000
6000   18 000

m   ft

Projection : Lambert's Equivalent Azimuthal

331 5 6 333 7

BELO HORIZONTE
CNF
Betim Contagem
Itabirito
Congonhas
Conselheiro Lafaiete
Ouro Prêto
Ponte Nova
Pico da Bandeira 2880
VITÓRIA
Vila Velha
Guarapari

MATO GROSSO DO SUL
Sidrolândia
Nioaque
Maracaju
Dourados
Ponta Porã
Pedro Juan Caballero
Amambaí

Três Lagoas
Andradina
Xavantina
Mirandópolis
Panorama
Presidente Epitácio
Adamantina
Santo Anastácio
Martinópolis
Rancharia
Presidente Prudente
Euclides da Cunha Paulista
Mirassol
Araçatuba
Birigüi
Penápolis
Lins
Tupã
Marília
Garça
Pompéia
Bauru
Pirajuí

Olímpia
São José do Rio Preto
Catanduva
Jaboticabal
Araraquara
São Carlos
Rio Claro
Limeira
Piracicaba

Batatais
Passos
Ribeirão Prêto
São Sebastião do Paraíso
Guaxupé
Mococa
Casa Branca
Poços de Caldas
Mogi Guaçu
Americana
Sumaré
CAMPINAS
Jundiaí

Oliveira
Campo Belo
Lavras
Varginha
Três Corações
São João del Rei
Barbacena
Juiz de Fora
Alfenas
Pouso Alegre
Itajubá
Cruzeiro

Ubá
Cataguases
Leopoldina
Muriaé
Três Rios
Além Paraíba
Carangola
Alegre
Castelo
Cachoeiro de Itapemirim
Itaperuna
Campos
São João da Barra

SÃO PAULO
RIO DE JANEIRO
Niterói
São Gonçalo
Duque de Caxias
Nova Iguaçu
Petrópolis
Nova Friburgo
Macaé
Cabo Frio

Guarulhos
Osasco
São Bernardo do Campo
Santo André
São Vicente
SANTOS
Guarujá
Praia Grande
Itanhaém

Sorocaba
Itapetininga
Tatuí
Itapeva
Registro
Iguape
Ilha Comprida
Ilha do Cardoso

BRAZIL
PARANÁ
Maringá
Cianorte
Umuarama
Londrina
Apucarana
Arapongas
Mandaguari
Cornélio Procópio
Jacarèzinho
Cascavel
Foz do Iguaçu
Ciudad del Este
Guarapuava
Ponta Grossa
CURITIBA
Antonina
Paranaguá
Guaratuba

Medianeira
Francisco Beltrão
Pato Branco
Palmas
União da Vitória
Porto União
São Mateus do Sul
Rio Negro
Mafra
JOINVILLE
São Francisco do Sul
Itajaí

SANTA CATARINA
Chapecó
Concórdia
Joaçaba
Campos Novos
Curitibanos
Rio do Sul
Blumenau
Brusque
São José
Ilha de Santa Catarina
FLORIANÓPOLIS

Xanxerê
Caçador
Santa Cecília
Lages
Vacaria
São Joaquim
Tubarão
Laguna
Criciúma
Araranguá
Torres

RIO GRANDE DO SUL
Santa Maria
Santa Cruz do Sul
Caxias do Sul
Bento Gonçalves
Novo Hamburgo
São Leopoldo
Canoas
Viamão
PORTO ALEGRE
Osório

Erechim
Passo Fundo
Carazinho
Cruz Alta
Ijuí
Santa Rosa
Santo Ângelo
São Luís Gonzaga
Horizontina
Frederico Westphalen

Santiago
São Borja
Alegrete
São Gabriel
Dom Pedrito
Bagé
Pelotas
Rio Grande
São José do Norte

Santana do Livramento
Rivera
Tacuarembó
Melo
Rio Branco
Jaguarão
Vergara
Treinta y Tres
Chuy
Rocha
Maldonado
Pta. del Este
MONTEVIDEO

URUGUAY
Santa Vitória do Palmar
Aiguá
Minas
San Carlos

A T L A N T I C

O C E A N

▼ 5304

Tropic of Capricorn

25

30

35

55 West from Greenwich 50 45 40

5 6 7

COPYRIGHT PHILIP'S

1:6 400 000

50 0 50 100 150 200 250 300 km
50 0 50 100 150 200 miles

2 334 **3** **4** 335 **5**

PACIFIC OCEAN

ATLANTIC OCEAN

LA PAMPA
BUENOS AIRES
RÍO NEGRO
NEUQUÉN
LA ARAUCANÍA
LOS RÍOS
LOS LAGOS
CHUBUT
SANTA CRUZ
MAGALLANES Y ANTÁRTICA CHILENA

CHILE
ARGENTINA

Cities and towns:
Temuco, Valdivia, Osorno, Puerto Montt, Ancud, Castro, Quellón, Chaitén, Coyhaique, Puerto Aisén, Cochrane, Puerto Natales, Punta Arenas, Porvenir, Puerto Williams, Ushuaia

Neuquén, San Carlos de Bariloche, Esquel, Trelew, Puerto Madryn, Rawson, Comodoro Rivadavia, Caleta Olivia, Puerto Deseado, Puerto San Julián, Puerto Santa Cruz, Río Gallegos, Río Grande, El Calafate

Bahía Blanca, Punta Alta, Carmen de Patagones, Viedma, Necochea, General Roca, Cipolletti, Colonia 25 de Mayo

Golfo San Matías
Golfo San Jorge
Península Valdés
Golfo de Penas
Bahía Grande
Estrecho de Magallanes (Magellan's Strait)
Canal Beagle
Isla Grande de Tierra del Fuego
TIERRA DEL FUEGO
CABO DE HORNOS (Cape Horn)
Islas Diego Ramírez

Cerro Aconcagua, Cerro Fitz Roy, San Valentín 4058, San Lorenzo 3706, Cerro Paine 3248, Monte Darwin 2488

FALKLAND ISLANDS (U.K.)
(ISLAS MALVINAS)
West Falkland, East Falkland
Jason Is., Pebble I., King George B., Queen Charlotte B., Weddell I., Port Darwin, Stanley
Mt. Adam 700, Mt. Usborne 705
Beauchêne I.

LOS GLACIARES
TORRES DEL PAINE
Lago Argentino, Lago Viedma, Lago Buenos Aires (L. General Carrera), L. San Martín, L. Cardiel

Projection: Lambert's Equivalent Azimuthal

West from Greenwich

COPYRIGHT PHILIP'S

GEOGRAPHICAL GLOSSARY

This is a list of the geographical terms from various foreign languages that are found in the place names on the maps and in the index. Each is followed by the language and its English meaning.

Afr. Afrikaans
Alb. Albanian
Amh. Amharic
Ar. Arabic
Belo. Belorussian
Berb. Berber
Bulg. Bulgarian
Burm. Burmese
Cam. Cambodian
Cat. Catalan
Chin. Chinese
Czec. Czech
Dan. Danish
Dut. Dutch
Est. Estonian
Fin. Finnish
Fr. French
Gae. Gaelic
Ger. German
Gr. Greek
Heb. Hebrew
Hin. Hindi
Hung. Hungarian
I.-C. Indo-Chinese
Ice. Icelandic
It. Italian
Indo. Indonesian
Jap. Japanese
Kaz. Kazakh
Kor. Korean
Kyrg. Kyrgyz
Lapp. Lapp (Sami)
Lat. Latvian
Lith. Lithuanian
Malag. Malagasy
Mong. Mongolian
Nor. Norway
Pash. Pashto
Per. Persian
Pol. Polish
Port. Portuguese
Rom. Romanian
Russ. Russian
Sin. Sinhalese
Ser.-Cr. Serbo-Croat
Slov. Slovene
Som. Somali
Span. Spanish
Swe. Swedish
Tib. Tibetan
Turk. Turkish
Ukr. Ukrainian
Viet. Vietnamese

-á *Ice.* river
-å *Dan., Nor., Swe.* stream
-abad *Farsi, Russ.* town
Abyad *Ar.* white mountain
Ada, Adasi *Turk.* island
Addis *Amh.* new
Adrar *Ar., Berb.* mountains
Aiguille *Fr.* peak
Aïn, Aïn (A.) *Ar.* spring
Åkra *Gr.* cape, point
Akrotiri *Gr.* cape, point
Alb *Ger.* mountains
Albufera *Span.* lagoon
-ålen *Nor.* islands
Alpen *Ger.* mountain ranges
Alpes *Fr.* mountains
Alpi *It.* mountains
Alt *Ger.* old
Alta, Alto *Port.* high, upper
Altos *Span.* mountains
-älv, -älven *Swe.* stream, river
Amtskommune (Amt.) *Dan.* first-order administrative division
-ån *Swe.* river
Anse *Fr.* bay
Ao *Thai* bay
Appennino *It.* mountain range
Archipel *Fr.* archipelago
Archipiélago (Arch.) *Span.* archipelago
Arcipelago *It.* archipelago
Arquipélago (Arq.) *Port.* archipelago
Arrecife *Span.* reef
Arroyo (Arr.) *Span.* stream
-ås, -åsen *Nor., Swe.* hill
Ayios *Gr.* island
Ayn *Ar.* well, waterhole

Baai, -baai *Afr., Dut.* bay
Bāb *Ar.* gate, strait
Bäck, -bäcken *Swe.* stream
Back, -backen, *Swe.* hill
Bad, -baden *Ger.* spa
Badia *Cat.* bay
Bādiyah, Bādiyat *Ar.* desert
Bæk *Dan.* stream
Bælt *Dan.* strait
Baharu *Malay* new
Bahia (B.) *Span.* bay
Bahiret *Ar.* lagoon
Bahr *Ar.* sea, lake, river
Bahra Bahrat *Ar.* lake
Baía (B.) *Port.* bay
Baie (B.) *Fr.* bay
Baixa, Baixo *Port.* lower
Baja, Bajo *Span.* lower
Bakke *Nor.* hill
Bala *Farsi* upper
Ballon *Fr.* dome
Baltă *Rom.* marsh, lake
Ban *Lao, Thai* village
-Bana *Jap.* cape
Banc *Fr.* bank
Banco *Span.* bank
Bandao *Chin.* peninsula
Bandar *Ar., Malay* port, harbour
Bandar *Farsi* bay
Banja *Ser.-Cr.* spa, resort
Banjaran *Malay* mountain range
Baraji *Turk.* dam
Barat *Indo., Malay* western
Barrage (Barr.) *Fr.* dam
Barragem (Barr.) *Port.* dam, reservoir
Bas, basse *Fr.* lower
Bassin *Fr.* basin
-batang *Indo.* river
Baṭlaq *Farsi* marsh
Batu *Malay* mountain
Bayt *Heb.* house, village
Bazar *Hin.* market, bazaar
-beek *Afr., Dut.* river
Be'er *Heb.* well
Bei *Chin.* north, northern
Beinn, Ben *Gae.* mountain
Beit *Heb.* village
Belaya, Belo, Beloye, Belyy *Russ.* white
Belogorye *Russ.* hills, mountain range
Bender *Som.* harbour
Berg(e), -berg(e) *Afr., Ger.* mountain(s)
-berg, -en, -et *Nor., Swe.* hill, mountain, rock
Besar *Indo., Malay* big
Bet *Heb.* house, village
Bir, Bîr, Bi'r *Ar.* well
Birkat, Birket *Ar.* lake, marsh, well
Bishti *Alb.* cape
-bjerg *Dan.* hill, point
Blaenau *Welsh* upland
-bo *Chin.* lake
Boca *Port., Span.* river mouth, inlet
Bodden *Ger.* bay, inlet
Bogaz, Boğazı *Turk.* channel, strait
Bogd *Mong.* mountain range
Bois *Fr.* woods
Boka *Ser.-Cr.* gulf, inlet
Bolshoi, Bolshaya, Bolshoye (Bol.) *Russ.* great, large
Bordj (Bj.) *Ar.* fort
-borg *Dan., Nor., Swe.* castle, fort
Bory *Pol.* woods
Bosque *Span.* woods
-botn *Nor.* valley floor
Bouche(s) *Fr.* mouth(s)
Braţul *Rom.* distributary stream, branch
-bre, -breen *Nor.* glacier
Bredning *Dan.* bay
Brücke *Ger.* bridge
-brug *Dut.* bridge
-brunn *Swe.* well, spring
Bucht *Ger.* bay
Bugt *Dan.* bay
-bugten *Dan.* bay
Buheirat *Ar.* lake, reservoir
Bukit *Malay* hill
-bukt, -a *Nor.* bay
-bukten *Swe.* bay
-bulag *Mong.* spring
Bulag *Chin.* lake
Bulu *Malay* mountain
Bum *Burm.* mountain
Bûr *Ar.* port
Burg. *Ar.* fort
Burg, -burg *Ger.* castle
Burnu, Burun *Turk.* cape
Butt *Gae.* promontory
Büyük *Turk.* big
-by *Dan., Nor., Swe.* town
-byen *Nor., Swe.* town

Cabeza *Span.* peak, hill
Cabo (C.) *Port., Span.* headland, cape
Cachoeira *Port.* waterfall
Cala Cat. *It.* bay
Camp Port. *Span.* land, field
Câmpia *Rom.* plain
Campo *It., Port., Span.* plain
Campos *Span.* upland
Canal (Can.) *Fr., Port., Span.* canal, channel
Canale (Can.) *It.* channel
Canalul (Can.) *Ser.-Cr.* canal
Cao Nguyen *Thai* plateau, tableland
Cap (C.) *Cat., Fr.* cape
Capo (C) *It.* cape
Carn *Gae.* hill
Carse *Gae.* valley
Catarata *Port., Span.* cataract
Cauce *Span.* intermittent stream
Causse *Fr.* limestone plateau
Cay, Cayi, -cay, -cayi *Turk.* river
Cayo(s) *Span.* rock(s), islet(s)
Cefn *Welsh* hill
Cerro *Span.* hill, peak
Česká, Český, České *Czec.* Czech
Chaco *Span.* jungle
Chaîne(s) *Fr.* mountain range(s)
Chang *Chin.* mountain
Chapa *Span.* hills, upland
Chapada *Port.* hills, upland
Chaung *Burm.* stream, river
Chi *Chin.* small lake
-ch'ŏn *Kor.* river
-chŏsuji *Kor.* reservoir
Chott *Ar.* salt lake, depression
Chu *Tib.* river
Chute *Fr.* waterfall
Città *It.* city
Ciudad *Span.* city
Co *Tib.* lake
Cochilla (Coch.) *Port.* hills
Col *Fr., It.* pass
Colina(s) *Span.* hill(s)
Colle *It.* pass
Colline(s) *Fr.* hill(s)
Conca *It.* plain, basin
Cordillera (Cord.) *Span.* mountain range
Costa *It., Port., Span.* coast
Côte *Fr.* coast, slope, hill
Coteaux *Fr.* hills
Cuchilla *Span.* hills
Cuenca *Span.* river basin
Cu-Lao *Viet.* island

Da *Chin.* big
Da *Viet.* river
Daban *Mong.* pass
Dağ(ı) *Turk.* mountain(s)
Dāgh *Farsi* mountain
Dağları *Turk.* mountain range
-dai, -daichi *Jap.* plateau
-Dake *Jap.* mountain
-dal, -e *Dan., Swe.* valley
-dal, -en *Swe., Nor.* valley, stream
Dalay Mong. large lake
-ðalir, -ðalur *Ice.* valley
-damm, -en *Swe.* lake
Danau *Malay* lake
Dao *Chin., Viet.* island
Dar *Ar.* region
Darya *Russ.* river
Daryācheh *Farsi* marshy lake, lake
Dasht *Farsi* desert, steppe
Daung *Burm.* mountain, hill
Dayr *Ar.* monastery
Debre *Amh.* hill
Deli *Ser.-Cr.* mountain
Deniz, -i *Turk.* sea
Département (Dépt.) *Fr.* first-order administrative division
Dere *Turk.* stream
Desierto (Des.) *Span.* desert
Détroit *Fr.* strait
Dhar *Ar.* region, mountain range
Diep *Dut.* channel
Dijk *Dut.* dyke
Ding *Chin.* mountain
Dingzi *Chin.* hill, mountain
Djebel (Dj.) *Ar.* mountain
-djúp *Ice.* fjord
-djupet *Swe.* channel, sound
-Do *Jap., Kor.* island
Dolina *Russ.* valley
Dolna, Dolni *Bulg.* lower
Dolna, Dolne, Dolny *Russ.* lower
Dolni *Czec.* lower
Dolok (D.) *Malay* mountain
-dong *Kor.* village, town
Dong *Chin.* east, eastern
Donja, Donji *Ser.-Cr.* lower
-dorf *Ger.* village
-dorp *Afr.* village
-drif *Afr.* ford
-dybet *Dan.* marine channel
Dzong *Tib.* town, settlement
Dzüün *Mong.* east, eastern

-egga *Nor.* peak
-eiland, -en (eil.) *Afr., Dut.* island(s)
Eilean *Gae.* island
-elv, -a *Nor.* river
Embalse *Span.* reservoir
'Emeq *Heb.* plain, valley
Ensenada *Span.* bay
Erg *Ar.* sand desert
Estero *Span.* estuary
Estrada *Span.* bay
Estrecho *Span.* strait
Estuaire *Fr.* estuary
Estuario *Span.* estuary
Étang *Fr.* lagoon, lake
-ey, -jar *Ice.* island(s)
-ežeras *Lith.* lake
-ezers *Lat.* lake

Falaise *Fr.* cliff
-fallet *Swe.* waterfall
Farihy *Malag.* lake
Faro *Span.* lighthouse
-feld *Ger.* field
-fell *Ice.* mountain, hill
Feng *Chin.* mountain range
Fiume (F.) *It.* river
-fjäll, -en, -et *Swe.* hill(s), mountain(s), ridge
-fjärden *Swe.* fjord
Fjeld *Dan.* mountain
-fjell, -et *Nor.* mountain range
-fjord, -en *Dan., Nor., Swe.* fjord
-fjorður *Ice.* fjord, bay, inlet
Fleuve (Fl.) *Fr.* river
-flói *Ice.* bay, marshy country
Fluss (F.) *Ger.* river
Foce, Foci *It.* mouth(s)
Folyó (F.) *Hung.* river
-fonn *Nor.* glacier
-fontein *Afr.* fountain, spring
Forêt *Fr.* forest
-fors, -en *Swe.* waterfall, rapids
-foss, -en *Ice., Nor.* waterfall
Forst *Ger.* forest
Foum *Ar.* pass
Fuente *Span.* source
-furt *Ger.* ford
Fylke *Nor.* first-order administrative division

-gang *Chin.* bay, harbour
-gang *Kor.* river
Ganga *Hin., Sin.* river
Gangri *Tib.* mountain
Gaoyuan *Chin.* plateau
-gat *Dan.* sound
-Gata *Jap.* lake
-gau *Ger.* district
-Gawa *Jap.* river
Gebel (G.) *Ar.* mountain
Gebirge (Geb.) *Ger.* hills, mountains
Gezirat, Geziret *Ar.* island
Ghat *Hin.* range of hills
Ghiol *Rom.* lake
Ghubbat *Ar.* bay, inlet
Gjiri *Alb.* bay
Gjol *Alb.* lagoon, lake
Glava (Gl.) *Ser.-Cr.* mountain, peak
Glen *Gae.* valley
Gletscher (Gl.) *Ger.* glacier
Gobi *Mong.* desert
Gol *Mong.* river
Göl *Azeri, Turk.* lake
Golfe (G.) *Fr.* gulf
Golfo (G.) *It., Span.* gulf
Gölü *Turk.* lake
Gomba *Tib.* settlement
Gora, Góra *Bulg., Russ., Ser.-Cr., Pol.* mountain
Gorje *Ser.-Cr.* hills, mountains
Gorno *Russ.* mountainous
-gorod *Russ.* small town
Gory, Góry *Pol., Russ.* mountain
-grad *Bulg. Russ., Ser.-Cr.* town, city
-grada *Russ.* ridge
Gran *It., Span.* big, great
Grand, -e *Fr.* big, great
Groot (Gt.) *Afr., Dut.* big, great
Gross, -e, -en, -er *Ger.* big, great(er)
Grupo *Span.* group
Gruppo *It.* group
Guan *Chin.* pass
Guba (G.) *Russ.* bay
-Guntō *Jap.* island group
Gunong, Gunung (G.) *Indo., Malay* mountain
Gură *Rom.* passage

Hadabat *Ar.* plateau
Hadjer *Ar.* mountain
-hafen *Ger.* harbour, port
Haff *Ger.* bay, lagoon
Hai *Chin.* lake, sea
Haixia *Chin.* channel, strait
Halbinsel *Ger.* peninsula
Halvø *Dan.* peninsula
Halvøya *Nor.* peninsula
Hāmad, Hamada, Hammādah, Hammādat *Ar.* stony desert, plateau
-hamn *Swe., Nor.* harbour, anchorage
Hāmūn *Farsi* marsh, lake
-Hantō *Jap.* peninsula
Har(e) *Heb.* hill(s), mountain(s)
Hassi (Hi.) *Ar.* well
-haug *Nor.* hill
Hav, Havet *Nor., Swe.* sea
-havn *Dan., Nor.* bay, harbour
Havre *Fr.* harbour
Hawd *Ar.* oasis
Hawr *Ar.* lake, marsh
He *Chin.* river
-hegység *Hung.* hills, forest
Heide *Ger.* heath, moor
Helodranon' *Malag.* bay
Higashi *Jap.* east, eastern
-ho *Kor.* lake
-hø *Nor.* peak
Hoch *Ger.* high
Hochland *Afr.* highland
Hoek, -hoek *Afr., Dut.* cape, point
-höfn *Ice.* harbour, port
-hög, -en, -högar, -högarna *Swe.* hill(s), peak, mountain
Höhe *Ger.* height
Hohen *Ger.* high, upper
-hoi *Chin.* bay
-høj, -e *Dan.* hills
-holm, -holme, -holmen *Dan., Nor., Swe.* island
Hon *Viet.* island
Hoog *Dut.* high
Hora *Czec., Ukr.* mountain
-horn *Ger.* peak
Hory *Czec.* mountains, hills
-hot *Mong.* town
-hoved *Dan.* point, headland, peninsula
-hrad *Czec.* town
Hráun *Ice.* lava
-hsi *Chin.* river
-hsia *Chin.* gorge, strait
-hsien *Chin.* district
Hu *Chin.* lake, reservoir
Huk *Dan., Ger.* cape
-huk *Swe.* cape
Huken *Nor.* cape

Idd *Ar.* well
Idehan *Ar., Berb.* sandy plain, dunes
-ike *Jap.* lake
Île(s) (I(s).) *Fr.* island(s)
Ilha(s) (I(s).) *Port.* island(s)
imeni *Russ.* 'in the name of'
Inish *Gae.* island
Insel(n) (I.) *Ger.* island(s)
Irmak *Turk.* river
'Irq *Ar.* dunes
Isla(s) (I(s).) *Span.* island(s)
Iso *Fin.* big, great
Isol, -a, -e (I.) *It.* island(s)
Isthme *Fr.* isthmus
Istmo *Span.* isthmus
-iwa *Jap.* island

Jabal *Ar.* mountain range
Järv *Est.* lake
järvi *Fin.* lake, bay, pond
-jaur, -javre *Lapp.* lake
Jazā'ir *Ar.* islands
Jazīra, jazīrat *Ar.* island
Jazireh *Farsi* island
Jebel *Ar.* mountain
Jezero *Ser.-Cr.* lake
Jezioro *Pol.* lake
Jiang *Chin.* river
Jiao *Chin.* cape
-Jima *Jap.* island
Jøkulen *Nor.* glacier, ice cap
-joki *Fin.* river
-jökull *Ice.* glacier, ice cap
Jūras Līcis *Lat.* bay, gulf

Kaap (K.) *Afr.* cape
-kai *Jap.* bay, channel, sea
-kaikyō *Jap.* strait
-kaise *Lapp.* mountain
kalnas *Lith.* hill
Kamennyy *Russ.* stony
Kampong *Cam.* village
Kampung *Malay* village
-kanaal *Dut.* canal
Kanal *Dan.* channel, gulf
Kanal *Ger., Swe.* canal
-kanal *Ser.-Cr.* channel, canal
Kanava *Fin.* canal
Kang *Kor.* river, bay
Kap (K.) *Dan., Ger.* cape, point
-kapp *Nor.* cape, point
-kaupstaður *Ice.* market town
-kaupunki *Fin.* town
Kavīr *Farsi* salt desert
Kébir *Ar.* great
Kecil *Malay* lesser, little
Kefar *Heb.* village, hamlet
-Ken *Jap.* first-order administrative division
Kep, -i (K.) *Alb.* cape
Kepulauan (Kep.) *Indo., Malay* archipelago
Keski- *Fin.* middle, central
Khalīg, Khalīj *Ar.* gulf
-khamba *Tib.* source, spring
Khawr *Ar.* bay, channel, wadi
Khlong *Thai* river
Kho Khot *Thai* isthmus
Khōr *Farsi* bay, estuary
Khrebet *Russ.* mountain range
Kita- *Jap.* north
Klein,-e, -er *Ger.* small
-klint *Dan.* cliff
Klintar *Swe.* hills
-kloof *Afr.* gorge, pass
Knude *Dan.* point
-Ko *Jap.* lake
Ko *Thai* island
-kōchi *Jap.* mountainous region
-kōgen *Jap.* plateau
Kohi *Pash.* mountains
Kol *Kaz., Kyrg.* lake
Kólpos *Gr., Turk.* gulf, bay
Kolymskoye *Russ.* mountain range
Kompong *Malay* landing place
-kop *Afr.* hill
-kopf *Ger.* hill
-köping *Swe.* market town
Körfäzi *Azeri* gulf
Körfezi *Turk.* gulf
Kosa *Russ., Ukr.* spit
-koski *Fin.* rapids
-kraal *Afr.* native village
-kraj *Czec., Pol., Ser.-Cr.* region
Krasnyy *Russ.* red
Kryazh *Russ.* ridge, hills
Kuala *Malay* bay
-kuan *Chin.* pass
Kūh(ha) *Farsi* mountain(s)
Kul *Russ.* lake
-kulle *Swe.* hill
Kum *Russ.* sandy desert
Kumpu *Fin.* hill
Kwe *Burm.* bay, gulf
-kylä *Fin.* village
Kyst, -en *Dan., Nor.* coast
Kyun(zu) *Burm.* island(s)

La *Tib.* pass
-laagte *Afr.* watercourse

Lääni *Fin.* first-order administrative division
Lac (L.) *Fr.* lake
Lacul (L.) *Rom.* lake, lagoon
Lago (L.) *It., Port., Span.* lake, lagoon
Lagoa (L.) *Port.* lagoon
Lagos *Port., Span.* lakes
Laguna (L.) *It., Span.* lagoon, lake
Lagune (L.) *Fr.* lake
-laht *Est.* bay
Lahti *Fin.* bay, gulf, cove
Lakhti *Russ.* bay, gulf
Lam *Thai* river
Lampi *Fin.* lake
Län *Swe.* first-order administrative division
Land *Ger.* first-order administrative division
-land *Dan.* region
-land *Afr., Nor.* land, province
Lande *Fr.* heath
Laut *Indo.* sea
Law *Gae.* hill, mountain
Līcis *Lat.* gulf
Lido *It.* beach, shore
Liedao *Chin.* islands
Lilla *Swe.* small
Lille *Dan., Nor.* small
Liman *Russ.* bay, gulf
Limni (L.) *Gr.* lake
Ling *Chin.* mountain range
-linna *Fin.* fort
Llano *Span.* prairie, plain
Llyn *Welsh* lake
Loch (L.) *Gae.* lake, inlet
Lough (L.) *Gae.* lake, inlet
Lum *Alb.* river
Lund *Dan.* forest
-lund, -en *Swe.* wood(s)
-luoto *Fin.* island

-maa *Est.* island
Madīnat *Ar.* town, city
Madiq *Ar.* strait
Maja *Alb.* mountains
-mäki *Fin.* hill, hillside
Mal *Alb.* mountain
Maloye, Malyy, Malyya *Russ.* little, small
Mala, Mali, Malo *Ser.-Cr.* little, small
Malaya *Belo.* small
Malé *Czec., Slovak* small
Mali *Alb.* mountain
-man *Kor.* bay
Mar *Span.* lagoon, sea
Marais *Fr.* marsh
Mare *It.* sea
Mare *Rom.* great
Marisma *Span.* marsh
-mark *Dan., Nor.* land
Marsâ *Ar.* anchorage, bay, inlet
Masabb *Ar.* river mouth, estuary
Massif *Fr.* upland, mountains
Mato *Port.* forest
Mazar *Farsi* shrine, tomb
Meer, -meer *Afr., Dut., Ger.* lake, sea
-men *Chin.* bay, gorge, channel
Mesto *Ser.-Cr., Czec.* town
Mezzo *It.* middle
Midbar *Heb.* wilderness
Mierzeja *Pol.* spit
Mifraz *Heb.* bay
Mina *Ar.* port
Minami *Jap.* south, southern
-misaki *Jap.* cape, point
Mittel *Ger.* central, middle
-mo *Nor., Swe.* heath, island
-mon *Swe.* heath
Mong *Burm.* town
Mont(s) (Mt(s).) *Fr.* hill(s), mountain(s)
Montagna (Mt.) *It.* mountain
Montagne(s) (Mt(s).) *Fr.* hill(s), mountain(s)
Montaña(s) (Mt(s).) *Span.* mountain(s)
Montanyes *Cat.* mountains
Monte(s) (Mte(s).) *It., Port., Span.* mountain(s)
Monti (Mti.) *It.* mountains
More *Russ.* sea
Mörön *Mong.* river
Moyen *Fr.* central, middle
Muang *Malay* town
Mui *Viet.* cape
Mull *Gae.* promontory
Mund, -mund *Afr.* mouth
Munkhafed *Ar.* depression
Munte (Mte.) *Rom.* mount
Munţi(i) (Mţi.) *Rom.* mountain(s)
Muong *Malay* village
Myit *Burm.* river
Myitwanya *Burm.* mouths of river
Mynydd *Welsh* mountain
-myr *Nor., Swe.* swamp
-mýri *Ice.* swamp
Mys (M.) *Russ.* cape

-Nada *Jap.* bay, gulf
-næs *Dan.* point, cape
Nafūd *Ar.* sandy desert
Nagorye *Russ.* hills, mountains
Nagy *Hung.* big
Nahal (N.) *Heb.* river
Nahr (N.) *Ar.* river, stream
Najd *Ar.* plateau, pass
Nakhon *Thai* town
Nam *Kor., Viet.* river
-nam *Kor.* south
Namakzār *Per.* salt flat
Nan *Chin.* south, southern
-nao *Chin.* lake
-näs *Swe.* cape
Neder *Dut.* lower
Nedre *Nor.* lower
Nei *Chin.* inner
Nek *Afr.* pass
-nes *Ice., Nor.* cape
Ness, -ness *Gae.* promontory, cape
Nevada, Nevado *Span.* snow-capped mountain
Nez *Fr.* cape
Nieder *Ger.* lower
-niemi *Fin.* cape, point, peninsula, island
Nieuw, -e *Dut.* new
Nishi *Jap.* west, western
Nisos, Nisoi *Gr.* island(s)
Nizhneye, Nizhniy *Russ.* lower
Nizina *Belo., Pol.* lowland
Nizmennost *Russ.* plain, lowland
Nizní *Czec.* lower
Noord *Dut.* north, northern
Nord *Fr.* north, northern
Norra *Swe.* north, northern
Nørre *Dan.* north, northern
Norte *Port., Span.* north, northern
Nos *Bulg., Russ.* cape, point
Nosy *Malag.* island
Nouveau, Nouvelle *Fr.* new
Nova, Novi *Bulg., Port., Serb.-Cr.* new
Novaya, Novo, Novoye, Novyy *Russ.* new
Nové, Novy *Czec., Slovak* new
Novo *Port.* new
Nowa, Nowe, Nowy *Pol.* new
Nudo *Span.* mountain
Nueva, Nuevo *Span.* new
Nur *Chin.* lake
Nur *Tib.* peak
Nuruu *Mong.* mountain range
Nusa *Indo.* island
Nuur *Mong.* lake
Ny *Dan., Nor., Swe.* new

-ø *Dan., Nor.* island
-ö *Swe.* island,
-öar, -na *Swe.* islands
Ober *Ger., Ukr.* upper
Oblast *Russ.* administrative division
Öbor *Mong.* inner
Occidental *Fr., Span.* western
-odde *Dan., Nor.* point, peninsula, cape
Oeste *Span.* west, western
Oglat *Ar.* well
Oji *Alb.* bay
Ojo *Span.* spring
-Oki *Jap.* bay
-ön *Swe.* island
Ondör *Mong.* upper
Oost(er) *Dut.* east(ern)
Oraşu *Rom.* city
Ord *Gae.* point
Óri *Gr.* mountains
Oriental, -e *Fr., Span.* east, eastern
Órmos *Gr.* bay
Óros *Gr.* mountain(s)
Ort *Ger.* point, cape
Ost *Ger.* east
Øst(er) *Den., Nor.* east(ern)
Öst(ra) *Swe.* east(ern)
Ostriv *Ukr.* island
Ostrov(a) *Russ.* island(s)
Otok(i) *Ser.-Cr.* island(s)
Ouabi, Ouadi (O.) *Ar.* dry watercourse, wadi
Oud, -e *Dut.* old
Oued, -i (O.) *Ar.* watercourse
Ouest *Fr.* west, western
Ouzan *Farsi* river
Ova, -si *Turk.* plains, lowlands
Over- *Dan., Dut.* upper
Över-, Övre *Nor., Swe.* upper
-øy, -a *Nor.* island(s)
Oya *Hin.* point
Oya *Sin.* river
Ozero, Ozera (Oz.) *Russ., Ukr.* lake(s)

-pää *Fin.* hill(s), mountain
Pahta *Lapp.* hill
Pampa(s) *Span.* plain(s)
Pantanal *Port.* marsh
Pantano *Span.* reservoir
Pantao *Chin.* peninsula
Parbat *Urdu* mountain
Pas *Fr.* strait
Paso (P.) *Span.* pass
Passage *Fr.* channel
Passe *Fr.* channel
Passo (P.) *It.* pass
Pasul (P.) *Rom.* pass
Patam *Hin.* small village
Patna, -patnam *Hin.* small village
Pegunungan *Indo., Malay* mountain range
Pei, -pei *Chin.* north
Pélagos *Gr.* sea
Pen *Welsh* hill
Peña *Span.* rock, peak
Pendi *Chin.* basin, depression
Péninsule *Fr.* peninsula
Penisola (Pen.) *It.* peninsula
Pereval (Per.) *Russ.* pass
Pervo-, Pervyy- *Russ.* first
Pertuis *Fr.* channel, strait
Peski *Russ.* sand desert
Petit, -e *Fr.* small
Phanom *Thai* mountain
Phnum *Cam.* mountain
Phou *Lao.* mountain
Phu *Thai, Viet.* mountain
Piano *It.* plain
Pic *Cat., Fr.* peak
Pico(s) *Span.* peak(s)
-piggen *Dan.* peak
Pik *Russ.* peak
Pingyuan *Chin.* plain
Pique *Fr.* peak
Piton *Fr.* peak
Pivostriv *Ukr.* peninsula
Piz, Pizzo *It.* peak
Plage *Fr.* beach
Plaine *Fr.* plain
Planalto *Port.* plateau
Planina (Pl.) *Bulg., Ser.-Cr.* mountain range
Plato *Russ., Bulg.* plateau
Playa *Span.* beach
-po *Chin.* lake, wetland
Pointe (Pte.) *Fr.* point, cape
Pojezierze *Pol.* lakes
Polder *Dut.* reclaimed farmland
-pólis *Gr.* city, town
Poluostrov (Pov.) *Russ.* peninsula
Połwysep *Pol.* peninsula
Pont *Fr.* bridge
Ponta (Pta.) *Port.* point, cape
Ponte *Port.* bridge
Poort *Afr.* passage, gate
-poort *Dut.* port
Porta *Port.* pass
Porţile *Rom.* gate
Portillo *Span.* pass
Porto *It., Port., Span.* port
Potámi, Potamós *Gr.* river
Pradesh *Hin.* state
Praia *Port.* beach, shore
Presa *Span.* reservoir
Presqu'ile *Fr.* peninsula
Prokhod *Bulg.* pass
Proliv *Russ.* strait
Promontorio *Span.* promontory
Průsmyk (Pr.) *Czec.* pass
Pueblo *Span.* village
Puerto (Pto.) *Span.* port
Puig *Cat.* peak
Pulau (P.) *Indo., Malay* island
Puna *Span.* desert plateau
Puncak *Indo.* peak
Punta (Pta.) *It., Span.* point, peak
Puy *Fr.* peak

Qal'at *Ar.* fort
Qanat *Ar.* canal
Qasr *Ar.* fort
Qiryat *Heb.* town
Qiuling *Chin.* plateau
Qolleh *Farsi* mountain
-qundao *Chin.* islands

Rach *Viet.* river
Rags *Lat.* cape
Rambla *Cat.* river
Ramlat *Ar.* sandy desert
Rão (R.) *Port.* river
Rann *Hin.* swampy region
Rao *I.-C.* river
Ras *Amh., Ar., Farsi* cape, point
Récif(s) *Fr.* reef(s)
Recife(s) *Port.* reef(s)
Reka *Bulg.* river
Repede *Rom.* rapids
Represa *Port.* reservoir
Reshteh *Farsi* mountain range
-rettō *Jap.* group of islands, chain
Ria *Port., Span.* estuary, bay
Ribeirão (R.) *Port.* river
Ribera (R.) *Span.* river bank
Rijeka *Ser.-Cr.* river
Rio (R.) *Port., Span.* river
Rivier (R.) *Afr., Dut.* river
Riviera *It.* coastal plain, coast
Rivière (R.) *Fr.* river
Roca *Span.* rock
Rocca *It.* rock, peak
Roche *Fr.* rock
Rt *Ser.-Cr.* cape, point
Rubh', Rubha *Gae.* cape, point
-rück *Ger.* ridge
Rūd *Farsi* stream, river
Rudohorie *Slovak* mountains
Rzeka (R.) *Pol.* river

-saar *Est.* island
-saari *Fin.* island
Sabkhat, Sabkhet *Ar.* salt flats
Sadd *Ar.* dam
Sagar,-a *Hin., Urdu* lake
Sahrâ *Ar.* desert
-Saki *Jap.* cape, point
Salar *Span.* salt flat
Salina(s) *Span.* salt marsh(es)
-salmi *Fin.* strait, sound, lake, channel
Saltsjöbad *Swe.* resort
-Sammyaku *Jap.* mountain range
Samut *Thai* gulf
San (S.) *It., Port., Span.* saint
-San *Jap., Kor.* hill, mountain
-Sanchi *Jap.* mountain range
Sankt (St.) *Ger., Russ.* saint
-sanmaek *Kor.* mountain range
-sanmyaku *Jap.* mountain range
Santa (Sta.) *It., Port., Span.* saint
Santo (Sto.) *It. Port., Span.* saint
São (S.) *Port.* saint
Sarīr *Ar.* desert
Sasso *It.* mountain
Satu *Rom.* village
Saurums *Lat.* strait
Sebkha, Sebkhet *Ar.* salt flat
See, -see *Ger.* lake
-şehir *Turk.* town
Selat *Indo., Malay* strait
Selatan *Indo.* southern
-selkä *Fin.* bay, lake, ridge, hills
Selo *Ser.-Cr., Russ.* village
Selva *Port., Span.* forest, wood
Seno *Span.* bay, sound
Serir *Ar.* stony desert
Serra (Sa.) *Cat., Port.* range of hills
Serranía *Span.* mountain ridge
Severo, Severnaya, Severnoye, Severnyy (Sev.) *Russ.* north, northern
Sfântu *Rom.* saint
Shahr, -shahr *Farsi* city, town
Shamo *Chin.* desert
Shan *Chin.* hills, mountains
Shankou *Chin.* pass
Shanmo *Chin.* mountain range
Sharm *Ar.* bay
Shatt *Ar.* river mouth, estuary
-Shima *Jap.* island
Shimāli *Ar.* northern
-Shotō *Jap.* group of islands
-shui *Chin.* river
-shuiku *Chin.* reservoir
Sierra (Sa.) *Span.* mountain range
-sjö, -sjön, -sjø *Swe., Nor.* lake
-sjøen *Dan.* sea
-sjór *Ice.* lake
-sker *Ice.* island
-skär *Swe.* island, rock, cape
-skog, -skogen *Nor., Swe.* wood(s)
-skov *Dan.* forest
Slieve *Gae.* hill, mountain
Sø *Dan., Nor.* lake
Söder, Södra *Swe.* south, southern
Sør *Nor.* south, southern
Solonchak *Russ.* salt lake, marsh
Sønder, Søndra *Dan.* south, southern
Song *Viet.* river
Souk *Ar.* market
-spitze *Ger.* peak, mountain
-spruit *Afr.* stream
Sredna, Sredno *Bulg.* middle, central
Sredne, Sredneye *Russ.* middle, central
Srednja *Ser.-Cr.* middle, central
-stad *Afr., Nor., Swe.* town
-stadt *Ger.* town
-staður *Ice.* town
Stara, Stari *Ser.-Cr.* old
Stará, Staré, Stary *Czec.* old
Staraya, Staroye, Staryy *Russ.* old
Stare, Staro, Stary *Ukr.* old
Stausee *Ger.* reservoir
Stenón *Gr.* strait, pass
Step *Russ.* steppe
Stor, -a *Swe.* big
Store *Dan.* big
-strand *Dan., Ger., Nor., Swe.* beach
-strede *Nor.* straits
Strelka *Russ.* spit
-strete *Nor.* straits
Stretto (Str.) *It.* strait
Strædet (Str.) *Dan.* strait
-ström, -strömmen *Swe.* stream(s)
-stroom *Afr.* large river
Sud *Fr.* south, southern
Süd, -er *Ger.* south, southern
Suid *Afr.* south, southern
-Suidō *Jap.* strait, channel
Sul *Port.* south, southern
Sûn *Burm.* cape
-sund, -et *Swe., Nor.* sound, estuary, inlet
Sungai *Indo., Malay* river
Sur *Span.* south, southern
Sveti *Bulg.* saint
Syd *Dan., Swe.* south, southern
Sýsla *Ice.* first-order administrative division

-tag *Uighur* mountain
Tai -tai *Chin.* tower
-Take *Jap.* mountain
Tal *Mong.* plain, steppe
-tal *Ger.* valley
Tall *Ar.* hills
Tanjona *Malag.* cape, point
Tanjung, Tanjong (Tg.) *Indo., Malay.* cape, point
Tao *Chin.* island
Tasik *Malay* lake
Tassili *Ar.* rocky plateau
Tau *Russ.* mountain range
Taung *Burm.* mountain
Taungdan. *Burm.* mountain range
Taunggya *Burm.* pass
-tekojärvi *Fin.* reservoir
Teluk *Indo., Malay* bay, gulf
Ténéré *Berb.* desert
Tengah *Indo.* middle, central
-thal *Ger.* valley
Thok *Tib.* town
Tien *Chin.* lake, marsh
Tierra *Span.* land, country
Timur *Indo.* eastern
-tind *Nor.* peak
-ting *Chin.* mountain
Tjärn, -en, -et *Swe.* lake
-Tō *Jap.* island
Tong *Kor.* village, town
Tong *Burm., Thai, Kor.* mountain range
Tonlé *Cam.* lake
Top *Dut.* peak
-topp, -en *Nor.* peak
-träsk *Swe.* lake, swamp
Tsangpo *Tib.* large river
Tso *Tib.* lake
Tsu *Jap.* entrance, bay
Tsui *Chin.* cape, point
Tulur *Ar.* hill
-tunturi *Fin.* hill(s), mountain(s), ridge

Uad *Ar.* dry watercourse, wadi
Über *Ger.* upper
-udde, -udden *Swe.* point, cape
Uebi *Som.* river
Ujung *Indo., Malay* cape
Unter- *Ger.* lower
Us *Mong.* water
Ust, Ustye *Russ.* river mouth
Utara *Indo.* north, northern
Uttar *Hin.* north, northern
Uul *Mong., Russ.* mountain range

-vaara *Fin.* hill, mountain ridge, peak
Vaart *Dut.* canal
-våg *Nor.* bay
Val *Fr., Port., Span.* valley
Valea *Rom.* valley
-vall, -en *Swe.* mountain
Valle *It., Span.* valley
Vallée *Fr.* valley
Valli *It.* lake, lagoon
-város *Hung.* town
-varre *Nor.* mountain
Väst, Västra *Swe.* west, western
-vatn *Ice., Nor.* lake
-vatnet *Nor.* lake
-vatten, vattnet *Swe.* lake
-vecchio *It.* old
Vechi *Rom.* old
-ved, -veden *Swe.* hills
Veld, -veld *Afr.* field
Velha, Velho *Port.* old
Velika, Velike, Veliki, Veliko *Ser.-Cr., Slov.* big, large
Velikaya, Velikiy *Russ.* big, large
Velká, Velké, Velký *Czec.* big, large
Verkhne, Verkhniy *Russ.* upper
-vesi *Fin.* water, lake, bay, sound, strait
Vest, Vester, Vestre *Dan., Nor.* west, western
-vidda *Nor.* plateau
Vieille, Vieux *Fr.* old
Vieja, Vejo *Span.* old
Vig *Dan.* bay, inlet, cove, lagoon, lake
-vik *Ice.* bay
-vik, -a, -en *Nor., Swe.* bay, gulf, inlet, lake
Vila *Port.* small town
Villa *Span.* town
Ville *Fr.* town
Vinh *Viet.* bay
Vîrful (Vf.) *Rom.* peak, mountain
-viz *Hung.* river
-víztároló *Hung.* reservoir
-vlei *Afr.* lake, salt pan
-vliet *Dut.* canal
-vloer *Afr.* salt pan
Vodokhranilishche (Vdkhr.) *Russ.* reservoir
Vodoskovyshche (Vdskh.) *Ukr.* reservoir
Volcán (Vol.) *Span.* volcano, mountain
Vorota *Russ.* pass, channel, strait
Vostochno, Vostochnyy *Russ.* east, eastern
-vötn *Ice.* lakes
Vozvyshennost *Russ.* heights, uplands
Vozyera *Belo.* lake
Vrata *Bulg.* gate, pass
Vrchovina *Czec.* mountainous country
Vrch(y) *Czec.* mountain (range)
Vung *Viet.* bay, gulf
-vuori *Fin.* mountain, hill
Vychodné *Slovak* east, eastern
Vysochyna *Ukr.* upland

-waard *Dut.* polder
Wadi (W.) *Ar.* dry watercourse
Wâhât *Ar.* oasis
Wald *Ger.* forest, mountains
-Wan *Chin., Jap.* bay, harbour
Wāw *Ar.* well
Webi *Amh.* river
Wes *Afr.* west, western
Wielka, Wielki, Wielko *Pol.* big, large
Woestyn *Afr.* desert
Wysoka, Wysoki *Pol.* upper
Wyżyna *Pol.* plateau

Xi *Chin.* river
Xia *Chin.* gorge, strait
Xiao *Chin.* small

Yam *Heb.* sea
-Yama *Jap.* mountain
-yan *Chin.* gorge, island
Yang *Chin.* bay, sea, sound
Yangi *Russ.* new
Yazovir *Bulg.* reservoir
Yeni *Turk.* new
Yli *Fin.* upper
Ynys *Welsh* island
Yoma *Burm.* mountain range
Ytre-, Ytter- *Nor., Swe.* outer
-yuan *Chin.* stream
Yugo- *Ser.-Cr.* south, southern
Yunhe *Chin.* canal
Yuzhni, Yuzhno *Russ.* south, southern

-Zaki *Jap.* point
Zalew *Pol.* lagoon, swamp
Zaliv *Russ.* bay, gulf
-Zan *Jap.* mountain
Zangbo *Tib.* stream, river
Zapadnaya, Zapadno, Zapadnyi (Zap.) *Russ.* west, western
Zatoka *Pol., Ukr.* bay, gulf
-zee *Dut.* lake, sea
Zemlya *Russ.* land, island(s)
Zhang *Chin.* mountain
-zhou *Chin.* island
Zhong *Chin.* middle, central
Zhou *Chin.* island
Zizhiqu *Chin.* autonomous region
Zuid, Zuider *Dut.* south, southern

INDEX TO WORLD MAPS

HOW TO USE THE INDEX

The index contains the names of all the principal places and features shown on the World and City Maps. Each name is followed by an additional entry in italics giving the country or region within which it is located. The alphabetical order of names composed of two or more words is governed primarily by the first word, then by the second, and then by the country or region name that follows. This is an example of the rule:

Mir *Niger*	14°5N 11°59E	**259**	F2
Mīr Kūh *Iran*	26°22N 58°55E	**247**	E8
Mīr Shahdād *Iran*	26°15N 58°29E	**247**	E8
Mira *Italy*	45°26N 12°8E	**199**	C9

Physical features composed of a proper name (Erie) and a description (Lake) are positioned alphabetically by the proper name. The description is positioned after the proper name and is usually abbreviated:

Erie, L. *N. Amer.*	42°15N 81°0W	**312**	D4

Where a description forms part of a settlement or administrative name, however, it is always written in full and put in its true alphabetical position:

Mount Olive *U.S.A.*	39°4N 89°44W	**310**	E7

Names beginning with M' and Mc are indexed as if they were spelled Mac. Names beginning St. are alphabetized under Saint, but Sankt, Sint, Sant', Santa and San are all spelt in full and are alphabetized accordingly. If the same place name occurs two or more times in the index and all are in the same country, each is followed by the name of the administrative subdivision in which it is located.

The geographical co-ordinates which follow each name in the index give the latitude and longitude of each place. The first co-ordinate indicates latitude – the distance north or south of the Equator. The second co-ordinate indicates longitude – the distance east or west of the Greenwich Meridian. Both latitude and longitude are measured in degrees and minutes (there are 60 minutes in a degree). Latitude and longitude references are not used on the Central Area City Maps.

The latitude is followed by N(orth) or S(outh) and the longitude by E(ast) or W(est).

The number in bold type which follows the geographical co-ordinates refers to the number of the map page where that feature or place will be found. This is usually the largest scale at which the place or feature appears.

The letter and figure that are immediately after the page number give the grid square on the map page, within which the feature is situated. The letter represents the latitude and the figure the longitude. A lower-case letter immediately after the page number refers to an inset map on that page.

In some cases the feature itself may fall within the specified square, while the name is outside. This is usually the case only with features that are larger than a grid square.

Rivers are indexed to their mouths or confluences, and carry the symbol ➔ after their names. The following symbols are also used in the index: ■ country, ☑ overseas territory or dependency, ☐ first-order administrative area, ☆ U.S. county, △ national park, ◠ other park (provincial park, nature reserve or game reserve), ⊛ Australian aboriginal land, ▲ U.S. Indian reservation ✈ (LHR) principal airport (and location identifier).

HOW TO PRONOUNCE PLACE NAMES

English-speaking people usually have no difficulty in reading and pronouncing correctly English place names. However, foreign place name pronunciations may present many problems. Such problems can be minimized by following some simple rules. However, these rules cannot be applied to all situations, and there will be many exceptions.

1. In general, stress each syllable equally, unless your experience suggests otherwise.
2. Pronounce the letter 'a' as a broad 'a' as in 'arm'.
3. Pronounce the letter 'e' as a short 'e' as in 'elm'.
4. Pronounce the letter 'i' as a cross between a short 'i' and long 'e', as the two 'i's in 'California'.
5. Pronounce the letter 'o' as an intermediate 'o' as in 'soft'.
6. Pronounce the letter 'u' as an intermediate 'u' as in 'sure'.
7. Pronounce consonants hard, except in the Romance-language areas where 'g's are likely to be pronounced softly like 'j' in 'jam'; 'j' itself may be pronounced as 'y'; and 'x's may be pronounced as 'h'.
8. For names in mainland China, pronounce 'q' like the 'ch' in 'chin', 'x' like the 'sh' in 'she', 'zh' like the 'j' in 'jam', and 'z' as if it were spelled 'dz'. In general, pronounce 'a' as in 'father', 'e' as in 'but', 'i' as in 'keep', 'o' as in 'or', and 'u' as in 'rule'.

Moreover, English has no diacritical marks (accent and pronunciation signs), although some languages do. The following is a brief and general guide to the pronunciation of those most frequently used in the principal Western European languages.

Pronunciation as in

French	é	day and shows that the 'e' is to be pronounced; e.g. Orléans.
	è	mare
	î	used over any vowel and does not affect pronunciation; shows contraction of the name, usually omission of 's' following a vowel.
	ç	's' before 'a', 'o' and 'u'.
	ë, ï, ü	over 'e', 'i' and 'u' when they are used with another vowel and shows that each is to be pronounced.
German	ä	fate
	ö	fur
	ü	no English equivalent; like French 'tu'.
Italian	à, é	over vowels and indicates stress.
Portuguese	ã, õ	vowels pronounced nasally.
	ç	boss
	á	shows stress.
	ô	shows that a vowel has an 'i' or 'u' sound combined with it.
Spanish	ñ	canyon
	ü	pronounced as 'w' and separately from adjoining vowels.
	á	usually indicates that this is a stressed vowel.

ABBREVIATIONS

A.C.T. – Australian Capital Territory
A.R. – Autonomous Region
Afghan. – Afghanistan
Afr. – Africa
Ala. – Alabama
Alta. – Alberta
Amer. – America(n)
Ant. – Antilles
Arch. – Archipelago
Ariz. – Arizona
Ark. – Arkansas
Atl. Oc. – Atlantic Ocean
B. – Baie, Bahía, Bay, Bucht, Bugt
B.C. – British Columbia
Bangla. – Bangladesh
Barr. – Barrage
Bos.-H. – Bosnia-Herzegovina
C. – Cabo, Cap, Cape, Coast
C.A.R. – Central African Republic
C. Prov. – Cape Province
Calif. – California
Cat. – Catarata
Cent. – Central
Chan. – Channel
Colo. – Colorado
Conn. – Connecticut
Cord. – Cordillera
Cr. – Creek
Czech. – Czech Republic
D.C. – District of Columbia
Del. – Delaware
Dem. – Democratic
Dep. – Dependency
Des. – Desert
Dét. – Détroit
Dist. – District
Dj. – Djebel
Dom. Rep. – Dominican Republic
E. – East

El Salv. – El Salvador
Eq. Guin. – Equatorial Guinea
Est. – Estrecho
Falk. Is. – Falkland Is.
Fd. – Fjord
Fla. – Florida
Fr. – French
G. – Golfe, Golfo, Gulf, Guba, Gebel
Ga. – Georgia
Gt. – Great, Greater
Guinea-Biss. – Guinea-Bissau
H.K. – Hong Kong
H.P. – Himachal Pradesh
Hants. – Hampshire
Harb. – Harbor, Harbour
Hd. – Head
Hts. – Heights
I.(s). – Île, Ilha, Insel, Isla, Island, Isle
Ill. – Illinois
Ind. – Indiana
Ind. Oc. – Indian Ocean
Ivory C. – Ivory Coast
J. – Jabal, Jebel
Jaz. – Jazīrah
Junc. – Junction
K. – Kap, Kapp
Kans. – Kansas
Kep. – Kepulauan
Ky. – Kentucky
L. – Lac, Lacul, Lago, Lagoa, Lake, Limni, Loch, Lough
La. – Louisiana
Ld. – Land
Liech. – Liechtenstein
Lux. – Luxembourg
Mad. P. – Madhya Pradesh
Madag. – Madagascar

Man. – Manitoba
Mass. – Massachusetts
Md. – Maryland
Me. – Maine
Medit. S. – Mediterranean Sea
Mich. – Michigan
Minn. – Minnesota
Miss. – Mississippi
Mo. – Missouri
Mont. – Montana
Mozam. – Mozambique
Mt.(s) – Mont, Montaña, Mountain
Mte. – Monte
Mti. – Monti
N. – Nord, Norte, North, Northern, Nouveau, Nahal, Nahr
N.B. – New Brunswick
N.C. – North Carolina
N. Cal. – New Caledonia
N. Dak. – North Dakota
N.H. – New Hampshire
N.I. – North Island
N.J. – New Jersey
N. Mex. – New Mexico
N.S. – Nova Scotia
N.S.W. – New South Wales
N.W.T. – North West Territory
N.Y. – New York
N.Z. – New Zealand
Nac. – Nacional
Nat. – National
Nebr. – Nebraska
Neths. – Netherlands
Nev. – Nevada
Nfld & L... – Newfoundland and Labrador
Nic. – Nicaragua
O. – Oued, Ouadi
Occ. – Occidentale

Okla. – Oklahoma
Ont. – Ontario
Or. – Orientale
Oreg. – Oregon
Os. – Ostrov
Oz. – Ozero
P. – Pass, Passo, Pasul, Pulau
P.E.I. – Prince Edward Island
Pa. – Pennsylvania
Pac. Oc. – Pacific Ocean
Papua N.G. – Papua New Guinea
Pass. – Passage
Peg. – Pegunungan
Pen. – Peninsula, Péninsule
Phil. – Philippines
Pk. – Peak
Plat. – Plateau
Prov. – Province, Provincial
Pt. – Point
Pta. – Ponta, Punta
Pte. – Pointe
Qué. – Québec
Queens. – Queensland
R. – Rio, River
R.I. – Rhode Island
Ra. – Range
Raj. – Rajasthan
Recr. – Recreational, Récréatif
Reg. – Region
Rep. – Republic
Res. – Reserve, Reservoir
Rhld-Pfz. – Rheinland-Pfalz
S. – South, Southern, Sur
Si. Arabia – Saudi Arabia
S.C. – South Carolina
S. Dak. – South Dakota
S.I. – South Island
S. Leone – Sierra Leone
Sa. – Serra, Sierra

Sask. – Saskatchewan
Scot. – Scotland
Sd. – Sound
Sev. – Severnaya
Sib. – Siberia
Sprs. – Springs
St. – Saint
Sta. – Santa
Ste. – Sainte
Sto. – Santo
Str. – Strait, Stretto
Switz. – Switzerland
Tas. – Tasmania
Tenn. – Tennessee
Terr. – Territory, Territoire
Tex. – Texas
Tg. – Tanjung
Trin. & Tob. – Trinidad & Tobago
U.A.E. – United Arab Emirates
U.K. – United Kingdom
U.S.A. – United States of America
Univ. – University, Université, Universidad
Ut. P. – Uttar Pradesh
Va. – Virginia
Vdkhr. – Vodokhranilishche
Vdskh. – Vodoskhovyshche
Vf. – Vîrful
Vic. – Victoria
Vol. – Volcano
Vt. – Vermont
W. – Wadi, West
W. Va. – West Virginia
Wall. & F. Is. – Wallis and Futuna Is.
Wash. – Washington
Wis. – Wisconsin
Wlkp. – Wielkopolski
Wyo. – Wyoming
Yorks. – Yorkshire

A

A ʻÂli an Nîl = Upper Nile □ South Sudan 9°30N 33°0E 257 F3
A Baña Spain 42°58N 8°46W 194 C2
A Cañiza Spain 42°13N 8°16W 194 C2
A Coruña Spain 43°20N 8°25W 194 B2
A Coruña □ Spain 43°10N 8°30W 194 B2
A Cruz do Incio Spain 42°39N 7°21W 194 C3
A Estrada Spain 42°43N 8°27W 194 C2
A Fonsagrada Spain 43°8N 7°4W 194 B3
A Guarda Spain 41°56N 8°52W 194 D2
A Gudiña Spain 42°4N 7°8W 194 C3
A Pobre Spain 42°35N 7°3W 194 C3
A Ramallosa Spain 42°45N 8°30W 194 C2
A Rúa Spain 42°24N 7°6W 194 C3
A Serra de Outes Spain 42°52N 8°55W 194 C2
A Shau Vietnam 16°6N 107°22E 236 D6
A.R.M.M. = Muslim Mindanao □ Phil. 8°0N 123°0E 233 H3
Aabenraa Denmark 55°3N 9°25E 163 J3
Aabybro Denmark 57°10N 9°44E 163 G3
Aachen Germany 50°45N 6°6E 178 E2
Aalâm Iraq 33°19N 44°23E 113 B2
Aalborg Denmark 57°2N 9°54E 163 G3
Aalborg Bugt Denmark 56°50N 10°35E 163 H4
Aalen Germany 48°51N 10°6E 179 G6
Aalestrup Denmark 56°42N 9°29E 163 H3
Aalsmeer Neths. 52°16N 4°46E 112 B1
Aalst Belgium 50°56N 4°2E 170 D4
Aalten Neths. 51°56N 6°35E 170 C6
Aalter Belgium 51°5N 3°28E 170 C3
Äänekoski Finland 62°36N 25°44E 160 E21
Aarau Switz. 47°23N 8°4E 179 H4
Aarberg Switz. 47°2N 7°16E 179 H3
Aare → Switz. 47°33N 8°14E 179 H4
Aargau □ Switz. 47°26N 8°10E 179 H4
Aarhus Denmark 56°8N 10°11E 163 H4
Aarlen = Arlon Belgium 49°42N 5°49E 170 E5
Aars Denmark 56°48N 9°30E 163 H3
Aarschot Belgium 50°59N 4°49E 170 D4
Aasiaat Greenland 68°43N 52°56W 154 D5
Ab-i-Istada Afghan. 32°29N 67°55E 240 B3
Ab-i-Panja = Pyandzh → Asia 37°6N 68°20E 240 A2
Aba Sichuan, China 32°59N 101°42E 228 A3
Aba Dem. Rep. of the Congo 3°58N 30°17E 268 B3
Aba Nigeria 5°10N 7°19E 263 D6
Âbâ, Jazîrat Sudan 13°30N 32°31E 257 E3
Abacaxis → Brazil 3°54S 58°47W 329 D6
Abaco I. Bahamas 26°25N 77°10W 320 A4
Abadab, J. Sudan 18°54N 35°56E 256 D4
Ābādān Iran 30°22N 48°20E 247 D6
Abade Ethiopia 9°22N 38°3E 257 F4
Ābādeh Iran 31°8N 52°40E 247 D7
Abadín Spain 43°21N 7°29W 194 B3
Abadla Algeria 31°2N 2°45W 261 B4
Abaeté Brazil 19°9S 45°27W 333 E2
Abaeté → Brazil 18°2S 45°12W 333 E2
Abaetetuba Brazil 1°40S 48°50W 332 B2
Abagnar Qi = Xilinhot China 43°52N 116°2E 226 C9
Abah, Tanjung Indonesia 8°46S 115°38E 231 K18
Abai Paraguay 25°58S 55°54W 335 B4
Abakaliki Nigeria 6°22N 8°2E 263 D6
Abakan Russia 53°40N 91°10E 217 B12
Abala Congo 1°17S 15°35E 264 C3
Abala Niger 14°56N 3°22E 263 C5
Abalak Niger 15°22N 6°21E 263 B6
Abalemma Algeria 20°51N 5°59E 261 D6
Abalemma Niger 16°12N 7°50E 263 B6
Abalessa Algeria 22°58N 4°47E 261 D5
Abana Turkey 41°59N 34°1E 212 B6
Abancay Peru 13°35S 72°55W 330 C3
Abang, Gunung Indonesia 8°16S 115°25E 231 J18
Abanga → Gabon 0°20S 10°30E 264 C2
Abano Terme Italy 45°22N 11°46E 199 C8
Abapó Bolivia 18°48S 63°25W 331 D5
Abarán Spain 38°12N 1°23W 197 G3
Abariringa Kiribati 2°50S 171°40W 277 A16
Abarqū Iran 31°10N 53°20E 247 D7
Abasha Georgia 42°11N 42°13E 191 J6
Abashiri Japan 44°0N 144°15E 220 B12
Abashiri-Wan Japan 44°0N 144°30E 220 C12
Abau Papua N. G. 10°11S 148°46E 286 F5
Abaújszántó Hungary 48°16N 21°12E 182 B6
Abava → Latvia 57°6N 21°54E 184 A8
Ābay = Nîl el Azraq → Sudan 15°38N 32°31E 257 D3
Abay Kazakhstan 49°38N 72°53E 217 C8
Abaya, L. Ethiopia 6°30N 37°50E 257 F4
Abaza Russia 52°39N 90°6E 217 B12
Abba C.A.R. 5°20N 15°11E 264 A3
Abbadia di Fiastra △ Italy 43°12N 13°24E 199 E10
Abbadia San Salvatore Italy 42°53N 11°41E 199 F8
ʻAbbāsābād Iran 33°34N 58°23E 247 C8
Abbay = Nîl el Azraq → Sudan 15°38N 32°31E 257 D3
Abbaye, Pt. U.S.A. 46°58N 88°8W 308 B9
Abbazia = Opatija Croatia 45°21N 14°17E 199 C11
Abbé, L. Ethiopia 11°8N 41°47E 257 E5
Abbeville France 50°6N 1°49E 173 B8
Abbeville Ala., U.S.A. 31°34N 85°15W 316 D4
Abbeville Ga., U.S.A. 31°59N 83°18W 316 D6
Abbeville La., U.S.A. 29°58N 92°8W 314 G8
Abbeville S.C., U.S.A. 34°11N 82°23W 316 A7
Abbey Wood U.K. 51°29N 0°7E 125 B4
Abbeyfeale Ireland 52°23N 9°18W 166 D2
Abbeyleix Ireland 52°54N 7°22W 166 D4
Abbiategrasso Italy 45°24N 8°54E 198 C5
Abbot Ice Shelf Antarctica 73°0S 92°0W 151 D16
Abbotsford Canada 49°5N 122°20W 296 D4
Abbottabad Pakistan 34°10N 73°15E 242 B5
Abbou, O. ben → Algeria 28°32N 5°14E 261 C5
ABC Islands W. Indies 12°15N 69°0W 322 g
Abcoude Neths. 52°17N 4°59E 112 B2
Abd al Kūrī Yemen 12°5N 52°20E 249 D6
Ābdānān Iran 32°56N 47°28E 213 F12
Ābdar Iran 30°16N 55°19E 247 D7
Ābdīn Egypt 30°2N 31°14E 117 A2
ʻAbdolābād Iran 34°12N 56°30E 247 C8
Abdulino Russia 53°42N 53°40E 216 B4
Abdullah South Sudan 5°30N 29°55E 257 F3
Abdulpur Bangla. 24°15N 88°59E 243 G13
Abéché Chad 13°50N 20°35E 259 F4
Abejar Spain 41°48N 2°47W 196 D2
Abekr Sudan 12°45N 28°50E 257 E2
Abel Tasman △ N.Z. 40°59S 173°3E 285 A8
Abengourou Ivory C. 6°42N 3°27W 262 D4
Abeno Japan 34°38N 135°31E 222 E11
Abenójar Spain 38°53N 4°21W 195 G6
Åbenrå = Aabenraa Denmark 55°3N 9°25E 163 J3
Abensberg Germany 48°48N 11°51E 179 G7
Abeokuta Nigeria 7°3N 3°19E 263 D5
Aberaeron U.K. 52°15N 4°15W 169 E3
Aberayron = Aberaeron U.K. 52°15N 4°15W 169 E3
Aberchirder U.K. 57°34N 2°37W 167 D6
Abercorn = Mbala Zambia 8°46S 31°24E 269 D3
Abercorn Australia 25°12S 151°5E 281 D5
Abercrombie River △ Australia 34°5S 149°40E 283 C8
Aberdare U.K. 51°43N 3°27W 169 F4
Aberdare △ Kenya 0°22S 36°44E 268 C4
Aberdare Ra. Kenya 0°15S 36°50E 268 C4
Aberdaugleddau = Milford Haven U.K. 51°42N 5°7W 169 F2
Aberdeen N.S.W., Australia 32°9S 150°56E 283 B9
Aberdeen Sask., Canada 52°20N 106°8W 297 C7
Aberdeen Hong Kong, China 22°14N 114°8E 122 B1
Aberdeen Eastern Cape, S. Africa 32°28S 24°2E 270 D3
Aberdeen C. of Aberd., U.K. 57°9N 2°5W 167 D6
Aberdeen Idaho, U.S.A. 42°57N 112°50W 304 E7
Aberdeen Md., U.S.A. 39°31N 76°10W 309 F15
Aberdeen Miss., U.S.A. 33°49N 88°33W 315 E10
Aberdeen Ohio, U.S.A. 38°39N 83°46W 311 F13
Aberdeen S. Dak., U.S.A. 45°28N 98°29W 308 C4
Aberdeen Wash., U.S.A. 46°59N 123°50W 306 D3
Aberdeen, City of □ U.K. 57°10N 2°10W 167 D6
Aberdeen L. Canada 64°30N 99°0W 294 E12
Aberdeenshire □ U.K. 57°17N 2°36W 167 D6
Aberdour U.K. 56°3N 3°18W 121 A2
Aberdour Castle U.K. 56°3N 3°18W 121 A2
Aberdovey = Aberdyfi U.K. 52°33N 4°3W 169 E3
Aberdyfi U.K. 52°33N 4°3W 169 E3
Aberfeldy U.K. 56°37N 3°51W 167 E5
Aberfoyle U.K. 56°11N 4°23W 167 E4
Abergavenny U.K. 51°49N 3°1W 169 F4
Abergele U.K. 53°17N 3°35W 168 D4
Abergwaun = Fishguard U.K. 52°0N 4°58W 169 E3
Aberhonddu = Brecon U.K. 51°57N 3°23W 169 F4
Abermaw = Barmouth U.K. 52°44N 4°4W 168 E3
Abernathy U.S.A. 33°50N 101°51W 314 E4
Aberpennar = Mountain Ash U.K. 51°40N 3°23W 169 F4
Abert, L. U.S.A. 42°38N 120°14W 304 E3
Abertawe = Swansea U.K. 51°37N 3°57W 169 F4
Aberteifi = Cardigan U.K. 52°5N 4°40W 169 E3
Aberystwyth U.K. 52°25N 4°5W 169 E3
Abfanggraben → Germany 48°10N 11°41E 131 A3
Abhā Si. Arabia 18°0N 42°34E 248 C3
Abhar Iran 36°9N 49°13E 213 D13
Abhayapuri India 26°24N 90°38E 241 B3
Abia □ Nigeria 5°30N 7°35E 263 D6
Abide Turkey 38°55N 29°20E 205 C11
Abidiya Sudan 18°18N 34°3E 256 D3
Abidjan Ivory C. 5°26N 3°58W 262 D4
Abilene Kans., U.S.A. 38°55N 97°13W 308 F5
Abilene Tex., U.S.A. 32°28N 99°43W 314 E5
Abingdon Oxon., U.K. 51°40N 1°17W 169 F6
Abingdon Ill., U.S.A. 40°48N 90°24W 310 D6
Abingdon Va., U.S.A. 36°43N 81°59W 309 G13
Abingdon, I. = Pinta, I. Ecuador 0°35N 90°44W 330 a
Abington Reef Australia 18°0S 149°35E 280 B4
Abiod, Remel el Tunisia 31°45N 9°35E 261 B6
Abitau → Canada 59°53N 109°3W 297 B7
Abitibi → Canada 51°3N 80°55W 298 B3
Abitibi, L. Canada 48°40N 79°40W 298 C4
Abiy Adi Ethiopia 13°39N 39°3E 257 E4
Abiyata, L. Ethiopia 7°37N 38°36E 266 C4
Abiyata-Shala △ Ethiopia 7°40N 38°37E 257 F4
Abkhaz Republic = Abkhazia □ Georgia 43°12N 41°5E 191 J5
Abkhazia □ Georgia 43°12N 41°5E 191 J5
Ablon-sur-Seine France 48°43N 2°25E 134 B3
Abminga Australia 26°8S 134°51E 281 D1
Abnûb Egypt 27°18N 31°4E 256 B3
Åbo = Turku Finland 60°30N 22°19E 162 B8
Abo, Massif d' Chad 21°41N 16°8E 259 D3
Abohar India 30°10N 74°10E 242 D6
Aboisso Ivory C. 5°30N 3°5W 262 D4
Abolo Congo 0°8N 14°16E 264 B2
Abomey Benin 7°10N 2°5E 263 D5
Abong-Mbang Cameroon 4°0N 13°8E 264 B2
Abongabong Indonesia 4°15N 96°48E 234 B1
Abonnema Nigeria 4°41N 6°49E 263 E6
Abony Hungary 47°12N 20°3E 182 C5
Abor Hills India 28°25N 94°46E 241 A5
Aborlan Phil. 9°26N 118°33E 233 G2
Aboso Ghana 5°23N 1°57W 262 D4
Abou-Deïa Chad 11°20N 19°20E 259 F3
Abou-Goulem Chad 13°37N 21°38E 259 F4
Abou-Telfan △ Chad 12°2N 18°58E 259 F3
Abovyan Armenia 40°16N 44°37E 191 K7
Aboyne U.K. 57°4N 2°47W 167 D6
Abra □ Phil. 17°35N 120°45E 232 C3
Abra de Ilog Phil. 13°27N 120°44E 232 E3
Abra Pampa Argentina 22°43S 65°42W 334 A2
Abraham L. Canada 52°15N 116°35W 296 C5
Abramtsevo Russia 55°49N 37°49E 129 B3
Abrantes Portugal 39°24N 8°7W 195 F2
Abreojos, Pta. Mexico 26°50N 113°40W 318 B2
Abri Esh Shamâliya, Sudan 20°50N 30°27E 256 C3
Abri Janub Kordofân, Sudan 11°40N 30°21E 257 E3
Abrolhos, Banco dos Brazil 18°0S 38°0W 333 E4
Abrud Romania 46°19N 23°5E 182 D8
Abruzzo □ Italy 42°15N 14°0E 199 F10
Absaroka Range U.S.A. 44°45N 109°50W 304 D9
Abşeron Yarımadası Azerbaijan 40°28N 49°57E 191 K9
Abtenau Austria 47°33N 13°21E 180 D6
Abu India 24°41N 72°50E 242 G5
Abū al Ḍuhūr Syria 35°44N 37°2E 250 C8
Abū al Abyad U.A.E. 24°11N 53°50E 247 E7
Abū al Khaṣīb Iraq 30°25N 48°0E 246 D5
Abū ʻAlī Si. Arabia 27°20N 49°27E 247 E6
Abū ʻAlī → Lebanon 34°25N 35°50E 250 D6
Abū ʻArīsh Si. Arabia 16°53N 42°48E 248 C3
Abū ʻAweigîla Egypt 30°50N 34°7E 251 H5
Abū Ballas Egypt 24°26N 27°36E 256 C2
Abu Deleiq Sudan 15°57N 33°48E 257 D3
Abu Dhabi = Abū Ẓāby U.A.E. 24°28N 54°22E 247 E7
Abû Dis Sudan 19°12N 33°38E 256 D3
Abû Dis West Bank 31°46N 35°16E 123 B2
Abu Dom Sudan 16°18N 32°25E 257 D3
Abū Duʼān Syria 36°25N 38°15E 213 D8
Abu el Gaīn, W. → Egypt 29°35N 33°30E 251 J4
Abu en Numrus Egypt 29°57N 31°12E 117 B2
Abu Fatma, Ras Sudan 22°25N 36°25E 256 C4
Abû Gabra Sudan 11°2N 26°50E 257 E2
Abu Gaʼda, W. → Egypt 29°15N 32°53E 251 J3
Abu Gelba Sudan 13°11N 31°52E 257 E3
Abu Ghosh Israel 31°48N 35°6E 123 B1
Abu Gubeiha Sudan 11°30N 31°15E 257 E3
Abu Habl, Khawr → Sudan 12°37N 31°0E 257 E3
Abū Ḥadrīyah Si. Arabia 27°20N 48°58E 247 E6
Abu Hail U.A.E. 25°17N 55°20E 119 A2
Abu Hamed Sudan 19°32N 33°13E 256 D3
Abû Haraz An Nîl el Azraq, Sudan 14°35N 33°30E 257 E3
Abû Haraz El Gezira, Sudan 14°35N 33°30E 257 E3
Abû Haraz Esh Shamâliya, Sudan 19°8N 32°18E 256 D3
Abû Higar Sudan 12°50N 33°59E 257 E3
Abū Kamāl Syria 34°30N 41°0E 213 E9
Abu Kebîr Egypt 30°43N 31°40E 251 H2
Abu Kuleiwat Sudan 12°20N 26°0E 257 E2
Abū Madd, Raʼs Si. Arabia 24°50N 37°7E 246 E3
Abu Mataria Sudan 10°59N 26°9E 257 E2
Abu Mena = Abu Mina Egypt 30°51N 29°40E 256 H6
Abu Mendi Ethiopia 11°48N 35°42E 257 E4
Abu Mina Egypt 30°51N 29°40E 256 H6
Abū Mūsā U.A.E. 25°52N 55°3E 247 E7
Abū Nujaym Libya 30°35N 15°24E 258 B3
Abū Qaṣr Si. Arabia 30°21N 38°34E 246 D3
Abu Qireiya Egypt 24°5N 35°28E 256 C4
Abu Qurqâs Egypt 28°1N 30°44E 256 B3
Abū Raṣāṣ, Raʼs Oman 20°10N 58°38E 249 B7
Abu Rudeis Egypt 28°54N 33°11E 251 K4
Abu Shagara, Ras Sudan 21°4N 37°19E 256 C4
Abû Shanab Janub Kordofân, Sudan 10°47N 29°32E 266 B2
Abû Shanab Shamâl Kordofân, Sudan 13°58N 27°49E 257 E2
Abu Simbel Egypt 22°18N 31°40E 256 C3
Abu Soma, Râs Egypt 26°51N 33°58E 256 B3
Abū Şukhayr Iraq 31°54N 44°30E 213 G11
Abu Sultân Egypt 30°24N 32°21E 256 H8
Abu Tabari Sudan 17°32N 28°32E 256 D2
Abu Tig Egypt 27°4N 31°15E 256 B3
Abu Tiga Sudan 12°47N 34°12E 257 E3
Abu Tineitin Sudan 14°24N 31°1E 257 E3
Abû Uruq Sudan 15°52N 30°25E 257 D3
Abû Zabad Sudan 12°25N 29°10E 257 E2
Abū Ẓāby U.A.E. 24°28N 54°22E 247 E7
Abū Zeydābād Iran 33°54N 51°45E 247 C6
Abufari Brazil 5°25S 62°59W 331 B5
Abuja Nigeria 9°5N 7°32E 263 D6
Abukuma-Gawa → Japan 38°6N 140°52E 220 E10
Abukuma-Sammyaku Japan 37°30N 140°45E 220 F10
Abulug Phil. 18°27N 121°27E 232 B3
Abumombazi Dem. Rep. of the Congo 3°42N 22°10E 264 B4
Abunã Brazil 9°40S 65°20W 331 B4
Abunã → Brazil 9°41S 65°20W 331 B4
Abune Yosef Ethiopia 12°5N 39°12E 257 E4
Aburatsu Japan 31°34N 131°24E 222 F3
Aburo Dem. Rep. of the Congo 2°4N 30°53E 268 B3
Abut Hd. N.Z. 43°7S 170°15E 285 D5
Abuye Meda Ethiopia 10°30N 39°49E 257 E4
Abuyog Phil. 10°45N 125°0E 233 F5
Abwong South Sudan 9°2N 32°14E 257 F3
Åby Sweden 58°40N 16°10E 163 F10
Aby, Lagune Ivory C. 5°15N 3°14W 262 D4
Abyad Sudan 13°47N 26°24E 257 E2
Abyān □ Yemen 13°50N 46°0E 248 D4
Abyei Sudan 9°36N 28°26E 257 F2
Abyei ☒ Sudan 9°30N 28°30E 257 F2
Ābyek Iran 36°4N 50°33E 247 B6
Acacias Colombia 3°59N 73°46W 328 C3
Acacias Madrid, Spain 127 c2
Academy Gletscher Greenland 82°2N 34°0W 154 A7
Acadia △ U.S.A. 44°20N 68°13W 309 C19
Açailandia Brazil 5°0S 47°30W 332 C2
Acajutla El Salv. 13°36N 89°50W 320 D2
Acámbaro Mexico 20°2N 100°44W 318 D4
Acandí Colombia 8°32N 77°14W 328 B2
Acanthus Greece 40°27N 23°47E 202 F7
Acaponeta Mexico 22°30N 105°22W 318 C3
Acapulco Mexico 16°51N 99°55W 319 D5
Acapulco Trench Pac. Oc. 12°0N 88°0W 320 D2
Acará Brazil 1°57S 48°11W 332 B2
Acarai, Serra Brazil 1°50N 57°50W 329 C6
Acaraú Brazil 2°53S 40°7W 332 B3
Acari Brazil 6°31S 36°38W 332 C4
Acari Peru 15°25S 74°36W 330 D3
Acarigua Venezuela 9°33N 69°12W 328 B4
Acassuso Argentina 34°29S 58°30W 117 A2
Acatlán Mexico 18°12N 98°3W 319 D5
Acayucán Mexico 17°57N 94°55W 319 D6
Accademia, Galleria dell' Venice, Italy 142 b2
Accademia, Ponte dell' Venice, Italy 142 b2
Accéglio Italy 44°28N 7°0E 198 D4
Accomac U.S.A. 37°43N 75°40W 309 G16
Accous France 43°0N 0°36W 174 E3
Accra Ghana 5°35N 0°6W 263 D4
Accrington U.K. 53°45N 2°22W 168 D5
Acebal Argentina 33°20S 60°50W 334 C3
Aceh □ Indonesia 4°15N 97°30E 234 B1
Acerra Italy 40°57N 14°22E 201 B7
Acequias Spain 37°30N 3°55W 195 H5
Achacachi Bolivia 16°3S 68°43W 330 D4
Achaguas Venezuela 7°46N 68°14W 328 B4
Achaia □ Greece 38°5N 21°45E 204 C3
Achalpur India 21°22N 77°32E 244 D3
Achao Chile 42°28S 73°30W 336 B2
Acharnes Greece 38°5N 23°44E 204 C5
Achegour Niger 19°10N 11°54E 259 E2
Acheloos → Greece 38°19N 21°7E 204 C3
Achelouma Niger 22°12N 12°50E 259 D2
Achelouma, Enneri → Niger 21°55N 13°35E 259 D2
Acheng China 45°30N 126°58E 227 B14
Achenkirch Austria 47°32N 11°45E 180 D4
Achénouma Niger 19°7N 12°55E 259 E2
Achensee Austria 47°26N 11°45E 180 D4
Achentrias Greece 34°59N 25°13E 205 G7
Acher India 23°10N 72°32E 242 H5
Achères France 48°57N 2°3E 134 A1
Achern Germany 48°37N 8°4E 179 G4
Acheron → N.Z. 42°16S 173°4E 285 C8
Achill Hd. Ireland 53°58N 10°15W 166 C1
Achill I. Ireland 53°58N 10°1W 166 C1
Achim Germany 53°1N 9°3E 178 B5
Achinsk Russia 56°20N 90°20E 215 D10
Achladokampos Greece 37°31N 22°35E 204 D4
Achouka Gabon 0°52S 9°45E 264 C2
Acıgöl Turkey 37°50N 29°50E 205 D11
Acilia Italy 41°47N 12°21E 136 C1
Acıpayam Turkey 37°26N 29°22E 205 D11
Acireale Italy 37°37N 15°10E 201 E8
Ackerman U.S.A. 33°19N 89°11W 315 E10
Ackley U.S.A. 42°33N 93°3W 310 B3
Acklins I. Bahamas 22°30N 74°0W 321 B5
Aclimação Brazil 23°34S 46°37W 137 B2
Acme Alta., Canada 51°33N 113°30W 296 C6
Acme Pa., U.S.A. 40°8N 79°26W 312 F5
Acobamba Peru 12°52S 74°35W 330 C3
Acomayo Peru 13°55S 71°38W 330 C3
Aconcagua, Cerro Argentina 32°39S 70°0W 334 C2
Aconquija, Mt. Argentina 27°0S 66°0W 334 B2
Acopiara Brazil 6°6S 39°27W 332 C4
Açores, Is. dos Atl. Oc. 38°0N 27°0W 153 d1
Acorizal Brazil 15°12S 56°22W 331 D6
Acornhoek S. Africa 24°37S 31°2E 271 B5
Acoua Mayotte 12°43S 45°4E 272 b
Acquapendente Italy 42°44N 11°52E 199 F8
Acquasanta Terme Italy 42°46N 13°24E 199 F10
Acquasparta Italy 42°41N 12°33E 199 F9
Acquaviva delle Fonti Italy 40°54N 16°50E 201 B9
Acqui Terme Italy 44°41N 8°28E 198 D5
Acraman, L. Australia 32°2S 135°23E 281 E2
Acre = ʻAkko Israel 32°55N 35°4E 250 F6
Acre □ Brazil 9°1S 71°0W 330 B3
Acre → Brazil 8°45S 67°22W 330 B4
Acri Italy 39°29N 16°23E 201 C9
Acropolis Athens, Greece 112 c2
Acs Hungary 47°42N 18°2E 182 C3
Actæon Mt. St. Helena 15°58S 5°42W 153 h
Actéon, Groupe French Polynesia 21°20S 136°30W 289 f
Actinolite Canada 44°32N 77°19W 312 B7
Actium Greece 38°57N 20°45E 207 B2
Acton Ont., Canada 43°38N 80°3W 312 C4
Acton London, U.K. 51°30N 0°16W 125 A2
Açu Brazil 5°34S 36°54W 332 C4
Açúcar, Pão de Brazil 22°56S 43°9W 135 B2
Acul = Vidin Bulgaria 43°59N 22°50E 202 C6
Acworth U.S.A. 34°4N 84°41W 316 A5
Ad Dafinah Si. Arabia 23°18N 41°58E 248 B3
Ad Ḍafrah U.A.E. 23°30N 54°30E 249 B6
Ad Dahna Si. Arabia 24°30N 48°10E 249 A5
Ad Dākhilīyah □ Oman 22°30N 57°30E 249 B7
Ad Ḍālīʻ Yemen 13°42N 44°44E 248 D4
Ad Ḍālīʻ □ Yemen 13°42N 44°44E 248 D4
Ad Dammām Si. Arabia 26°20N 50°5E 247 E6
Ad Dāmūr Lebanon 33°43N 35°27E 250 E6
Ad Darb Si. Arabia 18°2N 43°7E 248 C3
Ad Dawādimī Si. Arabia 24°35N 44°15E 246 E5
Ad Dawḥah Qatar 25°15N 51°35E 247 E6
Ad Dawr Iraq 34°27N 43°47E 213 E10
Ad Dhakhīrah Qatar 25°44N 51°33E 247 E6
Ad Ḍiffah Libya 30°30N 24°30E 258 B4
Ad Dilam Si. Arabia 23°55N 47°10E 248 B4
Ad Dirʻīyah Si. Arabia 24°44N 46°35E 246 E5
Ad Dīwānīyah Iraq 32°0N 45°0E 213 F11
Ad Dujayl Iraq 33°51N 44°14E 213 F11
Ad Duqm Oman 19°39N 57°42E 249 C7
Ad Duwayd Si. Arabia 30°15N 42°17E 246 D4
Ada Ghana 5°44N 0°40E 263 D5
Ada Serbia 45°49N 20°9E 182 E5
Ada Minn., U.S.A. 47°18N 96°31W 308 B5
Ada Ohio, U.S.A. 40°46N 83°49W 311 D13
Ada Okla., U.S.A. 34°46N 96°41W 314 D6
Ada Beja Portugal 38°47N 9°13W 126 A1
Adad Somalia 9°27N 46°32E 267 C6
Adado, Ras Somalia 11°19N 48°39E 267 B6
Adair, C. Canada 71°30N 71°34W 295 C17
Adaja → Spain 41°32N 4°52W 194 D6
Adak U.S.A. 51°45N 176°45W 303 L3
Adak I. U.S.A. 51°45N 176°45W 303 L3
Ådalsbruk Norway 60°43N 11°19E 164 D8
Adam Oman 22°15N 57°28E 249 B7
Adam, Mt. Falk. Is. 51°34S 60°4W 153 f
Adamantina Brazil 21°42S 51°4W 333 F1
Adamaoua □ Cameroon 6°30N 13°30E 263 D7
Adamaoua, Massif de l' Cameroon 7°20N 12°20E 263 D7
Adamawa □ Nigeria 9°20N 12°30E 263 D7
Adamawa Highlands = Adamaoua, Massif de l' Cameroon 7°20N 12°20E 263 D7
Adamello, Mte. Italy 46°9N 10°30E 198 B7
Adamello △ Italy 46°4N 10°28E 198 B7
Adami Tulu Ethiopia 7°53N 38°41E 257 F4
Adaminaby Australia 36°0S 148°45E 283 D8
Adams Mass., U.S.A. 42°38N 73°7W 313 D11
Adams N.Y., U.S.A. 43°49N 76°1W 313 C8
Adams Wis., U.S.A. 43°57N 89°49W 308 D9
Adams, Mt. U.S.A. 46°12N 121°30W 306 D5
Adam's Bridge Sri Lanka 9°15N 79°40E 245 K4
Adams L. Canada 51°10N 119°40W 296 C5
Adams Park U.S.A. 33°43N 84°27W 118 B2
Adam's Peak Sri Lanka 6°48N 80°30E 245 L5
Adamuz Spain 38°2N 4°32W 195 G6
ʻAdan Yemen 12°45N 45°0E 248 D4
Adana Turkey 37°0N 35°16E 250 B6
Adana □ Turkey 37°0N 35°30E 250 B6
Adanero Spain 40°56N 4°36W 194 E6
Adang, Ko Thailand 6°33N 99°18E 237 J2
Adapazarı = Sakarya Turkey 40°48N 30°25E 212 B4
Adar Gwagwa, J. Sudan 22°15N 35°20E 256 C4
Adarama Sudan 17°10N 34°52E 257 D3
Adare Ireland 52°34N 8°47W 166 D3
Adare, C. Antarctica 71°0S 171°0E 151 D11
Adarte Eritrea 13°18N 42°8E 257 E5
Adaut Indonesia 8°8S 131°7E 231 F8
Adavale Australia 25°52S 144°32E 281 D3
Adda → Italy 45°8N 9°53E 198 C6
Addatigala India 17°31N 82°3E 244 F6
Addax △ Niger 19°17N 9°22E 259 E1
Addis Ababa = Addis Abeba Ethiopia 9°2N 38°42E 257 F4
Addis Abeba Ethiopia 9°2N 38°42E 257 F4
Addis Alem Ethiopia 9°0N 38°17E 257 F4
Addis Zemen Ethiopia 12°7N 37°47E 257 E4
Addiscombe U.K. 51°22N 0°4W 125 B3
Addison Ill., U.S.A. 41°55N 88°0W 311 C8
Addison N.Y., U.S.A. 42°1N 77°14W 312 D7
Addo S. Africa 33°32S 25°45E 270 D4
Addo △ S. Africa 33°30S 25°50E 270 D4
Addu Atoll Maldives 0°38S 73°10E 272 d
Adebour Niger 13°17N 11°50E 259 F2
Ādeh Iran 37°42N 45°11E 246 B5
Adel Ga., U.S.A. 31°8N 83°25W 316 D6
Adel Iowa, U.S.A. 41°37N 94°1W 310 C2
Adel Bagrou Mauritania 15°29N 6°57W 262 B3
Adelaide S. Austral., Australia 34°52S 138°30E 282 C3
Adelaide Eastern Cape, S. Africa 32°42S 26°20E 270 D4
Adelaide I. Antarctica 67°15S 68°30W 151 C17
Adelaide Pen. Canada 68°15N 97°30W 294 D12
Adelaide River Australia 13°15S 131°7E 278 B5
Adelaide Village Bahamas 25°0N 77°31W 153 b
Adelanto U.S.A. 34°35N 117°22W 307 L9
Adelaye C.A.R. 7°7N 22°49E 264 A4
Adele I. Australia 15°32S 123°9E 278 C3
Adélie, Terre Antarctica 68°0S 140°0E 151 C10
Adélie Land = Adélie, Terre Antarctica 68°0S 140°0E 151 C10
Adelong Australia 35°16S 148°4E 283 C8
Adelphi U.S.A. 39°0N 76°58W 143 A3
Adelsk Belarus 53°24N 23°47E 184 E10
Ademuz Spain 40°5N 1°13W 196 E3
Aden = ʻAdan Yemen 12°45N 45°0E 248 D4
Aden, G. of Ind. Oc. 12°30N 47°30E 267 B6
Adendorp S. Africa 32°15S 24°30E 270 D3
Aderbissinat Niger 15°34N 7°54E 263 B6
Aderklaa Austria 48°17N 16°32E 142 A3
Adh Dhayd U.A.E. 25°17N 55°53E 247 E7
Adhoi India 23°26N 70°32E 242 H4
Adi Indonesia 4°15S 133°30E 231 E8
Adi Arkai Ethiopia 13°35N 37°57E 257 E4
Adi Daro Ethiopia 14°20N 38°14E 257 E4
Adi Keyih Eritrea 14°51N 39°22E 257 E4
Adi Kwala Eritrea 14°38N 38°48E 257 E4
Adi Ugri Eritrea 14°58N 38°48E 257 E4
Adieu, C. Australia 32°0S 132°10E 279 F5
Adieu Pt. Australia 15°14S 124°35E 278 C3
Adigala Ethiopia 10°24N 42°15E 257 E5
Adige → Italy 45°9N 12°20E 199 C9
Adigrat Ethiopia 14°20N 39°26E 257 E4
Adıgüzel Barajı Turkey 38°13N 29°14E 205 C11
Adilabad India 19°33N 78°20E 244 E4
Adilcevaz Turkey 38°47N 42°43E 213 C10
Adīrī Libya 27°32N 13°2E 258 C2
Adirondack △ U.S.A. 44°0N 74°20W 313 C10
Adirondack Mts. U.S.A. 44°0N 74°0W 313 C10
Adis Abeba = Addis Abeba Ethiopia 9°2N 38°42E 257 F4
Adıyaman Turkey 37°45N 38°16E 213 D8
Adıyaman □ Turkey 37°30N 38°10E 213 D8
Adjim Tunisia 33°47N 10°50E 258 B2
Adjohon Benin 6°41N 2°32E 263 D5
Adjud Romania 46°7N 27°10E 183 D12
Adjumani Uganda 3°20N 31°50E 268 B3
Adjuntas Puerto Rico 18°10N 66°43W 321 b
Adlavik Is. Canada 55°0N 58°40W 299 B8
Adler Russia 43°28N 39°52E 191 J4
Adler Planetarium U.S.A. 41°51N 87°36W 119 B3
Admer Algeria 20°21N 5°27E 261 D6
Admer, Erg d' Algeria 24°0N 9°5E 261 D6
Admiralteyskaya Storona Russia 59°56N 30°17E 137 B2
Admiralty G. Australia 14°20S 125°55E 278 B4
Admiralty Gulf ✪ Australia 14°16S 125°52E 278 B4
Admiralty I. U.S.A. 57°30N 134°30W 296 B2
Admiralty Inlet Canada 72°30N 86°0W 295 C14
Admiralty Is. Papua N. G. 2°0S 147°0E 286 B4
Admiralty Island △ U.S.A. 57°40N 134°10W 303 H14
Adnan Menderes, İzmir ✈ (ADB) Turkey 38°23N 27°6E 205 C9
Ado Nigeria 6°36N 2°56E 263 D5
Ado-Ekiti Nigeria 7°38N 5°12E 263 D6
Adok South Sudan 8°10N 30°20E 257 F3
Adola Ethiopia 11°14N 41°44E 257 E5
Adolfo González Chaves Argentina 38°2S 60°5W 334 D3
Adolfo Ruiz Cortines, Presa Mexico 27°15N 109°6W 318 B3
Adonara Indonesia 8°15S 123°5E 231 F6
Adoni India 15°33N 77°18E 245 G3
Adony Hungary 47°6N 18°52E 182 C3
Adour → France 43°32N 1°32W 174 E2
Adra India 23°30N 86°42E 243 H12
Adra Spain 36°43N 3°3W 195 J7
Adrano Italy 37°40N 14°50E 201 E7
Adrar Algeria 27°51N 0°11E 261 C4
Adrar □ Algeria 25°45N 1°0E 261 C5
Adrar □ Mauritania 21°0N 10°0W 260 D3
Adrar des Iforas Africa 19°40N 1°40E 261 D5
Adré Chad 13°40N 22°20E 259 F4
Adria Italy 45°3N 12°3E 199 C9
Adrian Ga., U.S.A. 32°33N 82°35W 316 C7
Adrian Mich., U.S.A. 41°54N 84°2W 311 C12
Adrian Mo., U.S.A. 38°24N 94°21W 310 F2
Adrian Tex., U.S.A. 35°16N 102°40W 314 D3
Adrianople = Edirne Turkey 41°40N 26°34E 203 E10
Adriatic Sea Medit. S. 43°0N 16°0E 193 C7
Adua Indonesia 1°45S 129°50E 231 E7
Adung Long Burma 28°7N 97°42E 241 A6
Adur India 9°8N 76°40E 245 K3
Adwa Ethiopia 14°15N 38°52E 257 E4
Adygea □ Russia 45°0N 40°0E 191 H5
Adzhar Republic = Ajaria □ Georgia 41°30N 42°0E 191 K6
Adzhibakul = Qazımämmäd Azerbaijan 40°3N 49°0E 191 K9
Adzopé Ivory C. 6°7N 3°49W 262 D4
Aegae = Aigai Greece 40°28N 22°19E 202 F6
Ægean Sea Medit. S. 38°30N 25°0E 205 C7
Aerhtai Shan Mongolia 46°40N 92°45E 217 C12
Ærø Denmark 54°52N 10°25E 163 K4
Ærøskøbing Denmark 54°53N 10°24E 163 K4
Aetos Greece 37°15N 21°50E 204 D3
Afaahiti Tahiti 17°45S 149°17W 289 e
Afafi, Massif d' Niger 22°11N 15°10E 259 D3
ʻAfak Iraq 32°4N 45°15E 213 F11
Afandou Greece 36°18N 28°12E 206 E12
Afar □ Ethiopia 12°0N 41°0E 257 E5
Afarag, Erg Algeria 23°50N 2°47E 261 D5
Afareaitu Moorea 17°33S 149°47W 289 e
Åfarnes Norway 62°40N 7°32E 164 B4
Afdega Ethiopia 6°4N 43°30E 267 C5
Afdem Ethiopia 9°28N 41°0E 267 C5
Åffori Italy 45°31N 9°11E 128 A2
Afton U.S.A. 38°33N 90°20W 310 F6
Afghanistan ■ Asia 33°0N 65°0E 240 B2
Afgooye Somalia 2°7N 44°59E 267 D5
ʻAfīf Si. Arabia 23°53N 42°56E 248 B3
Afikpo Nigeria 5°53N 7°54E 263 D6
Aflandshage Denmark 55°33N 12°35E 118 B3
Aflisses, O. → Algeria 28°40N 0°50E 261 C5
Aflou Algeria 34°7N 2°3E 261 B5
Afmadow Somalia 0°31N 42°4E 267 D5
Afogados da Ingàzeira Brazil 7°45S 37°39W 332 C4
Afognak I. U.S.A. 58°15N 152°30W 303 G9
Afono B. Amer. Samoa 14°15S 170°38W 302 f
Afore Papua N. G. 9°9S 148°23E 286 E5
Afragóla Italy 40°55N 14°18E 201 B7
Afram → Ghana 7°0N 0°52W 263 D4
Afrera Ethiopia 13°16N 41°5E 257 E5
Africa 10°0N 20°0E 254 E6
ʻAfrīn Syria 36°32N 36°50E 250 B7
ʻAfrīn → Syria 36°20N 36°35E 250 B7
Afşar → Turkey 37°2N 32°25E 250 A3
Afşarīyeh Iran 35°39N 51°30E 141 B2
Afşin Turkey 38°14N 36°55E 212 C7
Afton Iowa, U.S.A. 41°2N 94°12W 310 C2
Afton N.Y., U.S.A. 42°14N 75°32W 313 D9
Afton Wyo., U.S.A. 42°44N 110°56W 304 E8
Afuá Brazil 0°15S 50°20W 329 D7
ʻAfula Israel 32°37N 35°17E 250 F6
Afumba Zambia 15°38S 24°56E 265 F4
Afyon Turkey 38°45N 30°33E 205 C12
Afyon □ Turkey 38°25N 30°30E 205 C12
Afyonkarahisar = Afyon Turkey 38°45N 30°33E 205 C12
Aga Egypt 30°55N 31°10E 256 H7
Aga I. Micronesia 7°29N 151°43E 287 T18
Āgā Jarī Iran 30°42N 49°50E 247 D6
Agadem Niger 16°50N 13°11E 259 E2
Agadès = Agadez Niger 16°58N 7°59E 259 E1
Agadez Niger 16°58N 7°59E 259 E1
Agadir Morocco 30°28N 9°55W 260 B3
Agaete Canary Is. 28°6N 15°43W 153 e1
Agaie Nigeria 9°1N 6°18E 263 D6
Agalas Greece 37°43N 20°47E 207 D2
Agalega Is. Mauritius 11°0S 57°0E 273 F4
Agana Guam 13°28N 144°45E 302 d
Agana B. Guam 13°29N 144°45E 302 d
Ağapınar Turkey 39°48N 30°47E 205 B12
Agar India 23°40N 76°2E 242 H7
Agar → India 21°0N 82°57E 244 D6
Agâraktem Mali 23°8N 6°22W 260 D3
Agaro Ethiopia 7°50N 36°38E 257 F4
Agartala India 23°50N 91°23E 241 D3
Agaş Romania 46°28N 26°15E 183 D11
Agassiz Canada 49°14N 121°46W 296 D4
Agassiz Icecap Canada 80°15N 76°0W 295 A16
Agat Guam 13°25N 144°40E 302 d
Agats Indonesia 5°33S 138°0E 231 F9
Agatti I. India 10°50N 72°12E 245 J1
Agattu I. U.S.A. 52°25N 173°35E 303 K1
Agawam U.S.A. 42°5N 72°37W 313 D12
Agbélouvé Togo 6°35N 1°14E 263 D5
Agboville Ivory C. 5°55N 4°15W 262 D4
Agboyi Cr. → Nigeria 6°33N 3°24E 124 A2
Ağcabädi Azerbaijan 40°5N 47°27E 191 K8
Ağdam Azerbaijan 40°0N 46°58E 191 K8
Ağdara Azerbaijan 40°13N 46°49E 191 K8
Ağdaş Azerbaijan 40°44N 47°22E 191 K8
Agde France 43°19N 3°28E 174 E7
Agde, C. d' France 43°16N 3°28E 174 E7
Agdz Morocco 30°47N 6°30W 260 B3
Agdzhabedi = Ağcabädi Azerbaijan 40°5N 47°27E 191 K8
Agen France 44°12N 0°38E 174 D4
Ageo Japan 35°58N 139°36E 223 B11
Ager Tay Chad 20°0N 17°41E 259 E3
Agerbæk Denmark 55°36N 8°48E 163 J2
Agersø Denmark 55°13N 11°12E 163 J5
Ågerup Denmark 55°43N 12°19E 118 A1
Ågesta Sweden 59°12N 18°6E 139 B2
Ageyevo Russia 54°10N 36°27E 188 E9
Aggteleki △ Hungary 48°27N 20°36E 182 B5
Āgh Kand Iran 37°15N 48°4E 213 D13
Aghathonisi Greece 37°28N 27°0E 205 D8
Aghia Anna Greece 38°52N 23°24E 204 C5
Aghia Deka Greece 35°3N 24°58E 207 E5
Aghia Ekaterinis, Akra Greece 39°50N 19°50E 206 B9
Aghia Galini Greece 35°6N 24°41E 207 E5
Aghia Marina Athina, Greece 37°48N 23°51E 112 C3
Aghia Marina Kasos, Greece 35°27N 26°53E 205 F8
Aghia Marina Leros, Greece 37°11N 26°48E 205 D8
Aghia Paraskevi Athina, Greece 38°1N 23°49E 112 A2
Aghia Paraskevi Voreio Aigaio, Greece 39°14N 26°21E 205 B8
Aghia Roumeli Greece 35°14N 23°58E 207 E4
Aghia Varvara Greece 35°8N 25°1E 207 E6
Aghiasos Greece 39°5N 26°23E 205 B8
Aghio Theodori Greece 37°55N 23°9E 204 D5
Aghion Oros □ Greece 40°25N 24°6E 203 F8
Aghios Andreas Greece 37°21N 22°45E 204 D4
Aghios Dimitrios Greece 37°53N 23°44E 112 B2
Aghios Efimia Greece 38°18N 20°36E 207 C2
Aghios Efstratios Greece 39°34N 24°58E 204 B6
Aghios Georgios Greece 37°28N 23°57E 204 D5
Aghios Ioannis, Akra Greece 35°20N 25°40E 207 E6
Aghios Ioannis Rendis Greece 37°57N 23°39E 112 B1
Aghios Isidoros Greece 36°9N 27°51E 206 E11
Aghios Kirikos Greece 37°34N 26°17E 205 D8
Aghios Leon Greece 37°47N 20°43E 207 D2
Aghios Matheos Greece 39°30N 19°47E 206 C9
Aghios Mironas Greece 35°15N 25°1E 207 E6
Aghios Nikolaos Etoloakarnania, Greece 38°52N 20°48E 207 B2
Aghios Nikolaos Kriti, Greece 35°11N 25°41E 207 E6
Aghios Nikolaos Lefkada, Greece 38°36N 20°34E 207 B2
Aghios Oros = Athos Greece 40°9N 24°22E 203 F8
Aghios Petros Greece 38°40N 20°36E 207 B2
Aghios Stephanos Greece 39°46N 19°39E 206 B9
Aghios Thekli Greece 38°15N 20°23E 207 C1
Aghios Thomas Greece 38°58N 20°47E 207 B2
Aghiou Orous, Kolpos Greece 40°6N 24°0E 202 F7
Aghireşu Romania 46°53N 23°15E 183 D8
Aghoueyyit Mauritania 21°10N 15°6W 260 D1
Aghreïjit Mauritania 21°58N 12°11W 260 D2
Agia Greece 39°43N 22°45E 204 B4
Agincourt Canada 43°47N 79°16W 141 A3
Aginskoye Russia 51°6N 114°32E 215 D12
Agjert Mauritania 16°23N 9°17W 262 B3
Ağlasun Turkey 37°39N 30°31E 205 D12
Agly → France 42°46N 3°3E 174 F7
Agmar Mauritania 25°18N 10°50W 260 C2
Agnew Australia 28°1S 120°31E 279 E3
Agnibilékrou Ivory C. 7°10N 3°11W 262 D4
Agnita Romania 45°59N 24°40E 183 E9
Agnone Italy 41°48N 14°22E 199 G11
Ago Japan 34°20N 136°51E 223 C8
Ago-Are Nigeria 8°30N 3°25E 263 D5
Agofie Ghana 8°27N 0°15E 263 D5
Agogna → Italy 45°4N 8°54E 198 C5
Agoitz = Aoiz Spain 42°46N 1°22W 196 C3
Agön Sweden 61°34N 17°23E 162 C11
Agon Coutainville France 49°2N 1°34W 172 C5
Agoo Phil. 16°20N 120°22E 232 C3
Agora Athens, Greece 112 c1
Agordo Italy 46°18N 12°2E 199 B9
Agori India 24°33N 82°57E 243 G10
Agouifa Mauritania 19°57N 16°10W 260 E1
Agouna Benin 7°39N 1°47E 263 D5
Agout → France 43°47N 1°41E 174 E5
Agra India 27°17N 77°58E 242 F7
Agra Canal India 28°33N 77°17E 120 B2
Agrakhanskiy Poluostrov Russia 43°42N 47°36E 191 J8
Agram = Zagreb Croatia 45°50N 15°58E 199 C12
Agramunt Spain 41°48N 1°6E 196 D6
Agreda Spain 41°51N 1°55W 196 D3
Ağri Turkey 39°44N 43°3E 213 C10
Ağri □ Turkey 39°45N 43°5E 213 C10
Agri → Italy 40°13N 16°44E 201 B9
Ağrı Dağı Turkey 39°50N 44°15E 213 C11
Ağrı Karakose = Ağri Turkey 39°44N 43°3E 213 C10
Agria Greece 39°20N 23°1E 204 B5
Agricola Oriental Mexico 19°23N 99°4W 128 B2
Agrigento Italy 37°19N 13°34E 200 E6
Agrihan N. Marianas 18°46N 145°40E 302 a
Agrinio Greece 38°37N 21°27E 204 C3
Agrópoli Italy 40°21N 14°59E 201 B7
Ağstafa Azerbaijan 41°7N 45°27E 191 K7
Água Branca Brazil 5°50S 42°40W 332 C3
Agua Caliente Mexico 32°29N 116°59W 307 N10
Agua Caliente Springs U.S.A. 32°56N 116°19W 307 N10
Água Clara Brazil 20°25S 52°45W 331 E7
Agua Espraiada → Brazil 23°36S 46°41W 137 B2
Agua Fria △ U.S.A. 34°14N 112°0W 305 J8
Agua Hechicera Mexico 32°28N 116°15W 307 N10
Agua Preta → Brazil 1°41S 63°48W 329 D5
Agua Prieta Mexico 31°18N 109°34W 318 A3
Aguachica Colombia 8°19N 73°38W 328 B3
Aguada Puerto Rico 18°23N 67°11W 321 b
Aguada Cecilio Argentina 40°51S 65°51W 336 B3
Aguadas Colombia 5°40N 75°38W 328 B2
Aguadilla Puerto Rico 18°26N 67°10W 321 C6
Aguadulce Panama 8°15N 80°32W 320 E3
Agualva-Cacem Portugal 38°46N 9°15W 126 A1
Aguanga U.S.A. 33°27N 116°51W 307 M10
Aguanish Canada 50°14N 62°2W 299 B7
Aguanish → Canada 50°13N 62°5W 299 B7
Aguapeí Brazil 16°12S 59°43W 331 D6
Aguapeí → Brazil 21°0S 51°0W 333 F1
Aguapey → Argentina 29°7S 56°36W 334 B4
Aguaray Guazú → Paraguay 24°47S 57°19W 334 A4
Aguarico → Ecuador 0°59S 75°11W 328 D2
Aguaro-Guariquito △ Venezuela 8°20N 66°35W 328 B4
Aguas → Spain 41°20N 0°30W 196 D4
Aguas Blancas Chile 24°15S 69°55W 334 A2
Aguas Calientes, Sierra de Argentina 25°26S 66°40W 334 B2
Aguas Formosas Brazil 17°5S 40°57W 333 E3
Aguas Lindas de Goiás Brazil 15°46S 48°15W 333 E2
Aguascalientes Mexico 21°53N 102°18W 318 C4

INDEX
Alba 341

Aguascalientes □ Mexico 22°0N 102°20W 318 C4
Agudo Spain 38°59N 4°52W 195 G6
Águeda Portugal 40°34N 8°27W 194 E2
Agueda → Spain 41°2N 6°56W 194 D4
Aguelhok Mali 19°29N 0°52E 261 E5
Aguelt el Melah
Mauritania 23°3N 10°40W 260 D2
Agüenit W. Sahara 22°11N 13°8W 260 D2
Aguié Niger 13°31N 7°46E 263 C6
Aguila, Punta Puerto Rico 17°57N 67°13W 321 b
Aguilafuente Spain 41°13N 4°7W 194 D6
Aguilar de Campóo Spain 42°47N 4°15W 194 C6
Aguilar de la Frontera
Spain 37°31N 4°40W 195 H6
Aguilares Argentina 27°26S 65°35W 334 B2
Águilas Spain 37°23N 1°35W 197 H3
Agüimes Canary Is. 27°58N 15°27W 153 e1
Aguja, C. de la Colombia 11°18N 74°12W 328 A3
Agujereada, Pta.
Puerto Rico 18°30N 67°8W 321 b
Agulaa Ethiopia 13°40N 39°40E 257 E4
Agulhas, C. S. Africa 34°52S 20°0E 270 D3
Agulhas Ridge Atl. Oc. 42°0S 15°0E 152 L13
Agulo Canary Is. 28°11N 17°12W 153 e1
Agung, Gunung
Indonesia 8°20S 115°28E 231 J18
Aguni-Jima Japan 26°30N 127°10E 221 L3
Agur Uganda 2°28N 32°55E 268 B3
Agurei → South Sudan 7°45N 33°0E 257 F3
Agusan → Phil. 9°0N 125°30E 233 G5
Agusan del Norte □ Phil. 9°20N 125°10E 233 G5
Agusan del Sur □ Phil. 8°30N 125°30E 233 G5
Agustín Codazzi Colombia 10°2N 73°14W 328 A3
Agutaya I. Phil. 11°9N 120°58E 233 F3
Ağva Turkey 41°8N 29°51E 203 E13
Agvali Russia 42°36N 46°8E 191 J8
Aha Mts. Botswana 19°45S 21°0E 270 A3
Ahad Rifaydah Si. Arabia 17°50N 42°50E 248 C3
Ahaggar Algeria 23°0N 6°30E 261 D6
Ahaggar △ Algeria 23°0N 4°50E 261 D5
Ahai Dam China 27°21N 100°30E 228 D3
Ahal □ Turkmenistan 37°0N 57°0E 216 E5
Ahamansu Ghana 7°38N 0°35E 263 D5
Ahar Iran 38°35N 47°0E 213 C12
Ahat Turkey 38°39N 29°47E 205 C11
Ahaura → N.Z. 42°21S 171°34E 285 C6
Ahaus Germany 52°4N 7°0E 178 C2
Ahé French Polynesia 14°30S 146°18W 289 f
Åheim Norway 62°2N 5°13E 164 B2
Ahelledjem Algeria 26°37N 6°58E 261 C6
Ahimanawa Ra. N.Z. 39°3S 176°30E 284 F5
Ahioma Papua N. G. 10°20S 150°33E 286 F6
Ahipara B. N.Z. 35°5S 173°5E 284 B2
Ahir Dağı Turkey 38°45N 30°10E 205 C12
Ahiri India 19°30N 80°0E 244 E5
Ahlat Turkey 38°45N 42°29E 213 C10
Ahlen Germany 51°45N 7°53E 178 D3
Ahmad Wal Pakistan 29°18N 65°58E 242 E1
Ahmadabad India 23°0N 72°40E 242 H5
Aḩmadābād Khorāsān, Iran 35°3N 60°50E 247 C9
Aḩmadābād Khorāsān,
Iran 35°49N 59°42E 247 C8
Aḩmadī Iran 27°56N 56°42E 247 E8
Ahmadnagar India 19°7N 74°46E 244 E2
Ahmadpur India 18°40N 76°57E 244 E3
Ahmadpur East Pakistan 29°12N 71°10E 242 E4
Ahmadpur Lamma
Pakistan 28°19N 70°3E 242 E4
Ahmanson Theater Los Angeles, U.S.A. 127 b2
Ahmar, Mts. Ethiopia 9°20N 41°15E 257 F5
Ahmedabad = Ahmadabad
India 23°0N 72°40E 242 H5
Ahmednagar = Ahmadnagar
India 19°7N 74°46E 244 E2
Ahmetbey Turkey 41°26N 27°34E 203 E11
Ahmetler Turkey 38°28N 29°5E 205 C11
Ahmetli Turkey 38°32N 27°57E 205 C9
Ahmeyim Mauritania 20°51N 14°25W 260 D2
Ahoada Nigeria 5°8N 6°36E 263 D6
Ahome Mexico 25°55N 109°11W 318 B3
Ahon, Tarso Chad 20°23N 18°18E 259 D3
Ahoskie U.S.A. 36°17N 76°59W 315 C16
Ahr → Germany 50°32N 7°16E 178 E3
Ahram Iran 28°52N 51°16E 247 D6
Ahrax Pt. Malta 36°0N 14°22E 206 F7
Ahrensbök Germany 54°2N 10°35E 178 A6
Ahrensburg Germany 53°40N 10°13E 178 B6
Ahrensfelde Germany 52°34N 13°34E 115 A4
Ahu Akivi Chile 27°7S 109°24W 330 b
Ahu Tepeu Chile 27°6S 109°25W 330 b
Ahu Tongariki Chile 27°8S 109°17W 330 b
Ahu Vinapu Chile 27°10S 109°25W 330 b
Ahuachapán El Salv. 13°54N 89°52W 320 D2
'Āhuimanu U.S.A. 21°26N 157°50W 302 K14
Ahun France 46°4N 2°5E 173 F9
Ahuntsic Canada 45°32N 73°41W 130 A1
Ahunui French Polynesia 19°39S 140°25W 289 f
Ahuriri → N.Z. 44°31S 170°12E 285 E5
Åhus Sweden 55°56N 14°18E 163 J8
Ahvāz Iran 31°20N 48°40E 247 D6
Ahvenanmaa = Åland
Finland 60°15N 20°0E 161 F19
Aḩwar Yemen 13°30N 46°40E 248 D4
Ahzar → Mali 15°30N 3°20E 263 B5
Ai → India 26°26N 90°44E 241 B3
Ai → Ōsaka, Japan 34°46N 135°35E 133 A2
Ai-Ais Namibia 27°54S 17°59E 270 C2
Ai-Ais and Fish River Canyon △
Namibia 24°45S 17°15E 270 B2
Aiari → Brazil 1°22N 68°36W 328 C4
Aichach Germany 48°27N 11°8E 179 G7
Aichi □ Japan 35°0N 137°15E 223 C9
'Aiea U.S.A. 21°23N 157°56W 302 K14
Aigai Greece 40°28N 22°19E 202 F6
Aigle Switz. 46°18N 6°58E 179 J2
Aignay-le-Duc France 47°40N 4°43E 173 E11
Aigoual, Mt. France 44°8N 3°35E 174 D7
Aigre France 45°54N 0°1E 174 C4
Aigremont France 48°54N 2°1E 134 A1
Aigrettes, Île aux Mauritius 20°25S 57°43E 272 e
Aiguá Uruguay 34°13S 54°46W 335 C5
Aigueperse France 46°3N 3°13E 173 F10
Aigues → France 44°7N 4°43E 175 D8
Aigues-Mortes France 43°35N 4°12E 175 E8
Aigues-Mortes, G. d' France 43°31N 4°3E 175 E8
Aigües-Tortes i Estany de St.
Maurici △ Spain 42°38N 0°31E 196 C4
Aiguilles France 44°47N 6°51E 175 D10
Aiguillon France 44°18N 0°21E 174 D4
Aigurande France 46°27N 1°49E 173 F8
Aihui = Heihe China 50°10N 127°30E 219 A14
Aija Peru 9°50S 77°45W 330 B2
Aikawa Japan 38°2N 138°15E 220 E9
Aiken U.S.A. 33°34N 81°43W 316 B8
Ailao Shan China 24°0N 101°20E 228 E3
Aileron Australia 22°39S 133°20E 280 C1
Ailey U.S.A. 32°11N 82°34W 316 C7
Ailigandí Panama 9°14N 78°1W 328 B2
Aillant-sur-Tholon France 47°52N 3°20E 173 E10
Aillik Canada 55°11N 59°18W 299 A8
Ailsa Craig Ont., Canada 43°8N 81°33W 312 C3
Ailsa Craig S. Ayrs., U.K. 55°15N 5°6W 167 F3
Ailuilual Papua N. G. 9°38S 150°35E 286 E6
Aim Russia 59°0N 133°55E 215 D14
Aimogasta Argentina 28°33S 66°50W 334 B2
Aimorés Brazil 19°30S 41°4W 333 E3
Ain □ France 46°5N 5°20E 173 F12
Ain → France 45°45N 5°11E 175 C9
Aïn Beïda Algeria 35°50N 7°29E 261 A6
Aïn Ben Khellil Algeria 33°15N 0°49W 261 B4
Aïn Ben Tili Mauritania 25°59N 9°27W 260 C3
Aïn Beni Mathar Morocco 34°1N 2°0W 261 B4
Aïn Benian Algeria 36°48N 2°55E 261 A5
Aïn Dalla Egypt 27°20N 27°23E 256 B2
Aïn Defla Algeria 36°16N 1°58E 261 A5
Aïn Defla □ Algeria 36°10N 2°10E 261 A5
Aïn el Akhḍar Egypt 28°50N 33°55E 251 K4
Aïn el Mafki Egypt 27°30N 28°15E 256 B2
Aïn Girba Egypt 29°20N 25°14E 256 B2
Aïn M'lila Algeria 36°2N 6°35E 261 A6
Aïn Murr Sudan 21°50N 25°9E 256 C2
Aïn Qeiqab Egypt 29°42N 24°55E 256 B1
Aïn Salah = In Salah
Algeria 27°10N 2°32E 261 C5
Aïn Sefra Algeria 32°47N 0°37W 261 B4
Aïn Sheikh Murzûk
Egypt 26°47N 27°45E 256 B2
Aïn Sudr Egypt 29°50N 33°6E 251 J4
Aïn Sukhna Egypt 29°32N 32°20E 256 J8
Aïn Tédelès Algeria 36°0N 0°21E 261 A5
Aïn Témouchent Algeria 35°16N 1°8W 261 A4
Aïn Témouchent □ Algeria 35°20N 1°5W 261 A4
Aïn Tikkidine Algeria 25°33N 1°24E 261 C5
Aïn Touta Algeria 35°26N 5°54E 261 A6
Aïn Zeitûn Egypt 29°10N 25°48E 256 B2
Aïn Zorah Morocco 34°37N 3°32W 261 B4
Ainaži Latvia 57°50N 24°24E 188 D3
Ainos Oros Greece 38°5N 20°40E 207 C2
Ainsworth U.S.A. 42°33N 99°52W 308 D4
Aintab = Gaziantep Turkey 37°6N 37°23E 250 A8
Aioi Japan 34°48N 134°28E 222 C6
Aiome Papua N. G. 5°8S 144°44E 286 C3
Aipe Colombia 3°13N 75°15W 328 C2
Aiquile Bolivia 18°10S 65°10W 331 D4
Aïr Niger 18°30N 8°0E 259 E1
Air Canada Centre Toronto, Canada 141 c2
Aïr et Ténéré △ Niger 18°12N 9°56E 263 B6
Air Force I. Canada 67°58N 74°5W 295 D17
Air Hitam Malaysia 1°55N 103°11E 237 M4
Air View Park Singapore 1°20N 103°46E 138 A2
Aira Japan 31°43N 130°43E 222 F2
Airaines France 49°53N 1°55E 173 C8
Airão Brazil 1°56S 61°22W 329 D5
Airbangis Indonesia 0°12N 99°22E 234 B1
Airdrie Alta., Canada 51°18N 114°2W 296 C6
Airdrie N. Lanarks., U.K. 55°52N 3°57W 167 F5
Aire → Meuse, France 49°18N 4°49E 173 C11
Aire → N. Yorks., U.K. 53°43N 0°55W 168 D7
Aire, I. de l' Spain 39°48N 4°16E 206 B5
Aire-sur-la-Lys France 50°37N 2°22E 173 B9
Aire-sur-l'Adour France 43°42N 0°15W 174 E3
Aireys Inlet Australia 38°29S 144°5E 282 E6
Airlie Beach Australia 20°16S 148°43E 280 b
Airport West Australia 37°42S 144°52E 128 A1
Airvault France 46°50N 0°8W 172 F6
Aisch → Germany 49°49N 10°58E 179 F6
Aisén □ Chile 46°30S 73°0W 336 C2
Aisne □ France 49°42N 3°40E 173 C10
Aisne → France 49°26N 2°50E 173 C9
Ait India 25°54N 79°14E 243 G8
Ait Ben Haddou Morocco 31°3N 7°7W 260 B3
Aitana, Sierra de Spain 38°35N 0°24W 197 G4
Aitape Papua N. G. 3°11S 142°22E 286 B2
Aitkin U.S.A. 46°32N 93°42W 308 B7
Aitutaki Cook Is. 18°52S 159°45W 289 J12
Aiuaba Brazil 6°38S 40°7W 332 C3
Aiud Romania 46°19N 23°44E 183 D8
Aix-en-Provence France 43°32N 5°27E 175 E9
Aix-la-Chapelle = Aachen
Germany 50°45N 6°6E 178 E2
Aix-les-Bains France 45°41N 5°53E 175 C9
Aixe-sur-Vienne France 45°47N 1°9E 174 C5
Aiyang, Mt. Papua N. G. 5°10S 141°20E 286 C1
Aíyina = Egina Greece 37°45N 23°26E 204 D5
Aizawl India 23°40N 92°44E 241 D4
Aizenay France 46°44N 1°38W 172 F5
Aizkraukle Latvia 56°36N 25°11E 188 D3
Aizpute Latvia 56°43N 21°40E 184 B8
Aizuwakamatsu Japan 37°30N 139°56E 220 F9
Ajabshir Iran 37°28N 45°54E 213 D11
Ajaccio France 41°55N 8°40E 175 G12
Ajaccio, G. d' France 41°52N 8°40E 175 G12
Ajai △ Uganda 2°52N 31°16E 268 B3
Ajaigarh India 24°52N 80°16E 243 G9
Ajajú → Colombia 0°59N 72°20W 328 C3
Ajalpan Mexico 18°22N 97°15W 319 D5
Ajanta India 20°30N 75°48E 244 D2
Ajanta Ra. India 20°28N 75°50E 244 D2
Ajaokuta Nigeria 7°28N 6°42E 263 D6
Ajari Rep. = Ajaria □
Georgia 41°30N 42°0E 191 K6
Ajaria □ Georgia 41°30N 42°0E 191 K6
Ajax Canada 43°50N 79°1W 312 C5
Ajax, Mt. N.Z. 42°35S 172°5E 285 C7
Ajdābiyā Libya 30°54N 20°4E 258 B4
Ajdovščina Slovenia 45°54N 13°54E 199 C10
Ajegunle Nigeria 6°26N 3°20E 124 B2
Aji Japan 34°40N 135°27E 133 A1
Ajibar Ethiopia 10°35N 38°36E 257 E4
Ajka Hungary 47°4N 17°31E 182 C2
'Ajlūn Jordan 32°18N 35°47E 251 F6
'Ajmān U.A.E. 25°25N 55°30E 247 E7
Ajmer India 26°28N 74°37E 242 F6
Ajnala India 31°50N 74°48E 242 D6
Ajo U.S.A. 32°22N 112°52W 305 K7
Ajo, C. de Spain 43°31N 3°35W 194 B7
Ajoupa-Bouillon Martinique 14°49N 61°7W 322 j
Ajuda Portugal 38°42N 9°12W 126 A1
Ajuda, Pta. da Azores 37°52N 25°19W 153 d3
Ajuy Phil. 11°10N 123°1E 233 F4
Ak Dağ Turkey 36°30N 29°32E 205 E11
Ak Dağlar Turkey 39°32N 36°12E 212 C7
Ak Dağları Turkey 36°30N 29°30E 205 E11
Ak-Dovurak Russia 51°11N 90°36E 217 B12
Ak-Mechet = Qyzylorda
Kazakhstan 44°48N 65°28E 217 D7
Ak-Mednet = Chornomorske
Ukraine 45°31N 32°40E 189 K7
Ak-Sheikh = Razdolnoye
Ukraine 45°46N 33°29E 189 K7
Akaba Togo 8°10N 1°2E 263 D5
Akabira Japan 43°33N 142°5E 220 C11
Akabli Algeria 26°49N 1°31E 261 C5
Akademika Obrucheva, Khrebet
Russia 51°50N 96°0E 217 B13
Akagera △ Rwanda 1°31S 30°33E 268 C3
Akaishi-Dake Japan 35°27N 138°9E 223 B10
Akaishi-Sammyaku
Japan 35°25N 138°10E 223 B10
Akaki Beseka Ethiopia 8°55N 38°45E 257 F4
Akäküs, J. Libya 25°20N 10°30E 258 C2
Akalkot India 17°32N 76°13E 244 F3
Akalla Sweden 59°24N 17°55E 139 A1
Akamas Cyprus 35°3N 32°18E 207 E8
Akan △ Japan 43°20N 144°20E 220 C12
Akanthou Cyprus 35°22N 33°45E 207 E9
Akarca Turkey 38°35N 29°35E 205 C11
Akaroa N.Z. 43°49S 172°59E 285 D7
Akaroa Harbour N.Z. 43°50S 172°55E 285 D7
Akasaka Tokyo, Japan 140 b3
Akasha Sudan 21°10N 30°32E 256 C3
Akashi Japan 34°45N 134°58E 222 C6
Akbarābād Iran 35°40N 51°20E 141 A2
Akbarpur Bihar, India 24°39N 83°58E 243 G10
Akbarpur Ut. P., India 26°25N 82°32E 243 F10
Akbou Algeria 36°31N 4°31E 261 A5
Akbulak Russia 51°1N 55°37E 216 B5
Akçaabat Turkey 41°1N 39°34E 213 B8
Akçadağ Turkey 38°27N 37°43E 212 C7
Akçakale Turkey 36°41N 38°56E 213 D8
Akçakoca Turkey 41°5N 31°8E 212 B4
Akçalı Dağları Turkey 36°18N 33°21E 250 B4
Akçaova Turkey 41°3N 29°57E 203 E13
Akçay Turkey 36°36N 29°45E 205 E11
Akçay → Turkey 37°50N 28°15E 205 D10
Akchâr Mauritania 20°20N 14°28W 260 D2
Akchi-Karasu = Toktogul
Kyrgyzstan 41°50N 72°50E 217 D8
Akdağ Antalya, Turkey 37°0N 32°0E 250 B3
Akdağ İzmir, Turkey 38°33N 26°30E 205 C8
Akdağmadeni Turkey 39°39N 35°53E 212 C6
Akdere Turkey 36°14N 33°46E 250 B4
Akdoğan = Lysi Cyprus 35°6N 33°41E 207 E9
Akechi Japan 35°18N 137°23E 223 B9
Akelamo Indonesia 1°35N 129°40E 231 D7
Åkernes = Åknes Norway 58°45N 7°30E 164 F4
Åkers styckebruk Sweden 59°15N 17°5E 162 E11
Åkersberga Sweden 59°29N 18°18E 162 E12
Akershus □ Norway 60°0N 11°10E 164 D8
Akershus Slott Oslo, Norway 133 c1
Akeru → India 17°25N 80°5E 244 F5
Aketi Dem. Rep. of the Congo 2°38N 23°47E 264 B4
Akhali Atoni Georgia 43°7N 40°50E 191 J5
Akhalkalaki Georgia 41°27N 43°25E 191 K6
Akhaltsikhe Georgia 41°40N 43°0E 191 K6
Akhḍar, W. al →
Si. Arabia 28°36N 36°36E 251 K7
Akhiok U.S.A. 56°57N 154°10W 303 H9
Akhisar Turkey 38°56N 27°48E 205 C9
Akhmîm Egypt 26°31N 31°47E 256 B3
Akhna Cyprus 35°3N 33°47E 207 E9
Akhnur India 32°52N 74°45E 243 C6
Akhtarīn Syria 36°31N 37°20E 250 B8
Akhtopol Bulgaria 42°6N 27°56E 203 D11
Akhtuba → Russia 47°41N 46°55E 191 G8
Akhtubinsk Russia 48°13N 46°7E 191 F8
Akhty Russia 41°30N 47°45E 191 K8
Akhtyrka = Okhtyrka
Ukraine 50°25N 35°0E 189 G8
Aki Japan 33°30N 133°54E 222 D5
Aki-Nada Japan 34°5N 132°40E 222 C4
Akiachak U.S.A. 60°55N 161°26W 303 F7
Akiak U.S.A. 60°55N 161°13W 303 F7
Akiéni Gabon 1°11S 13°53E 264 C2
Akihabara Tokyo, Japan 140 a5
Akimiski I. Canada 52°50N 81°30W 298 B3
Akıncı Burnu Turkey 36°19N 35°46E 250 B6
Akıncılar = Louroujina
Cyprus 35°0N 33°28E 207 F9
Akiōta Japan 34°36N 132°19E 222 C4
Åkirkeby Denmark 55°4N 14°55E 163 J8
Akita Japan 39°45N 140°7E 220 E10
Akita □ Japan 39°40N 140°30E 220 E10
Akjoujt Mauritania 19°45N 14°15W 262 B2
Akka Mali 15°24N 4°11W 262 B4
Akka Morocco 29°22N 8°9W 260 C3
Akkaraipattu Sri Lanka 7°13N 81°51E 245 L5
Akkaya Tepesi Turkey 37°25N 29°38E 205 D11
Akkerman = Bilhorod-
Dnistrovskyy Ukraine 46°11N 30°23E 189 J6
Akkeshi Japan 43°2N 144°51E 220 C12
'Akko Israel 32°55N 35°4E 250 F6
Akköy Turkey 37°29N 27°15E 205 D9
Akkuş Turkey 40°47N 37°0E 212 B7
Aklampa Benin 8°15N 2°10E 263 D5
Aklan □ Phil. 11°50N 122°30E 233 F4
Aklavik Canada 68°12N 135°0W 294 D4
Aklera India 24°26N 76°32E 242 G7
Akmenė Lithuania 56°15N 22°45E 184 B9
Akmenrags Latvia 56°50N 21°4E 184 B8
Akmolinsk = Astana
Kazakhstan 51°10N 71°30E 217 B8
Akmonte = Almonte
Spain 37°13N 6°38W 195 H4
Åknes Norway 58°45N 7°30E 164 F4
Aknoul Morocco 34°40N 3°55W 261 B4
Akō Japan 34°45N 134°24E 222 C6
Ako Nigeria 10°19N 10°48E 263 C7
Akobo South Sudan 7°47N 33°3E 257 F3
Akobo → Ethiopia 7°48N 33°3E 257 F3
Akola Maharashtra, India 20°42N 77°2E 244 D3
Akola Maharashtra, India 19°32N 74°3E 244 E2
Akolmiut U.S.A. 60°55N 162°20W 303 F7
Akonolinga Cameroon 3°50N 12°18E 263 E7
Akor Mali 14°59N 6°58W 262 C3
Akordat Eritrea 15°30N 37°40E 257 D4
Akosombo Dam Ghana 6°20N 0°5E 263 D5
Akot India 21°10N 77°10E 244 D3
Akot South Sudan 6°31N 30°9E 257 F3
Akoupé Ivory C. 6°23N 3°54W 262 D4
Akourousoulba C.A.R. 8°58N 20°46E 264 A4
Akpatok I. Canada 60°25N 68°8W 295 E18
Åkrahamn Norway 59°15N 5°10E 164 E2
'Akramah Libya 32°2N 23°41E 258 B4
Akranes Iceland 64°19N 22°5W 155 C4
Akreïjit Mauritania 18°19N 9°11W 262 B3
Akritas, Akra Greece 36°43N 21°54E 204 E3
Akron Colo., U.S.A. 40°10N 103°13W 304 F12
Akron Ind., U.S.A. 41°2N 86°1W 311 C10
Akron Ohio, U.S.A. 41°5N 81°31W 312 E3
Akrotiri Cyprus 34°36N 32°57E 207 F8
Akrotiri, Akra Greece 40°26N 25°27E 203 F9
Akrotiri Bay Cyprus 34°35N 33°10E 207 F9
Aksai Chin China 35°15N 79°55E 243 B8
Aksaray Turkey 38°25N 34°2E 212 C6
Aksaray □ Turkey 38°20N 33°45E 212 C5
Aksay = Aqsay Kazakhstan 51°11N 53°0E 187 D9
Akşehir Turkey 38°18N 31°30E 212 C4
Akşehir Gölü Turkey 38°30N 31°25E 212 C4
Akseki Turkey 37°2N 31°47E 250 A2
Akstafa = Ağstafa
Azerbaijan 41°7N 45°27E 191 K7
Aksu Xinjiang Uygur, China 41°5N 80°10E 217 D10
Aksu Turkey 36°57N 30°50E 250 B1
Aksu → Turkey 36°52N 30°57E 250 B1
Aksu He → China 40°26N 80°59E 217 D10
Aksum Ethiopia 14°5N 38°40E 257 E4
Aktash Russia 55°2N 52°2E 190 C11
Aktepe Turkey 36°42N 36°27E 250 B7
Aktio Greece 38°57N 20°46E 207 B2
Akto China 39°5N 75°59E 217 E9
Aktsyabrski Belarus 52°38N 28°53E 177 B15
Aktyubinsk = Aqtöbe
Kazakhstan 50°17N 57°10E 187 D10
Aku Nigeria 6°40N 7°18E 263 D6
Akula Dem. Rep. of the Congo 2°22N 20°12E 264 B4
Akun I. U.S.A. 54°11N 165°32W 303 J6
Akune Japan 32°1N 130°12E 222 E2
Akure Nigeria 7°15N 5°5E 263 D6
Akurenan Eq. Guin. 1°2N 10°40E 264 B2
Akuressa Sri Lanka 6°5N 80°29E 245 L5
Akureyri Iceland 65°40N 18°6W 155 B8
Akuseki-Shima Japan 29°27N 129°37E 221 K4
Akusha Russia 42°18N 47°30E 191 J8
Akutan U.S.A. 54°8N 165°46W 303 J6
Akutan I. U.S.A. 54°7N 165°55W 303 J6
Akwa-Ibom □ Nigeria 4°30N 7°30E 263 E6
Akwanga Nigeria 8°55N 8°23E 263 D6
Akyab = Sittwe Burma 20°18N 92°45E 241 E4
Akyazı Turkey 40°40N 30°38E 212 B4
Ål Norway 60°38N 8°33E 164 D5
Al Abyaḍ Libya 26°49N 14°1E 258 C2
Al Abyār Libya 32°9N 20°29E 258 B4
Al 'Adam Libya 31°51N 23°55E 258 B4
Al 'Adan = 'Adan Yemen 12°45N 45°0E 248 D4
Al Aḩsā = Hasa Si. Arabia 25°50N 49°0E 247 E6
Al Ajfar Si. Arabia 27°26N 43°0E 246 E4
Al Akhḍar, al Jabal Libya 32°30N 21°30E 258 B4
Al Amādīyah Iraq 37°5N 43°30E 213 D10
Al 'Amārah Iraq 31°55N 47°15E 213 G12
Al Anbār □ Iraq 33°25N 42°0E 246 C4
Al 'Aqabah Jordan 29°31N 35°0E 251 J6
Al 'Aqabah □ Jordan 29°30N 35°0E 251 J6
Al 'Aqīq Si. Arabia 20°39N 41°25E 248 B3
Al Arak Syria 34°38N 38°35E 213 E8
Al 'Aramah Si. Arabia 25°30N 46°0E 246 E5
Al 'Ariḍah Si. Arabia 17°3N 43°5E 248 C3
Al 'Arṭāwīyah Si. Arabia 26°31N 45°20E 246 E5
Al Ashkhara Oman 21°50N 59°30E 249 B7
Al 'Āṣimah = 'Ammān □
Jordan 31°40N 36°30E 251 G7
Al 'Assāfīyah Si. Arabia 28°17N 38°59E 246 D3
Al Atārib Syria 36°9N 36°49E 250 B7
Al 'Awdah Si. Arabia 25°32N 45°41E 246 E5
Al 'Ayn Si. Arabia 25°4N 38°6E 246 E3
Al 'Ayn U.A.E. 24°15N 55°45E 247 E7
Al 'Aẓamīyah Iraq 33°22N 44°22E 113 A2
Al 'Azīzīyah Iraq 32°54N 45°4E 213 F11
Al 'Azīzīyah Libya 32°30N 13°1E 258 B2
Al Bāb Syria 36°23N 37°29E 250 B8
Al Bad' Si. Arabia 28°28N 35°1E 246 D2
Al Bada U.A.E. 25°13N 55°16E 119 B2
Al Badā'i' Si. Arabia 26°2N 43°33E 246 E4
Al Bādī Iraq 35°56N 41°32E 246 C4
Al Badī' Si. Arabia 22°0N 46°35E 248 B4
Al Bāḩah Si. Arabia 20°1N 41°28E 256 C5
Al Bāḩah □ Si. Arabia 20°30N 41°30E 248 B3
Al Baḩrah Kuwait 29°40N 47°52E 246 D5
Al Baḩral Mayyit = Dead Sea
Asia 31°30N 35°30E 251 G6
Al Balqā' □ Jordan 32°5N 35°45E 251 F6
Al Barkāt Libya 24°56N 10°14E 258 D2
Al Barsha U.A.E. 25°6N 55°11E 119 B1
Al Bārūk, J. Lebanon 33°39N 35°40E 250 E6
Al Baṣrah Iraq 30°30N 47°50E 246 D5
Al Baṭḩā Iraq 31°6N 45°53E 246 D5
Al Bāṭinah □ Oman 24°0N 57°0E 249 B7
Al Batrūn Lebanon 34°15N 35°40E 250 D6
Al Bayāḍ Si. Arabia 22°0N 47°0E 248 B4
Al Bayḍā Libya 32°50N 21°44E 258 B4
Al Bayḍā' Yemen 14°5N 45°42E 248 D4
Al Bayḍā' □ Yemen 14°5N 45°42E 248 D4
Al Bi'ār Si. Arabia 22°39N 39°40E 248 B2
Al Biqā Lebanon 34°10N 36°10E 250 D7
Al Biqā □ Lebanon 34°0N 36°5E 250 E7
Al Bi'r Si. Arabia 28°51N 36°16E 251 K7
Al Birk Si. Arabia 18°13N 41°33E 248 C3
Al Bu'ayrāt al Ḩasūn
Libya 31°24N 15°44E 258 B3
Al Bukayrīyah Si. Arabia 26°9N 43°40E 246 E4
Al Bumbah Libya 32°24N 23°8E 258 B4
Al Burayj Syria 34°15N 36°46E 250 D7
Al Buṭnān □ Libya 31°40N 24°30E 258 B4
Al Buwayqāt Yemen 15°22N 48°30E 249 D5
Al Faḍilī Si. Arabia 26°58N 49°10E 247 E6
Al Fallūjah Iraq 33°20N 43°55E 213 F10
Al Fatḩah Iraq 35°3N 43°33E 213 E10
Al Fāw Iraq 30°0N 48°30E 247 D6
Al Faydamī Yemen 16°25N 52°26E 249 C6
Al Fujayrah U.A.E. 25°7N 56°18E 247 E8
Al Ghadaf, W. → Jordan 31°26N 36°43E 251 G7
Al Ghammās Iraq 31°45N 44°37E 246 D5
Al Gharīb Libya 32°35N 21°11E 258 B4
Al Ghaydah Yemen 16°13N 52°11E 249 C6
Al Ghayl Yemen 15°30N 50°54E 249 D5
Al Ghazālah Si. Arabia 26°48N 41°19E 246 E4
Al Ḩadd Oman 22°32N 59°48E 249 B7
Al Ḩaddār Si. Arabia 21°58N 45°57E 248 B4
Al Ḩadīthah Iraq 34°0N 41°13E 213 E10
Al Ḩadīthah Si. Arabia 31°28N 37°8E 246 D3
Al Ḩaḍr Iraq 35°35N 42°44E 213 E10
Al Ḩaffah Syria 35°36N 36°1E 250 C7
Al Ḩājānah Syria 33°20N 36°33E 250 E7
Al Ḩajar al Gharbī Oman 24°10N 56°15E 247 E8
Al Ḩallānīyah Oman 17°30N 56°1E 249 C7
Al Ḩāmad Si. Arabia 31°30N 39°30E 246 D3
Al Ḩamar Si. Arabia 22°26N 46°12E 248 B4
Al Ḩamdānīyah Syria 35°25N 36°50E 250 C7
Al Ḩamī Yemen 14°48N 49°49E 249 D5
Al Ḩamīdīyah Syria 34°50N 35°57E 250 D6
Al Ḩammār Iraq 30°57N 46°51E 246 D5
Al Ḩamrā' Si. Arabia 24°2N 38°55E 246 E3
Al Ḩamrā' Syria 35°19N 37°5E 250 C8
Al Ḩamrā', al Ḩamādah
Libya 29°30N 12°0E 258 C2
Al Hamriya Port U.A.E. 25°18N 55°20E 119 A2
Al Ḩamzah Iraq 31°43N 44°58E 246 D5
Al Ḩanākīyah Si. Arabia 24°51N 40°31E 246 E4
Al Ḩariq Si. Arabia 23°29N 46°27E 248 B4
Al Ḩarūj al Aswad Libya 27°0N 17°10E 258 C3
Al Ḩasakah Syria 36°35N 40°45E 213 D9
Al Ḩasakah □ Syria 36°40N 40°50E 213 D9
Al Ḩāshimīyah Iraq 32°22N 44°39E 213 G11
Al Ḩāsikīyah Oman 17°28N 55°36E 249 C6
Al Ḩawīyah Ash Sharqīyah,
Si. Arabia 24°45N 49°6E 249 A5
Al Ḩawīyah Makkah,
Si. Arabia 21°26N 40°30E 248 B3
Al Ḩawrah Yemen 13°50N 47°35E 248 D4
Al Ḩawṭah = Labij Yemen 13°4N 44°53E 248 D4
Al Ḩawṭah Yemen 15°58N 48°26E 249 D5
Al Ḩayy Iraq 32°5N 46°5E 213 F12
Al Ḩazm = Al Jawf Yemen 16°10N 44°37E 248 C4
Al Ḩijarah Asia 30°0N 44°0E 246 D4
Al Ḩillah Iraq 32°30N 44°25E 213 F11
Al Ḩillah Si. Arabia 23°35N 46°50E 248 B4
Al Ḩindīyah Iraq 32°30N 44°10E 213 F11
Al Ḩirmil Lebanon 34°26N 36°24E 250 D7
Al Hoceïma Morocco 35°8N 3°58W 261 A4
Al Hudaiba U.A.E. 25°14N 55°16E 119 B2
Al Ḩudaydah Yemen 14°50N 43°0E 248 D3
Al Ḩudaydah □ Yemen 14°50N 43°0E 248 D3
Al Ḩudūd ash Shamālīyah □
Si. Arabia 29°10N 42°30E 246 D4
Al Ḩufrah Libya 25°32N 14°1E 258 C2
Al Ḩufūf Si. Arabia 25°25N 49°45E 247 E6
Al Ḩulwah Si. Arabia 23°24N 46°48E 248 B4
Al Ḩumaydah Si. Arabia 29°14N 34°56E 251 J5
Al Ḩunayy Si. Arabia 25°58N 48°45E 247 E6
Al Ḩurayḍah Yemen 15°36N 48°11E 249 D5
Al Ḩusayyāt Libya 30°24N 20°37E 258 B4
Al 'Irqah Yemen 13°39N 47°22E 248 D4
Al 'Īsāwīyah Si. Arabia 30°43N 37°59E 246 D3
Al Ittihad = Madīnat ash Sha'b
Yemen 12°50N 45°0E 248 D4
Al Jabal al Akhḍar □
Libya 32°30N 21°41E 258 B4
Al Jabal al Gharbī □ Libya 31°26N 12°59E 258 B2
Al Jafiliya U.A.E. 25°14N 55°17E 119 B2
Al Jafr Jordan 30°18N 36°14E 251 H7
Al Jāfūrah Si. Arabia 25°0N 50°15E 247 E7
Al Jaghbūb Libya 29°42N 24°38E 258 C4
Al Jahrah Kuwait 29°25N 47°40E 246 D5
Al Jalāmīd Si. Arabia 31°20N 40°6E 246 D3
Al Jamalīyah Qatar 25°37N 51°5E 247 E6
Al Janūb □ Lebanon 33°20N 35°20E 250 E6
Al Jawf Libya 24°10N 23°24E 258 D4
Al Jawf Si. Arabia 29°55N 39°40E 246 D3
Al Jawf Yemen 16°10N 44°37E 248 C4
Al Jawf □ Si. Arabia 29°30N 39°30E 246 D3
Al Jawf □ Yemen 16°15N 45°0E 248 C4
Al Jazair = Algeria ■ Africa 28°30N 2°0E 261 C5
Al Jazirah Iraq 33°30N 44°0E 213 E10
Al Jithāmīyah Si. Arabia 27°41N 41°43E 246 E4
Al Jubayl Si. Arabia 27°0N 49°50E 247 E6
Al Jubaylah Si. Arabia 24°55N 46°25E 246 E5
Al Jubb Si. Arabia 27°11N 42°17E 246 E4
Al Jufrah Libya 29°10N 16°0E 258 C3
Al Jufrah □ Libya 27°30N 17°30E 258 C3
Al Jumūm Si. Arabia 21°37N 39°42E 248 B2
Al Junaynah Sudan 13°27N 22°45E 259 F4
Al Kabā'ish Iraq 30°58N 47°0E 246 D5
Al Kāmil Oman 22°13N 59°12E 249 B7
Al Karak Jordan 31°11N 35°42E 251 G6
Al Karak □ Jordan 31°0N 36°0E 251 H7
Al Kāẓimīyah Iraq 33°22N 44°18E 213 F11
Al Khābūrah Oman 23°57N 57°5E 247 F8
Al Khafji Si. Arabia 28°24N 48°29E 247 E6
Al Khalīl West Bank 31°32N 35°6E 251 G6
Al Khāliş Iraq 33°49N 44°32E 213 F11
Al Khamāsīn Si. Arabia 20°29N 44°46E 248 B4
Al Kharj Si. Arabia 24°0N 47°0E 248 B4
Al Kharsānīyah Si. Arabia 27°13N 49°18E 247 E6
Al Khaṣab Oman 26°14N 56°15E 247 E8
Al Khāṣirah Si. Arabia 23°30N 43°47E 248 B3
Al Khawr Qatar 25°41N 51°30E 247 E6
Al Khiḍr Iraq 31°12N 45°33E 246 D5
Al Khiyām Lebanon 33°20N 35°36E 250 E6
Al Khubar Si. Arabia 26°17N 50°12E 247 E6
Al Khums Libya 32°40N 14°17E 258 B2
Al Kifl Iraq 32°13N 44°22E 213 G11
Al Kiswah Syria 33°23N 36°14E 250 E7
Al Kūfah Iraq 32°2N 44°24E 213 F11
Al Kufrah Libya 24°17N 23°15E 258 D4
Al Kuhayfīyah Si. Arabia 27°12N 43°3E 246 E4
Al Kumayt Iraq 32°2N 46°52E 213 G12
Al Kūt Iraq 32°30N 46°0E 213 F11
Al Kuwayt Kuwait 29°30N 48°0E 246 D5
Al Labwah Lebanon 34°11N 36°20E 250 D7
Al Lādhiqīyah Syria 35°30N 35°45E 250 C6
Al Lādhiqīyah □ Syria 35°45N 36°0E 250 C7
Al Līth Si. Arabia 20°9N 40°15E 248 B3
Al Liwā' Oman 24°31N 56°36E 247 E8
Al Luḩayyah Yemen 15°45N 42°40E 248 D3
Al Madīnah Iraq 30°57N 47°16E 246 D5
Al Madīnah Si. Arabia 24°35N 39°52E 246 E3
Al Madīnah □ Si. Arabia 25°50N 40°0E 248 D3
Al Mafraq Jordan 32°17N 36°14E 251 F7
Al Mafraq □ Jordan 32°17N 36°15E 251 F7
Al Maghreb = Morocco ■
N. Afr. 32°0N 5°50W 260 B3
Al Maḩābishah Yemen 15°55N 43°24E 248 D3
Al Mahbes W. Sahara 27°10N 9°50W 260 C3
Al Maḩfidh Yemen 14°5N 46°55E 248 D4
Al Maḩmūdīyah Iraq 33°3N 44°21E 213 F11
Al Mahrah Yemen 16°0N 51°20E 249 D5
Al Mahrah □ Yemen 17°0N 52°0E 249 C6
Al Maḩwīt Yemen 15°29N 43°33E 248 D3
Al Majma'ah Si. Arabia 25°57N 45°22E 246 E5
Al Makhruq, W. → Jordan 31°28N 37°0E 251 G8
Al Makḩūl Si. Arabia 26°37N 42°39E 246 E4
Al Mālikīyah Syria 37°10N 42°8E 213 D10
Al Manāmah Bahrain 26°10N 50°30E 247 E6
Al Manara U.A.E. 25°9N 55°14E 119 B1
Al Maqwa' Kuwait 29°10N 47°59E 246 D5
Al Marāḩ Si. Arabia 25°35N 49°35E 247 E6
Al Marāwi'ah Yemen 14°50N 43°9E 248 D3
Al Marj Libya 32°25N 20°30E 258 B4
Al Marj □ Libya 32°20N 21°0E 258 B4
Al Marqab □ Libya 32°32N 14°35E 258 B2
Al Masana'a Oman 23°46N 57°39E 249 B7
Al Maṭlā Kuwait 29°24N 47°40E 246 D5
Al Mawṣil Iraq 36°15N 43°5E 213 D10
Al Mayādin Syria 35°1N 40°27E 213 E9
Al Mazār Jordan 31°4N 35°41E 251 G6
Al Midhnab Si. Arabia 25°50N 44°18E 246 E5
Al Minā' Lebanon 34°24N 35°49E 250 D6
Al Mina U.A.E. 25°15N 55°16E 119 B2
Al Miqdādīyah Iraq 34°0N 45°0E 213 E11
Al Mubarraz Si. Arabia 25°30N 49°40E 247 E6
Al Mudawwarah Jordan 29°19N 36°0E 251 J7
Al Muḍaybī Oman 22°34N 58°7E 249 B7
Al Mughayrā' U.A.E. 24°5N 53°32E 247 E7
Al Muḩarraq Bahrain 26°15N 50°40E 247 E6
Al Mukallā Yemen 14°33N 49°2E 249 D5
Al Mukhā Yemen 13°18N 43°15E 248 D3
Al Mukhaylī Libya 32°10N 22°17E 258 B4
Al Musayjīd Si. Arabia 24°5N 39°5E 246 E3
Al Musayyib Iraq 32°49N 44°20E 213 F11
Al Muthannā □ Iraq 30°30N 45°15E 246 D5
Al Muwayh Si. Arabia 22°41N 41°37E 256 C5
Al Muwayliḩ Si. Arabia 27°40N 35°30E 246 E2
Al Muzāḩimīyah
Si. Arabia 24°29N 46°18E 248 A4
Al Nasr U.A.E. 25°15N 55°19E 119 B2
Al Owuho = Otukpa Nigeria 7°9N 7°41E 263 D6
Al Qaddāḩīyah Libya 31°15N 15°9E 258 B3
Al Qādimah Si. Arabia 22°20N 39°13E 248 B2
Al Qādisīyah □ Iraq 32°0N 45°0E 246 D5
Al Qadmūs Syria 35°5N 36°10E 250 C7
Al Qaḩmah Si. Arabia 18°0N 41°41E 248 C3
Al Qā'idah Yemen 13°45N 44°10E 248 D4
Al Qā'im Iraq 34°21N 41°7E 213 E9
Al Qā'īyah Si. Arabia 24°33N 43°15E 246 E4
Al Qalībah Si. Arabia 28°24N 37°42E 246 D3
Al Qāmishlī Syria 37°2N 41°14E 213 D9
Al Qardāḩah Syria 35°27N 36°3E 250 C7
Al Qaryah ash Sharqīyah
Libya 30°28N 13°40E 258 B2
Al Qaryatayn Syria 34°12N 37°13E 250 D8
Al Qaṣabāt Libya 32°39N 14°1E 258 B2
Al Qaṣīm □ Si. Arabia 26°0N 43°0E 246 E4
Al Qaṭ'ā Syria 34°40N 40°48E 213 E9
Al Qaṭīf Si. Arabia 26°35N 50°0E 247 E6
Al Qaṭn Yemen 15°51N 48°26E 249 D5
Al Qaṭrānah Jordan 31°12N 36°6E 251 G7
Al Qaṭrūn Libya 24°56N 15°3E 258 D2
Al Qawz Si. Arabia 18°58N 41°26E 248 C3
Al Qayṣūmah Si. Arabia 28°20N 46°7E 246 D5
Al Qiblīyah Oman 17°30N 56°20E 249 C7
Al Quds = Jerusalem
Israel/West Bank 31°47N 35°10E 123 B2
Al Qunayṭirah Syria 33°5N 35°45E 250 F6
Al Qunfudhah Si. Arabia 19°3N 41°4E 248 C3
Al Quoz U.A.E. 25°8N 55°14E 119 B1
Al Qurayyāt Oman 23°17N 58°53E 249 B7
Al Qurayyāt Si. Arabia 31°20N 37°20E 246 D3
Al Qurḩ Yemen 16°44N 51°29E 249 C5
Al Qurnah Iraq 31°1N 47°25E 246 D5
Al Quṣayr Iraq 30°39N 45°50E 246 D5
Al Quṣayr Syria 34°31N 36°34E 250 D7
Al Quṭayfah Syria 33°44N 36°36E 250 E7
Al Quwayʻīyah Si. Arabia 24°3N 45°15E 248 A4
Al Quwayr Iraq 36°2N 43°29E 213 D10
Al Quwaysimah Jordan 31°55N 35°57E 251 G6
Al Safa U.A.E. 25°10N 55°14E 119 B1
Al Satwa U.A.E. 25°13N 55°16E 119 B2
Al Seeb = As Sīb Oman 23°41N 58°11E 249 B7
Al Sufouh U.A.E. 25°7N 55°12E 119 B1
Al 'Ubaylah Si. Arabia 21°59N 50°57E 249 B5
Al 'Uḑayliyah Si. Arabia 25°8N 49°18E 247 E6
Al 'Ulā Si. Arabia 26°35N 38°0E 246 E3
Al 'Ulayyah Si. Arabia 19°39N 41°54E 248 C3
Al Uqaylah ash Sharqīgah
Libya 30°12N 19°10E 258 B3
Al 'Uqayr Si. Arabia 25°40N 50°15E 247 E6
Al 'Urūq al Mutariḑah
Si. Arabia 21°0N 53°30E 249 B6
Al 'Uwaynāt Libya 25°47N 10°33E 261 C7
Al 'Uwaynid Si. Arabia 24°50N 46°0E 246 E5
Al 'Uwayqīlah Si. Arabia 30°30N 42°10E 246 D4
Al Uweinat Libya 21°34N 24°50E 259 D4
Al 'Uyūn Ḩijāz, Si. Arabia 24°33N 39°35E 246 E3
Al 'Uyūn Najd, Si. Arabia 26°30N 43°50E 246 E4
Al 'Uzayr Iraq 31°19N 47°25E 246 D5
Al Wāḩāt □ Libya 29°0N 22°0E 258 C4
Al Wajh Si. Arabia 26°10N 36°30E 246 E3
Al Wakrah Qatar 25°10N 51°40E 247 E6
Al Walaja West Bank 31°44N 35°9E 123 B1
Al Waqbah Si. Arabia 28°48N 45°33E 246 D5
Al Wari'āh Si. Arabia 27°51N 47°25E 246 E5
Al Wasl U.A.E. 25°12N 55°16E 119 B2
Al Wāţīyah Libya 32°28N 11°57E 258 B2
Al Wīgh Libya 24°16N 15°30E 258 D3
Al Wusţā □ Oman 20°0N 57°0E 249 C7
Al Yaman = Yemen ■ Asia 15°0N 44°0E 248 D4
Ala Italy 45°45N 11°0E 198 C8
Ala Dağ Turkey 37°44N 35°9E 246 B2
Ala Dağları Turkey 39°15N 43°33E 213 C10
Ala Tau Asia 45°30N 80°40E 217 C10
Ala Tau Shankou = Dzungarian
Gate Asia 45°10N 82°0E 217 C10
Alabama □ U.S.A. 33°0N 87°0W 315 E11
Alabama → U.S.A. 31°8N 87°57W 315 F11
Alabaster U.S.A. 33°15N 86°49W 315 E11
Alabat I. Phil. 14°7N 122°3E 232 D4
Alabel Phil. 6°4N 125°16E 233 H5
Alabule → Papua N. G. 8°31S 146°56E 286 E4
Alaca Turkey 40°10N 34°51E 212 B6
Alacaatlı Turkey 39°15N 28°3E 205 B10
Alaçam Turkey 41°36N 35°36E 212 B6
Alaçam Dağları Turkey 39°18N 28°49E 205 B10
Alacant = Alicante Spain 38°23N 0°30W 197 G4
Alaçatı Turkey 38°15N 26°22E 205 C8
Alachua U.S.A. 29°47N 82°30W 316 F7
Alaejos Spain 41°18N 5°13W 194 D5
Alagir Russia 43°3N 44°14E 191 J7
Alagna Valsésia Italy 45°51N 7°56E 198 C4
Alagoa de Baixo = Sertânia
Brazil 8°5S 37°20W 332 C4
Alagoa Grande Brazil 7°3S 35°35W 332 C4
Alagoas = Marechal Deodoro
Brazil 9°43S 35°54W 332 C4
Alagoas □ Brazil 9°0S 36°0W 332 C4
Alagoinhas Brazil 12°7S 38°20W 333 D4
Alagón Spain 41°46N 1°12W 196 D3
Alagón → Spain 39°44N 6°53W 194 F4
Alaguntan Nigeria 6°25N 3°29E 124 B2
Alagyoz = Aragats
Armenia 40°30N 44°15E 191 K7
Alahan Turkey 36°46N 33°19E 250 B4
Alaheaieatnu = Altaelva →
Norway 69°54N 23°17E 160 B20
Alai Range Asia 39°45N 72°0E 217 E8
Alaior Spain 39°57N 4°8E 206 B5
Alajero Canary Is. 28°3N 17°13W 153 e1
Alajuela Costa Rica 10°2N 84°8W 320 D3
Alajuela, L. Panama 9°14N 79°34W 320 c
Alakamisy Madag. 21°19S 47°14E 272 C2
Alakanuk U.S.A. 62°41N 164°37W 303 E6
Alaknanda → India 30°8N 78°36E 243 D8
Alaköl Kazakhstan 46°10N 81°35E 217 C10
Alakurtti Russia 66°58N 30°25E 160 C24
'Alalākeiki Channel
U.S.A. 20°30N 156°30W 302 C5
Alalapura Suriname 2°20N 56°25W 329 C6
Alalaú → Brazil 0°30S 61°9W 329 D5
Alamagan N. Marianas 17°36N 145°50E 302 a
Alamarvdasht Iran 27°37N 52°59E 247 E7
Alamata Ethiopia 12°25N 39°33E 257 E4
Alameda Calif., U.S.A. 37°46N 122°15W 136 B3
Alameda N. Mex.,
U.S.A. 35°11N 106°37W 305 J10
Alameda, Parque Mexico City, Mexico 128 b2
Alameda Memorial State Beach
Park U.S.A. 37°45N 122°16W 136 B3
Alaminos Phil. 16°10N 119°59E 232 C2
Alamo Ga., U.S.A. 32°9N 82°47W 316 C7
Alamo Nev., U.S.A. 37°22N 115°10W 307 H11
Alamogordo U.S.A. 32°54N 105°57W 305 K11
Alamos Mexico 27°1N 108°56W 318 B3
Alamosa U.S.A. 37°28N 105°52W 305 H11
Alampur India 15°55N 78°6E 245 G4
Åland Finland 60°15N 20°0E 161 F19
Aland India 17°36N 76°35E 244 F3
Alandroal Portugal 38°41N 7°24W 195 G3
Ålands hav Europe 60°0N 19°30E 161 G18
Ålandsbro Sweden 62°40N 17°51E 162 B11
Alandur India 13°0N 80°15E 245 H5
Alang Indonesia 4°7N 117°0E 235 B5
Alange, Embalse d' Spain 38°45N 6°18W 195 G4
Alania = North Ossetia □
Russia 43°30N 44°30E 191 J7
Alanis Spain 38°3N 5°43W 195 G5
Alanya Turkey 36°38N 32°0E 250 B3
Alaotra, Farihin' Madag. 17°30S 48°30E 272 B2
Alapaha U.S.A. 31°23N 83°13W 316 D6
Alapayevsk Russia 57°52N 61°42E 214 D7
Alappuzha India 9°30N 76°28E 245 K3
'Alāqān Si. Arabia 29°10N 35°21E 251 J6
Alar del Rey Spain 42°38N 4°20W 194 C6
Alara → Turkey 36°38N 31°39E 250 B2
Alaraz Spain 40°45N 5°17W 194 E5
Alarcón, Embalse de Spain 39°36N 2°10W 196 F2
Alaró Spain 39°42N 2°47E 206 B3
Alarobia-Vohiposa Madag. 20°59S 47°9E 272 C2
Alas Indonesia 8°29S 117°0E 235 E5
Alas, Selat Indonesia 8°40S 116°40E 235 D5
Alaşehir Turkey 38°23N 28°30E 205 C10
Alashtar Iran 33°51N 48°15E 213 F13
Alaska □ U.S.A. 64°0N 154°0W 303 D9
Alaska, G. of Pac. Oc. 58°0N 145°0W 303 G11
Alaska Maritime Nat. Wildlife
Refuge △ U.S.A. 52°0N 174°0W 303 L4
Alaska Peninsula U.S.A. 56°0N 159°0W 303 H8
Alaska Peninsula Nat. Wildlife
Refuge △ U.S.A. 56°0N 159°0W 303 J8
Alaska Range U.S.A. 62°50N 151°0W 303 E10
Alássio Italy 44°0N 8°10E 198 E5
Älät Azerbaijan 39°58N 49°25E 191 L9
Alatau Shan = Ala Tau
Asia 45°30N 80°40E 217 C10
Alatri Italy 41°43N 13°21E 199 G10
Alatyr Russia 54°55N 46°35E 190 C8
Alatyr → Russia 54°52N 46°36E 190 C8
Alaungdaw Kathapa △
Burma 22°30N 94°30E 241 D5
Alausí Ecuador 2°0S 78°50W 328 D2
Álava □ Spain 42°48N 2°28W 196 C2
Alava, C. U.S.A. 48°10N 124°44W 306 B2
Alaverdi Armenia 41°15N 44°37E 191 K7
Alavo = Alavus Finland 62°35N 23°36E 160 E20
Alavus Finland 62°35N 23°36E 160 E20
Alawa ⊙ Australia 15°42S 134°39E 280 B1
Alawoona Australia 34°45S 140°30E 282 C4
Alayawarra ⊙ Australia 22°0S 134°30E 280 C1
'Alayh Lebanon 33°46N 35°33E 250 E6
Alayköy = Yerolakkos
Cyprus 35°11N 33°15E 207 E9
Alazani → Azerbaijan 41°5N 46°40E 191 K8
Alba Italy 44°42N 8°2E 198 D5
Alba □ Romania 46°10N 23°30E 183 D8

Alba Adriática *Italy* 42°50N 13°56E **199** F10
Alba de Tormes *Spain* 40°50N 5°30W **194** E5
Alba-Iulia *Romania* 46°8N 23°39E **183** D8
Albac *Romania* 46°28N 22°58E **182** D7
Albacete *Spain* 39°0N 1°50W **197** F3
Albacete ☐ *Spain* 38°50N 2°0W **197** G3
Albacutya, L. *Australia* 35°45S 141°58E **282** C4
Ålbæk *Denmark* 57°36N 10°25E **163** G4
Ålbæk Bugt *Denmark* 57°35N 10°40E **163** G4
Albaida *Spain* 38°51N 0°31W **197** G4
Albalate de las Nogueras *Spain* 40°22N 2°18W **196** E2
Albalate del Arzobispo *Spain* 41°6N 0°31W **196** D4
Alban *France* 43°53N 2°28E **174** E6
Albanel, L. *Canada* 50°55N 73°12W **298** B5
Albania ■ *Europe* 41°0N 20°0E **202** E4
Albano Laziale *Italy* 41°44N 12°39E **199** G9
Albany *W. Austral., Australia* 35°1S 117°58E **279** G2
Albany *Ga., U.S.A.* 31°35N 84°10W **316** D5
Albany *Ind., U.S.A.* 40°18N 85°14W **311** D11
Albany *Mo., U.S.A.* 40°15N 94°20W **310** D2
Albany *N.Y., U.S.A.* 42°39N 73°45W **313** D11
Albany *Oreg., U.S.A.* 44°38N 123°6W **304** D2
Albany *Tex., U.S.A.* 32°44N 99°18W **314** E5
Albany *Wis., U.S.A.* 42°42N 89°26W **310** B7
Albany → *Canada* 52°17N 81°31W **298** B3
Albarca, C. d' *Spain* 39°4N 1°22E **206** C1
Albardón *Argentina* 31°20S 68°30W **334** C2
Albarracín *Spain* 40°25N 1°26W **196** E3
Albarracín, Sierra de *Spain* 40°30N 1°30W **196** E3
Albatera *Spain* 38°11N 0°52W **197** G4
Albatross B. *Australia* 12°45S 141°30E **280** A3
Albatross Pt. *N.Z.* 38°7S 174°44E **284** E3
Albay ☐ *Phil.* 13°13N 123°33E **232** E4
Albegna → *Italy* 42°30N 11°11E **199** F8
Albemarle *U.S.A.* 35°21N 80°12W **315** D14
Albemarle, I. = Isabela, I. *Ecuador* 0°30S 91°4W **330** a
Albemarle, Pta. *Ecuador* 0°11N 91°21W **330** a
Albemarle Sd. *U.S.A.* 36°5N 76°0W **315** C16
Albenga *Italy* 44°3N 8°13E **198** D5
Alberche → *Spain* 39°58N 4°46W **194** F6
Alberdi *Paraguay* 26°14S 58°20W **334** B4
Albères, Mts. *France* 42°28N 2°56E **174** F6
Ålberga *Sweden* 58°44N 16°35E **163** F10
Alberga → *Australia* 27°6S 135°33E **281** D2
Albern *Austria* 48°9N 16°29E **142** B2
Albersdorf *Germany* 54°8N 9°17E **178** A5
Albert *France* 50°0N 2°38E **173** C9
Albert, L. *Africa* 1°30N 31°0E **268** B3
Albert, L. *S. Austral., Australia* 35°30S 139°10E **282** C3
Albert Edward, Mt. *Papua N. G.* 8°20S 147°24E **286** E4
Albert Edward Ra. *Australia* 18°17S 127°57E **278** C4
Albert Lea *U.S.A.* 43°39N 93°22W **308** D7
Albert Nat. Park = Virunga △ *Dem. Rep. of the Congo* 0°5N 29°38E **268** B2
Albert Nile → *Uganda* 3°36N 32°2E **268** B3
Albert Park *Australia* 37°51S 144°58E **128** B1
Albert Town *Bahamas* 22°37N 74°33W **321** B5
Albert Town *Jamaica* 18°17N 77°33W **320** a
Alberta ☐ *Canada* 54°40N 115°0W **296** C6
Alberti *Argentina* 35°1S 60°16W **334** D3
Albertinia *S. Africa* 34°11S 21°34E **270** D3
Albertirsa *Hungary* 47°14N 19°37E **182** C4
Alberto de Agostini △ *Chile* 54°38S 71°37W **336** D2
Alberton *P.E.I., Canada* 46°50N 64°0W **299** C7
Alberton *Gauteng, S. Africa* 26°15S 28°7E **123** B2
Albertslund *Denmark* 55°39N 12°21E **118** B2
Albertville = Kalemie *Dem. Rep. of the Congo* 5°55S 29°9E **268** D2
Albertville *Savoie, France* 45°40N 6°22E **175** C10
Albertville *Ala., U.S.A.* 34°16N 86°13W **315** D11
Albi *France* 43°56N 2°9E **174** E6
Albia *U.S.A.* 41°2N 92°48W **310** C4
Albina *Suriname* 5°37N 54°15W **329** B7
Albina, Ponta *Angola* 15°52S 11°44E **265** F2
Albino *Italy* 45°46N 9°47E **198** C6
Albion *Ill., U.S.A.* 38°23N 88°4W **311** F8
Albion *Ind., U.S.A.* 41°24N 85°25W **311** C11
Albion *Mich., U.S.A.* 42°15N 84°45W **311** B12
Albion *Nebr., U.S.A.* 41°42N 98°0W **308** E4
Albion *Pa., U.S.A.* 41°53N 80°22W **312** E4
Albocásser *Spain* 40°21N 0°1E **196** E5
Albolote *Spain* 37°14N 3°39W **195** H7
Alborán *Medit. S.* 35°57N 3°0W **195** K7
Alborea *Spain* 39°17N 1°24W **197** F3
Ålborg = Aalborg *Denmark* 57°2N 9°54E **163** G3
Ålborg Bugt = Aalborg Bugt *Denmark* 56°50N 10°35E **163** H4
Alborz, Reshteh-ye Kūhhā-ye *Iran* 36°0N 52°0E **247** C7
Albox *Spain* 37°23N 2°8W **197** H2
Albuera *Phil.* 10°55N 124°42E **233** F5
Albufeira *Portugal* 37°5N 8°15W **195** H2
Albula → *Switz.* 46°38N 9°28E **179** J5
Albuñol *Spain* 36°48N 3°11W **195** J7
Albuquerque *Brazil* 19°23S 57°26W **331** D6
Albuquerque *N. Mex., U.S.A.* 35°5N 106°39W **305** J10
Albuquerque, Cayos de *Caribbean* 12°10N 81°50W **320** D3
Alburg *U.S.A.* 44°59N 73°18W **313** B11
Alburno, Mte. *Italy* 40°33N 15°17E **201** B8
Alburquerque *Spain* 39°15N 6°59W **195** F4
Albury *Australia* 36°3S 146°56E **283** D7
Alby *Sweden* 62°30N 15°28E **162** B9
Alcácer do Sal *Portugal* 38°22N 8°33W **195** G2
Alcáçovas *Portugal* 38°23N 8°9W **195** G2
Alcala *Phil.* 17°54N 121°39E **232** C3
Alcalá de Guadaira *Spain* 37°20N 5°50W **195** H5
Alcalá de Henares *Spain* 40°28N 3°22W **194** E7
Alcalá de los Gazules *Spain* 36°29N 5°43W **195** J5
Alcalá de Xivert *Spain* 40°19N 0°13E **196** E5
Alcalá del Júcar *Spain* 39°12N 1°26W **197** F3
Alcalá del Río *Spain* 37°31N 5°59W **195** H5
Alcalá del Valle *Spain* 36°54N 5°10W **195** J5
Alcalá la Real *Spain* 37°27N 3°57W **195** H7
Álcamo *Italy* 37°59N 12°55E **200** E5
Alcanadre *Spain* 42°24N 2°7W **196** C2
Alcanadre → *Spain* 41°43N 0°12W **196** D4
Alcanar *Spain* 40°33N 0°28E **196** E5
Alcanede *Portugal* 39°25N 8°49W **195** F2
Alcanena *Portugal* 39°27N 8°40W **195** F2
Alcañices *Spain* 41°41N 6°21W **194** D4
Alcañiz *Spain* 41°2N 0°8W **196** D4
Alcântara *Brazil* 2°20S 44°30W **332** B3
Alcantara *Lisboa, Portugal* 38°43N 9°10W **126** A1
Alcántara *Spain* 39°41N 6°57W **194** F4
Alcántara, Embalse de *Spain* 39°44N 6°50W **194** F4
Alcantarilla *Spain* 37°59N 1°12W **197** H3
Alcaracejos *Spain* 38°24N 4°58W **195** G6
Alcaraz *Spain* 38°40N 2°29W **197** G2
Alcaraz, Sierra de *Spain* 38°40N 2°20W **197** G2
Alcatraz I. *U.S.A.* 37°49N 122°25W **136** B2
Alcaudete *Spain* 37°35N 4°5W **195** H6
Alcázar de San Juan *Spain* 39°24N 3°12W **195** F7
Alcazarquivir = Ksar el Kebir *Morocco* 35°0N 6°0W **260** B3
Alcedo, Volcán *Ecuador* 0°24S 91°6W **330** a
Alchevsk *Ukraine* 48°30N 38°45E **189** H10
Alcira = Alzira *Spain* 39°9N 0°30W **197** F4
Alcobaça = Tucuruí *Brazil* 3°42S 49°44W **332** B2
Alcobaça *Portugal* 39°32N 8°58W **195** F2
Alcobendas *Spain* 40°32N 3°38W **127** A2
Alcolea del Pinar *Spain* 41°2N 2°28W **196** D2
Alcoma *U.S.A.* 27°54N 81°29W **317** H8
Alcorcón *Spain* 40°20N 3°48W **127** B1
Alcoutim *Portugal* 37°25N 7°28W **195** H3
Alcova *U.S.A.* 42°34N 106°43W **304** E10
Alcoy *Spain* 38°43N 0°30W **197** G4
Alcubierre, Sierra de *Spain* 41°45N 0°22W **196** D4
Alcublas *Spain* 39°48N 0°43W **196** F4
Alcúdia *Spain* 39°51N 3°7E **206** B4
Alcúdia, B. d' *Spain* 39°47N 3°15E **206** B4
Alcúdia, Sierra de la *Spain* 38°34N 4°30W **195** G6
Aldabra Is. *Seychelles* 9°22S 46°28E **255** G8
Aldama *Mexico* 22°55N 98°4W **319** C5
Aldan *Russia* 58°40N 125°30E **215** D13
Aldan → *Russia* 63°28N 129°35E **215** C13
Aldea, Pta. de la *Canary Is.* 28°0N 15°50W **153** e1
Aldeburgh *U.K.* 52°10N 1°37E **169** E9
Alden *Norway* 61°19N 4°45E **164** C1
Alder Pk. *U.S.A.* 35°53N 121°22W **306** K5
Alderney *U.K.* 49°42N 2°11W **169** H5
Aldershof *Germany* 52°26N 13°33E **115** B4
Aldershot *U.K.* 51°15N 0°44W **169** F7
Aldinga Beach *Australia* 35°17S 138°27E **282** C3
Aldo Bonzi *Argentina* 34°42S 58°31W **117** C1
Åled *Sweden* 56°44N 12°57E **163** H6
Aledo *U.S.A.* 41°12N 90°45W **310** C6
Alefa *Ethiopia* 11°55N 36°55E **257** E4
Aleg *Mauritania* 17°3N 13°55W **262** B2
Alegranza *Canary Is.* 29°23N 13°32W **260** C2
Alegranza, I. *Canary Is.* 29°23N 13°32W **153** e2
Alegre *Brazil* 20°50S 41°30W **333** F3
Alegrete *Brazil* 29°40S 56°0W **335** B4
Aleknagik *U.S.A.* 59°17N 158°36W **303** G8
Aleksandriya = Oleksandriya *Kirovohrad, Ukraine* 48°42N 33°3E **189** H7
Aleksandriya = Oleksandriya *Rivne, Ukraine* 50°37N 26°19E **177** C14
Aleksandriyskaya *Russia* 43°58N 47°14E **191** J8
Aleksandropol = Gyumri *Armenia* 40°47N 43°50E **191** K6
Aleksandrov *Russia* 56°23N 38°44E **188** D10
Aleksandrov Gay *Russia* 50°9N 48°34E **190** E9
Aleksandrovac *Serbia* 43°28N 21°3E **202** C5
Aleksandrovac *Serbia* 44°28N 21°13E **202** B5
Aleksandrovka = Oleksandrivka *Ukraine* 48°55N 32°20E **189** H7
Aleksandrovka = Ordzhonikidze *Ukraine* 47°39N 34°3E **189** J8
Aleksandrovo *Bulgaria* 43°14N 24°51E **203** C8
Aleksandrovsk = Belogorsk *Russia* 51°0N 128°20E **215** D13
Aleksandrovsk = Polyarny *Russia* 69°8N 33°20E **160** B25
Aleksandrovsk = Zaporizhzhya *Ukraine* 47°50N 35°10E **189** J8
Aleksandrovsk-Grushevsky = Shakhty *Russia* 47°40N 40°16E **191** G5
Aleksandrovsk-Sakhalinskiy *Russia* 50°50N 142°20E **219** A17
Aleksandrovskoye *Russia* 59°51N 30°20E **137** B2
Aleksandrów Kujawski *Poland* 52°53N 18°43E **185** F5
Aleksandrów Łódźki *Poland* 51°49N 19°17E **185** G6
Aleksandry, Zemlya *Russia* 80°25N 48°0E **214** A5
Alekseyevka *Samara, Russia* 52°35N 51°17E **190** D10
Alekseyevka *Voronezh, Russia* 50°43N 38°40E **189** G10
Alekseyevsk = Svobodnyy *Russia* 51°20N 128°0E **215** D13
Alekseyevskoye = Qazyghurt *Kazakhstan* 41°45N 69°23E **217** D7
Aleksin *Russia* 54°31N 37°9E **188** E9
Aleksinac *Serbia* 43°31N 21°42E **202** C5
Além Paraíba *Brazil* 21°52S 42°41W **333** F3
Alemania *Argentina* 25°40S 65°30W **334** B2
Alemania *Chile* 25°10S 69°55W **334** B2
Alen *Eq. Guin.* 1°58N 11°19E **264** B2
Alençon *France* 48°27N 0°4E **172** D7
'Alenuihähä Channel *U.S.A.* 20°30N 156°0W **302** C5
Alépé *Ivory C.* 5°29N 3°40W **262** D4
Aleppo = Ḥalab *Syria* 36°10N 37°15E **250** B8
Alerce Andino △ *Chile* 41°33S 72°29W **336** B2
Aléria *France* 42°5N 9°26E **175** F13
Alert *Canada* 83°2N 60°0W **295** A20
Aleru *India* 17°39N 79°3E **244** F4
Alès *France* 44°9N 4°5E **175** D8
Aleşd *Romania* 47°3N 22°22E **182** C7
Alessándria *Italy* 44°54N 8°37E **198** D5
Ålesund *Norway* 62°28N 6°12E **164** B3
Alet-les-Bains *France* 42°59N 2°14E **174** F6
Aletschhorn *Switz.* 46°28N 8°0E **179** J4
Aleutian Basin *Pac. Oc.* 57°0N 177°0E **288** B9
Aleutian Is. *Pac. Oc.* 52°0N 175°0W **303** K3
Aleutian Range *U.S.A.* 60°0N 154°0W **303** G9
Aleutian Trench *Pac. Oc.* 48°0N 180°0E **150** D17
Alexander *Ga., U.S.A.* 33°1N 81°53W **316** B8
Alexander *N. Dak., U.S.A.* 47°51N 103°39W **308** B2
Alexander, C. *Solomon Is.* 6°34S 156°32E **287** L9
Alexander, Mt. *Australia* 28°58S 120°16E **279** E3
Alexander Arch. *U.S.A.* 56°0N 136°0W **303** J14
Alexander Bay *S. Africa* 28°40S 16°30E **270** C2
Alexander City *U.S.A.* 32°56N 85°58W **316** C4
Alexander I. *Antarctica* 69°0S 70°0W **151** C17
Alexander Nevsky Abbey *Russia* 59°54N 30°23E **137** B2
Alexander Soutzos Museum *Athens, Greece* **112** b3
Alexandra *Vic., Australia* 37°8S 145°40E **283** D6
Alexandra *N.Z.* 45°14S 169°25E **285** F4
Alexandra *Singapore, Singapore* 1°17N 103°49E **138** B2
Alexandra *Gauteng, S. Africa* 26°6S 28°5E **123** A2
Alexandra Channel *Burma* 14°7N 93°13E **245** G11
Alexandra Falls *Canada* 60°29N 116°18W **296** A5
Alexandretta = İskenderun *Turkey* 36°32N 36°10E **250** B7
Alexandria = El Iskandarîya *Egypt* 31°13N 29°58E **256** H7
Alexandria *B.C., Canada* 52°35N 122°27W **296** C4
Alexandria *Ont., Canada* 45°19N 74°38W **313** A10
Alexandria *Romania* 43°57N 25°24E **183** G10
Alexandria *Eastern Cape, S. Africa* 33°38S 26°28E **270** D4
Alexandria *W. Dunb., U.K.* 55°59N 4°35W **167** F4
Alexandria *Ind., U.S.A.* 40°16N 85°41W **311** D11
Alexandria *Ky., U.S.A.* 38°58N 84°23W **311** F12
Alexandria *La., U.S.A.* 31°18N 92°27W **314** F8
Alexandria *Minn., U.S.A.* 45°53N 95°22W **308** C6
Alexandria *Mo., U.S.A.* 40°27N 91°28W **310** D5
Alexandria *S. Dak., U.S.A.* 43°39N 97°47W **308** D5
Alexandria *Va., U.S.A.* 38°49N 77°5W **143** C2
Alexandria Bay *U.S.A.* 44°20N 75°55W **313** B9
Alexandrina, L. *Australia* 35°25S 139°10E **282** C3
Alexandroupoli *Greece* 40°50N 25°54E **203** F9
Alexis *U.S.A.* 41°4N 90°33W **310** C6
Alexis → *Canada* 52°33N 56°8W **299** B8
Alexis Creek *Canada* 52°10N 123°20W **296** C4
Aley → *Russia* 52°51N 83°36E **217** B10
Aleysk *Russia* 52°40N 83°0E **217** B10
Alfabia *Spain* 39°44N 2°44E **206** B3
Alfama *Lisbon, Portugal* **126** c3
Alfambra *Spain* 40°33N 1°5W **196** E3
Alfândega da Fé *Portugal* 41°20N 6°59W **194** D4
Alfaro *Spain* 42°10N 1°50W **196** C3
Alfatar *Bulgaria* 43°59N 27°13E **203** C11
Alfeld *Germany* 51°59N 9°50E **178** D5
Alfenas *Brazil* 21°20S 46°10W **335** A6
Alföld *Hungary* 46°30N 20°0E **182** D5
Alfonsine *Italy* 44°30N 12°3E **199** D9
Alford *Aberds., U.K.* 57°14N 2°41W **167** D6
Alford *Lincs., U.K.* 53°15N 0°10E **168** D8
Alford *Fla., U.S.A.* 30°42N 85°24W **316** E4
Alfortville *France* 48°48N 2°24E **134** B3
Ålfotbreen *Norway* 61°45N 5°39E **164** C2
Ålfoten *Norway* 61°51N 5°41E **164** C2
Alfred *Maine, U.S.A.* 43°29N 70°43W **313** C14
Alfred *N.Y., U.S.A.* 42°16N 77°48W **312** D7
Alfredton *N.Z.* 40°41S 175°54E **284** G4
Alfreton *U.K.* 53°6N 1°24W **168** D6
Alfta *Sweden* 61°21N 16°4E **162** C10
Algaida *Spain* 39°33N 2°53E **206** B3
Algar *Spain* 36°40N 5°39W **195** J5
Ålgård *Norway* 58°46N 5°53E **164** F2
Algarinejo *Spain* 37°19N 4°9W **195** H6
Algarve *Portugal* 36°58N 8°20W **195** J2
Algeciras *Spain* 36°9N 5°28W **195** J5
Algemesí *Spain* 39°11N 0°27W **197** F4
Alger *Algeria* 36°42N 3°8E **261** A5
Alger ☐ *Algeria* 36°45N 3°10E **197** J8
Alger ✈ **(ALG)** *Algeria* 36°39N 3°13E **197** J8
Algeria ■ *Africa* 28°30N 2°0E **261** C5
Algés *Portugal* 38°42N 9°13W **126** A1
Algha *Kazakhstan* 49°53N 57°20E **187** E10
Alghero *Italy* 40°33N 8°19E **200** B1
Älghult *Sweden* 57°0N 15°35E **163** G9
Algiers = Alger *Algeria* 36°42N 3°8E **261** A5
Algiers *U.S.A.* 29°56N 90°2W **131** B2
Algoa B. *S. Africa* 33°50S 25°45E **270** D4
Algodonales *Spain* 36°54N 5°24W **195** J5
Algodor → *Spain* 39°55N 3°53W **194** F7
Algoma *U.S.A.* 44°36N 87°26W **308** C10
Algona *U.S.A.* 43°4N 94°14W **310** A2
Algonac *U.S.A.* 42°37N 82°32W **312** D2
Algonquin ⌓ *Canada* 45°50N 78°30W **298** C4
Alhama de Almería *Spain* 36°57N 2°34W **195** J8
Alhama de Aragón *Spain* 41°18N 1°54W **196** D3
Alhama de Granada *Spain* 37°0N 3°59W **195** H7
Alhama de Murcia *Spain* 37°51N 1°25W **197** H3
Alhambra *U.S.A.* 34°5N 118°7W **126** B4
Alhaurín el Grande *Spain* 36°39N 4°41W **195** J6
Alhucemas = Al Hoceïma *Morocco* 35°8N 3°58W **261** A4
'Alī al Gharbī *Iraq* 32°30N 46°45E **213** F12
'Alī ash Sharqī *Iraq* 32°7N 46°44E **213** F12
Äli Bayramlı = Şirvan *Azerbaijan* 39°59N 48°52E **191** L9
'Alī Khēl *Afghan.* 33°57N 69°43E **242** C3
Ali Sahîh *Djibouti* 11°10N 42°44E **257** E5
Alī Shāh *Iran* 38°9N 45°50E **246** B5
Ália *Italy* 37°47N 13°43E **200** E6
'Alīābād *Golestān, Iran* 36°40N 54°33E **247** B7
'Alīābād *Khorāsān, Iran* 32°30N 57°30E **247** C8
'Alīābād *Kordestān, Iran* 35°4N 46°58E **246** C5
'Alīābād *Yazd, Iran* 31°41N 53°49E **247** D7
Aliade *Nigeria* 7°18N 8°29E **263** D6
Aliaga *Spain* 40°40N 0°42W **196** E4
Aliağa *Turkey* 38°47N 26°59E **205** C8
Aliakmonas → *Greece* 40°30N 22°36E **202** F6
Alibag *India* 18°38N 72°56E **244** E1
Alibey → *Turkey* 41°3N 28°56E **122** B1
Alibey Barajı *Turkey* 41°8N 28°53E **122** B1
Alibeyköy *Turkey* 41°4N 28°56E **122** B1
Alibo *Ethiopia* 9°52N 37°5E **257** F4
Alibori → *Benin* 11°56N 3°17E **263** C5
Alibunar *Serbia* 45°5N 20°57E **182** E5
Alicante *Spain* 38°23N 0°30W **197** G4
Alicante ☐ *Spain* 38°30N 0°37W **197** G4
Alicante ✈ **(ALC)** *Spain* 38°14N 0°36W **197** G4
Alice *Eastern Cape, S. Africa* 32°48S 26°55E **270** D4
Alice *Tex., U.S.A.* 27°45N 98°5W **314** H5
Alice → *Queens., Australia* 24°2S 144°50E **280** C3
Alice → *Queens., Australia* 15°35S 142°20E **280** B3
Alice → *Papua N. G.* 6°10S 141°8E **286** D1
Alice, Punta *Italy* 39°24N 17°9E **201** C10
Alice Arm *Canada* 55°29N 129°31W **296** B3
Alice Springs *Australia* 23°40S 133°50E **280** C1
Alicedale *S. Africa* 33°15S 26°4E **270** D4
Aliceville *U.S.A.* 33°8N 88°9W **315** E10
Alicia *Bohol, Phil.* 9°54N 124°26E **233** G5
Alicia *Isabela, Phil.* 16°46N 121°42E **232** C3
Alicudi *Italy* 38°33N 14°20E **201** D7
Alien *Taiwan* 22°52N 120°19E **225** D2
Aliganj *India* 27°30N 79°10E **243** F8
Aligarh *Raj., India* 25°55N 76°15E **242** G7
Aligarh *Ut. P., India* 27°55N 78°10E **242** F8
Alīgūdarz *Iran* 33°25N 49°45E **247** C6
Alijó *Portugal* 41°16N 7°27W **194** D3
Alikanas *Greece* 37°51N 20°47E **207** D2
Alima → *Congo* 1°35S 16°37E **264** C3
Alimia *Greece* 36°16N 27°43E **206** E11
Alimodian *Phil.* 10°49N 122°26E **233** F4
Alimos *Greece* 37°52N 23°43E **112** B2
Alindao *C.A.R.* 5°2N 21°13E **264** A4
Alingsås *Sweden* 57°56N 12°31E **163** G6
Alipur *W. Bengal, India* 22°43N 88°12E **124** B1
Alipur *Pakistan* 29°25N 70°55E **242** E4
Alipur Duar *India* 26°30N 89°35E **241** B2
Aliquippa *U.S.A.* 40°37N 80°15W **312** F4
Alishan *Taiwan* 23°31N 120°48E **225** C2
Aliste → *Spain* 41°34N 5°58W **194** D5
Alitus = Alytus *Lithuania* 54°24N 24°3E **188** E3
Aliveri *Greece* 38°24N 24°2E **204** C6
Aliwal North *S. Africa* 30°45S 26°45E **270** D4
Alix *Canada* 52°24N 113°11W **296** C6
Aljezur *Portugal* 37°18N 8°49W **195** H2
Aljustrel *Portugal* 37°55N 8°10W **195** H2
Alkamari *Niger* 13°27N 11°10E **259** F2
Alkmaar *Neths.* 52°37N 4°45E **170** B4
All American Canal *U.S.A.* 32°45N 115°15W **307** N11
Allacapan *Phil.* 18°15N 121°35E **232** B3
Allach *Germany* 48°11N 11°27E **131** A1
Allada *Benin* 6°41N 2°9E **263** D5
Allagadda *India* 15°8N 78°30E **245** G4
Allagash → *U.S.A.* 47°5N 69°3W **309** B19
Allah Dad *Pakistan* 25°38N 67°34E **242** G2
Allahabad *India* 25°25N 81°58E **243** G9
Allakaket *U.S.A.* 66°34N 152°39W **303** C9
Allambie Heights *Australia* 33°46S 151°15E **139** A2
Allan *Canada* 51°53N 106°4W **297** C7
Allanche *France* 45°14N 2°57E **174** C6
Allanmyo *Burma* 19°30N 95°17E **241** F5
Allanridge *S. Africa* 27°45S 26°40E **270** C4
Allansford *Australia* 38°26S 142°39E **282** E5
Allanton *N.Z.* 45°55S 170°15E **285** F5
Allaqi, Wadi → *Egypt* 23°7N 32°47E **256** C3
Allariz *Spain* 42°11N 7°50W **194** C3
Allassac *France* 45°15N 1°29E **174** C5
Allatoona L. *U.S.A.* 34°10N 84°44W **316** A5
Ålleberg *Sweden* 58°8N 13°36E **163** F7
Allegan *U.S.A.* 42°32N 85°51W **311** B11
Allegany *U.S.A.* 42°6N 78°30W **312** D6
Allegheny → *U.S.A.* 40°27N 80°1W **312** F5
Allegheny Mts. *U.S.A.* 38°15N 80°10W **309** F13
Allegheny Plateau *U.S.A.* 41°30N 78°30W **309** E14
Allegheny Res. *U.S.A.* 41°50N 79°0W **312** E6
Allègre *France* 45°12N 3°41E **174** C7
Allègre, Pte. *Guadeloupe* 16°22N 61°46W **322** e
Allen *Argentina* 38°58S 67°50W **336** A3
Allen *Phil.* 12°30N 124°17E **232** E5
Allen, Bog of *Ireland* 53°15N 7°0W **166** C5
Allen, L. *Ireland* 54°8N 8°4W **166** B3
Allendale *U.S.A.* 33°1N 81°18W **316** B8
Allende *Mexico* 28°20N 100°51W **318** B4
Allenstein = Olsztyn *Poland* 53°48N 20°29E **184** E7
Allentown *U.S.A.* 40°37N 75°29W **313** F9
Allentsteig *Austria* 48°41N 15°20E **180** C8
Alleppey = Alappuzha *India* 9°30N 76°28E **245** K3
Allepuz *Spain* 40°29N 0°44W **196** E4
Aller → *Germany* 52°56N 9°12E **178** C5
Allermuir Hill *U.K.* 55°53N 3°14W **121** B2
Alley, The *Jamaica* 17°48N 77°17W **320** a
Alliance *Suriname* 5°50N 54°50W **329** B7
Alliance *Nebr., U.S.A.* 42°6N 102°52W **308** D2
Alliance *Ohio, U.S.A.* 40°55N 81°6W **312** F3
Allier ☐ *France* 46°25N 2°40E **173** F9
Allier → *France* 46°57N 3°4E **173** F10
Alliford Bay *Canada* 53°12N 131°58W **296** C2
Alligator Pond *Jamaica* 17°52N 77°34W **320** a
Allinagaram *India* 10°2N 77°30E **245** J3
Allinge *Denmark* 55°17N 14°50E **163** J8
Allison *U.S.A.* 42°45N 92°48W **310** B4
Alliston *Canada* 44°9N 79°52W **312** B5
Alloa *U.K.* 56°7N 3°47W **167** E5
Allones *France* 48°20N 1°40E **172** D8
Allora *Australia* 28°2S 152°0E **281** D5
Allos *France* 44°15N 6°38E **175** D10
Allston *U.S.A.* 42°21N 71°7W **116** A2
Alluitsup Paa *Greenland* 60°30N 45°35W **154** E6
Allur *India* 14°40N 80°4E **245** G5
Alluru Kottapatnam *India* 15°24N 80°7E **245** G5
Alma *Qué., Canada* 48°35N 71°40W **299** C5
Alma *Ga., U.S.A.* 31°33N 82°28W **316** D7
Alma *Kans., U.S.A.* 39°1N 96°17W **308** F5
Alma *Mich., U.S.A.* 43°23N 84°39W **309** D11
Alma *Nebr., U.S.A.* 40°6N 99°22W **308** E4
Alma *Wis., U.S.A.* 44°20N 91°55W **308** C8
Alma Ata = Almaty *Kazakhstan* 43°15N 76°57E **217** D9
Alma Hill *U.S.A.* 42°2N 78°0W **312** D7
Almacelles *Spain* 41°43N 0°27E **196** D5
Almada *Portugal* 38°41N 9°8W **126** A2
Almaden *Queens., Australia* 17°22S 144°40E **280** B3
Almadén *Spain* 38°49N 4°52W **195** G6
Almagro *Argentina* 34°38S 58°24W **117** B2
Almagro I. *Phil.* 11°55N 124°18E **233** F5
Almalyk = Olmaliq *Uzbekistan* 40°50N 69°35E **217** D7
Almanor, L. *U.S.A.* 40°14N 121°9W **304** F3
Almansa *Spain* 38°51N 1°5W **197** G3
Almanza *Spain* 42°39N 5°3W **194** C5
Almanzor, Pico *Spain* 40°15N 5°18W **194** E5
Almanzora → *Spain* 37°14N 1°46W **197** H3
Almargem do Bispo *Portugal* 38°49N 9°17W **126** A1
Almas *Brazil* 11°33S 47°9W **333** D2
Almaş, Munţii *Romania* 44°49N 22°12E **182** F7
Almassora *Spain* 39°57N 0°3W **196** F4
Almaty *Kazakhstan* 43°15N 76°57E **217** D9
Almaty ☐ *Kazakhstan* 44°30N 78°0E **217** D9
Almazán *Spain* 41°30N 2°30W **196** D2
Almeirim *Brazil* 1°30S 52°34W **329** D7
Almeirim *Portugal* 39°12N 8°37W **195** F2
Almelo *Neths.* 52°22N 6°42E **170** B6
Almenar de Soria *Spain* 41°43N 2°12W **196** D2
Almenara *Brazil* 16°11S 40°42W **333** E3
Almenara *Spain* 39°46N 0°14W **196** F4
Almenara, Sierra de *Spain* 37°34N 1°32W **197** H3
Almendra, Embalse de *Spain* 41°10N 6°5W **194** D4
Almendralejo *Spain* 38°41N 6°26W **195** G4
Almere *Neths.* 52°20N 5°15E **170** B5
Almería *Spain* 36°52N 2°27W **195** J8
Almería ☐ *Spain* 37°20N 2°20W **197** H2
Almería, G. de *Spain* 36°41N 2°28W **197** J2
Almetyevsk *Russia* 54°53N 52°20E **190** C11
Älmhult *Sweden* 56°33N 14°8E **163** H8
Almirante *Panama* 9°10N 82°30W **320** E3
Almirante G. Brown, Parque *Argentina* 34°40S 58°28W **117** C2
Almirante Montt, G. *Chile* 51°52S 72°50W **336** D2
Almiropotamos *Greece* 38°16N 24°11E **204** C6
Almiros *Greece* 39°11N 22°45E **204** B4
Almodôvar *Portugal* 37°31N 8°2W **195** H2
Almodóvar del Campo *Spain* 38°43N 4°10W **195** G6
Almodóvar del Río *Spain* 37°48N 5°1W **195** H5
Almon *West Bank* 31°49N 35°17E **123** B2
Almond *U.S.A.* 42°19N 77°44W **312** D7
Almond → *U.K.* 55°58N 3°18W **121** B2
Almont *U.S.A.* 42°55N 83°3W **312** D1
Almonte *Ont., Canada* 45°14N 76°12W **313** A8
Almonte *Spain* 37°13N 6°38W **195** H4
Almora *India* 29°38N 79°40E **243** E8
Almoradí *Spain* 38°7N 0°46W **197** G4
Almorox *Spain* 40°14N 4°24W **194** E6
Almoustarat *Mali* 17°35N 0°8E **263** B5
Älmsta *Sweden* 59°58N 18°50E **162** E12
Almudévar *Spain* 42°3N 0°35W **196** C4
Almuñécar *Spain* 36°43N 3°41W **195** J7
Almunge *Sweden* 59°53N 18°3E **162** E12
Almuradiel *Spain* 38°32N 3°28W **195** G7
Almus *Turkey* 40°22N 36°54E **212** B7
Almvik *Sweden* 57°49N 16°30E **163** G10
Almyrou, Ormos *Greece* 35°23N 24°20E **207** E5
Alna *Norway* 59°55N 10°50E **133** A4
Alness *U.K.* 57°41N 4°16W **167** D4
Alnif *Morocco* 31°10N 5°8W **260** B3
Alnmouth *U.K.* 55°24N 1°37W **168** B6
Alnsjøen *Norway* 59°57N 10°51E **133** A4
Alnwick *U.K.* 55°24N 1°42W **168** B6
Alofau *Amer. Samoa* 14°16S 170°36W **302** f
Alofi *Niue* 19°1S 169°55W **289** g
Alofi, I. *Wall. & F. Is.* 14°27S 178°5W **277** C15
Alofi B. *Niue* 19°1S 169°56W **289** g
Aloi *Uganda* 2°16N 33°10E **268** B3
Alon *Burma* 22°12N 95°5E **241** D5
Along *India* 28°10N 94°46E **241** A5
Alonissos *Greece* 39°12N 23°50E **204** B5
Alonissos-Northern Sporades △ *Greece* 39°15N 24°5E **204** B6
Alor *Indonesia* 8°15S 124°30E **231** F6
Alor Setar *Malaysia* 6°7N 100°22E **237** J3
Álora *Spain* 36°49N 4°46W **195** J6
Alosno *Spain* 37°33N 7°7W **195** H3
Alost = Aalst *Belgium* 50°56N 4°2E **170** D4
Alot *India* 23°56N 75°40E **242** H6
Alotau *Papua N. G.* 10°16S 150°30E **286** F6
Alougoum *Morocco* 30°17N 6°56W **260** B3
Aloum *Cameroon* 2°16N 10°34E **264** B2
Aloysius, Mt. *Australia* 26°0S 128°38E **279** E4
Alpaugh *U.S.A.* 35°53N 119°29W **306** K7
Alpe Apuane ⌓ *Italy* 44°4N 10°15E **198** D7
Alpedrinha *Portugal* 40°6N 7°27W **194** E3
Alpena *U.S.A.* 45°4N 83°27W **312** A1
Alpercatas → *Brazil* 6°2S 44°19W **332** C3
Alperton *U.K.* 51°32N 0°17W **125** A2
Alpes-de-Haute-Provence ☐ *France* 44°8N 6°10E **175** D10
Alpes-Maritimes ☐ *France* 43°55N 7°10E **175** E11
Alpha *Queens., Australia* 23°39S 146°37E **280** C4
Alpha *Ill., U.S.A.* 41°12N 90°23W **310** C6
Alpha Ridge *Arctic* 84°0N 118°0W **150** A2
Alpharetta *U.S.A.* 34°5N 84°18W **316** A5
Alphen aan den Rijn *Neths.* 52°7N 4°40E **170** B4
Alphios → *Greece* 37°40N 21°33E **204** D3
Alphonse *Seychelles* 7°0S 52°45E **273** E4
Alpiarça *Portugal* 39°15N 8°35W **195** F2
Alpine *Ariz., U.S.A.* 33°51N 109°9W **305** K9
Alpine *Calif., U.S.A.* 32°50N 116°46W **307** N10
Alpine *N.J., U.S.A.* 40°57N 73°57W **132** A2
Alpine *Tex., U.S.A.* 30°22N 103°40W **314** F3
Alpine △ *Australia* 36°56S 148°10E **283** D7
Alps *Europe* 46°30N 9°30E **176** E5
Alpu *Turkey* 39°46N 30°58E **212** C4
Alpurrurulam *Australia* 20°59S 137°50E **280** C2
Alqueta, Barragem do *Portugal* 38°20N 7°25W **195** G3
Alrø *Denmark* 55°52N 10°5E **163** J4
Alrode *S. Africa* 26°17S 28°7E **123** B2
Als *Denmark* 54°59N 9°55E **163** K3
Alsace ☐ *France* 48°15N 7°25E **173** D14
Alsask *Canada* 51°21N 109°59W **297** C7
Alsasua *Spain* 42°54N 2°10W **196** C2
Alsek → *U.S.A.* 59°10N 138°12W **296** B1
Alsemberg *Belgium* 50°44N 4°20E **116** B2
Alsergrund *Austria* 48°13N 16°21E **142** A2
Alsfeld *Germany* 50°44N 9°16E **178** E5
Alsip *U.S.A.* 41°40N 87°44W **119** C2
Alsta *Norway* 65°58N 12°40E **160** D15
Ålsten *Sweden* 59°19N 17°57E **139** B1
Alsterbro *Sweden* 56°57N 15°55E **163** H9
Alstermo *Sweden* 56°58N 15°38E **163** H9
Alston *U.K.* 54°49N 2°25W **168** C5
Alta *Finnmark, Norway* 69°57N 23°10E **160** B20
Älta *Sweden* 59°15N 18°11E **139** B3
Alta, Sierra *Spain* 40°31N 1°30W **196** E3
Alta Floresta *Brazil* 9°57S 55°58W **331** B6
Alta Gracia *Argentina* 31°40S 64°30W **334** C3
Alta Sierra *U.S.A.* 35°42N 118°33W **307** K8
Altadena *U.S.A.* 34°11N 118°8W **126** A4
Altaelva → *Norway* 69°54N 23°17E **160** B20
Altafjorden *Norway* 70°5N 23°5E **160** A20
Altagracia *Nueva Esparta, Venezuela* 11°6N 63°57W **329** a
Altagracia *Zulia, Venezuela* 10°45N 71°30W **328** A3
Altagracia de Orituco *Venezuela* 9°52N 66°23W **328** B4
Altai = Aerhtai Shan *Mongolia* 46°40N 92°45E **217** C12
Altai = Gorno-Altay ☐ *Russia* 51°0N 86°0E **217** B11
Altai △ *Russia* 50°30N 85°30E **217** B11
Altamachi → *Bolivia* 16°8S 66°50W **330** D4
Altamaha → *U.S.A.* 31°20N 81°20W **316** D8
Altamira *Brazil* 3°12S 52°10W **329** D7
Altamira *Chile* 25°47S 69°51W **334** B2
Altamira *Colombia* 2°3N 75°47W **328** C2
Altamira *Tamaulipas, Mexico* 22°24N 97°55W **319** C5
Altamira, Cuevas de *Spain* 43°20N 4°5W **194** B6
Altamont *Ill., U.S.A.* 39°4N 88°45W **311** E8
Altamont *N.Y., U.S.A.* 42°42N 74°2W **313** D10
Altamura *Italy* 40°49N 16°33E **201** B9
Altanbulag *Mongolia* 50°16N 106°30E **218** A10
Altar *Mexico* 30°43N 111°44W **318** A2
Altar, Gran Desierto de *Mexico* 31°50N 114°10W **318** B2
Altata *Mexico* 24°40N 107°55W **318** C3
Altavas *Phil.* 11°32N 122°29E **233** F4
Altavista *U.S.A.* 37°6N 79°17W **309** G14
Altay *Xinjiang Uygur, China* 47°48N 88°10E **217** C11
Altay *Mongolia* 46°22N 96°15E **218** B8
Altdorf *Switz.* 46°52N 8°36E **179** J4
Alte-Donau → *Austria* 48°14N 16°25E **142** A2
Alte Mellum *Germany* 53°43N 8°10E **178** B4
Altea *Spain* 38°38N 0°2W **197** G4
Altenberg *Germany* 50°45N 13°45E **178** E9
Altenbruch *Germany* 53°49N 8°46E **178** B4
Altenburg *Germany* 50°59N 12°25E **178** E8
Altenkirchen *Mecklenburg-Vorpommern, Germany* 54°38N 13°22E **178** A9
Altenkirchen *Rhld-Pfz., Germany* 50°41N 7°39E **178** E3
Altenmarkt *Austria* 47°43N 14°39E **180** D7
Alter do Chão *Brazil* 2°31S 54°57W **329** D6
Alter do Chão *Portugal* 39°12N 7°40W **195** F3
Alter Finkenkrug *Germany* 52°35N 13°3E **115** A1
Altes Rathaus *Munich, Germany* **131** b3
Altglienicke *Germany* 52°25N 13°32E **115** B4
Altha *U.S.A.* 30°34N 85°8W **316** E4
Altınkaya Barajı *Turkey* 41°18N 35°30E **212** B6
Altınoluk *Turkey* 39°34N 26°45E **205** B8
Altınova *Turkey* 39°12N 26°47E **205** B8
Altınözü *Turkey* 36°7N 36°14E **250** B7
Altıntaş *Turkey* 39°4N 30°7E **205** B12
Altınyaka *Turkey* 36°33N 30°20E **205** E12
Altınyayla *Turkey* 37°0N 29°33E **205** D11
Altiplano *Bolivia* 17°0S 68°0W **330** D4
Altkirch *France* 47°37N 7°15E **173** E14
Altlandsberg *Germany* 52°33N 13°43E **115** A5
Altlandsberg Nord *Germany* 52°34N 13°43E **115** A5
Altmannsdorf *Austria* 48°9N 16°18E **142** B1
Altmark *Germany* 52°45N 11°30E **178** C7
Altmühl → *Germany* 48°54N 11°52E **179** G7
Altmühltal ⌓ *Germany* 48°55N 11°15E **179** G7
Altmunster *Austria* 47°54N 13°45E **180** D6
Alto Adige = Trentino-Alto Adige ☐ *Italy* 46°30N 11°20E **199** B8
Alto Alegre *Brazil* 2°50N 61°20W **329** C5
Alto Araguaia *Brazil* 17°15S 53°20W **331** D7
Alto Chicapa *Angola* 10°52S 19°17E **265** E3
Alto Cuchumatanes = Cuchumatanes, Sierra de los *Guatemala* 15°35N 91°25W **320** C1
Alto Cuito = Tempué *Angola* 13°27S 18°49E **265** E3
Alto da Boa Vista *Brazil* 22°57S 43°16W **135** B1
Alto da Moóca *Brazil* 23°34S 46°33W **137** B2
Alto del Carmen *Chile* 28°46S 70°30W **334** B1
Alto do Pina *Portugal* 38°44N 9°7W **126** A2
Alto Douro *Portugal* 41°6N 7°47W **194** D3
Alto Garças *Brazil* 16°56S 53°32W **331** D7
Alto Garda Bresciano ⌓ *Italy* 45°42N 10°38E **198** C7
Alto Iriri → *Brazil* 8°50S 53°25W **331** B7
Alto Ligonha *Mozam.* 15°30S 38°11E **269** F4
Alto Molocue *Mozam.* 15°50S 37°35E **269** F4
Alto Paraguai *Brazil* 14°30S 56°31W **331** C6
Alto Paraguay ☐ *Paraguay* 21°0S 58°30W **334** A4
Alto Paraiso de Goiás *Brazil* 14°7S 47°31W **333** D2
Alto Paraná ☐ *Paraguay* 25°30S 54°50W **335** B5
Alto Parnaíba *Brazil* 9°6S 45°57W **332** C2
Alto Purús → *Peru* 9°12S 70°28W **330** B3
Alto Río Senguerr *Argentina* 45°2S 70°50W **336** C2
Alto Santo *Brazil* 5°31S 38°15W **332** C4
Alto Sucuriú *Brazil* 19°19S 52°47W **331** D7
Alton *Ont., Canada* 43°54N 80°5W **312** C4
Alton *Hants., U.K.* 51°9N 0°59W **169** F7
Alton *Ill., U.S.A.* 38°53N 90°11W **310** F6
Alton *N.H., U.S.A.* 43°27N 71°13W **313** C13
Altona *Vic., Australia* 37°51S 144°49E **128** B1
Altona *Man., Canada* 49°6N 97°33W **297** D9
Altoona *Ala., U.S.A.* 34°2N 86°20W **316** A3
Altoona *Iowa, U.S.A.* 41°39N 93°28W **310** C3
Altoona *Pa., U.S.A.* 40°31N 78°24W **312** F6
Altos *Brazil* 5°3S 42°28W **332** C3
Altötting *Germany* 48°12N 12°39E **179** G8
Altstätten *Switz.* 47°22N 9°33E **179** H5
Altun Kupri *Iraq* 35°45N 44°9E **213** E11
Altun Shan *China* 38°30N 88°0E **217** E11
Alturas *U.S.A.* 41°29N 120°32W **304** F3
Altus *U.S.A.* 34°38N 99°20W **314** D5
Alubijid *Phil.* 8°35N 124°29E **233** G5
Alucra *Turkey* 40°22N 38°47E **213** B8
Aluk *South Sudan* 8°25N 27°30E **257** F2
Alūksne *Latvia* 57°24N 27°3E **188** D4
Alunda *Sweden* 60°4N 18°5E **162** D12
Alunite *U.S.A.* 35°59N 114°55W **307** K12
Aluoro → *Ethiopia* 8°26N 33°24E **257** F3
Alupka *Ukraine* 44°23N 34°2E **189** K8
Alur *India* 15°24N 77°15E **245** E3
Alur Gajah *Malaysia* 2°23N 102°13E **234** B2
Alushta *Ukraine* 44°40N 34°25E **189** K8
Alusi *Indonesia* 7°35S 131°40E **231** F8
Alustante *Spain* 40°36N 1°40W **196** E3
Alutgama *Sri Lanka* 6°26N 79°59E **245** L4
Alutnuwara *Sri Lanka* 7°19N 80°59E **245** L5
Aluva = Alwaye *India* 10°8N 76°24E **245** J3
Alva *U.S.A.* 36°48N 98°40W **314** C5
Alvaiázere *Portugal* 39°49N 8°23W **194** F2
Alvalade *Portugal* 38°45N 9°8W **126** A2
Älvängen *Sweden* 57°58N 12°8E **163** G6
Alvão ⌓ *Portugal* 41°22N 7°48W **194** D3
Alvarado *Veracruz, Mexico* 18°46N 95°46W **319** D5
Alvarado *Tex., U.S.A.* 32°24N 97°13W **314** E6
Alvarães *Brazil* 3°12S 64°50W **329** D5
Alvaro Obregón, Presa *Mexico* 27°52N 109°52W **318** B3
Alvdal *Norway* 62°6N 10°37E **164** B7
Älvdalen *Sweden* 61°13N 14°4E **162** C8
Alvear *Argentina* 29°5S 56°30W **334** B4
Alverca *Portugal* 38°56N 9°1W **195** G1
Alvesta *Sweden* 56°54N 14°35E **163** H8
Alvik *Sweden* 59°19N 17°58E **139** B1
Alvin Callendar Naval Air Station *U.S.A.* 29°50N 90°1W **131** B2
Alvinston *Canada* 42°49N 81°52W **312** D3
Alvito *Portugal* 38°15N 7°58W **195** G3
Älvkarleby *Sweden* 60°34N 17°26E **162** D11
Alvorado *Brazil* 12°28S 49°6W **333** D2
Alvord Desert *U.S.A.* 42°30N 118°25W **304** E4
Älvros *Sweden* 62°3N 14°38E **162** B8
Älvsbyn *Sweden* 65°40N 21°0E **160** D19
Älvsjo *Sweden* 59°16N 18°0E **139** B2
Ålvundeid *Norway* 62°45N 8°33E **164** B5
Älvvik *Sweden* 59°21N 18°15E **139** A3
Alwar *India* 27°38N 76°34E **242** F7
Alwaye *India* 10°8N 76°24E **245** J3
Alxa Zuoqi *China* 38°50N 105°40E **226** E3
Alyangula *Australia* 13°55S 136°30E **280** A2
Alyata = Älät *Azerbaijan* 39°58N 49°25E **191** L9
Alyth *U.K.* 56°38N 3°13W **167** E5
Alytus *Lithuania* 54°24N 24°3E **188** E3
Alzada *U.S.A.* 45°2N 104°25W **304** D11
Alzamay *Russia* 55°33N 98°39E **215** D10
Alzey *Germany* 49°45N 8°7E **179** F4
Alzira *Spain* 39°9N 0°30W **197** F4
Am Dam *Chad* 12°40N 20°35E **259** F4
Am Géréda *Chad* 12°53N 21°14E **259** F4
Am Hasenbergl *Germany* 48°12N 11°33E **131** A2
Am Sak *Chad* 13°39N 20°8E **259** F4
Am Steinhof *Austria* 48°12N 16°17E **142** A1
Am Timan *Chad* 11°0N 20°10E **259** F4
Am Wald *Germany* 48°3N 11°36E **131** B2
Ama Keng *Singapore* 1°23N 103°41E **138** A2
Amacayacu △ *Colombia* 3°21S 70°8W **328** D3
Amada Gaza *C.A.R.* 4°46N 15°9E **264** B3
Amådalen *Sweden* 61°20N 14°44E **162** C8
Amadeus, L. *Australia* 24°54S 131°0E **279** D5
Amadi *Dem. Rep. of the Congo* 3°40N 26°40E **268** B2
Amâdi *South Sudan* 5°29N 30°25E **257** F3
Amadjuak L. *Canada* 65°0N 71°8W **295** E17
Amadora *Portugal* 38°45N 9°13W **126** A1
Amagansett *U.S.A.* 40°59N 72°9W **313** F12
Amagasaki *Japan* 34°42N 135°23E **133** A1
Amager *Denmark* 55°36N 12°35E **118** B3
Amagi *Japan* 33°25N 130°39E **222** D2
Amagunze *Nigeria* 6°20N 7°40E **263** D6
Amahai *Indonesia* 3°20S 128°55E **231** E7
Amaile *Samoa* 13°59S 171°22W **287** V20
Amaimon *Papua N. G.* 5°12S 145°30E **286** C3
Amaiun-Maia *Spain* 43°12N 1°29W **196** B3
Amakusa = Hondo *Japan* 32°27N 130°12E **222** E2
Amakusa-Nada *Japan* 32°35N 130°5E **222** E2
Amakusa-Shotō *Japan* 32°15N 130°10E **222** E2
Amal *Oman* 18°21N 55°39E **249** C6
Åmål *Sweden* 59°3N 12°42E **162** E6
Amāl Qādisiya *Iraq* 33°16N 44°20E **113** B2
Amalapuram *India* 16°35N 81°55E **245** F5
Amalfi *Colombia* 6°55N 75°4W **328** B2
Amalfi *Italy* 40°38N 14°36E **201** B7
Amaliada *Greece* 37°47N 21°22E **204** D3
Amalienborg Slot *Copenhagen, Denmark* **118** b3
Amalner *India* 21°5N 75°5E **244** D2
Amamapare *Indonesia* 4°53S 136°38E **231** E9
Amambaí *Brazil* 23°5S 55°13W **335** A4
Amambaí → *Brazil* 23°22S 53°56W **335** A5
Amambay ☐ *Paraguay* 23°0S 56°0W **335** A4
Amambay, Cordillera de *S. Amer.* 23°0S 55°45W **335** A4
Amami *Japan* 28°22N 129°27E **221** K4
Amami-Guntō *Japan* 27°16N 129°21E **221** L4
Amami-Ō-Shima *Japan* 28°16N 129°21E **221** K4
Aman, Pulau *Malaysia* 5°16N 100°24E **237** c
Amana → *Venezuela* 9°45N 62°39W **329** B5
Amaná, L. *Brazil* 2°35S 64°40W **329** D5
Amanab *Papua N. G.* 3°40S 141°14E **286** B1
Amanat → *India* 24°7N 84°4E **243** G11
Amanave *Amer. Samoa* 14°20S 170°50W **302** f
Amanda Park *U.S.A.* 47°28N 123°55W **306** C3
Amankeldi *Kazakhstan* 50°10N 65°10E **217** B7
Amanohashidate *Japan* 35°40N 135°15E **223** B7
Amantea *Italy* 39°8N 16°4E **201** C9
Amanu *French Polynesia* 17°48S 140°46W **289** f
Amapá *Brazil* 2°5N 50°50W **329** C7
Amapá ☐ *Brazil* 1°40N 52°0W **329** C7
Amapari = Ferreira Gomes *Brazil* 0°48N 51°8W **329** C7
Amara *Sudan* 10°25N 34°10E **257** E3
Amara ☐ *Ethiopia* 12°30N 37°30E **257** E4
Amaração = Luís Correia *Brazil* 3°0S 41°35W **332** B3
Amarante *Brazil* 6°14S 42°50W **332** C3
Amarante *Portugal* 41°16N 8°5W **194** D2
Amarante do Maranhão *Brazil* 5°36S 46°45W **332** C2
Amaranth *Canada* 50°36N 98°43W **297** C9
Amarapura *Burma* 21°54N 96°3E **241** E6
Amaravati → *India* 11°0N 78°15E **245** J4

Amareleja *Portugal* 38°12N 7°13W **195** G3
Amargosa *Brazil* 13°2S 39°36W **333** D4
Amargosa ➜ *U.S.A.* 36°14N 116°51W **307** J10
Amargosa Desert
  U.S.A. 36°40N 116°30W **307** J10
Amargosa Range
  U.S.A. 36°20N 116°45W **307** J10
Amari *Greece* 35°13N 24°40E **205** D7
Amarillo *U.S.A.* 35°13N 101°50W **314** D4
Amarkantak *India* 22°40N 81°45E **243** H9
'Amârna, Tell el *Egypt* 27°38N 30°52E **256** B3
Amarnath *India* 19°12N 73°22E **244** E1
Amarpur *Bihar, India* 25°5N 87°0E **243** G12
Amarpur *Tripura, India* 23°31N 91°39E **241** D3
Amarti *Eritrea* 14°17N 41°6E **257** E5
Amarwara *India* 22°18N 79°10E **243** H8
Amasin *W. Sahara* 25°45N 13°20W **260** C2
Amasra *Turkey* 41°45N 32°23E **212** B5
Amassama *Nigeria* 5°1N 6°2E **263** D6
Amasya *Turkey* 40°40N 35°50E **212** B6
Amasya □ *Turkey* 40°40N 35°50E **212** B6
Amata *S. Austral., Australia* 26°9S 131°9E **279** E5
Amata *Piemonte, Italy* 45°34N 9°8E **128** A1
Amataurá *Brazil* 3°29S 68°6W **328** D4
Amatignak I. *U.S.A.* 51°16N 179°6W **303** L3
Amatikulu *S. Africa* 29°3S 31°33E **271** C5
Amatitlán *Guatemala* 14°29N 90°38W **320** D1
Amau *Papua N. G.* 10°2S 148°34E **286** F5
Amay *Belgium* 50°33N 5°19E **170** D5
Amazon = Amazonas ➜
  S. Amer. 0°5S 50°0W **329** D8
Amazonas □ *Brazil* 5°0S 65°0W **331** B5
Amazonas □ *Peru* 5°0S 78°0W **330** B2
Amazonas □ *Venezuela* 3°30N 66°0W **328** C4
Amazonas ➜ *S. Amer.* 0°5S 50°0W **329** D8
Amba Ferit *Ethiopia* 10°55N 38°50E **257** E4
Ambagarh Chowki *India* 20°47N 80°43E **244** D5
Ambah *India* 19°38N 75°50E **244** E2
Ambahakily *Madag.* 21°36S 43°41E **272** C1
Ambahita *Madag.* 24°1S 45°16E **272** C2
Ambajogal *India* 18°44N 76°23E **244** E3
Ambala *India* 30°23N 76°56E **242** D7
Ambalangoda *Sri Lanka* 6°15N 80°5E **245** L5
Ambalantota *Sri Lanka* 6°7N 81°1E **245** L5
Ambalapulai *India* 9°25N 76°25E **245** K3
Ambam *Cameroon* 2°20N 11°15E **264** B2
Ambanja *Madag.* 13°40S 48°27E **272** A2
Ambararata *Madag.* 15°3S 48°33E **272** B2
Ambarchik *Russia* 69°40N 162°20E **215** C17
Ambarijeby *Madag.* 14°56S 47°41E **272** A2
Ambaro, Helodranon'
  Madag. 13°23S 48°38E **272** A2
Ambasamudram *India* 8°43N 77°25E **245** K3
Ambato *Ecuador* 1°5S 78°42W **328** D2
Ambato *Madag.* 13°24S 48°29E **272** A2
Ambato, Sierra de
  Argentina 28°25S 66°10W **334** B2
Ambato Boeny *Madag.* 16°28S 46°43E **272** B2
Ambatofinandrahana
  Madag. 20°33S 46°48E **272** C2
Ambatolampy *Madag.* 19°20S 47°35E **272** B2
Ambatomainty *Madag.* 17°41S 45°40E **272** B2
Ambatomanoina *Madag.* 18°18S 47°37E **272** B2
Ambatondrazaka *Madag.* 17°55S 48°28E **272** B2
Ambatosoratra *Madag.* 17°37S 48°31E **272** B2
Ambelokipi *Greece* 39°45N 22°22E **204** B4
Ambelonas *Greece* 15°17S 46°58E **272** B2
Ambenja *Madag.* 15°17S 46°58E **272** B2
Amberg *Germany* 49°26N 11°52E **179** F7
Ambergris Cay *Belize* 18°0N 87°55W **320** C2
Ambérieu-en-Bugey
  France 45°57N 5°20E **175** C9
Amberley *Ont., Canada* 44°2N 81°42W **312** B3
Amberley *N.Z.* 43°9S 172°44E **285** F7
Ambert *France* 45°33N 3°44E **174** C7
Ambidédi *Mali* 14°35N 11°47W **262** C2
Ambikapur *India* 23°15N 83°15E **243** H10
Ambikol *Sudan* 21°20N 30°50E **256** C3
Ambil I. *Phil.* 13°48N 120°18E **232** E4
Ambilobé *Madag.* 13°10S 49°3E **272** A2
Ambinanindrano *Madag.* 20°5S 48°23E **272** C2
Ambinanitelo *Madag.* 15°21S 49°35E **272** B2
Ambinda *Madag.* 16°25S 45°52E **272** B2
Ambitle I. *Papua N. G.* 4°5S 153°37E **286** C7
Amble *U.K.* 55°20N 1°36W **168** B6
Ambler *U.S.A.* 67°5N 157°52W **303** C8
Ambleside *U.K.* 54°26N 2°58W **168** C5
Ambo *Peru* 10°5S 76°10W **330** C2
Amboahangy *Madag.* 24°15S 46°43E **272** C2
Amboasary *Madag.* 25°1S 46°45E **272** D2
Ambodifototra *Madag.* 16°59S 49°52E **272** B2
Ambodilazana *Madag.* 18°6S 49°10E **272** B2
Ambodiriana *Madag.* 17°55S 49°18E **272** B2
Ambohidratrimo *Madag.* 18°50S 47°26E **272** B2
Ambohidray *Madag.* 18°36S 48°18E **272** B2
Ambohimahamasina
  Madag. 21°56S 47°11E **272** C2
Ambohimahasoa *Madag.* 21°7S 47°13E **272** C2
Ambohimanga
  Antananarivo,
  Madag. 18°45S 47°33E **272** B2
Ambohimanga *Fianarantsoa,*
  Madag. 20°52S 47°36E **272** C2
Ambohimitombo *Madag.* 20°43S 47°26E **272** C2
Ambohitra *Madag.* 12°30S 49°10E **272** A2
Amboise *France* 47°24N 1°2E **172** E8
Amboiva *Angola* 11°33S 14°43E **265** D2
Ambon *Indonesia* 3°43S 128°12E **231** E7
Ambondro *Madag.* 25°13S 45°44E **272** D2
Amboró □ *Bolivia* 17°39S 64°34W **331** D5
Amboseli, L. *Kenya* 2°40S 37°10E **268** C4
Amboseli △ *Kenya* 2°37S 37°13E **268** C4
Ambositra *Madag.* 20°31S 47°25E **272** C2
Ambovombe *Madag.* 25°11S 46°5E **272** D2
Amboy *Calif., U.S.A.* 34°33N 115°45W **307** L11
Amboy *Ill., U.S.A.* 41°44N 89°20W **310** C7
Amboyna Cay *S. China Sea* 7°50N 112°50E **230** C4
Ambre, Île d' *Mauritius* 20°2S 57°41E **272** e
Ambridge *U.S.A.* 40°36N 80°14W **316** F4
Ambriz *Angola* 7°48S 13°8E **265** D2
Ambriz □ *Angola* 7°56S 10°27E **265** D2
Ambrolauri *Georgia* 42°31N 43°9E **213** A10
Ambrym *Vanuatu* 16°15S 168°10E **287** F6
Ambur *India* 12°48N 78°43E **245** H4
Ambunti *Papua N. G.* 4°13S 142°22E **286** C2
Amby *Australia* 26°30S 148°11E **281** D4
Amchitka I. *U.S.A.* 51°32N 179°0E **303** L2
Amderma *Russia* 69°45N 61°30E **214** C7
Amdhi *India* 23°51N 81°27E **243** H9
Amdo *China* 32°20N 91°40E **218** E7
Ameca *Mexico* 20°33N 104°2W **318** C4
Ameca ➜ *Mexico* 20°41N 105°18W **318** C3
Amecameca de Juárez
  Mexico 19°8N 98°46W **319** D5
Amed *Indonesia* 8°19S 115°39E **231** J18
Ameixoeira *Portugal* 38°46N 9°9E **196** b
Ameland *Neths.* 53°27N 5°45E **170** A5
Amélia *Italy* 42°33N 12°25E **199** F9
Amelia City *U.S.A.* 30°35N 81°28W **316** E6
Amelia Earhart Park
  U.S.A. 25°53N 80°16W **129** C1
Amelia I. *U.S.A.* 30°40N 81°25W **316** E6
Amendolara *Italy* 39°57N 16°35W **201** C9
Amenia *U.S.A.* 41°51N 73°33W **313** E11

América *Brazil* 23°35S 46°41W **137** B1
America-Antarctica Ridge
  S. Ocean 59°0S 16°0W **151** B2
American Falls *U.S.A.* 42°47N 112°51W **304** E7
American Falls Res.
  U.S.A. 42°47N 112°52W **304** E7
American Fork *U.S.A.* 40°23N 111°48W **304** F8
American Highland
  Antarctica 73°0S 75°0E **151** D6
American Indian Museum
  Washington, D.C., U.S.A. **143** b3
American Museum of Natural
  History *New York, U.S.A.* **132** b2
American River *Australia* 35°47S 137°46E **282** C2
American Samoa ☑
  Pac. Oc. 14°20S 170°0W **302** f
American Samoa △
  Amer. Samoa 14°15S 170°28W **302** g
American Univ. *U.S.A.* 38°56N 77°5W **143** B2
Americana *Brazil* 22°45S 47°20W **335** A6
Americus *U.S.A.* 32°4N 84°14W **316** C5
Amerigo Vespucci, Firenze ✈ (FLR)
  Italy 43°49N 11°13E **199** E8
Amerika = Nakhodka
  Russia 42°53N 132°54E **220** C6
Amersfoort *Neths.* 52°9N 5°23E **170** B5
Amersfoort *Mpumalanga,*
  S. Africa 26°55S 29°53E **271** C4
Amery Basin *S. Ocean* 68°15S 74°30E **151** C6
Amery Ice Shelf *Antarctica* 69°30S 72°0E **151** C6
Amerzgane *Morocco* 31°4N 7°14W **260** B3
Ames = Bertamirans
  Spain 42°54N 8°38W **194** C2
Ames *U.S.A.* 42°2N 93°37W **310** D3
Amesbury *U.S.A.* 42°51N 70°56W **313** D14
Amet *India* 25°18N 73°56E **242** G5
Amfiklia *Greece* 38°38N 22°35E **204** C4
Amfilochia *Greece* 38°52N 21°9E **204** C3
Amfipoli *Greece* 40°48N 23°52E **202** F7
Amfissa *Greece* 38°32N 22°22E **204** C4
Amga *Russia* 60°50N 132°0E **215** C14
Amga ➜ *Russia* 62°38N 134°32E **215** C14
Amgaon *India* 21°22N 80°22E **244** D5
Amgu *Russia* 45°45N 137°15E **220** B8
Amguid *Algeria* 26°26N 5°22E **261** C6
Amgun ➜ *Russia* 52°56N 139°38E **215** D14
Amherst *Burma* 16°4N 97°34E **241** G6
Amherst *N.S., Canada* 45°48N 64°8W **299** C7
Amherst *Mass., U.S.A.* 42°23N 72°31W **313** D12
Amherst *N.Y., U.S.A.* 42°59N 78°48W **312** D6
Amherst *Ohio, U.S.A.* 41°24N 82°14W **312** E2
Amherst I. *Canada* 44°8N 76°43W **313** B8
Amherstburg *Canada* 42°6N 83°6W **311** B13
Amiata, Mte. *Italy* 42°53N 11°37E **199** F8
Amidon *U.S.A.* 46°29N 103°19W **308** B2
Amiens *France* 49°54N 2°16E **173** C9
Amik Gölü *Turkey* 36°22N 36°17E **250** B7
Amili *India* 28°25N 95°52E **241** A5
Amiin *Iraq* 33°19N 44°29E **213** B2
Aminadav *Israel* 31°45N 35°8E **123** B1
Amindeo *Greece* 40°42N 21°42E **202** F5
Amindivi Is. *India* 11°23N 72°23E **245** J1
Amini I. *India* 11°6N 72°46E **245** J1
Amino *Ethiopia* 23°43S 19°21E **270** B2
Amintsi *Namibia* 23°43S 19°21E **270** B2
Âmir, Ra's *Libya* 32°57N 21°43E **258** B4
Amirabad *Iran* 33°20N 46°16E **246** C5
Amirabad *Tehran, Iran* 35°43N 51°24E **247** C6
Amirante Is. *Seychelles* 6°0S 53°0E **210** J7
Amisk ➜ *Canada* 56°43N 98°0W **297** B9
Amisk L. *Canada* 54°35N 102°15W **297** C8
Amistad, Presa de la
  Mexico 29°26N 101°3W **318** B4
Amistad △ *U.S.A.* 29°32N 101°12W **314** G4
Amite *U.S.A.* 30°44N 90°30W **315** F9
Amizmiz *Morocco* 31°12N 8°15W **260** B3
Amla *India* 21°56N 78°7E **242** J8
Amlapura *Indonesia* 8°27S 115°37E **231** J18
Amli *Norway* 58°45N 8°32E **164** F5
Amlia I. *U.S.A.* 52°4N 173°30W **303** K4
Amlwch *U.K.* 53°24N 4°20W **168** D3
Amm Adam *Sudan* 16°20N 36°1E **257** D4
'Ammān *Jordan* 31°57N 35°52E **251** G6
'Ammān □ *Jordan* 31°40N 36°30E **251** G7
Ammanford *U.K.* 51°48N 3°59W **169** F4
Ammassalik = Tasiilaq
  Greenland 65°40N 37°20W **154** D7
Ammerån ➜ *Sweden* 63°9N 16°13E **162** A10
Ammersee *Germany* 48°0N 11°7E **179** G7
Ammochostos = Famagusta
  Cyprus 35°8N 33°55E **207** E9
Ammon *U.S.A.* 43°28N 111°58W **304** E8
Amnat Charoen *Thailand* 15°51N 104°38E **236** E5
Amnura *Bangla.* 24°37N 88°25E **243** G13
Amo Jiang ➜ *China* 23°0N 101°50E **228** F3
Amol *Iran* 36°23N 52°20E **247** B7
Amora *Portugal* 38°37N 9°6W **196** D1
Amoreira *Portugal* 38°48N 9°11W **126** A1
Amoret *U.S.A.* 38°15N 94°35W **310** F2
Amorgos *Greece* 36°50N 25°57E **205** D6
Amory *U.S.A.* 33°59N 88°29W **315** E10
Amos *Canada* 48°35N 78°5W **298** C4
Âmot *Buskerud, Norway* 59°57N 9°54E **164** E6
Âmot *Oppland, Norway* 61°0N 10°2E **164** D7
Âmot *Telemark, Norway* 59°34N 8°0E **164** E5
Âmot *Sweden* 60°58N 16°27E **162** D10
Amotfors *Sweden* 59°47N 12°22E **162** E6
Amotsdal *Norway* 59°37N 8°26E **164** E5
Amour, Djebel *Algeria* 33°42N 1°37E **261** B5
Amoy = Xiamen *China* 24°25N 118°4E **229** E12
Ampah *Indonesia* 1°46S 115°7E **235** C5
Ampanavoana *Madag.* 15°41S 50°22E **272** B3
Ampang *Malaysia* 3°8N 101°45E **237** L3
Ampanganalana, Lakandranon'
  Madag. 14°35S 48°0E **272** C2
Ampani *India* 19°35N 82°38E **244** E6
Ampanihy *Madag.* 24°40S 44°45E **272** C1
Amparafaravola *Madag.* 17°35S 48°13E **272** B2
Amparai *Indonesia* 8°31S 114°31E **231** K18
Ampasinambo, Helodranon'
  Madag. 20°35S 48°0E **272** C2
Ampasindava, Helodranon'
  Madag. 13°42S 47°55E **272** A2
Ampasindava, Saikanosy
  Madag. 13°40S 47°55E **272** A2
Ampatero, Nevado *Peru* 15°40S 71°56W **330** D3
Ampenan *Indonesia* 8°34S 116°4E **231** K18
Amper *Nigeria* 9°25N 9°40E **263** C6
Amper ➜ *Germany* 48°29N 11°55E **179** G7
Ampezo *Italy* 46°25N 12°48E **199** B9
Amphoe Kathu *Thailand* 7°55N 98°21E **234** a
Amphoe Thalang *Thailand* 8°1N 98°20E **234** a
Ampitsikinana *Madag.* 12°51S 49°49E **272** A2
Ampombiantambo
  Madag. 12°42S 48°57E **272** A2
Amposta *Spain* 40°43N 0°34E **196** B6
Ampotaka *Madag.* 25°3S 44°41E **272** D1
Ampoza *Madag.* 22°20S 44°44E **272** C1
Amqui *Canada* 48°28N 67°27W **299** C6
Amrabad *India* 16°23N 78°50E **245** F4
'Amrān *Yemen* 15°41N 43°54E **254** D3
'Amrān □ *Yemen* 15°40N 43°55E **254** D3
Amravati = Amravati
  India 20°55N 77°45E **244** D3

Amravati *India* 20°55N 77°45E **244** D3
Amreli *India* 21°35N 71°17E **242** J4
Amrenene el Kasba *Algeria* 22°10N 0°30E **261** D5
Amritsar *India* 31°35N 74°57E **242** H5
Amroha *India* 28°53N 78°30E **243** E8
Amrum *Germany* 54°38N 8°22E **178** A4
Amsâga *Mauritania* 20°7N 14°10W **260** D2
Amsel *Algeria* 22°47N 5°29E **261** D6
Amstel *Amsterdam, Neths.* **112** b2
Amstel ➜ *Amsterdam, Neths.* **112** b3
Amsterdam *N.Y., U.S.A.* 52°18N 4°54E **112** B2
Amstelveen *Neths.* 52°18N 4°51E **112** B2
Amsterdam *Neths.* 52°23N 4°54E **112** B2
Amsterdam *N.Y., U.S.A.* 42°56N 74°11W **313** D10
Amsterdam ✈ (AMS)
  Neths. 52°18N 4°45E **112** B2
Amsterdam I. = Nouvelle
  Amsterdam, Î. *Ind. Oc.* 38°30S 77°30E **273** H6
Amsterdam-Rijnkanaal
  Neths. 52°17N 5°1E **112** B3
Amsterdam Zuidoost
  Neths. 52°18N 4°58E **112** B2
Amsterdamse Bos *Neths.* 52°19N 4°50E **112** B1
Amstetten *Austria* 48°7N 14°51E **180** C7
'Amûdah *Syria* 37°6N 40°55E **213** D9
Amudarya *Turkmenistan* 37°53N 65°15E **216** E7
Amudarya ➜ *Uzbekistan* 43°30N 59°0E **216** E6
Amukta I. *U.S.A.* 52°30N 171°16W **303** K5
Amukta Pass *U.S.A.* 52°0N 171°0W **303** K5
Amulung *Phil.* 17°50N 121°43E **232** C3
Amund Ringnes I.
  Canada 78°20N 96°25W **295** B12
Amundsen Abyssal Plain
  S. Ocean 65°0S 120°0W **151** C14
Amundsen Basin *Arctic* 87°30N 80°0E **153** A9
Amundsen Gulf *Canada* 71°0N 124°0W **294** C7
Amundsen Ridges
  S. Ocean 69°15S 123°0W **151** C14
Amundsen-Scott *Antarctica* 90°0S 166°0E **151** E
Amundsen Sea *Antarctica* 72°0S 115°0W **151** D15
Amungen *Sweden* 61°10N 15°40E **162** D9
Amuntai *Indonesia* 2°28S 115°25E **235** C5
Amur ➜ *Russia* 52°56N 141°10E **215** D15
Amur, W. ➜ *Sudan* 18°56N 33°34E **256** D3
Amurang *Indonesia* 1°5N 124°40E **231** D6
Amurrio *Spain* 43°3N 3°0W **196** B1
Amursk *Russia* 50°14N 136°54E **215** D14
Amusco *Spain* 42°10N 4°28E **194** C6
Amvrakikos Kolpos *Greece* 39°0N 20°55E **204** C2
Amvrosiyivka *Ukraine* 47°43N 38°50E **189** J10
Amyderya = Amudarya ➜
  Uzbekistan 43°58N 59°34E **216** D5
An Bien *Vietnam* 9°45N 105°0E **237** H5
An Hoa *Vietnam* 15°40N 108°5E **236** E7
An Khe *Vietnam* 13°57N 108°51E **236** F7
An Nabatîyah at Tahta
  Lebanon 33°23N 35°27E **250** B4
An Nabk *Syria* 34°2N 36°44E **250** D7
An Nafud *Si. Arabia* 28°15N 41°0E **246** D4
An Nâjiyah *Iraq* 34°26N 41°33E **213** D9
An Najaf *Iraq* 32°3N 44°15E **213** G11
An Namâş *Si. Arabia* 19°7N 42°8E **248** C3
An Nâşiriyah *Iraq* 31°0N 46°15E **246** D5
An Nawfaliyah *Libya* 30°54N 17°58E **258** B3
An Nhon = Binh Dinh
  Vietnam 13°55N 109°7E **236** F7
An Nîl □ *Sudan* 19°30N 33°0E **256** D3
An Nîl el Abyad □ *Sudan* 14°0N 32°15E **257** E3
An Nîl el Azraq □ *Sudan* 11°30N 34°30E **257** E3
An Nu'ayrîyah *Si. Arabia* 27°30N 48°30E **247** E6
An Nu'mânîyah *Iraq* 32°32N 45°25E **213** F11
An Nuqat al Khams □
  Libya 32°42N 11°57E **258** B2
An Ros = Rush *Ireland* 53°31N 6°6W **166** C5
An Thoi, Quan Dao
  Vietnam 9°58N 104°0E **237** H5
Âna-Sira *Norway* 58°17N 6°25E **164** F3
Anaa *French Polynesia* 17°25S 145°30W **289** f
Anabar ➜ *Russia* 73°8N 113°36E **215** B12
Anaco *Venezuela* 9°27N 64°28W **329** B5
Anaconda *U.S.A.* 46°8N 112°57W **306** C7
Anacortes *U.S.A.* 48°30N 122°37W **306** B4
Anacostia *U.S.A.* 38°51N 76°59W **143** B3
Anacostia ➜ *U.S.A.* 38°52N 77°1W **143** B3
Anacuao, Mt. *Phil.* 16°16N 121°53E **232** C3
Anadarko *U.S.A.* 35°4N 98°15W **314** D5
Anadia *Brazil* 9°42S 36°18W **332** C4
Anadia *Portugal* 40°26N 8°27W **194** E2
Anadolu *Turkey* 39°0N 30°0E **212** C5
Anadoluhisarı *Turkey* 41°4N 29°3E **128** B2
Anadyr *Russia* 64°35N 177°20E **215** C18
Anadyr ➜ *Russia* 64°55N 176°5E **215** C18
Anadyrskiy Zaliv *Russia* 64°0N 180°0E **215** C19
Anafi *Greece* 36°22N 25°48E **205** E7
Anafonitria *Greece* 37°50N 20°38E **207** D2
Anaga, Pta. de *Canary Is.* 28°34N 16°9W **153** d1
Anagni *Italy* 41°44N 13°9E **199** G10
'Ânah *Iraq* 34°25N 42°0E **213** D9
Anaheim *U.S.A.* 33°50N 117°55W **307** M9
Anaheim Lake *Canada* 52°28N 125°18W **296** C3
Anahola *U.S.A.* 22°9N 159°19W **302** A2
'Anahulu ➜ *U.S.A.* 21°37N 158°6W **302** J13
Anai Mudi *India* 10°12N 77°4E **245** J3
Anaichak *U.S.A.* 56°50N 158°15W **303** H8
Anaimalai Hills *India* 10°20N 76°40E **245** J3
Anajás *Brazil* 0°59S 49°57W **332** B2
Anajatuba *Brazil* 3°16S 44°37W **332** B3
Anakao *Madag.* 23°40S 43°39E **272** C1
Anakapalle *India* 17°42N 83°6E **244** F6
Anakena *Chile* 27°5S 109°20W **338** B2
Anakie *Australia* 23°32S 147°45E **280** C4
Anaklia *Georgia* 42°24N 41°35E **191** J5
Anakuturuk Pass *U.S.A.* 68°8N 151°45W **303** B10
Analalava *Madag.* 14°35S 48°0E **272** A2
Analavoka *Madag.* 39°36N 19°55E **272** B2
Anamā *Brazil* 3°35S 61°22W **329** D5
Anambar ➜ *Pakistan* 30°15N 68°50E **242** D3
Anambas, Kepulauan
  Indonesia 3°20N 106°30E **234** B3
Anambas Is. = Anambas,
  Kepulauan *Indonesia* 3°20N 106°30E **234** B3
Anambra □ *Nigeria* 6°20N 7°0E **263** C6
Aname *Vanuatu* 20°8S 169°47E **287** K7
Anamosa *U.S.A.* 42°7N 91°17W **310** D5
Anamur *Turkey* 36°8N 32°58E **250** B5
Anamur Burnu *Turkey* 36°4N 32°4E **250** B5
Anan *Japan* 33°54N 134°40E **222** D6
Anand *India* 22°32N 72°59E **242** H5
Anandapuram *India* 14°15N 79°1E **245** G4
Anandpur *India* 21°16N 86°13E **244** D8
Anantnag *Spain* 9°20N 27°48E **204** B2
Ananes *Greece* 36°33N 24°40E **205** E6
Anang Pitjantjatjara ☉
  Australia 27°0S 132°0E **279** E5
Anantapur *India* 14°39N 77°42E **245** G3
Anantnag *India* 33°45N 75°10E **243** C6
Ananyiv *Ukraine* 47°44N 29°58E **183** C13
Anapa *Russia* 44°53N 37°20E **191** K9
Anápodiaris ➜ *Greece* 34°59N 25°20E **207** F6
Anápolis = Simão Dias
  Brazil 10°44S 37°49W **332** C4
Anápolis *Brazil* 16°15S 48°50W **333** E2
Anapu ➜ *Brazil* 1°53S 50°53W **329** D7
Anár *Iran* 30°55N 55°13E **247** D7

Anär Darreh *Afghan.* 32°46N 61°39E **240** B1
Anárak *Iran* 33°25N 53°40E **247** C7
Anarisfjällen *Sweden* 63°6N 13°10E **162** A7
Anas ➜ *India* 23°26N 74°0E **242** H5
Añasco *Puerto Rico* 18°17N 67°8W **321** b
Anata *West Bank* 31°49N 35°16E **123** B2
Anatolia = Anadolu *Turkey* 39°0N 30°0E **212** C5
Anatsogno *Madag.* 23°33S 43°46E **272** C1
Añatuya *Argentina* 28°20S 62°50W **334** B3
Anatye ☉ *Australia* 22°29S 137°3E **280** C2
Anauá ➜ *Brazil* 0°58N 61°21W **329** C5
Anaunethad L. *Canada* 60°55N 104°25W **297** A8
Anavilhanas, Arquipélago das
  Brazil 2°42S 60°45W **329** D5
Anbyŏn *N. Korea* 39°1N 127°35E **226** C3
Ancares, Sierra dos *Spain* 42°51N 6°52W **194** C4
Ancaster *Canada* 43°13N 79°59W **312** C5
Ancenis *France* 47°21N 1°10W **172** E5
Anchieta = Piatã *Brazil* 13°9S 41°48W **333** D3
Anch'ing = Anqing
  China 30°30N 117°3E **229** B11
Ancho, Canal *Chile* 50°0S 74°20W **336** D2
Anchor Bay *U.S.A.* 38°48N 123°34W **306** G2
Anchorage *U.S.A.* 61°13N 149°54W **303** F10
Anchorage ✈ (ANC) *U.S.A.* 61°10N 150°0W **303** F10
Anchuthengu *India* 8°40N 76°46E **245** K3
Anci *China* 39°20N 116°40E **226** E9
Ancohuma, Nevado
  Bolivia 16°0S 68°50W **330** D4
Ancol *Indonesia* 6°7S 106°49E **122** A1
Ancón *Peru* 11°50S 77°10W **330** C2
Ancona *Italy* 43°38N 13°30E **199** E10
Ancud *Chile* 42°0S 73°50W **336** B2
Ancud, G. de *Chile* 42°0S 73°0W **336** B2
Ancy-le-Franc *France* 47°46N 4°10E **173** E11
Anda *Heilongjiang, China* 46°24N 125°19E **219** B14
Anda *China* 16°17N 119°57E **232** C2
Andacollo *Argentina* 37°10S 70°42W **334** D1
Andacollo *Chile* 30°14S 71°6W **334** C1
Andahuaylas *Peru* 13°40S 73°25W **330** C3
Andaingo *Madag.* 18°12S 48°17E **272** B2
Andalgalá *Argentina* 27°40S 66°30W **334** B2
Ândalsnes *Norway* 62°35N 7°43E **164** B4
Andalucía □ *Spain* 37°35N 5°0W **195** H6
'Andalus *Iraq* 33°19N 44°18E **113** B1
Andalusia = Andalucía □
  Spain 37°35N 5°0W **195** H6
Andalusia *U.S.A.* 31°18N 86°29W **315** F11
Andaman & Nicobar Is. □
  India 10°0N 93°0E **245** K11
Andaman Is. *Ind. Oc.* 12°30N 92°45E **245** H11
Andaman Sea *Ind. Oc.* 13°0N 96°0E **230** B1
Andamooka *Australia* 30°27S 137°9E **281** E2
Andara *Namibia* 18°2S 21°9E **270** B3
Andaraí *Bahia, Brazil* 12°48S 41°20W **333** D3
Andaraí *Rio de J., Brazil* 22°55N 44°15E **135** B1
Andelot-Blancheville
  France 48°15N 5°18E **173** D12
Andenes *Norway* 69°19N 16°18E **160** B7
Andéranboukane *Mali* 15°26N 3°2E **263** B5
Anderlecht *Belgium* 50°50N 4°19E **116** A1
Andermatt *Switz.* 46°38N 8°35E **179** J4
Andernach *Germany* 50°26N 7°24E **178** E3
Andernos-les-Bains *France* 44°44N 1°6W **174** D2
Andersen Air Force Base ○ (UAM)
  Guam 13°35N 144°55E **302** d
Anderslöv *Sweden* 55°26N 13°19E **163** J7
Anderson *Vic., Australia* 38°31S 145°26E **283** E6
Anderson *Alaska,*
  U.S.A. 64°25N 149°15W **303** D10
Anderson *Calif., U.S.A.* 40°27N 122°18W **304** F2
Anderson *Ind., U.S.A.* 40°10N 85°41W **311** D11
Anderson *Mo., U.S.A.* 36°39N 94°27W **308** G6
Anderson *S.C., U.S.A.* 34°31N 82°39W **315** D13
Anderson ➜ *Canada* 12°42N 129°0W **294** C6
Anderson I. *India* 12°46N 92°43E **245** H11
Anderson Park *U.S.A.* 33°45N 84°27W **113** B2
Andersonville *U.S.A.* 32°12N 84°9W **316** C5
Andersonville △ *U.S.A.* 32°12N 84°9W **316** C5
Anderstorp *Sweden* 57°19N 13°39E **163** G7
Andes, Colombia 5°39N 75°54E **328** B2
Andes, Cord. de los *S. Amer.* 20°0S 68°0W **330** D4
Andfjorden *Norway* 69°10N 16°20E **160** B17
Andhra, I. *India* 18°54N 73°32E **244** B1
Andhra Pradesh □ *India* 18°0N 79°0E **244** F4
Andijon *Uzbekistan* 41°10N 72°15E **217** D8
Andijon □ *Uzbekistan* 40°45N 72°20E **217** D8
Andikithira = Antikythira
  Greece 35°52N 23°15E **204** F5
Andilamena *Madag.* 17°1S 48°35E **272** B2
Andímeshk *Iran* 32°27N 48°21E **213** F12
Andimilos = Antimilos
  Greece 36°47N 24°12E **204** E6
Andiparos = Antiparos
  Greece 37°0N 25°3E **205** D7
Andipaxoi = Antipaxi
  Greece 39°9N 20°13E **204** C2
Andípsara *Greece* 38°30N 25°29E **205** C7
Andizhan = Andijon
  Uzbekistan 41°10N 72°15E **217** D8
Andkhvoy *Afghan.* 36°52N 65°8E **240** A2
Andoain *Spain* 43°13N 2°1W **196** B2
Andoany *Madag.* 13°25S 48°16E **272** A2
Andoas *Peru* 2°55S 76°25W **328** D2
Andol *India* 17°51N 78°4E **244** F4
Andola *India* 16°57N 76°50E **244** F3
Andong *S. Korea* 36°40N 128°43E **226** C4
Andongwei *China* 35°8N 119°20E **227** G10
Andorra ■ *Europe* 42°30N 1°30E **196** A6
Andorra La Vella *Andorra* 42°31N 1°32E **174** F5
Andorra la Vieja = Andorra
  La Vella *Andorra* 42°31N 1°32E **174** F5
Andover *Hants., U.K.* 51°12N 1°29W **169** F6
Andover *N.B., Canada* 46°36N 67°45W **299** C6
Andover *Kans., U.S.A.* 37°43N 97°7W **308** G5
Andover *Maine, U.S.A.* 44°40N 70°45W **313** B14
Andover *Mass., U.S.A.* 42°40N 71°8W **313** D13
Andover *N.J., U.S.A.* 40°59N 74°45W **313** F10
Andover *N.Y., U.S.A.* 42°10N 77°48W **312** D7
Andover *Ohio, U.S.A.* 41°36N 80°34W **312** E4
Andoya *Norway* 69°10N 15°50E **160** B16
Andradas *Brazil* 22°4S 46°34W **137** A2
Andradina *Brazil* 20°54S 51°23W **333** H1
Andrahary, Mt. *Madag.* 13°37S 49°17E **272** A2
Andramasina *Madag.* 19°11S 47°35E **272** B2
Andranopasy *Madag.* 21°17S 43°44E **272** C1
Andratx *Spain* 39°39N 2°25E **193** B9
André Félix △ *C.A.R.* 9°29N 23°18E **266** A4
Andreapol *Russia* 56°40N 32°17E **188** D6
Andrée Land *Greenland* 73°40N 26°0W **154** C8
Andreevka *Russia* 45°16N 41°53E **191** K6
Andrews *Tex., U.S.A.* 32°19N 102°33W **314** E3
Andria *Italy* 41°13N 16°17E **201** A9
Andriamena *Madag.* 17°26S 47°30E **272** B2
Andriandampy *Madag.* 22°45S 45°41E **272** C2
Andriba *Madag.* 17°30S 46°58E **272** B2

Anivorano *Toamasina,*
  Madag. 18°44S 48°58E **272** B2
Aniwa *Vanuatu* 19°17S 169°35E **287** F7
Anjalankoski *Finland* 60°45N 26°51E **188** B4
Anjangaon *India* 21°10N 77°20E **244** D3
Anjar = Hawsh Mûssá
  Lebanon 33°45N 35°55E **250** E6
Anjar *India* 23°6N 70°10E **242** H4
Anjengo = Anchuthengu
  India 8°40N 76°46E **245** K3
Anji *China* 30°36N 119°40E **229** B12
Anjidiv I. *India* 14°40N 74°10E **245** G2
Anjou *France* 47°20N 0°15W **172** E6
Anjou *Qué., Canada* 45°36N 73°33W **130** A2
Anjou *Maine-et-Loire,*
  France 47°20N 0°15W **172** E6
Anjouan *Comoros Is.* 12°15S 44°20E **272** a
Anjozorobe *Madag.* 18°22S 47°52E **272** B2
Anju *N. Korea* 39°36N 125°40E **226** C3
Anka *Nigeria* 12°13N 5°58E **263** C6
Ankaboa, Tanjona
  Madag. 21°58S 43°20E **272** C1
Ankang *China* 32°40N 109°1E **226** H5
Ankara *Turkey* 39°57N 32°54E **212** C5
Ankara □ *Turkey* 39°55N 32°50E **212** C5
Ankarafantsika △ *Madag.* 16°38S 47°5E **272** B2
Ankaramena *Madag.* 21°57S 46°39E **272** C2
Ankarata *Madag.* 9°20S 47°0E **272** B2
Ankarsrum *Sweden* 57°41N 16°20E **163** G10
Ankasakasa *Madag.* 16°21S 44°52E **272** B1
Ankavandra *Madag.* 18°46S 45°18E **272** B2
Ankazoabo *Madag.* 22°18S 44°31E **272** C1
Ankazobe *Madag.* 18°20S 47°10E **272** B2
Ankeny *U.S.A.* 41°44N 93°36W **310** C3
Ankhialo = Pomorie
  Bulgaria 42°32N 27°41E **203** D11
Ankililoaka *Madag.* 22°58S 43°45E **272** C1
Ankilizato *Madag.* 20°25S 45°1E **272** C2
Anking = Anqing *China* 30°30N 117°3E **229** B11
Ankisabe *Madag.* 19°17S 46°29E **272** B2
Anklam *Germany* 53°51N 13°41E **178** B9
Ankleshwar *India* 21°38N 73°3E **244** D1
Ankober *Ethiopia* 9°35N 39°40E **257** F4
Ankola *India* 14°40N 74°18E **245** G2
Ankoro
  Dem. Rep. of the Congo 6°45S 26°55E **268** D2
Ankororoka *Madag.* 25°30S 45°11E **272** D2
Ankpa *Nigeria* 7°22N 7°38E **263** D6
Anlong *China* 25°2N 105°27E **228** E5
Anlong Veng *Cambodia* 14°14N 104°5E **236** E5
Anlu *China* 31°15N 113°45E **229** B9
Anmyeondo *S. Korea* 36°25N 126°25E **224** D3
Ann *Burma* 19°48N 94°0E **241** F5
Ann *Sweden* 63°19N 12°33E **162** A6
Ann, C. *U.S.A.* 42°38N 70°35W **313** D14
Ann Arbor *U.S.A.* 42°17N 83°45W **311** B13
Anna *Russia* 51°28N 40°23E **190** E5
Anna *Ill., U.S.A.* 37°28N 89°15W **308** G9
Anna *U.S.A.* 40°24N 84°11W **311** D12
Anna Regina *Guyana* 7°10N 58°30W **329** B6
Annaba *Algeria* 36°50N 7°46E **261** A6
Annaba □ *Algeria* 36°12N 7°46E **261** A6
Annaberg-Buchholz
  Germany 50°34N 13°0E **178** E9
Annai *Guyana* 3°57N 59°8W **329** C6
Annaka *Japan* 36°9N 138°54E **223** A10
Annalee ➜ *Ireland* 54°2N 7°24W **166** B4
Annalee Heights *U.S.A.* 38°51N 77°10W **143** B1
Annam = Trung-Phan
  Vietnam 7°0N 109°0E **236** D6
Annamitique, Chaîne
  Asia 17°0N 106°0E **236** D6
Annan *U.K.* 54°59N 3°16W **167** G5
Annan ➜ *U.K.* 54°58N 3°16W **167** G5
Annanberg *Papua N. G.* 4°52S 144°42E **286** C3
Annapolis *U.S.A.* 38°59N 76°30W **309** F11
Annapolis Royal *Canada* 44°44N 65°32W **299** D6
Annapurna *Nepal* 28°34N 83°50E **243** E10
Anne Frankhuis *Amsterdam, Neths.* **112** a1
Annean, L. *Australia* 26°54S 118°14E **279** E2
Anneberg *Sweden* 57°44N 14°49E **163** G8
Annecy *France* 45°55N 6°8E **175** C10
Annecy, Lac d' *France* 45°52N 6°10E **175** C10
Annemasse *France* 46°12N 6°16E **175** C10
Annenfeld = Şämkir
  Azerbaijan 40°50N 46°0E **191** K8
Annenskiy Most *Russia* 6°C°45N 37°10E **188** B9
Annette I. *U.S.A.* 55°9N 131°28W **296** B2
Annette Island ▲ *U.S.A.* 55°9N 131°28W **303** J15
Annigeri *India* 15°26N 75°26E **245** G2
Anniston *U.S.A.* 33°39N 85°50W **316** B4
Annobón *Atl. Oc.* 1°25S 5°36E **255** G4
Annonay *France* 45°15N 4°40E **175** C8
Annotto B. *Jamaica* 18°17N 76°45W **320** a
Annotto Bay *Jamaica* 18°16N 76°47W **320** a
Annsjön *Sweden* 63°19N 12°34E **162** A6
Annville *Germany* 49°12N 77°5E **179** F3
Annweiler *Germany* 49°12N 7°58E **179** F3
Ano Poroia *Greece* 41°17N 23°2E **202** E7
Ano Siros *Greece* 37°29N 24°56E **204** D6
Anogi *Greece* 38°25N 20°40E **207** C2
Anogia *Greece* 35°16N 24°52E **207** D6
Anorotsangana *Madag.* 13°56S 47°55E **272** A2
Anosibe *Madag.* 19°26S 48°13E **272** B2
Anou Mellene *Mali* 17°29N 0°53E **263** B5
Anoumaba *Ivory C.* 6°23N 4°38W **262** D4
Anping *Hebei, China* 38°15N 115°30E **226** E8
Anping *Liaoning, China* 41°5N 123°30E **227** D12
Anpu Gang *China* 21°25N 109°50E **228** G7
Anqing *China* 30°30N 117°3E **229** B11
Anqiu *China* 36°25N 119°10E **227** F10
Anren *China* 26°43N 113°18E **229** D9
Ansager *Denmark* 55°43N 8°45E **163** J2
Ansai *China* 36°50N 109°20E **226** F5
Ansan *S. Korea* 37°21N 126°52E **224** D3
Ansbach *Germany* 49°28N 10°34E **179** F6
Anse-Bertrand *Guadeloupe* 16°28N 61°32W **322** e
Anse Boileau *Seychelles* 4°43S 55°29E **272** f
Anse La Raye *St. Lucia* 13°55N 61°3W **323** m
Anse Royale *Seychelles* 4°44S 55°31E **272** f
Anseba ➜ *Eritrea* 16°0N 38°30E **257** D4
Anseong *S. Korea* 37°0N 127°16E **224** D3
Anserma *Colombia* 5°13N 75°48W **328** B2
Ansfelden *Austria* 48°12N 14°17E **180** C7
Anshan *China* 41°5N 122°58E **227** D12
Anshun *China* 26°18N 105°57E **228** D5
Ansião *Portugal* 3°56N 8°27W **194** F2
Ansley *U.S.A.* 41°18N 99°23W **308** E4
Anshō *Spain* 42°51N 0°48W **196** C5
Ansoáin *Spain* 42°50N 1°37W **196** C2
Anson *U.S.A.* 32°45N 99°54W **314** E5
Anson B. *Australia* 13°20S 130°6E **278** B5
Ansongo *Mali* 15°25N 0°35E **263** B5
Ansonia *U.S.A.* 41°21N 73°5W **313** E11
Ansonia *Ohio, U.S.A.* 40°13N 84°38W **316** A3
Anstruther *U.K.* 56°14N 2°41W **167** E6
Ansudu *Indonesia* 2°11S 139°22E **231** E9
Antabamba *Peru* 14°40S 73°0W **330** C3
Antah *India* 25°2N 76°14E **242** G7
Antakya = Hatay *Turkey* 36°14N 36°10E **250** B7
Antalaha *Madag.* 14°57S 50°20E **272** A3
Antalät *Libya* 3°8N 20°42E **258** B4

Antalya *Turkey* 36°52N 30°45E **250** B1
Antalya □ *Turkey* 36°50N 30°45E **250** B1
Antalya Körfezi *Turkey* 36°15N 31°30E **250** B2
Antambohobe *Madag.* 22°20S 46°47E **272** C2
Antanambao-Manampotsy *Madag.* 19°29S 48°34E **272** B2
Antanambe *Madag.* 16°26S 49°52E **272** B2
Antananarivo *Madag.* 18°55S 47°31E **272** B2
Antananarivo □ *Madag.* 19°0S 47°0E **272** B2
Antanifotsy *Madag.* 19°39S 47°19E **272** B2
Antanimbaribe *Madag.* 21°30S 44°48E **272** C1
Antanimora *Madag.* 24°49S 45°40E **272** C2
Antarctic Pen. *Antarctica* 67°0S 60°0W **151** C18
Antarctica 90°0S 0°0 **151** E3
Antécume Pata *Fr. Guiana* 3°17N 54°4W **329** C7
Antelope *Zimbabwe* 21°2S 28°31E **269** G2
Antep = Gaziantep *Turkey* 37°6N 37°23E **250** A8
Antequera *Paraguay* 24°8S 57°7W **334** A4
Antequera *Spain* 37°5N 4°33W **195** H6
Antero, Mt. *U.S.A.* 38°41N 106°15W **304** G10
Antevamena *Madag.* 21°2S 44°8E **272** C1
Anthony *Fla., U.S.A.* 29°18N 82°7W **317** F7
Anthony *Kans., U.S.A.* 37°9N 98°2W **308** G4
Anthony *N. Mex., U.S.A.* 32°0N 106°36W **305** K10
Anti Atlas *Morocco* 30°0N 8°30W **260** C3
Anti-Lebanon = Sharqi, Al Jabal ash *Lebanon* 33°40N 36°10E **250** E7
Antibes *France* 43°34N 7°6E **175** E11
Antibes, C. d' *France* 43°31N 7°7E **175** E11
Anticosti, Î. d' *Canada* 49°30N 63°0W **299** C7
Antifer, C. d' *France* 49°41N 0°10E **172** C7
Antigo *U.S.A.* 45°9N 89°9W **308** C9
Antigonish *Canada* 45°38N 61°58W **299** C7
Antigua *Canary Is.* 28°24N 14°1W **153** e2
Antigua *Guatemala* 14°34N 90°41W **320** D1
Antigua *W. Indies* 17°0N 61°50W **322** b
Antigua & Barbuda ■ *W. Indies* 17°20N 61°48W **322** b
Antigua Int. ✕ (ANU) *Antigua & B.* 17°8N 61°47W **322** b
Antigues, Pte. d' *Guadeloupe* 16°26N 61°32W **322** e
Antikythira *Greece* 35°52N 23°15E **204** F5
Antilla *Cuba* 20°40N 75°50W **320** B4
Antilles = West Indies *Cent. Amer.* 15°0N 65°0W **321** D7
Antimilos *Greece* 36°47N 24°12E **204** E6
Anting *Taiwan* 23°7N 120°14E **225** C2
Antioch = Hatay *Turkey* 36°14N 36°10E **250** B7
Antioch *U.S.A.* 38°1N 121°48W **306** G5
Antioche, Pertuis d' *France* 46°6N 1°20W **174** B2
Antioquia *Colombia* 6°40N 75°55W **328** B2
Antioquia □ *Colombia* 7°0N 75°30W **328** B2
Antiparos *Greece* 37°0N 25°3E **205** D7
Antipaxi *Greece* 39°9N 20°14E **204** B2
Antipodes Is. *Pac. Oc.* 49°45S 178°40E **288** M9
Antipolo *Phil.* 14°35N 121°10E **232** D3
Antique □ *Phil.* 11°10N 122°5E **233** F4
Antirio *Greece* 38°20N 21°46E **204** C3
Antlers *U.S.A.* 34°14N 95°37W **314** D7
Antoetra *Madag.* 20°46S 47°20E **272** C2
Antofagasta *Chile* 23°50S 70°30W **334** A1
Antofagasta □ *Chile* 24°0S 69°0W **334** A2
Antofagasta de la Sierra *Argentina* 26°5S 67°20W **334** B2
Antofalla *Argentina* 25°30S 68°5W **334** B2
Antofalla, Salar de *Argentina* 25°40S 67°45W **334** B2
Antoine, L. *Grenada* 12°11N 61°36W **323** q
Anton *U.S.A.* 33°49N 102°10W **314** E3
Antongila, Helodrano *Madag.* 15°30S 49°50E **272** B2
Antonibé *Madag.* 15°7S 47°24E **272** B2
Antonina *Brazil* 25°26S 48°42W **335** B6
Antonio B. Won Pat Int. ✕ (GUM) *Guam* 13°29N 144°48E **302** d
Antônio Enes = Angoche *Mozam.* 16°8S 39°55E **269** F4
Antony *France* 48°44N 2°17E **134** B2
Antrain *France* 48°28N 1°30W **172** D5
Antrim *Antrim, U.K.* 54°43N 6°14W **166** B5
Antrim *Ohio, U.S.A.* 40°7N 81°21W **312** F3
Antrim □ *U.K.* 54°56N 6°25W **166** B5
Antrim, Mts. of *U.K.* 55°3N 6°14W **166** A5
Antrim Plateau *Australia* 18°8S 128°20E **278** C4
Antriol *Bonaire* 12°12N 68°16W **322** h
Antrodoco *Italy* 42°25N 13°5E **199** F10
Antropovo *Russia* 58°24N 43°6E **190** A6
Antsakabary *Madag.* 15°3S 48°56E **272** B2
Antsalova *Madag.* 18°40S 44°37E **272** B1
Antsenavolo *Madag.* 21°24S 48°3E **272** C2
Antsiafabositra *Madag.* 17°18S 46°57E **272** B2
Antsirabe *Antananarivo, Madag.* 19°55S 47°2E **272** B2
Antsirabe *Antsiranana, Madag.* 14°0S 49°59E **272** A2
Antsirabe *Mahajanga, Madag.* 15°57S 48°58E **272** B2
Antsiranana *Madag.* 12°25S 49°20E **272** A2
Antsiranana □ *Madag.* 12°16S 49°17E **272** A2
Antsohihy *Madag.* 14°50S 47°59E **272** A2
Antsohimbondrona Seranana *Madag.* 13°7S 48°48E **272** A2
Antu *China* 42°30N 128°20E **227** C15
Antufash *Yemen* 15°42N 42°25E **248** D3
Antung *Taiwan* 23°18N 121°20E **225** C3
Antwerp = Antwerpen *Belgium* 51°13N 4°25E **170** C4
Antwerp *N.Y., U.S.A.* 44°12N 75°37W **313** B9
Antwerp *Ohio, U.S.A.* 41°11N 84°45W **311** C12
Antwerpen *Belgium* 51°13N 4°25E **170** C4
Antwerpen □ *Belgium* 51°15N 4°40E **170** C4
Anukur, C. *Papua N. G.* 6°18S 149°37E **286** D5
Anupgarh *India* 29°10N 73°10E **242** E5
Anuppur *India* 23°6N 81°41E **243** H9
Anuradhapura *Sri Lanka* 8°22N 80°28E **245** K5
Anurrete ⊙ *Australia* 20°50S 135°38E **280** C2
Anveh *Iran* 27°23N 54°11E **247** E7
Anvers = Antwerpen *Belgium* 51°13N 4°25E **170** C4
Anvers I. *Antarctica* 64°30S 63°40W **151** C17
Anvik *U.S.A.* 62°39N 160°13W **303** E7
Anwen *China* 29°4N 120°26E **229** C13
Anxi *Fujian, China* 25°2N 118°12E **229** E12
Anxi *Gansu, China* 40°30N 95°43E **218** C8
Anxian *China* 31°40N 104°25E **228** B5
Anxiang *China* 29°27N 112°11E **229** C9
Anxious B. *Australia* 33°24S 134°45E **281** E1
Anyama *Ivory C.* 5°30N 4°3W **262** D4
Anyang *Henan, China* 36°5N 114°21E **226** F8
Anyang *S. Korea* 37°23N 126°55E **224** D3
Anyer *Indonesia* 6°4S 105°53E **234** D3
Anyi *Jiangxi, China* 28°49N 115°25E **229** C10
Anyi *Shanxi, China* 35°2N 111°2E **226** G6
Anyuan *China* 25°9N 115°21E **229** E10
Anyue *China* 30°9N 105°50E **228** B5
Anza *U.S.A.* 33°35N 116°39W **307** M10
Anze *China* 36°10N 112°12E **226** F7
Anzegloul *Algeria* 26°50N 0°1E **261** C5
Anzhero-Sudzhensk *Russia* 56°10N 86°0E **214** D9
Ánzio *Italy* 41°27N 12°37E **200** A5
Anzoátegui □ *Venezuela* 9°0N 64°30W **329** B5
Ao Makham *Thailand* 7°50N 98°24E **237** a
Ao Phangnga △ *Thailand* 8°10N 98°32E **237** a
Aoba *Vanuatu* 15°25S 167°50E **287** E5
Aoga-Shima *Japan* 32°28N 139°46E **223** E11
Aohan Qi *China* 43°18N 119°43E **227** C10
Aoiz *Spain* 42°46N 1°22W **196** C3
Aoji *N. Korea* 42°31N 130°23E **224** A5
Aola *Solomon Is.* 9°30S 160°30E **287** M11
Aomen = Macau *China* 22°12N 113°33E **229** F9
Aomori *Japan* 40°45N 140°45E **220** D10
Aomori □ *Japan* 40°45N 140°40E **220** D10
AON Center *U.S.A.* **119** b2
tAonach, An = Nenagh *Ireland* 52°52N 8°11W **166** D3
Aonla *India* 28°16N 79°11E **243** E8
Aono-Yama *Japan* 34°28N 131°48E **222** C3
Aorai, Mt. *Tahiti* 17°34S 149°30W **289** e
Aoraki Mount Cook *N.Z.* 43°36S 170°9E **285** D5
Aoral, Phnum *Cambodia* 12°0N 104°15E **237** G5
Aorangi Ra. *N.Z.* 41°28S 175°22E **284** H4
Aore *Vanuatu* 15°35S 167°10E **287** E5
Aoreora *Morocco* 28°51N 10°53W **260** C2
Aosta *Italy* 45°45N 7°20E **198** C4
Aotea Harbour *N.Z.* 38°0S 174°50E **284** E3
Aotearoa = New Zealand ■ *Oceania* 40°0S 176°0E **284** G5
Aoudéras *Niger* 17°45N 8°20E **259** E1
Aouinet Torkoz *Morocco* 28°31N 9°46W **260** C3
Aouk, Bahr ➜ *Africa* 8°51N 18°53E **259** G3
Aouk-Aoukalé ⌂ *C.A.R.* 9°52N 21°25E **264** A4
Aoukar *Mali* 23°50N 2°45W **260** D4
Aoukâr *Mauritania* 17°40N 10°0W **262** B3
Aoulef el Arab *Algeria* 26°55N 1°2E **261** C5
Aousred *W. Sahara* 22°32N 14°17W **260** D2
Aoyama *Tokyo, Japan* **140** b2
Aozou *Chad* 21°45N 17°28E **259** D3
Aozou, Couloir d' *Chad* 22°0N 19°0E **259** D3
Ap Lei Chau *China* 22°14N 114°9E **122** B1
Apá ➜ *S. Amer.* 22°6S 58°2W **334** A4
Apache *U.S.A.* 34°54N 98°22W **314** D5
Apache Junction *U.S.A.* 33°25N 111°33W **305** K8
Apalachee B. *U.S.A.* 30°0N 84°0W **316** E5
Apalachicola *U.S.A.* 29°43N 84°59W **316** F5
Apalachicola ➜ *U.S.A.* 29°43N 84°58W **316** F5
Apalachicola B. *U.S.A.* 29°40N 85°0W **316** F3
Apam *Ghana* 5°19N 0°42W **263** D4
Apamea *Syria* 35°31N 36°28E **250** C7
Apapa *Nigeria* 6°26N 3°21E **124** B2
Apapa Quays *Nigeria* 6°26N 3°23E **124** B2
Apaporis ➜ *Colombia* 1°23S 69°25W **328** D4
Aparados da Serra △ *Brazil* 29°10S 50°8W **335** B5
Aparecida = Bertolinia *Brazil* 7°38S 43°57W **332** C3
Aparecida de Goiânia *Brazil* 16°45S 49°16W **333** E2
Aparecida do Taboado *Brazil* 20°5S 51°5W **333** F1
Aparri *Phil.* 18°22N 121°38E **232** B3
Aparurén *Venezuela* 5°6N 62°8W **329** B5
Apataki *French Polynesia* 15°26S 146°20W **289** f
Apateu *Romania* 46°36N 21°47E **182** D6
Apatin *Serbia* 45°40N 19°0E **182** E4
Apatity *Russia* 67°34N 33°22E **160** C25
Apatou *Fr. Guiana* 5°9N 54°20W **329** B7
Apatula = Finke *Australia* 25°34S 134°35E **280** D1
Apatzingán *Mexico* 19°5N 102°21W **318** D4
Apayao □ *Phil.* 18°10N 121°10E **232** B3
Apelação *Portugal* 38°48N 9°7W **126** A2
Apeldoorn *Neths.* 52°13N 5°57E **170** B5
Apen *Germany* 53°13N 7°48E **178** B3
Apennines = Appennini *Italy* 44°30N 10°0E **198** D7
Apenrade = Aabenraa *Denmark* 55°3N 9°25E **163** J3
Apere ➜ *Bolivia* 13°44S 65°18W **331** C4
Aphrodisias *Turkey* 37°42N 28°46E **205** D10
Api *Nepal* 30°0N 80°57E **218** F5
Apia *Samoa* 13°50S 171°50W **287** V20
Apiacás, Serra dos *Brazil* 9°50S 57°0W **331** B6
Apiaí *Brazil* 24°31S 48°50W **333** F2
Apiaú ➜ *Brazil* 2°39N 61°12W **329** C5
Apiaú, Serra do *Brazil* 2°30N 62°0W **329** C5
Apidiá ➜ *Brazil* 11°39S 61°11W **331** C5
Apies ➜ *S. Africa* 25°15S 28°8E **271** C4
Apinajé *Brazil* 11°31S 48°18W **333** D2
Apiti *N.Z.* 39°58S 175°54E **284** F4
Apizaco *Mexico* 19°25N 98°8W **319** D5
Aplao *Peru* 16°0S 72°40W **330** D3
Apo, Mt. *Phil.* 6°53N 125°14E **233** H5
Apo East Pass. *Phil.* 12°40N 120°40E **232** E3
Apo Reef ⌂ *Phil.* 12°50N 120°50E **232** E3
Apo West Pass. *Phil.* 12°31N 120°22E **232** E3
Apodi *Brazil* 5°39S 37°48W **332** C4
Apoera *Suriname* 5°12N 57°10W **329** B6
Apokalia *Greece* 36°5N 27°48E **206** E11
Apokalia, Ormos *Greece* 36°5N 27°45E **206** E11
Apolda *Germany* 51°2N 11°32E **178** D7
Apollo Bay *Australia* 38°45S 143°40E **282** E5
Apollonia = Sūsah *Libya* 32°52N 21°59E **258** B4
Apollonia *Greece* 36°15N 27°58E **206** E11
Apolo *Bolivia* 14°30S 68°30W **330** C4
Apolonia *Greece* 36°58N 24°43E **204** E6
Apónguao ➜ *Venezuela* 4°48N 61°36W **329** C5
Apopa *El Salv.* 13°48N 89°10W **320** D2
Apopka *U.S.A.* 28°40N 81°31W **317** G8
Apopka, L. *U.S.A.* 28°37N 81°37W **133** A1
Apoquindo *Chile* 33°24S 70°32W **137** B2
Aporé *Brazil* 18°58S 52°1W **331** D7
Aporé ➜ *Brazil* 19°27S 50°57W **333** E1
Aporema *Brazil* 1°14N 50°49W **332** A1
Apostle Is. *U.S.A.* 47°0N 90°40W **308** B8
Apostle Islands ⌂ *U.S.A.* 46°55N 91°0W **308** B8
Apóstoles *Argentina* 28°0S 56°0W **335** B4
Apostolos Andreas, C. *Cyprus* 35°42N 34°35E **207** E10
Apostolovo *Ukraine* 47°39N 33°39E **189** J7
Apoteri *Guyana* 4°2N 58°32W **329** C6
Appalachian Mts. *U.S.A.* 38°0N 80°0W **309** G14
Äppelbo *Sweden* 60°29N 14°1E **162** D8
Appennini *Italy* 44°30N 10°0E **198** D7
Appennino Ligure *Italy* 44°30N 9°0E **198** D6
Appenzell-Ausser Rhoden □ *Switz.* 47°23N 9°23E **179** H5
Appenzell-Inner Rhoden □ *Switz.* 47°20N 9°25E **179** H5
Appiano *Italy* 46°28N 11°15E **199** B8
Apple Hill *Canada* 45°13N 74°46W **313** A10
Apple Valley *U.S.A.* 34°32N 117°14W **307** L9
Appleby-in-Westmorland *U.K.* 54°35N 2°29W **168** C5
Appledore *U.K.* 51°3N 4°13W **169** F3
Appleton *U.S.A.* 44°16N 88°25W **308** C9
Appleton City *U.S.A.* 38°11N 94°2W **310** F6
Appleton Rum Distillery *Jamaica* 18°10N 77°44W **320** a
Appling *U.S.A.* 33°33N 82°19W **316** B7
Approuague *Fr. Guiana* 4°20N 52°0W **329** C7
Approuague ➜ *Fr. Guiana* 4°30N 51°57W **329** C7
Apra Harbor *Guam* 13°26N 144°40E **302** d
Apricena *Italy* 41°47N 15°27E **199** G12
Aprill ➜ *Papua N. G.* 4°18S 142°26E **286** C2
Aprilia *Italy* 41°36N 12°39E **200** A5
Apsheronsk *Russia* 44°28N 39°42E **191** H4
Apsley *Canada* 44°45N 78°6W **312** B6
Apt *France* 43°53N 5°24E **175** E9
Apterkarskiy Ostrov *Russia* 59°57N 30°20E **137** B2
Apuane, Alpi *Italy* 44°7N 10°14E **198** D7
Apuaú *Brazil* 2°25S 60°53W **329** D5
Apucarana *Brazil* 23°55S 51°33W **335** A5
Apulia = Púglia □ *Italy* 41°15N 16°15E **201** A9
Apurashokoru *Palau* 7°16N 134°17E **288** c
Apurauan *Phil.* 9°35N 118°20E **233** G2
Apure □ *Venezuela* 7°10N 68°50W **328** B4
Apure ➜ *Venezuela* 7°37N 66°25W **328** B4
Apurímac □ *Peru* 14°0S 73°0W **330** C3
Apurímac ➜ *Peru* 12°17S 73°56W **330** C3
Apuseni, Munţii *Romania* 46°30N 22°45E **182** D7
Āq Qālā *Iran* 37°10N 54°30E **247** B7
Aqaba = Al 'Aqabah *Jordan* 29°31N 35°0E **251** J6
Aqaba, G. of *Red Sea* 29°0N 34°40E **251** K5
'Aqabah, Khalīj al = Aqaba, G. of *Red Sea* 29°0N 34°40E **251** K5
Aqadyr *Kazakhstan* 48°17N 74°50E **217** C8
Āqchah *Afghan.* 36°56N 66°11E **240** A2
'Aqdā *Iran* 32°26N 53°37E **247** C7
Aqiq *Sudan* 18°14N 38°12E **256** D4
Aqiq, Khalîg *Sudan* 18°20N 38°10E **256** D4
'Aqiq, W. al ➜ *Si. Arabia* 20°16N 41°40E **248** B3
Aqköl *Kazakhstan* 51°59N 70°56E **217** B8
Aqmola = Astana *Kazakhstan* 51°10N 71°30E **217** B8
Aqmola □ *Kazakhstan* 51°30N 70°0E **217** B8
'Aqrah *Iraq* 36°46N 43°45E **213** D10
Aqsay *Kazakhstan* 51°11N 53°0E **187** D9
Aqshatau *Kazakhstan* 47°59N 74°3E **217** C8
Aqsū *Ongtüstik Qazaqstan, Kazakhstan* 42°25N 69°50E **217** D7
Aqsū *Pavlodar, Kazakhstan* 52°2N 76°55E **217** B9
Aqsügek *Kazakhstan* 44°37N 74°30E **217** D8
Aqtaū *Mangghystaū, Kazakhstan* 43°39N 51°12E **187** F9
Aqtaū *Qaraghandy, Kazakhstan* 50°14N 73°3E **217** C8
Aqtöbe *Kazakhstan* 50°17N 57°10E **187** D10
Aqtoghay *Kazakhstan* 46°57N 79°40E **217** C9
Aqua = Sokhumi *Georgia* 43°0N 41°0E **191** J5
Aquarium of the Americas *New Orleans, U.S.A.* **131** b3
Aquidauana *Brazil* 20°30S 55°50W **331** E6
Aquidauana ➜ *Brazil* 19°44S 56°50W **331** D6
Aquila *Mexico* 18°36N 103°30W **318** D4
Aquileia *Italy* 45°46N 13°22E **199** C10
Aquiles Serdán *Mexico* 28°36N 105°53W **318** B3
Aquin *Haiti* 18°16N 73°24W **321** C5
Aquitain, Bassin *France* 44°0N 0°30W **171** D3
Aquitaine □ *France* 44°25N 0°30W **174** D3
Ar Horqin Qi *China* 43°45N 120°0E **227** C11
Ar Kazimiyah *Iraq* 33°22N 44°20E **113** B1
Ar Rafid *Syria* 32°57N 35°52E **250** F6
Ar Raḥḥālīyah *Iraq* 32°44N 43°23E **213** F10
Ar Rāhidah *Yemen* 13°23N 44°19E **248** D4
Ar Ram *West Bank* 31°51N 35°15E **123** A2
Ar Ramādī *Iraq* 33°25N 43°20E **213** F10
Ar Raml *Libya* 26°45N 19°40E **258** C3
Ar Ramthā *Jordan* 32°34N 36°0E **251** F7
Ar Raqqah *Syria* 35°59N 39°8E **213** E8
Ar Raqqah □ *Syria* 36°20N 39°10E **213** D8
Ar Rashidiya = Er Rachidia *Morocco* 31°58N 4°20W **260** B4
Ar Rass *Si. Arabia* 25°50N 43°40E **246** E4
Ar Rastan *Syria* 34°55N 36°43E **250** D7
Ar Rawḍah *Si. Arabia* 21°16N 42°50E **248** B3
Ar Rawḍah *Ṣan'ā', Yemen* 15°26N 44°13E **248** D4
Ar Rawḍah *Shabwah, Yemen* 14°28N 47°17E **248** D4
Ar Rayyan *Qatar* 25°17N 51°25E **247** E6
Ar Rifā'ī *Iraq* 31°50N 46°10E **246** D5
Ar Riyāḍ *Si. Arabia* 24°41N 46°42E **246** E5
Ar Riyāḍ □ *Si. Arabia* 23°0N 45°50E **248** B4
Ar Riyān *Yemen* 14°39N 49°19E **267** B6
Ar Rmās, W. ➜ *Syria* 35°47N 36°50E **250** C7
Ar Ru'ays *Qatar* 26°8N 51°12E **247** E6
Ar Rukhaymīyah *Iraq* 29°22N 45°38E **246** D5
Ar Rumaythah *Iraq* 31°31N 45°12E **246** D5
Ar Ruṣāfah *Syria* 35°45N 38°49E **213** E8
Ar Ruṣayfah *Jordan* 32°1N 36°3E **251** F7
Ar Rustāq *Oman* 23°23N 57°26E **249** B7
Ar Rutbah *Iraq* 33°0N 40°15E **213** F9
Ar Ruwayḍah *Si. Arabia* 23°40N 44°40E **248** B4
Ara *India* 25°35N 84°32E **243** G11
Ara ➜ *Japan* 35°41N 139°50E **140** A4
Ara Goro *Ethiopia* 5°48N 41°18E **257** F5
Ara Tera *Ethiopia* 6°38N 40°57E **257** F5
Arab *U.S.A.* 34°19N 86°30W **315** D11
'Arab, Bahr el ➜ *South Sudan* 9°0N 29°30E **257** F2
Arab, Khalîg el *Egypt* 30°55N 29°0E **256** A2
Arab, Shatt al ➜ *Asia* 29°57N 48°34E **247** D6
'Araba, W. ➜ *Egypt* 28°19N 33°31E **256** J8
'Arabābād *Iran* 33°2N 57°41E **247** C8
'Arabah, W. ➜ *Yemen* 18°5N 51°26E **249** C5
Araban *Turkey* 37°28N 37°44E **212** D7
Arabatskaya Strelka *Ukraine* 45°40N 35°0E **189** K8
Arabba *Italy* 46°30N 11°52E **199** B8
Arabelo *Venezuela* 4°55N 64°13W **329** C5
Arabi *U.S.A.* 31°50N 83°44W **316** D6
Arabia *Asia* 25°0N 45°0E **210** F6
Arabian Basin *Ind. Oc.* 11°30N 65°0E **273** C5
Arabian Desert = Es Sahrâ' Esh Sharqîya *Egypt* 27°30N 32°30E **256** B3
Arabian Gulf = Persian Gulf *Asia* 27°0N 50°0E **247** E6
Arabian Sea *Ind. Oc.* 16°0N 65°0E **238** F9
Arabistan = Khūzestān □ *Iran* 31°0N 49°0E **247** D6
Araç *Turkey* 41°15N 33°21E **212** B5
Aracaju *Brazil* 10°55S 37°4W **332** D4
Aracataca *Colombia* 10°38N 74°9W **328** A3
Aracati *Brazil* 4°30S 37°44W **332** B4
Araçatuba *Brazil* 21°10S 50°30W **335** A5
Araceli *Phil.* 10°33N 119°59E **233** F2
Aracena *Spain* 37°53N 6°38W **195** H4
Aracena, Sierra de *Spain* 37°50N 6°50W **195** H4
Arachova *Greece* 38°28N 22°35E **204** C4
Arachthos ➜ *Greece* 39°20N 21°4E **204** B3
Aracides, C. *Solomon Is.* 8°21S 161°0E **287** M11
Aračinovo *Macedonia* 42°1N 21°34E **202** D5
Araçuaí *Brazil* 16°52S 42°4W **333** E3
Araçuaí ➜ *Brazil* 16°46S 42°2W **333** E3
'Arad *Israel* 31°15N 35°12E **251** G6
Arad *Romania* 46°10N 21°20E **182** D6
Arad □ *Romania* 46°20N 22°0E **182** D6
Arada *Chad* 15°0N 20°20E **259** F4
Arādān *Iran* 35°21N 52°30E **247** C7
Aradhippou *Cyprus* 34°57N 33°36E **207** E12
Arafura Sea *E. Indies* 9°0S 135°0E **288** H5
Aragarças *Brazil* 15°55S 52°15W **331** D7
Aragats *Armenia* 40°30N 44°15E **191** K7
Aragon *U.S.A.* 34°2N 85°3W **316** A4
Aragón □ *Spain* 41°25N 0°40W **196** D4
Aragón ➜ *Spain* 42°13N 1°44W **196** C3
Aragona *Italy* 37°24N 13°37E **200** E6
Aragua □ *Venezuela* 10°0N 67°10W **328** A4
Aragua de Barcelona *Venezuela* 9°28N 64°49W **329** B5
Araguacema *Brazil* 8°50S 49°20W **332** C2
Araguaçu = Paraguaçu Paulista *Brazil* 22°22S 50°35W **335** A5
Araguaçu *Brazil* 12°49S 49°51W **333** D2
Araguaia ➜ *Brazil* 5°21S 48°41W **332** C2
Araguaiana *Brazil* 15°43S 51°51W **331** D7
Araguaína *Brazil* 7°12S 48°12W **332** C2
Araguari *Brazil* 18°38S 48°11W **333** E2
Araguari ➜ *Brazil* 1°15N 49°55W **329** C8
Araguatins *Brazil* 5°38S 48°7W **332** C2
Arahal *Spain* 37°15N 5°33W **195** H5
Arain *India* 26°27N 75°2E **242** F6
Araioses *Brazil* 2°53S 41°55W **332** B3
Arak *Algeria* 25°20N 3°45E **261** C5
Arāk *Iran* 34°0N 49°40E **247** C6
Araka *South Sudan* 4°20N 30°23E **257** G3
Arakan = Rakhine □ *Burma* 19°0N 94°15E **241** F5
Arakan Coast *Burma* 19°0N 94°0E **241** F4
Arakan Yoma *Burma* 20°0N 94°40E **241** F5
Arakawa *Japan* 35°44N 139°48E **140** A3
Arakkonam *India* 13°7N 79°43E **245** H4
Araklı *Turkey* 41°6N 40°2E **213** B9
Araks = Aras, Rūd-e ➜ *Asia* 40°5N 48°29E **213** B13
Araks ➜ *Iran* 39°10N 47°10E **216** E3
Aral *Kazakhstan* 46°41N 61°45E **216** C6
Aral Mangy Qaraqumy *Kazakhstan* 46°50N 63°10E **216** C6
Aral Sea *Asia* 45°0N 58°20E **216** C5
Aral Tengizi = Aral Sea *Asia* 45°0N 58°20E **216** C5
Aralık *Turkey* 39°52N 44°31E **213** C11
Aralkum *Asia* 44°30N 60°35E **216** D6
Aralsk = Aral *Kazakhstan* 46°41N 61°45E **216** C6
Aralskoye More = Aral Sea *Asia* 45°0N 58°20E **216** C5
Aralsor, Ozero = Aralsor Köli *Kazakhstan* 49°5N 48°12E **191** F9
Aralsor Köli *Kazakhstan* 49°5N 48°12E **191** F9
Aramac *Australia* 22°58S 145°14E **280** C4
Aramia ➜ *Papua N. G.* 7°55S 143°22E **286** D2
Aran ➜ *India* 19°55N 78°12E **244** E4
Aran Areh *Ethiopia* 9°2N 43°54E **267** C5
Aran I. = Arranmore *Ireland* 55°0N 8°30W **166** A3
Aran Is. *Ireland* 53°6N 9°38W **166** C2
Aranda de Duero *Spain* 41°39N 3°42W **194** D7
Arandān *Iran* 35°23N 46°55E **246** C5
Aranđelovac *Serbia* 44°18N 20°34E **202** B4
Aranga *N.Z.* 35°44S 173°40E **284** B2
Arani *Bolivia* 17°34S 65°46W **331** D4
Arani *India* 12°43N 79°19E **245** H4
Aranjuez *Spain* 40°1N 3°40W **194** E7
Aranos *Namibia* 24°9S 19°7E **270** B2
Aransas Pass *U.S.A.* 27°55N 97°9W **314** H6
Arany-hegyi-patak ➜ *Hungary* 47°34N 19°4E **117** A2
Aranyaprathet *Thailand* 13°41N 102°30E **236** F4
Arao *Japan* 32°59N 130°25E **222** E2
Araouane *Mali* 18°55N 3°30W **262** B4
Arapahoe *U.S.A.* 40°18N 99°54W **308** E4
Arapari *Brazil* 5°34S 49°15W **332** C2
Arapawa I. *N.Z.* 41°11S 174°17E **285** B9
Arapey Grande ➜ *Uruguay* 30°55S 57°49W **334** C4
Arapgir *Turkey* 39°5N 38°30E **213** C8
Arapiraca *Brazil* 9°45S 36°39W **332** C4
Arapis, Akra *Greece* 40°27N 24°0E **203** F8
Arapongas *Brazil* 23°29S 51°28W **335** A5
Arapuni *N.Z.* 38°4S 175°39E **284** E4
Ar'ar *Si. Arabia* 30°59N 41°2E **246** D4
Araracuara *Colombia* 0°24S 72°17W **328** D3
Araranguá *Brazil* 29°0S 49°30W **335** B6
Araraquara *Brazil* 21°50S 48°0W **333** F2
Araras *Brazil* 22°22S 47°23W **333** F2
Araras, Serra das *Brazil* 25°0S 53°10W **335** B5
Ararat *Armenia* 39°48N 44°50E **213** C11
Ararat *Vic., Australia* 37°16S 142°58E **282** D5
Ararat, Mt. = Ağrı Dağı *Turkey* 39°50N 44°15E **213** C11
Arari *Brazil* 3°28S 44°47W **332** B3
Araria *India* 26°9N 87°33E **243** F12
Araripe, Chapada do *Brazil* 7°20S 40°0W **332** C4
Araripina *Brazil* 7°33S 40°34W **332** C3
Araruama, L. de *Brazil* 22°53S 42°12W **333** F3
Araruna *Brazil* 6°52S 35°44W **332** C4
Aras, Rūd-e ➜ *Asia* 40°5N 48°29E **213** B13
Arataane *Mauritania* 18°24N 8°32W **262** B3
Araticu = Oeiras do Pará *Brazil* 1°58S 49°51W **329** D8
Arauca *Colombia* 7°0N 70°40W **328** B3
Arauca □ *Colombia* 6°40N 71°0W **328** B3
Arauca ➜ *Venezuela* 7°24N 66°35W **328** B4
Arauco *Chile* 37°16S 73°25W **334** D1
Araújos *Brazil* 19°56S 45°14W **333** E2
Arauquita *Colombia* 7°2N 71°25W **328** B3
Araure *Venezuela* 9°34N 69°13W **328** B4
Aravaca *Spain* 40°27N 3°47W **127** B1
Aravalli Range *India* 25°0N 73°30E **242** G5
Arawa *Ethiopia* 9°57N 41°58E **257** F5
Arawale ⌂ *Kenya* 1°24S 40°9E **268** C5
Arawe Is. *Papua N. G.* 6°6S 149°0E **286** D5
Arawhata ➜ *N.Z.* 44°0S 168°40E **285** E3
Araxá *Brazil* 19°35S 46°55W **333** E2
Araya, Pen. de *Venezuela* 10°40N 64°0W **329** A5
Arayat *Phil.* 15°10N 120°46E **232** D3
Arba Gugu *Ethiopia* 8°40N 40°15E **257** F5
Arba Minch *Ethiopia* 6°0N 37°30E **257** F4
Arbat *Iraq* 35°25N 45°35E **213** E11
Arbataash *Iraq* 33°20N 44°19E **113** A1
Arbatax *Italy* 39°56N 9°42E **200** C2
Arbi *Ethiopia* 9°4N 35°7E **257** F4
Arbīl *Iraq* 36°15N 44°5E **213** D11
Arbīl □ *Iraq* 36°20N 44°20E **213** D11
Arboga *Sweden* 59°24N 15°52E **162** E9
Arbois *France* 46°55N 5°46E **173** F12
Arboletes *Colombia* 8°51N 76°26W **328** B2
Arbore *Ethiopia* 5°3N 36°50E **257** F4
Arborëa *Italy* 39°46N 8°35E **200** C1
Arborfield *Canada* 53°6N 103°39W **297** C8
Arborg *Canada* 50°54N 97°13W **297** C9
Arbre du Ténéré *Niger* 17°50N 10°4E **259** E2
Arbroath *U.K.* 56°34N 2°35W **167** E6
Arbuckle *U.S.A.* 39°1N 122°3W **306** F4
Arbus *Italy* 39°30N 8°33E **200** C1
Arc ➜ *France* 45°34N 6°12E **175** C10
Arc de Triomphe *Paris, France* **134** a2
Arc-lès-Gray *France* 47°28N 5°34E **173** E12
Arcachon *France* 44°40N 1°10W **174** D2
Arcachon, Bassin d' *France* 44°42N 1°10W **174** D2
Arcade *U.S.A.* 42°32N 78°25W **312** D6
Arcadia *Calif., U.S.A.* 34°7N 118°1W **136** B3
Arcadia *Fla., U.S.A.* 27°13N 81°52W **317** H8
Arcadia *Ind., U.S.A.* 40°11N 86°1W **311** D10
Arcadia *Iowa, U.S.A.* 42°5N 95°3W **310** B1
Arcadia *La., U.S.A.* 32°33N 92°55W **314** E8
Arcadia *Pa., U.S.A.* 40°47N 78°51W **312** F6
Arcadia *Wis., U.S.A.* 44°15N 91°30W **308** C8
Arcanum *U.S.A.* 39°59N 84°33W **311** E11
Arcata *U.S.A.* 40°52N 124°5W **304** F1
Arcévia *Italy* 43°30N 12°56E **199** E9
Archanes *Greece* 35°16N 25°11E **205** F7
Archangel = Arkhangelsk *Russia* 64°38N 40°36E **186** B7
Archangelos *Preveza, Greece* 39°6N 20°42E **207** A2
Archangelos *Rhodes, Greece* 36°13N 28°7E **206** E12
Archar *Bulgaria* 43°50N 22°54E **202** C6
Archbald *U.S.A.* 41°30N 75°32W **313** E9
Archbold *U.S.A.* 41°31N 84°18W **311** C12
Archena *Spain* 38°9N 1°16W **197** G3
Archenu, J. *Libya* 22°15N 24°45E **259** D4
Archer *U.S.A.* 29°32N 82°32W **317** F7
Archer ➜ *Australia* 13°28S 141°41E **280** A3
Archer B. *Australia* 13°20S 141°30E **280** A3
Archer Bend = Mungkan Kandju △ *Australia* 13°35S 142°52E **280** A3
Archers Post *Kenya* 0°35N 37°35E **268** B4
Arches △ *U.S.A.* 38°45N 109°25W **304** G9
Archidona *Spain* 37°6N 4°22W **195** H6
Archipel-de-Mingan △ *Canada* 50°13N 63°10W **299** B7
Archipiélago Chinijo △ *Canary Is.* 29°20N 13°30W **153** e2
Archipiélago Los Roques △ *Venezuela* 11°50N 66°44W **321** D6
Archives Navy Memorial *Washington, D.C., U.S.A.* **143** b2
Arci, Mte. *Italy* 39°47N 8°45E **200** C1
Arcidosso *Italy* 42°52N 11°33E **199** F8
Arcila = Asilah *Morocco* 35°29N 6°0W **260** A3
Arcipelago de la Maddalena △ *Italy* 41°14N 9°24E **200** A2
Arcipelago Toscano △ *Italy* 42°45N 10°15E **198** F7
Arcis-sur-Aube *France* 48°32N 4°10E **173** D11
Arckaringa Cr. ➜ *Australia* 28°10S 135°22E **281** D2
Arco *Italy* 45°55N 10°53E **198** C7
Arco *Idaho, U.S.A.* 43°38N 113°18W **304** E7
Arco Plaza *Los Angeles, U.S.A.* **127** b1
Arcola *U.S.A.* 39°41N 88°19W **311** E8
Arcoona *Australia* 31°2S 137°1E **282** A2
Arcos de Jalón *Spain* 41°12N 2°16W **196** D2
Arcos de la Frontera *Spain* 36°45N 5°49W **195** J5
Arcos de Valdevez *Portugal* 41°55N 8°22W **194** D2
Arcot *India* 12°53N 79°20E **245** H4
Arcoverde *Brazil* 8°25S 37°4W **332** C4
Arcozelo *Portugal* 40°32N 7°47W **194** E3
Arctic Bay *Canada* 73°1N 85°7W **295** C14
Arctic Mid-Ocean Ridge *Arctic* 87°0N 90°0E **150** A
Arctic Ocean *Arctic* 78°0N 160°0W **150** B18
Arctic Red River = Tsiigehtchic *Canada* 67°15N 134°0W **294** D5
Arctic Village *U.S.A.* 68°8N 145°32W **303** B11
Arctowski *Antarctica* 62°30S 58°0W **151** C18
Arcueil *France* 48°48N 2°19E **134** B2
Arda ➜ *Bulgaria* 41°40N 26°30E **203** E10
Arda ➜ *Italy* 45°3N 10°2E **198** C7
Ardabīl *Iran* 38°15N 48°18E **213** C13
Ardabīl □ *Iran* 38°15N 48°20E **247** B6
Ardahan *Turkey* 41°7N 42°41E **213** B10
Ardahan □ *Turkey* 41°10N 42°50E **213** B10
Ardakān = Sepīdān *Iran* 30°20N 52°5E **247** D7
Ardakān *Iran* 32°19N 53°59E **247** C7
Ardala *Sweden* 58°22N 13°19E **163** F7
Ardales *Spain* 36°53N 4°51W **195** J6
Årdalstangen *Norway* 61°14N 7°43E **164** C4
Ardamata *Sudan* 13°29N 22°28E **259** F4
Ardara *Ireland* 54°46N 8°25W **166** B3
Ardas ➜ *Greece* 41°40N 26°30E **203** E10
Ardèche □ *France* 44°42N 4°16E **175** D8
Ardèche ➜ *France* 44°16N 4°39E **175** D8
Ardee *Ireland* 53°52N 6°33W **166** C5
Arden *Ont., Canada* 44°43N 76°56W **312** B8
Arden *Denmark* 56°46N 9°52E **163** H3
Arden *Calif., U.S.A.* 38°36N 121°33W **306** G5
Arden *Nev., U.S.A.* 36°1N 115°14W **307** J11
Ardenne *Belgium* 49°50N 5°5E **170** E5
Ardennes = Ardenne *Belgium* 49°50N 5°5E **170** E5
Ardennes □ *France* 49°35N 4°40E **173** C11
Ardentes *France* 46°45N 1°50E **173** F8
Arderin *Ireland* 53°2N 7°39W **166** C4
Ardeşen *Turkey* 41°12N 41°2E **213** B9
Ardestān *Iran* 33°20N 52°25E **247** C7
Ardfert *Ireland* 52°20N 9°47W **166** D2
Ardglass *U.K.* 54°16N 5°36W **166** B6
Ardhéa = Aridea *Greece* 40°58N 22°3E **202** F6
Ardila ➜ *Portugal* 38°12N 7°28W **195** G3
Ardino *Bulgaria* 41°34N 25°9E **203** E9
Ardivachar Pt. *U.K.* 57°23N 7°26W **167** D1
Ardlethan *Australia* 34°22S 146°53E **283** C7
Ardmore *Okla., U.S.A.* 34°10N 97°8W **314** D6
Ardmore *Pa., U.S.A.* 40°2N 75°17W **313** F9
Ardnamurchan, Pt. of *U.K.* 56°43N 6°14W **167** E2
Ardnave Pt. *U.K.* 55°53N 6°20W **167** F2
Ardon *Russia* 43°10N 44°18E **191** J7
Ardore *Italy* 38°11N 16°10E **201** D9
Ardres *France* 50°50N 1°59E **173** B8
Ardrossan *S. Austral., Australia* 34°26S 137°53E **282** C2
Ardrossan *N. Ayrs., U.K.* 55°39N 4°49W **167** F4
Ards Pen. *U.K.* 54°33N 5°34W **166** B6
Arduan *Sudan* 19°54N 30°20E **256** D3
Ardud *Romania* 47°37N 22°52E **182** C7
Åre *Sweden* 63°22N 13°15E **162** A7
Arecibo *Puerto Rico* 18°29N 66°43W **321** C6
Areia Branca *Brazil* 5°0S 37°0W **332** C4
Arena, Pt. *U.S.A.* 38°57N 123°44W **306** G3
Arena I. *Phil.* 9°14N 120°45E **233** G3
Arenal *Honduras* 15°21N 86°50W **320** C2
Arenales, Cerro *Chile* 47°5S 73°40W **336** C2
Arenápolis *Brazil* 14°26S 56°49W **331** C6
Arenas = Las Arenas *Spain* 43°17N 4°50W **194** B6
Arenas, Pta. *Venezuela* 10°58N 64°24W **329** a
Arenas de San Pedro *Spain* 40°12N 5°5W **194** E5
Arendal *Norway* 58°28N 8°46E **164** F5
Arendsee *Germany* 52°52N 11°27E **178** C7
Arenillas *Ecuador* 3°33S 80°10W **328** D1
Arensburg = Kuressaare *Estonia* 58°15N 22°30E **188** C2
Arenys de Mar *Spain* 41°35N 2°33E **196** D7
Arenzano *Italy* 44°24N 8°41E **198** D5
Arenzville *U.S.A.* 39°53N 90°22W **310** E6
Areopoli *Greece* 36°40N 22°22E **204** E4
Arequipa *Peru* 16°20S 71°30W **330** D3
Arequipa □ *Peru* 16°0S 72°50W **330** D3
Arere *Brazil* 0°16S 53°52W **329** D7
Arero *Ethiopia* 4°41N 38°50E **257** G4
Arès *France* 44°47N 1°8W **174** D2
Arese *Italy* 45°32N 9°4E **128** A1
Arévalo *Spain* 41°3N 4°43W **194** D6
Arezzo *Italy* 43°25N 11°53E **199** E8
Arga *Turkey* 38°21N 37°59E **246** B3
Arga ➜ *Spain* 42°18N 1°47W **196** C3
Argalasti *Greece* 39°13N 23°13E **204** B5
Argamasilla de Alba *Spain* 39°8N 3°5W **195** F7
Argamasilla de Calatrava *Spain* 38°44N 4°4W **195** G6
Arganda del Rey *Spain* 40°19N 3°26W **194** E7
Arganil *Portugal* 40°13N 8°3W **194** E2
Arganzuela *Spain* 40°23N 3°42W **127** B1
Argao *Phil.* 9°52N 123°36E **233** G4
Argarapa ⊙ *Australia* 22°20S 134°58E **280** C1
Argasi *Greece* 37°45N 20°56E **207** D2
Argedeb *Ethiopia* 6°11N 41°13E **257** F5
Argelès-Gazost *France* 43°0N 0°6W **174** E3
Argelès-sur-Mer *France* 42°34N 3°1E **174** F7
Argens ➜ *France* 43°24N 6°44E **175** E10
Argent-sur-Sauldre *France* 47°33N 2°25E **173** E9
Argenta = North Little Rock *U.S.A.* 34°45N 92°16W **314** D8
Argenta *B.C., Canada* 50°11N 116°56W **296** C5
Argenta *Italy* 44°37N 11°50E **199** D8
Argenta *Ill., U.S.A.* 39°59N 88°49W **311** E8
Argentan *France* 48°45N 0°1W **172** D6
Argentário, Mte. *Italy* 42°24N 11°9E **199** F8
Argentat *France* 45°6N 1°56E **174** C5
Argentera *Italy* 44°12N 7°5E **198** D4
Argenteuil *France* 48°56N 2°15E **134** A2
Argentia *Canada* 47°18N 53°58W **299** C9
Argentiera, C. dell' *Italy* 40°44N 8°8E **200** B1
Argentina ■ *S. Amer.* 35°0S 66°0W **327** G4
Argentine Abyssal Plain *Atl. Oc.* 46°0S 52°0W **152** L6
Argentine Basin *Atl. Oc.* 45°0S 45°0W **152** L7
Argentino, L. *Argentina* 50°10S 73°0W **336** D2
Argenton-Château *France* 46°59N 0°27W **172** F6
Argenton-sur-Creuse *France* 46°36N 1°30E **173** F8
Argeș □ *Romania* 45°0N 24°45E **183** F9
Argeș ➜ *Romania* 44°5N 26°38E **183** F11
Arghandab ➜ *Afghan.* 31°30N 64°15E **242** D1
Argheile *Ethiopia* 5°19N 42°4E **257** F5
Argirades *Greece* 39°27N 19°58E **206** C9
Argiroupoli *Athina, Greece* 37°52N 23°44E **112** B2
Argiroupoli *Kriti, Greece* 35°17N 24°20E **207** E5
Argo *Sudan* 19°28N 30°30E **256** D3
Argolida □ *Greece* 37°38N 22°50E **204** D4
Argolikos Kolpos *Greece* 37°20N 22°52E **204** D4
Argonne *France* 49°10N 5°0E **173** C12
Argos *Greece* 37°40N 22°43E **204** D4
Argos *Ind., U.S.A.* 41°14N 86°15W **311** C10
Argos Orestiko *Greece* 40°27N 21°18E **202** F5
Argostoli *Greece* 38°11N 20°29E **207** C2
Argostoliou, Kolpos *Greece* 38°10N 20°27E **207** C1
Arguedas *Spain* 42°11N 1°36W **196** C3
Argüelles *Madrid, Spain* **127** a1
Arguello, Pt. *U.S.A.* 34°35N 120°39W **307** L6
Arguineguín *Canary Is.* 27°46N 15°41W **153** e1
Argun *Russia* 43°18N 45°52E **191** J7
Argun ➜ *Russia* 53°20N 121°28E **219** A13
Argungu *Nigeria* 12°40N 4°31E **263** C5
Argus Pk. *U.S.A.* 35°52N 117°26W **307** K9
Argyle, L. *Australia* 16°20S 128°40E **278** C4
Argyle Waterfalls *Trin. & Tob.* 11°15N 60°35W **323** s
Argyll & Bute □ *U.K.* 56°13N 5°28W **167** E3
Arhavi *Turkey* 41°21N 41°18E **213** B9
Århus = Aarhus *Denmark* 56°8N 10°11E **163** H4
Ari Atoll *Maldives* 3°53N 72°50E **272** d
Aria *N.Z.* 38°33S 175°0E **284** E4
Ariadnoye *Russia* 45°8N 134°25E **220** B7
Ariamsvlei *Namibia* 28°9S 19°51E **270** C2
Ariana *Tunisia* 36°52N 10°12E **258** A2
Ariana □ *Tunisia* 36°50N 9°52E **261** A6
Ariano Irpino *Italy* 41°9N 15°5E **201** A8
Ariari ➜ *Colombia* 2°35N 72°47W **328** C3
Aribinda *Burkina Faso* 14°17N 0°52W **263** C4
Arica *Chile* 18°32S 70°20W **330** D3
Arica *Colombia* 2°0S 71°50W **328** D3
Arica y Parinacota □ *Chile* 17°40S 69°50W **330** D4
Arico *Canary Is.* 28°9N 16°29W **153** e1
Arid, C. *Australia* 34°1S 123°10E **279** F3
Arida *Japan* 34°5N 135°8E **223** C7
Aridal *W. Sahara* 25°59N 13°54W **260** C2
Aride *Seychelles* 4°13S 55°40E **272** c
Aridea *Greece* 40°58N 22°3E **202** F6
Ariège □ *France* 42°56N 1°30E **174** F5
Ariège ➜ *France* 43°30N 1°25E **174** E5
Arieș ➜ *Romania* 46°24N 23°20E **183** D8
Arigat el Fersig *Algeria* 27°35N 2°7W **261** C4
Arihā *Israel* 31°51N 35°27E **256** A4
Arīḥā *Syria* 35°49N 36°35E **250** C7
Arikok △ *Aruba* 12°31N 69°56W **322** f
Arila, Akra *Greece* 39°43N 19°39E **206** B9
Arilje *Serbia* 43°44N 20°7E **202** C4
Arima *Kanagawa, Japan* 35°33N 139°32E **140** B2
Arima *Trin. & Tob.* 10°38N 61°17W **323** t
Arima ➜ *Trin. & Tob.* 10°35N 61°16W **323** t
Aringay *Phil.* 16°26N 120°21E **232** C3
Arinos ➜ *Brazil* 10°25S 58°20W **331** C6
Ario de Rosales *Mexico* 19°12N 101°43W **318** D4
Ariogala *Lithuania* 55°16N 23°28E **184** C10
Arios Pagos *Athens, Greece* **112** c1
Aripo ➜ *Trin. & Tob.* 10°35N 61°14W **323** t
Aripo, Mt. *Trin. & Tob.* 10°45N 61°15W **323** t
Aripo Caves *Trin. & Tob.* 10°43N 61°14W **323** t
Aripuanã *Brazil* 9°25S 60°30W **331** B5
Aripuanã ➜ *Brazil* 5°7S 60°25W **331** B5
Ariquemes *Brazil* 9°55S 63°6W **331** B5
Arisaig *U.K.* 56°55N 5°51W **167** E3
Arish, W. el ➜ *Egypt* 31°9N 33°49E **256** A3
Arissa *Ethiopia* 11°10N 41°35E **257** E5
Aristazabal I. *Canada* 52°40N 129°10W **296** C3
Arita *Japan* 33°11N 129°54E **222** D1
Aritao *Phil.* 16°18N 121°2E **232** C3
Ariton *U.S.A.* 31°36N 85°43W **316** D4
Arivonimamo *Madag.* 19°1S 47°11E **272** B2
Ariyalur *India* 11°8N 79°8E **245** J4
Ariza *Spain* 41°19N 2°3W **196** D2
Arizaro, Salar de *Argentina* 24°40S 67°50W **334** A2
Arizona *Argentina* 35°45S 65°25W **334** D2
Arizona □ *U.S.A.* 34°0N 112°0W **305** J8
Arizpe *Mexico* 30°20N 110°10W **318** A2
'Arjah *Si. Arabia* 24°43N 44°17E **246** E5
Årjäng *Sweden* 59°24N 12°8E **162** E6
Arjeplog *Sweden* 66°3N 17°54E **160** C17
Arjeplouvve = Arjeplog *Sweden* 66°3N 17°54E **160** C17
Arjona *Colombia* 10°14N 75°22W **328** A2
Arjona *Spain* 37°56N 4°4W **195** H6
Arjuna *Indonesia* 7°49S 112°34E **235** D4
Arka *Russia* 60°15N 142°0E **215** C15
Arkadak *Russia* 51°58N 43°30E **190** E6
Arkadelphia *U.S.A.* 34°7N 93°4W **314** D8
Arkadia □ *Greece* 37°30N 22°20E **204** D4
Arkaig, L. *U.K.* 56°59N 5°10W **167** E3
Arkalgud *India* 12°46N 76°3E **245** H3
Arkalyk = Arqalyk *Kazakhstan* 50°13N 66°50E **217** B7
Arkansas □ *U.S.A.* 35°0N 92°30W **314** D8
Arkansas ➜ *U.S.A.* 33°47N 91°4W **314** E9
Arkansas City *U.S.A.* 37°4N 97°2W **308** G5
Arkaroola *Australia* 30°20S 139°22E **281** E2
Arkavāz *Iran* 33°22N 46°35E **213** F12
Arkhangelsk *Russia* 64°38N 40°36E **186** B7
Arkhangelskoye *Russia* 51°32N 40°58E **190** E5
Arki *Greece* 37°24N 26°44E **205** D8
Arki *India* 31°9N 76°58E **242** D7
Arkiko *Eritrea* 15°33N 39°33E **257** D4
Arklow *Ireland* 52°48N 6°10W **166** D5
Arkona, Kap *Germany* 54°42N 13°26E **178** A9
Arkösund *Sweden* 58°29N 16°56E **163** F10
Arkoudi *Greece* 38°33N 20°43E **207** B2
Arkport *U.S.A.* 42°24N 77°42W **312** D7
Arkticheskiy, Mys *Russia* 81°10N 95°0E **215** A10
Arkul *Russia* 57°17N 50°3E **190** B10
Arkville *U.S.A.* 42°9N 74°37W **313** D10
Ärla *Sweden* 59°17N 16°40E **162** E10
Arlanda, Stockholm ✕ (ARN) *Sweden* 59°41N 17°56E **139** A1
Arlanza ➜ *Spain* 42°6N 4°9W **194** C6
Arlanzón ➜ *Spain* 42°3N 4°17W **194** C6
Arlbergpass *Austria* 47°9N 10°12E **180** D3
Arlbergtunnel *Austria* 47°9N 10°12E **180** D3
Arles *France* 43°41N 4°40E **175** E8
Arli *Burkina Faso* 11°35N 1°28E **263** C5
Arli △ *Burkina Faso* 11°35N 1°28E **263** C5
Arlington *Free State, S. Africa* 28°1S 27°53E **271** C4

Arlington Ga., U.S.A. 31°26N 84°44W **316** D5
Arlington Mass., U.S.A. 42°24N 71°10W **116** A1
Arlington N.Y., U.S.A. 41°42N 73°54W **313** E11
Arlington Oreg., U.S.A. 45°43N 120°12W **304** D3
Arlington S. Dak., U.S.A. 44°22N 97°8W **308** C5
Arlington Tex., U.S.A. 32°44N 97°6W **316** E6
Arlington Va., U.S.A. 38°53N 77°7W **143** B2
Arlington Vt., U.S.A. 43°5N 73°9W **313** C11
Arlington Wash., U.S.A. 48°12N 122°8W **306** B4
Arlington Heights Ill., U.S.A. 42°5N 87°59W **311** B9
Arlington Heights Mass., U.S.A. 42°25N 71°10W **116** A1
Arlington Nat. Cemetery U.S.A. 38°52N 77°4W **143** B2
Arlon Belgium 49°42N 5°49E **170** E5
Arlparra Australia 22°11S 134°30E **280** C1
Arltunga Australia 23°26S 134°41E **280** C1
Armação Brazil 22°52S 43°6W **135** B2
Armadale Vic., Australia 37°51S 145°0E **128** B2
Armadale W. Austral., Australia 32°9S 116°0E **279** F2
Armagh U.K. 54°21N 6°39W **166** B5
Armagh □ U.K. 54°18N 6°37W **166** B5
Armagnac France 43°50N 0°10E **174** E4
Armançon → France 47°59N 3°30E **173** E10
Armando Bermúdez △ Dom. Rep. 19°3N 71°0W **321** C5
Armant Egypt 25°37N 32°32E **256** B3
Armatree Australia 31°26S 148°28E **283** A4
Armavir Russia 45°2N 41°7E **191** H5
Armenia Colombia 4°35N 75°45W **328** C2
Armenia ■ Asia 40°20N 45°0E **191** K7
Armenian Quarter Jerusalem **182** E7
Armeniş Romania 45°13N 22°17E **182** E7
Armenistís, Ákra Greece 36°8N 27°42E **206** E11
Armenteros Spain 40°54N 5°23W **194** B3
Armentières France 50°40N 2°50E **173** B9
Armero Colombia 4°58N 74°54W **328** C3
Armidale Australia 30°30S 151°40E **283** A9
Armilla Spain 37°9N 3°37W **195** H7
Armori India 20°28N 79°59E **244** D4
Armorique △ France 48°22N 3°50W **172** D2
Armour U.S.A. 43°19N 98°21W **308** D4
Armour Heights Canada 43°45N 79°25W **141** A2
Armstrong B.C., Canada 50°25N 119°10W **296** D5
Armstrong Ont., Canada 50°18N 89°4W **298** C2
Armur India 18°48N 78°16E **244** E4
Armutlu Bursa, Turkey 40°31N 28°50E **203** F12
Armutlu İzmir, Turkey 38°24N 27°34E **205** C9
Arnarfjörður Iceland 65°48N 23°40W **155** D2
Arnaud → Canada 59°59N 69°46W **295** F18
Árnauti, C. Cyprus 35°6N 32°17E **207** D8
Arnay-le-Duc France 47°10N 4°27E **173** E11
Arncliffe Australia 33°56S 151°8E **139** B1
Arnedillo Spain 42°13N 2°14W **196** D2
Arnedo Spain 42°12N 2°5W **196** C2
Árnes Iceland 66°1N 21°31W **155** A5
Ârnes Akershus, Norway 60°7N 11°28E **164** D8
Árnessýsla Iceland 64°15N 20°30W **155** C6
Arnett U.S.A. 36°8N 99°46W **314** C5
Arnhem Neths. 51°58N 5°55E **170** C5
Arnhem, C. Australia 12°20S 137°30E **280** A2
Arnhem B. Australia 12°20S 136°10E **280** A2
Arnhem Land Australia 13°10S 134°30E **280** A1
Arnhem Land △ N. Terr., Australia 12°50S 134°50E **280** A1
Arnhem Land △ N. Terr., Australia 12°50S 134°50E **280** A1
Arníssa Greece 40°47N 21°49E **202** F5
Arno → Italy 43°41N 10°17E **198** E7
Arno Bay Australia 33°54S 136°34E **282** D2
Arnold Notts., U.K. 53°1N 1°7W **168** D6
Arnold Calif., U.S.A. 38°15N 120°21W **306** G6
Arnold Mo., U.S.A. 38°26N 90°23W **310** F6
Arnold Arboretum U.S.A. 42°18N 71°8W **116** B3
Arnoldstein Austria 46°33N 13°43E **180** E6
Arnon → France 47°13N 2°1E **173** E9
Arnos Vale Trin. & Tob. 11°13N 60°45W **323** s
Arnot Canada 55°56N 96°41W **297** B9
Arnoya Norway 70°9N 20°40E **160** A19
Arnprior Canada 45°26N 76°21W **313** A8
Arnsberg Germany 51°24N 8°5E **178** D4
Arnsberger Wald △ Germany 51°25N 8°20E **178** D4
Arnstadt Germany 50°50N 10°56E **178** E6
Arnswalde = Choszczno Poland 53°7N 15°25E **185** E2
Aro → Venezuela 8°1N 64°11W **329** B5
Aroa, Pte. Moorea 17°28S 149°46W **289** e
Aroab Namibia 26°41S 19°39E **270** C2
Aroania Óros Greece 37°56N 22°12E **204** D4
Aroche Spain 37°56N 6°57W **195** H4
Arochuku Nigeria 5°21N 7°56E **263** D6
Aroeiras Brazil 7°31S 35°41W **332** C4
Arolsen Germany 51°23N 9°2E **178** D5
Aron India 25°57N 77°56E **242** G6
Aron → France 46°50N 3°28E **173** F10
Arona Canary Is. 28°6N 16°40W **153** d
Arona Italy 45°46N 8°34E **198** C5
Arorae Kiribati 2°38S 176°49E **277** A14
Arorangi Cook Is. 21°13S 159°49W **289** h
Aroroy Phil. 12°31N 123°24E **232** E4
Aros → Mexico 29°9N 107°57W **318** B3
Arousa, Ría de → Spain 42°28N 8°57W **194** C2
Åroysund Norway 59°10N 10°27E **164** E7
Arpa → Asia 39°28N 44°56E **213** C11
Arpaçay Turkey 40°50N 43°19E **213** D10
Árpádföld Hungary 47°32N 19°8E **117** A3
Arpajon France 48°36N 2°15E **173** D9
Arpajon-sur-Cère France 44°53N 2°28E **174** D6
Arpaşu de Jos Romania 45°47N 24°37E **183** E9
Arqalyk Kazakhstan 50°13N 66°50E **217** B7
Arque Bolivia 17°48S 66°32W **334** D3
Arrabury Australia 26°45S 141°0E **283** A3
Arrah = Ara India 25°35N 84°32E **243** G11
Arrah Ivory C. 6°40N 3°58W **262** D4
Arraias Brazil 12°56S 46°57W **333** D2
Arraias → Mato Grosso, Brazil 11°10S 53°35W **331** C7
Arraias → Pará, Brazil 7°30S 49°20W **332** C2
Arraiján Panama 8°56N 79°36W **320** c
Arraiolos Portugal 38°44N 7°59W **195** G3
Arran U.K. 55°34N 5°12W **167** F3
Arranmore Ireland 55°0N 8°30W **166** A3
Arras France 50°17N 2°46E **173** B9
Arrasate Spain 43°3N 2°30W **196** B2
Arrats → France 44°6N 0°52E **174** E4
Arreau France 42°54N 0°22E **174** F4
Arrecife Canary Is. 28°57N 13°37W **153** e2
Arrecifes Argentina 34°6S 60°9W **334** C3
Arrée, Mts. d' France 48°26N 3°55W **172** D3
Arrentela Portugal 38°37N 9°6W **196** D1
Arreso Denmark 55°58N 12°6E **163** J6
Arriaga Mexico 16°14N 93°54W **319** D6
Arribes del Duero △ Spain 41°11N 6°39W **194** D4
Arrilalah Australia 23°43S 143°54E **280** C3
Arrino Australia 29°30S 115°40E **279** E2
Arrochar Spain 43°20N 4°6W **196** B1
Arrojado → Brazil 13°24S 44°20W **333** D2

Arroyo de la Luz Spain 39°30N 6°38W **195** F4
Arroyo del Puerco = Arroyo de la Luz Spain 39°30N 6°38W **195** F4
Arroyo Grande U.S.A. 35°7N 120°35W **307** K6
Arroyo Seco Park U.S.A. 34°6N 118°11W **126** B3
Ars Iran 37°9N 47°46E **246** B5
Ars-sur-Moselle France 49°5N 6°4E **173** C13
Arsenale Venice, Italy **142** b4
Arsenault L. Canada 55°6N 108°32W **297** B7
Arseno Russia 44°10N 133°15E **220** B6
Arsiero Italy 45°48N 11°21E **199** C8
Arsikere India 13°15N 76°15E **245** H3
Arsin Turkey 41°8N 39°55E **213** D8
Arsk Russia 56°10N 49°50E **190** B9
Árslanköy Turkey 37°0N 34°17E **250** B5
Arta Greece 39°8N 21°2E **204** B3
Artà Spain 39°41N 3°21E **206** B10
Arta → Greece 39°15N 21°5E **204** B3
Artà, Coves d' Spain 39°40N 3°24E **206** B4
Artane Ireland 53°22N 6°12W **120** A2
Artashat Armenia 37°41N 35°11E **123** B2
Arteaga Mexico 18°28N 102°25W **318** D4
Arteche Phil. 12°17N 125°22E **232** E5
Arteijo = Arteixo Spain 43°19N 8°29W **194** B2
Arteixo Spain 43°19N 8°29W **194** B2
Artem Azerbaijan 40°28N 50°20E **191** K10
Artem Russia 43°22N 132°13E **220** C6
Artemovsk Sib., Russia 54°45N 93°35E **215** D10
Artemovsk Ukraine 48°35N 38°0E **189** H9
Artemovskiy Russia 47°45N 40°16E **191** G5
Artenay France 48°5N 1°50E **173** D8
Artern Germany 51°22N 11°18E **178** D7
Artesa de Segre Spain 41°54N 1°3E **196** D6
Artesia = Mosomane Botswana 24°2S 26°19E **270** B4
Artesia Italy 32°51N 104°24W **305** K11
Arthington Liberia 6°35N 10°45W **262** D2
Arthur Ont., Canada 43°50N 80°32W **312** C4
Arthur Ill., U.S.A. 39°43N 88°28W **311** E8
Arthur → Australia 41°2S 144°40E **281** G3
Arthur Cr. → Australia 22°30S 136°25E **280** C2
Arthur Pt. Australia 22°7S 150°3E **280** C5
Arthur River Australia 33°20S 117°2E **279** F2
Arthur's Pass N.Z. 42°54S 171°35E **285** C6
Arthur's Pass △ N.Z. 42°53S 171°42E **285** C6
Arthur's Seat U.K. 55°56N 3°9W **121** B3
Arthur's Town Bahamas 24°38N 75°42W **321** B4
Artigas = Rio Branco Uruguay 32°40S 53°40W **335** C5
Artigas Antarctica 62°30S 58°0W **151** C18
Artigas Uruguay 30°20S 56°30W **334** C4
Artik Armenia 40°38N 43°58E **191** K6
Artillery L. Canada 63°9N 107°52W **297** A7
Artois France 50°20N 2°30E **173** B9
Artotina Greece 38°42N 22°2E **204** C4
Artova Turkey 40°5N 36°28E **212** B7
Artrutx, C. de Spain 39°55N 3°49E **206** B4
Arts, Place des Montréal, Canada **130** b2
Arts Bogd Uul Mongolia 44°40N 102°20E **226** B2
Artsyz Ukraine 46°4N 29°26E **183** D14
Artux China 39°40N 76°10E **217** E9
Artux Turkey 41°14N 41°44E **213** D9
Artvin Turkey 41°10N 41°50E **213** D9
Artyk Russia 64°12N 145°25E **215** C15
Artyom = Artyom Azerbaijan 40°28N 50°20E **191** K10
Aru, Kepulauan Indonesia 6°0S 134°30E **231** F8
Aru Is. = Aru, Kepulauan Indonesia 6°0S 134°30E **231** F8
Arua Uganda 3°1N 30°58E **268** B3
Aruanã Brazil 14°54S 51°10W **333** D1
Aruba ☑ W. Indies 12°30N 70°0W **322** f
Arudy France 43°7N 0°28W **174** E3
Arué Tahiti 17°31S 149°30W **289** e
Aruma Brazil 4°44S 62°8W **329** D5
Arumpo Australia 33°48S 142°55E **282** B5
Arun → Nepal 26°55N 87°10E **243** F12
Arun → W. Susx., U.K. 50°49N 0°33W **169** G7
Arunachal Pradesh □ India 28°0N 95°0E **241** B5
Aruppukkottai India 9°31N 78°8E **245** K4
Arusha Tanzania 3°20S 36°40E **268** C4
Arusha □ Tanzania 3°20S 36°30E **268** C4
Arusha △ Tanzania 3°16S 36°47E **268** C4
Arusha Chini Tanzania 3°32S 37°20E **268** C4
Arut → Indonesia 2°42S 111°34E **235** E4
Aruvi → Sri Lanka 8°48N 79°53E **245** K4
Aruwimi → Dem. Rep. of the Congo 1°13N 23°36E **264** D4
Arvada Colo., U.S.A. 39°48N 105°5W **304** G11
Arvada Wyo., U.S.A. 44°39N 106°8W **304** D10
Arvakalu Sri Lanka 8°20N 79°58E **245** K4
Arvayheer Mongolia 46°15N 102°48E **218** B9
Arve → France 46°11N 6°8E **173** F13
Arvi Kriti, Greece 34°59N 25°28E **207** F6
Arvi India 20°59N 78°16E **244** D4
Arviat Canada 61°6N 93°59W **297** A10
Arvidsjaur Sweden 65°35N 19°10E **160** D18
Arvika Sweden 59°40N 12°36E **162** E6
Arvin U.S.A. 35°12N 118°50W **307** K8
Arwad Syria 34°51N 35°51E **250** D6
Arwal India 25°15N 84°41E **243** G11
Arxan China 47°11N 119°57E **219** B12
Áryd Sweden 56°49N 14°59E **163** H8
Arys Kazakhstan 42°26N 68°48E **217** D7
Arzachena Italy 41°5N 9°23E **200** A2
Arzanah U.A.E. 24°47N 52°34E **247** E7
Arzew Algeria 35°50N 0°23W **261** A4
Arzgir Russia 45°18N 44°23E **191** H7
Arzignano Italy 45°31N 11°20E **199** C8
Arzúa Spain 42°56N 8°9W **194** C2
Aš Czech Rep. 50°13N 12°12E **180** A5
As Sweden 63°15N 14°34E **162** A8
As Pontes de García Rodríguez Spain 43°27N 7°50W **194** B3
As Sa'an Syria 35°16N 37°22E **250** C8
Aş Şafā Syria 33°10N 37°0E **250** B8
Aş Şaffānīyah Si. Arabia 27°55N 48°50E **247** E6
As Safīrah Syria 36°5N 37°21E **250** B8
Aş Şahm Oman 24°10N 56°53E **247** E8
Aş Sājir Si. Arabia 25°11N 44°36E **246** E5
As Salamīyah Syria 35°1N 37°2E **250** C8
Aş Şalif Yemen 15°18N 42°41E **248** D3
As Salmān Iraq 30°30N 44°32E **246** D5
As Salt Jordan 32°2N 35°43E **251** F6
As Sal'w'a Qatar 24°23N 50°50E **247** E6
As Samāwah Iraq 31°15N 45°15E **246** D5
As Sanamayn Syria 33°3N 36°10E **251** B5
As Sawādah Si. Arabia 22°24N 44°28E **248** B4
Aş Şawrah Yemen 14°5N 45°48E **248** E4
As Sayl al Kabīr Si. Arabia 21°41N 40°12E **246** E3
As Sib Oman 23°41N 58°11E **247** F8
As Sohar = Şuḩār Oman 24°20N 56°40E **247** E8
As Sukhnah Syria 34°52N 38°52E **246** C3
As Sulaymānīyah Iraq 35°35N 45°29E **246** C5
As Sulaymī Si. Arabia 26°17N 41°21E **246** E4
As Sulaymīyah □ Iraq 35°50N 45°30E **213** E11

As Sulaymī Si. Arabia 26°17N 41°21E **246** E4
As Sulayyil Si. Arabia 20°27N 45°34E **248** B4
As Sulṭān Libya 31°4N 17°8E **258** B3
As Summān Si. Arabia 25°0N 47°0E **246** E5
Aş Şurrah Yemen 13°57N 46°14E **248** D4
Aş Şuwar Syria 35°30N 40°38E **213** E9
As Suwaydā' Syria 32°40N 36°30E **250** F7
As Suwaydā' □ Syria 32°45N 36°45E **250** F7
As Suwayq Oman 23°51N 57°26E **247** F8
Aş Şuwayrah Iraq 32°55N 45°0E **213** F11
Aş Şuwayrah Iraq 32°55N 45°0E **213** F11
Asab Namibia 25°30S 18°0E **270** C2
Asaba Nigeria 6°12N 6°38E **263** D6
Asad, Buḩayrat al Syria 36°0N 38°15E **213** D8
Asadābād Iran 34°47N 48°7E **213** E13
Asafo Ghana 6°20N 2°40W **262** D4
Asaga Str. Amer. Samoa 14°10S 169°37W **302** g
Asagaya Japan 35°41N 139°38E **140** A2
Asahi Chiba, Japan 35°43N 140°39E **223** B12
Asahi Ōsaka, Japan 34°43N 135°31E **133** A2
Asahi-Gawa → Japan 34°36N 133°58E **222** C5
Asahigawa = Asahikawa Japan 43°46N 142°22E **220** C11
Asahikawa Japan 43°46N 142°22E **220** C11
Asakusa Japan 35°42N 139°47E **140** A3
Asakusabashi Tokyo, Japan **140** d5
Asale, L. Ethiopia 14°0N 40°20E **257** F5
Asaluyeh Iran 27°29N 52°37E **247** E7
Asamankese Ghana 5°50N 0°40W **263** D4
Asan S. Korea 36°48N 127°1E **224** D3
Asan → India 26°37N 78°24E **243** F8
Asansol India 23°40N 87°1E **243** H12
Āsarna Sweden 62°39N 14°22E **162** B7
Asati India 22°28N 88°15E **124** C1
Asbe Teferi Ethiopia 9°4N 40°49E **257** F5
Asbesberg S. Africa 29°0S 23°0E **270** C3
Asbestos Canada 45°47N 71°58W **299** C5
Asbury Park U.S.A. 40°13N 74°1W **313** F10
Åsby Sweden 57°14N 12°18E **163** G6
Ascea Italy 40°8N 15°11E **201** B8
Ascensión Mexico 31°6N 107°59W **318** A3
Ascensión, B. de la Mexico 19°40N 87°30W **319** D7
Ascension I. Atl. Oc. 7°57S 14°23W **153** g
Aschach an der Donau Austria 48°22N 14°2E **180** C7
Aschaffenburg Germany 49°58N 9°6E **179** F5
Aschendorf Germany 53°3N 7°19E **178** B3
Aschersleben Germany 51°45N 11°29E **178** D7
Aschheim Germany 48°10N 11°42E **131** A3
Asciano Italy 43°14N 11°33E **199** E8
Ascó Spain 41°11N 0°32E **196** D5
Áscoli Piceno Italy 42°51N 13°34E **199** F10
Áscoli Satriano Italy 41°11N 15°32E **201** A8
Ascope Peru 7°46S 79°8W **330** B2
Ascot Vale Australia 37°46S 144°53E **128** A1
Ascotán Chile 21°45S 68°17W **334** A2
Ascuncion I. Atl. Oc. 7°35N 125°45E **233** H5
Aseb Eritrea 13°0N 42°40E **257** E5
Asedjrad Algeria 24°51N 1°29E **261** D5
Aseki Papua N. G. 7°21S 146°12E **286** D4
Asela Ethiopia 8°0N 39°0E **257** F4
Asenovgrad Bulgaria 42°1N 24°51E **203** D8
Aseral Norway 58°37N 7°25E **163** G3
Asfeld France 49°27N 4°5E **173** C11
Asfūn el Matā'na Egypt 25°26N 32°30E **256** B3
Aşgabat Turkmenistan 37°58N 58°24E **247** B8
Åsgårdhamna Norway 59°22N 10°27E **164** E7
Asgata Cyprus 34°46N 33°15E **207** E9
Ash Fork U.S.A. 35°13N 112°29W **305** J7
Ash Grove U.S.A. 37°19N 93°35W **308** G7
Ash Shabakah Iraq 30°49N 43°39E **246** D4
Ash Shafa Si. Arabia 21°29N 39°49E **248** B2
Ash Shamāl □ Lebanon 34°25N 36°0E **250** D7
Ash Shāmīyah Iraq 31°55N 44°35E **213** F11
Ash Sha'rā' Si. Arabia 24°16N 44°11E **248** A4
Ash Shāriqah U.A.E. 25°23N 55°26E **247** E7
Ash Shariqah □ Si. Arabia 25°15N 55°26E **247** E7
Ash Sharmah Si. Arabia 28°1N 35°16E **251** K6
Ash Sharqāṭ Iraq 35°27N 43°16E **213** E10
Ash Sharqīyah □ Oman 22°30N 59°0E **249** B7
Ash Sharqīyah □ Si. Arabia 23°0N 50°0E **249** B6
Ash Shawbak Jordan 30°30N 35°35E **251** G6
Ash Shawmarah Si. Arabia 25°43N 45°44E **246** E5
Ash Shaykh Ḩumayd Si. Arabia 28°6N 34°33E **251** K5
Ash Shifā' Si. Arabia 28°6N 34°33E **251** K5
Ash Shiḩr Yemen 14°45N 49°36E **249** D5
Ash Shināfīyah Iraq 31°35N 44°39E **246** D5
Ash Shu'bah Si. Arabia 28°54N 44°44E **246** D5
Ash Shumlūl Si. Arabia 26°31N 47°20E **246** E5
Ash Shuqayq Si. Arabia 17°44N 42°1E **248** D3
Ash Shūr'ā Iraq 35°58N 43°13E **246** C4
Ash Shurayf Si. Arabia 25°43N 45°47E **246** E5
Ash Shuwayrif Libya 29°59N 14°16E **258** C2
Asha Russia 55°0N 57°16E **186** D10
Ashanti □ Ghana 7°30N 1°30W **262** D4
Ashbourne U.K. 53°2N 1°43W **168** D6
Ashbridge's Bay Park Canada 43°40N 79°18W **141** B3
Ashburn Ga., U.S.A. 31°43N 83°39W **316** D6
Ashburn Ill., U.S.A. 41°45N 87°43W **119** C2
Ashburton Vic., Australia 37°51S 145°4E **128** B2
Ashburton N.Z. 43°53S 171°48E **285** D6
Ashburton → Australia 21°40S 114°56E **278** D1
Ashburton, North Branch → N.Z. 43°54S 171°44E **285** D6
Ashburton, South Branch → N.Z. 43°54S 171°44E **285** D6
Ashcroft Canada 50°40N 121°20W **296** C4
Ashdod Israel 31°49N 34°35E **251** G5
Ashdown U.S.A. 33°40N 94°8W **314** E7
Asheboro U.S.A. 35°43N 79°49W **316** B6
Asheim Norway 61°42N 11°11E **164** D8
Ashern Canada 51°11N 98°21W **297** C9
Asherton U.S.A. 28°27N 99°46W **314** G5
Asheville U.S.A. 35°36N 82°33W **315** D13
Ashewat Pakistan 31°22N 68°32E **242** D3
Asheweig → Canada 54°17N 87°12W **298** B2
Ashford Australia 29°15S 151°3E **283** A9
Ashford Kent, U.K. 51°8N 0°53E **169** F8
Ashford N.S.W., Australia 29°15S 151°3E **281** D5
Ashford Surrey, U.K. 51°25N 0°27W **118** D5
Ashford Ala., U.S.A. 31°11N 85°14W **316** D4
Ashgabat Turkmenistan 37°58N 58°24E **247** B8
Ashhurst N.Z. 40°16S 175°45E **284** D4
Ashibetsu Japan 43°31N 142°11E **220** C11
Ashikaga Japan 36°28N 139°29E **223** A11
Ashington U.K. 55°11N 1°33W **168** B6
Ashio Japan 36°38N 139°27E **223** A11
Ashizuri-Uwakai △ Japan 32°56N 132°32E **222** E5
Ashizuri-Zaki Japan 32°44N 133°0E **222** E5
Ashkarkot Afghan. 33°3N 67°58E **242** C2
Ashkhabad = Ashgabat Turkmenistan 37°58N 58°24E **247** B8
Åshkhāneh Iran 37°26N 56°55E **247** B8
Ashland Kans., U.S.A. 37°11N 99°46W **308** G4
Ashland Ky., U.S.A. 38°28N 82°38W **309** F12
Ashland Maine, U.S.A. 46°38N 68°24W **309** B19
Ashland Mont., U.S.A. 45°36N 106°16W **304** D10
Ashland Ohio, U.S.A. 40°52N 82°19W **312** F2
Ashland Oreg., U.S.A. 42°12N 122°43W **304** E2
Ashland Pa., U.S.A. 40°45N 76°22W **313** F8
Ashland Va., U.S.A. 37°46N 77°29W **309** G15
Ashland Wis., U.S.A. 46°35N 90°53W **308** B8
Ashland, L. U.S.A. 38°20N 89°11W **310** F7
Ashley N. Dak., U.S.A. 46°2N 99°22W **308** B4
Ashley Pa., U.S.A. 41°12N 75°55W **313** E9
Ashley → N.Z. 43°17S 172°44E **285** D7

Astorga Davao del S., Phil. 6°54N 125°27E **233** H5
Astorga Spain 42°29N 6°8W **194** C4
Astoria Ill., U.S.A. 40°14N 90°21W **310** D6
Astoria N.Y., U.S.A. 40°46N 73°55W **132** B7
Astoria Oreg., U.S.A. 46°11N 123°50W **306** D3
Åstorp Sweden 56°6N 12°55E **163** H6
Astrakhan Russia 46°25N 48°5E **191** G9
Astrakhan □ Russia 46°25N 48°0E **191** G8
Astrebla Downs Australia 24°12S 140°34E **280** C3
Astrolabe, Récifs de l' N. Cal. 19°48S 165°37E **288** d
Astrolabe Park Australia 33°57S 151°12E **139** B2
Astudillo Spain 42°12N 4°22W **194** C6
Asturias □ Spain 43°15N 6°0W **194** B5
Asturias ✕ (OVD) Spain 43°33N 6°3W **194** B4
Asunción Bolivia 11°46S 67°50W **330** C4
Asuncion N. Marianas 19°40N 145°24E **302** c
Asunción Paraguay 25°10S 57°30W **334** B4
Asunción Nochixtlán Mexico 17°28N 97°14W **319** D5
Åsunden Sweden 58°0N 15°51E **163** F9
Asutri Sudan 15°25N 35°45E **257** D4
Aswa → Uganda 3°43N 31°55E **268** B3
Aswa-Lolim △ Uganda 2°43N 31°35E **268** B3
Aswad, Ra's al Si. Arabia 21°20N 39°0E **248** B2
Aswān Egypt 24°4N 32°57E **256** C3
Aswân High Dam = Sadd el Aali Egypt 23°54N 32°54E **256** C3
Asyût Egypt 27°11N 31°4E **256** B3
Asyûti, Wadi → Egypt 27°11N 31°4E **256** B3
Aszód Hungary 47°39N 19°28E **182** C4
At-Bashy Kyrgyzstan 41°32N 75°46E **217** C9
Aṭ Ṭafīlah Jordan 30°45N 35°30E **251** H6
Aṭ Ṭafīlah □ Jordan 30°45N 35°30E **251** H6
Aṭ Ṭa'if Si. Arabia 21°5N 40°27E **248** B3
Aṭ Ṭāj Libya 24°13N 23°18E **258** D4
Aṭ Ṭa'mīm □ Iraq 35°30N 44°0E **246** C5
Aṭ Tamīmī Libya 32°20N 23°4E **258** B4
Aṭ Ṭīraq Si. Arabia 27°19N 44°33E **246** E4
Aṭ Ṭubayq Si. Arabia 29°30N 37°0E **251** J8
Aṭ Tuhaythat Yemen 14°18N 43°15E **248** D3
Aṭ Tunayb Jordan 31°48N 35°57E **251** G6
Aṭ Turbah Lahij, Yemen 12°40N 43°30E **248** E3
Aṭ Turbah Ta'izz, Yemen 13°13N 44°7E **248** E4
Atabey Turkey 37°57N 30°39E **205** D12
Atacama □ Chile 27°30N 70°0W **334** B2
Atacama, Desierto de Chile 24°0S 69°20W **334** A2
Atacama, Salar de Chile 23°30S 68°20W **334** A2
Ataco Colombia 3°35N 75°23W **328** C2
Atafu Pac. Oc. 8°35S 172°30W **277** B16
Atakeye △ Australia 22°30S 133°45E **278** D5
Atakor Algeria 23°27N 5°31E **261** D6
Atakpamé Togo 7°31N 1°13E **263** D5
Atalaia do Norte Brazil 4°20S 70°12W **328** D3
Atalándi Greece 38°39N 22°58E **204** C4
Atalaya Peru 10°45S 73°50W **330** C3
Atalaya de Femes Canary Is. 28°56N 13°47W **153** e2
Atâleia Brazil 18°3S 41°6W **333** E3
Atami Japan 35°5N 139°4E **223** B11
Atamyrat Turkmenistan 37°50N 65°12E **217** F7
Atankawng Burma 25°50N 97°47E **241** G4
Atap Indonesia 3°51N 117°1E **235** B5
Atapupu Indonesia 9°0S 124°51E **231** F6
Atâr Mauritania 20°30N 13°5W **260** D2
Ataram, Erg n- Algeria 23°57N 2°0E **261** D5
Atarfe Spain 37°13N 3°40W **195** H7
Atari Pakistan 30°56N 74°2E **242** D6
Atarot ✕ (JRS) West Bank 31°52N 35°14E **123** A2
Atascadero U.S.A. 35°29N 120°40W **307** K6
Atasū Kazakhstan 48°30N 71°0E **217** C8
Atatürk, İstanbul ✕ (IST) Turkey 40°59N 28°49E **203** F12
Atatürk Baraji Turkey 37°28N 38°30E **213** D8
Atauro E. Timor 8°10S 125°30E **231** F7
Ataviros Greece 36°12N 27°50E **206** E11
Atbara Sudan 17°42N 33°59E **256** D3
'Atbara, Nahr → Sudan 17°40N 33°56E **256** D3
Atbasar Kazakhstan 51°48N 68°20E **217** B7
Atça Turkey 37°53N 28°13E **205** D10
Atchafalaya B. U.S.A. 29°25N 91°25W **314** G9
Atchison U.S.A. 39°34N 95°7W **308** F6
Atebubu Ghana 7°47N 1°0W **263** D4
Ateca Spain 41°20N 1°49W **196** D2
Aterno → Italy 42°11N 13°51E **199** F10
Ateshan Iran 35°35N 52°37E **247** C7
Atesine, Alpi Italy 46°55N 11°30E **199** B8
Atessa Italy 42°6N 14°27E **199** F11
Ath Belgium 50°38N 3°47E **170** D3
Athabasca Canada 54°45N 113°20W **296** D6
Athabasca → Canada 58°40N 110°50W **297** B6
Athabasca, L. Canada 59°15N 109°15W **297** B7
Athabasca Sand Dunes △ Canada 59°4N 108°43W **297** B7
Athagarh India 20°43N 85°33E **244** D7
Athamanon Oros Greece 39°30N 21°6E **204** B3
Athboy Ireland 53°37N 6°56W **166** C5
Athena U.S.A. 45°49N 118°30W **304** D4
Athenry Ireland 53°18N 8°44W **166** C3
Athens = Athína Greece 37°58N 23°43E **204** D5
Athens Ala., U.S.A. 34°48N 86°58W **315** D11
Athens Ga., U.S.A. 33°57N 83°23W **316** B6
Athens N.Y., U.S.A. 42°16N 73°49W **313** D11
Athens Ohio, U.S.A. 39°20N 82°6W **312** F6
Athens Pa., U.S.A. 41°57N 76°31W **313** E8
Athens Tenn., U.S.A. 35°27N 84°36W **315** D12
Athens Tex., U.S.A. 32°12N 95°51W **314** E7
Atherley Canada 44°37N 79°20W **141** A4
Atherton Australia 17°17S 145°30E **280** B4
Athi River Kenya 1°28S 36°58E **268** C4
Athiémé Benin 6°37N 1°40E **263** D5
Athienou Cyprus 35°3N 33°47E **207** D9
Athína Greece 37°58N 23°43E **204** D5
Athína ✕ (ATH) Greece 37°58N 23°43E **204** D5
Athínai = Athína Greece 37°58N 23°43E **204** D5
Athis-Mons France 48°42N 2°23E **134** B3
Athlone Ireland 53°25N 7°56W **166** C4
Athni India 16°44N 75°6E **245** F2
Atholl, Forest of U.K. 56°51N 3°50W **167** E5
Atholl, Kap Greenland 76°25N 69°30W **154** B4
Atholville Canada 47°59N 66°43W **305** A6
Athos Greece 40°9N 24°22E **203** D8
Athy Ireland 53°0N 7°0W **166** C5
Ati Sudan 13°5N 29°2E **265** F11
Ati, J. Egypt 22°10N 34°53E **256** C3
Atiak Uganda 3°12N 32°2E **268** B3
Atico Peru 16°14S 73°40W **330** D3

Atienza Spain 41°12N 2°52W **196** D2
Atifiya Iraq 33°21N 44°21E **113** A2
Atiir South Sudan 6°10N 30°35E **257** F3
Atikaki △ Canada 51°30N 95°31W **297** C9
Atikameg → Canada 52°30N 82°46W **298** B3
Atikokan Canada 48°45N 91°37W **298** C1
Atikonak L. Canada 52°40N 64°32W **299** B6
Atimaono Tahiti 17°46S 149°28W **289** e
Atimonan Phil. 14°0N 121°56E **232** D3
'Ātinah, W. = Oman 18°23N 53°28E **249** C6
Atirampattinam India 10°28N 79°20E **245** J4
Atişalen Turkey 41°3N 28°52E **122** B1
Atitlán △ Guatemala 14°38N 91°10W **320** D1
Atiu Cook Is. 20°0S 158°10W **289** J12
Atka Russia 60°50N 151°48E **215** C16
Atka Alaska, U.S.A. 52°12N 174°12W **303** K4
Atka I. U.S.A. 52°7N 174°30W **303** K5
Atkarsk Russia 51°55N 45°2E **190** E7
Atkinson Ga., U.S.A. 31°13N 81°47W **316** D5
Atkinson Ill., U.S.A. 41°25N 90°1W **310** D6
Atkinson Nebr., U.S.A. 42°32N 98°59W **308** D4
Atlanta Ga., U.S.A. 33°45N 84°23W **113** C2
Atlanta Ill., U.S.A. 40°16N 89°14W **310** D7
Atlanta Mo., U.S.A. 39°54N 92°29W **310** E4
Atlanta Tex., U.S.A. 33°7N 94°10W **314** E7
Atlanta Hartsfield-Jackson Int. ✕ (ATL) U.S.A. 33°38N 84°26W **113** C2
Atlanta History Center U.S.A. 33°44N 84°22W **113** B2
Atlanta Zoo U.S.A. 33°44N 84°22W **113** B2
Atlantic U.S.A. 41°24N 95°1W **310** C2
Atlantic Beach U.S.A. 30°20N 81°24W **316** E6
Atlantic City U.S.A. 39°21N 74°27W **309** F16
Atlantic-Indian Basin Antarctica 60°0S 30°0E **151** B4
Atlantic Ocean 0°0 20°0W **152** F8
Atlántico □ Colombia 10°45N 75°0W **328** A3
Atlantis S. Africa 33°34S 18°29E **270** D2
Atlas Mts. = Haut Atlas Morocco 32°30N 5°0W **260** B4
Atlin Canada 59°31N 133°41W **296** B2
Atlin, L. Canada 59°26N 133°45W **296** B2
Atlin △ Canada 59°10N 134°30W **296** B2
Atløyna Norway 61°21N 4°58E **164** C1
Atmakur Andhra Pradesh, India 18°45N 78°39E **244** E4
Atmakur Andhra Pradesh, India 14°37N 79°40E **245** G4
Atmore U.S.A. 31°2N 87°29W **317** D2
Atna → Norway 61°44N 10°49E **164** C7
Atna → Norway 61°44N 10°49E **164** C7
Atō Japan 34°25N 131°40E **222** C3
Atocha Bolivia 20°56S 66°14W **330** E4
Atok Phil. 16°35N 120°43E **232** C3
Atoka U.S.A. 34°23N 96°8W **314** D6
Atokos Greece 38°28N 20°49E **204** C2
Atolia U.S.A. 35°19N 117°37W **307** K9
Atomium Belgium 50°54N 4°20E **116** A2
Atongo-Bakari C.A.R. 5°49N 21°35E **264** A4
Atori Solomon Is. 8°42S 160°59E **287** M11
Atqasuk → U.S.A. 70°28N 157°24W **303** A8
Atqasuk U.S.A. 70°52N 155°55W **303** A9
Atrak → Norway 59°59N 8°45E **164** E5
Atrai → Bangla. 24°7N 89°22E **241** C2
Atrak = Atrek → Turkmenistan 37°35N 53°58E **247** B8
'Ātran Sweden 57°7N 12°57E **163** G6
Ātran → Sweden 56°53N 12°30E **163** H6
Atrato → Colombia 8°17N 76°58W **328** B2
Atrauli India 28°2N 78°20E **242** E8
Atrek → Turkmenistan 37°35N 53°58E **247** B8
Atri Italy 42°35N 13°58E **199** F10
Atsiki Greece 39°56N 25°13E **205** B7
Atsoum, Mts. Cameroon 6°41N 12°57E **263** D7
Atsugi Japan 35°25N 139°21E **223** B11
Atsuta Japan 43°24N 141°26E **220** C10
Attalla U.S.A. 34°1N 86°6W **316** B3
Attapeu Laos 14°48N 106°50E **236** E6
Attapulgus U.S.A. 30°45N 84°29W **316** E5
Attawapiskat Canada 52°56N 82°24W **298** B3
Attawapiskat → Canada 52°57N 82°18W **298** B3
Attawapiskat L. Canada 52°18N 87°54W **298** B2
Attersee Austria 47°55N 13°32E **180** D6
Attica Ind., U.S.A. 40°18N 87°15W **311** D9
Attica Ohio, U.S.A. 41°4N 82°53W **312** E2
Attichy France 49°28N 3°3E **173** C11
Attigny France 49°28N 4°35E **173** C11
Attika = Attikí □ Greece 38°10N 23°40E **204** D5
Attikamagen L. Canada 55°0N 66°30W **298** B5
Attikí □ Greece 38°10N 23°40E **204** D5
Attleboro U.S.A. 41°57N 71°17W **313** E13
Attock Pakistan 33°52N 72°20E **242** C5
Attopu = Attapeu Laos 14°48N 106°50E **236** E6
Attu U.S.A. 52°56N 173°15E **303** K1
Attu I. U.S.A. 52°55N 172°55E **303** K1
Attunga Australia 30°55S 150°50E **283** A9
Attur India 11°35N 78°30E **245** J4
'Atūd Yemen 14°53N 48°10E **249** D5
Atuel → Argentina 36°17S 66°50W **334** C2
Atura Uganda 2°3N 32°20E **268** B3
Åtvidaberg Sweden 58°12N 16°0E **163** F10
Atwater U.S.A. 37°21N 120°37W **306** H6
Atwood Ont., Canada 43°40N 81°1W **312** C3
Atwood Ill., U.S.A. 39°48N 88°28W **311** E8
Atwood Kans., U.S.A. 39°48N 101°3W **308** F3
Atyraū Kazakhstan 47°5N 52°0E **187** E18
Atzgersdorf Austria 48°9N 16°18E **142** B1
Au Sable → U.S.A. 44°25N 83°20W **312** B1
Au Sable → U.S.A. 44°25N 83°20W **312** B1
Au Sable Forks U.S.A. 44°27N 73°41W **313** B11
Au Sable Pt. U.S.A. 44°20N 83°20W **312** B1
Au Vent, Région Réunion 21°0S 55°35E **272** f
Aua Amer. Samoa 14°17S 170°40W **302** f
Auas Honduras 15°29N 84°20W **320** C3
Auasberg Namibia 22°37S 17°13E **270** B2
Aubagne France 43°17N 5°37E **175** E6
Aube □ France 48°15N 4°10E **173** D11
Aube → France 48°34N 3°43E **173** D10
Aubel Belgium 50°42N 5°52E **170** D5
Aubenas France 44°37N 4°24E **175** D8
Aubenton France 49°50N 4°12E **173** C11
Auberry U.S.A. 37°7N 119°29W **306** H7
Aubigny-sur-Nère France 47°30N 2°24E **173** E9
Aubin France 44°31N 2°15E **174** D6
Aubrac, Mts. d' France 44°40N 3°0E **174** D7

Auburn S. Austral., Australia 34°1S 138°42E **282** C3
Auburn Ala., U.S.A. 32°36N 85°29W **316** C4
Auburn Calif., U.S.A. 38°54N 121°4W **306** G5
Auburn Ill., U.S.A. 39°36N 89°45W **310** E6
Auburn Ind., U.S.A. 41°22N 85°4W **311** C11
Auburn Maine, U.S.A. 44°6N 70°14W **309** C18
Auburn N.Y., U.S.A. 42°56N 76°34W **313** D9
Auburn Nebr., U.S.A. 40°23N 95°51W **308** E6
Auburn Wash., U.S.A. 47°18N 122°13W **306** C4
Auburn Ra. Australia 25°15S 150°30E **281** D5
Auburndale Fla., U.S.A. 28°4N 81°48W **316** F6
Auburndale Mass., U.S.A. 42°20N 71°14W **116** A1
Aubusson France 45°57N 2°11E **174** C6
Auce Latvia 56°28N 22°53E **184** B9

Auch France 43°39N 0°36E 174 E4
Auchendinny U.K. 55°51N 3°11W 121 B2
Auchi Nigeria 7°6N 6°13E 263 D6
Auchterarder U.K. 56°18N 3°41E 167 E5
Auchtermuchty U.K. 56°18N 3°13W 167 E5
Auckland N.Z. 36°52S 174°46E 284 C3
Auckland □ N.Z. 36°50S 175°0E 284 C3
Auckland Is. Pac. Oc. 50°40S 166°5E 288 N8
Auckland Park S. Africa 26°11S 28°0E 123 B2
Aude □ France 43°8N 2°28E 174 E6
Aude → France 43°13N 3°14E 174 E7
Auden Canada 50°14N 87°53W 298 B2
Auderghem Belgium 50°49N 4°26E 116 B2
Auderville France 49°43N 1°57W 172 C5
Audincourt France 47°30N 6°50E 173 E13
Audo Ra. Ethiopia 6°20N 41°50E 257 F5
Audubon U.S.A. 41°43N 94°56W 310 C2
Audubon Park U.S.A. 29°55N 90°8W 131 B2
Aue Germany 50°35N 12°41E 178 E8
Auerbach Germany 50°30N 12°24E 178 E8
Aufist W. Sahara 25°44N 14°39W 260 C2
Agathella Australia 25°48S 146°35E 281 D4
Aughnacloy U.K. 54°25N 6°59E 166 C5
Aughrim Ireland 53°18N 8°19W 166 C3
Augrabies Falls S. Africa 28°35S 20°20E 270 C3
Augrabies Falls □
  S. Africa 28°40S 20°22E 270 C3
Augsburg Germany 48°25N 10°52E 179 G6
Augsburg-Westliche Wälder △
  Germany 48°22N 10°40E 179 G6
August Town Jamaica 17°59N 76°44W 320 a
Augusta W. Austral.,
  Australia 34°19S 115°9E 279 F2
Augusta Italy 37°13N 15°13E 201 E8
Augusta Ark., U.S.A. 35°17N 91°22W 314 D9
Augusta Ga., U.S.A. 33°28N 81°58W 316 B8
Augusta Ill., U.S.A. 40°14N 90°57W 310 D6
Augusta Kans., U.S.A. 37°41N 96°59W 308 G5
Augusta Ky., U.S.A. 38°47N 84°0W 311 F12
Augusta Maine, U.S.A. 44°19N 69°47W 309 C19
Augusta Mont., U.S.A. 47°30N 112°24W 304 C7
Augusta, Mausoleo di Rome, Italy 136 b2
Augustenborg Denmark 54°57N 9°53E 163 K3
Augustine I. U.S.A. 59°22N 153°26W 303 D9
Augusto Cardosa = Metangula
  Mozam. 12°40S 34°50E 269 E3
Augustów Poland 53°51N 23°0E 184 E9
Augustówka Poland 52°11N 21°5E 143 B2
Augustus, Mt. Australia 24°20S 116°50E 279 D2
Augustus I. Australia 15°20S 124°30E 278 C3
Aujuittuq = Grise Fiord
  Canada 76°25N 82°57W 295 B15
Aukan Eritrea 15°29N 40°50E 257 D5
Auki Solomon Is. 8°45S 160°42E 287 M11
Aukra Norway 62°47N 6°55E 164 B3
Aukrug □ Germany 54°5N 9°45E 178 A5
Aukštaitija △ Lithuania 55°15N 26°0E 161 J22
Aukum U.S.A. 38°34N 120°43W 306 G6
Aul India 20°41N 86°39E 244 D8
Aulavik △ Canada 73°42N 119°55W 294 C8
Auld, L. Australia 22°25S 123°50E 278 D3
Aŭliekŏl Kazakhstan 52°31N 62°45E 216 B6
Aulifeltet Norway 60°30N 11°21E 162 D5
Auliye-Ata = Taraz
  Kazakhstan 42°54N 71°22E 217 D8
Aulla Italy 44°12N 9°58E 198 D6
Aulnay France 46°2N 0°22N 174 B3
Aulnay-sous-Bois France 48°56N 2°29E 134 A3
Aulne → France 48°17N 4°16E 172 D2
Aulnoye-Aymeries France 50°12N 3°50E 173 B10
Aulong Palau 7°16N 134°17E 288 c
Ault Somme, France 50°8N 1°26E 172 B8
Ault Colo., U.S.A. 40°35N 104°44W 304 F11
Aulus-les-Bains France 42°49N 1°19E 174 F5
Aumale = Sour el Ghozlane
  Algeria 36°10N 3°45E 261 A5
Aumale France 49°46N 1°46E 172 C8
Aumo Papua N. G. 5°44S 148°30E 286 C5
Aumont-Aubrac France 44°43N 3°17E 174 D7
Auna Nigeria 10°9N 4°42E 263 C5
Aundah India 19°32N 77°3E 244 E3
Aundh India 17°33N 74°23E 244 F2
Auning Denmark 56°26N 10°22E 163 H4
Aunis France 46°5N 0°50W 174 B3
Aunu'u Amer. Samoa 14°20S 170°31W 302 f
Auponhia Indonesia 1°58S 125°27E 231 E7
Aups France 43°37N 6°15E 175 E10
Aur, Pulau Malaysia 2°35N 104°10E 237 L5
Aura Burma 26°59N 97°57E 241 A6
Auraiya India 26°28N 79°33E 243 F8
Aurangabad Bihar, India 24°45N 84°18E 243 G11
Aurangabad Maharashtra,
  India 19°50N 75°23E 244 E2
Auray France 47°40N 2°59W 172 E4
Aurdal Norway 60°55N 9°26E 164 D4
Aure Norway 63°16N 8°33E 164 A5
Aurelio Italy 41°54N 12°26E 261 G5
Aurès Algeria 35°8N 6°30E 261 A6
Aurich Germany 53°28N 7°28E 178 B3
Aurilândia Brazil 16°44S 50°28W 333 E1
Aurillac France 44°55N 2°26E 174 D6
Aurlandsfjorden Norway 61°3N 7°1E 164 C4
Aurlandsvangen Norway 60°55N 7°12E 164 D4
Auronzo di Cadore Italy 46°33N 12°26E 199 B9
Aurora = Maéwo
  Vanuatu 15°10S 168°10E 287 E6
Aurora = San Francisco
  Phil. 13°21N 122°31E 232 E4
Aurora Ont., Canada 44°0N 79°28W 312 C5
Aurora Isabela, Phil. 16°59N 121°38E 232 C3
Aurora Zamboanga del S.,
  Phil. 7°57N 123°36E 233 H4
Aurora Western Cape,
  S. Africa 32°40S 18°29E 270 D2
Aurora Colo., U.S.A. 39°43N 104°49W 304 G11
Aurora Ill., U.S.A. 41°45N 88°19W 311 C8
Aurora Mo., U.S.A. 36°58N 93°43W 308 G7
Aurora Nebr., U.S.A. 40°52N 98°0W 308 E5
Aurora Ohio, U.S.A. 41°21N 81°20W 312 D3
Aurora □ Phil. 15°30N 121°30E 232 D3
Aurora Memorial △
  Phil. 15°40N 121°20E 232 D3
Aursmoen Norway 59°55N 11°26E 164 E8
Aursunden Norway 62°40N 11°40E 164 E5
Aurukun Australia 13°20S 141°45E 280 A3
Aurukun □ Australia 13°30S 141°45E 280 A3
Aus Namibia 26°35S 16°12E 270 C2
Ausa India 18°19N 81°46W 312 C3
Ausable → Canada 43°19N 81°46W 312 C3
Auschwitz = Oświęcim
  Poland 50°2N 19°11E 185 H6
Ausim Egypt 30°7N 31°8E 117 A1
Auski Roadhouse
  Australia 22°22S 118°41E 278 D2
Auspitz = Hustopeče
  Czech Rep. 48°57N 16°43E 181 C9
Aussig = Ústí nad Labem
  Czech Rep. 50°41N 14°3E 180 A7
Aust-Agder □ Norway 58°45N 8°0E 164 F4
Austad Norway 58°58N 7°37E 164 F4
Austen Harbour India 12°55N 92°45E 245 H11
Austerlitz = Slavkov u Brna
  Czech Rep. 49°10N 16°52E 181 C9
Austerlitz, Gare d' France 48°50N 2°22E 134 A3
Austevoll Norway 60°5N 5°13E 164 D2

Austin Ill., U.S.A. 41°53N 87°45W 119 B2
Austin Ind., U.S.A. 38°45N 85°49W 311 F11
Austin Minn., U.S.A. 43°40N 92°58W 308 D7
Austin Nev., U.S.A. 39°30N 117°4W 304 G5
Austin Pa., U.S.A. 41°38N 78°6W 312 E6
Austin Tex., U.S.A. 30°17N 97°45W 314 D6
Austin I. Canada 61°10N 94°0W 297 A10
Austin, L. Australia 27°40S 118°0E 279 E2
Austmarka Norway 60°6N 12°21E 164 D9
Austnes Norway 62°38N 6°16E 164 B3
Austra Norway 65°8N 11°55E 160 D14
Austral Is. = Tubuaï, Îs.
  French Polynesia 25°0S 150°0W 289 f
Austral Seamount Chain
  Pac. Oc. 24°0S 150°0W 289 K13
Australia ■ Oceania 23°0S 135°0E 276 C3
Australian-Antarctic Basin
  S. Ocean 60°0S 120°0E 151 C9
Australian Capital Territory □
  Australia 35°30S 149°0E 283 C8
Australind Australia 33°17S 115°42E 279 F2
Austria ■ Europe 47°0N 14°0E 180 E7
Austur-skaftafellssýsla
  Iceland 64°15N 16°0W 155 C10
Austurland □ Iceland 64°55N 15°30W 155 C11
Austvågøya Norway 68°20N 14°40E 160 B16
Autazes Brazil 3°35S 59°8W 329 D6
Auterive France 43°21N 1°29E 174 E5
Authie → France 50°22N 1°38E 173 B8
Authon-du-Perche France 48°12N 0°54E 172 D7
Autlán de Navarro
  Mexico 19°46N 104°22W 318 D4
Autun France 46°58N 4°17E 173 F11
Auvergne □ France 45°20N 3°15E 174 C6
Auvergne, Mts. d' France 45°20N 2°55E 174 C6
Auvézère → France 45°12N 0°50E 174 C4
Auxerre France 47°48N 3°32E 173 E10
Auxi-le-Château France 50°15N 2°8E 173 B9
Auxonne France 47°10N 5°20E 173 E12
Auyuittuq △ Canada 67°30N 66°0W 295 D18
Auzances France 46°2N 2°30E 174 B6
Auzat France 42°21N 1°29E 174 F5
Av-Dovurak Russia 51°17N 91°35E 215 D10
Ava Mo., U.S.A. 36°57N 92°40W 308 G7
Ava, L. Mo., U.S.A. 36°57N 92°40W 308 G7
Avaldsnes Norway 59°21N 5°20E 164 E2
Avallon France 47°30N 3°53E 173 E10
Avalon U.S.A. 33°21N 118°20W 307 M8
Avalon Pen. Canada 47°30N 53°20W 299 C9
Avana → Cook Is. 21°14S 159°43W 289 h
Avanavero Suriname 4°51N 57°22W 329 C6
Avanigadda India 16°0N 80°56E 245 G5
Avannaarsua □ Greenland 80°0N 55°0W 154 B5
Avanos Turkey 38°43N 34°51E 212 C6
Avantas Greece 40°57N 25°56E 203 F9
Avaré Brazil 23°4S 48°58W 335 A6
Avarua Cook Is. 21°12S 159°46W 289 h
Avarua Harb. Cook Is. 21°12S 159°46W 289 h
Avatele Cook Is. 19°6S 169°55W 289 h
Avatiu Cook Is. 21°12S 159°47W 289 h
Avawatz Mts. U.S.A. 35°40N 116°30W 307 K10
Ave, Is. las Venezuela 12°0N 67°40W 321 D6
Aviemore U.K. 57°12N 3°50W 167 D5
Aviemore, L. N.Z. 44°31S 170°15E 285 L3
Avigliana Italy 45°5N 7°23E 198 C4
Avigliano Italy 40°44N 15°43E 201 B8
Avignon France 43°57N 4°50E 175 E8
Aylmer Canada 64°5N 108°30W 294 E10
Ávila Spain 40°39N 4°43W 194 E6
Ávila □ Spain 40°39N 5°0W 194 E5
Ávila, Sierra de Spain 40°40N 5°15W 194 E5
Avila Beach U.S.A. 35°11N 120°44W 307 K6
Avilés Spain 43°35N 5°57W 194 B5
Avintes Portugal 41°7N 8°33W 194 D2
Avis Portugal 39°4N 7°53W 195 F3
Avis Pa., U.S.A. 41°11N 77°19W 312 E7
Aviz = Avis Portugal 39°4N 7°53W 195 F3
Avize France 48°59N 4°1E 173 D11
Avlóna Greece 38°13N 24°8E 204 C6
Avlonári Greece 38°31N 24°5E 204 C6
Avlum Denmark 56°16N 8°47E 163 H2
Avoca Vic., Australia 37°5S 143°26E 282 D3
Avoca N.Y., U.S.A. 42°25N 77°25W 312 D7
Avoca Vic., Australia 35°40S 143°43E 282 C5
Avoca → Wicklow, Ireland 52°48N 6°10W 166 D5
Avoca B.C., Canada 51°45N 119°19W 296 C5
Avola Italy 36°56N 15°7E 201 F8
Avon Ill., U.S.A. 40°40N 90°26W 310 D6
Avon N.Y., U.S.A. 42°55N 77°45W 312 D7
Avon → W. Austral.,
  Australia 31°40S 116°7E 279 F2
Avon → Bristol, U.K. 51°29N 2°41W 169 F5
Avon → Dorset, U.K. 50°44N 1°46W 169 G6
Avon → Warks., U.K. 52°0N 2°8W 169 E5
Avon Park U.S.A. 27°36N 81°31W 317 H8
Avondale Ill., U.S.A. 41°56N 87°41W 119 B2
Avondale U.S.A. 39°45N 75°12W 313 F10
Avondale Zimbabwe 17°43S 30°58E 269 F3
Avondale Heights
  Australia 37°45S 144°52E 128 A1
Avonlea Canada 50°0N 105°0W 313 A10
Avonmore Canada 45°10N 74°58W 313 A10
Avonmouth U.K. 51°30N 2°42W 169 F5
Avranches France 48°40N 1°20W 172 D5
Avre → France 48°47N 1°22E 172 D8
Avrillé France 47°30N 0°35W 172 E6
Avtovac Bos.-H. 43°9N 18°35E 202 C2
Avtovo Russia 59°51N 30°16E 137 B1
Avu Avu Solomon Is. 9°50S 160°22E 287 M11
Awa-Shima Japan 38°27N 139°14E 220 E6
Awag il Baqar
  South Sudan 9°30N 30°10E 257 E3
A'waj → Syria 33°23N 36°20E 250 B5
Awaji Japan 34°28N 134°56E 222 C6

Awaji-Shima Japan 34°30N 134°50E 222 C6
'Awali Bahrain 26°0N 50°30E 247 E6
Awantipur India 33°55N 75°3E 243 C6
Awanui N.Z. 35°4S 173°17E 284 B5
Aware Ethiopia 8°16N 44°9E 267 C5
Awarja → India 17°5N 76°15E 244 F3
Awarua B. N.Z. 44°28S 168°4E 285 E3
Awarua Pt. N.Z. 44°15S 168°5E 285 E3
Awasa Ethiopia 7°2N 38°28E 257 F4
Awasa, L. Ethiopia 7°0N 38°30E 257 F4
Awash Ethiopia 9°1N 40°10E 257 F5
Awash → Ethiopia 11°45N 41°5E 257 E5
Awash △ Ethiopia 9°8N 40°0E 257 F5
Awaso Ghana 6°15N 2°22W 262 D4
Awat China 40°30N 80°24E 217 D10
Awatere → N.Z. 41°37S 174°10E 285 B9
Awbārī Libya 26°46N 12°57E 258 C2
Awbārī, Idehan Libya 27°10N 11°30E 258 C2
Awdal □ Somalia 10°30N 43°30E 267 B5
Awe, L. U.K. 56°17N 5°16W 167 E3
Aweil South Sudan 8°42N 27°20E 257 F2
Awgu Nigeria 6°4N 7°24E 263 D6
Awjilah Libya 29°8N 21°7E 258 C4
Awka Nigeria 6°12N 7°5E 263 D6
Aworro Papua N. G. 1°58N 10°24E 286 D2
Awsard Mauritania 22°37N 14°22W 260 D2
Ax-les-Thermes France 42°44N 1°50E 174 F5
Axat France 42°48N 2°13E 174 F6
Axe → U.K. 50°42N 3°4W 169 F5
Axel Heiberg I. Canada 80°0N 90°0W 295 B14
Axim Ghana 4°51N 2°15W 262 E4
Axinim Brazil 4°2S 59°22W 329 D6
Axintele Romania 44°37N 26°47E 183 F11
Axioma Brazil 6°45S 64°31W 331 B5
Áxios → Greece 40°57N 22°35E 202 F6
Axminster U.K. 50°46N 3°0W 169 G4
Axson U.S.A. 31°17N 82°44W 316 B7
Axvall Sweden 58°23N 13°34E 163 F7
Ay France 49°3N 4°1E 173 C11
Ayaantang Eq. Guin. 1°58N 10°24E 264 B2
Ayabaca Peru 4°40S 79°53W 330 A2
Ayabe Japan 35°20N 135°20E 223 B7
Ayacucho Argentina 37°5S 58°20W 334 D4
Ayacucho Peru 13°0S 74°0W 330 C3
Ayacucho □ Peru 14°0S 74°0W 330 C3
Ayaguz = Ayaköz
  Kazakhstan 48°10N 80°10E 217 C10
Ayakkum Hu China 37°30N 89°20E 217 E11
Ayaköz Kazakhstan 48°10N 80°10E 217 C10
Ayaköz → Kazakhstan 46°40N 79°14E 217 C9
Ayakudi India 10°28N 77°56E 245 J3
Ayala Phil. 6°57N 121°57E 233 H3
Ayamé Ivory C. 5°35N 3°9W 262 D4
Ayamonte Spain 37°12N 7°24W 195 H3
Ayan Russia 56°30N 138°16E 215 D14
Ayancık Turkey 41°57N 34°35E 212 B6
Ayangba Nigeria 7°31N 7°8E 263 D6
Ayapel Colombia 8°19N 75°9W 328 B2
Ayas Turkey 40°2N 32°21E 212 B5
Ayaviri Peru 14°50S 70°35W 330 C3
Ayazağa Turkey 41°6N 28°59E 122 B1
Aybak Afghan. 36°15N 68°5E 240 A3
Aybastı Turkey 40°41N 37°23E 212 B7
Aydarkŏl Uzbekistan 40°50N 67°10E 217 D7
Aydın Turkey 37°51N 27°51E 212 D2
Aydın □ Turkey 37°50N 28°0E 205 D9
Aydın Dağları Turkey 38°0N 28°0E 205 D10
Aydıncık Turkey 36°9N 33°21E 250 B4
Aydıngkŏl Hu China 42°40N 89°15E 217 D11
Ayelu Ethiopia 10°5N 40°42E 257 E5
Ayenngré Togo 8°40N 1°16E 263 D5
Ayer U.S.A. 42°34N 71°35W 313 D13
Ayer Chawan, Pulau
  Singapore 1°16N 103°41E 138 B2
Ayer Hitam Malaysia 5°24N 100°16E 237 c
Ayer Merbau, Pulau
  Singapore 1°16N 103°42E 138 B2
Ayerbe Spain 42°17N 0°41W 196 C4
Ayer's Cliff Canada 45°10N 72°3W 313 A12
Ayers Rock = Uluru
  Australia 25°23S 131°5E 279 E5
Ayeyarwady = Irrawaddy →
  Burma 15°50N 95°6E 241 G5
Áyia Napa Cyprus 34°59N 34°0E 207 E9
Áyia Phyla Cyprus 34°43N 33°1E 207 F9
Áyios Amvrósios Cyprus 35°20N 33°35E 207 E9
Áyios Seríyios Cyprus 35°12N 33°53E 207 D9
Áyios Theodhoros Cyprus 35°22N 34°1E 207 E10
Áyios Yeóryios = Aghios Georgios
  Greece 37°28N 23°57E 204 D5
Aykhal Russia 66°0N 111°30E 215 C12
Aykino Russia 62°15N 49°56E 186 B8
Aykırıkçi Turkey 39°8N 30°9E 205 B12
Aylesbury U.K. 51°49N 0°49W 169 F7
Aylmer Canada 42°46N 80°59W 312 D4
Aylmer, L. Canada 64°5N 108°30W 294 E10
'Ayn, Wādī al Oman 22°15N 55°28E 247 F7
'Ayn al Ghazālah Libya 32°10N 23°20E 258 B4
Ayn Dār Si. Arabia 25°55N 49°10E 247 E6
Ayn Sifni Iraq 36°51N 43°20E 246 B4
Ayn Zālah Iraq 36°45N 42°35E 246 B4
Ayna Spain 38°34N 2°3W 197 G2
'Aynat Yemen 16°4N 49°9E 249 C5
'Aynūnah Si. Arabia 28°5N 35°8E 246 E3
Ayod South Sudan 8°7N 31°26E 257 F3
Ayolas Paraguay 27°10S 56°59W 334 B4
Ayon, Ostrov Russia 69°50N 169°0E 215 C17
Ayora Spain 39°3N 1°3W 197 F3
Ayorou Niger 14°53N 1°0E 263 C5
Ayos Cameroon 3°53N 12°31E 264 B2
'Ayoûn el 'Atroûs
  Mauritania 16°38N 9°37W 262 B3
Ayr Queens., Australia 19°35S 147°25E 280 B4
Ayr Ont., Canada 43°17N 80°27W 312 C4
Ayr Ayr, U.K. 55°28N 4°38W 167 F4
Ayr → U.K. 55°28N 4°38W 167 F4
Ayrancı Turkey 37°21N 33°41E 212 D5
Ayrancılar Turkey 38°15N 27°18E 205 C9
Ayre, Pt. of I. of Man 54°25N 4°21W 168 C3
Ayribaba Turkmenistan 37°50N 66°34E 217 E7
Aysha Ethiopia 10°50N 42°42E 257 E5
Ayton Australia 15°56S 145°22E 280 B4
Aytos Bulgaria 42°42N 27°16E 203 D11
Aytoska Planina
  Bulgaria 42°45N 27°30E 203 D11
Ayu, Kepulauan Indonesia 0°35N 131°5E 231 D8
Ayutla Guatemala 14°40N 92°10W 320 D1
Ayutla de los Libres
  Mexico 16°54N 99°13W 319 D5
Ayutthaya = Phra Nakhon Si
  Ayutthaya Thailand 14°25N 100°30E 236 E3
Ayvacık Turkey 39°36N 26°24E 212 C2
Ayvalık Turkey 39°20N 26°46E 205 C8
Az Zabadānī Syria 33°43N 36°5E 250 B5
Az Zāhirīyah West Bank 31°25N 34°58E 251 D5
Az Zahrān Si. Arabia 26°10N 50°7E 247 E6
Az Zarqā Jordan 32°5N 36°4E 251 C5
Az Zarqā □ Jordan 32°5N 36°4E 251 C5
Az Zarqā' U.A.E. 24°53N 53°4E 247 E7
Az Zāwiyah Libya 32°52N 12°56E 258 B2
Az Zāwiyah □ Libya 32°50N 12°40E 258 B2
Az Zaydīyah Yemen 15°20N 43°1E 248 D3
Az Zilfī Si. Arabia 26°12N 44°52E 246 E5
Az Zubayr Iraq 30°26N 47°40E 246 D6
Az Zuhrah Yemen 15°44N 43°0E 248 D3

Az Zuqur Yemen 14°0N 42°45E 248 D3
Az Zuwaytīnah Libya 30°58N 20°7E 258 B4
Azabu Tokyo, Japan 140 c3
Azad Kashmir □ Pakistan 33°50N 73°50E 243 C5
Azamgarh India 26°5N 83°13E 243 F10
Azambuja Portugal 39°4N 8°51W 195 F2
Azángaro Peru 14°55S 70°13W 330 C3
Azaouad Mali 19°0N 3°0W 262 B4
Azaouak → Mali 15°50N 3°18E 263 B5
Azaouak, Vallée de l' Mali 15°50N 3°20E 263 B5
Āzar Shahr Iran 37°45N 45°59E 246 B6
Azara Nigeria 8°22N 9°12E 263 D6
Azārān Iran 32°55N 47°16E 246 C6
Azarbāijān = Azerbaijan ■
  Asia 40°20N 48°0E 191 K9
Āzarbāyjān-e Gharbī □
  Iran 37°0N 44°30E 246 B5
Āzarbāyjān-e Sharqī □
  Iran 37°20N 47°0E 246 B6
Azare Nigeria 11°55N 10°10E 263 C7
Azay-le-Rideau France 47°16N 0°30E 172 E7
A'zāz Syria 36°36N 37°4E 250 B8
Azazga Algeria 36°48N 4°22E 261 A5
Azcapotzalco Mexico 19°28N 99°10W 128 E1
Azefal Mauritania 21°0N 14°45W 260 D2
Azeffoun Algeria 36°51N 4°26E 261 A5
Azemmour Morocco 33°20N 9°20E 260 B3
Azennezal Algeria 22°58N 0°43E 261 D5
Azerbaijan ■ Asia 40°20N 48°0E 191 K9
Azezo Ethiopia 12°28N 37°15E 257 E4
Aznalcóllar Spain 37°32N 6°17W 195 H4
Azogues Ecuador 2°35S 78°0W 328 D2
Azores = Açores, Is. dos
  Atl. Oc. 38°0N 27°0W 153 d1
Azores-Biscay Rise Atl. Oc. 42°0N 20°0W 152 B9
Azoum, B. → Chad 10°53N 20°15E 259 F4
Azov Russia 47°3N 39°25E 191 G4
Azov, Sea of Europe 46°0N 36°30E 189 J9
Azovskoye More = Azov, Sea of
  Europe 46°0N 36°30E 189 J9
Azpeitia Spain 43°12N 2°19W 196 B2
Azrak, B. → Chad 10°53N 20°15E 259 F4
Azraq ash Shīshān Jordan 31°50N 36°49E 251 C7
Azrou Morocco 33°28N 5°19W 260 B3
Aztec U.S.A. 36°49N 107°59W 305 H10
Azteca, Estadia Mexico 19°19N 99°9W 128 C2
Azua de Compostela
  Dom. Rep. 18°25N 70°44W 321 C5
Azuaga Spain 38°16N 5°39W 195 G5
Azuara Spain 41°15N 0°53W 196 D4
Azuay □ Ecuador 2°55S 79°0W 328 D2
Azúcar, Cerro Pan de
  Chile 33°19S 70°41W 137 A1
Azuer → Spain 39°8N 3°36W 195 F7
Azuero, Pen. de Panama 7°30N 80°30W 320 E3
Azuga Romania 45°27N 25°33E 183 E10
Azul Argentina 36°42S 59°43W 334 D4
Azul, Lagoa Azores 37°52N 25°47W 153 d3
Azul, Serra Brazil 14°50S 54°50W 331 C7
Azumino Japan 36°20N 137°50E 223 A9
Azurduy Bolivia 19°59S 64°29W 331 D5
Azusa U.S.A. 34°8N 117°54W 307 L9
Azzaba Algeria 36°48N 7°6E 261 A6
Azzano Décimo Italy 45°53N 12°46E 199 C9
Azzel Matti, Sebkra Algeria 26°10N 0°43E 261 C5

B

Ba Be △ Vietnam 22°25N 105°37E 236 A5
Ba Don Vietnam 17°45N 106°26E 236 D6
Ba Dong Vietnam 9°40N 106°33E 237 H6
Ba Ngoi Vietnam 11°54N 109°10E 237 G7
Ba Ria Vietnam 10°30N 107°10E 237 G6
Ba Tri Vietnam 10°2N 106°36E 237 G6
Ba Xian = Bazhou China 39°8N 116°22E 226 E9
Baa Indonesia 10°50S 123°0E 278 B3
Baalbek = Ba'labakk
  Lebanon 34°0N 36°10E 250 E7
Baambrugge Neths. 52°15N 4°59E 112 B2
Baamonde Spain 43°7N 7°44W 194 B3
Baao Phil. 13°27N 123°22E 232 E4
Baardheere Somalia 2°20N 42°27E 267 C5
Baarle-Nassau Belgium 51°27N 4°56E 170 C4
Bab el Mandeb Red Sea 12°35N 43°25E 248 E3
Baba Bulgaria 42°44N 23°59E 202 D7
Baba, B. do Angola 14°50S 12°14E 265 C2
Baba Budan Hills India 13°30N 75°44E 245 H2
Baba Burnu Turkey 39°29N 26°2E 205 C8
Baba Channel Pakistan 24°48N 66°58E 242 H1
Baba L. Pakistan 24°49N 66°57E 242 H1
Babaçulândia Brazil 7°13S 47°46W 332 D2
Babadag Romania 44°55N 28°44E 183 F13
Babadayhan Turkm. 37°29N 60°32E 247 B8
Babaeski Turkey 41°26N 27°6E 203 F11
Babahoyo Ecuador 1°40S 79°30W 328 D2
Babai = Sarju → India 27°21N 81°23E 243 F9
Babai Nepal 28°10N 82°1E 243 E9
Babak = Sarju → India 27°21N 81°23E 243 F9
Babak Phil. 7°8N 125°41E 233 H5
Babana Nigeria 10°31N 3°46E 263 C5
Babanusa Sudan 11°20N 27°48E 257 E2
Babar Algeria 35°10N 7°6E 261 A6
Babar Indonesia 8°0S 129°30E 231 F7
Babar Pakistan 31°7N 69°32E 242 D3
Babarkach Pakistan 29°45N 68°0E 242 E3
Babarpur India 28°41N 77°16E 120 A2
Babase I. Papua N. G. 4°0S 153°42E 286 C7
Babayevo Russia 59°24N 35°55E 188 C8
Babb U.S.A. 48°51N 113°27W 304 B7
Babelthuap Palau 7°30N 134°30E 288 c
Babenhausen Germany 49°57N 8°57E 179 F4
Bābeni Romania 45°2N 24°11E 183 F9
Baberu India 25°33N 80°43E 243 G9
Babi Indonesia 2°5N 96°39E 234 B1
Babi Besar, Pulau
  Malaysia 2°25N 103°59E 237 L4
Babia Gora Europe 49°38N 19°38E 185 J6
Babian Jiang → China 22°35N 101°47E 228 F7
Bábil □ Iraq 32°30N 44°30E 246 C5
Babile Ethiopia 9°16N 42°11E 257 F5
Babīle → Ethiopia 8°45N 42°0E 267 C5
Babimost Poland 52°12N 15°49E 185 F2
Babinda Australia 17°20S 145°56E 280 B4
Babine → Canada 55°45N 127°44W 296 B3
Babine Canada 55°45N 126°37W 296 B3
Babine L. Canada 54°48N 126°0W 296 B3
Babiogórski □ Poland 49°38N 19°39E 185 J6
Babo Indonesia 2°30S 133°30E 231 E8
Bābol Iran 36°40N 52°50E 247 B7
Bābol Sar Iran 36°45N 52°45E 247 B7
Baborów Poland 50°7N 17°53E 185 H4
Baboua C.A.R. 5°49N 14°58E 264 A2
Babruysk Belarus 53°10N 29°15E 177 B15
Babson Park U.S.A. 27°49N 81°32E 317 H8
Babuhri India 26°49N 69°43E 242 F3
Babuna Macedonia 41°30N 21°40E 202 G5
Babura Nigeria 12°51N 9°0E 263 C6
Babusar Pass Pakistan 35°12N 73°59E 243 C5
Babushkin Russia 55°51N 37°42E 129 A3

Babušnica Serbia 43°7N 22°27E 202 C6
Bača → Slovenia 46°8N 13°54E 199 B10
Babadag Romania 42°30N 35°0E 246 D5
Badampahar India 22°10N 86°10E 244 C8
Badanah Si. Arabia 30°58N 41°30E 246 D4
Badarinath India 30°45N 79°30E 243 D8
Badarpur India 24°54N 92°38E 241 C4
Badas, Kepulauan
  Indonesia 0°45N 107°5E 234 B3
Badas → Pakistan 28°0N 64°20E 242 D2
Badegi Nigeria 9°1N 6°8E 263 D6
Badéguichéri Niger 14°30N 5°2E 263 C6
Baden Austria 48°1N 16°13E 181 C9
Baden Switz. 47°28N 8°18E 179 H4
Baden Pa., U.S.A. 40°38N 80°14W 312 F4
Baden-Baden Germany 48°44N 8°13E 179 G4
Baden-Württemberg □
  Germany 48°20N 8°40E 179 G4
Badgam India 34°1N 74°45E 243 B6
Badgastein Austria 47°7N 13°9E 180 D6
Badger Nfld. & L., Canada 49°0N 56°30W 299 C8
Badger Calif., U.S.A. 36°38N 119°1W 306 J7
Badgingarra △ Australia 30°23S 115°22E 279 F2
Badhoevedorp Neths. 52°20N 4°47E 112 A1
Badia Polésine Italy 45°5N 11°29E 199 C8
Badian □ Guinea 13°37N 13°11W 262 C2
Badin Pakistan 24°38N 68°54E 242 G3
Badinka = Mali 13°31N 9°28W 262 C3
Badjokola
  Dem. Rep. of the Congo 3°54N 20°17E 264 B4
Badlands U.S.A. 43°55N 102°30W 308 D2
Badlands △ U.S.A. 43°38N 102°56W 308 D2
Badli India 28°44N 77°8E 120 A1
Badnera India 20°48N 77°44E 244 J10
Badoc Phil. 17°56N 120°28E 232 C3
Badogo Mali 11°2N 8°13W 262 C3
Badoumbé Mali 13°42N 10°15W 262 C2
Badr Hunayn Si. Arabia 23°44N 38°46E 248 B2
Badrah Iraq 33°6N 45°58E 213 F11
Badrain Jaran Shamo
  China 40°40N 103°20E 226 D2
Badrinath India 30°44N 79°29E 243 D8
Badu Sri Lanka 7°1N 81°7E 245 L5
Badulla Sri Lanka 7°1N 81°7E 245 L5
Badung, Bukit Indonesia 8°49S 115°10E 231 K18
Badung, Selat Indonesia 8°40S 115°22E 231 K18
Badvel India 14°45N 79°3E 245 G4
Baena Spain 37°37N 4°20W 195 H6
Baengnyeongdo S. Korea 37°57N 124°40E 224 D2
Bærami Australia 32°27S 150°27E 283 B9
Bærum Norway 59°54N 10°30E 164 E6
Baetov Kyrgyzstan 41°13N 74°54E 217 D8
Baeza Spain 37°57N 3°25W 195 H7
Bafang Cameroon 5°9N 10°11E 263 D7
Bafatá Guinea-Biss. 12°8N 14°40W 262 C2
Baffin B. N. Amer. 72°0N 64°0W 292 B13
Baffin I. Canada 68°0N 75°0W 295 C13
Bafia Cameroon 4°40N 11°10E 263 F7
Bafilo Togo 9°22N 1°22E 263 D5
Bafing → Mali 12°38N 10°50W 262 C2
Bafing △ Mali 12°38N 10°50W 262 C2
Bafliyûn Syria 36°37N 36°59E 246 B3
Bafoulabé Mali 13°50N 10°55W 262 C2
Bafoussam Cameroon 5°28N 10°25E 263 D7
Bafq Iran 31°40N 55°25E 247 D7
Bafra Turkey 41°34N 35°54E 212 B6
Bäft Iran 29°15N 56°38E 247 D8
Bafut Cameroon 6°6N 10°2E 263 D7
Bafwasende
  Dem. Rep. of the Congo 1°3N 27°5E 268 C2
Bagabag Brazil
Bagabag I. Papua N. G. 4°48S 146°14E 286 C4
Bagac Phil. 14°36N 120°23E 232 D3
Bagac B. Phil. 14°36N 120°20E 232 D3
Bagaha India 27°6N 84°5E 243 F11
Bagalkot India 16°10N 75°40E 245 F2
Bagam Niger 15°43N 6°35E 263 B6
Bagamanoc Phil. 13°57N 124°17E 232 E5
Bagamoyo Tanzania 6°28S 38°55E 268 D4
Bagan = Pagan Burma 21°10N 94°55E 241 E5
Bagan Datoh Malaysia 3°59N 100°47E 237 L3
Bagan Serai Malaysia 5°1N 100°32E 237 K3
Baganga Phil. 7°34N 126°33E 233 H6
Bagani Namibia 18°7N 21°41E 270 A3
Baganupiapi Indonesia 2°12N 100°50E 234 B2
Bagasra India 21°30N 71°0E 242 J4
Bagata
  Dem. Rep. of the Congo 3°44S 17°57E 264 C3
Bagaud Brazil 12°20N 34°18E 257 D3
Bagawi Sudan 12°20N 34°18E 257 D3
Bagbag Sudan 15°23N 31°30E 257 D3
Bağçılar Turkey 41°2N 28°49E 122 B1
Bagdad Calif., U.S.A. 34°35N 115°53W 307 L11
Bagdarin Russia 54°26N 113°36E 215 D12
Bagé Brazil 31°20S 54°15W 335 C5
Bagenalstown Ireland 52°42N 6°58W 166 D5
Bagepalli India 13°47N 77°47E 245 H3
Bagerhat Bangla. 22°40N 89°47E 243 H12
Bageshwar India 29°51N 79°46E 243 E8
Bagevadi India 16°35N 75°58E 245 F2
Baggao Phil. 17°56N 121°46E 232 C3
Bággio Italy 45°27N 9°6E 128 A1
Baggs U.S.A. 41°2N 107°39W 304 F10
Bagh Pakistan 33°59N 73°45E 243 C5
Bāgh-e Feyz Iran 35°44N 51°19E 141 A1
Bagha India 25°32N 81°1E 243 G9
Baghain → India 25°32N 81°1E 243 G9
Baghdad = Baghdād Iraq 33°20N 44°23E 113 A2
Baghdād Iraq 33°20N 44°23E 113 A2
Baghdad al Muthana ✈ (BGW)
  Iraq 33°14N 44°30E 113 B2
Baghdad Int. ✈ (SDA)
  Iraq 33°15N 44°14E 113 B1
Bagheria Italy 38°5N 13°30E 200 D6
Baghlān Afghan. 36°12N 68°46E 240 A3
Baghlān □ Afghan. 36°0N 68°30E 240 A3
Bagley U.S.A. 47°32N 95°24W 308 B6
Baglung Nepal 28°16N 83°24E 243 E10
Bagmari India 23°40N 88°23E 124 B2
Bagnara Cálabra Italy 38°17N 15°48E 201 D8
Bagnasco Italy 44°18N 8°2E 198 D5
Bagnell Dam U.S.A. 38°14N 92°36W 310 F4
Bagnères-de-Bigorre France 43°5N 0°9E 174 E4
Bagnères-de-Luchon
  France 42°47N 0°38E 174 F4
Bagneux France 48°47N 2°18E 134 B3
Bagni di Lucca Italy 44°1N 10°35E 198 D7
Bagno di Romagna Italy 43°50N 11°58E 199 E8
Bagnol-sur-Cèze France 44°10N 4°37E 175 D8
Bagnolet France 48°52N 2°25E 134 A3
Bagnols-sur-Cèze France 44°10N 4°37E 175 D8
Bagnorégio Italy 42°37N 12°5E 199 G9
Bago = Pegu Burma 17°20N 96°29E 241 G6
Bago Phil. 10°32N 122°50E 233 F4
Bagodar India 24°5N 85°52E 243 G11
Bagrationovsk Russia 54°23N 20°39E 161 J19
Bagrdan Serbia 44°5N 21°11E 202 B5
Bagsværd Denmark 55°46N 12°27E 118 A2
Bagsværd Sø Denmark 55°45N 12°26E 118 A2
Bagua Peru 5°35S 78°22W 330 B2
Baguiati India 22°36N 88°25E 124 B2
Bagumbayan Phil. 14°28N 121°3E 232 D3

Bağyurdu *Turkey* 38°25N 27°41E **205** C9
Bagzane, Monts *Niger* 17°43N 8°45E **259** E1
Bahabón de Esgueva
Spain 41°52N 3°43W **194** D7
Bahadurabad Ghat
Bangla. 25°11N 89°44E **241** C2
Bahadurganj *India* 26°16N 87°49E **243** F12
Bahadurgarh *India* 28°40N 76°57E **242** E7
Bahā'i Temple *U.S.A.* 42°4N 87°41W **119** A2
Bahaja *Somalia* 11°16N 49°50E **267** B6
Baham, Pte. *Martinique* 14°24N 60°50W **322** j
Bahama, Canal Viejo de
W. Indies 22°10N 77°30W **320** B4
Bahamas ■ *N. Amer.* 24°0N 75°0W **321** B5
Bahār *Iran* 34°54N 48°26E **213** E13
Bahārak *Afghan.* 37°0N 70°53E **240** A3
Baharampur *India* 24°2N 88°27E **243** G13
Baharîya, El Wâhât al
Egypt 28°0N 28°50E **256** B2
Baharu Pandan = Pandan
Malaysia 1°32N 103°46E **237** d
Bahawalnagar *Pakistan* 30°0N 73°15E **242** E5
Bahawalpur *Pakistan* 29°24N 71°40E **242** E4
Bahçe *Turkey* 37°13N 36°34E **212** D7
Bahçecik *Turkey* 40°41N 29°44E **203** F13
Bahçeköy *Turkey* 41°10N 28°59E **122** A1
Bahçelievler *Turkey* 41°0N 28°50E **122** B1
Baheli *Phil.* 10°0N 118°47E **233** F2
Bäherden *Turkmenistan* 38°25N 57°26E **247** B8
Baheri *India* 28°45N 79°34E **243** E8
Bahgul → *India* 27°45N 79°36E **243** F8
Bahi *Tanzania* 5°58S 35°21E **268** D4
Bahi Swamp *Tanzania* 6°10S 35°0E **268** D4
Bahia = Salvador *Brazil* 13°0S 38°30W **333** D4
Bahia □ *Brazil* 12°0S 42°0W **333** D3
Bahía, Is. de la *Honduras* 16°45N 86°15W **320** C2
Bahía Blanca *Argentina* 38°35S 62°13W **334** D3
Bahía de Caráquez
Ecuador 0°40S 80°27W **328** D1
Bahía de Los Angeles
Mexico 28°56N 113°34W **318** B2
Bahía Kino *Mexico* 28°47N 111°58W **318** B2
Bahía Laura *Argentina* 48°10S 66°30W **336** C3
Bahía Mansa *Chile* 40°33S 73°46W **336** B2
Bahía Negra *Paraguay* 20°5S 58°5W **331** E6
Bahía Solano *Colombia* 6°14N 77°25W **328** B2
Bahir Dar *Ethiopia* 11°37N 37°10E **257** E4
Bahlā' *Oman* 22°58N 57°18E **249** B7
Bahmanzād *Iran* 31°15N 51°47E **247** D6
Bahmer *Algeria* 27°32N 0°10W **261** C4
Bahr el Ahmar □ *Egypt* 28°40N 31°30E **251** K2
Bahr el Ahmar □ *Sudan* 20°0N 35°0E **256** D4
Bahr el Ghazal = Kanem □
Chad 15°0N 16°0E **259** F3
Bahr el Jebel = Central Equatoria □
South Sudan 4°0N 31°0E **257** G3
Bahraich *India* 27°38N 81°37E **243** F9
Bahrain ■ *Asia* 26°0N 50°35E **247** E6
Bahror *India* 27°51N 76°20E **242** F7
Bahtīm *Egypt* 30°8N 31°16E **117** A2
Bāhū Kalāt *Iran* 25°43N 61°25E **247** E9
Bai *Mali* 13°35N 3°28W **262** C4
Bai Bung, Mui = Ca Mau, Mui
Vietnam 8°38N 104°44E **237** H5
Bai Thuong *Vietnam* 19°54N 105°23E **236** C5
Baia de Aramă *Romania* 45°0N 22°50E **182** E7
Baía dos Tigres *Angola* 16°40S 11°47E **265** F2
Baia Farta *Angola* 12°40S 13°11E **265** E2
Baia Mare *Romania* 47°40N 23°35E **183** C8
Baia-Sprie *Romania* 47°41N 23°43E **183** C8
Baião *Brazil* 2°40S 49°40W **332** B2
Baïbokoum *Chad* 7°46N 15°43E **259** G3
Baicheng *Jilin, China* 45°38N 122°42E **227** B12
Baicheng *Xinjiang Uygur,*
China 41°46N 81°52E **217** D10
Băicoi *Romania* 45°3N 25°52E **183** E10
Baidoa = Baydhabo *Somalia* 3°8N 43°30E **267** D5
Baie-Comeau *Canada* 49°12N 68°10W **299** C6
Baie du Cap *Mauritius* 20°29S 57°22E **272** e
Baie-Mahault *Guadeloupe* 16°16N 61°35W **322** e
Baie-St-Paul *Canada* 47°28N 70°32W **299** C5
Baie Ste-Anne *Seychelles* 4°18S 55°45E **272** c
Baie-Trinité *Canada* 49°25N 67°20W **299** C6
Baie Verte *Canada* 49°55N 56°12W **299** C8
Baignes-Ste-Radegonde
France 45°23N 0°25W **174** C3
Baigneux-les-Juifs *France* 47°31N 4°39E **173** E11
Baihar *India* 22°6N 80°33E **243** H9
Baihe *Hubei, China* 32°50N 110°5E **226** H6
Baihe *Jilin, China* 42°27N 128°9E **227** C15
Baihetan Dam *China* 27°11N 102°54E **228** D4
Ba'ījī *Iraq* 35°0N 43°30E **213** E10
Baijnath *India* 29°55N 79°37E **243** E8
Baikal, L. = Baykal, Oz.
Russia 53°0N 108°0E **215** D11
Baikonur = Bayqonyr
Kazakhstan 45°40N 63°20E **216** C6
Baikunthpur *India* 23°15N 82°33E **243** H10
Bailadila, Mt. *India* 18°43N 81°15E **244** E5
Baile Átha Cliath = Dublin
Ireland 53°21N 6°15W **120** A2
Baile Átha Fhirdhia = Ardee
Ireland 53°52N 6°33W **166** C5
Baile Átha Í = Athy *Ireland* 53°0N 7°0W **166** C5
Baile Átha Luain = Athlone
Ireland 53°25N 7°56W **166** C4
Baile Átha Troim = Trim
Ireland 53°33N 6°48W **166** C5
Baile Brigín = Balbriggan
Ireland 53°37N 6°11W **166** C5
Băile Govora *Romania* 45°5N 24°11E **183** E9
Băile Herculane *Romania* 44°53N 22°26E **182** F7
Băile Olănești *Romania* 45°12N 24°14E **183** E9
Baile Sear = Baleshare
U.K. 57°31N 7°22W **167** D1
Băile Tușnad *Romania* 46°9N 25°51E **183** D10
Bailén *Spain* 38°8N 3°48W **195** G7
Băilești *Romania* 44°1N 23°20E **183** F8
Baileys Crossroads *U.S.A.* 38°50N 77°6W **143** B2
Bailhongal *India* 15°55N 74°53E **245** G2
Baillieborough *Ireland* 53°56N 6°59W **166** C5
Bailique, Ilha *Brazil* 1°2N 49°58W **332** A2
Baille-Argent *Guadeloupe* 16°15N 61°48W **322** e
Baillif *Guadeloupe* 16°1N 61°44W **322** e
Bailly *France* 48°50N 2°4E **134** A1
Bailugh *Afghan.* 32°40N 66°47E **240** B2
Bailundo = Luau *Angola* 10°40S 22°10E **265** E4
Bailundo *Angola* 12°10S 15°50E **265** E3
Baima *China* 33°0N 100°26E **228** A3
Baimuru *Papua N. G.* 7°35S 144°51E **286** D3
Bain-de-Bretagne *France* 47°50N 1°40W **172** E5
Bainbridge *Ga., U.S.A.* 30°55N 84°35W **316** E5
Bainbridge *Ind., U.S.A.* 39°46N 86°49W **311** E10
Bainbridge *N.Y., U.S.A.* 42°18N 75°29W **313** D9
Bainbridge *Ohio, U.S.A.* 39°14N 83°16W **311** E13
Bainbridge Island *U.S.A.* 47°38N 122°32W **316** C4
Baine *China* 42°0N 128°0E **219** C14
Baing *Indonesia* 10°14S 120°34E **231** F6
Bainiu *China* 32°50N 112°15E **226** H7
Bainyik *Papua N. G.* 3°40S 143°4E **286** B2
Baiona *Spain* 42°6N 8°52W **194** C2
Bā'ir *Jordan* 30°45N 36°55E **251** H7
Bā'ir, W. → *Jordan* 30°59N 37°24E **251** H8
Baird Mts. *U.S.A.* 67°0N 160°0W **303** C7
Bairiki = Tarawa *Kiribati* 1°30N 173°0E **288** G9
Bairin Youqi *China* 43°30N 118°35E **227** C10
Bairin Zuoqi *China* 43°58N 119°15E **227** C10
Bairnsdale *Australia* 37°48S 147°36E **283** D7
Bairro Alto *Lisbon, Portugal* **126** c1
Bairro Lopes *Lisbon, Portugal* **126** b3
Bais *Phil.* 9°35N 123°7E **233** G4
Baisha *Guangdong, China* 23°8N 113°11E **121** B2
Baisha *Henan, China* 34°20N 112°32E **226** G7
Baisha Li *China* 19°12N 109°20E **236** C7
Baishan = Hunjiang
China 41°54N 126°26E **224** B3
Baishan *China* 42°43N 127°14E **227** C14
Baissa *Nigeria* 7°14N 10°38E **263** D7
Baitadi *Nepal* 29°35N 80°25E **243** E9
Baitarani → *India* 20°45N 86°48E **244** D8
Baixa *Lisbon, Portugal* **126** c2
Baixa Grande *Brazil* 11°57S 40°11W **333** D3
Baixa Limia-Sierra do Xurés ⌂
Spain 41°59N 8°2W **194** D2
Baixo-Longa *Angola* 15°41S 18°45E **265** F3
Baiyer River *Papua N. G.* 5°32S 144°9E **286** C3
Baiyin *China* 36°45N 104°14E **226** F3
Baiyü *China* 31°16N 98°50E **228** B2
Baiyu Shan *China* 37°15N 107°30E **226** F4
Baiyuda *Sudan* 17°35N 32°7E **256** D3
Baiyun *China* 23°11N 113°16E **121** A2
Baiyun Mountain Scenic Area
China 23°11N 113°17E **121** A2
Baj Baj *India* 22°30N 88°5E **243** H13
Baja *Hungary* 46°12N 18°59E **182** D3
Baja, Pta. *Easter I., Chile* 27°10S 109°22W **330** b
Baja, Pta. *Baja Calif.,*
Mexico 29°58N 115°49W **318** B1
Baja California *Mexico* 31°10N 115°12W **318** A1
Baja California □ *Mexico* 30°0N 115°0W **318** B2
Baja California Sur □
Mexico 25°50N 111°50W **318** B2
Bajag *India* 22°40N 81°21E **243** H9
Bajamar *Canary Is.* 28°33N 16°20W **153** e1
Bajana *India* 23°7N 71°49E **242** H4
Bajatrejo *Indonesia* 8°29S 114°19E **231** J17
Bajawa *Indonesia* 8°47S 120°59E **231** F6
Bajera *Indonesia* 8°31S 115°2E **231** J18
Bājgīrān *Iran* 37°36N 58°24E **247** B8
Bājil *Yemen* 15°4N 43°17E **248** D3
Bajimba, Mt. *Australia* 29°17S 152°6E **281** D5
Bajina Bašta *Serbia* 43°58N 19°35E **202** C3
Bajmok *Serbia* 45°57N 19°24E **182** E4
Bajo Boquete *Panama* 8°46N 82°27W **320** E3
Bajo Caracoles *Argentina* 47°27S 70°56W **336** C2
Bajo Nuevo *Caribbean* 15°40N 78°50W **320** C4
Bajoga *Nigeria* 10°57N 11°20E **263** C7
Bajool *Australia* 23°40S 150°35E **280** C5
Bak *Hungary* 46°43N 16°51E **182** D1
Bakala *C.A.R.* 6°15N 20°20E **264** A4
Bakar *Croatia* 45°18N 14°32E **199** C11
Bakassi Pen. *Cameroon* 4°42N 8°20E **263** E6
Bakel *Senegal* 14°56N 12°20W **262** C2
Baker *Calif., U.S.A.* 35°16N 116°4W **307** K10
Baker *Fla., U.S.A.* 30°48N 86°41W **317** E3
Baker *Mont., U.S.A.* 46°22N 104°17W **304** C11
Baker, Canal *Chile* 47°45S 74°45W **336** C2
Baker, L. *Canada* 64°0N 96°0W **294** E12
Baker, Mt. *U.S.A.* 48°50N 121°49W **304** B3
Baker City *U.S.A.* 44°47N 117°50W **304** D5
Baker I. *Pac. Oc.* 0°10N 176°35W **277** A15
Baker I. *Alaska, U.S.A.* 55°20N 133°40W **296** B2
Baker L. *Australia* 26°54S 126°5E **279** E4
Baker Lake *Canada* 64°20N 96°3W **294** E12
Bakere
Dem. Rep. of the Congo 1°36N 23°50E **264** B4
Bakerhill *U.S.A.* 31°47N 85°18W **316** D4
Bakers Creek *Australia* 21°13S 149°7E **280** C4
Bakers Dozen Is. *Canada* 56°45N 78°45W **298** A4
Bakersfield *Calif., U.S.A.* 35°23N 119°1W **307** K8
Bakersfield *Vt., U.S.A.* 44°45N 72°48W **313** B12
Bakharden = Bäherden
Turkmenistan 38°25N 57°26E **247** B8
Bakhchysaray *Ukraine* 44°40N 33°45E **189** K7
Bakhmach *Ukraine* 51°10N 32°45E **189** G7
Bakhmut = Artemovsk
Ukraine 48°35N 38°0E **189** H9
Bākhtarān = Kermānshāh
Iran 34°23N 47°0E **213** E12
Bākhtarān = Kermānshāh □
Iran 34°0N 46°30E **246** C5
Bakhtegān, Daryācheh-ye
Iran 29°40N 53°50E **247** D7
Bakhtegān △ *Iran* 29°51N 53°40E **247** D7
Baki = Krasnyye Baki
Russia 57°8N 45°10E **190** B7
Bakı *Azerbaijan* 40°29N 49°56E **191** K9
Baki *Somalia* 10°30N 43°48E **267** B5
Bakır → *Turkey* 38°55N 27°0E **205** C9
Bakırdaği *Turkey* 38°13N 35°46E **212** C6
Bakırköy *Turkey* 40°58N 28°52E **122** C1
Bakkafjörður *Iceland* 66°2N 14°48W **155** A12
Bakkaflói *Iceland* 66°10N 14°45W **155** A12
Bakkagerði *Iceland* 65°31N 13°49W **155** B13
Baklan *Turkey* 38°0N 29°36E **205** C11
Bako *Ethiopia* 5°51N 36°23E **257** F4
Bako *Ivory C.* 9°8N 7°40W **262** D3
Bako △ *Malaysia* 1°43N 110°28E **235** B4
Bakony *Hungary* 47°10N 17°30E **182** C2
Bakony Forest = Bakony
Hungary 47°10N 17°30E **182** C2
Bakool □ *Somalia* 4°0N 44°0E **267** D5
Bakori *Nigeria* 11°34N 7°25E **263** C6
Bakouma *C.A.R.* 5°40N 22°56E **264** A4
Baksan *Russia* 43°42N 43°32E **191** J6
Bakswaho *India* 24°15N 79°18E **243** G8
Baku = Bakı *Azerbaijan* 40°29N 49°56E **191** K9
Bakun Dam *Malaysia* 2°50N 113°50E **235** B4
Bakundi *Nigeria* 8°2N 10°45E **263** D7
Bakung *Indonesia* 0°5N 104°26E **234** B2
Bakungan *Indonesia* 2°55N 97°28E **234** B1
Bakuriani *Georgia* 41°44N 43°31E **213** B10
Bakutis Coast *Antarctica* 74°0S 120°0W **151** D15
Bakwa-Kenge
Dem. Rep. of the Congo 4°51S 22°4E **265** C4
Bakwanga = Mbuji-Mayi
Dem. Rep. of the Congo 6°9S 23°40E **265** D4
Baky = Bakı *Azerbaijan* 40°29N 49°56E **191** K9
Bal Harbor *U.S.A.* 25°53N 80°7W **129** C3
Bala *Ont., Canada* 45°1N 79°37W **312** A5
Bala *Senegal* 14°1N 13°8W **262** C2
Bala *Turkey* 39°32N 33°6E **212** C5
Bala *Gwynedd, U.K.* 52°54N 3°36W **168** E4
Bala, L. *U.K.* 52°53N 3°37W **168** E4
Bālā Morghāb *Afghan.* 35°35N 63°20E **240** B1
Balabac *Phil.* 7°59N 117°4E **233** H1
Balabac I. *Phil.* 8°0N 117°0E **233** H1
Balabac Str. *E. Indies* 7°53N 117°5E **230** C5
Balabagh *Afghan.* 34°25N 70°12E **242** B4
Ba'labakk *Lebanon* 34°0N 36°10E **250** E7
Balabalangan, Kepulauan
Indonesia 2°20S 117°30E **235** C5
Balabio, Î. *N. Cal.* 20°7S 164°11E **288** d
Bălăcița *Romania* 44°23N 23°8E **183** F8
Balad *Iraq* 34°0N 44°9E **213** F11
Balad Rūz *Iraq* 33°42N 45°5E **213** F11
Bālādeh *Fārs, Iran* 29°17N 51°56E **247** D6
Bālādeh *Māzandaran, Iran* 36°12N 51°48E **247** B6
Balaghat *India* 21°49N 80°12E **244** D5
Balaghat Ra. *India* 18°50N 76°30E **244** E3
Balaguer *Spain* 41°50N 0°50E **196** D5
Balaikarangan *Indonesia* 0°49N 110°25E **235** B4
Balaipungut *Indonesia* 1°3N 101°17E **234** B2
Balaisabut *Indonesia* 0°28N 110°49E **235** B4
Balaka
Dem. Rep. of the Congo 4°52S 19°57E **265** C3
Balakän *Azerbaijan* 41°43N 46°24E **191** K8
Balakété *C.A.R.* 6°56N 19°54E **264** A3
Balakhna *Russia* 56°25N 43°32E **190** B6
Balaklava *S. Austral.,*
Australia 34°7S 138°22E **282** C3
Balaklava *Ukraine* 44°30N 33°30E **189** K7
Balakliya *Ukraine* 49°28N 36°55E **189** H9
Balakovo *Russia* 52°4N 47°55E **190** D8
Balamau *India* 27°10N 80°21E **243** F9
Balamban *Phil.* 10°30N 123°43E **233** F4
Balambangan, Pulau
Malaysia 7°17N 116°55E **235** A5
Bălan *Romania* 46°39N 25°49E **183** D10
Balancán *Mexico* 17°48N 91°32W **319** D6
Balanda = Kalininsk
Russia 51°30N 44°40E **190** E7
Balandra B. *Trin. & Tob.* 10°42N 61°0W **323** t
Balanga *Phil.* 14°41N 120°32E **232** D3
Balangala
Dem. Rep. of the Congo 0°30N 19°56E **264** B3
Balangiga *Phil.* 11°7N 125°23E **233** F5
Balangir *India* 20°43N 83°35E **244** D6
Balaoan *Phil.* 16°49N 120°24E **232** C3
Balapur *India* 20°40N 76°45E **244** D3
Balara *Phil.* 14°39N 121°3E **127** B2
Balashikha *Russia* 55°48N 37°58E **188** E9
Balashov *Russia* 51°30N 43°10E **190** E6
Balasinor *India* 22°57N 73°23E **242** H5
Balasore = Baleshwar
India 21°35N 87°3E **244** D8
Balassagyarmat *Hungary* 48°4N 19°15E **182** B4
Balât *Egypt* 25°36N 29°19E **256** B2
Balaton *Hungary* 46°50N 17°40E **182** D2
Balaton-Felvidéki △
Hungary 46°52N 17°30E **182** D2
Balatonboglár *Hungary* 46°46N 17°40E **182** D2
Balatonfüred *Hungary* 46°58N 17°54E **182** D2
Balatonszentgyörgy
Hungary 46°41N 17°19E **182** D2
Balayan *Phil.* 13°57N 120°44E **232** E3
Balayan B. *Phil.* 13°51N 120°48E **232** E3
Balazote *Spain* 38°54N 2°9W **197** G2
Balbalan *Phil.* 17°27N 121°12E **232** C3
Balbalasang-Balbalan △
Phil. 17°23N 121°1E **232** C3
Balbi, Mt. *Papua N. G.* 5°55S 154°58E **286** C8
Balbieriškis *Lithuania* 54°32N 23°53E **184** D10
Balbigny *France* 45°49N 4°11E **175** C8
Balbina *Brazil* 1°58S 59°29W **329** D6
Balbina, Represa de *Brazil* 2°0S 59°30W **329** D6
Balboa *Panama* 8°57N 79°34W **320** c
Balbriggan *Ireland* 53°37N 6°11W **166** C5
Balcarce *Argentina* 38°0S 58°10W **334** D4
Balcarres *Canada* 50°50N 103°35W **297** C8
Bălcești *Romania* 44°37N 23°57E **183** F8
Balchik *Bulgaria* 43°28N 28°11E **203** C12
Balclutha *N.Z.* 46°15S 169°45E **285** G4
Balcones Escarpment
U.S.A. 29°30N 99°15W **314** G5
Balçova *Turkey* 38°22N 27°4E **205** C9
Bald I. *Australia* 34°57S 118°27E **279** F2
Bald Knob *U.S.A.* 35°19N 91°34W **314** D9
Baldenburg = Biały Bór
Poland 53°53N 16°51E **184** E3
Baldia *Pakistan* 24°54N 66°58E **123** A1
Baldock L. *Canada* 56°33N 97°57W **297** B9
Baldoyle *Ireland* 53°24N 6°8W **120** A3
Baldwin *Fla., U.S.A.* 30°18N 81°59W **316** E8
Baldwin *Mich., U.S.A.* 43°54N 85°51W **309** D11
Baldwin *Pa., U.S.A.* 40°21N 79°58W **312** F5
Baldwin, L. *U.S.A.* 28°34N 81°19W **133** A3
Baldwin Hills *U.S.A.* 34°0N 118°21W **126** B2
Baldwin Hills Res. *U.S.A.* 34°0N 118°21W **126** B2
Baldwinsville *U.S.A.* 43°10N 76°20W **313** C8
Baldy Peak *U.S.A.* 33°54N 109°34W **305** K9
Bale *Croatia* 45°4N 13°46E **199** C10
Bale *Oromiya, Ethiopia* 6°57N 40°8E **257** F5
Bale *Oromiya, Ethiopia* 6°20N 41°30E **257** F5
Bale Mts. △ *Ethiopia* 6°59N 39°52E **257** F4
Baleares, Is. *Spain* 39°30N 3°0E **206** B4
Balearic Is. = Baleares, Is.
Spain 39°30N 3°0E **206** B4
Baleh → *Malaysia* 2°1N 113°1E **235** B4
Baleia, Pta. da *Brazil* 17°40S 39°7W **333** E4
Baleine → *Canada* 58°15N 67°40W **299** A6
Baleine, Petite R. de la →
Canada 56°0N 76°45W **298** A4
Băleni *Romania* 45°48N 27°51E **183** E12
Baler *Phil.* 15°46N 121°34E **232** D3
Baler B. *Phil.* 15°50N 121°35E **232** D3
Baleshare *U.K.* 57°31N 7°22W **167** D1
Baleshwar *India* 21°35N 87°3E **244** D8
Balestrand *Norway* 61°11N 6°31E **164** C3
Baley *Russia* 51°36N 116°37E **215** D12
Balezino *Russia* 58°2N 53°6E **190** B11
Balfate *Honduras* 15°48N 86°25W **320** C2
Balfour Channel
Solomon Is. 8°43S 157°27E **287** M9
Balgo *Australia* 20°9S 127°58E **278** D4
Balgowlah *Australia* 33°47S 151°16E **139** A2
Balgowlah Heights
Australia 33°48S 151°16E **139** A2
Balham *U.K.* 51°26N 0°8W **125** B3
Balharshah *India* 19°50N 79°23E **244** E4
Bali *Cameroon* 5°54N 10°0E **263** D7
Bali *Dem. Rep. of the Congo* 2°50S 16°12E **264** C3
Bali *Kriti, Greece* 35°25N 24°47E **207** E5
Bali *Raj., India* 25°11N 73°17E **242** G5
Bali *W. Bengal, India* 22°39N 88°20E **124** B1
Bali *Indonesia* 8°20S 115°0E **231** J18
Bali □ *Indonesia* 8°20S 115°0E **231** J17
Bali, Selat *Indonesia* 8°18S 114°25E **231** J17
Bali Barat △ *Indonesia* 8°12S 114°35E **231** J17
Bali Sea *Indonesia* 8°0S 115°0E **231** J17
Balia *S. Leone* 9°22N 11°1W **262** D2
Baliapal *India* 21°40N 87°17E **243** J12
Baliceaux *St. Vincent* 12°57N 61°8W **323** n
Balicuatro Is. *Phil.* 12°39N 124°24E **232** E5
Baliganja *India* 22°31N 88°22E **124** B2
Balige *Indonesia* 2°14N 99°2E **234** B1
Baligród *Poland* 49°20N 22°17E **185** J9
Baliguda *India* 20°12N 83°55E **244** D6
Balik Pulau *Malaysia* 5°21N 100°14E **237** c
Balıkesir *Turkey* 39°39N 27°53E **205** B9
Balıkesir □ *Turkey* 39°45N 28°0E **205** B9
Balīkh → *Syria* 35°52N 39°12E **213** E8
Balıklıçeşme *Turkey* 40°18N 27°5E **203** F11
Balikpapan *Indonesia* 1°10S 116°55E **235** C5
Balimbing *Phil.* 5°5N 119°58E **233** J2
Balimo *Papua N. G.* 8°6S 142°57E **286** E2
Baling *Malaysia* 5°41N 100°55E **237** K3
Balingasag *Phil.* 8°45N 124°47E **233** G5
Bålinge *Sweden* 59°57N 17°33E **162** E11
Balingen *Germany* 48°16N 8°51E **179** G4
Balingsnäs *Sweden* 59°13N 18°0E **139** B2
Balingsta *Sweden* 59°12N 18°3E **139** B2
Balinsasayao Twin Lakes △
Phil. 9°21N 123°9E **233** G4
Balinț *Romania* 45°48N 21°54E **182** E6
Balintang Channel *Phil.* 19°49N 121°40E **232** B3
Balintang I. *Phil.* 19°58N 122°9E **232** B4
Balintawak *Phil.* 14°39N 120°59E **127** B1
Baliza *Brazil* 16°0S 52°20W **331** D7
Baljurashī *Si. Arabia* 19°51N 41°33E **248** C3
Balkan □ *Turkmenistan* 40°0N 54°30E **216** D5
Balkan Mts. = Stara Planina
Bulgaria 43°15N 23°0E **202** C7
Balkanabat *Turkmenistan* 39°30N 54°22E **247** B7
Balkh *Afghan.* 36°44N 66°47E **217** E7
Balkh □ *Afghan.* 36°50N 67°0E **240** A2
Balkhash = Balqash
Kazakhstan 46°50N 74°50E **214** E8
Balkhash, Ozero = Balqash Köli
Kazakhstan 46°0N 74°50E **217** C8
Balkonda *India* 18°52N 78°21E **244** E4
Ballachulish *U.K.* 56°41N 5°8W **167** E3
Balladonia *Australia* 32°27S 123°51E **279** F3
Ballaghaderreen *Ireland* 53°55N 8°34W **166** C3
Ballan *Australia* 37°35S 144°13E **282** D6
Ballarat *Australia* 37°33S 143°50E **282** D5
Ballard, L. *Australia* 29°20S 120°40E **279** E3
Ballater *U.K.* 57°3N 3°3W **167** D5
Ballé *Mali* 15°18N 8°33W **262** B3
Ballena, Pta. *Venezuela* 11°11N 63°47W **329** a
Ballenas, Canal de
Mexico 29°10N 113°29W **318** B2
Balleny Is. *Antarctica* 66°30S 163°0E **151** C11
Balleroy *France* 49°11N 0°50W **172** C6
Ballerup *Denmark* 55°43N 12°21E **118** A2
Ballestas, Is. *Peru* 13°44S 76°25W **330** C2
Ballı *Turkey* 40°50N 27°3E **203** F11
Ballia *India* 25°46N 84°12E **243** G11
Ballina *N.S.W., Australia* 28°50S 153°31E **281** D5
Ballina *Mayo, Ireland* 54°7N 9°9W **166** B2
Ballinasloe *Ireland* 53°20N 8°13W **166** C3
Ballincollig *Ireland* 51°53N 8°33W **166** E3
Ballinger *U.S.A.* 31°45N 99°57W **314** F5
Ballinrobe *Ireland* 53°38N 9°13W **166** C2
Ballinskelligs B. *Ireland* 51°48N 10°13W **166** E1
Ballinteer *Ireland* 53°17N 6°15W **120** B2
Ballon *France* 48°10N 0°14E **172** D7
Ballons des Vosges ⌂ *France* 48°0N 7°0E **173** E14
Ballsh *Albania* 40°36N 19°44E **202** F3
Ballston Spa *U.S.A.* 43°0N 73°51W **313** D11
Ballyboden *Ireland* 53°17N 6°18W **120** B2
Ballyboghil *Ireland* 53°32N 6°16W **166** C5
Ballybrack *Ireland* 53°15N 6°7W **120** B3
Ballybunion *Ireland* 52°31N 9°40W **166** D2
Ballycanew *Ireland* 52°37N 6°19W **166** D5
Ballycastle *U.K.* 55°12N 6°15W **166** A5
Ballyclare *U.K.* 54°46N 6°0W **166** B5
Ballycroy △ *Ireland* 54°5N 9°50W **166** B2
Ballydehob *Ireland* 51°34N 9°28W **166** E2
Ballyfermot *Ireland* 53°20N 6°21W **120** A1
Ballygawley *U.K.* 54°27N 7°2W **166** B4
Ballyhaunis *Ireland* 53°46N 8°46W **166** C3
Ballyheige *Ireland* 52°23N 9°49W **166** D2
Ballymena *U.K.* 54°52N 6°17W **166** B5
Ballymoney *U.K.* 55°5N 6°31W **166** A5
Ballymorefinn Hill *Ireland* 53°14N 6°22W **120** B1
Ballymote *Ireland* 54°5N 8°31W **166** B3
Ballymun *Ireland* 53°23N 6°16W **120** A2
Ballynahinch *U.K.* 54°24N 5°54W **166** B6
Ballyporeen *Ireland* 52°16N 8°6W **166** D3
Ballyquintin Pt. *U.K.* 54°20N 5°30W **166** B6
Ballyshannon *Ireland* 54°30N 8°11W **166** B3
Balmaceda *Chile* 46°0S 71°50W **336** C2
Balmain *Australia* 33°51S 151°11E **139** B2
Balmaseda *Spain* 43°11N 3°12W **196** B1
Balmazújváros *Hungary* 47°37N 21°21E **182** C6
Balmertown *Canada* 51°4N 93°41W **297** C10
Balmoral *Australia* 37°15S 141°48E **282** D4
Balmorhea *U.S.A.* 30°59N 103°45W **314** F3
Balochistan = Baluchistan □
Pakistan 27°30N 65°0E **240** D2
Balod *India* 20°44N 81°13E **244** D5
Balombo *Angola* 12°21S 14°46E **265** E2
Balombo → *Angola* 11°57S 13°46E **265** E2
Balonne → *Australia* 28°47S 147°56E **281** D4
Balotra *India* 25°50N 72°14E **242** G5
Balpyq Bī *Kazakhstan* 44°52N 78°12E **217** D9
Balqash *Kazakhstan* 46°50N 74°50E **214** E8
Balqash Köli *Kazakhstan* 46°0N 74°50E **217** C8
Balrampur *India* 27°30N 82°20E **243** F10
Balranald *Australia* 34°38S 143°33E **282** C5
Balş *Romania* 44°22N 24°5E **183** F9
Balsapuerto *Peru* 5°48S 76°33W **330** B2
Balsas → *Maranhão, Brazil* 7°15S 44°35W **332** C3
Balsas → *Tocantins, Brazil* 9°58S 47°52W **332** C2
Balsas → *Michoacan,*
Mexico 17°55N 102°10W **318** D4
Balsas del Norte *Mexico* 18°0N 99°46W **319** D5
Bålsta *Sweden* 59°35N 17°30E **162** E11
Balta *Romania* 44°54N 22°38E **182** F7
Balta *Ukraine* 47°56N 29°45E **183** C14
Baltaköl *Kazakhstan* 43°7N 67°46E **217** D7
Baltanás *Spain* 41°56N 4°15W **194** D6
Bălți *Moldova* 47°48N 27°58E **183** C12
Baltic Sea *Europe* 57°0N 19°0E **161** H18
Baltîm *Egypt* 31°35N 31°10E **256** H7
Baltimore *Cork, Ireland* 51°29N 9°22W **166** E2
Baltimore *Md., U.S.A.* 39°17N 76°36W **309** F15
Baltimore *Ohio, U.S.A.* 39°51N 82°36W **312** G2
Baltinglass *Ireland* 52°56N 6°43W **166** D5
Baltit *Pakistan* 36°15N 74°40E **243** A6
Baltiysk *Russia* 54°41N 19°58E **184** D6
Baltiyskiy = Paldiski
Estonia 59°23N 24°9E **188** C3
Baltra, I. *Ecuador* 0°26S 90°16W **330** a
Baltrum *Germany* 53°43N 7°24E **178** B3
Baluan I. *Papua N. G.* 2°33S 147°17E **286** B4
Baluchistan □ *Pakistan* 27°30N 65°0E **240** D2
Balud *Phil.* 12°2N 123°12E **232** E4
Baluhati *India* 22°39N 88°15E **124** B1
Baluqtybulaq *Kazakhstan* 50°51N 51°8E **190** E10
Baluran △ *Indonesia* 7°50S 114°23E **235** D4
Balurghat *India* 25°15N 88°44E **241** C2
Balut I. *Phil.* 5°24N 125°23E **233** J5
Balvanera *Argentina* 34°37S 58°23W **117** B2
Balvi *Latvia* 57°8N 27°15E **188** D4
Balwyn *Australia* 37°48S 145°4E **128** A2
Balwyn North *Australia* 37°47S 145°4E **128** A2
Balya *Turkey* 39°44N 27°35E **205** B9
Balykchy *Kyrgyzstan* 42°26N 76°12E **217** D9
Balyqshy *Kazakhstan* 47°4N 51°52E **187** E9
Balzar *Ecuador* 2°2S 79°54W **328** D2
Bam *Iran* 29°7N 58°14E **247** D8
Bama *Guangxi Zhuangzu,*
China 24°8N 107°12E **228** E6
Bama *Nigeria* 11°33N 13°41E **263** C7
Bamaga *Australia* 10°50S 142°25E **280** A3
Bamaji L. *Canada* 51°9N 91°25W **298** B1
Bamako *Mali* 12°34N 7°55W **262** C3
Bamba
Dem. Rep. of the Congo 5°45S 18°23E **265** D3
Bamba *Mali* 17°5N 1°24W **263** B4
Bambama *Congo* 2°32S 13°32E **264** C2
Bambamarca *Peru* 6°36S 78°32W **330** B2
Bambang *Phil.* 16°23N 121°6E **232** C3
Bambannan I. *Phil.* 5°37N 120°17E **233** J3
Bambao *Comoros Is.* 12°11S 44°31E **272** a
Bambara Maoundé *Mali* 15°26N 4°3W **262** B4
Bambari *C.A.R.* 5°40N 20°35E **264** A4
Bambaroo *Australia* 18°50S 146°10E **280** B4
Bambaya *Guinea* 10°55N 13°38W **262** D2
Bamberg *Bayern, Germany* 49°54N 10°54E **179** F6
Bamberg *S.C., U.S.A.* 33°18N 81°2W **316** B8
Bambesi *Ethiopia* 9°45N 34°40E **257** F3
Bambey *Senegal* 14°42N 16°28W **262** C1
Bambili
Dem. Rep. of the Congo 3°40N 26°0E **268** B2
Bambinga
Dem. Rep. of the Congo 3°43S 18°53E **264** C3
Bambio *C.A.R.* 3°55N 16°57E **264** B3
Bamboi *Ghana* 8°13N 2°1W **262** D4
Bamboo Avenue *Jamaica* 18°6N 77°47W **320** a
Bambous *Mauritius* 20°15S 57°24E **272** e
Bambouti *C.A.R.* 5°24N 27°12E **264** A5
Bambuí *Brazil* 20°1S 45°58W **333** F2
Bamburgh *U.K.* 55°37N 1°43W **168** B6
Bamenda *Cameroon* 5°57N 10°11E **263** D7
Bamendjing, L. de
Cameroon 5°50N 10°30E **263** D7
Bamfield *Canada* 48°45N 125°10W **296** D3
Bāmīān *Afghan.* 34°49N 67°49E **240** B2
Bāmīān □ *Afghan.* 35°0N 67°0E **240** B2
Bamiancheng *China* 43°15N 124°2E **227** C13
Bamingui *C.A.R.* 7°34N 20°11E **264** A4
Bamingui → *C.A.R.* 8°33N 19°5E **264** A3
Bamingui-Bangoran △
C.A.R. 8°30N 19°46E **264** A3
Bamkin *Cameroon* 6°3N 11°27E **263** D7
Bamou △ *Iran* 29°45N 52°35E **247** D7
Bampūr *Iran* 27°15N 60°21E **247** E9
Bampūr → *Iran* 27°24N 59°0E **247** E8
Bamu → *Papua N. G.* 8°1S 143°33E **286** E2
Ban *Burkina Faso* 14°5N 2°27W **262** C4
Ban Ao Tu Khun *Thailand* 8°9N 98°20E **237** a
Ban Ban *Laos* 19°31N 103°30E **236** C4
Ban Bang Hin *Thailand* 9°32N 98°35E **237** H2
Ban Bang Khu *Thailand* 7°57N 98°23E **237** a
Ban Bang Rong *Thailand* 8°3N 98°25E **237** a
Ban Bo Phut *Thailand* 9°33N 100°2E **237** b
Ban Chaweng *Thailand* 9°32N 100°3E **237** b
Ban Chiang *Thailand* 17°30N 103°10E **236** D4
Ban Chiang Klang
Thailand 19°25N 100°55E **236** C3
Ban Choho *Thailand* 15°2N 102°9E **236** E4
Ban Dan Lan Hoi *Thailand* 17°0N 99°35E **236** D2
Ban Don = Surat Thani
Thailand 9°6N 99°20E **237** H2
Ban Don *Vietnam* 12°53N 107°48E **236** F6
Ban Don, Ao → *Thailand* 9°20N 99°25E **237** H2
Ban Dong *Thailand* 19°30N 100°59E **236** C3
Ban Hong *Thailand* 18°18N 98°50E **236** C2
Ban Hua Thanon *Thailand* 9°26N 100°1E **237** b
Ban Kantang *Thailand* 7°25N 99°31E **237** J2
Ban Karon *Thailand* 7°51N 98°18E **237** a
Ban Kata *Thailand* 7°50N 98°18E **237** a
Ban Keun *Laos* 18°22N 102°35E **236** C4
Ban Khai *Thailand* 12°46N 101°18E **236** F3
Ban Kheun *Laos* 20°13N 101°7E **236** B3
Ban Khlong Khian *Thailand* 8°10N 98°26E **237** a
Ban Khlong Kua *Thailand* 6°57N 100°8E **237** J3
Ban Khuan *Thailand* 8°20N 98°25E **237** a
Ban Ko Yai Chim *Thailand* 11°17N 99°26E **237** G2
Ban Laem *Thailand* 13°13N 99°59E **236** F2
Ban Lamai *Thailand* 9°28N 100°3E **237** b
Ban Lao Ngam *Laos* 15°28N 106°10E **236** E6
Ban Le Kathe *Thailand* 15°49N 98°53E **236** E2
Ban Lo Po Noi *Thailand* 8°1N 98°34E **237** a
Ban Mae Chedi *Thailand* 19°11N 99°31E **236** C2
Ban Mae Nam *Thailand* 9°34N 100°0E **237** b
Ban Mae Sariang *Thailand* 18°10N 97°56E **236** C1
Ban Mê Thuôt = Buon Ma Thuot
Vietnam 12°40N 108°3E **236** F7
Ban Mi *Thailand* 15°3N 100°32E **236** E3
Ban Muang Mo *Laos* 19°4N 103°58E **236** C4
Ban Na Bo *Thailand* 9°19N 99°41E **237** b
Ban Na San *Thailand* 8°53N 99°52E **237** H2
Ban Na Tong *Laos* 20°56N 101°47E **236** B3
Ban Nam Bac *Laos* 20°38N 102°20E **236** B4
Ban Nammi *Laos* 17°7N 105°40E **236** D5
Ban Nong Bok *Laos* 17°5N 104°48E **236** D5
Ban Nong Pling *Thailand* 15°40N 100°10E **236** E3
Ban Pak Chan *Thailand* 10°32N 98°51E **237** G2
Ban Patong *Thailand* 7°54N 98°18E **237** a
Ban Phai *Thailand* 16°4N 102°44E **236** D4
Ban Phak Chit *Thailand* 8°0N 98°24E **237** a
Ban Pong *Thailand* 13°50N 99°55E **236** F2
Ban Rawai *Thailand* 7°47N 98°20E **237** a
Ban Ron Phibun *Thailand* 8°9N 99°51E **237** H2
Ban Sakhu *Thailand* 8°4N 98°18E **237** a
Ban Sanam Chai *Thailand* 7°33N 100°25E **237** J3
Ban Tak *Thailand* 17°2N 99°4E **236** D2
Ban Tako *Thailand* 14°5N 102°40E **236** E4
Ban Tha Nun *Thailand* 8°12N 98°18E **237** a
Ban Tha Rua *Thailand* 7°59N 98°22E **237** a
Ban Tha Yu *Thailand* 8°17N 98°22E **237** a
Ban Thong Krut *Thailand* 9°25N 99°57E **237** b
Ban Xien Kok *Laos* 20°54N 100°39E **236** B3
Ban Yen Nhan *Vietnam* 20°57N 106°2E **236** B6
Banā, W. → *Yemen* 13°3N 45°24E **248** D4
Banaadir □ *Somalia* 2°7N 45°24E **267** D6
Banaba *Kiribati* 0°45S 169°50E **288** H8
Banagher *Ireland* 53°11N 7°59W **166** C3
Banalia
Dem. Rep. of the Congo 1°32N 25°5E **268** B2
Banam *Cambodia* 11°20N 105°17E **237** G5
Banamba *Mali* 13°29N 7°22W **262** C3
Banana Is. *S. Leone* 8°7N 13°15W **262** D2
Banana Island *Nigeria* 6°28N 3°27E **124** B2
Bananal, I. do *Brazil* 11°30S 50°30W **333** D1
Bananga *India* 6°57N 93°54E **245** L11
Banaras = Varanasi *India* 25°22N 83°0E **243** G10
Banas → *Gujarat, India* 23°45N 71°25E **242** H4
Banas → *Mad. P., India* 24°15N 81°30E **243** G9
Bânâs, Ras *Egypt* 23°57N 35°59E **256** C4
Banática *Portugal* 38°40N 9°11W **126** A1
Banaue *Phil.* 16°55N 121°4E **232** C3
Banaz *Turkey* 38°46N 29°46E **205** C11
Banaz → *Turkey* 38°12N 29°14E **205** C11
Banbridge *U.K.* 54°22N 6°16W **166** B5
Banbury *U.K.* 52°4N 1°20W **169** E6
Banc d'Arguin △
Mauritania 20°10N 16°20W **260** D1
Banchory *U.K.* 57°3N 2°29W **167** D6
Banco *Ethiopia* 6°12N 38°13E **257** F4
Banco do Brazil, Centro Cultural
Rio de J., Brazil **135** a2
Bancoran *Phil.* 7°45N 118°30E **233** H2
Bancroft = Chililabombwe
Zambia 12°18S 27°43E **269** E2
Bancroft *Canada* 45°3N 77°51W **312** A7
Band *Romania* 46°30N 24°25E **183** D9
Band Bonī *Iran* 25°30N 59°33E **247** E8
Band-e Amīr *Afghan.* 34°50N 67°10E **240** B2
Band-e Torkestan *Afghan.* 35°30N 64°0E **240** B2
Band Qīr *Iran* 31°39N 48°53E **247** D6
Banda *Cameroon* 3°58N 14°32E **264** B2
Banda *Mad. P., India* 24°3N 78°57E **243** G8
Banda *Maharashtra, India* 15°49N 73°52E **245** G1
Banda *Ut. P., India* 25°30N 80°26E **243** G9
Banda, Kepulauan
Indonesia 4°37S 129°50E **231** E7
Banda Aceh *Indonesia* 5°35N 95°20E **234** A1
Banda Banda, Mt.
Australia 31°10S 152°28E **283** A10
Banda Elat *Indonesia* 5°40S 133°5E **231** F8
Banda Is. = Banda, Kepulauan
Indonesia 4°37S 129°50E **231** E7
Banda Kani
Dem. Rep. of the Congo 4°48S 13°52E **265** C2
Banda Sea *Indonesia* 6°0S 130°0E **231** F8
Bandai-Asahi △ *Japan* 37°38N 140°5E **220** F10
Bandai-San *Japan* 37°36N 140°4E **220** F10
Bandak *Norway* 59°23N 8°29E **164** E5
Bandama → *Ivory C.* 6°32N 4°30W **262** D3
Bandama Blanc → *Ivory C.* 6°55N 5°30W **262** D4
Bandama Rouge →
Ivory C. 6°55N 5°30W **262** D4
Bandamadji *Comoros Is.* 11°47S 43°26E **272** a
Bandān *Iran* 31°23N 60°44E **247** D9
Bandanaira *Indonesia* 4°32S 129°54E **231** E7
Bandanwara *India* 26°9N 74°38E **242** F6
Bandar = Machilipatnam
India 16°12N 81°8E **245** F5
Bandar-e Abbās *Iran* 27°15N 56°15E **247** E8
Bandar-e Anzalī *Iran* 37°30N 49°30E **213** D13
Bandar-e Bushehr = Būshehr
Iran 28°55N 50°55E **247** D6
Bandar-e Chārak *Iran* 26°45N 54°20E **247** E7
Bandar-e Deylam *Iran* 30°5N 50°10E **247** D6
Bandar-e Emām Khomeynī
Iran 30°30N 49°5E **247** D6
Bandar-e Lengeh *Iran* 26°35N 54°58E **247** E7
Bandar-e Maqām *Iran* 26°56N 53°29E **247** E7
Bandar-e Ma'shur *Iran* 30°35N 49°10E **247** D6
Bandar-e Rīg *Iran* 29°29N 50°38E **247** D6
Bandar-e Torkeman *Iran* 37°0N 54°10E **247** B7
Bandar Labuan *Malaysia* 5°20N 115°14E **235** A5
Bandar Lampung
Indonesia 5°20S 105°10E **234** D3
Bandar Maharani = Muar
Malaysia 2°3N 102°34E **237** L4
Bandar Penggaram = Batu Pahat
Malaysia 1°50N 102°56E **237** M4
Bandar Seri Begawan
Brunei 4°52N 115°0E **235** B4
Bandar Sri Aman
Malaysia 1°15N 111°32E **235** B4
Bandawe *Malawi* 11°58S 34°5E **269** E3
Bande *Spain* 42°3N 7°58W **194** C3
Bandeira, Pico da *Brazil* 20°26S 41°47W **333** F3
Bandeirante *Brazil* 13°41S 50°48W **333** D1
Bandera *Argentina* 28°55S 62°20W **334** B3
Banderas, B. de *Mexico* 20°40N 105°25W **318** C3
Bandhavgarh *India* 23°40N 81°2E **243** H9
Bandhavgarh △ *India* 23°45N 81°10E **243** H9
Bandi → *India* 26°12N 75°47E **242** F6
Bandi → *India* 19°2N 80°28E **244** E5
Bandiagara *Mali* 14°12N 3°29W **262** C4
Bandikui *India* 27°3N 76°34E **242** F7
Bandingilo △ *South Sudan* 5°26N 32°17E **257** F3
Bandipur △ *India* 11°45N 76°30E **245** J3
Bandırma *Turkey* 40°20N 28°0E **203** F11
Bandjarmasin = Banjarmasin
Indonesia 3°20S 114°35E **235** C4
Bandol *France* 43°8N 5°46E **175** E9
Bandon *Ireland* 51°44N 8°44W **166** E3
Bandon → *Ireland* 51°43N 8°37W **166** E3
Bandra *India* 19°3N 72°49E **130** A1
Bandra Pt. *India* 19°3N 72°49E **130** A1
Bandraboua *Mayotte* 12°42S 45°8E **272** b
Bandrélé *Mayotte* 12°54S 45°11E **272** b
Bandula *Mozam.* 19°0S 33°7E **269** F3
Bandundu
Dem. Rep. of the Congo 3°15S 17°22E **264** C3
Bandundu □
Dem. Rep. of the Congo 3°30S 17°30E **264** C3
Bandung *Indonesia* 6°54S 107°36E **235** D3
Bané *Burkina Faso* 11°42N 0°15W **263** C4
Băneasa *Romania* 45°56N 27°55E **183** E12
Bāneh *Iran* 35°59N 45°53E **213** E11
Banes *Cuba* 21°0N 75°42W **320** B4
Banff *Alta., Canada* 51°10N 115°34W **296** C5
Banff *Aberds., U.K.* 57°40N 2°33W **167** D6
Banff △ *Canada* 51°30N 116°15W **296** C5
Banfora *Burkina Faso* 10°40N 4°40W **262** C4
Bang Fai → *Laos* 16°57N 104°45E **236** D5
Bang Hieng → *Laos* 16°10N 105°10E **236** D5
Bang Kapi *Thailand* 13°45N 100°38E **113** B2
Bang Krathum *Thailand* 16°34N 100°18E **236** D3
Bang Lamung *Thailand* 13°3N 100°56E **236** F3
Bang Lang △ *Thailand* 5°58N 101°19E **237** K3
Bang Lang Res. *Thailand* 6°6N 101°17E **237** J3
Bang Mun Nak *Thailand* 16°2N 100°23E **236** D3
Bang Na *Thailand* 13°40N 100°36E **113** B2
Bang Pa In *Thailand* 14°14N 100°35E **236** E3
Bang Phlad *Bangkok, Thailand* **113** a1
Bang Rakam *Thailand* 16°45N 100°7E **236** D3
Bang Saphan *Thailand* 11°14N 99°28E **237** G2
Bang Thao *Thailand* 7°59N 98°18E **237** a
Banga *Angola* 8°43S 15°13E **265** D3
Banga *Dem. Rep. of the Congo* 5°25S 20°28E **265** D4
Banga *Aklan, Phil.* 11°38N 122°20E **233** F4
Banga *S. Cotabato, Phil.* 6°21N 124°47E **233** H5
Bangaduni I. *India* 21°34N 88°52E **241** E2
Bangala Dam *Zimbabwe* 21°7S 31°25E **269** G3
Bangalore *India* 12°59N 77°40E **245** H3
Banganapalle *India* 15°19N 78°14E **245** G4
Banganga → *India* 27°6N 77°25E **242** F6
Bangangté *Cameroon* 5°8N 10°32E **263** D7
Bangaon *India* 23°0N 88°47E **243** H13
Bangar *Brunei* 4°43N 115°4E **235** B4
Bangar *La Union, Phil.* 16°54N 120°25E **232** C3
Bangassou *C.A.R.* 4°55N 23°7E **264** B4
Bangbae *S. Korea* 37°29N 126°59E **137** C1
Bangeta, Mt. *Papua N. G.* 6°21S 147°3E **286** D4
Banggai *Indonesia* 1°34S 123°30E **231** E6
Banggai, Kepulauan
Indonesia 1°40S 123°30E **231** E6
Banggai Arch. = Banggai,
Kepulauan *Indonesia* 1°40S 123°30E **231** E6
Banggi, Pulau *Malaysia* 7°17N 117°12E **235** A5
Banghāzī *Libya* 32°11N 20°3E **258** B4
Banghāzī □ *Libya* 32°7N 20°4E **258** B4
Bangil *Indonesia* 7°36S 112°50E **235** D4
Bangjang *South Sudan* 11°23N 32°41E **257** E3
Bangka *Sulawesi, Indonesia* 1°50N 125°5E **231** D7
Bangka *Sumatera, Indonesia* 2°0S 105°50E **234** C3
Bangka, Selat *Indonesia* 2°30S 105°30E **234** C3
Bangka-Belitung □
Indonesia 2°30S 107°0E **234** C3
Bangkalan *Indonesia* 7°2S 112°46E **235** D4
Bangkang *Burma* 22°4N 99°1E **228** F2
Bangkaru *Indonesia* 2°4N 97°7E **234** B1
Bangkhen *Thailand* 13°52N 100°36E **113** A2
Bangkinang *Indonesia* 0°18N 101°5E **234** B2
Bangko *Indonesia* 2°5S 102°9E **234** C2
Bangkok *Thailand* 13°45N 100°35E **236** F3
Bangkok, Bight of
Thailand 12°55N 100°30E **236** F3
Bangkok Don Muang Int. ✈ (BKK)
Thailand 13°53N 100°36E **113** A2
Bangkok Noi *Thailand* 13°45N 100°29E **113** B1
Bangkok Yai *Thailand* 13°43N 100°29E **113** B1
Bangla = Paschimbanga □
India 23°0N 88°0E **243** H13
Bangladesh ■ *Asia* 24°0N 90°0E **241** D3
Bangli *Indonesia* 8°27S 115°21E **231** J18
Banglo *India* 22°31N 88°14E **124** B1
Bangoi-Kouni *Comoros Is.* 11°22S 43°21E **272** a
Bangolo *Ivory C.* 7°1N 7°29W **262** D3
Bangong Co *China* 33°45N 78°43E **243** C8
Bangor *Down, U.K.* 54°40N 5°40W **166** B6
Bangor *Gwynedd, U.K.* 53°14N 4°8W **168** D3
Bangor *Maine, U.S.A.* 44°48N 68°46W **309** C19
Bangor *Mich., U.S.A.* 42°18N 86°7W **311** B10
Bangor *Pa., U.S.A.* 40°52N 75°13W **313** F9
Bangoran → *C.A.R.* 8°42N 19°6E **264** A3
Bangrak *Thailand* 13°43N 100°31E **113** B2
Bangsu *Thailand* 13°49N 100°31E **113** B2
Bangu *Dem. Rep. of the Congo* 0°3S 19°12E **264** C3

Bangued Phil. 17°40N 120°37E 232 C3
Bangui C.A.R. 4°23N 18°35E 264 B3
Bangui Phil. 18°32N 120°46E 232 B3
Bangui B. Phil. 18°33N 120°43E 232 B3
Banguru
Dem. Rep. of the Congo 0°30N 27°10E 268 B2
Bangweulu, L. Zambia 11°0S 30°0E 269 E3
Bangweulu Swamp
Zambia 11°20S 30°15E 269 E3
Banhine △ Mozam. 22°49S 32°55E 271 B5
Bani Burkina Faso 13°43N 0°10W 263 C4
Bani C.A.R. 7°6N 22°50E 264 A4
Bani Dom. Rep. 18°16N 70°22W 321 C5
Bani Phil. 16°11N 119°52E 232 C2
Bani → Mali 14°30N 4°12W 262 C4
Bani, Jebel Morocco 29°16N 8°0W 260 C3
Bani Bangou Niger 15°3N 2°42E 263 B5
Banī Sa'd Iraq 33°34N 44°32E 213 F11
Banī Walīd Libya 31°36N 13°53E 258 B2
Bania C.A.R. 4°1N 16°7E 264 B3
Bania Ivory C. 9°4N 3°6W 262 D4
Baniara Papua N. G. 9°44S 149°54E 286 E5
Banihal Pass India 33°30N 75°12E 243 C6
Banikoara Benin 11°18N 2°26E 263 C5
Banīnah Libya 32°0N 20°12E 258 B4
Banissa Kenya 3°55N 40°19E 257 G5
Bāniyās Syria 35°10N 36°0E 250 C7
Banja Luka Bos.-H. 44°49N 17°11E 182 F2
Banjar India 31°38N 77°21E 242 D7
Banjar → India 22°36N 80°22E 243 H9
Banjarbaru Indonesia 3°25S 114°49E 235 C4
Banjarmasin Indonesia 3°20S 114°35E 235 C4
Banjul Gambia 13°28N 16°40W 262 C1
Bank London, U.K. 125 b5
Bank of China Tower Hong Kong, China 122 c1
Banka India 24°53N 86°55E 243 G12
Bankas Mali 14°4N 3°31W 262 C4
Bankeryd Sweden 57°53N 14°6E 163 G8
Banket Zimbabwe 17°27S 30°19E 269 F3
Bankilaré Niger 14°35N 0°44E 263 C5
Bankot India 17°58N 73°2E 244 F1
Banks U.S.A. 31°49N 85°51W 316 D4
Banks, C. Australia 34°0S 151°16E 139 C2
Banks I. = Moa Australia 10°11S 142°16E 280 a
Banks I. B.C., Canada 53°20N 130°0W 296 C3
Banks I. N.W.T., Canada 73°15N 121°30W 294 C7
Banks Is. Vanuatu 13°50S 167°30E 287 C5
Banks L. U.S.A. 31°2N 83°6W 316 D6
Banks Pen. N.Z. 43°45S 173°15E 285 D8
Banks Str. Australia 40°40S 148°10E 281 G4
Banksmeadow Australia 33°57S 151°12E 139 B2
Bankumuna
Dem. Rep. of the Congo 4°28S 19°57E 265 C3
Bankura India 23°11N 87°18E 243 H12
Bankya Bulgaria 42°43N 23°8E 202 D7
Banmankhi India 25°53N 87°11E 243 G12
Banmauk Burma 24°24N 95°51E 241 C5
Bann → Armagh, U.K. 54°30N 6°31W 166 B5
Bann → L'derry., U.K. 55°8N 6°41W 166 A5
Bannaanka Saraar Somalia 9°25N 46°17E 267 C6
Bannalec France 47°57N 3°42W 172 E3
Bannang Sata Thailand 6°16N 101°16E 237 J3
Bannerton Australia 34°42S 142°47E 282 C5
Banning U.S.A. 33°56N 116°53W 307 M10
Banningville = Bandundu
Dem. Rep. of the Congo 3°15S 17°22E 264 C3
Banno Ethiopia 4°51N 37°24E 257 G4
Banno-saki Japan 26°33N 128°8E 288 a
Bannockburn Ont., Canada 44°39N 77°33W 312 B7
Bannockburn Stirling, U.K. 56°5N 3°55W 167 E5
Bannockburn Zimbabwe 20°17S 29°48E 269 G2
Bannu Pakistan 33°0N 70°18E 240 B3
Bano India 22°40N 84°55E 243 H11
Bañolas = Banyoles Spain 42°16N 2°44E 196 C7
Banon France 44°2N 5°38E 175 D9
Baños de la Encina Spain 38°10N 3°46W 195 G7
Baños de Molgas Spain 42°15N 7°40W 194 C3
Bánovce nad Bebravou
Slovak Rep. 48°44N 18°16E 181 C11
Banovići Bos.-H. 44°25N 18°32E 182 F3
Bansagar Dam India 24°11N 81°17E 244 B5
Bansalan Phil. 6°55N 125°13E 233 H5
Bansgaon India 26°33N 83°21E 243 F10
Banská Bystrica
Slovak Rep. 48°46N 19°14E 181 C12
Banská Štiavnica
Slovak Rep. 48°25N 18°55E 181 C11
Bansko Bulgaria 41°52N 23°28E 202 E7
Banskobystrický □
Slovak Rep. 48°20N 19°0E 181 C12
Banstala India 22°31N 88°24E 124 B2
Banswara India 23°32N 74°24E 242 H6
Bantaeng Indonesia 5°32S 119°56E 235 D5
Bantaji → Nigeria 8°6N 10°6E 263 D7
Bantayan Phil. 11°10N 123°43E 233 F4
Bantayan I. Phil. 11°13N 123°44E 233 F4
Banteay Prei Nokor
Cambodia 11°56N 105°40E 237 G5
Banten Indonesia 6°5S 106°8E 234 D3
Banten □ Indonesia 6°30S 106°0E 234 D3
Banton I. Phil. 12°56N 122°4E 232 E4
Bantra India 22°35N 88°18E 124 B1
Bantry Ireland 51°41N 9°27W 166 E2
Bantry B. Ireland 51°37N 9°44W 166 E2
Bantva India 21°29N 70°12E 242 J4
Bantval India 12°55N 75°0E 245 H2
Banya Bulgaria 42°33N 24°50E 203 D8
Banyak, Kepulauan
Indonesia 2°10N 97°10E 234 B1
Banyalbufar Spain 39°42N 2°31E 206 B3
Banyeres de Mariola Spain 38°44N 0°38W 197 G4
Banyo Cameroon 6°52N 11°45E 263 D7
Banyoles Spain 42°16N 2°44E 196 C7
Banyuls-sur-Mer France 42°28N 3°8E 174 F7
Banyuwangi Indonesia 8°13S 114°21E 231 J17
Banz Papua N. G. 5°47S 144°37E 286 C3
Banza Dem. Rep. of the Congo 0°28N 20°10E 264 B4
Banzare Coast Antarctica 68°0S 125°0E 151 C9
Banzyville = Mobayi
Dem. Rep. of the Congo 4°15N 21°8E 264 B4
Bao Ha Vietnam 22°11N 104°21E 228 F5
Bao Lac Vietnam 22°57N 105°40E 236 A5
Bao Loc Vietnam 11°32N 107°48E 237 G6
Bao'an China 22°34N 113°52E 219 a
Baocheng China 33°12N 106°56E 228 A6
Baode China 39°1N 111°5E 226 E6
Baodi China 39°38N 117°20E 227 E9
Baoding China 38°50N 115°28E 226 E8
Baoji China 34°20N 107°5E 226 G4
Baojing China 28°45N 109°41E 228 C7
Baokang China 31°54N 111°12E 229 B8
Baoro C.A.R. 5°40N 15°58E 264 A3
Baoshan Shanghai, China 31°24N 121°28E 138 A1
Baoshan Yunnan, China 25°10N 99°5E 228 E2
Baotou China 40°32N 110°2E 226 D6
Baotow = Baotou China 40°32N 110°2E 226 D6
Baoulé → Mali 12°36N 9°45W 262 C3
Baoxing China 30°24N 102°50E 228 B4
Baoying China 33°17N 119°20E 227 H10
Baoyou = Ledong China 18°41N 109°5E 236 C7
Bap India 27°23N 72°18E 242 F5
Bapatla India 15°55N 80°30E 245 G5
Bapaume France 50°7N 2°50E 173 B9
Baqar, Bahr el → Egypt 31°7N 32°6E 251 G3
Bāqerābād Iran 33°2N 51°58E 247 C6
Ba'qūbah Iraq 33°45N 44°50E 213 F11
Baquedano Chile 23°20S 69°52W 334 A2
Bar Montenegro 42°8N 19°6E 202 D3
Bar Ukraine 49°4N 27°40E 177 D14
Bar Bigha India 25°21N 85°47E 243 G11
Bar Giyora Israel 31°45N 35°5E 123 B1
Bar Harbor U.S.A. 44°23N 68°13W 309 C19
Bar-le-Duc France 48°47N 5°10E 173 D12
Bar-sur-Aube France 48°14N 4°40E 173 D11
Bar-sur-Seine France 48°7N 4°20E 173 D11
Bara India 25°16N 81°43E 243 G9
Bâra Romania 47°2N 27°3E 183 C12
Bara Sudan 13°42N 30°20E 266 B3
Bara Banki India 26°55N 81°12E 243 F9
Baraawe Somalia 1°20N 44°8E 267 D5
Barabai Indonesia 2°32S 115°34E 235 C5
Baraboo U.S.A. 43°28N 89°45W 308 D9
Baracoa Cuba 20°20N 74°30W 321 B5
Baradā → Syria 33°33N 36°34E 250 E7
Baradero Argentina 33°52S 59°29W 334 C4
Baradine Australia 30°56S 149°4E 283 A8
Baraga U.S.A. 46°47N 88°30W 308 B9
Bărăganul Romania 44°49N 27°31E 183 F12
Baragoi Kenya 1°47N 36°47E 268 B4
Barah → India 27°42N 77°5E 242 F6
Barahanagar India 22°39N 88°22E 124 B2
Barahona Dom. Rep. 18°13N 71°7W 321 C5
Barail Range India 25°15N 93°20E 241 C4
Barajas Spain 40°28N 3°34W 127 B2
Barajas, Madrid ✕ (MAD)
Spain 40°26N 3°34W 127 B2
Barak → India 24°52N 92°30E 241 C4
Baraka Sudan 10°59N 27°59E 257 E2
Baraka → Sudan 18°13N 37°35E 256 D4
Barakaldo Spain 43°18N 2°59W 196 B2
Barakar → India 24°7N 86°14E 243 G12
Barakee △ Australia 31°37S 151°53E 283 A9
Barakī Afghan. 33°56N 68°55E 240 B3
Barakot India 21°33N 84°59E 243 J11
Barakpur India 22°47N 88°21E 124 A2
Baralaba Australia 24°13S 149°50E 280 C4
Baralla Spain 42°53N 7°15W 194 C3
Baralzon L. Canada 60°0N 98°3W 297 B9
Baram → Malaysia 4°35N 113°58E 235 B4
Baramati India 18°11N 74°33E 244 E2
Baramba India 20°25N 85°23E 244 D7
Barameiya Sudan 18°32N 36°38E 256 D4
Baramula India 34°15N 74°20E 243 B6
Baran India 25°9N 76°40E 242 G7
Baran → Pakistan 25°13N 68°17E 242 G3
Barañain Spain 42°48N 1°40W 196 C3
Baranavichy Belarus 53°10N 26°0E 177 B14
Barani Burkina Faso 13°9N 3°51W 262 C4
Baranoa Colombia 10°48N 74°55W 328 A3
Baranof U.S.A. 57°5N 134°50W 296 B2
Baranof I. U.S.A. 57°0N 135°0W 303 H14
Baranów Sandomierski
Poland 50°29N 21°30E 185 H8
Baranowicze = Baranavichy
Belarus 53°10N 26°0E 177 B14
Baranya □ Hungary 46°0N 18°15E 182 E3
Barão de Cocais Brazil 19°56S 43°28W 333 E3
Barão de Grajaú Brazil 6°45S 43°1W 332 C3
Barão de Melgaço Mato Grosso,
Brazil 16°14S 55°52W 331 D6
Barão de Melgaço Rondônia,
Brazil 11°50S 60°45W 331 C5
Baraolt Romania 46°5N 25°34E 183 D10
Baraona Spain 41°17N 2°39W 196 D2
Barapasi Indonesia 2°15S 137°5E 231 E9
Barapina = Panguna
Papua N. G. 6°21S 155°25E 286 D8
Baras Phil. 13°40N 124°22E 232 E5
Barasat India 22°46N 88°31E 243 H13
Barat Daya, Kepulauan
Indonesia 7°30S 128°0E 231 F7
Baratang I. India 12°13N 92°45E 245 H11
Barataria B. U.S.A. 29°20N 89°55W 315 G10
Barauda India 23°33N 75°15E 242 H6
Baraut India 29°13N 77°7E 242 E7
Baraya Colombia 3°10N 75°4W 328 C2
Barbacan = Roxas Phil. 10°20N 119°21E 233 F2
Barbacena Brazil 21°15S 43°56W 333 F3
Barbacoas Colombia 1°45N 78°0W 328 C2
Barbados ■ W. Indies 13°10N 59°30W 323 r
Barbalha Brazil 7°19S 39°17W 332 C4
Barban Croatia 45°5N 14°2E 199 C11
Barbària, C. de Spain 38°39N 1°24E 206 D1
Barbarigo, Palazzo Venice, Italy 142 b2
Barbaros Turkey 40°54N 27°27E 203 F11
Barbas, C. W. Sahara 22°20N 16°42W 260 D1
Barbastro Spain 42°2N 0°5E 196 C5
Barbate Spain 36°13N 5°56W 195 J5
Barbaza Phil. 11°12N 122°2E 233 F4
Barbeau Pk. Canada 81°54N 75°1W 295 A16
Barber Curaçao 12°17N 69°4W 322 g
Barberini, Palazzo Rome, Italy 136 b3
Barberino di Mugello Italy 44°0N 11°15E 199 E8
Barbers Pt. U.S.A. 21°18N 158°7W 302 K13
Barberton Mpumalanga,
S. Africa 25°42S 31°2E 271 C5
Barberton Ohio, U.S.A. 41°1N 81°39W 312 E3
Barberville U.S.A. 29°11N 81°26W 317 F8
Barbezieux-St-Hilaire
France 45°28N 0°9W 174 C3
Barbican London, U.K. 125 a4
Barbosa Colombia 5°57N 73°37W 328 B3
Barbourville U.S.A. 36°52N 83°53W 309 G12
Barbuda W. Indies 17°30N 61°40W 322 c
Bărca Romania 43°59N 23°36E 183 G8
Barcaldine Australia 23°43S 145°6E 280 C4
Barcarena Brazil 1°30S 48°40W 332 B2
Barcarena Lisboa, Portugal 38°43N 9°16W 126 A1
Barcarena, Rib. de →
Portugal 38°41N 9°16W 126 A1
Barcarrota Spain 38°31N 6°51W 195 G4
Barce = Al Marj Libya 32°25N 20°30E 258 B4
Barcellona Pozzo di Gotto
Italy 38°9N 15°13E 201 D8
Barcelona Spain 41°22N 2°10E 114 A2
Barcelona Venezuela 10°10N 64°40W 329 A5
Barcelona □ Spain 41°30N 2°0E 196 D7
Barcelona ✕ (BCN) Spain 41°18N 2°5E 114 B1
Barceloneta Puerto Rico 18°27N 66°32W 321 b
Barcelonette France 44°23N 6°40E 175 D10
Barcelos Brazil 1°0S 63°0W 329 D5
Barcin Poland 52°52N 17°55E 185 F4
Barclayville Liberia 4°48N 8°10W 262 E3
Barcoo → Australia 25°30S 142°50E 280 D3
Barcroft, L. U.S.A. 38°52N 77°9W 143 B2
Barcs Hungary 45°58N 17°28E 182 E2
Barczewo Poland 53°50N 20°42E 184 E7
Bärdä Azerbaijan 40°25N 47°10E 191 K8
Barda del Medio
Argentina 38°45S 68°11W 336 A3
Bardaï Chad 21°25N 17°0E 259 D3
Bardas Blancas Argentina 35°49S 69°45W 334 D2
Bardawîl, Sabkhet el
Egypt 31°10N 33°15E 251 G4
Barddhaman India 23°14N 87°39E 243 H12
Bardejov Slovak Rep. 49°18N 21°15E 181 B14
Bardera = Baardheere
Somalia 2°20N 42°27E 267 D5
Barð Iceland 66°3N 19°8W 155 A7
Bárðarbunga Iceland 64°38N 17°32W 155 C9
Barðastrandarsýsla
Iceland 65°40N 23°0W 155 B3
Bardi Italy 44°38N 9°44E 198 D6
Bardīyah Libya 31°45N 25°5E 258 B5
Bardoli India 21°12N 73°5E 244 D1
Bardolino Italy 45°33N 10°43E 198 C7
Bardonécchia Italy 45°5N 6°42E 198 C3
Bardsey I. U.K. 52°45N 4°47W 168 E3
Bardstown U.S.A. 37°49N 85°28W 311 G11
Bare Ethiopia 4°37N 42°43E 267 D5
Bareilly India 28°22N 79°27E 243 E8
Barela India 23°6N 80°3E 243 H9
Barellan Australia 34°16S 146°24E 283 C7
Barentin France 49°33N 0°58E 172 C7
Barenton France 48°38N 0°50W 172 D6
Barents Sea Arctic 73°0N 39°0E 150 B9
Barentsøya Svalbard 78°25N 21°20E 154 B13
Barentu Eritrea 15°2N 37°35E 257 D4
Barfleur France 49°40N 1°17W 172 C5
Barfleur, Pte. de France 49°42N 1°16W 172 C5
Barfurush = Bābol Iran 36°40N 52°50E 247 B7
Barga Italy 44°4N 10°29E 198 D7
Bargaal Somalia 11°25N 51°0E 267 B7
Bargara Australia 24°50S 152°25E 280 C5
Bargarh India 21°20N 83°37E 244 D6
Bargas Spain 39°56N 4°3W 194 F6
Barge Italy 44°43N 7°20E 198 D4
Bargi Dam India 22°59N 80°0E 244 C5
Bargnop Sudan 9°32N 28°25E 257 F2
Bargo Australia 34°18S 150°35E 283 C9
Bargteheide Germany 53°44N 10°14E 178 B6
Barguzin Russia 53°37N 109°37E 215 D11
Barh India 25°29N 85°46E 243 G11
Barhaj India 26°18N 83°44E 243 F10
Barham Australia 35°36S 144°8E 282 C6
Barharwa India 24°52N 87°47E 243 G12
Barhi India 24°15N 85°25E 243 G11
Bari Dem. Rep. of the Congo 3°20N 19°25E 264 B3
Bari India 26°39N 77°39E 242 F7
Bari Italy 41°8N 16°51E 201 A9
Bari □ Somalia 10°0N 50°0E 267 B6
Bari Doab Pakistan 30°20N 73°0E 242 D5
Bari Sadri India 24°28N 74°30E 242 G6
Bari Sardo Italy 39°50N 9°38E 200 C2
Barīdī, Ra's Si. Arabia 24°17N 37°31E 246 E3
Barim Yemen 12°39N 43°25E 248 D3
Barima → Guyana 8°33N 60°25W 329 B5
Barinas Venezuela 8°36N 70°15W 328 B3
Barinas □ Venezuela 8°10N 69°50W 328 B4
Baring U.S.A. 40°15N 92°12W 310 D4
Baring, C. Canada 70°0N 117°30W 294 D8
Baringa
Dem. Rep. of the Congo 0°45N 20°52E 264 B4
Baringo Kenya 0°38N 36°16E 266 D4
Baringo, L. Kenya 0°47N 36°16E 268 B4
Barinitas Venezuela 8°45N 70°25W 328 B3
Baripada India 21°57N 86°45E 244 D8
Bariri Brazil 22°4S 48°44W 333 F2
Bârîs Egypt 24°42N 30°31E 256 C3
Barisal Bangla. 22°45N 90°20E 241 D3
Barisal □ Bangla. 22°45N 90°20E 241 D3
Barisan, Pegunungan
Indonesia 3°30S 102°15E 234 C2
Barit I. Phil. 18°51N 121°15E 232 B3
Barito → Indonesia 4°0S 114°50E 235 C4
Barítú △ Argentina 23°43S 64°40W 334 A3
Barjac France 44°20N 4°22E 175 D8
Barjols France 43°34N 6°2E 175 E10
Barjūj, Wadi → Libya 25°26N 12°12E 258 C2
Bark L. Canada 45°27N 77°51W 312 A7
Barka = Baraka → Sudan 18°13N 37°35E 256 D4
Barkā' Oman 23°40N 58°0E 249 B7
Barkakana India 23°37N 85°29E 243 H11
Barkal, J. Sudan 18°32N 31°50E 256 D3
Barkald Norway 61°59N 10°53E 164 C7
Barkam China 31°51N 102°28E 228 B4
Barker U.S.A. 43°20N 78°33W 312 C6
Barking U.K. 51°32N 0°5E 125 A4
Barkingside U.K. 51°35N 0°4E 125 A4
Barkley, L. U.S.A. 37°1N 88°14W 315 C10
Barkley Sound Canada 48°50N 125°10W 296 D3
Barkly East S. Africa 30°58S 27°33E 270 D4
Barkly Homestead
Australia 19°52S 135°50E 280 B2
Barkly Tableland
Australia 17°50S 136°40E 280 B2
Barkly West S. Africa 28°5S 24°31E 270 C3
Barkol, Wadi → Sudan 17°40N 32°0E 256 D3
Barkol Kazak Zizhixian
China 43°37N 93°2E 218 C7
Barla Dağı Turkey 38°5N 30°40E 205 C12
Bârlad Romania 46°15N 27°38E 183 D12
Bârlad → Romania 45°38N 27°32E 183 E12
Barlee, L. Australia 29°15S 119°30E 279 E2
Barlee, Mt. Australia 24°38S 128°13E 279 D4
Barletta Italy 41°19N 16°17E 201 A9
Barlinek Poland 53°0N 15°15E 185 F2
Barlovento Canary Is. 28°48N 17°48W 153 e1
Barlovento C. Verde Is. 17°0N 25°0W 153 j
Barlow L. Canada 62°0N 103°0W 297 A8
Barmedman Australia 34°9S 147°21E 283 C7
Barmer India 25°45N 71°20E 242 G4
Barmera Australia 34°15S 140°28E 282 C4
Barmouth U.K. 52°44N 4°4W 168 E3
Barmstedt Germany 53°47N 9°46E 178 B5
Barn, The St. Helena 15°55S 5°40W 153 h
Barna → India 25°21N 83°3E 243 G10
Barnagar India 23°7N 75°19E 242 H6
Barnala India 30°23N 75°33E 242 D6
Barnard → Australia 31°34S 151°25E 283 A9
Barnard Castle U.K. 54°33N 1°55W 168 C6
Barnato Australia 31°38S 145°0E 283 A6
Barnaul Russia 53°20N 83°40E 217 B10
Barnes N.S.W., Australia 36°2S 144°49E 282 D6
Barnes London, U.K. 51°28N 0°14W 125 B2
Barnesville Ga., U.S.A. 33°3N 84°9W 316 B5
Barnesville Minn., U.S.A. 46°43N 96°28W 308 B5
Barnet U.K. 51°39N 0°11W 125 A2
Barnet □ U.K. 51°38N 0°9W 169 F7
Barneveld Neths. 52°7N 5°36E 170 B5
Barneville-Cartevert
France 49°23N 1°46W 172 C5
Barnhart U.S.A. 31°8N 101°10W 314 F4
Barnsley U.K. 53°34N 1°27W 168 D6
Barnstable U.S.A. 41°42N 70°18W 309 E18
Barnstaple U.K. 51°5N 4°4W 169 F3
Barnstaple Bay = Bideford Bay
U.K. 51°5N 4°20W 169 F3
Barnum B. Palau 7°6N 134°15E 288 c
Barnwell U.S.A. 33°15N 81°23W 316 B8
Baro Nigeria 8°35N 6°18E 263 D6
Baro → Ethiopia 8°26N 33°13E 257 F3
Barobo Phil. 8°33N 126°7E 233 G6
Baroda = Vadodara India 22°20N 73°10E 242 H5
Baroda India 25°29N 76°35E 242 G7
Baroe S. Africa 33°13S 24°33E 270 D3
Baron Ra. Australia 23°30S 127°45E 278 D4
Barong China 31°3N 99°20E 228 B2
Barora Solomon Is. 7°30S 158°20E 287 L10
Barora Ite Solomon Is. 7°36S 158°24E 287 L10
Barotse = Western □
Zambia 15°0S 24°4E 265 F4
Barotseland Zambia 15°0S 24°0E 265 F4
Barouéli Mali 13°4N 6°50W 262 C3
Barpali India 21°11N 83°35E 244 D6
Barpathar India 26°17N 93°53E 241 B4
Barpeta India 26°20N 91°10E 241 B3
Barqa Libya 27°0N 23°0E 258 B4
Barqin Libya 27°33N 13°34E 258 C2
Barques, Pt. Aux U.S.A. 44°4N 82°58W 312 B2
Barquisimeto Venezuela 10°4N 69°19W 328 A4
Barr, Ras el Egypt 31°32N 31°50E 256 H7
Barr Smith Range
Australia 27°4S 120°20E 279 E3
Barra Brazil 11°5S 43°10W 332 D3
Barra Gambia 13°28N 16°32W 262 C1
Barra W. Isles, U.K. 57°0N 7°29W 167 E1
Barra, Sd. of U.K. 57°4N 7°25W 167 D1
Barra Andai Pakistan 24°47N 66°59E 123 B2
Barra Bonita = Ibaiti
Brazil 23°50S 50°10W 333 F1
Barra da Estiva Brazil 13°38S 41°19W 333 D3
Barra de Navidad
Mexico 19°12N 104°41W 318 D4
Barra de São Manuel Brazil 7°19S 58°5W 331 B6
Barra do Bugres Brazil 15°0S 57°11W 331 D6
Barra do Corda Brazil 5°30S 45°10W 332 C2
Barra do Dande Angola 8°28S 13°22E 265 D2
Barra do Garças Brazil 15°54S 52°16W 331 D7
Barra do Mendes Brazil 11°43S 42°4W 333 D3
Barra do Piraí Brazil 22°30S 43°50W 333 F3
Barra Falsa, Pta. da
Mozam. 22°58S 35°37E 271 B6
Barra Funda Brazil 23°31S 46°39W 137 B2
Barra Hd. U.K. 56°47N 7°40W 167 E1
Barra Mansa Brazil 22°35S 44°12W 333 F3
Barraba Australia 30°21S 150°35E 283 A9
Barracão do Barreto Brazil 8°48S 58°24W 331 B6
Barracas Argentina 34°39S 58°24W 117 B2
Barracas al Sur = Avellaneda
Argentina 34°40S 58°22W 117 C2
Barrackpur = Barakpur
India 22°47N 88°21E 124 A2
Barrafranca Italy 37°22N 14°12E 201 E7
Barrāmīya Egypt 25°4N 33°47E 256 B3
Barranca Lima, Peru 10°45S 77°50W 330 C2
Barranca Loreto, Peru 4°50S 76°50W 328 D2
Barranca del Cobre △
Mexico 27°18N 107°40W 318 B3
Barrancabermeja Colombia 7°0N 73°50W 328 B3
Barrancas Colombia 10°57N 72°50W 328 A3
Barrancas Venezuela 8°55N 62°5W 329 B5
Barranco Peru 12°9S 77°2W 124 B2
Barrancones Pt.
Trin. & Tob. 10°31N 61°28W 323 t
Barrancos Portugal 38°10N 6°58W 195 G4
Barranqueras Argentina 27°30S 59°0W 334 B4
Barranquilla Colombia 11°0N 74°50W 328 A3
Barranquitas Puerto Rico 18°11N 66°19W 321 b
Barras Brazil 4°15S 42°18W 332 B3
Barras Colombia 1°45S 73°13W 328 D3
Barraute Canada 48°26N 77°38W 298 C4
Barre Mass., U.S.A. 42°25N 72°6W 313 D12
Barre Vt., U.S.A. 44°12N 72°30W 313 B12
Barre de l'Isle Ridge
St. Lucia 13°55N 60°58W 323 m
Barreal Argentina 31°33S 69°28W 334 C2
Barrei Ethiopia 6°10N 42°49E 257 F5
Barreiras Brazil 12°8S 45°0W 333 D3
Barreirinha Brazil 2°47S 57°3W 329 D6
Barreirinhas Brazil 2°30S 42°50W 332 B3
Barreiro Portugal 38°39N 9°5W 126 B2
Barreiros Brazil 8°49S 35°12W 332 C4
Barrême France 43°57N 6°23E 175 E10
Barren, Nosy Madag. 18°25S 43°40E 272 B1
Barren I. India 12°16N 93°51E 245 H11
Barren Is. U.S.A. 58°55N 152°15W 303 G9
Barreto Brazil 22°50S 43°15W 133 B3
Barretos Brazil 20°30S 48°35W 333 F2
Barrhead Canada 54°10N 114°24W 296 C6
Barrie Canada 44°24N 79°40W 312 B5
Barrier, C. N.Z. 36°25S 175°32E 284 C4
Barrier Ra. N.S.W.,
Australia 31°0S 141°30E 282 A4
Barrier Ra. Otago, N.Z. 44°15S 169°32E 285 E4
Barrier Ra. W. Coast, N.Z. 44°30S 168°30E 285 E3
Barrière Canada 51°12N 120°7W 296 C4
Barrière-la-Croix
Martinique 14°27N 60°51W 322 j
Barrigada Guam 13°28N 144°48E 302 d
Barrineau Park U.S.A. 30°42N 87°26W 317 E2
Barrington U.S.A. 41°44N 71°18W 313 E13
Barrington, I. = Santa Fé, I.
Ecuador 0°49S 90°5W 330 a
Barrington L. Canada 56°55N 100°15W 297 B8
Barrington Tops Australia 32°6S 151°28E 283 B9
Barrington Tops △
Australia 32°4S 151°25E 283 B9
Barringun Australia 29°1S 145°41E 281 D4
Barrit-Luluno = Luba
Phil. 17°19N 120°42E 232 C3
Barron U.S.A. 45°24N 91°51W 308 C8
Barrouallie St. Vincent 13°14N 61°17W 323 n
Barroui = Salisbury
Dominica 15°26N 61°27W 323 k
Barrow U.S.A. 71°18N 156°47W 303 A8
Barrow → Ireland 52°25N 6°58W 166 D5
Barrow, Pt. U.S.A. 71°23N 156°29W 303 A8
Barrow Creek Australia 21°30S 133°55E 280 C1
Barrow I. Australia 20°45S 115°20E 278 D2
Barrow-in-Furness U.K. 54°7N 3°14W 168 C4
Barrow Pt. Australia 14°20S 144°40E 280 A3
Barrow Ra. Australia 26°0S 127°40E 279 E4
Barrow Str. Canada 74°20N 95°0W 150 B3
Barruecopardo Spain 41°4N 6°40W 194 D4
Barruelo de Santullán
Spain 42°54N 4°17W 194 C6
Barry V. of Glam., U.K. 51°24N 3°16W 169 F4
Barry Ill., U.S.A. 39°42N 91°2W 310 E5
Barry's Bay Canada 45°29N 77°41W 312 A7
Barsalogho Burkina Faso 13°25N 1°3W 263 C4
Barsat Pakistan 36°10N 72°45E 243 A5
Barsham Syria 35°21N 40°33E 213 E9
Barshatas Kazakhstan 48°10N 78°39E 217 C9
Barsi India 18°10N 75°50E 244 E2
Barsinghausen Germany 52°18N 9°28E 178 C5
Barsoi India 25°48N 87°57E 241 C1
Barstow U.S.A. 34°54N 117°1W 307 L9
Bartala India 22°32N 88°15E 124 B1
Bartenstein = Bartoszyce
Poland 54°15N 20°55E 184 D7
Bartfeld = Bardejov
Slovak Rep. 49°18N 21°15E 181 B14
Barth Germany 54°22N 12°42E 178 A8
Bartica Guyana 6°25N 58°40W 329 B6
Bartin Turkey 41°38N 32°21E 212 B5
Bartle Frere Australia 17°27S 145°50E 280 B4
Bartlesville U.S.A. 36°45N 95°59W 314 C7
Bartlett Calif., U.S.A. 36°29N 118°2W 306 J8
Bartlett Tenn., U.S.A. 35°12N 89°52W 315 D10
Bartlett, L. Canada 63°5N 118°20W 296 A5
Bartolbaai Curaçao 12°20N 69°2W 322 g
Bartolo = Betanzos
Bolivia 19°34S 65°27W 331 D4
Bartolomeu Dias Mozam. 21°10S 35°8E 269 G4
Barton Phil. 10°24N 119°8E 233 F2
Barton Vt., U.S.A. 44°45N 72°11W 313 B12
Barton Park Australia 33°56S 151°9E 139 B1
Barton upon Humber
U.K. 53°41N 0°25W 168 D7
Bartonville U.S.A. 40°39N 89°39W 310 D7
Bartoszyce Poland 54°15N 20°55E 184 D7
Bartow Fla., U.S.A. 27°54N 81°50W 317 H8
Bartow Ga., U.S.A. 32°53N 82°29W 316 C7
Bartyki Poland 52°10N 21°6E 143 C2
Barú, I. de Colombia 10°15N 75°35W 328 A2
Barú, Volcan Panama 8°55N 82°35W 320 E3
Barumba
Dem. Rep. of the Congo 1°3N 23°37E 268 B1
Barumbu
Dem. Rep. of the Congo 1°14N 23°31E 264 B4
Barúmini Italy 39°42N 8°59E 200 C1
Barung, Nusa Indonesia 8°30S 113°30E 235 D4
Barus Indonesia 2°0N 98°24E 234 B1
Baruth Germany 52°4N 13°30E 178 C9
Baruun Urt Mongolia 46°46N 113°15E 219 B11
Baruunsuu Mongolia 43°43N 105°35E 226 C3
Barvinkove Ukraine 48°57N 37°0E 189 H9
Bärwalde = Barwice
Poland 53°44N 16°21E 184 E3
Barwani India 22°2N 74°57E 242 H6
Barwice Poland 53°44N 16°21E 184 E3
Barwick U.S.A. 30°54N 83°44W 316 E6
Barycz → Poland 51°42N 16°15E 185 G3
Barysaw Belarus 54°17N 28°28E 177 A15
Barysh Russia 53°39N 47°8E 190 D8
Barzān Iraq 36°55N 44°3E 246 B5
Bârzava Romania 46°7N 21°59E 182 D6
Bas-Congo □
Dem. Rep. of the Congo 5°0S 15°0E 265 D2
Bas du Fort Guadeloupe 16°13N 61°30W 322 e
Bas-Kouilou Congo 4°28S 11°42E 265 C2
Bas-Rhin □ France 48°40N 7°30E 173 D14
Bašaid Serbia 45°38N 20°25E 182 E5
Bāsa'idū Iran 26°35N 55°20E 247 E7
Basal Pakistan 33°33N 72°13E 242 C5
Basankusa
Dem. Rep. of the Congo 1°5N 19°50E 264 B3
Basarabeasca Moldova 46°21N 28°58E 183 D13
Basarabi Romania 44°10N 28°26E 183 F13
Basarabia = Bessarabiya
Moldova 47°0N 28°10E 177 E15
Basauri Spain 43°13N 2°53W 196 B2
Basawa Afghan. 34°15N 70°50E 242 B4
Basco Phil. 20°27N 121°58E 232 A3
Bascuñán, C. Chile 28°52S 71°35W 334 B1
Basekpio
Dem. Rep. of the Congo 4°43N 24°36E 264 B4
Basel Switz. 47°35N 7°35E 179 H3
Basel, Euroairport ✕ (BSL)
Europe 47°36N 7°32E 173 E14
Basel-Landschaft □ Switz. 47°26N 7°45E 179 H3
Basento → Italy 40°20N 16°49E 201 B9
Baserah Indonesia 0°25S 101°43E 234 C2
Basey Phil. 11°17N 125°4E 233 F5
Bashākerd, Kūhhā-ye
Iran 26°42N 58°35E 247 E8
Bashanta = Gorodovikovsk
Russia 46°8N 41°58E 191 G5
Bashaw Canada 52°35N 112°58W 296 C6
Bāshī Iran 28°41N 51°4E 247 D6
Bashi Channel Asia 21°25N 121°30E 225 E2
Bashkir Republic =
Bashkortostan □ Russia 54°0N 57°0E 186 D10
Bashkortostan □ Russia 54°0N 57°0E 186 D10
Bashtanivka Ukraine 45°46N 29°29E 183 E14
Basibasy Madag. 22°10S 43°40E 272 C1
Basilaki I. Papua N. G. 10°35S 151°0E 286 F6
Basilan Phil. 6°33N 122°4E 233 H3
Basilan I. Phil. 6°35N 122°0E 233 H4
Basilan Str. Phil. 6°50N 122°0E 233 H4
Basildon U.K. 51°34N 0°28E 169 F8
Basilé Eq. Guin. 3°42N 8°48E 263 E6
Basilé, Pico de Eq. Guin. 3°36N 8°49E 263 E6
Basilicata □ Italy 40°30N 16°30E 201 B9
Basim = Washim India 20°3N 77°0E 244 D3
Basin U.S.A. 44°23N 108°2W 304 D9
Basinger U.S.A. 27°23N 81°2W 317 H8
Basingstoke U.K. 51°15N 1°5W 169 F6
Basirhat Bangla. 22°40N 88°54E 241 D2
Basīt, Ra's al Syria 35°51N 35°48E 250 C6
Baška Croatia 44°58N 14°45E 199 D11
Başkale Turkey 38°2N 43°59E 213 C10
Baskatong, Rés. Canada 46°46N 75°50W 298 C4
Basle = Basel Switz. 47°35N 7°35E 179 H3
Başmakçı Turkey 37°54N 30°1E 205 D12
Basmat India 19°15N 77°12E 244 E3
Basoda India 23°52N 77°54E 242 H7
Basoko
Dem. Rep. of the Congo 1°16N 23°40E 264 B4
Basongo
Dem. Rep. of the Congo 4°15S 20°20E 265 C4
Basora, Pta. Aruba 12°25N 69°51W 322 f
Basque, Pays France 43°15N 1°20W 174 E2
Basque Provinces = País Vasco □
Spain 42°50N 2°45W 196 C2
Basra = Al Başrah Iraq 30°30N 47°50E 246 D5
Bass, Îs. de
French Polynesia 27°55S 143°26W 289 f
Bass Str. Australia 39°15S 146°30E 281 F4
Bassae Greece 37°26N 21°53E 204 D3
Bassano Canada 50°48N 112°20W 296 C6
Bassano del Grappa Italy 45°46N 11°44E 199 C8
Bassar Togo 9°19N 0°57E 263 D5
Bassas da India Ind. Oc. 22°0S 39°0E 269 G4
Basse-Normandie □
France 48°45N 0°30W 172 D6
Basse-Pointe Martinique 14°52N 61°8W 322 j
Basse Santa-Su Gambia 13°13N 14°15W 262 C2
Basse-Terre Guadeloupe 16°0N 61°44W 322 e
Basse Terre Trin. & Tob. 10°7N 61°19W 323 t
Bassein Burma 16°45N 94°30E 241 G5
Basses, Pte. des Guadeloupe 15°52N 61°17W 322 e
Basses-Alpes = Alpes-de-Haute-
Provence □ France 44°8N 6°10E 175 D10
Basses-Pyrénées = Pyrénées-
Atlantiques □ France 43°10N 0°50W 174 E3
Basseterre St. Kitts & Nevis 17°17N 62°43W 322 d
Bassett U.S.A. 42°35N 99°32W 308 D4
Bassi India 30°44N 76°21E 242 D7
Bassigny France 48°0N 5°30E 173 E12
Bassikounou Mauritania 15°55N 6°1W 262 B3
Bassila Benin 9°1N 1°46E 263 D5
Bassum Germany 52°50N 8°40E 178 C4
Båstad Sweden 56°25N 12°51E 163 H6
Bastak Iran 27°15N 54°25E 247 E7
Baştām Iran 36°29N 55°4E 247 B7
Bastar India 19°15N 81°40E 244 E5
Bastelica France 42°1N 9°3E 175 F13
Basti India 26°52N 82°55E 243 F10
Bastia France 42°40N 9°30E 175 F13
Bastille, Place de la Paris, France 134 c5
Bastogne Belgium 50°1N 5°43E 170 D5
Bastrop La., U.S.A. 32°47N 91°55W 314 E9
Bastrop Tex., U.S.A. 30°7N 97°19W 314 F6
Basu Indonesia 0°18S 103°36E 234 C2
Basud Phil. 14°4N 122°58E 232 D4
Basuo = Dongfang China 18°50N 108°33E 236 C7
Basus Egypt 30°7N 31°12E 117 A2
Basutoland = Lesotho ■
Africa 29°40S 28°0E 271 C4
Başyayla Turkey 36°45N 32°40E 250 B3
Bat al Khutm & Al 'Ayn
Oman 23°16N 56°44E 249 B7
Bat-ongan Caves Phil. 12°20N 123°15E 232 E4
Bat Yam Israel 32°2N 34°44E 251 F5
Bata Eq. Guin. 1°57N 9°50E 264 B1
Bata Romania 46°1N 22°4E 182 D7
Bataan □ Phil. 14°40N 120°25E 232 D3
Bataan △ Phil. 14°45N 120°27E 232 D3
Batabanó Cuba 22°41N 82°18W 320 B3
Batabanó, G. de Cuba 22°30N 82°30W 320 B3
Batac Phil. 18°3N 120°34E 232 B3
Batagai Russia 67°38N 134°38E 215 C14
Batajnica Serbia 44°54N 20°17E 202 B4
Batak Bulgaria 41°57N 24°12E 203 E8
Batakan Indonesia 4°5S 114°37E 235 C4
Batala India 31°48N 75°12E 242 D6
Batalha Portugal 39°40N 8°50W 194 F2
Batalpashinsk = Cherkessk
Russia 44°15N 42°5E 191 H6
Batam Indonesia 1°5N 104°3E 234 B2
Batama
Dem. Rep. of the Congo 0°58N 26°33E 268 B2
Batamay Russia 63°30N 129°15E 215 C13
Batan I. Albay, Phil. 13°15N 124°0E 232 E4
Batan I. Batanes, Phil. 20°26N 121°58E 232 A3
Batan Is. Phil. 20°30N 122°0E 232 A3
Batanagar India 22°31N 88°15E 124 B1
Batanes □ Phil. 20°40N 121°55E 232 A3
Batang Sichuan, China 30°1N 99°0E 228 B2
Batang Indonesia 6°55S 109°45E 235 D3
Batang Ai △ Malaysia 1°32N 112°2E 235 B4
Batang Gadis △ Indonesia 0°28N 99°12E 234 B1
Batanga Gabon 0°21S 9°18E 264 C1
Batangafo C.A.R. 7°25N 18°20E 264 A3
Batangas Phil. 13°35N 121°10E 232 E3
Batangas □ Phil. 13°40N 121°5E 232 E3
Batanta Indonesia 0°55S 130°40E 231 E8
Batarasa Phil. 8°40N 117°37E 233 G1
Batas I. Phil. 11°10N 119°36E 233 F2
Batatais Brazil 20°54S 47°37W 335 A6
Batavia = Jakarta Indonesia 6°9S 106°52E 122 A2
Batavia Ill., U.S.A. 41°51N 88°19W 311 C8
Batavia N.Y., U.S.A. 43°0N 78°11W 312 D6
Batavia Ohio, U.S.A. 39°5N 84°11W 311 E12
Bataysk Russia 47°3N 39°45E 189 J10
Batbakara = Amankeldi
Kazakhstan 50°10N 65°10E 217 B7
Batchelor Australia 13°4S 131°1E 278 B5
Batdambang Cambodia 13°7N 103°12E 236 F4
Batéké, Plateau Congo 3°30S 15°45E 264 C3
Batemans B. Australia 35°40S 150°12E 283 C9
Batemans Bay Australia 35°44S 150°11E 283 C9
Batesburg-Leesville
U.S.A. 33°54N 81°33W 316 B8
Batesville Ark., U.S.A. 35°46N 91°39W 314 D9
Batesville Ind., U.S.A. 39°18N 85°13W 311 E11
Batesville Miss., U.S.A. 34°19N 89°57W 315 D10
Batesville Tex., U.S.A. 28°58N 99°37W 314 G5
Bath Ont., Canada 44°11N 76°47W 313 B8
Bath St. Kitts & Nevis 17°8N 62°37W 322 d
Bath Bath & N.E. Somerset,
U.K. 51°23N 2°22W 169 F5
Bath Maine, U.S.A. 43°55N 69°49W 309 D19
Bath N.Y., U.S.A. 42°20N 77°19W 312 D7
Bath & North East Somerset □
U.K. 51°21N 2°27W 169 F5
Bath Beach U.S.A. 40°36N 74°0W 132 C1
Bath I. Pakistan 24°49N 67°1E 123 B2
Batha □ Chad 14°0N 19°0E 259 F3
Batha → Chad 12°47N 17°34E 259 F3
Batheay Cambodia 11°59N 104°57E 237 G5
Bathsheba Barbados 13°13N 59°32W 323 r
Bathurst = Banjul
Gambia 13°28N 16°40W 262 C1
Bathurst N.S.W.,
Australia 33°25S 149°31E 283 B8
Bathurst N.B., Canada 47°37N 65°43W 299 C6
Bathurst Eastern Cape,
S. Africa 33°30S 26°50E 270 D4
Bathurst, C. Canada 70°34N 128°0W 294 C6
Bathurst B. Australia 14°16S 144°25E 280 A3
Bathurst Harb. Australia 43°15S 146°10E 281 G4
Bathurst I. N. Terr.,
Australia 11°30S 130°10E 278 B5
Bathurst I. Nunavut,
Canada 76°0N 100°30W 295 B11
Bathurst Inlet Canada 66°50N 108°1W 294 D10
Bati Ethiopia 11°10N 40°0E 257 E5
Batie Burkina Faso 9°53N 2°53W 262 D4
Batiki Fiji 17°48S 179°10E 287 A2
Batir West Bank 31°43N 35°8E 123 B1
Batken Kyrgyzstan 40°3N 70°50E 217 D8
Batken □ Kyrgyzstan 39°50N 71°0E 217 E8
Batlow Australia 35°31S 148°9E 283 C8
Batman Turkey 37°55N 41°5E 213 D9
Baṭn al Ghūl Jordan 29°36N 35°56E 251 J6
Batna Algeria 35°34N 6°15E 261 A6
Batna □ Algeria 35°30N 5°55E 261 A6
Batnfjordsøra Norway 62°53N 7°42E 164 B4
Bato Catanduanes, Phil. 13°36N 124°18E 232 E5
Bato Leyte, Phil. 10°13N 124°48E 233 F5
Bato Bato Phil. 5°6N 119°49E 233 J2
Batoala Gabon 0°48N 13°27E 264 B2
Batobato = San Isidro Phil. 6°50N 126°5E 233 H6
Batočina Serbia 44°7N 21°5E 202 B5
Batok, Bukit Singapore 1°21N 103°46E 138 A2
Batoka Zambia 16°45S 27°15E 269 F2
Baton Rouge U.S.A. 30°27N 91°11W 314 F9
Batong, Ko Thailand 6°32N 99°12E 237 J2
Bátonyterenye Hungary 47°59N 19°50E 182 C4
Batopilas Mexico 27°1N 107°44W 318 B3
Batouri Cameroon 4°30N 14°25E 264 B2
Batovany = Partizánske
Slovak Rep. 48°38N 18°23E 181 C11
Båtsfjord Norway 70°38N 29°39E 160 A23
Batsi Greece 37°52N 24°47E 204 D6
Battambang = Batdambang
Cambodia 13°7N 103°12E 236 F4
Battersea U.K. 51°28N 0°9W 125 B3
Battery Park New York, U.S.A. 132 f1
Batti Malv India 8°50N 92°51E 245 K11
Batticaloa Sri Lanka 7°43N 81°45E 245 L5
Battipáglia Italy 40°37N 14°58E 201 B7
Battle U.K. 50°55N 0°30E 169 G8
Battle → Canada 52°43N 108°15W 297 C7
Battle Creek U.S.A. 42°19N 85°11W 311 B11
Battle Ground U.S.A. 45°47N 122°32W 306 E4
Battle Harbour Canada 52°16N 55°35W 299 B8
Battle Lake U.S.A. 46°17N 95°43W 308 B6
Battle Mountain U.S.A. 40°38N 116°56W 304 F5
Battlefields Zimbabwe 18°37S 29°47E 269 F2
Battleford Canada 52°45N 108°15W 297 C7
Battonya Hungary 46°16N 21°3E 182 D6
Batu Ethiopia 6°55N 39°45E 257 F4
Batu Malaysia 3°15N 101°40E 237 L3
Batu, Bukit Malaysia 2°16N 113°43E 235 B4
Batu, Kepulauan Indonesia 0°30S 98°25E 234 C1
Batu Bora, Bukit Malaysia 2°43N 114°43E 235 B4
Batu Ferringhi Malaysia 5°28N 100°15E 237 c
Batu Gajah Malaysia 4°28N 101°3E 237 K3
Batu Is. = Batu, Kepulauan
Indonesia 0°30S 98°25E 234 C1
Batu Pahat Malaysia 1°50N 102°56E 237 M4
Batu Puteh, Gunung
Malaysia 4°15N 101°31E 237 K3
Batuan Phil. 12°25N 123°46E 232 E4
Batuata Indonesia 6°12S 122°42E 231 F6
Batugondang, Tanjung
Indonesia 8°6S 114°29E 231 J17
Batukaru, Gunung
Indonesia 8°20S 115°5E 231 J18
Batulaki Phil. 5°34N 125°19E 233 J5
Batuli = San Isidro Phil. 6°50N 126°5E 233 H6
Batumi Georgia 41°39N 41°44E 191 K5
Batuputih Indonesia 1°2N 118°28E 235 B5
Batur, Gunung Indonesia 8°14S 115°23E 231 J18
Batura Sar Pakistan 36°30N 74°31E 243 A6
Baturaja Indonesia 4°11S 104°15E 234 C2

Baturité Brazil 4°28S 38°45W 332 B4
Baturiti Indonesia 8°19S 115°11E 231 J18
Batusangkar Indonesia 0°27S 100°35E 234 C2
Batys Qazaqstan □
Kazakhstan 50°00N 50°00E 216 C3
Bau Malaysia 1°25N 110°9E 235 B4
Bauang Phil. 16°31N 120°20E 232 C3
Baubau Indonesia 5°25S 122°38E 231 F6
Baucau E. Timor 8°27S 126°27E 231 F7
Bauchi Nigeria 10°22N 9°48E 263 C6
Bauchi □ Nigeria 10°30N 10°0E 263 C7
Baud France 47°52N 3°1W 172 E3
Bauda India 20°50N 84°25E 244 D7
Baudette U.S.A. 48°43N 94°36W 308 A6
Bauer, C. Australia 32°44S 134°4E 281 E1
Bauerwitz = Baborów
Poland 50°7N 18°1E 185 H5
Bauguen = Salcedo Phil. 11°9N 125°40E 233 F5
Bauhinia Australia 24°35S 149°18E 280 C4
Baukau = Baucau
E. Timor 8°27S 126°27E 231 F7
Bauko Phil. 17°0N 120°52E 232 C3
Baulai → Bangla. 24°22N 91°1E 241 C3
Bauld, C. Canada 51°38N 55°26W 295 G20
Bauman Russia 55°45N 37°40E 129 B3
Baume-les-Dames France 47°22N 6°22E 173 E13
Baumgarten Austria 48°12N 16°17E 142 A1
Baunatal Germany 51°14N 9°24E 178 D5
Baunei Italy 40°2N 9°40E 200 B2
Baure Nigeria 12°52N 8°50E 263 C6
Baures Bolivia 13°35S 63°35W 331 C5
Bauru Brazil 22°10S 49°0W 335 A6
Baús Brazil 18°22S 52°47W 331 D7
Bausi India 24°48N 87°1E 243 G12
Bauska Latvia 56°24N 24°15E 184 B11
Bautino Kazakhstan 44°35N 50°14E 191 H10
Bautzen Germany 51°10N 14°26E 178 D10
Bauya S. Leone 8°12N 12°38W 262 D2
Bavānāt Iran 30°28N 53°27E 247 D7
Bavanište Serbia 44°49N 20°55E 182 F5
Bavaria = Bayern □
Germany 48°50N 12°0E 179 G7
Båven Sweden 59°0N 16°56E 162 E10
Bavispe → Mexico 29°15N 109°11W 318 B3
Baw Baw △ Australia 37°50S 146°17E 283 D7
Bawal Indonesia 7°52S 111°13E 235 D4
Bawan Indonesia 1°42S 113°55E 235 C4
Bawdwin Burma 23°5N 97°20E 241 D6
Bawean Indonesia 5°46S 112°35E 235 D4
Bawku Ghana 11°3N 0°19W 263 C4
Bawlakhe Burma 19°11N 97°21E 241 F6
Bawolung China 28°50N 101°16E 228 C3
Bawomataluwo Indonesia 0°38N 97°44E 234 B1
Baxley U.S.A. 31°47N 82°21W 316 D7
Baxter Iowa, U.S.A. 41°49N 93°9W 310 C3
Baxter Minn., U.S.A. 46°21N 94°17W 308 B6
Baxter Springs U.S.A. 37°2N 94°44W 308 G6
Baxter State △ U.S.A. 46°5N 68°57W 309 B19
Bay □ Somalia 3°0N 43°30E 267 D5
Bay, L. U.S.A. 28°25N 81°34W 133 A2
Bay, Laguna de Phil. 14°20N 121°11E 232 D3
Bay City Mich., U.S.A. 43°36N 83°54W 309 D12
Bay City Tex., U.S.A. 28°59N 95°58W 314 G7
Bay Harbor Islands U.S.A. 25°53N 80°7W 129 C3
Bay Hill U.S.A. 28°28N 81°30W 133 B1
Bay Minette U.S.A. 30°53N 87°46W 315 F11
Bay of Plenty □ N.Z. 38°0S 177°0E 284 D5
Bay Ridge U.S.A. 40°37N 74°1W 132 C1
Bay Roberts Canada 47°36N 53°16W 299 C9
Bay St. Louis U.S.A. 30°19N 89°20W 315 F10
Bay Springs U.S.A. 31°59N 89°17W 315 F10
Bay View N.Z. 39°25S 176°50E 284 F5
Baya Dem. Rep. of the Congo 11°53S 27°25E 269 E2
Bayambang Phil. 15°49N 120°27E 232 D3
Bayamo Cuba 20°20N 76°40W 320 B4
Bayamón Puerto Rico 18°24N 66°9W 321 C6
Bayan Har Shan China 34°0N 98°0E 218 E8
Bayan Hot = Alxa Zuoqi
China 38°50N 105°40E 226 E3
Bayan Lepas Malaysia 5°17N 100°16E 237 c
Bayan Obo China 41°52N 109°59E 226 D5
Bayan-Ovoo = Erdenetsogt
Mongolia 42°55N 106°5E 226 C4
Bayan-Tumen = Choybalsan
Mongolia 48°4N 114°30E 219 B11
Bayana India 26°55N 77°18E 242 F7
Bayanaūyl Kazakhstan 50°45N 75°45E 217 B9
Bayanhongor Mongolia 46°8N 102°43E 218 B9
Bayard N. Mex., U.S.A. 32°46N 108°8W 305 K9
Bayard Nebr., U.S.A. 41°45N 103°20W 308 E2
Bayawan Phil. 9°46N 122°45E 233 G4
Baybay Phil. 10°40N 124°55E 233 F5
Bayburt Turkey 40°15N 40°20E 213 B9
Bayburt □ Turkey 40°35N 39°25E 213 B8
Baydaratskaya Guba
Russia 69°0N 67°30E 214 C7
Baydhabo Somalia 3°8N 43°30E 267 D5
Bayelsa □ Nigeria 4°30N 6°0E 263 E6
Bayerische Alpen
Germany 47°35N 11°30E 179 H7
Bayerische Rhön ⌓
Germany 50°15N 10°5E 179 E6
Bayerischer Spessart ⌓
Germany 49°58N 10°15E 179 F6
Bayerischer Wald
Germany 48°56N 12°50E 179 G8
Bayern □ Germany 48°50N 12°0E 179 G7
Bayeux France 49°17N 0°42W 172 C6
Bayfield Ont., Canada 43°34N 81°42W 312 C3
Bayfield Wis., U.S.A. 46°49N 90°49W 308 B8
Bayḥān al Qiṣāb Yemen 15°48N 45°44E 248 D4
Bayındır Turkey 38°13N 27°39E 205 C9
Bayit Va-Gan Israel 31°46N 35°11E 123 B2
Baykal, Oz. Russia 53°0N 108°0E 215 D11
Baykan Turkey 38°7N 41°44E 213 C9
Baykit Russia 61°50N 95°50E 215 ...
Baymak Russia 52°36N 58°19E 186 D10
Baynes Mts. Namibia 17°15S 13°0E 270 A1
Bayombong Phil. 16°30N 121°10E 232 C3
Bayon France 48°30N 6°20E 173 D13
Bayona = Baiona Spain 42°6N 8°52W 194 C2
Bayonet Point U.S.A. 28°20N 82°41W 317 G7
Bayonne Pyrénées-Atlantiques,
France 43°30N 1°28W 174 E2
Bayonne N.J., U.S.A. 40°40N 74°6W 132 B1
Bayou Boeuf U.S.A. 29°50N 90°10W 131 B1
Bayou Segnette State Park ⌓
U.S.A. 29°53N 90°10W 131 B2
Bayovar Peru 5°50S 81°0W 330 B1
Bayport U.S.A. 28°32N 82°39W 317 G7
Bayqonyr Kazakhstan 45°40N 63°20E 216 C6
Bayram-Ali = Baýramaly
Turkmenistan 37°37N 62°10E 247 B9
Baýramaly Turkmenistan 37°37N 62°10E 247 B9
Bayramiç Turkey 39°48N 26°36E 205 B8
Bayrampaşa Turkey 41°1N 28°56E 122 B1
Bayreuth Germany 49°56N 11°35E 179 F7
Bayrischzell Germany 47°41N 12°0E 179 H8
Bayrūt Lebanon 33°53N 35°31E 250 E6
Bays, L. of Canada 45°15N 79°4W 312 A5
Bayshore Calif., U.S.A. 37°42N 122°24W 136 B2
Bayshore Fla., U.S.A. 26°43N 81°50W 317 J8
Baysville Canada 45°9N 79°7W 312 A5
Bayswater London, U.K. 125 b2
Bayt al Faqīh Yemen 14°31N 43°19E 248 D3
Bayt Lahm West Bank 31°43N 35°12E 123 B2
Baytik Shan China 45°15N 90°50E 217 C12
Baytown U.S.A. 29°43N 94°59W 314 G7
Bayugan Phil. 8°43N 125°42E 233 G5
Bayview U.S.A. 37°44N 122°23W 136 B2
Bayville = Kirkwood
S. Africa 33°22S 25°15E 270 D4
Bayy al Kabir, W. Libya 31°10N 15°53E 258 B3
Bayy al Khā'ib, Wādī →
Libya 30°55N 15°29E 258 B3
Bayzo Niger 13°52N 4°35E 263 C5
Baza Spain 37°33N 2°47W 195 H8
Bāzār Iran 35°40N 51°25E 141 A2
Bazar Dyuzi Russia 41°12N 47°50E 191 K8
Bazardüzü = Bazar Dyuzi
Russia 41°12N 47°50E 191 K8
Bāzargān Iran 39°22N 44°26E 213 C11
Bazargic = Dobrich
Bulgaria 43°37N 27°49E 203 C11
Bazarny Karabulak
Russia 52°20N 46°29E 190 D8
Bazarnyy Syzgan Russia 53°45N 46°40E 190 D8
Bazaruto, I. do Mozam. 21°40S 35°28E 271 B6
Bazaruto △ Mozam. 21°42S 35°26E 271 B6
Bazas France 44°27N 0°13W 174 D3
Bazhong China 31°52N 106°46E 228 B6
Bazhou China 39°8N 116°22E 226 E9
Bazin Guadeloupe 16°22N 61°26W 322 e
Bazmān, Kūh-e Iran 28°4N 60°1E 247 D9
Baztan = Elizondo Spain 43°12N 1°30W 196 B3
Bé, Nosy Madag. 13°25S 48°15E 272 A2
Beach U.S.A. 46°58N 104°0W 308 B2
Beach City U.S.A. 40°39N 81°35W 312 F3
Beachport Australia 37°29S 140°0E 282 D4
Beachville Canada 43°5N 80°49W 312 C4
Beachy Hd. U.K. 50°44N 0°15E 169 G8
Beacon W. Austral.,
Australia 30°26S 117°52E 279 F2
Beacon N.Y., U.S.A. 41°30N 73°58W 313 E11
Beacon Hill Hong Kong,
China 22°21N 114°10E 122 A2
Beacon Hill Boston, U.S.A. 116 b1
Beaconsfield Australia 41°11S 146°48E 281 G4
Beagle, Canal S. Amer. 55°0S 68°30W 336 E3
Beagle Bay Australia 16°58S 122°40E 278 C3
Beagle Bay ◎ Australia 16°53S 122°40E 278 C3
Beagle G. Australia 12°15S 130°25E 278 B5
Béal an Átha = Ballina
Ireland 54°7N 9°9W 166 B2
Béal Átha na Sluaighe = Ballinasloe
Ireland 53°20N 8°13W 166 C3
Bealanana Madag. 14°33S 48°44E 272 A2
Beals Cr. → U.S.A. 32°10N 100°51W 314 E4
Beamsville Canada 43°12N 79°28W 312 C5
Bear → Calif., U.S.A. 38°56N 121°36W 306 G5
Bear → Utah, U.S.A. 41°30N 112°8W 300 G17
Béar, C. France 42°31N 3°8E 174 F7
Bear I. Ireland 51°38N 9°50W 166 E2
Bear L. Man., Canada 55°8N 96°0W 297 B9
Bear L. Utah, U.S.A. 41°59N 111°21W 304 F8
Bear Lake Canada 45°27N 79°35W 312 A5
Beardmore Canada 49°36N 87°57W 298 C2
Beardmore Glacier
Antarctica 84°30S 170°0E 151 E11
Beardstown U.S.A. 40°1N 90°26W 310 E6
Bearma → India 24°20N 79°51E 243 G8
Béarn France 43°20N 0°30W 174 E3
Bearpaw Mts. U.S.A. 48°12N 109°30W 304 B9
Bearskin Lake Canada 53°58N 91°2W 298 B1
Beas → India 31°10N 74°59E 242 D6
Beas de Segura Spain 38°15N 2°53W 195 G8
Beasain Spain 43°3N 2°11W 196 B2
Beata, C. Dom. Rep. 17°40N 71°30W 321 C5
Beata, I. Dom. Rep. 17°34N 71°31W 321 C5
Beata Ridge W. Indies 16°0N 72°30W 321 C5
Beato Portugal 38°44N 9°5W 126 A2
Beatrice Nebr., U.S.A. 40°16N 96°45W 308 E5
Beatrice Zimbabwe 18°15S 30°55E 269 F3
Beatrice, C. Australia 14°20S 136°55E 280 A2
Beatton → Canada 56°15N 120°45W 296 B4
Beatton River Canada 57°26N 121°20W 296 B4
Beatty U.S.A. 36°54N 116°46W 306 J10
Beau Bassin Mauritius 20°13S 57°27E 272 e
Beauaraba = Pittsworth
Australia 27°41S 151°37E 281 D5
Beaucaire France 43°48N 4°39E 175 E8
Beauce, Plaine de la France 48°10N 1°45E 173 D8
Beauceville Canada 46°13N 70°46W 299 C5
Beauchêne, I. Falk. Is. 52°55S 59°15W 153 f
Beaudesert Australia 27°59S 153°0E 281 D5
Beaufort Vic., Australia 37°25S 143°25E 282 D5
Beaufort Savoie, France 45°44N 6°34E 175 C10
Beaufort Malaysia 5°30N 115°40E 235 A5
Beaufort N.C., U.S.A. 34°43N 76°40W 315 D16
Beaufort S.C., U.S.A. 32°26N 80°40W 316 C9
Beaufort Sea Arctic 72°0N 140°0W 292 B5
Beaufort West S. Africa 32°18S 22°36E 270 D3
Beaugency France 47°47N 1°38E 173 E8
Beauharnois Canada 45°20N 73°52W 313 A11
Beaujeu France 46°10N 4°35E 173 F11
Beaujolais France 46°0N 4°22E 173 F11
Beaulieu → Canada 62°3N 113°11W 296 A6
Beaulieu-sur-Dordogne
France 44°58N 1°50E 174 D5
Beaulieu-sur-Mer France 43°42N 7°20E 175 E11
Beauly U.K. 57°30N 4°28W 167 D4
Beauly → U.K. 57°29N 4°27W 167 D4
Beaumaris U.K. 53°16N 4°6W 168 D3
Beaumont Belgium 50°15N 4°14E 170 D4
Beaumont Dordogne, France 44°45N 0°46E 174 D4
Beaumont Dublin, Ireland 53°23N 6°13W 120 A2
Beaumont N.Z. 45°50S 169°33E 285 F4
Beaumont Calif., U.S.A. 33°57N 115°59W 307 M9
Beaumont Tex., U.S.A. 30°5N 94°6W 314 F7
Beaumont-de-Lomagne
France 43°53N 1°0E 174 E5
Beaumont-le-Roger France 49°4N 0°47E 172 C7
Beaumont-sur-Sarthe
France 48°13N 0°8E 172 D7
Beaumont Heights
Canada 43°45N 79°34W 141 A1
Beaune France 47°2N 4°50E 173 E11
Beaune-la-Rolande France 48°4N 2°25E 173 D9
Beauport Guadeloupe 16°25N 61°30W 322 e
Beaupré Canada 47°3N 70°54W 299 C5
Beaupréau France 47°12N 1°0W 172 E6
Beauraing Belgium 50°7N 4°57E 170 D4
Beaurepaire France 45°22N 5°1E 175 C9
Beausejour Man., Canada 50°5N 96°35W 297 C9
Beauséjour Guadeloupe 16°18N 61°4W 322 e
Beauséjour Martinique 14°44N 60°57W 322 j
Beauvais France 49°25N 2°8E 173 C9
Beauval Canada 55°9N 107°37W 297 B7
Beauvoir-sur-Mer France 46°55N 2°2W 172 F4
Beauvoir-sur-Niort France 46°12N 0°30W 174 B3
Beaver Alaska, U.S.A. 66°22N 147°24W 303 C11
Beaver Okla., U.S.A. 36°49N 100°31W 314 C4
Beaver Pa., U.S.A. 40°42N 80°19W 312 F4
Beaver Utah, U.S.A. 38°17N 112°38W 304 G7
Beaver → B.C., Canada 59°52N 124°20W 296 B4
Beaver → Ont., Canada 55°55N 87°48W 298 A2
Beaver → Sask., Canada 55°26N 107°45W 297 B7
Beaver → Okla., U.S.A. 36°35N 99°30W 314 C5
Beaver City U.S.A. 40°8N 99°50W 308 E4
Beaver Creek Canada 63°0N 141°0W 294 E3
Beaver Dam U.S.A. 43°28N 88°50W 308 D9
Beaver Falls U.S.A. 40°46N 80°20W 312 F4
Beaver Hill L. Canada 54°5N 94°50W 297 C10
Beaver I. U.S.A. 45°40N 85°33W 309 C11
Beavercreek U.S.A. 39°43N 84°11W 311 E12
Beaverhill L. Canada 53°27N 112°32W 296 C6
Beaverlodge Canada 55°11N 119°29W 296 B5
Beaverstone → Canada 54°59N 89°25W 298 B2
Beaverton Ont., Canada 44°26N 79°9W 312 B5
Beaverton Oreg., U.S.A. 45°29N 122°48W 306 E4
Beawar India 26°3N 74°18E 242 F6
Bebedouro Brazil 21°0S 48°25W 335 A6
Bebek Turkey 41°4N 29°2E 122 B2
Bebera, Tanjung
Indonesia 8°44S 115°51E 231 K18
Beboa Madag. 17°22S 44°33E 272 B1
Beboto Chad 8°16N 16°56E 259 G3
Bebra Germany 50°58N 9°48E 178 E5
Becán Mexico 18°34N 89°31W 319 D7
Bécancour Canada 46°20N 72°26W 309 B17
Beccles U.K. 52°27N 1°35E 169 E9
Bečej Serbia 45°36N 20°3E 182 E5
Beceni Romania 45°23N 26°48E 183 E11
Becerreá Spain 42°51N 7°10W 194 C3
Béchar Algeria 31°38N 2°18W 261 B4
Béchar □ Algeria 30°15N 3°5E 261 B5
Becharof L. U.S.A. 57°56N 156°23W 303 H8
Becharof Nat. Wildlife Refuge ⌓
U.S.A. 58°0N 156°15W 303 H8
Becharre = Bsharri
Lebanon 34°15N 36°0E 250 D7
Běchovice Czech Rep. 50°4N 14°36E 135 B3
Bechuanaland = Botswana ■
Africa 22°0S 24°0E 270 B3
Bechyně Czech Rep. 49°17N 14°29E 180 B7
Beckenham U.K. 51°24N 0°1W 125 B3
Bečkerek = Zrenjanin
Serbia 45°22N 20°23E 182 E5
Beckley U.S.A. 37°47N 81°11W 309 G13
Beckton U.K. 51°30N 0°4E 125 A4
Beckum Germany 51°45N 8°3E 178 D4
Beclean Romania 47°11N 24°11E 183 C9
Becontree U.K. 51°33N 0°7E 125 A4
Bečov nad Teplou
Czech Rep. 50°5N 12°49E 180 A5
Bečva → Czech Rep. 49°31N 17°20E 181 B10
Bédar Spain 37°11N 1°59W 197 H3
Bédarieux France 43°37N 3°10E 174 E7
Beddington Corner U.K. 51°23N 0°9W 125 B3
Beddouza, C. Morocco 32°33N 9°9W 260 B3
Bedeau = Râs el Ma
Algeria 34°26N 0°50W 261 B4
Bedele Ethiopia 8°31N 36°23E 257 F4
Bederkesa Germany 53°37N 8°50E 178 B4
Bederwanak Somalia 9°34N 44°23E 267 C5
Bedeso Ethiopia 9°58N 40°52E 257 F5
Bedford Qué., Canada 45°7N 72°59W 313 A12
Bedford Eastern Cape,
S. Africa 32°40S 26°10E 270 D4
Bedford Beds., U.K. 52°8N 0°28W 169 E7
Bedford Ind., U.S.A. 38°52N 86°29W 311 F10
Bedford Iowa, U.S.A. 40°40N 94°44W 310 D2
Bedford Ky., U.S.A. 38°36N 85°19W 311 F11
Bedford Mass., U.S.A. 42°27N 71°15W 116 A1
Bedford Ohio, U.S.A. 41°23N 81°32W 312 E3
Bedford Pa., U.S.A. 40°1N 78°30W 312 F6
Bedford Va., U.S.A. 37°20N 79°31W 309 G14
Bedford □ U.K. 52°4N 0°28W 169 E7
Bedford, C. Australia 15°14S 145°21E 280 B4
Bedford Park Ill., U.S.A. 41°46N 87°46W 119 C2
Bedford Park N.Y., U.S.A. 40°52N 73°52W 132 A2
Bedford Stuyvesant
U.S.A. 40°41N 73°56W 132 B2
Bedford View S. Africa 26°10S 28°7E 123 B2
Bedi Chad 11°6N 18°33E 259 F3
Będków Poland 51°36N 19°44E 185 G6
Bednja → Croatia 46°20N 16°52E 199 B13
Bednodemyanovsk
Russia 53°55N 43°15E 190 D6
Bedok Singapore 1°19N 103°56E 138 B3
Bedok, Res. Singapore 1°20N 103°56E 138 A3
Bedónia Italy 44°30N 9°38E 198 D6
Bedourie Australia 24°30S 139°30E 280 C2
Bedti → India 14°50N 74°44E 245 G2
Bedugul Indonesia 8°17S 115°10E 231 J18
Bedum Neths. 53°18N 6°36E 170 A6
Będzin Poland 50°19N 19°7E 185 H6
Bee Ridge U.S.A. 27°17N 82°29W 317 H7
Beebe Plain Canada 45°1N 72°9W 313 A12
Beech Creek U.S.A. 41°5N 77°36W 312 E7
Beech Fork → U.S.A. 37°46N 85°41W 311 G11
Beech Grove U.S.A. 39°43N 86°5W 311 E10
Beecher U.S.A. 41°21N 87°38W 311 C9
Beechey Point U.S.A. 70°29N 149°9W 303 A10
Beechworth Australia 36°22S 146°43E 283 D7
Beechy Canada 50°53N 107°24W 297 C7
Beed = Bir India 19°4N 75°46E 244 E2
Beef I. Br. Virgin Is. 18°26N 64°30W 321 b
Beelitz Germany 52°14N 12°58E 178 C8
Beenleigh Australia 27°43S 153°10E 281 D5
Be'er Menuha Israel 30°19N 35°8E 246 D2
Be'er Sheva Israel 31°15N 34°48E 251 G5
Beerenberg Norway 71°0N 8°20W 154 C10
Beersel Belgium 50°46N 4°18E 116 B1
Beersheba = Be'er Sheva
Israel 31°15N 34°48E 251 G5
Beeskow Germany 52°10N 14°15E 178 C10
Beestekraal S. Africa 25°23S 27°38E 271 C4
Beeston U.K. 52°56N 1°14W 168 E6
Beeton Canada 44°5N 79°47W 312 B5
Beetzendorf Germany 52°42N 11°6E 178 C7
Beeville U.S.A. 28°24N 97°45W 314 G6
Befale Dem. Rep. of the Congo 0°25N 20°45E 264 B4
Befandriana Mahajanga,
Madag. 15°16S 48°32E 272 B2
Befandriana Toliara, Madag. 21°55S 44°0E 272 C1
Befasy Madag. 20°33S 44°23E 272 C1
Befori Dem. Rep. of the Congo 0°8N 22°22E 264 B4
Befotaka Antsiranana,
Madag. 13°15S 48°16E 272 A2
Befotaka Fianarantsoa,
Madag. 23°49S 47°0E 272 C2
Bega Australia 36°41S 149°51E 283 D8
Bega, Canalul Romania 45°37N 20°46E 182 E5
Begamganj Bangla. 22°56N 91°6E 241 D3
Bégard France 48°38N 3°18W 172 D3
Beğendik Turkey 40°55N 26°34E 203 F10
Beggars Pt. Antigua & B. 17°10N 61°48W 322 b
Begndal Norway 60°49N 9°46E 164 D6
Begoro Ghana 6°23N 0°23W 263 D4
Begusarai India 25°24N 86°9E 243 G12
Behābād Iran 32°24N 59°47E 247 C8
Behala India 22°30N 88°18E 124 B1
Behara Madag. 24°55S 46°20E 272 C2
Behbehān Iran 30°30N 50°15E 247 D6
Beheloka Madag. 23°54S 43°40E 272 C1
Behm Canal U.S.A. 55°10N 131°0W 296 B2
Behshahr Iran 36°45N 53°35E 247 B7
Bei Hai Beijing, China 114 b2
Bei Hai Park Beijing, China 114 b2
Bei Jiang → China 23°2N 112°58E 229 F9
Bei Shan China 41°30N 96°0E 218 C8
Bei'an China 48°10N 126°20E 219 B14
Beibei China 29°47N 106°22E 228 C6
Beicai China 31°11N 121°32E 138 B2
Beichuan China 31°55N 104°39E 228 B5
Beihai China 21°28N 109°6E 228 G7
Beijing China 39°53N 116°21E 114 B1
Beijing □ China 39°55N 116°20E 226 E9
Beijing Zoo Beijing, China 114 a1
Beilau = Piława Poland 51°57N 21°32E 185 G8
Beilen Neths. 52°52N 6°27E 170 B6
Beiliu China 22°41N 110°21E 229 F8
Beilngries Germany 49°2N 11°28E 179 F7
Beilpajah Australia 32°54S 143°52E 282 B5
Beilul Eritrea 13°2N 42°20E 257 E5
Béinamar Chad 8°40N 15°23E 259 G3
Beinn na Faoghla = Benbecula
U.K. 57°26N 7°21W 167 D1
Beipan Jiang → China 24°55N 106°5E 228 E6
Beipiao China 41°52N 120°32E 227 D11
Beira Mozam. 19°50S 34°52E 269 F3
Beirut = Bayrūt Lebanon 33°53N 35°31E 250 E6
Beiseker Canada 51°23N 113°32W 296 C6
Beit Duqu West Bank 31°51N 35°6E 123 A1
Beit Ghur at-Taht
West Bank 31°54N 35°5E 123 A1
Beit Ghur el-Fawqa
West Bank 31°53N 35°5E 123 A1
Beit Hanina West Bank 31°50N 35°12E 123 B2
Beit Ij'za West Bank 31°51N 35°9E 123 A1
Beit Iksa West Bank 31°49N 35°11E 123 B2
Beit I'nan West Bank 31°51N 35°7E 123 A1
Beit Jala West Bank 31°43N 35°11E 123 B2
Beit Lāhīyā Gaza Strip 31°33N 34°30E 251 G5
Beit Lekhem = Bayt Lahm
West Bank 31°43N 35°12E 123 B2
Beit Liqya West Bank 31°52N 35°4E 123 A1
Beit Nekofa Israel 31°49N 35°7E 123 B1
Beit Sahur West Bank 31°42N 35°13E 123 B2
Beit Sofafa West Bank 31°45N 35°12E 123 B2
Beit Surik West Bank 31°50N 35°9E 123 B1
Beit Ur al-Fawqa
West Bank 31°53N 35°7E 123 A1
Beit Zayit Israel 31°47N 35°9E 123 B1
Beitaipingzhuan China 39°57N 116°20E 114 B1
Beitaolaizhao China 44°58N 125°58E 227 B13
Beitar Ilit West Bank 31°42N 35°7E 123 B1
Beitbridge Zimbabwe 22°12S 30°0E 269 G3
Beitin West Bank 31°56N 35°14E 123 A2
Beitsun China 23°7N 113°10E 121 B2
Beitunya West Bank 31°53N 35°10E 123 A2
Beiuş Romania 46°40N 22°21E 182 D7
Beixing Jing Park China 37°12N 121°21E 138 B1
Beizhen = Binzhou China 37°20N 118°2E 227 F10
Beizhen China 41°38N 121°54E 227 D11
Beizhengzhen China 44°31N 123°30E 227 B12
Beja Portugal 38°2N 7°53W 195 G3
Béja Tunisia 36°43N 9°12E 258 A1
Beja □ Portugal 37°55N 7°55W 195 H3
Béja □ Tunisia 36°40N 9°29E 261 A6
Bejaïa Algeria 36°42N 5°2E 261 A5
Bejaïa □ Algeria 36°40N 4°55E 261 A5
Béjar Spain 40°23N 5°46W 194 E5
Bejestān Iran 34°30N 58°5E 247 C8
Bek-Budi = Qarshi
Uzbekistan 38°53N 65°48E 217 E7
Bekaa Valley = Al Biqā
Lebanon 34°10N 36°10E 250 D7
Bekasi Indonesia 6°14S 106°59E 234 D3
Békásmegyer Hungary 47°35N 19°3E 117 A2
Bekçiler Turkey 36°56N 29°44E 205 E11
Bekdash Turkmenistan 41°34N 52°32E 216 D4
Békés Hungary 46°47N 21°9E 182 D6
Békés □ Hungary 46°45N 21°0E 182 D6
Békéscsaba Hungary 46°40N 21°5E 182 D6
Bekilli Turkey 38°17N 29°27E 205 C11
Bekily Madag. 24°13S 45°19E 272 C2
Bekisopa Madag. 21°40S 45°54E 272 C2
Bekitro Madag. 24°33S 45°18E 272 C2
Bekkelaget Norway 59°53N 10°47E 133 A3
Bekkestua Norway 59°55N 10°35E 133 A2
Bekodoka Madag. 16°58S 45°7E 272 B2
Bekoji Ethiopia 7°40N 39°17E 257 F4
Bekok Malaysia 2°20N 103°7E 237 L4
Bekopaka Madag. 19°9S 44°48E 272 B1
Bekwai Ghana 6°30N 1°34W 262 D4
Bel Air Mauritius 20°15S 57°44E 272 e
Bel Air Calif., U.S.A. 34°4N 118°27W 128 B2
Bela India 25°50N 82°0E 243 G10
Bela Pakistan 26°12N 66°20E 242 F2
Bela Aliança = Rio do Sul
Brazil 27°13S 49°37W 335 B6
Bela Bela S. Africa 24°51S 28°19E 271 B4
Bela Crkva Serbia 44°55N 21°27E 182 F6
Bela Palanka Serbia 43°13N 22°17E 202 C6
Bela Vista Mato Grosso do Sul,
Brazil 22°12S 56°20W 334 A4
Bela Vista São Paulo,
Brazil 23°33S 46°38W 137 B2
Bela Vista Mozam. 26°10S 32°44E 271 C5
Bélabo Cameroon 4°56N 13°18E 264 B2
Bélâbre France 46°34N 1°8E 174 B5
Belaga Malaysia 2°42N 113°47E 235 B4
Belalcázar Spain 38°35N 5°10W 195 G5
Belan → India 24°2N 81°45E 243 G9
Bélanger Canada 45°35N 73°42W 130 A1
Belanovica Serbia 44°15N 20°23E 202 B4
Belarus ■ Europe 53°30N 27°0E 177 B14
Belas Angola 8°55S 13°9E 265 D2
Belas Lisboa, Portugal 38°46N 9°17W 126 A1
Belau = Palau ■ Palau 7°30N 134°30E 288 c
Belavenona Madag. 24°50S 47°4E 272 C2
Belawan Indonesia 3°33N 98°32E 234 B1
Belaya Ethiopia 11°25N 36°8E 257 E4
Belaya → Russia 54°40N 56°0E 186 C9
Belaya Glina Russia 46°5N 40°48E 191 G5
Belaya Kalitva Russia 48°13N 40°50E 191 F5
Belaya Tserkov = Bila Tserkva
Ukraine 49°45N 30°10E 177 D16
Belaya Zemlya, Ostrova
Russia 81°36N 62°18E 214 A7
Belayan → Indonesia 0°14S 116°36E 235 C5
Belceşti Romania 47°19N 27°7E 183 C12
Bełchatów Poland 51°21N 19°22E 185 G6
Belcher Is. Canada 56°15N 78°45W 298 A3
Belchite Spain 41°18N 0°43W 196 D4
Belden U.S.A. 40°2N 121°17W 306 E5
Beldibi Turkey 36°25N 32°26E 250 B3
Belding U.S.A. 43°6N 85°14W 311 A11
Belebey Russia 54°7N 54°7E 186 D9
Beledweyne Somalia 4°30N 45°5E 267 D6
Beleghata India 22°33N 88°22E 124 B2
Belém = Palmeirais Brazil 6°0S 43°0W 332 C3
Belém Brazil 1°20S 48°30W 332 B2
Belém Lisboa, Portugal 38°41N 9°12W 126 A1
Belém, Torre de Portugal 38°41N 9°12W 126 A1
Belém de São Francisco
Brazil 8°46S 38°58W 332 C4
Belén Argentina 27°40S 67°5W 334 B2
Belén Colombia 1°26N 75°56W 328 C2
Belén Paraguay 23°30S 57°6W 334 A4
Belén Peru 3°45S 73°15W 330 B3
Belen N. Mex., U.S.A. 34°40N 106°46W 305 J10
Belene Bulgaria 43°39N 25°10E 203 C9
Belênzinho Brazil 23°32S 46°34W 137 B2
Belep, Îs. N. Cal. 19°45S 163°40E 288 d
Bélesta France 42°55N 1°56E 174 F5
Belet Uen = Beledweyne
Somalia 4°30N 45°5E 267 D6
Belev Russia 53°50N 36°5E 188 F9
Belevi Turkey 38°0N 27°28E 205 C9
Belfair U.S.A. 47°27N 122°50W 306 C4
Belfast = eMakhazeni
S. Africa 25°42S 30°2E 271 C5
Belfast N.Z. 43°27S 172°39E 285 D7
Belfast Antrim, U.K. 54°37N 5°56W 166 B6
Belfast Maine, U.S.A. 44°26N 69°1W 309 C19
Belfast N.Y., U.S.A. 42°21N 78°7W 312 D6
Belfast L. U.K. 54°40N 5°50W 166 B6
Belfield U.S.A. 46°53N 103°12W 308 B2
Belfort France 47°38N 6°50E 173 E13
Belfort, Territoire de □
France 47°40N 6°55E 173 E13
Belfry U.S.A. 45°9N 109°1W 304 D9
Belgachiya India 22°36N 88°23E 124 B2
Belgard = Białogard Poland 54°2N 15°58E 184 D2
Belgaum India 15°55N 74°35E 245 G2
Belgavi = Belgaum India 15°55N 74°35E 245 G2
Belgharia India 22°39N 88°22E 124 B2
Belgian Congo = Congo, Dem. Rep.
of the ■ Africa 3°0S 23°0E 265 C4
Belgioioso Italy 45°10N 9°19E 198 C6
Belgium ■ Europe 50°30N 5°0E 170 D4
Belgodère France 42°35N 9°1E 175 F13
Belgorod Russia 50°35N 36°35E 189 G9
Belgorod □ Russia 50°45N 36°45E 189 G9
Belgorod-Dnestrovskiy = Bilhorod-
Dnistrovskyy Ukraine 46°11N 30°23E 189 J6
Belgrade = Beograd Serbia 44°50N 20°37E 202 B4
Belgrade U.S.A. 45°47N 111°11W 304 D8
Belgrano Antarctica 77°52S 34°37W 151 D1
Belgrano B. Aires,
Argentina 34°33S 58°27W 117 B2
Belgravia London, U.K. 125 c3
Belgrove N.Z. 41°27S 172°59E 285 B7
Belhaven U.S.A. 35°33N 76°37W 315 D16
Béli Guinea-Biss. 11°51N 13°56W 262 C2
Beli Nigeria 7°52N 10°55E 263 D7
Beli Drim → Europe 42°6N 20°25E 202 D4
Beli Manastir Croatia 45°45N 18°36E 182 E3
Beli Timok → Serbia 43°53N 22°14E 202 C6
Bélice → Italy 37°35N 12°55E 200 E5
Belimbing Indonesia 8°24S 115°2E 231 J18
Bélinga Gabon 1°10N 13°2E 264 B2
Belinskiy Russia 53°0N 43°25E 190 D6
Belinyu Indonesia 1°35S 105°50E 234 C3
Beliton Is. = Belitung
Indonesia 3°10S 107°50E 235 C3
Belitung Indonesia 3°10S 107°50E 235 C3
Beliu Romania 46°30N 22°0E 182 D6
Belize Angola 4°39S 12°46E 265 C2
Belize ■ Cent. Amer. 17°0N 88°30W 320 C2
Belize Barrier Reef Belize 17°9N 88°3W 319 D7
Belize City Belize 17°25N 88°10W 320 C2
Beljakovci Macedonia 42°6N 21°59E 202 D5
Beljanica Serbia 44°8N 21°43E 202 B5
Belkovskiy, Ostrov
Russia 75°32N 135°44E 215 B14
Bell Calif., U.S.A. 33°58N 118°11W 126 C3
Bell Fla., U.S.A. 29°45N 82°52W 316 F7
Bell → Canada 49°48N 77°38W 298 C4
Bell Gardens U.S.A. 33°58N 118°9W 126 C4
Bell I. Canada 50°46N 55°35W 299 B8
Bell-Irving → Canada 56°12N 129°5W 296 B3
Bell Peninsula Canada 63°50N 82°0W 295 E15
Bell Tower Beijing, China 114 a3
Bell Ville Argentina 32°40S 62°40W 334 C3
Bella Italy 40°45N 15°32E 201 B8
Bella Bella Canada 52°10N 128°10W 296 C3
Bella Coola Canada 52°25N 126°40W 296 C3
Bella Flor Bolivia 11°9S 67°49W 330 C4
Bella Unión Uruguay 30°15S 57°40W 334 C4
Bella Vista Corrientes,
Argentina 28°33S 59°0W 334 B4
Bella Vista Tucuman,
Argentina 27°10S 65°25W 334 B2
Bella Vista Ark., U.S.A. 36°28N 94°16W 308 G6
Bellac France 46°7N 1°3E 174 B5
Bellágio Italy 45°59N 9°15E 198 C6
Bellaire U.S.A. 40°1N 80°45W 312 F4
Bellária Italy 44°9N 12°28E 199 D9
Bellary India 15°10N 76°56E 245 G3
Bellata Australia 29°53S 149°46E 281 D4
Bellavista Santiago, Chile 33°31S 70°35W 137 C2
Bellavista Galápagos Is.,
Ecuador 0°41S 90°18W 330 a
Bellavista Lima, Peru 12°4S 77°8W 124 B2
Belle U.S.A. 38°17N 91°43W 310 F5
Belle → Trin. & Tob. 11°14N 60°37W 323 s
Belle Fille → Dominica 15°25N 61°16W 323 k
Belle Fourche U.S.A. 44°40N 103°51W 308 C2
Belle Fourche → U.S.A. 44°26N 102°18W 308 C2
Belle Glade U.S.A. 26°41N 80°40W 317 J9
Belle Harbor U.S.A. 40°34N 73°51W 132 C2
Belle-Île France 47°20N 3°10W 172 E3
Belle Isle Nfld. & L.,
Canada 51°57N 55°25W 299 B8
Belle Isle Fla., U.S.A. 28°27N 81°12W 317 G8
Belle Isle, Str. of Canada 51°30N 56°30W 299 B8
Belle Plaine U.S.A. 41°54N 92°17W 310 C4
Belle Rive U.S.A. 38°14N 88°45W 311 F8
Belle River Canada 42°18N 82°43W 312 D2
Belle Vue Maurel Mauritius 20°7S 57°39E 272 e
Belle Yella Liberia 7°24N 10°0W 262 D3
Belledonne France 45°20N 6°10E 175 C10
Bellefontaine Martinique 14°39N 61°10W 322 j
Bellefontaine Ohio,
U.S.A. 40°22N 83°46W 311 D13
Bellefonte U.S.A. 40°55N 77°47W 312 F7
Bellegarde France 47°59N 2°26E 173 E9
Bellegarde-en-Marche
France 45°59N 2°18E 174 C6
Bellegarde-sur-Valserine
France 46°4N 5°50E 173 F12
Bellême France 48°22N 0°34E 172 D7
Belleoram Canada 47°31N 55°25W 299 C8
Belleplaine Barbados 13°15N 59°34W 323 r
Belleview U.S.A. 29°4N 82°3W 317 F7
Belleville Ont., Canada 44°10N 77°23W 312 B7
Belleville Rhône, France 46°7N 4°45E 173 F11
Belleville Ill., U.S.A. 38°31N 89°59W 310 F7
Belleville Kans., U.S.A. 39°50N 97°38W 308 F5
Belleville N.J., U.S.A. 40°47N 74°9W 313 F10
Belleville N.Y., U.S.A. 43°46N 76°10W 313 C8
Belleville-sur-Vie France 46°46N 1°25W 172 F5
Bellevue Idaho, U.S.A. 43°28N 114°16W 304 E6
Bellevue Iowa, U.S.A. 42°16N 90°26W 310 B6
Bellevue Mich., U.S.A. 42°27N 85°1W 311 B11
Bellevue Nebr., U.S.A. 41°9N 95°54W 308 E6
Bellevue Ohio, U.S.A. 41°17N 82°51W 312 E2
Bellevue Wash., U.S.A. 47°37N 122°12W 306 C4
Bellevue, Col de Réunion 21°9S 55°36E 272 f
Bellevue, Schloss Berlin, Germany 115 a2
Belley France 45°46N 5°41E 175 C9
Bellin = Kangirsuk Canada 60°0N 70°0W 295 F18
Bellinge Denmark 55°20N 10°20E 163 J4
Bellingen Australia 30°25S 152°50E 283 A10
Bellingham London, U.K. 51°25N 0°1W 125 B3
Bellingham Wash.,
U.S.A. 48°46N 122°29W 306 B4
Bellingshausen Abyssal Plain
S. Ocean 64°0S 90°0W 151 C16
Bellingshausen Sea
Antarctica 66°0S 80°0W 151 C17
Bellinzona Switz. 46°11N 9°1E 179 J5
Bello Colombia 6°20N 75°33W 328 B2
Bellona Solomon Is. 11°17S 159°47E 287 N10
Bellows Falls U.S.A. 43°8N 72°27W 313 C12
Bellpat Pakistan 29°0N 68°5E 242 E3
Bellpuig Spain 41°37N 1°1E 196 D6
Belluno Italy 46°9N 12°13E 199 B9
Belluno Dominica 15°25N 61°21W 323 k
Bellville U.S.A. 32°9N 81°59W 316 C8
Bellwood U.S.A. 40°36N 78°20W 312 F6
Belmanier Dominica 15°35N 61°24W 323 k
Bélmez Spain 38°17N 5°17W 195 G5
Belmond U.S.A. 42°51N 93°37W 310 B3
Belmont N.S.W., Australia 33°4S 151°42E 283 B9
Belmont Ont., Canada 42°53N 81°5W 312 D3
Belmont Grenada 12°6N 61°45W 323 q
Belmont Northern Cape,
S. Africa 29°28S 24°22E 270 C3
Belmont London, U.K. 51°36N 0°18W 125 A2
Belmont Mass., U.S.A. 42°23N 71°10W 116 A1
Belmont N.Y., U.S.A. 42°14N 78°2W 312 D6
Belmont Cragin U.S.A. 41°55N 87°45W 119 B2
Belmont Harbor U.S.A. 41°56N 87°38W 119 B3
Belmonte Brazil 16°0S 39°0W 333 E4
Belmonte Portugal 40°21N 7°20W 194 E3
Belmonte Spain 39°34N 2°43W 197 F2
Belmopan Belize 17°18N 88°30W 320 C2
Belmore Australia 33°55S 151°5E 139 B1
Belmullet Ireland 54°14N 9°58W 166 B2
Belo Dem. Rep. of the Congo 0°32S 23°13E 264 C4
Belo Madag. 20°44S 44°0E 272 C1
Belo Horizonte Brazil 19°55S 43°56W 333 E3
Belo Jardim Brazil 8°20S 36°26W 332 C4
Belo Monte Brazil 3°5S 51°46W 329 D7
Belo-Tsiribihina Madag. 19°40S 44°30E 272 B1
Belogorsk = Bilohirsk
Ukraine 45°3N 34°35E 189 K8
Belogorsk Russia 51°0N 128°20E 215 D13
Belogradchik Bulgaria 43°53N 22°42E 202 C6
Belogradets Bulgaria 43°22N 27°18E 203 C11
Beloha Madag. 25°10S 45°3E 272 D2
Beloit Kans., U.S.A. 39°28N 98°6W 308 F4
Beloit Wis., U.S.A. 42°31N 89°2W 310 B7
Belokalitvenskaya = Belaya Kalitva
Russia 48°13N 40°50E 191 F5
Belokorovichi Ukraine 51°7N 28°2E 177 C15
Belomorsk Russia 64°35N 34°54E 186 B5
Belondo
Dem. Rep. of the Congo 0°19S 19°31E 264 C3
Belonge
Dem. Rep. of the Congo 2°7S 19°33E 264 C3
Belonia India 23°15N 91°30E 241 D3
Belopolye = Bilopillya
Ukraine 51°14N 34°20E 189 G8
Belorechensk Russia 44°46N 39°52E 191 H4
Beloretsk Russia 53°58N 58°24E 186 D10
Belorussia = Belarus ■
Europe 53°30N 27°0E 177 B14
Beloshchelye = Naryan-Mar
Russia 67°42N 53°12E 186 A9
Beloslav Bulgaria 43°11N 27°42E 203 C11
Belotsarsk = Kyzyl
Russia 51°50N 94°30E 217 B12
Beloūsovka Kazakhstan 50°8N 82°31E 217 B10
Belovo Bulgaria 42°13N 24°1E 203 D8
Belovo Russia 54°30N 86°0E 217 B11
Beloyarskiy Russia 63°42N 66°40E 214 C7
Beloye, Ozero Russia 60°10N 37°35E 188 B9
Beloye More Russia 66°30N 38°0E 186 A6
Belozem Bulgaria 42°12N 25°2E 203 D9
Belozersk Russia 60°1N 37°45E 188 B9
Belpasso Italy 37°35N 14°58E 201 E7
Belpre U.S.A. 39°17N 81°34W 309 F13
Belrain India 28°23N 80°55E 243 E9
Belt U.S.A. 47°23N 110°55W 304 C8
Beltana Australia 30°48S 138°25E 282 A3
Belterra Brazil 2°45S 55°0W 329 D7
Beltinci Slovenia 46°37N 16°20E 199 B13
Belton Mo., U.S.A. 38°49N 94°32W 310 F2
Belton Tex., U.S.A. 31°3N 97°28W 314 F6
Belton L. U.S.A. 31°6N 97°28W 314 F6
Beltsy = Bălţi Moldova 47°48N 27°58E 183 C12
Belturbet Ireland 54°6N 7°26W 166 B4
Belukha Russia 49°50N 86°50E 217 C11
Belur India 22°37N 88°21E 124 B2
Beluran Malaysia 5°48N 117°35E 235 A5
Beluša Slovak Rep. 49°5N 18°17E 181 B11
Belushya Guba Russia 71°32N 52°19E 214 B6
Belušić Serbia 43°50N 21°10E 202 C5
Belvedere St. Vincent 13°8N 61°11W 323 n
Belvedere London, U.K. 51°29N 0°9E 125 B4
Belvedere Calif., U.S.A. 37°52N 122°27W 136 A2
Belvedere Marittimo Italy 39°37N 15°52E 201 C8
Belvedere Park U.S.A. 33°45N 84°16W 113 B3
Belvès France 44°46N 1°0E 174 D5
Belvidere Ill., U.S.A. 42°15N 88°50W 311 B8
Belvidere N.J., U.S.A. 40°50N 75°5W 313 F9
Belvis de la Jara Spain 39°45N 4°57W 194 F6
Bely Bychek = Chagoda
Russia 59°10N 35°15E 188 C8
Belyando → Australia 21°38S 146°50E 280 C4
Belyando Crossing
Australia 21°32S 146°51E 280 C4
Belyayevo Bogorodskoye
Russia 55°39N 37°31E 129 C2
Belyuen Australia 12°34S 130°42E 278 B5
Belyy Russia 55°49N 32°51E 188 E7
Belyy, Ostrov Russia 73°30N 71°0E 214 B8
Belyy Yar Russia 58°26N 84°39E 214 D9
Belyye Vody = Aqsū
Kazakhstan 42°25N 69°50E 217 D7
Belz Ukraine 50°23N 24°1E 185 H11
Bełżec Poland 50°23N 23°26E 185 H10
Belzig Germany 52°8N 12°35E 178 C8
Belzoni U.S.A. 33°11N 90°29W 315 E9
Bełżyce Poland 51°11N 22°17E 185 G9
Bemaraha, Lembalemban' i
Madag. 18°40S 44°45E 272 B1
Bemarivo Madag. 21°45S 44°45E 272 C1
Bemarivo → Antsiranana,
Madag. 14°9S 50°9E 272 A3
Bemarivo → Mahajanga,
Madag. 15°27S 47°40E 272 B2
Bemavo Madag. 21°33S 45°25E 272 C2
Bembe Angola 7°3S 14°25E 265 D2
Bembéréke Benin 10°11N 2°43E 263 C5
Bembesi Zimbabwe 20°0S 28°58E 269 G2
Bembesi → Zimbabwe 18°57S 27°47E 269 F2
Bembézar → Spain 37°45N 5°13W 195 H5
Bembibre Spain 42°37N 6°25W 194 C4
Bemboka △ Australia 36°35S 149°41E 283 D8
Bement U.S.A. 39°55N 88°34W 311 E8
Bemetara India 21°42N 81°32E 243 J9
Bemidji U.S.A. 47°28N 94°53W 308 B6
Bemolanga Madag. 17°44S 45°6E 272 B2
Bemowo Poland 52°15N 20°53E 143 B1
Ben Iran 32°32N 50°45E 247 C6
Ben Boyd △ Australia 37°0S 149°55E 283 D8
Ben Cruachan U.K. 56°26N 5°8W 167 E3
Ben Dearg U.K. 57°47N 4°56W 167 D4
Ben En △ Vietnam 19°37N 105°30E 236 C5
Ben Gardane Tunisia 33°11N 11°11E 258 B2
Ben Halls Gap △ Australia 31°37S 151°1E 283 A9
Ben Hope U.K. 58°25N 4°36W 167 C4
Ben Lawers U.K. 56°32N 4°14W 167 E4
Ben Lomond N.S.W.,
Australia 30°1S 151°43E 281 E5
Ben Lomond Tas.,
Australia 41°33S 147°42E 281 G4
Ben Lomond Stirling, U.K. 56°11N 4°38W 167 E4
Ben Lomond △ Australia 41°33S 147°39E 281 G4
Ben Luc Vietnam 10°39N 106°29E 237 G6
Ben Macdhui U.K. 57°4N 3°40W 167 D5
Ben Mhor U.K. 57°15N 7°18W 167 D1
Ben More Argyll & Bute,
U.K. 56°26N 6°1W 167 E2
Ben More Stirling, U.K. 56°23N 4°32W 167 E4
Ben More Assynt U.K. 58°8N 4°52W 167 C4

Ben Nevis U.K. 56°48N 5°1W 167 E3
Ben Ohau Ra. N.Z. 44°1S 170°4E 285 E5
Ben Quang Vietnam 17°3N 106°55E 236 D6
Ben Slimane Morocco 33°38N 7°7W 260 B3
Ben Tadjine, Djebel Algeria 29°0N 3°30W 260 C4
Ben Tre Vietnam 10°14N 106°23E 237 G6
Ben Vorlich U.K. 56°21N 4°14W 167 E4
Ben Wyvis U.K. 57°40N 4°35W 167 D4
Bena Nigeria 11°20N 5°50E 263 C6
Bena-Dibele
Dem. Rep. of the Congo 4°4S 22°50E 265 C4
Bena-Leka
Dem. Rep. of the Congo 5°8S 22°10E 265 D4
Bena-Tshadi
Dem. Rep. of the Congo 4°40S 22°49E 265 C4
Benagerie Australia 31°25S 140°22E 282 A4
Benahmed Morocco 33°4N 7°9W 260 B3
Benaki Museum Athens, Greece 112 b3
Benalla Australia 36°30S 146°0E 283 D7
Benalmádena Spain 36°36N 4°34W 195 J6
Benambra, Mt. Australia 36°31S 147°34E 283 D7
Benanee Australia 34°31S 142°52E 282 C5
Benangin Indonesia 0°58S 115°19E 235 D5
Bénara Mayotte 12°53S 45°9E 272 b
Benares = Varanasi India 25°22N 83°0E 243 G10
Bénat, C. France 43°5N 6°22E 175 E10
Benavente Portugal 38°59N 8°49W 195 G2
Benavente Spain 42°2N 5°43W 194 C5
Benavides U.S.A. 27°36N 98°25W 314 H5
Benavides de Órbigo Spain 42°30N 5°54W 194 C5
Benbecula U.K. 57°26N 7°21W 167 D1
Benbonyathe Hill
Australia 30°25S 139°11E 282 A3
Bend U.S.A. 44°4N 121°19W 304 D3
Bendale Canada 43°45N 79°13W 141 A3
Bendela
Dem. Rep. of the Congo 3°18S 17°36E 264 C3
Bendemeer Australia 30°53S 151°8E 283 A9
Bender Beyla Somalia 9°30N 50°48E 267 C7
Bendery = Tighina
Moldova 46°50N 29°30E 183 D14
Bendigo Australia 36°40S 144°15E 282 D6
Bendin = Będzin Poland 50°19N 19°7E 185 H6
Bendorf Germany 50°25N 7°35E 178 E3
Bendsburg = Będzin Poland 50°19N 19°7E 185 H6
Benë Beraq Israel 32°6N 34°51E 251 F5
Benedittinos Brazil 5°27S 42°22W 332 C3
Benedito Leite Brazil 7°13S 44°34W 332 C3
Benefica Brazil 22°52S 43°14W 135 B1
Bénéna Mali 13°9N 4°17W 262 C4
Benenitra Madag. 23°27S 45°5E 272 C2
Benešov Czech Rep. 49°46N 14°41E 180 B7
Benevento Italy 41°8N 14°45E 201 A7
Benfeld France 48°22N 7°34E 173 D14
Benfica Portugal 38°45N 9°11W 126 A1
Beng Mealea Cambodia 13°28N 104°14E 236 F5
Benga Mozam. 16°11S 33°40E 269 F3
Bengal = Paschimbanga □
India 23°0N 88°0E 243 H13
Bengal, Bay of Ind. Oc. 15°0N 90°0E 239 F14
Bengaluru = Bangalore
India 12°59N 77°40E 245 H3
Bengbis Cameroon 3°27N 12°36E 263 E7
Bengbu China 32°58N 117°20E 227 H9
Benghazi = Banghāzī Libya 32°11N 20°3E 258 B4
Benghisa Point Malta 35°49N 14°33E 206 F8
Bengkalis Indonesia 1°30N 102°10E 237 M4
Bengkayang Indonesia 0°49N 109°28E 235 B3
Bengkulu Indonesia 3°50S 102°12E 234 C2
Bengkulu □ Indonesia 3°48S 102°16E 234 C2
Bengo Dem. Rep. of the Congo 2°11S 19°5E 264 C3
Bengo □ Angola 9°0S 13°10E 265 D2
Bengough Canada 49°25N 105°10W 297 D7
Bengtsfors Sweden 59°2N 12°14E 162 E6
Benguela Angola 12°37S 13°25E 265 E2
Benguela □ Angola 13°0S 13°30E 265 E2
Benguerir Morocco 32°16N 7°56W 260 B3
Benguérua, I. Mozam. 21°58S 35°28E 271 B6
Benguet □ Phil. 16°30N 120°40E 232 C3
Benha Egypt 30°26N 31°8E 256 H7
Benham Seamount
Pac. Oc. 15°40N 124°30E 232 D5
Beni Dem. Rep. of the Congo 0°30N 29°27E 268 B2
Beni □ Bolivia 14°0S 65°0W 331 C5
Beni → Bolivia 10°23S 65°24W 331 C4
Beni Abbès Algeria 30°5N 2°5W 261 B4
Beni Hammad Algeria 35°49N 4°47E 261 A5
Beni Haoua Algeria 36°30N 1°30E 261 A5
Beni Mazâr Egypt 28°32N 30°44E 256 B3
Beni Mellal Morocco 32°21N 6°21W 260 B3
Beni Ounif Algeria 32°0N 1°10W 261 B4
Beni Saf Algeria 35°17N 1°15W 261 A4
Beni Suef Egypt 29°5N 31°6E 256 J7
Beniah L. Canada 63°23N 112°17W 296 A6
Benicarló Spain 40°23N 0°23E 196 E5
Benicàssim Spain 40°3N 0°4E 196 E5
Benidorm Spain 38°33N 0°9W 197 G4
Benin ■ Africa 10°0N 2°0E 263 D5
Benin → Nigeria 5°45N 5°4E 263 D6
Benin, Bight of W. Afr. 5°0N 3°0E 263 E5
Benin City Nigeria 6°20N 5°31E 263 D6
Benissa Spain 38°43N 0°3E 197 G5
Benitez Int. ✕ (SCL) Chile 33°33S 70°42W 137 B1
Bénitiers, Île aux Mauritius 20°24S 57°20E 272 e
Benito Juárez Argentina 37°40S 59°43W 334 D4
Benito Juárez, Int. ✕ (MEX)
Mexico 19°25N 99°5W 128 B2
Benitses Greece 39°32N 19°55E 206 B9
Benjamin Aceval
Paraguay 24°58S 57°34W 334 A4
Benjamin Constant Brazil 4°40S 70°15W 328 D3
Benjamin Hill Mexico 30°9N 111°7W 318 A2
Benkelman U.S.A. 40°3N 101°32W 308 E3
Benkovac Croatia 44°2N 15°37E 199 D12
Benmore Pk. N.Z. 44°25S 170°8E 285 E5
Bennett Canada 59°51N 135°0W 296 B2
Bennett, L. Australia 22°50S 131°2E 278 D5
Bennetta, Ostrov Russia 76°21N 148°56E 215 B15
Bennettsville U.S.A. 34°37N 79°41W 315 D15
Bennichchâb Mauritania 19°32N 15°12W 262 B1
Bennington N.H., U.S.A. 43°0N 71°55W 313 D11
Bennington Vt., U.S.A. 42°53N 73°12W 313 D11
Beno Dem. Rep. of the Congo 3°41S 17°49E 264 C3
Bénodet France 47°53N 4°7W 172 E2
Benom Malaysia 3°50N 102°6E 237 L4
Benoni S. Africa 26°11S 28°18E 271 C4
Benoud Algeria 32°20N 0°16E 261 B5
Bénoué △ Cameroon 8°30N 13°55E 264 A2
Benoy Chad 8°59N 16°19E 259 G3
Benque Viejo del Carmen
Belize 17°5N 89°8W 320 C2
Bense Dominica 15°35N 61°22W 323 k
Bensheim Germany 49°41N 8°38E 179 F4
Benson Ariz., U.S.A. 31°58N 110°18W 305 L8
Benson Minn., U.S.A. 45°19N 95°36W 308 C6
Bensonhurst U.S.A. 40°35N 73°59W 132 C2
Bent Iran 26°20N 59°31E 247 E8
Benteng Indonesia 6°10S 120°30E 231 F6
Bentiaba Angola 14°15S 12°21E 265 E2
Bentinck I. Queens.,
Australia 17°3S 139°35E 280 B2
Bentinck I. Burma 11°45N 98°3E 237 G2
Bentiu South Sudan 9°10N 29°55E 257 F2
Bentley Subglacial Trench
Antarctica 80°0S 115°0W 151 E15
Bento Gonçalves Brazil 29°10S 51°31W 335 B5
Benton Ark., U.S.A. 34°34N 92°35W 314 D8
Benton Calif., U.S.A. 37°48N 118°32W 306 H8
Benton Ill., U.S.A. 38°0N 88°55W 310 G8
Benton Pa., U.S.A. 41°12N 76°23W 313 E8
Benton Harbor U.S.A. 42°6N 86°27W 311 B10
Benton Heights U.S.A. 42°7N 86°24W 311 B10
Bentong Malaysia 3°31N 101°55E 237 L3
Bentonville U.S.A. 36°22N 94°13W 314 C7
Bentu Liben Ethiopia 8°32N 38°21E 257 F4
Benue □ Nigeria 7°20N 8°45E 263 D6
Benue → Nigeria 7°48N 6°46E 263 D6
Benxi China 41°20N 123°48E 224 B1
Benza Dem. Rep. of the Congo 4°49S 13°17E 265 D2
Benzdorp Suriname 3°44N 54°5W 329 C7
Beo Indonesia 4°25N 126°50E 231 D7
Beograd Serbia 44°50N 20°37E 202 B4
Beograd ✕ (BEG) Serbia 43°49N 20°17E 202 C4
Beolgyo S. Korea 34°51N 127°21E 224 E3
Beoumi Ivory C. 7°45N 5°23W 262 D3
Beppu Japan 33°15N 131°30E 222 D3
Beppu-Wan Japan 33°18N 131°34E 222 D3
Beqa Fiji 18°23S 178°8E 287 B2
Beqaa Valley = Al Biqā
Lebanon 34°10N 36°10E 250 D7
Bequia St. Vincent 13°0N 61°15W 323 n
Ber Mota India 23°27N 68°34E 242 H3
Bera, Tasik Malaysia 3°5N 102°38E 237 L4
Berach → India 25°15N 75°2E 242 G6
Beraketa Madag. 23°7S 44°25E 272 C1
Béran-Djoko Congo 3°15N 17°0E 264 B3
Berane Montenegro 42°51N 19°52E 202 D3
Berastagi Indonesia 3°11N 98°31E 237 L2
Berat Albania 40°43N 19°59E 202 F3
Berau = Tanjungredeb
Indonesia 2°9N 117°29E 235 B5
Berau → Indonesia 2°10N 117°42E 235 B5
Berau, Teluk Indonesia 2°30S 132°30E 231 E8
Beravina Madag. 18°10S 45°14E 272 B2
Berbak △ Indonesia 1°27S 104°19E 234 C2
Berber Sudan 18°0N 34°0E 256 D3
Berbera Somalia 10°30N 45°2E 267 B6
Berbérati C.A.R. 4°15N 15°40E 264 B3
Berbice → Guyana 6°20N 57°32W 329 B6
Berceto Italy 44°31N 9°51E 198 D6
Berchem-Ste-Agathe
Belgium 50°52N 4°17E 116 A1
Berchidda Italy 40°47N 9°10E 200 B2
Berchtesgaden Germany 47°38N 13°0E 179 H8
Berchtesgaden △
Germany 47°34N 12°55E 179 H8
Berck France 50°25N 1°36E 173 B8
Berdaale Bay, Somalia 7°4N 47°51E 267 D6
Berdaale Mudug, Somalia 3°14N 43°11E 267 D5
Berdichev = Berdychiv
Ukraine 49°57N 28°30E 177 D15
Berdsk Russia 54°47N 83°2E 217 B10
Berdyansk Ukraine 46°45N 36°50E 189 J9
Berdychiv Ukraine 49°57N 28°30E 177 D15
Béré Chad 9°20N 16°9E 259 G3
Berea U.S.A. 37°34N 84°17W 309 G11
Berebere Indonesia 2°25N 128°45E 231 D7
Bereeda Somalia 11°45N 51°0E 267 B7
Berehomet Ukraine 48°10N 25°19E 183 B10
Berehove Ukraine 48°15N 22°35E 182 B7
Bereina Papua N. G. 8°39S 146°30E 286 E4
Bereket Turkmenistan 39°16N 55°32E 247 B7
Berekua Dominica 15°14N 61°19W 323 k
Berekum Ghana 7°29N 2°34W 262 D4
Berenice Egypt 24°2N 35°25E 256 C4
Berens → Canada 52°25N 97°2W 297 C9
Berens I. Canada 52°18N 97°18W 297 C9
Berens River Canada 52°25N 97°0W 297 C9
Beresfield Australia 32°50S 151°40E 283 B9
Beresford U.S.A. 43°5N 96°47W 308 D5
Berestechko Ukraine 50°22N 25°5E 177 C13
Berești Romania 46°6N 27°50E 183 D12
Berețău → Romania 47°10N 21°50E 182 C6
Berettyó → Hungary 46°59N 21°7E 182 D6
Berettyóújfalu Hungary 47°13N 21°33E 182 C6
Berevo Mahajanga, Madag. 17°14S 44°17E 272 B1
Berevo Toliara, Madag. 19°44S 44°58E 272 B1
Bereza = Byaroza Belarus 52°31N 24°51E 177 B13
Berezhany Ukraine 49°26N 24°58E 177 D13
Berezina = Byarezina →
Belarus 52°33N 30°14E 177 B16
Berezivka Ukraine 47°14N 30°55E 189 J6
Berezna Ukraine 51°35N 31°46E 189 G6
Bereznik Russia 62°51N 42°40E 186 B7
Berezniki Russia 59°24N 56°46E 186 C10
Berezovo Russia 64°0N 65°0E 214 C7
Berezyne Ukraine 46°14N 29°12E 183 D14
Berg am Laim Germany 48°7N 11°38E 131 B2
Berga Spain 42°6N 1°48E 196 C6
Berga Kalmar, Sweden 57°14N 16°3E 163 G10
Bergama Turkey 39°8N 27°11E 205 B9
Bérgamo Italy 45°41N 9°43E 198 C6
Bergaon India 20°41N 80°27E 244 D5
Bergara Spain 43°9N 2°28W 196 B2
Bergby Sweden 60°57N 17°2E 162 D11
Berge Norway 59°34N 8°10E 162 E2
Bergedorf Germany 53°28N 10°6E 178 B6
Bergeforsen Sweden 62°32N 17°23E 162 B11
Bergen Mecklenburg-Vorpommern,
Germany 54°25N 13°25E 178 A9
Bergen Niedersachsen,
Germany 52°49N 9°57E 178 C5
Bergen Neths. 52°40N 4°43E 170 B4
Bergen Hordaland, Norway 60°20N 5°20E 164 D2
Bergen N.Y., U.S.A. 43°5N 77°57W 312 C7
Bergen ✕ (BGO) Norway 60°17N 5°19E 164 D2
Bergen op Zoom Neths. 51°28N 4°18E 170 C4
Bergenfield U.S.A. 40°55N 73°59W 132 A2
Bergerac France 44°51N 0°30E 174 D4
Bergham Germany 48°2N 11°37E 131 B2
Bergheim Germany 50°57N 6°38E 178 E2
Bergholz U.S.A. 40°31N 80°53W 312 F4
Bergisch Gladbach Germany 50°59N 7°8E 178 E3
Bergisches Land ⌂ Germany 51°20N 7°30E 178 E3
Bergkamen Germany 51°37N 7°38E 178 D3
Bergkvara Sweden 56°23N 16°5E 163 H10
Bergshamra Sweden 59°38N 18°37E 162 E12
Bergsjö Sweden 61°59N 17°3E 162 C11
Bergstadt = Leśnica
Poland 50°26N 18°11E 185 H5
Bergstrasse-Odenwald ⌂
Germany 49°45N 5°55E 179 F1
Bergues France 50°58N 2°24E 173 B9
Bergviken Sweden 61°15N 16°40E 162 C10
Bergville S. Africa 28°52S 29°18E 271 C4
Bergvliet S. Africa 34°2S 18°25E 118 B1
Berhala, Selat Indonesia 1°0S 104°15E 234 C2
Berhampore = Baharampur
India 24°2N 88°27E 243 G13
Berhampur = Brahmapur
India 19°15N 84°54E 244 E7
Berheci → Romania 45°58N 27°28E 183 E12
Beri Spain 41°20N 2°1E 114 A1
Berikat, Tanjung
Indonesia 2°34S 106°52E 234 C3
Bering Glacier U.S.A. 60°20N 143°30W 303 F12
Bering Land Bridge ⌂
U.S.A. 66°20N 165°0W 303 C6
Bering Sea Pac. Oc. 58°0N 171°0W 292 D2
Bering Strait Pac. Oc. 65°30N 169°0W 303 D5
Beringovskiy Russia 63°3N 179°19E 215 C18
Berisso Argentina 34°56S 57°50W 334 C4
Berja Spain 36°50N 2°56W 195 J8
Berkåk Norway 62°50N 10°0E 164 B6
Berkane Morocco 34°52N 2°20W 261 B4
Berkeley U.S.A. 37°51N 122°16W 136 A3
Berkeley, C. Ecuador 0°1N 91°35W 330 a
Berkner I. Antarctica 79°30S 50°0W 151 D18
Berkovitsa Bulgaria 43°16N 23°8E 202 C7
Berkshire U.S.A. 42°19N 76°11W 313 D8
Berkshire Downs U.K. 51°33N 1°29W 169 F6
Berlanga Spain 38°17N 5°50W 195 G5
Berlenga, I. Portugal 39°25N 9°30W 195 F1
Berlengas = Valença do Piauí
Brazil 6°20S 41°45W 332 C3
Berlin = Kitchener
Canada 43°27N 80°29W 312 C4
Berlin Berlin, Germany 52°31N 13°23E 115 A3
Berlin Ga., U.S.A. 31°4N 83°37W 316 D6
Berlin Md., U.S.A. 38°20N 75°13W 309 F16
Berlin N.H., U.S.A. 44°28N 71°11W 313 B13
Berlin N.Y., U.S.A. 42°42N 73°23W 313 D11
Berlin Wis., U.S.A. 43°58N 88°57W 308 D9
Berlin □ Germany 52°30N 13°20E 178 C9
Berlin Brandenburg ✕ (BER)
Germany 52°22N 13°30E 115 B4
Berlin Dom Germany 52°31N 13°24E 115 A3
Berlin L. U.S.A. 41°3N 81°0W 312 E4
Berlinchen = Barlinek
Poland 53°0N 15°15E 185 F2
Bermagui Australia 36°25S 150°4E 283 D9
Bermeja, Sierra Spain 36°30N 5°11W 195 J5
Bermejo → Formosa,
Argentina 26°51S 58°23W 334 B4
Bermejo → San Juan,
Argentina 32°30S 67°30W 334 C2
Bermejo, Paso = Uspallata, P. de
Argentina 32°37S 69°22W 334 C2
Bermen, L. Canada 53°35N 68°55W 299 B6
Bermeo Spain 43°25N 2°47W 196 B2
Bermillo de Sayago Spain 41°22N 6°8W 194 D4
Bermondsey U.K. 51°29N 0°3W 125 B3
Bermuda ☒ Atl. Oc. 32°18N 64°45W 153 a
Bermuda Int. ✕ (BDA)
Bermuda 32°22N 64°41W 153 a
Bermuda Rise Atl. Oc. 32°30N 65°0W 152 C5
Bern Switz. 46°57N 7°28E 179 J3
Bern □ Switz. 46°45N 7°40E 179 J3
Bernabeu, Estadio Spain 40°27N 3°41W 127 B1
Bernal Heights U.S.A. 37°44N 122°24W 136 B2
Bernalda Italy 40°24N 16°41E 201 B9
Bernalillo U.S.A. 35°18N 106°33W 305 J10
Bernam → Malaysia 3°45N 101°5E 234 B2
Bernardo, Palazzo Venice, Italy 142 b2
Bernardo de Irigoyen
Argentina 26°15S 53°40W 335 B5
Bernardo O'Higgins △
Chile 48°50S 75°36W 336 C1
Bernardsville U.S.A. 40°43N 74°34W 313 F10
Bernasconi Argentina 37°55S 63°44W 334 D3
Bernau Bayern, Germany 47°47N 12°22E 179 H8
Bernau Brandenburg,
Germany 52°40N 13°35E 178 C9
Bernay France 49°5N 0°35E 172 C7
Bernburg Germany 51°47N 11°44E 178 D7
Berndorf Austria 47°59N 16°1E 180 D9
Berne = Bern Switz. 46°57N 7°28E 179 J3
Berne = Bern □ Switz. 46°45N 7°40E 179 J3
Berne U.S.A. 40°39N 84°57W 311 D12
Berner Alpen Switz. 46°27N 7°35E 179 J3
Berneray U.K. 57°43N 7°11W 167 D1
Bernier I. Australia 24°50S 113°12E 279 D1
Bernina, Piz Switz. 46°20N 9°54E 179 J5
Bernkastel-Kues Germany 49°55N 7°3E 179 F3
Bernstadt = Bierutów
Poland 51°7N 17°32E 185 G4
Bernstein = Pelczyce
Poland 53°3N 15°16E 185 E2
Bero → Angola 15°10S 12°9E 265 F2
Beroroha Madag. 21°40S 45°10E 272 C2
Béroubouay Benin 10°34N 2°46E 263 C5
Beroun Czech Rep. 49°57N 14°5E 180 B7
Berounka → Czech Rep. 50°0N 14°22E 180 B7
Berovo Macedonia 41°38N 22°51E 202 E6
Berre, Étang de France 43°27N 5°5E 175 E9
Berre-l'Étang France 43°27N 5°10E 175 E9
Berrechid Morocco 33°18N 7°36W 260 B3
Berri Australia 34°14S 140°35E 282 C4
Berriane Algeria 32°50N 3°46E 261 B5
Berridale Australia 36°22S 148°48E 283 D8
Berrien Springs U.S.A. 41°57N 86°20W 311 C10
Berrigan Australia 35°38S 145°49E 283 C6
Berriwillock Australia 35°36S 142°59E 282 C5
Berrouaghia Algeria 36°10N 2°53E 261 A5
Berry N.S.W., Australia 34°46S 150°43E 283 C9
Berry Indre, France 46°50N 2°0E 173 F8
Berry Is. Bahamas 25°40N 77°50W 320 A4
Berrydale U.S.A. 30°53N 87°3W 317 E2
Berryessa, L. U.S.A. 38°31N 122°6W 306 G4
Berryville U.S.A. 36°22N 93°34W 314 C8
Berseba Namibia 26°0S 17°46E 270 C2
Bersenbrück Germany 52°34N 7°56E 178 C3
Bershad Ukraine 48°22N 29°31E 183 B14
Bertamirans Spain 42°54N 8°38W 194 C2
Berthold U.S.A. 48°19N 101°44W 308 A3
Berthoud U.S.A. 40°19N 105°5W 304 F11
Bertincourt France 50°5N 2°58E 173 B9
Bertolinia Brazil 7°38S 43°57W 332 C3
Bertoua Cameroon 4°30N 13°45E 264 B2
Bertraghboy B. Ireland 53°22N 9°54W 166 C2
Bertys = Balqash
Kazakhstan 46°50N 74°50E 214 E8
Beru Kiribati 1°20S 176°0E 277 A14
Berufjörður Iceland 64°48N 14°29W 155 C12
Berunes Iceland 64°42N 14°16W 155 C12
Beruni Uzbekistan 41°41N 60°45E 216 D6
Beruri Brazil 3°54S 61°22W 329 D5
Beruwala Sri Lanka 6°30N 80°0E 245 L4
Berwick U.S.A. 41°3N 76°14W 313 E8
Berwick-upon-Tweed U.K. 55°46N 2°0W 168 B6
Berwyn U.S.A. 41°50N 87°47W 119 B2
Berwyn Heights U.S.A. 38°59N 76°55W 143 B3
Berwyn Mts. U.K. 52°54N 3°26W 168 E4
Beryslav Ukraine 46°50N 33°30E 189 J7
Berzasca Romania 44°39N 21°58E 182 F6
Berzence Hungary 46°12N 17°11E 182 D2
Besal Pakistan 35°4N 73°56E 243 B5
Besalampy Madag. 16°43S 44°29E 272 B1
Besançon France 47°15N 6°2E 173 E13
Besar Indonesia 2°40S 116°0E 235 C5
Besar, Gunung Malaysia 5°10N 101°18E 234 A2
Beshenkovichi Belarus 55°2N 29°29E 188 E5
Besiktas Turkey 41°2N 29°0E 122 B2
Beška Serbia 45°8N 20°6E 182 E5
Beslan Russia 43°15N 44°28E 191 J7
Besna Kobila Serbia 42°31N 22°10E 202 D6
Besnard L. Canada 55°25N 106°0W 297 B7
Besni Turkey 37°41N 37°52E 212 D7
Besor, N. → Egypt 31°28N 34°22E 251 G5
Besòs → Spain 41°24N 2°13E 114 A2
Bessa Monteiro Angola 7°7S 13°44E 265 D2
Bessarabiya Moldova 47°0N 28°10E 177 E15
Bessarabka = Basarabeasca
Moldova 46°21N 28°58E 183 D13
Bessèges France 44°18N 4°8E 175 D8
Bessemer Ala., U.S.A. 33°24N 86°58W 315 E11
Bessemer Mich., U.S.A. 46°29N 90°3W 308 B8
Bessemer Pa., U.S.A. 40°59N 80°30W 312 F4
Bessie, L. U.S.A. 28°29N 81°31W 133 B1
Bessin France 49°18N 1°0W 172 C6
Bessines-sur-Gartempe
France 46°6N 1°22E 174 B5
Beswick Australia 14°34S 132°53E 278 B5
Beswick ☼ Australia 14°31S 132°51E 278 B5
Bet Horon West Bank 31°52N 35°7E 123 A1
Bet She'an Israel 32°30N 35°30E 251 F6
Bet Shemesh Israel 31°44N 35°0E 251 G6
Betafo Madag. 19°50S 46°51E 272 B2
Betamba
Dem. Rep. of the Congo 2°17S 21°24E 264 C4
Betancuria Canary Is. 28°25N 14°3W 153 e2
Betancuria, Mt. Canary Is. 28°25N 14°6W 153 e2
Betania Colombia 4°22N 72°54W 328 C3
Betanzos Bolivia 19°34S 65°27W 331 D4
Betanzos Spain 43°15N 8°12W 194 B2
Bétaré Oya Cameroon 5°40N 14°5E 264 A2
Betatao Madag. 18°11S 47°52E 272 B2
Bétera Spain 39°35N 0°28W 197 F4
Bétérou Benin 9°12N 2°16E 263 D5
Bethal S. Africa 26°27S 29°28E 271 C4
Bethalto U.S.A. 38°55N 90°2W 310 F6
Bethanien Namibia 26°31S 17°8E 270 C2
Bethany Ont., Canada 44°11N 78°34W 312 B6
Bethany Ill., U.S.A. 39°39N 88°45W 310 F8
Bethany Mo., U.S.A. 40°16N 94°2W 310 D2
Bethany Okla., U.S.A. 35°31N 97°38W 314 D6
Bethel Montserrat 16°44N 62°9W 323 p
Bethel Alaska, U.S.A. 60°48N 161°45W 303 F7
Bethel Conn., U.S.A. 41°22N 73°25W 313 E11
Bethel Maine, U.S.A. 44°25N 70°47W 313 B14
Bethel Ohio, U.S.A. 38°58N 84°5W 311 F12
Bethel Vt., U.S.A. 43°50N 72°38W 313 C12
Bethel Park U.S.A. 40°19N 80°2W 312 F4
Béthenville France 49°18N 4°23E 173 C11
Bethesda U.S.A. 38°59N 77°6W 143 B2
Bethlehem = Bayt Lahm
West Bank 31°43N 35°12E 123 B2
Bethlehem Free State,
S. Africa 28°14S 28°18E 271 C4
Bethlehem Pa., U.S.A. 40°37N 75°23W 313 F9
Bethnal Green U.K. 51°31N 0°2W 125 A3
Bethulie S. Africa 30°30S 25°59E 270 D4
Béthune France 50°30N 2°38E 173 B9
Béthune → France 49°53N 1°9E 172 C8
Bethungra Australia 34°45S 147°51E 283 C7
Betijoque Venezuela 9°23N 70°44W 328 B3
Betim Brazil 19°58S 44°13W 333 E3
Betioky Toliara, Madag. 23°48S 44°20E 272 C1
Betioky Toliara, Madag. 22°27S 43°43E 272 C1
Betong Malaysia 1°24N 111°31E 235 B4
Betong Thailand 5°45N 101°5E 237 K3
Betoota Australia 25°45S 140°42E 280 D3
Betor Ethiopia 11°37N 39°2E 257 E4
Betor W. Bengal, India 22°34N 88°17E 124 B1
Bétou Congo 3°2N 18°32E 264 B3
Betpaqdala Kazakhstan 45°45N 70°30E 217 C8
Betroka Madag. 23°16S 46°0E 272 C2
Betsiamites Canada 48°56N 68°40W 299 C6
Betsiamites → Canada 48°56N 68°38W 299 C6
Betsiboka → Madag. 16°3S 46°36E 272 B2
Bettendorf U.S.A. 41°32N 90°30W 310 C6
Bettiah India 26°48N 84°33E 243 F11
Bettna Sweden 58°55N 16°38E 163 F10
Bèttola Italy 44°47N 9°36E 198 D6
Betul India 21°58N 77°59E 244 D3
Betung Indonesia 3°58S 104°34E 234 C2
Betung Kerihun △
Indonesia 1°11N 113°38E 235 B4
Betws-y-Coed U.K. 53°5N 3°48W 168 D4
Betxi Spain 39°56N 0°12W 196 F4
Betzdorf Germany 50°46N 7°52E 178 E3
Béu Angola 6°15S 15°32E 265 D3
Beuil France 44°6N 6°59E 175 D10
Beulah Vic., Australia 35°58S 142°29E 282 C5
Beulah Fla., U.S.A. 28°32N 81°34W 133 A1
Beulah Mich., U.S.A. 44°38N 86°6W 308 C10
Beulah N. Dak., U.S.A. 47°16N 101°47W 308 B3
Beulah, L. U.S.A. 28°32N 81°33W 133 A1
Beurkia Chad 15°20N 17°56E 259 E3
Beurs van Berlage Amsterdam, Neths. 112 a2
Beuthen = Bytom Poland 50°25N 18°54E 185 H5
Beuthen an der Oder = Bytom
Odrzański Poland 51°44N 15°48E 185 G2
Beuvron → France 47°29N 1°15E 172 E8
Beveren Belgium 51°12N 4°16E 170 C4
Beverley W. Austral.,
Australia 32°9S 116°56E 279 F2
Beverley E. Riding, U.K. 53°51N 0°26W 168 D7
Beverley Hills Australia 33°56S 151°5E 139 B1
Beverley Park Australia 33°58S 151°8E 139 B1
Beverly Ill., U.S.A. 41°42N 87°39W 119 C3
Beverly Mass., U.S.A. 42°33N 70°53W 313 D14
Beverly Arts Center
U.S.A. 41°41N 87°40W 119 C2
Beverly Glen U.S.A. 34°6N 118°26W 126 B2
Beverly Hills Calif., U.S.A. 34°5N 118°24W 126 B2
Beverly Hills Fla., U.S.A. 28°55N 82°28W 317 G7
Beverly Hills-Morgan Park Historic
District U.S.A. 41°41N 87°40W 119 C2
Beverungen Germany 51°39N 9°22E 178 D5
Bevoalavo Madag. 25°13S 44°26E 272 D2
Bewas → India 23°59N 79°21E 243 H8
Bewdley Canada 44°5N 78°19W 312 B6
Bex Switz. 46°15N 7°1E 179 J3
Bexhill U.K. 50°51N 0°29E 169 G8
Bexley Australia 33°56S 151°7E 139 B1
Bexley □ U.K. 51°27N 0°9E 125 B4
Bexleyheath U.K. 51°27N 0°8E 125 B4
Bexon St. Lucia 13°57N 60°59W 323 m
Bey Dağları Turkey 36°38N 30°29E 205 E12
Beyānlū Iran 36°0N 47°51E 246 C5
Beyazköy Turkey 41°21N 27°42E 203 E11
Beyçayırı Turkey 40°15N 26°55E 203 F10
Beydağ Turkey 38°5N 28°13E 205 C10
Beyeğaç Turkey 37°14N 28°53E 205 D10
Beyin Ghana 5°1N 2°41W 262 D4
Beykoz Turkey 41°7N 29°7E 122 B2
Beyla Guinea 8°30N 8°38W 262 D3
Beylerbeyi Turkey 41°2N 29°2E 122 B2
Beynat France 45°8N 1°44E 174 C5
Beyneu Kazakhstan 45°18N 55°9E 187 G10
Beyoba Turkey 38°48N 27°47E 205 C9
Beyoğlu Turkey 41°1N 28°58E 122 B1
Beyoneisu Retsugan
Japan 31°55N 139°55E 223 F11
Beypazarı Turkey 40°10N 31°56E 212 B4
Beypore → India 11°10N 75°47E 245 J2
Beyra Somalia 6°57N 47°19E 267 C6
Beyşehir Turkey 37°41N 31°43E 212 D4
Beyşehir Gölü Turkey 37°41N 31°33E 212 D4
Beytüşşebap Turkey 37°35N 43°10E 213 D10
Bezdan Serbia 45°50N 18°57E 182 E3
Bezhetsk Russia 57°47N 36°39E 188 D9
Béziers France 43°20N 3°12E 174 E7
Bezons France 48°56N 2°13E 134 A2
Bezuidenhout Park
S. Africa 26°10S 28°5E 123 B2
Bezwada = Vijayawada
India 16°31N 80°39E 244 F5
Bhabua India 25°3N 83°37E 243 G10
Bhachau India 23°20N 70°16E 242 H4
Bhadar → Gujarat, India 22°17N 72°20E 242 H5
Bhadar → Gujarat, India 21°27N 69°47E 242 J3
Bhadarwah India 32°58N 75°46E 243 C6
Bhadgaon = Bhaktapur
Nepal 27°38N 85°24E 243 F11
Bhadohi India 25°25N 82°34E 243 G10
Bhadra India 29°8N 75°14E 242 E6
Bhadra → India 14°0N 75°20E 245 H2
Bhadrachalam India 17°40N 80°53E 244 F5
Bhadrak India 21°10N 86°30E 244 D8
Bhadrakali India 22°40N 88°20E 124 A2
Bhadran India 22°19N 72°6E 242 H5
Bhadravati India 13°49N 75°40E 245 H2
Bhag Pakistan 29°2N 67°49E 242 E2
Bhagalpur India 25°10N 87°0E 243 G12
Bhagirathi → Paschimbanga,
India 23°25N 88°23E 243 H13
Bhagirathi → Uttarakhand,
India 30°8N 78°35E 243 D8
Bhainsa India 19°10N 77°58E 244 E3
Bhairab → Bangla. 22°51N 89°34E 241 D2
Bhairab Bazar Bangla. 24°4N 90°58E 241 C3
Bhakkar Pakistan 31°40N 71°5E 242 D4
Bhakra Dam India 31°30N 76°45E 242 D7
Bhaktapur Nepal 27°38N 85°24E 243 F11
Bhalki India 18°2N 77°13E 244 E3
Bhalswa India 28°44N 77°10E 120 A2
Bhambo Khan Qarmati
Pakistan 24°49N 67°7E 123 B2
Bhamo Burma 24°15N 97°15E 241 C6
Bhamragarh India 19°30N 80°40E 244 E5
Bhandara India 21°5N 79°42E 244 D4
Bhanpura India 24°31N 75°44E 242 G6
Bhanrer Ra. India 23°40N 79°45E 243 H8
Bhaptiahi India 26°19N 86°44E 243 F12
Bharat = India ■ Asia 20°0N 78°0E 239 F11
Bharatpur Chhattisgarh,
India 23°44N 81°46E 243 H9
Bharatpur Raj., India 27°15N 77°30E 242 F7
Bharatpur Nepal 27°34N 84°10E 243 F11
Bharno India 23°14N 84°53E 243 H11
Bharraig = Barra U.K. 57°0N 7°29W 167 E1
Bharraig, Caolas = Barra, Sd. of
U.K. 57°4N 7°25W 167 D1
Bharuch India 21°47N 73°0E 244 D1
Bhatarsaigh = Vatersay
U.K. 56°55N 7°32W 167 E1
Bhatghar L. India 18°10N 73°48E 244 E1
Bhatiapara Ghat Bangla. 23°13N 89°42E 241 D2
Bhatinda India 30°15N 74°57E 242 D6
Bhatkal India 13°58N 74°35E 245 H2
Bhatpara India 22°50N 88°25E 243 H13
Bhatsala India 22°30N 88°16E 124 B1
Bhattu India 29°36N 75°19E 242 E6
Bhaun Pakistan 32°55N 72°40E 242 C5
Bhaunagar = Bhavnagar
India 21°45N 72°10E 244 D1
Bhavani India 11°27N 77°43E 245 J3
Bhavnagar India 21°45N 72°10E 244 D1
Bhawanipatna India 19°55N 83°10E 244 E6
Bhawanipur India 22°32N 88°21E 124 B2
Bhawari India 25°42N 73°4E 242 G5
Bhayavadar India 21°51N 70°15E 242 J4
Bhearnaraigh = Berneray
U.K. 57°43N 7°11W 167 D1
Bhendkhal India 18°52N 72°59E 130 B2
Bhera Pakistan 32°29N 72°57E 242 C5
Bheri → Nepal 28°47N 81°18E 243 E9
Bhikangaon India 21°52N 75°57E 242 J6
Bhilai = Bhilainagar-Durg
India 21°13N 81°26E 244 D5
Bhilainagar-Durg India 21°13N 81°26E 244 D5
Bhilsa = Vidisha India 23°28N 77°53E 242 H7
Bhilwara India 25°25N 74°38E 242 G6
Bhima → India 16°25N 77°17E 244 F3
Bhimavaram India 16°30N 81°30E 245 F5
Bhimbar Pakistan 32°59N 74°3E 243 C6
Bhind India 26°30N 78°46E 243 F8
Bhinga India 27°43N 81°56E 243 F9
Bhinmal India 25°0N 72°15E 242 G5
Bhisho S. Africa 32°50S 27°23E 270 D4
Bhit I. Pakistan 24°49N 67°0E 123 B1
Bhiwandi India 19°20N 73°0E 244 E1
Bhiwani India 28°50N 76°9E 242 E7
Bhogava → India 22°26N 72°20E 242 H5
Bhojpur Nepal 27°10N 87°3E 243 F12
Bhokardan India 20°16N 75°46E 244 D2
Bhola Bangla. 22°45N 90°35E 241 D3
Bholari Pakistan 25°19N 68°13E 242 G3
Bhongir India 17°30N 78°56E 244 F4
Bhopal India 23°20N 77°30E 242 H7
Bhopalpatnam India 18°52N 80°23E 244 E5
Bhor India 18°12N 73°53E 244 E1
Bhuban India 20°53N 85°50E 244 D7
Bhubaneshwar India 20°15N 85°50E 244 D7
Bhuj India 23°15N 69°49E 242 H3
Bhuleshwar Mumbai, India 130 b2
Bhumiphol Res. Thailand 17°20N 98°40E 236 D2
Bhusawal India 21°3N 75°46E 244 D2
Bhutan ■ Asia 27°25N 90°30E 241 B3
Biá → Brazil 3°28S 67°23W 328 D4
Biafra, B. of = Bonny, Bight of
Africa 3°30N 9°20E 263 E6
Biak Indonesia 1°10S 136°6E 231 E9
Biała Poland 50°24N 17°40E 185 H4
Biała → Poland 50°3N 20°55E 185 H7
Biała Piska Poland 53°37N 22°5E 184 E9
Biała Podlaska Poland 52°4N 23°6E 185 F10
Biała Rawska Poland 51°48N 20°29E 185 G7
Białobrzegi Poland 51°39N 20°58E 185 G7
Białogard Poland 54°2N 15°58E 184 D2
Białołeka Dworska Poland 52°19N 21°1E 143 B2
Białowieski △ Poland 52°43N 23°50E 185 F10
Białowieża Poland 52°41N 23°49E 185 F10
Biały Bór Poland 53°53N 16°51E 184 E3
Białystok Poland 53°10N 23°10E 185 E10
Biancavilla Italy 37°38N 14°52E 201 E7
Bianco Italy 38°5N 16°9E 201 D9
Biankouma Ivory C. 7°50N 7°40W 262 D3
Biaora India 23°56N 76°56E 242 H7
Bīārjmand Iran 36°6N 55°53E 247 B7
Biaro Indonesia 2°5N 125°26E 231 D7
Biarritz France 43°29N 1°33W 174 E2
Biasca Switz. 46°22N 8°58E 179 J4
Biavela Angola 14°43S 19°45E 265 E3
Biba Egypt 28°55N 31°0E 256 J7
Bibai Japan 43°19N 141°52E 220 C10
Bibala Angola 14°44S 13°24E 265 E2
Bibane, Bahiret el Tunisia 33°16N 11°13E 258 B2
Bibassé Gabon 1°27N 11°37E 264 B2
Bibbiena Italy 43°42N 11°49E 199 E8
Bibby I. Canada 61°55N 93°0W 297 A10
Bibei → Spain 42°24N 7°13W 194 C3
Biberach Germany 48°5N 9°47E 179 G5
Bibi Papua N. G. 5°30S 146°2E 286 C4
Bibiani Ghana 6°30N 2°8W 262 D4
Bibile Sri Lanka 7°10N 81°25E 245 L5
Bibungwa
Dem. Rep. of the Congo 2°40S 28°15E 268 C2
Bicaj Albania 41°58N 20°25E 202 E4
Bicaz Romania 46°53N 26°5E 183 D11
Bicazu Ardelean
Romania 46°51N 25°56E 183 D10
Biccari Italy 41°23N 15°12E 201 A8
Bicentennial Park N.S.W.,
Australia 33°51S 151°5E 139 B1
Bicentennial Park Calif.,
U.S.A. 34°1N 118°1W 126 B4
Bicester U.K. 51°54N 1°9W 169 F6
Biche Trin. & Tob. 10°26N 61°8W 323 t
Bichena Ethiopia 10°28N 38°10E 257 E4
Bicheno Australia 41°52S 148°18E 281 G4
Bichia India 22°27N 80°42E 243 H9
Bichvinta Georgia 43°9N 40°21E 191 J5
Bickerton I. Australia 13°45S 136°10E 280 A2
Bickley U.K. 51°23N 0°2E 125 B4
Bicknell U.S.A. 38°47N 87°19W 311 F9
Bicol △ Phil. 13°55N 122°58E 232 E4
Bicske Hungary 47°29N 18°38E 182 C3
Bicuari △ Angola 15°14S 14°45E 265 F2
Bicutan Phil. 14°30N 121°3E 127 C2
Bid = Bir India 19°4N 75°46E 244 E2
Bida Dem. Rep. of the Congo 4°55N 19°56E 264 B3
Bida Nigeria 9°3N 5°58E 263 D6
Bidar India 17°55N 77°35E 244 F3
Bidde Somalia 0°58N 42°37E 267 D5
Biddeford U.S.A. 43°30N 70°28W 309 D18
Biddwara Ethiopia 5°11N 38°34E 257 F4
Bideford U.K. 51°1N 4°13W 169 F3
Bideford Bay U.K. 51°5N 4°20W 169 F3
Bidhan Nagar India 22°35N 88°25E 124 B2
Bidhuna India 26°49N 79°31E 243 F8
Bīdokht Iran 34°20N 58°46E 247 C8
Bidor Malaysia 4°6N 101°15E 237 K3
Bidu West Bank 31°50N 35°9E 123 B1
Bidyadanga Australia 18°45S 121°43E 278 C3
Bidzar Cameroon 9°54N 14°7E 264 A2
Bie Sweden 59°5N 16°12E 162 E10
Bié □ Angola 12°30S 17°0E 265 E3
Bié, Planalto de Angola 12°0S 16°0E 265 E3
Bieber U.S.A. 41°7N 121°8W 304 F3
Biebrza → Poland 53°13N 22°25E 185 E9
Biebrzański △ Poland 53°36N 22°45E 184 E9
Biecz Poland 49°44N 21°15E 185 J8
Biel Switz. 47°8N 7°14E 179 H3
Bielany Poland 52°17N 20°57E 143 B1
Bielawa Dolnośląskie,
Poland 50°43N 16°37E 185 H3
Bielawa Warszawa, Poland 52°8N 21°9E 143 C2
Bielefeld Germany 52°1N 8°33E 178 C4
Bielersee Switz. 47°6N 7°5E 179 H3
Bielitz = Bielsko-Biała
Poland 49°50N 19°2E 185 J6
Biella Italy 45°34N 8°3E 198 C5
Bielsk Podlaski Poland 52°47N 23°12E 185 F10
Bielsko-Biała Poland 49°50N 19°2E 185 J6
Bien Hoa Vietnam 10°57N 106°49E 237 G6
Bienne = Biel Switz. 47°8N 7°14E 179 H3
Bienvenida Spain 38°18N 6°12W 195 G4
Bienvenue Fr. Guiana 3°0N 52°30W 329 C7
Bienville, L. Canada 55°5N 72°40W 298 A5
Bierné France 47°48N 0°33W 172 E6
Bierun Poland 50°6N 19°6E 185 H6
Bierutów Poland 51°7N 17°32E 185 G4
Biesbosch △ Neths. 51°45N 4°48E 170 C4
Biescas Spain 42°37N 0°20W 196 C4
Biesdorf Germany 52°30N 13°33E 115 A4
Biese → Germany 52°53N 11°46E 178 C7
Biesiesfontein S. Africa 30°57S 17°58E 270 D2
Bieszczadzki △ Poland 49°5N 22°43E 185 J9
Bietigheim-Bissingen
Germany 48°58N 9°8E 179 G5
Bièvre → France 48°44N 2°9E 134 B1
Bièvres France 48°45N 2°13E 134 B2
Bieżuń Poland 52°58N 19°55E 185 F6
Biferno → Italy 41°59N 15°2E 199 G12
Bifoum Gabon 0°20S 10°23E 264 C2
Big → Nfld. & L., Canada 54°50N 58°55W 299 B8
Big → Mo., U.S.A. 38°28N 90°37W 310 F6
Big B. = Awarua B. N.Z. 44°28S 168°4E 285 E3
Big B. Canada 55°43N 60°35W 299 A7
Big Bear City U.S.A. 34°16N 116°51W 307 L10
Big Bear Lake U.S.A. 34°15N 116°56W 307 L10
Big Belt Mts. U.S.A. 46°30N 111°25W 304 C8
Big Bend Swaziland 26°50S 31°58E 271 C5
Big Bend △ U.S.A. 29°20N 103°5W 314 G3
Big Black → U.S.A. 32°3N 91°4W 315 E9
Big Blue → Ind., U.S.A. 39°12N 85°56W 311 E11
Big Blue → Kans., U.S.A. 39°35N 96°34W 308 F5
Big Buddha
Hong Kong, China 22°15N 113°54E 219 a
Big Creek U.S.A. 37°11N 119°14W 306 H7
Big Cypress ⌂ U.S.A. 26°0N 81°10W 317 J8
Big Cypress Swamp
U.S.A. 26°15N 81°30W 317 J8
Big Delta U.S.A. 64°10N 145°51W 303 D11
Big Desert Australia 35°45S 141°10E 281 F3
Big Falls U.S.A. 48°12N 93°48W 308 A7
Big Fork → U.S.A. 48°31N 93°43W 308 A7
Big Horn Mts. = Bighorn Mts.
U.S.A. 44°25N 107°0W 304 D10
Big I. Canada 61°7N 116°45W 296 A5
Big Lake Alaska, U.S.A. 61°20N 150°20W 303 F10
Big Lake Tex., U.S.A. 31°12N 101°28W 314 F4
Big Moose U.S.A. 43°49N 74°58W 313 C10
Big Muddy → U.S.A. 37°33N 89°32W 310 G8
Big Muddy Cr. →
U.S.A. 48°8N 104°36W 304 B11
Big Pine U.S.A. 37°10N 118°17W 306 H8
Big Pine Key U.S.A. 24°40N 81°21W 317 L8
Big Piney U.S.A. 42°32N 110°7W 304 E8
Big Quill L. Canada 51°55N 104°30W 297 C8
Big Rapids U.S.A. 43°42N 85°29W 309 D11
Big Rideau L. Canada 44°40N 76°15W 313 B8
Big River Canada 53°50N 107°0W 297 C7
Big Run U.S.A. 40°57N 78°55W 312 F6
Big Sable Pt. U.S.A. 44°3N 86°1W 308 C10
Big Salmon → Canada 61°52N 134°55W 296 A2
Big Sand L. Man., Canada 57°45N 99°45W 297 B9
Big Sand L. Fla., U.S.A. 28°25N 81°29W 133 B2
Big Sandy U.S.A. 48°11N 110°7W 304 B8
Big Sandy → U.S.A. 38°25N 82°36W 309 F12
Big Sandy Cr. = Sandy Cr. →
U.S.A. 41°51N 109°47W 304 F9
Big Sandy Cr. → U.S.A. 38°7N 102°29W 304 G12
Big Satilla Cr. → U.S.A. 31°27N 82°3W 316 D7
Big Sioux → U.S.A. 42°29N 96°27W 308 D5
Big South Fork △ U.S.A. 36°27N 84°47W 315 C12
Big Spring U.S.A. 32°15N 101°28W 314 E4
Big Stone City U.S.A. 45°18N 96°28W 308 C5
Big Stone Gap U.S.A. 36°52N 82°47W 309 G12
Big Stone L. U.S.A. 45°18N 96°27W 308 C5
Big Sur U.S.A. 36°15N 121°48W 306 J5
Big Timber U.S.A. 45°50N 109°57W 304 D9
Big Trout L. Canada 53°40N 90°0W 298 B2
Big Trout Lake Canada 53°45N 90°0W 298 B2
Biğa Turkey 40°13N 27°14E 203 F11
Biga → Turkey 40°20N 27°14E 203 F11
Bigadiç Turkey 39°22N 28°7E 205 B10
Biganos France 44°39N 0°59W 174 D3
Bigeumdo S. Korea 34°45N 125°56E 224 E3
Biggar Sask., Canada 52°4N 108°0W 297 C7
Biggar S. Lanarks., U.K. 55°38N 3°32W 167 F5
Bigge I. Australia 14°35S 125°10E 278 B4
Biggenden Australia 25°31S 152°4E 281 D5
Biggleswade U.K. 52°5N 0°14W 169 E7
Biggs U.S.A. 39°25N 121°43W 306 F5
Bighorn U.S.A. 46°10N 107°27W 304 C10
Bighorn → U.S.A. 46°10N 107°28W 304 C10
Bighorn Canyon ⌂
U.S.A. 45°10N 108°0W 304 D10
Bighorn L. U.S.A. 44°55N 108°15W 304 D9
Bighorn Mts. U.S.A. 44°25N 107°0W 304 D10
Bigi Dem. Rep. of the Congo 3°2N 22°25E 264 B3
Bignona Senegal 12°52N 16°14W 262 C1
Bigorre France 43°10N 0°5E 174 E4
Bigstone L. Canada 53°42N 95°44W 297 C9
Biguglia, Étang de France 42°36N 9°29E 175 F13
Bigwa Tanzania 7°10S 39°10E 268 D4
Bihać Bos.-H. 44°49N 15°57E 199 D12
Bihar India 25°5N 85°40E 243 G11

Bihar □ *India* 25°0N 86°0E 243 G12
Biharamulo *Tanzania* 2°25S 31°25E 268 C3
Biharamulo △ *Tanzania* 2°24S 31°26E 268 C3
Bihariganj *India* 25°44N 86°59E 243 G12
Biharkeresztes *Hungary* 47°8N 21°44E 182 C6
Bihor □ *Romania* 47°0N 22°10E 182 D7
Bihor, Munţii *Romania* 46°29N 22°47E 182 D7
Bijagós, Arquipélago dos *Guinea-Biss.* 11°15N 16°10W 262 C1
Bijaipur *India* 26°2N 77°20E 242 F7
Bijapur *Chhattisgarh, India* 18°50N 80°50E 244 E5
Bijapur *Karnataka, India* 16°50N 75°55E 244 F2
Bījār *Iran* 35°52N 47°35E 213 E12
Bijauri *Nepal* 28°6N 82°20E 243 E10
Bijawar *India* 24°38N 79°30E 243 G8
Bijbels Museum *Amsterdam, Neths.* 112 b1
Bijela *Montenegro* 42°28N 18°39E 202 D2
Bijeljina *Bos.-H.* 44°46N 19°14E 182 F4
Bijelo Polje *Montenegro* 43°1N 19°45E 202 C3
Bijie *China* 27°20N 105°16E 228 D5
Bijnor *India* 29°27N 78°11E 242 E8
Bikaner *India* 28°2N 73°18E 242 E5
Bikapur *India* 26°30N 82°7E 243 F10
Bikeqi *China* 40°43N 111°20E 226 D6
Bikfayyā *Lebanon* 33°55N 35°41E 250 E6
Bikié *Congo* 3°7S 13°52E 264 C2
Bikin *Russia* 46°50N 134°20E 220 A7
Bikin → *Russia* 46°51N 134°2E 220 A7
Bikini Atoll *Marshall Is.* 12°0N 167°30E 288 F8
Bikita *Zimbabwe* 20°6S 31°41E 271 B5
Bīkkū Bīttī *Libya* 22°0N 19°12E 259 D3
Bikoro *Dem. Rep. of the Congo* 0°48S 18°15E 264 C3
Bikoué *Cameroon* 3°55N 11°50E 263 E7
Bila Tserkva *Ukraine* 49°45N 30°10E 177 D16
Bilād Banī Bū 'Alī *Oman* 22°1N 59°19E 249 B7
Bilanga *Burkina Faso* 12°40N 0°1W 263 C4
Bilara *India* 26°14N 73°53E 242 F5
Bilasipara *India* 26°13N 90°14E 241 B3
Bilaspur *Chhattisgarh, India* 22°2N 82°15E 243 H10
Bilaspur *Punjab, India* 31°19N 76°50E 242 D7
Biläsuvar *Azerbaijan* 39°27N 48°32E 213 C13
Bilauk Taungdan *Thailand* 13°0N 99°0E 236 F2
Bilauri *Nepal* 28°41N 80°21E 243 E9
Bilbao *Spain* 43°16N 2°56W 196 B2
Bilbao ✈ (BIO) *Spain* 43°18N 2°57W 196 B2
Bilbeis *Egypt* 30°25N 31°34E 256 H7
Bilbo = Bilbao *Spain* 43°16N 2°56W 196 B2
Bilbor *Romania* 47°6N 25°30E 183 C10
Bilche-Zolote *Ukraine* 48°47N 25°53E 183 B10
Bilciureşti *Romania* 44°44N 25°48E 183 F10
Bíldudalur *Iceland* 65°41N 23°36W 155 B3
Bílé Karpaty *Europe* 49°5N 18°0E 181 B11
Bileća *Bos.-H.* 42°53N 18°27E 202 D2
Bilecik *Turkey* 40°5N 30°5E 212 B4
Bilecik □ *Turkey* 40°0N 30°0E 212 B3
Bilećko Jezero *Bos.-H.* 42°48N 18°28E 202 D2
Bileh Savār *Iran* 39°21N 48°21E 213 C13
Biłgoraj *Poland* 50°33N 22°42E 185 H9
Bilgram *India* 27°11N 80°2E 243 F9
Bilhaur *India* 26°51N 80°5E 243 F9
Bilhorod-Dnistrovskyy *Ukraine* 46°11N 30°23E 189 J6
Bili → *Dem. Rep. of the Congo* 4°9N 22°29E 264 B4
Bilibino *Russia* 68°3N 166°20E 215 C17
Bilibiza *Mozam.* 12°30S 40°20E 269 E5
Bilimora *India* 20°45N 72°57E 244 D1
Bilin *Burma* 17°14N 97°15E 241 G6
Biliran *Phil.* 11°28N 124°28E 233 F5
Biliran □ *Phil.* 11°35N 124°28E 233 F5
Bilisht *Albania* 40°37N 21°2E 202 F5
Bill Baggs Cape Florida State Recr. Area △ *U.S.A.* 25°40N 80°9W 129 D3
Billabong Cr. → *Australia* 35°5S 144°2E 282 C6
Billdal *Sweden* 57°35N 11°57E 163 G5
Billiluna *Australia* 19°37S 127°41E 278 C4
Billings *U.S.A.* 45°47N 108°30W 304 D9
Billiton Is. = Belitung *Indonesia* 3°10S 107°50E 235 C3
Billsta *Sweden* 63°20N 18°28E 162 A12
Billund *Denmark* 55°44N 9°6E 163 J3
Billy Pt. *Antigua & B.* 17°44N 61°52W 322 c
Bilma *Niger* 18°50N 13°30E 259 E2
Bilma, Grand Erg de *Niger* 18°30N 14°0E 259 E2
Bilo Gora *Croatia* 45°53N 17°15E 182 E2
Biloela *Australia* 24°24S 150°31E 280 C5
Bilohirsk *Ukraine* 45°3N 34°35E 189 K8
Biloku *Guyana* 1°50N 58°25W 329 C6
Biloli *India* 18°46N 77°44E 244 E3
Bilopillya *Ukraine* 51°14N 34°20E 189 G8
Bilovodsk *Ukraine* 49°13N 39°36E 189 H10
Biloxi *U.S.A.* 30°24N 88°53W 315 F10
Bilpa Morea Claypan *Australia* 25°0S 140°0E 280 D3
Bilqās Qism Auwal *Egypt* 31°12N 31°21E 251 G2
Bilston *U.K.* 55°52N 3°10W 121 B2
Biltine *Chad* 14°40N 20°50E 259 F4
Bilugyun *Burma* 16°24N 97°32E 241 G6
Bilyarsk *Russia* 54°58N 50°22E 190 C10
Bim Son *Vietnam* 20°4N 105°51E 236 B5
Bima *Indonesia* 8°22S 118°49E 235 D5
Bimban *Egypt* 24°24N 32°54E 256 C3
Bimbe *Angola* 11°50S 15°50E 265 E3
Bimberi Pk. *Australia* 35°44S 148°51E 283 C8
Bimbila *Ghana* 8°54N 0°5E 263 D5
Bimbini *Comoros Is.* 12°11S 44°14E 272 a
Bimbo *C.A.R.* 4°15N 18°33E 264 B3
Bimini Is. *Bahamas* 25°42N 79°25W 320 A4
Bin Ghunaymah, Jabal *Libya* 25°0N 15°30E 258 D3
Bin Jawwād *Libya* 30°47N 18°4E 258 B3
Bin Xian *Heilongjiang, China* 45°42N 127°32E 227 B14
Bin Xian *Shaanxi, China* 35°2N 108°4E 226 G5
Bin Yauri *Nigeria* 10°46N 4°45E 263 C5
Bina-Etawah *India* 24°13N 78°14E 242 G8
Binacayan *Phil.* 14°27N 120°55E 127 C1
Binalbagan *Phil.* 10°12N 122°50E 233 F4
Binalong *Australia* 34°40S 148°39E 283 C8
Bīnālūd, Kūh-e *Iran* 36°30N 58°30E 247 B8
Binanga *Indonesia* 1°24N 99°46E 234 B1
Binangonan de Lampon = Infanta *Phil.* 14°45N 121°39E 232 D3
Binatang = Bintangau *Malaysia* 2°10N 111°40E 235 B4
Binche *Belgium* 50°26N 4°10E 170 D4
Binchuan *China* 25°42N 100°38E 228 E3
Binda *Dem. Rep. of the Congo* 5°52S 13°14E 265 D2
Binder *Chad* 9°56N 14°27E 259 G2
Bindki *India* 26°2N 80°36E 243 F9
Bindloe, I. = Marchena, I. *Ecuador* 0°19N 90°29W 330 a
Bindoy *Phil.* 9°48N 123°5E 233 G4
Bindslev *Denmark* 57°33N 10°11E 163 G4
Bindura *Zimbabwe* 17°18S 31°18E 269 F3
Binéfar *Spain* 41°51N 0°18E 196 D5
Bingara *Australia* 29°52S 150°36E 281 D5
Bingaram I. *India* 10°56N 72°17E 245 J1
Bingen *Germany* 49°57N 7°55E 179 F3
Bingerau = Węgrów *Poland* 52°24N 22°0E 185 F9
Bingerville *Ivory C.* 5°18N 3°49W 262 D4
Bingham *U.S.A.* 45°3N 69°53W 309 C19
Binghamton *U.S.A.* 42°6N 75°55W 313 D9
Bingo-Ochiai *Japan* 34°59N 133°8E 222 C4
Bingöl *Turkey* 38°53N 40°29E 213 C9
Bingöl □ *Turkey* 38°55N 40°30E 213 C9
Bingöl Dağları *Turkey* 39°16N 41°9E 213 C9
Bingsjö *Sweden* 61°1N 15°39E 162 C9
Binh Dinh *Vietnam* 13°55N 109°7E 236 F7
Binh Son *Vietnam* 15°20N 108°40E 236 E7
Binhai *China* 34°2N 119°49E 227 G10
Bini Erde *Chad* 20°6N 18°1E 259 D3
Binic *France* 48°36N 2°50W 172 D4
Binisatua *Spain* 39°50N 4°11E 206 B5
Binissalem *Spain* 39°41N 2°50E 206 B3
Binjai *Kepulauan Riau, Indonesia* 3°48N 108°13E 235 B3
Binjai *Sumatera Utara, Indonesia* 3°20N 98°30E 234 B1
Binji *Nigeria* 13°10N 4°55E 263 C5
Binka *India* 21°2N 83°48E 244 D6
Binnah, Ras *Somalia* 11°59N 51°10E 267 B7
Binnaway *Australia* 31°28S 149°24E 283 A8
Binondo *Phil.* 14°36N 120°58E 127 B1
Binongko *Indonesia* 5°57S 124°2E 231 F6
Binscarth *Canada* 50°37N 101°17W 297 C8
Binshangul Gumuz □ *Ethiopia* 11°0N 35°30E 257 E4
Bint Goda *Sudan* 13°17N 31°33E 257 E3
Bintan *Indonesia* 1°0N 104°0E 234 B2
Bintangau *Malaysia* 2°10N 111°40E 235 B4
Bintaro Jaya *Indonesia* 6°16S 106°44E 122 B1
Bintuhan *Indonesia* 4°48S 103°22E 234 C2
Bintulu *Malaysia* 3°10N 113°0E 235 B4
Bintuni *Indonesia* 2°7S 133°32E 231 E8
Binyang *China* 23°12N 108°47E 228 F7
Binz *Germany* 54°24N 13°35E 178 A9
Binza *Dem. Rep. of the Congo* 4°21S 15°14E 265 C3
Binzert = Bizerte *Tunisia* 37°15N 9°50E 258 A1
Binzhou *China* 37°20N 118°2E 227 F10
Bío Bío □ *Chile* 37°35S 72°0W 334 D1
Biobío → *Chile* 36°49S 73°10W 334 D1
Biograd na Moru *Croatia* 43°56N 15°29E 199 E12
Biogradska Gora △ *Montenegro* 42°55N 19°40E 202 D3
Bioko *Eq. Guin.* 3°30N 8°40E 263 E6
Biokovo *Croatia* 43°23N 17°0E 199 E14
Biougra *Morocco* 30°15N 9°14W 260 B3
Bipindi *Cameroon* 3°6N 10°30E 263 E7
Bir *India* 19°4N 75°46E 244 E2
Bir, Ras *Djibouti* 12°0N 43°20E 257 E5
Bîr Abu Hashim *Egypt* 23°42N 34°6E 256 C3
Bîr Abu Minqar *Egypt* 26°33N 27°33E 256 B2
Bîr Abu Muḥammad *Egypt* 29°44N 34°14E 251 J5
Bîr Abu Sandûq *Egypt* 29°24N 32°30E 251 J3
Bi'r Adal Deib *Sudan* 22°35N 36°10E 256 C4
Bi'r al Butayyihāt *Jordan* 29°47N 35°20E 251 J6
Bi'r al Ḩamdh *Si. Arabia* 28°30N 34°55E 251 K5
Bi'r al Mārī *Jordan* 30°4N 35°33E 251 H6
Bi'r al Musallam *Si. Arabia* 28°56N 35°38E 251 K6
Bi'r al Qattār *Jordan* 29°47N 35°32E 251 J6
Bir 'Ali *Yemen* 14°1N 48°20E 249 D5
Bîr 'Amrâne *Mauritania* 22°45N 8°39W 260 D3
Bîr Aouine *Tunisia* 32°25N 9°18E 258 B1
Bîr 'Asal *Egypt* 25°55N 34°20E 256 B3
Bi'r ash Shakkūsīyah *Syria* 35°23N 37°26E 250 C8
Bir Atrun *Sudan* 18°15N 26°40E 256 D2
Bîr Beida *Egypt* 30°25N 34°29E 251 H5
Bir Bel Guerdâne *Mauritania* 25°24N 10°31W 260 C2
Bîr Bireida *Egypt* 29°8N 32°7E 251 J3
Bîr Buerât *Egypt* 28°59N 32°11E 251 K3
Bi'r Dhu'fān *Libya* 31°59N 14°32E 258 B2
Bîr Di *South Sudan* 7°34N 28°49E 257 F2
Bîr Diqnash *Egypt* 31°3N 25°23E 256 A2
Bir el Abbes *Algeria* 26°7N 6°9W 260 C3
Bîr el 'Abd *Egypt* 31°2N 33°0E 251 G4
Bîr el 'Agramîya *Egypt* 29°38N 31°50E 251 J2
Bir el Ater *Algeria* 34°46N 8°3E 261 B6
Bîr el Basur *Egypt* 29°51N 25°49E 256 B2
Bîr el Biarât *Egypt* 29°30N 34°43E 251 J5
Bîr el Dakhal *Egypt* 28°39N 32°23E 251 K3
Bîr el Duweidar *Egypt* 30°56N 32°32E 251 H3
Bîr el Garârât *Egypt* 31°3N 33°34E 251 G4
Bîr el Gâreb *Mauritania* 20°33N 16°12W 260 D1
Bîr el Gellaz *Egypt* 30°50N 26°40E 256 A2
Bîr el Ghamr *Egypt* 28°43N 31°20E 251 K2
Bîr el Heisi *Egypt* 29°22N 34°36E 251 J5
Bîr el Jafir *Egypt* 30°50N 32°41E 251 H3
Bîr el Mâlḥi *Egypt* 30°38N 33°19E 251 H4
Bîr el Manâyif *Egypt* 30°31N 32°12E 251 H3
Bîr el-Naṣb *Egypt* 29°3N 33°2E 251 J4
Bîr el Ṣafra *Egypt* 28°45N 34°21E 251 K5
Bîr el-Saura *Egypt* 29°9N 34°30E 251 J5
Bîr el Shaqqa *Egypt* 30°54N 25°1E 256 A2
Bîr el Thamâda *Egypt* 30°12N 33°27E 251 H4
Bîr Enzarân *W. Sahara* 23°53N 14°32W 260 D2
Bîr Fuad *Egypt* 30°35N 26°28E 256 A2
Bîr Gandûs *W. Sahara* 21°36N 16°30W 260 D1
Bîr Gebeil Ḥiṣn *Egypt* 30°2N 33°18E 251 H4
Bi'r Ghadīr *Syria* 34°6N 37°3E 250 D8
Bîr Ghalla *Egypt* 28°23N 32°19E 251 K3
Bi'r Gharr *Si. Arabia* 28°7N 35°32E 251 K6
Bîr Gindali *Egypt* 29°55N 31°40E 251 J2
Bîr Haimur *Egypt* 22°45N 33°40E 256 C3
Bîr Ḩasana *Egypt* 30°29N 33°46E 251 H4
Bîr Hööker *Egypt* 30°22N 30°21E 256 H7
Bi'r Ïdimah *Si. Arabia* 18°31N 44°12E 248 C4
Bi'r Jadīd *Si. Arabia* 29°10N 35°6E 251 J6
Bîr Kanayis *Egypt* 24°59N 33°15E 256 C3
Bîr Kaseiba *Egypt* 31°0N 33°17E 251 H4
Bîr Kerawein *Egypt* 27°10N 28°25E 256 B2
Bîr Lahfân *Egypt* 31°0N 33°51E 251 H4
Bir Lahrache *Algeria* 32°1N 8°12E 261 B6
Bîr Madkûr *Egypt* 30°44N 32°33E 251 H3
Bîr Maql *Egypt* 23°7N 33°40E 256 C3
Bîr Mîneiga *Sudan* 22°47N 35°12E 256 C4
Bîr Misaha *Egypt* 22°13N 27°59E 256 C2
Bir Mogreïn *Mauritania* 25°10N 11°25W 260 C2
Bîr Mureir *Egypt* 28°25N 31°15E 251 K2
Bîr Murr *Egypt* 23°28N 30°10E 256 C3
Bi'r Muṭribah *Kuwait* 29°54N 47°17E 246 D5
Bîr Nabala *West Bank* 31°51N 35°12E 123 A2
Bîr Nakheila *Egypt* 24°1N 30°50E 256 C3
Bîr Nakhul *Egypt* 29°5N 33°16E 251 J4
Bîr Qatia *Egypt* 30°58N 32°45E 251 H3
Bîr Qatrani *Egypt* 30°55N 26°10E 256 A2
Bîr Ranga *Egypt* 24°25N 35°15E 256 C4
Bîr Sahara *Egypt* 22°54N 28°40E 256 C2
Bîr Sa'îd *Egypt* 29°38N 31°24E 251 J2
Bîr Seiyâla *Egypt* 26°10N 33°50E 256 B3
Bîr Shalatein *Egypt* 23°5N 35°25E 256 C4
Bîr Shebb *Egypt* 22°25N 29°40E 256 C2
Bîr Shût *Egypt* 23°50N 35°15E 256 C4
Bîr Sidri *Egypt* 28°53N 33°28E 251 K4
Bîr Tâba *Egypt* 29°29N 34°53E 251 J5
Bîr Terfawi *Egypt* 22°57N 28°55E 256 C2
Bîr Umm Qubûr *Egypt* 24°35N 34°2E 256 C3
Bîr Ungât *Egypt* 22°8N 33°48E 256 C3
Bîr Wuseit *Egypt* 29°14N 33°1E 251 J4
Bîr Za'farâna *Egypt* 29°10N 32°40E 256 J8
Bîr Zeidûn *Egypt* 25°45N 33°40E 256 B3
Birāk *Libya* 27°31N 14°20E 258 C2
Birak el Kiyam *Egypt* 30°2N 31°9E 117 A1
Biramféro *Guinea* 11°40N 9°10W 262 C3
Birao *C.A.R.* 10°20N 22°47E 264 A4
Biratnagar *Nepal* 26°27N 87°17E 243 F12
Birawa *Dem. Rep. of the Congo* 2°20S 28°48E 268 C2
Birch → *Canada* 58°28N 112°17W 296 B6
Birch Cliff *Canada* 43°41N 79°16W 141 A3
Birch Grove *Grenada* 12°6N 61°40W 323 q
Birch Hills *Canada* 52°59N 105°25W 297 C7
Birch I. *Canada* 52°26N 99°54W 297 C9
Birch L. *N.W.T., Canada* 62°4N 116°33W 296 A5
Birch L. *Ont., Canada* 51°23N 92°18W 298 B1
Birch Mts. *Canada* 57°30N 113°10W 296 B6
Birch River *Canada* 52°24N 101°6W 297 C8
Birchip *Australia* 35°56S 142°55E 282 C5
Birchiş *Romania* 45°58N 22°9E 182 E7
Birchwood *N.Z.* 45°55S 167°53E 285 F2
Birchwood *Alaska, U.S.A.* 61°24N 149°28W 303 F10
Bird *Canada* 56°30N 94°13W 297 B10
Bird I. = Aves, I. de *W. Indies* 15°45N 63°55W 321 C7
Bird I. *S. Georgia* 54°0S 38°3W 151 B1
Birds Creek *Canada* 45°6N 77°52W 312 A7
Birdseye *U.S.A.* 38°19N 86°42W 311 F10
Birdsville *Australia* 25°51S 139°20E 280 D2
Birdum Cr. → *Australia* 15°14S 133°0E 278 C5
Birdwood *Australia* 34°51S 138°58E 282 C3
Birecik *Turkey* 37°2N 38°0E 213 D8
Birein *Israel* 30°50N 34°28E 251 H5
Bireuen *Indonesia* 5°14N 96°39E 234 A1
Birganj *Nepal* 27°1N 84°52E 243 F11
Birgu = Vittoriosa *Malta* 35°54N 14°31E 206 D2
Birhan *Ethiopia* 10°45N 38°4E 266 B4
Biri *Norway* 60°58N 10°35E 164 D7
Biri → *South Sudan* 7°56N 26°33E 257 F2
Birifo *Gambia* 13°30N 14°0W 262 C2
Birigüi *Brazil* 21°18S 50°16W 335 A5
Birini *C.A.R.* 7°51N 22°24E 264 A4
Bīrjand *Iran* 32°53N 59°13E 247 C8
Birka *Sweden* 59°20N 17°32E 162 E11
Birkeland *Norway* 58°24N 7°12E 164 F4
Birkenfeld *Germany* 49°38N 7°9E 179 F3
Birkenhead *U.K.* 53°23N 3°2W 168 D4
Birkenstein *Germany* 52°31N 13°40E 115 A5
Birkerød *Denmark* 55°50N 12°25E 163 J6
Birket Fatmé *Chad* 12°55N 19°7E 259 F3
Birket Qârûn *Egypt* 29°30N 30°40E 256 J7
Birkfeld *Austria* 47°21N 15°45E 180 D8
Birkhadem *Algeria* 36°43N 3°3E 261 A5
Birkholz *Germany* 52°37N 13°34E 115 A4
Birkholzaue *Germany* 52°38N 13°36E 115 A4
Birkirkara *Malta* 35°54N 14°28E 206 F7
Bîrlad = Bârlad *Romania* 46°15N 27°38E 183 D12
Birmingham *W. Mids., U.K.* 52°29N 1°52W 169 E6
Birmingham *Ala., U.S.A.* 33°31N 86°48W 315 E11
Birmingham *Iowa, U.S.A.* 40°53N 91°57W 310 D5
Birmingham Int. ✈ (BHX) *U.K.* 52°26N 1°45W 169 E6
Birmitrapur *India* 22°24N 84°46E 244 C7
Birni Ngaouré *Niger* 13°5N 2°51E 263 C5
Birni Nkonni *Niger* 13°55N 5°15E 263 C6
Birnie *Kiribati* 3°35S 171°31W 277 A16
Birnin Gwari *Nigeria* 11°0N 6°45E 263 C6
Birnin Kebbi *Nigeria* 12°32N 4°12E 263 C5
Birnin Kudu *Nigeria* 11°30N 9°29E 263 C6
Birobidzhan *Russia* 48°50N 132°50E 219 B15
Birougou, Mts. *Gabon* 1°51S 12°20E 264 C2
Birr *Ireland* 53°6N 7°54W 166 C4
Birrarung Park *Australia* 37°45S 145°4E 128 A2
Birrie → *Australia* 29°43S 146°37E 281 D4
Birsilpur *India* 28°11N 72°15E 242 E5
Birsk *Russia* 55°25N 55°30E 186 C10
Birtle *Canada* 50°30N 101°5W 297 C8
Biryuchiy *Ukraine* 46°10N 35°0E 189 J8
Biržai *Lithuania* 56°11N 24°45E 188 D3
Birzebbugga *Malta* 35°50N 14°32E 206 F8
Birzhi → *Latvia* 56°53N 26°5E 188 D4
Birzula = Kotovsk *Ukraine* 47°45N 29°35E 177 E15
Bisa *Indonesia* 1°15S 127°28E 231 E7
Bisáccia *Italy* 41°1N 15°22E 201 A8
Bisacquino *Italy* 37°42N 13°15E 200 E6
Bisai *Japan* 35°16N 136°44E 223 B8
Bisalpur *India* 28°14N 79°48E 243 E8
Bisbee *U.S.A.* 31°27N 109°55W 305 L9
Biscarrosse *France* 44°22N 1°20W 174 D2
Biscarrosse et de Parentis, Étang de *France* 44°21N 1°10W 174 D2
Biscay, B. of *Atl. Oc.* 45°0N 2°0W 171 D1
Biscay Abyssal Plain *Atl. Oc.* 45°0N 8°0W 152 B11
Biscayne △ *U.S.A.* 25°25N 80°12W 317 K9
Biscayne B. *U.S.A.* 25°40N 80°12W 317 K9
Biscayne Bay Aquatic Reserve *U.S.A.* 25°40N 80°16W 129 E2
Biscayne Park *U.S.A.* 25°52N 80°10W 129 C2
Biscéglie *Italy* 41°14N 16°30E 201 A9
Bischheim *France* 48°37N 7°46E 173 D14
Bischoflack = Škofja Loka *Slovenia* 46°9N 14°19E 199 B11
Bischofsburg = Biskupiec *Poland* 53°53N 20°58E 184 E7
Bischofshofen *Austria* 47°26N 13°14E 180 D6
Bischofstal = Ujazd *Poland* 50°23N 18°21E 185 H5
Bischofstein = Bisztynek *Poland* 54°8N 20°53E 184 D7
Bischofswerda *Germany* 51°7N 14°10E 178 D10
Bischwiller *France* 48°46N 7°50E 173 D14
Biscoe Is. *Antarctica* 66°0S 67°0W 151 C17
Biscoitos *Azores* 38°47N 27°15W 153 d1
Biscotasing *Canada* 47°18N 82°9W 298 C3
Biševo *Croatia* 42°57N 16°3E 199 F13
Bisha *Eritrea* 15°30N 37°31E 257 D4
Bishah, W. → *Si. Arabia* 21°24N 43°26E 248 B3
Bishan *China* 29°33N 106°12E 228 C6
Bishanga *Dem. Rep. of the Congo* 4°31S 21°2E 265 C4
Bishkek *Kyrgyzstan* 42°54N 74°46E 217 D8
Bishnath *India* 26°40N 93°10E 241 B4
Bishnupur *India* 23°8N 87°20E 243 H12
Bisho = Bhisho *S. Africa* 32°50S 27°23E 270 D4
Bishop *Calif., U.S.A.* 37°22N 118°24W 306 H8
Bishop *Ga., U.S.A.* 33°49N 83°26W 316 B6
Bishop *Tex., U.S.A.* 27°35N 97°48W 314 H6
Bishop Auckland *U.K.* 54°39N 1°40W 168 C6
Bishop Lavis *S. Africa* 33°56S 18°35E 118 A2
Bishop Museum *U.S.A.* 21°20N 157°52W 302 K14
Bishop's Falls *Canada* 49°2N 55°30W 299 C8
Bishop's Stortford *U.K.* 51°52N 0°10E 169 F8
Bishopscourt *S. Africa* 33°59S 18°27E 118 A1
Bisignano *Italy* 39°31N 16°17E 201 C9
Bisina, L. *Uganda* 1°38N 33°56E 268 B3
Biskra *Algeria* 34°50N 5°44E 261 B6
Biskra *Malta* 35°58N 14°21E 206 F7
Biskra □ *Algeria* 34°40N 5°25E 261 B6
Biskupiec *Poland* 53°53N 20°58E 184 E7
Bislig *Phil.* 8°12N 126°18E 233 G6
Bismarck *Mo., U.S.A.* 37°46N 90°38W 310 G6
Bismarck *N. Dak., U.S.A.* 46°48N 100°47W 308 B3
Bismarck Arch. *Papua N. G.* 2°30S 150°0E 286 B6
Bismarck Ra. *Papua N. G.* 5°35S 145°0E 286 C3
Bismarck Sea *Papua N. G.* 4°10S 146°50E 286 C4
Bismarckburg = Kasanga *Tanzania* 8°30S 31°10E 269 D3
Bismark *Germany* 52°40N 11°33E 178 C7
Bismil *Turkey* 37°51N 40°40E 213 D9
Bismo *Norway* 61°54N 8°15E 164 C5
Biso *Uganda* 1°44N 31°26E 268 B3
Bison *U.S.A.* 45°31N 102°28W 308 C2
Bīsotūn *Iran* 34°23N 47°26E 213 E12
Bispebjerg *Denmark* 55°42N 12°31E 118 A3
Bispgården *Sweden* 63°2N 16°40E 162 A10
Bissagos = Bijagós, Arquipélago dos *Guinea-Biss.* 11°15N 16°10W 262 C1
Bissam Cuttack *India* 19°31N 83°31E 244 E6
Bissau *Guinea-Biss.* 11°45N 15°45W 262 C1
Bissaula *Nigeria* 7°0N 10°27E 263 D7
Bissigh, Lach → *Somalia* 0°45N 41°33E 267 D5
Bissikrima *Guinea* 10°50N 10°58W 262 C2
Bissonet Plaza *U.S.A.* 30°1N 90°13W 131 A1
Bissorã *Guinea-Biss.* 12°16N 15°35W 262 C1
Bistcho L. *Canada* 59°45N 118°50W 296 B5
Bistreţ *Romania* 43°54N 23°23E 183 G8
Bistrica = Ilirska-Bistrica *Slovenia* 45°34N 14°14E 199 C11
Bistriţa *Romania* 47°9N 24°35E 183 C9
Bistriţa → *Romania* 46°30N 26°57E 183 D11
Bistriţa Năsăud □ *Romania* 47°15N 24°30E 183 C9
Bistriţei, Munţii *Romania* 47°15N 25°40E 183 C10
Biswan *India* 27°29N 81°2E 243 F9
Bisztynek *Poland* 54°8N 20°53E 184 D7
Bita → *C.A.R.* 6°26N 24°43E 264 A4
Bitam *Gabon* 2°5N 11°25E 264 B2
Bitburg *Germany* 49°58N 6°31E 179 F2
Bitche *France* 49°2N 7°25E 173 C14
Bithynia *Turkey* 40°40N 31°0E 212 B4
Bitkine *Chad* 11°59N 18°13E 259 F3
Bitlis *Turkey* 38°20N 42°3E 213 C10
Bitlis □ *Turkey* 38°20N 42°5E 213 C10
Bitola *Macedonia* 41°1N 21°20E 202 E5
Bitolj = Bitola *Macedonia* 41°1N 21°20E 202 E5
Bitonto *Italy* 41°6N 16°41E 201 A9
Bitra I. *India* 11°33N 72°9E 245 J1
Bitter Creek *U.S.A.* 41°33N 108°33W 304 F9
Bitter L. = Buheirat-Murrat-el-Kubra *Egypt* 30°18N 32°26E 256 H8
Bitterfeld *Germany* 51°37N 12°20E 178 D8
Bitterfontein *S. Africa* 31°1S 18°32E 270 D2
Bitterroot → *U.S.A.* 46°52N 114°7W 304 C6
Bitterroot Range *U.S.A.* 46°0N 114°20W 304 C6
Bitterwater *U.S.A.* 36°23N 121°0W 306 J6
Bitti *Italy* 40°29N 9°23E 200 B2
Bittou *Burkina Faso* 11°17N 0°18W 263 C4
Bittsevsky Forest Park *Russia* 55°38N 37°35E 129 C2
Biu *Nigeria* 10°40N 12°3E 263 C7
Bivolari *Romania* 47°31N 27°27E 183 C12
Bivolu, Vf. *Romania* 47°16N 25°58E 183 C10
Biwa-Ko *Japan* 35°15N 136°10E 223 B8
Biwabik *U.S.A.* 47°32N 92°21W 308 B7
Bixad *Romania* 47°56N 23°28E 183 C8
Bixby *U.S.A.* 35°57N 95°53W 314 D7
Biya → *Russia* 52°25N 85°0E 217 B11
Biyala *Egypt* 31°10N 31°13E 251 G2
Biyang *China* 32°38N 113°21E 226 H7
Biysk *Russia* 52°40N 85°0E 217 B11
Bizana *S. Africa* 30°50S 29°52E 271 D4
Bizen *Japan* 34°43N 134°8E 222 C6
Bizerte *Tunisia* 37°15N 9°50E 258 A1
Bizerte □ *Tunisia* 37°5N 9°35E 261 A6
Bjåen fjellstove *Norway* 59°37N 7°26E 164 E4
Bjargtangar *Iceland* 65°30N 24°30W 155 B2
Bjarkalundur *Iceland* 65°33N 22°9W 155 B3
Bjärnum *Sweden* 56°17N 13°43E 163 H7
Bjästa *Sweden* 63°12N 18°29E 162 A12
Bjelasica *Montenegro* 42°50N 19°40E 202 D3
Bjelašnica *Bos.-H.* 43°43N 18°9E 182 G3
Bjelland *Norway* 58°23N 7°32E 164 F4
Bjelovar *Croatia* 45°56N 16°49E 199 C13
Bjerringbro *Denmark* 56°23N 9°39E 163 H3
Bjervamoen *Norway* 59°17N 9°5E 164 E6
Bjøberg *Norway* 60°56N 8°13E 164 D5
Björbo *Sweden* 60°27N 14°44E 162 D8
Bjørkelangen *Norway* 59°53N 11°34E 164 E8
Björklinge *Sweden* 60°2N 17°33E 162 D11
Björknäs *Sweden* 59°19N 18°12E 139 B3
Björkö *Sweden* 59°52N 19°2E 162 E13
Bjørnafjorden *Norway* 60°7N 5°28E 164 D2
Björneborg = Pori *Finland* 61°29N 21°48E 188 B1
Björneborg *Sweden* 59°14N 14°16E 162 E8
Bjørnevatn *Norway* 69°40N 30°0E 160 B24
Bjørnøya *Arctic* 74°30N 19°0E 150 B8
Bjursås *Sweden* 60°44N 15°25E 162 D9
Bjuv *Sweden* 56°5N 12°55E 163 H6
Bla *Mali* 12°56N 5°47W 262 C3
Blå Jungfrun △ *Sweden* 57°16N 16°47E 163 G10
Blace *Serbia* 43°18N 21°17E 202 C5
Blachownia *Poland* 50°49N 18°56E 185 H5
Black = Da → *Vietnam* 21°15N 105°20E 228 G5
Black → *Ont., Canada* 44°42N 79°19W 312 B5
Black → *Alaska, U.S.A.* 66°42N 144°42W 303 C11
Black → *Ariz., U.S.A.* 33°44N 110°13W 305 K8
Black → *Ark., U.S.A.* 35°38N 91°20W 314 D9
Black → *La., U.S.A.* 31°16N 91°50W 314 F9
Black → *Mich., U.S.A.* 42°59N 82°27W 312 D2
Black → *N.Y., U.S.A.* 43°59N 76°4W 313 C8
Black → *Wis., U.S.A.* 43°57N 91°22W 308 D8
Black Bay Pen. *Canada* 48°38N 88°21W 298 C2
Black Birch L. *Canada* 56°53N 107°45W 297 B7
Black Canyon of the Gunnison △ *U.S.A.* 38°40N 107°35W 304 G10
Black Cr. → *Canada* 43°40N 79°30W 141 A2
Black Creek Pioneer Village *Canada* 43°46N 79°30W 141 A1
Black Diamond = Pittsburg *U.S.A.* 38°2N 121°53W 306 G5
Black Diamond *Canada* 50°45N 114°14W 296 C6
Black Duck → *Canada* 56°51N 89°2W 298 A2
Black Forest = Schwarzwald *Germany* 48°30N 8°20E 179 G4
Black Forest *U.S.A.* 39°0N 104°43W 304 G11
Black Hd. *Ireland* 53°9N 9°16W 166 C2
Black Hills *U.S.A.* 44°0N 103°45W 308 D2
Black I. *Canada* 51°12N 96°30W 297 C9
Black L. *Sask., Canada* 59°12N 105°15W 297 B7
Black L. *Mich., U.S.A.* 45°28N 84°16W 309 C11
Black L. *N.Y., U.S.A.* 44°31N 75°36W 313 B9
Black Lake *Canada* 59°11N 105°20W 297 B7
Black Mesa *U.S.A.* 36°58N 102°58W 314 C3
Black Mountain *Australia* 30°18S 151°39E 283 A9
Black Mt. = Mynydd Du *U.K.* 51°52N 3°50W 169 F4
Black Mt. *Bhutan* 27°20N 90°25E 241 B3
Black Mts. *U.K.* 51°55N 3°7W 169 F4
Black Range *U.S.A.* 33°15N 107°50W 305 K10
Black River *Jamaica* 18°0N 77°50W 320 a
Black River *N.Y., U.S.A.* 44°0N 75°47W 313 C9
Black River B. *Jamaica* 18°0N 77°51W 320 a
Black River Falls *U.S.A.* 44°18N 90°51W 308 C8
Black River Gorges *Mauritius* 20°24S 57°25E 272 e
Black Rock *S. Austral., Australia* 32°50S 138°44E 282 B3
Black Rock *Barbados* 13°7N 59°37W 323 r
Black Rock Desert *U.S.A.* 41°10N 118°50W 304 F4
Black Sea *Eurasia* 43°30N 35°0E 187 F6
Black Tickle *Canada* 53°28N 55°45W 299 B8
Black Volta → *Africa* 8°41N 1°33W 262 D4
Black Warrior → *U.S.A.* 32°32N 87°51W 315 E11
Blackall *Australia* 24°25S 145°45E 280 C4
Blackball *N.Z.* 42°22S 171°26E 285 C6
Blackbraes △ *Australia* 19°10S 144°10E 280 B3
Blackbull *Australia* 17°55S 141°45E 280 B3
Blackburn *U.K.* 53°45N 2°29W 168 D5
Blackburn, Mt. *U.S.A.* 61°44N 143°26W 303 F12
Blackburn with Darwen □ *U.K.* 53°45N 2°29W 168 D5
Blackdown Tableland △ *Australia* 23°52S 149°8E 280 C4
Blackfen *U.K.* 51°26N 0°6E 125 B4
Blackfoot *U.S.A.* 43°11N 112°21W 304 E7
Blackfoot → *U.S.A.* 46°52N 113°53W 304 C7
Blackfoot Res. *U.S.A.* 42°55N 111°39W 304 E8
Blackheath *U.K.* 51°28N 0°0 125 B4
Blackman *U.S.A.* 30°56N 86°38W 317 E3
Blackpool *U.K.* 53°49N 3°3W 168 D4
Blackpool □ *U.K.* 53°49N 3°3W 168 D4
Blackriver *U.S.A.* 44°46N 83°17W 312 B1
Blackrock *Ireland* 53°18N 6°11W 120 B2
Blacks Harbour *Canada* 45°3N 66°49W 299 C6
Blacksburg *U.S.A.* 37°14N 80°25W 309 G13
Blackshear *U.S.A.* 31°18N 82°14W 316 D7
Blackshear, L. *U.S.A.* 31°51N 83°56W 316 D6
Blacksod B. *Ireland* 54°6N 10°0W 166 B1
Blackstairs Mt. *Ireland* 52°33N 6°48W 166 D5
Blackstone *U.S.A.* 37°5N 78°0W 309 G14
Blackstone Ra. *Australia* 26°0S 128°30E 279 E4
Blackville *U.S.A.* 33°22N 81°16W 316 B8
Blackwater = West Road → *Canada* 53°18N 122°53W 296 C4
Blackwater *Australia* 23°35S 148°53E 280 C4
Blackwater → *Meath, Ireland* 53°39N 6°41W 166 C4
Blackwater → *Waterford, Ireland* 52°4N 7°52W 166 D4
Blackwater → *Armagh, U.K.* 54°31N 6°35W 166 B5
Blackwater → *Fla., U.S.A.* 30°36N 87°2W 317 E2
Blackwater → *Mo., U.S.A.* 38°56N 92°57W 310 F4
Blackwell *U.S.A.* 36°48N 97°17W 314 C6
Blackwells Corner *U.S.A.* 35°37N 119°47W 307 K7
Blackwood, C. *Papua N. G.* 7°49S 144°31E 286 D3
Bladensburg *U.S.A.* 38°55N 76°55W 143 B3
Bladensburg △ *Australia* 22°30S 142°59E 280 C3
Blaenau Ffestiniog *U.K.* 53°0N 3°56W 168 E4
Blaenau Gwent □ *U.K.* 51°48N 3°12W 169 F4
Blåfell *Iceland* 64°30N 19°51W 155 C7
Bláfjall *Iceland* 65°26N 16°50W 155 B10
Blagaj *Bos.-H.* 43°16N 17°55E 202 C1
Blagnac *France* 43°37N 1°23E 174 E5
Blagnac, Toulouse ✈ (TLS) *France* 43°37N 1°22E 174 E5
Blagodarnoye = Blagodarnyy *Russia* 45°7N 43°37E 191 H6
Blagodarnyy *Russia* 45°7N 43°37E 191 H6
Blagoevgrad *Bulgaria* 42°2N 23°5E 202 D7
Blagoevgrad □ *Bulgaria* 42°2N 23°5E 202 D7
Blagoveshchensk *Russia* 50°20N 127°30E 219 A14
Blahkiuh *Indonesia* 8°31S 115°12E 231 J18
Blain *Loire-Atlantique, France* 47°29N 1°45W 172 E5
Blain *Pa., U.S.A.* 40°20N 77°31W 312 F7
Blaine *Minn., U.S.A.* 45°10N 93°13W 308 C7
Blaine *Wash., U.S.A.* 48°59N 122°45W 306 B4
Blaine Lake *Canada* 52°51N 106°52W 297 C7
Blair *U.S.A.* 41°33N 96°8W 308 E5
Blair Athol *Australia* 22°42S 147°31E 280 C4
Blair Atholl *U.K.* 56°46N 3°50W 167 E5
Blair Village *U.S.A.* 33°40N 84°23W 113 C2
Blairgowrie *Gauteng, S. Africa* 26°6S 28°0E 123 A2
Blairgowrie *Perth & Kinr., U.K.* 56°35N 3°21W 167 E5
Blairsden *U.S.A.* 39°47N 120°37W 306 F6
Blairsville *U.S.A.* 40°26N 79°16W 312 F5
Blaj *Romania* 46°10N 23°57E 183 D8
Blaka *Niger* 21°21N 12°47E 259 D2
Blakang Mati, Pulau *Singapore* 1°15N 103°50E 237 d
Blake House *U.S.A.* 42°19N 71°3W 116 B2
Blake Pt. *U.S.A.* 48°11N 88°25W 308 A9
Blakehurst *Australia* 33°59S 151°6E 139 B1
Blakely *Ga., U.S.A.* 31°23N 84°56W 316 D5
Blakely *Pa., U.S.A.* 41°28N 75°37W 313 E9
Blakesburg *U.S.A.* 40°58N 92°38W 310 D4
Blakstad *Akershus, Norway* 59°49N 10°28E 133 B1
Blakstad *Aust-Agder, Norway* 58°30N 8°39E 164 F5
Blambangan, Semenanjung *Indonesia* 8°42S 114°29E 231 K17
Blâmont *France* 48°35N 6°50E 173 D13
Blanc, C. *Spain* 39°21N 2°51E 206 B3
Blanc, C. *Tunisia* 37°15N 9°56E 258 A1
Blanc, Mont *Europe* 45°48N 6°50E 175 C10
Blanca, B. *Argentina* 39°10S 61°30W 336 A4
Blanca Peak *U.S.A.* 37°35N 105°29W 305 H11
Blanchardville *U.S.A.* 42°49N 89°52W 310 B7
Blanche, C. *Australia* 33°1S 134°9E 281 E1
Blanche, L. *S. Austral., Australia* 29°15S 139°40E 281 D2
Blanche, L. *W. Austral., Australia* 22°25S 123°17E 278 D3
Blanche, L. *U.S.A.* 28°28N 81°30W 133 B1
Blanche, Pte. *St. Lucia* 13°53N 61°5W 323 m
Blanche, Pte. *St.-Maarten* 18°0N 63°2W 322 a
Blanche Channel *Solomon Is.* 8°30S 157°30E 287 M9
Blanchester *U.S.A.* 39°17N 83°59W 311 E13
Blanchisseuse *Trin. & Tob.* 10°48N 61°18W 323 t
Blanco *Western Cape, S. Africa* 33°55S 22°23E 270 D3
Blanco *Tex., U.S.A.* 30°6N 98°25W 314 F5
Blanco → *Argentina* 30°20S 68°42W 334 C2
Blanco → *Bolivia* 12°30S 64°18W 331 C5
Blanco, C. *Costa Rica* 9°34N 85°8W 320 E2
Blanco, C. *Oreg., U.S.A.* 42°51N 124°34W 304 E1
Blanco, Pta. *Bonaire* 12°13N 68°14W 322 h
Blanda → *Iceland* 65°37N 20°9W 155 B6
Blandford Forum *U.K.* 50°51N 2°9W 169 G5
Blanding *U.S.A.* 37°37N 109°29W 305 H9
Blandinsville *U.S.A.* 40°33N 90°52W 310 D6
Blanes *Spain* 41°40N 2°48E 196 D7
Blangkejeren *Indonesia* 3°59N 97°20E 234 B1
Blangpidie *Indonesia* 3°44N 96°49E 234 B1
Blangy-sur-Bresle *France* 49°55N 1°37E 173 C8
Blanice → *Czech Rep.* 49°10N 14°5E 180 B7
Blankaholm *Sweden* 57°36N 16°33E 163 G10
Blankenberge *Belgium* 51°20N 3°9E 170 C3
Blankenburg *Berlin, Germany* 52°35N 13°27E 115 A3
Blankenburg *Sachsen-Anhalt, Germany* 51°47N 10°57E 178 D6
Blankenfelde *Germany* 52°37N 13°23E 115 A3
Blanku, I. *Curaçao* 12°2N 68°47W 322 g
Blanquefort *France* 44°55N 0°38W 174 D3
Blanquilla, I. *Venezuela* 11°51N 64°37W 321 D7
Blanquillo *Uruguay* 32°53S 55°37W 335 C4
Blansko *Czech Rep.* 49°22N 16°40E 181 B9
Blantyre *Malawi* 15°45S 35°0E 269 F4
Blarney *Ireland* 51°56N 8°33W 166 E3
Blasdell *U.S.A.* 42°48N 78°50W 312 D6
Blåsjø *Norway* 59°20N 6°50E 164 E3
Błaszki *Poland* 51°38N 18°30E 185 G5
Blatná *Czech Rep.* 49°25N 13°52E 180 B6
Blato *Croatia* 42°56N 16°48E 199 F13
Blaubeuren *Germany* 48°24N 9°46E 179 G5
Blaustein *Germany* 48°25N 9°53E 179 G5
Blåvands Huk *Denmark* 55°33N 8°4E 163 J2
Blaydon *U.K.* 54°58N 1°42W 168 C6
Blaye *France* 45°8N 0°40W 174 C3
Blaye-les-Mines *France* 44°1N 2°8E 174 D6
Blayney *Australia* 33°32S 149°14E 283 B8
Blaze, Pt. *Australia* 12°56S 130°11E 278 B5
Błażowa *Poland* 49°53N 22°7E 185 J9
Blechhammer = Blachownia *Poland* 50°49N 18°56E 185 H5
Bleckede *Germany* 53°17N 10°43E 178 B6
Bled *Slovenia* 46°27N 14°7E 199 B11
Blefjell *Norway* 59°48N 9°10E 164 E6
Bleiburg *Austria* 46°35N 14°49E 180 E7
Blejeşti *Romania* 44°19N 25°27E 183 F10
Blekinge *Sweden* 56°25N 15°20E 161 H16
Blekinge län □ *Sweden* 56°20N 15°20E 163 H9
Blenheim *Ont., Canada* 42°20N 82°0W 312 D3
Blenheim *N.Z.* 41°38S 173°57E 285 B8
Bléone → *France* 44°5N 6°0E 175 D10
Blérancourt *France* 49°31N 3°9E 173 C10
Bletchley *U.K.* 51°59N 0°44W 169 F7
Bleus, Monts *Dem. Rep. of the Congo* 1°30N 30°30E 268 B3
Blida *Algeria* 36°30N 2°49E 261 A5
Blida □ *Algeria* 36°35N 3°0E 261 A5
Blidet Amor *Algeria* 32°59N 5°58E 261 B6
Blidö *Sweden* 59°37N 18°53E 162 E12
Blidsberg *Sweden* 57°56N 13°30E 163 G7
Blieskastel *Germany* 49°14N 7°12E 179 F3
Bligh Sound *N.Z.* 44°47S 167°32E 285 E2
Bligh Water *Fiji* 17°0S 178°0E 287 A2
Blind River *Canada* 46°10N 82°58W 298 C3
Blinisht *Albania* 41°52N 19°59E 202 E3
Bliss *Idaho, U.S.A.* 42°56N 114°57W 304 E6
Bliss *N.Y., U.S.A.* 42°34N 78°15W 312 D6
Blissfield *Mich., U.S.A.* 41°50N 83°52W 311 C13
Blissfield *Ohio, U.S.A.* 40°24N 81°58W 312 F3
Blitar *Indonesia* 8°5S 112°11E 235 D4
Blitchton *U.S.A.* 32°12N 81°26W 316 C8
Blitta *Togo* 8°23N 1°6E 263 D5
Blizne *Poland* 52°14N 20°52E 143 B1
Block I. *U.S.A.* 41°11N 71°35W 313 E13
Block Island Sd. *U.S.A.* 41°15N 71°40W 313 E13
Bloemenmarkt *Amsterdam, Neths.* 112 b2
Bloemfontein *S. Africa* 29°6S 26°7E 270 C4
Bloemhof *S. Africa* 27°38S 25°32E 270 C4
Blois *France* 47°35N 1°20E 172 E8
Blomskog *Sweden* 59°16N 12°2E 162 E6
Blomstermåla *Sweden* 56°59N 16°21E 163 H10
Blomvåg *Norway* 60°32N 4°50E 164 D1
Blönduós *Iceland* 65°40N 20°12W 155 B6
Blongas *Indonesia* 8°53S 116°2E 231 K19
Blonie *Poland* 52°12N 20°37E 185 F7
Bloodvein → *Canada* 51°47N 96°43W 297 C9
Bloody B. *Trin. & Tob.* 11°18N 60°38W 323 s
Bloody Foreland *Ireland* 55°10N 8°17W 166 A3
Bloom = Chicago Heights *U.S.A.* 41°30N 87°38W 311 C9
Bloomer *U.S.A.* 45°6N 91°29W 308 C8
Bloomfield *Ont., Canada* 43°59N 77°14W 312 C7
Bloomfield *Ind., U.S.A.* 39°1N 86°57W 311 E10
Bloomfield *Iowa, U.S.A.* 40°45N 92°25W 310 D4
Bloomfield *Ky., U.S.A.* 37°55N 85°19W 311 G11
Bloomfield *N. Mex., U.S.A.* 36°43N 107°59W 305 H10
Bloomfield *Nebr., U.S.A.* 42°36N 97°39W 308 D5
Bloomingburg *U.S.A.* 39°36N 83°24W 311 E13
Bloomington *Ill., U.S.A.* 40°28N 89°0W 310 D8
Bloomington *Ind., U.S.A.* 39°10N 86°32W 311 E10
Bloomington *Minn., U.S.A.* 44°50N 93°17W 308 C7
Bloomington *Wis., U.S.A.* 42°53N 90°55W 310 B6
Bloomsburg *U.S.A.* 41°0N 76°27W 313 F8
Bloomsbury *Australia* 20°48S 148°38E 280 b
Bloomsbury *London, U.K.* 125 a3
Blora *Indonesia* 6°57S 111°25E 235 D4
Blossburg *U.S.A.* 41°41N 77°4W 312 E7
Blosseville Kyst *Greenland* 68°50N 26°30W 154 D8
Blota *Poland* 52°9N 21°1E 143 C3
Blouberg *S. Africa* 23°8S 28°59E 271 B4
Blountstown *U.S.A.* 30°27N 85°3W 316 E4
Blowing Point Village *Anguilla* 18°11N 63°6W 322 a
Blowing Rock *Anguilla* 18°9N 63°10W 322 a
Bludenz *Austria* 47°10N 9°50E 180 D2
Blue → *U.S.A.* 38°11N 86°19W 311 F10
Blue Cypress L. *U.S.A.* 27°44N 80°45W 317 H9
Blue Earth *U.S.A.* 43°38N 94°6W 308 D6
Blue Hole *Jamaica* 18°10N 76°24W 320 a
Blue Hole △ *Belize* 17°24N 87°30W 320 C2
Blue Island *U.S.A.* 41°40N 87°40W 119 D2
Blue Lagoon △ *Zambia* 15°28S 27°26E 269 F2
Blue Lagoon L. *U.S.A.* 25°46N 80°17W 129 D1
Blue Mesa Res. *U.S.A.* 38°28N 107°20W 304 G10
Blue Mosque = Sultanahme Camii *Turkey* 41°0N 28°58E 122 B1
Blue Mound *U.S.A.* 39°42N 89°7W 310 E7
Blue Mountain Lake *U.S.A.* 43°51N 74°27W 313 C10
Blue Mountain Pk. *Jamaica* 18°3N 76°36W 320 a
Blue Mountains and John Crow Mountains △ *Jamaica* 18°5N 76°34W 320 a
Blue Mt. *U.S.A.* 40°30N 76°30W 313 F8
Blue Mts. *N.S.W., Australia* 33°40S 150°15E 283 B9
Blue Mts. *Jamaica* 18°3N 76°36W 320 a
Blue Mts. *Maine, U.S.A.* 44°50N 70°35W 313 B14
Blue Mts. *Oreg., U.S.A.* 45°0N 118°20W 304 D4
Blue Mts. △ *Australia* 34°2S 150°15E 283 B9
Blue Mud B. *Australia* 13°30S 136°0E 280 A2
Blue Mud Bay © *Australia* 13°25S 136°2E 280 A2
Blue Nile = Nîl el Azraq → *Sudan* 15°38N 32°31E 257 D3
Blue Nile Falls = Tis Issat *Ethiopia* 11°25N 37°45E 257 E4
Blue Rapids *U.S.A.* 39°41N 96°39W 308 F5
Blue Ridge *U.S.A.* 36°40N 80°50W 309 G13
Blue River *Canada* 52°6N 119°18W 296 C5
Blue Springs *U.S.A.* 39°1N 94°17W 310 E2
Bluebell *Ireland* 53°19N 6°21W 120 B1
Bluefield *U.S.A.* 37°15N 81°17W 309 G13
Bluefields *Nic.* 12°20N 83°50W 320 D3
Bluevale *Canada* 43°51N 81°15W 312 C3
Bluff *Queens., Australia* 23°35S 149°4E 280 C4
Bluff *N.Z.* 46°37S 168°20E 285 G3
Bluff *Utah, U.S.A.* 37°17N 109°33W 305 H9
Bluff Harbour *N.Z.* 46°36S 168°21E 285 G3
Bluff Hd. *China* 22°11N 114°12E 122 B2
Bluff Knoll *Australia* 34°24S 118°15E 279 F2
Bluff Pt. *Australia* 27°50S 114°5E 279 E1
Bluffers Park *Canada* 43°43N 79°14W 141 A3
Bluffs *U.S.A.* 39°45N 90°32W 310 E6
Bluffton *Ga., U.S.A.* 31°31N 84°52W 316 D5
Bluffton *Ind., U.S.A.* 40°44N 85°11W 311 D11
Bluffton *Ohio, U.S.A.* 40°54N 83°54W 311 D13
Bluffton *S.C., U.S.A.* 32°14N 80°52W 316 C9
Blumberg *Germany* 52°36N 13°39E 115 A4
Blumenau = Stettler *Canada* 52°19N 112°40W 296 C6
Blumenau *Brazil* 27°0S 49°0W 335 B6
Blunt *U.S.A.* 44°31N 99°59W 308 C4
Blunt Pt. *U.S.A.* 37°51N 122°25W 136 A2
Blutenberg *Germany* 48°9N 11°27E 131 B1
Bly *U.S.A.* 42°24N 121°3W 304 E3
Blyde River Canyon △ *S. Africa* 24°37S 31°2E 271 B5
Blylaget *Norway* 59°46N 10°41E 133 B3
Blyth *S. Austral., Australia* 33°49S 138°28E 282 B3
Blyth *Ont., Canada* 43°44N 81°26W 312 C3
Blyth *Northumberland, U.K.* 55°8N 1°31W 168 B6

Blythe *Calif., U.S.A.* 33°37N 114°36W **307** M12
Blythe *Ga., U.S.A.* 33°17N 82°12W **316** B7
Blytheville *U.S.A.* 35°56N 89°55W **315** D10
Bø *Telemark, Norway* 59°25N 9°3E **164** E6
Bo *S. Leone* 7°55N 11°50W **262** D2
Bo Duc *Vietnam* 11°58N 106°50E **237** G6
Bo-eun *S. Korea* 36°29N 127°43E **224** D3
Bo Hai *China* 39°0N 119°0E **227** E10
Bo Hai Haixia *Asia* 38°25N 121°10E **227** E11
Bo-Kaap Museum *Cape Town, S. Africa* **118** c2
Bō-no-Misaki *Japan* 31°15N 130°13E **222** F2
Bo Xian = Bozhou *China* 33°55N 115°41E **226** H8
Boa Esperança *Brazil* 3°21N 61°23W **329** C5
Boa Esperança, Represa
Brazil 6°50S 43°50W **332** C3
Boa Nova *Brazil* 14°22S 40°10W **333** D3
Boa Viagem *Brazil* 5°7S 39°44W **332** C4
Boa Vista = Tocantinópolis
Brazil 6°20S 47°25W **332** C2
Boa Vista *Brazil* 2°48N 60°30W **329** C5
Boa Vista *C. Verde Is.* 16°0N 22°49W **153** j
Boa Vista, Alto do *Brazil* 22°58S 43°16W **135** B1
Boa Vista do Erechim = Erechim
Brazil 27°35S 52°15W **335** B5
Boac *Phil.* 13°27N 121°50E **232** E3
Boaco *Nic.* 12°29N 85°35W **320** D2
Bo'ai *China* 35°10N 113°3E **226** G7
Boal *Spain* 43°25N 6°49W **194** B4
Boali *C.A.R.* 4°48N 18°7E **264** B3
Boalsburg *U.S.A.* 40°47N 77°49W **312** F7
Boane *Mozam.* 26°6S 32°19E **271** C5
Boang I. *Papua N. G.* 3°23S 153°18E **286** B7
Boao *China* 19°8N 110°34E **236** C8
Boardman *U.S.A.* 41°2N 80°40W **312** E4
Boardwalk *U.S.A.* 40°34N 73°49W **132** C3
Boath *India* 19°20N 78°20E **244** E4
Boatswain Bird I.
Ascension I. 7°56S 14°18W **153** g
Boavista *Portugal* 38°48N 9°8W **126** A2
Boayan I. *Phil.* 10°34N 119°9E **233** F2
Boaz I. *Bermuda* 32°18N 64°51W **153** a
Bob Marley Mausoleum
Jamaica 18°18N 77°18W **320** a
Bobadah *Australia* 32°19S 146°41E **283** B7
Bobai *China* 22°17N 109°59E **228** F7
Bobbili *India* 18°35N 83°30E **244** E6
Bòbbio *Italy* 44°46N 9°23E **198** D6
Bobcaygeon *Canada* 44°33N 78°33W **312** B6
Bobigny *France* 48°54N 2°26E **134** A3
Boblad *India* 17°13N 75°26E **244** F2
Böblingen *Germany* 48°40N 9°1E **179** G5
Bobo-Dioulasso
Burkina Faso 11°8N 4°13W **262** C4
Bobolice *Poland* 53°58N 16°37E **184** E3
Bobon *Phil.* 12°32N 124°34E **232** E5
Bobonaza → *Ecuador* 2°36S 76°38W **328** D2
Bobonong *Botswana* 21°58S 28°20E **271** B4
Boboshevo *Bulgaria* 42°9N 23°0E **202** D7
Bobov Dol *Bulgaria* 42°20N 23°0E **202** D6
Bóbr → *Poland* 52°4N 15°4E **185** F2
Bobraomby, Tanjon' i
Madag. 12°40S 49°10E **272** A2
Bobrov *Russia* 51°5N 40°2E **190** E5
Bobrovytsya *Ukraine* 50°45N 31°23E **189** G6
Bobruysk = Babruysk
Belarus 53°10N 29°15E **177** B15
Bobrynets *Ukraine* 48°4N 32°5E **189** H7
Bobures *Venezuela* 9°15N 71°11W **328** B3
Boby, Pic *Madag.* 22°12S 46°55E **272** C2
Boca de Pozo *Venezuela* 11°0N 64°23W **329** a
Boca del Río *Veracruz,*
Mexico 19°5N 96°4W **319** D5
Boca del Rio *Venezuela* 10°58N 64°11W **329** a
Boca do Acre *Brazil* 8°50S 67°27W **330** B4
Boca do Jari *Brazil* 1°7S 51°58W **329** D7
Boca Grande *Fla., U.S.A.* 26°45N 82°16W **317** J7
Boca Grande *Venezuela* 8°40N 60°40W **329** B5
Boca Raton *U.S.A.* 26°21N 80°5W **317** J9
Boca Slagbaai *Bonaire* 12°16N 68°24W **322** h
Bocaiúva *Brazil* 17°7S 43°49W **333** E3
Bocanda *Ivory C.* 7°5N 4°31W **262** D4
Bocanegra *Peru* 12°1S 77°7W **124** B2
Bocaranga *C.A.R.* 7°0N 15°35E **264** A3
Bocas del Dragón = Dragon's
Mouths *Trin. & Tob.* 11°0N 61°50W **323** t
Bocas del Toro *Panama* 9°15N 82°20W **320** E3
Boceguillas *Spain* 41°20N 3°39W **194** D7
Bochkarevo = Belogorsk
Russia 51°0N 128°20E **215** D13
Bochmanivka *Ukraine* 47°40N 29°34E **183** C14
Bochnia *Poland* 49°58N 20°27E **185** J7
Bocholt *Germany* 51°50N 6°36E **178** D2
Bochum = Senwabarana
S. Africa 23°17S 29°7E **271** B4
Bochum *Germany* 51°28N 7°13E **178** D3
Bockenem *Germany* 52°1N 10°8E **178** C6
Boćki *Poland* 52°39N 23°3E **185** F10
Bocognano *France* 42°5N 9°4E **175** F13
Bocoio *Angola* 12°28S 14°10E **265** E2
Boconó *Venezuela* 9°15N 70°16W **328** B3
Boconó → *Venezuela* 8°43N 69°34W **328** B4
Bocoyna *Mexico* 27°52N 107°35W **318** B3
Bocşa *Romania* 45°21N 21°47E **182** E6
Boda *C.A.R.* 4°19N 17°26E **264** B3
Boda *Dalarna, Sweden* 61°1N 15°13E **162** C9
Böda *Kalmar, Sweden* 57°15N 17°3E **163** G11
Boda *Västernorrland,*
Sweden 62°52N 16°39E **162** B10
Bodafors *Sweden* 57°48N 14°23E **163** G8
Bodaybo *Russia* 57°50N 114°0E **215** D12
Boddam *U.K.* 59°56N 1°17W **167** B7
Boddington *Australia* 32°50S 116°30E **279** F2
Bode Sadu *Nigeria* 9°0N 4°47E **263** D5
Bodega Bay *U.S.A.* 38°20N 123°3W **306** G3
Boden *Sweden* 65°50N 21°42E **160** D19
Bodensee *Europe* 47°35N 9°25E **179** H5
Bodenteich *Germany* 52°50N 10°42E **178** C6
Bodh Gaya *India* 24°41N 84°59E **243** G11
Bodhan *India* 18°40N 77°44E **244** E3
Bodinayakkanur *India* 10°2N 77°10E **245** J3
Bodinga *Nigeria* 12°58N 5°10E **263** C6
Bodmin *U.K.* 50°28N 4°43W **169** G3
Bodmin Moor *U.K.* 50°33N 4°36W **169** G3
Bodø *Norway* 67°17N 14°24E **160** C16
Bodoquena, Serra da
Brazil 21°0S 56°50W **331** E6
Bodoupa *C.A.R.* 5°43N 17°36E **264** A3
Bodrichi *Chad* 19°11N 15°54E **259** E3
Bodrog → *Hungary* 48°11N 21°22E **182** B6
Bodrum *Turkey* 37°3N 27°30E **205** D9
Boduna
Dem. Rep. of the Congo 5°5N 19°44E **264** A3
Bódva → *Hungary* 48°19N 20°45E **182** B5
Boedo *Argentina* 34°38S 58°26W **117** B2
Boembé *Congo* 2°54S 15°39E **264** C3
Boën *France* 45°44N 4°1E **175** C8
Boende
Dem. Rep. of the Congo 0°24S 21°12E **264** C4
Boerne *U.S.A.* 29°47N 98°44W **314** G5
Boesmans → *S. Africa* 33°42S 26°39E **270** D4
Boffa *Guinea* 10°16N 14°3W **262** C2
Bog Walk *Jamaica* 18°6N 77°1W **320** a
Bogal, Lagh → *Kenya* 0°41N 40°57E **267** D5
Bogale *Burma* 16°17N 95°24E **241** G5
Bogalusa *U.S.A.* 30°47N 89°52W **315** F10
Bogan → *Australia* 30°20S 146°55E **283** A7
Bogan Gate *Australia* 33°7S 147°49E **283** B7
Bogandé *Burkina Faso* 13°2N 0°8W **263** C4
Bogangolo *C.A.R.* 5°34N 18°15E **264** A3
Bogantungan *Australia* 23°41S 147°17E **280** C4
Bogata *U.S.A.* 33°28N 95°13W **314** E7
Bogatić *Serbia* 44°51N 19°30E **202** B3
Boğazkale *Turkey* 40°2N 34°37E **212** B6
Boğazlıyan *Turkey* 39°11N 35°14E **212** C6
Bogbonga
Dem. Rep. of the Congo 1°36N 19°24E **264** B3
Bogda Shan *China* 43°35N 89°40E **217** D11
Bogen *Sweden* 60°4N 12°33E **162** D6
Bogenhausen *Germany* 48°8N 11°36E **131** B2
Bogense *Denmark* 55°34N 10°5E **163** J4
Bogetići *Montenegro* 42°41N 18°58E **202** D2
Boggabilla *Australia* 28°36S 150°24E **281** D5
Boggabri *Australia* 30°45S 150°5E **283** A9
Boggeragh Mts. *Ireland* 52°2N 8°55W **166** D3
Boghari = Ksar el Boukhari
Algeria 35°51N 2°52E **261** A5
Bogia *Papua N. G.* 4°9S 145°0E **286** C3
Bogildo *S. Korea* 34°9N 126°32E **224** E3
Boglan = Solhan *Turkey* 38°57N 41°3E **213** C9
Bogles *Grenada* 12°30N 61°26W **323** q
Bognor Regis *U.K.* 50°47N 0°40W **169** G7
Bogo *Phil.* 11°3N 124°0E **233** F4
Bogodukhov = Bohodukhiv
Ukraine 50°9N 35°33E **189** G8
Bogol Manya *Ethiopia* 4°34N 41°29E **257** G5
Bogong, Mt. *Australia* 36°47S 147°17E **283** D7
Bogor *Indonesia* 6°36S 106°48E **234** D3
Bogoroditsk *Russia* 53°47N 38°8E **188** F10
Bogorodsk *Russia* 56°4N 43°30E **190** B6
Bogorodskoye = Kamskoye Ustye
Russia 55°10N 49°20E **190** C9
Bogorodskoye = Leninskoye
Russia 58°23N 47°3E **190** A8
Bogorodskoye *Russia* 55°48N 37°42E **129** B3
Bogoslovsky = Karpinsk
Russia 59°45N 60°1E **186** C11
Bogoso *Ghana* 5°38N 2°3W **262** D4
Bogotá *Colombia* 4°34N 74°0W **328** C3
Bogota *N.J., U.S.A.* 40°52N 74°2W **132** A1
Bogotol *Russia* 56°15N 89°50E **214** D9
Bogou *Togo* 10°40N 0°12E **263** C5
Bogra *Bangla.* 24°51N 89°22E **241** C2
Bogstadvatnet *Norway* 59°58N 10°37E **133** A2
Boguchany *Russia* 58°40N 97°30E **215** D10
Boguchar *Russia* 49°55N 40°32E **190** F5
Bogué *Mauritania* 16°45N 14°10W **262** B2
Boguszów-Gorce *Poland* 50°45N 16°12E **185** H3
Bohain-en-Vermandois
France 49°59N 3°28E **173** C10
Bohdan *Ukraine* 48°2N 24°22E **183** B9
Bohemian Forest = Böhmerwald
Germany 49°8N 13°14E **179** F9
Bohena Cr. → *Australia* 30°17S 149°42E **283** A8
Bohinjska Bistrica
Slovenia 46°17N 14°1E **199** B11
Böhmerwald *Germany* 49°8N 13°14E **179** F9
Böhmisch-Brod = Český Brod
Czech Rep. 50°4N 14°52E **180** A7
Böhmisch-Leipa = Česká Lípa
Czech Rep. 50°45N 14°30E **180** A7
Böhmisch-Trübau = Česká Třebová
Czech Rep. 49°54N 16°27E **181** B9
Bohmte *Germany* 52°22N 8°19E **178** C4
Bohnsdorf *Germany* 52°23N 13°34E **115** B4
Bohodukhiv *Ukraine* 50°9N 35°33E **189** G8
Bohol *Somalia* 5°45N 46°9E **267** C6
Bohol □ *Phil.* 9°50N 124°10E **233** G5
Bohol Sea *Phil.* 9°0N 124°0E **233** G5
Bohol Str. *Phil.* 9°45N 123°40E **233** G4
Bohongou *Burkina Faso* 12°30N 0°40E **263** C5
Böhönye *Hungary* 46°25N 17°28E **182** D2
Bohorodchany *Ukraine* 48°48N 24°32E **183** B9
Bohorok *Indonesia* 3°30N 98°12E **237** L2
Böhöt *Mongolia* 45°13N 108°16E **226** B5
Bohu *China* 41°58N 86°37E **217** D11
Bohuslän *Sweden* 58°25N 12°0E **163** F5
Bohuslav *Ukraine* 49°33N 30°56E **189** H6
Boi *Nigeria* 9°35N 9°27E **263** D6
Boi, Pta. do *Brazil* 23°55S 45°15W **335** A6
Boiaçu *Brazil* 0°27S 61°46W **329** D5
Boigu *Australia* 9°16S 142°13E **280** a
Boigu I. *Australia* 9°15S 142°14E **286** E2
Boileau, C. *Australia* 17°40S 122°7E **278** C3
Boim *Brazil* 2°49S 55°10W **329** D6
Boing'o *South Sudan* 9°58N 33°44E **257** F3
Boipariguda *India* 18°46N 82°26E **244** E6
Boipeba, I. de *Brazil* 13°39S 38°55W **333** D4
Boiro *Spain* 42°39N 8°54W **194** C2
Bois → *Brazil* 18°35S 50°2W **333** E1
Bois-Blanc *Réunion* 21°11S 55°49E **272** f
Bois-Colombes *France* 48°55N 2°16E **134** A2
Bois-d'Arcy *France* 48°48N 2°1E **134** B1
Boise *U.S.A.* 43°37N 116°13W **304** E5
Boise City *U.S.A.* 36°44N 102°31W **314** C3
Boissevain *Canada* 49°15N 100°5W **297** D8
Boissy-St-Léger *France* 48°44N 2°31E **134** B4
Bôite → *Italy* 46°5N 12°5E **199** B9
Boitzenburg *Germany* 53°16N 13°35E **178** B9
Boizenburg *Germany* 53°23N 10°43E **178** B6
Bojador *W. Sahara* 23°56N 15°49W **260** D1
Bojador, C. *W. Sahara* 26°0N 14°30W **260** C2
Bojana → *Albania* 41°52N 19°22E **202** E3
Bojano *Italy* 41°29N 14°29E **201** A7
Bojanowo *Poland* 51°43N 16°42E **185** G3
Bøjden *Denmark* 55°6N 10°7E **163** J4
Bojnūrd *Iran* 37°30N 57°20E **247** B8
Bojonegoro *Indonesia* 7°11S 111°54E **235** D4
Boju *Nigeria* 7°22N 7°55E **263** D6
Boka *Serbia* 45°22N 20°52E **182** E5
Boka Kotorska
Montenegro 42°23N 18°32E **202** D2
Boka Tabla *Curaçao* 12°22N 69°8W **322** g
Bokada
Dem. Rep. of the Congo 4°8N 19°23E **264** B3
Bokala *Dem. Rep. of the Congo* 3°8S 17°4E **264** C3
Bokala *Ivory C.* 8°31N 4°33W **262** D4
Bokani *Nigeria* 9°28N 5°10E **263** D6
Bokaro *India* 23°46N 85°55E **243** H11
Bokatola
Dem. Rep. of the Congo 0°38S 18°46E **264** C3
Boké *Guinea* 10°56N 14°17W **262** C2
Bokela
Dem. Rep. of the Congo 1°10S 21°59E **264** C4
Bokenda
Dem. Rep. of the Congo 1°16N 21°22E **264** B4
Bokhara → *Australia* 29°55S 146°42E **281** D4
Bokkos *Nigeria* 9°17N 9°1E **263** D6
Boklar Dağları *Turkey* 37°5N 33°55E **250** A4
Boknafjorden *Norway* 59°14N 5°40E **164** E2
Boko *Congo* 4°46S 14°36E **265** C2
Bokode
Dem. Rep. of the Congo 3°55N 19°30E **264** B3
Bokoko *Gabon* 2°40S 10°10E **264** C2
Bokondo
Dem. Rep. of the Congo 0°15N 22°32E **264** B4
Bokor △ *Cambodia* 10°50N 104°1E **237** G5
Bokora ⌂ *Uganda* 2°12N 31°32E **268** B3
Bokoro *Chad* 12°25N 17°14E **259** F3
Bokota
Dem. Rep. of the Congo 0°56S 22°24E **264** C4
Bokote *Dem. Rep. of the Congo* 0°12S 21°8E **264** C4
Bokpyin *Burma* 11°18N 98°42E **237** G2
Boksitogorsk *Russia* 59°22N 33°50E **188** C7
Boku *Papua N. G.* 6°34S 155°21E **286** D8
Bokungu
Dem. Rep. of the Congo 0°35S 22°50E **264** C4
Bol *Chad* 13°30N 14°40E **259** F2
Bol *Croatia* 43°18N 16°38E **199** E13
Bolama *Guinea-Biss.* 11°30N 15°30W **262** C1
Bolan → *Pakistan* 28°38N 67°42E **242** E2
Bolan Pass *Pakistan* 29°50N 67°20E **240** C2
Bolaños → *Mexico* 21°12N 104°5W **318** C4
Bolaños de Calatrava
Spain 38°54N 3°40W **195** G7
Bolayır *Turkey* 40°31N 26°45E **203** F10
Bolbec *France* 49°30N 0°30E **172** C7
Boldājī *Iran* 31°56N 51°3E **247** D6
Boldeşti-Scăeni *Romania* 45°3N 26°2E **183** E11
Boldinasco *Italy* 45°29N 9°8E **128** B1
Bole *Xinjiang Uygur, China* 44°55N 81°37E **217** C10
Bole *Ethiopia* 6°36N 37°20E **257** F4
Bole *Ghana* 9°3N 2°23W **262** D4
Bolekhiv *Ukraine* 49°0N 23°57E **177** D12
Boleko
Dem. Rep. of the Congo 1°35S 19°50E **264** C3
Bøler *Norway* 59°53N 10°50E **133** A4
Bolesławiec *Poland* 51°17N 15°37E **185** G2
Bolgatanga *Ghana* 10°44N 0°53W **263** C4
Bolgrad = Bolhrad
Ukraine 45°40N 28°32E **183** E13
Bolhrad *Ukraine* 45°40N 28°32E **183** E13
Bolia *Dem. Rep. of the Congo* 1°36S 18°22E **264** C3
Bolinao *Phil.* 16°23N 119°54E **232** C2
Bolinao, C. *Phil.* 16°23N 119°55E **232** C2
Bolingbroke *U.S.A.* 32°57N 83°48W **316** C6
Bolingbrook *U.S.A.* 41°42N 88°4W **311** C8
Bolingo
Dem. Rep. of the Congo 3°31S 21°43E **264** C4
Bolintin-Vale *Romania* 44°27N 25°46E **183** F10
Bolívar *Antioquia, Colombia* 5°50N 76°1W **328** B2
Bolívar *Cauca, Colombia* 2°0N 77°0W **328** C2
Bolívar *Peru* 7°18S 77°48W **330** B2
Bolivar *Mo., U.S.A.* 37°37N 93°25W **308** G7
Bolivar *N.Y., U.S.A.* 42°4N 78°10W **312** D6
Bolivar *Tenn., U.S.A.* 35°12N 89°0W **315** D10
Bolívar □ *Colombia* 9°0N 74°40W **328** B3
Bolívar □ *Ecuador* 1°15S 79°5W **328** D2
Bolívar □ *Venezuela* 6°20N 63°30W **329** B5
Bolivia ■ *S. Amer.* 17°6S 64°0W **331** D5
Bolivian Plateau = Altiplano
Bolivia 17°0S 68°0W **330** D4
Boljevac *Serbia* 43°51N 21°58E **202** C5
Bolkhov *Russia* 53°25N 36°0E **188** F9
Bolków *Poland* 50°55N 16°6E **185** H3
Bollate *Italy* 45°32N 9°7E **128** A1
Bollebygd *Sweden* 57°40N 12°35E **163** G6
Bollène *France* 44°18N 4°45E **175** D8
Bollensdorf *Germany* 52°30N 13°42E **115** A5
Bollmora *Sweden* 59°14N 18°14E **139** B3
Bollnäs *Sweden* 61°21N 16°24E **162** C10
Bollon *Australia* 28°2S 147°29E **281** D4
Bollstabruk *Sweden* 62°59N 17°40E **162** B11
Bolmen *Sweden* 56°55N 13°40E **163** H7
Bolnisi *Georgia* 41°26N 44°32E **191** K7
Bolobo *Dem. Rep. of the Congo* 2°6S 16°20E **264** C3
Bologna *Italy* 44°29N 11°20E **199** D8
Bologna ✕ (BLQ) *Italy* 44°34N 11°16E **199** D8
Bologoye *Russia* 57°55N 34°5E **188** D8
Bolomba
Dem. Rep. of the Congo 0°35N 19°0E **264** B3
Bolombo →
Dem. Rep. of the Congo 1°32N 21°14E **264** B4
Bolonchén *Mexico* 20°1N 89°45W **319** D7
Bolondo
Dem. Rep. of the Congo 2°12S 18°42E **264** C3
Bolong *Chad* 12°3N 17°45E **259** F3
Bolong *Phil.* 7°6N 122°14E **233** H4
Bolongongo *Angola* 8°28S 15°16E **265** D3
Bolotana *Italy* 40°20N 8°52E **200** B1
Boloven, Cao Nguyen
Laos 15°10N 106°30E **236** E6
Bolpur *India* 23°40N 87°45E **243** H12
Bolsena *Italy* 42°39N 11°59E **199** F8
Bolsena, L. di *Italy* 42°36N 11°56E **199** F8
Bolshakovo *Russia* 54°53N 21°40E **184** D8
Bolshaya Chernigovka
Russia 52°6N 50°52E **190** D10
Bolshaya Garmanda = Evensk
Russia 62°12N 159°30E **215** C16
Bolshaya Glushitsa
Russia 52°28N 50°30E **190** D10
Bolshaya Martynovka
Russia 47°19N 41°37E **191** G5
Bolshaya Okhta *Russia* 59°56N 30°26E **137** B2
Bolshaya Tsaryovshchina =
Volzhskiy *Russia* 48°56N 44°46E **191** F7
Bolshaya Vradiyevka
Ukraine 47°50N 30°40E **189** J6
Bolshevik, Ostrov *Russia* 78°30N 102°0E **215** B11
Bolshoy Anyuy →
Russia 68°30N 160°49E **215** C17
Bolshoy Begichev, Ostrov
Russia 74°20N 112°30E **215** B12
Bolshoy Kamen *Russia* 43°7N 132°19E **220** C6
Bolshoy Kavkas = Caucasus
Mountains *Eurasia* 42°50N 44°0E **191** J7
Bolshoy Lyakhovskiy, Ostrov
Russia 73°35N 142°0E **215** B15
Bolshoy Theatre *Moscow, Russia* **129** b2
Bolshoy Tokmak = Tokmak
Kyrgyzstan 42°49N 75°15E **217** D9
Bolshoy Tyuters, Ostrov
Russia 59°51N 27°13E **188** C4
Bólstaðarhlíð *Iceland* 65°31N 19°49W **155** B7
Bolsward *Neths.* 53°3N 5°32E **170** A5
Bolt Head *U.K.* 50°12N 3°48W **169** G4
Boltaña *Spain* 42°28N 0°4E **196** C5
Boltigen *Switz.* 46°38N 7°24E **179** J3
Bolton *Ont., Canada* 43°54N 79°45W **312** C5
Bolton *Gt. Man., U.K.* 53°35N 2°26W **168** D5
Bolton *Georgia, U.S.A.* 33°48N 84°28W **113** B2
Bolton Landing *U.S.A.* 43°32N 73°35W **313** C11
Bolu *Turkey* 40°45N 31°35E **212** B4
Bolu □ *Turkey* 40°40N 31°30E **212** B4
Bolubolu *Papua N. G.* 9°21S 150°20E **286** E6
Bolungavík *Iceland* 66°9N 23°15W **155** A3
Boluo *China* 23°3N 114°21E **229** F10
Bolvadin *Turkey* 38°45N 31°4E **212** C4
Bolzano *Italy* 46°31N 11°22E **199** B8
Bom Comércio *Brazil* 9°45S 65°54W **331** B4
Bom Conselho *Brazil* 9°10S 36°41W **332** C4
Bom Despacho *Brazil* 19°43S 45°15W **333** E2
Bom Jesus *Angola* 9°11S 13°34E **265** D2
Bom Jesus *Brazil* 9°4S 44°22W **332** C3
Bom Jesus da Gurguéia, Serra
Brazil 9°0S 43°0W **332** C3
Bom Jesus da Lapa *Brazil* 13°15S 43°25W **333** D3
Bom Retiro *Brazil* 23°31S 46°38W **137** B2
Boma *Dem. Rep. of the Congo* 5°50S 13°4E **265** D2
Boma △ *South Sudan* 7°0N 34°0E **257** F3
Bomaderry *Australia* 34°52S 150°37E **283** C9
Bomandjokou *Congo* 0°34N 14°23E **264** B2
Bomaneh
Dem. Rep. of the Congo 1°18N 23°47E **264** B4
Bomassa *Congo* 2°12N 16°12E **264** B3
Bomate
Dem. Rep. of the Congo 2°14N 25°15E **264** C3
Bombala *Australia* 36°56S 149°15E **283** D8
Bombarral *Portugal* 39°15N 9°9W **195** F1
Bombay = Mumbai *India* 18°56N 72°50E **130** B2
Bombay *U.S.A.* 44°56N 74°34W **313** B10
Bombedor, Pta. *Venezuela* 9°53N 61°37W **329** G9
Bomberai, Semenanjung
Indonesia 3°0S 133°0E **231** E8
Bombo Kasani
Dem. Rep. of the Congo 5°51S 21°54E **265** D4
Bomboma
Dem. Rep. of the Congo 2°25N 18°55E **264** B3
Bombombwa
Dem. Rep. of the Congo 1°40N 25°40E **268** B2
Bomboyo *Chad* 12°1N 15°28E **259** F3
Bomdila *India* 27°18N 92°22E **241** B4
Bomdo *India* 28°44N 94°54E **241** A5
Bomet *Kenya* 0°47S 35°21E **266** E4
Bomi *China* 29°50N 95°45E **218** F8
Bomi Hills *Liberia* 7°1N 10°38W **262** D2
Bomili *Dem. Rep. of the Congo* 1°45N 27°5E **268** B2
Bømlo *Norway* 59°37N 5°13E **164** E2
Bomokandi →
Dem. Rep. of the Congo 3°39N 26°8E **268** B2
Bomongo
Dem. Rep. of the Congo 1°27N 18°21E **264** B3
Bompoka *India* 8°15N 93°13E **245** K11
Bomputu
Dem. Rep. of the Congo 0°23S 20°6E **264** C4
Bomst = Babimost *Poland* 52°10N 15°49E **185** F2
Bomu → *C.A.R.* 4°40N 22°30E **264** B4
Bomu Occidentale ⌂
Dem. Rep. of the Congo 4°48N 24°17E **264** B4
Bomu Orientale ⌂
Dem. Rep. of the Congo 5°0N 25°50E **264** B2
Bon, C. = Ra's aṭ Ṭib *Tunisia* 37°1N 11°2E **258** A2
Bon Acceuil *Mauritius* 20°10S 57°39E **272** e
Bon Echo ⌂ *Canada* 44°55N 77°16W **312** B7
Bon Sar Pa *Vietnam* 12°24N 107°35E **236** F6
Bona, Mt. *U.S.A.* 61°23N 141°45W **303** F12
Bonāb *Āzarbājān-e Sharqī,*
Iran 37°20N 46°4E **213** D12
Bonāb *Zanjān, Iran* 36°35N 48°41E **213** D13
Bonaigarh *India* 21°50N 84°57E **243** J11
Bonaire *Ga., U.S.A.* 32°33N 83°36W **316** C6
Bonaire *W. Indies* 12°10N 68°15W **322** h
Bonampak *Mexico* 16°44N 91°5W **319** D6
Bonang *Australia* 37°11S 148°41E **283** D8
Bonanza *Nic.* 13°54N 84°35W **320** D3
Bonaparte Arch. *Australia* 14°0S 124°30E **278** B3
Bonaparte Rocks *Grenada* 12°24N 61°30W **323** q
Boñar *Spain* 42°52N 5°19W **194** C5
Bonar Bridge *U.K.* 57°54N 4°20W **167** D4
Bonasse *Trin. & Tob.* 10°5N 61°54W **323** t
Bonaventure *Canada* 48°5N 65°32W **299** C6
Bonaventure, Place *Montréal, Canada* **130** c2
Bonavista *Canada* 48°40N 53°5W **299** C9
Bonavista, C. *Canada* 48°42N 53°5W **299** C9
Bonavista B. *Canada* 48°45N 53°25W **299** C9
Bondeno *Italy* 44°53N 11°25E **199** D8
Bondi *Australia* 33°53S 151°16E **139** B2
Bondo *Équateur,*
Dem. Rep. of the Congo 1°22S 23°54E **264** C4
Bondo *Orientale,*
Dem. Rep. of the Congo 3°55N 23°53E **264** B4
Bondoc Pen. *Phil.* 13°26N 122°33E **232** E4
Bondokodi *Indonesia* 9°33S 119°0E **278** A2
Bondoukou *Ivory C.* 8°2N 2°47W **262** D4
Bondowoso *Indonesia* 7°55S 113°49E **235** D4
Bondy *France* 48°54N 2°28E **134** A3
Bondy, Forêt de *France* 48°54N 2°33E **134** A4
Bône = Annaba *Algeria* 36°50N 7°46E **261** A6
Bone, Teluk *Indonesia* 4°10S 120°50E **231** E6
Bonefish Pond *Bahamas* 24°59N 77°23W **153** b
Bonerate *Indonesia* 7°25S 121°5E **231** F6
Bonerate, Kepulauan
Indonesia 6°30S 121°10E **231** F6
Bo'ness *U.K.* 56°1N 3°37W **167** E5
Bonete, Cerro *Argentina* 27°55S 68°40W **334** B2
Bonfim = Senhor-do-Bonfim
Brazil 10°30S 40°10W **332** D3
Bonfim *Brazil* 3°33N 59°25W **329** C6
Bong Son = Hoai Nhon
Vietnam 14°28N 109°1E **236** E7
Bonga *Ethiopia* 7°15N 36°14E **257** F4
Bongabon *Phil.* 15°38N 121°8E **232** D3
Bongabong *Phil.* 12°45N 121°29E **232** E3
Bongaigaon *India* 26°28N 90°34E **241** B3
Bongandanga
Dem. Rep. of the Congo 1°24N 21°3E **264** B4
Bongao *Phil.* 5°2N 119°46E **233** J2
Bongo *Dem. Rep. of the Congo* 1°47S 17°41E **264** C3
Bongo, Sa. de *Angola* 10°35S 15°15E **265** E3
Bongo I. *Phil.* 7°20N 124°13E **233** H5
Bongor *Chad* 10°35N 15°20E **259** F3
Bongos, Massif des *C.A.R.* 8°40N 22°25E **264** A4
Bongouanou *Ivory C.* 6°42N 4°15W **262** D4
Bonham *U.S.A.* 33°35N 96°11W **314** E6
Boni *Mali* 15°3N 2°10W **262** B4
Boni ⌂ *Kenya* 1°35S 41°18E **268** C5
Bonifacio *France* 41°24N 9°10E **175** G13
Bonifacio, Bouches de
Medit. S. 41°12N 9°15E **200** A2
Bonifacio Monument
Phil. 14°38N 120°58E **127** B1
Bonifay *U.S.A.* 30°47N 85°41W **316** E4
Bonin Is. = Ogasawara Gunto
Pac. Oc. 27°0N 142°0E **288** E6
Bonita Springs *U.S.A.* 26°21N 81°47W **317** J8
Bonito *Brazil* 21°8S 56°28W **331** E6
Bonjol *Indonesia* 0°1S 100°13E **234** C2
Bonke *Ethiopia* 6°5N 37°16E **257** F4
Bonkoukou *Niger* 14°0N 3°15E **263** C5
Bonn *Germany* 50°46N 7°6E **178** E3
Bonnabel Place *U.S.A.* 30°0N 90°8W **131** A2
Bonnat *France* 46°20N 1°54E **173** F8
Bonne Terre *U.S.A.* 37°55N 90°33W **310** G6
Bonneau *U.S.A.* 33°16N 79°58W **316** B10
Bonners Ferry *U.S.A.* 48°42N 116°19W **304** B5
Bonnétable *France* 48°11N 0°25E **172** D7
Bonneuil-sur-Marne
France 48°46N 2°30E **134** B4
Bonneval *France* 45°22N 7°3E **175** C11
Bonneval-sur-Arc *France* 48°11N 1°24E **172** D8
Bonneville *France* 46°4N 6°24E **173** F13
Bonney, L. *Australia* 37°50S 140°20E **282** D4
Bonnie Doon *Australia* 37°2S 145°53E **283** D6
Bonnie Rock *Australia* 30°29S 118°22E **279** F2
Bonnington *U.K.* 55°54N 3°25W **121** B1
Bonny *Nigeria* 4°25N 7°13E **263** E6
Bonny → *Nigeria* 4°20N 7°10E **263** E6
Bonny, Bight of *Africa* 3°30N 9°20E **263** E6
Bonny Hills *Australia* 31°36S 152°51E **283** A10
Bonny-sur-Loire *France* 47°33N 2°50E **173** E9
Bonnyrigg *U.K.* 55°53N 3°6W **167** F5
Bonnyrigg and Lasswade
U.K. 55°52N 3°6W **121** B3
Bonnyville *Canada* 54°20N 110°45W **297** C6
Bono *Italy* 40°25N 9°2E **200** B2
Bonoi *Indonesia* 1°45S 137°41E **231** E9
Bonorva *Italy* 40°25N 8°46E **200** B1
Bonsall *U.S.A.* 33°16N 117°14W **307** M9
Bonsucesso *Brazil* 22°51S 43°15W **135** B1
Bontang *Indonesia* 0°10N 117°30E **235** C5
Bontebok △ *S. Africa* 34°5S 20°28E **270** D3
Bontheuwel *S. Africa* 33°57S 18°33E **118** A2
Bonthe *S. Leone* 7°30N 12°33W **262** D2
Bontoc *Phil.* 17°7N 120°58E **232** C3
Bontosunggu *Indonesia* 5°41S 119°42E **235** D5
Bonyeri *Ghana* 5°1N 2°46W **262** D4
Bonyhád *Hungary* 46°18N 18°32E **182** D3
Bonython Ra. *Australia* 23°40S 128°45E **278** D4
Boo *Sweden* 59°20N 18°16E **139** A3
Booderee △ *Australia* 35°12S 150°42E **283** C9
Boodjamulla △ *Australia* 18°15S 138°6E **280** B2
Bookabie *Australia* 31°50S 132°41E **279** F5
Booke *Dem. Rep. of the Congo* 2°34S 22°3E **264** C4
Booker *U.S.A.* 36°27N 100°32W **314** C4
Bool Lagoon *Australia* 37°7S 140°40E **282** D4
Boola *Guinea* 8°22N 8°41W **262** D3
Boolcoomata *Australia* 31°57S 140°33E **282** A4
Booleroo Centre *Australia* 32°53S 138°21E **282** B3
Booligal *Australia* 33°58S 144°53E **283** B6
Boon Pt. *Antigua & B.* 17°10N 61°50W **322** b
Böön Tsagaan Nuur
Mongolia 45°35N 99°9E **218** B8
Boonah *Australia* 27°58S 152°41E **281** D5
Boone *Iowa, U.S.A.* 42°4N 93°53W **310** B3
Boone *N.C., U.S.A.* 36°13N 81°41W **315** C14
Booneville *Ark., U.S.A.* 35°8N 93°55W **314** D8
Booneville *Miss., U.S.A.* 34°39N 88°34W **315** D10
Boonville *Calif., U.S.A.* 39°1N 123°22W **306** F3
Boonville *Ind., U.S.A.* 38°3N 87°16W **311** F9
Boonville *Mo., U.S.A.* 38°58N 92°44W **310** F4
Boonville *N.Y., U.S.A.* 43°29N 75°20W **313** C9
Boorabbin △ *Australia* 31°30S 120°10E **279** F3
Boorama *Somalia* 9°55N 43°7E **267** C5
Boorindal *Australia* 30°22S 146°11E **281** E4
Boorowa *Australia* 34°28S 148°44E **283** C8
Boort *Australia* 36°7S 143°46E **282** D5
Boosaaso *Somalia* 11°12N 49°18E **267** B6
Booterstown *Ireland* 53°19N 6°12W **120** B2
Boothia, Gulf of *Canada* 71°0N 90°0W **294** C14
Boothia Pen. *Canada* 71°0N 94°0W **294** C13
Bootle *U.K.* 53°28N 3°1W **168** D4
Booué *Gabon* 0°5S 11°55E **264** C2
Bopako
Dem. Rep. of the Congo 1°53N 21°13E **264** B4
Boppard *Germany* 50°13N 7°35E **179** E3
Boquerón □ *Paraguay* 23°0S 60°0W **331** E6
Boquilla, Presa de la
Mexico 27°31N 105°30W **318** B3
Boquillas del Carmen
Mexico 29°11N 102°58W **318** B4
Bor *Czech Rep.* 49°41N 12°45E **180** B5
Bor *Russia* 56°28N 43°59E **190** B7
Bor *Serbia* 44°5N 22°7E **202** B6
Bôr *South Sudan* 6°10N 31°40E **257** F3
Bor *Sweden* 57°9N 14°10E **163** G8
Bor *Turkey* 37°54N 34°32E **212** D6
Bor, Lagh → *Kenya* 1°18N 40°40E **267** D5
Bor Mashash *Israel* 31°7N 34°50E **251** G5
Bor u Ceske Lipy = Nový Bor
Czech Rep. 50°46N 14°35E **180** A7
Bora Bora *French Polynesia* 16°30S 151°45W **289** f
Borah Peak *U.S.A.* 44°8N 113°47W **304** D7
Boraha, Nosy *Madag.* 16°50S 49°55E **272** B2
Borang *South Sudan* 4°50N 30°59E **257** G3
Borangapara *India* 25°14N 90°14E **241** C3
Borankul *Kazakhstan* 46°11N 54°25E **216** C4
Borås *Sweden* 57°43N 12°56E **163** G6
Borāzjān *Iran* 29°22N 51°10E **247** D6
Borba *Brazil* 4°12S 59°34W **329** D6
Borba *Portugal* 38°50N 7°26W **195** G3
Borbon *Phil.* 10°50N 124°2E **233** F5
Borborema, Planalto da
Brazil 7°0S 37°0W **332** C4
Borcea *Romania* 44°20N 27°45E **183** F12
Borchalo = Marneuli
Georgia 41°30N 44°48E **191** K7
Borçka *Turkey* 41°25N 41°41E **213** B9
Bord Khūn-e Now *Iran* 28°3N 51°28E **247** D6
Borda, C. *Australia* 35°45S 136°34E **282** C2
Bordeaux *France* 44°50N 0°36W **174** D3
Bordeaux ✕ (BOD) *France* 44°50N 0°35W **174** D3
Borden *Australia* 34°3S 118°12E **279** F2
Borden-Carleton *Canada* 46°18N 63°47W **299** C7
Borden I. *Canada* 78°30N 111°30W **295** B9
Borden Pen. *Canada* 73°0N 83°0W **295** C15
Borden Springs *U.S.A.* 33°56N 85°28W **316** B4
Border Ranges △
Australia 28°24S 152°56E **281** D5
Borders = Scottish Borders □
U.K. 55°35N 2°50W **167** F6
Bordertown *Australia* 36°19S 140°45E **282** D4
Borðeyri *Iceland* 65°12N 21°6W **155** B5
Bordj bou Arreridj *Algeria* 36°4N 4°45E **261** A5
Bordj Bourguiba *Tunisia* 32°12N 10°2E **258** B2
Bordj Flye Ste-Marie
Algeria 27°19N 2°32W **260** C4
Bordj in Eker *Algeria* 24°9N 5°3E **261** D6
Bordj Menaïel *Algeria* 36°46N 3°43E **261** A5
Bordj Messouda *Algeria* 30°12N 9°25E **261** B6
Bordj Mokhtar *Algeria* 21°20N 0°56E **261** D5
Bordj Nili *Algeria* 33°28N 3°2E **261** B5
Bordj Omar Driss *Algeria* 28°10N 6°40E **261** C6
Bordj Sif Fatima *Algeria* 31°6N 8°41E **261** B6
Bordj Tarat *Algeria* 25°55N 9°3E **261** C6
Borduttighat *India* 26°57N 93°58E **241** B4
Bore *Ethiopia* 4°39N 37°39E **257** G4
Borehamwood *U.K.* 51°40N 0°15W **169** F7
Borek Wielkopolski
Poland 51°54N 17°11E **185** G4
Borensberg *Sweden* 58°34N 15°17E **163** F9
Borgå = Porvoo *Finland* 60°24N 25°40E **188** B3
Borgampad *India* 17°39N 80°52E **244** F5
Borgarfjarðarsýsla
Iceland 64°30N 21°30W **155** C5
Borgarfjörður *Austurland*
Iceland 65°33N 13°47W **155** B13
Borgarfjörður *Vesturland*
Iceland 64°30N 22°0W **155** C4
Borgarnes *Iceland* 64°32N 21°55W **155** C5
Børgefjellet *Norway* 65°20N 13°45E **160** D15
Borger *Neths.* 52°54N 6°44E **170** B6
Borger *Tex., U.S.A.* 35°39N 101°24W **314** D4
Borgholm *Sweden* 56°52N 16°39E **163** H10
Borgia *Italy* 38°49N 16°30E **201** D9
Borgnesse, Pte. *Martinique* 14°26N 60°54W **322** j
Borgo San Dalmazzo *Italy* 44°20N 7°30E **198** D4
Borgo San Donnino = Fidenza
Italy 44°52N 10°3E **198** D7
Borgo San Lorenzo *Italy* 43°57N 11°23E **199** E8
Borgo Val di Taro *Italy* 44°29N 9°46E **198** D6
Borgo Valsugana *Italy* 46°3N 11°27E **199** B8
Borgomanero *Italy* 45°42N 8°28E **198** C5
Borgorose *Italy* 42°11N 13°13E **199** F10
Borgosésia *Italy* 45°43N 8°16E **198** C5
Borgotaro = Borgo Val di Taro
Italy 44°29N 9°46E **198** D6
Borgund *Norway* 61°3N 7°48E **164** C4
Borhoyn Tal *Mongolia* 43°50N 111°58E **226** C6
Bori *Nigeria* 4°42N 7°21E **263** E6
Borigumma *India* 19°3N 82°33E **244** E6
Borikhane *Laos* 18°33N 103°43E **236** C4
Borisoglebsk *Russia* 51°27N 42°5E **190** E6
Borisov = Barysaw
Belarus 54°17N 28°28E **177** A15
Borisovgrad = Pŭrvomay
Bulgaria 42°8N 25°17E **203** D9
Borisovka *Russia* 50°36N 36°1E **189** G9
Borisovo *Russia* 55°38N 37°44E **129** C3
Borj Jeneïn *Tunisia* 31°45N 10°9E **258** B2
Borja *Peru* 4°20S 77°40W **328** D2
Borja *Spain* 41°48N 1°34W **196** D3
Borjas Blancas = Les Borges
Blanques *Spain* 41°31N 0°52E **196** D5
Borjomi *Georgia* 41°48N 43°28E **191** K6
Børkop *Denmark* 55°39N 9°39E **163** J3
Borkou *Chad* 18°15N 18°50E **259** E3
Borkou-Ennedi-Tibesti □
Chad 18°0N 19°0E **259** E3
Borkum *Germany* 53°34N 6°40E **178** B2
Borlänge *Sweden* 60°29N 15°26E **162** D9
Borle *India* 19°2N 72°54E **130** A2
Borley, C. *Antarctica* 66°15S 52°30E **151** C5
Borlu *Turkey* 38°44N 28°27E **205** C10
Bormida → *Italy* 44°23N 8°13E **198** D5
Bórmio *Italy* 46°28N 10°22E **198** B7
Borna *Germany* 51°7N 12°29E **178** D8
Borne Sulinowo *Poland* 53°32N 16°33E **184** E3
Borneo *E. Indies* 1°0N 115°0E **235** B4
Bornholm *Denmark* 55°10N 15°0E **163** J8
Bornholmsgattet *Europe* 55°15N 14°20E **163** J8
Borno □ *Nigeria* 11°30N 13°0E **263** C7
Bornos *Spain* 36°48N 5°42W **195** J5
Bornova *Turkey* 38°27N 27°14E **205** C9
Bornu Yassa *Nigeria* 12°14N 12°25E **263** C7
Boro → *South Sudan* 8°52N 26°11E **257** F2
Borobudur △ *Indonesia* 7°36S 110°12E **231** G14
Borobudur *Indonesia* 7°40S 110°11E **235** D4
Borocay I. *Phil.* 11°58N 121°55E **233** F3
Borodino *Russia* 55°31N 35°40E **188** E8
Borodino *Ukraine* 46°18N 29°15E **183** D14
Borogontsy *Russia* 62°42N 131°8E **215** C14
Borohoro Shan *China* 44°6N 83°10E **217** D10
Boromo *Burkina Faso* 11°45N 2°58W **262** C4
Boron *U.S.A.* 35°0N 117°39W **307** L9
Boronga Is. *Burma* 19°58N 93°6E **241** F4
Borongan *Phil.* 11°37N 125°26E **233** F5
Boronia Park *Australia* 33°49S 151°8E **139** A1
Borotangba Mts. *C.A.R.* 6°30N 25°0E **257** F2
Borotou *Ivory C.* 8°46N 7°30W **262** D3
Borovan *Bulgaria* 43°27N 23°45E **202** C7
Borovichi *Russia* 58°25N 33°55E **188** C7
Borovsk *Russia* 55°12N 36°24E **188** E9
Borovskoy *Kazakhstan* 53°48N 64°9E **216** B6
Borrby *Sweden* 55°27N 14°10E **163** J8
Borrego Springs *U.S.A.* 33°15N 116°23W **307** M10
Borriol *Spain* 40°4N 0°4W **196** E4
Borrisokane *Ireland* 53°0N 8°7W **166** D3
Borroloola *Australia* 16°4S 136°17E **280** B2
Borşa *Cluj, Romania* 46°56N 23°40E **183** D8
Borşa *Maramureş, Romania* 47°41N 24°50E **183** C9
Borsad *India* 22°25N 72°54E **242** H5
Borsec *Romania* 46°57N 25°34E **183** D10
Borshchiv *Ukraine* 48°48N 26°3E **183** B11
Borsod-Abaúj-Zemplén □
Hungary 48°20N 21°0E **182** B6
Bort-les-Orgues *France* 45°24N 2°29E **174** C6
Bortala = Bole *China* 44°55N 81°37E **217** C10
Borth *U.K.* 52°29N 4°2W **169** E3
Börtnan *Sweden* 62°45N 13°50E **162** B7
Borūjerd *Iran* 33°55N 48°50E **213** F13
Boryeong *S. Korea* 36°21N 126°36E **224** D3
Borynya *Ukraine* 49°4N 23°0E **185** J10
Boryslav *Ukraine* 49°18N 23°28E **185** J10
Boryspil *Ukraine* 50°21N 30°59E **189** G6
Borzhomi = Borjomi
Georgia 41°48N 43°28E **191** K6
Borzna *Ukraine* 51°18N 32°26E **189** G7
Borzya *Russia* 50°24N 116°31E **219** A12
Bosa *Italy* 40°18N 8°30E **200** B1
Bosa Monene
Dem. Rep. of the Congo 1°16S 23°40E **264** C4
Bosaga *Turkmenistan* 37°33N 65°41E **240** A2
Bosambi
Dem. Rep. of the Congo 2°24N 22°39E **264** B4
Bosanska Dubica
Bos.-H. 45°10N 16°50E **199** C13
Bosanska Gradiška
Bos.-H. 45°10N 17°15E **182** E2
Bosanska Kostajnica
Bos.-H. 45°11N 16°33E **199** C13
Bosanska Krupa *Bos.-H.* 44°53N 16°10E **199** D13
Bosanski Brod *Bos.-H.* 45°10N 18°0E **182** E2
Bosanski Novi *Bos.-H.* 45°2N 16°22E **199** C13
Bosanski Petrovac
Bos.-H. 44°35N 16°21E **199** D13
Bosanski Šamac *Bos.-H.* 45°3N 18°29E **182** E3
Bosansko Grahovo
Bos.-H. 44°12N 16°26E **199** D13
Bosavi, Mt. *Papua N. G.* 6°30S 142°49E **286** D2
Boscastle *U.K.* 50°41N 4°42W **169** G3
Boscobel *U.S.A.* 43°8N 90°42W **310** A6
Boscobelle *Barbados* 13°17N 59°35W **323** r
Bose *China* 23°53N 106°35E **228** F6
Boseki *Dem. Rep. of the Congo* 2°34S 19°38E **264** C3
Boseong *S. Korea* 34°46N 127°5E **224** E3
Boshan *China* 36°28N 117°49E **227** F9
Boshof *S. Africa* 28°31S 25°13E **270** C4
Boshrūyeh *Iran* 33°50N 57°30E **247** C8
Bosilegrad *Serbia* 42°30N 22°27E **202** D6
Boskovice *Czech Rep.* 49°29N 16°40E **181** B9
Bosmont *S. Africa* 26°10S 27°57E **123** B1
Bosna → *Bos.-H.* 45°4N 18°29E **182** E3
Bosna i Hercegovina = Bosnia-
Herzegovina ■ *Europe* 44°0N 18°0E **182** G2
Bosnia-Herzegovina ■
Europe 44°0N 18°0E **182** G2
Bosnik *Indonesia* 1°5S 136°10E **231** E9
Bōsō-Hantō *Japan* 35°20N 140°20E **223** B12
Bosobolo
Dem. Rep. of the Congo 4°15N 19°50E **264** B3
Boson *Sweden* 59°22N 18°11E **139** A3
Bosporus = İstanbul Boğazı
Turkey 41°5N 29°3E **122** B2
Bosque Farms *U.S.A.* 35°51N 106°42W **305** J10
Bosra = Buşra ash Shām
Syria 32°30N 36°25E **251** F7
Bossangoa *C.A.R.* 6°35N 17°30E **264** A3
Bossé Bangou *Niger* 13°20N 1°18E **263** C5
Bossembélé *C.A.R.* 5°25N 17°40E **264** A3
Bossemtélé *C.A.R.* 5°41N 16°38E **264** A3
Bossier City *U.S.A.* 32°31N 93°44W **314** E8
Bossiesvlei *Namibia* 25°1S 16°44E **270** C2
Bosso *Niger* 13°43N 13°19E **259** F2
Bosso, Dallol → *Niger* 12°25N 2°50E **263** C5
Bostan *Pakistan* 30°26N 67°2E **242** D2
Bostānābād *Iran* 37°50N 46°50E **213** D12
Bostancı *Turkey* 40°57N 29°5E **122** C2
Bosten Hu *China* 41°55N 87°40E **217** D11
Boston *Phil.* 7°52N 126°22E **233** H6
Boston *Lincs., U.K.* 52°59N 0°2W **168** E7
Boston *Ga., U.S.A.* 30°47N 83°47W **316** E6
Boston *Mass., U.S.A.* 42°22N 71°3W **116** A2
Boston Bar *Canada* 49°52N 121°30W **296** D4
Boston Bay *Jamaica* 18°9N 76°22W **320** a
Boston Common *Boston, U.S.A.* **116** c1
Boston Logan Int. ✕ (BOS)
U.S.A. 42°22N 71°1W **116** A2
Boston Mts. *U.S.A.* 35°42N 93°15W **314** D8
Boston Tea Party Ship & Museum
Boston, U.S.A. **116** c3
Bostwick *U.S.A.* 29°46N 81°38W **316** F8
Bosumtwi, L. *Ghana* 6°30N 1°25W **263** D4
Bosusulu
Dem. Rep. of the Congo 0°50N 20°45E **264** B4
Bosut → *Croatia* 45°20N 18°45E **182** E3
Boswell *B.C., Canada* 49°28N 116°45W **296** D5
Boswell *Ind., U.S.A.* 40°31N 87°23W **311** D9
Boswell *Pa., U.S.A.* 40°10N 79°2W **312** F5
Bosworth *U.S.A.* 39°28N 93°20W **310** E3
Botad *India* 22°15N 71°40E **242** H4

Botafogo Brazil 22°56S 43°10W 135 B1
Botan → Turkey 37°57N 42°2E 213 D10
Botanic Gardens
Washington, D.C., U.S.A. 143 b3
Botanisk Have Copenhagen, Denmark 118 b2
Botany Australia 33°56S 151°12E 139 B2
Botany B. Australia 33°58S 151°11E 139 B2
Botany Bay △ Australia 34°0S 151°14E 139 B2
Botene Laos 17°35N 101°12E 236 D3
Botera Angola 11°37S 14°16E 265 E2
Botev Bulgaria 42°44N 24°52E 203 D8
Botevgrad Bulgaria 42°55N 23°47E 202 D7
Bothaville S. Africa 27°23S 26°34E 270 C4
Bothnia, G. of Europe 62°0N 20°0E 160 F19
Bothwell Tas., Australia 42°20S 147°1E 281 G4
Bothwell Ont., Canada 42°38N 81°52W 312 D3
Botič → Czech Rep. 50°4N 14°26E 135 B3
Botica Sete Portugal 38°49N 9°10W 126 A1
Boticas Portugal 41°41N 7°40W 194 D3
Botletle → Botswana 20°10S 23°15E 270 B3
Botlikh Russia 42°39N 46°11E 191 J8
Botna → Moldova 46°45N 29°34E 183 D14
Botola Dem. Rep. of the Congo 1°17S 18°13E 264 C3
Botolan Phil. 15°17N 120°1E 232 D3
Botoroaga Romania 44°8N 25°32E 183 F10
Botoşani Romania 47°42N 26°41E 183 C11
Botoşani □ Romania 47°50N 26°50E 183 C11
Botou Burkina Faso 12°42N 1°59E 263 C5
Botou China 38°4N 116°34E 226 E9
Botricello Italy 38°56N 16°51E 201 D9
Botro Ivory C. 7°51N 5°19W 262 D3
Botshabelo S. Africa 29°14S 26°44E 270 C4
Botswana ■ Africa 22°0S 24°0E 270 B3
Bottelier Curaçao 12°6N 68°54W 322 g
Bottineau U.S.A. 48°50N 100°27W 308 A3
Bottnaryd Sweden 57°47N 13°50E 163 G7
Bottom, The Saba 17°38N 63°15W 322 a
Bottopassi Suriname 4°14N 55°27W 329 C6
Bottrop Germany 51°31N 6°58E 178 D2
Botucatu Brazil 22°55S 48°30W 335 A6
Botum Sakor △ Cambodia 11°5N 103°15E 237 G4
Botwood Canada 49°6N 55°23W 299 C8
Bou Alam Algeria 33°50N 1°26E 261 B5
Bou Ali Algeria 27°11N 0°4W 261 C4
Bou Djébéha Mali 18°25N 2°45W 262 B4
Bou Guema Algeria 28°49N 0°19E 261 C5
Bou Ismaïl Algeria 36°38N 2°42E 261 A5
Bou Izakarn Morocco 29°12N 9°46W 260 C3
Boû Lanouâr Mauritania 21°12N 16°34W 260 D1
Boû Naga Mauritania 18°49N 13°20W 262 B2
Bou Noura Algeria 32°29N 3°43E 261 B5
Boû Rjeïmât Mauritania 19°4N 15°3W 262 B1
Bou Saâda Algeria 35°11N 4°9E 261 A5
Bou Salem Tunisia 36°45N 9°2E 258 A1
Bouaflé Ivory C. 7°1N 5°47W 262 D3
Bouaké Ivory C. 7°40N 5°2W 262 D3
Bouanga Congo 2°7S 16°8E 264 C3
Bouar C.A.R. 6°0N 15°40E 264 A3
Bouârfa Morocco 32°32N 1°58W 261 B4
Bouba Ndjida △ Cameroon 8°50N 14°45E 264 A2
Bouboût Algeria 27°26N 4°30W 260 C4
Bouca C.A.R. 6°45N 18°25E 264 A3
Boucaut B. Australia 12°0S 134°25E 280 A1
Boucherville Canada 45°36N 73°28W 130 A3
Boucherville, Îs. de
Canada 45°36N 73°28W 130 A3
Bouches-du-Rhône □
France 43°37N 5°2E 175 E9
Boucle de Baoulé △ Mali 13°53N 9°0W 262 C3
Boucles de la Seine Normande △
France 49°32N 0°35E 172 C7
Bouctouche Canada 46°30N 64°45W 299 C7
Bouda Algeria 27°50N 0°27W 261 C4
Boudenib Morocco 31°59N 3°31W 260 B4
Bouéni Mayotte 12°54S 45°4E 272 b
Bouéni, B. de Mayotte 12°55S 45°7E 272 b
Boufarik Algeria 36°34N 2°58E 261 A5
Bougainville, C. Australia 13°57S 126°4E 278 B4
Bougainville I. Papua N. G. 6°0S 155°0E 287 L8
Bougainville Reef
Australia 15°30S 147°5E 280 B4
Bougainville Str.
Solomon Is. 6°40S 156°10E 287 L9
Bougaroun, C. Algeria 37°6N 6°30E 261 A6
Bougie = Bejaïa Algeria 36°42N 5°2E 261 A6
Bougival France 48°51N 2°8E 134 A1
Bougouni Mali 11°30N 7°20W 262 C3
Bougtob Algeria 34°2N 0°5E 261 B5
Bouillante Guadeloupe 16°8N 61°46W 322 e
Bouillante, Pitons de
Guadeloupe 16°8N 61°43W 322 e
Bouillon Belgium 49°44N 5°3E 170 E5
Bouïra Algeria 36°20N 3°59E 261 A5
Bouïra □ Algeria 36°15N 3°55E 261 A5
Boukombé Benin 10°13N 1°9E 263 C5
Boulal Mali 15°8N 8°21W 262 B3
Boulazac France 45°10N 0°47E 174 C4
Boulder Colo., U.S.A. 40°1N 105°17W 304 F11
Boulder Mont., U.S.A. 46°14N 112°7W 304 C7
Boulder City U.S.A. 35°58N 114°49W 307 K12
Boulder Creek U.S.A. 37°7N 122°7W 306 H4
Boulder Dam = Hoover Dam
U.S.A. 36°1N 114°44W 307 K12
Boulder Pt. China 22°14N 114°6E 122 B1
Boulembo Gabon 1°26S 12°0E 264 C2
Boulí Mauritania 15°17N 12°18W 262 B2
Boulia Australia 22°52S 139°51E 280 C2
Bouligny France 49°17N 5°45E 173 C12
Boulogne → France 47°12N 1°47W 172 E5
Boulogne, Bois de France 48°51N 2°14E 134 A2
Boulogne-Billancourt
France 48°50N 2°14E 134 A2
Boulogne-sur-Gesse France 43°18N 0°38E 174 E4
Boulogne-sur-Mer France 50°42N 1°36E 173 B8
Bouloire France 47°59N 0°45E 172 E7
Boulou → C.A.R. 6°45N 24°16E 264 A4
Boulouli Mali 15°30N 9°25W 262 B3
Bouloupari N. Cal. 21°52S 166°4E 288 d
Bouloupessé Congo 1°58S 12°40E 264 C2
Boulsa Burkina Faso 12°39N 0°34W 263 C4
Boultoum Niger 14°45N 10°25E 259 F2
Bouma △ Fiji 16°50S 179°52E 287 A2
Boumalne Dadès Morocco 31°25N 6°0W 260 B3
Boumba → Cameroon 2°2N 15°12E 264 B2
Boumbé → C.A.R. 4°4N 15°23E 264 B3
Boûmdeïd Mauritania 17°25N 11°50W 262 B2
Boumerdès Algeria 36°46N 3°28E 261 A5
Boumerdès □ Algeria 36°45N 3°40E 261 A5
Boun Neua Laos 21°38N 101°54E 236 B3
Boun Tai Laos 21°23N 101°58E 236 B3
Bouna Ivory C. 9°10N 3°0W 262 D4
Boundary U.S.A. 64°5N 141°1W 303 D12
Boundary Peak U.S.A. 37°51N 118°21W 306 H8
Boundiali Ivory C. 9°30N 6°20W 262 D3
Boungou → C.A.R. 8°21N 23°48E 264 A4
Bountiful U.S.A. 40°53N 111°52W 304 F8
Bounty Is. Pac. Oc. 48°0S 178°30E 288 M9
Bounty Trough Pac. Oc. 46°0S 178°0E 288 M9
Boura Mali 12°25N 4°33W 262 C4
Bourail N. Cal. 21°34S 165°30E 288 d
Bourbeuse → U.S.A. 38°24N 90°53W 310 F6
Bourbon U.S.A. 41°18N 86°7W 311 C10
Bourbon-Lancy France 46°37N 3°45E 173 F10
Bourbon-l'Archambault
France 46°36N 3°4E 173 F10
Bourbon Street New Orleans, U.S.A. 131 b2
Bourbonnais Allier, France 46°28N 3°0E 173 F10
Bourbonnais Ill., U.S.A. 41°9N 87°52W 311 C9
Bourbonne-les-Bains
France 47°54N 5°45E 173 E12
Bourbourg France 50°56N 2°12E 173 B9
Bourdel L. Canada 56°43N 74°10W 298 A5
Bourem Mali 17°0N 0°24W 263 B4
Bouressa Mali 20°0N 2°15E 261 E5
Bourg France 45°3N 0°34W 174 C3
Bourg-Argental France 45°18N 4°32E 175 C8
Bourg-de-Péage France 45°2N 5°3E 175 C9
Bourg-en-Bresse France 46°13N 5°12E 173 F12
Bourg-la-Reine France 48°46N 2°19E 134 B2
Bourg-Lastic France 45°39N 2°35E 174 C6
Bourg-Madame France 42°25N 1°55E 174 F5
Bourg-St-Andéol France 44°23N 4°39E 175 D8
Bourg-St-Maurice France 45°35N 6°46E 175 C10
Bourganeuf France 45°57N 1°45E 174 C5
Bourgas = Burgas
Bulgaria 42°33N 27°29E 203 D11
Bourges France 47°9N 2°25E 173 E9
Bourget Canada 45°26N 75°9W 313 A9
Bourget, Lac du France 45°44N 5°52E 175 C9
Bourgneuf, B. de France 47°3N 2°10W 172 E4
Bourgneuf-en-Retz France 47°2N 1°58W 172 E5
Bourgogne □ France 47°0N 4°50E 173 F11
Bourgoin-Jallieu France 45°36N 5°17E 175 C9
Bourgueil France 47°17N 0°10E 172 E7
Bourke Australia 30°8S 145°55E 281 E4
Bourne U.K. 52°47N 0°22W 168 E7
Bournemouth U.K. 50°43N 1°52W 169 G6
Bournemouth □ U.K. 50°43N 1°52W 169 G6
Bouroum Burkina Faso 13°37N 0°39W 263 C4
Bouse U.S.A. 33°56N 114°0W 307 M13
Boussac France 46°22N 2°13E 173 F9
Boussé Burkina Faso 12°39N 1°53W 263 C4
Bousso Chad 10°34N 16°52E 259 F3
Boussouma Burkina Faso 12°52N 1°13W 263 C4
Bout, Pte. du Martinique 14°33N 61°3W 322 j
Bout Stable Bay Dominica 15°21N 61°15W 323 k
Boutilimit Mauritania 17°45N 14°40W 262 B2
Boutonne → France 45°54N 0°50W 174 C3
Bouvet I. = Bouvetøya
Antarctica 54°26S 3°24E 152 M12
Bouvetøya Antarctica 54°26S 3°24E 152 M12
Bouviers France 48°46N 2°4E 134 B1
Bouxwiller France 48°49N 7°27E 173 D14
Bouza Niger 14°29N 6°2E 263 C6
Bouznika Morocco 33°46N 7°6W 260 B3
Bouzonville France 49°17N 6°32E 173 C13
Bova Marina Italy 37°56N 15°55E 201 E8
Bovalino Marina Italy 38°10N 16°10E 201 D9
Bovec Slovenia 46°20N 13°33E 199 B10
Boven Kapuas, Pegunungan
Malaysia 1°25N 113°15E 235 B4
Bovenkerk Neths. 52°18N 4°51E 112 B2
Bovenkerker Polder Neths. 52°16N 4°52E 112 B2
Bøverdal Norway 61°44N 8°20E 164 C5
Bøverfjorden Norway 63°1N 8°32E 164 A5
Bovill U.S.A. 46°51N 116°24W 304 C5
Bovino Italy 41°15N 15°20E 201 A8
Bovisa Italy 45°30N 9°10E 128 A2
Bovril Argentina 31°21S 59°26W 334 C4
Bow U.K. 51°31N 0°1W 125 A3
Bow → Canada 49°57N 111°41W 296 C6
Bow Island Canada 49°50N 111°23W 304 B8
Bowbells U.S.A. 48°48N 102°15W 308 A2
Bowdle U.S.A. 45°27N 99°39W 308 C4
Bowdon U.S.A. 33°32N 85°15W 316 B4
Bowdon Junction U.S.A. 33°40N 85°9W 316 B4
Bowelling Australia 33°25S 116°30E 279 F2
Bowen Argentina 35°0S 67°31W 334 D2
Bowen Queens., Australia 20°0S 148°16E 280 J6
Bowen Mts. Australia 37°0S 147°50E 283 D7
Bowers Basin Pac. Oc. 53°45N 176°0E 150 D16
Bowers Ridge Pac. Oc. 54°0N 180°0E 150 D17
Bowery New York, U.S.A. 132 e2
Bowie Ariz., U.S.A. 32°19N 109°29W 305 K9
Bowie Tex., U.S.A. 33°34N 97°51W 314 E6
Bowkān Iran 36°31N 46°12E 213 D12
Bowland, Forest of U.K. 54°0N 2°30W 168 D5
Bowling Green Fla.,
U.S.A. 27°38N 81°50W 317 H8
Bowling Green Ky.,
U.S.A. 36°59N 86°27W 308 G10
Bowling Green Mo.,
U.S.A. 39°21N 91°12W 310 E5
Bowling Green Ohio,
U.S.A. 41°23N 83°39W 311 C13
Bowling Green, C.
Australia 19°19S 147°25E 280 B4
Bowling Green Bay △
Australia 19°26S 146°57E 280 B4
Bowman N. Dak., U.S.A. 46°11N 103°24W 308 B2
Bowman S.C., U.S.A. 33°21N 80°41W 316 B9
Bowman I. Antarctica 65°0S 104°0E 151 C8
Bowmanville = Clarington
Canada 43°55N 78°41W 312 C6
Bowmore U.K. 55°45N 6°17W 167 F2
Bowral Australia 34°26S 150°27E 283 C9
Bowraville Australia 30°37S 152°52E 281 E5
Bowron → Canada 54°3N 121°50W 296 C4
Bowron Lake △ Canada 53°10N 121°5W 296 C4
Bowser L. Canada 56°30N 129°30W 296 B3
Bowsman Canada 52°14N 101°12W 297 C8
Bowutu Mts. Papua N. G. 7°45S 147°10E 286 D4
Bowwood Zambia 17°5S 26°20E 269 F2
Box Cr. → Australia 34°10S 143°50E 281 E3
Boxholm Sweden 58°12N 15°3E 163 F9
Boxmeer Neths. 51°38N 5°56E 170 C5
Boxtel Neths. 51°36N 5°20E 170 C5
Boyabat Turkey 41°28N 34°47E 212 B6
Boyabo
Dem. Rep. of the Congo 3°43N 18°46E 264 B3
Boyacá □ Colombia 5°30N 72°30W 328 B3
Boyacıköy Turkey 41°5N 29°2E 122 B2
Boyalıca Turkey 40°29N 29°33E 203 F13
Boyang China 29°0N 116°38E 229 C11
Boyany Ukraine 48°17N 26°8E 183 B11
Boyasegese
Dem. Rep. of the Congo 3°29N 20°33E 264 B4
Boyce U.S.A. 31°23N 92°40W 314 F8
Boyd U.S.A. 30°11N 83°37W 316 E6
Boyd Conservation Area
Canada 43°49N 79°35W 141 A1
Boyd L. Canada 52°46N 76°42W 298 B4
Boyenge
Dem. Rep. of the Congo 0°14N 18°55E 264 B3
Boyer, C. N. Cal. 21°37S 168°6E 288 d
Boyera
Dem. Rep. of the Congo 0°40S 19°23E 264 C3
Boyle Alta., Canada 54°35N 112°49W 296 C6
Boyle Roscommon, Ireland 53°59N 8°18W 166 C3
Boyle Heights U.S.A. 34°1N 118°12W 126 B3
Boyne → Ireland 53°43N 6°15W 166 C5
Boyne, Bend of the Ireland 53°41N 6°27W 166 C5
Boyne City U.S.A. 45°13N 85°1W 309 C11
Boyni Qara Afghan. 36°20N 67°0E 240 A2
Boynitsa Bulgaria 43°58N 22°32E 202 C6
Boynton Beach U.S.A. 26°32N 80°4W 317 J9
Boyoma, Chutes
Dem. Rep. of the Congo 0°35N 25°23E 264 B5
Boysen Res. U.S.A. 43°25N 108°11W 304 E9
Boyup Brook Australia 33°50S 116°23E 279 F2
Boz Burun Turkey 40°32N 28°46E 203 F12
Boz Dağ Turkey 37°18N 29°11E 205 D11
Boz Dağları Turkey 38°20N 28°0E 205 C10
Bozai Gumbaz Afghan. 37°8N 74°0E 240 A4
Bozburun Turkey 36°43N 28°4E 205 E10
Bozcaada Turkey 39°49N 26°3E 212 C2
Bozdağ Turkey 36°50N 36°22E 250 B7
Bozdoğan Turkey 37°40N 28°17E 205 D10
Boze Papua N. G. 9°3S 143°3E 286 E2
Bozeman U.S.A. 45°41N 111°2W 304 D8
Bozen = Bolzano Italy 46°31N 11°22E 199 B8
Bozene
Dem. Rep. of the Congo 2°56N 19°12E 264 B3
Boževac Serbia 44°32N 21°24E 202 B5
Bozhou China 33°55N 115°41E 226 H8
Bozkır Turkey 37°11N 32°14E 212 D5
Bozkurt Turkey 37°50N 29°37E 205 D11
Bozouls France 44°28N 2°43E 174 D6
Bozoum C.A.R. 6°25N 16°35E 264 A3
Bozova Antalya, Turkey 37°13N 30°18E 205 D12
Bozova Sanlıurfa, Turkey 37°21N 38°32E 213 D8
Bozovici Romania 44°56N 22°0E 182 F7
Bozüyük Turkey 39°54N 30°3E 205 B12
Bozyazı Turkey 36°6N 33°0E 250 B4
Bra Italy 44°42N 7°51E 198 D4
Braås Sweden 57°4N 15°3E 163 G9
Brabant □ Belgium 50°46N 4°30E 170 D4
Brabant L. Canada 55°58N 103°43W 297 B8
Brabrand Denmark 56°9N 10°7E 163 H4
Brač Croatia 43°20N 16°40E 199 E13
Bracadale, L. U.K. 57°20N 6°30W 167 D2
Bracciano Italy 42°6N 12°10E 199 F9
Bracciano, L. di Italy 42°7N 12°14E 199 F9
Bracebridge Canada 45°2N 79°19W 312 A5
Bracieux France 47°30N 1°30E 172 E8
Bräcke Sweden 62°45N 15°26E 162 B9
Brackettville U.S.A. 29°19N 100°25W 314 G4
Brački Kanal Croatia 43°24N 16°40E 199 E13
Bracknell U.K. 51°25N 0°43W 169 F7
Bracknell Forest □ U.K. 51°25N 0°44W 169 F7
Brad Romania 46°10N 22°50E 182 D7
Brádano → Italy 40°23N 16°51E 201 B9
Bradbury Building Los Angeles, U.S.A. 127 b2
Bradenton U.S.A. 27°30N 82°34W 317 H7
Brades Montserrat 16°47N 62°13W 323 p
Bradford Ont., Canada 44°7N 79°34W 312 B5
Bradford W. Yorks., U.K. 53°47N 1°45W 168 D6
Bradford Ill., U.S.A. 41°11N 89°39W 310 C7
Bradford Ohio, U.S.A. 40°8N 84°27W 311 D12
Bradford Pa., U.S.A. 41°58N 78°38W 312 E6
Bradford Vt., U.S.A. 43°59N 72°9W 313 C12
Bradley Ark., U.S.A. 33°6N 93°39W 314 E8
Bradley Calif., U.S.A. 35°52N 120°48W 306 K6
Bradley Ill., U.S.A. 41°9N 87°52W 311 C9
Bradley Institute Zimbabwe 17°7S 31°25E 269 F3
Bradley Junction U.S.A. 27°48N 81°59W 317 H8
Bradner U.S.A. 41°20N 83°26W 311 C13
Brady U.S.A. 31°9N 99°20W 314 F5
Brædstrup Denmark 55°58N 9°37E 163 J3
Braemar Australia 33°12S 139°35E 282 B3
Braepark U.K. 55°58N 3°18W 121 B2
Braeside Canada 45°28N 76°24W 313 A8
Braeton Jamaica 17°57N 76°53W 320 a
Braga Portugal 41°35N 8°25W 194 D2
Braga □ Portugal 41°30N 8°30W 194 D2
Bragadiru Romania 43°46N 25°31E 183 G10
Bragado Argentina 35°2S 60°27W 334 D3
Bragança Brazil 1°0S 47°2W 332 B2
Bragança Portugal 41°48N 6°50W 194 D4
Bragança □ Portugal 41°30N 6°45W 194 D4
Bragança Paulista Brazil 22°55S 46°32W 335 A6
Bragg's Spur = West Memphis
U.S.A. 35°8N 90°10W 315 D9
Brahestad = Raahe
Finland 64°40N 24°28E 160 D21
Brahmakund India 27°52N 96°22E 241 B6
Brahmanbaria Bangla. 23°58N 91°15E 241 D3
Brahmani → India 20°39N 86°46E 244 D8
Brahmapur India 19°15N 84°54E 244 E7
Brahmaputra → Asia 23°40N 90°35E 241 D3
Braich-y-pwll U.K. 52°47N 4°46W 168 E3
Braid U.K. 55°55N 3°11W 121 B2
Braidwood Australia 35°27S 149°49E 283 C8
Brăila Romania 45°19N 27°59E 183 E12
Brăila □ Romania 45°5N 27°30E 183 E12
Brainerd U.S.A. 46°22N 94°12W 308 B6
Braintree Essex, U.K. 51°53N 0°34E 169 F8
Braintree Mass., U.S.A. 42°13N 71°0W 313 D14
Brak → S. Africa 29°35S 22°55E 270 C3
Brake Germany 53°20N 8°28E 178 B4
Brakel Germany 51°42N 9°11E 178 D5
Brakna □ Mauritania 17°0N 13°20W 262 B2
Bräkne-Hoby Sweden 56°14N 15°6E 163 H9
Brakwater Namibia 22°28S 17°3E 270 B2
Brålanda Sweden 58°34N 12°21E 163 F6
Bramberg Germany 50°6N 10°40E 179 E6
Bramdrupdam Denmark 55°31N 9°28E 163 J3
Bramhapuri India 20°36N 79°52E 244 D4
Bramley S. Africa 26°7S 28°4E 123 A2
Bramming Denmark 55°28N 8°42E 163 J2
Brämön Sweden 62°14N 17°40E 162 B11
Brampton Ont., Canada 43°45N 79°45W 312 C5
Brampton Cumb., U.K. 54°57N 2°44W 168 C5
Brampton I. Australia 20°49S 149°16E 280 b
Bramsche Germany 52°24N 7°59E 178 C3
Branchville U.S.A. 33°15N 80°49W 316 B9
Branco → Brazil 1°20S 61°50W 329 D5
Branco, C. Brazil 7°9S 34°47W 332 C5
Brandaris Bonaire 12°16N 68°23W 322 h
Brandberg Namibia 21°10S 14°33E 270 B1
Brandberg △ Namibia 21°10S 14°30E 270 B1
Brandbu Norway 60°26N 10°28E 164 D7
Brande Denmark 55°57N 9°8E 163 J3
Brandeis Univ. U.S.A. 42°21N 71°17W 116 A1
Brandenburg = Neubrandenburg
Germany 53°33N 13°15E 178 B9
Brandenburg Brandenburg,
Germany 52°25N 12°33E 178 C8
Brandenburg Ky., U.S.A. 38°0N 86°10W 311 G10
Brandenburg □ Germany 52°50N 13°0E 178 C9
Brandenburger Tor
Germany 52°30N 13°21E 115 A3
Brandfort S. Africa 28°40S 26°30E 270 C4
Brando France 42°47N 9°27E 175 F13
Brandon Man., Canada 49°50N 99°57W 297 D9
Brandon Fla., U.S.A. 27°56N 82°17W 317 H7
Brandon Vt., U.S.A. 43°48N 73°6W 313 C11
Brandon B. Ireland 52°17N 10°8W 166 D1
Brandon Mt. Ireland 52°15N 10°15W 166 D1
Brandsen Argentina 35°10S 58°15W 334 D4
Brandvlei S. Africa 30°25S 20°30E 270 D3
Brandýs nad Labem
Czech Rep. 50°10N 14°40E 180 A7
Brăneşti Romania 44°27N 26°20E 183 F11
Branford Conn., U.S.A. 41°17N 72°49W 313 E12
Branford Fla., U.S.A. 29°58N 82°56W 316 F7
Brani, Pulau Singapore 1°15N 103°50E 138 B3
Braniewo Poland 54°25N 19°50E 184 D6
Branik Czech Rep. 50°1N 14°25E 135 B2
Brännkyrka Sweden 59°17N 18°1E 139 B2
Bransfield Str. Antarctica 63°0S 59°0W 151 C18
Brańsk Poland 52°45N 22°50E 185 F9
Branson U.S.A. 36°39N 93°13W 308 G7
Brantford Canada 43°10N 80°15W 312 C4
Brantley U.S.A. 31°35N 86°16W 316 D3
Brantôme France 45°22N 0°39E 174 C4
Branxholme Australia 37°52S 141°49E 282 D4
Branxton Australia 32°38S 151°21E 283 B9
Branzi Italy 46°1N 9°46E 198 B6
Brás Amazonas, Brazil 2°5S 58°10W 329 D6
Brás São Paulo, Brazil 23°32S 46°36W 137 B2
Bras d'Or L. Canada 45°50N 60°50W 299 C7
Bras-Panon Réunion 20°59S 55°41E 272 f
Brasher Falls U.S.A. 44°49N 74°47W 313 B10
Brasil = Brazil ■ S. Amer. 12°0S 50°0W 327 E6
Brasil, Planalto Brazil 18°0S 46°30W 326 E6
Brasiléia Brazil 11°0S 68°45W 330 C4
Brasília Distrito Federal,
Brazil 15°47S 47°55W 333 E2
Brasília Minas Gerais,
Brazil 16°12S 44°26W 333 E3
Brasília △ Brazil 15°41S 48°8W 333 E2
Brasília Legal Brazil 3°49S 55°36W 329 D6
Braskereidfoss Norway 60°44N 11°46E 164 D8
Braslaw Belarus 55°38N 27°0E 188 E4
Braslovče Slovenia 46°21N 15°3E 199 B12
Braşov Romania 45°38N 25°35E 183 E10
Braşov □ Romania 45°45N 25°15E 183 E10
Brass Nigeria 4°35N 6°14E 263 E6
Brass → Nigeria 4°15N 6°13E 263 E6
Brassac-les-Mines France 45°24N 3°20E 174 C7
Brasschaat Belgium 51°19N 4°27E 170 C4
Brassey, Banjaran
Malaysia 5°0N 117°15E 235 B5
Brassey Ra. Australia 25°8S 122°15E 279 E3
Brasso Seco Trin. & Tob. 10°45N 61°16W 323 t
Brasstown Bald U.S.A. 34°53N 83°49W 315 D13
Brastad Sweden 58°23N 11°30E 163 F5
Brastavățu Romania 43°55N 24°24E 183 G9
Bratan = Morozov
Bulgaria 42°30N 25°10E 203 D9
Brateş Romania 45°50N 26°4E 183 E11
Brateyevo Russia 55°39N 37°45E 129 C3
Bratislava Slovak Rep. 48°10N 17°7E 181 C10
Bratislava M.R. Stefanik ✕ (BTS)
Slovak Rep. 48°11N 17°9E 181 C10
Bratislavský □
Slovak Rep. 48°15N 17°20E 181 C10
Bratsberg = Telemark □
Norway 59°25N 8°30E 164 E5
Bratsigovo Bulgaria 42°1N 24°22E 203 D8
Bratsk Russia 56°10N 101°30E 215 D11
Bratskoye Vdkhr. Russia 56°0N 101°40E 215 D11
Brattleboro U.S.A. 42°51N 72°34W 313 D12
Brattvåg Norway 62°37N 6°25E 164 B3
Bratunac Bos.-H. 44°13N 19°21E 182 F4
Braunau Austria 48°15N 13°3E 180 C6
Braunsberg = Braniewo
Poland 54°25N 19°50E 184 D6
Braunschweig Germany 52°15N 10°31E 178 C6
Braunton U.K. 51°7N 4°10W 169 F3
Brava = Baraawe Somalia 1°20N 44°8E 267 D5
Brava Cabo Verde Is. 15°0N 24°40W 153 j
Bravicea Moldova 47°22N 28°27E 183 C13
Bråviken Sweden 58°38N 16°32E 163 F10
Bravo del Norte, Rio = Grande,
Rio → N. Amer. 25°58N 97°9W 314 J6
Brawley U.S.A. 32°59N 115°31W 307 N11
Bray Ireland 53°13N 6°7W 166 C5
Bray, Mt. Australia 14°0S 134°30E 280 A1
Bray, Pays de France 49°46N 1°26E 171 B4
Bray-sur-Seine France 48°25N 3°14E 173 D10
Braybrook Australia 37°46S 144°51E 128 A1
Braymer U.S.A. 39°35N 93°48W 310 E3
Brázdim Czech Rep. 50°10N 14°35E 135 A3
Brazeau → Canada 52°55N 115°14W 296 C5
Brazil U.S.A. 39°32N 87°8W 311 E9
Brazil ■ S. Amer. 12°0S 50°0W 327 E6
Brazil Basin Atl. Oc. 15°0S 25°0W 152 H9
Brazilian Highlands = Brasil,
Planalto Brazil 18°0S 46°30W 326 E6
Brazo Sur → S. Amer. 25°21S 57°42W 334 B4
Brazos → U.S.A. 28°53N 95°23W 314 G7
Brazzaville Congo 4°9S 15°12E 265 C3
Brčko Bos.-H. 44°54N 18°46E 182 F3
Brda → Poland 53°8N 18°8E 185 E5
Brdy Czech Rep. 49°43N 13°55E 180 B6
Bré = Bray Ireland 53°13N 6°7W 166 C5
Breach Candy Mumbai, India 130 a1
Breaden, L. Australia 25°51S 125°28E 279 E4
Breakheart Reservation
U.S.A. 42°28N 71°1W 116 A2
Breaksea Sd. N.Z. 45°35S 166°35E 285 F1
Bream B. N.Z. 35°56S 174°28E 284 B3
Bream Hd. N.Z. 35°51S 174°36E 284 B3
Bream Tail N.Z. 36°3S 174°36E 284 C3
Breas Chile 25°29S 70°24W 334 B1
Breaza Romania 45°11N 25°40E 183 E10
Brebes Indonesia 6°52S 109°3E 235 D3
Brechin Ont., Canada 44°32N 79°10W 312 B5
Brechin Angus, U.K. 56°44N 2°39W 167 E6
Brecht Belgium 51°21N 4°38E 170 C4
Breckenridge Colo.,
U.S.A. 39°29N 106°3W 304 G10
Breckenridge Minn.,
U.S.A. 46°16N 96°35W 308 B5
Breckenridge Tex., U.S.A. 32°45N 98°54W 314 E5
Breckland U.K. 52°30N 0°40E 169 E8
Brecknock, Pen. Chile 54°35S 71°30W 336 D2
Břeclav Czech Rep. 48°46N 16°53E 181 C9
Brecon U.K. 51°57N 3°23W 169 F4
Brecon Beacons U.K. 51°53N 3°26W 169 F4
Brecon Beacons △ U.K. 51°50N 3°30W 169 F4
Breda Neths. 51°35N 4°45E 170 C4
Bredaryd Sweden 57°10N 13°45E 163 G7
Bredasdorp S. Africa 34°33S 20°2E 270 D3
Bredbo Australia 35°58S 149°10E 283 C8
Brede Denmark 55°47N 12°30E 118 A3
Bredebro Denmark 55°4N 8°50E 163 J2
Bredstedt Germany 54°37N 8°55E 178 A4
Bredy Russia 52°26N 60°21E 216 B6
Bree Belgium 51°8N 5°35E 170 C5
Breezy Point U.S.A. 40°33N 73°56W 132 C2
Brega = Marsá al Burayqah
Libya 30°24N 19°37E 258 B3
Bregalnica → Macedonia 41°43N 22°9E 202 E6
Bregenz Austria 47°30N 9°45E 180 D2
Bregovo Bulgaria 44°9N 22°39E 202 B6
Bréhal France 48°53N 1°30W 172 D5
Bréhat, Î. de France 48°51N 3°0W 172 D4
Breiðafjörður Iceland 65°15N 23°15W 155 B3
Breiðdalsvík Iceland 64°44N 14°0W 155 C13
Breil-sur-Roya France 43°56N 7°31E 175 E11
Breim Norway 61°44N 6°25E 164 C3
Breisach Germany 48°1N 7°36E 179 G3
Breitenlee Austria 48°15N 16°30E 142 A3
Brejinho de Nazaré Brazil 11°1S 48°34W 332 D2
Brejo Brazil 3°41S 42°47W 332 B3
Brekke Norway 61°1N 5°26E 164 C2
Brekken Norway 62°40N 11°51E 164 B8
Brekkestø Norway 58°11N 8°22E 164 F5
Bremanger Norway 61°51N 4°58E 164 C1
Bremangerlandet Norway 61°51N 5°0E 164 C1
Bremen Bremen, Germany 53°4N 8°47E 178 B4
Bremen Ga., U.S.A. 33°43N 85°9W 316 B4
Bremen Ind., U.S.A. 41°27N 86°9W 311 C10
Bremen □ Germany 53°4N 8°50E 178 B4
Bremer Bay Australia 34°21S 119°20E 279 F2
Bremer I. Australia 12°5S 136°45E 280 A2
Bremerhaven Germany 53°33N 8°36E 178 B4
Bremersdorp = Manzini
Swaziland 26°30S 31°25E 271 C5
Bremerton U.S.A. 47°34N 122°37W 306 C4
Bremervörde Germany 53°29N 9°8E 178 B5
Bremnes Norway 59°47N 5°8E 164 E2
Bremsnes Norway 63°6N 7°40E 164 A4
Breña Peru 12°3S 77°3W 124 B2
Brenes Spain 37°32N 5°54W 195 H5
Brenham U.S.A. 30°10N 96°24W 314 F6
Brenne France 46°44N 1°14E 174 B5
Brenne △ France 46°40N 1°15E 174 B5
Brennerpass Austria 47°2N 11°30E 180 D4
Brennhaug Norway 61°54N 9°21E 164 C6
Breno Italy 45°57N 10°18E 198 C7
Brent U.S.A. 32°56N 87°10W 315 E11
Brent □ U.K. 51°33N 0°16W 125 A2
Brent Res. U.K. 51°34N 0°14W 125 A2
Brenta → Italy 45°11N 12°18E 199 C9
Brentford U.K. 51°28N 0°18W 125 B2
Brentwood Essex, U.K. 51°37N 0°19E 169 F8
Brentwood Calif., U.S.A. 34°3N 118°28W 126 B2
Brentwood Calif., U.S.A. 37°56N 121°42W 306 H5
Brentwood N.Y., U.S.A. 40°47N 73°15W 313 F11
Brentwood Park U.S.A. 34°3N 118°29W 126 B2
Brera Italy 45°28N 9°11E 128 B2
Brereton Barbados 13°7N 59°30W 323 r
Bréscia Italy 45°33N 10°15E 198 C7
Breskens Neths. 51°23N 3°33E 170 C3
Breslau = Wrocław Poland 51°5N 17°5E 185 G4
Bresle → France 50°4N 1°22E 172 B8
Bressanone Italy 46°43N 11°39E 199 B8
Bressay U.K. 60°9N 1°6W 167 A7
Bresse France 46°50N 5°10E 173 F12
Bresso Italy 45°32N 9°11E 128 A2
Bressuire France 46°51N 0°30W 172 F6
Brest Belarus 52°10N 23°40E 177 B12
Brest Finistère, France 48°24N 4°31W 172 D2
Brest □ Belarus 52°30N 26°10E 177 B13
Brest-Litovsk = Brest
Belarus 52°10N 23°40E 177 B12
Bretagne □ France 48°10N 3°0W 172 D3
Bretanha, Pta. da Azores 37°54N 25°47W 153 d3
Bretçu Romania 46°7N 26°18E 183 D11
Bretenoux France 44°54N 1°51E 174 D5
Breteuil Eure, France 48°50N 0°57E 172 D7
Breteuil Oise, France 49°38N 2°18E 173 C9
Breton Canada 53°7N 114°28W 296 C6
Breton, Pertuis France 46°17N 1°25W 174 B2
Breton Sd. U.S.A. 29°35N 89°15W 315 G10
Brett, C. N.Z. 35°10S 174°20E 284 B3
Bretten Germany 49°2N 8°42E 179 F4
Breueh Indonesia 5°44N 95°3E 234 A1
Breuil-Cervinia Italy 45°56N 7°38E 198 C4
Brevard U.S.A. 35°14N 82°44W 315 D13
Breves Brazil 1°40S 50°29W 332 B1
Brevig Mission U.S.A. 65°20N 166°29W 303 D6
Brevik Telemark, Norway 59°4N 9°42E 164 E6
Brevik Stockholm, Sweden 59°20N 18°12E 139 A3
Břevnov Czech Rep. 50°4N 14°22E 135 B2
Brewarrina Australia 30°0S 146°51E 281 E4
Brewer U.S.A. 44°48N 68°46W 309 C19
Brewer, Mt. U.S.A. 36°44N 118°28W 306 J8
Brewerville Liberia 6°26N 10°47W 262 D2
Brewster N.Y., U.S.A. 41°24N 73°36W 313 E11
Brewster Ohio, U.S.A. 40°43N 81°36W 312 F3
Brewster Wash., U.S.A. 48°6N 119°47W 304 B4
Brewster, Kap = Kangikajik
Greenland 70°7N 22°0W 154 C8
Brewton U.S.A. 31°7N 87°4W 315 F11
Breyten S. Africa 26°16S 30°0E 271 C5
Breza Bos.-H. 44°2N 18°16E 182 F3
Brežice Slovenia 45°54N 15°35E 199 C12
Brézina Algeria 33°4N 1°14E 261 B5
Březnice Czech Rep. 49°32N 13°57E 180 B6
Breznik Bulgaria 42°44N 22°55E 202 D6
Brezno Slovak Rep. 48°50N 19°40E 181 C12
Brezoi Romania 45°21N 24°15E 183 E9
Brezovica Kosovo 42°15N 21°3E 202 D5
Brezovo Bulgaria 42°21N 25°5E 203 D9
Bria C.A.R. 6°30N 21°58E 264 A4
Briançon France 44°54N 6°39E 175 D10
Briare France 47°38N 2°45E 173 E9
Briars, The St. Helena 15°56S 5°43W 153 h
Briático Italy 38°43N 16°2E 201 D9
Bribie I. Australia 27°0S 153°10E 281 D5
Bribri Costa Rica 9°38N 82°50W 320 E3
Briceni Moldova 48°22N 27°6E 183 B12
Brickyard, The U.S.A. 41°55N 87°47W 119 B2
Bricquebec France 49°28N 1°38W 172 C5
Bridge City U.S.A. 29°55N 90°9W 131 B2
Bridge of Sighs = Sospiri, Ponte dei
Venice, Italy 142 b3
Bridgehampton U.S.A. 40°56N 72°19W 313 F12
Bridgend U.K. 51°30N 3°34W 169 F4
Bridgend □ U.K. 51°36N 3°36W 169 F4
Bridgenorth Canada 44°23N 78°23W 312 B6
Bridgeport Calif., U.S.A. 38°15N 119°14W 306 G7
Bridgeport Conn., U.S.A. 41°11N 73°12W 313 E11
Bridgeport Ill., U.S.A. 41°50N 87°38W 119 B3
Bridgeport Ill., U.S.A. 38°43N 87°46W 311 F9
Bridgeport N.Y., U.S.A. 43°9N 75°58W 313 C9
Bridgeport Nebr., U.S.A. 41°40N 103°6W 308 E2
Bridgeport Tex., U.S.A. 33°13N 97°45W 314 E6
Bridger U.S.A. 45°18N 108°55W 304 D9
Bridgeton U.S.A. 39°26N 75°14W 309 F16
Bridgetown W. Austral.,
Australia 33°58S 116°7E 279 F2
Bridgetown Barbados 13°6N 59°37W 323 r
Bridgetown N.S., Canada 44°55N 65°18W 299 D6
Bridgetown Western Cape,
S. Africa 33°58S 18°33E 118 A2
Bridgeview U.S.A. 41°45N 87°48W 119 C2
Bridgewater Tas.,
Australia 42°44S 147°14E 281 G4
Bridgewater Vic.,
Australia 36°36S 143°59E 282 D5
Bridgewater N.S., Canada 44°25N 64°31W 299 D7
Bridgewater Mass.,
U.S.A. 41°59N 70°58W 313 E14
Bridgewater N.Y., U.S.A. 42°53N 75°15W 313 D9
Bridgewater, C. Australia 38°23S 141°23E 282 E4
Bridgman U.S.A. 41°57N 86°33W 311 C10
Bridgnorth U.K. 52°32N 2°25W 169 E5
Bridgton U.S.A. 44°3N 70°42W 313 B14
Bridgwater U.K. 51°8N 2°59W 169 F5
Bridgwater B. U.K. 51°15N 3°15W 169 F4
Bridlington U.K. 54°5N 0°12W 168 C7
Bridlington B. U.K. 54°4N 0°10W 168 C7
Bridport Tas., Australia 40°59S 147°23E 281 G4
Bridport Dorset, U.K. 50°44N 2°45W 169 G5
Briec France 48°6N 4°0W 172 D2
Brieg = Brzeg Poland 50°52N 17°30E 185 H4
Brienne-le-Château
France 48°24N 4°30E 173 D11
Brienon-sur-Armançon
France 47°59N 3°38E 173 E10
Brienz Switz. 46°46N 8°2E 179 J4
Brienzersee Switz. 46°44N 7°53E 179 J3
Brier Cr. → U.S.A. 32°44N 81°26W 316 C8
Brière △ France 47°22N 2°13W 172 E4
Brievengat Curaçao 12°9N 68°54W 322 g
Brig Switz. 46°18N 7°59E 179 J3
Brigg U.K. 53°34N 0°28W 168 D7
Brigham City U.S.A. 41°31N 112°1W 304 F7
Bright Australia 36°42S 146°56E 283 D7
Brighton S. Austral.,
Australia 35°5S 138°30E 282 C3
Brighton Vic., Australia 37°55S 144°59E 128 B1
Brighton Ont., Canada 44°2N 77°44W 312 B7
Brighton Trin. & Tob. 10°15N 61°39W 323 t
Brighton Brighton & Hove,
U.K. 50°49N 0°7W 169 G7
Brighton Fla., U.S.A. 27°14N 81°6W 317 H8
Brighton Ill., U.S.A. 39°2N 90°8W 310 E6
Brighton Iowa, U.S.A. 41°10N 91°49W 310 C5
Brighton Mass., U.S.A. 42°21N 71°9W 116 A2
Brighton Mich., U.S.A. 42°32N 83°47W 311 B13
Brighton N.Y., U.S.A. 43°8N 77°34W 312 C7
Brighton Beach U.S.A. 40°34N 73°57W 132 C2
Brighton-Le-Sands
Australia 33°57S 151°9E 139 B1
Brighton Park U.S.A. 41°48N 87°41W 119 C2
Brightside Canada 45°7N 76°29W 313 A8
Brightwater N.Z. 41°22S 173°9E 285 B8
Brightwood U.S.A. 38°57N 77°1W 143 B2
Brigittenau Austria 48°14N 16°22E 142 A2
Brignogan-Plage France 48°40N 4°20W 172 D2
Brignoles France 43°25N 6°5E 175 E10
Brihuega Spain 40°45N 2°52W 196 E2
Brikama Gambia 13°15N 16°45W 262 C1
Brilliant U.S.A. 40°15N 80°39W 312 F4
Brilon Germany 51°23N 8°35E 178 D4
Brim Australia 36°3S 142°27E 282 D5
Brimbank Park Australia 37°43S 144°50E 128 A1
Brimfield U.S.A. 40°50N 89°53W 310 D7
Brimstone Hill Fort
St. Kitts & Nevis 17°20N 62°50W 322 d
Brindabella △ Australia 35°14S 148°5E 283 C8
Brindisi Italy 40°39N 17°55E 201 B10
Brinje Croatia 44°59N 15°9E 199 D12
Brinkley U.S.A. 34°53N 91°12W 314 D9
Brinkworth Australia 33°42S 138°26E 282 B3
Brinnon U.S.A. 47°41N 122°54W 306 C4
Brinson U.S.A. 30°59N 84°44W 316 E5
Brion, Î. Canada 47°46N 61°26W 299 C7
Brionne France 49°11N 0°43E 172 C7
Brionski Croatia 44°55N 13°45E 199 D10
Brioude France 45°18N 3°24E 174 C7
Briouze France 48°42N 0°23W 172 D6
Brisay Canada 54°26N 70°31W 299 B5
Brisbane Queens., Australia 27°25S 153°2E 281 D5
Brisbane Calif., U.S.A. 37°40N 122°23W 136 B2
Brisbane → Australia 27°24S 153°9E 281 D5
Brisbane Ranges △
Australia 37°47S 144°16E 282 D6
Brisbane Water △
Australia 33°26S 151°13E 283 B9
Brisighella Italy 44°13N 11°46E 199 D8
Bristol Bristol, U.K. 51°26N 2°35W 169 F5
Bristol Conn., U.S.A. 41°40N 72°57W 313 E12
Bristol Fla., U.S.A. 30°26N 84°59W 316 E5
Bristol Pa., U.S.A. 40°6N 74°51W 313 F10
Bristol R.I., U.S.A. 41°40N 71°16W 313 E13
Bristol Tenn., U.S.A. 36°36N 82°11W 315 C13
Bristol Vt., U.S.A. 44°8N 73°4W 313 B11
Bristol, City of □ U.K. 51°27N 2°36W 169 F5
Bristol B. U.S.A. 58°0N 160°0W 303 H8
Bristol Channel U.K. 51°18N 4°30W 169 F3
Bristol I. Antarctica 58°45S 28°0W 151 B1
Bristol L. U.S.A. 34°28N 115°41W 307 L11
Bristow U.S.A. 35°50N 96°23W 314 D6
Bristow I. Papua N. G. 9°8S 143°14E 286 E2
Britain = Great Britain
Europe 54°0N 2°15W 158 E5
Britânia Brazil 15°14S 51°9W 331 D7
British Central Africa = Malawi ■
Africa 11°55S 34°0E 269 E3
British Columbia □
Canada 55°0N 125°15W 296 C3
British East Africa = Kenya ■
Africa 1°0N 38°0E 268 B4
British Guiana = Guyana ■
S. Amer. 5°0N 59°0W 329 C6
British Honduras = Belize ■
Cent. Amer. 17°0N 88°30W 320 C2
British Indian Ocean Terr. = Chagos
Arch. ☒ Ind. Oc. 6°0S 72°0E 211 J9
British Isles Europe 54°0N 4°0W 165 D5
British Mts. N. Amer. 68°50N 140°0W 300 B12
British Museum London, U.K. 125 a3
British Virgin Is. ☒
W. Indies 18°30N 64°30W 321 C7
Brits S. Africa 25°37S 27°48E 271 C4
Britstown S. Africa 30°37S 23°30E 270 D3
Britt Ont., Canada 45°46N 80°34W 298 C3
Britt Iowa, U.S.A. 43°6N 93°48W 310 A3
Brittany = Bretagne □
France 48°10N 3°0W 172 D3
Britton U.S.A. 45°48N 97°45W 308 C5
Britz Germany 52°26N 13°27E 115 B3
Brive-la-Gaillarde France 45°10N 1°32E 174 C5
Briviesca Spain 42°32N 3°19W 194 C7
Brixen = Bressanone Italy 46°43N 11°39E 199 B8
Brixham U.K. 50°23N 3°31W 169 G4
Brixton U.K. 51°27N 0°8W 125 B3
Brnaze Croatia 43°41N 16°40E 199 E13
Brněnský □ Czech Rep. 49°10N 16°40E 181 B9
Brno Czech Rep. 49°10N 16°35E 181 B9
Broach = Bharuch India 21°47N 73°0E 244 D1
Broad → Ga., U.S.A. 33°59N 82°39W 316 B7
Broad → S.C., U.S.A. 34°1N 81°4W 315 D14
Broad Arrow Australia 30°23S 121°15E 279 F3
Broad B. U.K. 58°14N 6°18W 167 C2
Broad Haven Ireland 54°20N 9°55W 166 B2
Broad Law U.K. 55°30N 3°21W 167 F5
Broad Pk. = Faichan Kangri
India 35°48N 76°34E 243 B7
Broad Sd. Australia 22°0S 149°45E 280 C4
Broadalbin U.S.A. 43°4N 74°12W 313 C10
Broadback → Canada 51°21N 78°52W 298 B4
Broadford Australia 37°14S 145°4E 283 D6
Broadhurst Ra. Australia 22°30S 122°30E 278 D3
Broadmeadows Australia 37°40S 144°55E 128 A1
Broadmoor U.S.A. 37°41N 122°29W 136 B2
Broads, The U.K. 52°45N 1°30E 168 E9
Broadus U.S.A. 45°27N 105°25W 304 D11
Broadview U.S.A. 41°51N 87°52W 119 B1
Broadview Park U.S.A. 26°5N 80°12W 129 B2
Broadway New York, U.S.A. 132 d2
Broager Denmark 54°53N 9°40E 163 K3
Broby Sweden 56°15N 14°4E 163 H8
Broceni Latvia 56°42N 22°32E 184 B9
Brochet Canada 57°53N 101°40W 297 B8
Brochet, L. Canada 58°36N 101°35W 297 B8
Brock I. Canada 77°52N 114°19W 295 B9
Brocken Germany 51°47N 10°37E 178 D6
Brocklehurst Australia 32°9S 148°38E 283 B8
Brocklesby Australia 35°48S 146°40E 283 C7
Brockley U.K. 51°27N 0°2W 125 B3
Brockport U.S.A. 43°13N 77°56W 312 C7
Brockton U.S.A. 42°5N 71°1W 313 D13
Brockville Canada 44°35N 75°41W 313 B9
Brockway Mont.,
U.S.A. 47°18N 105°45W 304 C11
Brockway Pa., U.S.A. 41°15N 78°47W 312 E6
Brocton U.S.A. 42°23N 79°26W 312 D5
Brod Macedonia 41°32N 21°17E 202 E5
Brodarevo Serbia 43°14N 19°44E 202 C3
Brodeur Pen. Canada 72°30N 88°10W 295 C14
Brodhead U.S.A. 42°37N 89°22W 310 B7
Brodick U.K. 55°35N 5°9W 167 F3
Brodnica Poland 53°15N 19°25E 185 E6
Bródno Poland 52°17N 21°1E 143 B2
Bródnowski, Kanal Poland 52°17N 21°3E 143 B2
Brody Ukraine 50°5N 25°10E 177 C13
Broek Neths. 52°26N 5°0E 112 A2
Brogan U.S.A. 44°15N 117°31W 304 D5
Broglie France 49°2N 0°30E 172 C7
Brok Poland 52°43N 21°52E 185 F8
Broken Arrow U.S.A. 36°3N 95°48W 314 C7

Broken Bow *Nebr., U.S.A.* 41°24N 99°38W **308** E4
Broken Bow *Okla., U.S.A.* 34°2N 94°44W **314** D7
Broken Bow Lake *U.S.A.* 34°9N 94°40W **314** D7
Broken Hill = Kabwe *Zambia* 14°30S 28°29E **269** E2
Broken Hill *Australia* 31°58S 141°29E **282** A4
Broken River Ra. *Australia* 21°0S 148°22E **280** b
Brokind *Sweden* 58°13N 15°42E **163** F9
Brokopondo *Suriname* 5°3N 54°59W **329** B7
Bromberg = Bydgoszcz *Poland* 53°10N 18°0E **185** E5
Bromley □ *U.K.* 51°24N 0°2E **125** B4
Bromley Common *U.K.* 51°22N 0°2E **125** B4
Bromma *Sweden* 59°21N 17°55E **139** A1
Bromma ✈ **(BMA)** *Sweden* 59°21N 17°56E **139** A1
Bromo Tengger Semeru △ *Indonesia* 7°56S 112°57E **235** D4
Bromölla *Sweden* 56°5N 14°28E **163** H8
Brompton *London, U.K.* **125** c2
Bromsgrove *U.K.* 52°21N 2°2W **169** E5
Bronaugh *U.S.A.* 37°41N 94°28W **310** G2
Brøndby Strand *Denmark* 55°36N 12°25E **118** B2
Brøndbyøster *Denmark* 55°39N 12°26E **118** B2
Brøndbyvester *Denmark* 55°37N 12°23E **118** B2
Brønderslev *Denmark* 57°16N 9°57E **163** G3
Brondesbury *U.K.* 51°32N 0°12W **125** A2
Brong-Ahafo □ *Ghana* 7°50N 2°0W **262** D4
Broni *Italy* 45°4N 9°16E **198** C6
Bronkhorstspruit *S. Africa* 25°46S 28°45E **271** C4
Brønnøya *Norway* 59°51N 10°32E **133** A2
Brønnøysund *Norway* 65°28N 12°14E **160** D15
Brønshøj *Denmark* 55°41N 12°29E **118** A2
Bronson *Fla., U.S.A.* 29°27N 82°39W **317** F7
Bronson *Mich., U.S.A.* 41°52N 85°12W **311** C11
Bronte *Italy* 37°47N 14°50E **201** E7
Bronwood *U.S.A.* 31°50N 84°22W **316** D5
Bronxville *U.S.A.* 40°56N 73°49W **132** A3
Brook Park *U.S.A.* 41°23N 81°48W **312** E4
Brooke's Point *Phil.* 8°47N 117°50E **233** G1
Brookfield *Mo., U.S.A.* 39°47N 93°4W **310** E3
Brookfield *Wis., U.S.A.* 43°4N 88°9W **311** A8
Brookfield Zoo *U.S.A.* 41°50N 87°50W **119** B1
Brookhaven *Georgia, U.S.A.* 33°52N 84°19W **113** A2
Brookhaven *Miss., U.S.A.* 31°35N 90°26W **315** F9
Brookings *Oreg., U.S.A.* 42°3N 124°17W **304** E1
Brookings *S. Dak., U.S.A.* 44°19N 96°48W **308** C5
Brookland = West Columbia *U.S.A.* 33°59N 81°4W **316** B8
Brooklet *U.S.A.* 32°23N 81°40W **316** C8
Brooklin *Canada* 43°55N 78°55W **312** C6
Brookline *U.S.A.* 42°19N 71°8W **116** B2
Brooklyn *Western Cape, S. Africa* 33°54S 18°29E **118** A1
Brooklyn *Iowa, U.S.A.* 41°44N 92°27W **310** C4
Brooklyn *N.Y., U.S.A.* 40°37N 73°57W **132** C2
Brooklyn-Battery Tunnel *New York, U.S.A.* **132** f1
Brooklyn Bridge *New York, U.S.A.* **132** f2
Brooklyn Heights *New York, U.S.A.* **132** f2
Brooklyn Park *U.S.A.* 45°6N 93°23W **308** C7
Brookmont *U.S.A.* 38°57N 77°7W **143** B2
Brooks *Canada* 50°35N 111°55W **296** C6
Brooks Range *U.S.A.* 68°0N 152°0W **303** C9
Brookston *U.S.A.* 40°36N 86°52W **311** D10
Brooksville *Fla., U.S.A.* 28°33N 82°23W **317** G7
Brooksville *Ky., U.S.A.* 38°41N 84°4W **311** F12
Brookton *Australia* 32°22S 117°0E **279** F2
Brookville *Ind., U.S.A.* 39°25N 85°1W **311** E12
Brookville *Ohio, U.S.A.* 39°50N 84°24W **311** E12
Brookville *Pa., U.S.A.* 41°10N 79°5W **312** E5
Brookville L. *U.S.A.* 39°28N 85°0W **311** E11
Broom, L. *U.K.* 57°55N 5°15W **167** D3
Broome *Australia* 18°0S 122°15E **278** C3
Broons *France* 48°20N 2°16W **172** D4
Brora *U.K.* 58°0N 3°52W **167** C5
Brora → *U.K.* 58°0N 3°51W **167** C5
Brørup *Denmark* 55°29N 9°1E **163** J2
Brösarp *Sweden* 55°43N 14°6E **163** J8
Brosna → *Ireland* 53°14N 7°58W **166** C4
Brossard *Canada* 45°27N 73°28W **130** B3
Broşteni *Mehedinţi, Romania* 44°45N 22°59E **182** F7
Broşteni *Suceava, Romania* 47°14N 25°43E **183** C10
Brøsterud *Norway* 60°18N 8°34E **164** D5
Brotas de Macaúbas *Brazil* 12°0S 42°38W **333** D3
Brothers *U.S.A.* 43°49N 120°36W **304** E3
Brothers, The *Yemen* 12°8N 53°10E **249** D6
Brøttum *Norway* 61°2N 10°34E **164** C7
Brou *France* 48°13N 1°11E **172** D8
Brou-sur-Chantereine *France* 48°53N 2°37E **134** A4
Brouage *France* 45°52N 1°4W **174** C2
Brough *U.K.* 54°32N 2°18W **168** C5
Brough Hd. *U.K.* 59°8N 3°20W **167** B5
Broughton *U.S.A.* 37°56N 88°27W **311** G8
Broughton Island = Qikiqtarjuaq *Canada* 67°33N 63°0W **295** D19
Broumov *Czech Rep.* 50°35N 16°20E **181** A9
Brovary *Ukraine* 50°34N 30°48E **189** G6
Brovst *Denmark* 57°6N 9°31E **163** G3
Brown *Canada* 43°48N 79°14W **141** A3
Brown, L. *Australia* 31°5S 118°15E **279** F2
Brown, Mt. *Australia* 32°30S 138°0E **282** B3
Brown, Pt. *Australia* 32°32S 133°50E **281** E1
Brown City *U.S.A.* 43°13N 82°59W **312** C2
Brown Willy *U.K.* 50°35N 4°37W **169** G3
Brownfield *U.S.A.* 33°11N 102°17W **314** E3
Browning *Ill., U.S.A.* 40°8N 90°22W **310** D6
Browning *Mo., U.S.A.* 40°3N 93°12W **310** D3
Browning *Mont., U.S.A.* 48°34N 113°1W **304** B7
Browns Town *Jamaica* 18°24N 77°22W **320** a
Brownsburg *U.S.A.* 39°51N 86°24W **311** E10
Brownstown *U.S.A.* 38°53N 86°3W **311** F10
Brownsville *Fla., U.S.A.* 25°49N 80°15W **129** D1
Brownsville *Oreg., U.S.A.* 44°24N 122°59W **304** D2
Brownsville *Pa., U.S.A.* 40°1N 79°53W **312** F5
Brownsville *Tenn., U.S.A.* 35°36N 89°16W **315** D10
Brownsville *Tex., U.S.A.* 25°54N 97°30W **314** J6
Brownsweg *Suriname* 5°5N 55°15W **329** B6
Brownville *U.S.A.* 44°0N 75°59W **313** C9
Brownwood *U.S.A.* 31°43N 98°59W **314** F5
Browse I. *Australia* 14°7S 123°33E **278** B3
Broxton *U.S.A.* 31°38N 82°53W **316** D7
Bru *Norway* 61°32N 5°11E **164** C2
Bruas *Malaysia* 4°30N 100°47E **237** K3
Bruay-la-Buissière *France* 50°29N 2°33E **173** B9
Bruce *U.S.A.* 30°28N 85°58W **316** E4
Bruce, Mt. *Australia* 22°37S 118°8E **278** D2
Bruce B. *N.Z.* 43°35S 169°42E **285** D4
Bruce Pen. *Canada* 45°0N 81°30W **312** B3
Bruce Peninsula △ *Canada* 45°14N 81°36W **312** A3
Bruce Rock *Australia* 31°52S 118°8E **279** F2
Bruche → *France* 48°34N 7°43E **173** D14
Bruchsal *Germany* 49°7N 8°35E **179** F4
Bruck an der Leitha *Austria* 48°1N 16°47E **181** C9
Bruck an der Mur *Austria* 47°24N 15°16E **180** D8
Brue → *U.K.* 51°13N 2°59W **169** F5
Bruflat *Norway* 60°53N 9°37E **164** D6
Bruges = Brugge *Belgium* 51°13N 3°13E **170** C3
Brugg *Switz.* 47°29N 8°11E **179** H4
Brugge *Belgium* 51°13N 3°13E **170** C3
Brughério *Italy* 45°33N 9°17E **128** A2
Bruin *U.S.A.* 41°3N 79°43W **312** E5
Bruini *India* 29°10N 96°11E **241** A6
Bruit, Pulau *Malaysia* 2°35N 111°20E **235** B4
Brûk, W. el → *Egypt* 30°15N 33°50E **251** H4
Bruksvallarna *Sweden* 62°38N 12°27E **162** B6
Brûlé *Canada* 53°15N 117°58W **296** C5
Brûlé, L. *Canada* 53°35N 64°4W **299** B7
Brûlon *France* 47°58N 0°15W **172** E6
Brumado *Brazil* 14°14S 41°40W **333** D3
Brumado → *Brazil* 14°13S 41°40W **333** D3
Brumath *France* 48°43N 7°40E **173** D14
Brumunddal *Norway* 60°53N 10°56E **164** D7
Brundidge *U.S.A.* 31°43N 85°49W **316** D4
Bruneau *U.S.A.* 42°53N 115°48W **304** E6
Bruneau → *U.S.A.* 42°56N 115°57W **304** E6
Bruneck = Brunico *Italy* 46°48N 11°56E **199** B8
Brunei = Bandar Seri Begawan *Brunei* 4°52N 115°0E **235** B4
Brunei ■ *Asia* 4°50N 115°0E **235** B4
Brunflo *Sweden* 63°5N 14°50E **162** A8
Brunico *Italy* 46°48N 11°56E **199** B8
Brünn = Brno *Czech Rep.* 49°10N 16°35E **181** B9
Brunnen *Switz.* 46°59N 8°37E **179** J4
Brunner, L. *N.Z.* 42°37S 171°27E **285** C6
Brunnhóll *Iceland* 64°17N 15°26W **155** C11
Brunnsberg *Sweden* 61°17N 13°56E **162** C8
Brunsbüttel *Germany* 53°53N 9°6E **178** B5
Brunssum *Neths.* 50°57N 5°59E **170** D5
Brunswick = Braunschweig *Germany* 52°15N 10°31E **178** C6
Brunswick *Vic., Australia* 37°45S 144°57E **128** A1
Brunswick *Ga., U.S.A.* 31°10N 81°30W **316** D8
Brunswick *Maine, U.S.A.* 43°55N 69°58W **309** D19
Brunswick *Md., U.S.A.* 39°19N 77°38W **309** F15
Brunswick *Mo., U.S.A.* 39°26N 93°8W **310** E3
Brunswick *Ohio, U.S.A.* 41°14N 81°51W **312** E3
Brunswick, Pen. de *Chile* 53°30S 71°30W **336** D2
Brunswick B. *Australia* 15°15S 124°50E **278** C3
Brunswick Junction *Australia* 33°15S 115°50E **279** F2
Brunt Ice Shelf *Antarctica* 75°30S 25°0W **151** D2
Bruntál *Czech Rep.* 49°59N 17°27E **181** B10
Brus Laguna *Honduras* 15°47N 84°35W **320** C3
Brusa = Bursa *Turkey* 40°15N 29°5E **203** F13
Brusartsi *Bulgaria* 43°40N 23°5E **202** C7
Brush *U.S.A.* 40°15N 103°37W **304** F12
Brushton *U.S.A.* 44°50N 74°31W **313** B10
Brusio *Switz.* 46°14N 10°8E **179** J6
Brusque *Brazil* 27°5S 49°0W **335** B6
Brussegem *Belgium* 50°56N 4°16E **116** A1
Brussel *Belgium* 50°51N 4°21E **116** A2
Brussel ✈ **(BRU)** *Belgium* 50°54N 4°29E **116** A2
Brussels = Brussel *Belgium* 50°51N 4°21E **116** A2
Brussels *Canada* 43°44N 81°15W **312** C3
Brusy *Poland* 53°53N 17°43E **184** E4
Bruthen *Australia* 37°42S 147°50E **283** D7
Bruvoll *Norway* 60°27N 11°29E **164** D8
Bruxelles = Brussel *Belgium* 50°51N 4°21E **116** A2
Bruyères *France* 48°10N 6°40E **173** D13
Bruz *France* 48°1N 1°46W **172** D5
Bruzzano *Italy* 45°31N 9°10E **128** A2
Brwinów *Poland* 52°9N 20°40E **185** F7
Bry-sur-Marne *France* 48°50N 2°32E **134** A4
Bryagovo *Bulgaria* 41°58N 25°8E **203** E9
Bryan *Ohio, U.S.A.* 41°28N 84°33W **311** C12
Bryan *Tex., U.S.A.* 30°40N 96°22W **314** F6
Bryan, L. *U.S.A.* 28°22N 81°29W **133** B2
Bryan, Mt. *Australia* 33°30S 139°5E **282** B3
Bryanka *Ukraine* 48°32N 38°45E **189** H10
Bryansk *Bryansk, Russia* 53°13N 34°25E **189** F8
Bryansk *Dagestan, Russia* 44°20N 47°10E **191** H8
Bryansk □ *Russia* 53°10N 33°10E **189** F7
Bryanskoye = Bryansk *Russia* 44°20N 47°10E **191** H8
Bryanston *S. Africa* 26°4S 28°0E **123** A1
Bryant Park *New York, U.S.A.* **132** c2
Bryce Canyon △ *U.S.A.* 37°30N 112°10W **305** H7
Bryn *Norway* 59°55N 10°27E **133** A1
Bryne *Norway* 58°44N 5°38E **164** F2
Bryson City *U.S.A.* 35°26N 83°27W **315** D13
Bryukhovetskaya *Russia* 45°48N 39°0E **189** K10
Brza Palanka *Serbia* 44°28N 22°27E **202** B6
Brzeg *Poland* 50°52N 17°30E **185** H4
Brzeg Dolny *Poland* 51°16N 16°41E **185** G3
Brześć Kujawski *Poland* 52°36N 18°55E **185** F5
Brzešč nad Bugiem = Brest *Belarus* 52°10N 23°40E **177** B12
Brzesko *Poland* 49°59N 20°34E **185** J7
Brzeziny *Łódzkie, Poland* 51°49N 19°42E **185** G6
Brzeziny *Warszawa, Poland* 52°19N 21°2E **143** B2
Brzozów *Poland* 49°41N 22°3E **185** J9
Bsharri *Lebanon* 34°15N 36°0E **250** D7
Bū al Ḩijān, W. → *Libya* 27°25N 19°22E **258** C3
Bū Athlah *Libya* 30°9N 15°39E **258** B3
Bū Baqarah *U.A.E.* 25°35N 56°25E **247** E8
Bu Craa *W. Sahara* 26°45N 12°50W **260** C2
Bū Ḩasā *U.A.E.* 23°30N 53°20E **247** F7
Bū Tummayyim, W. → *Libya* 26°56N 19°13E **258** C3
Bua *Fiji* 16°48S 178°37E **287** A2
Bua *Sweden* 57°14N 12°7E **163** G6
Bua → *Malaysia* 12°45S 34°16E **269** E3
Bua Yai *Thailand* 15°33N 102°26E **236** E4
Bu'aale *Somalia* 1°5N 42°35E **267** D5
Buad I. *Phil.* 11°40N 124°51E **233** F5
Buala *Solomon Is.* 8°10S 159°35E **287** M10
Buan *S. Korea* 35°44N 126°44E **224** E3
Buapinang *Indonesia* 4°40S 121°30E **231** E6
Buatan *Indonesia* 0°44N 101°49E **234** B2
Buayan = General Santos *Phil.* 6°5N 125°14E **233** H5
Buba *Guinea-Biss.* 11°40N 14°59W **262** C2
Bubali Bird Sanctuary *Aruba* 12°33N 70°2W **322** f
Bubanda *Dem. Rep. of the Congo* 4°14N 19°38E **264** B3
Bubanza *Burundi* 3°6S 29°23E **268** C2
Bubaque *Guinea-Biss.* 11°16N 15°51W **262** C1
Bube *Ethiopia* 8°46N 35°48E **257** F4
Bubeneč *Czech Rep.* 50°6N 14°24E **135** B2
Bubi → *Zimbabwe* 22°20S 31°7E **271** B5
Būbiyān *Kuwait* 29°45N 48°15E **247** D6
Buc *France* 48°46N 2°7E **134** B1
Buca *Fiji* 16°38S 179°52E **287** A2
Buca *Turkey* 38°22N 27°11E **205** C9
Bucaco *Angola* 11°26S 20°10E **265** E4
Bucak *Turkey* 37°28N 30°36E **205** D12
Bucakkışla *Turkey* 36°57N 33°1E **250** B4
Bucaramanga *Colombia* 7°0N 73°0W **328** B3
Bucas Grande I. *Phil.* 9°40N 125°57E **233** G5
Bucasia *Australia* 21°2S 149°10E **280** b
Bucay *Phil.* 17°32N 120°43E **232** C3
Buccaneer Arch. *Australia* 16°7S 123°20E **278** C3
Buccino *Italy* 40°38N 15°22E **201** B8
Buccoo Reef *Trin. & Tob.* 11°10N 60°51W **323** s
Bucecea *Romania* 47°47N 26°28E **183** C11
Bucegi △ *Romania* 45°25N 25°25E **183** E10
Buchach *Ukraine* 49°5N 25°25E **177** D13
Buchan *Vic., Australia* 37°30S 148°12E **283** D8
Buchan *Aberds., U.K.* 57°32N 2°21W **167** D6
Buchan Ness *U.K.* 57°29N 1°46W **167** D7
Buchanan *Sask., Canada* 51°40N 102°45W **297** C8
Buchanan *Liberia* 5°57N 10°2W **262** D2
Buchanan *Ga., U.S.A.* 33°48N 85°11W **316** B4
Buchanan *Mich., U.S.A.* 41°50N 86°22W **311** C10
Buchanan, L. *Queens., Australia* 21°35S 145°52E **280** C4
Buchanan, L. *W. Austral., Australia* 25°33S 123°2E **279** E3
Buchanan, L. *Tex., U.S.A.* 30°45N 98°25W **314** F5
Buchanan Cr. → *Australia* 19°13S 136°33E **280** B2
Buchans *Canada* 48°50N 56°52W **299** C8
Bucharest = Bucureşti *Romania* 44°27N 26°10E **183** F11
Buchen *Germany* 49°32N 9°20E **179** F5
Buchenhain *Germany* 48°1N 11°29E **131** B1
Bucheon *S. Korea* 37°28N 126°45E **224** D3
Buchholz *Berlin, Germany* 52°36N 13°25E **115** A3
Buchholz *Niedersachsen, Germany* 53°19N 9°52E **178** B5
Buchloe *Germany* 48°1N 10°44E **179** G6
Buchon, Pt. *U.S.A.* 35°15N 120°54W **306** K6
Buciumi *Romania* 47°3N 23°1E **182** C8
Buck Hill Falls *U.S.A.* 41°11N 75°16W **313** E9
Bückeburg *Germany* 52°16N 9°7E **178** C5
Buckeye Lake *U.S.A.* 39°55N 82°29W **312** G2
Buckhannon *U.S.A.* 39°0N 80°8W **309** F13
Buckhaven *U.K.* 56°11N 3°3W **167** E5
Buckhead *U.S.A.* 33°51N 84°24W **113** A2
Buckhorn L. *Canada* 44°29N 78°23W **312** B6
Buckie *U.K.* 57°41N 2°58W **167** D6
Buckingham *Qué., Canada* 45°37N 75°24W **298** C4
Buckingham *Bucks., U.K.* 51°59N 0°57W **169** F7
Buckingham B. *Australia* 12°10S 135°40E **280** A2
Buckingham Canal *India* 14°0N 80°5E **245** H5
Buckingham Fountain *U.S.A.* **119** d2
Buckingham Palace *London, U.K.* **125** b3
Buckinghamshire □ *U.K.* 51°53N 0°55W **169** F7
Buckland *U.S.A.* 65°59N 161°8W **303** D7
Buckle Hd. *Australia* 14°26S 127°52E **278** B4
Buckleboo *Australia* 32°54S 136°12E **282** B2
Buckley *Flints., U.K.* 53°10N 3°5W **168** D4
Buckley *Ill., U.S.A.* 40°36N 88°2W **311** D8
Buckley → *Australia* 20°10S 138°49E **280** C2
Bucklin *Kans., U.S.A.* 37°33N 99°38W **308** G4
Bucklin *Mo., U.S.A.* 39°47N 92°53W **310** E4
Buckow *Germany* 52°25N 13°26E **115** B3
Bucks L. *U.S.A.* 39°54N 121°12W **306** F5
Bucktown *U.S.A.* 30°1N 90°8W **131** A2
Buco Zau *Angola* 4°46S 12°33E **265** C2
Bucquoy *France* 50°9N 2°43E **173** B9
Bucureşti *Romania* 44°27N 26°10E **183** F11
Bucureşti Otopeni ✈ **(OTP)** *Romania* 44°30N 26°11E **183** F11
Bucyrus *U.S.A.* 40°48N 82°59W **311** D14
Bud *Norway* 62°55N 6°55E **164** B3
Bud Bud *Somalia* 4°11N 46°28E **267** D6
Buda *Hungary* 47°30N 19°2E **117** A2
Buda Castle = Budaváripalota *Budapest, Hungary* **117** b2
Budacu, Vf. *Romania* 47°7N 25°41E **183** C10
Budafok *Hungary* 47°25N 19°2E **117** B2
Budalin *Burma* 22°20N 95°10E **241** D5
Budaörs *Hungary* 47°27N 18°57E **117** B1
Budapest *Hungary* 47°29N 19°3E **117** B2
Budapest □ *Hungary* 47°29N 19°5E **182** C4
Budapest ✈ **(BUD)** *Hungary* 47°26N 19°14E **117** B3
Budatétény *Hungary* 47°25N 19°1E **117** B2
Budaun *India* 28°5N 79°10E **243** E8
Budaváripalota *Budapest, Hungary* **117** b2
Budawang △ *Australia* 35°10S 150°12E **283** C9
Budd Coast *Antarctica* 68°0S 112°0E **151** C8
Buddenbrock = Brodnica *Poland* 53°15N 19°25E **185** E6
Budderoo △ *Australia* 35°40S 150°41E **283** C9
Buddinge *Denmark* 55°44N 12°30E **118** A3
Buddusò *Italy* 40°35N 9°15E **200** B2
Bude *U.K.* 50°49N 4°34W **169** G3
Budennovsk *Russia* 44°50N 44°10E **191** H7
Budeşti *Romania* 44°13N 26°30E **183** F11
Budeyi *Ukraine* 48°3N 29°16E **183** B14
Budge Budge = Baj Baj *India* 22°30N 88°5E **243** H13
Budgewoi *Australia* 33°13S 151°34E **283** B9
Búðardalur *Iceland* 65°7N 21°46W **155** B5
Budia *Spain* 40°38N 2°46W **196** E2
Büdingen *Germany* 50°16N 9°7E **179** E5
Budjala *Dem. Rep. of the Congo* 2°50N 19°40E **264** B3
Budo-Sungai Padi △ *Thailand* 6°19N 101°42E **237** J3
Budokan *Tokyo, Japan* **140** a4
Budoni *Italy* 40°40N 9°45E **200** B2
Búdrio *Italy* 44°32N 11°32E **199** D8
Bűdszentmihály = Tiszavasvári *Hungary* 47°58N 21°18E **182** C6
Budva *Montenegro* 42°17N 18°50E **202** D2
Budweis = České Budějovice *Czech Rep.* 48°55N 14°25E **180** C7
Budyonnovka = Novoazovsk *Ukraine* 47°15N 38°4E **189** J10
Budzyń *Poland* 52°54N 16°59E **185** F3
Bue *Norway* 58°40N 5°58E **164** F2
Buea *Cameroon* 4°10N 9°9E **263** E6
Buela *Angola* 5°54S 14°40E **265** D2
Buellton *U.S.A.* 34°37N 120°12W **307** L6
Buena Esperanza *Argentina* 34°45S 65°15W **334** C2
Buena Park *U.S.A.* 33°52N 117°59W **307** M9
Buena Vista *Bolivia* 17°27S 63°40W **331** D5
Buena Vista *Curaçao* 12°8N 68°57W **322** g
Buena Vista *Solomon Is.* 8°52S 160°3E **287** M11
Buena Vista *Colo., U.S.A.* 38°51N 106°8W **304** G10
Buena Vista *Ga., U.S.A.* 32°19N 84°31W **316** C5
Buena Vista *Va., U.S.A.* 37°44N 79°21W **309** G14
Buena Vista Lake Bed *U.S.A.* 35°12N 119°18W **307** K7
Buenaventura *Colombia* 3°53N 77°4W **328** C2
Buenaventura *Chihuahua, Mexico* 29°51N 107°29W **318** B3
Buenaventura, B. de *Colombia* 3°48N 77°17W **328** C2
Buenavista *Agusan del N., Phil.* 8°59N 125°24E **233** G5
Buenavista *Quezon, Phil.* 13°35N 122°34E **232** E4
Buendía, Embalse de *Spain* 40°25N 2°43W **196** E2
Buenópolis *Brazil* 17°54S 44°11W **333** E3
Buenos Aires *Argentina* 34°36S 58°22W **117** B2
Buenos Aires *Colombia* 1°36N 73°18W **328** C3
Buenos Aires *Costa Rica* 9°10N 83°20W **320** E3
Buenos Aires □ *Argentina* 36°30S 60°0W **334** D4
Buenos Aires, L. = General Carrera, L. *S. Amer.* 46°35S 72°0W **336** C2
Buenos Aires Ezeiza ✈ **(EZE)** *Argentina* 34°49S 58°32W **117** C1
Buenos Ayres *Trin. & Tob.* 10°6N 61°41W **323** t
Buesaco *Colombia* 1°23N 77°9W **328** C2
Bufalotta *Italy* 41°59N 12°33E **136** B2
Buff Bay *Jamaica* 18°14N 76°40W **320** a
Buffalo *Mo., U.S.A.* 37°39N 93°6W **310** G3
Buffalo *N.Y., U.S.A.* 42°53N 78°53W **312** D6
Buffalo *Okla., U.S.A.* 36°50N 99°38W **314** C5
Buffalo *S. Dak., U.S.A.* 45°35N 103°33W **308** C2
Buffalo *Wyo., U.S.A.* 44°21N 106°42W **304** D10
Buffalo → *Alta., Canada* 60°5N 115°5W **296** A5
Buffalo → *S. Africa* 28°43S 30°37E **271** C5
Buffalo ⌓ *U.S.A.* 36°14N 92°36W **314** C8
Buffalo Head Hills *Canada* 57°25N 115°55W **296** B5
Buffalo L. *Alta., Canada* 52°27N 112°54W **296** C6
Buffalo L. *N.W.T., Canada* 60°12N 115°25W **296** A5
Buffalo Narrows *Canada* 55°51N 108°29W **297** B7
Buffalo Springs ⌓ *Kenya* 0°32N 37°35E **268** B4
Buffels → *S. Africa* 29°36S 17°3E **270** C2
Buford *U.S.A.* 34°7N 83°59W **316** A6
Bug = Buh → *Ukraine* 46°59N 31°58E **189** J6
Bug → *Poland* 52°31N 21°5E **185** F8
Buga *Colombia* 4°0N 76°15W **328** C2
Bugala I. *Uganda* 0°40S 32°20E **268** C3
Buganda *Uganda* 0°0 31°30E **268** C3
Buganga *Uganda* 0°3S 32°0E **268** C3
Bugasong *Phil.* 11°3N 122°4E **233** F4
Bugda Acable *Somalia* 4°4N 45°15E **267** D6
Bugeat *France* 45°36N 1°55E **174** C5
Bugel, Tanjung *Indonesia* 6°26S 111°3E **235** D4
Búger *Spain* 39°45N 2°59E **206** B3
Bugibba *Malta* 35°57N 14°25E **206** F7
Bugio *Portugal* 38°39N 9°18W **126** B1
Bugojno *Bos.-H.* 44°2N 17°25E **182** F2
Bugsuk I. *Phil.* 8°12N 117°18E **233** G1
Buguey *Phil.* 18°17N 121°50E **232** B3
Buguias *Phil.* 16°43N 120°50E **232** C3
Bugulma *Russia* 54°33N 52°48E **186** D9
Buguma *Nigeria* 4°42N 6°55E **263** E6
Bugungu ⌓ *Uganda* 2°17N 31°50E **268** B3
Buguruslan *Russia* 53°39N 52°26E **186** D9
Buh → *Ukraine* 46°59N 31°58E **189** J6
Buharkent *Turkey* 37°58N 28°44E **205** D10
Buheirat-Murrat-el-Kubra *Egypt* 30°18N 32°26E **256** H8
Buhera *Zimbabwe* 19°18S 31°29E **271** A5
Bühl *Baden-W., Germany* 48°40N 8°8E **179** G4
Buhl *Idaho, U.S.A.* 42°36N 114°46W **304** E6
Buhuşi *Romania* 46°41N 26°45E **183** D11
Bui △ *Ghana* 8°21N 2°21W **262** D4
Buiksloot *Neths.* 52°24N 4°55E **112** A2
Builth Wells *U.K.* 52°9N 3°25W **169** E4
Buin *Papua N. G.* 6°48S 155°42E **287** L8
Buinsk *Russia* 55°0N 48°18E **190** C9
Buíque *Brazil* 8°37S 37°9W **332** C4
Buir Nur *Mongolia* 47°50N 117°42E **219** B12
Buis-les-Baronnies *France* 44°17N 5°16E **175** D9
Buitenveldert *Neths.* 52°20N 4°53E **112** B2
Buitenzorg = Bogor *Indonesia* 6°36S 106°48E **234** D3
Buitrago del Lozoya *Spain* 40°58N 3°38W **194** E7
Buizingen *Belgium* 50°44N 4°15E **116** B1
Bujalance *Spain* 37°54N 4°23W **195** H6
Bujanovac *Serbia* 42°28N 21°44E **202** D5
Bujaraloz *Spain* 41°29N 0°10W **196** D4
Buje *Croatia* 45°24N 13°39E **199** C10
Buji *China* 22°37N 114°5E **219** a
Bujumbura *Burundi* 3°16S 29°18E **268** C2
Bük *Hungary* 47°22N 16°45E **182** C1
Buk *Poland* 52°21N 16°30E **185** F3
Buka I. *Papua N. G.* 5°10S 154°35E **286** C8
Bukachacha *Russia* 52°55N 116°50E **215** D12
Bukama *Dem. Rep. of the Congo* 9°10S 25°50E **269** D2
Bukavu *Dem. Rep. of the Congo* 2°20S 28°52E **268** C2
Bukene *Tanzania* 4°15S 32°48E **268** C3
Bukhansan *S. Korea* 37°38N 126°58E **137** B1
Bukhara = Buxoro *Uzbekistan* 39°48N 64°25E **216** E6
Bukhoro = Buxoro *Uzbekistan* 39°48N 64°25E **216** E6
Bukhtarma Res. = Zaysan Köli *Kazakhstan* 48°0N 83°0E **217** C10
Bukidnon □ *Phil.* 8°0N 125°0E **233** G5
Bukima *Tanzania* 1°50S 33°25E **268** C3
Bukit Baka Bukit Raya △ *Indonesia* 0°43S 112°40E **235** C4
Bukit Barisan Selatan △ *Indonesia* 5°8S 104°4E **234** D2
Bukit Bendera *Malaysia* 5°25N 100°15E **237** c
Bukit Duabelas △ *Indonesia* 2°3S 102°48E **234** C2
Bukit Mertajam *Malaysia* 5°22N 100°28E **237** c
Bukit Nil *Malaysia* 1°22N 104°12E **237** d
Bukit Panjang *Singapore* 1°23N 103°46E **138** A2
Bukit Panjang Nature Reserve *Singapore* 1°22N 103°45E **138** A2
Bukit Tengah *Malaysia* 5°22N 100°25E **237** c
Bukit Tigapuluh △ *Indonesia* 1°15S 102°25E **234** C2
Bukit Timah Nature Reserve *Singapore* 1°20N 103°47E **138** A2
Bukitkemuning *Indonesia* 4°51S 104°33E **234** C2
Bukittinggi *Indonesia* 0°20S 100°20E **234** C2
Bükk *Hungary* 48°0N 20°30E **182** B5
Bukkapatnam *India* 14°14N 77°46E **245** G3
Bükki △ *Hungary* 48°3N 20°30E **182** B5
Bukoba *Tanzania* 1°20S 31°49E **268** C3
Bukum, Pulau *Singapore* 1°14N 103°46E **138** B2
Bukuru *Nigeria* 9°42N 8°48E **263** D6
Bukuya *Uganda* 0°40N 31°52E **268** B3
Būl, Kuh-e *Iran* 30°48N 52°45E **247** D7
Bula *Guinea-Biss.* 12°7N 15°43W **262** C1
Bula *Indonesia* 3°6S 130°30E **231** E8
Bula *Camarines S., Phil.* 13°28N 123°16E **232** E4
Bula-Atumba *Angola* 8°41S 14°52E **265** D2
Bulabog-Putian △ *Phil.* 11°2N 122°4E **233** F4
Bulacan □ *Phil.* 15°0N 121°5E **232** D3
Bülach *Switz.* 47°31N 8°32E **179** H4
Būlaevo *Kazakhstan* 54°54N 70°26E **217** B8
Bulahdelah *Australia* 32°23S 152°13E **283** B10
Bulalacao *Phil.* 12°31N 121°26E **232** E3
Bulan *Phil.* 12°40N 123°52E **232** E4
Bulancak *Turkey* 40°56N 38°14E **213** B8
Búland *Iceland* 63°46N 18°30W **155** D8
Bulanık *Turkey* 39°4N 42°14E **213** C10
Bûlâq *El Khârga, Egypt* 25°10N 30°38E **256** B3
Bûlâq *El Qâhira, Egypt* 30°3N 31°14E **117** A2
Bulawayo *Zimbabwe* 20°7S 28°32E **269** G2
Buldan *Turkey* 38°2N 28°50E **205** C10
Buldana *India* 20°30N 76°18E **244** D3
Buldir I. *U.S.A.* 52°21N 175°56E **303** K1
Buldon *Phil.* 7°33N 124°25E **233** H5
Bule *Phil.* 14°26N 121°2E **127** C2
Bulenga *Ghana* 9°56N 2°12W **262** D4
Bulgan *Mongolia* 48°45N 103°34E **218** B9
Bulgar *Russia* 54°57N 49°4E **190** C9
Bulgaria ■ *Europe* 42°35N 25°30E **203** D9
Bulgheria, Monte *Italy* 40°4N 15°26E **201** B8
Bulgurca *Turkey* 38°9N 27°9E **205** C9
Bulhale *Somalia* 5°20N 46°29E **267** C6
Bulhar *Somalia* 10°25N 44°30E **267** B5
Buli, Teluk *Indonesia* 0°48N 128°25E **231** D7
Buliluyan, C. *Phil.* 8°20N 117°15E **233** G1
Bulki *Ethiopia* 6°11N 36°31E **257** F4
Bulkley → *Canada* 55°15N 127°40W **296** B3
Bull Head *Jamaica* 18°10N 77°16W **320** a
Bull Savanna *Jamaica* 17°53N 77°35W **320** a
Bull Shoals L. *U.S.A.* 36°22N 92°35W **314** C8
Bullaque → *Spain* 38°59N 4°17W **195** G6
Bullard *U.S.A.* 32°38N 83°30W **316** C6
Bullas *Spain* 38°2N 1°40W **197** G3
Bulle *Switz.* 46°37N 7°3E **179** J3
Bullen Park *Australia* 37°46S 145°4E **128** A2
Bullenbaai *Curaçao* 12°11N 69°2W **322** g
Buller → *N.Z.* 41°44S 171°36E **285** B6
Buller, Mt. *Australia* 37°10S 146°28E **283** D7
Buller Gorge *N.Z.* 41°40S 172°10E **285** B7
Bulleringa △ *Australia* 17°39S 143°56E **280** B3
Bullhead City *U.S.A.* 35°8N 114°32W **307** K12
Bulli *Australia* 34°15S 150°57E **283** C9
Büllingen *Belgium* 50°25N 6°16E **170** D6
Bullock Creek *Australia* 17°43S 144°31E **280** B3
Bulloo → *Australia* 28°43S 142°30E **281** D3
Bulloo L. *Australia* 28°43S 142°25E **281** D3
Bulls *N.Z.* 40°10S 175°24E **284** G4
Bully-les-Mines *France* 50°27N 2°44E **173** B9
Bulman *Australia* 13°39S 134°20E **280** A1
Bulnes *Chile* 36°42S 72°19W **334** D1
Bulo Ghedudo *Somalia* 2°52N 43°1E **267** D5
Bulolo *Papua N. G.* 7°10S 146°40E **286** D4
Bulongo *Dem. Rep. of the Congo* 4°45S 21°30E **265** C4
Bulqizë *Albania* 41°30N 20°21E **202** E4
Bulsar = Valsad *India* 20°40N 72°58E **244** D1
Bultfontein *S. Africa* 28°18S 26°10E **270** C4
Buluan *Phil.* 6°44N 124°47E **233** H5
Buluan, L. *Phil.* 6°40N 124°49E **233** H5
Bulukumba *Indonesia* 5°33S 120°11E **231** F6
Bulun *Russia* 70°37N 127°30E **215** B13
Bulungkol *China* 38°36N 74°58E **217** E8
Bulungu *Bandundu, Dem. Rep. of the Congo* 4°33S 18°36E **265** C3
Bulungu *Kasai-Occ., Dem. Rep. of the Congo* 6°4S 21°54E **265** D4
Bulusan *Phil.* 12°45N 124°8E **232** E5
Bulusan Vol. *Phil.* 12°46N 124°3E **232** E5
Bumba *Bandundu, Dem. Rep. of the Congo* 6°58S 19°19E **265** D3
Bumba *Équateur, Dem. Rep. of the Congo* 2°13N 22°30E **264** B4
Bumbah, Khalīj *Libya* 32°20N 23°15E **258** B4
Bumbeşti-Jiu *Romania* 45°10N 23°24E **183** E8
Bumbiri I. *Tanzania* 1°40S 31°55E **268** C3
Bumbuna *S. Leone* 9°2N 11°49W **262** D2
Bumhkang *Burma* 26°51N 97°40E **241** B6
Bumhpa Bum *Burma* 26°51N 97°14E **241** B6
Bumi → *Zimbabwe* 17°0S 28°20E **269** F2
Bumtang = Jakar Dzong *Bhutan* 27°33N 90°43E **241** B3
Bumtang → *Bhutan* 26°56N 90°53E **241** B3
Buna *Dem. Rep. of the Congo* 3°14S 18°59E **264** C3
Buna *North Eastern, Kenya* 2°58N 39°30E **268** B4
Buna *Papua N. G.* 8°42S 148°27E **286** E5
Bunaken *Indonesia* 1°37N 124°46E **231** D6
Bunama *Papua N. G.* 10°9S 151°9E **286** F6
Bunawan *Phil.* 8°12N 125°57E **233** G5
Bunazi *Tanzania* 1°3S 31°23E **268** C3
Bunbury *Australia* 33°20S 115°35E **279** F2
Bunclody *Ireland* 52°39N 6°40W **166** D5
Buncrana *Ireland* 55°8N 7°27W **166** A4
Bund, The *China* 31°14N 121°30E **138** B1
Bunda *Dem. Rep. of the Congo* 4°58S 14°29E **265** C3
Bundaberg *Australia* 24°54S 152°22E **281** C5
Bundanoon *Australia* 34°40S 150°16E **283** C9
Bünde *Germany* 52°11N 8°35E **178** C4
Bundestag = Reichstag *Berlin, Germany* **115** a3
Bundey → *Australia* 21°46S 135°37E **280** C2
Bundi *India* 25°30N 75°35E **242** G6
Bundjalung △ *Australia* 29°16S 153°21E **281** D5
Bundoora North *Australia* 37°41S 145°2E **128** A2
Bundoora Park *Australia* 37°42S 145°2E **128** A2
Bundoran *Ireland* 54°28N 8°18W **166** B3
Bundukia *South Sudan* 5°14N 30°55E **257** F3
Bundure *Australia* 35°10S 146°1E **283** C7
Bung Kan *Thailand* 18°23N 103°37E **236** C4
Bunga → *Nigeria* 11°23N 9°56E **263** C6
Bungalaut, Selat *Indonesia* 2°0S 99°25E **234** C1
Bungay *U.K.* 52°27N 1°28E **169** E9
Bungendore *Australia* 35°14S 149°30E **283** C8
Bungil Cr. → *Australia* 27°5S 149°5E **281** D4
Bungle Bungle = Purnululu △ *Australia* 17°20S 128°20E **278** C4
Bungo *Angola* 7°26S 15°33E **265** D3
Bungo, Gunung *Malaysia* 1°16N 110°9E **235** B4
Bungo-Suidō *Japan* 33°0N 132°15E **222** E4
Bungoma *Kenya* 0°34N 34°34E **268** B3
Bungotakada *Japan* 33°35N 131°25E **222** D3
Bungu *Tanzania* 7°35S 39°0E **268** D4
Bunia *Dem. Rep. of the Congo* 1°35N 30°20E **268** B3
Bunianga *Dem. Rep. of the Congo* 3°28S 20°11E **264** C4
Bunji *Pakistan* 35°45N 74°40E **243** B6
Bunker Hill *Ill., U.S.A.* 39°3N 89°57W **310** E7
Bunker Hill *Ind., U.S.A.* 40°40N 86°6W **311** D10
Bunker Hill Memorial *U.S.A.* 42°22N 71°4W **116** A2
Bunker I. *Pakistan* 24°48N 66°57E **123** B1
Bunkie *U.S.A.* 30°57N 92°11W **314** F8
Bunkyō *Japan* 35°42N 139°45E **140** A3
Bunnefjorden *Norway* 59°50N 10°44E **133** A3
Bunnell *U.S.A.* 29°28N 81°16W **317** F8
Bunnythorpe *N.Z.* 40°16S 175°39E **284** G4
Buñol *Spain* 39°25N 0°47W **197** F4
Bunsuru → *Nigeria* 13°21N 6°23E **263** C5
Buntok *Indonesia* 1°40S 114°58E **235** C4
Bununu Dass *Nigeria* 10°5N 9°31E **263** C6
Bununu Kasa *Nigeria* 9°51N 9°32E **263** D6
Bunya Mts. △ *Australia* 26°51S 151°34E **281** D5
Bünyan *Turkey* 38°51N 35°51E **212** C6
Bunyola *Spain* 39°41N 2°42E **206** B3
Bunyu *Indonesia* 3°35N 117°50E **235** B5
Bunza *Nigeria* 12°8N 4°0E **263** C5
Bunzlau = Boleslawiec *Poland* 51°17N 15°37E **185** G2
Buol *Indonesia* 1°15N 121°32E **231** D6
Buon Brieng *Vietnam* 13°9N 108°12E **236** F7
Buon Ho *Vietnam* 12°57N 108°18E **236** F7
Buon Ma Thuot *Vietnam* 12°40N 108°3E **236** F7
Buona Vista Park *Singapore* 1°16N 103°47E **138** B2
Buong Long *Cambodia* 13°44N 106°59E **236** F6
Buorkhaya, Mys *Russia* 71°50N 132°40E **215** B14
Buqayq *Si. Arabia* 26°0N 49°45E **247** E6
Buqbuq *Egypt* 31°29N 25°29E **256** A2
Bur Acaba = Buurhakaba *Somalia* 3°12N 44°20E **267** D5
Bur Dubai *U.A.E.* 25°15N 55°17E **119** A2
Bûr Fuad *Egypt* 31°15N 32°20E **256** H8
Bûr Safâga *Egypt* 26°43N 33°57E **246** E2
Bûr Sa'îd *Egypt* 31°16N 32°18E **256** H8
Bûr Sûdân *Sudan* 19°32N 37°9E **256** D4
Bûr Taufiq *Egypt* 29°54N 32°32E **256** J8
Bura *Kenya* 1°4S 39°58E **268** C4
Buraan *Somalia* 10°14N 48°44E **267** B6
Burakin *Australia* 30°31S 117°10E **279** F2
Buram *Sudan* 10°51N 25°9E **257** E2
Buran = Buraan *Somalia* 10°14N 48°44E **267** B6
Burang *China* 30°15N 81°10E **218** E5
Burao = Burco *Somalia* 9°32N 45°32E **267** C6
Burāq *Syria* 33°11N 36°29E **250** E7
Burathum *Nepal* 28°4N 84°50E **243** E11
Burauen *Phil.* 10°58N 124°53E **233** F5
Buraydah *Si. Arabia* 26°20N 43°59E **246** E4
Burbank *Calif., U.S.A.* 34°12N 118°18W **126** A3
Burbank *Ill., U.S.A.* 41°44N 87°46W **119** C2
Burç *Turkey* 36°59N 37°8E **250** B8
Burcher *Australia* 33°30S 147°16E **283** B7
Burco *Somalia* 9°32N 45°32E **267** C6
Burda *India* 25°50N 77°35E **242** G7
Burdekin → *Australia* 19°38S 147°25E **280** B4
Burden, L. *U.S.A.* 28°27N 81°33W **133** B1
Burdeos *Phil.* 14°50N 121°58E **232** D3
Burdeos B. *Phil.* 14°44N 122°6E **232** D4
Burdur *Turkey* 37°45N 30°17E **205** D12
Burdur □ *Turkey* 37°45N 30°0E **205** D12
Burdur Gölü *Turkey* 37°44N 30°10E **205** D12
Burdwan = Barddhaman *India* 23°14N 87°39E **243** H12
Burdwood Bank *Atl. Oc.* 54°0S 59°0W **152** M6
Bure *Gojam, Ethiopia* 10°40N 37°4E **257** E4
Bure *Ilubabor, Ethiopia* 8°19N 35°8E **257** F4
Bure → *U.K.* 52°38N 1°43E **168** E9
Büren *Germany* 51°33N 8°35E **178** D4
Bureskoye Vdkhr. *Russia* 50°16N 130°20E **215** D14
Bureya → *Russia* 49°27N 129°30E **215** E13
Burford *Canada* 43°7N 80°27W **312** C4
Burg *Germany* 52°16N 11°51E **178** C7
Burg auf Fehmarn *Germany* 54°28N 11°9E **178** A7
Burg el Arab *Egypt* 30°54N 29°32E **256** H6
Burg et Tuyur *Sudan* 20°55N 27°56E **256** C2
Burg Stargard *Germany* 53°29N 13°18E **178** B9
Burgas *Bulgaria* 42°33N 27°29E **203** D11
Burgas □ *Bulgaria* 42°30N 27°20E **203** D11
Burgaski Zaliv *Bulgaria* 42°30N 27°39E **203** D11
Burgdorf *Niedersachsen, Germany* 52°27N 10°1E **178** C6
Burgdorf *Switz.* 47°3N 7°37E **179** H3
Burgenland □ *Austria* 47°20N 16°20E **181** D9
Burgeo *Canada* 47°37N 57°38W **299** C8
Burgersdorp *S. Africa* 31°0S 26°20E **270** D4
Burgess, Mt. *Australia* 30°50S 121°5E **279** F3
Burghausen *Germany* 48°9N 12°49E **179** G8
Burghead *U.K.* 57°43N 3°30W **167** D5
Búrgio *Italy* 37°36N 13°17E **200** E6
Burglengenfeld *Germany* 49°12N 12°2E **179** F8
Burgohondo *Spain* 40°26N 4°47W **194** E6
Burgos *Ilocos N., Phil.* 18°31N 120°39E **232** B3
Burgos *Pangasinan, Phil.* 16°4N 119°52E **232** C2
Burgos *Spain* 42°21N 3°41W **194** C7
Burgos □ *Spain* 42°21N 3°42W **194** C7
Burgstädt *Germany* 50°54N 12°49E **178** E8
Burgsvik *Sweden* 57°3N 18°19E **163** G12
Burguillos del Cerro *Spain* 38°23N 6°35W **195** G4
Burgundy = Bourgogne □ *France* 47°0N 4°50E **173** F11
Burhaniye *Turkey* 39°30N 26°58E **205** B8
Burhanpur *India* 21°18N 76°14E **244** D3
Burhi Gandak → *India* 25°20N 86°37E **243** G12
Burhner → *India* 22°43N 80°31E **243** H9
Buri Pen. *Eritrea* 15°25N 39°55E **257** D4
Burias I. *Phil.* 12°55N 123°5E **232** E4
Burias Pass. *Phil.* 13°0N 123°15E **232** E4
Burica, Pta. *Costa Rica* 8°3N 82°51W **320** E3
Burien *U.S.A.* 47°28N 122°20W **306** C4
Burigi, L. *Tanzania* 2°2S 31°22E **268** C3
Burigi ⌓ *Tanzania* 2°20S 31°6E **268** C3
Burim *Kosovo* 42°45N 20°24E **202** D4
Burin *Canada* 47°1N 55°14W **299** C8
Buriram *Thailand* 15°0N 103°0E **236** E4
Buriti Alegre *Brazil* 18°9S 49°3W **333** E2
Buriti Bravo *Brazil* 5°50S 43°50W **332** C3
Buriti dos Lopes *Brazil* 3°10S 41°52W **332** B3
Burj Al Arab *U.A.E.* 25°8N 55°11E **119** B1
Burj Dubai *U.A.E.* 25°12N 55°16E **119** B2
Burji *Ethiopia* 5°29N 37°51E **257** F4
Burkburnett *U.S.A.* 34°6N 98°34W **314** D5
Burke → *Australia* 23°12S 139°33E **280** C2
Burke Chan. *Canada* 52°10N 127°30W **296** C3
Burketown *Australia* 17°45S 139°33E **280** B2
Burkina Faso ■ *Africa* 12°0N 1°0W **262** C4
Burk's Falls *Canada* 45°37N 79°24W **298** C4
Burlada *Spain* 42°49N 1°36W **196** C3
Burleigh Falls *Canada* 44°33N 78°12W **312** B6
Burley *U.S.A.* 42°32N 113°48W **304** E7
Burlingame *U.S.A.* 37°35N 122°21W **306** H4
Burlington *Ont., Canada* 43°18N 79°45W **312** C5
Burlington *Colo., U.S.A.* 39°18N 102°16W **304** G12
Burlington *Iowa, U.S.A.* 40°49N 91°14W **310** D5
Burlington *Kans., U.S.A.* 38°12N 95°45W **308** F6
Burlington *Ky., U.S.A.* 39°2N 84°43W **311** E12
Burlington *Mass., U.S.A.* 42°30N 71°13W **116** A1
Burlington *N.C., U.S.A.* 36°6N 79°26W **315** C15
Burlington *N.J., U.S.A.* 40°4N 74°51W **313** F10
Burlington *Vt., U.S.A.* 44°29N 73°12W **313** B11
Burlington *Wash., U.S.A.* 48°28N 122°20W **306** B4
Burlington *Wis., U.S.A.* 42°41N 88°17W **311** B8
Burma ■ *Asia* 21°0N 96°30E **241** E6
Burnaby I. *Canada* 52°25N 131°19W **296** C2
Burnet *U.S.A.* 30°45N 98°14W **314** F5
Burney *U.S.A.* 40°53N 121°40W **304** F3
Burnham *U.S.A.* 40°38N 77°34W **312** F7
Burnham-on-Sea *U.K.* 51°14N 3°0W **169** F5
Burnham Park *U.S.A.* 41°49N 87°35W **119** C3
Burnham Park Harbor *U.S.A.* 41°51N 87°36W **119** B3
Burnhamthorpe *Canada* 43°37N 79°35W **141** B1
Burnie *Australia* 41°4S 145°56E **281** G4
Burnley *U.K.* 53°47N 2°14W **168** D5
Burns *U.S.A.* 43°35N 119°3W **304** E4
Burns Junction *U.S.A.* 42°47N 117°51W **304** E5
Burns Lake *Canada* 54°14N 125°45W **296** C3
Burnside → *Canada* 66°51N 108°4W **294** D10
Burnside, L. *Australia* 25°22S 123°0E **279** E3
Burnsville *U.S.A.* 44°47N 93°17W **308** C7
Burnt Oak *U.K.* 51°36N 0°15W **125** A2
Burnt Paw *U.S.A.* 66°54N 143°44W **303** C12
Burnt River *Canada* 44°41N 78°42W **312** B6
Burntisland *U.K.* 56°4N 3°13W **121** A2
Burntwood → *Canada* 56°8N 96°34W **297** B9
Burntwood L. *Canada* 55°22N 100°26W **297** B8
Burnwynd *U.K.* 55°54N 3°23W **121** B1
Buronga *Australia* 34°18S 142°20E **282** C5
Burqa *West Bank* 31°54N 35°15E **123** A2
Burqān *Kuwait* 29°0N 47°57E **246** D5
Burqin *China* 47°43N 87°0E **217** C11
Burra *S. Austral., Australia* 33°40S 138°55E **282** B3
Burra *Nigeria* 11°0N 8°56E **263** C6
Burragorang, L. *Australia* 33°52S 150°37E **283** B9
Burray *U.K.* 58°51N 2°54W **167** C6
Burrel *Albania* 41°36N 20°1E **202** E4
Burren △ *Ireland* 53°9N 9°5W **166** C2
Burren Junction *Australia* 30°7S 148°58E **281** E4
Burrendong, L. *Australia* 32°45S 149°10E **283** B8
Burriana *Spain* 39°50N 0°4W **196** F4
Burrinjuck, L. *Australia* 35°0S 148°36E **283** C8
Burro, Serranías del *Mexico* 28°56N 102°5W **318** B4
Burrow Hd. *U.K.* 54°41N 4°24W **167** G4
Burrowa-Pine Mountain △ *Australia* 36°6S 147°45E **283** D7
Burrum Coast △ *Australia* 25°13S 152°36E **281** D5
Burruyacú *Argentina* 26°30S 64°40W **334** B3
Burry Port *U.K.* 51°41N 4°15W **169** F3
Bursa *Turkey* 40°15N 29°5E **203** F13
Bursa □ *Turkey* 40°10N 29°5E **212** B3
Burseryd *Sweden* 57°12N 13°17E **163** G7
Burstall *Canada* 50°39N 109°54W **297** C7
Burton *Mich., U.S.A.* 43°0N 83°40W **311** B13
Burton *Ohio, U.S.A.* 41°28N 81°8W **312** E3
Burton *S.C., U.S.A.* 32°26N 80°43W **316** C9
Burton, L. *Canada* 54°45N 78°20W **298** B4
Burton upon Trent *U.K.* 52°48N 1°38W **168** E6
Burtundy *Australia* 33°45S 142°15E **282** B5
Burtus *Egypt* 30°8N 31°8E **117** A1
Buru *Indonesia* 3°30S 126°30E **231** E7
Buruanga *Phil.* 11°51N 121°53E **233** F3
Burudvatn *Norway* 59°58N 10°35E **133** A2
Burullus, Bahra el *Egypt* 31°25N 31°0E **256** H7
Burūm *Yemen* 14°22N 48°59E **249** D5
Burûn, Râs *Egypt* 31°14N 33°7E **251** G4
Burundi ■ *Africa* 3°15S 30°0E **268** C3

Burunny = Tsagan Aman Russia 47°34N 46°43E 191 G8
Bururi Burundi 3°57S 29°37E 268 C2
Burutu Nigeria 5°20N 5°29E 263 D6
Burwell U.S.A. 41°47N 99°8W 308 E4
Burwick U.K. 58°45N 2°58W 167 C5
Burwood Australia 33°52S 151°5E 139 B1
Bury U.K. 53°35N 2°17W 168 D5
Bury St. Edmunds U.K. 52°15N 0°43E 169 E8
Buryatia □ Russia 53°0N 110°0E 215 D12
Bürylbaytal Kazakhstan 44°56N 74°0E 217 D8
Buryn Ukraine 51°13N 33°50E 189 G7
Burzenin Poland 51°28N 18°47E 185 G5
Busa, Mt. Phil. 6°8N 124°39E 233 H5
Busalla Italy 44°34N 8°57E 198 D5
Busan S. Korea 35°5N 129°0E 224 E4
Busanga Dem. Rep. of the Congo 0°53S 22°7E 264 C4
Busango Swamp Zambia 14°15S 25°45E 269 E2
Busaso = Boosaaso Somalia 11°12N 49°18E 267 B6
Buşayrah Syria 35°9N 40°26E 213 E9
Busca Italy 44°31N 7°29E 198 D4
Bûsh Egypt 29°9N 31°8E 251 J2
Bushat Albania 41°58N 19°34E 202 E3
Būshehr Iran 28°55N 50°55E 247 D6
Būshehr □ Iran 28°20N 51°45E 247 D6
Bushenyi Uganda 0°35S 30°10E 268 C3
Bushimaie ➜ Dem. Rep. of the Congo 6°2S 23°45E 265 D4
Bushire = Būshehr Iran 28°55N 50°55E 247 D6
Bushiribana Aruba 12°33N 69°58W 322 f
Bushnell Fla., U.S.A. 28°40N 82°7W 317 G7
Bushnell Ill., U.S.A. 40°33N 90°31W 310 D6
Bushtyna Ukraine 48°3N 23°28E 183 B8
Bushwick U.S.A. 40°41N 73°54W 132 B2
Bushy Park U.K. 51°24N 0°20W 125 B1
Busie Ghana 10°29N 2°22W 262 C4
Business Bay U.A.E. 25°11N 55°16E 119 B2
Businga Dem. Rep. of the Congo 3°16N 20°59E 264 B4
Büsingen Germany 47°42N 8°41E 179 H4
Buskerud □ Norway 60°20N 9°0E 164 D5
Busko-Zdrój Poland 50°28N 20°42E 185 H7
Buslei Ethiopia 5°28N 44°25E 267 C5
Busovača Bos.-H. 44°6N 17°53E 182 F2
Buşra ash Shām Syria 32°30N 36°25E 251 F7
Busselton Australia 33°42S 115°15E 279 F2
Busseri ➜ South Sudan 7°41N 28°3E 257 F2
Busseto Italy 44°59N 10°2E 198 D7
Bussière-Badil France 45°39N 0°36E 174 C4
Bussolengo Italy 45°28N 10°51E 198 C7
Bussum Neths. 52°16N 5°10E 170 B5
Bustamante, B. Argentina 45°5S 66°18W 336 C3
Buşteni Romania 45°24N 25°32E 183 E10
Busto, C. Spain 43°34N 6°28W 194 B4
Busto Arsizio Italy 45°37N 8°51E 198 C5
Busu Djanoa Dem. Rep. of the Congo 1°43N 21°23E 264 B4
Busu Kwanga Dem. Rep. of the Congo 1°48N 20°21E 264 B4
Busu Mandji Dem. Rep. of the Congo 2°52N 21°14E 264 B4
Busuanga Phil. 12°14N 119°52E 232 E2
Busuanga I. Phil. 12°10N 120°0E 232 E2
Büsum Germany 54°7N 8°51E 178 A4
Busungbiu Indonesia 8°16S 114°58E 231 J17
Busy Corner Trin. & Tob. 10°18N 61°17W 323 t
Buta Dem. Rep. of the Congo 2°50N 24°53E 264 B4
Butantã Brazil 23°34S 46°42W 137 B1
Butare Rwanda 2°31S 29°52E 268 C2
Butaritari Kiribati 3°30N 174°0E 288 G9
Butcher I. India 18°57N 72°53E 130 B2
Bute S. Australia, Australia 33°51S 138°0E 282 B3
Bute Scotland, U.K. 55°48N 5°2W 167 F3
Bute Inlet Canada 50°40N 124°53W 296 C4
Butembo Dem. Rep. of the Congo 0°9N 29°18E 268 B2
Buteni Romania 46°19N 22°7E 182 D7
Butera Italy 37°11N 14°11E 201 E7
Butere Kenya 0°13N 34°30E 268 B3
Butha-Buthe Lesotho 28°47S 28°14E 271 C4
Butha Qi China 48°0N 122°32E 219 B13
Buthidaung Burma 20°52N 92°32E 241 E4
Butiaba Uganda 1°50N 31°20E 268 B3
Butler Ga., U.S.A. 32°33N 84°14W 316 C5
Butler Ind., U.S.A. 41°26N 84°52W 311 C12
Butler Ky., U.S.A. 38°47N 84°22W 311 F12
Butler Mo., U.S.A. 38°16N 94°20W 310 F2
Butler Pa., U.S.A. 40°52N 79°54W 312 F5
Butler, L. U.S.A. 28°29N 81°33W 133 B1
Buton Indonesia 5°0S 122°45E 231 E6
Bütow = Bytów Poland 54°10N 17°30E 184 D4
Butrint Albania 39°45N 20°1E 206 B10
Butrintit, L. e Albania 39°43N 20°5E 206 B10
Butte Mont., U.S.A. 46°0N 112°32W 304 C7
Butte Nebr., U.S.A. 42°58N 98°51W 308 D4
Butte Creek ➜ U.S.A. 39°12N 121°56W 306 F5
Butterworth = Gcuwa S. Africa 32°20S 28°11E 271 D4
Butterworth Malaysia 5°24N 100°23E 237 c
Buttevant Ireland 52°14N 8°40W 166 D3
Buttfield, Mt. Australia 24°45S 128°9E 279 D4
Button B. Canada 58°45N 94°23W 297 B10
Buttonwillow U.S.A. 35°24N 119°28W 307 K7
Butty Hd. Australia 33°54S 121°39E 279 F3
Butuan Phil. 8°57N 125°33E 233 G5
Butuan B. Phil. 9°4N 125°21E 233 G5
Butuku-Luba Eq. Guin. 3°29N 8°33E 263 E6
Butung = Buton Indonesia 5°0S 122°45E 231 E6
Buturlinovka Russia 50°50N 40°35E 190 E5
Butwal Nepal 27°33N 83°31E 243 F10
Butzbach Germany 50°25N 8°40E 179 E4
Bützow Germany 53°50N 11°58E 178 B7
Buuhoodle Somalia 8°20N 46°25E 267 C6
Buulobarde Somalia 3°50N 45°33E 267 D6
Buur Gaabo Somalia 1°13S 41°51E 267 E5
Buurhakaba Somalia 3°12N 44°20E 267 D5
Buvika Norway 63°18N 10°11E 164 A7
Buxa Duar India 27°45N 89°35E 243 F13
Buxar India 25°34N 83°58E 243 G10
Buxoro Uzbekistan 39°48N 64°25E 216 E6
Buxtehude Germany 53°28N 9°39E 178 B5
Buxton U.K. 53°16N 1°54W 168 D6
Buxy France 46°44N 4°40E 173 F11
Buy Russia 58°28N 41°28E 190 A5
Buyant-Uhaa Mongolia 44°55N 110°11E 226 B6
Buynaksk Russia 42°48N 47°7E 191 J8
Buyo Ivory C. 6°21N 7°5W 262 D3
Buyo, L. de Ivory C. 6°16N 7°10W 262 D3
Büyük Menderes ➜ Turkey 37°28N 27°11E 205 D9
Büyükçekmece Turkey 41°2N 28°35E 203 E12
Büyükdere Turkey 41°9N 29°2E 122 B2
Büyükeğri Dağı Turkey 36°45N 33°33E 250 B4
Büyükkariştiran Turkey 41°18N 27°33E 203 E11
Büyükkemikli Burnu Turkey 40°18N 26°14E 203 F10
Büyükkonuk = Komi Cyprus 35°24N 34°0E 207 E10
Büyükorhan Turkey 39°46N 28°56E 205 B10
Büyükyoncalı Turkey 41°20N 27°55E 203 E11
Buyun Shan China 40°4N 122°43E 227 D12
Buzançais France 46°54N 1°25E 172 F8
Buzău Romania 45°10N 26°50E 183 E11
Buzău □ Romania 45°20N 26°30E 183 E11
Buzău ➜ Romania 45°26N 27°44E 183 E12
Buzău, Pasul Romania 45°35N 26°12E 183 E11
Buzaymah Libya 24°55N 22°2E 258 D4
Buzen Japan 33°35N 131°5E 222 D3
Buzet Croatia 45°24N 13°58E 199 C10
Buzi ➜ Mozam. 19°50S 34°43E 269 F3
Buziaş Romania 45°38N 21°36E 182 E6
Büzmeýin Turkmenistan 38°3N 58°12E 247 B8
Buzuluk Russia 52°48N 52°12E 186 D9
Buzuluk ➜ Russia 50°15N 42°7E 190 E6
Buzzards Bay U.S.A. 41°45N 70°37W 313 E14
Bwagaoia Papua N. G. 10°40S 152°52E 286 F7
Bwana Mkubwa Zambia 13°8S 28°38E 269 E2
Bwasa Dem. Rep. of the Congo 3°55S 18°24E 264 C3
Bwatnapné Vanuatu 15°41S 168°9E 287 E6
Bwindi △ Uganda 1°2S 29°42E 268 C2
Byakar Dzong = Jakar Dzong Bhutan 27°33N 90°43E 241 B3
Byala Ruse, Bulgaria 43°28N 25°44E 203 C9
Byala Varna, Bulgaria 42°53N 27°55E 203 D11
Byala Slatina Bulgaria 43°26N 23°58E 202 C7
Byam Martin I. Canada 75°15N 134°15W 295 B11
Byarezina ➜ Belarus 52°33N 30°14E 177 B16
Byaroza Belarus 52°31N 24°51E 177 B13
Byblos = Jubayl Lebanon 34°5N 35°39E 250 D6
Bychawa Poland 51°1N 22°36E 185 G9
Byculla India 18°58N 72°50E 130 B2
Byczyna Poland 51°7N 18°12E 185 G5
Bydgoszcz Poland 53°10N 18°0E 185 E5
Byelorussia = Belarus ■ Europe 53°30N 27°0E 177 B14
Byeonsan △ S. Korea 35°40N 126°30E 224 E3
Byers U.S.A. 39°43N 104°14W 304 G11
Byesville U.S.A. 39°58N 81°32W 312 G3
Byfield △ Australia 22°52S 150°45E 280 C5
Bygdin Norway 61°2N 8°32E 164 C5
Bygdøy Norway 59°54N 10°40E 133 A3
Bygland Norway 58°50N 7°48E 164 F4
Byglandsfjorden Norway 58°44N 7°50E 164 F4
Bygstad Norway 61°23N 5°40E 164 C2
Bykhaw Belarus 53°31N 30°14E 177 B16
Bykhov = Bykhaw Belarus 53°31N 30°14E 177 B16
Bykle Norway 59°20N 7°22E 164 E4
Bykovo Russia 49°50N 45°25E 190 F7
Bylas U.S.A. 33°8N 110°7W 305 K8
Bylot Canada 58°25N 94°8W 297 B10
Bylot I. Canada 73°13N 78°34W 295 C16
Byram U.S.A. 32°11N 90°15W 315 E9
Byrd, C. Antarctica 69°38S 76°7W 151 C17
Byrock Australia 30°40S 146°27E 283 A7
Byron Ga., U.S.A. 32°39N 83°46W 316 C6
Byron Ill., U.S.A. 42°8N 89°15W 310 B7
Byron, C. Australia 28°43S 153°38E 281 D5
Byron Bay Australia 28°43S 153°37E 281 D5
Byrranga, Gory Russia 75°0N 100°0E 215 B11
Byrranga Mts. = Byrranga, Gory Russia 75°0N 100°0E 215 B11
Byrum Denmark 57°16N 11°0E 163 G5
Byske Sweden 64°57N 21°11E 160 D19
Byskeälven ➜ Sweden 64°57N 21°13E 160 D19
Bystrytsya Ukraine 48°27N 24°14E 183 B9
Bystrzyca ➜ Dolnośląskie, Poland 51°12N 16°55E 185 G3
Bystrzyca ➜ Lubelskie, Poland 51°21N 22°46E 185 G9
Bystrzyca Kłodzka Poland 50°19N 16°39E 185 H3
Bytča Slovak Rep. 49°13N 18°34E 181 B11
Bytkiv Ukraine 48°38N 24°28E 183 B9
Bytom Poland 50°25N 18°54E 185 H5
Bytom Odrzański Poland 51°44N 15°48E 185 G2
Bytów Poland 54°10N 17°30E 184 D4
Byumba Rwanda 1°35S 30°4E 268 C3
Bywater U.S.A. 29°58N 90°2W 131 B2
Byzantine Museum = Vizandino, Moussio Athens, Greece 112 b3
Bzenec Czech Rep. 48°58N 17°18E 181 C10
Bzura ➜ Poland 52°25N 20°15E 185 F7

C

C.B.S. Fox Studios U.S.A. 34°9N 118°24W 126 B2
C.N. Tower Toronto, Canada 141 c1
C.W. McConaughy, L. U.S.A. 41°14N 101°40W 308 E3
Ca ➜ Vietnam 18°45N 105°45E 236 C5
Ca' da Mosto Venice, Italy 142 b3
Ca' d'Oro Venice, Italy 142 b2
Ca' Foscari Venice, Italy 142 b2
Ca Mau Vietnam 9°7N 105°8E 237 H5
Ca Mau, Mui Vietnam 8°38N 104°44E 237 H5
Ca Na Vietnam 11°20N 108°54E 237 G7
Ca' Pesaro Venice, Italy 142 b2
Ca' Rezzonico Venice, Italy 142 b2
Caacupé Paraguay 25°23S 57°5W 334 B4
Caaguazú △ Paraguay 26°5S 55°31W 335 B4
Caála Angola 12°46S 15°30E 265 E3
Caamaño Sd. Canada 52°55N 129°25W 296 C3
Caapiranga Brazil 3°18S 61°13W 329 D5
Caazapá Paraguay 26°8S 56°19W 334 B4
Caazapá □ Paraguay 26°10S 56°0W 335 B4
Cabaad, Ras Somalia 6°18N 49°4E 267 C6
Cabadbaran Phil. 9°10N 125°38E 233 G5
Cabagan Phil. 17°26N 121°46E 232 C3
Cabalete I. Phil. 14°16N 121°49E 232 D3
Cabalian = San Juan Phil. 10°16N 125°10E 233 F5
Caballeria, C. de Spain 40°5N 4°5E 206 A5
Caballito Argentina 34°37S 58°25W 117 B2
Cabana Peru 8°25S 78°5W 330 B2
Cabana de Bergantiños Spain 43°13N 8°54W 194 B2
Cabanaconde Peru 15°38S 71°58W 330 D3
Cabañaquinta Spain 43°10N 5°38W 194 B5
Cabanatuan Phil. 15°30N 120°58E 232 D3
Cabañeros ⌂ Spain 39°18N 4°35W 195 F6
Cabanes Spain 40°9N 0°2E 196 E5
Cabangon Phil. 15°10N 120°3E 232 D3
Cabanilla Peru 15°36S 70°28W 330 D3
Cabano Canada 47°40N 68°56W 299 C6
Čabar Croatia 45°36N 14°39E 199 C11
Cabarroguis Phil. 16°30N 121°30E 232 C3
Cabarruyan I. Phil. 16°18N 119°59E 232 C2
Cabazon U.S.A. 33°55N 116°47W 307 M10
Cabedelo Brazil 7°0S 34°50W 332 C5
Cabeza del Buey Spain 38°44N 5°13W 195 G5
Cabezón de la Sal Spain 43°18N 4°14W 194 B6
Cabhán, An = Cavan Ireland 54°0N 7°22W 166 B4
Cabildo Chile 32°30S 71°5W 334 C1
Cabimas Venezuela 10°23N 71°25W 328 A3
Cabin John U.S.A. 38°58N 77°10W 143 B1
Cabin John Regional Park ⌂ U.S.A. 39°0N 77°10W 143 A1
Cabinda Angola 5°33S 12°11E 265 D2
Cabinda □ Angola 5°0S 12°30E 265 D2
Cabinet Mts. U.S.A. 48°10N 115°50W 304 B6
Cabinteely Ireland 53°16N 6°9W 120 B3
Cabiri Angola 8°52S 13°39E 265 D2
Cable Beach Bahamas 25°4N 77°24W 153 b
Cabo Blanco Argentina 47°15S 65°47W 336 C3
Cabo de Gata-Níjar △ Spain 36°51N 2°6W 197 J2
Cabo de Hornos △ Chile 55°42S 67°20W 336 E3
Cabo de Santo Agostinho Brazil 8°20S 34°55W 332 C5
Cabo Frio Brazil 22°51S 42°3W 333 F3
Cabo Pantoja Peru 1°0S 75°10W 328 D2
Cabo Raso Argentina 44°20S 65°15W 336 B3
Cabo Rojo Puerto Rico 18°5N 67°9W 321 b
Cabo San Lucas Mexico 22°53N 109°54W 318 C3
Cabo Verde = Cape Verde Is. ■ Atl. Oc. 16°0N 24°0W 153 j
Cabo Yubi = Tarfaya Morocco 27°55N 12°55W 260 C2
Cabonga, Réservoir Canada 47°20N 76°40W 298 C4
Cabool U.S.A. 37°7N 92°6W 308 G7
Caboolture Australia 27°5S 152°58E 281 D5
Cabora Bassa Dam = Cahora Bassa, Lago de Mozam. 15°20S 32°50E 269 F3
Caborca Mexico 30°37N 112°6W 318 A2
Cabot, Mt. U.S.A. 44°30N 71°25W 313 B13
Cabot Hd. Canada 45°14N 81°17W 312 A3
Cabot Str. Canada 47°15N 59°40W 299 C8
Cabra Dublin, Ireland 53°21N 6°18W 120 A2
Cabra Spain 37°30N 4°28W 195 H6
Cabra del Santo Cristo Spain 37°42N 3°16W 195 H7
Cabra I. India 7°18N 93°50E 245 L11
Cabra I. Phil. 13°53N 120°2E 232 E3
Cábras Italy 39°56N 8°32E 200 C1
Cabras I. Guam 13°27N 144°44E 302 d
Cabrera Spain 39°8N 2°57E 206 B3
Cabrera, Sierra Spain 42°12N 6°40W 194 C4
Cabrera △ Spain 39°13N 2°53E 197 F7
Cabri Canada 50°35N 108°25W 297 C7
Cabriel ➜ Spain 39°14N 1°3W 197 F3
Cabrits, Î. Martinique 14°23N 60°52W 322 j
Cabrits △ Dominica 15°35N 61°26W 323 k
Cabruta Venezuela 7°50N 66°10W 328 B4
Cabuçú de Baixo ➜ Brazil 23°30S 46°40W 137 A1
Cabuçú de Cima ➜ Brazil 23°30S 46°33W 137 A2
Cabugao Phil. 17°48N 120°27E 232 C3
Cabulauan Is. Phil. 11°25N 120°8E 233 F3
Cabulo Angola 10°18S 16°22E 265 E3
Caburan = Jose Abad Santos Phil. 5°55N 125°39E 233 J5
Cabuta Angola 9°48S 14°58E 265 D2
Cabuyaro Colombia 4°18N 72°49W 328 C3
Cacabelos Spain 42°36N 6°44W 194 C4
Caçador Brazil 26°47S 51°0W 335 B5
Čačak Serbia 43°54N 20°20E 202 C4
Cacandee Settlement Trin. & Tob. 10°33N 61°26W 323 t
Cacao Fr. Guiana 4°33N 52°26W 329 C7
Caçapava do Sul Brazil 30°30S 53°30W 335 C5
Cáccamo Italy 37°56N 13°40E 200 E6
Cacém Portugal 38°46N 9°18W 195 G1
Cáceres Brazil 16°5S 57°40W 331 D6
Cáceres Colombia 7°35N 75°20W 328 B2
Cáceres Spain 39°26N 6°23W 195 F4
Cáceres □ Spain 39°45N 6°0W 194 F5
Cachan France 48°47N 2°19E 134 B2
Cache Bay Canada 46°22N 80°0W 298 C4
Cache Cr. ➜ U.S.A. 38°42N 121°42W 306 G5
Cache Creek Canada 50°48N 121°19W 296 C4
Cacheu Guinea-Biss. 12°14N 16°8W 262 C1
Cachi Argentina 25°5S 66°10W 334 B2
Cachimbo Brazil 8°57S 54°54W 331 B7
Cachimbo, Serra do Brazil 9°30S 55°30W 331 B6
Cachimo Angola 8°21S 21°24E 265 D4
Cachinal de la Sierra Chile 24°58S 69°32W 334 A2
Cachingues Angola 13°5S 16°43E 265 E3
Cachoeira = Solonópole Brazil 5°44S 39°1W 332 C4
Cachoeira Brazil 12°30S 39°0W 333 D4
Cachoeira, Rib. da ➜ Brazil 23°38S 46°43W 137 B1
Cachoeira Alta Brazil 18°48S 50°58W 333 E1
Cachoeira do Sul Brazil 30°3S 52°53W 335 C5
Cachoeiro de Itapemirim Brazil 20°51S 41°7W 333 F3
Cachoeiro do Arari Brazil 1°1S 48°58W 332 B2
Cachopo Portugal 37°20N 7°49W 195 H3
Cachuela Esperanza Bolivia 10°32S 65°38W 331 C4
Cacilhas Portugal 38°41N 9°8W 126 A2
Cacine Guinea-Biss. 11°8N 14°57W 262 C1
Cacoal Brazil 11°32S 61°18W 331 C5
Cacólo Angola 10°9S 19°21E 265 E3
Caconda Angola 13°48S 15°8E 265 E3
Cacongo Angola 5°11S 12°5E 265 D2
Caçu Brazil 18°37S 51°4W 333 E1
Cacuaco Angola 8°47S 13°21E 265 D2
Cacuchi ➜ Angola 14°26S 16°46E 265 E3
Cacula Angola 14°29S 14°10E 265 E2
Caculé Brazil 14°30S 42°13W 333 D3
Caculuvar ➜ Angola 16°47S 14°56E 265 F2
Cacuso Angola 9°25S 15°45E 265 D3
Cadale Somalia 2°45N 46°19E 267 D6
Čadca Slovak Rep. 49°26N 18°45E 181 B11
Caddo U.S.A. 34°7N 96°16W 314 D6
Cader Idris U.K. 52°42N 3°53W 169 E4
Cadereyta de Jiménez Mexico 25°36N 100°0W 318 B5
Cades U.S.A. 33°47N 79°47W 316 B10
Cadí, Sierra del Spain 42°17N 1°42E 196 C6
Cadí-Moixeró ⌂ Spain 42°17N 1°44W 196 C3
Cadibarrawirracanna, L. Australia 28°52S 135°27E 281 D2
Cadillac Gironde, France 44°38N 0°20W 174 D3
Cadillac Mich., U.S.A. 44°15N 85°24W 309 C11
Cadiz Phil. 10°57N 123°15E 233 F4
Cádiz Spain 36°30N 6°20W 195 J4
Cadiz Calif., U.S.A. 34°30N 115°28W 307 L11
Cadiz Ohio, U.S.A. 40°22N 81°0W 312 F4
Cádiz □ Spain 36°36N 5°45W 195 J5
Cádiz, G. de Spain 36°40N 7°0W 195 J3
Cadiz L. U.S.A. 34°18N 115°24W 307 L11
Cadley U.S.A. 33°32N 82°40W 316 B7
Cadney Park Australia 27°55S 134°3E 281 D1
Cadomin Canada 53°2N 117°20W 296 C5
Cadotte Lake Canada 56°26N 116°23W 296 B5
Cadours France 43°44N 1°2E 174 E5
Cadoux Australia 30°46S 117°7E 279 F2
Cadwell U.S.A. 32°20N 83°3W 316 C6
Caen France 49°10N 0°22W 172 C6
Caerdydd = Cardiff U.K. 51°29N 3°10W 169 F4
Caerfyrddin = Carmarthen U.K. 51°52N 4°19W 169 F3
Caergybi = Holyhead U.K. 53°18N 4°38W 168 D3
Caernarfon U.K. 53°8N 4°16W 168 D3
Caernarfon B. U.K. 53°4N 4°40W 168 D3
Caernarvon = Caernarfon U.K. 53°8N 4°16W 168 D3
Caerphilly U.K. 51°35N 3°13W 169 F4
Caerphilly □ U.K. 51°37N 3°12W 169 F4
Caesarea Israel 32°30N 34°53E 251 F5
Caeté Brazil 19°55S 43°40W 333 E3
Caetité Brazil 13°50S 42°32W 333 D3
Cafayate Argentina 26°2S 66°0W 334 B2
Cafu Angola 16°30S 15°8E 265 F3
Cagayan □ Phil. 18°0N 121°50E 232 C3
Cagayan ➜ Phil. 18°25N 121°42E 232 B3
Cagayan de Oro Phil. 8°30N 124°40E 233 G5
Cagayan Is. Phil. 9°40N 121°16E 233 G3
Cagayan Sulu I. Phil. 7°1N 118°30E 233 H2
Cagli Italy 43°33N 12°39E 199 E9
Cágliari Italy 39°13N 9°7E 200 C2
Cágliari, G. di Italy 39°8N 9°11E 200 C2
Cagnano Varano Italy 41°49N 15°47E 199 G12
Cagnes-sur-Mer France 43°40N 7°9E 175 E11
Caguán ➜ Colombia 0°8S 74°18W 328 D3
Caguas Puerto Rico 18°14N 66°2W 321 C6
Caha Mts. Ireland 51°45N 9°40W 166 E2
Cahama Angola 16°17S 14°19E 265 F2
Cahir Ireland 52°22N 7°56W 166 D4
Cahirciveen Ireland 51°56N 10°14W 166 E1
Cahora Bassa, Lago de Mozam. 15°20S 32°50E 269 F3
Cahore Pt. Ireland 52°33N 6°12W 166 D5
Cahors France 44°27N 1°27E 174 D5
Cahuapanas Peru 5°15S 77°0W 330 B2
Cahuenga Park U.S.A. 34°8N 118°19W 126 B3
Cahuinari ➜ Colombia 1°21S 70°44W 328 D3
Cahuinari △ Colombia 1°20S 71°10W 328 D3
Cahul Moldova 45°50N 28°15E 183 E13
Cai Bau, Dao Vietnam 21°10N 107°27E 228 G6
Cai Be Vietnam 10°20N 106°2E 237 G6
Cai Nuoc Vietnam 8°56N 105°1E 237 H5
Caia Mozam. 17°51S 35°24E 269 F4
Caiabis, Serra dos Brazil 11°30S 56°30W 331 C6
Caianda Angola 11°2S 23°31E 265 E4
Caiapó, Serra do Brazil 17°0S 52°0W 331 D7
Caiapônia Brazil 16°57S 51°49W 331 D7
Caibarién Cuba 22°30N 79°30W 320 B4
Caibiran Phil. 11°34N 124°35E 233 F5
Caiçara = Alvarães Brazil 3°12S 64°50W 329 D5
Caicara Bolivar, Venezuela 7°38N 66°10W 328 B4
Caicara Monagas, Venezuela 9°52N 63°38W 329 B5
Caicó Brazil 6°20S 37°0W 332 C4
Caicos Is. Turks & Caicos 21°40N 71°40W 321 B5
Caicos Passage W. Indies 22°45N 72°45W 321 B5
Caidian China 30°35N 114°2E 229 B10
Caiguna Australia 32°16S 125°29E 279 F4
Caillandre, Morne St. Lucia 13°46N 60°57W 323 m
Caille I. Grenada 12°16N 61°34W 323 q
Cailloma Peru 15°9S 71°45W 330 D3
Cain, L. U.S.A. 28°28N 81°28W 133 B2
Cainari Moldova 46°41N 29°3E 183 D14
Cainde Angola 15°29S 13°24E 265 F2
Caine ➜ Bolivia 18°23S 65°21W 331 D4
Caird Coast Antarctica 75°0S 25°0W 151 D1
Cairn Gorm U.K. 57°7N 3°39W 167 D5
Cairngorm Mts. U.K. 57°6N 3°42W 167 D5
Cairngorms △ U.K. 57°10N 3°50W 167 D5
Cairnryan U.K. 54°59N 5°1W 167 G3
Cairns Australia 16°57S 145°45E 280 B4
Cairns L. Canada 51°42N 94°30W 297 C10
Cairo = El Qâhira Egypt 30°2N 31°13E 117 A2
Cairo Ga., U.S.A. 30°52N 84°13W 316 E5
Cairo Ill., U.S.A. 37°0N 89°11W 308 G9
Cairo N.Y., U.S.A. 42°18N 74°0W 313 D10
Cairo Int. ✕ (CAI) Egypt 30°7N 31°24E 117 A3
Cairo Montenotte Italy 44°23N 8°16E 198 D5
Cairofa Angola 14°3S 12°54E 265 E2
Caiseal = Cashel Ireland 52°30N 7°53W 166 D4
Caisleán an Bharraigh = Castlebar Ireland 53°52N 9°18W 166 C2
Caithness U.K. 58°25N 3°35W 167 C5
Caithness, Ord of U.K. 58°8N 3°36W 167 C5
Caitou Angola 14°28S 13°7E 265 E2
Caiúás = Rio Brilhante Brazil 21°48S 54°33W 335 A5
Caiundo Angola 15°50S 17°28E 265 F3
Caiza Bolivia 20°2S 65°40W 331 E4
Caja de Muertos, I. Puerto Rico 17°54N 66°32W 321 b
Cajabamba Peru 7°38S 78°4W 330 B2
Cajamarca Peru 7°5S 78°28W 330 B2
Cajamarca □ Peru 6°15S 78°50W 330 B2
Cajamarquilla = Bolivar Peru 7°18S 77°48W 330 B2
Cajapió Brazil 2°58S 44°48W 332 B3
Cajarc France 44°29N 1°50E 174 D5
Cajas △ Ecuador 2°48S 79°15W 328 D2
Cajatambo Peru 10°30S 77°2W 330 C2
Cajazeiras Brazil 6°52S 38°30W 332 C4
Čajetina Serbia 43°47N 19°42E 202 C3
Cajidiocan Phil. 12°22N 122°41E 232 E4
Caju Brazil 22°52S 43°12W 135 B1
Çakirgol Turkey 40°33N 39°40E 213 B8
Çakırlar Turkey 36°52N 30°33E 205 E12
Čakovec Croatia 46°23N 16°26E 199 B13
Čakovice Czech Rep. 50°9N 14°31E 135 B3
Çal Turkey 38°4N 29°23E 205 C11
Cala Spain 37°59N 6°21W 195 H4
Cala ➜ Spain 37°38N 6°5W 195 H4
Cala Cadolar, Punta de = Rotja, Pta. Spain 38°38N 1°35E 206 D2
Cala d'Or Spain 39°23N 3°14E 206 B4
Cala en Porter Spain 39°52N 4°8E 206 B5
Cala Figuera Spain 39°20N 3°10E 206 B4
Cala Figuera, C. de Spain 39°27N 2°31E 206 B3
Cala Forcat Spain 40°0N 3°47E 206 B4
Cala Major Spain 39°33N 2°37E 206 B3
Cala Mezquida = Sa Mesquida Spain 39°55N 4°16E 206 B5
Cala Millor Spain 39°35N 3°22E 206 B4
Cala Murada Spain 39°27N 3°17E 206 B4
Cala Ratjada Spain 39°43N 3°27E 206 B4
Cala Santa Galdana Spain 39°56N 3°58E 206 B4
Calabanga Phil. 13°42N 123°17E 232 E4
Calabar Nigeria 4°57N 8°20E 263 E6
Calabogie Canada 45°18N 76°43W 313 A8
Calabozo Venezuela 9°0N 67°28W 328 B4
Calábria □ Italy 39°0N 16°30E 201 C9
Calábria △ Italy 39°6N 16°35E 201 C9
Calaburras, Pta. de Spain 36°30N 4°38W 195 J6
Calaceite Spain 41°1N 0°11E 196 D5
Calacoto Bolivia 17°16S 68°38W 330 D4
Calacuccia France 42°21N 9°1E 175 F13
Calafat Romania 43°58N 22°59E 182 G7
Calafell Spain 41°11N 1°34E 196 D6
Calagnaan I. Phil. 11°29N 123°12E 233 F4
Calagua Is. Phil. 14°30N 122°55E 232 D4
Calahorra Spain 42°18N 1°59W 196 C3
Calai Angola 17°47S 19°41E 265 F3
Calais Pas-de-Calais, France 50°57N 1°56E 173 B8
Calais Maine, U.S.A. 45°11N 67°17W 309 C20
Calakmul ⌂ Mexico 18°14N 89°48W 319 D7
Calalaste, Cord. de Argentina 25°0S 67°0W 334 B2
Calama Brazil 8°0S 62°50W 331 B5
Calama Chile 22°30S 68°55W 334 A2
Calamar Bolivar, Colombia 10°15N 74°55W 328 A3
Calamar Vaupés, Colombia 1°58N 72°32W 328 C3
Calamarca Bolivia 16°55S 68°9W 330 D4
Calamba Cavite, Phil. 14°13N 121°10E 232 D3
Calamba Mis. Occ., Phil. 8°35N 123°39E 233 G4
Calamian Group Phil. 11°50N 119°55E 233 F2
Calamocha Spain 40°50N 1°17W 196 E3
Calamonte Spain 38°53N 6°23W 195 G4
Calan Romania 45°44N 22°59E 182 E7
Calañas Spain 37°40N 6°53W 195 H4
Calanda Spain 40°56N 0°15W 196 E4
Calandagan I. Phil. 10°39N 120°15E 233 F3
Calandula Angola 9°6S 15°57E 265 D3
Calang Indonesia 4°37N 95°37E 234 B1
Calangiánus Italy 40°56N 9°11E 200 B2
Calanscio, Sarir Libya 27°30N 22°30E 258 C4
Calapan Phil. 13°25N 121°7E 232 E3
Călăraşi Moldova 47°16N 28°19E 183 C13
Călăraşi Romania 44°12N 27°20E 183 F12
Călăraşi □ Romania 44°10N 27°0E 183 F12
Calasparra Spain 38°14N 1°41W 197 G3
Calatafimi Italy 37°55N 12°52E 200 E5
Calatagan Phil. 13°50N 120°38E 232 E3
Calatayud Spain 41°20N 1°40W 196 D3
Călăţele Romania 46°46N 23°1E 182 D8
Calato = Kalathos Greece 36°9N 28°8E 206 E12
Calatrava Eq. Guin. 1°6N 9°25E 264 B1
Calatrava Phil. 10°35N 123°28E 233 F4
Calatrava, Ponte di Venice, Italy 142 b1
Calauag Phil. 13°55N 122°15E 232 E4
Calavà, C. Italy 38°11N 14°55E 201 D7
Calavite, C. Phil. 13°26N 120°20E 232 E3
Calavite Pass. Phil. 13°36N 120°25E 232 E3
Calayan Phil. 19°16N 121°28E 232 B3
Calayan I. Phil. 19°20N 121°27E 232 B3
Calbayog Phil. 12°4N 124°38E 232 E5
Calbiga Phil. 11°38N 125°0E 233 F5
Calca Peru 13°22S 72°0W 330 C3
Calcasieu L. U.S.A. 29°55N 93°18W 314 G8
Calcium U.S.A. 44°1N 75°50W 313 B9
Calcutta = Kolkata India 22°34N 88°21E 124 B2
Calcutta U.S.A. 40°40N 80°34W 312 F4
Caldaro Italy 46°25N 11°14E 199 B8
Caldas □ Colombia 5°15N 75°30W 328 B2
Caldas da Rainha Portugal 39°24N 9°8W 195 F1
Caldas de Reis Spain 42°36N 8°39W 194 C2
Caldas Novas Brazil 17°45S 48°38W 333 E2
Calder ➜ U.K. 53°44N 1°22W 168 D6
Caldera Chile 27°5S 70°55W 334 B1
Caldera de Taburiente △ Canary Is. 28°43N 17°52W 153 e1
Caldwell Idaho, U.S.A. 43°40N 116°41W 304 E5
Caldwell Kans., U.S.A. 37°2N 97°37W 308 G5
Caldwell Tex., U.S.A. 30°32N 96°42W 314 F6
Caledon Ont., Canada 43°51N 79°51W 312 C5
Caledon Western Cape, S. Africa 34°14S 19°26E 270 D2
Caledon ➜ S. Africa 30°31S 26°5E 270 D4
Caledon B. Australia 12°45S 137°0E 280 A2
Caledonia Ont., Canada 43°7N 79°58W 312 C5
Caledonia Mo., U.S.A. 37°45N 90°46W 310 G6
Caledonia N.Y., U.S.A. 42°58N 77°51W 312 D7
Calella Spain 41°37N 2°40E 196 D7
Calemba Angola 16°0S 15°44E 270 A2
Calen Australia 20°56S 148°48E 280 b
Calenzana France 42°31N 8°51E 175 F12
Caleta Olivia Argentina 46°25S 67°25W 336 C3
Caletones Chile 34°6S 70°27W 334 C1
Calexico U.S.A. 32°40N 115°30W 307 N11
Calf of Man I. of Man 54°3N 4°48W 168 C3
Calgary Canada 51°0N 114°10W 296 C6
Calheta Azores 38°36N 28°1W 153 d1
Calheta Madeira 32°44N 17°11W 153 c
Calheta de Nesquim Azores 38°24N 28°5W 153 d1
Calhoun U.S.A. 34°30N 84°57W 315 D12
Calhoun Falls U.S.A. 34°6N 82°36W 316 A7
Cali Colombia 3°25N 76°35W 328 C2
Calibishie Dominica 15°35N 61°21W 323 k
Calicoan I. Phil. 10°59N 125°48E 233 F5
Calicut = Kozhikode India 11°15N 75°43E 245 J2
Caliente U.S.A. 37°37N 114°31W 305 H6
California Trin. & Tob. 10°24N 61°28W 323 t
California Mo., U.S.A. 38°38N 92°34W 310 F4
California Pa., U.S.A. 40°4N 79°54W 312 F5
California □ U.S.A. 37°30N 119°30W 306 H7
California, Baja, T.N. = Baja California □ Mexico 30°0N 115°0W 318 B2
California, Baja, T.S. = Baja California Sur □ Mexico 25°50N 111°50W 318 B2
California, G. de Mexico 27°0N 111°0W 318 B2
California City U.S.A. 35°10N 117°55W 307 K9
California Hot Springs U.S.A. 35°51N 118°41W 307 K8
California Inst. of Tech. U.S.A. 34°8N 118°8W 126 B4
California Los Angeles, Univ. of U.S.A. 34°4N 118°27W 126 B2
California Plaza Los Angeles, U.S.A. 127 b1
California State Univ. U.S.A. 34°4N 118°10W 126 B3
Cälilabad Azerbaijan 39°12N 48°29E 213 C13
Calilegua △ Argentina 25°36S 64°50W 334 B3
Călimăneşti Romania 45°14N 24°20E 183 E9
Călimani, Munţii Romania 47°12N 25°0E 183 C10
Calingasta Argentina 31°15S 69°30W 334 C2
Calinog Phil. 11°7N 122°32E 233 F4
Calintaan Phil. 12°35N 120°57E 232 E3
Calipatria U.S.A. 33°8N 115°31W 307 M11
Calistoga U.S.A. 38°35N 122°35W 306 G4
Calitri Italy 40°54N 15°26E 201 B8
Calitzdorp S. Africa 33°33S 21°42E 270 D3
Calivigny I. Grenada 12°0N 61°43W 323 q
Callabonna, L. Australia 29°40S 140°5E 281 D3
Callac France 48°25N 3°27W 172 D3
Callahan U.S.A. 30°34N 81°50W 316 E8
Callahan Tunnel Boston, U.S.A. 116 a3
Callan Ireland 52°32N 7°24W 166 D4
Callander U.K. 56°15N 4°13W 167 E4
Callang = San Manuel Phil. 16°4N 120°40E 232 C3
Callao Peru 12°3S 77°8W 124 B2
Callaway U.S.A. 30°8N 85°36W 316 E4
Calliaqua St. Vincent 13°8N 61°12W 323 n
Callicoon U.S.A. 41°46N 75°3W 313 E9
Calling Lake Canada 55°15N 113°12W 296 B6
Calliope Australia 24°0S 151°16E 280 C5
Callosa de Segura Spain 38°7N 0°53W 197 G4
Callosa d'En Sarrià Spain 38°40N 0°8W 197 G4
Calma, Costa de la Spain 39°28N 2°26E 206 B3
Calmar U.S.A. 43°11N 91°52W 310 A5
Calne U.K. 51°26N 2°0W 169 F6
Calola Angola 16°25S 17°48E 265 F3
Calolbon = San Andres Phil. 13°36N 124°6E 232 E5
Calonge Spain 41°52N 3°5E 196 D8
Caloocan Phil. 14°39N 120°58E 127 B1
Caloosahatchee ➜ U.S.A. 26°31N 82°1W 317 J7
Calore ➜ Italy 41°11N 14°28E 201 A7
Caloundra Australia 26°45S 153°10E 281 D5
Calpe Spain 38°39N 0°3E 197 G5
Calpella U.S.A. 39°14N 123°12W 306 F3
Calpine U.S.A. 39°40N 120°27W 306 F6
Calstock Canada 49°47N 84°9W 298 C3
Caltabellotta Italy 37°34N 13°13E 200 E6
Caltagirone Italy 37°14N 14°31E 201 E7
Caltanissetta Italy 37°29N 14°4E 201 E7
Çaltılıbük Turkey 39°57N 28°36E 203 G12
Caluango Angola 8°20S 19°36E 265 D3
Calubian Phil. 11°27N 124°26E 233 F5
Calucinga Angola 11°18S 16°12E 265 E3
Caluire-et-Cuire France 45°48N 4°52E 173 G11
Calulo Angola 10°1S 14°56E 265 E2
Calumet, L. U.S.A. 41°41N 87°35W 119 C3
Calumet City U.S.A. 41°37N 87°32W 119 C3
Calumet Park U.S.A. 41°40N 87°39W 119 C3
Calumet Sag Channel ➜ U.S.A. 41°40N 87°47W 119 C2
Calunda Angola 12°7S 23°36E 265 E4
Caluquembe Angola 13°47S 14°44E 265 E2
Caluso Italy 45°18N 7°53E 198 C4
Caluula Somalia 11°50N 50°45E 267 B7
Caluya I. Phil. 11°55N 121°34E 233 F3
Calvados □ France 49°5N 0°15W 172 C6
Calvados Chain, The Papua N. G. 11°10S 152°45E 286 F7
Calvairate Italy 45°27N 9°13E 128 B2
Calvert ➜ Australia 16°17S 137°44E 280 B2
Calvert I. Canada 51°30N 128°0W 296 C3
Calvert Ra. Australia 24°0S 122°30E 278 D3
Calvi France 42°34N 8°45E 175 F12
Calvià Spain 39°34N 2°31E 206 B3
Calvillo Mexico 21°51N 102°43W 318 C4
Calvinia S. Africa 31°28S 19°45E 270 D2
Calvo, Mte. Italy 41°44N 15°46E 199 G12
Calwa U.S.A. 36°42N 119°46W 306 J7
Calzada Almuradiel = Almuradiel Spain 38°32N 3°28W 195 G7
Calzada de Calatrava Spain 38°42N 3°46W 195 G7
Cam ➜ U.K. 52°21N 0°16E 169 E8
Cam Lam = Ba Ngoi Vietnam 11°54N 109°10E 237 G7
Cam Pha Vietnam 21°7N 107°18E 228 G6
Cam Ranh Vietnam 11°54N 109°12E 237 G7
Cam Xuyen Vietnam 18°15N 106°0E 236 C6
Camabatela Angola 8°20S 15°26E 265 D3
Camacã Brazil 15°24S 39°30W 333 E4
Camaçari Brazil 12°41S 38°18W 333 D4
Camacha Madeira 32°41N 16°49W 153 c
Camacupa Angola 11°58S 17°22E 265 E3
Camaguán Venezuela 8°6N 67°36W 328 B4
Camagüey Cuba 21°20N 77°55W 320 B4
Camagüey, Arch. de Cuba 22°18N 78°0W 320 B4
Camaiore Italy 43°56N 10°18E 198 E7
Camamu Brazil 13°57S 39°7W 333 D4
Camaná Peru 16°30S 72°50W 330 D3
Camanche U.S.A. 41°47N 90°15W 310 C6
Camanche Res. U.S.A. 38°14N 121°1W 306 G6
Camapuã Brazil 19°30S 54°5W 331 D7
Camaquã Brazil 30°51S 51°49W 335 C5
Camaquã ➜ Brazil 31°17S 51°47W 335 C5
Câmara de Lobos Madeira 32°39N 16°59W 153 c
Camararé ➜ Brazil 12°15S 58°55W 331 C6
Camarat, C. France 43°12N 6°41E 175 E10
Camarate Portugal 38°48N 9°7W 126 A2
Çamardı Turkey 37°49N 34°58E 212 D6
Camarès France 43°49N 2°53E 174 E6
Camaret-sur-Mer France 48°16N 4°37W 172 D2
Camargo Bolivia 20°38S 65°15W 331 E4
Camargo Tamaulipas, Mexico 26°19N 98°50W 319 B5
Camargue France 43°34N 4°34E 175 E8
Camargue △ France 43°30N 4°40E 175 E8
Camarillo U.S.A. 34°13N 119°2W 307 L7
Camariñas Spain 43°8N 9°12W 194 B1
Camarines Norte □ Phil. 14°10N 122°45E 232 D4
Camarines Sur □ Phil. 13°40N 123°20E 232 E4
Camaroes Portugal 38°49N 9°14W 126 A1
Camarón, C. Honduras 16°0N 85°5W 320 C2
Camarones Argentina 44°50S 65°40W 336 B3
Camarones, B. Argentina 44°45S 65°35W 336 B3
Camas Spain 37°24N 6°2W 195 H4
Camas Wash., U.S.A. 45°35N 122°24W 306 E4
Camas Valley U.S.A. 43°2N 123°40W 304 E2
Camatambo Angola 6°31S 15°21E 265 D3
Camataquí = Villa Abecia Bolivia 21°0S 68°18W 334 A2
Camaxilo Angola 8°21S 18°56E 265 D3
Camba Cassai Angola 9°47S 19°9E 265 D3
Camballin Australia 17°59S 124°12E 278 C3
Cambamba Angola 8°53S 14°44E 265 D2
Cambará Brazil 23°2S 50°5W 335 A5
Cambay = Khambhat India 22°23N 72°33E 242 H5
Cambay, G. of = Khambhat, G. of India 20°45N 72°30E 239 E10
Camberwell Vic., Australia 37°50S 145°5E 128 B2
Camberwell London, U.K. 51°28N 0°5W 125 B3
Cambil Spain 37°40N 3°33W 195 H7
Cambo Angola 10°55S 20°6E 265 D3
Cambo-les-Bains France 43°22N 1°23W 174 E2
Cambodia ■ Asia 12°15N 105°0E 236 F5
Camborne U.K. 50°12N 5°19W 169 G2
Cambrai S. Austral., Australia 34°40S 139°16E 282 C3
Cambrai Nord, France 50°11N 3°14E 173 B10
Cambre Spain 43°17N 8°20W 194 B2
Cambria U.S.A. 35°34N 121°5W 306 K5
Cambrian Mts. U.K. 52°3N 3°57W 169 E4
Cambridge Ont., Canada 43°23N 80°15W 312 C4
Cambridge Jamaica 18°18N 77°54W 320 a
Cambridge N.Z. 37°54S 175°29E 284 D4
Cambridge Cambs., U.K. 52°12N 0°8E 169 E8
Cambridge Ill., U.S.A. 41°18N 90°12W 310 C6
Cambridge Iowa, U.S.A. 41°54N 93°32W 310 C3
Cambridge Mass., U.S.A. 42°23N 71°7W 116 A2
Cambridge Minn., U.S.A. 45°34N 93°13W 308 C7
Cambridge N.Y., U.S.A. 43°2N 73°22W 313 C11
Cambridge Nebr., U.S.A. 40°17N 100°10W 308 E3
Cambridge Ohio, U.S.A. 40°2N 81°35W 312 F3
Cambridge Bay Canada 69°10N 105°0W 294 D11
Cambridge City U.S.A. 39°49N 85°10W 311 E11
Cambridge G. Australia 14°55S 128°15E 278 B4
Cambridge Springs U.S.A. 41°48N 80°4W 312 E4
Cambridgeshire □ U.K. 52°25N 0°7W 169 E7
Cambrils Spain 41°8N 1°3E 196 D6
Cambuci Rio de J., Brazil 21°35S 41°55W 333 F3
Cambuci São Paulo, Brazil 23°33S 46°47W 137 B2
Cambulo Angola 7°49S 21°15E 265 D4
Cambundi-Catembo Angola 10°10S 17°35E 265 E3
Camdeboo △ S. Africa 32°28S 24°25E 270 D3
Camden N.S.W., Australia 34°1S 150°43E 283 C9
Camden Ala., U.S.A. 31°59N 87°17W 315 F11
Camden Ark., U.S.A. 33°35N 92°50W 314 E8
Camden Maine, U.S.A. 44°13N 69°4W 309 C19
Camden N.J., U.S.A. 39°55N 75°7W 313 G9
Camden N.Y., U.S.A. 43°20N 75°45W 313 C9
Camden Ohio, U.S.A. 39°38N 84°39W 311 E12
Camden S.C., U.S.A. 34°13N 80°36W 315 D14
Camden □ U.K. 51°32N 0°8W 125 A3
Camden Bay U.S.A. 70°10N 145°15W 303 A11
Camden Sd. Australia 15°27S 124°25E 278 C3
Camdenton U.S.A. 38°1N 92°45W 310 F4
Camelford U.K. 50°37N 4°42W 169 G3
Çameli Turkey 37°5N 29°24E 205 D11
Camenca Moldova 48°3N 28°42E 183 B13
Camerino Italy 43°8N 13°4E 199 E10
Camerón Chile 53°38S 69°39W 336 D3
Cameron Ariz., U.S.A. 35°53N 111°25W 305 J8
Cameron La., U.S.A. 29°48N 93°20W 314 G8
Cameron Mo., U.S.A. 39°44N 94°14W 310 E2
Cameron S.C., U.S.A. 33°34N 80°43W 316 B9
Cameron Tex., U.S.A. 30°51N 96°59W 314 F6
Cameron Highlands Malaysia 4°27N 101°22E 237 K3
Cameron Hills Canada 59°48N 118°0W 296 B5
Cameron Mts. N.Z. 46°1S 167°0E 285 G2
Cameroon ■ Africa 6°0N 12°30E 264 A2
Camerota Italy 40°2N 15°22E 201 B8
Cameroun ➜ Cameroon 4°0N 9°35E 263 E6
Cameroun, Mt. Cameroon 4°13N 9°10E 263 E6
Cametá Brazil 2°12S 49°30W 332 B2
Çamiçi Gölü Turkey 37°29N 27°28E 205 D9
Camiguin □ Phil. 9°11N 124°42E 233 G5
Camiguin I. Phil. 18°56N 121°55E 232 B3
Camiling Phil. 15°42N 120°24E 232 D3
Camilla U.S.A. 31°14N 84°12W 316 D5
Caminha Portugal 41°50N 8°50W 194 D2
Camino U.S.A. 38°44N 120°41W 306 G6
Camiranga Brazil 1°48S 46°17W 332 B2
Camiri Bolivia 20°3S 63°31W 331 E5

Camissombo Angola 8°7S 20°38E 265 D4
Camlıbel = Myrtou Cyprus 35°18N 33°4E 207 E9
Çamlıca Turkey 41°1N 29°3E 122 B2
Çamlıyayla Turkey 37°10N 34°36E 250 A5
Cammal U.S.A. 41°24N 77°28W 312 E7
Cammarata Italy 37°38N 13°38E 200 E6
Cammin = Kamień Pomorski Poland 53°57N 14°43E 184 E1
Camo Ethiopia 4°29N 38°24E 266 D4
Camocim Brazil 2°55S 40°50W 332 B3
Camonica, Val Italy 46°0N 10°20E 198 B7
Camooweal Australia 19°56S 138°7E 280 B2
Camooweal Caves △ Australia 20°1S 138°11E 280 C2
Camopi Fr. Guiana 3°12N 52°17W 329 C7
Camopi → Fr. Guiana 3°10N 52°20W 329 C7
Camorta India 8°8N 93°30E 245 K11
Camotes Is. Phil. 10°40N 124°24E 233 F5
Camotes Sea Phil. 10°30N 124°15E 233 F5
Camp Coulter = Powell U.S.A. 44°45N 108°46W 304 D9
Camp Hill Ala., U.S.A. 32°48N 85°39W 316 C4
Camp Hill Pa., U.S.A. 40°14N 76°55W 312 F8
Camp Nelson U.S.A. 36°8N 118°39W 307 J8
Camp Pendleton U.S.A. 33°13N 117°24W 307 M9
Camp Point U.S.A. 40°3N 91°4W 310 D5
Camp Springs U.S.A. 38°48N 76°55W 143 C3
Camp Verde U.S.A. 34°34N 111°51W 305 J8
Camp Wood U.S.A. 29°40N 100°1W 314 G4
Campagna Italy 40°40N 15°6E 201 B8
Campamento Spain 40°23N 3°46W 127 B1
Campana Argentina 34°10S 58°55W 334 C4
Campana, I. Chile 48°20S 75°20W 336 C1
Campanário Madeira 32°39N 17°2W 153 c
Campanario Spain 38°52N 5°36W 195 G5
Campanet Spain 39°46N 2°58E 206 B3
Campánia □ Italy 41°0N 14°30E 201 B7
Campbell Northern Cape, S. Africa 28°48S 23°44E 270 C3
Campbell Calif., U.S.A. 37°17N 121°57W 306 H5
Campbell Fla., U.S.A. 28°16N 81°27W 317 G8
Campbell Ohio, U.S.A. 41°5N 80°37W 312 E4
Campbell, C. N.Z. 41°47S 174°18E 285 B9
Campbell I. Pac. Oc. 52°30S 169°0E 288 N8
Campbell L. Canada 63°14N 106°55W 297 A7
Campbell Plateau S. Ocean 50°0S 170°0E 151 A11
Campbell River Canada 50°5N 125°20W 296 C3
Campbellfield Australia 37°41S 144°57E 128 A1
Campbellford Canada 44°18N 77°48W 312 B7
Campbellpur Pakistan 33°46N 72°26E 242 C5
Campbellsburg U.S.A. 38°39N 86°16W 311 F10
Campbellsville U.S.A. 37°21N 85°20W 309 G11
Campbellton N.B., Canada 47°57N 66°43W 299 C6
Campbellton Fla., U.S.A. 30°57N 85°24W 316 E4
Campbelltown = Bluff N.Z. 46°37S 168°20E 285 G3
Campbelltown Australia 34°4S 150°49E 283 C9
Campbeltown U.K. 55°26N 5°36W 167 F3
Campêche Guadeloupe 16°26N 61°26W 322 e
Campeche Campeche, Mexico 19°51N 90°32W 319 D6
Campeche □ Mexico 19°0N 90°30W 319 D6
Campeche, Banco Mexico 22°30N 88°0W 320 B2
Campeche, Golfo de Mexico 19°30N 93°0W 319 D6
Câmpeni Romania 46°22N 23°3E 182 D8
Camperdown N.S.W., Australia 33°53S 151°11E 139 B2
Camperdown Vic., Australia 38°14S 143°9E 282 E5
Camperville Canada 51°59N 100°9W 297 C8
Campi Salentina Italy 40°24N 18°1E 201 B11
Câmpia Turzii Romania 46°34N 23°53E 183 D8
Campidano Italy 39°30N 8°47E 200 C1
Campidoglio, Piazza de Rome, Italy 136 c3
Campíglia Maríttima Italy 43°4N 10°37E 198 E7
Campillo de Altobuey Spain 39°36N 1°49W 197 F3
Campillos Spain 37°4N 4°51W 195 H6
Câmpina Romania 45°10N 25°45E 183 E10
Campina Grande Brazil 7°20S 35°47W 332 C4
Campina Verde Brazil 19°31S 49°28W 333 E2
Campinas Brazil 22°50S 47°0W 335 A6
Campione Italy 45°58N 8°58E 175 C12
Campli Italy 42°43N 13°41E 199 F10
Campo = Ntem → Cameroon 2°21N 9°49E 264 B2
Campo Cameroon 2°22N 9°50E 264 B1
Campo Spain 42°25N 0°24E 196 C5
Campo, Casa de Spain 40°25N 3°45W 127 B1
Campo ⌓ Cameroon 2°23N 10°5E 264 B2
Campo Belo Brazil 20°52S 45°16W 333 F2
Campo de Criptana Spain 39°24N 3°7W 195 F7
Campo de Diauarum Brazil 11°12S 53°14W 331 C7
Campo de Gibraltar Spain 36°15N 5°25W 195 J5
Campo F.C. Barcelona Spain 41°22N 2°7E 114 A1
Campo Florido Brazil 19°47S 48°35W 333 E2
Campo Formoso = Campo Florido Brazil 19°47S 48°35W 333 E2
Campo Formoso Brazil 10°30S 40°20W 332 D3
Campo Grande Brazil 20°25S 54°40W 331 E7
Campo Grando Portugal 38°45N 9°9W 126 A2
Campo Maior Brazil 4°50S 42°12W 332 B3
Campo Maior Portugal 39°2N 7°7W 195 F3
Campo Mourão Brazil 24°3S 52°22W 335 A5
Campo Pequeño Portugal 38°44N 9°8W 126 A2
Campo Santa Margherita Venice, Italy 142 b2
Campo Túres Italy 46°53N 11°55E 199 B8
Campoalegre Colombia 2°41N 75°20W 328 C2
Campobasso Italy 41°34N 14°39E 201 A7
Campobello di Licata Italy 37°15N 13°55E 200 E6
Campobello di Mazara Italy 37°38N 12°45E 200 E5
Campofelice di Roccella Italy 37°59N 13°53E 200 E6
Campolide Portugal 38°43N 9°9W 126 A2
Campomarino Italy 41°57N 15°2E 199 G12
Camporeale Italy 37°54N 13°6E 200 E6
Camporrobles Spain 39°39N 1°24W 196 F3
Campos Brazil 21°50S 41°20W 333 F3
Campos Spain 39°26N 3°1E 206 B4
Campos Altos Brazil 19°47S 46°10W 333 E2
Campos Belos Brazil 13°10S 47°3W 333 D2
Campos del Paraíso = Carrascosa del Campo Spain 40°2N 2°45W 196 E2
Campos Novos Brazil 27°21S 51°50W 335 B5
Campos Sales Brazil 7°4S 40°23W 332 C3
Camprodon Spain 42°19N 2°23E 196 C7
Camps Bay S. Africa 33°57S 18°23E 118 A1
Campton Fla., U.S.A. 30°53N 86°31W 317 E3
Campton Ga., U.S.A. 33°52N 83°43W 316 B6
Campton Ky., U.S.A. 37°44N 83°33W 311 G13
Camptonville U.S.A. 39°27N 121°3W 306 F5
Camptown U.S.A. 41°44N 76°14W 313 E8
Câmpulung Argeş, Romania 45°17N 25°3E 183 E10
Câmpulung Suceava, Romania 47°32N 25°30E 183 C10
Câmpuri Romania 46°0N 26°50E 183 D11
Campuya → Peru 1°40S 73°30W 328 D3
Campville U.S.A. 29°40N 82°7W 316 F7
Camrose Canada 53°0N 112°50W 296 C6
Camsell Portage Canada 59°37N 109°15W 297 B7
Camucuio Angola 14°7S 13°15E 265 E2
Camuy Puerto Rico 18°29N 66°51W 321 b
Çamyuva Turkey 36°30N 30°30E 205 E12
Çan Turkey 40°2N 27°3E 203 F11
Can Clavo Spain 38°57N 1°27E 206 D1
Can Creu Spain 38°58N 1°28E 206 D1
Can Gio Vietnam 10°25N 106°58E 237 G6
Can Pastilla Spain 39°32N 2°42E 206 B3
C'an San Joan Spain 41°28N 2°11E 114 A2
Can Tho Vietnam 10°2N 105°46E 237 G5
Canaan Trin. & Tob. 11°9N 60°49W 323 s
Canaan Conn., U.S.A. 42°2N 73°20W 313 D11
Canaan Hill Jamaica 18°23N 77°14W 320 a
Cañacao B. Phil. 14°29N 120°54E 127 C1
Canacona India 15°1N 74°4E 245 G2
Canada ■ N. Amer. 60°0N 100°0W 294 G11
Canada Abyssal Plain Arctic 80°0N 140°0W 150 B18
Canada Basin Arctic 75°0N 145°0W 150 B18
Cañada de Gómez Argentina 32°40S 61°30W 334 C3
Canadian U.S.A. 35°55N 100°23W 314 D4
Canadian → U.S.A. 35°28N 95°3W 314 D7
Canadian Shield Canada 53°0N 75°0W 292 D12
Canadys U.S.A. 33°3N 80°37W 316 B9
Canajoharie U.S.A. 42°54N 74°35W 313 D10
Çanakkale Turkey 40°8N 26°24E 203 F10
Çanakkale □ Turkey 40°10N 26°25E 203 F10
Çanakkale Boğazı Turkey 40°17N 26°32E 203 F10
Canal Flats Canada 50°10N 115°48W 296 C5
Canal Grande Venice, Italy 142 b2
Canal Point U.S.A. 26°52N 80°38W 317 J9
Canal Street New Orleans, U.S.A. 131 b2
Canala N. Cal. 21°32S 165°57E 288 d
Canalejas Argentina 35°15S 66°34W 334 D2
Canals Argentina 33°35S 62°53W 334 C3
Canals Spain 38°58N 0°35W 197 G4
Canandaigua U.S.A. 42°54N 77°17W 312 D7
Canandaigua L. U.S.A. 42°47N 77°19W 312 D7
Cananea Mexico 31°0N 110°18W 318 A2
Cañar Ecuador 2°33S 78°56W 328 D2
Cañar □ Ecuador 2°30S 79°0W 328 D2
Canarias, Is. Atl. Oc. 28°30N 16°0W 153 e1
Canaries St. Lucia 13°55N 61°4W 323 m
Canarreos, Arch. de los Cuba 21°35N 81°40W 320 B3
Canarsie U.S.A. 40°38N 73°53W 132 C2
Canary Is. = Canarias, Is. Atl. Oc. 28°30N 16°0W 153 e1
Canary Wharf U.K. 51°30N 0°1W 125 A3
Canaseraga U.S.A. 42°27N 77°45W 312 D7
Canastra, Serra da Brazil 20°0S 46°20W 333 F2
Canatlán Mexico 24°31N 104°47W 318 C4
Cañaveral Peru 3°56S 80°39W 328 D1
Canaveral, C. U.S.A. 28°27N 80°32W 317 G9
Canaveral ⌓ U.S.A. 28°28N 80°34W 317 G9
Cañaveruelas Spain 40°24N 2°38W 196 E2
Canavieiras Brazil 15°39S 39°0W 333 E4
Canbelego Australia 31°32S 146°18E 283 A7
Canberra Australia 35°15S 149°8E 283 C8
Canby Calif., U.S.A. 41°27N 120°52W 304 F3
Canby Minn., U.S.A. 44°43N 96°16W 308 C5
Canby Oreg., U.S.A. 45°16N 122°42W 306 E4
Cancale France 48°40N 1°50W 172 D5
Cancelleria, Palazzo dei Rome, Italy 136 c2
Canche → France 50°31N 1°39E 173 B8
Canchungo = Teixeira Pinto Guinea-Biss. 12°3N 16°0W 262 C1
Canchungo Guinea-Biss. 12°26N 16°5W 262 C1
Canchyuaya, Cordillera de Peru 7°30S 74°0W 330 B3
Cancún Mexico 21°8N 86°44W 319 C7
Candanchú Spain 42°47N 0°32W 196 C4
Candarave Peru 17°15S 70°13W 330 D3
Çandarlı Turkey 38°56N 26°56E 205 C8
Çandarlı Körfezi Turkey 38°52N 26°55E 205 C8
Candás Spain 43°35N 5°45W 194 B5
Candé France 47°34N 1°2W 172 E5
Candeias → Brazil 8°39S 63°31W 331 B5
Candela Italy 41°8N 15°31E 201 A8
Candelaria Argentina 27°29S 55°44W 335 B4
Candelaria Canary Is. 28°22N 16°22W 153 e1
Candelaria Phil. 13°56N 121°25E 232 E3
Candelario ⌓ Spain 40°20N 5°46W 194 E5
Candeleda Spain 40°10N 5°14W 194 E5
Candelo Australia 36°47S 149°43E 283 D8
Candi Dasa Indonesia 8°30S 115°34E 231 J18
Candia = Iraklio Greece 35°20N 25°12E 207 E6
Candia, Sea of = Crete, Sea of Greece 36°0N 25°0E 205 E7
Candiac Canada 45°23N 73°29W 130 B3
Cândido de Abreu Brazil 24°35S 51°20W 333 F1
Cândido Mendes Brazil 1°27S 45°43W 332 B2
Candle U.S.A. 65°55N 161°56W 303 D7
Candle L. Canada 53°50N 105°18W 297 C7
Candlemas I. Antarctica 57°3S 26°40W 151 B1
Cando U.S.A. 48°32N 99°12W 308 A4
Candon Phil. 17°12N 120°27E 232 C3
Canea = Chania Greece 35°30N 24°4E 207 E5
Caneças Portugal 38°48N 9°13W 126 A1
Canefield Dominica 15°20N 61°24W 323 k
Canela Brazil 10°15S 48°25W 332 D2
Canelles → St. Lucia 13°47N 60°55W 323 m
Canelli Italy 44°43N 8°17E 198 D5
Canelones Uruguay 34°32S 56°17W 335 C4
Canet-Plage France 42°41N 3°2E 174 F7
Cañete Chile 37°50S 73°30W 334 D1
Cañete Spain 40°3N 1°54W 196 E3
Cañete de las Torres Spain 37°53N 4°19W 195 H6
Cangamba Angola 13°40S 19°54E 265 E3
Cangandala Angola 9°45S 16°33E 265 D3
Cangandala △ Angola 9°53S 16°42E 265 D3
Cangas Spain 42°16N 8°47W 194 C2
Cangas de Onís Spain 43°21N 5°8W 194 B5
Cangas de Tineo = Cangas del Narcea Spain 43°10N 6°32W 194 B4
Cangas del Narcea Spain 43°10N 6°32W 194 B4
Cangnan China 27°30N 120°23E 229 D13
Cangoa Angola 13°8S 18°30E 265 E3
Cangola Angola 7°58S 15°53E 265 D3
Cangolo Angola 15°0S 13°52E 265 E2
Cangombe Angola 14°24S 19°59E 265 E3
Cangongo Angola 9°24S 17°30E 265 D3
Cangshan China 34°50N 118°2E 227 G10
Canguaretama Brazil 6°20S 35°5W 332 C4
Canguçu Brazil 31°22S 52°43W 335 C5
Canguçu, Serra do Brazil 31°20S 52°40W 335 C5
Cangumbe Angola 11°58S 19°12E 265 E3
Cangxi China 31°47N 105°59E 228 B5
Cangyuan China 23°12N 99°14E 228 F2
Cangzhou China 38°19N 116°52E 226 E9
Canhoca Angola 9°15S 14°41E 265 D2
Cani, I. Tunisia 36°21N 10°5E 258 A2
Caniapiscau → Canada 56°40N 69°30W 299 A6
Caniapiscau, L. Canada 54°10N 69°55W 299 B6
Canicattì Italy 37°21N 13°51E 200 E6
Canicattini Bagni Italy 37°2N 15°4E 201 E8
Canigao Channel Phil. 10°15N 124°42E 233 F5
Caniles Spain 37°26N 2°43W 195 H8
Canillas Spain 40°27N 3°38W 127 B2
Canillejas Spain 40°26N 3°36W 127 B2
Canim Lake Canada 51°47N 120°54W 296 C4
Canindé Brazil 4°22S 39°19W 332 B4
Canindé → Brazil 6°15S 42°52W 332 C3
Canindeyu □ Paraguay 24°10S 55°0W 335 A5
Canino Italy 42°28N 11°45E 199 F8
Canisteo U.S.A. 42°16N 77°36W 312 D7
Canisteo → U.S.A. 42°7N 77°8W 312 D7
Cañitas de Felipe Pescador Mexico 23°36N 102°43W 318 C4
Cañizal Spain 41°12N 5°22W 194 D5
Canjáyar Spain 37°1N 2°44W 195 H8
Canjinge Angola 10°12S 21°17E 265 E4
Çankırı Turkey 40°40N 33°37E 212 B5
Çankırı □ Turkey 40°40N 33°30E 212 B5
Cankuzo Burundi 3°10S 30°31E 268 C3
Canlaon Phil. 10°22N 123°12E 233 F4
Canlaon Volcano Phil. 10°25N 123°8E 233 F4
Canmore Canada 51°7N 115°18W 296 C5
Cann River Australia 37°35S 149°7E 283 D8
Canna U.K. 57°3N 6°33W 167 D2
Cannanore = Kannur India 11°53N 75°27E 245 J2
Cannanore Is. India 10°30N 72°30E 245 J1
Cannaregio Venice, Italy 142 a2
Cannaregio, Canale di Venice, Italy 142 a2
Cannelton U.S.A. 37°55N 86°45W 311 G10
Cannery, The San Francisco, U.S.A. 136 a1
Cannes France 43°32N 7°1E 175 E11
Canning Town = Port Canning India 22°23N 88°40E 243 H13
Canning Town U.K. 51°30N 0°1E 125 A4
Cannington Canada 44°20N 79°2W 312 B5
Cannóbio Italy 46°4N 8°42E 198 B5
Cannock U.K. 52°41N 2°1W 169 E5
Cannonball → U.S.A. 46°26N 100°35W 308 B3
Cannondale Mt. Australia 25°13S 148°57E 280 D4
Cannonsville Res. U.S.A. 42°4N 75°22W 313 D9
Cannonvale Australia 20°17S 148°43E 280 b
Caño Colorado Colombia 2°18N 68°22W 328 C4
Canoas Brazil 29°56S 51°11W 335 B5
Canoe L. Canada 55°10N 108°15W 297 B7
Cañon City U.S.A. 38°27N 105°14W 304 G11
Cañón de Río Blanco △ Mexico 18°43N 97°15W 319 D5
Cañón del Río Lobos ⌓ Spain 41°46N 3°28W 194 D7
Canonnier, Pte. du St.-Martin 18°4N 63°7W 322 a
Canonniers Pt. Mauritius 20°2S 57°32E 272 e
Canoochee → U.S.A. 31°59N 81°19W 316 D8
Canopus Australia 33°29S 140°42E 282 B4
Canora Canada 51°40N 102°30W 297 C8
Canosa di Púglia Italy 41°13N 16°4E 201 A9
Canouan St. Vincent 12°43N 61°20W 323 n
Canowindra Australia 33°35S 148°38E 283 B8
Canso Canada 45°20N 61°0W 299 C7
Canta Peru 11°29S 76°37W 330 C2
Cantabria □ Spain 43°10N 4°0W 194 B7
Cantabria, Sierra de Spain 42°40N 2°30W 196 C2
Cantabrian Mts. = Cantábrica, Cordillera Spain 43°0N 5°10W 194 C5
Cantábrica, Cordillera Spain 43°0N 5°10W 194 C5
Cantal □ France 45°5N 2°45E 174 C6
Cantal, Plomb du France 45°3N 2°45E 174 C6
Cantanhede Portugal 40°20N 8°36W 194 E2
Cantaura Venezuela 9°19N 64°21W 329 B5
Cantavieja Spain 40°31N 0°25W 196 E4
Čantavir Serbia 45°55N 19°46E 182 E4
Cantemir Moldova 46°17N 28°14E 183 D13
Canteras de Vallecas Spain 40°20N 3°37W 127 B2
Canterbury = Invermere Canada 50°30N 116°2W 296 C5
Canterbury N.S.W., Australia 33°55S 151°7E 139 B1
Canterbury Queens., Australia 25°23S 141°53E 280 D3
Canterbury Vic., Australia 37°49S 145°4E 128 A2
Canterbury Kent, U.K. 51°16N 1°6E 169 F9
Canterbury □ N.Z. 43°45S 171°19E 285 D6
Canterbury Bight N.Z. 44°16S 171°55E 285 E6
Canterbury Plains N.Z. 43°55S 171°22E 285 D6
Cantil U.S.A. 35°18N 117°58W 307 K9
Cantilan Phil. 9°20N 125°58E 233 G5
Cantillana Spain 37°36N 5°50W 195 H5
Canto do Buriti Brazil 8°7S 42°58W 332 C3
Canton = Guangzhou China 23°6N 113°13E 121 B2
Canton Ga., U.S.A. 34°14N 84°29W 315 D12
Canton Ill., U.S.A. 40°33N 90°2W 310 D6
Canton Miss., U.S.A. 32°37N 90°2W 315 E9
Canton Mo., U.S.A. 40°8N 91°32W 310 D5
Canton N.Y., U.S.A. 44°36N 75°10W 313 B9
Canton Ohio, U.S.A. 40°48N 81°23W 312 F3
Canton Pa., U.S.A. 41°39N 76°51W 312 E8
Canton S. Dak., U.S.A. 43°18N 96°35W 308 D5
Canton L. U.S.A. 36°6N 98°35W 314 C5
Canton Tower China 23°6N 113°19E 121 B2
Cantonment U.S.A. 30°37N 87°20W 317 E2
Cantù Italy 45°44N 9°8E 198 C6
Cantwell U.S.A. 63°24N 148°57W 303 E10
Canudos Brazil 7°13S 58°5W 331 B6
Canumã Amazonas, Brazil 4°2S 59°4W 329 D6
Canumã Amazonas, Brazil 6°8S 60°10W 331 B5
Canumã → Brazil 3°55S 59°10W 331 A6
Canunda △ Australia 37°42S 140°16E 282 D4
Canutama Brazil 6°30S 64°20W 331 B5
Canutillo U.S.A. 31°55N 106°36W 314 F1
Canvey U.K. 51°31N 0°37E 169 F8
Canyon U.S.A. 34°59N 101°55W 314 D4
Canyon De Chelly ⌓ U.S.A. 36°10N 109°20W 305 H9
Canyonlands △ U.S.A. 38°15N 110°0W 305 G9
Canyons of the Ancients ⌓ U.S.A. 37°30N 108°55W 305 H9
Canyonville U.S.A. 42°56N 123°17W 304 E2
Canzar Angola 7°35S 21°34E 265 D4
Cao Bang Vietnam 22°40N 106°15E 228 F6
Cao He → China 40°10N 124°32E 227 D13
Cao Lanh Vietnam 10°27N 105°38E 237 G5
Cao Xian China 34°50N 115°35E 226 G8
Caoheijing China 31°10N 121°25E 138 B1
Caombo Angola 8°42S 16°33E 265 D3
Cáorle Italy 45°36N 12°53E 199 C9
Cap-aux-Meules Canada 47°23N 61°52W 299 C7
Cap-Chat Canada 49°6N 66°40W 299 C6
Cap-de-la-Madeleine Canada 46°22N 72°31W 298 C5
Cap-de-Ville Trin. & Tob. 10°9N 61°42W 323 t
Cap-Haïtien Haiti 19°40N 72°20W 321 C5
Cap I. Phil. 5°57N 120°6E 233 J3
Cap Pt. St. Lucia 14°7N 60°57W 323 m
Capac U.S.A. 43°1N 82°56W 312 C2
Capáccio Italy 40°25N 15°5E 201 B8
Capaci Italy 38°10N 13°14E 200 D6
Capaia Angola 8°27S 20°13E 265 D4
Capalonga Phil. 14°20N 122°30E 232 D4
Capanaparo → Venezuela 7°1N 67°7W 328 B4
Capanema Brazil 1°12S 47°11W 332 B2
Capangombe Angola 15°6S 13°8E 265 F2
Capánnori Italy 43°50N 10°34E 198 E7
Capão Redondo Brazil 23°39S 46°45W 137 B1
Caparaó △ Brazil 20°25S 41°46W 333 F3
Caparica Portugal 38°40N 9°9W 126 A2
Caparica, Costa da Portugal 38°38N 9°15W 126 B1
Caparo → Trin. & Tob. 10°31N 61°28W 323 t
Capas Phil. 15°38N 120°28E 232 D3
Capatárida Venezuela 11°11N 70°37W 328 A3
Capayas Phil. 10°28N 119°39E 233 F2
Capbreton France 43°39N 1°26W 174 E2
Capdenac France 44°34N 2°5E 174 D6
Capdepera Spain 39°42N 3°26E 206 B4
Cape → Australia 20°59S 146°51E 280 C4
Cape Arid △ Australia 33°58S 123°13E 279 F3
Cape Barren I. Australia 40°25S 148°15E 281 G4
Cape Basin Atl. Oc. 34°0S 7°0W 152 K12
Cape Breton Highlands △ Canada 46°50N 60°40W 299 C7
Cape Breton I. Canada 46°0N 60°30W 299 C7
Cape Canaveral U.S.A. 28°24N 80°36W 317 G9
Cape Charles U.S.A. 37°16N 76°1W 309 G15
Cape Coast Ghana 5°5N 1°15W 263 D4
Cape Cod ⌓ U.S.A. 41°56N 70°6W 309 E18
Cape Coral U.S.A. 26°33N 81°57W 317 J8
Cape Crawford Australia 16°41S 135°43E 280 B2
Cape Dorset = Kinngait Canada 64°14N 76°32W 295 E16
Cape Fear → U.S.A. 33°53N 78°1W 315 E15
Cape Flats S. Africa 34°3S 18°33E 118 B2
Cape Girardeau U.S.A. 37°19N 89°32W 308 G9
Cape Hatteras ⌓ U.S.A. 35°30N 75°28W 315 D17
Cape Hillsborough △ Australia 20°54S 149°2E 280 b
Cape Jervis Australia 35°40S 138°5E 282 C3
Cape Krusenstern ⌓ U.S.A. 67°30N 163°30W 303 C7
Cape Le Grand △ Australia 33°54S 122°26E 279 F3
Cape Lisburne = Wevok U.S.A. 68°53N 166°13W 303 B6
Cape Lookout ⌓ U.S.A. 35°45N 76°25W 315 D16
Cape May U.S.A. 38°56N 74°56W 309 F16
Cape May Point U.S.A. 38°56N 74°58W 309 F16
Cape Melville △ Australia 14°26S 144°28E 280 A3
Cape Mount △ Liberia 6°44N 11°24W 262 D2
Cape Pole U.S.A. 55°58N 133°48W 303 J14
Cape Range △ Australia 22°3S 114°0E 278 D1
Cape St. George Canada 48°28N 59°14W 299 C8
Cape Tormentine Canada 46°8N 63°47W 299 C7
Cape Town S. Africa 33°55S 18°22E 118 A1
Cape Town Int. ✈ (CPT) S. Africa 33°58S 18°35E 118 A2
Cape Upstart △ Australia 19°45S 147°48E 280 B4
Cape Verde Abyssal Plain Atl. Oc. 23°0N 26°0W 152 D9
Cape Verde Is. ■ Atl. Oc. 16°0N 24°0W 153 j
Cape Verde Plateau Atl. Oc. 18°0N 20°0W 152 E10
Cape Vincent U.S.A. 44°8N 76°20W 313 B8
Cape Yakataga U.S.A. 60°4N 142°26W 303 F12
Cape York Peninsula Australia 12°0S 142°30E 286 F2
Capela Brazil 10°30S 37°0W 332 D4
Capelas Azores 37°50N 25°41W 153 d3
Capele Angola 13°39S 14°53E 265 E2
Capelengue Angola 8°53S 19°42E 265 D3
Capelinha Brazil 17°42S 42°31W 333 E3
Capelinhos, Pta. dos Azores 38°36N 28°50W 153 d1
Capella Australia 23°2S 148°1E 280 C4
Capella, Mt. Papua N. G. 5°4S 141°8E 286 C1
Capelongo Angola 14°54S 15°8E 265 E3
Capenda Camulemba Angola 9°24S 18°27E 265 D3
Capendu France 43°11N 2°31E 174 E6
Capertree Australia 33°6S 149°58E 283 B8
Capestang France 43°20N 3°2E 174 E7
Capesterre, Grande Rivière de la → Guadeloupe 16°3N 61°33W 322 e
Capesterre, Pte. de la Guadeloupe 16°3N 61°33W 322 e
Capesterre-Belle-Eau Guadeloupe 16°4N 61°36W 322 e
Capesterre-de-Marie-Galante Guadeloupe 15°53N 61°14W 322 e
Capim → Brazil 1°40S 47°47W 332 B2
Capinópolis Brazil 18°41S 49°35W 333 E2
Capinota Bolivia 17°43S 66°14W 330 D4
Capira Panama 8°45N 79°53W 328 B2
Capistrello Italy 41°57N 13°23E 199 G10
Capitan U.S.A. 33°35N 105°35W 305 K11
Capitán Aracena, I. Chile 54°10S 71°20W 336 D2
Capitán Arturo Prat Antarctica 63°0S 61°0W 151 C17
Capitán Pastene Chile 38°13S 73°1W 336 A2
Capitão de Campos Brazil 4°40S 41°55W 332 B3
Capitol Heights U.S.A. 38°52N 76°55W 143 B3
Capitol Hill N. Marianas 15°13N 145°45E 302 e
Capitol Reef △ U.S.A. 38°15N 111°10W 305 G8
Capitola U.S.A. 36°59N 121°57W 306 J5
Capitolini, Musei Rome, Italy 136 c3
Capivara, Serra da Brazil 14°35S 45°0W 333 D3
Capiz □ Phil. 11°35N 122°30E 233 F4
Capizzi Italy 37°51N 14°29E 201 E7
Capoche → Mozam. 15°35S 33°0E 269 F3
Capodichino, Nápoli ✈ (NAP) Italy 40°53N 14°16E 201 B7
Capoeira Brazil 5°37S 59°33W 331 B6
Capolo Angola 10°22S 14°7E 265 E2
Caporetto = Kobarid Slovenia 46°15N 13°30E 199 B10
Caporolo → Angola 12°56S 12°58E 265 E2
Capot → Martinique 14°50N 61°5W 322 j
Capoterra Italy 39°11N 8°58E 200 C1
Cappadocia Turkey 39°0N 35°0E 212 C6
Capps U.S.A. 30°24N 83°54W 316 E6
Capraia Italy 43°2N 9°50E 198 E6
Caprara, Pta. Italy 41°7N 8°19E 200 A1
Caprarola Italy 42°19N 12°14E 199 F9
Caprera Italy 41°12N 9°28E 200 A2
Capri Italy 40°33N 14°14E 201 B7
Capricorn Coast Australia 23°16S 150°49E 280 C5
Capricorn Group Australia 23°30S 151°55E 280 C5
Capricorn Ra. Australia 23°20S 116°50E 278 D2
Caprino Veronese Italy 45°36N 10°47E 198 C7
Caprivi □ Namibia 18°0S 23°30E 270 A3
Caprivi ⌓ Namibia 17°55S 22°37E 270 A3
Caprivi Strip Namibia 18°0S 23°0E 270 A3
Caps et Marais d'Opale ⌓ France 50°40N 2°0E 173 B9
Captain Cook U.S.A. 19°30N 155°55W 302 D6
Captain Cook Bridge Australia 34°0S 151°7E 139 C1
Captain Cook Landing Place Park Australia 34°1S 151°14E 139 C2
Captains Flat Australia 35°35S 149°27E 283 C8
Captieux France 44°18N 0°16W 174 D3
Captiva U.S.A. 26°31N 82°11W 317 J7
Capuça Angola 17°22S 21°18E 265 F4
Capuchos Portugal 38°38N 9°16W 126 B1
Capucin Dominica 15°38N 61°28W 323 k
Capul I. Phil. 12°26N 124°10E 232 E5
Capulin Volcano ⌓ U.S.A. 36°47N 103°58W 314 C3
Capunda Angola 10°41S 17°23E 265 E3
Caquetá □ Colombia 1°0N 74°0W 328 C3
Caquetá → Colombia 1°15S 69°15W 328 D4
Car Nicobar India 9°10N 92°47E 245 K11
Cara-Paraná → Colombia 1°45S 73°13W 328 D3
Carabanchel Alto Spain 40°22N 3°44W 127 B1
Carabanchel Bajo Spain 40°23N 3°44W 127 B1
Carabao I. Phil. 12°4N 121°56E 232 E3
Carabobo □ Venezuela 10°10N 68°5W 328 A4
Caracal Romania 44°8N 24°22E 183 F9
Caracaraí Brazil 1°50N 61°8W 329 C5
Caracas Venezuela 10°30N 66°55W 328 A4
Caracol Belize 16°45N 89°6W 320 C2
Caracol Mato Grosso do Sul, Brazil 22°18S 57°1W 334 A4
Caracol Piauí, Brazil 9°15S 43°22W 332 C3
Caracoli, Pte. Martinique 14°45N 60°52W 322 j
Caracollo Bolivia 17°39S 67°10W 330 D4
Caraga Phil. 7°20N 126°34E 233 H6
Caraga □ Phil. 9°40N 125°30E 233 G6
Caragabal Australia 33°49S 147°45E 283 B7
Caráglio Italy 44°25N 7°26E 198 D4
Carahue Chile 38°43S 73°12W 336 A2
Caraí Brazil 17°12S 41°42W 333 E3
Caraïbes, Mts. Guadeloupe 15°58N 61°41W 322 e
Carajás Brazil 2°57S 51°22W 332 C1
Carajás, Serra dos Brazil 6°0S 51°30W 332 C1
Caral Peru 10°53S 77°31W 330 C2
Caramoan Phil. 13°46N 123°52E 232 E4
Caramoan Pen. Phil. 13°47N 123°44E 232 E4
Caramoran Phil. 14°0N 124°8E 232 D5
Caranapatuba Brazil 6°38S 62°34W 331 B5
Carandaiti Bolivia 20°45S 63°4W 331 E5
Carangola Brazil 20°44S 42°5W 333 F3
Caransebeş Romania 45°28N 22°18E 182 E7
Carantec France 48°40N 3°55W 172 D3
Carapachay Argentina 34°31S 58°32W 117 B1
Carapichaima Trin. & Tob. 10°28N 61°27W 323 t
Carapo → Barinas, Venezuela 7°46N 70°23W 328 B3
Carapo → Bolívar, Venezuela 7°30N 64°0W 329 B5
Carapuse B. Trin. & Tob. 11°14N 60°35W 323 s
Caraquet Canada 47°48N 64°57W 299 C6
Caraş Severin □ Romania 45°10N 22°10E 182 E7
Caraşova Romania 45°11N 21°51E 182 E6
Caratasca, L. de Honduras 15°20N 83°40W 320 C3
Caratinga Brazil 19°50S 42°10W 333 E3
Carauaí Brazil 4°52S 66°54W 328 D4
Caraúbas Brazil 5°43S 37°33W 332 C4
Caravaca de la Cruz Spain 38°8N 1°52W 197 G3
Caravággio Italy 45°30N 9°38E 198 C6
Caravela Guinea-Biss. 11°30N 16°30W 262 C1
Caravelas Brazil 17°45S 39°15W 333 E4
Caraveli Peru 15°45S 73°25W 330 D3
Caravelle, Presqu'île de la Martinique 14°46N 60°48W 322 j
Caraz Peru 9°3S 77°47W 330 B2
Caraza Argentina 34°41S 58°25W 117 C2
Carazinho Brazil 28°16S 52°46W 335 B5
Carballino = O Carballiño Spain 42°26N 8°5W 194 C2
Carballo Spain 43°13N 8°41W 194 B2
Carberry Canada 49°50N 99°25W 297 D9
Carbet, Chutes du Guadeloupe 16°2N 61°38W 322 e
Carbet, Pitons du Martinique 14°42N 61°7W 322 j
Carbó Mexico 29°42N 110°58W 318 B2
Carbón, L. del Argentina 49°35S 68°21W 336 C3
Carbonara, C. Italy 39°6N 9°31E 200 C2
Carbondale Colo., U.S.A. 39°24N 107°13W 304 G10
Carbondale Ill., U.S.A. 37°44N 89°13W 310 G7
Carbondale Pa., U.S.A. 41°35N 75°30W 313 E9
Carbonear Canada 47°42N 53°13W 299 C9
Carboneras Spain 36°59N 1°53W 197 J3
Carboneras de Guadazaón Spain 39°54N 1°50W 196 F3
Carbónia Italy 39°10N 8°30E 200 C1
Carcabuey Spain 37°27N 4°17W 195 H6
Carcagente = Carcaixent Spain 39°8N 0°28W 197 F4
Carcaixent Spain 39°8N 0°28W 197 F4
Carcajou Canada 57°47N 117°6W 296 B5
Carcar Phil. 10°6N 123°38E 233 F4
Carcarana → Argentina 32°27S 60°48W 334 C3
Carcasse, C. Haiti 18°30N 74°28W 321 C5
Carcassonne France 43°13N 2°20E 174 E6
Carchi □ Ecuador 0°45N 78°0W 328 C2
Carcoar Australia 33°36S 149°8E 283 B8
Carcross Canada 60°13N 134°45W 296 A2
Çardak Çanakkale, Turkey 40°22N 26°43E 203 F10
Çardak Denizli, Turkey 37°49N 29°39E 205 D11
Cardamon Hills India 9°30N 77°15E 245 K3
Cardamon Mts. = Kravanh, Chuor Phnum Cambodia 12°0N 103°32E 237 G4
Cardeña Spain 38°16N 4°20W 195 G6
Cárdenas Cuba 23°0N 81°30W 320 B3
Cárdenas San Luis Potosí, Mexico 22°0N 99°38W 319 C5
Cárdenas Tabasco, Mexico 17°59N 93°22W 319 D6
Cardener → Spain 41°41N 1°51E 196 D6
Cardenete Spain 39°46N 1°41W 196 F3
Cardiel, L. Argentina 48°55S 71°10W 336 C2
Cardiff U.K. 51°29N 3°10W 169 F4
Cardiff □ U.K. 51°31N 3°12W 169 F4
Cardiff-by-the-Sea U.S.A. 33°1N 117°17W 307 M9
Cardigan U.K. 52°5N 4°40W 169 E3
Cardigan B. U.K. 52°30N 4°30W 169 E3
Cardinal Canada 44°47N 75°23W 313 B9
Cardón, Punta Venezuela 11°37N 70°14W 328 A3
Cardona Spain 41°56N 1°40E 196 D6
Cardona Uruguay 33°53S 57°18W 334 C4
Cardoso, Ilha do Brazil 25°8S 47°58W 335 B5
Cardston Canada 49°15N 113°20W 296 D6
Cardwell Australia 18°14S 146°2E 280 B4
Careen L. Canada 57°0N 108°11W 297 B7
Carei Romania 47°40N 22°29E 182 C7
Careiro Brazil 3°12S 59°45W 329 D6
Carenage Trin. & Tob. 10°41N 61°36W 323 t
Carentan France 49°19N 1°15W 172 C5
Carey Idaho, U.S.A. 43°19N 113°57W 304 E7
Carey Ohio, U.S.A. 40°57N 83°23W 311 D13
Carey, L. Australia 29°0S 122°15E 279 E3
Carey L. Canada 62°12N 102°55W 297 A8
Careysburg Liberia 6°34N 10°30W 262 D2
Cargados Carajos Ind. Oc. 17°0S 59°0E 273 F4
Cargèse France 42°7N 8°35E 175 F12
Carhaix-Plouguer France 48°18N 3°36W 172 D3
Carhuamayo Peru 10°51S 76°4W 330 C2
Carhuas Peru 9°15S 77°39W 330 B2
Carhué Argentina 37°10S 62°50W 334 D3
Caria Turkey 37°20N 28°10E 205 D10
Cariacica Brazil 20°16S 40°25W 333 F3
Cariaco Venezuela 10°29N 63°33W 329 A5
Cariango Angola 10°37S 15°20E 265 E3
Cariati Italy 39°30N 16°57E 201 C9
Caribbean Sea W. Indies 15°0N 75°0W 320 C4
Cariboo Mts. Canada 53°0N 121°0W 296 C4
Caribou U.S.A. 46°52N 68°1W 309 B19
Caribou → Man., Canada 59°20N 94°44W 297 B10
Caribou → N.W.T., Canada 61°27N 125°45W 296 A3
Caribou I. Canada 47°22N 85°49W 298 C2
Caribou Is. Canada 61°55N 113°15W 296 A6
Caribou L. Man., Canada 59°21N 96°10W 297 B9
Caribou L. Ont., Canada 50°25N 89°5W 298 B2
Caribou Mts. Canada 59°12N 115°40W 296 B5
Caribou River ⌓ Canada 59°35N 96°35W 297 B9
Caribrod = Dimitrovgrad Serbia 43°2N 22°48E 202 C6
Carichíc Mexico 27°56N 107°3W 318 B3
Caridad Phil. 14°28N 120°53E 127 C1
Carigara Phil. 11°18N 124°41E 233 F5
Carigara B. Phil. 11°22N 124°37E 233 F5
Carignan France 49°38N 5°10E 173 C12
Carignano Italy 44°55N 7°40E 198 D4
Carinda Australia 30°28S 147°41E 283 A7
Cariñena Spain 41°20N 1°13W 196 D3
Carinhanha Brazil 14°15S 44°46W 333 D3
Carinhanha → Brazil 14°20S 43°47W 333 D3
Carini Italy 38°8N 13°11E 200 D5
Cariño Spain 43°45N 7°52W 194 B3
Carínola Italy 41°11N 13°58E 200 A6
Carinthia = Kärnten □ Austria 46°52N 13°30E 180 E6
Carioca, Sa. da Brazil 22°57S 43°13W 135 B1
Caripito Venezuela 10°8N 63°6W 329 A5
Cariré Brazil 3°57S 40°27W 332 B3
Caritianas Brazil 9°20S 63°6W 331 B5
Carles Phil. 11°34N 123°8E 233 F4
Carlet Spain 39°14N 0°31W 197 F4
Carleton, Mt. Canada 47°23N 66°53W 299 C6
Carleton Place Canada 45°8N 76°9W 313 A8
Carletonville S. Africa 26°23S 27°22E 270 C4
Cârlibaba Romania 47°35N 25°8E 183 C10
Carlin U.S.A. 40°43N 116°7W 304 F5
Carlingford L. U.K. 54°3N 6°9W 166 B5
Carlinville U.S.A. 39°17N 89°53W 310 E7
Carlisle Cumb., U.K. 54°54N 2°56W 168 C5
Carlisle Ind., U.S.A. 38°58N 87°24W 311 F9
Carlisle Ky., U.S.A. 38°19N 84°1W 311 F12
Carlisle Pa., U.S.A. 40°12N 77°12W 312 F7
Carlisle I. Australia 20°49S 149°18E 280 b
Carlit, Pic France 42°35N 1°55E 174 F5
Carloforte Italy 39°8N 8°18E 200 C1
Carlos Casares Argentina 35°32S 61°20W 334 D3
Carlos Chagas Brazil 17°43S 40°45W 333 E3
Carlos Tejedor Argentina 35°25S 62°25W 334 D3
Carlota I. Phil. 13°1N 121°53E 232 E3
Carlow Ireland 52°50N 6°56W 166 D5
Carlow □ Ireland 52°43N 6°50W 166 D5
Carlsbad = Karlovy Vary Czech Rep. 50°13N 12°51E 180 A5
Carlsbad Calif., U.S.A. 33°10N 117°21W 307 M9
Carlsbad N. Mex., U.S.A. 32°25N 104°14W 305 K11
Carlsbad Caverns △ U.S.A. 32°10N 104°35W 305 K11
Carlsberg Ridge Ind. Oc. 1°0N 66°0E 273 D5
Carlstadt U.S.A. 40°50N 74°6W 132 A1
Carlton Australia 37°47S 144°57E 128 A1
Carlton Gardens Australia 37°48S 144°58E 128 A1
Carluke U.K. 55°45N 3°50W 167 F5
Carlyle Sask., Canada 49°40N 102°20W 297 D8
Carlyle Ill., U.S.A. 38°37N 89°22W 310 F7
Carlyle L. U.S.A. 38°37N 89°21W 310 F7
Carmacks Canada 62°5N 136°16W 294 E4
Carmagnola Italy 44°51N 7°43E 198 D4
Carman Canada 49°30N 98°0W 297 D9
Carmarthen U.K. 51°52N 4°19W 169 F3
Carmarthen B. U.K. 51°40N 4°30W 169 F3
Carmarthenshire □ U.K. 51°55N 4°13W 169 F3
Carmaux France 44°3N 2°10E 174 D6
Carmel Ind., U.S.A. 39°58N 86°7W 311 E10
Carmel N.Y., U.S.A. 41°26N 73°41W 313 E11
Carmel, Mt. = Hä Karmel, Har Israel 32°44N 35°3E 250 F5
Carmel-by-the-Sea U.S.A. 36°33N 121°55W 306 J5
Carmel Valley U.S.A. 36°29N 121°43W 306 J5
Carmelitane Scalze, Monastero Venice, Italy 142 a2
Carmelo Uruguay 34°0S 58°20W 334 C4
Carmen Bolivia 11°40S 67°51W 330 C4
Carmen Paraguay 27°13S 56°12W 335 B4
Carmen Bohol, Phil. 9°50N 124°12E 233 G5
Carmen Cebu, Phil. 10°35N 124°1E 233 F5
Carmen N. Cotabato, Phil. 7°13N 124°45E 233 H5
Carmen Venezuela 1°16N 66°52W 328 C4
Carmen, I. Mexico 25°57N 111°12W 318 B2
Carmen de Huechuraba Chile 33°20S 70°40W 137 B1
Carmen de la Legua -Reynosa Peru 12°3S 77°7W 124 B2
Carmen de Patagones Argentina 40°50S 63°0W 336 B4
Cármenes Spain 42°58N 5°34W 194 C5
Carmensa Argentina 35°15S 67°40W 334 D2
Carmi B.C., Canada 49°36N 119°8W 296 D5
Carmi Ill., U.S.A. 38°5N 88°10W 311 F8
Carmichael Village Bahamas 25°0N 77°26W 153 b
Carmila Australia 21°55S 149°24E 280 C4
Carmini, Scuola dei Venice, Italy 142 b2
Carmona Costa Rica 10°0N 85°15W 320 E2
Carmona Spain 37°28N 5°42W 195 H5
Carn Ban U.K. 57°7N 4°15W 167 D4
Carn Eige U.K. 57°17N 5°8W 167 D3
Carnac France 47°35N 3°6W 172 E3
Carnamah Australia 29°41S 115°53E 279 E2
Carnarvon W. Austral., Australia 24°51S 113°42E 279 D1
Carnarvon Ont., Canada 45°3N 78°41W 312 A6
Carnarvon Northern Cape, S. Africa 30°56S 22°8E 270 D3
Carnarvon △ Australia 24°54S 148°2E 280 C4
Carnarvon Ra. Queens., Australia 25°15S 148°30E 280 D4
Carnarvon Ra. W. Austral., Australia 25°20S 120°45E 279 E3
Carnatic India 9°40N 77°50E 245 K3
Carnation U.S.A. 47°39N 121°55W 306 C5
Carnaxide Portugal 38°43N 9°14W 126 A1
Carncastle U.K. 54°54N 5°53W 166 B6
Carndonagh Ireland 55°16N 7°15W 166 A4
Carnduff Canada 49°10N 101°50W 297 D8
Carnegie Vic., Australia 37°53S 145°3E 128 B2
Carnegie Pa., U.S.A. 40°24N 80°5W 312 F4
Carnegie, L. Australia 26°5S 122°30E 279 E3
Carnegie Hall New York, U.S.A. 132 c2
Carnegie Ridge Pac. Oc. 1°0S 87°0W 289 H19
Carney I. Antarctica 74°0S 121°0W 151 D14
Carnic Alps = Karnische Alpen Europe 46°36N 13°0E 180 E6
Carniche Alpi = Karnische Alpen Europe 46°36N 13°0E 180 E6
Carnide Portugal 38°45N 9°10W 126 A1
Carnot C.A.R. 4°59N 15°56E 264 B3
Carnot, C. Australia 34°57S 135°38E 281 E2
Carnot B. Australia 17°20S 122°15E 278 C3
Carnoustie U.K. 56°30N 2°42W 167 E6
Carnsore Pt. Ireland 52°10N 6°22W 166 D5
Caro U.S.A. 43°29N 83°24W 309 D12
Caroço São Tomé & Príncipe 1°32N 7°27E 265 a
Caroga Lake U.S.A. 43°8N 74°28W 313 C10
Carol City U.S.A. 25°56N 80°14W 129 C1
Carolina Brazil 7°10S 47°30W 332 C2
Carolina Puerto Rico 18°23N 65°58W 321 C6
Carolina Mpumalanga, S. Africa 26°5S 30°6E 271 C5
Carolinas Pt. N. Marianas 14°55N 145°38E 302 e
Caroline I. Kiribati 9°58S 150°13W 289 H12
Caroline Is. Micronesia 8°0N 150°0E 288 G6
Caroline Pk. N.Z. 45°57S 167°15E 285 F2
Carollton U.S.A. 29°57N 90°8W 131 B2
Carondelet Reef Kiribati 5°33S 173°50E 277 B16
Caroni Trin. & Tob. 10°34N 61°23W 323 t
Caroni → Trin. & Tob. 10°37N 61°30W 323 t
Caroní → Venezuela 8°21N 62°43W 329 B5
Caroni Arena Res. Trin. & Tob. 10°33N 61°15W 323 t
Caroni Bird Sanctuary Trin. & Tob. 10°36N 61°28W 323 t
Caroni Swamp Trin. & Tob. 10°36N 61°27W 323 t
Caronie = Nébrodi, Monti Italy 37°54N 14°35E 201 E7
Caroona Australia 31°24S 150°26E 283 A9
Carora Venezuela 10°11N 70°5W 328 A3
Carpathians Europe 49°30N 21°0E 177 D11

Carpații Meridionali
  Romania 45°30N 25°0E ■ 183 E9
Carpentaria, G. of Australia 14°0S 139°0E 280 A2
Carpentersville U.S.A. 42°6N 88°17W 311 B8
Carpentras France 44°3N 5°2E 175 D9
Carpi Italy 44°47N 10°53E 198 D7
Carpina Brazil 7°51S 35°15W 332 C4
Cărpineni Moldova 46°46N 28°22E ■ 183 D13
Carpio Spain 41°13N 5°7W 194 D5
Carr Boyd Ra. Australia 16°15S 128°35E 278 C4
Carra, L. Ireland 53°41N 9°14W 166 C2
Carrabelle U.S.A. 29°51N 84°40W 316 F15
Carraig Mhachaire Rois =
  Carrickmacross Ireland 53°59N 6°43W 166 C5
Carraig na Siúire = Carrick-on-Suir
  Ireland 52°21N 7°24W 166 D4
Carral Spain 43°14N 8°21W 194 B2
Carranglan Phil. 15°58N 121°4E 232 D3
Carranya ▷ Australia 19°13S 127°46E 278 C4
Carrara Italy 44°5N 10°6E 198 D7
Carrascal Santiago, Chile 25°35S 70°42W 137 B1
Carrascal Phil. 9°22N 125°56E 233 G5
Carrasco △ Bolivia 17°23S 64°59W 331 D5
Carrascosa del Campo
  Spain 40°2N 2°45W 196 E2
Carrauntoohill Ireland 52°0N 9°45W 166 D2
Carretas, Punta Peru 14°12S 76°17W 330 C2
Carriacou Grenada 12°29N 61°26W 323 q
Carrick-on-Shannon
  Ireland 53°57N 8°7W 166 C3
Carrick-on-Suir Ireland 52°21N 7°24W 166 D4
Carrickfergus U.K. 54°43N 5°49W 166 B6
Carrickmacross Ireland 53°59N 6°43W 166 C5
Carrickmines Ireland 53°15N 6°10W 120 B3
Carrières-sous-Bois France 48°55N 2°6E 134 A1
Carrières-sous-Poissy
  France 48°56N 2°2E 134 A1
Carrieton Australia 32°25S 138°31E 282 B3
Carrigaline Ireland 51°48N 8°23W 166 E3
Carrigeen B. Ireland 53°24N 6°5W 120 A3
Carrillo Mexico 26°54N 103°55W 318 B4
Carrington U.S.A. 47°27N 99°8W 308 B4
Carrión → Spain 41°53N 4°32W 194 D6
Carrión de los Condes
  Spain 42°20N 4°37W 194 C6
Carrizal Bajo Chile 28°5S 71°20W 334 B1
Carrizalillo Chile 29°5S 71°30W 334 B1
Carrizo Cr. → U.S.A. 36°55N 103°55W 305 H12
Carrizo Plain △ U.S.A. 35°11N 119°47W 306 K7
Carrizo Springs U.S.A. 28°31N 99°52W 314 G5
Carrizozo U.S.A. 33°38N 105°53W 305 K11
Carroll U.S.A. 42°4N 94°52W 310 B2
Carrollton Ga., U.S.A. 33°35N 85°5W 316 B4
Carrollton Ill., U.S.A. 39°18N 90°24W 310 F8
Carrollton Ky., U.S.A. 38°41N 85°11W 311 F11
Carrollton Mo., U.S.A. 39°22N 93°30W 310 E3
Carrollton Ohio, U.S.A. 40°34N 81°5W 312 F3
Carron → U.K. 57°53N 4°22W 167 D4
Carron, L. U.K. 57°22N 5°35W 167 D3
Carrot → Canada 53°50N 101°17W 297 C8
Carrot River Canada 53°17N 103°35W 297 C8
Carrouges France 48°34N 0°10W 172 D6
Carrù Italy 44°29N 7°52E 198 D4
Carruthers Canada 52°52N 109°16W 297 C7
Carsa Dek Ethiopia 5°13N 39°50E 257 F4
Çarşamba Turkey 41°11N 36°44E 212 B7
Carsòli Italy 42°6N 13°5E 199 F10
Carson Calif., U.S.A. 33°49N 118°16W 307 M8
Carson N. Dak., U.S.A. 46°25N 101°34W 308 B3
Carson → U.S.A. 39°45N 118°40W 306 F8
Carson City Mich.,
  U.S.A. 43°11N 84°51W 311 A12
Carson City Nev., U.S.A. 39°10N 119°46W 306 F7
Carson Sink U.S.A. 39°50N 118°25W 304 G4
Carstensz Pyramid = Jaya, Puncak
  Indonesia 3°57S 137°17E 231 E9
Cartagena Colombia 10°25N 75°33W 328 A2
Cartagena Spain 37°38N 0°59W 197 H4
Cartago Colombia 4°45N 75°55W 328 C2
Cartago Costa Rica 9°50N 83°55W 320 E3
Cártama Spain 36°43N 4°39W 195 J6
Cartaxo Portugal 39°10N 8°47W 195 F2
Cartaya Spain 37°16N 7°9W 195 H3
Carteret Is. = Kilinailau Is.
  Papua N. G. 4°45S 155°20E 286 C8
Cartersville U.S.A. 34°10N 84°48W 316 A5
Carterton N.Z. 41°2S 175°31E 284 H4
Carterville U.S.A. 37°46N 89°5W 310 G7
Carthage Tunisia 36°52N 10°20E 200 F3
Carthage Ill., U.S.A. 40°25N 91°8W 310 D5
Carthage Mo., U.S.A. 37°11N 94°19W 308 G6
Carthage N.Y., U.S.A. 43°59N 75°37W 313 C9
Carthage Tex., U.S.A. 32°9N 94°20W 314 E7
Cartier I. Australia 12°31S 123°29E 278 B3
Cartierville Canada 45°31N 73°42W 130 A1
Cartwright Canada 53°41N 56°58W 299 B8
Caruaru Brazil 8°15S 35°55W 332 C4
Carúpano Venezuela 10°39N 63°15W 329 A5
Caruray Brazil 10°20N 119°0E 233 F2
Carutapera Brazil 1°13S 46°1W 332 B2
Caruthersville U.S.A. 36°11N 89°39W 308 G9
Carvalho Brazil 2°16S 51°29W 329 D7
Carvin France 50°30N 2°57E 173 B9
Carvoeiro Brazil 1°30S 61°59W 329 D5
Carvoeiro, C. Portugal 39°21N 9°24W 195 F1
Cary I., U.S.A. 42°13N 88°14W 311 B8
Cary N.C., U.S.A. 35°47N 78°46W 315 D15
Cas-gwent = Chepstow
  U.K. 51°38N 2°41W 169 F5
Casa, Pas de la = Envalira, Port d'
  Europe 42°31N 1°43E 196 C6
Casa Branca Brazil 21°46S 47°4W 333 F2
Casa Branca Portugal 38°29N 8°12W 195 G2
Casa de Piedra Argentina 38°5S 67°28W 334 D2
Casa de Piedra, Embalse
  Argentina 38°5S 67°32W 334 D2
Casa Grande U.S.A. 32°53N 111°45W 305 K8
Casa Loma Canada 43°41N 79°24W 141 A2
Casa Nova Brazil 9°25S 41°5W 332 C3
Casa Verde Brazil 23°29S 46°40W 137 A1
Casablanca Chile 33°20S 71°25W 334 C1
Casablanca Morocco 33°36N 7°36W 260 B3
Casablanca △ Morocco 33°38N 7°40W 260 B3
Casacalenda Italy 41°44N 14°51E 199 G11
Casal da Mira Portugal 38°47N 9°14W 126 A1
Casal Morena Italy 41°49N 12°37E 136 C2
Casalbordino Italy 42°9N 14°35E 199 F11
Casale Monferrato Italy 44°59N 10°0E 198 D7
Casalmaggiore Italy 45°0N 10°24E 198 D7
Casalotti Italy 41°54N 12°22E 136 B1
Casalpusterlengo Italy 45°11N 9°39E 198 E6
Casamance → Senegal 12°33N 16°46E 262 C1
Casanare □ Colombia 5°30N 72°0W 328 B3
Casanare → Colombia 6°2N 69°51W 328 B4
Casares Spain 40°0N 18°10E 201 B11
Casas Ibáñez Spain 39°17N 1°30W 197 F3
Casasimarro Spain 39°22N 2°3W 197 F2
Casatejada Spain 39°54N 5°40W 194 E5
Casavieja Spain 40°17N 4°46W 194 E6
Cascada de Basaseachic △
  Mexico 28°10N 108°15W 318 B3
Cascade Idaho, U.S.A. 44°31N 116°2W 304 D5
Cascade Iowa, U.S.A. 42°18N 91°0W 310 B6

Cascade Mont., U.S.A. 47°16N 111°42W 304 C8
Cascade Heights U.S.A. 33°43N 84°26W 113 B2
Cascade Locks U.S.A. 45°40N 121°54W 306 E5
Cascade Pt. N.Z. 44°1S 168°20E 285 E3
Cascade Ra. U.S.A. 47°0N 121°30W 306 D5
Cascade Res. U.S.A. 44°32N 116°3W 304 D5
Cascais Portugal 38°41N 9°25W 195 G1
Cascavel Ceará, Brazil 4°7S 38°14W 332 B4
Cascavel Paraná, Brazil 24°57S 53°28W 335 A5
Cáscina Italy 43°41N 10°33E 198 E7
Casco B. U.S.A. 43°45N 70°0W 309 D19
Case Noyale Mauritius 20°23S 57°22E 272 e
Case-Pilote Martinique 14°38N 61°9W 322 j
Caselle Torinese Italy 45°10N 7°39E 198 C4
Caserta Italy 41°4N 14°20E 201 A7
Casey Antarctica 66°0S 76°0E 151 C8
Casey Ill., U.S.A. 39°18N 87°59W 311 E9
Caseyr, Raas = Asir, Ras
  Somalia 11°55N 51°10E 267 B7
Cashel Ireland 52°30N 7°53W 166 D4
Casibare → Colombia 3°48N 72°18W 328 C3
Casiguran Phil. 16°22N 122°7E 232 C4
Casiguran Sound Phil. 16°6N 121°58E 232 C3
Casilda Argentina 33°10S 61°10W 334 C3
Casim = General Toshevo
  Bulgaria 43°42N 28°6E 203 C12
Casimcea Romania 44°45N 28°23E 183 F13
Casino Australia 28°52S 153°3E 281 D5
Casiquiare → Venezuela 2°1N 67°7W 328 C4
Casitas Peru 3°54S 80°39W 330 A1
Čáslav Czech Rep. 49°54N 15°22E 180 B8
Casma Peru 9°30S 78°20W 330 B2
Casmalia U.S.A. 34°50N 120°32W 307 L6
Casnewydd = Newport
  U.K. 51°35N 3°0W 169 F5
Cásola Valsénio Italy 44°12N 11°40E 199 D8
Cásoli Italy 42°7N 14°18E 199 F11
Caspe Spain 41°14N 0°1W 196 D4
Casper U.S.A. 42°51N 106°19W 304 E10
Caspian Depression Eurasia 47°0N 48°0E 191 G9
Caspian Sea Eurasia 43°0N 50°0E 187 F9
Cass City U.S.A. 43°36N 83°10W 312 C1
Cass Lake U.S.A. 47°23N 94°37W 308 B6
Cassà de la Selva Spain 41°53N 2°52E 196 D7
Cassadaga U.S.A. 42°20N 79°19W 312 D5
Cassai Angola 10°33S 21°59E 265 E4
Cassai → Angola 3°2S 16°57E 265 E4
Cassamba Angola 13°6S 20°18E 265 E4
Cassano allo Iónio Italy 39°47N 16°20E 201 C9
Cassel France 50°48N 2°30E 173 B9
Casselberry U.S.A. 28°41N 81°20W 317 G8
Casselton U.S.A. 46°54N 97°13W 308 B5
Cassiar Mts. Canada 59°30N 130°30W 296 B2
Cassilândia Brazil 19°9S 51°45W 331 D7
Cassilis Australia 32°3S 149°58E 283 B8
Cassinga Angola 15°5S 16°4E 265 F3
Cassino Italy 41°30N 13°49E 200 A6
Cassis France 43°14N 5°32E 175 E9
Cassoalala Angola 9°30S 14°2E 265 D2
Cassoango Angola 13°42S 20°56E 265 E4
Cassongue Angola 11°53S 15°2E 265 E3
Cassopolis U.S.A. 41°55N 86°1W 311 C10
Cassundi Angola 10°57S 21°3E 265 E4
Cassville Mo., U.S.A. 36°41N 93°52W 308 G7
Cassville Wis., U.S.A. 42°43N 90°59W 310 B6
Castagneto Carducci Italy 43°9N 10°36E 198 E7
Castaic U.S.A. 34°30N 118°38W 307 L8
Castália U.S.A. 41°24N 82°49W 312 E2
Castanhal Brazil 1°18S 47°55W 332 B2
Castara Trin. & Tob. 11°17N 60°42W 323 s
Castara B. Trin. & Tob. 11°17N 60°42W 323 s
Castéggio Italy 45°0N 9°7E 198 C6
Castejón de Monegros
  Spain 41°37N 0°15W 196 D4
Castel Guadeloupe 16°15N 61°35W 322 e
Castèl del Monte Italy 41°5N 16°16E 201 A9
Castèl di Leva Italy 41°46N 12°33E 136 c2
Castèl di Sangro Italy 41°47N 14°6E 199 G11
Castèl San Pietro Terme
  Italy 44°24N 11°35E 199 D8
Castèl Sant'Angelo Rome, Italy 136 b1
Castelbuono Italy 37°56N 14°5E 201 E7
Casteldidardo Italy 43°36N 10°58E 198 E7
Castelfiorentino Italy 43°36N 10°58E 198 E7
Castelfranco Emília Italy 44°37N 11°2E 198 D8
Castelfranco Véneto Italy 45°40N 11°56E 198 C8
Casteljaloux France 44°19N 0°6E 174 D4
Castell-Nedd = Neath U.K. 51°39N 3°48W 169 F4
Castellabate Italy 40°17N 14°57E 201 B7
Castellammare, G. di Italy 38°8N 12°54E 200 D5
Castellammare del Golfo
  Italy 38°2N 12°53E 200 D5
Castellammare di Stábia
  Italy 40°42N 14°29E 201 B7
Castellamonte Italy 45°23N 7°42E 198 C4
Castellane France 43°50N 6°31E 175 E10
Castellaneta Italy 40°38N 16°56E 201 B9
Castelli Argentina 36°7S 57°47W 334 D4
Castello Venice, Italy 142 b4
Castelló de la Plana Spain 39°58N 0°3W 196 F4
Castellón de la Plana □
  Spain 40°15N 0°5W 196 E4
Castellote Spain 40°48N 0°15W 196 E4
Castelmáuro Italy 41°50N 14°43E 199 G11
Castelnau-de-Médoc France 45°2N 0°48W 174 C3
Castelnau-Magnoac
  France 43°17N 0°31E 174 E4
Castelnaudary France 43°20N 1°58E 174 E5
Castelnovo ne' Monti
  Italy 44°26N 10°24E 198 D7
Castelnuovo di Val di Cécina
  Italy 43°12N 10°54E 198 E7
Castelo = Manuel Urbano
  Brazil 8°53S 69°18W 330 B4
Castelo Branco 20°33S 41°14W 333 F3
Castelo, Pta. do Azores 36°56N 25°1W 153 d4
Castelo Branco Brazil 38°51N 28°44W 153 d1
Castelo Branco Portugal 39°50N 7°31W 194 F3
Castelo Branco □ Portugal 39°52N 7°45W 194 F3
Castelo de Paiva Portugal 41°2N 8°16W 194 D2
Castelo de Vide Portugal 39°25N 7°27W 194 F3
Castelo do Piauí Brazil 5°20S 41°33W 332 C3
Castelrosso = Megisti
  Greece 36°8N 29°34E 205 E11
Castelsardo Italy 40°55N 8°43E 200 B1
Castelsarrasin France 44°2N 1°7E 174 D5
Casteltérmini Italy 37°41N 13°47E 200 E6
Castelvetrano Italy 37°38N 12°47E 200 E5
Castendo Angola 8°39S 14°10E 265 D2
Casterton Australia 37°30S 141°30E 282 D4
Castets France 43°52N 1°9W 174 E2
Castiglion Fiorentino Italy 43°20N 11°55E 199 E8
Castiglione = Bou Ismaïl
  Algeria 36°38N 2°42E 261 A5
Castiglione del Lago Italy 43°7N 12°3E 199 E9
Castiglione della Pescáia
  Italy 42°46N 10°53E 198 F7
Castiglione delle Stiviere
  Italy 45°23N 10°29E 198 C7
Castilblanco Spain 39°17N 5°5W 195 F5
Castile U.S.A. 42°38N 78°3W 312 D6
Castilla Peru 5°12S 80°38W 330 B1
Castilla, Playa de Spain 37°6N 6°33W 195 J4

Castilla-La Mancha □
  Spain 39°30N 3°30W 195 F7
Castilla y Leon □ Spain 42°0N 5°0W 194 D6
Castillo de Locubín Spain 37°32N 3°56W 195 H7
Castillo de San Marcos △
  U.S.A. 29°54N 81°19W 316 F8
Castillon-en-Couserans
  France 42°56N 1°1E 174 F5
Castillonès France 44°39N 0°37E 174 D4
Castillos Uruguay 34°12S 53°52W 335 C5
Castle Bruce Dominica 15°26N 61°16W 323 k
Castle Dale U.S.A. 39°13N 111°1W 304 G8
Castle Douglas U.K. 54°56N 3°56W 167 G5
Castle Harbour Bermuda 32°21N 64°39W 153 B5
Castle Mt. Jamaica 18°9N 76°22W 320 a
Castle of Good Hope Cape Town, S. Africa 118 c3
Castle Roads Bermuda 32°20N 64°40W 153 a
Castle Rock Colo.,
  U.S.A. 39°22N 104°51W 304 G11
Castle Rock Wash.,
  U.S.A. 46°17N 122°54W 306 D4
Castle Rock Pt. St. Helena 16°1S 5°45W 153 h
Castlebar Ireland 53°52N 9°18W 166 C2
Castleblayney Ireland 54°7N 6°44W 166 B5
Castlecliff N.Z. 39°57S 175°5E 284 F4
Castlecomer Ireland 52°48N 7°14W 166 D4
Castlederg U.K. 54°42N 7°36W 166 B4
Castleford U.K. 53°43N 1°21W 168 D6
Castlegar Canada 49°20N 117°40W 296 D5
Castleisland Ireland 52°14N 9°28W 166 D2
Castleknock Ireland 53°22N 6°21W 120 A1
Castlemaine Vic., Australia 37°2S 144°12E 282 D6
Castlemaine Kerry, Ireland 52°10N 9°42W 166 D2
Castlepoint N.Z. 40°54S 176°15E 284 G5
Castlepollard Ireland 53°46N 7°14W 166 C4
Castlerea Ireland 53°46N 8°29W 166 C3
Castlereagh → Australia 30°12S 147°32E 283 A7
Castlereagh B. Australia 12°10S 135°10E 280 A2
Castleton U.S.A. 43°37N 73°11W 313 C11
Castleton Corners U.S.A. 40°36N 74°8W 132 C1
Castleton-on-Hudson
  U.S.A. 42°31N 73°45W 313 D11
Castletown I. of Man 54°5N 4°38W 168 C3
Castletown Bearhaven
  Ireland 51°39N 9°55W 166 E2
Castor Canada 52°15N 111°50W 296 C6
Castor → Canada 53°24N 78°58W 298 B4
Castorland U.S.A. 43°53N 75°31W 313 C9
Castres France 43°37N 2°13E 174 E6
Castricum Neths. 52°33N 4°40E 170 B4
Castries St. Lucia 14°2N 60°58W 323 m
Castril Spain 37°48N 2°46W 195 H8
Castro Brazil 24°45S 50°0W 335 A6
Castro Chile 42°30S 73°50W 336 B2
Castro Alves Brazil 12°46S 39°33W 333 D4
Castro del Río Spain 37°41N 4°29W 195 H6
Castro-Urdiales Spain 43°23N 3°11W 194 B7
Castro Valley U.S.A. 37°41N 122°5W 306 H4
Castro Verde Portugal 37°41N 8°4W 195 H2
Castrogiovanni = Enna
  Italy 37°34N 14°16E 201 E7
Castrojeriz Spain 42°17N 4°9W 194 C6
Castropol Spain 43°32N 7°0W 194 B4
Castroreale Italy 38°6N 15°12E 201 D8
Castrovillari Italy 39°49N 16°12E 201 C9
Castroville U.S.A. 36°46N 121°45W 306 J5
Castrovirreyna Peru 13°20S 75°18W 330 C2
Castuera Spain 38°43N 5°37W 195 G5
Caswell Sound N.Z. 44°59S 167°8E 285 E2
Çat Turkey 39°40N 41°3E 213 C9
Cat Ba, Dao Vietnam 20°50N 107°0E 236 B6
Cat Ba △ Vietnam 20°47N 107°3E 236 B6
Cat I. Bahamas 24°30N 75°30W 321 B4
Cat L. Canada 51°40N 91°50W 298 B1
Cat Lake Canada 51°40N 91°50W 298 B1
Cat Tien △ Vietnam 11°25N 107°17E 237 G6
Čata Slovak Rep. 47°58N 18°38E 181 D11
Catacamas Honduras 14°54N 85°56W 320 D2
Catacaos Peru 5°20S 80°45W 330 B1
Cataguases Brazil 21°23S 42°39W 333 F3
Catagupan Phil. 8°1N 116°58E 233 G3
Cataingan Phil. 12°0N 124°0E 232 E4
Çatak Turkey 41°30N 31°59E 212 B4
Çatalagzı Turkey 41°30N 31°59E 212 B4
Çatalca Turkey 41°8N 28°27E 205 D12
Catalina Nfld. & L., Canada 48°31N 53°4W 299 C9
Catalina Chile 25°13S 69°43W 334 B2
Catalina Ariz., U.S.A. 32°30N 110°50W 305 K8
Catalonia = Cataluña □
  Spain 41°40N 1°15E 196 D6
Cataluña □ Spain 41°40N 1°15E 196 D6
Catamarca Argentina 28°30S 65°50W 334 B2
Catamarca □ Argentina 27°0S 65°50W 334 B2
Catanauan Phil. 13°36N 122°19E 232 E4
Catanduanes □ Phil. 13°50N 124°20E 232 E5
Catanduva Brazil 21°5S 48°58W 335 A6
Catánia Italy 37°30N 15°6E 201 E8
Catánia, G. di Italy 37°25N 15°8E 201 E8
Cataño Puerto Rico 18°27N 66°7W 321 b
Catanzaro Italy 38°54N 16°35E 201 D9
Cataouatche, L. U.S.A. 29°50N 90°14W 131 B1
Cataraman N. Samar., Phil. 9°8N 124°45E 233 G5
Catarman Camiguin, Phil. 9°8N 124°45E 233 G5
Catatumbo → Venezuela 9°21N 71°45W 328 B3
Catbalogan Phil. 11°46N 124°53E 232 E5
Catchacoma Canada 44°44N 78°19W 312 B6
Cateco Cangola Angola 10°9S 15°51E 265 D3
Cateel B. Phil. 7°54N 126°25E 233 H6
Cateel B. Phil. 7°54N 126°25E 233 H6
Catende Brazil 26°0S 32°33E 271 C5
Catende Brazil 8°40S 35°5W 332 D4
Caterham U.K. 51°15N 0°4W 169 F7
Catete Angola 9°6S 13°43E 265 D2
Cathair na Mart = Westport
  Ireland 53°48N 9°31W 166 C2
Cathcart S. Africa 32°18S 27°10E 270 D4
Cathcart N.S.W.,
  Australia 36°52S 149°24E 283 D8
Cathcart Eastern Cape,
  S. Africa 32°18S 27°10E 270 D4
Cathedral Rock △
  Australia 30°24S 152°15E 283 A10
Catherine, L. U.S.A. 34°28N 92°44W 133 B2
Cathlamet U.S.A. 46°12N 123°23W 306 D3
Catió Guinea-Biss. 11°17N 15°15W 262 C1
Catismiña Venezuela 5°3N 63°40W 329 C5
Catita Brazil 9°31S 43°1W 332 D3
Cativa Brazil 22°10S 79°49W 330 C2
Catlettsburg U.S.A. 38°25N 82°36W 309 F12
Catlin U.S.A. 40°4N 87°42W 311 E9
Catoche, C. Mexico 21°35N 87°5W 319 C7
Çatmon Phil. 10°43N 124°1E 233 F5
Catoca Angola 11°55N 20°48E 265 E4
Catole do Rocha Brazil 6°21S 37°45W 332 C4
Catria, Mte. Italy 43°28N 12°42E 199 E9
Catriló Argentina 36°26S 63°24W 334 D3
Catrimani Brazil 0°27N 61°41W 329 C5

Catrimani → Brazil 0°28N 61°44W 329 C5
Ceará-Mirim Brazil 5°38S 35°25W 332 C4
Ceara Rise Atl. Oc. 4°30S 43°0W 152 F7
Cearbharlach = Carlow
  Ireland 52°50N 6°56W 166 D5
Ceauru, I. Romania 44°58N 23°11E 183 F8
Cebaco, I. de Panama 7°33N 81°9W 320 E3
Cebecov Turkey 41°7N 28°52E 122 B1
Cebollar Argentina 29°10S 66°35W 334 B2
Cebollera, Sierra de Spain 42°0N 2°30W 194 C2
Cebreros Spain 40°27N 4°28W 194 E6
Cebu Phil. 10°18N 123°54E 233 F4
Cebu □ Phil. 10°20N 123°40E 233 F4
Čečava Bos.-H. 44°42N 17°44E 182 F2
Ceccano Italy 41°34N 13°20E 200 A6
Cechignola Italy 41°48N 12°29E 136 C2
Cece Hungary 46°46N 18°39E 182 D3
Cechi Ivory C. 6°15N 4°25E 262 D4
Cecil Plains Australia 27°30S 151°11E 281 D5
Cecilienhof, Schloss
  Germany 52°25N 13°5E 115 B1
Cécina Italy 43°19N 10°31E 198 E7
Cécina → Italy 43°18N 10°29E 198 E7
Ceclavin Spain 39°50N 6°45W 194 F4
Cedar → U.S.A. 41°17N 91°21W 310 C5
Cedar City U.S.A. 37°41N 113°4W 305 H7
Cedar Creek Res. U.S.A. 32°11N 96°4W 314 E6
Cedar Falls Iowa, U.S.A. 42°32N 92°27W 310 B4
Cedar Falls Wash.,
  U.S.A. 47°25N 121°45W 306 C5
Cedar Grove Georgia,
  U.S.A. 33°40N 84°16W 113 C3
Cedar Grove Ind., U.S.A. 39°22N 84°56W 311 E12
Cedar Key U.S.A. 29°8N 83°2W 317 F6
Cedar L. Canada 53°10N 100°0W 297 C9
Cedar Lake U.S.A. 41°22N 87°26W 311 C9
Cedar Park U.S.A. 30°30N 97°49W 314 F6
Cedar Point U.S.A. 41°44N 83°21W 311 C13
Cedar Rapids U.S.A. 41°59N 91°40W 310 C5
Cedar Tree Pt. Antigua & B. 17°42N 61°53W 322 c
Cedartown U.S.A. 34°1N 85°15W 316 A4
Cedarvale Canada 55°1N 128°22W 296 B3
Cedarville KwaZulu Natal,
  S. Africa 30°23S 29°3E 271 D4
Cedarville Ohio, U.S.A. 39°44N 83°49W 311 E13
Cedeira Spain 43°39N 8°2W 194 B2
Cedrino → Italy 40°23N 9°44E 200 B2
Cedro Brazil 6°34S 39°3W 332 C4
Cedros Azores 38°38N 28°42W 153 d1
Cedros, I. Mexico 28°12N 115°15W 318 B1
Cedros B. Trin. & Tob. 10°16N 61°54W 323 t
Cedros Pt. Trin. & Tob. 10°16N 61°49W 323 t
Ceduna Australia 32°7S 133°46E 281 E1
Cedynia Poland 52°53N 14°12E 185 B1
Cee Spain 42°57N 9°10W 194 C1
Ceel Baraf Somalia 2°20N 45°30E 267 G4
Ceel Buur = El Bur Somalia 4°40N 46°35E 267 G4
Ceelbuur Somalia 4°40N 46°35E 267 G4
Ceeldheere Galguduud,
  Somalia 3°50N 47°8E 267 G4
Ceeldheere Galguduud,
  Somalia 5°22N 46°11E 267 G4
Ceerigaabo Somalia 10°35N 47°20E 267 E4
Cefalù Italy 38°2N 14°1E 201 D7
Cega → Spain 41°33N 4°46W 194 D6
Cegléd Hungary 47°11N 19°47E 182 C4
Céglie Messápico Italy 40°39N 17°31E 201 B10
Cehegín Spain 38°6N 1°48W 197 G3
Cehimg China 24°58N 105°48E 228 E5
Cehu-Silvaniei Romania 47°24N 23°9E 183 C8
Ceica Romania 46°53N 22°10E 182 D7
Ceikaya → Portugal 40°13N 8°16W 194 E2
Cela Angola 11°25N 15°7E 265 E3
Celano Italy 42°5N 13°33E 199 F10
Celanova Spain 42°9N 7°58W 194 C3
Celaque △ Honduras 14°30N 88°42W 320 D2
Celaya Mexico 20°31N 100°37W 318 C4
Celbridge Ireland 53°20N 6°32W 166 C5
Celebes = Sulawesi □ Indonesia 2°0S 120°0E 233 E4
Celebes Sea Indonesia 3°0N 123°0E 233 D4
Celendín Peru 6°52S 78°10W 330 B2
Celestial Mts. = Tian Shan
  Asia 40°30N 76°0E 227 C6
Čelić Bos.-H. 44°43N 18°49E 182 F3
Celica Ecuador 4°7S 79°59W 328 D2
Celinac Bos.-H. 44°44N 17°22E 182 F2
Celje Slovenia 46°16N 15°18E 198 B12
Celldömölk Hungary 47°16N 17°10E 182 C2
Celle Germany 52°37N 10°4E 178 C6
Celorico da Beira Portugal 40°38N 7°24W 194 E3
Celtic Sea Atl. Oc. 50°9N 9°34W 165 F2
Cempi, Teluk Indonesia 8°44S 118°25E 235 F5
Cenderawasih, Teluk
  Indonesia 3°0S 135°20E 231 E9
Cenepa → Peru 4°30S 78°0W 330 A2
Cengkelǒ'öy Turkey 41°2N 29°2E 122 B2
Cengkareng Indonesia 6°9S 106°45E 122 A1
Cengong China 27°13N 108°44E 228 D7
Ceno → Italy 44°30N 10°2E 198 D7
Centallo Italy 44°30N 7°35E 198 D4
Centelles Spain 41°50N 2°13E 196 D7
Centenário do Sul Brazil 22°48S 51°36W 333 F1
Centennial U.S.A. 39°34N 104°52W 304 G11
Centennial Olympic Park
  U.S.A. 33°46N 84°23W 113 B2
Centennial Park
  Australia 33°53S 151°14E 139 B2
Center N. Dak., U.S.A. 47°7N 101°18W 308 B3
Center Tex., U.S.A. 31°48N 94°11W 314 F7
Center Hill Fla., U.S.A. 28°38N 82°3E 317 G7
Center Hill Georgia, U.S.A. 33°46N 84°29W 113 B2
Center Point U.S.A. 42°12N 91°47W 310 C5
Centerburg U.S.A. 40°18N 82°42W 312 F2
Centerville Calif., U.S.A. 36°44N 119°30W 306 J7
Centerville Iowa, U.S.A. 40°44N 92°52W 310 D4
Centerville Ohio, U.S.A. 39°38N 84°8W 311 E12
Centerville Pa., U.S.A. 40°3N 79°59W 312 F5
Centerville Tenn., U.S.A. 35°47N 87°28W 315 D11
Centerville Tex., U.S.A. 31°16N 95°59W 314 F7
Cento Italy 44°43N 11°16E 198 D8
Centocelle Italy 41°52N 12°34E 136 B2
Central U.S.A. 32°47N 108°9W 305 K9
Central □ Botswana 22°0S 26°30E 270 A4
Central □ Ghana 5°30N 1°0W 263 D4
Central □ Kenya 0°30S 37°30E 268 C4
Central □ Malawi 13°30S 33°30E 269 E3
Central □ Papua N. G. 10°0S 148°0E 286 E5
Central □ Zambia 14°25S 28°50E 269 E2
Central, Cordillera Colombia 18°30S Bolivia 18°30S 64°55W 331 D5
Central, Cordillera
  Costa Rica 10°10N 84°5W 320 D3

Central, Cordillera
  Dom. Rep. 19°15N 71°0W 321 C5
Central, Cordillera Peru 7°0S 77°30W 330 B2
Central, Cordillera Phil. 17°20N 120°57E 232 C3
Central, Cordillera
  Puerto Rico 18°8N 66°35W 321 b
Central African Empire = Central
  African Rep. ■ Africa 7°0N 20°0E 264 A4
Central African Rep. ■
  Africa 7°0N 20°0E 264 A4
Central America America 12°0N 85°0W 292 H11
Central Australia ◇
  Australia 22°30S 128°30E 278 D4
Central Bedfordshire ◇
  U.K. 52°5N 0°20W 169 E7
Central Butte Canada 50°48N 106°31W 297 C7
Central City Colo.,
  U.S.A. 39°48N 105°31W 304 G11
Central City Iowa, U.S.A. 42°12N 91°32W 310 B5
Central City Ky., U.S.A. 37°18N 87°7W 308 G10
Central City Nebr., U.S.A. 41°7N 98°0W 308 E4
Central Desert ◇
  Australia 19°55S 130°46E 278 C5
Central Equatoria □
  South Sudan 4°0N 31°0E 257 G3
Central I. Kenya 3°30N 36°0E 268 B4
Central I. Kenya 3°30N 36°1E 268 B4
Central Japan Int. ✈ (NGO)
  Japan 34°53N 136°45E 223 C8
Central Kalahari △
  Botswana 22°36S 23°58E 270 B3
Central Makran Range
  Pakistan 26°30N 64°15E 240 D2
Central Pacific Basin
  Pac. Oc. 8°0N 175°0W 288 G10
Central Park New York, U.S.A. 132 a3
Central Park Zoo New York, U.S.A. 132 b2
Central Patricia Canada 51°30N 90°9W 298 B1
Central Point U.S.A. 42°23N 122°55W 304 E2
Central Provinces = Madhya
  Pradesh □ India 22°50N 78°0E 242 J8
Central Ra. Papua N. G. 5°0S 143°0E 286 C2
Central Range Wildlife Sanctuary △
  Trin. & Tob. 10°27N 61°14W 323 t
Central Russian Uplands
  Europe 54°0N 36°0E 158 E13
Central Siberian Plateau
  Russia 65°0N 105°0E 210 B12
Central Square U.S.A. 43°17N 76°9W 313 C8
Central Village Jamaica 17°59N 76°55W 320 a
Centralia Ont., Canada 43°17N 81°43W 310 F7
Centralia Ill., U.S.A. 38°32N 89°8W 310 F7
Centralia Mo., U.S.A. 39°13N 92°8W 310 F4
Centralia Wash., U.S.A. 46°43N 122°58W 306 D4
Centre □ Cameroon 4°45N 12°0E 263 E7
Centre U.S.A. 34°9N 85°41W 316 A4
Centre de Flacq Mauritius 20°12S 57°43E 272 e
Centreville Mich., U.S.A. 41°55N 85°32W 311 C11
Centreville N.Y., U.S.A. 42°28N 78°14W 312 D6
Centreville Pa., U.S.A. 41°44N 79°45W 312 E5
Century U.S.A. 30°58N 87°16W 317 F2
Century City U.S.A. 34°3N 118°25W 126 B2
Cenxi China 22°57N 110°57E 229 F8
Ceotina → Bos.-H. 43°36N 18°50E 202 C2
Cephalonia = Kefalonia
  Greece 38°15N 20°30E 207 C2
Cepin Croatia 45°32N 18°34E 182 E3
Ceprano Italy 41°33N 13°31E 200 A6
Ceptia Angola 12°56S 17°35E 265 E3
Ceptura Romania 45°1N 26°21E 183 E11
Cepu Indonesia 7°9S 111°35E 235 D4
Ceram = Seram Indonesia 3°10S 129°0E 231 E7
Ceram Sea = Seram Sea
  Indonesia 2°30S 128°30E 231 E7
Cerbère France 42°26N 3°10E 174 F7
Cerbicales, Îs. France 4°33N 9°22E 175 G13
Cercal Portugal 37°48N 8°40W 195 H2
Cerdaña Spain 42°22N 1°35E 196 C6
Cerdanyola del Vallès Spain 41°27N 2°8W 114 A1
Cère → France 44°55N 1°49E 174 D5
Cerea Italy 45°12N 11°13E 199 C8
Ceredigion □ U.K. 52°16N 4°15W 169 E3
Ceres Argentina 29°55S 61°55W 334 B3
Ceres Brazil 1°17S 49°35W 333 E2
Ceres Western Cape,
  S. Africa 33°21S 19°18E 270 D2
Ceres Calif., U.S.A. 37°35N 120°57W 306 H6
Céret France 42°30N 2°42E 174 F6
Cereté Colombia 8°53N 75°48W 328 B2
Cerf Seychelles 4°38S 55°40E 272 e
Cerfs, Îs. aux Mauritius 20°16S 57°47E 272 e
Cergy France 49°2N 2°4E 173 C9
Cerignola Italy 41°17N 15°53E 201 A8
Cerigo = Kythira Greece 36°8N 23°0E 204 E5
Cérilly France 46°37N 2°50E 173 F9
Cerisiers France 48°8N 3°30E 173 D10
Cerizay France 46°50N 0°40W 172 F6
Çerkeş Turkey 40°49N 32°52E 212 B5
Çerkezköy Turkey 41°17N 28°0E 205 D12
Cerknica Slovenia 45°48N 14°21E 199 C11
Cerkovica Bulgaria 43°41N 24°50E 203 C8
Cermei Romania 46°35N 21°50E 182 D6
Çermik Turkey 38°8N 39°26E 213 C8
Cerna Romania 45°4N 28°17E 183 E13
Cerna → Romania 44°38N 23°58E 183 F8
Cernăuti = Chernivtsi
  Ukraine 48°15N 25°52E 183 D10
Cernavodă Romania 44°22N 28°17E 183 F13
Cernay France 47°44N 7°10E 182 E14
Černik Croatia 45°17N 17°22E 182 E2
Cerralvo, I. Mexico 24°15N 109°55W 318 C3
Cërrik Albania 41°2N 19°58E 202 E3
Cerritos Mexico 22°26N 100°16W 318 C4
Cerro Chato Uruguay 33°6S 55°8W 335 C4
Cerro Chovoreca
  Paraguay 19°19S 59°47W 331 D6
Cerro Cofre de Perote △
  Mexico 19°29N 97°8W 319 D5
Cerro Corá △ Paraguay 22°35S 56°2W 334 A4
Cerro de la Estrella △
  Mexico 19°20N 99°2W 127 B3
Cerro de los Angeles Spain 40°18N 3°41W 127 C1
Cerro de Pasco Peru 10°45S 76°10W 330 C2
Cerro El Copey △ Venezuela 11°1N 63°54W 329 a
Cerro Gordo U.S.A. 39°53N 88°44W 311 E8
Cerro Hoya △ Panama 7°17N 80°45W 320 E3
Cerro Navia Chile 33°25S 70°44W 137 B1
Cerro Saroche △ Venezuela 10°8N 69°35W 328 A4
Cerro Sombrero Chile 52°45S 69°15W 336 G3
Certaldo Italy 43°33N 11°2E 198 E8
Cervantes Phil. 17°0N 120°44E 232 C3
Cervaro → Italy 4°30N 15°52E 201 A8
Cervati, Monte Italy 40°15N 15°29E 201 B8
Cerventes Australia 30°31S 115°3E 279 F2
Cervera Spain 41°40N 1°16E 196 D6
Cervera de Pisuerga Spain 42°51N 4°30W 194 C6
Cervera del Rio Alhama
  Spain 42°2N 1°58W 196 C3
Cervéteri Italy 42°0N 12°6E 199 F9
Cérvia Italy 44°15N 12°22E 199 D9
Cervignano del Friuli
  Italy 45°49N 13°20E 199 C10
Cervione France 42°20N 9°29E 175 F13

Cervo *Spain* 43°40N 7°24W **194** B3
Cesano Boscone *Italy* 45°26N 9°5E **128** B1
César □ *Colombia* 9°0N 73°30W **328** B3
Cesate *Italy* 45°35N 9°4E **128** A1
Cesena *Italy* 44°8N 12°15E **199** D9
Cesenático *Italy* 44°12N 12°24E **199** D9
Cēsis *Latvia* 57°18N 25°15E **188** D3
Česká Lípa *Czech Rep.* 50°41N 14°30E **180** A7
Česká Rep. = Czech Rep. ■
  Europe 50°0N 15°0E **180** B8
Česká Třebová *Czech Rep.* 49°54N 16°27E **181** B9
České Budějovice
  Czech Rep. 48°55N 14°25E **180** C7
České Velenice *Czech Rep.* 48°46N 14°57E **180** C7
Českobudějovický □
  Czech Rep. 49°10N 14°30E **180** B7
Českomoravská Vrchovina
  Czech Rep. 49°30N 15°40E **180** B8
Český Brod *Czech Rep.* 50°4N 14°52E **180** A7
Český Krumlov *Czech Rep.* 48°43N 14°21E **180** C7
Český Těšín *Czech Rep.* 49°45N 18°39E **181** B11
Cesma → *Croatia* 45°35N 16°29E **199** C13
Çeşme *Turkey* 38°20N 26°23E **205** C8
Cessnock *Australia* 32°50S 151°21E **283** B9
Cesson-Sévigné *France* 48°7N 1°36W **172** D5
Cestas *France* 44°44N 0°41W **174** D3
Cestos → *Liberia* 5°40N 9°10W **262** D3
Cestos Sehnkwehn △
  Liberia 5°40N 9°10W **262** D3
Cetaceo, Mt. *Phil.* 17°42N 122°3E **232** C4
Cetate *Romania* 44°7N 23°2E **182** F8
Cetatea-Albă = Bilhorod-
  Dnistrovskyy *Ukraine* 46°11N 30°23E **189** J6
Cetin Grad *Croatia* 45°26N 15°45E **199** C12
Cetina → *Croatia* 43°26N 16°42E **199** E13
Cetinje *Montenegro* 42°23N 18°59E **202** D2
Çetmi *Turkey* 39°32N 32°38E **250** B3
Cetraro *Italy* 39°31N 15°55E **201** C8
Ceuta *N. Afr.* 35°52N 5°18W **260** A3
Ceva *Italy* 44°23N 8°2E **198** D5
Ceve-i-Ra *Fiji* 21°46S 174°31E **277** E13
Cévennes △ *France* 44°10N 3°50E **174** D7
Cévennes △ *France* 44°15N 3°45E **174** D7
Ceyhan *Turkey* 37°4N 35°47E **250** A6
Ceyhan → *Turkey* 36°38N 35°40E **250** B6
Ceylanpınar *Turkey* 36°50N 40°2E **251** B9
Ceylon = Sri Lanka ■ *Asia* 7°30N 80°50E **245** L5
Ceylon Plain *Ind. Oc.* 4°0S 82°0E **273** E7
Cēze → *France* 44°6N 4°43E **175** D8
Cha-am *Thailand* 12°48N 99°58E **236** C2
Cha Kwo Ling *China* 22°18N 114°13E **122** B2
Chá Pungana *Angola* 13°44S 18°39E **268** C3
Chabanais *France* 45°52N 0°48E **174** C4
Chabeuil *France* 44°54N 5°1E **175** D9
Chablais *France* 46°20N 6°36E **173** F13
Chablis *France* 47°47N 3°48E **173** E10
Chabounia *Algeria* 35°30N 2°38E **261** A5
Chacabuco *Argentina* 34°40S 60°27W **334** C3
Chacachacare *Venezuela* 10°58N 64°9W **329** a
Chacachacare I.
  Trin. & Tob. 10°41N 61°45W **323** t
Chacao, Canal *Chile* 41°47S 73°42W **336** B2
Chacarrita *Argentina* 34°35S 58°27W **117** B2
Chachani, Nevado *Peru* 16°11S 71°31W **330** D3
Chachapoyas *Peru* 6°15S 77°50W **330** B2
Chachasp *Peru* 15°30S 72°15W **330** D3
Chachoengsao *Thailand* 13°42N 101°5E **236** F3
Chachran *Pakistan* 28°55N 70°30E **242** G4
Chachro *Pakistan* 25°5N 70°15E **242** G4
Chaco □ *Argentina* 26°30S 61°0W **334** B3
Chaco □ *Paraguay* 26°0S 60°0W **334** B4
Chaco → *U.S.A.* 36°46N 108°39W **305** H9
Chaco △ *Argentina* 27°0S 59°30W **334** B4
Chaco Culture △ *U.S.A.* 36°3N 107°58W **305** H10
Chacon, C. *U.S.A.* 54°42N 132°0W **296** C2
Chad ■ *Africa* 15°0N 17°15E **259** F7
Chad, L. = Tchad, L. *Chad* 13°30N 14°30E **259** F2
Chadileuvú → *Argentina* 37°46S 66°0W **334** D2
Chadiza *Zambia* 14°45S 32°27E **269** E3
Chadron *U.S.A.* 42°50N 103°0W **308** D3
Chadwell Heath *U.K.* 51°34N 0°8E **125** A4
Chadyr-Lunga = Ciadâr-Lunga
  Moldova 46°3N 28°51E **183** D13
Chae Hom *Thailand* 18°43N 99°35E **236** C2
Chae Son △ *Thailand* 18°42N 99°20E **236** C2
Chaem → *Thailand* 18°11N 98°38E **236** C2
Chaerŏng *N. Korea* 38°24N 125°36E **224** C2
Chafe *Nigeria* 11°56N 6°55E **264** C2
Chagai Hills = Chāh Gay Hills
  Afghan. 29°30N 64°0E **240** C2
Chagang-do □ *N. Korea* 40°50N 126°30E **224** C4
Chagda *Russia* 58°45N 130°38E **215** D14
Chagdo Kangri *China* 34°15N 84°10E **217** F10
Chaghcharān *Afghan.* 34°31N 65°15E **240** B2
Chagne *Ethiopia* 11°35N 36°30E **268** B4
Chagny *France* 46°57N 4°45E **173** F11
Chagoda *Russia* 59°10N 35°15E **188** C8
Chagos Arch. ☑ *Ind. Oc.* 6°0S 72°0E **211** J9
Chagres → □ *Panama* 9°10N 79°40W **320** c
Chagres △ *Panama* 9°33N 79°37W **320** c
Chaguanas *Trin. & Tob.* 10°14N 61°26W **323** t
Chaguaramas *Trin. & Tob.* 10°41N 61°38W **323** t
Chāh Akhvor *Iran* 32°41N 59°40E **247** C8
Chāh Bahar *Iran* 25°20N 60°40E **247** E9
Chāh-e-Āb *Afghan.* 37°23N 69°48E **240** A3
Chāh-e Kavīr *Iran* 34°29N 56°52E **247** C8
Chāh Gay Hills *Afghan.* 29°30N 64°0E **240** C2
Chahār Borj *Iran* 37°6N 45°59E **213** D11
Chahār Borjak *Afghan.* 30°17N 62°3E **240** C1
Chāhār Mahāll va Bakhtīārī □
  Iran 32°0N 49°0E **247** C6
Chahtung *Burma* 26°41N 98°10E **241** A7
Chai Badan *Thailand* 15°12N 101°8E **236** E3
Chai Chee *Singapore* 1°19N 103°56E **138** B3
Chai Wan *China* 22°16N 114°14E **122** B2
Chai Wan Kok *China* 22°22N 114°6E **122** A1
Chaibasa *India* 22°42N 85°49E **243** H11
Chaidari *Greece* 38°2N 23°38E **112** A1
Chaillé-les-Marais *France* 46°25N 1°2W **174** B2
Chaillot *Paris, France* 134 b2
Chaillu, Massif du *Gabon* 2°32S 11°0E **264** C2
Chain Ridge *Ind. Oc.* 5°0S 90°0E **273** D4
Chainat *Thailand* 15°11N 100°8E **236** E3
Chainpur *Nepal* 27°17N 87°19E **243** F12
Chaires *U.S.A.* 42°55S 72°43W **336** B2
Chaitén *Chile* 9°23N 98°14E **237** H2
Chaiya *Thailand* 9°23N 99°14E **237** H2
Chaiyaphum *Thailand* 15°48N 102°2E **236** E4
Chaj Doab *Pakistan* 32°15N 73°0E **242** C5
Chajari *Argentina* 30°42S 58°0W **334** C3
Chak Amru *Pakistan* 32°22N 75°11E **242** C6
Chaka *South Sudan* 4°49N 31°14E **267** G3
Chakar → *Pakistan* 29°29N 68°2E **242** E3
Chakari *Zimbabwe* 18°5S 29°51E **271** A4
Chakaria *Bangla.* 21°45N 92°5E **241** E8
Chakdaha *India* 23°28N 88°19E **243** H13
Chake Chake *Tanzania* 5°15S 39°45E **266** D4
Chakhānsūr *Afghan.* 31°10N 62°0E **240** D1
Chakonipau, L. *Canada* 56°18N 68°30E **243** H11
Chakradharpur *India* 22°45N 85°40E **243** H11
Chakrata *India* 30°42N 77°51E **242** D7
Chakwadam *Burma* 29°8N 98°31E **241** A7
Chakwal *Pakistan* 32°56N 72°53E **242** C5

Cheonan S. Korea 36°48N 127°9E 224 D3
Cheongdam S. Korea 37°31N 127°2E 137 B2
Cheongdo S. Korea 35°38N 128°42E 224 E4
Cheongju S. Korea 36°39N 127°27E 224 D3
Cheongsando S. Korea 34°11N 126°53E 224 E3
Cheongseong S. Korea 36°25N 129°3E 224 D4
Cheonho S. Korea 37°32N 127°6E 137 B2
Cheonsumman S. Korea 36°33N 126°25E 224 D3
Cheops Egypt 29°58N 31°8E 117 B1
Cheorwon S. Korea 38°15N 127°10E 224 C3
Chepelare Bulgaria 41°44N 24°40E 203 E8
Chepén Peru 7°15S 79°23W 330 B2
Chépénéhé N. Cal. 20°47S 167°9E 288 d
Chepes Argentina 31°20S 66°35W 334 C2
Chepo Panama 9°10N 79°6W 320 E4
Chepstow U.K. 51°38N 2°41W 169 F5
Chequamegon B. U.S.A. 46°39N 90°51W 308 B8
Cher □ France 47°10N 2°30E 173 E9
Cher → France 47°21N 0°29E 172 E7
Chéradi Italy 40°27N 17°10E 201 B10
Cheran India 25°45N 90°44E 241 C3
Cherasco Italy 44°39N 7°51E 198 D4
Cherating Malaysia 3°35N 103°5E 234 B2
Cheraw U.S.A. 34°42N 79°53W 315 D15
Cherbourg France 49°39N 1°40W 172 C5
Cherchell Algeria 36°35N 2°12E 261 A5
Cherdakly Russia 54°25N 48°50E 190 C9
Cherdyn Russia 60°24N 56°29E 186 B10
Cheremkhovo Russia 53°8N 103°1E 218 A9
Cherepanovo Russia 54°15N 83°30E 217 B10
Cherepovets Russia 59°5N 37°55E 188 C9
Chergui, Chott ech Algeria 34°21N 0°25E 261 B5
Chergui, Zahrez Algeria 35°11N 3°31E 261 B5
Cherial India 17°55N 78°59E 244 F4
Cheribon = Cirebon Indonesia 6°45S 108°32E 235 D3
Cherikov = Cherykaw Belarus 53°32N 31°20E 188 F6
Cheriyam I. India 10°9N 73°40E 245 J1
Cherkasy Ukraine 49°27N 32°4E 189 H7
Cherkasy □ Ukraine 48°55N 30°50E 189 H6
Cherkessk Russia 44°15N 42°5E 191 H6
Cherla India 18°5N 80°49E 244 E5
Cherlak Russia 54°15N 74°55E 217 B8
Chernaya Russia 70°30N 89°10E 215 B9
Chernelytsya Ukraine 48°49N 25°26E 183 B10
Cherni Bulgaria 42°35N 23°18E 202 D7
Chernigov = Chernihiv Ukraine 51°28N 31°20E 189 G6
Chernigovka Russia 44°19N 132°34E 220 B6
Chernihiv Ukraine 51°28N 31°20E 189 G6
Chernihiv □ Ukraine 51°10N 32°5E 189 G7
Chernivtsi Chernivtsi, Ukraine 48°15N 25°52E 183 B10
Chernivtsi Vinnyts'ka, Ukraine 48°32N 28°9E 183 B13
Chernivtsi □ Ukraine 48°5N 25°30E 183 B10
Chernobyl = Chornobyl Ukraine 51°20N 30°15E 177 C16
Chernogorsk Russia 53°49N 91°18E 217 B12
Chernomorskoye = Chornomorske Ukraine 45°31N 32°40E 189 K7
Chernorechye = Dzerzhinsk Russia 56°14N 43°30E 190 B6
Chernovtsy = Chernivtsi Ukraine 48°15N 25°52E 183 B10
Chernyakhovsk Russia 54°36N 21°48E 184 D8
Chernyanka Russia 50°56N 37°49E 189 G9
Chernysheyskiy Russia 63°0N 112°30E 215 C12
Chernyye Zemli Russia 46°10N 46°0E 191 H8
Cherokee Iowa, U.S.A. 42°45N 95°33W 308 D6
Cherokee Okla., U.S.A. 36°45N 98°21W 314 C5
Cherokee Village U.S.A. 36°18N 91°31W 314 C9
Cherokees, Grand Lake O' The U.S.A. 36°28N 94°55W 314 C7
Cherquenco Chile 38°35S 72°0W 336 A2
Cherrapunji India 25°17N 91°47E 241 C3
Cherry Valley U.S.A. 42°48N 74°45W 313 D10
Cherryville U.S.A. 37°51N 91°16W 310 G5
Cherskiy Russia 68°45N 161°18E 215 C17
Cherskogo Khrebet Russia 65°0N 143°0E 215 C15
Cherso Greece 41°5N 22°47E 202 E6
Chersonisos Akrotiri Greece 35°30N 24°10E 207 E5
Chertanovka → Russia 55°38N 37°48E 129 C2
Chertanovo Russia 55°38N 37°36E 129 C2
Cherthala India 9°42N 76°20E 245 K3
Chertkov = Chortkiv Ukraine 49°2N 25°46E 177 D13
Chertkovo Russia 49°25N 40°19E 189 H11
Cherven Belarus 53°45N 28°28E 177 B15
Cherven-Bryag Bulgaria 43°17N 24°7E 203 C8
Chervonoarmiyske Ukraine 45°47N 28°44E 183 E13
Chervonohrad Ukraine 50°25N 24°10E 177 C13
Cherwell → U.K. 51°44N 1°14W 169 F6
Cherykaw Belarus 53°32N 31°20E 177 B16
Cheryomushki Russia 55°40N 37°35E 129 B2
Chesapeake U.S.A. 36°49N 76°16W 309 G15
Chesapeake B. U.S.A. 38°0N 76°10W 309 F14
Cheshire East □ U.K. 53°15N 2°15W 168 D5
Cheshire West and Chester □ U.K. 53°15N 2°40W 168 D5
Cheshskaya Guba Russia 67°20N 47°0E 186 A8
Cheshunt U.K. 51°43N 0°1W 169 F7
Chesil Beach U.K. 50°37N 2°33W 169 G5
Chesley Canada 44°17N 81°5W 312 B3
Chesnokovka = Novoaltaysk Russia 53°30N 84°0E 217 B10
Cheste Spain 39°30N 0°41W 197 F4
Chester Ches., U.K. 53°12N 2°53W 168 D5
Chester Calif., U.S.A. 40°19N 121°14W 304 F3
Chester Ga., U.S.A. 32°24N 83°9W 316 C6
Chester Ill., U.S.A. 37°55N 89°49W 310 G7
Chester Mont., U.S.A. 48°31N 110°58W 304 B8
Chester Pa., U.S.A. 39°51N 75°22W 309 F16
Chester S.C., U.S.A. 34°43N 81°12W 315 D14
Chester Vt., U.S.A. 43°16N 72°36W 313 C12
Chester W. Va., U.S.A. 40°37N 80°34W 312 F4
Chester-le-Street U.K. 54°51N 1°34W 168 C6
Chesterfield Derby, U.K. 53°15N 1°25W 168 D6
Chesterfield Mo., U.S.A. 38°40N 90°35W 310 F6
Chesterfield, Îs. N. Cal. 19°52S 158°15E 277 D10
Chesterfield Inlet Canada 63°30N 90°45W 294 E13
Chesterton Ra. Australia 25°30S 147°27E 281 D4
Chesterton Range △ Australia 26°16S 147°22E 281 D4
Chestertown U.S.A. 43°40N 73°48W 313 C11
Chesterville Canada 45°6N 75°14W 313 A9
Chestnut Hill U.S.A. 42°19N 71°10W 116 B1
Chesuncook L. U.S.A. 46°0N 69°21W 309 C19
Chetamale India 10°43N 92°33E 245 J11
Chéticamp Canada 46°37N 60°59W 299 C7
Chetlat I. India 11°42N 72°42E 245 J1
Chetrosu Moldova 48°5N 27°54E 183 B12
Chetumal Mexico 18°30N 88°20W 319 D7
Chetumal, B. de Cent. Amer. 18°40N 88°10W 319 D7
Chetwynd Canada 55°45N 121°36W 296 B4
Cheung Chau China 22°13N 114°1E 219 a
Cheung Sha Wan China 22°20N 114°8E 122 A1
Chevak U.S.A. 61°32N 165°35W 303 F6
Chevalier, Î. de Martinique 14°25N 60°50W 322 j
Chevanceaux France 45°18N 0°14W 174 C3
Cheverly U.S.A. 38°55N 76°54W 143 B3
Chevilly-Larue France 48°46N 2°21E 134 B3
Cheviot U.S.A. 39°9N 84°36W 311 E12
Cheviot, The U.K. 55°29N 2°9W 168 B5
Cheviot Hills Northumberland, U.K. 55°23N 2°30W 168 B5
Cheviot Hills Calif., U.S.A. 34°2N 118°24W 126 B2
Cheviot Ra. Australia 25°20S 143°45E 280 C3
Chevreau, Île St. Barts 17°56N 62°51W 322 a
Chevy Chase U.S.A. 38°59N 77°4W 143 B2
Chew Bahir Ethiopia 4°40N 36°50E 257 G4
Chewelah U.S.A. 48°17N 117°43W 304 B5
Chewore ⌓ Zimbabwe 16°0S 29°52E 269 F2
Cheyenne Okla., U.S.A. 35°37N 99°40W 314 D5
Cheyenne Wyo., U.S.A. 41°8N 104°49W 304 F11
Cheyenne → U.S.A. 44°41N 101°18W 308 C3
Cheyenne Wells U.S.A. 38°49N 102°21W 304 G12
Cheyne B. Australia 34°35S 118°50E 279 F2
Cheyur India 12°21N 80°0E 245 H5
Chhabra India 24°40N 76°54E 242 G7
Chhaktala India 22°6N 74°11E 242 H6
Chhapra India 25°48N 84°44E 243 G11
Chhata India 27°42N 77°30E 242 F7
Chhatak Bangla. 25°5N 91°37E 241 C3
Chhatarpur Jharkhand, India 24°23N 84°11E 243 G11
Chhatarpur Mad. P., India 24°55N 79°35E 243 G8
Chhati India 20°47N 81°40E 244 D5
Chhatrapati Shivaji, Mumbai ✕ (BOM) India 19°5N 72°51E 130 A2
Chhatrapati Shivaji Terminus India 18°56N 72°50E 130 B2
Chhattisgarh □ India 22°0N 82°0E 243 J10
Chhaygaon India 26°3N 91°24E 241 B3
Chhep Cambodia 13°45N 105°24E 236 F5
Chhindwara Mad. P., India 23°3N 79°29E 243 H8
Chhindwara Mad. P., India 22°2N 78°59E 243 H8
Chhinhdipada India 21°6N 84°52E 244 D7
Chhlong Cambodia 12°15N 105°58E 237 F5
Chhota Tawa → India 22°14N 76°36E 242 H7
Chhoti Kali Sindh → India 24°2N 75°31E 242 G6
Chhuikhadan India 21°32N 80°59E 243 J9
Chhuk Cambodia 10°46N 104°28E 237 G5
Chi → Thailand 15°11N 104°43E 236 E5
Chi Thanh Vietnam 13°17N 109°16E 236 F7
Chia Keng Singapore 1°21N 103°52E 138 A3
Chiahsien Taiwan 23°5N 120°35E 225 C2
Chiai Taiwan 23°29N 120°25E 225 C2
Chiai □ Taiwan 23°30N 120°30E 225 C2
Chiaksan △ S. Korea 37°15N 128°0E 224 D4
Chiali Taiwan 23°9N 120°10E 225 C2
Chialuantsun Taiwan 22°49N 121°11E 225 D3
Chiamboni Somalia 1°39S 41°35E 267 E5
Chiamussu = Jiamusi China 46°40N 130°26E 219 B15
Chian Taiwan 23°59N 121°33E 225 C3
Chianapu Taiwan 22°47N 120°36E 225 D2
Chianciano Terme Italy 43°2N 11°49E 199 E8
Chiang Dao Thailand 19°22N 98°58E 236 C2
Chiang Dao, Doi Thailand 19°23N 98°54E 236 C2
Chiang Kham Thailand 19°32N 100°18E 236 C3
Chiang Khan Thailand 17°52N 101°36E 236 D3
Chiang Khong Thailand 20°17N 100°24E 228 G3
Chiang Mai Thailand 18°47N 98°59E 236 C2
Chiang Rai Thailand 19°52N 99°50E 228 H2
Chiang Saen Thailand 20°16N 100°5E 228 G3
Chiangchun Taiwan 23°12N 120°9E 225 C2
Chiange Angola 15°35S 13°40E 265 F2
Chianti Italy 43°32N 11°25E 199 E8
Chiaohsi Taiwan 24°49N 121°46E 225 B3
Chiaotou Taiwan 22°45N 120°18E 225 D2
Chiapa de Corzo Mexico 16°42N 93°0W 319 D6
Chiapas □ Mexico 16°30N 92°30W 319 D6
Chiapas, Sa. Madre de Mexico 15°40N 93°0W 319 D6
Chiaramonte Gulfi Italy 37°2N 14°42E 201 E7
Chiaravalle Italy 43°36N 13°19E 199 E10
Chiaravalle Centrale Italy 38°41N 16°25E 201 D9
Chiaravalle Milanese Italy 45°24N 9°16E 128 B2
Chiari Italy 45°32N 9°56E 198 C6
Chiatung Taiwan 22°25N 120°32E 225 D2
Chiatura Georgia 42°15N 43°17E 191 J6
Chiautla de Tapia Mexico 18°18N 98°36W 319 D5
Chiavari Italy 44°19N 9°19E 198 D6
Chiavenna Italy 46°19N 9°24E 198 B6
Chiba Japan 35°30N 140°7E 223 B12
Chiba □ Japan 35°30N 140°20E 223 B12
Chibabava Mozam. 20°17S 33°35E 271 B5
Chibango Angola 13°38S 21°56E 265 E4
Chibemba Cunene, Angola 15°48S 14°8E 265 F2
Chibemba Huila, Angola 16°20S 15°20E 265 F3
Chibi Zimbabwe 20°18S 30°25E 271 B5
Chibia Angola 15°10S 13°42E 265 F2
Chibizovka = Zherdevka Russia 51°56N 41°29E 190 E5
Chibougamau Canada 49°56N 74°24W 298 C5
Chibougamau, L. Canada 49°50N 74°20W 298 C5
Chibuk Nigeria 10°52N 12°50E 263 C7
Chibuto Mozam. 24°40S 33°33E 271 B5
Chibyu = Ukhta Russia 63°34N 53°41E 186 B9
Chic-Chocs, Mts. Canada 48°55N 66°0W 299 C6
Chicacole = Srikakulam India 18°14N 83°58E 244 E6
Chicago U.S.A. 41°52N 87°38W 119 B3
Chicago, Univ. of U.S.A. 41°47N 87°35W 119 C3
Chicago Harbor U.S.A. 41°52N 87°36W 119 B3
Chicago Heights U.S.A. 41°30N 87°38W 311 C9
Chicago Lawn U.S.A. 41°47N 87°40W 119 C2
Chicago O'Hare Int. ✕ (ORD) U.S.A. 41°59N 87°54W 311 C9
Chicago Ridge U.S.A. 41°41N 87°46W 119 C2
Chicago River → U.S.A. 119 b2
Chicago River, North Branch → U.S.A. 41°53N 87°42W 119 B2
Chicago Sanitary and Ship Canal U.S.A. 41°49N 87°46W 119 C2
Chicago State Univ. U.S.A. 41°43N 87°36W 119 C3
Chicapa → Dem. Rep. of the Congo 6°25S 20°48E 265 D4
Chicha Chad 16°57N 18°34E 259 E3
Chichagof I. U.S.A. 57°30N 135°30W 303 H14
Chichaoua Morocco 31°32N 8°44W 260 B3
Chichawatni Pakistan 30°32N 72°42E 242 D5
Chichén-Itzá Mexico 20°37N 88°35W 319 C7
Chicheng China 40°55N 115°55E 226 D8
Chichester U.K. 50°50N 0°47W 169 G7
Chichester Ra. Australia 22°12S 119°15E 278 D2
Chichi Hualien, Taiwan 23°44N 121°33E 225 C3
Chichi Nant'ou, Taiwan 23°49N 120°47E 225 C2
Chichibu Japan 35°59N 139°10E 223 A11
Chichibu-Tama-Kai △ Japan 35°52N 138°42E 223 B10
Ch'ich'ihaerh = Qiqihar China 47°26N 124°0E 219 B13
Chicholi India 22°1N 77°40E 242 H8
Ch'ich'ou Taiwan 23°45N 120°33E 225 C2
Chickasaw ⌓ U.S.A. 34°26N 97°0W 314 D6
Chickasha U.S.A. 35°3N 97°58W 314 D6
Chicken U.S.A. 64°5N 141°56W 303 D12
Chiclana de la Frontera Spain 36°26N 6°9W 195 J4
Chiclayo Peru 6°42S 79°50W 330 B2
Chico U.S.A. 39°44N 121°50W 306 F5
Chico → Chubut, Argentina 44°0S 67°0W 336 B3
Chico → Santa Cruz, Argentina 50°0S 68°30W 336 D3
Chico → Phil. 17°57N 121°36E 232 C3
Chicoa Mozam. 15°36S 32°20E 269 F3
Chicomba Angola 14°10S 14°52E 265 E2
Chicomo Mozam. 24°31S 34°6E 271 B5
Chicomostoc Mexico 22°28N 102°46W 318 C4
Chiconi Mayotte 12°50S 45°7E 272 b
Chicontepec Mexico 20°58N 98°10W 319 C5
Chicopee U.S.A. 42°9N 72°37W 313 D12
Chicoutimi Canada 48°28N 71°5W 299 C5
Chicualacuala Mozam. 22°6S 31°42E 271 B5
Chicuma Angola 13°26S 14°50E 265 E2
Chidambaram India 11°20N 79°45E 245 J4
Chidenguele Mozam. 24°55S 34°11E 271 B5
Chidley, C. Canada 60°23N 64°26W 295 E19
Chiducuane Mozam. 24°35S 34°25E 271 B5
Chiede Angola 17°15S 16°22E 265 F3
Chiefland U.S.A. 29°29N 82°52W 317 F7
Chiefs Pt. Canada 44°41N 81°18W 312 B3
Chiehting Taiwan 22°54N 120°11E 225 D2
Chiem Hoa Vietnam 22°12N 105°17E 236 A5
Chiemsee Germany 47°53N 12°28E 179 H8
Chienchen Taiwan 22°35N 120°18E 225 D2
Chiengi Zambia 8°45S 29°10E 269 D2
Chiengmai = Chiang Mai Thailand 18°47N 98°59E 236 C2
Chiengo Angola 13°20S 21°55E 265 E4
Chienti → Italy 43°18N 13°45E 199 E10
Chienzui China 23°12N 113°22E 121 A3
Chieri Italy 45°1N 7°49E 198 C4
Chiers → France 49°39N 4°59E 173 C11
Chiesa in Valmalenco Italy 46°16N 9°51E 198 B6
Chiese → Italy 45°8N 10°25E 198 C7
Chieti Italy 42°21N 14°10E 199 F11
Chifeng China 42°18N 118°58E 227 C10
Chigasaki Japan 35°19N 139°24E 223 B11
Chigirin Ukraine 49°4N 32°38E 189 H7
Chignecto B. Canada 45°30N 64°40W 299 C7
Chignik U.S.A. 56°18N 158°24W 303 H8
Chigorodó Colombia 7°41N 76°42W 328 B2
Chiguana Bolivia 21°0S 67°58W 334 A2
Chigwell U.K. 51°37N 0°6E 169 F8
Chihli, G. of = Bo Hai China 39°0N 119°0E 227 E10
Ch'ihpen Taiwan 22°42N 121°2E 225 D3
Ch'ihshang Taiwan 23°7N 121°12E 225 C3
Chihsi = Jixi China 45°20N 130°50E 227 B16
Chihu Taiwan 23°54N 120°24E 225 C2
Chihuahua Mexico 28°38N 106°5W 318 B3
Chihuahua □ Mexico 28°30N 106°0W 318 B3
Chiili = Shieli Kazakhstan 44°20N 66°15E 217 D7
Chik Bollapur India 13°25N 77°45E 245 H3
Chik Sha China 22°17N 114°16E 122 B2
Chikalda India 21°24N 77°19E 244 D3
Chikhli Ahmadabad, India 20°45N 73°4E 244 D1
Chikhli Maharashtra, India 20°20N 76°18E 244 D3
Chikmagalur India 13°15N 75°45E 245 H2
Chiknayakanhalli India 13°26N 76°37E 245 H3
Chikodi India 16°26N 74°38E 245 F2
Chiku Taiwan 23°8N 120°7E 225 C2
Chikugo Japan 33°14N 130°28E 222 D2
Chikuma-Gawa → Japan 36°59N 138°35E 223 A10
Chikura Japan 34°55N 139°57E 223 C11
Chikushino Japan 33°30N 130°30E 222 D2
Chikwawa Malawi 16°2S 34°50E 269 F3
Chila Angola 12°3S 14°29E 265 E2
Chi'ilaichu Shan Taiwan 24°5N 121°20E 225 B3
Chilanga Zambia 15°33S 28°16E 269 F2
Chilapa Mexico 17°36N 99°10W 319 D5
Chilas Pakistan 35°25N 74°5E 243 B6
Chilaw Sri Lanka 7°30N 79°50E 245 L4
Chilcotin → Canada 51°44N 122°23W 296 C4
Childers Australia 25°15S 152°17E 281 D5
Childersburg U.S.A. 33°16N 86°21W 316 B3
Children's Museum Boston, U.S.A. 116 c3
Children's Palace Beijing, China 114 b1
Childress U.S.A. 34°25N 100°13W 314 D4
Child's Hill U.K. 51°33N 0°12W 125 A2
Chile ■ S. Amer. 35°0S 72°0W 327 G3
Chile, Univ. de Chile 33°26S 70°39W 132 C2
Chile Basin Pac. Oc. 33°0S 80°0W 289 L20
Chile Chico Chile 46°33S 71°44W 336 C2
Chile Rise Pac. Oc. 38°0S 92°0W 289 L18
Chilecito Argentina 29°10S 67°30W 334 B2
Chilengue, Serra do Angola 13°18S 15°22E 265 E2
Chilesso Angola 11°35S 16°34E 265 E3
Chilete Peru 7°10S 78°50W 330 B2
Chilhowee U.S.A. 38°36N 93°51W 310 F3
Chilia, Braţul → Romania 45°14N 29°42E 183 E14
Chilibre Panama 9°9N 79°37W 320 c
Chilik = Shelek Kazakhstan 43°33N 78°17E 217 D9
Chililabombwe Zambia 12°18S 27°43E 269 E2
Chilim Pakistan 35°5N 75°5E 243 B6
Chilin = Jilin China 43°44N 126°30E 227 C14
Chiliomodi Greece 37°48N 22°51E 204 D4
Chilka L. India 19°40N 85°25E 244 E7
Chilko → Canada 52°0N 123°40W 296 C4
Chilko L. Canada 51°20N 124°10W 296 C4
Chilla Saroda India 28°35N 77°18E 120 B2
Chillagoe Australia 17°7S 144°33E 280 B3
Chillán Chile 36°40S 72°10W 334 D1
Chillicothe Ill., U.S.A. 40°55N 89°29W 310 D7
Chillicothe Mo., U.S.A. 39°48N 93°33W 310 E3
Chillicothe Ohio, U.S.A. 39°20N 82°59W 309 F12
Chilliwack Canada 49°10N 121°54W 296 D4
Chillum U.S.A. 38°56N 76°58W 143 B3
Chilly-Mazarin France 48°42N 2°17E 134 B2
Chilmari Bangla. 25°33N 89°43E 241 C2
Chilo India 27°25N 73°32E 242 F5
Chiloane, I. Mozam. 20°40S 34°55E 271 B5
Chiloé, I. de Chile 42°30S 73°50W 336 B2
Chiloé △ Chile 42°11S 73°59W 336 B2
Chilonda Angola 11°19S 16°12E 265 E3
Chilongo Angola 13°55S 16°35E 265 E3
Chilpancingo Mexico 17°33N 99°30W 319 D5
Chiltern Australia 36°10S 146°36E 283 D7
Chiltern Hills U.K. 51°40N 0°53W 169 F7
Chilton U.S.A. 44°2N 88°10W 308 C9
Chiluage Angola 9°30S 21°50E 265 D4
Chilubi Zambia 11°5S 29°58E 269 E2
Chilubula Zambia 10°14S 30°51E 269 E3
Chilumba Malawi 10°28S 34°12E 269 E3
Chilung Taiwan 25°3N 121°45E 225 A3
Chilwa, L. Malawi 15°15S 35°40E 269 F4
Chimakela Angola 15°24S 16°58E 265 F3
Chimakuldi India 25°47N 93°48E 241 C4
Chimaltitán Mexico 21°35N 103°50W 318 C4
Chimán Panama 8°45N 78°40W 320 E4
Chimanimani Zimbabwe 19°48S 32°52E 271 A5
Chimanimani △ Zimbabwe 19°48S 33°0E 271 A5
Chimay Belgium 50°3N 4°20E 170 D4
Chimayo U.S.A. 36°0N 105°56W 305 J11
Chimba Zambia 9°54S 31°28E 269 D3
Chimborazo Ecuador 1°29S 78°55W 328 D2
Chimborazo □ Ecuador 1°0S 78°40W 328 D2
Chimbote Peru 9°0S 78°35W 330 B2
Chimboy Uzbekistan 42°57N 59°47E 216 D5
Chimbu □ Papua N. G. 6°15S 144°50E 286 D3
Ch'imei Taiwan 23°12N 119°25E 225 C1
Ch'imei Yü Taiwan 23°13N 119°26E 225 C1
Chimichagua Colombia 9°15N 73°49W 328 B3
Chimkent = Shymkent Kazakhstan 42°18N 69°36E 217 D7
Chimoio Mozam. 19°4S 33°30E 269 F3
Chimpembe Zambia 9°31S 29°33E 269 D2
Chimur India 20°30N 79°23E 244 D4
Chin □ Burma 22°0N 93°0E 241 E4
Chin Hills Burma 22°30N 93°30E 241 D4
Chin Ling Shan = Qinling Shandi China 33°50N 108°10E 226 H5
China Mexico 25°42N 99°14W 319 B5
China ■ Asia 30°0N 110°0E 219 E11
China, Great Plain of Asia 35°0N 115°0E 210 E13
China Basin San Francisco, U.S.A. 136 c3
China Lake U.S.A. 35°44N 117°37W 307 K9
China Town Toronto, Canada 141 b1
Chinacota Colombia 7°37N 72°36W 328 B3
Chinan = Jinan China 36°38N 117°1E 226 F9
Chinandega Nic. 12°35N 87°12W 320 D2
Chinati Peak U.S.A. 29°57N 104°29W 314 G2
Chinatown Singapore 138 c2
Chinatown Boston, U.S.A. 116 c2
Chinatown Los Angeles, U.S.A. 127 a3
Chinatown New York, U.S.A. 132 e2
Chinatown San Francisco, U.S.A. 136 b2
Chincha Alta Peru 13°25S 76°7W 330 C2
Chinchaga → Canada 58°53N 118°20W 296 B5
Chincheros Peru 13°30S 73°44W 330 C3
Chinchilla Australia 26°45S 150°38E 281 D5
Chinchilla de Monte Aragón Spain 38°53N 1°40W 197 G3
Chincholi India 17°28N 77°26E 244 E3
Chinchorro, Banco Mexico 18°35N 87°22W 319 D7
Chinchou = Jinzhou China 41°5N 121°3E 227 D11
Chinchoua Gabon 0°1N 9°48E 264 B1
Chincoteague U.S.A. 37°56N 75°23W 309 G16
Chinde Mozam. 18°35S 36°30E 269 F4
Chindwin → Burma 21°26N 95°15E 241 E5
Chineni India 33°2N 75°15E 243 C6
Chinga Mozam. 15°13S 38°35E 269 F4
Chingaza △ Colombia 4°30N 73°40W 328 C3
Chingola Zambia 12°31S 27°53E 269 E2
Chingole Malawi 13°4S 34°17E 269 E3
Chingoni Mayotte 12°48S 45°8E 272 b
Chingpu Taiwan 23°28N 121°29E 225 C3
Ch'ingshui Changhua, Taiwan 24°16N 120°34E 225 B2
Chingshui Hualien, Taiwan 24°13N 121°41E 225 B3
Chingshui Ilan, Taiwan 24°39N 121°35E 225 B3
Ch'ingtao = Qingdao China 36°5N 120°20E 227 F11
Chinguar Angola 12°25S 16°45E 265 E3
Chinguetti Mauritania 20°25N 12°24W 260 D2
Chingune Mozam. 20°33S 34°58E 271 B5
Chingupota India 22°29N 88°14E 124 C1
Chinhanguanine Mozam. 25°21S 32°30E 271 C5
Chinhoyi Zimbabwe 17°20S 30°8E 269 F3
Chinhsien = Jinxian China 28°26N 116°17E 229 C11
Chiniot Pakistan 31°45N 73°0E 242 D5
Chinipas Mexico 27°23N 108°32W 318 B3
Chinji Pakistan 32°42N 72°22E 242 C5
Chinju = Jinju S. Korea 35°12N 128°2E 224 E4
Chinkai Afghan. 31°57N 67°26E 240 C2
Chinkapook Australia 35°11S 142°57E 282 C5
Chinkiang = Zhenjiang China 32°11N 119°26E 229 A12
Chinko → C.A.R. 4°50N 23°53E 264 B4
Chinle U.S.A. 36°9N 109°33W 305 H9
Ch'inlun Taiwan 22°32N 120°57E 225 D2
Chinmen Taiwan 24°26N 118°19E 225 a
Chinmen Tao Taiwan 24°26N 118°22E 225 a
Chinna Cr. → Pakistan 24°50N 67°0E 123 B2
Chinnamanur India 9°50N 77°24E 245 K3
Chinnampo = Namp'o N. Korea 38°52N 125°10E 224 C2
Chino Japan 35°59N 138°9E 223 B10
Chino Calif., U.S.A. 34°1N 117°41W 307 L9
Chino Valley U.S.A. 34°45N 112°27W 305 J7
Chinois, Quartier Montréal, Canada 130 b2
Chinon France 47°10N 0°15E 172 E7
Chinook U.S.A. 48°35N 109°14W 304 B9
Chinook Trough Pac. Oc. 44°0N 175°0W 288 C10
Chinoya Zambia 13°55S 23°16E 265 E4
Chinsali Zambia 10°30S 32°2E 269 E3
Chinshan Taiwan 25°13N 121°38E 225 A3
Chinsura = Chunchura India 22°53N 88°27E 243 H13
Chintalapudi India 17°4N 80°59E 244 F5
Chintamani India 13°26N 78°3E 245 H4
Chinwangtao = Qinhuangdao China 39°56N 119°30E 227 E10
Chióggia Italy 45°13N 12°17E 199 C9
Chios Greece 38°27N 26°9E 205 C8
Chios □ Greece 38°27N 26°9E 205 C8
Chipata Zambia 13°38S 32°28E 269 E3
Chipei Tao Taiwan 23°45N 119°37E 225 C1
Chiperceni Moldova 47°31N 28°50E 183 C13
Chipindo Angola 13°49S 15°48E 265 E3
Chipinge Zimbabwe 20°13S 32°28E 269 G3
Chipinge ⌓ Zimbabwe 20°14S 33°0E 269 G3
Chipiona Spain 36°44N 6°26W 195 J4
Chipley U.S.A. 30°47N 85°32W 316 E4
Chiplun India 17°31N 73°34E 244 F1
Chipman Canada 46°6N 65°53W 299 C6
Chipoka Malawi 13°57S 34°28E 269 E3
Chippenham U.K. 51°27N 2°6W 169 F5
Chippewa → U.S.A. 44°25N 92°5W 308 C7
Chippewa Falls U.S.A. 44°56N 91°24W 308 C8
Chipping Norton U.K. 51°56N 1°32W 169 F6
Chiprovtsi Bulgaria 43°24N 22°52E 202 C6
Chiputneticook Lakes N. Amer. 45°35N 67°35W 309 C20
Chiputo = Vila Vasco da Gama Mozam. 14°54S 32°14E 269 E3
Chipwi Burma 25°53N 98°8E 241 C7
Chiquelequele Angola 16°44S 19°5E 265 F3
Chiquián Peru 10°10S 77°0W 330 C2
Chiquibul △ Belize 16°49N 88°52W 320 C2
Chiquimula Guatemala 14°51N 89°37W 320 D2
Chiquinquira Colombia 5°37N 73°50W 328 B3
Chiquitos, Llanos de Bolivia 18°0S 61°30W 331 D5
Chir → Russia 48°30N 43°0E 191 F6
Chira → Peru 4°54S 81°8W 328 D1
Chirala India 15°50N 80°26E 245 G5
Chiramba Mozam. 16°55S 34°39E 269 F3
Chirawa India 28°14N 75°42E 242 E6
Chirchiq Uzbekistan 41°29N 69°35E 217 D7
Chiredzi Zimbabwe 21°0S 31°38E 271 B5
Chirfa Niger 20°55N 12°22E 259 D2
Chiribiquete △ Colombia 0°31N 72°50W 328 C3
Chiricahua △ U.S.A. 32°0N 109°20W 305 K9
Chiricahua Peak U.S.A. 31°51N 109°18W 305 L9
Chirikof I. U.S.A. 55°50N 155°40W 300 D8
Chiriqui, G. de Panama 8°0N 82°10W 320 E3
Chiriqui, L. de Panama 9°10N 82°0W 320 E3
Chirisa ⌓ Zimbabwe 17°53S 28°15E 269 F2
Chirivira Falls Zimbabwe 21°10S 32°12E 269 G3
Chirmiri India 23°15N 82°20E 243 H10
Chirnogi Romania 44°7N 26°32E 183 F11
Chirongui Mayotte 12°55S 45°9E 272 b
Chirpan Bulgaria 42°10N 25°19E 203 D9
Chirripó Grande, Cerro Costa Rica 9°29N 83°29W 320 E3
Chirundu Zimbabwe 16°3S 28°50E 271 A4
Chisamba Zambia 14°55S 28°20E 269 E2
Chisapani Nepal 28°37N 81°16E 243 E9
Chisasa Zambia 12°6S 25°30E 265 E5
Chisasibi Canada 53°50N 79°0W 298 B4
Ch'ishan Taiwan 22°44N 120°31E 225 D2
Ch'ishan Hsi → Taiwan 22°51N 120°28E 225 C2
Chisholm Alta., Canada 54°55N 114°10W 296 C6
Chisholm Minn., U.S.A. 47°29N 92°53W 308 B7
Chishtian Mandi Pakistan 29°50N 72°55E 242 E5
Chishui China 28°30N 105°42E 228 C5
Chishui He → China 28°49N 105°50E 228 C5
Chisimaio = Kismaayo Somalia 0°22S 42°32E 267 E5
Chisimba Falls Zambia 10°12S 30°56E 269 E3
Chişinău Moldova 47°2N 28°50E 183 C13
Chişinău ✕ (KIV) Moldova 47°3N 28°46E 183 C13
Chişineu Criş Romania 46°32N 21°37E 182 D6
Chislehurst U.K. 51°24N 0°6E 125 B4
Chisone → Italy 44°49N 7°25E 198 D4
Chisos Mts. U.S.A. 29°5N 103°15W 314 G3
Chissengue Angola 9°13S 20°34E 265 D4
Chissilo Angola 13°48S 16°31E 265 E3
Chistochina U.S.A. 62°34N 144°40W 303 E11
Chistopol Russia 55°25N 50°38E 190 C10
Chiswick U.K. 51°29N 0°16W 125 B2
Chiswick House U.K. 51°29N 0°15W 125 B2
Chita Colombia 6°11N 72°28W 328 B3
Chita Russia 52°0N 113°35E 219 A11
Chitado Angola 17°10S 14°8E 265 F2
Chitaldrug = Chitradurga India 14°14N 76°24E 245 G3
Chitan Taiwan 24°35N 121°29E 225 B3
Chitanda → Angola 16°1S 15°12E 265 F3
Chitapur India 17°10N 77°5E 244 F3
Chitembo Angola 13°30S 16°50E 265 E3
Chitina U.S.A. 61°31N 144°26W 303 F11
Chitipa Malawi 9°41S 33°19E 269 D3
Chitose Hokkaidō, Japan 42°49N 141°39E 220 C10
Chitose Kanagawa, Japan 35°33N 139°37E 140 B2
Chitradurga India 14°14N 76°24E 245 G3
Chitrakot India 19°10N 81°40E 244 E5
Chitral Pakistan 35°50N 71°56E 240 B3
Chitralada Palace Thailand 13°45N 100°31E 113 B2
Chitravati → India 14°45N 78°15E 245 G4
Chitré Panama 7°59N 80°27W 320 E3
Chittagong Bangla. 22°19N 91°48E 241 D3
Chittagong □ Bangla. 24°5N 91°0E 241 C3
Chittaurgarh India 24°52N 74°38E 242 G6
Chittoor India 13°15N 79°5E 245 H4
Chittur India 10°40N 76°45E 245 J3
Chitungwiza Zimbabwe 18°0S 31°6E 269 F3
Chiuju Taiwan 22°44N 120°29E 225 D2
Chiumbe → Dem. Rep. of the Congo 6°59S 21°12E 265 D4
Chiumbo Angola 12°29S 16°8E 265 E3
Chiume Angola 15°3S 21°14E 265 F4
Chiusi Italy 43°1N 11°57E 199 E8
Chiva Spain 39°27N 0°41W 197 F4
Chivacoa Venezuela 10°10N 68°54W 328 A4
Chivasso Italy 45°11N 7°53E 198 C4
Chivay Peru 15°40S 71°35W 330 D3
Chive Bolivia 12°23S 68°35W 330 C4
Chivhu Zimbabwe 19°2S 30°52E 269 F3
Chivilcoy Argentina 34°55S 60°0W 334 C4
Chiwanda Tanzania 11°23S 34°55E 269 E3
Chixi China 22°0N 112°58E 229 G9
Chiyoda Tokyo, Japan 140 b4
Chizarira Zimbabwe 17°36S 27°45E 269 F2
Chizarira △ Zimbabwe 17°44S 27°52E 269 F2
Chizela Zambia 13°8S 25°0E 265 E4
Chizu Japan 35°16N 134°14E 222 B6
Chkalov = Orenburg Russia 51°45N 55°6E 186 D10
Chkolovsk Russia 56°50N 43°10E 190 B6
Chloride U.S.A. 35°25N 114°12W 307 K12
Chlumec nad Cidlinou Czech Rep. 50°9N 15°29E 180 A8
Chmielnik Poland 50°37N 20°43E 185 H7
Cho-do N. Korea 38°30N 124°40E 224 C2
Cho Phuoc Hai Vietnam 10°26N 107°18E 237 G6
Choa Chu Kang Singapore 1°22N 103°41E 138 A2
Choba Kenya 2°30N 38°5E 266 D4
Chobe △ Botswana 18°37S 24°23E 270 A4
Choc B. St. Lucia 14°3N 60°59W 323 m
Choch'i Taiwan 23°20N 121°26E 225 C3
Chocianów Poland 51°27N 15°55E 185 G2
Chociwel Poland 53°29N 15°21E 184 E2
Chocó □ Colombia 6°0N 77°0W 328 B2
Chocolate Hills Phil. 9°54N 124°10E 233 G5
Chocolate Mts. U.S.A. 33°15N 115°15W 307 M11
Chocontá Colombia 5°9N 73°41W 328 B3
Choctawhatchee → U.S.A. 30°25N 86°8W 316 E3
Choctawhatchee B. U.S.A. 30°20N 86°20W 317 E3
Chodavaram Andhra Pradesh, India 17°50N 82°57E 244 F6
Chodavaram Andhra Pradesh, India 17°27N 81°46E 244 F5
Chodecz Poland 52°24N 19°2E 185 F6
Chodov Czech Rep. 50°15N 12°45E 180 A5
Chodov u Prahy Czech Rep. 50°1N 14°30E 135 B3
Chodziez Poland 52°58N 16°58E 185 F3
Choele Choel Argentina 39°11S 65°40W 336 A3
Chōfu Japan 35°38N 139°32E 140 B2
Choghā Zanbīl Iran 32°1N 48°32E 247 C6
Choirokoitia Cyprus 34°47N 33°20E 207 F9
Choiseul St. Lucia 13°47N 61°3W 323 m
Choiseul Solomon Is. 7°0S 156°40E 287 L9
Choisy-le-Roi France 48°46N 2°24E 134 B3
Choix Mexico 26°43N 108°17W 318 B3
Chojna Poland 52°58N 14°25E 185 F1
Chojnice Poland 53°42N 17°32E 184 E4
Chojnów Poland 51°18N 15°58E 185 G2
Chok Chai Thailand 14°44N 102°10E 236 E4
Chōkai-San Japan 39°6N 140°3E 220 E10
Choke Canyon Res. U.S.A. 28°30N 98°20W 314 G5
Choke Mts. Ethiopia 11°18N 37°15E 257 E4
Chokurdakh Russia 70°38N 147°55E 215 B15
Chokwé Mozam. 24°32S 32°59E 271 B5
Cholame U.S.A. 35°44N 120°18W 306 K6
Cholan Taiwan 24°18N 120°49E 225 B2
Cholargos Greece 37°59N 23°48E 112 B2
Cholet France 47°4N 0°52W 172 E6
Cholguan Chile 37°10S 72°3W 334 D1
Choloma Honduras 15°37N 87°57W 320 C2
Cholpon-Ata Kyrgyzstan 42°40N 77°6E 217 D9
Cholupice Czech Rep. 49°59N 14°27E 135 C2
Choluteca Honduras 13°20N 87°14W 320 D2
Choluteca → Honduras 13°0N 87°20W 320 D2
Chom Bung Thailand 13°37N 99°36E 236 F2
Chom Thong Bangkok, Thailand 13°41N 100°29E 113 B1
Chom Thong Chiang Mai, Thailand 18°25N 98°41E 236 C2
Choma Zambia 16°48S 26°59E 269 F2
Chomo Lhari Asia 27°49N 89°16E 241 B2
Chomolungma = Everest, Mt. Nepal 28°5N 86°58E 243 E12
Chomun India 27°15N 75°40E 242 F6
Chomutov Czech Rep. 50°28N 13°23E 180 A6
Chon Buri Thailand 13°21N 101°1E 236 F3
Chon Thanh Vietnam 11°24N 106°36E 237 G6
Chone Ecuador 0°40S 80°0W 328 D2
Chong Kai Cambodia 13°57N 103°35E 236 F4
Chong Mek Thailand 15°10N 105°27E 236 E5
Chong Pang Singapore 1°26N 103°49E 138 A2
Chong Phangan Thailand 9°39N 100°0E 237 b
Chong Samui Thailand 9°21N 99°50E 237 b
Chongde China 30°32N 120°26E 229 B13
Ch'ŏngjin N. Korea 41°47N 129°50E 224 B4
Chŏngju N. Korea 39°40N 125°5E 224 C2
Chongli China 40°58N 115°15E 226 D8
Chongming China 31°38N 121°23E 229 B13
Chongming Dao China 31°40N 121°30E 229 B13
Chongoni Rock Art Malawi 14°17S 34°16E 269 E3
Chongoroi Angola 13°37S 14°1E 265 E2
Chongoyape Peru 6°35S 79°25W 330 B2
Chŏngp'yŏng N. Korea 39°47N 127°23E 224 C3
Chongqing Chongqing, China 29°35N 106°25E 228 C6
Chongqing Sichuan, China 30°38N 103°40E 228 B4
Chongqing Shi □ China 30°0N 108°0E 228 C6
Chongren China 27°46N 116°3E 229 D11
Chonguene Mozam. 25°3S 33°49E 271 C5
Chongwe Zambia 15°21S 28°42E 269 F2
Chongwen Beijing, China 114 c2
Chongyi China 25°45N 114°29E 229 E10
Chongzuo China 22°23N 107°20E 228 F6
Chonogol Mongolia 45°54N 115°22E 226 B8
Chonos, Arch. de los Chile 45°0S 75°0W 336 C2
Chop Ukraine 48°26N 22°12E 182 B7
Chopda India 21°20N 75°15E 244 D2
Chopim → Brazil 25°35S 53°5W 335 B5
Chopin Museum Warsaw, Poland 143 b2
Chor Pakistan 25°31N 69°46E 242 G3
Chora Greece 37°3N 21°42E 204 D3
Chora Sfakion Greece 35°15N 24°9E 207 E5
Chorbat La India 34°42N 76°37E 243 B7
Chorley U.K. 53°39N 2°38W 168 D5
Chorna Ukraine 47°36N 29°26E 183 C14
Chornobyl Ukraine 51°20N 30°15E 177 C16
Chornomorske Ukraine 45°31N 32°40E 189 K7
Chorolque, Cerro Bolivia 20°59S 66°5W 334 A2
Choroszcz Poland 53°10N 22°59E 185 E9
Chorregon Australia 22°40S 143°32E 280 C3
Chorrillos Peru 12°10S 77°1W 124 C2
Chortkiv Ukraine 49°2N 25°46E 177 D13
Chorzele Poland 53°15N 20°55E 185 E7
Chorzów Poland 50°18N 18°57E 185 H5
Chos-Malal Argentina 37°20S 70°15W 334 D1
Ch'osan N. Korea 40°50N 125°47E 224 B2
Chosheta Shan Taiwan 23°50N 121°6E 225 C3
Chōshi Japan 35°45N 140°51E 223 B12
Choshui Hsi → Taiwan 23°50N 120°15E 225 C2
Choszczno Poland 53°7N 15°25E 185 E2
Chota Peru 6°33S 78°39W 330 B2
Choteau U.S.A. 47°49N 112°11W 304 C7
Chotěboř Czech Rep. 49°43N 15°40E 180 B8
Chotila India 22°23N 71°15E 242 H4
Chotta Udepur India 22°19N 74°1E 242 H6
Choûm Mauritania 21°11N 13°3W 260 D2
Choungui Mayotte 12°57S 45°8E 272 b
Chowchilla U.S.A. 37°7N 120°16W 306 H6
Chowpatty Beach Mumbai, India 130 b1
Choybalsan Mongolia 48°4N 114°30E 219 B11
Choyr Mongolia 46°24N 108°30E 219 B10
Chrisman U.S.A. 39°48N 87°41W 311 E9
Chrisoupoli Greece 40°58N 24°42E 203 F8
Christ Church Cathedral Montréal, Canada 130 c2
Christburg = Dzierzgoń Poland 53°58N 19°20E 184 E6
Christchurch N.Z. 43°33S 172°47E 285 D7
Christchurch Dorset, U.K. 50°44N 1°47W 169 G6
Christian I. Canada 44°50N 80°12W 312 B4
Christian Quarter Jerusalem 123 b3
Christian Sd. U.S.A. 55°56N 134°40W 303 J14
Christiana Greece 36°14N 25°13E 205 E7
Christiana Jamaica 18°10N 77°29W 320 a
Christiana North West, S. Africa 27°52S 25°8E 270 C4
Christiansborg Slot Copenhagen, Denmark 118 c2
Christiansfeld Denmark 55°21N 9°29E 163 J3
Christianshåb = Qasigiannguit Greenland 68°50N 51°18W 154 D5
Christianshavn Denmark 55°40N 12°35E 118 A3
Christiansted U.S. Virgin Is. 17°45N 64°42W 321 C7
Christie B. Canada 62°32N 111°10W 297 A6
Christina → Canada 56°40N 111°3W 297 B6
Christmas Cr. → Australia 18°29S 125°23E 278 C4
Christmas I. = Kiritimati Kiribati 1°58N 157°27W 289 G12
Christmas I. Ind. Oc. 10°30S 105°40E 273 F9
Christoffel △ Curaçao 12°21N 69°8W 322 g
Christopher U.S.A. 37°59N 89°3W 310 G7
Christopher, L. Australia 24°49S 127°42E 279 D4
Christyakovo = Thorez Ukraine 48°4N 38°34E 189 H10
Chrudim Czech Rep. 49°58N 15°43E 180 B8
Chrysler Building New York, U.S.A. 132 c2
Chrzanów Małopolskie, Poland 50°10N 19°21E 185 H6
Chrzanów Warszawa, Poland 52°13N 20°53E 143 B1
Chtapodia Greece 37°24N 25°34E 205 D7
Chtimba Malawi 10°35S 34°13E 269 E3
Chū = Shū Kazakhstan 43°36N 73°42E 217 D8
Chū = Shū → Kazakhstan 45°0N 67°44E 217 D7
Chu → Vietnam 19°53N 105°45E 236 C5
Chu Lai Vietnam 15°28N 108°45E 236 E7
Chu Mom Ray △ Vietnam 14°29N 107°38E 236 E6
Chu Se Vietnam 13°40N 108°8E 236 F7
Chuadanga Bangla. 23°38N 88°51E 241 D2
Chuak, Ko Thailand 9°28N 99°41E 237 b
Ch'uanchou = Quanzhou China 24°55N 118°34E 229 E12
Chūanchow = Quanzhou China 24°55N 118°34E 229 E12
Chuangwei Taiwan 24°45N 121°47E 225 B3
Chuankou China 34°20N 110°59E 226 G6
Chuathbaluk U.S.A. 61°40N 159°15W 303 F8
Chubarovka = Pology Ukraine 47°29N 36°15E 189 J9
Chubbuck U.S.A. 42°55N 112°28W 304 E7
Chūbu □ Japan 36°45N 137°30E 223 A9
Chūbu-Sangaku △ Japan 36°30N 137°40E 223 A9
Chubut □ Argentina 43°30S 69°0W 336 B3
Chubut → Argentina 43°20S 65°5W 336 B3
Chuch'i Taiwan 23°31N 120°33E 225 C2
Chuchi L. Canada 55°12N 124°30W 296 B4
Chuchow = Zhuzhou China 27°49N 113°12E 229 D9
Chuda India 22°29N 71°41E 242 H4
Chudovo Russia 59°10N 31°41E 188 C6
Chudskoye, Ozero Russia 58°13N 27°30E 188 C4
Chuen Lung China 22°23N 114°6E 122 A1
Chugach Mts. U.S.A. 60°45N 147°0W 303 F11
Chuginadak I. U.S.A. 52°50N 169°45W 303 K5
Chūgoku □ Japan 35°0N 133°0E 222 C5
Chūgoku-Sanchi Japan 35°0N 133°0E 222 B5
Chuguyev = Chuhuiv Ukraine 49°55N 36°45E 189 H9
Chugwater U.S.A. 41°46N 104°50W 304 F11
Chuhuyiv Ukraine 49°55N 36°45E 189 H9
Chuk Kok China 22°20N 114°15E 122 A2
Chuka Kenya 0°20S 37°39E 268 C4
Chukchi Plateau Arctic 78°0N 165°0W 150 B17

Chukchi Sea Russia 68°0N 175°0W 215 C19
Chukotskiy Mys Russia 64°14N 173°8W 300 C5
Chukotskiy Poluostrov Russia 66°0N 174°0W 300 B5
Chukotskoye Nagorye Russia 68°0N 175°0E 215 C18
Chula U.S.A. 31°33N 83°32W 316 D6
Chula Vista U.S.A. 32°38N 117°5W 307 N9
Chulalongkorn Univ. Thailand 13°44N 100°31E 113 B2
Chulband → India 20°40N 79°54E 244 D4
Ch'ulin Taiwan 22°8N 120°42E 225 D2
Chulucanas Peru 5°8S 80°10W 330 B1
Chulumani Bolivia 16°24S 67°31W 330 D4
Chulym → Russia 57°43N 83°51E 214 D9
Chum Phae Thailand 16°40N 102°6E 236 D4
Chum Saeng Thailand 15°55N 100°15E 236 E3
Chuma Bolivia 15°24S 68°56W 330 D4
Chumar India 32°40N 78°35E 243 C8
Chumbicha Argentina 29°0S 66°10W 334 B2
Chumerna Bulgaria 42°45N 25°55E 203 D9
Chumikan Russia 54°40N 135°10E 215 D14
Chumphon Thailand 10°35N 99°14E 237 G2
Chumpi Peru 15°4S 73°46W 330 D3
Chumuare Mozam. 14°31S 31°50E 269 E3
Chuna → Russia 57°47N 94°37E 215 D10
Chun'an Zhejiang, China 29°35N 119°3E 229 C12
Chunan Taiwan 24°41N 120°52E 225 B2
Chuncheon S. Korea 37°58N 127°44E 224 D3
Chunchura India 22°53N 88°27E 243 H13
Chunga Zambia 15°0S 26°2E 269 F2
Chungcheongbuk-do □ S. Korea 36°45N 128°0E 224 D4
Chungcheongnam-do □ S. Korea 36°30N 127°0E 224 D3
Ch'ungch'ing = Chongqing China 29°35N 106°25E 228 C6
Chunggang-ŭp N. Korea 41°48N 126°48E 224 B3
Chungho Taiwan 25°0N 121°28E 225 A3
Chunghwa N. Korea 38°52N 125°47E 224 C2
Chungju S. Korea 36°58N 127°58E 224 D3
Chungjuho S. Korea 36°57N 128°3E 224 D4
Chungking = Chongqing China 29°35N 106°25E 228 C6
Chungli Taiwan 24°57N 121°13E 225 B3
Chungpu Taiwan 23°26N 120°31E 225 C2
Chungt'iaoshan = Zhongtiao Shan China 35°0N 111°10E 226 G6
Chungtungwan Taiwan 24°31N 120°40E 225 B2
Chungyang Shanmo Taiwan 23°10N 121°0E 225 C3
Chunian Pakistan 30°57N 74°0E 242 D6
Chunya Tanzania 8°30S 33°27E 269 D3
Chunyang China 43°38N 129°23E 227 C15
Chuō Tokyo, Japan 140 b5
Chupara B. Trin. & Tob. 10°48N 61°22W 323 t
Chupara Pt. Trin. & Tob. 10°49N 61°22W 323 t
Chupei Taiwan 24°50N 121°0E 225 B3
Chuquibamba Peru 15°47S 72°44W 330 D3
Chuquibambilla Peru 14°7S 72°41W 330 C3
Chuquicamata Chile 22°15S 69°0W 334 A2
Chuquisaca □ Bolivia 20°30S 63°30W 331 E5
Chur Switz. 46°52N 9°32E 179 J5
Churachandpur India 24°20N 93°40E 241 C4
Church End U.K. 51°35N 0°11W 125 A2
Church of our Lady = Frauenkirche Munich, Germany 131 b2
Church Stretton U.K. 52°32N 2°48W 169 E5
Churchill Vic., Australia 38°19S 146°25E 283 E7
Churchill Man., Canada 58°47N 94°11W 297 B10
Churchill → Man., Canada 58°47N 94°12W 297 B10
Churchill → Nfld. & L., Canada 53°19N 60°10W 299 B7
Churchill, C. Canada 58°46N 93°12W 297 B10
Churchill Falls Canada 53°36N 64°19W 299 B7
Churchill L. Canada 55°55N 108°20W 297 B7
Churchill Pk. Canada 58°10N 125°10W 296 B3
Churchtown Ireland 53°18N 6°16W 120 B2
Churdan U.S.A. 42°9N 94°29W 310 D2
Churki India 23°50N 83°12E 243 H10
Churu India 28°20N 74°50E 242 E6
Churubusco U.S.A. 41°14N 85°19W 311 C11
Churún Merú = Angel Falls Venezuela 5°57N 62°30W 329 B5
Chushal India 33°40N 78°40E 243 C8
Chushan Taiwan 23°45N 120°40E 225 C2
Chuska Mts. U.S.A. 36°15N 108°50W 305 H9
Chusovoy Russia 58°22N 57°50E 186 C10
Chusovskoy Zavod = Chusovoy Russia 58°22N 57°50E 186 C10
Chuspipata Bolivia 16°18S 67°48W 330 D4
Chust = Khust Ukraine 48°10N 23°18E 183 B8
Chust Uzbekistan 41°0N 71°13E 217 D8
Chute-aux-Outardes Canada 49°7N 68°24W 299 C6
Chutung Taiwan 24°44N 121°5E 225 B3
Chuuk = Truk Micronesia 7°25N 151°46E 287 T17
Chuuk Lagoon Micronesia 7°24N 151°45E 287 T18
Chuvash Republic = Chuvashia □ Russia 55°30N 47°0E 190 C8
Chuvashia □ Russia 55°30N 47°0E 190 C8
Chuwārtah Iraq 35°43N 45°34E 213 E11
Chuwei Taiwan 25°6N 121°14E 225 A3
Chuxiong China 25°2N 101°28E 228 E3
Chüy Kyrgyzstan 42°55N 75°15E 217 D9
Chuy Uruguay 33°41S 53°27W 335 C5
Chüy □ Kyrgyzstan 42°25N 75°16E 217 D9
Chuzenji-Ko Japan 36°44N 139°27E 223 A11
Chuzhou China 32°19N 118°20E 229 A12
Chynadiyeve Ukraine 48°29N 22°50E 182 B7
Ci Xian China 36°20N 114°25E 226 F8
Ciacova Romania 45°35N 21°10E 182 E6
Ciadâr-Lunga Moldova 46°3N 28°51E 183 D13
Ciales Puerto Rico 18°20N 66°28W 321 b
Ciamis Indonesia 7°20S 108°21E 235 D3
Ciampino Italy 41°47N 12°36E 136 C2
Ciampino ✈ (CIA) Italy 41°47N 12°36E 136 C2
Cianjur Indonesia 6°49S 107°8E 234 D3
Cianorte Brazil 23°37S 52°37W 335 A5
Cibola U.S.A. 33°17N 114°42W 307 M12
Çiçekdağı Turkey 39°36N 34°24E 212 C6
Cicero U.S.A. 41°51N 87°44W 119 B2
Cicero Dantas Brazil 10°36S 38°23W 332 D4
Ciceron St. Lucia 13°59N 61°1W 323 m
Cicia Fiji 17°45S 179°18W 287 A3
Cidacos → Spain 42°21N 1°38W 196 C3
Cidade de Minas = Belo Horizonte Brazil 19°55S 43°56W 333 E3
Cide Turkey 41°53N 33°1E 212 B5
Cidra Puerto Rico 18°11N 66°10W 321 b
Ciechanów Poland 52°52N 20°38E 185 F7
Ciechanowiec Poland 52°40N 22°31E 185 F9
Ciechocinek Poland 52°53N 18°45E 185 F5
Ciego de Ávila Cuba 21°50N 78°50W 320 B4
Ciénaga Colombia 11°1N 74°15W 328 A3
Ciénaga de Oro Colombia 8°53N 75°37W 328 B2
Ciénagas del Catatumbo △ Venezuela 9°26N 72°8W 328 B3
Cienfuegos Cuba 22°10N 80°30W 320 B3
Cierp-Gaud France 42°55N 0°40E 174 F4
Cies, Is. Spain 42°12N 8°55W 194 C2
Cieszanów Poland 50°14N 23°8E 185 H10
Cieszyn Poland 49°45N 18°35E 185 J5
Cieza Spain 38°17N 1°23W 197 G3
Çifteler Turkey 39°22N 31°2E 212 C4
Cifuentes Spain 40°47N 2°37W 196 E2
Cihanbeyli Turkey 38°40N 32°55E 212 C5
Cihuatlán Mexico 19°14N 104°35W 318 D4
Cijara, Embalse de Spain 39°18N 4°52W 195 F6
Cijara △ Spain 39°18N 4°35W 195 F6
Cijulang Indonesia 7°42S 108°27E 235 D3
Cilacap Indonesia 7°43S 109°0E 235 D3
Cilandak Indonesia 6°17S 106°47E 122 B1
Cilaos, Cirque de Réunion 21°7S 55°28E 272 f
Cilaos Réunion 21°8S 55°27E 272 f
Çıldır Turkey 41°7N 43°8E 213 B10
Çıldır Gölü Turkey 41°5N 43°15E 213 B10
Cilento e Vallo di Diano △ Italy 40°15N 15°20E 201 B8
Cili China 29°30N 111°8E 229 C8
Cilibia Romania 45°4N 27°4E 183 E12
Cilicia Turkey 36°30N 35°0E 250 B5
Cilincing Indonesia 6°6S 106°54E 122 A2
Ciliwung → Indonesia 6°6S 106°47E 122 B2
Cill Airne = Killarney Ireland 52°4N 9°30W 166 D2
Cill Chainnigh = Kilkenny Ireland 52°39N 7°15W 166 D4
Cill Dara = Kildare Ireland 53°9N 6°55W 166 C5
Cill Droichid = Celbridge Ireland 53°20N 6°32W 166 C5
Cill Mhantáin = Wicklow Ireland 52°59N 6°3W 166 D5
Cilo Dağı Turkey 37°28N 43°55E 213 D10
Cima U.S.A. 35°14N 115°30W 307 K11
Cimarron Kans., U.S.A. 37°48N 100°21W 308 G3
Cimarron N. Mex., U.S.A. 36°31N 104°55W 305 H11
Cimarron → U.S.A. 36°10N 96°16W 314 C6
Čimice Czech Rep. 50°8N 14°25E 135 B2
Cimişlia Moldova 46°34N 28°44E 183 D13
Cimone, Mte. Italy 44°12N 10°42E 198 D7
Cina, Tanjung Indonesia 5°55S 104°45E 234 D2
Çinar Turkey 37°46N 40°19E 213 D9
Çınarcık Turkey 40°38N 29°5E 203 F13
Cinaruco-Capanaparo △ Venezuela 6°51N 67°32W 328 B4
Cinca → Spain 41°26N 0°21E 196 D5
Cincar Bos.-H. 43°55N 17°5E 182 G2
Cincinnati Iowa, U.S.A. 40°38N 92°56W 310 E7
Cincinnati Ohio, U.S.A. 39°9N 84°27W 311 E12
Cincinnati-Northern Kentucky Int. ✈ (CVG) U.S.A. 39°3N 84°40W 311 E12
Cincinnatus U.S.A. 42°33N 75°54W 313 D9
Çine Turkey 37°37N 28°2E 205 D10
Cinecittà Italy 41°51N 12°34E 136 B2
Ciney Belgium 50°18N 5°5E 170 D5
Cingoli Italy 43°23N 13°10E 199 E10
Cinigiano Italy 42°53N 11°24E 199 F8
Cinisello Bálsamo Italy 45°33N 9°13E 128 A2
Cinkota Hungary 47°31N 19°14E 117 A3
Cinque I. India 11°16N 92°42E 245 J11
Cinque Terre △ Italy 44°10N 9°45E 198 D6
Cinto, Mte. France 42°24N 8°54E 175 F12
Cintra, G. de W. Sahara 23°0N 16°15W 260 D1
Cintruénigo Spain 42°5N 1°49W 196 C3
Ciocile Romania 44°49N 27°14E 183 F12
Ciolăneşti din Deal Romania 44°19N 25°5E 183 F10
Ciorani Romania 44°45N 26°25E 183 F11
Čiovo Croatia 43°30N 16°17E 199 E13
Cipero → Trin. & Tob. 10°16N 61°28W 323 t
Cipete Indonesia 6°15S 106°47E 122 B1
Cipó Brazil 11°6S 38°31W 332 D4
Cipolletti Argentina 38°56S 67°59W 336 A3
Circeo, Mte. Italy 41°14N 13°3E 200 A6
Çirçir Turkey 40°3N 36°47E 212 C7
Circle Alaska, U.S.A. 65°50N 144°4W 303 D11
Circle Mont., U.S.A. 47°25N 105°35W 304 C11
Circleville U.S.A. 39°36N 82°57W 309 F12
Circular Reef Papua N. G. 3°25S 147°47E 286 B4
Cirebon Indonesia 6°45S 108°32E 235 D3
Cirencester U.K. 51°43N 1°57W 169 F6
Cireşu Romania 44°47N 22°31E 182 F7
Cirey-sur-Vezouze France 48°35N 6°57E 173 D13
Ciriè Italy 45°14N 7°36E 198 C4
Cirium Cyprus 34°40N 32°53E 207 F8
Cirò Italy 39°23N 17°4E 201 C10
Cirò Marina Italy 39°22N 17°8E 201 C10
Ciron → France 44°36N 0°18W 174 D3
Cisco U.S.A. 32°23N 98°59W 314 E5
Cislău Romania 45°14N 26°20E 183 E11
Cisna Poland 49°12N 22°20E 185 J9
Cisnădie Romania 45°42N 24°9E 183 E9
Cisne U.S.A. 38°31N 88°26W 311 F8
Cisneros Colombia 6°33N 75°4W 328 B2
Cissna Park U.S.A. 40°34N 87°54W 311 D9
Cisterna di Latina Italy 41°35N 12°49E 200 A5
Cisternino Italy 40°44N 17°25E 201 B10
Cistierna Spain 42°48N 5°7W 194 C5
Citadel = Kastellet Copenhagen, Denmark 118 a3
Citadel Budapest, Hungary 117 c2
Citaré → Brazil 1°11N 54°41W 329 C7
Citeli-Ckaro = Dedoplis Tsqaro Georgia 41°33N 46°0E 191 K8
Citi Performing Arts Center Boston, U.S.A. 116 c2
Citlaltépetl = Orizaba, Pico de Mexico 18°58N 97°15W 319 D5
Citra U.S.A. 29°25N 82°7W 317 F7
Citron Fr. Guiana 4°44N 53°57W 329 C7
Citrus Heights U.S.A. 38°42N 121°17W 306 G5
Citrus Springs U.S.A. 29°2N 82°27W 317 F7
Citrusdal S. Africa 32°35S 19°0E 270 D2
Città degli Studi Italy 45°28N 9°12E 128 B2
Città del Vaticano = Vatican City ■ Europe 41°54N 12°27E 136 B1
Città della Pieve Italy 42°57N 12°1E 199 F9
Città di Castello Italy 43°27N 12°14E 199 E9
Città Sant' Angelo Italy 42°32N 14°5E 199 F11
Cittadella Italy 45°39N 11°47E 199 C8
Cittaducale Italy 42°23N 12°57E 199 F9
Cittanova Italy 38°21N 16°5E 201 D9
City, The U.K. 51°30N 0°6W 125 A3
City Hall = Rådhus Oslo, Norway 133 b1
City Hall = Stadshuset Stockholm, Sweden 139 b1
City of the Dead Egypt 30°0N 31°15E 117 A2
City Park U.S.A. 30°0N 90°5W 131 A2
City Terrace U.S.A. 34°3N 118°11W 126 B3
Ciuc, Munţii Romania 46°25N 26°5E 183 D11
Ciucaş, Vf. Romania 45°31N 25°56E 183 E10
Ciucea Romania 46°57N 22°49E 182 D7
Ciuciulea Moldova 47°40N 27°29E 183 C12
Ciuciuleni Moldova 47°2N 28°25E 183 C13
Ciudad Acuña Mexico 29°18N 100°55W 318 B4
Ciudad Altamirano Mexico 18°20N 100°40W 318 D4
Ciudad Anáhuac Mexico 27°14N 100°7W 318 B4
Ciudad Bolívar Venezuela 8°5N 63°36W 329 B5
Ciudad Bolivia Venezuela 8°21N 70°34W 328 B3
Ciudad Camargo Mexico 27°40N 105°10W 318 B3
Ciudad Cortés Costa Rica 8°55N 84°0W 320 E3
Ciudad de México Mexico 19°24N 99°9W 318 D5
Ciudad de Nutrias Venezuela 8°5N 69°18W 328 B4
Ciudad del Carmen Mexico 18°38N 91°50W 319 D6
Ciudad del Este Paraguay 25°30S 54°50W 335 B5
Ciudad Delicias = Delicias Mexico 28°13N 105°28W 318 B3
Ciudad Deportiva Mexico 19°24N 99°5W 128 B2
Ciudad Fin de Semana Spain 40°26N 3°34W 127 B2
Ciudad Frontera Mexico 26°56N 101°27W 318 B4
Ciudad General Belgrano Argentina 34°43S 58°33W 117 C1
Ciudad Guayana Venezuela 8°0N 62°30W 329 B5
Ciudad Guerrero Mexico 28°33N 107°30W 318 B3
Ciudad Guzmán Mexico 19°41N 103°29W 318 D4
Ciudad Juárez Mexico 31°44N 106°29W 318 A3
Ciudad Lerdo Mexico 25°32N 103°32W 318 B4
Ciudad Lineál Spain 40°26N 3°38W 127 B2
Ciudad Madero Mexico 22°19N 97°50W 319 C5
Ciudad Mante Mexico 22°44N 98°59W 319 C5
Ciudad Obregón Mexico 27°29N 109°56W 318 B3
Ciudad Ojeda Venezuela 10°12N 71°19W 328 A3
Ciudad Piar Venezuela 7°27N 63°19W 329 B5
Ciudad Porfirio Díaz = Piedras Negras Mexico 28°42N 100°31W 318 B4
Ciudad Real Spain 38°59N 3°55W 195 G7
Ciudad Real □ Spain 38°50N 4°0W 195 G7
Ciudad Rodrigo Spain 40°35N 6°32W 194 E4
Ciudad Satélite Mexico 19°30N 99°13W 128 A1
Ciudad Trujillo = Santo Domingo Dom. Rep. 18°30N 69°59W 321 C6
Ciudad Universitaria B. Aires, Argentina 34°33S 58°27W 117 B2
Ciudad Universitaria México, Mexico 19°20N 99°11W 128 C1
Ciudad Valles Mexico 21°59N 99°1W 319 C5
Ciudad Victoria Mexico 23°44N 99°8W 319 C5
Ciudadela Spain 40°0N 3°50E 206 B4
Ciulniţa Romania 44°26N 27°22E 183 F12
Ciumeghiu Romania 46°44N 21°35E 182 D6
Ciuperceni Romania 44°54N 23°4E 182 F8
Ciutadella, Parc de la Barcelona, Spain 114 b3
Civa Burnu Turkey 41°21N 36°38E 212 B7
Civic Center Los Angeles, U.S.A. 127 b2
Civico Correr, Museo Venice, Italy 142 b3
Cividale del Friuli Italy 46°6N 13°25E 199 B10
Civita Castellana Italy 42°18N 12°24E 199 F9
Civitanova Marche Italy 43°18N 13°44E 199 E10
Civitavécchia Italy 42°6N 11°48E 199 F8
Civray France 46°10N 0°17E 174 B4
Çivril Turkey 38°20N 29°43E 205 C11
Cixerri → Italy 39°17N 8°59E 200 C1
Cixi China 30°17N 121°9E 229 B13
Cizre Turkey 37°19N 42°10E 213 D10
Clackmannanshire □ U.K. 56°10N 3°43W 167 E5
Clacton-on-Sea U.K. 51°47N 1°11E 169 F9
Clain → France 46°47N 0°33E 172 F7
Claire, L. Canada 58°35N 112°5W 296 B6
Claireville Res. Canada 43°45N 79°39W 141 A1
Clairton U.S.A. 40°18N 79°53W 312 F5
Clairvaux-les-Lacs France 46°35N 5°45E 173 F12
Claise → France 46°56N 0°42E 174 B5
Clallam Bay U.S.A. 48°15N 124°16W 306 B2
Clam Gulch U.S.A. 60°15N 151°23W 303 F10
Clamart France 48°48N 2°15E 134 B2
Clamecy France 47°28N 3°30E 173 E10
Clanton U.S.A. 32°51N 86°38W 315 E11
Clanwilliam S. Africa 32°11S 18°52E 270 D2
Clapham U.K. 51°27N 0°8W 125 B3
Clapton U.K. 51°33N 0°3W 125 A3
Clara Ireland 53°21N 7°37W 166 C4
Claraville U.S.A. 35°24N 118°20W 307 K8
Clare S. Austral., Australia 33°50S 138°37E 282 B3
Clare Mich., U.S.A. 43°49N 84°46W 309 D11
Clare □ Ireland 52°45N 9°0W 166 D3
Clare → Ireland 53°20N 9°2W 166 C2
Clare I. Ireland 53°47N 10°0W 166 C1
Claremont Jamaica 18°19N 77°11W 320 a
Claremont Western Cape, S. Africa 34°8S 18°28E 118 A1
Claremont Calif., U.S.A. 34°6N 117°43W 307 L9
Claremont N.H., U.S.A. 43°23N 72°20W 313 C12
Claremont Pt. Australia 14°1S 143°41E 280 A3
Claremore U.S.A. 36°19N 95°36W 314 C7
Claremorris Ireland 53°45N 9°0W 166 C3
Clarence U.S.A. 39°45N 92°16W 310 E4
Clarence → N.S.W., Australia 29°25S 153°22E 281 D5
Clarence → N.Z. 42°10S 173°56E 285 C8
Clarence, I. Chile 54°0S 72°0W 336 D2
Clarence, Port U.S.A. 65°15N 166°40W 303 D6
Clarence Bay Ascension I. 7°55S 14°25W 153 g
Clarence I. Antarctica 61°10S 54°0W 151 C18
Clarence Str. Australia 12°0S 131°0E 278 B5
Clarence Town Bahamas 23°6N 74°59W 321 B5
Clarendon Pa., U.S.A. 41°47N 79°6W 312 E5
Clarendon Tex., U.S.A. 34°56N 100°53W 314 D4
Clarenville Canada 48°10N 54°1W 299 C9
Claresholm Canada 50°2N 113°33W 296 D6
Clarie Coast Antarctica 68°0S 135°0E 151 C9
Clarinda U.S.A. 40°44N 95°2W 308 E6
Clarington Canada 43°55N 78°41W 312 C6
Clarion Iowa, U.S.A. 42°44N 93°44W 310 B3
Clarion Pa., U.S.A. 41°13N 79°23W 312 E5
Clarion → U.S.A. 41°7N 79°41W 312 E5
Clarion Fracture Zone Pac. Oc. 20°0N 120°0W 292 H7
Clark Mo., U.S.A. 39°17N 92°21W 310 E4
Clark S. Dak., U.S.A. 44°53N 97°44W 308 C5
Clark, Pt. Canada 44°4N 81°45W 312 B3
Clark Fork U.S.A. 48°9N 116°11W 304 B5
Clark Fork → U.S.A. 48°9N 116°15W 304 B5
Clarkdale U.S.A. 34°46N 112°3W 305 J7
Clarke City Canada 50°12N 66°38W 299 B6
Clarke I. Australia 40°32S 148°10E 281 G4
Clarke Ra. Australia 20°40S 148°30E 280 b
Clarks Fork Yellowstone → U.S.A. 45°32N 108°50W 304 D9
Clark's Harbour Canada 43°25N 65°38W 299 D6
Clarks Hill L. = J. Strom Thurmond L. U.S.A. 33°40N 82°12W 316 B7
Clarks Point U.S.A. 58°51N 158°33W 303 G8
Clarks Summit U.S.A. 41°30N 75°42W 313 E9
Clarks Town Jamaica 18°25N 77°33W 320 a
Clarksburg U.S.A. 39°17N 80°30W 309 F13
Clarksdale U.S.A. 34°12N 90°35W 315 D9
Clarkston U.S.A. 46°25N 117°3W 304 C5
Clarksville Ark., U.S.A. 35°28N 93°28W 314 D8
Clarksville Ind., U.S.A. 38°17N 85°45W 311 F11
Clarksville Iowa, U.S.A. 42°47N 92°40W 310 B4
Clarksville Mo., U.S.A. 39°22N 90°54W 310 E6
Clarksville Tenn., U.S.A. 36°32N 87°21W 315 C11
Clarksville Tex., U.S.A. 33°37N 95°3W 314 E7
Claro → Brazil 19°8S 50°40W 333 E1
Clatskanie U.S.A. 46°6N 123°12W 306 D3
Claude U.S.A. 35°7N 101°22W 314 D4
Claveria Cagayan, Phil. 18°37N 121°4E 232 B3
Claveria Masbate, Phil. 12°54N 123°15E 232 E4
Claveria Mis. Or., Phil. 8°38N 124°55E 233 G5
Clavering Ø Greenland 74°15N 21°0W 154 C8
Claxton U.S.A. 32°10N 81°55W 316 C8
Claxton B. Trin. & Tob. 10°21N 61°28W 323 t
Claxton Bay Trin. & Tob. 10°21N 61°28W 323 t
Clay U.S.A. 38°17N 121°10W 306 G5
Clay Center U.S.A. 39°23N 97°8W 308 F5
Clay City Ind., U.S.A. 39°17N 87°7W 311 E10
Clay City Ky., U.S.A. 37°52N 83°55W 311 G13
Clayhall U.K. 51°35N 0°3E 125 A4
Claypool U.S.A. 33°25N 110°51W 305 K8
Claysburg U.S.A. 40°17N 78°27W 312 F6
Claysville U.S.A. 40°7N 80°25W 312 F4
Clayton Ont., Canada 45°11N 76°19W 313 A8
Clayton Ala., U.S.A. 31°53N 85°27W 316 D4
Clayton Ind., U.S.A. 39°41N 86°31W 311 E10
Clayton N. Mex., U.S.A. 36°27N 103°11W 305 H12
Clayton N.Y., U.S.A. 44°14N 76°5W 313 B8
Clear, C. Ireland 51°25N 9°32W 166 E2
Clear, L. Ont., Canada 45°26N 77°12W 312 A7
Clear, L. Fla., U.S.A. 28°31N 81°24W 133 A2
Clear Hills Canada 56°40N 119°30W 296 B5
Clear I. Ireland 51°26N 9°30W 166 E2
Clear L. U.S.A. 39°2N 122°47W 306 F4
Clear Lake Iowa, U.S.A. 43°8N 93°23W 310 A3
Clear Lake S. Dak., U.S.A. 44°45N 96°41W 308 C5
Clear Lake Res. U.S.A. 41°56N 121°5W 304 F3
Clearfield Pa., U.S.A. 41°2N 78°27W 312 E6
Clearfield Utah, U.S.A. 41°7N 112°2W 304 F7
Clearlake U.S.A. 38°57N 122°38W 306 G4
Clearwater B.C., Canada 51°38N 120°2W 296 C4
Clearwater Fla., U.S.A. 27°59N 82°48W 317 H7
Clearwater → Alta., Canada 52°22N 114°57W 296 C6
Clearwater → Alta., Canada 56°44N 111°23W 297 B6
Clearwater L. Canada 53°34N 99°49W 297 C9
Clearwater Lake △ Canada 54°0N 101°0W 297 C8
Clearwater Mts. U.S.A. 46°5N 115°20W 304 C6
Clearwater River △ Canada 56°55N 109°10W 297 B7
Cleburne U.S.A. 32°21N 97°23W 314 E6
Clee Hills U.K. 52°26N 2°35W 169 E5
Cleethorpes U.K. 53°33N 0°3W 168 D7
Cleeve Cloud U.K. 51°56N 2°0W 169 F6
Clelles France 44°50N 5°38E 175 D9
Clemson U.S.A. 34°41N 82°50W 315 D13
Cleopatra Needle Phil. 10°7N 118°58E 233 F2
Clerke Reef Australia 17°22S 119°20E 278 C2
Clerkenwell London, U.K. 125 a4
Clermiston U.K. 55°57N 3°17W 121 B2
Clermont Queens., Australia 22°49S 147°39E 280 C4
Clermont Oise, France 49°23N 2°24E 173 C9
Clermont Fla., U.S.A. 28°33N 81°46W 317 G8
Clermont-en-Argonne France 49°5N 5°4E 173 C12
Clermont-Ferrand France 45°46N 3°4E 174 C7
Clermont-l'Hérault France 43°38N 3°26E 174 E7
Clerval France 47°25N 6°30E 173 E13
Clervaux Lux. 50°4N 6°2E 170 D6
Cles Italy 46°22N 11°2E 198 B8
Cleve Australia 33°43S 136°30E 282 B2
Clevedon U.K. 51°26N 2°52W 169 F5
Cleveland Miss., U.S.A. 33°45N 90°43W 315 E9
Cleveland Ohio, U.S.A. 41°29N 81°41W 312 E3
Cleveland Okla., U.S.A. 36°19N 96°28W 314 C6
Cleveland Tenn., U.S.A. 35°10N 84°53W 315 D12
Cleveland Tex., U.S.A. 30°21N 95°5W 314 F7
Cleveland, C. Australia 19°11S 147°1E 280 B4
Cleveland, Mt. U.S.A. 48°56N 113°51W 304 B7
Cleveland Heights U.S.A. 41°31N 81°33W 312 E3
Clevelândia Brazil 26°24S 52°23W 335 B5
Clevelândia do Norte Brazil 3°49N 51°52W 329 C7
Cleves U.S.A. 39°10N 84°45W 311 E12
Clew B. Ireland 53°50N 9°49W 166 C2
Clewiston U.S.A. 26°45N 80°56W 317 J9
Clichy France 48°54N 2°18E 134 A2
Clichy-sous-Bois France 48°54N 2°32E 134 A4
Clifden Galway, Ireland 53°29N 10°1W 166 C1
Clifden N.Z. 46°1S 167°42E 285 G2
Cliffdell U.S.A. 46°56N 121°5W 306 D5
Cliffside Canada 43°44N 79°14W 141 A3
Cliffside Park U.S.A. 40°49N 73°59W 132 B2
Cliffy Hd. Australia 35°1S 116°29E 279 G2
Clifton Queens., Australia 27°59S 151°53E 281 D5
Clifton Sindh, Pakistan 24°48N 67°1E 123 B2
Clifton Western Cape, S. Africa 33°56S 18°22E 118 A1
Clifton Ariz., U.S.A. 33°3N 109°18W 305 K9
Clifton Colo., U.S.A. 39°7N 108°25W 304 G9
Clifton Ill., U.S.A. 40°56N 87°56W 311 D9
Clifton N.Y., U.S.A. 40°37N 74°4W 132 C1
Clifton Tex., U.S.A. 31°47N 97°35W 314 F6
Clifton Beach Queens., Australia 16°46S 145°39E 280 B4
Clifton Beach Sindh, Pakistan 24°48N 67°2E 123 B2
Clifton Pt. Bahamas 25°1N 77°34W 153 b
Cliftondale U.S.A. 42°26N 71°0W 116 A2
Climax U.S.A. 30°53N 84°26W 316 E5
Clinch → U.S.A. 35°53N 84°29W 315 D12
Clingmans Dome U.S.A. 35°34N 83°30W 315 D13
Clint U.S.A. 31°35N 106°14W 314 F1
Clinton B.C., Canada 51°6N 121°35W 296 C4
Clinton Ont., Canada 43°37N 81°32W 312 C3
Clinton N.Z. 46°12S 169°23E 285 G4
Clinton Ark., U.S.A. 35°36N 92°28W 314 D8
Clinton Conn., U.S.A. 41°17N 72°32W 313 E12
Clinton Ill., U.S.A. 40°9N 88°57W 310 D8
Clinton Ind., U.S.A. 39°40N 87°24W 311 E9
Clinton Iowa, U.S.A. 41°51N 90°12W 310 C6
Clinton Mass., U.S.A. 42°25N 71°41W 313 D13
Clinton Mich., U.S.A. 42°4N 83°58W 311 B13
Clinton Miss., U.S.A. 32°20N 90°20W 315 E9
Clinton Mo., U.S.A. 38°22N 93°46W 310 F3
Clinton N.C., U.S.A. 35°0N 78°22W 315 D15
Clinton Okla., U.S.A. 35°31N 98°58W 314 D5
Clinton S.C., U.S.A. 34°29N 81°53W 315 D14
Clinton Tenn., U.S.A. 36°6N 84°8W 315 C12
Clinton Wash., U.S.A. 47°59N 122°21W 306 C4
Clinton Wis., U.S.A. 42°34N 88°52W 311 B8
Clinton, C. Australia 22°30S 150°45E 280 C5
Clinton, L. U.S.A. 40°10N 88°45W 311 D8
Clinton Colden L. Canada 63°58N 107°27W 294 E10
Clio U.S.A. 31°43N 85°37W 316 D4
Clipperton, Î. Pac. Oc. 10°18N 109°13W 289 F17
Clipperton Fracture Zone Pac. Oc. 19°0N 122°0W 289 G16
Clisham U.K. 57°58N 6°49W 167 D2
Clisson France 47°5N 1°16W 172 E5
Clitheroe U.K. 53°53N 2°22W 168 D5
Clive N.Z. 39°36S 176°58E 284 F5
Clive Iowa, U.S.A. 41°36N 93°43W 310 C3
Clive L. Canada 63°13N 118°54W 296 A5
Cliza Bolivia 17°36S 65°56W 331 D4
Clo-oose Canada 48°39N 124°49W 306 B2
Cloates, Pt. Australia 22°43S 113°40E 278 D1
Clocolan S. Africa 28°55S 27°34E 271 C4
Clodomira Argentina 27°35S 64°14W 334 B3
Cloghaneely Ireland 55°8N 8°5W 166 A3
Clogher Hd. Ireland 53°48N 6°14W 166 C5
Cloghran Ireland 53°27N 6°14W 120 A2
Clonakilty Ireland 51°37N 8°53W 166 E3
Clonakilty B. Ireland 51°35N 8°51W 166 E3
Cloncurry Queens., Australia 20°40S 140°28E 280 C3
Cloncurry Kildare, Ireland 53°25N 6°48W 166 C5
Cloncurry → Australia 18°37S 140°40E 280 B3
Clondalkin Ireland 53°19N 6°25W 166 C5
Clones Ireland 54°11N 7°15W 166 B4
Clonmel Ireland 52°21N 7°42W 166 D4
Clonskeagh Ireland 53°19N 6°14W 120 B2
Clontarf N.S.W., Australia 33°48S 151°16E 139 A2
Clontarf Dublin, Ireland 53°22N 6°11W 120 B2
Cloppenburg Germany 52°51N 8°1E 178 C4
Cloquet U.S.A. 46°43N 92°28W 308 B7
Clorinda Argentina 25°16S 57°45W 334 B4
Cloud Peak U.S.A. 44°23N 107°11W 304 D10
Cloudcroft U.S.A. 32°58N 105°45W 305 K11
Cloudy B. N.Z. 41°25S 174°10E 285 B9
Clovelly Australia 33°54S 151°15E 139 B2
Cloverdale Calif., U.S.A. 38°48N 123°1W 306 G4
Cloverdale Ind., U.S.A. 39°31N 86°48W 311 E10
Cloverport U.S.A. 37°50N 86°38W 311 G10
Clovis Calif., U.S.A. 36°49N 119°42W 306 J7
Clovis N. Mex., U.S.A. 34°24N 103°12W 305 J12
Cloyes-sur-le-Loir France 48°0N 1°14E 172 E8
Cloyne Canada 44°49N 77°11W 312 B7
Cluain Meala = Clonmel Ireland 52°21N 7°42W 166 D4
Club Terrace Australia 37°35S 148°58E 283 D8
Cluj □ Romania 46°45N 23°30E 183 D8
Cluj-Napoca Romania 46°47N 23°38E 183 D8
Clunes Australia 37°20S 143°45E 282 D5
Cluny France 46°26N 4°38E 173 F11
Cluses France 46°5N 6°35E 173 F13
Clusone Italy 45°53N 9°57E 198 C6
Clutha → N.Z. 46°20S 169°49E 285 G4
Clwyd → U.K. 53°19N 3°31W 168 D4
Clyattville U.S.A. 30°42N 83°19W 316 E6
Clyde Alta., Canada 54°9N 113°39W 296 C6
Clyde N.Z. 45°12S 169°20E 285 F4
Clyde N.Y., U.S.A. 43°5N 76°52W 312 C8
Clyde Ohio, U.S.A. 41°18N 82°59W 311 C14
Clyde → U.K. 55°55N 4°30W 167 F4
Clyde, Firth of U.K. 55°22N 5°1W 167 F3
Clyde River Canada 70°30N 68°30W 295 C18
Clydebank U.K. 55°54N 4°23W 167 F4
Clymer N.Y., U.S.A. 42°1N 79°37W 312 D5
Clymer Pa., U.S.A. 40°40N 79°1W 312 D5
Clyo U.S.A. 32°29N 81°16W 316 C8
Ćmielów Poland 50°53N 21°31E 185 H8
CNN Center U.S.A. 33°45N 84°23W 113 B2
Côa → Portugal 41°5N 7°6W 194 D3
Coachella U.S.A. 33°41N 116°10W 307 M10
Coachella Canal U.S.A. 32°43N 114°57W 307 N12
Coahoma U.S.A. 32°18N 101°18W 314 E4
Coahuayana → Mexico 18°41N 103°45W 318 D4
Coahuila □ Mexico 27°20N 102°0W 318 B4
Coal → Canada 59°39N 126°57W 296 B3
Coal City U.S.A. 41°17N 88°17W 311 C8
Coal I. N.Z. 46°8S 166°40E 285 G1
Coalane Mozam. 17°48S 37°2E 269 F4
Coalcomán Mexico 18°47N 103°9W 318 D4
Coaldale Canada 49°45N 112°35W 296 D6
Coalgate U.S.A. 34°32N 96°13W 314 D6
Coalinga U.S.A. 36°9N 120°21W 306 J6
Coalisland U.K. 54°33N 6°42W 166 B5
Coalville Leics., U.K. 52°44N 1°23W 168 E6
Coalville Utah, U.S.A. 40°55N 111°24W 304 F8
Coamo Puerto Rico 18°5N 66°22W 321 b
Coaraci Brazil 14°38S 39°32W 333 D4
Coari Brazil 4°8S 63°7W 329 D5
Coari → Brazil 4°30S 63°33W 329 D5
Coari, L. Brazil 4°15S 63°22W 329 D5
Coast □ Kenya 2°40S 39°45E 268 C4
Coast Mts. Canada 55°0N 129°20W 296 C3
Coast Ranges U.S.A. 39°0N 123°0W 306 G4
Coatbridge U.K. 55°52N 4°6W 167 F4
Coatepec Mexico 19°27N 96°58W 319 D5
Coatepeque Guatemala 14°46N 91°55W 320 D1
Coatesville U.S.A. 39°59N 75°50W 309 F16
Coaticook Canada 45°10N 71°46W 313 A13
Coats I. Canada 62°30N 83°0W 295 E15
Coats Land Antarctica 77°0S 25°0W 151 D1
Coatzacoalcos Mexico 18°7N 94°25W 319 D6
Cobá Mexico 20°31N 87°45W 319 C7
Cobadin Romania 44°5N 28°13E 183 F13
Cobalt Canada 47°25N 79°42W 298 C4
Cobán Guatemala 15°30N 90°21W 320 C1
Çobanlar Turkey 38°41N 30°47E 205 C12
Cobar Australia 31°27S 145°48E 283 A6
Cobargo Australia 36°20S 149°55E 283 D8
Cobbannah Australia 37°37S 147°13E 283 D7
Cobberas, Mt. Australia 36°53S 148°12E 283 D8
Cobden Australia 38°20S 143°3E 282 E5
Cobh Ireland 51°51N 8°17W 166 E3
Cóbh, An = Cobh Ireland 51°51N 8°17W 166 E3
Cobija Bolivia 11°0S 68°50W 330 C4
Cobleskill U.S.A. 42°41N 74°29W 313 D10
Coboconk Canada 44°39N 78°48W 312 B6
Cobourg Canada 43°58N 78°10W 312 C6
Cobourg Pen. Australia 11°20S 132°15E 278 B5
Cobram Australia 35°54S 145°40E 283 C6
Cobras, I. das Brazil 22°53S 43°9W 135 B2
Cóbué Mozam. 12°0S 34°58E 269 E3
Coburg Vic., Australia 37°44S 144°56E 128 A1
Coburg Bayern, Germany 50°15N 10°58E 179 E6
Coburg I. Canada 75°57N 79°26W 295 B16
Coca Spain 41°13N 4°32W 194 D6
Coca → Ecuador 0°29S 76°58W 328 D2
Cocachacra Peru 17°5S 71°45W 330 D3
Cocal Brazil 3°28S 41°34W 332 B3
Cocanada = Kakinada India 16°57N 82°11E 244 F6
Cocentaina Spain 38°45N 0°27W 197 G4
Cochabamba Bolivia 17°26S 66°10W 331 D4
Coche, I. Venezuela 10°47N 63°56W 329 A5
Cochem Germany 50°9N 7°9E 179 E3
Cochemane Mozam. 17°0S 32°54E 269 F3
Cochin = Kochi India 9°58N 76°20E 245 K3
Cochin China = Nam-Phan Vietnam 10°30N 106°0E 237 G6
Cochran U.S.A. 32°23N 83°21W 316 C6
Cochrane Alta., Canada 51°11N 114°30W 296 C6
Cochrane Ont., Canada 49°0N 81°0W 298 C3
Cochrane Chile 47°15S 72°33W 336 C2
Cochrane → Canada 59°0N 103°40W 297 B8
Cochrane, L. Chile 47°10S 72°0W 336 C2
Cochranton U.S.A. 41°31N 80°3W 312 E4
Cockburn Australia 32°5S 141°0E 282 B4
Cockburn, Canal Chile 54°30S 72°0W 336 D2
Cockburn I. Canada 45°55N 83°22W 298 C3
Cockburn Ra. Australia 15°46S 128°0E 278 C4
Cockermouth U.K. 54°40N 3°22W 168 C4
Cocklebiddy Australia 32°0S 126°3E 279 F4
Cockpit Jamaica 18°16N 77°39W 320 a
Cockpit Country, The Jamaica 18°15N 77°45W 320 a
Côco → Brazil 9°27S 50°2W 332 C2
Coco → Cent. Amer. 15°0N 83°8W 320 D3
Coco, I. del Pac. Oc. 5°25N 87°55W 289 G19
Coco, Pta. Colombia 2°58N 77°43W 328 C2
Coco Channel Asia 13°45N 93°10E 245 H11
Cocoa U.S.A. 28°21N 80°44W 317 G9
Cocoa Beach U.S.A. 28°20N 80°37W 317 G9
Cocoa Point Antigua & B. 17°33N 61°46W 322 c
Cocobeach Gabon 0°59N 9°34E 264 B1
Coconut Grove U.S.A. 25°42N 80°15W 129 D2
Cocoparra △ Australia 34°10S 146°12E 283 C7
Cocora Romania 44°45N 27°3E 183 F12
Côcos Brazil 14°10S 44°33W 333 D3
Côcos → Brazil 12°44S 44°48W 333 D3
Cocos B. Trin. & Tob. 10°24N 61°2W 323 t
Cocos Basin Ind. Oc. 5°0S 96°0E 273 D8
Cocos I. = Coco, I. del Pac. Oc. 5°25N 87°55W 289 G19
Cocos I. Guam 13°14N 144°39E 302 d
Cocos Is. Ind. Oc. 12°10S 96°55E 273 E9
Cocos Ridge Pac. Oc. 4°0N 88°0W 289 G19
Cocotá Brazil 22°48S 43°11W 135 A2
Cod, C. U.S.A. 42°5N 70°10W 309 D18
Codajás Brazil 3°55S 62°0W 329 D5
Codera, C. Venezuela 10°35N 66°4W 328 A4
Codfish I. N.Z. 46°47S 167°38E 285 G2
Codigoro Italy 44°49N 12°8E 199 D9
Codlea Romania 45°42N 25°27E 183 E10
Codó Brazil 4°30S 43°55W 332 B3
Codogno Italy 45°9N 9°42E 198 C6
Codpa Chile 18°50S 69°44W 330 D4
Codrington Antigua & B. 17°38N 61°50W 322 c
Codrington Lagoon Antigua & B. 17°39N 61°50W 322 c
Codróipo Italy 45°58N 13°0E 199 C10
Codru, Munţii Romania 46°30N 22°15E 182 D7
Cody U.S.A. 44°32N 109°3W 304 D9
Coe Hill Canada 44°52N 77°50W 312 B7
Coelemu Chile 36°30S 72°48W 334 D1
Coelho Neto Brazil 4°15S 43°0W 332 B3
Coen Australia 13°52S 143°12E 280 A3
Coeroeni Suriname 3°22N 57°21W 329 C6
Coeroeni → Suriname 3°21N 57°31W 329 C6
Coesfeld Germany 51°56N 7°10E 178 D3
Coetivy Is. Seychelles 7°8S 56°16E 273 E4
Cœuilly France 48°48N 2°32E 134 B4
Coeur d'Alene U.S.A. 47°41N 116°46W 304 C5
Coeur d'Alene L. U.S.A. 47°32N 116°49W 304 C5
Coevorden Neths. 52°40N 6°44E 170 B6
Cofete Canary Is. 28°6N 14°23W 153 e2
Coffeyville U.S.A. 37°2N 95°37W 308 G6
Coffin B. Australia 34°38S 135°28E 281 E2
Coffin Bay Australia 34°37S 135°29E 281 E2
Coffin Bay △ Australia 34°34S 135°19E 281 E2
Coffin Bay Peninsula Australia 34°32S 135°15E 281 E2
Coffs Harbour Australia 30°16S 153°5E 283 A10
Cofrentes Spain 39°13N 1°5W 197 F3
Cogalnic = Kohylnyk → Ukraine 45°49N 29°40E 183 E14
Cogealac Romania 44°36N 28°36E 183 F13
Coghinas → Italy 40°55N 8°48E 200 B1
Coghinas, L. del Italy 40°46N 9°3E 200 B2
Cognac France 45°41N 0°20W 174 C3
Cogne Italy 45°37N 7°21E 198 C4
Cogolin France 43°15N 6°32E 175 E10
Cogolludo Spain 40°59N 3°10W 196 E1
Cohocton U.S.A. 42°30N 77°30W 312 D7
Cohocton → U.S.A. 42°9N 77°6W 312 D7
Cohoes U.S.A. 42°46N 73°42W 313 D11
Cohuna Australia 35°45S 144°15E 282 C6
Coiba, I. de Panama 7°30N 81°40W 320 E3
Coig → Argentina 51°0S 69°10W 336 D3
Coigeach, Rubha U.K. 58°6N 5°26W 167 C3
Coihaique Chile 45°30S 71°45W 336 C2
Coimbatore India 11°2N 76°59E 245 J3
Coimbra Mato Grosso, Brazil 19°55S 57°48W 331 D6
Coimbra Portugal 40°15N 8°27W 194 E2
Coimbra □ Portugal 40°12N 8°25W 194 E2
Coin Spain 36°40N 4°48W 195 J6
Coina Portugal 38°39N 9°5W 126 B2
Coipasa, L. de Bolivia 19°12S 68°7W 330 D4
Coipasa, Salar de Bolivia 19°26S 68°9W 330 D4
Coit Tower San Francisco, U.S.A. 136 a2
Cojata Peru 15°2S 69°25W 330 D4
Cojedes □ Venezuela 9°20N 68°20W 328 B4
Cojedes → Venezuela 8°34N 68°5W 328 B4
Cojimies Ecuador 0°20N 80°0W 328 C1
Cojocna Romania 46°45N 23°50E 183 D8
Cojutepequé El Salv. 13°41N 88°54W 320 D2
Čoka Serbia 45°57N 20°12E 182 E5
Coker Nigeria 6°28N 3°20E 124 B2
Cokeville U.S.A. 42°5N 110°57W 304 E8
Colaba India 18°53N 72°48E 130 B1
Colaba Pt. India 18°53N 72°48E 130 B1
Colac Australia 38°21S 143°35E 282 E5
Colachel = Kolachel India 8°10N 77°15E 245 K3
Colán Peru 5°0S 81°0W 330 B1
Colatina Brazil 19°32S 40°37W 333 E3
Colbeck, C. Antarctica 77°6S 157°48W 151 D13
Colbert U.S.A. 34°2N 83°13W 316 A6
Colborne Canada 44°0N 77°53W 312 C7
Colby U.S.A. 39°24N 101°3W 308 F3
Colca, Cañón del Peru 15°50S 72°20W 330 D3
Colchester Essex, U.K. 51°54N 0°55E 169 F8
Colchester Conn., U.S.A. 41°35N 72°20W 313 E12
Cold Bay U.S.A. 55°12N 162°42W 303 J7
Cold L. Canada 54°33N 110°5W 297 C7
Cold Lake Canada 54°27N 110°10W 297 C6
Coldstream B.C., Canada 50°13N 119°11W 296 C5
Coldstream Borders, U.K. 55°39N 2°15W 167 F6
Coldwater Ont., Canada 44°42N 79°40W 312 B5
Coldwater Kans., U.S.A. 37°16N 99°20W 308 G4
Coldwater Mich., U.S.A. 41°57N 85°0W 311 C11
Coldwater Ohio, U.S.A. 40°29N 84°38W 311 D12
Coldwater, L. U.S.A. 41°48N 84°59W 311 C12
Cole Camp U.S.A. 38°28N 93°12W 310 F3
Coleambally Australia 34°49S 145°52E 283 C6
Colebrook U.S.A. 44°54N 71°30W 313 B13
Colegiales Argentina 34°34S 58°27W 117 B2
Coleman Alta., Canada 49°40N 114°30W 296 D6
Coleman Fla., U.S.A. 28°48N 82°4W 317 G7
Coleman Tex., U.S.A. 31°50N 99°26W 314 F5
Coleman → Australia 15°6S 141°38E 280 B3
Colenso S. Africa 28°44S 29°50E 271 C4
Coleraine Vic., Australia 37°36S 141°40E 282 D4
Coleraine L'derry., U.K. 55°8N 6°41W 166 A5
Coleridge, L. N.Z. 43°17S 171°30E 285 D6
Coleroon → India 11°25N 79°50E 245 J4
Colesberg S. Africa 30°45S 25°5E 270 D4
Coleville U.S.A. 38°34N 119°30W 306 G7
Colfax Calif., U.S.A. 39°6N 120°57W 306 F6
Colfax Ill., U.S.A. 40°34N 88°37W 311 D8
Colfax Ind., U.S.A. 40°12N 86°40W 311 D10
Colfax Iowa, U.S.A. 41°41N 93°14W 310 C3
Colfax La., U.S.A. 31°31N 92°42W 314 F8
Colfax Wash., U.S.A. 46°53N 117°22W 304 C5
Colhué Huapi, L. Argentina 45°30S 69°0W 336 C3
Colibaşi = Mioveni Romania 44°56N 24°54E 183 F9
Colibaşi Moldova 45°43N 28°11E 183 E13
Colibris, Pte. des Guadeloupe 16°17N 61°5W 322 e
Cólico Italy 46°8N 9°22E 198 B6
Colider Brazil 10°45S 55°25W 331 C6
Coligny Ain, France 46°23N 5°21E 173 F12
Coligny North West, S. Africa 26°17S 26°15E 271 C4
Colihaut Dominica 15°29N 61°29W 323 k
Colima Mexico 19°14N 103°43W 318 D4
Colima □ Mexico 19°10N 104°0W 318 D4
Colima, Nevado de Mexico 19°33N 103°38W 318 D4
Colina Chile 33°13S 70°45W 334 C1
Colina do Norte Guinea-Biss. 12°28N 15°0W 262 C2
Colinas Goiás, Brazil 14°15S 48°2W 333 D2
Colinas Maranhão, Brazil 6°0S 44°10W 332 C3
Colindale U.K. 51°35N 0°15W 125 A2
Colindres Spain 43°24N 3°27W 194 B7
Colinton U.K. 55°55N 3°14W 121 B2
Coll U.K. 56°39N 6°34W 167 E2
Collahuasi Chile 21°5S 68°45W 334 A2
Collarada, Peña Spain 42°43N 0°29W 196 C4
Collarenebri Australia 29°33S 148°34E 281 D4
Colle di Val d'Elsa Italy 43°25N 11°7E 198 E8
Collécchio Italy 44°45N 10°13E 198 D7
Colleen Bawn Zimbabwe 21°0S 29°12E 269 G2
College U.S.A. 64°52N 147°49W 303 D11
College Park Ga., U.S.A. 33°39N 84°27W 113 C2
College Park Md., U.S.A. 38°59N 76°55W 143 B3
College Point U.S.A. 40°47N 73°50W 132 B2
College Station U.S.A. 30°37N 96°21W 314 F6
Collégien France 48°50N 2°41E 134 A4
Collesalvetti Italy 43°34N 10°27E 198 E7

Colli Euganei ⌂ Italy 45°18N 11°43E 199 C8
Collie N.S.W., Australia 31°41S 148°18E 283 A8
Collie W. Austral., Australia 33°22S 116°8E 279 F2
Collier B. Australia 16°10S 124°15E 278 C3
Collier Ra. Australia 24°45S 119°10E 279 D2
Collier Range △ Australia 24°39S 119°7E 279 D2
Collier Row U.K. 51°35N 0°9E 125 A4
Colliers Wood U.K. 51°24N 0°10W 125 B2
Collierville U.S.A. 35°3N 89°40W 315 D10
Collina, Passo di Italy 44°2N 10°56E 198 D7
Collingwood Ont., Canada 44°29N 80°13W 312 B4
Collingwood N.Z. 40°41S 172°40E 285 A7
Collins Ont., Canada 50°17N 89°27W 298 B2
Collins Ga., U.S.A. 32°11N 82°7W 316 C7
Collins Mo., U.S.A. 37°54N 93°37W 310 G3
Collins Bay Canada 44°14N 76°36W 313 B8
Collinson Pen. Canada 69°58N 101°24W 294 D11
Collinsville Queens., Australia 20°30S 147°56E 280 C4
Collinsville Ill., U.S.A. 38°40N 89°59W 310 F7
Collipulli Chile 37°55S 72°30W 334 D1
Collo Algeria 36°58N 6°37E 261 A6
Collooney Ireland 54°11N 8°29W 166 B3
Colma U.S.A. 37°40N 122°27W 136 B2
Colmar France 48°5N 7°20E 173 D14
Colmars France 44°11N 6°39E 175 D10
Colmenar Spain 36°54N 4°20W 195 J6
Colmenar de Oreja Spain 40°6N 3°25W 194 E7
Colmenar Viejo Spain 40°39N 3°47W 194 E7
Colney Hatch U.K. 51°36N 0°9W 125 A3
Colo → Australia 33°25S 150°52E 283 B9
Cologne = Köln Germany 50°56N 6°57E 178 E2
Cologno Monzese Italy 45°31N 9°16E 128 A2
Colom, I. d'en Spain 39°58N 4°16E 206 B5
Coloma Calif., U.S.A. 38°48N 120°53W 306 G6
Coloma Mich., U.S.A. 42°11N 86°19W 311 B10
Colomb-Béchar = Béchar Algeria 31°38N 2°18W 261 B4
Colombes France 48°55N 2°15E 134 A2
Colombey-les-Belles France 48°32N 5°54E 173 D12
Colombey-les-Deux-Églises France 48°13N 4°50E 173 D11
Colômbia Brazil 20°10S 48°40W 333 F2
Colombia ■ S. Amer. 3°45N 73°0W 328 C3
Colombian Basin Caribbean 14°0N 76°0W 321 D5
Colombier St.-Martin 18°5N 63°4W 322 a
Colombo Sri Lanka 6°56N 79°58E 245 L4
Colomiers France 43°36N 1°21E 174 E5
Colón B. Aires, Argentina 33°53S 61°7W 334 C3
Colón Entre Ríos, Argentina 32°12S 58°10W 334 C4
Colón Cuba 22°42N 80°54W 320 B3
Colón Panama 9°20N 79°54W 320 c
Colón, Arch. de Ecuador 0°0 91°0W 330 a
Colón, Monumente a Barcelona, Spain 114 c3
Colón, Plaza de Madrid, Spain 127 a3
Colón Ridge Pac. Oc. 2°0N 96°0W 289 G18
Colonarie St. Vincent 13°14N 61°8W 323 n
Colonia Micronesia 9°30N 138°10E 287 R16
Colonia 25 de Mayo Argentina 37°48S 67°41W 336 A3
Colònia de Sant Jordi Spain 39°19N 2°59E 206 B3
Colonia del Sacramento Uruguay 34°25S 57°50W 334 C4
Colonia Dora Argentina 28°34S 62°59W 334 B3
Colonia Güell Spain 41°21N 2°2E 114 A1
Colonial Beach U.S.A. 38°15N 76°58W 309 F15
Colonie U.S.A. 42°43N 73°50W 313 D11
Colonna, C. Italy 39°2N 17°12E 201 C10
Colonsay Sask., Canada 51°59N 105°52W 297 C7
Colonsay Argyll & Bute, U.K. 56°5N 6°12W 167 E2
Colorado □ U.S.A. 39°30N 105°30W 304 G11
Colorado → Argentina 39°50S 62°8W 336 A4
Colorado → N. Amer. 31°45N 114°40W 305 L6
Colorado → Tex., U.S.A. 28°36N 95°59W 314 G7
Colorado City U.S.A. 32°24N 100°52W 314 E4
Colorado Plateau U.S.A. 37°0N 111°0W 305 H8
Colorado River Aqueduct U.S.A. 33°50N 117°23W 307 L12
Colorado Springs U.S.A. 38°50N 104°49W 304 G11
Colorno Italy 44°56N 10°23E 198 D7
Colosseo Rome, Italy 136 c3
Colosseum = Colosseo Rome, Italy 136 c3
Colotlán Mexico 22°6N 103°16W 318 C4
Colquechaca Bolivia 18°40S 66°1W 331 D4
Colquitt U.S.A. 31°10N 84°44W 316 D5
Colstrip U.S.A. 45°53N 106°38W 304 D10
Colton U.S.A. 44°33N 74°56W 313 B10
Columbia Ala., U.S.A. 31°18N 85°7W 316 D4
Columbia Ill., U.S.A. 38°27N 90°12W 310 F6
Columbia Ky., U.S.A. 37°6N 85°18W 309 G11
Columbia La., U.S.A. 32°6N 92°5W 314 E8
Columbia Miss., U.S.A. 31°15N 89°50W 315 F10
Columbia Mo., U.S.A. 38°57N 92°20W 310 F4
Columbia Pa., U.S.A. 40°2N 76°30W 313 F8
Columbia S.C., U.S.A. 34°0N 81°2W 316 A8
Columbia Tenn., U.S.A. 35°37N 87°2W 315 D11
Columbia → N. Amer. 46°15N 124°5W 306 D2
Columbia, C. Canada 83°6N 69°57W 295 A18
Columbia, District of □ U.S.A. 38°55N 77°0W 309 F15
Columbia, Mt. Canada 52°8N 117°20W 296 C5
Columbia Basin U.S.A. 46°45N 119°5W 304 C4
Columbia City U.S.A. 41°10N 85°29W 311 C11
Columbia Falls U.S.A. 48°23N 114°11W 304 B6
Columbia Mts. Canada 52°0N 119°0W 296 C5
Columbia Plateau U.S.A. 44°0N 117°30W 304 E5
Columbiana U.S.A. 40°53N 80°42W 312 F4
Columbretes, Is. Spain 39°50N 0°50E 196 F5
Columbus Ga., U.S.A. 32°28N 84°59W 316 C5
Columbus Ind., U.S.A. 39°13N 85°55W 311 E11
Columbus Kans., U.S.A. 37°10N 94°50W 308 G6
Columbus Miss., U.S.A. 33°30N 88°25W 315 E10
Columbus Mont., U.S.A. 45°38N 109°15W 304 D9
Columbus N. Mex., U.S.A. 31°50N 107°38W 305 L10
Columbus Nebr., U.S.A. 41°26N 97°22W 308 E5
Columbus Ohio, U.S.A. 39°58N 83°0W 311 E13
Columbus Tex., U.S.A. 29°42N 96°33W 314 G6
Columbus Circle Washington, D.C., U.S.A. 143 b3
Columbus Circle New York, U.S.A. 132 b2
Columbus Grove U.S.A. 40°55N 84°4W 311 D12
Columbus Junction U.S.A. 41°17N 91°22W 310 C5
Columbus Monument = Colón, Monumente a Barcelona, Spain 114 c3
Columbus Park Jamaica 18°28N 77°25W 320 a
Columbus Park Boston, U.S.A. 116 b3
Colunga Spain 43°29N 5°16W 194 B5
Colusa U.S.A. 39°13N 122°1W 306 F4
Colville U.S.A. 48°33N 117°54W 304 B5
Colville → U.S.A. 70°25N 150°30W 303 A10
Colville, C. N.Z. 36°29S 175°21E 284 C4
Colville Channel N.Z. 36°25S 175°27E 284 C4
Colville Ridge Pac. Oc. 30°0S 180°0E 277 G15
Colwood Canada 48°26N 123°29W 306 B3
Colwyn Bay U.K. 53°18N 3°44W 168 D4
Coma Ethiopia 8°29N 36°53E 257 F4
Comácchio Italy 44°42N 12°11E 199 D9
Comalcalco Mexico 18°16N 93°13W 319 D6
Comallo Argentina 41°0S 70°5W 336 B2
Comana Romania 44°10N 26°10E 183 F11
Comanche U.S.A. 31°54N 98°36W 314 F5
Comandante Arbues = Mirandópolis Brazil 21°9S 51°6W 335 A5
Comandante Ferraz Antarctica 62°30S 58°0W 151 C18
Comandante Luis Piedrabuena Argentina 49°59S 68°54W 336 C3
Comănești Romania 46°25N 26°26E 183 D11
Comarapa Bolivia 17°54S 64°29W 331 D5
Comarnic Romania 45°15N 25°38E 183 E10
Comayagua Honduras 14°25N 87°37W 320 D2
Combahee → U.S.A. 32°31N 80°31W 316 C9
Combara Australia 31°10S 148°22E 283 A8
Combarbalá Chile 31°11S 71°2W 334 C1
Combault France 48°48N 2°37E 134 B4
Combe Martin U.K. 51°12N 4°3W 169 F3
Combeaufontaine France 47°38N 5°54E 173 E12
Comber Ont., Canada 42°14N 82°33W 312 D2
Comber Down, U.K. 54°33N 5°45W 166 B6
Combermere Canada 45°22N 77°37W 312 A7
Combermere Bay Burma 19°37N 93°34E 241 F4
Comblain-au-Pont Belgium 50°29N 5°35E 170 D5
Combourg France 48°25N 1°46W 172 D5
Comboyne Australia 31°34S 152°27E 283 A10
Combrailles France 46°30N 2°8E 173 F9
Combronde France 45°58N 3°5E 174 C7
Comer Ala., U.S.A. 32°2N 85°23W 316 C4
Comer Ga., U.S.A. 34°4N 83°8W 316 A6
Comeragh Mts. Ireland 52°18N 7°34W 166 D4
Comércio, Praça do Portugal 38°41N 9°9W 126 A2
Comerio Puerto Rico 18°12N 66°12W 321 b
Comet Australia 23°36S 148°38E 280 C4
Comilla Bangla. 23°28N 91°10E 241 D3
Comino Malta 36°1N 14°20E 206 E7
Comino, C. Italy 40°32N 9°49E 200 B2
Cómiso Italy 36°56N 14°36E 201 F7
Comitán de Domínguez Mexico 16°15N 92°8W 319 D6
Commentry France 46°20N 2°46E 173 F9
Commerce Calif., U.S.A. 34°0N 118°9W 126 B4
Commerce Ga., U.S.A. 34°12N 83°28W 316 A6
Commerce Tex., U.S.A. 33°15N 95°54W 314 E7
Commercy France 48°43N 5°34E 173 D12
Commissioner's Pt. Bermuda 32°19N 64°49W 153 a
Committee B. Canada 68°30N 86°30W 295 D14
Commodore, C. Canada 44°47N 80°54W 312 B4
Commonwealth B. Antarctica 67°0S 144°0E 151 C10
Commoron Cr. → Australia 28°22S 150°8E 281 D5
Communism Pk. = imeni Ismail Samani, Pik Tajikistan 39°0N 72°2E 217 E8
Como Italy 45°47N 9°5E 198 C6
Como, Lago di Italy 46°0N 9°11E 198 B6
Comodoro Rivadavia Argentina 45°50S 67°40W 336 C3
Comoé → Ivory C. 5°12N 3°44W 262 D4
Comoé △ Ivory C. 9°0N 3°35W 262 D4
Comorâște Romania 45°10N 21°35E 182 E6
Comorin, C. = Kannyakumari India 8°3N 77°40E 245 K3
Comoros ■ Ind. Oc. 12°10S 44°15E 272 a
Comox Canada 49°42N 124°55W 296 D4
Company's Gardens Cape Town, S. Africa 118 c2
Compass Lake U.S.A. 30°36N 85°24W 316 E4
Compiègne France 49°24N 2°50E 173 C9
Comporta Portugal 38°22N 8°46W 195 G2
Compostela Nayarit, Mexico 21°14N 104°55W 318 C4
Compostela Phil. 7°40N 126°2E 233 H6
Comprida, I. Brazil 24°50S 47°42W 335 A6
Compton Qué., Canada 45°14N 71°49W 313 A13
Compton Calif., U.S.A. 33°53N 118°13W 307 M8
Comrat Moldova 46°18N 28°40E 183 D13
Comunidad Peru 13°59S 69°20W 330 C4
Con Cuong Vietnam 19°2N 104°54E 236 C5
Con Dao △ Vietnam 8°42N 106°35E 237 H6
Con Son, Dao Vietnam 8°41N 106°37E 237 H6
Cona Niyeu Argentina 41°58S 67°0W 336 B3
Conakry Guinea 9°29N 13°49W 262 D2
Conara Australia 41°50S 147°26E 281 G4
Conargo Australia 35°16S 145°10E 283 C6
Concarneau France 47°52N 3°56W 172 E3
Conceição Paraíba, Brazil 7°33S 38°31W 332 C4
Conceição Mozam. 18°47S 36°7E 269 F4
Conceição, I. da Brazil 22°52S 43°6W 135 B2
Conceição da Barra Brazil 18°35S 39°45W 333 E4
Conceição do Araguaia Brazil 8°0S 49°2W 332 C2
Conceição do Canindé Brazil 7°54S 41°34W 332 C3
Conceição do Maú Brazil 3°35N 59°53W 329 C6
Conceição do Paraíba = Capela Brazil 10°30S 37°0W 332 D4
Concepción Argentina 27°20S 65°35W 334 B2
Concepción Bolivia 16°15S 62°8W 331 D5
Concepción Chile 36°50S 73°0W 334 D1
Concepción Paraguay 23°22S 57°26W 334 A4
Concepción Peru 11°54S 75°19W 330 C2
Concepción Tarlac, Phil. 15°27N 120°47E 232 D3
Concepción □ Chile 37°0S 72°30W 334 D1
Concepción, Est. de Chile 50°30S 74°55W 336 D2
Concepción, L. Bolivia 17°20S 61°20W 331 D5
Concepción, Pta. Mexico 26°53N 111°50W 318 B2
Concepción del Oro Mexico 24°38N 101°25W 318 C4
Concepción del Uruguay Argentina 32°35S 58°20W 334 C4
Conception, Pt. U.S.A. 34°27N 120°28W 307 L6
Conception B. Nfld. & L., Canada 47°45N 53°0W 299 C9
Conception B. Namibia 23°55S 14°22E 270 B1
Conception I. Bahamas 23°52N 75°9W 321 B4
Concession Zimbabwe 17°27S 30°56E 269 F3
Conchali Chile 33°22S 70°39W 137 B2
Conchas Dam U.S.A. 35°22N 104°11W 305 J11
Conches-en-Ouche France 48°58N 0°56E 172 D7
Concho U.S.A. 34°28N 109°36W 305 J9
Concho → U.S.A. 31°34N 99°43W 314 F5
Conchos → Chihuahua, Mexico 29°35N 104°25W 318 B4
Conchos → Tamaulipas, Mexico 24°55N 97°38W 319 B5
Concord N.S.W., Australia 33°52S 151°6E 139 B1
Concord Ont., Canada 43°48N 79°29W 141 A2
Concord Grenada 12°7N 61°44W 323 q
Concord Calif., U.S.A. 37°59N 122°2W 306 H4
Concord Ga., U.S.A. 33°5N 84°27W 316 B5
Concord Mich., U.S.A. 42°11N 84°38W 311 B12
Concord Mo., U.S.A. 38°32N 90°23W 310 F6
Concord N.C., U.S.A. 35°25N 80°35W 315 D14
Concord N.H., U.S.A. 43°12N 71°32W 313 C13
Concorde, Place de la Paris, France 134 b3
Concordia Antarctica 75°6S 123°23E 151 D9
Concordia Argentina 31°20S 58°2W 334 C4
Concórdia Amazonas, Brazil 4°36S 66°36W 328 D4
Concórdia Sta. Catarina, Brazil 27°14S 52°1W 335 B5
Concordia Sinaloa, Mexico 23°17N 106°4W 318 C3
Concordia Kans., U.S.A. 39°34N 97°40W 308 F5
Concordia Mo., U.S.A. 38°59N 93°34W 310 F3
Concordia Univ. Montréal, Canada 130 c1
Concorezzo Italy 45°35N 9°19E 128 A2
Concrete U.S.A. 48°32N 121°45W 304 B3
Conda Angola 11°9S 14°20E 265 E2
Condah Australia 37°57S 141°44E 282 D4
Condamine Australia 26°56S 150°9E 281 D5
Condat France 45°21N 2°46E 174 C6
Condé Angola 10°50S 14°37E 265 E2
Conde Brazil 11°49S 37°37W 333 D4
Conde S. Dak., U.S.A. 45°9N 98°6W 308 C4
Condé-sur-Noireau France 48°51N 0°33W 172 D6
Condet Indonesia 6°17S 106°51E 122 A2
Condeúba Brazil 14°52S 42°0W 333 D3
Condobolin Australia 33°4S 147°6E 283 B7
Condom France 43°57N 0°22E 174 E4
Condon U.S.A. 45°14N 120°11W 304 D3
Conegliano Italy 45°53N 12°18E 199 C9
Conejera, I. = Conills, I. des Spain 39°11N 2°58E 206 B3
Conejos Mexico 26°14N 103°53W 318 B4
Conemaugh → U.S.A. 40°28N 79°19W 312 F5
Conero ⌂ Italy 43°32N 13°35E 199 E10
Coney I. = Serangoon, Pulau Singapore 1°23N 103°55E 138 A3
Coney Island U.S.A. 40°34N 74°0W 132 C2
Conflict Group Papua N. G. 10°47S 151°45E 286 F6
Confolens France 46°2N 0°40E 174 B4
Confuso → Paraguay 25°9S 57°34W 334 B4
Congaree → U.S.A. 33°44N 80°38W 316 B9
Congaree △ U.S.A. 33°47N 80°47W 316 B9
Congaz Moldova 46°7N 28°36E 183 D13
Congerville U.S.A. 40°38N 89°11W 310 D7
Conghua China 23°36N 113°31E 229 F9
Congjiang China 25°43N 108°52E 228 E7
Congleton U.K. 53°10N 2°13W 168 D5
Congo Brazil 7°48S 36°40W 332 C4
Congo (Brazzaville) = Congo ■ Africa 1°0S 16°0E 264 C3
Congo (Kinshasa) = Congo, Dem. Rep. of the ■ Africa 3°0S 23°0E 265 C4
Congo ■ Africa 1°0S 16°0E 264 C3
Congo → Africa 6°4S 12°24E 265 D2
Congo, Dem. Rep. of the ■ Africa 3°0S 23°0E 265 C4
Congo Basin Africa 0°10S 24°30E 254 G6
Congo Free State = Congo, Dem. Rep. of the ■ Africa 3°0S 23°0E 265 C4
Congonhas Brazil 20°30S 43°52W 333 F3
Congonhas São Paulo ✈ (CGH) Brazil 23°38S 46°39W 137 B2
Congress U.S.A. 34°9N 112°51W 305 J7
Conguillio △ Chile 38°40S 71°42W 336 A2
Conil de la Frontera Spain 36°17N 6°10W 195 J4
Conills, I. des Spain 39°11N 2°58E 206 B3
Conimbla △ Australia 33°45S 148°28E 283 B8
Coniston Canada 46°29N 80°51W 298 C3
Conjeeveram = Kanchipuram India 12°52N 79°45E 245 H4
Conklin Alta., Canada 55°38N 111°5W 297 B6
Conklin N.Y., U.S.A. 42°2N 75°49W 313 D9
Conkouati ⌂ Congo 3°50S 11°28E 264 C2
Conlendas, Pta. das Azores 38°38N 27°14W 153 d1
Conley → U.S.A. 33°40N 84°17W 113 C3
Conn, L. Ireland 54°3N 9°15W 166 B2
Connaught □ Ireland 53°43N 9°12W 166 C2
Connaught Place Delhi, India 120 b2
Conneaut U.S.A. 41°57N 80°34W 312 E4
Conneautville U.S.A. 41°45N 80°22W 312 E4
Connecticut □ U.S.A. 41°30N 72°45W 313 E12
Connecticut → U.S.A. 41°16N 72°20W 313 E12
Connell U.S.A. 46°40N 118°52W 304 C4
Connellsville U.S.A. 40°1N 79°35W 312 F5
Connemara Ireland 53°29N 9°45W 166 C2
Connemara △ Ireland 53°32N 9°52W 166 C2
Conner Phil. 17°48N 121°19E 232 C3
Connerré France 48°3N 0°30E 172 D7
Connersville U.S.A. 39°39N 85°8W 311 E11
Connors Ra. Australia 21°40S 149°10E 280 C4
Conoble Australia 32°55S 144°33E 283 B6
Conococha Peru 10°7S 77°18W 330 C2
Cononaco → Ecuador 1°32S 75°35W 328 D2
Conques France 44°36N 2°23E 174 D6
Conquest Canada 51°32N 107°14W 297 C7
Conquista = Vitória da Conquista Brazil 14°51S 40°51W 333 D3
Conrad Iowa, U.S.A. 42°14N 92°52W 310 B4
Conrad Mont., U.S.A. 48°10N 111°57W 304 B8
Conrad Rise S. Ocean 53°0S 41°0E 151 B5
Conran, C. Australia 37°49S 148°44E 283 D8
Conroe U.S.A. 30°19N 95°27W 314 F7
Conselheiro Lafaiete Brazil 20°40S 43°48W 333 F3
Conselheiro Pena Brazil 19°10S 41°30W 333 E3
Consell Spain 39°40N 2°49E 206 B3
Conselve Italy 45°14N 11°52E 199 C8
Conservatori, Palazzo dei Rome, Italy 136 c3
Consett U.K. 54°51N 1°50W 168 C6
Consolação Brazil 23°32S 46°38W 137 B2
Consort Canada 52°1N 110°46W 297 C6
Constance = Konstanz Germany 47°40N 9°10E 179 H5
Constance, L. = Bodensee Europe 47°35N 9°25E 179 H5
Constanța Romania 44°14N 28°38E 183 F13
Constanța □ Romania 44°15N 28°15E 183 F13
Constantia S. Africa 34°2S 18°26E 118 B1
Constantina Spain 37°51N 5°40W 195 H5
Constantine Algeria 36°25N 6°42E 261 A6
Constantine Mich., U.S.A. 41°50N 85°40W 311 C11
Constantine □ Algeria 36°30N 6°40E 261 A6
Constantine, Arch of = Costantino, Arco di Rome, Italy 136 c3
Constantine, C. U.S.A. 58°24N 158°54W 303 G8
Constantinople = İstanbul Turkey 41°0N 28°58E 122 C1
Constitución B. Aires, Argentina 34°38S 58°23W 117 B2
Constitución Chile 35°20S 72°30W 334 D1
Constitución Uruguay 31°0S 57°50W 334 C4
Constitución de 1857 △ Mexico 32°4N 115°55W 318 A1
Constitution U.S.A. 33°42N 84°20W 113 B2
Constitution Avenue Washington, D.C., U.S.A. 143 b2
Constitution Square = Syntagma Square Athens, Greece 112 b2
Consuegra Spain 39°28N 3°36W 195 F7
Consul Canada 49°20N 109°30W 297 D7
Contact U.S.A. 41°46N 114°45W 304 F6
Contagem Brazil 19°55S 44°6W 333 E3
Contai India 21°54N 87°46E 243 J12
Contamana Peru 7°19S 74°55W 330 B3
Contarina Italy 45°1N 12°13E 199 C9
Contarini Dal Zaffo, Palazzo Venice, Italy 142 c2
Contas → Brazil 14°17S 39°1W 333 D4
Contes France 43°49N 7°19E 175 E11
Continental U.S.A. 41°6N 84°16W 311 C12
Contoocook U.S.A. 43°13N 71°45W 313 C13
Contra Costa Mozam. 25°9S 33°30E 271 C5
Contres France 47°24N 1°26E 172 E8
Contrexéville France 48°10N 5°53E 173 D12
Controller B. U.S.A. 60°7N 144°15W 303 F11
Contumaza Peru 7°23S 78°57W 330 B2
Contwoyto L. Canada 65°42N 110°50W 294 D9
Convención Colombia 8°28N 73°21W 328 B3
Conversano Italy 40°58N 17°7E 201 B10
Converse U.S.A. 40°35N 85°52W 311 D11
Convoy U.S.A. 40°55N 84°43W 311 D12
Conway = Conwy U.K. 53°17N 3°50W 168 D4
Conway = Conwy → U.K. 53°17N 3°50W 168 D4
Conway Australia 20°24S 148°41E 280 b
Conway Ont., Canada 44°6N 76°54W 312 B8
Conway Ark., U.S.A. 35°5N 92°26W 314 D8
Conway Fla., U.S.A. 28°30N 81°19W 133 B2
Conway N.H., U.S.A. 43°59N 71°7W 313 C13
Conway S.C., U.S.A. 33°51N 79°3W 315 E15
Conway, C. Australia 20°34S 148°46E 280 b
Conway, L. S. Austral., Australia 28°17S 135°35E 281 D2
Conway, L. Fla., U.S.A. 28°28N 81°21W 133 B2
Conwy U.K. 53°17N 3°50W 168 D4
Conwy □ U.K. 53°10N 3°44W 168 D4
Conwy → U.K. 53°17N 3°50W 168 D4
Conyers U.S.A. 33°40N 84°1W 316 B5
Coober Pedy Australia 29°1S 134°43E 281 D1
Cooch Behar = Koch Bihar India 26°22N 89°29E 241 B2
Coogee Australia 33°55S 151°16E 139 B2
Cooinda Australia 13°15S 130°5E 278 B5
Cook S. Austral., Australia 30°37S 130°25E 279 F5
Cook Minn., U.S.A. 47°51N 92°41W 308 B7
Cook, B. Chile 55°10S 70°0W 336 E3
Cook, C. Canada 50°8N 127°55W 296 C3
Cook, Mt. = Aoraki Mount Cook N.Z. 43°36S 170°9E 285 D5
Cook, Récif de N. Cal. 19°25S 163°50E 288 d
Cook Bay Vanuatu 18°46S 169°15E 287 H7
Cook Inlet U.S.A. 60°0N 152°0W 303 G10
Cook Is. ☒ Pac. Oc. 17°0S 160°0W 289 J12
Cook Strait N.Z. 41°15S 174°29E 284 H3
Cooke Plains Australia 35°23S 139°34E 282 C3
Cookeville U.S.A. 36°10N 85°30W 315 C12
Cookhouse S. Africa 32°44S 25°47E 270 D4
Cooks Hammock U.S.A. 29°56N 83°17W 316 F6
Cooks Harbour Canada 51°36N 55°52W 299 B8
Cookshire Canada 45°25N 71°38W 313 A13
Cookstown Ont., Canada 44°11N 79°42W 312 B5
Cookstown Tyrone, U.K. 54°38N 6°45W 166 B5
Cooksville Canada 43°35N 79°38W 141 B1
Cooktown Australia 15°30S 145°16E 280 B4
Coolabah Australia 31°1S 146°43E 283 A7
Cooladdi Australia 26°37S 145°23E 281 D4
Coolah Australia 31°48S 149°41E 283 A8
Coolah Tops △ Australia 31°52S 150°0E 283 A9
Coolamon Australia 34°46S 147°8E 283 C7
Coolgardie Australia 30°55S 121°8E 279 F3
Coolidge Ariz., U.S.A. 32°59N 111°31W 305 K8
Coolidge Ga., U.S.A. 31°1N 83°52W 316 D6
Coolidge Dam U.S.A. 33°10N 110°32W 305 K8
Coolock Ireland 53°22N 6°12W 120 A2
Cooma Australia 36°12S 149°8E 283 D8
Coon Rapids Iowa, U.S.A. 41°53N 94°41W 310 C2
Coon Rapids Minn., U.S.A. 45°9N 93°19W 308 C7
Coonabarabran Australia 31°14S 149°18E 283 A8
Coonalpyn Australia 35°43S 139°52E 282 C3
Coonamble Australia 30°56S 148°27E 283 A8
Coonana Australia 31°0S 123°0E 279 F3
Coonana ⊙ Australia 30°51S 122°53E 279 F3
Coondapoor India 13°42N 74°40E 245 H2
Cooninnie, L. Australia 26°4S 139°59E 281 D2
Coonoor India 11°21N 76°45E 245 J3
Cooper U.S.A. 33°23N 95°42W 314 E7
Cooper → U.S.A. 32°50N 79°56W 316 C10
Cooper City U.S.A. 26°3N 80°16W 129 B1
Cooper Cr. → Australia 28°29S 137°46E 281 D2
Cooper Ridge Pac. Oc. 10°0N 150°30W 289 G12
Cooper's Hill Jamaica 18°4N 76°51W 320 a
Cooperstown N. Dak., U.S.A. 47°27N 98°8W 308 B4
Cooperstown N.Y., U.S.A. 42°42N 74°56W 313 D10
Coopersville U.S.A. 43°4N 85°57W 311 A11
Coopracambra △ Australia 37°20S 149°20E 283 D8
Coora → Trin. & Tob. 10°10N 61°28W 323 t
Coorabie Australia 31°54S 132°18E 279 F5
Coorong, The Australia 35°50S 139°20E 282 C3
Coorong △ Australia 36°0S 139°29E 282 D3
Coorow Australia 29°53S 116°2E 279 E2
Cooroy Australia 26°22S 152°54E 281 D5
Coos Bay U.S.A. 43°22N 124°13W 304 E1
Coosa → U.S.A. 32°30N 86°16W 315 E11
Cootamundra Australia 34°36S 148°1E 283 C8
Cootehill Ireland 54°4N 7°5W 166 B4
Copacabana Brazil 22°58S 43°11W 135 B1
Copahue Paso Argentina 37°49S 71°8W 334 D1
Copainalá Mexico 17°4N 93°18W 319 D6
Copake U.S.A. 42°7N 73°31W 313 D11
Copalnic Mănăștur Romania 47°30N 23°41E 183 C8
Copán Honduras 14°50N 89°9W 320 D2
Copatana Brazil 2°48S 67°4W 328 D4
Cope Colo., U.S.A. 39°40N 102°51W 304 G12
Cope S.C., U.S.A. 33°23N 81°0W 316 B8
Cope, C. Spain 37°26N 1°28W 197 H3
Copeland U.S.A. 25°57N 81°22W 317 K8
Copenhagen = København Denmark 55°40N 12°26E 118 A2
Copenhagen U.S.A. 43°54N 75°41W 313 C9
Copertino Italy 40°16N 18°3E 201 B11
Copiapó Chile 27°30S 70°20W 334 B1
Copiapó → Chile 27°19S 70°56W 334 B1
Coplay U.S.A. 40°44N 75°29W 313 F9
Copley Australia 30°36S 138°26E 282 A3
Copo △ Argentina 25°53S 61°41W 334 B3
Copp L. Canada 60°14N 114°40W 296 A6
Copparo Italy 44°54N 11°49E 199 D8
Coppename → Suriname 5°48N 55°55W 329 B6
Copper → U.S.A. 60°18N 145°3W 303 F11
Copper Canyon = Barranca del Cobre △ Mexico 27°18N 107°40W 318 B3
Copper Center U.S.A. 61°58N 145°18W 303 F11
Copper City = Invermere Canada 50°30N 116°2W 296 C5
Copper Harbor U.S.A. 47°28N 87°53W 308 B10
Copper Queen Zimbabwe 17°29S 29°18E 269 F2
Copperas Cove U.S.A. 31°8N 97°54W 314 F6
Copperbelt □ Zambia 13°15S 27°30E 269 E2
Coppermine = Kugluktuk Canada 67°50N 115°5W 294 D8
Coppermine → Canada 67°49N 116°4W 294 D8
Copperopolis U.S.A. 37°58N 120°38W 306 H6
Copșa Mică Romania 46°7N 24°15E 183 D9
Coquet → U.K. 55°20N 1°32W 168 B6
Coquilhatville = Mbandaka Dem. Rep. of the Congo 0°1N 18°18E 264 B3
Coquille U.S.A. 43°11N 124°11W 304 E1
Coquimbo Chile 30°0S 71°20W 334 C1
Coquimbo □ Chile 31°0S 71°0W 334 C1
Coquitlam Canada 49°17N 122°45W 296 D4
Corabia Romania 43°48N 24°30E 183 G9
Coração de Jesus Brazil 16°43S 44°22W 333 E3
Coracora Peru 15°5S 73°45W 330 D3
Coraki Australia 28°59S 153°17E 281 D5
Coral U.S.A. 40°29N 79°10W 312 F5
Coral B. Phil. 8°25N 117°26E 233 G1
Coral Bay Australia 23°8S 113°46E 278 D1
Coral Gables U.S.A. 25°43N 80°16W 129 D1
Coral Harbour Bahamas 24°58N 77°28W 153 b
Coral Harbour Nunavut, Canada 64°8N 83°10W 295 E15
Coral Heights Bahamas 25°0N 77°27W 153 b
Coral Hills U.S.A. 38°51N 76°55W 143 B3
Coral Sea Pac. Oc. 15°0S 150°0E 276 C9
Coral Sea Basin Pac. Oc. 14°0S 152°0E 288 J7
Coral Sea Islands Terr. □ Australia 20°0S 155°0E 276 D9
Coral Springs U.S.A. 26°16N 80°16W 317 J9
Corales del Rosario △ Colombia 10°8N 75°46W 328 A2
Coralville U.S.A. 41°40N 91°35W 310 C5
Coralville L. U.S.A. 41°42N 91°33W 310 C5
Corangamite, L. Australia 38°5S 143°30E 282 E5
Corantijn → Suriname 5°50N 57°8W 329 B6
Coraopolis U.S.A. 40°31N 80°10W 312 F4
Corato Italy 41°9N 16°25E 201 A9
Corbeil-Essonnes France 48°36N 2°26E 173 D9
Corbeiro, C. W. Sahara 21°50N 17°0W 260 D1
Corbett △ India 29°20N 79°0E 243 E8
Corbie France 49°54N 2°30E 173 C9
Corbières France 42°55N 2°35E 174 F6
Corbigny France 47°16N 3°40E 173 E10
Corbin U.S.A. 36°57N 84°6W 309 G11
Corbones → Spain 37°36N 5°39W 195 H5
Corbu Romania 44°25N 28°39E 183 F13
Corby U.K. 52°30N 0°41W 169 E7
Corcaigh = Cork Ireland 51°54N 8°29W 166 E3
Corcoran U.S.A. 36°6N 119°33W 306 J7
Corcovado, Cristo Redentor Brazil 22°57S 43°12W 135 B1
Corcovado △ Costa Rica 8°33N 83°35W 320 E3
Cordele U.S.A. 31°58N 83°47W 316 D6
Cordell U.S.A. 35°17N 98°59W 314 D5
Cordenòns Italy 45°59N 12°42E 199 C9
Cordes-sur-Ciel France 44°5N 1°57E 174 D5
Cordillera Azul △ Peru 7°30S 76°30W 330 B2
Cordillera de los Picachos △ Colombia 2°39N 74°30W 328 C3
Cordisburgo Brazil 19°7S 44°21W 333 E3
Córdoba Argentina 31°20S 64°10W 334 C3
Córdoba Veracruz, Mexico 18°53N 96°56W 319 D5
Córdoba Spain 37°50N 4°50W 195 H6
Córdoba □ Argentina 31°22S 64°15W 334 C3
Córdoba □ Colombia 8°20N 75°40W 328 B2
Córdoba □ Spain 38°5N 5°0W 195 G6
Córdoba, Sierra de Argentina 31°10S 64°25W 334 C3
Cordon Phil. 16°42N 121°32E 232 C3
Cordova U.S.A. 60°33N 145°45W 303 F11
Corduff Ireland 53°23N 6°21W 120 A1
Corella Spain 42°7N 1°48W 196 C3
Corella → Australia 19°34S 140°47E 280 B3
Coremas Brazil 7°1S 37°58W 332 C4
Corentyne → Guyana 5°50N 57°8W 329 B6
Corfield Australia 21°40S 143°21E 280 C3
Corfu = Kerkyra Greece 39°38N 19°50E 206 B9
Corfu U.S.A. 42°57N 78°24W 312 D6
Corfu ✈ (CFU) Greece 39°35N 19°54E 204 B1
Corfu, Str. of = Kerkyras, Notio Steno Greece 39°34N 20°0E 206 B10
Corgo = O Corgo Spain 42°56N 7°25W 194 C3
Corguinho Brazil 19°53S 54°52W 331 D7
Cori Italy 41°39N 12°55E 200 A5
Coria Spain 39°58N 6°33W 194 F4
Coria del Río Spain 37°16N 6°3W 195 H4
Coricudgy Australia 32°51S 150°24E 283 B9
Corigliano Cálabro Italy 39°36N 16°31E 201 C9
Corimba, Barra de Angola 8°52S 13°9E 265 D2
Coringa Is. Australia 16°58S 149°58E 280 B4
Corinth = Korinthos Greece 37°56N 22°55E 204 D4
Corinth Grenada 12°2N 61°40W 323 q
Corinth Ky., U.S.A. 38°30N 84°34W 311 F12
Corinth Miss., U.S.A. 34°56N 88°31W 315 D10
Corinth N.Y., U.S.A. 43°15N 73°49W 313 C11
Corinth, G. of = Korinthiakos Kolpos Greece 38°16N 22°30E 204 C4
Corinth Canal Greece 37°58N 23°0E 204 D4
Corinto Brazil 18°20S 44°30W 333 E3
Corinto Nic. 12°30N 87°10W 320 D2
Coriole Somalia 1°47N 44°32E 267 D5
Corisco Eq. Guin. 0°55N 9°18E 264 B1
Cork Ireland 51°54N 8°29W 166 E3
Cork □ Ireland 51°57N 8°40W 166 E3
Cork Harbour Ireland 51°47N 8°16W 166 E3
Corlay France 48°20N 3°5W 172 D3
Corleone Italy 37°49N 13°18E 200 E6
Corleto Perticara Italy 40°23N 16°2E 201 B9
Çorlu Turkey 41°11N 27°49E 203 E11
Cormack L. Canada 60°56N 121°37W 296 A4
Cormano Italy 45°32N 9°10E 128 A2
Cormòns Italy 45°58N 13°28E 199 C10
Cormorant Canada 54°14N 100°35W 297 C8
Cormorant L. Canada 54°15N 100°50W 297 C8
Corn Is. = Maíz, Is. del Nic. 12°15N 83°4W 320 D3
Cornalvo △ Spain 39°1N 6°13W 195 F4
Cornaredo Italy 45°30N 9°1E 128 A1
Cornélio Procópio Brazil 23°7S 50°40W 335 A5
Cornell U.S.A. 41°0N 88°44W 311 D8
Corner Brook Canada 48°57N 57°58W 299 C8
Corner della Regina, Palazzo Venice, Italy 142 b2
Corner Inlet Australia 38°45S 146°20E 283 E7
Corner Seamounts Atl. Oc. 35°0N 52°0W 152 C6
Corner Spinelli, Palazzo Venice, Italy 142 b2
Cornești Moldova 47°21N 28°1E 183 C13
Corneto = Tarquinia Italy 42°15N 11°45E 199 F8
Corníglio Italy 44°29N 10°5E 198 D7
Corning Ark., U.S.A. 36°25N 90°35W 315 C9
Corning Calif., U.S.A. 39°56N 122°11W 304 G2
Corning Iowa, U.S.A. 40°59N 94°44W 310 D2
Corning N.Y., U.S.A. 42°9N 77°3W 312 D7
Corno Grande Italy 42°28N 13°34E 199 F10
Cornwall Ont., Canada 45°2N 74°44W 313 A10
Cornwall Pa., U.S.A. 40°17N 76°25W 313 F8
Cornwall □ Jamaica 18°15N 77°54W 320 a
Cornwall □ U.K. 50°26N 4°40W 169 G3
Cornwall I. Canada 77°37N 94°38W 295 B13
Cornwallis I. Canada 75°8N 95°0W 295 B13
Cornwell U.S.A. 27°23N 81°6W 317 H8
Corny Pt. Australia 34°55S 137°0E 282 C2
Coro Venezuela 11°25N 69°41W 328 A4
Coroaci Brazil 18°35S 42°17W 333 E3
Coroatá Brazil 4°8S 44°0W 332 B3
Corocoro Bolivia 17°15S 68°28W 330 D4
Corocoro, I. Venezuela 8°30N 60°10W 329 B5
Coroico Bolivia 16°0S 67°50W 330 D4
Coromandel Brazil 18°28S 47°13W 333 E2
Coromandel N.Z. 36°45S 175°31E 284 C4
Coromandel Coast India 12°30N 81°0E 245 H5
Coromandel Pen. N.Z. 37°0S 175°45E 284 D4
Coromandel Ra. N.Z. 37°0S 175°40E 284 D4
Coron Phil. 12°1N 120°12E 232 E3
Coron B. Phil. 11°54N 120°8E 233 F3
Coron I. Phil. 11°55N 120°14E 233 F3
Corona Calif., U.S.A. 33°53N 117°34W 307 M9
Corona N. Mex., U.S.A. 34°15N 105°36W 305 J11
Coronado U.S.A. 32°41N 117°10W 307 N9
Coronado, B. de Costa Rica 9°0N 83°40W 320 E3
Coronados, G. de los Chile 41°40S 74°0W 336 B2
Coronados, Is. Los Mexico 32°26N 117°19W 307 N9
Coronation Canada 52°5N 111°27W 296 C6
Coronation Gulf Canada 68°25N 110°0W 294 D10
Coronation I. Antarctica 60°45S 46°0W 151 C18
Coronation Is. Australia 14°57S 124°55E 278 B3
Coronda Argentina 31°58S 60°56W 334 C3
Coronel Chile 37°0S 73°10W 334 D1
Coronel Bogado Paraguay 27°11S 56°18W 334 B4
Coronel Dorrego Argentina 38°40S 61°10W 334 D3
Coronel Fabriciano Brazil 19°31S 42°38W 333 E3
Coronel Murta Brazil 16°37S 42°11W 333 E3
Coronel Oviedo Paraguay 25°24S 56°30W 334 B4
Coronel Ponce Brazil 15°34S 55°1W 331 D6
Coronel Pringles Argentina 38°0S 61°30W 334 D3
Coronel Suárez Argentina 37°30S 61°52W 334 D3
Coronel Vidal Argentina 37°28S 57°45W 334 D4
Corongo Peru 8°30S 77°53W 330 B2
Coropuna, Nevado Peru 15°30S 72°41W 330 D3
Çorovodë Albania 40°31N 20°14E 202 F4
Corowa Australia 35°58S 146°21E 283 C7
Corozal Colombia 9°19N 75°18W 328 B2
Corozal □ Belize 18°23N 88°23W 319 D7
Corozal Pt. Trin. & Tob. 10°45N 61°37W 323 t
Corps France 44°50N 5°56E 175 D9
Corpus Argentina 27°10S 55°30W 335 B4
Corpus Christi U.S.A. 27°47N 97°24W 314 H6
Corpus Christi, L. U.S.A. 28°2N 97°52W 314 G6
Corque Bolivia 18°20S 67°41W 330 D4
Corral Chile 39°52S 73°26W 336 A2
Corral de Almaguer Spain 39°45N 3°10W 194 F7
Corralejo Canary Is. 28°43N 13°53W 153 e2
Corraun Pen. Ireland 53°54N 9°54W 166 C2
Corréggio Italy 44°46N 10°47E 198 D7
Corregidor Phil. 14°23N 120°35E 232 D3
Corrente Brazil 10°27S 45°10W 332 D2
Corrente → Brazil 13°8S 43°28W 333 D3
Correntes → Brazil 17°38S 55°8W 331 D6
Correntes, C. das Mozam. 24°6S 35°34E 271 B6
Correntina Brazil 13°20S 44°39W 333 D3
Corrèze □ France 45°20N 1°45E 174 C5
Corrèze → France 45°10N 1°28E 174 C5
Corrib, L. Ireland 53°27N 9°16W 166 C2
Corridónia Italy 43°15N 13°30E 199 E10
Corrientes Argentina 27°30S 58°45W 334 B4
Corrientes □ Argentina 28°0S 57°0W 334 B4
Corrientes → Argentina 30°42S 59°38W 334 C4
Corrientes → Peru 3°43S 74°35W 328 D3
Corrientes, C. Colombia 5°30N 77°34W 328 B2
Corrientes, C. Cuba 21°43N 84°30W 320 B3
Corrientes, C. Jalisco, Mexico 20°25N 105°42W 318 C3
Corrigan U.S.A. 31°0N 94°52W 314 F7
Corrigin Australia 32°20S 117°53E 279 F2
Corriverton Guyana 5°55N 57°20W 329 B6
Corry U.S.A. 41°55N 79°39W 312 E5
Corryong Australia 36°12S 147°53E 283 D7
Corse □ France 42°0N 9°0E 175 G13
Corse, C. France 43°1N 9°25E 175 E13
Corse ⌂ France 42°14N 9°10E 175 F13
Corse-du-Sud □ France 41°45N 9°0E 175 G13
Corsica = Corse □ France 42°0N 9°0E 175 G13
Corsicana U.S.A. 32°6N 96°28W 314 E6
Córsico Italy 45°25N 9°6E 128 B1
Corsini, Palazzo Rome, Italy 136 c1
Corstorphine U.K. 55°56N 3°17W 121 B2
Corte France 42°19N 9°11E 175 F13
Corte Pinto Portugal 37°42N 7°29W 195 H3
Cortegana Spain 37°52N 6°49W 195 H4
Cortes Phil. 9°17N 126°11E 233 G6
Cortés, Mar de = California, G. de Mexico 27°0N 111°0W 318 B2
Cortez U.S.A. 37°21N 108°35W 305 H9
Córthaidh, Inis = Enniscorthy Ireland 52°30N 6°34W 166 D5
Cortina d'Ampezzo Italy 46°32N 12°8E 199 B9
Cortland N.Y., U.S.A. 42°36N 76°11W 313 D8
Cortland Ohio, U.S.A. 41°20N 80°44W 312 E4
Cortona Italy 43°16N 11°59E 199 E8
Corubal → Guinea-Biss. 11°57N 15°5W 262 C2
Coruche Portugal 38°57N 8°30W 195 G2
Çoruh → Turkey 41°38N 41°38E 191 K5
Çorum Turkey 40°30N 34°57E 212 B6
Çorum □ Turkey 40°40N 35°0E 212 B6
Corumbá Brazil 19°0S 57°30W 331 D6
Corumbá → Brazil 18°19S 48°55W 333 E2
Corumbá de Goiás Brazil 16°0S 48°50W 333 E2
Corumbaíba Brazil 18°9S 48°34W 333 E2
Corund Romania 46°30N 25°13E 183 D10
Corunna = A Coruña Spain 43°20N 8°25W 194 B2
Corunna U.S.A. 42°59N 84°7W 311 B12
Corvallis U.S.A. 44°34N 123°16W 304 D2
Corvette, L. de la Canada 53°25N 74°3W 298 B5
Corviale Italy 41°51N 12°25E 136 B1
Corvo Azores 39°42N 31°6W 153 d2
Coryal Trin. & Tob. 10°30N 61°11W 323 t
Corydon Ind., U.S.A. 38°13N 86°7W 311 F10
Corydon Iowa, U.S.A. 40°46N 93°19W 310 D3
Corydon Ky., U.S.A. 37°44N 87°43W 311 G9
Cosalá Mexico 24°23N 106°41W 318 C3
Cosamaloapan de Carpio Mexico 18°22N 95°48W 319 D5
Cosenza Italy 39°18N 16°15E 201 C9
Coșereni Romania 44°38N 26°35E 183 F11
Coshocton U.S.A. 40°16N 81°51W 312 F3
Coslada Spain 40°25N 3°35W 127 B2
Cosmo Newberry Australia 28°0S 122°54E 279 E3
Cosmo Newberry ⊙ Australia 27°59S 122°53E 279 E3
Cosmonaut Sea S. Ocean 66°30S 40°0E 151 C5
Cosne-Cours-sur-Loire France 47°24N 2°54E 173 E9
Coso Junction U.S.A. 36°3N 117°57W 307 J9
Coso Pk. U.S.A. 36°13N 117°44W 307 J9
Cospeito Spain 43°12N 7°34W 194 B3
Cosquín Argentina 31°15S 64°30W 334 C3
Cossato Italy 45°34N 8°10E 198 C5
Cossé-le-Vivien France 47°57N 0°54W 172 E6
Cossigny France 48°43N 2°40E 134 B4
Cosson → France 47°30N 1°15E 172 E8
Costa Blanca Spain 38°25N 0°10W 197 G4
Costa Brava Spain 41°30N 3°0E 196 D8
Costa Cálida Spain 37°30N 1°30W 197 H3
Costa Daurada Spain 41°12N 1°15E 196 D6
Costa del Sol Spain 36°30N 4°30W 195 J6
Costa dels Pins Spain 39°38N 3°26E 206 B4
Costa Maya Mexico 18°44N 87°42W 319 D7
Costa Mesa U.S.A. 33°38N 117°55W 307 M9
Costa Rica ■ Cent. Amer. 10°0N 84°0W 320 E3
Costa Smeralda Italy 41°5N 9°35E 200 A2
Costa Teguise Canary Is. 29°0N 13°31W 153 e2
Costantino, Arco di Rome, Italy 136 c3
Costermansville = Bukavu Dem. Rep. of the Congo 2°20S 28°52E 268 C2
Costești Romania 44°40N 24°53E 183 F9
Costigliole d'Asti Italy 44°47N 8°11E 198 D5
Cosumnes → U.S.A. 38°16N 121°26W 306 G5
Coswig Sachsen, Germany 51°7N 13°34E 178 D9
Coswig Sachsen-Anhalt, Germany 51°53N 12°27E 178 D8
Cotabato Phil. 7°14N 124°15E 233 H5
Cotacajes → Bolivia 16°0S 67°1W 330 D4
Cotagaita Bolivia 20°45S 65°40W 334 A2
Cotahuasi Peru 15°12S 72°50W 330 D3
Cotao Portugal 38°45N 9°17W 126 A1
Côte d'Azur France 43°25N 7°10E 175 E11
Côte-d'Ivoire = Ivory Coast ■ Africa 7°30N 5°0W 262 D4
Côte d'Or France 47°10N 4°50E 173 E11
Côte-d'Or □ France 47°30N 4°50E 173 E11
Côte-St-Luc Canada 45°28N 73°39W 130 B2
Coteau des Prairies U.S.A. 45°20N 97°50W 308 C5

Coteau du Missouri U.S.A. 47°0N 100°0W 308 B4
Cotegipe Brazil 12°2S 44°15W 333 D3
Cotentin France 49°15N 1°30W 172 C5
Côtes-d'Armor □ France 48°25N 2°40W 172 D4
Côtes de Meuse France 49°15N 5°22E 173 C12
Côtes-du-Nord = Côtes-d'Armor □ France 48°25N 2°40W 172 D4
Cotiella Spain 42°31N 0°19E 196 C5
Cotillo Canary Is. 28°41N 14°1W 153 e2
Cotiujeni Moldova 47°51N 28°33E 183 C13
Cotoca Bolivia 17°49S 63°3W 331 D5
Cotonou Benin 6°20N 2°25E 263 D5
Cotopaxi Ecuador 0°40S 78°30W 328 D2
Cotopaxi □ Ecuador 0°5S 78°55W 328 D2
Cotopaxi △ Ecuador 0°39S 78°24W 328 D2
Cotronei Italy 39°9N 16°47E 201 C9
Cotswold Hills U.K. 51°42N 2°10W 169 F5
Cottage Grove U.S.A. 43°48N 123°3W 304 E2
Cottageville U.S.A. 32°56N 80°29W 316 C9
Cottam Canada 42°8N 82°45W 312 D2
Cottbus Germany 51°45N 14°20E 178 D10
Cotton Ground St. Kitts & Nevis 17°11N 62°36W 322 d
Cottondale U.S.A. 30°48N 85°23W 316 E4
Cottonwood Ala., U.S.A. 31°3N 85°18W 316 D4
Cottonwood Ariz., U.S.A. 34°45N 112°1W 305 J7
Cotulla U.S.A. 28°26N 99°14W 314 G5
Cotunduba, I. de Brazil 22°57S 43°8W 135 B2
Coubre, Pte. de la France 45°42N 1°15W 174 C2
Coubron France 48°54N 2°34E 134 A4
Couches France 46°53N 4°30E 173 F11
Couço Portugal 38°59N 8°17W 195 G2
Coudersport U.S.A. 41°46N 78°1W 312 E6
Couedic, C. du Australia 36°5S 136°40E 282 D2
Couëron France 47°13N 1°44W 172 E5
Couesnon → France 48°38N 1°32W 172 D5
Couhé France 46°17N 0°11E 174 B4
Coulanges-sur-Yonne France 47°31N 3°33E 173 E10
Coulee City U.S.A. 47°37N 119°17W 304 C4
Coulee Dam Nat. Recr. Area = Lake Roosevelt ⌂ U.S.A. 48°5N 118°14W 304 B4
Coulibistrie Dominica 15°27N 61°28W 323 k
Coulman I. Antarctica 73°35S 170°0E 151 D11
Coulommiers France 48°50N 3°3E 173 D10
Coulon → France 43°51N 5°6E 175 E9
Coulonge → Canada 45°52N 76°46W 298 C4
Coulonges-sur-l'Autize France 46°29N 0°36W 174 B3
Coulounieix-Chamiers France 45°11N 0°42E 174 C4
Coulterville Calif., U.S.A. 37°43N 120°12W 306 H6
Coulterville Ill., U.S.A. 38°11N 89°36W 310 F7
Council Alaska, U.S.A. 64°53N 163°41W 303 D7
Council Ga., U.S.A. 30°37N 82°31W 316 E7
Council Idaho, U.S.A. 44°44N 116°26W 304 D5
Council Bluffs U.S.A. 41°16N 95°52W 308 E6
Council Grove U.S.A. 38°40N 96°29W 308 F5
Coupeville U.S.A. 48°13N 122°41W 306 B4
Courantyne = Corentyne → Guyana 5°50N 57°8W 329 B6
Courantyne → S. Amer. 5°55N 57°5W 329 B6
Courbevoie France 48°53N 2°14E 134 A2
Courcelles Belgium 50°28N 4°22E 170 D4
Courchevel France 45°25N 6°36E 175 C10
Courçon France 46°15N 0°50W 174 B3
Courland → Trin. & Tob. 11°13N 60°47W 323 s
Courmayeur Italy 45°47N 6°58E 198 C3
Couronne, C. France 43°19N 5°3E 175 E9
Cours-la-Ville France 46°7N 4°19E 173 F11
Coursan France 43°14N 3°4E 174 E7
Courseulles-sur-Mer France 49°20N 0°29W 172 C6
Courtenay B.C., Canada 49°45N 125°0W 296 D4
Courtenay Loiret, France 48°2N 3°3E 173 D10
Courtland Ont., Canada 42°51N 80°38W 312 D4
Courtland Calif., U.S.A. 38°20N 121°34W 306 G5
Courtrai = Kortrijk Belgium 50°50N 3°17E 170 D3
Courtright Canada 42°49N 82°28W 312 D2
Courtry France 48°55N 2°35E 134 A4
Coushatta U.S.A. 32°1N 93°21W 314 E8
Coutances France 49°3N 1°28W 172 C5
Coutras France 45°3N 0°8W 174 C3
Coutts Crossing Australia 29°49S 152°55E 281 D5
Couva Trin. & Tob. 10°25N 61°27W 323 t
Couva □ Trin. & Tob. 10°25N 61°27W 323 t
Couvin Belgium 50°3N 4°29E 170 D4
Covarrubias Spain 42°4N 3°31W 194 C7
Covasna Romania 45°50N 26°10E 183 E11
Covasna □ Romania 45°50N 26°0E 183 E10
Cove I. Canada 45°17N 81°44W 312 A3
Coveñas Colombia 9°24N 75°44W 328 B2
Covent Garden London, U.K. 125 b4
Coventry U.K. 52°25N 1°28W 169 E6
Coverdale U.S.A. 31°38N 83°58W 316 D6
Covilhã Portugal 40°17N 7°31W 194 E3
Covington Ga., U.S.A. 33°36N 83°51W 316 B6
Covington Ind., U.S.A. 40°9N 87°24W 311 D9
Covington Ky., U.S.A. 39°5N 84°30W 311 E12
Covington Ohio, U.S.A. 40°7N 84°21W 311 D12
Covington Tenn., U.S.A. 35°34N 89°39W 315 D10
Covington Va., U.S.A. 37°47N 79°59W 309 G14
Cowal, L. Australia 33°40S 147°25E 283 B7
Cowan, Cerro Ecuador 0°12S 90°48W 330 a
Cowan, L. Australia 31°45S 121°45E 279 F3
Cowan L. Canada 54°0N 107°15W 297 C7
Cowangie Australia 35°12S 141°26E 282 C4
Cowansville Canada 45°14N 72°46W 313 A12
Coward Springs Australia 29°24S 136°49E 281 D2
Cowcowing Lakes Australia 30°55S 117°20E 279 F2
Cowden U.S.A. 39°15N 88°52W 311 E8
Cowdenbeath U.K. 56°7N 3°21W 167 E5
Cowell Australia 33°39S 136°56E 282 B2
Cowes Vic., Australia 38°28S 145°14E 283 E6
Cowes I. of W., U.K. 50°45N 1°18W 169 G6
Cowgate Edinburgh, U.K. 121 b3
Cowichan L. Canada 48°53N 124°17W 306 B2
Cowley U.K. 51°31N 0°28W 125 A1
Cowlitz → U.S.A. 46°6N 122°55W 306 D4
Cowra Australia 33°49S 148°42E 283 B8
Cox Spain 38°8N 0°53W 197 G4
Coxilha Grande Brazil 28°18S 51°30W 335 B5
Coxim Brazil 18°30S 54°55W 331 D7
Coxim → Brazil 18°34S 54°46W 331 D7
Cox's Bazar Bangla. 21°26N 91°59E 241 E3
Coyah Guinea 9°42N 13°22W 262 D2
Coyoacán Mexico 19°21N 99°9W 128 B2
Coyote Wells U.S.A. 32°44N 115°58W 307 N11
Coyuca de Benitez Mexico 17°2N 100°4W 319 D4
Coyuca de Catalán Mexico 18°20N 100°39W 318 D4
Cozad U.S.A. 40°52N 99°59W 308 E4
Cozes France 45°34N 0°49W 174 C3
Cozumel Mexico 20°31N 86°55W 319 C7
Cozumel, Isla Mexico 20°30N 86°40W 319 C7
Crab Hill Barbados 13°19N 59°38W 323 r
Crabs Pen. Antigua & B. 17°7N 61°45W 322 b
Crac des Chevaliers Syria 34°47N 36°18E 250 D7
Cracow = Kraków Poland 50°4N 19°57E 185 H6
Cracow Australia 25°17S 150°17E 281 D5
Craddock Channel N.Z. 36°10S 175°13E 284 C4
Cradle Mt.-Lake St. Clair △ Australia 41°49S 147°56E 281 G4
Cradock S. Austral., Australia 32°6S 138°31E 281 E2
Cradock Eastern Cape, S. Africa 32°8S 25°36E 270 D4
Crafers Australia 35°0S 138°42E 282 C3
Craig Alaska, U.S.A. 55°29N 133°9W 303 J14
Craig Colo., U.S.A. 40°31N 107°33W 304 F10
Craigavon U.K. 54°27N 6°23W 166 B5
Craighall Park S. Africa 26°7S 28°1E 123 A2
Craigieburn Australia 37°36S 144°56E 283 D6
Craiglockhart U.K. 55°55N 3°14W 121 B2
Craigmillar U.K. 55°56N 3°9W 121 B3
Craigmore Zimbabwe 20°28S 32°50E 269 G3
Craik Canada 51°3N 105°49W 297 C7
Crailsheim Germany 49°8N 10°5E 179 F6
Craiova Romania 44°21N 23°48E 183 F8
Cramond U.K. 55°58N 3°18W 121 B2
Cramond Bridge U.K. 55°57N 3°19W 121 B1
Cramond I. U.K. 55°59N 3°17W 121 B2
Cramsie Australia 23°20S 144°15E 280 C3
Cranberry L. U.S.A. 44°11N 74°50W 313 B10
Cranberry Portage Canada 54°35N 101°23W 297 C8
Cranbrook W. Austral., Australia 34°18S 117°33E 279 F2
Cranbrook B.C., Canada 49°30N 115°46W 296 D5
Crandon U.S.A. 45°34N 88°54W 308 C9
Crandon Park U.S.A. 25°42N 80°9W 129 D3
Crane Oreg., U.S.A. 43°25N 118°35W 304 E4
Crane Tex., U.S.A. 31°24N 102°21W 314 F3
Crane, The Barbados 13°6N 59°27W 323 r
Cranford U.K. 51°29N 0°25W 125 B1
Cranganore India 10°13N 76°13E 245 J3
Cranston U.S.A. 41°47N 71°26W 313 E13
Craon France 47°50N 0°58W 172 E6
Craonne France 49°27N 3°46E 173 C10
Craponne-sur-Arzon France 45°19N 3°51E 174 C7
Crasna Romania 46°32N 27°51E 183 D12
Crasna → Romania 47°44N 22°35E 182 C7
Crasnei, Munţii Romania 47°0N 23°20E 183 C8
Crater L. St. Vincent 13°17N 61°13W 323 n
Crater L. Oreg., U.S.A. 42°56N 122°6W 304 E2
Crater Lake △ U.S.A. 42°55N 122°10W 304 E2
Crater Mt. Papua N. G. 6°37S 145°7E 286 D3
Crater Pt. Papua N. G. 5°25S 152°9E 286 C7
Craters of the Moon ⌂ U.S.A. 43°25N 113°30W 304 E7
Crateús Brazil 5°10S 40°39W 332 C3
Crati → Italy 39°43N 16°31E 201 C9
Crato Brazil 7°10S 39°25W 332 C4
Crato Portugal 39°16N 7°39W 195 F3
Craven, L. Canada 54°20N 76°56W 298 B4
Cravo Norte Colombia 6°18N 70°12W 328 B3
Cravo Norte → Colombia 6°18N 70°12W 328 B3
Crawford Western Cape, S. Africa 33°59S 18°30E 118 A2
Crawford Ala., U.S.A. 32°27N 85°11W 316 C4
Crawford Nebr., U.S.A. 42°41N 103°25W 308 D2
Crawfordsville Ind., U.S.A. 40°2N 86°54W 311 D10
Crawfordsville Iowa, U.S.A. 41°12N 91°32W 310 C5
Crawfordville Fla., U.S.A. 30°11N 84°23W 316 E5
Crawfordville Ga., U.S.A. 33°33N 82°54W 316 B7
Crawley U.K. 51°7N 0°11W 169 F7
Crayford U.K. 51°27N 0°11E 125 B5
Crazy Mts. U.S.A. 46°12N 110°20W 304 C8
Crean L. Canada 54°5N 106°9W 297 C7
Crécy-en-Ponthieu France 50°15N 1°53E 173 B8
Crediton Ont., Canada 43°17N 81°33W 312 C3
Crediton Devon, U.K. 50°47N 3°40W 169 G4
Cree → Sask., Canada 58°57N 105°47W 297 B7
Cree → Dumf. & Gall., U.K. 54°55N 4°25W 167 G4
Cree L. Canada 57°30N 106°30W 297 B7
Creede U.S.A. 37°51N 106°56W 305 H10
Creekmouth U.K. 51°30N 0°6E 125 A4
Creekside U.S.A. 40°40N 79°11W 312 F5
Creel Mexico 27°45N 107°38W 318 B3
Creemore Canada 44°19N 80°6W 312 B4
Creighton Sask., Canada 54°45N 101°54W 297 C8
Creighton Nebr., U.S.A. 42°28N 97°54W 308 D5
Creil France 49°15N 2°29E 173 C9
Crema Italy 45°22N 9°41E 198 C6
Cremona Italy 45°7N 10°2E 198 C7
Crepaja Serbia 45°1N 20°38E 182 E5
Crepori → Brazil 5°42S 57°8W 331 B6
Crépy France 49°35N 3°32E 173 C10
Crépy-en-Valois France 49°14N 2°54E 173 C9
Cres Croatia 44°58N 14°25E 199 D11
Crescent, L. U.S.A. 28°30N 81°33W 133 A1
Crescent Beach U.S.A. 29°46N 81°15W 316 F8
Crescent City Calif., U.S.A. 41°45N 124°12W 304 F1
Crescent City Fla., U.S.A. 29°26N 81°31W 317 F8
Crescent Hd. Australia 31°11S 152°59E 283 A10
Crescent L. U.S.A. 29°28N 81°30W 317 F8
Crescentino Italy 45°11N 8°6E 198 C5
Crescenzago Italy 45°30N 9°14E 128 A2
Crespi d'Adda Italy 45°35N 9°32E 198 C6
Crespo Argentina 32°2S 60°19W 334 C3
Cressely France 48°44N 2°6E 134 B1
Cresskill U.S.A. 40°56N 73°57W 132 A2
Cresson U.S.A. 40°28N 78°36W 312 F6
Cressy Australia 38°2S 143°40E 282 E5
Crest France 44°44N 5°2E 175 D9
Cresta, Mt. Phil. 17°17N 122°6E 232 C4
Crestline Calif., U.S.A. 34°14N 117°18W 307 L9
Crestline Ohio, U.S.A. 40°47N 82°44W 312 F2
Creston B.C., Canada 49°10N 116°31W 296 D5
Creston Calif., U.S.A. 35°32N 120°33W 306 K6
Creston Iowa, U.S.A. 41°4N 94°22W 310 C2
Crestview Calif., U.S.A. 37°46N 118°58W 306 H8
Crestview Fla., U.S.A. 30°46N 86°34W 317 E3
Crestwood U.S.A. 41°38N 87°46W 119 D2
Creswick Australia 37°25S 143°58E 282 D5
Crêt de la Neige France 46°16N 5°58E 173 F12
Crete = Kriti Greece 35°15N 25°0E 207 E6
Crete Ill., U.S.A. 41°27N 87°38W 311 C9
Crete Nebr., U.S.A. 40°38N 96°58W 308 E5
Crete, Sea of Greece 36°0N 25°0E 205 E7
Créteil France 48°47N 2°27E 134 B3
Cretin, C. Papua N. G. 6°40S 147°53E 286 D4
Creus, C. de Spain 42°20N 3°19E 196 C8
Creuse □ France 46°10N 2°0E 173 F9
Creuse → France 47°0N 0°34E 174 B4
Creutzwald France 49°12N 6°42E 173 C13
Creuzburg Germany 51°3N 10°14E 178 D6
Crèvecœur-le-Grand France 49°37N 2°5E 173 C9
Crevillent Spain 38°12N 0°48W 197 G4
Crewe U.K. 53°6N 2°26W 168 D5
Crewkerne U.K. 50°53N 2°48W 169 G5
Crianlarich U.K. 56°24N 4°37W 167 E4
Criciúma Brazil 28°40S 49°23W 335 B6
Cricklewood U.K. 51°33N 0°13W 125 A2
Cricova Moldova 47°8N 28°52E 183 C13
Cridersville U.S.A. 40°39N 84°9W 311 D12
Crieff U.K. 56°22N 3°50W 167 E5
Crikvenica Croatia 45°11N 14°40E 199 C11
Crimea □ Ukraine 45°30N 33°10E 189 K8
Crimean Pen. = Krymskyy Pivostriv Ukraine 45°0N 34°0E 189 K8
Crimmitschau Germany 50°48N 12°24E 178 E8
Cristal, Mts. de Gabon 0°30N 10°30E 264 B2
Cristalândia Brazil 10°36S 49°11W 332 D2
Cristino Castro Brazil 8°49S 44°13W 332 C3
Cristo Redentor, Corcovado Brazil 22°56S 43°12W 135 B1
Cristobal Panama 9°19N 79°54W 320 c
Cristóbal, Pta. Ecuador 0°54S 91°31W 330 a
Cristuru Secuiesc Romania 46°17N 25°2E 183 D10
Crişul Alb → Romania 46°42N 21°17E 182 D6
Crişul Negru → Romania 46°42N 21°16E 182 D6
Crişul Repede → Romania 46°55N 20°59E 182 D5
Crittenden U.S.A. 38°47N 84°36W 311 F12
Criuleni Moldova 47°13N 29°10E 183 C14
Crivitz Germany 53°34N 11°39E 178 B7
Crixás Brazil 14°27S 49°58W 333 D2
Crna → Macedonia 41°33N 21°59E 202 E5
Crna Gora = Montenegro ■ Europe 42°40N 19°20E 202 D3
Crna Gora Macedonia 42°10N 21°30E 202 D5
Crna Reka = Crna → Macedonia 41°33N 21°59E 202 E5
Crna Trava Serbia 42°49N 22°19E 202 D6
Crni Drim → Macedonia 41°17N 20°40E 202 E4
Crni Timok → Serbia 43°53N 22°15E 202 C6
Crnoljeva Planina = Zhar, Mali Kosovo 42°20N 21°0E 202 D5
Črnomelj Slovenia 45°33N 15°10E 199 C12
Croagh Patrick Ireland 53°46N 9°40W 166 C2
Croajingolong △ Australia 37°45S 149°26E 283 D8
Croatia ■ Europe 45°20N 16°0E 199 C13
Croce, Ex Chiesa della Venice, Italy 142 c3
Crockenhill U.K. 51°22N 0°9E 125 B4
Crocker U.S.A. 37°57N 92°16W 310 G4
Crocker, Banjaran Malaysia 5°40N 116°30E 235 A5
Crocker, Cerro Ecuador 0°36S 90°21W 330 a
Crocker Range △ Malaysia 5°33N 116°8E 235 A5
Crockett U.S.A. 31°19N 95°27W 314 F7
Crocodile = Umgwenya → Mozam. 25°14S 32°18E 271 C5
Crocodile → S. Africa 24°12S 26°53E 270 B4
Crocodile Is. Australia 12°3S 134°58E 280 A1
Crocq France 45°52N 2°21E 174 C6
Crocus B. Anguilla 18°13N 63°5W 322 a
Crodo Italy 46°13N 8°19E 198 B5
Crohy Hd. Ireland 54°55N 8°26W 166 B3
Croisette, C. France 43°14N 5°22E 175 E9
Croisic, Pte. du France 47°19N 2°31W 172 E4
Croissy-Beaubourg France 48°49N 2°39E 134 B4
Croissy-sur-Seine France 48°52N 2°8E 134 A1
Croix, L. la Canada 48°20N 92°15W 298 C1
Croker, C. N. Terr., Australia 10°58S 132°35E 278 B5
Croker, C. Ont., Canada 44°58N 80°59W 312 B4
Croker I. Australia 11°12S 132°32E 278 B5
Croker Islands Seas ☼ Australia 11°20S 132°30E 278 B5
Cromarty U.K. 57°40N 4°2W 167 D4
Cromer U.K. 52°56N 1°17E 168 E9
Crompton Pt. Dominica 15°35N 61°19W 323 k
Cromwell N.Z. 45°3S 169°14E 285 F4
Cromwell Conn., U.S.A. 41°36N 72°39W 313 E12
Cronat France 46°43N 3°40E 173 F10
Crook U.K. 54°43N 1°45W 168 C6
Crooked → B.C., Canada 54°50N 122°54W 296 C4
Crooked → Oreg., U.S.A. 44°32N 121°16W 304 D3
Crooked Creek U.S.A. 61°52N 158°7W 303 F8
Crooked I. Bahamas 22°50N 74°10W 321 B5
Crooked Island Passage Bahamas 22°55N 74°35W 321 B5
Crookston Minn., U.S.A. 47°47N 96°37W 308 B5
Crookston Nebr., U.S.A. 42°56N 100°45W 308 D3
Crookwell Australia 34°28S 149°24E 283 C8
Cropane-Micone ⌂ Italy 38°31N 16°18E 201 D9
Crosby Gauteng, S. Africa 26°11S 27°59E 123 B1
Crosby Mersey., U.K. 53°30N 3°3W 168 D4
Crosby N. Dak., U.S.A. 48°55N 103°18W 308 A2
Crosby Pa., U.S.A. 41°45N 78°23W 312 E6
Crosbyton U.S.A. 33°40N 101°14W 314 E4
Crosía Italy 39°35N 16°45E 201 C9
Crosne France 48°43N 2°27E 134 B3
Cross → Nigeria 4°42N 8°21E 263 E6
Cross City U.S.A. 29°38N 83°7W 317 F6
Cross Fell U.K. 54°43N 2°28W 168 C5
Cross I. India 18°56N 72°51E 130 B2
Cross L. Canada 54°45N 97°30W 297 C9
Cross Lake Canada 54°37N 97°47W 297 C9
Cross River □ Nigeria 6°0N 8°0E 263 D6
Cross River △ Nigeria 5°50N 9°50E 263 D6
Cross Sound U.S.A. 58°0N 135°0W 303 G14
Cross Timbers U.S.A. 38°1N 93°14W 310 F3
Crossen = Krosno Odrzańskie Poland 52°3N 15°7E 185 F2
Crossett U.S.A. 33°8N 91°58W 314 E9
Crosshaven Ireland 51°47N 8°17W 166 E3
Crossley, Mt. N.Z. 42°50S 172°5E 285 C7
Crossmaglen U.K. 54°5N 6°36W 166 B5
Crossmolina Ireland 54°6N 9°20W 166 B2
Crossville Ill., U.S.A. 38°10N 88°4W 311 F8
Crossville Tenn., U.S.A. 35°57N 85°2W 315 D12
Croswell U.S.A. 43°16N 82°37W 312 C2
Croton-on-Hudson U.S.A. 41°12N 73°55W 313 E11
Crotone Italy 39°5N 17°8E 201 C10
Crouch End U.K. 51°34N 0°7W 125 A3
Crow → Canada 59°41N 124°20W 296 B4
Crow Agency U.S.A. 45°36N 107°28W 304 D10
Crow Hd. Ireland 51°35N 10°9W 166 E1
Crowdy Bay △ Australia 31°45S 152°45E 283 A10
Crowell U.S.A. 33°59N 99°43W 314 E5
Crowl Cr. → Australia 32°0S 145°30E 283 B6
Crowley U.S.A. 30°13N 92°22W 314 F8
Crowley, L. U.S.A. 37°35N 118°42W 306 H8
Crown I. Papua N. G. 5°7S 146°58E 286 C4
Crown Mine S. Africa 26°12S 27°57E 123 B1
Crown Point Ind., U.S.A. 41°25N 87°22W 311 C9
Crown Point N.Y., U.S.A. 43°57N 73°26W 313 C11
Crown Point ✈ (TAB) Trin. & Tob. 11°9N 60°50W 323 s
Crown Pt. Trin. & Tob. 11°18N 60°51W 323 s
Crownpoint U.S.A. 35°41N 108°9W 305 J9
Crows Landing U.S.A. 37°23N 121°6W 306 H5
Crows Nest N.S.W., Australia 33°49S 151°12E 139 A2
Crows Nest Queens., Australia 27°16S 152°4E 281 D5
Crowsnest Pass Canada 49°40N 114°40W 296 D6
Croydon Queens., Australia 18°13S 142°14E 280 B3
Croydon London, U.K. 51°22N 0°5W 125 B3
Croydon □ U.K. 51°22N 0°5W 169 F7
Croydon Park Australia 33°55S 151°7E 139 B1
Crozet, Îs. Ind. Oc. 46°27S 52°0E 273 J4
Crozet Basin Ind. Oc. 39°0S 60°0E 273 H5
Crozon France 48°15N 4°30W 172 D2
Cruagh Mt. Ireland 53°14N 6°17W 120 B2
Cruce de Sardina Canary Is. 27°52N 15°22W 153 e1
Cruces, Punta Colombia 6°39N 77°32W 328 B2
Crumlin Ireland 53°19N 6°19W 120 B2
Crusheen Ireland 52°57N 8°53W 166 D3
Cruz, C. Cuba 19°50N 77°50W 320 C4
Cruz Alta Brazil 28°45S 53°40W 335 B5
Cruz Bay U.S. Virgin Is. 18°20N 64°48W 321 b
Cruz das Almas Brazil 12°0S 39°6W 333 D4
Cruz de Pau Portugal 38°37N 9°7W 126 B2
Cruz del Eje Argentina 30°45S 64°50W 334 C3
Cruzeiro Brazil 22°33S 45°0W 333 F3
Cruzeiro do Oeste Brazil 23°46S 53°4W 335 A5
Cruzeiro do Sul = Joaçaba Brazil 27°5S 51°31W 335 B5
Cruzeiro do Sul Brazil 7°35S 72°35W 330 B3
Cry L. Canada 58°45N 129°0W 296 B3
Crystal B. U.S.A. 28°50N 82°45W 317 G7
Crystal Bay U.S.A. 39°15N 120°0W 306 F7
Crystal Brook Australia 33°21S 138°12E 282 B3
Crystal City Mo., U.S.A. 38°13N 90°23W 310 F6
Crystal City Tex., U.S.A. 28°41N 99°50W 314 G5
Crystal Falls U.S.A. 46°5N 88°20W 308 B9
Crystal Lake Fla., U.S.A. 30°26N 85°42W 316 E4
Crystal Lake Ill., U.S.A. 42°14N 88°19W 311 B8
Crystal Palace U.K. 51°25N 0°4W 125 B3
Crystal River U.S.A. 28°54N 82°35W 317 G7
Crystal Springs U.S.A. 31°59N 90°21W 315 F9
Csenger Hungary 47°50N 22°41E 182 C7
Csepel Hungary 47°25N 19°4E 117 B2
Csepelsziget Hungary 47°25N 19°4E 117 B2
Csillaghegy Hungary 47°35N 19°2E 117 A2
Csillagtelep Hungary 47°24N 19°5E 117 B2
Csömör Hungary 47°33N 19°14E 117 A3
Csömöri-patak → Hungary 47°35N 19°5E 117 A3
Csongrád Hungary 46°43N 20°12E 182 D5
Csongrád □ Hungary 46°32N 20°15E 182 D5
Csorna Hungary 47°38N 17°18E 182 C2
Csurgo Hungary 46°16N 17°9E 182 D2
Cu Lao Hon Vietnam 10°54N 108°18E 237 G7
Cua Rao Vietnam 19°16N 104°27E 236 C5
Cuácua → Mozam. 17°54S 37°0E 269 F4
Cuále Angola 8°22S 16°10E 265 D3
Cuále → Angola 8°29S 15°1E 265 D3
Cuamato Angola 17°2S 15°7E 265 F3
Cuamba Mozam. 14°45S 36°22E 269 E4
Cuando Angola 14°34S 19°1E 265 E3
Cuando → Angola 17°30S 23°15E 265 F4
Cuando Cubango □ Angola 16°25S 20°0E 265 F4
Cuangar Angola 17°36S 18°39E 265 F3
Cuango = Kwango → Dem. Rep. of the Congo 3°14S 17°22E 264 C3
Cuango Lunda Norte, Angola 9°8S 18°3E 265 D3
Cuango Moxico, Angola 14°30S 19°0E 265 E3
Cuango Uíge, Angola 6°15S 16°42E 265 D3
Cuanza → Angola 9°21S 13°9E 265 D2
Cuanza Norte □ Angola 8°50S 14°30E 265 D2
Cuanza Sul □ Angola 10°50S 14°50E 265 E2
Cuao → Venezuela 4°55N 67°40W 328 C4
Cuare → Trin. & Tob. 10°36N 61°6W 323 t
Cuarto → Argentina 33°25S 63°2W 334 C3
Cuatir → Angola 17°1S 18°9E 265 F3
Cuatro Vientos Spain 40°22N 3°47W 127 B1
Cuatrociénegas Mexico 26°59N 102°5W 318 B4
Cuauhtémoc Chihuahua, Mexico 28°25N 106°52W 318 B3
Cuauhtémoc México, Mexico 19°25N 99°9W 128 B2
Cuba Portugal 38°10N 7°54W 195 G3
Cuba Mo., U.S.A. 38°4N 91°24W 310 F5
Cuba N. Mex., U.S.A. 36°1N 107°4W 305 H10
Cuba N.Y., U.S.A. 42°13N 78°17W 312 D6
Cuba ■ W. Indies 22°0N 79°0W 320 B4
Cuba City U.S.A. 42°36N 90°26W 310 B6
Cubagua, I. Venezuela 10°49N 64°11W 329 a
Cubal Angola 12°26S 14°3E 265 E2
Cubal → Angola 15°9S 12°9E 265 F2
Cubango → Africa 18°50S 22°25E 265 F4
Cubanja Angola 14°49S 21°20E 265 E4
Cubao Phil. 14°37N 121°3E 127 B2
Cubia Angola 15°58S 21°42E 265 F4
Çubuk Turkey 40°14N 33°3E 212 B5
Çubuklu Turkey 41°5N 29°4E 122 B2
Cuc Phuong △ Vietnam 20°17N 105°38E 236 B5
Cuche Trin. & Tob. 10°22N 61°10W 323 t
Cuchi Angola 14°37S 16°58E 265 E3
Cuchi → Angola 15°13S 17°20E 265 F3
Cuchillo-Co Argentina 38°20S 64°37W 336 A4
Cuchivero → Venezuela 7°40N 65°57W 328 B4
Cuchumatanes, Sierra de los Guatemala 15°35N 91°25W 320 C1
Cuckfield U.K. 51°1N 0°8W 169 F7
Cucuí Brazil 1°12N 66°50W 328 C4
Cucumbi Angola 10°17S 19°5E 265 E3
Cucurpé Mexico 30°20N 110°43W 318 A2
Cucurrupí Colombia 4°23N 76°56W 328 C2
Cúcuta Colombia 7°54N 72°31W 328 B3
Cudahy Calif., U.S.A. 33°57N 118°11W 126 C3
Cudahy Wis., U.S.A. 42°57N 87°51W 311 B9
Cudalbi Romania 45°46N 27°41E 183 E12
Cudarebe = Kudarebe Aruba 12°37N 70°4W 322 f
Cuddalore India 11°46N 79°45E 245 J4
Cuddapah India 14°30N 78°47E 245 G4
Cuddapan, L. Australia 25°45S 141°26E 280 D3
Cudgewa Australia 36°10S 147°42E 283 D7
Cudillero Spain 43°33N 6°9W 194 B4
Cudjoehead Montserrat 16°47N 62°12W 323 p
Cue Australia 27°25S 117°54E 279 E2
Cuebe → Angola 15°46S 17°32E 265 F3
Cuéllar Spain 41°23N 4°21W 194 D6
Cuemba Angola 11°50S 17°42E 265 E3
Cuenca Ecuador 2°50S 79°9W 328 D2
Cuenca Spain 40°5N 2°10W 196 E2
Cuenca □ Spain 40°0N 2°0W 196 F3
Cuenca, Serranía de Spain 39°55N 1°50W 196 F3
Cuenca Alta del Manzanares ⌂ Spain 40°40N 3°55W 194 E7
Cuerda del Pozo, Embalse de la Spain 41°51N 2°44W 196 D2
Cuernavaca Mexico 18°55N 99°15W 319 D5
Cuero U.S.A. 29°6N 97°17W 314 G6
Cuers France 43°14N 6°5E 175 E10
Cueva de la Quebrada del Toro △ Venezuela 10°46N 69°3W 328 A4
Cueva de los Guácharos △ Colombia 1°35N 76°1W 328 C2
Cuevas, Cerro Bolivia 22°0S 65°12W 331 E4
Cuevas de Vera = Cuevas del Almanzora Spain 37°18N 1°58W 197 H3
Cuevas del Almanzora Spain 37°18N 1°58W 197 H3
Cuevo Bolivia 20°15S 63°30W 331 E5
Cugir Romania 45°48N 23°25E 183 E8
Cugnaux France 43°32N 1°20E 174 E5
Cuhai-Bakony → Hungary 47°35N 17°54E 182 C2
Cuiabá Brazil 15°30S 56°0W 331 D6
Cuiabá → Brazil 17°5S 56°36W 331 D6
Cuicuilco, Pirámide de Mexico 19°18N 99°11W 128 C1
Cuihangcun China 22°27N 113°32E 219 a
Cuijk Neths. 51°44N 5°50E 170 C5
Cuilco Guatemala 15°24N 91°58W 320 C1
Cuillin Hills U.K. 57°13N 6°15W 167 D2
Cuillin Sd. U.K. 57°4N 6°20W 167 D2
Cuilo = Kwilu → Dem. Rep. of the Congo 3°22S 17°22E 265 C3
Cuilo Angola 8°12S 19°28E 265 D3
Cuilo-Futa Angola 6°28S 15°51E 265 D3
Cuima Angola 13°25S 15°45E 265 E3
Cuimba Angola 6°10S 14°41E 265 D2
Cuiseaux France 46°30N 5°22E 173 F12
Cuité Brazil 6°29S 36°9W 332 C4
Cuito → Angola 18°1S 20°48E 265 F4
Cuito Cuanavale Angola 15°10S 19°10E 265 F3
Cuitzeo, L. de Mexico 19°55N 101°5W 318 D4
Cuiuni → Brazil 0°45S 63°7W 329 D5
Cuivre → U.S.A. 38°56N 90°41W 310 F6
Cujmir Romania 44°13N 22°57E 182 F7
Cukai Malaysia 4°13N 103°25E 237 K4
Çukurca Turkey 37°14N 43°36E 213 D10
Cul-de-Sac St.-Maarten 18°2N 63°4W 322 a
Cul de Sac St.-Martin 18°6N 63°2W 322 a
Culasi Phil. 11°26N 122°3E 233 F4
Culbertson U.S.A. 48°9N 104°31W 304 B11
Culburra N.S.W., Australia 34°56S 150°46E 283 C9
Culburra S. Austral., Australia 35°50S 139°58E 282 C3
Culcairn Australia 35°41S 147°3E 283 C7
Culebra Puerto Rico 18°19N 65°18W 321 b
Culebra, Sierra de la Spain 41°55N 6°20W 194 D4
Culfa Azerbaijan 38°57N 45°38E 213 C11
Culgoa Australia 35°44S 143°6E 282 C5
Culgoa → Australia 29°56S 146°20E 281 D4
Culgoa Flood Plain △ Australia 28°58S 147°5E 281 D4
Culiacán Mexico 24°50N 107°23W 318 C3
Culiacán → Mexico 24°30N 107°42W 318 C3
Culik Indonesia 8°21S 115°37E 231 J18
Culion Phil. 11°54N 119°58E 233 F3
Culion I. Phil. 11°50N 120°0E 233 F2
Culiseu → Brazil 12°14S 53°17W 331 C7
Cúllar Spain 37°35N 2°34W 195 H8
Cullarin Ra. Australia 34°30S 149°30E 283 C8
Cullen U.K. 57°42N 2°49W 167 D6
Cullen Bullen Australia 33°18S 150°2E 283 B9
Cullen Pt. Australia 11°57S 141°54E 286 F1
Cullera Spain 39°9N 0°17W 197 F4
Cullman U.S.A. 34°11N 86°51W 315 D11
Culloden U.S.A. 32°52N 84°6W 316 C5
Cullom U.S.A. 40°53N 88°16W 311 D8
Cullompton U.K. 50°51N 3°24W 169 G4
Culmore U.S.A. 38°51N 77°8W 143 B2
Culo → Angola 6°13S 15°34E 265 D3
Culoz France 45°47N 5°46E 175 C9
Culpeper U.S.A. 38°30N 78°0W 309 F14
Culuene → Brazil 12°56S 52°51W 331 C7
Culver U.S.A. 41°13N 86°25W 311 C10
Culver, Pt. Australia 32°54S 124°43E 279 F3
Culver City U.S.A. 34°1N 118°24W 126 B2
Culverden N.Z. 42°47S 172°49E 285 C7
Culverton U.S.A. 33°19N 82°54W 316 B7
Cuma Angola 12°52S 15°5E 265 E3
Cumaná Venezuela 10°30N 64°5W 329 A5
Cumana B. Trin. & Tob. 10°48N 60°56W 323 t
Cumaovası Turkey 38°15N 27°9E 205 C9
Cumari Brazil 18°16S 48°11W 333 E2
Cumballa Hill Mumbai, India 130 a1
Cumbe = Euclides da Cunha Brazil 10°31S 39°1W 332 D4
Cumberland B.C., Canada 49°40N 125°0W 296 D4
Cumberland Ont., Canada 45°29N 75°24W 313 A9
Cumberland St. Vincent 13°16N 61°16W 323 n
Cumberland Iowa, U.S.A. 41°16N 94°52W 310 C2
Cumberland Md., U.S.A. 39°39N 78°46W 309 F14
Cumberland → U.S.A. 37°9N 88°25W 308 G9
Cumberland, B. Chile 33°37S 78°49W 330 c
Cumberland, C. Vanuatu 14°39S 166°37E 287 D4
Cumberland, L. U.S.A. 36°52N 85°9W 309 G11
Cumberland Gap ⌂ U.S.A. 36°36N 83°40W 309 G12
Cumberland I. U.S.A. 30°50N 81°25W 316 E8
Cumberland Is. Australia 20°35S 149°10E 280 b
Cumberland Island ⌂ U.S.A. 30°12N 81°24W 316 E8
Cumberland L. Canada 54°3N 102°18W 297 C8
Cumberland Pen. Canada 67°0N 64°0W 295 D19
Cumberland Plateau U.S.A. 36°0N 85°0W 315 D12
Cumberland Sd. Canada 65°30N 66°0W 295 D18
Cumbernauld U.K. 55°57N 3°58W 167 F5
Cumbira Angola 12°11S 15°8E 265 E3
Cumborah Australia 29°40S 147°45E 281 D4
Cumbres de Majalca △ Mexico 28°48N 106°30W 318 B3
Cumbres de Monterrey △ Mexico 25°26N 100°25W 318 B4
Cumbres Mayores Spain 38°4N 6°39W 195 G4
Cumbria □ U.K. 54°42N 2°52W 168 C5
Cumbrian Mts. U.K. 54°30N 3°0W 168 C5
Cumbum India 15°40N 79°10E 245 G4
Cuminá Brazil 1°57S 56°2W 329 D6
Cuminá → Brazil 1°30S 56°0W 329 D6
Cuminapanema → Brazil 1°9S 54°54W 329 D7
Cumming, C. Chile 27°6S 109°14W 330 b
Cummings Mt. U.S.A. 35°2N 118°34W 307 K8
Cummins Australia 34°16S 135°43E 281 E2
Cumnock N.S.W., Australia 32°59S 148°46E 283 B8
Cumnock E. Ayrs., U.K. 55°28N 4°17W 167 F4
Cumpas Mexico 30°2N 109°48W 318 B3
Cumplida, Pta. Canary Is. 28°50N 17°48W 153 e1
Çumra Turkey 37°34N 32°45E 212 D5
Cumuto Trin. & Tob. 10°35N 61°12W 323 t
Cunapo → Trin. & Tob. 10°35N 61°8W 323 t
Cuñare Colombia 0°49N 72°32W 328 C3
Cunaripa Trin. & Tob. 10°33N 61°10W 323 t
Cuncumén Chile 31°53S 70°38W 334 C1
Cundeelee ☼ Australia 30°43S 123°25E 279 F3
Cunderdin Australia 31°37S 117°12E 279 F2
Cundinamarca □ Colombia 5°0N 74°0W 328 C3
Cunene □ Angola 16°30S 15°0E 265 F3
Cunene → Angola 17°20S 11°50E 265 F2
Cúneo Italy 44°23N 7°32E 198 D4
Cung Son Vietnam 13°2N 108°58E 236 F7
Çüngüş Turkey 38°13N 39°17E 246 B3
Cunhinga Angola 12°11S 16°47E 265 E3
Cunhinga → Angola 10°42S 16°41E 265 E3
Cunillera, I. = Sa Conillera Spain 38°59N 1°13E 206 D1
Cunjamba Angola 15°27S 20°10E 265 F4
Cunlhat France 45°38N 3°32E 174 C7
Cunnamulla Australia 28°2S 145°38E 281 D4
Cunningham Bahamas 25°5N 77°26W 153 b
Cunupia Trin. & Tob. 10°32N 61°22W 323 t
Cuorgnè Italy 45°23N 7°39E 198 C4
Cupar Sask., Canada 50°57N 104°10W 297 C8
Cupar Fife, U.K. 56°19N 3°1W 167 E5
Cupcini Moldova 48°6N 27°23E 183 B12
Cupecé → Brazil 23°39S 46°40W 137 B1
Cupertino U.S.A. 37°19N 122°2W 306 H4
Cupica, G. de Colombia 6°25N 77°30W 328 B2
Ćuprija Serbia 43°57N 21°26E 202 C5
Curaçá Brazil 8°59S 39°54W 332 C4
Curaçao W. Indies 12°10N 69°0W 322 g
Curaçao Int. ✈ (CUR) Curaçao 12°11N 68°57W 322 g
Curacautín Chile 38°26S 71°53W 336 A2
Curador = Presidente Dutra Brazil 5°15S 44°30W 332 C3
Curahuara de Carangas Bolivia 17°52S 68°26W 330 D4
Curalhinho = Coelho Neto Brazil 4°15S 43°0W 332 B3
Curamata → Trin. & Tob. 10°11N 61°28W 323 t
Curanilahue Chile 37°29S 73°28W 334 D1
Curaray → Peru 2°20S 74°5W 328 D3
Curatabaca Venezuela 6°19N 62°51W 329 B5
Cure → France 47°40N 3°41E 173 E10
Curepipe Mauritius 20°19S 57°31E 272 e
Curepipe Point Mauritius 20°21S 57°31E 272 e
Curepto Chile 35°8S 72°1W 334 D1
Curiapo Venezuela 8°33N 61°5W 329 B5
Curicó Chile 34°55S 71°20W 334 C1
Curicuriari → Brazil 0°14S 66°48W 328 D4
Curieuse Seychelles 4°15S 55°44E 272 c
Curimatá Brazil 10°2S 44°17W 332 D3
Curinga Italy 38°49N 16°19E 201 D9
Curiplaya Colombia 0°16N 74°52W 328 C3
Curitiba Brazil 25°20S 49°10W 335 B6
Curitibanos Brazil 27°18S 50°36W 335 B5
Curlewis Australia 31°7S 150°16E 283 A9
Curoca → Angola 15°43S 11°55E 265 F2
Curonian Spit = Kuršių Nerijos △ Lithuania 55°30N 21°6E 184 C8
Currabubula Australia 31°16S 150°44E 283 A9
Currais Novos Brazil 6°13S 36°30W 332 C4
Curral Velho C. Verde Is. 16°8N 22°48W 153 j
Curralinho Brazil 1°45S 49°46W 332 B2
Currane, L. Ireland 51°49N 10°4W 166 E1
Currant U.S.A. 38°44N 115°28W 304 G6
Curraweena Australia 30°47S 145°54E 283 A6
Currawinya △ Australia 28°55S 144°27E 281 D3
Current → U.S.A. 36°15N 90°55W 314 C9
Currie Tas., Australia 39°56S 143°53E 281 F3
Currie Edinburgh, U.K. 55°54N 3°17W 121 B2
Currie Nev., U.S.A. 40°16N 114°45W 304 F6
Curt-Bunar = Tervel Bulgaria 43°45N 27°28E 203 C11
Curtea de Argeş Romania 45°12N 24°42E 183 E9
Curtici Romania 46°21N 21°18E 182 D6
Curtin Springs Australia 25°20S 131°45E 279 E5
Curtis U.S.A. 40°38N 100°31W 308 E3
Curtis Group Australia 39°30S 146°37E 281 F4
Curtis I. Queens., Australia 23°35S 151°10E 280 C5
Curtis I. Pac. Oc. 30°30S 178°34W 277 G15
Curuá → Pará, Brazil 2°24S 54°5W 329 D7
Curuá → Pará, Brazil 5°23S 54°22W 331 B7
Curuá, I. Brazil 0°48N 50°10W 332 A1
Curuaés → Brazil 7°30S 54°45W 331 B7
Curuaí Brazil 2°17S 55°29W 329 D6
Curuápanema → Brazil 2°25S 55°2W 329 D6
Curuçá Brazil 0°43S 47°50W 332 B2
Curuçá → Brazil 4°27S 71°23W 330 B3
Curuguaty Paraguay 24°31S 55°42W 335 A4
Çürüksu Çayi = Büyük Menderes → Turkey 37°28N 27°11E 205 D9
Curup Indonesia 3°26S 102°13E 234 C2
Curupira, Serra S. Amer. 1°25N 64°30W 329 C5
Cururu → Brazil 7°12S 58°3W 331 B6
Cururupu Brazil 1°50S 44°50W 332 B3
Curuzú Cuatiá Argentina 29°50S 58°5W 334 B4
Curvelo Brazil 18°45S 44°27W 333 E3
Cusago Italy 45°26N 9°1E 128 B1
Cusano Milanino Italy 45°33N 9°11E 128 A2
Cusco Peru 13°32S 72°0W 330 C3
Cusco □ Peru 13°31S 71°59W 330 C3
Cushendall U.K. 55°5N 6°4W 166 A5
Cushing U.S.A. 35°59N 96°46W 314 D6
Cushing, Mt. Canada 57°35N 126°57W 296 B3
Cusihuiriáchic Mexico 28°14N 106°50W 318 B3
Cusna, Mte. Italy 44°17N 10°23E 198 D7
Cussabat = Al Qaşabāt Libya 32°39N 14°1E 258 B2
Cusset France 46°8N 3°28E 173 F10
Cusseta U.S.A. 32°18N 84°47W 316 C5
Cusso, Sa. do Angola 6°30S 14°58E 265 D2
Custer U.S.A. 43°46N 103°36W 308 D2
Custom House Dublin, Ireland 120 b3
Cut Bank U.S.A. 48°38N 112°20W 304 B7
Cutchogue U.S.A. 41°1N 72°30W 313 E12
Cutervo Peru 6°25S 78°55W 330 B2
Cuthbert U.S.A. 31°46N 84°48W 316 D5
Cutler U.S.A. 36°31N 119°17W 306 J7
Cutler Park U.S.A. 42°17N 71°12W 116 B1
Cutler Ridge U.S.A. 25°35N 80°20W 317 K9
Cutlerville U.S.A. 42°50N 85°40W 311 B11
Cutral-Có Argentina 38°58S 69°15W 336 A3
Cutro Italy 39°2N 16°59E 201 C9
Cuttaburra → Australia 29°43S 144°22E 281 D3
Cuttack India 20°25N 85°57E 244 D7
Cuva → Angola 11°42S 14°52E 265 E2
Cuvelai Angola 15°44S 15°50E 265 F3
Cuvier, C. Australia 23°14S 113°22E 279 D1
Cuvier I. N.Z. 36°27S 175°50E 284 C4
Çuvuşabaşi → Turkey 40°58N 28°51E 122 B1
Cuwei China 39°54N 116°15E 114 B1
Cuxhaven Germany 53°51N 8°41E 178 B4
Cuyabeno Ecuador 0°16S 75°53W 328 D2
Cuyahoga Falls U.S.A. 41°8N 81°29W 312 E3
Cuyahoga Valley △ U.S.A. 41°24N 81°33W 312 E3
Cuyapo Phil. 15°46N 120°40E 232 D3
Cuyo Phil. 10°51N 121°2E 233 F3
Cuyo East Pass. Phil. 11°0N 121°28E 233 F3
Cuyo Islands Phil. 11°4N 120°57E 233 F3
Cuyo West Pass. Phil. 11°0N 120°30E 233 F3
Cuyuni → Guyana 6°23N 58°41W 329 B6
Cuzco = Cusco Peru 13°32S 72°0W 330 C3
Cuzco Bolivia 20°0S 66°50W 330 E4
Čvrsnica Bos.-H. 43°36N 17°35E 182 G2
Cwmbran U.K. 51°39N 3°2W 169 F4
Cyangugu Rwanda 2°29S 28°54E 268 C2
Cybinka Poland 52°12N 14°46E 185 F1
Cyclades Greece 37°0N 24°30E 204 E6
Cyclades □ Greece 37°0N 25°0E 204 D6
Cygnet Australia 43°8S 147°1E 281 G4
Cynthiana U.S.A. 38°23N 84°18W 311 F12
Cypress Hills Sask., Canada 49°40N 109°30W 297 D7
Cypress Hills N.Y., U.S.A. 40°41N 73°53W 132 B2
Cypress Hills ⌂ Canada 49°40N 109°30W 297 D7
Cypress Park U.S.A. 34°6N 118°13W 126 B3
Cyprus ■ Asia 35°0N 33°0E 207 F9
Cyrenaica = Barqa Libya 27°0N 23°0E 258 B4
Cyrene Libya 32°53N 21°52E 258 B4
Czaplinek Poland 53°34N 16°14E 184 E3
Czar Canada 52°27N 110°50W 297 C6
Czarna → Łódzkie, Poland 51°18N 19°55E 185 G6
Czarna → Świętokrzyskie, Poland 50°28N 21°21E 185 H8
Czarna Białostocka Poland 53°18N 23°17E 185 E10
Czarna Woda Poland 53°51N 18°6E 184 E5
Czarne Poland 53°42N 16°58E 184 E3
Czarnków Poland 52°55N 16°38E 185 F3
Czaslau = Čáslav Czech Rep. 49°54N 15°22E 180 B8
Czech Rep. ■ Europe 50°0N 15°0E 180 B8
Czechowice-Dziedzice Poland 49°54N 18°59E 185 J5
Czempiń Poland 52°9N 16°43E 185 F3
Czeremcha Poland 52°31N 23°21E 185 F10
Czerniejewo Poland 52°26N 17°30E 185 F4
Czernowitz = Chernivtsi Ukraine 48°15N 25°52E 183 B10
Czernriaków Poland 52°11N 21°3E 143 B2
Czersk Poland 53°46N 17°58E 184 E4
Czerwieńsk Poland 52°1N 15°23E 185 F2
Czerwionka-Leszczyny Poland 50°7N 18°37E 185 H5
Częstochowa Poland 50°49N 19°7E 185 H6
Człopa Poland 53°6N 16°6E 185 E3
Człuchów Poland 53°41N 17°22E 184 E4
Czortów = Chortkiv Ukraine 49°2N 25°46E 177 D13
Czyste Poland 52°13N 20°57E 143 B1
Czyżew-Osada Poland 52°48N 22°19E 185 F9

D

D.C. War Memorial *Washington, D.C., U.S.A.* **143** b1
D.H.A. Phase VIII *Pakistan* 24°47N 67°2E **123** B2
Da → *Vietnam* 21°15N 105°20E **228** G5
Da Hinggan Ling *China* 48°0N 121°0E **219** B13
Da Lat *Vietnam* 11°56N 108°25E **237** G7
Da Moóca → *Brazil* 23°35S 46°35W **137** B2
Da Nang *Vietnam* 16°4N 108°13E **236** D7
Da Qaidam *China* 37°50N 95°15E **218** D8
Da Yunhe → *Hopei, China* 39°10N 117°10E **227** E9
Da Yunhe → *Jiangsu, China* 34°25N 120°5E **227** G11
Da'an *China* 45°30N 124°7E **227** B13
Daan Viljoen ⌂ *Namibia* 22°2S 16°45E **270** B2
Daanbantayan *Phil.* 11°17N 124°2E **233** F5
Dab'a, Ras el *Egypt* 31°3N 28°31E **256** H6
Daba Shan *China* 32°0N 109°0E **228** B7
Dabai *Nigeria* 11°25N 5°15E **263** C6
Dabajuro *Venezuela* 11°2N 70°40W **328** A3
Dabakala *Ivory C.* 8°15N 4°20W **262** D4
Dabaka *India* 26°7N 92°52E **241** B4
Dabaro *Somalia* 6°21N 48°43E **267** C6
Dabas *Hungary* 47°11N 19°19E **182** C4
Dabat *Ethiopia* 12°58N 37°41E **257** E4
Dabbagh, Jabal *Si. Arabia* 27°52N 35°45E **246** E2
Dabeiba *Colombia* 7°1N 76°16W **328** B2
Daber = Dobra *Poland* 53°34N 15°20E **184** E2
Dabhoi *India* 22°10N 73°20E **242** H5
Dąbie *Poland* 52°5N 18°50E **185** F5
Dabie Shan *China* 31°20N 115°20E **229** B10
Dabilda *Cameroon* 12°45N 14°35E **259** F2
Dabl, W. → *Si. Arabia* 29°5N 36°16E **251** J7
Ďáblice *Czech Rep.* 50°8N 14°29E **135** B2
Dabnou *Niger* 14°10N 5°22E **263** C6
Dabo *Indonesia* 0°30S 104°33E **234** C2
Dabola *Guinea* 10°50N 11°5W **262** C2
Dabou *Ivory C.* 5°20N 4°23W **262** D4
Daboya *Ghana* 9°30N 1°20W **263** D4
Dabravolya *Belarus* 52°55N 23°59E **185** F10
Dąbrowa *Poland* 52°19N 20°52E **143** B1
Dąbrowa Białostocka *Poland* 53°40N 23°21E **184** E10
Dąbrowa Górnicza *Poland* 50°15N 19°10E **185** H6
Dąbrowa Tarnowska *Poland* 50°10N 20°59E **185** H7
Dabu *China* 24°22N 116°41E **229** E11
Dabugam *India* 19°27N 82°26E **244** E6
Dabung *Malaysia* 5°23N 102°1E **237** K4
Dabus → *Ethiopia* 10°48N 35°10E **257** E4
Dacato → *Ethiopia* 7°25N 42°40E **257** F5
Dacca = Dhaka *Bangla.* 23°43N 90°26E **241** D3
Dachang *Jiangsu, China* 32°13N 118°45E **229** A12
Dachang *Shanghai, China* 31°17N 121°24E **138** B1
Dachang ✈ *China* 31°18N 121°25E **138** B1
Dachaoshan Dam *China* 24°1N 100°22E **228** E3
Dachau *Germany* 48°15N 11°26E **131** A1
Dachau-Ost *Germany* 48°15N 11°27E **131** A1
Dachauer Moos *Germany* 48°13N 11°27E **131** A1
Dachigam △ *India* 34°10N 75°0E **242** B6
Dachstein, Hoher *Austria* 47°28N 13°35E **180** D6
Dačice *Czech Rep.* 49°5N 15°26E **180** B8
Dacre *Canada* 45°22N 76°57W **312** A8
Dacula *U.S.A.* 33°59N 83°54W **316** B6
Dadanawa *Guyana* 2°50N 59°30W **329** C6
Dadar *India* 19°0N 72°49E **130** A1
Daday *Turkey* 41°28N 33°27E **212** B5
Dade City *U.S.A.* 28°22N 82°11W **317** G7
Dadès, Oued → *Morocco* 30°58N 6°44W **260** B3
Dadeville *U.S.A.* 32°50N 85°46W **316** C4
Dadhar *Pakistan* 29°28N 67°39E **242** E2
Dadiya *Nigeria* 9°35N 11°24E **263** D7
Ḍadnah *U.A.E.* 25°32N 56°22E **247** E8
Dadohae △ *S. Korea* 34°0N 126°0E **224** E3
Dadra = Achalpur *India* 21°22N 77°32E **244** D3
Dadra & Nagar Haveli □ *India* 20°5N 73°0E **244** D1
Dadri = Charkhi Dadri *India* 28°37N 76°17E **242** E7
Dadu *Pakistan* 26°45N 67°45E **242** F2
Dadu He → *China* 29°31N 103°46E **228** C4
Daebang *S. Korea* 37°30N 126°55E **137** B1
Daebudo *S. Korea* 37°14N 126°35E **224** D3
Daecheongdo *S. Korea* 37°49N 124°42E **224** D2
Daechi *S. Korea* 37°30N 127°2E **137** B2
Daegu *S. Korea* 35°50N 128°37E **224** E4
Daejeon *S. Korea* 36°20N 127°28E **224** D3
Daejeon □ *S. Korea* 36°20N 127°25E **224** D3
Daejeong *S. Korea* 33°8N 126°17E **224** a
Daemodo *S. Korea* 34°11N 126°45E **224** E3
Daet *Phil.* 14°2N 122°55E **232** D4
Daeyeonpyeong = Yeonpyeongdo *S. Korea* 37°40N 125°45E **224** D2
Dafang *China* 27°9N 105°39E **228** D5
Dafdaf, J. *Si. Arabia* 28°16N 35°35E **251** K6
Dafeng *China* 33°3N 120°45E **227** H11
Dafnes *Greece* 35°13N 25°3E **207** E6
Dafni *Athina, Greece* 37°55N 23°44E **112** B2
Dafni *Pelóponnese, Greece* 37°48N 22°1E **204** D4
Dafnoudi, Akra *Greece* 38°28N 20°32E **207** C2
Dağ *Turkey* 37°12N 30°31E **205** D12
Daga Post *South Sudan* 9°13N 33°58E **266** C3
Dagali *Norway* 60°25N 8°28E **164** D5
Dagana *Senegal* 16°30N 15°35W **262** B1
Dagash *Sudan* 19°19N 33°25E **256** D3
Dagenham *U.K.* 51°32N 0°8E **125** A4
Dagestan □ *Russia* 42°30N 47°0E **191** J8
Dagestanskiye Ogni *Russia* 42°6N 48°12E **191** J9
Dagg Sd. *N.Z.* 45°23S 166°45E **285** F1
Daggett *U.S.A.* 34°52N 116°52W **307** L10
Daghestan Republic = Dagestan □ *Russia* 42°30N 47°0E **191** J8
Daghfeli *Sudan* 19°18N 32°40E **256** D3
Daglfing *Germany* 48°8N 11°39E **131** B2
Dağlıq Qarabağ = Nagorno-Karabakh □ *Azerbaijan* 39°55N 46°45E **213** C12
Dagö = Hiiumaa *Estonia* 58°50N 22°45E **188** C2
Dagu *China* 38°59N 117°40E **227** E9
Dagua *Papua N. G.* 3°27S 143°20E **286** B2
Daguan *China* 27°43N 103°56E **228** D4
Dagupan *Phil.* 16°3N 120°20E **232** C3
Daguragu *Australia* 17°33S 130°30E **278** C5
Daguragu ⊙ *Australia* 17°24S 130°48E **278** C5
Dahab *Egypt* 28°31N 34°31E **251** K5
Dahab, Geziret el *Egypt* 29°59N 31°13E **117** B2
Dahanu *India* 19°58N 72°44E **244** E1
Daheisha *West Bank* 31°42N 35°11E **252** B4
Dahivadi *India* 17°43N 74°33E **244** F2
Dahlak Kebir *Eritrea* 15°50N 40°10E **257** D5
Dahlak Marine △ *Eritrea* 15°35N 40°15E **257** D5
Dahlem *Germany* 52°27N 13°16E **115** B2
Dahlenburg *Germany* 53°11N 10°44E **178** B6
Dahlonega *U.S.A.* 34°32N 83°59W **315** D13
Dahlwitz-Hoppegarten *Germany* 52°30N 13°41E **115** A5
Dahme *Germany* 51°52N 13°25E **178** D9
Dahod *India* 22°50N 74°15E **242** H6
Dahomey = Benin ■ *Africa* 10°0N 2°0E **263** C5
Dahong Shan *China* 31°25N 113°0E **229** B9
Dahongliutan *China* 35°45N 79°20E **243** B8
Dahongmen *China* 39°48N 116°21E **114** C2
Dahra *Libya* 29°30N 17°50E **258** C3
Dahra *Senegal* 15°22N 15°30W **262** B1
Dahra, Massif de *Algeria* 36°7N 1°21E **261** A5
Dahshûr *Egypt* 29°45N 31°14E **256** J7
Dahūk *Iraq* 36°50N 43°1E **213** D10
Dahūk □ *Iraq* 36°50N 42°50E **213** D10
Dahuofan Shuiku *China* 41°52N 124°12E **224** B2
Daḥy, Nafūd ad *Si. Arabia* 22°0N 45°25E **248** B4
Dai *Solomon Is.* 7°54S 160°40E **287** L11
Dai Hao *Vietnam* 18°1N 106°25E **236** C6
Dai-Sen *Japan* 35°22N 133°32E **222** B5
Dai Shan *China* 30°25N 122°10E **229** B14
Dai Xian *China* 39°4N 112°58E **226** E7
Daiba = Odaiba *Japan* 35°38N 139°47E **140** B3
Daicheng *China* 38°42N 116°38E **226** E9
Daigo *Japan* 36°46N 140°21E **223** A12
Daik-u *Burma* 17°47N 96°40E **241** G6
Daikondi = Dāykondī □ *Afghan.* 34°0N 66°0E **240** B2
Dailekh *Nepal* 28°50N 81°44E **243** E9
Daimanji-San *Japan* 36°14N 133°20E **222** A5
Daimiel *Spain* 39°5N 3°35W **195** F7
Daingean *Ireland* 53°18N 7°17W **166** C4
Daingean, An = Dingle *Ireland* 52°9N 10°17W **166** D1
Daingkog *China* 32°30N 97°58E **228** A1
Daintree *Australia* 16°20S 145°20E **280** B4
Daintree △ *Australia* 16°8S 145°2E **280** B4
Daiō-Misaki *Japan* 34°15N 136°45E **223** C8
Dair, J. ed *Sudan* 12°27N 30°42E **257** E3
Dairen = Dalian *China* 38°50N 121°40E **227** E11
Dairûṭ *Egypt* 27°34N 30°43E **256** B3
Daisen *Japan* 39°27N 140°29E **220** E10
Daisen-Oki △ *Japan* 35°23N 133°34E **222** B5
Daisetsu-Zan *Japan* 43°30N 142°57E **220** C11
Daisetsu-Zan △ *Japan* 43°30N 142°55E **220** C11
Daitari *India* 21°10N 85°46E **244** D7
Daitō *Japan* 35°19N 132°58E **222** B4
Daiyun Shan *China* 25°50N 118°15E **229** E12
Dajarra *Australia* 21°42S 139°30E **280** C2
Dajiaoting *China* 39°51N 116°27E **114** B2
Dajiawa *China* 37°9N 119°0E **227** F10
Dajin Chuan → *China* 31°16N 101°59E **228** B3
Dak Dam *Cambodia* 12°20N 107°21E **236** F6
Dak Nhe *Vietnam* 15°28N 107°48E **236** E6
Dak Pek *Vietnam* 15°4N 107°44E **236** E6
Dak Song *Vietnam* 12°19N 107°35E **237** F6
Dak Sui *Vietnam* 14°55N 107°43E **236** E6
Dakar *Senegal* 14°34N 17°29W **262** C1
Dakar □ *Senegal* 14°45N 17°20W **262** C1
Dakhal, W. el → *Egypt* 28°48N 32°47E **251** K3
Dakhin *Bangla.* 22°30N 90°45E **241** D3
Dakhla *W. Sahara* 23°50N 15°53W **260** D1
Dakhla, El Wâhât el *Egypt* 25°30N 28°50E **256** B2
Dakhnoye *Russia* 59°49N 30°15E **137** C1
Dakingari *Nigeria* 11°37N 4°1E **263** C5
Dakoank *India* 7°2N 93°43E **245** L11
Dakor *India* 22°45N 73°11E **242** H5
Dakoro *Niger* 14°31N 6°46E **263** C6
Dakota City *Iowa, U.S.A.* 42°43N 94°12W **310** B2
Dakota City *Nebr., U.S.A.* 42°25N 96°25W **308** D5
Đakovica = Gjakovë *Kosovo* 42°22N 20°26E **202** D4
Đakovo *Croatia* 45°19N 18°24E **182** E3
Dal *Norway* 59°53N 8°40E **164** E5
Dala *Lunda Sul, Angola* 11°3S 20°17E **265** E4
Dala *Uíge, Angola* 8°5S 15°49E **265** D3
Dala *Solomon Is.* 8°30S 160°41E **287** M11
Dala-Cachibo *Angola* 10°30S 14°41E **265** E2
Dala-Järna *Sweden* 60°33N 14°26E **162** D8
Dalaba *Guinea* 10°47N 12°12W **262** C2
Dalachi *China* 36°48N 105°0E **226** F3
Dalagan = San Antonio *Phil.* 14°57N 120°5E **232** D3
Dalaguete *Phil.* 9°46N 123°32E **233** G4
Dalai Nur *China* 43°20N 116°45E **226** C9
Dālakī *Iran* 29°26N 51°17E **247** D6
Dalälven → *Sweden* 60°12N 16°43E **162** D10
Dalaman *Turkey* 36°48N 28°47E **205** E10
Dalaman → *Turkey* 36°41N 28°43E **205** E10
Dalandzadgad *Mongolia* 43°27N 104°30E **226** C3
Dalanganem Is. *Phil.* 10°40N 120°17E **233** F3
Dalap-Uliga-Darrit = Majuro *Marshall Is.* 7°9N 171°12E **288** G9
Dalarna *Sweden* 61°0N 14°0E **162** D8
Dalarnas län □ *Sweden* 61°0N 14°15E **162** C8
Dalasýsla *Iceland* 65°15N 22°0W **155** B4
Dalat *Malaysia* 2°44N 111°56E **235** B4
Dalay *Mongolia* 43°28N 103°30E **226** C2
Dālbandīn *Pakistan* 29°0N 64°23E **240** C2
Dalbeattie *U.K.* 54°56N 3°50W **167** G5
Dalbeg *Australia* 20°16S 147°18E **280** C4
Dalbosjön *Sweden* 58°40N 12°45E **163** F6
Dalby *Queens., Australia* 27°10S 151°17E **281** D5
Dalby *Skåne, Sweden* 55°40N 13°22E **163** J7
Dalby Söderskog △ *Sweden* 55°41N 13°21E **163** J7
Dale *Sogn og Fjordane, Norway* 61°22N 5°23E **164** C2
Dale *Ind., U.S.A.* 33°10N 86°59W **311** F10
Dale City *U.S.A.* 33°38N 77°19W **309** F15
Dale Hollow L. *U.S.A.* 36°32N 85°27W **315** C12
Dalejsky potok → *Czech Rep.* 50°2N 14°24E **135** B2
Dalen *Norway* 59°25N 8°0E **164** E4
Dalet *Burma* 19°59N 93°51E **241** F4
Daletme *Burma* 21°36N 92°46E **241** E4
Daleville *Ala., U.S.A.* 31°19N 85°43W **316** D4
Daleville *Ind., U.S.A.* 40°7N 85°33W **311** D11
Dalga *Egypt* 27°39N 30°41E **256** B3
Dalgān *Iran* 27°31N 59°19E **247** E8
Dalgety Bay *U.K.* 56°2N 3°20W **121** A1
Dalhart *U.S.A.* 36°4N 102°31W **314** C3
Dalhousie *N.B., Canada* 48°5N 66°26W **299** C6
Dalhousie *India* 32°38N 75°58E **242** C6
Dali *Shaanxi, China* 34°48N 109°58E **226** G5
Dali *Yunnan, China* 25°40N 100°10E **228** E3
Dalian *China* 38°50N 121°40E **227** E11
Dalian Shang *China* 38°55N 121°40E **228** ...
Daliang Shan *China* 28°0N 102°45E **228** D4
Daling He → *China* 40°55N 121°40E **227** D11
Dalj *Croatia* 45°29N 18°59E **182** E3
Dalkeith *Midloth., U.K.* 55°54N 3°4W **121** B3
Dalkeith *Fla., U.S.A.* 30°0N 85°9W **316** E4
Dalkey *Ireland* 53°16N 6°6W **120** B3
Dalkey I. *Ireland* 53°17N 6°5W **120** B3
Dallas *Ga., U.S.A.* 33°55N 84°51W **316** B5
Dallas *Oreg., U.S.A.* 44°55N 123°19W **304** D2
Dallas *Tex., U.S.A.* 32°47N 96°48W **314** E6
Dallas City *U.S.A.* 40°38N 91°10W **310** D5
Dalle = Yirga Alem *Ethiopia* 6°48N 38°22E **257** F4
Dalles, The *U.S.A.* 45°36N 121°10W **304** D3
Dallgow *Germany* 52°32N 13°5E **115** A1
Dallol *Ethiopia* 14°14N 40°17E **257** E5
Dalmā *U.A.E.* 24°30N 52°20E **247** E7
Dalmacija *Croatia* 43°20N 17°0E **199** E13
Dalmas, L. *Canada* 53°30N 71°50W **299** B5
Dalmatia = Dalmacija *Croatia* 43°20N 17°0E **199** E13
Dalmau *India* 26°4N 81°2E **243** F9
Dalmellington *U.K.* 55°19N 4°23W **167** F4
Dalmeny *N.S.W., Australia* 36°10S 150°8E **283** D9
Dalmeny *Edinburgh, U.K.* 55°59N 3°22W **121** B1
Dalnegorsk *Russia* 44°32N 135°33E **220** B7
Dalnerechensk *Russia* 45°50N 133°40E **220** B6
Dalnevostochnyy □ *Russia* 67°0N 140°0E **215** C14
Dalny = Dalian *China* 38°50N 121°40E **227** E11
Daloa *Ivory C.* 7°0N 6°30W **262** D3
Dalou Shan *China* 28°15N 107°0E **228** C6
Dalry *U.K.* 55°42N 4°43W **167** F4
Dalrymple, L. *Australia* 20°40S 147°0E **280** C4
Dalrymple, Mt. *Australia* 21°1S 148°39E **280** b
Dals Långed *Sweden* 58°56N 12°18E **163** F6
Dalsætra *Norway* 61°28N 9°26E **164** C6
Dalsjöfors *Sweden* 57°46N 13°5E **163** G7
Dalsland *Sweden* 58°50N 12°15E **163** F6
Dalsmynni *Iceland* 64°48N 21°29W **155** C5
Dalston *U.K.* 51°32N 0°4W **125** A3
Daltenganj *India* 24°0N 84°4E **243** H11
Dalton *Ga., U.S.A.* 34°46N 84°58W **315** D12
Dalton *Mass., U.S.A.* 42°28N 73°11W **313** D11
Dalton *Nebr., U.S.A.* 41°25N 102°58W **308** E2
Dalton, Kap *Greenland* 69°25N 24°3W **154** D8
Dalton-in-Furness *U.K.* 54°10N 3°11W **168** C4
Daludalu *Indonesia* 1°4N 100°15E **234** B2
Dalupiri I. *Cagayan, Phil.* 19°5N 121°12E **232** B3
Dalupiri I. *N. Samar, Phil.* 12°25N 124°16E **232** E5
Dalvik *Iceland* 65°58N 18°32W **155** B8
Dálvvadis = Jokkmokk *Sweden* 66°35N 19°50E **160** C18
Dalwallinu *Australia* 30°17S 116°40E **279** F2
Daly → *Australia* 13°35S 130°19E **278** B5
Daly City *U.S.A.* 37°42N 122°27W **136** B2
Daly L. *Canada* 56°32N 105°39W **297** B7
Daly River *Australia* 13°46S 130°42E **278** B5
Daly River-Port Keats ⊙ *Australia* 14°13S 129°36E **278** B4
Daly Waters *Australia* 16°15S 133°24E **280** B1
Dalyan *Turkey* 36°50N 28°39E **205** E10
Dam *Amsterdam, Neths.* **112** a2
Dam Doi *Vietnam* 8°50N 105°12E **237** H5
Dam Ha *Vietnam* 21°21N 107°36E **236** B6
Damachova *Belarus* 51°45N 23°36E **185** G10
Damaia *Portugal* 38°44N 9°12W **126** A1
Daman *India* 20°25N 72°57E **244** D1
Daman & Diu □ *India* 20°25N 72°58E **244** D1
Dāmaneh *Iran* 33°1N 50°29E **247** C6
Damanganga → *India* 20°25N 72°56E **244** D1
Damanhûr *Egypt* 31°0N 30°30E **256** H7
Damant L. *Canada* 61°45N 105°5W **297** A7
Damaq *Iran* 35°25N 48°49E **213** E13
Damar *Indonesia* 7°7S 128°40E **231** F7
Damara *C.A.R.* 4°58N 18°42E **264** B3
Damarakia *Greece* 37°58N 23°39E **112** C1
Damaraland *Namibia* 20°0S 15°0E **270** B2
Damascus = Dimashq *Syria* 33°30N 36°18E **250** E7
Damascus *U.S.A.* 31°18N 84°43W **316** D5
Damasi *Greece* 39°43N 22°11E **204** B4
Damatura *Nigeria* 11°45N 11°55E **263** C7
Damāvand *Iran* 35°47N 52°0E **247** C7
Damāvand, Qolleh-ye *Iran* 35°56N 52°10E **247** C7
Damba *Angola* 6°44S 15°20E **265** D3
Damboa *Nigeria* 11°15N 12°55E **259** F2
Dâmboviţa □ *Romania* 45°0N 25°30E **183** E10
Dâmboviţa → *Romania* 44°12N 26°26E **183** F11
Dâmbovnic → *Romania* 44°28N 25°18E **183** F10
Dambrowica = Dubrovytsya *Ukraine* 51°31N 26°35E **177** C14
Dambulla *Sri Lanka* 7°51N 80°39E **245** L5
Dame Marie *Haiti* 18°34N 74°26W **321** C5
Dämeritzsee *Germany* 52°34N 13°43E **115** B5
Dāmghān *Iran* 36°10N 54°17E **247** B7
Dămienesti *Romania* 46°44N 26°59E **183** D11
Damietta = Dumyât *Egypt* 31°24N 31°48E **251** G2
Daming *China* 36°15N 115°6E **226** F8
Damīr Qābū *Syria* 36°58N 41°51E **246** B4
Dammai I. *Phil.* 5°47N 120°25E **233** J3
Dammam = Ad Dammām *Si. Arabia* 26°20N 50°5E **247** E6
Dammarie-les-Lys *France* 48°31N 2°39E **173** D9
Dammartin-en-Goële *France* 49°3N 2°41E **173** C9
Damme *Germany* 52°32N 8°11E **178** C4
Damodar → *India* 23°17N 87°35E **243** H12
Damoh *India* 23°50N 79°28E **243** H8
Damous *Algeria* 36°31N 1°42E **261** A5
Dampier *Australia* 20°41S 116°42E **278** D2
Dampier, Selat *Indonesia* 0°40S 131°0E **231** E8
Dampier Arch. *Australia* 20°38S 116°32E **278** D2
Dampier Str. *Papua N. G.* 5°50S 148°0E **286** C5
Damqawt *Yemen* 16°34N 52°50E **249** C4
Damrak *Amsterdam, Neths.* **112** a2
Damrani *Algeria* 27°45N 2°56W **260** C4
Damrei, Chuor Phnum *Cambodia* 11°30N 103°0E **237** G4
Damroh *India* 28°26N 95°14E **241** A5
Damvillers *France* 49°20N 5°21E **173** C12
Damyang *S. Korea* 35°19N 126°59E **224** E3
Dan Gorayo *Somalia* 8°43N 49°20E **267** C6
Dan-Gulbi *Nigeria* 11°40N 6°15E **263** C6
Dan Ryan Woods *U.S.A.* 41°44N 87°40W **119** C2
Dan-Sadau *Nigeria* 11°17N 6°29E **263** C6
Dana *Indonesia* 11°0S 121°15E **231** F6
Dana *Jordan* 30°41N 35°37E **251** H6
Dana *Nepal* 28°32N 83°37E **243** E10
Dana, L. *Canada* 50°53N 77°20W **298** B4
Dana, Mt. *U.S.A.* 37°54N 119°12W **306** H7
Danakil Depression *Ethiopia* 13°0N 41°0E **267** B5
Danakil Desert *Ethiopia* 12°45N 41°0E **257** E5
Danan *Ethiopia* 6°31N 43°30E **267** C5
Danané *Ivory C.* 7°16N 8°9W **262** D3
Danao *Phil.* 10°31N 124°1E **233** F5
Danau Sentarum △ *Indonesia* 0°51N 112°6E **235** B4
Danba *China* 30°54N 101°48E **228** B3
Danbury *U.S.A.* 41°24N 73°28W **313** E11
Danby L. *U.S.A.* 34°13N 115°5W **307** L11
Dand *Afghan.* 31°28N 65°32E **242** D1
Dande → *Angola* 8°28S 13°21E **265** D2
Dande ⌂ *Zimbabwe* 15°56S 30°16E **269** F3
Dandeldhura *Nepal* 29°20N 80°35E **243** E9
Dandeli *India* 15°5N 74°30E **245** G2
Dandenong *Australia* 38°0S 145°15E **283** E6
Danderhall *U.K.* 55°55N 3°7W **121** B3
Danderyd *Sweden* 59°24N 18°1E **139** A2
Dandī *Iran* 36°32N 47°37E **246** B5
Dandîl *Egypt* 29°10N 31°2E **256** J7
Dandong *China* 40°10N 124°20E **224** B2
Daneborg *Greenland* 74°18N 20°14W **154** C8
Danfeng *China* 33°45N 110°25E **226** H6
Danforth *Canada* 43°43N 79°16W **141** A3
Dangan Liedao *China* 22°2N 114°8E **229** F10
Dangcagan *Phil.* 7°36N 125°0E **233** H5
Dange *Angola* 7°56S 15°3E **265** D3
Dangé-St-Romain *France* 46°56N 0°36E **174** B4
Dângeni *Romania* 47°51N 26°58E **183** C11
Danger Is. = Pukapuka *Cook Is.* 10°53S 165°49W **289** J11
Danger Pt. *S. Africa* 34°40S 19°17E **270** D2
Dangjin *S. Korea* 36°53N 126°37E **224** D3
Dangla *Ethiopia* 11°18N 36°56E **257** E4
Dangla Shan = Tanggula Shan *China* 32°40N 92°10E **218** E7
Dangora *Nigeria* 11°30N 8°7E **263** C6
Dangouadougou *Burkina Faso* 10°9N 4°56W **262** D4
Dangrek, Mts. = Dangrek, Phnom *Thailand* 14°20N 104°0E **236** E5
Dangrek, Phnom *Thailand* 14°20N 104°0E **236** E5
Dangriga *Belize* 17°0N 88°13W **320** C2
Dangshan *China* 34°27N 116°22E **226** G9
Dangtu *China* 31°32N 118°25E **229** B12
Dangyang *China* 30°52N 111°44E **229** B8
Dania Beach *U.S.A.* 26°3N 80°8W **129** B3
Daniel *U.S.A.* 42°52N 110°4W **304** E8
Daniel's Harbour *Canada* 50°13N 57°35W **299** B8
Danielskuil *S. Africa* 28°11S 23°33E **270** C3
Danielson *U.S.A.* 41°48N 71°53W **313** E13
Danielsville *U.S.A.* 34°8N 83°13W **316** A6
Danilov *Russia* 58°16N 40°13E **188** C11
Danilovgrad *Montenegro* 42°38N 19°4E **202** D3
Danilovka *Russia* 50°25N 44°12E **190** E7
Daning *China* 36°28N 110°45E **226** F6
Danish West Indies = Virgin Is. (U.S.) ☐ *W. Indies* 18°20N 65°0W **321** C7
Danissa *Kenya* 3°17N 40°59E **267** D5
Danja *Nigeria* 11°21N 7°30E **263** C6
Danje-la-Menha *Angola* 9°32S 14°39E **265** D2
Danjiangkou *China* 32°31N 111°30E **229** A8
Danjiangkou Shuiku *China* 32°37N 111°30E **229** A8
Ḍank *Oman* 23°33N 56°16E **247** F8
Dankalwa *Nigeria* 11°52N 12°12E **263** C7
Dankama *Nigeria* 13°20N 7°44E **263** C6
Dankhar Gompa *India* 32°10N 78°10E **242** C8
Dankov *Russia* 53°20N 39°5E **188** F10
Danleng *China* 30°1N 103°31E **228** B4
Danlí *Honduras* 14°4N 86°35W **320** D2
Danmark = Denmark ■ *Europe* 55°45N 10°0E **163** J3
Danmark Fjord *Greenland* 81°30N 22°0W **154** A8
Danmarkshavn *Greenland* 76°45N 18°50W **154** B9
Dannemora *U.S.A.* 44°43N 73°44W **313** B11
Dannenberg *Germany* 53°6N 11°5E **178** B7
Dannevirke *N.Z.* 40°12S 176°8E **284** G5
Dannhauser *S. Africa* 28°0S 30°3E **271** C5
Danot *Ethiopia* 7°33N 45°17E **267** C6
Dansalan = Marawi City *Phil.* 8°0N 124°21E **233** G5
Dansville *U.S.A.* 42°34N 77°42W **312** D7
Danta *India* 24°11N 72°46E **242** G5
Dantan *India* 21°57N 87°20E **243** J12
Dante = Xaafuun *Somalia* 10°25N 51°16E **267** B7
Dantewara *India* 18°54N 81°21E **244** E5
Danube = Dunărea → *Europe* 45°20N 29°40E **183** E14
Danubyu *Burma* 17°15N 95°35E **241** G5
Danvers *U.S.A.* 42°34N 70°56W **313** D14
Danville *Ga., U.S.A.* 32°37N 83°15W **316** C6
Danville *Ill., U.S.A.* 40°8N 87°37W **311** D9
Danville *Ind., U.S.A.* 39°46N 86°32W **311** E10
Danville *Ky., U.S.A.* 37°39N 84°46W **311** G12
Danville *Pa., U.S.A.* 40°58N 76°37W **313** F8
Danville *Va., U.S.A.* 36°36N 79°23W **309** G14
Danville *Vt., U.S.A.* 44°25N 72°9W **313** B12
Danyang *China* 32°0N 119°31E **229** B12
Danzhai *China* 26°11N 107°48E **228** D6
Danzhou *China* 19°31N 109°33E **236** C7
Danzig = Gdańsk *Poland* 54°22N 18°40E **184** D5
Dao *Antique, Phil.* 10°30N 121°57E **233** F3
Dao *Capiz, Phil.* 11°24N 122°41E **233** F4
Dão → *Portugal* 40°20N 8°11W **194** E2
Dao Xian *China* 25°36N 111°31E **229** E8
Daocheng *China* 29°0N 100°10E **228** C3
Daora *W. Sahara* 27°5N 12°59W **260** C2
Daoud = Aïn Beïda *Algeria* 35°50N 7°29E **261** A6
Daoukro *Ivory C.* 7°10N 3°58W **262** D4
Dapa *Phil.* 9°46N 126°3E **233** G6
Dapaong *Togo* 10°55N 0°16E **263** C5
Dapchi *Nigeria* 12°32N 11°31E **263** C7
Dapiak, Mt. *Phil.* 8°15N 123°28E **233** G4
Dapitan *Phil.* 8°39N 123°25E **233** G4
Dapoli *India* 17°46N 73°11E **244** F1
Daporijo *India* 27°59N 94°13E **241** B5
Daqahlîya □ *Egypt* 30°55N 31°30E **251** H2
Daqing *China* 46°35N 125°0E **219** B13
Daqing Shan *China* 40°40N 111°0E **226** D6
Daqq-e Sorkh, Kavīr *Iran* 33°45N 52°50E **247** C7
Daqu Shan *China* 30°25N 122°20E **229** B14
Dar Banda *Africa* 8°0N 23°0E **254** F6
Dar el Beida = Casablanca *Morocco* 33°36N 7°36W **260** B3
Dar es Salaam *Tanzania* 6°50S 39°12E **268** D4
Dar Mazār *Iran* 29°14N 57°20E **247** D8
Dar Rounga *C.A.R.* 0°45N 22°20E **264** A4
Dār Ta'izzah *Syria* 36°20N 36°52E **250** B7
Dar'ā *Syria* 32°36N 36°7E **250** F7
Dar'ā □ *Syria* 32°55N 36°10E **250** F7
Dara Dere = Zlatograd *Bulgaria* 41°22N 25°7E **203** E9
Dārāb *Iran* 28°50N 54°30E **247** D7
Daraban *Pakistan* 31°44N 70°20E **242** D4
Darabani *Romania* 48°10N 26°39E **183** B11
Darai Hills *Papua N. G.* 7°8S 143°33E **286** D2
Daraina *Madag.* 13°12S 49°40E **272** A2
Daraj *Libya* 30°10N 10°28E **258** B2
Darakeh *Iran* 35°49N 51°22E **141** A2
Daram *Phil.* 11°38N 124°48E **233** F5
Dārān *Iran* 32°59N 50°24E **247** C6
Đaravica = Gjeravicë *Kosovo* 42°32N 20°8E **202** D4
Darawr *Egypt* 24°22N 32°51E **256** C3
Dārayyā *Syria* 33°28N 36°15E **250** E7
Darazo *Nigeria* 11°1N 10°24E **263** C7
Darband *Tehrān, Iran* 35°49N 51°27E **141** A2
Darband *Pakistan* 34°20N 72°50E **242** B5
Darband, Kūh-e *Iran* 31°34N 57°8E **247** D8
Darbhanga *India* 26°15N 85°55E **243** F11
Darburruk *Somalia* 9°44N 44°31E **267** C5
Darby, C. *U.S.A.* 64°19N 162°47W **303** D7
D'Arcy *Canada* 50°33N 122°29W **296** C4
Darda *Croatia* 45°40N 18°41E **182** E3
Dardanë *Kosovo* 42°35N 21°35E **202** D5
Dardanelle *Ark., U.S.A.* 35°13N 93°9W **314** D8
Dardanelle *Calif., U.S.A.* 38°20N 119°50W **306** G7
Dardanelles = Çanakkale Boğazı *Turkey* 40°17N 26°32E **203** F10
Dare → *Ethiopia* 7°20N 42°11E **257** F5
Darende *Turkey* 38°31N 37°30E **212** C7
Dārestān *Iran* 29°9N 58°42E **247** D8
Darfield *N.Z.* 43°29S 172°7E **285** D7
Darfo *Italy* 45°53N 10°11E **198** C7
Dârfûr *Sudan* 13°40N 24°0E **259** F4
Dargai *Pakistan* 34°25N 71°55E **242** B4
Dargaville *N.Z.* 35°57S 173°52E **284** B2
Dargol *Niger* 13°54N 1°22E **263** C5
Darhan *Mongolia* 49°37N 106°21E **218** B10
Darhan Muminggan *China* 41°40N 110°28E **226** D6
Dari *South Sudan* 5°48N 30°26E **257** F3
Darıca *Turkey* 40°45N 29°23E **212** B3
Darién, G. del *Colombia* 9°0N 77°0W **320** E4
Darién, Serranía del *Colombia* 8°30N 77°30W **320** E4
Darién △ *Panama* 7°36N 77°57W **320** E4
Dariganga = Ovoot *Mongolia* 45°21N 113°45E **226** B7
Daringbadi *India* 19°54N 84°8E **244** E7
Dario, Palazzo *Venice, Italy* **142** c2
Darjeeling = Darjiling *India* 27°3N 88°18E **241** B2
Darjiling *India* 27°3N 88°18E **241** B2
Darkan *Australia* 33°20S 116°43E **279** F2
Darke Peak *Australia* 33°27S 136°12E **282** B2
Darkhana *Pakistan* 30°39N 72°11E **242** D5
Darkhazīneh *Iran* 31°54N 48°39E **247** D6
Darkot Pass *Pakistan* 36°45N 73°26E **243** A5
Darling → *Australia* 34°4S 141°54E **282** C4
Darling Downs *Australia* 27°30S 150°30E **281** D5
Darling Harbour *Sydney, Australia* **139** b1
Darling Point *Australia* 33°52S 151°15E **139** B2
Darling Ra. *Australia* 32°30S 116°20E **279** F2
Darlington *Durham, U.K.* 54°32N 1°33W **168** C6
Darlington *Fla., U.S.A.* 30°57N 86°3W **316** E3
Darlington *S.C., U.S.A.* 34°18N 79°52W **315** D15
Darlington *Wis., U.S.A.* 42°41N 90°7W **310** B6
Darlington □ *U.K.* 54°32N 1°33W **168** C6
Darlington, L. *S. Africa* 33°10S 25°9E **270** D4
Darlington Point *Australia* 34°37S 146°1E **283** C7
Darlot, L. *Australia* 27°48S 121°35E **279** E3
Darłowo *Poland* 54°25N 16°25E **184** D3
Dărmăneşti *Bacău, Romania* 46°21N 26°33E **183** D11
Dărmăneşti *Suceava, Romania* 47°44N 26°9E **183** C11
Darmstadt *Germany* 49°51N 8°39E **179** F4
Darnah *Libya* 32°45N 22°45E **258** B4
Darnah □ *Libya* 31°0N 23°40E **258** B4
Darnall *S. Africa* 29°23S 31°18E **271** C5
Darndale *Ireland* 53°23N 6°12W **120** A2
Darney *France* 48°5N 6°2E **173** D13
Darnick *Australia* 32°48S 143°38E **282** B5
Darnley *Australia* 9°35S 143°46E **280** a
Darnley, C. *Antarctica* 68°0S 69°0E **151** C6
Darnley B. *Canada* 69°30N 123°30W **297** D7
Daroca *Spain* 41°9N 1°25W **196** D3
Daror *Ethiopia* 8°14N 44°42E **267** C5
Darou-Mousti *Senegal* 15°3N 16°3W **262** B1
Darr → *Australia* 23°39S 143°50E **280** C3
Darra Pezu *Pakistan* 32°19N 70°44E **242** C4
Darran Mts. *N.Z.* 44°37S 167°59E **285** E2
Darreh Shahr *Iran* 33°7N 47°22E **213** F12
Darrequeira *Argentina* 37°42S 63°10W **334** D3
Darrington *U.S.A.* 48°15N 121°36W **304** B3
Darrūs *Iran* 35°46N 51°27E **141** A2
Darsah *Yemen* 12°6N 53°16E **249** D6
Darsana *Bangla.* 23°35N 88°48E **241** D2
Darsi *India* 15°46N 79°44E **245** G4
Darsser Ort *Germany* 54°28N 12°32E **178** A8
Dart → *U.K.* 50°24N 3°39W **169** G4
Dartford *U.K.* 51°26N 0°13E **125** B5
Dartmoor *Vic., Australia* 37°56S 141°19E **282** D4
Dartmoor *Devon, U.K.* 50°38N 3°57W **169** G4
Dartmoor △ *U.K.* 50°37N 3°59W **169** G4
Dartmouth *N.S., Canada* 44°40N 63°30W **299** D7
Dartmouth *Devon, U.K.* 50°21N 3°36W **169** G4
Dartmouth, L. *Queens., Australia* 26°4S 145°18E **281** D4
Dartmouth, L. *Vic., Australia* 36°34S 147°32E **283** D7
Dartuch, C. = Artrutx, C. de *Spain* 39°55N 3°49E **206** B4
Daru *Papua N. G.* 9°3S 143°13E **286** E2
Daruvar *Croatia* 45°35N 17°14E **182** E2
Darvaza = Içoguz *Turkmenistan* 40°11N 58°24E **216** D5
Darvel, Teluk = Lahad Datu, Teluk *Malaysia* 4°50N 118°20E **235** B5
Darvi *Mongolia* 46°27N 94°7E **217** C12
Darwen *U.K.* 53°42N 2°29W **168** D5
Darwendale *Zimbabwe* 17°41S 30°33E **271** A5
Darwha *India* 20°15N 77°45E **244** D3
Darwin *N. Terr., Australia* 12°25S 130°51E **278** B5
Darwin *Calif., U.S.A.* 36°15N 117°35W **307** J9
Darwin, Mt. *Chile* 54°47S 69°55W **336** D3
Darwin, Volcán *Ecuador* 0°10S 91°18W **330** a
Darya Ganj *Delhi, India* **120** a3
Darya Khan *Pakistan* 31°48N 71°6E **242** D4
Daryapur *India* 20°55N 77°20E **244** D3
Daryoi Amu = Amudarya → *Uzbekistan* 43°58N 59°34E **216** D5
Dās *U.A.E.* 25°20N 53°30E **247** E7
Dashahe *China* 42°44N 128°10E **224** A4
Dashen, Ras *Ethiopia* 13°8N 38°26E **257** E4
Dasher *U.S.A.* 30°45N 83°13W **316** E6
Dashetai *China* 41°0N 109°5E **226** D5
Dashi *China* 23°1N 113°17E **121** B2
Dashiqiao *China* 40°38N 122°30E **227** D12
Dashkesan = Daşkäsän *Azerbaijan* 40°25N 46°0E **191** K7
Dashköpri *Turkmenistan* 36°16N 62°8E **247** B9
Dasht → *Pakistan* 25°10N 61°40E **240** D1
Dasht-i-Tahlab *Pakistan* 28°40N 62°25E **240** C1
Daska *Pakistan* 32°20N 74°20E **242** C6
Daşkäsän *Azerbaijan* 40°25N 46°0E **191** K7
Dasmariñas *Phil.* 14°20N 120°56E **232** D3
Daşoguz *Turkmenistan* 41°49N 59°58E **216** D5
Dasol B. *Phil.* 15°52N 119°50E **232** D2
Dassa *Benin* 7°46N 2°14E **263** D5
Dasuya *India* 31°49N 75°38E **242** D6
Datadian *Indonesia* 2°1N 115°13E **235** B5
Datansha *China* 23°8N 113°12E **121** B2
Datça *Turkey* 36°46N 27°40E **205** E9
Date *Japan* 42°28N 140°52E **220** C10
Datia *India* 25°39N 78°27E **243** G8
Datian *China* 25°40N 117°50E **229** E11
Datong *Anhui, China* 30°48N 117°44E **229** B11
Datong *Qinghai, China* 36°20N 102°50E **218** D9
Datong *Shanxi, China* 40°6N 113°18E **226** D7
Dattakhel *Pakistan* 32°54N 69°46E **242** C3
Dattapur = Dhamangaon *India* 20°48N 78°9E **244** D4
Datteln *Germany* 51°39N 7°21E **178** D3
Datu, Tanjung *Indonesia* 2°5N 109°39E **235** B3
Datu Piang *Phil.* 7°2N 124°30E **233** H5
Datuk, Tanjong = Datu, Tanjung *Indonesia* 2°5N 109°39E **235** B3
Datun *China* 40°0N 116°23E **114** B2
Daua = Dawa → *Africa* 4°11N 42°6E **257** G5
Daud Khel *Pakistan* 32°53N 71°34E **242** C4
Daudnagar *India* 25°2N 84°24E **243** G11
Daugava → *Latvia* 57°4N 24°3E **188** D3
Daugavpils *Latvia* 55°53N 26°32E **188** E4
Daulatabad *India* 19°57N 75°15E **244** E2
Daulatpur *India* 28°44N 77°6E **120** A1
Daule *Ecuador* 1°56S 79°56W **328** D2
Daule → *Ecuador* 2°10S 79°52W **328** D2
Daule-Peripa, Presa *Ecuador* 1°0S 79°35W **328** D2
Daulpur *India* 26°45N 77°59E **242** F7
Daun *Germany* 50°11N 6°49E **179** E2
Daund *India* 18°26N 74°40E **244** E2
Daung Kyun *Burma* 12°13N 98°4E **237** F1
Dauphin *Man., Canada* 51°9N 100°5W **297** C8
Dauphin *Pa., U.S.A.* 40°22N 76°56W **312** F8
Dauphin L. *Canada* 51°20N 99°45W **297** C9
Dauphiné *France* 45°15N 5°25E **175** C9
Daura *Borno, Nigeria* 11°31N 11°24E **263** C7
Daura *Katsina, Nigeria* 13°2N 8°21E **263** C6
Dausa *India* 26°52N 76°20E **242** F7
Däväçi *Azerbaijan* 41°15N 48°57E **191** K9
Davangere *India* 14°25N 75°55E **245** G2
Davao *Phil.* 7°0N 125°40E **233** H5
Davao □ *Phil.* 7°0N 125°55E **233** H5
Davao del Sur □ *Phil.* 6°30N 125°25E **233** H5
Davao G. *Phil.* 6°30N 125°48E **233** H5
Davao Oriental □ *Phil.* 7°10N 126°30E **233** H6
Dāvar Panāh = Sarāvān *Iran* 27°25N 62°15E **247** E9
Davenport *Calif., U.S.A.* 37°1N 122°12W **306** H4
Davenport *Fla., U.S.A.* 28°10N 81°36W **317** G8
Davenport *Iowa, U.S.A.* 41°32N 90°35W **310** C6
Davenport *Wash., U.S.A.* 47°39N 118°9W **304** C4
Davenport Ra. *Australia* 20°28S 134°0E **280** C1
Davenport Range △ *Australia* 20°36S 134°22E **280** C1
Daventry *U.K.* 52°16N 1°10W **169** E6
David *Panama* 8°30N 82°30W **320** E3
David City *U.S.A.* 41°15N 97°8W **308** E5
David Glacier *Antarctica* 75°20S 162°0E **151** D11
David Gorodok = Davyd Haradok *Belarus* 52°4N 27°8E **177** B14
David's Citadel *Jerusalem* **123** b3
David's Tomb *Jerusalem* **123** b3
Davidson *Canada* 51°16N 105°59W **297** C7
Davidson, Mt. *U.S.A.* 37°44N 122°27W **136** B2
Davidson Mts. *U.S.A.* 68°41N 142°22W **303** B12
Davidson's Mains *U.K.* 55°58N 3°16W **121** B2
Davie *U.S.A.* 26°3N 80°14W **129** B2
Davis *Antarctica* 68°34S 77°55E **151** C6
Davis *Calif., U.S.A.* 38°33N 121°44W **306** G5
Davis Dam *U.S.A.* 35°12N 114°34W **307** K12
Davis Inlet *Canada* 55°50N 60°59W **299** A7
Davis Mts. *U.S.A.* 30°50N 103°55W **314** F3
Davis Sea *Antarctica* 66°0S 92°0E **151** C7
Davis Str. *N. Amer.* 65°0N 58°0W **295** D19
Davisboro *U.S.A.* 32°59N 82°36W **316** C7
Davison *U.S.A.* 43°2N 83°31W **311** A13
Davlos *Cyprus* 35°25N 33°54E **207** E9
Davo → *Ivory C.* 5°0N 6°10W **262** D3
Davos *Switz.* 46°48N 9°49E **179** J5
Dăvudiyeh *Iran* 35°45N 51°25E **141** A2
Davutlar *Turkey* 37°43N 27°17E **205** D9
Davy L. *Canada* 58°53N 108°18W **297** B7
Davyd Haradok *Belarus* 52°4N 27°8E **177** B14
Davydkovo *Russia* 55°43N 37°29E **129** B1
Dawa → *Africa* 4°11N 42°6E **257** G5
Dawaki *Bauchi, Nigeria* 9°25N 9°33E **263** D6
Dawaki *Kano, Nigeria* 12°5N 8°23E **263** C6
Dawei = Tavoy *Burma* 14°2N 98°12E **236** E2
Dawes Ra. *Australia* 24°40S 150°40E **280** C5
Dawidy *Poland* 52°8N 20°58E **143** C1
Dawkah *Oman* 18°39N 54°5E **249** C6
Dawley = Telford *U.K.* 52°40N 2°27W **169** E5
Dawlish *U.K.* 50°35N 3°28W **169** G4
Dawna Ra. *Burma* 16°30N 98°30E **236** D2
Dawnyein *Burma* 15°54N 95°36E **241** G5
Dawqah *Si. Arabia* 19°36N 40°54E **248** C3
Dawran *Yemen* 14°45N 44°17E **248** D4
Dawros Hd. *Ireland* 54°50N 8°33W **166** B3
Dawson *U.S.A.* 31°46N 84°27W **316** D5
Dawson, I. *Chile* 53°50S 70°50W **336** D2
Dawson B. *Canada* 52°53N 100°49W **297** C8
Dawson City *Canada* 64°10N 139°30W **294** E4
Dawson Creek *Canada* 55°45N 120°15W **296** B4
Dawson Inlet *Canada* 61°50N 93°25W **297** A10
Dawson Ra. *Australia* 24°30S 149°48E **280** C4
Dawu *Hubei, China* 31°34N 114°7E **229** B9
Dawu *Sichuan, China* 30°55N 101°10E **228** B3
Dawwah *Oman* 20°33N 58°48E **249** B7
Dawwara, Ras id- *Malta* 35°52N 14°21E **206** F7
Dax *France* 43°44N 1°3W **174** E2
Daxian *China* 31°15N 107°23E **228** B6
Daxin *China* 22°50N 107°11E **228** F6
Daxindian *China* 37°30N 120°50E **227** F11
Daxing *China* 39°47N 116°24E **114** C2
Daxinggou *China* 43°25N 129°40E **227** C15
Daxue Shan *Sichuan, China* 30°30N 101°30E **228** B3
Daxue Shan *Yunnan, China* 23°42N 99°48E **228** F2
Day *U.S.A.* 30°12N 83°17W **316** E6
Daya el Khadra *Mauritania* 25°1N 6°2W **260** C3
Dayang He → *China* 39°51N 123°38E **224** C1
Dayao *China* 25°43N 101°20E **228** E3
Daye *China* 30°6N 114°58E **229** B10
Dayet en Naharat *Mali* 17°39N 3°10W **262** B4
Dayi *China* 30°41N 103°29E **228** B4
Dāykondī □ *Afghan.* 34°0N 66°0E **240** B2
Daylesford *Australia* 37°21S 144°9E **282** D6
Dayong *China* 29°11N 110°30E **229** C8
Dayr az Zawr *Syria* 35°20N 40°5E **213** E9
Dayr az Zawr □ *Syria* 34°50N 40°10E **213** E9
Daysland *Canada* 52°50N 112°20W **296** C6
Dayton *Iowa, U.S.A.* 42°16N 94°4W **310** B2
Dayton *Nev., U.S.A.* 39°14N 119°36W **306** F7
Dayton *Ohio, U.S.A.* 39°45N 84°12W **311** E12
Dayton *Pa., U.S.A.* 40°53N 79°15W **312** F5
Dayton *Tenn., U.S.A.* 35°30N 85°1W **315** D12
Dayton *Wash., U.S.A.* 46°19N 117°59W **304** C5
Dayton *Wyo., U.S.A.* 44°53N 107°16W **304** D10
Daytona Beach *U.S.A.* 29°13N 81°1W **317** F8
Dayu *China* 25°24N 114°22E **229** E10
Dayville *U.S.A.* 44°28N 119°32W **304** D4
Dazaifu *Japan* 33°32N 130°32E **222** D2
Dazhu *China* 30°41N 107°15E **228** B6
Dazkırı *Turkey* 37°57N 29°52E **205** D11
Dazu *China* 29°40N 105°42E **228** C5
De Aar *S. Africa* 30°39S 24°0E **270** D3
De Armanville *U.S.A.* 33°38N 85°45W **316** B4
De Bary *U.S.A.* 28°54N 81°18W **317** G8
De Forest *U.S.A.* 43°15N 89°20W **310** A7
De Funiak Springs *U.S.A.* 30°43N 86°7W **316** E3
De Grey → *Australia* 20°12S 119°13E **278** D2
De Haan *Belgium* 51°16N 3°2E **170** C3
De Hoop ⌂ *S. Africa* 34°30S 20°28E **270** D3
De Kalb Junction *U.S.A.* 44°30N 75°16W **313** B9
De Land *U.S.A.* 29°2N 81°18W **317** F8
De Leon *U.S.A.* 32°7N 98°32W **314** E5
De Leon Springs *U.S.A.* 29°7N 81°21W **317** F8
De Long Mts. *U.S.A.* 68°10N 163°30W **303** B7
De Panne *Belgium* 51°6N 2°34E **170** C2
De Pere *U.S.A.* 44°27N 88°4W **308** C9
De Queen *U.S.A.* 34°2N 94°21W **314** D7
De Quincy *U.S.A.* 30°27N 93°26W **314** F8
De Ruyters *U.S.A.* 42°45N 75°53W **313** D9
De Smet *U.S.A.* 44°23N 97°33W **308** C5
De Soto *U.S.A.* 38°8N 90°34W **310** F6
De Soto City *U.S.A.* 27°27N 81°24W **317** H8
De Tour Village *U.S.A.* 46°0N 83°56W **309** B12
De Witt *Ark., U.S.A.* 34°18N 91°20W **314** D9
De Witt *Iowa, U.S.A.* 41°49N 90°33W **310** C6
De Witt *Mich., U.S.A.* 42°51N 84°34W **311** B12
Dead L. *U.S.A.* 30°10N 85°10W **316** E4
Dead Sea *Asia* 31°30N 35°30E **251** G6
Deadhorse *U.S.A.* 70°11N 148°27W **303** A10
Deadman B. *U.S.A.* 29°30N 83°30W **317** F6
Deadwood *U.S.A.* 44°23N 103°44W **308** C2
Deadwood L. *Canada* 59°10N 128°30W **296** B3
Deal *U.K.* 51°13N 1°25E **169** F9
Deal I. *Australia* 39°30S 147°20E **282** E7
Dealesville *S. Africa* 28°41S 25°44E **270** C4
De'an *China* 29°21N 115°46E **229** C10
Dean → *Canada* 52°49N 126°58W **296** C3
Dean, Forest of *U.K.* 51°45N 2°33W **169** F5
Dean Chan. *Canada* 52°30N 127°15W **296** C3
Deán Funes *Argentina* 30°20S 64°20W **334** C3
Dearborn *Mich., U.S.A.* 42°19N 83°10W **311** B13
Dearborn *Mo., U.S.A.* 39°32N 94°46W **310** E2
Dease → *Canada* 59°56N 128°32W **296** B3
Dease Inlet *U.S.A.* 71°2N 155°26W **303** A9
Dease L. *Canada* 58°40N 130°5W **296** B2
Dease Lake *Canada* 58°25N 130°6W **296** B2
Death Valley *U.S.A.* 36°15N 116°50W **307** J10
Death Valley △ *U.S.A.* 36°29N 117°6W **307** J9
Death Valley Junction *U.S.A.* 36°20N 116°25W **307** J10
Deatnu = Tana → *Norway* 70°30N 28°14E **160** A23

Deauville *France* 49°23N 0°2E **172** C7
Deba *Spain* 43°18N 2°21W **196** B2
Deba Habe *Nigeria* 10°14N 11°20E **263** C7
Debagram *India* 23°41N 88°18E **243** H13
Debak *Malaysia* 1°34N 111°25E **235** B4
Debaltsevo *Ukraine* 48°22N 38°26E **189** H10
Debao *China* 23°21N 106°46E **228** F6
Debar *Macedonia* 41°31N 20°30E **202** E4
Debark *Ethiopia* 13°1N 37°48E **257** E4
Debden *Canada* 53°30N 106°50W **297** C8
Debdou *Morocco* 33°59N 3°0W **261** B4
Debe *Trin. & Tob.* 10°12N 61°27W **323** t
Dębica *Poland* 50°2N 21°25E **185** H8
Dęblin *Poland* 51°34N 21°50E **185** G8
Dębno *Poland* 52°44N 14°41E **185** F1
Débo, L. *Mali* 15°14N 4°15W **262** B4
DeBolt *Canada* 55°12N 118°1W **296** B5
Deborah East, L. *Australia* 30°45S 119°30E **279** F2
Deborah West, L. *Australia* 30°45S 119°5E **279** F2
Deboyne Is. *Papua N. G.* 10°43S 152°22E **286** F7
Debrc *Serbia* 44°38N 19°53E **202** B3
Debre Birhan *Ethiopia* 9°41N 39°31E **257** F4
Debre Markos *Ethiopia* 10°20N 37°40E **257** E4
Debre May *Ethiopia* 11°20N 37°25E **257** E4
Debre Sina *Ethiopia* 9°51N 39°50E **257** F4
Debre Tabor *Ethiopia* 11°50N 38°26E **257** E4
Debre Zebit *Ethiopia* 11°48N 38°30E **257** E4
Debre Zeyit *Ethiopia* 8°50N 39°0E **257** F4
Debrecen *Hungary* 47°33N 21°42E **182** C6
Debrzno *Poland* 53°31N 17°14E **184** E4
Deçan *Kosovo* 42°30N 20°18E **202** D4
Decatur *Ala., U.S.A.* 34°36N 86°59W **315** D11
Decatur *Ga., U.S.A.* 33°46N 84°16W **113** B3
Decatur *Ill., U.S.A.* 39°51N 88°57W **310** E8
Decatur *Ind., U.S.A.* 40°50N 84°56W **311** D12
Decatur *Mich., U.S.A.* 42°7N 85°58W **311** B11
Decatur *Tex., U.S.A.* 33°14N 97°35W **314** E6
Decazeville *France* 44°34N 2°15E **174** D6
Deccan *India* 18°0N 79°0E **244** F4
Deception, Mt. *Australia* 30°42S 138°16E **282** A3
Deception B. *Papua N. G.* 7°45S 144°40E **286** D3
Deception Bay *Australia* 27°10S 153°5E **281** D5
Deception I. *Antarctica* 63°0S 60°15W **151** C17
Deception L. *Canada* 56°33N 104°13W **297** B8
Dechang *China* 27°25N 102°11E **228** D4
Dechhu *India* 26°46N 72°20E **242** F5
Děčín *Czech Rep.* 50°47N 14°12E **180** A7
Decize *France* 46°50N 3°28E **173** F10
Deckerville *U.S.A.* 43°32N 82°44W **312** C2
Decollatura *Italy* 39°3N 16°21E **201** C9
Decorah *U.S.A.* 43°18N 91°48W **308** D8
Deda *Romania* 46°56N 24°50E **183** D9
Dedaye *Burma* 16°24N 95°53E **241** G5
Dedeágach = Alexandroupoli *Greece* 40°50N 25°54E **203** F9
Dededo *Guam* 13°31N 144°50E **302** d
Deder *Ethiopia* 9°19N 41°27E **257** F5
Dedham *U.S.A.* 42°15N 71°10W **116** B1
Dedopolis Tsqaro *Georgia* 41°33N 46°0E **191** K8
Dédougou *Burkina Faso* 12°30N 3°25W **262** C4
Dedovichi *Russia* 57°32N 29°56E **188** D5
Dedza *Malawi* 14°20S 34°20E **269** E3
Dee → *Aberds., U.K.* 57°9N 2°5W **167** D6
Dee → *Dumf. & Gall., U.K.* 54°51N 4°3W **167** G4
Dee → *Wales, U.K.* 53°22N 3°17W **168** D4
Deep B. *Canada* 61°15N 116°35W **296** A5
Deep Bay = Chilumba *Malawi* 10°28S 34°12E **269** E3
Deep Bay = Shenzhen Wan *China* 22°27N 113°55E **219** a
Deep Lead *Australia* 37°0S 142°43E **282** D5
Deepwater *N.S.W., Australia* 29°25S 151°51E **281** D5
Deepwater *Mo., U.S.A.* 38°16N 93°47W **310** F3
Deer → *Canada* 58°23N 94°13W **297** B10
Deer I. *U.S.A.* 54°55N 162°18W **303** J7
Deer L. *Canada* 52°40N 94°20W **297** C10
Deer Lake *Nfld. & L., Canada* 49°11N 57°27W **299** C8
Deer Lake *Ont., Canada* 52°36N 94°20W **297** C10
Deer Lodge *U.S.A.* 46°24N 112°44W **304** C7
Deer Park *Fla., U.S.A.* 28°6N 80°54W **317** G9
Deer Park *Ohio, U.S.A.* 39°12N 84°23W **311** E12
Deer Park *Wash., U.S.A.* 47°57N 117°28W **304** C5
Deer River *U.S.A.* 47°20N 93°48W **308** B7
Deeragun *Australia* 19°16S 146°33E **280** B4
Deerfield *Ill., U.S.A.* 42°10N 87°51W **311** B9
Deerfield *Mo., U.S.A.* 37°50N 94°30W **310** G2
Deerfield Beach *U.S.A.* 26°19N 80°6W **317** J9
Deering *U.S.A.* 66°4N 162°42W **303** C7
Defensores del Chaco △ *Paraguay* 20°13S 60°27W **331** E5
Defiance *U.S.A.* 41°17N 84°22W **311** C12
Dega Medo *Ethiopia* 7°59N 43°1E **267** C5
Degana *India* 26°50N 74°20E **242** F6
Dêgê *China* 31°44N 98°39E **228** B2
Degebe → *Portugal* 38°13N 7°29W **195** G3
Degeberga *Sweden* 55°51N 14°5E **163** J8
Degeh Bur *Ethiopia* 8°11N 43°31E **267** C5
Dégelis *Canada* 47°30N 68°35W **299** C6
Degema *Nigeria* 4°50N 6°48E **263** E6
Degerfors *Sweden* 59°15N 14°27E **162** E8
Degerhamn *Sweden* 56°20N 16°24E **163** H10
Deggendorf *Germany* 48°50N 12°57E **179** G8
Degh → *Pakistan* 31°3N 73°21E **242** D5
Değirmendere *Turkey* 40°42N 29°47E **203** F13
Degirmenlik = Kythréa *Cyprus* 35°15N 33°29E **207** E9
Degunino *Russia* 55°52N 37°33E **129** A2
Deh Bīd *Iran* 30°39N 53°11E **247** D7
Deh Dasht *Iran* 30°47N 50°33E **247** D6
Deh-e Shīr *Iran* 31°29N 53°45E **247** D7
Deh Nugaled = Nugaaleed, Dooxo *Somalia* 8°35N 48°35E **267** C6
Dehaj *Iran* 30°42N 54°53E **247** D7
Dehak *Iran* 27°11N 62°37E **240** D1
Déhane *Cameroon* 3°30N 10°5E **264** B2
Dehdez *Iran* 31°43N 50°17E **247** D6
Dehej *India* 21°44N 72°40E **242** J5
Dehestān *Iran* 28°30N 55°35E **247** D7
Dehgolān *Iran* 35°17N 47°25E **213** E12
Dehibat *Tunisia* 32°0N 10°47E **258** B2
Dehiwala *Sri Lanka* 6°50N 79°51E **245** L4
Dehlorān *Iran* 32°41N 47°16E **213** F12
Dehnow-e Kūhestān *Iran* 27°58N 58°32E **247** E8
Dehra Dun *India* 30°20N 78°4E **242** D8
Dehri *India* 24°50N 84°15E **243** G11
Dehua *China* 25°26N 118°14E **229** E12
Dehui *China* 44°30N 125°40E **227** B13
Deim Zubeir *South Sudan* 7°49N 26°16E **257** F2
Deinze *Belgium* 50°59N 3°32E **170** D3
Deir al Balah *Gaza Strip* 31°25N 34°21E **251** G5
Deir Dibwan *West Bank* 31°55N 35°16E **123** A2
Deir Ibzi'e *West Bank* 31°55N 35°7E **123** A1
Deira *U.A.E.* 25°16N 55°18E **119** A2
Dej *Romania* 47°10N 23°52E **183** C8
Deje *Sweden* 59°35N 13°29E **162** E7
Dejiang *China* 28°18N 108°7E **228** C7
Dejvice *Czech Rep.* 50°6N 14°23E **135** B2
Deka → *Zimbabwe* 18°4S 26°42E **270** A4
Dekabristov, Ostrov *Russia* 59°56N 30°15E **137** B1
DeKalb *U.S.A.* 41°56N 88°46W **311** C8
Dekemhare *Eritrea* 15°6N 39°0E **257** D4
Dekese *Dem. Rep. of the Congo* 3°24S 21°24E **264** C4
Dekoa *C.A.R.* 6°19N 19°4E **264** A3
Del Caño Rise *Ind. Oc.* 45°15S 44°15E **273** J3
Del Carmen *Phil.* 9°50N 126°0E **233** G6
Del Mar *U.S.A.* 32°58N 117°16W **307** N9
Del Norte *U.S.A.* 37°41N 106°21W **305** H10
Del Rey *U.S.A.* 33°59N 118°25W **126** C2
Del Rio *U.S.A.* 29°22N 100°54W **314** G4
Delai *Sudan* 17°21N 36°6E **256** D4
Delambre I. *Australia* 20°26S 117°5E **278** D2
Delami *Sudan* 11°38N 30°23E **257** E3
Delano *U.S.A.* 35°46N 119°15W **307** K7
Delano Peak *U.S.A.* 38°22N 112°22W **304** G7
Delārām *Afghan.* 32°9N 63°25E **240** B1
Delareyville *S. Africa* 26°41S 25°26E **270** C4
Delaronde L. *Canada* 54°3N 107°3W **297** C7
Delavan *Ill., U.S.A.* 40°22N 89°33W **310** D7
Delavan *Wis., U.S.A.* 42°38N 88°39W **311** B8
Delaware *U.S.A.* 40°18N 83°4W **311** D13
Delaware □ *U.S.A.* 39°0N 75°20W **309** F16
Delaware → *U.S.A.* 39°15N 75°20W **313** G9
Delaware B. *U.S.A.* 39°0N 75°10W **309** F16
Delaware Water Gap △ *U.S.A.* 41°10N 74°55W **313** E10
Delay → *Canada* 56°56N 71°28W **299** A5
Delbrück *Germany* 51°46N 8°34E **178** D4
Delčevo *Macedonia* 41°58N 22°46E **202** E6
Delegate *Australia* 37°4S 148°56E **283** D8
Delémont *Switz.* 47°22N 7°20E **179** H3
Delevan *U.S.A.* 42°29N 78°29W **312** D6
Delft *Neths.* 52°1N 4°22E **170** B4
Delft I. *Sri Lanka* 9°30N 79°40E **245** K4
Delfzijl *Neths.* 53°20N 6°55E **170** A6
Delgada, Punta *Chile* 52°28S 69°32W **336** D3
Delgado, C. *Mozam.* 10°45S 40°40E **269** E5
Delgerhet *Mongolia* 45°50N 110°30E **226** B6
Delgo *Sudan* 20°6N 30°40E **256** C3
Delhi *Ont., Canada* 42°51N 80°30W **312** D4
Delhi *India* 28°39N 77°13E **120** B2
Delhi *La., U.S.A.* 32°28N 91°30W **314** E9
Delhi *N.Y., U.S.A.* 42°17N 74°55W **313** D10
Delhi Gate *Delhi, India* **120** b3
Delhi Indira Gandhi Int. ✕ (DEL) *India* 28°34N 77°5E **120** B1
Deli Jovan *Serbia* 44°13N 22°9E **202** B6
Delia *Canada* 51°38N 112°23W **296** C6
Delice *Turkey* 39°54N 34°2E **212** C6
Delice → *Turkey* 40°45N 34°15E **212** B6
Délices *Dominica* 15°17N 61°17W **323** k
Delicias *Mexico* 28°13N 105°28W **318** B3
Delījān *Iran* 33°59N 50°40E **247** C6
Delimara Point *Malta* 35°49N 14°34E **206** F8
Déline *Canada* 65°11N 123°25W **294** D7
Delingha *China* 37°23N 97°23E **218** D8
Delisle *Canada* 51°55N 107°8W **297** C7
Delitzsch *Germany* 51°31N 12°20E **178** D8
Deliverance I. *Australia* 9°31S 141°34E **280** a
Dell City *U.S.A.* 31°56N 105°12W **314** F2
Dell Rapids *U.S.A.* 43°50N 96°43W **308** D5
Delle *France* 47°30N 7°2E **173** E14
Dellys *Algeria* 36°57N 3°57E **261** A5
Delmar *Iowa, U.S.A.* 42°0N 90°37W **310** C6
Delmar *N.Y., U.S.A.* 42°37N 73°47W **313** D11
Delmenhorst *Germany* 53°3N 8°37E **178** B4
Delmiro Gouveia *Brazil* 9°24S 38°6W **332** C4
Delnice *Croatia* 45°23N 14°50E **199** C11
Delonga, Ostrova *Russia* 76°40N 149°20E **215** B15
Deloraine *Tas., Australia* 41°30S 146°40E **281** G4
Deloraine *Man., Canada* 49°15N 100°29W **297** D8
Delos = Dilos *Greece* 37°23N 25°15E **205** D7
Delphi *Greece* 38°28N 22°30E **204** C4
Delphi *Ind., U.S.A.* 40°36N 86°41W **311** D10
Delphos *U.S.A.* 40°51N 84°21W **311** D12
Delportshoop *S. Africa* 28°22S 24°20E **270** C3
Delray Beach *U.S.A.* 26°28N 80°4W **317** J9
Delsbo *Sweden* 61°48N 16°32E **162** C10
Delta *Ala., U.S.A.* 33°26N 85°42W **316** B4
Delta *Colo., U.S.A.* 38°44N 108°4W **304** G9
Delta *Utah, U.S.A.* 39°21N 112°35W **304** G7
Delta □ *Nigeria* 5°30N 6°0E **263** D6
Delta Amacuro □ *Venezuela* 8°30N 61°30W **329** B5
Delta del Ebre △ *Spain* 40°43N 0°43E **196** E5
Delta del Po △ *Italy* 44°50N 12°15E **199** D9
Delta du Saloum △ *Senegal* 13°42N 16°43W **262** C1
Delta Dunărea △ *Romania* 45°15N 29°25E **183** E14
Delta Junction *U.S.A.* 64°2N 145°44W **303** D11
Deltona *U.S.A.* 28°54N 81°16W **317** G8
Delungra *Australia* 29°39S 150°51E **281** D5
Delvada *India* 20°46N 71°2E **242** J4
Delvinaki *Greece* 39°57N 20°32E **204** B2
Delvinë *Albania* 39°59N 20°6E **202** G4
Delyatyn *Ukraine* 48°32N 24°38E **183** B9
Demagiri *India* 22°55N 92°28E **241** E4
Demak *Indonesia* 6°53S 110°38E **235** D4
Demanda, Sierra de la *Spain* 42°15N 3°0W **196** C2
Demarcation Pt. *U.S.A.* 69°41N 141°18W **303** B12
Demarest *U.S.A.* 40°57N 73°57W **132** A2
Demavend = Damāvand, Qolleh-ye *Iran* 35°56N 52°10E **247** C7
Demba *Dem. Rep. of the Congo* 5°28S 22°15E **265** D4
Demba Chio *Angola* 9°41S 13°41E **265** D2
Dembecha *Ethiopia* 10°32N 37°30E **257** E4
Dembéni *Comoros Is.* 11°52S 43°23E **272** a
Dembéni *Mayotte* 12°50S 45°11E **272** b
Dembi *Ethiopia* 8°5N 36°25E **257** F4
Dembia *C.A.R.* 4°56N 23°53E **264** B4
Dembia *Dem. Rep. of the Congo* 3°33N 25°48E **268** B2
Dembica = Dębica *Poland* 50°2N 21°25E **185** H8
Dembidolo *Ethiopia* 8°34N 34°50E **257** F3
Demchok *India* 32°42N 79°29E **243** C8
Demer → *Belgium* 50°57N 4°42E **170** D4
Demerara Abyssal Plain *Atl. Oc.* 10°0N 48°0W **152** F7
Demetrias *Greece* 39°22N 23°1E **204** B5
Demidov *Russia* 55°16N 31°30E **188** E6
Deming *N. Mex., U.S.A.* 32°16N 107°46W **305** K10
Deming *Wash., U.S.A.* 48°50N 122°13W **306** B4
Demini → *Brazil* 0°46S 62°56W **329** D5
Demirci *Turkey* 39°2N 28°38E **205** B10
Demirköprü Barajı *Turkey* 38°42N 28°25E **205** C10
Demirköy *Turkey* 41°49N 27°45E **203** E11
Demirtas *Turkey* 36°25N 32°11E **250** B3
Demmin *Germany* 53°54N 13°2E **178** B9
Demnate *Morocco* 31°44N 6°59W **260** B3
Democracia *Brazil* 5°48S 61°26W **331** B5
Demonte *Italy* 44°19N 7°17E **198** D4
Demopolis *U.S.A.* 32°31N 87°50W **315** E11
Dempo *Indonesia* 4°2S 103°15E **234** C2
Demyansk *Russia* 57°40N 32°27E **188** D7
Den Bosch = 's-Hertogenbosch *Neths.* 51°42N 5°17E **170** C5
Den Burg *Neths.* 53°3N 4°47E **170** A4
Den Chai *Thailand* 17°59N 100°4E **236** D3
Den Haag = 's-Gravenhage *Neths.* 52°7N 4°17E **170** B4
Den Helder *Neths.* 52°57N 4°45E **170** B4
Den Ilp *Neths.* 52°27N 4°55E **112** A2
Den Lille Havfrue *Copenhagen, Denmark* **118** a3
Den Oever *Neths.* 52°56N 5°2E **170** B5
Denain *France* 50°20N 3°22E **173** B10
Denair *U.S.A.* 37°32N 120°48W **306** H6
Denali = McKinley, Mt. *U.S.A.* 63°4N 151°0W **303** E10
Denali △ *U.S.A.* 63°30N 152°0W **303** E10
Denau = Denov *Uzbekistan* 38°16N 67°54E **217** E7
Denbigh *Ont., Canada* 45°8N 77°15W **312** A7
Denbigh *Denbs., U.K.* 53°12N 3°25W **168** D4
Denbigh, C. *U.S.A.* 64°23N 161°32W **303** D7
Denbighshire □ *U.K.* 53°8N 3°22W **168** D4
Dendang *Indonesia* 3°7S 107°56E **235** C3
Dendé = Ndindi *Gabon* 3°46S 11°9E **264** C2
Dendermonde *Belgium* 51°2N 4°5E **170** C4
Deneba *Ethiopia* 9°47N 39°10E **257** F4
Deng Deng *Cameroon* 5°12N 13°31E **264** A2
Dengchuan *China* 25°59N 100°3E **228** E3
Denge *Nigeria* 12°52N 5°21E **263** C6
Dengfeng *China* 34°25N 113°2E **226** G7
Dengi *Nigeria* 9°25N 9°55E **263** D6
Dengkou *China* 40°18N 106°55E **226** D4
Dengzhou *China* 32°34N 112°4E **229** A9
Denham *Australia* 25°56S 113°31E **279** E1
Denham, Mt. *Jamaica* 18°13N 77°32W **320** a
Denham Ra. *Australia* 21°55S 147°46E **280** C4
Denham Sd. *Australia* 25°45S 113°15E **279** E1
Denholm *Canada* 52°39N 108°1W **297** C7
Denia *Spain* 38°49N 0°8E **197** G5
Denial B. *Australia* 32°14S 133°32E **281** E1
Deniliquin *Australia* 35°30S 144°58E **283** C6
Denimoo = Fort Resolution *Canada* 61°10N 113°40W **296** A6
Denis *Gabon* 0°19N 9°22E **264** B1
Denison *Iowa, U.S.A.* 42°1N 95°21W **308** D6
Denison *Tex., U.S.A.* 33°45N 96°33W **314** E6
Denison Plains *Australia* 18°35S 128°0E **278** C4
Denisovka *Kazakhstan* 52°27N 61°39E **216** B6
Denistone Heights *Australia* 33°48S 151°5E **139** A1
Deniyaya *Sri Lanka* 6°21N 80°33E **245** L5
Denizli *Turkey* 37°42N 29°2E **205** D11
Denizli □ *Turkey* 37°45N 29°5E **205** D11
Denman *Australia* 32°24S 150°42E **283** B9
Denman Glacier *Antarctica* 66°45S 100°0E **151** C8
Denmark *W. Austral., Australia* 34°59S 117°25E **279** F2
Denmark *S.C., U.S.A.* 33°19N 81°9W **316** B8
Denmark ■ *Europe* 55°45N 10°0E **163** J3
Denmark Str. *Atl. Oc.* 66°0N 30°0W **154** D8
Dennery *St. Lucia* 13°55N 60°54W **323** m
Dennison *U.S.A.* 40°24N 81°19W **312** F3
Denny *U.K.* 56°1N 3°55W **167** E5
Denov *Uzbekistan* 38°16N 67°54E **217** E7
Denpasar *Indonesia* 8°39S 115°13E **231** K18
Denpasar ✕ (DPS) *Indonesia* 8°44S 115°10E **231** K18
Denton *Ga., U.S.A.* 31°44N 82°42W **316** D7
Denton *Mont., U.S.A.* 47°19N 109°57W **304** C9
Denton *Tex., U.S.A.* 33°13N 97°8W **314** E6
Dentonia Park *Canada* 43°42N 79°17W **141** A3
D'Entrecasteaux, Îs. *N. Cal.* 18°0S 163°0E **277** D11
D'Entrecasteaux, Pt. *Australia* 34°50S 115°57E **279** F2
D'Entrecasteaux △ *Australia* 34°20S 115°33E **279** F2
D'Entrecasteaux Is. *Papua N. G.* 9°0S 151°0E **286** E6
Dentsville *U.S.A.* 34°4N 80°58W **316** A9
Denu *Ghana* 6°4N 1°8E **263** D5
Denver *Colo., U.S.A.* 39°42N 104°59W **304** G11
Denver *Ind., U.S.A.* 40°52N 86°5W **311** D10
Denver *Iowa, U.S.A.* 42°40N 92°20W **310** B4
Denver *Pa., U.S.A.* 40°14N 76°8W **313** F8
Denver City *U.S.A.* 32°58N 102°50W **314** E3
Denwood = Wainwright *Canada* 52°50N 110°50W **297** C6
Deoband *India* 29°42N 77°43E **242** E7
Deobhog *India* 19°53N 82°44E **244** E6
Deodrug *India* 16°26N 76°55E **245** F3
Deogarh *Odisha, India* 21°32N 84°45E **244** D7
Deogarh *Raj., India* 25°32N 73°54E **242** G5
Deoghar *India* 24°30N 86°42E **243** G12
Deogyusan △ *S. Korea* 35°45N 127°40E **224** E3
Deokjeokdo *S. Korea* 37°13N 126°7E **224** D3
Deolali *India* 19°58N 73°50E **244** E1
Deoli = Devli *India* 25°50N 75°20E **242** G6
Déols *France* 46°50N 1°43E **173** F8
Deora *India* 26°22N 70°55E **242** F4
Deorha = Jubbal *India* 31°5N 77°40E **242** D7
Deori *India* 23°24N 79°1E **243** H8
Deoria *India* 26°31N 83°48E **243** F10
Deosai Mts. *Pakistan* 35°40N 75°0E **243** B6
Deosri *India* 26°46N 90°29E **241** B3
Depalpur *India* 22°51N 75°33E **242** H6
DePaul Univ. *U.S.A.* 41°55N 87°39W **119** B3
Deposit *U.S.A.* 42°4N 75°25W **313** D9
Deptford *U.K.* 51°28N 0°1W **125** B3
Depuch I. *Australia* 20°37S 117°44E **278** D2
Deputati, Camera dei *Rome, Italy* **136** b2
Deputatskiy *Russia* 69°18N 139°54E **215** C14
Dêqên *China* 28°34N 98°51E **228** C2
Deqing *China* 23°8N 111°42E **229** F8
Dera, Lach → *Somalia* 0°15N 42°17E **267** D5
Dera Ghazi Khan *Pakistan* 30°5N 70°43E **242** D4
Dera Ismail Khan *Pakistan* 31°50N 70°50E **242** D4
Derabugti *Pakistan* 29°2N 69°9E **242** E3
Derawar Fort *Pakistan* 28°46N 71°20E **242** E4
Derbent *Russia* 42°5N 48°15E **191** J9
Derbent *Turkey* 38°11N 28°33E **205** C10
Derby *W. Austral., Australia* 17°18S 123°38E **278** C3
Derby *Derby City, U.K.* 52°56N 1°28W **168** E6
Derby *Conn., U.S.A.* 41°19N 73°5W **313** E11
Derby *Kans., U.S.A.* 37°33N 97°16W **308** G5
Derby *N.Y., U.S.A.* 42°41N 78°58W **312** D6
Derby City □ *U.K.* 52°56N 1°28W **168** E6
Derby Line *U.S.A.* 45°0N 72°6W **313** B12
Derbyshire □ *U.K.* 53°11N 1°38W **168** D6
Derdap △ *Serbia* 44°40N 22°23E **202** B6
Derdepoort *S. Africa* 24°38S 26°24E **270** B4
Derecske *Hungary* 47°20N 21°33E **182** C6
Dereham *U.K.* 52°41N 0°57E **169** E8
Dereköy *Turkey* 41°55N 27°21E **203** E11
Dereli *Turkey* 40°44N 38°26E **213** B8
Derg → *U.K.* 54°44N 7°26W **166** B4
Derg, L. *Ireland* 53°0N 8°20W **166** D3
Dergachi = Derhaci *Ukraine* 50°9N 36°11E **189** G9
Derhaci *Ukraine* 50°9N 36°11E **189** G9
Deridder *U.S.A.* 30°51N 93°17W **314** F8
Derik *Turkey* 37°21N 40°18E **213** D9
Derinkuyu *Turkey* 38°22N 34°45E **212** C6
Dermantsi *Bulgaria* 43°8N 24°17E **203** C8
Dermott *U.S.A.* 33°32N 91°26W **314** E9
Dernière Rivière *St. Lucia* 13°57N 60°55W **323** m
Dêrong *China* 28°44N 99°9E **228** C2
Derri *Somalia* 4°20N 46°37E **267** D6
Derrinallum *Australia* 37°57S 143°15E **282** D5
Derry = Londonderry *U.K.* 55°0N 7°20W **166** B4
Derry = Londonderry □ *U.K.* 55°0N 7°20W **166** B4
Derry *N.H., U.S.A.* 42°53N 71°19W **313** D13
Derry *Pa., U.S.A.* 40°20N 79°18W **312** F5
Derryveagh Mts. *Ireland* 54°56N 8°11W **166** B3
Derudub *Sudan* 17°31N 36°7E **256** D4
Derval *France* 47°40N 1°41W **172** E5
Derveni *Greece* 38°8N 22°25E **204** C4
Derventa *Bos.-H.* 44°59N 17°55E **182** F2
Derwent → *Cumb., U.K.* 54°39N 3°33W **168** C4
Derwent → *Derby, U.K.* 52°57N 1°28W **168** E6
Derwent → *N. Yorks., U.K.* 53°45N 0°58W **168** D7
Derwent Water *U.K.* 54°35N 3°9W **168** C4
Derzhavinsk *Kazakhstan* 51°6N 66°19E **217** B7
Des Moines *Iowa, U.S.A.* 41°35N 93°37W **310** C3
Des Moines *N. Mex., U.S.A.* 36°46N 103°50W **305** H12
Des Moines *Wash., U.S.A.* 47°24N 122°19W **306** C4
Des Moines → *U.S.A.* 40°23N 91°25W **310** D5
Des Moines ✕ (DSM) *U.S.A.* 41°32N 93°40W **310** C3
Des Plaines *U.S.A.* 42°2N 87°54W **311** B9
Des Plaines → *U.S.A.* 41°23N 88°15W **311** C8
Desa *Romania* 43°52N 23°2E **182** G8
Desaguadero *Peru* 16°34S 69°3W **330** D4
Desaguadero → *Argentina* 34°30S 66°46W **334** C2
Desaguadero → *Bolivia* 16°35S 69°5W **330** D4
Desantne *Ukraine* 45°34N 29°32E **183** E14
Désappointement, Is. du *French Polynesia* 14°10S 141°20W **289** f
Desaru *Malaysia* 1°31N 104°17E **237** d
Descanso, Pta. *Mexico* 32°21N 117°3W **307** N9
Descartes *France* 46°59N 0°42E **174** B4
Deschaillons-sur-St-Laurent *Canada* 46°32N 72°7W **299** C5
Deschambault L. *Canada* 54°50N 103°30W **297** C8
Deschutes → *U.S.A.* 45°38N 120°55W **304** D3
Descobrimento △ *Brazil* 16°53S 39°21W **333** E4
Dese *Ethiopia* 11°5N 39°40E **257** E4
Deseado, C. *Chile* 52°45S 74°42W **336** D2
Desenzano del Garda *Italy* 45°28N 10°32E **198** C7
Deseronto *Canada* 44°12N 77°3W **312** B7
Desert Center *U.S.A.* 33°43N 115°24W **307** M11
Desert Hot Springs *U.S.A.* 33°58N 116°30W **307** M10
Desert Wetlands Park *U.S.A.* 36°7N 115°2W **124** B2
Desertas, Ilhas *Madeira* 32°30N 16°30W **260** B1
Deset *Norway* 61°20N 11°26E **164** C8
Desfina *Greece* 38°25N 22°31E **204** C4
Deshaies *Guadeloupe* 16°18N 61°47W **322** e
Deshauteur *Guadeloupe* 16°15N 61°25W **322** e
Deshnok *India* 27°48N 73°21E **242** F5
Desierto Central de Baja California △ *Mexico* 29°40N 114°50W **318** B2
Desjardins, Complexe *Montréal, Canada* **130** b2
Deskati *Greece* 39°55N 21°49E **202** G5
Desna → *Ukraine* 50°33N 30°32E **177** C16
Desnățui → *Romania* 43°53N 23°35E **183** G8
Desolación, I. *Chile* 53°0S 74°0W **336** D2
Despeñaperros, Paso *Spain* 38°24N 3°30W **195** G7
Despeñaperros △ *Spain* 38°23N 3°32W **195** G7
Despotiko *Greece* 36°57N 24°58E **204** E6
Despotovac *Serbia* 44°6N 21°30E **202** B5
Dessau *Germany* 51°51N 12°14E **178** D8
Dessye = Dese *Ethiopia* 11°5N 39°40E **257** E4
Destin *U.S.A.* 30°24N 86°30W **317** E3
D'Estrees B. *Australia* 35°55S 137°45E **282** C2
Desuri *India* 25°18N 73°35E **242** G5
Desvres *France* 50°40N 1°48E **173** B8
Det Udom *Thailand* 14°54N 105°5E **236** E5
Deta *Romania* 45°24N 21°13E **182** E6
Dete *Zimbabwe* 18°38S 26°50E **270** A4
Đetinja → *Serbia* 43°51N 20°5E **202** C4
Detmold *Germany* 51°56N 8°52E **178** D4
Detour, Pt. *U.S.A.* 45°40N 86°40W **308** C10
Detroit *U.S.A.* 42°19N 83°12W **312** D1
Detroit Lakes *U.S.A.* 46°49N 95°51W **308** B6
Detroit Metropolitan Wayne County ✕ (DTW) *U.S.A.* 42°13N 83°21W **311** B13
Detskoye Selo = Pushkin *Russia* 59°45N 30°25E **188** C6
Dettifoss *Iceland* 65°48N 16°24W **155** B10
Detva *Slovak Rep.* 48°34N 19°25E **181** C12
Deua △ *Australia* 35°32S 149°46E **283** C8
Deurne *Neths.* 51°27N 5°49E **170** C5
Deutsch = Przemyśl *Poland* 49°50N 22°45E **185** J9
Deutsch Brod = Havlíčkův Brod *Czech Rep.* 49°36N 15°33E **180** B8
Deutsch-Eylau = Iława *Poland* 53°36N 19°34E **184** E6
Deutsch Krone = Wałcz *Poland* 53°17N 16°27E **185** E3
Deutsch-Luxemburgischer △ *Germany* 49°58N 6°12E **179** F2
Deutsche Bucht *Germany* 54°15N 8°0E **178** A4
Deutsche Oper *Germany* 52°30N 13°19E **115** A2
Deutsches Museum *Germany* 48°7N 11°35E **131** B2
Deutschland = Germany ■ *Europe* 51°0N 10°0E **178** E6
Deutschlandsberg *Austria* 46°49N 15°14E **180** E8
Deux-Sèvres □ *France* 46°35N 0°20W **172** F6
Deva *Romania* 45°53N 22°55E **182** E7
Devakottai *India* 9°55N 78°45E **245** K4
Devaprayag *India* 30°13N 78°35E **243** D8
Devarkonda *India* 16°42N 78°56E **244** F4
Dévaványa *Hungary* 47°2N 20°59E **182** C5
Deveci Dağları *Turkey* 40°10N 36°0E **212** B7
Devecikonağı *Turkey* 39°55N 28°34E **203** G12
Devecser *Hungary* 47°6N 17°26E **182** C2
Develi *Turkey* 38°23N 35°29E **212** C6
Deventer *Neths.* 52°15N 6°10E **170** B6
Devereux *U.S.A.* 33°13N 83°50W **316** B6
Deveron → *U.K.* 57°41N 2°32W **167** D6
Devesel *Romania* 44°28N 22°41E **182** F7
Devgad I. *India* 14°48N 74°5E **245** G2
Devgadh Bariya *India* 22°40N 73°55E **242** H5
Devgarh *India* 26°13N 73°52E **245** F1
Devi → *India* 19°59N 86°24E **244** E8
Devikot *India* 26°42N 71°12E **242** F4
Devil River Pk. *N.Z.* 40°56S 172°37E **285** A7
Devil's Bridge *Antigua & B.* 17°6N 61°41W **322** b
Devils Den *U.S.A.* 35°46N 119°58W **306** K7
Devils Hole = Death Valley △ *U.S.A.* 36°29N 117°6W **307** J9
Devils Island, I. = Diable, Île du *Fr. Guiana* 5°16N 52°34W **329** B7
Devils Lake *U.S.A.* 48°7N 98°52W **308** A4
Devils Paw *Canada* 58°47N 134°0W **296** B2
Devil's Peak *S. Africa* 33°57S 18°27E **118** A1
Devils Postpile △ *U.S.A.* 37°37N 119°5W **306** H7
Devil's Pt. *Sri Lanka* 9°26N 80°6E **245** K5
Devils Tower *U.S.A.* 44°35N 104°42W **304** D11
Devils Tower △ *U.S.A.* 44°48N 104°55W **304** D11
Devil's Woodyard Mud Volcano *Trin. & Tob.* 10°16N 61°22W **323** t
Devin *Bulgaria* 41°44N 24°24E **203** E8
Devine *U.S.A.* 29°8N 98°54W **314** G5
Devipattinam *India* 9°29N 78°54E **245** K4
Devizes *U.K.* 51°22N 1°58W **169** F6
Devli *India* 25°50N 75°20E **242** G6
Devnya *Bulgaria* 43°13N 27°33E **203** C11
Devoll → *Albania* 40°57N 20°15E **202** F4
Devon *Canada* 53°24N 113°44W **296** C6
Devon □ *U.K.* 50°50N 3°40W **169** G4
Devon I. *Canada* 75°10N 85°0W **295** B15
Devonport *Australia* 41°10S 146°22E **281** G4
Devrek *Turkey* 41°13N 31°57E **212** B4
Devrekâni *Turkey* 41°36N 33°50E **212** B5
Devrez → *Turkey* 41°6N 34°25E **212** B6
Devrukh *India* 17°3N 73°37E **244** F1
Dewas *India* 22°59N 76°3E **242** H7
Dewetsdorp *S. Africa* 29°33S 26°39E **270** C4
Dewey *Puerto Rico* 18°18N 65°18W **321** b
Dexing *China* 28°46N 117°30E **229** C11
Dexter *Maine, U.S.A.* 45°1N 69°18W **309** C19
Dexter *Mich., U.S.A.* 42°20N 83°53W **311** B13
Dexter *Mo., U.S.A.* 36°48N 89°57W **308** G9
Dexter *N. Mex., U.S.A.* 33°12N 104°22W **305** K11
Dey-Dey, L. *Australia* 29°12S 131°4E **279** E5
Deyang *China* 31°3N 104°27E **228** B5
Deyhūk *Iran* 33°15N 57°30E **247** C8
Deyyer *Iran* 27°55N 51°55E **247** E6
Dez → *Iran* 31°39N 48°52E **213** F13
Dezadeash L. *Canada* 60°28N 136°58W **296** A1
Dezfūl *Iran* 32°20N 48°30E **213** F13
Dezhneva, Mys *Russia* 66°5N 169°40W **215** C19
Dezhou *China* 37°26N 116°18E **226** F9
Dhadhar → *India* 24°56N 85°24E **243** G11
Dhahabān *Si. Arabia* 21°58N 39°3E **248** B2
Dhahiriya = Az̧ Z̧āhirīyah *West Bank* 31°25N 34°58E **251** G5
Dhahran = Az̧ Z̧ahrān *Si. Arabia* 26°10N 50°7E **247** E6
Dhak *Pakistan* 32°25N 72°33E **242** C5
Dhaka *Bangla.* 23°43N 90°26E **241** D3
Dhaka □ *Bangla.* 24°25N 90°25E **241** C3
Dhakuria *India* 22°30N 88°22E **124** B2
Dhali *Cyprus* 35°1N 33°25E **207** E9
Dhamangaon *India* 20°48N 78°9E **244** D4
Dhamār *Yemen* 14°30N 44°20E **248** D4
Dhamār □ *Yemen* 14°30N 44°20E **248** D4
Dhampur *India* 29°19N 78°33E **243** E8
Dhamra → *India* 20°47N 86°58E **244** D8
Dhamtari *India* 20°42N 81°35E **244** D5
Dhanbad *India* 23°50N 86°30E **243** H12
Dhangarhi *Nepal* 28°55N 80°40E **243** E9
Dhankuta *Nepal* 26°55N 87°40E **243** F12
Dhanora *India* 20°20N 80°22E **244** D5
Dhanpuri *India* 23°13N 81°30E **244** C5
Dhanushkodi *India* 9°11N 79°24E **245** K4
Dhar *India* 22°35N 75°26E **242** H6
Dharampur *India* 22°13N 75°18E **242** H6
Dharamsala = Dharmsala *India* 32°16N 76°23E **242** C7
Dharan *Nepal* 26°49N 87°17E **243** F12
Dharangaon *India* 21°1N 75°16E **244** D2
Dharapuram *India* 10°45N 77°34E **245** J3
Dharavi *India* 19°1N 72°51E **130** A2
Dhariwal *India* 31°57N 75°19E **242** D6
Dharla → *Bangla.* 25°46N 89°42E **243** G13
Dharmanagar *India* 24°22N 92°10E **241** C4
Dharmapuri *India* 12°10N 78°10E **245** H4
Dharmavaram *India* 14°29N 77°44E **245** G3
Dharmjaygarh *India* 22°28N 83°13E **243** H10
Dharmsala *India* 32°16N 76°23E **242** C7
Dharni *India* 21°33N 76°53E **242** J7
Dharug △ *Australia* 33°20S 151°2E **283** B9
Dharur *India* 18°3N 76°8E **244** E3
Dharwad *India* 15°30N 75°4E **245** G2
Dhasan → *India* 25°48N 79°24E **243** G8
Dhaulagiri *Nepal* 28°39N 83°28E **243** E10
Dhebar, L. *India* 24°10N 74°0E **242** G6
Dheftera *Cyprus* 35°5N 33°16E **207** E9
Dhemaji *India* 27°29N 94°35E **241** B5
Dhenkanal *India* 20°45N 85°35E **244** D7
Dherinia *Cyprus* 35°3N 33°57E **207** E9
Dheskáti = Deskati *Greece* 39°55N 21°49E **202** G5
Dhī Qār □ *Iraq* 31°0N 46°15E **246** D5
Dhiarrizos → *Cyprus* 34°41N 32°34E **207** F8
Dhībān *Jordan* 31°30N 35°46E **251** G6
Dhilwan *India* 31°31N 75°21E **242** D6
Dhimarkhera *India* 23°28N 80°22E **243** H9
Dhodhekánisos = Dodecanese *Greece* 36°35N 27°0E **205** E8
Dholka *India* 22°44N 72°29E **242** H5
Dhomokós = Domokos *Greece* 39°10N 22°18E **204** B4
Dhond = Daund *India* 18°26N 74°40E **244** E2
Dhone *India* 15°25N 77°53E **245** G3
Dhoraji *India* 21°45N 70°37E **242** J4
Dhorpatan *Nepal* 28°29N 83°4E **243** E10
Dhragonisi = Tragonhsi *Greece* 37°27N 25°29E **205** D7
Dhrangadhra *India* 22°59N 71°31E **242** H4
Dhrol *India* 22°33N 70°25E **242** H4
Dhubāb *Yemen* 12°56N 43°25E **248** D3
Dhuburi *India* 26°2N 89°59E **241** B2
Dhulasar *Bangla.* 21°52N 90°14E **241** E3
Dhule *India* 20°58N 74°50E **244** D2
Dhupdhara *India* 26°10N 91°4E **241** B3
Dhurbo *Somalia* 11°37N 50°20E **267** B7
Dhuusamarreeb *Somalia* 5°30N 46°15E **267** C6
Di-ib, W. → *Sudan* 22°38N 36°6E **256** C4
Di Linh *Vietnam* 11°35N 108°4E **237** G7
Di Linh, Cao Nguyen *Vietnam* 11°30N 108°0E **237** G7
Dia *Greece* 35°28N 25°14E **207** D6
Dia Deva = Butcher I. *India* 18°57N 72°53E **130** B2
Diabakania *Guinea* 10°38N 10°58W **262** C2
Diable, Île du *Fr. Guiana* 5°16N 52°34W **329** B7
Diable, Pte. du *Martinique* 14°46N 60°53W **322** j
Diables, Morne aux *Dominica* 15°37N 61°27W **323** k
Diablo Pt. *N. Marianas* 15°0N 145°35E **302** e
Diablo Range *U.S.A.* 37°20N 121°25W **306** J5
Diablotins, Morne *Dominica* 15°30N 61°24W **323** k
Diadema *Brazil* 23°41S 46°37W **137** C2
Diafarabé *Mali* 14°9N 4°57W **262** C4
Diala *Mali* 14°10N 9°58W **262** C3
Dialakoro *Mali* 12°18N 7°54W **262** C3
Dialakoto *Senegal* 13°21N 13°19W **262** C2
Diallassagou *Mali* 13°47N 3°41W **262** C4
Diamant, Pte. du *Martinique* 14°27N 61°3W **322** j
Diamant, Rocher du *Martinique* 14°27N 61°2W **322** j
Diamante *Argentina* 32°5S 60°40W **334** C3
Diamante *Italy* 39°41N 15°49E **201** C8
Diamante → *Argentina* 34°30S 66°46W **334** C2
Diamantina *Brazil* 18°17S 43°40W **333** E3
Diamantina → *Australia* 26°45S 139°10E **281** D2
Diamantina △ *Australia* 23°33S 141°23E **280** C3
Diamantino *Brazil* 14°30S 56°30W **331** C6
Diamond Bar *U.S.A.* 34°1N 117°48W **307** L9
Diamond Harbour *India* 22°11N 88°14E **243** H13
Diamond Head *U.S.A.* 21°16N 157°49W **302** K14
Diamond I. *Grenada* 12°20N 61°35W **323** q
Diamond Is. *Australia* 17°25S 151°5E **280** B5
Diamond Mts. *U.S.A.* 39°40N 115°50W **304** G6
Diamond Springs *U.S.A.* 38°42N 120°49W **306** G6
Diamou *Mali* 14°5N 11°16W **262** C2
Dian Chi *China* 24°50N 102°43E **228** E4
Dianalund *Denmark* 55°32N 11°30E **163** J5
Dianbai *China* 21°33N 111°0E **229** G8
Diancheng *China* 21°30N 111°4E **229** G8
Dianjiang *China* 30°24N 107°20E **228** B6
Diano Marina *Italy* 43°54N 8°5E **198** E5
Dianópolis *Brazil* 11°38S 46°50W **333** D2
Dianra *Ivory C.* 8°45N 6°14W **262** D3
Diaoyu Dao = Senkaku-Shotō *E. China Sea* 25°45N 123°30E **221** M1
Diaoyu Tai = Senkaku-Shotō *E. China Sea* 25°45N 123°30E **221** M1
Diapaga *Burkina Faso* 12°5N 1°46E **263** C5
Diapangou *Burkina Faso* 12°5N 0°10E **263** C5
Diariguila *Guinea* 10°35N 10°2W **262** C2
Diavolo, Mt. *India* 12°40N 92°56E **245** H11
Dibā = Dibbā al Ḩiṣn *U.A.E.* 25°45N 56°16E **247** E8
Dibagah *Iraq* 35°52N 43°48E **213** E10
Dibai *India* 28°13N 78°15E **242** E8
Dibaya *Dem. Rep. of the Congo* 6°30S 22°57E **265** D4
Dibaya-Lubue *Dem. Rep. of the Congo* 4°12S 19°54E **265** C3
Dibbā al Ḩiṣn *U.A.E.* 25°45N 56°16E **247** E8
Dibbeen △ *Jordan* 32°20N 35°45E **251** F6
Dibella *Niger* 17°32N 13°6E **259** E2
D'Iberville, Lac *Canada* 55°55N 73°15W **298** A5
Dibete *Botswana* 23°45S 26°32E **270** B4
Dibi *Cameroon* 7°8N 13°43E **264** A2
Dibru-Saikhowa △ *India* 27°40N 95°25E **241** B5
Dibrugarh *India* 27°29N 94°55E **241** B5
Diciosânmartin = Târnăveni *Romania* 46°19N 24°13E **183** D9
Dickens *U.S.A.* 33°37N 100°50W **314** E4
Dickeyville *U.S.A.* 42°38N 90°36W **310** B6
Dickinson *U.S.A.* 46°53N 102°47W **308** B2
Dickinson B. *Antigua & B.* 17°10N 61°51W **322** b
Dick's Pt. *Bahamas* 25°4N 77°18W **153** b
Dickson = Dikson *Russia* 73°40N 80°5E **214** B9
Dickson *U.S.A.* 36°5N 87°23W **315** C11
Dickson City *U.S.A.* 41°28N 75°36W **313** E9
Dicle Barajı *Turkey* 38°20N 40°11E **213** C9
Dicle Nehri → *Turkey* 37°44N 41°10E **213** D9
Dicomano *Italy* 43°53N 11°31E **199** E8
Didesa, W. → *Ethiopia* 10°2N 35°32E **257** E4
Didiéni *Mali* 13°53N 8°6W **262** C3
Didim *Turkey* 37°22N 27°16E **205** D9
Didimbo *Angola* 17°30S 21°45E **265** F4
Didimoticho *Greece* 41°22N 26°29E **203** E10
Didsbury *Canada* 51°35N 114°10W **296** C6
Didwana *India* 27°23N 74°36E **242** F6
Die *France* 44°47N 5°22E **175** D9
Diébougou *Burkina Faso* 11°0N 3°15W **262** C4
Diecke *Guinea* 7°27N 8°54W **262** D3
Diedenhofen = Thionville *France* 49°20N 6°10E **173** C13
Diefenbaker, L. *Canada* 51°0N 106°55W **297** C7
Diegem *Belgium* 50°53N 4°26E **116** A2
Diego de Almagro *Chile* 26°22S 70°3W **334** B1
Diego Garcia *Ind. Oc.* 7°50S 72°50E **273** E6
Diego Martin *Trin. & Tob.* 10°43N 61°34W **323** t
Diego Ramírez, Islas *Chile* 56°30S 68°44W **336** E3
Diego Suarez = Antsiranana *Madag.* 12°25S 49°20E **272** A2
Diekirch *Lux.* 49°52N 6°10E **170** E6
Diéma *Mali* 14°32N 9°12W **262** C3
Diembéring *Senegal* 12°29N 16°47W **262** C1
Diemelsee △ *Germany* 51°20N 8°40E **178** D4
Diemen *Neths.* 52°21N 4°58E **112** A2
Dien Ban *Vietnam* 15°53N 108°16E **236** E7
Dien Bien Phu *Vietnam* 21°20N 103°0E **228** G4
Dien Chau, Vinh *Vietnam* 19°0N 105°55E **236** C5
Dien Khanh *Vietnam* 12°15N 109°6E **237** F7
Diepholz *Germany* 52°37N 8°22E **178** C4
Diepkloof *S. Africa* 26°14S 27°57E **123** B1
Dieppe *France* 49°54N 1°4E **172** C8
Dieppe Bay Town *St. Kitts & Nevis* 17°25N 62°48W **322** d
Dieprivier *S. Africa* 34°2S 18°27E **118** B1
Dierks *U.S.A.* 34°7N 94°1W **314** D7
Diest *Belgium* 50°58N 5°4E **170** D5
Dieterich *U.S.A.* 39°4N 88°23W **311** E8
Dietikon *Switz.* 47°24N 8°24E **179** H4
Dieulefit *France* 44°32N 5°4E **175** D9
Dieuze *France* 48°49N 6°43E **173** D13
Dievenow = Dziwnów *Poland* 54°2N 14°45E **184** D1
Dif *Somalia* 0°59N 40°58E **267** D5
Diffa *Niger* 13°18N 12°36E **263** C7
Diffa □ *Niger* 14°0N 12°30E **263** C7
Differdange *Lux.* 49°31N 5°54E **170** E5
Diffun *Phil.* 16°36N 121°33E **232** C3
Dig *India* 27°28N 77°20E **242** F7
Digba *Dem. Rep. of the Congo* 4°25N 25°48E **268** B2
Digboi *India* 27°23N 95°38E **241** B5
Digby *Canada* 44°38N 65°50W **299** D6
Digges Is. *Canada* 62°40N 77°50W **295** E16
Diggi *India* 26°22N 75°26E **242** F6
Dighinala *Bangla.* 23°15N 92°5E **241** D4
Dighton *U.S.A.* 38°29N 100°28W **308** F3
Digity Mud Volcanoes *Trin. & Tob.* 10°12N 61°25W **323** t
Diglur *India* 18°34N 77°33E **244** E3
Digna *Mali* 14°48N 8°10W **262** C3
Digne-les-Bains *France* 44°5N 6°12E **175** D10
Digoin *France* 46°29N 4°1E **173** F11
Digor *Turkey* 40°22N 43°25E **213** B10
Digos *Phil.* 6°45N 125°20E **233** H5
Digranes *Iceland* 66°4N 14°44W **155** A12
Digras *India* 20°6N 77°45E **244** D3
Digul → *Indonesia* 7°7S 138°42E **231** F9
Digya △ *Ghana* 7°15N 0°5E **263** D5
Dihang = Brahmaputra → *Asia* 23°40N 90°35E **241** D3
Diinsoor *Somalia* 2°24N 42°59E **267** D5
Dijlah, Nahr → *Asia* 31°0N 47°25E **246** D5
Dijon *France* 47°20N 5°3E **173** E12
Dikhil *Djibouti* 11°8N 42°20E **257** E5
Dikili *Turkey* 39°4N 26°53E **205** B8
Dikirnis *Egypt* 31°6N 31°35E **256** H7
Dikkil = Dikhil *Djibouti* 11°8N 42°20E **257** E5
Dikodougou *Ivory C.* 9°4N 5°45W **262** D3
Diksmuide *Belgium* 51°2N 2°52E **170** C2
Dikson *Russia* 73°40N 80°5E **214** B9
Dikti Oros *Greece* 35°8N 25°30E **207** E6
Dikwa *Nigeria* 12°4N 13°30E **263** C7
Dila *Ethiopia* 6°21N 38°22E **257** F4
Dilasag *Phil.* 16°25N 122°11E **232** C4
Dilbeek *Belgium* 50°51N 4°17E **116** A1
Dilek Yarimadisi △ *Turkey* 37°40N 27°10E **205** D9
Dili *E. Timor* 8°39S 125°34E **231** F7
Diligent Strait *India* 12°11N 92°57E **245** H11
Dilijan *Armenia* 40°46N 44°57E **191** K7
Dilinata *Greece* 38°13N 20°31E **207** C2
Dilizhan = Dilijan *Armenia* 40°46N 44°57E **191** K7
Dilj *Croatia* 45°29N 18°1E **182** E3
Dillenburg *Germany* 50°43N 8°17E **178** E4
Dilley *U.S.A.* 28°40N 99°10W **314** G5
Dilli = Delhi *India* 28°39N 77°13E **120** B2
Dilli *Mali* 15°1N 7°40W **262** C3
Dillia → *Niger* 14°9N 12°50E **259** F2
Dilling *Sudan* 12°3N 29°35E **257** E2
Dillingen *Bayern, Germany* 48°36N 10°30E **179** G6
Dillingen *Saarland, Germany* 49°22N 6°43E **179** F2
Dillingham *U.S.A.* 59°3N 158°28W **303** G8
Dillon *Sask., Canada* 55°56N 108°35W **297** B7
Dillon *Mont., U.S.A.* 45°13N 112°38W **304** D7
Dillon *S.C., U.S.A.* 34°25N 79°22W **315** D15
Dillon → *Canada* 55°56N 108°56W **297** B7
Dillsboro *U.S.A.* 39°1N 85°4W **311** E11

Dillsburg *U.S.A.* 40°7N 77°2W **312** F7
Dilolo
  Dem. Rep. of the Congo 10°28S 22°18E **265** E4
Dilos *Greece* 37°23N 25°15E **205** D7
Dilove *Ukraine* 47°56N 24°11E **183** C9
Dimapur *India* 25°54N 93°45E **241** C4
Dimas *Mexico* 23°43N 106°47W **318** C3
Dimasalang *Phil.* 12°12N 123°51E **232** E4
Dimashq *Syria* 33°30N 36°18E **250** E7
Dimashq □ *Syria* 33°30N 36°30E **250** E7
Dimbaza *S. Africa* 32°50S 27°14E **271** D4
Dimbelenge
  Dem. Rep. of the Congo 5°33S 23°7E **265** D4
Dimbokro *Ivory C.* 6°45N 4°46W **262** D4
Dimboola *Australia* 36°28S 142°7E **282** D5
Dîmboviţa = Dâmboviţa →
  Romania 44°12N 26°26E **183** F11
Dimbulah *Australia* 17°8S 145°4E **280** B4
Dimitrovgrad *Bulgaria* 42°5N 25°35E **203** D9
Dimitrovgrad *Russia* 54°14N 49°39E **190** C9
Dimitrovgrad *Serbia* 43°2N 22°48E **202** C6
Dimitrovo = Pernik
  Bulgaria 42°35N 23°2E **202** D7
Dimitsana *Greece* 37°36N 22°3E **204** D4
Dimmitt *U.S.A.* 34°33N 102°19W **314** D3
Dimona *Israel* 31°2N 35°1E **246** D4
Dimonika *↑ Congo* 4°13S 12°21E **264** C2
Dimovo *Bulgaria* 43°43N 22°50E **202** C6
Dinagat *↑ Phil.* 10°0N 125°35E **233** F5
Dinagat I. *Phil.* 10°10N 125°40E **233** F5
Dinaig *Phil.* 7°11N 124°10E **233** H5
Dinajpur *Bangla.* 25°33N 88°43E **241** C2
Dinalupihan *Phil.* 14°52N 120°28E **232** D3
Dinan *France* 48°28N 2°2W **172** D4
Dīnān Āb *Iran* 32°4N 56°49E **247** C8
Dinant *Belgium* 50°16N 4°55E **170** D4
Dinapur *India* 25°38N 85°5E **243** G11
Dinar *Turkey* 38°5N 30°10E **205** C12
Dīnār, Kūh-e *Iran* 30°42N 51°46E **247** D6
Dinara Planina *Croatia* 44°0N 16°30E **199** D13
Dinard *France* 48°38N 2°6W **172** D4
Dinaric Alps = Dinara Planina
  Croatia 44°0N 16°30E **199** D13
Dinas *Phil.* 7°38N 123°20E **233** H4
Dinbych-y-Pysgod = Tenby
  U.K. 51°40N 4°42W **169** F3
Dindanko *Mali* 14°8N 9°30W **262** C3
Dinde *Angola* 14°17S 13°42E **265** G2
Dinder, Nahr ed → *Sudan* 14°6N 33°40E **257** E3
Dinder △ *Sudan* 12°30N 35°10E **257** F4
Dindi → *India* 16°24N 78°15E **245** F4
Dindigul *India* 10°25N 78°0E **245** G4
Dindori *India* 22°57N 81°5E **243** H9
Ding Xian = Dingzhou
  China 38°30N 114°59E **226** E8
Dinga *Dem. Rep. of the Congo* 5°17S 16°42E **265** D3
Dinga *Pakistan* 32°26N 67°10E **242** G2
Dingalan *Phil.* 15°18N 121°25E **232** D3
Dingalan B. *Phil.* 15°18N 121°25E **232** D3
Ding'an *China* 19°42N 110°19E **236** C8
Dingbian *China* 37°35N 107°32E **226** E4
Dingelstädt *Germany* 51°18N 10°19E **178** D6
Dingle *Kerry, Ireland* 52°9N 10°17W **166** D1
Dingle *Sweden* 58°32N 11°35E **163** F5
Dingle B. *Ireland* 52°3N 10°20W **166** D1
Dingle Pen. *Ireland* 52°12N 10°5W **166** D1
Dingli *Malta* 35°52N 14°23E **206** F7
Dingmans Ferry *U.S.A.* 41°13N 74°55W **313** C10
Dingo *Australia* 23°38S 149°19E **280** C4
Dingolfing *Germany* 48°37N 12°30E **179** G8
Dingras *Phil.* 18°6N 120°42E **232** B3
Dingtao *China* 35°5N 115°35E **226** G8
Dinguiraye *Guinea* 11°18N 10°49W **262** C2
Dingwall *U.K.* 57°36N 4°26W **167** D4
Dingxi *China* 35°30N 104°33E **226** G3
Dingxiang *China* 38°30N 112°58E **226** E7
Dingyuan *China* 32°32N 117°41E **229** A11
Dingzhou *China* 38°30N 114°59E **226** E8
Dinh, Mui *Vietnam* 11°22N 109°1E **237** G7
Dinh Lap *Vietnam* 21°33N 107°6E **236** B6
Dinhata *India* 26°8N 89°27E **241** B2
Dinin → *Ireland* 52°43N 7°18W **166** D4
Dinira △ *Venezuela* 9°57N 70°6W **333** B5
Dinokwe *Botswana* 23°29S 26°37E **270** B4
Dinorwic *Canada* 49°41N 92°30W **297** D10
Dinosaur △ *Alta.,*
  Canada 50°47N 111°30W **296** D6
Dinosaur △ *Colo., U.S.A.* 40°30N 108°45W **304** F9
Dinuba *U.S.A.* 36°32N 119°23W **306** K8
Diö *Sweden* 56°37N 14°15E **163** H8
Dioila *Mali* 12°23N 6°50W **262** C3
Dioka *Mali* 14°57N 10°4W **262** C2
Diomede *U.S.A.* 65°47N 169°0W **303** D5
Diona *Chad* 17°51N 22°36E **259** E4
Diongoï *Mali* 14°38N 8°34W **262** C3
Dionisades *Greece* 35°20N 26°10E **207** E7
Dionysos, Theatro *Athens, Greece* **112** C2
Diósgyör *Hungary* 48°7N 20°43E **182** B5
Diosig *Romania* 47°18N 22°2E **182** C7
Diougani *Mali* 14°19N 2°44W **262** C4
Dioulouloou *Senegal* 13°5N 16°38W **262** C1
Dioura *Mali* 14°59N 5°12W **262** C3
Diourbel *Senegal* 14°39N 16°12W **262** C1
Diourbel □ *Senegal* 14°45N 16°15W **262** C1
Dipaculao *Phil.* 15°51N 121°32E **232** D3
Dipalpur *Pakistan* 30°40N 73°39E **242** D5
Diphu *India* 25°50N 93°26E **241** C4
Dipkarpaz = Rizokarpaso
  Cyprus 35°36N 34°23E **207** E10
Diplo *Pakistan* 24°35N 69°35E **242** G3
Dipolog *Phil.* 8°36N 123°20E **233** G4
Dipperu △ *Australia* 21°56S 148°42E **280** C4
Dipton *N.Z.* 45°54S 168°22E **285** F3
Dir *Pakistan* 35°8N 71°59E **240** B3
Dirë *Mali* 16°20N 3°25W **262** B4
Dire Dawa *Ethiopia* 9°35N 41°45E **257** F5
Dirfis Oros *Greece* 38°40N 23°54E **204** C5
Diriamba *Nic.* 11°51N 86°19W **320** D2
Dirico *Angola* 17°50S 20°42E **265** H4
Dirk Hartog I. *Australia* 25°50S 113°5E **279** E1
Dirkou *Niger* 19°1N 12°52E **259** E2
Dirnismaning *Germany* 48°13N 11°38E **131** A2
Dirranbandi *Australia* 28°33S 148°17E **283** A4
Dirs *Si. Arabia* 17°58N 42°19E **257** F4
Dirschau = Tczew *Poland* 54°8N 18°50E **184** D5
Disa *India* 24°18N 72°10E **242** G5
Disa *Sudan* 12°5N 34°15E **257** E3
Disappointment, C.
  U.S.A. 46°18N 124°5W **306** D2
Disappointment, L.
  Australia 23°20S 122°40E **278** D3
Disaster B. *Australia* 37°15S 149°58E **283** D8
Discovery B. *Vic.,*
  Australia 38°10S 140°40E **282** E4
Discovery B. *China* 22°18N 114°1E **219** a
Discovery B. △ *Australia* 38°9S 141°16E **282** E4
Discovery Seamount
  Atl. Oc. 42°0S 0°10E **152** L12
Disentis Muster *Switz.* 46°42N 8°50E **179** J4
Dishna *Egypt* 26°9N 32°23E **256** B3
Disina *Nigeria* 11°35N 9°50E **263** C6
Disko = Qeqertarsuaq
  Greenland 69°45N 53°30W **154** D5
Disko Bugt *Greenland* 69°10N 52°0W **154** D5

Disna = Dzisna →
  Belarus 55°34N 28°12E **188** E5
Disney-M.G.M. Studios
  U.S.A. 28°21N 81°33W **133** B1
Disney Reef *Tonga* 19°17S 174°7W **287** P13
Disney Studios *U.S.A.* 34°9N 118°19W **126** B3
Disneyland Hong Kong
  China 22°18N 114°2E **219** a
Dispur *India* 26°3N 91°52E **241** B3
Diss *U.K.* 52°23N 1°7E **169** E9
Disteghil Sar *Pakistan* 36°20N 75°12E **243** A6
District of Columbia □
  U.S.A. 38°55N 77°0W **309** F15
Distrito Federal □ *Brazil* 15°45S 47°45W **333** E2
Distrito Federal □ *Mexico* 19°15N 99°10W **319** D5
Distrito Federal □
  Venezuela 10°30N 66°55W **328** A4
Disûq *Egypt* 31°8N 30°35E **256** H7
Ditan Park *Beijing, China* **114** a2
Diu *India* 20°45N 70°58E **242** J4
Diuata Mts. *Phil.* 9°0N 125°50E **233** G5
Divândarreh *Iran* 35°55N 47°2E **213** E12
Divarata *Greece* 38°20N 20°33E **207** C2
Divenié *Congo* 2°43S 12°1E **264** C2
Dives → *France* 49°18N 0°7W **172** C6
Dives-sur-Mer *France* 49°18N 0°8W **172** C6
Divi Pt. *India* 15°59N 81°9E **245** G5
Divichi = Dâvâçi
  Azerbaijan 41°15N 48°57E **191** K9
Divide *U.S.A.* 45°45N 112°45W **304** D7
Dividing Ra. *Australia* 27°45S 116°0E **279** E2
Divilican B. *Phil.* 17°21N 122°19E **232** C4
Divinópolis *Brazil* 20°10S 44°54W **333** F3
Divisões, Serra dos *Brazil* 17°0S 51°0W **333** E1
Divjake *Albania* 41°0N 19°32E **202** F3
Divnoye *Russia* 45°55N 43°21E **191** H6
Divo *Ivory C.* 5°48N 5°15W **262** D3
Divriği *Turkey* 39°22N 38°7E **213** C8
Dīwāl Kol *Afghan.* 34°23N 67°52E **242** B2
Dix → *U.S.A.* 37°49N 84°43W **311** G12
Dixie Mt. *U.S.A.* 39°55N ‐20°16W **306** F6
Dixie Union *U.S.A.* 31°20N 82°28W **316** D7
Dixmoor *U.S.A.* 41°37N 87°41W **119** D2
Dixon *Calif., U.S.A.* 38°27N 121°49W **306** G5
Dixon *Ill., U.S.A.* 41°50N 89°29W **310** C7
Dixon *N.M., U.S.A.* 37°59N 92°6W **310** G4
Dixon Entrance *U.S.A.* 54°30N ‐32°0W **303** J14
Dixville *Canada* 45°4N 71°46W **313** A13
Diyadin *Turkey* 39°33N 43°40E **213** C10
Diyālā □ *Iraq* 33°45N 44°50E **246** C5
Diyālā → *Iraq* 33°13N 44°30E **213** F11
Diyarb Nigm *Egypt* 30°45N 31°26E **251** H2
Diyarbakır *Turkey* 37°55N 40°18E **213** D9
Diyarbakır □ *Turkey* 38°0N 40°10E **213** D9
Diyodar *India* 24°8N 71°50E **242** G4
Dizangué *Cameroon* 3°46N 9°59E **264** B1
Dja → *Cameroon* 3°10N 12°58E **264** B2
Djadié → *Gabon* 0°46N 12°58E **264** B2
Djado *Niger* 21°4N 12°14E **259** D2
Djado, Plateau du *Niger* 21°29N 12°21E **259** D2
Djakarta = Jakarta
  Indonesia 6°9S ‐06°52E **122** A2
Djamâa *Algeria* 33°32N 5°59E **261** B6
Djamba *Angola* 16°45S 13°58E **265** H2
Djambala *Congo* 2°32S 14°30E **264** C2
Djanet *Algeria* 24°35N 9°32E **261** D6
Djaul I. *Papua N. G.* 2°58S 150°57E **286** B6
Djawa = Jawa *Indonesia* 7°0S 110°0E **235** D4
Djebel Tazzeka △ *Morocco* 34°6N 4°11W **260** B4
Djebiniana *Tunisia* 35°1N 11°0E **261** A8
Djédaa *Chad* 13°31N 18°34E **259** F3
Djelfa *Algeria* 34°40N 3°15E **261** B5
Djelfa □ *Algeria* 34°20N 3°40E **261** B5
Djema *C.A.R.* 6°3N 25°15E **264** A5
Djember *Chad* 10°25N 17°50E **259** F3
Djembo
  Dem. Rep. of the Congo 9°54S 22°18E **265** D4
Djémila *Algeria* 36°19N 5°44E **261** A6
Djendel *Algeria* 36°15N 2°25E **261** A5
Djenné *Mali* 14°0N 4°30W **262** C4
Djenoun, Garet el *Algeria* 25°4N 5°31E **261** C6
Djerba *Tunisia* 33°48N 10°54E **258** B2
Djerba, Î. de *Tunisia* 33°50N 10°48E **258** B2
Djérème → *Cameroon* 5°20N 13°24E **264** A2
Djerid, Chott *Tunisia* 33°42N 8°30E **258** B1
Djermaya *Chad* 12°24N 15°3E **259** F3
Djibo *Burkina Faso* 14°9N 1°35W **263** C4
Djibouti *Djibouti* 11°30N 43°5E **257** E5
Djibouti ■ *Africa* 12°0N 43°0E **257** E5
Djohong *Cameroon* 6°47N 14°20E **264** B4
Djolu *Dem. Rep. of the Congo* 0°35N 22°5E **264** B4
Djouab → *Gabon* 1°13N 13°12E **264** B2
Djoudj △ *Senegal* 16°24N 16°14W **262** B1
Djougou *Benin* 9°40N 1°45E **263** D5
Djoum *Cameroon* 2°41N 12°35E **264** B2
Djouna *Chad* 10°27N 20°4E **259** F4
Djugu *Dem. Rep. of the Congo* 1°55N 30°35E **266** B3
Djukbinj △ *Australia* 12°11S 131°2E **278** B5
Djúpavík *Iceland* 65°57N 21°33W **155** B4
Djúpivogur *Iceland* 64°39N 14°17W **155** C12
Djupvasshytta *Norway* 62°2N 7°16E **154** B3
Djurås *Sweden* 60°34N 15°8E **162** D9
Djurdjura △ *Algeria* 35°20N 4°15E **261** A5
Djūrö △ *Sweden* 58°52N 13°28E **163** F7
Djursholm *Sweden* 59°24N 18°5E **139** A2
Djursland *Denmark* 56°27N 10°45E **163** H4
Dmitriya Lapteva, Proliv
  Russia 73°0N 140°0E **215** B15
Dmitriyev Lgovskiy *Russia* 52°10N 35°0E **189** F8
Dmitriyevsk = Makiyivka
  Ukraine 48°0N 38°0E **189** H9
Dmitrov *Russia* 56°25N 37°32E **188** B9
Dmitrovsk-Orlovskiy
  Russia 52°29N 35°10E **188** F9
Dnepr = Dnipro →
  Ukraine 46°30N 32°18E **189** J7
Dneprodzerzhinsk =
  Dniprodzerzhynsk
  Ukraine 48°32N 34°37E **189** H8
Dneprodzerzhinskoye Vdkhr. =
  Dniprodzerzhynske Vdskh.
  Ukraine 48°49N 34°8E **189** H8
Dnepropetrovsk = Dnipropetrovsk
  Ukraine 48°30N 35°0E **189** H8

Dnipropetrovsk □
  Ukraine 48°15N 34°50E **189** H8
Dniprorudne *Ukraine* 47°21N 34°58E **189** J8
Dnister → *Europe* 46°18N 30°17E **177** E16
Dnistrovskyy Lyman
  Ukraine 46°15N 30°17E **189** J6
Dno *Russia* 57°50N 29°58E **188** D5
Dnyapro = Dnipro →
  Ukraine 46°30N 32°18E **189** J7
Do Gonbadān = Gachsārān
  Iran 30°15N 50°45E **247** D6
Doaba *Afghan.* 36°1N 69°32E **240** A3
Doabi *Afghan.* 36°11N 69°32E **240** A3
Doaktown *Canada* 46°33N 66°8W **299** C6
Doan Hung *Vietnam* 21°30N 105°10E **236** B5
Doany *Madag.* 14°21S 49°30E **272** A2
Doba *Chad* 8°40N 16°50E **259** G3
Dobandi *Pakistan* 31°13N 66°50E **242** D2
Dobbiaco *Italy* 46°44N 12°14E **199** B7
Dobbyn *Australia* 19°44S 140°2E **280** B3
Dobele *Latvia* 56°37N 23°16E **186** B10
Dobele *Latvia* 56°35N 23°15E **184** B10
Döbeln *Germany* 51°6N 13°7E **178** D9
Doberai, Jazirah *Indonesia* 1°25S 133°0E **231** E8
Döberitz *Germany* 52°32N 13°3E **115** A4
Dobiegniew *Poland* 52°59N 15°45E **185** F2
Doblas *Argentina* 37°5S 64°0W **334** D3
Döbling *Germany* 48°14N 16°20E **142** A2
Dobo *Dem. Rep. of the Congo* 2°20N 22°11E **264** B4
Dobo *Indonesia* 5°45S 134°15E **231** F8
Doboj *Bos.-H.* 44°46N 18°4E **182** F3
Dobong *S. Korea* 37°39N 127°2E **137** B2
Dobongsan *S. Korea* 37°40N 127°0E **137** A2
Dobra *Wielkopolskie, Poland* 51°55N 18°37E **185** G5
Dobra *Zachodnio-Pomorskie,*
  Poland 53°34N 15°20E **184** E2
Dobra *Dâmbovita,*
  Romania 44°52N 25°40E **183** F10
Dobra *Hunedoara, Romania* 45°54N 22°36E **182** E7
Dobre Miasto *Poland* 53°58N 20°26E **184** E7
Dobreşti *Romania* 46°51N 22°18E **182** D7
Dobrich *Bulgaria* 43°37N 27°49E **203** C11
Dobrich □ *Bulgaria* 43°37N 27°49E **203** C11
Dobrinishta *Bulgaria* 41°49N 23°34E **202** E7
Dobříš *Czech Rep.* 49°46N 14°10E **180** B7
Dobrodzień *Poland* 50°45N 18°25E **185** H5
Dobromyl *Ukraine* 49°34N 22°46E **185** D9
Dobron *Ukraine* 48°25N 22°32E **182** B8
Dobropole *Ukraine* 48°25N 37°2E **189** H9
Dobrovolsk *Russia* 54°46N 22°31E **184** D9
Dobruja *Europe* 44°30N 28°15E **183** F13
Dobrush *Belarus* 52°25N 31°22E **177** B16
Dobrzany *Poland* 53°22N 15°25E **184** E2
Dobrzyń nad Wisłą *Poland* 52°39N 19°22E **185** F6
Doc, Mui *Vietnam* 17°58N 106°30E **236** D6
Doc Can I. *Phil.* 5°55N 119°56E **233** J2
Doce → *Brazil* 19°37S 39°49W **333** E3
Docker River = Kaltukatjara
  Australia 24°52S 129°5E **279** D4
Docklands *U.K.* 51°30N 0°1W **125** A3
Docksta *Sweden* 63°3N 18°18E **162** A12
Doctor Arroyo *Mexico* 23°40N 100°11W **318** C4
Doctor Pedro P. Peña
  Paraguay 22°27S 62°21W **331** E5
Doctor Phillips *U.S.A.* 28°26N 81°29W **133** B2
Doctors Inlet *U.S.A.* 30°6N 81°47W **316** E8
Doda *India* 33°10N 75°34E **243** C6
Doda, L. *Canada* 49°25N 75°13W **298** C4
Doda Betta *India* 11°24N 76°44E **245** J3
Dodballapur *India* 13°18N 77°32E **245** H3
Dodder → *Ireland* 53°20N 6°13W **167** C5
Dodecanese *Greece* 36°35N 27°0E **205** E8
Dodekanisa = Dodecanese
  Greece 36°35N 27°0E **205** E8
Dodekanisa □ *Greece* 36°35N 27°0E **205** E8
Dodge City *U.S.A.* 37°45N 100°1W **308** H3
Dodge L. *Canada* 59°50N 105°36W **297** B7
Dodgeville *U.S.A.* 42°58N 90°8W **310** B8
Dodman Pt. *U.K.* 50°13N 4°48W **169** G3
Dodo *Cameroon* 7°30N 12°5E **263** D7
Dodo *South Sudan* 5°10N 29°57E **257** F2
Dodola *Ethiopia* 6°59N 39°11E **257** F4
Dodoma *Tanzania* 6°8S 35°45E **268** D4
Dodoma □ *Tanzania* 6°0S 36°0E **268** D4
Dodori △ *Kenya* 1°55S 41°7E **268** C5
Dodsland *Canada* 51°50N 108°45W **297** C7
Dodson *U.S.A.* 48°24N 108°15W **304** B9
Doerun *U.S.A.* 31°19N 83°55W **316** D6
Doesburg *Neths.* 52°1N 6°9E **170** B6
Dog Creek *Canada* 51°35N 122°14W **296** C4
Dog I. *U.S.A.* 29°48N 84°36W **316** F5
Dog L., *Man., Canada* 51°2N 98°31W **297** C9
Dog L., *Ont., Canada* 48°48N 89°30W **298** C2
Dogana di Mare, Palazzo *Venice, Italy* **142** c3
Doğankent *Turkey* 36°52N 35°18E **250** D7
Doğanşehir *Turkey* 38°5N 37°55E **212** C7
Dogliani *Italy* 44°32N 7°56E **198** D4
Dōgo *Japan* 36°15N 133°16E **222** A5
Dōgo-San *Japan* 35°2N 133°13E **222** B5
Dogondoutchi *Niger* 13°38N 4°2E **263** C5
Dogran *Pakistan* 31°48N 73°35E **242** D5
Dogs, Isle of *U.K.* 51°29N 0°1W **125** B3
Doğubayazıt *Turkey* 39°31N 44°5E **213** C11
Doğuéraoua *Niger* 14°0N 5°31E **263** C6
Dogura *Papua N. G.* 10°6S 150°9E **286** F6
Doha = Ad Dawḩah
  Qatar 25°15N 51°35E **247** E6
Dohazari *Bangla.* 22°10N 92°5E **241** D4
Dohinog = Manukan
  Phil. 8°32N 123°12E **233** G4
Dohrighat *India* 26°16N 83°31E **243** F10
Doi *Indonesia* 2°14N 127°49E **231** D7
Doi Inthanon *Thailand* 18°33N 98°34E **236** C2
Doi Inthanon △ *Thailand* 18°33N 98°34E **236** C2
Doi Khuntan △ *Thailand* 18°33N 99°14E **236** C2
Doi Luang *Thailand* 18°30N 101°0E **236** C3
Doi Luang △ *Thailand* 19°22N 99°35E **236** C2
Doi Phukha △ *Thailand* 19°8N 101°9E **236** C3
Doi Saket *Thailand* 18°52N 99°9E **236** C2
Doi Suthep Pui △ *Thailand* 18°49N 98°53E **236** C2
Doi Toa *Thailand* 17°55N 98°30E **236** D2
Dois Irmãos, Sa. *Brazil* 9°0S 42°30W **332** D5
Dojransko Jezero
  Macedonia 41°13N 22°44E **202** E6
Doka *Sudan* 13°31N 35°46E **257** E4
Dokdo = Liancourt Rocks
  Asia 37°15N 131°52E **221** F5
Dokka *Norway* 60°49N 10°7E **164** D7
Dokka → *Norway* 60°49N 10°7E **164** D7
Dokkum *Neths.* 53°20N 5°59E **170** A5
Dokos *Greece* 37°20N 23°20E **204** D5
Dokri *Pakistan* 27°25N 68°7E **242** F3
Dokshukino = Nartkala
  Russia 43°33N 43°51E **191** J6
Dokuchayevsk *Ukraine* 47°44N 37°40E **189** J9
Dol-de-Bretagne *France* 48°34N 1°47W **172** D5
Dolak, Pulau *Indonesia* 8°0S 138°30E **231** F9
Dolbeau-Mistassini
  Canada 48°53N 72°14W **299** B5
Dole *France* 47°7N 5°31E **173** E12
Doleib, Wadi → *Sudan* 12°56N 33°35E **257** E3
Dolenji Logatec = Logatec
  Slovenia 45°56N 14°15E **199** C11

Dolgellau *U.K.* 52°45N 3°53W **168** E4
Dolgelley = Dolgellau *U.K.* 52°45N 3°53W **168** E4
Doncaster *U.K.* 53°32N 1°6W **168** D6
Dondo *Angola* 9°45S 14°25E **265** D2
Dondo
  Dem. Rep. of the Congo 4°11N 21°39E **264** B4
Dondo *Mozam.* 19°33S 34°46E **269** F3
Dondo, Teluk *Indonesia* 0°50N 120°30E **231** D6
Dondra Head *Sri Lanka* 5°55N 80°40E **245** M5
Dondușeni *Moldova* 48°14N 27°36E **183** B12
Dondușeni *Moldova* 48°14N 27°36E **183** B12
Donegal *Ireland* 54°39N 8°5W **166** B3
Donegal □ *Ireland* 54°53N 8°0W **166** B3
Donegal B. *Ireland* 54°31N 8°49W **166** B3
Donets → *Russia* 47°33N 40°55E **191** G5
Donets Basin *Ukraine* 49°0N 38°0E **158** F13
Donetsk *Ukraine* 48°0N 37°45E **189** J9
Donetsk □ *Ukraine* 48°0N 37°45E **189** J9
Dong Ba Thin *Vietnam* 12°8N 109°13E **237** F7
Dong Dang *Vietnam* 21°54N 106°42E **236** B6
Dong Giam *Vietnam* 19°25N 105°31E **236** C5
Dong Ha *Vietnam* 16°55N 107°8E **236** D6
Dong Hene *Laos* 16°40N 105°18E **236** D5
Dong Hoi *Vietnam* 17°29N 106°36E **236** D6
Dong Jiang → *China* 23°6N 114°0E **229** F10
Dong Khe *Vietnam* 22°26N 106°27E **236** A6
Dong Phayayen *Thailand* 14°20N 101°22E **236** E3
Dong Ujimqin Qi *China* 45°32N 116°55E **226** B8
Dong Van *Vietnam* 23°16N 105°22E **236** A5
Dong Xoai *Vietnam* 11°32N 106°55E **237** G6
Donga *Nigeria* 7°45N 10°2E **263** D7
Donga → *Nigeria* 8°20N 9°58E **263** D7
Dong'an *China* 26°23N 111°12E **229** D8
Dongan Hills *U.S.A.* 40°35N 74°5W **123** F10
Dongara *Australia* 29°14S 114°57E **279** E1
Dongargarh *India* 21°10N 80°40E **244** D5
Dongbei *China* 45°0N 125°0E **227** D13
Dongcheng *Beijing, China* **114** b2
Dongchuan *China* 26°8N 103°1E **228** D4
Dongdaemung *S. Korea* 37°34N 127°2E **137** B2
Dongducheon *S. Korea* 37°54N 127°3E **137** A1
Donges *France* 47°18N 2°4W **172** E4
Dongfang *China* 18°50N 108°33E **236** C7
Dongfeng *China* 42°40N 125°34E **226** C13
Donggala *Indonesia* 0°30S 119°40E **235** C5
Donggan *China* 23°22N 105°9E **236** A5
Donggang *China* 39°52N 124°10E **224** C2
Donggou *China* 31°17N 121°33E **228** B8
Dongguan *China* 22°58N 113°44E **229** F9
Dongguang *China* 37°50N 116°30E **226** F9
Donghae *S. Korea* 37°29N 129°7E **224** C4
Donghai Dao *China* 21°0N 110°15E **229** G8
Dongjak *S. Korea* 37°30N 126°56E **137** B1
Dongjiao *China* 23°5N 113°12E **121** B2
Dongjingcheng *China* 44°5N 129°10E **227** B15
Dongkou *China* 27°6N 110°35E **229** D8
Donglan *China* 24°30N 107°21E **228** E6
Dongliao He → *China* 42°58N 123°32E **227** C12
Dongliu *China* 30°13N 116°55E **229** C11
Dongmen *China* 22°20N 107°48E **228** F6
Dongnae *S. Korea* 35°12N 129°5E **224** E4
Dongning *China* 44°2N 131°5E **227** B16
Dongnyi *China* 28°3N 100°15E **228** C3
Dongo *Angola* 14°36S 15°48E **265** E3
Dongobe
  Dem. Rep. of the Congo 4°35N 23°13E **264** B4
Dongola *Sudan* 19°9N 30°22E **256** D2
Dongou *Congo* 2°0N 18°5E **264** B3
Dongping *China* 35°55N 116°20E **226** G9
Dongri *India* 18°53N 72°57E **130** B2
Dongsha Dao
  S. China Sea 20°45N 116°43E **229** G11
Dongshan *China* 23°43N 117°30E **229** F11
Dongshanhu Park *China* 23°7N 113°17E **121** B2
Dongsheng *China* 39°50N 110°0E **226** E6
Dongsi Mosque *Beijing, China* **114** b2
Dongtai *China* 32°51N 120°21E **227** H11
Dongting Hu *China* 29°18N 112°45E **229** C9
Dongtou *China* 27°51N 121°10E **229** D13
Dongxiang *China* 28°11N 116°34E **229** C11
Dongxing *China* 21°34N 108°0E **228** G7
Dongyang *China* 29°13N 120°15E **229** C13
Dongyin *China* 37°33N 118°37E **227** F10
Dongyinggang *China* 37°55N 118°58E **227** F10
Dongzhi *China* 30°9N 117°0E **229** C11
Dongzhimen *China* 39°55N 116°24E **114** B2
Donington, C. *Australia* 34°45S 136°0E **282** C2
Doniphan *U.S.A.* 36°37N 90°50W **308** G8
Donja Stubica *Croatia* 45°59N 15°59E **199** C12
Donji Dušnik *Serbia* 43°12N 22°5E **202** C6
Donji Miholjac *Croatia* 45°45N 18°10E **182** E3
Donji Milanovac *Serbia* 44°28N 22°6E **202** B6
Donji Vakuf *Bos.-H.* 44°8N 17°24E **182** F2
Donna *Nordland, Norway* 66°6N 12°30E **160** C15
Donna *Tex., U.S.A.* 26°9N 98°4W **314** J5
Donnaconna *Canada* 46°41N 71°41W **299** C5
Donnelly's Crossing *N.Z.* 35°42S 173°38E **284** B2
Donner Pass *U.S.A.* 39°19N 120°20W **306** F6
Donnybrook *W. Austral.,*
  Australia 33°34S 115°48E **279** F2
Donnybrook *Dublin,*
  Ireland 53°19N 6°14W **120** D2
Donnybrook *KwaZulu Natal,*
  S. Africa 29°59S 29°48E **271** D4
Donora *U.S.A.* 40°11N 79°52W **312** F5
Donostia = Donostia-San Sebastián
  Spain 43°17N 1°58W **196** B3
Donostia-San Sebastián
  Spain 43°17N 1°58W **196** B3
Donousa *Greece* 37°5N 25°48E **205** D7
Donovan *U.S.A.* 40°53N 87°37W **311** D9
Donque *Angola* 15°28S 14°6E **265** E2
Donskoy *Russia* 53°55N 38°15E **188** F10
Donsol *Phil.* 12°54N 123°38E **232** E4
Donwood *Canada* 44°19N 78°16W **312** B6
Donzère *France* 44°28N 4°43E **175** D8
Donzy *France* 47°20N 3°6E **173** E10
Dookie *Australia* 36°20S 145°41E **283** D6
Doon → *U.K.* 55°27N 4°39W **167** F4
Doon Doon ◎ *Australia* 16°5S 128°5E **278** C4
Doornfontein *S. Africa* 26°11S 28°3E **123** B2
Doon → *U.K.* 55°27N 4°39W **167** F4
Dora, L. *Australia* 22°0S 123°0E **278** D3
Dora Báltea → *Italy* 45°11N 8°3E **198** C5
Dora Ripária → *Italy* 45°5N 7°44E **198** C4
Doran L. *Canada* 61°13N 108°6W **297** A7
Doraville *U.S.A.* 33°54N 84°17W **316** B5
Dorchester *Dorset, U.K.* 50°42N 2°27W **169** G5
Dorchester *Oxon., U.K.* 51°38N 1°10W **169** F6
Dorchester, C. *Canada* 65°27N 77°27W **295** B13
Dorchester Heights Nat. Historical
  Site *U.S.A.* 42°20N 71°2W **124** B3
Dordabis *Namibia* 22°57S 17°38E **270** C2
Dordogne □ *France* 45°5N 0°40E **174** C4
Dordogne → *France* 45°2N 0°36W **174** C2
Dordrecht *Neths.* 51°48N 4°39E **170** C4
Dordrecht *Eastern Cape,*
  S. Africa 31°20S 27°3E **270** D4
Dore → *France* 45°50N 3°35E **175** C7
Dore, Mts. *France* 45°32N 2°50E **175** C6
Doré L. *Canada* 54°46N 107°17W **297** C7
Dorée → *St. Lucia* 13°46N 61°3W **323** m

Donaustadt *Austria* 48°13N 16°29E **142** A2
Donauwörth *Germany* 48°43N 10°47E **179** G6
Doncaster *U.K.* 53°32N 1°6W **168** D6
Dondo *Angola* 9°45S 14°25E **265** D2
Dondo
  Dem. Rep. of the Congo 4°11N 21°39E **264** B4
Dores da Boa Esperança = Boa
  Esperança *Brazil* 3°21N 61°23W **329** C5
Dores do Indaiá *Brazil* 19°27S 45°36W **333** E3
Dorfen *Germany* 48°15N 12°8E **179** G8
Dorgali *Italy* 40°17N 9°35E **200** B2
Dori *Burkina Faso* 14°3N 0°2W **263** C4
Doring → *S. Africa* 31°54S 18°39E **270** D2
Doringbos *S. Africa* 31°59S 19°16E **270** D2
Dorking *U.K.* 51°14N 0°19W **169** F7
Dormaa-Ahenkro *Ghana* 7°15N 2°52W **262** D4
Dormans *France* 49°4N 3°38E **173** C10
Dormo, Ras *Eritrea* 13°14N 42°35E **257** E5
Dornach *Germany* 48°9N 11°41E **131** B3
Dornakal *India* 17°27N 80°10E **244** F5
Dornbirn *Austria* 47°25N 9°45E **180** D2
Dornes *France* 46°48N 3°18E **173** F10
Dorneşti *Romania* 47°52N 26°1E **183** C11
Dornie *U.K.* 57°17N 5°31W **167** D3
Dornoch *Ont., Canada* 44°18N 80°51W **312** B4
Dornoch *Highl., U.K.* 57°53N 4°2W **167** D4
Dornoch Firth *U.K.* 57°51N 4°4W **167** D4
Dornogovĭ □ *Mongolia* 44°0N 110°0E **226** C6
Doro *Mali* 16°9N 0°51W **263** B4
Doro, Kavo *Greece* 38°9N 24°38E **204** C6
Dorog *Hungary* 47°42N 18°45E **182** C3
Dorogobuzh *Russia* 54°50N 33°18E **188** E7
Dorohoi *Romania* 47°56N 26°23E **183** C11
Döröö Nuur *Mongolia* 48°0N 93°0E **217** C12
Dorpat = Tartu *Estonia* 58°20N 26°44E **188** C4
Dorr *Iran* 33°17N 50°38E **247** C6
Dorre I. *Australia* 25°13S 113°12E **279** E1
Dorrigo *Australia* 30°20S 152°44E **283** A10
Dorrigo □ *Australia* 30°22S 152°47E **283** A10
Dorris *U.S.A.* 41°58N 121°55W **304** F3
Dorset *Ont., Canada* 45°14N 78°54W **312** A6
Dorset *Vt., U.S.A.* 43°15N 73°5W **313** C11
Dorset □ *U.K.* 50°45N 2°26W **169** G5
Dorsoduro *Venice, Italy* **142** B1
Dorsten *Germany* 51°40N 6°58E **178** D2
Dortmund *Germany* 51°30N 7°28E **178** D3
Dortmund-Ems-Kanal →
  Germany 51°50N 7°26E **178** D3
Dörtyol *Turkey* 36°50N 36°13E **250** B7
Doruk *Turkey* 36°53N 35°45E **250** B6
Dorum *Germany* 53°41N 8°34E **178** B4
Doruma
  Dem. Rep. of the Congo 4°42N 27°33E **268** B2
Dorüneh *Iran* 35°10N 57°18E **247** C8
Dorval Int.. Montréal ✈ (YUL)
  Canada 45°28N 73°44W **130** B1
Dos Bahías, C. *Argentina* 44°58S 65°32W **336** B3
Dos d'Âne *Réunion* 20°58S 55°23E **272** f
Dos Hermanas *Spain* 37°16N 5°55W **195** H5
Dos Moninos → *Brazil* 22°9S 54°50S **335** A5
Dos Palos *U.S.A.* 36°59N 120°37W **306** J6
Dösemealtı *Turkey* 37°4N 30°36E **205** D12
Dosso *Niger* 13°0N 3°13E **263** C5
Dosso □ *Niger* 13°30N 3°30E **263** C5
Dosso → *Niger* 12°36N 2°36E **263** C5
Dostyq *Kazakhstan* 45°15N 82°29E **217** C10
Dot Lake *U.S.A.* 63°40N 144°4W **303** E11
Dothan *U.S.A.* 31°13N 85°24W **316** D4
Doty *U.S.A.* 46°38N 123°17W **306** D3
Douai *France* 50°21N 3°4E **173** B10
Douako *Guinea* 9°45N 10°8W **262** D2
Douala *Cameroon* 4°0N 9°45E **264** B1
Douala-Edéa △ *Cameroon* 3°20N 9°41E **264** B1
Douaumongo, C. *Mayotte* 12°38S 45°8E **272** b
Douaouir *Mali* 20°45N 3°0W **260** D4
Douarnenez *France* 48°6N 4°21W **172** D2
Doubabougou *Mali* 14°13N 7°59W **262** C3
Double Cove *N.Z.* 45°4S 168°49E **285** F3
Double Island Pt.
  Australia 25°56S 153°11E **281** D5
Double Mountain Fork →
  U.S.A. 33°16N 100°0W **314** E4
Doubrava → *Czech Rep.* 53°2N 15°20E **180** A8
Doubs □ *France* 47°10N 6°20E **173** E13
Doubs → *France* 46°53N 5°1E **173** F12
Doubtful Sd. *N.Z.* 45°20S 166°49E **285** F1
Doubtless B. *N.Z.* 34°55S 173°26E **284** A2
Doudeville *France* 49°43N 0°47E **172** C7
Doué-la-Fontaine *France* 47°11N 0°16W **172** E6
Douentza *Mali* 14°58N 2°48W **262** C4
Douentza □ *Mali* 15°40N 2°25W **262** C4
Dougga *Tunisia* 36°25N 9°13E **258** A1
Doughboy B. *N.Z.* 47°2S 167°40E **285** G1
Douglas *Ont., Canada* 45°31N 76°56W **312** A8
Douglas *I. of Man* 54°10N 4°28W **168** C3
Douglas *Northern Cape,*
  S. Africa 29°4S 23°46E **270** D3
Douglas *Alaska, U.S.A.* 58°17N 134°24W **303** E14
Douglas *Ariz., U.S.A.* 31°21N 109°33W **305** L9
Douglas *Ga., U.S.A.* 31°31N 82°51W **316** D7
Douglas *Mich., U.S.A.* 42°33N 86°14W **311** B10
Douglas *Wyo., U.S.A.* 42°45N 105°24W **304** D11
Douglas Apsley □
  Australia 41°45S 148°11E **281** G4
Douglas B. *Dominica* 15°36N 61°29W **323** k
Douglas C. *Canada* 58°51N 153°15W **303** D9
Douglas Chan. *Canada* 53°40N 129°20W **296** C3
Douglas Park *U.S.A.* 41°51N 87°42W **119** B2
Douglasville *U.S.A.* 33°45N 84°45W **316** B5
Douirat *Morocco* 33°2N 4°11W **260** B4
Doukaton, Akra *Greece* 38°34N 20°33E **207** B2
Doukkala-Abda □
  Morocco 32°10N 8°50W **260** B3
Doukoula *Cameroon* 10°10N 15°0E **259** F2
Doulevant-le-Château
  France 48°23N 4°55E **173** D11
Doullens *France* 50°10N 2°20E **173** B9
Doumé *Cameroon* 4°15N 13°25E **264** B2
Doumen *China* 22°10N 113°18E **229** F9
Douna *Mali* 13°13N 6°0W **262** C3
Dounreay *U.K.* 58°35N 3°44W **167** C5
Dourada, Serra *Brazil* 13°⁻0S 48°45W **333** D2
Dourados *Brazil* 22°9S 54°50S **335** A5
Dourados □ *Brazil* 21°58S 54°18W **335** A5
Dourados, Serra dos
  Brazil 23°30S 53°30W **335** A5
Dourbali *Chad* 11°49N 15°52E **259** F3
Dourdan *France* 48°30N 2°1E **173** D9
Douro → *Europe* 41°8N 8°40W **194** D2
Douvaine *France* 46°19N 6°16E **173** F13
Douville *Guadeloupe* 16°13N 61°32W **322** e
Douvres-la-Délivrande
  France 49°17N 0°23W **172** C6
Douz *Tunisia* 33°25N 9°0E **258** B1
Dove → *U.K.* 52°51N 1°36W **168** E6
Dove Creek *U.S.A.* 37°46N 108°54W **305** H9
Dover *Australia* 43°18S 147°2E **281** G4
Dover *Kent, U.K.* 51°7N 1°19E **169** F9
Dover *Del., U.S.A.* 39°10N 75°32W **309** F16
Dover *Ky., U.S.A.* 38°43N 83°54W **311** F12
Dover *N.H., U.S.A.* 43°12N 70°56W **313** C14
Dover *N.J., U.S.A.* 40°53N 74°34W **313** F10
Dover *Ohio, U.S.A.* 40°32N 81°29W **312** F3
Dover, Pt. *Australia* 32°32S 125°32E **279** F4
Dover, Str. of *Europe* 51°0N 1°30E **169** G9
Dover-Foxcroft *U.S.A.* 45°11N 69°13W **302** C7
Dover Plains *U.S.A.* 41°43N 73°35W **313** E11
Dovey = Dyfi → *U.K.* 52°32N 4°0W **169** E3
Dovhe *Ukraine* 48°22N 23°17E **183** B8

Dovlen = Devin Bulgaria 41°44N 24°24E 203 E8
Dovre Norway 61°58N 9°15E 164 C6
Dovre △ Norway 62°10N 9°30E 164 B6
Dovrefjell Norway 62°15N 9°33E 164 B6
Dovrefjell-Sunndalsfjella △ Norway 62°23N 9°11E 164 B6
Dow Rūd Iran 33°28N 49°4E 247 C6
Dowa Malawi 13°38S 33°58E 269 E3
Dowagiac U.S.A. 41°59N 86°6W 311 C10
Dowerin Australia 31°12S 117°2E 279 F2
Dowgha'i Iran 36°54N 58°32E 247 B8
Dowlat Yār Afghan. 34°30N 65°45E 240 B2
Dowlatābād Farāh, Afghan. 32°47N 62°40E 240 B1
Dowlatābād Fāryāb, Afghan. 36°26N 64°55E 240 A2
Dowlatābād Kermān, Iran 28°20N 56°40E 247 D8
Dowlatābād Khorāsān, Iran 35°16N 59°29E 247 C8
Dowlatābād Tehrān, Iran 35°38N 51°27E 141 B2
Dowling Park U.S.A. 30°15N 83°15W 316 E6
Down □ U.K. 54°23N 6°2W 166 B5
Down, L. U.S.A. 28°30N 81°31W 133 A1
Downers Grove U.S.A. 41°48N 88°1W 311 C8
Downey Calif., U.S.A. 33°56N 118°9W 126 C4
Downey Idaho, U.S.A. 42°26N 112°7W 304 E7
Downham Market U.K. 52°37N 0°23E 169 E8
Downieville U.S.A. 39°34N 120°50W 306 F6
Downing U.S.A. 40°29N 92°22W 310 D4
Downpatrick U.K. 54°20N 5°43W 166 B6
Downpatrick Hd. Ireland 54°20N 9°21W 166 B2
Downsview Canada 43°43N 79°30W 141 A2
Downsview Park Canada 43°45N 79°29W 141 A2
Downsville U.S.A. 42°5N 75°0W 313 D10
Downton, Mt. Canada 52°42N 124°52W 296 C4
Dowsārī Iran 28°25N 57°59E 247 D8
Dowshī Afghan. 35°35N 68°43E 240 B3
Doxato Greece 41°9N 24°16E 203 E8
Doyle U.S.A. 40°2N 120°6W 306 E6
Doylestown U.S.A. 40°21N 75°10W 313 F9
Dōzen Japan 36°5N 133°5E 222 A5
Dozois, Rés. Canada 47°30N 77°5W 298 C4
Dra Khel Pakistan 27°58N 66°45E 242 F2
Drâa, C. Morocco 28°47N 11°0W 260 C2
Drâa, Hamada du Algeria 28°0N 7°0W 260 C3
Drâa, Oued → Morocco 28°40N 11°10W 260 C2
Drac → France 45°12N 5°42E 175 C9
Drac, Coves del Spain 39°31N 3°19E 206 B4
Dračevo Macedonia 41°56N 21°31E 202 E5
Drachten Neths. 53°7N 6°5E 170 A6
Drăgănești Moldova 47°43N 28°15E 183 C13
Drăgănești-Olt Romania 44°9N 24°32E 183 F9
Drăgănești-Vlașca Romania 44°5N 25°33E 183 F10
Dragaš = Sharr Kosovo 42°5N 20°41E 202 D4
Drăgășani Romania 44°39N 24°17E 183 F9
Dragichyn Belarus 52°15N 25°8E 177 B13
Dragocvet Serbia 43°58N 21°15E 202 C5
Dragon's Mouths Trin. & Tob. 11°0N 61°50W 323 t
Dragør Denmark 55°35N 12°38E 118 B3
Dragovishtitsa Bulgaria 42°22N 22°39E 202 D6
Draguignan France 43°32N 6°27E 175 E10
Drahove Ukraine 48°14N 23°33E 183 B8
Drain U.S.A. 43°40N 123°19W 304 E2
Drake U.S.A. 47°55N 100°23W 308 B3
Drake Passage S. Ocean 58°0S 68°0W 151 B17
Drakensberg S. Africa 31°0S 28°0E 271 D4
Drama Greece 41°9N 24°10E 203 E8
Drama □ Greece 41°20N 24°0E 203 E8
Dramburg = Drawsko Pomorskie Poland 53°35N 15°50E 184 E2
Drammen Norway 59°42N 10°12E 164 E7
Drancy France 48°55N 2°26E 134 A3
Drangajökull Iceland 66°9N 22°15W 155 A4
Drangedal Norway 59°6N 9°3E 164 E6
Drangsnes Iceland 65°41N 21°27W 155 A5
Dranov, Ostrov Romania 44°55N 29°30E 183 F14
Drapetsona Greece 37°56N 23°37E 112 B1
Dras India 34°25N 75°48E 243 B6
Drastis, Akra Greece 39°48N 19°40E 206 B9
Drau = Drava → Croatia 45°33N 18°55E 182 E3
Drava → Croatia 45°33N 18°55E 182 E3
Dravograd Slovenia 46°36N 15°5E 199 B12
Drawa → Poland 52°52N 15°59E 185 F2
Drawieński △ Poland 53°6N 15°58E 185 E2
Drawno Poland 53°13N 15°46E 185 E2
Drawsko Pomorskie Poland 53°35N 15°50E 184 E2
Drayton Canada 43°46N 80°40W 312 C4
Drayton Plains U.S.A. 42°41N 83°23W 311 B13
Drayton Valley Canada 53°12N 114°58W 296 C6
Dreieich Germany 50°1N 8°41E 179 E4
Dreikikir Papua N. G. 3°35S 142°46E 286 B2
Dreilinden Germany 52°24N 13°10E 115 B2
Drenthe □ Neths. 52°52N 6°40E 170 B6
Drepano, Akra Greece 35°28N 24°14E 207 E5
Drepanum, C. Cyprus 34°54N 32°19E 207 F8
Dresden Ont., Canada 42°35N 82°11W 312 D2
Dresden Sachsen, Germany 51°3N 13°44E 178 D9
Dresden N.Y., U.S.A. 42°41N 76°57W 312 D8
Dreux France 48°44N 1°23E 172 D8
Drevsjø Norway 61°53N 12°1E 164 C9
Drewnica Poland 52°18N 21°6E 143 B2
Drexel U.S.A. 39°45N 84°18W 311 E12
Drezdenko Poland 52°50N 15°49E 185 F2
Driesen = Drezdenko Poland 52°50N 15°49E 185 F2
Driffield U.K. 54°0N 0°26W 168 C7
Driftwood U.S.A. 41°20N 78°8W 312 E6
Driggs U.S.A. 43°44N 111°6W 304 E8
Drigh Road Pakistan 24°52N 67°7E 123 A2
Drimnagh Ireland 53°19N 6°19W 120 B2
Drin → Albania 42°1N 19°38E 202 D3
Drin i Zi → Albania 41°37N 20°28E 202 E4
Drina → Bos.-H. 44°53N 19°21E 202 B3
Drincea → Romania 44°20N 22°55E 182 F7
Drinjača → Bos.-H. 44°15N 19°8E 182 F4
Driopida Greece 37°25N 24°26E 204 D6
Drissa = Vyerkhnyadzvinsk Belarus 55°45N 27°58E 188 E4
Driva → Norway 62°41N 9°31E 164 B6
Drivstoggo Norway 62°26N 9°47E 164 B6
Drniš Croatia 43°51N 16°10E 199 E13
Drøbak Norway 59°39N 10°39E 164 E7
Drobeta-Turnu Severin Romania 44°39N 22°41E 182 F7
Drobin Poland 52°42N 19°58E 185 F6
Drochia Moldova 48°2N 27°48E 183 B12
Drogenbos Belgium 50°47N 4°19E 116 B1
Drogheda Ireland 53°43N 6°22W 166 C5
Drogichin = Dragichyn Belarus 52°15N 25°8E 177 B13
Drogobych = Drohobych Ukraine 49°20N 23°30E 185 J10
Drohiczyn Poland 52°24N 22°39E 185 F9
Drohobych Ukraine 49°20N 23°30E 185 J10
Droichead Átha = Drogheda Ireland 53°43N 6°22W 166 C5
Droichead na Bandan = Bandon Ireland 51°44N 8°44W 166 E3
Droichead Nua = Newbridge Ireland 53°11N 6°48W 166 C5
Droitwich U.K. 52°16N 2°8W 169 E5
Drôme □ France 44°38N 5°15E 175 D9
Drôme → France 44°46N 4°46E 175 D8
Dromedary, C. Australia 36°17S 150°10E 283 D9
Drömling ⌓ Germany 52°29N 11°5E 178 C7
Dromore Down, U.K. 54°25N 6°9W 166 B5
Dromore Tyrone, U.K. 54°31N 7°28W 166 B4
Dromore West Ireland 54°15N 8°52W 166 B3
Dronero Italy 44°28N 7°22E 198 D4
Dronfield U.K. 53°19N 1°27W 168 D6
Dronne → France 45°2N 0°9W 174 C3
Dronning Ingrid Land Greenland 64°25N 52°5W 154 E5
Dronning Maud Land Antarctica 72°30S 12°0E 151 D3
Dronninglund Denmark 57°10N 10°19E 163 G4
Dronten Neths. 52°32N 5°43E 170 B5
Dropt → France 44°35N 0°6W 174 D3
Drosendorf Austria 48°52N 15°37E 180 C8
Drosh Pakistan 35°33N 71°48E 240 B3
Drottningholm Sweden 59°19N 17°53E 139 B1
Droué France 48°3N 1°6E 172 D8
Drouin Australia 38°10S 145°53E 283 E6
Druid Hills U.S.A. 33°47N 84°21W 113 B2
Drujba Uzbekistan 41°13N 61°18E 216 D6
Druk Yul = Bhutan ■ Asia 27°25N 90°30E 241 B3
Drum Tower Beijing, China 114 a3
Drumbo Canada 43°16N 80°35W 312 C4
Drumcliff Ireland 54°20N 8°29W 166 B3
Drumcondra Ireland 53°21N 6°16W 120 A2
Drumheller Canada 51°25N 112°40W 296 C6
Drummond U.S.A. 46°40N 113°9W 304 C7
Drummond I. U.S.A. 46°1N 83°39W 309 B12
Drummond Pt. Australia 34°9S 135°16E 281 E2
Drummond Ra. Australia 23°45S 147°10E 280 C4
Drummondville Canada 45°55N 72°25W 298 C5
Drummoyne Australia 33°51S 151°8E 139 B1
Drumright U.S.A. 35°59N 96°36W 314 D6
Druskeniki = Druskininkai Lithuania 54°3N 23°58E 188 E2
Druskininkai Lithuania 54°3N 23°58E 188 E2
Drut → Belarus 53°8N 30°5E 177 B16
Druya Belarus 55°45N 27°28E 188 E4
Druzhba Bulgaria 43°15N 28°1E 203 C12
Druzhina Russia 68°14N 145°18E 215 C15
Drvar Bos.-H. 44°21N 16°23E 199 D13
Drvenik Croatia 43°27N 16°3E 199 E13
Drwęca → Poland 53°0N 18°42E 185 E5
Dry Harbour Mts. Jamaica 18°19N 77°24W 320 a
Dry Tortugas U.S.A. 24°38N 82°55W 315 J13
Dryander △ Australia 20°13S 148°34E 280 b
Dryanovo Bulgaria 42°59N 25°28E 203 D9
Dryden Ont., Canada 49°47N 92°50W 297 D10
Dryden N.Y., U.S.A. 42°30N 76°18W 313 D8
Drygalski I. Antarctica 66°0S 92°0E 151 C7
Drygalski Ice Tongue Antarctica 75°24S 163°30E 151 D11
Drylaw U.K. 55°58N 3°15W 121 B2
Drysdale → Australia 13°59S 126°51E 278 B4
Drysdale I. Australia 11°41S 136°0E 280 A2
Drysdale River △ Australia 14°56S 127°2E 278 B4
Drzewica Poland 51°27N 20°29E 185 G7
Drzewiczka → Poland 51°36N 20°36E 185 G7
Dschang Cameroon 5°32N 10°3E 263 D7
Du Gué → Canada 57°21N 70°45W 298 A5
Du He → China 32°48N 110°40E 229 A8
Du Quoin U.S.A. 38°1N 89°14W 310 G7
Du'an China 23°59N 108°3E 228 F7
Duanesburg U.S.A. 42°45N 74°11W 313 D10
Duaringa Australia 23°42S 149°42E 280 C4
Duarte, Pico Dom. Rep. 19°2N 70°59W 321 C5
Dubai = Dubayy U.A.E. 25°18N 55°20E 119 A2
Dubai Creek U.A.E. 25°15N 55°19E 119 A2
Dubai Int. ✕ (DXB) U.A.E. 25°15N 55°21E 119 A2
Dubai Int. Financial Centre U.A.E. 25°12N 55°17E 119 B2
Dubai Internet City U.A.E. 25°6N 55°10E 119 B1
Dubai Maritime City U.A.E. 25°16N 55°16E 119 A2
Dubăsari Moldova 47°15N 29°10E 183 C14
Dubăsari Vdkhr. Moldova 47°30N 29°0E 183 C13
Dubawnt → Canada 64°33N 100°6W 297 A8
Dubawnt L. Canada 63°8N 101°28W 297 A8
Dubayy U.A.E. 25°18N 55°20E 119 A2
Dubbo Australia 32°11S 148°35E 283 B8
Dube → Liberia 5°16N 7°29W 262 D3
Dubeč Czech Rep. 50°3N 14°35E 135 B3
Dubele Dem. Rep. of the Congo 2°56N 29°35E 268 B2
Dübendorf Switz. 47°24N 8°37E 179 H4
Dubica Croatia 45°11N 16°48E 199 C13
Dublanc Dominica 15°31N 61°28W 323 k
Dublin Dublin, Ireland 53°21N 6°15W 120 A2
Dublin Ga., U.S.A. 32°32N 82°54W 316 C7
Dublin Ohio, U.S.A. 40°5N 83°7W 311 D13
Dublin Tex., U.S.A. 32°5N 98°21W 314 E5
Dublin □ Ireland 53°24N 6°20W 166 C5
Dublin ✕ (DUB) Ireland 53°26N 6°15W 120 A2
Dublin B. Ireland 53°19N 6°7W 120 B3
Dublin Castle Dublin, Ireland 120 c2
Dublin Harbour Ireland 53°21N 6°11W 120 A2
Dubna Russia 56°44N 37°10E 188 D9
Dubnica nad Váhom Slovak Rep. 48°58N 18°11E 181 C11
Dubno Ukraine 50°25N 25°45E 177 C13
Dubois Idaho, U.S.A. 44°10N 112°14W 304 D7
Dubois Ind., U.S.A. 38°27N 86°48W 311 F10
DuBois Pa., U.S.A. 41°7N 78°46W 312 E6
Dubossary = Dubăsari Moldova 47°15N 29°10E 183 C14
Dubossary Vdkhr. = Dubăsari Vdkhr. Moldova 47°30N 29°0E 183 C13
Dubove Ukraine 48°10N 23°53E 183 B8
Dubovka Russia 49°5N 44°50E 191 F7
Dubovskoye Russia 47°28N 42°46E 191 G6
Dubrajpur India 23°48N 87°25E 243 H12
Dubréka Guinea 9°46N 13°31W 262 D2
Dubrovitsa = Dubrovytsya Ukraine 51°31N 26°35E 177 C14
Dubrovnik Croatia 42°39N 18°6E 202 D2
Dubrovytsya Ukraine 51°31N 26°35E 177 C14
Dubulu Dem. Rep. of the Congo 4°18N 20°16E 264 B4
Dubuque U.S.A. 42°30N 90°41W 310 B6
Dubysa → Lithuania 55°5N 23°26E 184 C10
Duc de Gloucester, Îs. French Polynesia 20°38S 143°20W 289 f
Duc Tho Vietnam 18°32N 105°35E 236 C5
Ducale, Palazzo Venice, Italy 142 b3
Ducassous, Pte. Martinique 14°32N 60°50W 322 j
Duchang China 29°18N 116°12E 229 C11
Duchesne U.S.A. 40°10N 110°24W 304 F8
Duchess Australia 21°20S 139°50E 280 C2
Ducie I. Pac. Oc. 24°40S 124°48W 289 K15
Duck → U.S.A. 36°2N 87°52W 315 C11
Duck Cr. → Australia 22°37S 116°53E 278 D2
Duck Lake Canada 52°50N 106°16W 297 C7
Duck Mountain ⌓ Canada 51°45N 101°0W 297 C8
Duckwall, Mt. U.S.A. 37°58N 120°7W 306 H6
Ducos Martinique 14°33N 60°59W 322 j
Duda → Colombia 2°34N 74°3W 328 C3
Duddington U.K. 55°56N 3°8W 121 B3
Duderstadt Germany 51°31N 10°15E 178 D6
Dudhi India 24°15N 83°10E 243 G10
Dudhnoi India 25°59N 90°47E 241 C3
Dudinka Russia 69°30N 86°13E 215 C9
Dudley W. Mids., U.K. 52°31N 2°5W 169 E5
Dudley Ga., U.S.A. 32°32N 83°5W 316 C6
Dudna → India 19°17N 76°54E 244 E3
Dudo Somalia 9°20N 50°12E 267 C7
Dudo, W. → Somalia 9°14N 50°40E 267 C7
Dudub Ethiopia 6°55N 46°43E 267 C6
Dudwa India 28°30N 80°41E 243 E9
Dudwa △ India 28°30N 80°40E 243 E9
Duékoué Ivory C. 6°40N 7°15W 262 D3
Duenas Phil. 11°4N 122°37E 233 F4
Dueñas Spain 41°52N 4°33W 194 D6
Dueré Brazil 11°20S 49°17W 333 D2
Duero = Douro → Europe 41°8N 8°40W 194 D2
Duff Is. Pac. Oc. 9°50S 167°10E 277 B12
Dufftown U.K. 57°27N 3°8W 167 D5
Dufourspitz Switz. 45°56N 7°52E 179 K3
Dugger U.S.A. 39°4N 87°18W 311 E9
Dugi Otok Croatia 44°0N 15°3E 199 D11
Dugiuma Somalia 1°15N 42°34E 267 D5
Dugo Selo Croatia 45°51N 16°18E 199 C13
Duida-Marahuaca △ Venezuela 3°33N 65°33W 328 C4
Duisburg Germany 51°26N 6°45E 178 D2
Duitama Colombia 5°50N 73°2W 328 B3
Duivendrecht Neths. 52°20N 4°55E 112 B2
Duiwelskloof = Modjadjiskloof S. Africa 23°42S 30°10E 271 B5
Dujiangyan China 31°2N 103°38E 228 B4
Duk Fadiat South Sudan 7°45N 31°25E 257 F3
Duk Faiwil South Sudan 7°30N 31°29E 257 F3
Dukat Albania 40°16N 19°32E 202 F3
Dūkdamīn Iran 35°59N 57°43E 247 C8
Dukelský Průsmyk Slovak Rep. 49°25N 21°42E 181 B14
Dukhān Qatar 25°25N 50°50E 247 E6
Dukhovshchina Russia 55°15N 32°27E 188 E7
Duki Pakistan 30°14N 68°25E 240 C3
Dukla Poland 49°30N 21°35E 185 J8
Duku Bauchi, Nigeria 10°43N 10°43E 263 C7
Duku Sokoto, Nigeria 11°11N 4°55E 263 C5
Dula Dem. Rep. of the Congo 4°40N 20°21E 264 B4
Dūlāb Iran 35°39N 51°27E 141 B2
Dulag Phil. 10°57N 125°2E 233 F5
Dulan China 36°0N 97°11E 218 D8
Dulawan = Datu Piang Phil. 7°2N 124°30E 233 H5
Dulce U.S.A. 36°56N 107°0W 305 H10
Dulce → Argentina 30°32S 62°33W 334 C3
Dulce, G. Costa Rica 8°40N 83°20W 320 E3
Dulcina Antigua & B. 17°35N 61°49W 322 c
Dulf Iraq 35°7N 45°51E 246 C5
Dŭlgopol Bulgaria 43°3N 27°22E 203 C11
Duliu China 39°2N 116°55E 226 E9
Dullabchara India 24°30N 92°26E 241 C4
Dullewala Pakistan 31°50N 71°25E 242 D4
Dullstroom S. Africa 25°27S 30°7E 271 C5
Dülmen Germany 51°49N 7°17E 178 D3
Dulovo Bulgaria 43°48N 27°9E 203 C11
Dulpetorpet Norway 60°34N 12°19E 164 D9
Dulq Maghār Syria 36°22N 38°39E 213 D8
Duluth Ga., U.S.A. 34°0N 84°9W 316 A5
Duluth Minn., U.S.A. 46°47N 92°6W 308 B7
Dulwich U.K. 51°27N 0°5W 125 B3
Dum Dum India 22°39N 88°26E 124 B2
Dum Duma India 27°40N 95°40E 241 B5
Dūmā Syria 33°34N 36°24E 250 E7
Dumaguete Phil. 9°17N 123°15E 233 G4
Dumai Indonesia 1°35N 101°28E 234 B2
Dumalinao Phil. 7°49N 123°23E 233 H4
Dumanjug Phil. 10°4N 123°26E 233 F4
Dumanquilas B. Phil. 7°34N 123°4E 233 H4
Dumaran Phil. 10°33N 119°50E 233 F2
Dumaran I. Phil. 10°33N 119°51E 233 F2
Dumarao Phil. 11°16N 122°41E 233 F4
Dumas Ark., U.S.A. 33°53N 91°29W 314 E9
Dumas Tex., U.S.A. 35°52N 101°58W 314 D4
Ḑumayr Syria 33°39N 36°42E 250 E7
Dumbarton U.K. 55°57N 4°33W 167 F4
Dumbéa N. Cal. 22°10S 166°27E 288 d
Ďumbier Slovak Rep. 48°56N 19°38E 181 C12
Dumbleyung Australia 33°17S 117°42E 279 F2
Dumbo Angola 14°6S 17°24E 265 E3
Dumbrăveni Romania 46°14N 24°34E 183 D9
Dumfries U.K. 55°4N 3°37W 167 F5
Dumfries & Galloway □ U.K. 55°9N 3°58W 167 F5
Dumingag Phil. 8°20N 123°20E 233 G4
Dumitrești Romania 45°33N 26°55E 183 E11
Dumka India 24°12N 87°15E 243 G12
Dumlupınar Turkey 38°53N 30°0E 205 C12
Dümmer Germany 52°31N 8°20E 178 C4
Dümmer ⌓ Germany 52°31N 8°21E 178 C4
Dumoine → Canada 46°13N 77°51W 298 C4
Dumoine, L. Canada 46°55N 77°55W 298 C4
Dumont d'Urville Antarctica 66°40S 140°0E 151 C10
Dumont d'Urville Sea S. Ocean 63°30S 138°0E 151 C9
Dumoulin Is. Papua N. G. 10°54S 150°46E 286 F6
Dumpu Papua N. G. 5°53S 145°44E 286 C3
Dumyât Egypt 31°24N 31°48E 251 G2
Dumyât, Far → Egypt 31°32N 31°51E 251 G2
Dumyât, Masabb Egypt 31°28N 31°51E 251 G2
Dún Dealgan = Dundalk Ireland 54°1N 6°24W 166 B5
Dún Garbhán = Dungarvan Ireland 52°5N 7°37W 166 D4
Dún Laoghaire Ireland 53°17N 6°8W 120 B3
Dun-le-Palestel France 46°18N 1°39E 173 F8
Dun-sur-Auron France 46°53N 2°33E 173 F9
Dun-sur-Meuse France 49°23N 5°11E 173 C12
Duna = Dunărea → Europe 45°20N 29°40E 183 E14
Duna-Drava △ Hungary 46°15N 18°50E 182 D3
Duna Dzong Bhutan 27°2N 89°24E 241 B2
Duna-völgyi-főcsatorna Hungary 46°40N 19°14E 182 D4
Dünaburg = Daugavpils Latvia 55°53N 26°32E 188 E4
Dunaföldvár Hungary 46°50N 18°57E 182 D3
Dunagiri India 30°31N 79°52E 243 D8
Dunaj = Dunărea → Europe 45°20N 29°40E 183 E14
Dunajec → Poland 50°15N 20°44E 185 H7
Dunajská Streda Slovak Rep. 48°0N 17°37E 181 C10
Dunakeszi Hungary 47°37N 19°8E 182 C4
Dunapataj Hungary 46°39N 19°4E 182 D4
Dunărea → Europe 45°20N 29°40E 183 E14
Dunaszekcső Hungary 46°6N 18°45E 182 D3
Dunaújváros Hungary 46°58N 18°57E 182 D3
Dunav = Dunărea → Europe 45°20N 29°40E 183 E14
Dunavațu de Jos Romania 44°59N 29°13E 183 F14
Dunavtsi Bulgaria 43°57N 22°53E 202 C6
Dunay Russia 42°52N 132°22E 220 C6
Dunayivtsi Ukraine 48°54N 26°50E 183 B11
Dunback N.Z. 45°23S 170°36E 285 F5
Dunbar U.K. 56°0N 2°31W 167 E6
Dunblane U.K. 56°11N 3°58W 167 E5
Duncan B.C., Canada 48°45N 123°40W 306 B3
Duncan Ariz., U.S.A. 32°43N 109°6W 305 K9
Duncan Okla., U.S.A. 34°30N 97°57W 314 D6
Duncan, L. Canada 53°29N 77°58W 298 B4
Duncan Dock Cape Town, S. Africa 118 a3
Duncan L. Canada 62°51N 113°58W 296 A6
Duncan Passage India 11°0N 92°0E 245 J11
Duncan Town Bahamas 22°15N 75°45W 320 B4
Duncannon U.S.A. 40°23N 77°2W 312 F7
Duncans Jamaica 18°27N 77°32W 320 a
Duncansby Head U.K. 58°38N 3°1W 167 C5
Duncansville U.S.A. 40°25N 78°26W 312 F6
Dund-Us Mongolia 48°1N 91°38E 217 C12
Dundaga Latvia 57°31N 22°21E 184 A9
Dundalk Ont., Canada 44°10N 80°24W 312 B4
Dundalk Louth, Ireland 54°1N 6°24W 166 B5
Dundalk Md., U.S.A. 39°15N 76°31W 309 F15
Dundalk Bay Ireland 53°55N 6°15W 166 C5
Dundas = Uummannaq Greenland 77°33N 68°52W 154 B4
Dundas Canada 43°17N 79°59W 312 C5
Dundas, L. Australia 32°35S 121°50E 279 F3
Dundas I. Canada 54°30N 130°50W 296 C2
Dundas Str. Australia 11°15S 131°35E 278 B5
Dundee KwaZulu Natal, S. Africa 28°11S 30°15E 271 C5
Dundee Dundee C., U.K. 56°28N 2°59W 167 E6
Dundee Mich., U.S.A. 41°57N 83°40W 311 C13
Dundee N.Y., U.S.A. 42°32N 76°59W 312 D8
Dundee City □ U.K. 56°30N 2°58W 167 E6
Dundgovĭ □ Mongolia 45°10N 106°0E 226 B4
Dundrum Dublin, Ireland 53°18N 6°14W 120 B2
Dundrum Down, U.K. 54°16N 5°52W 166 B6
Dundrum B. U.K. 54°13N 5°47W 166 B6
Dunearn Singapore 1°19N 103°49E 138 B2
Dunedin N.Z. 45°50S 170°33E 285 F5
Dunedin Fla., U.S.A. 28°1N 82°46W 317 G7
Dunedoo Australia 32°0S 149°25E 283 A8
Dunfanaghy Ireland 55°11N 7°58W 166 A4
Dunfermline U.K. 56°5N 3°27W 167 E5
Dungannon Ont., Canada 43°51N 81°36W 312 C3
Dungannon Tyrone, U.K. 54°31N 6°46W 166 B5
Dungarpur India 23°52N 73°45E 242 H5
Dungarvan Ireland 52°5N 7°37W 166 D4
Dungarvan Harbour Ireland 52°4N 7°35W 166 D4
Dungeness U.K. 50°54N 0°59E 169 G8
Dungiven U.K. 54°56N 6°56W 166 B5
Dunglow Ireland 54°57N 8°21W 166 B3
Dungo, L. do Angola 17°15S 19°0E 265 F3
Dungog Australia 32°22S 151°46E 283 B9
Dungu Dem. Rep. of the Congo 3°40N 28°32E 268 B2
Dungun Malaysia 4°45N 103°25E 237 K4
Dungunâb Sudan 21°10N 37°9E 256 C4
Dungunâb, Khalîg Sudan 21°5N 37°12E 256 C4
Dunhua China 43°20N 128°14E 227 C15
Dunhuang China 40°8N 94°36E 218 C7
Dunk I. Australia 17°59S 146°29E 280 B4
Dunkassa Benin 10°21N 3°10E 263 C5
Dunkeld Queens., Australia 33°25S 149°29E 281 E4
Dunkeld Vic., Australia 37°40S 142°22E 282 D5
Dunkeld Perth & Kinr., U.K. 56°34N 3°35W 167 E5
Dunkerque France 51°2N 2°20E 173 A9
Dunkery Beacon U.K. 51°9N 3°36W 169 F4
Dunkirk = Dunkerque France 51°2N 2°20E 173 A9
Dunkirk U.S.A. 42°29N 79°20W 312 D5
Dunkuj Sudan 12°50N 32°49E 257 E3
Dunkwa Central, Ghana 6°0N 1°47W 262 D4
Dunkwa Central, Ghana 5°30N 1°0W 263 D4
Dunleary = Dún Laoghaire Ireland 53°17N 6°8W 120 B3
Dunleer Ireland 53°50N 6°24W 166 C5
Dunmanus B. Ireland 51°31N 9°50W 166 E2
Dunmanway Ireland 51°43N 9°6W 166 E2
Dunmarra Australia 16°42S 133°25E 280 B1
Dunmore U.S.A. 41°25N 75°38W 313 E9
Dunmore East Ireland 52°9N 7°0W 166 D5
Dunmore Town Bahamas 25°30N 76°39W 320 A4
Dunn U.S.A. 35°19N 78°37W 315 D15
Dunnellon U.S.A. 29°3N 82°28W 317 F7
Dunnet Hd. U.K. 58°40N 3°21W 167 C5
Dunning Ill., U.S.A. 41°56N 87°48W 119 B2
Dunning Nebr., U.S.A. 41°50N 100°6W 308 E3
Dunn's River Falls Jamaica 18°25N 77°8W 320 a
Dunnville Canada 42°54N 79°36W 312 D5
Dunolly Australia 36°51S 143°44E 282 D5
Dunoon U.K. 55°57N 4°56W 167 F4
Dunqul Egypt 23°26N 31°37E 256 C3
Duns U.K. 55°47N 2°20W 167 F6
Dunseith U.S.A. 48°50N 100°3W 308 A3
Dunshaughlin Ireland 53°31N 6°33W 166 C5
Dunsmuir U.S.A. 41°13N 122°16W 304 F2
Dunstable U.K. 51°53N 0°32W 169 F7
Dunstan Mts. N.Z. 44°53S 169°35E 285 E4
Dunster Canada 53°8N 119°50W 296 C5
Duntroon N.Z. 44°51S 170°40E 285 E5
Dunvegan Gauteng, S. Africa 26°9S 28°8E 123 A2
Dunvegan Highl., U.K. 57°27N 6°35W 167 D2
Dunvegan L. Canada 60°8N 107°10W 297 A7
Duolun China 42°12N 116°28E 226 C9
Duomo Italy 45°28N 9°11E 128 B2
Duomula China 34°8N 82°29E 217 E10
Duong Dong Vietnam 10°13N 103°58E 237 G4
Dupax del Norte Phil. 16°17N 121°5E 232 C3
Dupree U.S.A. 45°4N 101°35W 308 C3
Dupuyer U.S.A. 48°13N 112°30W 304 B7
Duque de Caxias Brazil 22°46S 43°18W 135 A1
Duque de York, I. Chile 50°37S 75°25W 336 D1
Durack → Australia 15°33S 127°52E 278 C4
Durack Ra. Australia 16°50S 127°40E 278 C4
Durack River Australia 15°32S 127°39E 278 C4
Durağan Turkey 41°25N 35°3E 212 B6
Durak Turkey 39°42N 28°17E 205 B10
Durakovac = Gjurakoc Kosovo 42°43N 20°29E 202 D4
Durance → France 43°55N 4°45E 175 E8
Durand Ga., U.S.A. 32°55N 84°46W 316 C5
Durand Ill., U.S.A. 42°26N 89°20W 310 B7
Durand Mich., U.S.A. 42°55N 83°59W 311 B13
Durand Wis., U.S.A. 44°38N 91°58W 308 C8
Durandeau St. Lucia 13°56N 60°59W 323 m
Durango Mexico 24°3N 104°39W 318 C4
Durango Colo., U.S.A. 37°16N 107°53W 305 H10
Durango □ Mexico 24°50N 105°20W 318 C4
Durankulak Bulgaria 43°41N 28°32E 203 C12
Durant Iowa, U.S.A. 41°36N 90°54W 310 C6
Durant Miss., U.S.A. 33°4N 89°51W 315 E10
Durant Okla., U.S.A. 33°59N 96°25W 314 E6
Duratón → Spain 41°37N 4°7W 194 D6
Durazno Uruguay 33°25S 56°31W 334 C4
Durazzo = Durrës Albania 41°19N 19°28E 202 E3
Durban Aude, France 42°59N 2°49E 174 F6
Durban KwaZulu Natal, S. Africa 29°49S 31°1E 271 C5
Durban ✕ (DIA) S. Africa 29°37S 31°7E 271 C5
Durbuy Belgium 50°21N 5°28E 170 D5
Dúrcal Spain 36°59N 3°34W 195 J7
Đurđevac Croatia 46°2N 17°3E 182 D2
Düren Germany 50°48N 6°29E 178 E2
Duren Sawit Indonesia 6°13S 106°54E 122 B2
Durg = Bhilainagar-Durg India 21°13N 81°26E 244 D5
Durgapur India 23°30N 87°20E 243 H12
Durham Canada 44°10N 80°49W 312 B4
Durham Darlington, U.K. 54°47N 1°34W 168 C6
Durham Calif., U.S.A. 39°39N 121°48W 306 F5
Durham N.C., U.S.A. 35°59N 78°54W 315 D15
Durham N.H., U.S.A. 43°8N 70°56W 313 C14
Durham □ U.K. 54°42N 1°45W 168 C6
Duri Indonesia 1°27N 101°15E 234 B2
Durlas = Thurles Ireland 52°41N 7°49W 166 D4
Durlești Moldova 47°1N 28°46E 183 C13
Ḑurmā Si. Arabia 24°37N 46°8E 246 E5
Durmitor Montenegro 43°10N 19°0E 202 C3
Durmitor △ Montenegro 43°15N 19°5E 202 C3
Durness U.K. 58°34N 4°45W 167 C4
Durnford, Pta. W. Sahara 23°37N 16°0W 260 D1
Durrës Albania 41°19N 19°28E 202 E3
Durrow Ireland 52°51N 7°24W 166 D4
Dursey I. Ireland 51°36N 10°12W 166 E1
Dursley U.K. 51°40N 2°21W 169 F5
Dursunbey Turkey 39°35N 28°37E 205 B10
Durtal France 47°40N 0°18W 172 E6
Duru Dem. Rep. of the Congo 4°14N 28°50E 268 B2
Duru Gölü Turkey 41°20N 28°35E 203 E12
Durukhsi Ethiopia 8°31N 45°28E 267 C6
Durusu Turkey 41°17N 28°41E 203 E12
Durūz, Jabal ad Jordan 32°35N 36°40E 250 F7
D'Urville, Tanjung Indonesia 1°28S 137°54E 231 E9
D'Urville I. N.Z. 40°50S 173°55E 285 A8
Duryea U.S.A. 41°20N 75°45W 313 E9
Dusa Mareb = Dhuusamarreeb Somalia 5°30N 46°15E 267 C6
Dûsh Egypt 24°35N 30°41E 256 C3
Dushak Turkmenistan 37°13N 60°1E 247 B9
Dushan China 25°48N 107°30E 228 E6
Dushanbe Tajikistan 38°33N 68°48E 217 E7
Dusheti Georgia 42°10N 44°42E 191 J7
Dushore U.S.A. 41°31N 76°24W 313 E8
Dusit Bangkok, Thailand 113 a2
Dusit Zoo Bangkok, Thailand 113 a2
Dusky Sd. N.Z. 45°47S 166°30E 285 F1
Dussejour, C. Australia 14°45S 128°13E 278 B4
Düsseldorf Germany 51°14N 6°47E 178 D2
Düsseldorf Rhein-Ruhr ✕ (DUS) Germany 51°17N 6°46E 178 D2
Dusti Tajikistan 37°20N 68°40E 217 E7
Duszniki-Zdrój Poland 50°24N 16°24E 185 H3
Dutch East Indies = Indonesia ■ Asia 5°0S 115°0E 235 C4
Dutch Guiana = Suriname ■ S. Amer. 4°0N 56°0W 329 C6
Dutch Harbor U.S.A. 53°53N 166°32W 303 K6
Dutlwe Botswana 23°58S 23°46E 270 B3
Dutsan Wai Nigeria 10°50N 8°10E 263 C6
Dutse Nigeria 11°46N 9°20E 263 C6
Dutton Canada 42°39N 81°30W 312 D3
Dutton → Australia 20°44S 143°10E 280 C3
Dutywa S. Africa 32°8S 28°18E 271 D4
Duved Sweden 63°23N 12°55E 162 A6
Düvertepe Turkey 39°14N 28°27E 205 B10
Dúvida = Roosevelt → Brazil 7°35S 60°20W 331 B5
Duwayhin, Khawr U.A.E. 24°20N 51°25E 247 E6
Duyfken Pt. Australia 12°33S 141°38E 280 A3
Duyun China 26°18N 107°29E 228 D6
Düzağaç Turkey 38°48N 30°10E 205 C12
Düzce = Akhna Cyprus 35°3N 33°47E 207 E9
Düzce Turkey 40°50N 31°10E 212 B4
Düzce □ Turkey 40°50N 31°10E 212 B4
Duzdab = Zāhedān Iran 29°30N 60°50E 247 D9
Duzer Guadeloupe 16°20N 61°44W 322 e
Düziçi Turkey 37°15N 36°28E 212 D7
Dve Mogili Bulgaria 43°35N 25°55E 203 C9
Dvigatelstroy = Kaspiysk Russia 42°52N 47°40E 191 J8
Dvina, Severnaya → Russia 64°32N 40°30E 186 B7
Dvinsk = Daugavpils Latvia 55°53N 26°32E 188 E4
Dvinskaya Guba Russia 65°0N 39°0E 186 B6
Dvor Croatia 45°4N 16°22E 199 C13
Dvůr Králové nad Labem Czech Rep. 50°27N 15°50E 180 A8
Dwarka India 22°18N 69°8E 242 H3
Dwellingup Australia 32°43S 116°4E 279 F2
Dwight Ont., Canada 45°20N 79°1W 312 A5
Dwight Ill., U.S.A. 41°5N 88°26W 311 C8
Dworp Belgium 50°44N 4°18E 116 B1
Dyakove Ukraine 48°1N 23°10E 182 B7
Dyakovo Russia 55°40N 37°39E 129 B2
Dyatkovo Russia 53°40N 34°27E 188 F8
Dyatlovo = Dzyatlava Belarus 53°28N 25°28E 177 B13
Dyce U.K. 57°13N 2°12W 167 D6
Dyer, C. Canada 66°37N 61°16W 295 D19
Dyer Bay Canada 45°10N 81°20W 312 A3
Dyer Plateau Antarctica 70°45S 65°30W 151 D17
Dyersburg U.S.A. 36°3N 89°23W 315 C10
Dyersville U.S.A. 42°29N 91°8W 310 B5
Dyfi → U.K. 52°32N 4°3W 169 E3
Dyhernfurth = Brzeg Dolny Poland 51°16N 16°41E 185 G3
Dyje → Czech Rep. 48°37N 16°56E 181 C9
Dyke Ackland B. Papua N. G. 9°0S 148°45E 286 E5
Dyker Beach Park U.S.A. 40°36N 74°1W 132 C1
Dykh Tau Russia 43°3N 43°8E 191 J6
Dymer Ukraine 50°47N 30°18E 177 C16
Dynów Poland 49°50N 22°11E 185 J9
Dyranut Norway 60°22N 7°31E 164 D4
Dyrhólaey Iceland 63°24N 19°8W 155 D7
Dyrnes Norway 63°25N 7°52E 164 A4
Dysart Queens., Australia 22°32S 148°23E 280 C4
Dysart Iowa, U.S.A. 42°10N 92°18W 310 B4
Dyushambe = Dushanbe Tajikistan 38°33N 68°48E 217 E7
Dyviziya Ukraine 45°55N 29°59E 183 E14
Dzamin Üüd = Borhoyn Tal Mongolia 43°50N 111°58E 226 C6
Dzaoudzi Mayotte 12°47S 45°16E 272 b
Dzaoudzi ✕ (DZA) Mayotte 12°48S 45°18E 272 b
Dzaudzhikau = Vladikavkaz Russia 43°0N 44°35E 191 J7
Dzavhan □ Mongolia 48°0N 96°0E 217 C13
Dzavhan Gol → Mongolia 48°54N 93°23E 218 B7
Dzerzhinsk Russia 56°14N 43°30E 190 B6
Dzerzhinskiy Russia 55°37N 37°50E 129 B2
Dzerzhinskiy Park Russia 55°50N 37°37E 129 B2
Dzhalal-Abad = Jalal-Abad Kyrgyzstan 40°56N 73°0E 217 D8
Dzhalal-Ogly = Stepanavan Armenia 41°1N 44°23E 191 K7
Dzhalinda Russia 53°26N 124°0E 215 D13
Dzhambeyty = Zhympity Kazakhstan 50°16N 52°35E 216 B4
Dzhambul = Taraz Kazakhstan 42°54N 71°22E 217 D8
Dzhankoy Ukraine 45°40N 34°20E 189 K8
Dzhanybek = Zhänibek Kazakhstan 49°25N 46°50E 190 F8
Dzhargalantu = Hovd □ Mongolia 48°2N 91°37E 217 C12
Dzharkent = Zharkent Kazakhstan 44°10N 80°0E 217 D10
Dzharylhach, Ostriv Ukraine 46°2N 32°55E 189 J7
Dzhezkazgan = Zhezqazghan Kazakhstan 47°44N 67°40E 217 C7
Dzhibkhalantu = Uliastay Mongolia 47°56N 97°28E 218 B8
Dzhizak = Jizzax Uzbekistan 40°6N 67°50E 217 D7
Dzhugdzur, Khrebet Russia 57°30N 138°0E 215 D14
Dzhulynk Ukraine 48°26N 29°45E 183 B14
Dzhumgoltau, Khrebet Kyrgyzstan 42°15N 74°30E 217 D8
Dzhungarskiye Vorota = Dzungarian Gate Asia 45°10N 82°0E 217 C10
Dzhuryn Ukraine 48°41N 28°18E 183 B13
Dzhvari = Jvari Georgia 42°42N 42°4E 191 J6
Działdowo Poland 53°15N 20°15E 185 E7
Działoszyce Poland 50°22N 20°20E 185 H7
Działoszyn Poland 51°6N 18°50E 185 G5
Dzibilchaltún Mexico 21°10N 89°35W 319 C7
Dzierzgoń Poland 53°58N 19°20E 184 E6
Dzierżoniów Poland 50°45N 16°39E 185 H3
Dzilam de Bravo Mexico 21°24N 88°53W 319 C7
Dzioua Algeria 33°14N 5°14E 261 B6
Dzisna Belarus 55°34N 28°12E 188 E5
Dzisna → Belarus 55°34N 28°12E 188 E5
Dziwnów Poland 54°2N 14°45E 184 D1
Dzūkija △ Lithuania 54°10N 24°30E 161 J21
Dzungarian Basin = Junggar Pendi China 44°30N 86°0E 217 D11
Dzungarian Gate Asia 45°10N 82°0E 217 C10
Dzur Mongolia 49°39N 95°46E 217 C13
Dzüünbayan Mongolia 44°29N 110°2E 226 B6
Dzüünharaa Mongolia 48°52N 106°28E 218 B10
Dzüünmod Mongolia 47°45N 106°58E 218 B10
Dzyarzhynsk Belarus 53°40N 27°1E 177 B14
Dzyatlava Belarus 53°28N 25°28E 177 B13

E

E.C. Manning ⌓ Canada 49°5N 120°45W 296 D4
E.T. Joshua ✕ (SVD) St. Vincent 13°8N 61°13W 323 n
E.U.R. = Esposizione Universale di Roma Italy 41°49N 12°28E 136 C1
Eabamet L. Canada 51°30N 87°46W 298 B2
Eabametoong Canada 51°30N 88°0W 298 B2
Éadan Doire = Edenderry Ireland 53°21N 7°4W 166 C4
Eads U.S.A. 38°29N 102°47W 304 G12
Eagar U.S.A. 34°6N 109°17W 305 J9
Eagle Alaska, U.S.A. 64°47N 141°12W 303 D12
Eagle Colo., U.S.A. 39°39N 106°50W 304 G10
Eagle → Canada 53°36N 57°26W 299 B8
Eagle, Mt. U.S. Virgin Is. 17°46N 64°49W 321 b
Eagle Beach Aruba 12°32N 70°3W 322 f
Eagle Butte U.S.A. 45°0N 101°10W 308 C3
Eagle Cr. → U.S.A. 38°36N 85°4W 311 F11
Eagle Grove U.S.A. 42°40N 93°54W 310 B3
Eagle L. Ont., Canada 49°42N 93°13W 297 D10
Eagle L. Calif., U.S.A. 40°39N 120°45W 304 F3
Eagle L. Maine, U.S.A. 46°20N 69°22W 309 B19
Eagle Lake Ont., Canada 45°8N 78°29W 312 A6
Eagle Lake Maine, U.S.A. 47°3N 68°36W 309 B19
Eagle Lake Tex., U.S.A. 29°35N 96°20W 314 G6
Eagle Mountain U.S.A. 33°49N 115°27W 307 M11
Eagle Nest U.S.A. 36°33N 105°16W 305 H11
Eagle Pass U.S.A. 28°43N 100°30W 314 G4
Eagle Pk. U.S.A. 38°10N 119°25W 306 G7
Eagle Pt. Australia 16°11S 124°23E 278 C3
Eagle River Mich., U.S.A. 47°25N 88°18W 308 B9
Eagle River Wis., U.S.A. 45°55N 89°15W 308 C9
Eagle Rock U.S.A. 34°8N 118°12W 126 B3
Eaglehawk Australia 36°44S 144°15E 282 D6
Eagles Mere U.S.A. 41°25N 76°33W 313 E8
Eagleville U.S.A. 40°28N 93°59W 310 D3
Ealing □ U.K. 51°31N 0°20W 125 A2
Ear Falls Canada 50°38N 93°13W 297 C10
Earlimart U.S.A. 35°53N 119°16W 307 K7
Earl's Court London, U.K. 125 c1
Earlsfield U.K. 51°26N 0°10W 125 B2
Earlville Ill., U.S.A. 41°35N 88°55W 311 C8
Earlville N.Y., U.S.A. 42°44N 75°32W 313 D9
Earlwood Australia 33°55S 151°8E 139 B1
Early Branch U.S.A. 32°45N 80°55W 316 C9
Earn → U.K. 56°21N 3°18W 167 E5
Earn, L. U.K. 56°23N 4°13W 167 E4
Earnslaw, Mt. N.Z. 44°32S 168°27E 285 E3
Earth U.S.A. 34°14N 102°24W 314 D3
Eas Vanuatu 16°20S 168°15E 287 F6
Easley U.S.A. 34°50N 82°36W 315 D13
East Anglia U.K. 52°30N 1°0E 168 E9
East Angus Canada 45°30N 71°40W 299 C5
East Antarctica Antarctica 80°0S 90°0E 151 D7
East Arlington Mass., U.S.A. 42°24N 71°8W 116 A2
East Arlington Va., U.S.A. 38°51N 77°4W 143 B2
East Aurora U.S.A. 42°46N 78°37W 312 D6
East Ayrshire □ U.K. 55°26N 4°11W 167 F4
East Bedfont U.K. 51°26N 0°28W 125 B1
East Beskids = Vychodné Beskydy Europe 49°20N 22°0E 181 B15
East Boston U.S.A. 42°22N 71°1W 116 A2
East Brady U.S.A. 40°59N 79°37W 312 F5
East Branch Clarion River L. U.S.A. 41°35N 78°35W 312 E6
East C. = Dezhneva, Mys Russia 66°5N 169°40W 215 C19
East C. N.Z. 37°42S 178°35E 284 D7
East C. Papua N. G. 10°13S 150°53E 286 F6
East Caroline Basin Pac. Oc. 4°0N 146°45E 288 G6
East Chicago U.S.A. 41°38N 87°27W 311 C9
East China Sea Asia 30°0N 126°0E 219 F14
East Coulee Canada 51°23N 112°27W 296 C6
East Dereham = Dereham U.K. 52°41N 0°57E 169 E8
East Don → Canada 43°48N 79°25W 141 A2
East Don Parkland Canada 43°47N 79°22W 141 A2
East Dublin U.S.A. 32°32N 82°52W 316 C7
East Dubuque U.S.A. 42°30N 90°39W 310 B6
East Dunbartonshire □ U.K. 55°57N 4°13W 167 F4
East Elmhurst U.S.A. 40°45N 73°52W 132 B2
East End Pt. Bahamas 25°3N 77°16W 153 b
East Falkland Falk. Is. 51°30S 58°30W 153 f
East Finchley U.K. 51°35N 0°10W 125 A2
East Flatbush U.S.A. 40°39N 73°55W 132 C2
East Fork White → U.S.A. 38°33N 87°14W 311 F9
East Grand Forks U.S.A. 47°56N 97°1W 308 B5
East Grand Rapids U.S.A. 42°58N 85°37W 311 B11
East Greenwich U.S.A. 41°40N 71°27W 313 E13
East Grinstead U.K. 51°7N 0°0 169 F8
East Ham U.K. 51°32N 0°3E 125 A4
East Hartford U.S.A. 41°46N 72°39W 313 E12
East Haydon Australia 18°0S 141°30E 280 B3
East Helena U.S.A. 46°35N 111°56W 304 C8
East Humber → Canada 43°47N 79°35W 141 A1
East Indies Asia 0°0 120°0E 210 J14
East Kilbride U.K. 55°47N 4°11W 167 F4
East Lamma Channel China 22°14N 114°9E 122 B1
East Lansing U.S.A. 42°44N 84°29W 311 B12
East Las Vegas = Whitney U.S.A. 36°4N 115°5W 124 B2
East Lexington U.S.A. 42°25N 71°12W 116 A2
East Livermore = Livermore Falls U.S.A. 44°29N 70°11W 309 C18
East Liverpool U.S.A. 40°37N 80°35W 312 F4
East London S. Africa 33°0S 27°55E 271 D4
East Los Angeles U.S.A. 34°1N 118°10W 126 B3
East Lothian □ U.K. 55°58N 2°44W 167 F6

East Main = Eastmain Canada 52°10N 78°30W 298 B4
East Mariana Basin Pac. Oc. 12°0N 153°0E 288 F7
East Milwaukee = Shorewood U.S.A. 43°5N 87°53W 311 A9
East Molesey U.K. 51°24N 0°21W 125 B1
East Moline U.S.A. 41°32N 90°26W 310 C6
East Naples U.S.A. 26°8N 81°46W 317 J8
East New Britain □ Papua N. G. 6°30S 152°30E 286 D7
East New York U.S.A. 40°40N 73°53W 132 B2
East Northport U.S.A. 40°53N 73°20W 313 F11
East Orange U.S.A. 40°46N 74°12W 313 F10
East Pacific Rise Pac. Oc. 15°0S 110°0W 289 J17
East Pakistan = Bangladesh ■ Asia 24°0N 90°0E 241 D3
East Palatka U.S.A. 29°39N 81°36W 316 F8
East Palestine U.S.A. 40°50N 80°33W 312 F4
East Peoria U.S.A. 40°40N 89°34W 310 D7
East Pine Canada 55°48N 120°12W 296 B4
East Pines U.S.A. 38°57N 76°54W 143 B3
East Point U.S.A. 33°41N 84°25W 113 B2
East Potomac Park Washington, D.C., U.S.A. 143 c1
East Providence U.S.A. 41°49N 71°23W 313 E13
East Pt. Br. Virgin Is. 18°40N 64°18W 321 b
East Pt. N.S., Canada 46°27N 61°58W 299 C7
East Pt. U.S. Virgin Is. 17°45N 64°34W 321 b
East Renfrewshire □ U.K. 55°46N 4°21W 167 F4
East Retford = Retford U.K. 53°19N 0°56W 168 D7
East Riding of Yorkshire □ U.K. 53°55N 0°30W 168 D7
East River → New York, U.S.A. 132 e3
East Rochester U.S.A. 43°7N 77°29W 312 C7
East Rutherford U.S.A. 40°50N 74°5W 132 A1
East St. Louis U.S.A. 38°37N 90°9W 310 F6
East Schelde = Oosterschelde → Neths. 51°33N 4°0E 170 C4
East Sea = Japan, Sea of Asia 40°0N 135°0E 220 E7
East Sepik □ Papua N. G. 4°0S 143°45E 286 C2
East Sheen U.K. 51°27N 0°16W 125 B2
East Siberian Sea Russia 73°0N 160°0E 215 B17
East Stroudsburg U.S.A. 41°1N 75°11W 313 E9
East Sussex □ U.K. 50°56N 0°19E 169 G8
East Talpiyot West Bank 31°45N 35°13E 123 B2
East Tasman Plateau Pac. Oc. 43°30S 152°0E 288 M7
East Tawas U.S.A. 44°17N 83°29W 309 C12
East Timor ■ Asia 8°50S 126°0E 231 F7
East Toorale Australia 30°27S 145°28E 281 E4
East Troy U.S.A. 42°47N 88°24W 311 B8
East Village New York, U.S.A. 132 e2
East Walker → U.S.A. 38°52N 119°10W 306 G7
East Wickham U.K. 51°28N 0°5E 125 B4
East Windsor U.S.A. 40°17N 74°34W 313 F10
East York Canada 43°40N 79°22W 141 A2
East Youngstown = Campbell U.S.A. 41°5N 80°37W 312 E4
Eastbourne N.Z. 41°19S 174°55E 284 H3
Eastbourne E. Sussex, U.K. 50°46N 0°18E 169 G8
Eastcote U.K. 51°34N 0°23W 125 A1
Eastend Canada 49°32N 108°50W 297 D7
Easter Fracture Zone Pac. Oc. 25°0S 115°0W 289 K16
Easter Howgate U.K. 55°52N 3°12W 121 B2
Easter I. = Pascua, I. de Chile 27°7S 109°23W 330 b
Eastern □ Ghana 6°30N 0°30W 263 D4
Eastern □ Kenya 0°0 38°30E 268 C4
Eastern □ S. Leone 8°15N 11°0W 262 D2
Eastern Cape □ S. Africa 32°0S 26°0E 270 D4
Eastern Cr. → Australia 20°40S 141°35E 280 C3
Eastern Desert = Es Sahrâ' Esh Sharqîya Egypt 27°30N 32°30E 256 B3
Eastern Equatoria □ South Sudan 5°0N 33°0E 257 G3
Eastern Ghats India 14°0N 78°50E 245 H4
Eastern Group = Lau Group Fiji 17°0S 178°30W 287 A3
Eastern Group Australia 33°30S 124°30E 279 F3
Eastern Guruma ☼ Australia 22°0S 117°30E 278 D2
Eastern Highlands □ Papua N. G. 6°30S 145°35E 286 D3
Eastern I. Midway Is. 28°12N 177°19W 302 c
Eastern Samar □ Phil. 11°40N 125°40E 233 F5
Eastern Transvaal = Mpumalanga □ S. Africa 26°0S 30°0E 271 C5
Easterville Canada 53°8N 99°49W 297 C9
Easthampton U.S.A. 42°16N 72°40W 313 D12
Eastlake U.S.A. 41°40N 81°26W 312 E3
Eastland U.S.A. 32°24N 98°49W 314 E5
Eastleigh U.K. 50°58N 1°21W 169 G6
Eastmain Canada 52°10N 78°30W 298 B4
Eastmain → Canada 52°27N 78°26W 298 B4
Eastman Qué., Canada 45°18N 72°19W 313 A12
Eastman Ga., U.S.A. 32°12N 83°11W 316 C6
Eastman Wis., U.S.A. 43°10N 91°1W 310 A5
Easton Md., U.S.A. 38°47N 76°5W 309 F15
Easton Pa., U.S.A. 40°41N 75°13W 313 F9
Easton Wash., U.S.A. 47°14N 121°11W 306 C5
Eastover U.S.A. 33°52N 80°41W 316 B9
Eastpoint U.S.A. 29°44N 84°53W 316 F5
Eastpoint Park Canada 43°46N 79°10W 141 A4
Eastport U.S.A. 44°56N 67°0W 309 C20
Eastsound U.S.A. 48°42N 122°55W 306 B4
Eastwood Australia 33°47S 151°4E 139 A1
Eaton Colo., U.S.A. 40°32N 104°42W 304 F11
Eaton Ohio, U.S.A. 39°45N 84°38W 311 E12
Eaton Canyon Park U.S.A. 34°10N 118°7W 126 A4
Eaton Centre Toronto, Canada 141 a2
Eaton Rapids U.S.A. 42°31N 84°39W 311 B12
Eatonia Canada 51°13N 109°25W 297 C7
Eatonton U.S.A. 33°20N 83°23W 316 B6
Eatontown U.S.A. 40°19N 74°4W 313 F10
Eatonville U.S.A. 46°52N 122°16W 306 D4
Eau Claire Fr. Guiana 3°30N 53°40W 329 C7
Eau Claire Wis., U.S.A. 44°49N 91°30W 308 C8
Eau Claire, L. à l' Canada 56°10N 74°25W 298 A5
Eauripik Rise Pac. Oc. 2°0N 142°0E 288 G6
Eauze France 43°53N 0°7E 174 E4
Eban Nigeria 9°40N 4°50E 263 D5
Ebanga Angola 12°45S 14°45E 265 E2
Ebangalakata Dem. Rep. of the Congo 0°29S 21°29E 264 C4
Ebano Mexico 22°13N 98°24W 319 C5
Ebara Japan 35°35N 139°42E 140 B3
Ebbegebirge ⌓ Germany 51°10N 7°55E 178 D3
Ebbw Vale U.K. 51°46N 3°12W 169 F4
Ebebiyín Eq. Guin. 2°9N 11°20E 264 B2
Ebel Gabon 0°7N 11°5E 264 B2
Ebeltoft Denmark 56°12N 10°41E 163 H4
Ebeltoft Vig Denmark 56°10N 10°35E 163 H4
Ebensburg U.S.A. 40°29N 78°44W 312 F6
Ebensee Austria 47°48N 13°46E 180 D6
Eber Gölü Turkey 38°38N 31°11E 212 C4
Eberbach Germany 49°28N 8°59E 179 F4
Eberswalde-Finow Germany 52°50N 13°49E 178 C9
Ebetsu Japan 43°7N 141°34E 220 C10
Ebey's Landing ⌓ U.S.A. 48°12N 122°41W 306 B4
Ebian China 29°11N 103°13E 228 C4
Ebingen Germany 48°13N 9°1E 179 G5
Ebino Japan 32°2N 130°48E 222 E2
Ebinur Hu China 44°55N 82°55E 217 D10
Ebisu Japan 35°38N 139°42E 140 B3
Ebla Syria 35°50N 36°48E 250 C7
Ebo Angola 11°40S 14°40E 265 E2
Ebola → Dem. Rep. of the Congo 3°20N 20°57E 264 B4
Éboli Italy 40°39N 15°2E 201 B8
Ebolowa Cameroon 2°55N 11°10E 263 E7
Ebonda Dem. Rep. of the Congo 2°12N 22°21E 264 B4
Ebonyi □ Nigeria 6°20N 8°0E 263 D6
Eboy Dem. Rep. of the Congo 2°50N 23°11E 264 B4
Ebrach Germany 49°51N 10°29E 179 F6
Ebre = Ebro → Spain 40°43N 0°54E 196 E5
Ébrié, Lagune Ivory C. 5°12N 4°26W 262 D4
Ebro → Spain 40°43N 0°54E 196 E5
Ebro, Embalse del Spain 43°0N 3°58W 194 C7
Ebstorf Germany 53°2N 10°24E 178 B6
Ebute-Metta Nigeria 6°23N 3°23E 124 B2
Ecatepec de Morelos Mexico 19°36N 99°3W 319 D5
Ecbatana = Hamadān Iran 34°52N 48°32E 213 E13
Ecclesville Trin. & Tob. 10°19N 61°8W 323 t
Eceabat Turkey 40°11N 26°21E 203 F10
Ech Chéliff Algeria 36°10N 1°20E 261 A5
Ech Chéliff □ Algeria 36°15N 1°30E 261 A5
Echague Phil. 16°42N 121°38E 232 C3
Echechonnee → U.S.A. 32°39N 83°36W 316 C6
Echigo-Sammyaku Japan 36°50N 139°50E 221 F9
Echinades Greece 38°25N 21°2E 207 C3
Echinos Greece 41°16N 25°1E 203 E9
Échirolles France 45°8N 5°44E 175 C9
Echizen Japan 35°50N 136°10E 223 B8
Echizen-Misaki Japan 35°59N 135°57E 223 B7
Echmiadzin = Ejmiatsin Armenia 40°12N 44°19E 191 K7
Echo U.S.A. 31°29N 85°28W 316 D4
Echo Bay N.W.T., Canada 66°5N 117°55W 294 D8
Echo Bay Ont., Canada 46°29N 84°4W 298 C3
Echo Park Los Angeles, U.S.A. 127 a1
Echoing → Canada 55°51N 92°5W 298 B1
Echterdingen, Stuttgart ✈ (STR) Germany 48°42N 9°11E 179 G5
Echternach Lux. 49°49N 6°25E 170 E6
Echuca Australia 36°10S 144°45E 283 D6
Écija Spain 37°30N 5°10W 195 H5
Eckental Germany 49°35N 11°12E 179 F7
Eckernförde Germany 54°26N 9°50E 178 A5
Eclectic U.S.A. 32°38N 86°2W 316 C3
Eclipse I. Australia 35°5S 117°58E 279 G2
Eclipse Is. Australia 13°54S 126°19E 278 B4
Eclipse Sd. Canada 72°38N 79°0W 295 C16
Écommoy France 47°50N 0°17E 172 E7
Economy = Ambridge U.S.A. 40°36N 80°14W 312 F4
Ecoporanga Brazil 18°23S 40°50W 333 E3
Écouché France 48°42N 0°10W 172 D6
Ecrins △ France 44°54N 6°18E 175 D10
Ecuador ■ S. Amer. 2°0S 78°0W 328 D2
Ecuador, Volcán Ecuador 1°1S 91°32W 330 a
Écueillé France 47°5N 1°21E 172 E8
Ed Sweden 58°55N 11°55E 163 F5
Ed Dabbura Sudan 17°40N 34°15E 256 D3
Ed Da'ein Sudan 11°26N 26°9E 257 E2
Ed Damazin Sudan 11°46N 34°21E 266 B3
Ed Dâmer Sudan 17°27N 34°0E 256 D3
Ed Dar el Beida = Casablanca Morocco 33°36N 7°36W 260 B3
Ed Debba Sudan 18°0N 30°51E 256 D3
Ed Déffa Egypt 30°40N 26°30E 256 A2
Ed Deim Sudan 10°10N 28°20E 257 E2
Ed Dibeikir Sudan 10°23N 29°9E 266 B2
Ed Dueim Sudan 14°0N 32°10E 257 E3
Eda Japan 35°33N 139°33E 140 B2
Edam Sask., Canada 53°11N 108°46W 297 C7
Edam Neths. 52°31N 5°3E 170 B5
Edane Sweden 59°38N 12°49E 162 E6
Edapally India 11°19N 78°3E 245 J4
Eday U.K. 59°11N 2°47W 167 B6
Edchera W. Sahara 27°2N 13°4W 260 C2
Edd Eritrea 14°0N 41°38E 257 E5
Eddrachillis B. U.K. 58°17N 5°14W 167 C3
Eddystone U.K. 50°11N 4°16W 169 G3
Eddystone Pt. Australia 40°59S 148°20E 281 G4
Eddyville U.S.A. 41°9N 92°38W 310 C4
Ede Neths. 52°4N 5°40E 170 B5
Ede Nigeria 7°45N 4°29E 263 D5
Édéa Cameroon 3°51N 10°9E 263 E7
Edebäck Sweden 60°4N 13°32E 162 D7
Edehon L. Canada 60°25N 97°15W 297 A9
Edelény Hungary 48°18N 20°44E 182 B5
Eden = Bar Harbor U.S.A. 44°23N 68°13W 309 C19
Eden N.S.W., Australia 37°3S 149°55E 283 D8
Eden N.C., U.S.A. 36°29N 79°53W 315 C15
Eden N.Y., U.S.A. 42°39N 78°55W 312 D6
Eden Tex., U.S.A. 31°13N 99°51W 314 F5
Eden → U.K. 54°57N 3°1W 168 C4
Edenburg S. Africa 29°43S 25°58E 270 C4
Edendale N.Z. 46°19S 168°48E 285 G3
Edendale Gauteng, S. Africa 26°8S 28°9E 123 A2
Edendale KwaZulu Natal, S. Africa 29°39S 30°18E 271 C5
Edenderry Ireland 53°21N 7°4W 166 C4
Edenhope Australia 37°4S 141°19E 282 D4
Edenmore Ireland 53°22N 6°11W 120 A2
Edenton U.S.A. 36°4N 76°39W 315 C16
Edenville S. Africa 27°37S 27°34E 271 C4
Eder → Germany 51°12N 9°28E 178 D5
Eder-Stausee Germany 51°10N 8°57E 178 D4
Edessa Greece 40°48N 22°5E 202 F6
Edewecht Germany 53°8N 7°58E 178 B3
Edfu = Idfû Egypt 24°55N 32°49E 256 C3
Edgar U.S.A. 40°22N 97°58W 308 E5
Edgars Cr. → Australia 37°43S 144°58E 128 A1
Edgartown U.S.A. 41°23N 70°31W 313 E14
Edge Hill U.K. 52°8N 1°26W 169 E6
Edgecumbe N.Z. 37°59S 176°47E 284 D5
Edgefield U.S.A. 33°47N 81°56W 316 B8
Edgeley Ont., Canada 43°47N 79°31W 141 A1
Edgeley N. Dak., U.S.A. 46°22N 98°43W 308 B4
Edgemar U.S.A. 37°39N 122°29W 136 C2
Edgemont U.S.A. 43°18N 103°50W 308 D2
Edgeøya Svalbard 77°45N 22°30E 150 B9
Edgerton Ohio, U.S.A. 41°27N 84°45W 311 C12
Edgerton Wis., U.S.A. 42°50N 89°4W 310 B7
Edgewater Fla., U.S.A. 28°59N 80°54W 317 G9
Edgewater N.J., U.S.A. 40°49N 73°58W 132 B2
Edgewood Fla., U.S.A. 28°29N 81°22W 133 B2
Edgewood Ill., U.S.A. 38°55N 88°40W 311 F8
Édhessa = Edessa Greece 40°48N 22°5E 202 F6
Edievale N.Z. 45°49S 169°22E 285 F4
Edina Liberia 6°0N 10°10W 262 D2
Edina Mo., U.S.A. 40°10N 92°11W 310 D4
Edinboro U.S.A. 41°52N 80°8W 312 E4
Edinburg Ill., U.S.A. 39°39N 89°23W 310 E7
Edinburg Tex., U.S.A. 26°18N 98°10W 314 H5
Edinburgh Edinburgh, U.K. 55°57N 3°13W 121 B2
Edinburgh Ind., U.S.A. 39°21N 85°58W 311 E11
Edinburgh ✈ (EDI) U.K. 55°54N 3°22W 121 B1
Edinburgh, City of □ U.K. 55°57N 3°17W 167 F5
Edinburgh Castle Edinburgh, U.K. 121 b2
Edineț Moldova 48°9N 27°18E 183 B12
Edirne Turkey 41°40N 26°34E 203 E10
Edirne □ Turkey 41°12N 26°30E 203 E10
Edison Ga., U.S.A. 31°34N 84°44W 316 D5
Edison Wash., U.S.A. 48°33N 122°27W 306 B4
Edison Park U.S.A. 42°1N 87°48W 119 A2
Edisto → U.S.A. 32°29N 80°21W 316 C9
Edisto Beach U.S.A. 32°29N 80°20W 316 C9
Edisto I. U.S.A. 32°35N 80°20W 316 C9
Edithburgh Australia 35°5S 137°43E 282 C2
Edjeleh Algeria 28°38N 9°50E 261 C6
Edmeston U.S.A. 42°42N 75°15W 313 D9
Edmond U.S.A. 35°39N 97°29W 314 D6
Edmonds U.S.A. 47°48N 122°22W 306 C4
Edmondston U.S.A. 38°56N 76°54W 143 B3
Edmondstown Ireland 53°17N 6°18W 120 B2
Edmonton Queens., Australia 17°2S 145°46E 280 B4
Edmonton Alta., Canada 53°30N 113°30W 296 C6
Edmund L. Canada 54°45N 93°17W 298 B1
Edmundston Canada 47°23N 68°20W 299 C6
Edna U.S.A. 28°59N 96°39W 314 G6
Edo □ Nigeria 6°30N 6°0E 263 D6
Edo → Japan 35°38N 139°52E 140 B4
Edogawa Japan 35°43N 139°52E 140 A4
Edolo Italy 46°10N 10°21E 198 B7
Edøya Norway 63°18N 8°10E 164 A5
Edremit Turkey 39°34N 27°0E 205 B9
Edremit Körfezi Turkey 39°30N 26°45E 205 B8
Edsberg Sweden 59°26N 17°57E 139 A1
Edsbro Sweden 59°54N 18°29E 162 E12
Edsbruk Sweden 58°1N 16°29E 163 F10
Edsbyn Sweden 61°23N 15°49E 162 C9
Edson Canada 53°35N 116°28W 296 C5
Eduardo Castex Argentina 35°50S 64°18W 334 D3
Eduardo Frei Antarctica 62°30S 58°0W 151 C18
Edward → Australia 35°5S 143°30E 282 C5
Edward, L. Africa 0°25S 29°40E 268 C2
Edward VII Land Antarctica 80°0S 150°0W 151 E13
Edwardesabad = Bannu Pakistan 33°0N 70°18E 240 B3
Edwards Calif., U.S.A. 34°50N 117°40W 307 L9
Edwards N.Y., U.S.A. 44°20N 75°15W 313 B9
Edwards → U.S.A. 41°9N 90°59W 310 C6
Edwards L. Australia 37°42S 144°59E 128 A1
Edwards Plateau U.S.A. 30°45N 101°20W 314 F4
Edwardsburg U.S.A. 41°48N 86°6W 311 C10
Edwardsville Ill., U.S.A. 38°49N 89°58W 310 F7
Edwardsville Pa., U.S.A. 41°15N 75°56W 313 E9
Edzná Mexico 19°39N 90°19W 319 D6
Edzo Canada 62°49N 116°4W 296 A5
Eek U.S.A. 60°14N 162°2W 303 F7
Eeklo Belgium 51°11N 3°33E 170 C3
Eel → Ind., U.S.A. 39°7N 86°57W 311 E10
Eel → Ind., U.S.A. 40°45N 86°22W 311 D10
Eenhana Namibia 17°30S 16°23E 270 A2
Eesti = Estonia ■ Europe 58°30N 25°30E 188 C3
Efate, I. Vanuatu 17°40S 168°25E 287 G6
Eferding Austria 48°18N 14°1E 180 C7
Effigy Mounds ⌓ U.S.A. 43°5N 91°11W 310 A5
Effingham U.S.A. 39°7N 88°33W 311 E8
Eforie Romania 44°1N 28°37E 183 F13
Efoulen Cameroon 2°46N 10°43E 264 B2
Efteløt Norway 59°33N 9°49E 164 E6
Efxinoupoli Greece 39°12N 22°42E 204 B4
Efzonos Greece 37°55N 23°49E 112 B2
Ega → Spain 42°19N 1°55W 196 C3
Égadi, Ísole Italy 37°55N 12°16E 200 E5
Egaleo Greece 37°59N 23°40E 112 B2
Egaleo, Oros Greece 38°0N 23°36E 112 B1
Egan Range U.S.A. 39°35N 114°55W 304 G6
Eganville Canada 45°32N 77°5W 312 A7
Egedesminde = Aasiaat Greenland 68°43N 52°56W 154 D5
Egegik U.S.A. 58°13N 157°22W 303 G8
Eger = Cheb Czech Rep. 50°9N 12°28E 180 A5
Eger Hungary 47°53N 20°27E 182 C5
Eger → Hungary 47°38N 20°50E 182 C5
Egersund Norway 58°26N 6°1E 164 F3
Egg I. St. Helena 15°58S 5°47W 153 h
Egg L. Canada 55°5N 105°30W 297 B7
Eggedal Norway 60°14N 9°22E 164 D6
Eggegebirge Südlicher Teutoburger Wald ⌓ Germany 51°40N 8°59E 178 D4
Eggenburg Austria 48°38N 15°50E 180 C8
Eggenfelden Germany 48°23N 12°46E 179 G8
Egherta Somalia 2°4N 43°11E 267 D5
Éghezée Belgium 50°35N 4°55E 170 D4
Egholo Solomon Is. 8°25S 157°25E 287 M9
Egilsstaðir Iceland 65°16N 14°25W 155 B12
Egina Greece 37°45N 23°26E 204 D5
Eginio Greece 40°28N 22°28E 202 F6
Egio Greece 38°15N 22°5E 204 C4
Egito Angola 12°4S 13°58E 265 E2
Égletons France 45°24N 2°3E 174 C6
Eglinton I. Canada 75°48N 118°30W 295 B8
Egmont Canada 49°45N 123°56W 296 D4
Egmont, C. N.Z. 39°16S 173°45E 284 F2
Egmont, Mt. = Taranaki, Mt. N.Z. 39°17S 174°5E 284 F3
Egmont △ N.Z. 39°17S 174°4E 284 F3
Egra India 21°54N 87°32E 243 J12
Eğridir Turkey 37°52N 30°51E 212 D4
Eğridir Gölü Turkey 37°53N 30°50E 212 D4
Egtved Denmark 55°38N 9°18E 163 J3
Éguas → Brazil 13°26S 44°14W 333 D3
Egum Atoll Papua N. G. 9°25S 152°0E 286 E7
Éguzon-Chantôme France 46°27N 1°33E 173 F8
Egvekinot Russia 66°19N 179°50W 215 C19
Egyek Hungary 47°39N 20°52E 182 C5
Egypt ■ Africa 28°0N 31°0E 256 B3
Eha Amufu Nigeria 6°30N 7°46E 263 D6
Eheli Algeria 22°26N 4°40E 261 D5
Ehime □ Japan 33°30N 132°40E 222 D4
Ehingen Germany 48°16N 9°43E 179 G5
Ehrenberg U.S.A. 33°36N 114°31W 307 M12
Ehrhardt U.S.A. 33°6N 81°1W 316 B8
Ehrwald Austria 47°24N 10°56E 180 D3
Eiao French Polynesia 8°0S 140°40W 289 f
Eibar Spain 43°11N 2°28W 196 B2
Eibenschitz = Ivančice Czech Rep. 49°6N 16°23E 181 B9
Eiche Germany 52°33N 13°35E 115 A4
Eiche Süd Germany 52°33N 13°35E 115 A4
Eichstätt Germany 48°54N 11°11E 179 G7
Eide Hordaland, Norway 60°31N 6°44E 164 D3
Eide Møre og Romsdal, Norway 62°55N 7°27E 164 B4
Eider → Germany 54°19N 8°57E 178 A4
Eidsbugarden Norway 61°23N 8°16E 164 C5
Eidsbygda Norway 62°36N 7°30E 164 B4
Eidsdalen Norway 62°16N 7°10E 164 B4
Eidsvåg Norway 62°46N 8°2E 164 B5
Eidsvold Australia 25°25S 151°12E 281 D5
Eidsvoll Norway 60°19N 11°14E 164 D8
Eielson U.S.A. 64°40N 147°4W 303 D11
Eifel Germany 50°15N 6°50E 179 E2
Eiffel, Tour Paris, France 134 c2
Eiffel Flats Zimbabwe 18°20S 30°0E 269 F3
Eiger Switz. 46°34N 8°1E 198 B5
Eigg U.K. 56°54N 6°10W 167 E2
Eighty Mile Beach Australia 19°30S 120°40E 278 C3
Eikefjord Norway 61°35N 5°27E 164 C2
Eikelandsosen Norway 60°15N 5°43E 164 D2
Eiken Norway 58°29N 7°14E 164 F4
Eikeren Norway 59°38N 9°58E 164 E6
Eikesdalen Norway 62°28N 8°12E 164 B5
Eil, L. U.K. 56°51N 5°16W 167 E3
Eil Malk Palau 7°10N 134°23E 288 c
Eildon Australia 37°14S 145°55E 283 D6
Eildon, L. Australia 37°10S 146°0E 283 D7
Eilean Siar □ U.K. 57°30N 7°10W 167 D1
Eilenburg Germany 51°27N 12°36E 178 D8
Ein Arik West Bank 31°54N 35°8E 123 A1
Ein el Luweiqa Sudan 14°5N 33°50E 257 E3
Ein Naquba Israel 31°47N 35°7E 123 B1
Ein Rafa Israel 31°47N 35°7E 123 B1
Eina Norway 60°38N 10°35E 164 D7
Einarsstaðir Iceland 65°44N 17°24W 155 B9
Einasleigh Australia 18°32S 144°5E 280 B3
Einasleigh → Australia 17°30S 142°17E 280 B3
Einbeck Germany 51°49N 9°53E 178 D5
Eindhoven Neths. 51°26N 5°28E 170 C5
Einsiedeln Switz. 47°7N 8°46E 179 H4
Eire = Ireland ■ Europe 53°50N 7°52W 166 C4
Eiríksjökull Iceland 64°46N 20°24W 155 C6
Eiríksstaðir Iceland 65°7N 15°25W 155 B11
Eiriosgaigh = Eriskay U.K. 57°4N 7°18W 167 D1
Eirunepé Brazil 6°35S 69°53W 330 B4
Eiseb → Namibia 20°33S 20°59E 270 B2
Eisenach Germany 50°58N 10°19E 178 E6
Eisenberg Germany 50°58N 11°54E 178 E7
Eisenerz Austria 47°32N 14°54E 180 D7
Eisenhüttenstadt Germany 52°9N 14°38E 178 C10
Eisenkappel Austria 46°29N 14°36E 180 E7
Eisenstadt Austria 47°51N 16°31E 181 D9
Eisenstein = Železná Ruda Czech Rep. 49°8N 13°15E 180 B6
Eisfeld Germany 50°25N 10°54E 179 E6
Eisleben Germany 51°32N 11°32E 178 D7
Eislingen Germany 48°41N 9°42E 179 G5
Eivindvik Norway 60°59N 5°5E 164 D2
Eivissa Spain 38°54N 1°26E 206 D1
Eixe, Serra do Spain 42°24N 6°54W 194 C4
Eizariya West Bank 31°46N 35°16E 123 B2
Ejby Denmark 55°41N 12°24E 118 A2
Ejea de los Caballeros Spain 42°7N 1°9W 196 C3
Ejeda Madag. 24°20S 44°31E 272 C1
Ejigbo Nigeria 6°33N 3°18E 124 A1
Ejmiatsin Armenia 40°12N 44°19E 191 K7
Ejura Ghana 7°23N 1°15W 263 D4
Ejutla Mexico 16°34N 96°44W 319 D5
Ekalaka U.S.A. 45°53N 104°33W 304 D11
Ekalla Gabon 1°27S 14°0E 264 C2
Ekanga Dem. Rep. of the Congo 2°23S 23°14E 264 C4
Ekaterinburg = Yekaterinburg Russia 56°50N 60°30E 214 D7
Ekeberg Norway 59°53N 10°46E 133 A3
Ekenäs = Raasepori Finland 60°0N 23°26E 188 B2
Ekenässjön Sweden 57°28N 15°1E 163 G9
Ekerö Sweden 59°16N 17°45E 162 E11
Eket Nigeria 4°38N 7°56E 263 E6
Eketahuna N.Z. 40°38S 175°43E 284 G4
Ekibastuz Kazakhstan 51°50N 75°10E 217 B9
Ekiti □ Nigeria 7°25N 5°20E 263 D6
Eklutna U.S.A. 61°27N 149°22W 303 F10
Eknäs Sweden 59°18N 18°13E 139 B3
Ekoli Dem. Rep. of the Congo 0°23S 24°13E 264 C4
Ekoln Sweden 59°45N 17°37E 162 E11
Ekouamou Congo 0°8N 16°31E 264 B3
Ekoungounou Congo 1°10S 15°52E 264 C3
Ekshärad Sweden 60°10N 13°30E 162 D7
Eksjö Sweden 57°40N 14°58E 163 G8
Ekukola Dem. Rep. of the Congo 0°31S 18°56E 264 C3
Ekuku Dem. Rep. of the Congo 0°41S 21°42E 264 C4
Ekukula Dem. Rep. of the Congo 0°15N 21°30E 264 B4
Ekuma → Namibia 18°40S 16°2E 270 A2
Ekuta Dem. Rep. of the Congo 3°0N 18°50E 264 B3
Ekwan → Canada 53°12N 82°15W 298 B3
Ekwan Pt. Canada 53°16N 82°7W 298 B3
Ekwok U.S.A. 59°22N 157°30W 303 G8
El Aaiún W. Sahara 27°9N 13°12W 260 C2
El Aargub Mauritania 23°37N 15°52W 260 D1
El Abanico Chile 37°20S 71°31W 334 D1
El 'Abbasiya El Qâhira, Egypt 30°3N 31°16E 117 A2
El Abbasiya Sudan 12°10N 31°18E 257 E3
El Abiodh-Sidi-Cheikh Algeria 32°53N 0°31E 261 B5
El Adde Somalia 2°35N 46°9E 267 D6
El Adeb Larache Algeria 27°22N 8°52E 261 C6
El 'Agrûd Egypt 30°14N 34°24E 251 H5
El Agua Venezuela 11°8N 63°52W 329 a
El Agustino Peru 12°2S 77°0W 124 B2
El Agustino, Cerro Peru 12°3S 76°59W 124 B3
El Aïoun Morocco 34°33N 2°30W 261 B4
El Ait Sudan 12°22N 27°27E 257 E2
El 'Aiyat Egypt 29°36N 31°15E 256 J7
El Alamein Egypt 30°48N 28°58E 256 A2
El Alto Peru 4°15S 81°14W 330 A1
El Aouj Mauritania 22°53N 12°49W 260 D2
El 'Aqaba, W. → Egypt 30°7N 33°54E 251 H4
El 'Arag Egypt 28°40N 26°20E 256 B2
El Aricha Algeria 34°13N 1°10W 261 B4
El Arīḥā West Bank 31°52N 35°27E 251 G6
El 'Arîsh Egypt 31°8N 33°50E 251 G4
El 'Arîsh, W. → Egypt 31°8N 33°47E 251 G4
El Arrouch Algeria 36°37N 6°53E 261 A6
El Asnam = Ech Chéliff Algeria 36°10N 1°20E 261 A5
El Astillero Spain 43°24N 3°49W 194 B7
El Avagi Somalia 3°36N 46°57E 267 D6
El Badâri Egypt 27°4N 31°25E 256 B3
El Badrshein Egypt 29°51N 31°16E 251 J2
El Bagur Egypt 30°25N 31°2E 251 H2
El Bahrein Egypt 28°30N 26°25E 256 B2
El Ballâs Egypt 26°2N 32°43E 256 B3
El Balyana Egypt 26°10N 32°3E 256 B3
El Banco Colombia 9°0N 73°58W 328 B3
El Baqeir Sudan 18°40N 33°40E 256 D3
El Baragil Egypt 30°4N 31°9E 117 A1
El Barco de Ávila Spain 40°21N 5°31W 194 E5
El Barco de Valdeorras = O Barco Spain 42°23N 6°58W 194 C4
El Basâlîn Egypt 29°58N 31°16E 117 B2
El Bauga Sudan 18°18N 33°52E 256 D3
El Baúl Venezuela 8°57N 68°17W 328 B4
El Bawiti Egypt 28°25N 28°45E 256 B2
El Bayadh Algeria 33°40N 1°1E 261 B5
El Bayadh □ Algeria 32°30N 1°10E 261 B5
El Bichar Venezuela 10°46N 63°58W 329 a
El Bierzo Spain 42°45N 6°30W 194 C4
El Bira West Bank 31°54N 35°13E 123 A2
El Bluff Nic. 11°59N 83°40W 320 D3
El Bolsón Argentina 41°55S 71°30W 336 B2
El Bonillo Spain 38°57N 2°35W 197 G2
El Bosque Chile 33°32S 70°40W 137 C2
El Buheirat = Lakes □ South Sudan 7°0N 30°0E 257 F3
El Bur Somalia 4°40N 46°37E 267 D6
El Burgo de Osma Spain 41°35N 3°4W 196 D1
El Caín Argentina 41°38S 68°19W 336 B3
El Cajon U.S.A. 32°48N 116°58W 307 N10
El Calafate Argentina 50°19S 72°15W 336 D2
El Callao Venezuela 7°18N 61°50W 329 B5
El Campello Spain 38°26N 0°24W 197 G4
El Campo U.S.A. 29°12N 96°16W 314 G6
El Capitan U.S.A. 37°44N 119°38E 306 H7
El Carbón Honduras 15°25N 85°32W 320 C2
El Cardón Venezuela 11°6N 63°51W 329 a
El Carmen Bolivia 13°40S 63°55W 331 C5
El Carmen Santiago, Chile 33°22S 70°43W 137 B1
El Carmen Colombia 9°43N 75°8W 328 B2
El Centro U.S.A. 32°48N 115°34W 307 N11
El Cerro Bolivia 17°30S 61°40W 331 D5
El Cerro de Andévalo Spain 37°45N 6°57W 195 H4
El Cocuy Colombia 6°25N 72°27W 328 B3
El Cocuy △ Colombia 6°33N 72°5W 328 B3
El Compadre Mexico 32°20N 116°14W 307 N10
El Copey, Cerro Venezuela 11°11N 63°55W 329 a
El Corcovado Argentina 43°25S 71°35W 336 B2
El Coronil Spain 37°5N 5°38W 195 H5
El Cortijo Chile 33°22S 70°42W 137 B1
El Cristo, Vaso Regulador Mexico 19°30N 99°5W 128 B1
El Cuy Argentina 39°55S 68°25W 336 A3
El Cuyo Mexico 21°31N 87°41W 319 C7
El Dab'a Egypt 31°0N 28°27E 256 H6
El Daheir Egypt 31°13N 34°10E 251 G5
El Dambahaddo Somalia 3°17N 46°40E 267 D6
El Deir Egypt 25°25N 32°20E 256 B3
El Dere = Ceeldheere Somalia 5°22N 46°11E 267 C6
El Dere Ethiopia 5°6N 43°5E 267 C5
El Descanso Mexico 32°12N 116°58W 307 N10
El Desemboque Mexico 30°33N 113°1W 318 A2
El Dilingat Egypt 30°50N 30°31E 256 H7
El Diviso Colombia 1°22N 78°14W 328 C2
El Djouf Mauritania 21°25N 6°40W 260 D3
El Dorado Sinaloa, Mexico 24°17N 107°21W 318 C3
El Dorado Ark., U.S.A. 33°12N 92°40W 314 E8
El Dorado Kans., U.S.A. 37°49N 96°52W 308 G5
El Dorado Venezuela 6°55N 61°37W 329 B5
El Dorado Springs U.S.A. 37°52N 94°1W 310 G2
El Duqqi Egypt 30°1N 31°12E 117 A2
El Eglab Algeria 26°20N 4°30W 260 C4
El 'Ein Sudan 16°35N 29°22E 257 D2
El Ejido Spain 36°47N 2°49W 195 J8
El Encinar de los Reyes Spain 40°30N 3°39W 127 A2
El Escorial Spain 40°35N 4°7W 194 E6
El Espinal Venezuela 10°58N 63°59W 329 a
El Espinar Spain 41°43N 4°15W 194 D6
El Eulma Algeria 36°9N 5°42E 261 A6
El Faiyûm Egypt 29°19N 30°50E 256 J7
El Faourar Tunisia 33°22N 8°45E 258 B1
El Fâsher Sudan 13°33N 25°26E 257 E2
El Fashn Egypt 28°50N 30°54E 256 J7
El Ferrol = Ferrol Spain 43°29N 8°15W 194 B2
El Fifi Sudan 10°4N 25°0E 257 E2
El Fud Ethiopia 7°15N 42°52E 267 C5
El Fuerte Mexico 26°25N 108°39W 318 B3
El Ga'a Sudan 14°16N 29°59E 257 E2
El Gamâlîya Egypt 31°10N 31°52E 251 G2
El Garef Sudan 12°3N 34°19E 257 E3
El Gebir Sudan 13°40N 29°40E 257 E2
El Gedida Egypt 25°40N 28°30E 256 B2
El Geneina = Al Junaynah Sudan 13°27N 22°45E 259 F4
El Geteina Sudan 14°50N 32°27E 257 E3
El Gezira Egypt 30°2N 31°13E 117 A2
El Gezira □ Sudan 15°0N 33°0E 257 E3
El Gharbîya □ Egypt 30°50N 31°0E 251 H2
El Ghurîya Egypt 30°2N 31°15E 117 A2
El Gir Sudan 19°50N 28°18E 256 D2
El Gîza Egypt 30°0N 31°12E 117 A2
El Gogorrón △ Mexico 21°49N 100°57W 318 C4
El Goléa Algeria 30°30N 2°50E 261 B5
El Gouna Egypt 27°5N 33°47E 256 B3
El Grau Spain 39°0N 0°7W 197 G4
El Guamache Nueva Esparta, Venezuela 10°44N 63°54W 329 a
El Guamache Nueva Esparta, Venezuela 10°54N 64°3W 329 a
El Hadjira Algeria 32°36N 5°30E 261 B6
El Hagiz Sudan 15°15N 35°50E 257 D4
El Hâi Egypt 29°39N 31°18E 256 J7
El Hajeb Morocco 33°43N 5°13W 260 B3
El Hamma Tunisia 33°54N 9°48E 258 B1
El Hammam Egypt 30°52N 29°25E 256 A2
El Hammâmi Mauritania 23°3N 11°30W 260 D2
El Hâmûl Egypt 31°18N 31°9E 251 G2
El Hamurre Somalia 7°13N 48°54E 267 C6
El Hank Mauritania 24°30N 7°0W 260 D3
El Hasian W. Sahara 26°20N 14°0W 260 C2
El Hawata Sudan 13°25N 34°42E 257 E3
El Hideib Sudan 13°0N 32°50E 257 E3
El Hilla Sudan 13°24N 27°2E 257 E2
El Homr Algeria 29°43N 1°45E 261 C5
El 'Idisât Egypt 25°30N 32°35E 256 B3
El Iskandarîya Egypt 31°13N 29°58E 256 H7
El Jadida Morocco 33°11N 8°17W 260 B3
El Jardal Honduras 14°54N 88°50W 320 D2
El Jebelein Sudan 12°40N 32°55E 257 E3
El Jebha Morocco 35°11N 4°43W 260 A4
El Jem Tunisia 35°19N 10°41E 258 A2
El Kab Sudan 19°27N 32°46E 256 D3
El Kafr el Sharqi Egypt 31°16N 31°10E 256 H7
El Kala Algeria 36°53N 8°26E 261 A6
El Kamlin Sudan 15°3N 33°11E 257 D3
El Kantara Algeria 35°14N 5°45E 261 A6
El Kantara Tunisia 33°45N 10°58E 258 B2
El Karaba Sudan 18°32N 33°41E 256 D3
El Kef Tunisia 36°12N 8°47E 258 A1
El Kef □ Tunisia 36°0N 9°0E 261 A6
El Kelaâ de Srahna Morocco 32°4N 7°27W 260 B3
El Kelaâ M'Gouna Morocco 31°14N 6°7W 260 B3
El Kere Ethiopia 5°50N 42°5E 257 F5
El Khadr West Bank 31°42N 35°10E 123 B1
El Khalîfa Egypt 30°0N 31°15E 117 A2
El Khandaq Sudan 18°30N 30°30E 256 D3
El Khanka Egypt 30°13N 31°21E 251 H2
El Khârga Egypt 25°30N 30°33E 256 B3
El Khartûm Sudan 15°31N 32°35E 257 D3
El Khartûm □ Sudan 16°0N 33°0E 257 D3
El Khartûm Bahrî Sudan 15°40N 32°31E 257 D3
El Khroub Algeria 36°10N 6°55E 261 A6
El Kôm el Ahmar Egypt 30°6N 31°10E 117 A2
El Kseur Algeria 36°46N 4°49E 261 A5
El Ksiba Morocco 32°45N 6°1W 260 B3
El Kuntilla Egypt 30°1N 34°45E 251 H5
El Laqâwa Sudan 11°25N 29°1E 257 E2
El Leh Ethiopia 3°46N 39°13E 257 G4
El Leiya Sudan 16°15N 35°28E 257 D4
El Leoncito △ Argentina 31°58S 69°10W 334 C2
El Limón Panama 9°15N 79°49W 320 c
El Lucero Mexico 30°37N 106°31W 318 A3
El Ma'âdi Egypt 29°57N 31°15E 117 B2
El Maestrazgo Spain 40°30N 0°25W 196 E4
El Mafâza Sudan 13°38N 34°30E 257 E3
El Maghra Egypt 30°15N 28°55E 256 A2
El Mahalla el Kubra Egypt 31°0N 31°0E 256 H7
El Mahârîq Egypt 25°35N 30°35E 256 B3
El Maîmûn Egypt 29°14N 31°12E 256 J7
El Maitén Argentina 42°3S 71°10W 336 B2
El Maiz Algeria 28°19N 0°9W 261 C4
El Maks el Bahari Egypt 24°30N 30°40E 256 C3
El Malpais ⌓ U.S.A. 34°53N 108°0W 305 J10
El Manshâh Egypt 26°26N 31°50E 256 B3
El Mansour Algeria 27°47N 0°14W 261 C4
El Mansûra Egypt 31°0N 31°19E 256 H7
El Manteco Venezuela 7°38N 62°45W 329 B5
El Manzala Egypt 31°10N 31°50E 256 H7
El Marâgha Egypt 26°35N 31°10E 256 B3
El Masid Sudan 15°15N 33°0E 257 D3
El Masnou Spain 41°28N 2°20E 196 D7
El Matarîya El Mansûra, Egypt 31°15N 32°0E 256 H8
El Matarîya El Qâhira, Egypt 30°7N 31°18E 117 A2
El Meda Ethiopia 5°39N 41°47E 257 F5
El Medano Canary Is. 28°3N 16°32W 153 e1
El Meghaier Algeria 33°55N 5°58E 261 B6
El Ménia = El Goléa Algeria 30°30N 2°50E 261 B5
El Meraguen Algeria 28°0N 0°7W 261 C4
El Metemma Sudan 16°50N 33°10E 257 D3
El Miamo Venezuela 7°39N 61°46W 329 B5
El Milagro Argentina 30°59S 65°59W 334 C2
El Milia Algeria 36°51N 6°13E 261 A6
El Minufîya □ Egypt 30°30N 31°0E 251 H2
El Minyâ Egypt 28°7N 30°33E 256 B3
El Mohandessin Egypt 30°2N 31°11E 117 A2
El Monte U.S.A. 34°4N 118°1W 126 B4
El Montseny Spain 41°55N 2°25E 196 D7
El Mreiti Mauritania 23°29N 7°51W 260 D3
El Mreyye Mauritania 18°0N 6°0W 262 B3
El Muqattam Egypt 30°1N 31°17E 117 A2
El Mûskî Egypt 30°3N 31°15E 117 A2
El Nido Phil. 11°10N 119°25E 233 F2
El Niybo Ethiopia 4°40N 39°55E 257 G4
El Obeid Sudan 13°8N 30°10E 257 E3
El Odaiya Sudan 12°8N 28°12E 257 E2
El Oro Mexico 19°51N 100°7W 319 D4
El Oro □ Ecuador 3°30S 79°50W 328 D2
El Oued Algeria 33°20N 6°58E 261 B6
El Oued □ Algeria 33°10N 7°15E 261 B6
El Palmar Bolivia 17°50S 63°9W 331 D5
El Palmar Venezuela 7°58N 61°53W 329 B5
El Palmar △ Argentina 32°10S 58°31W 334 C4
El Pardo Spain 40°30N 3°46W 127 A1
El Paso = Derby U.S.A. 37°33N 97°16W 308 G5
El Paso Ill., U.S.A. 40°44N 89°1W 310 D7
El Paso Tex., U.S.A. 31°45N 106°29W 314 F1
El Paso de Robles = Paso Robles U.S.A. 35°38N 120°41W 306 K6
El Pedernoso Spain 39°29N 2°45W 197 F2
El Pedroso Spain 37°51N 5°45W 195 H5
El Pilar Venezuela 10°32N 63°9W 329 A5
El Pinacate y Gran Desierto de Altar = Gran Desierto del Pinacate ⌓ Mexico 31°51N 113°32W 318 A2
El Pobleneu Spain 41°23N 2°11E 114 A2
El Pobo de Dueñas Spain 40°46N 1°39W 196 E3
El Portal Calif., U.S.A. 37°41N 119°47W 306 H7
El Portal Fla., U.S.A. 25°51N 80°11W 129 C2
El Porvenir Mexico 31°15N 105°51W 318 A3
El Prat Barcelona ✈ (BCN) Spain 41°18N 2°5E 114 B1
El Prat de Llobregat Spain 41°19N 2°5E 114 B1
El Progreso Galápagos Is., Ecuador 0°54S 89°33W 330 a
El Progreso Honduras 15°26N 87°51W 320 C2
El Pueblo Canary Is. 28°36N 17°47W 153 e1
El Pueblo de Los Angeles Historic Park Los Angeles, U.S.A. 127 b2
El Puente del Arzobispo Spain 39°48N 5°10W 194 F5
El Puerto de Santa María Spain 36°36N 6°13W 195 J4
El Qâhira Egypt 30°2N 31°13E 117 A2
El Qanâyat Egypt 30°37N 31°27E 251 H2
El Qantara Egypt 30°51N 32°20E 251 H3
El Qasr Egypt 25°44N 28°42E 256 B2
El Qassâsîn Egypt 30°33N 31°55E 251 H2
El Qubâbât Egypt 29°28N 31°16E 256 J7
El Qubba Egypt 30°4N 31°16E 117 A2
El Quseima Egypt 30°40N 34°15E 251 H5
El Qusîya Egypt 27°29N 30°44E 256 B3
El Râshda Egypt 25°36N 28°57E 256 B2
El Reloj Mexico 19°19N 99°9W 128 C2
El Reno U.S.A. 35°32N 97°57W 301 H20
El Retiro Spain 40°25N 3°41W 127 B1
El Rey △ Argentina 24°40S 64°34W 334 A3
El Rîdisiya Egypt 24°56N 32°51E 256 C3
El Rio U.S.A. 34°14N 119°10W 307 L7
El Ronquillo Spain 37°44N 6°10W 195 H4
El Roque, Pta. Canary Is. 28°10N 15°25W 153 e1
El Rosario Mexico 30°1N 115°45W 318 A1
El Rubio Spain 37°22N 5°0W 195 H5
El Saff Egypt 29°34N 31°16E 256 J7
El Salto Santiago, Chile 33°22S 70°38W 137 B2
El Salto Durango, Mexico 23°47N 105°22W 318 C3
El Salvador ■ Cent. Amer. 13°50N 89°0W 320 D2
El Sauce Nic. 13°0N 86°40W 320 D2
El Saucejo Spain 37°4N 5°6W 195 H5
El Sereno U.S.A. 34°4N 118°10W 126 B3
El Shallal Egypt 24°0N 32°53E 256 C3
El Simbillawein Egypt 30°48N 31°13E 256 H7
El Sombrero Venezuela 9°23N 67°3W 328 B4
El Suweis Egypt 29°58N 32°31E 256 B3
El Suweis □ Egypt 29°30N 32°15E 251 J3
El Tabbîn Egypt 29°47N 31°18E 256 J7
El Talibîya Egypt 29°59N 31°10E 117 B2
El Tamá △ S. Amer. 7°25N 72°25W 328 B3
El Tamarâni, W. → Egypt 30°7N 34°43E 251 H5
El Tarf Algeria 36°46N 8°19E 261 A6
El Tarf □ Algeria 36°45N 8°10E 261 A6
El Thamad Egypt 29°40N 34°28E 251 J5
El Tigre Venezuela 8°44N 64°15W 329 B5
El Tîh, Gebel Egypt 29°40N 33°50E 251 J4
El Tîna Egypt 31°3N 32°22E 256 H8
El Tirano Puerte Fermín Venezuela 11°7N 63°51W 329 a
El Tocuyo Venezuela 9°47N 69°48W 328 B4
El Tofo Chile 29°22S 71°18W 334 B1
El Tránsito Chile 28°52S 70°17W 334 B1
El Tucuche Trin. & Tob. 10°43N 61°25W 323 t
El Tuey Venezuela 11°1N 63°57W 329 a
El Tunal Venezuela 11°4N 64°18W 329 a
El Tuparro △ Colombia 5°19N 68°28W 328 B4
El Tûr Egypt 28°14N 33°36E 251 K4
El Turbio Argentina 51°45S 72°5W 336 D2
El Uarre Somalia 3°4N 45°20E 267 D6
El Uqsur Egypt 25°41N 32°38E 256 B3
El Valle ⌓ Spain 37°56N 1°6W 197 H3
El Valle del Espíritu Santo Venezuela 10°49N 63°53W 329 a
El Vendrell Spain 41°10N 1°30E 196 D6
El Vergel Chihuahua, Mexico 26°28N 106°22W 318 B3
El Vergel Distrito Federal, Mexico 19°18N 99°5W 128 C2
El Vigía Venezuela 8°38N 71°39W 328 B3
El Viso del Alcor Spain 37°23N 5°43W 195 H5
El Wabeira Egypt 29°34N 33°6E 251 J4
El Wâhli Egypt 30°3N 31°16E 117 A2
El Wak Somalia 2°44N 41°1E 267 D5
El Weguet Ethiopia 5°28N 42°17E 257 F5
El Wuz Sudan 15°5N 30°7E 257 D3
El Yaque Venezuela 10°54N 63°57W 329 a
El Yunque, Cerro Chile 33°39S 78°50W 330 c
El Yunque Puerto Rico 18°19N 65°48W 321 b
El Zamâlik Egypt 30°3N 31°12E 117 A2
El Zeitûn Egypt 30°6N 31°18E 117 A2
Elafonisos Greece 36°29N 22°56E 204 E4
Elamanchili India 17°33N 82°50E 244 F6
Élancourt France 48°47N 1°58E 173 D8
Elands Australia 31°37S 152°20E 283 A10
Elandsfontein Junc. = Germiston S. Africa 26°13S 28°10E 123 B2
Elasa Greece 35°18N 26°21E 205 F8
Elassona Greece 39°53N 22°12E 204 B4
Elat Israel 29°30N 34°56E 251 J5

Elati Oros Greece 38°43N 20°39E 207 B2
Elatia Greece 38°37N 22°46E 204 C4
Elâzığ Turkey 38°37N 39°14E 213 C8
Elâzığ □ Turkey 38°40N 39°15E 213 C8
Elba Italy 42°46N 10°17E 198 F7
Elba Ala., U.S.A. 31°25N 86°4W 316 D3
Elbasan Albania 41°9N 20°9E 202 E4
Elbe U.S.A. 46°45N 122°10W 306 D4
Elbe → Europe 53°50N 9°0E 178 B4
Elbe-Seitenkanal Germany 52°45N 10°32E 178 C6
Elberfeld U.S.A. 38°10N 87°27W 311 F9
Elbert, Mt. U.S.A. 39°7N 106°27W 304 G10
Elberton U.S.A. 34°7N 82°52W 316 A7
Elbeuf France 49°17N 1°2E 172 C8
Elbeyli Turkey 36°40N 37°27E 250 B8
Elbing = Elbląg Poland 54°10N 19°25E 184 D6
Elbistan Turkey 38°13N 37°15E 212 C7
Elbląg Poland 54°10N 19°25E 184 D6
Elbow Canada 51°7N 106°35W 297 C7
Elbrus Russia 43°21N 42°30E 191 J6
Elbufer-Drawehn △
Germany 53°8N 10°58E 178 B6
Elburn U.S.A. 41°54N 88°28W 311 C8
Elburz Mts. = Alborz, Reshteh-ye
Kūhhā-ye Iran 36°0N 52°0E 247 C7
Elche Spain 38°15N 0°42W 197 G4
Elche de la Sierra Spain 38°27N 2°3W 197 G2
Elcho I. Australia 11°55S 135°45E 280 A2
Elda Spain 38°29N 0°47W 197 G4
Eldama Ravine Kenya 0°3N 35°43E 268 B4
Elde → Germany 53°7N 11°15E 178 B7
Eldey Iceland 63°45N 22°55W 155 D4
Eldon Iowa, U.S.A. 40°55N 92°13W 310 D4
Eldon Mo., U.S.A. 38°21N 92°35W 310 F4
Eldon Wash., U.S.A. 47°33N 123°3W 306 C3
Eldora U.S.A. 42°22N 93°5W 310 B3
Eldorado = Echo Bay
Canada 66°5N 117°55W 294 D8
Eldorado Argentina 26°28S 54°43W 335 B5
Eldorado Ont., Canada 44°35N 77°31W 312 B7
Eldorado Ill., U.S.A. 37°49N 88°26W 311 G8
Eldorado Tex., U.S.A. 30°52N 100°36W 314 F4
Eldorendo U.S.A. 31°3N 84°39W 316 D5
Eldoret Kenya 0°30N 35°17E 268 B4
Eldred U.S.A. 41°58N 78°23W 312 E6
Eldridge U.S.A. 41°39N 90°35W 310 C6
Elea, C. Cyprus 35°19N 34°4E 207 E10
Eleanora, Pk. Australia 32°57S 121°9E 279 F3
Eleao U.S.A. 21°27N 157°52W 302 K14
Elefantes → Africa 24°10S 32°40E 271 B5
Elefantes, B. das Angola 13°13S 12°44E 265 E2
Elefantes, G. Chile 46°28S 73°49W 336 C2
Elefsina Greece 38°4N 23°26E 204 C5
Eleftherios Venizelos ✕ (ATH)
Greece 37°56N 23°56E 112 A3
Elektrogorsk Russia 55°56N 38°50E 188 E10
Elektroperedacha = Elektrogorsk
Russia 55°56N 38°50E 188 E10
Elektrostal Russia 55°41N 38°32E 188 E10
Elektrovoz = Stupino
Russia 54°57N 38°2E 188 E10
Elele Nigeria 5°5N 6°50E 263 D6
Elemi Triangle Africa 5°0N 35°20E 257 G4
Elena Bulgaria 42°55N 25°53E 203 D9
Elephant Butte Res.
U.S.A. 33°9N 107°11W 305 K10
Elephant I. Antarctica 61°0S 55°0W 151 C18
Elephant Pass Sri Lanka 9°35N 80°25E 245 K5
Elephanta Caves India 18°57N 72°57E 130 B2
Elephanta I. India 18°57N 72°56E 130 B2
Elesbão Veloso Brazil 6°13S 42°8W 332 C3
Eleshnitsa Bulgaria 41°52N 23°36E 202 E7
Eleşkirt Turkey 39°50N 42°50E 213 C10
Eleuthera I. Bahamas 25°0N 76°20W 320 B4
Eleutheroupoli Greece 40°52N 24°20E 203 F8
Elfin Cove U.S.A. 58°12N 136°22W 303 G13
Elgå Norway 62°10N 11°56E 164 B8
Elgin Ont., Canada 44°36N 76°13W 313 B8
Elgin Moray, U.K. 57°39N 3°19W 167 D5
Elgin Ill., U.S.A. 42°2N 88°17W 311 B8
Elgin N. Dak., U.S.A. 46°24N 101°51W 308 B3
Elgin Oreg., U.S.A. 45°34N 117°55W 304 D5
Elgin S.C., U.S.A. 34°10N 80°48W 316 A9
Elgin Tex., U.S.A. 30°21N 97°22W 314 F6
Elgoibar Spain 43°13N 2°24W 196 B2
Elgon, Mt. Africa 1°10N 34°30E 268 B3
Elgspiggen Norway 62°10N 11°21E 164 B8
Eliase Indonesia 8°21S 130°48E 231 F8
Elikonos Oros Greece 38°18N 22°45E 204 C4
Elim Namibia 17°48S 15°31E 270 A2
Elim Western Cape, S. Africa 34°35S 19°45E 270 D2
Elim Alaska, U.S.A. 64°37N 162°15W 303 D7
Elin Pelin Bulgaria 42°40N 23°36E 202 D7
Elingampangu
Dem. Rep. of the Congo 2°0S 24°4E 264 C4
Elipa Dem. Rep. of the Congo 1°3S 24°20E 264 C4
Eliseu Martins Brazil 8°13S 43°42W 332 C3
Elista Russia 46°16N 44°14E 191 G7
Eliza, L. Australia 37°15S 139°50E 282 D3
Elizabeth S. Austral.,
Australia 34°42S 138°41E 282 C3
Elizabeth Ill., U.S.A. 42°19N 90°13W 310 B6
Elizabeth N.J., U.S.A. 40°39N 74°12W 313 F10
Elizabeth, B. Ecuador 0°36S 91°12W 330 a
Elizabeth City U.S.A. 36°18N 76°14W 315 C16
Elizabethton U.S.A. 36°21N 82°13W 315 C13
Elizabethtown Ky.,
U.S.A. 37°42N 85°52W 311 G11
Elizabethtown N.Y.,
U.S.A. 44°13N 73°36W 313 B11
Elizabethtown Pa., U.S.A. 40°9N 76°36W 313 F8
Elizabethville = Lubumbashi
Dem. Rep. of the Congo 11°40S 27°28E 269 E2
Elizondo Spain 43°12N 1°30W 196 B3
Ełk Poland 53°50N 22°21E 184 E9
Elk → B.C., Canada 49°11N 115°14W 296 C5
Ełk → Poland 53°41N 22°28E 184 E9
Elk → Ala., U.S.A. 34°46N 87°16W 315 D11
Elk City U.S.A. 35°25N 99°25W 314 D5
Elk Creek U.S.A. 39°36N 122°32W 306 F4
Elk Grove U.S.A. 38°25N 121°22W 306 G5
Elk Island △ Canada 53°35N 112°59W 296 C6
Elk Lake Canada 47°40N 80°25W 298 C3
Elk Point Canada 53°54N 110°55W 297 C6
Elk River Idaho, U.S.A. 46°47N 116°11W 304 C5
Elk River Minn., U.S.A. 45°18N 93°35W 308 C7
Elkader U.S.A. 42°51N 91°24W 310 B5
Elkedra → Australia 21°8S 136°22E 280 C2
Elkhart Ind., U.S.A. 41°41N 85°58W 311 C11
Elkhart Kans., U.S.A. 37°0N 101°54W 308 G3
Elkhart → U.S.A. 41°41N 85°58W 311 C11
Elkhorn Man., Canada 49°59N 101°14W 297 D8
Elkhorn Wis., U.S.A. 42°40N 88°33W 311 B8
Elkhorn → U.S.A. 41°8N 96°19W 308 E5
Elkhovo Bulgaria 42°10N 26°35E 203 D10
Elkin U.S.A. 36°15N 80°51W 315 C14
Elkins U.S.A. 38°55N 79°51W 309 F14
Elkland U.S.A. 41°59N 77°19W 312 E7
Elko B.C., Canada 49°20N 115°10W 296 D5
Elko Nev., U.S.A. 40°50N 115°46W 304 F6
Elkton U.S.A. 43°49N 83°11W 312 C1
Ellas = Greece ■ Europe 40°0N 23°0E 204 B3
Ellaville Fla., U.S.A. 30°23N 83°10W 316 E6
Ellaville Ga., U.S.A. 32°14N 84°19W 316 C5
Ellboda Sweden 59°24N 18°15E 139 A3
Ellef Ringnes I. Canada 78°30N 102°2W 295 B11
Ellen, Mt. U.S.A. 44°9N 72°56W 313 B12
Ellenburg U.S.A. 44°54N 73°48W 313 B11
Ellendale U.S.A. 46°0N 98°32W 308 B4
Ellenor, L. U.S.A. 28°28N 81°25W 133 B2
Ellensburg U.S.A. 46°59N 120°34W 304 C3
Ellenville U.S.A. 41°43N 74°24W 313 E10
Ellerton Barbados 13°7N 59°33W 323 r
Ellery, Mt. Australia 37°28S 148°47E 283 D8
Ellesmere = Scottsdale
Australia 41°9S 147°31E 281 G4
Ellesmere, L. N.Z. 43°47S 172°28E 285 H7
Ellesmere I. Canada 79°30N 80°0W 295 B16
Ellesmere Island = Quttinirpaaq △
Canada 82°13N 72°13W 295 A17
Ellesmere Port U.K. 53°17N 2°54W 168 D5
Ellettsville U.S.A. 39°14N 86°38W 311 E10
Ellice Is. = Tuvalu ■
Pac. Oc. 8°0S 178°0E 277 B14
Ellicottville U.S.A. 42°17N 78°40W 312 D6
Ellington U.S.A. 42°13N 79°6W 312 D5
Elliniko Olympic Complex
Greece 37°50N 23°45E 112 B2
Elliot N. Terr., Australia 17°33S 133°32E 280 B1
Elliot Eastern Cape, S. Africa 31°22S 27°48E 271 D4
Elliot Lake Canada 46°25N 82°35W 298 C3
Elliotdale = Xhora
S. Africa 31°55S 28°38E 271 D4
Elliott U.S.A. 34°6N 80°10W 316 A9
Elliott Key U.S.A. 25°27N 80°12W 317 K9
Ellipse, The Washington, D.C., U.S.A. 143 b1
Ellis U.S.A. 38°56N 99°34W 308 F4
Ellis I. U.S.A. 40°41N 74°2W 132 B1
Elliston Australia 33°39S 134°53E 281 E1
Ellisville U.S.A. 31°36N 89°12W 315 F10
Ellon U.K. 57°22N 2°4W 167 D6
Ellora India 20°1N 75°10E 244 D2
Ellore = Eluru India 16°48N 81°8E 244 F5
Elloree U.S.A. 33°32N 80°34W 316 B9
Ellsworth Kans., U.S.A. 38°44N 98°14W 308 F4
Ellsworth Maine, U.S.A. 44°33N 68°25W 309 C19
Ellsworth Land Antarctica 76°0S 89°0W 151 D16
Ellsworth Mts. Antarctica 78°30S 85°0W 151 D16
Ellwangen Germany 48°57N 10°8E 179 G6
Ellwood City U.S.A. 40°52N 80°17W 312 F4
Ellzey U.S.A. 29°19N 82°48W 317 F7
Elm Switz. 46°54N 9°10E 179 J5
Elm-Lappwald △ Germany 52°15N 10°50E 178 C6
Elma Man., Canada 49°52N 95°55W 297 D9
Elma Wash., U.S.A. 47°0N 123°25W 306 D3
Elmadağ Turkey 39°55N 33°14E 212 C5
Elmalı Turkey 36°44N 29°56E 205 E11
Elmers End U.K. 51°23N 0°2W 125 B3
Elmhurst Ill., U.S.A. 41°53N 87°56W 311 C9
Elmhurst N.Y., U.S.A. 40°44N 73°53W 132 B2
Elmina Ghana 5°5N 1°21W 263 D4
Elmira Ont., Canada 43°36N 80°33W 312 C4
Elmira N.Y., U.S.A. 42°6N 76°48W 312 D8
Elmira Heights U.S.A. 42°8N 76°50W 312 D8
Elmodel U.S.A. 31°21N 84°29W 316 D5
Elmore Vic., Australia 36°30S 144°37E 282 D6
Elmore Ala., U.S.A. 32°32N 86°19W 316 C3
Elmore Ohio, U.S.A. 41°29N 83°18W 311 C13
Elmshorn Germany 53°43N 9°40E 178 B5
Elmstead U.K. 51°24N 0°2E 125 B4
Elmvale Canada 44°35N 79°52W 312 B5
Elmwood Ill., U.S.A. 40°47N 89°58W 310 D7
Elmwood La., U.S.A. 29°57N 90°11W 131 B1
Elmwood Park Ill., U.S.A. 41°55N 87°48W 119 B2
Elmwood Park N.J., U.S.A. 40°54N 74°7W 132 A1
Elne France 42°36N 2°58E 174 F6
Elnesvågen Norway 62°52N 7°10E 164 B4
Elnora U.S.A. 38°53N 87°5W 311 F9
Eloaua I. Papua N. G. 1°38S 149°40E 286 A5
Elobey, Is. Eq. Guin. 1°1N 9°29E 264 B1
Elongo
Dem. Rep. of the Congo 0°19S 21°39E 264 C4
Elora Canada 43°41N 80°26W 312 C4
Elorza Venezuela 7°3N 69°31W 328 B4
Elos Greece 36°46N 22°43E 204 E4
Elounda Greece 35°16N 25°42E 207 E6
Eloy U.S.A. 32°45N 111°33W 305 K8
Éloyes France 48°6N 6°36E 173 D13
Elphin Canada 44°55N 76°37W 313 B8
Elpitiya Sri Lanka 6°17N 80°10E 245 L5
Elrose Canada 51°12N 108°0W 297 C7
Elsberry U.S.A. 39°10N 90°47W 310 E6
Elsby △ Australia 14°55S 133°10E 278 B5
Elsdorf Germany 50°55N 6°34E 178 E2
Elsie Mich., U.S.A. 43°5N 84°23W 311 A12
Elsie Oreg., U.S.A. 45°52N 123°36W 306 E3
Elsiesrivier S. Africa 33°55S 18°35E 118 A2
Elsinore = Helsingør
Denmark 56°2N 12°35E 163 H6
Elster → Germany 51°25N 11°57E 178 D7
Elsternwick Australia 37°52S 145°0E 128 B2
Elsterwerda Germany 51°27N 13°31E 178 D9
Eltanin Fracture Zone System
S. Ocean 54°0S 130°0W 151 B14
Eltham N.Z. 39°26S 174°19E 284 F3
Eltham London, U.K. 51°27N 0°3E 125 B4
Elton Russia 49°5N 46°52E 191 F8
Elton, Ozero Russia 49°5N 46°42E 191 F8
Eltville Germany 50°2N 8°7E 179 E4
Eluru India 16°48N 81°8E 244 F5
Elvas Portugal 38°50N 7°10W 195 G3
Elven France 47°44N 2°36W 172 E4
Elverum Norway 60°53N 11°34E 164 D8
Elvire → Australia 17°51S 128°11E 278 C4
Elvire, Mt. Australia 29°22S 119°36E 279 E2
Elvo → Italy 45°23N 8°21E 198 C5
Elwell, L. = Tiber Res.
U.S.A. 48°19N 111°6W 304 B8
Elwood Vic., Australia 37°53S 144°59E 128 B1
Elwood Ill., U.S.A. 41°24N 88°7W 311 C8
Elwood Ind., U.S.A. 40°17N 85°50W 311 D11
Elwood Nebr., U.S.A. 40°36N 99°52W 308 E4
Elx = Elche Spain 38°15N 0°42W 197 G4
Ely Cambs., U.K. 52°24N 0°16E 169 E8
Ely Minn., U.S.A. 47°55N 91°51W 308 B8
Ely Nev., U.S.A. 39°15N 114°54W 304 G6
Elyria U.S.A. 41°22N 82°7W 312 E2
Elyros Greece 35°15N 23°45E 204 F5
Élysée France 48°52N 2°19E 134 A2
Elysian Park Los Angeles, U.S.A. 127 a3
Elz → Germany 48°18N 7°44E 179 G3
Émaé Vanuatu 17°4S 168°24E 287 G6
eMakhazeni S. Africa 25°42S 30°2E 271 C5
eMalahleni S. Africa 25°51S 29°14E 271 C4
Emāmrūd Iran 36°30N 55°0E 247 B7
Emāmzādeh Sāleh Iran 35°48N 51°26E 141 A2
Emån → Sweden 57°8N 16°30E 163 G10
Emao Vanuatu 17°29S 168°30E 287 G6
Emas △ Brazil 18°2S 52°50W 331 D7
Emateloa
Dem. Rep. of the Congo 1°16N 18°42E 264 B3
Embajadores Madrid, Spain 127 c2
eMbalenhle S. Africa 26°32S 29°4E 271 C4
Embarcación Argentina 23°10S 64°0W 334 A3
Embarcadero, The San Francisco, U.S.A. 136 b3
Embarras → U.S.A. 38°39N 87°37W 311 F9
Embetsu Japan 44°44N 141°47E 220 B10
Embi Kazakhstan 48°50N 58°8E 216 C5
Embi → Kazakhstan 46°55N 53°28E 187 E9
Embonas Greece 36°13N 27°51E 206 E11
Embro Canada 43°9N 80°54W 312 C4
Embrun France 44°34N 6°30E 175 D10
Embu Kenya 0°32S 37°38E 268 C4
Emden Germany 53°21N 7°12E 178 B3
Emecik Turkey 36°46N 27°49E 205 E9
Emei Shan China 29°32N 103°24E 228 C4
Emeishan China 29°31N 103°23E 228 C4
Emek Refa'im Jerusalem 123 c2
Émerainville France 48°48N 2°37E 134 B4
Emerald Queens., Australia 23°32S 148°10E 280 C4
Emerald Vic., Australia 37°56S 145°29E 276 E8
Emerald Buddha = Phra Kaeo
Bangkok, Thailand 113 b1
Emerald I. Canada 76°48N 114°10W 295 B9
Emerson Man., Canada 49°0N 97°10W 297 D9
Emerson Ga., U.S.A. 34°8N 84°45W 316 A5
Emeryville U.S.A. 37°49N 122°17W 136 A3
Emet Turkey 39°20N 29°15E 205 B11
Emeti Papua N. G. 7°53S 143°15E 286 D2
Emgwenya S. Africa 25°40S 30°18E 271 C5
Emi Koussi Chad 19°45N 18°55E 259 E3
Emilia-Romagna □ Italy 44°45N 11°0E 198 D8
Emilius, Mte. Italy 45°45N 7°20E 198 C4
Emin China 46°34N 83°36E 217 C10
Eminabad Pakistan 32°2N 74°8E 242 C6
Emine, Nos Bulgaria 42°40N 27°56E 203 D11
Eminence U.S.A. 38°22N 85°11W 311 F11
Eminönü Turkey 41°0N 28°57E 122 B1
Emirates, Mall of the
U.A.E. 25°7N 55°12E 119 B1
Emirau I. Papua N. G. 1°40S 150°0E 286 A6
Emirdağ Turkey 39°2N 31°8E 212 C4
Emirgan Turkey 41°6N 29°2E 122 B2
Emissi, Tarso Chad 21°27N 18°36E 259 D3
Emlenton U.S.A. 41°11N 79°43W 312 E5
Emlichheim Germany 52°37N 6°51E 178 C2
Emmaboda Sweden 56°37N 15°32E 163 H9
Emmalane U.S.A. 32°46N 82°0W 316 C7
Emmarentia S. Africa 26°9S 28°0E 123 A2
Emmastad Curaçao 12°8N 68°55W 322 g
Emmaus S. Africa 29°2S 25°15E 270 C4
Emmaus Pa., U.S.A. 40°32N 75°30W 313 F9
Emme → Switz. 47°14N 7°32E 179 H3
Emmeloord Neths. 52°44N 5°46E 170 B5
Emmen Neths. 52°48N 6°57E 170 B6
Emmen Switz. 47°5N 8°18E 179 H4
Emmendingen Germany 48°6N 7°51E 179 G3
Emmental Switz. 46°55N 7°40E 179 J3
Emmerich Germany 51°50N 6°14E 178 D2
Emmet Australia 24°45S 144°30E 280 C3
Emmetsburg U.S.A. 43°7N 94°41W 310 A2
Emmett Idaho, U.S.A. 43°52N 116°30W 304 E5
Emmett Mich., U.S.A. 42°59N 82°46W 312 D2
Emmiganuru = Yemmiganur
India 15°44N 77°29E 245 G3
Emmonak U.S.A. 62°47N 164°31W 303 E6
Emo Canada 48°38N 93°50W 297 D10
Emőd Hungary 47°57N 20°47E 182 C5
Emona Bulgaria 42°43N 27°53E 203 D11
Empalme Mexico 27°58N 110°51W 318 B2
Empangeni S. Africa 28°50S 31°52E 271 C5
Empedrado Argentina 28°0S 58°46W 334 B4
Emperor Seamount Chain
Pac. Oc. 40°0N 170°0E 288 D9
Emperor Trough Pac. Oc. 43°0N 175°30E 288 C9
Empingham Res. = Rutland Water
U.K. 52°39N 0°38W 169 E7
Empire U.S.A. 32°21N 83°18W 316 C6
Empire State Building New York, U.S.A. 132 c2
Empoli Italy 43°43N 10°57E 198 E7
Emporia Kans., U.S.A. 38°25N 96°11W 308 F5
Emporia Va., U.S.A. 36°42N 77°32W 309 G15
Emporium U.S.A. 41°31N 78°14W 312 E6
Empress Canada 50°57N 110°0W 297 C7
Empty Quarter = Rub' al Khālī
Si. Arabia 19°0N 48°0E 249 C5
Ems → Germany 53°20N 7°12E 178 B3
Emsdale Canada 45°32N 79°19W 312 A5
Emsdetten Germany 52°10N 7°32E 178 C3
Emu China 43°40N 128°6E 227 C15
Emu Park Australia 23°13S 150°50E 280 C5
eMuziwezinto S. Africa 30°15S 30°45E 271 D5
'En 'Avrona Israel 29°43N 35°0E 251 J6
'En Boqeq Israel 31°12N 35°21E 251 G6
En Gannim = Ramat Gan
Israel 32°4N 34°48E 251 F5
'En Gedi Israel 31°28N 35°25E 251 G6
En Na'am Sudan 10°21N 27°58E 266 B2
En Nahrat Mali 22°55N 3°36W 260 D4
En Nahud Sudan 12°45N 28°25E 257 E2
En Nofalab Sudan 15°52N 32°32E 257 D3
En Nuqra Sudan 10°4N 28°10E 266 B2
Ena Japan 35°25N 137°25E 223 B9
Ena-San Japan 35°26N 137°36E 223 B9
Enambú Colombia 1°1N 70°17W 328 C3
Enånger Sweden 61°30N 17°9E 162 C11
Enard B. U.K. 58°5N 5°20W 167 C3
Enare träsk = Inarijärvi
Finland 69°0N 28°0E 160 B23
Enarotali Indonesia 3°55S 136°21E 231 E9
Encampment U.S.A. 41°12N 106°47W 304 F10
Encantadas, Serra Brazil 30°40S 53°0W 335 C5
Encantado Brazil 22°53S 43°19W 135 B1
Encarnación Paraguay 27°15S 55°50W 335 B4
Encarnación de Diaz
Mexico 21°31N 102°14W 318 C4
Enchi Ghana 5°53N 2°48W 262 D4
Encinitas U.S.A. 33°3N 117°17W 307 M9
Encino Calif., U.S.A. 34°9N 118°28W 126 B2
Encino N. Mex., U.S.A. 34°39N 105°28W 305 J11
Encino Res. U.S.A. 34°8N 118°30W 126 B1
Encontrados Venezuela 9°3N 72°14W 328 B3
Encounter B. Australia 35°45S 138°45E 282 C3
Encruzilhada Brazil 15°31S 40°54W 333 E3
Encs Hungary 48°20N 21°8E 182 B6
Endako Canada 54°6N 125°2W 296 C3
Endau Kenya 1°18S 38°31E 268 C4
Endau Rompin △
Malaysia 2°27N 103°45E 237 L4
Ende Indonesia 8°45S 121°40E 231 F6
Endeavour Str. Australia 10°45S 142°0E 286 F2
Endelave Denmark 55°46N 10°18E 163 J4
Enden Norway 61°47N 10°15E 164 C7
Enderbury Kiribati 3°8S 171°5W 277 A16
Enderby Canada 50°35N 119°10W 296 C5
Enderby Abyssal Plain
S. Ocean 60°0S 40°0E 151 C5
Enderby I. Australia 20°35S 116°30E 278 D2
Enderby Land Antarctica 66°0S 53°0E 151 C5
Enderlin U.S.A. 46°38N 97°36W 308 B5
Enderrocat, C. Spain 39°28N 2°43E 206 B3
Endicott U.S.A. 42°6N 76°4W 313 D8
Endicott Mts. U.S.A. 68°0N 152°0W 303 C9
Endimari → Brazil 8°46S 66°7W 330 B4
Endwell U.S.A. 42°6N 76°2W 313 D8
Endyalgout I. Australia 11°40S 132°35E 278 B5
Ené → Peru 11°10S 74°18W 330 C3
Eneabba Australia 29°49S 115°16E 279 E2
Enebyberg Sweden 59°25N 17°59E 139 A1
Enerhodar Ukraine 47°30N 34°28E 189 J8
Enewetak Atoll
Marshall Is. 11°30N 162°15E 288 F8
Enez Turkey 40°45N 26°5E 203 F10
Enfer, Pte. d' Martinique 14°22N 60°54W 322 j
Enfield N.S.W., Australia 33°53S 151°6E 139 B1
Enfield N.S., Canada 44°56N 63°32W 299 D7
Enfield Conn., U.S.A. 41°58N 72°36W 313 E12
Enfield Ill., U.S.A. 38°6N 88°20W 311 F8
Enfield N.C., U.S.A. 36°11N 77°41W 315 C16
Enfield N.H., U.S.A. 43°39N 72°9W 313 C12
Enga □ Papua N. G. 5°30S 143°30E 286 C2
Engadin Switz. 46°45N 10°10E 179 J6
Engan Norway 63°8N 8°31E 164 A5
Engaño, C. Dom. Rep. 18°30N 68°20W 321 C6
Engaño, C. Phil. 18°35N 122°23E 232 B4
Engaru Japan 44°3N 143°31E 220 B11
Engcobo = Ngcobo
S. Africa 31°37S 28°0E 271 D4
Engelberg Switz. 46°48N 8°26E 179 J4
Engels Russia 51°28N 46°6E 190 E8
Engelsberg = Ängelsberg
Sweden 59°58N 16°0E 162 E10
Engemann L. Canada 58°0N 106°55W 297 B7
Engenho, I. do Brazil 22°50S 43°6W 135 B2
Engerdal Norway 61°45N 11°58E 164 C8
Engershatu Eritrea 16°7N 38°34E 257 D4
Enggano Indonesia 5°20S 102°40E 234 D2
Engineer Group
Papua N. G. 10°35S 151°20E 286 F6
Engkilili Malaysia 1°3N 111°42E 235 B4
England U.S.A. 34°33N 91°58W 314 D9
England □ U.K. 53°0N 2°0W 169 E5
Englee Canada 50°45N 56°5W 299 B8
Englehart Canada 47°49N 79°52W 298 C4
Englewood Fla., U.S.A. 26°58N 82°21W 317 J7
Englewood Ill., U.S.A. 41°46N 87°38W 119 C3
Englewood N.J., U.S.A. 40°54N 73°58W 132 A2
Englewood Ohio, U.S.A. 39°53N 84°18W 311 E12
Englewood Cliffs U.S.A. 40°53N 73°59W 132 A2
English U.S.A. 38°20N 86°28W 311 F10
English → Ont., Canada 49°12N 91°5W 297 C10
English → Iowa, U.S.A. 41°29N 91°32W 310 C5
English B. Ascension I. 7°54S 14°23W 153 g
English Bazar = Ingraj Bazar
India 24°58N 88°10E 243 G13
English Channel Europe 50°0N 2°0W 169 G6
English Company's Is., The
Australia 11°50S 136°32E 280 A2
English Harbour Town
Antigua & B. 17°1N 61°46W 322 b
English River Canada 49°14N 91°0W 298 C1
Engures ezers Latvia 57°16N 23°6E 184 A10
Enguri → Georgia 42°27N 41°38E 191 J5
Enid U.S.A. 36°24N 97°53W 314 C6
Enipeas → Greece 39°22N 22°17E 204 B4
Eniwa Japan 43°0N 141°30E 220 C10
Enkhuizen Neths. 52°42N 5°17E 170 B5
Enköping Sweden 59°37N 17°4E 162 E11
Enle China 24°0N 101°9E 228 F3
Enmore Australia 33°54S 151°10E 139 B2
Enna Italy 37°34N 14°16E 201 E7
Ennadai L. Canada 60°58N 101°20W 297 A8
Enné, O. → Chad 14°24N 18°45E 259 F4
Ennedi Chad 17°15N 22°0E 259 E4
Enneri Achelouma →
Niger 21°55N 13°35E 261 D7
Enngonia Australia 29°21S 145°50E 281 D4
Ennigerloh Germany 51°50N 8°2E 178 D4
Ennis Clare, Ireland 52°51N 8°59W 166 D3
Ennis Mont., U.S.A. 45°21N 111°44W 304 D8
Ennis Tex., U.S.A. 32°20N 96°38W 314 E6
Enniscorthy Ireland 52°30N 6°34W 166 D5
Enniskillen U.K. 54°21N 7°39W 166 B4
Ennistimon Ireland 52°57N 9°17W 166 D2
Enns Austria 48°12N 14°28E 180 C7
Enns → Austria 48°14N 14°32E 180 C7
Eno Finland 62°47N 30°10E 160 E24
Enosburg Falls U.S.A. 44°55N 72°48W 313 B12
Enping China 22°16N 112°21E 229 F9
Enrekang Indonesia 3°34S 119°47E 235 C5
Enrile Phil. 17°34N 121°42E 232 C3
Enriquillo, L. Dom. Rep. 18°20N 71°40W 321 C5
Enschede Neths. 52°13N 6°53E 170 B6
Ensenada Argentina 34°55S 57°55W 334 C4
Ensenada Chile 41°12S 72°33W 336 B2
Ensenada Baja Calif.,
Mexico 31°52N 116°37W 318 A1
Ensenada de los Muertos
Mexico 23°59N 109°51W 318 C2
Ensenada La Guardia
Venezuela 11°2N 64°5W 329 a
Enshi China 30°18N 109°29E 228 B7
Enshū-Nada Japan 34°27N 137°38E 223 C9
Ensiola, Pta. de n' Spain 39°7N 2°55E 206 B3
Ensisheim France 47°50N 7°20E 173 E14
Enskede Sweden 59°17N 18°4E 139 B2
Ensley U.S.A. 30°31N 87°16W 317 E2
Entebbe Uganda 0°4N 32°28E 268 B3
Enterprise N.W.T.,
Canada 60°47N 115°45W 296 A5
Enterprise Ala., U.S.A. 31°19N 85°51W 316 D4
Enterprise Nev., U.S.A. 36°13N 115°14W 124 B1
Enterprise Oreg., U.S.A. 45°25N 117°17W 304 D5
Entorno de Doñana △
Spain 37°0N 6°26W 195 J4
Entrance, The Australia 33°21S 151°30E 283 B9
Entraygues-sur-Truyère
France 44°38N 2°35E 174 D6
Entre-Deux Réunion 21°14S 55°28E 272 f
Entre Rios = Rio Brilhante
Brazil 21°48S 54°33W 335 A5
Entre Rios = Três Rios
Brazil 22°6S 43°15W 333 F3
Entre Rios Bolivia 21°30S 64°25W 334 A3
Entre Rios Bahia, Brazil 11°56S 38°5W 333 D4
Entre Rios Pará, Brazil 5°24S 54°21W 331 B7
Entre Rios □ Argentina 30°30S 58°30W 334 C4
Entrepeñas, Embalse de
Spain 40°34N 2°42W 196 E2
Entrevias Spain 40°22N 3°40W 127 B1
Entroncamento Portugal 39°28N 8°28W 195 F2
Enugu Nigeria 6°30N 7°30E 263 D6
Enugu □ Nigeria 6°30N 7°45E 263 D6
Enugu Ezike Nigeria 7°0N 7°29E 263 D6
Enumclaw U.S.A. 47°12N 121°59W 306 C5
Envalira, Port d' Europe 42°33N 1°43E 196 C6
Envermeu France 49°53N 1°15E 172 C8
Envigado Colombia 6°10N 75°35W 328 B2
Enviken Sweden 60°49N 15°46E 162 D9
Envira Brazil 7°18S 70°13W 330 B3
Envira → Brazil 7°9S 70°15W 330 B3
Enying Hungary 46°56N 18°15E 182 D3
Enyonga Gabon 0°59S 9°22E 264 C1
Enza → Italy 44°54N 10°31E 198 D7
Enzan = Kōshū Japan 35°42N 138°44E 223 B10
Eochaill = Youghal Ireland 51°56N 7°52W 166 E4
Eólie, Ís. Italy 38°30N 14°57E 201 D7
Eot I. Micronesia 7°23N 151°44E 287 T17
Epanomi Greece 40°25N 22°59E 202 F6
Epcot U.S.A. 28°21N 81°32W 133 B1
Epe Neths. 52°21N 5°59E 170 B5
Epe Nigeria 6°36N 3°59E 263 D5
Épéna Congo 1°22N 17°29E 264 B3
Épernay France 49°3N 3°56E 173 C10
Épernon France 48°35N 1°40E 173 D8
Ephesus Turkey 37°55N 27°22E 205 D9
Ephraim U.S.A. 39°22N 111°35W 304 G8
Ephrata Pa., U.S.A. 40°11N 76°11W 313 F8
Ephrata Wash., U.S.A. 47°19N 119°33W 304 C4
Epi Vanuatu 16°43S 168°15E 287 F6
Epidaurus = Epidavros
Greece 37°40N 23°7E 204 D5
Epidavros Greece 37°40N 23°7E 204 D5
Epidavros Limira Greece 36°46N 23°0E 204 E5
Épila Spain 41°36N 1°17W 196 D3
Épinac France 46°59N 4°31E 173 F11
Épinal France 48°10N 6°27E 173 D13
Epira Guyana 5°5N 57°20W 329 B6
Epiros □ Greece 39°30N 20°30E 204 B2
Episkopi Cyprus 34°40N 32°54E 207 F8
Episkopi Kriti, Greece 35°20N 24°20E 207 E5
Episkopi Bay Cyprus 34°35N 32°50E 207 F8
Epitalio Greece 37°37N 21°30E 204 D3
Eppalock, L. Australia 36°52S 144°34E 282 D6
Eppan = Appiano Italy 46°28N 11°15E 199 B8
Epping Australia 33°46S 151°5E 139 A1
Eppingen Germany 49°8N 8°53E 179 F4
Epsom U.K. 51°19N 0°16W 169 F7
Epukiro Namibia 21°40S 19°9E 270 B2
Equality U.S.A. 37°44N 88°20W 311 G8
Équateur □
Dem. Rep. of the Congo 2°0N 21°0E 264 B4
Equatorial Channel Maldives 0°0 73°10E 272 d
Equatorial Guinea ■ Africa 2°0N 8°0E 264 B1
Equeipa Venezuela 5°22N 62°43W 329 B5
Er Hai China 25°48N 100°11E 228 E3
Er Rachidia Morocco 31°58N 4°20W 260 B4
Er Rahad Sudan 12°45N 30°32E 257 E3
Er Rif Morocco 35°1N 4°1W 261 A4
Er Rogel Sudan 18°10N 35°25E 256 D4
Er Roseires Sudan 11°55N 34°30E 257 E3
Er Rua'at Sudan 12°21N 32°17E 257 E3
Eraclea Italy 45°35N 12°40E 199 C9
Eran Phil. 9°4N 117°42E 233 G1
Eran B. Phil. 9°5N 117°43E 233 G1
Erandol India 20°56N 75°20E 244 D2
Eranga
Dem. Rep. of the Congo 1°52S 18°56E 264 C3
Erap Papua N. G. 6°37S 146°51E 286 D4
Erasmus = Bronkhorstspruit
S. Africa 25°46S 28°45E 271 C4
Erave Papua N. G. 6°39S 144°0E 286 D2
Erave → Papua N. G. 6°54S 144°47E 286 D3
Erāwadī Myit = Irrawaddy →
Burma 15°50N 95°6E 241 G5
Erāwadī Myitwanya = Irrawaddy,
Mouths of the Burma 15°30N 95°0E 241 H5
Erawan △ Thailand 14°25N 98°58E 236 E2
Erba Italy 45°48N 9°15E 198 C6
Erba Sudan 19°5N 36°51E 256 D4
Erba, J. Sudan 20°48N 36°47E 256 C4
Erbaa Turkey 40°42N 36°36E 212 B7
Erbeng Shan China 42°50N 84°59E 217 D10
Erbeskopf Germany 49°44N 7°2E 179 F3
Erbil = Arbīl Iraq 36°15N 44°5E 213 D11
Erbu Ethiopia 6°44N 34°53E 257 E3
Ercan, Nicosia ✕ (ECN)
Cyprus 35°10N 33°30E 207 E9
Erçek Turkey 38°39N 43°36E 246 B4
Erciş Turkey 39°2N 43°21E 213 C10
Erciyaş Dağı Turkey 38°30N 35°30E 246 B2
Érd Hungary 47°22N 18°56E 182 C3
Erdao Jiang → China 42°37N 128°0E 224 A3
Erdek Turkey 40°23N 27°47E 203 F11
Erdély = Transilvania
Romania 46°30N 24°0E 183 D9
Erdemli Turkey 36°36N 34°19E 250 B5
Erdene = Ulaan-Uul
Mongolia 46°4N 100°49E 226 B6
Erdenet Mongolia 49°2N 104°5E 218 B9
Erdenetsogt Mongolia 42°55N 106°5E 226 C4
Erding Germany 48°18N 11°54E 179 G7
Erdre → France 47°13N 1°32W 172 E5
Erebato → Venezuela 5°54N 64°16W 329 B5
Erebus, Mt. Antarctica 77°35S 167°0E 151 D11
Erechim Brazil 27°35S 52°15W 335 B5
Ereğli Konya, Turkey 37°31N 34°4E 212 D6
Ereğli Zonguldak, Turkey 41°15N 31°24E 212 B4
Erei, Monti Italy 37°20N 14°20E 201 E7
Erenhot China 43°48N 112°2E 226 C7
Erenköy = Kokkina
Cyprus 35°11N 32°36E 207 E8
Erenköy Turkey 40°58N 29°3E 122 C2
Eresfjord Norway 62°40N 8°8E 164 B5
Eresma → Spain 41°26N 4°45W 194 D6
Eresos Greece 39°11N 25°57E 205 B7
Ereymentaū Kazakhstan 51°37N 73°6E 217 B8
Erfelek Turkey 41°53N 34°55E 212 B6
Erfenisdam S. Africa 28°30S 26°50E 270 C4
Erfjord Norway 59°20N 6°14E 164 E3
Erfoud Morocco 31°30N 4°15W 260 B4
Erftstadt Germany 50°50N 6°50E 178 E2
Erft → Germany 51°11N 6°44E 178 D2
Erfurt Germany 50°58N 11°2E 178 E7
Ergani Turkey 38°17N 39°49E 213 C8
Ergel Mongolia 43°8N 109°5E 226 C5
Ergene → Turkey 41°1N 26°22E 203 E10
Ergeni Vozvyshennost
Russia 47°0N 44°0E 191 G7
Ērgli Latvia 56°54N 25°38E 188 D3
Ergun He = Argun →
Russia 53°20N 121°28E 219 A13
Ergun Youqi China 50°15N 120°11E 219 A13
Erhlin Taiwan 23°54N 120°22E 225 C2
Erhshui Taiwan 23°45N 120°37E 225 C2
Eria → Spain 42°3N 5°44W 194 C5
Eriba Sudan 16°40N 36°10E 257 D4
Eriboll, L. U.K. 58°30N 4°42W 167 C4
Érice Italy 38°2N 12°35E 200 D5
Eridu U.S.A. 30°18N 83°50W 316 E6
Erie Mich., U.S.A. 41°47N 83°31W 311 C13
Erie Pa., U.S.A. 42°8N 80°5W 312 D4
Erie, L. N. Amer. 42°15N 81°0W 312 D4
Erie Canal U.S.A. 43°5N 78°43W 312 C7
Erieau Canada 42°16N 81°57W 312 D3
Erigavo = Ceerigaabo
Somalia 10°35N 47°20E 267 B6
Erikoussa Greece 39°53N 19°34E 206 B9
Eriksdale Canada 50°52N 98°7W 297 C9
Erimanthos Greece 37°57N 21°50E 204 D3
Erimo-Misaki Japan 41°50N 143°15E 220 D11
Erin Ont., Canada 43°45N 80°7W 312 C4
Erin Trin. & Tob. 10°5N 61°39W 323 t
Erin B. Trin. & Tob. 10°4N 61°43W 323 t
Erin Pt. Trin. & Tob. 10°3N 61°39W 323 t
Erinpura India 25°9N 73°3E 242 G5
Eriskay U.K. 57°4N 7°18W 167 D1
Erith U.K. 51°28N 0°11E 125 B5
Erithres Greece 38°13N 23°20E 204 C5
Eritrea ■ Africa 14°0N 38°30E 257 E4
Erivan = Yerevan
Armenia 40°10N 44°31E 191 K7
Erjas → Portugal 39°40N 7°1W 194 F3
Erkech-Tam Pass Asia 39°46N 74°2E 217 E8
Erkelenz Germany 51°4N 6°19E 178 D2
Erkner Germany 52°25N 13°44E 178 C9
Erlaa Austria 48°9N 16°19E 142 B1
Erlangen Germany 49°36N 11°0E 179 F6
Erlanger U.S.A. 39°1N 84°36W 311 E12
Erldunda Australia 25°14S 133°12E 280 D1
Ermelo Neths. 52°18N 5°35E 170 B5
Ermelo Mpumalanga,
S. Africa 26°31S 29°59E 271 C4
Ermenek Turkey 36°38N 33°0E 250 B4
Ermenek → Turkey 36°35N 33°23E 250 B4
Ermil Sudan 13°35N 27°40E 257 E2
Ermington Australia 33°48S 151°4E 139 A1
Ermioni Greece 37°23N 23°15E 204 D5
Ermita Phil. 14°35N 120°59E 127 B1
Ermones Greece 39°37N 19°46E 206 B9
Ermoupoli Greece 37°28N 24°57E 204 D6
Ernakulam India 9°59N 76°22E 245 K3
Erne → Ireland 54°30N 8°16W 166 B3
Erne, Lower L. U.K. 54°28N 7°47W 166 B4
Erne, Upper L. U.K. 54°14N 7°32W 166 B4
Ernée France 48°18N 0°56W 172 D6
Ernest Giles Ra. Australia 27°0S 123°45E 279 E3
Ernest N. Morial Convention Center
New Orleans, U.S.A. 131 c3
Ernstberg Germany 50°13N 6°47E 179 E2
Erode India 11°24N 77°45E 245 J3
Eromanga Australia 26°40S 143°11E 281 D3
Erongo Namibia 21°39S 15°58E 270 B2
Erongo □ Namibia 22°20S 15°0E 270 B2
Erquy France 48°38N 2°29W 172 D4
Erramala Hills India 15°30N 78°15E 245 G4
Errenteria Spain 43°19N 1°54W 196 B3
Errer → Ethiopia 7°32N 42°35E 257 F5
Errigal Ireland 55°2N 8°6W 166 A3
Errinundra △ Australia 37°20S 148°47E 283 D8
Erris Hd. Ireland 54°17N 10°0W 166 B1
Erromango Vanuatu 18°45S 169°5E 287 H7
Ersekë Albania 40°22N 20°40E 202 F4
Érsekújvár = Nové Zámky
Slovak Rep. 48°2N 18°8E 181 C11
Ershatou China 23°6N 113°18E 121 B2
Erskine U.S.A. 47°40N 96°0W 308 B6
Erskineville Australia 33°54S 151°12E 139 B2
Erstein France 48°25N 7°38E 173 D14
Ertai China 46°3N 90°5E 217 C12
Ertan Shuiku China 27°5N 101°52E 228 D3
Ertholmene Denmark 55°19N 15°11E 163 J9
Ertil Russia 51°55N 40°50E 190 E5
Ertis = Irtysh → Russia 61°4N 68°52E 214 C7
Ertis Kazakhstan 53°20N 75°27E 217 B9
Ertis → Kazakhstan 47°52N 84°16E 217 C10
Ertvågøy Norway 63°13N 8°26E 164 A5
Eruh Turkey 37°46N 42°13E 213 D10
Erunkan Nigeria 6°36N 3°23E 124 A2
Ervy-le-Châtel France 48°2N 3°55E 173 D10
Erwin U.S.A. 36°9N 82°25W 315 C13
Eryuan China 26°7N 99°57E 228 D2
Erzgebirge Germany 50°27N 12°55E 178 E8
Erzin Russia 50°15N 95°10E 217 B13
Erzin Turkey 36°57N 36°12E 250 B7
Erzincan Turkey 39°46N 39°30E 213 C8
Erzincan □ Turkey 39°45N 39°30E 213 C8
Erzsébet-Telep Hungary 47°27N 19°10E 117 B3
Erzurum Turkey 39°57N 41°15E 213 C9
Erzurum □ Turkey 39°55N 41°15E 213 C9
Es Caló Spain 38°40N 1°30E 206 D2
Es Canar Spain 39°2N 1°36E 206 C2
Es Mercadal Spain 39°59N 4°5E 206 B5
Es Migjorn Gran Spain 39°57N 4°3E 206 B5
Es Safiya Sudan 15°31N 30°7E 257 D3
Es Sahrā al Beida Egypt 27°50N 28°45E 256 B2
Es Sahrā' Esh Sharqīya
Egypt 27°30N 32°30E 256 B3
Es Sînâ' Egypt 29°0N 34°0E 246 D2
Es Sûkî Sudan 13°20N 33°58E 257 E3
Es Vedrà Spain 38°52N 1°12E 206 D1
Es'ala Papua N. G. 9°45S 150°49E 286 E6
Esambo
Dem. Rep. of the Congo 3°48S 23°30E 264 C4
Esan-Misaki Japan 41°40N 141°10E 220 D10
Esashi Hokkaidō, Japan 44°56N 142°35E 220 B11
Esashi Hokkaidō, Japan 41°52N 140°7E 220 D10
Esbjerg Denmark 55°29N 8°29E 163 J2
Esbo = Espoo Finland 60°12N 24°40E 188 B3
Escada Brazil 8°22S 35°8W 332 C4
Escalante Phil. 10°50N 123°33E 233 F4
Escalante Utah, U.S.A. 37°47N 111°36W 305 H8
Escalante → U.S.A. 37°24N 110°57W 305 H8
Escalón Mexico 26°45N 104°20W 318 B4
Escambia → U.S.A. 30°32N 87°11W 317 E2
Escanaba U.S.A. 45°45N 87°4W 308 C10
Escárcega Mexico 18°37N 90°43W 319 D6
Escarpada Pt. Phil. 18°31N 122°13E 232 B4
Escarpé, C. N. Cal. 20°41S 167°13E 288 d
Escaut = Schelde →
Belgium 51°15N 4°16E 170 C4
Esch-sur-Alzette Lux. 49°32N 6°0E 170 E6
Eschede Germany 52°44N 10°14E 178 C6
Eschenried Germany 48°13N 11°24E 131 A1
Eschwege Germany 51°11N 10°2E 178 D6
Eschweiler Germany 50°49N 6°15E 178 E2
Escobal Panama 9°6N 80°1W 320 c
Escoma Bolivia 15°40S 69°8W 330 D4
Escondido U.S.A. 33°7N 117°5W 307 M9
Escravos → Nigeria 5°35N 5°10E 263 D6
Escuinapa de Hidalgo
Mexico 22°50N 105°50W 318 C3
Escuintla Guatemala 14°20N 90°48W 320 D1
Eséka Cameroon 3°41N 10°44E 263 E7
Eşen → Turkey 36°27N 29°16E 205 E11
Esenguly Turkmenistan 37°37N 53°59E 216 E4
Esenler Turkey 41°1N 28°52E 122 B1
Esens Germany 53°38N 7°36E 178 B3
Esentepe = Áyios Amvrósios
Cyprus 35°20N 33°35E 207 E9
Esenyurt Turkey 41°3N 28°48E 203 E12
Esera → Spain 42°6N 0°15E 196 C5
Eşfahān Iran 32°39N 51°43E 247 C6
Eşfahān □ Iran 32°50N 51°50E 247 C6
Esfarāyen Iran 37°4N 57°30E 247 B8
Esfideh Iran 33°39N 59°46E 247 C8
Esgueva → Spain 41°40N 4°43W 194 D6
Esh Sham = Dimashq
Syria 33°30N 36°18E 250 E7
Esh Shamâlîya □ Sudan 19°0N 29°0E 256 D2
Esha Ness U.K. 60°29N 1°38W 167 A7
Eshan China 24°11N 102°24E 228 E4
Esher U.K. 51°21N 0°20W 125 B1
Eshkāshem = Ishkashim
Tajikistan 36°44N 71°37E 217 E8
Eshkol △ Israel 31°20N 34°30E 251 G5
Eshowe S. Africa 28°50S 31°30E 271 C5
Esiama Ghana 4°56N 2°25W 262 E4
Esigodini Zimbabwe 20°18S 28°56E 271 B4
Esil = Ishim → Russia 57°45N 71°10E 214 D8
Esil Kazakhstan 51°57N 66°24E 217 B7
Esino → Italy 43°39N 13°22E 199 E10
Esira Madag. 24°20S 46°42E 272 C2
Esk → Dumf. & Gall., U.K. 54°58N 3°2W 167 G5
Esk → N. Yorks., U.K. 54°30N 0°37W 168 C7
Eskān Iran 26°48N 63°9E 240 D1
Eskbank U.K. 55°52N 3°4W 121 B3
Esker Siding Canada 53°53N 66°25W 299 B6
Eskifjörður Iceland 65°3N 13°55W 155 B13
Eskije = Xanthi Greece 41°10N 24°58E 203 E8
Eskilsäter Sweden 58°57N 13°10E 163 F7
Eskilstuna Sweden 59°22N 16°32E 162 E10
Eskimalatya Turkey 38°24N 38°22E 213 C8
Eskimo Point = Arviat
Canada 61°6N 93°59W 297 A10
Eskişehir Turkey 39°50N 30°30E 205 B12
Eskişehir □ Turkey 39°40N 31°0E 205 B12
Esla → Spain 41°29N 6°3W 194 D4
Eslāmābād-e Gharb Iran 34°10N 46°30E 213 E12
Eslāmshahr Iran 35°40N 51°10E 247 C6
Eslöv Sweden 55°50N 13°20E 163 J7
Eşme Turkey 38°23N 28°58E 205 C10
Esmeralda, I. Chile 48°55S 75°25W 336 C1
Esmeraldas Ecuador 1°0N 79°40W 328 C2
Esmeraldas □ Ecuador 0°40N 79°30W 328 C2
Esmeraldas → Ecuador 0°58N 79°38W 328 C2
Esna = Isna Egypt 25°17N 32°30E 256 B3
Esnagi L. Canada 48°36N 84°33W 298 C3
Esom Hill U.S.A. 33°57N 85°23W 316 B4
Espa Norway 60°34N 11°16E 164 D8
Espada, Pta. Colombia 12°5N 71°7W 328 A3
Espalion France 44°32N 2°47E 174 D6

España = Spain ■ Europe 39°0N 4°0W 192 D3
Espanola Ont., Canada 46°15N 81°46W 298 C3
Espanola N. Mex., U.S.A. 35°59N 106°5W 305 J10
Española, I. Ecuador 1°23S 89°39W 330 a
Espanya, Plaça d' Barcelona, Spain 114 c1
Esparreguera Spain 41°33N 1°52E 196 D6
Esparza Costa Rica 9°59N 84°40W 320 E3
Espeland Norway 60°23N 5°28E 164 D2
Espelkamp Germany 52°24N 8°36E 178 C4
Espenberg, C. U.S.A. 66°33N 163°36W 303 C7
Esperança Amazonas, Brazil 4°24S 69°52W 328 D4
Esperança Paraíba, Brazil 7°1S 35°51W 332 C4
Esperance Australia 33°45S 121°55E 279 F3
Esperance, C. Solomon Is. 9°15S 159°43E 287 M10
Esperance B. Australia 33°48S 121°55E 279 F3
Esperantinópolis Brazil 4°53S 44°53W 332 B3
Esperanza Antarctica 65°0S 55°0W 151 C18
Esperanza Santa Cruz, Argentina 51°1S 70°49W 336 D2
Esperanza Santa Fe, Argentina 31°29S 61°3W 334 C3
Esperanza Mexico City, Mexico 128 c3
Esperanza Agusan del S., Phil. 8°43N 125°36E 233 G5
Esperanza Masbate, Phil. 11°45N 124°3E 233 F5
Esperanza Puerto Rico 18°6N 65°28W 321 b
Espéraza France 42°56N 2°14E 174 F6
Espevær Norway 59°35N 5°7E 164 E2
Espichel, C. Portugal 38°22N 9°16W 195 G1
Espiel Spain 38°11N 5°1W 195 G5
Espigão, Serra do Brazil 26°35S 50°30W 335 B5
Espinal Colombia 4°9N 74°53W 328 C3
Espinar Peru 14°51S 71°24W 330 C3
Espinazo, Sierra del = Espinhaço, Serra do Brazil 17°30S 43°30W 333 E3
Espinhaço, Serra do Brazil 17°30S 43°30W 333 E3
Espinho Portugal 41°1N 8°38W 194 D2
Espinilho, Serra do Brazil 28°30S 55°0W 335 B5
Espinosa de los Monteros Spain 43°5N 3°34W 194 B7
Espírito Santo □ Brazil 20°0S 40°45W 333 F3
Espírito Santo do Pinhal Brazil 22°10S 46°46W 335 A6
Espíritu Santo Vanuatu 15°15S 166°50E 287 E4
Espíritu Santo, B. del Mexico 19°20N 87°35W 319 D7
Espíritu Santo, I. Mexico 24°30N 110°22W 318 C2
Espita Mexico 21°1N 88°19W 319 C7
Espiye Turkey 40°56N 38°43E 213 B8
Esplanada Brazil 11°47S 37°57W 333 D4
Esplanade Singapore 138 c3
Esplugas Spain 41°22N 2°5E 114 A1
Espoo Finland 60°12N 24°40E 188 B3
Esposizione Universale di Roma Italy 41°49N 12°28E 136 C1
Espuña, Sierra de Spain 37°51N 1°35W 197 H3
Espungabera Mozam. 20°29S 32°45E 271 B5
Esquel Argentina 42°55S 71°20W 336 B2
Esquimalt Canada 48°26N 123°25W 306 B3
Esquina Argentina 30°0S 59°30W 334 C4
Essandsjøen Norway 63°0N 12°0E 164 A8
Essaouira Morocco 31°32N 9°42W 260 B3
Essen Belgium 51°28N 4°28E 170 C4
Essen Nordrhein-Westfalen, Germany 51°28N 7°2E 178 D3
Essendon Australia 37°44S 144°55E 128 A1
Essendon ✈ (MEB) Australia 37°43S 144°54E 128 A1
Essendon, Mt. Australia 25°0S 120°29E 279 E3
Essequibo → Guyana 6°50N 58°30W 329 B6
Essex Ont., Canada 42°10N 82°49W 312 D2
Essex Calif., U.S.A. 34°44N 115°15W 307 L11
Essex N.Y., U.S.A. 44°19N 73°21W 313 B11
Essex □ U.K. 51°54N 0°27E 169 F8
Essex Junction U.S.A. 44°29N 73°7W 313 B11
Essingen Sweden 59°19N 17°59E 139 B1
Essling Austria 48°12N 16°30E 142 A3
Esslingen Germany 48°44N 9°18E 179 G5
Essonne □ France 48°30N 2°20E 173 D9
Est, Gare de l' Paris, France 134 a5
Estaca de Bares, C. de Spain 43°46N 7°42W 194 B3
Estación Camacho Mexico 24°25N 102°18W 318 C4
Estación Simón Mexico 24°42N 102°35W 318 C4
Estadilla Spain 42°4N 0°16E 196 C5
Estado, Parque do Brazil 23°38S 46°38W 137 B2
Estados, I. de Los Argentina 54°40S 64°30W 336 D4
Estagel France 42°47N 2°40E 174 F6
Estagno Pt. Phil. 17°20N 122°24E 232 C4
Eşţahbānāt Iran 29°8N 54°4E 247 D7
Estância Brazil 11°16S 37°26W 332 D4
Estancia N. Mex., U.S.A. 34°46N 106°4W 305 J10
Estancia Monte León Argentina 50°14S 68°55W 336 D3
Estārm Iran 28°21N 58°21E 247 D8
Estarreja Portugal 40°45N 8°35W 194 E2
Estats, Pic d' Spain 42°40N 1°24E 196 C6
Estcourt S. Africa 29°0S 29°53E 271 C4
Este Italy 45°14N 11°39E 199 C8
Este △ Dom. Rep. 18°14N 68°42W 321 C6
Estefânia Lisbon, Portugal 126 a2
Estelí Nic. 13°9N 86°22W 320 D2
Estella Spain 42°40N 2°2W 196 C2
Estelle U.S.A. 29°50N 90°6W 131 B2
Estellencs Spain 39°39N 2°29E 206 B3
Estena → Spain 39°23N 4°44W 195 F6
Estepa Spain 37°17N 4°52W 195 H6
Estepona Spain 36°24N 5°7W 195 J5
Esterhazy Canada 50°37N 102°5W 297 C8
Esterias, C. Gabon 0°40N 9°20E 264 B1
Esternay France 48°44N 3°33E 173 D10
Esterri d'Aneu Spain 42°38N 1°5E 196 C6
Estevan Canada 49°10N 102°59W 297 D8
Estevan Group Canada 53°3N 129°38W 296 C3
Estherville U.S.A. 43°24N 94°50W 308 D6
Estill U.S.A. 32°45N 81°15W 316 C8
Estissac France 48°16N 3°48E 173 D10
Eston Canada 51°8N 108°40W 297 C7
Estonia ■ Europe 58°30N 25°30E 188 C3
Estoril Portugal 38°42N 9°23W 195 G1
Estouk Mali 18°14N 1°2E 263 B5
Estrela, Basilica da Portugal 38°42N 9°9W 126 A2
Estrela, Serra da Portugal 40°10N 7°45W 194 E3
Estrella Spain 38°25N 3°35W 195 G7
Estremoz Portugal 38°51N 7°39W 195 G3
Estrondo, Serra do Brazil 7°20S 48°0W 332 C2
Esutoru = Uglegorsk Russia 49°5N 142°2E 215 E15
Esztergom Hungary 47°47N 18°44E 182 C3
Et Tîdra Mauritania 19°45N 16°20W 262 B1
Etah India 27°35N 78°40E 243 F8
Étain France 49°13N 5°38E 173 C12
Étampes France 48°26N 2°10E 173 D9
Étang-Salé-les-Bains Réunion 21°15S 55°20E 272 f
Etanga Namibia 17°55S 13°0E 270 A1
Étaples France 50°30N 1°39E 173 B8
Etawah India 26°48N 79°6E 243 F8
Etawney L. Canada 57°50N 96°50W 297 B9
Etchojoa Mexico 26°55N 109°38W 318 B3
Ete Nigeria 7°2N 7°28E 263 D6
Etéké Gabon 1°29S 11°35E 264 C2
eThekwini = Durban S. Africa 29°49S 31°1E 271 C5
Ethel U.S.A. 46°32N 122°46W 306 D4
Ethelbert Canada 51°32N 100°25W 297 C8
Ethiopia ■ Africa 8°0N 40°0E 267 C4
Ethiopian Highlands Ethiopia 10°0N 37°0E 254 E7
Etili Turkey 39°59N 26°54E 203 G10
Etive, L. U.K. 56°29N 5°10W 167 E3
Etna Italy 37°50N 14°55E 201 E7
Etna → Norway 60°49N 10°7E 164 C6
Etne Norway 59°40N 5°58E 164 E2
Etobicoke Canada 43°39N 79°34W 141 B1
Etobicoke Cr. → Canada 43°35N 79°32W 141 B1
Etoile Dem. Rep. of the Congo 11°33S 27°30E 269 E2
Etoliko Greece 38°26N 21°21E 204 C3
Etolin Strait U.S.A. 60°20N 165°15W 303 F6
Etoloakarnania □ Greece 38°45N 21°18E 204 C3
Etosha △ Namibia 19°0S 16°0E 270 A2
Etosha Pan Namibia 18°40S 16°30E 270 A2
Etoumbi Congo 0°1S 14°57E 264 C2
Etowah U.S.A. 35°20N 84°32W 315 D12
Étréchy France 48°30N 2°12E 173 D9
Etrek Turkmenistan 37°36N 54°46E 247 B7
Étrépagny France 49°18N 1°36E 173 C8
Étretat France 49°42N 0°12E 172 C7
Etropole Bulgaria 42°50N 24°0E 203 D8
Ettelbruck Lux. 49°51N 6°5E 170 E6
Etterbeek Belgium 50°50N 4°23E 116 B2
Ettlingen Germany 48°56N 8°25E 179 G4
Ettrick Water → U.K. 55°31N 2°55W 167 F6
Etuku Dem. Rep. of the Congo 3°42S 25°45E 264 C5
Etulia Moldova 45°32N 28°27E 183 E13
Etzná-Tixmucuy = Edzná Mexico 19°39N 90°19W 319 D6
Eu France 50°3N 1°26E 172 B8
Eua Tonga 21°22S 174°56W 287 Q13
Euboea = Evia Greece 38°30N 24°0E 204 C6
Eucaliptus = Tomás Barrón Bolivia 17°35S 67°31W 330 D4
Euchareena Australia 32°57S 149°6E 283 B8
Eucla Australia 31°41S 128°52E 279 F4
Euclid U.S.A. 41°34N 81°32W 312 E3
Euclides da Cunha Brazil 10°31S 39°1W 332 D4
Eucumbene, L. Australia 36°2S 148°40E 283 D8
Eudora U.S.A. 33°7N 91°16W 314 E9
Eudunda Australia 34°12S 139°7E 282 C3
Eufaula Ala., U.S.A. 31°54N 85°9W 316 D4
Eufaula Okla., U.S.A. 35°17N 95°35W 314 D7
Eufaula L. U.S.A. 35°18N 95°21W 314 D7
Eugene U.S.A. 44°5N 123°4W 304 D2
Eugowra Australia 33°22S 148°24E 283 B8
Eulo Australia 28°10S 145°3E 281 D4
Eulonia U.S.A. 31°32N 81°26W 316 D8
Eumungerie Australia 31°56S 148°36E 283 A8
Eung-am S. Korea 37°34N 126°55E 137 B1
Eungella △ Australia 20°57S 148°40E 280 b
Eunice La., U.S.A. 30°30N 92°25W 314 F8
Eunice N. Mex., U.S.A. 32°26N 103°10W 305 K12
Eunpyeong S. Korea 37°36N 126°56E 137 B1
Eupen Belgium 50°37N 6°3E 170 D6
Euphrates = Furāt, Nahr al → Asia 31°0N 47°25E 246 D5
Eure □ France 49°10N 1°0E 172 C8
Eure → France 49°18N 1°12E 172 C8
Eure-et-Loir □ France 48°22N 1°30E 172 D8
Eureka Nunavut, Canada 80°0N 85°56W 295 B14
Eureka Calif., U.S.A. 40°47N 124°9W 304 F1
Eureka Ill., U.S.A. 40°43N 89°16W 310 D7
Eureka Kans., U.S.A. 37°49N 96°17W 308 G5
Eureka Mo., U.S.A. 38°30N 90°38W 310 F6
Eureka Mont., U.S.A. 48°53N 115°3W 304 B6
Eureka Nev., U.S.A. 39°31N 115°58W 304 G6
Eureka S.C., U.S.A. 33°42N 81°46W 316 B8
Eureka S. Dak., U.S.A. 45°46N 99°38W 308 C4
Eureka, Mt. Australia 26°35S 121°35E 279 E3
Eureka Sd. Canada 79°0N 85°0W 295 B15
Eurelia Australia 32°33S 138°35E 282 B3
Eurinilla Cr. → Australia 30°53S 140°11E 282 A4
Euroa Australia 36°44S 145°35E 283 D6
Europa, Île Ind. Oc. 22°20S 40°22E 271 B7
Europa, Picos de Spain 43°10N 4°49W 194 B6
Europa, Pt. Gib. 36°3N 5°21W 195 J5
Europe 50°0N 20°0E 158 E10
Europoort Neths. 51°57N 4°10E 170 C4
Euskirchen Germany 50°39N 6°48E 178 E2
Eustis U.S.A. 28°51N 81°41W 317 G8
Euston N.S.W., Australia 34°30S 142°46E 282 C5
Euston London, U.K. 125 a3
Eutawville U.S.A. 33°24N 80°21W 316 B9
Eutin Germany 54°8N 10°36E 178 A6
Eutsuk L. Canada 53°20N 126°45W 296 C3
Eva Perón = La Pampa □ Argentina 36°50S 66°0W 334 D2
Eva Perón = La Plata Argentina 35°0S 57°55W 334 C4
Evale Angola 16°33S 15°44E 265 F3
Evanger Norway 60°39N 6°7E 164 D3
Evanlı Turkey 36°46N 34°26E 250 B5
Evans U.S.A. 40°23N 104°41W 304 F11
Evans, L. Canada 50°50N 77°0W 298 B4
Evans City U.S.A. 40°46N 80°4W 312 F4
Evans Head Australia 29°7S 153°27E 281 D5
Evansburg Canada 53°36N 114°59W 296 C5
Evansdale U.S.A. 42°30N 92°17W 310 B4
Evanston Ill., U.S.A. 42°3N 87°40W 119 A2
Evanston Wyo., U.S.A. 41°16N 110°58W 304 F8
Evansville Ill., U.S.A. 38°5N 89°56W 310 F7
Evansville Ind., U.S.A. 37°58N 87°35W 311 G9
Evansville Wis., U.S.A. 42°47N 89°18W 310 B7
Évaux-les-Bains France 46°12N 2°29E 173 F9
Evaz Iran 27°46N 53°59E 247 E7
Evciler Afyon, Turkey 38°4N 29°54E 205 C11
Evciler Çanakkale, Turkey 39°47N 26°44E 205 B8
Eveleth U.S.A. 47°28N 92°32W 308 B7
Even Sapir Israel 31°46N 35°8E 123 B1
Evensk Russia 62°12N 159°30E 215 C16
Evenstad Norway 61°25N 11°7E 164 C8
Everard, L. Australia 31°30S 135°0E 281 E2
Everard Ranges Australia 27°5S 132°28E 279 E5
Evere Belgium 50°52N 4°25E 116 A2
Everest, Mt. Nepal 28°5N 86°58E 243 E12
Everett Ga., U.S.A. 31°24N 81°38W 316 D8
Everett Mass., U.S.A. 42°24N 71°3W 116 A2
Everett Pa., U.S.A. 40°1N 78°23W 312 F6
Everett Wash., U.S.A. 47°59N 122°12W 306 C4
Everglades, The U.S.A. 25°50N 81°0W 317 K9
Everglades △ U.S.A. 25°30N 81°0W 317 K9
Everglades City U.S.A. 25°52N 81°23W 317 K8
Evergreen Ala., U.S.A. 31°26N 86°57W 315 F11
Evergreen Mont., U.S.A. 48°14N 114°17W 304 B6
Evergreen Park U.S.A. 41°43N 87°42W 119 C2
Everöd Sweden 55°53N 14°5E 163 J8
Everton Australia 36°25S 146°33E 283 D7
Evertsberg Sweden 61°8N 13°58E 162 C7
Evesham U.K. 52°6N 1°56W 169 E6
Evia Greece 38°30N 24°0E 204 C6
Evia □ Greece 38°40N 23°40E 204 C5
Évian-les-Bains France 46°24N 6°35E 173 F13
Evīn Iran 35°47N 51°23E 141 A2
Evinayong Eq. Guin. 1°26N 10°35E 264 B2
Evinos → Greece 38°27N 21°40E 204 C3
Évisa France 42°15N 8°48E 175 F12
Evje Norway 58°36N 7°51E 164 F4
Évora Portugal 38°33N 7°57W 195 G3
Évora □ Portugal 38°33N 7°50W 195 G3
Evowghlī Iran 38°43N 45°13E 213 C11
Évreux France 49°3N 1°8E 172 C8
Evritania □ Greece 39°5N 21°30E 204 B3
Évron France 48°10N 0°24W 172 D6
Evros □ Greece 41°10N 26°0E 203 E10
Evros → Greece 41°40N 26°34E 203 F10
Evrotas → Greece 36°50N 22°40E 204 E4
Évry France 48°38N 2°27E 173 D9
Évvoia = Evia Greece 38°30N 24°0E 204 C6
'Ewa Beach U.S.A. 21°19N 158°1W 302 K13
'Ewa District U.S.A. 21°25N 158°0W 302 K14
'Ewa Villages U.S.A. 21°20N 158°3W 302 K13
Ewarton Jamaica 18°11N 77°6W 320 a
Ewasse Papua N. G. 5°19S 151°1E 286 C6
Ewe, L. U.K. 57°49N 5°38W 167 D3
Ewing Mo., U.S.A. 40°6N 91°43W 310 E5
Ewing Nebr., U.S.A. 42°16N 98°21W 308 D4
Ewo Congo 0°48S 14°45E 264 C2
Ewu Nigeria 6°33N 3°19E 124 A1
Exaltación Bolivia 13°10S 65°20W 331 C4
Excelsior Springs U.S.A. 39°20N 94°13W 310 E2
Exchange Square Hong Kong, China 122 c1
Excideuil France 45°20N 1°4E 174 C5
Exe → U.K. 50°41N 3°29W 169 G4
Exeter Ont., Canada 43°21N 81°29W 312 C3
Exeter Devon, U.K. 50°43N 3°31W 169 G4
Exeter Calif., U.S.A. 36°18N 119°9W 306 J7
Exeter N.H., U.S.A. 42°59N 70°57W 313 D14
Exhibition Place Canada 43°38N 79°25W 141 B2
Exira U.S.A. 41°35N 94°52W 310 C2
Exmoor U.K. 51°12N 3°45W 169 F4
Exmoor △ U.K. 51°8N 3°42W 169 F4
Exmouth W. Austral., Australia 21°54S 114°10E 278 D1
Exmouth Devon, U.K. 50°37N 3°25W 169 G4
Exmouth G. Australia 22°15S 114°15E 278 D1
Exmouth Plateau Ind. Oc. 19°0S 114°0E 288 J3
Expedition △ Australia 25°41S 149°7E 281 D4
Expedition Ra. Australia 24°30S 149°12E 280 C4
Experiment = Highland Mills U.S.A. 33°17N 84°17W 316 B5
Expo 2010 China 31°11N 121°29E 138 B1
Exposições, Palácio das Brazil 22°53S 43°13W 135 B1
Extremadura □ Spain 39°30N 6°5W 195 F4
Extrême-Nord □ Cameroon 11°0N 14°30E 259 F2
Exuma Sound Bahamas 24°30N 76°20W 320 B4
Eyak U.S.A. 60°32N 145°36W 303 F11
Eyasi, L. Tanzania 3°30S 35°0E 268 C4
Eydehavn Norway 58°30N 8°53E 164 F5
Eydhafushi Maldives 5°7N 73°2E 272 d
Eye Pen. U.K. 58°13N 6°10W 167 C2
Eyemouth U.K. 55°52N 2°5W 167 F6
Eygues = Aigues → France 44°7N 4°43E 175 D8
Eygurande France 45°40N 2°26E 173 G9
Eyjafjallajökull Iceland 63°38N 19°36W 155 D7
Eyjafjarðarsýsla Iceland 65°30N 18°30W 155 B8
Eyjafjörður Iceland 66°15N 18°30W 155 A8
Eyl Somalia 8°0N 49°50E 267 C6
Eymet France 44°40N 0°25E 174 D4
Eymoutiers France 45°40N 1°45E 174 C5
Eynesil Turkey 41°4N 39°9E 213 B8
Eyrarbakki Iceland 63°52N 21°9W 155 D5
Eyre (North), L. Australia 28°30S 137°20E 281 D2
Eyre (South), L. Australia 29°18S 137°25E 281 D2
Eyre, L. Australia 29°30S 137°26E 276 F6
Eyre Mts. N.Z. 45°25S 168°25E 285 F3
Eyre Pen. Australia 33°30S 136°17E 282 C1
Eysturoy Færoe Is. 62°13N 6°54W 160 E9
Eyüp Turkey 41°2N 28°55E 122 B1
Eyvān = Jūy Zar Iran 33°50N 46°18E 213 F12
Eyvānkī Iran 35°24N 51°56E 247 C6
Ez Zeidab Sudan 17°25N 33°55E 256 D3
Ezcaray Spain 42°19N 3°0W 196 C1
Ezeiza ✈ (EZE) Argentina 34°49S 58°32W 117 C1
Ežerėlis Lithuania 54°53N 23°37E 184 D10
Ezhou China 30°23N 114°50E 229 B10
Ezine Turkey 39°48N 26°20E 205 B8
Ezouza → Cyprus 34°44N 32°27E 207 F8

F

F.Y.R.O.M. = Macedonia ■ Europe 41°53N 21°40E 202 E5
Faaa Tahiti 17°34S 149°35W 289 e
Faaborg Denmark 55°6N 10°15E 163 J4
Faaone Tahiti 17°40S 149°21W 289 e
Fabala Guinea 9°44N 9°5W 262 D3
Fabbriche Nuove Venice, Italy 142 b2
Fabens U.S.A. 31°30N 106°10W 314 F1
Faber, Mt. Singapore 1°16N 103°49E 138 B2
Fåberg Norway 61°10N 10°25E 164 C7
Fabero Spain 42°46N 6°37W 194 C4
Fabius U.S.A. 42°50N 75°59W 313 D9
Fabriano Italy 43°20N 12°54E 199 E9
Făcăeni Romania 44°32N 27°53E 183 F12
Facatativá Colombia 4°49N 74°22W 328 C3
Faceville U.S.A. 30°45N 84°38W 316 E5
Fachi Niger 18°6N 11°34E 259 E2
Facundo Argentina 45°18S 69°58W 336 C3
Fada Chad 17°13N 21°34E 259 E4
Fada-n-Gourma Burkina Faso 12°10N 0°30E 263 C5
Fadd Hungary 46°28N 18°49E 182 D3
Faddeyevskiy, Ostrov Russia 76°0N 144°0E 215 B15
Faddor South Sudan 8°7N 32°17E 257 F3
Fadghāmī Syria 35°53N 40°52E 213 E9
Fadiffolu Atoll Maldives 5°23N 73°29E 272 d
Fadlab Sudan 17°42N 34°2E 256 D3
Fadwel South Sudan 8°11N 29°20E 266 C2
Fælledparken Denmark 55°42N 12°34E 118 A3
Faenza Italy 44°17N 11°53E 199 D8
Færingehavn = Kangerluarsoruseq Greenland 63°45N 51°27W 154 E5
Færoe Is. = Føroyar ⧄ Atl. Oc. 62°0N 7°0W 160 F9
Fafa Mali 15°22N 0°48E 263 B5
Fafe Portugal 41°27N 8°11W 194 D2
Fafen → Ethiopia 5°59N 44°25E 267 C5
Fagam Nigeria 11°1N 10°1E 263 C7
Fagamalo Amer. Samoa 14°18S 170°48W 302 f
Făgăras Romania 45°48N 24°58E 183 E9
Făgăras, Munţii Romania 45°40N 24°40E 183 E9
Fagasa Amer. Samoa 14°17S 170°43W 302 f
Fagatogo Amer. Samoa 14°16S 170°41W 302 f
Fågelfors Sweden 57°12N 15°51E 163 H9
Fågelmara Sweden 56°16N 15°58E 163 H9
Fågelön Sweden 59°18N 17°55E 139 B1
Fagerheim Norway 60°26N 7°46E 164 D4
Fagerhult Sweden 57°8N 15°40E 163 G9
Fagernes Norway 60°59N 9°14E 164 D6
Fagersjö Sweden 59°14N 18°4E 139 B2
Fagersta Sweden 60°1N 15°46E 162 D9
Făget Romania 45°52N 22°10E 182 E7
Făget, Munţii Romania 47°40N 23°10E 183 C8
Faggo Nigeria 11°21N 9°57E 263 C6
Faghmah Yemen 16°9N 49°26E 249 C5
Fagnano, L. Argentina 54°30S 68°0W 336 D3
Fagnières France 48°58N 4°20E 173 D11
Faguibine, L. Mali 16°45N 4°0W 262 B4
Fahlīān Iran 30°11N 51°28E 247 D6
Fahraj Kermān, Iran 29°0N 59°0E 247 D8
Fahraj Yazd, Iran 31°46N 54°36E 247 D7
Fai Tsi Long Vietnam 21°0N 107°30E 228 G6
Faial Azores 38°34N 28°42W 153 d1
Faial Madeira 32°47N 16°53W 153 c
Faial, Canal do Azores 38°33N 28°35W 153 d1
Faichan Kangri India 35°48N 76°34E 243 B7
Faichuk Micronesia 7°21N 151°38E 287 T17
Fair Haven N.Y., U.S.A. 43°18N 76°42W 313 C8
Fair Haven Vt., U.S.A. 43°36N 73°16W 313 C11
Fair Hd. U.K. 55°14N 6°9W 166 A5
Fair Isle U.K. 59°32N 1°38W 165 B6
Fair Oaks U.S.A. 38°39N 121°16W 306 G5
Fairbank U.S.A. 42°38N 92°3W 310 B4
Fairbanks Alaska, U.S.A. 64°51N 147°43W 303 D11
Fairbanks Fla., U.S.A. 29°44N 82°16W 316 F7
Fairborn U.S.A. 39°49N 84°2W 311 E12
Fairburn U.S.A. 33°34N 84°35W 316 B5
Fairbury Ill., U.S.A. 40°45N 88°31W 311 D8
Fairbury Nebr., U.S.A. 40°8N 97°11W 308 E5
Fairfax Ohio, U.S.A. 39°5N 83°37W 311 E13
Fairfax S.C., U.S.A. 32°59N 81°15W 316 C8
Fairfax Vt., U.S.A. 44°40N 73°1W 313 B11
Fairfield N.S.W., Australia 33°53S 150°57E 283 B9
Fairfield Calif., U.S.A. 38°15N 122°3W 306 G4
Fairfield Conn., U.S.A. 41°9N 73°16W 313 E11
Fairfield Idaho, U.S.A. 43°21N 114°44W 304 E6
Fairfield Ill., U.S.A. 38°23N 88°22W 311 F8
Fairfield Iowa, U.S.A. 40°56N 91°57W 310 D5
Fairfield Ohio, U.S.A. 39°20N 84°34W 311 E12
Fairfield Tex., U.S.A. 31°44N 96°10W 314 F6
Fairford Canada 51°37N 98°38W 297 C9
Fairhope U.S.A. 30°31N 87°54W 315 F11
Fairland S. Africa 26°8S 27°57E 123 A1
Fairlie N.Z. 44°5S 170°49E 285 E5
Fairmead U.S.A. 37°5N 120°10W 306 H6
Fairmilehead U.K. 55°54N 3°11W 121 B2
Fairmont Minn., U.S.A. 43°39N 94°28W 308 D6
Fairmont W. Va., U.S.A. 39°29N 80°9W 309 F13
Fairmount Calif., U.S.A. 34°45N 118°26W 307 L8
Fairmount N.Y., U.S.A. 43°5N 76°12W 313 C8
Fairplay U.S.A. 39°15N 106°2W 304 G10
Fairport Ont., Canada 43°49N 79°4W 141 A4
Fairport N.Y., U.S.A. 43°6N 77°27W 312 C7
Fairport Harbor U.S.A. 41°45N 81°17W 312 E3
Fairview Alta., Canada 56°5N 118°25W 296 B5
Fairview Mont., U.S.A. 47°51N 104°3W 304 C11
Fairview N.J., U.S.A. 40°48N 73°59W 132 B2
Fairview Okla., U.S.A. 36°16N 98°29W 314 C5
Fairview, L. U.S.A. 28°35N 81°24W 133 A2
Fairweather, Mt. U.S.A. 58°55N 137°32W 296 B1
Faisalabad Pakistan 31°30N 73°5E 242 D5
Faith U.S.A. 45°2N 102°2W 308 C2
Faizabad India 26°45N 82°10E 243 F10
Faizpur India 21°14N 75°49E 244 D2
Fajã Grande Azores 39°27N 31°16W 153 d2
Fajardo Puerto Rico 18°20N 65°39W 321 C6
Fajou, Îlet à Guadeloupe 16°21N 61°35W 322 e
Fajr, W. → Si. Arabia 29°10N 38°10E 246 D3
Fakaofo Pac. Oc. 9°23S 171°15W 277 B16
Fakarava French Polynesia 16°20S 145°37W 289 f
Fakenham U.K. 52°51N 0°51E 168 E8
Fåker Sweden 63°0N 14°34E 162 A8
Fakfak Indonesia 2°55S 132°18E 231 E8
Fakiya Bulgaria 42°10N 27°6E 203 D11
Fakobli Ivory C. 7°23N 7°23W 262 D3
Fakse Denmark 55°15N 12°8E 163 J6
Fakse Bugt Denmark 55°11N 12°15E 163 J6
Fakse Ladeplads Denmark 55°11N 12°9E 163 J6
Faku China 42°32N 123°21E 224 A1
Fala Beguets I. Micronesia 7°21N 151°41E 287 U17
Falaba S. Leone 9°54N 11°22W 262 D2
Falaise France 48°54N 0°12W 172 D6
Falakro Oros Greece 41°15N 23°58E 202 E7
Falam Burma 23°0N 93°45E 241 D4
Falas I. Micronesia 7°31N 151°44E 287 T18
Falces Spain 42°24N 1°48W 196 C3
Fălciu Romania 46°17N 28°7E 183 D13
Falcó, C. des Spain 38°50N 1°23E 206 D1
Falcón □ Venezuela 11°0N 69°50W 328 A4
Falcon, C. Algeria 35°50N 0°50W 261 A4
Falcón, Presa Mexico 26°35N 99°10W 319 B5
Falcon Lake Canada 49°42N 95°15W 297 D9
Falcon Res. U.S.A. 26°34N 99°10W 314 H5
Falconara Maríttima Italy 43°37N 13°24E 199 E10
Falcone, C. del Italy 40°58N 8°12E 200 B1
Falconer U.S.A. 42°7N 79°12W 312 D5
Faléa Mali 12°16N 11°17W 262 C2
Falefa Samoa 13°54S 171°31W 287 V20
Falelatai Samoa 13°55S 171°59W 287 V20
Falelima Samoa 13°32S 172°41W 287 V19
Falémé → Senegal 14°46N 12°14W 262 C2
Faleniu Amer. Samoa 14°19S 170°44W 302 f
Falenty Poland 52°8N 20°55E 143 C1
Falerum Sweden 58°8N 16°13E 163 F10
Faleshty = Făleşti Moldova 47°32N 27°44E 183 C12
Făleşti Moldova 47°32N 27°44E 183 C12
Falfurrias U.S.A. 27°14N 98°9W 314 H5
Falher Canada 55°44N 117°15W 296 B5
Faliraki Greece 36°22N 28°12E 206 E12
Faliro Greece 37°55N 23°39E 112 B1
Faliro, Ormos Greece 37°54N 23°40E 112 B2
Falkenberg Brandenburg, Germany 51°35N 13°14E 178 D9
Falkenberg Sweden 56°54N 12°30E 163 H6
Falkenburg = Niemodlin Poland 50°38N 17°38E 185 H4
Falkenburg Germany 52°34N 13°32E 115 A4
Falkenhagen Germany 52°34N 13°5E 115 A1
Falkensee Germany 52°34N 13°4E 115 A1
Falkirk U.K. 56°0N 3°47W 167 F5
Falkirk □ U.K. 55°58N 3°49W 167 F5
Falkland U.K. 56°16N 3°12W 167 E5
Falkland, East, I. Falk. Is. 51°40S 58°30W 336 D5
Falkland, West, I. Falk. Is. 51°40S 60°0W 336 D5
Falkland Is. ⧄ Atl. Oc. 51°30S 59°0W 153 f
Falkland Plateau Atl. Oc. 51°0S 50°0W 152 M7
Falkland Ridge Atl. Oc. 49°20S 40°0W 152 L8
Falkland Sd. Falk. Is. 52°0S 60°0W 153 f
Falknov nad Ohří = Sokolov Czech Rep. 50°12N 12°40E 180 A5
Falkonera Greece 36°50N 23°52E 204 E5
Falköping Sweden 58°12N 13°33E 163 F7
Fall River U.S.A. 41°43N 71°10W 313 E13
Fallbrook U.S.A. 33°23N 117°15W 307 M9
Fallon U.S.A. 39°28N 118°47W 304 G4
Falls City U.S.A. 40°3N 95°36W 308 E6
Falls Creek U.S.A. 41°9N 78°48W 312 E6
Falmouth Jamaica 18°30N 77°40W 320 a
Falmouth Corn., U.K. 50°9N 5°5W 169 G2
Falmouth Ky., U.S.A. 38°41N 84°20W 311 F12
Falmouth Mass., U.S.A. 41°33N 70°37W 313 E14
Falo I. Micronesia 7°28N 151°52E 287 T18
Falomo Nigeria 6°26N 3°26E 124 B2
Falsa, Pta. Mexico 27°51N 115°3W 318 B1
False B. S. Africa 34°15S 18°40E 270 D2
False Bay S. Africa 34°6S 18°33E 118 B2
False Divi Pt. India 15°43N 80°50E 245 G5
False Pass U.S.A. 54°51N 163°25W 303 J7
False Pt. India 20°18N 86°48E 244 D8
Falso, C. Honduras 15°12N 83°21W 320 C3
Falster Denmark 54°45N 11°55E 163 K5
Fălticeni Romania 47°21N 26°20E 183 C11
Falun Sweden 60°37N 15°37E 162 D9
Famagusta Cyprus 35°8N 33°55E 207 E9
Famagusta Bay Cyprus 35°15N 34°0E 207 E10
Famatina, Sierra de Argentina 27°30S 68°0W 334 B2
Famenin Iran 35°5N 48°58E 213 E13
Family L. Canada 51°54N 95°27W 297 C9
Famões Portugal 38°47N 9°13W 126 A1
Famoso U.S.A. 35°37N 119°12W 307 K7
Fan Xian China 35°55N 115°38E 226 G8
Fana Mali 13°0N 6°56W 262 C3
Fanad Hd. Ireland 55°17N 7°38W 166 A4
Fanahammaren Norway 60°16N 5°20E 164 D2
Fanari Greece 39°24N 21°47E 204 B3
Fandriana Madag. 20°14S 47°21E 272 C2
Fánes-Sénnes e Braies ⌂ Italy 46°38N 12°4E 199 B9
Faneuil Hall Marketplace Boston, U.S.A. 116 b3
Fang Thailand 19°55N 99°13E 236 C2
Fang Xian China 32°3N 110°40E 229 A8
Fangaga Sudan 17°40N 37°50E 256 D4
Fangak South Sudan 9°4N 30°53E 257 F3
Fangatau French Polynesia 15°22S 138°45W 289 f
Fangataufa French Polynesia 15°50S 140°52W 289 f
Fangchang China 31°5N 118°4E 229 B12
Fangcheng China 33°18N 112°59E 226 H7
Fangchenggang China 21°42N 108°21E 228 G7
Fangcun China 23°6N 113°13E 121 B2
Fangliao Taiwan 22°22N 120°38E 225 D2
Fangshan Beijing, China 39°41N 116°0E 226 E9
Fangshan Shanxi, China 38°3N 111°25E 226 E6
Fangshan Taiwan 22°15N 120°39E 225 D2
Fangyüan Taiwan 23°56N 120°19E 225 C2
Fangzi China 36°33N 119°10E 227 F10
Fani i Madh → Albania 41°56N 20°16E 202 E4
Fanjakana Madag. 21°10S 46°53E 272 C2
Fanjiatun China 43°40N 125°15E 227 C13
Fanling China 22°30N 114°8E 219 a
Fannich, L. U.K. 57°38N 4°59W 167 D4
Fannrem Norway 63°16N 9°50E 164 A6
Fannūj Iran 26°35N 59°38E 247 E8
Fanø Denmark 55°25N 8°25E 163 J2
Fano Italy 43°50N 13°1E 199 E10
Fanshi China 39°12N 113°20E 226 E7
Fantzuliao Hsi → Taiwan 22°42N 120°28E 225 D2
Fanuet I. Micronesia 7°32N 151°48E 287 T18
Fao = Al Fāw Iraq 30°0N 48°30E 247 D6
Faqirwali Pakistan 29°27N 73°0E 242 E5
Fâqûs Egypt 30°44N 31°47E 256 H7
Far East = Dalnevostochnyy □ Russia 67°0N 140°0E 215 C14
Far East Asia 40°0N 130°0E 210 E14
Fara in Sabina Italy 42°12N 12°43E 199 F9
Faradje Dem. Rep. of the Congo 3°50N 29°45E 268 B2
Farafangana Madag. 22°49S 47°50E 272 C2
Farafenni Gambia 13°34N 15°36W 262 C1
Farâfra, El Wâhât el Egypt 27°15N 28°20E 256 B2
Farāh Afghan. 32°20N 62°7E 240 B1
Farāh □ Afghan. 32°25N 62°10E 240 B1
Farāh → Afghan. 31°27N 61°28E 240 C1
Faraḩābād Iran 35°41N 51°30E 141 A2
Farahalana Madag. 14°26S 50°10E 272 A3
Faraid, Gebel Egypt 23°33N 35°19E 256 C4
Farako Ivory C. 10°45N 6°50W 262 D4
Farallon de Medinilla N. Marianas 16°1N 146°4E 302 a
Farallon de Pajaros N. Marianas 20°32N 144°54E 302 a
Farallones de Cali △ Colombia 3°13N 76°46W 328 C2
Faramana Burkina Faso 11°56N 4°45W 262 C4
Faranah Guinea 10°3N 10°45W 262 C2
Farap Turkmenistan 39°9N 63°36E 216 E6
Fararah Oman 17°55N 55°38E 249 C6
Farasān, Jazā'ir Si. Arabia 16°45N 41°55E 248 C3
Farasan Is. = Farasān, Jazā'ir Si. Arabia 16°45N 41°55E 248 C3
Faratsiho Madag. 19°24S 46°57E 272 B2
Farbaraki Somalia 2°30N 45°30E 267 D6
Fardes → Spain 37°35N 3°0W 195 H7
Fareham U.K. 50°51N 1°11W 169 G6
Farewell U.S.A. 62°31N 153°54W 303 E9
Farewell, C. N.Z. 40°29S 172°43E 285 A7
Farewell C. = Nunap Isua Greenland 59°48N 43°55W 154 F6
Farewell Spit N.Z. 40°35S 173°0E 285 A8
Farforovskaya Russia 59°52N 30°27E 137 B2
Färgelanda Sweden 58°34N 12°0E 163 F5
Farghona Uzbekistan 40°23N 71°19E 217 D8
Farghona □ Uzbekistan 40°30N 71°15E 217 D8
Farghona Vodiysi Asia 40°46N 71°30E 217 D8
Fargo Ga., U.S.A. 30°41N 82°34W 316 E7
Fargo N. Dak., U.S.A. 46°53N 96°48W 308 B5
Fār'iah, W. al → West Bank 32°12N 35°27E 251 F6
Faribault U.S.A. 44°18N 93°16W 308 C7
Faridabad India 28°26N 77°19E 242 E6
Faridkot India 30°44N 74°45E 242 D6
Faridpur Bangla. 23°15N 89°55E 241 D2
Faridpur India 28°13N 79°33E 243 E8
Fārigh, W. al → Libya 30°28N 20°44E 258 B3
Färila Sweden 61°48N 15°50E 162 C9
Farim Guinea-Biss. 12°27N 15°9W 262 C1
Farīmān Iran 35°40N 59°49E 247 C8
Farinha → Brazil 6°51S 47°30W 332 C2
Fariones, Pta. Canary Is. 29°13N 13°28W 153 e2
Fâriskûr Egypt 31°20N 31°43E 256 H7
Färjestaden Sweden 56°39N 16°27E 163 H10
Farkadona Greece 39°36N 22°4E 204 B4
Farleigh Australia 21°4S 149°8E 280 b
Farley U.S.A. 42°27N 91°0W 310 B6
Farmakonisi Greece 37°17N 27°5E 205 D9
Farmer City U.S.A. 40°15N 88°39W 311 D8
Farmersburg U.S.A. 39°15N 87°23W 311 E9
Farmerville U.S.A. 32°47N 92°24W 314 E8
Farmingdale U.S.A. 40°12N 74°10W 313 F10
Farmington B.C., Canada 55°54N 120°30W 296 B4
Farmington Calif., U.S.A. 37°55N 120°59W 306 H6
Farmington Ga., U.S.A. 33°47N 83°26W 316 B6
Farmington Ill., U.S.A. 40°42N 90°0W 310 D7
Farmington Iowa, U.S.A. 40°38N 91°44W 310 D5
Farmington Maine, U.S.A. 44°40N 70°9W 309 C18
Farmington Mo., U.S.A. 37°47N 90°25W 310 G6
Farmington N.H., U.S.A. 43°24N 71°4W 313 C13
Farmington N. Mex., U.S.A. 36°44N 108°12W 305 H9
Farmington Utah, U.S.A. 40°59N 111°53W 304 F8
Farmington → U.S.A. 41°51N 72°38W 313 E12
Farmland U.S.A. 40°15N 85°5W 311 D11
Farmville U.S.A. 37°18N 78°24W 309 G14
Färnäs Sweden 61°0N 14°39E 162 D8
Farne Is. U.K. 55°38N 1°37W 168 B6
Färnebofjärden △ Sweden 60°10N 16°48E 162 D10
Farnham Canada 45°17N 72°59W 313 A12
Farnham, Mt. Canada 50°29N 116°30W 296 C5
Farningham U.K. 51°23N 0°12E 125 B5
Faro Brazil 2°10S 56°39W 329 D6
Faro Yukon, Canada 62°11N 133°22W 294 E5
Faro Portugal 37°2N 7°55W 195 H3
Fårö Gotland, Sweden 57°55N 19°5E 163 G13
Faro □ Portugal 37°12N 8°10W 195 H2
Faro ✈ (FAO) Portugal 37°2N 7°57W 195 H3
Faro ⌂ Cameroon 8°15N 12°37E 264 A2
Fårösund Sweden 57°52N 19°2E 163 G13
Farquhar, C. Australia 23°50S 113°36E 279 D1
Farquhar Is. Seychelles 11°0S 52°0E 273 F4
Farrars Cr. → Australia 25°35S 140°43E 280 D3
Farrāshband Iran 28°57N 52°5E 247 D7
Farrell U.S.A. 41°13N 80°30W 312 E4
Farrell Flat Australia 33°48S 138°48E 282 B3
Farrokhī Iran 33°50N 59°31E 247 C8
Farruch, C. = Ferrutx, C. de Spain 39°47N 3°21E 206 B4
Farrukhabad India 27°24N 79°34E 244 A4
Fārs □ Iran 29°30N 55°0E 247 D7
Farsala Greece 39°17N 22°23E 204 B4
Fārsī Afghan. 33°47N 63°15E 240 B1
Fārsī Iran 27°58N 50°11E 247 E6
Farsø Denmark 56°46N 9°19E 163 H3
Farson U.S.A. 42°7N 109°26W 304 E9
Farsta Sweden 59°14N 18°5E 139 B2
Farsund Norway 58°5N 6°55E 164 F3
Fartak, Râs Si. Arabia 28°5N 34°34E 246 D2
Fartak, Ra's Yemen 15°38N 52°15E 249 D6
Fârţăneşti Romania 45°49N 27°59E 183 E12
Fartura, Serra da Brazil 26°21S 52°52W 335 B5
Faru Nigeria 12°48N 6°12E 263 C6
Fārūj Iran 37°14N 58°14E 247 B8
Fårup Denmark 56°33N 9°51E 163 H3
Farvel, Kap = Nunap Isua Greenland 59°48N 43°55W 154 F6
Farwell U.S.A. 34°23N 103°2W 314 D3
Fāryāb □ Afghan. 36°0N 65°0E 240 B2
Fasā Iran 29°0N 53°39E 247 D7
Fasanerie-Nord Germany 48°11N 11°32E 131 A2
Fasangarten Germany 48°5N 11°36E 131 B2
Fasano Italy 40°50N 17°22E 201 B10
Fashoda South Sudan 9°50N 32°2E 257 F3
Fasil Ghebbi Ethiopia 12°36N 37°28E 266 B4
Fáskrúðsfjörður Iceland 64°56N 14°1W 155 C12
Fassa Mali 13°26N 8°15W 262 C3
Fastiv Ukraine 50°7N 29°57E 177 C15
Fastnet Rock Ireland 51°22N 9°37W 166 E2
Fastov = Fastiv Ukraine 50°7N 29°57E 177 C15
Fatagartuting, Tanjung Indonesia 2°46S 131°57E 231 E8
Fataka Solomon Is. 11°55S 170°12E 277 C12
Fatatsu Ne Iwo Jima 24°45N 141°18E 288 b
Fatehabad Haryana, India 29°31N 75°27E 242 E6
Fatehabad Ut. P., India 27°1N 78°19E 242 F8
Fatehgarh India 27°25N 79°35E 243 F8
Fatehpur Bihar, India 24°38N 85°14E 243 G11
Fatehpur Raj., India 28°0N 74°40E 242 F6
Fatehpur Ut. P., India 25°56N 81°13E 243 G9
Fatehpur Ut. P., India 27°10N 81°13E 243 F9
Fatehpur Sikri India 27°6N 77°40E 242 F6
Fatesh Russia 52°8N 35°57E 189 F8
Fathai South Sudan 8°5N 31°48E 257 F3
Fathom Five ⌂ Canada 45°17N 81°40W 312 A3
Fatick Senegal 14°19N 16°27W 262 C1
Fatick □ Senegal 14°15N 16°30W 262 C1
Fatih Turkey 41°0N 28°56E 122 B1
Fatima Qué., Canada 47°24N 61°53W 299 C7
Fátima Portugal 39°37N 8°39W 195 F2
Fatoya Guinea 11°37N 9°10W 262 C3
Fatsa Turkey 41°2N 37°31E 212 B7
Fatshan = Foshan China 23°3N 113°9E 121 B1
Faucille, Col de la France 46°22N 6°2E 173 F13
Faulkton U.S.A. 45°2N 99°8W 308 C4
Faulquemont France 49°3N 6°36E 173 C13
Faure I. Australia 25°52S 113°50E 279 E1
Făurei Romania 45°6N 27°19E 183 E12
Fauresmith S. Africa 29°44S 25°17E 270 C4
Fauro Solomon Is. 6°55S 156°7E 287 L9
Fauske Norway 67°17N 15°25E 160 C16
Fåvang Norway 61°27N 10°11E 164 C7
Favânia Brazil 3°7S 51°48W 329 D7
Favara Italy 37°19N 13°39E 200 E6
Faváritx, C. de Spain 40°0N 4°15E 206 B5
Faverges France 45°45N 6°17E 175 C10
Favignana Italy 37°56N 12°20E 200 E5
Favignana, I. Italy 37°56N 12°19E 200 E5
Favoriten Austria 48°9N 16°23E 142 B2
Fawcett, Pt. Australia 11°46S 130°2E 278 B5
Fawkner Australia 37°42S 144°56E 128 A1
Fawkner Park Australia 37°50S 144°58E 128 B1
Fawn → Canada 55°20N 87°35W 298 A2
Fawnskin U.S.A. 34°16N 116°56W 307 L10
Faxaflói Iceland 64°29N 23°0W 155 C3
Faxälven → Sweden 63°13N 17°13E 162 A10
Faya-Largeau Chad 17°58N 19°6E 259 E3
Fayaoué N. Cal. 20°38S 166°33E 288 d
Fayd Si. Arabia 27°1N 42°52E 246 E4
Fayence France 43°38N 6°42E 175 E10
Fayette Ala., U.S.A. 33°41N 87°50W 315 E11
Fayette Iowa, U.S.A. 42°51N 91°48W 310 B5
Fayette Mo., U.S.A. 39°9N 92°41W 310 E4
Fayette N.Y., U.S.A. 42°48N 76°48W 313 D8
Fayette Ohio, U.S.A. 41°40N 84°20W 311 C12
Fayetteville Ark., U.S.A. 36°4N 94°10W 314 C7
Fayetteville Ga., U.S.A. 33°27N 84°27W 316 B5
Fayetteville N.C., U.S.A. 35°3N 78°53W 315 D15
Fayetteville N.Y., U.S.A. 43°1N 76°0W 313 C9
Fayetteville Tenn., U.S.A. 35°9N 86°34W 315 D11
Fayied Egypt 30°18N 32°16E 256 H8
Faylakah Kuwait 29°27N 48°20E 247 D6
Fayón Spain 41°15N 0°20E 196 D5
Fazao-Malfakassa △ Togo 8°45N 0°50E 263 D5
Fazenda Libongo Angola 8°24S 13°24E 265 D2
Fazenda Nova Brazil 16°11S 50°48W 333 E1
Fazilka India 30°27N 74°2E 242 D6
Fazilpur Pakistan 29°18N 70°29E 242 E4
Fdérik Mauritania 22°40N 12°45W 260 D2
Feakle Ireland 52°56N 8°40W 166 D3
Feale → Ireland 52°27N 9°37W 166 D2
Fear, C. U.S.A. 33°50N 77°58W 315 E16
Feather → U.S.A. 38°47N 121°36W 306 G5
Feather Falls U.S.A. 39°36N 121°16W 306 F5
Featherston N.Z. 41°6S 175°20E 284 H4
Featherstone Zimbabwe 18°42S 30°55E 269 F3
Fécamp France 49°45N 0°22E 172 C7
Feda Norway 58°17N 6°50E 164 F3
Fedala = Mohammedia Morocco 33°44N 7°21W 260 B3
Federación Argentina 31°0S 57°55W 334 C4
Federal Capital Terr. □ Nigeria 9°0N 7°10E 263 D6
Federal Way U.S.A. 47°18N 122°19W 306 C4
Fedeshkūh Iran 28°49N 53°50E 247 D7
Fedje Norway 60°47N 4°43E 164 D1
Fedorovka Kazakhstan 53°37N 62°42E 216 B6
Fefan I. Pac. Oc. 7°21N 151°51E 287 T18
Fehérgyarmat Hungary 47°58N 22°30E 182 C7
Fehmarn Germany 54°27N 11°7E 178 A7
Fehmarn Bælt Europe 54°35N 11°20E 163 K5
Fehmarn Belt = Fehmarn Bælt Europe 54°35N 11°20E 163 K5
Fei Xian China 35°18N 117°59E 227 G9
Feicheng China 36°14N 116°45E 226 F9
Feidong China 32°0N 117°35E 229 B11
Feijó Brazil 8°9S 70°21W 330 B3
Feilding N.Z. 40°13S 175°35E 284 G4
Feira de Santana Brazil 12°15S 38°57W 333 D4
Feirân, W. → Egypt 28°39N 33°12E 251 K4
Feirâni, G. Egypt 28°31N 34°19E 251 K5
Feiring Norway 60°30N 11°10E 164 D8
Feixi China 31°43N 117°59E 229 B11
Feixiang China 36°30N 114°45E 226 F8
Fejaj, Chott el Tunisia 33°52N 9°14E 258 B1
Fejér □ Hungary 47°9N 18°30E 182 C3
Fejø Denmark 54°55N 11°30E 163 K5
Feke Turkey 37°48N 35°56E 212 D6
Fekete → Hungary 45°47N 18°15E 182 E3
Felanitx Spain 39°28N 3°9E 206 B4
Felda U.S.A. 26°34N 81°26W 317 J8

Feldbach Austria 46°57N 15°52E 180 E8
Feldberg Baden-W., Germany 47°52N 8°0E 179 H3
Feldberg Mecklenburg-Vorpommern, Germany 53°20N 13°25E 178 B9
Feldkirch Austria 47°15N 9°37E 180 D2
Feldkirchen Austria 46°44N 14°6E 180 E7
Feldkirchen Oberbayern, Germany 48°8N 11°43E 131 B3
Feldmoching Germany 48°14N 11°32E 131 A2
Félicité Seychelles 4°19S 55°52E 272 c
Felicity U.S.A. 38°51N 84°6W 311 F12
Felidhoo Maldives 3°29N 73°32E 272 d
Felidu Atoll Maldives 3°29N 73°29E 272 d
Felipe Carrillo Puerto Mexico 19°38N 88°3W 319 D7
Felixburg Zimbabwe 19°29S 30°51E 271 A5
Felixlândia Brazil 18°47S 44°55W 333 E3
Felixstowe U.K. 51°58N 1°23E 169 F9
Felletin France 45°53N 2°11E 174 C6
Fellingsbro Sweden 59°26N 15°37E 162 E9
Fellsmere U.S.A. 27°46N 80°36W 317 H9
Felshtin = Gvardeyskoye Ukraine 45°7N 34°1E 189 K8
Felsogalla = Tatabánya Hungary 47°32N 18°25E 182 C3
Feltham U.K. 51°26N 0°24W 125 B1
Felton U.S.A. 37°3N 122°4W 306 H4
Feltre Italy 46°1N 11°54E 199 B8
Femer Bælt = Fehmarn Bælt Europe 54°35N 11°20E 163 K5
Femø Denmark 54°58N 11°35E 163 K5
Femunden Norway 62°10N 11°53E 164 B8
Femundsmarka △ Norway 62°18N 12°6E 164 B9
Fen He → China 35°36N 110°42E 226 G6
Fenchih Taiwan 23°30N 120°40E 225 C2
Fene Spain 43°27N 8°9W 194 B2
Fenelon Falls Canada 44°32N 78°45W 312 B6
Fener Turkey 41°1N 28°56E 122 B1
Fener Burnu Turkey 36°58N 27°18E 205 E9
Fenerbahçe Turkey 40°58N 29°2E 122 C2
Feneroa Ethiopia 13°5N 39°3E 257 E4
Feng Xian Jiangsu, China 34°43N 116°35E 226 G9
Feng Xian Shaanxi, China 33°54N 106°40E 226 H4
Fengari Greece 40°25N 25°32E 203 F9
Fengcheng Jiangxi, China 28°12N 115°48E 229 C10
Fengcheng Liaoning, China 40°28N 124°5E 224 B2
Fengdu China 29°55N 107°48E 228 C6
Fengfeng China 36°28N 114°8E 226 F8
Fenggang China 27°57N 107°47E 228 D6
Fenghua China 29°40N 121°25E 229 C13
Fenghuang China 27°57N 109°29E 228 D7
Fengjie China 31°3N 109°31E 228 B7
Fengkai China 23°24N 111°30E 229 F8
Fengkang Taiwan 22°12N 120°41E 225 D2
Fengle China 31°29N 112°29E 229 B9
Fenglin Taiwan 23°45N 121°26E 225 C3
Fengning China 41°10N 116°33E 226 D9
Fengpin Taiwan 23°36N 121°31E 225 C3
Fengqing China 24°38N 99°55E 228 E2
Fengqiu China 35°2N 114°25E 226 G8
Fengrun China 39°48N 118°8E 227 E10
Fengshan Guangxi Zhuangzu, China 24°39N 109°15E 228 E7
Fengshan Guangxi Zhuangzu, China 24°31N 107°3E 228 E6
Fengshan Taiwan 22°38N 120°21E 225 D2
Fengshun China 23°46N 116°10E 229 F11
Fengtai Anhui, China 32°50N 116°40E 229 A11
Fengtai Beijing, China 39°49N 116°14E 114 C1
Fengtai Stadium China 39°51N 116°15E 114 B1
Fengtongzhai △ China 30°32N 102°54E 228 B4
Fengxiang China 34°29N 107°25E 226 G4
Fengxin China 28°41N 115°18E 229 C10
Fengyang China 32°51N 117°29E 227 H9
Fengyi China 25°37N 100°20E 228 E3
Fengyüan Taiwan 24°15N 120°35E 225 B2
Fengzhen China 40°25N 113°2E 226 D7
Feni Bangla. 22°55N 91°32E 241 D3
Feni Is. Papua N. G. 4°0S 153°40E 286 C7
Fennimore U.S.A. 42°59N 90°39W 310 B6
Feno, C. de France 41°58N 8°33E 175 G12
Fenoarivo Fianarantsoa, Madag. 21°43S 46°24E 272 C2
Fenoarivo Fianarantsoa, Madag. 20°52S 46°53E 272 C2
Fenoarivo Afovoany Madag. 18°26S 46°34E 272 B2
Fenoarivo Atsinanana Madag. 17°22S 49°25E 272 B2
Fens, The U.K. 52°38N 0°2W 168 E7
Fensmark Denmark 55°17N 11°48E 163 J5
Fenton U.S.A. 42°48N 83°42W 311 B13
Fenxi China 36°40N 111°31E 226 F6
Fenyang China 37°18N 111°48E 226 F6
Fenyi China 27°45N 114°47E 229 D10
Fenyuan Taiwan 24°1N 120°37E 225 B2
Feodosiya Ukraine 45°2N 35°16E 189 K8
Fer, C. de Algeria 37°3N 7°10E 261 A6
Fera Solomon Is. 8°6S 159°37E 287 M10
Ferbane Ireland 53°16N 7°50W 166 C4
Ferdows Iran 33°58N 58°2E 247 C8
Fère-Champenoise France 48°45N 3°59E 173 D10
Fère-en-Tardenois France 49°10N 3°30E 173 C10
Ferencváros Hungary 47°29N 19°5E 117 B2
Ferentino Italy 41°42N 13°15E 199 G10
Feres Greece 40°53N 26°10E 203 F10
Ferfer Somalia 5°4N 45°9E 267 C6
Fergana = Farghona Uzbekistan 40°23N 71°19E 217 D8
Fergana Range Asia 41°0N 73°50E 217 D8
Fergus Canada 43°43N 80°24W 312 C4
Fergus Falls U.S.A. 46°17N 96°4W 308 B5
Ferguson U.S.A. 38°44N 90°18W 310 F6
Fergusson I. Papua N. G. 9°30S 150°45E 286 E6
Fériana Tunisia 34°59N 8°33E 258 B1
Feričanci Croatia 45°32N 18°0E 182 E2
Ferihegy, Budapest ✈ (BUD) Hungary 47°26N 19°14E 117 B3
Ferizaj Kosovo 42°23N 21°10E 202 D5
Ferkane Algeria 34°37N 7°26E 261 B6
Ferkéssédougou Ivory C. 9°35N 5°6W 262 D3
Ferlach Austria 46°32N 14°18E 180 E7
Ferland Canada 50°19N 88°27W 298 B2
Ferlo, Vallée du Senegal 15°15N 14°15W 262 B2
Ferlo-Nord ⌂ Senegal 15°43N 14°0W 262 B2
Ferlo-Sud ⌂ Senegal 15°43N 14°0W 262 B2
Fermanagh □ U.K. 54°21N 7°40W 166 B4
Fermo Italy 43°9N 13°43E 199 E10
Fermont Canada 52°47N 67°5W 299 B6
Fermoselle Spain 41°19N 6°27W 194 D4
Fermoy Ireland 52°9N 8°16W 166 D3
Fern Creek U.S.A. 38°9N 85°36W 311 G11
Fern Gully Jamaica 18°22N 77°5W 320 a
Fernán Núñez Spain 37°40N 4°44W 195 H6
Fernández Argentina 27°55S 63°50W 334 B3
Fernandina, I. Ecuador 0°25S 91°30W 330 a
Fernandina Beach U.S.A. 30°40N 81°27W 316 E8
Fernando de Noronha Brazil 4°0S 33°10W 152 G8
Fernando Póo = Bioko Eq. Guin. 3°30N 8°40E 263 E6
Fernandópolis Brazil 20°16S 50°14W 333 F1
Ferndale Ont., Canada 44°58N 81°17W 312 B3
Ferndale Gauteng, S. Africa 26°5S 28°0E 123 A2
Ferndale Wash., U.S.A. 48°51N 122°36W 306 B4
Fernie Canada 49°30N 115°5W 296 D5
Fernlees Australia 23°51S 148°7E 280 C4
Fernley U.S.A. 39°36N 119°15W 304 G4
Fernwood U.S.A. 43°16N 73°38W 313 C11
Feroke India 11°9N 75°46E 245 J2
Feroz Shah Kotla Cricket Stadium Delhi, India 120 b3
Ferozepore = Firozpur India 30°55N 74°40E 242 D6
Ferrandina Italy 40°29N 16°27E 201 B9
Ferrara Italy 44°50N 11°35E 199 D8
Ferrato, C. Italy 39°18N 9°38E 200 C2
Ferré, C. Martinique 14°27N 60°49W 322 j
Ferreira do Alentejo Portugal 38°4N 8°6W 195 G2
Ferreira Gomes Brazil 0°48N 51°8W 329 C7
Ferreñafe Peru 6°42S 79°50W 330 B2
Ferrerías Spain 39°59N 4°1E 206 B5
Ferret, C. France 44°38N 1°15W 174 D2
Ferrette France 47°30N 7°20E 173 E14
Ferriday U.S.A. 31°38N 91°33W 314 F9
Ferriere Italy 44°40N 9°30E 198 D6
Ferrières France 48°5N 2°48E 173 D9
Ferro, Capo Italy 41°9N 9°31E 200 A2
Ferrol Spain 43°29N 8°15W 194 B2
Ferrol, Pen. de Peru 9°10S 78°35W 330 B2
Ferron U.S.A. 39°5N 111°8W 304 G8
Ferros Brazil 19°14S 43°2W 333 E3
Ferrutx, C. de Spain 39°47N 3°21E 206 B4
Ferry Pass U.S.A. 30°31N 87°13W 317 E2
Ferryland Canada 47°2N 52°53W 299 C9
Ferrysburg U.S.A. 43°5N 86°13W 311 A10
Ferryville = Menzel-Bourguiba Tunisia 37°9N 9°49E 258 A1
Fertile U.S.A. 47°32N 96°17W 308 B5
Fertő-Hanság △ Hungary 47°25N 16°50E 182 C1
Fertőszentmiklós Hungary 47°35N 16°53E 182 C1
Fès Morocco 34°0N 5°0W 260 B4
Fès □ Morocco 34°1N 5°0W 260 B4
Feshi Dem. Rep. of the Congo 6°8S 18°10E 265 D3
Fessenden U.S.A. 47°39N 99°38W 308 B4
Festenberg = Twardogóra Poland 51°23N 17°28E 185 G4
Festøya Norway 62°22N 6°19E 164 B3
Festus U.S.A. 38°13N 90°24W 310 F6
Feté Bowé Senegal 14°56N 13°30W 262 C2
Feteşti Romania 44°22N 27°51E 183 F12
Fethiye Turkey 36°36N 29°6E 205 E11
Fethiye Körfezi Turkey 36°40N 28°50E 205 E10
Fetlar U.K. 60°36N 0°52W 167 A8
Fetsund Norway 59°56N 11°10E 164 E8
Feuilles → Canada 58°47N 70°4W 295 F17
Feurs France 45°45N 4°13E 175 C8
Fevik Norway 58°22N 8°39E 164 F5
Fevzipaşa Turkey 37°6N 36°37E 250 A7
Feyẕābād Badākhshān, Afghan. 37°7N 70°33E 240 A3
Feyẕābād Fāryāb, Afghan. 36°17N 64°52E 240 A2
Fez = Fès Morocco 34°0N 5°0W 260 B4
Fezzan Libya 27°0N 13°0E 258 C2
Fia Congo 3°25S 14°49E 264 C2
Fiambalá Argentina 27°45S 67°37W 334 B2
Fianarantsoa Madag. 21°26S 47°5E 272 C2
Fianarantsoa □ Madag. 22°30S 47°0E 272 B2
Fianga Cameroon 9°55N 15°9E 259 G3
Fiche Ethiopia 9°50N 38°46E 257 F4
Fichtelgebirge Germany 50°2N 11°55E 179 E7
Fichtelgebirge ⌂ Germany 50°8N 12°0E 179 E8
Fichtenau Germany 52°27N 13°42E 115 B5
Ficksburg S. Africa 28°51S 27°53E 271 C4
Fidenza Italy 44°52N 10°3E 198 D7
Fiditi Nigeria 7°45N 3°53E 263 D5
Fidjeland Norway 58°57N 6°56E 164 F3
Field → Australia 23°48S 138°0E 280 C2
Field I. Australia 12°5S 132°23E 278 B5
Field Museum of Natural History U.S.A. 41°51N 87°37W 119 B3
Fields Corner U.S.A. 42°18N 71°3W 116 B2
Fieni Romania 45°8N 25°25E 183 E10
Fier Albania 40°43N 19°33E 202 F3
Fiera Camp Italy 45°28N 9°9E 128 B1
Fierzë Albania 42°15N 20°1E 202 D4
Fife □ U.K. 56°16N 3°1W 167 E5
Fife Ness U.K. 56°17N 2°35W 167 E6
Fifth Cataract Sudan 18°22N 33°50E 256 D3
Fig Tree St. Kitts & Nevis 17°8N 62°35W 322 d
Figari France 41°29N 9°7E 175 G13
Figeac France 44°37N 2°2E 174 D6
Figeholm Sweden 57°22N 16°33E 163 G10
Figino Italy 45°29N 9°4E 128 B1
Figline Valdarno Italy 43°37N 11°28E 199 E8
Figtree Zimbabwe 20°22S 28°20E 269 G2
Figueira = Governador Valadares Brazil 18°15S 41°57W 333 E3
Figueira Castelo Rodrigo Portugal 40°57N 6°58W 194 E4
Figueira da Foz Portugal 40°7N 8°54W 194 E2
Figueiró dos Vinhos Portugal 39°55N 8°16W 194 F2
Figueres Spain 42°18N 2°58E 196 C7
Figuig Morocco 32°5N 1°11W 261 B4
Fihaonana Madag. 18°36S 47°12E 272 B2
Fiherenana Madag. 18°29S 48°24E 272 B2
Fiherenana → Madag. 23°19S 43°37E 272 C1
Fiji ■ Pac. Oc. 17°20S 179°0E 287 A2
Fijir Iraq 33°21N 44°21E 113 A2
Fik Ethiopia 8°10N 42°19E 257 F5
Fika Nigeria 11°15N 11°13E 263 C7
Filabres, Sierra de los Spain 37°13N 2°20W 195 H8
Filabusi Zimbabwe 20°34S 29°20E 271 B4
Filadelfia Bolivia 11°20S 68°46W 330 C4
Filadélfia Brazil 7°21S 47°30W 332 C2
Filadelfia Athina, Greece 38°2N 23°43E 112 A2
Filadélfia Italy 38°47N 16°17E 201 D9
Filadelfia Paraguay 22°21S 60°2W 334 A3
Fil'akovo Slovak Rep. 48°17N 19°50E 181 C12
Filchner Ice Shelf Antarctica 79°0S 40°0W 151 D1
Filefjell Norway 61°8N 8°10E 164 C5
Filey U.K. 54°12N 0°18W 168 C7
Filey B. U.K. 54°12N 0°15W 168 C7
Filfla Malta 35°47N 14°24E 206 F7
Fili-Mazilovo Russia 55°44N 37°29E 129 B1
Filiaşi Romania 44°32N 23°31E 183 F8
Filiates Greece 39°38N 20°16E 206 B10
Filiatra Greece 37°9N 21°35E 204 D3
Filicudi Italy 38°35N 14°33E 201 D7
Filim Oman 20°37N 58°12E 249 B7
Filingué Niger 14°21N 3°22E 263 C5
Filiourí = Lissos → Greece 41°15N 25°40E 203 E9
Filipada Greece 39°12N 20°53E 204 B2
Filipstad Sweden 59°43N 14°9E 162 E8
Filisur Switz. 46°41N 9°40E 179 J5
Fillmore Calif., U.S.A. 34°24N 118°55W 307 L8
Fillmore Utah, U.S.A. 38°58N 112°20W 304 G7
Filothei Greece 38°2N 23°46E 112 A2
Filotio Greece 37°3N 25°30E 205 D7
Filottrano Italy 43°26N 13°21E 199 E10
Filtu Ethiopia 5°8N 40°35E 257 F5
Filyos Cayı → Turkey 41°35N 32°10E 212 B5
Fimbul Ice Shelf S. Ocean 69°30S 1°0W 151 C2
Fimi → Dem. Rep. of the Congo 3°1S 16°58E 264 C3
Fina ⌂ Mali 13°15N 8°46W 262 C3
Finale Emília Italy 44°50N 11°18E 199 D8
Finale Lígure Italy 44°10N 8°20E 198 D5
Finalmarina = Finale Lígure Italy 44°10N 8°20E 198 D5
Fiñana Spain 37°10N 2°50W 195 H8
Financial District San Francisco, U.S.A. 136 b3
Finch Canada 45°11N 75°7W 313 A9
Finch Hatton Australia 20°25S 148°39E 280 b
Finchaa, L. Ethiopia 9°35N 37°20E 266 C4
Finchley U.K. 51°36N 0°11W 125 A2
Findhorn → U.K. 57°38N 3°38W 167 D5
Fındıklı Turkey 41°16N 41°9E 213 B9
Findlay U.S.A. 41°2N 83°39W 311 C13
Fine U.S.A. 44°14N 75°8W 313 B9
Fine Art, Museum of = Kunsthistorischesmuseum Vienna, Austria 142 b1
Fine Arts, Museum of U.S.A. 42°20N 71°5W 116 A2
Finger L. Canada 53°33N 93°30W 298 B1
Finger Lakes U.S.A. 42°40N 76°30W 313 D8
Finglas Ireland 53°23N 6°19W 120 A2
Fíngoè Mozam. 15°55S 31°50E 269 F3
Finike Turkey 36°21N 30°10E 205 E12
Finike Körfezi Turkey 36°17N 30°16E 205 E12
Finiq Albania 39°54N 20°3E 202 G4
Finistère □ France 48°20N 4°0W 172 D3
Finisterre = Fisterra Spain 42°54N 9°16W 194 C1
Finisterre, C. = Fisterra, C. Spain 42°50N 9°19W 194 C1
Finisterre Ra. Papua N. G. 6°0S 146°30E 286 D4
Finke Australia 25°34S 134°35E 280 D1
Finke Gorge △ Australia 24°8S 132°49E 278 D5
Finland ■ Europe 63°0N 27°0E 160 E22
Finland, G. of Europe 60°0N 26°0E 188 C3
Finlay → Canada 57°0N 125°10W 296 B3
Finley N.S.W., Australia 35°38S 145°35E 283 C6
Finley N. Dak., U.S.A. 47°31N 97°50W 308 B5
Finn → Ireland 54°51N 7°28W 166 B4
Finnerödja Sweden 58°57N 14°24E 163 F8
Finnigan, Mt. Australia 15°49S 145°17E 280 B4
Finniss, C. Australia 33°8S 134°51E 281 E1
Finnmark Norway 69°37N 23°57E 160 B20
Finnsnes Norway 69°14N 18°0E 160 B18
Finsbury U.K. 51°31N 0°6W 125 A3
Finsbury Park U.K. 51°34N 0°6W 125 A3
Finschhafen Papua N. G. 6°33S 147°50E 286 D4
Finse Norway 60°36N 7°30E 164 D4
Finspång Sweden 58°43N 15°47E 163 F9
Finsteraarhorn Switz. 46°31N 8°10E 179 J4
Finsterwalde Germany 51°37N 13°42E 178 D9
Fiora → Italy 42°20N 11°34E 199 F8
Fiordland △ N.Z. 45°46S 167°0E 285 F2
Fiorenzuola d'Arda Italy 44°56N 9°55E 198 D6
Fiorito Argentina 34°42S 58°26W 117 C2
Fīq Syria 32°46N 35°41E 250 F6
Firat = Furāt, Nahr al → Asia 31°0N 47°25E 246 D5
Fire Island ⌂ U.S.A. 40°38N 73°8W 313 F11
Firebag → Canada 57°45N 111°21W 297 B6
Firebaugh U.S.A. 36°52N 120°27W 306 J6
Firedrake L. Canada 61°25N 104°30W 297 A8
Firenze Italy 43°46N 11°15E 199 E8
Firenze Amerigo Vespucci ✈ (FLR) Italy 43°49N 11°13E 199 E8
Firenze Pisa ✈ (PSA) Italy 43°40N 10°22E 198 E7
Firenzuola Italy 44°7N 11°23E 199 D8
Firhouse Ireland 53°17N 6°20W 120 B2
Firk, Sha'ib → Iraq 30°59N 44°34E 246 D5
Firkachi Niger 15°40N 14°20E 259 E2
Firmi France 44°33N 2°19E 174 D6
Firminy France 45°23N 4°18E 175 C8
Firozabad India 27°10N 78°25E 243 F8
Firozpur India 30°55N 74°40E 242 D6
Firozpur-Jhirka India 27°48N 76°57E 242 F7
Fīrūzābād Iran 28°52N 52°35E 247 D7
Fīrūzkūh Iran 35°50N 52°50E 247 C7
Firvale Canada 52°27N 126°13W 296 C3
Fischerhäuser Germany 48°14N 11°41E 131 A3
Fish → Namibia 28°7S 17°10E 270 C2
Fish → Northern Cape, S. Africa 31°30S 20°16E 270 D3
Fish River Canyon Namibia 27°40S 17°35E 270 C2
Fisheating Cr. → U.S.A. 26°57N 81°7W 317 J8
Fisher B. Canada 51°35N 97°13W 297 C9
Fisher I. U.S.A. 25°45N 80°8W 129 D3
Fishermans Bend Australia 37°49S 144°55E 128 A1
Fisherman's Village U.S.A. 33°58N 118°27W 126 C2
Fisherman's Wharf San Francisco, U.S.A. 136 a1
Fishers U.S.A. 39°57N 86°0W 311 E11
Fishers I. U.S.A. 41°15N 72°0W 313 E13
Fisherville Canada 43°46N 79°28W 141 A2
Fishguard U.K. 52°0N 4°58W 169 E3
Fishing L. Canada 52°10N 95°24W 297 C9
Fishkill U.S.A. 41°32N 73°54W 313 E11
Fiskardo Greece 38°28N 20°35E 207 C2
Fiskenæsset = Qeqertarsuatsiaat Greenland 63°5N 50°45W 154 E5
Fisksätra Sweden 59°17N 18°13E 139 B3
Fismes France 49°20N 3°40E 173 C10
Fisterra Spain 42°54N 9°16W 194 C1
Fisterra, C. Spain 42°50N 9°19W 194 C1
Fitchburg Mass., U.S.A. 42°35N 71°48W 313 D13
Fitchburg Wis., U.S.A. 42°58N 89°28W 310 B7
Fitjar Iceland 64°28N 21°18W 155 C5
Fitjar Hordaland, Norway 59°55N 5°17E 164 E2
Fitri, L. Chad 12°50N 17°28E 259 F3
Fitz Roy Argentina 47°0S 67°0W 336 C3
Fitz Roy, Cerro Argentina 49°17S 73°5W 336 C2
Fitzgerald Alta., Canada 59°51N 111°36W 296 B6
Fitzgerald Ga., U.S.A. 31°43N 83°15W 316 D6
Fitzgerald River △ Australia 33°53S 119°55E 279 F3
Fitzmaurice → Australia 14°45S 130°5E 278 B5
Fitzroy → Queens., Australia 23°32S 150°52E 280 C5
Fitzroy → W. Austral., Australia 17°31S 123°35E 278 C3
Fitzroy Crossing Australia 18°9S 125°38E 278 C4
Fitzroy Gardens Australia 37°48S 144°58E 128 A1
Fitzwilliam I. Canada 45°30N 81°45W 312 A3
Fiuggi Italy 41°48N 13°13E 199 G10
Fiume = Rijeka Croatia 45°20N 14°21E 199 C11
Fiumicino, Roma ✈ (FCO) Italy 41°48N 12°15E 199 G9
Five Cowrie Cr. → Nigeria 6°26N 3°24E 124 B2
Five Dock Australia 33°52S 151°8E 139 B1
Five Island Harbour Antigua & B. 17°6N 61°54W 322 b
Five Points U.S.A. 36°26N 120°6W 306 J6
Fivizzano Italy 44°14N 10°8E 198 D7
Fizi Dem. Rep. of the Congo 4°17S 28°55E 268 C2
Fjæra Norway 59°52N 6°22E 164 E3
Fjærland Norway 61°24N 6°43E 164 C3
Fjærlandsfjorden Norway 61°17N 6°40E 164 C3
Fjällbacka Sweden 58°36N 11°17E 163 F5
Fjällnäs Sweden 62°36N 12°11E 162 B6
Fjärdhundra Sweden 59°47N 16°56E 162 E10
Fjellerup Denmark 56°29N 10°34E 163 H4
Fjellstrand Norway 59°47N 10°36E 133 B2
Fjerritslev Denmark 57°5N 9°15E 163 G3
Fjugesta Sweden 59°11N 14°52E 162 E8
Fkih ben Salah Morocco 32°32N 6°45W 260 B3
Flå Norway 60°25N 9°28E 164 D6
Flacq Plain Mauritius 20°13S 57°43E 272 e
Flagler Beach U.S.A. 29°29N 81°8W 317 F8
Flagstaff U.S.A. 35°12N 111°39W 305 J8
Flagstaff B. St. Helena 15°54S 5°41W 153 h
Flagstaff L. U.S.A. 45°12N 70°18W 313 A14
Flaherty I. Canada 56°15N 79°15W 298 A4
Flåm Norway 60°50N 7°7E 164 D4
Flamands St. Barts 17°55N 62°51W 322 a
Flambeau → U.S.A. 45°18N 91°14W 308 C8
Flamborough Hd. U.K. 54°7N 0°5W 168 C7
Flamengo Brazil 22°56S 43°11W 135 B1
Flamengos Azores 38°33N 28°39W 153 d1
Fläming Germany 52°6N 12°23E 178 C8
Flaming Gorge ⌂ U.S.A. 41°10N 109°25W 304 F9
Flaming Gorge Res. U.S.A. 41°10N 109°25W 304 F9
Flamingo Fla., U.S.A. 28°22N 81°22W 133 B2
Flamingo Fla., U.S.A. 25°8N 80°57W 317 K9
Flamingo, Teluk Indonesia 5°30S 138°0E 221 F9
Flaminio Italy 41°55N 12°28E 136 B1
Flanagan U.S.A. 40°53N 88°52W 311 D8
Flanagin Town Trin. & Tob. 10°25N 61°19W 323 t
Flanders = Flandre Europe 50°50N 2°30E 173 B9
Flandre Europe 50°50N 2°30E 173 B9
Flandre-Occidentale = West-Vlaanderen □ Belgium 51°0N 3°0E 170 D2
Flandre-Orientale = Oost-Vlaanderen □ Belgium 51°5N 3°50E 170 C3
Flandreau U.S.A. 44°3N 96°36W 308 C5
Flanigan U.S.A. 40°10N 119°53W 306 E7
Flannan Is. U.K. 58°9N 7°52W 167 C1
Flåsjön Sweden 64°5N 15°40E 160 D16
Flaskebekk Norway 59°51N 10°39E 133 A2
Flat U.S.A. 62°28N 158°1W 303 E8
Flat → N.W.T., Canada 61°33N 125°18W 296 A3
Flat → Mich., U.S.A. 42°56N 85°20W 311 B11
Flat Pt. N.Z. 41°14S 175°57E 284 H4
Flat Rock U.S.A. 42°6N 83°17W 311 B13
Flatbush U.S.A. 40°39N 73°56W 132 C2
Flateby Norway 59°50N 11°10E 164 E8
Flaten Sweden 59°15N 18°9E 139 B2
Flatey Iceland 66°10N 17°52W 155 A9
Flateyri Iceland 66°3N 23°31W 155 A3
Flathead L. U.S.A. 47°51N 114°8W 304 C6
Flatiron Building New York, U.S.A. 132 d2
Flatlands U.S.A. 40°37N 73°56W 132 C2
Flatow = Złotów Poland 53°22N 17°2E 184 E4
Flatrock → U.S.A. 39°12N 85°56W 311 F10
Flattery, C. Queens., Australia 14°58S 145°21E 280 A4
Flattery, C. Wash., U.S.A. 48°23N 124°29W 306 B2
Flatts Village Bermuda 32°18N 64°43W 153 a
Flatwoods U.S.A. 38°31N 82°43W 309 F12
Flecha Pt. Phil. 7°22N 123°24E 233 H4
Flechas Pt. Phil. 10°22N 119°34E 233 F2
Fleetwood Lancs., U.K. 53°55N 3°1W 168 D4
Fleetwood Pa., U.S.A. 40°27N 75°49W 313 F9
Flekke Norway 61°19N 5°20E 164 C2
Flekkefjord Norway 58°18N 6°39E 164 F3
Flemingsburg U.S.A. 38°25N 83°45W 311 F13
Flemington U.S.A. 41°7N 77°28W 312 E7
Flemington Racecourse Australia 37°47S 144°54E 128 A1
Flemish Cap Atl. Oc. 47°0N 45°0W 152 B7
Flen Sweden 59°4N 16°35E 162 E10
Flensburg Germany 54°47N 9°27E 178 A5
Flers France 48°47N 0°33W 172 D6
Flesberg Norway 59°51N 9°27E 164 E6
Flesherton Canada 44°16N 80°33W 312 B4
Flesko, Tanjung Indonesia 0°29N 124°30E 231 D6
Fletcher = Aurora U.S.A. 39°43N 104°49W 304 G11
Fleurance France 43°52N 0°40E 174 E4
Fleurier Switz. 46°54N 6°35E 179 J2
Fleurieu Pen. Australia 35°40S 138°5E 282 C3
Flevoland □ Neths. 52°30N 5°30E 170 B5
Flin Flon Canada 54°46N 101°53W 297 C8
Flinders → Australia 17°36S 140°36E 280 B3
Flinders B. Australia 34°19S 115°19E 279 F2
Flinders Chase △ Australia 35°50S 136°42E 282 C2
Flinders Group Australia 14°11S 144°15E 280 A3
Flinders I. S. Austral., Australia 33°44S 134°41E 281 E1
Flinders I. Tas., Australia 40°0S 148°0E 281 G4
Flinders Ranges Australia 31°30S 138°30E 282 A3
Flinders Ranges △ Australia 31°30S 138°40E 282 A3
Flinders Reefs Australia 17°37S 148°31E 280 B4
Flint Flints., U.K. 53°15N 3°8W 168 D4
Flint Mich., U.S.A. 43°1N 83°41W 311 A13
Flint → U.S.A. 30°57N 84°34W 316 E5
Flint I. Kiribati 11°26S 151°48W 289 f
Flint Pk. U.S.A. 34°9N 118°11W 126 B3
Flintshire □ U.K. 53°17N 3°17W 168 D4
Flipper Pt. Wake I. 19°18N 166°37E 302 b
Flisa Norway 60°37N 12°0E 164 D9
Flisa → Norway 60°37N 12°0E 164 D9
Fliseryd Sweden 57°6N 16°15E 163 G10
Flix Spain 41°14N 0°32E 196 D5
Flixecourt France 50°1N 2°5E 173 B9
Floby Sweden 58°8N 13°20E 163 F7
Floda Sweden 57°49N 12°22E 163 G6
Flodden U.K. 55°37N 2°8W 168 B5
Flogny-la-Chapelle France 47°57N 3°57E 173 E10
Floodplains △ Sri Lanka 8°10N 81°10E 245 K5
Floodwood U.S.A. 46°56N 92°55W 308 B7
Flora Apayao, Phil. 18°14N 121°5E 232 B3
Flora Ill., U.S.A. 38°40N 88°29W 310 F8
Flora Ind., U.S.A. 40°33N 86°31W 311 D10
Florac France 44°20N 3°37E 174 D7
Florahome U.S.A. 29°44N 81°54W 316 F8
Floral City U.S.A. 28°45N 82°17W 317 G7
Florala U.S.A. 31°0N 86°20W 315 F11
Florânia Brazil 6°8S 36°49W 332 C4
Floreana, I. = Santa María, I. Ecuador 1°17S 90°26W 330 a
Florence = Firenze Italy 43°46N 11°15E 199 E8
Florence Ala., U.S.A. 34°48N 87°41W 315 D11
Florence Ariz., U.S.A. 33°2N 111°23W 305 K8
Florence Calif., U.S.A. 33°57N 118°13W 126 C3
Florence Colo., U.S.A. 38°23N 105°8W 304 G11
Florence Oreg., U.S.A. 43°58N 124°7W 304 D1
Florence S.C., U.S.A. 34°12N 79°46W 315 D15
Florence, L. Australia 28°53S 138°9E 281 D2
Florence Bay = Chtimba Malawi 10°35S 34°13E 269 E3
Florence Bloom Bird Sanctuary ⌂ S. Africa 26°7S 28°0E 123 A2
Florencia Colombia 1°36N 75°36W 328 C2
Florennes Belgium 50°15N 4°35E 170 D4
Florensac France 43°23N 3°28E 174 E7
Florentia S. Africa 26°16S 28°8E 123 B2
Florenville Belgium 49°40N 5°19E 170 E5
Flores = Florânia Brazil 6°8S 36°49W 332 C4
Flores = Timon Brazil 5°8S 42°52W 332 C3
Flores B. Aires, Argentina 34°38S 58°27W 117 B2
Flores Azores 39°26N 31°13W 153 d2
Flores Brazil 7°51S 37°59W 332 C4
Flores Guatemala 16°59N 89°50W 320 C2
Flores Indonesia 8°35S 121°0E 235 D5
Flores, Mercado de Mexico 19°19N 99°5W 128 C2
Flores I. Canada 49°20N 126°10W 296 D3
Flores Sea Indonesia 6°30S 120°0E 231 F6
Floresta B. Aires, Argentina 34°37S 58°27W 117 B2
Floresta Brazil 8°40S 37°26W 332 C4
Floreşti Moldova 47°53N 28°17E 183 C13
Floresville U.S.A. 29°8N 98°10W 314 G5
Floriano Brazil 6°50S 43°0W 332 C3
Florianópolis Brazil 27°30S 48°30W 335 B6
Florida B. Aires, Argentina 34°31S 58°28W 117 B2
Florida Cuba 21°32N 78°14W 320 B4
Florida Puerto Rico 18°22N 66°34W 321 b
Florida Gauteng, S. Africa 26°10S 27°55E 123 B1
Florida Uruguay 34°7S 56°10W 335 C4
Florida □ U.S.A. 28°0N 82°0W 317 H8
Florida, Straits of U.S.A. 25°0N 80°0W 320 B4
Florida B. U.S.A. 25°0N 80°45W 320 B3
Florida City U.S.A. 25°27N 80°29W 317 K9
Florida Is. Solomon Is. 9°55S 160°15E 287 M11
Florida Keys U.S.A. 24°40N 81°0W 317 L8
Floridablanca Phil. 14°59N 120°31E 232 D3
Florídia Italy 37°5N 15°9E 201 E8
Floridsdorf Austria 48°15N 16°26E 142 A2
Florin U.S.A. 38°30N 121°24W 306 G5
Florina Greece 40°48N 21°26E 202 F5
Florina □ Greece 40°45N 21°20E 202 F5
Florissant U.S.A. 38°47N 90°19W 310 F6
Florø Norway 61°35N 5°1E 164 C2
Flotte, C. de N. Cal. 21°10S 167°25E 288 d
Flower Station Canada 45°10N 76°41W 313 A8
Flowerpot I. Canada 45°18N 81°38W 312 A3
Floydada U.S.A. 33°59N 101°20W 314 E4
Fludir Iceland 64°7N 20°6W 155 C6
Flugumyri Iceland 65°34N 19°19W 155 B7
Fluk Indonesia 1°42S 127°44E 231 E7
Flúmen → Spain 41°43N 0°9W 196 D4
Flumendosa → Italy 39°26N 9°37E 200 C2
Fluminimaggiore Italy 39°26N 8°30E 200 C1
Flushing = Vlissingen Neths. 51°26N 3°34E 170 C3
Flushing Mich., U.S.A. 43°4N 83°51W 311 A13
Flushing N.Y., U.S.A. 40°45N 73°49W 132 B3
Flushing Meadows Corona Park U.S.A. 40°44N 73°50W 132 B2
Fluvià → Spain 42°12N 3°7E 196 C8
Fly → Papua N. G. 8°25S 143°0E 286 E2
Flying Fish, C. Antarctica 72°6S 102°29W 151 D15
Flysta Sweden 59°22N 17°54E 139 A1
Fo Tan China 22°23N 114°11E 122 A2
Foa Tonga 19°45S 174°18W 287 P13
Foam Lake Canada 51°40N 103°32W 297 C8
Foča Bos.-H. 43°31N 18°47E 202 C2
Foça Turkey 38°39N 26°46E 205 C8
Fochabers U.K. 57°37N 3°6W 167 D5
Focşani Romania 45°41N 27°15E 183 E12
Fodé C.A.R. 5°29N 23°18E 264 A4
Fodécontéa Guinea 10°50N 14°22W 262 C2
Fogang China 23°52N 113°30E 229 F9
Foggaret el Arab Algeria 27°13N 2°49E 261 C5
Foggaret ez Zoua Algeria 27°20N 2°53E 261 C5
Fóggia Italy 41°27N 15°34E 201 A8
Foggy Bottom U.S.A. 38°54N 77°3W 143 B2
Foglia → Italy 43°55N 12°54E 199 E9
Fogo Nfld. & L., Canada 49°43N 54°17W 299 C9
Fogo C. Verde Is. 15°5N 24°20W 153 j
Fogo I. Canada 49°40N 54°5W 299 C9
Fohnsdorf Austria 47°12N 14°40E 180 D7
Föhr Germany 54°43N 8°30E 178 A4
Föhrenhain Austria 48°19N 16°26E 142 A2
Foia Portugal 37°19N 8°37W 195 H2
Foix France 42°58N 1°38E 174 E5
Fojnica Bos.-H. 43°59N 17°51E 182 G2
Fokida □ Greece 38°30N 22°15E 204 C4
Fokino Russia 53°30N 34°22E 188 F8
Fokku Nigeria 11°36N 4°32E 263 C5
Fokstugu Norway 62°7N 9°17E 164 B6
Folda Nord-Trøndelag, Norway 64°32N 10°30E 160 D14
Folda Nordland, Norway 67°38N 14°50E 160 C16
Földeák Hungary 46°19N 20°30E 182 D5
Folegandros Greece 36°40N 24°55E 204 E6
Foley Botswana 21°34S 27°21E 270 B4
Foley Ala., U.S.A. 30°24N 87°41W 315 F11
Foley Fla., U.S.A. 30°4N 83°32W 316 E6
Foleyet Canada 48°15N 82°25W 298 C3
Folgefonna Norway 60°3N 6°23E 164 D3
Folgefonna △ Norway 60°5N 6°15E 164 D3
Foligno Italy 42°57N 12°42E 199 F9
Folkestad Norway 62°7N 6°1E 164 B3
Folkestone U.K. 51°5N 1°12E 169 F9
Folkestone Marine Park △ Barbados 13°11N 59°38W 323 r
Folkston U.S.A. 30°50N 82°0W 316 E7
Folla → Norway 62°7N 10°37E 164 B7
Follansbee U.S.A. 40°19N 80°35W 312 F4
Folldal Norway 62°8N 10°0E 164 B6
Folle Anse, Pte. de Guadeloupe 15°56N 61°19W 322 e
Follebu Norway 61°13N 10°16E 164 C7
Follónica Italy 42°55N 10°45E 198 F7
Follónica, G. di Italy 42°54N 10°43E 198 F7
Folsom U.S.A. 38°40N 121°9W 306 G5
Folsom L. U.S.A. 38°42N 121°9W 306 G5
Folteşti Romania 45°45N 28°3E 183 E13
Fomboni Comoros Is. 12°18S 43°46E 272 a
Fomm ir-Rih Bay Malta 35°54N 14°20E 206 F7
Fond-du-Lac Sask., Canada 59°19N 107°12W 297 B7
Fond du Lac Wis., U.S.A. 43°47N 88°27W 308 D9
Fond-du-Lac → Canada 59°17N 106°0W 297 B7
Fond Rousseau Martinique 14°38N 61°6W 322 j
Fond St. Jacques St. Lucia 13°50N 61°1W 323 m
Fonda Iowa, U.S.A. 42°35N 94°51W 310 B2
Fonda N.Y., U.S.A. 42°57N 74°22W 313 D10
Fondamenta Nuove Venice, Italy 142 a3
Fondi Italy 41°21N 13°25E 200 A6
Fonds-St-Denis Martinique 14°44N 61°8W 322 j
Fonfría Spain 41°37N 6°9W 194 D4
Fongafale Tuvalu 8°31S 179°13E 277 B14
Fongen Norway 63°11N 11°38E 164 A8
Fonni Italy 40°7N 9°15E 200 B2
Fonsagrada = A Fonsagrada Spain 43°8N 7°4W 194 B3
Fonseca, G. de Cent. Amer. 13°10N 87°40W 320 D2
Font-Romeu-Odeillo-Via France 42°31N 2°3E 174 F5
Fontaine-Française France 47°32N 5°21E 173 E12
Fontainebleau Seine-et-Marne, France 48°24N 2°40E 173 D9
Fontainebleau Gauteng, S. Africa 26°6S 27°57E 123 A1
Fontana U.S.A. 34°6N 117°26W 307 L9
Fontana, L. Argentina 44°55S 71°30W 336 B2
Fontas → Canada 58°14N 121°48W 296 B4
Fonte Boa Brazil 2°33S 66°0W 328 D4
Fontem Cameroon 5°32N 9°52E 263 D6
Fontenay-aux-Roses France 48°47N 2°17E 134 B2
Fontenay-le-Comte France 46°28N 0°48W 174 B3
Fontenay-le-Fleury France 48°48N 2°2E 134 B1
Fontenay-sous-Bois France 48°51N 2°28E 134 A3
Fontenelle Res. U.S.A. 42°1N 110°3W 304 E8
Fontur Iceland 66°23N 14°32W 155 A12
Fonuafo'ou Tonga 20°19S 175°25W 287 Q13
Fonuakula Cook Is. 19°2S 169°55W 289 g
Fonualei Tonga 18°1S 174°19W 287 P13
Fonyód Hungary 46°44N 17°33E 182 D2
Foochow = Fuzhou China 26°5N 119°16E 229 D12
Foots Cray U.K. 51°24N 0°7E 125 B4
Footscray Australia 37°48S 144°56E 128 A1
Foping China 33°41N 108°0E 226 H5
Foraker, Mt. U.S.A. 62°58N 151°24W 303 E10
Forari Vanuatu 17°40S 168°31E 287 G6
Forbach France 49°10N 6°52E 173 C13
Forbes Australia 33°22S 148°5E 283 B8
Forbesganj India 26°17N 87°18E 243 F12
Forbidden City = Imperial Palace Museum Beijing, China 114 b3
Forcados Nigeria 5°26N 5°26E 263 D6
Forcados → Nigeria 5°25N 5°19E 263 D6
Forcalquier France 43°58N 5°47E 175 E9
Forchheim Germany 49°43N 11°2E 179 F7
Ford City Calif., U.S.A. 35°9N 119°27W 307 K7
Ford City Pa., U.S.A. 40°46N 79°32W 312 F5
Ford d'Or B. St. Lucia 13°56N 60°54W 323 m
Ford I. U.S.A. 21°22N 157°58W 302 K14
Forda → Norway 62°57N 10°40E 164 B7
Førde Hordaland, Norway 59°36N 5°27E 164 E2
Førde Rogaland, Norway 59°26N 5°23E 164 E2
Førde Sogn og Fjordane, Norway 61°27N 5°53E 164 C2
Førdefjorden Norway 61°29N 5°18E 164 C2
Fords Bridge Australia 29°41S 145°29E 281 D4
Ford's Theater Washington, D.C., U.S.A. 143 b2
Fordyce U.S.A. 33°49N 92°25W 314 E8
Forécariah Guinea 9°28N 13°10W 262 D2
Forel, Mt. Greenland 66°52N 36°55W 154 D7
Foremost Canada 49°26N 111°34W 296 D6
Foreshore Cape Town, S. Africa 118 a3
Forest Belgium 50°49N 4°20E 116 B1
Forest Ont., Canada 43°6N 82°0W 312 C3
Forest Miss., U.S.A. 32°22N 89°29W 315 E10
Forest Acres U.S.A. 34°1N 80°58W 316 A9
Forest City Iowa, U.S.A. 43°16N 93°39W 308 D7
Forest City N.C., U.S.A. 35°20N 81°52W 315 D14
Forest City Pa., U.S.A. 41°39N 75°28W 313 E9
Forest Gate U.K. 51°32N 0°1E 125 A4
Forest Grove U.S.A. 45°31N 123°7W 306 E3
Forest Heights U.S.A. 38°48N 77°0W 143 C2
Forest Hill Ont., Canada 43°41N 79°25W 141 A2
Forest Hill London, U.K. 51°26N 0°2W 125 B3
Forest Hills U.S.A. 40°42N 73°51W 132 B2
Forest Park Ga., U.S.A. 33°37N 84°22W 316 B5
Forest Park Ill., U.S.A. 41°51N 87°47W 119 B2
Forest Park N.Y., U.S.A. 40°42N 73°51W 132 B2
Forest Park Ohio, U.S.A. 39°17N 84°30W 311 E12
Forest View U.S.A. 41°48N 87°47W 119 C2
Forestburg Canada 52°35N 112°1W 296 C6
Foreste Casentinesi-Monte Falterona-Campigna △ Italy 43°50N 11°48E 199 E8
Foresthill U.S.A. 39°1N 120°49W 306 F6
Forestier Pen. Australia 43°0S 148°0E 281 G4
Forestville Qué., Canada 48°48N 69°2W 299 C6
Forestville Calif., U.S.A. 38°28N 122°54W 306 G4
Forestville N.Y., U.S.A. 42°28N 79°10W 312 D5
Forêt d'Orient ⌂ France 48°16N 4°25E 173 D11
Forêt du Day △ Djibouti 11°56N 42°40E 267 B5
Forez, Mts. du France 45°40N 3°50E 174 C7
Forfar U.K. 56°39N 2°53W 167 E6
Forillon △ Canada 48°46N 64°12W 299 C7
Forks U.S.A. 47°57N 124°23W 306 C2
Forks, The = Merritt Canada 50°10N 120°45W 296 C4
Forksville U.S.A. 41°29N 76°35W 313 E8
Forlì Italy 44°13N 12°3E 199 D9
Forman U.S.A. 46°7N 97°38W 308 B5
Formazza Italy 46°22N 8°26E 198 B5
Formby Pt. U.K. 53°33N 3°6W 168 D4
Formentera Spain 38°43N 1°27E 206 D1
Formentor, C. de Spain 39°58N 3°13E 206 B4
Formentor, Pen. de Spain 39°56N 3°11E 206 B4
Former Yugoslav Republic of Macedonia = Macedonia ■ Europe 41°53N 21°40E 202 E5
Fórmia Italy 41°15N 13°37E 200 A6
Formiga Brazil 20°27S 45°25W 333 F2
Formígine Italy 44°37N 10°51E 198 D7
Formosa = Taiwan ■ Asia 23°30N 121°0E 225 C3
Formosa Argentina 26°15S 58°10W 334 B4
Formosa Brazil 15°32S 47°20W 333 E2
Formosa □ Argentina 25°0S 60°0W 334 B4
Formosa, Serra Brazil 12°0S 55°0W 331 C7
Formosa B. = Ungwana B. Kenya 2°45S 40°20E 268 C5
Formosa do Rio Prêto Brazil 11°2S 45°3W 332 D2
Formosa Strait = Taiwan Strait Asia 24°40N 120°0E 229 E12
Formoso → Brazil 10°34S 49°56W 333 D2
Fornebu Norway 59°53N 10°36E 133 A2
Fornells Spain 40°3N 4°7E 206 A5
Fornos de Algodres Portugal 40°38N 7°32W 194 E3
Fornovo di Taro Italy 44°42N 10°6E 198 D7
Foro Romano Rome, Italy 136 c3
Forollhogna △ Norway 62°39N 10°41E 164 B7
Føroyar ☒ Atl. Oc. 62°0N 7°0W 160 F9
Forres U.K. 57°37N 3°37W 167 D5
Forrest Vic., Australia 38°33S 143°47E 282 E5
Forrest W. Austral., Australia 30°51S 128°6E 279 F4
Forrest, Mt. Australia 24°48S 127°45E 279 D4
Forrest City U.S.A. 35°1N 90°47W 315 D9
Forreston U.S.A. 42°8N 89°35W 310 B7
Fors Sweden 60°14N 16°20E 162 D10
Forsand Norway 58°54N 6°5E 164 F3
Forsayth Australia 18°33S 143°34E 280 B3
Forserum Sweden 57°42N 14°30E 163 G8
Forshaga Sweden 59°33N 13°29E 162 E7
Förslöv Sweden 56°21N 12°48E 163 H6
Forsmo Sweden 63°16N 17°11E 162 A11
Forssa Finland 60°49N 23°38E 188 B2
Forst Germany 51°45N 14°37E 178 D10
Forstenried Germany 48°5N 11°29E 131 B1
Forstenrieder Park Germany 48°3N 11°27E 131 B1
Forster Australia 32°12S 152°31E 283 B10
Forsvik Sweden 58°35N 14°26E 163 F8
Forsyth Ga., U.S.A. 33°2N 83°56W 316 B6
Forsyth Mont., U.S.A. 46°16N 106°41W 304 C10
Forsyth I. N.Z. 40°58S 174°5E 285 A9
Fort Mumbai, India 130 c2
Fort Abbas Pakistan 29°12N 72°52E 242 E5
Fort Albany Canada 52°15N 81°35W 298 B3
Fort-Aleksandrovsky = Fort Shevchenko Kazakhstan 44°35N 50°23E 191 H10
Fort Archambault = Sarh Chad 9°5N 18°23E 259 G3
Fort Assiniboine Canada 54°20N 114°45W 296 C6
Fort Atkinson U.S.A. 42°56N 88°50W 311 B8
Fort Augustus U.K. 57°9N 4°42W 167 D4
Fort Bay Saba 17°37N 63°15W 322 a
Fort Bayard = Zhanjiang China 21°15N 110°20E 229 G8
Fort Beaufort S. Africa 32°46S 26°40E 270 D4
Fort Benton U.S.A. 47°49N 110°40W 304 C8
Fort Bragg U.S.A. 39°26N 123°48W 304 G2
Fort Bridger U.S.A. 41°19N 110°23W 304 F8
Fort Canning Park Singapore 138 b2
Fort Caroline ⌂ U.S.A. 30°23N 81°30W 316 E8
Fort Charles Jamaica 17°55N 76°50W 320 a
Fort Charlotte St. Lucia 13°59N 61°0W 323 m
Fort Chipewyan Canada 58°42N 111°8W 297 B6
Fort Clatsop = Lewis and Clark ⌂ U.S.A. 46°8N 123°53W 306 D3
Fort Collins U.S.A. 40°35N 105°5W 304 F11
Fort-Coulonge Canada 45°50N 76°45W 298 C4

Fort Covington U.S.A. 44°59N 74°29W 313 B10
Fort Dauphin = Taolanaro Madag. 25°2S 47°0E 272 D2
Fort Davis Ala., U.S.A. 32°15N 85°43W 316 C4
Fort Davis Tex., U.S.A. 30°35N 103°54W 314 F3
Fort-de-France Martinique 14°36N 61°5W 322 j
Fort-de-France, B. de Martinique 14°34N 61°4W 322 j
Fort de Kock = Bukittinggi Indonesia 0°20S 100°20E 234 C2
Fort de Polignac = Illizi Algeria 26°31N 8°32E 261 C6
Fort de Possel = Possel C.A.R. 5°5N 19°10E 264 A3
Fort Defiance U.S.A. 35°45N 109°5W 305 J9
Fort Dodge U.S.A. 42°30N 94°11W 310 B2
Fort Drum U.S.A. 27°32N 80°48W 317 H9
Fort Dupont Park U.S.A. 38°52N 76°56W 143 B3
Fort Edward U.S.A. 43°16N 73°35W 313 C11
Fort Erie Canada 42°54N 78°56W 312 D6
Fort Fairfield U.S.A. 46°46N 67°50W 309 B20
Fort Flatters = Bordj Omar Driss Algeria 28°10N 6°40E 261 C6
Fort Foote Village U.S.A. 38°46N 77°1W 143 C2
Fort Foureau = Kousseri Cameroon 12°0N 14°55E 259 F2
Fort Frances Canada 48°36N 93°24W 297 D10
Fort Franklin = Déline Canada 65°11N 123°25W 294 D7
Fort Frederica ⌂ U.S.A. 31°13N 81°23W 316 D8
Fort Gaines U.S.A. 31°36N 85°3W 316 D4
Fort Garland U.S.A. 37°26N 105°26W 305 H11
Fort George = Chisasibi Canada 53°50N 79°0W 298 B4
Fort George = Prince George Canada 53°55N 122°50W 296 C4
Fort George Grenada 12°3N 61°45W 323 q
Fort Good Hope Canada 66°14N 128°40W 294 D6
Fort Gouraud = Fdérik Mauritania 22°40N 12°45W 260 D2
Fort Hancock U.S.A. 31°18N 105°51W 314 F2
Fort Hertz = Putao Burma 27°28N 97°30E 241 B6
Fort Hill = Chitipa Malawi 9°41S 33°19E 269 D3
Fort Hope = Eabametoong Canada 51°30N 88°0W 298 B2
Fort Irwin U.S.A. 35°16N 116°41W 307 K10
Fort Jameson = Chipata Zambia 13°38S 32°28E 269 E3
Fort Jeudy, Pt. of Grenada 11°59N 61°42W 323 q
Fort Johnston = Mangoche Malawi 14°25S 35°16E 269 E4
Fort Kent U.S.A. 47°15N 68°36W 309 B19
Fort Klamath U.S.A. 42°42N 122°0W 304 D3
Fort Lamy = Ndjamena Chad 12°10N 15°0E 259 F3
Fort-Laperrine = Tamanrasset Algeria 22°50N 5°30E 261 D6
Fort Laramie U.S.A. 42°13N 104°31W 304 E11
Fort Lauderdale U.S.A. 26°7N 80°8W 129 B3
Fort Lauderdale Executive ✕ (FXE) U.S.A. 26°11N 80°10W 129 A2
Fort Lauderdale-Hollywood Int. ✕ (FLL) U.S.A. 26°4N 80°10W 129 B3
Fort Lee U.S.A. 40°50N 73°58W 132 A2
Fort Liard Canada 60°14N 123°30W 296 A4
Fort Liberté Haiti 19°42N 71°51W 321 C5
Fort Lupton U.S.A. 40°5N 104°49W 304 F11
Fort MacKay Canada 57°12N 111°41W 296 B6
Fort Macleod Canada 49°45N 113°30W 296 D6
Fort MacMahon = El Homr Algeria 29°43N 1°45E 261 C5
Fort McMurray Canada 56°44N 111°7W 296 B6
Fort McPherson Canada 67°30N 134°55W 294 D5
Fort Madison U.S.A. 40°38N 91°27W 310 D5
Fort Manning = Mchinji Malawi 13°47S 32°58E 269 E3
Fort Marlborough Indonesia 3°48S 102°15E 234 C2
Fort Mason Center San Francisco, U.S.A. 136 a1
Fort Matanzas ⌂ U.S.A. 29°43N 81°14W 316 F8
Fort Meade U.S.A. 27°45N 81°48W 317 H8
Fort Mitchell U.S.A. 32°20N 85°1W 316 C4
Fort Morgan U.S.A. 40°15N 103°48W 304 F12
Fort Myers U.S.A. 26°39N 81°52W 317 J8
Fort Myers Beach U.S.A. 26°26N 81°52W 317 J8
Fort Myers Villas U.S.A. 26°33N 81°52W 317 J8
Fort Napoléon Guadeloupe 15°52N 61°35W 322 e
Fort Nelson Canada 58°50N 122°44W 296 B4
Fort Nelson → Canada 59°32N 124°0W 296 B4
Fort Norman = Tulita Canada 64°57N 125°30W 294 E6
Fort Ogden U.S.A. 27°5N 81°57W 317 H8
Fort Payne U.S.A. 34°26N 85°43W 315 D12
Fort Peck U.S.A. 48°1N 106°27W 304 B10
Fort Peck Dam U.S.A. 48°0N 106°26W 304 C10
Fort Peck L. U.S.A. 48°0N 106°26W 304 C10
Fort Pierce U.S.A. 27°27N 80°20W 317 H9
Fort Pierre U.S.A. 44°21N 100°22W 308 C3
Fort Pierre Bordes = Ti-n-Zaouatene Algeria 19°55N 2°55E 261 E5
Fort Plain U.S.A. 42°56N 74°37W 313 D10
Fort Portal Uganda 0°40N 30°20E 268 B3
Fort Providence Canada 61°3N 117°40W 296 A5
Fort Pulaski ⌂ U.S.A. 32°2N 80°56W 316 C9
Fort Qu'Appelle Canada 50°45N 103°50W 297 C8
Fort Recovery U.S.A. 40°25N 84°47W 311 D12
Fort Resolution Canada 61°10N 113°40W 296 A6
Fort Rixon Zimbabwe 20°2S 29°17E 269 G2
Fort Rosebery = Mansa Zambia 11°13S 28°55E 269 E2
Fort Ross U.S.A. 38°32N 123°13W 306 G3
Fort-Rousset = Owando Congo 0°29S 15°55E 264 C3
Fort Rupert = Waskaganish Canada 51°30N 78°40W 298 B4
Fort St. James Canada 54°30N 124°10W 296 C4
Fort St. John Canada 56°15N 120°50W 296 B4
Fort Sandeman = Zhob Pakistan 31°20N 69°31E 242 D3
Fort Saskatchewan Canada 53°40N 113°15W 296 C6
Fort Scott U.S.A. 37°50N 94°42W 308 G6
Fort Severn Canada 56°0N 87°40W 298 A2
Fort Shevchenko Kazakhstan 44°35N 50°23E 191 H10
Fort Simpson Canada 61°45N 121°15W 296 A4
Fort Smith Alta., Canada 60°0N 111°51W 296 B6
Fort Smith Ark., U.S.A. 35°23N 94°25W 314 D7
Fort Stockton U.S.A. 30°53N 102°53W 314 F3
Fort Sumner U.S.A. 34°28N 104°15W 305 J11
Fort Thomas U.S.A. 39°4N 84°26W 311 E12
Fort Thompson U.S.A. 44°3N 99°26W 308 C4
Fort Trinquet = Bir Mogreïn Mauritania 25°10N 11°25W 260 C2
Fort Union ⌂ U.S.A. 35°54N 105°1W 305 J11
Fort Uritskogo = Fort Shevchenko Kazakhstan 44°35N 50°23E 191 H10
Fort Valley U.S.A. 32°33N 83°53W 316 C6
Fort Vermilion Canada 58°24N 116°0W 296 B5
Fort Walton Beach U.S.A. 30°25N 86°36W 317 E3
Fort Ware Canada 57°26N 125°41W 296 B3
Fort Wayne U.S.A. 41°4N 85°9W 311 C11
Fort White U.S.A. 29°55N 82°43W 316 F7
Fort William U.K. 56°49N 5°7W 167 E3
Fort Worth U.S.A. 32°43N 97°19W 314 E6
Fort Yates U.S.A. 46°5N 100°38W 308 B3
Fort Yukon U.S.A. 66°34N 145°16W 303 C11
Fortaleza = Pôrto Azul Brazil 16°2S 41°17W 333 E3
Fortaleza Bolivia 12°6S 66°49W 330 C4
Fortaleza Brazil 3°45S 38°35W 332 B4
Forteau Canada 51°28N 56°58W 299 B8
Fortescue → Australia 21°0S 116°4E 278 D2
Fortescue River Roadhouse Australia 21°17S 116°8E 278 D2
Forth → U.K. 56°9N 3°50W 167 E5
Forth, Firth of U.K. 56°5N 2°55W 121 A3
Forth Rail Bridge U.K. 56°0N 3°23W 121 A1
Forth Road Bridge U.K. 56°0N 3°24W 121 A1
Forthassa Rharbia Algeria 32°52N 1°18W 261 B4
Fortín General Pando Paraguay 19°45S 59°47W 331 D6
Fortín Madrejón Paraguay 20°45S 59°52W 331 E6
Fortín Teniente Primero Ramiro Espínola Paraguay 21°27S 61°30W 331 E5
Fortín Uno Argentina 38°50S 65°18W 336 A3
Fortore → Italy 41°55N 15°17E 199 G12
Fortrose N.Z. 46°38S 168°45E 285 G3
Fortrose Highl., U.K. 57°35N 4°9W 167 D4
Fortuna Spain 38°11N 1°7W 197 G3
Fortuna Calif., U.S.A. 40°36N 124°9W 304 F1
Fortuna N. Dak., U.S.A. 48°55N 103°47W 308 A2
Fortuna Ledge = Marshall U.S.A. 61°53N 162°5W 303 F7
Fortune Canada 47°4N 55°50W 299 C8
Fortune B. Canada 47°30N 55°22W 299 C8
Forūr Iran 26°17N 54°32E 247 E7
Fos-sur-Mer France 43°26N 4°56E 175 E8
Fosen Norway 63°50N 10°20E 160 E14
Foshan China 23°3N 113°9E 121 B1
Fosnavåg Norway 62°22N 5°38E 164 B2
Foso Ghana 5°43N 1°15W 263 D4
Foss Iceland 63°51N 17°52W 155 D9
Fossano Italy 44°33N 7°43E 198 D4
Fossil U.S.A. 45°0N 120°9W 304 D3
Fossil Butte ⌂ U.S.A. 41°50N 110°27W 304 F8
Fossombrone Italy 43°41N 12°48E 199 E9
Fossvellir Iceland 65°27N 14°37W 155 B12
Foster Vic., Australia 38°40S 146°15E 283 E7
Foster Qué., Canada 45°17N 72°30W 313 A12
Foster Ky., U.S.A. 38°48N 84°13W 311 F12
Foster → Canada 55°47N 105°49W 297 B7
Foster Village U.S.A. 21°21N 157°55W 302 K14
Fosters Ra. Australia 21°35S 133°48E 280 C1
Fostoria U.S.A. 41°10N 83°25W 311 C13
Fót Hungary 47°35N 19°11E 117 A3
Fotadrevo Madag. 24°3S 45°1E 272 C2
Fouesnant France 47°53N 4°1W 172 E2
Fougamou Gabon 1°16S 10°30E 264 C2
Fougères France 48°21N 1°14W 172 D5
Foul Pt. Sri Lanka 8°35N 81°18E 245 K5
Foula U.K. 60°10N 2°5W 167 A6
Foulalaba Mali 10°40N 7°20W 262 C3
Foulness I. U.K. 51°36N 0°55E 169 F8
Foulpointe Madag. 17°41S 49°31E 272 B2
Foulwind, C. N.Z. 41°45S 171°28E 285 B6
Foum Assaka Morocco 29°8N 10°24W 260 C2
Foum Zguid Morocco 30°2N 6°59W 260 B3
Foumban Cameroon 5°45N 10°50E 263 D7
Foumbot Cameroon 5°31N 10°28E 263 D7
Foumbouni Comoros Is. 11°51S 43°29E 272 a
Foumirate Algeria 27°30N 3°12W 260 C4
Foundiougne Senegal 14°5N 16°32W 262 C1
Fountain Colo., U.S.A. 38°41N 104°42W 304 G11
Fountain Fla., U.S.A. 30°29N 85°25W 316 E4
Fountain Hills U.S.A. 33°37N 111°43W 305 K8
Fountain Springs U.S.A. 35°54N 118°51W 307 K8
Four Mountains, Is. of U.S.A. 53°0N 170°0W 303 K5
Four Roads Trin. & Tob. 10°41N 61°33W 323 t
Fourchambault France 47°2N 3°3E 173 E10
Fourchue, Île St. Barts 17°58N 62°54W 322 a
Fouriesburg S. Africa 28°38S 28°14E 270 C4
Fourmies France 50°1N 4°2E 173 B11
Fourna Greece 39°3N 21°52E 204 B3
Fournaise, Piton de la Réunion 21°14S 55°43E 272 f
Fourni Greece 37°36N 26°32E 205 D8
Fourqueux France 48°53N 2°3E 134 A1
Fours France 46°50N 3°42E 173 F10
Fous, Pte. des Dominica 15°12N 61°20W 323 k
Fousinshin = Fuxin China 42°5N 121°48E 227 C11
Fouta Djallon Guinea 11°20N 12°10W 262 C2
Foux, Cap-à- Haiti 19°43N 73°27W 321 C5
Foveaux Str. N.Z. 46°42S 168°10E 285 G3
Fowey U.K. 50°20N 4°39W 169 G3
Fowler Calif., U.S.A. 36°38N 119°41W 306 J7
Fowler Colo., U.S.A. 38°8N 104°2W 304 G11
Fowler Ind., U.S.A. 40°37N 87°19W 311 D9
Fowler Mich., U.S.A. 43°0N 84°45W 311 B12
Fowler, Pt. Australia 32°2S 132°3E 279 F5
Fowlers B. Australia 31°59S 132°34E 279 F5
Fowlerville U.S.A. 42°40N 84°4W 311 B12
Fowman Iran 37°13N 49°19E 213 D13
Fox → Canada 56°3N 93°18W 297 B10
Fox Creek Canada 54°24N 116°48W 296 C5
Fox Is. U.S.A. 53°0N 168°0W 303 K6
Fox Lake Alta., Canada 58°28N 114°31W 296 B6
Fox Lake Ill., U.S.A. 42°24N 88°11W 311 B8
Fox Studios Australia 33°55S 151°13E 139 B2
Fox Valley Canada 50°30N 109°25W 297 C7
Foxboro Ont., Canada 44°14N 77°26W 312 B7
Foxboro Mass., U.S.A. 42°4N 71°16W 313 D13
Foxdale Australia 20°22S 148°35E 280 b
Foxe Basin Canada 66°0N 77°0W 295 D16
Foxe Chan. Canada 65°0N 80°0W 295 E16
Foxe Pen. Canada 65°0N 76°0W 295 E16
Foxen Sweden 59°25N 11°55E 162 E5
Foxford Ireland 53°59N 9°7W 166 C2
Foxrock Ireland 53°17N 6°11W 120 B2
Foxton N.Z. 40°29S 175°18E 284 G4
Foyle, Lough U.K. 55°7N 7°4W 166 A4
Foynes Ireland 52°37N 9°7W 166 D2
Foz Spain 43°33N 7°20W 194 B3
Foz do Copeá Brazil 3°52S 63°19W 329 D5
Foz do Cunene Angola 17°15S 11°48E 265 F2
Foz do Gregório Brazil 6°47S 70°44W 330 B3
Foz do Iguaçu Brazil 25°30S 54°30W 335 B5
Foz do Mamoriá Brazil 2°27S 66°32W 328 D4
Frackville U.S.A. 40°47N 75°14W 313 F8
Fraga Spain 41°32N 0°21E 196 D5
Fraile Muerto Uruguay 32°31S 54°32W 335 C5
Framingham U.S.A. 42°18N 71°24W 313 D13
Framnes Iceland 66°1N 20°26W 155 A6
Frampol Poland 50°41N 22°40E 185 H9
Franca Brazil 20°33S 47°30W 333 F2
Francavilla al Mare Italy 42°25N 14°17E 199 F11
Francavilla Fontana Italy 40°32N 17°35E 201 B10
France ■ Europe 47°0N 3°0E 171 C5
Frances Australia 36°41S 140°55E 282 D4
Frances → Canada 60°16N 129°10W 296 A3
Frances L. Canada 61°23N 129°30W 296 A3
Francesville U.S.A. 40°59N 86°53W 311 D10
Franceville Gabon 1°40S 13°32E 264 C2
Franche-Comté □ France 46°50N 5°55E 173 F12
Francis Case, L. U.S.A. 43°4N 98°34W 308 D4
Francisco Beltrão Brazil 26°5S 53°4W 335 B5
Francisco de Orellana Ecuador 0°28S 76°58W 328 D2
Francisco Ignacio Madero Coahuila, Mexico 25°48N 103°18W 318 B4
Francisco Ignacio Madero Durango, Mexico 24°26N 104°18W 318 C4
Francisco Ignacio Madero, Presa Mexico 28°10N 105°37W 318 B3
Francisco Sá Brazil 16°28S 43°30W 333 E3
Francistown Botswana 21°7S 27°33E 271 B4
Francofonte Italy 37°14N 14°53E 201 E7
François Canada 47°35N 56°45W 299 C8
François, B. du Martinique 14°38N 60°54W 322 j
François-Joseph, Chutes Dem. Rep. of the Congo 7°37S 17°17E 265 D3
François L. Canada 54°0N 125°30W 296 C3
Francois Peron △ Australia 25°42S 113°33E 279 E1
Franconia U.S.A. 38°47N 77°7W 143 C2
Francs Pk. U.S.A. 43°58N 109°20W 304 E9
Franeker Neths. 53°12N 5°33E 170 A5
Frank Hann △ Australia 32°52S 120°19E 279 F3
Frank Lloyd Wright Home U.S.A. 41°53N 87°47W 119 B2
Frankel Singapore 1°18N 103°55E 138 B3
Frankenberg Germany 51°3N 8°48E 178 D4
Frankenhöhe ⌂ Germany 49°20N 10°25E 179 F6
Frankenstein = Ząbkowice Śląskie Poland 50°35N 16°50E 185 H3
Frankenwald Germany 50°20N 11°30E 179 E7
Frankenwald ⌂ Germany 50°15N 11°30E 179 E7
Frankfield Jamaica 18°8N 77°22W 320 a
Frankford Ont., Canada 44°12N 77°36W 312 B7
Frankford Mo., U.S.A. 39°29N 91°19W 310 E5
Frankfort Free State, S. Africa 27°17S 28°30E 271 C4
Frankfort Ind., U.S.A. 40°17N 86°31W 311 D10
Frankfort Kans., U.S.A. 39°42N 96°25W 308 F5
Frankfort Ky., U.S.A. 38°12N 84°52W 311 F12
Frankfort N.Y., U.S.A. 43°2N 75°4W 313 C9
Frankfort Ohio, U.S.A. 39°24N 83°11W 311 E13
Frankfurt Brandenburg, Germany 52°20N 14°32E 178 C10
Frankfurt Hessen, Germany 50°7N 8°41E 179 E4
Frankfurt ✕ (FRA) Germany 50°1N 8°34E 179 E4
Fränkische Alb Germany 49°10N 11°23E 179 F7
Fränkische Rezat → Germany 49°11N 11°1E 179 F7
Fränkische Saale → Germany 50°3N 9°42E 179 E5
Fränkische Schweiz Germany 49°50N 11°16E 179 F7
Fränkische Schweiz-Veldensteiner Forst ⌂ Germany 49°45N 11°22E 179 F7
Frankland → Australia 35°0S 116°48E 279 G2
Franklin Ga., U.S.A. 33°17N 85°6W 316 B4
Franklin Ind., U.S.A. 39°29N 86°3W 311 E10
Franklin Ky., U.S.A. 36°43N 86°35W 308 G10
Franklin La., U.S.A. 29°48N 91°30W 314 G9
Franklin Mass., U.S.A. 42°5N 71°24W 313 D13
Franklin N.H., U.S.A. 43°27N 71°39W 313 C13
Franklin N.Y., U.S.A. 42°20N 75°9W 313 D9
Franklin Nebr., U.S.A. 40°6N 98°57W 308 E4
Franklin Ohio, U.S.A. 39°34N 84°18W 311 E12
Franklin Pa., U.S.A. 41°24N 79°50W 312 E5
Franklin Va., U.S.A. 36°41N 76°56W 309 G15
Franklin W. Va., U.S.A. 38°39N 79°20W 309 F14
Franklin, Pt. U.S.A. 70°55N 158°48W 303 A8
Franklin B. Canada 69°45N 126°0W 294 D6
Franklin D. Roosevelt L. U.S.A. 48°18N 118°9W 304 B4
Franklin-Gordon Wild Rivers △ Australia 42°19S 145°51E 281 G4
Franklin Harb. Australia 33°43S 136°55E 282 B2
Franklin I. Antarctica 76°10S 168°30E 151 D11
Franklin I. Ont., Canada 45°24N 80°20W 312 A4
Franklin L. U.S.A. 40°25N 115°22W 304 F6
Franklin Mts. N.W.T., Canada 65°0N 125°0W 294 D6
Franklin Mts. N.Z. 44°55S 167°45E 285 E2
Franklin Park Mass., U.S.A. 42°18N 71°5W 116 B2
Franklin Park Va., U.S.A. 38°55N 77°9W 143 B2
Franklin Res. U.S.A. 34°5N 118°24W 126 B2
Franklin Str. Canada 72°0N 96°0W 294 C12
Franklinton U.S.A. 30°51N 90°9W 315 F9
Franklinville U.S.A. 42°20N 78°27W 312 D6
Franklyn Mt. N.Z. 42°4S 172°42E 285 C7
Franks Pk. U.S.A. 43°58N 109°18W 304 E9
Frankston Australia 38°8S 145°8E 283 E6
Frånö Sweden 62°55N 17°50E 162 B11
Fransfontein Namibia 20°12S 15°1E 270 B2
Fränsta Sweden 62°30N 16°11E 162 B10
Frantsa Iosifa, Zemlya Arctic 82°0N 55°0E 214 A6
Franz Canada 48°25N 84°30W 298 C3
Franz Josef Land = Frantsa Iosifa, Zemlya Arctic 82°0N 55°0E 214 A6
Franz Josef Strauss ✕ (MUC) Germany 48°21N 11°47E 131 A2
Franzburg Germany 54°11N 12°51E 178 A8
Frascati Italy 41°48N 12°41E 199 G9
Fraser U.S.A. 42°32N 82°57W 312 D2
Fraser → B.C., Canada 49°7N 123°11W 306 A3
Fraser → Nfld. & L., Canada 56°39N 62°10W 299 A7
Fraser, Mt. Australia 25°35S 118°20E 279 E2
Fraser I. Australia 25°15S 153°10E 281 D5
Fraser Lake Canada 54°0N 124°50W 296 C4
Fraserburg S. Africa 31°55S 21°30E 270 D3
Fraserburg Road = Leeu Gamka S. Africa 32°47S 21°59E 270 D3
Fraserburgh U.K. 57°42N 2°1W 167 D6
Fraserdale Canada 49°55N 81°37W 298 C3
Fraserpet = Kushalnagar India 12°14N 75°57E 245 H2
Frasertown N.Z. 38°58S 177°28E 284 E6
Fraserville = Rivière-du-Loup Canada 47°50N 69°30W 299 C6
Frashër Albania 40°23N 20°30E 202 F4
Frasne France 46°50N 6°10E 173 F13
Frăteşti Romania 43°58N 25°58E 183 G10
Frauenfeld Switz. 47°34N 8°54E 179 H4
Frauenkirche Munich, Germany 131 b2
Frauenstadt = Wadowice Poland 49°52N 19°30E 185 J6
Fraustadt = Wschowa Poland 51°48N 16°20E 185 G3
Fray Bentos Uruguay 33°10S 58°15W 334 C4
Fray Jorge ⌂ Chile 30°42S 71°40W 334 C1
Frazier Downs ◎ Australia 18°48S 121°42E 278 C3
Frechilla Spain 42°8N 4°50W 194 C6
Fredericia Denmark 55°34N 9°45E 163 J3
Frederick Md., U.S.A. 39°25N 77°25W 309 F15
Frederick Okla., U.S.A. 34°23N 99°1W 314 D5
Frederick S. Dak., U.S.A. 45°50N 98°31W 308 C4
Frederick E. Hyde Fjord Greenland 83°25N 29°0W 154 A8
Fredericksburg Pa., U.S.A. 40°27N 76°26W 313 F8
Fredericksburg Tex., U.S.A. 30°16N 98°52W 314 F5
Fredericksburg Va., U.S.A. 38°18N 77°28W 309 F15
Fredericktown Mo., U.S.A. 37°34N 90°18W 308 G8
Fredericktown Ohio, U.S.A. 40°29N 82°33W 312 F2
Frederico Westphalen Brazil 27°22S 53°24W 335 B5
Fredericton Canada 45°57N 66°40W 299 C6
Fredericton Junction Canada 45°41N 66°40W 299 C6
Frederiksberg Denmark 55°40N 12°32E 118 A3
Frederiksdal Denmark 55°46N 12°25E 118 A2
Frederikshåb = Paamiut Greenland 62°0N 49°43W 154 E6
Frederikshald = Halden Norway 59°9N 11°23E 164 E8
Frederikshamn = Hamina Finland 60°34N 27°12E 188 B4
Frederikshavn Denmark 57°28N 10°31E 163 G4
Frederikssund Denmark 55°50N 12°3E 163 J6
Frederiksted U.S. Virgin Is. 17°43N 64°53W 321 C7
Frederiksværk Denmark 55°58N 12°4E 163 J6
Fredersdorf Germany 52°31N 13°45E 115 A5
Fredonia Ariz., U.S.A. 36°57N 112°32W 305 H7
Fredonia Kans., U.S.A. 37°32N 95°49W 308 G6
Fredonia N.Y., U.S.A. 42°26N 79°20W 312 D5
Fredriksberg Sweden 60°8N 14°23E 162 D8
Fredrikstad Norway 59°13N 10°57E 164 E7
Fredriksvern = Stavern Norway 59°0N 10°1E 164 F7
Free State □ S. Africa 28°30S 27°0E 270 C4
Freeburg U.S.A. 38°19N 91°56W 310 F5
Freehold U.S.A. 40°16N 74°17W 313 F10
Freeland U.S.A. 41°1N 75°54W 313 E9
Freels, C. Nfld. & L., Canada 49°15N 53°30W 299 C9
Freels, C. Nfld. & L., Canada 46°37N 53°32W 299 C9
Freeman Calif., U.S.A. 35°35N 117°53W 307 K9
Freeman Mo., U.S.A. 38°37N 94°30W 310 F2
Freeman S. Dak., U.S.A. 43°21N 97°26W 308 D5
Freeport Bahamas 26°30N 78°47W 320 A4
Freeport Trin. & Tob. 10°27N 61°25W 323 t
Freeport Fla., U.S.A. 30°30N 86°8W 316 E3
Freeport Ill., U.S.A. 42°17N 89°36W 310 B7
Freeport N.Y., U.S.A. 40°39N 73°35W 313 F11
Freeport Ohio, U.S.A. 40°12N 81°15W 312 F3
Freeport Pa., U.S.A. 40°41N 79°41W 312 F5
Freeport Tex., U.S.A. 28°57N 95°21W 314 G7
Freetown Antigua & B. 17°3N 61°42W 322 b
Freetown S. Leone 8°30N 13°17W 262 D2
Freeville U.S.A. 42°30N 76°20W 313 D8
Frégate, L. de la Canada 53°15N 74°45W 298 B5
Fregate Island Nature Reserve St. Lucia 13°52N 60°53W 323 m
Fregenal de la Sierra Spain 38°10N 6°39W 195 G4
Fregene Italy 41°51N 12°12E 199 G9
Fregon Australia 26°45S 132°1E 279 E5
Freguesia Brazil 22°48S 43°10W 135 A1
Fréhel, C. France 48°40N 2°20W 172 D4
Freiberg Germany 50°55N 13°20E 178 E9
Freibourg = Fribourg Switz. 46°49N 7°9E 179 J3
Freiburg Baden-W., Germany 47°59N 7°51E 179 H3
Freiburg Niedersachsen, Germany 53°49N 9°16E 178 B5
Freiburg in Schlesien = Świebodzice Poland 50°51N 16°20E 185 H3
Freidrichshain, Volkspark Germany 52°31N 13°25E 115 A3
Freienwalde = Chociwel Poland 53°29N 15°21E 184 E2
Freiham Germany 48°8N 11°25E 131 B1
Freilassing Germany 47°50N 12°58E 179 H8
Freimann Germany 48°11N 11°37E 131 A2
Freire Chile 38°54S 72°38W 336 A2
Freirina Chile 28°30S 71°10W 334 B1
Freising Germany 48°24N 11°45E 179 G7
Freistadt Austria 48°30N 14°30E 180 C7
Freital Germany 51°1N 13°39E 178 D9
Freiwaldau = Jeseník Czech Rep. 50°14N 17°8E 181 A10
Fréjus France 43°25N 6°44E 175 E10
Fremantle Australia 32°7S 115°47E 279 F2
Fremont Calif., U.S.A. 37°32N 121°57W 306 H4
Fremont Ind., U.S.A. 41°44N 84°56W 311 C12
Fremont Iowa, U.S.A. 41°13N 92°26W 310 C4
Fremont Mich., U.S.A. 43°28N 85°57W 309 D11
Fremont Nebr., U.S.A. 41°26N 96°30W 308 E5
Fremont Ohio, U.S.A. 41°21N 83°7W 311 C13
Fremont → U.S.A. 38°24N 110°42W 304 G8
French Camp U.S.A. 37°53N 121°16W 306 H5
French Cays = Plana Cays Bahamas 22°38N 73°30W 321 B5
French Creek → U.S.A. 41°24N 79°50W 312 E5
French Frigate Shoals U.S.A. 23°45N 166°10W 302 G10
French Guiana ⊠ S. Amer. 4°0N 53°0W 329 C7
French Guinea = Guinea ■ W. Afr. 10°20N 11°30W 262 C2
French I. Australia 38°20S 145°22E 283 E6
French Island △ Australia 38°20S 145°22E 283 E6
French Lick U.S.A. 38°33N 86°37W 311 F10
French Market New Orleans, U.S.A. 131 a3
French Pass N.Z. 40°55S 173°55E 285 A8
French Polynesia ⊠ Pac. Oc. 20°0S 145°0W 289 f
French Quarter New Orleans, U.S.A. 131 a2
French Riviera = Côte d'Azur France 43°25N 7°10E 175 E11
French Sudan = Mali ■ Africa 17°0N 3°0W 262 B4
French Territory of the Afars and Issas = Djibouti ■ Africa 12°0N 43°0E 257 E5
French Togoland = Togo ■ W. Afr. 8°30N 1°35E 263 D5
Frenchburg U.S.A. 37°57N 83°38W 311 G13
Frenchman Cr. → N. Amer. 48°31N 107°10W 304 B10
Frenchman Cr. → Nebr., U.S.A. 40°14N 100°50W 308 E3
Frenda Algeria 35°2N 1°1E 261 A5
Frenštát pod Radhoštěm Czech Rep. 49°33N 18°13E 181 B11
Fresco Ivory C. 5°3N 5°31W 262 D3
Fresco → Brazil 7°15S 51°30W 331 B7
Fresh Pond U.S.A. 42°22N 71°8W 116 A2
Freshfield, C. Antarctica 68°25S 151°10E 151 C10
Fresnay-sur-Sarthe France 48°17N 0°1E 172 D7
Fresnes France 48°45N 2°18E 134 B2
Fresnillo Mexico 23°10N 102°53W 318 C4
Fresno U.S.A. 36°44N 119°47W 306 J7
Fresno Alhándiga Spain 40°42N 5°37W 194 E5
Fresno Res. U.S.A. 48°36N 109°57W 304 B9
Fresvik Norway 61°4N 6°55E 164 C3
Freudenau Austria 48°11N 16°25E 142 A2
Freudenstadt Germany 48°27N 8°24E 179 G4
Freudenthal = Bruntál Czech Rep. 49°59N 17°27E 181 B10
Frévent France 50°15N 2°17E 173 B9
Frew → Australia 20°0S 135°38E 280 C2
Frewsburg U.S.A. 42°3N 79°10W 312 D5
Freycinet ⌂ Australia 42°11S 148°19E 281 G4
Freycinet Pen. Australia 42°10S 148°25E 281 G4
Freyming-Merlebach France 49°8N 6°48E 173 C13
Freystadt = Kisielice Poland 53°36N 19°16E 184 E6
Freystadt = Kożuchów Poland 51°45N 15°31E 185 G2
Freyung Germany 48°48N 13°31E 179 G9
Fria Guinea 10°27N 13°38W 262 C2
Fria, C. Namibia 18°0S 12°0E 270 A1
Friant U.S.A. 36°59N 119°43W 306 J7
Friar's B. St. Kitts & Nevis 17°16N 62°40W 322 d
Friarstown Ireland 53°15N 6°21W 120 B1
Frías Argentina 28°40S 65°5W 334 B2
Fribourg Switz. 46°49N 7°9E 179 J3
Fribourg □ Switz. 46°40N 7°0E 179 J3
Frick Collection New York, U.S.A. 132 b3
Fridafors Sweden 56°25N 14°39E 163 H8
Friday Harbor U.S.A. 48°32N 123°1W 306 B3
Friedberg Bayern, Germany 48°21N 10°59E 179 G6
Friedberg Hessen, Germany 50°19N 8°45E 179 E4
Friedeberg = Mirsk Poland 50°58N 15°23E 185 H2
Friedeberg in Neumark = Strzelce Krajeńskie Poland 52°52N 15°33E 185 F2
Friedenau Germany 52°28N 13°22E 115 B3
Friedens U.S.A. 40°3N 78°59W 312 F6
Friedland = Mieroszów Poland 50°40N 16°11E 185 H3
Friedland = Pravdinsk Russia 56°29N 43°28E 190 B6
Friedland Germany 53°40N 13°33E 178 B9
Friedrichsfelde Germany 52°29N 13°33E 115 B4
Friedrichshafen Germany 47°39N 9°30E 179 H5
Friedrichshagen Germany 52°27N 13°37E 115 B4
Friedrichshain Germany 52°31N 13°25E 115 A3
Friedrichskoog Germany 54°1N 8°53E 178 A4
Friedrichslust Germany 52°33N 13°43E 115 A5
Friedrichstadt Germany 54°23N 9°6E 178 A5
Friendly Is. = Tonga ■ Pac. Oc. 19°50S 174°30W 287 P13
Friendship U.S.A. 42°12N 78°8W 312 D6
Friesach Austria 46°57N 14°24E 180 E7
Friesack Germany 52°44N 12°34E 178 C8
Friesland □ Neths. 53°5N 5°50E 170 A5
Friesoythe Germany 53°1N 7°51E 178 B3
Frigate Seychelles 4°35S 55°56E 272 c
Frigate Bay St. Kitts & Nevis 17°16N 62°41W 322 d
Frigate I. Grenada 12°25N 61°29W 323 q
Friggesund Sweden 61°54N 16°33E 162 C10
Friherrs Finland 60°16N 24°49E 121 B1
Frillesås Sweden 57°20N 12°12E 163 G6
Frilufts Museum Finland 60°11N 24°52E 121 B2
Frinnaryd Sweden 57°55N 14°50E 163 G8
Frio → U.S.A. 28°26N 98°11W 314 G5
Frio, C. Brazil 22°50S 41°50W 326 F6
Friol Spain 43°2N 7°47W 194 B3
Friona U.S.A. 34°38N 102°43W 314 D3
Frisches Haff = Zalew Wiślany Poland 54°20N 19°50E 184 D6
Frisco U.S.A. 33°8N 96°49W 314 E6
Fristad Sweden 57°50N 13°0E 163 G6
Fritch U.S.A. 35°38N 101°36W 314 D4
Fritsla Sweden 57°33N 12°47E 163 G6
Fritzlar Germany 51°7N 9°16E 178 D5
Friuli-Venézia Giulia □ Italy 46°0N 13°0E 199 C10
Frobisher B. Canada 62°30N 66°0W 295 E18
Frobisher Bay = Iqaluit Canada 63°44N 68°31W 295 E18
Frobisher L. Canada 56°20N 108°15W 297 B7
Frohavet Norway 64°0N 9°30E 160 E13
Frohenbruck = Veselí nad Lužnicí Czech Rep. 49°12N 14°43E 180 B7
Frohnleiten Austria 47°16N 15°19E 180 D8
Frolovo Russia 49°45N 43°40E 190 F6
Frombork Poland 54°21N 19°41E 184 D6
Frome U.K. 51°14N 2°19W 169 F5
Frome → U.K. 50°41N 2°6W 169 G5
Frome, L. Australia 30°45S 139°45E 282 A3
Frome Downs Australia 31°13S 139°45E 282 A3
Frómista Spain 42°16N 4°25W 194 C6
Front Range U.S.A. 40°25N 105°45W 304 F11
Front Royal U.S.A. 38°55N 78°12W 309 F14
Fronteira Portugal 39°3N 7°39W 195 F3
Fronteiras Brazil 7°5S 40°37W 332 C3
Frontenac ⌂ Canada 44°32N 76°30W 313 B8
Frontera Canary Is. 27°47N 17°59W 153 e1
Frontera Tabasco, Mexico 18°32N 92°38W 319 D6
Fronteras Mexico 30°56N 109°31W 318 A3
Frontignan France 43°27N 3°45E 174 E7
Frontón, I. Peru 12°7S 77°11W 124 B1
Frosinone Italy 41°38N 13°19E 200 A6
Frostburg U.S.A. 39°39N 78°56W 309 F14
Frostisen Norway 68°14N 17°10E 160 B17
Frostproof U.S.A. 27°45N 81°32W 317 H8
Frouard France 48°47N 6°8E 173 D13
Frövi Sweden 59°28N 15°24E 162 E9
Frøya Norway 63°43N 8°40E 160 E13
Fruita U.S.A. 39°9N 108°44W 304 G9
Fruithurst U.S.A. 33°44N 85°26W 316 B4
Fruitland Park U.S.A. 28°51N 81°54W 317 G8
Frumoasa Romania 46°28N 25°48E 183 D10
Frunze = Bishkek Kyrgyzstan 42°54N 74°46E 217 D8
Frunze Russia 55°47N 37°33E 129 B2
Frunzivka Ukraine 47°20N 29°45E 183 C14
Fruška Gora Serbia 45°7N 19°30E 182 E4
Fruška Gora ⌂ Serbia 45°8N 19°40E 202 A3
Frutal Brazil 20°0S 49°0W 333 F2
Frutigen Switz. 46°35N 7°38E 179 J3
Frýdek-Místek Czech Rep. 49°40N 18°20E 181 B11
Frýdlant Czech Rep. 50°56N 15°9E 180 A8
Fryeburg U.S.A. 44°1N 70°59W 313 B14
Fryvaldov = Jeseník Czech Rep. 50°14N 17°8E 181 A10
Fthiotida □ Greece 38°50N 22°25E 204 C4
Fu Jiang → China 30°0N 106°16E 228 C6
Fu Xian = Wafangdian China 39°38N 121°58E 227 E11
Fu Xian China 36°0N 109°20E 226 G5
Fua Mulaku Maldives 0°17S 73°26E 272 d
Fu'an China 27°11N 119°36E 229 D12
Fubian China 31°17N 102°22E 228 B4
Fucécchio Italy 43°44N 10°48E 198 E7
Fucheng China 37°50N 116°10E 226 F9
Fuchou = Fuzhou China 26°5N 119°16E 229 D12
Fuchū Hiroshima, Japan 34°34N 133°14E 222 C5
Fuchū Tōkyō, Japan 35°40N 139°29E 140 A1
Fuchuan China 24°50N 111°5E 229 E8
Fuchun Jiang → China 30°5N 120°5E 229 B13
Fúcino, Piana del Italy 41°2N 13°31E 199 F10
Fuding China 27°20N 120°12E 229 D13
Fuencaliente Canary Is. 28°28N 17°50W 153 e1
Fuencaliente Spain 38°25N 4°18W 195 G6
Fuencaliente, Pta. Canary Is. 28°27N 17°51W 153 e1
Fuencarral Spain 40°29N 3°42W 127 B1
Fuengirola Spain 36°32N 4°41W 195 J6
Fuenlabrada Spain 40°17N 3°48W 127 C1
Fuensalida Spain 40°3N 4°12W 194 E6
Fuente-Álamo Spain 38°44N 1°24W 197 G3
Fuente Álamo de Murcia Spain 37°42N 1°6W 197 H3
Fuente de Cantos Spain 38°15N 6°18W 195 G4
Fuente del Maestre Spain 38°31N 6°28W 195 G4
Fuente el Fresno Spain 39°14N 3°46W 195 F7
Fuente Obejuna Spain 38°15N 5°25W 195 G5
Fuente Palmera Spain 37°42N 5°6W 195 H5
Fuentes de Andalucía Spain 37°28N 5°20W 195 H5
Fuentes de Ebro Spain 41°31N 0°38W 196 D4
Fuentes de León Spain 38°5N 6°32W 195 G4
Fuentes de Oñoro Spain 40°33N 6°52W 194 E4
Fuentesaúco Spain 41°15N 5°30W 194 D5
Fuerte → Mexico 25°54N 109°22W 318 B3
Fuerte Olimpo Paraguay 21°0S 57°51W 334 A4
Fuerteventura Canary Is. 28°30N 14°0W 153 e2
Fuerteventura ✕ (FUE) Canary Is. 28°24N 13°52W 153 e2
Fufeng China 34°22N 108°0E 226 G5
Fuga I. Phil. 18°52N 121°20E 232 B3
Fugong China 27°5N 98°47E 228 D2
Fugou China 34°3N 114°25E 226 G8
Fugu China 39°2N 111°3E 226 E6
Fuhai China 47°2N 87°25E 217 C11
Fuḩaymī Iraq 34°16N 42°10E 213 E10
Fuhlsbüttel, Hamburg ✕ (HAM) Germany 53°35N 9°59E 178 B5
Fuhsien = Fu Xian China 33°0N 109°20E 226 G5
Fuhsing Changhua, Taiwan 24°3N 120°25E 225 B2
Fuhsing Kaohsiung, Taiwan 23°13N 120°48E 225 C2
Fuhsing Taoyüan, Taiwan 24°49N 121°21E 225 B3
Fuidhaigh = Wiay U.K. 57°24N 7°13W 167 D1
Fuji Japan 35°9N 138°39E 223 B10
Fuji-Hakone-Izu △ Japan 35°15N 138°45E 223 B10
Fuji-San Japan 35°22N 138°44E 223 B10
Fuji-Yoshida Japan 35°30N 138°46E 223 B10
Fujian □ China 26°0N 118°0E 229 E12
Fujieda Japan 34°52N 138°16E 223 C10
Fujin China 47°16N 132°1E 219 B15
Fujinomiya Japan 35°10N 138°40E 223 B10
Fujioka Japan 36°15N 139°5E 223 A11
Fujisawa Japan 35°22N 139°29E 223 B11
Fujiyama, Mt. = Fuji-San Japan 35°22N 138°44E 223 B10
Fukagawa Hokkaidō, Japan 43°43N 142°2E 220 C11
Fukagawa Tōkyō, Japan 35°39N 139°48E 140 B3
Fukang China 44°10N 87°59E 217 D11
Fukaya Japan 36°12N 139°12E 223 A11
Fukiage Japan 31°27N 130°17E 222 F2
Fukiage Imperial Garden Tokyo, Japan 140 a4
Fukien = Fujian □ China 26°0N 118°0E 229 E12
Fukuchiyama Japan 35°19N 135°9E 223 B7
Fukue Japan 32°41N 128°51E 221 H4
Fukue-Shima Japan 32°40N 128°45E 221 H4
Fukuei Chiao Taiwan 25°17N 121°32E 225 A3
Fukui Japan 36°5N 136°10E 223 A8
Fukui □ Japan 36°0N 136°12E 223 B8
Fukuma Japan 33°46N 130°28E 222 D2
Fukuoka Japan 33°39N 130°21E 222 D2
Fukuoka □ Japan 33°30N 131°0E 222 D3
Fukuoka Int. ✕ (FUK) Japan 33°34N 130°28E 222 D2
Fukuroi Japan 34°45N 137°55E 223 C9
Fukushima Fukushima, Japan 37°44N 140°28E 220 F10
Fukushima Ōsaka, Japan 34°41N 135°28E 133 A1
Fukushima □ Japan 37°30N 140°15E 220 F10
Fukuyama Japan 34°35N 133°20E 222 C5
Ful Bura South Sudan 7°50N 31°50E 257 F3
Fulacunda Guinea-Biss. 11°44N 15°3W 262 C1
Fulaga Fiji 19°8S 178°33W 287 B3
Fulan → Sweden 61°18N 13°4E 162 C7
Fulda Germany 50°32N 9°40E 178 E5
Fulda → Germany 51°25N 9°39E 178 D5
Fulford = North Miami Beach U.S.A. 25°55N 80°9W 129 C2
Fulford Harbour Canada 48°47N 123°27W 306 B3
Fulham U.K. 51°28N 0°12W 125 B2
Fuli Taiwan 23°1N 121°1E 225 C3
Fuliang China 29°23N 117°14E 229 C11
Fuling China 29°39N 107°17E 228 C6
Fullarton Trin. & Tob. 10°5N 61°54W 323 t
Fullerton Calif., U.S.A. 33°53N 117°56W 307 M9
Fullerton Nebr., U.S.A. 41°22N 97°58W 308 E5
Fulongquan China 44°20N 124°42E 227 B13
Fülöpszállás Hungary 46°49N 19°15E 182 D4
Fulton Ill., U.S.A. 41°52N 90°11W 310 C6
Fulton Ind., U.S.A. 40°57N 86°16W 311 D10
Fulton Mo., U.S.A. 38°52N 91°57W 310 F5
Fulton N.Y., U.S.A. 43°19N 76°25W 313 C8
Fulufjället Sweden 61°32N 12°41E 162 C6
Fumay France 49°58N 4°40E 173 C11
Fumel France 44°30N 0°58E 174 D4
Fumin China 25°10N 102°20E 228 E4
Funabashi Japan 35°45N 140°0E 223 B12
Funabori Japan 35°41N 139°52E 140 A4
Funafuti = Fongafale Tuvalu 8°31S 179°13E 277 B14
Funafuti Pac. Oc. 8°31S 179°13E 277 B14
Funan China 32°39N 115°42E 229 A10
Funäsdalen Sweden 62°33N 12°32E 162 B6
Funchal Madeira 32°38N 16°54W 153 c
Funchal ✕ (FNC) Madeira 32°42N 16°45W 153 c
Fundación Colombia 10°31N 74°11W 328 A3
Fundão Brazil 19°55S 40°24W 333 E3
Fundão Portugal 40°8N 7°30W 194 E3
Fundão, I. do Brazil 22°51S 43°13W 135 B1
Fundong Cameroon 6°15N 10°16E 264 A2
Fundu Moldovei Romania 47°32N 25°24E 183 C10
Fundulea Romania 44°28N 26°31E 183 F11
Fundy, B. of Canada 45°0N 66°0W 299 D6
Fundy △ Canada 45°35N 65°10W 299 C6
Fünfhaus Austria 48°11N 16°20E 142 A2
Fünfkirchen = Pécs Hungary 46°5N 18°15E 182 D3
Funhalouro Mozam. 23°3S 34°25E 271 B5
Funing Hebei, China 39°53N 119°12E 227 E10
Funing Jiangsu, China 33°45N 119°50E 227 H10
Funing Yunnan, China 23°35N 105°45E 228 F5
Funiu Shan China 33°30N 112°20E 226 H7
Funsi Ghana 10°21N 1°54W 262 C4
Funtua Nigeria 11°30N 7°18E 263 C6
Fuping Hebei, China 38°48N 114°12E 226 E8
Fuping Shaanxi, China 34°42N 109°10E 226 G5
Fuqing China 25°41N 119°21E 229 E12
Fuquan China 26°40N 107°27E 228 D6
Furano Japan 43°21N 142°23E 220 C11
Furāt, Nahr al → Asia 31°0N 47°25E 246 D5
Fureso Denmark 55°47N 12°25E 118 A2
Fūrg Iran 28°18N 55°13E 247 D7
Furkating India 26°28N 93°59E 241 B4
Furman U.S.A. 32°41N 81°11W 316 C8
Furmanov Russia 57°10N 41°9E 190 B5
Furnas Azores 37°46N 25°19W 153 d3
Furnás Spain 39°3N 1°32E 206 C2
Furnas, Represa de Brazil 20°50S 45°30W 333 F2
Furneaux Group Australia 40°10S 147°50E 281 G4
Furqlus Syria 34°36N 37°8E 250 D8
Fürstenau Germany 52°31N 7°40E 178 C3
Fürstenberg = Eisenhüttenstadt Germany 52°9N 14°38E 178 C10
Fürstenberg Germany 53°10N 13°8E 178 B9
Fürstenfeld Austria 47°3N 16°3E 180 D9
Fürstenfeldbruck Germany 48°10N 11°15E 179 G7
Fürstenwalde Germany 52°22N 14°3E 178 C10
Fürth Mittelfranken, Germany 49°28N 10°59E 179 F6
Fürth Oberbayern, Germany 48°2N 11°35E 131 B2
Fürth im Wald Germany 49°18N 12°50E 179 F8
Furtwangen Germany 48°2N 8°12E 179 G4
Furudal Sweden 61°10N 15°11E 162 C9
Furukawa = Hida Japan 36°14N 137°11E 223 A9

Furukawa = Ōsaki
Japan 38°34N 140°58E 220 E10
Furulund Sweden 55°46N 13°6E 163 J7
Furuvik Sweden 61°38N 17°20E 162 D11
Fury and Hecla Str.
Canada 69°56N 84°0W 295 D15
Fusagasugá Colombia 4°21N 74°22W 328 C3
Fuscaldo Italy 39°25N 16°2E 201 C9
Fushan Shandong, China 37°30N 121°15E 227 F11
Fushan Shanxi, China 35°58N 111°51E 226 G6
Fushë Arrëz Albania 42°4N 20°2E 202 D4
Fushë Kosovë Kosovo 42°40N 21°5E 202 D5
Fushë Krujë Albania 41°29N 19°43E 202 E3
Fushun Liaoning, China 41°50N 123°56E 224 B11
Fushun Sichuan, China 29°13N 104°52E 228 C5
Fusong China 42°20N 127°15E 224 A3
Füssen Germany 47°34N 10°42E 179 H6
Fusui China 22°40N 107°56E 228 F6
Futago-tamagawaen
Japan 35°36N 139°39E 140 B2
Futago-Yama Japan 33°35N 131°36E 222 D3
Futian China 22°32N 114°4E 219 a
Futiga Amer. Samoa 14°21S 170°45W 302 f
Futog Serbia 45°15N 19°42E 182 E4
Futrono Chile 40°8S 72°24W 336 B2
Futtsu Japan 35°13N 139°49E 223 B11
Fuwa Egypt 31°12N 30°33E 256 H7
Fuxian Hu China 24°30N 102°53E 228 E4
Fuxin China 42°5N 121°48E 227 C11
Fuxing Dao China 31°16N 121°33E 138 B2
Fuxing Park China 31°13N 121°27E 138 B1
Fuxinglu China 39°52N 116°16E 114 B1
Fuyang Anhui, China 33°0N 115°48E 226 H8
Fuyang Zhejiang, China 30°5N 119°57E 229 B12
Fuyang He → China 38°12N 117°0E 226 E9
Fuying Dao China 26°34N 120°9E 229 D13
Fuyong China 22°40N 113°49E 219 a
Fuyot Springs △ Phil. 17°1N 121°58E 232 C3
Fuyu Heilongjiang, China 47°49N 124°27E 219 B13
Fuyu Jilin, China 45°12N 124°43E 227 B13
Fuyuan China 25°40N 104°16E 228 E5
Fuyun China 47°0N 89°28E 217 C11
Füzesgyarmat Hungary 47°6N 21°14E 182 C6
Fuzhou = Linchuan
China 27°57N 116°15E 229 D11
Fuzhou China 26°5N 119°16E 229 D12
Füzuli Azerbaijan 39°36N 47°8E 213 C12
Fyn Denmark 55°20N 10°30E 163 J4
Fyne, L. U.K. 55°59N 5°23W 167 F3
Fynshav Denmark 54°59N 9°59E 163 K3
Fyresdal Norway 59°11N 8°5E 164 E5
Fyresvatn Norway 59°6N 8°10E 164 E5
Fyzabad = Faizabad India 26°45N 82°10E 243 F10
Fyzabad Trin. & Tob. 10°12N 61°33W 323 t

G

G. Ross Lord Park Canada 43°47N 79°28W 141 A2
Ga Ghana 9°47N 2°30W 262 D4
Ga-eun S. Korea 36°38N 128°5E 224 D4
Gaa Faru Atoll Maldives 4°45N 73°26E 272 d
Gaalkacyo Somalia 6°30N 47°30E 267 C6
Gaanda Nigeria 10°10N 12°27E 263 C7
Gabaldon Phil. 15°37N 121°20E 232 D3
Gabas → France 43°46N 0°42W 174 E3
Gabba Australia 9°45S 142°38E 280 a
Gabela Angola 11°0S 14°24E 265 E2
Gaberones = Gaborone
Botswana 24°45S 25°57E 270 B4
Gabès Tunisia 33°53N 10°2E 258 B2
Gabès □ Tunisia 33°35N 9°30E 261 B6
Gabès, G. de Tunisia 34°0N 10°30E 258 B2
Gabgaba, W. → Egypt 22°10N 33°5E 256 C3
Gabia Dem. Rep. of the Congo 4°37S 17°14E 265 C3
Gabia la Grande Spain 37°8N 3°40W 195 H7
Gąbin Poland 52°23N 19°41E 185 F6
Gablonz = Jablonec nad Nisou
Czech Rep. 50°43N 15°10E 180 A8
Gabon ■ Africa 0°10S 10°0E 264 C2
Gabon → Gabon 0°25N 9°20E 264 B1
Gaborone Botswana 24°45S 25°57E 270 B4
Gabrat Sa'id Sudan 16°16N 31°50E 266 A3
Gabriels U.S.A. 44°26N 74°12W 313 B10
Gābrīk Iran 25°44N 58°28E 247 E8
Gabro Ethiopia 6°18N 43°16E 267 C5
Gabrovo Bulgaria 42°52N 25°19E 203 D9
Gabú = Nova Lamego
Guinea-Biss. 12°19N 14°11W 262 C2
Gacé France 48°49N 0°20E 172 D7
Gāch Sār Iran 36°7N 51°19E 247 B6
Gachsārān Iran 30°15N 50°45E 247 D6
Gacko Bos.-H. 43°10N 18°33E 202 C2
Gad Hinglaj India 16°14N 74°21E 245 F2
Gadag India 15°30N 75°45E 245 G2
Gadaisu Papua N. G. 10°22S 149°46E 286 F5
Gadamai Sudan 17°11N 36°10E 257 D4
Gadap Pakistan 25°5N 67°28E 242 G2
Gadarwara India 22°50N 78°50E 243 H8
Gadebusch Germany 53°42N 11°7E 178 B7
Gadein South Sudan 8°10N 28°45E 257 F2
Gadhada India 22°0N 71°35E 242 J4
Gadis → Indonesia 1°2N 98°55E 234 B1
Gádor, Sierra de Spain 36°57N 2°45W 195 J8
Gadra Pakistan 25°40N 70°38E 242 G4
Gadsden Ala., U.S.A. 34°1N 86°1W 316 A3
Gadsden S.C., U.S.A. 33°51N 80°46W 316 B9
Gadwal India 16°10N 77°50E 245 F3
Gadyach = Hadyach
Ukraine 50°21N 34°0E 189 G8
Gadzi C.A.R. 4°47N 16°42E 264 B3
Gaebong S. Korea 37°29N 126°52E 137 C1
Găeşti Romania 44°48N 25°19E 183 F10
Gaeta Italy 41°12N 13°35E 200 A6
Gaeta, G. di Italy 41°6N 13°30E 200 A6
Gaffney U.S.A. 35°5N 81°39W 315 D14
Gafsa Tunisia 34°24N 8°43E 258 B1
Gafsa □ Tunisia 34°30N 8°48E 261 B6
Gagarawa Nigeria 12°25N 9°32E 263 C6
Gagarin India 25°43N 70°46E 242 G4
Gagarin Russia 55°38N 35°0E 188 E8
Găgăuzia □ Moldova 46°10N 28°40E 183 D13
Gage Park U.S.A. 41°47N 87°42W 119 C2
Gaggenau Germany 48°48N 8°18E 179 G4
Gaghamni Sudan 11°41N 28°19E 257 E2
Gagil-Tomil, I. Pac. Oc. 9°31N 138°12E 287 R16
Gagino Russia 55°15N 45°1E 190 C7
Gagliano del Capo Italy 39°50N 18°22E 201 C11
Gagnef Sweden 60°36N 15°5E 162 D9
Gagnoa Ivory C. 6°56N 5°16W 262 D3
Gagnon Canada 51°50N 68°5W 299 B6
Gagnon, L. Canada 62°3N 110°27W 297 A6
Gagny France 48°53N 2°32E 144 A2
Gago Coutinho
São Tomé & Principe 0°1S 6°32E 265 a
Gagra Georgia 43°20N 40°10E 191 J5
Gahini Rwanda 1°50S 30°30E 268 C3
Gahmar India 25°27N 83°49E 243 G10
Gai Xian = Gaizhou
China 40°22N 122°20E 224 B1
Gaibandha Bangla. 25°20N 89°36E 241 C2
Gaidouronisi Greece 34°53N 25°41E 207 F6
Gail U.S.A. 32°46N 101°27W 314 E4
Gail → Austria 46°36N 13°53E 180 E6
Gaillac France 43°54N 1°54E 174 E5
Gaillard Cut Panama 9°3N 79°40W 320 c
Gaillimh = Galway Ireland 53°17N 9°3W 166 C2
Gaillon France 49°10N 1°20E 172 C8
Gaimán Argentina 43°10S 65°25W 336 B3
Gaines U.S.A. 41°46N 77°35W 312 E7
Gainesville Fla., U.S.A. 29°40N 82°20W 317 F7
Gainesville Ga., U.S.A. 34°18N 83°50W 315 D13
Gainesville Mo., U.S.A. 36°36N 92°26W 308 G7
Gainesville Tex., U.S.A. 33°38N 97°8W 314 E6
Gainsborough U.K. 53°24N 0°46W 168 D7
Gairdner, L. Australia 31°30S 136°0E 282 A2
Gairloch U.K. 57°43N 5°41W 167 D3
Gairloch, L. U.K. 57°43N 5°45W 167 D3
Gaizhou China 40°22N 122°20E 224 B1
Gaj Croatia 45°28N 17°3E 182 E2
Gaj → Pakistan 26°26N 67°21E 242 F2
Gajendragarh India 15°44N 75°59E 245 G2
Gakona U.S.A. 62°18N 145°18W 303 E11
Gakuch Pakistan 36°7N 73°45E 243 A5
Gal Oya △ Sri Lanka 7°0N 81°20E 245 L5
Gal Oya Res. Sri Lanka 7°5N 81°30E 245 L5
Gal Tardo Somalia 3°34N 45°58E 267 D6
Galachipa Bangla. 22°8N 90°26E 241 D3
Galâla, Gebel el Egypt 29°21N 32°22E 256 J8
Galâla el Baharîya, G. el
Egypt 29°22N 32°23E 251 J3
Galâla el Qiblîya, G. el
Egypt 28°42N 32°22E 251 K3
Galán, Cerro Argentina 25°55S 66°52W 334 B2
Galana → Kenya 3°9S 40°8E 268 C5
Galangue Angola 13°42S 16°9E 265 E3
Galangue, Serra Angola 14°18S 15°22E 265 E3
Galanta Slovak Rep. 48°11N 17°45E 181 C10
Galapagar Spain 40°36N 3°58W 194 E7
Galápagos = Colón, Arch. de
Ecuador 0°0 91°0W 330 a
Galapagos Fracture Zone
Pac. Oc. 3°0N 110°0W 289 G17
Galapagos Rise Pac. Oc. 15°0S 95°0W 289 J18
Galashiels U.K. 55°37N 2°49W 167 F6
Galata Turkey 41°1N 28°58E 122 B1
Galata Tower Turkey 41°1N 28°59E 122 B1
Galatas Greece 37°30N 23°26E 204 D5
Galatea N.Z. 38°24S 176°45E 284 E5
Galateia Cyprus 35°25N 34°4E 207 E10
Galaţi Romania 45°27N 28°2E 183 E13
Galaţi □ Romania 45°45N 27°30E 183 E12
Galatia Turkey 39°30N 33°0E 212 C5
Galatina Italy 40°10N 18°10E 201 B11
Galátone Italy 40°9N 18°4E 201 B11
Galatsi Greece 38°1N 23°45E 112 A2
Galax U.S.A. 36°40N 80°56W 309 G13
Galaxidi Greece 38°22N 22°23E 204 C4
Galbīn Govĭ Mongolia 43°0N 107°0E 226 C4
Galcaio = Gaalkacyo
Somalia 6°30N 47°30E 267 C6
Gáldar Canary Is. 28°9N 15°39W 153 e1
Galdhøpiggen Norway 61°38N 8°18E 164 C5
Galeana Chihuahua,
Mexico 30°7N 107°38W 318 A3
Galeana Nuevo León,
Mexico 24°50N 100°4W 318 A3
Galeão, Int. de ✕ (GIG)
Brazil 22°49S 43°15W 135 A1
Galegu Sudan 12°36N 35°2E 257 E4
Galela Indonesia 1°50N 127°49E 231 D7
Galena Alaska, U.S.A. 64°44N 156°56W 303 D8
Galena Ill., U.S.A. 42°25N 90°26W 310 B6
Galeota Pt. Trin. & Tob. 10°8N 60°59W 323 t
Galera Spain 37°45N 2°33W 197 H2
Galera, Pta. Chile 39°59S 73°43W 336 A2
Galera, Pta. da Azores 37°42N 25°30W 153 d3
Galera Pt. Trin. & Tob. 10°49N 60°54W 323 t
Galesburg Ill., U.S.A. 40°57N 90°22W 310 D6
Galesburg Mich., U.S.A. 42°17N 85°26W 311 B11
Galestan △ Iran 37°30N 56°0E 247 B8
Galeton U.S.A. 41°44N 77°39W 312 E7
Galets → Réunion 20°56S 55°17E 272 f
Galga Ethiopia 6°39N 37°47E 257 F4
Galgasc Somalia 0°11N 41°38E 267 D5
Galguduud □ Somalia 5°0N 47°0E 267 D6
Galheirão → Brazil 12°23S 45°5W 333 D2
Gali Georgia 42°37N 41°46E 191 J5
Galicea Mare Romania 44°4N 23°19E 183 F8
Galich Russia 58°22N 42°24E 190 A6
Galiche Bulgaria 43°34N 23°53E 202 C7
Galicia □ Spain 42°43N 7°45W 194 C3
Galičica △ Macedonia 41°2N 20°55E 202 E4
Galien U.S.A. 41°48N 86°30W 311 C10
Galilee = Hagalil Israel 32°53N 35°18E 250 F6
Galilee, L. Australia 22°20S 145°50E 280 C4
Galilee, Sea of = Yam Kinneret
Israel 32°45N 35°35E 250 F6
Galim Cameroon 7°6N 12°25E 263 D7
Galina Pt. Jamaica 18°24N 76°58W 320 a
Galinoporni Cyprus 35°31N 34°18E 207 E10
Galion U.S.A. 40°44N 82°47W 312 F2
Galion, B. du Martinique 14°44N 60°56W 322 j
Galite, Îs. de la Tunisia 37°30N 8°59E 261 A6
Galiuro Mts. U.S.A. 32°30N 110°20W 305 K8
Galiwinku Australia 12°2S 135°34E 280 A2
Gallābāt Sudan 12°58N 36°11E 257 E4
Gallan Hd. U.K. 58°15N 7°2W 167 C1
Gallarate Italy 45°40N 8°48E 198 C5
Gallatin Mo., U.S.A. 39°55N 93°58W 310 E3
Gallatin Tenn., U.S.A. 36°24N 86°27W 315 C11
Galle Sri Lanka 6°5N 80°10E 245 L5
Gállego → Spain 41°39N 0°51W 196 D4
Gallegos → Argentina 51°35S 69°0W 336 D3
Gallery of Inuit Art = Dominion
Centre Toronto, Canada 141 b2
Galletti → Ethiopia 8°46N 41°10E 257 F5
Galley Hd. Ireland 51°32N 8°55W 166 E3
Galliate Italy 45°29N 8°42E 198 C5
Gallinas, Pta. Colombia 12°28N 71°40W 328 A3
Gallipoli = Gelibolu
Turkey 40°28N 26°43E 203 F10
Gallípoli Italy 40°3N 17°58E 201 B10
Gallipolis U.S.A. 38°49N 82°12W 309 F12
Gällivare Sweden 67°9N 20°40E 160 C19
Gallneukirchen Austria 48°21N 14°25E 180 C7
Gällö Sweden 62°55N 15°13E 162 B9
Gallo, C. Italy 38°13N 13°19E 200 D6
Gallocanta, L. de Spain 40°58N 1°30W 196 E3
Galloo I. U.S.A. 43°55N 76°25W 313 C8
Galloway U.K. 55°1N 4°29W 167 F4
Galloway, Mull of U.K. 54°39N 4°52W 167 G4
Gallup U.S.A. 35°32N 108°45W 305 J9
Gallur Spain 41°52N 1°19W 196 D3
Galma Galla Kenya 1°11S 40°47E 267 E5
Galmudug Somalia 6°30N 48°0E 267 C6
Galong Australia 34°37S 148°34E 283 C8
Galool Somalia 3°38N 43°49E 267 D5
Galoya Sri Lanka 8°10N 80°55E 245 K5
Galt Calif., U.S.A. 38°15N 121°18W 306 G5
Galt Mo., U.S.A. 40°8N 93°23W 310 D3
Galten Denmark 56°9N 9°54E 163 H3
Galtür Austria 46°58N 10°11E 180 E3
Galty Mts. Ireland 52°22N 8°10W 166 D3
Galtymore Ireland 52°21N 8°11W 166 D3
Galugāh Iran 36°43N 53°48E 247 B7
Galva U.S.A. 41°10N 90°3W 310 C6
Galvarino Chile 38°24S 72°47W 336 A2
Galve de Sorbe Spain 41°13N 3°10W 196 D1
Galveston Ind., U.S.A. 40°35N 86°11W 311 D10
Galveston Tex., U.S.A. 29°18N 94°48W 314 G7
Galveston B. U.S.A. 29°36N 94°50W 314 G7
Gálvez Argentina 32°0S 61°14W 334 C3
Galway Ireland 53°17N 9°3W 166 C2
Galway □ Ireland 53°22N 9°1W 166 C2
Galway B. Ireland 53°13N 9°10W 166 C2
Galyanovo Russia 55°48N 37°47E 129 B3
Gam → Vietnam 21°55N 105°12E 236 B5
Gamagōri Japan 34°50N 137°14E 223 C9
Gamari, L. Ethiopia 11°32N 41°40E 257 E5
Gamawa Nigeria 12°10N 10°31E 263 C7
Gamay Phil. 12°23N 125°18E 232 E5
Gamay B. Phil. 12°21N 125°21E 232 E5
Gamba Angola 11°42S 17°14E 265 E3
Gambaga Ghana 10°30N 0°28W 263 C4
Gambat Pakistan 27°17N 68°26E 242 F3
Gambela Ethiopia 8°14N 34°38E 257 F3
Gambela △ Ethiopia 8°0N 34°0E 257 F3
Gambela Hizboch □ Ethiopia 8°0N 34°0E 257 F3
Gambell U.S.A. 63°47N 171°45W 303 E5
Gambhir → India 26°58N 77°27E 242 F6
Gambia ■ W. Afr. 13°25N 16°0W 262 C1
Gambia → W. Afr. 13°28N 16°34W 262 C1
Gambier U.S.A. 40°22N 82°23W 312 F2
Gambier, C. Australia 11°56S 130°57E 278 B5
Gambier, Îs.
French Polynesia 23°8S 134°58W 289 f
Gambier Is. Australia 35°3S 136°30E 282 C2
Gambier Village Bahamas 25°4N 77°30W 153 b
Gambir Indonesia 6°9S 106°48E 122 A1
Gambo C.A.R. 4°39N 22°16E 264 B4
Gambo Canada 48°47N 54°13W 299 C9
Gamboa Rio de J., Brazil 22°53S 43°11W 135 B1
Gamboa Panama 9°7N 79°42W 320 c
Gamboli Pakistan 29°53N 68°24E 242 E3
Gambolòita Italy 45°26N 9°13E 128 B2
Gamboma Congo 1°55S 15°52E 264 C3
Gamboula C.A.R. 4°8N 15°9E 264 B3
Gamka → S. Africa 33°18S 21°39E 270 D3
Gamkab → Namibia 28°4S 17°54E 270 C2
Gamla Stan Stockholm, Sweden 139 c2
Gamla Uppsala Sweden 59°54N 17°40E 162 E11
Gamlakarleby = Kokkola
Finland 63°50N 23°8E 160 E20
Gamleby Sweden 57°54N 16°24E 163 G10
Gamlebyen Norway 59°54N 10°46E 133 A3
Gammon → Canada 51°24N 95°44W 297 C9
Gammon Ranges △
Australia 30°38S 139°8E 281 E2
Gamo-Gofa Ethiopia 5°40N 36°40E 257 F4
Gamoda-Saki Japan 33°50N 134°45E 222 D6
Gamou Niger 14°20N 9°55E 259 F1
Gampaha Sri Lanka 7°5N 79°59E 245 L4
Gampo S. Korea 35°48N 129°31E 224 E4
Gampola Sri Lanka 7°10N 80°34E 245 L5
Gamtoos → S. Africa 33°58S 25°1E 270 D4
Gamzigrad-Romuliana
Serbia 43°53N 22°11E 202 C6
Gan France 43°12N 0°27W 174 E3
Gan Gan Argentina 42°30S 68°10W 336 B3
Gan Goriama, Mts.
Cameroon 7°44N 12°45E 263 D7
Gan Jiang → China 29°15N 116°0E 229 C11
Ganado U.S.A. 35°43N 109°33W 305 J9
Gananita Sudan 18°22N 33°50E 256 D3
Gananoque Canada 44°20N 76°10W 313 B8
Ganassi Phil. 7°49N 124°6E 233 H5
Ganāveh Iran 29°35N 50°35E 247 D6
Gäncä Azerbaijan 40°45N 46°20E 191 K8
Gancheng China 18°51N 108°37E 236 C7
Gand = Gent Belgium 51°2N 3°42E 170 C3
Ganda Angola 13°3S 14°35E 265 E2
Gandajika
Dem. Rep. of the Congo 6°46S 23°58E 265 D4
Gandak → India 25°39N 85°13E 243 G11
Gandara Phil. 12°1N 124°49E 232 E5
Gandava Pakistan 28°32N 67°32E 242 E2
Gander Canada 48°58N 54°35W 299 C9
Gander L. Canada 48°58N 54°35W 299 C9
Ganderkesee Germany 53°2N 8°32E 178 B4
Ganderowe Falls Zimbabwe 17°20S 29°10E 269 F2
Gandesa Spain 41°3N 0°26E 196 D5
Gandhi Sagar India 24°40N 75°40E 242 G6
Gandhinagar India 23°15N 72°45E 242 H5
Gandi Nigeria 12°55N 5°49E 263 C6
Gandia Spain 38°58N 0°9W 197 G4
Gandino Italy 45°49N 9°54E 198 C6
Gando, Pta. Canary Is. 27°55N 15°22W 153 e1
Gandole Nigeria 8°28N 11°35E 263 D7
Gandou Congo 2°25N 17°25E 264 B3
Gandu Brazil 13°45S 39°30W 333 D4
Gâneb Mauritania 18°29N 10°8W 262 B2
Ganedidalem = Gani
Indonesia 0°48S 128°14E 231 E7
Ganga → India 23°20N 90°30E 243 H14
Ganga Sagar India 21°38N 88°5E 243 J13
Gangafani Mali 14°20N 2°20W 262 C4
Gangakher India 18°57N 76°45E 244 E3
Gangan → India 28°38N 78°58E 243 E8
Ganganagar India 29°56N 73°56E 242 E5
Gangapur Maharashtra,
India 19°41N 75°1E 244 E2
Gangapur Raj., India 26°32N 76°49E 242 F7
Gangara Niger 14°35N 8°29E 259 F1
Gangaw Burma 22°5N 94°5E 241 D5
Gangaw Taungdan
Burma 24°55N 96°35E 241 C6
Gangawati India 15°30N 76°36E 245 G3
Gangdisê Shan China 31°20N 81°0E 243 D9
Gangdong S. Korea 37°30N 127°5E 137 B2
Ganges = Ganga →
India 23°20N 90°30E 243 H14
Ganges Canada 48°51N 123°31W 296 D4
Ganges Hérault, France 43°56N 3°42E 174 E7
Ganges, Mouths of the
India 21°30N 90°0E 241 E3
Ganggyeong S. Korea 36°10N 127°0E 224 D3
Gånghester Sweden 57°42N 13°1E 163 G7
Ganghwa S. Korea 37°45N 126°30E 224 D3
Gangi Italy 37°48N 14°12E 201 E7
Gângiova Romania 43°54N 23°50E 183 G8
Gangnam S. Korea 37°30N 126°59E 137 B1
Gangneung S. Korea 37°45N 128°54E 224 D4
Gangoh India 29°46N 77°18E 242 E7
Gangotri India 30°50N 79°10E 243 D8
Gangotri △ India 30°50N 79°10E 243 D8
Gangseo S. Korea 37°32N 126°51E 137 B1
Gangseong S. Korea 38°24N 128°30E 224 C4
Gangtok India 27°20N 88°37E 241 B2
Gangtou China 23°12N 113°8E 121 A1
Gangu China 34°40N 105°15E 226 G3
Gangwa
Dem. Rep. of the Congo 3°30S 20°54E 264 C4
Gangwei China 23°4N 113°11E 121 B2
Gangwon-do □ S. Korea 37°45N 128°15E 224 D4
Gangyao China 44°12N 126°37E 227 B14
Gani Indonesia 0°48S 128°14E 231 E7
Ganj India 27°45N 78°57E 243 F8
Ganjam India 19°23N 85°4E 244 E7
Ganjiakou China 39°54N 116°16E 114 B1
Ganluo China 28°58N 102°59E 228 C4
Ganmain Australia 34°47S 147°1E 283 C7
Ganna South Sudan 7°30N 28°0E 266 C2
Gannat France 46°7N 3°11E 173 F10
Gannett Peak U.S.A. 43°11N 109°39W 304 E9
Ganquan China 36°20N 109°20E 226 F5
Gänserdorf Austria 48°20N 16°43E 181 C9
Ganshoren Belgium 50°52N 4°18E 116 A1
Ganshui China 28°40N 106°40E 228 C6
Gansu □ China 36°0N 104°0E 226 G3
Ganta Liberia 7°15N 8°59W 262 D3
Gantheaume, C. Australia 36°4S 137°32E 282 D2
Gantheaume B. Australia 27°40S 114°10E 279 E1
Gants Hill U.K. 51°34N 0°4E 125 A4
Gantsevichi = Hantsavichy
Belarus 52°49N 26°30E 177 B14
Gantung Indonesia 2°58S 108°9E 235 C3
Ganye Nigeria 8°25N 12°4E 263 D7
Ganyem = Genyem
Indonesia 2°46S 140°12E 231 E10
Ganyu China 34°50N 119°8E 227 G10
Ganyushkino Kazakhstan 46°35N 49°20E 191 G9
Ganzhou China 25°51N 114°56E 229 E10
Gao Mali 16°15N 0°5W 263 B4
Gao Xian China 28°21N 104°32E 228 C5
Gao'an China 28°26N 115°17E 229 C10
Gaobeidian China 39°19N 115°51E 226 E8
Gaocheng China 38°2N 114°49E 226 E8
Gaochun China 31°20N 118°49E 229 B12
Gaohang China 31°20N 121°36E 138 B2
Gaohebu China 30°43N 116°49E 229 B11
Gaokeng China 27°40N 113°58E 229 D9
Gaolan Dao China 21°55N 113°10E 229 G9
Gaoligong Shan China 24°45N 98°45E 228 E2
Gaomi China 36°20N 119°42E 227 F10
Gaoping China 35°45N 112°55E 226 G7
Gaoqiao China 31°21N 121°34E 138 A2
Gaotang China 36°50N 116°15E 226 F9
Gaoua Burkina Faso 10°20N 3°8W 262 C4
Gaoual Guinea 11°45N 13°25W 262 C2
Gaoxiong = Kaohsiung
Taiwan 22°35N 120°16E 225 D2
Gaoyang China 38°40N 115°45E 226 E8
Gaoyao China 23°3N 112°27E 229 F9
Gaoyou China 32°47N 119°26E 229 A12
Gaoyou Hu China 32°45N 119°20E 227 H10
Gaoyuan China 37°8N 117°58E 227 F9
Gaozhou China 21°58N 110°50E 229 G8
Gap France 44°33N 6°5E 175 D10
Gapan Phil. 15°19N 120°57E 232 D3
Gapat → India 24°30N 82°28E 243 G10
Gapuwiyak Australia 12°25S 135°43E 280 A2
Gar China 32°10N 79°58E 218 E4
Gara, L. Ireland 53°57N 8°26W 166 C3
Garāb Iran 33°27N 47°16E 213 F12
Garabogazköl Aylagy
Turkmenistan 41°0N 53°30E 187 F9
Garacad Somalia 6°57N 49°24E 267 C6
Garachico Canary Is. 28°22N 16°46W 153 e1
Garachiné Panama 8°0N 78°12W 320 E4
Garafía Canary Is. 28°48N 17°57W 153 e1
Garagum Turkmenistan 39°30N 60°0E 247 B8
Garah Australia 29°5S 149°38E 281 D4
Garaina Papua N. G. 7°53S 147°8E 286 D4
Garajonay Canary Is. 28°7N 17°14W 153 e1
Garajonay △ Canary Is. 28°7N 17°14W 153 e1
Garamba △
Dem. Rep. of the Congo 4°10N 29°40E 268 B2
Garango Burkina Faso 11°48N 0°34W 263 C4
Garanhuns Brazil 8°50S 36°30W 332 C4
Garapan N. Marianas 15°12N 145°43E 302 e
Garautha India 25°34N 79°18E 243 G8
Garawa ☉ Australia 16°43S 136°51E 280 B2
Garawe Liberia 4°35N 8°0W 262 E3
Garba Harre = Garbahaarrey
Somalia 3°19N 42°13E 267 D5
Garba Tula Kenya 0°30N 38°32E 268 B4
Garbagnate Milanese Italy 45°34N 9°4E 128 A1
Garbagududu Ethiopia 6°12N 43°50E 267 C5
Garbahaarrey Somalia 3°19N 42°13E 267 D5
Garbatella Italy 41°51N 12°30E 136 B2
Garberville U.S.A. 40°6N 123°48W 304 F2
Garbiyang India 30°8N 80°54E 243 D9
Garbsen Germany 52°26N 9°31E 178 C5
Garça Brazil 22°14S 49°37W 333 F2
Garças → Mato Grosso,
Brazil 15°54S 52°16W 331 D7
Garças → Pernambuco,
Brazil 8°43S 39°41W 332 C4
Garches France 48°50N 2°11E 134 A2
Garching Germany 48°14N 11°39E 131 A3
Garchitorena Phil. 13°52N 123°40E 232 E4
Garcia Hernandez Phil. 9°37N 124°18E 233 G5
Garcias Brazil 20°34S 52°13W 331 E7
Gard □ France 44°2N 4°10E 175 D8
Gard → France 43°51N 4°37E 175 E8
Garda, L. di Italy 45°40N 10°41E 198 C7
Gardabani Georgia 41°27N 45°5E 191 K7
Gardanne France 43°27N 5°27E 175 E9
Gårdby Sweden 56°36N 16°38E 163 H10
Garde L. Canada 62°50N 106°13W 297 A7
Gardelegen Germany 52°32N 11°24E 178 C7
Garden City El Qâhira,
Egypt 30°2N 31°14E 117 A2
Garden City Ga., U.S.A. 32°6N 81°9W 316 C8
Garden City Kans.,
U.S.A. 37°58N 100°53W 308 G3
Garden City Mo., U.S.A. 38°34N 94°12W 310 F2
Garden City Tex., U.S.A. 31°52N 101°29W 314 F4
Garden District U.S.A. 29°56N 90°5W 131 B2
Garden Grove U.S.A. 33°47N 117°55W 307 M9
Garden Reach India 22°33N 88°15E 124 B1
Gardens of Stone △
Australia 33°14S 150°11E 283 B9
Garder Norway 59°45N 10°38E 133 B2
Gardēz Afghan. 33°37N 69°9E 242 C3
Garðabær Iceland 64°5N 21°55W 155 C5
Garðskagi Iceland 64°5N 22°43W 155 C4
Garður Iceland 66°4N 16°46W 155 A10
Gardiki Greece 38°50N 21°55E 204 C3
Gardiner Maine, U.S.A. 44°14N 69°47W 309 C19
Gardiner Mont., U.S.A. 45°2N 110°22W 304 D8
Gardiners I. U.S.A. 41°6N 72°6W 313 E12
Gardner Fla., U.S.A. 27°21N 81°48W 317 H8
Gardner Ill., U.S.A. 41°12N 88°17W 311 C8
Gardner Mass., U.S.A. 42°34N 71°59W 313 D13
Gardner Canal Canada 53°27N 128°8W 296 C3
Gardner Pinnacles
U.S.A. 25°0N 167°55W 302 F10
Gardnerville U.S.A. 38°56N 119°45W 306 G7
Gardno, Jezioro Poland 54°40N 17°7E 184 D4
Gardo = Qardho Somalia 9°30N 49°6E 267 C6
Gardone Val Trómpia
Italy 45°41N 10°11E 198 C7
Gárdony Hungary 47°12N 18°39E 182 C3
Gare Tigre Fr. Guiana 4°58N 53°9W 329 C7
Gareloi I. U.S.A. 51°48N 178°48W 303 L3
Gares = Puente la Reina
Spain 42°40N 1°49W 196 C3
Garešnica Croatia 45°36N 16°56E 199 C13
Garéssio Italy 44°12N 8°2E 198 D5
Garey U.S.A. 34°53N 120°19W 307 L6
Garfield N.J., U.S.A. 40°52N 74°7W 132 A1
Garfield Wash., U.S.A. 47°1N 117°9W 304 C5
Garfield Park U.S.A. 41°52N 87°42W 119 B2
Garforth U.K. 53°47N 1°24W 168 D6
Gargaliani Greece 37°4N 21°38E 204 D3
Gargan, Mt. France 45°37N 1°39E 174 C5
Gargano △ Italy 41°43N 15°52E 199 G12
Gargantua, C. Canada 47°36N 85°2W 309 B11
Gargareta Greece 37°57N 23°43E 112 B2
Gargett Australia 21°9S 148°46E 280 b
Gargouna Mali 15°56N 0°13E 263 B5
Gargždai Lithuania 55°43N 21°24E 184 C8
Garhchiroli India 20°10N 80°0E 244 D5
Garibaldi ⌂ Canada 49°50N 122°40W 296 D4
Garibong S. Korea 37°29N 126°54E 137 C1
Gariep, L. S. Africa 30°40S 25°40E 270 D4
Garies S. Africa 30°32S 17°59E 270 D2
Garig Gunak Barlu △
Australia 11°26S 131°58E 278 B5
Garigliano → Italy 41°13N 13°45E 200 A6
Garissa Kenya 0°25S 39°40E 268 C4
Garkida Nigeria 10°27N 12°36E 263 C7
Garko Nigeria 11°45N 8°35E 263 C6
Garland Tex., U.S.A. 32°54N 96°38W 314 E6
Garland Utah, U.S.A. 41°45N 112°10W 304 F7
Garlasco Italy 45°12N 8°55E 198 C5
Garliava Lithuania 54°49N 23°52E 184 D10
Garlin France 43°33N 0°16W 174 E3
Garmāb Semnān, Iran 35°25N 56°45E 247 C8
Garmāb Zanjān, Iran 35°50N 48°11E 213 E13
Garmisch-Partenkirchen
Germany 47°30N 11°6E 179 H7
Garmo, Qullai = imeni Ismail
Samani, Pik Tajikistan 39°0N 72°2E 217 E8
Garmsār Iran 35°20N 52°25E 247 C7
Garner U.S.A. 43°6N 93°36W 310 A3
Garnett U.S.A. 38°17N 95°14W 308 F6
Garnpung L. Australia 33°25S 143°10E 282 B5
Garo Hills India 25°30N 90°30E 241 C3
Garoe = Garoowe Somalia 8°25N 48°33E 267 C6
Garonne → France 45°2N 0°36W 174 C3
Garonne, Canal Latéral à la
France 44°15N 0°18E 174 D4
Garoowe Somalia 8°25N 48°33E 267 C6
Garorimman S. Korea 36°54N 126°21E 224 D3
Garot India 24°19N 75°41E 242 G6
Garou, L. Mali 16°2N 2°45W 262 B4
Garoua Cameroon 9°19N 13°21E 263 D7
Garoua Boulaï Cameroon 5°53N 14°33E 264 A2
Garove I. Papua N. G. 4°42S 149°30E 286 C5
Garpenberg Sweden 60°19N 16°12E 162 D10
Garphyttan Sweden 59°18N 14°56E 162 E8
Garrauli India 25°5N 79°22E 243 G8
Garrel Germany 52°57N 8°1E 178 C4
Garreru Palau 7°19N 134°32E 288 c
Garrett U.S.A. 41°21N 85°8W 311 C11
Garrigues France 43°40N 3°55E 174 E7
Garrison Ky., U.S.A. 38°36N 83°10W 311 F13
Garrison Mont., U.S.A. 46°31N 112°49W 304 C7
Garrison N. Dak., U.S.A. 47°40N 101°25W 308 B3
Garrison Res. = Sakakawea, L.
U.S.A. 47°30N 101°25W 308 B3
Garron Pt. U.K. 55°3N 5°59W 166 A6
Garrovillas de Alconétar
Spain 39°40N 6°33W 195 F4
Garrucha Spain 37°11N 1°49W 197 H3
Garry → U.K. 56°44N 3°47W 167 E5
Garry, L. Canada 65°58N 100°18W 294 D11
Garrygala Turkmenistan 38°31N 56°29E 247 B8
Garsen Kenya 2°20S 40°5E 268 C5
Gärsnäs Sweden 55°32N 14°10E 163 J8
Garson L. Canada 56°19N 110°2W 297 B6
Garstang U.K. 53°55N 2°46W 168 D5
Gartempe → France 46°47N 0°49E 174 B4
Gartz Germany 53°13N 14°22E 178 B10
Garu Ghana 10°55N 0°11W 263 C4
Garu India 23°40N 84°14E 243 H11
Garub Namibia 26°37S 16°0E 270 C2
Garusuun Palau 7°21N 134°31E 288 c
Garut Indonesia 7°14S 107°53E 235 D3
Garvanza U.S.A. 34°6N 118°11W 126 B3
Garvão Portugal 37°42N 8°21W 195 H2
Garvie Mts. N.Z. 45°30S 168°50E 285 F3
Garwa = Garoua Cameroon 9°19N 13°21E 263 D7
Garwa India 24°11N 83°47E 243 G10
Garwolin Poland 51°55N 21°38E 185 G8
Gary U.S.A. 41°36N 87°20W 311 C9
Garz Germany 54°19N 13°20E 178 A9
Garzê China 31°38N 100°1E 228 B3
Garzón Colombia 2°10N 75°40W 328 C2
Gas City U.S.A. 40°29N 85°37W 311 D11
Gas-San Japan 38°32N 140°1E 220 E10
Gasa Bhutan 27°55N 89°40E 241 B2
Gasan Phil. 13°19N 121°51E 232 E3
Gasan Kuli = Esenguly
Turkmenistan 37°37N 53°59E 216 E4
Gascogne France 43°45N 0°20E 174 E4
Gascogne, G. de Europe 44°0N 2°0W 174 E2
Gasconade U.S.A. 38°40N 91°34W 310 F5
Gasconade → U.S.A. 38°41N 91°33W 310 F5
Gascony = Gascogne
France 43°45N 0°20E 174 E4
Gascoyne → Australia 24°52S 113°37E 279 D1
Gascoyne Junction
Australia 25°2S 115°17E 279 E2
Gascueña Spain 40°18N 2°31W 196 E2
Gash, Wadi → Africa 16°48N 35°51E 257 D4
Gash Setit ⌂ Eritrea 15°12N 36°58E 257 D4
Gåshaga Sweden 59°21N 18°13E 139 A3
Gashagar Nigeria 13°22N 12°47E 263 C7
Gashaka Nigeria 7°20N 11°29E 263 D7
Gashaka-Gumti △ Nigeria 7°23N 11°34E 263 D7
Gasherbrum Pakistan 35°40N 76°40E 243 B7
Gashua Nigeria 12°54N 11°0E 263 C7
Gasmata Papua N. G. 6°17S 150°20E 286 D6
Gaspar Grande Trin. & Tob. 10°40N 61°39W 323 t
Gasparilla I. U.S.A. 26°46N 82°16W 317 J7
Gasparillo Trin. & Tob. 10°18N 61°26W 323 t
Gasparito Curaçao 12°8N 68°56W 322 g
Gaspé Canada 48°52N 64°30W 299 C7
Gaspé, C. de Canada 48°48N 64°7W 299 C7
Gaspé Pen. = Gaspésie, Pén. de la
Canada 48°45N 65°40W 299 C6
Gaspésie, Pén. de la
Canada 48°45N 65°40W 299 C6
Gaspésie ⌂ Canada 48°55N 66°10W 299 C6
Gassan Burkina Faso 12°49N 3°12W 262 C4
Gassaway U.S.A. 38°41N 80°47W 309 F13
Gassen = Jasień Poland 51°46N 15°0E 185 G2
Gassol Nigeria 8°34N 10°25E 263 D7
Gasteiz = Vitoria-Gasteiz
Spain 42°50N 2°41W 196 C2
Gaston U.S.A. 33°49N 81°5W 316 B8
Gastonia U.S.A. 35°16N 81°11W 315 D14
Gastouni Greece 37°51N 21°15E 204 D3
Gastouri Greece 39°34N 19°54E 206 B9
Gastre Argentina 42°20S 69°15W 336 B3
Gästrikland Sweden 60°45N 16°40E 162 D10
Gata, C. Cyprus 34°34N 33°2E 207 F9
Gata, C. de Spain 36°41N 2°13W 197 J2
Gata, Sierra de Spain 40°20N 6°45W 194 E4
Gataga → Canada 58°35N 126°59W 296 B3
Gătaia Romania 45°26N 21°30E 182 E6
Gatchina Russia 59°35N 30°9E 188 C6
Gatehouse of Fleet U.K. 54°53N 4°12W 167 G4
Gates U.S.A. 43°9N 77°42W 312 C7
Gates of the Arctic ⌂
U.S.A. 67°45N 153°15W 303 C9
Gateshead U.K. 54°57N 1°35W 168 C6
Gateshead I. Canada 70°36N 100°26W 294 C11
Gatesville U.S.A. 31°26N 97°45W 314 F6
Gateway ⌂ U.S.A. 40°38N 73°51W 132 C2
Gateway of India India 18°55N 72°50E 130 B2
Gaths Zimbabwe 20°2S 30°32E 269 G3
Gâtinais France 48°5N 2°40E 173 D9
Gâtine, Hauteurs de
France 46°35N 0°45W 174 B3
Gatineau Canada 45°29N 75°39W 313 A9
Gatineau → Canada 45°27N 75°42W 298 C4
Gatineau ⌂ Canada 45°40N 76°0W 298 C4
Gatow Germany 52°29N 13°11E 115 B1
Gattaran Phil. 18°4N 121°38E 232 B3
Gattinara Italy 45°37N 8°22E 198 C5
Gatton Australia 27°32S 152°17E 281 D5
Gatún, L. Panama 9°7N 79°56W 320 c
Gatún Dam Panama 9°16N 79°55W 320 c
Gatún Locks Panama 9°16N 79°55W 320 c
Gatwick, London ✕ (LGW)
U.K. 51°10N 0°11W 169 F7
Gatyana S. Africa 32°16S 28°31E 271 D4
Gau Fiji 18°2S 179°18E 287 B2
Gaua Vanuatu 14°15S 167°30E 287 D5
Gaucín Spain 36°31N 5°19W 195 J5
Gauer L. Canada 57°0N 97°50W 297 B9
Gauhati = Guwahati
India 26°10N 91°45E 241 B3
Gauja → Latvia 57°10N 24°16E 188 D3
Gaujas △ Latvia 57°10N 24°50E 161 H21
Gaula → Norway 63°21N 10°14E 164 A7
Gaupne Norway 61°25N 7°18E 164 C4
Gaurdak = Gowurdak
Turkmenistan 37°50N 66°4E 217 E7
Gauri Phanta India 28°41N 80°36E 243 E9
Gauribidanur India 13°37N 77°32E 245 H3
Gaustatoppen Norway 59°48N 8°40E 164 E5
Gauteng □ S. Africa 26°0S 28°0E 271 C4
Gāv Koshī Iran 28°38N 57°12E 247 D8
Gavà Spain 41°18N 2°1W 114 B1
Gāvakān Iran 29°37N 53°10E 247 D7
Gavamar Spain 41°15N 2°1E 114 B1
Gavarnie France 42°44N 0°1W 174 F3
Gavāter Iran 25°10N 61°31E 247 E9
Gāvbandī Iran 27°12N 53°4E 247 E7
Gavdopoula Greece 34°56N 24°0E 207 F5
Gavdos Greece 34°50N 24°5E 207 F5
Gávea Brazil 22°58S 43°13W 135 B1
Gávea, Pedra da Brazil 22°59S 43°18W 135 B1
Gavi Italy 44°41N 8°49E 198 D5
Gavião Portugal 39°28N 7°56W 195 F3
Gaviota U.S.A. 34°29N 120°13W 307 L6
Gāvkhūnī, Bāţlāq-e Iran 32°6N 52°52E 247 C7
Gävle Sweden 60°40N 17°9E 162 D11
Gävleborgs län □ Sweden 61°30N 16°15E 162 C10
Gävlebukten Sweden 60°40N 17°20E 162 D11
Gavorrano Italy 42°55N 10°54E 198 F7
Gavray France 48°55N 1°20W 172 D5
Gavrilov Yam Russia 57°18N 39°49E 188 D10
Gavrio Greece 37°54N 24°44E 204 D6
Gawachab Namibia 27°4S 17°55E 270 C2
Gawai Burma 27°56N 97°30E 241 B6
Gawilgarh Hills India 21°15N 76°45E 244 D3
Gawler Australia 34°30S 138°42E 282 C3
Gawler Ranges Australia 32°30S 135°45E 282 B2
Gawu Nigeria 9°14N 6°52E 263 D6
Gaxun Nur China 42°22N 100°30E 218 C9
Gay Russia 51°27N 58°27E 186 D10
Gay Ga., U.S.A. 33°6N 84°35W 316 B5
Gaya India 24°47N 85°4E 243 G11
Gaya Niger 11°52N 3°28E 263 C5
Gaya Nigeria 11°57N 9°0E 263 C6
Gayasan △ S. Korea 35°45N 128°10E 224 E4
Gayéri Burkina Faso 12°39N 0°29E 263 C5
Gaylord U.S.A. 45°2N 84°41W 309 C11
Gayndah Australia 25°35S 151°32E 281 D5
Gaysin = Haysyn
Ukraine 48°57N 29°25E 183 B14
Gayvoron = Hayvoron
Ukraine 48°22N 29°52E 183 B14
Gaza Gaza Strip 31°30N 34°28E 251 G5
Gaza □ Mozam. 23°10S 32°45E 271 B5
Gaza Strip ■ Asia 31°29N 34°25E 251 G5
Gazanjyk = Bereket
Turkmenistan 39°16N 55°32E 247 B7
Gazaoua Niger 13°32N 7°55E 263 C6
Gāzbor Iran 28°5N 58°51E 247 D8
Gazdagrét Hungary 47°29N 19°0E 117 B1
Gazelle Pen. Papua N. G. 4°40S 152°0E 286 C7
Gazi Dem. Rep. of the Congo 1°3N 24°30E 264 B4
Gaziantep Turkey 37°6N 37°23E 250 A8
Gaziantep □ Turkey 37°0N 37°0E 250 B8
Gazimağusa = Famagusta
Cyprus 35°8N 33°55E 207 E9
Gaziosmanpaşa Turkey 41°5N 28°50E 122 B1
Gazipaşa Turkey 36°16N 32°18E 250 B3
Gazipur Bangla. 23°48N 90°39E 241 D3
Gazli Uzbekistan 40°8N 63°27E 216 D6
Gbadolite
Dem. Rep. of the Congo 4°17N 21°1E 264 B4
Gbarnga Liberia 7°19N 9°13W 262 D3
Gboko Nigeria 7°17N 9°4E 263 D6
Gcoverega Botswana 19°8S 24°18E 270 A3
Gcuwa S. Africa 32°20S 28°11E 271 D4
Gdańsk Poland 54°22N 18°40E 184 D5
Gdańsk ✕ (GDN) Poland 54°22N 18°30E 184 D5
Gdańska, Zatoka Poland 54°30N 19°20E 184 D6
Gdingen = Gdynia Poland 54°35N 18°33E 184 D5
Gdov Russia 58°48N 27°55E 188 C4
Gdynia Poland 54°35N 18°33E 184 D5
Geba → Guinea-Biss. 11°46N 15°36W 262 C1
Gebe Indonesia 0°5N 129°25E 231 D7
Gebeciler Turkey 38°46N 30°46E 205 C12
Gebeit Mine Sudan 21°3N 36°29E 256 C4
Gebel Abyad Sudan 19°0N 28°0E 256 D2
Gebel el Ahmar Egypt 30°2N 31°21E 117 A3
Gebel el Muqattam Egypt 30°1N 31°17E 117 A2
Gebel el Tura Egypt 29°56N 31°15E 117 B2
Gebel Iweibid Egypt 30°8N 32°13E 256 H8
Gebiley Somalia 9°42N 43°37E 267 C5
Gebze Turkey 40°47N 29°25E 203 F13
Gecha Ethiopia 7°30N 35°18E 257 F4
Geçitkale = Lefkoniko
Cyprus 35°18N 33°44E 207 E9
Gedaref Sudan 14°2N 35°28E 257 E4
Gedaref □ Sudan 14°0N 35°0E 257 E4
Gede, Tanjung Indonesia 6°46S 105°12E 234 D3
Gediz Turkey 39°1N 29°24E 205 B11
Gediz → Turkey 38°35N 26°48E 205 C8
Gedo Ethiopia 9°2N 37°25E 257 F4
Gedo □ Somalia 3°15N 42°10E 267 D5
Gèdre France 42°47N 0°2E 174 F4
Gedser Denmark 54°35N 11°55E 163 K5
Gedung, Pulau Malaysia 5°17N 100°23E 237 c
Geegully Cr. → Australia 18°32S 123°41E 278 C3
Geel Belgium 51°10N 4°59E 170 C4
Geelong Australia 38°10S 144°22E 282 E6
Geelvink B. = Cenderawasih, Teluk
Indonesia 3°0S 135°20E 231 E9
Geelvink Chan. Australia 28°30S 114°0E 279 E1
Geesthacht Germany 53°26N 10°22E 178 B6
Geidam Nigeria 12°57N 11°57E 263 C7
Geikie → Canada 57°45N 103°52W 297 B8
Geikie Gorge △ Australia 18°3S 125°41E 278 C4
Geilenkirchen Germany 50°57N 6°8E 178 E2
Geili Sudan 16°1N 32°37E 257 D3
Geilo Norway 60°32N 8°14E 164 D5
Geirangerfjorden Norway 62°7N 7°10E 164 B4
Geiselgasteig Germany 48°3N 11°33E 131 B2
Geisingen Germany 47°54N 8°38E 179 H4
Geislingen Germany 48°37N 9°50E 179 G5
Geistown U.S.A. 40°18N 78°52W 312 F6
Geita Tanzania 2°48S 32°12E 268 C3
Geitastrand Norway 63°22N 9°56E 164 A6
Geithus Norway 59°57N 9°59E 164 E6
Gejiu China 23°20N 103°10E 228 F4
Gel → South Sudan 7°5N 29°10E 257 F2
Gel, Meydān-e Iran 29°4N 54°50E 247 D7
Gel River South Sudan 7°5N 29°10E 257 F2
Gela Italy 37°4N 14°15E 201 E7
Gela, G. di Italy 37°0N 14°20E 201 F7
Geladi Ethiopia 6°59N 46°30E 267 C6
Gelahun Liberia 7°55N 10°28W 262 D2

Gelam Indonesia 2°54S 110°11E 235 C4
Gelang Patah Malaysia 1°27N 103°35E 237 d
Gelderland □ Neths. 52°5N 6°10E 170 B6
Geldern Germany 51°31N 6°20E 178 D2
Geldrop Neths. 51°25N 5°32E 170 C5
Geleen Neths. 50°57N 5°49E 170 D5
Gelehun S. Leone 8°20N 11°40W 262 D2
Gelembe Turkey 39°10N 27°50E 205 B9
Gelemso Ethiopia 8°49N 40°31E 257 F5
Gelendost Turkey 38°7N 31°1E 212 C4
Gelendzhik Russia 44°33N 38°10E 189 K10
Gelib = Jilib Somalia 0°29N 42°46E 267 D5
Gelibolu Turkey 40°28N 26°43E 203 F10
Gelibolu Yarımadası Turkey 40°20N 26°30E 203 F10
Gelidonya Burnu Turkey 36°12N 30°24E 212 D4
Gellinsoor Somalia 6°28N 46°39E 267 C6
Gelnhausen Germany 50°11N 9°11E 179 E5
Gelnica Slovak Rep. 48°51N 20°55E 181 C13
Gelsenkirchen Germany 51°32N 7°6E 178 D3
Gelting Germany 54°45N 9°53E 178 A5
Gelugur Malaysia 5°22N 100°18E 237 c
Gemas Malaysia 2°37N 102°36E 237 L4
Gembloux Belgium 50°34N 4°43E 170 D4
Gembu Nigeria 6°42N 11°10E 263 D7
Gemena Dem. Rep. of the Congo 3°13N 19°48E 264 B3
Gemerek Turkey 39°15N 36°10E 212 C7
Gemikonagı = Karavostasi Cyprus 35°8N 32°50E 207 E8
Gemla Sweden 56°52N 14°39E 163 H8
Gemlik Turkey 40°26N 29°9E 203 F13
Gemlik Körfezi Turkey 40°25N 28°55E 203 F12
Gemona del Friuli Italy 46°16N 13°9E 199 B10
Gemsa Egypt 27°39N 33°35E 256 B3
Gemsbok △ Botswana 25°5S 21°1E 270 C3
Gemünden Germany 50°3N 9°42E 179 E5
Genadi Greece 36°2N 27°56E 206 E11
Genale ➔ Ethiopia 6°2N 39°1E 257 F4
Genç Turkey 38°44N 40°34E 213 C9
Gençay France 46°23N 0°23E 174 B4
General Acha Argentina 37°20S 64°38W 334 D3
General Alvear B. Aires, Argentina 36°0S 60°0W 334 D4
General Alvear Mendoza, Argentina 35°0S 67°40W 334 D2
General Artigas Paraguay 26°52S 56°16W 334 B4
General Belgrano Argentina 36°35S 58°47W 334 D4
General Bernardo O'Higgins Antarctica 63°0S 58°3W 151 C18
General Cabrera Argentina 32°53S 63°52W 334 C3
General Carrera, L. S. Amer. 46°35S 72°0W 336 C2
General Cepeda Mexico 25°21N 101°22W 318 B4
General Conesa Argentina 40°6S 64°25W 336 B4
General Eugenio A. Garay Paraguay 20°31S 62°8W 331 E5
General Germán Busch = Villa Abecia Bolivia 21°0S 68°18W 334 A2
General Guido Argentina 36°40S 57°50W 334 D4
General Juan Madariaga Argentina 37°0S 57°0W 334 D4
General La Madrid Argentina 37°17S 61°20W 334 D3
General Lorenzo Vintter Argentina 40°45S 64°26W 336 B4
General Luna Phil. 13°41N 122°10E 232 E4
General MacArthur Phil. 11°18N 125°28E 233 F5
General Martin Miguel de Güemes Argentina 24°50S 65°0W 334 A3
General Pico Argentina 35°45S 63°50W 334 D3
General Pinedo Argentina 27°15S 61°20W 334 B3
General Pinto Argentina 34°45S 61°50W 334 C3
General Roca Argentina 39°2S 67°35W 336 A3
General Sampaio Brazil 4°2S 39°29W 332 B4
General San Martin Argentina 34°35S 58°32W 117 B1
General Santos Phil. 6°5N 125°14E 233 H5
General Tinio Phil. 15°39N 121°10E 232 D3
General Toshevo Bulgaria 43°42N 28°6E 203 C12
General Treviño Mexico 26°14N 99°29W 319 B5
General Trias Mexico 28°21N 106°22W 318 B3
General Uriburu = Zárate Argentina 34°7S 59°0W 334 C4
General Viamonte Argentina 35°1S 61°3W 334 D3
General Villegas Argentina 35°5S 63°0W 334 D3
General Vintter, L. Argentina 43°55S 71°40W 336 B2
Generoso Ponce = Jaci-Paraná Brazil 9°15S 64°23W 331 B5
Genesee Idaho, U.S.A. 46°33N 116°56W 304 C5
Genesee Pa., U.S.A. 41°59N 77°54W 312 E7
Genesee ➔ U.S.A. 43°16N 77°36W 312 C7
Geneseo Ill., U.S.A. 41°27N 90°9W 310 C6
Geneseo N.Y., U.S.A. 42°48N 77°49W 312 D7
Geneva = Genève Switz. 46°12N 6°9E 179 J2
Geneva Ala., U.S.A. 31°2N 85°52W 316 D4
Geneva Ga., U.S.A. 32°35N 84°33W 316 C5
Geneva Ill., U.S.A. 41°53N 88°18W 311 C8
Geneva Ind., U.S.A. 40°36N 84°58W 311 D12
Geneva N.Y., U.S.A. 42°52N 76°59W 312 D8
Geneva Nebr., U.S.A. 40°32N 97°36W 308 E5
Geneva Ohio, U.S.A. 41°48N 80°57W 312 E4
Geneva, L. = Léman, L. Europe 46°26N 6°30E 173 F13
Geneva, L. U.S.A. 42°38N 88°30W 311 B8
Genève Switz. 46°12N 6°9E 179 J2
Geng Afghan. 31°22N 61°28E 240 C1
Gengenbach Germany 48°24N 8°1E 179 G4
Gengma China 23°32N 99°20E 228 F2
Genhe China 50°47N 121°31E 219 A13
Genichesk = Henichesk Ukraine 46°12N 34°50E 189 J8
Genil ➔ Spain 37°42N 5°19W 195 H5
Génipa, B. de Martinique 14°33N 61°0W 322 j
Genisea Greece 40°45N 24°57E 203 E8
Genk Belgium 50°58N 5°32E 170 D5
Genkai-Nada Japan 34°0N 130°0E 222 D2
Genlis France 47°11N 5°12E 173 E12
Gennargentu, Mti. del Italy 40°1N 9°19E 200 B2
Gennes France 47°20N 0°17W 172 E6
Gennevilliers France 48°56N 2°17E 134 A2
Genoa = Génova Italy 44°25N 8°57E 198 D5
Genoa Vic., Australia 37°29S 149°35E 283 D8
Genoa Ill., U.S.A. 42°6N 88°42W 311 B8
Genoa N.Y., U.S.A. 42°40N 76°32W 313 D8
Genoa Nebr., U.S.A. 41°27N 97°44W 308 E5
Genoa Nev., U.S.A. 39°2N 119°50W 306 F7
Genoa ➔ Argentina 44°55S 70°5W 336 B2
Genoa City U.S.A. 42°30N 88°20W 311 B8
Génova Italy 44°25N 8°57E 198 D5
Génova ✕ (GOA) Italy 44°25N 8°56E 198 D5
Génova, G. di Italy 44°0N 9°0E 198 E6
Genovesa, I. Ecuador 0°20N 89°58W 330 a
Genriyetty, Ostrov Russia 77°6N 156°30E 215 B16
Gent Belgium 51°2N 3°42E 170 C3
Genteng Jawa Barat, Indonesia 7°22S 106°24E 234 D3
Genteng Jawa Timur, Indonesia 8°22S 114°9E 231 J17
Genthin Germany 52°25N 12°9E 178 C8
Gentilly Val-de-Marne, France 48°48N 2°21E 134 B3
Gentilly La., U.S.A. 30°0N 90°2W 131 A2
Gentio do Ouro Brazil 11°25S 42°30W 332 D3
Gentofte Denmark 55°44N 12°32E 118 A3
Gentryville U.S.A. 38°6N 87°2W 311 F9
Genval Belgium 50°43N 4°29E 116 B2
Genyem Indonesia 2°46S 140°12E 231 E10
Genzano di Lucània Italy 40°51N 16°2E 201 B9
Genzano di Roma Italy 41°42N 12°41E 199 G9
Geoagiu Romania 45°55N 23°12E 183 E8
Geochang S. Korea 35°41N 127°55E 224 E3
Geogeumdo S. Korea 34°27N 127°10E 224 E3
Geographe B. Australia 33°30S 115°15E 279 F2
Geographe Chan. Australia 24°30S 113°0E 279 D1
Geographical Society Ø Greenland 72°57N 23°15W 154 C8
Geoje S. Korea 34°51N 128°35E 224 E4
Geojedo S. Korea 34°51N 128°38E 224 E4
Geokchay = Göyçay Azerbaijan 40°42N 47°43E 191 K8
Georga, Zemlya Russia 80°30N 49°0E 214 A5
George S. Africa 33°58S 22°29E 270 D3
George ➔ Canada 58°49N 66°10W 299 A6
George, L. N.S.W., Australia 35°10S 149°25E 283 C8
George, L. S. Austral., Australia 37°25S 140°0E 282 D4
George, L. W. Austral., Australia 22°45S 123°40E 278 D3
George, L. Uganda 0°5N 30°10E 268 B3
George, L. Fla., U.S.A. 29°17N 81°36W 317 F8
George, L. N.Y., U.S.A. 43°37N 73°33W 313 C11
George Gill Ra. Australia 24°22S 131°45E 278 D5
George I. Hong Kong, China 22°13N 114°7E 122 B1
George I. St. Helena 15°58S 5°38W 153 h
George Pt. Australia 20°6S 148°36E 280 b
George River = Kangiqsualujjuaq Canada 58°30N 65°59W 295 F18
George Rogers Clark Nat. Memorial ⌂ U.S.A. 38°41N 87°32W 311 F9
George Sound N.Z. 44°52S 167°25E 285 E2
George Town Tas., Australia 41°6S 146°49E 281 G4
George Town Bahamas 23°33N 75°47W 320 B4
George Town Cayman Is. 19°20N 81°24W 320 C3
George Town Malaysia 5°25N 100°20E 237 c
George V Land Antarctica 69°0S 148°0E 151 C10
George VI Sound Antarctica 71°0S 68°0W 151 D17
George West U.S.A. 28°20N 98°7W 314 G5
Georges River Bridge Australia 34°0S 151°6E 139 C1
Georgetown = Janjanbureh Gambia 13°30N 14°47W 262 C2
Georgetown Ascension I. 7°56S 14°25W 153 g
Georgetown Queens., Australia 18°17S 143°33E 280 B3
Georgetown Ont., Canada 43°40N 79°56W 312 C5
Georgetown P.E.I., Canada 46°13N 62°24W 299 C7
Georgetown Guyana 6°50N 58°12W 329 B6
Georgetown St. Vincent 13°15N 61°7W 323 n
Georgetown Calif., U.S.A. 38°54N 120°50W 306 G6
Georgetown Colo., U.S.A. 39°42N 105°42W 304 G11
Georgetown D.C., U.S.A. 38°54N 77°3W 143 B2
Georgetown Fla., U.S.A. 29°23N 81°38W 317 F8
Georgetown Ga., U.S.A. 31°53N 85°6W 316 D4
Georgetown Ill., U.S.A. 39°59N 87°38W 311 E9
Georgetown Ky., U.S.A. 38°13N 84°33W 311 F12
Georgetown N.Y., U.S.A. 42°46N 75°44W 313 D9
Georgetown Ohio, U.S.A. 38°52N 83°54W 311 F12
Georgetown S.C., U.S.A. 33°23N 79°17W 315 E15
Georgetown Tex., U.S.A. 30°38N 97°41W 314 F6
Georgia □ U.S.A. 32°50N 83°15W 316 C6
Georgia ■ Asia 42°0N 43°0E 191 J6
Georgia, Str. of N. Amer. 49°25N 124°0W 306 A3
Georgia Basin S. Ocean 50°45S 35°30W 151 B1
Georgia Dome U.S.A. 33°45N 84°23W 113 B2
Georgian B. Canada 45°15N 81°0W 312 A4
Georgian Bay Islands △ Canada 44°53N 79°52W 312 B5
Georgievka Kazakhstan 49°19N 84°34E 217 C10
Georgina ➔ Australia 23°30S 139°47E 280 C2
Georgina I. Canada 44°22N 79°17W 312 B5
Georgioupoli Greece 35°20N 24°15E 207 E5
Georgiu-Dezh = Liski Russia 51°3N 39°30E 189 G10
Georgiyevsk Russia 44°12N 43°28E 191 H6
Georgsmarienhütte Germany 52°13N 8°3E 178 C4
Gera Germany 50°53N 12°4E 178 E8
Geraardsbergen Belgium 50°45N 3°53E 170 D3
Geraki Greece 37°0N 22°42E 204 D4
Geraki, Akra Greece 37°42N 20°59E 207 D2
Geral, Serra Bahia, Brazil 14°0S 41°0W 333 D3
Geral, Serra Goiás, Brazil 11°15S 46°30W 332 D2
Geral, Serra Sta. Catarina, Brazil 26°25S 50°0W 335 B6
Geral de Goiás, Serra Brazil 12°0S 46°0W 333 D2
Geral do Paranã, Serra Brazil 15°0S 47°30W 333 E2
Gerald U.S.A. 38°24N 91°20W 310 F5
Geraldine N.Z. 44°5S 171°15E 285 E6
Geraldine Mont., U.S.A. 47°36N 110°16W 304 C8
Geraldton = Innisfail Australia 17°33S 146°5E 280 B4
Geraldton W. Austral., Australia 28°48S 114°32E 279 E1
Geraldton Ont., Canada 49°44N 87°10W 298 C2
Geranium Australia 35°23S 140°11E 282 C4
Gérardmer France 48°3N 6°50E 173 D13
Gerasdorf bei Wien Austria 48°17N 16°28E 142 A2
Gerberau Germany 48°12N 11°27E 131 A1
Gercüş Turkey 37°34N 41°23E 213 D9
Gerdine, Mt. U.S.A. 61°35N 152°27W 303 F9
Gerede Turkey 40°45N 32°10E 212 B5
Gerês, Sierra do Portugal 41°48N 8°0W 194 D3
Gereshk Afghan. 31°47N 64°35E 240 C2
Geretsried Germany 47°51N 11°28E 179 H7
Gérgal Spain 37°7N 2°31W 197 H2
Gerik Malaysia 5°50N 101°15E 237 K3
Gering U.S.A. 41°50N 103°40W 308 E2
Geriş Turkey 36°57N 31°43E 250 B2
Gerlach U.S.A. 40°39N 119°21W 304 F4
Gerlachovský štít Slovak Rep. 49°11N 20°7E 181 B13
Gerli Argentina 34°41S 58°22W 117 C2
Gerlogubi Ethiopia 6°53N 45°3E 267 C6
German Bight = Deutsche Bucht Germany 54°15N 8°0E 178 A4
German East Africa = Tanzania ■ Africa 6°0S 34°0E 268 D3
German Planina Macedonia 42°20N 22°0E 202 D6
German South West Africa = Namibia ■ Africa 22°0S 18°9E 270 B2
Germania Land Greenland 77°5N 19°30W 154 B9
Germansen Landing Canada 55°43N 124°40W 296 B4
Germantown Ohio, U.S.A. 39°38N 84°22W 311 E12
Germantown Tenn., U.S.A. 35°5N 89°49W 315 D10
Germantown Wis., U.S.A. 43°14N 88°6W 311 A8
Germany ■ Europe 51°0N 10°0E 178 E6
Germencik Turkey 37°52N 27°37E 205 D9
Germering Germany 48°8N 11°22E 179 G7
Germersheim Germany 49°12N 8°22E 179 F4
Germī Iran 39°1N 48°3E 213 C13
Germiston S. Africa 26°13S 28°10E 123 B2
Gern Germany 48°10N 11°32E 131 B2
Gernene Algeria 21°40N 2°24E 261 D5
Gernika-Lumo Spain 43°19N 2°40W 196 B2
Gernsheim Germany 49°45N 8°30E 179 F4
Gero Japan 35°48N 137°14E 223 B9
Gerogery Australia 35°50S 147°1E 283 C7
Gerokgak Indonesia 8°11S 114°27E 231 J17
Gerolzhofen Germany 49°54N 10°21E 179 F6
Gerona = Girona Spain 41°58N 2°46E 196 D7
Gerona Phil. 15°36N 120°36E 232 D3
Geropotamos ➔ Greece 35°3N 24°50E 207 E5
Gerrard Canada 50°30N 117°17W 296 C5
Gerringong Australia 34°46S 150°47E 283 C9
Gers □ France 43°35N 0°30E 174 E4
Gers ➔ France 44°9N 0°39E 174 D4
Gersfeld Germany 50°27N 9°56E 178 E5
Gersoppa Falls India 14°12N 74°46E 245 G2
Gersthofen Germany 48°25N 10°53E 179 G6
Gertak Sanggul Malaysia 5°17N 100°12E 237 c
Gertak Sanggul, Tanjung Malaysia 5°16N 100°11E 237 c
Gerung Indonesia 8°43S 116°7E 231 K19
Géryville = El Bayadh Algeria 33°40N 1°1E 261 B5
Gerzat France 45°48N 3°8E 174 C7
Gerze Turkey 41°48N 35°12E 212 B6
Geseke Germany 51°38N 8°31E 178 D4
Geser Indonesia 3°50S 130°54E 231 E8
Gesira △ Somalia 1°58N 44°59E 267 D5
Gesso ➔ Italy 44°24N 7°33E 198 D4
Gestro, Wabi ➔ Ethiopia 4°12N 42°2E 257 G5
Gesuit, Ex Convento dei Venice, Italy 142 a3
Getafe Spain 40°18N 3°43W 127 C1
Getinge Sweden 56°49N 12°44E 163 H6
Getty Center, The U.S.A. 34°4N 118°29W 126 B2
Gettysburg Pa., U.S.A. 39°50N 77°14W 309 F15
Gettysburg S. Dak., U.S.A. 45°1N 99°57W 308 C4
Getxo Spain 43°21N 2°59W 196 B2
Getz Ice Shelf Antarctica 75°0S 130°0W 151 D14
Geumodo S. Korea 34°31N 127°45E 224 E3
Geumpang Indonesia 4°52N 96°6E 234 B1
Geunjeong S. Korea 37°28N 126°54E 137 C1
Geureudong, Gunung Indonesia 4°13N 96°42E 234 B1
Geurie Australia 32°22S 148°50E 283 B8
Geva Binyamin West Bank 31°51N 35°17E 123 A2
Gevaş Turkey 38°15N 43°6E 213 C10
Gévaudan France 44°40N 3°40E 174 D7
Gevgelija Macedonia 41°9N 22°30E 202 E6
Gévora ➔ Spain 38°53N 6°57W 195 G4
Gevrai India 19°16N 75°45E 244 E2
Gewani Ethiopia 10°12N 40°40E 257 E5
Gex France 46°21N 6°3E 173 F13
Geyikli Turkey 39°48N 26°12E 205 B8
Geylang Serai Singapore 1°19N 103°53E 138 B3
Geyser U.S.A. 47°16N 110°30W 304 C8
Geyserville U.S.A. 38°42N 122°54W 306 G4
Geysir Iceland 64°19N 20°18W 155 C6
Geyve Turkey 40°30N 30°18E 212 B4
Gezhouba Dam China 30°40N 111°20E 229 B8
Ghâbat el Arab = Wang Kai South Sudan 9°3N 29°23E 257 F2
Ghabeish Sudan 12°9N 27°21E 257 E2
Ghadāf, W. al ➔ Iraq 32°56N 43°30E 213 F10
Ghadāmis Libya 30°11N 9°29E 258 B1
Ghaddūwah Libya 26°26N 14°19E 258 C2
Ghaggar ➔ India 29°30N 74°53E 242 E6
Ghaghara ➔ India 25°45N 84°40E 243 G11
Ghaghat ➔ Bangla. 25°19N 89°38E 241 C2
Ghaghe Solomon Is. 7°24S 158°15E 287 L10
Ghagra India 23°17N 84°33E 243 H11
Ghagra ➔ India 27°29N 81°9E 243 F9
Ghajn Tuffieha Bay Malta 35°56N 14°21E 206 F7
Ghajnsielem Malta 36°2N 14°17E 206 E7
Ghalla, Wadi el ➔ Sudan 10°25N 27°32E 257 E2
Ghallamane Mauritania 23°15N 10°0W 260 D3
Ghallamane, Sebkhet Mauritania 23°41N 9°50W 260 D3
Ghamid az Zenad S. Arabia 19°35N 41°24E 248 C3
Ghana ■ W. Afr. 8°0N 1°0W 263 D4
Ghanpokhara Nepal 28°17N 84°14E 243 E11
Ghansor India 22°39N 80°1E 243 H9
Ghanzi Botswana 21°50S 21°34E 270 B3
Ghanzi □ Botswana 22°30S 22°30E 270 B3
Gharapuri = Elephanta I. India 18°57N 72°56E 130 B2
Gharapuri India 18°57N 72°57E 130 B2
Gharb = Shahrak-e Qods Iran 35°47N 51°22E 141 A2
Gharb Malta 36°4N 14°13E 206 E6
Gharb Bahr el Ghazâl = Western Bahr el Ghazâl □ South Sudan 7°30N 25°30E 257 F2
Gharb-Chrarda-Beni Hssen □ Morocco 35°35N 6°0W 260 A3
Gharb Dârfûr □ Sudan 13°0N 23°0E 259 F4
Gharb el Istiwa'iya = Western Equatoria □ South Sudan 5°0N 30°0E 257 G3
Gharb Kordofân □ Sudan 12°0N 28°0E 257 E2
Gharbîya, Es Sahrâ el Egypt 27°40N 26°30E 256 B2
Ghardaïa Algeria 32°20N 3°37E 261 B5
Ghardaïa □ Algeria 31°5N 3°10E 261 B5
Ghârib, G. Egypt 28°6N 32°54E 256 B3
Gharig Sudan 10°47N 27°33E 257 E2
Gharm Tajikistan 39°0N 70°20E 214 F8
Gharm, W. ➔ Oman 19°57N 57°38E 249 C7
Gharyān Libya 32°10N 13°0E 258 B2
Ghāt Libya 24°59N 10°11E 258 D2
Ghāt □ Libya 25°35N 10°15E 258 C2
Ghatal India 22°40N 87°46E 243 H12
Ghatampur India 26°8N 80°13E 243 F9
Ghatgaon India 21°24N 85°53E 244 D7
Ghatkopar India 19°4N 72°54E 130 A2
Ghatprabha ➔ India 16°15N 75°20E 245 F2
Ghats, Eastern India 14°0N 78°50E 245 H4
Ghats, Western India 14°0N 75°0E 245 H2
Ghatsila India 22°36N 86°29E 243 H12
Ghaṭṭī Si. Arabia 31°16N 37°31E 246 D3
Ghawdex = Gozo Malta 36°3N 14°15E 206 E7
Ghayl Si. Arabia 21°40N 46°20E 248 B4
Ghayl Bā Wazīr Yemen 14°46N 49°22E 249 D5
Ghazal, Bahr el ➔ Chad 13°0N 15°47E 259 F3
Ghazal, Bahr el ➔ South Sudan 9°31N 30°25E 257 F3
Ghazaouet Algeria 35°8N 1°50W 261 A4
Ghaziabad India 28°42N 77°26E 242 E7
Ghazipur Delhi, India 28°37N 77°19E 120 B2
Ghazipur Ut. P., India 25°38N 83°35E 243 G10
Ghaznī Afghan. 33°30N 68°28E 242 C3
Ghaznī □ Afghan. 32°10N 68°20E 240 C3
Ghedi Italy 45°24N 10°16E 198 C7
Ghelari Romania 45°38N 22°45E 182 E7
Ghent = Gent Belgium 51°2N 3°42E 170 C3
Gheorghe Gheorghiu-Dej = Onești Romania 46°17N 26°47E 183 D11
Gheorgheni Romania 46°43N 25°41E 183 D10
Gherla Romania 47°2N 23°57E 183 C8
Ghidigeni Romania 46°3N 27°30E 183 D12
Ghilarza Italy 40°7N 8°50E 200 B1
Ghimeș-Făget Romania 46°35N 26°2E 183 D11
Ghīnah, Wādī al ➔ Si. Arabia 30°27N 38°14E 246 D3
Ghīrān, W. ➔ Si. Arabia 20°52N 47°10E 248 B4
Ghirardelli Square San Francisco, U.S.A. 136 a1
Ghisonaccia France 42°1N 9°26E 175 F13
Ghisoni France 42°7N 9°12E 175 F13
Ghizar ➔ Pakistan 36°15N 73°43E 243 A5
Ghizri Pakistan 24°49N 67°2E 123 B2
Ghizri Cr. ➔ Pakistan 24°47N 67°5E 123 B2
Gho ➔ India 18°30N 74°35E 244 E2
Ghogha India 21°40N 72°20E 244 D1
Ghonda India 28°41N 77°16E 120 A2
Ghot Ogrein Egypt 31°10N 25°20E 256 A2
Ghotaru India 27°20N 70°1E 242 F4
Ghotki Pakistan 28°5N 69°21E 242 E3
Ghowr □ Afghan. 34°0N 64°20E 240 B2
Ghubbet el Bûs Egypt 29°35N 32°21E 251 J3
Ghughri India 22°39N 80°41E 243 H9
Ghugus India 19°58N 79°12E 244 E4
Ghulam Mohammad Barrage Pakistan 25°30N 68°20E 242 G3
Ghurayrah Si. Arabia 18°37N 42°41E 248 C3
Ghūriān Afghan. 34°17N 61°25E 240 B1
Ghusuri India 22°37N 88°21E 124 B2
Ghuzzawīl, Sabkhat Libya 29°30N 19°30E 258 C3
Gia Dinh Vietnam 10°49N 106°42E 237 G6
Gia Lai = Plei Ku Vietnam 13°57N 108°0E 236 F7
Gia Nghia Vietnam 11°58N 107°42E 237 G6
Gia Ngoc Vietnam 14°50N 108°58E 236 E7
Gia Vuc Vietnam 14°42N 108°34E 236 E7
Giali Greece 36°41N 27°11E 205 E9
Gialtra Greece 38°51N 22°59E 204 C4
Giamama = Jamaame Somalia 0°4N 42°44E 267 D5
Gian Phil. 5°49N 125°12E 233 J5
Gianicolense Italy 41°53N 12°28E 136 B1
Gianicolo Rome, Italy 136 c1
Gianitsa Greece 40°46N 22°24E 202 F6
Giannutri Italy 42°15N 11°6E 198 F8
Giant Forest U.S.A. 36°36N 118°43W 306 J8
Giant Mts. = Krkonoše Czech Rep. 50°50N 15°35E 180 A8
Giant Sequoia ⌂ U.S.A. 36°10N 118°35W 306 K8
Giant Wheel = Riesenrad Austria 48°14N 16°23E 142 A2
Giants Causeway U.K. 55°16N 6°29W 166 A5
Giant's Tank Sri Lanka 8°51N 80°2E 245 K5
Gianyar Indonesia 8°32S 115°20E 231 K18
Giarabub = Al Jaghbūb Libya 29°42N 24°38E 258 C4
Giaros Greece 37°32N 24°40E 204 D6
Giarre Italy 37°43N 15°11E 201 E8
Giaveno Italy 45°2N 7°21E 198 C4
Gibara Cuba 21°9N 76°11W 320 B4
Gibbon U.S.A. 40°45N 98°51W 308 E4
Gibe ➔ Ethiopia 7°20N 37°36E 257 F4
Gibe I Ethiopia 8°7N 37°0E 257 F4
Gibe II Ethiopia 8°0N 37°30E 257 F4
Gibe III Ethiopia 7°0N 37°30E 257 F4
Gibellina Nuova Italy 37°47N 12°58E 200 E5
Gibeon Namibia 25°9S 17°43E 270 C2
Gibraleón Spain 37°23N 6°58W 195 H4
Gibraltar ☑ Europe 36°7N 5°22W 195 J5
Gibraltar, Str. of Medit. S. 35°55N 5°40W 195 K5
Gibraltar Pt. Canada 43°36N 79°23W 141 B2
Gibraltar Range △ Australia 29°31S 152°19E 281 D5
Gibson U.S.A. 33°14N 82°36W 316 B7
Gibson City U.S.A. 40°28N 88°22W 311 D8
Gibson Desert Australia 24°0S 126°0E 278 D4
Gibsonburg U.S.A. 41°23N 83°19W 311 C13
Gibsons Canada 49°24N 123°32W 296 D4
Gibsonton U.S.A. 27°51N 82°23W 317 H7
Gibsonville U.S.A. 39°46N 120°54W 306 F6
Gidami Ethiopia 8°59N 34°37E 266 C3
Giddalur India 15°20N 78°57E 245 G4
Giddings U.S.A. 30°11N 96°56W 314 F6
Gidea Park U.K. 51°35N 0°11E 125 A5
Gidole Ethiopia 5°40N 37°25E 257 F4
Giebnegáisi = Kebnekaise Sweden 67°53N 18°33E 160 C18
Gien France 47°40N 2°36E 173 E9
Giengen Germany 48°37N 10°14E 179 G6
Giesing Germany 48°6N 11°35E 131 B2
Giessen Germany 50°34N 8°41E 178 E4
Gīfān Iran 37°54N 57°28E 247 B8
Gifatin, Geziret Egypt 27°10N 33°50E 256 B3
Gifford U.S.A. 27°40N 80°25W 317 H9
Gifhorn Germany 52°29N 10°32E 178 C6
Gift Lake Canada 55°53N 115°49W 296 B5
Gifu Japan 35°30N 136°45E 223 B8
Gifu □ Japan 35°40N 137°0E 223 B9
Gigant Russia 46°28N 41°20E 191 G5
Giganta, Sa. de la Mexico 26°0N 111°39W 318 B2
Gigen Bulgaria 43°40N 24°28E 203 C8
Gigha U.K. 55°42N 5°44W 167 F3
Giglio Italy 42°20N 10°52E 198 F7
Gignac France 43°39N 3°32E 174 E7
Gigüela ➔ Spain 39°8N 3°44W 195 F7
Gijang S. Korea 35°14N 129°12E 224 E4
Gijón Spain 43°32N 5°42W 194 B5
Gikongoro Rwanda 2°28S 29°34E 268 C2
Gil I. Canada 53°12N 129°15W 296 C3
Gila ➔ U.S.A. 32°43N 114°33W 305 K6
Gila Bend U.S.A. 32°57N 112°43W 305 K7
Gila Bend Mts. U.S.A. 33°10N 113°0W 305 K7
Gila Cliff Dwellings ⌂ U.S.A. 33°12N 108°16W 305 K9
Gīlān □ Iran 37°0N 50°0E 247 B6
Gīlān-e Gharb Iran 34°8N 45°55E 213 E11
Gilău Romania 46°45N 23°23E 183 D8
Gilbert ➔ Australia 16°35S 141°15E 280 B3
Gilbert Is. Kiribati 1°0N 172°0E 277 A14
Gilbert River Australia 18°9S 142°52E 280 B3
Gilbert Seamounts Pac. Oc. 52°50N 150°10W 150 D18
Gilbués Brazil 9°50S 45°21W 332 C2
Gilead U.S.A. 44°24N 70°59W 313 B14
Gilf el Kebîr, Hadabat el Egypt 23°50N 25°50E 256 C2
Gilford I. Canada 50°40N 126°30W 296 C3
Gilgandra Australia 31°43S 148°39E 283 A8
Gilgil Kenya 0°30S 36°20E 268 C4
Gilgit India 35°50N 74°15E 243 B6
Gilgit ➔ Pakistan 35°44N 74°37E 243 B6
Gilgit-Baltistan □ Pakistan 36°30N 73°0E 243 A5
Gilgunnia Australia 32°26S 146°2E 283 B7
Gili, Pulau 10°0S 115°0E 235 D5
Gili ⌂ Mozam. 16°39S 38°27E 269 F4
Gilimanuk Indonesia 8°10S 114°26E 231 J17
Giljeva Planina Europe 43°9N 20°0E 202 C3
Gill Pt. St. Helena 15°58S 5°38W 153 h
Gillam Canada 56°20N 94°40W 297 B10
Gilleleje Denmark 56°8N 12°19E 163 H6
Gillen, L. Australia 26°11S 124°38E 279 E3
Gilles, L. Australia 32°50S 136°45E 282 B2
Gillespie U.S.A. 39°8N 89°49W 310 E7
Gillespies Pt. N.Z. 43°24S 169°49E 285 D4
Gillette U.S.A. 44°18N 105°30W 304 D11
Gilliat Australia 20°40S 141°28E 280 C3
Gillingham U.K. 51°23N 0°33E 169 F8
Gilman U.S.A. 40°46N 88°0W 311 D9
Gilman City U.S.A. 40°8N 93°53W 310 D3
Gilmer U.S.A. 32°44N 94°57W 314 E7
Gilmerton U.K. 55°54N 3°7W 121 B3
Gilmore, L. Australia 32°29S 121°37E 279 F3
Gilmour Canada 44°48N 77°37W 312 B7
Gilo West Bank 31°44N 35°11E 123 B2
Gilo ➔ Ethiopia 8°10N 33°15E 257 F3
Gilort ➔ Romania 44°38N 23°32E 183 F8
Gilroy U.S.A. 37°1N 121°34W 306 H5
Giluwe, Mt. Papua N. G. 6°8S 143°52E 286 D2
Gimbi Ethiopia 9°3N 35°42E 257 F4
Gimcheon S. Korea 36°11N 128°4E 224 D4
Gimhae S. Korea 35°14N 128°53E 224 E4
Gimhwa S. Korea 38°17N 127°28E 224 C3
Gimie, Mt. St. Lucia 13°54N 61°0W 323 m
Gimje S. Korea 35°48N 126°45E 224 E3
Gimli Canada 50°40N 97°0W 297 C9
Gimmersta Sweden 59°14N 18°14E 139 B3
Gimo Sweden 60°11N 18°12E 162 D12
Gimone ➔ France 44°0N 1°6E 174 E5
Gimont France 43°38N 0°52E 174 E4
Gin ➔ Sri Lanka 6°5N 80°7E 245 L5
Gin Gin Australia 25°0S 151°58E 281 D5
Ginâh Egypt 25°21N 30°30E 256 B3
Ginatilan Phil. 9°34N 123°19E 233 G4
Gineifa Egypt 30°12N 32°25E 256 H8
Gingee India 12°15N 79°25E 245 H4
Gingin Australia 31°22S 115°54E 279 F2
Gingindlovu S. Africa 29°2S 31°30E 271 C5
Gingoog Phil. 8°50N 125°7E 233 G5
Gingoog B. Phil. 8°54N 125°7E 233 G5
Ginir Ethiopia 7°6N 40°40E 257 F5
Ginosa Italy 40°35N 16°45E 201 B9
Ginowan Japan 26°15N 127°45E 288 a
Ginza Tokyo, Japan 140 b5
Ginzo de Limia = Xinzo de Limia Spain 42°3N 7°47W 194 C3
Giofyros ➔ Greece 35°20N 25°6E 207 E6
Giohar = Jawhar Somalia 2°48N 45°30E 267 D6
Gióia, G. di Italy 38°30N 15°45E 201 D8
Gióia del Colle Italy 40°48N 16°55E 201 B9
Gióia Táuro Italy 38°25N 15°54E 201 D8
Gioiosa Iónica Italy 38°20N 16°18E 201 D9
Gioiosa Marea Italy 38°10N 14°54E 201 D7
Giona, Oros Greece 38°38N 22°14E 204 C4
Giovi, Passo dei Italy 44°33N 8°57E 198 D5
Giovinazzo Italy 41°11N 16°40E 201 A9
Gippsland Australia 37°52S 147°0E 283 D7
Gir △ India 21°0N 71°0E 242 J4
Gir Hills India 21°0N 71°0E 242 J4
Girab India 26°2N 70°38E 242 F4
Girâfi, W. ➔ Egypt 29°58N 34°39E 251 J5
Giraltovce Slovak Rep. 49°7N 21°32E 181 B14
Girapetra, Akra Greece 38°51N 20°41E 207 B2
Girard St. Lucia 13°59N 60°57W 323 m
Girard Ga., U.S.A. 33°3N 81°43W 316 B8
Girard Ill., U.S.A. 39°27N 89°47W 310 E7
Girard Kans., U.S.A. 37°31N 94°51W 308 G6
Girard Ohio, U.S.A. 41°9N 80°42W 312 E4
Girard Pa., U.S.A. 42°0N 80°19W 312 E4
Girardot Colombia 4°18N 74°48W 328 C3
Giraud, Pte. Dominica 15°20N 61°5W 323 k
Girdle Ness U.K. 57°9N 2°3W 167 D6
Giresun Turkey 40°55N 38°30E 213 B8
Giresun □ Turkey 40°30N 38°30E 213 B8
Girga Egypt 26°17N 31°55E 256 B3
Girgaum Mumbai, India 130 b2
Girgenti = Agrigento Italy 37°19N 13°34E 200 E6
Girgir, C. Papua N. G. 3°50S 144°35E 286 B3
Giri ➔ Dem. Rep. of the Congo 0°28N 17°59E 264 B3
Giri ➔ India 30°28N 77°41E 242 D7
Giridih India 24°10N 86°21E 243 G12
Girifalco Italy 38°49N 16°25E 201 D9
Giriftu Kenya 1°59N 39°46E 268 B4
Girilambone Australia 31°16S 146°57E 283 A7
Girne = Kyrenia Cyprus 35°20N 33°20E 207 E9
Giro Nigeria 11°7N 4°42E 263 C5
Giromagny France 47°45N 6°50E 173 E13
Giron = Kiruna Sweden 67°52N 20°15E 160 C19
Girona Spain 41°58N 2°46E 196 D7
Girona □ Spain 42°11N 2°38E 196 C7
Gironde □ France 44°45N 0°30W 174 D3
Gironde ➔ France 45°32N 1°7W 174 C2
Gironella Spain 42°2N 1°53E 196 C6
Girraween △ Australia 28°46S 151°54E 281 D5
Girringun △ Australia 18°15S 145°32E 280 B4
Giru Australia 19°30S 147°5E 280 B4
Girvan U.K. 55°14N 4°51W 167 F4
Gisborne Vic., Australia 37°29S 144°36E 282 D6
Gisborne N.Z. 38°39S 178°5E 284 E7
Gisborne □ N.Z. 38°39S 178°5E 284 E6
Gisenyi Rwanda 1°41S 29°15E 268 C2
Gislaved Sweden 57°19N 13°32E 163 G7
Gisors France 49°15N 1°47E 173 C8
Gitarama Rwanda 2°4S 29°45E 268 C2
Gitega Burundi 3°26S 29°56E 268 C2
Githio Greece 36°46N 22°34E 204 E4
Gitschin = Jičín Czech Rep. 50°25N 15°28E 180 A8
Giuba = Juba ➔ Somalia 1°30N 42°35E 267 D5
Giudecca, Canale della Venice, Italy 142 c2
Giugliano in Campania Italy 40°56N 14°12E 201 B7
Giulianova Italy 42°45N 13°57E 199 F10
Giura Greece 39°23N 24°10E 204 B6
Giurgeni Romania 44°45N 27°48E 183 F12
Giurgiu Romania 43°52N 25°57E 183 G10
Giurgiu □ Romania 44°20N 26°0E 183 F10
Giurgiulești Moldova 45°29N 28°12E 183 E13
Giustizia, Palazzo Venice, Italy 142 b3
Giv'at Ram Israel 31°47N 35°12E 123 B2
Giv'at Ye'arim Israel 31°47N 35°5E 123 B1
Giv'at Ze'ev West Bank 31°52N 35°10E 123 A2
Give Denmark 55°51N 9°13E 163 J3
Givet France 50°8N 4°49E 173 B11
Giv'on West Bank 31°51N 35°10E 123 A1
Givors France 45°35N 4°45E 175 C8
Givry France 46°41N 4°46E 173 F11
Giyani S. Africa 23°19S 30°43E 271 B5
Giyon Ethiopia 8°33N 38°1E 257 F4
Giza = El Giza Egypt 30°0N 31°12E 117 A2
Giza Pyramids Egypt 29°58N 31°9E 117 B1
Gizab Afghan. 33°22N 66°17E 242 C1
Gizhiga Russia 62°3N 160°30E 215 C17
Gizhiginskaya Guba Russia 61°0N 158°0E 215 C16
Gizo Solomon Is. 8°7S 156°50E 287 M9
Giżycko Poland 54°2N 21°48E 184 D8
Gizzeria Italy 38°59N 16°12E 201 D9
Gjakovë Kosovo 42°22N 20°26E 202 D4
Gjalicë e Lumës, Mal. Albania 42°2N 20°25E 202 D4
Gjantija Malta 36°2N 14°16E 206 E7
Gjegjan Albania 41°58N 20°3E 202 E4
Gjendesheim Norway 61°30N 8°48E 164 C5
Gjeravicë Kosovo 42°32N 20°8E 202 D4
Gjermundshamn Norway 60°40N 5°55E 164 D2
Gjersjøen Norway 59°47N 10°47E 133 B3
Gjerstad Norway 58°54N 9°1E 164 F6
Gjevilvatnet Norway 62°43N 9°23E 164 B6
Gjilan Kosovo 42°28N 21°29E 202 D5
Gjirokastër Albania 40°7N 20°10E 202 F4
Gjoa Haven Canada 68°38N 95°53W 294 D12
Gjøra Norway 62°33N 9°4E 164 B6
Gjøvik Norway 60°47N 10°43E 164 D7
Gjuhës, Kep i Albania 40°28N 19°15E 202 F3
Gjurakoc Kosovo 42°43N 20°29E 202 D4
Glace Bay Canada 46°11N 59°58W 299 C8
Glacier △ B.C., Canada 51°15N 117°30W 296 C5
Glacier △ Mont., U.S.A. 48°42N 113°48W 304 B7
Glacier Bay U.S.A. 58°40N 136°0W 303 G14
Glacier Bay ⌂ U.S.A. 58°45N 136°30W 296 B1
Glacier Peak U.S.A. 48°7N 121°7W 304 B3
Gladesville Australia 33°50S 151°8E 139 B1
Gladewater U.S.A. 32°33N 94°56W 314 E7
Gladsakse Denmark 55°45N 12°25E 118 A2
Gladstone Queens., Australia 23°52S 151°16E 280 C5
Gladstone S. Austral., Australia 33°15S 138°22E 282 B3
Gladstone Man., Canada 50°13N 98°57W 297 C9
Gladstone Ill., U.S.A. 43°52N 90°57W 310 D6
Gladstone Mich., U.S.A. 45°51N 87°1W 308 C10
Gladstone Mo., U.S.A. 39°13N 94°35W 310 E2
Gladwin U.S.A. 43°59N 84°29W 309 D11
Glafsfjorden Sweden 59°30N 12°37E 162 E6
Glagah Indonesia 8°13S 114°18E 231 J17
Glagów Małopolski Poland 50°10N 21°56E 185 H8
Glåma = Glomma ➔ Norway 59°12N 10°57E 164 E7
Gláma Iceland 65°48N 23°0W 155 B4
Glamis U.S.A. 32°55N 115°5W 307 N11
Glamoč Bos.-H. 44°3N 16°51E 199 D13
Glamorgan, Vale of □ U.K. 51°28N 3°25W 169 F4
Glåmos Norway 62°41N 11°25E 164 B8
Glamsbjerg Denmark 55°17N 10°6E 163 J4
Glanvillia Dominica 15°34N 61°28W 323 k
Glarus Switz. 47°3N 9°4E 179 H5
Glarus □ Switz. 47°0N 9°5E 179 J5
Glasco Kans., U.S.A. 39°22N 97°50W 308 F5
Glasco N.Y., U.S.A. 42°3N 73°57W 313 D11
Glasgow C. of Glasg., U.K. 55°51N 4°15W 167 F4
Glasgow Ky., U.S.A. 37°0N 85°55W 309 G11
Glasgow Mo., U.S.A. 39°14N 92°51W 310 E4
Glasgow Mont., U.S.A. 48°12N 106°38W 304 B10
Glasgow, City of □ U.K. 55°51N 4°12W 167 F4
Glasgow Int. ✕ (GLA) U.K. 55°51N 4°21W 167 F4
Glaslyn Canada 53°22N 108°21W 297 C7
Glasnevin Ireland 53°22N 6°15W 120 A2
Glassmoor U.S.A. 38°49N 77°0W 143 C3
Glasthule Ireland 53°17N 6°7W 120 B3
Glastonbury Somst., U.K. 51°9N 2°43W 169 F5
Glastonbury Conn., U.S.A. 41°43N 72°37W 313 E12
Glatz = Kłodzko Poland 50°28N 16°38E 185 H3
Glauchau Germany 50°49N 12°31E 178 E8
Glava Sweden 59°33N 12°35E 162 E6
Glavice Croatia 43°43N 16°41E 199 E13
Glazov Russia 58°9N 52°40E 190 A11
Gleichen Canada 50°52N 113°3W 296 C6
Gleisdorf Austria 47°6N 15°44E 180 D8
Gleiwitz = Gliwice Poland 50°22N 18°41E 185 H5
Glen U.S.A. 44°7N 71°11W 313 B13
Glen Affric U.K. 57°17N 5°1W 167 D3
Glen Afton N.Z. 37°37S 175°4E 284 D4
Glen Canyon U.S.A. 37°30N 110°40W 305 H8
Glen Canyon ⌂ U.S.A. 37°15N 111°0W 305 H8
Glen Canyon Dam U.S.A. 36°57N 111°29W 305 H8
Glen Coe U.K. 56°40N 5°0W 167 E3
Glen Cove U.S.A. 40°51N 73°38W 313 F11
Glen Garry U.K. 57°3N 5°7W 167 D3
Glen Innes Australia 29°44S 151°44E 281 D5
Glen Iris Australia 37°51S 145°3E 128 B2
Glen Lyon U.S.A. 41°10N 76°5W 313 E8
Glen Mar Park U.S.A. 38°57N 77°7W 143 B2
Glen Massey N.Z. 37°38S 175°2E 284 D4
Glen Mor U.K. 57°9N 4°37W 167 D4
Glen Moriston U.K. 57°11N 4°52W 167 D4
Glen Robertson Canada 45°22N 74°30W 313 A10
Glen Rouge Park Canada 43°49N 79°10W 141 A4
Glen Spean U.K. 56°53N 4°40W 167 E4
Glen Ullin U.S.A. 46°49N 101°50W 308 B3
Glénan, Îs. de France 47°42N 4°0W 172 E3
Glenasmole Reservoirs Ireland 53°15N 6°21W 120 B1
Glenavy N.Z. 44°54S 171°7E 285 E6
Glenbeigh Ireland 52°3N 9°58W 166 D2
Glenburn Australia 37°27S 145°26E 283 D6
Glencoe Ont., Canada 42°45N 81°43W 312 D3
Glencoe KwaZulu Natal, S. Africa 28°11S 30°11E 271 C5
Glencoe Ala., U.S.A. 33°57N 85°56W 316 B4
Glencoe Ill., U.S.A. 42°8N 87°45W 119 A2
Glencoe Minn., U.S.A. 44°46N 94°9W 308 C6
Glencolumbkille Ireland 54°43N 8°42W 166 B3
Glencorse Res. U.K. 55°51N 3°15W 121 B2
Glencullen Ireland 53°14N 6°12W 120 B2
Glendale Ariz., U.S.A. 33°32N 112°11W 305 K7
Glendale Calif., U.S.A. 34°9N 118°15W 126 B3
Glendale Fla., U.S.A. 30°52N 86°7W 316 E3
Glendale Zimbabwe 17°22S 31°5E 269 F3
Glendive U.S.A. 47°7N 104°43W 304 C11
Glendo U.S.A. 42°30N 105°2W 304 E11
Glendoo Mt. Ireland 53°14N 6°16W 120 B2
Glenelg Australia 34°58S 138°31E 282 C3
Glenelg ➔ Australia 38°4S 140°59E 282 E4
Glenfield U.S.A. 43°43N 75°24W 313 C9
Glengad Hd. Ireland 55°20N 7°10W 166 A4
Glengarriff Ireland 51°45N 9°34W 166 E2
Glengoffe Jamaica 18°10N 76°53W 320 a
Glenham N.Z. 46°26S 168°52E 285 G3
Glenhope N.Z. 41°40S 172°39E 285 B7
Glenhuntly Australia 37°52S 145°1E 128 B2
Glenmary, Mt. N.Z. 43°55S 169°55E 285 D4
Glenmont U.S.A. 40°31N 82°6W 312 F2
Glenmorgan Australia 27°14S 149°42E 281 D4
Glenn U.S.A. 39°31N 122°1W 306 F4
Glennallen U.S.A. 62°7N 145°33W 303 E11
Glennamaddy Ireland 53°37N 8°33W 166 C3
Glenns Ferry U.S.A. 42°57N 115°18W 304 E6
Glennville U.S.A. 31°56N 81°56W 316 D8
Glenora Canada 44°2N 77°3W 312 B7
Glenorchy Tas., Australia 42°49S 147°18E 281 G4
Glenorchy Vic., Australia 36°55S 142°41E 282 D5
Glenorchy N.Z. 44°51S 168°24E 285 E3
Glenore Australia 17°50S 141°12E 280 B3
Glenreagh Australia 30°2S 153°1E 281 E5
Glenrock U.S.A. 42°52N 105°52W 304 E11
Glenrothes U.K. 56°12N 3°10W 167 E5
Glenrowan Australia 36°29S 146°13E 283 D7
Glens Falls U.S.A. 43°19N 73°39W 313 C11
Glenside U.S.A. 40°6N 75°9W 313 F9
Glenthompson Australia 37°38S 142°38E 282 D5
Glenties Ireland 54°48N 8°17W 166 B3
Glenveagh △ Ireland 55°3N 8°1W 166 A3
Glenview U.S.A. 42°3N 87°48W 119 A2
Glenview Countryside U.S.A. 42°3N 87°49W 119 A2
Glenville U.S.A. 38°56N 80°50W 309 F13
Glenvista S. Africa 26°17S 28°3E 123 B2
Glenwood Nfld. & L., Canada 49°0N 54°58W 299 C9
Glenwood Ark., U.S.A. 34°20N 93°33W 314 D8
Glenwood Ga., U.S.A. 32°11N 82°40W 316 C7
Glenwood Hawai'i, U.S.A. 19°29N 155°9W 302 D6
Glenwood Iowa, U.S.A. 41°3N 95°45W 308 E6
Glenwood Minn., U.S.A. 45°39N 95°23W 308 C6
Glenwood Wash., U.S.A. 46°1N 121°17W 306 D5
Glenwood Springs U.S.A. 39°33N 107°19W 304 G10
Glettinganes Iceland 65°30N 13°37W 155 B13
Glidden U.S.A. 42°4N 94°44W 310 B2
Glifada Greece 37°52N 23°45E 112 B2
Glimåkra Sweden 56°19N 14°7E 163 H8
Glin Ireland 52°34N 9°17W 166 D2

Glina Croatia 45°20N 16°6E 199 C13
Glinojeck Poland 52°49N 20°21E 185 F7
Glittertind Norway 61°40N 8°32E 164 C5
Gliwice Poland 50°22N 18°41E 185 H5
Globe U.S.A. 33°24N 110°47W 305 K8
Glodeanu Siliştea Romania 44°50N 26°48E 183 F11
Glodeni Moldova 47°45N 27°31E 183 C12
Glödnitz Austria 46°53N 14°7E 180 E7
Glogau = Głogów Poland 51°37N 16°5E 185 G3
Gloggnitz Austria 47°41N 15°56E 180 D8
Głogów Poland 51°37N 16°5E 185 G3
Głogówek Poland 50°21N 17°53E 185 H4
Glomma → Norway 59°12N 10°57E 164 E7
Gloria Phil. 12°59N 121°30E 232 E3
Glorieuses, Îs. Ind. Oc. 11°30S 47°20E 272 A2
Glosa Greece 39°10N 23°45E 204 B5
Glossop U.K. 53°27N 1°56W 168 D6
Glostrup Denmark 55°39N 12°23E 118 B2
Gloucester N.S.W., Australia 32°0S 151°59E 283 B9
Gloucester Papua N. G. 5°31S 148°31E 286 C5
Gloucester Gloucs., U.K. 51°53N 2°15W 169 F5
Gloucester Mass., U.S.A. 42°37N 70°40W 313 D14
Gloucester, C. Papua N. G. 5°26S 148°21E 286 C5
Gloucester I. Australia 20°0S 148°30E 280 b
Gloucester Island △ Australia 20°2S 148°30E 280 b
Gloucester Point U.S.A. 37°15N 76°30W 309 G15
Gloucestershire □ U.K. 51°46N 2°15W 169 F5
Glover I. Grenada 11°59N 61°47W 323 q
Gloversville U.S.A. 43°3N 74°21W 313 C10
Glovertown Canada 48°40N 54°3W 299 C9
Gloverville = Warrenville U.S.A. 33°33N 81°48W 316 B8
Głowno Poland 51°59N 19°42E 185 G6
Głubczyce Poland 50°13N 17°52E 185 H4
Glubokiy Russia 48°35N 40°25E 191 F5
Glūbokoe Kazakhstan 50°8N 82°18E 217 B10
Glubokoye = Hlybokaye Belarus 55°10N 27°45E 188 E4
Głuchołazy Poland 50°19N 17°24E 185 H4
Glücksburg Germany 54°50N 9°33E 178 A5
Glückstadt Germany 53°45N 9°25E 178 B5
Glukhov = Hlukhiv Ukraine 51°40N 33°58E 189 G7
Glusk Belarus 52°53N 28°41E 177 B15
Głuszyca Poland 50°41N 16°23E 185 H3
Glyn Ebwy = Ebbw Vale U.K. 51°46N 3°12W 169 F4
Glyngøre Denmark 56°46N 8°52E 163 H2
Gmünd Kärnten, Austria 46°54N 13°31E 180 E6
Gmünd Niederösterreich, Austria 48°45N 15°0E 180 C8
Gmunden Austria 47°55N 13°48E 180 D6
Gnali Gabon 2°34S 11°18E 264 C2
Gnarp Sweden 62°3N 17°16E 162 B11
Gnesen = Gniezno Poland 52°30N 17°35E 185 F4
Gnesta Sweden 59°3N 17°17E 162 E11
Gniew Poland 53°50N 18°50E 184 E5
Gniewkowo Poland 52°54N 18°25E 185 F5
Gniezno Poland 52°30N 17°35E 185 F4
Gnjilane = Gjilan Kosovo 42°28N 21°29E 202 D5
Gnoien Germany 53°58N 12°41E 178 B8
Gnosjö Sweden 57°22N 13°43E 163 G7
Gnowangerup Australia 33°58S 117°59E 279 F2
Go Cong Vietnam 10°22N 106°40E 237 G6
Gō-Gawa → Japan 35°2N 132°13E 222 B4
Gō-no-ura Japan 33°44N 129°40E 222 D1
Goa India 15°33N 73°59E 245 G1
Goa Phil. 13°42N 123°29E 232 E4
Goa □ India 15°33N 73°59E 245 G1
Goalen Hd. Australia 36°33S 150°4E 283 D9
Goalpara India 26°10N 90°40E 241 B3
Goaltor India 22°43N 87°10E 243 H12
Goalundo Ghat Bangla. 23°50N 89°47E 243 H13
Goaso Ghana 6°48N 2°30W 262 D4
Goat Fell U.K. 55°38N 5°11W 167 F3
Goat I. Antigua & B. 17°43N 61°51W 322 c
Goat Pt. Antigua & B. 17°44N 61°51W 322 c
Goba Ethiopia 7°1N 39°59E 257 F4
Goba Mozam. 26°15S 32°13E 271 C5
Gobabis Namibia 22°30S 19°0E 270 B2
Gobe Papua N. G. 9°4S 149°0E 286 E5
Göbel Turkey 40°0N 28°9E 203 F12
Gobernador Gregores Argentina 48°46S 70°15W 336 C2
Gobi Asia 44°0N 110°0E 226 C6
Gobichettipalayam India 11°31N 77°21E 245 J3
Gobles U.S.A. 42°22N 85°53W 311 B11
Gobō Japan 33°53N 135°10E 223 D7
Gobo South Sudan 5°40N 31°10E 257 F3
Gobustan Azerbaijan 40°7N 49°22E 213 B13
Göçbeyli Turkey 39°13N 27°25E 205 B9
Goch Germany 51°41N 6°9E 178 D2
Gochang S. Korea 35°26N 126°42E 224 E3
Gochas Namibia 24°59S 18°55E 270 B2
God Dere Ethiopia 5°12N 44°1E 267 C5
Godalming U.K. 51°11N 0°36W 169 F7
Godavari → India 16°25N 82°18E 244 F6
Godavari Pt. India 17°0N 82°20E 244 F6
Godbout Canada 49°20N 67°38W 299 C6
Godda India 24°50N 87°13E 243 G12
Gode Ethiopia 5°53N 43°35E 267 C5
Godech Bulgaria 43°1N 23°4E 202 C7
Goderich Canada 43°45N 81°41W 312 C3
Goderville France 49°38N 0°22E 172 C7
Godfrey U.S.A. 38°58N 90°11W 310 F6
Godfrey Ra. Australia 24°0S 117°0E 279 D2
Goðafoss Iceland 65°41N 17°33W 155 B9
Godhavn = Qeqertarsuaq Greenland 69°15N 53°38W 154 D5
Goðdalir Iceland 65°20N 19°6W 155 B7
Godhra India 22°49N 73°40E 242 H5
Godinlabe Somalia 5°54N 46°38E 267 C6
Gödöllő Hungary 47°38N 19°25E 182 C4
Godoy Cruz Argentina 32°56S 68°52W 334 C2
Gods → Canada 56°22N 92°51W 298 A1
Gods L. Canada 54°40N 94°15W 298 B1
Gods River Canada 54°50N 94°5W 297 C10
Godthåb = Nuuk Greenland 64°10N 51°35W 154 E5
Godwin Austen = K2 Pakistan 35°58N 76°32E 243 B7
Goeie Hoop, Kaap die = Good Hope, C. of S. Africa 34°24S 18°30E 270 D2
Goéland, L. au Canada 49°50N 76°48W 298 C4
Goélands, L. aux Canada 55°27N 64°17W 299 A7
Goeree Neths. 51°50N 4°0E 170 C3
Goes Neths. 51°30N 3°55E 170 C3
Gofca → Somalia 1°10N 43°43E 267 D5
Goffstown U.S.A. 43°1N 71°36W 313 C13
Gogama Canada 47°35N 81°43W 298 C3
Gogar U.K. 55°56N 3°20W 121 B2
Gogebic, L. U.S.A. 46°30N 89°35W 308 B9
Goggetti Ethiopia 8°11N 38°35E 257 F4
Gogolin Poland 50°30N 18°0E 185 H5
Gogonou Benin 10°50N 2°50E 263 C5
Gogra = Ghaghara → India 25°45N 84°40E 243 G11
Gogriâl South Sudan 8°30N 28°8E 257 F2
Gogti Ethiopia 10°7N 42°51E 257 E5
Gohana India 29°8N 76°42E 242 E7
Goharganj India 23°1N 77°41E 242 H7
Goheung S. Korea 34°36N 127°17E 224 E3
Goi → India 22°4N 74°46E 242 H6
Goiana Brazil 7°33S 34°59W 332 C5
Goianésia Brazil 15°18S 49°7W 333 E2
Goiânia Brazil 16°43S 49°20W 333 E2
Goiás Brazil 15°55S 50°10W 333 E1
Goiás □ Brazil 12°10S 48°0W 332 D2
Goiatins Brazil 7°42S 47°10W 332 C2
Goiatuba Brazil 18°1S 49°23W 333 E2
Goidu Atoll Maldives 4°53N 72°54E 272 d
Goio-Erê Brazil 24°12S 53°1W 335 A5
Góis Portugal 40°10N 8°6W 194 E2
Gojam Ethiopia 10°55N 36°30E 257 E4
Gojeb, Wabi → Ethiopia 7°12N 36°40E 257 F4
Gojō Japan 34°21N 135°42E 223 C7
Gojra Pakistan 31°10N 72°40E 242 D5
Gokak India 16°11N 74°52E 245 F2
Gokarn India 14°33N 74°17E 245 G2
Gökçe = Sevana Lich Armenia 40°30N 45°20E 191 K7
Gökçe Turkey 40°10N 25°55E 203 F9
Gökçeada Turkey 40°10N 25°50E 203 F9
Gökçedağ Turkey 39°33N 28°56E 205 B10
Gökçen Turkey 38°7N 27°53E 205 C9
Gökçeören Turkey 38°37N 28°35E 205 C10
Gökçeyazı Turkey 39°40N 27°40E 205 B9
Gökırmak → Turkey 41°25N 35°8E 212 B6
Gökova Turkey 37°1N 28°17E 205 D10
Gökova Körfezi Turkey 36°55N 27°50E 205 E9
Göksu → Turkey 36°19N 34°5E 250 B5
Göksun Turkey 38°2N 36°30E 212 C7
Gokteik Burma 22°26N 97°0E 241 D6
Göktepe Karaman, Turkey 36°37N 32°37E 250 B3
Göktepe Muğla, Turkey 37°25N 28°34E 205 D10
Göktürk Turkey 41°10N 28°53E 122 A1
Gokurt Pakistan 29°40N 67°26E 242 E2
Gokwe Zimbabwe 18°7S 28°58E 271 A4
Gol Norway 60°42N 8°55E 164 D5
Gol Gol Australia 34°12S 142°14E 282 C5
Gola India 28°3N 80°32E 243 E9
Golabari India 22°35N 88°20E 124 B2
Golabki Poland 52°12N 20°52E 143 B1
Golaghat India 26°30N 94°0E 241 B5
Golakganj India 26°8N 89°52E 241 B2
Golan Heights = Hagolan Syria 33°0N 35°45E 250 F6
Gołańcz Poland 52°57N 17°18E 185 F4
Golāshkerd Iran 27°59N 57°16E 247 E8
Golaya Pristen = Hola Prystan Ukraine 46°29N 32°32E 189 J7
Gölbaşı Adiyaman, Turkey 37°43N 37°25E 212 D7
Gölbaşı Ankara, Turkey 39°47N 32°49E 212 C5
Golconda India 17°24N 78°23E 244 F4
Golconda Nev., U.S.A. 40°58N 117°30W 304 F5
Gölcük Kocaeli, Turkey 40°42N 29°48E 203 F13
Gölcük Niğde, Turkey 38°14N 34°47E 212 C6
Gold U.S.A. 41°52N 77°50W 312 E7
Gold Beach U.S.A. 42°25N 124°25W 304 E1
Gold Coast = Ghana ■ W. Afr. 8°0N 1°0W 263 D4
Gold Coast Queens., Australia 28°0S 153°25E 276 F9
Gold Coast Ill., U.S.A. 41°54N 87°37W 119 a2
Gold Coast W. Afr. 4°0N 1°40W 263 E4
Gold Creek U.S.A. 62°46N 149°41W 303 E10
Gold Hill U.S.A. 42°26N 123°3W 304 E2
Gold River Canada 49°46N 126°3W 296 D3
Gołdap Poland 54°19N 22°18E 184 D9
Goldberg = Złotoryja Poland 51°8N 15°55E 185 G2
Goldberg Germany 53°35N 12°4E 178 B8
Golden B.C., Canada 51°20N 116°59W 296 C5
Golden Ill., U.S.A. 40°7N 91°1W 310 D5
Golden B. N.Z. 40°40S 172°50E 285 A7
Golden Beach U.S.A. 25°57N 80°7W 129 C3
Golden Buddha = Traimit Bangkok, Thailand 113 c2
Golden Gate U.S.A. 37°48N 122°29W 136 B2
Golden Gate ⌓ U.S.A. 37°49N 122°31W 136 A2
Golden Gate Bridge U.S.A. 37°49N 122°28W 136 B2
Golden Gate Highlands △ S. Africa 28°40S 28°40E 271 C4
Golden Gate Park U.S.A. 37°46N 122°28W 136 B2
Golden Grove Middlesex, Jamaica 18°19N 77°9W 320 a
Golden Grove Surrey, Jamaica 17°55N 76°16W 320 a
Golden Hinde Canada 49°40N 125°44W 296 D3
Golden Horn = Haliç Turkey 41°1N 28°57E 122 B1
Golden Lake Canada 45°34N 77°21W 312 A7
Golden Rock India 10°45N 78°48E 245 J4
Golden Spike ⌓ U.S.A. 41°37N 112°33W 304 F7
Golden Vale Ireland 52°33N 8°17W 166 D3
Goldendale U.S.A. 45°49N 120°50W 304 D3
Golders Green U.K. 51°34N 0°11W 125 A2
Goldfield U.S.A. 37°42N 117°14W 305 H5
Goldingen = Kuldīga Latvia 56°58N 21°59E 184 B8
Goldoni, Casa Venice, Italy 142 b2
Goldoni, Teatro Venice, Italy 142 b3
Goldsand L. Canada 57°2N 101°8W 297 B8
Goldsboro U.S.A. 35°23N 77°59W 315 D16
Goldsmith U.S.A. 31°59N 102°37W 314 F3
Goldthwaite U.S.A. 31°27N 98°34W 314 F5
Golegã Portugal 39°24N 8°29W 195 F2
Goleniów Poland 53°35N 14°50E 184 E1
Golestān □ Iran 37°20N 55°25E 247 B7
Golestan Palace Iran 35°41N 51°25E 141 A2
Golestānak Iran 30°36N 54°14E 247 D7
Goleta U.S.A. 34°27N 119°50W 307 L7
Golf U.S.A. 42°3N 87°46W 119 A2
Golfito Costa Rica 8°41N 83°5W 320 E3
Golfo Aranci Italy 40°59N 9°38E 200 B2
Golfo de Santa Clara Mexico 31°42N 114°30W 318 A2
Golfo di Orosei e del Gennargentu △ Italy 40°5N 9°15E 200 B2
Gölgeli Dağları Turkey 37°10N 28°55E 205 D10
Gölhisar Turkey 37°8N 29°31E 205 D11
Goliad U.S.A. 28°40N 97°23W 314 G6
Golija Montenegro 43°5N 18°45E 202 C2
Golija Serbia 43°22N 20°15E 202 C4
Golina Poland 52°15N 18°4E 185 F5
Goljam Bratan = Morozov Bulgaria 42°30N 25°10E 203 D9
Gölköy Turkey 40°41N 37°37E 212 B7
Gollel = Lavumisa Swaziland 27°20S 31°55E 271 C5
Göllersdorf Austria 48°29N 16°7E 180 C9
Gollnow = Goleniów Poland 53°35N 14°50E 184 E1
Gölmarmara Turkey 38°42N 27°55E 205 C9
Golmud China 36°25N 94°53E 218 D7
Golo → France 42°31N 9°32E 175 F13
Golo I. Phil. 13°39N 120°22E 232 E3
Gölova Turkey 36°48N 30°5E 205 E12
Golovin U.S.A. 64°33N 163°2W 303 D7
Golpāyegān Iran 33°27N 50°18E 247 C6
Gölpazarı Turkey 40°16N 30°18E 212 B4
Golra Pakistan 33°37N 72°56E 242 C5
Golspie U.K. 57°58N 3°59W 167 D5
Golub-Dobrzyń Poland 53°7N 19°2E 185 E6
Golubac Serbia 44°38N 21°38E 202 B5
Golungo Alto Angola 9°8S 14°46E 265 D2
Golyam Perelik Bulgaria 41°36N 24°33E 203 E8
Golyama Kamchiya → Bulgaria 43°10N 27°55E 203 C11
Golyshi = Vetluzhskiy Russia 58°23N 45°26E 190 A7
Goma Dem. Rep. of the Congo 1°37S 29°10E 268 C2
Gomal Pass Pakistan 31°56N 69°20E 242 D3
Gomantong Caves Malaysia 5°40N 118°6E 235 A5
Gomati → India 25°32N 83°11E 243 G10
Gombari Dem. Rep. of the Congo 2°45N 29°3E 268 B2
Gombe Dem. Rep. of the Congo 0°45S 17°36E 264 C3
Gombe Nigeria 10°19N 11°2E 263 C7
Gömbe Turkey 36°33N 29°38E 205 E11
Gombe □ Nigeria 10°0N 11°10E 263 C7
Gombe → Tanzania 4°38S 31°40E 268 C3
Gombe Stream △ Tanzania 4°42S 29°37E 268 C2
Gombi Nigeria 10°12N 12°30E 263 C7
Gomel = Homyel Belarus 52°28N 31°0E 177 B16
Gomera Canary Is. 28°7N 17°14W 153 e1
Gómez Palacio Mexico 25°34N 103°30W 318 B4
Gomfi Greece 39°26N 21°36E 204 B3
Gomīshān Iran 37°4N 54°6E 247 B7
Gommern Germany 52°4N 11°50E 178 C7
Gomogomo Indonesia 6°39S 134°43E 231 F8
Gomoh India 23°52N 86°10E 243 H12
Gomotartsi Bulgaria 44°6N 22°57E 202 B6
Gompa = Ganta Liberia 7°15N 8°59W 262 D3
Gonābād Iran 34°15N 58°45E 247 C8
Gonaïves Haiti 19°20N 72°42W 321 C5
Gonarezhou △ Zimbabwe 21°32S 31°55E 269 G3
Gonâve, G. de la Haiti 19°29N 72°42W 321 C5
Gonâve, Île de la Haiti 18°51N 73°3W 321 C5
Gonbad-e Kāvūs Iran 37°20N 55°25E 247 B7
Gönc Hungary 48°28N 21°14E 182 B6
Gonda India 27°9N 81°58E 243 F9
Gondal India 21°58N 70°52E 242 J4
Gonder Ethiopia 12°39N 37°30E 257 E4
Gondia India 21°23N 80°10E 244 D5
Gondola Mozam. 19°10S 33°37E 269 F3
Gondomar Portugal 41°10N 8°35W 194 D2
Gondrecourt-le-Château France 48°31N 5°30E 173 D12
Gonen Israel 31°46N 35°13E 123 B2
Gönen Balıkesir, Turkey 40°6N 27°39E 203 F11
Gönen İsparta, Turkey 37°57N 30°31E 205 D12
Gönen → Turkey 40°6N 27°39E 203 F11
Gong Xian China 28°23N 104°47E 228 C5
Gong'an China 30°7N 112°12E 229 B9
Gongbei China 22°12N 113°32E 219 a
Gongchangling China 41°7N 123°27E 224 B1
Gongcheng China 24°50N 110°49E 229 E8
Gongga Shan China 29°40N 101°55E 228 C3
Gonggar China 29°23N 91°7E 218 F7
Gongguan China 21°48N 109°36E 228 G7
Gonghe China 36°18N 100°32E 218 D9
Gongju S. Korea 36°27N 127°7E 224 D3
Gongliu China 43°28N 82°8E 217 D10
Gongming China 22°47N 113°53E 219 a
Gongneung S. Korea 37°36N 127°3E 137 B2
Gongo Yembe Dem. Rep. of the Congo 1°58S 18°40E 264 C3
Gongola → Nigeria 9°30N 12°4E 263 D7
Gongolgon Australia 30°21S 146°54E 281 E4
Gongoué Gabon 0°31S 9°13E 264 C1
Gongshan China 27°43N 98°29E 228 D2
Gongtan China 28°55N 108°20E 228 C7
Gongyi China 34°45N 112°58E 226 G7
Gongzhuling China 43°30N 124°40E 227 C13
Goni Greece 39°52N 22°29E 204 B4
Goniadz Poland 53°30N 22°44E 184 E9
Goniri Nigeria 11°30N 12°15E 263 C7
Gonjo China 30°52N 98°17E 228 B2
Gonnesa Italy 39°16N 8°28E 200 C1
Gonnosfanádiga Italy 39°29N 8°39E 200 C1
Gonzaga Phil. 18°16N 122°0E 232 B4
Gonzales Calif., U.S.A. 36°30N 121°26W 306 J5
Gonzales Tex., U.S.A. 29°30N 97°27W 314 G6
González Mexico 22°48N 98°25W 319 C5
Goobang △ Australia 33°0S 148°32E 283 B8
Good Hope, C. of S. Africa 34°24S 18°30E 270 D2
Good Hope Lake Canada 59°16N 129°18W 296 B3
Good Hope Plantation Jamaica 18°25N 77°41W 320 a
Goodenough I. Papua N. G. 9°20S 150°15E 286 E6
Gooderham Canada 44°54N 78°21W 312 B6
Goodhouse S. Africa 28°57S 18°13E 270 C2
Gooding U.S.A. 42°56N 114°43W 304 E6
Goodland U.S.A. 39°21N 101°43W 308 F3
Goodlands Mauritius 20°2S 57°39E 272 e
Goodlow Canada 56°20N 120°8W 296 B4
Goodmayes U.K. 51°33N 0°6E 125 A4
Goodnews Bay U.S.A. 59°7N 161°35W 303 G7
Goodooga Australia 29°3S 147°28E 281 D4
Goodsprings U.S.A. 35°49N 115°27W 307 K11
Goodwater U.S.A. 33°4N 86°3W 316 B3
Goodwood S. Africa 33°55S 18°32E 118 A2
Goole U.K. 53°42N 0°53W 168 D7
Goolgowi Australia 33°58S 145°41E 283 B6
Goolwa Australia 35°30S 138°47E 282 C3
Goomalling Australia 31°15S 116°49E 279 F2
Goomeri Australia 26°12S 152°6E 281 D5
Goonda Mozam. 19°48S 33°57E 269 F3
Goondiwindi Australia 28°30S 150°21E 281 D5
Goongarrie, L. Australia 30°3S 121°9E 279 F3
Goongarrie △ Australia 30°7S 121°30E 279 F3
Goonyella Australia 21°47S 147°58E 280 C4
Goose → Canada 53°20N 60°35W 299 B7
Goose Creek U.S.A. 32°59N 80°2W 316 C9
Goose L. Calif., U.S.A. 41°56N 120°26W 304 F3
Goose L. Ill., U.S.A. 40°55N 89°27W 310 D7
Gooty India 15°7N 77°41E 245 G3
Gop India 22°5N 69°50E 242 H3
Gopalganj Bangla. 23°1N 89°50E 241 D2
Gopalganj India 26°28N 84°30E 243 F11
Gopalpur India 22°38N 88°26E 124 B2
Göppingen Germany 48°42N 9°39E 179 G5
Goqên China 29°7N 97°14E 241 A6
Gor Spain 37°23N 2°58W 195 H8
Góra Dolnośląskie, Poland 51°40N 16°31E 185 G3
Góra Mazowieckie, Poland 52°39N 20°6E 185 F7
Góra Kalwaria Poland 51°59N 21°14E 185 G8
Gorakhpur India 26°47N 83°23E 243 F10
Goražde Bos.-H. 43°38N 18°58E 182 G3
Gorbatov Russia 56°12N 43°2E 190 B6
Gorbea, Peña Spain 43°1N 2°50W 196 B2
Górce Poland 52°15N 20°55E 143 B1
Gorczański △ Poland 49°30N 20°10E 185 J7
Gorda, Banco Caribbean 15°40N 80°27W 320 C3
Gorda, Pta. Canary Is. 28°45N 18°0W 153 e1
Gorda, Pta. Nic. 14°20N 83°10W 320 D3
Gordan B. Australia 11°35S 130°10E 278 B5
Gördes Turkey 38°54N 28°17E 205 C10
Gordon Ga., U.S.A. 32°54N 83°20W 316 C6
Gordon Nebr., U.S.A. 42°48N 102°12W 308 D2
Gordon → Australia 42°27S 145°30E 281 G4
Gordon, I. Chile 54°55S 69°30W 336 D3
Gordon Bay Canada 45°12N 79°47W 312 A5
Gordon L. Alta., Canada 56°30N 110°25W 297 B6
Gordon L. N.W.T., Canada 63°5N 113°11W 296 A6
Gordonvale Australia 17°5S 145°50E 280 B4
Goré Chad 7°59N 16°31E 259 G3
Gore Ethiopia 8°12N 35°32E 257 F4
Gore N.Z. 46°5S 168°58E 285 G3
Gore Bay Canada 45°57N 82°28W 298 C3
Gore Hill Australia 33°49S 151°10E 139 A2
Gorée, Île de Senegal 14°40N 17°23W 262 C1
Görele Turkey 41°2N 39°0E 213 B8
Gorelyy → Russia 60°1N 30°30E 137 A3
Göreme Turkey 38°35N 34°52E 212 C6
Gorey Ireland 52°41N 6°18W 166 D5
Gorg Iran 29°29N 59°43E 247 D8
Gorgān Iran 36°55N 54°30E 247 B7
Gorgie U.K. 55°56N 3°14W 121 B2
Gorgol □ Mauritania 15°45N 13°0W 262 B2
Gorgona Italy 43°26N 9°54E 198 E6
Gorgora Ethiopia 12°15N 37°17E 257 E4
Gorgoram Nigeria 12°40N 10°45E 263 C7
Gorham U.S.A. 44°23N 71°10W 313 B13
Gori Georgia 42°0N 44°7E 191 J7
Goribidnur = Gauribidanur India 13°37N 77°32E 245 H3
Goriganga → India 29°45N 80°23E 243 E9
Gorinchem Neths. 51°50N 4°59E 170 C4
Gorinhatã Brazil 19°15S 49°45W 333 E2
Goris Armenia 39°31N 46°22E 213 C12
Goritsy Russia 57°4N 36°43E 188 D9
Gorízia Italy 45°56N 13°37E 199 C10
Gorj □ Romania 45°5N 23°25E 183 E8
Gorki = Horki Belarus 54°17N 30°59E 188 E6
Gorkiy = Nizhniy Novgorod Russia 56°20N 44°0E 190 B7
Gorkovskoye Vdkhr. Russia 57°2N 43°4E 190 B6
Gorky Park Russia 55°43N 37°36E 129 B2
Gorleston U.K. 52°35N 1°44E 169 E9
Gorlice Poland 49°35N 21°11E 185 J8
Görlitz Germany 51°9N 14°58E 178 D10
Gorlovka = Horlivka Ukraine 48°19N 38°5E 189 H10
Gorman U.S.A. 34°47N 118°51W 307 L8
Gorna Djumaya = Blagoevgrad Bulgaria 42°2N 23°5E 202 D7
Gorna Dzhumayo = Blagoevgrad Bulgaria 42°2N 23°5E 202 D7
Gorna Oryakhovitsa Bulgaria 43°7N 25°40E 203 C9
Gornja Radgona Slovenia 46°40N 16°2E 199 B13
Gornja Tuzla Bos.-H. 44°35N 18°46E 182 F3
Gornji Grad Slovenia 46°20N 14°52E 199 B11
Gornji Milanovac Serbia 44°3N 20°29E 202 B4
Gornji Vakuf Bos.-H. 43°57N 17°34E 182 G2
Gorno Ablanovo Bulgaria 43°37N 25°43E 203 C9
Gorno-Altay □ Russia 51°0N 86°0E 217 B11
Gorno-Altaysk Russia 51°50N 86°5E 217 B11
Gorno-Badakhshan = Kŭhiston-Badakhshon □ Tajikistan 38°30N 73°0E 217 E8
Gornozavodsk Russia 46°33N 141°50E 215 E15
Gornyak Russia 50°59N 81°27E 217 B10
Gornyatski Russia 67°32N 64°3E 186 A11
Gornyatskiy Russia 48°18N 40°56E 191 F5
Gornyy Primorsk, Russia 44°57N 133°59E 220 B6
Gornyy Saratov, Russia 51°50N 48°30E 190 E9
Goro → C.A.R. 9°14N 21°16E 264 A4
Gorodenka = Horodenka Ukraine 48°41N 25°29E 183 B10
Gorodets Russia 56°38N 43°28E 190 B6
Gorodishche = Horodyshche Ukraine 49°17N 31°27E 189 H6
Gorodishche Russia 53°13N 45°40E 190 D7
Gorodnya = Horodnya Ukraine 51°55N 31°33E 189 G6
Gorodok = Haradok Belarus 55°30N 30°3E 188 E6
Gorodok = Horodok Ukraine 49°46N 23°32E 177 D12
Gorodok = Zakamensk Russia 50°23N 103°17E 215 D11
Gorodovikovsk Russia 46°8N 41°58E 191 G5
Goroka Papua N. G. 6°7S 145°25E 286 D3
Goroke Australia 36°43S 141°29E 282 D4
Gorokhov = Horokhiv Ukraine 50°30N 24°45E 177 C13
Gorokhovets Russia 56°13N 42°39E 190 B6
Gorom Gorom Burkina Faso 14°26N 0°14W 263 C4
Goromonzi Zimbabwe 17°52S 31°22E 269 F3
Gorong, Kepulauan Indonesia 3°59S 131°25E 231 E8
Gorongose → Mozam. 20°30S 34°40E 271 B5
Gorongoza Mozam. 18°44S 34°2E 269 F3
Gorongoza, Sa. da Mozam. 18°27S 34°2E 269 F3
Gorongoza △ Mozam. 18°50S 34°29E 271 A5
Gorontalo Indonesia 0°35N 123°5E 231 D6
Gorontalo □ Indonesia 0°50N 122°20E 231 D6
Goronyo Nigeria 13°29N 5°39E 263 C6
Górowo Iławeckie Poland 54°17N 20°30E 184 D7
Gorron France 48°25N 0°50W 172 D6
Gorror Micronesia 9°26N 138°4E 287 S16
Gorshechnoye Russia 51°31N 38°2E 189 G10
Gort Ireland 53°3N 8°49W 166 C3
Gortis Greece 35°4N 24°58E 207 E5
Gorumahisani India 22°20N 86°24E 244 C8
Gorumara △ India 26°42N 88°55E 241 B2
Góry Bystrzyckie Poland 50°16N 16°33E 185 H3
Goryachiy Klyuch Russia 44°38N 39°8E 191 H4
Goryeong S. Korea 35°44N 128°15E 224 E4
Gorzkowice Poland 51°13N 19°36E 185 G6
Górzno Poland 53°12N 19°38E 185 E6
Gorzów Śląski Poland 51°3N 18°22E 185 G5
Gorzów Wielkopolski Poland 52°43N 15°15E 185 F2
Gose Japan 34°27N 135°44E 223 C7
Gosen Germany 52°23N 13°43E 115 B5
Gosener kanal Germany 52°24N 13°42E 115 B5
Goseong S. Korea 34°58N 128°19E 224 E4
Gosford Australia 33°23S 151°18E 283 B9
Goshen Calif., U.S.A. 36°21N 119°25W 306 J7
Goshen Ind., U.S.A. 41°35N 85°50W 311 C11
Goshen N.Y., U.S.A. 41°24N 74°20W 313 E10
Goshogawara Japan 40°48N 140°27E 220 D10
Goskopi = Kopeysk Russia 55°7N 61°37E 216 A6
Goslar Germany 51°54N 10°25E 178 D6
Gospel Oak U.K. 51°32N 0°9W 125 A3
Gospič Croatia 44°35N 15°23E 199 D12
Gosport Hants., U.K. 50°48N 1°9W 169 G6
Gosport Ind., U.S.A. 39°21N 86°40W 311 E10
Gossa Norway 62°52N 6°50E 164 B3
Gossas Senegal 14°28N 16°0W 262 C1
Gosse → Australia 19°32S 134°37E 280 B1
Gossi Mali 15°48N 1°20W 263 B4
Gossinga South Sudan 8°36N 25°59E 257 F2
Gostingen = Gostyń Poland 51°50N 17°3E 185 G4
Gostinopolye = Volkhov Russia 59°55N 32°15E 188 C7
Gostivar Macedonia 41°48N 20°57E 202 E4
Gostyń Poland 51°50N 17°3E 185 G4
Gostynin Poland 52°26N 19°29E 185 F6
Göta älv → Sweden 57°42N 11°54E 163 G5
Göta kanal Sweden 58°30N 15°58E 163 F10
Götaland Sweden 57°30N 14°30E 163 G8
Gotanda Japan 35°37N 139°43E 140 B3
Göteborg Sweden 57°43N 11°59E 163 G5
Gotemba Japan 35°18N 138°56E 223 B10
Götene Sweden 58°32N 13°30E 163 F7
Gotenhafen = Gdynia Poland 54°35N 18°33E 184 D5
Goteşti Moldova 46°9N 28°10E 183 D13
Goth Goli Mar Pakistan 24°53N 67°1E 123 A2
Goth Sher Shah Pakistan 24°53N 66°59E 123 A1
Gotha Thüringen, Germany 50°56N 10°42E 178 E6
Gotha Fla., U.S.A. 28°31N 81°31W 133 A1
Gothenburg = Göteborg Sweden 57°43N 11°59E 163 G5
Gothenburg U.S.A. 40°56N 100°10W 308 E3
Gothèye Niger 13°52N 1°34E 263 C5
Gotland Sweden 57°30N 18°33E 163 G12
Gotlands län □ Sweden 57°15N 18°30E 163 G12
Gotō = Fukue Japan 32°41N 128°51E 221 H4
Goto Meer Bonaire 12°14N 68°22W 322 h
Gotō-Rettō Japan 32°55N 129°5E 221 H4
Gotse Delchev Bulgaria 41°36N 23°46E 202 E7
Gotska Sandön Sweden 58°24N 19°15E 163 F13
Gōtsu Japan 35°0N 132°14E 222 C4
Góttero, Monte Italy 44°22N 9°42E 198 D6
Gottesberg = Boguszów-Gorce Poland 50°45N 16°12E 185 H3
Göttingen Germany 51°31N 9°55E 178 D5
Gottschee = Kočevje Slovenia 45°39N 14°50E 199 C11
Gottskär Sweden 57°25N 12°2E 163 G6
Gottwald = Zmiyev Ukraine 49°39N 36°27E 189 H9
Gottwaldov = Zlín Czech Rep. 49°14N 17°40E 181 B10
Goubangzi China 41°20N 121°52E 227 D11
Gouda Neths. 52°1N 4°42E 170 B4
Goudiri Senegal 14°15N 12°45W 262 C2
Goudoumaria Niger 13°40N 11°10E 259 F2
Goudouras, Akra Greece 34°59N 26°6E 207 F7
Gouéké Guinea 8°2N 8°43W 262 D3
Gough I. Atl. Oc. 40°10S 9°45W 152 L11
Gouin, Rés. Canada 48°35N 74°40W 298 C5
Gouitafla Ivory C. 7°30N 5°53W 262 D3
Goulburn Australia 34°44S 149°44E 283 C8
Goulburn Is. Australia 11°40S 133°20E 280 A1
Goulburn River △ Australia 32°19S 150°10E 283 B9
Goulds U.S.A. 25°33N 80°23W 317 K9
Goulia Ivory C. 10°1N 7°11W 262 C3
Goulimine Morocco 28°56N 10°0W 260 C3
Goulimine □ Morocco 29°8N 9°2W 260 C3
Goulmima Morocco 31°41N 4°57W 260 B4
Goumbou Mali 15°2N 7°25W 262 B3
Goumenissa Greece 40°56N 22°37E 202 F6
Gounatolo Solomon Is. 8°25S 160°52E 287 M11
Goundam Mali 16°27N 3°40W 262 B4
Goundi Chad 9°22N 17°21E 259 G3
Gounou-Gaya Chad 9°38N 15°31E 259 G3
Goura Greece 37°56N 22°20E 204 D4
Gouraya Algeria 36°31N 1°56E 261 A5
Gourbassi Mali 13°24N 11°38W 262 C2
Gourbeyre Guadeloupe 16°0N 61°41W 322 e
Gourde, Pt. Trin. & Tob. 10°40N 61°38W 323 t
Gourdon France 44°44N 1°23E 174 D5
Gouré Niger 14°0N 10°10E 259 F2
Gouri Chad 18°50N 16°49E 259 E3
Gourin France 48°8N 3°37W 172 D3
Gourits → S. Africa 34°21S 21°52E 270 D3
Gourma-Rharous Mali 16°55N 1°50W 263 B4
Gournay-en-Bray France 49°29N 1°44E 173 C8
Gournay-sur-Marne France 48°51N 2°34E 134 A4
Gournes Greece 35°19N 25°16E 207 E6
Gouro Chad 19°36N 19°36E 259 E3
Gourock U.K. 55°57N 4°49W 167 F4
Gourock Ra. Australia 36°0S 149°25E 283 D8
Goursi Burkina Faso 12°42N 2°37W 262 C4
Gouvea Brazil 18°27S 43°44W 333 E3
Gouverneur U.S.A. 44°20N 75°28W 313 B9
Gouvia Greece 39°39N 19°50E 206 B9
Gouyave Grenada 12°10N 61°44W 323 q
Gouzon France 46°12N 2°14E 173 F9
Gove, Barragem do Angola 13°26S 15°53E 265 E3
Gove Peninsula Australia 12°17S 136°49E 280 A2
Governador, I. do Brazil 22°48S 43°13W 135 A1
Governador Valadares Brazil 18°15S 41°57W 333 E3
Governor Generoso Phil. 6°39N 126°5E 233 H6
Governor's Harbour Bahamas 25°10N 76°14W 320 A4
Governors I. New York, U.S.A. 132 f1
Govĭaltay □ Mongolia 45°30N 96°0E 217 C13
Govindgarh India 24°23N 81°18E 243 G9
Gowan Ra. Australia 25°0S 145°0E 280 D4
Gowanda U.S.A. 42°28N 78°56W 312 D6
Gower U.K. 51°35N 4°10W 169 F3
Gowers Corner U.S.A. 28°20N 82°30W 317 G7
Gowna, L. Ireland 53°51N 7°34W 166 C4
Gowrie U.S.A. 42°17N 94°17W 310 B2
Gowurdak Turkmenistan 37°50N 66°4E 217 E7
Goya Argentina 29°10S 59°10W 334 B4
Goyang S. Korea 37°39N 126°50E 224 D3
Goyave Guadeloupe 16°8N 61°34W 322 e
Goyaves, Grande Rivière → Guadeloupe 16°18N 61°36W 322 e
Göyçay Azerbaijan 40°42N 47°43E 191 K8
Goyder Lagoon Australia 27°3S 138°58E 281 D2
Goygöl Azerbaijan 40°37N 46°12E 191 K8
Goyllarisquizga Peru 10°31S 76°24W 330 C2
Göynük Antalya, Turkey 36°41N 30°33E 205 E12
Göynük Bolu, Turkey 40°24N 30°48E 212 B4
Goz Beïda Chad 12°10N 21°20E 259 F4
Goz Regeb Sudan 16°3N 35°33E 257 D4
Gozdnica Poland 51°28N 15°4E 185 G2
Gözneköy Turkey 36°58N 34°33E 250 B5
Gozo Malta 36°3N 14°15E 206 E7
Graaff-Reinet S. Africa 32°13S 24°32E 270 D3
Graben Vienna, Austria 142 b2
Grabill U.S.A. 41°13N 84°57W 311 C12
Grabo Ivory C. 4°57N 7°30W 262 D3
Grabow Mecklenburg-Vorpommern, Germany 53°17N 11°34E 178 B7
Grabów Warszawa, Poland 52°8N 20°59E 143 C1
Grabów nad Prosną Poland 51°31N 18°7E 185 G5
Graça Lisbon, Portugal 126 b3
Gračac Croatia 44°18N 15°57E 199 D12
Gračanica Bos.-H. 44°43N 18°18E 182 F3
Graçay France 47°10N 1°50E 173 E8
Grace Cathedral San Francisco, U.S.A. 136 b2
Graceville U.S.A. 30°58N 85°31W 316 E4
Gracewood U.S.A. 33°22N 82°2W 316 B7
Gràcia Spain 41°24N 2°10E 114 A2
Gracias a Dios, C. Honduras 15°0N 83°10W 320 D3
Graciosa Azores 39°4N 28°0W 153 d1
Graciosa, I. Canary Is. 29°15N 13°32W 153 e2
Grad Sofiya □ Bulgaria 42°35N 23°20E 202 D7
Gradac Montenegro 43°23N 19°9E 202 C3
Gradačac Bos.-H. 44°52N 18°26E 182 F3
Gradaús Brazil 7°43S 51°11W 332 C1
Gradaús, Serra dos Brazil 8°0S 50°45W 332 C1
Gradeška Planina Macedonia 41°30N 22°15E 202 E6
Gradets Bulgaria 42°46N 26°30E 203 D10
Gradišče Slovenia 46°37N 15°50E 199 B12
Grădiştea de Munte Romania 45°37N 23°13E 183 E8
Grado Italy 45°40N 13°23E 199 C10
Grado Spain 43°23N 6°4W 194 B4
Grady U.S.A. 34°49N 103°19W 305 J12
Graeca, Lacul Romania 44°5N 26°10E 183 F11
Grafarnes Iceland 64°55N 23°16W 155 C3
Gräfelfing Germany 48°7N 11°25E 131 B1
Grafenau Germany 48°51N 13°22E 179 G9
Gräfenberg Germany 49°39N 11°14E 179 F7
Grafham Water U.K. 52°19N 0°18W 169 E7
Grafton N.S.W., Australia 29°38S 152°58E 281 D5
Grafton Ill., U.S.A. 38°58N 90°26W 310 F6
Grafton N. Dak., U.S.A. 48°25N 97°25W 308 A5
Grafton W. Va., U.S.A. 39°21N 80°2W 309 F13
Grafton Caledonia Wildlife Estate Trin. & Tob. 11°11N 60°47W 323 s
Grafton's Pt. Anguilla 18°20N 62°54W 322 a
Gragoatá Brazil 22°53S 43°8W 135 B2
Graham Ont., Canada 49°20N 90°30W 298 C1
Graham Ga., U.S.A. 31°50N 82°30W 316 D7
Graham Tex., U.S.A. 33°6N 98°35W 314 E5
Graham, Mt. U.S.A. 32°42N 109°52W 305 K9
Graham Bell, Ostrov = Greem-Bell, Ostrov Russia 81°0N 62°0E 214 A7
Graham I. B.C., Canada 53°40N 132°30W 296 C2
Graham I. Nunavut, Canada 77°25N 90°30W 295 B13
Graham Land Antarctica 65°0S 64°0W 151 C17
Grahamstown S. Africa 33°19S 26°31E 270 D4
Grahamsville U.S.A. 41°51N 74°33W 313 E10
Grahovo Montenegro 42°40N 18°40E 202 D2
Graïba Tunisia 34°30N 10°13E 258 B2
Graie, Alpi Europe 45°30N 7°10E 175 C11
Grain Coast W. Afr. 4°20N 10°0W 262 E3
Grajagan Indonesia 8°35S 114°13E 231 K17
Grajaú Brazil 5°50S 46°4W 332 C2
Grajaú → Brazil 3°41S 44°48W 332 B3
Grajewo Poland 53°39N 22°30E 184 E9
Gramada Bulgaria 43°49N 22°39E 202 C6
Gramat France 44°48N 1°43E 174 D5
Grammichele Italy 37°13N 14°38E 201 E7
Grámmos, Óros Greece 40°18N 20°47E 202 F4
Grampian U.S.A. 40°58N 78°37W 312 F6
Grampian Highlands = Grampian Mts. U.K. 56°50N 4°0W 167 E5
Grampian Mts. U.K. 56°50N 4°0W 167 E5
Grampians, The Australia 37°15S 142°20E 282 D5
Grampians △ Australia 37°15S 142°28E 282 D5
Gramsh Albania 40°52N 20°12E 202 F4
Gran Norway 60°23N 10°31E 164 D7
Gran → Suriname 4°1N 55°30W 329 C6
Gran Altiplanicie Central Argentina 49°0S 69°30W 336 C3
Gran Canaria Canary Is. 27°55N 15°35W 153 e1
Gran Chaco S. Amer. 25°0S 61°0W 334 B3
Gran Couva Trin. & Tob. 10°24N 61°22W 323 t
Gran Desierto del Pinacate ⌓ Mexico 31°51N 113°32W 318 A2
Gran Laguna Salada Argentina 44°24S 67°23W 336 B3
Gran Pajonal Peru 10°45S 74°30W 330 C3
Gran Paradiso Italy 45°33N 7°17E 198 C4
Gran Sasso d'Itália Italy 42°27N 13°42E 199 F10
Gran Sasso e Monti Della Laga △ Italy 42°32N 13°22E 199 F10
Granada Nic. 11°58N 86°0W 320 D2
Granada Spain 37°10N 3°35W 195 H7
Granada Colo., U.S.A. 38°4N 102°19W 304 G12
Granada □ Spain 37°18N 3°0W 195 H7
Granadilla de Abona Canary Is. 28°7N 16°33W 153 e1
Granard Ireland 53°47N 7°30W 166 C4
Granbury U.S.A. 32°27N 97°47W 314 E6
Granby Qué., Canada 45°25N 72°45W 313 A12
Granby Colo., U.S.A. 40°5N 105°56W 304 F11
Grand → Ont., Canada 42°51N 79°34W 312 D5
Grand → Mich., U.S.A. 43°4N 86°15W 311 A10
Grand → Mo., U.S.A. 39°23N 93°7W 310 E3
Grand → S. Dak., U.S.A. 45°40N 100°45W 308 C3
Grand Abaque, Pte.du Guadeloupe 16°21N 61°0W 322 e
Grand-Anse = Portsmouth Dominica 15°34N 61°27W 323 k
Grand Anse Grenada 12°1N 61°45W 323 q
Grand Anse B. Grenada 12°2N 61°45W 323 q
Grand B. Dominica 15°14N 61°18W 323 k
Grand Bahama I. Bahamas 26°40N 78°30W 320 A4
Grand Baie Mauritius 20°0S 57°35E 272 e
Grand Bank Canada 47°6N 55°48W 299 C8
Grand Banks Atl. Oc. 45°0N 52°0W 152 B6
Grand Bassam Ivory C. 5°10N 3°49W 262 D4
Grand Bassin Réunion 21°10S 55°32E 272 f
Grand Batanga Cameroon 2°50N 9°55E 264 B1
Grand Bazaar = Kapali Carsi Turkey 41°1N 28°58E 122 B1
Grand Bénare Réunion 21°6S 55°25E 272 f
Grand Bend Canada 43°18N 81°45W 312 C3
Grand Béréby Ivory C. 4°38N 6°55W 262 E3
Grand Blanc U.S.A. 42°56N 83°38W 311 B13
Grand Bois Mauritius 20°25S 57°32E 272 e
Grand-Bourg Guadeloupe 15°53N 61°19W 322 e
Grand Canal = Canal Grande Venice, Italy 142 b2
Grand Canal = Da Yunhe → China 39°10N 117°10E 227 E9
Grand Canyon U.S.A. 36°3N 112°9W 305 H7
Grand Canyon △ U.S.A. 36°15N 112°30W 305 H7
Grand Canyon-Parashant ⌓ U.S.A. 36°30N 113°45W 305 H7
Grand Case St.-Martin 18°6N 63°4W 322 a
Grand Cayman Cayman Is. 19°20N 81°20W 320 C3
Grand Central Station New York, U.S.A. 132 c2
Grand Cess Liberia 4°40N 8°12W 262 E3
Grand Coulee U.S.A. 47°57N 119°0W 304 C4
Grand Coulee Dam U.S.A. 47°57N 118°59W 304 C4
Grand Cul-de-Sac Marin Guadeloupe 16°20N 61°35W 322 e
Grand Étang △ Grenada 12°5N 61°42W 323 q
Grand Falls Canada 47°3N 67°44W 299 C6
Grand Falls-Windsor Canada 48°56N 55°40W 299 C8
Grand Fond St. Barts 17°53N 62°48W 322 a
Grand Forks B.C., Canada 49°0N 118°30W 296 D5
Grand Forks N. Dak., U.S.A. 47°55N 97°3W 308 B5
Grand Galet Réunion 21°17S 55°38E 272 f
Grand Gaube Mauritius 20°0S 57°39E 272 e
Grand Gorge U.S.A. 42°21N 74°29W 313 D10
Grand Haven U.S.A. 43°4N 86°13W 311 A10
Grand I. Mich., U.S.A. 46°31N 86°40W 308 B10
Grand I. N.Y., U.S.A. 43°0N 78°58W 312 D6
Grand Îlet Guadeloupe 15°50N 61°35W 322 e
Grand Îlet Réunion 21°1S 55°29E 272 f
Grand Island U.S.A. 40°55N 98°21W 308 E4
Grand Isle La., U.S.A. 29°14N 90°0W 315 G9
Grand Isle Vt., U.S.A. 44°43N 73°18W 313 B11
Grand Junction Colo., U.S.A. 39°4N 108°33W 304 G9
Grand Junction Iowa, U.S.A. 42°2N 94°14W 310 B2
Grand L. N.B., Canada 45°57N 66°7W 299 C6
Grand L. Nfld. & L., Canada 49°0N 57°30W 299 C8
Grand L. Nfld. & L., Canada 53°40N 60°30W 299 B7
Grand L. La., U.S.A. 29°55N 92°47W 314 G8
Grand L. Ohio, U.S.A. 40°32N 84°25W 311 D12
Grand Lahou Ivory C. 5°10N 5°5W 262 D3
Grand Lake U.S.A. 40°15N 105°49W 304 F11
Grand Ledge U.S.A. 42°45N 84°45W 311 B12
Grand-Lieu, L. de France 47°6N 1°40W 172 E5
Grand Mal B. Grenada 12°4N 61°45W 323 q
Grand Manan I. Canada 44°45N 66°52W 299 D6
Grand Marais Mich., U.S.A. 46°40N 85°59W 309 B11
Grand Marais Minn., U.S.A. 47°45N 90°25W 298 C1
Grand Marigot B. Dominica 15°25N 61°16W 323 k
Grand-Mère Canada 46°36N 72°40W 298 C5
Grand Palace Bangkok, Thailand 113 b1

Grand Place Belgium 50°50N 4°21E 116 A2
Grand Popo Benin 6°15N 1°57E 263 D5
Grand Portage U.S.A. 47°58N 89°41W 308 B9
Grand Prairie U.S.A. 32°44N 96°59W 314 E6
Grand Rapids = Wisconsin Rapids U.S.A. 44°23N 89°49W 308 C9
Grand Rapids Man., Canada 53°12N 99°19W 297 C9
Grand Rapids Mich., U.S.A. 42°58N 85°40W 311 B10
Grand Rapids Minn., U.S.A. 47°14N 93°31W 308 B7
Grand Rapids ✈ (GRR) U.S.A. 42°53N 85°31W 311 B11
Grand Récif Sud N. Cal. 22°47S 166°55E 288 d
Grand Ridge U.S.A. 30°43N 85°1W 316 E4
Grand River U.S.A. 40°49N 93°58W 310 D3
Grand River Bay Mauritius 20°9S 57°27E 272 e
Grand River South East → Mauritius 20°17S 57°46E 272 e
Grand' Rivière Martinique 14°52N 61°11W 322 j
Grand Roy Grenada 12°8N 61°45W 323 q
Grand St-Bernard, Col du Europe 45°50N 7°10E 179 K3
Grand Santi Fr. Guiana 4°20N 54°24W 329 C7
Grand Staircase-Escalante △ U.S.A. 37°25N 111°33W 305 H8
Grand Teton U.S.A. 43°54N 110°50W 304 E8
Grand Teton △ U.S.A. 43°50N 110°50W 304 E8
Grand Union Canal U.K. 52°7N 0°53W 169 E7
Grandas de Salime Spain 43°13N 6°53W 194 B4
Grande → Jujuy, Argentina 24°20S 65°2W 334 A2
Grande → Mendoza, Argentina 36°52S 69°45W 334 D2
Grande → Bolivia 15°51S 64°39W 331 D5
Grande → Bahia, Brazil 11°30S 44°30W 332 D3
Grande → Minas Gerais, Brazil 20°6S 51°4W 333 F1
Grande → Venezuela 8°36N 61°39W 329 B5
Grande, B. Argentina 50°30S 68°20W 336 D3
Grande, Darsena Venice, Italy 142 b4
Grande, I. Brazil 23°9S 44°14W 333 F3
Grande, Rio → N. Amer. 25°58N 97°9W 314 J6
Grande, Serra Piauí, Brazil 8°0S 45°10W 332 C2
Grande, Serra Tocantins, Brazil 11°15S 46°30W 332 D2
Grande Anse = Beauséjour Guadeloupe 16°18N 61°4W 322 e
Grande Anse Guadeloupe 16°19N 61°47W 322 e
Grande Anse Martinique 14°30N 61°5W 322 j
Grande Anse St. Lucia 14°1N 60°54W 323 m
Grande Anse Seychelles 4°18S 55°45E 272 c
Grande Baleine → Canada 55°16N 77°47W 298 A4
Grande Cache Canada 53°53N 119°8W 296 C5
Grande Casse, Pte. de la France 45°24N 6°49E 175 C10
Grande Comore Comoros Is. 11°35S 43°20E 272 a
Grande Cul de Sac B St. Lucia 13°59N 61°2W 323 m
Grande-Entrée Canada 47°30N 61°40W 299 C7
Grande Matelot Pt. Trin. & Tob. 10°49N 61°9W 323 t
Grande Place Brussels, Belgium 116 b2
Grande Prairie Canada 55°10N 118°50W 296 B5
Grande Pte. Guadeloupe 15°58N 61°37W 322 e
Grande-Rivière Qué., Canada 48°26N 64°30W 299 C7
Grande Riviere Trin. & Tob. 10°50N 61°3W 323 t
Grande Rivière, Pte. de la Guadeloupe 16°18N 61°36W 322 e
Grande Rivière Noire Mauritius 20°21S 57°21E 272 e
Grande Rivière Sud Est Mauritius 20°17S 57°46E 272 e
Grande Sertão Veredas △ Brazil 15°10S 45°40W 333 E2
Grande-Terre Guadeloupe 16°20N 61°25W 322 e
Grande Terre Mayotte 12°46S 45°7E 272 b
Grande-Vallée Canada 49°14N 65°8W 299 C6
Grande Vigie, Pte. de la Guadeloupe 16°32N 61°27W 322 e
Grandfalls U.S.A. 31°20N 102°51W 314 F3
Grândola Portugal 38°12N 8°35W 195 G2
Grandpré France 49°20N 4°50E 173 C11
Grands Causses △ France 44°5N 2°58E 174 D6
Grands-Jardins △ Canada 47°41N 70°51W 299 C5
Grandview Man., Canada 51°10N 100°42W 297 C8
Grandview Mo., U.S.A. 38°53N 94°32W 310 F2
Grandview Wash., U.S.A. 46°15N 119°54W 304 C4
Grandview Heights U.S.A. 39°58N 83°2W 311 E13
Grandvilliers France 49°40N 1°57E 173 C8
Graneros Chile 34°5S 70°45W 334 C1
Grange Hill Jamaica 18°18N 78°11W 320 a
Grangemouth U.K. 56°1N 3°42W 167 E5
Granger U.S.A. 41°35N 109°58W 304 F9
Grängesberg Sweden 60°6N 15°1E 162 D9
Grangeville U.S.A. 45°56N 116°7W 304 D5
Granisle Canada 54°53N 126°13W 296 C3
Granite City U.S.A. 38°42N 90°8W 310 F6
Granite Falls U.S.A. 44°49N 95°33W 308 C6
Granite L. Canada 48°8N 57°5W 299 C8
Granite Mt. U.S.A. 33°5N 116°28W 307 M10
Granite Pk. U.S.A. 45°10N 109°48W 304 D9
Graniteville S.C., U.S.A. 33°34N 81°49W 316 B8
Graniteville Vt., U.S.A. 44°8N 72°29W 313 B12
Granitola, C. Italy 37°34N 12°39E 200 E5
Granity N.Z. 41°39S 171°51E 285 B6
Granja Brazil 3°7S 40°50W 332 B3
Granja de Moreruela Spain 41°48N 5°44W 194 D5
Granja de Torrehermosa Spain 38°19N 5°35W 195 G5
Grankulla = Kauniainen Finland 60°13N 24°44E 121 B1
Gränna Sweden 58°1N 14°28E 163 F8
Granollers Spain 41°39N 2°18E 196 D7
Gransee Germany 53°1N 13°8E 178 B9
Grant Fla., U.S.A. 27°56N 80°32W 317 H9
Grant Nebr., U.S.A. 40°50N 101°43W 308 E3
Grant, Mt. U.S.A. 38°34N 118°48W 304 G4
Grant City U.S.A. 40°29N 94°25W 310 D2
Grant I. Australia 11°10S 132°52E 278 B5
Grant Park U.S.A. 41°52N 87°37W 119 c2
Grant Range U.S.A. 38°30N 115°25W 304 G6
Grantham U.K. 52°55N 0°38W 168 E7
Grantley Adams Int. ✈ (BGI) Barbados 13°4N 59°29W 323 r
Granton U.K. 55°58N 3°14W 121 B2
Grantown-on-Spey U.K. 57°20N 3°36W 167 D5
Grants U.S.A. 35°9N 107°52W 305 J10
Grants Pass U.S.A. 42°26N 123°19W 304 E2
Grantsville U.S.A. 40°36N 112°28W 304 F7
Grantville U.S.A. 33°14N 84°50W 316 B5
Granville Manche, France 48°50N 1°35W 172 D5
Granville Trin. & Tob. 10°7N 61°48W 323 t
Granville Ill., U.S.A. 41°16N 89°14W 310 C7
Granville N. Dak., U.S.A. 48°16N 100°47W 308 A4
Granville N.Y., U.S.A. 43°24N 73°16W 313 C11
Granville Ohio, U.S.A. 40°4N 82°31W 312 F2
Granville L. Canada 56°18N 100°30W 297 B8
Granvin Norway 60°33N 6°45E 164 D3
Graskop S. Africa 24°56S 30°49E 271 B5
Gräsö Sweden 60°28N 18°35E 162 D12
Grass → Canada 56°3N 96°33W 297 B9
Grass Range U.S.A. 47°2N 108°48W 304 C9
Grass River △ Canada 54°40N 100°50W 297 C8
Grass Valley Calif., U.S.A. 39°13N 121°4W 306 F6
Grass Valley Oreg., U.S.A. 45°22N 120°47W 304 D3
Grassano Italy 40°38N 16°17E 201 B9
Grasse France 43°38N 6°56E 175 E10
Grassflat U.S.A. 41°0N 78°6W 312 E6
Grassi, Palazzo Venice, Italy 142 b2
Grasslands △ Canada 49°11N 107°38W 297 D7
Grassy Australia 40°3S 144°5E 281 G3
Grassy Park S. Africa 34°3S 18°30E 118 B2
Gråsten Denmark 54°55N 9°35E 163 K3
Grästorp Sweden 58°20N 12°40E 163 F6
Gratis U.S.A. 39°38N 84°32W 311 E12
Gratkorn Austria 47°8N 15°21E 180 D8
Gratosóglio Italy 45°24N 9°1E 128 B2
Gratz U.S.A. 38°28N 84°57W 311 F12
Gratzwalde Germany 52°28N 13°42E 115 B5
Graubünden □ Switz. 46°45N 9°30E 179 J5
Graudenz = Grudziądz Poland 53°30N 18°47E 184 E5
Graulhet France 43°45N 1°59E 174 E5
Graus Spain 42°11N 0°20E 196 C5
Gravberget Norway 60°53N 12°14E 164 D9
Grave, Pte. de France 45°34N 1°4W 174 C2
Gravelbourg Canada 49°50N 106°35W 297 D7
Gravelines France 51°1N 2°10E 173 A9
's-Gravenhage Neths. 52°7N 4°17E 170 B4
Gravenhurst Canada 44°52N 79°20W 312 B5
Gravesend N.S.W., Australia 29°35S 150°20E 281 D5
Gravesend Kent, U.K. 51°26N 0°22E 169 F8
Gravesend N.Y., U.S.A. 40°36N 73°56W 132 C2
Gravina in Púglia Italy 40°49N 16°25E 201 B9
Gravois, Pointe-à- Haiti 18°2N 73°56W 321 C5
Gravone → France 41°58N 8°45E 175 G12
Gray Haute-Saône, France 47°22N 5°35E 173 E12
Gray Ga., U.S.A. 33°1N 83°32W 316 B6
Grayling Alaska, U.S.A. 62°57N 160°3W 303 E7
Grayling Mich., U.S.A. 44°40N 84°43W 309 C11
Grays U.K. 51°28N 0°21E 169 F8
Grays Harbor U.S.A. 46°59N 124°1W 306 D2
Grays L. U.S.A. 43°4N 111°26W 304 E8
Grays River U.S.A. 46°21N 123°37W 306 D3
Grayville U.S.A. 38°15N 88°0W 311 F9
Grayvoron Russia 50°29N 35°41E 189 G8
Graz Austria 47°4N 15°27E 180 D8
Grazhdanka Russia 59°59N 30°24E 137 B2
Grdelica Serbia 42°55N 22°3E 202 D6
Greåker Norway 59°16N 11°12E 164 E8
Greasy L. Canada 62°55N 122°12W 296 A4
Great Abaco I. = Abaco I. Bahamas 26°25N 77°10W 320 A4
Great Artesian Basin Australia 23°0S 144°0E 280 C3
Great Australian Bight Australia 33°30S 130°0E 279 F5
Great Bacolet Bay Grenada 12°4N 61°37W 323 q
Great Bahama Bank Bahamas 23°15N 78°0W 320 B4
Great Barrier I. N.Z. 36°11S 175°25E 284 C4
Great Barrier Reef Australia 18°0S 146°50E 280 B4
Great Barrier Reef △ Australia 20°0S 150°0E 280 B4
Great Barrington U.S.A. 42°12N 73°22W 313 D11
Great Basalt Wall △ Australia 19°52S 145°43E 280 B4
Great Basin U.S.A. 40°0N 117°0W 304 G5
Great Basin △ U.S.A. 38°56N 114°15W 304 G6
Great Basses Sri Lanka 6°11N 81°29E 245 L5
Great Bear → Canada 65°0N 126°0W 294 E7
Great Bear L. Canada 65°30N 120°0W 294 D8
Great Belt = Store Bælt Denmark 55°20N 11°0E 163 J4
Great Bend Kans., U.S.A. 38°22N 98°46W 308 F4
Great Bend Pa., U.S.A. 41°58N 75°45W 313 E9
Great Blasket I. Ireland 52°6N 10°32W 166 D1
Great Britain Europe 54°0N 2°15W 158 E5
Great Camanoe Br. Virgin Is. 18°30N 64°35W 321 b
Great Channel Asia 6°0N 94°0E 245 L11
Great Coco I. = Koko Kyunzu Burma 14°7N 93°22E 245 G11
Great Codroy Canada 47°51N 59°16W 299 C8
Great Divide, The = Great Dividing Ra. Australia 23°0S 146°0E 280 C4
Great Divide Basin U.S.A. 42°0N 108°0W 304 E9
Great Dividing Ra. Australia 23°0S 146°0E 280 C4
Great Driffield = Driffield U.K. 54°0N 0°26W 168 C7
Great Exuma I. Bahamas 23°30N 75°50W 320 B4
Great Falls Guyana 5°35N 61°0W 329 B5
Great Falls Mont., U.S.A. 47°30N 111°17W 304 C8
Great Fish = Groot-Vis → S. Africa 33°28S 27°5E 270 D4
Great Goat I. Jamaica 17°52N 77°3W 320 a
Great Guana Cay Bahamas 24°0N 76°20W 320 B4
Great Hall of the People Beijing, China 114 c3
Great Himalayan △ India 31°30N 77°30E 242 D7
Great Inagua I. Bahamas 21°0N 73°20W 321 B5
Great Indian Desert = Thar Desert India 28°0N 72°0E 242 F5
Great Karoo S. Africa 31°55S 21°0E 270 D3
Great Khingan Mts. = Da Hinggan Ling China 48°0N 121°0E 219 B13
Great Lake Australia 41°50S 146°40E 281 G4
Great Lakes N. Amer. 46°0N 84°0W 292 E11
Great Limpopo Transfrontier △ Africa 23°0S 31°45E 271 B5
Great Malvern U.K. 52°7N 2°18W 169 E5
Great Miami → U.S.A. 39°7N 84°49W 311 E12
Great Nicobar India 7°0N 93°50E 245 L11
Great Ormes Head U.K. 53°20N 3°52W 168 D4
Great Otway △ Australia 38°50S 143°50E 282 E5
Great Ouse → U.K. 52°48N 0°21E 168 E8
Great Palm I. Australia 18°45S 146°40E 280 B4
Great Pedro Bluff Jamaica 17°51N 77°44W 320 a
Great Pee Dee → U.S.A. 33°21N 79°10W 315 E15
Great Plains N. Amer. 47°0N 105°0W 292 E9
Great Ruaha → Tanzania 7°56S 37°52E 268 D4
Great Sacandaga L. U.S.A. 43°6N 74°16W 313 C10
Great Saint Bernard Pass = Grand St-Bernard, Col du Europe 45°50N 7°10E 179 K3
Great Salt Desert = Kavīr, Dasht-e Iran 34°30N 55°0E 247 C7
Great Salt L. U.S.A. 41°15N 112°40W 304 F7
Great Salt Lake Desert U.S.A. 40°50N 113°30W 304 F7
Great Salt Plains L. U.S.A. 36°45N 98°8W 314 C5
Great Salt Pond St. Kitts & Nevis 17°14N 62°40W 322 d
Great Sand Dunes △ U.S.A. 37°48N 105°45W 305 H11
Great Sand Sea N. Afr. 29°0N 24°0E 258 C4
Great Sandy △ Australia 26°13S 153°2E 281 D5
Great Sandy Desert Australia 21°0S 124°0E 278 D3
Great Sangi = Sangihe, Pulau Indonesia 3°35N 125°30E 231 D7
Great Scarcies → S. Leone 9°0N 13°0W 262 D2
Great Sd. Bermuda 32°17N 64°51W 153 a
Great Sea Reef Fiji 16°15S 179°0E 287 A2
Great Sitkin I. U.S.A. 52°3N 176°6W 303 K3
Great Skellig Ireland 51°47N 10°33W 166 E1
Great Slave L. Canada 61°23N 115°38W 296 A5
Great Smoky Mts. △ U.S.A. 35°40N 83°40W 315 D13
Great Stour = Stour → U.K. 51°18N 1°22E 169 F9
Great Victoria Desert Australia 29°30S 126°30E 279 E4
Great Wall Antarctica 62°30S 58°0W 151 C18
Great Wall China 38°30N 109°30E 226 E5
Great Western Forum U.S.A. 33°57N 118°20W 126 C2
Great Whale River = Kuujjuarapik Canada 55°20N 77°35W 298 A4
Great Whernside U.K. 54°10N 1°58W 168 C6
Great Yarmouth U.K. 52°37N 1°44E 169 E9
Great Zab = Zāb al Kabīr → Iraq 36°1N 43°24E 213 D10
Great Zimbabwe Zimbabwe 20°16S 30°54E 269 G3
Greater Antilles W. Indies 17°40N 74°0W 321 C5
Greater London □ U.K. 51°31N 0°6W 169 F7
Greater Manchester □ U.K. 53°30N 2°15W 168 D5
Greater Sunda Is. Indonesia 7°0S 112°0E 230 F4
Grebbestad Sweden 58°42N 11°15E 163 F5
Grebenka = Hrebenka Ukraine 50°9N 32°22E 189 G7
Greco Italy 45°30N 9°12E 128 A2
Greco, C. Cyprus 34°57N 34°5E 207 F10
Greco, Mte. Italy 41°48N 13°58E 199 G10
Gredos, Sierra de Spain 40°20N 5°0W 194 E6
Greece U.S.A. 43°13N 77°41W 312 C7
Greece ■ Europe 40°0N 23°0E 204 B3
Greeley Colo., U.S.A. 40°25N 104°42W 304 F11
Greeley Nebr., U.S.A. 41°33N 98°32W 308 E4
Greeleyville U.S.A. 33°40N 79°59W 316 B10
Greely Fd. Canada 80°30N 85°0W 295 A15
Greem-Bell, Ostrov Russia 81°0N 62°0E 214 A7
Green → Ky., U.S.A. 37°54N 87°30W 308 G10
Green → Utah, U.S.A. 38°11N 109°53W 304 G9
Green B. U.S.A. 45°0N 87°30W 308 C10
Green Bay U.S.A. 44°31N 88°0W 308 C9
Green C. Australia 37°13S 150°1E 283 D9
Green City U.S.A. 40°16N 92°57W 310 D4
Green Cove Springs U.S.A. 29°59N 81°42W 316 F8
Green I. = Lütao Taiwan 22°40N 121°30E 225 D3
Green I. Antigua & B. 17°2N 61°40W 322 b
Green I. Hong Kong, China 22°17N 114°6E 122 B1
Green I. Grenada 12°13N 61°35W 323 q
Green Is. Papua N. G. 4°35S 154°10E 286 C8
Green Island Jamaica 18°23N 78°17W 320 a
Green Island B. Phil. 10°12N 119°22E 233 F2
Green Lake Canada 54°17N 107°47W 297 C7
Green Mts. U.S.A. 43°45N 72°45W 313 C12
Green Point S. Africa 33°54S 18°25E 118 A1
Green Point Stadium S. Africa 33°54S 18°25E 118 A1
Green Pond U.S.A. 32°44N 80°37W 316 C9
Green River Papua N. G. 3°54S 141°11E 286 B1
Green River Utah, U.S.A. 38°59N 110°10W 304 G8
Green River Wyo., U.S.A. 41°32N 109°28W 304 F9
Green Valley U.S.A. 31°52N 110°56W 305 L8
Greenacres U.S.A. 26°38N 80°7W 317 J9
Greenbank U.S.A. 48°6N 122°34W 306 B4
Greenbush Mich., U.S.A. 44°35N 83°19W 312 B1
Greenbush Minn., U.S.A. 48°42N 96°11W 308 A5
Greencastle U.S.A. 39°38N 86°52W 311 E10
Greene Iowa, U.S.A. 42°54N 92°48W 310 B4
Greene N.Y., U.S.A. 42°20N 75°46W 313 D9
Greeneville U.S.A. 36°10N 82°50W 315 C13
Greenfield Calif., U.S.A. 36°19N 121°15W 306 J5
Greenfield Calif., U.S.A. 35°15N 119°0W 307 K8
Greenfield Ill., U.S.A. 39°21N 90°12W 310 E6
Greenfield Ind., U.S.A. 39°47N 85°46W 311 E11
Greenfield Iowa, U.S.A. 41°18N 94°28W 310 C2
Greenfield Mass., U.S.A. 42°35N 72°36W 313 D12
Greenfield Mo., U.S.A. 37°25N 93°51W 308 G7
Greenfield Ohio, U.S.A. 39°21N 83°23W 311 E13
Greenfield Park Canada 45°29N 73°28W 130 B3
Greenford U.K. 51°31N 0°21W 125 B2
Greenhill U.K. 51°34N 0°18W 125 A2
Greenhills Ireland 53°18N 6°20W 120 B1
Greenland ☒ N. Amer. 66°0N 45°0W 154 D6
Greenland Sea Arctic 73°0N 10°0W 154 B10
Greenmarket Square Cape Town, S. Africa 118 c2
Greenock U.K. 55°57N 4°46W 167 F4
Greenore Ireland 54°1N 6°9W 166 B5
Greenore Pt. Ireland 52°14N 6°19W 166 D5
Greenough Australia 28°58S 114°43E 279 E1
Greenough → Australia 28°51S 114°38E 279 E1
Greenough Pt. Canada 44°58N 81°26W 312 B3
Greenpoint New York, U.S.A. 132 e3
Greenport U.S.A. 41°6N 72°22W 313 E12
Greensboro Fla., U.S.A. 30°34N 84°45W 316 E5
Greensboro Ga., U.S.A. 33°35N 83°11W 316 B6
Greensboro N.C., U.S.A. 36°4N 79°48W 315 C15
Greensboro Vt., U.S.A. 44°36N 72°18W 313 B12
Greensburg Ind., U.S.A. 39°20N 85°29W 311 E11
Greensburg Kans., U.S.A. 37°36N 99°18W 308 G4
Greensburg Pa., U.S.A. 40°18N 79°33W 312 F5
Greenstone = Geraldton Canada 49°44N 87°10W 298 C2
Greenstone Pt. U.K. 57°55N 5°37W 167 D3
Greentown U.S.A. 40°29N 85°58W 311 D11
Greenup U.S.A. 39°15N 88°10W 311 E8
Greenvale Australia 18°59S 145°7E 280 B4
Greenville Liberia 5°1N 9°6W 262 D3
Greenville Ala., U.S.A. 31°50N 86°38W 315 F11
Greenville Calif., U.S.A. 40°8N 120°57W 306 E6
Greenville Fla., U.S.A. 30°28N 83°38W 316 E6
Greenville Ga., U.S.A. 33°2N 84°43W 316 B5
Greenville Ill., U.S.A. 38°53N 89°25W 310 F7
Greenville Ind., U.S.A. 38°22N 85°59W 311 F11
Greenville Maine, U.S.A. 45°28N 69°35W 309 C19
Greenville Mich., U.S.A. 43°11N 85°15W 311 A11
Greenville Miss., U.S.A. 33°24N 91°4W 315 E9
Greenville Mo., U.S.A. 37°8N 90°27W 308 G8
Greenville N.C., U.S.A. 35°37N 77°23W 315 D16
Greenville N.H., U.S.A. 42°46N 71°49W 313 D13
Greenville N.Y., U.S.A. 42°25N 74°1W 313 D10
Greenville Ohio, U.S.A. 40°6N 84°38W 311 D12
Greenville Pa., U.S.A. 41°24N 80°23W 312 E4
Greenville S.C., U.S.A. 34°51N 82°24W 315 D13
Greenville Tex., U.S.A. 33°8N 96°7W 314 E6
Greenwater Lake △ Canada 52°32N 103°30W 297 C8
Greenwich Conn., U.S.A. 41°2N 73°38W 313 E11
Greenwich N.Y., U.S.A. 43°5N 73°30W 313 C11
Greenwich Ohio, U.S.A. 41°2N 82°31W 312 E2
Greenwich □ U.K. 51°29N 0°1E 125 B4
Greenwich Observatory U.K. 51°28N 0°0 125 B3
Greenwich Village New York, U.S.A. 132 d1
Greenwood B.C., Canada 49°10N 118°40W 296 D5
Greenwood Ark., U.S.A. 35°13N 94°16W 314 D7
Greenwood Fla., U.S.A. 30°52N 85°10W 316 E4
Greenwood Ind., U.S.A. 39°37N 86°7W 311 E10
Greenwood Mass., U.S.A. 42°29N 71°2W 116 A2
Greenwood Miss., U.S.A. 33°31N 90°11W 315 E9
Greenwood S.C., U.S.A. 34°12N 82°10W 316 A7
Greenwood, Mt. Australia 13°48S 130°4E 278 B5
Greenwood Great House Jamaica 18°29N 77°44W 320 a
Grefsen Norway 59°56N 10°47E 133 A3
Gregbe Ivory C. 6°48N 6°43W 262 D3
Gregório → Brazil 6°50S 70°46W 330 B3
Gregory U.S.A. 43°14N 99°26W 308 D4
Gregory → Australia 17°53S 139°17E 280 B2
Gregory, L. S. Austral., Australia 28°55S 139°0E 281 D2
Gregory, L. W. Austral., Australia 20°0S 127°40E 278 D4
Gregory, L. W. Austral., Australia 25°38S 119°58E 279 E2
Gregory △ Australia 15°38S 131°15E 278 C5
Gregory Downs Australia 18°35S 138°45E 280 B2
Gregory Ra. Queens., Australia 19°30S 143°40E 280 B3
Gregory Ra. W. Austral., Australia 21°20S 121°12E 278 D3
Greifenberg = Gryfice Poland 53°55N 15°13E 184 E2
Greifenhagen = Gryfino Poland 53°16N 14°29E 185 E1
Greiffenberg = Gryfów Śląski Poland 51°2N 15°24E 185 G2
Greiffenberg Germany 53°5N 13°57E 178 B9
Greifswald Germany 54°5N 13°23E 178 A9
Greifswalder Bodden Germany 54°12N 13°35E 178 A9
Grein Austria 48°14N 14°51E 180 C7
Greiz Germany 50°39N 12°10E 178 E8
Gremikha Russia 67°59N 39°47E 186 A6
Grenaa Denmark 56°25N 10°53E 163 H4
Grenada U.S.A. 33°47N 89°49W 315 E10
Grenada ■ W. Indies 12°10N 61°40W 322 q
Grenade France 43°47N 1°17E 174 E5
Grenadier I. U.S.A. 44°3N 76°22W 313 B8
Grenadines, The St. Vincent 12°40N 61°20W 323 n
Grenchen Switz. 47°12N 7°24E 179 H3
Grenen Denmark 57°44N 10°40E 163 G4
Grenfell N.S.W., Australia 33°52S 148°8E 283 B8
Grenfell Sask., Canada 50°30N 102°56W 297 C8
Grenivík Iceland 65°57N 18°11W 155 B8
Grenjaðarstaður Iceland 65°49N 17°21W 155 B9
Grenoble France 45°12N 5°42E 175 C9
Grenville Grenada 12°7N 61°37W 323 q
Grenville, C. Australia 12°0S 143°13E 286 F2
Grenville Chan. Canada 53°40N 129°46W 296 C3
Gréoux-les-Bains France 43°45N 5°52E 175 E9
Gresham U.S.A. 45°30N 122°25W 306 E4
Gresham Park U.S.A. 33°43N 84°20W 113 B2
Gresik Indonesia 7°13S 112°38E 235 D4
Gretna Dumf. & Gall., U.K. 55°0N 3°3W 167 F5
Gretna Fla., U.S.A. 30°37N 84°40W 316 E5
Gretna La., U.S.A. 29°54N 90°3W 131 B2
Gretna City Park U.S.A. 29°54N 90°3W 131 B2
Greve Strand Denmark 55°34N 12°18E 118 B1
Greven Germany 52°6N 7°37E 178 C3
Grevena Greece 40°4N 21°25E 202 F5
Grevena □ Greece 40°2N 21°25E 202 F5
Grevenbroich Germany 51°5N 6°35E 178 D2
Grevenmacher Lux. 49°41N 6°26E 170 E6
Grevesmühlen Germany 53°52N 11°12E 178 B7
Grey → Nfld. & L., Canada 47°34N 57°6W 299 C8
Grey → N.Z. 42°27S 171°12E 285 C6
Grey, C. Australia 13°0S 136°35E 280 A2
Grey Is. Canada 50°50N 55°35W 295 G20
Grey Ra. Australia 27°0S 143°30E 281 D3
Greybull U.S.A. 44°30N 108°3W 304 D9
Greyfriars Kirk Edinburgh, U.K. 121 c3
Greymouth N.Z. 42°29S 171°13E 285 C6
Greynolds Park U.S.A. 25°56N 80°9W 129 C3
Greystones Ireland 53°9N 6°5W 166 C5
Greytown N.Z. 41°5S 175°29E 284 H4
Greytown KwaZulu Natal, S. Africa 29°1S 30°36E 271 C5
Gribanovskiy Russia 51°28N 41°50E 190 E5
Gribbell I. Canada 53°23N 129°0W 296 C3
Gribës, Mal i Albania 40°17N 19°45E 202 F3
Gribingui → C.A.R. 8°33N 19°5E 264 A3
Gribingui-Bamingui △ C.A.R. 7°45N 19°17E 264 A3
Gridley U.S.A. 39°22N 121°42W 306 F5
Griebeg, Ras il- Malta 35°58N 14°23E 206 F7
Griebnitzsee Germany 52°23N 13°8E 115 B1
Griekwastad S. Africa 28°49S 23°15E 270 C3
Griesheim Germany 49°51N 8°33E 179 F4
Grieskirchen Austria 48°16N 13°48E 180 C6
Griffin U.S.A. 33°15N 84°16W 316 B5
Griffin, L. U.S.A. 28°52N 81°51W 317 G8
Griffith N.S.W., Australia 34°18S 146°2E 283 C7
Griffith Ont., Canada 45°15N 77°10W 312 A7
Griffith I. Canada 44°50N 80°55W 312 B4
Griffith Park U.S.A. 34°8N 118°17W 126 B3
Griggsville U.S.A. 39°43N 90°43W 310 E6
Grignols France 44°23N 0°2W 174 D3
Grigoriopol Moldova 47°9N 29°18E 183 C14
Grimari C.A.R. 5°43N 20°6E 264 A4
Grimaylov = Hrymayliv Ukraine 49°20N 26°5E 177 D14
Grimbergen Belgium 50°56N 4°22E 116 A2
Grimes U.S.A. 39°4N 121°54W 306 F5
Grimm = Kamenskiy Russia 50°48N 45°25E 190 E7
Grimma Germany 51°14N 12°43E 178 D8
Grimmen Germany 54°7N 13°3E 178 A9
Grimsay U.K. 57°29N 7°14W 167 D1
Grimsby Ont., Canada 43°12N 79°34W 312 C5
Grimsby N.E. Lincs., U.K. 53°34N 0°5W 168 D7
Grímsey Iceland 66°33N 17°58W 155 A9
Grimshaw Canada 56°10N 117°40W 296 B5
Grimslöv Sweden 56°44N 14°34E 163 H8
Grímsstaðir Iceland 65°39N 16°7W 155 B10
Grimstad Norway 58°20N 8°35E 164 F5
Grímsvötn Iceland 64°26N 17°22W 155 C9
Grindavík Iceland 63°50N 22°26W 155 D4
Grindelwald Switz. 46°38N 8°2E 179 J4
Grindsted Denmark 55°46N 8°55E 163 J2
Grindstone I. U.S.A. 44°17N 76°27W 313 B8
Grindu Romania 44°44N 26°50E 183 F11
Grinnell U.S.A. 41°45N 92°43W 310 C4
Grinnell Pen. Canada 76°40N 95°0W 295 B13
Grintavec Slovenia 46°22N 14°32E 199 B11
Grinzing Austria 48°15N 16°20E 142 A2
Griomasaigh = Grimsay U.K. 57°29N 7°14W 167 D1
Gris-Nez, C. France 50°52N 1°35E 173 B8
Grise Fiord Canada 76°25N 82°57W 295 B15
Grishino = Krasnoarmeisk Ukraine 48°18N 37°11E 189 H9
Grisolles France 43°49N 1°19E 174 E5
Grisons = Graubünden □ Switz. 46°45N 9°30E 179 J5
Grisslehamn Sweden 60°5N 18°49E 162 D12
Grmeč Planina Bos.-H. 44°43N 16°16E 199 D13
Groais I. Canada 50°55N 55°35W 299 B8
Gröbenried Germany 48°13N 11°25E 131 A1
Grobiņa Latvia 56°33N 21°10E 184 B8
Groblersdal S. Africa 25°15S 29°25E 271 C4
Grobming Austria 47°27N 13°54E 180 D6
Grochów Poland 52°15N 21°5E 143 B2
Grocka Serbia 44°40N 20°42E 202 B4
Gródek Poland 53°6N 23°40E 185 E10
Gródek Jagielloński = Horodok Ukraine 49°46N 23°32E 177 D12
Grodekovo = Pogranichnyy Russia 44°25N 131°24E 220 B5
Grodków Poland 50°43N 17°21E 185 H4
Grodno = Hrodna Belarus 53°42N 23°52E 184 E10
Grodzisk Poland 52°19N 21°4E 143 B2
Grodzisk Mazowiecki Poland 52°7N 20°37E 185 F7
Grodzisk Wielkopolski Poland 52°15N 16°22E 185 F3
Grodzyanka = Hrodzyanka Belarus 53°31N 28°42E 177 B15
Groenendaal Belgium 50°46N 4°26E 116 B2
Groesbeck U.S.A. 31°31N 96°32W 314 F6
Grogol Petamburin Indonesia 6°9S 106°46E 122 A1
Groix France 47°38N 3°29W 172 E3
Groix, Î. de France 47°38N 3°28W 172 E3
Grójec Poland 51°50N 20°58E 185 G7
Gronau Niedersachsen, Germany 52°5N 9°47E 178 C5
Gronau Nordrhein-Westfalen, Germany 52°12N 7°2E 178 C3
Grong Norway 64°25N 12°8E 160 D15
Grönhögen Sweden 56°16N 16°24E 163 H10
Groningen Neths. 53°15N 6°35E 170 A6
Groningen Suriname 5°48N 55°28W 329 B6
Groningen □ Neths. 53°16N 6°40E 170 A6
Grønnedal = Kangilinnguit Greenland 61°20N 47°57W 154 E6
Gronsdorf Germany 48°7N 11°42E 131 B3
Groom U.S.A. 35°12N 101°6W 314 D4
Groot → S. Africa 33°45S 24°36E 270 D3
Groot-Berg → S. Africa 32°47S 18°8E 270 D2
Groot-Brakrivier S. Africa 34°2S 22°18E 270 D3
Groot Karasberge Namibia 27°20S 18°40E 270 C2
Groot Kei → S. Africa 32°41S 28°22E 271 D4
Groot-Vis → S. Africa 33°28S 27°5E 270 D4
Grootdrink S. Africa 28°33S 21°42E 270 C3
Groote Eylandt Australia 14°0S 136°40E 280 A2
Groote Peel △ Neths. 51°22N 5°49E 170 C5
Grootfontein Namibia 19°31S 18°6E 270 A2
Grootlaagte → Africa 20°55S 21°27E 270 B3
Grootvloer → S. Africa 30°0S 20°40E 270 D3
Grorud Norway 59°57N 10°52E 133 A4
Gros C. Canada 61°59N 113°32W 296 A6
Gros Cap Guadeloupe 16°24N 61°25W 322 e
Gros Islet St. Lucia 14°5N 60°58W 323 m
Gros-Morne Martinique 14°43N 61°2W 322 j
Gros Morne △ Canada 49°40N 57°50W 299 C8
Gros Piton St. Lucia 13°49N 61°5W 323 m
Grósio Italy 46°18N 10°16E 198 B7
Grosne → France 46°42N 4°56E 173 F11
Gross-Glienicke Germany 52°28N 13°6E 115 B1
Gross-Hadern Germany 48°6N 11°29E 131 B1
Gross-Lappen Germany 48°11N 11°35E 131 A2
Gross-Meseritsch = Velké Meziříčí Czech Rep. 49°21N 16°1E 180 B9
Gross-Strehlitz = Strzelce Opolskie Poland 50°31N 18°18E 185 H5
Gross Wartenberg = Syców Poland 51°19N 17°40E 185 G4
Grossa, Pta. Spain 39°6N 1°36E 206 C2
Grosse I. U.S.A. 42°8N 83°9W 311 B13
Grosse Krampe Germany 52°23N 13°40E 115 B5
Grosse Müggelsee Germany 52°26N 13°38E 115 B4
Grosse Point U.S.A. 42°23N 82°54W 312 D2
Grosse Point Lighthouse U.S.A. 42°2N 87°41W 119 A2
Grosse Pte. Guadeloupe 16°1N 61°17W 322 e
Grossenbrode Germany 54°21N 11°4E 178 A7
Grossenhain Germany 51°17N 13°32E 178 D9
Grossenzersdorf Austria 48°12N 16°33E 142 A3
Grossenzersdorfer Arm → Austria 48°12N 16°31E 142 A3
Grosser Arber Germany 49°6N 13°8E 179 F9
Grosser Biberhaufen Austria 48°12N 16°28E 142 A2
Grosser Plöner See Germany 54°10N 10°22E 178 A6
Grosser Wannsee Germany 52°25N 13°10E 115 B2
Grosseto Italy 42°46N 11°8E 199 F8
Grossfeld-Siedlung Austria 48°16N 16°26E 142 A2
Grossgerungs Austria 48°34N 14°57E 180 C7
Grossglockner Austria 47°5N 12°40E 180 D5
Grosshesselohe Germany 48°3N 11°32E 131 B2
Grossjedlersdorf Austria 48°16N 16°23E 142 A2
Grosswardein = Oradea Romania 47°2N 21°58E 182 C6
Grossziethen Germany 52°23N 13°26E 115 B3
Groswater B. Canada 54°20N 57°40W 299 B8
Grotli Norway 62°2N 7°42E 164 B4
Groton Conn., U.S.A. 41°21N 72°5W 313 E12
Groton N.Y., U.S.A. 42°36N 76°22W 313 D8
Groton S. Dak., U.S.A. 45°27N 98°6W 308 C4
Grottáglie Italy 40°32N 17°26E 201 B10
Grottaminarda Italy 41°4N 15°2E 201 A8
Grottammare Italy 42°59N 13°52E 199 F10
Grottkau = Grodków Poland 50°43N 17°21E 185 H4
Grouard Mission Canada 55°33N 116°9W 296 B5
Grouin, Pte. du France 48°43N 1°51W 172 D5
Ground Zero = National September 11 Memorial and Museum New York, U.S.A. 132 e1
Groundhog → Canada 48°45N 82°58W 298 C3
Grouw Neths. 53°5N 5°51E 170 A5
Grove City Fla., U.S.A. 26°56N 82°19W 317 J7
Grove City Ohio, U.S.A. 39°53N 83°6W 311 E13
Grove City Pa., U.S.A. 41°10N 80°5W 312 E4
Grove Hall U.S.A. 42°18N 71°4W 116 B2
Grove Hill U.S.A. 31°42N 87°47W 315 F11
Grove Park Hounslow, U.K. 51°28N 0°15W 125 B2
Grove Park Lewisham, U.K. 51°25N 0°1E 125 B4
Grove Park Georgia, U.S.A. 33°46N 84°26W 113 B2
Groveland Calif., U.S.A. 37°50N 120°14W 306 H6
Groveland Fla., U.S.A. 28°34N 81°51W 317 G8
Grover = Tiltonsville U.S.A. 40°10N 80°41W 312 F4
Grover Beach U.S.A. 35°7N 120°37W 307 K6
Groves U.S.A. 29°57N 93°54W 314 G8
Groveton N.H., U.S.A. 44°36N 71°31W 313 B13
Groveton Va., U.S.A. 38°46N 77°6W 143 C2
Grovetown U.S.A. 33°27N 82°12W 316 B7
Grožnjan Croatia 45°22N 13°43E 199 C10
Groznyy Russia 43°20N 45°45E 191 J7
Grua Norway 60°16N 10°40E 164 D7
Grubišno Polje Croatia 45°44N 17°12E 182 E2
Grudovo Bulgaria 42°21N 27°10E 203 D11
Grudusk Poland 53°3N 20°38E 185 E7
Grudziądz Poland 53°30N 18°47E 184 E5
Gruinard B. U.K. 57°56N 5°35W 167 D3
Gruissan France 43°8N 3°7E 174 E7
Grumo Áppula Italy 41°1N 16°42E 201 A9
Grums Sweden 59°22N 13°5E 162 E7
Grünau Germany 52°25N 13°34E 115 B4
Grünberg Germany 50°35N 8°58E 178 E4
Grünberg in Schlesien = Zielona Góra Poland 51°57N 15°31E 185 G2
Grund Iceland 65°31N 18°9W 155 B8
Gründau Germany 50°10N 9°9E 179 E5
Grundy Center U.S.A. 42°22N 92°47W 310 B4
Grunewald Germany 52°28N 13°13E 115 B2
Grungedal Norway 59°44N 7°43E 164 E4
Grünstadt Germany 49°34N 8°9E 179 F4
Grünwald Germany 48°2N 11°31E 131 B2
Grünwalder Forst Germany 48°2N 11°33E 131 B2
Gruppo di Tessa △ Italy 46°47N 11°0E 198 B8
Gruvberget Sweden 61°6N 16°10E 162 C10
Gruver U.S.A. 36°16N 101°24W 314 C4
Gruyères Switz. 46°35N 7°4E 179 J3
Gruža Serbia 43°54N 20°46E 202 C4
Gryazi Russia 52°30N 39°58E 189 F10
Gryazliv = Borovichi Russia 58°25N 33°55E 188 C7
Gryazovets Russia 58°50N 40°10E 188 C11
Grybów Poland 49°36N 20°55E 185 J7
Grycksbo Sweden 60°40N 15°29E 162 D9
Gryfice Poland 53°55N 15°13E 184 E2
Gryfino Poland 53°16N 14°29E 185 E1
Gryfów Śląski Poland 51°2N 15°24E 185 G2
Grymes Hill U.S.A. 40°36N 74°6W 132 C1
Gryt Sweden 58°12N 16°48E 163 F10
Grythyttan Sweden 59°41N 14°32E 162 E8
Grytviken S. Georgia 54°19S 36°33W 152 M8
Gstaad Switz. 46°28N 7°18E 179 J3
Gua India 22°18N 85°20E 243 H11
Gua Musang Malaysia 4°53N 101°58E 237 K3
Guabún, Pta. Chile 41°48S 74°2W 336 B2
Guacanayabo, G. de Cuba 20°40N 77°20W 320 B4
Guacara Venezuela 10°14N 67°53W 328 A4
Guachípas → Argentina 25°40S 65°30W 334 B2
Guadajoz → Spain 37°50N 4°51W 195 H6
Guadalajara Jalisco, Mexico 20°40N 103°20W 318 C4
Guadalajara Spain 40°37N 3°12W 196 E1
Guadalajara □ Spain 40°47N 2°30W 196 E2
Guadalcanal Solomon Is. 9°32S 160°12E 287 M11
Guadalcanal Spain 38°5N 5°52W 195 G5
Guadalén → Spain 38°5N 3°32W 195 G7
Guadales Argentina 34°30S 67°55W 334 C2
Guadalete → Spain 36°35N 6°13W 195 J4
Guadalimar → Spain 38°5N 3°28W 195 G7
Guadalmena → Spain 38°19N 2°56W 195 G8
Guadalmez → Spain 38°46N 5°4W 195 G5
Guadalope → Spain 41°15N 0°3W 196 D4
Guadalquivir → Spain 36°47N 6°22W 195 J4
Guadalupe = Guadeloupe ☒ W. Indies 16°15N 61°40W 322 e
Guadalupe Brazil 6°44S 43°47W 332 C3
Guadalupe Zacatecas, Mexico 22°45N 102°31W 318 C4
Guadalupe Manila, Phil. 14°34N 121°2E 127 B2
Guadalupe Spain 39°27N 5°17W 195 F5
Guadalupe Calif., U.S.A. 34°58N 120°34W 307 L6
Guadalupe → U.S.A. 28°27N 96°47W 314 G6
Guadalupe, Basilica de Mexico 19°29N 99°7W 128 B2
Guadalupe, Sierra de Spain 39°28N 5°30W 195 F5
Guadalupe de Bravo Mexico 31°23N 106°7W 318 A3
Guadalupe I. Pac. Oc. 29°0N 118°50W 292 G8
Guadalupe Mts. △ U.S.A. 31°40N 104°30W 314 F2
Guadalupe Peak U.S.A. 31°50N 104°52W 314 F2
Guadalupe y Calvo Mexico 26°6N 106°58W 318 B3
Guadarrama, Sierra de Spain 41°0N 4°0W 194 E7
Guadeloupe ☒ W. Indies 16°15N 61°40W 322 e
Guadeloupe △ Guadeloupe 16°10N 61°40W 322 e
Guadeloupe Passage W. Indies 16°50N 62°15W 322 e
Guadelupe Peru 7°15S 79°29W 330 B2
Guadiamar → Spain 36°55N 6°24W 195 J4
Guadiana → Portugal 37°14N 7°22W 195 H3
Guadiana Menor → Spain 37°56N 3°15W 195 H7
Guadiaro → Spain 36°17N 5°17W 195 J5
Guadiato → Spain 37°48N 5°5W 195 H5
Guadiela → Spain 40°22N 2°49W 196 E2
Guadix Spain 37°18N 3°11W 195 H7
Guafo, Boca del Chile 43°35S 74°0W 336 B2
Guafo, I. Chile 43°35S 74°50W 336 B2
Guaico Trin. & Tob. 10°35N 61°9W 323 t
Guainía □ Colombia 2°30N 69°0W 328 C4
Guainía → Colombia 2°1N 67°7W 328 C4
Guaíra Brazil 24°5S 54°10W 335 A5
Guaíra □ Paraguay 25°45S 56°30W 334 B4
Guaire = Gorey Ireland 52°41N 6°18W 166 D5
Guaitecas, Is. Chile 44°0S 74°30W 336 B2
Guajará-Mirim Brazil 10°50S 65°20W 331 C4
Guajira □ Colombia 11°30N 72°30W 328 A3
Guajira, Pen. de la Colombia 12°0N 72°0W 328 A3
Gualaceo Ecuador 2°54S 78°47W 328 D2
Gualán Guatemala 15°8N 89°22W 320 C2
Gualdo Tadino Italy 43°14N 12°47E 199 E9
Gualeguay Argentina 33°10S 59°14W 334 C4
Gualeguaychú Argentina 33°3S 59°31W 334 C4
Gualequay → Argentina 33°19S 59°39W 334 C4
Gualicho, Salina Argentina 40°25S 65°20W 336 B3
Gualjaina Argentina 42°45S 70°30W 336 B2
Guam ☒ Pac. Oc. 13°27N 144°45E 302 d
Guamá → Brazil 1°29S 48°30W 332 B2
Guamache, B. de Venezuela 10°53N 64°5W 329 a
Guamblin, I. Chile 44°50S 75°0W 336 B2
Guamini Argentina 37°1S 62°28W 334 D3
Guamote Ecuador 1°56S 78°43W 328 D2
Guampi, Sierra de Venezuela 6°0N 65°35W 329 B4
Guamúchil Mexico 25°28N 108°6W 318 B3
Guana I. Br. Virgin Is. 18°30N 64°30W 321 b
Guanabacoa Cuba 23°8N 82°18W 320 B3
Guanabara, B. de Brazil 22°52S 43°10W 135 B1
Guanabara, Jardim Brazil 22°48S 43°11W 135 A1
Guanabara, Palácio da Brazil 22°56S 43°11W 135 B1
Guanacaste, Cordillera de Costa Rica 10°40N 85°4W 320 D2
Guanacaste △ Costa Rica 10°57N 85°30W 320 D2
Guanaceví Mexico 25°56N 105°57W 318 B3
Guanahani = San Salvador I. Bahamas 24°0N 74°30W 321 B5
Guanaja Honduras 16°30N 85°55W 320 C2
Guanajay Cuba 22°56N 82°42W 320 B3
Guanajuato Mexico 21°1N 101°15W 318 C4
Guanajuato □ Mexico 21°0N 101°0W 318 C4
Guanambi Brazil 14°13S 42°47W 333 D3
Guanapo Trin. & Tob. 10°36N 61°15W 323 t
Guanare Venezuela 8°42N 69°12W 328 B4
Guanare → Venezuela 8°13N 67°46W 328 B4
Guandacol Argentina 29°30S 68°40W 334 B2
Guandi Shan China 37°53N 111°29E 226 F6
Guane Cuba 22°10N 84°7W 320 B3
Guang'an China 30°28N 106°35E 228 B6
Guang'anmen China 39°51N 116°18E 114 B1
Guangchang China 26°50N 116°21E 229 D11
Guangde China 30°54N 119°25E 229 B12
Guangdong □ China 23°0N 113°0E 229 F9
Guangfeng China 28°20N 118°15E 229 C12
Guanghan China 30°58N 104°17E 228 B5
Guangling China 39°47N 114°22E 226 E8
Guangnan China 24°5N 105°4E 228 E5
Guangning China 23°40N 112°22E 229 F9
Guangqumen China 39°52N 116°25E 114 B2
Guangrao China 37°5N 118°25E 227 F10
Guangshui China 31°37N 114°0E 229 B9
Guangshun China 26°8N 106°21E 228 D6
Guangwu China 37°48N 105°57E 226 F3
Guangxi Zhuangzu Zizhiqu □ China 24°0N 109°0E 228 F7
Guangyuan China 32°26N 105°51E 226 H3
Guangze China 27°30N 117°12E 229 D11
Guangzhou China 23°6N 113°13E 121 B2

Guanhães *Brazil* 18°47S 42°57W **333** E3
Guanica *Puerto Rico* 17°58N 66°55W **321** b
Guanipa → *Venezuela* 9°56N 62°26W **329** B5
Guanling *China* 25°56N 105°35E **228** E5
Guannan *China* 34°8N 119°21E **227** G10
Guanshuo *China* 23°4N 113°22E **121** B3
Guanta *Venezuela* 10°14N 64°36W **329** A5
Guantánamo *Cuba* 20°10N 75°14W **321** B4
Guantánamo B. *Cuba* 19°59N 75°10W **321** C4
Guantao *China* 36°42N 115°25E **226** F8
Guanting Shuiku *China* 40°14N 115°35E **226** D8
Guanyang *China* 25°30N 111°8E **229** E8
Guanyun *China* 34°20N 119°18E **227** G10
Guapay = Grande → *Bolivia* 15°51S 64°39W **331** D5
Guapí *Colombia* 2°36N 77°54W **328** C2
Guápiles *Costa Rica* 10°10N 83°46W **320** D3
Guapo → *Trin. & Tob.* 10°11N 61°40W **323** t
Guapo B. *Trin. & Tob.* 10°12N 61°41W **323** t
Guaporé = Rondônia *Brazil* 10°52S 61°57W **331** C5
Guaporé *Brazil* 28°51S 51°54W **335** B5
Guaporé → *Brazil* 11°55S 65°4W **331** C4
Guaqui *Bolivia* 16°41S 68°54W **330** D4
Guara, Sierra de *Spain* 42°19N 0°15W **196** C4
Guarabira *Brazil* 6°51S 35°29W **332** C4
Guaracara → *Trin. & Tob.* 10°18N 61°28W **323** t
Guarachirá → *Colombia* 5°27N 70°36W **328** B3
Guaranda *Ecuador* 1°36S 79°0W **328** D2
Guarani = Pacajus *Brazil* 4°10S 38°31W **332** B4
Guarapari *Brazil* 20°40S 40°30W **333** F3
Guarapuava *Brazil* 25°20S 51°30W **333** G1
Guaratinguetá *Brazil* 22°49S 45°9W **335** A6
Guaratuba *Brazil* 25°53S 48°38W **335** B6
Guarda *Portugal* 40°32N 7°20W **194** E3
Guarda □ *Portugal* 40°40N 7°20W **194** E3
Guardafui, C. = Asir, Ras *Somalia* 11°55N 51°10E **267** B7
Guardamar del Segura *Spain* 38°5N 0°39W **197** G4
Guardavalle *Italy* 38°30N 16°30E **201** D9
Guárdia Sanframondi *Italy* 41°15N 14°36E **201** A7
Guardiagrele *Italy* 42°11N 14°13E **199** F11
Guardo *Spain* 42°47N 4°50W **194** C6
Guareña *Spain* 38°51N 6°6W **195** G4
Guareña → *Spain* 41°29N 5°23W **194** D5
Guari *Papua N. G.* 8°3S 146°52E **286** E4
Guárico □ *Venezuela* 8°40N 66°35W **328** B4
Guarrojo → *Colombia* 4°6N 70°42W **328** C3
Guarujá *Brazil* 24°2S 46°25W **335** A6
Guarulhos *Brazil* 23°29S 46°33W **335** A6
Guasave *Mexico* 25°34N 108°27W **318** B3
Guascama, Pta. *Colombia* 2°32N 78°24W **328** C2
Guasdualito *Venezuela* 7°15N 70°44W **328** B3
Guasipati *Venezuela* 7°28N 61°54W **329** B5
Guasopa *Papua N. G.* 9°12S 152°56E **286** E7
Guastalla *Italy* 44°55N 10°39E **198** D7
Guatemala *Guatemala* 14°40N 90°22W **320** D1
Guatemala ■ *Cent. Amer.* 15°40N 90°30W **320** C1
Guatemala Basin *Pac. Oc.* 11°0N 95°0W **289** F18
Guatemala Trench *Pac. Oc.* 14°0N 95°0W **292** H10
Guatire *Venezuela* 10°28N 66°32W **328** A4
Guatopo △ *Venezuela* 10°5N 66°30W **328** A4
Guatuaro Pt. *Trin. & Tob.* 10°19N 60°59W **323** t
Guavi → *Papua N. G.* 7°48S 143°16E **286** D2
Guaviare □ *Colombia* 2°0N 72°30W **328** C3
Guaviare → *Colombia* 4°3N 67°44W **328** C4
Guaxupé *Brazil* 21°10S 47°5W **335** A6
Guayabero → *Colombia* 2°36N 72°47W **328** C3
Guayacán *Venezuela* 11°8N 63°55W **329** a
Guayacancito *Venezuela* 10°56N 64°13W **329** a
Guayaguayare *Trin. & Tob.* 10°8N 61°2W **323** t
Guayaguayare B. *Trin. & Tob.* 10°7N 61°2W **323** t
Guayama *Puerto Rico* 17°59N 66°7W **321** C6
Guayamuri, Cerro *Venezuela* 11°4N 63°51W **329** a
Guayaneco, Arch. *Chile* 47°45S 75°10W **336** C1
Guayanilla *Puerto Rico* 18°1N 66°47W **321** b
Guayaquil *Ecuador* 2°15S 79°52W **328** D2
Guayaquil *Baja Calif., Mexico* 29°59N 115°4W **318** B1
Guayaquil, G. de *Ecuador* 3°10S 81°0W **328** D1
Guayaramerín *Bolivia* 10°48S 65°23W **331** C4
Guayas → *Ecuador* 2°36S 79°52W **328** D2
Guaymas *Mexico* 27°56N 110°54W **318** B2
Guaynabo *Puerto Rico* 18°22N 66°7W **321** b
Guba *Dem. Rep. of the Congo* 10°38S 26°27E **269** E2
Guba *Ethiopia* 11°17N 35°20E **257** E4
Gûbâl, Madîq *Egypt* 27°30N 34°0E **256** B3
Gubam *Papua N. G.* 8°39S 141°53E **286** E1
Guban *Somalia* 10°30N 44°0E **267** B5
Gubat *Phil.* 12°55N 124°7E **232** E5
Gubbi *India* 13°19N 76°56E **245** H3
Gúbbio *Italy* 43°21N 12°35E **199** E9
Guben *Germany* 51°57N 14°42E **178** D10
Gubin *Poland* 51°57N 14°43E **185** G1
Gubio *Nigeria* 12°30N 12°42E **263** C7
Gubkin *Russia* 51°17N 37°32E **189** G9
Gubkinskiy *Russia* 64°27N 76°36E **214** C8
Guča *Serbia* 43°46N 20°15E **202** C4
Gucheng *China* 32°20N 111°30E **229** A8
Gucun *China* 31°21N 121°22E **138** A1
Gudå *Norway* 63°27N 11°36E **164** A8
Gudalur *India* 11°30N 76°29E **245** J3
Gudauta *Georgia* 43°7N 40°32E **191** J5
Gudbrandsdalen *Norway* 61°33N 10°10E **164** C7
Guddu Barrage *Pakistan* 28°30N 69°50E **242** E3
Gudenå → *Denmark* 56°29N 10°13E **163** H4
Gudermes *Russia* 43°24N 46°5E **191** J8
Gudhjem *Denmark* 55°12N 14°58E **163** J8
Gudivada *India* 16°30N 81°3E **245** F5
Gudiyattam *India* 12°57N 78°55E **245** H4
Gudö *Sweden* 59°12N 18°12E **139** B3
Gudur *India* 14°12N 79°55E **245** G4
Gudvangen *Norway* 60°52N 6°49E **164** D3
Guebwiller *France* 47°55N 7°12E **173** E14
Guecho = Getxo *Spain* 43°21N 2°59W **196** B2
Guékédou *Guinea* 8°40N 10°5W **262** D2
Guelb er Rîchât *Mauritania* 21°7N 11°24W **260** D2
Guéle Mendouka *Cameroon* 4°23N 12°55E **263** E7
Guélengdeng *Chad* 10°55N 15°31E **259** F3
Güell, Parque de *Spain* 41°24N 2°10E **114** A2
Guelma *Algeria* 36°25N 7°29E **261** A6
Guelma □ *Algeria* 36°25N 7°25E **261** A6
Guelmine = Goulimine *Morocco* 28°56N 10°0W **260** C3
Guelph *Canada* 43°35N 80°20W **312** C4
Guelta Zemmur *W. Sahara* 25°8N 12°22W **260** C2
Guemar *Algeria* 33°30N 6°49E **261** B6
Guéméné-Penfao *France* 47°38N 1°50W **172** E5
Guéméné-sur-Scorff *France* 48°4N 3°13W **172** D3
Guéné *Benin* 11°44N 3°16E **263** C5
Güeppí *Peru* 0°7S 75°15W **328** D2
Guer *France* 47°54N 2°8W **172** E4
Güer Aike *Argentina* 51°39S 69°35W **336** D3
Guera *Chad* 11°55N 18°12E **259** F3
Guéra □ *Chad* 11°30N 18°30E **259** F3
Guérande *France* 47°20N 2°26W **172** E4
Guerara *Algeria* 32°51N 4°22E **261** B5
Guercif *Morocco* 34°14N 3°21W **261** B4
Guéréda *Chad* 14°31N 22°5E **259** F4
Guéret *France* 46°11N 1°51E **173** F8
Guérigny *France* 47°6N 3°10E **173** E10
Guerneville *U.S.A.* 38°30N 123°0W **306** G4
Guernica = Gernika-Lumo *Spain* 43°19N 2°40W **196** B2
Guernsey *Chan. Is., U.K.* 49°26N 2°35W **169** H5
Guernsey *Wyo., U.S.A.* 42°16N 104°45W **304** E11
Guerrara *Algeria* 28°5N 0°8W **261** C4
Guerrero *Mexico City, Mexico* **128** a1
Guerrero □ *Mexico* 17°40N 100°0W **319** D5
Guerzim *Algeria* 29°39N 1°40W **261** C4
Guessou-Sud *Benin* 10°3N 2°38E **263** C5
Gueugnon *France* 46°36N 4°4E **173** F11
Guéyo *Ivory C.* 5°25N 6°5W **262** D3
Gufuðalur *Iceland* 65°34N 22°25W **155** B4
Guggenheim Museum *New York, U.S.A.* **132** b3
Gughe *Ethiopia* 6°12N 37°30E **257** F4
Gūgher *Iran* 29°28N 56°27E **247** D8
Guglionesi *Italy* 41°55N 14°55E **199** G11
Guguan *N. Marianas* 17°18N 145°51E **302** a
Guhrau = Góra *Poland* 51°40N 16°31E **185** G3
Gui Jiang → *China* 23°30N 111°15E **229** F8
Guia *Canary Is.* 28°8N 15°38W **153** e1
Guia de Isora *Canary Is.* 28°12N 16°46W **153** e1
Guia Lopes da Laguna *Brazil* 21°26S 56°7W **335** A4
Guiana *Venezuela* 5°9N 63°36W **329** B5
Guiana Highlands *S. Amer.* 5°10N 60°40W **326** C4
Guiana I. *Antigua & B.* 17°6N 61°44W **322** b
Guibéroua *Ivory C.* 6°14N 6°10W **262** D3
Guichen B. *Australia* 37°10S 139°45E **282** D3
Guichi *China* 30°39N 117°27E **229** B11
Guider *Cameroon* 9°56N 13°57E **263** D7
Guidiguir *Niger* 13°40N 9°50E **259** F1
Guidimaka □ *Mauritania* 15°20N 12°0W **262** B2
Guidimouni *Niger* 13°42N 9°31E **259** F1
Guiding *China* 26°34N 107°11E **228** D6
Guidong *China* 26°7N 113°57E **229** D9
Guidónia-Montecélio *Italy* 42°1N 12°45E **199** F9
Guiers, L. de *Senegal* 16°10N 15°50W **262** B1
Guigang *China* 23°8N 109°35E **228** F7
Guiglo *Ivory C.* 6°45N 7°30W **262** D3
Guihulngan *Phil.* 10°7N 123°16E **233** F4
Guijá *Mozam.* 24°27S 33°0E **271** B5
Guijuelo *Spain* 40°33N 5°40W **194** E5
Guildford *U.K.* 51°14N 0°34W **169** F7
Guilford *U.S.A.* 41°17N 72°41W **313** E12
Guilin *China* 25°18N 110°15E **229** E8
Guillaume-Delisle, L. *Canada* 56°15N 76°17W **298** A4
Guillaumes *France* 44°5N 6°52E **175** D10
Guillestre *France* 44°39N 6°40E **175** D10
Guilvinec *France* 47°48N 4°17W **172** E2
Güimar *Canary Is.* 28°18N 16°24W **153** e1
Guimarães *Brazil* 2°9S 44°42W **332** B3
Guimarães *Portugal* 41°28N 8°24W **194** D2
Guimaras □ *Phil.* 10°35N 122°37E **233** F4
Guimaras Str. *Phil.* 10°38N 122°48E **233** F4
Guimba *Phil.* 15°40N 120°46E **232** D3
Guinardó *Spain* 41°24N 2°10E **114** A2
Guinayangan *Phil.* 13°54N 122°27E **232** E4
Guinda *U.S.A.* 38°50N 122°12W **306** G4
Guindulman *Phil.* 9°46N 124°29E **233** G5
Guinea *Africa* 8°0N 8°0E **254** F4
Guinea ■ *W. Afr.* 10°20N 11°30W **262** C2
Guinea, Gulf of *Atl. Oc.* 3°0N 2°30E **263** E5
Guinea Basin *Atl. Oc.* 0°0 5°0W **152** G11
Guinea-Bissau ■ *Africa* 12°0N 15°0W **262** C2
Güines *Cuba* 22°50N 82°0W **320** B3
Guingamp *France* 48°34N 3°10W **172** D3
Guinguinéo *Senegal* 14°20N 15°57W **262** C1
Güinima *Venezuela* 10°44N 63°55W **329** a
Guinobatan *Phil.* 13°11N 123°36E **232** E4
Guipavas *France* 48°26N 4°29W **172** D2
Guiping *China* 23°21N 110°2E **229** F8
Guipúzcoa □ *Spain* 43°12N 2°15W **196** B2
Guir *Mali* 18°52N 2°52W **262** B4
Guir, O. → *Algeria* 31°29N 2°17W **261** B4
Guiratinga *Brazil* 16°21S 53°45W **331** D7
Guirel *Mauritania* 15°30N 7°3W **262** B3
Güiria *Venezuela* 10°32N 62°18W **329** F8
Guiscard *France* 49°40N 3°1E **173** C10
Guise *France* 49°52N 3°35E **173** C10
Guita-Koulouba *C.A.R.* 5°58N 23°21E **264** A4
Guitiriz *Spain* 43°11N 7°50W **194** B3
Guitri *Ivory C.* 5°30N 5°14W **262** D3
Guiuan *Phil.* 11°5N 125°55E **233** F5
Guixi *China* 28°16N 117°15E **229** C11
Guiyang *Guizhou, China* 26°32N 106°40E **228** D6
Guiyang *Hunan, China* 25°46N 112°42E **229** E9
Guizhou □ *China* 27°0N 107°0E **228** D6
Gujan-Mestras *France* 44°38N 1°4W **174** D2
Gujar Khan *Pakistan* 33°16N 73°19E **242** C5
Gujarat □ *India* 23°20N 71°0E **242** H4
Gujiang *China* 27°11N 114°47E **229** D10
Gujiao *China* 37°54N 112°8E **226** F7
Gujō *Japan* 35°45N 136°57E **223** B8
Gujranwala *Pakistan* 32°10N 74°12E **242** C6
Gujrat *Pakistan* 32°40N 74°2E **242** C6
Gukovo *Russia* 48°1N 39°58E **191** F5
Gulargambone *Australia* 31°20S 148°30E **283** A8
Gulbai *Pakistan* 24°52N 66°58E **123** A1
Gulbarga *India* 17°20N 76°50E **244** F3
Gulbene *Latvia* 57°8N 26°52E **188** D4
Gülchö *Kyrgyzstan* 40°19N 73°26E **217** D8
Guledagudda *India* 16°3N 75°48E **245** F2
Gülek *Turkey* 37°12N 34°48E **250** A5
Gulf □ *Papua N. G.* 8°0S 145°0E **286** D3
Gulf, The = Persian Gulf *Asia* 27°0N 50°0E **247** E6
Gulf Breeze *U.S.A.* 30°21N 87°9W **317** E2
Gulf Hammock *U.S.A.* 29°15N 82°43W **317** F7
Gulf Islands ⌓ *U.S.A.* 30°10N 87°10W **317** K2
Gulfport *Fla., U.S.A.* 27°44N 82°42W **317** H7
Gulfport *Miss., U.S.A.* 30°22N 89°6W **315** F10
Gulgong *Australia* 32°20S 149°49E **283** B8
Gulian *China* 52°56N 122°21E **219** A13
Gulin *China* 28°1N 105°50E **228** C5
Gulistan *Pakistan* 30°30N 66°35E **242** D2
Guliston *Uzbekistan* 40°29N 68°46E **217** D7
Gulja = Yining *China* 43°58N 81°10E **217** D10
Gulkana *U.S.A.* 62°16N 145°23W **303** E11
Gull Lake *Canada* 50°10N 108°29W **297** C7
Gullbrå *Norway* 60°50N 6°17E **164** D3
Gullbrandstorp *Sweden* 56°42N 12°43E **163** H6
Gullbringusýsla *Iceland* 64°0N 22°0W **155** D4
Gullfoss *Iceland* 64°20N 20°8W **155** C6
Gullhaug *Norway* 59°30N 10°15E **164** E7
Gullivan B. *U.S.A.* 25°45N 81°40W **317** K8
Gullspång *Sweden* 58°59N 14°6E **163** F8
Gullstein *Norway* 63°13N 8°9E **164** A5
Güllük *Turkey* 37°14N 27°35E **205** D9
Güllük Dağı △ *Turkey* 37°0N 30°30E **205** E12
Güllük Korfezi *Turkey* 37°12N 27°30E **205** D9
Gulma *Nigeria* 12°40N 4°23E **263** C5
Gulmarg *India* 34°3N 74°25E **243** B6
Gülnar *Turkey* 36°19N 33°24E **250** B4
Gulnare *Australia* 33°27S 138°27E **282** B3
Gülpınar *Turkey* 39°32N 26°7E **205** B8
Gülşehir *Turkey* 38°44N 34°37E **212** C6
Gulshan-e Iqbal *Pakistan* 24°54N 67°5E **123** A2
Gülshat *Kazakhstan* 46°38N 74°21E **217** C8
Gulsvik *Norway* 60°24N 9°38E **164** D6
Gulu *Uganda* 2°48N 32°17E **268** B3
Gŭlŭbovo *Bulgaria* 42°8N 25°55E **203** D9
Gulud, J. *Sudan* 11°41N 29°31E **257** E2
Gulwe *Tanzania* 6°30S 36°25E **268** D4
Gulyaypole = Hulyaypole *Ukraine* 47°45N 36°21E **189** J9
Gum Lake *Australia* 32°42S 143°9E **282** B5
Gumaca *Phil.* 13°55N 122°6E **232** E4
Gumal → *Pakistan* 31°40N 71°50E **242** D4
Gumbaz *Pakistan* 30°2N 69°0E **242** D3
Gumbinnen = Gusev *Russia* 54°35N 22°10E **184** D9
Gumdag *Turkmenistan* 39°9N 54°56E **216** E4
Gumel *Nigeria* 12°39N 9°22E **263** C6
Gumi *S. Korea* 36°10N 128°12E **224** D4
Gumiel de Hizán *Spain* 41°46N 3°41W **194** D7
Gumla *India* 23°3N 84°33E **243** H11
Gumlu *Australia* 19°53S 147°41E **280** B4
Gumma □ *Japan* 36°30N 138°20E **223** A10
Gummersbach *Germany* 51°1N 7°34E **178** D3
Gummi *Nigeria* 12°4N 5°9E **263** C6
Gümüldür *Turkey* 38°6N 27°0E **205** C9
Gumuljina = Komotini *Greece* 41°9N 25°26E **203** E9
Gümüşçay *Turkey* 40°16N 27°17E **203** F11
Gümüşhacıköy *Turkey* 40°50N 35°18E **212** B6
Gümüşhane *Turkey* 40°30N 39°30E **213** B8
Gümüşsu *Turkey* 38°14N 29°1E **205** C11
Gumzai *Indonesia* 5°28S 134°42E **231** F8
Gun Hill Tower *Barbados* 13°8N 59°33W **323** r
Gun Pt. *Grenada* 12°32N 61°37W **323** q
Guna *Amara, Ethiopia* 11°43N 38°14E **266** B4
Guna *Oromiya, Ethiopia* 8°18N 39°52E **257** F4
Guna *India* 24°40N 77°19E **242** G7
Gunbalanya *Australia* 12°20S 133°4E **278** B5
Gundabooka △ *Australia* 30°30S 145°20E **281** E4
Gundagai *Australia* 35°3S 148°6E **283** C8
Gundarehi *India* 20°57N 81°17E **244** D5
Gundelfingen *Germany* 48°34N 10°22E **179** G6
Gundji *Dem. Rep. of the Congo* 2°5N 21°27E **264** B4
Gundlakamma → *India* 15°30N 80°15E **245** G5
Gundlupet *India* 11°48N 76°41E **245** J3
Gündoğmuş *Turkey* 36°48N 32°0E **250** B3
Gunebang *Australia* 33°1S 146°38E **283** B7
Güney *Burdur, Turkey* 37°29N 29°34E **205** D11
Güney *Denizli, Turkey* 38°9N 29°4E **205** C11
Güneydoğu Toroslar *Turkey* 38°20N 40°30E **213** C9
Gungal *Australia* 32°17S 150°32E **283** B9
Gungo *Angola* 10°58S 15°30E **265** E2
Güngören *Turkey* 41°1N 28°52E **122** B1
Gungu *Dem. Rep. of the Congo* 5°43S 19°20E **265** D3
Gunisao → *Canada* 53°56N 97°53W **297** C9
Gunisao L. *Canada* 53°33N 96°15W **297** C9
Gunjur *Gambia* 13°12N 16°44W **262** C1
Gunjyal *Pakistan* 32°20N 71°55E **242** C4
Günlüce *Turkey* 36°50N 28°20E **205** E10
Gunnarskog *Sweden* 59°49N 12°34E **162** E6
Gunnbjørn Fjeld *Greenland* 68°55N 29°47W **154** D8
Gunnebo *Sweden* 57°44N 16°32E **163** G10
Gunnedah *Australia* 30°59S 150°15E **283** A9
Gunnersbury *U.K.* 51°29N 0°17W **125** B2
Gunnewin *Australia* 25°59S 148°33E **281** D4
Gunningbar Cr. → *Australia* 31°14S 147°6E **283** A7
Gunnison *Colo., U.S.A.* 38°33N 106°56W **304** G10
Gunnison *Utah, U.S.A.* 39°9N 111°49W **304** G8
Gunnison → *U.S.A.* 39°4N 108°35W **304** G9
Gunsan *S. Korea* 35°59N 126°45E **224** E3
Guntakal *India* 15°11N 77°27E **245** G3
Gunter *Canada* 44°52N 77°32W **312** B7
Guntersville *U.S.A.* 34°21N 86°18W **315** D11
Guntong *Malaysia* 4°36N 101°3E **237** K3
Guntur *India* 16°23N 80°30E **245** F5
Gunung Buda △ *Malaysia* 4°12N 114°57E **235** B4
Gunung Ciremay △ *Indonesia* 6°53S 108°24E **235** D3
Gunung Gading △ *Malaysia* 2°2N 109°52E **235** B3
Gunung Leuser △ *Indonesia* 3°39N 97°32E **234** B1
Gunung Mulu △ *Malaysia* 4°6N 114°53E **235** B4
Gunung Palung △ *Indonesia* 1°9S 110°13E **235** C4
Gunungapi *Indonesia* 6°45S 126°30E **231** F7
Gunungsitoli *Indonesia* 1°15N 97°30E **234** B1
Gunungtua *Indonesia* 1°30N 99°37E **234** B1
Gunupur *India* 19°5N 83°50E **244** E6
Günz → *Germany* 48°27N 10°16E **179** G6
Gunza *Angola* 10°50S 13°50E **265** E2
Günzburg *Germany* 48°26N 10°17E **179** G6
Gunzenhausen *Germany* 49°7N 10°44E **179** F6
Guo He → *China* 32°59N 117°10E **227** H9
Guomao *China* 39°54N 116°26E **114** B2
Guoyang *China* 33°32N 116°12E **226** H9
Gupis *Pakistan* 36°15N 73°20E **243** A5
Gura Humorului *Romania* 47°35N 25°53E **183** C10
Gura-Teghii *Romania* 45°30N 26°25E **183** E11
Gurabo *Puerto Rico* 18°16N 65°58W **321** b
Gurag *Ethiopia* 8°20N 38°20E **257** F4
Gurahonț *Romania* 46°16N 22°21E **182** D7
Gurbantünggüt Shamo *China* 45°8N 87°20E **217** C11
Gurdaspur *India* 32°5N 75°31E **242** C6
Gurdon *U.S.A.* 33°55N 93°9W **314** E8
Güre *Balıkesir, Turkey* 39°36N 26°54E **205** B8
Güre *Uşak, Turkey* 38°39N 29°10E **205** C11
Gurgaon *India* 28°27N 77°1E **242** E7
Gürgentepe *Turkey* 40°51N 37°50E **212** B7
Gurghiu, Munții *Romania* 46°41N 25°15E **183** D10
Gurgueia → *Brazil* 6°50S 43°24W **332** C3
Gurha *India* 25°12N 71°39E **242** G4
Guri, Embalse de *Venezuela* 7°50N 62°52W **329** B5
Gurimatu *Papua N. G.* 6°45S 144°45E **286** D3
Gurin *Nigeria* 9°5N 12°54E **263** D7
Gurinhatã *Brazil* 19°14S 49°48W **333** E2
Gurjaani *Georgia* 41°43N 45°52E **191** K7
Gurk → *Austria* 46°35N 14°31E **180** E7
Gurkfeld = Krško *Slovenia* 45°57N 15°30E **199** C12
Gurkha *Nepal* 28°5N 84°40E **243** E11
Gurla Mandhata = Naimona'nyi Feng *China* 30°26N 81°18E **243** D9
Gurley *Australia* 29°45S 149°48E **281** D4
Gurnee *U.S.A.* 42°22N 87°55W **311** B9
Gurnet Point *U.S.A.* 42°1N 70°34W **313** D14
Guro *Mozam.* 17°26S 32°30E **269** F3
Gürpınar *İstanbul, Turkey* 40°59N 28°37E **203** F12
Gürpınar *Van, Turkey* 38°18N 43°25E **213** C10
Gürsu *Turkey* 40°13N 29°11E **203** F13
Gurué *Mozam.* 15°25S 36°58E **269** F4
Gurueragu *Ethiopia* 6°23N 45°31E **267** C6
Gurun *Malaysia* 5°49N 100°27E **237** K3
Gürün *Turkey* 38°43N 37°15E **212** C7
Gurupá *Brazil* 1°25S 51°35W **329** D7
Gurupá, I. Grande de *Brazil* 1°25S 51°45W **329** D7
Gurupi *Brazil* 11°43S 49°4W **333** D2
Gurupi → *Brazil* 1°13S 46°6W **332** B2
Gurupi, Serra do *Brazil* 5°0S 47°50W **332** C2
Guruwe *Zimbabwe* 16°40S 30°42E **271** A5
Gurvan Sayhan Uul *Mongolia* 43°50N 104°0E **226** C3
Guryev = Atyraū *Kazakhstan* 47°5N 52°0E **187** E9
Guryevsk *Russia* 54°47N 20°38E **184** D7
Gus-Khrustalnyy *Russia* 55°42N 40°44E **190** C5
Gusau *Nigeria* 12°12N 6°40E **263** C6
Gusev *Russia* 54°35N 22°10E **184** D9
Gushan *China* 39°50N 123°35E **224** C1
Gushgy = Serhetabat *Turkmenistan* 35°20N 62°18E **247** C9
Gushi *China* 32°11N 115°41E **229** A10
Gushiago *Ghana* 9°55N 0°15W **263** D4
Gushikami *Japan* 26°7N 127°44E **288** a
Gushikawa = Uruma *Japan* 26°21N 127°52E **288** a
Gusinje *Montenegro* 42°35N 19°50E **202** D3
Gusinoozersk *Russia* 51°16N 106°27E **215** D11
Gúspini *Italy* 39°32N 8°37E **200** C1
Güssing *Austria* 47°3N 16°20E **181** D9
Gustav Holm, Kap *Greenland* 66°36N 34°15W **154** D7
Gustavia *St. Barts* 17°53N 62°51W **322** a
Gustavo A. Madero *Mexico* 19°29N 99°8W **128** B2
Gustavus *U.S.A.* 58°25N 135°44W **296** B1
Gustine *U.S.A.* 37°16N 121°0W **306** H6
Güstrow *Germany* 53°47N 12°10E **178** B8
Gusum *Sweden* 58°16N 16°30E **163** F10
Guta = Kolárovo *Slovak Rep.* 47°54N 18°0E **181** D10
Gütersloh *Germany* 51°54N 8°24E **178** D4
Gutha *Australia* 28°58S 115°55E **279** E2
Guthalungra *Australia* 19°52S 147°50E **280** B4
Guthrie *Ont., Canada* 44°28N 79°32W **312** B5
Guthrie *Okla., U.S.A.* 35°53N 97°25W **314** D6
Guthrie *Tex., U.S.A.* 33°37N 100°19W **314** E4
Guthrie Center *U.S.A.* 41°41N 94°30W **310** C2
Gutian *China* 26°32N 118°43E **229** D12
Gutiérrez *Bolivia* 19°25S 63°34W **331** D5
Guttenberg *Iowa, U.S.A.* 42°47N 91°6W **310** B5
Guttenberg *New York, U.S.A.* **132** a1
Guttentag = Dobrodzień *Poland* 50°45N 18°25E **185** H5
Guttstadt = Dobre Miasto *Poland* 53°58N 20°26E **184** E7
Gutu *Zimbabwe* 19°41S 31°9E **271** A5
Gutulia △ *Norway* 62°2N 12°11E **164** B9
Gutuyevskiy, Ostrov *Russia* 59°53N 30°15E **137** B1
Guwahati *India* 26°10N 91°45E **241** B3
Guy Fawkes River △ *Australia* 30°0S 152°20E **281** D5
Guy-Fayreau, Complexe *Montréal, Canada* **130** b2
Guyana ■ *S. Amer.* 5°0N 59°0W **329** C6
Guyancourt *France* 48°46N 2°4E **134** B1
Guyane française = French Guiana ⊠ *S. Amer.* 4°0N 53°0W **329** C7
Guyang *China* 41°0N 110°5E **226** D6
Guyenne *France* 44°30N 0°40E **174** D4
Guymon *U.S.A.* 36°41N 101°29W **314** C4
Guyotville = Aïn Benian *Algeria* 36°48N 2°55E **261** A5
Guyra *Australia* 30°15S 151°40E **281** E5
Guyton *U.S.A.* 32°20N 81°24W **316** C8
Guyuan *Hebei, China* 41°37N 115°40E **226** D8
Guyuan *Ningxia Huizu, China* 36°0N 106°20E **226** F4
Guzar *Uzbekistan* 38°36N 66°15E **217** E7
Güzelbağ *Turkey* 36°44N 31°53E **250** B2
Güzelbahçe *Turkey* 38°21N 26°54E **205** C8
Güzeloluk *Turkey* 36°47N 34°4E **250** B5
Güzelsu *Turkey* 36°53N 31°51E **250** B2
Güzelyurt = Morphou *Cyprus* 35°12N 32°59E **207** E8
Guzhang *China* 28°42N 109°58E **228** C7
Guzhen *China* 33°22N 117°18E **227** H9
Guzmán, L. de *Mexico* 31°20N 107°30W **318** A3
Gvardeysk *Russia* 54°39N 21°5E **184** D8
Gvardeyskoye *Ukraine* 45°7N 34°1E **189** K8
Gvarv *Norway* 59°23N 9°9E **164** E6
Gwa *Burma* 17°36N 94°34E **241** G5
Gwaai *Zimbabwe* 19°15S 27°45E **269** F2
Gwaai → *Zimbabwe* 17°59S 26°52E **269** F2
Gwabegar *Australia* 30°37S 148°59E **283** A8
Gwadabawa *Nigeria* 13°28N 5°15E **263** C6
Gwādar *Pakistan* 25°10N 62°18E **240** D1
Gwagwada *Nigeria* 10°15N 7°15E **263** C6
Gwaii Haanas △ *Canada* 52°21N 131°26W **296** C2
Gwalior *India* 26°12N 78°10E **242** F8
Gwanak *S. Korea* 37°29N 126°57E **137** C1
Gwanaksan *S. Korea* 37°27N 126°58E **137** C1
Gwanara *Nigeria* 8°55N 3°9E **263** D5
Gwanda *Zimbabwe* 20°55S 29°0E **269** G2
Gwandu *Nigeria* 12°30N 4°41E **263** C5
Gwane *Dem. Rep. of the Congo* 4°45N 25°48E **268** B2
Gwang-yang *S. Korea* 34°58N 127°35E **224** E3
Gwangju *S. Korea* 35°9N 126°54E **224** E3
Gwangju □ *S. Korea* 35°10N 126°45E **224** E3
Gwanju = Gwangju *S. Korea* 35°9N 126°54E **224** E3
Gwaram *Nigeria* 10°15N 10°25E **263** C7
Gwarzo *Nigeria* 12°20N 8°55E **263** C6
Gwasero *Nigeria* 9°29N 3°30E **263** D5
Gwda → *Poland* 53°3N 16°44E **185** E3
Gweebarra B. *Ireland* 54°51N 8°23W **166** B3
Gweedore *Ireland* 55°3N 8°14W **166** A3
Gweru *Zimbabwe* 19°28S 29°45E **269** F2
Gwi *Nigeria* 9°0N 7°10E **263** D6
Gwinn *U.S.A.* 46°19N 87°27W **308** B10
Gwio Kura *Nigeria* 12°40N 11°2E **263** C7
Gwoza *Nigeria* 11°5N 13°40E **263** C7
Gwydir → *Australia* 29°27S 149°48E **281** D4
Gwynedd □ *U.K.* 52°52N 4°10W **168** E3
Gyál *Hungary* 47°23N 19°13E **117** B3
Gyáli-patak → *Hungary* 47°23N 19°7E **117** B2
Gyandzha = Gäncä *Azerbaijan* 40°45N 46°20E **191** K8
Gyangzê *China* 29°5N 89°47E **218** F6
Gyaring Hu *China* 34°50N 97°40E **218** E8
Gydanskiy Poluostrov *Russia* 70°0N 78°0E **214** C8
Gyeonggi-do □ *S. Korea* 36°37N 127°15E **224** D3
Gyeongju *S. Korea* 35°51N 129°14E **224** E4
Gyeongsan *S. Korea* 35°49N 128°44E **224** E4
Gyeongsangbuk-do □ *S. Korea* 36°20N 128°45E **224** D4
Gyeongsangnam-do □ *S. Korea* 35°15N 128°15E **224** E4
Gyeryongsan △ *S. Korea* 36°20N 127°15E **224** D3
Gyigang *China* 28°40N 97°31E **241** A6
Gyl *Norway* 62°57N 8°7E **164** B5
Gyldenløve Fjord *Greenland* 64°15N 40°30W **154** E6
Gympie *Australia* 26°11S 152°38E **281** D5
Gyobingauk *Burma* 18°13N 95°39E **241** F5
Gyōda *Japan* 36°10N 139°30E **223** A11
Gyodongdo *S. Korea* 37°47N 126°15E **224** D3
Gyomaendrőd *Hungary* 46°56N 20°50E **182** D5
Gyöngyös *Hungary* 47°48N 19°56E **182** C4
Győr *Hungary* 47°41N 17°40E **182** C2
Győr-Moson-Sopron □ *Hungary* 47°40N 17°20E **182** C2
Gypsum Pt. *Canada* 61°53N 114°35W **296** A6
Gypsumville *Canada* 51°45N 98°40W **297** C9
Gyueshevo *Bulgaria* 42°14N 22°28E **202** D6
Gyula *Hungary* 46°38N 21°17E **182** D6
Gyumri *Armenia* 40°47N 43°50E **191** K6
Gyzylarbat = Serdar *Turkmenistan* 39°4N 56°23E **247** B8
Gyzyletrek = Etrek *Turkmenistan* 37°36N 54°46E **247** B7
Gzhatsk = Gagarin *Russia* 55°38N 35°0E **188** E8
Gzira *Malta* 35°54N 14°29E **206** F7

H

H. Neely Henry L. *U.S.A.* 33°55N 86°2W **316** B3
Ha 'Arava → *Israel* 30°50N 35°20E **251** H6
Ha Coi *Vietnam* 21°26N 107°46E **228** G6
Ha Dong *Vietnam* 20°58N 105°46E **228** G5
Ha Giang *Vietnam* 22°50N 104°59E **228** F5
Hä Karmel, Har *Israel* 32°44N 35°3E **250** F5
Ha Karmel △ *Israel* 32°45N 35°5E **250** F6
Ha Long = Hong Gai *Vietnam* 20°57N 107°5E **228** G6
Ha Long, Vinh *Vietnam* 20°56N 107°3E **236** B6
Ha Tien *Vietnam* 10°23N 104°29E **237** G5
Ha Tinh *Vietnam* 18°20N 105°54E **236** C5
Ha Trung *Vietnam* 19°58N 105°50E **236** C5
Haaga *Finland* 60°13N 24°53E **121** B2
Haakon VII Topp = Beerenberg *Norway* 71°0N 8°20W **154** C10
Haaksbergen *Neths.* 52°9N 6°45E **170** B6
Ha'ano *Tonga* 19°41S 174°18W **287** P13
Ha'apai Group *Tonga* 19°47S 174°27W **287** P13
Haapiti *Moorea* 17°34S 149°52W **289** e
Haapsalu *Estonia* 58°56N 23°30E **188** C2
Haar *Germany* 48°6N 11°43E **131** B3
Haarby *Denmark* 55°13N 10°7E **163** J4
Haarlem *Neths.* 52°23N 4°39E **170** B4
Haas-Lilienthal House *San Francisco, U.S.A.* **136** b1
Haast *N.Z.* 43°51S 169°1E **285** D4
Haast → *N.Z.* 43°50S 169°2E **285** D4
Haast Pass *N.Z.* 44°6S 169°21E **285** E4
Haasts Bluff *Australia* 23°22S 132°0E **278** D5
Haasts Bluff ❂ *Australia* 23°39S 130°34E **278** D5
Hab → *Pakistan* 24°53N 66°41E **242** G3
Hab Nadi Chauki *Pakistan* 25°0N 66°50E **242** G2
Habahe *China* 48°3N 86°23E **217** C11
Ḩabarūt *Yemen* 17°18N 52°44E **249** C6
Habaswein *Kenya* 1°2N 39°30E **268** B4
Ḩabawnah, W. → *Si. Arabia* 17°57N 44°58E **248** C4
Habay *Alta., Canada* 58°50N 118°44W **296** B5
Habay *Manila, Phil.* 14°27N 120°56E **127** C1
Ḩabbān *Yemen* 14°21N 47°5E **248** D4
Ḩabbānīyah *Iraq* 33°17N 43°29E **213** F10
Ḩabbānīyah, Hawr al *Iraq* 33°17N 43°29E **213** F10
Habelschwerdt = Bystrzyca Kłodzka *Poland* 50°19N 16°39E **185** H3
Habibas, Îles *Algeria* 35°44N 1°8W **197** K3
Habichtswald ⌓ *Germany* 51°15N 9°15E **178** D5
Habiganj *Bangla.* 24°24N 91°30E **241** C3
Habirag *China* 42°17N 115°42E **226** C8
Habisa *Sudan* 15°38N 31°18E **266** A3
Habo *Sweden* 57°55N 14°6E **163** G8
Haboro *Japan* 44°22N 141°42E **220** B10
Ḩabshān *U.A.E.* 23°50N 53°37E **247** F7
Hachenburg *Germany* 50°40N 7°49E **178** E3
Hachi *India* 27°48N 94°2E **241** B5
Hachijō-Jima *Japan* 33°5N 139°45E **223** D11
Hachiman = Gujō *Japan* 35°45N 136°57E **223** B8
Hachinohe *Japan* 40°30N 141°29E **220** D10
Hachiōji *Japan* 35°40N 139°20E **223** B11
Hacı Zeynalabdin *Azerbaijan* 40°37N 49°33E **191** K9
Hacıbektaş *Turkey* 38°56N 34°33E **212** C6
Hacılar *Turkey* 38°38N 35°26E **212** C6
Hack, Mt. *Australia* 30°45S 138°55E **282** A3
Hackås *Sweden* 62°56N 14°30E **162** B8
Hackbridge *U.K.* 51°23N 0°9W **125** B3
Hackensack *U.S.A.* 40°52N 74°4W **132** A1
Hackensack → *U.S.A.* 40°42N 74°7W **132** B1
Hackettstown *U.S.A.* 40°51N 74°50W **313** F10
Hackney □ *U.K.* 51°33N 0°3W **125** A3
Hackney Wick *U.K.* 51°32N 0°1W **125** A3
Håckrenmagasinet *Sweden* 63°15N 13°30E **162** C7
Haco *Angola* 10°15S 15°44E **265** E3
Hadali *Pakistan* 32°16N 72°11E **242** C5
Hadano *Japan* 35°22N 139°14E **223** B11
Hadarba, Ras *Sudan* 22°4N 36°51E **256** C4
Hadarom □ *Israel* 31°0N 35°0E **251** H6
Ḩadbaram *Oman* 17°27N 55°15E **249** C6
Ḩadd, Ra's al *Oman* 22°35N 59°50E **249** B7
Ḩaddā *Si. Arabia* 21°27N 39°34E **248** B2
Haddington *U.K.* 55°57N 2°47W **167** F6
Haddock *U.S.A.* 33°2N 83°26W **316** B6
Haddummati Atoll *Maldives* 2°0N 73°30E **272** d
Hadejia *Nigeria* 12°30N 10°5E **263** C7
Hadejia → *Nigeria* 12°50N 10°51E **263** C7
Hadera *Israel* 32°27N 34°55E **251** F5
Hadersleben = Haderslev *Denmark* 55°15N 9°30E **163** J3
Haderslev *Denmark* 55°15N 9°30E **163** J3
Hadgaon *India* 19°30N 77°40E **244** E3
Hadhramaut = Ḩaḑramawt □ *Yemen* 15°30N 49°30E **249** D5
Hadīboh *Yemen* 12°39N 54°2E **249** D6
Hadilik *China* 37°56N 86°6E **217** E11
Hadım *Turkey* 36°58N 32°26E **250** B3
Hadithah *Si. Arabia* 31°27N 37°9E **251** G8
Hadjadj, O. el → *Algeria* 28°18N 5°20E **261** C6
Hadjeb el Aïoun *Tunisia* 35°21N 9°32E **258** A1
Hadjer Kamaran *Chad* 12°41N 21°46E **259** F4
Hadjer-Lamis □ *Chad* 12°55N 16°0E **259** F3
Hadjer Mornou *Chad* 17°12N 23°8E **259** E4
Hadlaskar *Norway* 60°15N 7°9E **164** D4
Hadley B. *Canada* 72°31N 108°12W **294** C10
Hadong *S. Korea* 35°5N 127°44E **224** E3
Hadr, Warrâq el *Egypt* 30°5N 31°12E **117** A2
Ḩaḑramawt □ *Yemen* 15°30N 49°30E **249** D5
Ḩaḑramawt, W. → *Yemen* 15°10N 51°8E **249** D5
Ḩadrānīyah *Iraq* 35°38N 43°14E **246** C4
Hadrian's Wall *U.K.* 55°0N 2°30W **168** B5
Hadsten *Denmark* 56°19N 10°3E **163** H4
Hadsund *Denmark* 56°44N 10°8E **163** H4
Hadyach *Ukraine* 50°21N 34°0E **189** G8
Hae, Ko *Thailand* 7°44N 98°22E **237** a
Hægeland *Norway* 58°22N 7°45E **164** F4
Haeinsa △ *S. Korea* 35°47N 128°5E **224** E4
Haeju *N. Korea* 38°3N 125°45E **224** C2
Haeju-man *N. Korea* 37°54N 125°45E **224** D2
Hä'ena *U.S.A.* 22°14N 159°34W **302** A2
Haenam *S. Korea* 34°34N 126°35E **224** E3
Haenertsburg *S. Africa* 24°0S 29°50E **271** B4
Haerhpin = Harbin *China* 45°48N 126°40E **227** B14
Hafar al Bāţin *Si. Arabia* 28°32N 45°52E **246** D5
Hafik *Turkey* 39°51N 37°23E **212** C7
Ḩafīrat al 'Aydā *Si. Arabia* 26°26N 39°12E **246** E3
Ḩafit *Oman* 23°59N 55°49E **247** F7
Hafizabad *Pakistan* 32°5N 73°40E **242** C5
Haflong *India* 25°10N 93°5E **241** C4
Hafnarfjörður *Iceland* 64°4N 21°57W **155** C5
Hafnir *Iceland* 63°56N 22°41W **155** D4
Hafslo *Norway* 61°19N 7°10E **164** C4
Haft Gel *Iran* 31°30N 49°32E **247** D6
Haga *Sweden* 59°21N 18°1E **139** A2
Hagalil *Israel* 32°53N 35°18E **250** F6
Hagari → *India* 15°40N 77°0E **245** G3
Hagby *Sweden* 56°34N 16°11E **163** H10
Hagemeister I. *U.S.A.* 58°39N 160°54W **303** G7
Hagen *Germany* 51°21N 7°27E **178** D3
Hagenbrunn *Austria* 48°19N 16°27E **142** A2
Hagenow *Germany* 53°26N 11°12E **178** B7
Hagere Hiywet *Ethiopia* 8°59N 37°51E **266** C4
Hagerman *U.S.A.* 33°7N 104°20W **305** K11
Hagerman Fossil Beds ⌓ *U.S.A.* 42°48N 114°57W **304** E6
Hägersten *Sweden* 59°18N 17°59E **139** B1
Hagerstown *Ind., U.S.A.* 39°55N 85°10W **311** E11
Hagerstown *Md., U.S.A.* 39°39N 77°43W **309** F15
Hagersville *Canada* 42°58N 80°3W **312** D4
Hagetmau *France* 43°39N 0°37W **174** E3
Hagfors *Sweden* 60°3N 13°45E **162** D7
Häggvik *Sweden* 59°26N 17°56E **139** A1
Hagi *Iceland* 65°28N 23°25W **155** B3
Hagi *Japan* 34°30N 131°22E **222** C3
Hagolan *Syria* 33°0N 35°45E **250** F6
Hagondange *France* 49°16N 6°11E **173** C13
Hágöngulón *Iceland* 64°35N 18°8W **155** C8
Hagonoy *Bulacan, Phil.* 14°50N 120°44E **232** D3
Hagonoy *Manila, Phil.* 14°31N 121°3E **127** B2
Hags Hd. *Ireland* 52°57N 9°28W **166** D2
Hague, C. de la *France* 49°44N 1°56W **172** C5
Hague, The = 's-Gravenhage *Neths.* 52°7N 4°17E **170** B4
Hague Park *Canada* 43°45N 79°14W **141** A3
Haguenau *France* 48°49N 7°47E **173** D14
Hagunía *W. Sahara* 27°26N 12°24W **260** C2
Hahira *U.S.A.* 30°59N 83°22W **316** E6
Hai Duong *Vietnam* 20°56N 106°19E **228** G6
Hai'an *Guangdong, China* 20°18N 110°11E **229** G8
Hai'an *Jiangsu, China* 32°37N 120°27E **229** A13
Haian Shanmo *Taiwan* 23°25N 121°25E **225** C3
Haicheng *China* 40°50N 122°45E **224** B1
Haida Gwaii *Canada* 53°20N 132°10W **296** C2
Haidar Khel *Afghan.* 33°58N 68°38E **242** C3
Haidarâbâd = Hyderabad *India* 17°22N 78°29E **244** F4
Haidargarh *India* 26°37N 81°22E **243** F9
Haidari = Chaidari *Greece* 38°2N 23°38E **112** A1
Haidarpur *India* 28°43N 77°8E **120** A1
Haidhausen *Germany* 48°7N 11°36E **131** B2
Haidian *China* 39°59N 116°16E **114** B1
Haifa = Ḩefa *Israel* 32°46N 35°0E **250** F6
Haifeng *China* 22°58N 115°10E **229** F10
Haiger *Germany* 50°43N 8°12E **178** E4
Haight-Ashbury *U.S.A.* 37°46N 122°26W **136** B2
Haikou *China* 20°1N 110°16E **236** B8
Haiku-Pauwela *U.S.A.* 20°56N 156°19W **302** C5
Ḩā'īl *Si. Arabia* 27°28N 41°45E **246** E4
Ḩā'īl □ *Si. Arabia* 26°40N 41°40E **246** E4
Hailakandi *India* 24°42N 92°34E **241** C4
Hailar *China* 49°10N 119°38E **219** B12
Hailey *U.S.A.* 43°31N 114°19W **304** E6
Haileybury *Canada* 47°30N 79°38W **298** C4
Hailin *China* 44°37N 129°30E **227** B15
Hailing Dao *China* 21°35N 111°47E **229** G8
Hailun *China* 47°28N 126°50E **219** B14
Hailuoto *Finland* 65°3N 24°45E **160** D21
Haimen *Guangdong, China* 23°15N 116°38E **229** F11
Haimen *Jiangsu, China* 31°52N 121°10E **229** B13
Hainan □ *China* 19°0N 109°30E **236** C7
Hainan Dao *China* 19°0N 109°30E **236** C7
Hainan Str. = Qiongzhou Haixia *China* 20°10N 110°15E **236** B8
Hainault *U.K.* 51°36N 0°6E **125** A4
Hainaut □ *Belgium* 50°30N 4°0E **170** D4
Hainburg *Austria* 48°9N 16°56E **181** C9
Haines *Alaska, U.S.A.* 59°14N 135°26W **296** B1
Haines *Oreg., U.S.A.* 44°55N 117°56W **304** D5
Haines City *U.S.A.* 28°7N 81°38W **317** G8
Haines Junction *Canada* 60°45N 137°30W **296** A1
Hainfeld *Austria* 48°3N 15°48E **180** C8
Haining *China* 30°28N 120°40E **229** B13
Haiphong *Vietnam* 20°47N 106°41E **228** G6
Haitan Dao *China* 25°30N 119°45E **229** E12
Haiti ■ *W. Indies* 19°0N 72°30W **321** C5
Haiya *Sudan* 18°20N 36°21E **256** D4
Haiyan *Qinghai, China* 36°53N 100°59E **218** D9
Haiyan *Zhejiang, China* 30°28N 120°58E **229** B13
Haiyang *China* 36°47N 121°9E **227** F11
Haiyang Dao *China* 39°2N 123°10E **224** C1
Haiyuan *Guangxi Zhuangzu, China* 22°8N 107°35E **228** F6
Haiyuan *Ningxia Huizu, China* 36°35N 105°52E **226** F3
Haizhou *Guangdong, China* 23°5N 113°18E **121** B2
Haizhou *Jiangsu, China* 34°37N 119°7E **227** G10
Haizhou Wan *China* 34°50N 119°20E **227** G10
Haizhu Guangchang *China* 23°6N 113°14E **121** B2
Haj Ali Qoli, Kavīr *Iran* 35°55N 54°50E **247** C7
Hajar Bangar *Sudan* 10°40N 22°45E **259** F4
Hajdú-Bihar □ *Hungary* 47°30N 21°30E **182** C6
Hajdúböszörmény *Hungary* 47°40N 21°30E **182** C6
Hajdúdorog *Hungary* 47°48N 21°30E **182** C6
Hajdúhadház *Hungary* 47°40N 21°40E **182** C6
Hajdúnánás *Hungary* 47°50N 21°26E **182** C6
Hajdúsámson *Hungary* 47°37N 21°42E **182** C6
Hajdúszoboszló *Hungary* 47°27N 21°22E **182** C6
Haji Ibrahim *Iraq* 36°40N 44°30E **213** D11
Hājīābād *Iran* 33°37N 60°0E **247** C9
Hajipur *India* 25°45N 85°13E **243** G11
Ḩajjah *Yemen* 15°42N 43°36E **248** D3
Ḩajjah □ *Yemen* 15°42N 43°36E **248** D3
Ḩājjīābād *Iran* 28°19N 55°55E **247** D7
Ḩājjīābād-e Zarrīn *Iran* 33°9N 54°51E **247** C7
Hajnówka *Poland* 52°47N 23°35E **185** F10
Hajo *India* 26°15N 91°32E **241** B3
Hajodo *S. Korea* 34°17N 126°3E **224** E3
Ḩajrah *Si. Arabia* 20°14N 41°3E **248** B3
Haka *Burma* 22°39N 93°37E **241** D4
Hakansson, Mts. *Dem. Rep. of the Congo* 8°40S 25°45E **265** D5
Hakataramea *N.Z.* 44°43S 170°30E **285** E5
Hakkâri *Turkey* 37°34N 43°44E **213** D10
Hakkâri □ *Turkey* 37°30N 44°0E **213** D10
Hakkâri Dağları *Turkey* 38°2N 42°58E **213** C10
Hakken-Zan *Japan* 34°10N 135°54E **223** C7
Hakkōda San *Japan* 40°50N 141°0E **220** D10
Hakodate *Japan* 41°45N 140°44E **220** D10
Hakos *Namibia* 23°13S 16°21E **270** B2
Hakota *Japan* 36°5N 140°30E **223** A12
Håksberg *Sweden* 60°11N 15°12E **162** D9
Hakskeenpan *S. Africa* 26°48S 20°13E **270** C3
Haku-San *Japan* 36°9N 136°46E **223** A8
Haku-San △ *Japan* 36°15N 136°45E **223** A8
Hakuba *Japan* 36°42N 137°51E **223** A9
Hakui *Japan* 36°53N 136°47E **221** F8
Hakun *Burma* 26°46N 95°42E **241** B5
Hakunila *Finland* 60°16N 25°6E **121** B3
Hakupu *Cook Is.* 19°6S 169°50W **289** g
Hakusan *Japan* 36°31N 136°34E **223** A8
Hal Saflieni *Malta* 35°52N 14°30E **206** F8
Hala *Pakistan* 25°43N 68°20E **240** D3
Ḩalab *Syria* 36°10N 37°15E **250** B8
Ḩalab □ *Syria* 36°10N 37°10E **250** B8
Ḩalaban *Si. Arabia* 23°29N 44°23E **248** B4
Ḩalabjah *Iraq* 35°10N 45°58E **213** E11
Halaib *Sudan* 22°12N 36°30E **256** C4
Halaib Triangle *Africa* 22°30N 35°20E **256** C4
Halandri = Chalandri *Greece* 38°3N 23°48E **112** A2
Halangingie Pt. *Cook Is.* 19°2S 169°58W **289** g
Halasa *Sudan* 14°26N 30°39E **257** E3
Halásztelek *Hungary* 47°22N 19°0E **117** B1
Hālat 'Ammār *Si. Arabia* 29°10N 36°4E **251** J7
Hālawa, C. *U.S.A.* 21°10N 156°43W **302** B5
Hālawa Heights *U.S.A.* 21°23N 157°55W **302** K14

Halbā *Lebanon* 34°34N 36°6E **250** D7
Halberstadt *Germany* 51°54N 11°3E **178** D7
Halcombe *N.Z.* 40°8S 175°30E **284** G4
Halcon, Mt. *Phil.* 13°16N 121°0E **232** E3
Halden Fjäll = Haltiatunturi
Finland 69°17N 21°18E **160** B19
Halden *Norway* 59°9N 11°23E **164** E8
Haldensleben *Germany* 52°17N 11°24E **178** C7
Haldia *Bangla.* 22°1N 88°3E **243** H13
Haldwani *India* 29°31N 79°30E **243** E8
Hale *U.S.A.* 39°36N 93°20W **310** E3
Hale → *Australia* 24°56S 135°53E **280** C2
Haleakalā △ *U.S.A.* 20°40N 156°15W **302** C5
Hale'iwa *U.S.A.* 21°36N 158°6W **302** J13
Halesowen *U.K.* 52°27N 2°3W **169** E5
Halesworth *U.K.* 52°20N 1°31E **169** E9
Haleyville *U.S.A.* 34°14N 87°37W **315** D11
Half Assini *Ghana* 5°1N 2°50W **262** D4
Half Dome *U.S.A.* 37°44N 119°32E **306** H7
Half Way Tree *Jamaica* 18°0N 76°48W **320** a
Halfa al Jadidah *Sudan* 15°20N 35°35E **266** A4
Halfeti *Turkey* 37°15N 37°52E **212** D7
Halfmoon Bay *N.Z.* 46°50S 168°5E **285** G3
Halfway → *Canada* 56°12N 121°32W **296** B4
Halia *India* 24°50N 82°19E **243** G10
Haliburton *Canada* 45°3N 78°30W **312** A6
Haliç *Turkey* 41°1N 28°57E **122** B1
Halifax *Queens., Australia* 18°32S 146°22E **280** B4
Halifax *N.S., Canada* 44°38N 63°35W **299** D7
Halifax *W. Yorks., U.K.* 53°43N 1°52W **168** D6
Halifax *Pa., U.S.A.* 40°25N 76°55W **312** F8
Halifax B. *Australia* 18°50S 147°0E **280** B4
Halifax Harbour *Grenada* 12°6N 61°45W **323** q
Halifax I. *Namibia* 26°38S 15°4E **270** C2
Halik Shan *China* 42°20N 81°22E **217** D10
Halīl → *Iran* 27°40N 58°30E **247** E8
Halim Perdana Kusuma Int. ✈
(HLP) *Indonesia* 6°16S 106°53E **122** B2
Halimun △ *Indonesia* 6°42S 106°26E **234** D3
Halkett, C. *U.S.A.* 70°48N 152°11W **303** A9
Halki = Chalki *Greece* 36°17N 27°35E **205** E9
Halkida = Chalkida
Greece 38°27N 23°42E **204** C5
Halkidiki = Chalkidiki □
Greece 40°25N 23°20E **202** F7
Halkirk *U.K.* 58°30N 3°29W **167** C5
Hall Beach *Canada* 68°46N 81°12W **295** D15
Hall I. *U.S.A.* 60°40N 173°6W **303** F4
Hall in Tirol *Austria* 47°17N 11°30E **180** D4
Hall Pen. *Canada* 63°30N 66°0W **295** E18
Hall Pt. *Australia* 15°40S 124°23E **278** C3
Hallabro *Sweden* 56°22N 15°5E **163** H9
Halland *Sweden* 57°8N 12°47E **161** H15
Hallandale Beach *U.S.A.* 25°58N 80°8W **129** C3
Hallands län □ *Sweden* 57°0N 12°40E **163** H6
Hallands Väderö *Sweden* 56°27N 12°34E **163** H6
Hallandsås *Sweden* 56°22N 13°0E **163** H7
Ḥallāniyat, Ghubbat al
Oman 17°40N 55°45E **249** C6
Ḥallāniyat, Jazā'ir al
Oman 17°30N 55°58E **249** C6
Hallasan *S. Korea* 33°22N 126°32E **224** a
Hallasan △ *S. Korea* 33°20N 126°30E **224** a
Hällbybrunn *Sweden* 59°24N 16°25E **162** E10
Halle *Belgium* 50°44N 4°13E **116** B1
Halle *Nordrhein-Westfalen,*
Germany 52°3N 8°22E **178** C4
Halle *Sachsen-Anhalt,*
Germany 51°30N 11°56E **178** D7
Hällefors *Sweden* 59°47N 14°31E **162** E8
Hälleforsnäs *Sweden* 59°10N 16°30E **162** E10
Hallein *Austria* 47°40N 13°5E **180** D6
Hällekis *Sweden* 58°38N 13°27E **163** F7
Hallen *Sweden* 63°11N 14°4E **162** A8
Hallett *Australia* 33°25S 138°55E **282** B3
Hallettsville *U.S.A.* 29°27N 96°57W **314** G6
Halley *Antarctica* 75°35S 26°39W **151** D1
Hallia → *India* 16°55N 79°20E **244** F4
Hallim *S. Korea* 33°24N 126°15E **224** a
Hallingby *Norway* 60°7N 10°10E **164** D7
Hallingdal *Norway* 60°40N 9°8E **164** D6
Hallingdalselva → *Norway* 60°23N 9°35E **164** D6
Hallingskarvet *Norway* 60°36N 7°47E **164** D4
Hallingskarvet △ *Norway* 60°37N 7°45E **164** D4
Hallingskeid *Norway* 60°40N 7°17E **164** D4
Hallock *U.S.A.* 48°47N 96°57W **308** A5
Hallormsstaður *Iceland* 65°6N 14°45W **155** B12
Halls Creek *Australia* 18°16S 127°38E **278** C4
Halls Gap *Australia* 37°8S 142°34E **281** F3
Halls Lake *Canada* 45°7N 78°45W **312** A6
Hallsberg *Sweden* 59°5N 15°7E **162** E9
Hallstahammar *Sweden* 59°38N 16°15E **162** E10
Hallstatt *Austria* 47°33N 13°38E **180** D6
Hallstavik *Sweden* 60°5N 18°37E **162** D12
Hallstead *U.S.A.* 41°58N 75°45W **313** E9
Hallyeo △ *S. Korea* 34°45N 128°25E **224** E4
Halmahera *Indonesia* 0°40N 128°0E **231** D7
Halmeu *Romania* 47°57N 23°2E **182** C8
Halmstad *Sweden* 56°41N 12°52E **163** H6
Halong Bay = Ha Long, Vinh
Vietnam 20°56N 107°3E **236** B6
Halq el Oued *Tunisia* 36°53N 10°18E **258** A2
Hals *Denmark* 57°0N 10°18E **163** H4
Halsa *Norway* 63°3N 8°14E **164** A5
Halsafjorden *Norway* 63°5N 8°10E **164** A5
Hälsingborg = Helsingborg
Sweden 56°3N 12°42E **163** H6
Hälsingland *Sweden* 61°40N 16°5E **162** C10
Halstead *U.K.* 51°57N 0°40E **169** F8
Haltdalen *Norway* 62°56N 11°8E **164** B8
Haltern *Germany* 51°44N 7°11E **178** D3
Haltiala *Finland* 60°16N 24°57E **121** B2
Haltiatunturi *Finland* 69°17N 21°18E **160** B19
Haltiavuori *Finland* 60°16N 24°56E **121** B2
Halton □ *U.K.* 53°22N 2°45W **168** D5
Haltwhistle *U.K.* 54°58N 2°26W **168** C5
Ḥālūl *Qatar* 25°40N 52°40E **247** E7
Halvad *India* 23°1N 71°11E **242** H4
Halvān *Iran* 33°57N 56°15E **247** C8
Halve Dag, Pt. *Curaçao* 12°14N 69°7W **322** g
Ham *Chad* 10°1N 15°35E **259** F3
Ham *Somme, France* 49°45N 3°4E **173** C10
Ham *London, U.K.* 51°25N 0°18W **125** B2
Hamab *Namibia* 28°7S 19°16E **270** D2
Hamad *Sudan* 15°20N 33°32E **257** D3
Hamada *Japan* 34°56N 132°4E **222** C4
Hamadān *Iran* 34°52N 48°32E **213** E13
Hamadān □ *Iran* 35°0N 49°0E **247** C6
Hamadia *Algeria* 35°28N 1°57E **261** A5
Ḥamāh *Syria* 35°5N 36°40E **250** C7
Ḥamāh □ *Syria* 35°10N 37°0E **250** C8
Hamakita *Japan* 34°45N 137°47E **223** C9
Hamamatsu *Japan* 34°45N 137°45E **223** C9
Haman *S. Korea* 35°14N 128°28E **224** E4
Hamar *Norway* 60°48N 11°7E **164** D8
Hamâta, Gebel *Egypt* 24°17N 35°0E **246** E2
Hamatonbetsu *Japan* 45°10N 142°20E **220** B11
Hambantota *Sri Lanka* 6°10N 81°10E **245** L5
Hamber △ *Canada* 52°20N 118°0W **296** C5
Hamburg *Hamburg,*
Germany 53°33N 9°59E **178** B5
Hamburg *Ark., U.S.A.* 33°14N 91°48W **314** E9
Hamburg *N.Y., U.S.A.* 42°43N 78°50W **312** D6
Hamburg *Pa., U.S.A.* 40°33N 75°59W **313** F9
Hamburg □ *Germany* 53°30N 10°0E **178** B5
Hamburg Fuhlsbüttel ✈ (HAM)
Germany 53°35N 9°59E **178** B5
Ḥamd, W. al → *Si. Arabia* 24°55N 36°20E **246** E3
Ḥamḍah *Si. Arabia* 19°2N 43°36E **248** C3
Ḥamdānah *Si. Arabia* 19°59N 40°34E **248** C3
Hamden *U.S.A.* 41°23N 72°54W **313** E12
Hamdibey *Turkey* 39°50N 27°15E **205** B9
Häme *Finland* 61°38N 25°10E **160** F21
Hämeenkylä *Finland* 60°16N 24°48E **121** B1
Hämeenlinna *Finland* 61°0N 24°28E **188** B3
Hamélé *Ghana* 10°56N 2°45W **262** C4
Hamelin Pool *Australia* 26°22S 114°20E **279** E1
Hameln *Germany* 52°6N 9°21E **178** C5
Hamerkaz □ *Israel* 32°15N 34°55E **251** F5
Hamero Hadad *Ethiopia* 7°27N 42°14E **267** C5
Hamersley Ra. *Australia* 22°0S 117°45E **278** D2
Hamgyŏng-sanmaek
N. Korea 41°35N 129°15E **224** B4
Hamgyŏngbuk-do □
N. Korea 41°50N 129°25E **224** B4
Hamgyŏngnam-do □
N. Korea 40°0N 127°30E **224** C3
Hamhŭng *N. Korea* 39°54N 127°30E **224** C3
Hamhŭng-man *N. Korea* 39°48N 127°37E **224** C3
Hami *China* 42°55N 93°25E **218** C7
Hamilton = Churchill →
Canada 53°19N 60°10W **299** B7
Hamilton *Vic., Australia* 37°45S 142°2E **282** D5
Hamilton *Bermuda* 32°17N 64°47W **153** a
Hamilton *Ont., Canada* 43°15N 79°50W **312** C5
Hamilton *N.Z.* 37°47S 175°19E **284** D4
Hamilton *S. Lanarks., U.K.* 55°46N 4°2W **167** F4
Hamilton *Ala., U.S.A.* 34°9N 87°59W **315** D11
Hamilton *Alaska, U.S.A.* 62°54N 163°53W **303** E7
Hamilton *Ga., U.S.A.* 32°45N 84°53W **316** C5
Hamilton *Ill., U.S.A.* 40°24N 91°21W **310** D5
Hamilton *Ind., U.S.A.* 41°33N 84°56W **311** C12
Hamilton *Mo., U.S.A.* 39°45N 94°0W **310** E2
Hamilton *Mont., U.S.A.* 46°15N 114°10W **304** C6
Hamilton *N.Y., U.S.A.* 42°50N 75°33W **313** D9
Hamilton *Ohio, U.S.A.* 39°24N 84°34W **311** E12
Hamilton *Tex., U.S.A.* 31°42N 98°7W **314** F5
Hamilton → *Queens.,*
Australia 23°30S 139°47E **280** C2
Hamilton → *S. Austral.,*
Australia 26°40S 135°19E **281** D2
Hamilton City *U.S.A.* 39°45N 122°1W **306** F4
Hamilton I. *Australia* 20°21S 148°56E **280** b
Hamilton Inlet *Canada* 54°0N 57°30W **299** B8
Hamilton Mt. *U.S.A.* 43°25N 74°22W **313** C10
Hamina *Finland* 60°34N 27°12E **188** B4
Hamirpur *H.P., India* 31°41N 76°31E **242** D7
Hamirpur *Ut. P., India* 25°57N 80°9E **243** G9
Hamitabat *Turkey* 41°30N 27°17E **203** E11
Hamju *N. Korea* 39°51N 127°26E **224** C3
Hamlet *U.S.A.* 34°53N 79°42W **315** D15
Hamley Bridge *Australia* 34°17S 138°35E **282** C3
Hamlin = Hameln *Germany* 52°6N 9°21E **178** C5
Hamlin *N.Y., U.S.A.* 43°17N 77°55W **312** C7
Hamlin *Tex., U.S.A.* 32°53N 100°8W **314** E4
Hamm *Germany* 51°40N 7°50E **178** D3
Ḥammām al Alī *Iraq* 36°9N 43°15E **213** D10
Hammam Bouhadjar
Algeria 35°23N 0°58W **261** A4
Ḥammām Damt *Yemen* 14°5N 44°40E **248** D4
Hammamet *Tunisia* 36°24N 10°38E **258** A2
Hammamet, G. de *Tunisia* 36°10N 10°48E **258** A2
Ḥammār, Hawr al *Iraq* 30°50N 47°10E **246** D5
Hammarby *Sweden* 59°17N 18°5E **139** B2
Hammarstrand *Sweden* 63°7N 16°20E **162** A10
Hamme *Belgium* 50°55N 4°17E **116** A1
Hammelburg *Germany* 50°6N 9°53E **179** E5
Hammeren *Denmark* 55°18N 14°47E **163** J8
Hammerfest *Norway* 70°39N 23°41E **160** A20
Hammersmith *U.K.* 51°29N 0°14W **125** B2
Hammerstein = Czarne
Poland 53°42N 16°58E **184** E3
Hammerum *Denmark* 56°8N 9°3E **163** H3
Hamminkeln *Germany* 51°43N 6°35E **178** D2
Hammond *Ind., U.S.A.* 41°38N 87°30W **311** C9
Hammond *La., U.S.A.* 30°30N 90°28W **315** F9
Hammond *N.Y., U.S.A.* 44°27N 75°42W **313** B9
Hammondsport *U.S.A.* 42°25N 77°13W **312** D7
Hammonton *U.S.A.* 39°39N 74°48W **309** F16
Hamoyet, Jebel *Sudan* 17°33N 38°2E **256** D4
Hampden *N.Z.* 45°18S 170°50E **285** F5
Hampi *India* 15°18N 76°28E **245** G3
Hampshire □ *U.K.* 51°7N 1°23W **169** F6
Hampshire Downs *U.K.* 51°15N 1°10W **169** F6
Hampstead *Qué., Canada* 45°28N 73°37W **130** B2
Hampstead *Dominica* 15°36N 61°23W **323** k
Hampstead *London, U.K.* 51°33N 0°10W **125** A2
Hampstead Garden Suburb
U.K. 51°34N 0°11W **125** A2
Hampstead Heath *U.K.* 51°33N 0°10W **125** A2
Hampton *N.B., Canada* 45°32N 65°51W **299** C6
Hampton *Ont., Canada* 43°58N 78°45W **312** C6
Hampton *London, U.K.* 51°24N 0°21W **125** B1
Hampton *Ark., U.S.A.* 33°32N 92°28W **314** E8
Hampton *Ga., U.S.A.* 33°23N 84°17W **316** B5
Hampton *Iowa, U.S.A.* 42°45N 93°13W **310** B3
Hampton *N.H., U.S.A.* 42°57N 70°50W **313** D14
Hampton *S.C., U.S.A.* 32°52N 81°7W **316** C8
Hampton *Va., U.S.A.* 37°2N 76°21W **309** G15
Hampton Bays *U.S.A.* 40°53N 72°30W **313** F12
Hampton Court Palace
U.K. 51°24N 0°20W **125** B1
Hampton Springs *U.S.A.* 30°5N 83°40W **316** E6
Hampton Tableland
Australia 32°0S 127°0E **279** F4
Hampton Wick *U.K.* 51°24N 0°18W **125** B2
Hampyeong *S. Korea* 35°3N 126°31E **224** E3
Hampyeongman *S. Korea* 35°6N 126°23E **224** E3
Hamrā' *Baghdād, Iraq* 33°18N 44°18E **113** B1
Hamra *Gävleborg, Sweden* 61°39N 14°59E **162** C8
Hamra → *Chad* 12°52N 21°15E **259** F4
Hamrat esh Sheykh
Sudan 14°38N 27°55E **257** E2
Ḥamrīn, Jabal *Iraq* 34°30N 44°30E **213** E11
Hamrun *Malta* 35°53N 14°29E **206** F8
Hamtik *Phil.* 10°42N 121°59E **233** F3
Hamur *Turkey* 39°37N 43°3E **213** C10
Hamyang *S. Korea* 35°32N 127°42E **224** E3
Hamzalar *Turkey* 37°7N 32°33E **250** A3
Han i Hotit *Albania* 42°19N 19°27E **202** D3
Han Jiang → *China* 23°25N 116°40E **229** F11
Han Shui → *China* 30°34N 114°17E **229** B10
Hāna *U.S.A.* 20°45N 155°59W **302** C6
Hanahan *U.S.A.* 32°55N 80°0W **316** C10
Hanak *Si. Arabia* 25°32N 37°0E **246** E3
Hanak *Turkey* 41°14N 42°50E **213** B10
Hanaka *Finland* 60°20N 25°4E **121** A3
Hanalei *U.S.A.* 22°12N 159°30W **302** A2
Hanamaki *Japan* 39°23N 141°7E **220** E10
Hanamaulu *U.S.A.* 21°59N 159°22W **302** B2
Hanang *Tanzania* 4°30S 35°25E **268** C4
Hanapēpē *U.S.A.* 21°55N 159°35W **302** B2
Hanare Iwa *Iwo Jima* 24°48N 141°21E **288** b
Hanau *Germany* 50°7N 8°56E **179** E4
Hanauma B. *U.S.A.* 21°15N 157°40W **302** K14
Hanbogd = Ihbulag
Mongolia 43°11N 107°10E **226** C4
Hançalar *Turkey* 38°8N 29°24E **205** C11
Hâncești *Moldova* 46°50N 28°36E **183** D13
Hancheng *China* 35°31N 110°25E **226** G6
Hanchuan *China* 30°40N 113°50E **229** B9
Hanchung = Hanzhong
China 33°10N 107°1E **228** A6
Hancock *Mich., U.S.A.* 47°8N 88°35W **308** B9
Hancock *N.Y., U.S.A.* 41°57N 75°17W **313** E9
Hancock *Vt., U.S.A.* 43°55N 72°50W **313** C12
Handa *Japan* 34°53N 136°55E **223** C8
Handa I. *U.K.* 58°23N 5°11W **167** C3
Handan *China* 36°35N 114°28E **226** F8
Handeni *Tanzania* 5°25S 38°2E **268** D4
Handlová *Slovak Rep.* 48°45N 18°35E **181** C11
Handub *Sudan* 19°15N 37°16E **256** D4
Handwara *India* 34°21N 74°20E **243** B6
Haneda *Japan* 35°32N 139°44E **140** B3
Haneda, Tōkyō ✈ (HND)
Japan 35°33N 139°46E **140** B3
Hanegev *Israel* 30°50N 35°0E **251** H6
Hanford *U.S.A.* 36°20N 119°39W **306** J7
Hanford Reach △
U.S.A. 46°40N 119°30W **304** C4
Hang Chat *Thailand* 18°20N 99°21E **236** C2
Hang Hau *China* 22°19N 114°16E **122** B2
Hanga Roa *Chile* 27°8S 109°26W **330** b
Hangang → *S. Korea* 37°50N 126°30E **227** F14
Hangayn Nuruu *Mongolia* 47°30N 99°0E **218** B8
Hangchou = Hangzhou
China 30°18N 120°11E **229** B13
Hanger *Sweden* 57°6N 13°58E **163** G7
Hanggin Houqi *China* 40°58N 107°4E **226** D4
Hanggin Qi *China* 39°52N 108°50E **226** E5
Hanging Gardens *Mumbai, India* **130** b1
Hangkow = Wuhan
China 30°31N 114°18E **229** B10
Hangu = Hangu *China* 39°18N 117°53E **227** E9
Hangu *China* 39°18N 117°53E **227** E9
Hangzhou *China* 30°18N 120°11E **229** B13
Hangzhou Wan *China* 30°15N 120°45E **229** B13
Hanh *Mongolia* 51°32N 100°35E **218** A9
Hanhöhiy Uul *Mongolia* 49°30N 94°30E **217** C12
Hanhongor *Mongolia* 43°55N 104°28E **226** C3
Hani *Turkey* 38°24N 40°23E **213** C9
Hania = Chania *Greece* 35°30N 24°4E **207** E5
Ḥanīdh *Si. Arabia* 26°35N 48°38E **247** E6
Ḥanīsh *Yemen* 13°45N 42°46E **248** D3
Haniska *Slovak Rep.* 48°37N 21°15E **181** C14
Hanjiang *China* 25°26N 119°6E **229** E12
Hankinson *U.S.A.* 46°4N 96°54W **308** B5
Hankö *Finland* 59°50N 22°57E **188** C2
Hankou *China* 30°35N 114°30E **229** B10
Hanksville *U.S.A.* 38°22N 110°43W **304** G8
Hanle *India* 32°42N 79°4E **243** C8
Hanlon *Canada* 43°38N 79°39W **141** B1
Hanmer Springs *N.Z.* 42°32S 172°50E **285** C7
Hann → *Australia* 17°26S 126°17E **278** C4
Hann, Mt. *Australia* 15°45S 126°0E **278** C4
Hanna *Alta., Canada* 51°40N 111°54W **296** C6
Hanna *Wyo., U.S.A.* 41°52N 106°34W **304** F10
Hannah B. *Canada* 51°40N 80°0W **298** B4
Hannibal *Mo., U.S.A.* 39°42N 91°22W **310** E5
Hannibal *N.Y., U.S.A.* 43°19N 76°35W **313** C8
Hannik *Sudan* 18°12N 32°20E **256** D3
Hannover *Germany* 52°22N 9°46E **178** C5
Hanö *Sweden* 56°1N 14°50E **163** H8
Hanöbukten *Sweden* 55°35N 14°30E **163** J8
Hanoi *Vietnam* 21°5N 105°55E **228** G5
Hanover = Hannover
Germany 52°22N 9°46E **178** C5
Hanover *Ont., Canada* 44°9N 81°2W **312** B3
Hanover *Northern Cape,*
S. Africa 31°4S 24°29E **270** D3
Hanover *Ind., U.S.A.* 38°43N 85°28W **311** F11
Hanover *N.H., U.S.A.* 43°42N 72°17W **313** C12
Hanover *Ohio, U.S.A.* 40°4N 82°16W **312** F2
Hanover *Pa., U.S.A.* 39°48N 76°59W **309** F15
Hanover, I. *Chile* 51°0S 74°50W **336** D2
Hanpan, C. *Papua N. G.* 5°0S 154°35E **286** C8
Hans Lollik I.
U.S. Virgin Is. 18°24N 64°53W **321** b
Hans Meyer Ra.
Papua N. G. 4°20S 152°55E **286** C7
Hansdiha *India* 24°36N 87°5E **243** G12
Hanshou *China* 28°56N 111°50E **229** C8
Hansi *H.P., India* 32°27N 77°50E **242** C7
Hansi *Haryana, India* 29°10N 75°57E **242** E6
Hanson, L. *Australia* 31°0S 136°15E **282** A2
Hanstholm *Denmark* 57°7N 8°36E **163** G2
Hantan = Handan *China* 36°35N 114°28E **226** F8
Hanting *China* 36°46N 119°12E **227** F10
Hantsavichy *Belarus* 52°49N 26°30E **177** B14
Hanumangarh *India* 29°35N 74°19E **242** E6
Hanwell *U.K.* 51°30N 0°20W **125** A1
Hanworth *U.K.* 51°26N 0°23W **125** B1
Hanyin *China* 32°54N 108°28E **226** H5
Hanyū *Japan* 36°10N 139°32E **223** A11
Hanyuan *China* 29°21N 102°40E **228** C4
Hanzhong *China* 33°10N 107°1E **228** A6
Hanzhuang *China* 34°33N 117°23E **227** G9
Hao *French Polynesia* 18°15S 140°54W **289** f
Haora *India* 22°34N 88°18E **124** B1
Haouach, O. → *Chad* 16°45N 19°35E **259** E4
Haoxue *China* 30°3N 112°24E **229** B9
Haparanda *Sweden* 65°52N 24°8E **160** D21
Hapdeok *S. Korea* 36°48N 126°46E **224** D3
Hapeville *U.S.A.* 33°39N 84°24W **113** C2
Happy *U.S.A.* 34°45N 101°52W **314** D4
Happy Camp *U.S.A.* 41°48N 123°23W **304** F2
Happy Valley *China* 22°16N 114°10E **122** B2
Happy Valley-Goose Bay
Canada 53°15N 60°20W **299** B7
Hapsu *N. Korea* 41°13N 128°51E **224** B4
Hapur *India* 28°45N 77°45E **242** E7
Ḥaql *Si. Arabia* 29°10N 34°58E **251** J5
Haquira *Peru* 14°14S 72°12W **330** C3
Har *Indonesia* 5°16S 133°14E **231** F8
Har Adar *West Bank* 31°49N 35°8E **123** B1
Har-Ayrag *Mongolia* 45°47N 109°16E **226** B5
Har Gilo *West Bank* 31°43N 35°10E **123** B2
Har Homa *West Bank* 31°44N 35°12E **123** B2
Har Hu *China* 38°20N 97°38E **218** D8
Har Nof *Israel* 31°47N 35°11E **123** B2
Har Tsiyon *Jerusalem* **123** b3
Har Us Nuur *Mongolia* 48°0N 92°0E **217** C12
Har Yehuda *Israel* 31°35N 34°57E **251** G5
Ḥaraḍ *Si. Arabia* 24°22N 49°0E **249** A5
Ḥaraḍ *Yemen* 16°26N 43°5E **248** C3
Haradok *Belarus* 55°30N 30°3E **188** E6
Häradsbäck *Sweden* 56°32N 14°26E **163** H8
Harahan *U.S.A.* 29°56N 90°12W **131** B1
Haraiki *French Polynesia* 17°38S 143°27W **289** f
Haramosh *Pakistan* 35°50N 74°54E **243** B6
Haranomachi = Minamisōma
Japan 37°38N 140°58E **220** F10
Harar = Harer *Ethiopia* 9°20N 42°8E **257** F5
Harare *Zimbabwe* 17°43S 31°2E **269** F3
Ḥarāsīs, Jiddat al *Oman* 19°30N 56°0E **249** C7
Harat *Eritrea* 16°5N 39°26E **257** D4
Harau *Indonesia* 0°7S 100°35E **234** C2
Haraz-Djombo *Chad* 14°20N 19°12E **259** F3
Harazé *Chad* 9°57N 20°48E **259** G4
Harbel *Liberia* 6°16N 10°20W **262** D2
Harbhanga *India* 20°38N 84°36E **244** D7
Harbin *China* 45°48N 126°40E **227** B14
Harbiye *Turkey* 36°10N 36°8E **250** B7
Harbo *Sweden* 60°7N 17°12E **162** D11
Harboøre *Denmark* 56°38N 8°10E **163** H2
Harbor Beach *U.S.A.* 43°51N 82°39W **312** C2
Harborcreek *U.S.A.* 42°9N 79°57W **312** D5
Harbour Breton *Canada* 47°29N 55°50W **299** C8
Harbour Deep *Canada* 50°25N 56°32W **299** B8
Harbour Front Centre
Singapore 1°16N 103°49E **138** B2
Harbour View *Jamaica* 17°59N 76°50W **320** a
Harburg *Germany* 53°27N 9°58E **178** B5
Harburger Berge △
Germany 53°26N 9°51E **178** B5
Harda *India* 22°27N 77°5E **242** H7
Hardangerfjorden *Norway* 60°5N 6°0E **164** D3
Hardangerjøkulen *Norway* 60°30N 7°27E **164** D4
Hardangervidda *Norway* 60°7N 7°20E **164** D4
Hardangervidda △ *Norway* 60°10N 7°25E **164** D4
Hardap □ *Namibia* 24°0S 17°0E **270** B2
Hardap △ *Namibia* 24°29S 17°45E **270** B2
Hardap Dam *Namibia* 24°32S 17°50E **270** B2
Hardeeville *U.S.A.* 32°17N 81°5W **316** C8
Harden *Australia* 34°32S 148°24E **283** C8
Hardenberg *Neths.* 52°34N 6°37E **170** B6
Harderwijk *Neths.* 52°21N 5°38E **170** B5
Hardey → *Australia* 22°45S 116°8E **278** D2
Hardin *Ill., U.S.A.* 39°10N 90°37W **310** E6
Hardin *Mont., U.S.A.* 45°44N 107°37W **304** D10
Harding *S. Africa* 30°35S 29°55E **271** D4
Harding, L. *U.S.A.* 32°40N 85°5W **316** C4
Harding Ra. *Australia* 16°17S 124°55E **278** C3
Hardinsburg *U.S.A.* 37°47N 86°28W **311** G10
Hardisty *Canada* 52°40N 111°18W **296** C6
Hardoi *India* 27°26N 80°6E **243** F9
Hardwar = Haridwar *India* 29°58N 78°9E **242** E8
Hardwick *Ga., U.S.A.* 33°4N 83°14W **316** B6
Hardwick *Vt., U.S.A.* 44°30N 72°22W **313** B12
Hardwicke B. *Australia* 34°55S 137°20E **282** C2
Hardwood Lake *Canada* 45°12N 77°26W **312** A7
Hardy, Pen. *Chile* 55°30S 68°20W **336** E3
Hardy, Pte. *St. Lucia* 14°6N 60°56W **323** m
Hare B. *Canada* 51°15N 55°45W **299** B8
Hareid *Norway* 62°22N 6°1E **164** B3
Haren *Brussels, Belgium* 50°53N 4°25E **116** A2
Haren *Niedersachsen,*
Germany 52°47N 7°13E **178** C3
Harer *Ethiopia* 9°20N 42°8E **257** F5
Harerge *Ethiopia* 7°12N 42°0E **257** F5
Hareskovby *Denmark* 55°45N 12°23E **118** A2
Harestua *Norway* 60°11N 10°44E **164** D7
Hareto *Ethiopia* 9°23N 37°6E **257** F4
Harfleur *France* 49°30N 0°10E **172** C7
Hargeisa *Somalia* 9°30N 44°2E **267** C5
Hargeisa △ *Somalia* 10°2N 44°2E **267** B5
Harghita □ *Romania* 46°30N 25°30E **183** D10
Harghita, Munţii
Romania 46°25N 25°35E **183** D10
Hargshamn *Sweden* 60°12N 18°30E **162** D12
Hari → *Indonesia* 1°16S 104°5E **234** C2
Haria *Canary Is.* 29°8N 13°32W **153** e2
Ḥarīb *Yemen* 14°56N 45°30E **248** D4
Haricha, Hamada el *Mali* 22°40N 3°15W **260** D4
Haridwar *India* 29°58N 78°9E **242** E8
Harihar *India* 14°32N 75°44E **245** G2
Harihari *N.Z.* 43°9S 170°33E **285** D5
Hariharpur Garhi *Nepal* 27°19N 85°29E **243** F11
Ḥārim *Syria* 36°14N 36°29E **250** B7
Harim, Jabal al *Oman* 25°58N 56°14E **247** E8
Harima-Nada *Japan* 34°30N 134°35E **222** C6
Haringey □ *U.K.* 51°34N 0°5W **125** A3
Haringhata → *Bangla.* 22°0N 89°58E **241** E2
Haripad *India* 9°14N 76°28E **245** K3
Harīr, W. al → *Syria* 32°44N 35°59E **250** F6
Harīrūd → *Asia* 37°24N 60°38E **240** A1
Härjedalen *Sweden* 62°22N 13°5E **162** B7
Harjusuo *Finland* 60°19N 25°0E **121** B3
Harlaching *Germany* 48°5N 11°33E **131** B2
Harlan *Iowa, U.S.A.* 41°39N 95°19W **308** E6
Harlan *Ky., U.S.A.* 36°51N 83°19W **309** G12
Hârlău *Romania* 47°23N 26°55E **183** C11
Harlaw Res. *U.K.* 55°52N 3°18W **121** B2
Harlech *U.K.* 52°52N 4°6W **168** E3
Harlem *Ga., U.S.A.* 33°25N 82°19W **316** B7
Harlem *Mont., U.S.A.* 48°32N 108°47W **304** B9
Harlem *New York, U.S.A.* **132** a3
Harlesden *U.K.* 51°32N 0°14W **125** A2
Hårlev *Denmark* 55°21N 12°14E **163** J6
Harleyville *U.S.A.* 33°13N 80°27W **316** B9
Harlingen *Neths.* 53°11N 5°25E **170** A5
Harlingen *Tex., U.S.A.* 26°12N 97°42W **314** H6
Harlington *U.K.* 51°29N 0°25W **125** B1
Harlow *U.K.* 51°46N 0°8E **169** F8
Harlowton *U.S.A.* 46°26N 109°50W **304** C9
Harmaja *Finland* 60°6N 24°58E **121** C2
Harmancık *Turkey* 39°41N 29°9E **205** B11
Harmånger *Sweden* 61°55N 17°20E **162** C11
Harmashatar hegy
Hungary 47°33N 19°0E **117** A2
Harmil *Eritrea* 16°30N 40°10E **257** D5
Harnai *India* 17°48N 73°6E **244** F1
Harnai *Pakistan* 30°6N 67°56E **242** D2
Harney, L. *U.S.A.* 28°45N 81°3W **317** G8
Harney Basin *U.S.A.* 43°0N 119°30W **304** E4
Harney L. *U.S.A.* 43°14N 119°8W **304** E4
Harney Peak *U.S.A.* 43°52N 103°32W **308** D2
Härnön *Sweden* 62°36N 18°0E **162** B12
Härnösand *Sweden* 62°38N 17°55E **162** B11
Haro *Spain* 42°35N 2°55W **196** C2
Harold *U.S.A.* 30°40N 86°53W **317** E3
Harold Pond *Bahamas* 25°2N 77°22W **153** b
Harolds Cross *Ireland* 53°19N 6°16W **120** B2
Haroldswick *U.K.* 60°48N 0°50W **167** A8
Háros *Hungary* 47°23N 19°2E **117** B2
Harp L. *Canada* 55°5N 61°50W **299** A7
Harpanahalli *India* 14°47N 76°2E **245** G3
Harper = Costa Mesa
U.S.A. 33°38N 117°55W **307** M9
Harper *Liberia* 4°25N 7°43W **262** E3
Harper, Mt. *U.S.A.* 64°14N 143°51W **303** D12
Harperrig Res. *U.K.* 55°50N 3°26W **121** B1
Harplinge *Sweden* 56°45N 12°45E **163** H6
Harrah's Casino *New Orleans, U.S.A.* **131** b2
Harrai *India* 22°37N 79°13E **243** H8
Harrand *Pakistan* 29°28N 70°3E **242** E4
Harricana → *Canada* 50°56N 79°32W **298** B4
Harriman *U.S.A.* 35°56N 84°33W **315** D12
Harrington *Australia* 31°52S 152°42E **283** A10
Harrington Harbour
Canada 50°31N 59°30W **299** B8
Harrington Sd. *Bermuda* 32°20N 64°44W **153** a
Harris *Montserrat* 16°44N 62°11W **322** p
Harris *W. Isles, U.K.* 57°50N 6°55W **167** D2
Harris, L. *S. Austral.,*
Australia 31°10S 135°10E **281** E2
Harris, L. *Fla., U.S.A.* 28°47N 81°49W **317** G8
Harris, Sd. of *U.K.* 57°44N 7°6W **167** D1
Harris Mts. *N.Z.* 44°49S 168°49E **285** E3
Harris Pt. *Canada* 43°6N 82°9W **312** C2
Harrisburg *Ill., U.S.A.* 37°44N 88°32W **311** G8
Harrisburg *Nebr., U.S.A.* 41°33N 103°44W **308** E2
Harrisburg *Pa., U.S.A.* 40°16N 76°53W **312** F8
Harrismith *S. Africa* 28°15S 29°8E **271** C4
Harrison *Ark., U.S.A.* 36°14N 93°7W **314** C8
Harrison *Maine, U.S.A.* 44°7N 70°39W **313** B14
Harrison *Nebr., U.S.A.* 42°41N 103°53W **308** D2
Harrison, C. *Canada* 54°55N 57°55W **299** B8
Harrison Bay *U.S.A.* 70°40N 151°0W **303** A10
Harrison L. *Canada* 49°33N 121°50W **296** D4
Harrisonburg *U.S.A.* 38°27N 78°52W **309** F14
Harrison's Cave *Barbados* 13°11N 59°34W **323** r
Harrisonville *U.S.A.* 38°39N 94°21W **310** F2
Harriston *Canada* 43°57N 80°53W **312** C4
Harrisville *Mich., U.S.A.* 44°39N 83°17W **312** B1
Harrisville *N.Y., U.S.A.* 44°9N 75°19W **313** B9
Harrisville *Pa., U.S.A.* 41°8N 80°0W **312** E5
Harrodsburg *Ind., U.S.A.* 39°1N 86°33W **311** E10
Harrodsburg *Ky., U.S.A.* 37°46N 84°51W **311** G12
Harrogate *U.K.* 54°0N 1°33W **168** C6
Harrow *Vic., Australia* 37°9S 141°35E **282** D4
Harrow *Ont., Canada* 42°2N 82°55W **312** D2
Harrow □ *U.K.* 51°35N 0°21W **125** A1
Harrow on the Hill *U.K.* 51°34N 0°21W **125** A1
Harrow School *U.K.* 51°34N 0°20W **125** A1
Harrow Weald *U.K.* 51°36N 0°20W **125** A1
Harrowsmith *Canada* 44°24N 76°40W **313** B8
Harry S. Truman Res.
U.S.A. 38°16N 93°24W **310** F3
Harsefeld *Germany* 53°27N 9°30E **178** B5
Harsewinkel *Germany* 51°56N 8°14E **178** D4
Harsīn *Iran* 34°18N 47°33E **213** E12
Hârșova *Romania* 44°40N 27°59E **183** F12
Harstad *Norway* 68°48N 16°30E **160** B17
Harsud *India* 22°6N 76°44E **242** H7
Hart *U.S.A.* 43°42N 86°22W **308** D10
Hart, L. *Australia* 31°10S 136°25E **282** A2
Hartbees → *S. Africa* 28°45S 20°32E **270** C3
Hartberg *Austria* 47°17N 15°58E **180** D8
Hårteigen *Norway* 60°11N 7°3E **164** D4
Hartford *Ala., U.S.A.* 31°6N 85°42W **316** D4
Hartford *Conn., U.S.A.* 41°46N 72°41W **313** E12
Hartford *Ky., U.S.A.* 37°27N 86°55W **308** G10
Hartford *Mich., U.S.A.* 42°13N 86°10W **311** B10
Hartford *S. Dak., U.S.A.* 43°38N 96°57W **308** D5
Hartford *Vt., U.S.A.* 43°40N 72°20W **313** C12
Hartford *Wis., U.S.A.* 43°19N 88°22W **308** D9
Hartford City *U.S.A.* 40°27N 85°22W **311** D11
Hartingsburg = Bela Bela
S. Africa 24°51S 28°19E **271** B4
Hartland *N.B., Canada* 46°20N 67°32W **299** C6
Hartland *Wis., U.S.A.* 43°6N 88°21W **311** A8
Hartland Pt. *U.K.* 51°1N 4°32W **169** F3
Hartlepool *U.K.* 54°42N 1°13W **168** C6
Hartlepool □ *U.K.* 54°42N 1°17W **168** C6
Hartley Bay *Canada* 53°25N 129°15W **296** C3
Hartmannberge *Namibia* 17°0S 13°0E **270** A1
Hartney *Canada* 49°30N 100°35W **297** D8
Hârtop *Moldova* 46°39N 28°40E **183** D13
Harts → *S. Africa* 28°24S 24°17E **270** C3
Harts Range *Australia* 23°6S 134°55E **280** C1
Hartselle *U.S.A.* 34°27N 86°56W **315** D11
Hartsfield-Jackson Atlanta Int. ✈
(ATL) *U.S.A.* 33°38N 84°26W **113** C2
Hartshorne *U.S.A.* 34°51N 95°34W **314** D7
Hartstown *U.S.A.* 41°33N 80°23W **312** E4
Hartsville *U.S.A.* 34°23N 80°4W **315** D14
Hartswater *S. Africa* 27°34S 24°43E **270** C3
Hartwell *U.S.A.* 34°21N 82°56W **315** D13
Harumi *Tokyo, Japan* **140** c5
Harunabad *Pakistan* 29°35N 73°8E **242** E5
Harur *India* 12°3N 78°29E **245** H4
Harūt → *Afghan.* 31°29N 61°24E **240** C1
Harvand *Iran* 28°25N 55°43E **247** D7
Harvard *U.S.A.* 42°25N 88°37W **311** B8
Harvard Univ. *U.S.A.* 42°22N 71°7W **116** A2
Harvey *W. Austral.,*
Australia 33°5S 115°54E **279** F2
Harvey *Ill., U.S.A.* 41°36N 87°50W **119** D3
Harvey *La., U.S.A.* 29°54N 90°4W **131** B2
Harvey *N. Dak., U.S.A.* 47°47N 99°56W **308** B4
Harwich *U.K.* 51°56N 1°17E **169** F9
Harwood Heights *U.S.A.* 41°57N 87°46W **119** B2
Haryana □ *India* 29°0N 76°10E **242** E7
Haryn → *Belarus* 52°7N 27°17E **177** B14
Harz *Germany* 51°38N 10°44E **178** D6
Harz △ *Germany* 51°40N 10°18E **178** D6
Harzgerode *Germany* 51°38N 11°8E **178** D7
Hasa *Si. Arabia* 25°50N 49°0E **247** E6
Ḥasā, W. al → *Jordan* 31°4N 35°29E **251** G6
Hasaheisa *Sudan* 14°44N 33°20E **257** E3
Ḥasanābād *Eşfahan, Iran* 32°8N 52°44E **247** C7
Ḥasanābād *Tehrān, Iran* 35°44N 51°16E **141** A1
Hasankeyf *Turkey* 37°42N 41°24E **213** D9
Hasanparti *India* 18°4N 79°32E **244** E4
Hasawinah, Jabal al *Libya* 28°15N 14°0E **258** C2
Ḥasb, W. → *Iraq* 31°45N 44°17E **246** D5
Hasbrouck Heights *U.S.A.* 40°51N 74°6W **132** A1
Hasdo → *India* 21°44N 82°44E **243** J10
Haselhorst *Germany* 52°33N 13°14E **115** A2
Haselünne *Germany* 52°40N 7°29E **178** C3
Hashima *Japan* 35°20N 136°40E **223** B8
Hashimoto *Japan* 34°19N 135°37E **223** C7
Hashtjerd *Iran* 35°52N 50°40E **247** C6
Hashtpur = Tālesh *Iran* 37°58N 48°58E **213** D13
Hashtrud *Iran* 37°28N 47°4E **213** D12
Hasi Nueifed *W. Sahara* 24°54N 14°49W **260** D2
Ḥāsik *Oman* 17°22N 55°17E **249** C6
Haskell *U.S.A.* 33°10N 99°44W **314** E5
Haskovo = Khaskovo
Bulgaria 41°56N 25°30E **203** E9
Hasköy *Edirne, Turkey* 41°38N 26°52E **203** E10
Hasköy *İstanbul, Turkey* 41°2N 28°57E **122** B1
Haslach *Germany* 48°16N 8°5E **179** G4
Hasle *Denmark* 55°11N 14°44E **163** J8
Hasle *Oslo, Norway* 59°46N 10°38E **133** B2
Haslemere *U.K.* 51°5N 0°43W **169** F7
Haslev *Denmark* 55°18N 11°57E **163** J5
Haslum *Norway* 59°55N 10°34E **133** A2
Hasparren *France* 43°24N 1°18W **174** E2
Hassa *Turkey* 36°48N 36°29E **250** B7
Hassan *India* 13°0N 76°5E **245** H3
Hassberge △ *Germany* 50°8N 10°45E **179** E6
Hassela *Sweden* 62°7N 16°42E **162** B10
Hasselt *Belgium* 50°56N 5°21E **170** D5
Hassfurt *Germany* 50°2N 10°30E **179** E6
Hassi bel Guebbour *Algeria* 28°30N 6°41E **261** C6
Hassi bou Khelala *Algeria* 30°17N 0°18W **261** B4
Hassi Bourarchet *Algeria* 27°26N 9°19E **261** C6
Hassi Djafou *Algeria* 30°55N 3°35E **261** B5
Hassi el Hadjar *Algeria* 31°28N 4°45E **261** B5
Hassi Imoulaye *Algeria* 29°54N 9°10E **261** C6
Hassi Inifeg *Algeria* 29°15N 1°30W **261** C4
Hassi Inifel *Algeria* 29°50N 3°41E **261** C5
Hassi Mana *Algeria* 28°48N 2°37W **261** C4
Hassi Marroket *Algeria* 30°10N 3°0E **261** B5
Hassi Mengoub *Algeria* 29°49N 5°26W **260** C3
Hassi Messaoud *Algeria* 31°51N 6°1E **261** B6
Hassi Sougoued *Algeria* 26°50N 9°28E **261** C6
Hassi Tartrat *Algeria* 30°5N 6°28E **261** B6
Hassi Zerzour *Morocco* 30°51N 3°56W **260** B4
Hassi Zguilma *Algeria* 30°19N 6°10W **260** B3
Hässleholm *Sweden* 56°10N 13°46E **163** H7
Hasslö *Sweden* 56°7N 15°28E **163** H9
Hassloch *Germany* 49°22N 8°16E **179** F4
Hästhagen *Sweden* 59°18N 18°9E **139** B2
Hästholmen *Sweden* 58°17N 14°38E **163** F8
Hastings *Vic., Australia* 38°18S 145°12E **283** E6
Hastings *Barbados* 13°4N 59°36W **323** r
Hastings *N.Z.* 39°39S 176°52E **284** F6
Hastings *E. Sussex, U.K.* 50°51N 0°35E **169** G8
Hastings *Fla., U.S.A.* 29°43N 81°31W **316** F8
Hastings *Mich., U.S.A.* 42°39N 85°17W **311** B11
Hastings *Minn., U.S.A.* 44°44N 92°51W **308** C7
Hastings *Nebr., U.S.A.* 40°35N 98°23W **308** E4
Hastings Ra. *Australia* 31°15S 152°14E **283** A10
Hästveda *Sweden* 56°17N 13°55E **163** H7
Ḥaswayn *Yemen* 15°35N 52°6E **249** D6
Hat Ukraine 48°19N 22°38E **182** B7
Hat Head △ *Australia* 31°3S 153°1E **283** A10
Hat Lot *Vietnam* 21°15N 104°7E **236** B5
Hat Yai *Thailand* 7°1N 100°27E **237** J3
Hatanbulag = Ergel
Mongolia 43°8N 109°5E **226** C5
Hatay *Turkey* 36°14N 36°10E **250** B7
Hatay □ *Turkey* 36°25N 36°15E **250** B7
Hatch *U.S.A.* 32°40N 107°9W **305** K10
Hatch End *U.K.* 51°36N 0°22W **125** A1
Hatchet L. *Canada* 58°36N 103°40W **297** B8
Haţeg *Romania* 45°36N 22°55E **182** E7
Hateruma-Shima *Japan* 24°3N 123°47E **221** M1
Hatfield *Australia* 33°54S 143°49E **282** B5
Hatgal *Mongolia* 50°26N 100°9E **218** A9
Hathras *India* 27°36N 78°6E **242** F8
Hatia *Bangla.* 22°30N 91°5E **241** D3
Hatia *Nepal* 27°43N 87°21E **243** F12
Hatia Is. *Bangla.* 22°30N 91°0E **241** D3
Hatiara *India* 22°36N 88°26E **124** B2
Ḥāṭibah, Ra's *Si. Arabia* 21°55N 38°57E **256** C4
Hatid *India* 17°17N 75°3E **244** F2
Hatillo *Puerto Rico* 18°29N 66°50W **321** b
Hato *Bonaire* 12°11N 68°17W **322** h
Hato *Curaçao* 12°11N 68°57W **322** g
Hato Caves *Curaçao* 12°11N 68°57W **322** g
Hato Corozal *Colombia* 6°11N 71°45W **328** B3
Hato Mayor *Dom. Rep.* 18°46N 69°15W **321** C6
Hatra = Al Ḥaḍr *Iraq* 35°35N 42°44E **213** E10
Hatsukaichi *Japan* 34°22N 132°22E **222** C4
Hatta *India* 24°7N 79°36E **243** G8
Hatta *U.A.E.* 24°45N 56°4E **247** E8
Hattah *Australia* 34°48S 142°17E **282** C5
Hattah Kulkyne △
Australia 34°16S 142°33E **282** C5
Hatteras, C. *U.S.A.* 35°14N 75°32W **315** D17
Hatteras Abyssal Plain
Atl. Oc. 28°0N 72°0W **152** D4
Hattiesburg *U.S.A.* 31°20N 89°17W **315** F10
Hattusa *Turkey* 40°0N 34°37E **212** B6
Hatutu *French Polynesia* 7°56S 140°38W **289** f
Hatvan *Hungary* 47°40N 19°45E **182** C4
Hau → *Vietnam* 9°30N 106°13E **237** H6
Haubstadt *U.S.A.* 38°12N 87°34W **311** F9
Haud *Ethiopia* 8°0N 45°0E **267** C6
Hauganes *Iceland* 65°56N 18°27W **155** B8
Haugastøl *Norway* 60°30N 7°50E **164** D4
Hauge *Norway* 58°20N 6°15E **164** F3
Haugesund *Norway* 59°23N 5°13E **164** E2
Hauhui *Solomon Is.* 9°10S 160°59E **287** M11
Hauiti, Hauraki Haurangaroa Ra. *N.Z.* 38°42S 175°40E **284** E4
Haukeligrend *Norway* 59°44N 7°33E **164** E4
Hauketo *Norway* 59°50N 10°48E **133** A3
Haukipudas *Finland* 65°12N 25°20E **160** D21
Haultain → *Canada* 55°51N 106°46W **297** B7
Haungpa *Burma* 25°29N 96°7E **241** C6
Haura *Solomon Is.* 10°46S 161°59E **287** N11
Hauraki G. *N.Z.* 36°35S 175°5E **284** C4
Hauroko L. *N.Z.* 45°59S 167°21E **285** F2
Hausruck *Austria* 48°6N 13°30E **180** C6
Haut Atlas *Morocco* 32°30N 5°0W **260** B4
Haut de la Montagne
Guadeloupe 16°26N 61°28W **322** e
Haut-Jura △ *France* 46°23N 2°23E **173** F9
Haut-Languedoc △ *France* 43°30N 2°43E **174** E6
Haut-Niger △ *Guinea* 10°20N 10°20W **262** C2
Haut-Rhin □ *France* 48°0N 7°15E **173** E14
Haut-Zaïre = Orientale □
Dem. Rep. of the Congo 2°20N 26°0E **268** B2
Haute-Corse □ *France* 42°30N 9°30E **175** F13
Haute-Garonne □ *France* 43°30N 1°30E **174** E5
Haute-Loire □ *France* 45°5N 3°50E **174** C7
Haute-Marne □ *France* 48°10N 5°20E **173** D12
Haute-Normandie □ *France* 49°20N 1°0E **172** C7
Haute-Saône □ *France* 47°45N 6°10E **173** E13
Haute-Savoie □ *France* 46°0N 6°20E **175** C10
Haute-Vienne □ *France* 45°50N 1°10E **174** C5
Hautes-Alpes □ *France* 44°42N 6°20E **175** D10
Hautes Fagnes = Hohes Venn
Belgium 50°30N 6°5E **170** D6
Hautes-Pyrénées □ *France* 43°0N 0°10E **174** F4
Hauteville-Lompnès *France* 45°58N 5°36E **175** C9
Hautmont *France* 50°15N 3°55E **173** B10
Hauts-de-Seine □ *France* 48°52N 2°15E **173** D9
Hauts Plateaux *Algeria* 35°0N 1°0E **261** B5
Hau'ula *U.S.A.* 21°37N 157°55W **302** J14
Hauz Khas *India* 28°33N 77°11E **120** B2
Hauzenberg *Germany* 48°40N 13°37E **179** G9
Havana = La Habana
Cuba 23°8N 82°22W **320** B3
Havana *Fla., U.S.A.* 30°37N 84°25W **316** E5
Havana *Ill., U.S.A.* 40°18N 90°4W **310** D6
Havant *U.K.* 50°51N 0°58W **169** G7
Havârna *Romania* 48°4N 26°43E **183** B11
Havasor = Kığzı *Turkey* 38°18N 43°25E **246** B4
Havasu, L. *U.S.A.* 34°18N 114°28W **307** L12
Havdhem *Sweden* 57°10N 18°20E **163** G12
Havel → *Germany* 52°50N 12°3E **115** A2
Havelian *Pakistan* 34°2N 73°10E **242** B5
Havelkanal *Germany* 52°36N 13°10E **115** A2
Havelock *Ont., Canada* 44°26N 77°53W **312** B7
Havelock *N.Z.* 41°17S 173°48E **285** B8
Havelock *N.C., U.S.A.* 34°53N 76°54W **315** D16
Havelock I. *India* 11°58N 93°0E **245** J11
Havelock North *N.Z.* 39°40S 176°53E **284** F5
Haverfordwest *U.K.* 51°48N 4°58W **169** F3
Haverhill *Suffolk, U.K.* 52°5N 0°28E **169** E8
Haverhill *Fla., U.S.A.* 26°42N 80°7W **317** J9
Haverhill *Mass., U.S.A.* 42°47N 71°5W **313** D13
Haveri *India* 14°53N 75°24E **245** G2
Havering □ *U.K.* 51°34N 0°13E **125** A5
Havering-atte-Bower *U.K.* 51°37N 0°11E **125** A5
Haverö *Sweden* 62°18N 15°7E **162** B9
Haverstraw *U.S.A.* 41°12N 73°58W **313** E11
Håverud *Sweden* 58°50N 12°28E **163** F6
Havirga *Mongolia* 45°41N 113°5E **226** B7
Havířov *Czech Rep.* 49°46N 18°20E **181** B11
Havlíčkův Brod *Czech Rep.* 49°36N 15°33E **180** B8
Havneby *Denmark* 55°5N 8°34E **163** J2
Havran *Turkey* 39°33N 27°6E **205** B9
Havre *U.S.A.* 48°33N 109°41W **304** B9
Havre-Aubert *Canada* 47°12N 61°56W **299** C7
Havre-St.-Pierre *Canada* 50°18N 63°33W **299** B7
Havsa *Turkey* 41°31N 26°48E **203** E10
Havza *Turkey* 41°0N 35°35E **212** B6
Haw → *U.S.A.* 35°36N 79°3W **315** D15
Hawai'i *U.S.A.* 19°30N 155°30W **302** D6
Hawai'i □ *U.S.A.* 19°30N 156°30W **302** D5
Hawai'i County *U.S.A.* 19°30N 155°30W **302** D6
Hawai'i Kai *U.S.A.* 21°16N 157°42W **302** K14
Hawai'i Volcanoes △
U.S.A. 19°25N 155°18W **302** D6
Hawaiian Is. *Pac. Oc.* 20°30N 156°0W **302** G12
Hawaiian Ridge *Pac. Oc.* 24°0N 165°0W **289** E11
Hawarden *U.S.A.* 43°0N 96°29W **308** D5
Hawashiyah, W. *Egypt* 28°31N 32°58E **251** K3
Hawea, L. *N.Z.* 44°28S 169°19E **285** E4
Hawea Flat *N.Z.* 44°40S 169°19E **285** E4
Hawera *N.Z.* 39°35S 174°19E **284** F3
Hawesville *U.S.A.* 37°54N 86°45W **311** G10
Ḥawf *Yemen* 16°38N 53°2E **249** C6
Hawi *U.S.A.* 20°14N 155°50W **302** C6
Hawick *U.K.* 55°26N 2°47W **167** F6
Hawk Junction *Canada* 48°5N 84°38W **298** C3
Hawk Point *U.S.A.* 38°58N 91°8W **310** F5
Hawkdun Ra. *N.Z.* 44°53S 170°5E **285** E5
Hawke B. *N.Z.* 39°25S 177°20E **284** F6
Hawker *Australia* 31°59S 138°22E **282** A3
Hawke's Bay *Canada* 50°36N 57°10W **299** B8
Hawke's Bay □ *N.Z.* 39°45S 176°35E **284** F5
Hawkesbury *Canada* 45°37N 74°37W **298** C5
Hawkesbury I. *Canada* 53°37N 129°3W **296** C3
Hawkesbury Pt. *Australia* 11°55S 134°5E **280** A1
Hawkinsville *U.S.A.* 32°17N 83°28W **316** C6

Hawks Nest *Australia* 32°41S 152°11E **283** B10
Hawley *Minn., U.S.A.* 45°53N 96°19W **308** B5
Hawley *Pa., U.S.A.* 41°28N 75°11W **313** E9
Haworth *U.S.A.* 40°57N 73°59W **132** A2
Hawrā' *Yemen* 15°42N 48°16E **249** D5
Ḥawrān, W. → *Iraq* 33°58N 42°34E **213** F10
Hawthorne *Fla., U.S.A.* 29°36N 82°5W **317** F7
Hawthorne *Nev., U.S.A.* 38°32N 118°38W **304** G4
Hawthorne Racecourse
  U.S.A. 41°49N 87°44W **119** C2
Hay *Australia* 34°30S 144°51E **283** C6
Hay → *N. Terr., Australia* 24°50S 138°0E **280** C2
Hay → *Alta., Canada* 60°50N 116°26W **296** A5
Hay, C. *Australia* 14°55S 129°29E **278** B4
Hay I. *Canada* 44°53N 80°58W **302** A3
Hay L. *Canada* 58°50N 118°50W **296** B5
Hay-on-Wye *U.K.* 52°5N 3°8W **169** E4
Hay Point *Australia* 21°18S 149°17E **280** C4
Hay River *Canada* 60°51N 115°44W **296** B5
Hay Springs *U.S.A.* 42°41N 102°41W **308** D2
Hayachine-San *Japan* 39°34N 141°29E **222** E10
Hayange *France* 49°20N 6°2E **173** C13
Hayastan = Armenia ■
  Asia 40°20N 45°0E **191** K7
Hayato *Japan* 31°40N 130°43E **222** C7
Haydān, W. al → *Jordan* 31°29N 35°34E **251** G6
Haydarlı *Turkey* 38°16N 30°23E **205** C12
Hayden *U.S.A.* 40°30N 107°16W **304** F10
Hayes *Jamaica* 17°52N 77°14W **320** a
Hayes *Kent, U.K.* 51°22N 0°0 **125** A1
Hayes *Middlesex, U.K.* 51°30N 0°25W **125** A1
Hayes *S. Dak., U.S.A.* 44°23N 101°1W **308** C3
Hayes → *Canada* 57°3N 92°12W **298** A1
Hayes, Mt. *U.S.A.* 63°37N 146°43W **303** E11
Hayes Creek *Australia* 13°43S 131°22E **278** B5
Hayes End *U.S.A.* 51°31N 0°25W **125** A1
Hayford *U.S.A.* 41°45N 87°42W **119** C2
Hayle *U.K.* 50°11N 5°26W **169** G2
Hayling I. *U.K.* 50°48N 0°59W **169** G7
Haymā' *Oman* 19°56N 56°19E **249** C7
Hayman I. *Australia* 20°4S 148°53E **280** b
Haymana *Turkey* 39°26N 32°31E **212** C5
Haynan *Yemen* 15°50N 48°18E **249** D5
Haynau = Chojnów
  Poland 51°18N 15°58E **185** G2
Hayneville *U.S.A.* 32°23N 83°37W **316** G6
Hayrabolu *Turkey* 41°12N 27°5E **203** E11
Hays *Alta., Canada* 50°6N 111°48W **296** D6
Hays *Kans., U.S.A.* 38°53N 99°20W **308** F4
Ḥays *Yemen* 13°56N 43°29E **248** D3
Haysville *U.S.A.* 38°28N 86°55W **311** F10
Haysyn *Ukraine* 48°57N 29°25E **183** H14
Hayvoron *Ukraine* 48°22N 29°52E **183** H14
Hayward *Calif., U.S.A.* 37°40N 122°4W **306** H4
Hayward *Wis., U.S.A.* 46°1N 91°29W **308** B8
Haywards Heath *U.K.* 51°0N 0°5W **169** G7
Hazafon □ *Israel* 32°40N 35°20E **250** C4
Hazar *Turkmenistan* 39°34N 53°16E **187** G9
Hazārān, Kūh-e *Iran* 29°35N 57°20E **247** D8
Hazard *U.S.A.* 37°15N 83°12W **309** G12
Hazaribag *India* 23°58N 85°26E **243** H11
Hazaribag Road *India* 24°12N 85°57E **243** G11
Hazebrouck *France* 50°42N 2°31E **173** B9
Hazelton *B.C., Canada* 55°20N 127°42W **296** B3
Hazelton *N. Dak., U.S.A.* 46°29N 100°17W **308** B3
Hazen *U.S.A.* 47°18N 101°38W **308** B3
Hazen, L. *Canada* 81°47N 71°1W **154** A3
Hazlehurst *Ga., U.S.A.* 31°52N 82°36W **316** D7
Hazlehurst *Miss., U.S.A.* 31°52N 90°24W **315** F9
Hazlet *U.S.A.* 40°25N 74°12W **313** F10
Hazleton *Ind., U.S.A.* 38°29N 87°33W **311** F9
Hazleton *Pa., U.S.A.* 40°57N 75°59W **313** E9
Hazlett, L. *Australia* 21°30S 128°48E **278** D4
Hazro *Turkey* 38°15N 40°47E **246** B4
He Xian = Hezhou *China* 24°27N 111°30E **229** E8
He Xian *China* 31°45N 118°20E **229** B12
Head of Bight *Australia* 31°30S 131°25E **279** F5
Head-Smashed-In Buffalo Jump
  Canada 49°44N 113°37W **296** D6
Headland *U.S.A.* 31°21N 85°21W **316** D4
Headlands *Zimbabwe* 18°15S 32°2E **269** F3
Healdsburg *U.S.A.* 38°37N 122°52W **306** G4
Healdton *U.S.A.* 34°14N 97°29W **314** D6
Healesville *Australia* 37°35S 145°30E **283** D6
Healy *U.S.A.* 63°52N 148°58W **303** E10
Heany Junction *Zimbabwe* 20°6S 28°54E **271** B4
Heanza-shima *Japan* 26°20N 127°57E **288** a
Heard I. *Ind. Oc.* 53°6S 72°36E **273** K6
Hearne *U.S.A.* 30°53N 96°36W **314** F6
Hearst *Canada* 49°40N 83°41W **298** C3
Heart → *U.S.A.* 46°46N 100°50W **308** B3
Heart's Content *Canada* 47°54N 53°27W **299** C9
Heath → *Bolivia* 12°31S 68°38W **330** C4
Heath, Pte. *Canada* 49°8N 61°40W **299** B7
Heath Mts. *N.Z.* 45°39S 167°9E **285** F2
Heathcote *Australia* 36°56S 144°45E **283** D6
Heatherwood = Edson
  Canada 53°35N 116°28W **296** C5
Heathfield *S. Africa* 34°3S 18°27E **118** D1
Heathrow, London ✈ (LHR)
  U.K. 51°28N 0°27W **125** B1
Heavener *U.S.A.* 34°53N 94°36W **314** D7
Hebbronville *U.S.A.* 27°18N 98°41W **314** H5
Hebe Haven *China* 22°21N 114°15E **122** A2
Hebei □ *China* 39°0N 116°0E **226** E9
Hebel *Australia* 28°58S 147°47E **281** D4
Heber *U.S.A.* 32°44N 115°32W **307** N11
Heber Springs *U.S.A.* 35°30N 92°2W **314** D8
Hebgen L. *U.S.A.* 44°52N 111°20W **308** D8
Hebi *China* 35°57N 114°7E **226** G8
Hebrides *U.K.* 57°30N 7°0W **158** D4
Hebrides, Sea of the *U.K.* 57°5N 7°0W **167** D2
Hebron = Al Khalīl
  West Bank 31°32N 35°6E **251** G6
Hebron *Nfld. & L., Canada* 58°5N 62°30W **295** F19
Hebron *N. Dak., U.S.A.* 46°54N 102°3W **308** B3
Hebron *Nebr., U.S.A.* 40°10N 97°35W **308** E6
Heby *Sweden* 59°56N 16°53E **162** E10
Hecate Str. *Canada* 53°10N 130°30W **296** C2
Heceta I. *U.S.A.* 55°46N 133°40W **296** D2
Hechi *China* 24°40N 108°2E **228** E7
Hechingen *Germany* 48°21N 8°57E **179** G4
Hechuan *China* 30°2N 106°12E **228** B6
Hecla *U.S.A.* 45°53N 98°9W **308** C4
Hecla I. *Canada* 51°10N 96°43W **296** C10
Hedal *Norway* 60°37N 9°41E **162** D3
Heddal *Norway* 59°36N 9°9E **164** D3
Hédé *Ille-et-Vilaine, France* 48°18N 1°49W **172** D5
Hede *Jämtland, Sweden* 42°25N 13°30E **163** E6
Hedemora *Sweden* 60°18N 15°58E **162** D9
Hedenested *Denmark* 55°45N 9°42E **163** J3
Hedensunda *Sweden* 60°24N 17°0E **162** D10
Hedgehope *U.Z.* 46°12S 168°34E **285** G3
Hedmark □ *Norway* 61°17N 11°40E **164** C8
Hedo *Japan* 26°52N 128°16E **288** a
Hedo-misaki *Japan* 26°52N 128°16E **288** a
Hedong *China* 23°5N 112°14E **121** D2
Hedrick *U.S.A.* 41°11N 92°19W **310** D4
He'eia *U.S.A.* 21°25N 157°48W **302** K14
Heel Pt. *Wake I.* 19°18N 166°38E **302** b
Heerde *Neths.* 52°24N 6°2E **170** B6
Heerenveen *Neths.* 52°57N 5°55E **170** B5
Heerhugowaard *Neths.* 52°40N 4°51E **170** B4
Heerlen *Neths.* 50°55N 5°58E **170** D5
Heerwegen = Polkowice
  Poland 51°29N 16°3E **185** G3

Ḥefa *Israel* 32°46N 35°0E **250** C4
Ḥefa □ *Israel* 32°40N 35°0E **250** F6
Hefei *China* 31°52N 117°18E **229** B11
Hefeng *China* 29°55N 109°52E **228** C7
Heflin *U.S.A.* 33°39N 85°35W **316** B4
Hegalig *Sudan* 10°36N 31°54E **257** F3
Hegang *China* 47°20N 130°19E **219** B15
Heggenes *Norway* 61°9N 9°4E **164** C6
Heglig *Sudan* 10°0N 29°24E **257** F2
Hegra *Norway* 63°27N 11°8E **164** A8
Hei Ling Chau *China* 22°15N 114°2E **219** a
Heiban *Sudan* 11°13N 30°31E **257** E3
Heichengzhen *China* 36°24N 106°3E **226** F4
Heidal *Norway* 61°45N 9°19E **164** C6
Heide *Germany* 54°11N 9°9E **178** A5
Heidelberg *Baden-W.,
  Germany* 49°24N 8°42E **179** F4
Heidelberg *Western Cape,
  S. Africa* 34°6S 20°59E **270** D3
Heidelberg Heights
  Australia 37°45S 145°4E **128** A2
Heidelberg West *Australia* 37°43S 145°2E **128** A2
Heidelburg *S. Africa* 26°30S 28°21E **271** C4
Heidenau *Germany* 50°57N 13°40E **178** C8
Heideveld *S. Africa* 33°58S 18°32E **118** A2
Heidmühle *Germany* 48°41N 10°9E **179** G6
Heihe *China* 50°10N 127°30E **219** A14
Heijing *China* 25°22N 101°44E **228** E3
Heijo = P'yŏngyang
  N. Korea 39°0N 125°30E **224** C2
Heilbad Heiligenstadt
  Germany 51°22N 10°8E **178** D6
Heilbron *S. Africa* 27°16S 27°59E **271** C4
Heilbronn *Germany* 49°9N 9°13E **179** F5
Heiligenblut *Austria* 47°2N 12°51E **180** D5
Heiligenhafen *Germany* 54°22N 10°59E **178** A6
Heiligensee *Germany* 52°36N 13°13E **115** A2
Heiligenstadt *Austria* 48°14N 16°21E **142** A2
Heilongjiang □ *China* 48°0N 126°0E **219** B14
Heilprin Land *Greenland* 82°8N 33°0W **154** A7
Heilunkiang = Heilongjiang □
  China 48°0N 126°0E **219** B14
Heim *Norway* 63°26N 9°5E **164** A6
Heimaey *Iceland* 63°26N 20°17W **155** D6
Heimdal *Norway* 63°21N 10°22E **164** A7
Heineken Experience *Amsterdam, Neths.* 52°21N 4°53E **112** c2
Heinersdorf *Germany* 52°34N 13°26E **115** A3
Heinola *Finland* 61°13N 26°2E **188** B4
Heinsberg *Germany* 51°3N 6°5E **178** D2
Heinsun *Burma* 25°52N 95°35E **241** C5
Heinze Chaung *Burma* 14°42N 97°52E **236** E1
Heinze Kyun *Burma* 14°25N 97°45E **236** E1
Heinrkut *Burma* 25°14N 94°44E **241** C5
Heishan *China* 41°40N 122°5E **227** D12
Heishui *Liaoning, China* 42°8N 119°30E **227** C10
Heishui *Sichuan, China* 32°4N 103°2E **228** A4
Hejaz = Ḥijāz *Si. Arabia* 24°0N 40°0E **246** E3
Hejian *China* 38°25N 116°5E **226** E9
Hejiang *China* 28°43N 105°46E **228** C5
Hejin *China* 35°35N 110°42E **226** G6
Hejing *China* 42°18N 86°22E **217** D11
Hekimhan *Turkey* 38°50N 37°55E **212** C7
Hekinan *Japan* 34°52N 137°0E **223** G9
Hekla *Iceland* 63°56N 19°35E **155** D7
Hekou *Gansu, China* 36°10N 103°26E **226** F2
Hekou *Guangdong, China* 23°13N 112°45E **229** F9
Hekou *Yunnan, China* 22°30N 103°59E **228** F4
Hel *Poland* 54°37N 18°47E **184** D5
Helagsfjället *Sweden* 62°54N 12°25E **162** B6
Helan Shan *China* 38°30N 105°55E **226** E3
Heldenplatz *Vienna, Austria* **142** b1
Helen's Pt.
  St. Kitts & Nevis 17°25N 62°51W **322** d
Helechosa de los Montes
  Spain 39°22N 4°53W **195** F6
Helemano *U.S.A.* 21°35N 158°7W **302** J13
Helen Atoll *Palau* 2°40N 132°0E **231** D8
Helena *U.S.A.* 32°5N 82°55W **316** C7
Helena *Mont., U.S.A.* 46°36N 112°2W **304** C7
Helena -West Helena
  U.S.A. 34°32N 90°36W **315** D9
Hélène de Champlain, Parc △
  Canada 45°31N 73°32W **130** A2
Helenelund *Sweden* 59°24N 17°58E **139** A1
Helensburgh *N.S.W.,
  Australia* 34°11S 151°1E **283** C9
Helensburgh *Argyll & Bute,
  U.K.* 56°1N 4°43W **167** E4
Helensville *N.Z.* 36°41S 174°29E **284** B5
Helenvale *Australia* 15°43S 145°14E **280** B4
Helgasjön *Sweden* 56°55N 14°50E **163** H8
Helgeland *Norway* 66°7N 13°29E **160** C15
Helgoland *Germany* 54°10N 7°53E **178** A3
Helheim Gletscher
  Greenland 66°24N 38°12W **154** D7
Heligoland = Helgoland
  Germany 54°10N 7°53E **178** A3
Heligoland B. = Deutsche Bucht
  Germany 54°15N 8°0E **178** A4
Heliopolis = Masr el Gedida
  Egypt 30°5N 31°21E **117** A2
Hell *Norway* 63°26N 10°54E **164** A7
Hell-Bourg *Réunion* 21°3S 55°32E **272** f
Hell Hole Gorge △
  Australia 25°31S 144°12E **280** D3
Hella *Iceland* 63°50N 20°24W **155** D6
Hellas = Greece ■ *Europe* 40°0N 23°0E **204** D5
Helleland *Norway* 58°33N 6°7E **164** F3
Hellendoorn *Germany* 52°23N 13°35E **115** A4
Hellertown *U.S.A.* 40°35N 75°21W **313** F9
Hellerup *Denmark* 55°43N 12°33E **118** A3
Hellesylt *Norway* 62°7N 6°51E **164** B3
Hellevoetsluis *Neths.* 51°50N 4°8E **170** C4
Hellín *Spain* 38°31N 1°40W **197** G3
Helmand □ *Afghan.* 31°20N 64°0E **240** C2
Helmand → *Afghan.* 31°12N 61°34E **240** C1
Helme → *Germany* 51°20N 11°21E **178** D7
Helmeringhausen
  Namibia 25°54S 16°57E **270** C2
Helmond *Neths.* 51°29N 5°41E **170** C5
Helmsdale *U.K.* 58°7N 3°39W **167** C5
Helmsdale → *U.K.* 58°8N 3°43W **167** C5
Helmstedt *Germany* 52°12N 11°0E **178** C7
Helong *China* 42°40N 129°0E **227** C15
Helper *U.S.A.* 39°41N 110°51W **304** G8
Helsingborg *Sweden* 56°3N 12°42E **163** H6
Helsinge *Denmark* 56°2N 12°12E **163** H16
Helsingfors = Helsinki
  Finland 60°10N 24°55E **163** B21
Helsingør *Denmark* 56°2N 12°35E **163** H6
Helsinki *Finland* 60°10N 24°55E **163** B21
Helsinki-Vantaa ✈ (HEL)
  Finland 60°18N 24°58E **163** B21
Helska, Mierzeja *Poland* 54°45N 18°40E **184** D5
Helston *U.K.* 50°6N 5°17W **169** G2

Helvellyn *U.K.* 54°32N 3°1W **168** C4
Helwân *Egypt* 29°50N 31°20E **256** J7
Helwân □ *Egypt* 29°30N 31°30E **251** J2
Hemavati → *India* 12°30N 76°20E **245** H3
Hemel Hempstead *U.K.* 51°44N 0°28W **169** F7
Hemet *U.S.A.* 33°45N 116°58W **307** M10
Hemingford *U.S.A.* 42°19N 103°4W **308** D2
Hemis △ *India* 34°10N 77°15E **242** B7
Hemmingford *Canada* 45°3N 73°35W **313** A11
Hempe
  Dem. Rep. of the Congo 1°54N 22°42E **264** B4
Hempstead *N.Y., U.S.A.* 40°42N 73°37E **313** F11
Hempstead *Tex., U.S.A.* 30°6N 96°5W **314** F6
Hemse *Sweden* 57°15N 18°22E **163** G12
Hemsedal *Norway* 60°53N 8°30E **164** D5
Hemsön *Sweden* 62°42N 18°5E **162** B12
Hen *Norway* 60°13N 10°14E **164** D7
Hen and Chicken B.
  Australia 33°50S 151°7E **139** B1
Hen and Chickens Is.
  N.Z. 35°58S 174°45E **284** B3
Henán *Sweden* 58°6N 11°40E **163** F5
Henan □ *China* 34°0N 114°0E **226** H8
Henares → *Spain* 40°24N 3°30W **194** E7
Henashi-Misaki *Japan* 40°37N 139°51E **220** D9
Hendaye *France* 43°23N 1°47W **174** E2
Hendek *Turkey* 40°48N 30°44E **212** B4
Henderson *Argentina* 36°18S 61°43W **334** D3
Henderson *Ga., U.S.A.* 32°21N 83°47W **316** C6
Henderson *Ky., U.S.A.* 37°50N 87°35W **311** G9
Henderson *N.C., U.S.A.* 36°20N 78°25W **315** C15
Henderson *N.Y., U.S.A.* 43°50N 76°10W **313** C8
Henderson *Nev., U.S.A.* 36°2N 114°58W **304** J12
Henderson *Tenn., U.S.A.* 35°26N 88°38W **315** D10
Henderson I. *Pac. Oc.* 24°22S 128°19W **289** K15
Hendersonville *N.C.,
  U.S.A.* 35°19N 82°28W **315** C13
Hendersonville *Tenn.,
  U.S.A.* 36°18N 86°37W **315** C11
Hendijān *Iran* 30°14N 49°43E **247** D6
Hendon *U.K.* 51°35N 0°14W **125** A2
Hendorābī *Iran* 26°40N 53°37E **247** E7
Heng Jiang → *China* 22°40N 109°17E **228** F7
Heng Xian *China* 22°40N 109°17E **228** F7
Hengām *Iran* 26°38S 55°53E **247** D8
Henganofi *Papua N. G.* 6°15S 145°38E **286** B3
Hengcheng *China* 38°18N 106°28E **226** E4
Hengchun *Taiwan* 22°0N 120°44E **225** D2
Hengdaohezi *China* 44°52N 129°0E **227** B15
Hengelo *Neths.* 52°16N 6°48E **170** B6
Henggang *China* 22°39N 114°12E **219** a
Hengshan *Hunan, China* 27°16N 112°45E **229** D9
Hengshan *Shaanxi, China* 37°58N 109°5E **226** F5
Hengshui *China* 37°41N 115°40E **226** F8
Hengyang *China* 26°59N 112°22E **229** D9
Henichesk *Ukraine* 46°12N 34°50E **189** C8
Henima *India* 25°22N 93°36E **241** C4
Hénin-Beaumont *France* 50°25N 2°58E **173** B9
Hénin-Liétard = Hénin-Beaumont
  France 50°25N 2°58E **173** B9
Henley-on-Thames *U.K.* 51°32N 0°54W **169** F7
Henlopen, C. *U.S.A.* 38°48N 75°6W **309** F16
Henna *Japan* 26°19N 127°53E **288** a
Hennan *Sweden* 62°2N 15°54E **162** C9
Hennebont *France* 47°49N 3°19W **172** E3
Hennenman *S. Africa* 27°59S 27°1E **270** C4
Hennepin *U.S.A.* 41°15N 89°21W **310** C7
Hennessey *U.S.A.* 36°6N 97°54W **314** C6
Hennigsdorf *Germany* 52°38N 13°12E **115** A2
Henrietta *N.Y., U.S.A.* 43°4N 77°37W **312** C7
Henrietta *Tex., U.S.A.* 33°49N 98°12W **314** E5
Henrietta, Ostrov = Genriyetty,
  Ostrov *Russia* 77°6N 156°30E **215** B16
Henrietta Maria, C.
  Canada 55°9N 82°20W **298** A3
Henry *U.S.A.* 41°7N 89°22W **310** C7
Henry Ice Rise *Antarctica* 80°35S 62°0W **151** E17
Henry Lawrence I. *India* 12°9N 93°5E **245** H11
Henryetta *U.S.A.* 35°27N 95°59W **314** D7
Henryków *Poland* 52°19N 20°58E **143** B1
Henryville *Canada* 45°8N 73°11W **313** A11
Hensall *Canada* 43°26N 81°30W **312** C3
Henson Cr. → *U.S.A.* 38°47N 76°58W **143** C3
Henstedt-Ulzburg *Germany* 53°47N 10°0E **178** B6
Hentiesbaai *Namibia* 22°8S 14°18E **270** B1
Hentiyn Nuruu
  Mongolia 48°30N 108°30E **219** B10
Henttaa *Finland* 60°11N 24°45E **121** B1
Henty *Australia* 35°30S 147°3E **283** C7
Henzada *Burma* 17°38N 95°26E **241** G5
Hephaestia *Greece* 39°55N 25°14E **205** D7
Hephzibah *U.S.A.* 33°19N 82°6W **316** C7
Heping *China* 24°29N 115°0E **229** E10
Heping Park *China* 31°16N 121°30E **138** B2
Hepingli *China* 39°57N 116°23E **114** B2
Heppner *U.S.A.* 45°21N 119°33W **304** D4
Hepu *China* 21°40N 109°12E **228** G7
Hepworth *Canada* 44°37N 81°9W **312** B3
Heqing *China* 26°37N 100°11E **228** D3
Hequ *China* 39°20N 111°15E **226** E6
Hérádsflói *Iceland* 65°42N 14°12W **155** B12
Hérádsvötn → *Iceland* 65°45N 19°25W **155** B7
Heradsbygd *Norway* 60°49N 11°39E **164** C8
Heraklion = Iraklio
  Greece 35°20N 25°12E **207** E6
Herald Cays *Australia* 16°58S 149°9E **280** B4
Herand *Norway* 60°20N 6°22E **164** D3
Herangi R.z. *N.Z.* 38°33S 174°48E **284** C5
Herāt *Afghan.* 34°20N 62°7E **240** B1
Herāt □ *Afghan.* 35°0N 62°0E **240** B1
Hérault □ *France* 43°34N 3°15E **174** E7
Hérault → *France* 43°17N 3°26E **174** E7
Herault *France* 47°36N 1°8E **172** E8
Herbert → *Australia* 18°31S 146°17E **280** B4
Herbert Hoover Nat. Historic Site △
  U.S.A. 41°40N 91°21W **310** E9
Herbert I. *U.S.A.* 52°45N 170°7W **303** D2
Herbertabad *India* 11°43N 92°37E **245** J11
Herberton *Australia* 17°20S 145°25E **280** B4
Herbertsdale *S. Africa* 34°1S 21°46E **270** D3
Herbertville *N.Z.* 40°30S 176°33E **284** D5
Herbignac *France* 47°27N 2°18W **172** E4
Herborn *Germany* 50°40N 8°19E **178** E4
Herby *Poland* 50°45N 18°50E **185** H5
Herceg-Novi *Montenegro* 42°30N 18°33E **202** D2
Hercegfalva = Mezőfalva
  Hungary 46°55N 18°49E **182** D3
Herchmer *Canada* 57°22N 94°10W **297** B10
Herculana = Coxim
  Brazil 18°30S 54°55W **331** D7
Herðubreið *Iceland* 65°11N 16°21W **155** B10
Hereford *Hereford, U.K.* 52°4N 2°43W **169** E5
Hereford *Tex., U.S.A.* 34°49N 102°24W **314** D3
Herefordshire □ *U.K.* 52°8N 2°40W **169** E5
Hereñss *Norway* 58°32N 8°23E **164** F5
Hérehérétué
  French Polynesia 19°54S 144°58W **289** f
Hereroa *Sweden* 61°44N 12°28E **162** D6
Herekino *N.Z.* 35°18S 173°11E **284** B3
Herencia *Spain* 39°21N 3°21W **195** F7
Herentals *Belgium* 51°12N 4°51E **170** C4
Herford *Germany* 52°7N 8°39E **178** C4

Héricourt *France* 47°32N 6°45E **173** E13
Herington *U.S.A.* 38°40N 96°57W **308** F5
Heris *Iran* 38°14N 47°6E **213** C12
Herisau *Switz.* 47°22N 9°17E **179** H5
Hérisson *France* 46°32N 2°42E **173** C10
Herkimer *U.S.A.* 43°2N 74°59W **313** D10
Herlen → *Asia* 48°48N 117°0E **219** B12
Herlev *Denmark* 55°43N 12°27E **118** A2
Herlong *U.S.A.* 40°8N 120°8W **306** E6
Herm *U.K.* 49°30N 2°28W **169** H5
Hermakivka *Ukraine* 48°42N 26°11E **183** H11
Herman Eckstein Park
  S. Africa 26°9S 28°1E **123** A2
Hermana Mayor I. *Phil.* 15°47N 119°47E **232** D2
Hermannsburg *N. Terr.,
  Australia* 23°57S 132°45E **278** D5
Hermannsburg *Niedersachsen,
  Germany* 52°50N 10°5E **178** C6
Hermannskogel *Austria* 48°16N 16°18E **142** A1
Hermanník = Sibiu
  Romania 45°45N 24°9E **183** E9
Hermansverk *Norway* 61°11N 6°52E **164** C3
Hermanus *S. Africa* 34°27S 19°12E **270** D2
Herment *France* 45°45N 2°24E **174** C6
Hermidale *Australia* 31°30S 146°42E **283** E7
Hermiston *Edinburgh, U.K.* 55°55N 3°19W **121** B2
Hermiston *Oreg., U.S.A.* 45°51N 119°17W **304** D4
Hermitage *Grenada* 12°27N 61°28E **323** q
Hermitage *Mo., U.S.A.* 37°56N 93°19W **310** G8
Hermitage and Winter Palace
  Russia 59°56N 30°19E **137** B2
Hermon *N.Y., U.S.A.* 44°28N 75°14W **313** B9
Hermon, Mt. = Shaykh, J. ash
  Lebanon 33°25N 35°50E **250** E6
Hermosillo *Mexico* 29°10N 111°0W **318** B2
Hermosdorf *Germany* 52°37N 13°18E **115** A2
Hernád → *Hungary* 47°56N 21°8E **182** C6
Hernals *Austria* 48°13N 16°0E **142** A2
Hernandarias *Paraguay* 25°20S 54°40W **335** B5
Hernandez *U.S.A.* 36°24N 120°46W **306** J6
Hernando *Argentina* 32°28S 63°40W **334** C3
Hernando *Fla., U.S.A.* 28°54N 82°23W **317** G7
Hernando *Miss., U.S.A.* 34°50N 90°0W **315** D10
Herndon *U.S.A.* 40°43N 76°51W **312** F8
Herne *Germany* 51°32N 7°14E **178** D3
Herne Bay *U.K.* 51°21N 1°8E **169** F9
Herne Hill *U.K.* 51°27N 0°6W **125** B3
Herning *Denmark* 56°8N 8°58E **163** H2
Herod *U.S.A.* 31°42N 84°26W **316** D5
Héroes de Churubusco
  Mexico 19°21N 99°6W **128** B2
Heroica Caborca = Caborca
  Mexico 30°37N 112°6W **318** A2
Heroica Nogales = Nogales
  Mexico 31°19N 110°56W **318** A2
Heron Bay *Canada* 48°40N 86°25W **298** C2
Heron B. *Australia* 23°27S 151°55E **280** C5
Herons, Î. aux *Canada* 45°25N 73°34W **130** B2
Herradura, Pta. de la
  Canary Is. 28°26N 14°8W **153** e2
Herre *Norway* 59°6N 9°34E **164** E6
Herreid *U.S.A.* 45°50N 100°4W **308** C3
Herrenberg *Germany* 48°36N 8°52E **179** G4
Herrera *Spain* 37°26N 4°55W **195** H6
Herrera de Alcántara
  Spain 39°39N 7°25W **195** F3
Herrera de Pisuerga *Spain* 42°35N 4°20W **194** C6
Herrera del Duque *Spain* 39°10N 5°3W **195** F5
Herrestad *Sweden* 58°21N 11°50E **163** F5
Herrin *U.S.A.* 37°48N 89°2W **312** G7
Herriot *Canada* 56°22N 101°16W **297** B8
Herrljunga *Sweden* 58°5N 13°1E **163** F7
Hersbruck *Germany* 49°30N 11°26E **179** F7
Herschel I. *Canada* 69°35N 139°5W **150** C1
Herso = Cherso *Greece* 41°5N 22°47E **202** E6
Herstal *Belgium* 50°40N 5°38E **170** D5
Herstedoster *Denmark* 55°40N 12°22E **118** A2
Hertford *U.K.* 51°48N 0°4W **169** F7
Hertford *U.S.A.* 36°13N 76°28W **315** C16
Hertfordshire □ *U.K.* 51°51N 0°5W **169** F7
's-Hertogenbosch *Neths.* 51°42N 5°17E **170** C5
Hertsa *Ukraine* 48°9N 26°15E **183** H11
Hertsoniemi *Finland* 60°12N 25°2E **121** B3
Hertzogville *S. Africa* 28°9S 25°30E **270** C4
Hervás *Spain* 40°16N 5°52W **194** E5
Hervey B. *Australia* 25°0S 152°52E **280** C5
Herzberg *Brandenburg,
  Germany* 51°41N 13°14E **178** D9
Herzberg *Niedersachsen,
  Germany* 51°38N 10°20E **178** D6
Herzliyya *Israel* 32°10N 34°50E **251** C3
Herzogenburg *Austria* 48°17N 15°41E **180** C8
Heshrock L. *Canada* 50°50N 100°30W **297** B8
Heshan *Guangdong, China* 22°34N 113°4E **229** F9
Heshan *Guangxi Zhuangzu,
  China* 23°50N 108°53E **228** F7
Heshui *China* 35°48N 108°0E **226** G5
Heshun *China* 37°22N 113°32E **226** F7
Heskestad *Norway* 58°28N 6°22E **164** F3
Hesperia *U.S.A.* 34°25N 117°18W **307** L9
Hesperus Mt. *U.S.A.* 37°27N 108°7W **307** H9
Hesse = Hessen □ *Germany* 50°30N 9°0E **178** E4
Hessen □ *Germany* 50°30N 9°0E **178** E4
Hessenreuther und Manteler
  Wald △ *Germany* 49°45N 12°1E **179** F8
Hesso *Australia* 32°8S 137°27E **282** B2
Hestøyri *Iceland* 66°20N 22°53W **155** A4
Heston *U.K.* 51°28N 0°22W **125** B1
Hestra *Sweden* 57°33N 13°35E **163** G7
Hetauda *Nepal* 27°25N 85°2E **243** F11
Hetch Hetchy Aqueduct
  U.S.A. 37°29N 122°19W **306** H5
Hettinger *U.S.A.* 46°0N 102°42W **308** B2
Hettstedt *Germany* 51°39N 11°31E **178** D7
Heugueng → *S. Korea* 35°4N 126°34E **227** G14
Heukuro → *S. Korea* 34°37N 75°25W **313** B9
Heunghae *S. Korea* 36°12N 129°21E **224** D4
Heuvango → *S. Korea* 44°37N 75°25W **313** B9
Hevelândia *Brazil* 5°12S 61°50W **329** E5
Heves □ *Hungary* 47°50N 20°0E **182** C5
Hewitt *U.S.A.* 31°28N 97°12W **314** F6
Hexham *U.K.* 54°58N 2°4W **168** C5
Hexi *Yunnan, China* 24°10N 102°38E **228** E4
Hexigten Qi *China* 43°18N 117°30E **227** C9
Hextable *U.K.* 51°24N 0°10E **125** B5
Heydarābād *Iran* 30°33N 55°38E **247** D7
Heydebreck = Kędzierzyn-Koźle
  Poland 50°20N 18°12E **185** H5
Heyfield *Australia* 37°59S 146°47E **283** D7
Heysham *U.K.* 54°3N 2°53W **168** C5
Heyuan *China* 23°50N 114°42E **229** F10
Heywood *Australia* 38°8S 141°37E **282** D4
Heywood *U.K.* 53°36N 2°13W **168** D5
Heyworth *U.S.A.* 40°19N 88°59W **310** D8

Hillsboro *Ill., U.S.A.* 39°9N 89°29W **310** E7
Hillsboro *Kans., U.S.A.* 38°21N 97°12W **308** F5
Hillsboro *N. Dak., U.S.A.* 38°14N 90°34W **310** F6
Hillsboro *Ohio, U.S.A.* 39°12N 83°37W **311** E13
Hillsboro *Oreg., U.S.A.* 45°31N 122°59W **306** E3
Hillsboro *Tex., U.S.A.* 32°1N 97°8W **314** E6
Hillsboro Canal *U.S.A.* 26°30N 80°15W **317** J9
Hillsborough *Grenada* 12°28N 61°28W **323** q
Hillsborough *U.S.A.* 43°7N 71°54W **313** C12
Hillsborough Channel
  Australia 20°56S 149°15E **280** b
Hillsborough Dam
  Trin. & Tob. 11°13N 60°40W **323** J16
Hillsdale *U.S.A.* 26°41N 80°40W **317** J9
Hillsdale *Mich., U.S.A.* 41°56N 84°38W **311** C12
Hillsdale *N.Y., U.S.A.* 42°11N 73°32W **313** D11
Hillsport *Canada* 49°8S 85°34W **298** C2
Hillston *Australia* 33°30S 145°31E **283** B6
Hilltonia *U.S.A.* 32°53N 81°40W **316** C8
Hillwood *U.S.A.* 38°52N 77°9W **143** E7
Hilmiya *Egypt* 30°6N 31°19E **117** A2
Hilo ✈ (ITO) *U.S.A.* 19°43N 155°2W **302** D6
Hilo *U.S.A.* 19°43N 155°5W **302** D6
Hilongos *Phil.* 10°22N 124°44E **233** F5
Hilton *U.S.A.* 43°17N 77°48W **312** C7
Hilton Head Island
  U.S.A. 32°13N 80°45W **316** C9
Hilvan *Turkey* 37°34N 38°58E **213** D8
Hilversum *Neths.* 52°14N 5°10E **170** B5
Himachal Pradesh □ *India* 31°30N 77°0E **242** D7
Himalaya *Asia* 29°0N 84°0E **243** F11
Himamaylan *Phil.* 10°6N 122°52E **233** F4
Himarë *Albania* 40°8N 19°43E **202** F3
Himatnagar *India* 23°37N 72°57E **242** H5
Himchari △ *Bangla.* 21°28N 92°5E **241** E4
Hime-Jima *Japan* 33°43N 131°40E **222** D3
Himeji *Japan* 34°50N 134°40E **222** G6
Himi *Japan* 36°50N 136°55E **223** A8
Himmerland *Denmark* 56°45N 9°30E **163** H3
Hims *Syria* 34°40N 36°45E **250** A6
Hims □ *Syria* 34°30N 37°0E **250** D8
Hin Keng *China* 22°22N 114°10E **122** A2
Hin Khom, Laem *Thailand* 9°25N 99°56E **237** b
Hinatuan *Phil.* 8°22N 126°20E **233** G6
Hinatuan Passage *Phil.* 9°45S 125°47E **233** G5
Hinche *Haiti* 19°9N 72°1W **321** C5
Hinchinbrook I. *Australia* 18°20S 146°15E **280** B4
Hinchinbrook Island △
  Australia 18°14S 146°9E **280** B4
Hinckley *Leics., U.K.* 52°33N 1°22W **169** E6
Hinckley *Minn., U.S.A.* 46°1N 92°56W **308** B7
Hindaun *India* 26°44N 77°5E **242** F7
Hindenburg = Zabrze
  Poland 50°18N 18°50E **185** H5
Hindmarsh, L. *Australia* 36°5S 141°55E **282** C4
Hindol *India* 20°40N 85°10E **244** D7
Hinds *N.Z.* 43°59S 171°36E **285** D6
Hindsholm *Denmark* 55°30N 10°40E **163** H4
Hindu Bagh *Pakistan* 30°56N 67°50E **242** D2
Hindu Kush *Asia* 36°0N 71°0E **240** B3
Hindupur *India* 13°49N 77°32E **245** H3
Hines Creek *Canada* 56°20N 118°40W **296** B5
Hinesville *U.S.A.* 31°51N 81°36W **316** D8
Hinganghat *India* 20°30N 78°52E **244** D4
Hingham *U.S.A.* 48°33N 110°25W **304** B8
Hinghwa = Xinghua
  China 32°58N 119°48E **227** H10
Hingir *India* 21°57N 83°41E **243** J10
Hingoli *India* 19°41N 77°15E **244** E3
Hinganara *Phil.* 10°16N 122°50E **233** F4
Hinis *Turkey* 39°22N 41°44E **213** C9
Hinna = Imi *Ethiopia* 6°28N 42°10E **257** F5
Hinna *Nigeria* 10°25N 11°35E **263** C7
Hinnerup *Denmark* 56°16N 10°4E **163** H4
Hinnøya *Norway* 68°35S 15°50E **160** B9
Hino *Japan* 35°0N 136°15E **223** G8
Hinoba-an *Phil.* 9°35N 122°28E **233** G4
Hinojosa del Duque *Spain* 38°30N 5°9W **195** G5
Hinokage *Japan* 32°39N 131°14E **222** D3
Hinsdale *U.S.A.* 41°33N 87°28W **119** C2
Hinterrhein → *Switz.* 46°40N 9°25E **179** J5
Hinthada = Henzada
  Burma 17°38N 95°26E **241** G5
Hinton *Canada* 53°26N 117°34W **296** C5
Hinton *Okla., U.S.A.* 35°29N 98°21W **314** D5
Hinton *W. Va., U.S.A.* 37°40N 80°54W **309** G14
Hinubuan = Antipolo
  Phil. 14°35N 121°10E **232** D3
Hinunangan *Phil.* 10°25N 125°12E **233** F5
Hinzir Burnu *Turkey* 36°5N 35°53E **250** B6
Hios *Greece* 38°27N 26°9E **205** C8
Hirado *Japan* 33°22N 129°33E **222** D1
Hirado-Shima *Japan* 33°20N 129°26E **222** D1
Hirakata *Japan* 34°48N 135°40E **223** G7
Hirakud Dam *India* 21°32N 83°45E **244** D6
Hiran → *India* 23°6N 79°21E **243** H8
Hirapur *India* 24°22N 79°13E **243** G8
Hirara = Miyakojima
  Japan 24°48N 125°17E **221** M2
Hirata *Japan* 35°24N 132°49E **222** B4
Hiratsuka *Japan* 35°19N 139°21E **223** H9
Hirekerur *India* 14°28N 75°23E **245** G2
Hirfanlı Barajı *Turkey* 39°33N 33°31E **212** C5
Hirhafok *Algeria* 23°49N 5°45E **261** D6
Hiromi = Kihoku *Japan* 33°13N 132°36E **222** D2
Hiroo *Japan* 42°17N 143°19E **220** C11
Hirosaki *Japan* 40°34N 140°28E **220** D10
Hiroshima *Japan* 34°24N 132°30E **222** C3
Hiroshima □ *Japan* 34°50N 133°0E **222** G5
Hiroshima-Wan *Japan* 34°5N 132°5E **222** G5
Hirota *Japan* 34°45N 135°20E **133** A1
Hirschberg = Jelenia Góra
  Poland 50°50N 15°45E **185** H2
Hirschstetten *Austria* 48°13N 16°28E **142** A2
Hirson *France* 49°55N 4°4E **173** C11
Hirtshals *Denmark* 57°36N 9°57E **163** G3
Hisai *Japan* 34°40N 136°28E **223** G8
Hisar *India* 29°12N 75°45E **242** E6
Hisaria *Bulgaria* 42°30N 24°44E **203** D8

Hisb, Sha'ib → = Ḩasb, W. →
  Iraq 31°45N 44°17E **246** D5
Ḩismá *Si. Arabia* 28°30N 36°0E **251** K7
Ḩişn al 'Abr *Yemen* 16°9N 47°14E **248** C4
Hispaniola *W. Indies* 19°0N 71°0W **321** C5
Hit *Iraq* 33°38N 42°49E **246** C4
Hita *Japan* 33°20N 130°58E **222** D2
Hitachi *Japan* 36°36N 140°39E **223** E10
Hitachi-Ōta *Japan* 36°30N 140°30E **223** E10
Hitan, W. el *Egypt* 29°20N 30°10E **256** J7
Hitchin *U.K.* 51°58N 0°16W **169** F7
Hithadhoo *Maldives* 0°36S 73°5E **272** d
Hither Green *U.K.* 51°26N 0°0 **125** B3
Hitra *Norway* 63°30N 8°45E **164** A5
Hitoyoshi *Japan* 32°13N 130°45E **222** D2
Hitzacker *Germany* 53°9N 11°2E **178** B7
Hiu *Vanuatu* 13°10S 166°35E **287** C4
Hiva Oa *French Polynesia* 9°45S 139°0W **289** f
Hixon *Canada* 53°25N 122°35W **296** C4
Hiyoshi, N. → *Israel* 30°25N 35°10E **251** H6
Hizan *West Bank* 31°50N 35°16E **123** B2
Hjalmar L. *Canada* 61°33N 109°25W **297** A7

Hjälmaren *Sweden* 59°18N 15°40E **162** E9
Hjältevad *Sweden* 57°33N 15°20E **163** G9
Hjalteyri *Iceland* 65°55N 18°18W **155** B8
Hjartdal *Norway* 59°37N 8°41E **164** E5
Hjelmelandsvågen *Norway* 59°14N 6°10E **164** E3
Hjelset *Norway* 62°48N 7°30E **164** B4
Hjerkinn *Norway* 62°13N 9°33E **164** B6
Hjo *Sweden* 58°22N 14°17E **163** F8
Hjørsey *Iceland* 64°32N 22°21W **155** C4
Hjort Trench *S. Ocean* 58°0S 157°30E **151** B10
Hjortekær *Denmark* 55°47N 12°32E **118** A3
Hjortespring *Denmark* 55°44N 12°25E **118** A2
Hjortkvarn *Sweden* 58°54N 15°26E **163** F9
Hjukse *Norway* 59°31N 9°19E **164** E6
Hkakabo Razi *Burma* 28°25N 97°23E **228** C1
Hkakabo Razi △ *Burma* 28°0N 97°55E **241** A6
Hkamti *Burma* 26°0N 95°39E **241** C5
Hko-lam *Burma* 21°9N 98°5E **241** E7
Hko-ut *Burma* 20°58N 98°2E **241** E7
Hkyenhpa *Burma* 27°43N 97°22E **241** B6
Hlaingbwe *Burma* 17°8N 97°50E **241** G6
Hlinsko *Czech Rep.* 49°45N 15°54E **180** B8
Hlobane *S. Africa* 27°42S 31°0E **271** C5
Hlohovec *Slovak Rep.* 48°26N 17°49E **181** C10
Hlubočepy *Czech Rep.* 50°2N 14°23E **135** B2
Hlučín *Czech Rep.* 49°54N 18°11E **181** B11
Hluhluwe *S. Africa* 28°1S 32°15E **271** C5
Hluhluwe ≃ *S. Africa* 22°10S 32°5E **271** B5
Hlukhiv *Ukraine* 51°40N 33°58E **189** E5
Hlwaze *Burma* 18°54N 96°37E **241** F6
Hlyboka *Ukraine* 48°5N 25°56E **183** D10
Hlybokaye *Belarus* 55°10N 27°45E **188** E4
Hnappadalssýsla *Iceland* 64°50N 22°30W **155** D3
Hnífsdalur *Iceland* 66°7N 23°8W **155** A3
Hnúšťa *Slovak Rep.* 48°35N 19°58E **181** C12
Ho *Ghana* 6°37N 0°27E **263** D5
Ho Chi Minh City = Thanh Pho Ho
   Chi Minh *Vietnam* 10°58N 106°40E **237** G6
Ho Chung *China* 22°21N 114°14E **122** A2
Ho Hoa Binh *Vietnam* 20°50N 105°0E **228** G5
Ho Thac Ba *Vietnam* 21°42N 105°1E **236** A5
Ho Thuong *Vietnam* 19°32N 105°48E **236** C5
Hoa Binh *Vietnam* 20°50N 105°20E **228** G5
Hoa Hiep *Vietnam* 11°34N 105°51E **237** G5
Hoai Nhon *Vietnam* 14°28N 109°1E **236** E7
Hoang Lien ≃ *Vietnam* 21°30N 105°32E **236** B5
Hoang Lien Son *Vietnam* 22°0N 104°0E **228** F4
Hoanib ≃ *Namibia* 19°27S 12°46E **270** A2
Hoare B. *Canada* 65°17N 62°30W **295** D19
Hoarusib ≃ *Namibia* 19°3S 12°36E **270** A2
Hobart *Tas., Australia* 42°50S 147°21E **281** G4
Hobart *Ind., U.S.A.* 41°32N 87°15W **311** C9
Hobart *Okla., U.S.A.* 35°1N 99°6W **314** D5
Hobbs *U.S.A.* 32°42N 103°8W **305** K12
Hobbs Coast *Antarctica* 74°50S 131°0W **151** D14
Hobe Sound *U.S.A.* 27°4N 80°8W **317** H19
Hobo *Colombia* 2°35N 75°30W **328** C2
Hoboken *Ga., U.S.A.* 31°11N 82°8W **316** D7
Hoboken *New York, U.S.A.* **132** d1
Hobro *Denmark* 56°39N 9°46E **163** H3
Hobsons B. *Australia* 37°51S 144°55E **128** B1
Hoburgen *Sweden* 56°55N 18°7E **163** H12
Hobyo *Somalia* 5°25N 48°30E **267** G6
Hocalar *Turkey* 38°36N 30°0E **205** C11
Hochbrück *Germany* 48°14N 11°37E **131** A2
Hochelaga *Canada* 45°32N 73°33W **130** A2
Hochfeld *Namibia* 21°28S 17°58E **270** B2
Hochharz △ *Germany* 51°48N 10°38E **178** C6
Hochschwab *Austria* 47°35N 15°0E **180** D8
Höchstadt *Germany* 49°42N 10°47E **179** F6
Hochtaunus △ *Germany* 50°20N 8°30E **179** E4
Hoch'uan = Hechuan
   China 30°2N 106°12E **228** B6
Hochwan = Hechuan
   China 30°2N 106°12E **228** B6
Hockenheim *Germany* 49°19N 8°32E **179** F4
Hockley = Levelland
   U.S.A. 33°35N 102°23W **314** E3
Hodaka-Dake *Japan* 36°17N 137°39E **223** A9
Hodeida = Al Ḩudaydah
   Yemen 14°50N 43°0E **248** D3
Hodgeville *Canada* 50°7N 106°58W **297** C7
Hodgson *Canada* 51°13N 97°36W **297** C9
Hodh El Gharbi □
   Mauritania 16°30N 10°0W **262** B3
Hódmezővásárhely
   Hungary 46°28N 20°22E **182** D5
Hodna, Chott el *Algeria* 35°26N 4°43E **261** A6
Hodna, Monts du *Algeria* 35°52N 4°42E **261** A6
Hodonín *Czech Rep.* 48°50N 17°10E **181** C10
Hædic, Î. de *France* 47°20N 2°53W **172** E4
Hoegi *S. Korea* 37°35N 127°3E **142** D2
Hoeilaart *Belgium* 50°46N 4°28E **116** B2
Hoek van Holland *Neths.* 52°0N 4°7E **170** C4
Hoengseong *S. Korea* 37°29N 127°59E **224** D3
Hoeryong *N. Korea* 42°30N 129°45E **224** A4
Hoeyang *N. Korea* 38°43N 127°36E **224** D3
Hof *Bayern, Germany* 50°19N 11°55E **179** E7
Hof *Austurland Iceland* 65°33N 15°0W **155** B11
Hof *Austurland Iceland* 64°33N 14°40W **155** C12
Hof *Vestfold, Norway* 59°32N 10°5E **164** E7
Hofburg *Vienna, Austria* **142** b1
Hofei = Hefei *China* 31°52N 117°18E **229** D11
Hoffell *Iceland* 64°23N 15°20W **155** C11
Hoffman I. *U.S.A.* 40°34N 74°3W **132** C1
Hofgarten *Munich, Germany* **131** a3
Hofgeismar *Germany* 51°29N 9°23E **178** D5
Hofheim *Germany* 50°5N 8°26E **179** E4
Hofmeyr *S. Africa* 31°39S 25°50E **270** D4
Höfn *Iceland* 64°15N 15°13W **155** C11
Hofors *Sweden* 60°31N 16°15E **162** D10
Hofsjökull *Iceland* 64°49N 18°48W **155** C8
Hofsós *Iceland* 65°53N 19°26W **155** B7
Höfu *Japan* 34°3N 131°34E **222** C2
Hog Harbour *Vanuatu* 15°8S 167°6E **287** E5
Hog I. = Paradise I.
   Bahamas 25°6N 77°19W **153** b
Hog I. *Grenada* 12°0N 61°44E **323** j
Hog Pt. *Antigua & B.* 17°41N 61°47W **322** c
Hogan Group *Australia* 39°13S 147°1E **281** F4
Höganäs *Sweden* 56°12N 12°33E **163** H6
Hogansville *U.S.A.* 33°10N 84°55W **316** B5
Hogarth, Mt. *Australia* 21°48S 136°58E **280** C2
Hoge Kempen △ *Belgium* 51°6N 5°35E **170** C5
Hoge Veluwe △ *Neths.* 52°5N 5°46E **170** B5
Hogenakai Falls *India* 12°6N 77°50E **245** H3
Hoggar = Ahaggar *Algeria* 23°0N 6°30E **261** D6
Högsäter *Sweden* 58°38N 12°5E **163** F6
Högsby *Sweden* 57°10N 16°1E **163** G10
Högsjö *Sweden* 59°4N 15°44E **162** E9
Hogsty Reef *Bahamas* 21°41N 73°48W **325** B5
Hoh ≃ *U.S.A.* 47°45N 124°29W **306** C2
Hoh Xil Shan *China* 36°30N 89°0E **218** D6
Hohd ech Chargui □
   Mauritania 19°20N 7°15W **262** B2
Hohe Acht *Germany* 50°22N 7°0E **179** E3
Hohe Tauern *Austria* 47°11N 12°40E **180** D6
Hohe Tauern △ *Austria* 47°5N 12°0E **180** D5
Hohenau *Austria* 48°36N 16°55E **181** C10
Hohenbrunn *Germany* 48°2N 11°43E **131** B3
Hohenems *Austria* 47°22N 9°42E **180** D2
Hohenloher Ebene
   Germany 49°14N 9°36E **179** F5

Hohenmauth = Vysoké Mýto
   Czech Rep. 49°58N 16°10E **181** B9
Hohensalza = Inowrocław
   Poland 52°50N 18°12E **185** F5
Hohensalzburg = Lunino
   Russia 53°3N 45°18E **190** D7
Hohenschönhausen
   Germany 52°33N 13°30E **115** A4
Hohenstadt = Zábřeh
   Czech Rep. 49°53N 16°52E **181** B9
Hohenstein = Olsztynek
   Poland 53°34N 20°19E **184** E7
Hohenwald *U.S.A.* 35°33N 87°33W **315** D11
Hohenwestedt *Germany* 54°5N 9°40E **178** A5
Hoher Rhön = Rhön
   Germany 50°24N 9°58E **178** E5
Hoher Vogelsberg
   Germany 51°45N 9°35E **178** D5
Hohes Venn *Belgium* 50°30N 6°5E **170** D6
Hohes Venn-Eifel △ *Europe* 50°30N 6°10E **178** E2
Hohhot *China* 40°52N 111°40E **226** D6
Hohoe *Ghana* 7°8N 0°32E **263** D5
Hoi An *Vietnam* 15°53N 108°19E **236** E7
Hoi Xuan *Vietnam* 20°25N 105°9E **228** G5
Hoihow = Haikou *China* 20°1N 110°16E **236** B8
Hoisington *U.S.A.* 38°31N 98°47W **308** F4
Hojai *India* 26°2N 92°54E **241** B4
Hojambaz *Turkmenistan* 38°7N 65°0E **216** E6
Højer *Denmark* 54°58N 8°42E **163** K2
Hōjō *Japan* 33°58N 132°46E **222** D4
Hok *Sweden* 57°31N 14°16E **163** G8
Hokang = Hegang
   China 47°20N 130°19E **219** B15
Hökensås *Sweden* 58°0N 14°5E **163** G8
Hökerum *Sweden* 57°51N 13°16E **163** G7
Hokianga Harbour *N.Z.* 35°31S 173°22E **284** B2
Hokitika *N.Z.* 42°42S 171°0E **285** C6
Hokkaidō □ *Japan* 43°30N 143°0E **220** C11
Hoksund *Norway* 59°48N 9°54E **164** E6
Hokuto *Japan* 41°49N 140°39E **220** D10
Hol-Hol *Djibouti* 11°22N 42°50E **257** E5
Hola *Kenya* 1°29S 40°2E **268** B4
Hola Prystan *Ukraine* 46°29N 32°32E **189** J7
Holakas *Greece* 35°57N 27°53E **206** F11
Holalkere *India* 14°2N 76°11E **245** G3
Hólar *Iceland* 65°44N 19°8W **155** B7
Holargos = Cholargos
   Greece 37°59N 23°48E **112** B2
Holašovice *Czech Rep.* 48°57N 14°15E **180** C7
Holbæk *Denmark* 55°43N 11°43E **163** J5
Holborn *London, U.K.* **125** a4
Holbrook *N.S.W.,
   Australia* 35°42S 147°18E **283** C7
Holbrook *Ariz., U.S.A.* 34°54N 110°10W **305** J8
Holcomb *U.S.A.* 42°54N 77°25W **312** D7
Holden *Mo., U.S.A.* 38°43N 94°0W **310** F3
Holden *Utah, U.S.A.* 39°6N 112°16W **304** G7
Holden, L. *U.S.A.* 28°30N 81°23W **133** B2
Holdenville *U.S.A.* 35°5N 96°24W **314** D6
Holdrege *U.S.A.* 40°26N 99°23W **308** E4
Hole-Narsipur *India* 12°48N 76°16E **245** H3
Holešov *Czech Rep.* 49°20N 17°35E **181** B10
Holešovice *Czech Rep.* 13°11N 59°38W **323** r
Holgate *U.S.A.* 41°15N 84°8W **311** C12
Holguín *Cuba* 20°50N 76°20W **320** B4
Holič *Slovak Rep.* 48°49N 17°10E **181** C10
Holice *Czech Rep.* 50°6N 15°35E **181** B8
Holiday *U.S.A.* 28°11N 82°44W **317** G7
Holiday Park *U.S.A.* 26°8N 80°7W **129** B3
Höljes *Sweden* 60°50N 12°35E **162** D6
Hollabrunn *Austria* 48°34N 16°5E **180** C9
Hollams Bird I. *Namibia* 24°40S 14°30E **270** B1
Holland = Netherlands ■
   Europe 52°0N 5°30E **170** C5
Holland *Mich., U.S.A.* 42°47N 86°7W **311** B10
Holland *N.Y., U.S.A.* 42°38N 78°32W **312** D6
Holland B. *Jamaica* 17°57N 76°13W **320** a
Holland Centre *Canada* 44°23N 80°47W **312** B4
Holland Patent *U.S.A.* 43°14N 75°15W **313** C9
Holland Tunnel *New York, U.S.A.* **132** d1
Holland Village *Singapore* 1°18N 103°47E **138** E2
Hollandale *U.S.A.* 33°10N 90°51W **315** E9
Hollandia = Jayapura
   Indonesia 2°28S 140°38E **231** E10
Holley *U.S.A.* 43°14N 78°2W **312** C6
Hollfeld *Germany* 49°56N 11°18E **179** F7
Hollidaysburg *U.S.A.* 40°26N 78°24W **312** F6
Hollis *U.S.A.* 34°41N 99°55W **314** D5
Hollis Reservoir
   Trin. & Tob. 10°40N 61°10W **323** t
Hollister *Calif., U.S.A.* 36°51N 121°24W **306** J5
Hollister *Idaho, U.S.A.* 42°21N 114°35W **304** E6
Höllrigelskreuth *Germany* 48°2N 11°30E **131** B1
Hollum *Neths.* 53°35N 5°34E **170** A5
Hóllviken *Sweden* 55°25N 12°58E **163** K6
Hóllviksnäs = Höllviken
   Sweden 55°25N 12°58E **163** K6
Holly *U.S.A.* 42°48N 83°38W **311** B13
Holly Fla. *U.S.A.* 29°16N 81°3W **317** F8
Holly Hill *U.S.A.* 33°19N 80°25W **316** C8
Holly Springs Ga., U.S.A. 34°10N 84°30W **316** B5
Holly Springs Miss.,
   U.S.A. 34°46N 89°27W **315** D10
Hollywood *Wicklow, Ireland* 53°6N 6°35W **166** E4
Hollywood *Calif., U.S.A.* 34°5N 118°19W **126** B3
Hollywood *Fla., U.S.A.* 26°0N 80°8W **129** B3
Hollywood Bowl *U.S.A.* 34°7N 118°20E **126** B3
Holman *Canada* 70°44N 117°44W **294** C8
Hólmavík *Iceland* 65°42N 21°40W **155** B5
Holmen *Oppland, Norway* 60°40N 10°2E **164** D7
Holmen *Wis., U.S.A.* 43°58N 91°15W **308** D8
Holmenkollen *Norway* 59°57N 10°41E **113** A3
Holmes *Ch. Is., U.S.A.* 27°31N 82°43W **317** H7
Holmes Beach *U.S.A.* 27°31N 82°43W **317** H7
Holmes Cr. ≃ *U.S.A.* 30°30N 85°50W **316** E4
Holmes Reefs *Australia* 16°27S 148°0E **280** B4
Holmestrand *Norway* 59°31N 10°14E **164** E7
Holmfjord *Sweden* 59°14N 18°0E **139** B1
Holmlia *Norway* 59°49N 10°46E **113** A3
Holmsjö *Sweden* 56°25N 15°32E **163** H9
Holmsund *Västernorrland,
   Sweden* 62°26N 15°20E **162** B9
Holmsund *Västernorrland,
   Sweden* 63°41N 20°20E **160** E19
Holmsund *Västernorrland,
   Sweden* 63°41N 20°20E **160** E19
Holmudden *Sweden* 57°59N 19°5E **163** F12
Holod *Romania* 46°49N 22°8E **182** D7
Holon *Israel* 32°0N 34°46E **251** G5
Holopaw *U.S.A.* 28°8N 81°5W **317** G8
Holovne *Ukraine* 51°20N 24°5E **185** G11
Holoydal *Norway* 62°21N 11°23E **164** B7
Holozubyntsi *Ukraine* 48°50N 26°55E **183** B11
Holroyd ≃ *Australia* 14°10S 141°36E **280** A3
Holstebro *Denmark* 56°22N 8°37E **163** H2
Holsteinische Schweiz △
   Germany 54°8N 10°30E **178** A6
Holsteinsborg = Sisimiut
   Greenland 66°40N 53°30W **154** D5
Holsworthy *U.K.* 50°48N 4°22W **129** G3
Holt *Iceland* 63°33N 19°48W **155** D7
Holt *Fla., U.S.A.* 30°43N 86°45W **317** F2
Holt *Mich., U.S.A.* 42°39N 84°31W **311** B12
Holton *Nfld. & L., Canada* 54°31N 57°12W **299** B8

Holton *Kans., U.S.A.* 39°28N 95°44W **308** F6
Holts Summit *U.S.A.* 38°38N 92°7W **310** F4
Holtville *U.S.A.* 32°49N 115°23W **307** N11
Holualoa *U.S.A.* 19°37N 155°57W **302** D6
Holum *Norway* 58°6N 7°32E **164** F4
Holwerd *Neths.* 53°22N 5°54E **170** A5
Holy Cross *U.S.A.* 62°12N 159°46W **303** E8
Holy I. *Anglesey, U.K.* 53°17N 4°37W **168** D3
Holy I.,
   *Northumberland,
   U.K.* 55°40N 1°47W **168** B6
Holyhead *U.K.* 53°18N 4°38W **168** D3
Holyoke *Colo., U.S.A.* 40°35N 102°18W **304** F12
Holyoke *Mass., U.S.A.* 42°12N 72°37W **313** D12
Holyrood *Canada* 47°27N 53°8W **299** C9
Holyrood House, Palace of
   U.K. 55°57N 3°10W **121** B3
Holysloot *Neths.* 52°25N 5°2E **112** A3
Holzkirchen *Germany* 47°52N 11°42E **179** H7
Holzminden *Germany* 51°50N 9°28E **178** D5
Homa Bay *Kenya* 0°36S 34°30E **268** C3
Homalin *Burma* 24°55N 95°0E **241** C5
Homand *Iran* 32°28N 59°37E **247** C8
Homathko ≃ *Canada* 51°0N 124°56W **296** C4
Homberg *Germany* 51°2N 9°23E **178** D5
Homburg *Germany* 49°19N 7°21E **179** F3
Home B. *Canada* 68°40N 67°10W **295** C18
Home Hill *Australia* 19°43S 147°25E **280** B4
Home Reef *Tonga* 18°59S 174°47W **287** P13
Homedale *U.S.A.* 43°37N 116°56W **304** E5
Homei *Taiwan* 24°7N 120°29E **225** D2
Homeland *U.S.A.* 30°51N 82°1W **316** E7
Homer *Alaska, U.S.A.* 59°39N 151°33W **303** G10
Homer *Ill., U.S.A.* 40°4N 87°57W **311** D9
Homer *La., U.S.A.* 32°48N 93°4W **314** E8
Homer *Mich., U.S.A.* 42°9N 84°49W **311** B12
Homer *N.Y., U.S.A.* 42°38N 76°10W **313** D8
Homer City *U.S.A.* 40°32N 79°10W **312** F5
Homert △ *Germany* 51°15N 8°0E **178** D4
Homerton *U.K.* 51°32N 0°2W **125** A3
Homerville *U.S.A.* 31°2N 82°45W **316** D7
Homestead *Queens.,
   Australia* 20°20S 145°40E **280** C4
Homestead *Fla., U.S.A.* 25°28N 80°29W **317** K9
Homestead ◎ *U.S.A.* 41°17N 96°50W **308** E1
Hometown *U.S.A.* 41°44N 87°44W **119** C2
Homewood *U.S.A.* 41°34N 87°40W **311** C9
Hommelvik *Norway* 63°25N 10°48E **164** B4
Hommersåk *Norway* 58°56N 5°50E **164** F2
Homnabad *India* 17°42N 77°11E **244** F3
Homoine *Mozam.* 23°55S 35°8E **271** B6
Homoljske Planina *Serbia* 44°10N 21°45E **202** B5
Homonhon I. *Phil.* 10°44N 125°43E **233** F5
Homorod *Romania* 46°5N 25°15E **183** D10
Homosassa Springs
   U.S.A. 28°48N 82°35W **317** G7
Homs = Al Khums *Libya* 32°40N 14°17E **258** B2
Homs = Ḩimş *Syria* 34°40N 36°45E **250** D7
Homyel *Belarus* 52°28N 31°0E **177** B16
Homyel □ *Belarus* 52°40N 30°10E **189** F6
Hon Chong *Vietnam* 10°25N 104°30E **237** G5
Hon Me *Vietnam* 19°23N 105°56E **236** C5
Honan = Henan □ *China* 34°0N 114°0E **226** H8
Hōnanchō *Japan* 35°40N 139°39E **140** A2
Hōnaunau *U.S.A.* 19°26N 155°55W **302** D6
Honavar *India* 14°17N 74°27E **245** G2
Honaz *Turkey* 37°46N 29°18E **205** D11
Honbetsu *Japan* 43°7N 143°37E **220** C11
Honcho *Japan* 35°40N 139°41E **140** A3
Honcut *U.S.A.* 39°20N 121°32W **306** F5
Honda *Colombia* 5°12N 74°45W **328** B3
Honda, Bahia *Cuba* 22°54N 83°10W **320** B3
Honda B. *Phil.* 9°53N 118°49E **233** G2
Hondarribia *Spain* 43°22N 1°47W **196** B3
Hondeklipbaai *S. Africa* 30°19S 17°17E **270** D2
Honden *Japan* 35°43N 139°50E **140** A4
Hondo *Japan* 32°27N 130°12E **222** E2
Hondo *Tex., U.S.A.* 29°21N 99°9W **314** G5
Hondo, Río ≃ *Belize* 18°25N 88°21W **319** D7
Hondo, Río ≃ *Calif.,
   U.S.A.* 34°2N 118°15W **126** B4
Honduras ■ *Cent. Amer.* 14°40N 86°30W **320** D2
Honduras, G. de *Caribbean* 16°50N 87°0W **320** C2
Hønefoss *Norway* 60°10N 10°18E **164** D7
Honesdale *U.S.A.* 41°34N 75°16W **313** E9
Honey Harbour *Canada* 44°52N 79°49W **312** B5
Honey L. *U.S.A.* 40°15N 120°19W **306** E6
Honfleur *France* 49°25N 0°13E **172** C7
Høng *Denmark* 55°31N 11°18E **163** J5
Hong ≃ *Vietnam* 20°16N 106°34E **236** B5
Hong Gai *Vietnam* 20°57N 107°5E **228** G6
Hong He ≃ *China* 32°25N 115°35E **226** H8
Hong Hu *China* 29°54N 113°24E **229** C9
Hong Kong *China* 22°17N 114°11E **122** B2
Hong Kong □ *China* 22°11N 114°14E **219** a
Hong Kong I. *China* 22°16N 114°12E **122** B2
Hong Kong Int. ✈ (HKG)
   China 22°19N 113°57E **219** a
Hong Kong Park *Hong Kong, China* **122** c1
Honga *Angola* 15°9S 15°12E **265** F3
Hong'an *China* 31°20N 114°40E **229** B10
Hongcheon *S. Korea* 37°44N 127°53E **224** D3
Hongdo *S. Korea* 34°41N 125°12E **224** F2
Honghai Wan *China* 22°40N 115°0E **229** F10
Honghe *China* 23°25N 102°25E **228** F4
Honghu *China* 29°50N 113°30E **229** C9
Hongjie *S. Korea* 37°35N 126°56E **137** B1
Hongjiang *China* 27°7N 109°59E **228** D7
Hongjimun Tunnel
   S. Korea 37°37N 126°58E **137** B1
Hongkou *China* 31°16N 121°29E **138** B1
Hongliu He ≃ *China* 38°0N 109°50E **226** E5
Hongor *Mongolia* 45°45N 112°50E **226** B7
Hongqiao ≃ *China* 31°11N 121°22E **138** B1
Hongseong *S. Korea* 36°37N 126°38E **224** F2
Hongshan He ≃ *China* 23°48N 109°30E **228** F7
Hongtong *China* 36°16N 111°40E **226** F6
Honguedo, Détroit d'
   Canada 49°15N 64°0W **299** C7
Hongwon *N. Korea* 40°0N 127°56E **224** C3
Hongya *China* 29°51N 103°2E **228** B5
Hongze Hu *China* 33°15N 118°35E **227** H10
Honiara *Solomon Is.* 9°27S 159°57E **287** M10
Honiton *U.K.* 50°47N 3°11W **169** G4
Hönjō = Yurihonjō *Japan* 39°23N 140°3E **220** E10
Honjō *Japan* 36°14N 139°11E **223** A11
Honjyo *Japan* 35°55N 139°58E **140** A3
Honkawane *Japan* 35°5N 138°5E **223** B9
Honkorâb, Ras *Egypt* 24°35N 35°10E **256** C4
Honnali *India* 14°15N 75°40E **245** G2
Honningsvåg *Norway* 70°59N 25°59E **160** A21
Hōnō *Japan* 35°41N 139°33E **140** A2
Honoka'a *U.S.A.* 20°5N 155°28W **302** D6
Honokaa Hale *U.S.A.* 21°20N 158°6W **302** E13
Honolulu *U.S.A.* 21°19N 157°52W **302** E14
Honolulu District
   U.S.A. 21°19N 157°46W **302** K14
Honomu *U.S.A.* 19°52N 155°7W **302** D6

Honoré Mercier, Pont
   Canada 45°24N 73°39W **130** B1
Honouliuli *U.S.A.* 21°22N 158°2W **302** K13
Hōnow *Germany* 52°32N 13°38E **115** A4
Honshū *Japan* 36°0N 138°0E **223** A8
Hontoria del Pinar *Spain* 41°50N 3°10W **196** D1
Honu'apo Pt. *U.S.A.* 19°5N 155°33W **302** D6
Hood, Mt. *U.S.A.* 45°23N 121°42W **304** D3
Hood, Pt. *Papua N. G.* 10°4S 147°45E **286** F4
Hood River *U.S.A.* 45°43N 121°31W **304** D3
Hoodsport *U.S.A.* 47°24N 123°9W **306** C3
Hooge *Germany* 54°34N 8°33E **178** A4
Hoogeveen *Neths.* 52°44N 6°28E **170** B6
Hoogezand-Sappemeer
   Neths. 53°9N 6°45E **170** A6
Hooghly = Hugli ≃ *India* 21°56N 88°4E **243** J13
Hooghly-Chinsura = Chunchura
   India 22°53N 88°27E **243** H13
Hook *U.K.* 51°22N 0°17W **125** B2
Hook Hd. *Ireland* 52°7N 6°56W **166** D5
Hook I. *Australia* 20°4S 149°0E **280** b
Hook of Holland = Hoek van
   Holland *Neths.* 52°0N 4°7E **170** C4
Hooker *U.S.A.* 36°52N 101°13W **314** C4
Hooker Creek = Lajamanu
   Australia 18°23S 130°38E **278** C5
Hooker Creek ◎ *Australia* 18°6S 130°23E **278** C5
Ho'olehua *U.S.A.* 21°10N 157°5W **302** B4
Hoonah *U.S.A.* 58°7N 135°27W **296** B1
Hoop Bonaire 12°7N 68°17W **322** h
Hooper Bay *U.S.A.* 61°32N 166°6W **303** F6
Hoopeston *U.S.A.* 40°28N 87°40W **311** D9
Hoopstad *S. Africa* 27°50S 25°55E **270** C4
Höör *Sweden* 55°56N 13°33E **163** J7
Hoorn *Neths.* 52°38N 5°4E **170** B5
Hoover *U.S.A.* 33°24N 86°49W **315** E11
Hoover Dam *U.S.A.* 36°1N 114°44W **307** K12
Hooversville *U.S.A.* 40°9N 78°55W **312** F6
Hop Bottom *U.S.A.* 41°42N 75°46W **313** E9
Hopa *Turkey* 41°28N 41°30E **253** B9
Hope *B.C., Canada* 49°25N 121°25W **296** D4
Hope *Ark., U.S.A.* 33°40N 93°36W **314** E8
Hope *Ariz., U.S.A.* 33°40N 93°36W **314** E8
Hope *Ind., U.S.A.* 39°18N 85°46W **311** E11
Hope, L. *S. Austral.,
   Australia* 28°24S 139°18E **281** D2
Hope, L. *W. Austral.,
   Australia* 32°35S 120°15E **279** F3
Hope, Pt. *U.S.A.* 68°21N 166°47W **303** B6
Hope Bay *Jamaica* 18°12N 76°34W **320** a
Hope I. *Canada* 44°55N 80°11W **312** B4
Hope Town *Bahamas* 26°35N 76°57W **320** A4
Hope Vale *Australia* 15°16S 145°20E **280** B4
Hope Vale ◎ *Australia* 15°8S 145°15E **280** B4
Hopedale *Nfld. & L.,
   Canada* 55°28N 60°13W **299** A7
Hopedale *Mass., U.S.A.* 42°8N 71°33W **313** D13
Hopefield *S. Africa* 33°3S 18°22E **270** D2
Hopei = Hebei □ *China* 39°0N 116°0E **226** F9
Hopelchén *Mexico* 19°46N 89°51W **319** D7
Hopetoun *Vic., Australia* 35°42S 142°22E **282** C5
Hopetown *W. Austral.,
   Australia* 33°57S 120°7E **279** F3
Hopetown *S. Africa* 29°34S 24°3E **270** C3
Hopevale *U.S.A.* 37°18N 77°17W **309** G15
Hopewell *U.S.A.* 42°57N 12°10E **180** D5
Hopfgarten *Austria* 47°27N 12°10E **180** D5
Hopi *Burma* 24°58N 96°30E **241** C6
Hoping *Changhua, Taiwan* 24°10N 120°56E **225** D2
Hoping *Taitung, Taiwan* 23°4N 121°20E **225** C3
Hopkins *U.S.A.* 40°33N 94°49W **310** D2
Hopkins, L. *Australia* 24°15S 128°35E **278** D4
Hopkinsville *U.S.A.* 36°52N 87°29W **315** C10
Hopland *U.S.A.* 38°58N 123°7W **306** G3
Hopong *Burma* 20°47N 97°11E **241** E6
Hopwood's Ferry = Echuca
   Australia 36°10S 144°45E **283** B5
Hoque *Angola* 14°40S 13°55E **265** E2
Hoquiam *U.S.A.* 46°59N 123°53W **306** C3
Hôtel des Invalides *Paris, France* **134** c2
Hotham, C. *Australia* 12°3S 131°18E **278** B5
Hoting *Sweden* 64°8N 16°15E **160** D17
Hotolisht *Albania* 41°10N 20°25E **202** E4
Hotspur Seamount
   Atl. Oc. 17°55S 35°55W **152** H8
Hotte, Massif de la *Haiti* 18°30N 73°45W **321** C5
Hottentotsbaai *Namibia* 26°8S 14°59E **270** C1
Hou Hai *China* 22°45N 113°35E **122** c1
Houailou *N. Cal.* 21°17S 165°38E **288** d
Houat, Î. de *France* 47°24N 2°58W **172** E4
Houbétin *Czech Rep.* 50°6N 14°33E **135** B3
Houdan *France* 48°48N 1°35E **172** C8
Houei Sai *Laos* 20°18N 100°26E **228** G3
Houeillès *France* 44°12N 0°2E **174** D3
Houffalize *Belgium* 50°8N 5°48E **170** D5
Houghton *Gauteng, S. Africa* 26°10S 28°3E **123** B3
Houghton *Mich., U.S.A.* 47°7N 88°34W **308** B9
Houghton *N.Y., U.S.A.* 42°25N 78°9W **312** D6
Houghton L. *U.S.A.* 44°21N 84°44W **309** C11
Houghton-le-Spring *U.K.* 54°51N 1°28W **168** C6
Houhora Heads *N.Z.* 34°49S 173°9E **284** A2
Houilles *France* 48°56N 2°11E **134** A2
Houlton *U.S.A.* 46°8N 67°51W **309** B20
Houma *China* 35°36N 111°20E **226** G6
Houma *La., U.S.A.* 29°36N 90°43W **315** G9
Houmt Souk = Djerba
   Tunisia 33°48N 10°54E **258** B2
Houndé *Burkina Faso* 11°34N 3°31W **262** C4
Hounslow □ *U.K.* 51°28N 0°21W **125** C2
Houpu *Taiwan* 23°22N 120°21E **225** C2
Hourtin *France* 45°11N 1°4W **174** C2
Hourtin-Carcans, Étang d'
   France 45°10N 1°6W **174** C2
Housatonic ≃ *U.S.A.* 41°10N 73°7W **313** E11
House of Nobility =
   Riddarhuset
   Stockholm, Sweden **139** c2
House of Parliament =
   Riksdagshuset *Stockholm, Sweden* **139** b2
Houses of Parliament *London, U.K.* **125** c3
Houston *Canada* 54°25N 126°39W **296** B3
Houston *Mo., U.S.A.* 37°22N 91°58W **310** G8
Houston *Tex., U.S.A.* 29°45N 95°21W **314** G7
Hout ≃ Mogwadi ≃
   S. Africa 23°4S 29°36E **271** A4
Hout Bay *S. Africa* 34°2S 18°21E **123** B2
Houtkraal *S. Africa* 30°23S 24°5E **270** E3
Houtman Abrolhos
   Australia 28°43S 113°48E **279** E1
Hov *Norway* 60°42N 10°18E **164** D7
Hovd = Dund-Us
   Mongolia 48°1N 91°38E **217** C12
Hovd □ *Mongolia* 48°0N 91°0E **217** C12
Hovden *Aust-Agder, Norway* 59°33N 7°22E **164** D3
Hovden *Sogn og Fjordane,
   Norway* 61°41N 4°52E **164** D1
Hove *U.K.* 50°50N 0°10W **169** G7
Hove Å ≃ *Denmark* 56°24N 8°15E **163** H2
Hovedøya *Norway* 59°53N 10°43E **113** A3
Hovedstaden □ *Denmark* 55°50N 12°0E **163** J5
Hoveizeh *Iran* 31°27N 48°4E **247** D6
Hovgaard Ø *Greenland* 79°55N 18°50W **154** B9
Høvik *Norway* 59°54N 10°34E **133** A2
Hovin *Norway* 59°51N 9°0E **164** E6
Hovmantorp *Sweden* 56°47N 15°7E **163** H9
Hovorčovice *Czech Rep.* 50°10N 14°31E **135** A3
Hövsgöl *Mongolia* 43°37N 109°39E **226** C5
Hövsgöl Nuur *Mongolia* 51°0N 100°30E **218** A9
Hovsta *Sweden* 59°20N 15°15E **162** E9
Howakil *Eritrea* 15°10N 40°16E **257** D5
Howard *Queens., Australia* 25°16S 152°32E **281** D5
Howard *Pa., U.S.A.* 41°1N 77°40W **312** F7
Howard *S. Dak., U.S.A.* 44°1N 97°32W **308** C6
Howard Beach *U.S.A.* 40°39N 73°50W **132** C2
Howe *U.S.A.* 43°48N 113°0W **304** E7
Howe, C. *Australia* 37°30S 150°0E **283** D8
Howe, West Cape
   Australia 35°8S 117°36E **279** G2
Howe I. *Canada* 44°16N 76°17W **313** B8
Howell *U.S.A.* 42°36N 83°56W **311** B13
Howick *Qué., Canada* 45°11N 73°51W **313** A11
Howick *N.Z.* 36°54S 174°56E **284** e3
Howick *KwaZulu Natal,
   S. Africa* 29°28S 30°14E **271** C5
Howick Group *Australia* 14°20S 145°30E **280** A4
Howitt, L. *Australia* 27°40S 138°40E **281** D2
Howland I. *Pac. Oc.* 0°48N 176°38W **288** G10
Howlong *Australia* 35°59S 146°38E **283** C7
Howrah = Haora *India* 22°34N 88°18E **124** B1
Howth *Ireland* 53°23N 6°7W **120** A3
Howth Hd. *Ireland* 53°22N 6°4W **120** A3
Höxter *Germany* 51°46N 9°22E **178** D5
Hoxtolgay *China* 46°35N 85°59E **217** C11
Hoxton *London, U.K.* **125** a5
Hoxud *China* 42°15N 86°51E **217** D11
Hoy *U.K.* 58°50N 3°15W **167** C5
Hoya *Niedersachsen, Germany* 52°49N 9°8E **178** C5
Hōya *Tōkyō, Japan* 35°44N 139°34E **140** A2
Høyanger *Norway* 61°13N 6°4E **164** C3
Hoyerswerda *Germany* 51°26N 14°14E **178** D10
Hoylake *U.K.* 53°24N 3°10W **168** D4
Hōyo-Kaikyō *Japan* 33°20N 131°58E **222** D3
Hoyos *Spain* 40°9N 6°45W **194** E4
Hpa-an = Pa-an *Burma* 16°51N 97°40E **241** G6
Hpawlum *Burma* 27°12N 98°12E **241** B7
Hpettintha *Burma* 24°14N 95°23E **241** C5
Hpizow *Burma* 26°57N 98°24E **241** B7
Hpunan Pass *Asia* 27°30N 96°55E **241** A6
Hpyu = Pyu *Burma* 18°30N 96°28E **241** F6
Hradec Králové *Czech Rep.* 50°15N 15°50E **180** A8
Hrádek *Czech Rep.* 48°46N 16°16E **181** C9
Hrafnseyri *Iceland* 65°46N 23°28W **155** B3
Hranice *Czech Rep.* 49°34N 17°45E **181** B10
Hrazdan *Armenia* 40°30N 44°46E **191** K7
Hrebenka *Ukraine* 50°7N 32°24E **189** G7
Hrifunes *Iceland* 63°48N 18°30W **155** D8
Hrisey *Iceland* 66°0N 18°13W **155** B8
Hrisoupoli = Chrisoupoli
   Greece 40°58N 24°42E **203** F8
Hrodna *Belarus* 53°42N 23°52E **184** E10
Hrodna □ *Belarus* 53°20N 24°45E **188** F3
Hrodzyanka *Belarus* 53°31N 28°42E **177** B15
Hron ≃ *Slovak Rep.* 47°49N 18°45E **181** D10
Hrubieszów *Poland* 50°49N 23°51E **185** H10
Hrubý Jeseník *Czech Rep.* 50°5N 17°10E **181** A10
Hrvatska = Croatia ■
   Europe 45°20N 16°0E **199** C13
Hrymayliv *Ukraine* 49°20N 26°5E **177** D14
Hrynyava *Ukraine* 47°59N 24°53E **183** D9
Hsa-paw *Burma* 19°11N 97°30E **241** F6
Hsenwi *Burma* 23°22N 97°55E **241** C6
Hsi-hkip *Burma* 20°25N 96°42E **241** E6
Hsiafu *Taiwan* 25°7N 121°17E **225** A3
Hsiamen = Xiamen
   China 24°25N 118°4E **229** E12
Hsian = Xi'an *China* 34°15N 109°0E **226** G5
Hsiangshan *Taiwan* 24°46N 120°53E **225** B2
Hsiaochinmen Tao
   Taiwan 24°26N 118°14E **225** a
Hsiaohungt'ou Hsü
   Taiwan 21°57N 121°36E **225** D3
Hsiatashi *Taiwan* 22°28N 120°26E **225** D2
Hsiaying *Taiwan* 23°14N 120°15E **225** C2
Hsichih *Taiwan* 25°4N 121°39E **225** A3
Hsiho *Taiwan* 23°7N 120°12E **225** C2
Hsin'cheng *Taiwan* 24°10N 120°50E **225** B2
Hsinchu *Taiwan* 24°48N 120°58E **225** B2
Hsinchuang Kaohsiung,
   Taiwan 22°34N 120°29E **225** D2
Hsinchuang T'aipei,
   Taiwan 25°2N 121°27E **225** A3
Hsinfa *Taiwan* 22°52N 120°24E **225** D2
Hsinfeng *Taiwan* 24°54N 120°59E **225** B2
Hsinhailien = Lianyungang
   China 34°40N 119°11E **227** G10
Hsinhua *Taiwan* 23°3N 120°18E **225** C2
Hsini *Taiwan* 23°41N 120°15E **225** C2
Hsinkai = Bhamo *Burma* 24°15N 97°15E **241** C6
Hsinking = Changchun
   China 43°57N 125°17E **227** C13
Hsinpi *Taiwan* 22°28N 120°32E **225** D2
Hsinshih *Taiwan* 23°4N 120°17E **225** C2
Hsintien *Taiwan* 24°57N 121°32E **225** B3
Hsinwu *Taiwan* 24°59N 121°4E **225** B3
Hsinying *Taiwan* 23°21N 120°17E **225** C2
Hsinyuan *Taiwan* 22°30N 120°27E **225** D2
Hsiukuluan Hsi ≃
   Taiwan 23°28N 121°30E **225** C3
Hsiushui *Taiwan* 24°1N 120°30E **225** B2
Hsiushui *Taiwan* 23°41N 120°30E **225** C2
Hsopket *Burma* 23°11N 98°26E **228** F2
Hsüchou = Xuzhou
   China 34°18N 117°10E **227** G9
Hsüeh Shan *China* 24°23N 121°15E **225** a
Hsüehchia *Taiwan* 23°14N 120°10E **225** C2
Hsüehaitsun *Taiwan* 24°38N 120°50E **225** B2
Htawei = Tavoy *Burma* 14°2N 98°12E **241** H6
Hu Xian *China* 34°8N 108°42E **226** G5
Hua Hin *Thailand* 12°34N 99°58E **236** F2
Hua Lamphong Railway Station
   Bangkok, Thailand **113** c2
Hua Muang *Laos* 20°13N 103°52E **236** B4
Hua Xian *Henan, China* 35°30N 114°30E **226** G8
Hua Xian *Shaanxi, China* 34°30N 109°48E **226** G5
Hua Yü *Taiwan* 23°33N 119°34E **225** a
Hua'an *China* 25°1N 117°32E **229** E11
Huab ≃ *Namibia* 20°55N 13°26E **270** A2
Huacaya *Bolivia* 20°45S 63°43W **330** D3
Huachacalla *Bolivia* 18°45S 68°17W **330** D4
Huachinera *Mexico* 30°9N 108°55W **318** A3
Huachón *Peru* 11°10S 77°35W **330** C2
Huade *China* 41°55N 113°59E **226** C7
Huadian *China* 43°0N 126°40E **227** C14
Huadu *China* 23°22N 113°12E **229** F9
Huahine, Î.
   French Polynesia 16°46S 150°58W **289** f
Huai Hat *Thailand* 16°52N 104°17E **236** D5

Huai He → *China* 33°0N 118°30E 229 A12
Huai Kha Khaeng ⌓ *Thailand* 15°20N 98°55E 236 E2
Huai Nam Dang △ *Thailand* 19°30N 98°30E 236 C2
Huai Yot *Thailand* 7°45N 99°37E 237 J2
Huai'an *Hebei, China* 40°30N 114°20E 226 D8
Huai'an *Jiangsu, China* 33°30N 119°10E 227 H10
Huaibei *China* 34°0N 116°48E 226 G9
Huaibin *China* 32°32N 115°27E 229 A10
Huaicho = Puerto Acosta *Bolivia* 15°32S 69°15W 330 D4
Huaide = Gongzhuling *China* 43°30N 124°40E 227 C13
Huaidezhen *China* 43°48N 124°50E 227 C13
Huaihua *China* 27°32N 109°57E 228 D7
Huaiji *China* 23°55N 112°12E 229 F9
Huainan *China* 32°38N 116°58E 229 A11
Huaining *China* 30°24N 116°40E 229 B11
Huairen *China* 39°48N 113°20E 226 E7
Huairou *China* 40°20N 116°35E 226 D9
Huaiyang *China* 33°40N 114°52E 226 H8
Huaiyin *China* 33°30N 119°2E 227 H10
Huaiyuan *Anhui, China* 32°55N 117°10E 227 H9
Huaiyuan *Guangxi Zhuangzu, China* 24°31N 108°22E 228 E7
Huajuapán de León *Mexico* 17°48N 97°46W 319 D5
Hualālai *U.S.A.* 19°42N 155°52W 302 D6
Hualapai Peak *U.S.A.* 35°5N 113°54W 307 K13
Hualien *Taiwan* 23°59N 121°36E 225 C3
Hualien □ *Taiwan* 23°45N 121°25E 225 C3
Huallaga → *Peru* 5°15S 75°30W 330 B2
Huallanca *Peru* 8°50S 77°56W 330 B2
Huamachuco *Peru* 7°50S 78°5W 330 B2
Huambo *Angola* 12°42S 15°54E 265 E3
Huambo □ *Angola* 13°0S 16°0E 265 E3
Huan Jiang → *China* 34°28N 109°0E 226 G5
Huan Xian *China* 36°33N 107°7E 226 F4
Huancabamba *Peru* 5°10S 79°15W 330 B2
Huancane *Peru* 15°10S 69°44W 330 D4
Huancapi *Peru* 13°40S 74°0W 330 C3
Huancavelica *Peru* 12°50S 75°5W 330 C2
Huancavelica □ *Peru* 13°0S 75°0W 330 C3
Huancayo *Peru* 12°5S 75°12W 330 C2
Huanchaca *Bolivia* 20°15S 66°40W 330 E4
Huanchaca, Serranía de *Bolivia* 14°30S 60°39W 331 C5
Huang Hai = Yellow Sea *China* 35°0N 123°0E 227 G12
Huang He → *China* 37°55N 118°50E 227 F10
Huang Xian *China* 37°38N 120°30E 227 F11
Huangchuan *China* 32°15N 115°10E 229 A10
Huangdao *China* 36°0N 120°7E 227 G11
Huanggang *China* 30°29N 114°52E 229 B10
Huangguoshu *China* 26°0N 105°40E 228 E5
Huanghua *China* 38°22N 117°20E 227 E9
Huanghuagang *China* 38°20N 117°54E 227 E9
Huanghuagang Mausoleum *China* 23°9N 113°17E 121 B2
Huangling *China* 35°34N 109°15E 226 G5
Huanglong *China* 35°30N 109°59E 226 G5
Huanglong ⌓ *China* 32°44N 103°50E 228 A4
Huanglongtan *China* 32°40N 110°33E 229 A8
Huangmei *China* 30°5N 115°56E 229 B10
Huangpi *China* 30°50N 114°22E 229 B10
Huangping *China* 26°52N 107°54E 228 D6
Huangpu *China* 31°14N 121°30E 118 B2
Huangpu Jiang → *China* 31°11N 121°29E 118 B1
Huangshan *Anhui, China* 30°8N 118°9E 229 B12
Huangshan *Anhui, China* 29°42N 118°25E 229 C12
Huangshi *China* 30°10N 115°3E 229 B10
Huangsongdian *China* 43°45N 127°25E 227 C14
Huangtugang *China* 39°49N 116°15E 114 C1
Huangyan *China* 28°38N 121°19E 229 C13
Huangyangsi *China* 26°33N 111°39E 229 D8
Huaning *China* 24°17N 102°56E 228 E4
Huanjiang *China* 24°50N 108°18E 228 E7
Huanren *China* 41°23N 125°20E 224 B2
Huanren Shuiku *China* 41°17N 125°34E 224 B2
Huanta *Peru* 12°55S 74°20W 330 C3
Huantai *China* 36°58N 117°56E 227 F9
Huánuco *Peru* 9°55S 76°15W 330 B2
Huánuco □ *Peru* 9°55S 76°14W 330 B2
Huanuni *Bolivia* 18°16S 66°51W 330 D4
Huanzo, Cordillera de *Peru* 14°35S 73°20W 330 C3
Huaping *China* 26°46N 101°25E 228 D3
Huara *Chile* 19°59S 69°47W 330 D4
Huaral *Peru* 11°32S 77°13W 330 C2
Huaraz *Peru* 9°30S 77°32W 330 B2
Huari *Peru* 9°14S 77°14W 330 B2
Huarmey *Peru* 10°5S 78°5W 330 C2
Huarochiri *Peru* 12°9S 76°15W 330 C2
Huarocondo *Peru* 13°26S 72°14W 330 C3
Huarong *China* 29°29N 112°30E 229 C9
Huascar *Peru* 11°59S 77°1W 124 A2
Huascarán, Nevado *Peru* 9°7S 77°37W 330 B2
Huasco *Chile* 28°30S 71°15W 334 B1
Huasco → *Chile* 28°27S 71°13W 334 B1
Huasna *U.S.A.* 35°6N 120°24W 307 K6
Huatabampo *Mexico* 26°50N 109°38W 318 B3
Huauchinango *Mexico* 20°12N 98°3W 319 C5
Huautla de Jiménez *Mexico* 18°8N 96°51W 319 D5
Huaxi *China* 26°25N 106°40E 228 D6
Huay Khwang *Thailand* 13°47N 100°33E 113 B2
Huayhuash, Cordillera *Peru* 10°30S 76°45W 330 B2
Huayin *China* 34°35N 110°5E 226 G6
Huaying *China* 30°8N 106°44E 228 B6
Huayllay *Peru* 11°3S 76°21W 330 C2
Huayuan *China* 28°37N 109°29E 228 C7
Huazhou *China* 21°33N 110°33E 229 G8
Hubballi = Hubli *India* 15°22N 75°15E 245 G2
Hubbard *Iowa, U.S.A.* 42°18N 93°18W 310 B3
Hubbard *Ohio, U.S.A.* 41°9N 80°34W 312 E4
Hubbard *Tex., U.S.A.* 31°51N 96°48W 314 F6
Hubbard, Mt. *N. Amer.* 60°19N 139°4W 303 F13
Hubbard Glacier *Canada* 60°18N 139°22W 294 E4
Hubbart Pt. *Canada* 59°21N 94°41W 297 B10
Hubei □ *China* 31°0N 112°0E 229 B9
Hubli *India* 15°22N 75°15E 245 G2
Huch'ang *N. Korea* 41°25N 127°2E 224 B3
Huchow = Huzhou *China* 30°51N 120°8E 229 B13
Hucknall *U.K.* 53°3N 1°13W 168 D6
Huddersfield *U.K.* 53°39N 1°47W 168 D6
Huddinge *Sweden* 59°14N 18°0E 139 B2
Hude *Germany* 53°7N 8°26E 178 B4
Hudi *Sudan* 17°43N 34°18E 256 D3
Hudiksvall *Sweden* 61°43N 17°10E 162 C11
Hudson *Ont., Canada* 50°6N 92°9W 298 B1
Hudson *Fla., U.S.A.* 28°22N 82°42W 317 G7
Hudson *Mass., U.S.A.* 42°23N 71°34W 313 D13
Hudson *Mich., U.S.A.* 41°51N 84°21W 311 C12
Hudson *N.Y., U.S.A.* 42°15N 73°46W 313 D11
Hudson *Wis., U.S.A.* 44°58N 92°45W 308 C7
Hudson *Wyo., U.S.A.* 42°54N 108°35W 304 E9
Hudson → *U.S.A.* 40°42N 74°2W 313 F10
Hudson, C. *Antarctica* 68°21S 153°45E 151 C10
Hudson, Vol. *Chile* 46°4S 72°55W 336 C2
Hudson Bay *Nunavut, Canada* 60°0N 86°0W 295 F14
Hudson Bay *Sask., Canada* 52°51N 102°23W 297 C8
Hudson Falls *U.S.A.* 43°18N 73°35W 313 C11
Hudson Mts. *Antarctica* 74°32S 99°20W 151 D16
Hudson River Park *New York, U.S.A.* 132 e1
Hudson Str. *Canada* 62°0N 70°0W 295 E18
Hudson's Hope *Canada* 56°0N 121°54W 296 B4
Hudsonville *U.S.A.* 42°52N 85°52W 311 B11
Hue *Vietnam* 16°30N 107°35E 236 D6
Huebra → *Spain* 41°2N 6°48W 194 D4
Huechuraba *Chile* 33°22S 70°39W 137 B1
Huedin *Romania* 46°52N 23°2E 182 D8
Huehuetenango *Guatemala* 15°20N 91°28W 320 C1
Huejúcar *Mexico* 22°21N 103°13W 318 C4
Huélamo *Spain* 40°17N 1°48W 196 E3
Huelgoat *France* 48°22N 3°46W 172 D3
Huelma *Spain* 37°39N 3°28W 195 H7
Huelva *Spain* 37°18N 6°57W 195 H4
Huelva □ *Spain* 37°40N 7°0W 195 H4
Huelva → *Spain* 37°27N 6°0W 195 H5
Hueneme = Port Hueneme *U.S.A.* 34°7N 119°12W 307 L7
Huentelauquén *Chile* 31°38S 71°33W 334 C1
Huércal-Overa *Spain* 37°23N 1°57W 197 H3
Huerquehue △ *Chile* 39°6S 71°42W 336 A2
Huerta, Sa. de la *Argentina* 31°10S 67°30W 334 C2
Huertas, C. de las *Spain* 38°21N 0°24W 197 G4
Huerva → *Spain* 41°39N 0°52W 196 D4
Huesca *Spain* 42°8N 0°25W 196 C4
Huesca □ *Spain* 42°20N 0°1E 196 C5
Huéscar *Spain* 37°44N 2°35W 197 H2
Hueso Ballena, Pta. *Chile* 33°40S 78°46W 330 c
Huetamo *Mexico* 18°35N 100°53W 318 D4
Huete *Spain* 40°10N 2°43W 196 E2
Huevos I. *Trin. & Tob.* 10°42N 61°43W 323 t
Hugh Butler L. *U.S.A.* 33°6N 79°48W 316 B10
Hugh → *Australia* 25°1S 134°1E 280 D1
Hugh Taylor Birch State Recr. Area ⌓ *U.S.A.* 26°8N 80°6W 129 B3
Hughenden *Australia* 20°52S 144°10E 280 C3
Hughes *U.S.A.* 66°3N 154°15W 303 C9
Hughesville *U.S.A.* 41°14N 76°44W 313 E8
Hugli → *India* 21°56N 88°4E 243 J13
Hugo *Colo., U.S.A.* 39°8N 103°28W 304 G12
Hugo *Okla., U.S.A.* 34°1N 95°31W 314 D7
Hugoton *U.S.A.* 37°11N 101°21W 308 G3
Huguang Opera Museum *Beijing, China* 114 c2
Huhehaote = Hohhot *China* 40°52N 111°40E 226 D6
Huhsi *Taiwan* 23°35N 119°39E 225 C1
Hui Xian = Huixian *China* 35°27N 113°12E 226 G7
Hui Xian *China* 33°50N 106°4E 226 H4
Hui'an *China* 25°1N 118°43E 229 E12
Hui'anbu *China* 37°28N 106°38E 226 F4
Huiarau Ra. *N.Z.* 38°45S 176°55E 284 E5
Huichang *China* 25°32N 115°45E 229 E10
Huichapan *Mexico* 20°23N 99°39W 319 C5
Huichon *N. Korea* 40°10N 126°16E 224 B3
Huidong *Guangdong, China* 22°58N 114°43E 229 F10
Huidong *Sichuan, China* 26°34N 102°35E 228 D4
Huifa He → *China* 43°0N 127°50E 227 C14
Huila *Angola* 15°4S 13°32E 265 F2
Huíla □ *Angola* 14°0S 15°0E 265 E2
Huila □ *Colombia* 2°30N 75°45W 328 C2
Huila, Nevado del *Colombia* 3°0N 76°0W 328 C2
Huilai *China* 23°0N 116°18E 229 F11
Huili *China* 26°35N 102°17E 228 D4
Huimin *China* 37°27N 117°28E 227 F9
Huinan *China* 42°40N 126°2E 224 A3
Huinca Renancó *Argentina* 34°51S 64°22W 334 C3
Huining *China* 35°38N 105°0E 226 G3
Huinong *China* 39°5N 106°35E 226 E4
Huiroa *N.Z.* 39°15S 174°30E 284 F3
Huishui *China* 26°7N 106°38E 228 D6
Huisne → *France* 47°59N 0°11E 172 E7
Huiting *China* 34°5N 116°5E 226 G9
Huitong *China* 26°51N 109°45E 228 D7
Huixian *China* 35°27N 113°12E 226 G7
Huixtla *Mexico* 15°9N 92°28W 319 D6
Huize *China* 26°24N 103°15E 228 D4
Huizhou *China* 23°0N 114°23E 229 F10
Huizingen *Belgium* 50°45N 4°17E 116 B1
Hukawng Valley *Burma* 26°30N 96°30E 241 B6
Hukeri *India* 16°14N 74°36E 245 F2
Hukou *Jiangxi, China* 29°45N 116°21E 229 C11
Huk'ou *Taiwan* 24°54N 121°2E 225 B3
Hukuntsi *Botswana* 23°58S 21°45E 270 B3
Hula *Ethiopia* 6°33N 38°30E 257 F4
Hulan *China* 46°1N 126°44E 224 A3
Hulayfā' *Si. Arabia* 25°58N 40°45E 246 E4
Huld = Ulaanjirem *Mongolia* 45°5N 105°30E 226 B3
Hulin *China* 45°48N 132°59E 219 B15
Hulin He → *China* 45°0N 122°10E 227 B12
Hull = Kingston upon Hull *U.K.* 53°45N 0°21W 168 D7
Hull *Canada* 45°26N 75°43W 313 A9
Hull → *U.K.* 53°44N 0°20W 168 D7
Hulst *Neths.* 51°17N 4°2E 170 C4
Hultschin = Hlučín *Czech Rep.* 49°54N 18°11E 181 B11
Hultsfred *Sweden* 57°30N 15°52E 163 G9
Huludao *China* 40°45N 120°50E 227 D11
Hulun = Hailar *China* 49°10N 119°38E 219 B12
Hulun Nur *China* 49°0N 117°30E 219 B12
Hulunbuir = Hailar *China* 49°10N 119°38E 219 B12
Hulyaypole *Ukraine* 47°45N 36°21E 189 J9
Huma, Tanjung *Malaysia* 5°29N 100°16E 237 c
Humacao *Puerto Rico* 18°9N 65°50W 321 b
Humahuaca *Argentina* 23°10S 65°25W 334 A2
Humaitá = Porto Walter *Brazil* 8°15S 72°40W 330 B3
Humaitá *Brazil* 7°35S 63°1W 331 B5
Humaitá *Paraguay* 27°2S 58°31W 334 B4
Humansdorp *S. Africa* 34°2S 24°46E 270 D3
Humansville *U.S.A.* 37°48N 93°35W 310 G3
Humara, J. *Sudan* 16°16N 30°59E 257 D3
Humayun's Tomb *India* 28°35N 77°15E 120 B2
Humbe *Angola* 16°40S 14°55E 265 F2
Humbe, Serra do *Angola* 12°10S 15°25E 265 E3
Humber → *Ont., Canada* 43°47N 79°38W 141 A1
Humber → *England, U.K.* 53°42N 0°27W 168 D7
Humber B. *Canada* 43°37N 79°27W 141 B2
Humber Bay *Canada* 43°38N 79°29W 141 B2
Humber Bay Park *Canada* 43°37N 79°28W 141 B2
Humber College *Canada* 43°35N 79°30W 141 B1
Humber Summit *Canada* 43°45N 79°32W 141 A1
Humber Valley Village *Canada* 43°40N 79°31W 141 A1
Humberlea *Canada* 43°43N 79°31W 141 A1
Humberwood Park *Canada* 43°44N 79°37W 141 A1
Humboldt *Sask., Canada* 52°15N 105°9W 297 C7
Humboldt *Iowa, U.S.A.* 42°44N 94°13W 310 B2
Humboldt *Tenn., U.S.A.* 35°50N 88°55W 315 D10
Humboldt → *U.S.A.* 39°59N 118°36W 304 G4
Humboldt Gletscher = Sermersuaq *Greenland* 79°30N 62°0W 154 B4
Humboldt Mts. *N.Z.* 44°30S 168°15E 285 E3
Humboldt Park *U.S.A.* 41°54N 87°42W 119 B2
Humbolt, Mt. *N. Cal.* 21°53S 166°25E 288 d
Hume *U.S.A.* 36°48N 118°54W 306 J8
Hume, L. *Australia* 36°0S 147°5E 283 D7
Humen *China* 22°50N 113°40E 219 a
Humenné *Slovak Rep.* 48°55N 21°50E 181 C14
Humera *Spain* 40°25N 3°46W 127 B1
Humeston *U.S.A.* 40°52N 93°30W 310 D3
Hummelsta *Sweden* 59°34N 16°56E 162 E10
Hummelvika *Norway* 63°29N 8°19E 164 A5
Hummingbird Centre *Toronto, Canada* 141 b3
Hummock Hill = Whyalla *Australia* 33°2S 137°30E 282 B2
Humpata *Angola* 15°2S 13°24E 265 F2
Humphreys, Mt. *U.S.A.* 37°17N 118°40W 306 H8
Humphreys Peak *U.S.A.* 35°21N 111°41W 305 J8
Humpolec *Czech Rep.* 49°31N 15°20E 180 B8
Humptulips *U.S.A.* 47°14N 123°57W 306 C3
Humula *Australia* 35°30S 147°46E 283 C7
Hūn *Libya* 29°2N 16°0E 258 C3
Hun He → *China* 40°41N 122°8E 224 B1
Hun Jiang → *China* 40°50N 125°38E 227 D13
Húnaflói *Iceland* 65°50N 20°50W 155 B6
Hunan □ *China* 27°30N 112°0E 229 D9
Hunavatnssýsla *Iceland* 65°30N 20°25W 155 B6
Hunaydī Iraq 33°18N 44°29E 113 B2
Hunchun *China* 42°52N 130°28E 227 C16
Hundested *Denmark* 55°58N 11°52E 163 J5
Hundewali *Pakistan* 31°55N 72°38E 242 D5
Hundige *Denmark* 55°35N 12°18E 118 B1
Hundige Strand *Denmark* 55°35N 12°18E 118 B1
Hundorp *Norway* 61°33N 9°59E 164 C7
Hundred Islands △ *Phil.* 16°10N 120°2E 232 C3
Hundred Mile House *Canada* 51°38N 121°18W 296 C4
Hundvåg *Norway* 59°0N 5°43E 164 E2
Hunedoara *Romania* 45°40N 22°50E 182 E7
Hunedoara □ *Romania* 45°50N 22°54E 182 E7
Hunei *Taiwan* 22°53N 120°14E 225 D2
Hünfeld *Germany* 50°39N 9°46E 178 E5
Hung Hom *China* 22°18N 114°11E 122 B2
Hung Yen *Vietnam* 20°39N 106°4E 228 G6
Hunga Ha'apai *Tonga* 20°41S 175°7W 287 Q13
Hungary ■ *Europe* 47°20N 19°20E 181 D12
Hungary, Plain of *Europe* 47°0N 20°0E 158 F10
Hungerford *Australia* 28°58S 144°24E 281 D3
Hŭngnam *N. Korea* 39°49N 127°45E 224 C3
Hungt'ou Hsü = Lan Yü *Taiwan* 22°4N 121°25E 225 D3
Huni Valley *Ghana* 5°33N 1°56W 262 D4
Hunjiang *China* 41°54N 126°26E 224 B3
Hunneberg *Sweden* 58°18N 12°30E 163 F6
Hunnebostrand *Sweden* 58°27N 11°18E 163 F5
Hunsberge *Namibia* 27°45S 17°12E 270 C2
Hunsrück *Germany* 49°56N 7°27E 179 F3
Hunstanton *U.K.* 52°56N 0°29E 168 E8
Hunsur *India* 12°16N 76°16E 245 H3
Hunte → *Germany* 53°14N 8°28E 178 B4
Hunter *N.Z.* 44°36S 171°2E 285 E6
Hunter *N.Y., U.S.A.* 42°13N 74°13W 313 D10
Hunter → *N.S.W., Australia* 32°52S 151°46E 283 B9
Hunter → *N.Z.* 44°21S 169°27E 285 E4
Hunter, C. *Solomon Is.* 9°48S 159°50E 287 M10
Hunter Hills, The *N.Z.* 44°26S 170°46E 285 E5
Hunter I. *Tas., Australia* 40°30S 144°45E 281 G3
Hunter I. *B.C., Canada* 51°55N 128°0W 296 C3
Hunter Mts. *N.Z.* 45°43S 167°25E 285 F2
Hunter Ra. *Australia* 32°45S 150°15E 283 B9
Hunters Hill *Australia* 33°50S 151°9E 139 B1
Hunters Pt. *U.S.A.* 37°43N 122°21W 136 B2
Hunters Road *Zimbabwe* 19°9S 29°49E 269 F2
Hunterville *N.Z.* 39°56S 175°35E 284 F4
Huntingburg *U.S.A.* 38°18N 86°57W 311 F10
Huntingdon *Cambs., U.K.* 52°20N 0°11W 169 E7
Huntingdon *Pa., U.S.A.* 40°30N 78°1W 312 F6
Huntington = Shelton *U.S.A.* 41°19N 73°5W 313 E11
Huntington *Ind., U.S.A.* 40°53N 85°30W 311 D11
Huntington *N.Y., U.S.A.* 40°52N 73°26W 313 F11
Huntington *Oreg., U.S.A.* 44°21N 117°16W 304 D5
Huntington *Utah, U.S.A.* 39°20N 110°58W 304 G8
Huntington *Va., U.S.A.* 38°47N 77°4W 143 C2
Huntington *W. Va., U.S.A.* 38°25N 82°27W 309 F12
Huntington Beach *U.S.A.* 33°40N 118°5W 307 M9
Huntington Park *U.S.A.* 33°58N 118°13W 126 C3
Huntley *Jamaica* 18°4N 77°35W 320 a
Huntley *Ill., U.S.A.* 42°10N 88°26W 311 B8
Huntly *N.Z.* 37°34S 175°11E 284 D4
Huntly *Aberds., U.K.* 57°27N 2°47W 167 D6
Huntsville *Ont., Canada* 45°20N 79°14W 312 A5
Huntsville *Ala., U.S.A.* 34°44N 86°35W 315 D11
Huntsville *Mo., U.S.A.* 39°26N 92°33W 310 E4
Huntsville *Tex., U.S.A.* 30°43N 95°33W 314 F7
Hunyani → *Zimbabwe* 15°57S 30°39E 269 F3
Hunyuan *China* 39°42N 113°42E 226 E7
Hunza → *India* 35°54N 74°20E 243 B6
Huo Shan *China* 36°26N 111°52E 226 F6
Huo Xian = Huozhou *China* 36°36N 111°42E 226 F6
Huocheng *China* 44°0N 80°48E 217 D10
Huolin Gol *China* 45°32N 119°38E 227 B10
Huon G. *Papua N. G.* 7°0S 147°30E 286 D4
Huon Pen. *Papua N. G.* 6°20S 147°30E 286 D4
Huong Khe *Vietnam* 18°13N 105°41E 236 C5
Huonville *Australia* 43°0S 147°5E 281 G4
Huoqiu *China* 32°20N 116°12E 229 A11
Huoshan *China* 31°25N 116°20E 229 B11
Huoshao Dao = Lütao *Taiwan* 22°40N 121°30E 225 D3
Huozhou *China* 36°36N 111°42E 226 F6
Hupeh = Hubei □ *China* 31°0N 112°0E 229 B9
Hūr *Iran* 30°50N 57°7E 247 D8
Hurānd *Iran* 38°51N 47°22E 213 C12
Ḩuraymīla *Si. Arabia* 25°8N 46°8E 246 E5
Hurbanovo *Slovak Rep.* 47°51N 18°11E 181 D11
Hurd, C. *Canada* 45°13N 81°44W 312 A3
Hurdiyo *Somalia* 10°33N 51°6E 267 B7
Hure Qi *China* 42°45N 121°45E 227 C11
Hurezani *Romania* 44°49N 23°40E 183 F8
Hurghada *Egypt* 27°15N 33°50E 256 B3
Huriya *Iraq* 33°21N 44°19E 113 A1
Hurley *N. Mex., U.S.A.* 32°42N 108°8W 305 K9
Hurley *Wis., U.S.A.* 46°27N 90°11W 308 B8
Huron *Calif., U.S.A.* 36°12N 120°6W 306 J6
Huron *Ohio, U.S.A.* 41°24N 82°33W 312 E2
Huron *S. Dak., U.S.A.* 44°22N 98°13W 308 C4
Huron, L. *U.S.A.* 44°30N 82°40W 312 B2
Huron East *Canada* 43°37N 81°18W 312 C3
Hurricane *U.S.A.* 37°11N 113°17W 305 H7
Hurso *Ethiopia* 9°35N 41°33E 257 F5
Hurstville *Australia* 33°57S 151°6E 139 B1
Hurtsboro *U.S.A.* 32°15N 85°25W 316 C4
Hurungwe ⌓ *Zimbabwe* 16°7S 29°5E 269 F2
Hurunui → *N.Z.* 42°54S 173°18E 285 C8
Hurup *Denmark* 56°46N 8°25E 163 H2
Húsafell *Iceland* 64°42N 20°53W 155 C6
Husan *West Bank* 31°42N 35°8E 251 B1
Húsavík *Iceland* 66°3N 17°21W 155 A9
Husby *Sweden* 59°24N 17°56E 139 A1
Huşi *Romania* 46°41N 28°7E 183 D13
Huskisson *Australia* 35°2S 150°41E 283 C9
Huskvarna *Sweden* 57°47N 14°15E 163 G8
Huslia *U.S.A.* 65°41N 156°24W 303 D8
Husnes *Norway* 59°52N 5°45E 164 E2
Hustad *Norway* 62°57N 7°6E 164 B4
Hustadvika *Norway* 63°0N 7°0E 164 A3
Hustontown *U.S.A.* 40°3N 78°2W 312 F6
Hustopeče *Czech Rep.* 48°57N 16°43E 181 C9
Husum *København, Denmark* 55°42N 12°27E 118 A2
Husum *Schleswig-Holstein, Germany* 54°28N 9°4E 178 A5
Husum *Sweden* 63°21N 19°12E 162 A13
Huszt = Khust *Ukraine* 48°10N 23°18E 183 B8
Hutanopan *Indonesia* 0°40N 99°42E 234 B1
Hutchinson *Kans., U.S.A.* 38°5N 97°56W 308 F5
Hutchinson *Minn., U.S.A.* 44°54N 94°22W 308 C6
Ḩūth *Yemen* 16°14N 43°58E 248 C3
Hutiao Xia *China* 27°13N 100°9E 228 D3
Hutjena *Papua N. G.* 5°23S 154°42E 286 C8
Hutsonville *U.S.A.* 39°7N 87°40W 311 E9
Hutte Sauvage, L. de la *Canada* 56°15N 64°45W 299 A7
Hütteldorf *Austria* 48°12N 16°15E 142 A1
Hüttenberg *Austria* 46°56N 14°33E 180 E7
Hüttener Berge ⌓ *Germany* 54°24N 9°40E 178 A5
Hutton, Mt. *Australia* 25°51S 148°20E 281 D4
Huvadu Atoll *Maldives* 0°30N 73°15E 272 d
Hüvösvölgy *Hungary* 47°32N 19°0E 117 A2
Huwaki *Indonesia* 7°55S 126°30E 231 F7
Huwei *Taiwan* 23°42N 120°26E 225 C2
Huwei Hsü → *Taiwan* 23°37N 120°22E 225 C2
Huwon Secret Garden *S. Korea* 37°34N 126°59E 137 B1
Huwun *Ethiopia* 4°23N 40°6E 257 G5
Huy *Belgium* 50°31N 5°15E 170 D5
Huzhou *China* 30°51N 120°8E 229 B13
Huzurabad *India* 18°12N 79°25E 244 E4
Huzurnagar *India* 16°54N 79°53E 244 F4
Hvalpsund *Denmark* 56°42N 9°11E 163 H3
Hvalstad *Norway* 59°51N 10°27E 133 A1
Hvalstrand *Norway* 59°50N 10°30E 133 A2
Hvammsfjörður *Iceland* 65°4N 22°5W 155 B4
Hvammstangi *Iceland* 65°24N 20°57W 155 B6
Hvammur *Norðurland Vestra, Iceland* 65°53N 19°51W 155 B7
Hvammur *Vesturland, Iceland* 64°50N 21°21W 155 C5
Hvannadalshnúkur *Iceland* 64°1N 16°41W 155 C10
Hvanneyri *Iceland* 64°34N 21°36W 155 C5
Hvar *Croatia* 43°11N 16°28E 199 E13
Hvarski Kanal *Croatia* 43°15N 16°35E 199 E13
Hveragerði *Iceland* 64°0N 21°12W 155 C5
Hvidovre *Denmark* 55°38N 12°27E 118 B2
Hvítá → *Iceland* 64°30N 21°58W 155 C5
Hvítárvatn *Iceland* 64°37N 19°50W 155 C7
Hvittingfoss *Norway* 59°29N 10°0E 164 E7
Hvizdets *Ukraine* 48°35N 25°17E 183 B10
Hvolsvöllur *Iceland* 63°45N 20°14W 155 D6
Hwacheon-Cheosuji *S. Korea* 38°5N 127°50E 224 C3
Hwagok *S. Korea* 37°32N 126°51E 137 B1
Hwainan = Huainan *China* 32°38N 116°58E 229 A11
Hwaiyin = Huaiyin *China* 33°30N 119°2E 227 H10
Hwang Ho = Huang He → *China* 37°55N 118°50E 227 F10
Hwange *Zimbabwe* 18°18S 26°30E 269 F2
Hwange △ *Zimbabwe* 19°0S 26°30E 270 A4
Hwanghaebuk-do □ *N. Korea* 38°30N 126°25E 224 C3
Hwanghaenam-do □ *N. Korea* 38°15N 125°30E 224 C2
Hwangju *N. Korea* 38°40N 125°46E 224 C2
Hwangshih = Huangshi *China* 30°10N 115°3E 229 B10
Hwaseong *S. Korea* 37°12N 126°48E 224 D3
Hwasun *S. Korea* 35°3N 126°59E 224 E3
Hwekum *Burma* 26°7N 95°22E 241 B5
Hwllfordd = Haverfordwest *U.K.* 51°48N 4°58W 169 F3
Hyaing *Burma* 22°39N 94°44E 241 D5
Hyannis *Mass., U.S.A.* 41°39N 70°17W 309 E18
Hyannis *Nebr., U.S.A.* 42°0N 101°46W 308 E3
Hyargas Nuur *Mongolia* 49°0N 93°0E 217 C12
Hyattsville *U.S.A.* 38°57N 76°57W 143 B3
Hybo *Sweden* 61°49N 16°15E 162 C10
Hydaburg *U.S.A.* 55°15N 132°50W 296 B2
Hyde *N.Z.* 45°18S 170°16E 285 F5
Hyde Park *Sydney, Australia* 139 b2
Hyde Park *Guyana* 6°30N 58°16W 329 B6
Hyde Park *Gauteng, S. Africa* 26°6S 28°2E 123 A2
Hyde Park *London, U.K.* 51°30N 0°10W 125 C2
Hyde Park *Calif., U.S.A.* 33°58N 118°19W 126 C3
Hyde Park *Ill., U.S.A.* 41°47N 87°35W 119 C3
Hyde Park *Mass., U.S.A.* 42°15N 71°7W 116 B2
Hyde Park *N.Y., U.S.A.* 41°47N 73°56W 313 E11
Hyden *Australia* 32°24S 118°53E 279 F2
Hyder *U.S.A.* 55°55N 130°5W 296 B2
Hyderabad *India* 17°22N 78°29E 244 F4
Hyderabad *Pakistan* 25°23N 68°24E 242 G3
Hydra *Greece* 37°20N 23°28E 204 D5
Hyen *Norway* 61°44N 5°56E 164 C2
Hyères *France* 43°8N 6°9E 175 E10
Hyères, Îs. d' *France* 43°0N 6°20E 175 F10
Hyesan *N. Korea* 41°20N 128°10E 224 B4
Hyland → *Canada* 59°52N 128°12W 296 B3
Hylestad *Norway* 59°6N 7°29E 164 E5
Hyllestad *Norway* 61°10N 5°17E 164 C2
Hyltebruk *Sweden* 56°59N 13°15E 163 H7
Hyndman Peak *U.S.A.* 43°45N 114°8W 304 E6
Hynnekleiv *Norway* 58°36N 8°25E 164 F5
Hyōgo □ *Japan* 35°15N 134°50E 222 B6
Hyrra Banda *C.A.R.* 5°58N 22°4E 264 A4
Hyrum *U.S.A.* 41°38N 111°51W 304 F8
Hysham *U.S.A.* 46°18N 107°14W 304 C10
Hythe *U.K.* 51°4N 1°5E 169 F9
Hyūga *Japan* 32°25N 131°35E 222 E3
Hyvinge = Hyvinkää *Finland* 60°38N 24°50E 188 B3
Hyvinkää *Finland* 60°38N 24°50E 188 B3

I

I-n-Akhmed *Mali* 19°49N 0°56W 261 E4
I-n-Azaoua *Illizi, Algeria* 25°42N 6°54E 261 C6
I-n-Azaoua *Tamanrasset, Algeria* 20°46N 7°32E 261 D6
I-n-Échaï *Mali* 20°10N 2°5W 260 D4
I-n-Ezzane *Algeria* 23°29N 11°15E 261 D7
I-n-Gall *Niger* 16°51N 7°1E 263 B6
I-n-Kelemet *Algeria* 26°57N 5°47E 261 C5
I-n-Oudad *Algeria* 20°17N 4°38E 261 D5
I-n-Ouzzal *Algeria* 20°41N 2°34E 261 D5
I-n-Tadreft *Niger* 19°5N 6°38E 263 B6
Iabès, Erg *Algeria* 27°30N 0°0E 260 C4
Iablaniţa *Romania* 44°57N 22°19E 182 F7
Iaco → *Brazil* 9°3S 68°34W 330 B4
Iacobeni *Romania* 47°25N 25°20E 183 C10
Iaçu *Brazil* 12°45S 40°13W 333 C2
Iakora *Madag.* 23°6S 46°40E 272 C2
Ialibu *Papua N. G.* 6°17S 143°59E 286 D2
Ialissos *Greece* 36°24N 28°10E 206 E12
Ialomiţa □ *Romania* 44°30N 27°30E 183 F12
Ialomiţa → *Romania* 44°42N 27°51E 183 F12
Ialoveni *Moldova* 46°56N 28°47E 183 D13
Ialpug → *Moldova* 45°41N 28°35E 183 E13
Iamonia L. *U.S.A.* 30°38N 84°14W 316 E5
Ianca *Romania* 45°6N 27°29E 183 E12
Iara *Romania* 46°31N 23°35E 183 D8
Iarda *Ethiopia* 11°9N 35°53E 257 E4
Iargara *Moldova* 46°24N 28°23E 183 D13
Iaşi *Romania* 47°10N 27°40E 183 C12
Iaşi □ *Romania* 47°20N 27°0E 183 C12
Iasmos *Greece* 41°8N 25°11E 203 E9
Iauaretê *Colombia* 0°36N 69°12W 328 C4
Ib → *India* 21°34N 83°48E 243 J10
Iba *Phil.* 15°22N 120°0E 232 D2
Ibadan *Nigeria* 7°22N 3°58E 263 D5
Ibagué *Colombia* 4°20N 75°20W 328 C2
Ibaiti *Brazil* 23°50S 50°10W 333 F1
Ibajay *Phil.* 11°49N 122°10E 233 F4
Iballë *Albania* 42°12N 20°2E 202 D4
Ibăneşti *Botoşani, Romania* 48°4N 26°22E 183 B11
Ibăneşti *Mureş, Romania* 46°45N 24°57E 183 D9
Ibanshe *Dem. Rep. of the Congo* 4°58S 21°30E 265 C4
Ibar → *Serbia* 43°43N 20°45E 202 C4
Ibara *Japan* 34°36N 133°28E 222 C5
Ibaraki *Ibaraki, Japan* 36°20N 140°20E 223 A12
Ibaraki *Ōsaka, Japan* 34°49N 135°34E 223 C7
Ibaraki □ *Japan* 36°10N 140°10E 223 A12
Ibarra *Ecuador* 0°21N 78°7W 328 C2
Ibb *Yemen* 14°2N 44°10E 248 D4
Ibb □ *Yemen* 14°2N 44°10E 248 D4
Ibba *South Sudan* 4°49N 29°2E 257 G2
Ibba, Bahr el → *South Sudan* 5°30N 28°55E 257 F2
Ibbenbüren *Germany* 52°16N 7°43E 178 C3
Ibeke Gembo *Dem. Rep. of the Congo* 1°24S 18°51E 264 C3
Ibembo *Dem. Rep. of the Congo* 2°35N 23°35E 264 B4
Ibenga → *Congo* 2°19N 18°9E 264 B3
Ibera, L. *Argentina* 28°30S 57°9W 334 B4
Iberia *Peru* 11°21S 69°35W 330 C4
Iberia *Mo., U.S.A.* 38°5N 92°18W 310 F4
Iberian Peninsula *Europe* 40°0N 5°0W 158 H5
Iberville *Canada* 45°19N 73°17W 313 A11
Iberville, Mt. d' *Canada* 58°50N 63°50W 295 F19
Ibese *Nigeria* 6°33N 3°28E 124 A2
Ibeto *Nigeria* 10°29N 5°8E 263 C6
Ibi *Nigeria* 8°15N 9°44E 263 D6
Ibi *Spain* 38°38N 0°34W 197 G4
Ibiá *Brazil* 19°30S 46°30W 333 E2
Ibiapaba, Sa. da *Brazil* 4°0S 41°30W 332 B3
Ibicaraí *Brazil* 14°51S 39°36W 333 D4
Ibicuí *Brazil* 14°51S 39°59W 333 D4
Ibicuí → *Brazil* 29°25S 56°47W 335 B4
Ibicuy *Argentina* 33°55S 59°10W 334 C4
Ibirapuera *Brazil* 23°36S 46°40W 137 B1
Ibirapuera, Parque do *Brazil* 23°35S 46°38W 137 B2
Ibitiara *Brazil* 12°39S 42°13W 333 D3
Ibiza = Eivissa *Spain* 38°54N 1°26E 206 D1
Ibiza ✕ (IBZ) *Spain* 38°53N 1°22E 197 G6
Iblei, Monti *Italy* 37°15N 14°45E 201 E7
Ibn Hāni', Ra's *Syria* 35°35N 35°43E 250 C6
Ibo *Mozam.* 12°22S 40°40E 269 E5
Ibonma *Indonesia* 3°29S 133°31E 231 E8
Ibotirama *Brazil* 12°13S 43°12W 333 D3
Iboundji *Gabon* 1°0S 11°51E 264 C2
Ibrā' *Oman* 22°41N 58°33E 249 B7
İbradı *Turkey* 37°4N 31°35E 250 A2
Ibrāhīm → *Lebanon* 34°4N 35°38E 250 D6
'Ibrī *Oman* 23°14N 56°30E 249 B7
İbriktepe *Turkey* 41°0N 26°30E 203 E10
Ibshawâi *Egypt* 29°21N 30°40E 256 J7
Ibu *Indonesia* 1°35N 127°33E 231 D7
Ibuki-Sanchi *Japan* 35°25N 136°18E 223 B8
Ibusuki *Japan* 31°12N 130°40E 222 F2
Ica *Peru* 14°0S 75°48W 330 C2
Ica □ *Peru* 14°20S 75°30W 330 C2
Iça → *Brazil* 2°55S 67°58W 330 A4
Icabarú *Venezuela* 4°20N 61°45W 329 C5
Icabarú → *Venezuela* 4°45N 62°15W 329 C5
Icacos *Trin. & Tob.* 10°3N 61°54W 323 t
Icacos Pt. *Trin. & Tob.* 10°3N 61°57W 323 t
Içana *Brazil* 0°21N 67°19W 328 C4
Içana → *Brazil* 0°26N 67°19W 328 C4
Icaraí *Brazil* 22°54S 43°6W 135 B2
Icatu *Brazil* 2°46S 44°4W 332 B3
Icaturama = Santa Rosa de Viterbo *Colombia* 5°53N 72°59W 328 B3
İçel *Turkey* 36°51N 34°36E 250 B5
İçel □ *Turkey* 36°45N 34°0E 250 B5
Iceland ■ *Europe* 64°45N 19°0W 155 C8
Iceland Basin *Atl. Oc.* 61°0N 19°0W 150 C7
Icelandic Plateau *Arctic* 64°0N 10°0W 150 C7
İçerenköy *Turkey* 40°58N 29°6E 122 C2
İçeriçumra *Turkey* 37°34N 32°39E 212 D5
Ichalkaranji *India* 16°40N 74°33E 244 F2
Ich'ang = Yichang *China* 30°40N 111°20E 229 B8
Ichchapuram *India* 19°10N 84°40E 244 E7
Icheon *S. Korea* 37°17N 127°27E 224 D3
Ichgao *Japan* 35°32N 139°32E 140 B2
Ichhawar *India* 23°1N 77°1E 242 H7
Ichigaya *Tokyo, Japan* 140 a3
Ichihara *Japan* 35°28N 140°5E 223 B12
Ichikawa *Japan* 35°43N 139°54E 140 A4
Ichilo → *Bolivia* 15°57S 64°50W 331 D5
Ichinohe *Japan* 40°13N 141°17E 220 D10
Ichinomiya *Gifu, Japan* 35°18N 136°48E 223 B8
Ichinomiya *Kumamoto, Japan* 32°58N 131°5E 222 E3
Ichinoseki *Japan* 38°55N 141°8E 220 E10
Ichkeul △ *Tunisia* 37°9N 9°37E 258 A1
Ichnya *Ukraine* 50°52N 32°24E 189 G7
Icht *Morocco* 29°6N 8°54W 260 C3
Ichu *Taiwan* 23°20N 120°14E 225 C2
Ichun = Yichun *China* 47°44N 128°52E 219 B14
Ickenham *U.K.* 51°33N 0°26W 125 A1
Icó *Brazil* 6°24S 38°51W 332 C4
Icoca *Angola* 6°12S 16°20E 265 D3
Icod *Canary Is.* 28°22N 16°43W 153 e1
İçoğuz *Turkmenistan* 40°11N 58°24E 216 D5
Iconi *Comoros Is.* 12°21S 43°51E 272 a
Icoraci *Brazil* 1°18S 48°28W 332 B2
Icy C. *U.S.A.* 70°20N 161°52W 303 A7
Ida Grove *U.S.A.* 42°21N 95°28W 308 D6
Idan *Somalia* 6°10N 48°55E 267 C6
Idabel *U.S.A.* 33°54N 94°50W 314 E7
Idaga Hamus *Ethiopia* 14°13N 39°48E 257 E4
Idah *Nigeria* 7°5N 6°40E 263 D6
Idaho □ *U.S.A.* 45°0N 115°0W 304 D6
Idaho City *U.S.A.* 43°50N 115°50W 304 E6
Idaho Falls *U.S.A.* 43°30N 112°2W 304 E7
Idalia △ *Australia* 24°49S 144°36E 280 C3
Idanha-a-Nova *Portugal* 39°50N 7°15W 194 F3
Idar-Oberstein *Germany* 49°43N 7°16E 179 F3
Iday *Niger* 14°54N 11°33E 263 C7
'Idd el Ghanam *Sudan* 11°30N 24°19E 259 F4
Iddo *Nigeria* 6°28N 3°22E 124 B2
Idelès *Algeria* 23°50N 5°53E 261 D6
Idensalmi = Iisalmi *Finland* 63°32N 27°10E 160 E22
Idfû *Egypt* 24°55N 32°49E 256 C3
Ídhra = Hydra *Greece* 37°20N 23°28E 204 D5
Idi *Indonesia* 5°2N 97°37E 234 A1
Idi, Oros = Psiloritis, Oros *Greece* 35°15N 24°45E 207 E5
Idi Amin Dada, L. = Edward, L. *Africa* 0°25S 29°40E 268 C2
Idi-Oro *Nigeria* 6°31N 3°21E 124 A2
Idil *Turkey* 37°20N 41°53E 213 D9
Idiofa *Dem. Rep. of the Congo* 4°55S 19°42E 265 C3
Idjil = Fdérik *Mauritania* 22°40N 12°45W 260 D2
Idkerberget *Sweden* 60°22N 15°15E 162 D9
Idku *Egypt* 31°18N 30°17E 256 H7
Idku, Bahra el *Egypt* 31°18N 30°18E 256 H7
Idlib *Syria* 35°55N 36°36E 250 C7
Idlib □ *Syria* 35°45N 36°45E 250 C7
Idre *Sweden* 61°52N 12°42E 162 C6
Idria *U.S.A.* 36°25N 120°41W 306 J6
Idrija *Slovenia* 46°0N 14°5E 199 C11
Idritsa *Russia* 56°17N 28°53E 188 D5
Idutywa = Dutywa *S. Africa* 32°8S 28°18E 271 D4
Ie Shima *Japan* 26°43N 127°47E 288 a
Ie Suido *Japan* 26°42N 127°51E 288 a
Ieper *Belgium* 50°51N 2°53E 170 D2
Ierapetra *Greece* 35°1N 25°44E 207 F6
Ierissos *Greece* 40°22N 23°52E 202 F7
Ierissos Kolpos *Greece* 40°27N 23°57E 202 F7
Iernut *Romania* 46°27N 24°15E 183 D9
Ieshima-Shotō *Japan* 34°40N 134°32E 222 C6
Iesi *Italy* 43°31N 13°14E 199 E10
Iésolo *Italy* 45°32N 12°38E 199 C9
Iet *Ethiopia* 4°33N 43°1E 267 D5
Ifac, Penyal d' *Spain* 38°38N 0°5E 197 G5
'Ifāl, W. al → *Si. Arabia* 28°7N 35°3E 251 K6
Ifanadiana *Madag.* 21°19S 47°39E 272 C2
Ife *Nigeria* 7°30N 4°31E 263 D5
Iférouâne *Niger* 19°5N 8°24E 259 E1
Ifetesene *Algeria* 25°30N 4°33E 261 C5
Iffley *Australia* 18°53S 141°12E 280 B3
Ifon *Nigeria* 6°58N 5°40E 263 D6
Iforas, Adrar des *Africa* 19°40N 1°40E 261 D5
Ifould, L. *Australia* 30°52S 132°6E 279 F5
Ifrane *Morocco* 33°33N 5°7W 260 B3
Ifugao □ *Phil.* 16°40N 121°10E 232 C3
Iga *Japan* 34°45N 136°10E 223 C8
Igalo *Montenegro* 42°28N 18°30E 202 D2
Iganga *Uganda* 0°37N 33°28E 268 B3
Iganmu *Nigeria* 6°28N 3°22E 124 B2
Igara-Paraná → *Colombia* 2°9S 71°47W 328 D3
Igarapava *Brazil* 20°3S 47°47W 333 F2
Igarapé-Açu *Brazil* 1°4S 47°33W 332 B2
Igarapé-Miri *Brazil* 1°59S 48°58W 332 B2
Igarka *Russia* 67°30N 86°33E 214 C9
Igatpuri *India* 19°40N 73°35E 244 E1
Igbetti *Nigeria* 8°44N 4°8E 263 D5
Igbo-Ora *Nigeria* 7°29N 3°15E 263 D5
Igbobi *Nigeria* 6°31N 3°22E 124 A2
Igboho *Nigeria* 8°53N 3°50E 263 D5
Igbologun *Nigeria* 6°24N 3°19E 124 B1
Igbor *Nigeria* 7°27N 8°36E 263 D6
Iğdır *Turkey* 39°55N 44°2E 213 C11
Igelfors *Sweden* 58°52N 15°41E 163 F9
Iggesund *Sweden* 61°39N 17°10E 162 C11
Ighil Izane = Relizane *Algeria* 35°44N 0°31E 261 A5
Igiugig *U.S.A.* 59°20N 155°55W 303 G9
Iglau = Jihlava *Czech Rep.* 49°28N 15°35E 180 B8
Iglésias *Italy* 39°19N 8°32E 200 C1
Igli *Algeria* 30°25N 2°19W 261 B4
Igloolik = Iglulik *Canada* 69°20N 81°49W 295 D15
Iglulgaarjuk = Chesterfield Inlet *Canada* 63°30N 90°45W 294 E13
Iglulik *Canada* 69°20N 81°49W 295 D15
'Igma, G. el *Egypt* 29°10N 34°0E 251 J5
Ignace *Canada* 49°30N 91°40W 298 C1
İğneada *Turkey* 41°52N 27°59E 203 E11
İğneada Burnu *Turkey* 41°53N 28°2E 203 E12
Igny *France* 48°44N 2°13E 134 B2
Igoumenitsa *Greece* 39°32N 20°18E 206 B10
Igrim *Russia* 63°12N 64°30E 214 C7
Iguaçu → *Brazil* 25°36S 54°36W 335 B5
Iguaçu, Cat. del *Brazil* 25°41S 54°26W 335 B5
Iguaçu △ *Brazil* 25°30S 54°0W 335 B5
Iguaçu Falls = Iguaçu, Cat. del *Brazil* 25°41S 54°26W 335 B5
Iguala *Mexico* 18°21N 99°32W 319 D5
Igualada *Spain* 41°37N 1°37E 196 D6
Iguape *Brazil* 24°43S 47°33W 333 F2
Iguaratinga = São Francisco do Maranhão *Brazil* 6°15S 42°52W 332 C3
Iguassu = Iguaçu → *Brazil* 25°36S 54°36W 335 B5
Iguatu *Brazil* 6°20S 39°18W 332 C4
Iguazú △ *Argentina* 25°42S 54°22W 335 B5
Iguéla *Gabon* 2°0S 9°16E 264 C1
Iguéla, Lagune *Gabon* 1°48S 9°16E 264 C2
Iguidi, Erg *Africa* 27°0N 6°0W 260 C3
Iguig *Phil.* 17°45N 121°44E 232 C3
Igumen = Cherven *Belarus* 53°45N 28°28E 177 B15
Iharana *Madag.* 13°25S 50°0E 272 A3
Ihavandiffulu Atoll *Maldives* 7°0N 72°50E 272 d
Ihbulag *Mongolia* 43°11N 107°10E 226 C4
Iheya-Shima *Japan* 27°4N 127°58E 221 L3
Ihiala *Nigeria* 5°51N 6°55E 263 D6
Ihirene → *Algeria* 20°28N 4°37E 261 D5
Ihosy *Madag.* 22°24S 46°8E 272 C2
Ihotry, Farihy *Madag.* 21°56S 43°41E 272 C1
Ihu *Papua N. G.* 7°55S 145°24E 286 D3
Ihugh *Nigeria* 7°2N 9°0E 263 D6
Ii *Finland* 65°19N 25°22E 160 D21
Ii-Shima *Japan* 26°43N 127°47E 221 L3
Iida *Japan* 35°35N 137°50E 223 B9
Iijoki → *Finland* 65°20N 25°20E 160 D21
Iisalmi *Finland* 63°32N 27°10E 160 E22
Iiyama *Japan* 36°51N 138°22E 221 F9
Iizuka *Japan* 33°38N 130°42E 222 D2
IJ, Het → *Neths.* 52°23N 4°54E 112 A2
IJ-meer *Neths.* 52°23N 4°54E 112 A3
Ijâfene *Mauritania* 20°40N 8°0W 260 D3
Ijebu-Igbo *Nigeria* 6°56N 4°1E 263 D5
Ijebu-Ode *Nigeria* 6°47N 3°58E 263 D5
Ijesa-Tedo *Nigeria* 6°29N 3°19E 124 B1
Ijevan *Armenia* 40°52N 45°8E 191 K7
Ijill, Sebkhet *Mauritania* 22°47N 12°53W 260 D2
IJmuiden *Neths.* 52°28N 4°35E 170 B4
Ijo älv = Iijoki → *Finland* 65°20N 25°20E 160 D21
Ijora *Nigeria* 6°27N 3°22E 124 B2
IJssel → *Neths.* 52°35N 5°50E 170 B5
IJsselmeer *Neths.* 52°45N 5°20E 170 B5
Ijuí *Brazil* 28°23S 53°55W 335 B5
Ijuí → *Brazil* 27°58S 55°20W 335 B4
Ijûin *Japan* 31°37N 130°24E 222 F2
Ikalamavony *Madag.* 21°9S 46°35E 272 C2
Ikali *Dem. Rep. of the Congo* 2°2S 21°4E 264 C4
Ikamatua *N.Z.* 42°16S 171°41E 285 C6
Ikang *Nigeria* 4°49N 8°30E 263 E6
Ikanga *Kenya* 1°42S 38°4E 268 C4
Ikara *Nigeria* 11°12N 8°15E 263 C6
Ikare *Nigeria* 7°32N 5°40E 263 D6
Ikaria *Greece* 37°35N 26°10E 205 D8
Ikast *Denmark* 56°8N 9°10E 163 H3
Ikebe *Japan* 35°31N 139°34E 140 B2
Ikebukuro *Japan* 35°43N 139°42E 140 A3
Ikeda *Japan* 34°1N 133°48E 222 C5
Ikegami *Japan* 35°34N 139°42E 140 B3
Ikei-shima *Japan* 26°23N 127°59E 288 a
Ikeja *Nigeria* 6°36N 3°21E 124 A2
Ikela *Dem. Rep. of the Congo* 1°6S 23°6E 264 C4
Ikélemba *Congo* 1°12N 16°38E 264 B3
Ikélemba → *Dem. Rep. of the Congo* 0°7N 18°17E 264 B3
Ikengo *Dem. Rep. of the Congo* 0°8S 18°8E 264 C3
Ikere *Nigeria* 7°25N 5°19E 263 D6
Ikeuchi *Japan* 34°35N 135°32E 133 B2
Ikhtiman *Bulgaria* 42°27N 23°48E 202 D7
Iki *Japan* 33°45N 129°42E 222 D1
Iki-Kaikyō *Japan* 33°40N 129°45E 222 D1

Ikimba L. Tanzania 1°30S 31°20E 268 C3
Ikire Nigeria 7°23N 4°15E 263 D5
Ikitsuki-Shima Japan 33°23N 129°26E 222 D1
İkizdere Turkey 40°46N 40°32E 213 B9
Iko Congo 0°35S 16°0E 264 C3
Ikom Nigeria 6°0N 8°42E 263 D6
Ikoma Japan 34°30N 135°40E 223 C7
Ikomu
Dem. Rep. of the Congo 1°54S 19°40E 264 C3
Ikongo Madag. 21°52S 47°27E 272 C2
Ikopa → Madag. 16°45S 46°40E 272 B2
Ikorodu Nigeria 6°35N 3°29E 124 A2
Ikorongo ⌓ Tanzania 1°50S 34°53E 268 C3
Ikot Ekpene Nigeria 5°12N 7°40E 263 D6
Ikoyi Nigeria 6°27N 3°26E 124 B2
Ikparjuk = Arctic Bay
Canada 73°1N 85°7W 295 C14
Iksan S. Korea 35°59N 127°0E 224 E3
Ikuata Nigeria 6°24N 3°21E 124 B2
Ikungu Tanzania 1°33S 33°42E 268 C3
Ikuno Hyōgo, Japan 35°10N 134°48E 222 B6
Ikuno Ōsaka, Japan 34°40N 135°30E 133 A2
Ikuntji = Haasts Bluff
Australia 23°22S 132°0E 278 D5
Ikurun Nigeria 7°54N 4°40E 263 D5
Ikuta Japan 35°36N 139°32E 140 B2
Il-Kullana Malta 35°50N 14°24E 206 F7
Il-Munxar Malta 35°51N 14°34E 206 F8
Ila Dem. Rep. of the Congo 2°53S 21°7E 264 C4
Ila Nigeria 8°0N 4°39E 263 D5
Ila Oslo, Norway 59°57N 10°35E 133 A2
Ilafer Algeria 21°40N 1°58E 261 D5
Ilagan Phil. 17°7N 121°53E 232 C3
Ilaka Madag. 19°33S 48°52E 272 B2
Īlām Iran 33°36N 46°36E 213 F12
Ilam Nepal 26°58N 87°58E 243 F12
Īlām □ Iran 33°0N 47°0E 246 C5
Ilan Taiwan 24°45N 121°44E 225 B3
Ilan □ Taiwan 24°30N 121°35E 225 B3
Ilan, Mt. Phil. 10°26N 119°33E 233 F2
Ilanskiy Russia 56°14N 96°3E 215 D10
Ilaro Nigeria 6°53N 3°3E 263 D5
Ilatane Niger 16°30N 4°45E 263 B5
Ilave Peru 16°5S 69°40W 330 D4
Iława Poland 53°36N 19°34E 184 E6
Ilayangudi India 9°34N 78°37E 245 K4
Ile → Kazakhstan 45°53N 77°10E 217 C9
Île-à-la-Crosse Canada 55°27N 107°53W 297 B7
Île-à-la-Crosse, Lac
Canada 55°40N 107°45W 297 B7
Île-de-France □ France 49°0N 2°20E 173 D9
Ileanda Romania 47°20N 23°38E 183 C8
Ilebo Dem. Rep. of the Congo 4°17S 20°55E 265 C4
Ilek Russia 51°32N 53°21E 216 B4
Ilek → Russia 51°30N 53°22E 186 D9
Iler, O. → Algeria 20°59N 3°14E 261 D5
Ilero Nigeria 8°0N 3°20E 263 D5
Ilesha Kwara, Nigeria 8°57N 3°28E 263 D5
Ilesha Oyo, Nigeria 7°37N 4°40E 263 D5
Ilet = Krasnogorskiy
Russia 56°10N 48°28E 190 B9
Iletskaya = Sol Iletsk
Russia 51°10N 55°0E 186 D10
Iletsky Gorodok = Ilek
Russia 51°32N 53°21E 216 B4
Ilford Man., Canada 56°4N 95°35W 297 B9
Ilford London, U.K. 51°33N 0°4E 125 A4
Ilfracombe Queens.,
Australia 23°30S 144°30E 280 C3
Ilfracombe Devon, U.K. 51°12N 4°8W 169 F3
Ilgaz Turkey 40°55N 33°37E 212 B5
Ilgaz Dağları Turkey 41°10N 33°50E 212 B5
Ilgın Turkey 38°16N 31°55E 212 C4
Ilha, Pta. da Azores 38°25N 28°3W 153 d1
Ilha Grande Brazil 0°27S 65°2W 329 D4
Ilha Grande, B. da Brazil 23°9S 44°30W 333 F3
Ilha Grande, Represa
Brazil 23°10S 53°5W 335 A5
Ilha Grande △ Brazil 23°10S 53°20W 335 A5
Ílhavo Portugal 40°33N 8°43W 194 E2
Ilhéus Brazil 14°49S 39°2W 333 D4
Ili = Ile → Kazakhstan 45°53N 77°10E 217 C9
Ilia Romania 45°57N 22°40E 182 E7
Ilía □ Greece 37°45N 21°35E 204 D3
Iliamna U.S.A. 59°45N 154°55W 303 G9
Iliamna L. U.S.A. 59°30N 155°0W 303 G9
Ilias, Profitis Greece 36°17N 27°56E 206 E11
Iliç Turkey 39°27N 38°33E 213 C8
Ilıca Turkey 39°52N 27°46E 205 B9
Ilig, Ras Somalia 7°47N 49°50E 267 C6
Iligan Phil. 8°12N 124°13E 233 G5
Iligan B. Phil. 8°25N 124°5E 233 G5
Iligan Pt. Phil. 18°25N 122°25E 232 B4
Ilin I. Phil. 12°14N 121°5E 232 E3
ʻĪlio Pt. U.S.A. 21°13N 157°16W 302 B4
Ilion U.S.A. 43°1N 75°2W 313 D9
Ilioupoli Greece 37°54N 23°47E 112 B2
Ilirska-Bistrica Slovenia 45°34N 14°14E 199 C11
Iliwa = Rewa → Guyana 3°19N 58°42W 329 C6
Iliysk = Qapshaghay
Kazakhstan 43°51N 77°14E 217 D9
Ilkal India 15°57N 76°8E 245 G3
Ilkenau = Olkusz Poland 50°18N 19°33E 185 H6
Ilkeston U.K. 52°58N 1°19W 168 E6
Ilkley U.K. 53°56N 1°48W 168 D6
Illampu = Ancohuma, Nevado
Bolivia 16°0S 68°50W 330 D4
Illana B. Phil. 7°35N 123°45E 233 H4
Illapel Chile 32°0S 71°10W 334 C1
Ille-et-Vilaine □ France 48°10N 1°30W 172 D5
Ille-sur-Têt France 42°40N 2°38E 174 F6
Illéla Niger 14°32N 5°20E 263 C6
Iller → Germany 48°23N 9°58E 179 G5
Illertissen Germany 48°12N 10°7E 179 G6
Illescas Spain 40°8N 3°51W 194 E7
Illetas Spain 39°32N 2°35E 206 B3
Illichivsk Ukraine 46°20N 30°35E 189 J6
Illiers-Combray France 48°18N 1°15E 172 D8
Illimani, Nevado Bolivia 16°30S 67°50W 330 D4
Illinois □ U.S.A. 40°15N 89°30W 310 D7
Illinois → U.S.A. 38°58N 90°28W 310 F6
Illinois at Chicago, Univ. of
U.S.A. 41°52N 87°38W 119 B3
Illinois Institute of Technology
U.S.A. 41°50N 87°37W 119 B3
Illiopolis U.S.A. 39°51N 89°15W 310 E7
Illium = Troy Turkey 39°57N 26°12E 205 B8
Illizi Algeria 26°31N 8°32E 261 C6
Illizi □ Algeria 26°50N 8°10E 261 C6
Illkirch-Graffenstaden
France 48°34N 7°42E 173 D14
Íllora Spain 37°17N 3°53W 195 H7
Ilm → Germany 51°6N 11°40E 178 D7
Ilma, L. Australia 29°13S 127°46E 279 E4
Ilmajoki Finland 62°44N 22°34E 160 E20
Ilmen, Ozero Russia 58°15N 31°10E 188 C6
Ilmenau = Jordanów
Poland 49°41N 19°49E 185 J6
Ilmenau = Limanowa
Poland 49°42N 20°22E 185 J7
Ilmenau Germany 50°41N 10°54E 178 E6
Ilnytsya Ukraine 48°21N 23°5E 182 B8
Ilo Peru 17°40S 71°20W 330 D3
Ilobu Nigeria 7°45N 4°25E 263 D5
Iloc I. Phil. 11°17N 119°40E 233 F2
Ilocos Norte □ Phil. 18°10N 120°45E 232 B3
Ilocos Sur □ Phil. 17°20N 120°35E 232 C3
Iloilo Phil. 10°45N 122°33E 233 F4
Iloilo □ Phil. 11°0N 122°40E 233 F4
Ilomantsi Finland 62°38N 30°57E 160 E24
Ilora Nigeria 7°45N 3°50E 263 D5
Ilorin Nigeria 8°30N 4°35E 263 D5
Ilovatka Russia 50°30N 45°50E 190 E7
Ilovlya Russia 49°15N 44°2E 191 F7
Ilovlya → Russia 49°14N 44°10E 191 F7
Iłowa Poland 51°30N 15°10E 185 G2
Ilpendam Neths. 52°28N 4°57E 112 A2
Ilsos → Greece 37°55N 23°41E 112 B2
Ilubabor Ethiopia 7°25N 35°0E 257 F4
Ilulissat Greenland 69°12N 51°10W 154 D5
Ilva Mică Romania 47°17N 24°40E 183 C9
Ilwaco U.S.A. 46°19N 124°3W 306 D2
Ilyichevsk = Illichivsk
Ukraine 46°20N 30°35E 189 J6
Iłża Poland 51°10N 21°15E 185 G8
Iłżanka → Poland 51°14N 21°48E 185 G8
Imabari Japan 34°4N 133°0E 222 C5
Imagem e do Som, Museu da
Rio de J., Brazil 135 b3
Imaichi Japan 36°43N 139°46E 223 A11
Imaloto → Madag. 23°27S 45°13E 272 C2
İmamoğlu Turkey 37°15N 35°38E 212 D6
Iman = Dalnerechensk
Russia 45°50N 133°40E 220 B6
Imandra, Ozero Russia 67°30N 33°0E 160 C25
Imanombo Madag. 24°26S 45°49E 272 C2
Imari Japan 33°15N 129°52E 222 D1
Imasa Sudan 18°0N 36°12E 256 D4
Imathia □ Greece 40°30N 22°15E 202 F6
Imatra Finland 61°12N 28°48E 188 B5
Imbâbah Egypt 30°3N 31°12E 117 A2
Imbabura □ Ecuador 0°30N 78°45W 328 C2
Imbaimadai Guyana 5°44N 60°17W 329 B5
Imbiah Lookout Singapore 1°16N 103°49E 138 B2
Imbonga
Dem. Rep. of the Congo 0°43S 19°44E 264 C3
Iménas Mali 16°20N 0°40E 263 B5
imeni 26 Bakinskikh Komissarov =
Neftçala Azerbaijan 39°19N 49°12E 213 C13
imeni 26 Bakinskikh Komissarov
Turkmenistan 39°22N 54°10E 247 B7
imeni Dvadtsati Shesti Bakinskikh
Komissarov = Neftçala
Azerbaijan 39°19N 49°12E 213 C13
imeni Dzerzhinskogo =
Naryan-Mar Russia 67°42N 53°12E 186 A9
imeni Ismail Samani, Pik
Tajikistan 39°0N 72°2E 217 E8
imeni Mikoyana = Kara-Balta
Kyrgyzstan 42°50N 73°49E 217 D8
imeni Petrovskogo G.I. =
Horodyshche Ukraine 49°17N 31°27E 189 H6
imeni Sverdlova = Sverdlovsk
Ukraine 48°5N 39°47E 189 H10
imeni Tovarishcha Khateyevicha =
Synelnykove Ukraine 48°25N 35°30E 189 H8
imeni Tretyego Internatsionala =
Novoshakhtinsk
Russia 47°46N 39°58E 189 J10
Imeri, Serra Brazil 0°50N 65°25W 328 C4
Imerimandroso Madag. 17°26S 48°35E 272 B2
Imese Dem. Rep. of the Congo 2°6N 18°9E 264 B3
Imfolozi ⌓ S. Africa 28°18S 31°50E 271 C5
Imi Ethiopia 6°28N 42°10E 257 F5
Imielin Poland 52°9N 21°0E 143 C2
Imirim Brazil 23°29S 46°39W 137 A2
Imishly = İmişli Azerbaijan 39°55N 48°4E 191 L9
İmişli Azerbaijan 39°55N 48°4E 191 L9
Imitek Morocco 29°43N 8°10W 260 C3
Imitos Greece 37°55N 23°45E 112 B2
Imitos, Oros Greece 37°53N 23°48E 112 B2
Imizu Japan 36°47N 137°4E 223 A9
Imjado S. Korea 35°5N 126°5E 224 E3
Imjin-gang → N. Korea 37°47N 126°39E 224 D3
Imlay U.S.A. 40°40N 118°9W 304 F4
Imlay City U.S.A. 43°2N 83°5W 312 D1
Immaseri Sudan 15°40N 25°31E 257 D2
Immenstadt Germany 47°33N 10°13E 179 H6
Immingham U.K. 53°37N 0°13W 168 D7
Immokalee U.S.A. 26°25N 81°25W 317 J8
Imo □ Nigeria 5°30N 7°10E 263 D6
Imo → Nigeria 4°36N 7°35E 263 E6
Ímola Italy 44°20N 11°42E 199 D8
Imotski Croatia 43°27N 17°12E 199 E14
Impé Congo 2°45S 15°16E 264 C3
Imperatorskaya Gavan = Vanino
Russia 48°50N 140°5E 215 E15
Imperatriz Amazonas, Brazil 5°18S 67°11W 330 B4
Imperatriz Maranhão,
Brazil 5°30S 47°29W 332 C2
Impéria Italy 43°53N 8°3E 198 E5
Imperial Sask., Canada 51°21N 105°28W 297 C7
Imperial Peru 13°4S 76°21W 330 C2
Imperial Calif., U.S.A. 32°51N 115°34W 307 N11
Imperial Nebr., U.S.A. 40°31N 101°39W 308 E3
Imperial Beach U.S.A. 32°35N 117°6W 307 N9
Imperial Dam U.S.A. 32°55N 114°25W 307 N12
Imperial Palace = Paço Imperial
Rio de J., Brazil 135 a2
Imperial Palace Museum Beijing, China 114 b3
Imperial Res. U.S.A. 32°53N 114°28W 307 N12
Imperial Valley U.S.A. 33°0N 115°30W 307 N11
Imperieuse Reef Australia 17°36S 118°50E 278 C2
Impfondo Congo 1°40N 18°0E 264 B3
Imphal India 24°48N 93°56E 241 C4
Imphy France 46°55N 3°16E 173 F10
Impulo Angola 13°51S 13°39E 265 E2
İmranlı Turkey 39°54N 38°7E 213 C8
İmroz = Gökçeada Turkey 40°10N 25°50E 203 F9
Imst Austria 47°15N 10°44E 180 D3
Imuris Mexico 30°47N 110°52W 318 A2
Imuruan B. Phil. 10°40N 119°10E 233 F2
Imus Phil. 14°26N 120°56E 232 D3
In Aleï Mali 17°42N 2°30W 262 B4
In Amenas Algeria 28°5N 9°33E 261 C6
In Amguel Algeria 23°41N 5°9E 261 D6
In Atei Algeria 20°33N 6°4E 261 D6
In Belbel Algeria 27°55N 1°12E 261 C5
In Delimane Mali 15°52N 1°31E 263 B5
In Ghar Algeria 27°10N 1°59E 261 C5
In Guezzam Algeria 19°37N 5°52E 261 E6
In Koufi Mali 19°11N 1°25E 263 B5
In Salah Algeria 27°10N 2°32E 261 C5
In Tallak Mali 16°19N 3°15E 263 B5
In Tebezas Mali 17°49N 1°53E 263 B5
Ina Japan 35°50N 137°55E 223 B9
Ina Ill., U.S.A. 38°9N 88°54W 311 F8
Ina-Bonchi Japan 35°45N 137°58E 223 B9
Inabanga Phil. 10°2N 124°4E 233 F5
Inaccessible I. Atl. Oc. 37°18S 12°40W 152 K10
Inagauan Phil. 9°33N 118°39E 233 G2
Inagi Japan 35°38N 139°31E 140 B2
Inajá Brazil 8°54S 37°49W 332 C4
Inambari → Peru 12°41S 69°44W 330 C4
Inangahua N.Z. 41°52S 171°59E 285 B6
Inanwatan Indonesia 2°8S 132°10E 231 E8
Iñapari Peru 11°0S 69°40W 330 C4
Inarajan Guam 13°16N 144°45E 302 d
Inari Finland 68°54N 27°1E 160 B22
Inarijärvi Finland 69°0N 28°0E 160 B23
Inawashiro-Ko Japan 37°29N 140°6E 220 F10
Inazawa Japan 35°15N 136°47E 223 B8
Inbhear Mór, An = Arklow
Ireland 52°48N 6°10W 166 D5
Inbin Burma 18°6N 95°16E 241 F5
Inca Spain 39°43N 2°54E 206 B3
Inca de Oro Chile 26°45S 69°54W 334 B2
Incahuasi Argentina 27°2S 68°18W 334 B2
Incahuasi Chile 29°12S 71°5W 334 B1
İnce Burun Turkey 42°7N 34°56E 212 A6
İncekum Burnu Turkey 36°13N 33°57E 250 B4
İncesu Turkey 38°38N 35°11E 212 C6
Inchcolm U.K. 56°2N 3°18W 121 A2
Incheon S. Korea 37°27N 126°40E 224 D3
Inchicore Ireland 53°20N 6°20W 120 A1
Inchiri □ Mauritania 20°0N 15°0W 260 E2
Inchkeith U.K. 56°2N 3°8W 121 A3
Inchmickery U.K. 56°0N 3°16W 121 A2
Incio = A Cruz do Incio
Spain 42°39N 7°21W 194 C3
Incirano Italy 45°34N 9°9E 128 A1
İncirliova Turkey 37°50N 27°41E 205 D9
Incline Village U.S.A. 39°10N 119°58W 306 F7
Incomáti → Mozam. 25°46S 32°43E 271 C5
Incudine, Mte. France 41°50N 9°12E 175 G13
Inda Silase Ethiopia 14°10N 38°15E 257 E4
Indal Sweden 62°35N 17°5E 162 B11
Indalsälven → Sweden 62°36N 17°30E 162 B11
Indaw Burma 24°15N 96°5E 241 C6
Indawgyi In Burma 25°8N 96°20E 241 C6
Indbir Ethiopia 8°7N 37°52E 257 F4
Indefatigable, I. = Santa Cruz, I.
Ecuador 0°38S 90°23W 330 a
Independence Calif.,
U.S.A. 36°48N 118°12W 306 J8
Independence Iowa,
U.S.A. 42°28N 91°54W 310 B5
Independence Kans.,
U.S.A. 37°14N 95°42W 308 G6
Independence Ky.,
U.S.A. 38°57N 84°33W 311 F12
Independence Mo., U.S.A. 39°6N 94°25W 310 E2
Independence Avenue
Washington, D.C., U.S.A. 143 c2
Independence Fjord
Greenland 82°10N 29°0W 154 A8
Independence Mts.
U.S.A. 41°20N 116°0W 304 F5
Independência Brazil 5°23S 40°19W 332 C3
Independencia Santiago,
Chile 33°25S 70°39W 137 B2
Independencia Lima, Peru 11°59S 77°3W 124 A2
Independencia, I. Peru 14°16S 76°12W 330 C2
Independenţa Romania 45°25N 27°42E 183 E12
Inderbor Kazakhstan 48°33N 51°47E 216 C4
Index U.S.A. 47°50N 121°33W 306 C5
Indi India 17°10N 75°58E 244 F2
India ■ Asia 20°0N 78°0E 239 F11
India Gate Delhi, India 120 c2
Indialantic U.S.A. 28°6N 80°34W 317 G9
Indian → U.S.A. 27°59N 80°34W 317 G9
Indian Cabins Canada 59°52N 117°40W 296 B5
Indian Creek Village
U.S.A. 25°52N 80°8W 129 C3
Indian Harbour Canada 54°27N 57°13W 299 B8
Indian Harbour Beach
U.S.A. 28°10N 80°35W 317 G9
Indian Head Canada 50°30N 103°41W 297 C8
Indian L. U.S.A. 43°46N 74°16W 313 C10
Indian Lake U.S.A. 43°47N 74°16W 313 C10
Indian Ocean 5°0S 75°0E 273 E6
Indian Rocks Beach
U.S.A. 27°52N 82°51W 317 H7
Indian Springs U.S.A. 36°35N 115°40W 307 J11
Indian Town Pt.
Antigua & B. 17°6N 61°40W 322 b
Indian Walk Trin. & Tob. 10°16N 61°20W 323 t
Indiana U.S.A. 40°37N 79°9W 312 F5
Indiana □ U.S.A. 40°0N 86°0W 311 E11
Indiana Dunes ⌓ U.S.A. 41°40N 87°0W 311 C9
Indianapolis U.S.A. 39°46N 86°9W 311 E10
Indianapolis Int. ✈ (IND)
U.S.A. 39°43N 86°17W 311 E10
Indianola Iowa, U.S.A. 41°22N 93°34W 310 C3
Indianola Miss., U.S.A. 33°27N 90°39W 315 E9
Indianópolis Brazil 23°35S 46°38W 137 B2
Indiantown U.S.A. 27°1N 80°28W 317 H9
Indiapora Brazil 19°57S 50°17W 333 E1
Indiga Russia 67°38N 49°9E 186 A8
Indigirka → Russia 70°48N 148°54E 215 B15
Inđija Serbia 45°6N 20°7E 182 E5
Indio U.S.A. 33°43N 116°13W 307 M10
Indira Gandhi Canal India 28°0N 72°0E 242 F5
Indira Gandhi Int. ✈ (DEL)
India 28°34N 77°5E 120 B1
Indira Pt. India 6°44N 93°49E 245 L11
Indira Sagar India 22°15N 76°40E 242 H7
Indispensable Str.
Solomon Is. 9°0S 160°30E 287 M11
Indo-China Asia 15°0N 102°0E 210 G12
Indonesia ■ Asia 5°0S 115°0E 235 C4
Indore India 22°42N 75°53E 242 H6
Indramayu Indonesia 6°20S 108°19E 235 D3
Indrapura = Kerinci
Indonesia 1°40S 101°15E 234 C2
Indravati → India 19°20N 80°20E 244 E5
Indre □ France 46°50N 1°39E 173 F8
Indre → France 47°16N 0°11E 172 E7
Indre Ålvik Norway 60°26N 6°26E 164 D3
Indre Arna Norway 60°26N 5°30E 164 D2
Indre-et-Loire □ France 47°20N 0°40E 172 E7
Indrio U.S.A. 27°31N 80°21W 317 H9
Indulkana Australia 26°58S 133°5E 281 D1
Indungo Angola 14°48S 16°17E 265 E3
Indura Belarus 53°26N 23°53E 184 E10
Indus → Pakistan 24°20N 67°47E 242 G2
Indus, Mouths of the
Pakistan 24°0N 68°0E 242 H3
Industria S. Africa 26°11S 27°58E 123 B1
Industrial Canal U.S.A. 30°4N 90°4W 131 A2
Industry U.S.A. 40°20N 90°36W 310 D6
İnebolu Turkey 41°55N 33°40E 212 B5
İnecik Turkey 40°56N 27°16E 203 F11
İnegöl Turkey 40°5N 29°31E 203 F13
Inés, Mt. Argentina 48°30S 69°40W 336 C3
Ineu Romania 46°26N 21°51E 182 D6
Inezgane Morocco 30°25N 9°29W 260 B3
Infanta Phil. 14°45N 121°39E 232 D3
Infantes = Villanueva de los
Infantes Spain 38°43N 3°1W 195 G7
Infiernillo, Presa del
Mexico 18°35N 101°50W 318 D4
Infiesto Spain 43°21N 5°21W 194 B5
Inga, Barrage d'
Dem. Rep. of the Congo 5°39S 13°39E 265 D2
Ingabu Burma 17°37N 95°20E 241 G5
Inganda
Dem. Rep. of the Congo 0°5S 20°57E 264 C4
Ingapirca Ecuador 2°38S 78°56W 328 D2
Ingarö Sweden 59°12N 18°45E 162 E12
Ingelstad Sweden 56°45N 14°56E 163 H8
Ingende
Dem. Rep. of the Congo 0°12S 18°57E 264 C3
Ingeniero Jacobacci
Argentina 41°20S 69°36W 336 B3
Ingenio Canary Is. 27°55N 15°26W 153 e1
Ingenio Santa Ana
Argentina 27°25S 65°40W 334 B2
Ingersoll Canada 43°4N 80°55W 312 C4
Ingham Australia 18°43S 146°10E 280 B4
Ingierstrand Norway 59°49N 10°46E 133 B3
Ingleborough U.K. 54°10N 2°22W 168 C5
Inglefield Land Greenland 78°30N 70°0W 154 B4
Inglewood Queens.,
Australia 28°25S 151°2E 281 D5
Inglewood Vic., Australia 36°29S 143°53E 282 D5
Inglewood N.Z. 39°9S 174°14E 284 F3
Inglewood Calif., U.S.A. 33°58N 118°21W 126 C3
Inglis U.S.A. 29°2N 82°40W 317 F7
Ingliston U.K. 55°56N 3°23W 121 B1
Ingolf Fjord Greenland 80°35N 17°30W 154 A9
Ingólfshöfði Iceland 63°48N 16°39W 155 D10
Ingolstadt Germany 48°46N 11°26E 179 G7
Ingomar U.S.A. 46°35N 107°23W 304 C10
Ingonish Canada 46°42N 60°18W 299 C7
Ingore Guinea-Biss. 12°24N 15°48W 262 C1
Ingraj Bazar India 24°58N 88°10E 243 G13
Ingrid Christensen Coast
Antarctica 69°30S 76°0E 151 C6
Ingul = Inhul → Ukraine 46°50N 32°0E 189 J7
Ingulec = Inhulec Ukraine 47°42N 33°14E 189 J7
Ingulets = Inhulets →
Ukraine 46°46N 32°47E 189 J7
Inguri = Enguri →
Georgia 42°27N 41°38E 191 J5
Ingushetia □ Russia 43°20N 44°50E 191 J7
Ingwavuma S. Africa 27°9S 31°59E 271 C5
Inhaca Mozam. 26°1S 32°57E 271 C5
Inhaca Pen. Mozam. 26°13S 32°55E 271 C5
Inhafenga Mozam. 20°36S 33°53E 271 B5
Inhambane Mozam. 23°54S 35°30E 271 C6
Inhambane □ Mozam. 22°30S 34°20E 271 B5
Inhambupe Brazil 11°47S 38°21W 333 D4
Inhaminga Mozam. 18°26S 35°0E 269 F4
Inharrime Mozam. 24°30S 35°0E 271 B6
Inharrime → Mozam. 24°30S 35°0E 271 B6
Inhaúma Brazil 22°51S 43°17W 135 B1
Inhisar Turkey 40°3N 30°23E 205 A12
Inhul → Ukraine 46°50N 32°0E 189 J7
Inhulec Ukraine 47°42N 33°14E 189 J7
Inhulets → Ukraine 46°46N 32°47E 189 J7
Inhuma Brazil 6°40S 41°42W 332 C3
Inhumas Brazil 16°22S 49°30W 333 E2
Iniesta Spain 39°27N 1°45W 197 F3
Ining = Yining China 43°58N 81°10E 217 D10
Inini □ Fr. Guiana 4°0N 53°0W 329 C7
Inírida → Colombia 3°55N 67°52W 328 C4
Inis = Ennis Ireland 52°51N 8°59W 166 D3
Inishbofin Ireland 53°37N 10°13W 166 C1
Inisheer Ireland 53°3N 9°32W 166 C2
Inishfree B. Ireland 55°4N 8°23W 166 A3
Inishkea North Ireland 54°9N 10°11W 166 B1
Inishkea South Ireland 54°7N 10°12W 166 B1
Inishmaan Ireland 53°5N 9°35W 166 C2
Inishmore Ireland 53°8N 9°45W 166 C2
Inishmurray Ireland 54°26N 8°39W 166 B3
Inishowen Pen. Ireland 55°14N 7°15W 166 A4
Inishshark Ireland 53°37N 10°16W 166 C1
Inishturk Ireland 53°42N 10°7W 166 C1
Inishvickillane Ireland 52°3N 10°37W 166 D1
Initao Phil. 8°56N 124°20E 233 G5
Injāna Iraq 34°29N 44°38E 213 E11
Injibara Ethiopia 10°59N 37°0E 257 E4
Injinoo © Australia 10°56S 142°15E 280 A3
Injune Australia 25°53S 148°32E 281 D4
Inkisi →
Dem. Rep. of the Congo 4°46S 14°52E 265 D3
Inklin → N. Amer. 58°50N 133°10W 296 B2
Inland Kaikoura Ra.
N.Z. 41°59S 173°41E 285 B8
Inland Sea = Setonaikai
Japan 34°20N 133°30E 222 C5
Inle L. Burma 20°30N 96°58E 241 E6
Inlet U.S.A. 43°45N 74°48W 313 C10
Inn → Austria 48°35N 13°28E 180 C6
Innamincka Australia 27°44S 140°46E 281 D3
Innbygda Norway 61°19N 12°17E 164 C9
Inner Hebrides U.K. 57°0N 6°30W 167 E2
Inner Mongolia = Nei Monggol
Zizhiqu □ China 42°0N 112°0E 226 D7
Inner Port Shelter China 22°22N 114°17E 122 A2
Inner Sound U.K. 57°30N 5°55W 167 D3
Innerkip Canada 43°13N 80°42W 312 C4
Innes △ Australia 35°52S 136°53E 282 C2
Innetalling I. Canada 56°0N 79°0W 298 A4
Innisfail Queens., Australia 17°33S 146°5E 280 B4
Innisfail Alta., Canada 52°2N 113°57W 296 C6
Innoko Nat. Wildlife Refuge ⌓
U.S.A. 63°20N 158°25W 303 E8
In'noshima Japan 34°19N 133°10E 222 C5
Innsbruck Austria 47°16N 11°23E 180 D4
Innviertel Austria 48°15N 13°15E 180 C6
Innvik Norway 61°51N 6°37E 164 C3
Inny → Ireland 53°32N 7°51W 166 C4
Ino Japan 33°33N 133°26E 222 D5
Inocência Brazil 19°47S 51°48W 333 E1
Inongo
Dem. Rep. of the Congo 1°55S 18°30E 264 C3
Inoni Congo 3°4S 15°39E 264 C3
İnönü Turkey 39°48N 30°9E 205 B12
Inoucdjouac = Inukjuak
Canada 58°25N 78°15W 295 F16
Inousses Greece 38°33N 26°14E 205 C8
Inowrocław Poland 52°50N 18°12E 185 F5
Inquisivi Bolivia 16°50S 67°10W 330 D4
Inscription, C. Australia 25°29S 112°59E 279 E1
Insein Burma 16°50N 96°5E 241 G6
Insjön Sweden 60°41N 15°6E 162 D9
Ińsko Poland 53°25N 15°32E 184 E2
Insterberg = Chernyakhovsk
Russia 54°36N 21°48E 184 D8
Însurăţei Romania 44°50N 27°40E 183 F12
Inta Russia 66°5N 60°8E 186 A11
Intendente Alvear
Argentina 35°12S 63°32W 334 D3
İntepe Turkey 40°1N 26°20E 205 A8
Interlachen U.S.A. 29°37N 81°53W 317 F8
Interlagos Brazil 23°41S 46°42W 137 C1
Interlaken Switz. 46°41N 7°50E 179 J3
Interlaken N.Y., U.S.A. 42°37N 76°44W 313 D8
International Falls U.S.A. 48°36N 93°25W 308 A7
Interview I. India 12°55N 92°43E 245 H11
Intiyaco Argentina 28°43S 60°5W 334 B3
Întorsura Buzăului
Romania 45°41N 26°2E 183 E11
Intramuros Phil. 14°35N 120°57E 127 B1
Intrepid Air and Space Museum
New York, U.S.A. 132 b1
Intutu Peru 3°32S 74°48W 328 D3
Inubō-Zaki Japan 35°42N 140°52E 223 B12
Inukjuak Canada 58°25N 78°15W 295 F16
Inútil, B. Chile 53°30S 70°15W 336 D2
Inuvik Canada 68°16N 133°40W 294 D5
Inuyama Japan 35°23N 136°56E 223 B8
Invalides France 48°51N 2°18E 134 A2
Inveraray U.K. 56°14N 5°5W 167 E3
Inverbervie U.K. 56°51N 2°17W 167 E6
Invercargill N.Z. 46°24S 168°24E 285 G3
Inverclyde □ U.K. 55°55N 4°49W 167 F4
Inverell Australia 29°45S 151°8E 281 D5
Invergordon U.K. 57°41N 4°10W 167 D4
Inverkeithing U.K. 56°2N 3°24W 121 A1
Inverleigh Australia 38°6S 144°3E 282 E6
Inverloch Australia 38°38S 145°45E 281 F4
Invermere Canada 50°30N 116°2W 296 C5
Inverness N.S., Canada 46°15N 61°19W 299 C7
Inverness Highl., U.K. 57°29N 4°13W 167 D4
Inverness Ala., U.S.A. 32°1N 85°45W 316 C4
Inverness Fla., U.S.A. 28°50N 82°20W 317 G7
Inverurie U.K. 57°17N 2°23W 167 D6
Investigator Group
Australia 34°45S 134°20E 281 E1
Investigator Ridge Ind. Oc. 11°30S 98°10E 273 F8
Investigator Str. Australia 35°30S 137°0E 282 C2
Inya Russia 50°28N 86°37E 217 B11
Inyanga Zimbabwe 18°12S 32°40E 269 F3
Inyangani Zimbabwe 18°5S 32°50E 269 F3
Inyantue Zimbabwe 18°33S 26°39E 270 A4
Inyo Mts. U.S.A. 36°40N 118°0W 306 J9
Inyokern U.S.A. 35°39N 117°49W 307 K9
Inyonga Tanzania 6°45S 32°5E 268 D3
Inywa Burma 23°56N 96°17E 241 D6
Inza Russia 53°55N 46°25E 190 D8
Inzersdorf Austria 48°8N 16°21E 142 B2
Inzhavino Russia 52°22N 42°30E 190 D6
Inzia →
Dem. Rep. of the Congo 3°45S 17°57E 265 C3
Iō-Jima Japan 30°48N 130°18E 221 J5
Ioannina Greece 39°42N 20°47E 204 B2
Ioannina □ Greece 39°39N 20°57E 204 B2
Iokea Papua N. G. 8°25S 146°16E 286 E4
Iola U.S.A. 37°55N 95°24W 308 G6
Iolani Palace U.S.A. 21°18N 157°51W 302 K14
Ioma Papua N. G. 8°19S 147°52E 286 E4
Ion Corvin Romania 44°7N 27°50E 183 F12
Iona Angola 16°54S 12°34E 265 F2
Iona Argyll & Bute, U.K. 56°20N 6°25W 167 E2
Iona △ Angola 16°47S 12°20E 265 F2
Ione U.S.A. 38°21N 120°56W 306 G6
Iongo Angola 9°11S 17°45E 265 D3
Ionia U.S.A. 42°59N 85°4W 311 B11
Ionian Is. = Ionioi Nisoi
Greece 38°40N 20°0E 204 C2
Ionian Sea Medit. S. 37°30N 17°30E 193 D7
Ionioi Nisoi Greece 38°40N 20°0E 204 C2
Ionioi Nisoi □ Greece 38°40N 20°0E 207 B2
Ios Greece 36°41N 25°20E 205 E7
Iowa □ U.S.A. 42°18N 93°30W 310 C3
Iowa → U.S.A. 41°10N 91°1W 310 C5
Iowa City U.S.A. 41°40N 91°32W 310 C5
Iowa Falls U.S.A. 42°31N 93°16W 310 B3
Iowa Park U.S.A. 33°57N 98°40W 314 D5
Ipala Tanzania 4°30S 32°52E 268 C3
Ipameri Brazil 17°44S 48°9W 333 E2
Ipanema Minas Gerais,
Brazil 19°47S 41°44W 333 E3
Ipanema Rio de J., Brazil 22°59S 43°12W 135 B1
Iparía Peru 9°17S 74°29W 330 B3
Ipati Greece 38°52N 22°14E 204 C4
Ipatinga Brazil 19°32S 42°30W 333 E3
Ipatovo Russia 45°45N 42°50E 191 H6
Ipek = Pejë Kosovo 42°40N 20°17E 202 D4
Ipel' → Europe 47°48N 18°53E 181 D11
Ipiales Colombia 0°50N 77°37W 328 C2
Ipiaú Brazil 14°8S 39°44W 333 D4
Ipil Phil. 7°47N 122°35E 233 H4
Ipin = Yibin China 28°45N 104°32E 228 C5
Ipirá Brazil 12°10S 39°44W 333 D4
Ipiranga Brazil 23°35S 46°36W 137 B2
Ipiranga → Brazil 23°37S 46°37W 137 B2
Ipixuna Brazil 7°0S 71°40W 330 B3
Ipixuna → Amazonas,
Brazil 7°11S 71°51W 330 B3
Ipixuna → Amazonas, Brazil 5°45S 63°2W 331 B5
Ipoh Malaysia 4°35N 101°5E 237 K3
Iponri Nigeria 6°28N 3°22E 124 B2
Iporá Brazil 16°28S 51°7W 331 D7
Ipota Vanuatu 18°52S 169°20E 287 H7
Ippy C.A.R. 6°5N 21°7E 264 A4
İpsala Turkey 40°55N 26°23E 203 F10
Ipsario, Oros Greece 40°40N 24°40E 203 F8
Ipswich Queens., Australia 27°35S 152°40E 281 D5
Ipswich Suffolk, U.K. 52°4N 1°10E 169 E9
Ipswich Mass., U.S.A. 42°41N 70°50W 313 D14
Ipswich S. Dak., U.S.A. 45°27N 99°2W 308 C4
Ipu Brazil 4°23S 40°44W 332 B3
Ipueiras Brazil 4°33S 40°43W 332 B3
Ipuh Indonesia 3°0S 101°30E 234 C2
Ipupiara Brazil 11°49S 42°37W 333 D3
Iqaluit Canada 63°44N 68°31W 295 E18
Iqaluktuutiaq = Cambridge Bay
Canada 69°10N 105°0W 294 D11
Iquique Chile 20°19S 70°5W 330 E3
Iquitos Peru 3°45S 73°10W 328 D3
Ir Gannim = Bat Yam
Israel 32°2N 34°44E 251 F5
Irabu-Jima Japan 24°50N 125°10E 221 M2
Iracoubo Fr. Guiana 5°30N 53°10W 329 B7
Īrafshān Iran 26°42N 61°56E 247 E9
Irago-Suidō Japan 34°25N 137°0E 223 C8
Irahuan Phil. 9°48N 118°41E 233 G2
Iraklia Cyclades, Greece 36°50N 25°28E 205 E7
Iraklia Serres, Greece 41°10N 23°16E 202 E7
Iraklio Greece 35°20N 25°12E 207 E6
Iraklio □ Greece 35°10N 25°10E 207 E6
Iraklio ✈ (HER) Greece 35°20N 25°15E 207 E6
Iráklion = Iraklio Greece 35°20N 25°12E 207 E6
Irakliou, Kolpos Greece 35°23N 25°8E 207 E6
Irako-Zaki Japan 34°35N 137°1E 223 C9
Irala Paraguay 25°55S 54°35W 335 B5
Iran ■ Asia 33°0N 53°0E 247 C7
Iran, Pegunungan
Malaysia 2°20N 114°50E 235 B4
Iran Ra. = Iran, Pegunungan
Malaysia 2°20N 114°50E 235 B4
Iranamadu Tank Sri Lanka 9°23N 80°29E 245 K5
Īrānshahr Iran 27°15N 60°40E 247 E9
Irapa Venezuela 10°34N 62°35W 329 A5
Irapuato Mexico 20°41N 101°28W 318 C4
Iraq ■ Asia 33°0N 44°0E 213 F10
Irarrar, O. → Mali 20°0N 1°30E 261 E5
Irati Brazil 25°25S 50°38W 335 B5
Irazú, Volcan Costa Rica 10°28N 84°42W 320 D3
Irbes saurums Latvia 57°45N 22°5E 184 A9
Irbid Jordan 32°35N 35°48E 251 F6
Irbid □ Jordan 32°30N 35°50E 250 F6
Irebu Dem. Rep. of the Congo 0°40S 17°46E 264 C3
Irecê Brazil 11°18S 41°52W 332 D3
Iregua → Spain 42°27N 2°24E 196 C7
Ireland ■ Europe 53°50N 7°52W 166 C4
Ireland I. Bermuda 32°19N 64°50W 153 a
Ireland Island Bermuda 32°19N 64°50W 153 a
Ireland's Eye Ireland 53°24N 6°4W 120 A3
Irele Nigeria 7°40N 5°40E 263 D6
Ireng → Brazil 3°33N 59°51W 329 C6
Irerer, O. → Algeria 19°25N 5°47E 261 E6
Irgiz = Yrghyz Kazakhstan 48°37N 61°16E 216 C6
Irgiz = Yrghyz →
Kazakhstan 48°6N 62°30E 216 C6
Irgiz, Bolshaya → Russia 52°10N 49°10E 190 D9
Irharhar, O. → Algeria 28°3N 6°15E 261 C6
Irherm Morocco 30°7N 8°18W 260 B3
Irhil M'Goun Morocco 31°30N 6°28W 260 B3
Iri = Iksan S. Korea 35°59N 127°0E 224 E3
Irian Barat = Papua □
Indonesia 4°0S 137°0E 231 E9
Irian Jaya = Papua □
Indonesia 4°0S 137°0E 231 E9
Irian Jaya Barat □
Indonesia 2°5S 132°50E 231 E8
Iriba Chad 15°7N 22°15E 259 E4
Irié Guinea 8°15N 9°10W 262 D3
Iriga Phil. 13°25N 123°25E 232 E4
Iriklinskoye Vdkhr. Russia 52°0N 59°0E 216 B5
Iringa Tanzania 7°48S 35°43E 268 D4
Iringa □ Tanzania 7°48S 35°43E 268 D4
Irinjalakuda India 10°21N 76°14E 245 J3
Iriomote △ Japan 24°29N 123°53E 221 M1
Iriomote-Jima Japan 24°19N 123°48E 221 M1
Iriona Honduras 15°57N 85°11W 320 C2
Iriri → Brazil 3°52S 52°37W 329 D7
Iriri Novo → Brazil 8°46S 53°22W 331 B7
Irish Sea Europe 53°38N 4°48W 168 D3
Irkeshtam Pass = Erkech-Tam Pass
Asia 39°46N 74°2E 217 E8
Irkutsk Russia 52°18N 104°20E 218 A9
Irlığanlı Turkey 37°53N 29°12E 205 D11
Irma Canada 52°55N 111°14W 297 C6
Irō-Zaki Japan 34°36N 138°51E 223 C10
Irois B. Trin. & Tob. 10°9N 61°45W 323 t
Iroise, Mer d' France 48°15N 4°45W 172 D2
Iron Baron Australia 32°58S 137°11E 282 B2
Iron Gate = Portile de Fier
Europe 44°44N 22°30E 182 F7
Iron Knob Australia 32°46S 137°8E 282 B2
Iron Mountain U.S.A. 45°49N 88°4W 308 C9
Iron Range △ Australia 12°34S 143°18E 280 A3
Iron River U.S.A. 46°6N 88°39W 308 B9
Irondequoit U.S.A. 43°13N 77°35W 312 C7
Ironton Mo., U.S.A. 37°36N 90°38W 308 G8
Ironton Ohio, U.S.A. 38°32N 82°41W 309 F12
Ironwood U.S.A. 46°27N 90°9W 308 B8
Ironwood Forest ⌓
U.S.A. 32°32N 111°28W 305 K8
Iroquois Canada 44°51N 75°19W 313 B9
Iroquois → U.S.A. 41°5N 87°49W 311 C9
Iroquois Falls Canada 48°46N 80°41W 298 C3
Iroquois Point U.S.A. 21°19N 157°58W 302 K14
Irosin Phil. 12°42N 124°2E 232 E5
Irpin Ukraine 50°30N 30°15E 177 C16
Irqieqa, Ras I- Malta 35°56N 14°29E 206 F7
Irrara Cr. → Australia 29°35S 145°31E 281 D4
Irrawaddy □ Burma 17°0N 95°0E 241 G5
Irrawaddy → Burma 15°50N 95°6E 241 G5
Irrawaddy, Mouths of the
Burma 15°30N 95°0E 241 H5
Irricana Canada 51°19N 113°37W 296 C6
Irrunytju Australia 26°3S 128°56E 279 E4
Irshava Ukraine 48°19N 23°3E 182 B8
Irsina Italy 40°45N 16°14E 201 B9
Irtysh → Russia 61°4N 68°52E 214 C7
Irumu Dem. Rep. of the Congo 1°32N 29°53E 268 B2
Irún Spain 43°20N 1°52W 196 B3
Iruñea = Pamplona-Iruña
Spain 42°48N 1°38W 196 C3
Irurzun Spain 42°55N 1°50W 196 C3
Irvine Alta., Canada 49°57N 110°16W 297 D6
Irvine N. Ayrs., U.K. 55°37N 4°41W 167 F4
Irvine Calif., U.S.A. 33°41N 117°46W 307 M9
Irvine Ky., U.S.A. 37°42N 83°58W 311 G13
Irvinestown U.K. 54°28N 7°39W 166 B4
Irving U.S.A. 32°48N 96°56W 314 E6
Irving Park U.S.A. 41°57N 87°42W 119 B2
Irvington U.S.A. 37°53N 86°17W 311 G10
Irvona U.S.A. 40°46N 78°33W 312 F6
Irwin → Australia 29°15S 114°54E 279 E1
Irwinton U.S.A. 32°49N 83°10W 316 C6
Irwinville U.S.A. 31°39N 83°23W 316 D6
Irymple Australia 34°14S 142°8E 282 C5
Is, Jebel Sudan 22°3N 35°28E 256 C4
Is-sur-Tille France 47°30N 5°8E 173 E12
Isa Nigeria 13°14N 6°24E 263 C6
Isa Khel Pakistan 32°41N 71°17E 242 C4
Isaac → Australia 22°55S 149°20E 280 C4
Isabel Rio de J., Brazil 22°55S 43°14W 135 B1
Isabel S. Dak., U.S.A. 45°24N 101°26W 308 C3
Isabel, I. Mexico 21°51N 105°55W 318 C3
Isabel Segunda Puerto Rico 18°9N 65°27W 321 b
Isabela Basilan, Phil. 6°40N 121°59E 233 H3
Isabela Negros, Phil. 10°12N 122°59E 233 F4
Isabela Puerto Rico 18°30N 67°2W 321 b
Isabela □ Phil. 17°0N 122°0E 232 C4
Isabela, Canal Ecuador 0°20S 90°55W 330 a
Isabela, I. Ecuador 0°30S 91°4W 330 a
Isabella, Cord. Nic. 13°30N 85°25W 320 D2
Isabella Ra. Australia 21°0S 121°4E 278 D3
Isaccea Romania 45°16N 28°28E 183 E13
Isachsen, C. Canada 79°20N 105°28W 295 B10
Isachsen Mt. Antarctica 72°8S 26°5E 151 D4
Ísafjarðardjúp Iceland 66°10N 23°0W 155 A3
Ísafjarðarsýsla Iceland 66°0N 23°0W 155 B3
Ísafjörður Iceland 66°5N 23°9W 155 A3
Isagarh India 24°48N 77°51E 242 G7
Isagatedo Nigeria 6°31N 3°19E 124 A1
Isahaya Japan 32°52N 130°2E 222 E2
Isaka Dem. Rep. of the Congo 2°53S 18°54E 264 C3
Isaka Tanzania 3°56S 32°59E 268 C3
Işalnița Romania 44°24N 23°44E 183 F8
Isalo, Tangorombohitr'
Madag. 22°45S 45°15E 272 C2
Isalo △ Madag. 22°23S 45°16E 272 C2
Isan → India 26°51N 80°7E 243 F9
Isana = Içana → Brazil 0°26N 67°19W 328 C4
Isandja
Dem. Rep. of the Congo 2°59S 21°59E 264 C4
Isangano △ Zambia 11°8S 30°35E 269 E3
Isangi Dem. Rep. of the Congo 0°52N 24°10E 264 B4
Isanlu Makutu Nigeria 8°20N 5°50E 263 D6
Isar → Bayern, Germany 48°48N 12°57E 179 G8
Isar → Oberbayern,
Germany 48°15N 11°41E 131 A3
Isarco → Italy 46°27N 11°18E 199 B8
Isaris Greece 37°22N 22°0E 204 D3
Isarog, Mt. Phil. 13°39N 123°23E 232 E4
Isawa Japan 35°40N 138°35E 223 B10
Íscar Spain 41°22N 4°32W 194 D6
Iscayachi Bolivia 21°31S 65°3W 331 E4
İscehisar Turkey 38°51N 30°45E 205 C12
Íschia Italy 40°44N 13°57E 200 B6
Ischigualasto △ Argentina 30°0S 68°0W 334 B2
Iscuandé Colombia 2°28N 77°59W 328 C2
Isdell → Australia 16°27S 124°51E 278 C3
Ise Japan 34°25N 136°45E 223 C8
Ise-Shima △ Japan 34°25N 136°48E 223 C8
Ise-Wan Japan 34°43N 136°43E 223 C8
Isefjord Denmark 55°53N 11°50E 163 J5
Isel → Austria 46°50N 12°47E 180 E5
Iseo Italy 45°39N 10°3E 198 C7
Iseo, L. d' Italy 45°43N 10°4E 198 C7
Iseramagazi Tanzania 4°37S 32°10E 268 C3
Isère □ France 45°15N 5°40E 175 C9
Isère → France 44°59N 4°51E 175 D8
Iserlohn Germany 51°22N 7°41E 178 D3
Isérnia Italy 41°36N 14°14E 201 A7
Isesaki Japan 36°19N 139°12E 223 A11
Iseyin Nigeria 8°0N 3°36E 263 D5
Isfahan = Eşfahān Iran 32°39N 51°43E 247 C6
Isfjorden Norway 62°35N 7°49E 164 B4
Ishbīliya Iraq 33°21N 44°26E 113 A2
Ishëm Albania 41°33N 19°34E 202 E3
Isheng Oshwe
Dem. Rep. of the Congo 3°57S 22°33E 264 C4
Isherton Guyana 2°20N 59°25W 329 C6
Ishigaki Japan 24°26N 124°10E 221 M2
Ishigaki-Shima Japan 24°20N 124°10E 221 M2
Ishikari Japan 43°20N 141°15E 220 C10
Ishikari-Gawa → Japan 43°15N 141°23E 220 C10
Ishikari-Sammyaku
Japan 43°30N 143°0E 220 C11
Ishikari-Wan Japan 43°25N 141°1E 220 C10
Ishikawa Japan 26°25N 127°49E 288 a

Ishikawa □ Japan 36°30N 136°30E 223 A8
Ishim Russia 56°10N 69°30E 214 D7
Ishim → Russia 57°45N 71°10E 214 D8
Ishimbay Russia 53°28N 56°2E 216 B5
Ishinomaki Japan 38°32N 141°20E 220 E10
Ishioka Japan 36°11N 140°16E 223 A12
Ishizuchi-Yama Japan 33°45N 133°6E 222 D5
Ishkashim Tajikistan 36°44N 71°37E 217 E8
Ishkoman Pakistan 36°30N 73°50E 243 A5
Ishøj Strand Denmark 55°36N 12°20E 118 B2
Ishpeming U.S.A. 46°29N 87°40W 308 B10
Ishurdi Bangla. 24°9N 89°3E 241 C2
Isiboro Sécure △ Bolivia 16°15S 65°50W 331 D4
Isigny-sur-Mer France 49°19N 1°6W 172 C5
Isıklar Dağı Turkey 40°45N 27°15E 203 F11
Işıklı Turkey 38°19N 29°51E 205 C11
Isil Kul Russia 54°55N 71°16E 217 B8
Ísili Italy 39°44N 9°6E 200 C2
iSimangaliso ⌓ S. Africa 27°50S 32°32E 271 C5
Isiolo Kenya 0°24N 37°33E 268 B4
Isiro Dem. Rep. of the Congo 2°53N 27°40E 268 B2
Isisford Australia 24°15S 144°21E 280 C3
İskele = Trikomo Cyprus 35°17N 33°52E 207 E9
İskenderun Turkey 36°32N 36°10E 250 B7
İskenderun Körfezi Turkey 36°40N 35°50E 250 B6
İskilip Turkey 40°45N 34°29E 212 B6
Iskitim Russia 54°38N 83°18E 217 B10
Iskŭr → Bulgaria 43°45N 24°25E 203 C8
Iskŭr, Yazovir Bulgaria 42°23N 23°30E 202 D7
Iskushuban Somalia 10°18N 50°12E 267 B7
Iskut → Canada 56°45N 131°49W 296 B2
Isla → U.K. 56°32N 3°20W 167 E5
Isla Coiba △ Panama 7°33N 81°36W 320 E4
Isla Cristina Spain 37°13N 7°17W 195 H3
Isla de Salamanca △ Colombia 10°59N 74°40W 328 A3
Isla Gorge △ Australia 25°10S 149°57E 280 D4
Isla Gorgona △ Colombia 2°59N 78°10W 328 C2
Isla Guamblin △ Chile 44°50S 75°4W 336 B1
Isla Isabel △ Mexico 21°54N 105°58W 318 C3
Isla Magdalena △ Chile 44°20S 73°13W 336 B2
Isla Tiburón y San Estebán ⌓ Mexico 29°0N 112°27W 318 B2
Isla Vista U.S.A. 34°25N 119°53W 307 L7
İslahiye Turkey 37°0N 36°35E 250 B7
Islam Headworks Pakistan 29°49N 72°33E 242 E5
Islamabad Pakistan 33°40N 73°10E 242 C5
Islamgarh Pakistan 27°51N 70°48E 242 F4
Islamkot Pakistan 24°42N 70°13E 242 G4
Islamorada U.S.A. 24°56N 80°37W 317 L9
Islampur Bihar, India 25°9N 85°12E 243 G11
Islampur Maharashtra, India 17°2N 74°20E 244 F2
Islampur Paschimbanga, India 26°16N 88°12E 243 F13
Island = Iceland ■ Europe 64°45N 19°0W 155 C8
Island B. Phil. 9°6N 118°10E 233 G2
Island Harbour Anguilla 18°12N 63°0W 322 a
Island L. Canada 53°47N 94°25W 297 C10
Island Lagoon Australia 31°30S 136°40E 282 A2
Island Park Canada 43°37N 79°22W 141 B2
Island Pond U.S.A. 44°49N 71°53W 313 B13
Islands, B. of Nfld. & L., Canada 49°11N 58°15W 299 C8
Islands, B. of N.Z. 35°15S 174°6E 284 B3
Islay U.K. 55°46N 6°10W 167 F2
Isle → France 44°55N 0°15W 174 D3
Isle aux Morts Canada 47°35N 59°0W 299 C8
Isle of Hope U.S.A. 31°58N 81°5W 316 D8
Isle of Wight □ U.K. 50°41N 1°17W 169 G6
Isle Royale △ U.S.A. 48°0N 88°55W 308 B9
Isleton U.S.A. 38°10N 121°37W 306 G5
Islev Denmark 55°41N 12°27E 118 A2
Isleworth U.K. 51°28N 0°19W 125 B2
Islington Canada 43°38N 79°30W 141 B1
Islington □ U.K. 51°33N 0°5W 125 A3
Islote Pt. Trin. & Tob. 10°4N 61°47W 323 t
Ismail = Izmayil Ukraine 45°22N 28°46E 183 E13
Ismâ'ilîya Egypt 30°37N 32°18E 251 H3
Ismâ'ilîya □ Egypt 30°35N 32°16E 251 H3
Ismâ'ilîya, Qanâ el Egypt 30°7N 31°17E 117 A2
Ismâ'ilîya, Tir'at el → Egypt 30°4N 31°16E 251 H2
Ismaning Germany 48°13N 11°40E 131 A3
Ismayloskiy Park Russia 55°46N 37°46E 129 B3
Isna Egypt 25°17N 32°30E 256 B3
Isoanala Madag. 23°50S 45°44E 272 C2
Ísola del Liri Italy 41°41N 13°34E 199 G10
Ísola della Scala Italy 45°16N 11°0E 198 C7
Ísola di Capo Rizzuto Italy 38°58N 17°6E 201 D10
Isolo Nigeria 6°31N 3°19E 124 A1
Isparta Turkey 37°47N 30°30E 205 D12
Isparta □ Turkey 38°0N 31°0E 212 D4
Isperikh Bulgaria 43°43N 26°50E 203 C10
Íspica Italy 36°47N 14°55E 201 F7
İspir Turkey 40°28N 40°59E 213 B9
Israel ■ Asia 32°0N 34°50E 251 G5
Isratu Eritrea 16°20N 39°53E 257 D4
Issakly Russia 54°8N 51°32E 190 C10
Issano Guyana 5°49N 59°26W 329 B6
Issaouane, Erg Algeria 26°58N 8°42E 258 C1
Issia Ivory C. 6°33N 6°33W 262 D3
Issoire France 45°32N 3°15E 174 C7
Issoudun France 46°57N 1°59E 173 F8
Issy-les-Moulineaux France 48°49N 2°15E 134 B2
Issyk-Kul = Balykchy Kyrgyzstan 42°26N 76°12E 217 D9
Issyk-Kul, Ozero = Ysyk-Köl Kyrgyzstan 42°25N 77°15E 217 D9
Ist Croatia 44°17N 14°47E 199 D11
Istállós-kő Hungary 48°4N 20°26E 182 B5
İstanbul Turkey 41°0N 28°58E 122 C1
İstanbul □ Turkey 41°0N 29°0E 203 E12
İstanbul ✈ (IST) Turkey 40°59N 28°49E 203 F12
İstanbul Boğazı Turkey 41°5N 29°3E 122 B2
Istaravshān Tajikistan 39°55N 69°1E 217 E7
Isteren Norway 61°58N 11°47E 164 B8
Istiea Greece 38°57N 23°9E 204 C5
İstinye Turkey 41°6N 29°3E 122 B2
Istmina Colombia 5°10N 76°39W 328 B2
Isto, Mt. U.S.A. 69°12N 143°48W 303 B12
Istok = Burim Kosovo 42°45N 20°24E 202 D4
Istokpoga, L. U.S.A. 27°23N 81°17W 317 H8
Istra Croatia 45°10N 14°0E 199 C10
Istres France 43°31N 4°59E 175 E8
Istria = Istra Croatia 45°10N 14°0E 199 C10
Isugod Phil. 9°19N 118°5E 233 G2
Isulan Phil. 6°30N 124°29E 233 H5
Itá Paraguay 25°29S 57°21W 334 B4
Itä Hakkila Finland 60°17N 25°7E 121 B3
Itabaiana Paraíba, Brazil 7°18S 35°19W 332 C4
Itabaiana Sergipe, Brazil 10°41S 37°37W 332 D4
Itabaianinha Brazil 11°16S 37°47W 332 D4
Itaberaba Brazil 12°32S 40°18W 333 D3
Itaberaí Brazil 16°2S 49°48W 333 E2
Itabira Brazil 19°37S 43°13W 333 E3
Itabirito Brazil 20°15S 43°48W 333 F3
Itaboca Brazil 4°50S 62°40W 329 D5
Itabuna Brazil 14°48S 39°16W 333 D4
Itacajá Brazil 8°19S 47°46W 332 C2
Itacaunas → Brazil 5°21S 49°8W 332 C2
Itacoatiara Brazil 2°58S 58°30W 329 D6
Itaewon S. Korea 37°32N 126°58E 137 B1
Itaguari → Brazil 14°11S 44°40W 333 D3
Itaguatins Brazil 5°47S 47°29W 332 C2
Itaim → Brazil 7°2S 42°2W 332 C3
Itainópolis Brazil 7°24S 41°31W 332 C3
Itaipú, Represa de Brazil 25°30S 54°30W 335 B5
Itaituba Brazil 4°10S 55°50W 329 D6
Itajaí Brazil 27°50S 48°39W 335 B6
Itajany do Sul = Rio do Sul Brazil 27°13S 49°37W 335 B6
Itajubá Brazil 22°24S 45°30W 333 F2
Itajuípe Brazil 14°41S 39°22W 333 D4
Itaka Tanzania 8°50S 32°49E 269 D3
Itako Japan 35°56N 140°33E 223 B12
Itala ⌓ S. Africa 27°30S 31°7E 271 C5
Italy ■ Europe 42°0N 13°0E 192 C6
Itamaraju Brazil 17°4S 39°32W 333 E4
Itamarati Brazil 6°24S 68°15W 330 B4
Itamataré Brazil 2°16S 46°24W 332 B2
Itambacuri Brazil 18°1S 41°42W 333 E3
Itambé Brazil 15°15S 40°37W 333 E3
Itami Japan 34°46N 135°24E 133 A1
Itampolo Madag. 24°41S 43°57E 272 C1
Itanagar India 27°6N 93°37E 241 B4
Itandrano Madag. 21°47S 45°17E 272 C2
Itanhaém Brazil 24°11S 46°47W 333 F2
Itanhanga Brazil 22°59S 43°19W 135 B1
Itanhauã → Brazil 4°45S 63°48W 329 D5
Itanhém Brazil 17°9S 40°20W 333 E3
Itano Japan 34°7N 134°28E 222 C6
Itapaci Brazil 14°57S 49°34W 333 D2
Itapagé Brazil 3°41S 39°34W 332 B4
Itaparica = Petrolândia Brazil 9°5S 38°20W 332 C4
Itaparica, I. de Brazil 12°54S 38°42W 333 D4
Itaparica, Represa de Brazil 11°3S 42°47W 332 D3
Itapebi Brazil 15°56S 39°32W 333 E4
Itapecuru Mirim Brazil 3°24S 44°20W 332 B3
Itaperuna Brazil 21°10S 41°54W 333 F3
Itapetinga Brazil 15°15S 40°15W 333 E3
Itapetininga Brazil 23°36S 48°7W 335 A6
Itapeva Brazil 23°59S 48°59W 335 A6
Itapicuru → Bahia, Brazil 11°47S 37°32W 332 D4
Itapicuru → Maranhão, Brazil 2°52S 44°12W 332 B3
Itapipoca Brazil 3°30S 39°35W 332 B4
Itapira = Ubaitaba Brazil 14°18S 39°20W 333 D4
Itapiranga Brazil 2°45S 58°1W 329 D6
Itapiúna Brazil 4°33S 38°57W 332 B4
Itaporanga Paraíba, Brazil 7°18S 38°0W 332 C4
Itaporanga São Paulo, Brazil 23°42S 49°29W 333 F2
Itapuá □ Paraguay 26°40S 55°40W 335 B4
Itapuranga Brazil 15°40S 49°59W 333 E2
Itaquai → Brazil 4°20S 70°12W 330 A3
Itaquí Brazil 29°8S 56°30W 334 B4
Itararé Brazil 24°6S 49°23W 335 A6
Itarsi India 22°36N 77°51E 242 H7
Itarumã Brazil 18°42S 51°25W 333 E1
Itatí Argentina 27°16S 58°15W 334 B4
Itatiaia △ Brazil 22°22S 44°38W 335 A7
Itatira Brazil 4°30S 39°37W 332 B4
Itatuba Brazil 5°46S 63°20W 331 B5
Itatupã Brazil 0°37S 51°12W 329 D7
Itaueira Brazil 7°36S 43°2W 332 C3
Itaueira → Brazil 6°41S 42°55W 332 C3
Itaúna Brazil 20°4S 44°34W 333 F3
Itbayat Phil. 20°47N 121°51E 232 A3
Itbayat I. Phil. 20°45N 121°50E 232 A3
Itchen → U.K. 50°55N 1°22W 169 G6
Itchouma Niger 20°14N 13°32E 261 D7
Ite Peru 17°55S 70°57W 330 D3
Itea Greece 38°25N 22°25E 204 C4
Itezhi Tezhi, L. Zambia 15°30S 25°30E 269 F2
Ithaca = Ithaki Greece 38°25N 20°40E 207 C2
Ithaca U.S.A. 42°27N 76°30W 313 D8
Ithaki Greece 38°25N 20°40E 207 C2
Ithakis, Stenon Greece 38°22N 20°39E 207 C2
Iti △ Greece 38°50N 22°15E 204 C4
Itimbiri → Dem. Rep. of the Congo 2°2N 22°44E 264 B4
Itinga Brazil 16°36S 41°47W 333 E3
Itiquira Brazil 17°12S 54°7W 331 D7
Itiquira → Brazil 17°18S 56°44W 331 D6
Itiruçu Brazil 13°31S 40°9W 333 D3
Itiúba Brazil 10°43S 39°51W 332 D4
Itiyuro → Argentina 22°40S 63°50W 334 A3
Itkilik → U.S.A. 70°9N 150°56W 303 A10
Itō Japan 34°58N 139°5E 223 C11
Itogon Phil. 16°22N 120°41E 232 C3
Itoigawa Japan 37°2N 137°51E 221 F8
Itoko Dem. Rep. of the Congo 1°0S 21°48E 264 C4
Itoman Japan 26°7N 127°40E 288 a
Iton → France 49°9N 1°12E 172 C8
Itonamas → Bolivia 12°28S 64°24W 331 C5
Itri Italy 41°17N 13°32E 200 A6
Itsa Egypt 29°15N 30°47E 256 J7
Itsamia Comoros Is. 12°21S 43°52E 272 a
Itsandra Comoros Is. 11°40S 43°15E 272 a
Itsuki Japan 32°24N 130°50E 222 E2
Itsukushima Shrine Japan 34°17N 132°19E 222 C4
Íttiri Italy 40°36N 8°34E 200 B1
Ittoqqortoormiit Greenland 70°20N 23°0W 154 C8
Itu Brazil 23°17S 47°15W 335 A6
Itu Nigeria 5°10N 7°58E 263 D6
Itu Aba I. S. China Sea 10°23N 114°21E 230 B4
Ituaçu Brazil 13°50S 41°18W 333 D3
Ituango Colombia 7°4N 75°45W 328 B2
Ituí → Brazil 4°38S 70°19W 328 D3
Ituiutaba Brazil 19°0S 49°25W 333 E2
Itumbiara Brazil 18°20S 49°10W 333 E2
Ituna Canada 51°10N 103°24W 297 C8
Itunge Port Tanzania 9°40S 33°55E 269 D3
Ituni Guyana 5°28N 58°15W 329 B6
Itupiranga Brazil 5°9S 49°20W 332 C2
Iturama Brazil 19°44S 50°11W 333 E1
Iturbe Argentina 23°0S 65°25W 334 A2
Ituri → Dem. Rep. of the Congo 1°40N 27°1E 268 B2
Iturup, Ostrov Russia 45°0N 148°0E 215 E15
Ituverava Brazil 20°20S 47°47W 333 F2
Ituxi → Brazil 7°18S 64°51W 331 B5
Itzehoe Germany 53°55N 9°31E 178 B5
Iuka U.S.A. 38°37N 88°47W 311 F8
Iungsdalshytta Norway 60°49N 7°55E 164 D4
Ivahona Madag. 23°27S 46°10E 272 C2
Ivaí → Brazil 23°18S 53°42W 335 A5
Ivalo Finland 68°38N 27°35E 160 B22
Ivalojoki → Finland 68°40N 27°40E 160 B22
Ivanava Belarus 52°7N 25°29E 177 B13
Ivančice Czech Rep. 49°6N 16°23E 181 B9
Ivane-Puste Ukraine 48°39N 26°10E 183 B11
Ivăneşti Romania 46°39N 27°27E 183 D12
Ivangorod = Dęblin Poland 51°34N 21°50E 185 G8
Ivangorod Russia 59°27N 28°13E 188 C5
Ivanhoe N.S.W., Australia 32°56S 144°20E 282 B6
Ivanhoe Vic., Australia 37°45S 145°3E 128 A2
Ivanhoe Ont., Canada 44°23N 77°28W 312 B7
Ivanhoe Calif., U.S.A. 36°23N 119°13W 306 J7
Ivanhoe Minn., U.S.A. 44°28N 96°15W 308 C5
Ivanhorod Ukraine 48°48N 29°50E 183 B14
Ivanić Grad Croatia 45°41N 16°25E 199 C13
Ivanjica Serbia 43°35N 20°12E 202 C4
Ivanjska Bos.-H. 44°55N 17°4E 182 F2
Ivankoyskoye Vdkhr. Russia 56°37N 36°32E 188 D9
Ivano-Frankivsk Ukraine 48°40N 24°40E 183 B9
Ivano-Frankivsk □ Ukraine 48°45N 24°30E 183 B9
Ivanof Bay U.S.A. 55°54N 159°29W 303 J8
Ivanovo = Ivanava Belarus 52°7N 25°29E 177 B13
Ivanovo Bulgaria 43°43N 25°58E 203 C9
Ivanovo Russia 57°5N 41°0E 188 D11
Ivanovo □ Russia 57°10N 41°50E 190 B5
Ivanšćica Croatia 46°12N 16°13E 199 B13
Ivashchenkovo = Chapayevsk Russia 53°0N 49°40E 190 D9
Ivato Madag. 20°37S 47°10E 272 C2
Ivatsevichy Belarus 52°43N 25°21E 177 B13
Ivaylovgrad Bulgaria 41°32N 26°8E 203 E10
Ivdel Russia 60°42N 60°24E 186 B11
Iveragh Pen. Ireland 51°52N 10°15W 166 E1
Ives Estates U.S.A. 25°58N 80°10W 129 C2
Ivgres = Komsomolsk Russia 57°2N 40°20E 188 D11
Ivindo → Gabon 0°9S 12°9E 264 C2
Ivinheima → Brazil 23°14S 53°42W 335 A5
Ivinhema Brazil 22°10S 53°37W 335 A5
Ivittuut Greenland 61°14N 48°12W 154 E6
Iviza = Eivissa Spain 38°54N 1°26E 206 D1
Ivohibe Madag. 22°31S 46°57E 272 C2
Ivolândia Brazil 16°34S 50°51W 333 E1
Ivory Coast W. Afr. 4°20N 5°0W 262 E4
Ivory Coast ■ Africa 7°30N 5°0W 262 D4
Ivösjön Sweden 56°8N 14°25E 163 H8
Ivrea Italy 45°28N 7°52E 198 C4
İvrindi Turkey 39°34N 27°30E 205 B9
Ivry-sur-Seine France 48°49N 2°22E 134 B3
Ivujivik Canada 62°24N 77°55W 295 E16
Ivvavik △ Canada 69°6N 139°30W 294 D4
Ivybridge U.K. 50°23N 3°56W 169 G4
Iwa Japan 36°5N 139°52E 223 A11
Iwai-Jima Japan 33°47N 131°58E 222 D3
Iwaizumi Japan 39°50N 141°45E 220 E10
Iwaki Japan 37°3N 140°55E 221 F10
Iwakuni Japan 34°15N 132°8E 222 C4
Iwami Japan 35°32N 134°15E 222 B6
Iwami Ginzan Japan 35°6N 132°26E 222 B4
Iwamizawa Japan 43°12N 141°46E 220 C10
Iwanai Japan 42°58N 140°30E 220 C10
Iwase Japan 36°21N 140°6E 223 A12
Iwata Japan 34°42N 137°51E 223 C9
Iwate □ Japan 39°30N 141°30E 220 E10
Iwate-San Japan 39°51N 141°0E 220 E10
Iwo Nigeria 7°39N 4°9E 263 D5
Iwo Jima Pac. Oc. 24°47N 141°20E 288 b
Iwŏn N. Korea 40°19N 128°39E 224 B4
Iwonicz-Zdrój Poland 49°37N 21°47E 185 J8
Iwungu Dem. Rep. of the Congo 5°16S 19°17E 265 D3
Ixelles Belgium 50°50N 4°22E 116 B2
Ixiamas Bolivia 13°50S 68°5W 330 C4
Ixopo S. Africa 30°11S 30°5E 271 D5
Ixtepec Mexico 16°34N 95°6W 319 D5
Ixtlán del Río Mexico 21°2N 104°22W 318 C4
Iyal Bakhit Sudan 13°20N 28°39E 257 E2
Iyo Japan 33°45N 132°45E 222 D4
Iyo-Mishima Japan 33°58N 133°30E 222 D5
Iyo-Nada Japan 33°40N 132°20E 222 D4
Izabal, L. de Guatemala 15°30N 89°10W 320 C2
Izamal Mexico 20°56N 89°1W 319 C7
Izberbash Russia 42°35N 47°52E 191 J8
Izbica Poland 50°53N 23°10E 185 H10
Izbica Kujawska Poland 52°25N 18°40E 185 F5
Izbiceni Romania 43°45N 24°40E 183 G9
Izembek Nat. Wildlife Refuge ⌓ U.S.A. 55°15N 162°45W 303 J7
Izena-Shima Japan 26°56N 127°56E 221 L3
Izgrev Bulgaria 43°36N 26°58E 203 C10
Izhevsk Russia 56°51N 53°14E 186 C9
Izhma = Sosnogorsk Russia 63°37N 53°51E 186 B9
Izhma → Russia 65°19N 52°54E 186 A9
Izileg Algeria 20°20N 6°4E 261 D6
Izkī Oman 22°56N 57°46E 249 B7
Izmayil Ukraine 45°22N 28°46E 183 E13
Izmaylovo Russia 55°47N 37°47E 129 B3
İzmir Turkey 38°25N 27°8E 205 C9
İzmir □ Turkey 38°15N 27°40E 205 C9
İzmir Adnan Menderes ✈ (ADB) Turkey 38°23N 27°6E 205 C9
İzmir Körfezi Turkey 38°30N 26°50E 205 C8
İzmit = Kocaeli Turkey 40°45N 29°50E 203 F13
Iznájar Spain 37°15N 4°19W 195 H6
Iznalloz Spain 37°24N 3°30W 195 H7
İznik Turkey 40°23N 29°46E 212 B3
İznik Gölü Turkey 40°27N 29°30E 203 F13
Izobilno-Tishchenskoye = Izobil'nyy Russia 45°25N 41°44E 191 H5
Izobil'nyy Russia 45°25N 41°44E 191 H5
Izola Slovenia 45°32N 13°39E 199 C10
Izozog, Bañados de Bolivia 18°48S 62°10W 331 D5
Izra Syria 32°51N 36°15E 250 F7
Iztacalco Mexico 19°23N 99°5W 128 B2
Iztapalapa Mexico 19°21N 99°6W 128 B2
Iztochni Rodopi Bulgaria 41°45N 25°30E 203 E9
Izu Japan 34°58N 138°56E 223 C10
Izu-Hantō Japan 34°45N 139°0E 223 C11
Izu-Shotō Japan 34°30N 140°0E 221 G10
Izúcar de Matamoros Mexico 18°36N 98°28W 319 D5
Izuhara Japan 34°12N 129°17E 222 C1
Izumi Kagoshima, Japan 32°5N 130°22E 222 E2
Izumi Ōsaka, Japan 34°28N 135°24E 223 C7
Izumi-Sano Japan 34°23N 135°18E 223 C7
Izumo Japan 35°20N 132°46E 222 B4
Izunokuni Japan 35°2N 138°55E 223 B10
Izyaslav Ukraine 50°5N 26°50E 177 C14
Izyum Ukraine 49°12N 37°19E 189 H9

J

J.F.K. Int. ✈ (JFK) U.S.A. 40°38N 73°47W 313 F11
J.F. Rodrigues Brazil 2°55S 50°20W 332 B1
J.P. Koch Fjord Greenland 82°45N 44°0W 154 A6
J. Strom Thurmond L. U.S.A. 33°40N 82°12W 316 B7
Ja-ela Sri Lanka 7°5N 79°53E 245 L4
Ja-eundo S. Korea 34°53N 126°2E 224 E3
Ja'ār Yemen 13°13N 45°18E 248 D4
Jaba Ethiopia 6°20N 35°7E 257 F4
Jaba West Bank 31°51N 35°16E 123 A2
Jabal al Awliya' Sudan 15°14N 32°29E 266 A3
Jabal as Sirāj Afghan. 35°7N 69°16E 240 B3
Jabal at Ṭā'ir Red Sea 15°35N 41°52E 257 D5
Jabalón → Spain 38°53N 4°5W 195 G6
Jabalpur India 23°9N 79°58E 243 H8
Jabālya Gaza Strip 31°32N 34°29E 251 G5
Jabbūl Syria 36°4N 37°30E 246 B3
Jabiru Australia 12°40S 132°53E 278 B5
Jablah Syria 35°20N 36°0E 250 C7
Jablanac Croatia 44°42N 14°56E 199 D11
Jablanica Bos.-H. 43°40N 17°45E 182 G2
Jablonec nad Nisou Czech Rep. 50°43N 15°10E 180 A8
Jablonica Slovak Rep. 48°37N 17°26E 181 C10
Jabłonowo Pomorskie Poland 53°23N 19°10E 184 E6
Jablunkov Czech Rep. 49°35N 18°46E 181 B11
Jaboatão Brazil 8°7S 35°1W 332 C4
Jabonga Phil. 9°20N 125°32E 233 G5
Jabotabek = Jakarta Indonesia 6°9S 106°52E 122 A2
Jaboticabal Brazil 21°15S 48°17W 335 A6
Jabukovac Serbia 44°22N 22°21E 202 B6
Jaburu Brazil 5°30S 64°0W 331 B5
Jaca Spain 42°35N 0°33W 196 C4
Jacaré Brazil 22°53S 43°14W 135 B1
Jacaré → Brazil 10°3S 42°13W 332 D3
Jacareí Brazil 23°20S 46°0W 335 A6
Jacarèzinho Brazil 23°5S 49°58W 335 A6
Jaci-Paraná Brazil 9°15S 64°23W 331 B5
Jaciara Brazil 15°59S 54°57W 331 D7
Jacinto Brazil 16°10S 40°17W 333 E3
Jack River △ Australia 14°58S 144°19E 280 A3
Jackman U.S.A. 45°37N 70°15W 309 C18
Jacksboro U.S.A. 33°13N 98°10W 314 E5
Jackson Barbados 13°7N 59°36W 323 r
Jackson Ala., U.S.A. 31°31N 87°53W 315 F11
Jackson Calif., U.S.A. 38°21N 120°46W 306 G6
Jackson Ga., U.S.A. 33°20N 83°57W 316 B6
Jackson Ky., U.S.A. 37°33N 83°23W 309 G12
Jackson Mich., U.S.A. 42°15N 84°24W 311 B12
Jackson Minn., U.S.A. 43°37N 95°1W 308 D6
Jackson Miss., U.S.A. 32°18N 90°12W 315 E9
Jackson Mo., U.S.A. 37°23N 89°40W 308 G9
Jackson N.H., U.S.A. 44°10N 71°11W 313 B13
Jackson Ohio, U.S.A. 39°3N 82°39W 309 F12
Jackson S.C., U.S.A. 33°20N 81°47W 316 B8
Jackson Tenn., U.S.A. 35°37N 88°49W 315 D10
Jackson Wyo., U.S.A. 43°29N 110°46W 304 E8
Jackson, C. N.Z. 40°59S 174°20E 285 A9
Jackson B. N.Z. 43°58S 168°42E 285 D3
Jackson Center U.S.A. 40°27N 84°4W 311 D12
Jackson Hd. N.Z. 43°58S 168°37E 285 D3
Jackson Heights U.S.A. 40°44N 73°53W 132 B2
Jackson L. Fla., U.S.A. 30°30N 84°17W 316 E5
Jackson L. Ga., U.S.A. 33°19N 83°50W 316 B6
Jackson L. Wyo., U.S.A. 43°52N 110°36W 304 E8
Jackson Park U.S.A. 41°46N 87°34W 119 C3
Jacksons N.Z. 42°46S 171°32E 285 C6
Jackson's Arm Canada 49°52N 56°47W 299 C8
Jacksonville Ala., U.S.A. 33°49N 85°46W 316 B4
Jacksonville Ark., U.S.A. 34°52N 92°7W 314 D8
Jacksonville Calif., U.S.A. 37°52N 120°24W 306 H6
Jacksonville Fla., U.S.A. 30°20N 81°39W 316 E8
Jacksonville Ga., U.S.A. 31°49N 82°59W 316 D7
Jacksonville Ill., U.S.A. 39°44N 90°14W 310 E6
Jacksonville N.C., U.S.A. 34°45N 77°26W 315 D16
Jacksonville Tex., U.S.A. 31°58N 95°17W 314 F7
Jacksonville Beach U.S.A. 30°17N 81°24W 316 E8
Jacksonville Int. ✈ (JAX) U.S.A. 30°30N 81°41W 316 E8
Jacmel Haiti 18°14N 72°32W 321 C5
Jaco, Pte. Dominica 15°39N 61°24W 323 k
Jacob Lake U.S.A. 36°43N 112°13W 305 H7
Jacobabad Pakistan 28°20N 68°29E 242 E3
Jacobina Brazil 11°11S 40°30W 332 D3
Jacobshagen = Dobrzany Poland 53°22N 15°25E 184 E2
Jacon Javits Convention Center New York, U.S.A. 132 c1
Jacotet, B. Mauritius 20°30S 57°26E 272 e
Jacqueline Kennedy Onassis Res. New York, U.S.A. 132 a3
Jacques-Cartier Canada 45°31N 73°27W 130 A3
Jacques-Cartier, Dét. de Canada 50°0N 63°30W 299 C7
Jacques-Cartier, Mt. Canada 48°57N 66°0W 299 C6
Jacques-Cartier, Pont Canada 45°31N 73°32W 130 A2
Jacques-Cartier ⌓ Canada 47°15N 71°33W 299 C5
Jacqueville Ivory C. 5°12N 4°25W 262 D4
Jacuí → Brazil 30°2S 51°15W 335 C5
Jacumba U.S.A. 32°37N 116°11W 307 N10
Jacundá → Brazil 1°57S 50°26W 332 B1
Jadavpur India 22°28N 88°22E 124 C2
Jadcherla India 16°46N 78°9E 244 F4
Jade Germany 53°20N 8°14E 178 B4
Jade Buddha Temple China 31°15N 121°25E 138 B1
Jade City Canada 59°15N 129°37W 296 B3
Jade Dragon Snow Mt. = Yulong Xueshan China 27°6N 100°10E 228 D3
Jade Island Beijing, China 114 b2
Jade Mt. = Yü Shan Taiwan 23°25N 120°52E 225 C2
Jadebusen Germany 53°29N 8°12E 178 B4
Jadotville = Likasi Dem. Rep. of the Congo 10°55S 26°48E 269 E2
Jadovnik Serbia 43°20N 19°45E 202 C3
Jadraque Spain 40°55N 2°55W 196 E2
Jādū Libya 32°0N 12°0E 258 B2
Jægersborg Denmark 55°45N 12°31E 118 A3
Jægersborg Dyrehave Denmark 55°46N 12°33E 118 A3
Jaén Peru 5°25S 78°40W 330 B2
Jaén Spain 37°44N 3°43W 195 H7
Jaén □ Spain 37°50N 3°30W 195 H7
Jæren Norway 58°42N 5°47E 164 F2
Jærens Rev Norway 58°45N 5°45E 164 F2
Jafarabad India 20°52N 71°22E 242 J4
Jaffa = Tel Aviv-Yafo Israel 32°4N 34°48E 251 F5
Jaffa, C. Australia 36°58S 139°40E 282 D3
Jaffna Sri Lanka 9°45N 80°2E 245 K5
Jaffrey U.S.A. 42°49N 72°2W 313 D12
Jagadhri India 30°10N 77°20E 242 D7
Jagadishpur Bihar, India 25°30N 84°21E 243 G11
Jagadishpur W. Bengal, India 22°39N 88°17E 124 B1
Jagat Nepal 28°19N 84°53E 243 E11
Jagatpur India 28°44N 77°13E 120 A2
Jagdalpur India 19°3N 82°0E 244 E6
Jagdaqi China 50°25N 124°7E 219 A13
Jagersfontein S. Africa 29°44S 25°27E 270 C4
Jaghīn → Iran 27°17N 57°13E 247 E8
Jagna Phil. 9°39N 124°22E 233 G5
Jagodina Serbia 44°5N 21°15E 202 B5
Jagraon India 30°50N 75°25E 242 D6
Jagst → Germany 49°14N 9°10E 179 F5
Jagtial India 18°50N 79°0E 244 E4
Jaguaquara Brazil 13°32S 39°58W 333 D4
Jaguaré, Rib. do → Brazil 23°32S 46°45W 137 B1
Jaguariaíva Brazil 24°10S 49°50W 335 A6
Jaguaribe Brazil 5°53S 38°37W 332 C4
Jaguaribe → Brazil 4°25S 37°45W 332 B4
Jaguaruana Brazil 4°50S 37°47W 332 B4
Jagüey Grande Cuba 22°35N 81°7W 320 B3
Jagungal, Mt. Australia 36°8S 148°22E 283 D8
Jahanabad India 25°13N 84°59E 243 G11
Jahangirpur India 28°43N 77°12E 120 A2
Jahazpur India 25°37N 75°17E 242 G6
Jahrom Iran 28°30N 53°31E 247 D7
Jaicós Brazil 7°21S 41°8W 332 C3
Jaigarh India 17°17N 73°13E 244 F1
Jaijon India 31°21N 76°9E 242 D7
Jailolo Indonesia 1°5N 127°30E 231 D7
Jailolo, Selat Indonesia 0°5N 129°5E 231 D7
Jaintiapur Bangla. 25°8N 92°7E 241 C4
Jaipur Assam, India 27°16N 95°24E 241 B5
Jaipur Raj., India 27°0N 75°50E 242 F6
Jais India 26°15N 81°32E 243 F9
Jaisalmer India 26°55N 70°54E 242 F4
Jaisinghnagar India 23°38N 78°34E 243 H8
Jaitaran India 26°12N 73°56E 242 F5
Jaithari India 23°14N 78°37E 243 H8
Jajarkot Nepal 28°42N 82°14E 243 E10
Jājarm Iran 36°58N 56°27E 247 B8
Jajce Bos.-H. 44°19N 17°17E 182 F2
Jajpur India 20°53N 86°22E 244 D8
Jakam → India 23°54N 74°13E 242 H6
Jakar Dzong Bhutan 27°33N 90°43E 241 B3
Jakarta Indonesia 6°9S 106°52E 122 A2
Jakarta, Teluk Indonesia 6°5S 106°50E 122 A1
Jakarta Halim Perdana Kusuma Int. ✈ (HLP) Indonesia 6°16S 106°53E 122 B2
Jakhal India 29°48N 75°50E 242 E6
Jakharrah Libya 29°13N 21°34E 258 C4
Jakhau India 23°13N 68°43E 242 H3
Jakobshavn = Ilulissat Greenland 69°12N 51°10W 154 D5
Jakobstad = Pietarsaari Finland 63°40N 22°43E 160 E20
Jakupica Macedonia 41°45N 21°22E 202 E5
Jal U.S.A. 32°7N 103°12W 305 K12
Jalaihai Pt. Guam 13°18N 144°46E 302 d
Jalājil Si. Arabia 25°40N 45°27E 246 E5
Jalal-Abad Kyrgyzstan 40°56N 73°0E 217 D8
Jalal-Abad □ Kyrgyzstan 41°30N 72°30E 217 D8
Jalālābād Afghan. 34°30N 70°29E 242 B4
Jalalabad India 27°41N 79°42E 243 F8
Jalalpur Jattan Pakistan 32°38N 74°11E 242 C6
Jalama U.S.A. 34°29N 120°29W 307 L6
Jalan Kayu Singapore 1°24N 103°52E 138 A3
Jalandhar = Jullundur India 31°20N 75°40E 242 D6
Jalapa Guatemala 14°39N 89°59W 320 D2
Jalapa Enríquez = Xalapa Mexico 19°32N 96°55W 319 D5
Jalasjärvi Finland 62°29N 22°47E 160 E20
Jalaun India 26°8N 79°25E 243 F8
Jalāzin Afghan. 37°2N 64°49E 240 A2
Jaldak Afghan. 31°58N 66°43E 240 C2
Jaldhaka → Bangla. 26°16N 89°16E 241 B2
Jales Brazil 20°10S 50°33W 333 F1
Jalesar India 27°29N 78°19E 242 F8
Jaleswar Nepal 26°38N 85°48E 243 F11
Jalgaon India 21°0N 75°42E 244 D2
Jalībah Iraq 30°35N 46°32E 246 D5
Jalingo Nigeria 8°55N 11°25E 263 D7
Jalisco □ Mexico 20°20N 103°40W 318 D4
Jalkot Pakistan 35°14N 73°24E 243 B5
Jalna India 19°48N 75°38E 244 E2
Jalón → Spain 41°47N 1°4W 196 D3
Jalor India 25°21N 72°37E 242 G5
Jalpa Mexico 21°38N 102°58W 318 C4
Jalpaiguri India 26°32N 88°46E 241 B2
Jalpan Mexico 21°14N 99°29W 319 C5
Jālq Iran 27°35N 62°46E 240 D1
Jālū Libya 29°2N 21°33E 258 C4
Jaluit I. Marshall Is. 6°0N 169°30E 288 G8
Jalūlā Iraq 34°16N 45°10E 213 E11
Jam, Minaret of Afghan. 34°23N 64°30E 240 B2
Jamaame Somalia 0°4N 42°44E 267 D5
Jamaari Nigeria 11°44N 9°53E 263 C6
Jamaica ■ W. Indies 18°10N 77°30W 320 a
Jamaica B. U.S.A. 40°36N 73°50W 132 C3
Jamaica Channel Jamaica 17°0N 76°0W 321 C4
Jamaica Plain U.S.A. 42°18N 71°6W 116 B2
Jamakpuri India 28°37N 77°5E 120 B1
Jamalpur Bangla. 24°52N 89°56E 241 C2
Jamalpur India 25°18N 86°28E 243 G12
Jamalpurganj India 23°2N 87°59E 243 H13
Jamanota Aruba 12°29N 69°57W 322 f
Jamanxim → Brazil 4°43S 56°18W 331 A6
Jamari Brazil 8°45S 63°27W 331 B5
Jamari → Brazil 8°27S 63°30W 331 B5
Jamba Angola 14°40S 16°2E 265 E3
Jambewangi Indonesia 8°17S 114°7E 231 J17
Jambi Indonesia 1°38S 103°30E 234 C2
Jambi □ Indonesia 1°30S 102°30E 234 C2
Jambongan, Pulau Malaysia 6°45N 117°20E 235 A5
Jambusar India 22°3N 72°51E 242 H5
James U.S.A. 32°58N 83°29W 316 C6
James → S. Dak., U.S.A. 42°52N 97°18W 308 D5
James → Va., U.S.A. 36°56N 76°27W 309 G15
James, I. = San Salvador, I. Ecuador 0°16S 90°42W 330 a
James B. Canada 54°0N 80°0W 298 B3
James I. Gambia 13°19N 16°21W 262 C1
James Island U.S.A. 32°45N 79°55W 316 C10
James Ranges Australia 24°10S 132°30E 278 D5
James Ross I. Antarctica 63°58S 57°50W 151 C18
Jamesabad Pakistan 25°17N 69°15E 242 G3
Jameson Land Greenland 71°0N 23°30W 154 C8
Jamesport U.S.A. 39°58N 93°48W 310 E3
Jamestown = Wawa Canada 47°59N 84°47W 298 C3
Jamestown S. Austral., Australia 33°10S 138°32E 282 B3
Jamestown St. Helena 15°55S 5°43W 153 h
Jamestown Eastern Cape, S. Africa 31°6S 26°45E 270 D4
Jamestown Ind., U.S.A. 39°56N 86°38W 311 E10
Jamestown Mo., U.S.A. 38°48N 92°30W 310 F4
Jamestown N. Dak., U.S.A. 46°54N 98°42W 308 B4
Jamestown N.Y., U.S.A. 42°6N 79°14W 312 D5
Jamestown Ohio, U.S.A. 39°39N 83°33W 311 E13
Jamestown Pa., U.S.A. 41°29N 80°27W 312 E4
Jamestown S.C., U.S.A. 33°17N 79°42W 316 B10
Jamīlābād Iran 34°24N 48°28E 247 C6
Jamira → India 21°35N 88°28E 243 J13
Jämjö Sweden 56°12N 15°49E 163 H9
Jamkhandi India 16°30N 75°15E 244 F2
Jamkhed India 18°43N 75°19E 244 E2
Jammalamadugu India 14°51N 78°25E 245 G4
Jammerbugten Denmark 57°15N 9°20E 163 G3
Jammu India 32°43N 74°54E 242 C6
Jammu & Kashmir □ India 34°25N 77°0E 243 B7
Jamnagar India 22°30N 70°6E 242 H4
Jamner India 20°45N 75°52E 244 D2
Jamni → India 25°13N 78°35E 243 G8
Jampur Pakistan 29°39N 70°40E 242 E4
Jamrud Pakistan 33°59N 71°24E 242 C4
Jämsä Finland 61°53N 25°10E 188 B3
Jamshedpur India 22°44N 86°12E 243 H12
Jamshīdīyeh Iran 35°42N 51°22E 141 A2
Jamsil S. Korea 37°30N 127°4E 137 B2
Jamtara India 23°59N 86°49E 243 H12
Jämtland Sweden 63°31N 14°0E 160 E16
Jämtlands län □ Sweden 63°0N 14°40E 162 B7
Jamuna → Bangla. 23°51N 89°45E 241 D2
Jamurki Bangla. 24°9N 90°2E 241 C3
Jamwon S. Korea 37°30N 127°0E 137 B2
Jan L. Canada 54°56N 102°55W 297 C8
Jan Mayen Arctic 71°0N 9°0W 150 B7
Janakkala Finland 60°54N 24°36E 188 B3
Janakpur Nepal 26°42N 85°55E 244 A7
Janaúba Brazil 15°48S 43°19W 333 E3
Janaucu, I. Brazil 0°30N 50°10W 332 A1
Jand Pakistan 33°30N 72°6E 242 C5
Jandaia Brazil 17°6S 50°7W 333 E1
Jandanku ۞ Australia 16°20S 135°45E 280 B2
Jandaq Iran 34°3N 54°22E 247 C7
Jandía Canary Is. 28°6N 14°21W 153 e2
Jandía, Pta. de Canary Is. 28°3N 14°31W 153 e2
Jandía △ Canary Is. 28°4N 14°19W 153 e2
Jandiatuba → Brazil 3°28S 68°42W 328 D4
Jandola Pakistan 32°20N 70°9E 242 C4
Jandowae Australia 26°45S 151°7E 281 D5
Jándula → Spain 38°3N 4°6W 195 G6
Jane Pk. N.Z. 45°15S 168°20E 285 F3
Janesville U.S.A. 42°41N 89°1W 310 B7
Janga Ghana 10°5N 1°0W 263 C4
Jangamo Mozam. 24°6S 35°21E 271 B6
Janghai India 25°33N 82°19E 243 G10
Jangheung S. Korea 34°41N 126°52E 224 E3
Janghowon S. Korea 37°7N 127°37E 224 D3
Jangipur India 24°28N 88°4E 243 G12
Jangoon India 17°44N 79°5E 244 F4
Jangsu S. Korea 35°38N 127°31E 224 E3
Janhtang Ga Burma 26°32N 96°38E 241 B6
Jani Khel Afghan. 32°46N 68°24E 240 B3
Janikowo Poland 52°45N 18°7E 185 F5
Janinà = Ioannina □ Greece 39°39N 20°57E 204 B2
Janiuay Phil. 10°58N 122°30E 233 F4
Janja Bos.-H. 44°40N 19°14E 182 F4
Janjanbureh Gambia 13°30N 14°47W 262 C2
Janjevë Kosovo 42°35N 21°19E 202 D5
Janjgir India 22°1N 82°34E 243 J10
Janjina Croatia 42°58N 17°25E 199 F14
Janjina Madag. 20°30S 45°50E 272 C2
Jankau = Janikowo Poland 52°45N 18°7E 185 F5
Janki Poland 52°8N 20°52E 143 C1
Jannaale Somalia 1°48N 44°42E 267 D5
Janos Mexico 30°54N 108°10W 318 A3
Jánoshalma Hungary 46°18N 19°21E 182 D4
Jánosháza Hungary 47°8N 17°12E 182 C2
Jánossomorja Hungary 47°47N 17°11E 182 C2
Janów Poland 50°44N 19°27E 185 H6
Janów Lubelski Poland 50°48N 22°23E 185 H9
Janów Podlaski Poland 52°11N 23°11E 185 F10
Janowiec Wielkopolski Poland 52°45N 17°30E 185 F4
Jantho Indonesia 5°17N 95°38E 234 A1
Januária Brazil 15°25S 44°25W 333 E3
Janub = Southern △ South Sudan 6°50N 28°45E 257 F2
Janub Dârfûr □ Sudan 11°0N 25°0E 257 E2
Janub Kordofân □ Sudan 12°0N 30°0E 257 E3
Janûb Sînî □ Egypt 29°30N 33°50E 251 J4
Janubio Canary Is. 28°56N 13°50W 153 e2
Janville France 48°10N 1°50E 173 D8
Janwada India 18°0N 77°29E 244 E3
Janzé France 47°55N 1°28W 172 E5
Jaora India 23°40N 75°10E 242 H6
Japan ■ Asia 36°0N 136°0E 221 G8
Japan, Sea of Asia 40°0N 135°0E 220 E7
Japan Center San Francisco, U.S.A. 136 c1
Japan Trench Pac. Oc. 32°0N 142°0E 288 D6
Japen = Yapen Indonesia 1°50S 136°0E 231 E9
Japiim Brazil 7°37S 72°54W 330 B3
Japla India 24°33N 84°1E 243 G11
Japurá Brazil 1°48S 66°34W 328 D4
Japura Indonesia 0°19S 102°21E 234 C2
Japurá → Brazil 3°8S 65°46W 328 D4
Jaquarão Brazil 32°34S 53°23W 335 C5
Jaqué Panama 7°27N 78°8W 320 E4
Jarābulus Syria 36°49N 38°1E 213 D8
Jaraguá Goiás, Brazil 15°45S 49°20W 333 E2
Jaraguá São Paulo, Brazil 23°27S 46°44W 137 A1
Jaraguá, Pico de Brazil 23°27S 46°46W 137 A1
Jaraguari Brazil 20°9S 54°35W 331 E7
Jaraicejo Spain 39°40N 5°49W 195 F5
Jaraíz de la Vera Spain 40°4N 5°45W 194 E5
Jarama → Spain 40°24N 3°32W 194 E7
Jaramānah Syria 33°29N 36°21E 250 E7
Jaramillo Argentina 47°10S 67°7W 336 C3
Jarandilla de la Vera Spain 40°8N 5°39W 194 E5
Jaranwala Pakistan 31°15N 73°26E 242 D5
Jarash Jordan 32°17N 35°54E 251 F6
Jarash □ Jordan 32°17N 35°54E 251 F6
Jarauçu → Brazil 1°48S 52°22W 329 D7
Järbo Sweden 60°43N 16°36E 162 D10
Jarboesville = Lexington Park U.S.A. 38°16N 76°27W 309 F15
Jardas al 'Abīd Libya 32°18N 20°59E 258 B4
Jardim Brazil 21°28S 56°2W 334 A4
Jardim Paulista Brazil 23°34S 46°41W 137 B1
Jardín → Spain 38°50N 2°10W 197 G2
Jardín América Argentina 27°3S 55°14W 335 B4
Jardin Botanique Brussels, Belgium 116 a3
Jardine River △ Australia 11°9S 142°21E 280 A3
Jardines de la Reina, Arch. de los Cuba 20°50N 78°50W 320 B4
Jargalang China 43°5N 122°55E 227 C12
Jargalant = Hovd □ Mongolia 48°2N 91°37E 217 C12
Jari → Brazil 1°9S 51°54W 329 D7
Jaria Janjail Bangla. 25°0N 90°40E 241 C3
Jarīr, W. al → Si. Arabia 25°38N 42°30E 246 E4
Järlåsa Sweden 59°53N 17°12E 162 E11
Jarlsberg og Larvik = Vestfold □ Norway 59°15N 10°0E 164 E7
Jarmen Germany 53°54N 13°20E 178 B9
Järna Sweden 59°6N 17°34E 162 E11
Jarnac France 45°40N 0°11W 174 C3
Jarny France 49°9N 5°53E 173 C12
Jaro Phil. 11°11N 124°47E 233 F5
Jarocin Poland 51°59N 17°29E 185 G4
Jaroměř Czech Rep. 50°22N 15°52E 180 A8
Jarosław Poland 50°2N 22°42E 185 H9
Järpås Sweden 58°23N 12°57E 163 F6
Järpen Sweden 63°21N 13°26E 162 A7
Jarrahdale Australia 32°24S 116°5E 279 F2
Jarrahi → Iran 30°49N 48°48E 247 D6
Jarso Ethiopia 5°15N 37°30E 257 F4
Jartai China 39°45N 105°48E 226 E3
Jaru Brazil 10°26S 62°27W 331 C5
Jaru → Brazil 10°5S 61°59W 331 C5
Jarud Qi China 44°28N 120°50E 227 B11
Järvatältet Sweden 59°25N 17°54E 139 A1
Järvenpää Finland 60°29N 25°5E 188 B3
Jarvis Canada 42°53N 80°6W 312 D4
Jarvis I. Pac. Oc. 0°15S 160°5W 289 H12
Jarvorník Czech Rep. 50°23N 17°2E 181 A10
Järvsö Sweden 61°43N 16°10E 162 C10
Jarwa India 27°38N 82°30E 243 F10
Jaša Tomić Serbia 45°26N 20°50E 182 E5
Jasaan Phil. 8°39N 124°45E 233 G5
Jasdan India 22°2N 71°12E 242 H4
Jashpurnagar India 22°54N 84°9E 243 H11
Jasidih India 24°31N 86°39E 243 G12
Jasień Poland 51°46N 15°0E 185 G2
Jāsimīyah Iraq 33°45N 44°41E 213 F11
Jasin Malaysia 2°20N 102°26E 237 L4
Jāsk Iran 25°38N 57°45E 247 E8
Jaskhar India 18°54N 72°58E 130 B2
Jasło Poland 49°45N 21°30E 185 J8
Jasmund Germany 54°32N 13°35E 178 A9
Jasmund △ Germany 54°31N 13°38E 178 A9
Jaso India 24°30N 80°29E 243 G9
Jason Is. Falk. Is. 51°0S 61°0W 153 f
Jasonville U.S.A. 39°10N 87°12W 311 E9
Jasper Alta., Canada 52°55N 118°5W 296 C5
Jasper Ont., Canada 44°52N 75°57W 313 B9
Jasper Ala., U.S.A. 33°50N 87°17W 315 E11
Jasper Fla., U.S.A. 30°31N 82°57W 316 E7
Jasper Ind., U.S.A. 38°24N 86°56W 311 F10
Jasper Tex., U.S.A. 30°56N 94°1W 314 F7
Jasper △ Canada 52°50N 118°8W 296 C5
Jasrasar India 27°43N 73°49E 242 F5
Jassān Iraq 32°58N 45°52E 213 G11
Jassey = Iaşi Romania 47°10N 27°40E 183 C12
Jastarnia Poland 54°42N 18°40E 184 D5

Jastrebarsko Croatia 45°41N 15°39E 199 C12
Jastrow = Jastrowie Poland 53°26N 16°49E 184 E3
Jastrowie Poland 53°26N 16°49E 184 E3
Jastrzębie Zdrój Poland 49°57N 18°35E 185 J5
Jász-Nagykun-Szolnok □ Hungary 47°15N 20°30E 182 C5
Jászapáti Hungary 47°32N 20°10E 182 C5
Jászárokszállás Hungary 47°39N 19°58E 182 C4
Jászberény Hungary 47°30N 19°55E 182 C4
Jászkisér Hungary 47°27N 20°20E 182 C5
Jászladány Hungary 47°23N 20°10E 182 C5
Jataí Brazil 17°58S 51°48W 333 E1
Jatapu → Brazil 2°13S 58°17W 329 D6
Jath India 17°3N 75°13E 244 F2
Jati Pakistan 24°20N 68°19E 242 G3
Jatibarang Indonesia 6°28S 108°18E 235 D3
Jatiluwih Indonesia 8°23S 115°8E 231 J18
Jatinegara Indonesia 6°13S 106°52E 122 B2
Játiva = Xátiva Spain 38°59N 0°32W 197 G4
Jatobá = Petrolândia Brazil 9°5S 38°20W 332 C4
Jättendal Sweden 61°58N 17°15E 162 C11
Jaú Angola 15°12S 13°31E 265 F2
Jaú Brazil 22°10S 48°30W 335 A6
Jaú → Brazil 1°54S 61°26W 329 D5
Jauaperi → Brazil 1°26S 61°35W 329 D5
Jauer = Jawor Poland 51°4N 16°11E 185 G3
Jauja Peru 11°45S 75°15W 330 C2
Jaunpur India 25°46N 82°44E 243 G10
Jauru → Brazil 16°22S 57°46W 331 D6
Java = Jawa Indonesia 7°0S 110°0E 235 D4
Java Sea Indonesia 4°35S 107°15E 235 C3
Java Trench Ind. Oc. 9°0S 105°0E 234 D2
Javadi Hills India 12°40N 78°40E 245 H4
Javādīyeh Iran 35°39N 51°22E 141 B2
Javalambre, Sa. de Spain 40°6N 1°0W 196 E4
Javānrud Iran 34°47N 46°31E 213 E12
Jávea Spain 38°48N 0°10E 197 G5
Javhlant = Uliastay Mongolia 47°56N 97°28E 218 B8
Javier, I. Chile 47°5S 74°25W 336 C2
Javla India 17°18N 75°9E 244 F2
Jawa Indonesia 7°0S 110°0E 235 D4
Jawa Barat □ Indonesia 7°0S 107°0E 231 G12
Jawa Tengah □ Indonesia 7°0S 110°0E 235 D3
Jawa Timur □ Indonesia 8°0S 113°0E 235 D4
Jawad India 24°36N 74°51E 242 G6
Jawaharlal Nehru Port = Nhava Sheva India 18°58N 72°55E 130 B2
Jawf, W. al → Yemen 15°50N 45°30E 248 D4
Jawhar India 19°55N 73°14E 244 E1
Jawhar Somalia 2°48N 45°30E 267 D6
Jawor Poland 51°4N 16°11E 185 G3
Jaworowa Poland 52°9N 20°56E 143 C1
Jaworzno Poland 50°13N 19°11E 185 H6
Jaworzyna Śląska Poland 50°55N 16°28E 185 H3
Jawoyn ❂ Australia 14°16S 132°28E 278 B5
Jay U.S.A. 30°57N 87°9W 317 E2
Jay Peak U.S.A. 44°55N 72°32W 313 B12
Jaya, Puncak Indonesia 3°57S 137°17E 231 E9
Jayanca Peru 6°24S 79°50W 330 B2
Jayanti India 26°45N 89°40E 241 B2
Jayapura Indonesia 2°28S 140°38E 231 E10
Jayawijaya, Pegunungan Indonesia 5°0S 139°0E 231 F9
Jaynagar India 26°43N 86°9E 243 F12
Jaypur = Jeypore India 18°50N 82°38E 244 E6
Jayrūd Syria 33°49N 36°44E 250 E7
Jayton U.S.A. 33°15N 100°34W 314 E4
Jāz Mūrīān, Hāmūn-e Iran 27°20N 58°55E 247 E8
Jazīreh-ye Shīf Iran 29°4N 50°54E 247 D6
Jazminal Mexico 24°52N 101°24W 318 C4
Jazzīn Lebanon 33°31N 35°35E 250 E6
Jean U.S.A. 35°47N 115°20W 307 K11
Jean Lafitte Nat. Historical Park ⌓ U.S.A. 29°51N 90°9W 131 B1
Jean Marie River Canada 61°32N 120°38W 296 A4
Jean-Rabel Haiti 19°50N 73°5W 321 C5
Jeanerette U.S.A. 29°55N 91°40W 314 G9
Jeanette, Ostrov = Zhannetty, Ostrov Russia 76°43N 158°0E 215 B16
Jeanne-Mance, Parc Montréal, Canada 130 b1
Jeanneton, Morne Guadeloupe 16°14N 61°43W 322 e
Jeannette U.S.A. 40°20N 79°36W 312 F5
Jebāl Bārez, Kūh-e Iran 28°30N 58°20E 247 D8
Jebba Nigeria 9°9N 4°48E 263 D5
Jebel, Bahr el → South Sudan 9°30N 30°25E 257 F3
Jebel Ali = Minā' Jabal 'Alī U.A.E. 25°2N 55°8E 247 E7
Jebel Dud Sudan 13°25N 33°9E 257 E3
Jebel Elba △ Egypt 22°11N 36°22E 256 C4
Jebel Qerri Sudan 16°16N 32°50E 257 D3
Jeberos Peru 5°15S 76°10W 330 B2
Jebus Indonesia 1°43S 105°28E 234 C3
Jecheon S. Korea 37°8N 128°12E 224 D4
Jedburgh U.K. 55°29N 2°33W 167 F6
Jedda = Jiddah Si. Arabia 21°29N 39°10E 248 B2
Jeddore L. Canada 48°3N 55°55W 299 C8
Jedlesee Austria 48°15N 16°23E 142 A2
Jedlicze Poland 49°43N 21°40E 185 J8
Jędrzejów Poland 50°35N 20°15E 185 H7
Jedwabne Poland 53°17N 22°18E 185 E9
Jeetzel → Germany 53°9N 11°3E 178 B7
Jefferson Ga., U.S.A. 34°7N 83°35W 316 A6
Jefferson Iowa, U.S.A. 42°1N 94°23W 310 B2
Jefferson La., U.S.A. 29°57N 90°9W 131 B2
Jefferson Ohio, U.S.A. 41°44N 80°46W 312 E4
Jefferson Tex., U.S.A. 32°46N 94°21W 314 E7
Jefferson Wis., U.S.A. 43°0N 88°48W 311 B8
Jefferson, Mt. Nev., U.S.A. 38°47N 116°56W 304 G5
Jefferson, Mt. Oreg., U.S.A. 44°41N 121°48W 304 D3
Jefferson City Mo., U.S.A. 38°34N 92°10W 310 F4
Jefferson City Tenn., U.S.A. 36°7N 83°30W 315 C13
Jefferson Memorial Washington, D.C., U.S.A. 143 c1
Jefferson Park Calif., U.S.A. 34°2N 118°19W 126 B3
Jefferson Park Ill., U.S.A. 41°58N 87°46W 119 B2
Jeffersontown U.S.A. 38°12N 85°35W 311 F11
Jeffersonville Ga., U.S.A. 32°41N 83°20W 316 C6
Jeffersonville Ind., U.S.A. 38°17N 85°44W 311 F11
Jeffersonville Ohio, U.S.A. 39°39N 83°34W 311 E13
Jeffrey City U.S.A. 42°30N 107°49W 304 E10
Jega Nigeria 12°15N 4°23E 263 C5
Jegi S. Korea 37°34N 127°1E 137 B2
Jejevo Solomon Is. 8°6S 159°8E 287 M10
Jeju S. Korea 33°31N 126°32E 224 a
Jeju-do S. Korea 33°29N 126°34E 224 a
Jeju-do □ S. Korea 33°25N 126°30E 224 a
Jēkabpils Latvia 56°29N 25°57E 188 D3
Jekyll I. U.S.A. 31°4N 81°25W 316 D8
Jelambar Indonesia 6°9S 106°47E 122 A1
Jelcz-Laskowice Poland 51°2N 17°19E 185 G4
Jelenia Góra Poland 50°50N 15°45E 185 H2
Jelgava Latvia 56°41N 23°49E 184 B10
Jelgava □ Latvia 56°35N 23°45E 184 B10
Jelica Serbia 43°50N 20°17E 202 C4
Jelli South Sudan 5°25N 31°45E 257 F3
Jelonki Poland 52°14N 20°54E 143 B1
Jelšava Slovak Rep. 48°37N 20°15E 181 C13
Jema'a Mallam = Kafanchan Nigeria 9°40N 8°20E 263 D6
Jemaja Indonesia 3°5N 105°45E 234 B3
Jemaluang Malaysia 2°16N 103°52E 237 L4
Jember Indonesia 8°11S 113°41E 235 D4
Jempang, Danau Indonesia 0°25S 116°12E 235 C5
Jena Thüringen, Germany 50°54N 11°35E 178 E7
Jena La., U.S.A. 31°41N 92°8W 314 F8
Jenai Taiwan 24°2N 121°8E 225 B3
Jenbach Austria 47°24N 11°47E 180 D4
Jendouba Tunisia 36°29N 8°47E 258 A1
Jendouba □ Tunisia 36°34N 8°52E 261 A6
Jeneponto Indonesia 5°40S 119°44E 235 D5
Jengish Chokoso = Pobedy, Pik Kyrgyzstan 42°0N 79°58E 217 D9
Jenho Taiwan 23°54N 121°36E 225 C3
Jenīn West Bank 32°28N 35°18E 251 F6
Jenison U.S.A. 42°54N 85°47W 311 B11
Jenkins U.S.A. 37°10N 82°38W 309 G12
Jenner U.S.A. 38°27N 123°7W 306 G3
Jennings Fla., U.S.A. 30°36N 83°6W 316 E6
Jennings La., U.S.A. 30°13N 92°40W 314 F8
Jennings Mo., U.S.A. 38°43N 90°15W 310 F6
Jenny Pt. Dominica 15°28N 61°15W 323 k
Jensen Beach U.S.A. 27°15N 80°14W 317 H9
Jente Taiwan 22°58N 120°16E 225 D2
Jenwu Taiwan 22°42N 120°20E 225 D2
Jeollabuk-do □ S. Korea 35°45N 127°15E 224 E3
Jeollanam-do □ S. Korea 34°45N 127°0E 224 E3
Jeong-eup S. Korea 35°35N 126°50E 224 E3
Jeongseon S. Korea 37°20N 128°45E 227 F15
Jeonju S. Korea 35°50N 127°4E 224 E3
Jepara Indonesia 7°40S 109°14E 235 D3
Jeparit Australia 36°8S 142°1E 282 D5
Jequié Brazil 13°51S 40°5W 333 D3
Jequitaí → Brazil 17°4S 44°50W 333 E3
Jequitinhonha Brazil 16°30S 41°0W 333 E3
Jequitinhonha → Brazil 15°51S 38°53W 333 E4
Jerada Morocco 34°17N 2°10W 261 B4
Jerantut Malaysia 3°56N 102°22E 237 L4
Jerejak, Pulau Malaysia 5°19N 100°19E 237 c
Jérémie Haiti 18°40N 74°10W 321 C5
Jeremoabo Brazil 10°4S 38°21W 332 D4
Jerez, Pta. Mexico 22°58N 97°40W 319 C5
Jerez de García Salinas Mexico 22°39N 103°0W 318 C4
Jerez de la Frontera Spain 36°41N 6°7W 195 J4
Jerez de los Caballeros Spain 38°20N 6°45W 195 G4
Jericho = El Arīḩā West Bank 31°52N 35°27E 251 G6
Jericho Australia 23°38S 146°6E 280 C4
Jerichow Germany 52°30N 12°1E 178 C8
Jerico Springs U.S.A. 37°37N 94°1W 310 G2
Jerid, Chott el = Djerid, Chott Tunisia 33°42N 8°30E 258 B1
Jerilderie Australia 35°20S 145°41E 283 C6
Jermyn U.S.A. 41°32N 75°33W 313 E9
Jerningham Junction Trin. & Tob. 10°33N 61°23W 323 t
Jerome U.S.A. 42°44N 114°31W 304 E6
Jerónimos, Mosteiro dos Portugal 38°41N 9°11W 126 A1
Jerramungup Australia 33°55S 118°55E 279 F2
Jersey U.K. 49°11N 2°7W 169 H5
Jersey City U.S.A. 40°42N 74°4W 132 B1
Jersey Shore U.S.A. 41°12N 77°15W 312 E7
Jerseyville U.S.A. 39°7N 90°20W 310 E6
Jerumenha Brazil 7°5S 43°30W 332 C3
Jerusalem Israel/West Bank 31°47N 35°10E 123 B2
Jervis B. Australia 35°8S 150°46E 283 C9
Jervis Bay △ Australia 35°9S 150°40E 283 C9
Jervis Inlet Canada 50°0N 123°57W 296 C4
Jerzu Italy 39°47N 9°31E 200 C2
Jesenice Slovenia 46°28N 14°3E 199 B11
Jeseník Czech Rep. 50°14N 17°8E 181 A10
Jesenké Slovak Rep. 48°20N 20°10E 181 C13
Jesi = Iesi Italy 43°31N 13°14E 199 E10
Jessamine, L. U.S.A. 28°28N 81°23W 133 B2
Jessel = Jasło Poland 49°45N 21°30E 185 J8
Jesselton = Kota Kinabalu Malaysia 6°0N 116°4E 235 A5
Jessheim Norway 60°9N 11°10E 164 D8
Jessnitz Germany 51°40N 12°18E 178 D8
Jessore Bangla. 23°10N 89°10E 241 D2
Jesup Ga., U.S.A. 31°36N 81°53W 316 D8
Jesup Iowa, U.S.A. 42°29N 92°4W 310 B4
Jesup, L. U.S.A. 28°43N 81°14W 317 G8
Jesús Peru 7°15S 78°25W 330 B2
Jésus, Î. Canada 45°36N 73°44W 130 A1
Jesús Carranza Mexico 17°26N 95°2W 319 D5
Jesús María Argentina 30°59S 64°5W 334 C3
Jesús Maria Lima, Peru 12°4S 77°3W 124 B2
Jetmore U.S.A. 38°4N 99°54W 308 F4
Jetpur India 21°45N 70°10E 242 J4
Jette Belgium 50°53N 4°20E 116 A1
Jeumont France 50°18N 4°6E 173 B11
Jeungdo S. Korea 34°56N 126°9E 224 E3
Jeungpyeong S. Korea 36°47N 127°34E 224 D3
Jevnaker Norway 60°15N 10°26E 164 D7
Jewell U.S.A. 42°20N 93°39W 310 B3
Jewett U.S.A. 40°22N 81°2W 312 F3
Jewett City U.S.A. 41°36N 71°59W 313 E13
Jewish Quarter Jerusalem 123 b3
Jey Iran 35°41N 51°20E 141 B2
Jeyḩūnābād Iran 34°58N 48°59E 247 C6
Jeypore India 18°50N 82°38E 244 E6
Jeziorak, Jezioro Poland 53°40N 19°35E 184 E6
Jeziorany Poland 53°58N 20°46E 184 E7
Jeziorka → Poland 52°8N 21°9E 185 F8
Jha Jha India 24°46N 86°22E 243 G12
Jhaarkand = Jharkhand □ India 24°0N 85°50E 243 H11
Jhabua India 22°46N 74°36E 242 H6
Jhajjar India 28°37N 76°42E 242 E7
Jhal Pakistan 28°17N 67°27E 242 E2
Jhal Jhao Pakistan 26°20N 65°35E 240 D2
Jhalakati Bangla. 22°39N 90°12E 241 D3
Jhalawar India 24°40N 76°10E 242 G7
Jhalida India 23°22N 85°58E 243 H11
Jhalrapatan India 24°33N 76°10E 242 G7
Jhang Maghiana Pakistan 31°15N 72°22E 242 D5
Jhansi India 25°30N 78°36E 243 G8
Jhargram India 22°27N 86°59E 243 H12
Jharia India 23°45N 86°26E 243 H12
Jharkhand □ India 24°0N 85°50E 243 H11
Jharsuguda India 21°56N 84°5E 244 D7
Jhelum Pakistan 33°0N 73°45E 242 C5
Jhelum → Pakistan 31°20N 72°10E 242 D5
Jhenaidah Bangla. 23°33N 89°10E 241 D2
Jhilmilli India 23°24N 82°51E 243 H10
Jhudo Pakistan 24°58N 69°18E 242 G3
Jhunjhunun India 28°10N 75°30E 242 E6
Ji-Paraná Brazil 10°50S 61°58W 331 C5
Ji Xian China 36°7N 110°40E 226 F6
Jia Xian Henan, China 33°59N 113°12E 226 H7
Jia Xian Shaanxi, China 38°12N 110°28E 226 E6
Jiahe China 25°38N 112°19E 229 E9
Jiaji = Qionghai China 19°15N 110°26E 236 C8
Jialing Jiang → China 29°30N 106°20E 228 C6
Jiamusi China 46°40N 130°26E 219 B15
Ji'an Jiangxi, China 27°6N 114°59E 229 D10
Ji'an Jilin, China 41°5N 126°10E 227 D14
Jianchang China 40°55N 120°35E 227 D11
Jianchuan China 26°38N 99°55E 228 D2
Jiande China 29°23N 119°15E 229 C12
Jiang'an China 28°40N 105°3E 228 C5
Jiangbei China 29°40N 106°34E 228 C6
Jiangcheng China 22°36N 101°52E 228 F3
Jiangchuan China 24°8N 102°39E 228 E4
Jiangdi China 26°57N 103°37E 228 D4
Jiangdu China 32°27N 119°36E 229 A12
Jiange China 32°4N 105°32E 228 A5
Jianggao China 23°13N 113°13E 121 A2
Jianghua China 25°0N 111°47E 229 E8
Jiangjin China 29°14N 106°14E 228 C6
Jiangkou China 27°40N 108°49E 228 D7
Jiangle China 26°42N 117°23E 229 D11
Jiangmen China 22°32N 113°0E 229 F9
Jiangning China 31°55N 118°50E 229 B12
Jiangshan China 28°40N 118°37E 229 C12
Jiangsu □ China 33°0N 120°0E 227 H11
Jiangwan China 31°18N 121°28E 138 B1
Jiangxi □ China 27°30N 116°0E 229 D11
Jiangyan China 32°30N 120°7E 229 A13
Jiangyin China 31°54N 120°17E 229 B13
Jiangyong China 25°20N 111°22E 229 E8
Jiangyou China 31°44N 104°43E 228 B5
Jiangyuan China 42°2N 126°34E 227 C14
Jianhe China 26°37N 108°31E 228 D7
Jianli China 29°46N 112°56E 229 C9
Jianning China 26°50N 116°50E 229 D11
Jian'ou China 27°3N 118°17E 229 D12
Jianping China 41°53N 119°42E 227 D10
Jianshi China 30°37N 109°38E 228 B7
Jianshui China 23°36N 102°43E 228 F4
Jianyang Fujian, China 27°20N 118°5E 229 D12
Jianyang Sichuan, China 30°24N 104°33E 228 B5
Jiao Xian = Jiaozhou China 36°18N 120°1E 227 F11
Jiaohe Hebei, China 38°2N 116°20E 226 E9
Jiaohe Jilin, China 43°40N 127°22E 227 C14
Jiaoling China 24°41N 116°12E 229 E11
Jiaonan China 35°52N 119°58E 227 G10
Jiaozhou China 36°18N 120°1E 227 F11
Jiaozhou Wan China 36°5N 120°10E 227 F11
Jiaozuo China 35°16N 113°12E 226 G7
Jiawang China 34°28N 117°26E 227 G9
Jiaxiang China 35°25N 116°20E 226 G9
Jiaxing China 30°49N 120°45E 229 B13
Jiayi = Chiai Taiwan 23°29N 120°25E 225 C2
Jiayu China 29°55N 113°55E 229 C9
Jiayuguan China 39°49N 98°18E 218 D8
Jib West Bank 31°51N 35°11E 123 A2
Jibão, Serra do Brazil 14°48S 45°0W 333 D3
Jibiya Nigeria 13°5N 7°12E 263 C6
Jiblah Yemen 13°55N 44°9E 248 D4
Jibou Romania 47°15N 23°17E 183 C8
Jibuti = Djibouti ■ Africa 12°0N 43°0E 257 E5
Jicarón, I. Panama 7°10N 81°50W 320 E3
Jičín Czech Rep. 50°25N 15°28E 180 A8
Jiddah Si. Arabia 21°29N 39°10E 248 B2
Jido India 29°2N 94°58E 241 A5
Jido S. Korea 35°4N 126°14E 224 E3
Jieshou China 33°18N 115°22E 226 H8
Jiexiu China 37°2N 111°55E 226 F6
Jieyang China 23°35N 116°21E 229 F11
Jigalong Australia 23°21S 120°47E 278 D3
Jigalong ❂ Australia 23°21S 120°46E 278 D3
Jigawa □ Nigeria 12°0N 9°45E 263 C6
Jigme Dorje △ Bhutan 28°0N 89°40E 241 B2
Jigme Singye Wangchuck Bhutan 27°20N 90°25E 241 B3
Jigni India 25°45N 79°25E 243 G8
Jihād Iraq 33°17N 44°19E 113 B1
Jihlava Czech Rep. 49°28N 15°35E 180 B8
Jihlava → Czech Rep. 48°55N 16°36E 181 C9
Jihlavský □ Czech Rep. 49°30N 15°30E 180 B8
Jihnan Taiwan 24°22N 120°39E 225 B2
Jihočeský □ Czech Rep. 49°8N 14°35E 180 B7
Jihomoravský □ Czech Rep. 49°5N 16°30E 181 B9
Jiigley Somalia 5°25N 45°20E 267 C6
Jijel Algeria 36°52N 5°50E 261 A6
Jijel □ Algeria 36°45N 6°0E 261 A6
Jijiga Ethiopia 9°20N 42°50E 267 C5
Jikamshi Nigeria 12°12N 7°45E 263 C6
Jikau South Sudan 8°28N 33°47E 257 F3
Jilib Somalia 0°29N 42°46E 267 D5
Jilin China 43°44N 126°30E 227 C14
Jilin □ China 44°0N 127°0E 224 A3
Jiloca → Spain 41°21N 1°39W 196 D3
Jilong = Chilung Taiwan 25°3N 121°45E 225 A3
Jim Thompson's House Bangkok, Thailand 113 b3
Jim Thorpe U.S.A. 40°52N 75°44W 313 F9
Jima Ethiopia 7°40N 36°47E 257 F4
Jimbaran, Teluk Indonesia 8°46S 115°9E 231 K18
Jimbōchō Tokyo, Japan 140 a4
Jimbolia Romania 45°47N 20°43E 182 E5
Jimena de la Frontera Spain 36°27N 5°24W 195 J5
Jiménez Chihuahua, Mexico 27°8N 104°54W 318 B4
Jimenez Phil. 8°20N 123°50E 233 G4
Jimeta Nigeria 9°17N 12°28E 263 D7
Jimo China 36°23N 120°30E 227 F11
Jimsar China 43°59N 89°4E 217 D11
Jin Jiang → China 28°24N 115°48E 229 C10
Jin Xian = Jinzhou China 38°55N 121°42E 227 E11
Jinan China 36°38N 117°1E 226 F9
Jinchang China 38°30N 102°10E 218 D9
Jincheng China 35°29N 112°50E 226 G7
Jinchuan China 31°30N 102°3E 228 B4
Jind India 29°19N 76°22E 242 E7
Jindabyne Australia 36°25S 148°35E 283 D8
Jinding China 22°22N 113°33E 219 a
Jindo S. Korea 34°28N 126°15E 224 E3
Jindřichův Hradec Czech Rep. 49°10N 15°2E 180 B8
Jing He → China 34°27N 109°4E 226 G5
Jing Shan China 31°20N 111°35E 229 B8
Jing Xian China 30°38N 118°25E 229 B12
Jing'an Jiangxi, China 28°50N 115°17E 229 C10
Jingan Shanghai, China 31°14N 121°25E 138 B1
Jingbian China 37°20N 108°30E 226 F5
Jingchuan China 35°20N 107°20E 226 G4
Jingde China 30°15N 118°27E 229 B12
Jingdezhen China 29°20N 117°11E 229 C11
Jingdong China 24°23N 100°47E 228 E3
Jinggangshan China 26°58N 114°15E 229 D10
Jinggu China 23°35N 100°41E 228 F3
Jinghai Guangdong, China 22°59N 116°31E 229 F11
Jinghai Tianjin, China 38°55N 116°55E 226 E9
Jinghong China 22°0N 100°45E 228 G3
Jinghong Dam China 22°10N 100°46E 228 F3
Jingjiang China 32°2N 120°16E 229 A13
Jingle China 38°20N 111°55E 226 E6
Jingmen China 31°0N 112°10E 229 B9
Jingning China 35°30N 105°43E 226 G3
Jingpo Hu China 43°55N 128°55E 227 C15
Jingshan China 31°1N 113°7E 229 B9
Jingtai China 37°10N 104°6E 226 F3
Jingtanggang China 39°10N 119°5E 227 E10
Jingu Outer Garden Tokyo, Japan 140 b2
Jingxi China 23°8N 106°27E 228 F6
Jingyang China 34°30N 108°50E 226 G5
Jingyu China 42°25N 126°45E 224 A3
Jingyuan China 36°30N 104°40E 226 F3
Jingzhou Hubei, China 30°21N 112°11E 229 B9
Jingzhou Hunan, China 26°33N 109°40E 228 D7
Jingziguan China 33°15N 111°0E 226 H6
Jinhua China 29°8N 119°38E 229 C12
Jining Nei Monggol Zizhiqu, China 41°5N 113°0E 226 D7
Jining Shandong, China 35°22N 116°34E 226 G9
Jinja Uganda 0°25N 33°12E 268 B3
Jinjang Malaysia 3°13N 101°39E 237 L3
Jinji China 37°58N 106°8E 226 F4
Jinjiang Fujian, China 24°43N 118°33E 229 E12
Jinjiang Yunnan, China 26°14N 100°34E 228 D3
Jinjini Ghana 7°26N 2°42W 262 D4
Jinju S. Korea 35°12N 128°2E 224 E4
Jinkou China 30°20N 114°8E 229 B10
Jinkouhe China 29°18N 103°4E 228 C4
Jinmu Jiao China 18°9N 109°34E 236 C7
Jinnah Barrage Pakistan 32°58N 71°33E 242 C4
Jinning China 24°38N 102°38E 228 E4
Jinočany Czech Rep. 50°2N 14°16E 135 B1
Jinonice Czech Rep. 50°3N 14°22E 135 B2
Jinotega Nic. 13°6N 85°59W 320 D2
Jinotepe Nic. 11°50N 86°10W 320 D2
Jinping Guizhou, China 26°41N 109°10E 228 D7
Jinping Yunnan, China 22°45N 103°18E 228 F4
Jinqiao China 31°15N 121°36E 138 B2
Jinsha China 27°29N 106°12E 228 D6
Jinsha Jiang → China 28°50N 104°36E 228 C5
Jinshi China 29°40N 111°50E 229 C8
Jintan China 31°42N 119°36E 229 B12
Jintotolo Channel Phil. 11°48N 123°5E 233 F4
Jintotolo I. Phil. 11°51N 123°7E 233 F4
Jintur India 19°37N 76°42E 244 E3
Jinxi Jiangxi, China 27°56N 116°45E 229 D11
Jinxi Liaoning, China 40°52N 120°50E 227 D11
Jinxian China 28°26N 116°17E 229 C11
Jinxiang China 35°5N 116°22E 226 G9
Jinyang China 27°28N 103°5E 228 D4
Jinyun China 28°35N 120°5E 229 C13
Jinzhai China 31°40N 115°53E 229 B10
Jinzhong China 37°42N 112°46E 226 F7
Jinzhou Liaoning, China 38°55N 121°42E 227 E11
Jinzhou Liaoning, China 41°5N 121°3E 227 D11
Jiparaná → Brazil 8°3S 62°52W 331 B5
Jipijapa Ecuador 1°0S 80°40W 328 D1
Jiquilpan Mexico 19°59N 102°43W 318 D4
Jirisan S. Korea 35°20N 127°44E 224 E3
Jirisan △ S. Korea 35°15N 127°30E 224 E3
Jiroft Iran 28°45N 57°50E 247 D8
Jishan China 35°34N 110°58E 226 G6
Jishou China 28°21N 109°43E 228 C7
Jishui China 27°12N 115°8E 229 D10
Jisr ash Shughūr Syria 35°49N 36°18E 250 C7
Jitarning Australia 32°48S 117°57E 279 F2
Jitra Malaysia 6°16N 100°25E 237 J3
Jiu → Romania 43°47N 23°48E 183 G8
Jiudengkou China 39°56N 106°40E 226 E4
Jiujiang Guangdong, China 22°50N 113°0E 229 F9
Jiujiang Jiangxi, China 29°42N 115°58E 229 C10
Jiuling Shan China 28°40N 114°40E 229 C10
Jiulong = Kowloon China 22°19N 114°11E 122 B1
Jiulong China 28°57N 101°31E 228 C3
Jiuquan China 39°50N 98°20E 218 D8
Jiutai China 44°10N 125°50E 227 B13
Jiuxincheng China 39°17N 115°59E 226 E8
Jiuzhaigou ⌓ China 33°8N 103°52E 228 A4
Jiwani Pakistan 25°1N 61°44E 240 D1
Jiwani, Ras Pakistan 25°1N 61°44E 240 D1
Jixi Anhui, China 30°5N 118°34E 229 B12
Jixi Heilongjiang, China 45°20N 130°50E 227 B16
Jiyang China 37°0N 117°12E 227 F9
Jiyuan China 35°7N 112°57E 226 G7
Jiyūgaoka Japan 35°35N 139°40E 140 B3
Jiz', W. → Yemen 16°12N 52°14E 249 C6
Jizā'ir Iraq 33°15N 44°23E 113 B2
Jīzān Si. Arabia 17°0N 42°20E 248 C3
Jize China 36°54N 114°56E 226 F8
Jizera → Czech Rep. 50°10N 14°43E 180 A7
Jizhou China 37°35N 115°30E 226 F8
Jizīra Iraq 33°15N 44°25E 113 B2
Jizl, Wādī al → Si. Arabia 25°39N 38°25E 246 E3
Jizō-Zaki Japan 35°34N 133°20E 222 B5
Jizzax Uzbekistan 40°6N 67°50E 217 D7
Jizzax □ Uzbekistan 40°20N 67°40E 217 D7
Joaçaba Brazil 27°5S 51°31W 335 B5
Joaíma Brazil 16°39S 41°2W 333 E3
Joal Fadiout Senegal 14°9N 16°50W 262 C1
João Amaro Brazil 12°46S 40°22W 333 D3
João Belo = Xai-Xai Mozam. 25°6S 33°31E 271 C5
João Câmara Brazil 5°32S 35°48W 332 C4
João Neiva Brazil 19°45S 40°24W 333 E3
João Pessoa = Eirunepé Brazil 6°35S 69°53W 330 B4
João Pessoa = Porto Brazil 3°54S 42°42W 332 B3
João Pessoa Brazil 7°10S 34°52W 332 C5
João Pinheiro Brazil 17°45S 46°10W 333 E2
Joaquín V. González Argentina 25°10S 64°0W 334 B3
Jobat India 22°25N 74°34E 242 H6
Jobourg, Nez de France 49°41N 1°57W 172 C5
Jódar Spain 37°50N 3°21W 195 H7
Jodhpur India 26°23N 73°8E 242 F5
Jodiya India 22°42N 70°18E 242 H4
Joensuu Finland 62°37N 29°49E 160 E23
Jōetsu Japan 37°12N 138°10E 221 F9
Jœuf France 49°12N 6°0E 173 C12
Jofane Mozam. 21°15S 34°18E 271 B5
Joffre, Morne = Moustique, Morne Guadeloupe 16°7N 61°44W 322 e
Jog Falls = Gersoppa Falls India 14°12N 74°46E 245 G2
Jogbani India 26°25N 87°15E 243 F12
Jõgeva Estonia 58°45N 26°24E 188 C4
Jogjakarta = Yogyakarta Indonesia 7°49S 110°22E 235 D4
Joglo Indonesia 6°13S 106°45E 122 B1
Jōhana Japan 36°30N 136°57E 223 A8
Johannesburg Gauteng, S. Africa 26°11S 28°2E 123 B2
Johannesburg Calif., U.S.A. 35°22N 117°38W 307 K9
Johannesburg, Univ. of S. Africa 26°11S 28°0E 123 B2
Johanneskirchen Germany 48°10N 11°38E 131 A2
Johannesstift Germany 52°34N 13°12E 115 A2
Johannisburg = Pisz Poland 53°38N 21°49E 184 E8
Johannisthal Germany 52°26N 13°30E 115 B4
Johansfors Sweden 56°42N 15°32E 163 H9
Johilla → India 23°37N 81°14E 243 H9
John Crow Mts. Jamaica 18°5N 76°25W 320 a
John Day U.S.A. 44°25N 118°57W 304 D4
John Day → U.S.A. 45°44N 120°39W 304 D3
John Day Fossil Beds ⌓ U.S.A. 44°33N 119°38W 304 D4
John D'or Prairie Canada 58°30N 115°8W 296 B5
John F. Kennedy Nat. Historic Site ⌓ U.S.A. 42°20N 71°7W 116 A2
John F. Kennedy Space Center U.S.A. 28°40N 80°42W 317 G9
John H. Kerr Res. U.S.A. 36°36N 78°18W 315 C15
John Hancock Center U.S.A. 119 a2
John McLaren Park U.S.A. 37°43N 122°24W 136 B2
John o' Groats U.K. 58°38N 3°4W 167 C5
John U. Lloyd Beach ⌓ U.S.A. 26°4N 80°6W 129 B3
Johnnie U.S.A. 36°25N 116°5W 307 J10
Johns Creek U.S.A. 34°2N 84°12W 316 A5
Johns I. U.S.A. 32°47N 80°7W 316 C9
John's Ra. Australia 21°55S 133°23E 280 C1
Johnson U.S.A. 44°38N 72°41W 313 B12
Johnson City Kans., U.S.A. 37°34N 101°45W 308 G3
Johnson City N.Y., U.S.A. 42°7N 75°58W 313 D9
Johnson City Tenn., U.S.A. 36°19N 82°21W 315 C13
Johnson City Tex., U.S.A. 30°17N 98°25W 314 F5
Johnsonburg U.S.A. 41°29N 78°41W 312 E6
Johnsondale U.S.A. 35°58N 118°32W 307 K8
Johnsons Crossing Canada 60°29N 133°18W 296 A2
Johnsons Pt. Antigua & B. 17°2N 61°53W 322 b
Johnsonville N.Z. 41°13S 174°48E 284 H3
Johnston Iowa, U.S.A. 41°40N 93°42W 310 C3
Johnston S.C., U.S.A. 33°50N 81°48W 316 B8
Johnston, L. Australia 32°25S 120°30E 279 F3
Johnston City U.S.A. 37°49N 88°56W 310 G8
Johnston Falls = Mambilima Falls Zambia 10°31S 28°45E 269 E2
Johnston I. Pac. Oc. 17°10N 169°8W 289 F11
Johnstone Str. Canada 50°28N 126°0W 296 C3
Johnstown Kilkenny, Ireland 52°45N 7°33W 166 D4
Johnstown N.Y., U.S.A. 43°0N 74°22W 313 C10
Johnstown Ohio, U.S.A. 40°9N 82°41W 312 F2
Johnstown Pa., U.S.A. 40°20N 78°55W 312 F6
Johor □ Malaysia 2°5N 103°20E 237 M4
Johor, Selat Asia 1°28N 103°47E 237 d
Johor Bahru Malaysia 1°28N 103°46E 237 d
Jõhvi Estonia 59°22N 27°27E 188 C4
Joigny France 47°58N 3°20E 173 E10
Joinville Brazil 26°15S 48°55W 335 B6
Joinville Haute-Marne, France 48°27N 5°10E 173 D12
Joinville I. Antarctica 65°0S 55°30W 151 C18
Joinville-le-Pont France 48°49N 2°27E 134 B3
Jojutla Mexico 18°37N 99°11W 319 D5
Jøkelbugten Greenland 78°25N 20°20W 154 B9
Jokkmokk Sweden 66°35N 19°50E 160 C18
Jökulsá á Bru → Iceland 65°40N 14°16W 155 B12
Jökulsá á Fjöllum → Iceland 66°10N 16°30W 155 A10
Jökulsárgljúfur △ Iceland 65°56N 16°31W 155 B10
Jolfā Āzarbājān-e Sharqī, Iran 38°57N 45°38E 213 C11
Jolfā Eşfahan, Iran 32°58N 51°37E 247 C6
Joli-Bois Belgium 50°42N 4°24E 116 B2
Joliet U.S.A. 41°32N 88°5W 311 C8
Joliette Canada 46°3N 73°24W 298 C5
Jollas Finland 60°10N 25°5E 121 B3
Jolo Phil. 6°0N 121°0E 233 H3
Jolo Group Phil. 6°0N 121°9E 233 J3
Jolon U.S.A. 35°58N 121°9W 306 K5
Jølstravatnet Norway 61°32N 6°23E 164 C3
Jomalig I. Phil. 14°42N 122°22E 232 D4
Jombang Indonesia 7°33S 112°14E 235 D4
Jomda China 31°28N 98°12E 228 B2
Jonåker Sweden 58°45N 16°45E 163 F10
Jonava Lithuania 55°8N 24°12E 188 E3
Jondal Norway 60°16N 6°15E 164 D3
Jones Phil. 16°33N 121°42E 232 C3
Jones Sound Canada 76°0N 85°0W 295 B15
Jonesboro Ark., U.S.A. 35°50N 90°42W 315 D9
Jonesboro Ga., U.S.A. 33°31N 84°22W 316 B5
Jonesboro La., U.S.A. 32°15N 92°43W 314 E8
Jonesburg U.S.A. 38°51N 91°18W 310 F5
Jonesville Ind., U.S.A. 39°5N 85°54W 311 E11
Jonesville Mich., U.S.A. 41°59N 84°40W 311 C12
Jong → S. Leone 7°32N 12°23W 262 D2
Jonglei South Sudan 6°25N 31°30E 257 F3
Jonglei □ South Sudan 7°30N 32°30E 257 F3
Jonglei Canal South Sudan 9°20N 31°39E 266 C3
Jongmyo Royal Shrine S. Korea 37°34N 126°59E 137 B1
Jongno S. Korea 37°35N 126°59E 137 B1
Joniškis Lithuania 56°13N 23°35E 184 B10
Jönköping Sweden 57°45N 14°8E 163 G8
Jönköpings län □ Sweden 57°30N 14°30E 163 G8
Jonquière Canada 48°27N 71°14W 299 C5
Jonsered Sweden 57°45N 12°10E 163 G6
Jonstrup Denmark 55°45N 12°20E 118 A2
Jonzac France 45°27N 0°28W 174 C3
Joplin U.S.A. 37°6N 94°31W 308 G6
Joppa U.K. 55°57N 3°6W 121 B3
Jora India 26°20N 77°49E 242 F6
Jordan Guimaras, Phil. 10°40N 122°35E 233 F4
Jordan Mont., U.S.A. 47°19N 106°55W 304 C10
Jordan N.Y., U.S.A. 43°4N 76°29W 313 C8
Jordan ■ Asia 31°0N 36°0E 251 H7
Jordan → Asia 31°48N 35°32E 251 G6
Jordan Valley U.S.A. 42°59N 117°3W 304 E5
Jordânia Brazil 15°55S 40°11W 333 E3
Jordanów Poland 49°41N 19°49E 185 J6
Jordet Norway 61°25N 12°8E 164 C9
Jorge, C. Chile 51°40S 75°35W 336 D1
Jorge Chavez, Int. ✈ (LIM) Peru 12°2S 77°8W 124 B2
Jorge Newbery ✈ (AEP) Argentina 34°34S 58°25W 117 B2
Jorgen Brønlund Fjord Greenland 82°30N 31°0W 154 A7
Jorhat India 26°45N 94°12E 241 B5
Jori → Norway 62°4N 9°5E 162 B3
Jorm Afghan. 36°50N 70°52E 240 A3
Jörn Sweden 65°4N 20°1E 160 D19
Jorong Indonesia 3°58S 114°56E 235 C4
Jørpeland Norway 59°3N 6°1E 164 E3
Jorquera → Chile 28°3S 69°58W 334 B2
Joru S. Leone 7°41N 11°3W 262 D2
Jos Nigeria 9°53N 8°51E 263 D6
Jos Plateau Nigeria 9°55N 9°0E 263 D6
Jošanička Banja Serbia 43°24N 20°47E 202 C4
Jose Abad Santos Phil. 5°55N 125°39E 233 J5
José Batlle y Ordóñez Uruguay 33°20S 55°10W 335 C4
José Bonifácio = Erechim Brazil 27°35S 52°15W 335 B5
José de San Martín Argentina 44°4S 70°26W 336 B2
Jose Panganiban Phil. 14°17N 122°41E 232 D4
Józefa Piłsudskiego Park Poland 52°15N 21°2E 143 B1
Joseni Romania 46°42N 25°29E 183 D10
Joseph, L. Canada 45°10N 79°44W 312 A5
Joseph Banks Group Australia 34°36S 136°16E 282 C2
Joseph Bonaparte G. Australia 14°35S 128°50E 278 B4
Joseph L. Canada 52°45N 65°18W 299 B6
Joshinath India 30°34N 79°34E 243 D8
Joshinetsu-Kōgen △ Japan 36°42N 138°32E 223 A10
Joshua Tree U.S.A. 34°8N 116°19W 307 L10
Joshua Tree △ U.S.A. 33°55N 116°0W 307 M10
Josselin France 47°57N 2°33W 172 E4
Jost Van Dyke I. Br. Virgin Is. 18°29N 64°47W 321 b
Jostedal Norway 61°35N 7°15E 164 C4
Jostedalsbreen Norway 61°40N 6°59E 164 C3
Jōtō Japan 34°42N 135°33E 133 A2
Jotunheimen Norway 61°35N 8°25E 164 C5
Jotunheimen △ Norway 61°32N 8°25E 164 C5
Joubertberge Namibia 18°30S 14°0E 270 A1
Joué-lès-Tours France 47°21N 0°40E 172 E7
Jourdanton U.S.A. 28°55N 98°33W 314 G5
Joutseno Finland 61°7N 28°31E 188 B5
Jouy-en-Josas France 48°46N 2°10E 134 B2
Jovellanos Cuba 22°40N 81°10W 320 B3
Jovellar Phil. 13°4N 123°36E 232 E4
Jowai India 25°26N 92°12E 241 C4
Jowkār Iran 34°25N 48°40E 213 E13
Jowzjān □ Afghan. 36°10N 66°0E 240 A2
Joya de Cerén El Salv. 13°49N 89°22W 320 D2
Joyeuse France 44°29N 4°16E 175 D8
Jōyō Japan 34°50N 135°47E 223 C7
Józefów Lubelskie, Poland 50°28N 23°2E 185 H10
Józefów Mazowieckie, Poland 52°10N 21°11E 185 F8
Ju Xian China 36°35N 118°20E 227 F10
Juan Aldama Mexico 24°19N 103°21W 318 C4
Juan Anchorena Argentina 34°30S 58°29W 117 A2
Juan Bautista Alberdi Argentina 34°26S 61°48W 334 C3
Juan de Bolas Jamaica 18°5N 77°9W 320 a
Juan de Fuca, Str of. N. Amer. 48°15N 124°0W 306 B3
Juán de Nova Ind. Oc. 17°3S 43°45E 271 A7
Juan Fernández, Arch. de Pac. Oc. 33°50S 80°0W 326 G2
Juan Fernández △ Chile 33°38S 78°52W 330 c
Juan González Romero Mexico 19°30N 99°3W 128 A2
Juan José Castelli Argentina 25°27S 60°57W 334 B3
Juan L. Lacaze Uruguay 34°26S 57°25W 334 C4
Juana Días Puerto Rico 18°3N 66°31W 321 b
Juangriego Venezuela 11°5N 63°58W 329 a
Juangriego, B. de Venezuela 11°5N 63°59W 329 a
Juanjuí Peru 7°10S 76°45W 330 B2
Juankoski Finland 63°3N 28°19E 160 E23
Juara Brazil 11°20S 57°25W 331 C6
Juárez Mexico 27°37N 100°44W 318 B4
Juárez, Sa. de Mexico 32°0N 115°50W 318 A1
Juárez Int. ✈ (MEX) Mexico 19°25N 99°5W 128 B2
Juatinga, Pta. da Brazil 23°17S 44°30W 333 F3
Juàzeiro Brazil 9°30S 40°30W 332 C3
Juàzeiro do Norte Brazil 7°10S 39°18W 332 C4
Juazohn Liberia 5°22N 8°50W 262 D3
Juba South Sudan 4°50N 31°35E 257 G3
Juba → Somalia 1°30N 42°35E 267 D5
Jubail = Al Jubayl Si. Arabia 27°0N 49°50E 247 E6
Jubany Antarctica 62°30S 58°0W 151 C18
Jubayl Lebanon 34°5N 35°39E 250 D6
Jubbada Dhexe □ Somalia 2°0N 41°30E 267 D5
Jubbada Hoose □ Somalia 0°0 42°0E 267 E5
Jubbah Si. Arabia 28°2N 40°56E 246 D4
Jubbal India 31°5N 77°40E 242 D7
Jubbulpore = Jabalpur India 23°9N 79°58E 243 H8
Jübek Germany 54°33N 9°22E 178 A5
Jubga Russia 44°19N 38°48E 191 H4
Jubilee L. Australia 29°0S 126°50E 279 E4
Juby, C. Morocco 28°0N 12°59W 260 C2
Júcar = Xúquer → Spain 39°5N 0°10W 197 F4
Júcaro Cuba 21°37N 78°51W 320 B4
Juchitán de Zaragoza Mexico 16°26N 95°1W 319 D5
Judaberg Norway 59°10N 5°51E 164 E2
Judea = Har Yehuda Israel 31°35N 34°57E 251 G5
Judeira West Bank 31°52N 35°12E 123 A2
Judenburg Austria 47°12N 14°38E 180 D7
Judith → U.S.A. 47°44N 109°39W 304 C9
Judith, Pt. U.S.A. 41°22N 71°29W 313 E13
Judith Gap U.S.A. 46°41N 109°45W 304 C9
Juelsminde Denmark 55°43N 10°1E 163 J4
Jufari → Brazil 1°13S 62°0W 329 D5
Juhdum West Bank 31°42N 35°15E 123 B2
Juhu India 19°5N 73°0E 130 A2
Juifang Taiwan 25°7N 121°48E 225 A3
Juigalpa Nic. 12°6N 85°26W 320 D2
Juillac France 45°20N 1°19E 174 C5
Juist Germany 53°40N 6°59E 178 B2
Juisui Taiwan 23°30N 121°22E 225 C3
Juiz de Fora Brazil 21°43S 43°19W 333 F3
Jūjā Japan 35°45N 139°43E 140 A3
Jujuy □ Argentina 23°20S 65°40W 334 A2
Jukao = Rugao China 32°23N 120°31E 229 A13
Jukskeirivier → S. Africa 26°5S 28°6E 123 A2
Julesburg U.S.A. 40°59N 102°16W 304 F12
Juli Peru 16°10S 69°25W 330 D4
Julia Cr. → Australia 20°0S 141°11E 280 C3
Julia Creek Australia 20°39S 141°44E 280 C3
Juliaca Peru 15°25S 70°10W 330 D3
Julian U.S.A. 33°4N 116°38W 307 M10
Julian, L. Canada 54°25N 77°57W 298 B4
Julian Alps = Julijske Alpe Slovenia 46°15N 14°1E 199 B11
Juliana Top = Mandala, Puncak Indonesia 4°44S 140°20E 231 E10
Julianadorp Curaçao 12°9N 68°57W 322 g
Julianatop Suriname 3°40N 56°30W 329 C6
Julianehåb = Qaqortoq Greenland 60°43N 46°0W 154 E6
Julianów Poland 52°10N 21°9E 143 B2
Jülich Germany 50°55N 6°22E 178 E2
Juliette, L. U.S.A. 33°2N 83°50W 316 B6
Julijske Alpe Slovenia 46°15N 14°1E 199 B11
Julimes Mexico 28°25N 105°27W 318 B3
Jullundur India 31°20N 75°40E 242 D6
Julu China 37°15N 115°2E 226 F8
Jumbo Zimbabwe 17°30S 30°58E 269 F3
Jumbo Pk. U.S.A. 36°12N 114°11W 307 J12
Jumeirah U.A.E. 25°11N 55°14E 119 B1
Jumentos Cays Bahamas 23°0N 75°40W 320 B4
Jumilla Spain 38°28N 1°19W 197 G3
Jumla Nepal 29°15N 82°13E 243 E10
Jumna = Yamuna → India 25°30N 81°53E 243 G9
Jumunjin S. Korea 37°55N 128°54E 224 D4
Junagadh India 21°30N 70°30E 242 J4
Junan China 35°12N 118°53E 227 G10
Juncos Puerto Rico 18°14N 65°55W 321 b
Junction Tex., U.S.A. 30°29N 99°46W 314 F5
Junction Utah, U.S.A. 38°14N 112°13W 305 G7
Junction B. Australia 11°52S 133°55E 280 A1
Junction City Ga., U.S.A. 32°36N 84°28W 316 C5
Junction City Kans., U.S.A. 39°2N 96°50W 308 F5
Junction City Oreg., U.S.A. 44°13N 123°12W 304 D2
Junction Pt. Australia 11°45S 133°50E 280 A1
Jundah Australia 24°46S 143°2E 280 C3
Jundiaí Brazil 24°30S 47°0W 335 A6
Juneau U.S.A. 58°18N 134°25W 296 B2
Junee Australia 34°53S 147°35E 283 C7
Jung S. Korea 37°33N 126°59E 137 B1
Jungar Qi China 39°49N 110°57E 226 E6
Jungbunzlau = Mladá Boleslav Czech Rep. 50°27N 14°53E 180 A7
Jungfernheide, Volkspark Germany 52°32N 13°18E 115 A2
Jungfernsee Germany 52°25N 13°6E 115 B1
Jungfrau Switz. 46°32N 7°58E 179 J3
Junggar Pendi China 44°30N 86°0E 217 D11
Junghans, Teatro Venice, Italy 142 c2
Junghwa S. Korea 37°35N 127°3E 137 B2
Jungkat Indonesia 0°4N 109°13E 235 B3

Jungnang S. Korea 37°36N 127°5E 137 B2
Jungnangcheon →
S. Korea 37°32N 126°55E 137 B1
Jungsdalshytta = Iungsdalshytta
Norway 60°49N 7°55E 164 D4
Jungshahi Pakistan 24°52N 67°44E 242 G2
Juniata → U.S.A. 40°24N 77°1W 312 F7
Junín Argentina 34°33S 60°57W 334 C3
Junín Peru 11°12S 76°0W 330 C2
Junín □ Peru 11°30S 75°0W 330 C3
Junín, L. de Peru 11°2S 76°6W 330 C2
Junín de los Andes
Argentina 39°45S 71°0W 336 A2
Juniper Green U.K. 55°54N 3°16W 121 B2
Jūnīyah Lebanon 33°59N 35°38E 250 E6
Junk B. China 22°17N 114°15E 122 B2
Junlian China 28°8N 104°29E 228 C5
Junnar India 19°12N 73°58E 244 E1
Juno Beach U.S.A. 26°52N 80°3W 317 J9
Juntas Chile 28°24S 69°58W 334 B2
Juntura U.S.A. 43°45N 118°5W 304 E4
Juparanã, L. Brazil 19°16S 40°8W 333 E3
Jupiter U.S.A. 26°57N 80°6W 317 J9
Juquiá Brazil 24°19S 47°38W 333 F2
Jur, Nahr el → South Sudan 8°45N 29°15E 257 F2
Jura = Jura, Mts. du Europe 46°40N 6°5E 173 F13
Jura = Schwäbische Alb
Germany 48°20N 9°30E 179 G5
Jura U.K. 56°0N 5°50W 167 F3
Jura □ France 46°47N 5°45E 173 F12
Jura □ Switz. 47°20N 7°20E 179 H3
Jūra → Lithuania 55°3N 22°9E 184 C9
Jura, Mts. du Europe 46°40N 6°5E 173 F13
Jura, Sd. of U.K. 55°57N 5°45W 167 F3
Juradó Colombia 7°7N 77°46W 328 B2
Jurbarkas Lithuania 55°4N 22°46E 184 C9
Jurien Bay Australia 30°18S 115°2E 279 F2
Jurilovca Romania 44°46N 28°52E 183 F13
Jūrmala Latvia 56°58N 23°34E 184 B10
Jurong Jiangsu, China 31°57N 119°9E 229 B12
Jurong Singapore 1°19N 103°42E 138 B2
Jurong, Selat Singapore 1°17N 103°42E 138 B2
Jurong Industrial Estate
Singapore 1°19N 103°40E 138 B1
Juruá Brazil 3°27S 66°3W 328 D4
Juruá → Brazil 2°37S 65°44W 328 D4
Juruena Brazil 13°0S 58°10W 331 C6
Juruena → Brazil 7°20S 58°3W 331 B6
Jurujuba, Enseada de
Brazil 22°54S 43°6W 135 B2
Juruti Brazil 2°9S 56°4W 329 D6
Jūsō Japan 34°42N 135°27E 133 A1
Jussey France 47°50N 5°55E 173 E12
Justice U.S.A. 41°44N 87°49W 119 C2
Justicia Madrid, Spain 127 a3
Justo Daract Argentina 33°52S 65°12W 334 C2
Jutaí Amazonas, Brazil 2°44S 66°57W 328 D4
Jutaí Amazonas, Brazil 5°11S 68°54W 330 B4
Jutaí → Brazil 2°43S 66°57W 328 D4
Jüterbog Germany 51°59N 13°5E 178 D9
Juticalpa Honduras 14°40N 86°12W 320 D2
Jutland = Jylland Denmark 56°25N 9°30E 163 H3
Juuka Finland 63°13N 29°17E 160 E23
Juventud, I. de la Cuba 21°40N 82°40W 320 B3
Juvigny-sous-Andaine
France 48°32N 0°30W 172 D6
Juwangsan △ S. Korea 36°20N 129°15E 224 D4
Jūy Zar Iran 33°50N 46°18E 213 F12
Juye China 35°22N 116°5E 226 G9
Juzennecourt France 48°10N 4°58E 173 D11
Južni Brod = Brod
Macedonia 41°32N 21°17E 202 E5
Jvari Georgia 42°42N 42°4E 191 J6
Jwalahari India 28°40N 77°6E 120 B1
Jyderup Denmark 55°40N 11°26E 163 J5
Jylland Denmark 56°25N 9°30E 163 H3
Jyväskylä Finland 62°14N 25°50E 188 A3

K

K2 Pakistan 35°58N 76°32E 243 B7
Ka → Nigeria 11°40N 4°10E 263 C5
Kaa-Iya △ Bolivia 18°35S 61°40W 331 D5
Ka'a'awa U.S.A. 21°33N 157°51W 302 J14
Kaakha = Kaka
Turkmenistan 37°21N 59°36E 247 B8
Ka'ala U.S.A. 21°31N 158°9W 302 J13
Kaala-Gomén N. Cal. 20°40S 164°25E 288 d
Ka'alu'alu B. U.S.A. 18°58N 155°37W 302 E6
Kaap Plateau S. Africa 28°30S 24°0E 270 C3
Kaapkruis Namibia 21°55S 13°57E 270 B1
Kaapstad = Cape Town
S. Africa 33°55S 18°22E 118 A1
Kaashidhoo Atoll Maldives 4°58N 73°28E 272 d
Kaashidhoo Channel
Maldives 5°1N 73°28E 272 d
Kaataon, Mt. Phil. 8°10N 124°52E 233 G5
Kaba Guinea 10°9N 11°40W 262 C2
Kabacan Phil. 7°8N 124°49E 233 H5
Kabachishche = Zelenodolsk
Russia 55°55N 48°30E 190 C9
Kabaena Indonesia 5°15S 122°0E 231 F6
Kabala S. Leone 9°38N 11°37W 262 D2
Kabale Uganda 1°15S 30°0E 268 C3
Kabalo Dem. Rep. of the Congo 6°0S 27°0E 265 D5
Kabambare
Dem. Rep. of the Congo 4°41S 27°39E 268 C2
Kabango
Dem. Rep. of the Congo 8°35S 28°30E 269 D2
Kabanjahe Indonesia 3°6N 98°30E 234 B1
Kabankalan Phil. 9°59N 122°49E 233 G4
Kabara Fiji 18°59S 178°56W 287 B3
Kabara Mali 16°40N 2°50W 262 B4
Kabardinka Russia 44°40N 37°57E 189 K10
Kabardino-Balkaria □
Russia 43°30N 43°30E 191 J6
Kabarega Falls = Murchison Falls
Uganda 2°15N 31°30E 268 B3
Kabarnet Kenya 0°30N 35°45E 268 B4
Kabasalan Phil. 7°47N 122°44E 233 H4
Kabat Indonesia 8°16S 114°19E 231 J17
Kabaty Poland 52°21N 21°4E 143 C2
Kabba Nigeria 7°50N 6°3E 263 D6
Kabbani → India 12°13N 76°54E 245 H3
Kabi Niger 13°30N 12°35E 259 F2
Kabin Buri Thailand 13°57N 101°43E 236 F3
Kabinakagami L. Canada 48°54N 84°25W 298 C3
Kabinda
Dem. Rep. of the Congo 6°10S 24°29E 265 D4
Kabkabīyah Sudan 13°50N 24°0E 259 F4
Kablungu, C. Papua N. G. 6°20S 150°1E 286 D6
Kabna Sudan 19°6N 32°40E 256 D3
Kabo C.A.R. 7°35N 18°38E 264 A3
Kabompo Zambia 13°36S 24°14E 265 E4
Kabompo → Zambia 14°11S 23°11E 265 E4
Kabondo
Dem. Rep. of the Congo 8°58S 25°40E 265 D5
Kabongo
Dem. Rep. of the Congo 7°22S 25°33E 265 D5
Kabot Guinea 10°48N 14°57W 262 C2
Kabou Togo 9°28N 0°55E 263 D5
Kaboudia, Rass Tunisia 35°13N 11°10E 258 A2
Kabr Sudan 10°54N 26°50E 257 E2
Kabrît, G. el Egypt 29°42N 33°16E 251 J4
Kabrousse Senegal 12°25N 16°45W 262 C1
Kabubu
Dem. Rep. of the Congo 9°42S 24°40E 265 D4
Kabūd Gonbad Iran 37°5N 59°45E 247 B8
Kabudar Ahang Iran 35°11N 48°43E 213 E13
Kabugao Phil. 18°2N 121°11E 232 B3
Kābul Afghan. 34°28N 69°11E 242 B3
Kābul □ Afghan. 34°30N 69°0E 240 B3
Kābul → Pakistan 33°55N 72°14E 242 C5
Kabuli Papua N. G. 2°7S 146°40E 286 B4
Kabunga
Dem. Rep. of the Congo 1°38S 28°3E 268 C2
Kaburuang Indonesia 3°50N 126°30E 231 D7
Kabushiya Sudan 16°54N 33°41E 257 D3
Kabwanga
Dem. Rep. of the Congo 7°2S 22°36E 265 D4
Kabwe Zambia 14°30S 28°29E 269 E2
Kabwum Papua N. G. 6°11S 147°15E 286 D4
Kaçanik Kosovo 42°13N 21°12E 202 D5
Kačerginė Lithuania 54°56N 23°42E 184 D10
Kachar Kazakhstan 53°23N 62°55E 216 B6
Kachchh, Gulf of India 22°50N 69°15E 242 H3
Kachchh, Rann of India 24°0N 70°0E 242 H4
Kachchhidhana India 21°44N 78°46E 243 J8
Kachebera Zambia 13°50S 32°50E 269 E3
Kachia Nigeria 9°50N 7°55E 263 D6
Kachikau Botswana 18°8S 24°26E 270 A3
Kachin □ Burma 26°0N 97°30E 228 D1
Kachira, L. Uganda 0°40S 31°7E 268 C3
Kachīry Kazakhstan 53°10N 75°50E 217 B9
Kachisi Ethiopia 9°40N 37°50E 257 F4
Kachnara India 23°50N 75°6E 242 H6
Kachot Cambodia 11°30N 103°3E 237 G4
Kaçkar Turkey 40°45N 41°10E 213 B9
Kada Chad 19°20N 19°39E 259 E3
Kadaingti Burma 17°37N 97°32E 241 G6
Kadaiyanallur India 9°3N 77°22E 245 K3
Kadam, Mt. Uganda 1°45N 34°45E 268 B3
Kadan Czech Rep. 50°23N 13°16E 180 A6
Kadan Kyun Burma 12°30N 98°20E 236 F2
Kadanai → Afghan. 31°22N 65°45E 242 D1
Kadarkút Hungary 46°13N 17°39E 182 D2
Kadavu Fiji 19°0S 178°15E 287 B2
Kadavu Passage Fiji 18°45S 178°0E 287 B2
Kade Ghana 6°7N 0°56W 263 D4
Kadei → C.A.R. 3°31N 16°3E 264 B3
Kademlija = Triglav
Slovenia 46°21N 13°50E 199 B10
Kadena Japan 26°22N 127°45E 288 a
Kadhimain = Al Kāẓimīyah
Iraq 33°22N 44°18E 213 F11
Kadi India 23°18N 72°23E 242 H5
Kadiak I. = Kodiak I.
U.S.A. 57°30N 152°45W 303 H9
Kadiana Mali 10°45N 6°30W 262 C3
Kadıköy Turkey 40°59N 29°1E 122 C2
Kadina Australia 33°55S 137°43E 282 B2
Kadınhanı Turkey 38°14N 32°13E 212 C5
Kadiolo Mali 10°35N 7°41W 262 C3
Kadipur India 26°10N 82°23E 243 F10
Kadirabad India 19°51N 75°54E 244 E2
Kadiri India 14°12N 78°13E 245 G4
Kadirli Turkey 37°23N 36°5E 212 D7
Kadiyevka = Stakhanov
Ukraine 48°35N 38°40E 189 H10
Kadja, O. → Chad 12°2N 22°28E 259 F4
Kadmat I. India 11°14N 72°47E 245 J1
Kadodo Sudan 11°4N 29°31E 257 E2
Kadoka U.S.A. 43°50N 101°31W 308 D3
Kadom Russia 54°37N 42°30E 190 C6
Kadoma Ōsaka, Japan 34°44N 135°35E 133 A2
Kadoma Zimbabwe 18°20S 29°52E 269 F2
Kâdugli Sudan 11°0N 29°45E 257 E2
Kaduna Nigeria 10°30N 7°21E 263 C6
Kaduna □ Nigeria 11°0N 7°30E 263 C6
Kaduna → Nigeria 8°45N 5°48E 263 D6
Kadur India 13°34N 76°1E 245 H3
Kaduy Russia 59°12N 37°9E 188 C9
Kaédi Mauritania 16°9N 13°28W 262 B2
Kaélé Cameroon 10°7N 14°27E 259 F2
Ka'ena U.S.A. 21°34N 158°14W 302 J13
Ka'ena Pt. U.S.A. 21°35N 158°17W 302 J13
Kaeng Khoi Thailand 14°35N 101°0E 236 E3
Kaeng Krachan △
Thailand 12°57N 99°23E 236 F2
Kaeng Krung △ Thailand 9°30N 98°50E 237 H2
Kaeng Tana △ Thailand 15°25N 105°32E 236 E5
Kaeo N.Z. 35°6S 173°49E 284 B2
Kaesŏng N. Korea 37°58N 126°35E 224 D3
Kaesŏng □ N. Korea 38°0N 126°37E 224 D3
Kāf Si. Arabia 31°25N 37°29E 246 D3
Kafakumba
Dem. Rep. of the Congo 9°38S 23°46E 265 D4
Kafan = Kapan Armenia 39°18N 46°27E 213 C12
Kafanchan Nigeria 9°40N 8°20E 263 D6
Kafareti Nigeria 10°25N 11°12E 263 C7
Kaffrine Senegal 14°8N 15°36W 262 C1
Kafia Kingi Sudan 9°20N 24°25E 264 A4
Kafin Nigeria 9°30N 7°4E 263 D6
Kafin Madaki Nigeria 10°41N 9°46E 263 C6
Kafinda Zambia 12°32S 30°20E 269 E3
Kafr 'Aqab West Bank 31°52N 35°13E 123 A2
Kafr el Battikh Egypt 31°25N 31°44E 256 H7
Kafr el Dauwâr Egypt 31°8N 30°8E 256 H7
Kafr el Sheikh Egypt 31°15N 30°50E 251 G1
Kafr el Sheikh □ Egypt 31°15N 30°55E 251 G1
Kafr el Zaiyât Egypt 30°49N 30°48E 256 H7
Kafue Zambia 15°46S 28°9E 269 F2
Kafue △ Zambia 15°12S 25°38E 269 F2
Kafue Flats Zambia 15°40S 27°25E 269 F2
Kafulwe Zambia 9°0S 29°1E 269 D2
Kafumba
Dem. Rep. of the Congo 5°23S 18°55E 265 D3
Kaga Afghan. 34°14N 70°10E 242 B4
Kaga Japan 36°16N 136°15E 223 A8
Kaga Bandoro C.A.R. 7°0N 19°10E 264 A3
Kagamil I. U.S.A. 53°0N 169°43W 303 K5
Kaganovich = Tovarkovskiy
Russia 53°40N 38°14E 188 F10
Kagarko Nigeria 9°28N 7°36E 263 D6
Kagawa □ Japan 34°15N 134°0E 222 C6
Kagera □ Tanzania 2°0S 31°30E 268 C3
Kagera → Uganda 0°57S 31°47E 268 C3
Kâğıthane Turkey 41°4N 28°58E 122 B1
Kâğıthane → Turkey 41°9N 28°56E 122 B1
Kağızman Turkey 40°5N 43°10E 213 B10
Kagmar Sudan 14°24N 30°25E 257 E3
Kagologolo Indonesia 1°9S 98°37E 234 C1
Kagopal Chad 8°16N 16°23E 259 G3
Kagoro Nigeria 9°36N 8°23E 263 D6
Kagoshima Japan 31°35N 130°33E 222 F2
Kagoshima □ Japan 31°30N 130°30E 222 F2
Kagoshima-Wan Japan 31°25N 130°40E 222 F2
Kagran Austria 48°14N 16°26E 142 A2
Kagua Papua N. G. 6°26S 143°48E 286 D2
Kagul = Cahul Moldova 45°50N 28°15E 183 E13
Kahak Iran 36°6N 49°46E 247 B6
Kahala U.S.A. 21°16N 157°47W 302 K14
Kahalu'u U.S.A. 21°27N 157°50W 302 K14
Kahama Tanzania 4°8S 32°30E 268 C3
Kahan Pakistan 29°18N 68°54E 242 E3
Kahana U.S.A. 21°34N 157°53W 302 J14
Kahana B. U.S.A. 21°35N 157°50W 302 J14
Kahana Valley State Park ⌂
U.S.A. 21°32N 157°53W 302 J14
Kahang Malaysia 2°12N 103°32E 237 L4
Kahayan → Indonesia 3°40S 114°0E 235 C4
Kahe Tanzania 3°30S 37°25E 268 C4
Kahemba
Dem. Rep. of the Congo 7°18S 18°55E 265 D3
Kaherekoau Mts. N.Z. 45°45S 167°15E 285 F2
Kahil, Djebel bou Algeria 34°26N 4°0E 261 B5
Kahnawake Canada 45°24N 73°40W 130 B1
Kahnūj Iran 27°55N 57°40E 247 E8
Kahoka U.S.A. 40°25N 91°44W 310 D5
Kaho'olawe U.S.A. 20°33N 156°37W 302 C5
Kahouanne Guadeloupe 16°15N 61°12W 322 e
Kahouanne, Îlet à
Guadeloupe 16°22N 61°46W 322 e
Kahramanmaraş Turkey 37°37N 36°53E 212 D7
Kahramanmaraş □
Turkey 37°35N 36°33E 212 D7
Kâhta Turkey 37°46N 38°36E 213 D8
Kahuku U.S.A. 21°41N 157°57W 302 J14
Kahuku Pt. U.S.A. 21°43N 157°59W 302 J14
Kahul, Ozero Ukraine 45°24N 28°24E 183 E13
Kahului U.S.A. 20°54N 156°28W 302 C5
Kahului ✕ (OGG)
U.S.A. 20°54N 156°26W 302 C5
Kahurangi △ N.Z. 41°10S 172°32E 285 B7
Kahurangi Pt. N.Z. 40°50S 172°10E 285 A7
Kahuta Pakistan 33°35N 73°24E 242 C5
Kahuzi-Biega △
Dem. Rep. of the Congo 1°50S 27°55E 268 C2
Kai Japan 35°42N 138°30E 223 B10
Kai, Kepulauan Indonesia 5°55S 132°45E 231 F8
Kai Besar Indonesia 5°35S 133°0E 231 F8
Kai Is. = Kai, Kepulauan
Indonesia 5°55S 132°45E 231 F8
Kai Kecil Indonesia 5°45S 132°40E 231 F8
Kai Xian China 31°11N 108°21E 228 B7
Kaiama Nigeria 9°36N 4°1E 263 D5
Kaiapit Papua N. G. 6°18S 146°18E 286 D4
Kaiapoi N.Z. 43°24S 172°40E 285 D7
Kaidu He → China 41°46N 86°31E 218 C6
Kaieteur Falls Guyana 5°1N 59°10W 329 B6
Kaifeng China 34°48N 114°21E 226 G8
Kaihua China 29°12N 118°20E 229 C12
Kaijiang China 31°7N 107°55E 228 B6
Kaikohe N.Z. 35°25S 173°49E 284 B2
Kaikoura N.Z. 42°25S 173°43E 285 C8
Kaikoura Pen. N.Z. 42°25S 173°43E 285 C8
Kailahun S. Leone 8°18N 10°39W 262 D2
Kailash = Kangrinboqe Feng
China 31°0N 81°25E 243 D9
Kailashahar India 24°19N 92°0E 241 C4
Kaileuna I. Papua N. G. 8°32S 150°57E 286 E6
Kaili China 26°33N 107°59E 228 D6
Kailu China 43°38N 121°18E 227 C11
Kailua U.S.A. 21°24N 157°44W 302 K14
Kailua B. U.S.A. 21°25N 157°40W 302 K14
Kailua Kona U.S.A. 19°39N 155°59W 302 D6
Kaim → Papua N. G. 6°55S 141°33E 286 D1
Kaimaktsalan Oros = Voras Oros
Greece 40°57N 21°45E 202 F5
Kaimana Indonesia 3°39S 133°45E 231 E8
Kaimanawa Mts. N.Z. 39°15S 175°56E 284 F4
Kaimata N.Z. 42°34S 171°28E 285 C6
Kaimes U.K. 55°54N 3°10W 121 B2
Kaimganj India 27°33N 79°24E 243 F8
Kaimon-Dake Japan 31°11N 130°32E 222 F2
Kaimur Hills India 24°30N 82°0E 243 G10
Kainab → Namibia 28°32S 19°34E 270 C2
Kainan Japan 34°9N 135°12E 223 C7
Kainantu Papua N. G. 6°18S 145°52E 286 D3
Kainji Dam Nigeria 9°55N 4°35E 263 D5
Kainji Lake △ Nigeria 10°5N 4°6E 263 C5
Kainji Res. Nigeria 10°1N 4°40E 263 C5
Kainsk = Samara Russia 53°8N 50°6E 190 D10
Kainuu □ Finland 64°30N 29°7E 160 D23
Kaipara Harbour N.Z. 36°25S 174°14E 284 C3
Kaiping China 22°23N 112°42E 229 F9
Kaipokok B. Canada 54°54N 59°47W 299 B8
Kaira India 22°45N 72°50E 242 H5
Kairana India 29°24N 77°15E 242 E7
Kairiru I. Papua N. G. 3°21S 143°34E 286 B2
Kaironi Indonesia 0°47S 133°40E 231 E8
Kairouan Tunisia 35°45N 10°5E 258 A2
Kairouan □ Tunisia 35°30N 9°46E 261 A6
Kairuku Papua N. G. 8°51S 146°35E 286 E4
Kaiser Wilhelm Gedächtniskirche
Berlin, Germany 115 b2
Kaiser Wilhelm Kanal = Nord-
Ostsee-Kanal Germany 54°12N 9°32E 178 A5
Kaiser-Wilhelmsland = Papua □
Indonesia 4°0S 137°0E 231 E9
Kaiserebersdorf Austria 48°9N 16°26E 142 B2
Kaiserslautern Germany 49°26N 7°45E 179 F3
Kaiserstuhl Germany 48°4N 7°40E 179 G3
Kaitaia N.Z. 35°8S 173°17E 284 B2
Kaitangata N.Z. 46°17S 169°51E 285 G4
Kaithal India 29°48N 76°26E 242 E7
Kaitu → Pakistan 33°10N 70°30E 242 C4
Kaivoksela Finland 60°15N 24°53E 121 B2
Kaiwi Channel U.S.A. 21°15N 157°30W 302 K14
Kaiyang China 27°4N 106°59E 228 D6
Kaiyuan Liaoning, China 42°28N 124°1E 224 A2
Kaiyuan Yunnan, China 23°40N 103°12E 228 F4
Kaiyuh Mts. U.S.A. 64°30N 158°0W 303 D8
Kajaani Finland 64°17N 27°46E 160 D22
Kajabbi Australia 20°0S 140°1E 280 C3
Kajaki Afghan. 32°18N 65°5E 240 B2
Kajana = Kajaani
Finland 64°17N 27°46E 160 D22
Kajang Malaysia 2°59N 101°48E 237 L3
Kajaran Armenia 39°10N 46°7E 213 C12
Kajiado Kenya 1°53S 36°48E 268 C4
Kajo Kaji South Sudan 3°58N 31°40E 257 G3
Kajok South Sudan 8°19N 28°0E 257 F2
Kajuru Nigeria 10°15N 7°34E 263 C6
Kaka South Sudan 10°38N 32°10E 257 E3
Kaka Turkmenistan 37°21N 59°36E 247 B8
Kakabeka Falls Canada 48°24N 89°37W 298 C2
Kakadu △ Australia 12°0S 132°3E 278 B5
Kakamas S. Africa 28°45S 20°33E 270 C3
Kakamega Kenya 0°20N 34°46E 268 B3
Kakamigahara Japan 35°28N 136°48E 223 B8
Kakana India 9°7N 92°48E 245 K11
Kakanj Bos.-H. 44°4N 18°4E 182 F3
Kakanui Mts. N.Z. 45°10S 170°30E 285 F5
Kakata Liberia 6°35N 10°20W 262 D2
Kakching India 24°29N 94°0E 241 C5
Kakdwip India 21°53N 88°11E 243 J13
Kake = Akiōta Japan 34°36N 132°19E 222 C4
Kake U.S.A. 56°59N 133°57W 296 B2
Kakegawa Japan 34°45N 138°1E 223 C10
Kakeroma-Jima Japan 28°8N 129°14E 221 K4
Kākhak Iran 34°9N 58°38E 247 C8
Kakhib Russia 42°28N 46°34E 191 J8
Kakhonak U.S.A. 59°26N 154°51W 303 G9
Kakhovka Ukraine 46°45N 33°30E 189 J7
Kakhovske Vdskh. Ukraine 47°5N 34°0E 189 J7
Kakinada India 16°57N 82°11E 244 F6
Kakisa Canada 60°56N 117°25W 296 A5
Kakisa → Canada 61°3N 118°10W 296 A5
Kakisa L. Canada 60°56N 117°43W 296 A5
Kakisalmi = Priozersk
Russia 61°2N 30°7E 188 B6
Kakogawa Japan 34°46N 134°51E 222 C6
Kaktovik U.S.A. 70°8N 143°38W 303 A12
Kakum △ Ghana 5°24N 1°20W 263 D4
Kakuma Kenya 3°43N 34°52E 268 B3
Kakwa → Canada 54°37N 118°28W 296 C5
Kāl Gūsheh Iran 30°59N 58°12E 247 D8
Kal Sefīd Iran 34°52N 47°23E 213 E12
Kala Nigeria 12°2N 14°40E 263 C7
Kala Oya → Sri Lanka 8°20N 79°45E 245 K4
Kalaa-Kebira Tunisia 35°59N 10°32E 258 A2
Kalaallit Nunaat = Greenland ☑
N. Amer. 66°0N 45°0W 154 D6
Kalabagh Pakistan 33°0N 71°28E 242 C4
Kalabahi Indonesia 8°13S 124°31E 231 F6
Kalabak = Radomir
Bulgaria 42°37N 22°59E 202 D6
Kalabakan Malaysia 4°25N 117°29E 235 B5
Kalabana Mali 14°10N 8°35W 262 C3
Kalabo Zambia 14°58S 22°40E 265 E4
Kalach Russia 50°22N 41°0E 190 E5
Kalach na Donu Russia 48°43N 43°32E 191 F6
Kalachinsk Russia 55°3N 74°33E 217 A8
Kaladan → Burma 20°20N 93°5E 241 E4
Kaladar Canada 44°37N 77°5W 312 B7
Kalae U.S.A. 18°55N 155°41W 302 E6
Kalahari Africa 24°0S 21°30E 270 B3
Kalahari Gemsbok △
S. Africa 25°30S 20°30E 270 C3
Kalaheo U.S.A. 21°56N 159°32W 302 B2
Kalaikhum Tajikistan 38°28N 70°46E 217 E8
Kalajoki Finland 64°12N 24°10E 160 D21
Kalakamati Botswana 20°40S 27°25E 271 B4
Kalakan Russia 55°15N 116°45E 215 D12
Kalakol Kenya 3°33N 35°54E 266 D4
K'alak'unlun Shank'ou =
Karakoram Pass Asia 35°33N 77°50E 243 B7
Kalam Pakistan 35°34N 72°30E 243 B5
Kalama
Dem. Rep. of the Congo 2°52S 28°35E 268 C2
Kalama Wash., U.S.A. 46°1N 122°51W 306 E4
Kalamaki Greece 37°52N 23°43E 112 B2
Kalamalouè △ Cameroon 12°9N 14°58E 259 F2
Kalamansig Phil. 6°33N 124°3E 233 H5
Kalamaria Greece 40°33N 22°55E 202 F6
Kalamata Greece 37°3N 22°10E 204 D4
Kalamazoo U.S.A. 42°17N 85°35W 311 B11
Kalamazoo → U.S.A. 42°40N 86°10W 311 B10
Kalamb India 18°3N 74°48E 244 E2
Kalambaka Greece 39°42N 21°39E 204 B3
Kalambo Falls Tanzania 8°37S 31°35E 269 D3
Kalamitsi Greece 38°45N 20°36E 207 B2
Kalamnuri India 19°40N 77°20E 244 E3
Kalamos Attiki, Greece 38°17N 23°52E 204 C5
Kalamos Lefkada, Greece 38°37N 20°55E 207 B2
Kalan Turkey 39°7N 39°32E 246 B3
Kalangadoo Australia 37°34S 140°41E 282 D4
Kalankalan Guinea 10°7N 8°54W 262 C3
Kalannie Australia 30°22S 117°5E 279 F2
Kalāntarī Iran 32°10N 54°8E 247 C7
Kalao Indonesia 7°21S 121°0E 231 F6
Kalaoa U.S.A. 19°43N 155°58W 302 D6
Kalaotoa Indonesia 7°20S 121°50E 231 F6
Kalapana U.S.A. 19°21N 154°59W 302 D7
Kälarne Sweden 62°59N 16°8E 162 B10
Kalasin Thailand 16°26N 103°30E 236 D4
Kālat Iran 25°29N 59°22E 247 E8
Kalat Pakistan 29°8N 66°31E 240 C2
Kalāteh Iran 36°33N 55°41E 247 B7
Kalāteh-ye Ganj Iran 27°31N 57°55E 247 E8
Kalathos Greece 36°9N 28°8E 205 F10
Kalatungan, Mt. Phil. 7°54N 124°50E 233 H5
Kalaupapa U.S.A. 21°12N 156°59W 302 B5
Kalaupapa ⌂ U.S.A. 21°10N 156°59W 302 B5
Kalaus → Russia 45°40N 44°7E 191 H7
Kalavrita Greece 38°3N 22°8E 204 C4
Kalaw Burma 20°38N 96°34E 241 E6
Kalawao County U.S.A. 21°11N 156°58W 302 B5
Kalbā U.A.E. 25°5N 56°22E 247 E8
Kalbadevi Mumbai, India 130 b2
Kalbān Oman 20°18N 58°38E 249 B7
Kalbarri Australia 27°40S 114°10E 279 E1
Kalbarri △ Australia 27°51S 114°30E 279 E1
Kalburgi = Gulbarga
India 17°20N 76°50E 244 F3
Kalce Slovenia 45°54N 14°13E 176 F8
Kaldrananes Iceland 65°45N 21°25W 155 B5
Kale Antalya, Turkey 36°14N 30°0E 205 E12
Kale Denizli, Turkey 37°27N 28°49E 205 D10
Kaleburnu = Galinoporni
Cyprus 35°31N 34°18E 207 E10
Kalecik Turkey 40°4N 33°26E 212 B5
Kalegauk Kyun Burma 15°33N 97°35E 236 E1
Kalehe Dem. Rep. of the Congo 2°6S 28°50E 268 C2
Kalema Tanzania 1°12S 31°55E 268 C3
Kalemie
Dem. Rep. of the Congo 5°55S 29°9E 268 D2
Kalemyo Burma 23°11N 94°4E 241 D5
Kalety Poland 50°35N 18°52E 185 H5
Kalewa Burma 23°10N 94°15E 241 D5
Kaleybar Iran 38°47N 47°2E 213 C12
Kálfafell Iceland 63°57N 17°41W 155 D9
Kalgan = Zhangjiakou
China 40°48N 114°55E 226 D8
Kalghatgi India 15°11N 74°58E 245 G2
Kalgoorlie-Boulder
Australia 30°40S 121°22E 279 F3
Kalhovd Norway 60°4N 8°21E 164 D5
Kali → India 27°6N 79°55E 243 F8
Kali Sindh → India 25°32N 76°17E 242 G6
Kaliakra, Nos Bulgaria 43°21N 28°30E 203 C12
Kalianda Indonesia 5°50S 105°45E 234 D3
Kalibo Phil. 11°43N 122°22E 233 F4
Kaliganj Bangla. 22°25N 89°8E 241 D2
Kalihi U.S.A. 21°20N 157°53W 302 K14
Kalihi Valley U.S.A. 21°20N 157°52W 302 K14
Kalima
Dem. Rep. of the Congo 2°33S 26°32E 268 C2
Kalimantan Indonesia 0°0 114°0E 235 C4
Kalimantan Barat □
Indonesia 0°0 110°30E 235 C4
Kalimantan Selatan □
Indonesia 2°30S 115°30E 235 C5
Kalimantan Tengah □
Indonesia 2°0S 113°30E 235 C4
Kalimantan Timur □
Indonesia 1°30N 116°30E 235 B5
Kálimnos Greece 37°0N 27°0E 205 D8
Kalimpong India 27°4N 88°35E 241 B2
Kalinadi → India 14°50N 74°7E 245 G2
Kalinga □ Phil. 17°30N 121°20E 232 C3
Kalininkinsk Russia 51°29N 44°28E 216 B2
Kalinin = Tver Russia 56°55N 35°59E 188 D8
Kaliningrad Russia 54°42N 20°32E 184 D7
Kaliningrad ✕ (KGD)
Russia 54°45N 20°33E 184 D7
Kalininsk = Petrozavodsk
Russia 61°41N 34°20E 188 B8
Kalininsk Russia 51°30N 44°40E 190 E7
Kalinkavichy Belarus 52°12N 29°20E 177 B15
Kalinkovichi = Kalinkavichy
Belarus 52°12N 29°20E 177 B15
Kalinovik Bos.-H. 43°31N 18°29E 202 C2
Kalipetrovo Bulgaria 44°5N 27°14E 203 B11
Kalipur India 22°40N 88°17E 124 A1
Kalirachi Greece 40°40N 24°35E 203 F8
Kaliro Uganda 0°56N 33°30E 268 B3
Kalispell U.S.A. 48°12N 114°19W 304 B6
Kalisz Poland 51°45N 18°8E 185 G5
Kalisz Pomorski Poland 53°17N 15°55E 185 E2
Kalithea Greece 37°56N 23°43E 112 B2
Kaliua Tanzania 5°5S 31°48E 268 D3
Kaliveli Tank India 12°5N 79°50E 245 H4
Kalivia Thorikou Greece 37°50N 23°55E 204 D5
Kalix Sweden 65°53N 23°12E 160 D20
Kalixälven → Sweden 65°50N 23°11E 160 D20
Kalka India 30°46N 76°57E 242 D7
Kalkaji India 28°32N 77°12E 120 B2
Kalkaji Ghat India 24°36N 92°20E 241 C4
Kalkan Turkey 36°15N 29°23E 205 E11
Kalkarindji Australia 17°30S 130°47E 278 C5
Kalkaska U.S.A. 44°44N 85°11W 309 C11
Kalkfeld Namibia 20°57S 16°14E 270 B2
Kalkfontein Botswana 22°4S 20°57E 270 B3
Kalkım Turkey 39°48N 27°13E 205 B9
Kalkrand Namibia 24°1S 17°35E 270 B2
Kallakkurichchi India 11°44N 79°1E 245 J4
Kållandsö Sweden 58°40N 13°5E 163 F7
Kallavesi Finland 62°58N 27°30E 160 E22
Källby Sweden 58°30N 13°8E 163 F7
Kållered Sweden 57°32N 12°4E 163 G6
Kallidaikurichi India 8°38N 77°31E 245 K3
Kallies = Kalisz Pomorski
Poland 53°17N 15°55E 185 E2
Kallimasia Greece 38°18N 26°6E 205 C8
Kallinge Sweden 56°15N 15°18E 163 H9
Kallmet Albania 41°51N 19°41E 202 E3
Kallsjön Sweden 63°38N 13°0E 160 E15
Kalmalo Nigeria 13°40N 5°20E 263 C6
Kalmanstunga Iceland 64°44N 20°48W 155 C6
Kalmar Sweden 56°40N 16°20E 163 H10
Kalmar län □ Sweden 57°25N 16°0E 163 G10
Kalmar sund Sweden 56°40N 16°25E 163 H10
Kalmunai Sri Lanka 7°25N 81°49E 245 L5
Kalmykia □ Russia 46°5N 46°1E 191 G8
Kalna India 23°13N 88°25E 243 H13
Kalnai India 22°46N 83°30E 243 H10
Kalni → Bangla. 24°21N 91°13E 241 C3
Kalo Papua N. G. 10°1S 147°48E 286 F4
Kalo Nero Greece 37°20N 21°38E 204 D3
Kalocsa Hungary 46°32N 19°0E 182 D4
Kalofer Bulgaria 42°37N 24°59E 203 D8
Kalohi Channel U.S.A. 21°0N 157°0W 302 C5
Kalokhorio Cyprus 34°51N 33°2E 207 F9
Kaloko
Dem. Rep. of the Congo 6°47S 25°48E 265 D5
Kaloko-Honokōhau ⌂
U.S.A. 19°40N 156°1W 302 D5
Kalol Gujarat, India 22°37N 73°31E 242 H5
Kalol Gujarat, India 23°15N 72°33E 242 H5
Kalolimnos Greece 37°4N 27°5E 205 D9
Kalomo Zambia 17°0S 26°30E 269 F2
Kalona U.S.A. 41°29N 91°43W 310 C5
Kaloni Greece 39°14N 26°12E 205 B8
Kaloni, Kolpos Greece 39°10N 26°10E 205 B8
Kalookan = Caloocan
Phil. 14°39N 120°58E 127 B1
Kalpeni I. India 10°5N 73°38E 245 J1
Kalpi India 26°8N 79°47E 243 F8
Kalpitiya Sri Lanka 8°14N 79°46E 245 K4
Kalputhi I. India 10°49N 72°10E 245 J1
Kalrayan Hills India 11°45N 78°40E 245 J4
Kalsubai India 19°35N 73°45E 244 E1
Kaltag U.S.A. 64°20N 158°43W 303 D8
Kaltern = Caldaro Italy 46°25N 11°14E 199 B8
Kaltukatjara Australia 24°52S 129°5E 279 D4
Kaltungo Nigeria 9°48N 11°19E 263 D7
Kalu Pakistan 25°5N 67°39E 242 G2
Kaluga Russia 54°35N 36°10E 188 E9
Kaluga □ Russia 54°15N 34°50E 188 E8
Kalulong, Bukit Malaysia 3°14N 114°39E 235 B4
Kalulushi Zambia 12°50S 28°3E 269 E2
Kalumburu Australia 13°55S 126°35E 278 B4
Kalumburu ✪ Australia 14°17S 126°38E 278 B4
Kalundborg Denmark 55°41N 11°5E 163 J5
Kalush Ukraine 49°3N 24°23E 177 D13
Kałuszyn Poland 52°13N 21°52E 185 F8
Kalutara Sri Lanka 6°35N 80°0E 245 L5
Kalvåg Norway 61°46N 4°51E 164 C1
Kalvarija Lithuania 54°24N 23°14E 184 D10
Kalvebod Fælled Denmark 55°35N 12°31E 118 B3
Kalveboderne Denmark 55°37N 12°31E 118 B3
Kalwakurti India 16°41N 78°30E 244 F4
Kalya Russia 60°15N 59°59E 186 B10
Kalyan Maharashtra, India 20°30N 74°3E 244 D2
Kalyan Maharashtra, India 19°15N 73°9E 244 E1
Kalyandurg India 14°33N 77°6E 245 G3
Kalyani India 17°52N 76°57E 244 F3
Kalyansingapuram India 19°30N 83°19E 244 E6
Kalyazin Russia 57°15N 37°55E 188 D9
Kam Albania 42°17N 20°18E 202 D4
Kam → Nigeria 8°15N 1°10E 263 D7
Kama Burma 19°1N 95°4E 241 F5
Kama Dem. Rep. of the Congo 3°30S 27°5E 268 C2
Kama Fukuoka, Japan 33°33N 130°49E 222 D2
Kama → Russia 55°45N 52°0E 186 C9
Kama Iwa Iwo Jima 24°47N 141°17E 288 b
Kamachumu Tanzania 1°37S 31°37E 268 C3
Kamae Japan 32°48N 131°56E 222 E3
Kamaing Burma 25°26N 96°35E 241 C6
Kamaishi Japan 39°16N 141°53E 220 E10
Kamakou U.S.A. 21°7N 156°52W 302 B5
Kamakura Japan 35°19N 139°33E 223 B11
Kamalapurum India 14°35N 78°39E 245 G4
Kamalété Gabon 0°43S 11°49E 264 C2
Kamalia Pakistan 30°44N 72°42E 242 D5
Kamamaung Burma 17°21N 97°40E 241 G6
Kaman India 27°39N 77°16E 242 F6
Kaman Turkey 39°22N 33°44E 212 C5
Kamana
Dem. Rep. of the Congo 5°59S 24°58E 265 D4
Kamananui → U.S.A. 21°38N 158°4W 302 J13
Kamanjab Namibia 19°35S 14°51E 270 A2
Kamapanda Zambia 12°5S 24°0E 269 E1
Kamara Mali 14°38N 9°23W 262 C3
Kamarān Yemen 15°21N 42°35E 248 D3
Kamareddi India 18°19N 78°21E 244 E4
Kamarhati India 22°40N 88°23E 124 A2
Kamata Japan 35°33N 139°43E 140 B3
Kamativi Zimbabwe 18°20S 27°6E 270 A4
Kamba Dem. Rep. of the Congo 4°0S 22°22E 265 C4
Kamba Nigeria 11°50N 3°45E 263 C5
Kambalda West Australia 31°10S 121°37E 279 F3
Kambam India 9°45N 77°16E 245 K3
Kambangan, Nusa
Indonesia 7°40S 108°10E 235 D3
Kambar Pakistan 27°37N 68°1E 242 F3
Kambarka Russia 56°15N 54°11E 186 C9
Kambia S. Leone 9°3N 12°53W 262 D2
Kambolé Togo 8°43N 1°39E 263 D5
Kambolé Zambia 8°47S 30°48E 269 D3
Kambos Cyprus 35°2N 32°44E 207 E8
Kambove
Dem. Rep. of the Congo 10°51S 26°33E 269 E2
Kambuie
Dem. Rep. of the Congo 6°59S 22°19E 265 D4
Kambwatta Zambia 14°3S 23°43E 265 E4
Kamchatka, Poluostrov
Russia 57°0N 160°0E 215 D17
Kamchatka Pen. = Kamchatka,
Poluostrov Russia 57°0N 160°0E 215 D17
Kamchiya → Bulgaria 43°4N 27°44E 203 C11
Kame Ruins Zimbabwe 20°7S 28°25E 269 G2
Kameari Japan 35°45N 139°50E 140 A4
Kameda-Hantō Japan 41°50N 141°0E 220 D10
Kameido Japan 35°42N 139°50E 140 A4
Kamen Russia 53°50N 81°30E 217 B10
Kamen-Rybolov Russia 44°46N 132°2E 220 B5
Kamende
Dem. Rep. of the Congo 6°26S 24°35E 265 D4
Kamenica Serbia 43°27N 22°27E 202 C6
Kamenica Serbia 44°25N 19°40E 202 B3
Kamenice nad Lipou
Czech Rep. 49°18N 15°2E 180 B8
Kamenjak, Rt Croatia 44°47N 13°55E 199 D10
Kamenka = Kamyanka
Ukraine 49°3N 32°6E 189 H7
Kamenka Kazakhstan 51°7N 50°19E 190 E10
Kamenka Arkhangelsk,
Russia 65°58N 44°0E 186 A7
Kamenka Penza, Russia 53°10N 44°5E 190 D6
Kamenka Voronezh,
Russia 50°47N 39°20E 189 G10
Kamenka Bugskaya = Kamyanka-
Buzka Ukraine 50°8N 24°16E 177 C13
Kamenka Dneprovskaya =
Kamyanka-Dniprovska
Ukraine 47°29N 34°28E 189 J8
Kamenka-Shevchenkovskaya =
Kamyanka-Buzka
Ukraine 50°8N 24°16E 177 C13
Kamennomostskiy Russia 44°18N 40°13E 191 H5
Kameno Bulgaria 42°34N 27°18E 203 D11
Kamenolomini Russia 47°40N 40°14E 191 G5
Kamensk-Shakhtinskiy
Russia 48°23N 40°20E 191 F5
Kamensk Uralskiy Russia 56°25N 62°2E 214 D7
Kamenskaya = Kamensk-
Shakhtinskiy Russia 48°23N 40°20E 191 F5
Kamenskiy Russia 50°48N 45°25E 190 E7
Kamenskoye = Dniprodzerzhynsk
Ukraine 48°32N 34°37E 189 H8
Kamenskoye Russia 62°45N 165°30E 215 C17
Kamenyak Bulgaria 43°24N 26°57E 203 C10
Kamenz Germany 51°15N 14°5E 178 D10
Kameoka Japan 35°0N 135°35E 223 C7
Kamet India 30°55N 79°35E 243 D8
Kameyama Japan 34°51N 136°27E 223 C8
Kami Japan 33°36N 133°38E 222 D5
Kami-Itabashi Japan 35°45N 139°40E 140 A3
Kami-Jima Japan 32°27N 130°20E 222 E2
Kami-Koshiki-Jima
Japan 31°50N 129°52E 222 F1
Kamiagata Japan 34°47N 129°24E 222 C1
Kamiah U.S.A. 46°14N 116°2W 304 C5
Kamień Krajeński Poland 53°32N 17°32E 184 E4
Kamień Pomorski Poland 53°57N 14°43E 184 E1
Kamienna → Poland 51°6N 21°47E 185 G8
Kamienna Góra Poland 50°47N 16°2E 185 H3
Kamieńsk Poland 51°12N 19°29E 185 G6
Kamieskroon S. Africa 30°9S 17°56E 270 D2
Kamikitazawa Japan 35°39N 139°36E 140 B2
Kamilukuak L. Canada 62°22N 101°40W 297 A8
Kamin-Kashyrskyy
Ukraine 51°39N 24°56E 177 C13
Kamina
Dem. Rep. of the Congo 8°45S 25°0E 265 D5
Kaminak L. Canada 62°10N 95°0W 297 A10
Kaminoyama Japan 38°9N 140°17E 220 E10
Kamioka Japan 36°25N 137°15E 223 A9
Kamiros Greece 36°20N 27°56E 206 E11
Kamishak Bay U.S.A. 59°15N 153°45W 303 G9
Kamisu Japan 35°50N 140°45E 223 B12
Kamitsurumа Japan 35°30N 139°26E 140 B1
Kamitsushima Japan 34°50N 129°28E 222 C1
Kamituga
Dem. Rep. of the Congo 3°2S 28°10E 268 C2
Kamla → India 25°35N 86°36E 243 G12
Kamloops Canada 50°40N 120°20W 296 C4
Kamnik Slovenia 46°14N 14°37E 199 B11
Kamo Armenia 40°21N 45°7E 191 K7
Kamo Japan 37°39N 139°3E 220 F9
Kamo N.Z. 35°42S 174°20E 284 B3
Kamoa Mts. Guyana 1°30N 59°0W 329 C6
Kamogawa Japan 35°5N 140°5E 223 B12
Kamojima = Yoshinogawa
Japan 34°4N 134°21E 222 C6
Kamoke Pakistan 32°4N 74°4E 242 C6
Kamo'oloa U.S.A. 21°34N 158°7W 302 J13
Kamoshida Japan 35°33N 139°31E 140 B2
Kamp → Austria 48°23N 15°42E 180 C8
Kampala Uganda 0°20N 32°30E 268 B3
Kampar Malaysia 4°18N 101°9E 237 K3
Kampar → Indonesia 0°30N 103°8E 234 B2
Kampen Neths. 52°33N 5°53E 170 B5
Kamphaeng Phet
Thailand 16°28N 99°30E 236 D2
Kampinoski △ Poland 52°21N 20°40E 185 F7
Kampolombo, L. Zambia 11°37S 29°42E 269 E2
Kampong Cham Cambodia 12°0N 105°30E 237 G5
Kampong Chhnang
Cambodia 12°20N 104°35E 237 F5
Kampong Landang
Singapore 1°20N 103°55E 138 A3
Kampong Pengerang
Malaysia 1°22N 104°7E 237 d
Kampong Punggai
Malaysia 1°27N 104°18E 237 d
Kampong Saom
Cambodia 10°38N 103°30E 237 G4
Kampong Saom, Chaak
Cambodia 10°50N 103°32E 237 G4
Kampong Tanjong Langsat
Malaysia 1°28N 104°1E 237 d
Kampong Tanjong Penjuru
Singapore 1°18N 103°45E 138 B2
Kampong Telok Ramunia
Malaysia 1°22N 104°15E 237 d
Kampot Cambodia 10°36N 104°10E 237 G5
Kampsville U.S.A. 39°18N 90°37W 310 E6
Kampti Burkina Faso 10°7N 3°25W 262 C4
Kampuchea = Cambodia ■
Asia 12°15N 105°0E 236 F5
Kampung Air Putih
Malaysia 4°15N 103°10E 237 K4
Kampung Bali Indonesia 6°11S 106°48E 122 B1
Kampung Jerangau
Malaysia 4°50N 103°10E 237 K4
Kampung Raja Malaysia 5°45N 102°35E 237 K4
Kampungbaru = Tolitoli
Indonesia 1°5N 120°50E 231 D6
Kamrau, Teluk Indonesia 3°30S 133°36E 231 E8
Kamsack Canada 51°34N 101°54W 297 C8
Kamsar Guinea 10°40N 14°36W 262 C2
Kamskoye Ustye Russia 55°10N 49°20E 190 C9
Kamskoye Vdkhr. Russia 58°41N 56°7E 186 C10
Kamsuuma Somalia 0°15N 42°46E 267 D5
Kamthi India 21°9N 79°19E 244 D4
Kamuchawie L. Canada 56°18N 101°59W 297 B8
Kamuela U.S.A. 20°1N 155°41W 302 C6
Kamui-Misaki Japan 43°20N 140°21E 220 C10
Kamyanets-Podilskyy
Ukraine 48°45N 26°40E 183 B11
Kamyanka Ukraine 49°3N 32°6E 189 H7
Kamyanka-Buzka
Ukraine 50°8N 24°16E 177 C13
Kamyanka-Dniprovska
Ukraine 47°29N 34°28E 189 J8
Kamyanyets Belarus 52°23N 23°49E 185 F10
Kamyanyuki Belarus 52°32N 23°49E 185 F10
Kāmyārān Iran 34°47N 46°56E 213 E12
Kamyshin Russia 50°10N 45°24E 190 E7
Kamyzyak Russia 46°4N 48°10E 191 G9
Kan = Gan Jiang →
China 29°15N 116°0E 229 C11
Kan Burma 22°25N 94°5E 241 D5
Kan South Sudan 9°1N 31°47E 257 F3

Katavi Swamp Tanzania 6°50S 31°10E 268 D3
Katchall India 7°57N 93°22E 245 L11
Katchiungo Angola 12°35S 16°13E 265 E3
Katerini Greece 40°18N 22°37E 202 F6
Katghora India 22°30N 82°33E 243 H10
Katha Burma 24°10N 96°30E 241 C6
Katherîna, Gebel Egypt 28°30N 33°57E 251 K4
Katherine Australia 14°27S 132°20E 278 B5
Katherine Gorge = Nitmiluk △ Australia 14°6S 132°15E 278 B5
Kathi India 21°47N 74°3E 242 J6
Kathiawar India 22°20N 71°0E 242 H4
Kathikas Cyprus 34°55N 32°25E 207 F8
Kathleen U.S.A. 28°7N 82°2W 317 G7
Kathmandu Nepal 27°45N 85°20E 243 F11
Kathua India 32°23N 75°34E 242 C6
Kati Mali 12°41N 8°4W 262 C3
Katihar India 25°34N 87°36E 243 G12
Katikati N.Z. 37°32S 175°57E 284 D4
Katima Mulilo Namibia 17°28S 24°13E 270 A3
Katimbira Malawi 12°40S 34°0E 269 E3
Katingan = Mendawai → Indonesia 3°30S 113°0E 235 C4
Katiola Ivory C. 8°10N 5°10W 262 D3
Katipunan Phil. 8°31N 123°17E 233 G4
Katiti ◎ Australia 25°1S 131°11E 279 E5
Katla Iceland 63°36N 19°7W 155 D7
Katlabukh, Ozero Ukraine 45°28N 29°0E 183 E14
Katlanovo Macedonia 41°52N 21°40E 202 E5
Katmai △ U.S.A. 58°20N 155°0W 303 G9
Katmandu = Kathmandu Nepal 27°45N 85°20E 243 F11
Katni India 23°51N 80°24E 243 H9
Kato Achaia Greece 38°8N 21°33E 204 C3
Kato Chorio Greece 35°3N 25°47E 207 E6
Kato Korakiana Greece 39°42N 19°45E 206 B9
Káto Pyrgos Cyprus 35°11N 32°41E 207 E8
Katochi Greece 38°26N 21°15E 204 C3
Katol India 21°17N 78°38E 244 D4
Katompe Dem. Rep. of the Congo 6°2S 26°23E 265 D5
Katong Singapore 1°18N 103°53E 138 B3
Katonga → Uganda 0°34N 31°50E 268 B3
Katoomba Australia 33°41S 150°19E 283 B9
Katouna Greece 38°47N 21°7E 204 C3
Katowice Poland 50°17N 19°5E 185 H6
Katrancı Dağı Turkey 37°27N 30°25E 205 D12
Katrine, L. U.K. 56°15N 4°30W 167 E4
Katrineholm Sweden 59°0N 16°12E 162 E10
Katsepe Madag. 15°45S 46°15E 272 B2
Katsina Nigeria 13°0N 7°32E 263 C6
Katsina □ Nigeria 12°30N 7°30E 263 C6
Katsina Ala Nigeria 7°10N 9°30E 263 D6
Katsina Ala → Nigeria 7°10N 9°20E 263 D6
Katsumoto Japan 33°51N 129°42E 222 D1
Katsushika Japan 35°44N 139°51E 140 A4
Katsuta Japan 36°25N 140°31E 223 A12
Katsuura Japan 35°10N 140°20E 223 B12
Katsuyama Fukui, Japan 36°3N 136°30E 223 A8
Katsuyama Okayama, Japan 35°5N 133°41E 222 B5
Kattaqŭrghon Uzbekistan 39°55N 66°15E 217 E7
Kattavia Greece 35°57N 27°46E 206 F11
Kattegat Denmark 56°40N 11°20E 163 H5
Katthammarsvik Sweden 57°26N 18°51E 163 G12
Kattowitz = Katowice Poland 50°17N 19°5E 185 H6
Katul, J. Sudan 14°12N 29°25E 257 E2
Katumba Dem. Rep. of the Congo 7°40S 25°17E 265 D5
Katun → Russia 52°25N 85°1E 217 B11
Katwa India 23°30N 88°5E 243 H13
Katwijk Neths. 52°12N 4°24E 170 B4
Kąty Wrocławskie Poland 51°2N 16°45E 185 G3
Ka'ū Desert U.S.A. 19°21N 155°19W 302 D6
Kau Pai Chau China 22°12N 114°15E 122 B2
Kau-Ye Kyun Burma 11°1N 98°32E 237 G2
Kau Yi Chau China 22°17N 114°4E 122 B1
Kaua'i U.S.A. 22°3N 159°30W 302 A2
Kauai Channel U.S.A. 21°45N 158°50W 302 B3
Kauai Island Lihue Municipal ✕ (LIH) U.S.A. 21°58N 159°20W 302 B2
Kaub Germany 50°5N 7°46E 179 E3
Kaudom ⌂ Namibia 18°45S 20°51E 270 A3
Kauehi French Polynesia 15°49S 145°10W 289 f
Kaufbeuren Germany 47°53N 10°37E 179 H6
Kaufman U.S.A. 32°35N 96°19W 314 E6
Kauhajoki Finland 62°25N 22°10E 160 E20
Kaukauna U.S.A. 44°17N 88°17W 308 C9
Kaukauveld Namibia 20°0S 20°15E 270 B3
Kaukonahua → U.S.A. 21°35N 158°7W 302 J13
Ka'ula I. U.S.A. 21°40N 160°33W 302 B1
Kaulakahi Channel U.S.A. 22°0N 159°55W 302 B2
Kaulsdorf Germany 52°29N 13°34E 115 B4
Kaunā Pt. U.S.A. 19°2N 155°53W 302 D6
Kaunakakai U.S.A. 21°6N 157°1W 302 B4
Kaunas Lithuania 54°54N 23°54E 184 D10
Kaunas ✕ (KUN) Lithuania 54°57N 24°3E 184 D11
Kaunchi = Yangiyul Uzbekistan 41°0N 69°3E 217 D7
Kaunghein Burma 25°41N 95°26E 241 C5
Kaunia Bangla. 25°46N 89°26E 241 C2
Kauniainen Finland 60°13N 24°44E 121 B1
Kaunos Turkey 36°49N 28°39E 205 E10
Kaupangur Iceland 65°38N 18°2W 155 B8
Kaura Namoda Nigeria 12°37N 6°33E 263 C6
Kauru Nigeria 10°33N 8°12E 263 C6
Kautokeino Norway 69°0N 23°4E 160 B20
Kauwapur India 27°31N 82°18E 243 F10
Kavacha Russia 60°16N 169°51E 215 C17
Kavadarci Macedonia 41°26N 22°3E 202 E6
Kavajë Albania 41°11N 19°33E 202 E3
Kavak Turkey 41°4N 36°3E 212 B7
Kavak Dağı Turkey 37°10N 28°2E 205 D10
Kavaklı Turkey 41°39N 27°10E 203 E11
Kavaklıdere Turkey 37°27N 28°21E 205 D10
Kavaklii = Topolovgrad Bulgaria 42°5N 26°20E 203 D10
Kavala Greece 40°57N 24°28E 203 F8
Kavala □ Greece 41°5N 24°30E 203 E8
Kavala Kolpos Greece 40°50N 24°25E 203 F8
Kavalerovo Russia 44°15N 135°4E 220 B7
Kavali India 14°55N 80°1E 245 G5
Kavār Iran 29°11N 52°44E 247 D7
Kavaratti India 10°34N 72°37E 245 J1
Kavaratti I. India 10°33N 72°38E 245 J1
Kavarna Bulgaria 43°26N 28°22E 203 C12
Kavava Dem. Rep. of the Congo 8°52S 22°19E 265 D4
Kavi India 22°12N 72°38E 242 H5
Kavieng Papua N. G. 2°36S 150°51E 286 B6
Kavimba Botswana 18°2S 24°38E 270 A3
Kavīr, Dasht-e Iran 34°30N 55°0E 247 C7
Kavīr △ Iran 34°40N 52°0E 247 C7
Kavirondo G. = Winam G. Kenya 0°20S 34°15E 268 C3
Kavkaz Russia 45°20N 36°40E 189 K9
Kävlinge Sweden 55°47N 13°9E 163 J7
Kavos Greece 39°23N 20°3E 206 C10
Kavousi Greece 35°7N 25°51E 207 E6
Kavungo Angola 11°31S 23°3E 265 E4
Kaw Fr. Guiana 4°30N 52°15W 329 C7
Kawa Sudan 13°42N 32°34E 257 E3
Kawachi-Nagano Japan 34°28N 135°31E 223 C7
Kawagama L. Canada 45°18N 78°45W 312 A6
Kawagoe Japan 35°55N 139°29E 223 B11
Kawaguchi Japan 35°52N 139°45E 223 B11
Kawah Ijen △ Indonesia 8°3S 114°14E 235 D4
Kawaihae B. U.S.A. 20°0N 155°50W 302 C6
Kawaihoa Pt. U.S.A. 21°47N 160°12W 302 B1
Kawaikini U.S.A. 22°5N 159°29W 302 A2
Kawailoa U.S.A. 21°36N 158°3W 302 J13
Kawailoa Beach U.S.A. 21°37N 158°5W 302 J13
Kawakawa N.Z. 35°23S 174°6E 284 B3
Kawambwa Zambia 9°48S 29°3E 269 D2
Kawana Zambia 13°5S 25°58E 265 E5
Kawanabe Japan 31°23N 130°24E 222 F2
Kawanoe = Shikokochūō Japan 34°1N 133°34E 222 C5
Kawardha India 22°0N 81°17E 243 J9
Kawasaki Japan 35°31N 139°43E 140 B3
Kawasi Indonesia 1°38S 127°28E 231 E7
Kawau I. N.Z. 36°25S 174°52E 284 C3
Kawawa Japan 35°31N 139°33E 140 B2
Kawawachikamach Canada 54°48N 66°50W 299 B6
Kawęczyn Poland 52°16N 21°5E 143 B2
Kaweka Ra. N.Z. 39°17S 176°19E 284 F5
Kawela U.S.A. 21°42N 158°1W 302 J13
Kawerau N.Z. 38°7S 176°42E 284 E5
Kawhia N.Z. 38°4S 174°49E 284 E3
Kawhia Harbour N.Z. 38°5S 174°51E 284 E3
Kawio, Kepulauan Indonesia 4°30N 125°30E 231 D7
Kawkareik Burma 16°33N 98°14E 241 G7
Kawlin Burma 23°47N 95°41E 241 D5
Kawthaung Burma 10°5N 98°36E 237 H2
Kawthoolei = Kayin □ Burma 18°0N 97°30E 241 G6
Kawthule = Kayin □ Burma 18°0N 97°30E 241 G6
Kawya Burma 24°50N 94°58E 241 C5
Kaxgar He → China 39°45N 78°24E 217 E9
Kaxholmen Sweden 57°51N 14°19E 163 G8
Kaya Burkina Faso 13°4N 1°10W 263 C4
Kayah □ Burma 19°15N 97°15E 241 F6
Kayak I. U.S.A. 59°56N 144°23W 303 G11
Kayalıköy Barajı Turkey 41°50N 27°5E 203 E11
Kayamkulam India 9°10N 76°33E 245 K3
Kayan Burma 16°54N 96°34E 241 G6
Kayan → Indonesia 2°55N 117°35E 235 B5
Kayan Mentarang △ Indonesia 2°25N 115°30E 235 B5
Kaycee U.S.A. 43°43N 106°38W 304 E10
Kayeli Indonesia 3°20S 127°10E 231 E7
Kayenda Dem. Rep. of the Congo 10°48S 23°6E 265 E4
Kayenta U.S.A. 36°44N 110°15W 305 H8
Kayes Congo 4°25S 11°41E 265 C2
Kayes Mali 14°25N 11°30W 262 C2
Kayes □ Mali 14°0N 11°0W 262 C2
Kayı Turkey 39°12N 30°46E 205 B12
Kayima S. Leone 8°54N 11°15W 262 D2
Kayin □ Burma 18°0N 97°30E 241 G6
Kaymakçı Turkey 38°10N 28°8E 205 C10
Kayoa Indonesia 0°1N 127°28E 231 D7
Kayomba Zambia 13°11S 24°2E 269 E1
Kayombo Zambia 13°3S 23°51E 265 E4
Kaysatskoye Russia 49°47N 46°49E 190 F8
Kayseri Turkey 38°45N 35°30E 212 C6
Kayseri □ Turkey 38°40N 36°0E 212 C7
Kaysville U.S.A. 41°2N 111°56W 304 F8
Kayts Sri Lanka 9°42N 79°51E 245 K4
Kayu Putih Indonesia 6°10S 106°53E 122 B2
Kayuagung Indonesia 3°24S 104°50E 234 C2
Kaz Dağı Turkey 39°42N 26°50E 205 B8
Kazachye Russia 70°52N 135°58E 215 B14
Kazakhstan ■ Asia 50°0N 70°0E 217 C8
Kazan Russia 55°50N 49°10E 190 C9
Kazan → Canada 64°2N 95°29W 297 A9
Kazan-Rettō Pac. Oc. 25°0N 141°0E 288 E6
Kazancı Turkey 36°29N 32°51E 250 B3
Kazanlăk Bulgaria 42°38N 25°20E 203 D9
Kazanlı Turkey 36°49N 34°43E 250 B5
Kazanskaya Russia 49°50N 41°10E 190 F5
Kazatin = Kozyatyn Ukraine 49°45N 28°50E 177 D15
Kazaure Nigeria 12°42N 8°28E 263 C6
Kazbek Russia 42°42N 44°30E 191 J7
Kāzerūn Iran 29°38N 51°40E 247 D6
Kazi Magomed = Qazımämmäd Azerbaijan 40°3N 49°0E 191 K9
Kazimierz Dolny Poland 51°19N 21°57E 185 G8
Kazimierza Wielka Poland 50°15N 20°30E 185 H7
Kazincbarcika Hungary 48°17N 20°36E 182 B5
Kazipet India 17°58N 79°30E 244 F4
Kaziranga △ India 26°40N 93°30E 241 B4
Kaziza Dem. Rep. of the Congo 10°42S 23°52E 265 E4
Kazlų Rūda Lithuania 54°46N 23°30E 184 D10
Kazo Japan 36°7N 139°36E 223 A11
Kaztalovka Kazakhstan 49°47N 48°43E 190 F9
Kazu Burma 25°27N 97°46E 241 C6
Kazuma Pan △ Zimbabwe 18°20S 25°48E 269 F2
Kazumba Dem. Rep. of the Congo 6°25S 22°5E 265 D4
Kazungula Zambia 17°35S 25°15E 265 F5
Kazuno Japan 40°10N 140°45E 220 D10
Kazym → Russia 63°54N 65°50E 214 C7
Kbely Czech Rep. 50°8N 14°32E 135 B3
Kcynia Poland 53°0N 17°30E 185 F4
Ke-hsi Mansam Burma 21°56N 97°50E 241 E6
Ké-Macina Mali 13°58N 5°22W 262 C3
Kea Greece 37°35N 24°22E 204 D6
Kea'au U.S.A. 19°37N 155°2W 302 D6
Keady U.K. 54°15N 6°42W 166 B5
Keahi Pt. U.S.A. 21°19N 157°59W 302 K14
Keahole Pt. U.S.A. 19°44N 156°4W 302 D5
Kealaikahiki Channel U.S.A. 20°35N 156°50W 302 C5
Kealakekua U.S.A. 19°31N 155°55W 302 D6
Kearney Mo., U.S.A. 39°22N 94°22W 310 E2
Kearney Nebr., U.S.A. 40°42N 99°5W 308 E4
Kearney ◎ Australia 20°10S 128°4E 278 D4
Kearny U.S.A. 33°3N 110°55W 305 K8
Kearsarge, Mt. U.S.A. 43°22N 71°50W 313 C13
Keban Turkey 38°50N 38°50E 213 C8
Keban Barajı Turkey 38°41N 38°33E 213 C8
Kebara Congo 2°27S 14°25E 264 C2
Kebayoran Baru Indonesia 6°14S 106°47E 122 B1
Kebayoran Lama Indonesia 6°13S 106°46E 122 B1
Kebbi □ Nigeria 11°35N 4°0E 263 C5
Kébémèr Senegal 15°23N 16°34W 262 B1
Kébi Ivory C. 9°18N 6°37W 262 D3
Kebi, Mayo → Cameroon 9°18N 13°33E 264 A2
Kebili Tunisia 33°47N 9°0E 258 B1
Kebili □ Tunisia 33°30N 8°50E 261 B6
Kebnekaise Sweden 67°53N 18°33E 160 C18
Kebon Jeruk Indonesia 6°11S 106°46E 122 B1
Kebri Dehar Ethiopia 6°45N 44°17E 267 C5
Kebumen Indonesia 7°42S 109°40E 235 D3
Kecel Hungary 46°31N 19°16E 182 D4
Kechika → Canada 59°41N 127°12W 296 B3
Keçiborlu Turkey 37°57N 30°18E 205 D12
Kecskemét Hungary 46°57N 19°42E 182 D4
Kedada Ethiopia 5°25N 35°58E 257 F4
Kedah □ Malaysia 5°50N 100°40E 237 K3
Kėdainiai Lithuania 55°15N 24°2E 184 C11
Kedar West Bank 31°44N 35°18E 123 B2
Kedarnath India 30°44N 79°4E 243 D8
Kedgwick Canada 47°40N 67°20W 299 C6
Kediet Ijill Mauritania 22°38N 12°33W 260 D2
Kediri Indonesia 7°51S 112°1E 235 D4
Kedja Dem. Rep. of the Congo 4°50N 19°16E 264 B3
Kedjebi Ghana 8°12N 0°25E 263 D5
Kédougou Senegal 12°35N 12°10W 262 C2
Kedoya Indonesia 6°10S 106°45E 122 B1
Kedros Oros Greece 35°11N 24°37E 207 E5
Kędzierzyn-Koźle Poland 50°20N 18°12E 185 H5
Ke'ehi Lagoon U.S.A. 21°20N 157°54W 302 K14
Keeler U.S.A. 36°29N 117°52W 306 J9
Keeley L. Canada 54°54N 108°8W 297 C7
Keeling Is. = Cocos Is. Ind. Oc. 12°10S 96°55E 273 F8
Keelung = Chilung Taiwan 25°3N 121°45E 225 A3
Keenapusan Phil. 6°50N 118°50E 233 H2
Keene Ont., Canada 44°15N 78°10W 312 B6
Keene Calif., U.S.A. 35°13N 118°33W 307 K8
Keene N.H., U.S.A. 42°56N 72°17W 313 D12
Keene N.Y., U.S.A. 44°16N 73°46W 313 B11
Keep River △ Australia 15°49S 129°8E 278 C4
Keeper Hill Ireland 52°45N 8°16W 166 D3
Keepit, L. Australia 30°50S 150°30E 283 A9
Keerweer, C. Australia 14°0S 141°32E 280 A3
Keeseville U.S.A. 44°29N 73°30W 313 B11
Keetmanshoop Namibia 26°35S 18°8E 270 C2
Keewatin Canada 49°46N 94°34W 297 D10
Keewatin → Canada 56°29N 100°46W 297 B8
Kefa Ethiopia 6°55N 36°30E 257 F4
Kefalonia Greece 38°15N 20°30E 207 C2
Kefalonia □ Greece 38°15N 20°30E 207 C2
Kefalonia ✕ (EFL) Greece 38°10N 20°30E 207 C1
Kefalos Greece 36°45N 26°59E 205 E8
Kefamenanu Indonesia 9°28S 124°29E 231 F6
Kefar Sava Israel 32°11N 34°54E 251 F5
Keffi Nigeria 8°55N 7°43E 263 D6
Keffin Hausa Nigeria 12°13N 9°59E 263 C6
Keflavík Iceland 64°2N 22°35W 155 C4
Keflavík ✕ (KEF) Iceland 64°0N 22°45W 155 C4
Keftya Ethiopia 13°54N 37°7E 257 E4
Keg River Canada 57°54N 117°55W 296 B5
Kegalla Sri Lanka 7°15N 80°21E 245 L5
Kegaska Canada 50°9N 61°18W 299 B7
Kehancha Kenya 1°11S 34°37E 268 C3
Keheili Sudan 19°25N 32°50E 256 D3
Kehena U.S.A. 19°23N 154°55W 302 D7
Kehl Germany 48°34N 7°50E 179 G3
Keibul Lamjao △ India 24°30N 93°55E 241 C4
Keighley U.K. 53°52N 1°54W 168 D6
Keijo = Seoul S. Korea 37°31N 126°58E 137 B2
Keila Estonia 59°18N 24°25E 188 C3
Keilor Australia 37°42S 144°50E 128 A1
Keilor North Australia 37°44S 144°51E 128 A1
Keimoes S. Africa 28°41S 20°59E 270 C3
Keimola Finland 60°20N 24°49E 121 A1
Keita Niger 14°46N 5°56E 263 C6
Keïta, B. → Chad 9°14N 18°21E 259 G3
Keitele Finland 63°10N 26°20E 160 E22
Keith S. Austral., Australia 36°6S 140°20E 282 D4
Keith Moray, U.K. 57°32N 2°57W 167 D6
Keithsburg U.S.A. 41°6N 90°56W 310 C6
Keiyasi Fiji 17°53S 177°46E 287 A1
Keizer U.S.A. 44°57N 123°1W 304 D2
Kejimkujik △ Canada 44°25N 65°25W 299 D6
Kejserr Franz Joseph Fd. Greenland 73°30N 24°30W 154 C8
Kekaha U.S.A. 21°58N 159°43W 302 B2
Kekri India 26°0N 75°10E 242 G6
Keksgolm = Priozersk Russia 61°2N 30°7E 188 B6
Kelafo Ethiopia 5°37N 44°8E 267 C5
Kelam Ethiopia 4°48N 35°58E 257 G4
Kelamet Eritrea 16°0N 38°30E 257 D4
Kelan China 38°43N 111°31E 226 E6
Kelang = Klang Malaysia 3°2N 101°26E 237 L3
Kelani Ganga → Sri Lanka 6°58N 79°50E 245 L4
Kelantan □ Malaysia 5°10N 102°0E 237 K3
Kelantan → Malaysia 6°13N 102°14E 237 J4
Kelapa Gading Indonesia 6°9S 106°52E 122 A2
Këlcyrë Albania 40°20N 20°12E 202 F4
Kelekçi Turkey 37°15N 29°20E 205 D11
Kelenföld Hungary 47°27N 19°2E 117 B2
Keles Turkey 39°54N 29°14E 203 G13
Keleti-főcsatorna Hungary 47°45N 21°20E 182 C6
Kelheim Germany 48°54N 11°52E 179 G7
Kelibia Tunisia 36°50N 11°3E 258 A2
Kelkit Turkey 40°7N 39°16E 213 B8
Kelkit → Turkey 40°45N 36°32E 212 B7
Kellé Congo 0°8S 14°38E 264 C2
Kellé Niger 14°16N 10°7E 263 C7
Keller U.S.A. 31°50N 81°15W 316 D8
Kellerberrin Australia 31°36S 117°38E 279 F2
Kellett, C. Canada 72°0N 126°0W 150 B1
Kelleys I. U.S.A. 41°36N 82°42W 312 E2
Kellogg U.S.A. 47°32N 116°7W 304 C5
Kells Ireland 53°44N 6°53W 166 C5
Kelmė Lithuania 55°38N 22°56E 184 C9
Kelmentsi Ukraine 48°28N 26°50E 183 B11
Kélo Chad 9°10N 15°45E 259 G3
Kelokedhara Cyprus 34°48N 32°39E 207 F8
Kelowna Canada 49°50N 119°25W 296 D5
Kelsey Creek Australia 20°26S 148°31E 280 b
Kelseyville U.S.A. 38°59N 122°50W 306 G4
Kelso N.Z. 45°54S 169°15E 285 F4
Kelso Borders, U.K. 55°36N 2°26W 167 F6
Kelso Wash., U.S.A. 46°9N 122°54W 306 D4
Keluang = Kluang Malaysia 2°3N 103°18E 237 L4
Kelvin S. Africa 26°4S 28°5E 123 A2
Kelvington Canada 52°10N 103°30W 297 C8
Kem Russia 65°0N 34°38E 186 B5
Kem → Russia 64°57N 34°41E 186 B5
Kem-Kem Morocco 30°40N 4°30W 260 B4
Kema Indonesia 1°22N 125°8E 231 D7
Kemah Turkey 39°32N 39°5E 213 C8
Kemaliye Erzincan, Turkey 39°16N 38°29E 213 C8
Kemaliye Manisa, Turkey 38°27N 28°25E 205 C10
Kemalpaşa Turkey 38°25N 27°27E 205 C9
Kemaman Malaysia 4°12N 103°18E 237 K4
Kemang Indonesia 6°15S 106°48E 122 B1
Kemano Canada 53°35N 128°0W 296 C3
Kemapyu Burma 18°49N 97°19E 241 F6
Kemasik Malaysia 4°25N 103°27E 237 K4
Kemayoran Indonesia 6°10S 106°51E 122 B2
Kembé C.A.R. 4°36N 21°54E 264 B4
Kembolcha Ethiopia 11°2N 39°42E 257 E4
Kemer Antalya, Turkey 36°36N 30°34E 205 E12
Kemer Burdur, Turkey 37°21N 30°4E 205 D12
Kemer Muğla, Turkey 36°40N 29°22E 205 E11
Kemer Barajı Turkey 37°30N 28°37E 205 D10
Kemerburgaz Turkey 41°9N 28°54E 122 B1
Kemerovo Russia 55°20N 86°5E 214 D9
Kemerovo □ Russia 55°0N 86°0E 217 B11
Ķemeru △ Latvia 56°58N 23°25E 184 B10
Kemi Finland 65°44N 24°34E 160 D21
Kemi älv = Kemijoki → Finland 65°47N 24°32E 160 D21
Kemi träsk = Kemijärvi Finland 66°43N 27°22E 160 C22
Kemijärvi Finland 66°43N 27°22E 160 C22
Kemijoki → Finland 65°47N 24°32E 160 D21
Kemmerer U.S.A. 41°48N 110°32W 304 F8
Kemmuna = Comino Malta 36°1N 14°20E 206 E7
Kemp, L. U.S.A. 33°46N 99°9W 314 E5
Kemp Land Antarctica 69°0S 55°0E 151 C5
Kempas Malaysia 1°33N 103°42E 237 d
Kempen = Kępno Poland 51°18N 17°58E 185 G4
Kempsey Australia 31°1S 152°50E 283 A10
Kempt, L. Canada 47°25N 74°22W 298 C5
Kempten Germany 47°45N 10°17E 179 H6
Kempton Tas., Australia 42°31S 147°12E 281 G4
Kempton Ind., U.S.A. 40°17N 86°14W 311 D10
Kempton Park Races U.K. 51°24N 0°23W 125 B1
Kemptville Canada 45°0N 75°38W 313 B9
Ken → India 25°13N 80°27E 243 G9
Kenadsa Algeria 31°48N 2°26W 261 B4
Kenai U.S.A. 60°33N 151°16W 303 F10
Kenai Fjords △ U.S.A. 59°40N 149°50W 303 G10
Kenai Mts. U.S.A. 60°0N 150°0W 303 G10
Kenai Nat. Wildlife Refuge ⌂ U.S.A. 60°20N 150°30W 303 F10
Kenamuke Swamp South Sudan 5°55N 33°48E 257 F3
Kenansville U.S.A. 27°53N 80°59W 317 H9
Kendai India 22°45N 82°37E 243 H10
Kendal Indonesia 6°56S 110°14E 235 D4
Kendal Cumb., U.K. 54°20N 2°44W 168 C5
Kendall N.S.W., Australia 31°35S 152°44E 283 A10
Kendall Fla., U.S.A. 25°40N 80°19W 129 D1
Kendall → Australia 14°4S 141°35E 280 A3
Kendallville U.S.A. 41°27N 85°16W 311 C11
Kendari Indonesia 3°50S 122°30E 231 E6
Kendawangan Indonesia 2°32S 110°17E 235 C4
Kende Nigeria 11°30N 4°12E 263 C5
Kendégué Chad 10°0N 18°36E 259 F3
Kendi, Pulau Malaysia 5°13N 100°11E 237 c
Kendrapara India 20°35N 86°30E 244 D8
Këndrevicës, Maja e Albania 40°15N 19°52E 202 F3
Kendrew S. Africa 32°32S 24°30E 270 D3
Kendrick U.S.A. 29°15N 82°10W 317 F7
Kene Thao Laos 17°44N 101°10E 236 D3
Kenedy U.S.A. 28°49N 97°51W 314 G6
Kenema S. Leone 7°50N 11°14W 262 D2
Keng Kok Laos 16°26N 105°12E 236 D5
Keng Tawng Burma 20°45N 98°18E 241 E7
Keng Tung Burma 21°18N 99°39E 236 B2
Kengani Dem. Rep. of the Congo 2°59S 17°36E 264 C3
Kenge Dem. Rep. of the Congo 4°50S 17°4E 265 C3
Kengeja Tanzania 5°26S 39°45E 268 D4
Kenhardt S. Africa 29°19S 21°12E 270 C3
Kéniéba Mali 12°54N 11°17W 262 C2
Kenilworth Western Cape, S. Africa 33°59S 18°27E 118 A1
Kenilworth Ill., U.S.A. 42°5N 87°43W 119 A2
Keningau Malaysia 5°20N 116°10E 235 A5
Kenitra Morocco 34°15N 6°40W 260 B3
Kenli China 37°30N 118°20E 227 F10
Kenmare Kerry, Ireland 51°53N 9°36W 166 E2
Kenmare N. Dak., U.S.A. 48°41N 102°5W 308 A2
Kenmare River → Ireland 51°48N 9°51W 166 E2
Kennebago Lake U.S.A. 45°4N 70°40W 313 A14
Kennebec U.S.A. 43°54N 99°52W 308 D4
Kennebec → U.S.A. 43°45N 69°46W 309 D19
Kennebunk U.S.A. 43°23N 70°33W 313 C14
Kennedy Zimbabwe 18°52S 27°10E 270 A4
Kennedy, C. = Canaveral, C. U.S.A. 28°27N 80°32W 317 G9
Kennedy Channel Arctic 80°50N 66°0W 154 A4
Kennedy Entrance U.S.A. 59°1N 152°0W 303 G10
Kennedy Ra. Australia 24°45S 115°10E 279 D2
Kennedy Range △ Australia 24°34S 115°2E 279 D2
Kennedy Space Center U.S.A. 28°40N 80°42W 317 G9
Kennedy Town China 22°16N 114°6E 122 B1
Kennemerduinen △ Neths. 52°27N 4°33E 170 B4
Kenner U.S.A. 29°59N 90°14W 131 A1
Kennesaw U.S.A. 34°1N 84°37W 316 A5
Kennet → U.K. 51°27N 0°57W 169 F7
Kenneth Ra. Australia 23°50S 117°8E 279 D2
Kennett U.S.A. 36°14N 90°3W 308 G8
Kennewick U.S.A. 46°12N 119°7W 304 C4
Kennington London, U.K. 125 c4
Kennisis Lake Canada 45°13N 78°36W 312 A6
Kenogami → Canada 51°6N 84°28W 298 B3
Kenora Canada 49°47N 94°29W 297 D10
Kenosha U.S.A. 42°35N 87°49W 311 B9
Kensal Green U.K. 51°32N 0°13W 125 A2
Kensal Rise London, U.K. 125 a1
Kensington N.S.W., Australia 33°54S 151°13E 139 B2
Kensington P.E.I., Canada 46°28N 63°34W 299 C7
Kensington Gauteng, S. Africa 26°11S 28°6E 123 B2
Kensington London, U.K. 51°29N 0°10W 125 B2
Kensington N.Y., U.S.A. 40°38N 73°57W 132 C2
Kensington Palace U.K. 51°30N 0°11W 125 A2
Kent Ohio, U.S.A. 41°9N 81°22W 312 E3
Kent Tex., U.S.A. 31°4N 104°13W 314 F2
Kent Wash., U.S.A. 47°22N 122°14W 306 C4
Kent □ U.K. 51°12N 0°40E 169 F8
Kent Group Australia 39°30S 147°20E 281 F4
Kent Pen. Canada 68°30N 107°0W 294 D10
Kentaū Kazakhstan 43°32N 68°36E 217 D7
K'enting △ Taiwan 21°57N 120°48E 225 E2
Kentish Town U.K. 51°32N 0°8W 125 A3
Kentland U.S.A. 40°46N 87°27W 311 D9
Kenton London, U.K. 51°34N 0°17W 125 A2
Kenton Ohio, U.S.A. 40°39N 83°37W 311 D13
Kentucky □ U.S.A. 37°0N 84°0W 309 G11
Kentucky → U.S.A. 38°41N 85°11W 311 F11
Kentucky L. U.S.A. 37°1N 88°16W 308 G9
Kentville Canada 45°6N 64°29W 299 C7
Kentwood La., U.S.A. 30°56N 90°31W 315 F9
Kentwood Mich., U.S.A. 42°52N 85°39W 311 B11
Kenwood House U.K. 51°34N 0°9W 125 A3
Kenya ■ Africa 1°0N 38°0E 268 B4
Kenya, Mt. Kenya 0°10S 37°18E 268 C4
Kenyir, Tasik Malaysia 5°1N 102°54E 237 K4
Kenzou Cameroon 4°10N 15°2E 264 B3
Keo Neua, Deo Vietnam 18°23N 105°10E 236 C5
Keokuk U.S.A. 40°24N 91°24W 310 D5
Keoladeo △ India 27°0N 77°20E 242 F7
Keonjhargarh India 21°28N 85°35E 243 J11
Keosauqua U.S.A. 40°44N 91°58W 310 D5
Keota U.S.A. 41°22N 91°57W 310 C5
Kep Cambodia 10°29N 104°19E 237 G5
Kep Vietnam 21°24N 106°16E 236 B6
Kep △ Cambodia 10°30N 104°18E 237 G5
Kepa Poland 52°13N 21°3E 143 B2
Kepala Batas Malaysia 5°31N 100°26E 237 c
Kepez Turkey 40°5N 26°24E 203 F10
Kepi Indonesia 6°32S 139°19E 231 F9
Kępice Poland 54°16N 16°51E 184 D3
Kepler Mts. N.Z. 45°25S 167°20E 285 F2
Kępno Poland 51°18N 17°58E 185 G4
Keppel Harbour Singapore 1°15N 103°49E 138 B2
Keppel Pt. Papua N. G. 10°10S 147°58E 286 F4
Kepsut Turkey 39°40N 28°9E 205 B10
Kepuhi Pt. U.S.A. 21°29N 158°14W 302 K13
Kepulauan Karimunjawa △ Indonesia 5°50S 110°25E 235 D4
Kerala □ India 11°0N 76°15E 245 J3
Keram → Papua N. G. 4°7S 144°5E 286 C3
Kerama-Rettō Japan 26°5N 127°15E 221 L3
Keramikos Athens, Greece 112 b1
Keran Pakistan 34°35N 73°59E 243 B5
Keran △ Togo 10°9N 0°41E 263 C5
Kerang Vic., Australia 35°40S 143°55E 282 C5
Kerang Indonesia 2°15S 116°3E 235 C5
Keranyo Ethiopia 5°3N 38°18E 257 F4
Kerao → South Sudan 11°0N 32°41E 257 E3
Keratea Greece 37°48N 23°58E 204 D5
Keraudren, C. Australia 19°58S 119°45E 278 C2
Kerava Finland 60°25N 25°5E 188 B3
Keravat Papua N. G. 4°17S 152°2E 286 C7
Kerch Ukraine 45°20N 36°20E 189 K9
Kerchenskiy Proliv Black Sea 45°10N 36°30E 189 K9
Kerchoual Mali 17°12N 0°20E 263 B5
Kerema Papua N. G. 7°58S 145°50E 286 D3
Kerempe Burnu Turkey 42°2N 33°20E 212 A5
Keren Eritrea 15°45N 38°28E 257 D4
Kerepakupai-Meru = Angel Falls Venezuela 5°57N 62°30W 329 B5
Kerewan Gambia 13°29N 16°10W 262 C1
Kerguelen Ind. Oc. 49°15S 69°10E 273 J5
Kerguelen Plateau S. Ocean 55°0S 75°0E 273 K6
Keri Greece 37°40N 20°49E 207 D2
Keri Kera Sudan 12°21N 32°42E 257 E3
Kerian, Kuala Malaysia 5°10N 100°25E 237 c
Kericho Kenya 0°22S 35°15E 268 C4
Kerikeri N.Z. 35°12S 173°59E 284 B2
Kerinci Indonesia 1°40S 101°15E 234 C2
Kerinci Seblat △ Indonesia 2°30S 101°30E 234 C1
Kerintji = Kerinci Indonesia 1°40S 101°15E 234 C2
Keriya He → China 38°30N 82°10E 217 E10
Kerkenna, Îs. Tunisia 34°48N 11°11E 258 B2
Kerki = Atamyrat Turkmenistan 37°50N 65°12E 217 E7
Kerkini, L. Greece 41°12N 23°10E 202 E7
Kerkouane Tunisia 36°58N 11°2E 200 F4
Kerkrade Neths. 50°53N 6°4E 170 D6
Kerkyra Greece 39°38N 19°50E 206 B9
Kerkyra □ Greece 39°37N 19°50E 206 B9
Kerkyra ✕ (CFU) Greece 39°35N 19°54E 204 B1
Kerkyras, Notio Steno Greece 39°34N 20°0E 206 B10
Kerma Sudan 19°33N 30°32E 256 D3
Kermadec Is. Pac. Oc. 30°0S 178°15W 277 G15
Kermadec Trench Pac. Oc. 30°30S 176°0W 277 G15
Kermān Iran 30°15N 57°1E 247 D8
Kerman Calif., U.S.A. 36°43N 120°4W 306 J6
Kermān □ Iran 30°0N 57°0E 247 D8
Kermān, Bīābān-e Iran 28°45N 59°45E 247 D8
Kermānshāh Iran 34°23N 47°0E 213 E12
Kermānshāh □ Iran 34°0N 46°30E 246 C5
Kermen Bulgaria 42°30N 26°16E 203 D10
Kermine = Navoi Uzbekistan 40°9N 65°22E 217 D7
Kermit U.S.A. 31°52N 103°6W 314 F3
Kern → U.S.A. 35°16N 119°18W 307 K7
Kernavė Lithuania 54°53N 24°49E 188 E3
Kernhof Austria 47°49N 15°32E 180 D8
Kernow = Cornwall □ U.K. 50°26N 4°40W 169 G3
Kernville U.S.A. 35°45N 118°26W 307 K8
Keroh Malaysia 5°43N 101°1E 237 K3
Keros Greece 36°54N 25°40E 205 E7
Kérou Benin 10°50N 2°5E 263 C5
Kérouane Guinea 9°15N 9°0W 262 D3
Kerowagi Papua N. G. 5°51S 144°51E 286 C3
Kerpen Germany 50°51N 6°41E 178 E2
Kerrera U.K. 56°24N 5°33W 167 E3
Kerrobert Canada 51°56N 109°8W 297 C7
Kerrville U.S.A. 30°3N 99°8W 314 F5
Kerry □ Ireland 52°7N 9°35W 166 D2
Kerry Hd. Ireland 52°25N 9°56W 166 D2
Kersa Ethiopia 9°28N 41°48E 257 F5
Kertosono Indonesia 7°38S 112°9E 235 D4
Kerulen = Herlen → Asia 48°48N 117°0E 219 B12
Kervo = Kerava Finland 60°25N 25°5E 188 B3
Kerzaz Algeria 29°29N 1°37W 261 C4
Kesagami → Canada 51°40N 79°45W 298 B4
Kesagami L. Canada 50°23N 80°15W 298 B3
Keşan Turkey 40°49N 26°38E 203 F10
Kesariani Greece 37°57N 23°46E 112 B2
Kesennuma Japan 38°54N 141°35E 220 E10
Keshāvar Iran 36°50N 46°22E 213 D12
Keshit Iran 29°43N 58°17E 247 D8
Kesigi = Kosgi India 15°51N 77°16E 245 G3
Keşiş Dağ Turkey 39°47N 39°46E 213 C8
Keskal India 20°5N 81°35E 244 D5
Keskin Turkey 39°40N 33°36E 212 C5
Kestenga Russia 65°50N 31°45E 160 D24
Keswick U.K. 54°36N 3°8W 168 C4
Keszthely Hungary 46°50N 17°15E 182 D2
Ket → Russia 58°55N 81°32E 214 D9
Keta Ghana 5°49N 1°0E 263 D5
Keta Lagoon Ghana 5°55N 1°0E 263 D5
Ketapang Jawa Timur, Indonesia 8°9S 114°23E 231 J17
Ketapang Kalimantan Barat, Indonesia 1°55S 110°0E 235 C4
Ketchenery Russia 47°18N 44°32E 191 G7
Ketchikan U.S.A. 55°21N 131°39W 296 B2
Ketchum U.S.A. 43°41N 114°22W 304 E6
Kete Krachi Ghana 7°46N 0°1W 263 D4
Ketef, Khalîg Umm el Egypt 23°40N 35°35E 246 F2
Keti Bandar Pakistan 24°8N 67°27E 242 G2
Kétou Benin 7°25N 2°45E 263 D5
Ketri India 28°1N 75°50E 242 E6
Kętrzyn Poland 54°7N 21°22E 184 D8
Ketta Congo 1°28N 15°54E 264 B3
Kettering Northants., U.K. 52°24N 0°43W 169 E7
Kettering Ohio, U.S.A. 39°41N 84°10W 311 E12
Kettle → Canada 56°40N 89°34W 297 B11
Kettle Falls U.S.A. 48°37N 118°3W 304 B4
Kettle Point Canada 43°10N 82°1W 312 C2
Kettle Pt. Canada 43°13N 82°1W 312 C2
Kettleman City U.S.A. 36°1N 119°58W 306 J7
Kęty Poland 49°51N 19°16E 185 J6
Keuka L. U.S.A. 42°30N 77°9W 312 D7
Keuruu Finland 62°16N 24°41E 188 A3
Kevelaer Germany 51°36N 6°15E 178 D2
Kew Vic., Australia 37°48S 145°2E 128 A2
Kew London, U.K. 51°28N 0°17W 125 B2
Kew Gardens Ont., Canada 43°39N 79°18W 141 A3
Kew Gardens London, U.K. 51°28N 0°17W 125 B2
Kewanee U.S.A. 41°14N 89°56W 310 C7
Kewanna U.S.A. 41°1N 86°25W 311 C10
Keware Nepal 27°57N 83°47E 243 F10
Kewaunee U.S.A. 44°27N 87°31W 308 C10
Keweenaw B. U.S.A. 47°0N 88°15W 308 B9
Keweenaw Pen. U.S.A. 47°15N 88°15W 308 B9
Keweenaw Pt. U.S.A. 47°25N 87°43W 308 B10
Kexholm = Priozersk Russia 61°2N 30°7E 188 B6
Key, L. Ireland 54°0N 8°15W 166 C3
Key Biscayne U.S.A. 25°41N 80°9W 129 D3
Key Colony Beach U.S.A. 24°45N 80°57W 317 L9
Key Lake Mine Canada 57°5N 105°32W 297 B7
Key Largo U.S.A. 25°5N 80°27W 317 K9
Key West U.S.A. 24°33N 81°48W 317 L8
Keyala South Sudan 4°27N 32°52E 257 G3
Keynsham U.K. 51°24N 2°29W 169 F5
Keyser U.S.A. 39°26N 78°59W 309 F14
Keystone Heights U.S.A. 29°47N 82°2W 316 F7
Keytesville U.S.A. 39°26N 92°56W 310 E4
Kezhma Russia 58°59N 101°9E 215 D11
Kezi Zimbabwe 20°58S 28°32E 271 B4
Kežmarok Slovak Rep. 49°10N 20°28E 181 B13
Kgalagadi □ Botswana 24°30S 22°0E 270 B3
Kgalagadi Transfrontier ⌂ Africa 25°10S 21°0E 270 C3
Khabarovsk Russia 48°30N 135°5E 219 B16
Khabr △ Iran 28°51N 56°22E 247 D8
Khābūr → Syria 35°17N 40°35E 213 E9
Khachmas = Xaçmaz Azerbaijan 41°31N 48°42E 191 K9
Khachrod India 23°25N 75°20E 242 H6
Khadari, W. el → Sudan 10°29N 27°15E 257 E2
Khadro Pakistan 26°11N 68°50E 242 F3
Khadyzhensk Russia 44°26N 39°32E 191 H4
Khadzhilyangar = Dahongliutan China 35°45N 79°20E 243 B8
Khaga India 25°47N 81°7E 243 G9
Khagaria India 25°30N 86°32E 243 G12
Khagrachari Bangla. 23°6N 91°58E 241 D3
Khaipur Pakistan 29°34N 72°17E 242 E5
Khair India 27°57N 77°46E 242 F7
Khairabad India 27°33N 80°47E 243 F9
Khairagarh India 21°27N 81°2E 243 J9
Khairpur Pakistan 27°32N 68°49E 242 F3
Khairpur Nathan Shah Pakistan 27°6N 67°44E 242 F2
Khairwara India 23°58N 73°38E 242 H5
Khaisor → Pakistan 31°17N 68°59E 242 D3
Khajuraho India 24°51N 79°55E 243 G8
Khajuri Kach Pakistan 32°4N 69°51E 242 C3
Khāk Dow Afghan. 34°57N 67°16E 240 B2
Khakassia □ Russia 53°0N 90°0E 217 B12
Khakhea Botswana 24°48S 23°22E 270 B3
Khalafābād Iran 30°54N 49°24E 247 D6
Khalīj Iraq 33°18N 44°28E 113 B2
Khalilabad India 26°48N 83°5E 243 F10
Khalīlī Iran 27°38N 53°17E 247 E7
Khalkhāl Iran 37°37N 48°32E 213 D13
Khalkís = Chalkida Greece 38°27N 23°42E 204 C5
Khalmer-Sede = Tazovskiy Russia 67°30N 78°44E 214 C8
Khalmer Yu Russia 67°58N 65°1E 214 C7
Khalturin Russia 58°40N 48°50E 186 C8
Kham Keut Laos 18°15N 104°43E 236 C5
Khamaria India 23°5N 80°48E 243 H9
Khambhaliya India 22°14N 69°41E 242 H3
Khambhat India 22°23N 72°33E 242 H5
Khambhat, G. of India 20°45N 72°30E 239 E10
Khamgaon India 20°42N 76°37E 244 D3
Khami Ruins = Kame Ruins Zimbabwe 20°7S 28°25E 269 G2
Khamīr Iran 26°57N 55°36E 247 E7
Khamir Yemen 16°2N 44°0E 248 C4
Khamīs Mushayṭ Si. Arabia 18°18N 42°44E 248 C3
Khammam India 17°11N 80°6E 244 F5
Khamsa Egypt 30°27N 32°23E 251 H3
Khan → Namibia 22°37S 14°56E 270 B2
Khān Abū Shāmat Syria 33°39N 36°53E 250 E7
Khān al Baghdādī Iraq 33°51N 42°32E 213 G10
Khān al Ḩammād Iraq 32°19N 44°16E 213 G11
Khān Azād Iraq 33°7N 44°22E 246 C5
Khān Mujiddah Iraq 32°21N 43°48E 246 C4
Khān Shaykhūn Syria 35°26N 36°38E 212 E7
Khan Tengri, Pik Asia 42°12N 80°10E 217 D10
Khān Yūnis Gaza Strip 31°21N 34°18E 251 G5
Khānābād Afghan. 36°45N 69°5E 240 A3
Khanai Pakistan 30°30N 67°8E 242 D2
Khānaqīn Iraq 34°23N 45°25E 213 E11
Khanāşir Syria 35°45N 37°30E 250 C8
Khānbāghī Iran 36°10N 55°25E 247 B7
Khandwa India 21°49N 76°22E 244 D3
Khandyga Russia 62°42N 135°35E 215 C14
Khanewal Pakistan 30°20N 71°55E 242 D4
Khangah Dogran Pakistan 31°50N 73°37E 242 D5
Khangchendzonga = Kanchenjunga △ India 27°42N 88°8E 241 B2
Khanh Duong Vietnam 12°44N 108°44E 236 F7
Khaniá = Chania Greece 35°30N 24°4E 207 E5
Khaniadhana India 25°1N 78°8E 242 G8
Khanka, L. Asia 45°0N 132°24E 220 B6
Khankendy = Xankändi Azerbaijan 39°52N 46°49E 213 C12
Khanna India 30°42N 76°16E 242 D7
Khanozai Pakistan 30°37N 67°19E 242 D2
Khanpur Pakistan 28°42N 70°35E 242 E4
Khansā' Iraq 33°21N 44°28E 113 A2
Khanty-Mansiysk Russia 61°0N 69°0E 214 C7
Khanzira, Ras Somalia 10°52N 45°48E 267 B6
Khao Khitchakut △ Thailand 12°50N 102°10E 236 F4
Khao Laem △ Thailand 14°56N 98°31E 236 E2
Khao Laem Res. Thailand 14°50N 98°30E 236 E2
Khao Lak △ Malaysia 8°38N 98°18E 237 H2
Khao Luang △ Thailand 8°34N 99°42E 237 H2
Khao Nam Khang △ Thailand 6°32N 100°35E 237 J3
Khao Phlu Thailand 9°29N 99°59E 237 b
Khao Pu -Khao Ya △ Thailand 7°26N 99°57E 237 J2
Khao Sam Roi Yot △ Thailand 12°13N 99°57E 237 F2
Khao Sok △ Thailand 8°55N 98°38E 237 H2
Khao Yai △ Thailand 14°21N 101°29E 236 E3
Khaoen Si Nakarin △ Thailand 14°47N 99°0E 236 E2
Khapalu Pakistan 35°10N 76°20E 243 B7
Khapcheranga Russia 49°42N 112°24E 215 E12
Khaptao △ Nepal 29°20N 81°10E 243 E9
Kharabali Russia 47°25N 47°15E 191 G8
Kharagauli Georgia 42°1N 43°12E 191 J6
Kharaghoda India 23°11N 71°46E 242 H4
Kharagpur India 22°20N 87°25E 243 H12
Kharan Kalat Pakistan 28°34N 65°21E 240 C2
Kharānaq Iran 32°20N 54°45E 247 C7
Kharavli India 18°54N 72°55E 130 B2
Kharda India 18°40N 75°34E 244 E2
Khardung La India 34°20N 77°43E 243 B7
Kharg = Khārk, Jazīreh-ye Iran 29°15N 50°28E 247 D6
Khârga, El Wâhât el Egypt 25°10N 30°35E 256 B3
Khargon India 21°45N 75°40E 244 D2
Khari → India 25°54N 74°31E 242 G6
Kharian Pakistan 32°49N 73°52E 242 C5
Khariar India 20°17N 82°46E 244 D6
Kharit, Wadi el → Egypt 24°26N 33°3E 256 C3
Khārk, Jazīreh-ye Iran 29°15N 50°28E 247 D6
Kharkiv Ukraine 49°58N 36°20E 189 H9
Kharkiv □ Ukraine 48°20N 36°20E 189 H9
Kharkov = Kharkiv Ukraine 49°58N 36°20E 189 H9
Kharmanli Bulgaria 41°55N 25°55E 203 E9
Kharovsk Russia 59°56N 40°13E 188 C11
Kharsawangarh India 22°48N 85°50E 243 H11
Kharta Turkey 40°55N 29°7E 212 B3
Khartoum = El Khartûm Sudan 15°31N 32°35E 257 D3
Khartum Canada 45°15N 77°5W 312 A7
Khasan Russia 42°25N 130°40E 220 C5
Khasavyurt Russia 43°16N 46°40E 191 J8
Khāsh Iran 28°15N 61°15E 240 C1
Khāsh, Dasht-e Afghan. 31°50N 62°30E 240 C1
Khashm el Girba Sudan 14°59N 35°58E 257 E4
Khashum Sudan 12°27N 28°2E 257 E2
Khashuri Georgia 42°3N 43°35E 191 J6
Khasi Hills India 25°30N 91°30E 241 C3

Khaskovo *Bulgaria* 41°56N 25°30E **203** E9
Khaskovo □ *Bulgaria* 42°0N 25°40E **203** E9
Khat, Laem *Thailand* 8°6N 98°26E **237** a
Khatanga *Russia* 72°0N 102°20E **215** B11
Khatanga → *Russia* 72°55N 106°0E **215** B11
Khatauli *India* 29°17N 77°43E **242** E7
Khatlon □ *Tajikistan* 37°50N 69°0E **217** E7
Khatra *India* 22°59N 86°51E **243** H12
Khātūnābād *Iran* 30°1N 55°25E **247** D7
Khatyrka *Russia* 62°3N 175°15E **215** C18
Khavda *India* 23°51N 69°43E **242** H3
Khawlaf, Ra's *Yemen* 12°40N 54°7E **249** D6
Khawr Fakkān *U.A.E.* 25°21N 56°22E **247** E8
Khay' *Si. Arabia* 18°45N 41°24E **248** C3
Khaybar, Ḩarrat
Si. Arabia 25°30N 39°45E **246** E4
Khāzimiyah *Iraq* 34°46N 43°37E **246** C4
Khazzān Jabal al Awliyā
Sudan 15°24N 32°20E **257** D3
Khe Bo *Vietnam* 19°8N 104°41E **236** C5
Khe Long *Vietnam* 21°29N 104°46E **236** B5
Khe Sanh *Vietnam* 16°37N 106°45E **236** D6
Khed *Maharashtra, India* 17°43N 73°27E **244** F1
Khed *Maharashtra, India* 18°51N 73°56E **244** E1
Khed Brahma *India* 24°7N 73°5E **242** G5
Khefren *Egypt* 29°58N 31°8E **117** B1
Khekra *India* 28°52N 77°20E **242** E7
Khem-Beldyr = Kyzyl
Russia 51°50N 94°30E **217** B12
Khemarak Phouminville = Krong
Kaoh Kong *Cambodia* 11°37N 102°59E **237** G4
Khemisset *Morocco* 33°50N 6°1W **260** B3
Khemmarat *Thailand* 16°10N 105°15E **236** D5
Khenāmān *Iran* 30°27N 56°29E **247** D8
Khenchela *Algeria* 35°28N 7°11E **261** A6
Khenchela □ *Algeria* 35°0N 7°0E **261** B6
Khenifra *Morocco* 32°58N 5°46W **260** B3
Kherrata *Algeria* 36°27N 5°13E **261** A6
Khersān → *Iran* 31°33N 50°22E **247** D6
Kherson *Ukraine* 46°35N 32°35E **189** J7
Kherson □ *Ukraine* 46°15N 33°10E **189** J7
Kheta → *Russia* 71°54N 102°6E **215** B11
Khewari *Pakistan* 26°36N 68°52E **242** F3
Khibinogorsk = Kirovsk
Russia 67°32N 33°41E **186** A5
Khichripur *India* 28°37N 77°18E **120** B2
Khidirpur *India* 22°32N 88°19E **124** B1
Khilchipur *India* 24°2N 76°34E **242** G7
Khilok *Russia* 51°30N 110°45E **215** D12
Khimki *Russia* 55°50N 37°20E **188** E9
Khimki-Khovrino *Russia* 55°51N 37°31E **129** A2
Khíos = Chios *Greece* 38°27N 26°9E **205** C8
Khirbet Batin Abu Lihyah
West Bank 31°50N 35°6E **123** A1
Khirbet el-Misbah
West Bank 31°53N 35°4E **123** A1
Khirbet Jub e-Rum
West Bank 31°44N 35°16E **123** B2
Khirsadoh *India* 22°11N 78°47E **243** H8
Khiuma = Hiiumaa
Estonia 58°50N 22°45E **188** C2
Khiva = Xiva *Uzbekistan* 41°30N 60°18E **216** D6
Khlebarovo *Bulgaria* 43°37N 26°15E **203** C10
Khlong Khlung *Thailand* 16°12N 99°43E **236** D2
Khlong Lan △ *Thailand* 16°12N 99°13E **236** D2
Khlong Phanom △
Thailand 8°45N 98°38E **237** H2
Khlong San *Thailand* 13°43N 100°29E **113** B2
Khlong Toey *Thailand* 13°43N 100°36E **113** B2
Khmelnik *Ukraine* 49°33N 27°58E **177** D14
Khmelnytskyy *Ukraine* 49°23N 27°0E **177** D14
Khmelnytskyy □
Ukraine 49°50N 26°40E **177** D14
Khmer Rep. = Cambodia ■
Asia 12°15N 105°0E **236** F5
Khoai, Hon *Vietnam* 8°26N 104°50E **237** H5
Khobar = Al Khubar
Si. Arabia 26°17N 50°12E **247** E6
Khodoriv *Ukraine* 49°24N 24°19E **177** D13
Khodzent = Khŭjand
Tajikistan 40°17N 69°37E **217** D7
Khojak Pass *Afghan.* 30°51N 66°34E **242** D2
Khojayli = Xo'jayli
Uzbekistan 42°29N 59°31E **216** D5
Khok Kloi *Thailand* 8°17N 98°19E **237** a
Khok Pho *Thailand* 6°43N 101°6E **237** J3
Khok Samrong *Thailand* 15°3N 100°43E **236** E3
Khokhropār *Pakistan* 25°42N 70°12E **240** D3
Kholm *Afghan.* 36°45N 67°40E **240** A2
Kholm *Russia* 57°10N 31°15E **188** D6
Kholmsk *Russia* 47°40N 142°5E **215** E15
Khomārlu *Iran* 39°6N 47°3E **213** C12
Khomas □ *Namibia* 23°30S 17°0E **270** B2
Khomas Hochland *Namibia* 22°40S 16°0E **270** B2
Khombole *Senegal* 14°43N 16°42W **262** C1
Khomeyn *Iran* 33°40N 50°7E **247** C6
Khomeynī Shahr *Iran* 32°41N 51°31E **247** C6
Khomodino *Botswana* 22°46S 23°52E **270** B3
Khon Kaen *Thailand* 16°30N 102°47E **236** D4
Khong → *Cambodia* 13°32N 105°58E **236** F5
Khong Sedone *Laos* 15°34N 105°49E **236** E5
Khonsa *India* 26°57N 95°33E **241** B5
Khonuu *Russia* 66°30N 143°12E **215** C15
Khoper → *Russia* 49°30N 42°20E **190** F6
Khor el 'Atash *Sudan* 13°20N 34°15E **257** E3
Khorāsān-e Janūb □ *Iran* 32°0N 59°0E **247** C8
Khorāsān-e Razavī □ *Iran* 35°0N 57°0E **247** C8
Khorāsān-e Shemālī □ *Iran* 37°0N 57°0E **247** B8
Khorat = Nakhon Ratchasima
Thailand 14°59N 102°12E **236** E4
Khorat, Cao Nguyen
Thailand 15°30N 102°50E **236** E4
Khorazm □ *Uzbekistan* 43°0N 60°0E **216** D6
Khorb el Ethel *Algeria* 28°30N 6°17W **260** C3
Khorel *India* 22°41N 88°18E **124** A1
Khorixas *Namibia* 20°16S 14°59E **270** B1
Khorol *Ukraine* 49°48N 33°15E **189** H7
Khorosovo *Russia* 55°46N 37°27E **129** B1
Khorramābād *Khorāsān, Iran* 35°6N 57°57E **247** C8
Khorramābād *Lorestān, Iran* 33°30N 48°25E **213** F13
Khorramdarreh *Iran* 36°11N 49°11E **213** D13
Khorramshahr *Iran* 30°29N 48°15E **247** D6
Khorugh *Tajikistan* 37°30N 71°36E **240** A3
Khosravī *Iran* 30°48N 51°28E **247** D6
Khosrowābād *Khuzestān, Iran* 30°10N 48°25E **247** D6
Khosrowābād *Kordestān, Iran* 35°31N 47°38E **213** E12
Khost *Pakistan* 30°13N 67°35E **242** D2
Khosūyeh *Iran* 28°32N 54°26E **247** D7
Khotan = Hotan *China* 37°25N 79°55E **217** E9
Khotang *Nepal* 27°1N 86°51E **243** F12
Khotyn *Ukraine* 48°31N 26°27E **183** B11
Khouribga *Morocco* 32°58N 6°57W **260** B3
Khowai *Bangla.* 24°5N 91°40E **241** C3
Khowst *Afghan.* 33°22N 69°58E **242** C3
Khowst □ *Afghan.* 33°20N 70°0E **240** B3
Khoyniki *Belarus* 51°54N 29°55E **177** C15
Khram, Ko *Thailand* 12°42N 100°47E **236** F3
Khrami → *Georgia* 41°25N 45°0E **191** K7
Khrenovoye *Russia* 51°4N 40°16E **190** E5
Khromtaū *Kazakhstan* 50°17N 58°27E **216** B5
Khrysokhou B. *Cyprus* 35°6N 32°25E **207** E8
Khuan Wa *Thailand* 7°53N 98°17E **237** a
Khudrah, W. → *Yemen* 18°10N 50°20E **249** C5
Khudzhand = Khŭjand
Tajikistan 40°17N 69°37E **217** D7
Khuff *Si. Arabia* 24°55N 44°53E **246** E5
Khūgīānī *Afghan.* 31°34N 66°32E **242** D2
Khuis *Botswana* 26°40S 21°49E **270** C3
Khuiyala *India* 27°9N 70°25E **242** F4
Khŭjand *Tajikistan* 40°17N 69°37E **217** D7
Khujner *India* 23°47N 76°36E **242** H7
Khukhan *Thailand* 14°42N 104°12E **236** E5
Khulays *Si. Arabia* 22°9N 39°19E **248** B2
Khulna *Bangla.* 22°45N 89°34E **241** D2
Khulna □ *Bangla.* 22°25N 89°35E **241** D2
Khulo *Georgia* 41°33N 42°19E **191** K6
Khumago *Botswana* 20°26S 24°32E **270** B3
Khumrah *Si. Arabia* 21°22N 39°13E **248** B2
Khunjerab △ *Pakistan* 36°40N 75°30E **243** A6
Khunjerab Pass = Kinjirap Daban
Asia 36°40N 75°25E **240** A4
Khūnsorkh *Iran* 27°9N 56°7E **247** E8
Khunti *India* 23°5N 85°17E **243** H11
Khūr *Iran* 32°55N 58°18E **247** C8
Khurai *India* 24°3N 78°23E **242** G8
Khuraydah *Yemen* 15°33N 48°18E **249** D5
Khurayș *Si. Arabia* 25°6N 48°2E **247** E6
Khurda *India* 20°11N 85°37E **244** D7
Khureit *Sudan* 13°59N 26°3E **257** E2
Khurja *India* 28°15N 77°58E **242** E7
Khūrmāl *Iraq* 35°18N 46°2E **213** E12
Khurr, Wādī al *Iraq* 32°3N 43°52E **246** C4
Khūsf *Iran* 32°46N 58°53E **247** C8
Khushab *Pakistan* 32°20N 72°20E **242** C5
Khust *Ukraine* 48°10N 23°18E **183** B8
Khutse ⌓ *Botswana* 23°31S 24°12E **270** B3
Khuwei *Sudan* 13°5N 29°14E **257** E2
Khuzdar *Pakistan* 27°52N 66°30E **242** F2
Khūzestān □ *Iran* 31°0N 49°0E **247** D6
Khvāf *Iran* 34°33N 60°8E **247** C9
Khvājeh *Iran* 38°9N 46°35E **246** B5
Khvājeh Moḩammad, Kūh-e
Afghan. 36°22N 70°17E **240** A3
Khvalynsk *Russia* 52°30N 48°2E **190** D9
Khvānsār *Iran* 29°56N 54°8E **247** D7
Khvatovka *Russia* 52°24N 46°32E **190** D8
Khvor *Iran* 33°45N 55°0E **247** C7
Khvorgū *Iran* 27°34N 56°27E **247** E8
Khvormūj *Iran* 28°40N 51°30E **247** D6
Khvoy *Iran* 38°35N 45°0E **213** C11
Khvoynaya *Russia* 58°58N 34°28E **188** C8
Khwae Noi → *Thailand* 14°1N 99°32E **236** E2
Khyber Pakhtunkhwa □
Pakistan 34°0N 72°0E **242** C4
Khyber Pass *Afghan.* 34°10N 71°8E **242** B4
Khyriv *Ukraine* 49°32N 22°50E **185** J9
Kia *Fiji* 16°16S 179°8E **287** A2
Kia *Solomon Is.* 7°32S 158°26E **287** L10
Kiabukwa
Dem. Rep. of the Congo 8°40S 24°48E **265** D4
Kiadho → *India* 19°37N 77°40E **244** E3
Kiama *N.S.W., Australia* 34°40S 150°50E **283** C9
Kiamba
Dem. Rep. of the Congo 7°19S 17°49E **265** D3
Kiamari *Pakistan* 24°49N 66°58E **123** B1
Kiamba *Phil.* 6°2N 124°46E **233** H5
Kiambi *Dem. Rep. of the Congo* 7°15S 28°0E **268** D2
Kiamusze = Jiamusi
China 46°40N 130°26E **219** B15
Kian = Ji'an *China* 41°5N 126°10E **227** D14
Kiana *U.S.A.* 66°58N 160°26W **303** C7
Kiang West △ *Gambia* 13°25N 15°50W **262** C1
Kiangara *Madag.* 17°58S 47°2E **272** B2
Kiangsi = Jiangxi □
China 27°30N 116°0E **229** D11
Kiangsu = Jiangsu □
China 33°0N 120°0E **227** H11
Kiato *Greece* 38°1N 22°45E **204** C4
Kibæk *Denmark* 56°2N 8°51E **163** H2
Kibale △ *Uganda* 0°16N 30°18E **268** B3
Kibanga Port *Uganda* 0°10N 32°58E **268** B3
Kibangou *Congo* 3°26S 12°22E **264** C2
Kibara *Tanzania* 2°8S 33°30E **268** C3
Kibare, Mts.
Dem. Rep. of the Congo 8°25S 27°10E **268** D2
Kibawe *Phil.* 7°34N 125°0E **233** H5
Kibenga
Dem. Rep. of the Congo 7°56S 17°30E **265** D3
Kibira △ *Burundi* 3°6S 30°24E **268** C3
Kiboga *Uganda* 0°58N 31°45E **268** B3
Kibombo
Dem. Rep. of the Congo 3°57S 25°53E **265** C5
Kibondo *Tanzania* 3°35S 30°45E **268** C3
Kibre Mengist *Ethiopia* 5°54N 38°59E **257** F4
Kıbrıs = Cyprus ■ *Asia* 35°0N 33°0E **207** F9
Kibumbu *Burundi* 3°32S 29°45E **268** C2
Kibungo *Rwanda* 2°10S 30°32E **268** C3
Kibuye *Burundi* 3°39S 29°59E **268** C2
Kibuye *Rwanda* 2°3S 29°21E **268** C2
Kibwesa *Tanzania* 6°30S 29°58E **268** D2
Kibwezi *Kenya* 2°27S 37°57E **268** C4
Kicasalih *Turkey* 41°23N 26°48E **203** E10
Kičevo *Macedonia* 41°34N 20°59E **202** E4
Kichha → *India* 28°41N 79°18E **243** E8
Kichmengskiy Gorodok
Russia 59°59N 45°48E **186** B8
Kicking Horse Pass
Canada 51°28N 116°16W **296** C5
Kid, W. → *Egypt* 28°9N 34°27E **251** K5
Kid I. *Antigua & B.* 17°42N 61°49W **322** c
Kidal *Mali* 18°26N 1°22E **263** B5
Kidal □ *Mali* 19°55N 1°5E **261** E5
Kidapawan *Phil.* 7°1N 125°3E **233** H5
Kidderminster *U.K.* 52°24N 2°15W **169** E5
Kidepo Valley △ *Uganda* 3°52N 33°50E **268** B3
Kidete *Tanzania* 6°25S 37°17E **268** D4
Kidira *Senegal* 14°28N 12°13W **262** C2
Kidnappers, C. *N.Z.* 39°38S 177°5E **284** F6
Kidsgrove *U.K.* 53°5N 2°14W **168** D5
Kidston *Australia* 18°52S 144°8E **280** B3
Kidugallo *Tanzania* 6°49S 38°15E **268** D4
Kidurong, Tanjong
Malaysia 3°16N 113°3E **235** B4
Kiel *Germany* 54°19N 10°8E **178** A6
Kiel Canal = Nord-Ostsee-Kanal
Germany 54°12N 9°32E **178** A5
Kiel-Kanal = Nord-Ostsee-Kanal
Germany 54°12N 9°32E **178** A5
Kielce *Poland* 50°52N 20°42E **185** H7
Kielder Water *U.K.* 55°11N 2°31W **168** B5
Kieler Bucht *Germany* 54°35N 10°25E **178** A6
Kiembara *Burkina Faso* 13°15N 2°44W **262** C4
Kienge
Dem. Rep. of the Congo 10°30S 27°30E **269** E2
Kierling *Austria* 48°18N 16°16E **142** A1
Kierlingbach → *Austria* 48°18N 16°19E **142** A1
Kiessé *Niger* 13°29N 4°1E **263** C5
Kieta *Papua N. G.* 6°12S 155°36E **286** D8
Kiev = Kyyiv *Ukraine* 50°30N 30°28E **177** C16
Kifaya *Guinea* 12°10N 13°4W **262** C2
Kiffa *Mauritania* 16°37N 11°24W **262** B2
Kifisos → *Athina, Greece* 37°58N 23°42E **112** B2
Kifisos → *Voiotia, Greece* 38°35N 23°20E **204** C5
Kifissia *Greece* 38°4N 23°49E **204** C5
Kifrī *Iraq* 34°45N 45°0E **213** E11
Kigali *Rwanda* 1°59S 30°4E **268** C3
Kigarama *Tanzania* 1°1S 31°50E **268** C3
Kigelle *South Sudan* 8°40N 34°2E **257** F3
Kigezi ⌓ *Uganda* 0°34S 29°55E **268** C2
Kiğı *Turkey* 39°18N 40°21E **213** C9
Kigoma □ *Tanzania* 5°0S 30°0E **268** D3
Kigoma-Ujiji *Tanzania* 4°55S 29°36E **268** C2
Kigomasha, Ras *Tanzania* 4°58S 38°58E **268** C4
Kigosi ⌓ *Tanzania* 4°10S 31°45E **268** C3
Kığzı *Turkey* 38°18N 43°25E **246** B4
Kīhei *U.S.A.* 20°47N 156°28W **302** C5
Kihikihi *N.Z.* 38°2S 175°22E **284** E4
Kihnu *Estonia* 58°9N 24°1E **188** C3
Kihoku *Japan* 33°13N 132°36E **222** D4
Kiholo B. *U.S.A.* 19°50N 155°55W **302** D6
Kii-Hantō *Japan* 34°0N 135°45E **223** D7
Kii-Nagashima *Japan* 34°12N 136°20E **223** C8
Kii-Sanchi *Japan* 34°20N 136°0E **223** C8
Kii-Suidō *Japan* 33°40N 134°45E **222** D6
Kiira Dam *Uganda* 0°25N 33°0E **268** B3
Kiire *Japan* 31°22N 130°33E **222** F2
Kijik *U.S.A.* 60°20N 154°20W **303** F9
Kikaiga-Shima *Japan* 28°19N 129°59E **221** K4
Kikiak = Rigolet *Canada* 54°10N 58°23W **299** B8
Kikinda *Serbia* 45°50N 20°30E **182** E5
Kikládhes = Cyclades
Greece 37°0N 24°30E **204** E6
Kikoira *Australia* 33°39S 146°40E **283** B7
Kikombo *Bandundu, Dem. Rep. of the Congo* 5°37S 18°50E **265** D3
Kikombo *Bandundu, Dem. Rep. of the Congo* 5°49S 17°45E **265** D3
Kikongo
Dem. Rep. of the Congo 4°16S 17°17E **265** C3
Kikori *Papua N. G.* 7°25S 144°15E **286** D3
Kikori → *Papua N. G.* 7°38S 144°20E **286** D3
Kikuchi *Japan* 32°59N 130°47E **222** E2
Kikuna *Japan* 35°30N 139°37E **140** B2
Kikuyu *Kenya* 1°15S 36°40E **268** C4
Kikwit *Dem. Rep. of the Congo* 5°0S 18°45E **265** D3
Kil *Sweden* 59°30N 13°20E **162** E7
Kilafors *Sweden* 61°14N 16°36E **162** C10
Kilakkarai *India* 9°12N 78°47E **245** K4
Kilar *India* 33°6N 76°25E **242** C7
Kīlauea *U.S.A.* 22°13N 159°25W **302** A2
Kīlauea Caldera *U.S.A.* 19°25N 155°17W **302** D6
Kilbarrack *Ireland* 53°23N 6°9W **120** A3
Kilbeggan *Ireland* 53°22N 7°30W **166** C4
Kilbrannan Sd. *U.K.* 55°37N 5°26W **167** F3
Kilbuck Mts. *U.S.A.* 60°36N 159°53W **303** F8
Kilburn *U.K.* 51°32N 0°11W **125** A2
Kilchu *N. Korea* 40°57N 129°25E **224** B4
Kilcoy *Australia* 26°59S 152°30E **281** D5
Kildare *Ireland* 53°9N 6°55W **166** C5
Kildare □ *Ireland* 53°10N 6°50W **166** C5
Kildinstroy *Russia* 68°48N 33°6E **160** B25
Kileikli *Sudan* 11°25N 25°31E **257** E2
Kilembe
Dem. Rep. of the Congo 5°42S 19°55E **265** D3
Kilen *Norway* 59°20N 8°49E **164** E5
Kilfinnane *Ireland* 52°21N 8°28W **166** D3
Kilgarvan *Ireland* 51°54N 9°27W **166** E2
Kilgore *U.S.A.* 32°23N 94°53W **314** E7
Kilgoris *Kenya* 1°0S 34°53E **268** C3
Kilibo *Benin* 8°32N 2°38E **263** D5
Kilifi *Kenya* 3°40S 39°48E **268** C4
Kilimanjaro *Tanzania* 3°7S 37°20E **268** C4
Kilimanjaro □ *Tanzania* 4°0S 38°0E **268** C4
Kilimanjaro △ *Tanzania* 3°2S 37°19E **268** C4
Kilimli *Turkey* 41°28N 31°50E **212** B4
Kilinailau Is. *Papua N. G.* 4°45S 155°20E **286** C8
Kilindini *Kenya* 4°4S 39°40E **268** C4
Kilinochchi *Sri Lanka* 9°24N 80°25E **245** K5
Kilis *Turkey* 36°42N 37°6E **250** B8
Kilis □ *Turkey* 36°50N 37°10E **212** D7
Kiliya *Ukraine* 45°28N 29°16E **183** E14
Kilkee *Ireland* 52°41N 9°39W **166** D2
Kilkeel *U.K.* 54°7N 5°55W **166** B5
Kilkenny *Ireland* 52°39N 7°15W **166** D4
Kilkenny □ *Ireland* 52°35N 7°15W **166** D4
Kilkieran B. *Ireland* 53°20N 9°41W **166** C2
Kilkís *Greece* 40°58N 22°57E **202** F6
Kilkís □ *Greece* 41°5N 22°50E **202** E6
Killakee *Ireland* 53°15N 6°19W **120** B2
Killala *Ireland* 54°13N 9°13W **166** B2
Killala B. *Ireland* 54°16N 9°8W **166** B2
Killaloe *Ont., Canada* 45°33N 77°25W **312** A7
Killaloe *Clare, Ireland* 52°48N 8°28W **166** D3
Killarney *Queens., Australia* 28°20S 152°18E **281** D5
Killarney *Man., Canada* 49°10N 99°40W **297** D9
Killarney *Kerry, Ireland* 52°4N 9°30W **166** D2
Killarney, L. *Bahamas* 25°3N 77°27W **153** b
Killarney □ *Ireland* 52°0N 9°33W **166** D2
Killary Harbour *Ireland* 53°38N 9°52W **166** C2
Killdeer *U.S.A.* 47°22N 102°45W **308** B2
Killeberg *Sweden* 56°29N 14°5E **163** H8
Killeen *U.S.A.* 31°7N 97°44W **314** F6
Killester *Ireland* 53°22N 6°11W **120** A2
Killin *U.K.* 56°28N 4°19W **167** E4
Killiney *Ireland* 53°15N 6°7W **120** B3
Killiney B. *Ireland* 53°16N 6°5W **120** B3
Killington Pk. *U.S.A.* 43°36N 72°49W **313** C12
Killini = Kyllini *Greece* 37°55N 21°8E **207** D3
Killini *Greece* 37°54N 22°25E **204** D4
Killiniq I. *Canada* 60°24N 64°37W **295** E19
Killorglin *Ireland* 52°6N 9°47W **166** D2
Killybegs *Ireland* 54°38N 8°26W **166** B3
Kilmacud *Ireland* 53°17N 6°13W **120** B2
Kilmainham *Ireland* 53°20N 6°17W **120** A2
Kilmainham Gaol *Ireland* 53°21N 6°19W **120** A2
Kilmarnock *U.K.* 55°37N 4°29W **167** F4
Kilmashogue Mt. *Ireland* 53°15N 6°17W **120** B2
Kilmez *Russia* 56°58N 50°55E **190** B10
Kilmez → *Russia* 56°58N 50°28E **190** B10
Kilmore *Vic., Australia* 37°25S 144°53E **283** D6
Kilmore *Dublin, Ireland* 53°23N 6°13W **120** A2
Kilmore Quay *Ireland* 52°10N 6°36W **166** D5
Kilnamanagh *Ireland* 53°18N 6°22W **120** B1
Kilo *Finland* 60°13N 24°47E **121** B1
Kilokri *India* 28°34N 77°15E **120** B2
Kilómetro 1082 = Joaquín V.
González *Argentina* 25°10S 64°0W **334** B3
Kilondo *Tanzania* 9°45S 34°20E **269** D3
Kilosa *Tanzania* 6°48S 37°0E **268** D4
Kilrush *Ireland* 52°38N 9°29W **166** D2
Kiltan I. *India* 11°29N 73°0E **245** J1
Kiltiernan *Ireland* 53°15N 6°11W **120** B2
Kilwa Kisiwani *Tanzania* 8°58S 39°32E **269** D4
Kilwa Kivinje *Tanzania* 8°45S 39°25E **269** D4
Kilwa Masoko *Tanzania* 8°55S 39°30E **269** D4
Kilwinning *U.K.* 55°39N 4°43W **167** F4
Kim *U.S.A.* 37°15N 103°21W **305** H12
Kim → *Cameroon* 5°28N 11°7E **263** D7
Kimaam *Indonesia* 7°58S 138°53E **231** F9
Kimamba *Tanzania* 6°45S 37°10E **268** D4
Kimba *Australia* 33°8S 136°23E **282** B2
Kimball *Nebr., U.S.A.* 41°14N 103°40W **308** E2
Kimball *S. Dak., U.S.A.* 43°45N 98°57W **308** D4
Kimbanda
Dem. Rep. of the Congo 4°16S 18°30E **265** C3
Kimbe *Papua N. G.* 5°33S 150°11E **286** C6
Kimbe B. *Papua N. G.* 5°15S 150°30E **286** C6
Kimberley *W. Austral., Australia* 16°20S 127°0E **278** C4
Kimberley *B.C., Canada* 49°40N 115°59W **296** D5
Kimberley *Ont., Canada* 44°23N 80°32W **312** B4
Kimberley *Northern Cape, S. Africa* 28°43S 24°46E **270** C3
Kimberly *U.S.A.* 42°32N 114°22W **304** E6
Kimbongo
Dem. Rep. of the Congo 6°8S 18°1E **265** D3
Kimch'aek *N. Korea* 40°40N 129°10E **224** B4
Kimhae = Gimhae
S. Korea 35°14N 128°53E **224** E4
Kimhwa *N. Korea* 38°25N 127°36E **224** C3
Kimi *Greece* 38°38N 24°6E **204** C6
Kimitsu *Japan* 35°19N 139°54E **223** B11
Kimjŏngsugŭp *N. Korea* 41°24N 127°45E **224** B3
Kimmage *Ireland* 53°18N 6°17W **120** B2
Kimmirut *Canada* 62°50N 69°50W **295** E18
Kimolos *Greece* 36°48N 24°37E **204** E6
Kimongo *Congo* 4°27S 12°53E **265** C2
Kimovsk *Moskva, Russia* 55°21N 37°28E **188** E9
Kimovsk *Tula, Russia* 54°0N 38°29E **188** E10
Kimpangu
Dem. Rep. of the Congo 5°52S 15°3E **265** D3
Kimparana *Mali* 12°48N 5°0W **262** C4
Kimpese *Congo* 5°33S 14°26E **265** D2
Kimpese
Dem. Rep. of the Congo 5°35S 14°26E **265** D2
Kimry *Russia* 56°55N 37°15E **188** D9
Kimstad *Sweden* 58°35N 15°58E **163** F9
Kimvula
Dem. Rep. of the Congo 5°44S 15°58E **265** D3
Kin *Burma* 22°46N 94°42E **241** D5
Kin-u *Burma* 22°46N 95°37E **241** D5
Kin-wan *Japan* 26°23N 127°55E **288** a
Kinabalian, Mt. *Phil.* 8°12N 125°26E **233** G5
Kinabalu, Gunung
Malaysia 6°3N 116°14E **235** A5
Kinabalu △ *Malaysia* 6°0N 116°30E **235** A5
Kinango *Kenya* 4°8S 39°19E **268** C4
Kinard *U.S.A.* 30°16N 85°15W **316** E4
Kinaros *Greece* 36°59N 26°15E **205** E8
Kinaskan L. *Canada* 57°38N 130°8W **296** B2
Kinbasket L. *Canada* 52°0N 118°10W **296** C5
Kinbirila *Guinea* 39°35N 89°25W **310** F7
Kincardine *Canada* 44°10N 81°40W **312** B3
Kinchafoonee Cr. →
U.S.A. 31°38N 84°10W **316** D5
Kinchega △ *Australia* 32°27S 142°15E **282** B5
Kincolith *Canada* 55°0N 129°57W **296** C3
Kinda *Kasai-Or., Dem. Rep. of the Congo* 9°18S 25°4E **265** D5
Kinda *Katanga, Dem. Rep. of the Congo* 4°47S 21°48E **265** C4
Kindambi
Dem. Rep. of the Congo 5°6S 18°14E **265** D4
Kindberg *Austria* 47°30N 15°27E **180** D8
Kinde *U.S.A.* 43°56N 83°0W **312** C2
Kindele
Dem. Rep. of the Congo 8°39S 24°10E **265** D4
Kinder Scout *U.K.* 53°24N 1°52W **168** D6
Kinderhook *U.S.A.* 39°42N 91°10W **310** E5
Kindersley *Canada* 51°30N 109°10W **297** C7
Kindi *Iraq* 33°18N 44°22E **113** B2
Kindia *Guinea* 10°0N 12°52W **262** D2
Kindong
Dem. Rep. of the Congo 3°58S 17°30E **264** C3
Kindu *Dem. Rep. of the Congo* 2°55S 25°50E **264** C5
Kinel *Russia* 53°15N 50°40E **190** D10
Kineshma *Russia* 57°30N 42°5E **190** B6
Kinesi *Tanzania* 1°25S 33°50E **268** C3
King, L. *Australia* 33°10S 119°35E **279** F2
King, Mt. *Australia* 25°10S 147°30E **280** D4
King Christian I.
Canada 77°48N 101°40W **295** B11
King City *Calif., U.S.A.* 36°13N 121°8W **306** J5
King City *Mo., U.S.A.* 40°3N 94°31W **310** D2
King Cove *U.S.A.* 55°3N 162°19W **303** J7
King Cr. → *Australia* 24°35S 139°30E **280** C2
King Edward →
Australia 14°14S 126°35E **278** B4
King Edward Point
S. Georgia 54°17S 36°30W **151** B1
King Frederick VI Land = Kong
Frederik VI.s Kyst
Greenland 63°0N 43°0W **154** E6
King George B. *Falk. Is.* 51°30S 60°30W **153** f
King George I. *Antarctica* 60°0S 60°0W **151** C18
King George Is. *Canada* 57°20N 80°30W **295** F15
King George Sd. *Australia* 35°5S 118°0E **279** G2
King George VI Falls
Guyana 5°42N 61°5W **329** B5
King I. = Kadan Kyun
Burma 12°30N 98°20E **236** F2
King I. *Tas., Australia* 39°50S 144°0E **281** F3
King I. *B.C., Canada* 52°10N 127°40W **296** C3
King Khalid Military City =
Madinat al Malik Khālid al
Askarīyah *Si. Arabia* 27°54N 45°31E **246** E5
King Leopold Ranges
Australia 17°30S 125°45E **278** C4
King of Prussia *U.S.A.* 40°5N 75°23W **313** F9
King Salmon *U.S.A.* 58°42N 156°40W **303** G8
King Sd. *Australia* 16°50S 123°20E **278** C3
King Sejong *Antarctica* 62°30S 58°0W **151** C18
King Shaka = Durban ✕ (DIA)
S. Africa 29°37S 31°7E **271** C5
King William I. *Canada* 69°10N 97°25W **294** D12
King William's Town
S. Africa 32°51S 27°22E **270** D4
Kingaok = Bathurst Inlet
Canada 66°50N 108°1W **294** D10
Kingaroy *Australia* 26°32S 151°51E **281** D5
Kingdom City *U.S.A.* 38°56N 91°56W **310** F5
Kingfisher *U.S.A.* 35°52N 97°56W **314** D6
Kinghorn *U.K.* 56°5N 3°10W **121** A2
Kingirbān *Iraq* 34°40N 44°54E **246** C5
Kingisepp = Kuressaare
Estonia 58°15N 22°30E **188** C2
Kingisepp *Russia* 59°25N 28°40E **188** C5
Kingking = Pantukan
Phil. 7°9N 125°54E **233** H5
Kinglake △ *Australia* 37°30S 145°22E **283** D6
Kingman *Ariz., U.S.A.* 35°12N 114°4W **307** K12
Kingman *Ind., U.S.A.* 39°58N 87°18W **311** E9
Kingman *Kans., U.S.A.* 37°39N 98°7W **308** G4
Kingoonya *Australia* 30°55S 135°19E **281** E2
Kingri *Pakistan* 30°27N 69°49E **242** D3
Kings → *U.S.A.* 36°3N 119°50W **306** J7
Kings Canyon *Australia* 24°15S 131°34E **278** D5
Kings Canyon △ *U.S.A.* 36°50N 118°40W **306** J8
Kings County = Offaly □
Ireland 53°15N 7°30W **166** C4
Kings Cross *Sydney, Australia* **139** c3
King's Cross *London, U.K.* **125** a4
Kings Domain *Australia* 37°49S 144°58E **128** A1
Kings Forest = Kongelunden
Denmark 55°34N 12°34E **118** B3
King's Lynn *U.K.* 52°45N 0°24E **168** E8
Kings Park *U.S.A.* 40°53N 73°16W **313** F11
Kings Peak *U.S.A.* 40°46N 110°23W **304** F8
King's Trough *Atl. Oc.* 43°48N 22°0W **152** B9
Kingsbridge *U.K.* 50°17N 3°47W **169** G4
Kingsburg *U.S.A.* 36°31N 119°33W **306** J7
Kingsbury *Vic., Australia* 37°43S 145°2E **128** A2
Kingsbury *London, U.K.* 51°34N 0°15W **125** A2
Kingscote *Australia* 35°40S 137°38E **282** C2
Kingscourt *Ireland* 53°54N 6°48W **166** C5
Kingsford *N.S.W., Australia* 33°56S 151°14E **139** B2
Kingsford *Mich., U.S.A.* 45°48N 88°4W **308** C9
Kingsford Smith, Sydney ✕ (SYD)
Australia 33°57S 151°11E **139** B2
Kingsland *U.S.A.* 30°48N 81°41W **316** E8
Kingsport *U.S.A.* 36°33N 82°33W **315** C13
Kingston *Ont., Canada* 44°14N 76°30W **313** B8
Kingston *Jamaica* 17°55N 76°50W **320** a
Kingston *N.Z.* 45°20S 168°43E **285** F3
Kingston *N.H., U.S.A.* 42°56N 71°3W **313** D13
Kingston *N.Y., U.S.A.* 41°56N 73°59W **313** E11
Kingston *Pa., U.S.A.* 41°16N 75°54W **313** E9
Kingston *R.I., U.S.A.* 41°29N 71°30W **313** E13
Kingston Pk. *U.S.A.* 35°44N 115°55W **307** K11
Kingston South East
Australia 36°51S 139°55E **282** D3
Kingston upon Hull *U.K.* 53°45N 0°21W **168** D7
Kingston upon Hull □
U.K. 53°45N 0°21W **168** D7
Kingston-upon-Thames □
U.K. 51°24N 0°17W **125** B2
Kingston Vale *U.K.* 51°25N 0°25W **125** B2
Kingstown = Dún Laoghaire
Ireland 53°17N 6°8W **120** B3
Kingstown *N.S.W., Australia* 30°29S 151°6E **283** A9
Kingstown *St. Vincent* 13°10N 61°10W **323** n
Kingstree *U.S.A.* 33°40N 79°50W **316** B10
Kingsville *Ont., Canada* 42°2N 82°45W **312** D2
Kingsville *Tex., U.S.A.* 27°31N 97°52W **314** H6
Kingsway *Canada* 43°38N 79°32W **141** B1
Kingtechen = Jingdezhen
China 29°20N 117°11E **229** C11
Kingunda
Dem. Rep. of the Congo 6°36S 16°58E **265** D3
Kingussie *U.K.* 57°6N 4°2W **167** D4
Kingwood *U.S.A.* 30°2N 95°16W **314** F7
Kinhwa = Jinhua *China* 29°8N 119°38E **229** C12
Kınık *Antalya, Turkey* 36°20N 29°20E **205** E11
Kınık *İzmir, Turkey* 39°6N 27°24E **205** B9
Kinistino *Canada* 52°57N 105°2W **297** C7
Kinjirap Daban *Asia* 36°40N 75°25E **240** A4
Kinkala *Congo* 4°18S 14°49E **265** C2
Kinki □ *Japan* 33°45N 136°0E **223** D8
Kinkony, Farihin' *Madag.* 16°8S 45°50E **272** B2
Kinleith *N.Z.* 38°20S 175°56E **284** E4
Kinlochleven *U.K.* 56°43N 5°0W **167** E4
Kinmount *Canada* 44°48N 78°45W **312** B6
Kinmundy *U.S.A.* 38°46N 88°51W **311** F8
Kinn *Norway* 61°34N 4°45E **164** C1
Kinna *Sweden* 57°32N 12°42E **163** G6
Kinnairds Hd. *U.K.* 57°43N 2°1W **167** D6
Kinnared *Sweden* 57°2N 13°7E **163** G7
Kinnarp *Sweden* 58°5N 13°32E **163** F7
Kinneviken *Sweden* 58°35N 13°15E **163** F7
Kinngait *Canada* 64°14N 76°32W **295** E16
Kinniyai *Sri Lanka* 8°29N 81°11E **245** K5
Kino Nuevo *Mexico* 28°52N 112°3W **318** B2
Kinogitan *Phil.* 9°0N 124°48E **233** G5
Kinoje → *Canada* 52°8N 81°25W **298** B3
Kinokawa *Japan* 34°15N 135°20E **223** C7
Kinomoto *Japan* 35°30N 136°13E **223** B8
Kinoni *Uganda* 0°41S 30°28E **268** C3
Kinoosao *Canada* 57°5N 102°1W **297** B8
Kinross *U.K.* 56°13N 3°25W **167** E5
Kinsale *Cork, Ireland* 51°42N 8°31W **166** E3
Kinsale *Montserrat* 16°42N 62°13W **323** p
Kinsale, Old Hd. of *Ireland* 51°37N 8°33W **166** E3
Kinsaley *Ireland* 53°24N 6°11W **120** A2
Kinsarvik *Norway* 60°22N 6°43E **164** D3
Kinsha = Chang Jiang →
China 31°48N 121°10E **229** B13
Kinshasa
Dem. Rep. of the Congo 4°20S 15°15E **265** C3
Kinsley *U.S.A.* 37°55N 99°25W **308** G4
Kinsman *U.S.A.* 41°26N 80°35W **312** E4
Kinston *Ala., U.S.A.* 31°13N 86°10W **316** D3
Kinston *N.C., U.S.A.* 35°16N 77°35W **315** D16
Kintamani *Indonesia* 8°14S 115°19E **231** J18
Kintampo *Ghana* 8°5N 1°41W **263** D4
Kintap *Indonesia* 3°51S 115°13E **235** C5
Kintore *U.K.* 57°14N 2°20W **167** D6
Kintore Ra. *Australia* 23°15S 128°47E **278** D4
Kintshua
Dem. Rep. of the Congo 4°27S 19°38E **265** C3
Kintyre *U.K.* 55°30N 5°35W **167** F3
Kintyre, Mull of *U.K.* 55°17N 5°47W **167** F3
Kinu-Gawa → *Japan* 35°36N 139°57E **223** B11
Kinushseo → *Canada* 55°15N 83°45W **298** A3
Kinuso *Canada* 55°20N 115°25W **296** B5
Kinvarra *Ireland* 53°8N 8°56W **166** C3
Kinwat *India* 19°38N 78°12E **244** E4
Kinyangiri *Tanzania* 4°25S 34°37E **268** C3
Kinyeti *South Sudan* 3°57N 32°54E **257** G3
Kinzia *Dem. Rep. of the Congo* 3°36S 18°26E **264** C3
Kinzig → *Germany* 48°36N 7°49E **179** G3
Kinzua *U.S.A.* 41°52N 78°58W **312** E6
Kioni *Greece* 38°27N 20°41E **207** C2
Kiosk *Canada* 46°6N 78°53W **298** C4
Kiowa *Kans., U.S.A.* 37°1N 98°29W **308** G4
Kiowa *Okla., U.S.A.* 34°43N 95°54W **314** D7
Kipahigan L. *Canada* 55°20N 101°55W **297** B8
Kipanga *Tanzania* 6°15S 35°20E **268** D4
Kipapa → *U.S.A.* 21°24N 158°1W **302** K13
Kiparissia *Greece* 37°15N 21°40E **204** D3
Kiparissiakos Kolpos
Greece 37°25N 21°25E **204** D3
Kipawa, L. *Canada* 46°50N 79°0W **298** C4
Kipembawe *Tanzania* 7°38S 33°27E **268** D3
Kipengere Ra. *Tanzania* 9°12S 34°15E **269** D3
Kipili *Tanzania* 7°28S 30°32E **268** D3
Kipini *Kenya* 2°30S 40°32E **268** C5
Kipling *Canada* 50°6N 102°38W **297** C8
Kipling Heights *Canada* 43°43N 79°34W **141** A1
Kipnuk *U.S.A.* 59°56N 164°3W **303** G6
Kippure *Ireland* 53°11N 6°21W **166** C5
Kipseli *Athens, Greece* **112** a3
Kipushi
Dem. Rep. of the Congo 11°48S 27°12E **269** E2
Kira *Uganda* 0°24N 32°38E **268** B3
Kira Panagia *Greece* 39°17N 24°4E **204** B6
Kirakira *Solomon Is.* 10°27S 161°56E **287** N11
Kirandul *India* 18°33N 81°10E **244** E5
Kirane *Mali* 15°20N 10°20W **262** B2
Kiranomena *Madag.* 18°17S 46°2E **272** B2
Kiraz *Turkey* 38°14N 28°13E **205** C10
Kirazlı *Turkey* 40°2N 26°41E **203** F10
Kirchhain *Germany* 50°47N 8°56E **178** E4
Kirchheim *Germany* 48°39N 9°27E **179** G5
Kirchheimbolanden
Germany 49°40N 8°0E **179** F3
Kirchschlag *Austria* 47°30N 16°19E **181** D9
Kirchstockbach *Germany* 48°1N 11°40E **131** B3
Kirchtrudering *Germany* 48°7N 11°40E **131** B3
Kirdāsa *Egypt* 30°2N 31°6E **251** H2
Kirdimi *Chad* 18°11N 18°31E **259** E3
Kireç *Turkey* 39°33N 28°22E **205** B10
Kirensk *Russia* 57°50N 107°55E **215** D11
Kirghiz Range *Asia* 42°40N 73°40E **217** D8
Kirghizia = Kyrgyzstan ■
Asia 42°0N 75°0E **217** D9
Kirgiz-Kulak = Chirchiq
Uzbekistan 41°29N 69°35E **217** D7
Kirgiziya Steppe *Eurasia* 50°0N 55°0E **187** E10
Kiri *Dem. Rep. of the Congo* 1°29S 19°0E **264** C3
Kiri Buru *India* 22°0N 85°0E **244** D7
Kiribati ■ *Pac. Oc.* 3°0S 180°0E **277** A15
Kırıkhan *Turkey* 36°31N 36°21E **250** B7
Kirikiri *Nigeria* 6°26N 3°18E **124** B1
Kırıkkale *Turkey* 39°51N 33°32E **212** C5
Kirikopuni *N.Z.* 35°50S 174°1E **284** B3
Kirillov *Russia* 59°49N 38°24E **188** C10
Kirin = Jilin *China* 43°44N 126°30E **227** C14
Kirindi Oya → *Sri Lanka* 6°15N 81°20E **245** L5
Kirinyaga = Kenya, Mt.
Kenya 0°10S 37°18E **268** C4
Kirirom △ *Cambodia* 11°18N 104°5E **237** G5
Kirishi *Russia* 59°28N 32°0E **188** C7
Kirishima *Japan* 31°44N 130°46E **222** F2
Kirishima Yaku △ *Japan* 31°24N 130°50E **221** J5
Kirishima-Yama *Japan* 31°58N 130°55E **222** F2
Kiritimati *Kiribati* 1°58N 157°27W **289** G12
Kiriwina I. *Papua N. G.* 8°40S 151°6E **286** E6
Kırka *Turkey* 39°17N 30°33E **205** B12
Kırkağaç *Turkey* 39°8N 27°40E **205** B9
Kirkby *U.K.* 53°30N 2°54W **168** D5
Kirkby-in-Ashfield *U.K.* 53°6N 1°14W **168** D6
Kirkby Lonsdale *U.K.* 54°12N 2°36W **168** C5
Kirkby Stephen *U.K.* 54°29N 2°21W **168** C5
Kirkcaldy *U.K.* 56°7N 3°9W **167** E5
Kirkcudbright *U.K.* 54°50N 4°2W **167** G4
Kirke Værløse *Denmark* 55°47N 12°19E **118** A1
Kirkehamn *Norway* 58°14N 6°31E **164** F3
Kirkenær *Norway* 60°27N 12°3E **164** D9
Kirkenes *Norway* 69°40N 30°5E **160** B24
Kirkfield *Canada* 44°34N 78°59W **312** B6
Kirkhill *U.K.* 55°50N 3°13W **121** B2
Kirkintilloch *U.K.* 55°56N 4°8W **167** F4
Kirkjubæjarklaustur
Iceland 63°47N 18°4W **155** D8
Kirkkonummi *Finland* 60°8N 24°26E **188** B3
Kirkland *Ill., U.S.A.* 42°6N 88°51W **311** B8
Kirkland *Wash., U.S.A.* 47°40N 122°12W **306** C4
Kirkland Lake *Canada* 48°9N 80°2W **298** C3
Kırklareli *Turkey* 41°44N 27°15E **203** E11
Kırklareli □ *Turkey* 41°45N 27°15E **203** E11
Kirklin *U.S.A.* 40°12N 86°22W **311** D10
Kirkliston *U.K.* 55°57N 3°24W **121** B1
Kirkliston Ra. *N.Z.* 44°25S 170°34E **285** E5
Kirknewton *U.K.* 55°53N 3°25W **121** B1
Kirknitz = Cerknica
Slovenia 45°48N 14°21E **199** C11
Kirksville *U.S.A.* 40°12N 92°35W **310** D4
Kirkūk *Iraq* 35°30N 44°21E **213** E11
Kirkwall *U.K.* 58°59N 2°58W **167** C6
Kirkwood *Eastern Cape, S. Africa* 33°22S 25°15E **270** D4
Kirkwood *Mo., U.S.A.* 38°35N 90°24W **310** F6
Kirlampudi *India* 17°12N 82°12E **244** F6
Kirmasti = Mustafakemalpaşa
Turkey 40°2N 28°24E **203** F12
Kirn *Germany* 49°47N 7°26E **179** F3
Kirobası *Turkey* 36°43N 33°52E **250** B4
Kirov *Kaluga, Russia* 54°3N 34°20E **188** E8
Kirov *Kirov, Russia* 58°35N 49°40E **186** C8
Kirov Palace of Culture
Russia 59°55N 30°16E **137** B1
Kirovabad = Gäncä
Azerbaijan 40°45N 46°20E **191** K8
Kirovakan = Vanadzor
Armenia 40°48N 44°30E **191** K7
Kirovo = Kirovohrad
Ukraine 48°35N 32°20E **189** H7
Kirovograd = Kirovohrad
Ukraine 48°35N 32°20E **189** H7
Kirovohrad *Ukraine* 48°35N 32°20E **189** H7
Kirovohrad □ *Ukraine* 48°30N 31°30E **189** H6
Kirovsk *Russia* 67°32N 33°41E **186** A5
Kirovskiy = Balpyq Bī
Kazakhstan 44°52N 78°12E **217** D9
Kirovskiy *Astrakhan, Russia* 45°51N 48°11E **191** H9
Kirovskiy *Kamchatka, Russia* 54°27N 155°42E **215** D16
Kirovskiy *Primorsk, Russia* 45°7N 133°30E **220** B6
Kirriemuir *U.K.* 56°41N 3°1W **167** E5
Kirsanov *Russia* 52°35N 42°40E **190** D6
Kırşehir *Turkey* 39°14N 34°5E **212** C6
Kirtachi *Niger* 12°52N 2°30E **263** C5
Kirteh *Afghan.* 32°15N 63°0E **240** B1
Kirthar △ *Pakistan* 25°45N 67°30E **242** F2
Kirthar Range *Pakistan* 27°0N 67°0E **242** F2
Kirtland *U.S.A.* 36°44N 108°21W **305** H9
Kiruna *Sweden* 67°52N 20°15E **160** C19
Kirundu
Dem. Rep. of the Congo 0°50S 25°35E **264** C5
Kirya *Russia* 55°8N 46°55E **190** C8
Kiryat Anavim *Israel* 31°49N 35°6E **123** B1
Kiryat Ha Yovel *Israel* 31°46N 35°10E **123** B1
Kiryū *Japan* 36°24N 139°20E **223** A11
Kisa *Sweden* 58°0N 15°39E **163** G9
Kisaga *Tanzania* 4°30S 34°23E **268** C3
Kisalföld *Hungary* 47°30N 17°0E **182** C2
Kisambo
Dem. Rep. of the Congo 6°25S 18°14E **265** D3
Kisandji
Dem. Rep. of the Congo 6°18S 19°16E **265** D3
Kisanga
Dem. Rep. of the Congo 2°30N 26°35E **268** B2
Kisangani
Dem. Rep. of the Congo 0°35N 25°15E **268** B2
Kisantu *Dem. Rep. of the Congo* 5°7S 15°5E **265** D3
Kisar *Indonesia* 8°5S 127°10E **231** F7
Kisaran *Indonesia* 3°0N 99°37E **234** B1
Kisarawe *Tanzania* 6°53S 39°0E **268** D4
Kisarazu *Japan* 35°23N 139°55E **223** B11
Kisbér *Hungary* 47°30N 18°2E **182** C3
Kiselevsk *Russia* 54°5N 86°39E **217** B11
Kish = Qeys *Iran* 26°32N 53°58E **249** A6
Kishanganga → *Pakistan* 34°18N 73°28E **243** B5
Kishanganj *India* 26°3N 88°14E **241** B2
Kishangarh *Raj., India* 26°34N 74°52E **242** F6
Kishangarh *Raj., India* 27°50N 70°30E **242** F4
Kishb, Ḩarrat al *Si. Arabia* 22°30N 40°15E **248** B3
Kishi *Nigeria* 9°1N 3°52E **263** D5
Kishinev = Chişinău
Moldova 47°2N 28°50E **183** C13
Kishiwada *Japan* 34°28N 135°22E **223** C7
Kishkareny = Lazo
Moldova 47°33N 28°2E **183** C13
Kishkenekōl *Kazakhstan* 53°38N 72°20E **217** B8
Kishorganj *Bangla.* 24°26N 90°40E **241** C3
Kishtwar *India* 33°20N 75°48E **242** C6
Kishwaukee → *U.S.A.* 42°12N 89°8W **310** B7
Kisielice *Poland* 53°36N 19°16E **184** E6
Kisigo ⌓ *Tanzania* 6°27S 34°17E **268** D3
Kisii *Kenya* 0°40S 34°45E **268** C3
Kisiju *Tanzania* 7°23S 39°19E **268** D4
Kisır *Turkey* 41°0N 43°5E **213** B10
Kisizi *Uganda* 1°0S 29°58E **268** C2
Kiska I. *U.S.A.* 51°59N 177°30E **303** L2
Kiskomárom = Zalakomár
Hungary 46°33N 17°10E **182** D2
Kiskőrei-víztároló
Hungary 47°31N 20°36E **182** C5
Kiskőrös *Hungary* 46°37N 19°20E **182** D4
Kiskundorozsma *Hungary* 46°16N 20°5E **182** D5
Kiskunfélegyháza
Hungary 46°42N 19°53E **182** D4
Kiskunhalas *Hungary* 46°28N 19°37E **182** D4
Kiskunmajsa *Hungary* 46°30N 19°48E **182** D4
Kiskunsági △ *Hungary* 46°39N 19°30E **182** D4
Kislovodsk *Russia* 43°50N 42°45E **191** J6
Kismaayo *Somalia* 0°22S 42°32E **267** E5
Kismayu = Kismaayo *Somalia* 1°25N 41°30E **267** D5
Kiso-Gawa → *Japan* 35°20N 136°45E **223** B8
Kiso-Sammyaku *Japan* 35°45N 137°45E **223** B9
Kisofukushima *Japan* 35°52N 137°43E **223** B9

Kisoro Uganda 1°17S 29°48E 268 C2
Kispest Hungary 47°27N 19°8E 117 B2
Kissamos = Kasteli Greece 35°29N 23°38E 207 E4
Kissamos, Kolpos Greece 35°30N 23°38E 207 E4
Kissidougou Guinea 9°5N 10°5W 262 D2
Kissimmee U.S.A. 28°18N 81°24W 317 G8
Kissimmee → U.S.A. 27°9N 80°52W 317 H8
Kissimmee, L. U.S.A. 27°55N 81°17W 317 H8
Kississing L. Canada 55°10N 101°20W 297 B8
Kissónerga Cyprus 34°49N 32°24E 207 F8
Kissu, J. Sudan 21°37N 25°10E 256 C2
Kista Sweden 59°24N 17°57E 139 A1
Kistanje Croatia 43°58N 15°55E 199 E12
Kistna = Krishna → India 15°57N 80°59E 245 G5
Kisújszállás Hungary 47°12N 20°50E 182 C5
Kisuki Japan 35°17N 132°54E 222 B4
Kisumu Kenya 0°3S 34°45E 268 C3
Kisvárda Hungary 48°14N 22°4E 182 B7
Kiswani Tanzania 4°5S 37°57E 268 C4
Kiswere Tanzania 9°27S 39°30E 269 D4
Kit Carson U.S.A. 38°46N 102°48W 304 G12
Kita Ōsaka, Japan 34°41N 135°30E 133 A2
Kita Tōkyō, Japan 35°44N 139°44E 140 A3
Kita Mali 13°5N 9°25W 262 C3
Kita-Ura Japan 36°0N 140°34E 223 B12
Kitaa □ Greenland 70°0N 47°0W 154 C6
Kitaibaraki Japan 36°50N 140°45E 221 F10
Kitakami Japan 39°20N 141°10E 220 E10
Kitakami-Gawa → Japan 38°25N 141°19E 220 E10
Kitakami-Sammyaku Japan 39°30N 141°30E 220 E10
Kitakata Japan 37°39N 139°52E 220 F9
Kitakyūshū Japan 33°50N 130°50E 222 D2
Kitale Kenya 1°0N 35°0E 268 B4
Kitami Japan 43°48N 143°54E 220 C11
Kitami-Sammyaku Japan 44°22N 142°43E 220 B11
Kitangiri, L. Tanzania 4°5S 34°20E 268 C3
Kitanglad △ Phil. 8°57N 124°21E 233 G5
Kitano Hana Iwo Jima 24°49N 141°20E 288 b
Kitano-Kaikyō Japan 34°17N 134°58E 222 C6
Kitaotao Phil. 7°40N 125°1E 233 H5
Kitava I. Papua N. G. 8°40S 151°20E 286 E6
Kitaya Tanzania 10°38S 40°8E 269 E5
Kitazawa Japan 35°39N 139°40E 140 B3
Kitcharao Phil. 9°27N 125°36E 233 G5
Kitchener Canada 43°27N 80°29W 312 C4
Kitee Finland 62°5N 30°8E 188 A6
Kitega = Gitega Burundi 3°26S 29°56E 266 C2
Kitengo Dem. Rep. of the Congo 7°26S 24°8E 265 D4
Kitgum Uganda 3°17N 32°52E 268 B3
Kithira = Kythira Greece 36°8N 23°0E 204 E5
Kithnos Greece 37°26N 24°27E 204 D6
Kiti Cyprus 34°50N 33°34E 207 F9
Kiti, C. Cyprus 34°48N 33°36E 207 F9
Kitimat Canada 54°3N 128°38W 296 C3
Kitinen → Finland 67°14N 27°27E 160 C22
Kitiyab Sudan 17°13N 33°35E 257 D3
Kitombe Dem. Rep. of the Congo 5°22S 18°59E 265 D3
Kitridge Pt. Barbados 13°9N 59°25W 323 r
Kitros Greece 40°22N 22°34E 202 F6
Kitsman Ukraine 48°26N 25°46E 183 B10
Kitsuki Japan 33°25N 131°37E 222 D3
Kittakittaooloo, L. Australia 28°3S 138°14E 281 D2
Kittanning U.S.A. 40°49N 79°31W 312 F5
Kittatinny Mt. U.S.A. 41°19N 74°39W 313 F10
Kittery U.S.A. 43°5N 70°45W 313 C14
Kittilä Finland 67°40N 24°51E 160 C21
Kitui Kenya 1°17S 38°0E 268 C4
Kitwanga Canada 55°6N 128°4W 296 B3
Kitwe Zambia 12°54S 28°13E 269 E2
Kityang = Jieyang China 23°35N 116°21E 229 F11
Kitzbühel Austria 47°27N 12°24E 180 D5
Kitzbühler Alpen Austria 47°20N 12°20E 180 D5
Kitzingen Germany 49°44N 10°9E 179 F6
Kiu Tsiu China 22°22N 114°17E 122 A2
Kiukiang = Jiujiang China 29°42N 115°58E 229 C10
Kiunga Papua N. G. 6°7S 141°18E 286 D1
Kiunga Marine ⌂ Kenya 2°1S 41°14E 268 C5
Kivalina U.S.A. 67°44N 164°33W 303 C6
Kivarli India 24°33N 72°46E 242 G5
Kivertsi Ukraine 50°50N 25°28E 177 C13
Kividhes Cyprus 34°46N 32°51E 207 F8
Kivik Sweden 55°41N 14°13E 163 J8
Kivistö Finland 60°18N 24°50E 121 B2
Kivotos Greece 40°13N 21°26E 202 F5
Kivu, L. Dem. Rep. of the Congo 1°48S 29°0E 268 C2
Kiwai I. Papua N. G. 8°35S 143°30E 286 E2
Kiwirrkurra Australia 22°49S 127°45E 278 D4
Kiwirrkurra ◎ Australia 22°49S 127°45E 278 D4
Kiyev = Kyyiv Ukraine 50°30N 30°28E 177 C16
Kiyevskoye Vdkhr. = Kyyivske Vdskh. Ukraine 51°0N 30°25E 177 C16
Kıyıköy Turkey 41°38N 28°5E 203 E12
Kiza → Japan 34°37N 135°27E 133 B1
Kizel Russia 59°3N 57°40E 186 C10
Kizhi, Ostrov Russia 62°4N 35°13E 188 B8
Kiziba-Baluba ⌂ Congo 11°50S 28°0E 269 E2
Kiziguru Rwanda 1°46S 30°23E 268 C3
Kızıl Adalar Turkey 40°52N 29°5E 203 F13
Kızıl Dağ Turkey 36°19N 35°57E 250 B6
Kızıl Irmak → Turkey 41°44N 35°58E 212 B6
Kizil Jilga China 35°26N 78°50E 243 B8
Kizil Yurt Russia 43°13N 46°54E 191 J8
Kızılcabölük Turkey 37°37N 29°1E 205 D11
Kızılcadağ Turkey 37°1N 29°58E 205 D11
Kızılcahamam Turkey 40°30N 32°30E 212 B5
Kızıldağ △ Turkey 38°5N 31°20E 246 B1
Kızılhisar Turkey 37°32N 29°17E 212 D3
Kızılırmak Turkey 40°21N 33°59E 212 B5
Kızılkaya Turkey 37°18N 30°27E 205 D12
Kızılören Turkey 38°15N 30°10E 205 C12
Kızıltepe Turkey 37°12N 40°35E 213 D9
Kızıltoprak Turkey 40°58N 29°3E 122 C2
Kizimkazi Tanzania 6°28S 39°30E 268 D4
Kizlyar Russia 43°51N 46°40E 191 J8
Kizuri Japan 34°38N 135°34E 133 B2
Kizyl-Arvat = Serdar Turkmenistan 39°4N 56°23E 247 B8
Kjellerup Denmark 56°17N 9°25E 163 H3
Kjellmyra Norway 60°39N 12°1E 164 D9
Kjelsås Norway 59°57N 10°47E 133 A3
Kjølen Norway 62°3N 8°45E 164 C5
Kjölur Iceland 64°50N 19°25W 155 C7
Kjósarsýsla Iceland 64°15N 21°30W 155 C5
Kladanj Bos.-H. 44°14N 18°42E 182 F3
Kladnica Serbia 43°23N 20°2E 202 C4
Kladno Czech Rep. 50°10N 14°7E 180 A7
Kladovo Serbia 44°36N 22°33E 202 B6
Kladow Germany 52°27N 13°9E 115 B1
Klæbu Norway 63°18N 10°29E 164 A7
Klaeng Thailand 12°47N 101°39E 236 F3
Klagan Malaysia 5°58N 117°27E 235 A5
Klagenfurt Austria 46°38N 14°20E 180 E7
Klaipėda Lithuania 55°43N 21°10E 184 C8
Klaipėda □ Lithuania 55°43N 21°7E 184 C8
Klaksvík Færoe Is. 62°14N 6°35W 160 E9
Klamath → U.S.A. 41°33N 124°5W 304 F1
Klamath Falls U.S.A. 42°13N 121°46W 304 E3
Klamath Mts. U.S.A. 41°50N 123°20W 304 F2
Klamono Indonesia 1°8S 131°30E 231 E8
Klampenborg Denmark 55°46N 12°35E 118 A3
Klampo Indonesia 0°7N 116°58E 235 B5
Klang Malaysia 3°2N 101°26E 237 L3
Klangklang Burma 22°41N 93°26E 241 D4
Klanjec Croatia 46°3N 15°45E 199 B12
Klappan → Canada 58°0N 129°43W 296 B3
Klara = Trysilelva → Norway 61°2N 12°35E 164 C9
Klarälven → Sweden 59°23N 13°32E 162 E7
Klässbol Sweden 59°33N 12°45E 162 E6
Klaten Indonesia 7°43S 110°36E 235 D4
Klatovy Czech Rep. 49°23N 13°18E 180 B6
Klausenburg = Cluj-Napoca Romania 46°47N 23°38E 183 D8
Klawer S. Africa 31°44S 18°36E 270 D2
Klawock U.S.A. 55°33N 133°6W 303 J14
Klazienaveen Neths. 52°44N 7°0E 170 B6
Klé Mali 12°0N 6°28W 262 C3
Klečany Czech Rep. 50°10N 14°24E 135 A2
Klecko Poland 52°38N 17°25E 185 F4
Kleczew Poland 52°22N 18°9E 185 F5
Kledering Austria 48°8N 16°26E 142 B2
Kleena Kleene Canada 52°0N 124°59W 296 C4
Klein Bonaire Bonaire 12°9N 68°18W 322 h
Klein Jukskei → S. Africa 26°6S 27°57E 123 A1
Klein-Karas Namibia 27°33S 18°7E 270 C2
Klein-Schlatten = Zlatna Romania 46°8N 23°11E 183 D8
Kleinbegin S. Africa 28°54S 21°40E 270 C3
Kleinmachnow Germany 52°24N 13°14E 115 B2
Kleinschönebeck Germany 52°29N 13°42E 115 B5
Klekovača Bos.-H. 44°25N 16°32E 199 D13
Klembivka Ukraine 48°23N 28°25E 183 B13
Klemetsrud Norway 59°50N 10°51E 133 A4
Klender Indonesia 6°12S 106°54E 122 A2
Klenoec Macedonia 41°32N 20°49E 202 E4
Klenovec Slovak Rep. 48°36N 19°54E 181 C12
Klerksdorp S. Africa 26°53S 26°38E 270 C4
Kleszczele Poland 52°35N 23°19E 185 F10
Kletnya Russia 53°23N 33°12E 188 F7
Kletsk = Klyetsk Belarus 53°5N 26°45E 177 B14
Kletskiy Russia 49°16N 43°11E 191 F6
Kleve Germany 51°47N 6°7E 178 D2
Kličany Czech Rep. 50°11N 14°25E 135 A2
Klickitat U.S.A. 45°49N 121°9W 304 D3
Klickitat → U.S.A. 45°42N 121°17W 306 E5
Klidhes Cyprus 35°42N 34°36E 207 E10
Klimovichi Belarus 53°36N 32°0E 188 F6
Klin Russia 56°20N 36°48E 188 D9
Klinaklini → Canada 51°21N 125°40W 296 C3
Klinë Kosovo 42°37N 20°35E 202 D4
Klintehamn Sweden 57°24N 18°12E 163 G12
Klintsy Russia 52°50N 32°10E 189 F7
Klip → S. Africa 27°3S 29°3E 271 C4
Klipdale S. Africa 34°19S 19°57E 270 D2
Klippan Sweden 56°8N 13°10E 163 H7
Klipplaat S. Africa 33°1S 24°22E 270 D3
Kliprivierberg Nature Reserve S. Africa 26°16S 28°2E 123 B2
Klishkivtsi Ukraine 48°26N 26°16E 183 B11
Klisura Bulgaria 42°40N 24°28E 203 D8
Kljajićevo Serbia 45°45N 19°17E 182 E4
Ključ Bos.-H. 44°32N 16°48E 199 D13
Klobuck Poland 50°55N 18°55E 185 H5
Klockestrand Sweden 62°53N 17°55E 162 B11
Kłodawa Poland 52°15N 18°55E 185 F5
Kłodzko Poland 50°28N 16°38E 185 H3
Kløfta Norway 60°4N 11°6E 164 D8
Klondike Canada 64°0N 139°26W 294 E4
Klondike Goldrush ⌂ U.S.A. 59°27N 135°19W 303 G14
Klong Wang Chao △ Thailand 16°20N 99°9E 236 D2
Klos Albania 41°28N 20°10E 202 E4
Klosterneuburg Austria 48°18N 16°19E 142 A1
Klosters Switz. 46°52N 9°52E 179 J5
Klötze Germany 52°37N 11°10E 178 C7
Klouto Togo 6°57N 0°44E 263 D5
Klövsjö Sweden 62°32N 14°11E 162 B8
Kluane △ Canada 60°45N 139°30W 296 A1
Kluane L. Canada 61°15N 138°40W 294 E4
Kluang Malaysia 2°3N 103°18E 237 L4
Kluczbork Poland 50°58N 18°12E 185 H5
Klukhori = Karachayevsk Russia 43°50N 41°55E 191 J5
Klukwan U.S.A. 59°24N 135°54W 303 G14
Klungkung Indonesia 8°32S 115°24E 231 K18
Klyetsk Belarus 53°5N 26°45E 177 B14
Klyuchevskaya, Gora Russia 55°50N 160°30E 215 D17
Klyuchi Russia 56°18N 160°51E 215 D17
Knaben Norway 58°40N 7°4E 164 F4
Knappavellir Iceland 63°54N 16°36W 155 D10
Knäred Sweden 56°31N 13°19E 163 H7
Knaresborough U.K. 54°1N 1°28W 168 C6
Knarvik Norway 60°32N 5°19E 164 D2
Knee L. Man., Canada 55°3N 94°45W 298 A1
Knee L. Sask., Canada 55°51N 107°0W 297 B7
Kneïss, Îs. Tunisia 34°22N 10°18E 258 B2
Knesset Jerusalem 123 B1
Knezha Bulgaria 43°30N 24°5E 203 C8
Knight I. U.S.A. 60°21N 147°45W 303 F11
Knight Inlet Canada 50°45N 125°40W 296 C3
Knighton U.K. 52°21N 3°3W 169 E4
Knights Ferry U.S.A. 37°50N 120°40W 306 H6
Knights Landing U.S.A. 38°48N 121°43W 306 G5
Knightsbridge London, U.K. 125 c2
Knightstown U.S.A. 39°48N 85°32W 311 E11
Knin Croatia 44°3N 16°17E 199 D13
Knislinge Sweden 56°12N 14°5E 163 H8
Knittelfeld Austria 47°13N 14°51E 180 D7
Knivsta Sweden 59°43N 17°48E 162 E11
Knjaževac Serbia 43°35N 22°18E 202 C6
Knob, C. Australia 34°32S 119°16E 279 F2
Knob Lake = Kawawachikamach Canada 54°48N 66°50W 299 B6
Knob Noster U.S.A. 38°46N 93°33W 310 F3
Knock Ireland 53°48N 8°55W 166 C3
Knockmealdown Mts. Ireland 52°14N 7°56W 166 D4
Knokke-Heist Belgium 51°21N 3°17E 170 C3
Knossos Greece 35°16N 25°10E 207 D7
Knowlton Canada 45°13N 72°31W 313 A12
Knox U.S.A. 41°18N 86°37W 311 C10
Knox Coast Antarctica 66°30S 108°0E 151 C8
Knoxville Ga., U.S.A. 32°47N 83°59W 316 C6
Knoxville Ill., U.S.A. 40°55N 90°17W 310 D6
Knoxville Iowa, U.S.A. 41°19N 93°6W 310 C4
Knoxville Pa., U.S.A. 41°57N 77°27W 312 E7
Knoxville Tenn., U.S.A. 35°58N 83°55W 315 D13
Knud Rasmussen Land Greenland 78°0N 60°0W 154 B4
Knysna S. Africa 34°2S 23°2E 270 D3
Knyszyn Poland 53°20N 22°56E 184 E9
Ko Kha Thailand 18°11N 99°24E 236 C2
Kō-Saki Japan 34°5N 129°13E 222 C1
Ko Tarutao △ Thailand 6°31N 99°26E 237 J2
Ko Yao Thailand 8°7N 98°35E 237 a
Koartac = Quaqtaq Canada 60°55N 69°40W 295 E18
Koba Aru, Indonesia 6°37S 134°37E 231 F8
Koba Bangka, Indonesia 2°26S 106°14E 234 C3
Kőbánya Hungary 47°28N 19°9E 117 B2
Kobarid Slovenia 46°15N 13°30E 199 B10
Kobayashi Japan 31°56N 130°59E 222 F2
Kobbegem Belgium 50°55N 4°15E 116 A1
Kobdo = Hovd □ Mongolia 48°2N 91°37E 217 C12
Kōbe Japan 34°41N 135°13E 223 C7
Kobelyaky Ukraine 49°11N 34°9E 189 H8
København Denmark 55°40N 12°26E 118 A2
København ✈ (CPH) Denmark 55°37N 12°39E 118 B3
Kobenni Mauritania 15°58N 9°24W 262 B3
Kōbi-Sho E. China Sea 25°56N 123°41E 221 M1
Koblenz Germany 50°21N 7°36E 179 E3
Kobo Dem. Rep. of the Congo 4°54S 17°9E 265 C3
Kobo Ethiopia 12°2N 39°56E 257 E4
Kobryn Belarus 52°15N 24°22E 177 B13
Kobuchizawa Japan 35°52N 138°19E 223 B10
Kobuk U.S.A. 66°55N 156°52W 303 C8
Kobuk → U.S.A. 66°54N 160°38W 303 C7
Kobuk Valley △ U.S.A. 67°0N 160°0W 303 C7
Kobuleti Georgia 41°55N 41°45E 191 K5
Kobyletska Polyana Ukraine 48°3N 24°4E 183 B9
Kobylin Poland 51°43N 17°12E 185 G4
Kobylisy Czech Rep. 50°7N 14°26E 135 B2
Kobyłka Poland 52°20N 21°10E 143 A3
Kobylkino Russia 54°8N 43°56E 190 C6
Koca → Turkey 40°8N 27°57E 203 F11
Kocabaş Turkey 37°49N 29°20E 205 D11
Kocaeli Turkey 40°45N 29°50E 203 F13
Kocaeli □ Turkey 40°45N 29°55E 203 F13
Kočane Serbia 43°12N 21°52E 202 C5
Kočani Macedonia 41°55N 22°25E 202 E6
Koçarlı Turkey 37°45N 27°43E 205 D9
Koceljevo Serbia 44°28N 19°50E 202 B3
Kočevje Slovenia 45°39N 14°50E 199 C11
Koçgiri = Zara Turkey 39°58N 37°43E 212 C7
Koch Bihar India 26°22N 89°29E 241 B2
Kochas India 25°15N 83°56E 243 G10
Kocher → Germany 49°13N 9°12E 179 F5
Kochi India 9°58N 76°20E 245 K3
Kōchi Japan 33°30N 133°35E 222 D5
Kōchi □ Japan 33°40N 133°30E 222 D5
Kochiu = Gejiu China 23°20N 103°10E 228 F4
Kochkor Kyrgyzstan 42°13N 75°46E 217 D9
Kochubey Russia 44°23N 46°32E 191 H8
Kock Poland 51°38N 22°27E 185 G9
Kodaira Japan 35°43N 139°28E 140 A1
Kodala India 19°38N 84°57E 244 E7
Kodanaka Japan 35°34N 139°37E 140 B2
Kodarma India 24°28N 85°36E 243 G11
Koddiyar B. Sri Lanka 8°33N 81°15E 245 K5
Kode Sweden 57°57N 11°51E 163 G5
Kodenmacho Tokyo, Japan 140 a5
Kodi Dem. Rep. of the Congo 3°34S 22°12E 264 C4
Kodiak U.S.A. 57°47N 152°24W 303 H9
Kodiak I. U.S.A. 57°30N 152°45W 303 H9
Kodikkarai = Point Calimere India 10°17N 79°49E 245 J4
Kodinar India 20°46N 70°46E 242 J4
Kodinsk Russia 58°40N 99°10E 215 D10
Kodlipet India 12°48N 75°53E 245 H2
Kodok South Sudan 9°53N 32°7E 257 F3
Kodori → Georgia 42°47N 41°10E 191 J5
Kodoro Dem. Rep. of the Congo 1°16N 20°6E 264 B4
Kodungallur = Cranganore India 10°13N 76°13E 245 J3
Kodyma Ukraine 48°6N 29°7E 183 B14
Koedoesberge S. Africa 32°40S 20°11E 270 D3
Koekelberg Belgium 50°52N 4°20E 116 A1
Koes Namibia 26°0S 19°15E 270 C2
Kofarnihon Tajikistan 38°33N 69°1E 217 E7
Kofçaz Turkey 41°58N 27°12E 203 E11
Koffiefontein S. Africa 29°30S 25°0E 270 C4
Kofiau Indonesia 1°11S 129°50E 231 E7
Köflach Austria 47°4N 15°5E 180 D8
Koforidua Ghana 6°3N 0°17W 263 D4
Kōfu Japan 35°40N 138°30E 223 B10
Koga Fukuoka, Japan 33°45N 130°25E 222 D2
Koga Ibaraki, Japan 36°11N 139°43E 223 A11
Kogaluc → Canada 56°12N 61°44W 299 A7
Koganei Japan 35°42N 139°31E 140 A2
Kogarah Australia 33°57S 151°8E 139 B1
Køge Denmark 55°27N 12°11E 163 J6
Køge Bugt Denmark 55°34N 12°24E 163 J6
Kogi □ Nigeria 7°45N 6°45E 263 D6
Kogin Baba Nigeria 7°55N 11°35E 263 D7
Kogo Eq. Guin. 1°5N 9°42E 264 B1
Kogon Uzbekistan 39°43N 64°33E 216 E6
Koh-i-Khurd Afghan. 33°30N 65°59E 242 C1
Koh-i-Maran Pakistan 29°18N 66°50E 242 E2
Koh Ker Cambodia 13°47N 104°32E 236 F5
Koh Wai Thailand 11°54N 102°25E 237 H4
Kohala Mts. U.S.A. 20°5N 155°45W 302 C6
Kohat Pakistan 33°40N 71°29E 242 C4
Kohima India 25°35N 94°10E 241 C5
Kohkīlūyeh va Būyer Aḩmadi □ Iran 31°30N 50°30E 247 D6
Kohler Ra. Antarctica 77°0S 110°0W 151 D15
Kohlfurt = Węgliniec Poland 51°18N 15°10E 185 G2
Kohlu Pakistan 29°54N 69°15E 242 E3
Kohtla-Järve Estonia 59°20N 27°20E 188 C4
Kohukohu N.Z. 35°22S 173°38E 284 B2
Kohylnyk → Ukraine 45°49N 29°40E 183 E14
Koi Sanjaq Iraq 36°5N 44°38E 213 D11
Koidu S. Leone 8°38N 10°59W 262 D2
Koihoa India 8°12N 93°29E 245 K11
Koilkuntla India 15°14N 78°19E 245 G4
Koillismaa Finland 65°44N 28°36E 160 D23
Koimbani Comoros Is. 11°37S 43°21E 272 a
Koin N. Korea 40°28N 126°18E 224 B3
Koinare Bulgaria 43°21N 24°8E 203 C8
Koindu S. Leone 8°26N 10°19W 262 D2
Koivisto = Primorsk Russia 60°22N 28°37E 188 B5
Koivupää Finland 60°18N 24°53E 121 B2
Koja Indonesia 6°8S 106°52E 122 A2
Koja Utara Indonesia 6°5S 106°53E 122 A2
Kojetín Czech Rep. 49°21N 17°20E 181 B10
Kojo N. Korea 38°58N 127°58E 224 C3
Kojonup Australia 33°48S 117°10E 279 F2
Kojūr Iran 36°23N 51°43E 247 B6
Kokand = Qŭqon Uzbekistan 40°31N 70°56E 217 D8
Kokang Burma 23°45N 98°30E 228 F2
Kokas Indonesia 2°42S 132°26E 231 E8
Kokava Slovak Rep. 48°35N 19°50E 181 C12
Kokcha → Afghan. 37°9N 69°24E 240 A3
Kokchetav = Kökshetaū Kazakhstan 53°20N 69°25E 217 B7
Köke'e State Park ⌂ U.S.A. 22°6N 159°40W 302 A2
Kokemäenjoki → Finland 61°32N 21°44E 188 B1
Kokerite Guyana 7°12N 59°35W 329 B6
Kokhav Ya'akov West Bank 31°53N 35°14E 123 A2
Kokhma Russia 56°57N 41°8E 190 B5
Koki Senegal 15°30N 15°59W 262 B1
Kokiu = Gejiu China 23°20N 103°10E 228 F4
Kokkilai Sri Lanka 9°0N 80°57E 245 K5
Kokkina Cyprus 35°11N 32°36E 207 E8
Kokkola Finland 63°50N 23°8E 160 E20
Koko Nigeria 11°28N 4°29E 263 C5
Koko Head U.S.A. 21°16N 157°43W 302 K14
Koko Kyunzu Burma 14°7N 93°22E 245 G11
Kokobunji Japan 35°42N 139°27E 140 A1
Kokobunji-Temple Japan 35°44N 139°55E 140 A4
Kokoda Papua N. G. 8°54S 147°47E 286 E4
Kokologo Burkina Faso 12°11N 1°53W 262 C4
Kokolopozo Ivory C. 5°8N 6°5W 262 D3
Kokomo U.S.A. 40°29N 86°8W 311 D10
Kokopo Papua N. G. 4°22S 152°19E 286 C7
Kokoro Niger 14°12N 0°55E 263 C5
Koksan N. Korea 38°46N 126°40E 224 C3
Kökshetaū Kazakhstan 53°20N 69°25E 217 B7
Koksoak → Canada 58°30N 68°10W 295 F18
Kokstad S. Africa 30°32S 29°29E 271 D4
Köktal Kazakhstan 44°8N 79°48E 217 D9
Kokubu = Kirishima Japan 31°44N 130°46E 222 F2
Kokyar China 37°23N 77°10E 217 E9
Kola Indonesia 5°35S 134°30E 231 F8
Kola Russia 68°45N 33°8E 160 B25
Kola Pen. = Kolskiy Poluostrov Russia 67°30N 38°0E 186 A6
Kolachel India 8°10N 77°15E 245 K3
Kolachi → Pakistan 27°8N 67°2E 242 F2
Kolahoi India 34°12N 75°22E 243 B6
Kolahun Liberia 8°15N 10°4W 262 D2
Kolaka Indonesia 4°3S 121°46E 231 E6
Kolar India 13°12N 78°15E 245 H4
Kolar Gold Fields India 12°58N 78°16E 245 H4
Kolarängen Sweden 59°16N 18°10E 139 B3
Kolaras India 25°14N 77°36E 242 G6
Kolari Finland 67°20N 23°48E 160 C20
Kolarovgrad = Shumen Bulgaria 43°18N 26°55E 203 C10
Kolárovo Slovak Rep. 47°54N 18°0E 181 D10
Kolasib India 24°15N 92°45E 241 C4
Kolašin Montenegro 42°50N 19°31E 202 D3
Kolayat India 27°50N 72°50E 242 F5
Kolbäck Sweden 59°34N 16°15E 162 E10
Kolbäcksån → Sweden 59°36N 16°16E 162 E10
Kolbeinsstaðir Iceland 64°59N 22°16W 155 C4
Kolberg = Kołobrzeg Poland 54°10N 15°35E 184 D2
Kolbermoor Germany 47°51N 12°4E 179 H8
Kolbio Kenya 1°8S 41°12E 267 E5
Kolbotn Norway 59°48N 10°48E 133 B3
Kolbu Norway 60°39N 10°45E 164 D7
Kolbuszowa Poland 50°15N 21°46E 185 H8
Kolchugino = Leninsk-Kuznetskiy Russia 54°44N 86°10E 217 B11
Kolchugino Russia 56°17N 39°22E 188 D10
Kolda Senegal 12°55N 14°57W 262 C2
Kolda □ Senegal 13°5N 14°50W 262 C2
Koldegi Sudan 12°30N 30°16E 257 E3
Kolding Denmark 55°30N 9°29E 163 J3
Kole Dem. Rep. of the Congo 3°16S 22°42E 264 C4
Koléa Algeria 36°38N 2°46E 261 A5
Kolepom = Dolak, Pulau Indonesia 8°0S 138°30E 231 F9
Kolguyev, Ostrov Russia 69°20N 48°30E 186 A8
Kolhapur India 16°43N 74°15E 244 F2
Kolia Ivory C. 9°46N 6°28W 262 D3
Koliganek U.S.A. 59°48N 157°25W 303 G8
Kolimbia Greece 36°15N 28°10E 206 E12
Kolín Czech Rep. 50°2N 15°9E 180 A8
Kolind Denmark 56°21N 10°34E 163 H4
Kolkas rags Latvia 57°46N 22°37E 184 A9
Kolkata India 22°34N 88°21E 124 B2
Kolkata Maidan India 22°33N 88°21E 124 B1
Kolkata Netaji Subhash Chandra Bose Int. ✈ (CCU) India 22°38N 88°26E 124 B2
Kollam India 8°50N 76°38E 245 K3
Kölleda Germany 51°11N 11°15E 178 D7
Kollegal India 12°9N 77°9E 245 H3
Kolleru L. India 16°40N 81°10E 244 F5
Kollum Neths. 53°17N 6°10E 170 A6
Kolmanskop Namibia 26°45S 15°14E 270 C2
Köln Germany 50°56N 6°57E 178 E2
Kolno Poland 53°25N 21°56E 184 E8
Koło Warszawa, Poland 52°14N 20°56E 143 B1
Koło Wielkopolskie, Poland 52°14N 18°40E 185 F5
Kołobrzeg Poland 54°10N 15°35E 184 D2
Kolochava Ukraine 48°26N 23°41E 183 B8
Kologi Sudan 10°51N 30°58E 257 E3
Kolokani Mali 13°35N 7°45W 262 C3
Kolokinthou Greece 38°0N 23°42E 112 B2
Koloko Burkina Faso 11°5N 5°19W 262 C3
Kolola Ethiopia 7°29N 41°58E 257 F5
Kolombangara Solomon Is. 8°0S 157°5E 287 M9
Kolomna Russia 55°8N 38°45E 188 E10
Kolomyagi Russia 60°0N 30°19E 137 A1
Kolomyya Ukraine 48°31N 25°2E 183 B10
Kolondiéba Mali 11°5N 6°54W 262 C3
Kolonodale Indonesia 2°0S 121°19E 231 E6
Kolonos Greece 37°59N 23°43E 112 B2
Kolonowskie Poland 50°39N 18°22E 185 H5
Kolpashevo Russia 58°20N 83°5E 214 D9
Kolpino Russia 59°44N 30°39E 188 C6
Kolpny Russia 52°17N 37°1E 189 F9
Kolsås Norway 59°55N 10°30E 133 A2
Kolskiy Poluostrov Russia 67°30N 38°0E 186 A6
Kolskiy Zaliv Russia 69°23N 34°0E 160 B26
Kolsva Sweden 59°36N 15°51E 162 E9
Kolubara → Serbia 44°35N 20°15E 202 B4
Kolumadulu Atoll Maldives 2°22N 73°7E 272 d
Koluszki Poland 51°45N 19°46E 185 G6
Kolwezi Dem. Rep. of the Congo 10°40S 25°25E 269 E2
Kolyma → Russia 69°30N 161°0E 215 C17
Kolymskoye Nagorye Russia 63°0N 157°0E 215 C16
Kôm Hamâda Egypt 30°46N 30°41E 256 H7
Kôm Ombo Egypt 24°25N 32°52E 256 C3
Koma Tou Yialou Cyprus 35°25N 34°8E 207 E10
Komadugu Gana → Nigeria 13°5N 12°24E 263 C7
Komae Japan 35°37N 139°34E 140 B2
Komagane Japan 35°44N 137°58E 223 B9
Komagome Japan 35°43N 139°45E 140 A3
Komaki Japan 35°17N 136°55E 223 B8
Komandorskiye Is. = Komandorskiye Ostrova Russia 55°0N 167°0E 215 D17
Komandorskiye Ostrova Russia 55°0N 167°0E 215 D17
Komárno Slovak Rep. 47°49N 18°5E 181 D11
Komarnyky Ukraine 48°59N 23°3E 182 B8
Komárom Hungary 47°43N 18°7E 182 C3
Komárom-Esztergom □ Hungary 47°35N 18°20E 182 C3
Komárommújváros = Komárom Hungary 47°43N 18°7E 182 C3
Komatipoort S. Africa 25°25S 31°55E 271 C5
Komatsu Japan 36°25N 136°30E 223 A8
Komatsushima Japan 34°0N 134°35E 222 D6
Komavangard = Sobinka Russia 56°0N 40°0E 188 E11
Komazawa Japan 35°37N 139°40E 140 B3
Komba Dem. Rep. of the Congo 2°52N 24°3E 264 B4
Kombissiri Burkina Faso 12°4N 1°20W 263 C4
Kombo Gabon 0°20S 12°22E 264 C2
Kombong India 28°7N 94°51E 241 A5
Kombori Burkina Faso 13°26N 3°56W 262 C4
Komboti Greece 39°6N 21°5E 204 B3
Kome Channel Uganda 0°10S 32°35E 268 C3
Komebail Lagoon Palau 7°25N 134°25E 288 c
Komen Slovenia 45°49N 13°45E 199 C10
Komenda Ghana 5°4N 1°28W 263 D4
Komi Cyprus 35°24N 34°0E 207 E10
Komi □ Russia 64°0N 55°0E 186 B10
Kominter = Novoshakhtinsk Russia 47°46N 39°58E 189 J10
Komintern = Marhanets Ukraine 47°40N 34°40E 189 J8
Komiža Croatia 43°3N 16°11E 199 E13
Komló Hungary 46°15N 18°16E 182 D3
Kommamur Canal India 16°0N 80°25E 245 G5
Kommunarsk = Alchevsk Ukraine 48°30N 38°45E 189 H10
Kommunizma, Pik = imeni Ismail Samani, Pik Tajikistan 39°0N 72°2E 217 E8
Komodo Indonesia 8°37S 119°20E 235 D5
Komodo △ Indonesia 8°36S 119°34E 235 D5
Komono Congo 3°10S 13°20E 264 C2
Komoran, Pulau Indonesia 8°18S 138°45E 231 F9
Komoro Japan 36°19N 138°26E 223 A10
Komotau = Chomutov Czech Rep. 50°28N 13°23E 180 A6
Komotini Greece 41°9N 25°26E 203 E9
Komovi Montenegro 42°41N 19°39E 202 D3
Kompasberg S. Africa 31°45S 24°32E 270 D3
Kompong Chhnang = Kampong Chhnang Cambodia 12°20N 104°35E 237 F5
Kompong Chikreng Cambodia 13°5N 104°18E 236 F5
Kompong Kleang Cambodia 13°6N 104°8E 236 F5
Kompong Luong Cambodia 11°49N 104°48E 237 G5
Kompong Pranak Cambodia 13°35N 104°55E 236 F5
Kompong Som = Kampong Saom Cambodia 10°38N 103°30E 237 G4
Kompong Som, Chhung = Kampong Saom, Chaak Cambodia 10°50N 103°32E 237 G4
Kompong Speu Cambodia 11°26N 104°32E 237 G5
Kompong Sralau Cambodia 14°5N 105°46E 236 E5
Kompong Thom Cambodia 12°35N 104°51E 236 F5
Kompong Trabeck Cambodia 13°6N 105°14E 236 F5
Kompong Trach Cambodia 11°25N 105°48E 237 G5
Kompong Tralach Cambodia 11°54N 104°47E 237 G5
Komrat = Comrat Moldova 46°18N 28°40E 183 D13
Komsberg S. Africa 32°40S 20°45E 270 D3
Komsomolets = Qarabalyq Kazakhstan 53°45N 62°2E 216 B6
Komsomolets, Ostrov Russia 80°30N 95°0E 215 A10
Komsomolsk Ivanovo, Russia 57°2N 40°20E 188 D11
Komsomolsk Ukraine 49°1N 33°38E 189 H7
Komsomolsk-na-Amur Russia 50°30N 137°0E 219 A16
Komsomolskiy Russia 54°27N 45°33E 190 C7
Komsomolskoe Kazakhstan 50°25N 60°5E 216 B6
Komsomolsky = Chirchiq Uzbekistan 41°29N 69°35E 217 D7
Kömür Burnu Turkey 38°39N 26°12E 205 C8
Kon Ka Kinh △ Vietnam 14°19N 107°23E 236 E6
Kon Tum Vietnam 14°24N 108°0E 236 E7
Kon Tum, Plateau du Vietnam 14°30N 108°30E 236 E7
Kona W. Bengal, India 22°37N 88°18E 124 B1
Kona Mali 14°57N 3°53W 262 C4
Kona Nigeria 8°57N 11°21E 263 D7
Kona ✈ (KOA) U.S.A. 19°44N 156°3W 302 D5
Könähuanui U.S.A. 21°21N 157°47W 302 K14
Konakovo Russia 56°40N 36°51E 188 D9
Konala Finland 60°14N 24°52E 121 B2
Konar □ Afghan. 34°30N 71°3E 240 B3
Konarak India 19°54N 86°7E 244 E8
Konārak Iran 25°21N 60°23E 249 A8
Konārī Iran 28°13N 51°36E 247 D6
Konch India 26°0N 79°10E 243 G8
Kondagaon India 19°35N 81°35E 244 E5
Konde Tanzania 4°57S 39°45E 268 C4
Kondias Greece 39°49N 25°10E 205 B7
Kondinin Australia 32°34S 118°8E 279 F2
Kondli India 28°36N 77°19E 120 B2
Kondo Dem. Rep. of the Congo 5°35S 13°0E 265 D2
Kondoa Tanzania 4°55S 35°50E 268 C4
Kondopoga Russia 62°12N 34°17E 188 A8
Kondoz Afghan. 36°50N 68°50E 240 A3
Kondoz → Afghan. 37°0N 68°16E 240 A3
Kondratyevo Russia 57°22N 98°15E 215 D10
Kondrovo Russia 54°48N 35°56E 188 E8
Konduga Nigeria 11°35N 13°26E 263 C7
Kondukur India 15°12N 79°57E 245 G4
Kondūz □ Afghan. 36°50N 68°50E 240 A3
Koné Cameroon 8°50N 13°17E 259 G2
Koné N. Cal. 21°4S 164°52E 288 d
Köneürgench Turkmenistan 42°19N 59°10E 216 D5
Konevo Russia 62°8N 39°20E 188 A10
Kong = Khong → Cambodia 13°32N 105°58E 236 F5
Kong Ivory C. 8°54N 4°36W 262 D4
Kong, Koh Cambodia 11°20N 103°0E 237 G4
Kong Christian IX.s Land Greenland 68°0N 36°0W 154 D7
Kong Christian X.s Land Greenland 74°0N 29°0W 154 C8
Kong Frederik IX.s Land Greenland 67°0N 52°0W 154 D5
Kong Frederik VI.s Kyst Greenland 63°0N 43°0W 154 E6
Kong Frederik VIII.s Land Greenland 78°30N 26°0W 154 B8
Kong Karls Land Svalbard 79°0N 28°0E 154 B13
Kong Oscar Fjord Greenland 72°20N 24°0W 154 C8
Kongauru I. Palau 7°3N 134°16E 288 c
Kongbo C.A.R. 4°44N 21°23E 264 B4
Kongeå → Denmark 55°23N 8°39E 163 J2
Kongelunden Denmark 55°34N 12°34E 118 B3
Kongens Lyngby Denmark 55°46N 12°30E 118 A3
Kongernes Nordsjælland △ Denmark 56°5N 12°15E 163 H6
Kongerslev Denmark 56°54N 10°6E 163 H4
Kongkemul Indonesia 1°52N 116°10E 235 B5
Konglu Burma 27°13N 97°57E 241 B6
Kongmoon = Jiangmen China 22°32N 113°0E 229 F9
Kongo Finland 60°20N 24°47E 121 A1
Kongola Namibia 17°45S 23°20E 270 A3
Kongolo Kasai-Or., Dem. Rep. of the Congo 5°26S 24°49E 265 D4
Kongolo Katanga, Dem. Rep. of the Congo 5°22S 27°0E 268 D2
Kongor South Sudan 7°1N 31°27E 257 F3
Kongossambougou ⌂ Mali 14°0N 8°30W 262 C3
Kongoulou Cameroon 2°59N 11°7E 264 B2
Kongoussi Burkina Faso 13°19N 1°32W 263 C4
Kongsberg Norway 59°39N 9°39E 164 E6
Kongsvinger Norway 60°12N 12°2E 164 D9
Kongur Shan China 38°34N 75°18E 217 E9
Kongwa Tanzania 6°11S 36°26E 268 D4
Koni Dem. Rep. of the Congo 10°40S 27°11E 269 E2
Koniakari Mali 14°35N 10°50W 262 C2
Koniecpol Poland 50°46N 19°40E 185 H6
Königgrätz = Hradec Králové Czech Rep. 50°15N 15°50E 180 A8
Königs Wusterhausen Germany 52°19N 13°38E 178 C9
Königsberg = Chojna Poland 52°58N 14°25E 185 F1
Königsberg = Kaliningrad Russia 54°42N 20°32E 184 D7
Königsbrunn Germany 48°16N 10°54E 179 G6
Königshütte = Chorzów Poland 50°18N 18°57E 185 H5
Königslutter Germany 52°15N 10°49E 178 C6
Konin Poland 52°12N 18°15E 185 F5
Köninginhof an der Elbe = Dvůr Králové nad Labem Czech Rep. 50°27N 15°50E 180 A8
Koninklijk Paleis Amsterdam, Neths. 112 a2
Konispol Albania 39°42N 20°10E 206 B10
Konitsa Greece 40°5N 20°48E 204 A2
Konjic Bos.-H. 43°42N 17°58E 182 G2
Konkiep Namibia 26°49S 17°15E 270 C2
Konkō Japan 34°33N 133°36E 222 C4
Konkouré → Guinea 9°50N 13°42W 262 D2
Konnagar India 22°42N 88°21E 124 A2
Könnern Germany 51°41N 11°47E 178 D7
Konnur India 16°14N 74°49E 245 F2
Kono S. Leone 8°30N 11°5W 262 D2
Konogogo Papua N. G. 3°29S 152°10E 286 B7
Konohana Japan 34°40N 135°26E 133 A1
Konongo Ghana 6°40N 1°15W 263 D4
Konos Papua N. G. 3°10S 151°44E 286 B6
Konosha Russia 61°0N 40°5E 188 B11
Kōnosu Japan 36°3N 139°31E 223 A11
Konotop Ukraine 51°12N 33°7E 189 G7
Konqi He → China 41°0N 86°0E 217 D11
Konradshof = Skawina Poland 49°59N 19°50E 185 J6
Konradshöhe Germany 52°35N 13°13E 115 A2
Konrei Palau 7°43N 134°36E 288 c
Konsankoro Guinea 9°2N 9°0W 262 D3
Końskie Poland 51°15N 20°23E 185 G7
Konsmo Norway 58°16N 7°23E 164 F4
Konstadt = Wołczyn Poland 51°1N 18°3E 185 G5
Konstancin-Jeziorna Poland 52°5N 21°7E 185 F8
Konstantinograd = Krasnohrad Ukraine 49°27N 35°27E 189 H8
Konstantinovka = Kostyantynivka Ukraine 48°32N 37°39E 189 H9
Konstantinovsk Russia 47°33N 41°10E 191 G5
Konstantynów Łódźki Poland 51°45N 19°20E 185 G6
Konstanz Germany 47°40N 9°10E 179 H5
Kont Iran 26°55N 61°50E 247 E9
Konta India 17°48N 81°23E 244 F5
Kontagora Nigeria 10°23N 5°27E 263 C6
Kontcha Cameroon 7°59N 12°15E 263 D7
Kontiolahti Finland 62°46N 29°50E 160 E23
Kontokali Greece 39°38N 19°51E 206 B9
Konya Turkey 37°52N 32°35E 212 D5
Konya □ Turkey 37°46N 32°20E 250 A3
Konya Ovası Turkey 38°9N 33°5E 212 C5
Konyin Burma 22°58N 94°42E 241 D5
Konz Germany 49°42N 6°34E 179 F2
Konza Kenya 1°45S 37°7E 268 C4
Koo-wee-rup Australia 38°13S 145°28E 283 E6
Koocanusa, L. Canada 49°20N 115°15W 304 B6
Kookynie Australia 29°17S 121°22E 279 E3
Ko'olau Range U.S.A. 21°35N 157°50W 302 J14
Ko'olauloa District U.S.A. 21°35N 157°55W 302 J14
Ko'olaupoko District U.S.A. 21°25N 157°50W 302 K14
Kō'Ōlina U.S.A. 21°19N 158°7W 302 K13
Koolyanobbing Australia 30°48S 119°36E 279 F2
Koondrook Australia 35°33S 144°8E 282 C6
Koonibba Australia 31°54S 133°25E 281 E1
Koorawatha Australia 34°2S 148°33E 283 C8
Koorda Australia 30°48S 117°35E 279 F2
Kooskia U.S.A. 46°9N 115°59W 304 C6
Kootenay → U.S.A. 49°19N 117°39W 296 D5
Kootenay △ Canada 51°0N 116°0W 296 C5
Kootenay L. Canada 49°45N 116°50W 304 B5
Kootingal Australia 31°3S 151°4E 283 A9
Kootjieskolk S. Africa 31°15S 20°21E 270 D3
Kopanina Czech Rep. 50°3N 14°17E 135 B1
Kopanovka Russia 47°28N 46°50E 191 G8
Kopaonik Serbia 43°10N 20°50E 202 C4
Kopaonik △ Serbia 43°20N 20°50E 202 C4
Kopargaon India 19°51N 74°28E 244 E2
Koparkhairna India 19°6N 72°59E 130 A2
Kópasker Iceland 66°18N 16°27W 155 A10
Kópavogur Iceland 64°6N 21°55W 155 C5
Kopayhorod Ukraine 48°52N 27°53E 183 B12
Köpenick Germany 52°26N 13°35E 115 B4
Koper Slovenia 45°31N 13°44E 199 C10
Kopervik Norway 59°17N 5°17E 164 E2
Kopet Dagh Asia 38°0N 58°0E 247 B8
Kopeysk Russia 55°7N 61°37E 216 A6
Kopi Australia 33°24S 135°40E 281 E2
Köping Sweden 59°31N 16°3E 162 E10
Köpingsvik Sweden 56°53N 16°43E 163 H10
Kopište Croatia 42°48N 16°42E 199 F13
Koplik Albania 42°15N 19°25E 202 D3
Köpmanholmen Sweden 63°10N 18°35E 162 A12
Koppa India 13°33N 75°21E 245 H2
Koppal India 15°23N 76°5E 245 G3
Koppang Norway 61°34N 11°3E 164 C8
Kopparberg Sweden 59°52N 15°0E 162 E9
Koppeh Dāgh = Kopet Dagh Asia 38°0N 58°0E 247 B8
Kopperå Norway 63°24N 11°50E 164 A8
Koppies S. Africa 27°20S 27°30E 271 C4
Koppom Sweden 59°43N 12°10E 162 E6
Koprivlen Bulgaria 41°31N 23°53E 202 E7
Koprivnica Croatia 46°12N 16°45E 199 B13
Kopřivnice Czech Rep. 49°36N 18°9E 181 B11
Koprivshtitsa Bulgaria 42°40N 24°19E 203 D8
Köprü → Turkey 36°48N 31°11E 250 B2
Köprübaşı Turkey 38°43N 28°23E 205 C10
Köprülü Turkey 36°43N 32°10E 250 B3
Köprülü △ Turkey 37°20N 31°5E 246 B1
Kopychyntsi Ukraine 49°7N 25°58E 177 D13
Kor Aban Somalia 3°58N 42°44E 267 D5
Kora △ Kenya 0°14S 38°44E 268 C4
Koraa Shiir Somalia 3°16N 46°16E 267 D6
Korab Macedonia 41°44N 20°40E 202 E4
Korahe Ethiopia 6°39N 44°5E 267 C5
Koral India 21°50N 73°12E 242 J5
Korangal India 17°6N 77°38E 244 E3
Korangi Pakistan 24°47N 67°8E 123 B2
Koraput India 18°50N 82°40E 244 E6
Korarou, L. Mali 15°15N 3°15W 262 B4
Korba India 22°20N 82°45E 243 H10
Korbach Germany 51°16N 8°52E 178 D4
Korbu, Gunung Malaysia 4°41N 101°18E 237 K3
Korçë Albania 40°37N 20°50E 202 F4
Korčula Croatia 42°56N 16°57E 199 F13
Korčulanski Kanal Croatia 43°3N 16°40E 199 E13
Kord Kūy Iran 36°48N 54°7E 247 B7
Kord Sheykh Iran 28°31N 52°53E 247 D7
Kordestan = Kurdistan Asia 37°20N 43°30E 213 D10
Kordestān □ Iran 36°0N 47°0E 246 C5
Kordié Burkina Faso 12°36N 2°22W 262 C4
Koré Mayroua Niger 13°18N 3°55E 263 C5
Korea, North ■ Asia 40°0N 127°0E 224 C3
Korea, South ■ Asia 36°0N 128°0E 224 D4
Korea Bay Korea 39°0N 124°0E 224 C2
Korea Strait Asia 34°0N 129°30E 227 H15
Koregaon India 17°40N 74°10E 244 F2

Korem Ethiopia 12°30N 39°32E 257 E4
Koremasa Japan 35°39N 139°29E 140 B1
Korenevo Russia 51°27N 34°55E 189 G8
Korenica = Titova Korenica Croatia 44°45N 15°41E 199 D12
Korenovsk Russia 45°30N 39°22E 191 H4
Korets Ukraine 50°40N 27°5E 177 C14
Korfantów Poland 50°29N 17°36E 185 H4
Körfez Turkey 40°47N 29°44E 203 F13
Korff Ice Rise Antarctica 79°0S 69°30W 151 D17
Korgalzhyn = Qorghalzhyn Kazakhstan 50°25N 69°11E 217 B7
Korgan Turkey 40°44N 37°13E 212 B7
Korgus Sudan 19°16N 33°29E 256 D3
Korhogo Ivory C. 9°29N 5°28W 262 D3
Koribundu S. Leone 7°41N 11°46W 262 D2
Koridalos Greece 37°59N 23°39E 112 B1
Korienzé Mali 15°22N 3°50W 262 B4
Korinthia □ Greece 37°50N 22°35E 204 D4
Korinthiakos Kolpos Greece 38°16N 22°30E 204 C4
Korinthos Greece 37°56N 22°55E 204 D4
Korioumé Mali 16°35N 3°0W 262 B4
Korissia, L. Greece 39°27N 19°53E 206 C9
Korithi Greece 37°55N 20°42E 207 D2
Kōriyama Japan 37°24N 140°23E 220 F10
Korkino Russia 54°54N 61°23E 216 B6
Korkuteli Turkey 37°4N 30°13E 205 D12
Korla China 41°45N 86°4E 217 D11
Kormakiti, C. Cyprus 35°23N 32°56E 207 E8
Körmend Hungary 47°5N 16°35E 182 C1
Kormor Iraq 35°8N 44°50E 213 E11
Kornat Croatia 43°50N 15°20E 199 E12
Kornat △ Croatia 43°50N 15°12E 199 E12
Korneshty = Corneşti Moldova 47°21N 28°1E 183 C13
Korneuburg Austria 48°20N 16°20E 181 C9
Kórnik Poland 52°15N 17°6E 185 F4
Kornsjø Norway 58°57N 11°39E 164 F8
Koro Fiji 17°19S 179°23E 287 A2
Koro Ivory C. 8°32N 7°30W 262 D3
Koro Mali 14°1N 2°58W 262 C4
Koro Sea Fiji 17°30S 179°45W 287 A3
Koro Toro Chad 16°5N 18°30E 259 E3
Koroba Papua N. G. 5°44S 142°47E 286 C2
Korobkovo = Gubkin Russia 51°17N 37°32E 189 G9
Korocha Russia 50°54N 37°19E 189 G9
Köroğlu Dağları Turkey 40°38N 33°0E 212 B5
Korogwe Tanzania 5°5S 38°25E 268 D4
Koroit Australia 38°18S 142°24E 282 E5
Koroleve Ukraine 48°9N 23°8E 183 B8
Korolevu Fiji 18°12S 177°46E 287 B1
Koromiri Cook Is. 21°15S 159°43W 289 h
Korona U.S.A. 29°25N 81°12W 317 F8
Koronadal Phil. 6°12N 124°51E 233 H5
Korong Vale Australia 36°22S 143°45E 282 D5
Koroni Greece 36°48N 21°57E 204 E3
Koronia, L. Greece 40°47N 23°10E 202 F7
Koronos Greece 37°12N 25°35E 205 D7
Koronowo Poland 53°19N 17°55E 185 E4
Koropelé C.A.R. 4°44N 17°11E 264 B3
Koropets Ukraine 48°56N 25°10E 183 B10
Koror Palau 7°20N 134°28E 288 c
Körös → Hungary 46°43N 20°12E 182 D5
Körös Maros △ Hungary 47°8N 20°52E 182 C5
Köröstarcsa Hungary 46°53N 21°3E 182 D6
Korosten Ukraine 50°54N 28°36E 177 C15
Korostyshev Ukraine 50°19N 29°4E 177 C15
Korotoyak Russia 51°1N 39°2E 189 G10
Korovou Fiji 17°47S 178°32E 287 A2
Koroyanitu △ Fiji 17°40S 177°35E 287 A1
Korraraika, Helodranon' i Madag. 17°45S 43°57E 272 B1
Korror I. Palau 7°20N 134°29E 288 c
Korsakov Russia 46°36N 142°42E 215 E15
Korsberga Sweden 57°19N 15°7E 163 G9
Korshiv Ukraine 48°39N 25°1E 183 B10
Korshunovo Russia 58°37N 110°10E 215 D12
Korsør Denmark 55°20N 11°9E 163 J5
Korsun Shevchenkovskiy Ukraine 49°26N 31°16E 189 H6
Korsze Poland 54°11N 21°9E 184 D8
Korti Sudan 18°6N 31°33E 256 D3
Kortrijk Belgium 50°50N 3°17E 170 D3
Korucu Turkey 39°28N 27°22E 205 B9
Korumburra Australia 38°26S 145°50E 283 E6
Korup △ Cameroon 5°15N 9°2E 264 A1
Korwai India 24°7N 78°5E 242 G8
Koryakskoye Nagorye Russia 61°0N 171°0E 215 C18
Koryukovka Ukraine 51°46N 32°16E 189 G7
Kos Greece 36°50N 27°15E 205 E9
Kosa Ethiopia 7°50N 36°50E 257 F4
Kosai Japan 34°42N 137°32E 223 C9
Kosan N. Korea 38°52N 127°25E 224 C3
Kosaya Gora Russia 54°10N 37°30E 188 E9
Kościan Poland 52°5N 16°40E 185 F3
Kościerzyna Poland 54°8N 17°59E 184 D4
Kosciusko U.S.A. 33°4N 89°35W 315 E10
Kosciuszko, Mt. Australia 36°27S 148°16E 283 D8
Kosciuszko △ Australia 36°30S 148°20E 283 D8
Kösély → Hungary 47°25N 21°5E 182 C6
Kosgi Andhra Pradesh, India 16°58N 77°43E 244 F3
Kosgi Andhra Pradesh, India 15°51N 77°16E 245 G3
Kosha Sudan 20°50N 30°30E 256 C3
Koshava Bulgaria 44°4N 23°2E 202 B7
Kōshi Japan 32°53N 130°48E 222 E2
Koshigaya Japan 35°54N 139°48E 223 B11
K'oshih = Kashi China 39°30N 76°2E 217 E9
Koshiki-Kaikyo Japan 31°30N 130°0E 222 F1
Koshiki-Rettō Japan 31°45N 129°49E 222 F1
Koshim → Kazakhstan 49°20N 50°30E 190 F10
Koshkonong L. U.S.A. 42°52N 88°58W 311 B8
Kōshoku Japan 36°38N 138°6E 223 A10
Kōshū Japan 35°42N 138°44E 223 B10
Koshu-Kavak = Krumovgrad Bulgaria 41°29N 25°38E 203 E9
Kosi India 27°48N 77°29E 242 F7
Kosi → India 28°41N 78°57E 243 E8
Košice Slovak Rep. 48°42N 21°15E 181 C14
Košický □ Slovak Rep. 48°45N 21°0E 181 C14
Kosino Russia 55°43N 37°50E 129 B4
Kosiv Ukraine 48°19N 25°6E 183 B10
Kosjerić Serbia 44°0N 19°55E 202 B3
Köşk Turkey 37°50N 28°3E 205 D10
Koskinou Greece 36°23N 28°13E 206 E12
Koslan Russia 63°34N 49°14E 186 B8
Köslin = Koszalin Poland 54°11N 16°8E 184 D3
Kosmach Ukraine 48°20N 24°50E 183 B9
Kosŏng N. Korea 38°40N 128°22E 224 C4
Kosovo ■ Europe 42°30N 21°0E 202 D4
Kosovo Polje = Fushë Kosovë Kosovo 42°40N 21°5E 202 D5
Kosovska Kamenica = Dardanë Kosovo 42°35N 21°35E 202 D5
Kosovska Mitrovica = Mitrovicë Kosovo 42°54N 20°52E 202 D4
Kossou, L. de Ivory C. 6°59N 5°31W 262 D3
Kosta Sweden 56°50N 15°24E 163 H9
Kostajnica Croatia 45°17N 16°30E 199 C13
Kostanjevica Slovenia 45°51N 15°27E 199 C12
Kostenets = Pernik Bulgaria 42°35N 23°2E 202 D7
Kostenets Bulgaria 42°15N 23°52E 202 D7
Koster S. Africa 25°52S 26°54E 270 C4
Kôstî Sudan 13°8N 32°43E 257 E3
Kostinbrod Bulgaria 42°49N 23°13E 202 D7
Kostolac Serbia 44°37N 21°15E 202 B5
Kostopil Ukraine 50°51N 26°22E 177 C14
Kostroma Russia 57°50N 40°58E 188 D11
Kostromo □ Russia 58°10N 42°50E 190 A6
Kostromskoye Vdkhr. Russia 57°52N 40°49E 188 D11
Kostryzhivka Ukraine 48°39N 25°43E 183 B10
Kostrzyn Lubuskie, Poland 52°35N 14°39E 185 F1
Kostrzyn Wielkopolskie, Poland 52°24N 17°14E 185 F4
Kostyantynivka Ukraine 48°32N 37°39E 189 H9
Kostyukovichi = Kastsyukovichy Belarus 53°20N 32°4E 189 F7
Kosugi Japan 35°34N 139°39E 140 B2
Koszalin Poland 54°11N 16°8E 184 D3
Kőszeg Hungary 47°23N 16°33E 182 C1
Kot Addu Pakistan 30°30N 71°0E 242 D4
Kot Kapura India 30°35N 74°50E 242 D6
Kot Moman Pakistan 32°13N 73°0E 242 C5
Kot Sultan Pakistan 30°46N 70°56E 242 D4
Kota India 25°14N 75°49E 242 G6
Kota Jakarta, Indonesia 6°7S 106°48E 122 A1
Kota Barrage India 25°6N 75°51E 242 G6
Kota Belud Malaysia 6°21N 116°26E 235 A5
Kota Bharu Malaysia 6°7N 102°14E 237 J4
Kota Kinabalu Malaysia 6°0N 116°4E 235 A5
Kota Tinggi Malaysia 1°44N 103°53E 237 M4
Kotaagung Indonesia 5°38S 104°29E 234 D2
Kotabaru Kalimantan Barat, Indonesia 0°49S 111°31E 235 C4
Kotabaru Kalimantan Selatan, Indonesia 3°20S 116°20E 235 C5
Kotabaru Sumatera Barat, Indonesia 1°7S 101°43E 234 C2
Kotabesi Indonesia 2°24S 112°58E 235 C4
Kotabumi Indonesia 4°49S 104°54E 234 C2
Kotajawa Indonesia 5°37S 104°19E 234 D2
Kotamobagu Indonesia 0°57N 124°31E 231 D6
Kotapad India 19°9N 82°21E 244 E6
Kotapinang Indonesia 1°53N 100°5E 237 M3
Kotawaringin Indonesia 2°28S 111°27E 235 C4
Kotcho L. Canada 59°7N 121°12W 296 B4
Kotdwara India 29°45N 78°32E 243 E8
Kotel Bulgaria 42°52N 26°26E 203 D10
Kotelnich Russia 58°22N 48°24E 190 A9
Kotelnikovo Russia 47°38N 43°8E 191 G6
Kotelnyy, Ostrov Russia 75°10N 139°0E 215 B14
Kothapet India 19°21N 79°28E 244 E4
Kothari → India 25°20N 75°4E 242 G6
Köthen Germany 51°45N 11°59E 178 D7
Kothi Chhattisgarh, India 23°21N 82°3E 243 H10
Kothi Mad. P., India 24°45N 80°40E 243 G9
Kotiro Pakistan 26°17N 67°13E 242 F2
Kotka Finland 60°28N 26°58E 188 B4
Kotlas Russia 61°17N 46°43E 186 B8
Kotlenska Planina Bulgaria 42°56N 26°30E 203 D10
Kotli Pakistan 33°30N 73°55E 242 C5
Kotlik U.S.A. 63°2N 163°33W 303 E7
Kotma India 23°12N 81°58E 243 H9
Kōtō Japan 35°40N 139°48E 140 A3
Kotohira Japan 34°11N 133°49E 222 C5
Koton-Karifi Nigeria 8°0N 6°48E 263 D6
Kotonkoro Nigeria 11°3N 5°58E 263 C6
Kotor Montenegro 42°25N 18°47E 202 D2
Kotor Varoš Bos.-H. 44°38N 17°22E 182 F2
Kotoriba Croatia 46°23N 16°48E 199 B13
Kotovo Russia 50°22N 44°45E 190 E7
Kotovsk Russia 52°36N 41°32E 190 D5
Kotovsk Ukraine 47°45N 29°35E 177 E15
Kotputli India 27°43N 76°12E 242 F7
Kotri Pakistan 25°22N 68°22E 242 G3
Kotri → India 19°15N 80°35E 244 E5
Kotronas Greece 36°38N 22°29E 204 E4
Kotrung India 22°41N 88°20E 124 A2
Kötschach-Mauthen Austria 46°41N 13°1E 180 E6
Kottagudem India 17°30N 80°40E 244 F5
Kottayam India 9°35N 76°33E 245 K3
Kotto C.A.R. 4°14N 22°2E 264 B4
Kotto → C.A.R. 4°14N 22°2E 264 B4
Kottur India 10°34N 76°56E 245 J3
Kotturu India 14°45N 76°10E 245 G3
Kotu Group Tonga 20°0S 174°45W 287 Q13
Kotuy → Russia 71°54N 102°6E 215 B11
Kotyuzhany Ukraine 48°48N 27°42E 183 B12
Kotzebue U.S.A. 66°53N 162°39W 303 C7
Kotzebue Sound U.S.A. 66°20N 163°0W 303 C7
Kotzenau = Chocianów Poland 51°27N 15°55E 185 G2
Kouango C.A.R. 5°0N 20°10E 264 B4
Kouchibouguac △ Canada 46°50N 65°0W 299 C6
Koudougou Burkina Faso 12°10N 2°20W 262 C4
Koufey Niger 13°57N 7°56E 259 F1
Koufonisi Iraklio, Greece 34°56N 26°8E 207 F7
Koufonisi Notio Aigaio, Greece 36°57N 25°35E 205 E7
Kougaberge S. Africa 33°48S 23°50E 270 D3
K'ouhu Taiwan 23°35N 120°11E 225 C2
Kouibli Ivory C. 7°15N 7°14W 262 D3
Kouilou → Congo 4°10S 12°5E 265 C2
Koukdjuak → Canada 66°43N 73°0W 295 D17
Kouki C.A.R. 7°22N 17°3E 264 A3
Koukoulé, Mt. Comoros Is. 12°18S 43°41E 272 a
Koukourou C.A.R. 7°12N 20°2E 264 A4
Koula Greece 41°23N 24°44E 203 E8
Koula Moutou Gabon 1°15S 12°25E 264 C2
Koulen = Kulen Cambodia 13°50N 104°40E 236 F5
Koulikoro Mali 12°40N 7°50W 262 C3
Koulikoro □ Mali 14°0N 7°45W 262 C3
Kouloura Greece 39°42N 19°54E 206 B9
Koumac N. Cal. 20°33S 164°17E 288 d
Koumala Australia 21°38S 149°15E 280 C4
Koumameyeng Gabon 0°11N 11°51E 264 B2
Koumankou Mali 11°58N 6°6W 262 C3
Koumbia Burkina Faso 11°10N 3°50W 262 C4
Koumbia Guinea 11°48N 13°29W 262 C2
Koumboum Guinea 10°25N 13°0W 262 C2
Koumpenntoum Senegal 13°59N 14°34W 262 C2
Koumra Chad 8°50N 17°35E 259 G3
Koun-Fao Ivory C. 7°30N 3°15W 262 D4
Koundara Guinea 12°29N 13°18W 262 C2
Koundé C.A.R. 6°7N 14°38E 264 A2
Koungheul Senegal 14°0N 14°50W 262 C2
Koungou Mayotte 12°43S 45°12E 272 b
Koungoulou Congo 3°31S 13°20E 264 C2
Kountze U.S.A. 30°22N 94°19W 314 F7
Koupéla Burkina Faso 12°11N 0°21W 263 C4
Kouponia Greece 37°57N 23°47E 112 B2
Kourémalé Mali 11°59N 8°42W 262 C3
Kouri-shima Japan 26°42N 128°1E 288 a
Kouris → Cyprus 34°38N 32°54E 207 F8
Kourizo, P. de Chad 22°28N 15°27E 258 D3
Kourou Fr. Guiana 5°9N 52°39W 329 B7
Kourouba Mali 13°22N 10°57W 262 C2
Koûroudjél Mauritania 16°12N 11°30W 262 B2
Kouroukoto Mali 12°35N 10°5W 262 C2
Kourouma Burkina Faso 11°35N 4°50W 262 C4
Kourouninkoto Mali 13°52N 9°35W 262 C3
Kouroussa Guinea 10°45N 9°45W 262 C3
Koussanar Senegal 13°52N 14°5W 262 C2
Koussané Mali 14°53N 11°14W 262 C2
Koussané Senegal 14°10N 12°22W 262 C2
Kousseri Cameroon 12°0N 14°55E 259 F2
Koutiala Mali 12°25N 5°23W 262 C3
Kouto Ivory C. 9°53N 6°25W 262 D3
Kouts U.S.A. 41°19N 87°2W 311 C9
Kouvé Togo 6°25N 1°25E 263 D5
Kouvola Finland 60°52N 26°43E 188 B4
Kouyi Congo 2°29S 12°25E 264 C2
Kouyou → Congo 0°44S 16°38E 264 C3
Kovačica Serbia 45°5N 20°38E 182 E5
Kovdor Russia 67°34N 30°24E 160 C24
Kovel Ukraine 51°11N 24°38E 177 C13
Kovilpatti India 9°10N 77°50E 245 K3
Kovin Serbia 44°44N 20°59E 182 F5
Kovno = Kaunas Lithuania 54°54N 23°54E 184 D10
Kovrov Russia 56°25N 41°25E 190 B5
Kovur Andhra Pradesh, India 17°3N 81°39E 244 F5
Kovur Andhra Pradesh, India 14°30N 80°1E 245 G5
Kowal Poland 52°32N 19°7E 185 F6
Kowalewo Pomorskie Poland 53°10N 18°52E 185 E5
Kowanyama Australia 15°29S 141°44E 280 B3
Kowanyama ⚙ Australia 15°20S 141°47E 280 B3
Kowlīnī Afghan. 37°39N 65°58E 240 A2
Kowloon China 22°19N 114°11E 122 B1
Kowloon Park Hong Kong, China 122 a2
Kowloon Peak China 22°20N 114°13E 122 A2
Kowloon Res. China 22°21N 114°9E 122 A1
Kowloon Tong China 22°20N 114°10E 122 A2
Kowŏn N. Korea 39°26N 127°14E 224 C3
Kōyama Japan 31°20N 130°56E 222 F2
Koyampattur = Coimbatore India 11°2N 76°59E 245 J3
Köyceğiz Turkey 36°57N 28°40E 205 E10
Köyceğiz Gölü Turkey 36°56N 28°42E 205 E10
Köytendag Turkmenistan 37°30N 66°1E 240 A2
Koyuk U.S.A. 64°56N 161°9W 303 D7
Koyukuk U.S.A. 64°53N 157°42W 303 D8
Koyukuk → U.S.A. 64°55N 157°32W 303 D8
Koyukuk Nat. Wildlife Refuge ⌂ U.S.A. 65°35N 156°30W 303 D8
Koyulhisar Turkey 40°20N 37°52E 212 B7
Koyunyeri Turkey 40°50N 26°26E 203 F10
Koza = Okinawa Japan 26°19N 127°46E 288 a
Kozak Turkey 39°15N 27°6E 205 B9
Kozaklı Turkey 39°13N 34°49E 212 C6
Kozan Turkey 37°26N 35°50E 212 D6
Kozani Greece 40°19N 21°47E 202 F5
Kozani □ Greece 40°18N 21°45E 202 F5
Kozara Bos.-H. 45°0N 17°0E 199 D14
Kozara △ Bos.-H. 45°0N 17°0E 182 F2
Kozarac Bos.-H. 44°58N 16°48E 199 D13
Kozelets Ukraine 50°55N 31°7E 189 G6
Kozelsk Russia 54°2N 35°48E 188 E8
Kozhikode India 11°15N 75°43E 245 J2
Kozhva Russia 65°10N 57°0E 186 A10
Koziegłowy Poland 50°37N 19°8E 185 H6
Kozienice Poland 51°35N 21°34E 185 G8
Kozje Slovenia 46°5N 15°35E 199 B12
Kozloduy Bulgaria 43°45N 23°42E 202 C7
Kozlov = Michurinsk Russia 52°58N 40°27E 190 D5
Kozlovets Bulgaria 43°30N 25°20E 203 C9
Kozlovka Russia 55°52N 48°14E 190 C9
Kozlu Turkey 41°26N 31°45E 212 B4
Kozluk Turkey 38°11N 41°31E 213 C9
Koźmin Poland 51°48N 17°27E 185 G4
Kozmodemyansk Russia 56°20N 46°36E 190 B8
Kōzu-Shima Japan 34°13N 139°10E 223 C11
Kożuchów Poland 51°45N 15°31E 185 G2
Kozyatyn Ukraine 49°45N 28°50E 177 D15
Kozyrevsk Russia 56°3N 159°51E 215 D16
Kpabia Ghana 9°10N 0°20W 263 D4
Kpalimé Togo 6°57N 0°44E 263 D5
Kpandae Ghana 8°30N 0°2W 263 D4
Kpessi Togo 8°4N 1°16E 263 D5
Kra, Isthmus of = Kra, Kho Khot Thailand 10°15N 99°30E 237 G2
Kra, Kho Khot Thailand 10°15N 99°30E 237 G2
Kra Buri Thailand 10°22N 98°46E 237 G2
Kraai → S. Africa 30°40S 26°45E 270 D4
Kraainem Belgium 50°52N 4°28E 116 A2
Krabi Thailand 8°4N 98°55E 237 H2
Kracheh = Kratie Cambodia 12°32N 106°10E 236 F6
Kragan Indonesia 6°43S 111°38E 235 D4
Kragerø Norway 58°52N 9°25E 164 F6
Kragujevac Serbia 44°2N 20°56E 202 B4
Krailling Germany 48°5N 11°25E 131 B1
Krainburg = Kranj Slovenia 46°16N 14°22E 199 B11
Krajenka Poland 53°18N 16°59E 185 E3
Krak Castle = Crac des Chevaliers Syria 34°47N 36°18E 250 D7
Krakatau = Rakata, Pulau Indonesia 6°10S 105°20E 234 D3
Krakatoa = Rakata, Pulau Indonesia 6°10S 105°20E 234 D3
Krakau = Kraków Poland 50°4N 19°57E 185 H6
Krakor Cambodia 12°32N 104°12E 236 F5
Kraków Poland 50°4N 19°57E 185 H6
Kraków ✕ (KRK) Poland 50°5N 19°52E 185 H6
Kraksaan Indonesia 7°43S 113°23E 235 D4
Kralanh Cambodia 13°35N 103°25E 236 F4
Kralendijk Bonaire 12°9N 68°16W 322 h
Králíky Czech Rep. 50°6N 16°45E 181 A9
Kraljevo Serbia 43°44N 20°41E 202 C4
Kralovéhradecký □ Czech Rep. 50°25N 15°50E 180 A8
Královský Chlmec Slovak Rep. 48°27N 22°0E 181 C14
Kralupy nad Vltavou Czech Rep. 50°13N 14°20E 180 A7
Kramatorsk Ukraine 48°50N 37°30E 189 H9
Kramfors Sweden 62°55N 17°48E 162 B11
Kramis, C. Algeria 36°26N 0°45E 261 A5
Krampnitz Germany 52°27N 13°3E 115 B1
Krampnitzsee Germany 52°27N 13°3E 115 B1
Krania Greece 39°53N 21°18E 202 G5
Krania Elasonas Greece 39°57N 22°2E 204 B4
Kranidi Greece 37°20N 23°10E 204 D5
Kranj Slovenia 46°16N 14°22E 199 B11
Kranji Industrial Estate Singapore 1°26N 103°45E 138 A2
Kranji Res. Singapore 1°26N 103°44E 138 A2
Kranjska Gora Slovenia 46°29N 13°48E 199 B10
Krankskop S. Africa 28°0S 30°47E 271 C5
Kranz = Zelenogradsk Russia 54°53N 20°29E 184 D7
Krapina Croatia 46°10N 15°52E 199 B12
Krapina → Croatia 45°50N 15°50E 199 C12
Krapkowice Poland 50°29N 17°56E 185 H4
Krappitz = Krapkowice Poland 50°29N 17°56E 185 H4
Kras Croatia 45°35N 14°0E 199 C10
Krasavino Russia 60°58N 46°29E 186 B8
Krasieo Res. Thailand 14°49N 99°30E 236 E2
Kraskino Russia 42°44N 130°48E 220 C5
Krāslava Latvia 55°54N 27°10E 188 E4
Kraslice Czech Rep. 50°19N 12°31E 180 A5
Krasnaya Gorbatka Russia 55°52N 41°45E 190 C5
Krasnaya Polyana Russia 43°40N 40°13E 191 J5
Krasnaya Sloboda = Krasnoslobodsk Russia 48°42N 44°33E 191 F7
Krasne Ukraine 46°7N 29°15E 183 D14
Krasni Okny Ukraine 47°32N 29°27E 183 C14
Kraśnik Poland 50°55N 22°15E 185 H9
Krasno-Presnenskaya Russia 55°45N 37°32E 129 B2
Krasnoarmeisk Ukraine 48°18N 37°11E 189 H9
Krasnoarmeysk = Tayynsha Kazakhstan 53°50N 69°45E 217 B7
Krasnoarmeysk Russia 51°0N 45°42E 190 E7
Krasnoarmeyskiy Russia 47°0N 42°12E 191 G6
Krasnoarmeysky Rudnik = Dobropole Ukraine 48°25N 37°2E 189 H9
Krasnobrod Poland 50°33N 23°12E 185 H10
Krasnodar Russia 45°5N 39°0E 191 H4
Krasnodar □ Russia 46°30N 39°30E 191 G4
Krasnodarskoye Vdkhr. Russia 45°1N 39°23E 191 H4
Krasnodon Ukraine 48°17N 39°44E 189 H10
Krasnogorskiy Russia 56°10N 48°28E 190 B9
Krasnograd = Krasnohrad Ukraine 49°27N 35°27E 189 H8
Krasnogvardeysk = Gatchina Russia 59°35N 30°9E 188 C6
Krasnogvardeysk Ukraine 45°32N 34°16E 189 K8
Krasnogvardeyskoye Russia 45°52N 41°33E 191 H5
Krasnohrad Ukraine 49°27N 35°27E 189 H8
Krasnokamensk Russia 50°3N 118°0E 215 D12
Krasnokamsk Russia 58°4N 55°48E 186 C10
Krasnokokshaysk = Yoshkar Ola Russia 56°38N 47°55E 190 B8
Krasnokutsk Ukraine 50°10N 34°50E 189 G8
Krasnolesnyy Russia 51°53N 39°35E 189 G10
Krasnoperekopsk Ukraine 46°0N 33°54E 189 J7
Krasnorechenskiy Russia 44°41N 135°14E 220 B7
Krasnoselkup Russia 65°20N 82°10E 214 C9
Krasnoslobodsk Mordvinia, Russia 54°25N 43°45E 190 C6
Krasnoslobodsk Volgograd, Russia 48°42N 44°33E 191 F7
Krasnoturinsk Russia 59°46N 60°12E 186 C11
Krasnoufimsk Russia 56°36N 57°38E 186 C10
Krasnouralsk Russia 58°21N 60°3E 186 C11
Krasnovishersk Russia 60°23N 57°3E 186 B10
Krasnovodsk = Türkmenbashi Turkmenistan 40°5N 53°5E 247 A7
Krasnoyarsk Russia 56°8N 93°0E 215 D10
Krasnoyarskoye Russia 54°31N 21°56E 184 D8
Krasnoyarskoye Vdkhr. Russia 56°0N 92°30E 215 D10
Krasnoye = Krasnyy Russia 54°25N 31°30E 188 E6
Krasnoye = Ulan Erge Russia 46°19N 44°53E 191 G7
Krasnoyilsk Ukraine 47°59N 25°38E 183 C10
Krasnozavodsk Russia 56°27N 38°25E 188 D10
Krasnoznamensk Russia 54°57N 22°30E 184 D9
Krasny = Kyzyl Russia 51°50N 94°30E 217 B12
Krasny = Mozhga Russia 56°26N 52°15E 190 B11
Krasny Boyevik = Kotovsk Russia 52°36N 41°32E 190 D5
Krasny Sulin Russia 47°52N 40°8E 191 G5
Krasnystaw Poland 50°57N 23°5E 185 H10
Krasnyy Russia 54°25N 31°30E 188 E6
Krasnyy Kholm Russia 58°10N 37°10E 188 C9
Krasnyy Kut Russia 50°50N 47°0E 190 E8
Krasnyy Liman Ukraine 48°58N 37°50E 189 H9
Krasnyy Luch Ukraine 48°13N 39°0E 189 H10
Krasnyy Profintern Russia 57°45N 40°27E 188 D11
Krasnyy Yar Astrakhan, Russia 46°43N 48°23E 191 G9
Krasnyy Yar Samara, Russia 53°30N 50°22E 190 D10
Krasnyy Yar Volgograd, Russia 50°42N 44°45E 190 E7
Krasnyye Baki Russia 57°8N 45°10E 190 B7
Krasnyyoskolske Vdskh. Ukraine 49°27N 37°40E 189 H9
Kraszna → Hungary 48°4N 22°20E 182 B7
Kratie Cambodia 12°32N 106°10E 236 F6
Kratke Ra. Papua N. G. 6°45S 146°0E 286 D4
Kratovo Macedonia 42°6N 22°10E 202 D6
Krau Indonesia 3°19S 140°5E 231 E10
Kraulshavn = Nuussauq Greenland 74°8N 57°3W 154 C5
Kravanh, Chuor Phnum Cambodia 12°0N 103°32E 237 G4
Krč Czech Rep. 50°2N 14°26E 135 B2
Krefeld Germany 51°20N 6°33E 178 D2
Kremaston, L. Greece 38°52N 21°30E 204 C3
Kremen Croatia 44°28N 15°53E 199 D12
Kremenchuk Ukraine 49°5N 33°25E 189 H7
Kremenchuksk Vdskh. Ukraine 49°20N 32°30E 189 H7
Kremenets Ukraine 50°8N 25°43E 177 C13
Kremennaya Ukraine 49°1N 38°10E 189 H10
Kremges = Svitlovodsk Ukraine 49°2N 33°13E 189 H7
Kremlin Moscow, Russia 129 c2
Kremmen Germany 52°45N 13°1E 178 C9
Kremmling U.S.A. 40°4N 106°24W 304 F10
Kremnica Slovak Rep. 48°45N 18°50E 181 C11
Krems Austria 48°25N 15°36E 180 C8
Kremsmünster Austria 48°3N 14°8E 180 C7
Krenau = Chrzanów Poland 50°10N 19°21E 185 H6
Krestena Greece 37°35N 21°37E 204 D3
Krestovskiye, Ostrov Russia 59°57N 30°14E 137 B1
Kretinga Lithuania 55°53N 21°15E 184 C8
Krettamia Algeria 28°47N 3°27W 260 C4
Krettsy Russia 58°15N 32°30E 188 C7
Kreuzberg Bayern, Germany 50°22N 9°58E 179 E5
Kreuzberg Berlin, Germany 52°30N 13°24E 115 A3
Kreuzburg = Kluczbork Poland 50°58N 18°12E 185 H5
Kreuztal Germany 50°57N 8°0E 178 E4
Kria Vrisi Greece 40°41N 22°18E 202 F6
Kribi Cameroon 2°57N 9°56E 263 E6
Krichem Bulgaria 42°8N 24°28E 203 D8
Krichev = Krychaw Belarus 53°40N 31°41E 177 B16
Kril'on, Mys Russia 45°53N 142°5E 220 B11
Krim Slovenia 45°53N 14°30E 199 C11
Krim-Krim Chad 9°0N 15°24E 259 G3
Krindachyovka = Krasnyy Luch Ukraine 48°13N 39°0E 189 H10
Krios, Akra Greece 35°13N 23°34E 207 E4
Krishna → India 15°57N 80°59E 245 G5
Krishnagiri India 12°32N 78°16E 245 H4
Krishnanagar India 23°24N 88°33E 243 H13
Krishnaraja Sagar India 12°20N 76°30E 245 H3
Kristdala Sweden 57°24N 16°13E 163 G10
Kristians = Oppland □ Norway 61°15N 9°40E 164 C6
Kristiansand Norway 58°8N 8°1E 164 F5
Kristianstad Sweden 56°2N 14°9E 163 H8
Kristiansund Norway 63°7N 7°45E 164 A4
Kristiinankaupunki Finland 62°16N 21°21E 160 E19
Kristinehamn Sweden 59°18N 14°7E 162 E8
Kristinestad = Kristiinankaupunki Finland 62°16N 21°21E 160 E19
Kristinopol = Chervonohrad Ukraine 50°25N 24°10E 177 C13
Krithoti, Akra Greece 38°30N 21°2E 207 B3
Kriti Greece 35°15N 25°0E 207 E6
Kritsa Greece 35°10N 25°41E 207 E6
Kritzendorf Austria 48°19N 16°18E 142 A1
Kriva → Macedonia 42°5N 21°47E 202 D5
Kriva Palanka Macedonia 42°11N 22°19E 202 D6
Krivaja → Bos.-H. 44°27N 18°9E 182 F3
Krivelj Serbia 44°10N 22°5E 202 B6
Křivoklátsko ⌂ Czech Rep. 50°1N 13°51E 180 A6
Krivoy Rog = Kryvyy Rih Ukraine 47°51N 33°20E 189 J7
Križevci Croatia 46°3N 16°32E 199 B13
Krk Croatia 45°8N 14°40E 199 C11
Krka → Slovenia 45°50N 15°30E 199 C12
Krka △ Croatia 43°53N 15°56E 199 E12
Krkonoše Czech Rep. 50°50N 15°35E 180 A8
Krkonoše △ Czech Rep. 50°43N 15°39E 180 A8
Krnjaja = Kljajićevo Serbia 45°45N 19°17E 182 E4
Krnov Czech Rep. 50°5N 17°40E 181 A10
Krobia Poland 51°47N 16°59E 185 G3
Krøderen Norway 60°9N 9°49E 164 D6
Krokees Greece 36°53N 22°32E 204 E4
Krokek Sweden 58°40N 16°24E 163 F10
Krokodil = Umgwenya → Mozam. 25°14S 32°18E 271 C5
Krokom Sweden 63°20N 14°30E 162 A8
Krokowa Poland 54°47N 18°9E 184 D5
Króksfjarðarnes Iceland 65°27N 21°56W 155 B5
Krokstadelva Norway 59°56N 10°1E 164 E7
Krolevets Ukraine 51°35N 33°20E 189 G7
Królewska Huta = Chorzów Poland 50°18N 18°57E 185 H5
Kroměříž Czech Rep. 49°18N 17°21E 181 B10
Krompachy Slovak Rep. 48°54N 20°52E 181 C13
Kromy Russia 52°48N 35°48E 189 F8
Kronach Germany 50°14N 11°19E 179 E7
Kronau = Kranjska Gora Slovenia 46°29N 13°48E 199 B10
Krong Kaoh Kong Cambodia 11°37N 102°59E 237 G4
Kronobergs län □ Sweden 56°45N 14°30E 163 H8
Kronprins Christian Land Greenland 80°30N 22°0W 154 A8
Kronprins Frederik Land Greenland 81°0N 45°0W 154 A6
Kronprins Olav Kyst Antarctica 69°0S 42°0E 151 C5
Kronprinsesse Märtha Kyst Antarctica 73°30S 10°0W 151 D2
Kronshtadt Russia 59°57N 29°51E 188 C5
Kronstadt = Braşov Romania 45°38N 25°35E 183 E10
Kroonstad S. Africa 27°43S 27°19E 270 C4
Kröpelin Germany 54°4N 11°47E 178 A7
Kropotkin Russia 45°28N 40°28E 191 H5
Kropp Germany 54°24N 9°31E 178 A5
Krosna Lithuania 54°23N 23°33E 184 D10
Krośniewice Poland 52°15N 19°11E 185 F6
Krosno Poland 49°42N 21°46E 185 J8
Krosno Odrzańskie Poland 52°3N 15°7E 185 F2
Krotoszyn Poland 51°42N 17°23E 185 G4
Krotovka Russia 53°18N 51°10E 190 D10
Krousonas Greece 35°13N 24°59E 207 E5
Krrabë Albania 41°13N 20°0E 202 E3
Krško Slovenia 45°57N 15°30E 199 C12
Krstača Serbia 42°57N 20°8E 202 D4
Kruger △ S. Africa 24°50S 26°10E 271 B4
Krugersdorp S. Africa 26°5S 27°46E 271 C4
Krui Indonesia 5°10S 103°55E 234 D2
Kruisfontein S. Africa 33°59S 24°43E 270 D3
Krujë Albania 41°32N 19°46E 202 E3
Krulevshchina = Krulyewshchyna Belarus 55°5N 27°45E 188 E4
Krulyewshchyna Belarus 55°5N 27°45E 188 E4
Krumbach Germany 48°13N 10°22E 179 G6
Krumë Albania 42°14N 20°28E 202 D4
Krummau = Český Krumlov Czech Rep. 48°43N 14°21E 180 C7
Krumme Lanke Germany 52°27N 13°14E 115 B2
Krummensee Germany 52°35N 13°41E 115 A5
Krummhübel = Karpacz Poland 50°46N 15°46E 185 H2
Krumovgrad Bulgaria 41°29N 25°38E 203 E9
Krung Thep = Bangkok Thailand 13°45N 100°35E 113 B2
Krupanj Serbia 44°25N 19°22E 202 B3
Krupina Slovak Rep. 48°22N 19°5E 181 C12
Krupinica → Slovak Rep. 48°4N 18°55E 181 C11
Krupki Belarus 54°19N 29°8E 177 A15
Krusboda Sweden 59°13N 18°14E 139 B3
Krusenstern, C. U.S.A. 67°8N 163°45W 303 C7
Kruševac Serbia 43°35N 21°28E 202 C5
Kruševo Macedonia 41°23N 21°19E 202 E5
Krushchyov = Svitlovodsk Ukraine 49°2N 33°13E 189 H7
Krushë e Madhe Kosovo 42°19N 20°39E 202 D4
Krushelnyksya Ukraine 49°7N 23°29E 185 J10
Kruszwica Poland 52°40N 18°20E 185 F5
Krychaw Belarus 53°40N 31°41E 177 B16
Krymsk Russia 44°50N 38°0E 189 K10
Krymskiy Poluostrov = Krymskyy Pivostriv Ukraine 45°0N 34°0E 189 K8
Krymskyy Pivostriv Ukraine 45°0N 34°0E 189 K8
Krynica Poland 49°25N 20°57E 185 J7
Krynica Morska Poland 54°23N 19°28E 184 D6
Krynki Poland 53°17N 23°43E 185 E10
Krynychne Ukraine 45°32N 28°40E 183 E13
Kryvyy Rih Ukraine 47°51N 33°20E 189 J7
Kryzhopil Ukraine 48°23N 28°53E 183 B13
Krzemieniec = Kremenets Ukraine 50°8N 25°43E 177 C13
Krzepice Poland 50°58N 18°50E 185 H5
Krzeszów Poland 50°24N 22°21E 185 H9
Krzna → Poland 52°8N 23°32E 185 F10
Krzywiń Poland 51°58N 16°50E 185 G3
Krzyż Wielkopolski Poland 52°52N 16°0E 185 F2
Ksabi Morocco 32°51N 4°13W 260 B4
Ksar Chellala Algeria 35°13N 2°19E 261 A5
Ksar el Boukhari Algeria 35°51N 2°52E 261 A5
Ksar el Kebir Morocco 35°0N 6°0W 260 B3
Ksar es Souk = Er Rachidia Morocco 31°58N 4°20W 260 B4
Ksar Rhilane Tunisia 33°0N 9°39E 258 B1
Książ Wielkopolski Poland 52°4N 17°14E 185 F4
Ksour, Mts. des Algeria 32°45N 0°30W 261 B4
Kstovo Russia 56°12N 44°13E 190 B7
Ku, W. el → Sudan 13°37N 25°15E 257 E2
Ku-Ring-Gai Chase △ Australia 33°39S 151°14E 283 B9
Ku Tree Res. U.S.A. 21°30N 157°59W 302 J14
Kuah Malaysia 6°19N 99°51E 237 J2
Kuala Indonesia 2°55N 105°47E 234 B3
Kuala Belait Malaysia 4°35N 114°11E 235 B4
Kuala Berang Malaysia 5°5N 103°1E 237 K4
Kuala Dungun = Dungun Malaysia 4°45N 103°25E 237 K4
Kuala Kangsar Malaysia 4°46N 100°56E 237 K3
Kuala Kelawang Malaysia 2°56N 102°5E 237 L4
Kuala Kerai Malaysia 5°30N 102°12E 237 K4
Kuala Kubu Bharu Malaysia 3°34N 101°39E 237 L3
Kuala Lipis Malaysia 4°10N 102°3E 237 K4
Kuala Lumpur Malaysia 3°9N 101°41E 237 L3
Kuala Nerang Malaysia 6°16N 100°37E 237 J3
Kuala Pilah Malaysia 2°45N 102°15E 237 L4
Kuala Rompin Malaysia 2°49N 103°29E 237 L4
Kuala Selangor Malaysia 3°20N 101°15E 237 L3
Kuala Sepetang Malaysia 4°49N 100°28E 237 K3
Kuala Terengganu Malaysia 5°20N 103°8E 237 K4
Kualajelai Indonesia 2°58S 110°46E 235 C4
Kualakapuas Indonesia 2°55S 114°20E 235 C4
Kualakurun Indonesia 1°10S 113°50E 235 C4
Kualapembuang Indonesia 3°14S 112°38E 235 C4
Kualapesaguan Indonesia 2°1S 110°7E 235 C4
Kualapu'u U.S.A. 21°9N 157°2W 302 B4
Kualasimpang Indonesia 4°17N 98°3E 234 B1
Kualatungkal Indonesia 0°49S 103°28E 234 C2
Kualoa Pt. U.S.A. 21°31N 157°50W 302 J14
Kuamat Malaysia 5°13N 117°30E 235 A5
Kuan Shan Taiwan 23°14N 120°54E 225 C2
Kuanao Taiwan 24°31N 118°24E 225 a
Kuancheng China 40°37N 118°30E 227 D10
Kuandang Indonesia 0°56N 123°1E 231 D6
Kuandian China 40°45N 124°45E 224 B2
Kuangchou = Guangzhou China 23°6N 113°13E 121 B2
Kuangfu Taiwan 23°40N 121°25E 225 C3
Kuanhsi Taiwan 24°48N 121°10E 225 B3
Kuanmiao Taiwan 22°58N 120°19E 225 D2
Kuanshan Taiwan 23°3N 121°9E 225 C3
Kuantan Malaysia 3°49N 103°20E 237 L4
Kuanyin Ilan, Taiwan 24°23N 121°46E 225 B3
Kuanyin Taoyüan, Taiwan 25°2N 121°4E 225 A3
Kuapä Pond U.S.A. 21°17N 157°43W 302 K14
Kuapnit Balinsasayao △ Phil. 10°53N 124°55E 233 F5
Kuba = Quba Azerbaijan 41°21N 48°32E 191 K9
Kubah △ Malaysia 1°35N 110°9E 235 B4
Kuban → Russia 45°20N 37°30E 189 K9
Kuban Depression = Prikubanskaya Nizmennost Russia 45°39N 38°33E 191 H4
Kubaysah Iraq 33°35N 42°37E 213 G10
Kubenskoye, Ozero Russia 59°40N 39°25E 188 C10
Kuberle = Krasnoarmeyskiy Russia 47°0N 42°12E 191 G6
Kubokawa = Shimanto Japan 33°12N 133°8E 222 D5
Kubor, Mt. Papua N. G. 6°10S 144°44E 286 D3
Kubrat Bulgaria 43°49N 26°31E 203 C10
Kubu Indonesia 8°16S 115°35E 231 J18
Kubumesaai Indonesia 1°31N 115°6E 235 B5
Kubutambahan Indonesia 8°5S 115°10E 231 J18
Kucar, Tanjung Indonesia 8°39S 114°34E 231 K18
Kučevo Serbia 44°30N 21°40E 202 B5
Kuchaman India 27°13N 74°47E 242 F6
Kuchchaveli Sri Lanka 8°49N 81°6E 245 K5
Kuchenspitze Austria 47°7N 10°12E 180 D3
Kuchinda India 21°44N 84°21E 243 J11
Kuching Malaysia 1°33N 110°25E 235 B4
Kuchino-eruba-Jima Japan 30°28N 130°12E 221 J5
Kuchino-Shima Japan 29°57N 129°55E 221 K4
Kuchinotsu Japan 32°36N 130°11E 222 E2
Kuchl Austria 47°37N 13°9E 180 D6
Kūchnay Darvīshān Afghan. 30°59N 64°10E 240 C2
Kuchurhan → Ukraine 46°33N 29°57E 183 D14
Kucing = Kuching Malaysia 1°33N 110°25E 235 B4
Kuçovë Albania 40°47N 19°57E 202 F3
Küçükbahçe Turkey 38°33N 26°24E 205 C8
Küçükköy Balıkesir, Turkey 39°16N 26°42E 205 B8
Küçükköy İstanbul, Turkey 41°3N 28°52E 122 B1
Küçükkuyu Turkey 39°32N 26°36E 205 B8
Küçükmenderes → Turkey 37°57N 27°16E 205 D9
Küçüksu Turkey 41°5N 29°5E 122 B2
Kud → Pakistan 26°5N 66°20E 242 F2
Kuda India 23°10N 71°15E 242 H4
Kuda Indonesia 1°1N 112°58E 235 B4
Kudahuvadhoo Maldives 2°40N 72°54E 272 d
Kudahuvadhoo Channel Maldives 2°40N 73°0E 272 d
Kudaka-shima Japan 26°9N 127°53E 288 a
Kudal India 16°2N 73°41E 245 F1
Kudalier → India 18°35N 79°48E 244 E4
Kudamatsu Japan 34°0N 131°52E 222 D3
Kudankita Tokyo, Japan 140 a3
Kudarebe Aruba 12°37N 70°4W 322 f
Kudat Malaysia 6°55N 116°55E 235 A5
Kudirkos Naumiestis Lithuania 54°46N 22°53E 184 D9
Kudowa-Zdrój Poland 50°27N 16°15E 185 H3
Kudremukh India 13°15N 75°20E 245 H2
Kudrovo Russia 59°54N 30°30E 137 B3
Kudus Indonesia 6°48S 110°51E 235 D4
Kudymkar Russia 59°1N 54°39E 186 C9
Kueishan Tao Taiwan 24°51N 121°57E 225 B3
Kueiyang = Guiyang China 26°32N 106°40E 228 D6
Kufra Oasis = Al Kufrah Libya 24°17N 23°15E 258 D4
Kufstein Austria 47°35N 12°11E 180 D5
Kugaaruk = Pelly Bay Canada 68°38N 89°50W 295 D14
Kugluktuk Canada 67°50N 115°5W 294 D8
Kugong I. Canada 56°18N 79°50W 298 A4
Kūh Dasht Iran 33°32N 47°36E 213 F12
Kūh-e Sorkh Iran 35°30N 58°45E 216 E5
Kūhak Iran 27°12N 63°10E 240 D1
Kuhan Pakistan 28°19N 67°14E 242 E2
Kūhbonān Iran 31°23N 56°19E 247 D8
Kūhestak Iran 26°47N 57°2E 247 E8
Kūhestān Afghan. 34°39N 61°12E 240 B1
Kuhin Iran 36°22N 49°40E 247 B6
Kūhīrī Iran 26°55N 61°2E 247 E9
Kūhiston-Badakhshon □ Tajikistan 38°30N 73°0E 217 E8
Kuhmo Finland 64°7N 29°31E 160 D23
Kuhn Chae △ Thailand 19°8N 99°24E 236 C2
Kuhnsdorf Austria 46°37N 14°38E 180 E7
Kūhpāyeh Eşfahan, Iran 32°44N 52°20E 247 C7
Kūhpāyeh Kermān, Iran 30°35N 57°15E 247 D8
Kūhrān, Kūh-e Iran 26°46N 58°12E 247 E8
Kui Buri Thailand 12°3N 99°52E 237 F2
Kuiburi △ Thailand 12°10N 99°37E 237 F2
Kuichong China 22°38N 114°25E 219 a
Kuiseb → Namibia 22°59S 14°31E 270 B1
Kuito Angola 12°22S 16°55E 265 E3
Kuiu I. U.S.A. 57°45N 134°10W 296 B2
Kujang N. Korea 39°57N 126°1E 224 C3
Kujawsko-Pomorskie □ Poland 53°20N 18°30E 184 E5
Kuji Japan 40°11N 141°46E 220 D10
Kujū-San Japan 33°5N 131°15E 222 D3
Kuk Papua N. G. 5°47S 144°19E 286 C3
Kukarka = Sovetsk Russia 57°38N 48°53E 190 B9
Kukava Ukraine 48°37N 27°43E 183 B12
Kukavica Serbia 42°48N 21°57E 202 D5
Kukawa Nigeria 12°58N 13°27E 263 C7
Kuk'eng Taiwan 23°38N 120°33E 225 C2
Kukës Albania 42°5N 20°27E 202 D4
Kuki Japan 36°4N 139°40E 223 A11
Kukipi Papua N. G. 8°10S 146°6E 286 E4
Kukmor Russia 56°11N 50°54E 190 B10
Kükong = Shaoguan China 24°48N 113°35E 229 E9
Kuku Pt. Wake I. 19°18N 166°34E 302 b
Kukuan Taiwan 24°17N 121°2E 225 B3

Kukuihaele U.S.A. 20°5N 155°35W 302 C6
Kukup Malaysia 1°20N 103°27E 237 d
Kukup, Pulau Malaysia 1°18N 103°25E 237 d
Kukvidze Russia 50°40N 43°10E 190 E6
Kula Bulgaria 43°52N 22°36E 202 C6
Kula Serbia 45°37N 19°32E 182 E4
Kula Turkey 38°32N 28°40E 205 C10
Kula Gulf Solomon Is. 8°5S 157°18E 287 M9
K'ula Kangri Asia 28°14N 90°36E 241 A3
K'ula Shan Bhutan 28°14N 90°36E 241 A3
Kulachi Pakistan 31°56N 70°27E 242 D4
Kulai Malaysia 1°44N 103°35E 237 M4
Kulal, Mt. Kenya 2°43N 36°56E 266 D4
Kulaly, Ostrov = Kulaly Aral
Kazakhstan 45°0N 50°5E 191 H10
Kulaly Aral Kazakhstan 45°0N 50°5E 191 H10
Kulasekarappattinam India 8°20N 78°5E 245 K4
Kulassein I. Phil. 6°25N 120°41E 233 H3
Kulaura Bangla. 24°32N 92°3E 241 C4
Kulautuva Lithuania 54°56N 23°36E 184 D10
Kuldīga Latvia 56°58N 21°59E 184 B8
Kuldīga □ Latvia 56°55N 22°0E 184 B8
Kuldja = Yining China 43°58N 81°10E 217 D10
Kuldu Sudan 12°50N 28°30E 257 E2
Kulebaki Russia 55°22N 42°25E 190 C6
Kulen Cambodia 13°50N 104°40E 236 F5
Kulen Vakuf Bos.-H. 44°35N 16°2E 199 D13
Kulgam India 33°36N 75°2E 243 C6
Kulgera Australia 25°50S 133°18E 280 D1
Kulhudhuffushi Maldives 6°37N 73°3E 272 d
Kulim Malaysia 5°22N 100°34E 237 K3
Kulin Australia 32°40S 118°2E 279 F2
Kulittalai India 10°55N 78°25E 245 J4
Kulkayu = Hartley Bay
Canada 53°25N 129°15W 296 C3
Kullen Sweden 56°18N 12°26E 163 H6
Kullu India 31°58N 77°6E 242 D7
Kulmbach Germany 50°6N 11°26E 179 E7
Kŭlob Tajikistan 37°55N 69°50E 217 E7
Kulosaari Finland 60°11N 25°0E 121 B3
Kulp Turkey 38°29N 41°2E 213 C9
Kulpawn → Ghana 10°20N 1°5W 263 D4
Kulsary = Qulsary
Kazakhstan 46°59N 54°1E 187 E9
Kulti India 23°43N 86°50E 243 H12
Kulu Turkey 39°5N 33°4E 212 C5
Kulumadau Papua N. G. 9°3S 152°43E 286 E7
Kulunda Russia 52°35N 78°57E 217 B9
Kulundinskoye, Ozero
Russia 53°0N 79°36E 217 B9
Kulungar Afghan. 34°0N 69°2E 242 C3
Kŭlvand Iran 31°21N 54°35E 247 D7
Kulwin Australia 35°2S 142°42E 282 C5
Kulyab = Kŭlob Tajikistan 37°55N 69°50E 217 E7
Kuma Japan 33°39N 132°54E 222 D4
Kuma → Russia 44°55N 47°0E 191 H8
Kumafşarı Turkey 37°19N 29°32E 205 D11
Kumaganum Nigeria 13°8N 10°38E 263 C7
Kumagaya Japan 36°9N 139°22E 223 A11
Kumai Indonesia 2°44S 111°43E 235 C4
Kumai, Teluk Indonesia 3°0S 111°45E 235 C4
Kumalar Dağı Turkey 38°15N 30°20E 205 C12
Kumamba, Kepulauan
Indonesia 1°36S 138°45E 231 E9
Kumamoto Japan 32°45N 130°45E 222 E2
Kumamoto □ Japan 32°55N 130°55E 222 E2
Kumano Japan 33°54N 136°5E 223 D8
Kumano-Nada Japan 33°47N 136°20E 223 D8
Kumanovo Macedonia 42°9N 21°42E 202 D5
Kumar → Afghan. 34°30N 70°28E 240 B3
Kumara N.Z. 42°37S 171°12E 285 C6
Kumarina Roadhouse
Australia 24°41S 119°32E 279 D2
Kumarkhali Bangla. 23°51N 89°15E 241 D2
Kumasi Ghana 6°41N 1°38W 262 D4
Kumba Cameroon 4°36N 9°24E 263 E6
Kumbağ Turkey 40°51N 27°27E 203 F11
Kumbakonam India 10°58N 79°25E 245 J4
Kumbarilla Australia 27°15S 150°55E 281 D5
Kumbatine △ Australia 31°8S 152°35E 283 A10
Kumbhraj India 24°22N 77°3E 242 G7
Kumbia Australia 26°41S 151°39E 281 D5
Kumbo Cameroon 6°15N 10°36E 263 D7
Kumbukkan Oya →
Sri Lanka 6°35N 81°40E 245 L5
Kŭmch'on N. Korea 38°10N 126°29E 224 C3
Kumdah Si. Arabia 20°23N 45°5E 248 B4
Kume-Shima Japan 26°20N 126°47E 221 L3
Kumeny Russia 58°10N 49°47E 190 A9
Kumertau Russia 52°45N 55°57E 186 D10
Kumharsain India 31°19N 77°27E 242 D7
Kumi Uganda 1°30N 33°58E 268 B3
Kumkale Turkey 39°59N 26°11E 203 G10
Kumla Örebro, Sweden 59°8N 15°10E 162 E9
Kumla Stockholm, Sweden 59°13N 18°11E 139 B3
Kumlu Turkey 36°21N 36°37E 250 B7
Kumluca Turkey 36°22N 30°20E 205 E12
Kummerower See
Germany 53°49N 12°51E 178 B8
Kumo Nigeria 10°1N 11°12E 263 C7
Kumo älv = Kokemäenjoki →
Finland 61°32N 21°44E 188 B1
Kumon Bum Burma 26°30N 97°15E 241 B6
Kumotori-Yama Japan 35°51N 138°57E 223 B10
Kumta India 14°29N 74°25E 245 G2
Kumtag Shamo China 39°40N 92°0E 218 D7
Kumukahi, C. U.S.A. 19°31N 154°49W 302 D7
Kumusi → Papua N. G. 8°16S 148°13E 286 E5
Kumyalı = Koma Tou Yialou
Cyprus 35°25N 34°8E 207 E10
Kumylzhenskaya Russia 49°51N 42°38E 190 F6
Kuna U.S.A. 43°30N 116°25W 304 E5
Kunágota Hungary 46°26N 21°3E 182 D6
Kunak Malaysia 4°41N 118°15E 235 B5
Kunashir, Ostrov Russia 44°0N 146°0E 215 E15
Kunchaung Burma 23°50N 96°35E 241 D6
Kunchha Nepal 28°8N 84°20E 243 E11
Kunda Estonia 59°30N 26°34E 188 C4
Kunda India 25°43N 81°31E 243 G9
Kundar → Pakistan 31°56N 69°19E 242 D3
Kundelungu △
Dem. Rep. of the Congo 10°30S 27°40E 269 E2
Kundelungu Ouest △
Dem. Rep. of the Congo 9°55S 27°17E 269 D2
Kundian Pakistan 32°27N 71°28E 242 C4
Kundiawa Papua N. G. 6°2S 145°1E 286 D3
Kundla India 21°21N 71°25E 242 J4
Kundur Indonesia 0°45N 103°25E 234 B2
Kunene □ Namibia 20°0S 14°0E 270 A1
Kung, Ao Thailand 8°5N 98°24E 237 a
Kunga → Bangla. 21°46N 89°30E 241 E2
Kungälv Sweden 57°53N 11°59E 163 G5
Kungens kurva Sweden 59°15N 17°53E 139 B1
Kunghit I. Canada 52°6N 131°3W 296 C2
Kungkuan Taiwan 24°35N 120°44E 225 B2
Kungliao Taiwan 25°1N 121°54E 225 A3
Kungliga Slottet Stockholm, Sweden 139 b2
Kungrad = Qŭnghirot
Uzbekistan 43°2N 58°50E 216 D5
Kungsängen Sweden 59°29N 17°45E 162 E11
Kungsbacka Sweden 57°30N 12°5E 163 G6
Kungsgården Sweden 60°37N 16°35E 162 D10
Kungshamn Sweden 58°22N 11°15E 163 F5
Kungshatt Sweden 59°17N 17°53E 139 B1
Kungsholmen Sweden 59°20N 18°2E 139 A2
Kungsör Sweden 59°25N 16°5E 162 E10
Kungsuliao Taiwan 24°37N 120°45E 225 B2
Kungu
Dem. Rep. of the Congo 2°47N 19°12E 264 B3
Kungur Russia 57°25N 56°57E 186 C10
Kungurri Australia 21°4S 148°45E 280 b
Kungyangon Burma 16°27N 96°20E 241 G6
Kunhar → Pakistan 34°20N 73°30E 243 B5
Kunhegyes Hungary 47°22N 20°36E 182 C5
Kunia U.S.A. 21°28N 158°4W 302 K13
Kunigami Japan 26°46N 128°12E 288 a
Kunimi-Dake Japan 32°33N 131°1E 222 E3
Kuningan Jakarta,
Indonesia 6°13S 106°49E 122 B1
Kuningan Jawa Barat,
Indonesia 6°59S 108°29E 235 D3
Kunisaki Japan 33°33N 131°45E 222 D3
Kunitachi Japan 35°41N 139°27E 140 A1
Kunjirap Daban Pakistan 36°52N 75°27E 240 A4
Kunlara Australia 34°54S 139°55E 282 C3
Kunlong Burma 23°20N 98°50E 228 F2
Kunlun Shan Asia 36°0N 86°30E 217 E11
Kunlun Shankou China 35°38N 94°4E 218 D7
Kunmadaras Hungary 47°28N 20°45E 182 C5
Kunming China 25°1N 102°41E 228 E4
Kunming Hu China 39°59N 116°13E 114 B1
Kunmunya ⊘ Australia 15°26S 124°42E 278 C3
Kunnamkulam India 10°38N 76°7E 245 J3
Kunów Poland 50°57N 21°17E 185 H8
Kunratice Czech Rep. 50°0N 14°28E 135 B2
Kunshan China 31°22N 120°58E 229 B13
Kunsthistorischesmuseum
Vienna, Austria 142 b1
Kunszentmárton Hungary 46°50N 20°20E 182 D5
Kunszentmiklós Hungary 47°2N 19°8E 182 C4
Kuntaur Senegal 13°40N 14°48W 262 C2
Kunua Papua N. G. 5°46S 154°43E 286 C8
Kununurra Australia 15°40S 128°50E 278 C4
Kunwari → India 26°26N 79°11E 243 F8
Kunya-Urgench = Köneürgench
Turkmenistan 42°19N 59°10E 216 D5
Künzelsau Germany 49°17N 9°42E 179 F5
Kunzulu
Dem. Rep. of the Congo 3°28S 16°12E 264 C3
Kuohsing Taiwan 24°2N 120°51E 225 B2
Kuopio Finland 62°53N 27°35E 160 E22
Kupa → Croatia 45°28N 16°24E 199 C13
Kupang Indonesia 10°19S 123°39E 231 F6
Kupchino Russia 59°50N 30°23E 137 B2
Kupiano Papua N. G. 10°4S 148°14E 286 F5
Kūpikipikiʻō Pt. U.S.A. 21°15N 157°47W 302 K14
Kupino Russia 54°21N 77°16E 217 B9
Kupreanof I. U.S.A. 56°50N 133°30W 296 B2
Kupres Bos.-H. 43°56N 17°15E 182 G2
Kupyansk Ukraine 49°52N 37°35E 189 H9
Kupyansk-Uzlovoi
Ukraine 49°40N 37°43E 189 H9
Kuqa China 41°35N 82°30E 217 D10
Kür → Azerbaijan 39°29N 49°15E 213 C13
Kur → Bhutan 26°50N 91°0E 241 B3
Kür Dili Azerbaijan 39°3N 49°13E 213 C13
Kura = Kür →
Azerbaijan 39°29N 49°15E 213 C13
Kurahashi-Jima Japan 34°8N 132°31E 222 C4
Kuramo Waters Nigeria 6°25N 3°26E 124 B2
Kuranda Australia 16°48S 145°35E 280 B4
Kuranga India 22°4N 69°10E 242 H3
Kurashiki Japan 34°40N 133°50E 222 C5
Kurayn Si. Arabia 27°39N 49°50E 247 E6
Kurayoshi Japan 35°26N 133°50E 222 B5
Kurbağalı → Turkey 40°58N 29°1E 122 C2
Kŭrchatov Kazakhstan 50°45N 78°32E 217 B9
Kürdämir Azerbaijan 40°25N 48°3E 191 K9
Kurdistan Asia 37°20N 43°30E 213 D10
Kurduvadi India 18°8N 75°29E 244 E2
Kŭrdzhali Bulgaria 41°38N 25°21E 203 E9
Kŭrdzhali □ Bulgaria 41°38N 25°21E 203 E9
Kure Japan 34°14N 132°32E 222 C4
Küre Turkey 41°48N 33°43E 212 B5
Küre Dağları Turkey 41°50N 34°10E 212 B6
Kure I. U.S.A. 28°25N 178°25W 302 B4
Kuressaare Estonia 58°15N 22°30E 188 C2
Kurgan Russia 55°26N 65°18E 216 A7
Kurgan-Tyube = Qŭrghonteppa
Tajikistan 37°50N 68°47E 217 E7
Kurganinsk Russia 44°54N 40°34E 191 H5
Kurgannaya = Kurganinsk
Russia 44°54N 40°34E 191 H5
Kuri India 26°37N 70°43E 242 F4
Kuria Maria Is. = Ḩallāniyat, Jazā'ir
al Oman 17°30N 55°58E 249 C6
Kurichchi India 11°36N 77°35E 245 J3
Kuridala Australia 21°16S 140°29E 280 C3
Kurigram Bangla. 25°49N 89°39E 241 C2
Kurihara Japan 38°45N 140°56E 224 E10
Kurikka Finland 62°36N 22°24E 160 E20
Kuril Basin Pac. Oc. 47°0N 150°0E 150 E15
Kuril Is. = Kurilskiye Ostrova
Russia 45°0N 150°0E 215 E16
Kuril-Kamchatka Trench
Pac. Oc. 44°0N 153°0E 288 C7
Kurilsk Russia 45°14N 147°53E 215 E15
Kurilskiye Ostrova Russia 45°0N 150°0E 215 E16
Kurino Japan 31°57N 130°43E 222 F2
Kurinskaya Kosa = Kür Dili
Azerbaijan 39°3N 49°13E 213 C13
Kurisches Haff = Kurshskiy Zaliv
Russia 55°9N 21°6E 184 C8
Kürkçü Turkey 36°34N 33°39E 250 B4
Kurkheda India 20°37N 80°12E 244 D5
Kurkur Egypt 23°50N 32°0E 256 C3
Kurla India 19°4N 72°52E 130 A2
Kurlkuta ⊘ Australia 24°0S 127°5E 278 D4
Kurlovskiy Russia 55°25N 40°40E 190 C5
Kurmuk Sudan 10°33N 34°21E 257 E3
Kurmuri India 19°4N 72°53E 130 A2
Kurnool India 15°45N 78°0E 245 G4
Kuro-Shima Kagoshima,
Japan 30°50N 129°57E 221 J4
Kuro-Shima Okinawa,
Japan 24°14N 124°1E 221 M2
Kurobe-Gawe → Japan 36°55N 137°25E 223 A9
Kurogi Japan 33°12N 130°40E 222 D2
Kuror, J. Sudan 20°27N 31°30E 256 C3
Kurow N.Z. 44°44S 170°29E 285 E5
Kurów Poland 51°23N 22°12E 185 G9
Kurrajong Australia 33°33S 150°42E 283 B9
Kurram → Pakistan 32°36N 71°20E 242 C4
Kurri Kurri Australia 32°50S 151°28E 283 B9
Kurrimine Australia 17°47S 146°6E 280 B4
Kursavka Russia 44°29N 42°32E 191 H6
Kurse Korhi India 20°14N 80°46E 244 D5
Kurseong = Karsiyang
India 26°56N 88°18E 241 B2
Kurshim Kazakhstan 48°34N 83°39E 217 C10
Kurshskaya Kosa ⌂
Russia 55°7N 20°45E 184 C7
Kurshskiy Zaliv Russia 55°9N 21°6E 184 C8
Kuršių Nerijos ⌂ Lithuania 55°30N 21°6E 184 C8
Kursk Russia 51°42N 36°11E 189 G9
Kursk □ Russia 51°50N 36°10E 189 G9
Kursu = Salla Finland 66°50N 28°49E 160 C23
Kuršumlija Serbia 43°9N 21°19E 202 C5
Kuršumlijska Banja Serbia 43°3N 21°11E 202 C5
Kurşunlu Bursa, Turkey 40°39N 29°40E 203 F13
Kurşunlu Çankırı, Turkey 40°51N 33°15E 212 B5
Kurtalan Turkey 37°56N 41°44E 213 D9
Kurtbey Turkey 41°9N 26°35E 203 E10
Kurtistown U.S.A. 19°36N 155°4W 302 D6
Kuru South Sudan 7°43N 26°31E 257 F2
Kuru, Bahr el →
South Sudan 8°10N 26°50E 257 F2
Kurucaşile Turkey 41°49N 32°42E 212 B5
Kuruçay Turkey 39°39N 38°29E 246 B3
Kurukshetra = Thanesar
India 30°1N 76°52E 242 D7
Kuruktag China 41°0N 89°0E 217 D11
Kuruman S. Africa 27°28S 23°28E 270 C3
Kuruman → S. Africa 26°56S 20°39E 270 C3
Kurume Fukuoka, Japan 33°15N 130°30E 222 D2
Kurume Tōkyō, Japan 35°45N 139°31E 140 A2
Kurun → South Sudan 5°30N 34°17E 257 F3
Kurunegala Sri Lanka 7°30N 80°23E 245 L5
Kurupukari Guyana 4°43N 58°37W 329 C6
Kurya Russia 61°42N 57°9E 186 B10
Kuryanovo Russia 55°39N 37°42E 129 C3
Kus Gölü Turkey 40°10N 27°55E 203 F11
Kuşadası Turkey 37°52N 27°15E 212 D2
Kuşadası Körfezi Turkey 37°56N 27°0E 205 D8
Kusamba Indonesia 8°34S 115°27E 231 K18
Kusatsu Gunma, Japan 36°37N 138°36E 223 A10
Kusatsu Shiga, Japan 34°58N 135°57E 223 C7
Kusawa L. Canada 60°20N 136°13W 296 A1
Kusel Germany 49°32N 7°24E 179 F3
Kushaka Nigeria 10°32N 6°48E 263 C6
Kushalgarh India 23°10N 74°27E 242 H6
Kushalnagar India 12°14N 75°57E 245 H2
Kushchevskaya Russia 46°33N 39°35E 191 G4
Kusheriki Nigeria 10°33N 6°28E 263 C6
Kushikino Japan 31°44N 130°16E 222 F2
Kushima Japan 31°29N 131°14E 222 F3
Kushimoto Japan 33°28N 135°47E 223 D7
Kushiro Japan 43°0N 144°25E 220 C12
Kushiro-Gawa → Japan 42°59N 144°23E 220 C12
Kushiro Shitsugen △
Japan 43°9N 144°26E 220 C12
Kūshk Iran 28°46N 56°51E 247 D8
Kushka = Serhetabat
Turkmenistan 35°20N 62°18E 247 C9
Kushmurun = Qusmuryn
Kazakhstan 52°27N 64°36E 216 B6
Kushnytsya Ukraine 48°27N 23°15E 183 B8
Kushol India 33°40N 76°36E 243 C7
Kushtia Bangla. 23°55N 89°5E 241 D2
Kushva Russia 58°18N 59°45E 186 C10
Kuskan Turkey 36°29N 33°17E 250 B4
Kuskokwim → U.S.A. 60°5N 162°25W 303 F7
Kuskokwim B. U.S.A. 59°45N 162°25W 303 G7
Kuskokwim Mts. U.S.A. 62°30N 156°0W 303 E9
Kuskovo Russia 55°44N 37°48E 129 B3
Kusmi India 23°17N 83°55E 243 H10
Kusŏng N. Korea 39°59N 125°15E 224 C2
Kussharo-Ko Japan 43°38N 144°21E 220 C12
Kustanay = Qostanay
Kazakhstan 53°10N 63°35E 216 B6
Küstenje = Constanța
Romania 44°14N 28°38E 183 F13
Kustia India 22°31N 88°23E 124 B2
Küstrin = Kostrzyn
Poland 52°35N 14°39E 185 F1
Kusu Japan 33°16N 131°9E 222 D3
Kut, Ko Thailand 11°40N 102°35E 237 G4
Kuta Indonesia 8°43S 115°11E 231 K18
Kutacane Indonesia 3°50N 97°50E 234 B1
Kütahya Turkey 39°30N 30°2E 205 B12
Kütahya □ Turkey 39°10N 29°30E 205 B11
Kutai △ Indonesia 0°23N 117°16E 235 B5
Kutaisi Georgia 42°19N 42°40E 191 J6
Kutaraja = Banda Aceh
Indonesia 5°35N 95°20E 234 A1
Kutch, Gulf of = Kachchh, Gulf of
India 22°50N 69°15E 242 H3
Kutch, Rann of = Kachchh, Rann of
India 24°0N 70°0E 242 H4
Kutina Croatia 45°29N 16°48E 199 C13
Kutiyana India 21°36N 70°2E 242 J4
Kutjevo Croatia 45°23N 17°55E 182 E2
Kutkai Burma 23°27N 97°56E 241 D6
Kutkashen = Qäbälä
Azerbaijan 40°58N 47°47E 191 K8
Kutná Hora Czech Rep. 49°57N 15°16E 180 B8
Kutno Poland 52°15N 19°23E 185 F6
Kutru India 19°5N 80°46E 244 E5
Kutse Botswana 21°7S 22°16E 270 B3
Kuttabul Australia 21°1S 148°54E 280 b
Kutu Dem. Rep. of the Congo 2°40S 18°11E 264 C3
Kutu Moke
Dem. Rep. of the Congo 3°12S 17°21E 264 C3
Kutum Sudan 14°10N 24°40E 257 E1
Kúty Slovak Rep. 48°40N 17°3E 181 C10
Kuty Ukraine 48°16N 25°11E 183 B10
Kuujjuaq Canada 58°6N 68°15W 295 F18
Kuujjuarapik Canada 55°20N 77°35W 298 A4
Kuusamo Finland 65°57N 29°8E 160 D23
Kuusankoski Finland 60°55N 26°38E 188 B4
Kuvango Angola 14°28S 16°20E 265 E3
Kuvshinovo Russia 57°2N 34°11E 188 D8
Kuwait = Al Kuwayt
Kuwait 29°30N 48°0E 246 D5
Kuwait ■ Asia 29°30N 47°30E 246 D5
Kuwana Japan 35°5N 136°43E 223 B8
Kuwana → India 26°25N 83°15E 243 F10
Kuwol-san N. Korea 38°30N 125°15E 224 C2
Kuybyshev = Samara
Russia 53°8N 50°6E 190 D10
Kuybyshev Russia 55°27N 78°19E 216 B8
Kuybyshevka-Vostochnaya =
Belogorsk Russia 51°0N 128°20E 215 D13
Kuybyshevo Ukraine 47°25N 36°40E 189 J9
Kuybyshevskoye Vdkhr.
Russia 55°2N 49°30E 190 C9
Kuye He → China 38°23N 110°46E 226 E6
Kūyeh Iran 38°45N 47°57E 246 B5
Kuyto, Ozero Russia 65°6N 31°20E 160 D24
Kuytun China 44°25N 85°0E 217 D11
Kuyucak Turkey 37°55N 28°28E 205 D10
Kuyumba Russia 60°58N 96°59E 215 C10
Kuzey Anadolu Dağları
Turkey 41°0N 36°45E 212 B7
Kuzguncuk Turkey 41°2N 29°2E 122 B2
Kuzhitturai India 8°18N 77°11E 245 K3
Kuzitrin → U.S.A. 65°10N 165°25W 303 D6
Kuzmin Serbia 45°2N 19°25E 182 E4
Kuznetsk Russia 53°12N 46°40E 190 D8
Kuznetsovo = Konakovo
Russia 56°40N 36°51E 188 D9
Kuzomen Russia 66°22N 36°50E 186 A6
Kuzucubelen Turkey 36°51N 34°27E 250 B5
Kuzyminki Russia 55°42N 37°46E 129 B3
Kværangen Norway 70°5N 21°15E 160 A19
Kværndrup Denmark 55°10N 10°31E 163 J4
Kvaløya Norway 69°40N 18°30E 160 B18
Kvam Norway 61°40N 9°42E 164 C6
Kvänum Sweden 58°18N 13°11E 163 F7
Kvareli = Qvareli Georgia 41°57N 45°47E 191 K7
Kvarner Croatia 44°50N 14°10E 199 D11
Kvarnerič Croatia 44°43N 14°37E 199 D11
Kvås Norway 58°16N 7°14E 164 F4
Kvernaland Norway 58°47N 5°45E 164 F2
Kvichak B. U.S.A. 58°48N 157°30W 303 G8
Kvicksund Sweden 59°27N 16°19E 162 E10
Kvikne Norway 62°35N 10°16E 164 B7
Kvillsfors Sweden 57°24N 15°29E 163 G9
Kvina → Norway 58°17N 6°56E 164 F3
Kvinlog Norway 58°31N 6°55E 164 F3
Kvirily = Zestaponi Georgia 42°6N 43°0E 191 J6
Kvismare kanal Sweden 59°11N 15°35E 162 E9
Kvissleby Sweden 62°18N 17°22E 162 B11
Kviteseid Norway 59°24N 8°29E 164 E5
Kvitøya Svalbard 80°8N 32°35E 154 A14
Kwabhaca S. Africa 30°51S 29°0E 271 D4
Kwai = Khwae Noi →
Thailand 14°1N 99°32E 236 E2
Kwai Chung China 22°22N 114°7E 122 A1
Kwajalein Marshall Is. 9°5N 167°20E 288 G8
Kwakhanai Botswana 21°39S 21°16E 270 B3
Kwakoegron Suriname 5°12N 55°25W 329 B6
Kwale Coast, Kenya 4°15S 39°31E 268 C4
Kwale Nigeria 5°46N 6°26E 263 D6
Kwamalasamutu
Suriname 2°20N 56°47W 329 C6
KwaMashu S. Africa 29°45S 30°58E 271 C5
Kwamouth
Dem. Rep. of the Congo 3°9S 16°12E 264 C3
Kwando → Africa 18°27S 23°32E 265 F4
Kwangchow = Guangzhou
China 23°6N 113°13E 121 B2
Kwangdaeri N. Korea 40°34N 127°33E 227 D14
Kwango →
Dem. Rep. of the Congo 3°14S 17°22E 264 C3
Kwangsi-Chuang = Guangxi
Zhuangzu Zizhiqu □
China 24°0N 109°0E 228 F7
Kwangtung = Guangdong □
China 23°0N 113°0E 229 F9
Kwara □ Nigeria 8°45N 4°30E 263 D6
Kwataboahegan →
Canada 51°9N 80°50W 298 B3
Kwatisore Indonesia 3°18S 134°50E 231 E8
KwaZulu Natal □ S. Africa 29°0S 30°0E 271 C5
Kweichow = Guizhou □
China 27°0N 107°0E 228 D6
Kweilin = Guilin China 25°18N 110°15E 229 E8
Kweisui = Hohhot China 40°52N 111°40E 226 D6
Kweiyang = Guiyang
China 26°32N 106°40E 228 D6
Kwekwe Zimbabwe 18°58S 29°48E 269 F2
Kweneng □ Botswana 24°0S 25°0E 270 B3
Kwenge →
Dem. Rep. of the Congo 4°50S 18°44E 265 C3
Kwethluk U.S.A. 60°49N 161°26W 303 F7
Kwidzyn Poland 53°44N 18°55E 184 E5
Kwigillingok U.S.A. 59°51N 163°8W 303 G7
Kwiha Ethiopia 13°29N 39°32E 257 E4
Kwikila Papua N. G. 9°49S 147°38E 286 E4
Kwilu →
Dem. Rep. of the Congo 3°22S 17°22E 265 C3
Kwinana Australia 32°15S 115°47E 279 F2
Kwinbet Burma 16°20N 94°14E 241 G5
Kwisa → Poland 51°34N 15°24E 185 G2
Kwoka Indonesia 0°31S 132°27E 231 E8
Kwolla Nigeria 9°0N 9°15E 263 D6
Kwun Tong China 22°19N 114°13E 122 B2
Kya-in-Seikkyi Burma 16°2N 98°8E 241 G7
Kyabé Chad 9°30N 19°0E 259 G3
Kyabra Cr. → Australia 25°36S 142°55E 281 D3
Kyabram Australia 36°19S 145°4E 283 D6
Kyaikkami Burma 16°4N 97°34E 241 G6
Kyaiklat Burma 16°25N 95°40E 241 G5
Kyaikmaraw Burma 16°23N 97°44E 241 G6
Kyaikthin Burma 23°32N 95°40E 241 D5
Kyaikto Burma 17°20N 97°3E 236 D1
Kyaing Tong = Keng Tung
Burma 21°18N 99°39E 236 B2
Kyakhta Russia 50°30N 106°25E 215 D11
Kyambura ⌂ Uganda 0°7S 30°9E 268 C3
Kyan-zaki Japan 26°5N 127°39E 288 a
Kyancutta Australia 33°8S 135°33E 281 E2
Kyangin Burma 18°20N 95°20E 241 F5
Kyaukhnyat Burma 18°15N 97°31E 241 F6
Kyaukki Burma 18°27N 96°56E 241 F6
Kyaukkyi Burma 18°15N 94°29E 241 F5
Kyaukme Burma 22°32N 97°2E 241 D6
Kyaukpadaung Burma 20°52N 95°8E 241 E5
Kyaukpyu Burma 19°28N 93°30E 241 F4
Kyaukse Burma 21°36N 96°10E 241 E6
Kyauktaga Burma 18°10N 96°37E 241 F6
Kyauktan Burma 16°38N 96°19E 241 G6
Kyauktaw Burma 20°51N 92°59E 241 E4
Kyaunggon Burma 17°6N 95°11E 241 G5
Kyawkku Burma 21°48N 96°56E 241 E6
Kybartai Lithuania 54°39N 22°45E 184 D9
Kyburz U.S.A. 38°47N 120°18W 306 G6
Kyeintali Burma 18°0N 94°29E 241 G5
Kyelang India 32°35N 77°2E 242 C7
Kyenjojo Uganda 0°40N 30°37E 268 B3
Kyidaunggan Burma 19°53N 96°12E 241 F6
Kyjov Czech Rep. 50°6N 14°33E 135 B3
Kyjov Czech Rep. 49°1N 17°7E 181 B10
Kyle Sask., Canada 50°50N 108°2W 297 C7
Kyle Tex., U.S.A. 29°59N 97°53W 314 F6
Kyle Dam Zimbabwe 20°15S 31°0E 269 G3
Kyle of Lochalsh U.K. 57°17N 5°44W 167 D3
Kyll → Germany 49°48N 6°41E 179 F2
Kyllburg Germany 50°2N 6°34E 179 E2
Kyllini Greece 37°55N 21°8E 207 D3
Kyllini, Akra Greece 37°57N 21°8E 207 D3
Kymijoki → Finland 60°30N 26°55E 188 B4
Kymmene älv = Kymijoki →
Finland 60°30N 26°55E 188 B4
Kyneton Australia 37°10S 144°29E 282 D6
Kynuna Australia 21°37S 141°55E 280 C3
Kyō-ga-Saki Japan 35°45N 135°15E 223 B7
Kyoga, L. Uganda 1°35N 33°0E 268 B3
Kyogle Australia 28°40S 153°0E 281 D5
Kyom → South Sudan 8°58N 28°13E 257 F2
Kyŏngju = Gyeongju
S. Korea 35°51N 129°14E 224 E4
Kyŏngsŏng N. Korea 41°35N 129°36E 224 B4
Kyōtamba Japan 35°6N 135°17E 223 B7
Kyōto Japan 35°0N 135°45E 223 C7
Kyōto □ Japan 35°15N 135°45E 223 B7
Kyparissovouno Cyprus 35°19N 33°10E 207 E9
Kyperounda Cyprus 34°56N 32°58E 207 E8
Kypros = Cyprus ■ Asia 35°0N 33°0E 207 E9
Kyrenia Cyprus 35°20N 33°20E 207 D9
Kyrgyzstan ■ Asia 42°0N 75°0E 217 D9
Kyritz Germany 52°56N 12°24E 178 C8
Kyrkhult Sweden 56°22N 14°34E 163 H8
Kyrksæterøra Norway 63°18N 9°5E 164 A6
Kyrnasivka Ukraine 48°35N 28°58E 183 B13
Kyrnychky Ukraine 45°42N 29°4E 183 E14
Kyro älv = Kyrönjoki →
Finland 63°14N 21°45E 160 E19
Kyrönjoki → Finland 63°14N 21°45E 160 E19
Kystatyam Russia 67°20N 123°10E 215 C13
Kysucké Nové Mesto
Slovak Rep. 49°18N 18°47E 181 B11
Kytay, Ozero Ukraine 45°40N 29°13E 183 E14
Kythira Greece 36°8N 23°0E 204 E5
Kythréa Cyprus 35°15N 33°29E 207 D12
Kyu-hkok Burma 24°4N 98°4E 241 C7
Kyūhōji Japan 34°38N 135°33E 133 B2
Kyunhla Burma 23°25N 95°15E 241 D5
Kyuquot Sound Canada 50°2N 127°22W 296 D3
Kyurdamir = Kürdämir
Azerbaijan 40°25N 48°3E 191 K9
Kyūshū Japan 33°0N 131°0E 222 E3
Kyūshū □ Japan 33°0N 131°0E 222 E3
Kyushu-Palau Ridge
Pac. Oc. 20°0N 136°0E 288 E5
Kyūshū-Sanchi Japan 32°35N 131°17E 222 E3
Kyūshū Trench Japan 31°35N 134°10E 222 F6
Kyustendil Bulgaria 42°16N 22°41E 202 D6
Kyustendil □ Bulgaria 42°16N 22°41E 202 D6
Kyusyur Russia 70°19N 127°30E 215 B13
Kywong Australia 34°58S 146°44E 283 C7
Kyyiv Ukraine 50°30N 30°28E 177 C16
Kyyiv □ Ukraine 50°5N 30°45E 189 G6
Kyyivske Vdskh. Ukraine 51°0N 30°25E 177 C16
Kyzyl Russia 51°50N 94°30E 217 B12
Kyzyl-Adyr Kyrgyzstan 42°39N 71°35E 217 D8
Kyzyl-Burun = Siyäzän
Azerbaijan 41°3N 49°10E 191 K9
Kyzyl-Khoto = Kyzyl
Russia 51°50N 94°30E 217 B12
Kyzyl Kum Uzbekistan 42°30N 65°0E 217 D6
Kyzyl Kyya Kyrgyzstan 40°16N 72°8E 217 D8
Kyzyl Orda = Qyzylorda
Kazakhstan 44°48N 65°28E 217 D7
Kyzyl-Suu Kyrgyzstan 42°20N 78°0E 217 D9

L

L.A. County Art Museum
U.S.A. 34°4N 118°21W 126 B2
La Albuera Spain 38°45N 6°49W 195 G4
La Alcarria Spain 40°31N 2°45W 196 E2
La Almarcha Spain 39°41N 2°24W 196 F2
La Almunia de Doña Godina
Spain 41°29N 1°23W 196 D3
La Amistad △ Cent. Amer. 9°28N 83°18W 320 E3
La Asunción Venezuela 11°2N 63°51W 329 a
La Baie Canada 48°19N 70°53W 299 C5
La Banda Argentina 27°45S 64°10W 334 B3
La Bañeza Spain 42°17N 5°54W 194 C5
La Barca Mexico 20°17N 102°34W 318 C4
La Barceloneta Spain 41°22N 2°11E 114 A2
La Barge U.S.A. 42°16N 110°12W 304 E8
La Barra Nic. 12°54N 83°33W 320 D3
La Bastide-Puylaurent
France 44°35N 3°55E 174 D7
La Baule France 47°17N 2°24W 172 E4
La Belle Fla., U.S.A. 26°46N 81°26W 317 J8
La Belle Mo., U.S.A. 40°7N 91°55W 310 D5
La Biche → Canada 59°57N 123°50W 296 B4
La Biche, L. Canada 54°50N 112°3W 296 C6
La Bisbal d'Empordà Spain 41°58N 3°2E 196 D8
La Blanca Chile 33°30S 70°40W 137 C2
La Boca Argentina 34°38S 58°22W 117 B2
La Brea Peru 4°40S 81°7W 330 A1
La Brea Trin. & Tob. 10°15N 61°37W 323 t
La Brède France 44°41N 0°32W 174 D3
La Bresse France 48°2N 6°53E 173 D13
La Bretèche France 48°51N 2°1E 134 A1
La Bureba Spain 42°36N 3°24W 194 C7
La Cal → Bolivia 17°27S 58°15W 331 D6
La Calera Chile 32°50S 71°10W 334 C1
La Calle = El Kala Algeria 36°50N 8°26E 261 A6
La Campana △ Chile 32°58S 71°14W 334 C1
La Campiña Lima, Peru 12°11S 77°0W 124 C2
La Campiña Spain 37°45N 4°45W 195 H6
La Canal = Sa Canal Spain 38°51N 1°23E 206 D1
La Cañiza = A Cañiza
Spain 42°13N 8°16W 194 C2
La Canourgue France 44°26N 3°13E 174 D7
La Capelle France 49°59N 3°50E 173 C10
La Carlota Argentina 33°30S 63°20W 334 C3
La Carlota Phil. 10°25N 122°55E 233 F4
La Carlota Spain 37°40N 4°56W 195 H6
La Carolina Spain 38°17N 3°38W 195 G7
La Castellana Phil. 10°20N 123°3E 233 F4
La Cavalerie France 44°1N 3°10E 174 D7
La Ceiba Honduras 15°40N 86°50W 320 C2
La Ceiba Venezuela 9°28N 71°4W 328 B3
La Celle-St-Cloud France 48°50N 2°9E 134 A1
La Certosa, Isole Venice, Italy 142 b5
La Chaise-Dieu France 45°18N 3°42E 174 C7
La Chapelle d'Angillon
France 47°21N 2°25E 173 E9
La Chapelle-St-Luc France 48°20N 4°3E 173 D11
La Chapelle-sur-Erdre
France 47°18N 1°34W 172 E5
La Charité-sur-Loire France 47°10N 3°1E 173 E10
La Chartre-sur-le-Loir
France 47°44N 0°34E 172 E7
La Châtaigneraie France 46°39N 0°44W 174 B3
La Châtre France 46°35N 2°0E 173 F9
La Chaux → Mauritius 20°23S 57°41E 272 e
La Chaux-de-Fonds Switz. 47°7N 6°50E 179 H2
La Chorrera Colombia 0°44S 73°1W 328 D3
La Chorrera Panama 8°53N 79°47W 320 c
La Ciotat France 43°12N 5°36E 175 E9
La Cisterna Chile 33°32S 70°39W 137 C2
La Ciudadela Mexico City, Mexico 128 c2
La Clayette France 46°17N 4°19E 173 F11
La Cocha Argentina 27°50S 65°40W 334 B2
La Concepción = Ri-Aba
Eq. Guin. 3°28N 8°40E 263 E6
La Concepción Panama 8°31N 82°37W 320 E3
La Concepción Venezuela 10°30N 71°50W 328 A3
La Concordia Mexico 16°5N 92°38W 319 D6
La Constitución, Plaza de = Zócalo
Mexico City, Mexico 128 b3
La Coruña = A Coruña
Spain 43°20N 8°25W 194 B2
La Côte-St-André France 45°24N 5°15E 175 C9
La Courneuve France 48°55N 2°22E 134 A3
La Courtine France 45°41N 2°15E 174 C6
La Crau Bouches-du-Rhône,
France 43°32N 4°40E 175 E8
La Crau Var, France 43°9N 6°4E 175 E10
La Crescent U.S.A. 43°50N 91°18W 308 D8
La Crete Canada 58°11N 116°24W 296 B5
La Crosse Fla., U.S.A. 29°51N 82°24W 316 F7
La Crosse Kans., U.S.A. 38°32N 99°18W 308 F4
La Crosse Wis., U.S.A. 43°48N 91°15W 308 D8
La Cruz Costa Rica 11°4N 85°39W 320 D2
La Cruz Sinaloa, Mexico 23°55N 106°54W 318 C3
La Cumbre, Volcán Ecuador 0°21S 91°32W 330 a
La Dehesa Chile 33°21S 70°33W 137 B2
La Désirade Guadeloupe 16°18N 61°3W 322 e
La Digue Seychelles 4°20S 55°51E 272 c
La Dorada Colombia 5°30N 74°40W 328 B3
La Encantada Peru 12°13S 77°1W 124 C2
La Esperanza Argentina 40°26S 68°32W 336 B3
La Esperanza Cuba 22°46N 83°44W 320 B3
La Esperanza Honduras 14°15N 88°10W 320 D2
La Estación Spain 37°21N 3°48W 127 B1
La Estrada = A Estrada
Spain 42°43N 8°27W 194 C2
La Falaise, Gorges de
Martinique 14°49N 61°10W 322 j
La Faouët France 48°2N 3°30W 172 D3
La Fayette U.S.A. 34°42N 85°17W 315 D12
La Fé Cuba 22°2N 84°15W 320 B3
La Fenice, Teatro Venice, Italy 142 b2
La Fère France 49°39N 3°21E 173 C10
La Ferté-Bernard France 48°10N 0°40E 172 D7
La Ferté-Gaucher France 48°47N 3°19E 173 D10
La Ferté-Macé France 48°35N 0°22W 172 D6
La Ferté-St-Aubin France 47°42N 1°57E 173 E8
La Ferté-sous-Jouarre
France 48°56N 3°8E 173 D10
La Ferté-Vidame France 48°37N 0°53E 172 D7
La Flèche France 47°42N 0°4W 172 E6
La Floresta Spain 41°26N 2°3E 114 A1
La Florida Chile 33°33S 70°34W 137 C2
La Foa N. Cal. 21°43S 165°50E 288 d
La Follette U.S.A. 36°23N 84°7W 315 C12
La Fontaine U.S.A. 40°40N 85°43W 311 D11
La Fortuna Spain 40°21N 3°46W 127 B1
La França Spain 41°22N 2°9E 114 A1
La Fregeneda Spain 40°58N 6°54W 194 E4
La Fría Venezuela 8°13N 72°15W 328 B3
La Fuente Venezuela 11°4N 63°52W 329 a
La Fuente de San Esteban
Spain 40°49N 6°15W 194 E4
La Gacilly France 47°45N 2°8W 172 E4
La Garenne-Colombes
France 48°54N 2°15E 134 A2
La Gi Vietnam 10°40N 107°45E 237 G6
La Gineta Spain 39°8N 2°1W 197 F2
La Giudecca Venice, Italy 142 c2
La Giustiniana Italy 41°59N 12°24E 136 B1
La Glória Colombia 8°37N 73°48W 328 B3
La Goulette = Halq el Oued
Tunisia 36°53N 10°18E 258 A2
La Gran Sabana Venezuela 5°30N 61°30W 329 B5
La Grand'Combe France 44°13N 4°2E 175 D8
La Grande U.S.A. 45°20N 118°5W 304 D4
La Grande → Canada 53°50N 79°0W 298 B5
La Grande 3, Rés. Canada 53°40N 75°10W 298 B4
La Grande 4, Rés. Canada 54°0N 73°15W 298 B5
La Grande-Motte France 43°23N 4°5E 175 E8
La Grange Calif., U.S.A. 37°42N 120°27W 306 H6
La Grange Ga., U.S.A. 33°2N 85°2W 316 B4
La Grange Ky., U.S.A. 38°24N 85°22W 311 F11
La Grange Mo., U.S.A. 40°3N 91°35W 310 D5
La Grange Tex., U.S.A. 29°54N 96°52W 314 G6
La Granja Chile 33°31S 70°38W 137 C2
La Grave France 45°3N 6°18E 175 C10
La Grazia, Isola Venice, Italy 142 c3
La Grita Venezuela 8°8N 71°59W 328 B3
La Guaira Venezuela 10°36N 66°56W 328 A4
La Guardia = A Guarda
Spain 41°56N 8°52W 194 D2
La Guardia Venezuela 11°0N 64°1W 329 a
La Guardia, New York ✕ (LGA)
U.S.A. 40°46N 73°52W 132 B2
La Gudiña = A Gudiña Spain 42°4N 7°8W 194 C3
La Güera Mauritania 20°51N 17°0W 260 D1
La Guerche-de-Bretagne
France 47°57N 1°16W 172 E5
La Guerche-sur-l'Aubois
France 46°58N 2°56E 173 F9
La Habana Cuba 23°8N 82°22W 320 B3
La Harpe U.S.A. 40°35N 90°58W 310 D6
La Haute Vallée de Chevreuse ⌂
France 48°35N 1°58E 173 D8
La Haye-du-Puits France 49°17N 1°33W 172 C5
La Horqueta Venezuela 7°55N 60°20W 329 B5
La Horra Spain 41°44N 3°53W 194 D7
La Hulpe Belgium 50°43N 4°30E 116 B2
La Independencia Mexico 16°15N 92°1W 319 D6
La Isabela Dom. Rep. 19°58N 71°2W 321 C5
La Isleta Venezuela 10°54N 63°56W 329 a
La Jonquera Spain 42°25N 2°53E 196 C7
La Joya Peru 16°43S 71°52W 330 D3
La Junta U.S.A. 37°59N 103°33W 304 H12
La Laguna Canary Is. 28°28N 16°18W 153 e1
La Lézarde → Martinique 14°35N 61°1W 322 j
La Libertad = Puerto Libertad
Mexico 29°55N 112°43W 318 B2
La Libertad Guatemala 16°47N 90°7W 320 C1
La Libertad □ Peru 8°0S 78°30W 330 B2
La Ligua Chile 32°30S 71°16W 334 C1
La Línea de la Concepción
Spain 36°15N 5°23W 195 J5
La Llacuna Spain 41°24N 2°12E 114 A2
La Loche Canada 56°29N 109°26W 297 B7
La Loma Mexico 19°31N 99°11W 128 A1
La Londe-les-Maures
France 43°8N 6°14E 175 E10
La Lora Spain 42°45N 4°0W 194 C7
La Loupe France 48°29N 1°0E 172 D8
La Louvière Belgium 50°27N 4°10E 170 D4
La Lucila Argentina 34°30S 58°29W 117 B2
La Lune Trin. & Tob. 10°3N 61°22W 323 t
La Machine France 46°54N 3°27E 173 F10
La Maddalena Italy 41°13N 9°24E 200 A2
La Maladrerie France 48°54N 2°1E 134 A1
La Malbaie Canada 47°40N 70°10W 299 C5
La Malinche △ Mexico 19°15N 98°3W 319 D5
La Mancha Spain 39°10N 2°54W 197 F2
La Manche → Martinique 14°33N 61°0W 322 j
La Mariña Spain 43°30N 7°40W 194 B3
La Martre, L. Canada 63°15N 117°55W 296 A5
La Merced Peru 11°3S 75°19W 330 C2
La Mercy = Durban ✕ (DIA)
S. Africa 29°37S 31°7E 271 C5
La Mesa Baja Calif.,
Mexico 32°30N 116°57W 307 N10
La Mesa Calif., U.S.A. 32°46N 117°1W 307 N9
La Mesilla U.S.A. 32°16N 106°48W 305 K10
La Milla, Cerro Peru 12°2S 77°5W 124 B2
La Moille U.S.A. 41°32N 89°17W 310 C7
La Moine → U.S.A. 39°59N 90°31W 310 E6
La Monachina Italy 41°53N 12°21E 136 B1
La Montagne Réunion 20°53S 55°26E 272 f
La Monte U.S.A. 38°46N 93°26W 310 F3
La Moraleja Spain 40°30N 3°38W 127 A2
La Mothe-Achard France 46°37N 1°40W 172 F5
La Mothe-Chalançon
France 44°30N 5°21E 175 D9
La Motte-du-Caire France 44°20N 6°3E 175 D10
La Motte-Servolex France 45°35N 5°53E 175 C9
La Moure U.S.A. 46°21N 98°18W 308 B4
La Moustique →
Guadeloupe 16°10N 61°34W 322 e
La Muela Spain 41°36N 1°7W 196 D3
La Mure France 44°55N 5°48E 175 D9
La Negra Chile 23°46S 70°18W 334 A1
La Nopalera Mexico 19°18N 99°5W 128 C2
La Oliva Canary Is. 28°36N 13°57W 153 e2
La Oraya Peru 11°32S 75°54W 330 C2
La Orotava Canary Is. 28°22N 16°31W 153 e1
La Oroya Peru 11°32S 75°54W 330 C2
La Pacaudière France 46°11N 3°52E 173 F10
La Pagerie Martinique 14°32N 61°3W 322 j
La Palma Canary Is. 28°40N 17°50W 153 e1
La Palma Panama 8°15N 78°0W 320 E4
La Palma del Condado
Spain 37°21N 6°38W 195 H4
La Paloma Chile 30°35S 71°0W 334 C1
La Pampa □ Argentina 36°50S 66°0W 334 D2
La Paragua Venezuela 6°50N 63°20W 329 B5
La Pastora Trin. & Tob. 10°42N 61°19W 323 t
La Paternal Argentina 34°35S 58°28W 117 B2
La Paya △ Colombia 0°0 75°5W 328 C2
La Paz Entre Ríos,
Argentina 30°50S 59°45W 334 C4
La Paz San Luis, Argentina 33°30S 67°20W 334 C2
La Paz Bolivia 16°20S 68°10W 330 D4
La Paz Honduras 14°20N 87°47W 320 D2
La Paz Baja Calif. S.,
Mexico 24°10N 110°18W 318 C2
La Paz Abra, Phil. 17°40N 120°41E 232 C3
La Paz Tarlac, Phil. 15°26N 120°45E 232 D3
La Paz □ Bolivia 15°30S 68°0W 330 D4
La Paz Centro Nic. 12°20N 86°41W 320 D2
La Pedrera Colombia 1°18S 69°43W 328 D4
La Pérade Canada 46°35N 72°12W 299 C5
La Perla Chihuahua,
Mexico 28°18N 104°32W 318 B4
La Perla Lima, Peru 12°4S 77°7W 124 B2

La Perouse Australia 33°59S 151°14E 139 B2
La Perouse, Bahia Chile 27°5S 109°18W 330 b
La Perouse Str. Asia 45°40N 142°0E 220 B11
La Pesca Mexico 23°46N 97°47W 319 C5
La Piedad Mexico 20°21N 102°0W 318 C4
La Pine U.S.A. 43°40N 121°30W 304 E3
La Pisana Italy 41°51N 12°23E 136 B1
La Plaine Dominica 15°20N 61°15W 323 k
La Plaine des Cafres Réunion 21°13S 55°33E 272 f
La Plaine des Palmistes Réunion 21°7S 55°38E 272 f
La Plata Argentina 35°0S 57°55W 334 C4
La Plata Colombia 2°23N 75°53W 328 C2
La Plata Mo., U.S.A. 40°2N 92°29W 310 D4
La Plata, L. Argentina 44°55S 71°50W 336 B2
La Playa, Pta. Venezuela 10°48N 64°0W 329 a
La Plaza Venezuela 11°6N 63°52W 329 a
La Pobla de Lillet Spain 42°16N 1°59E 196 C6
La Pobla de Segur Spain 42°15N 0°58E 196 C5
La Pocatière Canada 47°22N 70°2W 299 C5
La Pola de Gordón Spain 42°51N 5°41W 194 C5
La Porta France 42°25N 9°21E 175 F13
La Porte U.S.A. 29°40N 95°1W 314 G7
La Porte City U.S.A. 42°19N 92°12W 310 B4
La Possession Réunion 20°55S 55°21E 272 f
La Prairie Canada 45°25N 73°29W 130 B3
La Presanella Italy 46°13N 10°40E 198 B7
La Puebla = Sa Pobla Spain 39°46N 3°1E 206 B4
La Puebla de Cazalla Spain 37°10N 5°20W 195 H5
La Puebla de los Infantes Spain 37°47N 5°24W 195 H5
La Puebla de Montalbán Spain 39°52N 4°22W 194 F6
La Puebla del Río Spain 37°16N 6°3W 195 H4
La Puerta de Segura Spain 38°22N 2°45W 195 G8
La Punta Peru 12°4S 77°10W 124 B1
La Puntigala Spain 41°27N 2°13E 114 A2
La Purísima Mexico 26°10N 112°4W 318 B2
La Push U.S.A. 47°55N 124°38W 306 C2
La Queue-en-Brie France 48°47N 2°34E 134 B4
La Quiaca Argentina 22°5S 65°35W 334 A2
La Rambla Barcelona, Spain 114 b2
La Reina Chile 33°26S 70°33W 137 B2
La Réole France 44°35N 0°1W 174 D3
La Republica, Plaza de Mexico City, Mexico 128 b1
La Restinga Canary Is. 27°38N 17°59W 153 e1
La Ribera Spain 41°21N 2°4E 114 A1
La Rioja Argentina 29°20S 67°0W 334 B2
La Rioja □ Argentina 29°30S 67°0W 334 B2
La Rioja □ Spain 42°20N 2°20W 196 C2
La Rivière des Pluies Réunion 20°54S 55°31E 272 f
La Robla Spain 42°50N 5°41W 194 C5
La Roche N. Cal. 21°26S 168°2E 288 d
La Roche-Bernard France 47°31N 2°19W 172 E4
La Roche-Canillac France 45°12N 1°57E 174 C5
La Roche-en-Ardenne Belgium 50°11N 5°35E 170 D5
La Roche-sur-Foron France 46°4N 6°19E 173 F13
La Roche-sur-Yon France 46°40N 1°25W 172 F5
La Rochefoucauld France 45°44N 0°24E 174 C4
La Rochelle France 46°10N 1°9W 174 B2
La Roda Spain 39°13N 2°15W 197 F2
La Roda de Andalucía Spain 37°12N 4°46W 195 H6
La Romaine Canada 50°13N 60°40W 299 B7
La Romana Dom. Rep. 18°27N 68°57W 321 C6
La Ronge Canada 55°5N 105°20W 297 B7
La Rue U.S.A. 40°35N 83°23W 311 D13
La Rumorosa Mexico 32°34N 116°6W 307 N10
La Sabina = Sa Savina Spain 38°44N 1°25E 206 D1
La Sagra Spain 37°57N 2°35W 197 H2
La Sagrera Spain 41°25N 2°11E 114 A2
La Salada Argentina 34°43S 58°28W 117 C2
La Saline Réunion 21°4S 55°16E 272 f
La Salle U.S.A. 41°20N 89°6W 310 C7
La Sanabria Spain 42°0N 6°30W 194 C4
La Santa Canary Is. 29°5N 13°40W 153 e2
La Sarre Canada 48°45N 79°15W 298 C4
La Scala Italy 45°28N 9°11E 128 B2
La Scie Canada 49°57N 55°36W 299 C8
La Selva Spain 42°0N 2°45E 196 C7
La Selva Beach U.S.A. 36°56N 121°51W 306 J5
La Selva del Camp Spain 41°13N 1°8E 196 D6
La Serena Chile 29°55S 71°10W 334 B1
La Serena Spain 38°45N 5°40W 195 G5
La Seu d'Urgell Spain 42°22N 1°23E 196 C6
La Seyne-sur-Mer France 43°7N 5°52E 175 E9
La Sila Italy 39°15N 16°35E 201 C9
La Solana Spain 38°59N 3°14W 195 G7
La Soufrière St. Vincent 13°20N 61°11W 323 n
La Souterraine France 46°15N 1°30E 173 F8
La Spézia Italy 44°7N 9°50E 198 D6
La Storta Italy 41°59N 12°20E 136 A1
La Suze-sur-Sarthe France 47°53N 0°2E 172 E7
La Tagua Colombia 0°3N 74°40W 328 C3
La Taxonera Spain 41°25N 2°10E 114 A2
La Teste-de-Buch France 44°37N 1°8W 174 D2
La Tortuga, I. Venezuela 11°0N 65°22W 321 D6
La Tour-du-Pin France 45°33N 5°27E 175 C9
La Tranche-sur-Mer France 46°20N 1°27W 172 F5
La Tremblade France 45°46N 1°8W 174 C2
La Trinidad Phil. 16°28N 120°35E 232 C3
La Trinité Martinique 14°45N 60°58W 322 j
La Tuque Canada 47°30N 72°50W 298 C5
La Unión Chile 40°10S 73°0W 336 B2
La Unión Colombia 1°35N 77°5W 328 C2
La Unión El Salv. 13°20N 87°50W 320 D2
La Unión Guerrero, Mexico 17°58N 101°49W 318 D4
La Unión Peru 9°43S 76°45W 330 B2
La Unión Spain 37°38N 0°53W 197 H4
La Union □ Phil. 16°30N 120°25E 232 C3
La Urbana Venezuela 7°8N 66°56W 328 B4
La Vache B. Trin. & Tob. 10°45N 61°29W 323 t
La Vache Pt. Trin. & Tob. 10°47N 61°28W 323 t
La Vall d'Uixó Spain 39°49N 0°15W 196 F4
La Vecilla Spain 42°51N 5°27W 194 C5
La Vecindad Venezuela 11°4N 63°56W 329 a
La Vega Dom. Rep. 19°20N 70°30W 321 C5
La Vega Peru 10°41S 77°44W 330 C2
La Vela de Coro Venezuela 11°27N 69°34W 328 A4
La Veleta Spain 37°1N 3°22W 195 H7
La Venta Mexico 18°5N 94°3W 319 D6
La Venturosa Colombia 6°8N 68°48W 328 B4
La Vergne U.S.A. 36°1N 86°35W 315 C11
La Veronica Trin. & Tob. 10°42N 61°21W 323 t
La Victoria Lima, Peru 12°3S 77°2W 124 B2
La Victoria Venezuela 10°14N 67°20W 328 A4
La Villa Joiosa = Villajoyosa Spain 38°30N 0°12W 197 G4
La Vista U.S.A. 33°48N 84°21W 113 B2
La Voulte-sur-Rhône France 44°48N 4°46E 175 D8
Laa an der Thaya Austria 48°43N 16°23E 181 C9
Laaber, Grosse → Germany 48°55N 12°30E 179 G8
Laage Germany 53°55N 12°21E 178 B8
Laajalahti Finland 60°11N 24°48E 121 B1
Laajasalo Finland 60°10N 25°1E 121 B3
Laaksolahti Finland 60°14N 24°45E 121 B1
Laas Dawaco Somalia 10°28N 49°0E 267 B6
Laascaanood = Las Anod Somalia 8°26N 47°19E 267 C6
Laasqoray Somalia 11°10N 48°20E 267 B6
Laatzen Germany 52°19N 9°48E 178 C5
Lā'au Pt. U.S.A. 21°6N 157°19W 302 B4
Laba → Russia 45°1N 39°42E 191 H4
Labagou Nat. Forest Park China 40°1N 116°22E 114 A2
Laban Burma 25°52N 96°40E 241 C6
Labasa Fiji 16°30S 179°27E 287 A2
Labason Phil. 8°4N 122°31E 233 G4
Labastide-Murat France 44°39N 1°33E 174 D5
Labastide-Rouairoux France 43°28N 2°39E 174 E6
Labbézenga Mali 15°2N 0°48E 263 B5
Labdah = Leptis Magna Libya 32°40N 14°12E 258 B2
Labe = Elbe → Europe 53°50N 9°0E 178 B4
Labé Guinea 11°24N 12°16W 262 C2
Laberge, L. Canada 61°11N 135°12W 296 A1
Labes = Łobez Poland 53°38N 15°39E 184 E2
Labia, Palazzo Venice, Italy 142 a2
Labian, Tanjong Malaysia 5°9N 119°13E 235 A5
Labiau = Polessk Russia 54°50N 21°8E 184 D8
Labig Pt. = Iligan Pt. Phil. 18°25N 122°25E 232 B4
Labin Croatia 45°5N 14°8E 199 C11
Labinsk Russia 44°40N 40°48E 191 H5
Labis Malaysia 2°22N 103°2E 237 L4
Labiszyn Poland 52°57N 17°54E 185 F4
Lablâba, W. el → Egypt 30°1N 31°19E 117 A2
Labo Phil. 14°9N 122°51E 232 D4
Laboe Germany 54°24N 10°13E 178 A6
Laborec → Slovak Rep. 48°37N 21°58E 181 C14
Laborie St. Lucia 13°45N 61°2W 323 m
Labouheyre France 44°13N 0°55W 174 D3
Laboulaye Argentina 34°10S 63°30W 334 C3
Labrador Canada 53°20N 61°0W 299 B7
Labrador City Canada 52°57N 66°55W 299 B6
Labrador Sea Atl. Oc. 57°0N 54°0W 295 F21
Lábrea Brazil 7°15S 64°51W 331 B5
Labruguière France 43°31N 2°16E 174 E6
Labuan □ Malaysia 5°20N 115°12E 235 A5
Labuan, Pulau Malaysia 5°21N 115°13E 235 A5
Labuha Indonesia 0°30S 127°30E 231 E7
Labuhan Indonesia 6°22S 105°50E 234 D3
Labuhanbajo Indonesia 8°28S 119°54E 235 D5
Labuhanbilik Indonesia 2°31N 100°10E 237 L3
Labuk, Telok Malaysia 6°10N 117°50E 235 A5
Labutta Burma 16°9N 94°46E 241 G5
Labyrinth, L. Australia 30°40S 135°11E 281 E2
Labytnangi Russia 66°39N 66°21E 186 A12
Laç Albania 41°38N 19°43E 202 E3
Lac □ Chad 13°30N 14°30E 259 F2
Lac Bay Bonaire 12°6N 68°13W 322 h
Lac-Bouchette Canada 48°16N 72°11W 299 C5
Lac-Édouard Canada 47°40N 72°16W 299 C5
Lac La Biche Canada 54°45N 111°58W 296 C6
Lac la Martre = Wha Ti Canada 63°8N 117°16W 294 E8
Lac La Ronge △ Canada 55°9N 104°41W 297 B7
Lac-Mégantic Canada 45°35N 70°53W 299 C5
Lac Thien Vietnam 12°25N 108°11E 236 F7
Lacanau France 44°58N 1°5W 174 D2
Lacanau, Étang de France 44°58N 1°7W 174 D2
Lacantún → Mexico 16°36N 90°39W 319 D6
Lácara → Spain 38°55N 6°25W 195 G4
Lacaune France 43°43N 2°40E 174 E6
Lacaune, Mts. de France 43°43N 2°50E 174 E6
Laccadive Is. = Lakshadweep Is. India 10°0N 72°30E 245 J1
Lacepede B. Australia 36°40S 139°40E 282 D3
Lacepede Is. Australia 16°55S 122°0E 278 C3
Lacerdónia Mozam. 18°3S 35°35E 269 F4
Lacey U.S.A. 47°7N 122°49W 306 C4
Lachania Greece 35°58N 27°54E 206 F11
Lachay, Pta. Peru 11°17S 77°44W 330 C2
Lachen India 27°46N 88°36E 241 B2
Lachhmangarh India 27°50N 75°4E 242 F6
Lachi Pakistan 33°25N 71°20E 242 C4
Lachia Taiwan 22°43N 120°53E 225 D2
Lachine Canada 45°26N 73°42W 130 B1
Lachine, Canal de Canada 45°26N 73°38W 130 B2
Lachlan → Australia 34°22S 143°55E 282 C5
Lachoc Peru 12°50S 75°6W 330 C2
Lachute Canada 45°39N 74°21W 298 C5
Laçın Azerbaijan 39°38N 46°33E 213 C12
Lackagh Hills Ireland 54°16N 8°10W 166 B3
Lackawanna U.S.A. 42°50N 78°50W 312 D6
Lackawaxen U.S.A. 41°29N 74°59W 313 E10
Lacolle Canada 45°5N 73°22W 313 A11
Lacombe Canada 52°30N 113°44W 296 C6
Lacon U.S.A. 41°2N 89°24W 310 C7
Lacona Iowa, U.S.A. 41°12N 93°23W 310 C3
Lacona N.Y., U.S.A. 43°39N 76°10W 313 C8
Láconi Italy 39°54N 9°4E 200 C2
Laconia U.S.A. 43°32N 71°28W 313 C13
Lacoochee U.S.A. 28°28N 82°11W 317 G7
Lacq France 43°25N 0°35W 174 E3
Lacre Punt Bonaire 12°1N 68°14W 322 h
Lad Phrao Thailand 13°47N 100°35E 113 B2
Ladakh Ra. India 34°0N 78°0E 243 C8
Ladário Brazil 19°1S 57°35W 331 D6
Ladd U.S.A. 41°23N 89°13W 310 C7
Laddonia U.S.A. 39°15N 91°39W 310 E5
Lądek-Zdrój Poland 50°21N 16°53E 185 H3
Ladera Heights U.S.A. 33°59N 118°22W 126 C2
Lâdik Turkey 40°57N 35°58E 212 B6
Ladismith S. Africa 33°28S 21°15E 270 D3
Ladispoli Italy 41°55N 12°5E 199 G9
Lādīz Iran 28°55N 61°15E 247 D9
Ladnun India 27°38N 74°25E 242 F6
Ladoga, L. = Ladozhskoye Ozero Russia 61°15N 30°30E 188 B6
Ladonas → Greece 37°40N 21°50E 204 D3
Ladozhskoye Ozero Russia 61°15N 30°30E 188 B6
Ladrillero, G. Chile 49°20S 75°35W 336 C1
Ladson U.S.A. 32°59N 80°6W 316 C9
Ladushkin Russia 54°34N 20°10E 184 D7
Ladvi Czech Rep. 50°8N 14°27E 135 B2
Lady Poland 52°8N 20°57E 143 C1
Lady Elliott I. Australia 24°7S 152°42E 280 C5
Lady Frere S. Africa 31°42S 27°14E 270 D4
Lady Grey S. Africa 30°43S 27°13E 270 D4
Lady Lake U.S.A. 28°55N 81°55W 317 G8
Ladybrand S. Africa 29°9S 27°29E 270 C4
Ladysmith B.C., Canada 49°0N 123°49W 306 B3
Ladysmith KwaZulu Natal, S. Africa 28°32S 29°46E 271 C4
Ladysmith Wis., U.S.A. 45°28N 91°12W 308 C8
Ladyznyn Ukraine 48°40N 29°15E 183 B14
Lae Papua N. G. 6°40S 147°2E 286 D4
Lae 'o Kealaikahiki U.S.A. 20°32N 156°42W 302 C5
Laem Ngop Thailand 12°10N 102°26E 237 F4
Laem Son △ Thailand 9°29N 98°24E 237 H2
Lærdalsøyri Norway 61°5N 7°28E 164 C4
Laerma Greece 36°9N 27°57E 206 E11
Læsø Denmark 57°15N 11°5E 163 G5
Læsø Rende Denmark 57°20N 10°45E 163 G4
Lafayette Ala., U.S.A. 32°54N 85°24W 316 C4
Lafayette Ind., U.S.A. 40°25N 86°54W 311 D10
Lafayette La., U.S.A. 30°14N 92°1W 314 F8
Lafayette Tenn., U.S.A. 36°31N 86°2W 315 C11
Lafayette Park San Francisco, U.S.A. 136 b1
Lafayette Square New Orleans, U.S.A. 131 b2
Laferte → Canada 61°53N 117°44W 296 A5
Lafia Nigeria 8°30N 8°34E 263 D6
Lafiagi Nigeria 8°52N 5°20E 263 D6
Lafkos Greece 39°9N 23°14E 204 B5
Lafleche Canada 49°45N 106°40W 297 D7
Lafon South Sudan 5°5N 32°29E 257 F3
Lafontaine Montréal, Canada 130 a1
Lafontaine, Parc Canada 45°33N 73°34W 130 A2
Laful India 7°10N 93°52E 245 L11
Lagaip → Papua N. G. 5°4S 142°52E 286 C2
Lagan = Kaspiyskiy Russia 45°22N 47°23E 191 H8
Lagan Sweden 56°56N 13°58E 163 H7
Lagan → Sweden 56°30N 12°58E 163 H6
Lagan → Antrim, U.K. 54°36N 5°55W 166 B6
Lagana, Kolpos Greece 37°42N 20°53E 207 D2
Laganas Greece 37°44N 20°53E 207 D2
Lagangilang Phil. 17°37N 120°44E 232 C3
Lagarfljót → Iceland 65°40N 14°18W 155 B12
Lagarto Brazil 10°54S 37°41W 332 D4
Lagawe Phil. 16°49N 121°6E 232 C3
Lagdo Cameroon 9°3N 13°44E 259 G2
Lagdo, L. de Cameroon 8°40N 14°0E 264 A2
Lage Germany 51°59N 8°48E 178 D4
Lågen → Oppland, Norway 61°8N 10°25E 164 C7
Lågen → Vestfold, Norway 59°3N 10°3E 164 E7
Lägerdorf Germany 53°53N 9°34E 178 B5
Lages Brazil 27°48S 50°20W 335 B5
Laggan = Lake Louise Canada 51°30N 116°10W 296 C5
Lagh Badana △ Somalia 1°16S 41°49E 267 E5
Laghmān □ Afghan. 34°20N 70°0E 240 B3
Laghouat Algeria 33°50N 2°59E 261 B5
Laghouat □ Algeria 33°35N 2°40E 261 B5
Lagnieu France 45°55N 5°20E 175 C9
Lagny-sur-Marne France 48°52N 2°44E 173 D9
Lago = Niassa □ Mozam. 13°30S 36°0E 269 E4
Lago Italy 39°10N 16°9E 201 C9
Lago Agrio Ecuador 0°5N 76°52W 328 C2
Lago de Sanabria y Entorno ⌂ Spain 42°9N 6°45W 194 C4
Lago Posadas Argentina 47°30S 71°40W 336 C2
Lago Puelo △ Argentina 42°30S 71°55W 336 B2
Lago Ranco Chile 40°19S 72°30W 336 B2
Lagoa Azores 37°45N 25°20W 153 d3
Lagoa Rio de J., Brazil 22°58S 43°11W 135 B1
Lagôa Portugal 37°8N 8°27W 195 H2
Lagoa do Peixe △ Brazil 31°12S 50°55W 335 C5
Lagoa Vermelha Brazil 28°13S 51°32W 335 B5
Lagoaça Portugal 41°11N 6°44W 194 D4
Lagodekhi Georgia 41°50N 46°22E 191 K8
Lagoña = Laguna Beach U.S.A. 33°33N 117°47W 307 M9
Lagónegro Italy 40°8N 15°45E 201 B8
Lagonoy G. Phil. 13°35N 123°50E 232 E4
Lagos Angola 16°3S 16°35E 265 F3
Lagos Greece 41°1N 25°6E 203 E9
Lagos Nigeria 6°25N 3°27E 124 B2
Lagos Portugal 37°5N 8°41W 195 H2
Lagos □ Nigeria 6°28N 3°25E 263 D5
Lagos de Moreno Mexico 21°21N 101°55W 318 C4
Lagos Harbour Nigeria 6°26N 3°23E 124 B2
Lagos-Ikeja ✈ (LOS) Nigeria 6°34N 3°19E 124 A1
Lagos Island Nigeria 6°26N 3°23E 124 B2
Lagos Lagoon Nigeria 6°30N 3°28E 124 B2
Lagrange = Bidyadanga Australia 18°45S 121°43E 278 C3
Lagrange U.S.A. 41°39N 85°25W 311 C11
Lagrange B. Australia 18°38S 121°42E 278 C3
Laguardia Spain 42°33N 2°35W 196 C2
Laguépie France 44°8N 1°57E 174 D5
Lagún Curaçao 12°19N 69°10W 322 g
Laguna = Padilla Bolivia 19°19S 64°20W 331 D5
Laguna Brazil 28°30S 48°50W 335 B6
Laguna N. Mex., U.S.A. 35°2N 107°25W 305 J10
Laguna □ Phil. 14°10N 121°20E 232 D3
Laguna, Sa. de la Mexico 23°35N 109°55W 318 C3
Laguna Beach U.S.A. 33°33N 117°47W 307 M9
Laguna Blanca △ Argentina 39°0S 70°5W 336 A2
Laguna de B. Phil. 14°29N 121°6E 127 C2
Laguna de Duera Spain 41°35N 4°43W 194 D6
Laguna de la Restinga △ Venezuela 11°0N 64°10W 329 a
Laguna de Lachuá △ Guatemala 15°55N 90°40W 320 C1
Laguna de Raya Venezuela 10°56N 64°7W 329 a
Laguna de Tacarigua △ Venezuela 10°59N 64°7W 328 A4
Laguna del Laja △ Chile 37°27S 71°20W 334 D1
Laguna del Tigre △ Guatemala 17°32N 90°56W 320 C1
Laguna Limpia Argentina 26°32S 59°45W 334 B4
Laguna San Rafael △ Chile 46°54S 73°31W 336 C2
Lagunas Chile 21°0S 69°45W 334 A2
Lagunas Peru 5°10S 75°35W 330 B2
Lagunas de Chacahua △ Mexico 16°0N 97°43W 319 D5
Lagunas de Montebello △ Mexico 16°4N 91°42W 319 D6
Lagunas de Ruidera ⌂ Spain 38°57N 2°52W 197 G2
Lagunillas Bolivia 19°38S 63°43W 331 D5
Lahad Datu Malaysia 5°0N 118°20E 235 A5
Lahad Datu, Telok Malaysia 4°50N 118°20E 235 B5
Lahaina U.S.A. 20°53N 156°41W 302 C5
Lahan Sai Thailand 14°25N 102°52E 236 E4
Lahanam Laos 16°16N 105°16E 236 D5
Lahar India 26°12N 78°57E 243 F8
Laharpur India 27°43N 80°56E 243 F9
Lahat Indonesia 3°45S 103°30E 234 C2
Lahe Burma 26°20N 95°26E 241 B5
Lahewa Indonesia 1°22N 97°12E 234 B1
Lahij Yemen 13°4N 44°53E 248 D4
Lahij □ Yemen 13°0N 44°30E 248 D4
Lāhījān Iran 37°10N 50°6E 247 B6
Lahilahi Pt. U.S.A. 21°28N 158°13W 302 K13
Lähn = Wleń Poland 51°2N 15°39E 185 G2
Lahn → Germany 50°19N 7°37E 179 E3
Lahnstein Germany 50°19N 7°37E 179 E3
Laholm Sweden 56°30N 13°2E 163 H7
Laholmsbukten Sweden 56°30N 12°45E 163 H6
Lahore Pakistan 31°32N 74°22E 242 D6
Lahpongsel Burma 27°7N 98°25E 241 B7
Lahr Germany 48°20N 7°52E 179 G3
Lahri Pakistan 29°11N 68°13E 242 E3
Lāhrūd Iran 38°30N 47°52E 213 C12
Lahti Finland 60°58N 25°40E 188 B3
Lahtis = Lahti Finland 60°58N 25°40E 188 B3
Lahugala Kitulana △ Sri Lanka 6°50N 81°40E 245 L5
Laï Chad 9°25N 16°18E 259 G3
Lai Chau Vietnam 22°5N 103°3E 228 F4
Lai-hka Burma 21°16N 97°40E 241 E6
Laiagam Papua N. G. 5°33S 143°30E 286 C2
Lai'an China 32°28N 118°30E 229 A12
Laibach = Ljubljana Slovenia 46°4N 14°33E 199 B11
Laibin China 23°42N 109°14E 228 F7
Lā'ie U.S.A. 21°39N 157°56W 302 J14
Laifeng China 29°27N 109°20E 228 C7
L'Aigle France 48°46N 0°38E 172 D7
Laignes France 47°50N 4°20E 173 E11
L'Aiguillon-sur-Mer France 46°20N 1°18W 174 B2
Laila = Layla Si. Arabia 22°10N 46°40E 248 B4
Laim Germany 48°7N 11°30E 131 B2
Lainate Italy 45°34N 9°1E 128 A1
Laingsburg S. Africa 33°9S 20°52E 270 D3
Lainioälven → Sweden 67°35N 22°40E 160 C20
Lainz Austria 48°10N 16°16E 142 B1
Lairg U.K. 58°2N 4°24W 167 C4
Laïri, B. de Chad 12°28N 16°45E 259 F3
Lais Indonesia 3°31S 102°3E 234 C2
Lais Phil. 6°20N 125°39E 233 H5
Laisamis Kenya 1°36N 37°48E 268 B4
Laissac France 44°23N 2°50E 174 D6
Láives Italy 46°26N 11°20E 199 B8
Laiwu China 36°15N 117°40E 227 F9
Laixi China 36°50N 120°31E 227 F11
Laiyang China 36°59N 120°45E 227 F11
Laiyuan China 39°20N 114°40E 226 E8
Laizhou China 37°8N 119°57E 227 F10
Laizhou Wan China 37°30N 119°30E 227 F10
Lajamanu Australia 18°23S 130°38E 278 C5
Lajeado = Guiratinga Brazil 16°21S 53°45W 331 D7
Lajedo Azores 39°23N 31°15W 153 d2
Lajere Nigeria 12°10N 11°25E 263 C7
Lajes Azores 38°46N 27°6W 153 d1
Lajes Rio Grande do N., Brazil 5°41S 36°14W 332 C4
Lajes das Flores Azores 39°23N 31°10W 153 d2
Lajes do Pico Azores 38°23N 28°16W 153 d1
Lajinha Brazil 20°9S 41°37W 333 F3
Lajkovac Serbia 44°27N 20°14E 202 B4
Lajosmizse Hungary 47°3N 19°32E 182 C4
Lak Sao Laos 18°11N 104°59E 236 C5
Lakaband Pakistan 31°2N 69°15E 242 D3
Lakamané Mali 14°35N 9°44W 262 C3
Lakatoro Vanuatu 16°6S 167°25E 287 F5
Lake U.S.A. 44°33N 110°24W 304 D8
Lake Alfred U.S.A. 28°6N 81°44W 317 G8
Lake Alpine U.S.A. 38°29N 120°0W 306 G7
Lake Andes U.S.A. 43°9N 98°32W 308 D4
Lake Arthur U.S.A. 30°5N 92°41W 314 F8
Lake Bindegolly △ Australia 28°0S 144°12E 281 D3
Lake Boga Australia 35°26S 143°38E 282 C5
Lake Buena Vista U.S.A. 28°23N 81°32W 133 B1
Lake Butig △ Phil. 7°45N 124°16E 233 H5
Lake Butler U.S.A. 30°1N 82°21W 316 E7
Lake Cain Hills U.S.A. 28°29N 81°28W 133 B2
Lake Cargelligo Australia 33°15S 146°22E 283 B7
Lake Charles U.S.A. 30°14N 93°13W 314 F8
Lake City Colo., U.S.A. 38°2N 107°19W 304 G10
Lake City Fla., U.S.A. 30°11N 82°38W 316 E7
Lake City Iowa, U.S.A. 42°16N 94°44W 310 B2
Lake City Mich., U.S.A. 44°20N 85°13W 309 C11
Lake City Minn., U.S.A. 44°27N 92°16W 308 C7
Lake City Pa., U.S.A. 42°1N 80°21W 312 D4
Lake City S.C., U.S.A. 33°52N 79°45W 316 B10
Lake Clark △ U.S.A. 61°0N 154°0W 303 F9
Lake Coleridge N.Z. 43°17S 171°30E 285 D6
Lake Cowichan Canada 48°49N 124°3W 296 D4
Lake District △ U.K. 54°30N 3°21W 168 C4
Lake Eildon △ Australia 37°10S 145°56E 283 D6
Lake Elsinore U.S.A. 33°38N 117°20W 307 M9
Lake Eyre △ Australia 28°40S 137°31E 281 D2
Lake Forest U.S.A. 42°15N 87°50W 311 B9
Lake Gairdner △ Australia 31°41S 135°51E 281 E2
Lake Geneva U.S.A. 42°36N 88°26W 311 B8
Lake George U.S.A. 43°26N 73°43W 313 C11
Lake Grace Australia 33°7S 118°28E 279 F2
Lake Gregory ◎ Australia 20°12S 127°27E 278 D4
Lake Harbor U.S.A. 26°42N 80°48W 317 J9
Lake Harbour = Kimmirut Canada 62°50N 69°50W 295 E18
Lake Havasu City U.S.A. 34°27N 114°22W 307 L12
Lake Helen U.S.A. 28°59N 81°14W 317 G8
Lake Hughes U.S.A. 34°41N 118°26W 307 L8
Lake Isabella U.S.A. 35°38N 118°28W 307 K8
Lake Jackson U.S.A. 29°3N 95°27W 314 G7
Lake King Australia 33°5S 119°45E 279 F2
Lake Kopiago Papua N. G. 5°23S 142°31E 286 C2
Lake Kutubu Papua N. G. 6°20S 143°18E 286 D2
Lake Lenore Canada 52°24N 104°59W 297 C8
Lake Louise Canada 51°30N 116°10W 296 C5
Lake Mackay ◎ Australia 21°48S 129°46E 278 D4
Lake Mburo △ Uganda 0°33S 30°56E 268 C3
Lake Mead ⌂ U.S.A. 36°30N 114°22W 307 K12
Lake Meredith ⌂ U.S.A. 35°50N 101°50W 314 D4
Lake Mills Iowa, U.S.A. 43°25N 93°32W 308 D7
Lake Mills Wis., U.S.A. 43°5N 88°55W 311 A8
Lake Murray Papua N. G. 6°48S 141°29E 286 D1
Lake Nakura △ Kenya 0°21S 36°8E 268 C4
Lake Odessa U.S.A. 42°47N 85°8W 311 B11
Lake Orion U.S.A. 42°47N 83°14W 311 B13
Lake Park Fla., U.S.A. 26°48N 80°3W 317 J9
Lake Park Ga., U.S.A. 30°41N 83°11W 316 E6
Lake Placid Fla., U.S.A. 27°18N 81°22W 317 H8
Lake Placid N.Y., U.S.A. 44°17N 73°59W 313 B11
Lake Pleasant U.S.A. 43°28N 74°25W 313 C10
Lake Point Tower U.S.A. 119 b3
Lake Providence U.S.A. 32°48N 91°10W 314 E9
Lake Pukaki N.Z. 44°11S 170°8E 285 E5
Lake Roosevelt ⌂ U.S.A. 48°5N 118°14W 304 B4
Lake St. Peter Canada 45°18N 78°2W 312 A6
Lake Shore Drive U.S.A. 119 a2
Lake Shore Park U.S.A. 119 a2
Lake Stevens U.S.A. 48°1N 122°4W 306 B4
Lake Superior ⌂ Canada 47°45N 84°45W 298 C3
Lake Tekapo N.Z. 44°0S 170°30E 285 E5
Lake Torrens △ Australia 30°55S 137°40E 281 E2
Lake View U.S.A. 42°18N 95°3W 310 B1
Lake Villa U.S.A. 42°25N 88°5W 311 B8
Lake Village U.S.A. 33°20N 91°17W 314 E9
Lake Wales U.S.A. 27°54N 81°35W 317 H8
Lake Worth U.S.A. 26°37N 80°3W 317 J9
Lake Zurich U.S.A. 42°12N 88°5W 311 B8
Lakeba Fiji 18°13S 178°47W 287 B3
Lakeba Passage Fiji 18°0S 178°45W 287 B3
Lakefield Canada 44°25N 78°16W 312 B6
Lakefield △ Australia 15°24S 144°26E 280 B3
Lakehurst U.S.A. 40°1N 74°19W 313 F10
Lakeland Queens., Australia 15°49S 144°57E 280 B3
Lakeland Fla., U.S.A. 28°3N 81°57W 317 G8
Lakeland Ga., U.S.A. 31°2N 83°4W 316 D6
Lakemba = Lakeba Fiji 18°13S 178°47W 287 B3
Lakemba Australia 33°55S 151°5E 139 B1
Lakepa Cook Is. 18°59S 169°48W 289 g
Lakeport Calif., U.S.A. 39°3N 122°55W 306 F4
Lakeport Mich., U.S.A. 43°7N 82°30W 312 C2
Lakes □ South Sudan 7°0N 30°0E 257 F3
Lakes Entrance Australia 37°50S 148°0E 283 D8
Lakeside Gauteng, S. Africa 26°5S 28°8E 123 A2
Lakeside Western Cape, S. Africa 34°5S 18°27E 118 B1
Lakeside Calif., U.S.A. 32°52N 116°55W 307 N10
Lakeside Nebr., U.S.A. 42°3N 102°26W 308 D2
Lakeside Ohio, U.S.A. 41°32N 82°46W 312 E2
Lakeview Ill., U.S.A. 41°56N 87°38W 119 B3
Lakeview La., U.S.A. 30°0N 90°6W 131 A2
Lakeview Oreg., U.S.A. 42°11N 120°21W 304 E3
Lakeville U.S.A. 44°39N 93°14W 308 C7
Lakewood Colo., U.S.A. 39°42N 105°4W 304 G11
Lakewood N.J., U.S.A. 40°6N 74°13W 313 F10
Lakewood N.Y., U.S.A. 42°6N 79°19W 312 D5
Lakewood Ohio, U.S.A. 41°28N 81°47W 312 E3
Lakewood Wash., U.S.A. 47°11N 122°32W 306 C4
Lakewood Park Fla., U.S.A. 27°33N 80°24W 317 H9
Lakewood Park Georgia, U.S.A. 33°43N 84°24W 113 B2
Lakha India 26°9N 70°54E 242 F4
Lakhimpur India 27°57N 80°46E 243 F9
Lakhipur Assam, India 24°48N 93°0E 241 C4
Lakhipur Assam, India 26°2N 90°18E 241 B3
Lakhisarai India 25°11N 86°5E 243 G12
Lakhnadon India 22°36N 79°36E 243 H8
Lakhnau = Lucknow India 26°50N 81°0E 243 F9
Lakhonpheng Laos 15°54N 105°34E 236 E5
Lakhpat India 23°48N 68°47E 242 H3
Lakhtinskiy Russia 59°59N 30°9E 137 B1
Lakhtinskiy Razliv, Oz. Russia 59°59N 30°12E 137 B1
Lâki Azerbaijan 40°34N 47°22E 191 K8
Laki Iceland 64°4N 18°14W 155 C8
Lakin U.S.A. 37°57N 101°15W 308 G3
Lakitusaki → Canada 54°21N 82°25W 298 B3
Lakka Greece 39°17N 20°9E 206 C10
Lakki Greece 35°24N 23°57E 207 E4
Lakki Pakistan 32°36N 70°55E 242 C4
Lakonia □ Greece 36°55N 22°30E 204 E4
Lakonikos Kolpos Greece 36°40N 22°40E 204 E4
Lakor Indonesia 8°15S 128°17E 231 F7
Lakota Ivory C. 5°50N 5°30W 262 D3
Lakota N. Dak., U.S.A. 48°2N 98°21W 308 A4
Laksar India 29°46N 78°3E 242 E8
Laksefjorden Norway 70°45N 26°50E 160 A22
Lakselv Norway 70°2N 25°0E 160 A21
Laksettipet India 18°52N 79°13E 244 E4
Lakshadweep □ India 10°0N 72°30E 245 J1
Lakshadweep Is. India 10°0N 72°30E 245 J1
Laksham Bangla. 23°14N 91°8E 241 D3
Lakshimpur Bangla. 22°58N 90°50E 241 D3
Lakshmanpur Chhattisgarh, India 22°58N 83°3E 243 H10
Lakshmanpur W. Bengal, India 22°38N 88°16E 124 B1
Lakshmeshwar India 15°9N 75°28E 245 G2
Lakshmikantapur India 22°5N 88°20E 243 H13
Laksi Thailand 13°53N 100°35E 113 A2
Lakuramau Papua N. G. 2°54S 151°15E 286 B6
Lal-lo Phil. 18°12N 121°40E 232 B3
Lal Qila Delhi, India 120 a3
Lala Dem. Rep. of the Congo 4°10S 20°30E 265 C4
Lala Phil. 7°59N 123°46E 233 H4
Lala Musa Pakistan 32°40N 73°57E 242 C5
Lalaghat India 24°30N 92°40E 241 C4
Lalago Tanzania 3°28S 33°58E 268 C3
Lalang → Indonesia 2°24S 104°39E 234 C2
Lalapanzi Zimbabwe 19°20S 30°15E 269 F3
Lalapaşa Turkey 41°49N 26°44E 203 E10
Lalara Gabon 0°19N 11°32E 264 B2
Lalbenque France 44°19N 1°34E 174 D5
Lalbert Australia 35°38S 143°20E 282 C5
L'Albufera Spain 39°20N 0°27W 197 F4
L'Alcora Spain 40°5N 0°14W 196 E4
L'Alfàs del Pi Spain 38°35N 0°5W 197 G4
Lalganj India 25°52N 85°13E 243 G11
Lalgola India 24°25N 88°15E 243 G13
Lālī Iran 32°21N 49°6E 247 C6
Lalibela Ethiopia 12°3N 39°0E 257 E4
Lalin Heilongjiang, China 45°12N 127°0E 227 B14
Lalín Spain 42°40N 8°5W 194 C2
Lalin He → China 45°32N 125°40E 227 B13
Lalinde France 44°50N 0°44E 174 D4
Lalitapur India 24°42N 78°28E 243 G8
Lalitpur Nepal 27°40N 85°20E 243 F11
Lalkua India 29°5N 79°31E 243 E8
Lalm Norway 61°50N 9°17E 164 C6
Lalmanir Hat Bangla. 25°54N 89°27E 241 C2
Lalsot India 26°34N 76°20E 242 F7
Lam Nam Nan △ Thailand 17°55N 100°28E 236 D3
Lam Pao Res. Thailand 16°50N 103°15E 236 D4
Lam Tin China 22°18N 114°14E 122 B1
Lama Kara Togo 9°30N 1°15E 263 D5
Lamae Thailand 9°51N 99°5E 237 H2
Lamag Malaysia 5°29N 117°49E 235 A5
Lamaing Burma 15°25N 97°53E 236 E1
Lamaipum Burma 25°40N 97°57E 241 C6
Lamap Vanuatu 16°26S 167°43E 287 F5
Lamar Colo., U.S.A. 38°5N 102°37W 304 G12
Lamar Mo., U.S.A. 37°30N 94°16W 308 G6
Lamarque Argentina 39°24S 65°40W 336 A3
Lamas Peru 6°28S 76°31W 330 B2
Lamastre France 44°59N 4°35E 175 D8
Lamayuru India 34°25N 76°56E 243 B7
Lambach Austria 48°6N 13°51E 180 C6
Lamballe France 48°29N 2°31W 172 D4
Lambaréné Gabon 0°41S 10°12E 264 C2
Lambasa = Labasa Fiji 16°30S 179°27E 287 A2
Lambay I. Ireland 53°29N 6°1W 166 C5
Lambayeque □ Peru 6°45S 80°0W 330 B2
Lambert Norway 59°52N 10°48E 133 A3
Lambert, C. Papua N. G. 4°11S 151°31E 286 C6
Lambert-St. Louis Int. ✈ (STL) U.S.A. 38°45N 90°22W 310 F6
Lambert's Bay S. Africa 32°5S 18°17E 270 D2
Lambertville U.S.A. 41°46N 83°35W 311 C13
Lambesc France 43°39N 5°16E 175 E9
Lambèse = Tazoult Algeria 35°29N 6°11E 261 A6
Lambeth Canada 42°54N 81°18W 312 D3
Lambeth □ U.K. 51°28N 0°6W 125 B3
Lambi Solomon Is. 9°22S 159°39E 287 M10
Lambia Greece 37°52N 21°53E 204 D3
Lambir Hills △ Malaysia 4°12N 114°1E 235 B4
Lambomakondro Madag. 22°41S 44°44E 272 C1
Lambon Papua N. G. 4°45S 152°48E 286 C7
Lambrate Italy 45°29N 9°16E 128 B2
Lambro → Italy 45°8N 9°32E 198 C6
Lambro, Parco Italy 45°29N 9°14E 128 B2
Lambton Mills Canada 43°39N 79°30W 141 B1
Lambu Papua N. G. 3°18S 151°43E 286 B6
Lambunao Phil. 11°3N 122°29E 233 F4
Lamé Chad 9°15N 14°32E 259 G2
Lame Nigeria 10°30N 9°20E 263 C6
Lame Deer U.S.A. 45°37N 106°40W 304 D10
Lamego Portugal 41°5N 7°52W 194 D3
Lamentin Guadeloupe 16°16N 61°38W 322 e
Lamèque Canada 47°45N 64°38W 299 C7
Lameroo Australia 35°19S 140°33E 282 C4
Lamesa U.S.A. 32°44N 101°58W 314 E4
Lamia Greece 38°55N 22°26E 204 C4
Lamigan Pt. Phil. 6°48N 126°21E 233 H6
Lamine → U.S.A. 38°59N 92°51W 310 F4
Lamington △ Australia 28°13S 153°12E 281 D5
Lamitan Phil. 6°39N 122°8E 233 H4
Lamlam, Mt. Guam 13°22N 144°41E 302 d
Lamma I. China 22°12N 114°7E 122 B1
Lammermuir Hills U.K. 55°50N 2°40W 167 F6
Lammeulo Indonesia 5°14N 95°56E 234 A1
Lammhult Sweden 57°10N 14°35E 163 G8
Lamoille → U.S.A. 44°38N 73°13W 313 B11
Lamon B. Phil. 14°30N 122°20E 232 D4
Lamongan Indonesia 7°7S 112°25E 235 D4
Lamoni U.S.A. 40°37N 93°56W 310 D3
Lamont Alta., Canada 53°46N 112°50W 296 C6
Lamont Calif., U.S.A. 35°15N 118°55W 307 K8
Lamont Fla., U.S.A. 30°23N 83°49W 316 E6
Lamont Iowa, U.S.A. 42°36N 91°39W 310 B5
Lamont Wyo., U.S.A. 42°13N 107°29W 304 E10
Lamotte-Beuvron France 47°36N 2°2E 173 E9
Lampa Peru 15°22S 70°22W 330 D3
Lampang Thailand 18°16N 99°32E 236 C2
Lampasas U.S.A. 31°4N 98°11W 314 F5
Lampazos de Naranjo Mexico 27°1N 100°31W 318 B4
Lampedusa Medit. S. 35°36N 12°40E 258 A2
Lampertheim Germany 49°35N 8°27E 179 F4
Lampeter U.K. 52°7N 4°4W 169 E3
Lamphun Thailand 18°40N 99°2E 236 C2
Lampione Medit. S. 35°33N 12°20E 258 A2
Lampman Canada 49°25N 102°50W 297 D8
Lamprechtshausen Austria 48°0N 12°58E 180 D5
Lampung □ Indonesia 5°30S 104°30E 234 D2
Lampung, Teluk Indonesia 5°40S 105°20E 234 D3
Lamta India 22°8N 80°7E 243 H9
Lamu Burma 19°14N 94°10E 241 F5
Lamu Coast, Kenya 2°16S 40°55E 268 C5
Lamu □ Kenya 2°0S 40°45E 268 C5
Lamud Peru 6°10S 77°57W 330 B2
Lamy U.S.A. 35°29N 105°53W 305 J11
Lan Xian China 38°15N 111°35E 226 E6
Lan Yü Taiwan 22°4N 121°25E 225 D3
Lāna'i U.S.A. 20°50N 156°55W 302 C5
Lāna'i City U.S.A. 20°50N 156°55W 302 C5
Lāna'ihale U.S.A. 20°49N 156°53W 302 C5
Lanak La China 34°27N 79°32E 243 B8
Lanak'o Shank'ou = Lanak La China 34°27N 79°32E 243 B8
Lanao, L. Phil. 7°52N 124°15E 233 H5
Lanao del Norte □ Phil. 8°0N 124°10E 233 H5
Lanao del Sur □ Phil. 7°40N 124°15E 233 H5
Lanark Ont., Canada 45°1N 76°22W 313 A8
Lanark S. Lanarks., U.K. 55°40N 3°47W 167 F5
Lanark Ill., U.S.A. 42°6N 89°50W 310 B7
Lanbi Kyun Burma 10°50N 98°20E 237 G2
Lancang China 22°36N 99°58E 228 F2
Lancang Jiang → China 21°40N 101°10E 228 G3
Lancashire □ U.K. 53°50N 2°48W 168 D5
Lancaster Ont., Canada 45°10N 74°30W 313 A10
Lancaster Lancs., U.K. 54°3N 2°48W 168 C5
Lancaster Calif., U.S.A. 34°42N 118°8W 307 L8
Lancaster Ky., U.S.A. 37°37N 84°35W 309 G11
Lancaster Mo., U.S.A. 40°31N 92°32W 310 D4
Lancaster N.H., U.S.A. 44°29N 71°34W 313 B13
Lancaster Ohio, U.S.A. 39°43N 82°36W 309 F12
Lancaster Pa., U.S.A. 40°2N 76°19W 313 F8
Lancaster S.C., U.S.A. 34°43N 80°46W 315 D14
Lancaster Wis., U.S.A. 42°51N 90°43W 310 B6
Lancaster, Récif = Neilson, Récif Pac. Oc. 27°1S 146°2W 289 f
Lancaster Sd. Canada 74°13N 84°0W 295 C15
Lancelin Australia 31°0S 115°18E 279 F2
Lanchow = Lanzhou China 36°1N 103°52E 226 F2
Lanchyn Ukraine 48°33N 24°45E 183 B9
Lanciano Italy 42°14N 14°23E 199 F11
Lanco Chile 39°24S 72°46W 336 A2
Lancones Peru 4°30S 80°30W 330 A1
Lancun China 36°25N 120°10E 227 F11
Łańcut Poland 50°10N 22°13E 185 H9
Land Between the Lakes ⌂ U.S.A. 36°25N 88°0W 315 C11
Landau Bayern, Germany 48°40N 12°41E 179 G8
Landau Rhld-Pfz., Germany 49°12N 8°6E 179 F4
Landay Afghan. 30°31N 63°47E 240 C1
Landeck Austria 47°9N 10°34E 180 D3
Lander U.S.A. 42°50N 108°44W 304 E9
Lander → Australia 22°0S 132°0E 278 D5
Landerneau France 48°28N 4°17W 172 D2
Landeryd Sweden 57°7N 13°15E 163 G7
Landes France 44°0N 1°0W 174 D2
Landes □ France 43°57N 0°48W 174 E3
Landes de Gascogne ⌂ France 44°23N 0°50W 174 D3
Landeshut = Kamienna Góra Poland 50°47N 16°2E 185 H3
Landete Spain 39°56N 1°25W 196 F3
Landfall I. India 13°40N 93°2E 245 H11
Landi Kotal Pakistan 34°7N 71°6E 242 B4
Landianchang China 39°56N 116°17E 114 B1
Landisburg U.S.A. 40°21N 77°19W 312 F7
Landivisiau France 48°31N 4°6W 172 D2
Landmannalaugar Iceland 63°59N 19°4W 155 D7
Landquart Switz. 46°58N 9°32E 179 J5
Landrecies France 50°7N 3°40E 173 B10
Land's End U.K. 50°4N 5°44W 169 G2
Landsberg = Górowo Iławeckie Poland 54°17N 20°30E 184 D7
Landsberg Germany 48°2N 10°53E 179 G6
Landsberg an der Warthe = Gorzów Wielkopolski Poland 52°43N 15°15E 185 F2
Landsberg in Oberschlesien = Gorzów Śląski Poland 51°3N 18°22E 185 G5
Landsborough Cr. → Australia 22°28S 144°35E 280 C3
Landsbro Sweden 57°24N 14°56E 163 G8
Landshut Germany 48°34N 12°8E 179 G8
Landskrona Sweden 55°53N 12°50E 163 J6
Landsmeer Neths. 52°26N 4°55E 112 A2
Landstrasse Austria 48°12N 16°23E 142 A2
Landstuhl Germany 49°24N 7°33E 179 F3
Landvetter Sweden 57°41N 12°17E 163 G6
Landwehr kanal Germany 52°29N 13°24E 115 B3
Lane U.S.A. 33°32N 79°53W 316 B10
Lane Cove Australia 33°48S 151°9E 139 A1
Lane Cove Nat. Park △ Australia 33°47S 151°8E 139 A1
Lanesboro U.S.A. 41°57N 75°34W 313 E9
Lanester France 47°46N 3°22W 172 E3
Lanett U.S.A. 32°52N 85°12W 316 C4
Lang Shan China 41°0N 106°30E 226 D4
Lang Son Vietnam 21°52N 106°42E 228 G6
Lang Suan Thailand 9°57N 99°4E 237 H2
Langå Midtjylland, Denmark 56°23N 9°54E 163 H3
Langa Western Cape, S. Africa 33°57S 18°31E 118 A2
La'nga Co China 30°45N 81°15E 243 D9
Langa-Langa Dem. Rep. of the Congo 3°50S 15°59E 264 C3
Langadas Greece 40°46N 23°6E 202 F7
Langadia Greece 37°43N 22°1E 204 D4
Långan → Sweden 63°19N 14°44E 162 A8
Langanes Iceland 66°20N 14°53W 155 A12
Langano, L. Ethiopia 7°36N 38°43E 257 F4
Langar Afghan. 37°2N 72°40E 240 A4
Langar Iran 35°23N 60°25E 247 C9
Langara I. Canada 54°14N 133°1W 296 C2
Langarūd Iran 37°11N 50°8E 247 B6
Långås Sweden 56°58N 12°26E 163 H6
Langatabbetje Suriname 4°59N 54°28W 329 C7
Langdai China 26°6N 105°21E 228 D5
Langdon U.S.A. 48°45N 98°22W 308 A4
Långe Jan = Ölands södra udde Sweden 56°12N 16°23E 163 H10
Langeac France 45°7N 3°29E 174 C7
Langeais France 47°20N 0°24E 172 E7
Langeb Baraka → Sudan 17°28N 36°50E 256 D4
Langeberg S. Africa 33°55S 21°0E 270 D3
Langeberge S. Africa 28°15S 22°33E 270 C3
Langeland Denmark 54°56N 10°48E 163 K4
Langelands Bælt Denmark 54°50N 10°55E 163 K4
Langen Hessen, Germany 49°59N 8°40E 179 F4
Langen Niedersachsen, Germany 53°36N 8°36E 178 B4
Langenbielau = Bielawa Poland 50°43N 16°37E 185 H3
Langenburg Canada 50°51N 101°43W 297 C8
Langeneß Germany 54°38N 8°36E 178 A4

Langenlois Austria 48°29N 15°40E 180 C8
Langenzersdorf Austria 48°18N 16°21E 142 A2
Langeoog Germany 53°45N 7°32E 178 B3
Langer See Germany 52°24N 13°37E 143 B4
Langeskov Denmark 55°22N 10°35E 163 J4
Langesund Norway 59°0N 9°45E 164 F6
Langevåg Norway 62°26N 6°13E 164 B3
Langfang China 39°30N 116°41E 222 B2
Langgapayung Indonesia 1°43N 99°58E 234 B1
Långhem Sweden 57°36N 13°14E 163 G7
Langhirano Italy 44°37N 10°16E 198 D7
Langholm U.K. 55°9N 3°0W 167 F5
Langisjór Iceland 64°11N 18°15W 155 C8
Langjökull Iceland 64°39N 20°12W 155 C6
Langkawi, Pulau Malaysia 6°25N 99°45E 237 J2
Langklip S. Africa 28°12S 20°20E 270 C3
Langkon Malaysia 6°30N 116°40E 235 A5
Langley B.C., Canada 49°7N 122°39W 306 A4
Langley Va., U.S.A. 38°57N 77°11W 143 B1
Langley Park U.S.A. 38°59N 76°58W 143 B3
Langnau Switz. 46°56N 7°47E 179 J3
Langogne France 44°43N 3°50E 174 D7
Langon France 44°33N 0°16W 174 D3
Langøya Norway 68°45N 14°50E 160 B16
Langreo Spain 43°18N 5°40W 194 B5
Langres France 47°52N 5°20E 173 E12
Langres, Plateau de France 47°45N 5°3E 173 E12
Langsa Indonesia 4°30N 97°57E 234 B1
Långsele Sweden 63°12N 17°4E 162 A11
Långshyttan Sweden 60°27N 16°2E 163 D10
Langtang △ Nepal 28°10N 85°30E 243 E11
Langtao Burma 27°15N 97°34E 241 B6
Langting India 25°31N 93°7E 241 C4
Langtou China 40°1N 124°19E 227 D13
Langtry U.S.A. 29°49N 101°34W 314 G4
Langu Thailand 6°53N 99°47E 237 J2
Langue de Barbarie △ Senegal 14°54N 16°30W 262 C1
Languedoc France 43°58N 3°55E 174 E7
Languedoc-Roussillon □ France 43°25N 3°0E 174 E6
Langwald Germany 48°10N 11°25E 131 A1
Langxi China 22°38N 113°27E 219 a
Langxi China 31°10N 119°12E 229 B12
Langzhong China 31°38N 105°58E 228 B5
Lanigan Canada 51°51N 105°2W 297 C7
Lanin △ Argentina 40°0S 71°58W 336 A2
Lanjigarh India 19°43N 83°23E 244 E6
Lankao China 34°48N 114°50E 226 G8
Lanikai U.S.A. 21°23N 157°42W 302 K14
Lanin □ Argentina 40°0S 71°58W 336 A2
Länkäran Azerbaijan 38°48N 48°52E 213 C13
Lankwitz Germany 52°25N 13°21E 115 B3
Lanmeur France 48°39N 3°43W 172 D7
Lannemezan France 43°8N 0°23E 174 E4
Lannilis France 48°35N 4°32W 172 D2
Lannion France 48°46N 3°29W 172 D3
L'Annonciation Canada 46°25N 74°55W 298 C5
L'Annunziatella Italy 41°49N 12°33E 136 C2
Lanouaille France 45°24N 1°9E 174 C5
Lanping China 26°28N 99°12E 236 D2
Lansang △ Thailand 16°45N 99°0E 236 D2
Lansdale U.S.A. 40°14N 75°17W 313 F9
Lansdowne N.S.W., Australia 31°48S 152°30E 283 A10
Lansdowne Ont., Canada 44°24N 76°1W 313 B8
Lansdowne India 29°50N 78°41E 243 E8
Lansdowne Western Cape. S. Africa 33°59S 18°30E 118 A2
Lansdowne House = Neskantaga Canada 52°14N 87°53W 298 B2
L'Anse U.S.A. 46°45N 88°27W 308 B9
L'Anse à l'Âne Martinique 14°32N 61°4W 322 j
L'Anse au Loup Canada 51°32N 56°50W 299 B8
L'Anse aux Epines Grenada 11°59N 61°45W 323 q
L'Anse aux Meadows Canada 51°36N 55°32W 299 B8
L'Anse Mitan Martinique 14°32N 61°4W 322 j
Lansford U.S.A. 40°50N 75°53W 313 F9
Lanshan China 25°24N 112°10E 229 E9
Lanshantou China 35°5N 119°20E 227 G10
Lansing Ont., Canada 43°45N 79°24W 141 A2
Lansing Mich., U.S.A. 42°44N 84°33W 311 B12
Lanslebourg-Mont-Cenis France 45°17N 6°52E 175 C10
Lanta, Ko Thailand 7°35N 99°3E 237 J2
Lantana U.S.A. 26°35N 80°3W 317 J9
Lantau I. China 22°15N 113°56E 219 a
Lantewa Nigeria 12°16N 11°44E 263 C7
Lantian China 34°11N 109°20E 226 G5
Lanus Argentina 34°42S 58°23W 117 C2
Lanusei Italy 39°52N 9°34E 200 C2
Lanuza Phil. 9°14N 126°4E 233 G6
Lanxi China 29°13N 119°28E 229 C12
Lanyang Hsi → Taiwan 24°43N 121°49E 225 D3
Lanyû China 22°2N 121°33E 225 F5
Lanzarote Canary Is. 29°0N 13°40W 153 e22
Lanzarote ✈ (ACE) Canary Is. 28°57N 13°40W 153 e22
Lanzhou China 36°1N 103°52E 226 F2
Lanzo Torinese Italy 45°16N 7°28E 198 C4
Lao → Italy 39°47N 15°48E 201 C8
Lao Cai Vietnam 22°30N 103°57E 228 F4
Laoag Phil. 18°7N 120°34E 232 B2
Laoang Phil. 12°32N 125°8E 232 E5
Laoha He → China 43°25N 120°35E 227 C11
Laohekou China 32°22N 111°38E 229 A8
Laois □ Ireland 52°57N 7°27W 166 D4
Laon France 49°33N 3°35E 173 C10
Laona U.S.A. 45°34N 88°40W 308 C9
Laoung Hsi → Taiwan 24°43N 120°27E 225 D2
Laos ■ Asia 17°45N 105°0E 236 D5
Lapa Paraná, Brazil 25°46S 49°44W 335 B6
Lapa Rio de J., Brazil 22°54S 43°10W 135 B1
Lapac I. Phil. 5°32N 120°47E 233 J3
Lapai Nigeria 9°5N 6°32E 263 D6
Lapalisse France 46°15N 3°38E 173 F10
Laparan I. Phil. 5°57N 120°0E 233 J2
Lapeer U.S.A. 43°3N 83°19W 311 A13
Lapeyrade France 44°2N 0°3W 174 E3
Lapithos Cyprus 35°21N 33°11E 207 E9
Lapland = Lappland Europe 68°7N 24°0E 160 B21
LaPorte Ind., U.S.A. 41°36N 86°43W 311 C10
Laporte Pa., U.S.A. 41°25N 76°30W 313 E8
Lapovo Serbia 44°10N 21°2E 202 B5
Lappeenranta Finland 61°3N 28°12E 188 B5
Lappland Europe 68°7N 24°0E 160 B21
Lappo = Lapua Finland 62°58N 23°0E 160 E20
Laprida Argentina 37°34S 60°45W 336 D3
Lâpseki Turkey 40°20N 26°41E 203 F10
Lapta = Lapithos Cyprus 35°21N 33°11E 207 E9
Laptev Sea Russia 76°0N 125°0E 215 B13
Lapu-Lapu Phil. 10°20N 123°55E 232 F4
Lapua Finland 62°58N 23°0E 160 E20
Lapuş, Munţii Romania 47°20N 23°50E 183 C3
Lăpuşna Moldova 46°53N 28°25E 183 D13
Lapy Poland 52°59N 22°52E 185 F9
L'Áquila Italy 42°22N 13°22E 198 F6
Lar Iran 27°40N 54°14E 247 E7
Lara Australia 38°2S 144°26E 283 F3
Lara □ Venezuela 10°10N 69°50W 328 A4
Larabanga Ghana 9°16N 1°56W 262 D4
Larache Morocco 35°10N 6°5W 260 A3

Laragaran = Plaridel Phil. 8°37N 123°43E 233 G4
Laragne-Montéglin France 44°18N 5°49E 175 D9
Lärak Iran 26°35N 56°21E 249 A7
Laramie U.S.A. 41°19N 105°35W 304 F11
Laramie Mts. U.S.A. 42°0N 105°30W 304 F11
Laranda = Karaman Turkey 37°14N 33°13E 206 C2
Laranjal do Jari Brazil 0°51S 52°32W 329 D7
Laranjeiras Brazil 22°55S 43°10W 135 B1
Laranjeiras do Sul Brazil 25°23S 52°23W 335 B5
Larantuka Indonesia 8°21S 122°55E 231 F6
Larat Indonesia 7°0S 132°0E 231 F8
L'Arbresle France 45°50N 4°36E 175 C8
Lårbro Sweden 57°47N 18°50E 163 G12
Lårdal Norway 59°25N 8°10E 164 F3
Larde Mozam. 16°28S 39°43E 269 F4
Larder Lake Canada 48°5N 79°40W 298 C4
Lardos Greece 36°6N 28°1E 206 C12
Lardos, Akra = Líndos, Akra Greece 36°4N 28°10E 206 C12
Lardos, Órmos Greece 36°4N 28°2E 206 C12
Laredo Spain 43°26N 3°28W 194 B7
Laredo Tex., U.S.A. 27°30N 99°30W 314 H5
Laredo Sd. Canada 52°30N 128°53W 296 C3
Larena Phil. 9°15N 123°3E 233 G4
Lares Puerto Rico 18°18N 66°53W 321 b
Large I. Grenada 12°24N 61°30W 323 q
Largentière France 44°34N 4°18E 175 D8
Largo U.S.A. 27°54N 82°47W 317 H7
Largo, Key U.S.A. 25°15N 80°15W 317 K9
Largs U.K. 55°47N 4°52W 167 F4
Lari Italy 43°34N 10°35E 198 E7
Lariang Indonesia 1°26S 119°17E 235 C5
Larimore U.S.A. 47°54N 97°38W 308 A6
Larino Italy 41°48N 14°54E 199 G11
Larisa Greece 39°36N 22°27E 204 B4
Lárisis Station Athens, Greece 112 a1
Larissa = Larisa Greece 39°36N 22°27E 204 B4
Larissos → Greece 39°39N 22°24E 204 B4
Larkana Pakistan 27°32N 68°18E 242 F3
Larkins = South Miami U.S.A. 25°42N 80°17W 129 D1
Larnaca Cyprus 34°55N 33°38E 207 E9
Larnaca ✈ (LCA) Cyprus 34°50N 33°34E 207 E9
Larnaca Bay Cyprus 34°53N 33°45E 207 F9
Larnare, Pte. Martinique 14°47N 61°13W 322 j
Larne U.K. 54°51N 5°51W 166 B6
Larned U.S.A. 38°11N 99°6W 308 F4
Laroquebrou France 44°58N 2°12E 174 D6
Larose U.S.A. 29°34N 90°23W 315 G9
Larose, Pte. Martinique 14°39N 60°53W 322 j
Larrimah Australia 15°35S 133°12E 280 B5
Larsen Bay U.S.A. 57°32N 153°59W 303 H9
Larsen Ice Shelf Antarctica 67°0S 62°0W 151 C17
Larsnes Norway 62°12N 5°35E 164 C2
Larvik Norway 59°4N 10°2E 164 F4
Larzac, Causse du France 43°50N 3°17E 174 E7
Las Alpujarras Spain 36°55N 3°20W 197 J1
Las Animas U.S.A. 38°4N 103°13W 304 G12
Las Anod Somalia 8°26N 47°19E 267 C6
Las Arenas Spain 43°17N 4°50W 194 B6
Las Batuecas △ Spain 40°32N 6°5W 194 E4
Las Bermúdez Venezuela 10°56N 64°1W 329 a
Las Bonitas Venezuela 7°52N 65°40W 328 B4
Las Brenãs Argentina 27°5S 61°7W 334 B3
Las Cabezas de San Juan Spain 36°57N 5°58W 196 J5
Las Cabreras Venezuela 11°3N 63°58W 329 a
Las Cañadas del Teide △ Canary Is. 28°15N 16°37W 153 e1
Las Chimeneas Mexico 32°8N 116°5W 307 N10
Las Coloradas Argentina 39°34S 70°36W 336 A2
Las Corts Spain 41°23N 2°9E 114 A1
Las Cruces U.S.A. 32°19N 106°47W 305 K10
Las Flores Argentina 36°10S 59°7W 334 D4
Las Gabias = Gabia la Grande Spain 37°8N 3°40W 195 H7
Las Heras Mendoza, Argentina 32°51S 68°49W 334 C2
Las Heras Santa Cruz, Argentina 46°33S 68°57W 336 C3
Las Hermosas △ Colombia 3°48N 75°51W 328 C2
Las Horquetas Argentina 48°14S 71°11W 336 C2
Las Kabacki Poland 52°6N 21°2E 143 C2
Las Khoreh = Laasqoray Somalia 11°10N 48°20E 267 B6
Las Lajas Argentina 38°30S 70°25W 336 A2
Las Lomas Peru 4°40S 80°10W 330 A1
Las Lomitas Argentina 24°43S 60°35W 334 A3
Las Manos, Cueva de Argentina 47°9S 70°40W 336 C2
Las Marismas Spain 37°5N 6°20W 196 H4
Las Médulas Spain 42°28N 6°46W 194 C4
Las Mercedes Venezuela 9°7N 66°24W 328 B4
Las Minas Spain 38°20N 1°41W 197 G3
Las Navas de la Concepción Spain 37°56N 5°30W 195 H5
Las Navas del Marqués Spain 40°36N 4°22W 194 E6
Las Nieves Phil. 8°46N 125°34E 233 G5
Las Orquídeas △ Colombia 6°36N 76°16W 328 B2
Las Palmas Argentina 27°8S 58°45W 334 B4
Las Palmas Canary Is. 28°7N 15°26W 153 e1
Las Palmas → Mexico 32°31N 116°58W 307 N10
Las Palmas ✈ (LPA) Canary Is. 27°55N 15°25W 153 e1
Las Pedroñas Spain 39°26N 2°40W 195 F2
Las Piedras Puerto Rico 18°11N 65°52W 321 b
Las Piedras Uruguay 34°44S 56°14W 335 C4
Las Pinas Phil. 14°29N 120°58E 127 C1
Las Pipinas Argentina 35°30S 57°19W 334 D4
Las Plumas Argentina 43°40S 67°15W 336 B3
Las Ramblas = La Rambla Barcelona, Spain 114 b2
Las Rejas Chile 33°27S 70°42W 137 B1
Las Rosas Argentina 32°30S 61°35W 334 C3
Las Rozas Spain 40°29N 3°52W 194 E7
Las Tablas Panama 7°49N 80°14W 320 E3
Las Toscas Argentina 28°21S 59°18W 334 B4
Las Tunas Cuba 20°58N 76°59W 320 B4
Las Varillas Argentina 31°50S 62°50W 334 C3
Las Vegas N. Mex., U.S.A. 35°36N 105°13W 305 J11
Las Vegas Nev., U.S.A. 36°10N 115°8W 124 A2
Las Vegas McCarran Int. ✈ (LAS) U.S.A. 36°5N 115°9W 124 B2
Lasa = Lhasa China 29°25N 90°58E 218 F7
LaSalle Canada 45°26N 73°39W 130 B2
LaSalle Street U.S.A. 119 a1
LaSalle Street Station U.S.A. 119 a1
Lasanga I. Papua N. G. 7°25S 147°15E 286 D4
Lasarte-Oria Spain 43°16N 2°1W 196 B2
Lascano Uruguay 33°35S 54°12W 335 C5
Lascelles Australia 35°35S 142°34E 282 C5
Lasek Bielański Poland 52°17N 20°57E 143 A1
Lasek Na Kole Poland 52°13N 20°54E 143 B1
Lash-e Joveyn Afghan. 31°45N 61°30E 240 C1
Lashburn Canada 53°10N 109°40W 297 C7
Lashio Burma 22°56N 97°45E 241 D6
Lashkar India 26°10N 78°10E 243 F7
Lashkar Gãh Afghan. 31°35N 64°21E 240 D1

Lasin Poland 53°30N 19°2E 184 E6
Lasíthi Greece 35°11N 25°31E 207 E6
Lasíthi □ Greece 35°5N 25°50E 207 E6
Läsjerd Iran 35°24N 53°4E 247 C7
Lask Poland 51°34N 19°8E 185 G6
Łaskarzew Poland 51°48N 21°36E 185 G8
Laško Slovenia 46°10N 15°16E 199 B12
Lassance Brazil 17°54S 44°34W 333 E3
Lassay-les-Châteaux France 48°27N 0°30W 172 D6
Lassen Pk. U.S.A. 40°29N 121°30W 304 F3
Lassen Volcanic △ U.S.A. 40°30N 121°20W 304 F3
Lassóngo Angola 12°5S 22°46E 265 E4
Last Mountain L. Canada 51°5N 105°14W 297 C7
Lastchance Cr. → U.S.A. 40°2N 121°15W 306 E5
Lastoursville Gabon 0°55S 12°38E 264 C2
Lastovo Croatia 42°46N 16°55E 199 F13
Lastovski Kanal Croatia 42°50N 17°0E 199 F13
Lat Yao Thailand 15°45N 99°48E 236 D1
Lata Mt. Amer. Samoa 14°14S 169°27W 302 f
Latacunga Ecuador 0°50S 78°35W 328 D2
Latady I. Antarctica 70°45S 74°35W 151 D17
Latakia = Al Lādhiqīyah Syria 35°30N 35°45E 250 C6
Latchford Canada 47°20N 79°50W 298 C4
Latehar India 23°45N 84°30E 243 H11
Laterza Italy 40°37N 16°48E 201 B9
Latham Australia 29°44S 116°20E 279 E2
Lathen Germany 52°52N 7°19E 178 C3
Lathi India 27°43N 71°23E 242 F4
Lathi Vanuatu 14°57S 167°8E 287 D5
Lathrop U.S.A. 39°33N 94°20W 310 E2
Lathrop Wells U.S.A. 36°39N 116°24W 307 J10
Latiano Italy 40°33N 17°43E 201 B10
Latin, Quartier Montréal, Canada 130 b2
Latina Italy 41°28N 12°52E 200 A5
Latina Madrid, Spain 40°24N 3°44W 127 B1
Latina Italy 45°47N 13°0E 199 C10
Latium = Lazio □ Italy 42°10N 12°30E 199 F9
Laton U.S.A. 36°26N 119°41W 306 J7
Latorytsya → Slovak Rep. 48°28N 21°50E 181 C14
Latouche Treville, C. Australia 18°27S 121°49E 278 C3
Latouma Niger 22°10N 14°50E 259 D2
Látrar Iceland 66°24N 23°3W 155 A3
Latrobe Tas., Australia 41°14S 146°30E 281 G4
Latrobe Pa., U.S.A. 40°19N 79°23W 312 F5
Latrónico Italy 40°5N 16°1E 201 B9
Latur India 18°25N 76°40E 244 E3
Latvia ■ Europe 56°50N 24°0E 188 D2
Lau Nigeria 9°11N 11°19E 263 D7
Lau Bsan Pac. Oc. 20°0S 177°0W 277 E15
Lau Group Fiji 17°0S 178°30W 287 A3
Lau Ridge Pac. Oc. 21°0S 178°30W 277 L15
Laubach Germany 50°33N 8°59E 178 E5
Lauca → Bolivia 19°9S 68°10W 330 D4
Lauchhammer Germany 51°29N 13°47E 178 D9
Lauda-Königshofen Germany 49°33N 9°42E 179 F5
Laudal Norway 58°15N 7°30E 164 F2
Laudat Dominica 15°20N 61°21W 323 a
Lauderdale Lakes U.S.A. 26°9N 80°12W 129 B1
Lauderhill U.S.A. 26°8N 80°12W 129 B1
Lauenburg = Lębork Poland 54°33N 17°46E 184 D4
Lauenburgische Seen △ Germany 53°38N 10°45E 178 B6
Lauf Germany 49°30N 11°16E 179 F7
Laufäs Iceland 65°53N 18°4W 155 B8
Laugar Iceland 65°15N 21°48W 155 B5
Laugarás Iceland 64°7N 20°30W 155 C6
Laugarbakki Iceland 65°20N 20°55W 155 B6
Laugarvatn Iceland 64°13N 20°44W 155 C6
Lauge Koch Kyst Greenland 75°45N 57°45W 295 B20
Laughlin U.S.A. 35°10N 114°34W 307 K12
Laujar de Andarax Spain 37°0N 2°54W 197 H2
Laukaa Finland 62°24N 25°56E 160 E21
Laukkaing Burma 23°52N 98°38E 241 D7
Laulau, Bahia N. Marianas 15°8N 145°45E 302 e
Launceston Tas., Australia 41°24S 147°8E 281 G4
Launceston Corn., U.K. 50°38N 4°22W 165 G3
Laune → Ireland 52°7N 9°47W 166 D2
Launglon Bok Burma 13°50N 97°54E 236 F1
Laupheim Germany 48°14N 9°52E 179 G5
Laura Queens., Australia 15°32S 144°32E 280 B3
Laura S. Austral., Australia 33°10S 138°18E 282 B3
Laureana di Borrello Italy 38°30N 16°5E 201 D9
Laurel Fla., U.S.A. 27°8N 82°27W 317 H7
Laurel Ind., U.S.A. 39°30N 85°11W 311 E11
Laurel Miss., U.S.A. 31°41N 89°8W 315 F10
Laurel Mont., U.S.A. 45°40N 108°46W 304 D9
Laurel Bay U.S.A. 32°27N 80°47W 317 E5
Laurel Hill U.S.A. 40°14N 79°6W 312 F5
Laurencekirk U.K. 56°50N 2°28W 167 E6
Laurens Iowa, U.S.A. 42°51N 94°52W 310 B2
Laurens S.C., U.S.A. 34°30N 82°1W 315 D13
Laurentian Plateau Canada 52°0N 70°0W 299 B6
Lauria Italy 40°2N 15°50E 201 B8
Laurie L. Canada 56°35N 101°57W 297 B8
Laurinburg U.S.A. 34°47N 79°28W 315 D15
Laurium U.S.A. 47°14N 88°27W 308 B9
Lausanne Switz. 46°32N 6°38E 179 J2
Laut, Pulau Indonesia 3°40S 116°10E 235 C5
Laut Kecil, Kepulauan Indonesia 4°45S 115°40E 235 C5
Lautaro Chile 38°31S 72°27W 336 A2
Lauterbach Germany 50°37N 9°24E 178 E5
Lauterecken Germany 49°38N 7°35E 179 F3
Lautoka Fiji 17°37S 177°27E 287 A1
L'Autre Bord Guadeloupe 16°20N 61°20W 322 e
Lauttasaari → Indonesia 4°45S 115°0E 235 C5
Lauwers → Neths. 53°22N 6°11E 170 A6
Lauwersmeer △ Neths. 53°22N 6°11E 170 A6
Lauzès France 44°34N 1°35E 174 D5
Lava → Russia 54°37N 21°14E 184 D8
Lava, Nosy Madag. 14°33S 47°36E 269 B8
Lava Beds △ U.S.A. 41°40N 121°30W 304 F3
Lavagh More Ireland 54°46N 8°6W 166 B3
Lavagna Italy 44°18N 9°22E 198 D6
Laval France 48°4N 0°48W 172 D6
Laval-des-Rapides Canada 45°33N 73°42W 130 A1
Lavalle Argentina 28°15S 65°15W 334 B2
Lāvān Iran 26°48N 53°22E 247 E7
Lavanggu Solomon Is. 11°36S 160°16E 287 N11
Lavant → France 48°46N 53°22E 247 D7
Lavara Greece 41°19N 26°22E 203 E10
Lavardac France 44°12N 0°20E 174 D4
Lavaur France 43°40N 1°49E 174 E5
Lavelanet France 42°57N 1°51E 174 F5
Lavello Italy 41°3N 15°48E 201 A8
Laventille □ Trin. & Tob. 10°39N 61°30W 323 t
L'Avérdy, C. Papua N. G. 4°57N 153°0E 288 C8
Lavers Hill Australia 38°40S 143°25E 282 E5
Laverton Australia 28°44S 122°29E 279 E3
Lavik Norway 61°6N 5°25E 164 D2
Lavis Italy 46°8N 11°7E 198 B8
Lavīzān Iran 35°47N 51°30E 141 A2
Lavos Portugal 40°6N 8°49W 194 D2
Lavoutte, Anse St. Lucia 14°5N 60°55W 323 a
Lavradio Portugal 38°40N 9°2W 126 A2
Lavras Brazil 21°20S 45°0W 333 H3

Lavre Portugal 38°46N 8°22W 195 G2
Lavrio Greece 37°40N 24°4E 204 D6
Lavris Greece 35°25N 24°40E 207 C5
Lāvūsh Manda △ Zambia 12°46S 31°0E 269 E3
Lawa → Phil. 12°6N 125°1E 233 E5
Lawa-an Phil. 11°5N 125°5E 233 F5
Lawachara △ Bangla. 24°20N 91°43E 241 C3
Lawak I. Phil. 10°46N 115°55E 235 A4
Lawas Malaysia 4°55N 115°25E 235 B5
Lawdar Yemen 13°53N 45°52E 248 D4
Lawele Indonesia 5°13S 122°57E 231 F6
Lawit Indonesia 1°23N 112°55E 235 B4
Lawler U.S.A. 43°4N 92°9W 310 B4
Lawn Hill = Boodjamulla △ Australia 18°15S 138°6E 280 B2
Lawndale U.S.A. 33°54N 118°24W 119 B2
Lawng Pit Burma 25°30N 97°25E 241 B3
Lawqah Si. Arabia 29°49N 42°45E 246 D4
Lawra Ghana 10°39N 2°51W 262 C4
Lawrence N.Z. 45°55S 169°41E 285 F4
Lawrence Ind., U.S.A. 39°50N 86°2W 311 E10
Lawrence Kans., U.S.A. 38°58N 95°14W 308 F6
Lawrence Mass., U.S.A. 42°43N 71°10W 313 D13
Lawrence Heights Canada 43°43N 79°25W 141 A2
Lawrenceburg Ind., U.S.A. 39°6N 84°52W 311 E12
Lawrenceburg Ky., U.S.A. 38°2N 84°54W 311 F12
Lawrenceburg Tenn., U.S.A. 35°14N 87°20W 315 D11
Lawrenceville Ga., U.S.A. 33°57N 83°59W 316 B6
Lawrenceville Ill., U.S.A. 38°44N 87°41W 311 F9
Lawrenceville Pa., U.S.A. 41°59N 77°8W 312 E7
Laws U.S.A. 37°24N 118°20W 306 H8
Lawson U.S.A. 39°26N 94°12W 310 E2
Lawtey U.S.A. 30°3N 82°5W 316 F7
Lawton Mich., U.S.A. 42°10N 85°50W 311 B11
Lawton Okla., U.S.A. 34°37N 98°25W 314 D5
Lawu Indonesia 7°40S 111°13E 235 D4
Lawz, J. al Si. Arabia 28°39N 35°18E 246 D2
Laxå Sweden 58°59N 14°37E 163 F8
Laxamýri Iceland 65°58N 17°24W 155 B8
Laxford, L. U.K. 58°24N 5°6W 167 C3
Laxiwa Dam China 36°4N 101°11E 218 D9
Laxou France 48°41N 6°8E 173 D13
Lay → France 46°18N 1°17W 174 B2
Layari Pakistan 24°52N 60°12E 123 A2
Layari → Pakistan 24°52N 66°58E 123 A2
Layla Si. Arabia 22°10N 46°40E 248 A4
Laylān Iraq 35°18N 44°31E 246 C5
Layon → France 47°20N 0°45W 172 E6
Layou St. Vincent 13°12N 61°17W 323 a
Layou → Dominica 15°23N 61°27W 323 k
Laysan I. Pac. Oc. 25°50N 171°50W 302 F9
Layton Fla., U.S.A. 24°50N 80°47W 317 L9
Layton Utah, U.S.A. 41°4N 111°58W 304 F8
Laytonville U.S.A. 39°41N 123°29W 304 G2
Laza Burma 26°30N 97°38E 241 B6
Lazarata Greece 38°47N 20°40E 207 B2
Lazarev Sea S. Ocean 67°30S 3°0W 151 C2
Lazarevac Serbia 44°23N 20°17E 202 B4
Lazarevskoye Russia 43°55N 39°21E 191 J4
Lázaro Cárdenas Mexico 17°55N 102°11W 318 D4
Lazdijai Lithuania 54°14N 23°31E 184 D10
Lazhuglung China 34°52N 81°24E 217 F10
Lazi Phil. 9°8N 123°38E 233 G4
Lázienki Palace Warsaw, Poland 143 c3
Lazienkowski Park Warsaw, Poland 52°13N 21°1E 143 B2
Lazio □ Italy 42°10N 12°30E 199 F9
Lazo Moldova 47°33N 28°27E 183 C13
Lazo Russia 43°25N 133°55E 226 C6
Lazy Lake U.S.A. 26°9N 80°8W 129 B3

Le Beausset France 43°12N 5°48E 175 E9
Le Bélier Réunion 21°2S 55°28E 272 f
Le Bic Canada 48°20N 68°41W 299 C6
Le Blanc France 46°37N 1°3E 174 B5
Le Blanc-Mesnil France 48°56N 2°30E 134 A3
Le Bleymard France 44°30N 3°42E 174 D7
Le Bourget France 48°56N 2°25E 134 A3
Le Bourgneuf-la-Fôret France 48°10N 0°59W 172 D6
Le Bugue France 44°55N 0°56E 174 D4
Le Carbet Martinique 14°43N 61°7W 322 j
Le Cateau Cambrésis France 50°7N 3°32E 173 B10
Le Caylar France 43°51N 3°19E 174 E7
Le Chambon-Feugerolles France 45°24N 4°19E 175 C8
Le Chameau Guadeloupe 15°51N 61°35W 322 e
Le Châtelet France 46°38N 2°16E 173 F9
Le Chenoi Belgium 50°41N 4°18E 116 B2
Le Chesnay France 48°49N 2°8E 134 B1
Le Cheylard France 44°55N 4°25E 175 D8
Le Claire U.S.A. 41°36N 90°21W 310 C6
Le Conquet France 48°21N 4°46W 172 D2
Le Creusot France 46°48N 4°24E 173 F11
Le Croisic France 47°18N 2°30W 172 E4
Le Diamant Martinique 14°28N 61°2W 322 j
Le Donjon France 46°20N 3°48E 173 F10
Le Dorat France 46°14N 1°5E 174 B5
Le François Martinique 14°38N 60°57W 322 j
Le Gosier Guadeloupe 16°14N 61°29W 322 f
Le Grand-Brûlé Réunion 21°14S 55°47E 272 f
Le Grand-Lucé France 47°52N 0°28E 172 E7
Le Grand-Pressigny France 46°55N 0°48E 172 F7
Le Grand-Quevilly France 49°24N 1°4E 172 D8
Le Gris Gris Mauritius 20°31S 57°32E 272 e
Le Gros Morne Réunion 21°5S 55°28E 272 f
Le Havre France 49°30N 0°5E 172 D7
Le Kremlin-Bicêtre France 48°48N 2°21E 134 B3
Le Lamentin Martinique 14°35N 61°2W 322 j
Le Lavandou France 43°8N 6°22E 175 E10
Le Lion-d'Angers France 47°38N 0°42W 172 E6
Le Lorrain Martinique 14°48N 61°3W 322 j
Le Louroux-Béconnais France 47°30N 0°55W 172 E6
Le Luc France 43°23N 6°17E 175 E10
Le Lude France 47°39N 0°9E 172 E7
Le Maire, Estr. de Argentina 54°50S 65°0W 336 D4
Le Mans France 48°0N 0°10E 172 E7
Le Marigot Martinique 14°50N 61°4W 322 j
Le Marin Martinique 14°27N 60°55W 322 j
Le Mars U.S.A. 42°47N 96°10W 308 D6
Le Mayet-de-Montagne France 46°4N 3°40E 173 F10
Le Mêle-sur-Sarthe France 48°31N 0°22E 172 D7
Le Mesnil-le-Roi France 48°56N 2°7E 134 A1
Le Monastier-sur-Gazeille France 44°57N 3°59E 174 D7
Le Monêtier-les-Bains France 44°58N 6°30E 175 D10
Le Mont-Dore France 45°35N 2°49E 174 C6
Le Mont-St-Michel France 48°40N 1°30W 172 D5
Le Morne Brabant Mauritius 20°27S 57°19E 272 e
Le Morne Rouge Martinique 14°47N 61°9W 322 j
Le Morne-Vert Martinique 14°42N 61°9W 322 j
Le Moule Guadeloupe 16°20N 61°22W 322 e
Le Moyne, L. Canada 56°45N 68°47W 299 A6
Le Muy France 43°28N 6°34E 175 E10

Le Palais France 47°20N 3°10W 172 E3
Le Pecq France 48°53N 2°6E 134 A1
Le Perreux France 48°50N 2°29E 134 A3
Le Perthus France 42°30N 2°53E 174 F6
Le Pin France 48°54N 2°37E 134 A4
Le Plessis-Robinson France 48°47N 2°15E 134 B2
Le Plessis-Trévise France 48°48N 2°34E 134 B4
Le Port Réunion 20°56S 55°18E 272 f
Le Port-Marly France 48°52N 2°6E 134 A1
Le Pré-St-Gervais France 48°53N 2°23E 134 A3
Le Prêcheur Martinique 14°50N 61°12W 322 j
Le Puy-en-Velay France 45°3N 3°52E 174 C7
Le Raincy France 48°53N 2°31E 134 A4
Le Raysville U.S.A. 41°50N 76°10W 313 E8
Le Robert Martinique 14°40N 60°56W 322 j
Le Roy U.S.A. 40°21N 88°46W 311 D9
Le Roy N.Y., U.S.A. 42°58N 77°59W 312 D7
Le St-Esprit Martinique 14°34N 60°56W 322 j
Le Soufflaur Guadeloupe 16°19N 61°2W 322 e
Le Sueur U.S.A. 44°28N 93°55W 308 C7
Le Tampon Réunion 21°16S 55°32E 272 f
Le Teil France 44°33N 4°40E 175 D8
Le Teilleul France 48°32N 0°53W 172 D6
Le Theil France 48°16N 0°42E 172 D7
Le Thillot France 47°53N 6°46E 173 E13
Le Touquet-Paris-Plage France 50°30N 1°36E 172 B8
Le Tréport France 50°3N 1°20E 172 B8
Le Trou à Diable Guadeloupe 15°57N 61°14W 322 e
Lège-Cap-Ferret France 44°48N 1°9W 174 D2
Lège Hida Ethiopia 7°56N 41°4E 257 F5
Legendre I. Australia 20°22S 116°55E 278 D2
Leghorn = Livorno Italy 43°33N 10°19E 198 E7
Legian Indonesia 8°42S 115°10E 231 K18
Legionowo Poland 52°25N 20°50E 185 F7
Legnago Italy 45°11N 11°18E 199 C8
Legnano Italy 45°36N 8°54E 198 C5
Legnica Poland 51°12N 16°10E 185 G3
Legrad Croatia 46°17N 16°51E 199 B13
Leh India 34°9N 77°35E 243 B7
Lehigh Acres U.S.A. 26°36N 81°39W 317 H8
Lehighton U.S.A. 40°50N 75°43W 313 F9
Lehliu Romania 44°29N 26°50E 183 F11
Leho South Sudan 7°7N 33°52E 257 F2
Lehrte Germany 52°22N 9°58E 178 C5
Lehtimäki Finland 60°10N 24°15E 121 B2
Lehua I. U.S.A. 22°1N 160°6W 302 A1
Lehututu Botswana 23°54S 21°55E 270 B3
Lei Shui → China 26°55N 112°35E 229 D9
Lei Yue Mun China 22°17N 114°14E 219 b
Leiah Pakistan 30°58N 70°58E 242 D4
Leião Portugal 38°40N 9°17W 126 A1
Leibnitz Austria 46°47N 15°34E 180 C8
Leibo China 28°11N 103°46E 228 C4
Leicester City □ U.K. 52°38N 1°8W 169 E6
Leicester Square London, U.K. 125 b3
Leicestershire □ U.K. 52°41N 1°17W 169 E6
Leichhardt Australia 33°53S 151°9E 130 B1
Leichhardt → Australia 17°35S 139°48E 280 B2
Leichhardt Ra. Australia 20°46S 147°40E 280 C4
Leiden Neths. 52°9N 4°30E 170 B4
Leie → Belgium 51°2N 3°45E 170 C3
Leifers = Láives Italy 46°26N 11°20E 199 B8
Leigh → U.K. 53°30N 2°18W 169 D5
Leigh Creek Australia 30°38S 138°26E 282 B3
Leikanger Norway 62°15N 5°47E 164 B2
Leikanger Sogn og Fjordane, Norway 61°10N 6°51E 164 D3
Leikanger Sogn og Fjordane, Norway 62°8N 5°18E 164 B2
Leiktho Burma 19°13N 96°35E 241 F6
Leimen Germany 49°21N 8°41E 179 F4
Leimus Nic. 14°40N 84°3W 320 D3
Leine → Germany 52°43N 9°36E 178 C5
Leinefelde Germany 51°23N 10°19E 178 D6
Leinster Australia 27°51S 120°36E 279 E3
Leinster □ Ireland 53°3N 7°8W 166 C4
Leinster, Mt. Ireland 52°37N 6°46W 166 D5
Leipalingis Lithuania 54°4N 23°51E 184 D10
Leipe = Lipno Poland 52°49N 19°15E 185 F6
Leipzig Germany 51°18N 12°22E 178 D8
Leira Norway 60°58N 9°17E 164 D6
Leiria Portugal 39°46N 8°53W 194 F2
Leiria □ Portugal 39°46N 8°53W 194 F2
Leirvik Norway 59°47N 5°28E 164 E2
Leishan China 26°15N 108°20E 228 D7
Leisler, Mt. Australia 23°23S 129°20E 278 D4
Leisure City U.S.A. 25°30N 80°26W 317 K9
Leith U.K. 55°59N 3°11W 121 B3
Leith Hill U.K. 51°11N 0°22W 169 F7
Leitha → Europe 47°50N 17°15E 181 D10
Leitir Ceanainn = Letterkenny Ireland 54°57N 7°45W 166 B4
Leitrim □ Ireland 54°8N 8°0W 166 B4
Leitza Spain 43°5N 1°55W 196 B2
Leixlip Ireland 53°22N 6°30W 166 C5
Leiyang China 26°27N 112°45E 229 D9
Leizhou China 20°52N 110°8E 228 G7
Leizhou Bandao China 21°0N 110°0E 228 G7
Leizhou Wan China 20°50N 110°20E 228 G8
Lek → Neths. 51°54N 4°35E 170 C4
Leka Norway 65°5N 11°35E 160 D14
Lekani Greece 41°10N 24°35E 203 D8
Lekbibaj Albania 42°17N 19°56E 202 D3
Lekeitio Spain 43°20N 2°32W 196 B2
Lékéti, Mt. Congo 2°34S 14°17E 264 C2
Lekki Nigeria 6°26N 3°28E 263 D5
Lekki Lagoon Nigeria 6°30N 4°7E 263 D5
Lekki Peninsula Nigeria 6°26N 3°29E 263 D5
Léko Mali 13°37N 9°2W 262 C3
Lékoli-Pandaka △ Congo 0°41N 14°50E 264 B2
Lékoni Gabon 1°35S 14°14E 264 C2
Lékoni → Gabon 1°11S 13°16E 264 C2
Lekoui Burkina Faso 12°37N 3°40W 262 C4
Leksand Sweden 60°44N 15°0E 163 D8
Leksura = Lentekhi Georgia 42°47N 42°45E 191 J6
Leland Mich., U.S.A. 45°1N 85°45W 309 C11
Leland Miss., U.S.A. 33°24N 90°54W 315 E9
Leläng Sweden 59°10N 12°8E 164 E5
Lelepa Vanuatu 17°35S 168°11E 287 G6
Leleque Argentina 42°28S 71°0W 336 B2
Leli Solomon Is. 8°42S 161°4E 287 M11
Lelia China 37°44N 117°13E 227 F9
Lelintah Indonesia 1°11S 130°50E 231 E8
Léliouna Guinea 11°1N 12°56E 262 B2
Lelu Burma 19°4N 95°30E 241 F5
Lelystad Neths. 52°30N 5°25E 170 B5
Lem Denmark 56°2N 8°22E 163 H2
Lema Nigeria 12°58N 4°13E 263 C5
Lema Shilindi Ethiopia 4°1N 35°45E 257 G5
Léman, L. Europe 46°26N 6°30E 179 J2
Lemankoa Papua N. G. 5°3S 154°37E 288 C8
Lembar Indonesia 8°45S 116°4E 231 K19
Lemberg = Lviv Ukraine 49°50N 24°0E 187 D3
Lembongan, Nusa Indonesia 8°40S 115°27E 231 K18
Lembuak Indonesia 8°36S 116°11E 231 K19
Lemera Dem. Rep. of the Congo 3°0S 28°55E 268 C2
Lemery Phil. 13°51N 120°55E 232 D2
Lemesós = Limassol Cyprus 34°42N 33°1E 207 F9
Lemfu Dem. Rep. of the Congo 5°18S 15°13E 265 D3

Lemhi Ra. U.S.A. 44°0N 113°0W 304 D7
Lemmer Neths. 52°51N 5°43E 170 B5
Lemmon U.S.A. 45°57N 102°10W 308 C2
Lemon Grove U.S.A. 32°44N 117°1W 307 N9
Lemoore U.S.A. 36°18N 119°46W 306 J7
Lemotol B. Micronesia 7°21N 151°35E 287 T17
Lemoyne Canada 45°29N 73°29W 130 B3
Lempdes France 45°22N 3°17E 174 C7
Lemsid W. Sahara 26°33N 13°51W 260 C2
Lemukutan Indonesia 0°45N 108°43E 235 B3
Lemvig Denmark 56°33N 8°20E 163 H2
Lemyethna Burma 17°36N 95°9E 241 G5
Lena U.S.A. 42°23N 89°49W 310 B7
Lena → Russia 72°52N 126°40E 215 B13
Lenadoon Pt. Ireland 54°18N 9°3W 166 B2
Lenakel Vanuatu 19°38S 169°16E 287 J7
Lenart Slovenia 46°36N 15°48E 199 B12
Lenartovce Slovak Rep. 48°18N 20°19E 181 C13
Lencloître France 46°50N 0°20E 172 F7
Lençóis Brazil 12°35S 41°24W 333 D3
Lençóis Maranhenses △ Brazil 2°30S 43°0W 332 B3
Lendava Slovenia 46°35N 16°25E 199 B13
Lendinara Italy 45°5N 11°36E 199 C8
Lenger Kazakhstan 42°12N 69°54E 217 D7
Lengerich Germany 52°11N 7°52E 178 C3
Lenggong Malaysia 5°6N 100°58E 237 K3
Lenggries Germany 47°41N 11°35E 179 H7
Léngoué Congo 1°15N 15°38E 264 B3
Lengshuijiang China 27°40N 111°26E 229 D8
Lengshuitan China 26°27N 111°35E 229 D8
Lengua de Vaca, Pta. Chile 30°14S 71°38W 334 C1
Lengwe △ Malawi 16°14S 34°45E 269 F3
Lengwethen = Lunino Russia 53°38N 45°18E 190 D7
Lengyeltóti Hungary 46°40N 17°40E 182 D2
Lengyeltótihács = Lengyeltóti Hungary 46°40N 17°40E 182 D2
Lenhovda Sweden 57°0N 15°16E 163 G9
Lenin Russia 55°43N 37°34E 129 B2
Lenin Mausoleum Moscow, Russia 129 b2
Lenina, Kanal → Russia 43°44N 45°17E 191 J7
Leninabad = Khŭjand Tajikistan 40°17N 69°37E 217 D7
Leninakan = Gyumri Armenia 40°47N 43°50E 191 K6
Lenine Ukraine 45°17N 35°46E 189 K8
Leningrad = Sankt-Peterburg Russia 59°55N 30°20E 137 B1
Leningrad □ Russia 59°40N 32°0E 188 C7
Lenino = Leninsk-Kuznetskiy Russia 54°44N 86°10E 217 B11
Lenino Russia 55°38N 37°39E 129 C2
Leninogorsk = Ridder Kazakhstan 50°20N 83°30E 217 B10
Leninogorsk Russia 54°36N 52°30E 216 B4
Leninsk = Petrodvorets Russia 59°52N 29°54E 188 C5
Leninsk Russia 48°40N 45°15E 191 F7
Leninsk-Kuznetskiy Russia 54°44N 86°10E 217 B11
Leninsk-Turkmensky = Türkmenabat Turkmenistan 39°6N 63°34E 247 B9
Leninskiye Gory Russia 55°41N 37°32E 129 B2
Leninskoye Russia 58°23N 47°3E 190 A8
Lenk Switz. 46°27N 7°28E 179 J3
Lenkoran = Länkäran Azerbaijan 38°48N 48°52E 213 C13
Lenmalu Indonesia 1°45S 130°15E 231 E8
Lennartsfors Sweden 59°20N 11°55E 162 E5
Lenne → Germany 51°25N 7°29E 178 D3
Lennestadt Germany 51°8N 8°2E 178 D4
Lennox Calif., U.S.A. 33°56N 118°20W 126 C2
Lennox S. Dak., U.S.A. 43°21N 96°53W 308 D5
Lennox, I. Chile 55°18S 66°50W 336 E3
Lennoxville Canada 45°22N 71°51W 313 A13
Leno Italy 45°22N 10°13E 198 C7
Lenoir U.S.A. 35°55N 81°32W 315 D14
Lenoir City U.S.A. 35°48N 84°16W 315 D12
Lenore L. Canada 52°30N 104°59W 297 C8
Lenox Ga., U.S.A. 31°16N 83°28W 316 D6
Lenox Iowa, U.S.A. 40°53N 94°34W 310 D2
Lenox Mass., U.S.A. 42°22N 73°17W 313 D11
Lens France 50°26N 2°50E 173 B9
Lensahn Germany 54°13N 10°53E 178 A6
Lensk Russia 60°48N 114°55E 215 C12
Lensvik Norway 63°31N 9°48E 164 A6
Lentas Greece 34°56N 24°56E 207 F5
Lentekhi Georgia 42°47N 42°45E 191 J6
Lenti Hungary 46°37N 16°33E 182 D1
Lentini Italy 37°17N 15°0E 201 E8
Lentschütz = Łęczyca Poland 52°5N 19°15E 185 F6
Lenwood U.S.A. 34°53N 117°7W 307 L9
Lenya Burma 11°33N 98°57E 237 G2
Lenzen Germany 53°5N 11°29E 178 B7
Léo Burkina Faso 11°3N 2°2W 262 C4
Leoben Austria 47°22N 15°5E 180 D8
Leobschütz = Głubczyce Poland 50°13N 17°52E 185 H4
Leodhais = Lewis U.K. 58°9N 6°40W 167 C2
Leola U.S.A. 45°43N 98°56W 308 C4
Leominster Hereford, U.K. 52°14N 2°43W 169 E5
Leominster Mass., U.S.A. 42°32N 71°46W 313 D13
León = Cotopaxi □ Ecuador 0°5S 78°55W 328 D2
Léon Landes, France 43°53N 1°18W 174 E2
León Guanajuato, Mexico 21°6N 101°41W 318 C4
León Nic. 12°27N 86°51W 320 D2
León Spain 42°38N 5°34W 194 C5
Leon Iowa, U.S.A. 40°44N 93°45W 310 D3
León □ Spain 42°40N 5°55W 194 C5
Leon → U.S.A. 31°14N 97°28W 314 F6
León, Montes de Spain 42°30N 6°18W 194 C4
Leonardo da Vinci, Roma ✈ (FCO) Italy 41°48N 12°15E 199 G9
Leonardtown U.S.A. 38°17N 76°38W 309 F15
Leonardville Namibia 23°29S 18°49E 270 B2
Leonárisso Cyprus 35°28N 34°8E 207 E10
Leonberg Germany 48°48N 9°1E 179 G5
Leonding Austria 48°16N 14°15E 180 C7
Leone Amer. Samoa 14°23S 170°48W 302 f
Leonessa Italy 42°34N 12°58E 199 F9
Leonforte Italy 37°38N 14°23E 201 E7
Leongatha Australia 38°30S 145°58E 283 E6
Leonia Fla., U.S.A. 30°55N 86°1W 316 E3
Leonia N.J., U.S.A. 40°51N 73°59W 132 A2
Leonidio Greece 37°9N 22°52E 204 D4
Leonora Australia 28°49S 121°19E 279 E3
Leopardstown Ireland 53°16N 6°11W 120 B2
Leopold II, L. = Mai-Ndombe, L. Dem. Rep. of the Congo 2°0S 18°20E 264 C3
Leopoldau Austria 48°15N 16°26E 142 A2
Leopoldina = Aruanã Brazil 14°54S 51°10W 333 D1
Leopoldina = Parnamirim Brazil 8°5S 39°34W 332 C4
Leopoldina Brazil 21°28S 42°40W 333 F3
Leopoldo Bulhões Brazil 16°37S 48°46W 333 E2
Leopoldsburg Belgium 51°7N 5°13E 170 C5
Leopoldsdorf Austria 48°7N 16°23E 142 B2
Leopoldstadt Austria 48°13N 16°22E 142 A2
Leopoldville = Kinshasa Dem. Rep. of the Congo 4°20S 15°15E 265 C3
Leoti U.S.A. 38°29N 101°21W 308 F3
Leova Moldova 46°28N 28°15E 183 D13
Leoville Canada 53°39N 107°33W 297 C7
Lepar Indonesia 2°57S 106°49E 234 C3
Lepe Spain 37°15N 7°12W 195 H3
Lepel = Lyepyel Belarus 54°50N 28°40E 188 E5
Lepenou Greece 38°42N 21°17E 204 C3
Leping China 28°47N 117°7E 229 C11
Lépo, L. do Angola 17°0S 19°0E 265 F3
Lepontine, Alpi Italy 46°22N 8°27E 198 B5
Leportovo Russia 55°45N 37°43E 129 B3
Leposavić Kosovo 43°6N 20°48E 202 C4
Leppävaara Finland 60°13N 24°49E 121 B1
Leppävirta Finland 62°29N 27°46E 160 E22
Lepsény Hungary 47°0N 18°15E 182 D3
Leptis Magna Libya 32°40N 14°12E 258 B2
Lequeitio = Lekeitio Spain 43°20N 2°32W 196 B2
Lercara Friddi Italy 37°45N 13°36E 200 E6
Léré C.A.R. 6°46N 17°25E 264 A3
Léré Chad 9°39N 14°13E 259 G2
Léré Mali 15°45N 4°55W 262 B4
Lere Bauchi, Nigeria 9°43N 9°18E 263 D6
Lere Kaduna, Nigeria 10°23N 8°35E 263 C6
Leribe Lesotho 28°51S 28°3E 271 C4
Lérici Italy 44°4N 9°55E 198 D6
Lérida = Lleida Spain 41°37N 0°39E 196 D5
Lérins, Îs. de France 43°31N 7°3E 175 E11
Lerma Spain 42°0N 3°47W 194 C7
Leros Greece 37°10N 26°50E 205 D8
Lérouville France 48°44N 5°30E 173 D12
Lerum Sweden 57°46N 12°16E 163 G6
Lerwick U.K. 60°9N 1°9W 167 A7
Leş Romania 46°58N 21°50E 182 D6
Les Abrets France 45°32N 5°35E 175 C9
Les Abymes Guadeloupe 16°17N 61°32W 322 e
Les Andelys France 49°15N 1°25E 172 C8
Les Anses-d'Arlets Martinique 14°28N 61°6W 322 j
Les Avirons Réunion 21°14S 55°20E 272 f
Les Borges Blanques Spain 41°31N 0°52E 196 D5
Les Cayes Haiti 18°15N 73°46W 321 C5
Les Coteaux Canada 45°15N 74°13W 313 A10
Les Escoumins Canada 48°21N 69°24W 299 C6
Les Essarts France 46°47N 1°12W 172 F5
Les Grands Fonds Guadeloupe 16°16N 61°26W 322 e
Les Herbiers France 46°52N 1°1W 172 F5
Les Lilas France 48°52N 2°25E 134 A3
Les Loges-en-Josas France 48°45N 2°8E 134 B1
Les Mangles Guadeloupe 16°23N 61°27W 322 e
Les Minquiers, Plateau des Chan. Is. 48°58N 2°8W 172 D4
Les Moroubas C.A.R. 6°11N 20°13E 264 A4
Les Pavillons-sous-Bois France 48°54N 2°30E 134 A4
Les Pieux France 49°30N 1°48W 172 C5
Les Ponts-de-Cé France 47°25N 0°30W 172 E6
Les Riceys France 47°59N 4°22E 173 E11
Les Sables-d'Olonne France 46°30N 1°45W 174 B2
Les Tantes Grenada 12°19N 61°33W 323 q
Les Trois-Bassins Réunion 21°5S 55°18E 272 f
Les Trois-Îlets Martinique 14°32N 61°2W 322 j
Les Vans France 44°25N 4°7E 175 D8
Lesbos Greece 39°10N 26°20E 205 B8
L'Escala Spain 42°7N 3°8E 196 C8
L'Escalier Mauritius 20°28S 57°36E 272 e
Leschnitz = Leśnica Poland 50°26N 18°11E 185 H5
Leshan China 29°33N 103°41E 228 C4
Leshukonskoye Russia 64°54N 45°46E 186 B8
Leshwe ⌓ Dem. Rep. of the Congo 12°45S 29°30E 269 E2
Lésigny France 48°44N 2°37E 134 B4
Lésina Italy 41°52N 15°21E 199 G12
Lésina, L. di Italy 41°53N 15°26E 199 G12
Lesjaskog Norway 62°14N 8°22E 164 B5
Lesjaverk Norway 62°12N 8°34E 164 B5
Lesjöfors Sweden 59°58N 14°11E 162 E8
Leskhimstroy = Syeverodonetsk Ukraine 48°58N 38°35E 189 H10
Lesko Poland 49°30N 22°23E 185 J9
Leskov I. Antarctica 56°0S 28°0W 151 B1
Leskovac Serbia 43°0N 21°58E 202 C5
Leskovik Albania 40°10N 20°34E 202 F4
Leslau = Włocławek Poland 52°40N 19°3E 185 F6
Leslie Ga., U.S.A. 31°57N 84°5W 316 D5
Leslie Mich., U.S.A. 42°27N 84°26W 311 B12
Leśna Poland 51°1N 15°15E 185 G2
Lesneven France 48°35N 4°20W 172 D2
Leśnica Poland 50°26N 18°11E 185 H5
Lešnica Serbia 44°39N 19°20E 202 B3
Lesnoi = Umba Russia 66°42N 34°11E 186 A5
Lesnoye Russia 58°15N 35°18E 188 C8
Lesnozavodskaya Russia 59°51N 30°29E 137 B2
Lesopilnoye Russia 46°44N 134°20E 220 A7
Lesotho ■ Africa 29°40S 28°0E 271 C4
Lesozavodsk Russia 45°30N 133°29E 220 B6
Lesparre-Médoc France 45°18N 0°57W 174 C3
L'Espluga de Francolí Spain 41°24N 1°7E 196 D6
Lessay France 49°14N 1°30W 172 C5
Lesse → Belgium 50°15N 4°54E 170 D4
Lesse et Lomme ⌓ Belgium 50°8N 5°9E 170 D5
Lessebo Sweden 56°45N 15°16E 163 H9
Lesser Antilles W. Indies 15°0N 61°0W 321 D7
Lesser Slave L. Canada 55°30N 115°25W 296 B5
Lesser Sunda Is. Indonesia 8°0S 120°0E 235 D5
Lessines Belgium 50°42N 3°50E 170 D3
Lester B. Pearson Int., Toronto ✈ (YYZ) Canada 43°46N 79°35W 141 A1
L'Esterre Grenada 12°28N 61°29W 323 q
Lestershire = Johnson City U.S.A. 42°7N 75°58W 313 D9
Lestock Canada 51°19N 103°59W 297 C8
Lesuer I. Australia 13°50S 127°17E 278 B4
Lesueur △ Australia 30°11S 115°10E 279 F2
Lesung Indonesia 0°42N 114°42E 235 B4
Lésvos = Lesbos Greece 39°10N 26°20E 205 B8
Leszno Poland 51°50N 16°30E 185 G3
Letaba S. Africa 23°59S 31°50E 271 B5
Letälven → Sweden 59°5N 14°20E 162 E8
L'Étang-la-Ville France 48°52N 2°4E 134 A1
L'Étang-Salé Réunion 21°15S 55°23E 272 f
Létavértes Hungary 47°23N 21°55E 182 C6
Letchworth U.K. 51°59N 0°13W 169 F7
Letea, Ostrov Romania 45°18N 29°20E 183 E14
Lethbridge Canada 49°45N 112°45W 296 D6
Lethem Guyana 3°20N 59°50W 329 C6
Leti, Kepulauan Indonesia 8°10S 128°0E 231 F7
Leti Is. = Leti, Kepulauan Indonesia 8°10S 128°0E 231 F7
Letiahau → Botswana 21°16S 24°0E 270 B3
Leticia Colombia 4°9S 70°0W 328 D4
Leting China 39°23N 118°55E 227 E10
Letjiesbos S. Africa 32°34S 22°16E 270 D3
Letlhakane Botswana 21°27S 25°30E 270 B4
Letlhakeng Botswana 24°0S 24°59E 270 B3
Letná Prague, Czech Rep. 135 a2
Letňany Czech Rep. 50°8N 14°30E 135 B3
Letopolis = Ausîm Egypt 30°7N 31°8E 117 A1
Letpadan Burma 17°45N 95°45E 241 G5
Letpan Burma 19°28N 94°10E 241 F5
Letsôk-aw Kyun Burma 11°30N 98°25E 237 G2
Letterkenny Ireland 54°57N 7°45W 166 B4
Leu Romania 44°10N 24°0E 183 F9
Léua Angola 11°34S 20°32E 265 E4
Leucadia U.S.A. 33°4N 117°18W 307 M9
Leucate France 42°56N 3°3E 174 F7
Leucate, Étang de France 42°50N 3°0E 174 F7
Leuchars U.K. 56°24N 2°53W 167 E6
Leuk Switz. 46°19N 7°37E 179 J3
Leuşeni Moldova 46°49N 28°12E 183 D13
Leuser, Gunung Indonesia 3°46N 97°12E 234 B1
Leusoalii Amer. Samoa 14°14S 169°25W 302 f
Leutkirch Germany 47°49N 10°1E 179 H6
Leutschau = Levoča Slovak Rep. 49°2N 20°35E 181 B13
Leuven Belgium 50°52N 4°42E 170 D4
Leuze-en-Hainaut Belgium 50°36N 3°37E 170 D3
Lev Tolstoy Russia 53°13N 39°29E 188 F10
Levallois-Perret France 48°53N 2°16E 134 A2
Levan Albania 40°40N 19°28E 202 F3
Levanger Norway 63°45N 11°19E 160 E14
Levant, Î. du France 43°3N 6°28E 175 E10
Lévanto Italy 44°10N 9°38E 198 D6
Lévanzo Italy 38°0N 12°20E 200 D5
Leveld Norway 60°44N 8°33E 164 D5
Levelland U.S.A. 33°35N 102°23W 314 E3
Levelock U.S.A. 59°7N 156°51W 303 G8
Leven U.K. 56°12N 3°0W 167 E6
Leven, L. U.K. 56°12N 3°22W 167 E5
Leven, Toraka Madag. 12°30S 47°45E 272 A2
Levent Turkey 41°5N 29°0E 122 B2
Leveque C. Australia 16°20S 123°0E 278 C3
Levera △ Grenada 12°13N 61°38W 323 q
Leverano Italy 40°17N 18°0E 201 B10
Leverger = Santo Antônio do Leverger Brazil 15°52S 56°5W 331 D6
Leverkusen Germany 51°1N 7°1E 178 D3
Levice Slovak Rep. 48°13N 18°35E 181 C11
Lévico Terme Italy 46°0N 11°18E 199 C8
Levie France 41°40N 9°7E 175 G13
Levier France 46°58N 6°8E 173 F13
Levin N.Z. 40°37S 175°18E 284 G4
Lévis Canada 46°48N 71°9W 299 C5
Levis, L. Canada 62°37N 117°58W 296 A5
Levitha Greece 37°0N 26°28E 205 D8
Levittown N.Y., U.S.A. 40°44N 73°31W 313 F11
Levittown Pa., U.S.A. 40°9N 74°51W 313 F10
Levka Bulgaria 41°52N 26°15E 203 E10
Levka Oros Greece 35°18N 24°3E 207 E5
Levkada □ Greece 38°45N 20°40E 207 B2
Levkás = Lefkada Greece 38°40N 20°43E 207 B2
Levoča Slovak Rep. 49°2N 20°35E 181 B13
Levroux France 46°59N 1°38E 173 F8
Levski Bulgaria 43°21N 25°10E 203 C9
Levskigrad = Karlovo Bulgaria 42°38N 24°47E 203 D8
Levuka Fiji 17°34S 179°0E 287 A2
Lewe Burma 19°38N 96°7E 241 F6
Lewes E. Sussex, U.K. 50°52N 0°1E 169 G8
Lewes Del., U.S.A. 38°46N 75°9W 309 F16
Lewin Brzeski Poland 50°45N 17°37E 185 H4
Lewis U.K. 58°9N 6°40W 167 C2
Lewis → U.S.A. 45°51N 122°48W 306 E4
Lewis, Butt of U.K. 58°31N 6°16W 167 C2
Lewis and Clark ⌓ U.S.A. 46°8N 123°53W 306 D3
Lewis Pass N.Z. 42°31S 172°11E 285 C7
Lewis Ra. Australia 20°3S 128°50E 278 D4
Lewis Range U.S.A. 48°5N 113°5W 304 B7
Lewis Run U.S.A. 41°52N 78°40W 312 E6
Lewisburg Ohio, U.S.A. 39°51N 84°33W 311 E12
Lewisburg Pa., U.S.A. 40°58N 76°54W 312 F8
Lewisburg Tenn., U.S.A. 35°27N 86°48W 315 D11
Lewisburg W. Va., U.S.A. 37°48N 80°27W 309 G13
Lewisdale U.S.A. 38°58N 76°59W 143 B3
Lewisham □ U.K. 51°27N 0°1W 125 B3
Lewisport U.S.A. 37°56N 86°54W 311 G10
Lewisporte Canada 49°15N 55°3W 299 C8
Lewiston Idaho, U.S.A. 46°25N 117°1W 304 C5
Lewiston Maine, U.S.A. 44°6N 70°13W 309 C18
Lewiston N.Y., U.S.A. 43°11N 79°3W 312 C5
Lewistown Ill., U.S.A. 40°24N 90°9W 310 D6
Lewistown Mo., U.S.A. 40°5N 91°49W 310 D5
Lewistown Mont., U.S.A. 47°4N 109°26W 304 C9
Lewistown Pa., U.S.A. 40°36N 77°34W 312 F7
Lexington Ga., U.S.A. 33°52N 83°7W 316 B6
Lexington Ill., U.S.A. 40°39N 88°47W 311 D8
Lexington Ky., U.S.A. 38°3N 84°30W 311 F12
Lexington Mass., U.S.A. 42°25N 71°12W 116 A1
Lexington Mich., U.S.A. 43°16N 82°32W 312 C2
Lexington Mo., U.S.A. 39°11N 93°52W 310 E3
Lexington N.C., U.S.A. 35°49N 80°15W 315 D14
Lexington N.Y., U.S.A. 42°15N 74°22W 313 D10
Lexington Nebr., U.S.A. 40°47N 99°45W 308 E4
Lexington Ohio, U.S.A. 40°41N 82°35W 312 F2
Lexington S.C., U.S.A. 33°59N 81°11W 316 B8
Lexington Tenn., U.S.A. 35°39N 88°24W 315 D10
Lexington Va., U.S.A. 37°47N 79°27W 309 G14
Lexington Park U.S.A. 38°16N 76°27W 309 F15
Leyburn U.K. 54°19N 1°48W 168 C6
Leye China 24°48N 106°29E 228 E6
Leyeh Taiwan 23°28N 120°42E 225 C2
Leyland U.K. 53°42N 2°43W 168 D5
Leyre → France 44°39N 1°1W 174 D2
Leyte Phil. 10°30N 125°0E 233 F5
Leyte □ Phil. 11°0N 125°0E 233 F5
Leyte Gulf Phil. 10°50N 125°25E 233 F5
Leyton U.K. 51°33N 0°1W 125 A3
Leytonstone U.K. 51°34N 0°0 125 A4
Leżajsk Poland 50°16N 22°25E 185 H9
Lezay France 46°15N 0°1W 174 B3
Lezhë Albania 41°47N 19°39E 202 E3
Lezhi China 30°19N 104°58E 228 B5
Lézignan-Corbières France 43°13N 2°43E 174 E6
Lezoux France 45°49N 3°21E 174 C7
Lgov Russia 51°42N 35°16E 189 G8
Lhasa China 29°25N 90°58E 218 F7
L'Haÿ-les-Roses France 48°46N 2°20E 134 B3
Lhazê China 29°5N 87°38E 218 F6
L'Hermite, I. Chile 55°50S 68°0W 336 E3
Lhokkruet Indonesia 4°55N 95°24E 234 B1
Lhokseumawe Indonesia 5°10N 97°10E 234 A1
Lhoksukon Indonesia 5°2N 97°19E 234 A1
L'Hospitalet de Llobregat Spain 41°21N 2°6E 114 A1
Lhotka Czech Rep. 50°1N 14°26E 135 B2
Lhuntsi Dzong Bhutan 27°39N 91°10E 241 B3
Lhut, W. → Somalia 10°17N 50°9E 267 B7
Li Thailand 17°48N 98°57E 236 D2
Li Jiang → China 24°40N 110°40E 229 E8
Li Jiang △ China 24°38N 110°38E 229 E8
Li Shan China 35°30N 111°56E 226 G6
Li Shui → China 29°24N 112°1E 229 C9
Li Xian Gansu, China 34°10N 105°5E 226 G3
Li Xian Hebei, China 38°30N 115°35E 226 E8
Li Xian Hunan, China 29°36N 111°42E 229 C8
Li Yuba South Sudan 5°23N 27°25E 266 C2
Lia-Moya C.A.R. 6°54N 16°17E 264 A3
Liadi Greece 36°50N 26°11E 205 E8
Liamuiga, Mt. St. Kitts & Nevis 17°22N 62°48W 322 d
Lian Phil. 14°3N 120°39E 232 D3
Liancheng China 25°42N 116°40E 229 E11
Liancourt Rocks Asia 37°15N 131°52E 221 F5
Liang Tao Taiwan 26°23N 128°28E 225 b
Lianga Phil. 8°38N 126°6E 233 G6
Lianga B. Phil. 8°37N 126°12E 233 G6
Liangcheng Nei Monggol Zizhiqu, China 40°28N 112°25E 226 D7
Liangcheng Shandong, China 35°32N 119°37E 227 G10
Liangdang China 33°56N 106°18E 226 H4
Lianghe China 24°50N 98°20E 228 E2
Lianghekou China 29°11N 108°44E 228 C7
Liangping China 30°38N 107°47E 228 B6
Liangpran Indonesia 1°4N 114°23E 235 B4
Liangshui He → China 39°48N 116°23E 114 C2
Lianhua China 27°3N 113°54E 229 D9
Lianhua Chi China 39°52N 116°16E 114 B1
Lianhua He → China 39°52N 116°13E 114 B1
Lianhua Shan China 23°40N 115°48E 229 F10
Lianjiang Fujian, China 26°12N 119°27E 229 D12
Lianjiang Guangdong, China 21°40N 110°20E 229 G8
Lianping China 24°26N 114°30E 229 E10
Lianshan China 24°38N 112°8E 229 E9
Lianshanguan China 40°53N 123°43E 224 B1
Lianshui China 33°42N 119°20E 227 H10
Lianyuan China 27°40N 111°38E 229 D8
Lianyungang China 34°40N 119°11E 227 G10
Lianzhou China 24°51N 112°22E 229 E9
Liao He → China 41°0N 121°50E 227 D11
Liaocheng China 36°28N 115°58E 226 F8
Liaodong Bandao China 40°0N 122°30E 227 E12
Liaodong Wan China 40°20N 121°10E 227 D11
Liaoning □ China 41°40N 122°30E 224 B1
Liaotung, G. of = Liaodong Wan China 40°20N 121°10E 227 D11
Liaoyang China 41°15N 122°58E 224 B1
Liaoyuan China 42°58N 125°2E 227 C13
Liaozhong China 41°23N 122°50E 224 B1
Liapades Greece 39°42N 19°40E 206 B9
Liard → Canada 61°51N 121°18W 296 A4
Liard River Canada 59°25N 126°5W 296 B3
Liari Pakistan 25°37N 66°30E 242 G2
Liat Indonesia 2°53S 107°5E 234 C3
Libanggaon Nepal 28°18N 82°38E 243 E10
Líbano Colombia 4°55N 75°4W 328 C2
Libau = Liepāja Latvia 56°30N 21°0E 184 B8
Libby U.S.A. 48°23N 115°33W 304 B6
Libčice nad Vitavou Czech Rep. 50°11N 14°22E 135 A2
Libeň Czech Rep. 50°6N 14°27E 135 B2
Libenge Dem. Rep. of the Congo 3°40N 18°55E 264 B3
Liberal U.S.A. 37°3N 100°55W 308 G3
Liberdade Acre, Brazil 10°5S 70°20W 330 C3
Liberdade São Paulo, Brazil 23°33S 46°37W 137 B2
Liberdade → Brazil 9°40S 52°17W 331 B7
Liberdade, Avenida da Lisbon, Portugal 126 b1
Liberec Czech Rep. 50°47N 15°7E 180 A8
Liberecký □ Czech Rep. 50°45N 15°0E 180 A8
Liberia Costa Rica 10°40N 85°30W 320 D2
Liberia ■ W. Afr. 6°30N 9°30W 262 D3
Libertà, Ponte della Venice, Italy 142 a1
Libertad Antique, Phil. 11°46N 121°55E 233 F3
Libertad Venezuela 8°20N 69°37W 328 B4
Libertador □ Chile 34°15S 70°45W 334 C1
Liberton U.K. 55°54N 3°9W 121 B3
Liberty Ind., U.S.A. 39°38N 84°56W 311 E12
Liberty Mo., U.S.A. 39°15N 94°25W 310 E2
Liberty N.Y., U.S.A. 41°48N 74°45W 313 E10
Liberty Pa., U.S.A. 41°34N 77°6W 312 E7
Liberty Tex., U.S.A. 30°3N 94°48W 314 F7
Liberty Center U.S.A. 41°27N 84°1W 311 C12
Liberty I. U.S.A. 40°41N 74°2W 132 B1
Liberty-Newark Int. ✈ (EWR) U.S.A. 40°42N 74°10W 313 F10
Liberty Ōsaka Museum Japan 34°38N 135°29E 133 B1
Liberty State Park ⌓ U.S.A. 40°42N 74°2W 132 B1
Libertyville U.S.A. 42°18N 87°57W 311 B9
Libeznice Czech Rep. 50°11N 14°29E 135 A2
Libiąż Poland 50°7N 19°21E 185 H6
Libibi Angola 14°42S 17°44E 265 E3
Lîbîya, Sahrâ' Africa 25°0N 25°0E 258 C4
Libjo Phil. 10°12N 125°32E 233 F5
Libmanan Phil. 13°42N 123°4E 232 E4
Libo China 25°22N 107°53E 228 E6
Libobo, Tanjung Indonesia 0°54S 128°28E 231 E7
Libode S. Africa 31°33S 29°2E 271 D4
Libohovë Albania 40°3N 20°10E 202 F4
Liboi Kenya 0°24N 40°57E 267 D5
Libona Phil. 8°20N 124°44E 233 G5
Libonda Zambia 14°28S 23°12E 265 E4
Libong, Ko Thailand 7°15N 99°23E 237 J2
Libourne France 44°55N 0°14W 174 D3
Libramont Belgium 49°55N 5°23E 170 E5
Library of Congress Washington, D.C., U.S.A. 143 b3
Librazhd Albania 41°12N 20°22E 202 E4
Libreville Gabon 0°25N 9°26E 264 B1
Libro Pt. Phil. 11°25N 119°28E 233 F2
Libuš Czech Rep. 50°0N 14°27E 135 B2
Libya ■ N. Afr. 27°0N 17°0E 258 C3
Libyan Desert = Lîbîya, Sahrâ' Africa 25°0N 25°0E 258 C4
Libyan Plateau = Ed Déffa Egypt 30°40N 26°30E 256 A2
Licantén Chile 35°55S 72°0W 334 D1
Licata Italy 37°6N 13°56E 200 E6
Lice Turkey 38°27N 40°39E 213 C9
Licheng China 36°28N 113°20E 226 F7
Lichfield U.K. 52°41N 1°49W 169 E6
Lichia Taiwan 22°47N 121°3E 225 D3
Lichiao China 23°3N 113°18E 121 B2
Lichinga Mozam. 13°13S 35°11E 269 E4
Lichtenburg Berlin, Germany 52°31N 13°30E 115 A4
Lichtenburg North West, S. Africa 26°8S 26°8E 270 C4
Lichtenfels Germany 50°8N 11°4E 179 E7
Lichterfelde Germany 52°25N 13°19E 115 B2
Lichuan Hubei, China 30°18N 108°57E 228 B7
Lichuan Jiangxi, China 27°18N 116°55E 229 D11
Licking → U.S.A. 39°6N 84°30W 311 F12
Licosa, Punta Italy 40°15N 14°54E 201 B7
Licungo → Mozam. 17°40S 37°15E 269 F4
Lida Belarus 53°53N 25°15E 177 B13
Liden Sweden 62°42N 16°48E 162 B10
Lidhult Sweden 56°50N 13°27E 163 H7
Lidingö Sweden 59°21N 18°8E 139 A2
Lidköping Sweden 58°31N 13°7E 163 F7
Lido Niger 12°54N 3°44E 263 C5
Lido di Roma = Óstia, Lido di Italy 41°43N 12°17E 199 G9
Lidoriki Greece 38°32N 22°12E 204 C4
Lidzbark Poland 53°15N 19°49E 185 E6
Lidzbark Warmiński Poland 54°7N 20°34E 184 D7
Liebenthal = Lubomierz Poland 51°1N 15°31E 185 G2
Liebenwalde Germany 52°52N 13°24E 178 C9
Lieberose Germany 51°59N 14°17E 178 D10
Liebig, Mt. Australia 23°18S 131°22E 278 D5
Liebling Romania 45°36N 21°20E 182 E6
Liechtenstein ■ Europe 47°8N 9°35E 179 H5
Liège Belgium 50°38N 5°35E 170 D5
Liège □ Belgium 50°32N 5°35E 170 D5
Liegnitz = Legnica Poland 51°12N 16°10E 185 G3
Lieksa Finland 63°18N 30°2E 160 E24
Lienart Dem. Rep. of the Congo 3°3N 25°31E 268 B2
Lienyünchiangshih = Lianyungang China 34°40N 119°11E 227 G10
Lienz Austria 46°50N 12°46E 180 E5
Liepāja Latvia 56°30N 21°0E 184 B8
Liepāja □ Latvia 56°30N 21°30E 184 B8
Liepājas ezers Latvia 56°27N 21°3E 184 B8
Lier Belgium 51°7N 4°34E 170 C4
Liernais France 47°13N 4°16E 173 E11
Lieshi Lingyuan China 23°7N 113°16E 121 B2
Liesing Austria 48°8N 16°17E 142 B1
Liesing → Austria 48°8N 16°28E 142 B2
Lieşti Romania 45°38N 27°34E 183 E12
Lietuva = Lithuania ■ Europe 55°30N 24°0E 188 E2
Liévin France 50°24N 2°47E 173 B9
Lièvre → Canada 45°31N 75°26W 298 C4
Liezen Austria 47°34N 14°15E 180 D7
Liffey → Ireland 53°21N 6°13W 166 C5
Lifford Ireland 54°51N 7°29W 166 B4
Liffré France 48°12N 1°30W 172 D5
Lifjell Norway 59°27N 8°45E 164 E5
Lifou, Î. N. Cal. 20°53S 167°13E 288 d
Lifudzin Russia 44°21N 134°58E 220 B7
Lifuka Tonga 19°48S 174°21W 287 P13
Ligao Phil. 13°14N 123°32E 232 E4
Ligasa Dem. Rep. of the Congo 0°44N 23°49E 264 B4
Lighthouse Point U.S.A. 26°15N 80°7W 317 J9
Lighthouse Pt. U.S.A. 29°54N 84°21W 316 F5
Lightning Ridge Australia 29°22S 148°0E 281 D4
Lignano Sabbiadoro Italy 45°42N 13°9E 199 C10
Ligny-en-Barrois France 48°36N 5°20E 173 D12
Ligonha → Mozam. 16°54S 39°9E 269 F4
Ligonier Ind., U.S.A. 41°28N 85°35W 311 C11
Ligonier Pa., U.S.A. 40°15N 79°14W 312 F5
Ligourio Greece 37°37N 23°4E 204 D5
Ligovo Russia 59°49N 30°10E 137 C1
Ligueil France 47°2N 0°49E 172 E7
Liguria □ Italy 44°30N 8°50E 198 D5
Ligurian Sea Medit. S. 43°20N 9°0E 198 E5
Lihir Group Papua N. G. 3°0S 152°35E 286 B7
Lihir I. Papua N. G. 3°5S 152°35E 286 B7
Lihou Reefs and Cays Australia 17°25S 151°40E 280 B5
Lihu'e U.S.A. 21°59N 159°23W 302 B2
Lihué Calel △ Argentina 38°0S 65°10W 334 D2
Lijiang China 26°55N 100°20E 228 D3
Lijordet Norway 59°56N 10°36E 133 A2
Lik → Laos 18°31N 102°30E 236 C4
Likala Dem. Rep. of the Congo 0°9N 19°12E 264 B3
Likang Taiwan 22°47N 120°29E 225 D2
Likasi Dem. Rep. of the Congo 10°55S 26°48E 269 E2
Likati Dem. Rep. of the Congo 3°20N 24°0E 264 B4
Likati → Dem. Rep. of the Congo 2°53N 24°3E 264 B4
Likenäs Sweden 60°37N 13°3E 162 D7
Likete Dem. Rep. of the Congo 0°48S 21°31E 264 C4
Likhaya = Likhovskoy Russia 48°10N 40°10E 191 F5
Likhoborka → Russia 55°50N 37°37E 129 A2
Likhoslavl Russia 57°12N 35°30E 188 D8
Likhovskoy Russia 48°10N 40°10E 191 F5
Likhvin = Chekalin Russia 54°10N 36°10E 188 E9
Likimi Dem. Rep. of the Congo 2°44N 20°47E 264 B4
Likita Dem. Rep. of the Congo 4°15N 23°36E 264 B4
Liknes Norway 58°19N 6°59E 164 F3
Likokou Gabon 0°12S 12°48E 264 C2
Likoma I. Malawi 12°3S 34°45E 269 E3
Likouala → Congo 0°2N 14°53E 264 C3
Likouala aux Herbes → Congo 0°52S 17°8E 264 C3
Liku Cook Is. 19°2S 168°47W 289 g
Likumburu Tanzania 9°43S 35°8E 269 D4
Lilanga Dem. Rep. of the Congo 0°34S 23°56E 264 C4
L'Île-Bouchard France 47°7N 0°26E 172 E7
L'Île-Rousse France 42°38N 8°57E 175 F12
Lilenga Dem. Rep. of the Congo 1°4N 22°2E 264 B4
Liling China 27°42N 113°29E 229 D9
Lilla Edet Sweden 58°9N 12°8E 163 F6
Lilla Värtan Sweden 59°20N 18°11E 139 A3
Lille France 50°38N 3°3E 173 B10
Lille Bælt Denmark 55°20N 9°45E 163 J3
Lille Værløse Denmark 55°47N 12°22E 118 A2
Lillebonne France 49°30N 0°32E 172 C7
Lillehammer Norway 61°8N 10°30E 164 C7
Lillesand Norway 58°15N 8°23E 164 F5
Lillestrøm Norway 59°58N 11°5E 164 E8
Lillhärdal Sweden 61°51N 14°5E 162 C8
Lillian Pt. Australia 27°40S 126°6E 279 E4
Lillo Spain 39°45N 3°20W 194 F7
Lillooet Canada 50°44N 121°57W 296 C4
Lillooet → Canada 49°15N 121°57W 296 D4
Lilongwe Malawi 14°0S 33°48E 269 E3
Liloy Phil. 8°4N 122°39E 233 G4
Liluah India 22°37N 88°19E 124 B1
Lim → Europe 43°45N 19°15E 202 C3
Lim Chu Kang Singapore 1°26N 103°43E 138 A2
Lima Brazil 4°36S 63°40W 329 D5
Lima Indonesia 3°39S 127°58E 231 E7
Lima Peru 12°3S 77°2W 124 B2
Lima Ill., U.S.A. 40°11N 91°23W 310 D5
Lima Mont., U.S.A. 44°38N 112°36W 304 D7
Lima N.Y., U.S.A. 42°54N 77°36W 312 D7
Lima Ohio, U.S.A. 40°44N 84°6W 311 D12
Lima □ Peru 12°3S 77°3W 330 C2
Lima → Portugal 41°41N 8°50W 194 D2
Lima Jorge Chavez, Int. ✈ (LIM) Peru 12°2S 77°8W 124 B2
Liman = Krasnyy Liman Ukraine 48°58N 37°50E 189 H9
Liman Russia 45°45N 47°12E 191 H8
Limanowa Poland 49°42N 20°22E 185 J7
Limassol Cyprus 34°42N 33°1E 207 F9
Limavady U.K. 55°3N 6°56W 166 A5
Limay → Argentina 39°0S 68°0W 336 A3
Limay Mahuida Argentina 37°10S 66°45W 334 D2
Limbach-Oberfrohna Germany 50°52N 12°43E 178 E8
Limbang Malaysia 4°42N 115°6E 235 B5
Limbara, Mte. Italy 40°51N 9°10E 200 B2
Limbaži Latvia 57°31N 24°42E 188 D3
Limbdi India 22°34N 71°51E 242 H4
Limbe Cameroon 4°1N 9°10E 263 E6
Limbiate Italy 45°35N 9°7E 128 A1
Limbueta Angola 12°30S 18°42E 265 E3
Limbuhan = Pio V. Corpuz Phil. 11°55N 124°2E 233 F5
Limburg Germany 50°22N 8°4E 179 E4
Limburg □ Belgium 51°2N 5°25E 170 C5
Limburg □ Neths. 51°20N 5°55E 170 C5
Lime Village U.S.A. 61°21N 155°28W 303 F9
Limedsforsen Sweden 60°52N 13°25E 162 D7
Limehouse U.K. 51°30N 0°1W 125 A3
Limeil-Brévannes France 48°44N 2°29E 134 B3
Limeira = Joaçaba Brazil 27°5S 51°31W 335 B5
Limeira Brazil 22°35S 47°28W 335 A6
Limenaria Greece 40°38N 24°32E 203 F8
Limenas Chersonisou Greece 35°18N 25°21E 207 E6
Limerick Limerick, Ireland 52°40N 8°37W 166 D3
Limerick Maine, U.S.A. 43°41N 70°48W 313 C14
Limerick □ Ireland 52°30N 8°50W 166 D3
Limestone U.S.A. 42°2N 78°38W 312 D6
Limestone → Canada 56°31N 94°7W 297 B10
Limestone Hill = Lackawanna U.S.A. 42°50N 78°50W 312 D6
Limfjorden Denmark 56°55N 9°0E 163 H3
Limia = Lima → Portugal 41°41N 8°50W 194 D2
Limingen Norway 64°48N 13°35E 160 D15
Limmared Sweden 57°34N 13°20E 163 G7
Limmen ✪ Australia 15°15S 135°30E 280 B2
Limmen Bight Australia 14°40S 135°35E 280 A2
Limmen Bight → Australia 15°7S 135°44E 280 B2
Limni Greece 38°43N 23°18E 204 C5
Limnos Greece 39°50N 25°5E 205 B7
Limoeiro Brazil 7°52S 35°27W 332 C4
Limoeiro do Norte Brazil 5°5S 38°0W 332 C4
Limoges Ont., Canada 45°20N 75°16W 313 A9
Limoges Haute-Vienne, France 45°50N 1°15E 174 C5
Limón Costa Rica 10°0N 83°2W 320 E3
Limon Colo., U.S.A. 39°16N 103°41W 304 G12
Limone Piemonte Italy 44°12N 7°34E 198 D4
Limonlu Turkey 36°34N 34°15E 250 B5
Limousin □ France 45°30N 1°30E 174 C5
Limousin, Plateaux du France 45°45N 1°15E 174 C5
Limoux France 43°4N 2°12E 174 E6
Limpopo □ S. Africa 24°5S 29°0E 271 B4
Limpopo → Africa 25°5S 33°30E 271 C5
Lin Xian China 37°57N 110°58E 226 F6
Lin'an China 30°15N 119°42E 229 B12
Linao Pt. Phil. 6°46N 123°58E 233 H4
Linapacan Phil. 11°30N 119°52E 233 F2
Linapacan I. Phil. 11°27N 119°49E 233 F2
Linapacan Str. Phil. 11°37N 119°56E 233 F2
Linares Chile 35°50S 71°40W 334 D1
Linares Colombia 1°23N 77°31W 328 C2
Linares Nuevo León, Mexico 24°52N 99°34W 319 C5
Linares Spain 38°10N 3°40W 195 G7
Linaria Greece 38°52N 24°31E 204 C6
Linaro, Capo Italy 42°2N 11°50E 199 F8
Línas Mte. Italy 39°25N 8°38E 200 C1
Linate, Milano ✈ (LIN) Italy 45°27N 9°16E 128 B2
Linbropark S. Africa 26°5S 28°7E 123 A2
Lincang China 23°58N 100°1E 228 F3
Lincheng China 37°25N 114°30E 226 F8
Linchuan China 27°57N 116°15E 229 D11
Lincoln = Beamsville Canada 43°12N 79°28W 312 C5
Lincoln Argentina 34°55S 61°30W 334 C3
Lincoln N.Z. 43°38S 172°30E 285 D7
Lincoln Lincs., U.K. 53°14N 0°32W 168 D7
Lincoln Calif., U.S.A. 38°54N 121°17W 306 G5
Lincoln Ill., U.S.A. 40°9N 89°22W 310 D7
Lincoln Kans., U.S.A. 39°3N 98°9W 308 F4
Lincoln Maine, U.S.A. 45°22N 68°30W 309 C19
Lincoln N.H., U.S.A. 44°3N 71°40W 313 B13
Lincoln N. Mex., U.S.A. 33°30N 105°23W 305 K11
Lincoln Nebr., U.S.A. 40°49N 96°41W 308 E5
Lincoln Boyhood ⌓ U.S.A. 38°7N 86°59W 311 F10
Lincoln Center for Performing Arts New York, U.S.A. 132 b2
Lincoln City U.S.A. 44°57N 124°1W 304 D1
Lincoln Hav = Lincoln Sea Arctic 84°0N 55°0W 154 A5
Lincoln Heights U.S.A. 34°4N 118°12W 126 B3
Lincoln Memorial U.S.A. 38°52N 77°4W 143 B2
Lincoln Park Calif., U.S.A. 37°47N 122°30W 136 B1
Lincoln Park Ga., U.S.A. 32°52N 84°20W 316 C5
Lincoln Park Ill., U.S.A. 41°57N 87°38W 119 B3
Lincoln Park Mich., U.S.A. 42°15N 83°11W 311 B13
Lincoln Park N.J., U.S.A. 40°55N 74°18W 132 B1
Lincoln Park Zoo U.S.A. 41°55N 87°38W 119 B3
Lincoln Sea Arctic 84°0N 55°0W 154 A5
Lincoln Tunnel New York, U.S.A. 132 c1
Lincolnshire □ U.K. 53°14N 0°32W 168 D7
Lincolnshire Wolds U.K. 53°26N 0°13W 168 D7
Lincolnton Ga., U.S.A. 33°48N 82°29W 316 B7
Lincolnton N.C., U.S.A. 35°29N 81°16W 315 D14
Lincolnwood U.S.A. 42°1N 87°43W 119 A2
Lind U.S.A. 46°58N 118°37W 304 C4
Linda U.S.A. 39°8N 121°34W 306 F5
Linda-a-Pastora Portugal 38°42N 9°15W 126 A1
Lindale U.S.A. 34°11N 85°11W 316 A4
Lindås Norway 60°44N 5°9E 164 D2
Lindau Germany 47°33N 9°42E 179 H5
Lindeman I. Australia 20°27S 149°3E 280 b
Lindeman Islands △ Australia 20°28S 149°5E 280 b
Linden = Gladstone U.S.A. 39°13N 94°35W 310 E2
Linden Guyana 6°0N 58°10W 329 B6
Linden Gauteng, S. Africa 26°8S 28°0E 123 A2
Linden Ala., U.S.A. 32°18N 87°48W 315 E11
Linden Calif., U.S.A. 38°1N 121°5W 306 G5
Linden Ind., U.S.A. 40°11N 86°54W 311 D10
Linden Mich., U.S.A. 42°49N 83°47W 311 B13
Linden Tex., U.S.A. 33°1N 94°22W 314 E7
Lindenberg Germany 52°36N 13°31E 115 A4
Lindenhurst U.S.A. 40°41N 73°23W 313 F11
Lindenow Fjord Greenland 60°30N 43°25W 154 E6
Lindesberg Sweden 59°36N 15°15E 162 E9
Lindesnes Norway 57°58N 7°3E 164 G4
Lindi Tanzania 9°58S 39°38E 269 D4
Lindi □ Tanzania 9°40S 38°30E 269 D4
Lindi → Dem. Rep. of the Congo 0°33N 25°5E 268 B2
Lindley U.S.A. 42°1N 77°8W 312 D7
Lindö Sweden 58°37N 16°15E 163 F10
Lindome Sweden 57°35N 12°5E 163 G6
Lindos Greece 36°6N 28°4E 206 E12
Lindos, Akra Greece 36°4N 28°10E 206 E12
Lindoso Portugal 41°52N 8°11W 194 D2
Lindow Germany 52°58N 12°59E 178 C8
Lindøya Norway 59°53N 10°42E 133 A3
Lindsay Ont., Canada 44°22N 78°43W 312 B6
Lindsay Calif., U.S.A. 36°12N 119°5W 306 J7
Lindsay Okla., U.S.A. 34°50N 97°38W 314 D6
Lindsborg U.S.A. 38°35N 97°40W 308 F5
Lindsdal Sweden 56°44N 16°18E 163 H10
Line Islands Pac. Oc. 7°0N 160°0W 289 H12
Linesville U.S.A. 41°39N 80°26W 312 E4
Lineville Ala., U.S.A. 33°19N 85°45W 316 B4
Lineville Iowa, U.S.A. 40°35N 93°32W 310 D3
Linfen China 36°3N 111°30E 226 F6
Ling Xian Hunan, China 26°29N 113°48E 229 D9
Ling Xian Shandong, China 37°22N 116°30E 226 F9
Lingal India 16°17N 78°31E 245 F4
Linganamakki Res. India 14°6N 74°52E 245 G2
Lingao China 19°56N 109°42E 236 C7
Lingayen Phil. 16°1N 120°14E 232 C3
Lingayen G. Phil. 16°10N 120°15E 232 C3
Lingbao China 34°31N 110°51E 226 G6
Lingbi China 33°33N 117°33E 227 H9
Lingbo Sweden 61°3N 16°41E 162 C10
Lingchuan Guangxi Zhuangzu, China 25°26N 110°21E 229 E8
Lingchuan Shanxi, China 35°45N 113°12E 226 G7
Lingding Yang China 22°25N 113°44E 219 a
Lingen Germany 52°31N 7°19E 178 C3
Lingga Indonesia 0°12S 104°37E 234 C2
Lingga, Kepulauan Indonesia 0°10S 104°30E 234 C2
Lingga Arch. = Lingga, Kepulauan Indonesia 0°10S 104°30E 234 C2
Linghai China 41°11N 121°22E 227 D11
Linghed Sweden 60°48N 15°55E 162 D9
Linghem Sweden 58°26N 15°47E 163 F9
Lingig Phil. 8°2N 126°24E 233 G6

Lingle U.S.A. 42°8N 104°21W 304 E11
Lingomo
Dem. Rep. of the Congo 0°38N 22°3E 264 B4
Lingqiu China 39°28N 114°22E 226 E8
Lingshan China 22°25N 109°18E 228 F7
Lingshi China 36°48N 111°48E 226 F6
Lingshou China 38°20N 114°20E 226 E8
Lingshui China 18°27N 110°0E 236 C8
Lingsugur India 16°10N 76°31E 245 F3
Lingtai China 35°0N 107°40E 226 G4
Linguère Senegal 15°25N 15°5W 262 B1
Lingui China 25°12N 110°2E 229 E8
Lingunda
Dem. Rep. of the Congo 0°49N 21°6E 264 C3
Lingwu China 38°6N 106°20E 226 E4
Lingyuan China 41°10N 119°15E 227 D10
Lingyun China 25°2N 106°35E 228 E6
Linhai China 28°50N 121°8E 229 C13
Linhares Brazil 19°25S 40°4W 333 E3
Linhe China 40°48N 107°20E 226 D4
Liniers Argentina 34°39S 58°30W 117 B1
Linjiang China 41°50N 127°0E 224 B3
Linkebeek Belgium 50°46N 4°20E 116 B2
Linköping Sweden 58°28N 15°36E 163 F9
Linkou China 45°15N 130°18E 227 B16
Linksfield S. Africa 26°9S 28°6E 123 A2
Linli China 29°27N 111°30E 229 C8
Linlithgow = West Lothian □
U.K. 55°54N 3°36W 167 F5
Linmeyer S. Africa 26°15S 28°4E 123 B2
Linn U.S.A. 38°29N 91°51W 310 F5
Linna Finland 60°20N 24°50E 121 A2
Linnei Taiwan 23°45N 120°36E 225 C2
Linneus U.S.A. 39°53N 93°11W 310 E3
Linnhe, L. U.K. 56°36N 5°25W 167 E3
Linosa Medit. S. 35°51N 12°50E 258 A2
Linpien Taiwan 22°26N 120°3E 225 D2
Linqi China 35°45N 113°52E 226 G7
Linqing China 36°50N 115°42E 226 F8
Linqu China 36°25N 118°30E 227 F10
Linquan China 33°5N 115°17E 229 A10
Lins Brazil 21°40S 49°44W 335 A6
Linshu China 34°53N 118°38E 227 G10
Linshui China 30°21N 106°57E 228 B6
Linsia = Linxia China 35°36N 103°10E 218 D9
Linstead Jamaica 18°8N 77°2W 320 a
Linta → Madag. 25°2S 44°5E 272 D1
Lintao China 35°26N 103°58E 226 G2
Linth → Switz. 47°7N 9°7E 179 H5
Linthal Switz. 46°54N 9°0E 179 J5
Linton Ind., U.S.A. 39°2N 87°10W 311 F9
Linton N. Dak., U.S.A. 46°16N 100°14W 308 B3
Lintong China 34°20N 109°10E 226 G5
Lintuvaara Finland 60°14N 24°45E 121 B1
Linwood Canada 43°35N 80°43W 312 C4
Linwu China 25°19N 112°31E 229 E9
Linxi Hebei, China 39°42N 118°26E 227 E10
Linxi Liaoning, China 43°36N 118°2E 227 C10
Linxia China 35°36N 103°10E 218 D9
Linxiang China 29°28N 113°23E 229 C9
Linyanti → Africa 17°50S 25°5E 270 A4
Linyi Shandong, China 37°13N 116°54E 226 F9
Linyi Shandong, China 35°5N 118°21E 227 G10
Linying China 33°48N 113°56E 226 H7
Linyuan Taiwan 22°30N 120°23E 225 D2
Linz Austria 48°18N 14°18E 180 C7
Linz Rhld-Pfz., Germany 50°34N 7°17E 178 E3
Linzhenzhen China 36°30N 109°59E 226 F5
Linzhou China 36°4N 113°49E 226 F7
Linzi China 36°50N 118°20E 227 F10
Lioko Équateur,
Dem. Rep. of the Congo 0°2N 22°4E 264 B4
Lioko Orientale,
Dem. Rep. of the Congo 1°25N 23°7E 264 B4
Liomseter Norway 61°15N 9°35E 164 C6
Lion, G. du France 43°10N 4°0E 174 E7
Lion Rock Country Park ⌂
China 22°21N 114°11E 122 A2
Lionel Town Jamaica 17°50N 77°15W 320 a
Lioni Italy 40°52N 15°11E 201 B8
Lions, G. of = Lion, G. du
France 43°10N 4°0E 174 E7
Lion's Den Zimbabwe 17°15S 30°5E 269 F3
Lion's Head Ont., Canada 44°58N 81°15W 312 B3
Lion's Head Western Cape,
S. Africa 33°56S 18°23E 118 A1
Liouesso Congo 1°2N 15°43E 264 B3
Lioumi Greece 38°0N 23°40E 112 B2
Liozno = Lyozna Belarus 55°0N 30°50E 188 E6
Lipa Phil. 13°57N 121°10E 232 E3
Lipali Mozam. 15°50S 35°50E 269 F4
Lipany Slovak Rep. 49°9N 20°58E 181 B13
Lipari Italy 38°26N 14°58E 201 D7
Lipari, I. Italy 38°29N 14°56E 201 D7
Lipari, Is. = Eólie, Ís. Italy 38°30N 14°57E 201 D7
Lipatkain Indonesia 0°1N 101°12E 234 B2
Lipcani Moldova 48°14N 26°48E 183 B11
Liperi Finland 62°31N 29°24E 160 E23
Lipetsk Russia 52°37N 39°35E 189 F10
Lipetsk □ Russia 52°50N 38°50E 190 D4
Lipiany Poland 53°2N 14°58E 185 E1
Liping China 26°15N 109°7E 228 D7
Lipisi Greece 37°19N 26°50E 205 D8
Lipjan Kosovo 42°31N 21°7E 202 D5
Lipkany = Lipcani
Moldova 48°14N 26°48E 183 B11
Lipnik nad Bečvou
Czech Rep. 49°32N 17°36E 181 B10
Lipno Poland 52°49N 19°15E 185 F6
Lipova Romania 46°8N 21°42E 182 D6
Lipovets Ukraine 49°12N 29°1E 177 D15
Lippe → Germany 51°39N 6°36E 178 D2
Lippehne = Lipiany Poland 53°2N 14°58E 185 E1
Lippstadt Germany 51°41N 8°22E 178 D4
Lipscomb U.S.A. 36°14N 100°16W 314 C4
Lipsk Poland 53°44N 23°24E 184 E10
Lipsko Poland 51°9N 21°40E 185 G8
Liptovský Hrádok
Slovak Rep. 49°2N 19°44E 181 B12
Liptovský Mikuláš
Slovak Rep. 49°6N 19°35E 181 B12
Liptrap, C. Australia 38°50S 145°55E 283 E6
Lipu China 24°30N 110°22E 229 E8
Lira Uganda 2°17N 32°57E 268 B3
Liranga Congo 0°43S 17°32E 264 C3
Liri → Italy 41°25N 13°52E 200 A6
Liria = Lliria Spain 39°37N 0°35W 197 F4
Lisakovsk Kazakhstan 52°33N 62°37E 216 B6
Lisala Dem. Rep. of the Congo 2°12N 21°38E 264 B4
Lisboa Portugal 38°42N 9°8W 126 A2
Lisboa □ Portugal 39°0N 9°12W 195 F1
Lisboa ✈ (LIS) Portugal 38°46N 9°8W 126 A2
Lisbon = Lisboa Portugal 38°42N 9°8W 126 A2
Lisbon N. Dak., U.S.A. 46°27N 97°41W 308 B5
Lisbon N.H., U.S.A. 44°13N 71°55W 313 B13
Lisbon N.Y., U.S.A. 44°43N 75°19W 313 B9
Lisbon Ohio, U.S.A. 40°46N 80°46W 312 F4
Lisbon Falls U.S.A. 44°0N 70°4W 309 D18
Lisburn U.K. 54°31N 6°3W 166 B5
Lisburn, C. Vanuatu 15°39S 166°46E 287 E4
Lisburne, C. U.S.A. 68°53N 166°13W 303 B6
Liscannor B. Ireland 52°55N 9°24W 166 D2
Liscia → Italy 41°11N 9°9E 200 A2
Lisdoonvarna Ireland 53°2N 9°18W 166 C2
Lishan Taiwan 24°16N 121°14E 225 B3
Lishe Jiang → China 24°15N 101°35E 228 E3
Lishi China 37°31N 111°8E 226 F6
Lishu China 43°20N 124°18E 227 C13
Lishui Guangdong, China 23°12N 113°9E 121 A1
Lishui Jiangsu, China 31°38N 119°2E 229 B12
Lishui Zhejiang, China 28°28N 119°54E 229 C12
Lisianski I. U.S.A. 26°2N 174°0W 302 F9
Lisichansk = Lysychansk
Ukraine 48°55N 38°30E 189 H10
Lisieux France 49°10N 0°12E 172 C7
Liski Russia 51°3N 39°30E 189 G10
L'Isle-Jourdain Gers, France 43°36N 1°5E 174 E5
L'Isle-Jourdain Vienne,
France 46°13N 0°31E 174 B4
L'Isle-sur-la-Sorgue France 43°54N 5°2E 175 E9
Lisle-sur-Tarn France 43°52N 1°49E 174 E5
Lismore N.S.W., Australia 28°44S 153°21E 281 D5
Lismore Waterford, Ireland 52°8N 7°55W 166 D4
Lissa = Leszno Poland 51°50N 16°30E 185 G3
Lissos → Greece 41°15N 25°40E 203 E9
Lista Norway 58°7N 6°39E 164 F3
Lister, Mt. Antarctica 78°0S 162°0E 151 D11
Lister og Mandals = Vest-Agder □
Norway 58°30N 7°15E 164 F4
Liston Australia 28°39S 152°6E 281 D5
Listowel Ont., Canada 43°44N 80°58W 312 C4
Listowel Kerry, Ireland 52°27N 9°29W 166 D2
Lit Sweden 63°19N 14°51E 162 A8
Lit-et-Mixe France 44°2N 1°15W 174 D2
Litang Guangxi Zhuangzu,
China 23°12N 109°8E 228 F7
Litang Sichuan, China 30°1N 100°17E 228 B3
Litang Malaysia 5°27N 118°31E 235 A5
Litang Qu → China 28°4N 101°32E 228 C3
Litani → Lebanon 33°20N 35°15E 250 E6
Litchfield Vic., Australia 36°18S 142°52E 282 D5
Litchfield Calif., U.S.A. 40°24N 120°23W 306 E6
Litchfield Conn., U.S.A. 41°45N 73°11W 313 E11
Litchfield Ill., U.S.A. 39°11N 89°39W 310 E7
Litchfield Minn., U.S.A. 45°8N 94°32W 308 C6
Litchfield △ Australia 13°14S 131°1E 278 B5
Liteni Romania 47°32N 26°32E 183 C11
Lithakia Greece 37°43N 20°50E 207 D2
Lithgow Australia 33°25S 150°8E 283 B9
Lithino, Akra Greece 34°55N 24°44E 207 F5
Lithuania ■ Europe 55°30N 24°0E 188 E2
Litija Slovenia 46°3N 14°50E 199 B11
Lititz U.S.A. 40°9N 76°18W 313 F8
Litochoro Greece 40°8N 22°34E 202 F6
Litoko Dem. Rep. of the Congo 1°13S 24°47E 264 C4
Litoměřice Czech Rep. 50°33N 14°10E 180 A7
Litomyšl Czech Rep. 49°52N 16°20E 181 B9
Litschau Austria 48°58N 15°4E 180 C8
Little Abaco Bahamas 26°50N 77°30W 320 A4
Little Andaman I. India 10°45N 92°30E 245 J11
Little Aral Sea = Northern Aral Sea
Kazakhstan 46°20N 60°30E 216 C6
Little B. N.S.W., Australia 33°58S 151°15E 139 B2
Little Barrier I. N.Z. 36°12S 175°8E 284 C4
Little Basses Sri Lanka 6°24N 81°43E 245 L5
Little Belt Mts. U.S.A. 46°40N 110°45W 304 C8
Little Bighorn Battlefield ⌂
U.S.A. 45°34N 107°25W 304 D10
Little Blue → U.S.A. 39°42N 96°41W 308 F5
Little Buffalo → Canada 61°0N 113°46W 296 A6
Little Calumet → U.S.A. 41°39N 87°34W 119 D3
Little Cayman Cayman Is. 19°41N 80°3W 320 C3
Little Churchill →
Canada 57°30N 95°22W 297 B9
Little Coco I. Burma 14°0N 93°13E 245 H11
Little Colorado →
U.S.A. 36°12N 111°48W 305 H8
Little Current Canada 45°55N 82°0W 298 C3
Little Current → Canada 50°57N 84°36W 298 B3
Little Desert △ Australia 37°25S 141°30E 282 D4
Little Diomede I. U.S.A. 65°45N 168°56W 303 C5
Little Falls Minn., U.S.A. 45°59N 94°22W 308 C6
Little Falls N.Y., U.S.A. 43°3N 74°51W 313 C10
Little Ferry U.S.A. 40°50N 74°2W 132 A1
Little Fork → U.S.A. 48°31N 93°35W 308 A7
Little Grand Rapids
Canada 52°0N 95°29W 297 C9
Little Haiti U.S.A. 25°50N 80°11W 129 C2
Little Havana U.S.A. 25°47N 80°15W 129 D1
Little Humboldt →
U.S.A. 41°1N 117°43W 304 F5
Little Inagua I. Bahamas 21°40N 73°50W 321 B5
Little India Singapore 138 a2
Little Italy New York, U.S.A. 132 e2
Little Karoo S. Africa 33°45S 21°0E 270 D3
Little Khingan Mts. = Xiao Hinggan
Ling China 49°0N 127°0E 219 B14
Little Lake U.S.A. 35°56N 117°55W 307 K9
Little Lake Conway
U.S.A. 28°29N 81°21W 133 B2
Little Laut Is. = Laut Kecil,
Kepulauan Indonesia 4°45S 115°40E 235 C5
Little London Jamaica 18°15N 78°13W 320 a
Little Mecatina = Petit-Mécatina →
Canada 50°40N 59°30W 299 B8
Little Mermaid = Den Lille Havfrue
Copenhagen, Denmark 118 a3
Little Minch U.K. 57°35N 6°45W 167 D2
Little Missouri →
U.S.A. 47°36N 102°25W 308 B2
Little Nicobar India 7°20N 93°40E 245 L11
Little Ouse → U.K. 52°22N 1°12E 169 E9
Little Rann India 23°25N 71°25E 242 H4
Little Red → U.S.A. 35°11N 91°27W 314 D9
Little River N.Z. 43°45S 172°49E 285 D7
Little Rock U.S.A. 34°45N 92°17W 314 D8
Little Rouge → Canada 43°45N 79°11W 141 A4
Little Ruaha → Tanzania 7°57S 37°53E 268 D4
Little Sable Pt. U.S.A. 43°38N 86°33W 308 D10
Little Scarcies → S. Leone 8°50N 13°10W 262 D2
Little Sioux → U.S.A. 41°48N 96°4W 308 E5
Little Sitkin I. U.S.A. 51°57N 178°31E 303 L2
Little Smoky → Canada 54°44N 117°11W 296 C5
Little Snake → U.S.A. 40°27N 108°26W 304 F9
Little Sound Bermuda 32°15N 64°50W 153 a
Little Tokyo Los Angeles, U.S.A. 127 c2
Little Valley U.S.A. 42°15N 78°48W 312 D6
Little Wabash → U.S.A. 37°55N 88°5W 311 G8
Little White → U.S.A. 43°40N 100°40W 308 D3
Little York U.S.A. 41°1N 90°45W 310 C6
Little Zab = Zāb aş Şaghīr →
Iraq 35°17N 43°29E 213 E10
Littlefield U.S.A. 33°55N 102°20W 314 E3
Littlehampton U.K. 50°49N 0°32W 169 G7
Littleton U.S.A. 44°18N 71°46W 313 B13
Littoral □ Cameroon 4°0N 10°0E 263 E7
Littoria = Latina Italy 41°28N 12°52E 200 A5
Litunga Angola 13°19S 16°48E 265 E3
Litvinov Czech Rep. 50°36N 13°37E 180 A6
Liu He → Jilin, China 42°46N 126°13E 224 A3
Liu He → Liaoning,
China 40°55N 121°35E 227 D11
Liu Jiang → China 23°55N 109°30E 228 F7
Liuba China 33°38N 106°55E 228 A6
Liucheng China 24°38N 109°14E 228 E7
Liuchia Taiwan 23°13N 120°21E 225 C2
Liuch'iu Taiwan 22°21N 120°22E 225 D2
Liuch'iu Yü Taiwan 22°21N 120°22E 225 D2
Liugou China 40°57N 118°15E 227 D10
Liuhang China 31°21N 121°21E 138 A1
Liuhe China 42°17N 125°43E 224 A2
Liuheng Dao China 29°40N 122°5E 229 C14
Liujiang China 24°26N 109°11E 228 E7
Liukang Tenggaja = Sabalana,
Kepulauan Indonesia 6°45S 118°50E 231 F5
Liuli Tanzania 11°3S 34°38E 269 E3
Liupan Shan China 35°39N 106°12E 226 G4
Liupanshui China 26°38N 104°48E 228 D5
Liurong Temple China 23°8N 113°15E 121 B2
Liuwa Plain Zambia 14°20S 22°30E 265 E4
Liuwa Plain △ Zambia 14°45S 22°35E 265 E4
Liuyang China 28°10N 113°37E 229 C9
Liuying Taiwan 23°17N 120°18E 225 C2
Liuzhou China 24°22N 109°22E 228 E7
Liuzhuang China 33°12N 120°18E 227 H11
Livada Romania 47°52N 23°5E 182 C8
Livadero Greece 40°2N 21°57E 202 F5
Livadhia Cyprus 34°57N 33°38E 207 F9
Livadhje Albania 39°47N 20°7E 206 B10
Livadi Greece 40°8N 22°9E 204 A4
Livadia Greece 38°27N 22°54E 204 C4
Livarot France 48°58N 0°9E 172 D7
Live Oak Calif., U.S.A. 39°17N 121°40W 306 F5
Live Oak Fla., U.S.A. 30°18N 82°59W 316 E7
Live Oak Manor U.S.A. 29°57N 90°14W 131 B1
Lively Canada 46°26N 81°9W 309 B13
Liveras Cyprus 35°23N 32°57E 207 E8
Livermore U.S.A. 37°41N 121°47W 306 H5
Livermore, Mt. U.S.A. 30°38N 104°11W 314 F2
Livermore Falls U.S.A. 44°29N 70°11W 309 C18
Liverpool N.S.W.,
Australia 33°54S 150°58E 283 B9
Liverpool N.S., Canada 44°5N 64°41W 299 D7
Liverpool Mersey., U.K. 53°25N 3°0W 168 D4
Liverpool N.Y., U.S.A. 43°6N 76°13W 313 C8
Liverpool Bay U.K. 53°30N 3°20W 168 D4
Liverpool Plains Australia 31°15S 150°15E 283 A9
Liverpool Ra. Australia 31°50S 150°30E 283 A9
Liverpool Street London, U.K. 125 a5
Livigno Italy 46°35N 10°10E 198 B7
Livingston Guatemala 15°50N 88°50W 320 C2
Livingston W. Loth., U.K. 55°54N 3°30W 167 F5
Livingston Ala., U.S.A. 32°35N 88°11W 315 E10
Livingston Calif., U.S.A. 37°23N 120°43W 306 H6
Livingston Mont., U.S.A. 45°40N 110°34W 304 D8
Livingston S.C., U.S.A. 33°38N 81°7W 316 B8
Livingston Tenn., U.S.A. 36°23N 85°19W 315 C12
Livingston Tex., U.S.A. 30°43N 94°56W 314 F7
Livingston Wis., U.S.A. 42°54N 90°26W 310 B6
Livingston, L. U.S.A. 30°50N 95°10W 314 F7
Livingston Manor
U.S.A. 41°54N 74°50W 313 E10
Livingstone Zambia 17°46S 25°52E 269 F2
Livingstone △ Australia 35°22S 147°22E 283 C7
Livingstone Mts. N.Z. 45°15S 168°9E 285 F3
Livingstone Mts. Tanzania 9°40S 34°20E 269 D3
Livingstonia Malawi 10°38S 34°5E 269 E3
Livno Bos.-H. 43°50N 17°1E 182 G2
Livny Russia 52°30N 37°30E 189 F9
Livonia Mich., U.S.A. 42°23N 83°23W 311 B13
Livonia N.Y., U.S.A. 42°49N 77°40W 312 D7
Livorno Italy 43°33N 10°19E 198 E7
Livradois-Forez ⌂ France 44°0N 3°0E 174 E7
Livramento = Nossa Senhora do
Livramento Brazil 15°48S 56°22W 331 D6
Livramento Brazil 30°55S 55°30W 335 C4
Livramento do Brumado
Brazil 13°39S 41°50W 333 D3
Livron-sur-Drôme France 44°46N 4°51E 175 D8
Livry-Gargan France 48°55N 2°31E 134 A4
Livyntsi Ukraine 48°25N 26°37E 183 B11
Liwā' U.A.E. 23°0N 54°10E 249 B6
Liwale Tanzania 9°48S 37°58E 269 D4
Liwan China 23°3N 113°13E 121 B2
Liwiec → Poland 52°36N 21°34E 185 F8
Liwonde Malawi 15°4S 35°13E 269 F4
Liwonde △ Malawi 14°48S 35°20E 269 E4
Lixi China 26°23N 101°59E 228 D3
Lixian China 31°23N 103°13E 228 B4
Lixin China 33°8N 116°13E 229 A11
Lixouri Greece 38°12N 20°26E 207 C2
Liyang China 31°26N 119°28E 229 B12
Lizard → Trin. & Tob. 10°9N 61°1W 323 t
Lizard I. Australia 14°42S 145°30E 280 A4
Lizard Pt. U.K. 49°57N 5°13W 169 H2
Lizarda Brazil 9°36S 46°41W 332 C2
Lizarra = Estella Spain 42°40N 2°2W 196 C2
Lizella U.S.A. 32°48N 83°49W 316 C6
Lizzano Italy 40°23N 17°27E 201 B10
Ljan Norway 59°50N 10°46E 133 A3
Ljig Serbia 44°13N 20°18E 202 B4
Ljøra → Norway 61°24N 12°35E 164 C9
Ljørdalen Norway 61°23N 12°41E 164 C9
Ljosland Norway 58°47N 7°22E 164 F4
Ljubija Bos.-H. 44°55N 16°35E 199 D13
Ljubinje Bos.-H. 42°58N 18°5E 202 D2
Ljubišnja Europe 43°18N 19°6E 202 C3
Ljubljana Slovenia 46°4N 14°33E 199 B11
Ljubljana ✈ (LJU)
Slovenia 46°14N 14°33E 199 B11
Ljubno Slovenia 46°25N 14°46E 199 B11
Ljubovija Serbia 44°11N 19°22E 202 B3
Ljugarn Sweden 57°20N 18°43E 163 G12
Ljung Sweden 57°59N 13°3E 163 G7
Ljungan → Sweden 62°18N 17°23E 162 B11
Ljungaverk Sweden 62°30N 16°5E 162 B10
Ljungby Sweden 56°49N 13°55E 163 H7
Ljungbyholm Sweden 56°39N 16°5E 163 H10
Ljungdalen Sweden 62°51N 12°47E 162 B6
Ljungsbro Sweden 58°31N 15°30E 163 F9
Ljungskile Sweden 58°14N 11°55E 163 F5
Ljusdal Sweden 61°46N 16°3E 162 C10
Ljusfallshammar Sweden 58°48N 15°30E 163 F9
Ljusnan → Sweden 61°12N 17°8E 162 C11
Ljusne Sweden 61°13N 17°7E 162 C11
Ljusterö Sweden 59°31N 18°37E 162 E12
Ljustorp Sweden 62°38N 17°19E 162 B11
Ljutomer Slovenia 46°31N 16°11E 199 B13
Llagostera Spain 41°50N 2°54E 196 D7
Llamellín Peru 9°0S 76°54W 330 B2
Llancanelo, Salina
Argentina 35°40S 69°8W 334 D2
Llandeilo U.K. 51°53N 3°59W 169 F4
Llandovery U.K. 51°59N 3°48W 169 F4
Llandrindod Wells U.K. 52°14N 3°22W 169 E4
Llandudno U.K. 53°19N 3°50W 168 D4
Llanelli U.K. 51°41N 4°10W 169 F3
Llanes Spain 43°25N 4°50W 194 B6
Llanfair-ym-Muallt = Builth Wells
U.K. 52°9N 3°25W 169 E4
Llanganates △ Ecuador 0°51S 72°20W 328 D3
Llangollen U.K. 52°58N 3°11W 168 E4
Llanidloes U.K. 52°27N 3°31W 169 E4
Llano U.S.A. 30°45N 98°41W 314 F5
Llano → U.S.A. 30°39N 98°26W 314 F5
Llano de Can Gineu Spain 41°27N 2°10E 114 A2
Llano Estacado U.S.A. 33°30N 103°0W 314 E3
Llanos S. Amer. 5°0N 71°35W 326 C3
Llanos de Challe △ Chile 28°8S 71°1W 334 B1
Llanquihue, L. Chile 41°10S 72°50W 336 B1
Llanwrtyd Wells U.K. 52°7N 3°38W 169 E4
Llata Peru 9°25S 76°47W 330 B2
Llebeig, C. des Spain 39°33N 2°18E 206 B3
Lleida Spain 41°37N 0°39E 196 D5
Lleida □ Spain 42°6N 1°0E 196 C6
Llentrisca, C. Spain 38°52N 1°15E 206 D1
Llera de Canales Mexico 23°19N 99°1W 319 C5
Llerena Spain 38°17N 6°0W 195 G5
Llevant, Sa. de Spain 39°35N 3°17E 206 B4
Lleyn Peninsula U.K. 52°51N 4°36W 168 E3
Llica Bolivia 19°52S 68°16W 330 D4
Llico Chile 34°46S 72°5W 334 C1
Lliria Spain 39°37N 0°35W 197 F4
Llivia Spain 42°28N 1°59E 174 F5
Llobregat → Spain 41°19N 2°5E 196 D7
Llodio Spain 43°9N 2°58W 196 B2
Llorente Phil. 11°25N 125°33E 233 F5
Llorente de Mar Spain 41°41N 2°53E 196 D7
Lloseta Spain 39°43N 2°52E 206 B3
Lloyd B. Australia 12°45S 143°27E 280 A3
Lloyd L. Canada 57°22N 108°57W 297 B7
Lloydminster Canada 53°17N 110°0W 297 C7
Llubí Spain 39°42N 3°0E 206 B4
Llucena del Cid Spain 40°9N 0°17W 196 E4
Llucmajor Spain 39°29N 2°53E 206 B3
Lluidas Vale Jamaica 18°6N 77°5W 320 a
Llullaillaco, Volcán
S. Amer. 24°43S 68°30W 334 A2
Llullaillaco △ Chile 24°50S 68°51W 334 A2
Lo → Vietnam 21°18N 105°25E 236 B5
Lo Aranguiz Chile 33°23S 70°40W 137 B2
Lo Boza Chile 33°23S 70°43W 137 B1
Lo Chau China 22°11N 114°15E 122 B2
Lo Chau Pak Mai China 22°11N 114°14E 122 B2
Lo Espejo Chile 33°31S 70°42W 137 C1
Lo Hermida Chile 33°28S 70°33W 137 B2
Lo Prado Chile 33°26S 70°42W 137 B1
Lo So Shing China 22°12N 114°7E 122 B1
Lo Wai China 22°22N 114°8E 122 A1
Loa U.S.A. 38°24N 111°39W 304 G8
Loa → Chile 21°26S 70°41W 334 A1
Loagan Bunut △ Malaysia 3°32N 114°40E 235 B4
Loaita I. S. China Sea 10°41N 114°25E 230 B4
Loakulu Indonesia 0°31S 117°2E 235 C5
Loange →
Dem. Rep. of the Congo 4°17S 20°2E 265 C4
Loango Congo 4°38S 11°50E 265 C2
Loanhead U.K. 55°53N 3°9W 121 B3
Loano Italy 44°8N 8°15E 198 D5
Loay Phil. 9°36N 124°1E 233 G5
Lobamba Swaziland 26°28S 31°12E 271 C5
Lobatse Botswana 25°12S 25°40E 270 C4
Lobau Wien, Austria 48°10N 16°31E 142 A3
Löbau Sachsen, Germany 51°5N 14°40E 178 D10
Lobaye → C.A.R. 3°41N 18°35E 264 B3
Loben = Lubliniec Poland 50°43N 18°45E 185 H5
Lobenstein Germany 50°25N 11°39E 178 E7
Lobería Argentina 38°10S 58°40W 334 D4
Löberöd Sweden 55°47N 13°31E 163 J7
Lobez Poland 53°38N 15°39E 184 E2
Lobito Angola 12°18S 13°35E 265 E2
Lobo Phil. 13°39N 121°13E 232 E3
Lobo → Ivory C. 6°2N 6°45W 262 D3
Lobos Argentina 35°10S 59°0W 334 D4
Lobos, I. Mexico 27°20N 110°36W 318 B2
Lobos, I. de Canary Is. 28°45N 13°50W 153 e2
Lobos, Pt. U.S.A. 37°46N 122°30W 136 B1
Lobos de Afuera, Islas
Peru 6°57S 80°42W 330 B1
Lobos de Tierra, I. Peru 6°27S 80°52W 330 B1
Łobżenica Poland 53°18N 17°15E 185 E4
Loc Binh Vietnam 21°46N 106°54E 236 B6
Loc Ninh Vietnam 11°50N 106°34E 237 G6
Locarno Switz. 46°10N 8°47E 179 J4
Loch Garman = Wexford
Ireland 52°20N 6°28W 166 D5
Loch Lomond and the Trossachs △
U.K. 56°10N 4°40W 167 E4
Lochaber U.K. 56°59N 5°1W 167 E3
Locham Germany 48°7N 11°26E 131 B1
Locharbriggs U.K. 55°7N 3°35W 167 F5
Lochboisdale U.K. 57°9N 7°20W 167 D1
Loche, L. La Canada 56°30N 109°30W 297 B7
Lochem Neths. 52°9N 6°26E 170 B6
Loches France 47°7N 1°0E 172 E7
Lochgilphead U.K. 56°2N 5°26W 167 E3
Lochinvar △ Zambia 15°55S 27°15E 269 F2
Lochinver U.K. 58°9N 5°14W 167 C3
Lochkov Czech Rep. 50°0N 14°21E 135 B2
Lochloosa L. U.S.A. 29°30N 82°7W 317 F7
Lochmaddy U.K. 57°36N 7°10W 167 D1
Lochnagar Queens.,
Australia 23°33S 145°38E 280 C4
Lochnagar Aberds., U.K. 56°57N 3°15W 167 E5
Lochów Poland 52°33N 21°42E 185 F8
Lochy, L. U.K. 57°0N 4°53W 167 E4
Lock Australia 33°34S 135°46E 281 E2
Lock Haven U.S.A. 41°8N 77°28W 312 E7
Lockeford U.S.A. 38°10N 121°9W 306 G5
Lockeport Canada 43°47N 65°4W 299 D6
Lockerbie U.K. 55°7N 3°21W 167 F5
Lockhart N.S.W.,
Australia 35°14S 146°40E 283 C7
Lockhart Tex., U.S.A. 29°53N 97°40W 314 G6
Lockhart, L. Australia 33°15S 119°3E 279 F2
Lockhart River Australia 12°58S 143°30E 280 A3
Lockhart River ☼
Australia 12°47S 143°20E 280 A3
Lockhausen Germany 48°10N 11°24E 131 A1
Lockney U.S.A. 34°7N 101°27W 314 D4
Lockport Ill., U.S.A. 41°35N 88°3W 311 C8
Lockport N.Y., U.S.A. 43°10N 78°42W 312 C6
Locminé France 47°54N 2°51W 172 E4
Locri Italy 38°14N 16°16E 201 D9
Locronan France 48°7N 4°15W 172 D2
Locust Cr. → U.S.A. 39°40N 93°17W 310 E3
Locust Grove U.S.A. 33°21N 84°7W 316 B5
Lod Israel 31°57N 34°54E 251 G5
Lodalskåpa Norway 61°47N 7°13E 164 C4
Lodeinoye Pole Russia 60°44N 33°33E 188 B7
Lodève France 43°44N 3°19E 174 E7
Lodge Bay Canada 52°14N 55°51W 299 B8
Lodge Grass U.S.A. 45°19N 107°22W 304 D10
Lodhran Pakistan 29°32N 71°30E 242 E4
Lodi Italy 45°19N 9°30E 198 C6
Lodi Calif., U.S.A. 38°8N 121°16W 306 G5
Lodi N.J., U.S.A. 40°52N 74°5W 132 A1
Lodi Ohio, U.S.A. 41°2N 82°1W 312 E3
Lodi Estate India 28°36N 77°15E 120 B2
Lodja Dem. Rep. of the Congo 3°30S 23°23E 264 C4
Lodosa Spain 42°25N 2°4W 196 C2
Lödöse Sweden 58°2N 12°9E 163 F6
Lodwar Kenya 3°7N 35°36E 268 B4
Łódź Poland 51°45N 19°27E 185 G6
Łódzkie □ Poland 51°30N 19°30E 185 G6
Loei Thailand 17°29N 101°35E 236 D3
Loengo
Dem. Rep. of the Congo 4°48S 26°30E 265 C5
Loeriesfontein S. Africa 31°0S 19°26E 270 D2
Lofa → Liberia 6°35N 11°8W 262 D2
Lofa Mano △ Liberia 7°55N 10°25W 262 D2
Lofer Austria 47°35N 12°41E 180 D5
Lofoten Norway 68°30N 13°59E 160 B16
Lofsdalen Sweden 62°10N 13°20E 162 B7
Lofsen → Sweden 62°7N 13°57E 162 B7
Loftahammar Sweden 57°54N 16°41E 163 G10
Loga Niger 13°40N 3°15E 263 C5
Logan Iowa, U.S.A. 41°39N 95°47W 308 E6
Logan Ohio, U.S.A. 39°32N 82°25W 309 F12
Logan Utah, U.S.A. 41°44N 111°50W 304 F8
Logan W. Va., U.S.A. 37°51N 81°59W 309 G13
Logan, Mt. Canada 60°34N 140°23W 294 E3
Logan Int., Boston ✈ (BOS)
U.S.A. 42°22N 71°1W 116 A2
Logan Martin L. U.S.A. 33°26N 86°20W 316 B3
Logan Square U.S.A. 41°55N 87°42W 119 B2
Logandale U.S.A. 36°36N 114°29W 307 J12
Logansport Ind., U.S.A. 40°45N 86°22W 311 D10
Logansport La., U.S.A. 31°58N 94°0W 314 F8
Loganville U.S.A. 33°50N 83°54W 316 B6
Logatec Slovenia 45°56N 14°15E 199 C11
Logirim South Sudan 4°43N 33°14E 257 G3
Lognes-Émerainville ✈ (XLG)
France 48°49N 2°37E 134 B4
Logo South Sudan 5°20N 30°18E 257 F3
Logone → Chad 12°6N 15°2E 259 F3
Logone Gana Chad 11°36N 15°4E 259 F3
Logone Occidental □ Chad 8°30N 16°0E 259 G3
Logone Occidental → Chad 8°50N 16°0E 259 G3
Logone Oriental □ Chad 8°30N 16°30E 259 G3
Logone Oriental → Chad 9°7N 16°26E 259 G3
Logroño Spain 42°28N 2°27W 196 C2
Logrosán Spain 39°20N 5°32W 195 F5
Løgstør Denmark 56°58N 9°14E 163 H3
Logtak L. India 24°33N 93°50E 241 C4
Løgumkloster Denmark 55°4N 8°57E 163 J2
Loh Vanuatu 13°21S 166°38E 287 C4
Lohals Denmark 55°8N 10°55E 163 J4
Lohardaga India 23°27N 84°45E 243 H11
Loharia India 23°45N 74°14E 242 H6
Loharu India 28°27N 75°49E 242 E6
Lohja Finland 60°12N 24°5E 188 B3
Löhme Germany 52°37N 13°40E 115 A5
Löhne Germany 52°11N 8°40E 178 C4
Loho = Luohe China 33°32N 114°2E 226 H8
Lohr Germany 49°59N 9°35E 179 F5
Lohri Wah → Pakistan 27°27N 67°37E 242 F2
Loi-lem Burma 20°52N 97°28E 241 E6
Loikaw Burma 19°40N 97°17E 241 F6
Loimaa Finland 60°50N 23°5E 188 B2
Loir → France 47°33N 0°32W 172 E6
Loir-et-Cher □ France 47°40N 1°20E 172 E8
Loire □ France 45°40N 4°5E 175 C8
Loire → France 47°16N 2°10W 172 E4
Loire Anjou Touraine ⌂
France 47°14N 0°5W 172 E6
Loire-Atlantique □ France 47°25N 1°40W 172 E5
Loire Inférieure = Loire-
Atlantique □ France 47°25N 1°40W 172 E5
Loiret □ France 47°55N 2°30E 173 E9
Loitz Germany 53°58N 13°8E 178 B9
Loja Ecuador 3°59S 79°16W 330 A2
Loja Spain 37°10N 4°10W 195 H6
Loja □ Ecuador 4°0S 79°13W 328 D2
Loje → Angola 7°49S 13°6E 265 D2
Loji = Kawasi Indonesia 1°38S 127°28E 231 E7
Lojo = Lohja Finland 60°12N 24°5E 188 B3
Løjt Kirkeby Denmark 55°7N 9°26E 163 J3
Lojung China 24°27N 109°36E 228 E7
Loka Dem. Rep. of the Congo 0°22N 18°2E 264 B3
Loka South Sudan 4°13N 31°0E 257 G3
Lokako
Dem. Rep. of the Congo 0°57S 18°55E 264 C4
Lokandu
Dem. Rep. of the Congo 2°30S 25°45E 264 C5
Lokaw
Dem. Rep. of the Congo 2°40S 20°12E 264 C4
Løken Norway 59°48N 11°29E 164 E8
Lokeren Belgium 51°6N 3°59E 170 C3
Lokgwabe Botswana 24°10S 21°50E 270 B3
Lokhvytsya Ukraine 50°25N 33°18E 189 G7
Lokichar Kenya 2°23N 35°39E 268 B4
Lokichokio Kenya 4°19N 34°13E 268 B3
Lokitaung Kenya 4°12N 35°48E 268 B4
Lokkan tekojärvi
Finland 67°55N 27°35E 160 C22
Løkken Denmark 57°22N 9°41E 163 G3
Løkken Sør-Trøndelag,
Norway 63°9N 9°41E 164 A6
Loknya Russia 56°49N 30°4E 188 D6
Loko C.A.R. 3°38N 18°2E 264 B3
Loko Nigeria 8°1N 7°53E 263 D6
Lokoja Nigeria 7°47N 6°45E 263 D6
Lokolama
Dem. Rep. of the Congo 2°35S 19°50E 264 C3
Lokolenge
Dem. Rep. of the Congo 1°12N 22°38E 264 B4
Lokolo →
Dem. Rep. of the Congo 1°43S 18°23E 264 C3
Lokot Russia 52°34N 34°36E 189 F8
Loktak L. = Logtak L.
India 24°33N 93°50E 241 C4
Lokuru Solomon Is. 8°20S 157°0E 287 M9
Lol South Sudan 6°26N 29°37E 257 F2
Lol → South Sudan 9°13N 26°30E 257 F2
Lola Angola 14°19S 13°37E 265 E2
Lola Guinea 7°52N 8°29W 262 D3
Lola, Mt. U.S.A. 39°26N 120°22W 306 F6
Lolgorien Kenya 1°14S 34°48E 268 C3
Lolibai, Gebel South Sudan 3°50N 33°0E 257 G3
Lolimi South Sudan 4°35N 34°0E 257 G3
Loliondo Tanzania 2°2S 35°39E 268 C4
Lolland Denmark 54°45N 11°30E 163 K5
Lollar Germany 50°37N 8°43E 178 E4
Lolo U.S.A. 46°45N 114°5W 304 C6
Lolo → Eq. Guin. 1°36N 9°37E 264 B1
Lolo → Gabon 0°18S 12°18E 264 C2
Lolobau I. Papua N. G. 4°55S 151°10E 286 C6
Lolodorf Cameroon 3°16N 10°49E 263 E7
Lolokhet Pakistan 24°54N 67°2E 123 A2
Loloma Zambia 13°24S 24°21E 265 E4
Lolotiqui Vanuatu 15°32S 168°10E 287 E6
Lom Bulgaria 43°48N 23°12E 202 C7
Lom Oppland, Norway 61°50N 8°34E 164 C5
Lom → Bulgaria 43°45N 23°15E 202 C7
Lom → Cameroon 5°20N 13°24E 264 A2
Lom Kao Thailand 16°53N 101°14E 236 D3
Lom Sak Thailand 16°47N 101°15E 236 D3
Loma U.S.A. 47°56N 110°30W 304 C8
Loma Linda U.S.A. 34°3N 117°16W 307 L9
Loma Mansa S. Leone 9°13N 11°7W 262 D2
Loma Mts. S. Leone 9°10N 11°7W 262 D2
Lomako →
Dem. Rep. of the Congo 0°50N 20°50E 264 B4
Lomaloma Fiji 17°17S 178°59W 287 A3
Lomami →
Dem. Rep. of the Congo 0°46N 24°16E 264 B4
Lomas Chapultepec
Mexico 19°25N 99°12W 128 B1
Lomas de San Angel Inn
Mexico 19°20N 99°13W 128 B1
Lomas de Zamora
Argentina 34°45S 58°24W 334 C4
Lombadina Australia 16°31S 122°54E 278 C3
Lombard U.S.A. 41°53N 88°1W 311 C8
Lombárdia □ Italy 45°40N 9°30E 198 C6
Lombardy = Lombárdia □
Italy 45°40N 9°30E 198 C6
Lombardy East S. Africa 26°6S 28°7E 123 A2
Lombe Angola 9°27S 16°13E 265 D3
Lombez France 43°29N 0°55E 174 E4
Lomblen Indonesia 8°30S 123°32E 231 F6
Lombok Indonesia 8°45S 116°30E 235 D5
Lombok, Selat Indonesia 8°30S 115°50E 231 K18
Lomé Togo 6°9N 1°20E 263 D5
Lomela
Dem. Rep. of the Congo 2°19S 23°15E 264 C4
Lomela →
Dem. Rep. of the Congo 0°15S 20°40E 264 C4
Lomianki Poland 52°21N 20°54E 143 A1
Lomié Cameroon 3°13N 13°38E 264 B2
Lomma Sweden 55°43N 13°6E 163 J7
Lommel Belgium 51°14N 5°19E 170 C5
Lomond Canada 50°24N 112°36W 296 C6
Lomond, L. U.K. 56°8N 4°38W 167 E4
Lomonosov Ridge Arctic 88°0N 140°0E 150 A
Lomphat Cambodia 13°30N 106°59E 236 F6
Lompobatang Indonesia 5°24S 119°56E 231 F5
Lompoc U.S.A. 34°38N 120°28W 307 L6
Lomseggje Norway 61°49N 8°21E 164 C5
Lomus Reforma Mexico 19°24N 99°14W 128 B1
Łomża Poland 53°10N 22°2E 185 E9
Lon, Ko Thailand 7°47N 98°23E 237 a
Lonavale India 18°46N 73°29E 244 E1
Loncoche Chile 39°20S 72°50W 336 A2
Loncopué Argentina 38°4S 70°37W 336 A2
Londa India 15°30N 74°30E 245 G2
Londiani Kenya 0°10S 35°33E 268 C4
Londinières France 49°50N 1°25E 172 C8
London Ont., Canada 42°59N 81°15W 312 D3
London London, U.K. 51°30N 0°3W 125 B3
London Ky., U.S.A. 37°8N 84°5W 309 G11
London Ohio, U.S.A. 39°53N 83°27W 311 E13
London, Greater □ U.K. 51°36N 0°5W 169 F7
London Avenue Canal
U.S.A. 30°3N 90°6W 131 A2
London Bridge Grenada 12°15N 61°35W 323 q
London Bridge London, U.K. 125 b5
London City ✈ (LCY) U.K. 51°30N 0°3E 125 A4
London Gatwick ✈ (LGW)
U.K. 51°10N 0°11W 169 F7
London Heathrow ✈ (LHR)
U.K. 51°28N 0°27W 125 B1
London Mills U.S.A. 40°43N 90°11W 310 D6
London Stansted ✈ (STN)
U.K. 51°54N 0°14E 169 F8
London Zoo U.K. 51°31N 0°9W 125 A3
Londonderry U.K. 55°0N 7°20W 166 B4
Londonderry □ U.K. 55°0N 7°20W 166 B4
Londonderry, C.
Australia 13°45S 126°55E 278 B4
Londonderry, I. Chile 55°0S 71°0W 336 E2
Londrina Brazil 23°18S 51°10W 335 A5
Londuimbale Angola 12°15S 15°19E 265 E3
Lone Pine U.S.A. 36°36N 118°4W 306 J8
Lonely Mine Zimbabwe 19°30S 28°49E 271 A4
Long, Î. Martinique 14°36N 60°51W 322 j
Long Akah Malaysia 3°19N 114°47E 235 B4
Long B. N.S.W., Australia 33°59S 151°15E 139 B2
Long B. Cornwall, Jamaica 18°20N 78°20W 320 a
Long B. S.C., U.S.A. 33°35N 78°45W 315 E15
Long Beach Calif.,
U.S.A. 33°46N 118°11W 307 M8
Long Beach N.Y., U.S.A. 40°35N 73°39W 313 F11
Long Beach Wash., U.S.A. 46°21N 124°3W 306 D2
Long Branch Ont., Canada 43°35N 79°31W 141 B1
Long Branch N.J., U.S.A. 40°18N 74°0W 313 F11
Long Cay Bahamas 25°6N 77°22W 153 b
Long Creek U.S.A. 44°43N 119°6W 304 D4
Long Ditton U.K. 51°22N 0°19W 125 B2
Long Eaton U.K. 52°53N 1°15W 168 E6
Long I. Antigua & B. 17°8N 61°45W 322 b
Long I. Queens., Australia 20°22S 148°51E 280 b
Long I. Bahamas 23°20N 75°10W 321 B4
Long I. Nunavut, Canada 54°50N 79°20W 298 B4
Long I. Cork, Ireland 51°30N 9°34W 166 E2
Long I. Papua N. G. 5°20S 147°5E 286 C4
Long I. N.Y., U.S.A. 40°45N 73°30W 313 F11
Long Island City U.S.A. 40°45N 73°56W 132 B2
Long Island Sd. U.S.A. 41°10N 73°0W 313 E12
Long L. Ont., Canada 49°30N 86°50W 298 C2
Long L. N.Y., U.S.A. 44°0N 74°23W 313 C10
Long Lake U.S.A. 43°58N 74°25W 313 C10
Long Mountain Mauritius 20°8S 57°32E 272 e
Long Point Canada 42°34N 80°25W 312 D4
Long Point B. Canada 42°40N 80°10W 312 D4
Long Prairie U.S.A. 45°59N 94°52W 308 C6
Long Prairie → U.S.A. 46°20N 94°36W 308 B6
Long Pt. Bahamas 25°1N 77°20W 153 b
Long Pt. Ont., Canada 42°35N 80°2W 312 D4
Long Pt. Ont., Canada 43°56N 76°53W 313 C8
Long Pt. Otago, N.Z. 46°34S 169°36E 285 G4
Long Range Mts. Canada 49°30N 57°30W 299 C8
Long Reef Australia 14°1S 125°48E 278 B4
Long Sault Canada 45°2N 74°53W 313 A10
Long Str. = Longa, Proliv
Russia 70°0N 175°0E 215 C18
Long Street Cape Town, S. Africa 118 c2
Long Thanh Vietnam 10°47N 106°57E 237 G6
Long Xian China 34°55N 106°55E 226 G4
Long Xuyen Vietnam 10°19N 105°28E 237 G5
Longa Angola 14°42S 18°32E 265 E3
Longa Greece 36°53N 21°55E 204 E3
Longa → Angola 10°15S 13°29E 265 E2
Longa, Proliv Russia 70°0N 175°0E 215 C18
Longa Mavinga △ Angola 16°20S 20°15E 265 F4
Longagung Indonesia 2°16N 115°16E 235 B5
Long'an China 23°10N 107°40E 228 F6
Longana Vanuatu 15°18S 168°0E 287 E5
Longarone Italy 46°16N 12°18E 199 B9
Longbenton U.K. 55°1N 1°31W 168 B6
Longberang Indonesia 3°43N 116°7E 235 B5
Longbia Indonesia 2°37N 116°42E 235 B5
Longboat Key U.S.A. 27°23N 82°39W 317 H7
Longboh Indonesia 0°52N 115°1E 235 B5
Longburn N.Z. 40°23S 175°35E 284 G4
Longchamp, Hippodrome de
France 48°51N 2°13E 134 A2
Longchang China 29°18N 105°15E 228 C5
Longchuan Guangdong,
China 24°5N 115°17E 229 E10
Longchuan Yunnan, China 24°23N 97°58E 228 E1
Longde China 35°30N 106°20E 226 G4
Longdenville Trin. & Tob. 10°31N 61°23W 323 t
Longeau France 47°47N 5°20E 173 E12
Longford Tas., Australia 41°32S 147°3E 281 G4
Longford Longf., Ireland 53°43N 7°49W 166 C4
Longford □ Ireland 53°42N 7°45W 166 C4
Longfort, An = Longford
Ireland 53°43N 7°49W 166 C4
Longgan Shan China 42°19N 126°30E 224 A3
Longhai China 24°25N 117°46E 229 E11
Longhua Guangdong, China 22°39N 114°0E 219 a
Longhua Hebei, China 41°18N 117°45E 227 D9
Longhua Pagoda China 31°10N 121°26E 138 B1
Longhua Park China 31°10N 121°26E 138 B1
Longhui China 27°7N 111°2E 229 D8
Longido Tanzania 2°43S 36°42E 268 C4
Longiram Indonesia 0°5S 115°45E 235 C5
Longjela Indonesia 2°28N 115°28E 235 B5
Longjing China 42°46N 129°25E 227 C15
Longkou Jiangxi, China 26°8N 115°10E 229 D10
Longkou Shandong,
China 37°40N 120°18E 227 F11
Longlac Canada 49°45N 86°25W 298 C2
Longli China 26°25N 106°58E 228 D6
Longlin China 24°47N 105°20E 228 E5
Longling China 24°37N 98°39E 228 E2
Longmeadow U.S.A. 42°3N 72°34W 313 D12
Longmen China 23°40N 114°18E 229 F10
Longmen Shiku China 34°28N 112°28E 226 G7
Longming China 22°59N 107°7E 228 F6
Longmont U.S.A. 40°10N 105°6W 304 F11
Longnan China 24°55N 114°47E 229 E10
Longnawan Indonesia 1°51N 114°55E 235 B4
Longobucco Italy 39°27N 16°37E 201 C9
Longoni, B. de Mayotte 12°41S 45°8E 272 b
Longonot △ Kenya 0°55S 36°28E 266 E4
Longos Greece 39°16N 20°7E 206 C10
Longquan China 28°7N 119°10E 229 C12

Longreach Australia 23°28S 144°14E 280 C3
Longshan China 29°29N 109°25E 228 C7
Longsheng China 25°48N 110°0E 229 E8
Longtan Dam China 25°5N 107°0E 228 E6
Longtan Hu ➔ China 39°51N 116°24E 114 B2
Longué-Jumelles France 47°22N 0°8W 172 E6
Longue-Pointe Canada 45°35N 73°31W 130 A2
Longueau France 49°52N 2°21E 173 C9
Longueuil Canada 45°31N 73°29W 130 A3
Longuy Cameroon 3°5N 9°58E 264 B1
Longuyon France 49°27N 5°35E 173 C12
Longvic France 47°17N 5°4E 173 E12
Longview Tex., U.S.A. 32°30N 94°44W 314 E7
Longview Wash., U.S.A. 46°8N 122°57W 306 D4
Longwood St. Helena 15°57S 5°41W 153 h
Longwood Fla., U.S.A. 28°42N 81°21W 317 G8
Longwy France 49°30N 5°46E 173 C12
Longxi China 34°53N 104°40E 226 G3
Longxue Dao China 22°41N 113°38E 219 a
Longyan China 25°10N 117°0E 229 E11
Longyearbyen Svalbard 78°13N 15°40E 150 B8
Longyou China 29°1N 119°8E 229 C12
Longzhou China 22°22N 106°50E 228 F6
Loni India 28°45N 77°17E 120 A2
Lonigo Italy 45°23N 11°23E 199 C8
Löningen Germany 52°44N 7°46E 178 C3
Lonja ➔ Croatia 45°22N 16°40E 199 C13
Lonkala
Dem. Rep. of the Congo 4°37S 23°14E 265 C4
Lonkin Burma 25°39N 96°22E 241 C6
Lonoke U.S.A. 34°47N 91°54W 314 D9
Lonquimay Chile 38°26S 71°14W 336 A2
Lons-le-Saunier France 46°40N 5°31E 173 F12
Lönsboda Sweden 56°24N 14°20E 163 H8
Lønset Norway 62°46N 7°24E 164 B4
Lonton Burma 25°6N 96°17E 241 C6
Looc Phil. 12°15N 121°59E 232 E3
Looe U.K. 50°22N 4°28W 169 G3
Loogootee U.S.A. 38°41N 86°55W 311 F10
Lookout, C. Canada 55°18N 83°56W 298 A3
Lookout, C. N.C., U.S.A. 34°35N 76°32W 315 D16
Loolmalasin Tanzania 3°0S 35°53E 268 C4
Loon ➔ Alta., Canada 57°8N 115°3W 296 B5
Loon ➔ Man., Canada 55°53N 101°59W 297 B8
Loon Lake Canada 54°2N 109°10W 297 C7
Loongana Australia 30°52S 127°5E 279 F4
Loop, The U.S.A. 41°52N 87°38W 119 c1
Loop Hd. Ireland 52°34N 9°56W 166 D2
Lop China 37°3N 80°11E 217 E10
Lop Nor = Lop Nur China 40°20N 90°10E 217 D12
Lop Nur China 40°20N 90°10E 217 D12
Lopare Bos.-H. 44°39N 18°46E 182 F3
Lopatin Russia 43°50N 47°35E 191 J8
Lopatina, Gora Russia 50°47N 143°10E 215 D15
Lopatino = Volzhsk
Russia 55°57N 48°23E 190 C9
Lopatka, Mys Russia 50°52N 156°40E 215 D16
Lopaye South Sudan 6°37N 33°40E 257 F3
Lopburi Thailand 14°48N 100°37E 236 E3
Lopé-Okanda △ Gabon 0°45S 11°34E 264 C2
Lopevi Vanuatu 16°30S 168°21E 287 F6
Lopez Phil. 13°53N 122°15E 232 E4
Lopez Pa., U.S.A. 41°27N 76°20W 313 E8
Lopez, C. Gabon 0°47S 8°40E 264 C1
López de Filippis = Mariscal
Estigarribia Paraguay 22°3S 60°40W 334 A3
Lopinot Trin. & Tob. 10°41N 61°19W 323 t
Lopori ➔
Dem. Rep. of the Congo 1°14N 19°49E 264 B3
Lopphavet Norway 70°27N 21°15E 160 A19
Lora Norway 62°8N 8°45E 164 B5
Lora ➔ Afghan. 31°35N 66°32E 240 C2
Lora ➔ Oppland, Norway 62°8N 8°42E 164 B5
Lora, Hāmūn-i- Pakistan 29°38N 64°58E 240 C2
Lora Cr. ➔ Australia 28°10S 135°22E 281 D2
Lora del Río Spain 37°39N 5°33W 195 H5
Lorain U.S.A. 41°28N 82°11W 312 E2
Loraine U.S.A. 40°9N 91°13W 310 D5
Loralai Pakistan 30°20N 68°41E 242 D3
Lorca Spain 37°41N 1°42W 197 H3
Lord Howe I. Pac. Oc. 31°33S 159°6E 277 G10
Lord Howe Rise Pac. Oc. 30°0S 162°30E 277 H12
Lord Howe Seamount Chain
Pac. Oc. 28°0S 159°0E 277 F10
Lord Loughborough I.
Burma 10°25N 97°54E 237 G1
Lord's Cricket Ground
U.K. 51°31N 0°10W 125 A2
Lordsburg U.S.A. 32°21N 108°43W 305 K9
Lorengau Papua N. G. 2°1S 147°15E 286 B4
Lorestān □ Iran 33°30N 48°40E 247 C6
Loreto Bolivia 15°13S 64°40W 331 D5
Loreto Brazil 7°5S 45°10W 332 C2
Loreto Marche, Italy 43°26N 13°36E 199 E10
Loreto Piemonte, Italy 45°29N 9°12E 128 B2
Loreto Baja Calif. S.,
Mexico 26°0N 111°21W 318 B2
Loreto Surigao N., Phil. 10°21N 125°34E 233 F5
Loreto □ Peru 5°0S 75°0W 328 E3
Lorgues France 43°28N 6°22E 175 E10
Lorhosso = Loropéni
Burkina Faso 10°17N 3°38W 262 C4
Lorian Swamp Kenya 0°40N 39°35E 267 D4
Lorica Colombia 9°14N 75°49W 328 B2
Lorient Morbihan, France 47°45N 3°23W 172 E3
Lorient St. Barts 17°54N 62°49W 322 a
Lorimor U.S.A. 41°8N 94°3W 310 C2
Lőrinci Hungary 47°44N 19°41E 182 C4
Lormi India 22°17N 81°41E 243 H9
Lorn U.K. 56°26N 5°10W 167 E3
Lorn, Firth of U.K. 56°20N 5°40W 167 E3
Lorne Australia 38°33S 143°59E 282 E5
Loronyo South Sudan 4°38N 32°38E 257 G3
Loropéni Burkina Faso 10°17N 3°38W 262 C4
Lorovouno Cyprus 35°8N 32°36E 207 E8
Lörrach Germany 47°36N 7°40E 179 H3
Lorrain ➔ Martinique 14°50N 61°3W 322 j
Lorraine = Baker
U.S.A. 46°22N 104°17W 304 C11
Lorraine □ France 48°53N 6°0E 173 D13
Lorraine △ France 48°55N 5°50E 173 D12
Los Sweden 61°45N 15°10E 162 C9
Los, Îles de Guinea 9°30N 13°50W 262 D2
Los Alamos Calif., U.S.A. 34°44N 120°17W 307 L6
Los Alamos N. Mex.,
U.S.A. 35°53N 106°19W 305 J10
Los Alcornocales △ Spain 36°21N 5°32W 195 J5
Los Alerces △ Argentina 42°55S 71°55W 336 B2
Los Altos U.S.A. 37°23N 122°7W 306 H4
Los Andes Chile 32°50S 70°40W 334 C1
Los Angeles Chile 37°28S 72°23W 336 A2
Los Angeles Calif., U.S.A. 34°4N 118°15W 126 B3
Los Angeles Aqueduct
U.S.A. 35°22N 118°5W 307 K9
Los Angeles Int. ✈ (LAX)
U.S.A. 33°57N 118°25W 126 C2
Los Antiguos Argentina 46°35S 71°40W 336 C2
Los Bagres Venezuela 10°57N 63°58W 329 a
Los Banos U.S.A. 37°4N 120°51W 306 H6
Los Barrios Spain 36°11N 5°30W 195 J5
Los Blancos Argentina 23°40S 62°30W 334 A3
Los Cabos Int. ✈ (SJD)
Mexico 23°9N 109°43W 318 C3
Los Cardones △ Argentina 25°8S 65°55W 334 B2
Los Cerrillos ✈ (ULC)
Chile 33°29S 70°42W 137 B1
Los Chiles Costa Rica 11°2N 84°43W 320 D3
Los Corrales de Buelna
Spain 43°16N 4°4W 194 B6
Los Cristianos Canary Is. 28°3N 16°42W 153 e1
Los Frailes, I. Venezuela 11°11N 63°44W 329 a
Los Gallardos Spain 37°10N 1°57W 197 H3
Los Gallos Pt. Trin. & Tob. 10°5N 61°55W 323 t
Los Gatos U.S.A. 37°14N 121°59W 306 H5
Los Glaciares △ Argentina 50°0S 73°55W 336 C2
Los Gómez Venezuela 10°57N 64°4W 329 a
Los Haïtises △ Dom. Rep. 19°4N 69°36W 321 C6
Los Hermanos, Is.
Venezuela 11°45N 64°25W 321 D7
Los Huemules △ Chile 46°10S 73°23W 336 C2
Los Islotes Canary Is. 29°4N 13°44W 153 e2
Los Katíos △ Colombia 7°50N 77°10W 328 B2
Los Lagos Chile 39°51S 72°50W 336 A2
Los Llanos de Aridane
Canary Is. 28°38N 17°54W 153 e1
Los Loros Chile 27°50S 70°6W 334 B1
Los Lunas U.S.A. 34°48N 106°44W 305 J10
Los Menucos Argentina 40°50S 68°10W 336 B3
Los Mochis Mexico 25°45N 108°57W 318 B3
Los Monegros Spain 41°29N 0°13W 196 D4
Los Monos Argentina 46°1S 69°36W 336 C3
Los Muermos Chile 41°24S 73°29W 336 B2
Los Nevados △ Colombia 4°41N 75°21W 328 C2
Los Nietos Spain 37°39N 0°47W 197 H4
Los Nietos Calif., U.S.A. 33°57N 118°4W 126 C4
Los Olivos Lima, Peru 11°59S 77°5W 124 A2
Los Olivos Calif., U.S.A. 34°40N 120°7W 307 L6
Los Palacios Cuba 22°35N 83°15W 320 B3
Los Palacios y Villafranca
Spain 37°10N 5°55W 195 H5
Los Queñes Chile 35°1S 70°48W 334 D1
Los Remedios △ Mexico 19°28N 99°17W 128 B1
Los Reyes Mexico 19°21N 99°6W 128 B2
Los Reyes de Salgado
Mexico 19°35N 102°29W 318 D4
Los Ríos □ Ecuador 1°30S 79°25W 328 D2
Los Roques, Is. Venezuela 11°50N 66°45W 321 D6
Los Santos de Maimona
Spain 38°27N 6°22W 195 G4
Los Teques Venezuela 10°21N 67°2W 328 A4
Los Testigos, Is. Venezuela 11°23N 63°6W 329 A5
Los Vilos Chile 32°10S 71°30W 334 C1
Los Yébenes Spain 39°36N 3°55W 195 F7
Loshan = Leshan China 29°33N 103°41E 228 C4
Łosice Poland 52°13N 22°43E 185 F9
Lošinj Croatia 44°30N 14°30E 199 D11
Losiny Ostrov △ Russia 55°50N 37°45E 129 A3
Loskop Dam S. Africa 25°23S 29°20E 271 C4
Løsning Denmark 55°48N 9°42E 163 J3
Losombo
Dem. Rep. of the Congo 1°2N 19°4E 264 B3
Lossiemouth U.K. 57°42N 3°17W 167 D5
Lossnen Sweden 62°26N 12°45E 162 B6
Lostwithiel U.K. 50°24N 4°41W 169 G3
Losuia Papua N. G. 8°30S 151°4E 286 E6
Lot Belgium 50°46N 4°16E 116 B1
Lot □ France 44°39N 1°40E 174 D5
Lot ➔ France 44°18N 0°20E 174 D4
Lot-et-Garonne □ France 44°22N 0°30E 174 D4
Lota Chile 37°5S 73°10W 334 D1
Lotagipi Swamp Kenya 4°36N 34°55E 257 G3
Løten Norway 60°51N 11°21E 164 D8
Lotfābād Iran 37°32N 59°20E 247 B8
Lothair S. Africa 26°22S 30°27E 271 C5
Loto Dem. Rep. of the Congo 2°48S 22°3E 264 C4
Lotoi ➔
Dem. Rep. of the Congo 1°35S 18°30E 264 C3
Lotorp Sweden 58°44N 15°50E 163 F9
Lötschbergtunnel Switz. 46°26N 7°43E 179 J3
Lotta ➔ Europe 68°42N 31°6E 160 B24
Lottefors Sweden 61°25N 16°24E 162 C10
Löttorp Sweden 57°10N 17°0E 163 G11
Lotung Taiwan 24°41N 121°46E 225 B3
Lotus River S. Africa 34°4S 18°31E 118 B2
Lotus Temple India 28°33N 77°15E 120 B2
Lötzen = Giżycko Poland 54°2N 21°48E 184 D8
Lou I. Papua N. G. 2°25S 147°22E 286 B4
Loubière Dominica 15°16N 61°23W 323 k
Loubomo Congo 4°9S 12°47E 264 C2
Loudéac France 48°11N 2°47W 172 D4
Loudi China 27°42N 111°59E 229 D8
Loudima Congo 4°6S 13°5E 264 C2
Loudonville U.S.A. 40°38N 82°14W 312 F2
Loudun France 47°3N 0°5E 172 E7
Loue ➔ France 47°1N 5°28E 173 E12
Louga Senegal 15°45N 16°5W 262 B1
Louga □ Senegal 15°20N 15°35W 262 B1
Loughborough U.K. 52°47N 1°11W 168 E6
Lougheed I. Canada 77°26N 105°6W 295 B10
Loughlinstown Ireland 53°15N 6°7W 120 B3
Loughman U.S.A. 28°14N 81°34W 317 G8
Loughrea Ireland 53°12N 8°33W 166 C3
Loughros More B. Ireland 54°48N 8°32W 166 B3
Louhans France 46°38N 5°12E 173 F12
Louis Armstrong New Orleans
Int. ✈ (MSY) U.S.A. 30°0N 90°15W 131 B1
Louis Armstrong Park
New Orleans, U.S.A. 131 a2
Louis-Gentil = Youssoufia
Morocco 32°16N 8°31W 260 B3
Louis Trichardt S. Africa 23°1S 29°43E 271 B4
Louis XIV, Pte. Canada 54°37N 79°45W 298 B4
Louisa U.S.A. 38°7N 82°36W 309 F12
Louisbourg Canada 45°55N 60°0W 299 C8
Louisburg U.S.A. 38°37N 94°41W 310 F2
Louisburgh Ireland 53°46N 9°49W 166 C2
Louise, L. U.S.A. 28°28N 81°32W 133 B1
Louise I. Canada 52°55N 131°50W 296 C2
Louiseville Canada 46°20N 72°56W 298 C5
Louisiade Arch.
Papua N. G. 11°10S 153°0E 286 F7
Louisiana U.S.A. 39°27N 91°3W 310 E6
Louisiana □ U.S.A. 30°50N 92°0W 314 F9
Louisiana Superdome
New Orleans, U.S.A. 131 b1
Louisville Ala., U.S.A. 31°47N 85°33W 316 D4
Louisville Ga., U.S.A. 33°0N 82°25W 316 B7
Louisville Ill., U.S.A. 38°46N 88°30W 311 F8
Louisville Ky., U.S.A. 38°15N 85°46W 311 F11
Louisville Miss., U.S.A. 33°7N 89°3W 315 E10
Louisville Ohio, U.S.A. 40°50N 81°16W 312 F3
Louisville Ridge Pac. Oc. 31°0S 172°30W 288 L10
Loukoléla Congo 1°4S 17°10E 264 C3
Loukouo Congo 3°38S 14°39E 264 C2
Loulay France 46°3N 0°30W 174 B3
Loulé Portugal 37°9N 8°0W 195 H3
Loulouni Mali 10°54N 5°36W 262 C3
Loum Cameroon 4°42N 9°44E 264 B1
Louny Czech Rep. 50°20N 13°48E 180 A6
Loup City U.S.A. 41°17N 98°58W 308 E4
Loups Marins, Lacs des
Canada 56°30N 73°45W 298 A5
Lourdes France 43°6N 0°3W 174 E3
Lourdes-de-Blanc-Sablon
Canada 51°24N 57°12W 299 B8
Lourenço Brazil 2°30N 51°40W 329 C7
Lourenço Marques = Maputo
Mozam. 25°58S 32°32E 271 C5
Loures Portugal 38°49N 9°10W 126 A1
Lourinhã Portugal 39°14N 9°17W 195 F1
Louros Greece 39°3N 20°47E 207 A2
Louroujina Cyprus 35°0N 33°28E 207 F9
Lousã Portugal 40°7N 8°14W 194 E2
Louta Burkina Faso 13°30N 3°10W 262 C4
Louth N.S.W., Australia 30°30S 145°8E 283 A6
Louth Louth, Ireland 53°58N 6°32W 166 C5
Louth Lincs., U.K. 53°22N 0°1W 168 D7
Louth □ Ireland 53°56N 6°34W 166 C5
Louth B. Australia 34°33S 135°56E 282 C1
Loutra Edipsou Greece 38°54N 23°2E 204 C5
Loutra Kyllinis Greece 37°52N 21°7E 207 D3
Loutraki Greece 37°58N 22°57E 204 D4
Loutropoli Thermis Greece 39°11N 26°29E 205 B8
Louvain = Leuven Belgium 50°52N 4°42E 170 D4
Louvale U.S.A. 32°10N 84°50W 316 C5
Louveciennes France 48°51N 2°8E 134 A1
Louviers France 49°12N 1°10E 172 C8
Louvre, Musée du Paris, France 134 b4
Louvre, Palais du Paris, France 134 b4
Louwsburg S. Africa 27°37S 31°7E 271 C5
Lovat ➔ Russia 58°14N 31°28E 188 C6
Lovćen Montenegro 42°23N 18°51E 202 D2
Lovćen △ Montenegro 42°20N 18°50E 202 D2
Lovech Bulgaria 43°8N 24°42E 203 C8
Lovech □ Bulgaria 43°0N 24°45E 203 D8
Loveland Colo., U.S.A. 40°24N 105°5W 304 F11
Loveland Ohio, U.S.A. 39°16N 84°16W 311 E12
Lovell U.S.A. 44°50N 108°24W 304 D9
Lovelock U.S.A. 40°11N 118°28W 304 F4
Lóvere Italy 45°49N 10°4E 198 C7
Lovers Leap Jamaica 17°52N 77°39W 320 a
Loves Park U.S.A. 42°19N 89°3W 310 B7
Lövestad Sweden 55°40N 13°54E 163 J7
Loviisa Finland 60°28N 26°12E 188 B4
Lovilia U.S.A. 41°8N 92°55W 310 C4
Lovina Indonesia 8°9S 115°1E 231 J18
Loving U.S.A. 32°17N 104°6W 305 K11
Lovington Ill., U.S.A. 39°43N 88°38W 311 E8
Lovington N. Mex.,
U.S.A. 32°57N 103°21W 305 K12
Lovisa = Loviisa Finland 60°28N 26°12E 188 B4
Lovosice Czech Rep. 50°30N 14°2E 180 A7
Lovran Croatia 45°18N 14°15E 199 C11
Lovrin Romania 45°58N 20°48E 182 E5
Lövstabruk Sweden 60°25N 17°53E 162 D11
Lövstabukten Sweden 60°35N 17°45E 162 D11
Lóvua Lunda Norte, Angola 7°19S 20°12E 265 D4
Lóvua Moxico, Angola 11°33S 23°33E 265 E4
Lóvua ➔
Dem. Rep. of the Congo 6°6S 20°37E 265 D4
Low, L. Canada 52°29N 76°17W 298 B4
Low B. Antigua & B. 17°39N 61°51W 322 b
Low Pt. Australia 32°25S 127°25E 279 F4
Low Tatra = Nízké Tatry
Slovak Rep. 48°55N 19°30E 181 C12
Lowa Dem. Rep. of the Congo 1°25S 25°47E 268 C2
Lowa ➔
Dem. Rep. of the Congo 1°24S 25°51E 268 C2
Lowden U.S.A. 41°52N 90°56W 310 C6
Lowell Ind., U.S.A. 41°18N 87°25W 311 C9
Lowell Mass., U.S.A. 42°38N 71°19W 313 D13
Lowell Mich., U.S.A. 42°56N 85°20W 311 B11
Lowellville U.S.A. 41°2N 80°32W 312 E4
Löwen = Lewin Brzeski
Poland 50°45N 17°37E 185 H4
Löwen ➔ Namibia 26°51S 18°17E 270 C2
Löwenberg = Lwówek Śląski
Poland 51°7N 15°38E 185 G2
Löwenstadt = Brzeziny
Poland 51°49N 19°42E 185 G6
Lower Alkali L. U.S.A. 41°16N 120°2W 304 F3
Lower Arrow L. Canada 49°40N 118°5W 296 D5
Lower Austria = Niederösterreich □
Austria 48°25N 15°40E 180 C8
Lower B. U.S.A. 40°32N 74°5W 132 C1
Lower California = Baja California
Mexico 31°10N 115°12W 318 A1
Lower East Side New York, U.S.A. 132 e2
Lower Glenelg △ Australia 38°4S 141°41E 282 E4
Lower Hutt N.Z. 41°10S 174°55E 284 H3
Lower Kalskag U.S.A. 61°31N 160°22W 303 F7
Lower Lake U.S.A. 38°55N 122°37W 306 G4
Lower Manhattan New York, U.S.A. 132 e1
Lower Manitou L. Canada 49°15N 93°0W 297 D10
Lower Manzanilla
Trin. & Tob. 10°31N 61°3W 323 t
Lower New York B. = Lower B.
U.S.A. 40°32N 74°5W 132 C1
Lower Paia U.S.A. 20°55N 156°23W 302 C5
Lower Peirce Res.
Singapore 1°22N 103°49E 138 A2
Lower Post Canada 59°58N 128°30W 296 B3
Lower Red L. U.S.A. 47°58N 95°0W 308 B6
Lower Saxony = Niedersachsen □
Germany 52°50N 9°0E 178 C4
Lower Shing Mun Res.
China 22°22N 114°9E 122 A1
Lower Tunguska = Tunguska,
Nizhnyaya ➔ Russia 65°48N 88°4E 215 C9
Lower Zambezi △ Zambia 15°25S 29°40E 269 F2
Lowestoft U.K. 52°29N 1°45E 169 E9
Lowgar □ Afghan. 34°0N 69°0E 240 B3
Łowicz Poland 52°6N 19°55E 185 F6
Lowly, Pt. Australia 33°0S 137°46E 282 B2
Lowry City U.S.A. 38°8N 93°44W 310 F3
Lowther I. Canada 74°33N 97°30W 295 C12
Lowville U.S.A. 43°47N 75°29W 313 C9
Loxton S. Austral.,
Australia 34°28S 140°31E 282 C4
Loxton Northern Cape,
S. Africa 31°30S 22°22E 270 D3
Loyalton U.S.A. 39°41N 120°14W 306 F6
Loyalty Is. = Loyauté, Îs.
N. Cal. 20°50S 166°30E 288 d
Loyang = Luoyang
China 34°40N 112°26E 226 G7
Loyauté, Îs. N. Cal. 20°50S 166°30E 288 d
Loyev = Loyew Belarus 51°56N 30°46E 177 C16
Loyew Belarus 51°56N 30°46E 177 C16
Loyola Univ. U.S.A. 42°0N 87°39W 119 B3
Loyoro Uganda 3°22N 34°14E 268 B3
Lož Slovenia 45°43N 14°30E 199 C11
Lozère □ France 44°35N 3°30E 174 D7
Loznica Serbia 44°32N 19°12E 202 B3
Lozova Ukraine 49°0N 36°20E 189 H9
Ltalaltuma ◎ Australia 23°57S 132°25E 278 D5
Lu India 26°58N 95°14E 241 B5
Lü Shan China 29°30N 115°55E 229 C10
Lü Shan △ China 29°26N 115°52E 229 C10
Lu Verne U.S.A. 42°55N 94°5W 310 B2
Lu Wo China 22°33N 114°6E 219 a
Lu Xun, Tomb of China 31°17N 121°29E 138 B1
Lu Xun Museum Beijing, China 114 b1
Lu Xun Park China 31°17N 121°28E 138 B1
Lua ➔
Dem. Rep. of the Congo 2°46N 18°26E 264 B3
Lua Makiki U.S.A. 20°33N 156°37W 302 C5
Luachimo Angola 7°23S 20°48E 265 D4
Luacono Angola 11°15S 21°37E 265 E4
Luajan ➔ India 24°44N 85°1E 243 G11
Lualaba ➔
Dem. Rep. of the Congo 0°26N 25°20E 264 B5
Luale Dem. Rep. of the Congo 1°9N 23°5E 264 B4
Luambe △ Zambia 12°30S 32°15E 269 E3
Luampa Zambia 15°4S 24°20E 265 F4
Lu'an China 31°45N 116°29E 229 B11
Luan Chau Vietnam 21°38N 103°24E 228 G4
Luan He ➔ China 39°20N 119°5E 227 E10
Luan Xian China 39°40N 118°40E 227 E10
Luancheng Guangxi Zhuangzu,
China 22°48N 108°55E 228 F7
Luancheng Hebei, China 37°53N 114°40E 226 F8
Luanco Spain 43°37N 5°48W 194 B5
Luanda Angola 8°50S 13°15E 265 D2
Luando ➔ Angola 10°21S 16°27E 265 E3
Luando ⌓ Angola 11°0S 17°32E 265 E3
Luang, Doi Thailand 18°30N 101°15E 236 C3
Luang, Thale Thailand 7°30N 100°15E 237 J3
Luang Nam Tha Laos 20°58N 101°30E 228 G3
Luang Prabang Laos 19°52N 102°10E 228 H4
Luanginga ➔ Zambia 15°11S 22°55E 265 F4
Luangwa Zambia 15°35S 30°16E 269 F3
Luangwa ➔ Zambia 14°25S 30°25E 269 E3
Luangwa Valley Zambia 13°30S 31°30E 269 E3
Luangwe = Loange ➔
Dem. Rep. of the Congo 4°17S 20°2E 265 C4
Luania-Bubi
Dem. Rep. of the Congo 7°28S 24°49E 265 D4
Luanne China 40°55N 117°40E 227 D9
Luanping China 40°53N 117°23E 227 D9
Luanshya Zambia 13°3S 28°28E 269 E2
Luapula □ Zambia 11°0S 29°0E 269 E2
Luapula ➔ Africa 9°26S 28°33E 269 D2
Luar, Danau Indonesia 0°55N 112°15E 235 B4
Luarca Spain 43°32N 6°32W 194 B4
Luashi
Dem. Rep. of the Congo 10°50S 23°36E 265 E4
Luatamba Angola 12°6S 20°19E 265 E4
Luatira Angola 12°52S 17°14E 265 E3
Luau Angola 10°40S 22°10E 265 E4
Luba Phil. 17°19N 120°42E 232 C3
Lubaczów Poland 50°10N 23°8E 185 H10
Lubalo Angola 9°10S 19°15E 265 D3
Lubamiti
Dem. Rep. of the Congo 2°28S 17°47E 264 C3
Lubań Poland 51°5N 15°15E 185 G2
Lubana, Ozero = Lubānas Ezers
Latvia 56°45N 27°0E 188 D4
Lubānas Ezers Latvia 56°45N 27°0E 188 D4
Lubang Phil. 13°52N 120°7E 232 E3
Lubang Is. Phil. 13°50N 120°12E 232 E3
Lubango Angola 14°55S 13°30E 265 E2
Lubao Dem. Rep. of the Congo 5°17S 25°42E 265 D5
Lubao Phil. 14°56N 120°36E 232 D3
Lübars Germany 52°37N 13°21E 115 A3
Lubartów Poland 51°28N 22°42E 185 G9
Lubawa Poland 53°30N 19°48E 184 E6
Lübbecke Germany 52°18N 8°37E 178 C4
Lübben Germany 51°56N 13°54E 178 D9
Lübbenau Germany 51°52N 13°57E 178 D9
Lubbock U.S.A. 33°35N 101°51W 314 E4
Lübeck Germany 53°52N 10°40E 178 B6
Lübecker Bucht Germany 54°3N 10°54E 178 A6
Lubefu
Dem. Rep. of the Congo 4°47S 24°27E 265 C4
Lubefu ➔
Dem. Rep. of the Congo 4°10S 23°0E 265 C4
Lubelskie □ Poland 51°20N 22°50E 185 G9
Lüben = Lubin Poland 51°24N 16°11E 185 G3
Lubero = Luofu
Dem. Rep. of the Congo 0°10S 29°15E 268 C2
Luberon △ France 43°52N 5°25E 175 E9
Lubersac France 45°26N 1°23E 174 C5
Lubicon L. Canada 56°23N 115°56W 296 B5
Lubień Kujawski Poland 52°23N 19°9E 185 F6
Lubilash ➔
Dem. Rep. of the Congo 6°2S 23°45E 265 D4
Lubin Poland 51°24N 16°11E 185 G3
Lublin Poland 51°12N 22°38E 185 G9
Lubliniec Poland 50°43N 18°45E 185 H5
Lubnān = Lebanon ■ Asia 34°0N 36°0E 250 E7
Lubnān, Jabal Lebanon 33°45N 35°40E 250 E6
Lubniewice Poland 52°31N 15°15E 185 F2
Lubny Ukraine 50°3N 32°58E 189 G7
Lubomierz Poland 51°1N 15°31E 185 G2
Luboń Poland 52°21N 16°51E 185 F3
Lubondaie
Dem. Rep. of the Congo 8°1S 26°32E 265 D4
Lubongola
Dem. Rep. of the Congo 2°35S 27°50E 268 C2
L'ubotín Slovak Rep. 49°17N 20°53E 181 B13
Lubraniec Poland 52°33N 18°50E 185 F5
Lubsko Poland 51°45N 14°57E 185 G1
Lübtheen Germany 53°18N 11°5E 178 B7
Lubuagan Phil. 17°21N 121°10E 232 C3
Lubudi
Dem. Rep. of the Congo 6°51S 21°18E 265 D4
Lubudi ➔ Kasai-Occ.,
Dem. Rep. of the Congo 4°19S 20°23E 265 C4
Lubudi ➔ Katanga,
Dem. Rep. of the Congo 9°0S 25°35E 265 D5
Lubuklinggau Indonesia 3°15S 102°55E 234 C2
Lubukpakam Indonesia 3°33N 98°52E 234 B1
Lubuksikaping Indonesia 0°10N 100°15E 234 B2
Lubumbashi
Dem. Rep. of the Congo 11°40S 27°28E 269 E2
Lubunda
Dem. Rep. of the Congo 5°12S 26°41E 265 D5
Lubungu Zambia 14°35S 26°24E 269 E2
Lubuskie □ Poland 52°10N 15°20E 185 F2
Lubutu
Dem. Rep. of the Congo 0°45S 26°30E 268 C2
Luc-en-Diois France 44°36N 5°28E 175 D9
Lucala Angola 9°7S 15°58E 265 D3
Lucala ➔ Angola 9°38S 14°16E 265 D2
Lucan Ont., Canada 43°11N 81°24W 312 C3
Lucan Dublin, Ireland 53°22N 6°28W 166 C5
Lucania, Mt. Canada 61°1N 140°27W 294 E3
Lucapa Angola 8°25S 20°45E 265 D4
Lucas U.S.A. 41°2N 93°29W 310 C3
Lucas Channel = Main Channel
Canada 45°21N 81°45W 312 A3
Lucban Phil. 14°6N 121°33E 232 D3
Lucca Italy 43°50N 10°29E 198 E7
Lucé France 48°26N 1°27E 172 D8
Luce Bay U.K. 54°45N 4°48W 167 G4
Lucea Jamaica 18°27N 78°10W 320 a
Lucedale U.S.A. 30°56N 88°35W 315 F10
Lucena Phil. 13°56N 121°37E 232 E3
Lucena Spain 37°27N 4°31W 195 H6
Lučenec Slovak Rep. 48°18N 19°42E 181 C12
Lucera Italy 41°30N 15°20E 201 A8
Lucerne = Lake Worth
U.S.A. 26°37N 80°3W 317 J9
Lucerne = Luzern Switz. 47°3N 8°18E 179 H4
Lucerne U.S.A. 39°6N 122°48W 306 F4
Lucerne Valley U.S.A. 34°27N 116°57W 307 L10
Luchena ➔ Spain 37°44N 1°50W 197 H3
Lucheng China 36°20N 113°11E 226 F7
Lucheringo ➔ Mozam. 11°43S 36°17E 269 E4
Luchow = Luzhou China 28°52N 105°20E 228 C5
Lüchow Germany 52°58N 11°8E 178 C7
Luchu Taiwan 22°52N 120°15E 225 D2
Luchuan China 22°21N 110°12E 229 F8
Lucia U.S.A. 36°2N 121°33W 306 J5
Lucie ➔ Suriname 3°35N 57°38W 329 C6
Lucinda Australia 18°32S 146°20E 280 B4
Lucindale Australia 36°58S 140°26E 282 D4
Lucira Angola 14°0S 12°35E 265 E2
Luciras, B. das Angola 13°52S 12°31E 265 E2
Luckau Germany 51°50N 13°42E 178 D9
Luckenwalde Germany 52°5N 13°10E 178 C9
Luckey U.S.A. 41°27N 83°29W 311 C13
Luckhoff S. Africa 29°44S 24°43E 270 C3
Lucknow Ont., Canada 43°57N 81°31W 312 C3
Lucknow India 26°50N 81°0E 243 F9
Luçon France 46°28N 1°10W 174 B2
Lucusse Angola 12°32S 20°48E 265 E4
Lucy, L. U.S.A. 28°34N 81°44W 133 A2
Lüda = Dalian China 38°50N 121°40E 227 E11
Luda Kamchiya ➔
Bulgaria 43°3N 27°29E 203 C11
Ludbreg Croatia 46°15N 16°38E 199 B13
Lüdenscheid Germany 51°13N 7°37E 178 D3
Lüderitz Namibia 26°41S 15°8E 270 C2
Lüderitzbaai Namibia 26°36S 15°8E 270 C2
Ludhiana India 30°57N 75°56E 242 D6
Ludian China 27°10N 103°33E 228 D4
Luding Qiao China 29°53N 102°12E 228 C4
Lüdinghausen Germany 51°46N 7°27E 178 D3
Ludington U.S.A. 43°57N 86°27W 308 D10
Ludlow Shrops., U.K. 52°22N 2°42W 169 E5
Ludlow Calif., U.S.A. 34°43N 116°10W 307 L10
Ludlow Pa., U.S.A. 41°43N 78°56W 312 E6
Ludlow Vt., U.S.A. 43°24N 72°42W 313 C12
Ludowici U.S.A. 31°43N 81°45W 316 D8
Luduş Romania 46°29N 24°5E 183 D9
Ludvika Sweden 60°8N 15°14E 162 D9
Ludwigsburg Germany 48°53N 9°11E 179 G5
Ludwigsfeld Germany 48°12N 11°27E 131 A1
Ludwigsfelde Germany 52°17N 13°17E 178 C9
Ludwigshafen Germany 49°29N 8°26E 179 F4
Ludwigslust Germany 53°19N 11°30E 178 B7
Ludza Latvia 56°32N 27°43E 188 D4
Lue Australia 32°38S 149°50E 283 B8
Luebo Dem. Rep. of the Congo 5°21S 21°23E 265 D4
Lueki Dem. Rep. of the Congo 3°20S 25°48E 264 C5
Luena Angola 12°13S 19°51E 265 E3
Luena Dem. Rep. of the Congo 9°28S 25°43E 269 D2
Luena Zambia 10°40S 30°25E 269 E3
Luena ➔ Angola 12°30S 22°34E 265 E4
Luena ➔ Zambia 14°46S 23°30E 265 E4
Luena Flats Zambia 14°47S 23°17E 265 E4
Luengué △ Angola 16°55S 19°55E 265 F3
Luenha = Ruenya ➔
Africa 16°24S 33°48E 269 F3
Luepa Venezuela 5°43N 61°31W 329 B5
Lueta ➔
Dem. Rep. of the Congo 7°4S 21°40E 265 D4
Luete ➔ Zambia 15°46S 23°10E 265 F4
Lüeyang China 33°22N 106°10E 228 A6
Lufeng Guangdong, China 22°57N 115°38E 229 F10
Lufeng Yunnan, China 25°0N 102°5E 228 E4
Lufico Angola 6°24S 13°23E 265 D2
Lufira ➔
Dem. Rep. of the Congo 9°30S 27°0E 269 D2
Lufkin U.S.A. 31°21N 94°44W 314 F7
Lufupa
Dem. Rep. of the Congo 10°37S 24°56E 265 E4
Luga Russia 58°40N 29°55E 188 C5
Luga ➔ Russia 59°40N 28°18E 188 C5
Lugano Switz. 46°1N 8°57E 179 J4
Lugano, L. di Switz. 46°0N 9°0E 198 C6
Lugansk = Luhansk
Ukraine 48°38N 39°15E 189 H10
Luganville Vanuatu 15°27S 167°10E 287 E5
Lugard's Falls Kenya 3°6S 38°41E 268 C4
Lugela Mozam. 16°25S 36°43E 269 F4
Lugenda ➔ Mozam. 11°25S 38°33E 269 E4
Lugh = Luuq Somalia 3°48N 42°34E 267 D5
Lugnaquilla Ireland 52°58N 6°28W 166 D5
Lugnvik Sweden 62°56N 17°55E 162 B11
Lugo Italy 44°25N 11°54E 199 D8
Lugo Spain 43°2N 7°35W 194 B3
Lugo □ Spain 43°0N 7°30W 194 C3
Lugoj Romania 45°42N 21°57E 182 E6
Lugovoy = Qulan
Kazakhstan 42°55N 72°43E 214 E8
Lugus I. Phil. 5°41N 120°50E 233 J3
Luhansk Ukraine 48°38N 39°15E 189 H10
Luhansk □ Ukraine 49°10N 38°40E 189 H10
Luhe China 32°19N 118°50E 229 A12
Luhe ➔ Germany 53°23N 10°13E 178 B6
Luhit ➔ India 27°48N 95°28E 241 B5
Luhu China 23°9N 113°16E 121 B2
Luhuo China 31°21N 100°48E 228 B3
Lui ➔ Angola 8°21S 17°33E 265 D3
Lui ➔ Zambia 16°18S 23°17E 265 F4
Luia Angola 8°10S 21°32E 265 D4
Luia ➔ Angola 8°32S 21°47E 265 D4
Luiana Angola 17°25S 22°59E 265 F4
Luiana ➔ Angola 17°24S 23°3E 265 F4
Luiana ⌓ Angola 16°55S 22°20E 265 F4
Luichow = Liuzhou
China 24°22N 109°22E 228 E7
Luichow Pen. = Leizhou Bandao
China 21°0N 110°0E 228 G7
Luikuei Taiwan 23°0N 120°38E 225 D2
Luilaka ➔
Dem. Rep. of the Congo 0°52S 20°12E 264 C4
Luimneach = Limerick
Ireland 52°40N 8°37W 166 D3
Luing U.K. 56°14N 5°39W 167 E3
Luino Italy 45°59N 8°44E 198 C5
Luio ➔ Angola 13°17S 21°37E 265 E4
Luís Correia Brazil 3°0S 41°35W 332 B3
Luís Gonçalves Brazil 5°37S 50°25W 332 C1
Luitpold Coast Antarctica 78°30S 32°0W 151 D1
Luiza Dem. Rep. of the Congo 7°40S 22°30E 265 D4
Luizi Dem. Rep. of the Congo 6°0S 27°25E 268 D2
Luján Argentina 34°45S 59°5W 334 C4
Lujiang China 31°20N 117°15E 229 B11
Lukala
Dem. Rep. of the Congo 5°31S 14°32E 265 D2
Lukang Taiwan 24°1N 120°22E 225 B2
Lukanga Bandundu,
Dem. Rep. of the Congo 1°41S 18°9E 264 C3
Lukanga Équateur,
Dem. Rep. of the Congo 1°0S 18°8E 264 C3
Lukanga Swamp Zambia 14°30S 27°40E 269 E2
Lukavac Bos.-H. 44°33N 18°32E 182 F3
Lukenie ➔
Dem. Rep. of the Congo 3°0S 18°50E 264 C3
Lŭki Bulgaria 41°50N 24°43E 203 E8
Lukk Libya 32°1N 24°46E 258 B4
Lukla Nepal 27°42N 86°43E 243 F12
Lukolela Équateur,
Dem. Rep. of the Congo 1°10S 17°12E 264 C3
Lukolela Kasai-Or.,
Dem. Rep. of the Congo 5°23S 24°32E 265 D4
Lukosi Zimbabwe 18°30S 26°30E 269 F2
Lukovë Albania 39°59N 19°54E 202 G3
Lukovit Bulgaria 43°13N 24°11E 203 C8
Łuków Poland 51°55N 22°23E 185 G9
Lukoyanov Russia 55°2N 44°29E 190 C7
Luksefjell Norway 59°23N 9°34E 164 E6
Luku Taiwan 23°44N 120°45E 225 C2
Lukulu Zambia 14°23S 23°15E 265 E4
Lukuni
Dem. Rep. of the Congo 5°50S 17°16E 265 D3
Lukusuzi △ Zambia 12°43S 32°36E 269 E3
Lula Dem. Rep. of the Congo 5°22S 16°2E 265 D3
Lülang Shan China 38°0N 111°15E 226 F6
Luleå Sweden 65°35N 22°10E 160 D20
Luleälven ➔ Sweden 65°35N 22°10E 160 D20
Lüleburgaz Turkey 41°23N 27°22E 203 E11
Luliang China 25°0N 103°40E 228 E4
Lulima
Dem. Rep. of the Congo 4°12S 25°36E 268 C2
Luling U.S.A. 29°41N 97°39W 314 G6
Lulong China 39°53N 118°51E 227 E10
Lulonga ➔
Dem. Rep. of the Congo 1°0N 18°10E 264 B3
Lulu U.S.A. 30°7N 82°29W 316 E7
Lulu ➔
Dem. Rep. of the Congo 1°18N 23°42E 264 B4
Lulua ➔
Dem. Rep. of the Congo 4°30S 20°30E 265 C4
Luluabourg = Kananga
Dem. Rep. of the Congo 5°55S 22°18E 265 D4
Luma Amer. Samoa 14°16S 169°33W 302 f
Lumai Angola 13°13S 21°25E 265 E4
Lumajang Indonesia 8°8S 113°13E 235 D4
Lumaku, Gunong
Malaysia 4°52N 115°38E 235 B5
Lumār Iran 33°33N 46°49E 213 F12
Lumbala ➔ Angola 12°39S 22°35E 265 E4
Lumbala Kaquengue
Angola 12°39S 22°34E 265 E4
Lumbala N'guimbo
Angola 14°18S 21°18E 265 E4
Lumbe ➔ Zambia 16°44S 23°41E 265 F4
Lumber City U.S.A. 31°56N 82°41W 316 D7
Lumberton N.C., U.S.A. 34°37N 79°0W 315 D15
Lumberton Tex., U.S.A. 30°16N 94°12W 314 F7
Lumbis Indonesia 4°18N 116°15E 235 B5
Lumding India 25°46N 93°10E 241 C4
Lumi Papua N. G. 3°30S 142°2E 286 B2
Lumiar Portugal 38°46N 9°10W 126 A2
Lumpkin U.S.A. 32°3N 84°48W 316 C5
Lumsden Sask., Canada 50°39N 104°52W 297 C8
Lumsden N.Z. 45°44S 168°27E 285 F3
Lumut Malaysia 4°13N 100°37E 237 K3
Lumut, Tanjung Indonesia 3°50S 105°58E 234 C3
Luna India 23°43N 69°16E 242 H3
Luna Apayao, Phil. 18°18N 121°21E 232 B3
Lunan China 24°40N 103°18E 228 E4
Lunavada India 23°8N 73°37E 242 H5
Lunca Romania 47°22N 25°1E 183 C10
Lunca Corbului Romania 44°42N 24°45E 183 F9
Lund Sweden 55°44N 13°12E 163 J7
Lunda Norte □ Angola 8°0S 20°0E 265 D4
Lunda Sul □ Angola 10°0S 20°0E 265 E4
Lundamo Norway 63°9N 10°19E 164 A7
Lundazi Zambia 12°20S 33°7E 269 E3
Lunde Sweden 62°53N 17°51E 162 B11
Lundenburg = Břeclav
Czech Rep. 48°46N 16°53E 181 C9
Lunderskov Denmark 55°29N 9°19E 163 J3
Lundi ➔ Zimbabwe 21°43S 32°34E 269 G3
Lundtofte Denmark 55°47N 12°32E 118 A3
Lundu Malaysia 1°40N 109°50E 235 B3
Lundy U.K. 51°10N 4°41W 169 F3
Lune ➔ U.K. 54°0N 2°51W 168 C5
Lüneburg Germany 53°15N 10°24E 178 B6
Lüneburg Heath = Lüneburger
Heide Germany 53°10N 10°12E 178 B6
Lüneburger Heide
Germany 53°10N 10°12E 178 B6
Lunel France 43°39N 4°9E 175 E8
Lünen Germany 51°37N 7°32E 178 D3
Lunenburg Canada 44°22N 64°18W 299 D7
Lunéville France 48°36N 6°30E 173 D13
Lung Mei China 22°23N 114°15E 122 A2
Lunga Dem. Rep. of the Congo 5°46S 12°14E 265 C4
Lunga ➔ Zambia 14°34S 26°25E 269 E2
Lunga Lunga Kenya 4°33S 39°7E 268 C4
Lungchin Taiwan 24°12N 120°31E 225 B2
Lunge Angola 12°13S 16°7E 265 E3
Lungga Solomon Is. 9°25S 160°3E 287 M11
Lungi S. Leone 8°40N 13°17W 262 D2
Lunglei India 22°55N 92°45E 241 D4
Lungngo Burma 21°57N 93°36E 241 E4
Lung'tan Taiwan 24°52N 121°12E 225 B3
Lungwebungu ➔ Zambia 14°19S 23°14E 265 E4
Luni India 26°0N 73°6E 242 G5
Luni ➔ India 24°41N 71°14E 242 G4
Luninets = Luninyets
Belarus 52°15N 26°50E 177 B14
Luning U.S.A. 38°30N 118°11W 304 G4
Lunino Russia 53°38N 45°18E 190 D7
Luninyets Belarus 52°15N 26°50E 177 B14
Lunkaransar India 28°29N 73°44E 242 E5
Lunner Norway 60°19N 10°35E 164 D7
Lunpei Taiwan 24°45N 120°21E 225 C2
Lunsar S. Leone 8°41N 12°32W 262 D2
Lunsemfwa ➔ Zambia 14°54S 30°12E 269 E3
Lunsemfwa Falls Zambia 14°30S 29°6E 269 E2
Luntai China 41°46N 84°14E 217 D10
Luo He ➔ China 34°35N 110°20E 226 G6
Luocheng China 24°48N 108°53E 228 E7
Luochuan China 35°45N 109°26E 226 G5
Luoci China 25°19N 102°18E 228 E4
Luodian China 25°24N 106°43E 228 E6
Luoding China 22°45N 111°40E 229 F8
Luofu Dem. Rep. of the Congo 0°10S 29°15E 268 C2
Luohe China 33°32N 114°2E 226 H8
Luojiang Guangdong, China 23°5N 113°17E 121 B2
Luojiang Sichuan, China 31°18N 104°33E 228 B5
Luonan China 34°5N 110°10E 226 G6
Luoning China 34°35N 111°40E 226 G6
Luoshan China 32°13N 114°30E 229 A10
Luotian China 30°46N 115°22E 229 B10
Luoxiao Shan China 26°30N 114°1E 229 D10
Luoyang China 34°40N 112°26E 226 G7
Luoyuan China 26°28N 119°30E 229 D12
Luozi Dem. Rep. of the Congo 4°54S 14°0E 265 C2
Luozigou China 43°42N 130°18E 227 C16
Lupeni Romania 45°21N 23°13E 183 E8
Lupilichi Mozam. 11°47S 35°13E 269 E4
Lupire Angola 14°36S 19°29E 265 E3
Łupków Poland 49°15N 22°4E 185 J9
Lupoing China 24°53N 104°21E 228 E5
Lupon Phil. 6°54N 126°0E 233 H6
Luputa Dem. Rep. of the Congo 7°7S 23°43E 265 D4
Luqa Malta 35°52N 14°29E 206 F7
Luquan Hebei, China 38°4N 114°17E 226 E8
Luquan Yunnan, China 25°35N 102°25E 228 E4
Luque Paraguay 25°19S 57°25W 334 B4
Luquembo Angola 10°44S 17°43E 265 E3
Luquillo Puerto Rico 18°23N 65°43W 321 b
Luquillo, Sierra de
Puerto Rico 18°20N 65°47W 321 b
Lúras Italy 40°56N 9°10E 200 B2
Luray U.S.A. 38°40N 78°28W 309 F14
Lure France 47°40N 6°30E 173 E13
Luremo Angola 8°30S 17°50E 265 D3
Lurgan U.K. 54°27N 6°20W 166 B5
Luribay Bolivia 17°6S 67°39W 330 D4
Lurín Peru 12°17S 76°52W 330 C2
Lúrio Mozam. 13°32S 40°30E 269 E5
Lurio ➔ Mozam. 13°35S 40°30E 269 E5
Lusaka Zambia 15°28S 28°16E 269 F2
Lusaka □ Zambia 15°30S 29°0E 269 F2
Lusambo
Dem. Rep. of the Congo 4°58S 23°28E 265 C4
Lusancay Is. and Reefs
Papua N. G. 8°30S 150°30E 286 E6
Lusangaye
Dem. Rep. of the Congo 4°54S 26°0E 265 C5
Luseland Canada 52°5N 109°24W 297 C7
Lusenga Plain △ Zambia 9°22S 29°14E 269 D2
Lusengo
Dem. Rep. of the Congo 1°47N 19°31E 264 B3
Lushan Henan, China 33°45N 112°55E 226 H7
Lushan Sichuan, China 30°12N 102°52E 228 B4
Lushi China 34°3N 111°3E 226 G6
Lushnjë Albania 40°55N 19°41E 202 F3
Lushoto Tanzania 4°47S 38°20E 268 C4
Lushui China 25°58N 98°44E 228 E2
Lushuihe China 42°31N 127°47E 224 A3
Lüshun China 38°45N 121°15E 227 E11

Lusignan France 46°26N 0°8E 174 B4
Lusigny-sur-Barse France 48°16N 4°15E 173 D11
Lusiye Zambia 15°30S 23°57E 265 F4
Lusk U.S.A. 42°46N 104°27W 304 E11
Lussac-les-Châteaux France 46°24N 0°43E 174 B4
Lustenau Austria 47°26N 9°39E 180 D2
Lustheim Germany 48°14N 11°34E 131 A2
Lustrafjorden Norway 61°23N 7°25E 164 C4
Lūt, Dasht-e Iran 31°30N 58°0E 247 D8
Luta = Dalian China 38°50N 121°40E 227 E11
Lütao Taiwan 22°40N 121°30E 225 D3
Lutembo Angola 13°26S 21°16E 265 E4
Lutherstadt Wittenberg Germany 51°53N 12°39E 178 D8
Luthersville U.S.A. 33°13N 84°45W 316 B5
Luti Solomon Is. 7°14S 157°0E 287 L9
Luton U.K. 51°53N 0°24W 169 F7
Luton ☐ U.K. 51°53N 0°24W 169 F7
Lutong Malaysia 4°28N 114°0E 235 B4
Lutsel K'e Canada 62°24N 110°44W 297 A6
Lutshima → Dem. Rep. of the Congo 5°22S 18°59E 265 D3
Lutsk Ukraine 50°50N 25°15E 177 C13
Luttenberg = Ljutomer Slovenia 46°31N 16°11E 199 B13
Lutto = Lotta → Europe 68°42N 31°6E 160 B24
Lutuai Angola 12°41S 20°7E 265 E4
Lutz U.S.A. 28°9N 82°28W 317 G7
Lützow Holmbukta Antarctica 69°10S 37°30E 151 C4
Lutzputs S. Africa 28°3S 20°40E 270 C3
Luuk Phil. 5°58N 121°18E 233 J3
Luuq Somalia 3°48N 42°34E 267 D5
Luverne Ala., U.S.A. 31°43N 86°16W 316 D3
Luverne Minn., U.S.A. 43°39N 96°13W 308 D5
Luvo Angola 5°51S 14°5E 265 D2
Luvua Dem. Rep. of the Congo 8°48S 25°17E 265 D5
Luvua → Dem. Rep. of the Congo 6°50S 27°30E 268 D2
Luvuvhu → S. Africa 22°25S 31°18E 271 B5
Luwan China 31°12N 121°27E 138 B1
Luwegu → Tanzania 8°31S 37°23E 269 D4
Luwero Uganda 0°50N 32°28E 268 B3
Luwuk Indonesia 0°56S 122°47E 231 E6
Luxembourg Lux. 49°37N 6°9E 170 E6
Luxembourg ☐ Belgium 49°58N 5°30E 170 E5
Luxembourg ■ Europe 49°45N 6°0E 170 E5
Luxembourg ✕ (LUX) Lux. 49°37N 6°10E 170 E6
Luxembourg, Palais du Paris, France 134 c4
Luxemburg U.S.A. 42°36N 91°5W 310 B5
Luxeuil-les-Bains France 47°49N 6°24E 173 E13
Luxi Hunan, China 28°20N 110°7E 229 C8
Luxi Yunnan, China 24°40N 103°55E 228 E4
Luxi Yunnan, China 24°27N 98°36E 228 E2
Luxian China 29°9N 105°24E 228 C5
Luxor = El Uqsur Egypt 25°41N 32°38E 256 B3
Luy-de-Béarn → France 43°39N 0°48W 174 E3
Luy-de-France → France 43°39N 0°48W 174 E3
Luyeh Hualien, Taiwan 23°35N 121°32E 225 C3
Luyeh T'aitung, Taiwan 22°55N 121°8E 225 D3
Luyi China 33°50N 115°35E 226 H8
Luykau = Loikaw Burma 19°40N 97°17E 241 F6
Luz Azores 39°1N 28°0W 153 d1
Luz-St-Sauveur France 42°53N 0°0 174 F4
Luza Russia 60°39N 47°10E 186 B8
Luzern Switz. 47°3N 8°18E 179 H3
Luzern ☐ Switz. 47°2N 7°55E 179 H3
Luzhai China 24°29N 109°42E 228 E7
Luzhany Ukraine 48°22N 25°47E 183 B10
Luzhi China 26°21N 105°16E 228 D5
Luzhniki Sports Centre Russia 55°43N 37°31E 129 B2
Luzhou China 28°52N 105°20E 228 C5
Luziânia Brazil 16°20S 48°0W 333 E2
Luzilândia Brazil 3°28S 42°22W 332 B3
Lužnice → Czech Rep. 49°14N 14°23E 180 B7
Luzon Phil. 16°0N 121°0E 232 C3
Luzon Strait Asia 21°0N 120°40E 229 G13
Luzy France 46°47N 3°58E 173 F10
Luzzi Italy 39°27N 16°17E 201 C9
Lviv Ukraine 49°50N 24°0E 177 D13
Lviv ☐ Ukraine 49°30N 23°45E 177 D12
Lvov = Lviv Ukraine 49°50N 24°0E 177 D13
Lwówek Poland 52°28N 16°10E 185 F3
Lwówek Śląski Poland 51°7N 15°38E 185 G2
Lyakhavichy Belarus 53°2N 26°32E 187 F14
Lyakhovskiye, Ostrova Russia 73°40N 141°0E 215 B15
Lyaki = Läki Azerbaijan 40°34N 47°22E 191 K8
Lyal I. Canada 44°57N 81°24W 312 B3
Lyall Mt. N.Z. 45°16S 167°32E 285 F2
Lyallpur = Faisalabad Pakistan 31°30N 73°5E 242 D5
Lyaskovets Bulgaria 43°6N 25°44E 203 C9
Lyasnaya → Belarus 52°9N 23°31E 185 F10
Lybster U.K. 58°18N 3°15W 167 C5
Lycabettus Athens, Greece 112 b3
Lycaonia Turkey 38°0N 33°0E 212 D5
Lychen Germany 53°12N 13°18E 178 B9
Lychkova Russia 57°55N 32°24E 188 D7
Lycia Turkey 36°30N 29°30E 205 E11
Lyck = Ełk Poland 53°50N 22°21E 184 E9
Lycksele Sweden 64°38N 18°40E 160 D18
Lyckebyån → Sweden 56°12N 15°39E 163 H9
Lycosura Greece 37°20N 22°3E 204 D4
Lydda = Lod Israel 31°57N 34°54E 251 G5
Lyddan I. Antarctica 74°0S 21°0W 151 D2
Lydenburg S. Africa 25°10S 30°29E 271 C5
Lydia Turkey 38°48N 28°19E 205 C10
Lydynia → Poland 52°43N 20°26E 185 F7
Lyell N.Z. 41°48S 172°4E 285 B7
Lyell I. Canada 52°40N 131°35W 296 C2
Lyepyel Belarus 54°50N 28°40E 188 E5
Lyford Cay Bahamas 25°2N 77°33W 153 b
Lygnern Sweden 57°30N 12°15E 163 G6
Lykavittos Hill = Lycabettus Athens, Greece 112 b3
Lykens U.S.A. 40°34N 76°42W 313 F8
Lyman Ukraine 45°41N 29°45E 183 E14
Lyman Wyo., U.S.A. 41°20N 110°18W 304 F8
Lymanske Ukraine 46°40N 29°58E 183 D14
Lyme B. U.K. 50°42N 2°53W 169 G4
Lyme Regis U.K. 50°43N 2°57W 169 G5
Lymington U.K. 50°45N 1°32W 169 G6
Lyna → Poland 54°37N 21°14E 184 D8
Lynchburg Ohio, U.S.A. 39°15N 83°48W 311 E13
Lynchburg S.C., U.S.A. 34°3N 80°4W 316 A9
Lynchburg Va., U.S.A. 37°25N 79°9W 309 G14
Lynd → Australia 16°28S 143°18E 280 B3
Lynd Ra. Australia 25°30S 149°20E 281 D4
Lynden Ont., Canada 43°14N 80°9W 312 C4
Lynden Wash., U.S.A. 48°57N 122°27W 306 B4
Lyndhurst S. Austral., Australia 30°15S 138°18E 281 E2
Lyndhurst N.J., U.S.A. 40°49N 74°7W 132 B1
Lyndon → Australia 23°29S 114°6E 279 D1
Lyndonville N.Y., U.S.A. 43°20N 78°23W 312 C6
Lyndonville Vt., U.S.A. 44°31N 72°1W 313 B12
Lyngdal Buskerud, Norway 59°54N 9°32E 164 E6
Lyngdal Vest-Agder, Norway 58°8N 7°7E 164 F4
Lyngen Norway 69°45N 20°30E 160 B19
Lyngør Norway 58°38N 9°8E 164 F6
Lynher Reef Australia 15°27S 121°55E 278 C3
Lynn Ind., U.S.A. 40°3N 84°56W 311 D12
Lynn Mass., U.S.A. 42°28N 70°57W 313 D14
Lynn Canal U.S.A. 58°50N 135°15W 303 G14
Lynn Haven U.S.A. 30°15N 85°39W 316 E4
Lynn Lake Canada 56°51N 101°3W 297 B8
Lynn Woods Res. U.S.A. 42°29N 71°0W 116 A2
Lynne U.S.A. 29°12N 81°55W 317 F8
Lynnville U.S.A. 38°12N 87°18W 311 F9
Lynnwood U.S.A. 47°49N 122°18W 306 C4
Lynton U.K. 51°13N 3°50W 169 F4
Lyntupy Belarus 55°4N 26°23E 188 E4
Lynx L. Canada 62°25N 106°15W 297 A7
Lyon France 45°46N 4°50E 175 C8
Lyon, Gare de Paris, France 134 c5
Lyon St-Exupery ✕ (LYS) France 45°44N 5°2E 175 C9
Lyonnais France 45°45N 4°15E 175 C8
Lyons = Lyon France 45°46N 4°50E 175 C8
Lyons Ga., U.S.A. 32°12N 82°19W 316 C7
Lyons Ill., U.S.A. 41°48N 87°49W 119 C2
Lyons Kans., U.S.A. 38°21N 98°12W 308 F4
Lyons N.Y., U.S.A. 43°5N 77°0W 312 C8
Lyons → Australia 25°2S 115°9E 279 E2
Lyons Falls U.S.A. 43°37N 75°22W 313 C9
Lyozna Belarus 55°0N 30°50E 188 E6
Lyra Reef Papua N. G. 1°50S 153°35E 286 A7
Lys = Leie → Belgium 51°2N 3°45E 170 C3
Lysá nad Labem Czech Rep. 50°11N 14°51E 180 A7
Lysaker Norway 59°54N 10°38E 133 A2
Lysakerselva → Norway 59°54N 10°38E 133 A2
Lysebotn Norway 59°3N 6°37E 164 E3
Lysefjorden Norway 59°0N 6°23E 164 E3
Lysekil Sweden 58°17N 11°26E 163 F5
Lysi Cyprus 35°6N 33°41E 207 E9
Lyskovo Russia 56°0N 45°3E 190 B7
Lyss Switz. 47°4N 7°19E 179 H3
Lysolaje Czech Rep. 50°8N 14°22E 135 B2
Lystrup Denmark 56°14N 10°14E 163 H4
Lysva Russia 58°7N 57°49E 186 C10
Lysvik Sweden 60°1N 13°9E 162 D7
Lysychansk Ukraine 48°55N 38°30E 189 H10
Lytham St. Anne's U.K. 53°45N 3°0W 168 D4
Lyttelton N.Z. 43°35S 172°44E 285 D7
Lytton Canada 50°13N 121°31W 296 C4
Lyuban Russia 59°16N 31°18E 188 C6
Lyubertsy Russia 55°40N 37°51E 188 E9
Lyubim Russia 58°20N 40°39E 188 C11
Lyubimets Bulgaria 41°50N 26°5E 203 E10
Lyublino Russia 55°41N 37°44E 129 B3
Lyuboml Ukraine 51°11N 24°4E 185 G11
Lyubotyn Ukraine 50°0N 36°0E 189 H8
Lyubytino Russia 58°50N 33°16E 188 C7
Lyudinovo Russia 53°52N 34°28E 188 F8

M

M.R. Štefánik, Bratislava ✕ (BTS) Slovak Rep. 48°11N 17°9E 181 C10
Ma → Vietnam 19°47N 105°56E 228 H5
Ma, O. el → Algeria 27°45N 7°52W 260 C3
Ma Nam Wat China 22°21N 114°16E 122 A2
Ma On Shan China 22°24N 114°10E 219 a
Ma On Shan Country Park ⌂ China 22°22N 114°14E 122 A2
Ma'adaba Jordan 31°43N 35°47E 251 H6
Maafushi Maldives 3°59N 73°27E 272 d
Maakhir Somalia 10°30N 47°30E 267 B6
Ma'ale Adumim West Bank 31°49N 35°17E 123 B2
Ma'ale Ha Khamisha Israel 31°49N 35°7E 123 B1
Ma'ale Mikhmas West Bank 31°52N 35°18E 123 A2
Ma'alot-Tarshiha Israel 33°1N 35°17E 250 E6
Maamba Zambia 17°17S 26°28E 270 A4
Ma'ān Jordan 30°12N 35°44E 251 H6
Ma'ān ☐ Jordan 30°0N 36°0E 251 J7
Maana'oba Solomon Is. 8°17S 160°50E 287 M11
Maanselkä Finland 63°52N 28°32E 160 C23
Ma'anshan China 31°44N 118°29E 229 B12
Maantiekylä Finland 60°20N 25°0E 121 A3
Maarianhamina = Mariehamn Finland 60°5N 19°55E 161 F18
Maarifa Iraq 33°15N 44°21E 113 B2
Maarmorilik Greenland 71°3N 51°0W 154 C5
Ma'arrat an Nu'mān Syria 35°43N 36°43E 250 C7
Maas → Neths. 51°45N 4°32E 170 C4
Maaseik Belgium 51°6N 5°45E 170 C5
Maasim Phil. 5°52N 125°0E 233 J5
Maasin Phil. 10°8N 124°50E 233 F5
Maastricht Neths. 50°50N 5°40E 170 D5
Maasupa Solomon Is. 9°16S 161°17E 287 M11
Maave Mozam. 21°4S 34°47E 271 B5
Mababe Depression Botswana 18°50S 24°15E 270 A3
Mabaia Angola 7°12S 14°2E 265 D2
Mabalane Mozam. 23°37S 32°31E 271 B5
Mabanga Dem. Rep. of the Congo 1°30N 19°6E 264 B3
Ma'bar Yemen 14°48N 44°17E 248 D4
Mabaruma Guyana 8°10N 59°50W 329 B6
Mabato Pt. Phil. 14°29N 121°3E 127 C2
Mabein Burma 23°29N 96°37E 241 D6
Mabel, L. U.S.A. 28°25N 81°32W 133 B1
Mabel L. Canada 50°35N 118°43W 296 C5
Mabenga Dem. Rep. of the Congo 3°39S 18°40E 264 C3
Mabenge Dem. Rep. of the Congo 4°15N 24°12E 264 B4
Maberly Canada 44°50N 76°32W 313 B8
Mabesi, L. S. Leone 7°10N 11°42W 262 D2
Mabian China 28°47N 103°37E 228 C4
Mabil Ethiopia 10°26N 36°52E 257 E4
Mabinay Phil. 9°48N 122°54E 233 G4
Mabirou Congo 1°3S 15°42E 264 C3
Mablethorpe U.K. 53°20N 0°15E 168 D8
Mableton U.S.A. 33°49N 84°35W 316 B5
Mably France 46°5N 4°4E 173 F11
Maboma Dem. Rep. of the Congo 2°30N 28°10E 268 B2
Mabonto S. Leone 8°53N 11°50W 262 D2
Maboukou Congo 3°39S 12°4E 264 C2
Mabouya I. Grenada 12°29N 61°30W 323 q
Mabroûk Mali 19°29N 1°15W 261 E4
Mabrous Niger 21°14N 13°35E 259 D2
Mabuasehube ⌂ Botswana 25°5S 21°10E 270 C3
Mabudis Phil. 20°55N 121°55E 232 A3
Mabuiag Australia 9°57S 142°11E 280 a
Mac Bac Vietnam 9°46N 106°7E 237 H6
Macachin Argentina 37°10S 63°43W 334 D3
Macaco, Morro do Brazil 22°56S 43°6W 135 B2
Macaé Brazil 22°20S 41°43W 333 F3
Macael Spain 37°20N 2°18W 197 H2
Macaíba Brazil 5°51S 35°21W 332 C4
Macajalar B. Phil. 8°55N 124°39E 233 G5
Macajuba Brazil 12°9S 40°22W 333 D3
McAlester U.S.A. 34°56N 95°46W 314 D7
McAllen U.S.A. 26°12N 98°14W 314 H5
McAlpin U.S.A. 30°8N 82°57W 316 E7
MacAlpine L. Canada 66°32N 102°45W 294 D11
Macamic Canada 48°45N 79°0W 298 C4
Macanao, B. de Venezuela 11°2N 64°23W 329 a
Macanao, Pen. de Venezuela 11°0N 64°18W 329 a
Macao = Macau China 22°12N 113°33E 229 F9
Macão Portugal 39°35N 7°59W 195 F3
Macapá Brazil 0°5N 51°4W 329 C7
Macaque, Morne Dominica 15°20N 61°20W 323 k
Macará Ecuador 4°23S 79°57W 328 D2
Macarani Brazil 15°33S 40°24W 333 E3
Macarena, Serranía de la Colombia 2°45N 73°55W 328 C3
Macareo, Caño → Venezuela 9°47N 61°36W 329 B5
Macarthur Australia 38°5S 142°0E 282 E5
McArthur → Australia 15°54S 136°40E 280 B2
McArthur, Port Australia 16°4S 136°23E 280 B2
Macas Ecuador 2°19S 78°7W 328 D2
Macate Peru 8°48S 78°7W 330 B2
Macau Brazil 5°15S 36°40W 332 C4
Macau China 22°12N 113°33E 229 F9
Macaúbas Brazil 13°2S 42°42W 333 D3
Macauley I. Pac. Oc. 30°12S 178°28W 277 G15
Macaya → Colombia 0°59N 72°20W 328 C3
McBride Canada 53°20N 120°19W 296 C4
McCall U.S.A. 44°55N 116°6W 304 D5
McCamey U.S.A. 31°8N 102°14W 314 F3
McCammon U.S.A. 42°39N 112°12W 304 E7
McCarran Int., Las Vegas ✕ (LAS) U.S.A. 36°5N 115°9W 124 B2
McCarthy U.S.A. 61°26N 142°56W 303 F12
McCauley I. Canada 53°40N 130°15W 296 C2
McCleary U.S.A. 47°3N 123°16W 306 C3
McClenny U.S.A. 30°17N 82°7W 316 E7
Macclesfield U.K. 53°15N 2°8W 168 D5
M'Clintock Chan. Canada 72°0N 102°0W 294 C11
McClintock Ra. Australia 18°44S 127°38E 278 C4
McCloud U.S.A. 41°15N 122°8W 304 F2
McCluer I. Australia 11°5S 133°0E 278 B5
McClure U.S.A. 40°42N 77°19W 312 F7
McClure, L. U.S.A. 37°35N 120°16W 306 H6
M'Clure Str. Canada 75°0N 119°0W 295 C8
McClusky U.S.A. 47°29N 100°27W 308 B3
McComb U.S.A. 31°15N 90°27W 315 F9
McCook Ill., U.S.A. 41°47N 87°49W 119 C2
McCook Nebr., U.S.A. 40°12N 100°38W 308 E3
McCormick U.S.A. 33°55N 82°17W 316 B7
McCreary Canada 50°47N 99°29W 297 C9
McCullough Mt. U.S.A. 35°35N 115°13W 307 K11
McCusker → Canada 55°32N 108°39W 297 B7
McDavid U.S.A. 30°52N 87°19W 317 E2
McDermitt U.S.A. 41°59N 117°43W 304 F5
McDonald U.S.A. 40°22N 80°14W 312 F4
Macdonald, L. Australia 23°30S 129°0E 278 D4
Macdonald, Mt. Vanuatu 17°36S 168°23E 287 G6
McDonald Is. Ind. Oc. 53°0S 73°0E 273 K6
MacDonnell Ranges Australia 23°40S 133°0E 278 D5
McDonough U.S.A. 33°27N 84°9W 316 B5
McDougalls Well Australia 31°8S 141°15E 282 A4
MacDowell L. Canada 52°15N 92°45W 298 B1
Macduff U.K. 57°40N 2°31W 167 D6
Maceda Spain 42°16N 7°39W 194 C3
Macedonia U.S.A. 41°19N 81°31W 312 E3
Macedonia ☐ Greece 41°53N 21°40E 202 E5
Macedonia ■ Europe 41°53N 21°40E 202 E5
Maceió Brazil 9°40S 35°41W 332 C4
Maceira Portugal 39°41N 8°55W 194 F2
Macenta Guinea 8°35N 9°32W 262 D3
Macerata Italy 43°18N 13°27E 199 E10
McFarland U.S.A. 35°41N 119°14W 307 K7
McFarlane → Canada 59°12N 107°58W 297 B7
Macfarlane, L. Australia 32°0S 136°40E 282 B2
McGehee U.S.A. 33°38N 91°24W 314 E9
McGill U.S.A. 39°23N 114°47W 304 G6
McGill Univ. Montréal, Canada 130 b1
Macgillycuddy's Reeks Ireland 51°58N 9°45W 166 E2
McGrath U.S.A. 62°58N 155°36W 303 E9
McGraw U.S.A. 42°36N 76°8W 313 D8
McGregor U.S.A. 43°1N 91°11W 310 A5
McGregor Ra. Australia 27°0S 142°45E 281 D3
McGuire, Mt. Australia 20°18S 148°23E 280 b
Mach Pakistan 29°50N 67°20E 242 E2
Māch Kowr Iran 25°48N 61°28E 247 E9
Machacalis Brazil 17°5S 40°45W 333 E3
Machado = Jiparaná → Brazil 8°3S 62°52W 331 B5
Machagai Argentina 26°56S 60°2W 334 B3
Machakos Kenya 1°30S 37°15E 268 C4
Machala Ecuador 3°20S 79°57W 328 D2
Machalilla △ Ecuador 1°24S 80°42W 328 D1
Machanbaw Burma 27°16N 97°36E 241 B6
Machanga Mozam. 20°59S 35°0E 271 B6
Machattie, L. Australia 24°50S 139°48E 280 C2
Machault France 49°21N 4°29E 173 C11
Machava Mozam. 25°54S 32°28E 271 C5
Machecoul France 47°0N 1°49W 172 F5
Macheke Zimbabwe 18°5S 31°51E 271 A5
Machelen Belgium 50°55N 4°26E 116 A2
Macheng China 31°12N 115°2E 229 B10
McHenry U.S.A. 42°21N 88°16W 311 B8
Macherado Greece 37°46N 20°49E 207 D2
Macherla India 16°29N 79°26E 244 F4
Machero Spain 39°21N 4°20W 195 F6
Machgaon India 20°5N 86°17E 244 D8
Machhu → India 23°6N 70°46E 242 H4
Machiara △ Pakistan 34°40N 73°30E 242 B5
Machias Maine, U.S.A. 44°43N 67°28W 309 C20
Machias N.Y., U.S.A. 42°25N 78°29W 312 D6
Machichi → Canada 57°3N 92°6W 297 B10
Machico Madeira 32°43N 16°44W 153 c
Machida Japan 35°32N 139°26E 140 B1
Machilipatnam India 16°12N 81°8E 245 F5
Machiques Venezuela 10°4N 72°34W 328 A3
Machu Picchu Peru 13°8S 72°30W 330 C3
Machynlleth U.K. 52°35N 3°50W 169 E4
Macia Mozam. 25°2S 33°8E 271 C5
Macias Nguema Biyoga = Bioko Eq. Guin. 3°30N 8°40E 263 E6
Maciejowice Poland 51°36N 21°26E 185 G8
McIlwraith Ra. Australia 13°50S 143°20E 280 A3
Măcin Romania 45°16N 28°8E 183 E13
Macina Mali 14°50N 5°0W 262 C4
McInnes L. Canada 52°13N 93°45W 297 C10
McIntosh U.S.A. 45°55N 101°21W 308 C3
McIntosh L. Canada 55°45N 105°0W 297 B8
Macintosh Ra. Australia 27°39S 125°32E 279 E4
Macintyre → Australia 28°37S 150°47E 281 D5
Maciołki Poland 52°19N 21°9E 129 B3
Macizo Galaico Spain 42°30N 7°30W 194 C3
Maçka Turkey 40°49N 39°36E 213 B8
Mackay Queens., Australia 21°8S 149°11E 280 K7
Mackay Idaho, U.S.A. 43°55N 113°37W 304 E7
MacKay → Canada 57°10N 111°38W 296 B6
Mackay, L. Australia 22°30S 129°0E 278 D4
McKay Ra. Australia 23°0S 122°30E 278 D3
McKean Kiribati 3°36S 174°8W 277 A16
McKeesport U.S.A. 40°20N 79°51W 312 F5
McKellar Canada 45°30N 79°55W 312 A5
McKenna U.S.A. 46°56N 122°33W 306 D4
Mackenzie = Linden Guyana 6°0N 58°10W 329 B6
Mackenzie Canada 55°20N 123°5W 296 B4
McKenzie U.S.A. 36°8N 88°31W 315 C10
Mackenzie → Queens., Australia 23°38S 149°46E 280 C4
Mackenzie → N.W.T., Canada 69°10N 134°20W 294 D5
McKenzie → U.S.A. 44°7N 123°6W 304 D2
Mackenzie Bay Canada 69°0N 137°30W 292 C6
Mackenzie King I. Canada 77°45N 111°0W 295 B9
Mackenzie Mts. Canada 64°0N 130°0W 292 C6
Mackenzie Plains N.Z. 44°10S 170°25E 285 E5
McKerrow, L. N.Z. 44°25S 168°5E 285 E3
Mackheim = Maków Mazowiecki Poland 52°52N 21°6E 185 F8
Mackinac, Straits of U.S.A. 45°50N 84°40W 309 C11
Mackinaw U.S.A. 40°32N 89°21W 310 D7
Mackinaw → U.S.A. 40°33N 89°44W 310 D7
Mackinaw City U.S.A. 45°47N 84°44W 309 C11
McKinlay Australia 21°16S 141°18E 280 C3
McKinlay → Australia 20°50S 141°28E 280 C3
McKinley, Mt. U.S.A. 63°4N 151°0W 303 E10
McKinley Park Alaska, U.S.A. 63°44N 148°55W 303 E10
McKinley Park Ill., U.S.A. 41°49N 87°40W 119 C2
McKinley Sea Arctic 82°0N 0°0 154 A11
McKinney U.S.A. 33°12N 96°37W 314 E6
Mackinnon Road Kenya 3°40S 39°1E 268 C4
McKittrick Calif., U.S.A. 35°18N 119°37W 307 K7
McKittrick Mo., U.S.A. 38°44N 91°27W 310 F5
Macklin Canada 52°20N 109°56W 297 C7
Macksville Australia 30°40S 152°56E 283 A10
McLaren Vale Australia 35°13S 138°31E 282 C3
McLaughlin U.S.A. 45°49N 100°49W 308 C3
Maclean Australia 29°26S 153°16E 281 D5
McLean Ill., U.S.A. 40°19N 89°10W 310 D7
McLean Tex., U.S.A. 35°14N 100°36W 314 D4
McLean Va., U.S.A. 38°56N 77°10W 143 B1
McLeansboro U.S.A. 38°6N 88°32W 311 F8
Maclear S. Africa 31°2S 28°23E 271 D4
Maclear, C. Malawi 13°58S 34°49E 269 E3
Macleay → Australia 30°56S 153°0E 283 A10
McLennan Canada 55°42N 116°50W 296 B5
MacLeod = Fort Macleod Canada 49°45N 113°30W 296 D6
McLeod → Canada 54°9N 115°44W 296 C5
McLeod, L. Australia 24°9S 113°47E 279 D1
MacLeod B. Canada 62°53N 110°0W 297 A7
McLeod Lake Canada 54°58N 123°0W 296 C4
McLoughlin, Mt. U.S.A. 42°27N 122°19W 304 E2
MacMahon = Aïn Touta Algeria 35°26N 5°54E 261 A6
McMechen U.S.A. 39°57N 80°44W 312 G4
McMinnville Oreg., U.S.A. 45°13N 123°12W 304 D2
McMinnville Tenn., U.S.A. 35°41N 85°46W 315 D12
McMurdo Antarctica 77°51S 166°37E 151 D11
McMurdo Sd. Antarctica 77°0S 170°0E 151 D11
McMurray = Fort McMurray Canada 56°44N 111°7W 296 B6
McMurray U.S.A. 48°19N 122°14W 306 B4
Maco Phil. 7°20N 125°50E 233 H5
Maçobere Mozam. 21°13S 32°47E 269 G3
Macocolo Angola 6°47S 16°8E 265 D3
Macodoene Mozam. 23°32S 35°5E 271 B6
Macolo Angola 7°5S 16°42E 265 D3
Macomb U.S.A. 40°27N 90°40W 310 D6
Macomer Italy 40°16N 8°47E 200 B1
Mâcon Saône-et-Loire, France 46°19N 4°50E 173 F11
Macon Ga., U.S.A. 32°51N 83°38W 316 C6
Macon Ill., U.S.A. 39°43N 89°0W 310 E8
Macon Miss., U.S.A. 33°7N 88°34W 315 E10
Macon Mo., U.S.A. 39°44N 92°28W 310 E4
Macondo Angola 12°37S 23°46E 265 E4
Macopocho → Chile 33°24S 70°40W 137 B1
Macossa Mozam. 17°55S 33°56E 269 F3
Macou → Dominica 15°25N 61°27W 323 k
Macou, Pte. Guadeloupe 16°21N 61°31W 322 e
Macouba Martinique 14°52N 61°9W 322 j
Macoun L. Canada 56°32N 103°40W 297 B8
Macoupin Cr. → U.S.A. 39°11N 90°38W 310 E6
Macovane Mozam. 21°30S 35°2E 271 B6
MacPherson = Kapuskasing Canada 49°25N 82°30W 298 C3
McPherson U.S.A. 38°22N 97°40W 308 F5
McPherson Pk. U.S.A. 34°53N 119°53W 307 L7
McPherson Ra. Australia 28°15S 153°15E 281 D5
Macquarie → Australia 30°7S 147°24E 283 A7
Macquarie Harbour Australia 42°15S 145°23E 281 G4
Macquarie I. Pac. Oc. 54°36S 158°55E 288 N7
Macquarie Ridge S. Ocean 57°0S 159°0E 151 B10
Macqueripe B. Trin. & Tob. 10°44N 61°37W 323 t
McRae U.S.A. 32°4N 82°54W 316 C7
MacRitchie Res. Singapore 1°20N 103°49E 138 A2
MacRobertson Land Antarctica 71°0S 64°0E 151 D6
Macroom Ireland 51°54N 8°57W 166 E3
MacTier Canada 45°8N 79°47W 312 A5
Macubela Mozam. 16°53S 37°49E 269 F4
Macugnaga Italy 45°58N 7°58E 198 C4
Macuira △ Colombia 12°9N 71°21W 328 A3
Macuje Colombia 0°24N 73°10W 328 C3
Macul Chile 33°30S 70°35W 137 C2
Macumba → Australia 27°52S 137°12E 281 D2
Macuro Venezuela 10°42N 61°55W 329 F9
Macusani Peru 14°4S 70°29W 330 C3
Macuse Mozam. 17°45S 37°10E 269 F4
Macuspana Mexico 17°46N 92°36W 319 D6
Macusse Angola 17°48S 20°23E 265 F4
Macy's on State Street U.S.A. 119 c2
Mada → Nigeria 7°59N 7°55E 263 D6
Ma'dabā ☐ Jordan 31°43N 35°47E 251 G6
Madadeni S. Africa 27°43S 30°3E 271 C5
Madadi Chad 18°28N 20°45E 255 E4
Madagali Nigeria 10°56N 13°33E 263 C7
Madagascar ■ Africa 20°0S 47°0E 272 C8
Madagoi → Somalia 0°49N 42°58E 267 D5
Madā'in Sālih Si. Arabia 26°46N 37°57E 246 E3
Madakasira India 13°56N 77°16E 245 H3
Madalena Azores 38°32N 28°32W 153 d1
Madama Niger 22°0N 13°40E 259 D2
Madame, I. Canada 45°30N 60°58W 299 C7
Madame Tussaud's London, U.K. 125 a3
Madan Bulgaria 41°30N 24°57E 203 E8
Madanapalle India 13°33N 78°28E 245 H4
Madang Papua N. G. 5°12S 145°49E 286 C3
Madang ☐ Papua N. G. 5°0S 145°30E 286 C3
Madaoua Niger 14°5N 6°27E 263 C6
Madara Bulgaria 43°17N 27°8E 203 C11
Madara Nigeria 11°45N 10°35E 263 C7
Madaripur Bangla. 23°19N 90°15E 241 D3
Madau I. Papua N. G. 8°58S 152°28E 286 E7
Madauk Burma 17°56N 96°52E 241 G6
Madawaska Canada 45°30N 78°0W 312 A7
Madawaska → Canada 45°27N 76°21W 312 A8
Madaxmaroodi Somalia 9°39N 44°36E 267 D5
Madaya Burma 22°12N 96°10E 241 D6
Madbar South Sudan 6°17N 30°45E 257 F3
Maddalena Italy 41°16N 9°23E 200 A2
Maddalena, Ex Monastero della Venice, Italy 142 c2
Maddaloni Italy 41°2N 14°23E 201 A7
Maddela Phil. 16°21N 121°41E 232 C3
Maddur India 12°36N 77°4E 245 H3
Madeira Atl. Oc. 32°50N 17°0W 153 c
Madeira Ohio, U.S.A. 39°11N 84°21W 311 E12
Madeira → Brazil 3°22S 58°45W 329 D6
Madeleine, Îs. de la Canada 47°30N 61°40W 299 C7
Maden Turkey 38°23N 39°40E 213 C8
Madera Chihuahua, Mexico 29°12N 108°7W 318 B3
Madera Calif., U.S.A. 36°57N 120°3W 306 J6
Madera Pa., U.S.A. 40°49N 78°26W 312 F6
Madgaon India 15°12N 73°58E 245 G1
Madha India 18°0N 75°30E 244 F2
Madhavpur India 21°15N 69°58E 242 J3
Madhira India 16°55N 80°22E 244 F5
Madhubani India 26°21N 86°7E 243 F12
Madhudaha India 22°30N 88°24E 124 B2
Madhugiri India 13°40N 77°12E 245 H3
Madhumati → Bangla. 22°53N 89°52E 241 D2
Madhupur Bangla. 24°37N 90°2E 241 C3
Madhupur India 24°16N 86°39E 243 G12
Madhupur △ Bangla. 24°43N 90°4E 241 C3
Madhya Pradesh ☐ India 22°50N 78°0E 242 J8
Madhyamgram India 22°41N 88°26E 124 A2
Madidi → Bolivia 12°32S 66°52W 330 C4
Madikeri India 12°30N 75°45E 245 H2
Madikwe ⌂ S. Africa 27°38S 32°15E 271 C5
Madill U.S.A. 34°6N 96°46W 314 D6
Madimba Angola 6°36S 14°23E 265 D2
Madimba Dem. Rep. of the Congo 4°58S 15°5E 265 C3
Madīn México, Mexico 19°32N 99°16W 128 A1
Ma'din Syria 35°45N 39°36E 213 E8
Madín, L. Mexico 19°31N 99°16W 128 A1
Madina Mali 13°25N 8°50W 262 C3
Madīnah Al Mansūr Iraq 33°18N 44°20E 113 B2
Madinani Ivory C. 9°37N 6°57W 262 D3
Madīnat al Malik Khālid al Askarīyah Si. Arabia 27°54N 45°31E 246 E5
Madīnat ash Sha'b Yemen 12°50N 45°0E 248 D4
Madīnat ath Thawrah Syria 35°50N 38°32E 213 E8
Mâdinet Nasr Egypt 30°4N 31°18E 117 A2
Madingo Congo 4°5S 11°24E 264 C2
Madingou Congo 4°10S 13°33E 264 C2
Madîq Gûbâl Egypt 27°47N 33°55E 251 L4
Madîq Tirân Egypt 27°55N 34°30E 251 L5
Madirovalo Madag. 16°26S 46°32E 272 B2
Madison Calif., U.S.A. 38°41N 121°59W 306 G5
Madison Fla., U.S.A. 30°28N 83°25W 316 E6
Madison Ga., U.S.A. 33°36N 83°28W 316 B6
Madison Ind., U.S.A. 38°44N 85°23W 311 F11
Madison Mo., U.S.A. 39°28N 92°13W 310 E4
Madison Nebr., U.S.A. 41°50N 97°27W 308 E5
Madison Ohio, U.S.A. 41°46N 81°3W 312 E3
Madison S. Dak., U.S.A. 44°0N 97°7W 308 C5
Madison Wis., U.S.A. 43°4N 89°24W 310 A7
Madison → U.S.A. 45°56N 111°31W 304 D8
Madison Avenue New York, U.S.A. 132 c2
Madison Heights U.S.A. 37°25N 79°8W 309 G14
Madison Square New York, U.S.A. 132 d2
Madison Square Garden New York, U.S.A. 132 c2
Madisonville Ky., U.S.A. 37°20N 87°30W 308 G10
Madisonville Tex., U.S.A. 30°57N 95°55W 314 F7
Madista Botswana 21°15S 25°6E 270 B4
Madiun Indonesia 7°38S 111°32E 235 D4
Madjingo Gabon 1°20N 14°4E 264 B2
Mado Gashi Kenya 0°44N 39°10E 268 B4
Madoc Canada 44°30N 77°28W 312 B7
Madoi China 34°46N 98°18E 218 E8
Madon → France 48°36N 6°6E 173 D13
Madona Latvia 56°53N 26°5E 188 D4
Madonie Italy 37°50N 13°50E 200 E6
Madonna dell' Orto Venice, Italy 142 a2
Madonna di Campiglio Italy 46°14N 10°49E 198 B7
Madra Dağı Turkey 39°23N 27°12E 205 B9
Madrakah, Ra's al Oman 19°0N 57°50E 249 C7
Madras = Chennai India 13°8N 80°19E 245 H5
Madras = Tamil Nadu ☐ India 11°0N 77°0E 245 J3
Madras U.S.A. 44°38N 121°8W 304 D3
Madre, L. U.S.A. 25°15N 97°30W 314 J6
Madre, Sierra Phil. 17°0N 122°0E 232 C4
Madre de Dios ☐ Peru 12°0S 70°15W 330 C3
Madre de Dios → Bolivia 10°59S 66°8W 330 C4
Madre de Dios, I. Chile 50°20S 75°10W 336 D1
Madre del Sur, Sierra Mexico 17°30N 100°0W 319 D5
Madre Occidental, Sierra Mexico 27°0N 107°0W 318 B3
Madre Oriental, Sierra Mexico 25°0N 100°0W 318 C5
Madri India 24°16N 73°32E 242 G5
Madrid Spain 40°24N 3°42W 127 B1
Madrid Ala., U.S.A. 31°2N 85°24W 316 D4
Madrid Iowa, U.S.A. 41°53N 93°49W 310 C3
Madrid N.Y., U.S.A. 44°45N 75°8W 313 B9
Madrid ☐ Spain 40°30N 3°45W 194 E7
Madrid Barajas ✕ (MAD) Spain 40°26N 3°34W 127 B2
Madridejos Spain 39°28N 3°33W 195 F7
Madrigal de las Altas Torres Spain 41°5N 5°0W 194 D6
Madrona Spain 41°27N 2°1E 114 A1
Madrona, Sierra Spain 38°27N 4°16W 195 G6
Madroñera Spain 39°26N 5°42W 195 F5
Madrusah Libya 24°48N 14°58E 258 D2
Madu Sudan 14°37N 26°4E 257 E2
Madula Dem. Rep. of the Congo 0°27N 25°22E 264 B5
Maduo Dem. Rep. of the Congo 1°24S 20°44E 264 C4
Madupi Burma 21°36N 93°27E 241 E4
Madura W. Austral., Australia 31°55S 127°0E 279 F4
Madura Indonesia 7°30S 114°0E 231 G15
Madura, Selat Indonesia 7°30S 113°20E 235 D4
Madura Oya △ Sri Lanka 7°20N 81°10E 245 L5
Madurai India 9°55N 78°10E 245 K4
Madurantakam India 12°30N 79°50E 245 H4
Madzhalis Russia 42°9N 47°47E 191 J8
Mae Chan Thailand 20°9N 99°52E 236 B2
Mae Charim △ Thailand 18°17N 100°59E 236 C3
Mae Hong Son Thailand 19°16N 97°56E 236 C2
Mae Khlong → Thailand 13°24N 100°0E 236 F3
Mae Moei △ Thailand 17°26N 98°7E 236 D2
Mae Phang △ Thailand 19°7N 99°13E 236 C2
Mae Phrik Thailand 17°27N 99°7E 236 D2
Mae Ping △ Thailand 17°37N 98°51E 236 D2
Mae Ramat Thailand 16°58N 98°31E 236 D2
Mae Rim Thailand 18°54N 98°57E 236 C2
Mae Sai Thailand 20°20N 99°55E 228 G2
Mae Sot Thailand 16°43N 98°34E 236 D2
Mae Suai Thailand 19°39N 99°33E 228 H2
Mae Tha Thailand 18°28N 99°8E 236 C2
Mae Tup Res. Thailand 17°52N 98°45E 236 D2
Mae Wa △ Thailand 17°23N 99°16E 236 D2
Mae Wong △ Thailand 15°54N 99°12E 236 E2
Mae Yom △ Thailand 18°43N 100°15E 236 C3
Maebaru Japan 33°33N 130°12E 222 D2
Maebashi Japan 36°24N 139°4E 223 A11
Maella Spain 41°8N 0°7E 196 D5
Maelpaeg L. Canada 48°20N 56°30W 299 C8
Maesawa Japan 35°44N 139°31E 140 A2
Maesteg U.K. 51°36N 3°40W 169 F4
Maestra, Sierra Cuba 20°15N 77°0W 320 B4
Maestre de Campo I. Phil. 12°56N 121°42E 232 E3
Maetambe, Mt. Solomon Is. 7°3S 157°1E 287 L9
Maevatanana Madag. 16°56S 46°49E 272 B2
Maéwo Vanuatu 15°10S 168°10E 287 E6
Mafadi S. Africa 29°12S 29°21E 271 C4
Mafate, Cirque de Réunion 21°3S 55°25E 272 f
Mafeking = Mafikeng S. Africa 25°50S 25°38E 270 C4
Mafeking Canada 52°40N 101°10W 297 C8
Maféré Ivory C. 5°30N 3°2W 262 D4
Mafeteng Lesotho 29°51S 27°15E 270 C4
Maffra Australia 37°53S 146°58E 283 D7
Mafia I. Tanzania 7°45S 39°50E 268 D4
Mafikeng S. Africa 25°50S 25°38E 270 C4
Mafra Brazil 26°10S 49°55W 335 B6
Mafra Portugal 38°55N 9°20W 195 G1
Mafungabusi Plateau Zimbabwe 18°30S 29°8E 269 F2
Magadan Russia 59°38N 150°50E 215 D16
Magadi Kenya 1°54S 36°19E 268 C4
Magadi Rift Valley, Kenya 1°54S 36°19E 268 C4
Magadi, L. Kenya 1°54S 36°19E 268 C4
Magaliesburg S. Africa 26°0S 27°32E 271 C4
Magallanes = Punta Arenas Chile 53°10S 71°0W 336 D2
Magallanes Phil. 12°50N 123°50E 232 E4
Magallanes, Estrecho de Chile 52°30S 75°0W 336 D2
Magallanes y Antártica Chilena ☐ Chile 52°0S 72°0W 336 D2
Magaluf Spain 39°29N 2°32E 206 B3
Magangué Colombia 9°14N 74°45W 328 B3
Maganoy Phil. 6°51N 124°31E 233 H5
Magaria Niger 13°4N 9°5E 259 F1
Magarida Papua N. G. 10°18S 149°20E 286 F5
Magburaka S. Leone 8°47N 12°0W 262 D2
Magdagachi Russia 53°27N 125°48E 215 D13
Magdalen Is. = Madeleine, Îs. de la Canada 47°30N 61°40W 299 C7
Magdalena Argentina 35°5S 57°30W 334 D4
Magdalena Bolivia 13°13S 63°57W 331 C5
Magdalena Lima, Peru 12°5S 77°5W 124 B2
Magdalena N. Mex., U.S.A. 34°7N 107°15W 305 J10
Magdalena ☐ Colombia 10°0N 74°0W 328 B3
Magdalena → Colombia 11°6N 74°51W 328 A3
Magdalena, B. Mexico 24°35N 112°0W 318 C2
Magdalena, I. Chile 44°40S 73°0W 336 B2
Magdalena, I. Mexico 24°40N 112°15W 318 C2
Magdalena, Llano de Mexico 25°0N 111°25W 318 C2
Magdalena Contreras Mexico 19°20N 99°13W 128 C1
Magdalena de Kino Mexico 30°38N 110°57W 318 A2
Magdeburg Germany 52°7N 11°38E 178 C7
Magdelaine Cays Australia 16°33S 150°18E 280 B5
Magdub Sudan 13°42N 25°5E 257 E2
Magee U.S.A. 31°52N 89°44W 315 F10
Magelang Indonesia 7°29S 110°13E 235 D4
Magellan's Str. = Magallanes, Estrecho de Chile 52°30S 75°0W 336 D2
Magelungen Sweden 59°13N 18°4E 139 B2
Magenta Italy 45°28N 8°53E 198 C5
Magenta, L. Australia 33°30S 119°2E 279 F2
Magerøya Norway 71°3N 25°40E 160 A21
Maggea Australia 34°28S 140°2E 282 C4
Maggia → Switz. 46°18N 8°36E 179 J4
Maggiorasca, Mte. Italy 44°33N 9°29E 198 D6
Maggiore, Lago Italy 45°57N 8°39E 198 C5
Maggotty Jamaica 18°9N 77°46W 320 a
Maghâgha Egypt 28°38N 30°50E 256 B3
Maghama Mauritania 15°32N 12°57W 262 B2
Maghera U.K. 54°51N 6°41W 166 B5
Magherafelt U.K. 54°45N 6°37W 166 B5
Maghnia Algeria 34°50N 1°43W 261 B4
Maghreb Baghdād, Iraq 33°23N 44°22E 113 A2
Maghreb N. Afr. 32°0N 4°0W 254 C3
Maginu Japan 35°34N 139°34E 140 B2
Magione Italy 43°8N 12°12E 199 E9
Magistralnyy Russia 56°16N 107°36E 215 D11
Maglaj Bos.-H. 44°33N 18°7E 182 F3
Magliana Italy 41°50N 12°26E 136 B1
Magliano in Toscana Italy 42°36N 11°17E 199 F8
Máglie Italy 40°7N 18°18E 201 B11
Magnac-Laval France 46°13N 1°11E 174 B5
Magnetic Pole (North) Arctic 82°18N 113°24W 150 A2
Magnetic Pole (South) Antarctica 64°8S 138°8E 151 C9
Magnisia ☐ Greece 39°15N 23°0E 204 B5
Magnitogorsk Russia 53°27N 59°4E 186 D10
Magnolia Ark., U.S.A. 33°16N 93°14W 314 E8
Magnolia Miss., U.S.A. 31°9N 90°28W 315 F9
Magnor Norway 59°56N 12°15E 164 E9
Magny-en-Vexin France 49°9N 1°47E 173 C8
Magny-les-Hameaux France 48°44N 2°3E 134 B1
Mago Fiji 17°26S 179°8W 287 A3
Mago △ Ethiopia 5°40N 36°18E 257 F4
Magog Canada 45°18N 72°9W 313 A12
Magoro Uganda 1°45N 34°12E 268 B3
Magoye Zambia 16°1S 27°30E 269 F2
Magpet Phil. 7°6N 125°6E 233 H5
Magpie, L. Canada 51°0N 64°41W 299 B7
Magrath Canada 49°25N 112°50W 296 D6
Magre → Spain 39°11N 0°25W 197 F4
Magrur Sudan 14°1N 30°27E 257 E3
Magrur, Wadi → Sudan 16°5N 26°30E 257 D2
Magsingal Phil. 17°41N 120°25E 232 C3
Magta Lahjar Mauritania 17°28N 13°17W 262 B2
Magu Tanzania 2°30S 33°30E 268 C3
Maguan China 23°0N 104°21E 228 F5
Maguarinho, C. Brazil 0°15S 48°30W 332 B2
Magude Mozam. 25°2S 32°40E 271 C5
Maguindanao ☐ Phil. 7°5N 124°40E 233 H5
Magura Bangla. 23°26N 89°26E 241 D2
Magurski △ Poland 49°30N 21°30E 185 J8
Maġusa = Famagusta Cyprus 35°8N 33°55E 207 E9
Maguse L. Canada 61°37N 95°10W 297 A9
Maguse Pt. Canada 61°20N 93°50W 297 A10
Magvana India 23°13N 69°22E 242 H3
Magwe Burma 20°10N 95°0E 241 E5
Magwe South Sudan 4°8N 32°17E 257 G3
Magwe ☐ Burma 20°0N 95°0E 241 F5
Magyarország = Hungary ■ Europe 47°20N 19°20E 181 D12
Maha Oya Sri Lanka 7°31N 81°22E 245 L5
Maha Sarakham Thailand 16°12N 103°16E 236 D4
Mahābād Iran 36°50N 45°45E 213 D11
Mahabaleshwar India 17°58N 73°43E 244 F1
Mahabalipuram India 12°37N 80°11E 245 H5
Mahabharat Lekh Nepal 28°30N 82°0E 243 E10
Mahabo Madag. 20°23S 44°40E 272 C1
Mahad India 18°6N 73°29E 244 E1
Mahaddayweyne Somalia 2°58N 45°32E 267 D6
Mahadeo Hills India 22°20N 78°30E 243 H8
Mahadeopur India 18°48N 80°0E 244 E5
Mahaffey U.S.A. 40°53N 78°44W 312 F6
Mahagi Dem. Rep. of the Congo 2°20N 31°0E 268 B3
Mahagnao Volcano △ Phil. 10°52N 124°51E 233 F5
Mahaicony Guyana 6°36N 57°48W 329 B6
Mahajamba → Madag. 15°33S 47°8E 272 B2
Mahajamba, Helodranon' i Madag. 15°24S 47°5E 272 B2
Mahajan India 28°48N 73°56E 242 E5
Mahajanga Madag. 15°40S 46°25E 272 B2
Mahajanga ☐ Madag. 17°0S 47°0E 272 B2
Mahajilo → Madag. 19°42S 45°22E 272 B2

Mahakam → *Indonesia* 0°35S 117°17E 235 C5
Mahalapye *Botswana* 23°1S 26°51E 270 B4
Mahalaxmi *Mumbai, India* 130 a1
Mahalchhar *Bangla.* 22°55N 92°2E 241 D4
Mahale Mts. *Tanzania* 6°20S 30°0E 268 D3
Mahale Mts. △ *Tanzania* 6°10S 29°50E 268 D2
Maḥallāt *Iran* 33°55N 50°30E 247 C6
Māhān *Iran* 30°5N 57°18E 247 D8
Mahan → *India* 23°30N 82°50E 243 H10
Mahanadi → *India* 20°20N 86°25E 244 D8
Mahananda → *India* 25°12N 87°52E 243 G12
Mahanoro *Madag.* 19°54S 48°48E 272 B2
Mahanoy City *U.S.A.* 40°49N 76°9W 313 F8
Mahaplag *Phil.* 10°35N 124°57E 233 F5
Mahar, L. *U.S.A.* 25°46N 80°18W 129 D1
Maharashtra □ *India* 20°30N 75°30E 244 D2
Maharès *Tunisia* 34°32N 10°29E 258 B2
Maharivo → *Madag.* 20°26S 44°10E 272 C1
Mahasamund *India* 21°6N 82°6E 244 D6
Mahasham, W. → *Egypt* 30°15N 34°10E 251 H5
Mahasoa *Madag.* 22°12S 46°6E 272 C2
Mahasolo *Madag.* 19°7S 46°22E 272 B2
Mahattat ash Shīdīyah
Jordan 29°55N 35°55E 251 J6
Mahattat 'Unayzah
Jordan 30°30N 35°47E 251 H6
Mahaut *Dominica* 15°21N 61°24W 323 k
Mahaut *Guadeloupe* 16°11N 61°46W 322 e
Mahavavy → *Madag.* 15°57S 45°54E 272 B2
Mahaweli Ganga →
Sri Lanka 8°27N 81°13E 245 K5
Mahaxay *Laos* 17°22N 105°12E 236 D5
Mahbubabad *India* 17°42N 80°2E 244 F5
Mahbubnagar *India* 16°45N 77°59E 244 F3
Mahd adh Dhahab
Si. Arabia 23°30N 40°52E 248 B3
Mahda *U.A.E.* 25°20N 56°15E 247 E8
Maḥḍah *Oman* 24°24N 55°59E 247 E7
Mahdia *Guyana* 5°13N 59°8W 329 B6
Mahdia *Tunisia* 35°28N 11°0E 258 A2
Mahdia □ *Tunisia* 35°20N 10°35E 261 A7
Mahe *Jammu & Kashmir, India* 33°10N 78°32E 243 C8
Mahé *Pondicherry, India* 11°42N 75°34E 245 J2
Mahé *Seychelles* 5°0S 55°30E 272 c
Mahé ✈ (SEZ) *Seychelles* 4°40S 55°31E 272 c
Mahébourg *Mauritius* 20°24S 57°42E 272 e
Mahendra Giri *India* 8°20N 77°30E 245 K3
Mahendragarh *India* 28°17N 76°14E 242 E7
Mahendranagar *Nepal* 28°55N 80°20E 243 E9
Mahenge *Tanzania* 8°45S 36°41E 269 D4
Maheno *N.Z.* 45°10S 170°50E 285 F5
Mahesana *India* 23°39N 72°26E 242 H5
Maheshtala *India* 22°29N 88°15E 124 C1
Maheshwar *India* 22°11N 75°35E 242 H6
Maheskhali I. *Bangla.* 21°36N 91°56E 241 E3
Mahgawan *India* 26°29N 78°37E 243 F8
Mahi → *India* 22°15N 72°55E 242 H5
Mahia Pen. *N.Z.* 39°9S 177°55E 284 F6
Mahibadhoo *Maldives* 3°47N 72°58E 272 d
Mahighe *Solomon Is.* 8°30S 159°58E 287 M10
Mahikeng = Mafikeng
S. Africa 25°50S 25°38E 270 C4
Mahilyow *Belarus* 53°55N 30°18E 177 B16
Mahilyow □ *Belarus* 54°10N 30°50E 188 E6
Mahim *Maharashtra, India* 19°2N 72°50E 130 A2
Mahim *Maharashtra, India* 19°39N 72°44E 244 E1
Mahim B. *India* 19°2N 72°49E 130 A1
Mahina *Tahiti* 17°30S 149°27W 289 e
Mahipalpur *India* 28°32N 77°7E 120 B1
Mahirija *Morocco* 34°0N 3°16W 261 B4
Mahlaing *Burma* 21°6N 95°39E 241 E5
Mahlsdorf *Germany* 52°30N 13°37E 115 A4
Mahmiya *Sudan* 17°12N 33°43E 257 D3
Mahmoodabad *Pakistan* 24°51N 67°4E 123 A2
Mahmud Kot *Pakistan* 30°16N 71°0E 242 D4
Mahmudia *Romania* 45°5N 29°5E 183 E14
Mahmudiye *Turkey* 39°48N 30°15E 205 B12
Mahmutbey *Turkey* 41°3N 28°49E 203 E12
Mahmutlar *Turkey* 36°29N 32°5E 250 B3
Māhneshān *Iran* 36°44N 47°39E 213 D12
Mahnomen *U.S.A.* 47°19N 95°58W 308 B6
Maho *Sri Lanka* 7°49N 80°16E 245 L5
Mahoba *India* 25°15N 79°55E 243 G8
Mahomet *U.S.A.* 40°12N 88°24W 311 D8
Mahón = Maó *Spain* 39°53N 4°16E 206 B5
Mahon, Menorca ✈ (MAH)
Spain 39°50N 4°16E 196 F9
Mahone Bay *Canada* 44°27N 64°23W 299 D7
Mahongo ⌓ *Namibia* 18°0S 23°15E 270 B3
Mahopac *U.S.A.* 41°22N 73°45W 313 E11
Mahoua *Chad* 11°49N 18°26E 259 F3
Mahrāt, Jabal *Yemen* 17°0N 51°0E 249 C5
Mahrauli *India* 28°31N 77°10E 120 B2
Mährisch-Budwitz = Moravské Budějovice *Czech Rep.* 49°4N 15°49E 180 B8
Mährisch-Schönberg = Šumperk
Czech Rep. 49°59N 16°59E 181 B9
Mährisch-Trubau = Moravská Třebová *Czech Rep.* 49°45N 16°40E 181 B9
Mahul *India* 19°0N 72°53E 130 A2
Mahuta *Nigeria* 11°32N 4°58E 263 C5
Mahuva *India* 21°5N 71°48E 242 J4
Mahya Dağı *Turkey* 41°47N 27°36E 203 E11
Mai-Ndombe, L.
Dem. Rep. of the Congo 2°0S 18°20E 264 C3
Mai Thon, Ko *Thailand* 7°40N 98°28E 237 a
Maia *Amer. Samoa* 14°13S 169°25W 302 g
Maia *Azores* 36°56N 25°1W 153 d4
Maia *Portugal* 41°14N 8°37W 194 D2
Maials *Spain* 41°22N 0°30E 196 D5
Maibong *India* 25°18N 93°10E 241 C4
Maicao *Colombia* 11°23N 72°13W 328 A3
Maîche *France* 47°16N 6°48E 173 E13
Maici → *Brazil* 6°30S 61°43W 331 B5
Maicuru → *Brazil* 2°14S 54°17W 329 D7
Máida *Italy* 38°51N 16°22E 201 D9
Maida Vale *London, U.K.* 125 a1
Maidan Khula *Afghan.* 33°36N 69°50E 242 C3
Maidenhead *U.K.* 51°31N 0°42W 169 F7
Maidstone *Vic., Australia* 37°47S 144°52E 128 A1
Maidstone *Sask., Canada* 53°5N 109°20W 297 C7
Maidstone *Kent, U.K.* 51°16N 0°32E 169 F8
Maiduguri *Nigeria* 12°0N 13°20E 263 C7
Maiella △ *Italy* 42°5N 14°5E 199 F11
Măieruş *Romania* 45°53N 25°31E 183 E10
Maigatari *Nigeria* 12°46N 9°27E 263 C6
Maigh Nuad = Maynooth
Ireland 53°23N 6°34W 166 C5
Maignelay Montigny
France 49°32N 2°30E 173 C9
Maigo *Phil.* 8°10N 123°57E 233 G4
Maigualida, Sierra
Venezuela 5°30N 65°10W 329 B4
Maigudo *Ethiopia* 7°30N 37°8E 257 F4
Maihar *India* 24°16N 80°45E 243 G9
Maihara *Japan* 35°19N 136°17E 223 B8
Maikala Ra. *India* 22°0N 81°0E 244 D5
Maiko △
Dem. Rep. of the Congo 0°30S 27°50E 268 C2
Mailani *India* 28°17N 80°21E 243 E9
Mā'ili *U.S.A.* 21°25N 158°11W 302 K13
Mā'ili Pt. *U.S.A.* 21°24N 158°11W 302 K13
Maillezais *France* 46°22N 0°45W 174 B3
Mailsi *Pakistan* 29°48N 72°15E 242 E5
Maimbung *Phil.* 5°56N 121°2E 233 J3
Main → *Bayern, Germany* 50°0N 8°18E 179 F4
Main → *Antrim, U.K.* 54°43N 6°18W 166 B5
Main Channel *Canada* 45°21N 81°45W 312 A3
Main Range △ *Australia* 28°11S 152°27E 281 D5
Main Ridge *Trin. & Tob.* 11°16N 60°40W 323 s
Mainburg *Germany* 48°38N 11°47E 179 G7
Maindargi *India* 17°28N 76°18E 244 F3
Maine *France* 48°20N 0°15W 172 D6
Maine □ *U.S.A.* 45°20N 69°0W 309 C19
Maine → *Ireland* 52°9N 9°45W 166 D2
Maine, G. of *U.S.A.* 43°0N 68°30W 301 G26
Maine-et-Loire □ *France* 47°31N 0°30W 172 E6
Maïne-Soroa *Niger* 13°13N 12°2E 263 C7
Maingkaing *Burma* 24°48N 95°16E 241 C5
Maingkwan *Burma* 26°15N 96°37E 241 B6
Mainistir na Corann = Midleton
Ireland 51°55N 8°10W 166 E3
Mainit *Phil.* 9°32N 125°32E 233 G5
Mainit, L. *Phil.* 9°31N 125°30E 233 G5
Mainland *Orkney, U.K.* 58°59N 3°8W 167 C5
Mainland *Shet., U.K.* 60°15N 1°22W 167 A7
Mainpuri *India* 27°18N 79°4E 243 F8
Maintal *Germany* 50°7N 8°52E 179 E4
Maintenon *France* 48°35N 1°35E 173 D8
Maintirano *Madag.* 18°3S 44°1E 272 B1
Mainz *Germany* 50°1N 8°14E 179 E4
Maio *C. Verde Is.* 15°13N 23°10W 153 j
Maipú *Argentina* 36°52S 57°50W 334 D4
Maipú *Santiago, Chile* 33°30S 70°45W 137 C1
Maiquetía *Venezuela* 10°36N 66°57W 328 A4
Máira → *Italy* 44°49N 7°38E 198 D4
Mairabari *India* 26°30N 92°22E 241 B4
Mairipotaba *Brazil* 17°18S 49°28W 333 E2
Maisi *Cuba* 20°17N 74°9W 321 B5
Maisí, Pta. de *Cuba* 20°10N 74°10W 321 B5
Maiskhal I. *Bangla.* 21°36N 91°56E 241 E3
Maison Coloniale
Guadeloupe 16°18N 61°16W 322 e
Maisonneuve, Parc
Canada 45°32N 73°33W 130 A2
Maisons-Alfort *France* 48°48N 2°26E 134 B3
Maisons-Laffitte *France* 48°57N 2°8E 134 A1
Maissoneuve *Canada* 45°32N 73°33W 130 A2
Maitland *N.S.W., Australia* 32°33S 151°36E 283 B9
Maitland *S. Austral., Australia* 34°23S 137°40E 282 C2
Maitland *Western Cape, S. Africa* 33°53S 18°29E 118 A1
Maitland → *Canada* 43°45N 81°43W 312 C3
Maitland, Banjaran
Malaysia 4°55N 116°37E 235 B5
Maitri *Antarctica* 70°0S 3°0W 151 D3
Maitum *Phil.* 6°2N 124°30E 233 H5
Maiyema *Nigeria* 12°5N 4°25E 263 C5
Maiyuan *China* 25°34N 117°28E 229 E11
Maiz, Is. del *Nic.* 12°15N 83°4W 320 D3
Maizuru *Japan* 35°25N 135°22E 223 B7
Majagual *Colombia* 8°33N 74°38W 328 B3
Majalengka *Indonesia* 6°50S 108°13E 235 D3
Majanji *Uganda* 0°16N 34°0E 268 B3
Majari → *Brazil* 3°29N 60°58W 329 C5
Majdūl *Libya* 25°51N 15°7E 258 C3
Majene *Indonesia* 3°38S 118°57E 235 C5
Majes → *Peru* 16°40S 72°44W 330 D3
Majete ⌓ *Malawi* 15°54S 34°34E 269 F3
Majevica *Bos.-H.* 44°45N 18°50E 182 F3
Maji *Ethiopia* 6°12N 35°30E 257 F4
Majiang *China* 26°28N 107°32E 228 D6
Majorca = Mallorca *Spain* 39°30N 3°0E 206 B4
Majors Creek *Australia* 35°33S 149°45E 283 C8
Majuli I. *India* 26°58N 94°14E 241 B5
Majuriã *Brazil* 7°30S 54°55W 331 B5
Majuro *Marshall Is.* 7°9N 171°12E 288 G9
Mak, Ko *Thailand* 11°49N 102°29E 237 G4
Maka *Senegal* 13°40N 14°10W 262 C2
Mākaha *Hawai'i, U.S.A.* 21°29N 153°13W 302 K13
Makaha *Zimbabwe* 17°20S 32°39E 271 A5
Makahoa Pt. *U.S.A.* 21°41N 157°56W 302 J14
Makak *Cameroon* 3°36N 11°0E 263 E7
Makaka *Congo* 3°45S 13°39E 264 C2
Makakilo City *U.S.A.* 21°22N 158°5W 302 K13
Makakou *Gabon* 0°11S 12°12E 264 C2
Makalamabedi *Botswana* 20°19S 23°51E 270 B3
Makale *Indonesia* 3°6S 119°51E 235 C5
Makalu *Asia* 27°55N 87°8E 243 F12
Makalu-Barun △ *Nepal* 27°45N 87°10E 243 F12
Makamba *Burundi* 4°8S 29°49E 268 C2
Makapu'u Pt. *U.S.A.* 21°19N 157°39W 302 K14
Makarewa Junction *N.Z.* 46°20S 168°21E 285 G3
Makari *Cameroon* 12°35N 10°27E 259 F2
Makarikari = Makgadikgadi Salt Pans *Botswana* 20°40S 25°45E 270 B4
Makarov Basin *Arctic* 87°0N 150°0W 150 A
Makarovo *Russia* 57°40N 107°45E 215 D11
Makarska *Croatia* 43°20N 17°2E 199 E14
Makaryev *Russia* 57°52N 43°50E 190 B6
Makasar *Indonesia* 6°17S 106°52E 122 A2
Makassar *Indonesia* 5°10S 119°20E 235 D5
Makassar, Selat *Indonesia* 1°0S 118°20E 235 C5
Makassar, Str. of = Makassar, Selat
Indonesia 1°0S 118°20E 235 C5
Makat = Maqat
Kazakhstan 47°39N 53°19E 187 E9
Makati *Phil.* 14°33N 121°7E 127 B2
Makaw
Dem. Rep. of the Congo 3°29S 18°20E 264 C3
Makawao *U.S.A.* 20°52N 156°17W 302 C5
Makaya
Dem. Rep. of the Congo 3°21S 18°1E 264 C3
Makedonija = Macedonia ■
Europe 41°53N 21°40E 202 E5
Makefu *Cook Is.* 18°59S 169°55W 289 g
Makemo *French Polynesia* 16°35S 143°40W 289 f
Makeni *S. Leone* 8°55N 12°5W 262 D2
Makeyevka = Makiyivka
Ukraine 48°0N 38°0E 189 H9
Makgadikgadi △
Botswana 20°27S 24°47E 270 B3
Makgadikgadi Salt Pans
Botswana 20°40S 25°45E 270 B4
Makhachkala *Russia* 43°0N 47°30E 191 J8
Makhado = Louis Trichardt
S. Africa 23°1S 29°43E 271 B4
Makham, Ao *Thailand* 7°51N 98°25E 237 a
Makharadze = Ozurgeti
Georgia 41°55N 42°0E 191 K5
Makhfar al Buşayyah *Iraq* 30°0N 46°10E 246 D5
Makhmūr *Iraq* 35°46N 43°35E 213 E10
Makhtal *India* 16°30N 77°31E 245 E3
Makhyah, W. → *Yemen* 17°40N 49°1E 249 C5
Makian *Indonesia* 0°20N 127°20E 231 D7
Makina *Solomon Is.* 9°50S 160°50E 287 M11
Makindu *Kenya* 2°18S 37°50E 268 C4
Mäkiniitty *Finland* 60°20N 24°58E 121 A2
Makinka = Makinsk
Kazakhstan 52°37N 70°26E 217 B8
Makinsk *Kazakhstan* 52°37N 70°26E 217 B8
Makira = San Cristóbal
Solomon Is. 10°30S 161°0E 287 N11
Makiyivka *Ukraine* 48°0N 38°0E 189 H9
Makkah *Si. Arabia* 21°30N 39°54E 248 B2
Makkah □ *Si. Arabia* 21°30N 42°30E 248 B3
Makkovik *Canada* 55°10N 59°10W 299 A8
Makó *Hungary* 46°14N 20°33E 182 D5
Mako *Senegal* 12°52N 12°20W 262 C2
Makogai *Fiji* 17°28S 179°0E 287 A2
Makok *Gabon* 0°1S 9°35E 264 C1
Makokou *Gabon* 0°40N 12°50E 264 B2
Makongo
Dem. Rep. of the Congo 3°25N 26°17E 268 B2
Makoro
Dem. Rep. of the Congo 3°10N 29°59E 268 B2
Makoua *Congo* 0°5S 15°50E 264 C3
Maków Mazowiecki
Poland 52°52N 21°6E 185 F8
Maków Podhalański
Poland 49°43N 19°45E 185 J6
Makra *Greece* 36°15N 25°54E 205 E7
Makrai *India* 22°2N 77°0E 242 H7
Makran *Asia* 26°13N 61°30E 240 D1
Makran Coast Range
Pakistan 25°40N 64°0E 240 D2
Makrana *India* 27°2N 74°46E 242 F6
Makrany *Belarus* 51°48N 24°17E 185 G11
Makri *Greece* 40°52N 25°40E 203 F9
Makri *India* 19°46N 81°55E 244 E5
Makrigialos *Greece* 35°2N 25°59E 207 E6
Makthar *Tunisia* 35°48N 9°12E 258 A1
Mākū *Iran* 39°15N 44°31E 213 C11
Mākua *U.S.A.* 21°32N 158°13W 302 J13
Makum *India* 27°30N 95°23E 241 B5
Makumbi
Dem. Rep. of the Congo 5°50S 20°43E 265 D4
Makunda *Botswana* 22°30S 20°7E 270 B3
Makung *Taiwan* 23°34N 119°34E 225 C1
Makungo *Somalia* 0°49N 42°35E 267 D5
Makunudu Atoll *Maldives* 6°20N 72°35E 272 d
Makunza
Dem. Rep. of the Congo 8°52S 24°19E 265 D4
Makurazaki *Japan* 31°15N 130°20E 222 D2
Makurdi *Nigeria* 7°43N 8°35E 263 D6
Makushin Volcano
U.S.A. 53°53N 166°55W 303 K6
Mākūyeh *Iran* 28°7N 53°9E 247 D7
Makwassie *S. Africa* 27°17S 26°0E 270 C4
Makwiro *Zimbabwe* 17°58S 30°25E 271 A5
Mal *India* 26°51N 88°45E 241 B2
Mâl *Mauritania* 16°58N 13°23W 262 B2
Mal B. *Ireland* 52°50N 9°30W 166 D2
Mala = Mallow *Ireland* 52°8N 8°39W 166 D3
Mala *Peru* 12°40S 76°38W 330 C2
Mala ⊙ *Australia* 21°39S 130°45E 278 D5
Mala, Pta. *Panama* 7°28N 80°2W 320 E3
Mala Belozërka *Ukraine* 47°12N 34°56E 189 J8
Malá Fatra △ *Slovak Rep.* 49°10N 19°0E 181 B12
Mala Kapela *Croatia* 44°45N 15°30E 199 D12
Mala Panew → *Poland* 50°43N 17°54E 185 H4
Malá Strana *Czech Rep.* 50°4N 14°24E 135 B2
Mala Vyska *Ukraine* 48°39N 31°36E 189 H6
Malabang *Phil.* 7°36N 124°3E 233 H5
Malabar *N.S.W., Australia* 33°58S 151°14E 139 B2
Malabar *Fla., U.S.A.* 28°0N 80°34W 317 H9
Malabar Coast *India* 11°0N 75°0E 245 J2
Malabar Hill *India* 18°57N 72°48E 130 B1
Malabar Pt. *India* 18°56N 72°48E 130 B1
Malabo = Rey Malabo
Eq. Guin. 3°45N 8°50E 263 E6
Malabon *Phil.* 14°39N 120°56E 127 B1
Malabrigo = Puerto Chicama
Peru 7°45S 79°20W 330 B2
Malabrigo Pt. *Phil.* 13°36N 121°15E 232 E3
Malabu *Nigeria* 9°32N 12°48E 263 D7
Malabuñgan *Phil.* 9°3N 117°38E 233 G1
Malacañang Palace *Phil.* 14°35N 120°59E 127 B1
Malacca, Straits of *Indonesia* 3°0N 101°0E 237 L3
Malacky *Slovak Rep.* 48°27N 17°0E 181 C10
Malad City *U.S.A.* 42°12N 112°15W 304 E7
Maladeta *Spain* 42°39N 0°39E 196 C5
Maladzyechna *Belarus* 54°20N 26°50E 177 A14
Málaga *Colombia* 6°42N 72°44W 328 B3
Málaga *Spain* 36°43N 4°23W 195 J6
Málaga □ *Spain* 36°38N 4°58W 195 J6
Malagarasi *Tanzania* 5°5S 30°50E 268 D3
Malagarasi → *Tanzania* 5°12S 29°47E 268 D3
Malagasy Rep. = Madagascar ■
Africa 20°0S 47°0E 272 B2
Malagón *Spain* 39°11N 3°52W 195 F7
Malagón → *Spain* 37°35N 7°29W 195 H3
Malah *Syria* 32°33N 36°54E 251 F7
Malahide *Ireland* 53°26N 6°9W 120 A3
Malaimbandy *Madag.* 20°20S 45°36E 272 C2
Malaita *Solomon Is.* 9°0S 161°0E 287 M11
Malakal *South Sudan* 9°33N 31°40E 257 F3
Malakal Harb. *Palau* 7°19N 134°27E 288 c
Malakanagiri *India* 18°21N 81°54E 244 E5
Malakand *Pakistan* 34°40N 71°55E 242 B4
Malakoff *France* 48°49N 2°18E 134 B2
Malakula *Vanuatu* 16°15S 167°30E 287 F5
Malakwal *Pakistan* 32°34N 73°13E 242 C5
Malalag *Phil.* 6°36N 125°24E 233 H5
Malalaua *Papua N. G.* 8°4S 146°10E 286 E4
Malam *Chad* 11°27N 20°59E 259 F4
Malamala *Indonesia* 3°21S 120°55E 231 E6
Malanda *Australia* 17°22S 145°35E 280 B4
Malang *Indonesia* 7°59S 112°45E 235 D4
Malanga *Mozam.* 13°28S 36°7E 269 E4
Malangas *Phil.* 7°37N 123°1E 233 H4
Malange ⌓ *Angola* 9°30S 16°0E 265 D3
Malangen *Norway* 69°24N 18°37E 160 B18
Malangwa *Nepal* 26°52N 85°34E 243 F11
Malanje *Angola* 9°36S 16°17E 265 D3
Malanut B. *Phil.* 9°15N 117°59E 233 G1
Malapatan *Phil.* 5°59N 125°18E 233 J5
Malappuram *India* 11°7N 76°11E 245 J3
Mälaren *Sweden* 59°30N 17°10E 162 E11
Malargüe *Argentina* 35°32S 69°30W 334 D2
Malarhöjaen *Sweden* 59°18N 17°58E 139 B1
Malartic *Canada* 48°9N 78°9W 298 C4
Malaryta *Belarus* 51°50N 24°3E 185 G11
Malasiqui *Phil.* 15°55N 120°24E 232 D3
Malaspina Glacier
U.S.A. 59°50N 140°30W 303 G12
Malate *Phil.* 14°34N 120°59E 127 B1
Malatya *Turkey* 38°25N 38°20E 213 C8
Malatya □ *Turkey* 38°15N 38°0E 212 C7
Malawali, Pulau *Malaysia* 7°3N 117°18E 235 A5
Malawi ■ *Africa* 11°55S 34°0E 269 E3
Malawi, L. *Africa* 12°30S 34°30E 269 E3
Malay *Phil.* 11°54N 121°55E 233 F3
Malay Pen. *Asia* 7°25N 100°0E 237 J3
Malay Quarter *Cape Town, S. Africa* 118 c2
Malaya Belozërka = Mala Belozërka
Ukraine 47°12N 34°56E 189 J8
Malaya Neva *Russia* 59°56N 30°16E 137 B1
Malaya Okhta *Russia* 59°55N 30°25E 137 B2
Malaya Vishera *Russia* 58°55N 32°25E 188 C7
Malaya Viska = Mala Vyska
Ukraine 48°39N 31°36E 189 H6
Malaybalay *Phil.* 8°5N 125°7E 233 G5
Malāyer *Iran* 34°19N 48°51E 213 E13
Malaysia ■ *Asia* 5°0N 110°0E 237 K4
Malazgirt *Turkey* 39°10N 42°33E 213 C10
Malbaza *Niger* 13°59N 5°38E 263 C6
Malbon *Australia* 21°5S 140°17E 280 C3
Malbooma *Australia* 30°41S 134°11E 281 E1
Malbork *Poland* 54°3N 19°1E 184 D6
Malca Dube *Ethiopia* 6°47N 42°4E 267 C5
Malcésine *Italy* 45°46N 10°48E 198 C7
Malchin *Germany* 53°44N 12°44E 178 B8
Malchow *Berlin, Germany* 52°34N 13°29E 115 A3
Malchow *Mecklenburg-Vorpommern, Germany* 53°28N 12°25E 178 B8
Malcolm *Australia* 28°51S 121°25E 279 E3
Malcolm, Pt. *Australia* 33°48S 123°45E 279 F3
Malczyce *Poland* 51°14N 16°29E 185 G3
Maldah *India* 25°2N 88°9E 243 G13
Maldegem *Belgium* 51°14N 3°26E 170 C3
Malden *London, U.K.* 51°23N 0°15W 125 B2
Malden *Mass., U.S.A.* 42°26N 71°3W 116 A2
Malden *Mo., U.S.A.* 36°34N 89°57W 308 G9
Malden I. *Kiribati* 4°3S 155°1W 289 H12
Maldives ■ *Ind. Oc.* 5°0N 73°0E 272 d
Maldon *Vic., Australia* 37°0S 144°6E 282 D6
Maldon *Essex, U.K.* 51°44N 0°42E 169 F8
Maldonado *Uruguay* 34°59S 55°0W 335 C5
Maldonado, Pta. *Mexico* 16°20N 98°33W 319 D5
Malè *Italy* 46°21N 10°55E 198 B7
Malé *Maldives* 4°10N 73°28E 272 d
Malé ✈ (MLE) *Maldives* 4°11N 73°28E 272 d
Malé Atoll *Maldives* 4°45N 73°15E 272 d
Malé Karpaty *Slovak Rep.* 48°30N 17°20E 181 C10
Maleas, Akra *Greece* 36°28N 23°7E 204 E5
Malebo, Pool *Africa* 4°17S 15°20E 265 C3
Malegaon *India* 20°30N 74°38E 244 D2
Malei *Mozam.* 17°12S 36°58E 269 F4
Maleizen *Belgium* 50°45N 4°31E 116 B3
Malek *South Sudan* 6°4N 31°36E 257 F3
Malek Kandī *Iran* 37°9N 46°6E 213 D12
Malela *Bas-Congo, Dem. Rep. of the Congo* 5°59S 12°37E 265 D2
Malela *Maniema, Dem. Rep. of the Congo* 4°22S 26°8E 265 C5
Malema *Mozam.* 14°57S 37°20E 269 E4
Maleme *Greece* 35°31N 23°49E 207 E4
Malendok I. *Papua N. G.* 3°28S 153°13E 286 B7
Maler Kotla *India* 30°32N 75°58E 242 D6
Målerås *Sweden* 56°54N 15°34E 163 H9
Males *Greece* 35°6N 25°35E 207 E6
Malesherbes *France* 48°15N 2°24E 173 D9
Maleshevska Planina
Europe 41°38N 23°7E 202 E7
Malešice *Czech Rep.* 50°5N 14°30E 135 B3
Malesina *Greece* 38°37N 23°14E 204 C5
Malestroit *France* 47°49N 2°25W 172 E4
Malfa *Italy* 38°35N 14°50E 201 D7
Malgobek *Russia* 43°30N 44°34E 191 J7
Malgomaj *Sweden* 64°40N 16°30E 160 D17
Malgrat de Mar *Spain* 41°39N 2°46E 196 D7
Malha *Sudan* 15°8N 25°10E 257 D2
Malhada *Brazil* 14°21S 43°47W 333 D3
Malhargarh *India* 24°17N 74°59E 242 G6
Malheur → *U.S.A.* 44°4N 116°59W 304 D5
Malheur L. *U.S.A.* 43°20N 118°48W 304 E4
Mali *Guinea* 12°10N 12°20W 262 C2
Mali ■ *Africa* 17°0N 3°0W 262 B4
Mali → *Burma* 25°42N 97°30E 241 C6
Mali Kanal *Serbia* 45°36N 19°24E 182 E4
Mali Kyun *Burma* 13°0N 98°20E 236 F2
Malia *Greece* 35°17N 25°32E 207 E6
Malia, Kolpos *Greece* 35°19N 25°27E 207 E6
Maliao *Taiwan* 23°48N 120°13E 225 C2
Malibran, Teatro *Venice, Italy* 142 b3
Malibu *U.S.A.* 34°2N 118°41W 307 L8
Maligaya = Gloria *Phil.* 12°59N 121°30E 232 E3
Maliku = Minicoy I. *India* 8°17N 73°2E 245 K1
Maliku *Indonesia* 0°39S 123°16E 231 E6
Malili *Indonesia* 2°42S 121°6E 231 E6
Målilla *Sweden* 57°23N 15°48E 163 G9
Malimba, Mts.
Dem. Rep. of the Congo 7°30S 29°30E 268 D2
Malin Hd. *Ireland* 55°23N 7°23W 166 A4
Malin Pen. *Ireland* 55°20N 7°17W 166 A4
Malindang, Mt. *Phil.* 8°13N 123°38E 233 G4
Malindi *Kenya* 3°12S 40°5E 268 C5
Malindi Marine ⌓ *Kenya* 3°15S 40°7E 268 C5
Malines = Mechelen
Belgium 51°2N 4°29E 170 C4
Malino *Indonesia* 1°0N 121°0E 231 D6
Malinyi *Tanzania* 8°56S 36°0E 269 D4
Malipo *China* 23°7N 104°42E 228 F5
Maliq *Albania* 40°45N 20°48E 202 F4
Malir → *Pakistan* 24°49N 67°4E 123 B2
Malita *Phil.* 6°19N 125°39E 233 H5
Maliwun *Burma* 10°17N 98°40E 237 G2
Maliya *India* 23°5N 70°46E 242 H4
Maljenik *Serbia* 43°54N 21°43E 202 C5
Malka Mari △ *Kenya* 4°11N 40°46E 268 B5
Malkapur *India* 20°53N 76°12E 244 D3
Malkara *Turkey* 40°53N 26°53E 203 F10
Malkhangiri = Malakanagiri
India 18°21N 81°54E 244 E5
Małkinia Górna *Poland* 52°42N 22°5E 185 F9
Malko Tŭrnovo *Bulgaria* 41°59N 27°31E 203 E11
Mall, The *Washington, D.C., U.S.A.* 143 b2
Mallacoota *Australia* 37°40S 149°40E 283 D8
Mallacoota Inlet
Australia 37°34S 149°40E 283 D8
Mallaig *U.K.* 57°0N 5°50W 167 D3
Mallala *Australia* 34°26S 138°30E 282 C3
Mallaoua *Niger* 13°2N 9°36E 263 C6
Mallard *U.S.A.* 42°56N 94°41W 310 B2
Mallawan *India* 27°4N 80°12E 243 F9
Mallawi *Egypt* 27°44N 30°44E 256 B3
Mallee Cliffs △ *Australia* 34°16S 142°32E 282 C5
Mallemort *France* 43°43N 5°11E 175 E9
Mallery Mills *U.K.* 55°52N 3°20W 121 B2
Málles Venosta *Italy* 46°41N 10°32E 198 B7
Mallicolo = Malakula
Vanuatu 16°15S 167°30E 287 F5
Mallorca *Spain* 39°30N 3°0E 206 B4
Mallorytown *Canada* 44°29N 75°53W 313 B9
Mallow *Ireland* 52°8N 8°39W 166 D3
Malmbäck *Sweden* 57°34N 14°28E 163 G8
Malmberget *Sweden* 67°11N 20°40E 160 C19
Malmédy *Belgium* 50°25N 6°2E 170 D6
Malmesbury *S. Africa* 33°28S 18°41E 270 D2
Malmi *Finland* 60°15N 24°59E 121 B2
Malmivaara = Malmberget
Sweden 67°11N 20°40E 160 C19
Malmköping *Sweden* 59°8N 16°44E 162 E10
Malmö *Sweden* 55°36N 12°59E 163 J7
Malmok *Aruba* 12°36N 70°4W 322 f
Malmøya *Norway* 59°52N 10°45E 133 A3
Malmslätt *Sweden* 58°27N 15°33E 163 F9
Malmyzh *Russia* 56°31N 50°41E 190 B10
Malnaş *Romania* 46°2N 25°49E 183 D10
Malo *Vanuatu* 15°40S 167°11E 287 E5
Malo Konare *Bulgaria* 42°12N 24°24E 203 D8
Maloarkhangelsk *Russia* 52°28N 36°30E 189 F9
Maloca *Brazil* 0°43N 55°57W 329 C6
Malolo *Fiji* 17°45S 177°11E 287 A1
Malolos *Phil.* 14°50N 120°49E 232 D3
Malolotja ⌓ *Swaziland* 26°4S 31°6E 271 C5
Malombe L. *Malawi* 14°40S 35°15E 269 E4
Malomice *Poland* 51°34N 15°29E 185 G2
Malomir *Bulgaria* 42°16N 26°32E 203 D10
Malone *Fla., U.S.A.* 30°57N 85°10W 316 E4
Malone *N.Y., U.S.A.* 44°51N 74°18W 313 B10
Malong *China* 25°24N 103°34E 228 E4
Malonga
Dem. Rep. of the Congo 10°24S 23°10E 265 E4
Małopolskie □ *Poland* 49°50N 20°20E 185 J7
Malorad *Bulgaria* 43°28N 23°41E 202 C7
Måløv *Denmark* 55°44N 12°20E 118 A1
Måløy *Norway* 61°57N 5°6E 164 C2
Maloyaroslovets *Russia* 55°2N 36°20E 188 E9
Malpartida de Cáceres
Spain 39°26N 6°30W 195 F4
Malpaso *Canary Is.* 27°43N 18°3W 153 e1
Malpaso, Presa = Netzahualcóyotl, Presa *Mexico* 17°8N 93°35W 319 D6
Malpelo, I. de *Colombia* 4°3N 81°35W 289 G19
Malpensa, Milano ✈ (MXP) = Milano Malpensa ✈ (MXP)
Italy 45°38N 8°43E 128 A1
Malpica de Bergantiños
Spain 43°19N 8°50W 194 B2
Malprabha → *India* 16°20N 76°5E 245 F3
Malpur *India* 23°21N 73°27E 242 H5
Malpura *India* 26°17N 75°23E 242 F6
Mals = Málles Venosta
Italy 46°41N 10°32E 198 B7
Malsiras *India* 17°52N 74°55E 244 F2
Malta *Brazil* 6°54S 37°31W 332 C4
Malta *Idaho, U.S.A.* 42°18N 113°22W 304 E7
Malta *Mont., U.S.A.* 48°21N 107°52W 304 B10
Malta ■ *Europe* 35°55N 14°26E 206 F7
Malta ✈ (MLA) *Malta* 35°52N 14°29E 206 F7
Maltahöhe *Namibia* 24°55S 17°0E 270 B2
Maltepe *Turkey* 40°55N 29°8E 203 F13
Malton *Ont., Canada* 43°42N 79°38W 141 A1
Malton *N. Yorks., U.K.* 54°8N 0°49W 168 C7
Malu'a *Solomon Is.* 8°20S 160°38E 287 M11
Maludam △ *Malaysia* 1°39N 111°2E 235 B4
Maluku = Manolo Fortich
Phil. 8°28N 124°50E 233 G5
Maluku *Indonesia* 1°0S 127°0E 231 E7
Maluku □ *Indonesia* 3°0S 128°0E 231 E7
Maluku Sea = Molucca Sea
Indonesia 0°0 125°0E 231 E6
Malumfashi *Nigeria* 11°48N 7°39E 263 C6
Malunda *Indonesia* 3°0S 118°50E 235 C5
Malundo *Angola* 14°51S 22°0E 265 E4
Malung *Sweden* 60°42N 13°44E 162 D7
Malungon *Phil.* 6°16N 125°14E 233 H5
Malungsfors *Sweden* 60°44N 13°33E 162 D7
Malur *India* 13°0N 77°55E 245 H3
Maluso *Phil.* 6°33N 121°53E 233 H3
Maluwe *Ghana* 8°40N 2°17W 262 D4
Malvalli *India* 12°28N 77°8E 245 H3
Malvan *India* 16°2N 73°30E 245 F1
Malvern *Vic., Australia* 37°50S 145°2E 128 B2
Malvern *Ont., Canada* 43°47N 79°13W 141 A3
Malvern *Gauteng, S. Africa* 26°11S 28°5E 123 B2
Malvern *Ark., U.S.A.* 34°22N 92°49W 314 D8
Malvern Hills *U.K.* 52°0N 2°19W 169 E5
Malvik *Norway* 63°25N 10°40E 164 A7
Malvinas, Is. = Falkland Is. ⊠
Atl. Oc. 51°30S 59°0W 153 f
Malwal *South Sudan* 9°19N 31°35E 257 F3
Malý Dunaj →
Slovak Rep. 47°45N 18°9E 181 D11
Malya *Tanzania* 3°5S 33°38E 268 C3
Malye Derbety *Russia* 47°57N 44°42E 191 G7
Malyn *Ukraine* 50°46N 29°3E 177 C15
Malyy Lyakhovskiy, Ostrov
Russia 74°7N 140°36E 215 B15
Malyy Taymyr, Ostrov
Russia 78°6N 107°15E 215 B11
Mama *Russia* 58°18N 112°54E 215 D12
Mamadysh *Russia* 55°44N 51°23E 190 C10
Mamaku *N.Z.* 38°5S 176°8E 284 E5
Māmala B. *U.S.A.* 21°15N 157°55W 302 K14
Mamanguape *Brazil* 6°50S 35°4W 332 C4
Mamanuca Group *Fiji* 17°35S 177°5E 287 A1
Mamarr Mitlā *Egypt* 30°2N 32°54E 251 H3
Mamasa *Indonesia* 2°55S 119°20E 235 C5
Mambajao *Phil.* 9°15N 124°43E 233 G5
Mambasa
Dem. Rep. of the Congo 1°22N 29°3E 268 B2
Mamberamo → *Indonesia* 2°0S 137°50E 231 E9
Mambéré → *C.A.R.* 3°31N 16°3E 264 B3
Mambili → *Congo* 0°6N 16°5E 264 B3
Mambilima Falls *Zambia* 10°31S 28°45E 269 E2
Mambirima
Dem. Rep. of the Congo 11°25S 27°33E 269 E2
Mambo *Tanzania* 4°52S 38°22E 268 C4
Mambrui *Kenya* 3°5S 40°5E 268 C5
Mamburao *Phil.* 13°13N 120°39E 232 E3
Mamedkala *Russia* 42°10N 48°7E 191 J9
Mameigwess L. *Canada* 52°35N 87°50W 298 B2
Mamers *France* 48°21N 0°22E 172 D7
Mamfé *Cameroon* 5°50N 9°15E 263 D6
Māmī, Ra's *Yemen* 12°32N 54°30E 249 D6
Mamili △ *Namibia* 18°2S 24°1E 270 A3
Mamiña *Chile* 20°5S 69°14W 330 E4
Mamlyutka *Kazakhstan* 54°56N 68°32E 217 B7
Mammoth *U.S.A.* 32°43N 110°39W 305 K8
Mammoth Cave △
U.S.A. 37°8N 86°13W 308 G10
Mamonovo *Russia* 54°28N 19°55E 184 D6
Mamoré → *Bolivia* 10°23S 65°53W 331 C4
Mamou *Guinea* 10°15N 12°0W 262 C2
Mamoudzou *Mayotte* 12°48S 45°14E 272 b
Mampang Prapatan
Indonesia 6°15S 106°49E 122 B1
Mampikony *Madag.* 16°6S 47°38E 272 B2
Mampoko
Dem. Rep. of the Congo 0°51N 18°42E 264 B3
Mampong *Ghana* 7°6N 1°26W 263 D4
Mampukuji *Japan* 35°36N 139°31E 140 B2
Mamry, Jezioro *Poland* 54°5N 21°50E 184 D8
Mamuil Malal, Paso
S. Amer. 39°35S 71°28W 336 A2
Mamuju *Indonesia* 2°41S 118°50E 235 C5
Ma'mūl *Oman* 18°8N 55°16E 249 C6
Mamuno *Botswana* 22°16S 20°1E 270 B3
Mamuras *Albania* 41°34N 19°41E 202 E3
Man *Ivory C.* 7°30N 7°40W 262 D3
Man → *India* 17°31N 75°32E 244 F2
Man, I. of *India* 8°28N 93°36E 245 K11
Man, I. of *U.K.* 54°15N 4°30W 168 C3
Man-Bazar *India* 23°4N 86°39E 243 H12
Man Budrukh *India* 19°2N 72°55E 130 A2
Man Kat *Burma* 22°5N 98°1E 241 D7
Man Khurd *India* 19°3N 72°55E 130 A2
Man Na *Burma* 23°27N 97°19E 241 D6
Man of War B. *Trin. & Tob.* 11°19N 60°34W 323 s
Mana *Fr. Guiana* 5°45N 53°55W 329 B7
Mānā *Hawai'i, U.S.A.* 22°2N 159°47W 302 A2
Mana → *Fr. Guiana* 5°45N 53°55W 329 B7
Mana Pools △ *Zimbabwe* 15°56S 29°25E 269 F2
Manaar, G. of = Mannar, G. of
Asia 8°30N 79°0E 245 K4
Manabí □ *Ecuador* 0°40S 80°5W 328 D1
Manacacias → *Colombia* 4°23N 72°4W 328 C3
Manacapuru *Brazil* 3°16S 60°37W 329 D5
Manacapuru → *Brazil* 3°18S 60°37W 329 D5
Manacor *Spain* 39°34N 3°13E 206 B4
Manadas *Azores* 38°38N 28°3W 153 d1
Manado *Indonesia* 1°29N 124°51E 231 D6
Managua *Nic.* 12°6N 86°20W 320 D2
Managua, L. de *Nic.* 12°20N 86°30W 320 D2
Manaia *N.Z.* 39°33S 174°8E 284 F3
Manakara *Madag.* 22°8S 48°1E 272 C2
Manākau *N.Z.* 42°15S 173°42E 285 C8
Manākhah *Yemen* 15°5N 43°44E 248 D3
Manakhat *Israel* 31°45N 35°11E 123 B2
Manali *India* 32°16N 77°10E 242 C7
Manam I. *Papua N. G.* 4°5S 145°0E 286 C3
Manama = Al Manāmah
Bahrain 26°10N 50°30E 247 E6
Manambao → *Madag.* 17°35S 44°0E 272 B1
Manambato *Madag.* 13°43S 49°7E 272 A2
Manambolo → *Madag.* 19°18S 44°22E 272 B1
Manambolosy *Madag.* 15°2S 49°40E 272 B2
Mánamo, Caño →
Venezuela 9°55N 62°16W 329 B5
Mānana I. *U.S.A.* 21°20N 157°40W 302 K14
Mananara *Madag.* 16°10S 49°46E 272 B2
Mananara → *Madag.* 23°21S 47°42E 272 C2
Mananara ⌓ *Madag.* 16°14S 49°45E 272 B2
Manangatang *Australia* 35°5S 142°54E 282 C5
Mananjary *Madag.* 21°13S 48°20E 272 C2
Manankoro *Mali* 10°28N 7°25W 262 C3
Manantali, L. de *Mali* 13°12N 10°28W 262 C2
Manantavadi *India* 11°49N 76°1E 245 J3
Manantenina *Madag.* 24°17S 47°19E 272 C2
Manaos = Manaus *Brazil* 3°0S 60°0W 329 D6
Manapire → *Venezuela* 7°42N 66°7W 328 B4
Manapla *Phil.* 10°58N 123°5E 233 F4
Manapouri *N.Z.* 45°34S 167°39E 285 F2
Manapouri, L. *N.Z.* 45°32S 167°32E 285 F2
Manapparai *India* 10°36N 78°25E 245 J4
Manaqil *Sudan* 14°15N 32°59E 257 E3
Manar → *India* 18°50N 77°20E 244 E3
Manār, Jabal *Yemen* 14°2N 44°17E 248 D4
Manaravolo *Madag.* 23°59S 45°39E 272 C2
Manas *Xinjiang Uygur, China* 44°17N 86°10E 217 D11
Manas *Somalia* 2°57N 43°28E 267 D5
Manas → *India* 26°12N 90°40E 241 B3
Manas ⌓ *India* 26°40N 91°0E 241 B3
Manas He → *China* 45°38N 85°12E 218 B6
Manas Hu *China* 45°45N 85°55E 217 C11
Manaslu *Nepal* 28°33N 84°33E 243 E11
Manasquan *U.S.A.* 40°8N 74°3W 313 F10
Manassa *U.S.A.* 37°11N 105°56W 305 H11
Manati *Puerto Rico* 18°26N 66°29W 321 b
Manati B. *St. Helena* 16°0S 5°46W 153 h
Manau *Papua N. G.* 8°4S 148°0E 286 E4
Manaus *Brazil* 3°0S 60°0W 329 D6
Manavgat *Turkey* 36°47N 31°26E 250 B2
Manavgat → *Turkey* 36°43N 31°27E 250 B2
Manawan = Rizal *Phil.* 17°51N 121°21E 232 C3
Manawan L. *Canada* 55°24N 103°14W 297 B8
Manawatu → *N.Z.* 40°28S 175°12E 284 G4
Manawatu-Wanganui □
N.Z. 39°50S 175°30E 284 F4
Manay *Phil.* 7°17N 126°33E 233 H6
Manbij *Syria* 36°31N 37°57E 212 D7
Mancha Real *Spain* 37°48N 3°39W 195 H7
Manche □ *France* 49°10N 1°20W 172 C5
Manchegorsk *Russia* 67°54N 32°58E 214 C4
Manchester *Gt. Man., U.K.* 53°29N 2°12W 168 D5
Manchester *Calif., U.S.A.* 38°58N 123°41W 306 G3
Manchester *Conn., U.S.A.* 41°47N 72°31W 313 E12
Manchester *Ga., U.S.A.* 32°51N 84°37W 316 C5
Manchester *Iowa, U.S.A.* 42°29N 91°27W 310 B5
Manchester *Ky., U.S.A.* 37°9N 83°46W 309 G12
Manchester *Mich., U.S.A.* 42°9N 84°2W 311 B12
Manchester *N.H., U.S.A.* 42°59N 71°28W 313 D13
Manchester *N.Y., U.S.A.* 42°56N 77°16W 312 D7
Manchester *Ohio, U.S.A.* 38°41N 83°36W 311 F13
Manchester *Pa., U.S.A.* 40°4N 76°43W 313 F8
Manchester *Tenn., U.S.A.* 35°29N 86°5W 315 D11
Manchester *Vt., U.S.A.* 43°10N 73°5W 313 C11
Manchester Int. ✈ (MAN)
U.K. 53°21N 2°17W 168 D5
Manchester L. *Canada* 61°28N 107°29W 297 A7
Manchhar L. *Pakistan* 26°25N 67°39E 242 F2
Manchineel Bay *Grenada* 12°26N 61°29W 323 q
Manchou *Taiwan* 22°1N 120°50E 225 D2
Manchuria = Dongbei
China 45°0N 125°0E 227 D13
Manchurian Plain *China* 47°0N 124°0E 210 D14
Manciano *Italy* 42°35N 11°31E 199 F8
Mancifa *Ethiopia* 6°53N 41°50E 257 F5
Máncora *Peru* 4°9S 81°1W 330 A1
Mand → *India* 21°42N 83°15E 243 J10
Mand → *Iran* 28°20N 52°30E 247 D7
Manda *Ludewe, Tanzania* 10°30S 34°40E 269 E3
Manda *Mbeya, Tanzania* 7°58S 32°29E 268 D3
Manda *Mbeya, Tanzania* 8°30S 32°49E 269 D3
Manda △ *Chad* 9°45N 17°52E 259 G3
Mandabé *Madag.* 21°0S 44°55E 272 C1
Mandaguari *Brazil* 23°32S 51°42W 335 A5
Mandah = Töhöm
Mongolia 44°27N 108°2E 226 B5
Mandai *Singapore* 1°24N 103°45E 138 A2
Mandal *Norway* 58°2N 7°25E 164 F4
Mandala, Puncak
Indonesia 4°44S 140°20E 231 E10
Mandalay *Burma* 22°0N 96°4E 241 E6
Mandalay □ *Burma* 22°0N 96°5E 241 E5
Mandale = Mandalay
Burma 22°0N 96°4E 241 E6
Mandalgarh *India* 25°12N 75°6E 242 G6
Mandalgovi *Mongolia* 45°45N 106°10E 226 B4
Mandalī *Iraq* 33°43N 45°28E 213 F11
Mandalselva → *Norway* 58°2N 7°28E 164 F4
Mandaluyong *Phil.* 14°35N 121°1E 127 B2
Mandan *U.S.A.* 46°50N 100°54W 308 B3
Mandaoli *India* 28°37N 77°17E 120 B2
Mandaon *Phil.* 12°13N 123°17E 232 E4
Mandaqui → *Brazil* 23°30S 46°40W 137 A2
Mandar, Teluk *Indonesia* 3°32S 119°21E 235 C5
Mandara Mts. *Nigeria* 10°40N 13°40E 259 F2
Mándas *Italy* 39°40N 9°8E 200 C2
Mandasor = Mandsaur
India 24°3N 75°8E 242 G6
Mandaue *Phil.* 10°20N 123°56E 233 F4
Mandel *Afghan.* 33°17N 61°53E 240 B1
Mandelieu-la-Napoule
France 43°34N 6°57E 175 E10
Mandera *Kenya* 3°55N 41°53E 268 B5
Mandeville *Jamaica* 18°2N 77°31W 320 a
Mandi *India* 31°39N 76°58E 242 D7
Mandi Burewala *Pakistan* 30°9N 72°41E 242 D5
Mandi Dabwali *India* 29°58N 74°42E 242 E6
Mandiana *Guinea* 10°37N 8°39W 262 C3
Mandigos = Manica
Mozam. 18°58S 32°59E 271 A5
Mandimba *Mozam.* 14°20S 35°40E 269 E4
Mandioli *Indonesia* 0°40S 127°20E 231 E7
Mandioré, L. *S. Amer.* 18°8S 57°33W 331 D6
Mandla *India* 22°39N 80°30E 243 H9
Mandø *Denmark* 55°18N 8°33E 163 J2
Mandoli *India* 28°41N 77°18E 120 A2
Mandorah *Australia* 12°32S 130°42E 278 B5
Mandoto *Madag.* 19°34S 46°17E 272 B2
Mandoudi *Greece* 38°48N 23°29E 204 C5
Mandoul *Chad* 9°40N 15°30E 259 G3
Mandra *Greece* 38°4N 23°30E 204 C5
Mandra *Pakistan* 33°23N 73°12E 242 C5
Mandraki *Greece* 36°36N 27°11E 205 E9
Mandrare → *Madag.* 25°10S 46°30E 272 D2
Mandritsara *Madag.* 15°50S 48°49E 272 B2
Mandronarivo *Madag.* 21°7S 45°38E 272 C2
Mandsaur *India* 24°3N 75°8E 242 G6
Mandurah *Australia* 32°36S 115°48E 279 F2
Mandúria *Italy* 40°24N 17°38E 201 B10
Mandvi *Gujarat, India* 22°51N 69°22E 242 H3
Mandvi *Maharashtra, India* 18°56N 72°50E 130 B2
Mandya *India* 12°30N 77°0E 245 H3
Mandzai *Pakistan* 30°55N 67°6E 242 D2
Mané *Burkina Faso* 12°59N 1°21W 263 C4
Maneh *Iran* 37°39N 57°7E 247 B8
Manenberg *S. Africa* 33°58S 18°33E 118 A2
Manengouba, Mts. *Cameroon* 5°0N 9°50E 263 E6
Maner → *India* 18°30N 79°40E 244 F4

Manera *Madag.* 22°55S 44°20E **272** C1
Manérbio *Italy* 45°21N 10°8E **198** C7
Maneroo Cr. → *Australia* 23°21S 143°53E **280** C3
Manfalût *Egypt* 27°20N 30°52E **256** B3
Manfred *Australia* 33°19S 143°45E **282** B5
Manfredónia *Italy* 41°38N 15°55E **199** G12
Manfredónia, G. di *Italy* 41°35N 16°5E **199** G13
Mang Kung Uk *China* 22°18N 114°16E **122** B2
Mang-won *S. Korea* 37°33N 126°55E **137** B1
Manga *Brazil* 14°46S 43°56W **333** D3
Manga *Burkina Faso* 11°40N 1°4W **263** C4
Manga *Congo* 0°13S 16°5E **264** C3
Manga *Niger* 15°0N 14°0E **259** F2
Mangabeiras, Chapada das
Brazil 10°0S 46°30W **332** D2
Mangai
Dem. Rep. of the Congo 4°2S 19°33E **265** C3
Mangaia *Cook Is.* 21°55S 157°55W **289** K12
Mangakino *N.Z.* 38°22S 175°47E **284** E4
Mangal *Phil.* 6°25N 121°58E **233** H3
Mangalagiri *India* 16°26N 80°36E **245** F5
Mangaldai *India* 26°26N 92°2E **241** B4
Mangaldan *Phil.* 16°4N 120°24E **232** C3
Mangalia *Romania* 43°50N 28°35E **183** G13
Mangalmé *Chad* 12°26N 19°37E **259** F3
Mangalore *India* 12°55N 74°47E **245** H2
Mangaluru = Mangalore
India 12°55N 74°47E **245** H2
Mangalvedha *India* 17°31N 75°28E **244** F2
Mangan *India* 27°31N 88°32E **241** B2
Mangaon *India* 18°15N 73°20E **244** E1
Mangarrayi ☼ *Australia* 15°5S 133°10E **280** B1
Mangawan *India* 24°41N 81°33E **243** G9
Mangaweka *N.Z.* 39°48S 175°47E **284** F4
Mangaweka, Mt. *N.Z.* 39°49S 176°5E **284** F5
Mange
Dem. Rep. of the Congo 0°54N 20°30E **264** B4
Manger *Norway* 60°38N 5°3E **164** D2
Manggar *Indonesia* 2°50S 108°10E **235** C3
Manggawitu *Indonesia* 4°8S 133°32E **231** E8
Mangghystaū *Kazakhstan* 43°40N 51°13E **216** D4
Mangghystaū □ *Kazakhstan* 45°0N 53°0E **216** D4
Mangghystaū Tübegi
Kazakhstan 44°30N 52°30E **216** D4
Manggis *Indonesia* 8°29S 115°31E **231** J18
Mangin Taungdan *Burma* 24°15N 95°45E **241** C5
Mangindrano *Madag.* 14°17S 48°58E **272** A2
Mangkalihat, Tanjung
Indonesia 1°2N 118°59E **235** B5
Mangkururrpa ☼
Australia 20°35S 129°43E **278** D4
Mangla *Pakistan* 33°7N 73°39E **242** C5
Mangla Dam *Pakistan* 33°9N 73°44E **243** C5
Manglares, C. *Colombia* 1°36N 79°2W **328** C2
Manglaur *India* 29°44N 77°49E **242** E7
Mangle, B. de *Venezuela* 10°57N 64°10W **329** a
Mangle, Pta. *Venezuela* 10°52N 64°3W **329** a
Manglillo *Venezuela* 10°57N 64°19W **329** a
Manglisi *Georgia* 41°41N 44°22E **191** K7
Mangnai *China* 37°52N 91°43E **218** D7
Mangnai Zhen *China* 38°24N 90°14E **217** E12
Mango *Togo* 10°20N 0°30E **263** C5
Mango *Tonga* 20°17S 174°29W **287** Q13
Mangoche *Malawi* 14°25S 35°16E **269** E4
Mangoky → *Madag.* 21°29S 43°41E **272** C1
Mangole *Indonesia* 1°50S 125°55E **231** E6
Mangolpuri *India* 28°41N 77°6E **120** A1
Mangombe
Dem. Rep. of the Congo 1°20S 26°48E **268** C2
Mangonui *N.Z.* 35°1S 173°32E **284** B2
Mangoro → *Madag.* 20°0S 48°45E **272** C2
Mangrol *Mad. P., India* 21°7N 70°7E **242** J4
Mangrol *Raj., India* 25°20N 76°31E **242** G6
Mangrul Pir *India* 20°19N 77°21E **244** D3
Manguaba = Pilar *Brazil* 9°36S 35°56W **332** C4
Mangualde *Portugal* 40°38N 7°48W **194** E3
Mangueigne *Chad* 10°30N 21°15E **259** F4
Mangueira, L. da *Brazil* 33°0S 52°50W **335** C5
Manguéni, Hamada
Niger 22°35N 12°40E **258** D2
Manguinhos ✕ *Brazil* 22°52S 43°14W **135** B1
Mangum *U.S.A.* 34°53N 99°30W **314** D5
Mangungu
Dem. Rep. of the Congo 5°16S 19°36E **265** D3
Manguri *Australia* 28°58S 134°22E **281** A1
Mangyshlak, Poluostrov =
Mangghystaū Tübegi
Kazakhstan 44°30N 52°30E **216** D4
Manhattan *Kans., U.S.A.* 39°11N 96°35W **308** F5
Manhattan *New York, U.S.A.* **132** d2
Manhattan Beach *U.S.A.* 40°34N 73°56W **132** C2
Manhattan Bridge *New York, U.S.A.* **132** f2
Manhatten *U.S.A.* 41°26N 87°59W **311** C9
Manhiça *Mozam.* 25°23S 32°49E **271** C5
Manhuaçu *Brazil* 20°15S 42°2W **333** F3
Manhumirim *Brazil* 20°22S 41°57W **333** F3
Maní *Colombia* 4°49N 72°17W **328** C3
Mania → *Madag.* 19°42S 45°22E **272** B2
Maniago *Italy* 46°10N 12°43E **199** B9
Manica *Mozam.* 18°58S 32°59E **271** A5
Manica □ *Mozam.* 19°10S 33°45E **271** A5
Manicahan *Phil.* 7°1N 122°12E **233** H4
Manicaland □ *Zimbabwe* 19°0S 32°30E **269** F3
Manicoré *Brazil* 5°48S 61°16W **331** B5
Manicoré → *Brazil* 5°51S 61°19W **331** B5
Manicouagan → *Canada* 49°30N 68°30W **299** C6
Manicouagan, Rés.
Canada 51°5N 68°40W **299** B6
Maniema □
Dem. Rep. of the Congo 3°0S 26°0E **268** C2
Manīfah *Si. Arabia* 27°44N 49°0E **247** E6
Manifold, C. *Australia* 22°41S 150°50E **280** C5
Maniganggo *China* 31°56N 99°10E **228** B2
Manigotagan *Canada* 51°6N 96°18W **297** C9
Manigotagan → *Canada* 51°7N 96°20W **297** C9
Manihari *India* 25°21N 87°38E **243** G12
Manihi *French Polynesia* 14°24S 145°56W **289** f
Manihiki *Cook Is.* 10°24S 161°1W **289** J11
Manihiki Plateau *Pac. Oc.* 11°0S 164°0W **289** J11
Maniitsoq *Greenland* 65°26N 52°55W **154** D5
Manika, Plateau de la
Dem. Rep. of the Congo 10°0S 25°5E **269** E2
Manikchhari *Bangla.* 22°51N 91°50E **241** D3
Manikganj *Bangla.* 23°52N 90°0E **241** D3
Manikpur *India* 25°4N 81°7E **243** G9
Manila *Phil.* 14°35N 120°58E **127** B1
Manila *Utah, U.S.A.* 40°59N 109°43W **304** F9
Manila B. *Phil.* 14°40N 120°35E **232** D3
Manila Ninoy Aquino Int. ✕ **(MNL)**
Phil. 14°31N 121°0E **127** B2
Manildra *Australia* 33°11S 148°41E **283** B8
Manilla *Australia* 30°45S 150°43E **283** A9
Manimpé *Mali* 14°11N 5°28W **262** C3
Maningrida *Australia* 12°3S 134°13E **280** A1
Maninian *Ivory C.* 10°3N 7°52W **262** C3
Maninjau, Danau
Indonesia 0°19S 100°11E **234** C2
Manipur □ *India* 25°0N 94°0E **241** C5
Manipur → *Burma* 23°45N 94°20E **241** D5
Manisa *Turkey* 38°38N 27°30E **205** C9
Manisa □ *Turkey* 38°40N 28°0E **205** C9
Manistee *U.S.A.* 44°15N 86°19W **308** C10
Manistee → *U.S.A.* 44°15N 86°21W **308** C10
Manistique *U.S.A.* 45°57N 86°15W **308** C10
Manito *U.S.A.* 40°26N 89°47W **310** D7
Manitoba □ *Canada* 53°30N 97°0W **297** B9
Manitoba, L. *Canada* 51°0N 98°45W **297** C9
Manitou *Canada* 49°15N 98°32W **297** D9
Manitou, L. *Canada* 50°55N 65°17W **299** B6
Manitou Beach *U.S.A.* 41°58N 84°19W **311** C12
Manitou Is. *U.S.A.* 45°8N 86°0W **308** C10
Manitou L. *Canada* 52°43N 109°43W **297** C7
Manitou Springs
U.S.A. 38°52N 104°55W **304** G11
Manitoulin I. *Canada* 45°40N 82°30W **298** C3
Manitouwadge *Canada* 49°8N 85°48W **298** C2
Manitowoc *U.S.A.* 44°5N 87°40W **308** C10
Manitsauá-Missu →
Brazil 10°58S 53°20W **331** C7
Maniyachi *India* 8°51N 77°55E **245** K3
Manizales *Colombia* 5°5N 75°32W **328** B2
Manja *Madag.* 21°26S 44°20E **272** C1
Manjacaze *Mozam.* 24°45S 34°0E **271** B5
Manjakandriana *Madag.* 18°55S 47°47E **272** B2
Manjhand *Pakistan* 25°50N 68°10E **242** G3
Manjiang *China* 41°56N 127°35E **224** B3
Manjimup *Australia* 34°15S 116°6E **279** F2
Manjlegaon *India* 19°9N 76°14E **244** E3
Manjo *Cameroon* 4°50N 9°49E **264** B1
Manjra → *India* 18°49N 77°52E **244** E3
Mankato *Kans., U.S.A.* 39°47N 98°13W **308** F4
Mankato *Minn., U.S.A.* 44°10N 94°0W **308** C6
Mankayan *Phil.* 16°52N 120°47E **232** C3
Mankayane *Swaziland* 26°40S 31°4E **271** C5
Mankera *Pakistan* 31°23N 71°26E **242** D4
Mankim *Cameroon* 5°6N 12°3E **263** D7
Mankkaa *Finland* 60°11N 24°47E **121** B1
Mankono *Ivory C.* 8°1N 6°10W **262** D3
Mankota *Canada* 49°25N 107°5W **297** D7
Mankulam *Sri Lanka* 9°8N 80°26E **245** K5
Manlay = Üydzin *Mongolia* 44°9N 107°0E **226** B4
Manleluag △ *Phil.* 15°4N 120°17E **232** D3
Manley Hot Springs
U.S.A. 65°0N 150°38W **303** D10
Manlleu *Spain* 42°2N 2°17E **196** C7
Manly *Australia* 33°47S 151°17E **139** A2
Manmad *India* 20°18N 74°28E **244** D2
Mann, L. *U.S.A.* 28°32N 81°35W **133** A2
Mann Ranges *Australia* 26°6S 130°5E **279** E5
Manna *Indonesia* 4°25S 102°55E **234** C2
Mannahill *Australia* 32°25S 140°0E **282** B4
Mannar *Sri Lanka* 9°1N 79°54E **245** K4
Mannar, G. of *Asia* 8°30N 79°0E **245** K4
Mannar I. *Sri Lanka* 9°5N 79°45E **245** K4
Mannargudi *India* 10°45N 79°51E **245** J4
Mannheim *Germany* 49°29N 8°29E **179** F4
Manning *Alta., Canada* 56°53N 117°39W **296** B5
Manning *Oreg., U.S.A.* 45°45N 123°13W **306** E3
Manning *S.C., U.S.A.* 33°42N 80°13W **316** B9
Manning → *Australia* 31°52S 152°43E **283** A10
Manning Str. *Solomon Is.* 7°30S 158°0E **287** L10
Mann's Chinese Theatre
U.S.A. 34°6N 118°20W **126** B2
Mannswörth *Austria* 48°8N 16°30E **142** B3
Mannu → *Italy* 39°16N 9°0E **200** C2
Mannu, C. *Italy* 40°3N 8°21E **200** B1
Mannum *Australia* 34°50S 139°20E **282** C3
Mano *S. Leone* 8°3N 12°2W **262** D2
Mano → *Liberia* 6°56N 11°30W **262** D2
Mano River *Liberia* 7°20N 11°6W **262** D2
Manoa *Bolivia* 9°40S 65°27W **331** B4
Manoharpur *India* 22°23N 85°12E **243** H11
Manokotak *U.S.A.* 58°58N 159°3W **303** G8
Manokwari *Indonesia* 0°54S 134°0E **231** E8
Manolada *Greece* 38°4N 21°21E **204** C3
Manolo Fortich *Phil.* 8°28N 124°50E **233** G5
Manombo *Madag.* 22°57S 43°28E **272** C1
Manono
Dem. Rep. of the Congo 7°15S 27°25E **268** D2
Manono *Samoa* 13°50S 172°5W **287** V19
Manoppello *Italy* 42°15N 14°3E **199** F11
Manor Park *U.K.* 51°32N 0°1E **125** A4
Manora *Pakistan* 24°47N 66°58E **123** B1
Manora Pt. *Pakistan* 24°47N 66°58E **123** B1
Manorhamilton *Ireland* 54°18N 8°11W **166** B3
Manosque *France* 43°49N 5°47E **175** E9
Manotick *Canada* 45°13N 75°41W **313** A9
Manouane → *Canada* 49°30N 71°10W **299** C5
Manouane, L. *Canada* 50°45N 70°45W **299** B5
Manovo-Gounda Saint Floris △
C.A.R. 9°30N 21°25E **264** A4
Manp'o *N. Korea* 41°6N 126°24E **224** B3
Manpojin = Manp'o
N. Korea 41°6N 126°24E **224** B3
Manpur *Chhattisgarh,*
India 23°17N 83°35E **243** H10
Manpur *Chhattisgarh, India* 20°22N 80°43E **244** D5
Manpur *Mad. P., India* 22°26N 75°37E **242** H6
Manquehue, Cerro *Chile* 33°21S 70°35W **137** B2
Manra *Kiribati* 4°27S 171°15W **277** A16
Manresa *Spain* 41°48N 1°50E **196** D6
Mansa *Gujarat, India* 23°27N 72°45E **242** H5
Mansa *Punjab, India* 30°0N 75°27E **242** E6
Mansa *Zambia* 11°13S 28°55E **269** E2
Mansa Konko *Gambia* 13°28N 15°33W **262** C1
Mansalay *Phil.* 12°31N 121°26E **232** E3
Månsåsen *Sweden* 63°5N 14°18E **162** A8
Mansehra *Pakistan* 34°20N 73°15E **242** B5
Mansel I. *Canada* 62°0N 80°0W **295** E15
Mansfield *Vic., Australia* 37°4S 146°6E **283** D7
Mansfield *Notts., U.K.* 53°9N 1°11W **168** D6
Mansfield *Ga., U.S.A.* 33°31N 83°44W **316** B6
Mansfield *La., U.S.A.* 32°2N 93°43W **314** E8
Mansfield *Mass., U.S.A.* 42°2N 71°13W **313** D13
Mansfield *Ohio, U.S.A.* 40°45N 82°31W **312** F2
Mansfield *Pa., U.S.A.* 41°48N 77°5W **312** E7
Mansfield *Tex., U.S.A.* 32°33N 97°8W **314** E6
Mansfield, Mt. *U.S.A.* 44°33N 72°49W **313** B12
Mansi *Burma* 24°48N 95°52E **241** C5
Mansidão *Brazil* 10°43S 44°2W **332** D3
Mansilla de las Mulas
Spain 42°30N 5°25W **194** C5
Mansle *France* 45°52N 0°12E **174** C4
Manso → *Brazil* 13°50S 47°0W **333** D2
Mansôa *Guinea-Biss.* 12°0N 15°20W **262** C1
Manson *U.S.A.* 42°32N 94°32W **310** B2
Manson Creek *Canada* 55°37N 124°32W **296** B4
Mansoura *Algeria* 36°1N 4°31E **261** A5
Manta *Ecuador* 1°0S 80°40W **328** D1
Manta, B. de *Ecuador* 0°54S 80°44W **328** D1
Mantalingajan, Mt. *Phil.* 8°55N 117°45E **233** G1
Mantantale
Dem. Rep. of the Congo 2°10S 20°11E **264** C4
Mantare *Tanzania* 2°42S 33°13E **268** C3
Mantaro → *Peru* 12°16S 73°57W **330** C3
Manteca *U.S.A.* 37°48N 121°13W **306** H5
Mantecal *Venezuela* 7°34N 69°17W **328** B4
Mantena *Brazil* 18°47S 40°59W **333** E3
Manteno *U.S.A.* 41°15N 87°50W **311** C9
Manteo *U.S.A.* 35°55N 75°40W **315** D17
Mantes-la-Jolie *France* 48°58N 1°41E **173** D8
Mantha *India* 19°40N 76°23E **244** E3
Manthani *India* 18°40N 79°35E **244** E4
Manti *U.S.A.* 39°16N 111°38W **304** G8
Mantiqueira, Serra da
Brazil 22°0S 44°0W **333** F3
Manton *U.S.A.* 44°25N 85°24W **309** C11
Mantorp *Sweden* 58°21N 15°20E **163** F9
Mántova *Italy* 45°9N 10°48E **198** C7
Mänttä Vilppula *Finland* 62°3N 24°40E **188** A3
Mantua = Mántova *Italy* 45°9N 10°48E **198** C7
Mantung *Australia* 34°35S 140°3E **282** C4
Manturovo *Russia* 58°23N 44°45E **190** A7
Manú *Peru* 12°10S 70°51W **330** C3
Manú → *Peru* 12°16S 70°55W **330** C3
Manu'a Is.
Amer. Samoa 14°13S 169°35W **287** W21
Manuel Alves → *Brazil* 11°19S 48°28W **333** D2
Manuel Alves Grande →
Brazil 7°27S 47°35W **332** C2
Manuel Urbano *Brazil* 8°53S 69°18W **330** B4
Manui *Indonesia* 3°35S 123°5E **231** E6
Manukan *Phil.* 8°32N 123°12E **233** G4
Manukau *N.Z.* 37°0S 174°52E **284** D3
Manukau Harbour *N.Z.* 37°3S 174°45E **284** D3
Manunui *N.Z.* 38°54S 175°21E **284** E4
Manuoha *N.Z.* 38°39S 177°7E **284** E6
Manuripi → *Bolivia* 11°6S 67°36W **330** C4
Manus □ *Papua N. G.* 2°0S 147°0E **286** B4
Manus I. *Papua N. G.* 2°0S 147°0E **286** B4
Manvi *India* 15°57N 76°59E **245** G3
Manwan Dam *China* 24°44N 100°20E **228** E3
Manwath *India* 19°19N 76°32E **244** E3
Many *U.S.A.* 31°34N 93°29W **314** F8
Manyallaluk ☼ *Australia* 14°16S 132°49E **278** B5
Manyani *Kenya* 3°5S 38°30E **268** C4
Manyara □ *Tanzania* 4°30S 37°10E **268** C4
Manyara, L. *Tanzania* 3°40S 35°50E **268** C4
Manyara △ *Tanzania* 3°35S 35°50E **268** C4
Manyas *Turkey* 40°2N 27°59E **203** F11
Manyas Gölü = Kus Gölü
Turkey 40°10N 27°55E **203** F11
Manyava *Ukraine* 48°39N 24°21E **183** B9
Manych → *Russia* 47°13N 40°40E **191** G5
Manych-Gudilo, Ozero
Russia 46°24N 42°38E **191** G6
Manyonga → *Tanzania* 4°10S 34°15E **268** C3
Manyoni *Tanzania* 5°45S 34°55E **268** D3
Manzai *Pakistan* 32°12N 70°15E **242** C4
Manzala, Bahra el *Egypt* 31°10N 31°56E **256** H7
Manzanar ⌂ *U.S.A.* 36°44N 118°9W **306** J7
Manzanares *Spain* 39°2N 3°22W **195** F7
Manzanares, Canal de
Spain 40°19N 3°38W **127** C2
Manzaneda *Spain* 42°12N 7°15W **194** C3
Manzanilla Pt. *Trin. & Tob.* 10°31N 61°1W **323** t
Manzanillo *Cuba* 20°20N 77°31W **320** B4
Manzanillo *Colima,*
Mexico 19°3N 104°20W **318** D4
Manzanillo *Venezuela* 11°9N 63°54W **329** a
Manzanillo, Pta. *Panama* 9°30N 79°40W **320** E4
Manzano Mts. *U.S.A.* 34°40N 106°20W **305** J10
Manzarīyeh *Iran* 34°53N 50°50E **247** C6
Manzhouli *China* 49°35N 117°25E **219** B12
Manzini *Swaziland* 26°30S 31°25E **271** C5
Manzouli = Manzhouli
China 49°35N 117°25E **219** B12
Manzur Vadisi △ *Turkey* 39°10N 39°30E **246** B3
Mao *Chad* 14°4N 15°19E **259** F3
Maó *Spain* 39°53N 4°16E **206** B5
Mao Mausoleum *Beijing, China* **114** c3
Maoka = Kholmsk
Russia 47°40N 142°5E **215** E15
Maoke, Pegunungan
Indonesia 3°40S 137°30E **231** E9
Maolin *China* 43°58N 123°30E **227** C12
Maoming *China* 21°50N 110°54E **229** G8
Maopi T'ou *China* 21°56N 120°43E **225** E2
Maouri, Dallol → *Niger* 12°5N 3°30E **263** C5
Maoxian *China* 31°41N 103°49E **228** B4
Maoxing *China* 45°28N 124°40E **227** B13
Map *Micronesia* 9°35N 138°10E **287** R16
Mapalma
Dem. Rep. of the Congo 2°3N 24°30E **264** B4
Mapam Yumco *China* 30°45N 81°28E **243** D9
Mapastepec *Mexico* 15°26N 92°54W **319** D6
Mapfongui *Gabon* 1°15S 12°59E **264** C2
Maphrao, Ko *Thailand* 7°56N 98°26E **237** a
Mapia, Kepulauan
Indonesia 0°50N 134°20E **231** D8
Mapimí *Mexico* 25°49N 103°51W **318** B4
Mapimí, Bolsón de
Mexico 27°0N 104°15W **318** B4
Maping *China* 31°34N 113°32E **229** B9
Mapinga *Tanzania* 6°40S 39°12E **268** D4
Mapinhane *Mozam.* 22°20S 35°0E **271** B6
Mapire *Venezuela* 7°45N 64°42W **329** B5
Maple → *U.S.A.* 42°59N 84°57W **311** B12
Maple Creek *Canada* 49°55N 109°29W **297** D7
Maple Valley *U.S.A.* 47°25N 122°3W **306** C4
Mapleton *U.S.A.* 44°2N 123°52W **304** D2
Mapo *S. Korea* 37°32N 126°56E **137** B1
Mapoon ☼ *Australia* 11°44S 142°8E **280** A3
Mapourika, L. *N.Z.* 43°16S 170°12E **285** D5
Maprik *Papua N. G.* 3°44S 143°3E **286** B2
Mapuca *India* 15°36N 73°46E **245** G1
Mapuera → *Brazil* 1°5S 57°2W **329** D6
Mapulanguene *Mozam.* 24°29S 32°6E **271** B5
Mapungubwe △ *S. Africa* 22°12S 29°22E **271** B4
Maputo *Mozam.* 25°58S 32°32E **271** C5
Maputo □ *Mozam.* 26°0S 32°25E **271** C5
Maputo, B. de *Mozam.* 25°50S 32°45E **271** C5
Maputo ⌂ *Mozam.* 26°23S 32°48E **271** C5
Maqanshy *Kazakhstan* 46°47N 82°1E **217** C10
Maqat *Kazakhstan* 47°39N 53°19E **187** E9
Maqên *China* 34°24N 100°6E **218** E9
Maqên Gangri *China* 34°55N 99°18E **218** E8
Maqiaohe *China* 44°40N 130°30E **227** B16
Maqnā *Si. Arabia* 28°25N 34°50E **251** K5
Maqran, W. → *Si. Arabia* 20°55N 47°12E **248** B4
Maqteïr *Mauritania* 21°50N 11°40W **260** D2
Maqu *China* 33°52N 101°42E **218** E9
Maquan He = Brahmaputra →
Asia 23°40N 90°35E **241** D3
Maqueda *Spain* 40°4N 4°22W **194** E6
Maqueda Channel *Phil.* 13°42N 124°1E **232** E5
Maquela do Zombo *Angola* 6°0S 15°15E **265** D3
Maquinchao *Argentina* 41°15S 68°50W **336** B3
Maquoketa *U.S.A.* 42°4N 90°40W **310** B6
Mar *Canada* 44°49N 81°12W **312** B3
Mar, Serra do *Brazil* 25°30S 49°0W **335** B6
Mar Chiquita, L.
Argentina 30°40S 62°50W **334** C3
Mar del Plata *Argentina* 38°0S 57°30W **334** D4
Mar Menor *Spain* 37°40N 0°45W **197** H4
Mar Vista *U.S.A.* 34°0N 118°25W **126** B2
Mara *Guyana* 6°0N 57°36W **329** B6
Mara *India* 28°11N 94°14E **241** A5
Mara *Tanzania* 1°30S 34°32E **268** C3
Mara □ *Tanzania* 1°45S 34°20E **268** C3
Maraã *Brazil* 1°52S 65°25W **328** D4
Maraa *Tahiti* 17°46S 149°34W **289** e
Marabá *Brazil* 5°20S 49°5W **332** C2
Marabahan *Indonesia* 3°0S 114°45E **235** C4
Maraboon, L. *Australia* 23°41S 148°0E **280** C4
Maracá, I. de *Brazil* 2°10N 50°30W **329** C7
Maracaibo *Venezuela* 10°40N 71°37W **328** A3
Maracaibo, L. de *Venezuela* 9°40N 71°30W **328** B3
Maracaju *Brazil* 21°38S 55°9W **335** A4
Maracajú, Serra de *Brazil* 20°57S 55°1W **331** E6
Maracanã *Pará, Brazil* 0°46S 47°27W **332** B2
Maracanã *Rio de J., Brazil* 22°54S 43°13W **135** B1
Maracanaú *Brazil* 3°52S 38°38W **332** B4
Maracás *Brazil* 13°26S 40°18W **333** D3
Maracas *Trin. & Tob.* 10°41N 61°24W **323** t
Maracas → *Trin. & Tob.* 10°34N 61°25W **323** t
Maracas B. *Trin. & Tob.* 10°45N 61°26W **323** t
Maracas Bay Village
Trin. & Tob. 10°46N 61°28W **323** t
Maracas Falls *Trin. & Tob.* 10°44N 61°24W **323** t
Maracay *Venezuela* 10°15N 67°28W **328** A4
Maracena *Spain* 37°12N 3°38W **195** H7
Marādah *Libya* 29°15N 19°15E **258** C3
Maradi *Niger* 13°29N 7°20E **263** C6
Maradi □ *Niger* 14°15N 7°15E **263** C6
Marāgheh *Iran* 37°30N 46°12E **213** D12
Maragogipe *Brazil* 12°46S 38°55W **333** D4
Marāh *Si. Arabia* 25°0N 45°35E **246** E5
Marahoue △ *Ivory C.* 8°0N 7°8W **262** D3
Marais du Cotentin et du Bessin ⌂
France 49°10N 1°30W **172** C5
Marais Poitevin, Val de Sèvre et
Vendée ⌂ *France* 46°18N 0°35W **174** B3
Maraisburg = Hofmeyr
S. Africa 31°39S 25°50E **270** D4
Marajó, B. de *Brazil* 1°0S 48°30W **332** B2
Marajo, I. de *Brazil* 1°0S 49°30W **332** B2
Marākand *Iran* 38°51N 45°16E **246** B5
Marakele △ *S. Africa* 24°30S 25°30E **271** D4
Maralal *Kenya* 1°0N 36°38E **268** B4
Maralinga *Australia* 30°13S 131°32E **279** F5
Maralinga Tjarutja ☼
Australia 29°30S 131°0E **279** E5
Maram *India* 25°25N 94°6E **241** C5
Marama *Australia* 35°10S 140°10E **282** C4
Maramag *Phil.* 7°46N 125°0E **233** H5
Maramaraereğlisi *Turkey* 40°57N 27°57E **203** F11
Maramasike *Solomon Is.* 9°30S 161°25E **287** M11
Marambio *Antarctica* 64°0S 56°0W **151** C18
Maramureş □ *Romania* 47°45N 24°0E **183** C9
Maran *Malaysia* 3°35N 102°45E **237** L4
Marana *U.S.A.* 32°27N 111°13W **305** K8
Maranboy *Australia* 14°40S 132°39E **278** B5
Maranchón *Spain* 41°6N 2°15W **196** D2
Marand *Iran* 38°30N 45°45E **213** C11
Marandochori *Greece* 38°38N 20°39E **207** B2
Maranello *Italy* 44°32N 10°52E **198** D7
Marang *Malaysia* 5°12N 103°13E **237** K4
Maranguape *Brazil* 3°55S 38°50W **332** B4
Maranhão = São Luís
Brazil 2°39S 44°15W **332** B3
Maranhão □ *Brazil* 5°0S 46°0W **332** C2
Marano, L. di *Italy* 45°44N 13°10E **199** C10
Maranoa → *Australia* 27°50S 148°37E **281** D4
Marañón → *Peru* 4°30S 73°35W **330** A3
Marão *Mozam.* 24°18S 34°2E **271** B5
Maraoli *India* 19°2N 72°53E **130** A2
Marapi → *Brazil* 0°37N 55°58W **329** C6
Marari *Brazil* 5°43S 67°47W **330** B4
Maraş = Kahramanmaraş
Turkey 37°37N 36°53E **212** D7
Mărăşeşti *Romania* 45°52N 27°14E **183** E12
Maratea *Italy* 39°59N 15°43E **201** C8
Marateca *Portugal* 38°34N 8°40W **195** G2
Marathasa *Cyprus* 34°59N 32°51E **207** F8
Marathia, Akra *Greece* 37°39N 20°50E **207** D2
Marathokambos *Greece* 37°43N 26°42E **205** D8
Marathon *Queens.,*
Australia 20°51S 143°32E **280** C3
Marathon *Ont., Canada* 48°44N 86°23W **298** C2
Marathon *Fla., U.S.A.* 24°43N 81°5W **317** L8
Marathon *N.Y., U.S.A.* 42°27N 76°2W **313** D8
Marathon *Tex., U.S.A.* 30°12N 103°15W **314** F3
Marathonas *Greece* 38°11N 23°58E **204** C5
Marathóvounos *Cyprus* 35°13N 33°37E **207** E9
Maratua *Indonesia* 2°10N 118°35E **235** B5
Maraú *Brazil* 14°6S 39°0W **333** D4
Marau *Indonesia* 2°9S 110°42E **235** C4
Marau *Solomon Is.* 10°31S 161°31E **287** N11
Maraval *Trin. & Tob.* 10°42N 61°31W **323** t
Maraval → *Trin. & Tob.* 10°39N 61°32W **323** t
Maravari *Solomon Is.* 7°50S 156°42E **287** L9
Maravatío *Mexico* 19°54N 100°27W **318** D4
Marawi City *Phil.* 8°0N 124°21E **233** G5
Marāwih *U.A.E.* 24°18N 53°18E **247** E7
Marazliyivka *Ukraine* 46°8N 30°3E **183** D15
Marbella *Spain* 36°30N 4°57W **195** J6
Marble Bar *Australia* 21°9S 119°44E **278** D2
Marblehead *Mass.,*
U.S.A. 42°29N 70°51W **313** D14
Marblehead *Ohio, U.S.A.* 41°32N 82°44W **312** E2
Mårbu *Norway* 60°11N 8°9E **164** D5
Marburg = Maribor
Slovenia 46°36N 15°40E **199** B12
Marburg *Germany* 50°47N 8°46E **178** E4
Marca, Pta. do *Angola* 16°31S 11°43E **265** F2
Marcal → *Hungary* 47°41N 17°40E **182** C2
Marcali *Hungary* 46°35N 17°25E **182** D2
Marcapata *Peru* 13°31S 70°52W **330** C3
Marcaria *Italy* 45°7N 10°32E **198** C7
Mărcăuţi *Moldova* 48°20N 27°14E **183** B12
Marcelin *Poland* 52°19N 20°59E **143** B1
Marceline *U.S.A.* 39°43N 92°57W **310** E4
March *U.K.* 52°33N 0°5E **169** E8
Marchal
Dem. Rep. of the Congo 5°16S 14°58E **265** D2
Marchand = Rommani
Morocco 33°31N 6°40W **260** B3
Marche *France* 46°5N 1°20E **174** B5
Marche □ *Italy* 43°30N 13°15E **199** E10
Marché Bonsecours *Montréal, Canada* **130** b3
Marche-en-Famenne
Belgium 50°14N 5°19E **170** D5
Marchena *Spain* 37°18N 5°23W **195** H5
Marchena, Canal de
Ecuador 0°19N 90°12W **330** a
Marchena, I. *Ecuador* 0°19N 90°29W **330** a
Marches = Marche □
Italy 43°30N 13°15E **199** E10
Marchesale ⌂ *Italy* 38°32N 16°13E **201** D9
Marciana Marina *Italy* 42°48N 10°12E **198** F7
Marcianise *Italy* 41°2N 14°17E **201** A7
Marcigny *France* 46°17N 4°2E **173** F11
Marcillat-en-Combraille
France 46°12N 2°38E **173** F9
Marck *France* 50°57N 1°57E **173** B8
Marckolsheim *France* 48°10N 7°30E **173** D14
Marco Island *U.S.A.* 25°58N 81°44W **317** K8
Marco Rondon *Brazil* 12°0S 60°56W **331** C5
Marcona *Peru* 15°10S 75°0W **330** D3
Marcos Juárez *Argentina* 32°42S 62°5W **334** C3
Mărculeşti *Moldova* 47°52N 28°14E **183** C13
Marcus Baker, Mt.
U.S.A. 61°26N 147°45W **303** F11
Marcus I. = Minami-Tori-Shima
Pac. Oc. 24°20N 153°58E **288** E7
Marcy, Mt. *U.S.A.* 44°7N 73°56W **313** B11
Mardan *Pakistan* 34°20N 72°0E **242** B5
Mardarivka *Ukraine* 47°32N 29°44E **183** C14
Mardie *Australia* 21°12S 115°59E **278** D2
Mardin *Turkey* 37°20N 40°43E **213** D9
Mårdsjö *Sweden* 63°18N 15°35E **162** A9
Maré, Î. *N. Cal.* 21°30S 168°0E **277** E12
Marécchia → *Italy* 44°4N 12°34E **199** D9
Marechal Deodoro *Brazil* 9°43S 35°54W **332** C4
Marechal Floriano = Piranhas
Brazil 9°27S 37°46W **332** C4
Maree, L. *U.K.* 57°40N 5°26W **167** D3
Mareeba *Australia* 16°59S 145°28E **280** B4
Mareeg *Somalia* 3°46N 47°18E **267** D6
Mareetsane *S. Africa* 26°9S 25°25E **270** C4
Mareil-Marly *France* 48°52N 2°4E **134** A1
Maremma *Italy* 42°30N 11°30E **199** F8
Maremma ⌂ *Italy* 42°35N 11°8E **198** F8
Maréna *Kayes, Mali* 14°36N 10°45W **262** C2
Maréna *Koulikouro, Mali* 13°55N 7°20W **262** C3
Marengo *Ind., U.S.A.* 38°22N 86°21W **311** F10
Marengo *Iowa, U.S.A.* 41°48N 92°4W **310** C4
Marennes *France* 45°49N 1°7W **174** C2
Marerano *Madag.* 21°23S 44°52E **272** C1
Maréttimo *Italy* 37°58N 12°4E **200** E5
Mareuil *France* 45°26N 0°29E **174** C4
Marfa *U.S.A.* 30°19N 104°1W **314** F2
Marganets = Marhanets
Ukraine 47°40N 34°40E **189** J8
Margao = Madgaon *India* 15°12N 73°58E **245** G1
Margaret → *Australia* 18°9S 125°41E **278** C4
Margaret Bay *Canada* 51°20N 127°35W **296** C3
Margaret I. = Margitsziget *Hungary* **117** a2
Margaret L. *Canada* 58°56N 115°25W **296** B5
Margaret River *Australia* 33°57S 115°4E **279** F2
Margareten *Austria* 48°11N 16°20E **142** A2
Margarita, I. de *Venezuela* 11°0N 64°0W **329** a
Margariti *Greece* 39°22N 20°26E **204** B2
Margaritovo *Russia* 43°25N 134°45E **220** C7
Margate *KwaZulu Natal,*
S. Africa 30°50S 30°20E **271** D5
Margate *Kent, U.K.* 51°23N 1°23E **169** F9
Margate *Fla., U.S.A.* 26°15N 80°12W **317** J9
Margeride, Mts. de la
France 44°43N 3°38E **174** D7
Marggrabowa = Olecko
Poland 54°2N 22°31E **184** D9
Margherita *India* 27°16N 95°40E **241** B5
Margherita di Savóia *Italy* 41°22N 16°9E **201** A9
Margherita Pk. *Uganda* 0°22N 29°51E **268** B3
Marghilon *Uzbekistan* 40°27N 71°42E **217** D8
Marghita *Romania* 47°22N 22°22E **182** C7
Margitsziget *Hungary* **117** a2
Margonin *Poland* 52°58N 17°5E **185** F4
Margosatubig *Phil.* 7°34N 123°10E **233** H4
Māргow, Dasht-e *Afghan.* 30°40N 62°30E **240** C1
Marguerite *Canada* 52°30N 122°25W **296** C4
Marhanets *Ukraine* 47°40N 34°40E **189** J8
Marhoum *Algeria* 34°27N 0°11W **261** B4
Mari *Papua N. G.* 9°11S 141°42E **286** E1
Mārī' *Syria* 36°29N 37°10E **250** B8
Mari El □ *Russia* 56°30N 48°0E **190** B8
Mari Indus *Pakistan* 32°57N 71°34E **242** C4
Mari Republic = Mari El □
Russia 56°30N 48°0E **190** B8
Maria *Austria* 48°11N 16°21E **142** A2
Maria, Îs. *French Polynesia* 21°48S 154°41W **289** f
María, Sa. de *Spain* 37°39N 2°14W **197** H2
Maria Aurora *Phil.* 15°48N 121°28E **232** D3
María de la Salut *Spain* 39°40N 3°5E **206** B4
María Elena *Chile* 22°18S 69°40W **334** A2
María Grande *Argentina* 31°45S 59°55W **334** C4
Maria I. *N. Terr., Australia* 14°52S 135°45E **280** A2
Maria I. *Tas., Australia* 42°35S 148°0E **281** G4
Maria Is. *St. Lucia* 13°44N 60°56W **323** m
Maria Island △ *Australia* 42°38S 148°5E **281** G4
Maria Pereira = Mombaça
Brazil 5°43S 39°45W **332** C4
Maria Theresiopel = Subotica
Serbia 46°6N 19°39E **182** D4
Maria van Diemen, C.
N.Z. 34°29S 172°40E **284** A1
Mariager *Denmark* 56°40N 9°59E **163** H3
Mariager Fjord *Denmark* 56°42N 10°19E **163** H4
Mariahilferstrasse *Vienna, Austria* **142** b1
Mariakani *Kenya* 3°50S 39°27E **268** C4
Mariala △ *Australia* 25°57S 145°2E **281** D4
Marian *Australia* 21°9S 148°57E **280** b
Marian L. *Canada* 63°0N 116°15W **296** A5
Mariana Islands *Pac. Oc.* 15°15N 145°48E **302** a
Mariana Trench *Pac. Oc.* 13°0N 145°0E **302** a
Mariani *India* 26°39N 94°19E **241** B5
Marianica, Cord. = Morena, Sierra
Spain 38°20N 4°0W **195** G7
Marianna *Ark., U.S.A.* 34°46N 90°46W **315** D9
Marianna *Fla., U.S.A.* 30°46N 85°14W **316** E4
Mariannelund *Sweden* 57°37N 15°35E **163** G9
Mariánské Lázně
Czech Rep. 49°58N 12°41E **180** B5
Marias → *U.S.A.* 47°56N 110°30W **304** C8
Marías, Is. *Mexico* 21°25N 106°28W **318** C3
Mariato, Punta *Panama* 7°12N 80°52W **320** E3
Mariazell *Austria* 47°47N 15°19E **180** D8
Ma'rib *Yemen* 15°25N 45°21E **248** D4
Ma'rib □ *Yemen* 15°25N 45°21E **248** D4
Maribo *Denmark* 54°48N 11°30E **163** K5
Maribor *Slovenia* 46°36N 15°40E **199** B12
Maricaban I. *Phil.* 13°39N 120°53E **232** E3
Maricao *Puerto Rico* 18°11N 66°59W **321** b
Marico → *Africa* 23°35S 26°57E **270** B4
Maricopa *Ariz., U.S.A.* 33°4N 112°3W **305** K7
Maricopa *Calif., U.S.A.* 35°4N 119°24W **307** K7
Maridalen *Norway* 59°59N 10°45E **133** A3
Maridalsvatnet *Norway* 59°59N 10°46E **133** A3
Marîdî *South Sudan* 4°55N 29°25E **257** G2
Marîdî, Wadi →
South Sudan 6°15N 29°21E **257** F2
Marié → *Brazil* 0°27S 66°26W **328** D4
Marie Byrd Land
Antarctica 79°30S 125°0W **151** D14
Marie-Galante *Guadeloupe* 15°56N 61°16W **322** e
Marie-Galante, Canal de
Guadeloupe 16°0N 61°25W **322** e
Mariecourt = Kangiqsujuaq
Canada 61°30N 72°0W **295** E17
Mariefred *Sweden* 59°15N 17°12E **162** E11
Mariehamn *Finland* 60°5N 19°55E **161** F18
Marieholm *Sweden* 55°53N 13°10E **163** J7
Mariembourg *Belgium* 50°6N 4°31E **170** D4
Marienbad = Mariánské Lázně
Czech Rep. 49°58N 12°41E **180** B5
Marienberg *Germany* 50°39N 13°9E **178** E9
Marienburg = Malbork
Poland 54°3N 19°1E **184** D6
Mariendorf *Germany* 52°26N 13°23E **115** B3
Marienfelde *Germany* 52°24N 13°23E **115** B3
Marienplatz *Munich, Germany* **131** b2
Mariental *Namibia* 24°36S 18°0E **270** B2
Marienville *U.S.A.* 41°28N 79°8W **312** E5
Mariestad *Sweden* 58°43N 13°50E **163** F7
Marietta *Ga., U.S.A.* 33°57N 84°33W **316** B5
Marietta *Ohio, U.S.A.* 39°25N 81°27W **309** F13
Marieville *Canada* 45°26N 73°10W **313** A11
Mariga → *Nigeria* 9°40N 5°55E **263** C6
Marignane *France* 43°25N 5°13E **175** E9
Marigot *Dominica* 15°33N 61°18W **323** k
Marigot *Guadeloupe* 16°5N 61°46W **322** e
Marigot *St.-Martin* 18°4N 63°5W **322** a
Marigot Bay *St. Lucia* 13°58N 61°1W **323** m
Marihatag *Phil.* 8°48N 126°18E **233** G6
Mariinsk *Russia* 56°10N 87°20E **214** D9
Mariinsk Water = Volgo-Baltiyskiy
Kanal *Russia* 60°0N 38°0E **188** B9
Mariinskiy Posad *Russia* 56°10N 47°45E **190** B8
Marijampolė *Lithuania* 54°33N 23°19E **184** D10
Marijampolė □ *Lithuania* 54°34N 23°21E **184** D10
Marikina *Phil.* 14°37N 121°5E **127** B2
Marikina → *Phil.* 14°33N 121°3E **127** B2
Marília *Brazil* 22°13S 50°0W **335** A6
Marimba *Angola* 8°28S 17°8E **265** D3
Marín *Spain* 42°23N 8°42W **194** C2
Marin, Cul-de-Sac du
Martinique 14°27N 60°53W **322** j
Marin City *U.S.A.* 37°52N 122°30W **136** A1
Marin Pen. *U.S.A.* 37°50N 122°30W **136** A1
Marina *U.S.A.* 36°41N 121°48W **306** J5
Marina Bay Sands
Singapore 1°17N 103°51E **138** B3
Marina del Rey *U.S.A.* 33°58N 118°27W **126** C2
Marinduque *Phil.* 13°25N 122°0E **231** B6
Marinduque □ *Phil.* 13°18N 122°0E **232** E4
Marine City *U.S.A.* 42°43N 82°30W **312** D2
Marine Drive *Mumbai, India* **130** b1
Marineland *U.S.A.* 29°40N 81°13W **316** F8
Marineo *Italy* 37°57N 13°25E **200** E6
Marinette *U.S.A.* 45°6N 87°38W **308** C10
Maringá *Brazil* 23°26S 52°2W **335** A5
Maringa →
Dem. Rep. of the Congo 1°14N 19°48E **264** B3
Marinha Grande *Portugal* 39°45N 8°56W **194** F2
Marinho dos Abrolhos △
Brazil 17°50S 39°0W **333** E4
Marino *Dublin, Ireland* 53°22N 6°14W **120** A2
Marino *Italy* 41°46N 12°39E **199** G9
Marion *Ala., U.S.A.* 32°38N 87°19W **315** E11
Marion *Ark., U.S.A.* 35°13N 90°12W **308** H8
Marion *Ill., U.S.A.* 37°44N 88°56W **310** G8
Marion *Ind., U.S.A.* 40°32N 85°40W **311** D11
Marion *Iowa, U.S.A.* 42°2N 91°36W **310** B5
Marion *Kans., U.S.A.* 38°21N 97°1W **308** F5
Marion *N.C., U.S.A.* 35°41N 82°1W **315** D13
Marion *Ohio, U.S.A.* 40°35N 83°8W **311** D13
Marion *S.C., U.S.A.* 34°11N 79°24W **315** D15
Marion *Va., U.S.A.* 36°50N 81°31W **309** G13
Marion, L. *U.S.A.* 33°28N 80°10W **316** B9
Marion Bay *Australia* 35°12S 136°59E **282** C2
Marion I. *Ind. Oc.* 47°0S 38°0E **273** J2
Maripa *Venezuela* 7°26N 65°9W **329** B4
Maripasoula *Fr. Guiana* 3°40N 54°4W **329** C7
Maripipi I. *Phil.* 11°47N 124°19E **233** F5
Mariposa *U.S.A.* 37°29N 119°58W **306** H7
Mariscal Estigarribia
Paraguay 22°3S 60°40W **334** A3
Marisco, Ponta do *Brazil* 23°1S 43°18W **135** C1
Maritas, Laguna de las
Venezuela 10°55N 63°56W **329** a
Maritime Alps = Maritimes, Alpes
Europe 44°10N 7°10E **175** D11
Maritimes, Alpes *Europe* 44°10N 7°10E **175** D11
Maritsa = Evros →
Greece 41°40N 26°34E **203** F10
Maritsa *Greece* 36°22N 28°8E **206** E12
Mariupol *Ukraine* 47°5N 37°31E **189** J9
Marīvān *Iran* 35°30N 46°25E **213** E12
Mariveles *Phil.* 14°26N 120°29E **232** D3
Marj 'Uyūn *Lebanon* 33°21N 35°34E **250** E6
Marjan = Wazikhwah
Afghan. 32°11N 68°21E **240** B3
Mark Twain L. *U.S.A.* 39°28N 91°55W **310** E5
Marka *Si. Arabia* 18°14N 41°19E **256** D5
Marka *Somalia* 1°48N 44°50E **267** D5
Markam *China* 29°42N 98°38E **228** C2
Markapur *India* 15°44N 79°19E **245** G4
Markaryd *Sweden* 56°28N 13°35E **163** H7
Markat *Albania* 39°44N 20°12E **206** B10
Markazī □ *Iran* 34°0N 49°30E **247** C6
Markdale *Canada* 44°19N 80°39W **312** B4
Marked Tree *U.S.A.* 35°32N 90°25W **315** D9
Markelsdorfer Huk
Germany 54°33N 11°4E **178** A7
Market Drayton *U.K.* 52°54N 2°29W **168** E5
Market Harborough *U.K.* 52°29N 0°55W **169** E7
Market Rasen *U.K.* 53°24N 0°20W **168** D7
Markham *Ont., Canada* 43°52N 79°16W **141** A2
Markham *Ill., U.S.A.* 41°36N 87°42W **119** D2
Markham → *Papua N. G.* 6°41S 147°2E **286** D4
Markham, Mt. *Antarctica* 83°0S 164°0E **151** E11
Marki *Poland* 52°19N 21°6E **143** B2
Märkisch Friedland = Mirosławiec
Poland 53°20N 16°5E **184** E3
Märkische Schweiz ⌂
Germany 52°34N 14°2E **178** C10
Markit *China* 38°54N 77°40E **217** E9
Markkleeberg *Germany* 51°16N 12°23E **178** D8
Markland Wood *Canada* 43°38N 79°34W **141** B1
Markleeville *U.S.A.* 38°42N 119°47W **306** G7
Markopoulo *Greece* 37°53N 23°57E **204** D5
Markounda *C.A.R.* 7°39N 16°55E **264** A3
Markovac *Serbia* 44°14N 21°7E **202** B5
Markovo *Russia* 64°40N 170°24E **215** C17
Markoye *Burkina Faso* 14°39N 0°2E **263** C5
Marks *Russia* 51°45N 46°50E **190** E8
Marksshtadt = Marks
Russia 51°45N 46°50E **190** E8
Marksville *U.S.A.* 31°8N 92°4W **314** F8
Markt Schwaben
Germany 48°11N 11°52E **179** G7
Marktoberdorf *Germany* 47°45N 10°37E **179** H6
Marktredwitz *Germany* 50°1N 12°6E **179** E8
Marl *Germany* 51°39N 7°4E **178** D3
Marla *Australia* 27°19S 133°33E **281** D1
Marlbank *Canada* 44°26N 77°6W **312** B7
Marlboro *U.S.A.* 41°36N 73°59W **313** E11
Marlborough *Queens.,*
Australia 22°46S 149°52E **280** C4
Marlborough *Wilts., U.K.* 51°25N 1°43W **169** F6
Marlborough *Mass.,*
U.S.A. 42°21N 71°33W **313** D13
Marlborough □ *N.Z.* 41°40S 173°50E **285** B8
Marlborough Downs *U.K.* 51°27N 1°53W **169** F6
Marle *France* 49°43N 3°47E **173** C10
Marlin *U.S.A.* 31°18N 96°54W **314** F6
Marlow *Mecklenburg-Vorpommern,*
Germany 54°9N 12°33E **178** A8
Marlow *Bucks., U.K.* 51°34N 0°46W **169** F7
Marlow *Okla., U.S.A.* 34°39N 97°58W **314** D6
Marly, Forêt de *France* 48°52N 2°2E **134** A1
Marly-le-Roi *France* 48°52N 2°5E **134** A1
Marmagao *India* 15°25N 73°56E **245** G1
Marmande *France* 44°30N 0°10E **174** D4
Marmara *Turkey* 40°35N 27°34E **203** F11
Marmara, Sea of = Marmara Denizi
Turkey 40°45N 28°15E **203** F12
Marmara Denizi *Turkey* 40°45N 28°15E **203** F12
Marmara Gölü *Turkey* 38°37N 28°2E **205** C10
Marmaris *Turkey* 36°50N 28°14E **205** E10
Marmaris Limanı *Turkey* 36°50N 28°19E **205** E10
Marmelos → *Brazil* 6°6S 61°46W **331** B5
Marmion, Mt. *Australia* 29°16S 119°50E **279** E2
Marmion L. *Canada* 48°55N 91°20W **298** C1
Marmolada, Mte. *Italy* 46°26N 11°51E **199** B8
Marmolejo *Spain* 38°3N 4°13W **195** G6
Marmora *Canada* 44°28N 77°41W **312** B7
Mármora, La *Italy* 39°59N 9°20E **200** C2
Marnay *France* 47°16N 5°48E **173** E12
Marne *Germany* 53°56N 9°2E **178** B5
Marne □ *France* 48°50N 4°10E **173** D11
Marne → *France* 48°47N 2°29E **173** D9
Marne-la-Vallée *France* 48°50N 2°37E **134** A4
Marneuli *Georgia* 41°30N 44°48E **191** K7
Marnia = Maghnia
Algeria 34°50N 1°43W **261** B4
Marnoo *Australia* 36°40S 142°52E **282** D5
Maro *Chad* 8°30N 19°0E **259** G3
Maro Reef *U.S.A.* 25°25N 170°35W **302** F9
Maro Rosa *Brazil* 13°58S 49°9W **333** D2
Maroa *Ill., U.S.A.* 40°2N 88°57W **310** D8
Maroa *Venezuela* 2°43N 67°33W **328** C4
Maroala *Madag.* 15°23S 47°59E **272** B2
Maroantsetra *Madag.* 15°26S 49°44E **272** B2
Maroelaboom *Namibia* 19°15S 18°53E **270** A2
Marofandilia *Madag.* 20°7S 44°34E **272** C1
Marojejy ⌂ *Madag.* 14°26S 49°21E **272** A2
Marokau *French Polynesia* 18°2S 142°17W **289** f
Marolambo *Madag.* 20°2S 48°7E **272** C2
Marolles-en-Brie *France* 48°44N 2°33E **134** B4

Maromandia *Madag.* 14°13S 48°5E **272** A2
Maromokotro *Madag.* 14°0S 49°0E **272** A2
Marondera *Zimbabwe* 18°5S 31°42E **269** F3
Maroni ➔ *Fr. Guiana* 5°30N 54°0W **329** B7
Maronia *Greece* 40°53N 25°30E **203** F9
Maronne ➔ *France* 45°5N 1°56E **174** C5
Maroochydore *Australia* 26°29S 153°5E **281** D5
Maroon Town *Jamaica* 18°22N 77°48W **320** a
Maroona *Australia* 37°27S 142°54E **282** D5
Maros *Indonesia* 5°0S 119°34E **235** C5
Maros ➔ *Hungary* 46°15N 20°13E **182** D5
Marosakoa *Madag.* 15°26S 46°38E **272** B2
Maroseranana *Madag.* 18°32S 48°51E **272** B2
Maróstica *Italy* 45°44N 11°40E **199** C8
Marotandrano *Madag.* 16°10S 48°50E **272** B2
Marotiri, Îs. = Bass, Îs. de
French Polynesia 27°55S 143°26W **289** f
Maroua *Cameroon* 10°40N 14°20E **259** F2
Maroubra *Australia* 33°56S 151°16E **139** B2
Marovato *Madag.* 15°48S 48°5E **272** B2
Marovoay *Madag.* 16°6S 46°39E **272** B2
Marowijne □ *Suriname* 4°0N 55°0W **329** C7
Marowijne ➔ *Suriname* 5°45N 53°58W **329** B7
Marqakōl *Kazakhstan* 48°45N 85°45E **217** C11
Marquard *S. Africa* 28°40S 27°28E **270** C4
Marquesas Fracture Zone
Pac. Oc. 9°0S 125°0W **289** H15
Marquesas Is. = Marquises, Îs.
French Polynesia 9°30S 140°0W **289** f
Marquesas Keys *U.S.A.* 24°35N 82°10W **317** L7
Marquette *U.S.A.* 46°33N 87°24W **308** B10
Marquette Park *U.S.A.* 41°46N 87°42W **119** C2
Marquis *St. Lucia* 14°2N 60°54W **323** m
Marquis, C. *St. Lucia* 14°3N 60°54W **323** m
Marquis I. *Grenada* 12°5N 61°37W **323** q
Marquise *France* 50°50N 1°40E **173** B8
Marquises, Îs.
French Polynesia 9°30S 140°0W **289** f
Marra, Gebel *South Sudan* 7°20N 27°35E **257** F2
Marra, Pta. da *Angola* 16°31S 11°43E **265** F2
Marra Cr. ➔ *Australia* 30°8S 147°15E **283** A7
Marra-Marra △ *Australia* 33°30S 151°4E **283** B9
Marracuene *Mozam.* 25°45S 32°35E **271** C5
Marradi *Italy* 44°4N 11°37E **199** D8
Marrakech *Morocco* 31°9N 8°0W **260** B3
Marratxí *Spain* 39°39N 2°48E **206** B3
Marrawah *Australia* 40°55S 144°42E **281** G3
Marrecas, Serra das *Brazil* 9°0S 41°0W **332** C3
Marree *Australia* 29°39S 138°1E **281** D2
Marrero *U.S.A.* 29°53N 90°6W **131** B2
Marrickville *Australia* 33°54S 151°9E **139** B1
Marrimane *Mozam.* 22°58S 33°34E **271** B5
Marromeu *Mozam.* 18°15S 36°25E **271** A6
Marromeu △ *Mozam.* 19°0S 36°0E **271** A6
Marroquí, Punta *Spain* 36°0N 5°37W **195** K5
Marrowie Cr. ➔
Australia 33°23S 145°40E **283** B6
Marruás = Porto *Brazil* 3°54S 42°42W **332** B3
Marrubane *Mozam.* 18°0S 37°0E **269** F4
Marrúbiu *Italy* 39°40N 8°35E **200** C1
Marrupa *Mozam.* 13°8S 37°30E **269** E4
Mars B. *Ascension I.* 7°59S 14°24W **153** g
Mars Hill *U.S.A.* 46°31N 67°52W **309** B20
Marsá al Burayqah *Libya* 30°24N 19°37E **258** B3
Marsá 'Alam *Egypt* 25°5N 34°54E **256** B3
Marsá Matrûh *Egypt* 31°19N 27°9E **256** A2
Marsá Sha'b *Sudan* 22°52N 35°47E **256** C4
Marsabit *Kenya* 2°18N 38°0E **268** B4
Marsabit △ *Kenya* 2°23N 37°56E **268** B4
Marsala *Italy* 37°48N 12°26E **200** E5
Marsalforn *Malta* 36°4N 14°16E **206** E7
Mărșani *Romania* 44°1N 24°1E **183** F9
Marsaskala *Malta* 35°52N 14°34E **206** F8
Marsaxlokk *Malta* 35°51N 14°33E **206** F8
Marsaxlokk Bay *Malta* 35°49N 14°33E **206** F8
Marsberg *Germany* 51°28N 8°52E **178** D4
Marsciano *Italy* 42°54N 12°20E **199** F9
Marsden *Australia* 33°47S 147°32E **283** B7
Marsden Point *N.Z.* 35°50S 174°31E **284** B3
Marseillan *France* 43°23N 3°31E **174** E7
Marseille *France* 43°18N 5°23E **175** E9
Marseille-Marignane ✈ (MRS)
France 43°26N 5°14E **175** E9
Marseilles = Marseille
France 43°18N 5°23E **175** E9
Marseilles *U.S.A.* 41°20N 88°43W **311** C8
Marsfield *Australia* 33°46S 151°7E **139** A1
Marsh I. *U.S.A.* 29°34N 91°53W **314** G9
Marsh L. *U.S.A.* 28°29N 81°29W **133** B2
Marshall *Liberia* 6°8N 10°22W **262** D2
Marshall *Alaska, U.S.A.* 61°53N 162°5W **303** F7
Marshall *Ark., U.S.A.* 35°55N 92°38W **314** D8
Marshall *Ill., U.S.A.* 39°23N 87°42W **311** E9
Marshall *Mich., U.S.A.* 42°16N 84°58W **311** B12
Marshall *Minn., U.S.A.* 44°27N 95°47W **308** C6
Marshall *Mo., U.S.A.* 39°7N 93°12W **310** E3
Marshall *Tex., U.S.A.* 32°33N 94°23W **314** E7
Marshall ➔ *Australia* 22°59S 136°59E **280** C2
Marshall, C. *Ecuador* 0°1S 91°12W **330** a
Marshall Bennett Is.
Papua N. G. 8°50S 151°55E **286** E6
Marshall Is. ■ *Pac. Oc.* 9°0N 171°0E **288** G9
Marshalltown *U.S.A.* 42°3N 92°55W **310** B4
Marshallville = Lewisporte
Canada 49°15N 55°3W **299** C8
Marshallville *U.S.A.* 32°27N 83°56W **316** C6
Marshbrook *Zimbabwe* 18°33S 31°9E **271** A5
Marshfield = Coos Bay
U.S.A. 43°22N 124°13W **304** E1
Marshfield *Mo., U.S.A.* 37°15N 92°54W **308** G7
Marshfield *Vt., U.S.A.* 44°20N 72°20W **313** B12
Marshfield *Wis., U.S.A.* 44°40N 90°10W **308** C8
Marshūn *Iran* 36°19N 49°23E **247** B6
Mársico Nuovo *Italy* 40°25N 15°44E **201** B8
Marsouins, R. des ➔
Réunion 21°1S 55°44E **272** f
Märsta *Sweden* 59°37N 17°52E **162** E11
Marstal *Denmark* 54°51N 10°30E **163** K4
Marstrand *Sweden* 57°53N 11°35E **163** G5
Mart *U.S.A.* 31°33N 96°50W **314** F6
Marta ➔ *Italy* 42°14N 11°42E **199** F8
Martaban *Burma* 16°30N 97°35E **241** G6
Martaban, G. of *Burma* 16°5N 96°30E **241** G6
Martano *Italy* 40°12N 18°18E **201** B11
Martapura *Kalimantan Selatan,*
Indonesia 3°22S 114°47E **235** C4
Martapura *Sumatera Selatan,*
Indonesia 4°19S 104°22E **234** C2
Marte *Nigeria* 12°23N 13°46E **263** C7
Marte, Campo de *Brazil* 23°30S 46°38W **137** B2
Marte, R. Gómez, Presa
Mexico 26°10N 99°0W **319** B5
Martel *France* 44°57N 1°37E **174** D5
Martelange *Belgium* 49°49N 5°43E **170** E5
Martellago *Italy* 45°33N 12°9E **199** C9
Martés, Sierra *Spain* 39°20N 1°0W **197** F4
Martesana, Naviglio della
Italy 45°31N 9°17E **128** A2
Martfű *Hungary* 47°1N 20°17E **182** C5
Marthaguy Cr. ➔
Australia 30°16S 147°35E **283** A7
Marthapal *India* 19°24N 81°37E **244** E5
Martha's Vineyard
U.S.A. 41°25N 70°38W **313** E14
Martigné-Ferchaud *France* 47°50N 1°20W **172** E5
Martigny *Switz.* 46°6N 7°3E **179** J3
Martigues *France* 43°24N 5°4E **175** E9
Martil *Morocco* 35°33N 5°15W **260** A3
Martin *Slovak Rep.* 49°6N 18°58E **181** B11
Martin *S. Dak., U.S.A.* 43°11N 101°44W **308** D3
Martin *Tenn., U.S.A.* 36°21N 88°51W **315** C10
Martin ➔ *Spain* 41°18N 0°19W **196** D4
Martin L. *U.S.A.* 32°41N 85°55W **316** C4
Martin Luther King Nat. Historic
Site △ *U.S.A.* 33°45N 84°22W **113** B2
Martin Pt. *U.S.A.* 70°8N 143°16W **303** A12
Martin Vaz *Atl. Oc.* 20°30S 28°51W **152** J9
Martina Franca *Italy* 40°42N 17°20E **201** B10
Martinborough *N.Z.* 41°14S 175°29E **284** H4
Martinez *B. Aires,*
Argentina 34°29S 58°31W **117** A1
Martinez *Calif., U.S.A.* 38°1N 122°8W **306** G4
Martinez *Ga., U.S.A.* 33°31N 82°5W **316** B7
Martinho Campos *Brazil* 19°20S 45°13W **333** E2
Martinique ☒ *W. Indies* 14°40N 61°0W **322** j
Martinique Channel
St. Vincent 12°34N 61°25W **323** n
Martinique Passage
W. Indies 15°15N 61°0W **321** C7
Martinkylä *Finland* 60°17N 24°51E **121** B2
Martinó *Greece* 38°35N 23°12E **204** C5
Martinópolis *Brazil* 22°11S 51°12W **335** A5
Martins Ferry *U.S.A.* 40°6N 80°44W **312** F4
Martinsberg *Austria* 48°22N 15°9E **180** C8
Martinsburg *Pa., U.S.A.* 40°19N 78°20W **312** F6
Martinsburg *W. Va.,*
U.S.A. 39°27N 77°58W **309** F15
Martinsicuro *Italy* 42°54N 13°54E **199** F10
Martinstein *Germany* 48°6N 11°27E **131** B1
Martinsville *Ill., U.S.A.* 39°20N 87°53W **311** E9
Martinsville *Ind., U.S.A.* 39°26N 86°25W **311** E10
Martinsville *Va., U.S.A.* 36°41N 79°52W **309** G14
Marton *N.Z.* 40°4S 175°23E **284** G4
Martorell *Spain* 41°28N 1°56E **196** D6
Martos *Spain* 37°44N 3°58W **195** H7
Martu ☼ *Australia* 22°30S 122°30E **278** D3
Martūbah *Libya* 32°35N 22°46E **258** B4
Martuni *Armenia* 40°8N 45°20E **191** K7
Maru *Nigeria* 12°22N 6°22E **263** C6
Marudi *Malaysia* 4°11N 114°19E **235** B4
Maruf *Afghan.* 31°30N 67°6E **240** C2
Marugame *Japan* 34°15N 133°40E **222** C5
Marui = Pagwi *Papua N. G.* 4°4S 143°2E **286** C2
Maruia ➔ *N.Z.* 41°47S 172°13E **285** B7
Maruim *Brazil* 10°45S 37°5W **332** D4
Maruko *Japan* 35°33N 139°40E **140** B3
Marulan *Australia* 34°43S 150°3E **283** C9
Marum, Mt. *Vanuatu* 16°15S 168°7E **287** F6
Marunga *Angola* 17°23S 20°2E **265** F4
Marungu, Mts.
Dem. Rep. of the Congo 7°30S 30°0E **268** D3
Marunouchi *Tokyo, Japan* **140** b4
Maruoka = Sakai *Japan* 36°9N 136°16E **223** A8
Maruwa ☼ *Australia* 22°30S 127°30E **278** D4
Marv Dasht *Iran* 29°50N 52°40E **247** D7
Marvão = Castelo do Piauí
Brazil 5°20S 41°33W **332** C3
Marvast *Iran* 30°30N 54°15E **247** D7
Marvejols *France* 44°33N 3°19E **174** D7
Marvel Loch *Australia* 31°28S 119°29E **279** F2
Marwar *India* 25°43N 73°45E **242** G5
Mary *Turkmenistan* 37°40N 61°50E **247** B9
Mary Esther *U.S.A.* 30°25N 86°40W **317** E3
Maryborough = Portlaoise
Ireland 53°2N 7°18W **166** C4
Maryborough *Queens.,*
Australia 25°31S 152°37E **281** D5
Maryborough *Vic.,*
Australia 37°3S 143°44E **282** D5
Maryfield *Canada* 49°50N 101°35W **297** D8
Maryino = Pristen *Russia* 51°15N 36°44E **189** G9
Maryino *Russia* 55°40N 37°45E **129** B3
Maryland *Singapore* 1°19N 103°47E **138** B2
Maryland □ *U.S.A.* 39°0N 76°30W **309** F15
Maryland Junction
Zimbabwe 17°45S 30°31E **269** F3
Marylebone *London, U.K.* **125** a2
Marymont *Poland* 52°16N 20°58E **143** B1
Maryport *U.K.* 54°44N 3°28W **168** C4
Mary's Harbour *Canada* 52°18N 55°51W **299** B8
Marysin Wawerski *Poland* 52°14N 21°6E **143** B2
Marystown *Canada* 47°10N 55°10W **299** C8
Marysville *Calif., U.S.A.* 39°9N 121°35W **306** F5
Marysville *Kans., U.S.A.* 39°51N 96°39W **308** F5
Marysville *Mich., U.S.A.* 42°54N 82°29W **312** D2
Marysville *Ohio, U.S.A.* 40°14N 83°22W **311** D13
Marysville *Wash., U.S.A.* 48°3N 122°11W **306** B4
Maryville *Mo., U.S.A.* 40°21N 94°52W **310** D2
Maryville *Tenn., U.S.A.* 35°46N 83°58W **315** D13
Marzahn *Germany* 52°32N 13°34E **115** A4
Marzo, Punta *Colombia* 6°50N 77°42W **328** B2
Masada *Israel* 31°18N 35°21E **251** G6
Mas'ada *Syria* 33°13N 35°45E **250** E6
Masahunga *Tanzania* 2°6S 33°18E **268** C3
Masai *Malaysia* 1°29N 103°55E **237** d
Masai Mara △ *Kenya* 1°25S 35°5E **268** C4
Masai Steppe *Tanzania* 4°30S 36°30E **268** C4
Masaka *Uganda* 0°21S 31°45E **268** C3
Māsāl *Iran* 37°23N 49°8E **213** D12
Masalembo, Kepulauan
Indonesia 5°35S 114°30E **235** D4
Masalima, Kepulauan
Indonesia 5°4S 117°5E **235** D5
Masallı *Azerbaijan* 39°3N 48°40E **213** C13
Masalog Pt. *N. Marianas* 15°1N 145°40E **302** e
Masamba *Indonesia* 2°30S 120°15E **231** E6
Masan *S. Korea* 35°11N 128°32E **224** E4
Masandam, Ra's *Oman* 26°30N 56°30E **247** E8
Masasi *Tanzania* 10°45S 38°52E **269** E4
Masaya *Nic.* 12°0N 86°7W **320** D2
Masba *Nigeria* 11°35N 13°1E **263** C7
Masbate *Phil.* 12°21N 123°36E **232** E4
Masbate □ *Phil.* 12°20N 123°30E **232** E4
Masbate Pass. *Phil.* 12°30N 123°35E **232** E4
Máscali *Italy* 37°45N 15°12E **201** E8
Mascara *Algeria* 35°26N 0°6E **261** A5
Mascara □ *Algeria* 35°25N 0°10E **261** A5
Mascarene Is. *Ind. Oc.* 22°0S 55°0E **254** J9
Mascot *Australia* 33°55S 151°12E **139** B2
Mascota *Mexico* 20°32N 104°49W **318** C4
Mascoutah *U.S.A.* 38°29N 89°48W **310** F7
Masefau B. *Amer. Samoa* 14°15S 170°37W **302** f
Masein *Burma* 23°22N 94°21E **241** D5
Masela *Indonesia* 8°9S 129°51E **231** F7
Maseru *Lesotho* 29°18S 27°30E **270** C4
Masfjorden *Norway* 60°48N 5°18E **164** D2
Mashaba *Zimbabwe* 20°2S 30°29E **269** G3
Mashābih *Si. Arabia* 25°35N 36°30E **246** E3
Mashan *China* 23°40N 108°11E **228** F7
Mashang *China* 36°48N 117°57E **227** F9
Mashar *South Sudan* 9°16N 26°51E **257** F2
Mashatu △ *Botswana* 22°45S 29°5E **271** B4
Mashegu *Nigeria* 10°0N 5°35E **263** D6
Masherbrum *Pakistan* 35°38N 76°18E **243** B7
Mashhad *Iran* 36°20N 59°35E **247** B8
Mashi *Nigeria* 13°0N 7°54E **263** C6
Mashiki *Japan* 32°51N 130°53E **222** E2
Mashīz *Iran* 29°56N 56°37E **247** D8
Mashkel ➔ *Pakistan* 26°2N 65°19E **240** D2
Māshkel, Hāmūn-i-
Pakistan 28°20N 62°56E **240** C1
Mashki Chāh *Pakistan* 29°5N 62°30E **240** C1
Mashonaland Central □
Zimbabwe 17°30S 31°0E **271** A5
Mashonaland East □
Zimbabwe 18°0S 32°0E **271** A5
Mashonaland West □
Zimbabwe 17°30S 29°30E **271** A4
Mashrakh *India* 26°7N 84°48E **243** F11
Mashtaga = Maştağa
Azerbaijan 40°35N 50°1E **191** K10
Masi Manimba
Dem. Rep. of the Congo 4°40S 17°54E **265** C3
Masibi *Angola* 11°6S 22°41E **265** E4
Masig *Australia* 9°45S 143°24E **280** a
Masindi *Uganda* 1°40N 31°43E **268** B3
Masindi Port *Uganda* 1°43N 32°2E **268** B3
Masinga Res. *Kenya* 0°58S 37°38E **268** C4
Masinloc *Phil.* 15°32N 119°57E **232** D2
Maşīrah, Jazīrat *Oman* 21°0N 58°50E **249** B7
Maşīrah, Khalīj *Oman* 20°10N 58°10E **249** B7
Maşīrah, Tur'at *Oman* 20°30N 58°40E **249** B7
Masisea *Peru* 8°35S 74°22W **330** B3
Masisi *Dem. Rep. of the Congo* 1°23S 28°49E **268** C2
Masjed Soleyman *Iran* 31°55N 49°18E **247** D6
Mask, L. *Ireland* 53°36N 9°22W **166** C2
Maskelyne Is. *Vanuatu* 16°32S 167°49E **287** F5
Maski *India* 15°56N 76°46E **245** G3
Maskin *Oman* 23°44N 56°52E **247** F8
Maslen Nos *Bulgaria* 42°18N 27°48E **203** D11
Maslinica *Croatia* 43°24N 16°13E **199** E13
Masmo *Sweden* 59°15N 17°53E **139** B1
Maşna'ah *Yemen* 14°27N 48°17E **249** D5
Masnou = El Masnou
Spain 41°28N 2°20E **196** D7
Masoala, Saikanosy
Madag. 15°45S 50°10E **272** B3
Masoala, Tanjon' i
Madag. 15°59S 50°13E **272** B3
Masoala △ *Madag.* 15°30S 50°12E **272** B3
Masoarivo *Madag.* 19°3S 44°19E **272** B1
Masohi = Amahai
Indonesia 3°20S 128°55E **231** E7
Masomeloka *Madag.* 20°17S 48°37E **272** C2
Mason *Mich., U.S.A.* 42°35N 84°27W **311** B12
Mason *Nev., U.S.A.* 38°56N 119°8W **306** G7
Mason *Ohio, U.S.A.* 39°22N 84°19W **311** E12
Mason *Tex., U.S.A.* 30°45N 99°14W **314** F5
Mason B. *N.Z.* 46°55S 167°45E **285** G2
Mason City *Ill., U.S.A.* 40°12N 89°42W **310** D7
Mason City *Iowa, U.S.A.* 43°9N 93°12W **310** A3
Mason Hall *Trin. & Tob.* 11°13N 60°43W **323** s
Maspalomas *Canary Is.* 27°46N 15°35W **153** e1
Maspalomas, Pta.
Canary Is. 27°43N 15°36W **153** e1
Maspeth *U.S.A.* 40°43N 73°55W **132** B2
Masqat *Oman* 23°37N 58°36E **249** B7
Masr el Gedida *Egypt* 30°5N 31°21E **117** A2
Masr el Qadima *Egypt* 30°0N 31°14E **117** A2
Massa *Congo* 3°45S 15°29E **264** C3
Massa *Italy* 44°1N 10°9E **198** D7
Massa, O. ➔ *Morocco* 30°2N 9°40W **260** B3
Massa Maríttima *Italy* 43°3N 10°52E **198** E7
Massachusetts □ *U.S.A.* 42°30N 72°0W **313** D13
Massachusetts Avenue
Washington, D.C., U.S.A. **143** a2
Massachusetts B. *U.S.A.* 42°25N 70°50W **313** D14
Massachusetts Inst. of Tech.
U.S.A. 42°21N 71°5W **116** A2
Massacre *Dominica* 15°20N 61°25W **323** k
Massafra *Italy* 40°35N 17°7E **201** B10
Massaguet *Chad* 12°28N 15°26E **259** F3
Massakory *Chad* 13°0N 15°49E **259** F3
Massamá *Portugal* 38°45N 9°16W **126** A1
Massamba *Mozam.* 15°58S 33°31E **269** F3
Massanella *Spain* 39°48N 2°51E **206** B3
Massangano *Angola* 9°40S 14°13E **265** D2
Massangena *Mozam.* 21°34S 33°0E **271** B5
Massango *Angola* 8°1S 16°10E **265** D3
Massapê *Brazil* 3°31S 40°19W **332** B3
Massat *France* 42°53N 1°21E **174** F5
Massawa = Mitsiwa
Eritrea 15°35N 39°25E **257** D4
Massena *U.S.A.* 44°56N 74°54W **313** B10
Massenya *Chad* 11°21N 16°9E **259** F3
Masset *Canada* 54°2N 132°10W **296** C2
Masseube *France* 43°25N 0°34E **174** E4
Massey ➔ *Canada* 43°42N 79°19W **141** A3
Massey Hall *Toronto, Canada* **141** a3
Massiac *France* 45°15N 3°11E **174** C7
Massif Central *France* 44°55N 3°0E **174** D7
Massif des Bauges △
France 45°40N 6°10E **173** G13
Massigui *Mali* 11°48N 6°50W **262** C3
Massillon *U.S.A.* 40°48N 81°32W **312** F3
Massima *Gabon* 1°27S 11°33E **264** C2
Massinie, O. ➔ *Algeria* 36°13N 2°12E **261** A5
Massinga *Mozam.* 23°15S 35°22E **271** B6
Massingir *Mozam.* 23°51S 32°4E **271** B5
Masson-Angers *Canada* 45°32N 75°25W **313** A9
Masson I. *Antarctica* 66°10S 93°20E **151** C7
Massouka *Gabon* 1°37S 9°56E **264** C1
Massow = Maszewo *Poland* 53°29N 15°3E **184** E2
Massy *France* 48°43N 2°16E **134** B2
Mastābah *Si. Arabia* 20°49N 39°26E **248** B2
Maştağa *Azerbaijan* 40°35N 50°1E **191** K10
Mastanli = Momchilgrad
Bulgaria 41°33N 25°23E **203** E9
Masterton *N.Z.* 40°56S 175°39E **284** G4
Mastic *U.S.A.* 40°47N 72°54W **313** F12
Mastuj *Pakistan* 36°20N 72°36E **243** A5
Mastung *Pakistan* 29°50N 66°56E **240** E5
Mastūrah *Si. Arabia* 23°7N 38°52E **248** B2
Masty *Belarus* 53°27N 24°38E **177** B13
Masuda *Japan* 34°40N 131°51E **222** C3
Masuika
Dem. Rep. of the Congo 7°37S 22°32E **265** D4
Masuku = Franceville
Gabon 1°40S 13°32E **264** C2
Masurai *Indonesia* 2°30S 101°51E **234** C2
Masurian Lakes = Mazurski,
Pojezierze *Poland* 53°50N 21°0E **184** E7
Masvingo *Zimbabwe* 20°8S 30°49E **269** G3
Masvingo □ *Zimbabwe* 21°0S 31°30E **269** G3
Maswa △ *Tanzania* 2°58S 34°19E **268** C3
Maşyāf *Syria* 35°4N 36°20E **250** C5
Maszewo *Poland* 53°29N 15°3E **184** E2
Mat ➔ *Albania* 41°40N 19°35E **202** E3
Mât ➔ *Réunion* 20°57S 55°42E **272** f
Mata *Israel* 31°43N 35°4E **123** B1
Mata-au = Clutha ➔
N.Z. 46°20S 169°49E **285** G4
Mata de São João *Brazil* 12°31S 38°17W **333** D4
Mata Redonda *Venezuela* 10°57N 64°7W **329** a
Mata-Utu *Wall. & F. Is.* 13°17S 176°8W **277** C15
Matabele Plain *Zambia* 16°20S 23°10E **265** F4
Matabeleland North □
Zimbabwe 19°0S 28°0E **269** F2
Matabeleland South □
Zimbabwe 21°0S 29°0E **269** G2
Matachel ➔ *Spain* 38°50N 6°17W **195** G4
Matachewan *Canada* 47°56N 80°39W **298** C3
Matacuni ➔ *Venezuela* 3°2N 65°16W **329** C4
Matadi
Dem. Rep. of the Congo 5°52S 13°31E **265** D2
Matafao, Mt. *Amer. Samoa* 14°17S 170°42W **302** f
Matagalpa *Nic.* 13°0N 85°58W **320** D2
Matagami *Canada* 49°45N 77°34W **298** C4
Matagami, L. *Canada* 49°50N 77°40W **298** C4
Matagorda B. *U.S.A.* 28°40N 96°12W **314** G6
Matagorda I. *U.S.A.* 28°15N 96°30W **314** G6
Matahiva *French Polynesia* 17°32S 149°20W **289** f
Mataiea *Tahiti* 17°46S 149°25W **289** e
Matak *Indonesia* 3°18N 106°16E **234** B3
Matakana *N.S.W.,*
Australia 32°59S 145°54E **283** B6
Matakana *N.Z.* 36°21S 174°43E **284** C3
Matala *Angola* 14°46S 15°4E **265** E3
Matala *Kriti, Greece* 34°59N 24°45E **207** F5
Matalaque *Peru* 16°26S 70°49W **330** D3
Matale *Sri Lanka* 7°30N 80°37E **245** L5
Matam *Senegal* 15°34N 13°17W **262** B2
Matam □ *Senegal* 15°37N 13°19W **262** B2
Matamata *N.Z.* 37°48S 175°47E **284** D4
Matameye *Niger* 13°26N 8°28E **259** F1
Matamoros *Coahuila,*
Mexico 25°32N 103°15W **318** B4
Matamoros *Tamaulipas,*
Mexico 25°53N 97°30W **319** B5
Ma'ṭan as Sarra *Libya* 21°45N 22°0E **259** D4
Ma'ṭan Bishārah *Libya* 23°0N 22°32E **258** D4
Matandu ➔ *Tanzania* 8°45S 34°19E **269** D3
Matane *Canada* 48°50N 67°33W **299** C6
Matang *China* 23°30N 104°7E **228** F5
Matankari *Niger* 13°46N 4°1E **263** C5
Matanomadh *India* 23°33N 68°57E **242** H3
Matanzas *Cuba* 23°0N 81°40W **320** B3
Matapa *Botswana* 23°11S 24°39E **270** B3
Matapan, C. = Tenaro, Akra
Greece 36°22N 22°27E **204** E4
Matapédia *Canada* 48°0N 66°59W **299** C6
Matapo △ *Zimbabwe* 20°30S 29°40E **269** G2
Matara *Sri Lanka* 5°58N 80°30E **245** M5
Mataram *Indonesia* 8°35S 116°7E **231** K19
Matarani *Peru* 17°0S 72°10W **330** D3
Mataranka *Australia* 14°55S 133°4E **278** B5
Matarinao B. *Phil.* 11°12N 125°33E **233** F5
Matarma, Râs *Egypt* 30°27N 32°44E **251** H3
Mataró *Spain* 41°32N 2°29E **196** D7
Matarraña ➔ *Spain* 41°14N 0°22E **196** D5
Mataruška Banja *Serbia* 43°40N 20°40E **202** C4
Matasiete, Cerro *Venezuela* 11°3N 63°51W **329** a
Mataso *Vanuatu* 17°14S 168°26E **287** G6
Matata *N.Z.* 37°54S 176°48E **284** D5
Matatiele *S. Africa* 30°20S 28°49E **271** D4
Matatila Dam *India* 25°0N 78°22E **244** B4
Matatula, C. *Amer. Samoa* 14°15S 170°33W **302** f
Mataura *N.Z.* 46°11S 168°51E **285** G3
Mataura ➔ *N.Z.* 46°34S 168°44E **285** G3
Matavai, B. de *Tahiti* 17°30S 149°23W **289** e
Matavera *Cook Is.* 21°13S 159°44W **289** h
Mataveri *Chile* 27°9S 109°27W **330** b
Mategua *Bolivia* 13°1S 62°48W **331** C5
Matehuala *Mexico* 23°39N 100°39W **318** C4
Mateke
Dem. Rep. of the Congo 4°52S 24°25E **264** C3
Mateke Hills *Zimbabwe* 21°48S 31°0E **269** G3
Matelot *Trin. & Tob.* 10°50N 61°7W **323** t
Matera *Italy* 40°40N 16°36E **201** B9
Matese, Monti del *Italy* 41°27N 14°22E **201** A7
Matese △ *Italy* 41°24N 14°23E **201** A7
Mátészalka *Hungary* 47°58N 22°20E **182** C7
Matetsi *Zimbabwe* 18°12S 26°0E **269** F2
Mateur *Tunisia* 37°0N 9°40E **258** A1
Matfors *Sweden* 62°21N 17°2E **162** B11
Matha *France* 45°52N 0°20W **174** C3
Matheniko △ *Uganda* 2°49N 34°27E **268** B3
Mathis *U.S.A.* 28°6N 97°50W **314** G6
Mathoura *Australia* 35°50S 144°55E **283** C6
Mathraki *Greece* 39°48N 19°31E **206** B9
Mathura *India* 27°30N 77°40E **242** F7
Mati *Phil.* 6°55N 126°15E **233** H6
Matiakoali *Burkina Faso* 12°28N 1°2E **263** C5
Matiali *India* 26°56N 88°49E **243** F13
Matías Romero *Mexico* 16°53N 95°2W **319** D5
Matibane *Mozam.* 14°49S 40°45E **269** E5
Matinha *Portugal* 38°45N 9°5W **126** A2
Matinhos *Brazil* 25°49S 48°32W **333** G2
Matiri Ra. *N.Z.* 41°38S 172°20E **285** B7
Matjiesfontein *S. Africa* 33°14S 20°35E **270** D3
Matla ➔ *India* 21°40N 88°40E **243** J13
Matlab Bazar *Bangla.* 23°20N 90°43E **241** D3
Matlamanyane *Botswana* 19°33S 25°57E **270** A4
Matli *Pakistan* 25°2N 68°39E **242** G3
Matlock *U.K.* 53°9N 1°33W **168** D6
Matmata *Tunisia* 33°37N 9°59E **258** B1
Matna *Sudan* 13°49N 35°10E **257** E4
Matnog *Phil.* 12°35N 124°5E **232** E5
Mato *Dem. Rep. of the Congo* 8°1S 24°24E **265** D4
Mato ➔ *Venezuela* 7°9N 65°7W **329** B4
Mato, Serrania de
Venezuela 6°25N 65°25W **328** B4
Mato Grosso □ *Brazil* 14°0S 55°0W **331** C7
Mato Grosso, Planalto do
Brazil 15°0S 55°0W **331** D7
Mato Grosso do Sul □
Brazil 18°0S 55°0W **331** D7
Matobo = Matapo △
Zimbabwe 20°30S 29°40E **269** G2
Matochkin Shar, Proliv
Russia 73°23N 55°12E **214** B6
Matola *Mozam.* 25°57S 32°27E **271** C5
Matong *Papua N. G.* 5°36S 151°50E **286** C6
Matopo Hills *Zimbabwe* 20°36S 28°20E **269** G2
Matopos *Zimbabwe* 20°20S 28°29E **269** G2
Matosinhos *Portugal* 41°11N 8°42W **194** D2
Matou *Taiwan* 23°11N 120°15E **225** C2
Matouba *Guadeloupe* 16°2N 61°41W **322** e
Matour *France* 46°19N 4°29E **173** F11
Matramam *Indonesia* 6°12S 106°51E **122** B2
Matroosberg *S. Africa* 33°23S 19°40E **270** D2
Maṭruḥ *Oman* 23°37N 58°30E **249** B7
Matsena *Nigeria* 13°5N 10°5E **263** C7
Matsesta *Russia* 43°34N 39°51E **191** J4
Matsu Tao *Taiwan* 26°8N 119°56E **225** b
Matsubara = Takahagi
Japan 36°43N 140°45E **221** F10
Matsubase *Japan* 32°40N 130°40E **222** E2
Matsudo *Japan* 35°47N 139°54E **223** B11
Matsue *Japan* 35°25N 133°10E **222** B5
Matsum, Ko *Thailand* 9°22N 99°59E **237** b
Matsumae *Japan* 41°26N 140°7E **220** D10
Matsumae-Hantō *Japan* 41°30N 140°15E **220** D10
Matsumoto *Japan* 36°15N 138°0E **223** A10
Matsusaka *Japan* 34°34N 136°32E **223** C8
Matsushima *Kumamoto,*
Japan 32°30N 130°25E **222** E2
Matsushima *Miyagi,*
Japan 38°20N 141°10E **220** E10
Matsuura *Japan* 33°20N 129°49E **222** D1
Matsuyama *Japan* 33°45N 132°45E **222** D4
Matsuzaki *Japan* 34°43N 138°50E **223** C10
Mattagami ➔ *Canada* 50°43N 81°29W **298** B3
Mattancheri *India* 9°50N 76°15E **245** K3
Mattapan *U.S.A.* 42°16N 71°6W **116** B2
Mattawa *Canada* 46°20N 78°45W **298** C4
Matterhorn *Switz.* 45°58N 7°39E **179** K3
Mattersburg *Austria* 47°44N 16°24E **181** D9
Matteson *U.S.A.* 41°30N 87°42W **311** C9
Matthew, Î. *N. Cal.* 22°29S 171°15E **277** E13
Matthew Town *Bahamas* 20°57N 73°40W **321** B5
Matthews *U.S.A.* 40°23N 85°30W **311** D11
Matthews Ridge *Guyana* 7°37N 60°10W **329** B5
Mattias Church *Budapest, Hungary* **117** b1
Mattice *Canada* 49°40N 83°20W **298** C3
Mattili *India* 18°33N 82°12E **244** E6
Mattituck *U.S.A.* 40°59N 72°32W **313** F12
Mattō = Hakusan *Japan* 36°31N 136°34E **223** A8
Mattoon *U.S.A.* 39°29N 88°23W **311** E8
Matuba *Mozam.* 24°28S 32°49E **271** B5
Matucana *Peru* 11°55S 76°25W **330** C2
Matugama *Sri Lanka* 6°31N 80°7E **245** L5
Matuguinao *Phil.* 12°5N 124°55E **232** E5
Matuka *Papua N. G.* 4°54S 145°47E **286** C3
Matuku *Fiji* 19°10S 179°44E **287** B2
Matūn = Khowst *Afghan.* 33°22N 69°58E **242** C3
Matura *Trin. & Tob.* 10°40N 61°4W **323** t
Matura B. *Trin. & Tob.* 10°39N 61°1W **323** t
Maturín *Venezuela* 9°45N 63°11W **329** B5
Matusadona △ *Zimbabwe* 16°58S 28°42E **269** F2
Matutum, Mt. *Phil.* 6°22N 125°5E **233** H5
Matveyev Kurgan *Russia* 47°35N 38°57E **189** J10
Matxitxako, C. *Spain* 43°28N 2°47W **196** B2
Mátyásföld *Hungary* 47°30N 19°12E **117** A3
Mau *Mad. P., India* 26°17N 78°41E **243** F8
Mau *Ut. P., India* 25°56N 83°33E **243** G10
Mau *Ut. P., India* 25°17N 81°23E **243** G9
Mau Escarpment *Kenya* 0°40S 36°0E **268** C4
Mau Ranipur *India* 25°16N 79°8E **243** G8
Mau Tso Ngam *China* 22°22N 114°1E **122** A2
Maua *Eastern, Kenya* 0°14N 37°56E **268** C4
Maua *Mozam.* 13°53S 37°10E **269** E4
Mauban *Phil.* 14°12N 121°44E **232** D3
Maubeuge *France* 50°17N 3°57E **173** B10
Maubin *Burma* 16°44N 95°39E **241** G5
Maubourguet *France* 43°29N 0°1E **174** E4
Maud, Pt. *Australia* 23°6S 113°45E **278** D1
Maud Rise *S. Ocean* 66°0S 3°0E **151** C3
Maude *Australia* 34°29S 144°18E **282** C6
Maudin Sun *Burma* 16°0N 94°30E **241** G5
Mauer *Austria* 48°9N 16°16E **142** B1
Maués *Brazil* 3°20S 57°45W **329** D6
Maués-Acu ➔ *Brazil* 3°22S 57°44W **329** D6
Maug Is. *N. Marianas* 20°1N 145°13E **302** a
Mauganj *India* 24°50N 81°55E **243** G9
Maughold Hd. *I. of Man* 54°18N 4°18W **168** C3
Mauguio *France* 43°37N 4°1E **174** E8
Maui *U.S.A.* 20°48N 156°20W **302** C5
Maulamyaing = Moulmein
Burma 16°30N 97°40E **241** G6
Maule □ *Chile* 36°5S 72°30W **334** D1
Mauléon-Licharre *France* 43°14N 0°54W **174** E3
Maullín *Chile* 41°38S 73°37W **336** B2
Maulvi Bazar *Bangla.* 24°29N 91°42E **241** C3
Maumee *U.S.A.* 41°34N 83°39W **311** C13
Maumee ➔ *U.S.A.* 41°42N 83°28W **311** C13
Maumere *Indonesia* 8°38S 122°13E **231** F6
Maumusson, Pertuis de
France 45°48N 1°14W **174** C2
Maun *Botswana* 20°0S 23°26E **270** B3
Mauna Kea *U.S.A.* 19°50N 155°28W **302** D6
Mauna Loa *U.S.A.* 19°30N 155°35W **302** D6
Mauna Loa Forest Reserve
U.S.A. 19°35N 155°33W **302** D6
Maunabo *Puerto Rico* 18°1N 65°54W **321** b
Maunaloa *U.S.A.* 21°8N 157°13W **302** B4
Maunalua B. *U.S.A.* 21°15N 157°45W **302** K14
Maunath Bhanjan = Mau
India 25°56N 83°33E **243** G10
Maunawili *U.S.A.* 21°23N 157°46W **302** K14
Maunga Orito *Chile* 27°10S 109°25W **330** b
Maunga Puakatiki *Chile* 27°6S 109°15W **330** b
Maunga Terevaka *Chile* 27°5S 109°23W **330** b
Maungaroa *Cook Is.* 21°13S 159°48W **289** h
Maungatongaiti *Cook Is.* 21°14S 159°48W **289** h
Maungaturoto *N.Z.* 36°6S 174°23E **284** C3
Maungdaw *Burma* 20°50N 92°21E **241** E4
Maungmagan Kyunzu
Burma 14°0N 97°48E **236** E1
Maungu *Kenya* 3°33S 38°45E **268** C4
Maupihaa
French Polynesia 16°50S 153°55W **289** f
Maupin *U.S.A.* 45°11N 121°5W **304** D3
Maupiti *French Polynesia* 16°27S 152°15W **289** f
Maure-de-Bretagne *France* 47°59N 1°58W **172** E5
Maurepas, L. *U.S.A.* 30°15N 90°30W **315** F9
Maures *France* 43°15N 6°15E **175** E10
Mauriac *France* 45°13N 2°19E **174** C6
Maurice, L. *Australia* 29°30S 131°0E **279** E5
Mauriceville *N.Z.* 40°45S 175°42E **284** G4
Mauricie △ *Canada* 46°45N 73°0W **298** C5
Maurienne *France* 45°13N 6°30E **175** C10
Mauripur *Pakistan* 24°52N 66°55E **123** A1
Mauritania ■ *Africa* 20°50N 10°0W **260** D3
Mauritius ■ *Ind. Oc.* 20°0S 57°0E **272** e
Mauritius ✈ (MRU)
Mauritius 20°25S 57°40E **272** e
Mauron *France* 48°9N 2°18W **172** D4
Maurs *France* 44°43N 2°12E **174** D6
Mauston *U.S.A.* 43°48N 90°5W **308** D8
Mauterndorf *Austria* 47°9N 13°40E **180** D6
Mauthen *Austria* 46°40N 13°0E **180** E6
Mauvezin *France* 43°44N 0°53E **174** E4
Mauzé-sur-le-Mignon
France 46°12N 0°41W **174** B3
Mavaca ➔ *Venezuela* 2°31N 65°11W **329** C4
Mavinga *Angola* 15°50S 20°21E **265** F4
Mavli *India* 24°45N 73°55E **242** G5
Mavoko = Athi River
Kenya 1°28S 36°58E **268** C4
Mavrata *Greece* 38°4N 20°44E **207** C2
Mavrovë *Albania* 40°26N 19°32E **202** F3
Mavrovo △ *Macedonia* 41°36N 20°45E **202** E4
Mavuradonha Mts.
Zimbabwe 16°30S 31°30E **269** F3
Mawa *Dem. Rep. of the Congo* 2°45N 26°40E **268** B2
Mawai *India* 22°30N 81°4E **243** H9
Mawana *India* 29°6N 77°58E **242** E7
Mawand *Pakistan* 29°33N 68°38E **242** E3
Mawat *Iraq* 35°54N 45°24E **213** E11
Mawjib, W. al ➔ *Jordan* 31°28N 35°36E **251** G6
Mawkmai *Burma* 20°14N 97°37E **241** E6
Mawlaik *Burma* 23°40N 94°26E **241** D5
Mawlamyine = Moulmein
Burma 16°30N 97°40E **241** G6
Mawlamyinegyun *Burma* 16°23N 95°16E **241** G6
Mawlawkho *Burma* 17°50N 97°38E **241** G6
Mawqaq *Si. Arabia* 27°25N 41°8E **246** E4
Mawson *Antarctica* 67°30S 62°53E **151** C6
Mawson Coast *Antarctica* 68°30S 63°0E **151** C6
Mawson Pk. *Heard I.* 53°6S 73°31E **273** K6
Mawsynram *India* 25°15N 91°30E **241** C3
Mawza' *Yemen* 13°16N 43°30E **248** D3
Max *U.S.A.* 47°49N 101°18W **308** B3
Maxambamba = Nova Iguaçu
Brazil 22°45S 43°28W **333** F3
Maxcanú *Mexico* 20°35N 90°0W **319** C6
Maxesibeni *S. Africa* 30°49S 29°23E **271** D4
Maxeys *U.S.A.* 33°45N 83°11W **316** B6
Maxhamish L. *Canada* 59°50N 123°17W **296** B4
Maxhof *Germany* 48°4N 11°29E **131** B1
Maxixe *Mozam.* 23°54S 35°17E **271** B6
Maxville *Canada* 45°17N 74°51W **313** A10
Maxwell *N.Z.* 39°51S 174°49E **284** F3
Maxwell *Calif., U.S.A.* 39°17N 122°11W **306** F4
Maxwelton *Australia* 20°43S 142°41E **280** C3
May, C. *U.S.A.* 38°56N 74°58W **309** F16
May Jirgui *Niger* 13°44N 8°8E **259** F1
May Pen *Jamaica* 17°58N 77°15W **320** a
May River *Papua N. G.* 4°19S 141°58E **286** C1
Maya *Indonesia* 1°10S 109°35E **235** C3
Maya ➔ *Russia* 60°28N 134°28E **215** D14
Maya Mts. *Belize* 16°30N 89°0W **320** C2
Mayabandar *India* 12°56N 92°56E **245** H11
Mayaguana I. *Bahamas* 22°30N 72°44W **321** B5
Mayagüez *Puerto Rico* 18°12N 67°9W **321** C6
Mayahi *Niger* 13°58N 7°40E **263** C6
Mayaky *Ukraine* 47°26N 29°33E **183** C14
Mayals = Maials *Spain* 41°22N 0°30E **196** D5
Mayama *Congo* 3°51S 14°54E **264** C2
Mayāmey *Iran* 36°24N 55°42E **247** B7
Mayang *China* 27°53N 109°49E **228** D7
Mayanup *Australia* 33°57S 116°27E **279** F2
Mayapán *Mexico* 20°29N 89°11W **319** C7
Mayari *Cuba* 20°40N 75°41W **321** B4
Mayaro *Trin. & Tob.* 10°17N 61°1W **323** t
Mayaro □ *Trin. & Tob.* 10°10N 61°5W **323** t
Mayaro B. *Trin. & Tob.* 10°14N 60°59W **323** t
Mayavaram = Mayiladuthurai
India 11°3N 79°42E **245** J4
Maybell *U.S.A.* 40°31N 108°5W **304** F9
Maybio *Phil.* 5°50N 125°35E **233** J5
Maybole *U.K.* 55°21N 4°42W **167** F4
Maychew *Ethiopia* 12°50N 39°31E **257** E4
Maydān *Iraq* 34°55N 45°37E **213** E11
Maydan *Ukraine* 48°36N 23°29E **183** B8
Mayen *Germany* 50°19N 7°13E **179** E3
Mayenne *France* 48°20N 0°38W **172** D6
Mayenne □ *France* 48°10N 0°40W **172** D6
Mayenne ➔ *France* 47°30N 0°32W **172** E6
Mayer *U.S.A.* 34°24N 112°14W **305** J7
Mayerthorpe *Canada* 53°57N 115°8W **296** C5
Mayesville *U.S.A.* 34°0N 80°12W **316** A9
Mayfair *Gauteng, S. Africa* 26°11S 28°0E **123** B2
Mayfair *London, U.K.* **125** b3
Mayfield *Ky., U.S.A.* 36°44N 88°38W **308** G9
Mayfield *N.Y., U.S.A.* 43°6N 74°16W **313** C10
Mayhill *U.S.A.* 32°53N 105°29W **305** K11
Mayiladuthurai *India* 11°3N 79°42E **245** J4
Maykop *Russia* 44°35N 40°10E **191** H5
Mayma *Russia* 52°3N 85°55E **217** B11
Maymyo *Burma* 22°2N 96°28E **236** A1
Maynard *Mass., U.S.A.* 42°26N 71°27W **313** D13
Maynard *Wash., U.S.A.* 47°59N 122°55W **306** C4
Maynard Hills *Australia* 28°28S 119°49E **279** E2
Mayne ➔ *Australia* 23°40S 141°55E **280** C3
Maynooth *Ont., Canada* 45°13N 77°56W **312** A7
Maynooth *Kildare, Ireland* 53°23N 6°34W **166** C5
Mayo *Yukon, Canada* 63°38N 135°57W **294** E4
Mayo *Trin. & Tob.* 10°21N 61°23W **323** t
Mayo *Fla., U.S.A.* 30°3N 83°10W **316** E6
Mayo □ *Ireland* 53°53N 9°3W **166** C2
Mayo ➔ *Argentina* 45°45S 69°45W **336** C3
Mayo ➔ *Peru* 6°38S 76°15W **330** B2
Mayo B. *Phil.* 6°56N 126°22E **233** H6
Mayo Daga *Nigeria* 6°59N 11°25E **263** D7
Mayo Faran *Nigeria* 8°57N 12°4E **263** D7
Mayo-Kébbi Est □ *Chad* 10°20N 15°30E **259** F3
Mayo-Kébbi Ouest □ *Chad* 9°40N 17°50E **259** G3
Mayoko *Congo* 2°18S 12°49E **264** C2
Mayoko
Dem. Rep. of the Congo 1°6S 23°50E **264** C4
Mayon Volcano *Phil.* 13°15N 123°41E **232** E4
Mayor Buratovich
Argentina 39°15S 62°37W **336** A4
Mayor I. *N.Z.* 37°16S 176°17E **284** D5
Mayor Pablo Lagerenza
Paraguay 19°55S 60°47W **331** D5
Mayorga *Spain* 42°10N 5°16W **194** C5
Mayotte ☒ *Ind. Oc.* 12°50S 45°10E **272** b
Mayoyao *Phil.* 16°59N 121°14E **232** C3
Mayqayyng *Kazakhstan* 51°27N 75°47E **217** B9
Mayraira Pt. *Phil.* 18°39N 120°51E **232** B3
Mayreau *St. Vincent* 12°39N 61°23W **323** n
Maysān □ *Iraq* 31°55N 47°15E **246** D5
Mayskiy *Russia* 43°47N 44°2E **191** J7
Maysville *Ky., U.S.A.* 38°39N 83°46W **311** F13
Maysville *Mo., U.S.A.* 39°53N 94°22W **310** E2
Maytiguid I. *Phil.* 11°30N 119°36E **233** F2
Mayu *Indonesia* 1°30N 126°30E **231** D7
Mayumba *Gabon* 3°25S 10°39E **264** C2
Mayuram = Mayiladuthurai
India 11°3N 79°42E **245** J4
Mayville *N. Dak., U.S.A.* 47°30N 97°20W **308** B5
Mayville *N.Y., U.S.A.* 42°15N 79°30W **312** D5
Maywood *Calif., U.S.A.* 33°59N 118°12W **126** C3
Maywood *Ill., U.S.A.* 41°52N 87°51W **119** B1
Maywood *N.J., U.S.A.* 40°53N 74°3W **132** A1
Maywood Park Race Track
U.S.A. 41°54N 87°50W **119** B1
Mazabuka *Zambia* 15°52S 27°44E **269** F2
Mazagān = El Jadida
Morocco 33°11N 8°17W **260** B3
Mazagão *Brazil* 0°7S 51°16W **329** D7
Mazagaon *Mumbai, India* **130** a2
Mazamet *France* 43°30N 2°20E **174** E6
Mazán *Peru* 3°30S 73°0W **328** D3
Māzandarān □ *Iran* 36°30N 52°0E **247** B7
Mazapil *Mexico* 24°39N 101°34W **318** C4
Mazar *China* 36°32N 77°1E **217** E9
Mazar, O. ➔ *Algeria* 31°50N 1°36E **261** B5
Mazār-e Sharīf *Afghan.* 36°41N 67°0E **240** A2
Mazara del Vallo *Italy* 37°39N 12°35E **200** E5
Mazarredo *Argentina* 47°10S 66°50W **336** C3
Mazarrón *Spain* 37°38N 1°19W **197** H3
Mazarrón, G. de *Spain* 37°27N 1°19W **197** H3
Mazaruni ➔ *Guyana* 6°25N 58°35W **329** B6
Mazatán *Mexico* 29°0N 110°8W **318** B2
Mazatenango *Guatemala* 14°35N 91°30W **320** D1
Mazatlán *Mexico* 23°13N 106°25W **318** C3
Mažeikiai *Lithuania* 56°20N 22°20E **184** B9
Mazhafa, J. *Si. Arabia* 28°52N 35°57E **251** K6
Māzhān *Iran* 32°30N 59°0E **247** C8
Mazıdağı *Turkey* 37°28N 40°29E **213** D9
Mazīnān *Iran* 36°19N 56°56E **247** B8
Mazo Cruz *Peru* 16°45S 69°44W **330** D4
Mazoe *Mozam.* 16°42S 33°7E **269** F3
Mazoe ➔ *Mozam.* 16°20S 33°30E **269** F3
Mazomanie *U.S.A.* 43°11N 89°48W **310** A7
Mazon *U.S.A.* 41°14N 88°25W **311** C8
Mazowe *Zimbabwe* 17°28S 30°58E **269** F3
Mazowieckie □ *Poland* 52°40N 21°0E **185** F8
Mazrûb *Sudan* 14°0N 29°20E **257** E2
Mazurski, Pojezierze
Poland 53°50N 21°0E **184** E7
Mazyr *Belarus* 51°59N 29°15E **177** B15
Mba *Fiji* 17°33S 177°41E **287** A1
Mbaba *Senegal* 14°59N 16°44W **262** C1
Mbabane *Swaziland* 26°18S 31°6E **271** C5
Mbaéré ➔ *C.A.R.* 3°47N 17°31E **264** B3
Mbagne *Mauritania* 16°6N 14°47W **262** B2
M'bahiakro *Ivory C.* 7°33N 4°19W **262** D4
Mbaïki *C.A.R.* 3°53N 18°1E **264** B3
Mbakana, Mt. de *Cameroon* 7°57N 15°6E **264** A3
Mbala *Zambia* 8°46S 31°24E **269** D3
Mbalabala *Zimbabwe* 20°27S 29°3E **271** B4
Mbalam *Cameroon* 2°13N 13°49E **264** B2
Mbale *Uganda* 1°8N 34°12E **268** B3
Mbali ➔ *C.A.R.* 4°27N 18°20E **264** B3
Mbalmayo *Cameroon* 3°33N 11°33E **263** E7
Mbam ➔ *Cameroon* 4°24N 11°17E **263** E7
Mbamba Bay *Tanzania* 11°13S 34°49E **269** E3
Mbandaka
Dem. Rep. of the Congo 0°1N 18°18E **264** B3
Mbandjok *Cameroon* 4°27N 11°54E **264** B2
Mbanga *Cameroon* 4°30N 9°33E **263** E6
Mbanika *Solomon Is.* 9°3S 159°13E **287** M10
M'Banio, Lagune *Gabon* 3°35S 11°0E **264** C2
Mbanza Congo *Angola* 6°18S 14°16E **265** D2

Mbanza Ngungu Dem. Rep. of the Congo 5°12S 14°53E 265 D2
Mbarangandu Tanzania 10°11S 36°48E 269 D4
Mbarara Uganda 0°35S 30°40E 268 C3
Mbari → C.A.R. 4°34N 22°43E 264 B4
Mbatto Ivory C. 6°28N 4°22W 262 D4
Mbava Solomon Is. 7°47S 156°33E 287 L9
Mbé Congo 3°14S 15°50E 264 C3
Mbe Eq. Guin. 1°47N 9°56E 264 B1
Mbengga = Beqa Fiji 18°23S 178°8E 287 B2
Mbengué Gabon 2°2S 11°7E 264 C2
Mbengui Gabon 2°3S 10°4E 264 C2
Mbéni Comoros Is. 11°30S 43°22E 272 a
Mbenkuru → Tanzania 9°25S 39°50E 269 D4
Mbéré → Cameroon 7°45N 15°36E 264 A3
Mberengwa Zimbabwe 20°29S 29°57E 269 G2
Mberengwa, Mt. Zimbabwe 20°37S 29°55E 269 G2
Mberubu Nigeria 6°10N 7°38E 263 D6
Mbesuma Zambia 10°0S 32°2E 269 E3
Mbeya Tanzania 8°54S 33°29E 269 D3
Mbeya □ Tanzania 8°15S 33°30E 268 D3
Mbhashe → S. Africa 32°15S 28°54E 271 D4
Mbigou Gabon 1°53S 11°56E 264 C2
M'bili South Sudan 7°35N 28°15E 257 F2
Mbinga Tanzania 10°50S 35°0E 269 E4
Mbini = Río Muni □ Eq. Guin. 1°30N 10°0E 264 B2
Mbini Eq. Guin. 1°35N 9°37E 264 B1
Mbizi Zimbabwe 21°23S 31°1E 269 G3
Mboi Dem. Rep. of the Congo 6°57S 21°54E 265 D4
Mboki C.A.R. 5°19N 25°58E 257 F2
Mbokonimbeti Solomon Is. 8°57S 160°7E 287 M11
Mboli Dem. Rep. of the Congo 4°8N 23°9E 264 B4
Mbombela S. Africa 25°29S 30°59E 271 C5
Mbomo Congo 0°25N 14°42E 264 B2
M'bonge Cameroon 4°33N 9°5E 263 E6
Mboro Senegal 15°9N 16°54W 262 B1
Mboua Cameroon 4°25N 14°16E 264 A2
Mbouda Cameroon 5°38N 10°15E 264 A2
M'boukou, L. de Cameroon 6°23N 12°50E 263 D7
Mboune Senegal 14°42N 13°34W 262 C2
Mbouoma Congo 0°52S 15°4E 264 C3
Mbour Senegal 14°22N 16°54W 262 C1
Mbout Mauritania 16°1N 12°38W 262 B2
Mbrés C.A.R. 6°40N 19°48E 264 A3
M'Bridge → Angola 7°12S 12°51E 265 D2
Mbuji-Mayi Dem. Rep. of the Congo 6°9S 23°40E 265 D4
Mbulu Tanzania 3°45S 35°30E 268 C4
Mbuma Dem. Rep. of the Congo 3°32N 24°50E 264 B4
Mbuma Solomon Is. 8°59S 160°46E 287 M11
Mburucuyá Argentina 28°1S 58°14W 334 B4
Mburucuyá △ Argentina 28°1S 58°12W 334 B4
M'bwat Cameroon 6°29N 10°45E 264 A2
Mcherrah Algeria 27°0N 4°30W 260 C4
Mchinga Tanzania 9°44S 39°45E 269 D4
Mchinji Malawi 13°47S 32°58E 269 E3
Mdantsane S. Africa 32°56S 27°46E 271 D4
Mdennah Mauritania 24°37N 6°0W 260 D3
Me'a She' Arim Jerusalem 123 a2
Mead, L. U.S.A. 36°0N 114°44W 307 J12
Meade = Atqasuk → U.S.A. 70°52N 155°55W 303 A9
Meade U.S.A. 37°17N 100°20W 308 G3
Meade River = Atqasuk U.S.A. 70°28N 157°24W 303 A8
Meadow Lake Canada 54°10N 108°26W 297 C7
Meadow Lake ⌓ Canada 54°27N 109°0W 297 C7
Meadow Valley Wash → U.S.A. 36°40N 114°34W 307 J12
Meadowbank Park Australia 33°49S 151°6E 139 A1
Meadville Mo., U.S.A. 39°47N 93°18W 310 E3
Meadville Pa., U.S.A. 41°39N 80°9W 312 E4
Meaford Canada 44°36N 80°35W 312 B4
Meakan Dake Japan 45°15N 144°0E 220 C11
Mealhada Portugal 40°22N 8°27W 194 E2
Mealy Mts. Canada 53°10N 58°0W 299 B8
Meander River Canada 59°2N 117°42W 296 B5
Meares, C. U.S.A. 45°37N 124°0W 304 D1
Mearim → Brazil 3°4S 44°35W 332 B3
Meath □ Ireland 53°40N 6°57W 166 C5
Meath Park Canada 53°27N 105°22W 297 C7
Meaulne France 46°36N 2°36E 173 F9
Meaux France 48°58N 2°50E 173 D9
Mebechi-Gawa → Japan 40°31N 141°31E 220 D10
Mebonden Norway 63°13N 11°2E 164 A8
Mebulu, Tanjung Indonesia 8°50S 115°5E 231 K18
Mecanhelas Mozam. 15°12S 35°54E 269 F4
Mecaya → Colombia 0°29N 75°11W 328 C2
Mecca = Makkah Si. Arabia 21°30N 39°54E 248 B2
Mecca U.S.A. 33°34N 116°5W 307 M10
Mechanicsburg Ohio, U.S.A. 40°4N 83°33W 311 D13
Mechanicsburg Pa., U.S.A. 40°13N 77°1W 312 F8
Mechanicsville U.S.A. 41°54N 91°16W 310 C5
Mechanicville U.S.A. 42°54N 73°41W 313 D11
Mechara Ethiopia 8°36N 40°20E 257 F5
Mechelen Belgium 51°2N 4°29E 170 C4
Mecheria Algeria 33°35N 0°18W 261 B4
Mechernich Germany 50°35N 6°39E 178 E2
Mechetinskaya Russia 46°45N 40°32E 191 G5
Mechol Micronesia 9°37N 138°9E 287 R16
Měcholupy Czech Rep. 50°3N 14°32E 135 B3
Mechra Bel Ksiri Morocco 34°34N 5°57W 260 B3
Mechra Benâbbou Morocco 32°39N 7°48W 260 B3
Měčice Czech Rep. 50°11N 14°31E 135 A3
Mecidiye Turkey 40°38N 26°32E 203 F10
Mecidiyeköy Turkey 41°4N 29°0E 122 B2
Mecitözü Turkey 40°32N 35°17E 212 B6
Mecklenburg Germany 53°33N 11°40E 176 B7
Mecklenburg-Vorpommern □ Germany 53°45N 12°15E 178 B8
Mecklenburger Bucht Germany 54°20N 11°40E 178 A7
Meconta Mozam. 14°59S 39°50E 269 E4
Mecsek Hungary 46°10N 18°18E 182 D3
Mecubúri Mozam. 14°39S 38°54E 269 E4
Mecubúri → Mozam. 14°10S 40°30E 269 E5
Mecúfi Mozam. 13°20S 40°32E 269 E5
Meda Portugal 40°57N 7°18W 194 E3
Medak India 18°1N 78°15E 244 E4
Medan Indonesia 3°40N 98°38E 234 B1
Medang Indonesia 8°9S 117°22E 235 D5
Médanos Argentina 38°50S 62°42W 336 A4
Médanos de Coro △ Venezuela 11°35N 69°44W 328 A4
Medanosa, Pta. Argentina 48°8S 66°0W 336 C3
Medart U.S.A. 30°5N 84°23W 316 E5
Medaryville U.S.A. 41°5N 86°55W 311 C10
Medawachchiya Sri Lanka 8°30N 80°30E 245 K5
Medchal India 17°37N 78°29E 244 F4
Mede Italy 45°6N 8°44E 198 C5
Médéa Algeria 36°12N 2°50E 261 A5
Médéa □ Algeria 35°0N 3°0E 261 B5
Mededa Bos.-H. 43°44N 19°10E 182 G4
Médégué Gabon 0°37N 10°8E 264 B2
Medeiros Neto Brazil 17°20S 40°14W 333 E3
Medellín Colombia 6°15N 75°35W 328 B2
Medelpad Sweden 62°33N 16°30E 162 B10
Medemblik Neths. 52°46N 5°8E 170 B5
Médenine Tunisia 33°21N 10°30E 258 B2
Médenine □ Tunisia 32°20N 10°0E 261 B7
Mederdra Mauritania 17°0N 15°38W 262 B1
Medford Mass., U.S.A. 42°25N 71°7W 116 A2
Medford Oreg., U.S.A. 42°19N 122°52W 304 E2
Medford Wis., U.S.A. 45°9N 90°20W 308 C8
Medgidia Romania 44°15N 28°19E 183 F13
Medi South Sudan 5°4N 30°42E 257 F3
Media Agua Argentina 31°58S 68°25W 334 C2
Media Luna Argentina 34°45S 66°44W 334 C2
Medianeira Brazil 25°17S 54°5W 335 B5
Mediapolis U.S.A. 41°0N 91°10W 310 D5
Mediaş Romania 46°9N 24°22E 183 D9
Medicilândia Brazil 3°33S 53°8W 329 D7
Medicina Italy 44°28N 11°38E 199 D8
Medicine Bow U.S.A. 41°54N 106°12W 304 F10
Medicine Bow Mts. U.S.A. 40°40N 106°0W 304 F10
Medicine Hat Canada 50°0N 110°45W 297 D6
Medicine Lake U.S.A. 48°30N 104°30W 304 B11
Medicine Lodge U.S.A. 37°17N 98°35W 308 G4
Medina = Al Madīnah Si. Arabia 24°35N 39°52E 246 E3
Medina Brazil 16°15S 41°29W 333 E3
Medina Colombia 4°30N 73°21W 328 C3
Medina Mis. Or., Phil. 8°55N 125°0E 233 G5
Medina N. Dak., U.S.A. 46°54N 99°18W 308 B4
Medina N.Y., U.S.A. 43°13N 78°23W 312 C6
Medina Ohio, U.S.A. 41°8N 81°52W 312 E3
Medina → U.S.A. 29°16N 98°29W 314 G5
Medina de Pomar Spain 42°56N 3°29W 194 C7
Medina de Rioseco Spain 41°53N 5°3W 194 D5
Medina del Campo Spain 41°18N 4°55W 194 D6
Médina Gounas Senegal 13°8N 13°45W 262 C2
Medina L. U.S.A. 29°32N 98°56W 314 G5
Medina Sidonia Spain 36°28N 5°57W 195 J5
Medinaceli Spain 41°12N 2°30W 196 D2
Medinipur India 22°25N 87°21E 243 H12
Mediodia Spain 40°22N 3°39W 127 B2
Mediterranean Sea Europe 35°0N 15°0E 193 E8
Medjerda, O. → Tunisia 37°7N 10°13E 258 A2
Mednogorsk Russia 51°24N 57°37E 216 B5
Medny = Mednogorsk Russia 51°24N 57°37E 216 B5
Médoc France 45°10N 0°50W 174 C3
Medog China 29°19N 95°19E 241 A5
Medora U.S.A. 38°49N 86°10W 311 F10
Médouneu Gabon 0°57N 10°47E 264 B2
Medulin Croatia 44°49N 13°55E 199 D10
Medveđa Serbia 42°50N 21°32E 202 D5
Medvedevo Russia 56°37N 47°47E 190 B8
Medveditsa → Tver, Russia 57°5N 37°30E 188 D9
Medveditsa → Volgograd, Russia 49°35N 42°41E 190 F6
Medvedok Russia 57°20N 50°1E 190 B10
Medvezhi, Ostrava Russia 71°0N 161°0E 215 B17
Medvezhye = Krasnogvardeyskoye Russia 45°52N 41°33E 191 H5
Medvezhyegorsk Russia 63°0N 34°25E 186 B5
Medway □ U.K. 51°25N 0°32E 169 F8
Medway → U.K. 51°27N 0°46E 169 F8
Medzev Slovak Rep. 48°43N 20°55E 181 C13
Medzilaborce Slovak Rep. 49°17N 21°52E 181 B14
Medžitlija Macedonia 40°56N 21°26E 202 F5
Meekatharra Australia 26°32S 118°29E 279 E2
Meeker U.S.A. 40°2N 107°55W 304 F10
Meeniyan Australia 38°35S 146°3E 283 E7
Meersburg Germany 47°41N 9°16E 179 H5
Meerut India 29°1N 77°42E 242 E7
Meeteetse U.S.A. 44°9N 108°52W 304 D9
Mega Ethiopia 3°57N 38°19E 257 G4
Mega Sumatera Barat, Indonesia 4°0S 101°2E 234 C2
Megalo Ethiopia 6°51N 40°47E 267 C5
Megalo Chorio Greece 36°27N 27°24E 205 E9
Megalonisos Greece 38°0N 24°15E 204 D6
Megalopoli Greece 37°25N 22°7E 204 D4
Meganisi Greece 38°38N 20°46E 207 B2
Megara Greece 37°58N 23°22E 204 D5
Megasini India 21°38N 86°21E 243 J12
Megdovas = Tavropos → Greece 39°10N 21°45E 204 B3
Megève France 45°51N 6°37E 175 C10
Meghalaya □ India 25°50N 91°0E 241 C3
Meghezez Ethiopia 9°18N 39°26E 257 F4
Meghna → Bangla. 22°50N 90°50E 241 D3
Megion Russia 61°3N 76°6E 214 C8
Mégiscane, L. Canada 48°35N 75°55W 298 C4
Megisti Greece 36°8N 29°34E 205 E11
Megra Russia 60°11N 37°14E 188 B9
Meguro Japan 35°37N 139°42E 140 B3
Meguro → Japan 35°37N 139°45E 140 B3
Mehadia Romania 44°56N 22°23E 182 F7
Mehaïguene, O. → Algeria 32°15N 2°59E 261 B5
Meharry, Mt. Australia 22°59S 118°35E 278 D2
Mehedeby Sweden 60°27N 17°25E 162 D11
Mehedinţi □ Romania 44°40N 22°45E 182 F7
Meheisa Sudan 19°38N 32°57E 256 D3
Mehekar India 20°9N 76°34E 244 D3
Méhétia French Polynesia 17°52S 148°3W 289 f
Mehlville U.S.A. 38°31N 90°19W 308 F8
Mehmetçik = Galateia Cyprus 35°25N 34°4E 207 E10
Mehndawal India 26°58N 83°5E 243 F10
Mehr Jān Iran 33°50N 55°6E 247 C7
Mehrābād Iran 36°53N 47°55E 213 D12
Mehrābād ✈ (THR) Iran 35°41N 51°18E 141 A1
Mehrābān Iran 38°4N 47°7E 213 C12
Mehram Nagar India 28°34N 77°8E 120 B1
Mehrān Iran 33°7N 46°10E 213 F12
Mehrān → Iran 26°45N 55°26E 247 E7
Mehrgarh Pakistan 29°30N 67°30E 242 E2
Mehrīz Iran 31°35N 54°28E 247 D7
Mehrow Germany 52°34N 13°37E 115 A4
Mehtar Lam Afghan. 34°39N 70°11E 240 B3
Mehun-sur-Yèvre France 47°10N 2°13E 173 E9
Mei Jiang → China 24°25N 116°35E 229 E11
Mei Lanfang, Pantheon of Beijing, China 114 a2
Mei Xian China 34°18N 107°55E 226 G4
Meia Ponte → Brazil 18°32S 49°36W 333 E2
Meicheng China 29°29N 119°16E 229 C12
Meichengzhen China 28°9N 111°40E 229 C8
Meichuan China 30°8N 115°31E 229 B10
Meidling Austria 48°10N 16°20E 142 A2
Meidougou Cameroon 6°25N 14°13E 264 A2
Méier Brazil 22°52S 43°15W 135 B1
Meiganga Cameroon 6°30N 14°25E 264 A2
Meighen I. Canada 80°0N 99°30W 295 B12
Meigs U.S.A. 31°4N 84°6W 316 D5
Meigu China 28°16N 103°20E 228 C4
Meihekou China 42°32N 125°40E 224 A2
Meiji Shrine Tokyo, Japan 140 b1
Meiktila Burma 20°53N 95°54E 241 E5
Meili Xue Shan China 28°30N 98°39E 228 C2
Meimyu = Maymyo Burma 22°2N 96°28E 236 A1
Meinerzhagen Germany 51°6N 7°38E 178 D3
Meiningen Germany 50°34N 10°25E 178 E6
Meinung Taiwan 22°54N 120°32E 225 D2
Meio → Brazil 13°36S 44°7W 333 D3
Meira, Serra de Spain 43°15N 7°15W 194 B3
Meiringen Switz. 46°43N 8°12E 179 J4
Meise Belgium 50°56N 4°20E 116 A1
Meishan Sichuan, China 30°3N 103°23E 228 B4
Meishan Taiwan 23°35N 120°33E 225 C2
Meissen Germany 51°9N 13°29E 178 D9
Meissner Germany 51°14N 9°50E 178 D5
Meissner-Kaufunger Wald ⌓ Germany 51°16N 9°45E 178 D5
Meitan China 27°45N 107°29E 228 D6
Meizhou China 24°16N 116°6E 229 E11
Meja India 25°9N 82°7E 243 G10
Mejillones Chile 23°10S 70°30W 334 A1
Mejiro Japan 35°43N 139°43E 140 A3
Mékambo Gabon 1°2N 13°50E 264 B2
Mekdela Ethiopia 11°24N 39°10E 257 E4
Mekele Ethiopia 13°33N 39°30E 257 E4
Mekerghene, Sebkra Algeria 26°21N 1°30E 261 C5
Mékhé Senegal 15°7N 16°38W 262 B1
Mekhomiya = Razlog Bulgaria 41°53N 23°28E 202 E7
Mekhtar Pakistan 30°30N 69°15E 240 C3
Meknès Morocco 33°57N 5°33W 260 B3
Meknès-Tafilalet □ Morocco 33°3N 5°35W 260 B3
Meko Nigeria 7°27N 2°52E 263 D5
Mekong → Asia 9°30N 106°15E 237 H6
Mekongga Indonesia 3°39S 121°15E 231 E6
Mekoryuk U.S.A. 60°23N 166°11W 303 F6
Mekrou → Benin 12°25N 2°50E 263 C5
Mekvari = Kür → Azerbaijan 39°29N 49°15E 213 C13
Mel Italy 46°4N 12°5E 199 B9
Melagiri Hills India 12°20N 77°30E 245 H3
Melah, Oued el → Algeria 32°20N 2°28E 261 B5
Melaka Malaysia 2°15N 102°15E 237 L4
Melaka □ Malaysia 2°15N 102°15E 237 L4
Melambes Greece 35°8N 24°40E 207 E5
Melanesia Pac. Oc. 4°0S 155°0E 277 A10
Melanesian Basin Pac. Oc. 0°5N 160°35E 288 G8
Melapalaiyam India 8°39N 77°44E 245 K3
Melawi → Indonesia 0°5N 111°29E 235 B4
Melaya Indonesia 8°17S 114°30E 231 J17
Melbourne Vic., Australia 37°48S 144°58E 128 A1
Melbourne Fla., U.S.A. 28°5N 80°37W 317 G9
Melbourne Iowa, U.S.A. 41°57N 93°6W 310 C3
Melbourne ✈ (MEL) Australia 37°40S 144°50E 128 A1
Melcher-Dallas U.S.A. 41°14N 93°15W 310 C3
Melchor Múzquiz Mexico 27°53N 101°31W 318 B4
Melchor Ocampo Mexico 24°51N 101°39W 318 C4
Meldal Norway 63°3N 9°44E 164 A6
Méldola Italy 44°7N 12°5E 199 D9
Meldorf Germany 54°5N 9°5E 178 A5
Mélé C.A.R. 9°46N 21°33E 264 A4
Mele B. Vanuatu 17°44S 168°14E 287 G6
Meleden Somalia 10°25N 49°51E 267 B6
Melegnano Italy 45°21N 9°19E 198 C6
Meleizem Mauritania 22°19N 11°24W 260 D2
Melekeok Palau 7°27N 134°38E 288 c
Melekess = Dimitrovgrad Russia 54°14N 49°39E 190 C9
Melenci Serbia 45°32N 20°20E 182 E5
Melenki Russia 55°20N 41°37E 190 C5
Meleuz Russia 52°58N 55°55E 216 B5
Mélèzes → Canada 57°40N 69°29W 298 A5
Melfi Chad 11°0N 17°59E 259 F3
Melfi Italy 41°0N 15°39E 201 B8
Melfort Sask., Canada 52°50N 104°37W 297 C8
Melfort Zimbabwe 18°0S 31°25E 269 F3
Melgaço Portugal 42°7N 8°15W 194 C2
Melgar de Fernamental Spain 42°27N 4°17W 194 C6
Melgraseyri Iceland 66°1N 22°27W 155 A4
Melhus Norway 63°17N 10°18E 164 A7
Melide Spain 42°55N 8°1W 194 C2
Meligales Greece 37°15N 21°59E 204 D3
Melilla N. Afr. 35°21N 2°57W 261 A4
Melilli Italy 37°11N 15°7E 201 E8
Melintang, Danau Indonesia 0°18S 116°20E 235 C5
Melipilla Chile 33°42S 71°15W 334 C1
Melissa Canada 45°24N 79°14W 312 A5
Melissa, Akra Greece 35°6N 24°33E 207 E5
Melissa Oros Greece 37°32N 26°4E 205 D8
Melissani Cave Greece 38°15N 20°38E 207 C2
Melita Canada 49°15N 101°0W 297 D8
Mélito di Porto Salvo Italy 37°55N 15°47E 201 E8
Melitopol Ukraine 46°50N 35°22E 189 J8
Melk Austria 48°13N 15°20E 180 C8
Melkki Finland 60°8N 24°53E 121 C2
Mellan Fryken Sweden 59°45N 13°10E 162 E7
Mellansel Sweden 63°26N 18°19E 160 E18
Mellbystrand Sweden 56°30N 12°56E 163 H6
Melle Deux-Sèvres, France 46°14N 0°10W 174 B3
Melle Niedersachsen, Germany 52°12N 8°20E 178 C4
Mellègue, O. → Tunisia 36°36N 9°14E 258 A1
Mellen U.S.A. 46°20N 90°40W 308 B8
Mellerud Sweden 58°41N 12°28E 163 F6
Mellette U.S.A. 45°9N 98°30W 308 C4
Mellid = Melide Spain 42°55N 8°1W 194 C2
Mellieha Malta 35°57N 14°22E 206 F7
Mellieha Bay Malta 35°59N 14°22E 206 F7
Mellit Sudan 14°7N 25°34E 257 E2
Mellizo Sur, Cerro Chile 48°33S 73°10W 336 C2
Mellrichstadt Germany 50°25N 10°17E 178 E6
Mellunkylä Finland 60°14N 25°5E 121 B3
Mellunmäki Finland 60°14N 25°6E 121 B3
Melnik Bulgaria 41°30N 23°25E 202 E7
Mělník Czech Rep. 50°22N 14°23E 180 A7
Melnytsya Podilska Ukraine 48°37N 26°10E 183 B11
Melo Uruguay 32°20S 54°10W 335 C5
Melolo Indonesia 9°53S 120°40E 231 F6
Melouprey Cambodia 13°48N 105°16E 236 F5
Melrhir, Chott Algeria 34°13N 6°30E 261 B6
Melrose N.S.W., Australia 32°42S 146°57E 283 B7
Melrose Borders, U.K. 55°36N 2°43W 167 F6
Melrose Mass., U.S.A. 42°27N 71°2W 116 A2
Melrose Minn., U.S.A. 45°40N 94°49W 308 C6
Melrose N. Mex., U.S.A. 34°26N 103°38W 305 J12
Melrose N.Y., U.S.A. 40°49N 73°55W 132 B2
Melrose Park U.S.A. 26°6N 80°11W 129 B3
Melsbroek Belgium 50°55N 4°29E 116 A2
Melsisi Vanuatu 15°46S 168°10E 287 E6
Melstone U.S.A. 46°36N 107°52W 304 C10
Melsungen Germany 51°7N 9°32E 178 D5
Melton Australia 37°41S 144°35E 282 D6
Melton Mowbray U.K. 52°47N 0°54W 168 E7
Melun France 48°32N 2°39E 173 D9
Melung Nepal 27°31N 86°3E 243 F12
Melur India 10°2N 78°23E 245 J4
Melut South Sudan 10°30N 32°13E 257 E3
Melville Sask., Canada 50°55N 102°50W 297 C8
Melville Gauteng, S. Africa 26°11S 28°1E 123 B2
Melville, C. Queens., Australia 14°11S 144°30E 280 A3
Melville, C. Phil. 7°49N 117°0E 233 H1
Melville, L. Canada 53°30N 60°0W 299 B8
Melville B. N. Terr., Australia 12°0S 136°45E 280 A2
Melville B. Greenland 75°30N 63°0W 154 B4
Melville I. N. Terr., Australia 11°30S 131°0E 278 B5
Melville I. Canada 75°30N 112°0W 295 B9
Melville Pen. Canada 68°0N 84°0W 295 D15
Melvin, Lough Ireland 54°26N 8°10W 166 B3
Mélykút Hungary 46°11N 19°25E 182 D4
Memaliaj Albania 40°25N 19°56E 202 F3
Memba Mozam. 14°11S 40°30E 269 E5
Membalong Indonesia 3°9S 107°37E 235 C3
Memboro Indonesia 9°30S 119°30E 278 A2
Membrilla Spain 38°59N 3°21W 195 G7
Memel = Klaipėda Lithuania 55°43N 21°10E 184 C8
Memel S. Africa 27°38S 29°36E 271 C4
Memmingen Germany 47°58N 10°10E 179 H6
Mempawah Indonesia 0°30N 109°5E 235 B3
Memphis Egypt 29°52N 31°12E 256 J7
Memphis Mich., U.S.A. 42°54N 82°46W 312 D2
Memphis Mo., U.S.A. 40°28N 92°10W 310 D4
Memphis Tenn., U.S.A. 35°8N 90°2W 315 D9
Memphis Tex., U.S.A. 34°44N 100°33W 314 D4
Memphrémagog, L. N. Amer. 45°8N 72°17W 313 B12
Mena Ukraine 51°31N 32°13E 189 G7
Mena Ark., U.S.A. 34°35N 94°15W 314 D7
Mena → Ethiopia 5°40N 40°50E 257 F5
Menado = Manado Indonesia 1°29N 124°51E 231 D6
Menai Strait U.K. 53°11N 4°13W 168 D3
Ménaka Mali 15°59N 2°18E 263 B5
Menan = Chao Phraya → Thailand 13°40N 100°31E 236 F3
Menarandra → Madag. 25°17S 44°30E 272 D1
Menard U.S.A. 30°55N 99°47W 314 F5
Menard Fracture Zone Pac. Oc. 43°0S 97°0W 289 M18
Menate Indonesia 0°12S 113°3E 235 C4
Menawashei Sudan 12°41N 24°59E 257 E1
Mendaña Fracture Zone Pac. Oc. 16°0S 91°0W 289 J18
Mendawai → Indonesia 3°30S 113°0E 235 C4
Mende France 44°31N 3°30E 174 D7
Mendebo Mts. Ethiopia 7°0N 39°22E 257 F4
Mendeleyev Ridge Arctic 80°0N 178°0W 150 B17
Menden Germany 51°26N 7°47E 178 D3
Mendenhall, C. U.S.A. 59°45N 166°10W 303 G6
Menderes Turkey 38°14N 27°8E 205 C9
Mendhar India 33°35N 74°10E 243 C6
Mendi Ethiopia 9°47N 35°4E 257 F4
Mendi Papua N. G. 6°11S 143°39E 286 D2
Mendip Hills U.K. 51°17N 2°40W 169 F5
Mendocino U.S.A. 39°19N 123°48W 304 G2
Mendocino, C. U.S.A. 40°26N 124°25W 304 F1
Mendocino Fracture Zone Pac. Oc. 40°0N 142°0W 289 D13
Mendol Indonesia 0°36N 103°13E 234 B2
Mendon U.S.A. 42°0N 85°27W 311 B11
Mendooran Australia 31°50S 149°6E 283 A8
Mendota Calif., U.S.A. 36°45N 120°23W 306 J6
Mendota Ill., U.S.A. 41°33N 89°7W 310 C7
Mendoyo Indonesia 8°23S 114°42E 231 J17
Mendoza Argentina 32°50S 68°52W 334 C2
Mendoza □ Argentina 33°0S 69°0W 334 C2
Mene Grande Venezuela 9°49N 70°56W 328 B3
Menemen Turkey 38°34N 27°3E 205 C9
Menen Belgium 50°47N 3°7E 170 D3
Menéndez, L. Argentina 42°40S 71°51W 336 B2
Menfi Italy 37°36N 12°58E 200 E5
Mengcheng China 33°12N 116°36E 226 H9
Mengdingjie China 23°31N 98°58E 228 F2
Mengeš Slovenia 46°10N 14°35E 199 B11
Menggala Indonesia 4°30S 105°15E 234 C3
Menghai China 21°49N 100°55E 228 G3
Mengíbar Spain 37°58N 3°48W 195 H7
Mengjin China 34°55N 112°45E 226 G7
Mengla China 21°20N 101°25E 228 G3
Menglian China 22°21N 99°27E 228 F2
Mengong Cameroon 2°56N 11°25E 264 B2
Mengshan China 24°14N 110°55E 229 E8
Mengyin China 35°40N 117°58E 227 G9
Mengzhe China 22°2N 100°15E 228 F3
Mengzi China 23°20N 103°22E 228 F4
Menifee U.S.A. 33°41N 117°10W 307 M9
Menihek Canada 54°28N 56°36W 299 B6
Menihek L. Canada 54°0N 67°0W 299 B6
Menin = Menen Belgium 50°47N 3°7E 170 D3
Menindee Australia 32°20S 142°25E 282 B5
Menindee L. Australia 32°20S 142°25E 282 B5
Meningie Australia 35°50S 139°18E 282 C3
Menjangan, Pulau Indonesia 8°7S 114°31E 231 J17
Menkrour Algeria 26°27N 8°9E 261 C6
Menlo Park U.S.A. 37°27N 122°12W 306 H4
Menngen ☼ Australia 15°21S 131°16E 278 C5
Menominee U.S.A. 45°6N 87°37W 308 C10
Menominee → U.S.A. 45°6N 87°35W 308 C10
Menomonee Falls U.S.A. 43°10N 88°7W 311 A8
Menomonie U.S.A. 44°53N 91°55W 308 C8
Menongue Angola 14°48S 17°52E 265 E3
Menorca Spain 40°0N 4°0E 206 B5
Menorca ✈ (MAH) Spain 39°50N 4°16E 196 F9
Mentakab Malaysia 3°29N 102°21E 237 L4
Mentasta Lake U.S.A. 62°55N 143°45W 303 E12
Mentawai, Kepulauan Indonesia 2°0S 99°0E 234 C1
Mentawai, Selat Indonesia 1°45S 100°0E 234 C2
Menteng Indonesia 6°11S 106°49E 122 B1
Menton France 43°50N 7°29E 175 E11
Mentone U.S.A. 41°10N 86°2W 311 C10
Mentor U.S.A. 41°40N 81°21W 312 E3
Menyamya Papua N. G. 7°10S 145°59E 286 D3
Menyapa Indonesia 1°4N 116°4E 235 B5
Menzel-Bourguiba Tunisia 37°9N 9°49E 258 A1
Menzel-Chaker Tunisia 35°0N 10°26E 258 B2
Menzel-Temime Tunisia 36°46N 11°0E 258 A2
Menzelinsk Russia 55°47N 53°11E 186 C9
Menzies Australia 29°40S 121°2E 279 E3
Meob B. Namibia 24°25S 14°34E 270 B1
Meoqui Mexico 28°17N 105°29W 318 B3
Mepaco Mozam. 15°57S 30°48E 269 F3
Meppel Neths. 52°42N 6°12E 170 B6
Meppen Germany 52°42N 7°17E 178 C3
Mequinenza Spain 41°22N 0°17E 196 D5
Mequinenza, Embalse de Spain 41°25N 0°15E 196 D5
Mequon U.S.A. 43°14N 87°59W 311 A9
Mer France 47°42N 1°30E 172 E8
Merai Papua N. G. 4°52S 152°19E 286 C7
Merak Indonesia 6°10N 106°26E 231 F12
Meråker Norway 63°25N 11°46E 164 A8
Meramangye, L. Australia 28°25S 132°13E 279 E5
Meramec → U.S.A. 38°24N 90°21W 310 F6
Meran = Merano Italy 46°40N 11°9E 199 B8
Merano Italy 46°40N 11°9E 199 B8
Mérantaise → France 48°42N 2°8E 134 B1
Merapi Indonesia 7°32S 110°26E 235 D4
Merate Italy 45°42N 9°25E 198 C6
Meratus, Pegunungan Indonesia 2°45S 115°40E 235 C5
Merauke Indonesia 8°29S 140°24E 231 F10
Merbein Australia 34°10S 142°2E 282 C5
Merca = Marka Somalia 1°48N 44°50E 267 D5
Mercamadrid Spain 40°21N 3°39W 127 B2
Mercantour △ France 44°16N 6°43E 175 D10
Mercato Saraceno Italy 43°57N 12°12E 199 E9
Merced U.S.A. 37°18N 120°29W 306 H6
Merced → U.S.A. 37°21N 120°59W 306 H6
Merced, L. U.S.A. 37°43N 122°29W 136 B2
Merced Pk. U.S.A. 37°36N 119°24W 306 H7
Mercedes B. Aires, Argentina 34°40S 59°30W 334 C4
Mercedes Corrientes, Argentina 29°10S 58°5W 334 B4
Mercedes San Luis, Argentina 33°40S 65°21W 334 C2
Mercedes Camarines N., Phil. 14°7N 123°1E 232 D4
Mercedes Uruguay 33°12S 58°0W 334 C4
Merceditas Chile 28°20S 70°35W 334 B1
Mercer N.Z. 37°16S 175°5E 284 D4
Mercer Mo., U.S.A. 40°31N 93°32W 310 D3
Mercer Pa., U.S.A. 41°14N 80°15W 312 E4
Mercer Island U.S.A. 47°34N 122°13W 306 C4
Merchandise Mart U.S.A. 119 b1
Mercier Bolivia 10°42S 68°5W 330 C4
Mercury U.S.A. 36°40N 115°59W 307 J11
Mercury B. N.Z. 36°48S 175°45E 284 C4
Mercury Is. N.Z. 36°37S 175°52E 284 C4
Mercy, C. Canada 65°0N 63°30W 295 E19
Merdrignac France 48°11N 2°27W 172 D4
Mere U.K. 51°6N 2°16W 169 F5
Mere Lava Vanuatu 14°25S 168°3E 287 D6
Merebuk, Gunung Indonesia 8°13S 114°39E 231 J17
Meredale S. Africa 26°16S 27°58E 123 B1
Meredith Australia 37°49S 144°5E 282 D6
Meredith, C. Falk. Is. 52°15S 60°40W 153 f
Meredith, L. U.S.A. 35°43N 101°33W 314 D4
Meredosia U.S.A. 39°50N 90°34W 310 E6
Merefa Ukraine 49°48N 36°3E 189 H9
Merei Romania 45°7N 26°43E 183 E11
Merga = Nukheila Sudan 19°1N 26°21E 256 D2
Mergui Burma 12°26N 98°34E 236 F2
Mergui Arch. = Myeik Kyunzu Burma 11°30N 97°30E 237 G1
Meribah Australia 34°43S 140°51E 282 C4
Méribel-les-Allues France 45°25N 6°34E 175 C10
Meriç Turkey 41°11N 26°25E 203 E10
Meriç → Turkey 40°52N 26°12E 203 F10
Mérida Yucatán, Mexico 20°58N 89°37W 319 C7
Merida Phil. 10°55N 124°32E 233 F5
Mérida Spain 38°55N 6°25W 195 G4
Mérida Venezuela 8°24N 71°8W 328 B3
Mérida □ Venezuela 8°30N 71°10W 328 B3
Mérida, Cord. de Venezuela 9°0N 71°0W 328 B3
Meriden W. Mids., U.K. 52°26N 1°38W 169 E6
Meriden Conn., U.S.A. 41°32N 72°48W 313 E12
Meridian Calif., U.S.A. 39°9N 121°55W 306 F5
Meridian Ga., U.S.A. 31°27N 81°23W 316 D8
Meridian Idaho, U.S.A. 43°37N 116°24W 304 E5
Meridian Miss., U.S.A. 32°22N 88°42W 315 E10
Mérignac France 44°51N 0°39W 174 D3
Merimbula Australia 36°53S 149°54E 283 D8
Merin Gubai Somalia 1°26N 44°20E 267 D5
Merinda Australia 20°2S 148°11E 280 C4
Mering Germany 48°16N 10°59E 179 G6
Meringa Nigeria 10°44N 12°9E 263 C7
Meringur Australia 34°20S 141°19E 282 C4
Merir Palau 4°10N 132°30E 231 D8
Merirumã Brazil 1°15N 54°50W 329 C7
Merizo Guam 13°16N 144°40E 302 d
Merkel U.S.A. 32°28N 100°1W 314 E4
Merlimau, Pulau Singapore 1°17N 103°42E 138 B2
Mermaid Reef Australia 17°6S 119°36E 278 C2
Mero Dominica 15°25N 61°26W 323 k
Meroe India 7°33N 93°33E 245 L11
Merowe Sudan 18°29N 31°46E 256 D3
Merowe Dam Sudan 18°35N 31°56E 256 D3
Merredin Australia 31°28S 118°18E 279 F2
Merri Cr. → Australia 37°47S 144°59E 128 A1
Merrick U.K. 55°8N 4°28W 167 F4
Merrickville Canada 44°55N 75°50W 313 B9
Merrill Oreg., U.S.A. 42°1N 121°36W 304 E3
Merrill Wis., U.S.A. 45°11N 89°41W 308 C9
Merrillville U.S.A. 41°29N 87°20W 311 C9
Merrimack → U.S.A. 42°49N 70°49W 313 D14
Merriman U.S.A. 42°55N 101°42W 308 D3
Merrion Ireland 53°19N 6°12W 120 B2
Merrionette Park U.S.A. 41°41N 87°40W 119 C2
Merritt Canada 50°10N 120°45W 296 C4
Merritt Island U.S.A. 28°21N 80°42W 317 G9
Merriwa Australia 32°6S 150°22E 283 B9
Merriwagga Australia 33°47S 145°43E 283 B6
Merry I. Canada 55°29N 77°31W 298 A4
Merrygoen Australia 31°51S 149°12E 283 A8
Merryville U.S.A. 30°45N 93°33W 314 F8
Mersa Fatma Eritrea 14°57N 40°17E 257 E5
Mersch Lux. 49°44N 6°7E 170 E6
Merse → Italy 43°5N 11°22E 199 E8
Mersea I. U.K. 51°47N 0°58E 169 F8
Merseburg Germany 51°22N 11°59E 178 D7
Mersey → U.K. 53°25N 3°1W 168 D4
Merseyside □ U.K. 53°31N 3°2W 168 D4
Mersin = İçel Turkey 36°51N 34°36E 250 B5
Mersing Malaysia 2°25N 103°50E 237 L4
Merta India 26°39N 74°4E 242 F6
Merta Road India 26°43N 73°55E 242 F5
Merthyr Tydfil U.K. 51°45N 3°22W 169 F4
Merthyr Tydfil □ U.K. 51°46N 3°21W 169 F4
Merti Kenya 1°4N 38°40E 268 B4
Mértola Portugal 37°40N 7°40W 195 H3
Merton □ U.K. 51°25N 0°11W 125 B2
Mertz Glacier Antarctica 67°30S 144°45E 151 C10
Mertzon U.S.A. 31°16N 100°49W 314 F4
Méru Oise, France 49°13N 2°8E 173 C9
Meru Eastern, Kenya 0°3N 37°40E 268 B4
Meru Tanzania 3°15S 36°46E 268 C4
Meru △ Kenya 0°5N 38°10E 268 B4
Meru Betiri △ Indonesia 8°27S 113°51E 235 D4
Merv = Mary Turkmenistan 37°40N 61°50E 247 B9
Merville France 50°38N 2°38E 173 B9
Méry-sur-Seine France 48°31N 3°54E 173 D10
Merzifon Turkey 40°53N 35°32E 212 B6
Merzig Germany 49°26N 6°38E 179 F2
Merzouga, Erg Tin Algeria 24°0N 11°4E 261 D7
Mesa U.S.A. 33°25N 111°50W 305 K8
Mesa Verde △ U.S.A. 37°11N 108°29W 305 H9
Mesach Mellet Libya 24°30N 11°30E 258 D2
Mesada = Masada Israel 31°18N 35°21E 251 G6
Mesagne Italy 40°34N 17°48E 201 B10
Mesanagros Greece 36°1N 27°49E 206 E11
Mesaoría Cyprus 35°12N 33°14E 207 E9
Meschede Germany 51°20N 8°18E 178 D4
Mescit Turkey 40°21N 41°11E 213 B9
Mesemvriya = Nesebŭr Bulgaria 42°41N 27°46E 203 D11
Mesfinto Ethiopia 13°20N 37°22E 257 E4
Mesgarābād Iran 35°27N 51°30E 141 B3
Mesgouez, L. Canada 51°20N 75°0W 298 B5
Meshchovsk Russia 54°22N 35°17E 188 E8
Meshed = Mashhad Iran 36°20N 59°35E 247 B8
Meshgīn Shahr Iran 38°30N 47°45E 213 C12
Meshkede-Ser = Bābol Sar Iran 36°45N 52°45E 247 B7
Meshoppen U.S.A. 41°36N 76°3W 313 E8
Meshra er Req South Sudan 8°25N 29°18E 257 F2
Mesilinka → Canada 56°6N 124°30W 296 B4
Meslay-du-Maine France 47°58N 0°33W 172 E6
Mesocco Switz. 46°23N 9°12E 179 J5
Mesologi Greece 38°21N 21°28E 204 C3
Mesongi Greece 39°29N 19°56E 206 C9
Mesopotamia = Al Jazirah Iraq 33°30N 44°0E 213 E10
Mesopotamia U.S.A. 41°27N 80°57W 312 E4
Mesopotamo Greece 39°14N 20°32E 204 B2
Mesoraca Italy 39°5N 16°48E 201 C9
Mésou Volímais = Volimes Greece 37°52N 20°39E 207 D2
Mesquite U.S.A. 36°48N 114°4W 305 H6
Messaad Algeria 34°8N 3°30E 261 B5
Messac France 47°49N 1°50W 172 E5
Messalo → Mozam. 12°25S 39°15E 269 E4
Messaména Cameroon 3°48N 12°49E 264 B2
Messara, Kolpos Greece 35°6N 24°47E 207 E5
Messe Austria 48°13N 16°24E 142 A2
Messier, Canal Chile 48°20S 74°33W 336 C2
Messina = Musina S. Africa 22°20S 30°5E 271 B5
Messina Italy 38°11N 15°34E 201 D8
Messina, Str. di Italy 38°15N 15°35E 201 D8
Messini Greece 37°4N 22°1E 204 D4
Messinia □ Greece 37°10N 22°0E 204 D3
Messiniakos Kolpos Greece 36°45N 22°5E 204 E4
Messkirch Germany 47°59N 9°7E 179 H5
Messlingen Sweden 62°40N 12°50E 162 B6
Mesta = Nestos → Europe 40°54N 24°49E 203 F8
Mesta, Akra Greece 38°16N 25°53E 205 C7
Mestanza Spain 38°35N 4°4W 195 G6
Mestersvig Greenland 72°10N 23°40W 154 C8
Mestre Italy 45°29N 12°15E 199 C9
Mestre, Espigão Brazil 12°30S 46°10W 333 D2
Mesudiye Turkey 40°28N 37°46E 212 B7
Meta U.S.A. 38°19N 92°10W 310 F4
Meta □ Colombia 3°30N 73°0W 328 C3
Meta → S. Amer. 6°12N 67°28W 328 B4
Meta Incognita Pen. Canada 62°45N 68°30W 295 E18
Metabetchouan Canada 48°26N 71°52W 299 C5
Metairie U.S.A. 29°59N 90°9W 131 A2
Metalici, Munţii Romania 46°15N 22°50E 182 D7
Metaline Falls U.S.A. 48°52N 117°22W 304 B5
Metallifere, Colline Italy 43°10N 11°0E 198 E8
Metamora U.S.A. 40°47N 89°22W 310 D7
Metán Argentina 25°30S 65°0W 334 B3
Metangula Mozam. 12°40S 34°50E 269 E3
Metanópoli Italy 45°24N 9°15E 128 B2
Metauro → Italy 43°50N 13°3E 199 E10
Metcalf U.S.A. 30°43N 83°59W 316 E6
Metcalfe Canada 45°14N 75°28W 313 A9
Metema Ethiopia 12°58N 36°12E 257 E4
Metengobalame Mozam. 14°49S 34°30E 269 E3
Meteora Greece 39°43N 21°37E 204 B3
Methana Greece 37°35N 23°23E 204 D5
Methoni Greece 36°49N 21°42E 204 E3
Methven N.Z. 43°38S 171°40E 285 D6
Metil Mozam. 16°24S 39°0E 269 F4
Metkovets Bulgaria 43°37N 23°10E 202 C7
Metković Croatia 43°6N 17°39E 199 E14
Metlakatla U.S.A. 55°8N 131°35W 303 J15
Metlaoui Tunisia 34°24N 8°24E 258 B1
Metlik Papua N. G. 4°46S 152°55E 286 C7
Metlika Slovenia 45°40N 15°20E 199 C12
Metlili Chaamba Algeria 32°16N 3°38E 261 B5
Metro Indonesia 5°5S 105°20E 234 D3
Metro Toronto Zoo Canada 43°48N 79°10W 141 A3
Metropolis U.S.A. 37°9N 88°44W 308 G9
Metropolitan Museum of Art New York, U.S.A. 132 b3
Metropolitana □ Chile 33°30S 70°50W 334 C1
Metsovo Greece 39°48N 21°12E 204 B3
Metter U.S.A. 32°24N 82°3W 316 C7
Mettuppalaiyam India 11°18N 76°59E 245 J3
Mettur India 11°48N 77°47E 245 J3
Metu Ethiopia 8°18N 35°35E 257 F4
Metz France 49°8N 6°10E 173 C13
Metzingen Germany 48°31N 9°17E 179 G5
Meudon France 48°48N 2°14E 134 B2
Meulaboh Indonesia 4°11N 96°3E 234 B1
Meung-sur-Loire France 47°50N 1°40E 173 E8
Meureudu Indonesia 5°19N 96°10E 234 A1
Meurthe → France 48°47N 6°9E 173 D13
Meurthe-et-Moselle □ France 48°52N 6°0E 173 D13
Meuse □ France 49°8N 5°25E 173 C12
Meuse → Europe 50°45N 5°41E 170 D5
Meuselwitz Germany 51°2N 12°17E 178 D8
Meutapok, Mt. Malaysia 5°40N 117°0E 235 A5
Mevaseret Zion Israel 31°48N 35°9E 123 B1
Mevo Beitar Israel 31°43N 35°6E 123 B1
Mexia U.S.A. 31°41N 96°29W 314 F6
Mexiana, I. Brazil 0°0 49°30W 332 B2
Mexicali Mexico 32°40N 115°30W 307 N11
Mexican Plateau Mexico 25°0N 104°0W 292 G9
Mexican Water U.S.A. 36°57N 109°32W 305 H9
Mexico Maine, U.S.A. 44°34N 70°33W 313 B14
Mexico Mo., U.S.A. 39°10N 91°53W 310 E5
Mexico N.Y., U.S.A. 43°28N 76°14W 313 C8
México □ Mexico 19°20N 99°30W 319 D5
Mexico ■ Cent. Amer. 25°0N 105°0W 318 C4
México, Ciudad de Mexico 19°24N 99°9W 128 B2
Mexico, G. of Cent. Amer. 25°0N 90°0W 319 C7
Mexico B. U.S.A. 43°35N 76°20W 313 C8
Mexico Beach U.S.A. 29°57N 85°25W 316 F4
Mexico City Int. ✈ (MEX) Mexico 19°25N 99°5W 128 B2
Meydān-e Naftūn Iran 31°56N 49°18E 247 D6
Meydani, Ra's-e Iran 25°24N 59°6E 247 E8
Meyenburg Germany 53°18N 12°14E 178 B8
Meyers Chuck U.S.A. 55°45N 132°15W 296 B2
Meyersdal S. Africa 26°17S 28°5E 123 B2
Meymac France 45°32N 2°10E 174 C6
Meymaneh Afghan. 35°53N 64°38E 240 B2
Meyo Cameroon 2°50N 11°1E 264 B2
Meyrueis France 44°12N 3°27E 174 D7
Meyssac France 45°3N 1°40E 174 C5
Meyzieu France 45°46N 4°59E 175 C8
Mezdra Bulgaria 43°12N 23°42E 202 C7
Mèze France 43°27N 3°36E 174 E7
Mezen Russia 65°50N 44°20E 186 A7
Mezen → Russia 65°44N 44°22E 186 A7
Mézenc, Mt. France 44°54N 4°11E 175 D8
Mezeş, Munţii Romania 47°5N 23°5E 182 C8
Mezha → Russia 55°44N 31°33E 188 E6
Mezhdurechensk Russia 53°41N 88°3E 217 B11
Mezhdurechenskiy Russia 59°36N 65°56E 214 D7
Mezhdurechye = Shali Russia 43°9N 45°55E 191 J7
Mezhevaya Utka = Sinegorskiy Russia 47°55N 40°52E 191 G5
Mézidon-Canon France 49°5N 0°1W 172 C6
Mézières-en-Brenne France 46°49N 1°13E 174 B5
Mézilhac France 44°49N 4°21E 175 D8
Mézin France 44°4N 0°16E 174 D4
Mezitli Turkey 36°45N 34°29E 250 B5
Mezőberény Hungary 46°49N 21°3E 182 D6
Mezőfalva Hungary 46°55N 18°49E 182 D3
Mezőhegyes Hungary 46°19N 20°49E 182 D5
Mezőkövácsháza Hungary 46°25N 20°57E 182 D5
Mezőkövesd Hungary 47°49N 20°35E 182 C5
Mézos France 44°5N 1°10W 174 D2
Mezőtúr Hungary 47°1N 20°41E 182 C5
Mezquital Mexico 23°29N 104°23W 318 C4
Mezzate Italy 45°26N 9°17E 128 B2
Mezzolombardo Italy 46°13N 11°5E 198 B8
Mfolozi → S. Africa 28°25S 32°26E 271 C5
Mgarr Malta 35°55N 14°22E 206 F7
Mgarr Gozo, Malta 36°2N 14°18E 206 E7
Mgeta Tanzania 8°22S 36°6E 269 D4
Mglin Russia 53°2N 32°50E 189 F7
Mhamid Morocco 29°49N 5°43W 260 C3
Mhlaba Hills Zimbabwe 18°30S 30°30E 269 F3
Mhow India 22°33N 75°50E 242 H6

Mi-Shima Japan 34°46N 131°9E 222 C3
Miadong S. Korea 37°36N 127°0E 137 B2
Miagao Phil. 10°39N 122°14E 233 F4
Miahuatlán Mexico 16°20N 96°36W 319 D5
Miaich South Sudan 9°30N 30°30E 257 F3
Miajadas Spain 39°9N 5°54W 195 F5
Miami Fla., U.S.A. 25°46N 80°11W 129 D2
Miami Okla., U.S.A. 36°53N 94°53W 314 C7
Miami Tex., U.S.A. 35°42N 100°38W 314 D4
Miami ➔ U.S.A. 25°46N 80°11W 129 D1
Miami Beach U.S.A. 25°47N 80°7W 129 D3
Miami Canal U.S.A. 25°45N 80°12W 317 K9
Miami Gardens U.S.A. 25°56N 80°15W 129 C1
Miami Int. ✈ (MIA) U.S.A. 25°48N 80°17W 129 D1
Miami Lakes U.S.A. 25°54N 80°18W 129 C1
Miami Shores U.S.A. 25°51N 80°11W 129 C2
Miami Springs U.S.A. 25°49N 80°17W 129 D1
Miamisburg U.S.A. 39°38N 84°17W 311 E12
Mian Xian China 33°10N 106°32E 228 A6
Mianchi China 34°48N 111°48E 226 G6
Miāndarreh Iran 35°37N 53°39E 247 C7
Miāndowāb Iran 37°0N 46°5E 213 D12
Miandrivazo Madag. 19°31S 45°29E 272 B2
Mīāneh Iran 37°30N 47°40E 213 D12
Mianning China 28°32N 102°9E 228 C4
Mianwali Pakistan 32°38N 71°28E 242 C4
Mianyang China 31°22N 104°47E 228 B5
Mianzhu China 31°22N 104°7E 228 B5
Miao Ling China 26°5N 107°30E 228 D6
Miaodao Qundao China 38°10N 120°45E 227 E11
Miaoli Taiwan 24°37N 120°49E 225 B2
Miaoli □ Taiwan 24°30N 120°55E 225 B2
Miarinarivo Antananarivo, Madag. 18°57S 46°55E 272 B2
Miarinarivo Toamasina, Madag. 16°38S 48°15E 272 B2
Miariravaratra Madag. 20°13S 47°31E 272 C2
Miass Russia 54°59N 60°6E 186 D11
Miasteczko Krajeńskie Poland 53°7N 17°1E 185 E4
Miastko Poland 54°0N 16°58E 184 E3
Miasto Poland 52°15N 21°0E 143 B2
Mica S. Africa 24°10S 30°48E 271 B5
Micanopy U.S.A. 29°30N 82°17W 317 F7
Micăsasa Romania 46°7N 24°7E 183 D9
Micco U.S.A. 27°53N 80°30W 317 H9
Miccosukee U.S.A. 30°36N 84°3W 316 E5
Miccosukee, L. U.S.A. 30°33N 83°53W 316 E6
Michael, Mt. Papua N. G. 6°27S 145°22E 286 D3
Michalovce Slovak Rep. 48°47N 21°58E 181 C14
Michałowice Poland 52°10N 20°52E 143 B1
Michigan □ U.S.A. 44°0N 85°0W 309 C11
Michigan, L. U.S.A. 44°0N 87°0W 311 B9
Michigan Avenue U.S.A. 119 b2
Michigan Center U.S.A. 42°14N 84°20W 311 B12
Michigan City U.S.A. 41°43N 86°54W 311 C10
Michika Nigeria 10°36N 13°23E 263 C7
Michipicoten I. Canada 47°40N 85°40W 298 C2
Michle Czech Rep. 50°3N 14°28E 135 B2
Michoacán □ Mexico 19°10N 101°50W 318 D4
Michurin Bulgaria 42°9N 27°51E 203 D11
Michurinsk Russia 52°58N 40°27E 190 D5
Micoene Angola 4°26S 12°48E 265 C2
Micoud St. Lucia 13°49N 60°54W 323 m
Micronesia Pac. Oc. 11°0N 160°0E 288 G7
Micronesia, Federated States of ■ Pac. Oc. 9°0N 150°0E 288 G7
Mid-Atlantic Ridge Atl. Oc. 0°0 20°0W 152 J10
Mid City Calif., U.S.A. 34°4N 118°20W 126 B2
Mid City La., U.S.A. 29°58N 90°6W 131 B2
Mid-Indian Ocean Basin Ind. Oc. 10°0S 80°0E 273 F7
Mid-Indian Ridge Ind. Oc. 30°0S 75°0E 273 H6
Mid-Pacific Seamounts Pac. Oc. 18°0N 177°0W 288 F10
Midai Indonesia 3°0N 107°47E 235 B3
Midale Canada 49°25N 103°20W 297 D8
Middelburg Neths. 51°30N 3°36E 170 C3
Middelburg Eastern Cape, S. Africa 31°30S 25°0E 270 D4
Middelburg Mpumalanga, S. Africa 25°49S 29°28E 271 C4
Middelfart Denmark 55°30N 9°43E 163 J3
Middelpos S. Africa 31°55S 20°13E 270 D3
Middelwit S. Africa 24°51S 27°3E 270 B4
Middle ➔ U.S.A. 41°26N 93°30W 310 C3
Middle Alkali L. U.S.A. 41°27N 120°5W 304 F3
Middle America Trench = Guatemala Trench Pac. Oc. 14°0N 95°0W 292 H10
Middle Andaman I. India 12°30N 92°50E 245 H11
Middle Bass I. U.S.A. 41°41N 82°48W 312 E2
Middle East Asia 35°0N 40°0E 210 E5
Middle Fork Feather ➔ U.S.A. 38°33N 121°30W 306 F5
Middle Ground Midway Is. 28°14N 177°24W 302 c
Middle Harbour Australia 33°47S 151°14E 139 A2
Middle Hd. Australia 33°49S 151°16E 139 A2
Middle I. Australia 34°6S 123°11E 279 F3
Middle Island St. Kitts & Nevis 17°20N 62°48W 322 d
Middle Loup ➔ U.S.A. 41°17N 98°24W 308 E4
Middle Park Australia 37°50S 144°57E 128 B1
Middle Raccoon ➔ U.S.A. 41°35N 93°35W 310 C3
Middle Village U.S.A. 40°43N 73°52W 132 B2
Middleboro U.S.A. 41°54N 70°55W 313 E14
Middleburg Fla., U.S.A. 30°4N 81°52W 316 E8
Middleburg Pa., U.S.A. 40°47N 77°3W 312 F7
Middleburgh U.S.A. 42°36N 74°20W 313 D10
Middlebury Ind., U.S.A. 41°41N 85°42W 311 C11
Middlebury Vt., U.S.A. 44°1N 73°10W 313 B11
Middlefield U.S.A. 41°27N 81°4W 312 E3
Middlemarch N.Z. 45°30S 170°9E 285 F5
Middlemount Australia 22°50S 148°40E 280 C4
Middleport N.Y., U.S.A. 43°13N 78°29W 312 C6
Middleport Ohio, U.S.A. 39°0N 82°3W 309 F12
Middlesboro U.S.A. 36°36N 83°43W 309 G12
Middlesbrough U.K. 54°35N 1°13W 168 C6
Middlesbrough □ U.K. 54°28N 1°13W 168 C6
Middlesex Belize 17°2N 88°31W 320 C2
Middlesex N.J., U.S.A. 40°36N 74°30W 313 F10
Middlesex N.Y., U.S.A. 42°42N 77°16W 312 D7
Middlesex □ Jamaica 18°10N 77°5W 320 a
Middlesex Fells Reservation U.S.A. 42°27N 71°6W 116 A2
Middleton Queens., Australia 22°22S 141°32E 280 C3
Middleton N.S., Canada 44°57N 65°4W 299 D6
Middleton Wis., U.S.A. 43°6N 89°30W 310 A7
Middleton Cr. ➔ Australia 22°35S 141°51E 280 C3
Middleton I. U.S.A. 59°26N 146°20W 303 D11
Middletown Armagh, U.K. 54°17N 6°51W 166 B5
Middletown Calif., U.S.A. 38°45N 122°37W 306 G4
Middletown Conn., U.S.A. 41°34N 72°39W 313 E12
Middletown Ky., U.S.A. 38°14N 85°32W 311 F11
Middletown N.Y., U.S.A. 41°27N 74°25W 313 E10
Middletown Ohio, U.S.A. 39°31N 84°24W 311 E12
Middletown Pa., U.S.A. 40°12N 76°44W 313 F8
Middleville U.S.A. 42°43N 85°28W 311 B11
Midelt Morocco 32°46N 4°44W 260 B4
Midge Point Australia 20°39S 148°43E 280 b
Midhirst N.Z. 39°17S 174°18E 284 F3
Miðsandur Iceland 64°24N 21°28W 155 D3
Midhurst Ont., Canada 44°26N 79°43W 312 B5
Midhurst W. Susx., U.K. 50°59N 0°44W 169 G7
Midī Yemen 16°19N 42°48E 248 C3
Midi, Canal du ➔ France 43°45N 1°21E 174 E5
Midi, Gare du Brussels, Belgium 116 c1
Midi d'Ossau, Pic du France 42°50N 0°26W 174 F3
Midi-Pyrénées □ France 43°55N 1°45E 174 E5
Midland W. Austral., Australia 31°54S 116°1E 279 F2
Midland Ont., Canada 44°45N 79°50W 312 B5
Midland Calif., U.S.A. 33°52N 114°48W 307 M12
Midland Mich., U.S.A. 43°37N 84°14W 309 D11
Midland Pa., U.S.A. 40°39N 80°27W 312 F4
Midland Tex., U.S.A. 32°0N 102°3W 314 F3
Midland Beach U.S.A. 40°34N 74°6W 132 C1
Midlands □ Zimbabwe 19°40S 29°0E 269 F2
Midleton Ireland 51°55N 8°10W 166 E3
Midlothian U.S.A. 41°37N 87°45W 119 D2
Midlothian □ U.K. 55°51N 3°5W 167 F5
Midnapore = Medinipur India 22°25N 87°21E 243 H12
Midongy, Tangorombohitr' i Madag. 23°30S 47°0E 272 C2
Midongy Atsimo Madag. 23°35S 47°1E 272 C2
Midori Japan 36°30N 139°15E 223 A11
Midou ➔ France 43°54N 0°30W 174 E3
Midouze ➔ France 43°48N 0°51W 174 E3
Midsayap Phil. 7°12N 124°32E 233 H5
Midsund Norway 62°41N 6°40E 164 B3
Midtgulen Norway 61°44N 5°11E 164 C2
Midtjylland □ Denmark 56°30N 9°0E 163 H2
Midu China 25°18N 100°30E 228 E3
Midville U.S.A. 32°49N 82°14W 316 C7
Midway Ala., U.S.A. 32°5N 85°31W 316 C4
Midway Fla., U.S.A. 30°30N 84°27W 316 E5
Midway Is. Pac. Oc. 28°13N 177°22W 302 c
Midway Wells U.S.A. 32°41N 115°7W 307 N11
Midwest U.S.A. 42°0N 90°0W 301 G22
Midwest Wyo., U.S.A. 43°25N 106°16W 304 E10
Midwest City U.S.A. 35°27N 97°24W 314 D6
Midwood U.S.A. 40°37N 73°57W 132 C2
Midyat Turkey 37°25N 41°23E 213 D9
Midžor Bulgaria 43°24N 22°40E 202 C6
Mie Japan 32°58N 131°35E 222 E3
Mie □ Japan 34°30N 136°10E 223 C8
Miechów Poland 50°21N 20°5E 185 H7
Miedwie, Jezioro Poland 53°17N 14°54E 185 E1
Miedzeszyn Poland 52°13N 21°11E 143 B3
Międzybórz Poland 51°25N 17°34E 185 G4
Międzychód Poland 52°35N 15°53E 185 F2
Międzylesie Dolnośląskie, Poland 50°8N 16°40E 185 H3
Międzylesie Warszawa, Poland 52°12N 21°10E 143 B3
Międzyrzec Podlaski Poland 51°58N 22°45E 185 G9
Międzyrzecz Poland 52°26N 15°35E 185 F2
Międzyzdroje Poland 53°56N 14°26E 184 E1
Miejska Górka Poland 51°39N 16°58E 185 G3
Miélan France 43°27N 0°19E 174 E4
Mielau = Mława Poland 53°9N 20°25E 185 E7
Mielec Poland 50°15N 21°25E 185 H8
Mienga Angola 17°12S 19°48E 265 F3
Miercurea-Ciuc Romania 46°21N 25°48E 183 D10
Miercurea Sibiului Romania 45°53N 23°48E 183 E8
Mieres Spain 43°18N 5°48W 194 B5
Mieroszów Poland 50°40N 16°11E 185 H3
Mies = Stříbro Czech Rep. 49°44N 13°0E 180 A6
Mieso Ethiopia 9°15N 40°43E 257 F5
Miessaari Finland 60°8N 24°47E 121 C1
Mieszkowice Poland 52°47N 14°30E 185 F1
Mifflintown U.S.A. 40°34N 77°24W 312 F7
Mifraz Ḥefa Israel 32°52N 35°0E 250 F6
Migang Shan China 35°32N 106°13E 226 G4
Migennes France 47°58N 3°31E 173 E10
Migliarino Italy 44°46N 11°56E 199 D8
Migliarino-San Rossore-Massaciuccoli △ Italy 43°44N 10°20E 198 E7
Migori Kenya 1°4S 34°28E 268 C3
Miguasha △ Canada 48°5N 66°26W 299 C6
Miguel Alemán, Presa Mexico 18°15N 96°32W 319 D5
Miguel Alves Brazil 4°11S 42°55W 332 B3
Miguel Calmon Brazil 11°25S 40°36W 332 D3
Miguel Hidalgo Mexico 19°25N 99°12W 128 B1
Miguel Hidalgo, Presa Mexico 26°30N 108°34W 318 B3
Miguelturra Spain 38°58N 3°53W 195 G7
Mihăileni Romania 47°58N 26°9E 183 C11
Mihăileşti Romania 44°20N 25°54E 183 F10
Mihailovca Moldova 46°33N 28°56E 183 D13
Mihalgazi Turkey 40°2N 30°34E 205 A12
Mihalıççık Turkey 39°53N 31°30E 212 C4
Mihara Japan 34°24N 133°5E 222 C5
Mihara-Yama Japan 34°43N 139°23E 223 C11
Miheşu de Cîmpie Romania 46°41N 24°9E 183 D9
Mijas Spain 36°36N 4°40W 195 J6
Mikawa-Wan Japan 34°44N 137°13E 223 C9
Mikese Tanzania 6°48S 37°55E 268 D4
Mikha-Tskhakaya = Senaki Georgia 42°15N 42°1E 191 J6
Mikhailovka = Mykhaylivka Ukraine 47°12N 35°15E 189 J8
Mikhaylov Russia 54°14N 39°0E 188 E10
Mikhaylovgrad = Montana Bulgaria 43°27N 23°16E 202 C7
Mikhaylovka = Kimovsk Russia 54°0N 38°29E 188 E10
Mikhaylovka Russia 50°3N 43°5E 190 E6
Mikhnevo Russia 55°4N 37°59E 188 E9
Miki Hyōgo, Japan 34°48N 134°59E 222 C6
Miki Kagawa, Japan 34°12N 134°7E 222 C6
Mikines Greece 37°43N 22°46E 204 D4
Mikir Hills India 26°10N 93°30E 241 B4
Mikkeli Finland 61°43N 27°15E 188 B4
Mikkwa ➔ Canada 58°25N 114°46W 296 B6
Mikniya Sudan 17°0N 33°45E 257 D3
Mikołajki Poland 53°49N 21°37E 184 E8
Míkonos = Mykonos Greece 37°30N 25°25E 205 D7
Mikope Dem. Rep. of the Congo 4°58S 20°43E 265 C4
Mikoyan-Shakhar = Karachayevsk Russia 43°50N 41°55E 191 J5
Mikri Prespa, L. Greece 40°47N 21°3E 202 F5
Mikro Derio Greece 41°19N 26°6E 203 E10
Mikstat Poland 51°32N 17°59E 185 G4
Mikulov Czech Rep. 48°48N 16°39E 181 C9
Mikumi Tanzania 7°26S 37°0E 268 D4
Mikumi △ Tanzania 7°35S 37°15E 268 D4
Mikun Russia 62°20N 50°0E 186 B9
Mikuni Japan 36°13N 136°9E 223 A8
Mikuni-Tōge Japan 36°50N 138°50E 223 A10
Mikura-Jima Japan 33°52N 139°36E 223 D11
Mila Algeria 36°27N 6°16E 261 A6
Mila □ Algeria 36°25N 6°10E 261 A6
Milaca U.S.A. 45°45N 93°39W 308 C7
Miladummadulu Atoll Maldives 5°50N 73°30E 272 d
Milagro Ecuador 2°11S 79°36W 328 D2
Milagros Phil. 12°13N 123°30E 232 E4
Milan = Milano Italy 45°28N 9°10E 128 B1
Milan Ga., U.S.A. 32°1N 83°4W 316 C6
Milan Ill., U.S.A. 41°27N 90°34W 310 C6
Milan Mich., U.S.A. 42°5N 83°41W 311 B13
Milan Mo., U.S.A. 40°12N 93°7W 310 D3
Milan Tenn., U.S.A. 35°55N 88°46W 315 D10
Miland Norway 59°54N 8°45E 164 E5
Milando Angola 8°45S 17°36E 265 D3
Milando △ Angola 8°45S 17°10E 265 D3
Milanese, Parco Regionale △ Italy 45°35N 9°5E 128 A1
Milang Australia 35°24S 138°58E 282 C3
Milange Mozam. 16°3S 35°45E 269 F4
Milano Italy 45°28N 9°10E 128 B1
Milano Due Italy 45°29N 9°16E 128 B2
Milano Linate ✈ (LIN) Italy 45°27N 9°16E 128 B2
Milano Malpense ✈ (MXP) Italy 45°38N 8°43E 128 A1
Milano San Felice Italy 45°28N 9°18E 128 B2
Milanoa Madag. 13°35S 49°47E 272 A2
Milâs Turkey 37°20N 27°50E 205 D9
Milatos Greece 35°18N 25°34E 207 E6
Milazzo Italy 38°13N 15°15E 201 D8
Milbank U.S.A. 45°13N 96°38W 308 C5
Milbanke Sd. Canada 52°19N 128°33W 296 C3
Milbertshofen Germany 48°10N 11°34E 131 A2
Milden Canada 51°29N 107°32W 297 C7
Mildenhall U.K. 52°21N 0°32E 169 E8
Mildmay Canada 44°3N 81°7W 312 B3
Mildura Australia 34°13S 142°9E 282 C5
Mile China 24°28N 103°20E 228 E4
Mile and a Quarter Barbados 13°16N 59°37W 323 r
Miles Australia 26°40S 150°9E 281 D5
Miles City U.S.A. 46°25N 105°51W 304 C11
Mileşti Moldova 47°13N 28°3E 183 C13
Milestone Canada 49°59N 104°31W 297 D8
Mileto Italy 38°36N 16°4E 201 D9
Miletto, Mte. Italy 41°27N 14°22E 201 A7
Miletus Turkey 37°30N 27°18E 205 D9
Milevsko Czech Rep. 49°27N 14°21E 180 B7
Milford Calif., U.S.A. 40°10N 120°22W 306 E6
Milford Conn., U.S.A. 41°14N 73°3W 313 E11
Milford Del., U.S.A. 38°55N 75°26W 309 F16
Milford Ill., U.S.A. 40°38N 87°42W 311 D9
Milford Mass., U.S.A. 42°8N 71°31W 313 D13
Milford Mich., U.S.A. 42°35N 83°36W 311 B13
Milford N.H., U.S.A. 42°50N 71°39W 313 D13
Milford N.Y., U.S.A. 42°35N 74°56W 313 D10
Milford Pa., U.S.A. 41°19N 74°48W 313 E10
Milford Utah, U.S.A. 38°24N 113°1W 304 G7
Milford Haven U.K. 51°42N 5°7W 169 F2
Milford Sd. N.Z. 44°41S 167°47E 285 E2
Milḥ, Baḥr al = Razāzah, Buḥayrat ar Iraq 32°40N 43°35E 213 F10
Miliana Aïn Salah, Algeria 27°20N 2°32E 261 C5
Miliana Médéa, Algeria 36°20N 2°15E 261 A5
Milicz Poland 51°31N 17°19E 185 G4
Milies Greece 39°20N 23°9E 204 B5
Milikapiti Australia 11°26S 130°40E 278 B5
Miliani Town U.S.A. 21°28N 158°1W 302 K13
Miling Australia 30°30S 116°17E 279 F2
Militello in Val di Catánia Italy 37°16N 14°48E 201 E7
Militsch = Milicz Poland 51°31N 17°19E 185 G4
Milk, Wadi el ➔ Sudan 17°55N 30°20E 256 D3
Milk River Canada 49°10N 112°5W 296 D6
Milk River Spa Jamaica 17°50N 77°22W 320 a
Mill ➔ U.S.A. 42°57N 83°23W 312 D1
Mill Hill U.K. 51°37N 0°14W 125 A2
Mill I. Antarctica 66°0S 101°30E 151 C8
Mill I. Nunavut, Canada 63°58N 77°47W 295 E16
Mill Shoals U.S.A. 38°15N 88°21W 311 F8
Mill Valley U.S.A. 37°54N 122°32W 306 H4
Millárs ➔ Spain 39°55N 0°1W 196 F4
Millau France 44°8N 3°4E 174 D7
Millbridge Canada 44°41N 77°36W 312 B7
Millbrook Ont., Canada 44°10N 78°29W 312 B6
Millbrook Ala., U.S.A. 32°29N 86°22W 315 E11
Millbrook N.Y., U.S.A. 41°47N 73°42W 313 E11
Mille Lacs, L. des Canada 48°45N 90°35W 298 C1
Mille Lacs L. U.S.A. 46°15N 93°39W 308 B7
Milledgeville Ga., U.S.A. 33°5N 83°14W 316 B6
Milledgeville Ill., U.S.A. 41°58N 89°46W 310 C7
Millen U.S.A. 32°48N 81°57W 316 C8
Millennium Dome U.K. 51°30N 0°0 125 A4
Millennium I. = Caroline I. Kiribati 9°58S 150°13W 289 H12
Millennium Park U.S.A. 119 c2
Miller U.S.A. 44°31N 98°59W 308 C4
Miller Lake Canada 45°6N 81°26W 312 A3
Miller Meadow U.S.A. 41°51N 87°49W 119 B2
Millerhill U.K. 55°55N 3°5W 121 B3
Millerovo Russia 48°57N 40°28E 191 F5
Miller's Flat N.Z. 45°39S 169°23E 285 F4
Millers Point Sydney, Australia 139 a1
Millersburg Ind., U.S.A. 41°32N 85°42W 311 C11
Millersburg Ohio, U.S.A. 40°33N 81°55W 312 F3
Millersburg Pa., U.S.A. 40°32N 76°58W 312 F8
Millerton N.Z. 41°39S 171°54E 285 B6
Millerton N.Y., U.S.A. 41°57N 73°31W 313 E11
Millerton L. U.S.A. 37°1N 119°41W 306 J7
Millet St. Lucia 13°55N 60°59W 323 m
Millevaches, Plateau de France 45°45N 2°0E 174 C6
Millheim U.S.A. 40°54N 77°29W 312 F7
Millicent Australia 37°34S 140°21E 282 D4
Milligan U.S.A. 30°45N 86°38W 317 E3
Millington U.S.A. 35°20N 89°53W 315 D10
Millinocket U.S.A. 45°39N 68°43W 309 C19
Millmerran Australia 27°53S 151°16E 281 D5
Millom U.K. 54°13N 3°16W 168 C4
Mills L. Canada 61°30N 118°20W 296 A5
Millsboro U.S.A. 40°0N 80°0W 312 G5
Millstream Chichester △ Australia 21°35S 117°6E 278 D2
Millstreet Ireland 52°4N 9°4W 166 D2
Millthorpe Australia 33°26S 149°12E 283 B8
Milltown Ireland 53°19N 6°14W 120 B2
Milltown Malbay Ireland 52°52N 9°24W 166 D2
Millville N.J., U.S.A. 39°24N 75°2W 309 F16
Millville Pa., U.S.A. 41°7N 76°32W 313 E8
Millwood L. U.S.A. 33°42N 93°58W 314 E8
Milna Croatia 43°20N 16°28E 199 E13
Milne ➔ Australia 21°10S 137°33E 280 C2
Milne Bay □ Papua N. G. 10°0S 152°30E 286 E7
Milne Land Greenland 70°40N 26°30W 154 C8
Milnerton S. Africa 33°53S 18°29E 118 A1
Milo U.S.A. 45°15N 68°59W 309 C19
Milo ➔ Guinea 8°52N 9°0W 262 D3
Miloli'i U.S.A. 19°11N 155°55W 302 D6
Milon, Akra Greece 36°15N 28°11E 206 E12
Milon-la-Chapelle France 48°43N 2°3E 134 B1
Milos Greece 36°44N 24°25E 204 E6
Miłosław Poland 52°12N 17°32E 185 F4
Milot Albania 41°41N 19°43E 202 E3
Milparinka Australia 29°46S 141°57E 281 D3
Milpitas U.S.A. 37°26N 121°55W 306 H5
Milson U.S.A. 39°30N 85°28W 311 E11
Miltenberg Germany 49°41N 9°16E 179 F5
Milton N.S.W., Australia 35°20S 150°27E 283 C9
Milton N.S., Canada 44°4N 64°45W 299 D7
Milton Ont., Canada 43°31N 79°53W 312 C5
Milton N.Z. 46°7S 169°59E 285 G4
Milton Calif., U.S.A. 38°3N 120°51W 306 G6
Milton Fla., U.S.A. 30°38N 87°3W 317 E2
Milton Iowa, U.S.A. 40°41N 92°10W 310 D4
Milton Mass., U.S.A. 42°14N 71°2W 116 B2
Milton Pa., U.S.A. 41°1N 76°51W 312 F8
Milton Vt., U.S.A. 44°38N 73°7W 313 B11
Milton Wis., U.S.A. 42°47N 88°56W 311 B8
Milton Bridge U.K. 55°51N 3°11W 121 B2
Milton-Freewater U.S.A. 45°56N 118°23W 304 D4
Milton Keynes U.K. 52°1N 0°44W 169 E7
Milton Keynes □ U.K. 52°1N 0°44W 169 E7
Milton Park Montréal, Canada 130 b1
Miltou Chad 10°14N 17°26E 259 F3
Miluo China 29°0N 112°59E 229 C9
Milverton Canada 43°34N 80°55W 312 C4
Milwaukee U.S.A. 43°2N 87°54W 311 A9
Milwaukee Deep Atl. Oc. 19°50N 68°0W 321 C6
Milwaukie U.S.A. 45°26N 122°38W 306 E4
Mim Ghana 6°57N 2°33W 262 D4
Mima Japan 34°4N 134°9E 222 C6
Mimico Canada 43°36N 79°29W 141 B2
Mimico Creek ➔ Canada 43°37N 79°28W 141 B1
Mimili Australia 27°0S 132°42E 279 E5
Mimizan France 44°12N 1°13W 174 D2
Mimoň Czech Rep. 50°38N 14°43E 180 A7
Mimongo Gabon 1°11S 11°36E 264 C2
Mimoso Brazil 15°10S 48°5W 333 E2
Mims U.S.A. 28°40N 80°51W 317 G9
Min Jiang ➔ Fujian, China 26°0N 119°35E 229 E12
Min Jiang ➔ Sichuan, China 28°45N 104°40E 228 C5
Min Xian China 34°25N 104°5E 226 G3
Mināʾ Jabal ʿAlī U.A.E. 25°2N 55°8E 247 E7
Mīnā Suʿud Si. Arabia 28°45N 48°28E 247 D6
Mīnāʾ al Aḥmadī Kuwait 29°5N 48°10E 247 D6
Minago ➔ Canada 54°33N 98°59W 297 C9
Minakami Japan 36°49N 138°59E 223 A10
Minaki Canada 49°59N 94°40W 297 D10
Minakuchi Japan 34°58N 136°10E 223 C8
Minalungao △ Phil. 15°2N 121°8E 232 D3
Minamata Japan 32°10N 130°30E 222 E2
Minami Japan 34°40N 135°30E 133 A2
Minami-Arapusa △ Japan 35°30N 138°9E 223 B10
Minami-Tori-Shima Pac. Oc. 24°20N 153°58E 288 E7
Minamiaizu Japan 37°12N 139°46E 221 F9
Minamiawaji Japan 34°10N 134°42E 222 C6
Minamisōma Japan 37°38N 140°58E 220 F10
Minamitsunashima Japan 35°32N 139°37E 140 B2
Minas Indonesia 0°50N 101°26E 234 B2
Minas Uruguay 34°20S 55°10W 335 C4
Minas, Sierra de las Guatemala 15°9N 89°31W 320 C2
Minas Basin Canada 45°20N 64°12W 299 C7
Minas de Riotinto Spain 37°42N 6°35W 195 H4
Minas Gerais □ Brazil 18°50S 46°0W 333 E2
Minas Novas Brazil 17°15S 42°36W 333 E3
Minatitlán Mexico 17°59N 94°31W 319 D6
Minato Ōsaka, Japan 34°39N 135°25E 133 B1
Minato Tokyo, Japan 140 c3
Minbu Burma 20°10N 94°52E 241 E5
Minbya Burma 20°22N 93°16E 241 E4
Minchinabad Pakistan 30°10N 73°34E 242 D5
Mincio ➔ Italy 45°4N 10°59E 198 C7
Minčol Slovak Rep. 49°15N 20°58E 181 B13
Mindanao Phil. 8°0N 125°0E 233 H5
Mindanao Sea = Bohol Sea Phil. 9°0N 124°0E 233 G5
Mindanao Trench Pac. Oc. 12°0N 126°6E 232 E5
Mindel ➔ Germany 48°31N 10°23E 179 G6
Mindelheim Germany 48°2N 10°29E 179 G6
Mindelo C. Verde Is. 16°24N 25°0W 153 j
Minden Ont., Canada 44°55N 78°43W 312 B6
Minden Nordrhein-Westfalen, Germany 52°17N 8°55E 178 C4
Minden La., U.S.A. 32°37N 93°17W 314 E8
Minden Nev., U.S.A. 38°57N 119°46W 306 G7
Mindibungu = Billiluna Australia 19°37S 127°41E 278 C4
Mindiptana Indonesia 5°55S 140°22E 231 F10
Mindon Burma 19°21N 94°44E 241 F5
Mindona L. Australia 33°6S 142°6E 282 B5
Mindoro Phil. 13°0N 121°0E 232 E3
Mindoro Occidental □ Phil. 13°0N 120°55E 232 E3
Mindoro Oriental □ Phil. 13°0N 121°5E 232 E3
Mindoro Str. Phil. 12°30N 120°30E 232 E3
Mindouli Congo 4°12S 14°28E 265 C2
Mindourou Cameroon 3°29N 13°26E 264 B2
Mine Japan 34°12N 131°7E 222 C3
Minehead U.K. 51°12N 3°29W 169 F4
Mineiros Brazil 17°34S 52°34W 331 D7
Mineola N.Y., U.S.A. 40°44N 73°38W 313 F11
Mineola Tex., U.S.A. 32°40N 95°29W 314 E7
Mineral Bath Jamaica 17°58N 76°22W 320 a
Mineral King U.S.A. 36°27N 118°36W 306 J8
Mineral Point U.S.A. 42°52N 90°11W 310 B6
Mineral Wells U.S.A. 32°48N 98°7W 314 E5
Mineralnyye Vody Russia 44°15N 43°8E 191 H6
Miners Bay Canada 44°49N 78°46W 312 B6
Minersville U.S.A. 40°41N 76°16W 313 F8
Minerva N.Y., U.S.A. 43°47N 73°59W 313 C11
Minerva Ohio, U.S.A. 40°44N 81°6W 312 F3
Minervino Murge Italy 41°5N 16°5E 201 A9
Minetto U.S.A. 43°24N 76°28W 313 C8
Minfeng China 37°4N 82°46E 217 E10
Ming-Kush Kyrgyzstan 41°40N 74°28E 217 D8
Mingäçevir Azerbaijan 40°45N 47°0E 191 K8
Mingäçevir Su Anbarı Azerbaijan 40°57N 46°50E 191 K8
Mingala C.A.R. 5°6N 21°49E 264 A4
Mingan Canada 50°20N 64°0W 299 B7
Mingary Australia 32°8S 140°45E 282 B4
Mingchien Taiwan 23°50N 120°42E 225 C2
Mingechaur = Mingäçevir Azerbaijan 40°45N 47°0E 191 K8
Mingechaurskoye Vdkhr. = Mingäçevir Su Anbarı Azerbaijan 40°57N 46°50E 191 K8
Mingela Australia 19°52S 146°38E 280 B4
Mingenew Australia 29°12S 115°21E 279 E2
Mingera Cr. ➔ Australia 20°38S 137°45E 280 C2
Minggang China 32°24N 114°3E 229 A10
Mingguang China 32°46N 117°59E 229 A11
Mingin Burma 22°50N 94°30E 241 D5
Minglanilla Spain 39°34N 1°38W 197 F3
Minglun China 25°10N 108°21E 228 E7
Mingo Congo 1°55S 15°1E 264 C3
Mingo Junction U.S.A. 40°19N 80°37W 312 F4
Mingora Pakistan 34°48N 72°22E 243 B5
Mingorria Spain 40°45N 4°40W 194 E6
Mingshan China 30°6N 103°10E 228 B4
Mingteke Daban = Mintaka Pass Pakistan 37°0N 74°58E 243 A6
Mingxi China 26°18N 117°12E 229 D11
Mingyuegue China 43°2N 128°50E 227 C15
Minhe China 36°9N 102°45E 218 D9
Minhla Magwe, Burma 19°58N 95°3E 241 F5
Minhla Pegu, Burma 17°59N 95°43E 241 G5
Minho = Miño ➔ Spain 41°52N 8°40W 194 D2
Minhou China 26°0N 119°15E 229 E12
Minhsiung Taiwan 23°33N 120°35E 225 C2
Miničevo Serbia 43°42N 22°18E 182 G7
Minicoy I. India 8°17N 73°2E 245 K1
Minidoka U.S.A. 42°45N 113°29W 304 E7
Minier U.S.A. 40°26N 89°19W 310 D7
Minigwal, L. Australia 29°31S 123°14E 279 E3
Minilya ➔ Australia 23°45S 114°0E 279 D1
Minilya Roadhouse Australia 23°55S 114°0E 279 D1
Mininera Australia 37°37S 142°58E 282 D5
Minipi L. Canada 52°25N 60°45W 299 B7
Minj Papua N. G. 5°54S 144°37E 286 C3
Minjilang Australia 11°8S 132°33E 278 B5
Mink L. Canada 61°54N 117°40W 296 A5
Minkammen South Sudan 6°3N 31°32E 257 F3
Minkebé Gabon 1°45N 12°45E 264 B2
Minlaton Australia 34°45S 137°35E 282 C2
Minna Nigeria 9°37N 6°30E 263 D6
Minna-shima Japan 26°39N 127°49E 288 a
Minneapolis Kans., U.S.A. 39°8N 97°42W 308 F5
Minneapolis Minn., U.S.A. 44°57N 93°16W 308 C7
Minnedosa Canada 50°14N 99°50W 297 C9
Minnesota □ U.S.A. 46°0N 94°15W 308 B6
Minnesota ➔ U.S.A. 44°54N 93°9W 308 C7
Minnesund Norway 60°23N 11°14E 164 D8
Minnewaukan U.S.A. 48°4N 99°15W 308 A4
Minnipa Australia 32°51S 135°9E 281 E2
Minnitaki L. Canada 49°57N 92°10W 298 C1
Mino Japan 35°32N 136°55E 223 B8
Miño Spain 43°21N 8°12W 194 B2
Miño ➔ Spain 41°52N 8°40W 194 D2
Mino-Kamo Japan 35°23N 137°2E 223 B9
Mino-Mikawa-Kōgen Japan 35°10N 137°23E 223 B9
Minoa Greece 35°6N 25°45E 205 F7
Minobu Japan 35°22N 138°26E 223 B10
Minobu-Sanchi Japan 35°14N 138°20E 223 B10
Minonk U.S.A. 40°54N 89°2W 310 D7
Minooka U.S.A. 41°27N 88°16W 311 C8
Minorca = Menorca Spain 40°0N 4°0E 206 B5
Minore Australia 32°14S 148°27E 283 B8
Minot U.S.A. 48°14N 101°18W 308 A3
Minqin China 38°38N 103°20E 226 E2
Minqing China 26°15N 118°50E 229 D12
Minsen Germany 53°41N 7°58E 178 B3
Minshât el Bekkarî Egypt 30°0N 31°8E 117 A1
Minsk Belarus 53°52N 27°30E 177 B14
Minsk □ Belarus 53°15N 27°30E 188 F4
Mińsk Mazowiecki Poland 52°10N 21°33E 185 F8
Minster U.S.A. 40°24N 84°23W 311 D12
Mintabie Australia 27°15S 133°7E 281 D1
Mintaka Pass Pakistan 37°0N 74°58E 243 A6
Minthami Burma 23°55N 94°16E 241 D5
Minto N.B., Canada 46°5N 66°5W 299 C6
Minto Alaska, U.S.A. 64°53N 149°10W 303 D10
Minto, L. Canada 57°13N 75°0W 298 A5
Minton Canada 49°10N 104°35W 297 D8
Mintoum Gabon 0°27N 12°16E 264 B2
Minturn U.S.A. 39°35N 106°26W 304 G10
Minturno Italy 41°15N 13°45E 200 A6
Minudasht Iran 37°17N 56°7E 247 B8
Minûf Egypt 30°26N 30°52E 256 H7
Minusinsk Russia 53°43N 91°20E 217 B12
Minutang India 28°15N 96°30E 241 A6
Minvoul Gabon 2°9N 12°8E 264 B2
Minwakh Yemen 16°48N 48°6E 249 C5
Minyâ el Qamh Egypt 30°31N 31°21E 256 H7
Minya Konka = Gongga Shan China 29°40N 101°55E 228 C3
Minyip Australia 36°29S 142°36E 282 D5
Minzhong China 22°37N 113°30E 219 a
Mionica Bos.-H. 44°51N 18°29E 182 F3
Mionica Serbia 44°14N 20°6E 202 B4
Mioveni Romania 44°56N 24°54E 183 F9
Miquan China 43°58N 87°42E 217 D11
Miquelon Qué., Canada 49°25N 76°27W 298 C4
Miquelon St-P. & M. 47°8N 56°22W 299 C8
Mir Belarus 53°27N 26°28E 177 B14
Mir Niger 14°5N 11°59E 259 F2
Mīr Kūh Iran 26°22N 58°55E 247 E8
Mīr Shahdād Iran 26°15N 58°29E 247 E8
Mira Italy 45°26N 12°8E 199 C9
Mira Portugal 40°26N 8°44W 194 E2
Mira ➔ Colombia 1°36N 79°1W 328 C2
Mira ➔ Portugal 37°43N 8°47W 195 H2
Mira por vos Cay Bahamas 22°9N 74°30W 321 B5
Mirābād Afghan. 30°25N 61°50E 240 C1
Mirabella Eclano Italy 41°2N 14°59E 201 A7
Mirabello, Kolpos Greece 35°10N 25°50E 207 E6
Miracema do Norte Brazil 9°33S 48°24W 332 C2
Mirador Brazil 6°22S 44°22W 332 C3
Mirador-Río Azul △ Guatemala 17°45N 89°50W 320 C1
Miraflores = Rovira Colombia 4°15N 75°20W 328 C2
Miraflores Colombia 1°25N 72°13W 328 C3
Miraflores Lima, Peru 12°7S 77°2W 124 B2
Miraflores, L. Panama 9°1N 79°36W 320 c
Miraflores Locks Panama 9°0N 79°36W 320 c
Miraj India 16°50N 74°45E 244 F2
Miram Shah Pakistan 33°0N 70°2E 242 C4
Miramar Argentina 38°15S 57°50W 334 D4
Miramar Mozam. 23°50S 35°35E 271 B6
Miramar Fla., U.S.A. 25°59N 80°13W 129 C1
Miramas France 43°33N 4°59E 175 E8
Mirambeau France 45°23N 0°35W 174 C3
Miramichi Canada 47°2N 65°28W 299 C6
Miramichi B. Canada 47°15N 65°0W 299 C7
Miramont-de-Guyenne France 44°37N 0°21E 174 D4
Miranda Brazil 20°10S 56°15W 331 E6
Miranda □ Venezuela 10°15N 66°25W 328 A4
Miranda ➔ Brazil 19°25S 57°20W 331 D6
Miranda de Ebro Spain 42°41N 2°57W 196 C2
Miranda do Corvo Portugal 40°6N 8°20W 194 E2
Miranda do Douro Portugal 41°30N 6°16W 194 D4
Mirande France 43°31N 0°25E 174 E4
Mirandela Portugal 41°32N 7°10W 194 D3
Mirándola Italy 44°53N 11°4E 198 D8
Mirandópolis Brazil 21°9S 51°6W 335 A5
Mirango Malawi 13°32S 34°58E 269 E3
Mirani Australia 21°8S 148°53E 280 b
Mirano Italy 45°30N 12°7E 199 C9
Miras Albania 40°30N 20°56E 202 F4
Mirassol Brazil 20°46S 49°28W 335 A6
Mirbāṭ Oman 17°0N 54°45E 249 C6
Mirboo North Australia 38°24S 146°10E 283 E7
Mirear Egypt 23°15N 35°41E 256 C4
Mirebeau France 46°49N 0°10E 172 F7
Mirebeau-sur-Bèze France 47°25N 5°20E 173 E12
Mirecourt France 48°20N 6°10E 173 D13
Mires Greece 35°4N 24°56E 207 E5
Mirgorod = Myrhorod Ukraine 49°58N 33°37E 189 H7
Miri Malaysia 4°23N 113°59E 235 B4
Miriálguda India 16°52N 79°35E 244 F4
Miriam Vale Australia 24°20S 151°33E 280 C5
Miribel France 45°50N 4°57E 173 G11
Mirigama Sri Lanka 7°15N 80°8E 245 L5
Mirim, L. S. Amer. 32°45S 52°50W 335 C5
Mirimire Venezuela 11°10N 68°43W 328 A4
Miringoni Comoros Is. 12°17S 43°38E 272 a
Miriuwung Gajerrong ◎ Australia 15°0S 128°45E 278 C4
Mirjāveh Iran 29°1N 61°30E 247 D9
Mirnyy Antarctica 66°50S 92°30E 151 C14
Mirnyy Russia 62°33N 113°53E 215 C12
Miroč Serbia 44°32N 22°16E 202 B6
Mirokhan Pakistan 27°46N 68°6E 242 F3
Mirond L. Canada 55°6N 102°47W 297 B8
Mirosławiec Poland 53°20N 16°5E 184 E3
Mirpur Pakistan 33°32N 73°56E 243 C5
Mirpur Batoro Pakistan 24°44N 68°16E 242 G3
Mirpur Bibiwari Pakistan 28°33N 67°44E 242 E2
Mirpur Khas Pakistan 25°30N 69°0E 242 G3
Mirpur Sakro Pakistan 24°33N 67°41E 242 G2
Mirria Niger 13°43N 9°7E 259 F1
Mirrool Australia 34°19S 147°10E 283 C7
Mirs Bay = Tai Pang Wan China 22°33N 114°24E 219 a
Mirsale Somalia 5°57N 47°59E 267 C6
Mirsk Poland 50°58N 15°23E 185 H2
Mirtağ Turkey 38°23N 41°56E 246 B4
Mirtoo Sea Greece 37°0N 23°20E 204 D5
Mirtou, Kolpos Greece 38°20N 20°27E 207 C1
Miryang S. Korea 35°31N 128°44E 224 E4
Mirzaani Georgia 41°24N 46°5E 191 K8
Mirzachul = Guliston Uzbekistan 40°29N 68°46E 217 D7
Mirzapur India 25°10N 82°34E 243 G10
Mirzapur-cum-Vindhyachal = Mirzapur India 25°10N 82°34E 243 G10
Mirzoyan = Taraz Kazakhstan 42°54N 71°22E 217 D8
Misaki Japan 34°18N 135°9E 223 C7
Misamis = Ozamiz Phil. 8°15N 123°50E 233 G4
Misamis Occidental □ Phil. 8°20N 123°42E 233 G4
Misamis Oriental □ Phil. 8°45N 125°0E 233 G5
Misantla Mexico 19°56N 96°50W 319 D5
Misawa Japan 40°41N 141°24E 220 D10
Miscou I. Canada 47°57N 64°31W 299 C7
Misdroy = Międzyzdroje Poland 53°56N 14°26E 184 E1
Misericordia = Itaporanga Brazil 7°18S 38°0W 332 C4
Misericórdia, Sa. da Brazil 22°51S 43°17W 135 B1
Misha India 7°59N 93°20E 245 L10
Mish'āb, Ra's al Si. Arabia 28°15N 48°43E 247 D6
Mishagua ➔ Peru 11°12S 72°58W 330 C3
Mishamo Tanzania 5°41S 30°41E 268 D3
Mishan China 45°37N 131°48E 220 B5
Mishawaka U.S.A. 41°40N 86°11W 311 C10
Mishbih, Gebel Egypt 22°38N 34°44E 256 C3
Mishima Japan 35°10N 138°52E 223 B10
Mishmi Hills India 29°0N 96°0E 241 A6
Mishō Japan 32°57N 132°35E 222 E4
Misima I. Papua N. G. 10°40S 152°45E 286 F7
Misión Mexico 32°6N 116°53W 307 N10
Misión Fagnano Argentina 54°32S 67°17W 336 D3
Misiones □ Argentina 27°0S 55°0W 335 B5
Misiones □ Paraguay 27°0S 56°0W 334 B4
Miskah Si. Arabia 24°49N 42°56E 246 E4
Miski, E. ➔ Chad 20°0N 17°55E 259 E3
Miskitos, Cayos Nic. 14°26N 82°50W 320 D3
Miskolc Hungary 48°7N 20°50E 182 B5
Misoke Dem. Rep. of the Congo 0°42S 28°2E 268 C2
Misool Indonesia 1°52S 130°10E 231 E8
Miṣr = Egypt ■ Africa 28°0N 31°0E 256 B3
Miṣrātah Libya 32°24N 15°3E 258 B3
Miṣrātah □ Libya 33°30N 15°0E 258 C3
Missanabie Canada 48°20N 84°6W 298 C3
Missão Catrimani Brazil 2°48N 62°18W 329 C5
Missão Velha Brazil 7°15S 39°10W 332 C4
Missinaibi ➔ Canada 50°43N 81°29W 298 B3
Missinaibi L. Canada 48°23N 83°40W 298 C3
Mission B.C., Canada 49°10N 122°15W 296 D4
Mission Calif., U.S.A. 37°44N 122°25W 136 B2
Mission S. Dak., U.S.A. 43°18N 100°39W 308 D3
Mission Tex., U.S.A. 26°13N 98°20W 314 H5
Mission Beach Australia 17°53S 146°6E 280 B4
Mission Viejo U.S.A. 33°36N 117°40W 307 M9
Missirah Senegal 13°40N 16°30W 262 C1
Missisa L. Canada 52°20N 85°7W 298 B2
Missisicabi ➔ Canada 51°14N 79°31W 298 B4
Mississagi ➔ Canada 46°15N 83°9W 298 C3
Mississauga Canada 43°32N 79°35W 141 B1
Mississinewa L. U.S.A. 40°42N 85°52W 311 D10
Mississippi □ U.S.A. 33°0N 90°0W 315 E10
Mississippi ➔ U.S.A. 29°9N 89°15W 315 G10
Mississippi L. Canada 45°5N 76°10W 313 A8
Mississippi River Delta U.S.A. 29°10N 89°15W 315 G10
Mississippi Sd. U.S.A. 30°20N 89°0W 315 F10
Missoula U.S.A. 46°52N 114°1W 304 C6
Missour Morocco 33°3N 4°0W 260 B4
Missouri □ U.S.A. 38°25N 92°30W 310 E3
Missouri ➔ U.S.A. 38°49N 90°7W 310 F6
Missouri City U.S.A. 29°37N 95°32W 314 G7
Missouri Valley U.S.A. 41°34N 95°53W 308 E6
Mist U.S.A. 45°59N 123°15W 306 E3
Mistassibi ➔ Canada 48°53N 72°13W 299 B5
Mistassini Canada 48°53N 72°12W 299 C5
Mistassini ➔ Canada 48°42N 72°20W 299 C5
Mistassini, L. Canada 51°0N 73°30W 298 B5
Mistastin L. Canada 55°57N 63°20W 299 A7
Mistelbach Austria 48°34N 16°34E 181 C9
Misterbianco Italy 37°31N 15°1E 201 E8
Misteriosa Bank Caribbean 18°50N 83°50W 320 C3
Misti, Volcán Peru 16°18S 71°24W 330 D3
Mistinibi, L. Canada 55°56N 64°17W 299 A7
Mistissini Canada 48°53N 72°12W 299 C5
Mistras = Mystras Greece 37°4N 22°22E 204 D4
Mistretta Italy 37°56N 14°22E 201 E7
Misty Fjords Nat. Monument △ U.S.A. 55°40N 130°40W 303 J15
Misty L. Canada 58°53N 101°40W 297 B8
Misugi Japan 34°31N 136°16E 223 C8
Misumi Japan 32°37N 130°27E 222 E2
Misurata = Miṣrātah Libya 32°24N 15°3E 258 B3
Mit Ghamr Egypt 30°42N 31°12E 256 H7
Mitaka Japan 35°40N 139°34E 140 A2
Mitande Mozam. 14°6S 35°58E 269 E4
Mitatib Sudan 15°59N 36°12E 257 D4
Mitau = Jelgava Latvia 56°41N 23°49E 184 B10
Mitava = Jelgava Latvia 56°41N 23°49E 184 B10
Mitcham U.K. 51°23N 0°10W 125 B2
Mitcham Common U.K. 51°23N 0°8W 125 B2
Mitchell Queens., Australia 26°29S 147°58E 281 D4
Mitchell Ont., Canada 43°28N 81°12W 312 C3
Mitchell Ga., U.S.A. 33°13N 82°42W 316 B7
Mitchell Ind., U.S.A. 38°44N 86°28W 311 F10
Mitchell Nebr., U.S.A. 41°57N 103°49W 308 E2
Mitchell Oreg., U.S.A. 44°34N 120°9W 304 D3
Mitchell S. Dak., U.S.A. 43°43N 98°2W 308 D4
Mitchell ➔ Australia 15°12S 141°35E 280 B3
Mitchell, Mt. U.S.A. 35°46N 82°16W 315 D13
Mitchell-Alice Rivers △ Australia 15°28S 142°5E 280 B3
Mitchell Museum of the American Indian U.S.A. 42°4N 87°43W 119 A2
Mitchell Ra. Australia 12°49S 135°36E 280 A2
Mitchell River △ Australia 37°37S 147°22E 283 D7
Mitchell's Plain S. Africa 34°4S 18°35E 118 B2
Mitchelstown Ireland 52°15N 8°16W 166 D3
Mitha Tiwana Pakistan 32°13N 72°6E 242 C5
Mithi Pakistan 24°44N 69°48E 242 G3
Mithimna Greece 39°20N 26°12E 205 B8
Mithrao Pakistan 27°28N 69°40E 242 F3
Mitiamo Australia 36°12S 144°15E 282 D6

Mitikas *Etoloakarnania, Greece* 38°40N 20°56E **207** B2
Mitikas *Preveza, Greece* 39°0N 20°42E **207** B2
Mitilini *Greece* 39°6N 26°35E **205** B8
Mitilinii *Greece* 37°42N 26°56E **205** D8
Mitla Pass = Mamarr Mitlā *Egypt* 30°2N 32°54E **251** H3
Mito *Japan* 36°20N 140°30E **223** A12
Mitra, Mt. *Eq. Guin.* 1°23N 9°19E **264** B1
Mitre, Mt. *N.Z.* 40°50S 175°30E **284** G4
Mitrofanovka *Russia* 49°58N 39°42E **189** H10
Mitrovicë *Kosovo* 42°54N 20°52E **202** D4
Mitrowitz = Sremska Mitrovica *Serbia* 44°59N 19°38E **182** F4
Mitsamiouli *Comoros Is.* 11°20S 43°16E **272** a
Mitsang *Gabon* 0°42N 12°33E **264** B2
Mitsinjo *Madag.* 16°1S 45°52E **272** B2
Mitsio, Nosy *Madag.* 12°54S 48°36E **272** A2
Mitsiwa *Eritrea* 15°35N 39°25E **257** D4
Mitsiwa Channel *Eritrea* 15°30N 40°0E **257** D5
Mitsoudjé *Comoros Is.* 11°48S 43°16E **272** a
Mitsukaidō *Japan* 36°1N 139°59E **223** A11
Mitsushima *Japan* 34°15N 129°20E **222** C1
Mittagong *Australia* 34°28S 150°29E **283** C9
Mitte *Germany* 52°32N 13°24E **115** A3
Mittel Isarkanal → *Germany* 48°12N 11°40E **131** A3
Mittel Schreiberhau = Szklarska Poreba *Poland* 50°50N 15°33E **185** H2
Mittelberg *Austria* 47°20N 10°10E **180** D3
Mittelfranken □ *Germany* 49°25N 10°40E **179** F6
Mittellandkanal → *Germany* 52°20N 8°28E **178** C4
Mittelwalde = Międzylesie *Poland* 50°8N 16°40E **185** H3
Mittenwalde *Germany* 52°15N 13°31E **178** C9
Mittersill *Austria* 47°16N 12°29E **180** D5
Mitterteich *Germany* 49°57N 12°14E **179** F8
Mittimatalik = Pond Inlet *Canada* 72°40N 77°0W **295** C16
Mittweida *Germany* 50°59N 12°59E **178** E8
Mitú *Colombia* 1°15N 70°13W **328** C3
Mituas *Colombia* 3°52N 68°49W **328** C4
Mitumba *Tanzania* 7°8S 31°2E **268** D3
Mitumba, Mts. *Dem. Rep. of the Congo* 7°0S 27°30E **268** D2
Mitwaba *Dem. Rep. of the Congo* 8°2S 27°17E **269** D2
Mityana *Uganda* 0°23N 32°2E **268** B3
Mitzic *Gabon* 0°45N 11°40E **264** B2
Miura *Japan* 35°12N 139°40E **223** B11
Mixcoac *Mexico* 19°23N 99°11W **128** B1
Mixteco → *Mexico* 18°11N 98°30W **319** D5
Miyagi □ *Japan* 38°15N 140°45E **220** E10
Miyāh, W. el → *Egypt* 25°0N 33°23E **256** C3
Miyāh, W. el → *Syria* 34°44N 39°57E **246** C3
Miyake-Jima *Japan* 34°5N 139°30E **223** C11
Miyako *Japan* 39°40N 141°59E **220** E10
Miyako-Jima *Japan* 24°45N 125°20E **221** M2
Miyako-Rettō *Japan* 24°24N 125°0E **221** M2
Miyakojima *Okinawa, Japan* 24°48N 125°17E **221** M2
Miyakojima *Ōsaka, Japan* 34°42N 135°31E **133** A2
Miyakonojō *Japan* 31°40N 131°5E **222** F3
Miyān Rahan *Iran* 34°34N 47°26E **213** E12
Miyani *India* 21°50N 69°26E **242** J3
Miyanojō *Japan* 31°54N 130°27E **222** F2
Miyanoura-Dake *Japan* 30°20N 130°31E **221** J5
Miyata *Japan* 33°49N 130°42E **222** D2
Miyazaki *Japan* 31°56N 131°30E **222** F3
Miyazaki □ *Japan* 32°30N 131°30E **222** E3
Miyazu *Japan* 35°35N 135°10E **223** B7
Miyet, Bahr el = Dead Sea *Asia* 31°30N 35°30E **251** G6
Miyi *China* 26°47N 102°9E **228** D4
Miyoshi *Japan* 34°48N 132°51E **222** C4
Miyun *China* 40°28N 116°50E **226** D9
Miyun Shuiku *China* 40°30N 117°0E **227** D9
Mizan Teferi *Ethiopia* 6°57N 35°35E **257** F4
Mizdah *Libya* 31°30N 13°0E **258** B2
Mizen Hd. *Cork, Ireland* 51°27N 9°50W **166** E2
Mizen Hd. *Wicklow, Ireland* 52°51N 6°4W **166** D5
Mizhhirya *Ukraine* 48°32N 23°30E **183** B8
Mizhi *China* 37°47N 110°12E **226** F6
Mizil *Romania* 44°59N 26°29E **183** F11
Mizo Hills = Mizoram □ *India* 23°30N 92°40E **241** D4
Mizonokuchi *Japan* 35°35N 139°34E **140** B2
Mizoram □ *India* 23°30N 92°40E **241** D4
Mizpe Ramon *Israel* 30°34N 34°49E **251** H5
Mizue *Japan* 35°41N 139°54E **140** A4
Mizuho = Kyōtamba *Japan* 35°6N 135°17E **223** B7
Mizuho *Antarctica* 70°30S 41°0E **151** D5
Mizunami *Japan* 35°22N 137°15E **223** B9
Mizusawa = Ōshū *Japan* 39°8N 141°8E **220** E10
Mjällby *Sweden* 56°3N 14°40E **163** H8
Mjöbäck *Sweden* 57°28N 12°53E **163** G6
Mjölby *Sweden* 58°20N 15°10E **163** F9
Mjølfjell *Norway* 60°41N 6°55E **164** D3
Mjømna *Norway* 60°55N 4°55E **164** D1
Mjörn *Sweden* 57°55N 12°25E **163** G6
Mjøsa *Norway* 60°40N 11°0E **164** D8
Mkata *Tanzania* 5°45S 38°20E **268** D4
Mkhaya ⌓ *Swaziland* 26°34S 31°45E **271** C5
Mkhuze ⌓ *S. Africa* 29°27S 29°30E **271** C4
Mkokotoni *Tanzania* 5°55S 39°15E **268** D4
Mkomazi *Tanzania* 4°40S 38°7E **268** C4
Mkomazi → *S. Africa* 30°12S 30°50E **271** D5
Mkomazi ⌓ *Tanzania* 4°4S 30°2E **268** C3
Mkulwe *Tanzania* 8°37S 32°20E **269** D3
Mkumbi, Ras *Tanzania* 7°38S 39°55E **268** D4
Mkushi *Zambia* 14°25S 29°15E **269** E2
Mkushi River *Zambia* 13°32S 29°45E **269** E2
Mkuze *S. Africa* 27°10S 32°0E **271** C5
Mladá Boleslav *Czech Rep.* 50°27N 14°53E **180** A7
Mladenovac *Serbia* 44°28N 20°44E **202** B4
Mlala Hills *Tanzania* 6°50S 31°40E **268** D3
M'lang *Phil.* 6°56N 124°52E **233** H5
Mlange = Mulanje, Mt. *Malawi* 16°2S 35°33E **269** F4
Mlava → *Serbia* 44°45N 21°13E **202** B5
Mława *Poland* 53°9N 20°25E **185** E7
Mlawula ⌓ *Swaziland* 26°12S 32°2E **271** C5
Mlinište *Bos.-H.* 44°15N 16°50E **199** D13
Mljet *Croatia* 42°43N 17°30E **199** F14
Mljet △ *Croatia* 42°45N 17°25E **199** F14
Mljetski Kanal *Croatia* 42°48N 17°35E **199** F14
Młocinski, Park *Poland* 52°19N 20°57E **143** B1
Młociny *Poland* 52°18N 20°55E **143** B1
Mlynary *Poland* 54°12N 19°46E **184** D6
Mmabatho *S. Africa* 25°49S 25°30E **270** C4
Mme *Cameroon* 6°18N 10°14E **263** D7
Mnevniki *Russia* 55°45N 37°28E **129** B1
Mnichovo Hradiště *Czech Rep.* 50°32N 14°59E **180** A7
Mo *Hordaland, Norway* 60°49N 5°48E **164** D2
Mo *Møre og Romsdal, Norway* 63°0N 8°59E **164** A5
Mo *Telemark, Norway* 59°28N 7°50E **164** E4
Mo i Rana *Norway* 66°20N 14°7E **160** C16
Moa *Queens., Australia* 10°11S 142°16E **280** a
Moa *Cuba* 20°40N 74°56W **321** B4
Moa *Indonesia* 8°0S 128°0E **231** F7
Moa → *S. Leone* 6°59N 11°36W **262** D2
Moab *U.S.A.* 38°35N 109°33W **304** G9
Moabi *Gabon* 2°24S 10°59E **264** C2
Moaco → *Brazil* 7°41S 68°18W **330** B4
Moala *Fiji* 18°36S 179°53E **287** B2
Moama *Australia* 36°7S 144°46E **281** F3
Moamba *Mozam.* 25°36S 32°15E **271** C5
Moapa *U.S.A.* 36°40N 114°37W **307** J12
Moate *Ireland* 53°24N 7°44W **166** C4
Moba *Dem. Rep. of the Congo* 7°0S 29°48E **268** D2
Moba *Lagos, Nigeria* 6°26N 3°28E **124** B2
Mobara *Japan* 35°25N 140°18E **223** B12
Mobārakābād *Iran* 28°24N 53°20E **247** D7
Mobaye *C.A.R.* 4°25N 21°5E **264** B4
Mobayi *Dem. Rep. of the Congo* 4°15N 21°8E **264** B4
Mobeka *Dem. Rep. of the Congo* 1°52N 19°49E **264** B3
Mobenzélé *Congo* 0°56N 17°50E **264** B3
Moberly *U.S.A.* 39°25N 92°26W **310** E4
Moberly Lake *Canada* 55°50N 121°44W **296** B4
Mobile *U.S.A.* 30°41N 88°3W **315** F10
Mobile B. *U.S.A.* 30°30N 88°0W **315** F11
Mobridge *U.S.A.* 45°32N 100°26W **308** C3
Mobutu Sese Seko, L. = Albert, L. *Africa* 1°30N 31°0E **268** B3
Moc Chau *Vietnam* 20°50N 104°38E **236** B5
Moc Hoa *Vietnam* 10°46N 105°56E **237** G5
Moca *Puerto Rico* 18°24N 67°10W **321** b
Mocabe Kasari *Dem. Rep. of the Congo* 9°58S 26°12E **269** D2
Mocajuba *Brazil* 2°35S 49°30W **332** B2
Moçambique = Mozambique ■ *Africa* 19°0S 35°0E **269** F4
Moçambique *Mozam.* 15°3S 40°42E **269** F5
Moçâmedes = Namibe *Angola* 15°7S 12°11E **265** F2
Mocanaqua *U.S.A.* 41°9N 76°8W **313** E8
Mocapra → *Venezuela* 7°56N 66°46W **328** B4
Mocco, Morro de *Angola* 12°28S 15°11E **265** E3
Moce *Fiji* 18°40S 178°29W **287** B3
Mocenigo, Palazzo *Venice, Italy* **142** b2
Mocha = Al Mukhā *Yemen* 13°18N 43°15E **248** D3
Mocha, I. *Chile* 38°22S 73°56W **336** A2
Mochos *Greece* 35°16N 25°27E **207** E6
Mochudi *Botswana* 24°27S 26°7E **270** B4
Mocimboa da Praia *Mozam.* 11°25S 40°20E **269** E5
Mociu *Romania* 46°46N 24°3E **183** D9
Möckeln *Sweden* 56°40N 14°15E **163** H8
Mockfjärd *Sweden* 60°30N 14°57E **162** D8
Moclips *U.S.A.* 47°14N 124°13W **306** C2
Mocoa *Colombia* 1°7N 76°35W **328** C2
Mococa *Brazil* 21°28S 47°0W **335** A6
Mocorito *Mexico* 25°29N 107°55W **318** B3
Moctezuma *Mexico* 29°48N 109°42W **318** B3
Moctezuma → *Mexico* 21°59N 98°34W **319** C5
Mocuba *Mozam.* 16°54S 36°57E **269** F4
Moczydło *Poland* 52°8N 21°2E **143** C2
Moda *Burma* 24°22N 96°29E **241** C6
Modane *France* 45°12N 6°40E **175** C10
Modasa *India* 23°30N 73°21E **242** H5
Modder → *S. Africa* 29°2S 24°37E **270** C3
Modderfontein = Niekerkshoop *S. Africa* 29°19S 22°51E **270** C3
Modderfontein *S. Africa* 26°5S 28°10E **123** A2
Modderrivier *S. Africa* 29°2S 24°38E **270** C3
Módena *Italy* 44°40N 10°55E **198** D7
Modena *Utah, U.S.A.* 37°48N 113°56W **305** H7
Modernamuseet *Stockholm, Sweden* **139** b3
Modesto *U.S.A.* 37°39N 121°0W **306** H6
Möðrudalur *Iceland* 65°22N 15°53W **155** B11
Möðruvellir *Iceland* 65°46N 18°15W **155** B8
Módica *Italy* 36°52N 14°46E **201** F7
Modimolle *S. Africa* 24°42S 28°22E **271** B4
Modjadjiskloof *S. Africa* 23°42S 30°10E **271** B5
Modjamboli *Dem. Rep. of the Congo* 2°28N 22°6E **264** B4
Mödling *Austria* 48°5N 16°17E **181** C9
Modo *South Sudan* 5°31N 30°33E **257** F3
Modoc *U.S.A.* 33°44N 82°13W **316** B7
Modra *Slovak Rep.* 48°19N 17°20E **181** C10
Modřany *Czech Rep.* 50°0N 14°24E **135** B2
Modriča *Bos.-H.* 44°57N 18°17E **182** F3
Moe *Australia* 38°12S 146°19E **283** E7
Moebase *Mozam.* 17°3S 38°41E **269** F4
Moëlan-sur-Mer *France* 47°49N 3°38W **172** E3
Moelv *Norway* 60°56N 10°43E **164** D7
Moen I. = Weno *Pac. Oc.* 7°27N 151°52E **287** T18
Moengo *Suriname* 5°45N 54°20W **329** B7
Moenjodaro = Mohenjodaro *Pakistan* 27°19N 68°7E **242** F3
Moerewa *N.Z.* 35°8S 174°1E **284** B3
Moffat *U.K.* 55°21N 3°27W **167** F5
Moga *India* 30°48N 75°8E **242** D6
Mogadishu = Muqdisho *Somalia* 2°2N 45°25E **267** D6
Mogador = Essaouira *Morocco* 31°32N 9°42W **260** B3
Mogadouro *Portugal* 41°22N 6°47W **194** D4
Mogalakwena → *S. Africa* 22°38S 28°40E **271** B4
Mogami-Gawa → *Japan* 38°45N 140°0E **220** E10
Mogán *Canary Is.* 27°53N 15°43W **153** e1
Mogandjo *Dem. Rep. of the Congo* 1°23N 24°15E **264** B4
Mogaung *Burma* 25°20N 97°0E **241** C6
Mogen *Norway* 60°2N 7°52E **164** D4
Mogente = Moixent *Spain* 38°52N 0°45W **197** G4
Mogho *Ethiopia* 4°54N 40°16E **257** G5
Mogielnica *Poland* 51°42N 20°41E **185** G7
Mogige *Ethiopia* 5°24N 36°14E **257** F4
Mogilev = Mahilyow *Belarus* 53°55N 30°18E **177** B16
Mogilev-Podolskiy = Mohyliv-Podilskyy *Ukraine* 48°26N 27°48E **183** B12
Mogilno *Poland* 52°39N 17°55E **185** F4
Mogincual *Mozam.* 15°35S 40°25E **269** F5
Mogliano Véneto *Italy* 45°33N 12°14E **199** C9
Mogocha *Russia* 53°40N 119°50E **215** D12
Mogoditshane *Botswana* 24°37S 25°51E **270** B4
Mogok *Burma* 23°0N 96°40E **241** D6
Mogollon Rim *U.S.A.* 34°10N 110°50W **305** J8
Mógoro *Italy* 39°41N 8°47E **200** C1
Mograt *Sudan* 19°28N 33°16E **256** D3
Mogroum *Chad* 11°6N 15°25E **259** F3
Moguer *Spain* 37°15N 6°52W **195** H4
Mogumber *Australia* 31°2S 116°3E **279** F2
Mogwadi → *S. Africa* 23°4S 29°36E **271** B4
Mogyoród *Hungary* 47°35N 19°14E **117** A3
Mohács *Hungary* 45°58N 18°41E **182** E3
Mohaka → *N.Z.* 39°7S 177°12E **284** F6
Mohala *India* 20°35N 80°44E **244** D5
Mohales Hoek *Lesotho* 30°7S 27°26E **270** D4
Mohali *Congo* 0°15N 15°29E **264** B3
Mohali *Punjab, India* 30°47N 76°41E **242** D7
Mohall *U.S.A.* 48°46N 101°31W **308** A3
Moḥammadābād *Iran* 37°52N 59°5E **247** B8
Mohammadia *Algeria* 35°33N 0°3E **261** A5
Mohammedia *Morocco* 33°44N 7°21W **260** B3
Mohammerah = Khorramshahr *Iran* 30°29N 48°15E **247** D6
Mohana *India* 19°27N 84°16E **244** E7
Mohana → *India* 24°43N 85°0E **243** G11
Mohanganj *Bangla.* 24°54N 90°59E **241** C3
Mohanlalganj *India* 26°41N 80°58E **243** F9
Mohave, L. *U.S.A.* 35°12N 114°34W **307** K12
Mohawk → *U.S.A.* 42°47N 73°41W **313** D11
Moheda *Sweden* 57°1N 14°35E **163** G8
Mohéli *Comoros Is.* 12°20S 43°40E **272** a
Mohéli ✕ (NWA) *Comoros Is.* 12°19S 43°47E **272** a
Mohenjodaro *Pakistan* 27°19N 68°7E **242** F3
Moher, Cliffs of *Ireland* 52°58N 9°27W **166** D2
Mohican, C. *U.S.A.* 60°12N 167°25W **303** F6
Mohicanville Res. *U.S.A.* 40°45N 82°9W **312** F2
Möhne → *Germany* 51°29N 7°57E **178** D3
Mohns Ridge *Arctic* 72°30N 5°0W **150** B7
Mohnyin *Burma* 24°47N 96°22E **241** C6
Mohoro *Tanzania* 8°6S 39°8E **268** D4
Mohrin = Moryń *Poland* 52°51N 14°22E **185** F1
Mohsenābād *Iran* 36°40N 59°35E **247** B8
Mohyliv-Podilskyy *Ukraine* 48°26N 27°48E **183** B12
Moi *Norway* 58°27N 6°32E **164** F3
Moia *South Sudan* 5°3N 28°2E **257** F2
Moidart, L. *U.K.* 56°47N 5°52W **167** E3
Moinabad *India* 17°44N 77°16E **244** F3
Moinești *Romania* 46°28N 26°31E **183** D11
Moinho Velho, Cor. → *Brazil* 23°35S 46°35W **137** B2
Moira → *Canada* 44°21N 77°24W **312** B7
Moirang *India* 24°30N 93°46E **241** C4
Moirans *France* 45°20N 5°33E **175** C9
Moirans-en-Montagne *France* 46°26N 5°43E **173** F12
Moisakūla *Estonia* 58°3N 25°12E **188** C3
Moisie *Canada* 50°12N 66°1W **299** B6
Moisie → *Canada* 50°14N 66°5W **299** B6
Moissac *France* 44°7N 1°5E **174** D5
Moïssala *Chad* 8°21N 17°46E **259** G3
Moita *Portugal* 38°38N 8°58W **195** G2
Moixent *Spain* 38°52N 0°45W **197** G4
Mõja *Sweden* 59°26N 18°55E **162** E12
Mojácar *Spain* 37°6N 1°55W **197** H3
Mojados *Spain* 41°26N 4°40W **194** D6
Mojave *U.S.A.* 35°3N 118°10W **307** K8
Mojave ⌓ *U.S.A.* 35°7N 115°32W **307** K11
Mojave Desert *U.S.A.* 35°0N 116°30W **307** L10
Moji das Cruzes *Brazil* 23°31S 46°11W **335** A6
Moji-Guaçu *Brazil* 22°22S 46°57W **333** F2
Moji-Guaçu → *Brazil* 20°53S 48°10W **335** A6
Mojiang *China* 23°37N 101°35E **228** F3
Mojjo → *Ethiopia* 7°55N 42°0E **257** F5
Mojkovac *Montenegro* 42°58N 19°35E **202** D3
Mojo *Bolivia* 21°48S 65°33W **334** A2
Mojo *Ethiopia* 8°35N 39°5E **257** F4
Mojokerto *Indonesia* 7°28S 112°26E **235** D4
Mojos, Llanos de *Bolivia* 15°10S 65°0W **331** D5
Moju *Brazil* 1°53S 48°46W **332** B2
Moju → *Brazil* 1°40S 48°25W **332** B2
Mok *S. Korea* 37°32N 126°52E **137** B1
Moka *Mauritius* 20°13S 57°29E **272** e
Mokai *N.Z.* 38°32S 175°56E **284** E4
Mokala △ *S. Africa* 29°10S 24°10E **270** C3
Mokambo *Dem. Rep. of the Congo* 12°25S 28°20E **269** E2
Mokameh *India* 25°24N 85°55E **243** G11
Mokane *U.S.A.* 38°41N 91°53W **310** F5
Mōkapu Peninsula *U.S.A.* 21°25N 157°45W **302** K14
Mokau *N.Z.* 38°42S 174°39E **284** E3
Mokau → *N.Z.* 38°35S 174°35E **284** E3
Mokelumne → *U.S.A.* 38°13N 121°28W **306** G5
Mokelumne Hill *U.S.A.* 38°18N 120°43W **306** G6
Mokhotlong *Lesotho* 29°22S 29°2E **271** C4
Mokihinui → *N.Z.* 41°33S 171°58E **285** B6
Möklinta *Sweden* 60°4N 16°33E **162** D10
Moknine *Tunisia* 35°35N 10°58E **258** A2
Mokoan, L. *Australia* 36°27S 146°5E **283** D7
Mokokchung *India* 26°15N 94°30E **241** B5
Mōkōlea Rock *U.S.A.* 21°27N 157°44W **302** K14
Mokolo *Cameroon* 10°49N 13°54E **259** F2
Mokolo *Dem. Rep. of the Congo* 1°55N 18°6E **264** B3
Mokolo → *S. Africa* 23°14S 27°43E **271** B4
Mokombe *Dem. Rep. of the Congo* 0°14S 23°48E **264** C4
Mokopane *S. Africa* 24°10S 28°55E **271** B4
Mokotów *Poland* 52°12N 21°0E **143** B2
Mokpalin *Burma* 17°26N 96°53E **241** G6
Mokpo *S. Korea* 34°50N 126°25E **224** E3
Mokra Gora *Europe* 42°50N 20°30E **202** D4
Mokronog *Slovenia* 45°57N 15°9E **199** C12
Moksha → *Russia* 54°45N 41°53E **190** C6
Mokshan *Russia* 53°25N 44°35E **190** D7
Mokuauia I. *U.S.A.* 21°40N 157°56W **302** J14
Mokulē'ia *U.S.A.* 21°35N 158°9W **302** J13
Mokulua Is. *U.S.A.* 21°24N 157°42W **302** K14
Mokumanu *U.S.A.* 21°28N 157°43W **302** K14
Mokwa *Nigeria* 9°19N 5°0E **263** D6
Mol *Belgium* 51°11N 5°5E **170** C5
Mola di Bari *Italy* 41°4N 17°5E **201** A10
Molai *Greece* 36°49N 22°56E **204** E4
Molakalmuru *India* 14°55N 76°50E **245** G3
Molale *Ethiopia* 10°10N 39°41E **257** E4
Molaly *Kazakhstan* 45°27N 78°18E **217** C9
Molanda *Dem. Rep. of the Congo* 2°28N 20°48E **264** B4
Molara *Italy* 40°52N 9°43E **200** B2
Molat *Croatia* 44°15N 14°50E **199** D11
Molave *Phil.* 8°5N 123°30E **233** G4
Molchanovo *Russia* 57°40N 83°50E **214** D9
Mold *U.K.* 53°9N 3°8W **168** D4
Moldava nad Bodvou *Slovak Rep.* 48°38N 21°0E **181** C14
Moldavia = Moldova ■ *Europe* 47°0N 28°0E **183** C13
Moldavia *Romania* 46°30N 27°0E **183** D12
Molde *Norway* 62°45N 7°9E **164** B4
Moldova ■ *Europe* 47°0N 28°0E **183** C13
Moldova Nouă *Romania* 44°45N 21°41E **182** F6
Moldoveanu, Vf. *Romania* 45°36N 24°45E **183** E9
Moldovița *Romania* 47°41N 25°32E **183** C10
Mole → *U.K.* 51°24N 0°21W **169** F7
Mole △ *Ghana* 9°43N 1°44W **263** D4
Molegbwe *Dem. Rep. of the Congo* 4°12N 20°53E **264** B4
Molenbeek-St-Jean *Belgium* 50°51N 4°19E **116** A1
Molepolole *Botswana* 24°28S 25°28E **270** B4
Molesworth *N.Z.* 42°5S 173°16E **285** C8
Molfetta *Italy* 41°12N 16°36E **201** A9
Möli'i Pond *U.S.A.* 21°31N 157°51W **302** J14
Molina de Aragón *Spain* 40°46N 1°52W **196** E3
Molina de Segura *Spain* 38°3N 1°12W **197** G3
Moline *U.S.A.* 41°30N 90°31W **310** C6
Molinella *Italy* 44°37N 11°40E **199** D8
Molino *U.S.A.* 30°43N 87°20W **317** E2
Molino de Rosas *Mexico* 19°21N 99°14W **128** B1
Molinos *Argentina* 25°28S 66°15W **334** B2
Moliro *Dem. Rep. of the Congo* 8°12S 30°30E **268** D3
Moliterno *Italy* 40°14N 15°52E **201** B8
Molkom *Sweden* 59°37N 13°44E **162** E7
Mölle *Sweden* 56°17N 12°31E **163** H6
Molledo *Spain* 43°8N 4°6W **194** B6
Mollem *Belgium* 50°56N 4°13E **116** A1
Mollendo *Peru* 17°0S 72°0W **330** D3
Mollerin, L. *Australia* 30°30S 117°35E **279** F2
Mollerussa *Spain* 41°37N 0°54E **196** D5
Mollina *Spain* 37°8N 4°38W **195** H6
Molins de Rey *Spain* 41°24N 2°1E **114** A1
Mölln *Germany* 53°39N 10°32E **178** B6
Mölltorp *Sweden* 58°30N 14°26E **163** F8
Mölndal *Sweden* 57°40N 12°3E **163** G5
Mölnlycke *Sweden* 57°40N 12°8E **163** G6
Molo *Burma* 23°22N 96°53E **241** D6
Molo *Rift Valley, Kenya* 0°15S 35°44E **268** C4
Molochansk *Ukraine* 47°15N 35°35E **189** J8
Molochnoye, Ozero *Ukraine* 46°30N 35°20E **189** J8
Molodechno = Maladzyechna *Belarus* 54°20N 26°50E **177** A14
Molodezhnaya *Antarctica* 67°40S 45°51E **151** C9
Molodove *Ukraine* 46°13N 29°39E **183** D14
Moloka'i *U.S.A.* 21°8N 157°0W **302** B4
Molokai Fracture Zone *Pac. Oc.* 28°0N 125°0W **289** E15
Molokini I. *U.S.A.* 20°38N 156°30W **302** C5
Molong *Australia* 33°5S 148°54E **283** B8
Molopo → *Africa* 28°30S 20°12E **270** C3
Molos *Greece* 38°47N 22°37E **204** C4
Molotov = Perm *Russia* 58°0N 56°10E **186** C10
Molotov, Mys = Arkticheskiy, Mys *Russia* 81°10N 95°0E **215** A10
Molotovsk = Nolinsk *Russia* 57°28N 49°57E **190** B9
Molotovsk = Severodvinsk *Russia* 64°27N 39°58E **186** B6
Molotovskoye = Krasnogvardeyskoye *Russia* 45°52N 41°33E **191** H5
Moloundou *Cameroon* 2°8N 15°15E **264** B3
Molowaie *Dem. Rep. of the Congo* 5°47S 23°18E **265** D4
Molsheim *France* 48°33N 7°29E **173** D14
Molson L. *Canada* 54°22N 96°40W **297** C9
Molteno *S. Africa* 31°22S 26°22E **270** D4
Molu *Indonesia* 6°45S 131°40E **231** F8
Molucca Sea *Indonesia* 0°0 125°0E **231** E6
Moluccas = Maluku *Indonesia* 1°0S 127°0E **231** E7
Molundo *Phil.* 7°57N 124°23E **233** H5
Moma *Dem. Rep. of the Congo* 1°35S 23°52E **264** C4
Moma *Mozam.* 16°47S 39°4E **269** F4
Momba *Australia* 30°58S 143°30E **282** A5
Mombaça *Brazil* 5°43S 39°45W **332** C4
Mombango *Dem. Rep. of the Congo* 1°45N 24°26E **264** B4
Mombasa *Kenya* 4°3S 39°40E **268** C4
Mombetsu *Japan* 44°21N 143°22E **220** B11
Mombil *Burma* 27°46N 98°6E **241** B7
Momboyo → *Dem. Rep. of the Congo* 0°16S 19°0E **264** C3
Mombuey *Spain* 42°3N 6°20W **194** C4
Momchilgrad *Bulgaria* 41°33N 25°23E **203** E9
Momence *U.S.A.* 41°10N 87°40W **311** C9
Momi *Dem. Rep. of the Congo* 1°42S 27°0E **268** C2
Momote *Papua N. G.* 2°4S 147°27E **286** B4
Mompog Pass. *Phil.* 13°34N 122°13E **232** E4
Mompós *Colombia* 9°14N 74°26W **328** B3
Møn *Denmark* 54°57N 12°20E **163** K6
Mon *India* 26°45N 95°6E **241** B5
Mon *Hordaland, Norway* 60°37N 6°31E **164** D3
Mon □ *Burma* 16°0N 97°30E **241** G6
Mona, Canal de la = Mona Passage *W. Indies* 18°30N 67°45W **321** C6
Mona, Isla *Puerto Rico* 18°5N 67°54W **321** C6
Mona, Pta. *Costa Rica* 9°37N 82°36W **320** E3
Mona Passage *W. Indies* 18°30N 67°45W **321** C6
Mona Quimbundo *Angola* 9°55S 19°58E **265** D3
Monaca *U.S.A.* 40°41N 80°17W **312** F4
Monaco ■ *Europe* 43°46N 7°23E **175** E11
Monadhliath Mts. *U.K.* 57°10N 4°4W **167** D4
Monadnock, Mt. *U.S.A.* 42°52N 72°7W **313** D12
Monagas □ *Venezuela* 9°20N 63°0W **329** B5
Monaghan *Ireland* 54°15N 6°57W **166** B5
Monaghan □ *Ireland* 54°11N 6°56W **166** B5
Monahans *U.S.A.* 31°36N 102°54W **314** F3
Monapo *Mozam.* 14°56S 40°19E **269** E5
Monar, L. *U.K.* 57°26N 5°8W **167** D3
Monaragala *Sri Lanka* 6°52N 81°22E **245** L5
Monarch Mt. *Canada* 51°55N 125°57W **296** C3
Monashee Mts. *Canada* 51°0N 118°43W **296** C5
Monasterevin *Ireland* 53°8N 7°4W **166** C4
Monastir = Bitola *Macedonia* 41°1N 21°20E **202** E5
Monastir *Tunisia* 35°50N 10°49E **258** A2
Monastir ✕ *Tunisia* 35°37N 10°45E **261** A7
Monbetsu = Hidaka *Japan* 42°30N 142°10E **220** C11
Moncalieri *Italy* 45°0N 7°41E **198** D4
Moncalvo *Italy* 45°3N 8°16E **198** C5
Moncão *Portugal* 42°4N 8°27W **194** C2
Moncarapacho *Portugal* 37°5N 7°46W **195** H3
Moncayo, Sierra del *Spain* 41°48N 1°50W **196** D3
Moncha-Guba = Monchegorsk *Russia* 67°54N 32°58E **160** C25
Monchegorsk *Russia* 67°54N 32°58E **160** C25
Mönchengladbach *Germany* 51°11N 6°27E **178** D2
Monchique *Portugal* 37°19N 8°38W **195** H2
Moncks Corner *U.S.A.* 33°12N 80°1W **316** B9
Monclova *Mexico* 26°54N 101°25W **318** B4
Moncontour *France* 48°22N 2°38W **172** D4
Moncton *Canada* 46°7N 64°51W **299** C7
Mondariz *Spain* 42°14N 8°27W **194** C2
Mondego → *Portugal* 40°9N 8°52W **194** E2
Mondego, C. *Portugal* 40°11N 8°54W **194** E2
Mondeodo *Indonesia* 3°34S 122°9E **231** E6
Mondeor *S. Africa* 26°16S 28°0E **123** B2
Mondeville *France* 49°10N 0°18W **172** C6
Mondimbi *Dem. Rep. of the Congo* 1°48N 22°46E **264** B4
Mondjuku *Dem. Rep. of the Congo* 1°41S 21°12E **264** C4
Mondlo *S. Africa* 27°59S 30°43E **271** C5
Mondo *Chad* 13°47N 15°32E **259** F3
Mondolfo *Italy* 43°45N 13°6E **199** E10
Mondoñedo *Spain* 43°25N 7°23W **194** B3
Mondovì *Italy* 44°23N 7°49E **198** D4
Mondragó *Spain* 39°21N 3°12E **206** B4
Mondragon = Arrasate *Spain* 43°4N 2°30W **196** B2
Mondragon *Phil.* 12°31N 124°45E **232** E5
Mondragone *Italy* 41°7N 13°53E **200** A6
Mondrain I. *Australia* 34°9S 122°14E **279** F3
Moneague *Jamaica* 18°16N 77°7W **320** a
Moneda, Palacio de la *Chile* 33°26S 70°39W **137** B2
Monemvasia *Greece* 36°41N 23°3E **204** E5
Monerò *Brazil* 22°48S 43°11W **135** A1
Moneron, Ostrov *Russia* 46°15N 141°16E **220** A10
Monessen *U.S.A.* 40°9N 79°54W **312** F5
Monesterio *Spain* 38°6N 6°15W **195** G4
Monestier-de-Clermont *France* 44°55N 5°38E **175** D9
Monett *U.S.A.* 36°55N 93°55W **308** G7
Moneymore *U.K.* 54°41N 6°40W **166** B5
Monfalcone *Italy* 45°49N 13°32E **199** C10
Monflanquin *France* 44°32N 0°47E **174** D4
Monforte *Portugal* 39°6N 7°25W **195** F3
Monforte de Lemos *Spain* 42°31N 7°33W **194** C3
Mong Hpayak *Burma* 20°52N 99°55E **236** B2
Mong Hsat *Shan, Burma* 21°54N 98°30E **228** G2
Mong Hsat *Shan, Burma* 20°31N 99°15E **236** B2
Mong Hta *Burma* 19°50N 98°35E **241** F7
Mong Ket *Burma* 23°8N 98°22E **241** D7
Mong Kok *China* 22°19N 114°10E **122** B2
Mong Kung *Burma* 21°35N 97°35E **241** E6
Mong Kyawt *Burma* 19°56N 98°45E **241** F7
Mong Long *Burma* 22°47N 96°37E **241** D6
Mong Mit *Burma* 23°7N 96°41E **241** D6
Mong Nai *Burma* 20°32N 97°46E **241** E6
Mong Pan *Burma* 20°19N 98°22E **241** E7
Mong Ping *Burma* 21°22N 99°2E **228** G2
Mong Pu *Burma* 20°55N 98°44E **241** E7
Mong Tai = Shan □ *Burma* 21°30N 98°30E **241** E7
Mong Ton *Burma* 20°17N 98°45E **241** E7
Mong Tung *Burma* 22°2N 97°41E **241** D6
Mong Yai *Burma* 22°21N 98°3E **241** D7
Mong Yang *Burma* 21°50N 99°41E **236** B2
Mong Yu *Burma* 23°30N 97°47E **241** D6
Monga *Dem. Rep. of the Congo* 4°12N 22°49E **264** B4
Mongala → *Dem. Rep. of the Congo* 1°53N 19°46E **264** B3
Mongalla *South Sudan* 5°8N 31°42E **257** F3
Mongandia *Congo* 0°45N 17°11E **264** B3
Mongers, L. *Australia* 29°25S 117°5E **279** E2
Mongga *Solomon Is.* 7°52S 157°0E **287** L9
Monghyr = Munger *India* 25°23N 86°30E **243** G12
Mongibello = Etna *Italy* 37°50N 14°55E **201** E7
Mongla *Bangla.* 22°8N 89°35E **241** D2
Mongmong *Guam* 13°28N 144°45E **302** d
Mongngaw *Burma* 22°47N 96°59E **241** D6
Mongo *Chad* 12°14N 18°43E **259** F3
Mongó *Eq. Guin.* 1°52N 10°10E **264** B2
Mongo → *S. Leone* 9°35N 12°10W **262** D2
Mongolia ■ *Asia* 47°0N 103°0E **218** B9
Mongolia, Plateau of *Asia* 45°0N 105°0E **210** D12
Mongomo *Eq. Guin.* 1°38N 11°19E **264** B2
Mongonu *Nigeria* 12°40N 13°32E **263** C7
Mongororo *Chad* 12°3N 22°26E **259** F4
Mongstad *Norway* 60°49N 5°2E **164** D2
Mongu *Zambia* 15°16S 23°12E **265** F4
Mônguà *Angola* 16°43S 15°20E **265** F3
Moniac *U.S.A.* 30°31N 82°14W **316** E7
Monifieth *U.K.* 56°30N 2°48W **167** E6
Monistrol-sur-Loire *France* 45°17N 4°11E **175** C8
Monkayo *Phil.* 7°50N 126°5E **233** H6
Monkey Bay *Malawi* 14°7S 35°1E **269** E4
Monkey Mia *Australia* 25°48S 113°43E **279** E1
Monkey River *Belize* 16°22N 88°29W **320** C2
Monkey Town *Trin. & Tob.* 10°12N 61°25W **323** t
Mońki *Poland* 53°23N 22°48E **184** E9
Monkland *Canada* 45°11N 74°52W **313** A10
Monkoto *Dem. Rep. of the Congo* 1°38S 20°35E **264** C4
Monkstown *Ireland* 53°18N 6°10W **120** B3
Monkton *Canada* 43°35N 81°5W **312** C3
Monmouth *Monmouths., U.K.* 51°48N 2°42W **169** F5
Monmouth *Ill., U.S.A.* 40°55N 90°39W **310** D6
Monmouth *Oreg., U.S.A.* 44°51N 123°14W **304** D2
Monmouthshire □ *U.K.* 51°48N 2°54W **169** F5
Monnickendam *Neths.* 52°28N 5°2E **112** A3
Mono *Solomon Is.* 7°20S 155°35E **287** L8
Mono → *Togo* 6°17N 1°51E **263** D5
Mono, Pta. *Nic.* 12°0N 83°30W **320** D3
Mono L. *U.S.A.* 38°1N 119°1W **306** H7
Monolith *U.S.A.* 35°7N 118°22W **307** K8
Monolithos *Greece* 36°7N 27°45E **206** E11
Monon *U.S.A.* 40°52N 86°53W **311** D10
Monona *Iowa, U.S.A.* 43°3N 91°23W **310** A5
Monona *Wis., U.S.A.* 43°4N 89°20W **310** A7
Monongahela *U.S.A.* 40°12N 79°56W **312** F5
Monópoli *Italy* 40°57N 17°18E **201** B10
Monor *Hungary* 47°21N 19°27E **182** C4
Monos I. *Trin. & Tob.* 10°42N 61°44W **323** t
Monóvar *Spain* 38°28N 0°53W **197** G4
Monowai *N.Z.* 45°53S 167°31E **285** F2
Monowai, L. *N.Z.* 45°53S 167°25E **285** F2
Monqoumba *C.A.R.* 3°33N 18°40E **264** B3
Monreal del Campo *Spain* 40°47N 1°20W **196** E3
Monreale *Italy* 38°5N 13°17E **200** D6
Monroe *Ga., U.S.A.* 33°47N 83°43W **316** B6
Monroe *Iowa, U.S.A.* 41°31N 93°6W **310** C3
Monroe *La., U.S.A.* 32°30N 92°7W **314** E8
Monroe *Mich., U.S.A.* 41°55N 83°24W **311** C13
Monroe *N.C., U.S.A.* 34°59N 80°33W **315** D14
Monroe *N.Y., U.S.A.* 41°20N 74°11W **313** E10
Monroe *Ohio, U.S.A.* 39°27N 84°22W **311** E12
Monroe *Utah, U.S.A.* 38°38N 112°7W **304** G7
Monroe *Wash., U.S.A.* 47°51N 121°58W **306** C5
Monroe *Wis., U.S.A.* 42°36N 89°38W **310** B7
Monroe, L. *U.S.A.* 28°50N 81°19W **317** G8
Monroe City *Ind., U.S.A.* 38°37N 87°20W **311** F9
Monroe City *Mo., U.S.A.* 39°39N 91°44W **310** E5
Monroe L. *U.S.A.* 39°1N 86°31W **311** E10
Monroeton *U.S.A.* 41°43N 76°29W **313** E8
Monroeville *Ala., U.S.A.* 31°31N 87°20W **315** F11
Monroeville *Ind., U.S.A.* 40°59N 84°52W **311** D12
Monroeville *Pa., U.S.A.* 40°26N 79°45W **312** F5
Monrovia *Liberia* 6°18N 10°47W **262** D2
Monrovia *Calif., U.S.A.* 34°9N 118°1W **126** B4
Mons *Belgium* 50°27N 3°58E **170** D3
Møns Klint *Denmark* 54°57N 12°33E **163** K6
Monsanto *Portugal* 38°44N 9°12W **126** A1
Monsanto, Parque Florestal de *Portugal* 38°43N 9°11W **126** A1
Monsaraz *Portugal* 38°28N 7°22W **195** G3
Monse *Indonesia* 4°7S 123°15E **231** E6
Monsefú *Peru* 6°52S 79°52W **330** B2
Monségur *France* 44°38N 0°4E **174** D4
Monsélice *Italy* 45°14N 11°45E **199** C8
Mönsterås *Sweden* 57°3N 16°26E **163** G10
Mont Cenis, Col du *France* 45°15N 6°55E **175** C10
Mont-de-Marsan *France* 43°54N 0°31W **174** E3
Mont-Dore *N. Cal.* 22°16S 166°34E **288** d
Mont Fouari ⌓ *Congo* 2°52S 11°32E **264** C2
Mont-Joli *Canada* 48°37N 68°10W **299** C6
Mont-Laurier *Canada* 46°35N 75°30W **298** C4
Mont-Louis *Canada* 49°15N 65°44W **299** C6
Mont Peko ⌓ *Ivory C.* 9°5N 7°15W **262** D3
Mont-roig del Camp *Spain* 41°5N 0°58E **196** D5
Mont-Royal *Canada* 45°30N 73°38W **130** A2
Mont-Royal, Parc *Canada* 45°30N 73°36W **130** A2
Mont-St-Michel, Le *France* 48°40N 1°30W **172** D5
Mont Sangbé ⌓ *Ivory C.* 8°0N 7°10W **262** D3
Mont-Tremblant ⌓ *Canada* 46°30N 74°30W **298** C5
Montabaur *Germany* 50°25N 7°50E **178** E3
Montagnac = Remchi *Algeria* 35°2N 1°26W **261** A4
Montagnac *France* 43°29N 3°28E **174** E7
Montagnana *Italy* 45°13N 11°28E **199** C8
Montagne Blanche *Mauritius* 20°16S 57°39E **272** e
Montagne d'Ambre △ *Madag.* 12°37S 49°8E **272** A2
Montagne de Reims ⌓ *France* 49°8N 4°0E **173** C11
Montagu *S. Africa* 33°45S 20°8E **270** D3
Montagu I. *Antarctica* 58°25S 26°20W **151** B1
Montague *Canada* 46°10N 62°39W **299** C7
Montague, I. *Mexico* 31°45N 114°48W **318** A2
Montague I. *N.S.W., Australia* 36°16S 150°13E **283** D9
Montague I. *Alaska, U.S.A.* 60°0N 147°30W **303** G11
Montague Ra. *Australia* 27°15S 119°30E **279** E2
Montague Sd. *Australia* 14°28S 125°20E **278** B4
Montaigu *France* 46°59N 1°18W **172** F5
Montalbán *Spain* 40°50N 0°45W **196** E4
Montalbano Iónico *Italy* 40°17N 16°34E **201** B9
Montalbo *Spain* 39°53N 2°42W **196** F2
Montalcino *Italy* 43°3N 11°29E **199** E8
Montalegre *Angola* 8°45S 17°29E **265** D3
Montalegre *Portugal* 41°49N 7°47W **194** D3
Montalto *Italy* 38°10N 15°55E **201** D8
Montalto di Castro *Italy* 42°21N 11°37E **199** F8
Montalto Uffugo *Italy* 39°24N 16°9E **201** C9
Montalvo *U.S.A.* 34°15N 119°12W **307** L7
Montamarta *Spain* 41°39N 5°49W **194** D5
Montana *Bulgaria* 43°27N 23°16E **202** C7
Montaña *Peru* 6°0S 73°0W **330** B3
Montana □ *Bulgaria* 43°30N 23°10E **202** C7
Montana □ *U.S.A.* 47°0N 110°0W **304** C9
Montaña Clara, I. *Canary Is.* 29°17N 13°33W **153** e2
Montañas de Malaga ⌓ *Spain* 36°48N 4°32W **195** J6
Montánchez *Spain* 39°15N 6°8W **195** F4
Montanhas do Tumucumaque △ *Brazil* 2°5N 53°0W **329** C7
Montañita *Colombia* 1°22N 75°28W **328** C2
Montargil *Portugal* 39°5N 8°10W **195** F2
Montargis *France* 47°59N 2°43E **173** E9
Montauban *France* 44°2N 1°21E **174** D5
Montauk *U.S.A.* 41°3N 71°57W **313** E13
Montauk Pt. *U.S.A.* 41°4N 71°51W **313** E13
Montbard *France* 47°38N 4°20E **173** E11
Montbarrey *France* 47°1N 5°39E **173** E12
Montbéliard *France* 47°31N 6°48E **173** E13
Montblanc *Spain* 41°23N 1°4E **196** D6
Montbrison *France* 45°36N 4°3E **175** C8
Montcada i Reixac *Spain* 41°29N 2°12W **114** A2
Montcalm, Pic de *France* 42°40N 1°25E **174** F5
Montceau-les-Mines *France* 46°40N 4°23E **173** F11
Montcenis *France* 46°47N 4°23E **175** B8
Montclair *U.S.A.* 40°49N 74°12W **313** F10
Montcornet *France* 49°40N 4°1E **173** C11
Montcuq *France* 44°21N 1°13E **174** D5
Montdidier *France* 49°38N 2°35E **173** C9
Monte Albán *Mexico* 17°2N 96°46W **319** D5
Monte Alegre *Brazil* 2°0S 54°0W **329** D7
Monte Alegre de Goiás *Brazil* 13°14S 47°10W **333** D2
Monte Alegre de Minas *Brazil* 18°52S 48°52W **333** E2
Monte Alegre do Piauí *Brazil* 9°46S 45°18W **332** C2
Monte Azul *Brazil* 15°9S 42°53W **333** E3
Monte-Carlo *Monaco* 43°44N 7°25E **175** E11
Monte Carmelo *Brazil* 18°43S 47°29W **333** E2
Monte Caseros *Argentina* 30°10S 57°50W **334** C4
Monte Chingolo *Argentina* 34°43S 58°22W **117** C2
Monte Comán *Argentina* 34°40S 67°53W **334** C2
Monte Cristi *Dom. Rep.* 19°52N 71°39W **321** C5
Monte Cucco ⌓ *Italy* 43°22N 12°44E **199** E9
Monte Dinero *Argentina* 52°18S 68°33W **336** D3
Monte Dourado *Brazil* 0°52S 52°31W **329** D7
Monte Lindo → *Paraguay* 23°56S 57°12W **334** A4
Monte Palatino *Rome, Italy* **136** c3
Monte Pascoal △ *Brazil* 16°51S 39°21W **333** E4
Monte Patria *Chile* 30°42S 70°58W **334** C1
Monte Quemado *Argentina* 25°53S 62°41W **334** B3
Monte Redondo *Portugal* 39°53N 8°50W **194** F2
Monte Rio *U.S.A.* 38°28N 123°0W **306** G4
Monte San Giovanni Campano *Italy* 41°38N 13°31E **200** A6
Monte San Giuliano = Erice *Italy* 38°2N 12°35E **200** D5
Monte San Savino *Italy* 43°20N 11°43E **199** E8
Monte Sant' Ángelo *Italy* 41°42N 15°59E **199** G12
Monte Santu, C. di *Italy* 40°5N 9°44E **200** B2
Monte Sibillini △ *Italy* 42°55N 13°15E **199** F10
Monte Subasio ⌓ *Italy* 43°5N 12°40E **199** E9
Monte Vista *U.S.A.* 37°35N 106°9W **305** H10
Monteagudo *Argentina* 27°14S 54°8W **335** B5
Monteagudo *Bolivia* 19°49S 63°59W **331** D5
Montealegre del Castillo *Spain* 38°48N 1°17W **197** G3
Montebello *Qué., Canada* 45°40N 74°55W **298** C5
Montebello *Guadeloupe* 16°10N 61°36W **322** b
Montebello *Calif., U.S.A.* 34°1N 118°8W **126** B4
Montebello Iónico *Italy* 37°59N 15°45E **201** E8
Montebello Is. *Australia* 20°30S 115°45E **278** D2
Montebelluna *Italy* 45°47N 12°3E **199** C9
Montebourg *France* 49°30N 1°20W **172** C5
Montecarlo *Argentina* 26°34S 54°47W **335** B5
Montecastrilli *Italy* 42°39N 12°29E **199** F9
Montecatini Terme *Italy* 43°53N 10°46E **198** E7
Montecito *U.S.A.* 34°26N 119°40W **307** L7
Montecristi *Ecuador* 1°0S 80°40W **328** D1
Montecristo *Italy* 42°20N 10°19E **198** F7
Montefalco *Italy* 42°54N 12°39E **199** F9
Montefiascone *Italy* 42°32N 12°2E **199** F9
Montefrío *Spain* 37°20N 4°0W **195** H7
Montegiórgio *Italy* 43°6N 13°33E **199** E10
Montego B. *Jamaica* 18°28N 77°56W **320** a
Montego Bay *Jamaica* 18°28N 77°55W **320** a
Montehermoso *Spain* 40°5N 6°21W **194** E4
Monteiro *Brazil* 7°48S 37°2W **332** C4
Montejicar *Spain* 37°33N 3°30W **195** H7
Montelbaanstoren *Amsterdam, Neths.* **112** b3
Monteleone di Calabria = Vibo Valéntia *Italy* 38°40N 16°6E **201** D9
Montelíbano *Colombia* 8°5N 75°29W **328** B2
Montélimar *France* 44°33N 4°45E **175** D8
Montella *Italy* 40°51N 15°1E **201** B8
Montellano *Spain* 36°59N 5°29W **195** J5
Montello *U.S.A.* 43°48N 89°20W **308** D9
Montemayor, Meseta de *Argentina* 44°20S 66°10W **336** B3
Montemor *Portugal* 38°49N 9°12W **126** A1
Montemor-o-Novo *Portugal* 38°40N 8°12W **195** G2
Montemor-o-Velho *Portugal* 40°11N 8°40W **194** E2
Montemorelos *Mexico* 25°12N 99°49W **319** B5
Montendre *France* 45°16N 0°26W **174** C3
Montenegro *Brazil* 29°39S 51°29W **335** B5
Montenegro ■ *Europe* 42°40N 19°20E **202** D3
Montenero di Bisáccia *Italy* 41°57N 14°47E **199** G11
Montepuez *Mozam.* 13°8S 38°59E **269** E4
Montepuez → *Mozam.* 12°32S 40°27E **269** E5
Montepulciano *Italy* 43°5N 11°47E **199** E8
Montereale *Italy* 42°31N 13°15E **199** F10
Montereau-Fault-Yonne *France* 48°22N 2°57E **173** D9
Monterey *Calif., U.S.A.* 36°37N 121°55W **306** J5
Monterey *Ind., U.S.A.* 41°11N 86°30W **311** C10
Monterey B. *U.S.A.* 36°45N 122°0W **306** J5
Monterey Hills *U.S.A.* 34°6N 118°10W **126** B3
Monterey Park *U.S.A.* 34°3N 118°7W **126** B3
Montería *Colombia* 8°46N 75°53W **328** B2
Montero *Bolivia* 17°20S 63°15W **331** D5
Monteros *Argentina* 27°11S 65°30W **334** B2
Monterotondo *Italy* 42°3N 12°37E **199** F9
Monterrey *Mexico* 25°40N 100°19W **318** B4
Montes Altos *Brazil* 5°50S 47°4W **332** C2
Montes Azules ⌓ *Mexico* 16°21N 91°3W **319** D6
Montes Claros *Brazil* 16°30S 43°50W **333** E3
Montesano *U.S.A.* 46°59N 123°36W **306** D3
Montesano sulla Marcellana *Italy* 40°16N 15°42E **201** B8
Montesárchio *Italy* 41°4N 14°38E **201** A7

Montescaglioso Italy 40°33N 16°40E 201 B9
Montesilvano Italy 42°29N 14°8E 199 F11
Montesinho ⌂ Portugal 41°54N 6°52W 194 D4
Montespaccato Italy 41°54N 12°23E 136 B1
Montesson France 48°54N 2°8E 134 A1
Montevarchi Italy 43°31N 11°34E 199 E8
Monteverde Nuovo Italy 41°52N 12°26E 136 B1
Montevideo Uruguay 34°50S 56°11W 335 C4
Montevideo Minn., U.S.A. 44°57N 95°43W 308 C6
Montezuma Ga., U.S.A. 32°18N 84°2W 316 C5
Montezuma Ind., U.S.A. 39°48N 87°22W 311 E9
Montezuma Iowa, U.S.A. 41°35N 92°32W 310 C4
Montezuma Castle ⌂ U.S.A. 34°39N 111°45W 305 J8
Montfaucon France 47°6N 1°7W 172 E5
Montfaucon-d'Argonne France 49°16N 5°8E 173 C12
Montfaucon-en-Velay France 45°11N 4°20E 175 C8
Montfermeil France 48°54N 2°33E 134 A4
Montfort-le-Gesnois France 48°3N 0°25E 172 D7
Montfort-sur-Meu France 48°9N 1°58W 172 D5
Montfragüe ⌂ Spain 39°48N 5°52W 194 F5
Montgenèvre France 44°56N 6°43E 175 D10
Montgomery = Sahiwal Pakistan 30°45N 73°8E 242 D5
Montgomery Powys, U.K. 52°34N 3°8W 169 E4
Montgomery Ala., U.S.A. 32°23N 86°19W 316 C3
Montgomery Ill., U.S.A. 41°44N 88°21W 311 C8
Montgomery Pa., U.S.A. 41°10N 76°53W 312 E8
Montgomery W. Va., U.S.A. 38°11N 81°19W 309 F13
Montgomery City U.S.A. 38°59N 91°30W 310 F5
Montguyon France 45°12N 0°12W 174 C3
Monthermé France 49°52N 4°42E 173 C11
Monthey Switz. 46°15N 6°56E 179 J2
Monthois France 49°19N 4°43E 173 C11
Monti Italy 40°49N 9°19E 200 B2
Monti Lucrétili ⌂ Italy 42°5N 12°50E 199 F9
Monti Picentini ⌂ Italy 40°45N 15°2E 201 B8
Monti Simbruini ⌂ Italy 41°55N 13°13E 199 G10
Monticelli d'Ongina Italy 45°5N 9°56E 198 C6
Monticello Ark., U.S.A. 33°38N 91°47W 314 E9
Monticello Fla., U.S.A. 30°33N 83°52W 316 E6
Monticello Ga., U.S.A. 33°18N 83°40W 316 B6
Monticello Ill., U.S.A. 40°1N 88°34W 311 D8
Monticello Ind., U.S.A. 40°45N 86°46W 311 D10
Monticello Iowa, U.S.A. 42°15N 91°12W 310 B5
Monticello Ky., U.S.A. 36°50N 84°51W 309 G11
Monticello Minn., U.S.A. 45°18N 93°48W 308 C7
Monticello Miss., U.S.A. 31°33N 90°7W 315 F9
Monticello Mo., U.S.A. 40°7N 91°43W 310 D5
Monticello N.Y., U.S.A. 41°39N 74°42W 313 E10
Monticello Utah, U.S.A. 37°52N 109°21W 305 H9
Montichiari Italy 45°25N 10°23E 198 C7
Montier-en-Der France 48°30N 4°45E 173 D11
Montignac France 45°4N 1°10E 174 C5
Montigny-le-Bretonneux France 48°46N 2°1E 134 B1
Montigny-les-Metz France 49°7N 6°10E 173 C13
Montigny-sur-Aube France 47°57N 4°45E 173 E11
Montijo Portugal 38°41N 8°54W 195 G2
Montijo Spain 38°52N 6°39W 195 G4
Montilla Spain 37°36N 4°40W 195 H6
Montivilliers France 49°33N 0°12E 172 C7
Montjay-la-Tour France 48°54N 2°40E 134 A4
Montjuïc Spain 41°22N 2°10E 114 A2
Montjuïc, Parc de Barcelona, Spain 114 c1
Montluçon France 46°22N 2°36E 173 F9
Montmagny Canada 46°58N 70°34W 299 C5
Montmarault France 46°19N 2°57E 173 F9
Montmartre Canada 50°14N 103°27W 297 C8
Montmédy France 49°30N 5°20E 173 C12
Montmélian France 45°30N 6°4E 175 C10
Montmirail France 48°51N 3°30E 173 D10
Montmoreau-St-Cybard France 45°23N 0°8E 174 C4
Montmorillon France 46°26N 0°50E 174 B4
Montmort-Lucy France 48°55N 3°49E 173 D10
Monto Australia 24°52S 151°6E 280 C5
Montoire-sur-le-Loir France 47°45N 0°52E 172 E7
Montongbuwoh Indonesia 8°33S 116°4E 231 K19
Montório al Vomano Italy 42°35N 13°38E 199 F10
Montoro Spain 38°1N 4°27W 195 G6
Montour Falls U.S.A. 42°21N 76°51W 312 D8
Montoursville U.S.A. 41°15N 76°55W 312 E8
Montparnasse, Gare France 48°50N 2°19E 134 A2
Montpelier Idaho, U.S.A. 42°19N 111°18W 304 E8
Montpelier Ind., U.S.A. 40°33N 85°17W 311 D11
Montpelier Ohio, U.S.A. 41°35N 84°37W 311 C12
Montpelier Vt., U.S.A. 44°16N 72°35W 313 B12
Montpellier France 43°37N 3°52E 174 E7
Montpezat-de-Quercy France 44°15N 1°30E 174 D5
Montpon-Ménestérol France 45°0N 0°11E 174 D4
Montréal Qué., Canada 45°30N 73°33W 130 A2
Montréal Aude, France 43°13N 2°8E 174 E6
Montréal Gers, France 43°56N 0°11E 174 E4
Montreal → Canada 47°14N 84°39W 298 C3
Montréal, Î. de Canada 45°30N 73°40W 130 A2
Montréal, Univ. de Canada 45°29N 73°37W 130 B2
Montréal Est Canada 45°37N 73°31W 130 A2
Montréal L. Canada 54°20N 105°45W 297 C7
Montreal Lake Canada 54°3N 105°46W 297 C7
Montréal Nord Canada 45°36N 73°36W 130 A2
Montréal Ouest Canada 45°27N 73°39W 130 B1
Montréal Trudeau Int. ✈ (YUL) Canada 45°28N 73°44W 130 B1
Montredon-Labessonnié France 43°45N 2°18E 174 E6
Montrésor France 47°10N 1°10E 172 E8
Montret France 46°40N 5°7E 173 F12
Montreuil Pas-de-Calais, France 50°27N 1°45E 173 B8
Montreuil Seine-St-Denis, France 48°51N 2°27E 134 A3
Montreuil-Bellay France 47°8N 0°9W 172 E6
Montreux Switz. 46°26N 6°55E 179 J2
Montrevel-en-Bresse France 46°21N 5°8E 173 F12
Montrichard France 47°20N 1°10E 172 E8
Montrose Angus, U.K. 56°44N 2°27W 167 E6
Montrose Colo., U.S.A. 38°29N 107°53W 304 G10
Montrose Pa., U.S.A. 41°50N 75°53W 313 E9
Montrose, L. U.S.A. 38°18N 93°50W 310 F3
Montrouge France 48°48N 2°18E 134 B2
Monts, Pte. des Canada 49°20N 67°12W 299 C6
Montsalvy France 44°41N 2°30E 174 D6
Montsant, Serra de Spain 41°17N 1°0E 196 D6
Montsauche-les-Settons France 47°13N 4°2E 173 E11
Montsec, Serra del Spain 42°5N 0°45E 196 C5
Montseny ⌂ Spain 41°43N 2°22W 196 D2
Montserrat B. Aires, Argentina 34°37S 58°24W 117 B2
Montserrat Spain 41°36N 1°49E 196 D6
Montserrat ☑ W. Indies 16°40N 62°10W 323 p
Montserrat Hills Trin. & Tob. 10°23N 61°21W 323 t
Montuenga Spain 41°3N 4°38W 194 D6
Montuiri Spain 39°34N 2°59E 206 B3
Montvert-les-Bas Réunion 21°19S 55°32E 272 f
Monveda Dem. Rep. of the Congo 2°52N 21°30E 264 B4
Monyo Burma 17°59N 95°30E 241 G5
Monywa Burma 22°7N 95°11E 241 D5
Monza Italy 45°35N 9°16E 128 A2
Monze Zambia 16°17S 27°29E 269 F2
Monze, C. Pakistan 24°47N 66°37E 242 G2
Monzón Spain 41°52N 0°10E 196 D5
Monzoro Italy 45°27N 9°2E 128 B1
Moóca Brazil 23°33S 46°35W 137 B2
Moodyville = North Vancouver Canada 49°19N 123°4W 306 A3
Mooers U.S.A. 44°58N 73°35W 313 B11
Mooi → S. Africa 28°45S 30°34E 271 C5
Mooi River S. Africa 29°13S 29°50E 271 C4
Mo'oka Japan 36°26N 140°1E 223 A12
Mookgopong S. Africa 24°31S 28°44E 271 B4
Moomba Australia 28°6S 140°12E 281 A3
Moonachie U.S.A. 40°50N 74°2W 132 B1
Moonah → Australia 22°3S 138°33E 280 C2
Moonda, L. Australia 25°52S 140°25E 280 D3
Moonee Ponds Australia 37°45S 144°53E 128 A1
Moonee Valley Racecourse Australia 37°45S 144°55E 128 A1
Moonie Australia 27°46S 150°20E 281 D5
Moonie → Australia 29°19S 148°43E 281 D4
Moonta Australia 34°6S 137°32E 282 C2
Moora Australia 30°37S 115°58E 279 F2
Moorcroft U.S.A. 44°16N 104°57W 304 D11
Moore → Australia 31°22S 115°30E 279 F2
Moore, L. Australia 29°50S 117°35E 279 E2
Moore Falls Canada 44°48N 78°48W 312 B6
Moore Haven U.S.A. 26°50N 81°6W 317 J8
Moore Park Australia 24°43S 152°17E 280 C5
Moore Res. U.S.A. 44°20N 71°53W 313 B13
Moore River △ Australia 31°7S 115°39E 279 F2
Moorea French Polynesia 17°30S 149°50W 289 e
Moorefield U.S.A. 39°4N 78°58W 309 F14
Mooresville U.S.A. 39°37N 86°22W 311 E10
Moorfoot Hills U.K. 55°44N 3°8W 167 F5
Moorhead U.S.A. 46°53N 96°45W 308 B5
Moorland U.S.A. 42°26N 94°18W 310 B2
Moormerland Germany 53°20N 7°20E 178 B3
Moornanyah L. Australia 33°15S 143°42E 282 B5
Mooroopna Australia 36°25S 145°22E 283 D6
Moorpark U.S.A. 34°17N 118°53W 307 L8
Moorreesburg S. Africa 33°6S 18°38E 270 D2
Moorrinya △ Australia 21°42S 144°58E 280 C3
Moosach Germany 48°10N 11°30E 131 A2
Moosburg Germany 48°27N 11°56E 179 G7
Moose → Ont., Canada 51°20N 80°25W 298 B3
Moose → N.Y., U.S.A. 43°38N 75°24W 313 C9
Moose Creek Canada 45°15N 74°58W 313 A10
Moose Factory Canada 51°16N 80°32W 298 B3
Moose Jaw Canada 50°24N 105°30W 297 C7
Moose Jaw → Canada 50°34N 105°18W 297 C7
Moose Lake Man., Canada 53°46N 100°8W 297 C8
Moose Lake Minn., U.S.A. 46°27N 92°46W 308 B7
Moose Mountain ⌂ Canada 49°48N 102°25W 297 D8
Moose Pass U.S.A. 60°29N 149°22W 303 F10
Moosehead L. U.S.A. 45°38N 69°40W 309 C19
Mooselookmeguntic L. U.S.A. 44°55N 70°49W 313 B14
Moosilauke, Mt. U.S.A. 44°3N 71°40W 313 B13
Moosomin Canada 50°9N 101°40W 297 C8
Moosonee Canada 51°17N 80°39W 298 B3
Moosup U.S.A. 41°43N 71°53W 313 E13
Mootwingee △ Australia 31°10S 142°30E 282 A5
Mopane S. Africa 22°37S 29°52E 271 B4
Mopeia Velha Mozam. 17°30S 35°40E 269 F4
Mopipi Botswana 21°6S 24°55E 270 B3
Mopoi C.A.R. 5°6N 26°54E 268 A2
Mopti Mali 14°30N 4°0W 262 C4
Mopti □ Mali 14°40N 4°0W 262 C4
Moqatta Sudan 14°38N 35°50E 257 E4
Moqor Afghan. 32°50N 67°42E 242 C2
Moquegua Peru 17°15S 70°46W 330 D3
Moquegua □ Peru 16°50S 70°55W 330 D3
Mór Hungary 47°25N 18°12E 182 C3
Mora Cameroon 11°2N 14°7E 259 F2
Mora Maharashtra, India 18°54N 72°55E 130 B2
Móra Portugal 38°55N 8°10W 195 G2
Mora Spain 39°41N 3°46W 195 F7
Mora Sweden 61°2N 14°38E 162 C8
Mora Minn., U.S.A. 45°53N 93°18W 308 C7
Mora N. Mex., U.S.A. 35°58N 105°20W 305 J11
Móra de Rubielos Spain 40°15N 0°45W 196 E4
Móra d'Ebre Spain 41°6N 0°38E 196 D5
Móra la Nova Spain 41°7N 0°39E 196 D5
Morača → Montenegro 42°20N 19°9E 202 D3
Morada Nova Brazil 5°7S 38°23W 332 C4
Morada Nova de Minas Brazil 18°37S 45°22W 333 E2
Moradabad India 28°50N 78°50E 243 E8
Morafenobe Madag. 17°50S 44°53E 272 B1
Morąg Poland 53°55N 19°56E 184 E6
Moral de Calatrava Spain 38°51N 3°33W 195 G7
Moraleda, Canal Chile 44°30S 73°30W 336 B2
Moraleja Spain 40°6N 6°43W 194 E4
Morales Bolívar, Colombia 8°16N 73°51W 328 B3
Morales Cauca, Colombia 2°45N 76°38W 328 C2
Moramanga Madag. 18°56S 48°12E 272 B2
Moran Kans., U.S.A. 37°55N 95°10W 308 G6
Moran Wyo., U.S.A. 43°50N 110°31W 304 E8
Moranbah Australia 22°1S 148°6E 280 C4
Morané French Polynesia 23°10S 137°7W 289 f
Morang = Biratnagar Nepal 26°27N 87°17E 243 F12
Moranhat India 27°10N 94°50E 241 B5
Morano Cálabro Italy 39°50N 16°8E 201 C9
Morant Bay Jamaica 17°53N 76°25W 320 a
Morant Cays Jamaica 17°22N 76°0W 320 C4
Morant Pt. Jamaica 17°55N 76°12W 320 a
Morar India 26°14N 78°14E 242 F8
Morar, L. U.K. 56°57N 5°40W 167 E3
Moratalaz Spain 40°24N 3°39W 127 B2
Moratalla Spain 38°14N 1°49W 197 G3
Moratuwa Sri Lanka 6°45N 79°55E 245 L4
Morava → Slovak Rep. 48°10N 16°59E 181 C9
Moravia Iowa, U.S.A. 40°53N 92°49W 310 D4
Moravia N.Y., U.S.A. 42°43N 76°25W 313 D8
Moravian Hts. = Českomoravská Vrchovina Czech Rep. 49°30N 15°40E 180 B8
Moravica → Serbia 43°52N 20°8E 202 C4
Moravița Romania 45°17N 21°14E 182 E6
Moravská Třebová Czech Rep. 49°45N 16°40E 181 B9
Moravské Budějovice Czech Rep. 49°4N 15°49E 180 B8
Morawa Australia 29°13S 116°0E 279 E2
Morawhanna Guyana 8°30N 59°40W 329 B6
Moray □ U.K. 57°31N 3°18W 167 D5
Moray Firth U.K. 57°40N 3°52W 167 D5
Morbach Germany 49°48N 7°6E 179 F3
Morbegno Italy 46°8N 9°34E 198 B6
Morbi India 22°50N 70°42E 242 H4
Morbihan □ France 47°55N 2°50W 172 E4
Mörby Sweden 59°23N 18°3E 139 A2
Mörbylånga Sweden 56°32N 16°22E 163 H10
Morcenx France 44°3N 0°55W 174 D3
Morcone Italy 41°20N 14°40E 201 A7
Mordelles France 48°5N 1°52W 172 D5
Morden Man., Canada 49°15N 98°10W 297 D9
Morden London, U.K. 51°24N 0°13W 125 B2
Mordoğan Turkey 38°30N 26°37E 205 C8
Mordovian Republic = Mordvinia □ Russia 54°20N 44°30E 190 C7
Mordovo Russia 52°6N 40°50E 190 D5
Mordvinia □ Russia 54°20N 44°30E 190 C7
Mordy Poland 52°13N 22°31E 185 F9
Møre og Romsdal □ Norway 62°30N 8°0E 164 B4
Moreau → U.S.A. 45°18N 100°43W 308 C3
Morebeng S. Africa 23°30S 29°55E 271 B4
Morecambe U.K. 54°5N 2°52W 168 C5
Morecambe B. U.K. 54°7N 3°0W 168 C5
Moree Australia 29°28S 149°54E 281 D4
Morée → France 48°57N 2°25E 134 A3
Morehead Papua N. G. 8°41S 141°41E 286 E1
Morehead Ky., U.S.A. 38°11N 83°26W 311 F13
Morehead City U.S.A. 34°43N 76°43W 315 D16
Morel → India 26°13N 76°36E 242 F7
Moreland U.S.A. 33°17N 84°46W 316 B5
Morelia Mexico 19°42N 101°7W 318 D4
Morella Queens., Australia 23°0S 143°52E 280 C3
Morella Spain 40°35N 0°5W 196 E4
Morelos Mexico 26°42N 107°40W 318 B3
Morelos □ Mexico 18°45N 99°0W 319 D5
Moremi ⌂ Botswana 19°18S 23°10E 270 A3
Morena India 26°30N 78°4E 242 F8
Morena, Sierra Spain 38°20N 4°0W 195 G7
Morenci U.S.A. 41°43N 84°13W 311 C12
Moreni Romania 44°59N 25°36E 183 F10
Moreno Bolivia 11°9S 66°15W 330 C4
Moreno Valley U.S.A. 33°56N 117°14W 307 M10
Moreru → Brazil 10°10S 59°15W 331 C6
Moresby I. Canada 52°30N 131°40W 296 C2
Morestel France 45°40N 5°28E 175 C9
Moreton I. Australia 27°10S 153°25E 281 D5
Moreton Island △ Australia 27°2S 153°24E 281 D5
Moreuil France 49°46N 2°30E 173 C9
Morez France 46°31N 6°2E 173 F13
Morgan S. Austral., Australia 34°2S 139°35E 282 C3
Morgan Ga., U.S.A. 31°32N 84°36W 316 D5
Morgan Utah, U.S.A. 41°2N 111°41W 304 F8
Morgan City U.S.A. 29°42N 91°12W 314 G9
Morgan Hill U.S.A. 37°8N 121°39W 306 H5
Morgan Park U.S.A. 41°41N 87°38W 119 C3
Morganfield U.S.A. 37°41N 87°55W 308 G10
Morganton U.S.A. 35°45N 81°41W 315 D14
Morgantown Ind., U.S.A. 39°22N 86°16W 311 E10
Morgantown W. Va., U.S.A. 39°38N 79°57W 309 F14
Morgenzon S. Africa 26°45S 29°36E 271 C4
Morges Switz. 46°31N 6°29E 179 J2
Morghak Iran 29°7N 57°54E 247 D8
Morgongåva Sweden 59°57N 16°58E 162 E10
Morhange France 48°55N 6°38E 173 D13
Morhar → India 25°29N 85°11E 243 G11
Mori China 43°49N 90°11E 217 D12
Mori Italy 45°51N 10°59E 198 C7
Mori Japan 42°6N 140°35E 220 C10
Moriah Trin. & Tob. 11°15N 60°43W 323 s
Moriarty U.S.A. 34°59N 106°3W 305 J10
Moribaya Guinea 9°53N 9°32W 262 D3
Morice L. Canada 53°50N 127°40W 296 C3
Morichal Largo → Venezuela 9°27N 62°25W 329 B5
Morichal Viejo Colombia 2°13N 70°2W 328 C3
Moriguchi Japan 34°43N 135°34E 133 A2
Moriki Nigeria 12°52N 6°30E 263 C6
Morinville Canada 53°49N 113°41W 296 C6
Morioka Japan 39°45N 141°8E 220 E10
Moris Mexico 28°10N 108°32W 318 B3
Morisset Australia 33°6S 151°30E 283 B9
Morivione Italy 45°26N 9°12E 128 B2
Moriyama Japan 35°4N 135°59E 223 B7
Morlaàs France 43°21N 0°18W 174 E3
Morlaix France 48°36N 3°52W 172 D3
Mörlunda Sweden 57°19N 15°52E 163 G9
Mormanno Italy 39°53N 15°59E 201 C8
Mormant France 48°37N 2°52E 173 D9
Mormugao = Marmagao India 15°25N 73°56E 245 G1
Morne-à-l'Eau Guadeloupe 16°20N 61°27W 322 e
Morne des Esses Martinique 14°44N 61°1W 322 j
Morne Diablotins Dominica 15°30N 61°24W 323 k
Morne Fendue Grenada 12°12N 61°38W 323 q
Morne Raquette Dominica 15°27N 61°27W 323 k
Morne Trois Pitons △ Dominica 15°22N 61°20W 323 k
Morningside Gauteng, S. Africa 26°4S 28°3E 123 A2
Morningside Edinburgh, U.K. 55°56N 3°12W 121 B2
Morningside Park Ont., Canada 43°47N 79°12W 141 A3
Morningside Park Fla., U.S.A. 28°26N 81°24W 133 B2
Mornington Australia 38°15S 145°5E 283 E6
Mornington, I. Chile 49°50S 75°30W 336 C1
Mornington I. Australia 16°30S 139°30E 280 B2
Mornington Peninsula △ Australia 38°28S 144°53E 283 E6
Mornos → Greece 38°25N 21°50E 204 C3
Moro Pakistan 26°40N 68°0E 242 F2
Moro Sudan 10°50N 30°9E 257 E3
Moro → Pakistan 29°42N 67°22E 242 E2
Moro G. Phil. 6°30N 123°0E 233 H4
Morobe Papua N. G. 7°49S 147°38E 286 D4
Morobe □ Papua N. G. 7°0S 147°0E 286 D4
Morocco U.S.A. 40°57N 87°27W 311 D9
Morocco ■ N. Afr. 32°0N 5°50W 260 B3
Morococha Peru 11°40S 76°5W 330 C2
Morogoro Tanzania 6°50S 37°40E 268 D4
Morogoro □ Tanzania 8°0S 37°0E 268 D4
Moroleón Mexico 20°8N 101°12W 318 C4
Morombe Madag. 21°45S 43°22E 272 C1
Moron = Morong Phil. 14°41N 120°16E 232 D3
Moron Argentina 34°39S 58°37W 334 C4
Morón Cuba 22°8N 78°39W 320 B4
Mörön Mongolia 49°38N 100°9E 218 B9
Morón de Almazán Spain 41°29N 2°27W 196 D2
Morón de la Frontera Spain 37°6N 5°28W 195 H5
Morona → Peru 4°40S 77°10W 328 D2
Morona-Santiago □ Ecuador 2°30S 78°0W 328 D2
Morondava Madag. 20°17S 44°17E 272 C1
Morondo Ivory C. 8°57N 6°47W 262 D3
Morong Phil. 14°41N 120°16E 232 D3
Morongo Valley U.S.A. 34°3N 116°37W 307 L10
Moroni Comoros Is. 11°40S 43°16E 272 a
Moroni Utah, U.S.A. 39°32N 111°35W 304 G8
Moroni Iconi ✈ (YVA) Comoros Is. 11°32S 43°15E 272 a
Moronou Ivory C. 6°16N 4°59W 262 D4
Morotai Indonesia 2°10N 128°30E 231 D7
Moroto Uganda 2°28N 34°42E 268 B3
Moroto, Mt. Uganda 2°30N 34°43E 268 B3
Morozov Bulgaria 42°30N 25°10E 203 D9
Morozovsk Russia 48°25N 41°50E 191 F5
Morpeth Ont., Canada 42°23N 81°50W 312 D3
Morpeth Northumberland, U.K. 55°10N 1°41W 168 B6
Morphou Cyprus 35°12N 32°59E 207 E8
Morphou Bay Cyprus 35°15N 32°50E 207 E8
Morrelganj Bangla. 22°28N 89°51E 241 D2
Morrilton U.S.A. 35°9N 92°44W 314 D8
Morrinhos Ceará, Brazil 3°14S 40°7W 332 B3
Morrinhos Minas Gerais, Brazil 17°45S 49°10W 333 E2
Morrinsville N.Z. 37°40S 175°32E 284 D4
Morris Man., Canada 49°25N 97°22W 297 D9
Morris Ill., U.S.A. 41°22N 88°26W 311 C8
Morris Minn., U.S.A. 45°35N 95°55W 308 C6
Morris N.Y., U.S.A. 42°33N 75°15W 313 D9
Morris Pa., U.S.A. 41°35N 77°17W 312 E7
Morris, Mt. Australia 26°9S 131°4E 279 E5
Morris Jesup, Kap Greenland 83°40N 34°0W 154 A7
Morrisburg Canada 44°55N 75°7W 313 B9
Morrison U.S.A. 41°49N 89°58W 310 C7
Morrisonville U.S.A. 39°25N 89°27W 310 E7
Morristown Ariz., U.S.A. 33°51N 112°37W 305 K7
Morristown Ind., U.S.A. 39°40N 85°42W 311 E11
Morristown N.J., U.S.A. 40°48N 74°29W 313 F10
Morristown N.Y., U.S.A. 44°35N 75°39W 313 B9
Morristown Tenn., U.S.A. 36°13N 83°18W 315 C13
Morrisville N.Y., U.S.A. 42°53N 75°35W 313 D9
Morrisville Pa., U.S.A. 40°13N 74°47W 313 F10
Morrisville Vt., U.S.A. 44°34N 72°36W 313 B12
Morro, Pta. Chile 27°6S 71°0W 334 B1
Morro Bay U.S.A. 35°22N 120°51W 306 K6
Morro Chico Chile 52°2S 71°26W 336 D2
Morro del Jable Canary Is. 28°3N 14°23W 153 e2
Morro do Chapéu Brazil 11°33S 41°9W 333 D3
Morro Grande = Barão de Cocais Brazil 19°56S 43°28W 333 E3
Morro Jable, Pta. de Canary Is. 28°2N 14°20W 153 e2
Morro Solar, Cerro Peru 12°11S 77°1W 124 C2
Morrocoy △ Venezuela 10°48N 68°13W 328 A4
Morros Brazil 2°52S 44°3W 332 B3
Morrosquillo, G. de Colombia 9°35N 75°40W 320 E4
Morrow U.S.A. 39°21N 84°8W 311 E12
Mörrum Sweden 56°12N 14°45E 163 H8
Morrumbene Mozam. 23°31S 35°16E 271 B6
Mörrumsån → Sweden 56°10N 14°45E 163 H8
Mors Denmark 56°50N 8°45E 163 H2
Morshansk Russia 53°28N 41°50E 190 D5
Morsi India 21°21N 78°0E 244 D4
Mörsil Sweden 63°19N 13°40E 162 A7
Mortagne → France 48°33N 6°27E 173 D13
Mortagne-au-Perche France 48°31N 0°33E 172 D7
Mortagne-sur-Gironde France 45°28N 0°47W 174 C3
Mortagne-sur-Sèvre France 47°0N 0°59W 172 F6
Mortain France 48°40N 0°57W 172 D6
Mortara Italy 45°15N 8°44E 198 C5
Morteau France 47°3N 6°35E 173 E13
Morteros Argentina 30°50S 62°0W 334 C3
Mortes, R. das → Brazil 11°45S 50°44W 333 D1
Mortlach Canada 50°27N 106°4W 297 C7
Mortlake N.S.W., Australia 33°50S 151°6E 139 B1
Mortlake Vic., Australia 38°5S 142°50E 282 E5
Mortlake London, U.K. 51°27N 0°15W 125 B2
Morton Ill., U.S.A. 40°37N 89°28W 310 D7
Morton Tex., U.S.A. 33°44N 102°46W 314 E3
Morton Wash., U.S.A. 46°34N 122°17W 306 D4
Morton △ Australia 35°0S 150°12E 283 C9
Morton Grove U.S.A. 42°2N 87°46W 119 A2
Moruga Trin. & Tob. 10°4N 61°16W 323 t
Moruga → Trin. & Tob. 10°5N 61°16W 323 t
Morumbi Brazil 23°35S 46°42W 137 B1
Morundah Australia 34°57S 146°19E 283 C7
Morung Sudan 10°32N 31°3E 266 B3
Moruya Australia 35°58S 150°3E 283 C9
Morvan France 47°5N 4°3E 173 E11
Morvan ⌂ France 47°12N 4°3E 173 E11
Morvant Trin. & Tob. 10°40N 61°29W 323 t
Morven Queens., Australia 26°22S 147°5E 281 D4
Morven N.Z. 44°50S 171°6E 285 E6
Morven Ga., U.S.A. 30°57N 83°30W 316 E6
Morvern U.K. 56°38N 5°44W 167 E3
Morwell Australia 38°10S 146°22E 283 E7
Morwell △ Australia 38°14S 146°23E 283 E7
Moryń Poland 52°51N 14°22E 185 F1
Morzhovets, Ostrov Russia 66°44N 42°35E 186 A7
Morzine France 46°11N 6°42E 173 F13
Mosakahiken = Moose Lake Canada 53°46N 100°8W 297 C8
Mosalsk Russia 54°30N 34°55E 188 E8
Mosbach Germany 49°21N 9°9E 179 F5
Mosby Norway 58°12N 7°55E 164 F4
Moscavide Portugal 38°47N 9°6W 126 A2
Moščenice Croatia 45°17N 14°16E 199 C11
Moschato Greece 37°55N 23°40E 112 B2
Mosciano Sant' Ángelo Italy 42°42N 13°52E 199 F10
Moscone Convention Center San Francisco, U.S.A. 136 c2
Moscos Is. Burma 14°0N 97°30E 236 F1
Moscow = Moskva Russia 55°45N 37°37E 129 B2
Moscow Idaho, U.S.A. 46°44N 117°0W 304 C5
Moscow Mich., U.S.A. 42°3N 84°30W 311 B12
Moscow Pa., U.S.A. 41°20N 75°31W 313 E9
Moscow Mills U.S.A. 38°57N 90°55W 310 F6
Mosel → Europe 50°22N 7°36E 173 B14
Moselle = Mosel → Europe 50°22N 7°36E 173 B14
Moselle □ France 48°59N 6°33E 173 D13
Moses Lake U.S.A. 47°8N 119°17W 304 C4
Mosgiel N.Z. 45°53S 170°21E 285 F5
Moshaweng → S. Africa 26°35S 22°50E 270 C3
Moshchnyy, Ostrov Russia 60°1N 27°50E 188 B4
Moshi Tanzania 3°22S 37°18E 268 C4
Moshi → Nigeria 9°18N 4°38E 263 D5
Moshupa Botswana 24°46S 25°29E 270 B4
Mosi-oa-Tunya = Victoria Falls Zimbabwe 17°58S 25°52E 269 F2
Mosina Poland 52°15N 16°50E 185 F3
Mosite Dem. Rep. of the Congo 0°53N 23°40E 264 B4
Mosjøen Norway 65°51N 13°12E 160 D15
Moskenesøya Norway 67°58N 13°0E 160 C15
Moskenstraumen Norway 67°47N 12°45E 160 C15
Moskog Norway 61°26N 6°0E 164 C2
Moskva Russia 55°45N 37°37E 129 B2
Moskva □ Russia 56°20N 37°20E 188 D9
Moskva → Russia 55°5N 38°51E 188 E10
Moskvoretskiy Russia 55°42N 37°37E 129 B2
Moslavačka Gora Croatia 45°40N 16°37E 199 C13
Mosman Australia 33°49S 151°15E 139 B2
Moso Vanuatu 17°30S 168°15E 287 G6
Mosomane Botswana 24°2S 26°19E 270 B4
Mosonmagyaróvár Hungary 47°52N 17°18E 182 C2
Mošorin Serbia 45°19N 20°4E 182 E5
Mospyne Ukraine 47°52N 38°0E 189 J9
Mosqueiro Brazil 1°10S 48°28W 332 B2
Mosquera Colombia 2°35N 78°24W 328 C2
Mosquero U.S.A. 35°47N 103°58W 305 J12
Mosqueruela Spain 40°21N 0°27W 196 E4
Mosquitia Honduras 15°20N 84°10W 320 C3
Mosquito, Pta. Venezuela 10°53N 63°53W 329 a
Mosquito Creek L. U.S.A. 41°18N 80°46W 312 E4
Mosquito L. Canada 62°35N 103°20W 297 A8
Mosquitos, G. de los Panama 9°15N 81°10W 320 E3
Moss Norway 59°27N 10°40E 164 E7
Moss Vale Australia 34°32S 150°25E 283 C9
Mossaka Congo 1°15S 16°45E 264 C3
Mossâmedes Brazil 16°7S 50°11W 333 E1
Mossbank Canada 49°56N 105°56W 297 D7
Mossburn N.Z. 45°41S 168°15E 285 F3
Mosselbaai S. Africa 34°11S 22°8E 270 D3
Mossendjo Congo 2°55S 12°42E 264 C2
Mossfellsbær Iceland 64°11N 21°45W 155 C5
Mossgiel Australia 33°15S 144°5E 282 B6
Mössingen Germany 48°24N 9°4E 179 G5
Mossman Australia 16°21S 145°15E 280 B4
Mossoró Brazil 5°10S 37°15W 332 C4
Mossuril Mozam. 14°58S 40°42E 269 E5
Mossy Head U.S.A. 30°45N 86°19W 317 E3
Mossy Point Australia 35°50S 150°11E 283 C9
Most Czech Rep. 50°31N 13°38E 180 A6
Mosta Malta 35°55N 14°26E 206 F7
Mostaganem Algeria 35°54N 0°5E 261 A5
Mostaganem □ Algeria 35°40N 0°15E 261 A5
Mostar Bos.-H. 43°22N 17°50E 182 G2
Mostardas Brazil 31°2S 50°51W 335 C5
Mostefa, Rass Tunisia 36°55N 11°3E 258 A2
Mosteiros Azores 37°53N 25°49W 153 d3
Mosterhamn Norway 59°42N 5°21E 164 E2
Mostiska = Mostyska Ukraine 49°48N 23°4E 185 J10
Móstoles Spain 40°19N 3°53W 194 E7
Mosty = Masty Belarus 53°27N 24°38E 177 B13
Mostyska Ukraine 49°48N 23°4E 185 J10
Mosul = Al Mawşil Iraq 36°15N 43°5E 213 D10
Møsvatnet Norway 59°52N 8°5E 164 E5
Mota Ethiopia 11°5N 37°52E 257 E4
Mota Vanuatu 13°49S 167°42E 287 C5
Mota del Cuervo Spain 39°30N 2°52W 197 F2
Mota del Marqués Spain 41°38N 5°11W 194 D5
Mota Lava Vanuatu 13°40S 167°40E 287 C5
Motaba Congo 2°6N 18°2E 264 B3
Motagua → Guatemala 15°44N 88°14W 320 C2
Motala Sweden 58°32N 15°1E 163 F9
Motaze Mozam. 24°48S 32°52E 271 B5
Moţca Romania 47°15N 26°37E 183 C11
Motegi Japan 36°32N 140°11E 223 A12
Moth India 25°43N 78°57E 243 G8
Motherwell U.K. 55°47N 3°58W 167 F5
Moti Bagh India 28°33N 77°10E 120 B2
Motihari India 26°30N 84°55E 243 F11
Motilla del Palancar Spain 39°34N 1°55W 197 F3
Motiti I. N.Z. 37°38S 176°25E 284 D5
Motnik Slovenia 46°14N 14°54E 199 B11
Motobu Japan 26°39N 127°53E 288 a
Motocurunya Venezuela 4°24N 64°5W 329 C5
Motol Czech Rep. 50°3N 14°21E 135 B2
Motovun Croatia 45°20N 13°50E 199 C10
Motozintla de Mendoza Mexico 15°22N 92°14W 319 D6
Motril Spain 36°31N 3°37W 195 J7
Motru Romania 44°48N 22°59E 182 F7
Motru → Romania 44°32N 23°31E 183 F8
Motsa Israel 31°47N 35°9E 123 B2
Motsa Ilit Israel 31°48N 35°9E 123 B1
Motspur Park U.K. 51°23N 0°14W 125 B2
Mott U.S.A. 46°23N 102°20W 308 B2
Mottingham U.K. 51°26N 0°1E 125 B4
Möttling = Metlika Slovenia 45°40N 15°20E 199 C12
Móttola Italy 40°38N 17°2E 201 B10
Motu → N.Z. 37°52S 177°36E 284 D6
Motu Nui Chile 27°12S 109°28W 330 b
Motu Tapu Cook Is. 21°14S 159°43W 289 h
Motuba Dem. Rep. of the Congo 2°20N 18°34E 264 B3
Motueka N.Z. 41°7S 173°1E 285 B8
Motueka → N.Z. 41°5S 173°1E 285 B8
Motul Mexico 21°6N 89°17W 319 C7
Motupena Pt. Papua N. G. 6°30S 155°10E 286 D8
Mou N. Cal. 21°5S 167°26E 288 d
Mouanda Gabon 1°28S 13°7E 264 C2
Mouchalagane → Canada 50°56N 68°41W 299 B6
Mouchoir Bank W. Indies 20°57N 70°47W 321 B5
Mouding China 25°20N 101°28E 228 E3
Moudjeria Mauritania 17°50N 12°28W 262 B2
Moudon Switz. 46°40N 6°49E 179 J2
Moudros Greece 39°50N 25°18E 205 B7
Mougoundou Congo 2°40S 12°41E 264 C2
Mouhoun = Black Volta → Africa 8°41N 1°33W 262 D4
Mouila Gabon 1°50S 11°0E 264 C2
Mouka C.A.R. 7°16N 21°52E 264 A4
Moukalaba ⌂ Gabon 2°50S 10°35E 264 C2
Moukambo Gabon 3°5S 11°38E 264 C2
Moul Niger 15°5N 13°11E 259 F2
Moulamein Australia 35°3S 144°1E 282 C6
Moule à Chique, C. St. Lucia 13°43N 60°57W 323 m
Moulhoulé Djibouti 11°58N 42°58E 267 B5
Mouliana Greece 35°10N 25°59E 207 E6
Moulin Rouge Paris, France 134 a3
Moulins France 46°35N 3°19E 173 F10
Moulmein Burma 16°30N 97°40E 241 G6
Moulouya, O. → Morocco 35°5N 2°25W 261 A4
Moulton U.S.A. 40°41N 92°41W 310 D4
Moultrie U.S.A. 31°11N 83°47W 316 D6
Moultrie, L. U.S.A. 33°20N 80°5W 316 B9
Mounana Gabon 1°18S 13°13E 264 C2
Mound City Mo., U.S.A. 40°7N 95°14W 308 E6
Mound City S. Dak., U.S.A. 45°44N 100°4W 308 C3
Moundou Chad 8°40N 16°10E 259 G3
Moundsville U.S.A. 39°55N 80°44W 312 G4
Mounembé Congo 3°20S 12°32E 264 C2
Moung Cambodia 12°46N 103°27E 236 F4
Moungoudi Congo 2°45S 11°46E 264 C2
Mount Airy U.S.A. 36°31N 80°37W 315 C14
Mount Albert Canada 44°8N 79°19W 312 B5
Mount Apo △ Phil. 7°0N 125°10E 233 H5
Mount Arayat △ Phil. 15°39N 120°44E 232 D3
Mount Aspiring △ N.Z. 44°19S 168°47E 285 E3
Mount Ayliff = Maxesibeni S. Africa 30°49S 29°23E 271 D4
Mount Ayr U.S.A. 40°43N 94°14W 310 D2
Mount Barker S. Austral., Australia 35°5S 138°52E 282 C3
Mount Barker W. Austral., Australia 34°38S 117°40E 279 F2
Mount Barnett Roadhouse Australia 16°39S 125°57E 278 C4
Mount Beauty Australia 36°47S 147°10E 283 D7
Mount Brydges Canada 42°54N 81°29W 312 D3
Mount Buffalo △ Australia 36°43S 146°46E 283 D7
Mount Burr Australia 37°34S 140°26E 281 F3
Mount Carmel = Ha Karmel △ Israel 32°45N 35°5E 250 F6
Mount Carmel Ill., U.S.A. 38°25N 87°46W 311 F9
Mount Carmel Pa., U.S.A. 40°47N 76°26W 313 F8
Mount Carroll U.S.A. 42°6N 89°59W 310 B7
Mount Clemens U.S.A. 42°35N 82°53W 312 D2
Mount Cook N.Z. 43°44S 170°5E 285 D5
Mount Cook △ N.Z. 43°35S 170°15E 285 D5
Mount Coolon Australia 21°25S 147°25E 280 C4
Mount Darwin Zimbabwe 16°47S 31°38E 269 F3
Mount Dennis Canada 43°40N 79°28W 141 A2
Mount Desert I. U.S.A. 44°21N 68°20W 309 C19
Mount Dora U.S.A. 28°48N 81°38W 317 G8
Mount Ebenezer Australia 25°6S 132°34E 279 E5
Mount Eccles △ Australia 38°5S 141°54E 282 E4
Mount Eden U.S.A. 38°3N 85°9W 311 F11
Mount Edziza ⌂ Canada 57°30N 130°45W 296 B2
Mount Elgon △ E. Afr. 1°4N 34°42E 268 B3
Mount Field △ Australia 42°39S 146°35E 281 G4
Mount Fletcher S. Africa 30°40S 28°30E 271 D4
Mount Forest Canada 43°59N 80°43W 312 C4
Mount Frankland △ Australia 31°47S 116°37E 279 F2
Mount Frederick ☼ Australia 19°39S 129°18E 278 C4
Mount Frere = Kwabhaca S. Africa 30°51S 29°0E 271 D4
Mount Gambier Australia 37°50S 140°46E 282 D4
Mount Garnet Australia 17°37S 145°6E 280 B4
Mount Greenwood U.S.A. 41°42N 87°42W 119 C2
Mount Hagen Papua N. G. 5°52S 144°16E 286 C3
Mount Hamiguitan △ Phil. 6°44N 126°10E 233 H6
Mount Holly U.S.A. 39°59N 74°47W 313 G10
Mount Holly Springs U.S.A. 40°7N 77°12W 312 F7
Mount Hood Memorial Park ⌂ U.S.A. 42°26N 71°1W 116 A2
Mount Hope N.S.W., Australia 32°51S 145°51E 283 B6
Mount Hope S. Austral., Australia 34°7S 135°23E 281 E2
Mount Horeb U.S.A. 43°1N 89°44W 310 B7
Mount Iglit-Mount Baco △ Phil. 12°45N 121°8E 232 E3
Mount Isa Australia 20°42S 139°26E 280 C2
Mount Isarog △ Phil. 13°38N 123°24E 232 E4
Mount James ☼ Australia 24°51S 116°54E 279 D2
Mount Jewett U.S.A. 41°44N 78°39W 312 E6
Mount Ka'ala Nat. Area Reserve ⌂ U.S.A. 21°31N 158°7W 302 J13
Mount Kaputar △ Australia 30°16S 150°10E 281 E5
Mount Kenya △ Kenya 0°7S 37°21E 268 C4
Mount Kisco U.S.A. 41°12N 73°44W 313 E11
Mount Laguna U.S.A. 32°52N 116°25W 307 N10
Mount Larcom Australia 23°48S 150°59E 280 C5
Mount Lofty Ranges Australia 34°35S 139°5E 282 C3
Mount McKinley = Denali △ U.S.A. 63°30N 152°0W 303 E10
Mount Magnet Australia 28°2S 117°47E 279 E2
Mount Malindang △ Phil. 8°17N 123°32E 233 G4
Mount Manara Australia 32°29S 143°58E 282 B5
Mount Maunganui N.Z. 37°40S 176°14E 284 D5
Mount Merrion Ireland 53°18N 6°12W 120 B2
Mount Molloy Australia 16°42S 145°20E 280 B4
Mount Morgan Australia 23°40S 150°25E 280 C5
Mount Morris Mich., U.S.A. 43°7N 83°42W 311 A13
Mount Morris N.Y., U.S.A. 42°44N 77°52W 312 D7
Mount Olive U.S.A. 39°4N 89°44W 310 E7
Mount Olivet U.S.A. 38°32N 84°2W 311 F12
Mount Olympus U.S.A. 34°7N 118°21W 126 B2
Mount Orab U.S.A. 39°2N 83°55W 311 E13
Mount Pearl Canada 47°31N 52°47W 299 C9
Mount Penn U.S.A. 40°20N 75°54W 313 F9
Mount Perry Australia 25°13S 151°42E 281 D5
Mount Pleasant Iowa, U.S.A. 40°58N 91°33W 310 D5
Mount Pleasant Mich., U.S.A. 43°36N 84°46W 309 D11
Mount Pleasant Pa., U.S.A. 40°9N 79°33W 312 F5
Mount Pleasant S.C., U.S.A. 32°47N 79°52W 316 C10
Mount Pleasant Tenn., U.S.A. 35°32N 87°12W 315 D11
Mount Pleasant Tex., U.S.A. 33°9N 94°58W 314 E7
Mount Pleasant Utah, U.S.A. 39°33N 111°27W 304 G8
Mount Pocono U.S.A. 41°7N 75°22W 313 E9
Mount Pulaski U.S.A. 40°1N 89°17W 310 D7
Mount Pulog △ Phil. 16°35N 120°57E 232 C3
Mount Rainier U.S.A. 38°56N 76°57W 143 B3
Mount Rainier △ U.S.A. 46°55N 121°50W 306 D5
Mount Remarkable △ Australia 32°47S 138°3E 282 B3
Mount Revelstoke △ Canada 51°5N 118°30W 296 C5
Mount Robson ⌂ Canada 53°0N 119°0W 296 C5
Mount St. Helens ⌂ U.S.A. 46°14N 122°11W 306 D4
Mount Selinda Zimbabwe 20°24S 32°43E 271 B5
Mount Shasta U.S.A. 41°19N 122°19W 304 F2
Mount Signal U.S.A. 32°39N 115°37W 307 N11
Mount Somers N.Z. 43°45S 171°27E 285 D6
Mount Sterling Ill., U.S.A. 39°59N 90°45W 310 E6
Mount Sterling Ky., U.S.A. 38°4N 83°56W 311 F13
Mount Sterling Ohio, U.S.A. 39°43N 83°16W 311 E13
Mount Surprise Australia 18°10S 144°17E 280 B3
Mount Union U.S.A. 40°23N 77°53W 312 F7
Mount Upton U.S.A. 42°26N 75°23W 313 D9
Mount Vernon Ga., U.S.A. 32°11N 82°36W 316 C7
Mount Vernon Ill., U.S.A. 38°19N 88°55W 310 F8
Mount Vernon Ind., U.S.A. 37°56N 87°54W 311 G9
Mount Vernon Iowa, U.S.A. 41°55N 91°23W 310 C5
Mount Vernon N.Y., U.S.A. 40°54N 73°49W 132 A3
Mount Vernon Ohio, U.S.A. 40°23N 82°29W 312 F2
Mount Vernon Wash., U.S.A. 48°25N 122°20W 306 B4
Mount Vernon Square Washington, D.C., U.S.A. 143 a2
Mount Victor Australia 32°11S 139°44E 282 B3
Mount Washington U.S.A. 39°5N 84°24W 311 F11
Mount Wellington N.Z. 36°55S 174°52E 284 C3
Mount William △ Australia 40°56S 148°14E 281 G4
Mount Wynne St. Vincent 13°14N 61°16W 323 n
Mount Zion = Har Tsiyon Jerusalem 123 b3
Mount Zion U.S.A. 39°46N 88°53W 311 E8
Mounta, Akra Greece 38°3N 20°47E 207 C2
Mountain □ Phil. 17°20N 121°10E 232 C3
Mountain Ash U.K. 51°40N 3°23W 169 F4
Mountain Center U.S.A. 33°42N 116°44W 307 M10
Mountain City Nev., U.S.A. 41°50N 115°58W 304 F6
Mountain City Tenn., U.S.A. 36°29N 81°48W 315 C14
Mountain Dale U.S.A. 41°41N 74°32W 313 E10
Mountain Grove U.S.A. 37°8N 92°16W 308 G7
Mountain Home Ark., U.S.A. 36°20N 92°23W 314 C8
Mountain Home Idaho, U.S.A. 43°8N 115°41W 304 E6
Mountain Iron U.S.A. 47°32N 92°37W 308 B7
Mountain Pass U.S.A. 35°29N 115°35W 307 K11

Mountain View Ark., U.S.A. 35°52N 92°7W 314 D8
Mountain View Calif., U.S.A. 37°23N 122°5W 306 H4
Mountain View Hawai'i, U.S.A. 19°33N 155°7W 302 D6
Mountain Village U.S.A. 62°5N 163°43W 303 E7
Mountain Zebra △ S. Africa 32°14S 25°27E 270 D4
Mountainair U.S.A. 34°31N 106°15W 305 J10
Mountbellew Ireland 53°28N 8°31W 166 C3
Mountlake Terrace U.S.A. 47°47N 122°18W 306 C4
Mountmellick Ireland 53°7N 7°20W 166 C4
Mountrath Ireland 53°0N 7°28W 166 D4
Moura Queens., Australia 24°35S 149°58E 280 C4
Moura Brazil 1°32S 61°38W 329 D5
Moura Portugal 38°7N 7°30W 195 G3
Mourão Portugal 38°22N 7°22W 195 G3
Mourdi, Dépression du Chad 18°10N 23°0E 259 E4
Mourdiah Mali 14°35N 7°25W 262 C3
Mourenx France 43°22N 0°38W 174 E3
Mouri Ghana 5°6N 1°14W 263 D4
Mourilyan Australia 17°35S 146°3E 280 B4
Mourmelon-le-Grand France 49°8N 4°22E 173 C11
Mourne → U.K. 54°52N 7°26W 166 B4
Mourne Mts. U.K. 54°10N 6°0W 166 B5
Mournies Greece 35°29N 24°1E 207 E5
Mouscron Belgium 50°45N 3°12E 170 D3
Mousgougou Chad 10°47N 16°9E 259 F3
Moussa 'Ali Djibouti 12°27N 42°24E 267 B5
Moussoro Chad 13°41N 16°35E 259 F3
Moustique, Morne Guadeloupe 16°7N 61°44W 322 e
Mouthe France 46°44N 6°12E 173 F13
Moutier Switz. 47°16N 7°21E 179 H3
Moûtiers France 45°29N 6°32E 175 C10
Moutong Indonesia 0°28N 121°13E 231 D6
Mouy France 49°18N 2°20E 173 C9
Mouydir, Monts du Algeria 25°30N 4°10E 261 C5
Mouyondzi Congo 4°1S 13°59E 264 C2
Mouzaki Greece 39°25N 21°37E 204 B3
Mouzarak Chad 13°17N 15°58E 259 F3
Mouzon France 49°36N 5°3E 173 C12
Movas Mexico 28°10N 109°25W 318 B3
Moville Ireland 55°11N 7°3W 166 A4
Mowandjum Australia 17°22S 123°40E 278 C3
Moweaqua U.S.A. 39°38N 89°1W 310 E7
Moxico □ Angola 12°0S 20°30E 265 E4
Moxotó → Brazil 9°19S 38°14W 332 C4
Moy → Ireland 54°8N 9°8W 166 B2
Moya Comoros Is. 12°18S 44°18E 272 a
Moyale Ethiopia 3°34N 39°5E 266 D4
Moyale Kenya 3°30N 39°4E 257 G4
Moyamba S. Leone 8°4N 12°30W 262 D2
Moyen Atlas Morocco 33°0N 5°0W 260 B4
Moyen-Chari □ Chad 9°0N 18°0E 259 G3
Moyo Indonesia 8°10S 117°40E 235 D5
Moyobamba Peru 6°0S 77°0W 330 B2
Moyowosi ⌂ Tanzania 3°50S 31°0E 268 C3
Moyto Chad 12°35N 16°33E 259 F3
Moyu China 37°15N 79°44E 217 E9
Moyyero → Russia 68°44N 103°42E 215 C11
Moyynqum Zhambyl, Kazakhstan 44°17N 72°57E 217 D8
Moyynqum Zhambyl, Kazakhstan 44°12N 71°0E 217 D8
Moyynty Kazakhstan 47°10N 73°18E 217 C8
Mozambique = Moçambique Mozam. 15°3S 40°42E 269 F5
Mozambique ■ Africa 19°0S 35°0E 269 F4
Mozambique Basin Ind. Oc. 30°0S 40°0E 273 G2
Mozambique Chan. Africa 17°30S 42°30E 271 A7
Mozarthaus Vienna, Austria 142 b2
Mozdok Russia 43°45N 44°48E 191 J7
Mozdūrān Iran 36°9N 60°35E 247 B9
Mozhaysk Russia 55°30N 36°2E 188 E9
Mozhga Russia 56°26N 52°15E 190 B11
Mozhnābād Iran 34°7N 60°6E 247 C9
Mozirje Slovenia 46°22N 14°58E 199 B11
Mozyr = Mazyr Belarus 51°59N 29°15E 177 B15
Mpanda Tanzania 6°23S 31°1E 268 D3
Mpé Congo 2°58S 14°38E 264 C2
Mpese Dem. Rep. of the Congo 5°16S 15°30E 265 D3
Mpésoba Mali 12°31N 5°39W 262 C3
Mphoeng Zimbabwe 21°10S 27°51E 269 G2
Mpika Zambia 11°51S 31°25E 269 E3
Mpoko → C.A.R. 4°19N 18°33E 264 B3
Mpouya Congo 2°38S 16°13E 264 C3
Mpulungu Zambia 8°51S 31°5E 269 D3
Mpumalanga S. Africa 29°50S 30°33E 271 C5
Mpumalanga □ S. Africa 26°0S 30°0E 271 C5
Mpwapwa Tanzania 6°23S 36°30E 268 D4
Mqabba Malta 35°51N 14°28E 206 F7
Mqanduli S. Africa 31°49S 28°45E 271 D4
Mqinvartsveri = Kazbek Russia 42°42N 44°30E 191 J7
Mragowo Poland 53°52N 21°18E 184 E8
M'ramani Comoros Is. 12°20S 44°31E 272 a
Mramor Serbia 43°20N 21°45E 202 C5
Mrauk-u = Myohaung Burma 20°35N 93°11E 241 E4
Mrimina Morocco 29°50N 7°9W 260 C3
Mrkonjić Grad Bos.-H. 44°26N 17°4E 182 F2
Mrkopalj Croatia 45°21N 14°52E 199 C11
Mrocza Poland 53°16N 17°35E 185 E4
Msaken Tunisia 35°49N 10°33E 258 A2
Msambansovu Zimbabwe 15°50S 30°3E 269 F3
Msida Malta 35°54N 14°29E 206 F7
M'sila Algeria 35°46N 4°30E 261 A5
M'sila □ Algeria 35°20N 4°20E 261 A5
Msoro Zambia 13°35S 31°50E 269 E3
Msta → Russia 58°25N 31°20E 188 C6
Mstislavl = Mstsislaw Belarus 54°0N 31°50E 177 A16
Mstsislaw Belarus 54°0N 31°50E 177 A16
Mszana Dolna Poland 49°41N 20°5E 185 J7
Mszczonów Poland 51°58N 20°33E 185 G7
Mtama Tanzania 10°17S 39°21E 269 E4
Mtamvuna = Mthamvuna → S. Africa 31°6S 30°12E 271 D5
Mthamvuna → S. Africa 31°6S 30°12E 271 D5
Mthatha S. Africa 31°36S 28°49E 271 D4
Mtilikwe → Zimbabwe 21°9S 31°30E 269 G3
Mtima Congo 3°49S 12°7E 264 C2
Mtirala △ Georgia 41°50N 42°2E 191 K6
Mtito Andei Kenya 2°41S 38°10E 268 C4
Mtsamboro Mayotte 12°42S 45°4E 272 b
Mtsamboro, Î. Mayotte 12°38S 45°2E 272 b
Mtsangamouji Mayotte 12°45S 45°5E 272 b
Mtsapéré Mayotte 12°46S 45°11E 272 b
Mtsensk Russia 53°17N 36°36E 188 F9
Mtskheta Georgia 41°52N 44°45E 191 K7
Mtubatuba S. Africa 28°30S 32°8E 271 C5
Mtwalume S. Africa 30°30S 30°38E 271 D5
Mtwara-Mikindani Tanzania 10°20S 40°20E 269 E5
Mu → Burma 21°56N 95°38E 241 E5
Mu Gia, Deo Vietnam 17°40N 105°47E 236 D5
Mu Ko Chang △ Thailand 11°59N 102°22E 237 G4
Mu Ko Surin Thailand 9°30N 97°55E 237 H1
Mu-se Burma 23°59N 97°54E 241 D6
Mu Us Shamo China 39°0N 109°0E 226 E5
Muacandala Angola 10°2S 19°40E 265 E3
Muan S. Korea 34°59N 126°28E 224 E3
Muaná Brazil 1°25S 49°15W 332 B2
Muanda Dem. Rep. of the Congo 6°0S 12°20E 265 D2
Muang Beng Laos 20°23N 101°46E 228 G3
Muang Chiang Rai = Chiang Rai Thailand 19°52N 99°50E 228 H2
Muang Et Laos 20°49N 104°1E 236 B5
Muang Hiam Laos 20°5N 103°22E 236 B4
Muang Hongsa Laos 19°43N 101°20E 236 C3
Muang Houn Laos 20°8N 101°23E 228 G3
Muang Kau Laos 15°6N 105°47E 236 E5
Muang Khao Laos 19°38N 103°32E 236 C4
Muang Khong Laos 14°7N 105°51E 236 E5
Muang Khoua Laos 21°5N 102°31E 228 G4
Muang Liap Laos 18°29N 101°40E 236 C3
Muang Mai Thailand 8°5N 98°21E 237 a
Muang May Laos 14°49N 106°56E 236 E6
Muang Na Mo Laos 21°3N 101°49E 228 G3
Muang Ngeun Laos 20°36N 101°3E 228 G3
Muang Ngoi Laos 20°43N 102°41E 228 G4
Muang Nong Laos 16°22N 106°30E 236 D6
Muang Ou Neua Laos 22°18N 101°48E 228 F3
Muang Ou Tay Laos 22°7N 101°48E 228 F3
Muang Pak Beng Laos 19°54N 101°8E 228 H3
Muang Phalane Laos 16°39N 105°34E 236 D5
Muang Phiang Laos 19°6N 101°32E 236 C3
Muang Phine Laos 16°32N 106°2E 236 D6
Muang Saiapoun Laos 18°24N 101°31E 236 C3
Muang Sing Laos 21°11N 101°9E 228 G3
Muang Son Laos 20°27N 103°19E 236 B4
Muang Soui Laos 19°33N 102°52E 236 C4
Muang Va Laos 21°53N 102°19E 228 G4
Muang Va Laos 18°18N 101°20E 236 C3
Muang Xai Laos 20°42N 101°59E 228 G3
Muang Xamteu Laos 19°59N 104°38E 236 C5
Muangai Angola 12°32S 19°55E 265 E3
Muar Malaysia 2°3N 102°34E 237 L4
Muara Takus Indonesia 0°20N 100°39E 234 B2
Muarabadak Indonesia 0°20S 117°26E 235 C5
Muarabeliti Indonesia 3°15S 103°1E 234 C2
Muarabungo Indonesia 1°28S 102°52E 234 C2
Muaradua Indonesia 4°31S 104°4E 234 D2
Muaraenim Indonesia 3°40S 103°50E 234 C2
Muarajambi Indonesia 1°28S 103°40E 234 C2
Muarajuloi Indonesia 0°12S 114°3E 235 C4
Muarakaman Indonesia 0°2S 116°45E 235 C5
Muarapupit Indonesia 2°43S 102°54E 234 C2
Muarasabak Indonesia 1°7S 103°51E 234 C2
Muarasiberut Indonesia 1°35S 99°12E 234 C1
Muaratebo Indonesia 1°30S 102°26E 234 C2
Muaratembesi Indonesia 1°42S 103°8E 234 C2
Muarateweh Indonesia 0°58S 114°52E 235 C4
Muarawahau Indonesia 1°1N 116°52E 235 B5
Mubarakpur India 26°6N 83°18E 243 F10
Mubarraz = Al Mubarraz Si. Arabia 25°30N 49°40E 247 E6
Mubende Uganda 0°33N 31°22E 268 B3
Mubi Nigeria 10°18N 13°16E 263 C7
Mucaba, Sa. de Angola 7°12S 15°0E 265 D3
Mucajá Brazil 3°57S 57°32W 329 D6
Mucajaí → Brazil 2°25N 60°52W 329 C5
Mucajaí, Serra do Brazil 2°23N 61°10W 329 C5
Mucari Angola 9°30S 16°54E 265 D3
Muchachos, Roque de los Canary Is. 28°44N 17°52W 153 e1
Mücheln Germany 51°17N 11°47E 178 D7
Muchinga Mts. Zambia 11°30S 31°30E 269 E3
Muchkapskiy Russia 51°52N 42°28E 190 E6
Muchuan China 28°57N 103°55E 228 C5
Muck U.K. 56°50N 6°15W 167 E2
Muckadilla Australia 26°35S 148°23E 281 D4
Muckalee Cr. → U.S.A. 31°33N 84°9W 316 D5
Muckaty ✪ Australia 18°37S 133°52E 280 B1
Muckle Flugga U.K. 60°51N 0°54W 167 A8
Muco → Colombia 4°15N 70°21W 328 C3
Mucoma Angola 15°18S 13°39E 265 F2
Muconda Angola 10°31S 21°15E 265 E4
Mucope Angola 16°24S 14°52E 265 F2
Mucugê Brazil 13°0S 41°23W 333 D3
Mucuim → Brazil 6°33S 64°18W 329 E5
Mucur Turkey 39°3N 34°22E 212 C6
Mucura Brazil 2°31S 62°43W 329 D5
Mucuri Brazil 18°0S 39°36W 333 E4
Mucurici Brazil 18°6S 40°31W 333 E3
Mucusso Angola 18°1S 21°25E 265 F4
Mucusso ⌂ Angola 17°27S 21°0E 265 F4
Mucussueje Angola 10°18S 19°49E 265 E4
Muda Canary Is. 28°34N 13°57W 153 e2
Mudanjiang China 44°38N 129°30E 227 B15
Mudanya Turkey 40°25N 28°50E 203 F12
Muddebihal India 16°20N 76°8E 245 F3
Muddy Cr. → U.S.A. 38°24N 110°42W 304 G8
Mudgee Australia 32°32S 149°31E 283 B8
Mudhol Andhra Pradesh, India 18°58N 77°55E 244 E3
Mudhol Karnataka, India 16°21N 75°17E 245 F2
Mudiata Dem. Rep. of the Congo 7°15S 22°1E 265 D4
Mudigere India 13°8N 75°38E 245 H2
Mūdiyah Yemen 13°56N 46°57E 248 D4
Mudjatik → Canada 56°1N 107°36W 297 B7
Mudon Burma 16°15N 97°44E 241 G6
Mudug □ Somalia 7°0N 48°0E 267 C6
Mudukulattur India 9°21N 78°31E 245 K4
Mudumu △ Namibia 18°5S 23°29E 270 A3
Mudurnu Turkey 40°27N 31°12E 212 B4
Muecate Mozam. 14°55S 39°40E 269 E4
Mueda Mozam. 11°36S 39°28E 269 E4
Mueller Ranges Australia 18°18S 126°46E 278 C4
Muende Mozam. 14°28S 33°0E 269 E3
Muerto, Mar Mexico 16°10N 94°10W 319 D6
Mufu Shan China 29°20N 114°30E 229 C10
Mufulira Zambia 12°32S 28°15E 269 E2
Mufumbiro Range Africa 1°25S 29°30E 268 C2
Mugardos Spain 43°27N 8°15W 194 B2
Muge → Portugal 39°8N 8°44W 195 F2
Müggelberge Germany 52°25N 13°37E 115 B5
Müggelheim Germany 52°24N 13°40E 115 B5
Múggia Italy 45°36N 13°46E 199 C10
Muggiò Italy 45°35N 9°13E 128 A2
Mughal Gardens Delhi, India 120 c1
Mughal Sarai India 25°18N 83°7E 243 G10
Mughalzhar Taūy Kazakhstan 49°0N 58°40E 216 C5
Mughayrā' Si. Arabia 29°17N 37°41E 246 D3
Mugi Japan 33°40N 134°25E 222 D6
Mugia = Muxia Spain 43°3N 9°10W 194 B1
Mugila, Mts. Dem. Rep. of the Congo 7°0S 28°50E 268 D2
Muginga Angola 8°26S 17°46E 265 D3
Muğla Turkey 37°15N 28°22E 205 D10
Muğla □ Turkey 37°15N 28°20E 205 D10
Mugiad Sudan 11°1N 27°50E 257 E2
Müglizh Bulgaria 42°37N 25°32E 203 D9
Mugodzhary = Mughalzhar Taūy Kazakhstan 49°0N 58°40E 216 C5
Mugu Nepal 29°45N 82°30E 243 E10
Mugu Karnali → Nepal 29°38N 81°51E 243 E9
Muhagiriya Sudan 12°0N 25°38E 259 F5
Muhala Congo 5°40S 28°43E 268 D2
Muhammad, Râs Egypt 27°44N 34°16E 251 L5
Muhammad Qol Sudan 20°53N 37°9E 256 C4
Muhammadabad India 26°4N 83°25E 243 F10
Muḩayriqah Si. Arabia 23°59N 45°4E 248 B4
Muhesi → Tanzania 7°0S 35°20E 268 D4
Mühlacker Germany 48°57N 8°51E 179 G4
Mühldorf Germany 48°14N 12°32E 179 G8
Mühleiten Austria 48°10N 16°33E 142 A3
Mühlenfliess → Germany 52°32N 13°42E 115 A5
Mühlhausen = Milevsko Czech Rep. 49°27N 14°21E 180 B7
Mühlhausen Germany 51°12N 10°27E 178 D6
Mühlig Hofmann fjell Antarctica 72°30S 5°0E 151 D3
Mühlviertel Austria 48°30N 14°10E 180 C7
Muhoro Kenya 1°1S 34°7E 266 E3
Muhos Finland 64°47N 25°59E 160 D21
Muḩradah Syria 35°15N 36°35E 250 C7
Muhu Estonia 58°36N 23°11E 188 C2
Muhutwe Tanzania 1°35S 31°45E 268 C3
Mui Wo China 22°16N 113°59E 219 a
Muiden Neths. 52°20N 5°4E 112 A3
Muie Angola 14°23S 20°25E 265 E4
Muileann gCearr, An = Mullingar Ireland 53°31N 7°21W 166 C4
Muine Bheag = Bagenalstown Ireland 52°42N 6°58W 166 D5
Muineachán = Monaghan Ireland 54°15N 6°57W 166 B5
Muir, L. Australia 34°30S 116°40E 279 F2
Muir of Ord U.K. 57°32N 4°28W 167 D4
Muisné Ecuador 0°36N 80°2W 328 C1
Muizenberg S. Africa 34°5S 18°27E 118 B1
Mujahidpur India 28°33N 77°14E 120 B2
Mujeres, I. Mexico 21°13N 86°43W 320 B2
Muju do Campos Brazil 2°35S 54°41W 329 D7
Muka, Tanjung Malaysia 5°28N 100°11E 237 c
Mukacheve Ukraine 48°27N 22°45E 182 B7
Mukachevo = Mukacheve Ukraine 48°27N 22°45E 182 B7
Mukah Malaysia 2°55N 112°5E 235 B4
Mukandpur India 28°44N 77°11E 120 A2
Mukandwara India 24°49N 75°59E 242 G6
Mukawa Papua N. G. 9°48S 149°59E 286 E5
Mukawwa, Geziret Egypt 23°55N 35°53E 246 F2
Mukawwar Sudan 20°50N 37°17E 256 C4
Mukaylah Si. Arabia 19°16N 41°48E 248 C3
Mukdahan Thailand 16°32N 104°43E 236 D5
Mukdahan △ Thailand 16°26N 104°45E 236 D5
Mukden = Shenyang China 41°48N 123°27E 224 B1
Mukerian India 31°57N 75°37E 242 D6
Mukhavyets → Belarus 52°5N 23°39E 185 F10
Mukher India 18°42N 77°22E 244 E3
Mukhmas West Bank 31°52N 35°17E 123 A2
Mukhtolovo Russia 55°29N 43°15E 190 C6
Mukhtuya = Lensk Russia 60°48N 114°55E 215 C12
Mukinbudin Australia 30°55S 118°5E 279 F2
Mukishi Kasai-Occ., Dem. Rep. of the Congo 5°39S 21°3E 265 D4
Mukishi Katanga, Dem. Rep. of the Congo 8°30S 24°44E 265 D4
Muko Japan 34°55N 135°40E 223 C7
Muko → Japan 34°48N 135°22E 133 A1
Muko Phetra △ Thailand 6°57N 99°33E 237 J2
Mukojima Japan 35°43N 139°49E 140 A3
Mukomuko Indonesia 2°30S 101°10E 234 C2
Mukomwenze Dem. Rep. of the Congo 6°49S 27°15E 268 D2
Mukono Uganda 0°21N 32°45E 268 B3
Muktinath Nepal 28°49N 83°53E 243 E10
Muktsar India 30°30N 74°30E 242 D6
Mukur = Moqor Afghan. 32°50N 67°42E 242 C2
Mukutuwa → Canada 53°10N 97°24W 297 C9
Mukwela Zambia 17°0S 26°40E 269 F2
Mukwonago U.S.A. 42°52N 88°20W 311 B8
Mul India 20°4N 79°40E 244 D4
Mula Spain 38°3N 1°33W 197 G3
Mula → India 18°34N 74°21E 244 E2
Mula → Pakistan 27°57N 67°36E 242 F2
Mulaku Atoll Maldives 3°0N 73°30E 272 d
Mulamba Dem. Rep. of the Congo 6°21S 21°13E 265 D4
Mulanay Phil. 13°31N 122°24E 232 E4
Mulange Dem. Rep. of the Congo 3°40S 27°10E 268 C2
Mulanje, Mt. Malawi 16°2S 35°33E 269 F4
Mulâtre, Pte. Dominica 15°17N 61°15W 323 k
Mulatupo Sasardi Panama 8°57N 77°45W 328 B2
Mulbagal India 13°10N 78°24E 245 H4
Mulbarton S. Africa 26°17S 28°3E 123 B2
Mulberry U.S.A. 27°54N 81°59W 317 H8
Mulberry Grove U.S.A. 38°56N 89°16W 310 F7
Mulchatna → U.S.A. 59°40N 157°7W 303 G8
Mulchén Chile 37°45S 72°20W 334 D1
Mulde → Germany 51°53N 12°15E 178 D8
Muldraugh U.S.A. 37°56N 85°59W 311 G11
Mule Creek Junction U.S.A. 43°23N 104°13W 304 E11
Muleba Tanzania 1°50S 31°37E 268 C3
Mulegé Mexico 26°53N 111°59W 318 B2
Muleshoe U.S.A. 34°13N 102°43W 314 D3
Muletta, Gara Ethiopia 9°15N 41°44E 257 F5
Mulgrave Canada 45°38N 61°31W 299 C7
Mulgrave I. = Badu Australia 10°7S 142°11E 280 a
Mulhacén Spain 37°4N 3°20W 195 H7
Mülheim Germany 51°25N 6°54E 178 D2
Mulhouse France 47°40N 7°20E 173 E14
Muli Sichuan, China 27°52N 101°8E 228 D3
Muli Maldives 2°55N 73°34E 272 d
Mulifanua Samoa 13°50S 171°59W 287 V20
Muling China 44°35N 130°10E 227 B16
Mulki India 13°6N 74°48E 245 H2
Mull U.K. 56°25N 5°56W 167 E3
Mull, Sound of U.K. 56°30N 5°50W 167 E3
Mullach Íde = Malahide Ireland 53°26N 6°9W 120 A3
Mullaittivu Sri Lanka 9°15N 80°49E 245 K5
Mullen U.S.A. 42°3N 101°1W 308 D3
Mullengudgery Australia 31°43S 147°23E 281 B4
Mullens U.S.A. 37°35N 81°23W 309 G13
Muller, Pegunungan Indonesia 0°30N 113°30E 235 B4
Mullet Ra. Papua N. G. 5°35S 142°20E 286 C2
Mullet Pen. Ireland 54°13N 10°2W 166 B1
Mullettbaai St.-Maarten 18°4N 63°7W 322 a
Mullewa Australia 28°29S 115°30E 279 E2
Müllheim Germany 47°47N 7°36E 179 H3
Mulligan → Australia 25°0S 139°0E 280 D2
Mullingar Ireland 53°31N 7°21W 166 C4
Mullins U.S.A. 34°12N 79°15W 315 D15
Mullsjö Sweden 57°56N 13°55E 163 G7
Mullumbimby Australia 28°30S 153°30E 281 D5
Mulobezi Zambia 16°45S 25°7E 269 F2
Mulondo Angola 15°41S 15°12E 265 F3
Mulonga Plain Zambia 16°20S 22°40E 265 F4
Mulroy B. Ireland 55°15N 7°46W 166 A4
Mulshi L. India 18°30N 73°48E 244 E1
Multai India 21°50N 78°21E 244 D4
Multan Pakistan 30°15N 71°36E 242 D4
Mulu, Gunung Malaysia 4°3N 114°56E 235 B4
Mulug India 18°11N 79°57E 244 E4
Mulumbe, Mts. Dem. Rep. of the Congo 8°40S 27°30E 269 D2
Mulundu Dem. Rep. of the Congo 6°40S 20°33E 265 D4
Mulungushi Dam Zambia 14°48S 28°48E 269 E2
Mulurulu L. Australia 33°15S 143°20E 282 B5
Mulvane U.S.A. 37°29N 97°15W 308 G5
Mulwad Sudan 18°45N 30°39E 256 D3
Mulwala Australia 35°59S 146°0E 283 C7
Mulwala, L. Australia 35°59S 146°1E 281 C4
Muma Dem. Rep. of the Congo 3°25N 23°21E 264 B4
Mumbai India 18°56N 72°50E 130 B2
Mumbai Chhatrapati Shivaji Int. ✕ (BOM) India 19°5N 72°51E 130 A2
Mumbai Harbour India 18°58N 72°55E 130 B2
Mumbeji Zambia 13°51S 23°39E 265 E4
Mumbondo Angola 10°9S 14°15E 265 E2
Mumbwa Zambia 15°0S 27°0E 269 F2
Mumeng Papua N. G. 7°1S 146°37E 286 D4
Mumias Kenya 0°20N 34°29E 268 C4
Mummel Gulf △ Australia 31°17S 151°51E 283 A9
Mumra Russia 45°45N 47°41E 191 H8
Mun → Thailand 15°19N 105°30E 236 E5
Mun-gyeong S. Korea 36°35N 128°12E 224 D4
Muna Indonesia 5°0S 122°30E 231 F6
Munabao India 25°45N 70°17E 242 G4
Munakata Japan 33°48N 130°38E 222 D2
Munamagi Estonia 57°43N 27°4E 188 D4
Munaung Burma 18°45N 93°40E 241 F4
Munaung I. = Cheduba I. Burma 18°45N 93°40E 241 F4
Muncan Indonesia 8°34S 115°11E 231 K18
Muncar Indonesia 8°26S 114°20E 231 J17
Munch-museum Norway 59°55N 10°46E 133 A3
Münchberg Germany 50°11N 11°47E 179 E7
Müncheberg Germany 52°30N 14°9E 178 C10
Münchehofe Germany 52°29N 13°40E 115 B5
München Germany 48°8N 11°34E 131 B2
München Franz Josef Strauss Int. ✕ (MUC) Germany 48°21N 11°47E 131 A2
Munchen-Gladbach = Mönchengladbach Germany 51°11N 6°27E 178 D2
Munchique △ Colombia 2°44N 77°1W 328 C2
Muncho Lake Canada 59°0N 125°50W 296 B3
Munch'ŏn N. Korea 39°14N 127°19E 224 C3
Muncie U.S.A. 40°12N 85°23W 311 D11
Muncoonie L. West Australia 25°12S 138°40E 280 D2
Munda Solomon Is. 8°20S 157°16E 287 M9
Mundabbera Australia 25°36S 151°18E 281 D5
Mundakayam India 9°30N 76°50E 245 K3
Mundal Sri Lanka 7°48N 79°48E 245 L4
Munday U.S.A. 33°27N 99°38W 314 E5
Mundelein U.S.A. 42°16N 88°0W 311 B8
Mundemba Cameroon 4°57N 8°52E 264 B1
Münden Germany 51°25N 9°38E 178 D5
Münden ⌂ Germany 51°28N 9°42E 178 D5
Mundiwindi Australia 23°47S 120°9E 278 D3
Mundo → Spain 38°30N 2°15W 197 G2
Mundo Novo Brazil 11°50S 40°29W 333 D3
Mundo Nuevo Trin. & Tob. 10°28N 61°15W 323 t
Mundra India 22°54N 69°48E 242 H3
Mundrabilla Australia 31°52S 127°51E 279 F4
Munenga Angola 10°2S 14°41E 265 E2
Munera Spain 39°2N 2°29W 197 F2
Muneru → India 16°45N 80°3E 244 F5
Mungallala Australia 26°28S 147°34E 281 D4
Mungallala Cr. → Australia 28°53S 147°5E 281 D4
Mungana Australia 17°8S 144°27E 280 B3
Mungaoli India 24°24N 78°7E 242 G8
Mungari Mozam. 17°12S 33°30E 269 F3
Mungbere Dem. Rep. of the Congo 2°36N 28°28E 268 B2
Mungeli India 22°4N 81°41E 243 H9
Munger India 25°23N 86°30E 243 G12
Mungerannie Australia 28°1S 138°39E 281 A2
Mungilli ✪ Australia 25°14S 124°17E 279 E3
Mungkan Kandju △ Australia 13°35S 142°52E 280 A3
Mungkarta ✪ Australia 20°22S 134°2E 280 C1
Mungo Angola 11°49S 16°16E 265 E3
Mungo, L. Australia 33°45S 143°0E 282 B5
Mungo △ Australia 33°44S 143°6E 282 B5
Munhango Angola 12°10S 18°38E 265 E3
Munhango → Angola 11°17S 19°44E 265 E4
Munich = München Germany 48°8N 11°34E 131 B2
Munising U.S.A. 46°25N 86°40W 308 B10
Munka-Ljungby Sweden 56°16N 12°58E 163 H6
Munkebo Denmark 55°27N 10°34E 163 J4
Munkedal Sweden 58°28N 11°40E 163 F5
Munkfors Sweden 59°47N 13°30E 162 E7
Munkkiniemi Finland 60°11N 24°52E 121 B2
Munku-Sardyk Russia 51°45N 100°20E 215 D11
Münnerstadt Germany 50°14N 10°12E 179 E6
Munnsville U.S.A. 42°58N 75°35W 313 D9
Muñoz Phil. 15°43N 120°54E 232 D3
Muñoz Gamero, Pen. Chile 52°30S 73°5W 336 D2
Munro Argentina 34°31S 58°31W 117 B1
Munroe L. Canada 59°13N 98°35W 297 B9
Munsan S. Korea 37°51N 126°48E 224 D3
Munshiganj Bangla. 23°33N 90°32E 241 D3
Munson U.S.A. 30°52N 86°52W 317 E3
Münster Haut-Rhin, France 48°2N 7°8E 173 D14
Münster Niedersachsen, Germany 52°58N 10°5E 178 C6
Münster Nordrhein-Westfalen, Germany 51°58N 7°37E 178 D3
Munster □ Ireland 52°18N 8°44W 166 D3
Münsterberg = Ziębice Poland 50°37N 17°2E 185 H4
Muntadgin Australia 31°45S 118°33E 279 F2
Muntele Mare, Vf. Romania 46°30N 23°12E 183 D8
Muntinlupa Phil. 14°27N 121°2E 127 C2
Muntok Indonesia 2°5S 105°10E 234 C3
Munzur Dağları Turkey 39°30N 39°10E 213 C8
Muong Nhie Vietnam 22°12N 102°28E 228 F4
Muong Sen Vietnam 19°24N 104°8E 236 C5
Muong Te Vietnam 22°24N 102°49E 228 F4
Muong Xia Vietnam 20°19N 104°50E 236 B5
Muonio Finland 67°57N 23°40E 160 C20
Muonio älv = Muonionjoki → Finland 67°11N 23°34E 160 C20
Muonioälven = Muonionjoki → Finland 67°11N 23°34E 160 C20
Muonionjoki → Finland 67°11N 23°34E 160 C20
Mupa Angola 16°5S 15°50E 265 F3
Mupa → Mozam. 18°58S 35°54E 269 F4
Mupa △ Angola 15°55S 15°35E 265 F3
Muping China 37°22N 121°36E 227 F11
Mupoi South Sudan 5°28N 27°40E 257 F2
Muqaddam, Wadi → Sudan 18°4N 31°30E 256 D3
Muqaybirah Yemen 13°20N 46°5E 248 D4
Muqdisho Somalia 2°2N 45°25E 267 D6
Muqshin Oman 19°35N 54°55E 249 C6
Muqshin, W. → Oman 19°44N 55°14E 249 C6
Muquequete Angola 14°53S 14°58E 265 F2
Mur → Austria 46°18N 16°52E 181 E9
Mûr-de-Bretagne France 48°12N 3°0W 172 D4
Muradiye Manisa, Turkey 38°39N 27°21E 205 C9
Muradiye Van, Turkey 39°0N 43°44E 213 C10
Murai Res. Singapore 1°23N 103°40E 138 A2
Murakami Japan 38°14N 139°29E 220 E9
Muralag = Prince of Wales I. Australia 10°40S 142°10E 286 F2
Murallón, Cerro Chile 49°48S 73°30W 336 C2
Muranda Rwanda 1°52S 29°20E 268 C2
Murang'a Kenya 0°45S 37°9E 268 C4
Murano Venice, Italy 142 a4
Muranów Poland 52°14N 20°58E 143 B1
Murashi Russia 59°30N 49°0E 186 C8
Murat France 45°7N 2°53E 174 C6
Murat → Turkey 38°46N 40°0E 213 C9
Murat Bay = Ceduna Australia 32°7S 133°46E 281 E1
Murat Dağı Turkey 38°55N 29°43E 205 C11
Muratlı Turkey 41°10N 27°29E 203 E11
Murato France 42°35N 9°20E 175 F13
Murau Austria 47°6N 14°10E 180 D7
Murava Belarus 52°39N 24°15E 185 F11
Muravera Italy 39°25N 9°34E 200 C2
Muravyevo = Mažeikiai Lithuania 56°20N 22°20E 184 B9
Muravyovsky = Korsakov Russia 46°36N 142°42E 215 E15
Murayama Japan 38°30N 140°25E 220 E10
Murça Portugal 41°24N 7°28W 194 D3
Murcaayo Somalia 11°41N 50°34E 267 B7
Murchison N.Z. 41°49S 172°21E 285 B7
Murchison → Australia 27°45S 114°0E 279 E1
Murchison, Mt. Antarctica 73°25S 166°20E 151 D11
Murchison, Mt. N.Z. 43°0S 171°22E 285 D6
Murchison Falls Uganda 2°15N 31°30E 268 B3
Murchison Falls △ Uganda 2°17N 31°48E 268 B3
Murchison Mts. N.Z. 45°13S 167°23E 285 F2
Murchison Ra. Australia 20°0S 134°10E 280 C1
Murchison Rapids Malawi 15°55S 34°35E 269 F3
Murchison Roadhouse Australia 27°39S 116°14E 279 E2
Murcia Spain 38°5N 1°10W 197 G3
Murcia □ Spain 37°50N 1°30W 197 H3
Murdo U.S.A. 43°53N 100°43W 308 D3
Murdoch Pt. Australia 14°37S 144°55E 280 A3
Mürefte Turkey 40°40N 27°14E 203 F11
Mureş □ Romania 46°45N 24°40E 183 D9
Mureş → Romania 46°15N 20°13E 182 D5
Mureşul = Mureş → Romania 46°15N 20°13E 182 D5
Muret France 43°30N 1°20E 174 E5
Murewa Zimbabwe 17°39S 31°47E 271 A5
Murfreesboro N.C., U.S.A. 36°27N 77°6W 315 C16
Murfreesboro Tenn., U.S.A. 35°51N 86°24W 315 D11
Murgab Tajikistan 38°10N 74°2E 217 E8
Murgap → Turkmenistan 38°18N 61°12E 247 B9
Murgenella Australia 11°34S 132°56E 278 B5
Murgeni Romania 46°12N 28°1E 183 D13
Murgha Kibzai Pakistan 30°44N 69°25E 242 D3
Murghob = Murgab Tajikistan 38°10N 74°2E 217 E8
Murgon Australia 26°15S 151°54E 281 D5
Muri Cook Is. 21°15S 159°43W 289 h
Muri India 23°22N 85°52E 243 H11
Muria Indonesia 6°36S 110°53E 235 D4
Muriaé Brazil 21°8S 42°23W 333 F3
Murias de Paredes Spain 42°52N 6°11W 194 C4
Murici Brazil 9°19S 35°56W 332 C4
Muriége Angola 9°58S 21°11E 265 D4
Muriel Mine Zimbabwe 17°14S 30°40E 269 F3
Murien △ India 23°45N 93°20E 241 D4
Murila Angola 10°44S 20°20E 265 E4
Murino Russia 59°59N 30°29E 137 B2
Müritz Germany 53°25N 12°42E 178 B8
Müritz △ Germany 53°22N 12°55E 178 B8
Muriwai Beach N.Z. 36°50S 174°26E 284 C3
Murkong Selek India 27°44N 95°18E 241 B5
Murliganj India 25°54N 86°59E 243 G12
Murmansk Russia 68°57N 33°10E 160 B25
Murmashi Russia 68°47N 32°42E 160 B25
Murnau Germany 47°40N 11°12E 179 H7
Muro Haute-Corse, France 42°34N 8°54E 175 F12
Muro Spain 39°44N 3°3E 206 B4
Muro, C. de France 41°44N 8°37E 175 G12
Muro de Alcoy Spain 38°46N 0°26W 197 G4
Muro Lucano Italy 40°45N 15°29E 201 B8
Murom Russia 55°35N 42°3E 190 C6
Muroran Japan 42°25N 141°0E 220 C10
Muros Spain 42°45N 9°5W 194 C1
Muros e Noya, Ría de → Spain 42°45N 9°0W 194 C1
Muroto Japan 33°18N 134°9E 222 D6
Muroto-Misaki Japan 33°15N 134°10E 222 D6
Murovani Kurylivtsi Ukraine 48°44N 27°31E 183 B12
Murowana Goślina Poland 52°35N 17°0E 185 F3
Murphy U.S.A. 43°13N 116°33W 304 E5
Murphys U.S.A. 38°8N 120°28W 306 G6
Murphy's Station = Sunnyvale U.S.A. 37°23N 122°2W 306 H4
Murphysboro U.S.A. 37°46N 89°20W 310 G7
Murrat Sudan 18°51N 29°33E 256 D2
Murrat Wells Sudan 21°3N 32°55E 256 C3
Murray Queens., Australia 15°56S 144°2E 280 a
Murray Iowa, U.S.A. 41°3N 93°57W 310 C3
Murray Ky., U.S.A. 36°37N 88°19W 308 G9
Murray Utah, U.S.A. 40°40N 111°53W 304 F8
Murray → Australia 35°20S 139°22E 282 C3
Murray, L. Papua N. G. 7°0S 141°35E 286 D1
Murray, L. S.C., U.S.A. 34°3N 81°13W 316 A8
Murray Bridge Australia 35°6S 139°14E 282 C3
Murray Fracture Zone Pac. Oc. 35°0N 130°0W 289 D14
Murray Harbour Canada 46°0N 62°28W 299 C7
Murray River △ Australia 34°23S 140°32E 281 E3
Murray-Sunset △ Australia 34°45S 141°30E 282 C4
Murrayfield U.K. 55°57N 3°15W 121 B2
Murraysburg S. Africa 31°58S 23°47E 270 D3
Murrayville U.S.A. 39°35N 90°15W 310 E6
Murree Pakistan 33°56N 73°28E 242 C5
Murrieta U.S.A. 33°33N 117°13W 307 M9
Murro di Porco, Capo Italy 37°0N 15°20E 201 F8
Murrumbateman Australia 34°58S 149°0E 283 C8
Murrumbidgee → Australia 34°43S 143°12E 282 C5
Murrumburrah Australia 34°32S 148°22E 283 C8
Murrurundi Australia 31°42S 150°51E 283 A9
Murshid Sudan 21°40N 31°10E 256 C3
Murshidabad India 24°11N 88°19E 243 G13
Murska Sobota Slovenia 46°39N 16°12E 199 B13
Murtala Mohammed Int. ✕ (LOS) Nigeria 6°34N 3°19E 124 A1
Murtazapur India 20°40N 77°25E 244 D3
Murtle L. Canada 52°8N 119°38W 296 C5
Murtoa Australia 36°35S 142°28E 282 D5
Murtosa Portugal 40°44N 8°40W 194 E2
Muru → Brazil 8°9S 70°45W 330 B3
Murud India 18°19N 72°58E 244 E1
Murung → Indonesia 0°12N 114°3E 235 B4
Murungu Tanzania 4°12S 31°10E 268 C3
Murupara N.Z. 38°28S 176°42E 284 E5
Mururoa French Polynesia 21°52S 138°55W 289 f
Murwara India 23°46N 80°28E 243 H9
Murwillumbah Australia 28°18S 153°27E 281 D5
Mürz → Austria 47°30N 15°25E 180 D8
Murzūq Libya 25°53N 13°57E 258 C2
Murzūq □ Libya 25°0N 16°0E 258 D3
Murzūq, Idehān Libya 24°50N 13°51E 258 D2
Mürzzuschlag Austria 47°36N 15°41E 180 D8
Mus India 9°14N 92°47E 245 K11
Muş Turkey 38°45N 41°30E 213 C9
Muş □ Turkey 38°45N 41°30E 213 C9
Musa Dem. Rep. of the Congo 2°40N 19°18E 264 B3
Musa → Papua N. G. 9°3S 148°55E 286 E5
Mûsa, Gebel Egypt 28°33N 33°59E 251 K4
Musa Khel Pakistan 30°59N 69°52E 242 D3
Mūsa Qal'eh Afghan. 32°20N 64°50E 240 B2
Musabeyli Turkey 36°53N 36°55E 250 B7
Musadi Dem. Rep. of the Congo 2°31S 22°50E 264 C4
Musafirkhana India 26°22N 81°48E 243 F9
Musala Bulgaria 42°13N 23°37E 202 D7
Musala Indonesia 1°41N 98°28E 234 B1
Musan N. Korea 42°12N 129°12E 224 A4
Musandam □ Oman 26°0N 56°20E 249 A7
Musandam, Ra's Oman 26°20N 56°20E 249 A7
Musangu Dem. Rep. of the Congo 10°28S 23°55E 265 E4
Musasa Tanzania 3°25S 31°30E 268 C3
Musashino Japan 35°42N 139°33E 140 A2
Musay'id Qatar 25°0N 51°33E 247 E6
Musaymīr Yemen 13°27N 44°37E 248 D4
Muscat = Masqat Oman 23°37N 58°36E 249 B7
Muscat & Oman = Oman ■ Asia 23°0N 58°0E 249 B7
Muscatatuck → U.S.A. 38°46N 86°10W 311 F10
Muscatine U.S.A. 41°25N 91°3W 310 C5
Muschu I. Papua N. G. 3°25S 143°35E 286 B2
Muscle Shoals U.S.A. 34°45N 87°40W 315 D11
Muscoda U.S.A. 43°11N 90°27W 310 A6
Musengezi = Unsengedsi → Zimbabwe 15°43S 31°14E 269 F3
Museumquartier Vienna, Austria 142 c1
Museumsinsel Germany 52°30N 13°25E 115 A3
Musgrave Harbour Canada 49°27N 53°58W 299 C9
Musgrave Ranges Australia 26°0S 132°0E 279 E5
Mushie Dem. Rep. of the Congo 2°56S 16°55E 264 C3
Mushima Zambia 14°10S 24°56E 265 E4
Mushin Nigeria 6°31N 3°21E 124 A2
Musi → India 16°41N 79°40E 244 F4
Musi → Indonesia 2°20S 104°56E 234 C2
Musiektheater Amsterdam, Neths. 112 b3
Musina S. Africa 22°20S 30°5E 271 B5
Musiri India 10°56N 78°27E 245 J4
Muskauer Park Europe 51°34N 14°43E 178 D10
Muskeg → Canada 60°20N 123°20W 296 A4
Muskego U.S.A. 42°55N 88°8W 311 B8
Muskegon U.S.A. 43°14N 86°16W 311 A10
Muskegon → U.S.A. 43°14N 86°21W 308 D10
Muskegon Heights U.S.A. 43°12N 86°16W 311 A10
Muskogee U.S.A. 35°45N 95°22W 314 D7
Muskoka, L. Canada 45°0N 79°25W 312 B5
Muskoka Falls Canada 44°59N 79°17W 312 B5
Muskwa → Canada 58°47N 122°48W 296 B4
Muslim Mindanao □ Phil. 8°0N 123°0E 233 H3
Muslim Quarter Jerusalem 123 a3
Muslimiyah Syria 36°19N 37°12E 246 B3
Musmar Sudan 18°13N 35°40E 256 D4
Musocco Italy 45°29N 9°8E 128 B1
Musofu Zambia 13°30S 29°0E 269 E2
Musoma Tanzania 1°30S 33°48E 268 C3
Musquaro, L. Canada 50°38N 61°5W 299 B7
Musquodoboit Harbour Canada 44°50N 63°9W 299 D7
Mussau I. Papua N. G. 1°30S 149°40E 286 A5
Musselburgh U.K. 55°57N 3°2W 167 F5
Musselshell → U.S.A. 47°21N 107°57W 304 C10
Mussende Angola 10°32S 16°5E 265 E3
Musserra Angola 7°37S 13°2E 265 D2
Mussidan France 45°2N 0°22E 174 C4
Mussolinea di Sardegna = Arborèa Italy 39°46N 8°35E 200 C1
Mussolo Angola 9°59S 17°19E 265 D3
Mussomeli Italy 37°35N 13°45E 200 E6
Mussoorie India 30°27N 78°6E 242 D8
Mussuco Angola 17°2S 19°3E 265 F3
Mustafakemalpaşa Turkey 40°2N 28°24E 203 F12
Mustahil Ethiopia 5°16N 44°45E 267 C5
Mustang Nepal 29°10N 83°55E 243 E10
Mustansirīya Iraq 33°22N 44°24E 113 A2
Musters, L. Argentina 45°20S 69°25W 336 C3
Mustique I. St. Vincent 12°52N 61°11W 323 n
Musturud Egypt 30°8N 31°17E 117 A2
Musudan N. Korea 40°50N 129°43E 224 B4
Muswell Hill U.K. 51°35N 0°8W 125 A3
Muswellbrook Australia 32°16S 150°56E 283 B9
Muszyna Poland 49°22N 20°55E 185 J7
Mût Egypt 25°28N 28°58E 256 B2
Mut Turkey 36°40N 33°28E 250 B4
Mutalau Cook Is. 18°56S 169°50W 289 g
Mutanabi Iraq 33°19N 44°21E 113 B2
Mutanda Dem. Rep. of the Congo 5°17S 16°34E 265 D3
Mutanda Mozam. 21°0S 33°34E 271 B5
Mutanda Zambia 12°24S 26°13E 269 E2
Mutankiang = Mudanjiang China 44°38N 129°30E 227 B15
Mutanshe Taiwan 22°9N 120°48E 225 D2
Mutare Zimbabwe 18°58S 32°38E 269 F3
Mutawintji △ Australia 31°10S 142°30E 281 E3
Mutha Kenya 1°48S 38°26E 268 C4
Muthana Iraq 33°19N 44°27E 113 B2
Muting Indonesia 7°23S 140°20E 231 F10
Mutki = Mirtağ Turkey 38°23N 41°56E 246 B4
Mutoko Zimbabwe 17°24S 32°13E 271 A5
Mutomo Kenya 1°51S 38°12E 268 C4
Mutoray Russia 60°56N 101°0E 215 C11
Mutoto Dem. Rep. of the Congo 5°42S 22°42E 265 D4
Mutoxo Angola 12°17S 21°40E 265 E4
Mutsamudu Comoros Is. 12°10S 44°25E 272 a
Mutshatsha Dem. Rep. of the Congo 10°35S 24°20E 265 E4
Mutsu Japan 41°5N 140°55E 220 D10
Mutsu-Wan Japan 41°5N 140°55E 220 D10
Muttaburra Australia 22°38S 144°29E 280 C3
Muttalip Turkey 39°50N 30°32E 205 B12
Mutton I. Ireland 52°49N 9°32W 166 D2
Muttura = Mathura India 27°30N 77°40E 242 F7
Mutuáli Mozam. 14°55S 37°0E 269 E4
Mutum Biyu Nigeria 8°40N 10°50E 263 D7
Mutumba Burundi 3°25S 29°21E 268 C2
Mutunópolis Brazil 13°40S 49°15W 333 D2
Mutur Sri Lanka 8°27N 81°16E 245 K5
Muweilih Egypt 30°42N 34°19E 251 H5
Muxaluando Angola 8°8S 14°18E 265 D2
Muxia Spain 43°3N 9°10W 194 B1
Muxima Angola 9°33S 13°58E 265 D2
Muy Muy Nic. 12°39N 85°36W 320 D2
Muyinga Burundi 3°14S 30°33E 268 C3
Muynak Uzbekistan 43°44N 59°10E 216 D5
Muyunkum, Peski = Moyynqum Kazakhstan 44°12N 71°0E 217 D8
Muz Tag China 36°25N 87°25E 217 E11
Muzaffarabad Pakistan 34°25N 73°30E 243 B5
Muzaffargarh Pakistan 30°5N 71°14E 242 D4
Muzaffarnagar India 29°26N 77°40E 242 E7
Muzaffarpur India 26°7N 85°23E 243 F11
Muzafirpur Pakistan 30°58N 69°9E 242 D3
Mużakowski, Park = Muskauer Park Europe 51°34N 14°43E 178 D10
Muzeze Angola 15°3S 17°43E 265 F3
Muzhi Russia 65°25N 64°40E 186 A11

Muzillac France 47°35N 2°30W 172 E4
Muzon, C. U.S.A. 54°40N 132°42W 303 J14
Muztagh-Ata China 38°17N 75°7E 217 E9
Muztor = Toktogul Kyrgyzstan 41°50N 72°50E 217 D8
Muzūra Egypt 28°53N 30°48E 256 J7
Mvadhi-Ousyé Gabon 1°13N 13°12E 264 B2
Mvam Gabon 0°13S 9°39E 264 C1
Mvangan Cameroon 2°17N 11°43E 264 B2
Mvôlô South Sudan 6°2N 29°53E 257 F2
Mvuma Zimbabwe 19°16S 30°30E 269 F3
Mvurwi Zimbabwe 17°0S 30°57E 269 F3
Mwabvi ⌓ Malawi 16°42S 35°0E 269 F3
Mwadi-Kalumbu Dem. Rep. of the Congo 7°53S 18°43E 265 D3
Mwadui Tanzania 3°26S 33°32E 268 C3
Mwali = Mohéli Comoros Is. 12°20S 43°40E 272 a
Mwambo Tanzania 10°30S 40°22E 269 E5
Mwandi Zambia 17°30S 24°51E 269 F1
Mwanza Katanga, Dem. Rep. of the Congo 7°55S 26°43E 265 D5
Mwanza Tanzania 2°30S 32°58E 268 C3
Mwanza Zambia 16°58S 24°28E 265 F4
Mwanza □ Tanzania 2°0S 33°0E 268 C3
Mwaya Tanzania 9°32S 33°55E 269 D3
Mweelrea Ireland 53°39N 9°49W 166 C2
Mweka Dem. Rep. of the Congo 4°50S 21°34E 265 C4
Mwendjila Dem. Rep. of the Congo 7°12S 18°51E 265 D3
Mwene-Ditu Dem. Rep. of the Congo 6°35S 22°27E 265 D4
Mwenezi Zimbabwe 21°15S 30°48E 269 G3
Mwenezi → Mozam. 22°40S 31°50E 269 G3
Mwenga Dem. Rep. of the Congo 3°1S 28°28E 268 C2
Mweru, L. Zambia 9°0S 28°40E 269 D2
Mweru Wantipa △ Zambia 8°39S 29°25E 269 D2
Mwetshi Dem. Rep. of the Congo 4°50S 22°38E 265 C4
Mweza Range Zimbabwe 21°0S 30°0E 269 G3
Mwilambwe Dem. Rep. of the Congo 8°7S 25°5E 265 D5
Mwimbi Tanzania 8°38S 31°39E 269 D3
Mwingi Kenya 0°56S 38°4E 268 C4
Mwinilunga Zambia 11°43S 24°25E 265 E4
My Son Vietnam 15°48N 108°7E 236 E7
My Tho Vietnam 10°29N 106°23E 237 G6
Mya, O. → Algeria 30°46N 4°54E 261 B5
Myajlar India 26°15N 70°20E 242 F4
Myakka → U.S.A. 26°56N 82°11W 317 J7
Myall Lakes △ Australia 32°25S 152°30E 283 B10
Myanaung Burma 18°18N 95°22E 241 F5
Myanmar = Burma ■ Asia 21°0N 96°30E 241 E6
Myaung Burma 21°50N 95°25E 241 E5
Myaungmya Burma 16°30N 94°40E 241 G5
Mycenæ = Mikines Greece 37°43N 22°46E 204 D4
Myebon Burma 20°3N 93°22E 241 E4
Myedna Belarus 51°52N 23°42E 185 G10
Myeik = Mergui Burma 12°26N 98°34E 236 F2
Myeik Kyunzu Burma 11°30N 97°30E 237 G1
Myerstown U.S.A. 40°22N 76°19W 313 F8
Myingyan Burma 21°30N 95°20E 241 E5
Myitkyina Burma 25°24N 97°26E 241 C6
Myitson Burma 23°16N 96°34E 241 D6
Myittha Burma 21°25N 96°8E 241 E6
Myittha → Burma 23°12N 94°17E 241 D5
Myjava Slovak Rep. 48°41N 17°37E 181 C10
Mykhaylivka Ukraine 47°12N 35°15E 189 J8
Mykines Færoe Is. 62°7N 7°35W 160 E9
Myking Norway 60°41N 5°19E 164 D2
Mykolayiv Ukraine 46°58N 32°0E 189 J7
Mykolayiv □ Ukraine 47°20N 31°50E 189 J6
Mykonos Greece 37°30N 25°25E 205 D7
Mylius Erichsen Land Greenland 81°30N 27°0W 154 A8
Myllypuro Finland 60°13N 25°3E 121 B3
Mymensingh Bangla. 24°45N 90°24E 241 C3
Mynydd Du U.K. 51°52N 3°50W 169 F4
Myo-gyi Burma 21°27N 96°22E 241 E6
Myohaung Burma 20°35N 93°11E 241 E4
Myohla Burma 19°16N 95°25E 241 F5
Myotha Burma 21°41N 95°43E 241 E5
Myothit Kachin, Burma 24°24N 97°24E 241 C6
Myothit Magwe, Burma 20°12N 95°27E 241 E5
Myrasýsla Iceland 64°45N 21°30W 155 C5
Mýrdalsjökull Iceland 63°40N 19°6W 155 D7
Myrhorod Ukraine 49°58N 33°37E 189 H7
Mýri Iceland 65°23N 17°23W 155 B9
Myrtle Beach U.S.A. 33°42N 78°53W 315 E15
Myrtle Creek U.S.A. 43°1N 123°17W 304 E2
Myrtle Grove U.S.A. 30°23N 87°17W 317 E2
Myrtle Point U.S.A. 43°4N 124°8W 304 E1
Myrtleford Australia 36°34S 146°44E 283 D7
Myrtou Cyprus 35°18N 33°4E 207 E9
Myrviken Sweden 62°58N 14°20E 162 B8
Mysen Norway 59°33N 11°20E 164 E8
Mysia Turkey 39°50N 27°0E 203 G11
Myślenice Poland 49°51N 19°57E 185 J6
Myślibórz Poland 52°55N 14°50E 185 F1
Mysłowice Poland 50°15N 19°12E 185 H6
Myslowitz = Mysłowice Poland 50°15N 19°12E 185 H6
Mysore = Karnataka □ India 13°15N 77°0E 245 H3
Mysore India 12°17N 76°41E 245 H3
Mystic Conn., U.S.A. 41°21N 71°58W 313 E13
Mystic Iowa, U.S.A. 40°47N 92°57W 310 D4
Mystic → U.S.A. 42°22N 71°3W 116 A2
Mystras Greece 37°4N 22°22E 204 D4
Mysuru = Mysore India 12°17N 76°41E 245 H3
Myszków Poland 50°45N 19°22E 185 H6
Myszyniec Poland 53°23N 21°21E 184 E8
Mytishchi Russia 55°50N 37°50E 188 E9
Mývatn Iceland 65°36N 17°0W 155 B10
M'zab, Oued → Algeria 32°15N 5°0E 261 B6
M'Zab Valley = M'zab, Oued → Algeria 32°15N 5°0E 261 B6
Mže → Czech Rep. 49°46N 13°24E 180 B6
Mzimba Malawi 11°55S 33°39E 269 E3
Mzimkulu → S. Africa 30°44S 30°28E 271 D5
Mzimvubu → S. Africa 31°38S 29°33E 271 D4
Mzuzu Malawi 11°30S 33°55E 269 E3

N

N.S.C.B. Int. ✈ (CCU) India 22°38N 88°26E 124 B2
Na Clocha Liatha = Greystones Ireland 53°9N 6°5W 166 C5
Na Haeo △ Thailand 17°31N 100°58E 236 D3
Na Hearadh = Harris U.K. 57°50N 6°55W 167 D2
Na Hearadh, Caolas = Harris, Sd. of U.K. 57°44N 7°6W 167 D1
Na-lang Burma 22°42N 97°33E 241 D6
Na Noi Thailand 18°19N 100°43E 236 C3
Na Phao Laos 17°35N 105°44E 236 D5
Na Sam Vietnam 22°3N 106°37E 228 F6
Na Sceirí = Skerries Ireland 53°35N 6°8W 166 C5
Na Thon Thailand 9°32N 99°56E 237 b
Naab → Germany 49°1N 12°2E 179 F8
Nā'ālehu U.S.A. 19°4N 155°35W 302 D6
Na'am Sudan 9°42N 28°27E 257 F2
Na'am → South Sudan 6°48N 29°57E 257 F2
Naama Algeria 33°16N 0°19E 261 B5
Naama □ Algeria 33°15N 0°45E 261 B5
Naantali Finland 60°29N 22°2E 188 B1
Naas Ireland 53°12N 6°40W 166 C5
Nababeep S. Africa 29°36S 17°46E 270 C2
Nabadwip = Navadwip India 23°34N 88°20E 243 H13
Nabari Japan 34°37N 136°5E 223 C8
Nabawa Australia 28°30S 114°48E 279 E1
Nabberu, L. Australia 25°50S 120°30E 279 E3
Nabburg Germany 49°27N 12°11E 179 F8
Naberezhnaya Tower Russia 55°45N 37°32E 129 B2
Naberezhnyye Chelny Russia 55°42N 52°19E 190 C11
Nabesna U.S.A. 62°22N 143°0W 303 E12
Nabeul Tunisia 36°30N 10°44E 258 A2
Nabeul □ Tunisia 36°30N 10°40E 261 A7
Nabha India 30°26N 76°14E 242 D7
Nabi Sâlih Egypt 28°37N 33°59E 251 K4
Nabīd Iran 29°40N 57°38E 247 D8
Nabire Indonesia 3°15S 135°26E 231 E9
Nabisar Pakistan 25°8N 69°40E 242 G3
Nabisipi → Canada 50°14N 62°13W 299 B7
Nabiswera Uganda 1°27N 32°15E 268 B3
Nāblus = Nābulus West Bank 32°14N 35°15E 251 F6
Naboomspruit S. Africa 24°32S 28°40E 271 B4
Nabou Burkina Faso 11°25N 2°50W 262 C4
Nabouwalu Fiji 17°0S 178°45E 287 A2
Nabq Egypt 28°6N 34°25E 251 K5
Nabua Phil. 13°24N 123°22E 232 E4
Nābulus West Bank 32°14N 35°15E 251 F6
Nabunturan Phil. 7°35N 125°58E 233 H5
Nacala Mozam. 14°32S 40°34E 269 E5
Nacaome Honduras 13°31N 87°30W 320 D2
Nacaroa Mozam. 14°22S 39°56E 269 E4
Naches U.S.A. 46°44N 120°42W 304 C3
Naches → U.S.A. 46°38N 120°31W 306 D6
Nachicapau, L. Canada 56°40N 68°5W 299 A6
Nachikatsuura Japan 33°33N 135°58E 223 D7
Nachingwea Tanzania 10°23S 38°49E 269 E4
Nachna India 27°34N 71°41E 242 F4
Náchod Czech Rep. 50°25N 16°8E 180 A9
Nachuge India 10°47N 92°21E 245 J11
Nacimiento, L. U.S.A. 35°46N 120°53W 306 K6
Nacka Sweden 59°19N 18°10E 139 B3
Nackara Australia 32°48S 139°12E 282 B3
Naco Mexico 31°19N 109°56W 318 A3
Nacogdoches U.S.A. 31°36N 94°39W 314 F7
Nácori Chico Mexico 29°40N 108°57W 318 B3
Nacozari de García Mexico 30°25N 109°38W 318 A3
Nacula Fiji 16°54S 177°27E 287 A1
Nada = Danzhou China 19°31N 109°33E 236 C7
Nådendal = Naantali Finland 60°29N 22°2E 188 B1
Nadezhdinsky = Serov Russia 59°29N 60°35E 186 C11
Nadi Fiji 17°42S 177°20E 287 A1
Nadi Sudan 18°40N 33°41E 256 D3
Nadiad India 22°41N 72°56E 242 H5
Nădlac Romania 46°10N 20°50E 182 D5
Nador Morocco 35°14N 2°58W 261 A4
Nadur Malta 35°54N 14°22E 206 F7
Nadur Gozo, Malta 36°2N 14°18E 206 E7
Nadūshan Iran 32°2N 53°35E 247 C7
Nadvirna Ukraine 48°37N 24°30E 183 B9
Nadvoitsy Russia 63°52N 34°14E 186 B5
Nadvornaya = Nadvirna Ukraine 48°37N 24°30E 183 B9
Nadym Russia 65°35N 72°42E 214 C8
Nadym → Russia 66°12N 72°0E 214 C8
Nærbø Norway 58°40N 5°39E 164 F2
Nærøyfjorden Norway 60°55N 6°55E 164 D3
Nærsnes Norway 59°45N 10°27E 133 B1
Næstved Denmark 55°13N 11°44E 163 J5
Nafada Nigeria 11°8N 11°20E 263 C7
Nafpaktos Greece 38°24N 21°50E 204 C3
Nafplio Greece 37°33N 22°50E 204 D4
Naft-e Safīd Iran 31°40N 49°17E 247 D6
Naftan Pt. N. Marianas 15°5N 145°45E 302 e
Naftshahr Iran 34°0N 45°30E 213 E11
Nafud Desert = An Nafūd Si. Arabia 28°15N 41°0E 246 D4
Nafūsah, Jabal Libya 32°12N 12°30E 258 B2
Nag Hammâdi Egypt 26°2N 32°18E 256 B3
Naga Japan 26°34N 127°43E 288 a
Naga Camarines S., Phil. 13°33N 123°15E 232 E4
Naga Cebu, Phil. 10°13N 123°45E 233 F4
Naga Zamboanga del S., Phil. 7°46N 122°45E 233 H4
Naga, Kreb en Africa 24°12N 6°0W 260 D3
Naga Hills = Nagaland □ India 26°0N 94°30E 241 C5
Naga-Shima Kagoshima, Japan 32°10N 130°9E 222 E2
Naga-Shima Yamaguchi, Japan 33°49N 132°5E 222 D4
Nagagami Canada 50°23N 84°20W 298 B3
Nagahama Ehime, Japan 33°36N 132°29E 222 D4
Nagahama Shiga, Japan 35°23N 136°16E 223 B8
Nagai Japan 38°6N 140°2E 220 E10
Nagai I. U.S.A. 55°5N 160°0W 303 J8
Nagaland □ India 26°0N 94°30E 241 C5
Nagambie Australia 36°47S 145°10E 283 D6
Nagano Japan 36°40N 138°10E 223 A10
Nagano □ Japan 36°15N 138°0E 223 A10
Nagaoka Japan 37°27N 138°51E 221 F9
Nagaon India 26°20N 92°50E 241 B4
Nagappattinam India 10°46N 79°51E 245 J4
Nagar → Bangla. 24°27N 89°12E 241 C2
Nagar Karnul India 16°29N 78°20E 245 F4
Nagar Parkar Pakistan 24°28N 70°46E 242 G4
Nagara-Gawa → Japan 35°40N 136°43E 223 B8
Nagaram India 18°21N 80°26E 244 E5
Nagarhole △ India 12°0N 76°10E 245 J3
Nagari Hills India 13°3N 79°45E 245 H4
Nagarjuna Sagar India 16°30N 79°13E 245 F4
Nagasaki Japan 32°47N 129°50E 222 E1
Nagasaki □ Japan 32°50N 129°40E 222 E1
Nagato Japan 34°19N 131°5E 222 C3
Nagatsuta Japan 35°32N 139°31E 140 B2
Nagaur India 27°15N 73°45E 242 F5
Nagayo Japan 32°48N 129°50E 222 E1
Nagbhir India 20°34N 79°55E 244 D4
Nagda India 23°27N 75°25E 242 H6
Nagercoil India 8°12N 77°26E 245 K3
Nagina India 29°30N 78°30E 243 E8
Nagīneh Iran 34°20N 57°15E 247 C8
Naginimara India 26°49N 94°50E 241 B5
Nagir Pakistan 36°12N 74°42E 243 A6
Naglarby Sweden 60°25N 15°34E 162 D9
Nagles Mts. Ireland 52°8N 8°30W 166 D3
Nago-wan Japan 26°34N 127°57E 288 a
Nagod India 24°34N 80°36E 243 G9
Nagold Germany 48°32N 8°43E 179 G4
Nagold → Germany 48°52N 8°42E 179 G4
Nagoorin Australia 24°17S 151°15E 280 C5
Nagorno-Karabakh □ Azerbaijan 39°55N 46°45E 213 C12
Nagornyy Russia 55°58N 124°57E 215 D13
Nagoya Indonesia 1°15N 104°5E 234 B2
Nagoya Japan 35°10N 136°50E 223 B8
Nagoya ✈ (NGO) Japan 34°53N 136°45E 223 C8
Nagpartian = Burgos Phil. 18°31N 120°39E 232 B3
Nagpur India 21°8N 79°10E 244 D4
Nagqu China 31°29N 92°3E 218 E7
Nags Head St. Kitts & Nevis 17°13N 62°38W 322 d
Nagua Dom. Rep. 19°23N 69°50W 321 C6
Naguabo Puerto Rico 18°13N 65°44W 321 b
Nagurunguru ⚙ Australia 16°45S 129°45E 278 C4
Nagyatád Hungary 46°14N 17°22E 182 D2
Nagyecsed Hungary 47°53N 22°24E 182 C7
Nagykálló Hungary 47°53N 21°51E 182 C6
Nagykanizsa Hungary 46°28N 17°0E 182 D2
Nagykáta Hungary 47°25N 19°45E 182 C4
Nagykőrös Hungary 47°5N 19°48E 182 C4
Nagyszombat = Trnava Slovak Rep. 48°23N 17°35E 181 C10
Nagytétény Hungary 47°23N 18°59E 117 B1
Nagyvárad = Oradea Romania 47°2N 21°58E 182 C6
Naha Japan 26°13N 127°42E 288 a
Nahabuan Indonesia 0°49N 114°4E 235 B4
Nahalin West Bank 31°41N 35°7E 123 B1
Nahan India 30°33N 77°18E 242 D7
Nahanni △ Canada 61°36N 125°41W 296 A4
Nahanni Butte Canada 61°2N 123°31W 296 A4
Nahargarh Mad. P., India 24°10N 75°14E 242 G6
Nahargarh Raj., India 24°55N 76°50E 242 G7
Nahariyya Israel 33°1N 35°5E 250 F6
Nahāvand Iran 34°10N 48°22E 213 E13
Nahe → Germany 49°58N 7°54E 179 F3
Nahirne Ukraine 45°26N 28°27E 183 E13
Nahîya, W. → Egypt 28°55N 31°0E 256 B3
Nahuel Huapi, L. Argentina 41°0S 71°32W 336 B2
Nahuel Huapi △ Argentina 41°3S 71°59W 336 B2
Nahuelbuta △ Chile 37°44S 72°57W 334 D1
Nahunta U.S.A. 31°12N 81°59W 316 D8
Nai Yong Thailand 8°14N 98°22E 237 a
Naic Phil. 14°19N 120°46E 232 D3
Naicá Mexico 27°53N 105°31W 318 B3
Naicam Canada 52°30N 104°30W 297 C8
Naifaru Maldives 5°26N 73°20E 272 d
Naikoon ⌓ Canada 53°55N 131°55W 296 C2
Naikul India 21°20N 84°58E 244 D7
Naila Germany 50°19N 11°42E 179 E7
Naimisharanya India 27°21N 80°30E 243 F9
Naimona'nyi Feng China 30°26N 81°18E 243 D9
Nain Nfld. & L., Canada 56°34N 61°40W 299 A7
Nā'īn Iran 32°54N 53°0E 247 C7
Nain Jamaica 17°57N 77°38W 320 a
Naini Tal India 29°30N 79°30E 243 E8
Nainpur India 22°30N 80°10E 243 H9
Naintré France 46°46N 0°29E 172 F7
Nainwa India 25°46N 75°51E 242 G6
Naipu Romania 44°12N 25°47E 183 F10
Nairai Fiji 17°49S 179°15E 287 A2
Nairn U.K. 57°35N 3°53W 167 D5
Nairobi Kenya 1°17S 36°48E 268 C4
Nairobi △ Kenya 1°22S 36°50E 268 C4
Naissaar Estonia 59°34N 24°29E 188 C3
Naita, Mt. Ethiopia 5°30N 35°18E 257 F4
Naitaba Fiji 17°0S 179°16W 287 A3
Naivasha Kenya 0°40S 36°30E 268 C4
Naivasha, L. Kenya 0°48S 36°20E 268 C4
Najac France 44°14N 1°58E 174 D5
Najaf = An Najaf Iraq 32°3N 44°15E 213 G11
Najafābād Iran 32°40N 51°15E 247 C6
Najafgarh Drain → India 28°39N 77°4E 120 B1
Najd Si. Arabia 26°30N 42°0E 248 A3
Nájera Spain 42°26N 2°48W 196 C2
Najerilla → Spain 42°32N 2°48W 196 C2
Najibabad India 29°40N 78°20E 242 E8
Najin N. Korea 42°12N 130°15E 224 A5
Najmah Si. Arabia 26°42N 50°6E 247 E6
Najrān Si. Arabia 17°34N 44°18E 248 C4
Najrān □ Si. Arabia 18°30N 45°50E 248 C4
Naju S. Korea 35°3N 126°43E 224 E3
Naka Japan 36°30N 140°35E 223 A12
Naka-Gawa → Japan 36°20N 140°36E 223 A12
Nakadōri-Shima Japan 32°57N 129°4E 221 H4
Nakagusuku-wan Japan 26°14N 127°53E 288 a
Nakahara Japan 35°33N 139°37E 140 B2
Nakał = Nakło nad Notecią Poland 53°9N 17°38E 185 E4
Nakalagba Dem. Rep. of the Congo 2°50N 27°58E 268 B2
Nakalele Pt. U.S.A. 21°2N 156°35W 302 B5
Nakama Japan 33°56N 130°43E 222 D2
Nakambé = White Volta → Ghana 9°10N 1°15W 263 D4
Nakaminato Japan 36°21N 140°36E 223 A12
Nakamura = Shimanto Japan 32°59N 132°56E 222 E4
Nakanai Mts. Papua N. G. 5°40S 151°0E 286 C6
Nakano Nagano, Japan 36°45N 138°22E 223 A10
Nakano Tōkyō, Japan 35°42N 139°39E 140 A2
Nakano-Shima Japan 29°51N 129°52E 221 K4
Nakanojō Japan 36°35N 138°51E 223 A10
Nakashibetsu Japan 43°33N 144°59E 220 C12
Nakatsu Japan 33°34N 131°15E 222 D3
Nakatsugawa Japan 35°29N 137°30E 223 B9
Nakfa Eritrea 16°40N 38°32E 257 D4
Nakfa ⌓ Eritrea 17°28N 38°55E 257 D4
Nakha Yai, Ko Thailand 8°3N 98°28E 237 a
Nakhichevan = Naxçıvan Azerbaijan 39°12N 45°15E 213 C11
Nakhichevan Rep. = Naxçıvan □ Azerbaijan 39°25N 45°26E 213 C11
Nakhl Egypt 29°55N 33°43E 251 J4
Nakhl-e Taqī Iran 27°28N 52°36E 247 E7
Nakhodka Russia 42°53N 132°54E 220 C6
Nakhon Nayok Thailand 14°12N 101°13E 236 E3
Nakhon Pathom Thailand 13°49N 100°3E 236 F3
Nakhon Phanom Thailand 17°23N 104°43E 236 D5
Nakhon Ratchasima Thailand 14°59N 102°12E 236 E4
Nakhon Sawan Thailand 15°35N 100°10E 236 E3
Nakhon Si Thammarat Thailand 8°29N 100°0E 237 H3
Nakhon Thai Thailand 17°5N 100°44E 236 D3
Nakhtarana India 23°20N 69°15E 242 H3
Nakijin Japan 26°40N 127°58E 288 a
Nakina Canada 50°10N 86°40W 298 B2
Nakło nad Notecią Poland 53°9N 17°38E 185 E4
Naknek U.S.A. 58°44N 157°1W 303 G8
Nako Burkina Faso 10°40N 3°4W 262 C4
Nakodar India 31°8N 75°31E 242 D6
Nakskov Denmark 54°50N 11°8E 163 K5
Naktong → S. Korea 35°7N 128°57E 227 G15
Nakuru Kenya 0°15S 36°4E 268 C4
Nakuru, L. Kenya 0°23S 36°5E 268 C4
Nakusp Canada 50°20N 117°45W 296 C5
Nal Pakistan 27°40N 66°12E 242 F2
Nal → Pakistan 25°20N 65°30E 242 G1
Nalázi Mozam. 24°3S 33°20E 271 B5
Nalchik Russia 43°30N 43°33E 191 J6
Nałęczów Poland 51°17N 22°9E 185 G9
Nalerigu Ghana 10°35N 0°25W 263 C4
Nalgonda India 17°6N 79°15E 244 F4
Nalhati India 24°17N 87°52E 243 G12
Naliya India 23°16N 68°50E 242 H3
Nallamalai Hills India 15°30N 78°50E 245 G4
Nallıhan Turkey 40°11N 31°20E 212 B4
Nalolo Zambia 15°33S 23°7E 265 F4
Nalón → Spain 43°32N 6°4W 194 B4
Nalong Burma 24°44N 97°28E 241 C6
Nalubaale Dam Uganda 0°30N 33°5E 268 B3
Nalumasortoq Greenland 60°23N 44°28W 154 E6
Nālūt Libya 31°54N 11°0E 258 B2
Nālūt □ Libya 31°52N 10°58E 258 B2
Nam Can Vietnam 8°46N 104°59E 237 H5
Nam-ch'on N. Korea 38°15N 126°26E 224 C3
Nam Co China 30°30N 90°45E 218 E7
Nam Dinh Vietnam 20°25N 106°5E 228 G6
Nam Du, Quan Dao Vietnam 9°41N 104°21E 237 H5
Nam Hke → Burma 25°34N 95°41E 228 G2
Nam Loi → Burma 21°3N 98°27E 228 G3
Nam Nao △ Thailand 16°44N 101°32E 236 D3
Nam Ngum Res. Laos 18°35N 102°34E 236 C4
Nam-Phan Vietnam 10°30N 106°0E 237 G6
Nam Phong Thailand 16°42N 102°52E 236 D4
Nam Theun Res. Laos 17°51N 105°3E 236 D5
Nam Tok Thailand 14°21N 99°4E 236 E2
Nam Un Res. Thailand 17°13N 103°44E 236 D4
Namachire Angola 11°26S 22°43E 265 E4
Namacunde Angola 17°18S 15°50E 265 F3
Namacurra Mozam. 17°30S 36°50E 271 A6
Namadgi △ Australia 35°42S 149°0E 283 C8
Namai B. Palau 7°31N 134°38E 288 c
Namak, Daryācheh-ye Iran 34°30N 52°0E 247 C7
Namak, Kavir-e Iran 34°30N 57°30E 247 C8
Namakkal India 11°13N 78°13E 245 J4
Namakzār, Daryācheh-ye Iran 34°0N 60°30E 240 B1
Namaland Namibia 26°0S 17°0E 270 B2
Namanga Kenya 2°33S 36°47E 268 C4
Namangan Uzbekistan 41°0N 71°40E 217 D8
Namangan □ Uzbekistan 41°0N 71°15E 217 D8
Namapa Mozam. 13°43S 39°50E 269 E4
Namaqua △ S. Africa 30°0S 17°30E 270 D2
Namaqualand S. Africa 30°0S 17°25E 270 D2
Namasagali Uganda 1°2N 33°0E 268 B3
Namatanai Papua N. G. 3°40S 152°29E 286 B7
Namber Indonesia 1°2S 134°49E 231 E8
Nambour Australia 26°32S 152°58E 281 D5
Nambouwalu = Nabouwalu Fiji 17°0S 178°45E 287 A2
Nambuangongo Angola 8°1S 14°12E 265 D2
Nambucca Heads Australia 30°37S 153°0E 283 A10
Nambung △ Australia 30°30S 115°5E 279 F2
Namcha Barwa China 29°40N 95°10E 218 F8
Namche Bazar Nepal 27°51N 86°47E 243 F12
Namchonjŏm = Nam-ch'on N. Korea 38°15N 126°26E 224 C3
Namdapha △ India 27°30N 96°50E 241 B6
Namecunda Mozam. 14°54S 37°37E 269 E4
Nameh Indonesia 2°34N 116°21E 235 B5
Namen = Namur Belgium 50°27N 4°52E 170 D4
Namenalala Fiji 17°8S 179°9E 287 A2
Nameponda Mozam. 15°50S 39°50E 269 F4
Nameri △ India 26°55N 92°55E 241 B4
Namerikawa Japan 36°46N 137°20E 223 A9
Náměšť nad Oslavou Czech Rep. 49°12N 16°10E 181 B9
Námestovo Slovak Rep. 49°24N 19°25E 181 B12
Nametil Mozam. 15°40S 39°21E 269 F4
Namew L. Canada 54°14N 101°56W 297 C8
Namgia India 31°48N 78°40E 243 D8
Namhkam Burma 23°50N 97°41E 228 E1
Namhsan Burma 22°48N 97°2E 241 D6
Namialo Mozam. 14°55S 39°59E 269 E4
Namib Desert Namibia 22°30S 15°0E 270 B2
Namib-Naukluft ⌓ Namibia 24°40S 15°16E 270 B2
Namibe Angola 15°7S 12°11E 265 F2
Namibe □ Angola 16°35S 12°30E 265 F2
Namibe ⌓ Angola 16°35S 12°20E 265 F2
Namibia ■ Africa 22°0S 18°9E 270 B2
Namibia Abyssal Plain Atl. Oc. 30°0S 5°30E 152 J12
Namibwoestyn = Namib Desert Namibia 22°30S 15°0E 270 B2
Namīn Iran 38°25N 48°30E 213 C13
Namjeju S. Korea 33°14N 126°33E 224 a
Namlan Burma 22°15N 97°24E 241 D6
Namlea Indonesia 3°18S 127°5E 231 E7
Namoi → Australia 30°12S 149°30E 283 A9
Namous, O. en → Algeria 31°0N 0°15W 261 B4
Nampa U.S.A. 43°34N 116°34W 304 E5
Nampala Mali 15°20N 5°30W 262 B3
Namp'o N. Korea 38°52N 125°10E 224 C2
Namp'o □ N. Korea 38°52N 125°25E 224 C2
Nampō-Shotō Japan 32°0N 140°0E 221 J10
Nampula Mozam. 15°6S 39°15E 269 F4
Namrole Indonesia 3°46S 126°46E 231 E7
Namsan Park S. Korea 37°32N 126°59E 137 B1
Namse Shankou China 30°0N 82°25E 243 E10
Namsen → Norway 64°28N 11°37E 160 D14
Namslau = Namysłów Poland 51°6N 17°42E 185 G4
Namsos Norway 64°29N 11°30E 160 D14
Namtok Chat Trakan △ Thailand 17°17N 100°40E 236 D3
Namtok Huay Yang △ Thailand 11°35N 99°30E 237 G2
Namtok Mae Surin △ Thailand 18°55N 98°2E 236 C2
Namtok Ngao △ Thailand 9°58N 98°46E 237 H2
Namtok Phlew △ Thailand 12°32N 102°13E 236 F4
Namtok Yong △ Thailand 8°15N 98°45E 237 H2
Namtsy Russia 62°43N 129°37E 215 C13
Namtu Burma 23°5N 97°28E 241 D6
Namtumbo Tanzania 10°30S 36°4E 269 E4
Namu Canada 51°52N 127°50W 296 C3
Namuka-i-Lau Fiji 18°53S 178°37W 287 B3
Namukulu Cook Is. 18°57S 169°54W 289 g
Namumea Tuvalu 5°41S 176°9E 277 B14
Namur Belgium 50°27N 4°52E 170 D4
Namur □ Belgium 50°17N 5°0E 170 D4
Namuruputh Kenya 4°34N 35°57E 268 B4
Namutoni Namibia 18°49S 16°55E 270 A2
Namwala Zambia 15°44S 26°30E 269 F2
Namwon Jeju-do, S. Korea 33°16N 126°43E 224 a
Namwon Jeollabuk-do, S. Korea 35°23N 127°23E 224 E3
Namyang N. Korea 42°57N 129°52E 224 A4
Namyangju S. Korea 37°38N 127°12E 224 D3
Namyeong S. Korea 37°32N 126°57E 137 B1
Namysłów Poland 51°6N 17°42E 185 G4
Nan Thailand 18°48N 100°46E 236 C3
Nan → Thailand 15°42N 100°9E 236 E3
Nan-ch'ang = Nanchang China 28°42N 115°55E 229 C10
Nan Ling China 25°0N 112°30E 229 E8
Nan Xian China 29°20N 112°22E 229 C9
Nana C.A.R. 5°0N 15°50E 264 A3
Nana Romania 44°17N 26°34E 183 F11
Nana-Barya ⌓ C.A.R. 7°40N 17°29E 264 A3
Nana Kru Liberia 4°55N 8°45W 262 E3
Nanaimo Canada 49°10N 124°0W 296 D4
Nänäkuli U.S.A. 21°24N 158°9W 302 K13
Nanam N. Korea 41°44N 129°40E 224 B4
Nan'an China 24°59N 118°21E 229 E12
Nanango Australia 26°40S 152°0E 281 D5
Nan'ao Guangdong, China 23°28N 117°5E 229 F11
Nanao Japan 37°0N 137°0E 221 F8
Nanao Taiwan 24°28N 121°48E 225 B3
Nanbiancun China 23°4N 113°10E 121 B1
Nanbu China 31°18N 106°3E 228 B6
Nanchang China 28°42N 115°55E 229 C10
Nanchang He → China 39°58N 116°14E 114 B1
Nancheng China 27°33N 116°35E 229 D11
Nanching = Nanjing China 32°2N 118°47E 229 A12
Nanchong China 30°43N 106°2E 228 B6
Nanchuan China 29°9N 107°6E 228 C6
Nanchung = Nanchong China 30°43N 106°2E 228 B6
Nancowry India 7°59N 93°32E 245 L11
Nancy France 48°42N 6°12E 173 D13
Nanda Devi India 30°23N 79°59E 243 D8
Nanda Devi △ India 30°30N 79°50E 243 D8
Nanda Kot India 30°17N 80°5E 243 D9
Nandan = Minamiawaji Japan 34°10N 134°42E 222 C6
Nandan China 24°58N 107°29E 228 E6
Nandang China 23°6N 113°12E 121 B2
Nanded India 19°10N 77°20E 244 E3
Nandewar Ra. Australia 30°15S 150°35E 281 E5
Nandgaon India 20°19N 74°39E 244 D2
Nandi = Nadi Fiji 17°42S 177°20E 287 A1
Nandi Zimbabwe 20°58S 31°44E 269 G3
Nandigama India 16°47N 80°18E 244 F5
Nandigram India 22°1N 87°58E 243 H12
Nandikotkur India 15°52N 78°18E 245 G4
Nandura India 20°52N 76°25E 244 D3
Nandurbar India 21°20N 74°15E 244 D2
Nandyal India 15°30N 78°30E 245 G4
Nanfeng Guangdong, China 23°45N 111°47E 229 F8
Nanfeng Jiangxi, China 27°12N 116°28E 229 D11
Nang Rong Thailand 14°38N 102°48E 236 E4
Nanga-Eboko Cameroon 4°41N 12°22E 263 E7
Nanga Parbat Pakistan 35°10N 74°35E 243 B6
Nangade Mozam. 11°5S 39°36E 269 E4
Nangal Dewat India 28°33N 77°5E 120 B1
Nangalao I. Phil. 11°26N 120°10E 233 F3
Nangamau Indonesia 0°6S 111°55E 235 C4
Nangamentebah Indonesia 0°33N 112°46E 235 B4
Nangapinoh Indonesia 0°20S 111°44E 235 C4
Nangar △ Australia 33°23S 148°3E 283 B8
Nangarhār □ Afghan. 34°20N 70°0E 240 B3
Nangatayap Indonesia 1°32S 110°34E 235 C4
Nangbéto, L. de Togo 7°26N 1°25E 263 D5
Nangeya Mts. Uganda 3°30N 33°30E 268 B3
Nangis France 48°33N 3°1E 173 D10
Nangnim-sanmaek N. Korea 40°13N 126°51E 224 B3
Nangong China 37°23N 115°22E 226 F8
Nangtud, Mt. Phil. 11°17N 122°11E 233 F4
Nanguneri India 8°29N 77°40E 245 K3
Nangwarry Australia 37°33S 140°48E 282 D4
Nanhua Yunnan, China 25°13N 101°21E 228 E3
Nanhua Taiwan 23°2N 120°28E 225 C2
Nanhuang China 36°58N 121°48E 227 F11
Nanhui China 31°5N 121°44E 229 B13
Nanhunan Shan Taiwan 24°21N 121°26E 225 B3
Nanisivik Canada 73°2N 84°33W 295 C15
Naniwa Japan 34°39N 135°29E 133 B1
Nanjangud India 12°6N 76°43E 245 H3
Nanji Shan China 27°27N 121°4E 229 D13
Nanjian China 25°2N 100°25E 228 E3
Nanjiang China 32°28N 106°51E 228 A6
Nanjing Fujian, China 24°25N 117°20E 229 E11
Nanjing Jiangsu, China 32°2N 118°47E 229 A12
Nanjirinji Tanzania 9°41S 39°5E 269 D4
Nankana Sahib Pakistan 31°27N 73°38E 242 D5
Nankang Jiangxi, China 25°40N 114°45E 229 E10
Nankang Taiwan 25°3N 121°35E 225 A3
Nanking = Nanjing China 32°2N 118°47E 229 A12
Nankoku Japan 33°39N 133°44E 222 D5
Nanlang China 22°30N 113°32E 219 a
Nanliao Taiwan 24°50N 120°55E 225 B2
Nanling China 30°55N 118°20E 229 B12
Nannial India 19°4N 79°38E 244 E4
Nanning China 22°48N 108°20E 228 F7
Nannup Australia 33°59S 115°48E 279 F2
Nanole India 19°0N 72°55E 130 A2
Nanortalik Greenland 60°10N 45°17W 154 E6
Nanpan Jiang → China 25°10N 106°5E 228 E6
Nanpara India 27°52N 81°33E 243 F9
Nanping Fujian, China 26°38N 118°10E 229 D12
Nanping Henan, China 29°55N 112°3E 229 C9
Nanpu Bridge China 31°12N 121°30E 138 B2
Nanri Dao China 25°15N 119°25E 229 E12
Nansang Burma 20°53N 97°43E 241 E6
Nansei-Shotō = Ryūkyū-Rettō Japan 26°0N 126°0E 221 M3
Nansen Basin Arctic 84°0N 50°0E 150 A10
Nansen Land Greenland 83°0N 43°0W 154 A6
Nansen Sd. Canada 81°0N 91°0W 295 A13
Nansha China 22°45N 113°34E 219 a
Nansha Port China 22°40N 113°40E 219 a
Nanshan China 18°19N 109°10E 236 C7
Nanshan I. S. China Sea 10°45N 115°49E 230 B5
Nanshi China 31°12N 121°29E 138 B1
Nansio Tanzania 2°3S 33°4E 268 C3
Nant France 44°1N 3°18E 174 D7
Nantan Japan 35°6N 135°28E 223 B7
Nantawarrinna ⚙ Australia 30°49S 138°58E 281 B2
Nanterre France 48°53N 2°12E 134 A2
Nantes France 47°12N 1°33W 172 E5
Nantiat France 46°1N 1°11E 174 B5
Nanticoke U.S.A. 41°12N 76°0W 313 E8
Nanton Canada 50°21N 113°46W 296 C6
Nanton Pt. Antigua & B. 17°0N 61°45W 322 b
Nantong China 32°1N 120°52E 229 A13
Nantou China 22°32N 113°55E 219 a
Nant'ou Taiwan 23°55N 120°41E 225 C2
Nant'ou □ Taiwan 23°50N 121°0E 225 C3
Nantua France 46°10N 5°35E 173 F12
Nantucket U.S.A. 41°17N 70°6W 309 E18
Nantucket I. U.S.A. 41°16N 70°5W 309 E18
Nantulo Mozam. 12°32S 38°45E 269 E4
Nantung = Nantong China 32°1N 120°52E 229 A13
Nantwich U.K. 53°4N 2°31W 168 D5
Nanty Glo U.S.A. 40°28N 78°50W 312 F6
Nantzu Taiwan 22°44N 120°19E 225 D2
Nanuku Passage Fiji 16°45S 179°15W 287 A3
Nanumanga Pac. Oc. 6°18S 176°20E 277 B14
Nanuque Brazil 17°50S 40°21W 333 E3
Nanusa, Kepulauan Indonesia 4°45N 127°1E 231 D7
Nanutarra Roadhouse Australia 22°32S 115°30E 278 D2
Nanwan Taiwan 21°57N 120°46E 225 E2
Nanxi China 28°54N 104°59E 228 C5
Nanxiong China 25°6N 114°15E 229 E10
Nanyang China 33°11N 112°30E 226 H7
Nanyi Hu China 31°5N 119°0E 229 B12
Nanyuan China 39°47N 116°24E 226 E9
Nanyuki Kenya 0°2N 37°4E 268 B4
Nanzhang China 31°45N 111°50E 229 B8
Nanzhao China 33°30N 112°20E 226 H7
Nao, C. de la Spain 38°44N 0°14E 197 G5
Naococane, L. Canada 52°50N 70°45W 299 B5
Naogaon Bangla. 24°52N 88°52E 241 C2
Naoné Vanuatu 15°0S 168°8E 287 E6
Naoussa Cyclades, Greece 37°7N 25°14E 205 D7
Naoussa Imathia, Greece 40°42N 22°9E 202 F6
Naozhou Dao China 20°55N 110°20E 229 G8
Napa U.S.A. 38°18N 122°17W 306 G4
Napa → U.S.A. 38°10N 122°19W 306 G4
Napaimiut U.S.A. 61°33N 158°42W 303 F8
Napakiak U.S.A. 60°42N 161°57W 303 F7
Näpali Coast U.S.A. 22°11N 159°39W 302 A2
Napanee Canada 44°15N 77°0W 312 B8
Napanoch U.S.A. 41°44N 74°22W 313 E10
Napaskiak U.S.A. 60°43N 161°55W 303 F7
Nape Laos 18°18N 105°6E 236 C5
Nape Pass = Keo Neua, Deo Vietnam 18°23N 105°10E 236 C5
Naperville U.S.A. 41°46N 88°9W 311 C8
Napier N.Z. 39°30S 176°56E 284 F5
Napier Broome B. Australia 14°2S 126°37E 278 B4
Napier Mole Pakistan 24°49N 66°58E 123 B1
Napier Pen. Australia 12°4S 135°43E 280 A2
Napierville Canada 45°11N 73°25W 313 A11
Napili-Honokowai U.S.A. 20°58N 156°39W 302 C5
Naples = Nápoli Italy 40°50N 14°15E 201 B7
Naples U.S.A. 26°8N 81°48W 317 J8
Naples Park U.S.A. 26°17N 81°46W 317 J8
Napo China 23°22N 105°50E 228 F5
Napo □ Ecuador 0°30S 77°0W 328 D2
Napo → Peru 3°20S 72°40W 328 D3
Napoleon N. Dak., U.S.A. 46°30N 99°46W 308 B4
Napoleon Ohio, U.S.A. 41°23N 84°8W 311 C12
Napoleon's Tomb St. Helena 15°56S 5°42W 153 h
Nápoli Italy 40°50N 14°15E 201 B7
Nápoli, G. di Italy 40°43N 14°10E 201 B7
Nápoli Capodichino ✈ (NAP) Italy 40°53N 14°16E 201 B7
Napopo Dem. Rep. of the Congo 4°15N 28°0E 268 B2
Nappanee U.S.A. 41°27N 86°0W 311 C11
Napperby Australia 33°9S 138°7E 282 B3
Naqadeh Iran 36°57N 45°23E 213 D11
Naqb, Ra's an Jordan 29°48N 35°44E 251 J6
Naqqāsh Iran 35°40N 49°6E 247 C6
När Sweden 57°15N 18°35E 163 G10
Nara Japan 34°40N 135°49E 223 C7
Nara Mali 15°10N 7°20W 262 B3
Nara □ Japan 34°30N 136°0E 223 C8
Nara Canal Pakistan 24°30N 69°20E 242 G3
Nara Visa U.S.A. 35°37N 103°6W 305 J12
Naracoorte Australia 36°58S 140°45E 282 D4
Naradhan Australia 33°34S 146°17E 283 B7
Naraina India 28°36N 77°8E 120 B1
Naraini India 25°11N 80°29E 243 G9
Naranjos Mexico 21°21N 97°41W 319 C5
Narasannapeta India 18°25N 84°3E 244 E7
Narasapur India 16°26N 81°40E 245 F5
Narasaraopet India 16°14N 80°4E 245 F5
Narathiwat Thailand 6°30N 101°48E 237 J3
Narayanapatnam India 18°53N 83°10E 244 E6
Narayangadh = Bharatpur Nepal 27°34N 84°10E 243 F11
Narayanganj Bangla. 23°40N 90°33E 241 D3
Narayanpet India 16°45N 77°30E 244 F3
Narbada = Narmada → India 21°38N 72°36E 242 J5
Narberth U.K. 51°47N 4°44W 169 F3
Narbonne France 43°11N 3°0E 174 E7
Narborough, I. = Fernandina, I. Ecuador 0°25S 91°30W 330 a
Narbuvoll Norway 62°21N 11°27E 164 B8
Narcea → Spain 43°33N 6°44W 194 B4
Narcondam I. India 13°20N 94°16E 245 H12
Nardīn Iran 37°3N 55°59E 247 B7
Nardò Italy 40°11N 18°2E 201 B11
Narembeen Australia 32°7S 118°24E 279 F2
Nares Abyssal Plain Atl. Oc. 22°0N 67°0W 152 D5
Nares Str. Arctic 80°0N 70°0W 154 B3
Naretha Australia 31°0S 124°45E 279 F3
Narew → Poland 52°26N 20°41E 185 F7
Nari → Pakistan 28°0N 67°40E 242 F2
Nariman Pt. Maharashtra, India 18°55N 72°49E 130 B1
Nariman Pt. Mumbai, India 130 c1
Narin Afghan. 36°5N 69°0E 240 A3
Narindra, Helodranon' i Madag. 14°55S 47°30E 272 A2
Narino □ Colombia 1°30N 78°0W 328 C2
Narita Japan 35°47N 140°19E 223 B12
Narita, Tōkyō ✈ (NRT) Japan 35°45N 140°25E 223 B12
Nariva → Trin. & Tob. 10°24N 61°4W 323 t
Nariva Swamp Trin. & Tob. 10°26N 61°4W 323 t
Närke Sweden 59°10N 15°0E 162 E8
Narmada → India 21°38N 72°36E 242 J5
Narmada Canal India 22°20N 73°45E 244 C1
Nārmak Iran 35°42N 51°28E 141 A2
Narman Turkey 40°26N 41°57E 213 B9
Narnaul India 28°5N 76°11E 242 E7
Narni Italy 42°30N 12°30E 199 F9
Naro Ghana 10°22N 2°27W 262 C4
Naro Fominsk Russia 55°23N 36°43E 188 E9
Narodnaya Russia 65°5N 59°58E 186 A10
Narok Kenya 1°55S 35°52E 268 C4
Narón Spain 43°32N 8°9W 194 B2
Narooma Australia 36°14S 150°4E 283 D9
Narowal Pakistan 32°6N 74°52E 242 C6
Narrabri Australia 30°19S 149°46E 281 E4
Narran → Australia 28°37S 148°12E 281 D4
Narrandera Australia 34°42S 146°31E 283 C7
Narrogin Australia 32°58S 117°14E 279 F2
Narromine Australia 32°12S 148°12E 283 B8
Narrow Hills ⌓ Canada 54°0N 104°37W 297 C8
Narrows, The St. Kitts & Nevis 17°12N 62°40W 322 d
Narsampet India 17°57N 79°58E 244 F4
Narsaq Greenland 60°57N 46°4W 154 E6
Narsimhapur India 22°54N 79°14E 243 H8
Narsingdi Bangla. 23°55N 90°43E 241 D3
Narsinghgarh India 23°45N 76°40E 242 H7
Narsinghpur India 20°28N 85°5E 244 D7
Narsipatnam India 17°40N 82°37E 244 F6
Nartes, L. e Albania 40°32N 19°25E 202 F3
Nartkala Russia 43°33N 43°51E 191 J6
Naruo Japan 34°43N 135°22E 133 A1
Narutō = Sanmu Kantō, Japan 34°11N 134°37E 222 C6
Narutō = Sanmu Shikoku, Japan 35°36N 140°25E 223 B12
Naruto-Kaikyō Japan 34°14N 134°39E 222 C6
Narva Estonia 59°23N 28°12E 188 C5
Narva → Russia 59°27N 28°2E 188 C4
Narva Bay = Narva Laht Estonia 59°35N 27°35E 161 G22
Narva Laht Estonia 59°35N 27°35E 161 G22
Narvacan Phil. 17°25N 120°28E 232 C3
Narvik Norway 68°28N 17°26E 160 B17
Narvskoye Vdkhr. Russia 59°18N 28°14E 188 C5
Narwana India 29°39N 76°6E 242 E7
Narwiański △ Poland 52°5N 22°53E 185 F9
Narwinbi ⚙ Australia 16°7S 136°17E 280 B2
Naryan-Mar Russia 67°42N 53°12E 186 A9
Narym Russia 59°0N 81°30E 214 D9
Naryn Kyrgyzstan 41°26N 75°58E 217 D9
Naryn □ Kyrgyzstan 41°26N 75°58E 217 D9
Naryn → Uzbekistan 40°52N 71°36E 217 D8
Naryn Qum Kazakhstan 47°30N 49°0E 191 G9
Nás, An = Naas Ireland 53°12N 6°40W 166 C5
Nasa Norway 66°29N 15°23E 160 C16
Nasau Fiji 17°19S 179°27E 287 A2
Năsăud Romania 47°19N 24°29E 183 C9
Nasawa Vanuatu 15°12S 168°9E 287 E6
Naşb, W. → Egypt 28°29N 34°31E 251 K5
Näsby Sweden 59°25N 18°5E 139 A2
Näsbypark Sweden 59°25N 18°5E 139 A2

Nasca *Peru* 14°50S 74°57W **330** C3
Nasca Ridge *Pac. Oc.* 20°0S 80°0W **289** K19
Naseby *N.Z.* 45°1S 170°10E **285** F5
Naselle *U.S.A.* 46°22N 123°49W **306** D3
Naser, Buheirat en *Egypt* 23°0N 32°30E **256** C3
Nashik = Nasik *India* 19°58N 73°50E **244** E1
Nashua *Iowa, U.S.A.* 42°57N 92°32W **310** B4
Nashua *Mont., U.S.A.* 48°8N 106°22W **304** B10
Nashua *N.H., U.S.A.* 42°45N 71°28W **313** D13
Nashville *Ark., U.S.A.* 33°57N 93°51W **314** E8
Nashville *Ga., U.S.A.* 31°12N 83°15W **316** D6
Nashville *Ill., U.S.A.* 38°21N 89°23W **310** F7
Nashville *Ind., U.S.A.* 39°12N 86°15W **311** E10
Nashville *Mich., U.S.A.* 42°36N 85°5W **311** B11
Nashville *Tenn., U.S.A.* 36°10N 86°47W **315** C11
Našice *Croatia* 45°32N 18°4E **182** E3
Nasielsk *Poland* 52°35N 20°50E **185** F7
Nasik *India* 19°58N 73°50E **244** E1
Nasipit *Phil.* 8°57N 125°19E **233** G5
Nasir *South Sudan* 8°36N 33°4E **257** F3
Nasirabad = Mymensingh *Bangla.* 24°45N 90°24E **241** C3
Nasirabad *India* 26°15N 74°45E **242** F6
Nasirabad *Pakistan* 28°23N 68°24E **242** E3
Nasiri = Ahvāz *Iran* 31°20N 48°40E **247** D6
Nasiriyah = An Nāşirīyah *Iraq* 31°0N 46°15E **246** D5
Naskaupi → *Canada* 53°47N 60°51W **299** B7
Naso *Italy* 38°7N 14°47E **201** D7
Naso Pt. *Phil.* 10°25N 121°57E **233** F3
Naşrābād *Iran* 34°8N 51°26E **247** C6
Naşriān-e Pā'īn *Iran* 32°52N 46°52E **246** C5
Nass → *Canada* 55°0N 129°40W **296** C3
Nassarawa *Nigeria* 8°32N 7°41E **263** D6
Nassarawa □ *Nigeria* 8°30N 8°20E **263** D6
Nassau *Bahamas* 25°5N 77°20W **153** b
Nassau *N.Y., U.S.A.* 42°31N 73°37W **313** D11
Nassau, B. *Chile* 55°20S 68°0W **336** E3
Nassau Int. ✈ (NAS) *Bahamas* 25°3N 77°28W **153** b
Nasser, L. = Naser, Buheirat en *Egypt* 23°0N 32°30E **256** C3
Nasser City = Kôm Ombo *Egypt* 24°25N 32°52E **256** C3
Nassian *Ivory C.* 8°28N 3°28W **262** D4
Nässjö *Sweden* 57°39N 14°42E **163** G8
Nastapoka → *Canada* 56°55N 76°33W **298** A4
Nastapoka, Is. *Canada* 56°55N 76°50W **298** A4
Nasugbu *Phil.* 14°5N 120°38E **232** D3
Näsum *Sweden* 56°10N 14°29E **163** H8
Nasushiobara *Japan* 36°58N 140°3E **221** F10
Näsviken *Sweden* 61°46N 16°52E **162** C10
Nat Ma Taung △ *Burma* 21°30N 93°35E **241** E4
Nata *Botswana* 20°12S 26°12E **270** B4
Nata → *Botswana* 20°14S 26°10E **270** B4
Natagaima *Colombia* 3°37N 75°6W **328** C2
Natal *Brazil* 5°47S 35°13W **332** C4
Natal *Indonesia* 0°35N 99°7E **234** B1
Natal Drakensberg = uKhahlamba Drakensberg ⌓ *S. Africa* 29°27S 29°30E **271** C4
Natalinci *Serbia* 44°15N 20°49E **182** F5
Naţanz *Iran* 33°30N 51°55E **247** C6
Natashquan *Canada* 50°14N 61°46W **299** B7
Natashquan → *Canada* 50°7N 61°50W **299** B7
Natchez *U.S.A.* 31°34N 91°24W **314** F9
Natchitoches *U.S.A.* 31°46N 93°5W **314** F8
Natewa B. *Fiji* 16°35S 179°40E **287** A2
Nathalia *Australia* 36°1S 145°13E **283** D6
Nathan Philips Square *Toronto, Canada* **141** b2
Nathan Road *Hong Kong, China* **122** a2
Nathdwara *India* 24°55N 73°50E **242** G5
Nathu La *Asia* 27°24N 88°49E **241** B2
Nati, Pta. *Spain* 40°3N 3°50E **206** A4
Natimuk *Australia* 36°42S 142°0E **282** D5
Nation → *Canada* 55°30N 123°32W **296** B4
National Arboretum *U.S.A.* 38°54N 76°59W **143** B2
National Art Gallery *Beijing, China* **114** b2
National Capital District □ *Papua N. G.* 9°25S 147°10E **286** E4
National City *U.S.A.* 32°40N 117°5W **307** N9
National Grand Theatre *Beijing, China* **114** c2
National Maritime Museum *U.K.* 51°29N 0°0 **125** B3
National Place *Washington, D.C., U.S.A.* **143** b2
National September 11 Memorial and Museum *New York, U.S.A.* **132** e1
National University (N.U.S.) *Singapore* 1°19N 103°46E **138** B2
National Zoological Park *U.S.A.* 38°55N 77°4W **143** B2
Nationals Park *U.S.A.* 38°53N 77°1W **143** B2
Natitingou *Benin* 10°20N 1°26E **263** C5
Natividad, I. *Mexico* 27°52N 115°11W **318** B1
Natividade *Brazil* 11°43S 47°47W **333** D2
Nativity, Basilica of *West Bank* 31°42N 35°12E **123** B2
Natkyizin *Burma* 14°57N 97°59E **236** E1
Natmauk *Burma* 20°20N 95°24E **241** E5
Natogyi *Burma* 21°25N 95°39E **241** E5
Natolin *Poland* 52°8N 21°4E **143** C2
Natonin *Phil.* 17°6N 121°18E **232** C3
Nator *Bangla.* 24°21N 89°5E **241** C2
Natron, L. *Tanzania* 2°20S 36°0E **268** C4
Natrona Heights *U.S.A.* 40°37N 79°44W **312** F5
Natrûn, W. el → *Egypt* 30°25N 30°13E **256** H7
Nattai △ *Australia* 34°12S 150°22E **283** C9
Nättraby *Sweden* 56°13N 15°31E **163** H9
Natukanaoka Pan *Namibia* 18°40S 15°45E **270** A2
Natuna Besar, Kepulauan *Indonesia* 4°0N 108°15E **235** B3
Natuna Is. = Natuna Besar, Kepulauan *Indonesia* 4°0N 108°15E **235** B3
Natuna Selatan, Kepulauan *Indonesia* 2°45N 109°0E **235** B3
Natural Bridge *U.S.A.* 44°5N 75°30W **313** B9
Natural Bridges ⌓ *U.S.A.* 37°36N 110°0W **305** H9
Naturaliste, C. *Tas., Australia* 40°50S 148°15E **281** G4
Naturaliste, C. *W. Austral., Australia* 33°32S 115°0E **279** F2
Naturaliste Plateau *Ind. Oc.* 34°0S 112°0E **276** G1
Nau Qala *Afghan.* 34°5N 68°5E **242** B3
Naucalpan de Juárez *Mexico* 19°28N 99°14W **128** B1
Naucelle *France* 44°13N 2°20E **174** D6
Nauders *Austria* 46°54N 10°30E **180** E3
Nauen *Germany* 52°36N 12°52E **178** C8
Naugard = Nowogard *Poland* 53°41N 15°10E **184** E2
Naugatuck *U.S.A.* 41°30N 73°3W **313** E11
Naujaat = Repulse Bay *Canada* 66°30N 86°30W **295** D14
Naujan *Phil.* 13°20N 121°18E **232** E3
Naujan Lake △ *Phil.* 13°9N 121°20E **232** E3
Naujoji Akmenė *Lithuania* 56°19N 22°54E **184** B9
Naulila *Angola* 17°13S 14°39E **265** F2
Naumburg *Germany* 51°9N 11°47E **178** D7
Naumburg am Queis = Nowogrodziec *Poland* 51°12N 15°24E **185** G2
Naupada *Andhra Pradesh, India* 18°34N 84°18E **244** E7
Naupada *Maharashtra, India* 19°3N 72°50E **130** A2
Nā'ūr *Jordan* 31°53N 35°50E **251** G6
Nauru ■ *Pac. Oc.* 1°0S 166°0E **288** H8
Naushahra = Nowshera *Pakistan* 34°0N 72°0E **240** B4
Naushahro *Pakistan* 26°50N 68°7E **242** F3
Naushon I. *U.S.A.* 41°29N 70°45W **313** E14
Nausori *Fiji* 18°2S 178°32E **287** B2
Naustdal *Norway* 61°31N 5°43E **164** C2
Nauta *Peru* 4°31S 73°35W **328** D3
Nautanwa *India* 27°20N 83°25E **243** F10
Naute ⌓ *Namibia* 26°55S 17°57E **270** C2
Nautla *Mexico* 20°13N 96°47W **319** C5
Nauvoo *U.S.A.* 40°33N 91°23W **310** D5
Nava *Coahuila, Mexico* 28°25N 100°45W **318** B4
Nava *Spain* 43°21N 5°31W **194** B5
Nava del Rey *Spain* 41°22N 5°6W **194** D5
Navadwip *India* 23°34N 88°20E **243** H13
Navahermosa *Spain* 39°41N 4°28W **195** F6
Navahrudak *Belarus* 53°40N 25°50E **177** B13
Navai *Fiji* 17°36S 177°57E **287** A1
Navajo Res. *U.S.A.* 36°48N 107°36W **305** H10
Naval *Phil.* 11°34N 124°23E **233** F5
Navalcarnero *Spain* 40°17N 4°5W **194** E6
Navalgund *India* 15°34N 75°22E **245** G2
Navalmoral de la Mata *Spain* 39°52N 5°33W **194** F5
Navalvillar de Pela *Spain* 39°9N 5°24W **195** F5
Navan *Ireland* 53°39N 6°41W **166** C5
Navanagar = Jamnagar *India* 22°30N 70°6E **242** H4
Navapolatsk *Belarus* 55°32N 28°37E **188** E5
Navarin, Mys *Russia* 62°15N 179°5E **215** C18
Navarino, I. *Chile* 55°0S 67°40W **336** E3
Navarra □ *Spain* 42°40N 1°40W **196** C3
Navarre *Fla., U.S.A.* 30°24N 86°52W **317** E3
Navarre *Ohio, U.S.A.* 40°43N 81°31W **312** F3
Navarro → *U.S.A.* 39°11N 123°45W **306** F3
Navas de San Juan *Spain* 38°30N 3°19W **195** G7
Navasota *U.S.A.* 30°23N 96°5W **314** F6
Navassa I. *W. Indies* 18°30N 75°0W **321** C5
Nävekvarn *Sweden* 58°38N 16°49E **163** F10
Naver → *U.K.* 58°32N 4°14W **167** C4
Navet *Trin. & Tob.* 10°21N 61°10W **323** t
Navet → *Trin. & Tob.* 10°24N 61°5W **323** t
Navet Res. *Trin. & Tob.* 10°24N 61°15W **323** t
Navi Mumbai *India* 19°5N 73°0E **130** A2
Navia *Spain* 43°35N 6°42W **194** B4
Navia → *Spain* 43°15N 6°50W **194** B4
Navia de Suarna = A Pobre *Spain* 42°58N 7°3W **194** C3
Navibandar *India* 21°26N 69°48E **242** J3
Navidad *Chile* 33°57S 71°50W **334** C1
Navidad Bank *W. Indies* 20°0N 68°58W **321** B6
Navíglio di Pavia *Italy* 45°24N 9°9E **128** B1
Navíglio Grande *Italy* 45°25N 9°5E **128** B1
Naviraí *Brazil* 23°8S 54°13W **335** A5
Naviti *Fiji* 17°7S 177°15E **287** A1
Navlakhi *India* 22°58N 70°28E **242** H4
Navlya *Russia* 52°53N 34°30E **189** F8
Năvodari *Romania* 44°19N 28°36E **183** F13
Navoi *Uzbekistan* 40°9N 65°22E **217** D7
Navojoa *Mexico* 27°6N 109°26W **318** B3
Navolato *Mexico* 24°47N 107°42W **318** C3
Navona, Piazza *Rome, Italy* **136** b2
Navotas *Phil.* 14°39N 120°56E **127** B1
Navrongo *Ghana* 10°51N 1°3W **263** C4
Navsari *India* 20°57N 72°59E **244** D1
Navua *Fiji* 18°12S 178°11E **287** B2
Navy Pier *U.S.A.* 41°53N 87°36W **119** b3
Nawa Kot *Pakistan* 28°21N 71°24E **242** E4
Nawab Khan *Pakistan* 30°17N 69°12E **242** D3
Nawabganj *Bangla.* 24°35N 88°14E **241** C2
Nawabganj *Ut. P., India* 26°56N 81°14E **243** F9
Nawabganj *Ut. P., India* 28°32N 79°40E **243** E8
Nawabshah *Pakistan* 26°15N 68°25E **242** F3
Nawada *India* 24°50N 85°33E **243** G11
Nāwah *Afghan.* 32°19N 67°53E **240** B2
Nawakot *Nepal* 27°55N 85°10E **243** F11
Nawalgarh *India* 27°50N 75°15E **242** F6
Nawanshahr *India* 32°33N 74°48E **243** C6
Nawapara *India* 20°46N 82°33E **244** D6
Nawar, Dasht-i- *Afghan.* 33°52N 68°0E **242** C3
Nawāsīf, Ḩarrat *Si. Arabia* 21°20N 42°10E **248** B3
Nawi *Sudan* 18°32N 30°50E **256** D3
Nawng Hpa *Burma* 22°30N 98°30E **241** D7
Nawoiy = Navoi *Uzbekistan* 40°9N 65°22E **217** D7
Nawş, Ra's *Oman* 17°15N 55°16E **249** C6
Naxçıvan *Azerbaijan* 39°12N 45°15E **213** C11
Naxçıvan □ *Azerbaijan* 39°25N 45°26E **213** C11
Naxos *Greece* 37°8N 25°25E **205** D7
Naxxar *Malta* 35°55N 14°27E **206** F7
Nay *France* 43°10N 0°18W **174** E3
Nay, Mui *Vietnam* 12°54N 109°26E **236** F7
Nāy Band *Būshehr, Iran* 27°20N 52°40E **247** E7
Nāy Band *Khorāsān, Iran* 32°20N 57°34E **247** C8
Naya → *Colombia* 3°13N 77°22W **328** C2
Nayagarh *India* 20°8N 85°6E **244** D7
Nayakhan *Russia* 61°56N 159°0E **215** C16
Nayarit □ *Mexico* 22°0N 105°0W **318** C4
Nayé *Senegal* 14°28N 12°12W **262** C2
Nayong *China* 26°50N 105°20E **228** D5
Nayoro *Japan* 44°21N 142°28E **220** B11
Naypyidaw *Burma* 19°44N 96°12E **241** F6
Nayudupeta *India* 13°54N 79°54E **245** H4
Nayyāl, W. → *Si. Arabia* 28°35N 39°4E **246** D3
Nazal Hikmat Beg *Iraq* 33°23N 44°25E **113** A2
Nazar Kahrizi *Iran* 37°20N 46°45E **213** D12
Nazaré *Bahia, Brazil* 13°2S 39°0W **333** D4
Nazaré *Pará, Brazil* 6°25S 52°29W **331** B7
Nazaré *Tocantins, Brazil* 6°23S 47°40W **332** C2
Nazaré *Portugal* 39°36N 9°4W **195** F1
Nazareth = Nazerat *Israel* 32°42N 35°17E **250** F6
Nazareth *U.S.A.* 40°44N 75°19W **313** F9
Nazarovo *Russia* 57°2N 90°40E **215** D10
Nazas *Mexico* 25°14N 104°8W **318** B4
Nazas → *Mexico* 25°12N 104°12W **318** B4
Nazca = Nasca *Peru* 14°50S 74°57W **330** C3
Naze, The *U.K.* 51°53N 1°18E **169** F9
Nazerat *Israel* 32°42N 35°17E **250** F6
Nāzīk *Iran* 39°1N 45°4E **213** C11
Nazilli *Turkey* 37°55N 28°15E **205** D10
Nazimabad *Pakistan* 24°54N 67°1E **123** A2
Nazinon = Red Volta → *Africa* 10°34N 0°30W **263** C4
Nazir Hat *Bangla.* 22°35N 91°49E **241** D3
Nazko *Canada* 53°1N 123°37W **296** C4
Nazko → *Canada* 53°7N 123°34W **296** C4
Nazlet el Simmân *Egypt* 29°59N 31°9E **117** B1
Nāzlu *Iran* 37°41N 45°0E **213** D11
Nazret *Ethiopia* 8°32N 39°22E **257** F4
Ncama *Eq. Guin.* 1°55N 10°56E **264** B2
Nchanga *Zambia* 12°30S 27°49E **269** E2
Ncheu *Malawi* 14°50S 34°47E **269** E3
Ncue *Eq. Guin.* 2°1N 10°28E **264** B2
Ndala *Tanzania* 4°45S 33°15E **268** C3
Ndalatando *Angola* 9°12S 14°48E **265** D2
Ndali *Benin* 9°50N 2°46E **263** D5
Ndareda *Tanzania* 4°12S 35°30E **268** C4
Ndélé *C.A.R.* 8°25N 20°36E **264** A4
Ndendé *Gabon* 2°22S 11°23E **264** C2
Ndiael ⌓ *Senegal* 16°15N 16°0W **262** B1
Ndikinimeki *Cameroon* 4°46N 10°50E **263** E7
Ndim *Cameroon* 5°10N 10°41E **264** A2
Ndindi *Gabon* 3°46S 11°9E **264** C2
N'Dioum *Senegal* 16°31N 14°39W **262** B2
Ndjamena *Chad* 12°10N 15°0E **259** F3
Ndjolé *Gabon* 0°10S 10°45E **264** C2
Ndogo, Lagune *Gabon* 2°35S 10°0E **264** C2
Ndok *Cameroon* 7°57N 14°42E **264** A2
Ndoki-Nouabalé ⌓ *Congo* 2°32N 16°32E **264** B3
Ndola *Zambia* 13°0S 28°34E **269** E2
Ndomo ⌓ *S. Africa* 26°52S 32°15E **271** C5
Ndoto Mts. *Kenya* 2°0N 37°0E **268** B4
Ndoua, C. *N. Cal.* 22°24S 166°56E **288** d
Ndouba *Congo* 0°9S 14°4E **264** C2
Ndoukou *C.A.R.* 4°33N 20°39E **264** B4
Nduguti *Tanzania* 4°18S 34°41E **268** C3
Nea → *Norway* 63°15N 11°0E **164** A8
Nea Alexandria *Greece* 37°52N 23°46E **112** B2
Nea Alikarnassos *Greece* 35°18N 25°13E **205** F7
Nea Anchialos *Greece* 39°16N 22°49E **204** B4
Nea Epidavros *Greece* 37°40N 23°7E **204** D5
Nea Ionia *Athina, Greece* 38°3N 23°45E **112** A2
Nea Ionia *Magnisia, Greece* 39°21N 22°56E **204** B4
Nea Kalikratia *Greece* 40°21N 23°3E **202** F7
Nea Liosia *Greece* 38°3N 23°43E **112** A2
Nea Makri *Greece* 38°5N 23°59E **204** C5
Nea Moudania *Greece* 40°15N 23°17E **202** F7
Nea Peramos *Attiki, Greece* 38°0N 23°26E **204** C5
Nea Peramos *Kavala, Greece* 40°50N 24°18E **203** F8
Nea Samsounda *Greece* 39°5N 20°45E **207** A2
Nea Smirni *Greece* 37°54N 23°43E **112** B2
Nea Visa *Greece* 41°34N 26°33E **203** E10
Nea Zichni *Greece* 41°2N 23°49E **202** E7
Neagari = Nomi *Japan* 36°26N 136°25E **223** A8
Neagh, Lough *U.K.* 54°37N 6°25W **166** B5
Neah Bay *U.S.A.* 48°22N 124°37W **306** B2
Neale, L. *Australia* 24°15S 130°0E **278** D5
Neales → *Australia* 28°8S 136°47E **281** D2
Neamati *India* 26°50N 94°20E **241** B5
Neamţ □ *Romania* 47°0N 26°20E **183** C11
Neapoli *Athens, Greece* **112** a3
Neapoli *Kozani, Greece* 40°20N 21°24E **202** F5
Neapoli *Kriti, Greece* 35°15N 25°37E **207** E6
Neapoli *Lakonia, Greece* 36°27N 23°8E **204** E5
Near Is. *U.S.A.* 52°30N 174°0E **303** K1
Near North *U.S.A.* 41°54N 87°38W **119** b1
Neath *U.K.* 51°39N 3°48W **169** F4
Neath Port Talbot □ *U.K.* 51°42N 3°45W **169** F4
Nebbi *Uganda* 2°28N 31°6E **268** B3
Nebbou *Burkina Faso* 11°9N 1°51W **263** C4
Nebelat el Hagana *Sudan* 13°13N 29°2E **257** E2
Nebine Cr. → *Australia* 29°27S 146°56E **281** D4
Nebitdag = Balkanabat *Turkmenistan* 39°30N 54°22E **247** B7
Nebka *Algeria* 27°28N 3°12W **260** C4
Neblina, Pico da *Brazil* 0°48N 66°0W **328** C4
Nebo *Australia* 21°42S 148°42E **280** C4
Nebolchy *Russia* 59°8N 33°18E **188** C7
Nebraska □ *U.S.A.* 41°30N 99°30W **308** E4
Nebraska City *U.S.A.* 40°41N 95°52W **308** E6
Nébrodi, Monti *Italy* 37°54N 14°35E **201** E7
Nebušice *Czech Rep.* 50°6N 14°19E **135** B1
Necedah *U.S.A.* 44°2N 90°4W **308** C8
Nechako → *Canada* 53°55N 122°42W **296** C4
Neches → *U.S.A.* 29°58N 93°51W **314** G8
Nechisar △ *Ethiopia* 5°58N 37°55E **257** F4
Neckar → *Germany* 49°27N 8°29E **179** F4
Neckartal-Odenwald ⌓ *Germany* 49°30N 9°5E **179** F5
Necker I. *U.S.A.* 23°35N 164°42W **302** G11
Necochea *Argentina* 38°30S 58°50W **334** D4
Nectar Brook *Australia* 32°43S 137°57E **282** B2
Neda *Spain* 43°30N 8°9W **194** B2
Neda → *Greece* 37°25N 21°45E **204** D3
Nedalshytta *Norway* 62°59N 12°3E **164** B9
Nedelino *Bulgaria* 41°27N 25°3E **203** E9
Nedelišće *Croatia* 46°23N 16°22E **199** B13
Nederhorst *Neths.* 52°16N 5°3E **112** B3
Nederland = Netherlands ■ *Europe* 52°0N 5°30E **170** C5
Nedlitz *Germany* 52°25N 13°3E **115** B1
Nedoboyivtsi *Ukraine* 48°26N 26°21E **183** B11
Nedreberg *Norway* 60°59N 11°41E **164** D8
Nedroma *Algeria* 35°1N 1°45W **261** A4
Nedstrand *Norway* 59°21N 5°49E **164** E2
Nee Soon *Singapore* 1°24N 103°49E **138** A2
Needham *U.S.A.* 42°17N 71°14W **116** B1
Needham Heights *U.S.A.* 42°17N 71°14W **116** B1
Needles *B.C., Canada* 49°53N 118°7W **296** D5
Needles *Calif., U.S.A.* 34°51N 114°37W **307** L12
Needles, The *U.K.* 50°39N 1°35W **169** G6
Needles Pt. *N.Z.* 36°3S 175°25E **284** C4
Neembucú □ *Paraguay* 27°0S 58°0W **334** B4
Neemuch = Nimach *India* 24°30N 74°56E **242** G6
Neenah *U.S.A.* 44°11N 88°28W **308** C9
Neepawa *Canada* 50°15N 99°30W **297** C9
Neeses *U.S.A.* 33°33N 81°7W **316** B8
Nefta *Tunisia* 33°53N 7°50E **258** B1
Neftçala *Azerbaijan* 39°19N 49°12E **213** C13
Neftechala = Neftçala *Azerbaijan* 39°19N 49°12E **213** C13
Neftegorsk *Krasnodar, Russia* 44°25N 39°45E **191** H4
Neftegorsk *Sakhalin, Russia* 53°1N 142°58E **215** D15
Neftekumsk *Russia* 44°46N 44°50E **191** H7
Nefteyugansk *Russia* 61°5N 72°42E **214** C8
Nefyn *U.K.* 52°56N 4°31W **168** E3
Négala *Mali* 12°52N 8°30W **262** C3
Negapatam = Nagappattinam *India* 10°46N 79°51E **245** J4
Negara *Indonesia* 8°22S 114°37E **231** J17
Negaunee *U.S.A.* 46°30N 87°36W **308** B10
Negele *Oromiya, Ethiopia* 5°20N 39°36E **257** F4
Negele *Oromiya, Ethiopia* 7°21N 38°42E **266** C4
Negeri Sembilan □ *Malaysia* 2°45N 102°10E **237** L4
Negev Desert = Hanegev *Israel* 30°50N 35°0E **251** H6
Negoiul, Vf. *Romania* 45°38N 24°35E **183** E9
Negombo *Sri Lanka* 7°12N 79°50E **245** L4
Negotin *Serbia* 44°16N 22°37E **202** B6
Negotino *Macedonia* 41°29N 22°7E **202** E6
Negra, Peña *Spain* 42°11N 6°30W **194** C4
Negra, Pta. *Mauritania* 22°54N 16°18W **260** D1
Negra, Pta. *Peru* 6°6S 81°10W **330** B1
Negra Pt. *Phil.* 18°40N 120°50E **232** B3
Negra Pt. *Trin. & Tob.* 10°4N 61°23W **323** t
Negrais, C. = Maudin Sun *Burma* 16°0N 94°30E **241** G5
Nègres, Pte. des *Martinique* 14°35N 61°5W **322** j
Negreşti *Romania* 46°50N 27°30E **183** D12
Negreşti-Oaş *Romania* 47°52N 23°26E **183** C8
Negril *Jamaica* 18°22N 78°20W **320** a
Négrine *Algeria* 34°30N 7°30E **261** B6
Negro → *Argentina* 41°2S 62°47W **336** B4
Negro → *Bolivia* 14°11S 63°7W **331** C5
Negro → *Brazil* 3°0S 60°0W **329** D6
Negro → *Uruguay* 33°24S 58°22W **334** C4
Negro, C. = Tarf, Ras *Morocco* 35°40N 5°11W **260** A3
Negro, C. *Venezuela* 11°11N 63°53W **329** a
Negros *Phil.* 9°30N 122°40E **233** G4
Negros Occidental □ *Phil.* 10°0N 122°55E **233** F4
Negros Oriental □ *Phil.* 9°45N 123°0E **233** G4
Negru Vodă *Romania* 43°47N 28°21E **183** G13
Neguac *Canada* 47°15N 65°5W **299** C6
Nehalem → *U.S.A.* 45°40N 123°56W **306** E3
Nehāvand *Iran* 35°56N 49°31E **247** C6
Nehbandān *Iran* 31°35N 60°5E **247** D9
Nehe *China* 48°29N 124°50E **219** B13
Nehoiu *Romania* 45°24N 26°20E **183** E11
Nei Mongol Zizhiqu □ *China* 42°0N 112°0E **226** D7
Neiafu *Tonga* 18°39S 173°59W **287** P14
Neidenburg = Nidzica *Poland* 53°25N 20°28E **185** E7
Neiges, Piton des *Réunion* 21°5S 55°29E **272** f
Neijiang *China* 29°35N 104°55E **228** C5
Neikiang = Neijiang *China* 29°35N 104°55E **228** C5
Neilingding Dao *China* 22°25N 113°48E **219** a
Neill I. *India* 11°50N 93°3E **245** J11
Neillsville *U.S.A.* 44°34N 90°36W **308** C8
Neilson, Récif *Pac. Oc.* 27°1S 146°2W **289** f
Neilton *U.S.A.* 47°25N 123°53W **306** C3
Neipu *Taiwan* 22°37N 120°33E **225** D2
Neiqiu *China* 37°15N 114°30E **226** F8
Neisse = Nysa → *Europe* 52°4N 14°46E **178** C10
Neiva *Colombia* 2°56N 75°18W **328** C2
Neiwan *Taiwan* 24°42N 121°10E **225** B3
Neixiang *China* 33°10N 111°52E **226** H6
Nejanilini L. *Canada* 59°33N 97°48W **297** B9
Nejd = Najd *Si. Arabia* 26°30N 42°0E **248** A3
Nejo *Ethiopia* 9°30N 35°28E **257** F4
Nejrab *Afghan.* 34°58N 69°34E **240** B3
Nekā *Iran* 36°39N 53°19E **247** B7
Nekemte *Ethiopia* 9°4N 36°30E **257** F4
Nêkheb *Egypt* 25°10N 32°48E **256** B3
Neksø *Denmark* 55°4N 15°8E **163** J9
Nelamangala *India* 13°6N 77°24E **245** H3
Nelas *Portugal* 40°32N 7°52W **194** E3
Nelaug *Norway* 58°39N 8°40E **164** F5
Nelia *Australia* 20°39S 142°12E **280** C3
Nelidovo *Russia* 56°13N 32°49E **188** D7
Neligh *U.S.A.* 42°8N 98°2W **308** D4
Nelkan *Russia* 57°40N 136°4E **215** D14
Nellikuppam *India* 11°46N 79°43E **245** J4
Nellis Air Force Base ✈ (LSV) *U.S.A.* 36°14N 115°2W **124** A2
Nellore *India* 14°27N 79°59E **245** G4
Nelson *B.C., Canada* 49°30N 117°20W **296** D5
Nelson *N.Z.* 41°18S 173°16E **285** B8
Nelson *Lancs., U.K.* 53°50N 2°13W **168** D5
Nelson *Ariz., U.S.A.* 35°31N 113°19W **305** J7
Nelson *Nev., U.S.A.* 35°42N 114°49W **307** K12
Nelson □ *N.Z.* 41°20S 173°20E **285** B8
Nelson → *Canada* 54°33N 98°2W **297** C9
Nelson, C. *Vic., Australia* 38°26S 141°32E **282** E4
Nelson, C. *Papua N. G.* 9°0S 149°20E **286** E5
Nelson, Estrecho *Chile* 51°30S 75°0W **336** D2
Nelson Bay *Australia* 32°43S 152°9E **283** B10
Nelson Forks *Canada* 59°30N 124°0W **296** B4
Nelson House *Canada* 55°47N 98°51W **297** B9
Nelson L. *Canada* 55°48N 100°7W **297** B8
Nelson Lakes △ *N.Z.* 41°55S 172°44E **285** B7
Nelson's Dockyard *Antigua & B.* 17°1N 61°46W **322** b
Nelspoort *S. Africa* 32°7S 23°0E **270** D3
Nelspruit = Mbombela *S. Africa* 25°29S 30°59E **271** C5
Néma *Mauritania* 16°40N 7°15W **262** B3
Neman = Nemunas → *Lithuania* 55°25N 21°10E **184** C8
Neman *Russia* 55°2N 22°2E **184** C9
N'ematābād *Iran* 35°38N 51°21E **141** B2
Nembe *Nigeria* 4°32N 6°24E **263** E6
Nembrala *Indonesia* 10°53S 122°50E **278** B3
Nemea *Greece* 37°49N 22°40E **204** D4
Nemecký Brod = Havlíčkův Brod *Czech Rep.* 49°36N 15°33E **180** B8
Nemeiben L. *Canada* 55°20N 105°20W **297** B7
Nemërçkë, Mal *Albania* 40°15N 20°15E **202** F4
Nemira, Vf. *Romania* 46°17N 26°19E **183** D11
Nemiscau *Canada* 51°18N 76°54W **298** B4
Nemiscau, L. *Canada* 51°25N 76°40W **298** B4
Nemours = Ghazaouet *Algeria* 35°8N 1°50W **261** A4
Nemours *France* 48°16N 2°40E **173** D9
Nemrut Daği △ *Turkey* 38°0N 38°55E **213** C8
Nemšová *Slovak Rep.* 48°58N 18°7E **181** C11
Nemunas → *Lithuania* 55°25N 21°10E **184** C8
Nemuro *Japan* 43°20N 145°35E **220** C12
Nemuro-Kaikyō *Japan* 43°30N 145°30E **220** C12
Nemyriv *Ukraine* 50°7N 23°27E **185** H10
Nen Jiang → *China* 45°28N 124°30E **227** B13
Nenagh *Ireland* 52°52N 8°11W **166** D3
Nenana *U.S.A.* 64°34N 149°5W **303** D10
Nenasi *Malaysia* 3°9N 103°23E **237** L4
Nendo *Pac. Oc.* 10°45S 165°54E **277** C12
Nene → *U.K.* 52°49N 0°11E **169** E8
Nengkao Shan *Taiwan* 23°58N 121°16E **225** C3
Nengonengo *French Polynesia* 18°47S 141°48W **289** f
Nenita *Greece* 38°14N 26°6E **205** C8
Nenjiang *China* 49°10N 125°10E **219** B14
Neno *Malawi* 15°25S 34°40E **269** F3
Neo Chori *Greece* 38°25N 21°17E **204** C3
Neochori *Greece* 39°4N 21°0E **204** B2
Neodesha *U.S.A.* 37°25N 95°41W **308** G6
Neoga *U.S.A.* 39°19N 88°27W **311** E8
Neon Petritsi *Greece* 41°16N 23°15E **202** E7
Neópolis *Brazil* 10°18S 36°35W **332** D4
Neora Valley △ *India* 27°0N 88°45E **241** B2
Neosho *U.S.A.* 36°52N 94°22W **308** G6
Neosho → *U.S.A.* 36°48N 95°18W **314** C7
Nepal ■ *Asia* 28°0N 84°30E **243** F11
Nepalganj *Nepal* 28°5N 81°40E **243** E9
Nepalganj Road *India* 28°1N 81°41E **243** E9
Nepean B. *Australia* 35°42S 137°37E **282** C2
Nephi *U.S.A.* 39°43N 111°50W **304** G8
Nephin *Ireland* 54°1N 9°22W **166** B2
Nephin Beg Range *Ireland* 54°0N 9°40W **166** C2
Nepi *Italy* 42°14N 12°21E **199** F9
Nepomuk *Czech Rep.* 49°29N 13°35E **180** B6
Neppel = Moses Lake *U.S.A.* 47°8N 119°17W **304** C4
Neptune *U.S.A.* 40°13N 74°2W **313** F10
Neptune Is. *Australia* 35°17S 136°10E **282** C2
Neqāb *Iran* 36°42N 57°25E **247** B8
Nera → *Italy* 42°26N 12°24E **199** F9
Nera → *Romania* 44°48N 21°25E **182** F6
Nérac *France* 44°8N 0°21E **174** D4
Nerang *Australia* 27°58S 153°20E **281** D5
Nerastro, Sarīr *Libya* 24°20N 20°37E **258** D4
Neratovice *Czech Rep.* 50°16N 14°31E **180** A7
Nerchinsk *Russia* 52°0N 116°39E **215** D12
Nereju *Romania* 45°43N 26°43E **183** E11
Nerekhta *Russia* 57°26N 40°38E **188** D11
Neresnytsya *Ukraine* 48°7N 23°46E **183** B8
Néret, L. *Canada* 54°45N 70°44W **299** B5
Neretvanski Kanal *Croatia* 43°7N 17°10E **199** E14
Nerima *Japan* 35°44N 139°40E **140** A3
Neringa *Lithuania* 55°20N 21°5E **184** C8
Neris → *Lithuania* 55°8N 24°16E **188** E3
Nerja *Spain* 36°43N 3°55W **195** J7
Nerl → *Russia* 56°11N 40°34E **188** D11
Nerpio *Spain* 38°11N 2°16W **197** G2
Nerva *Spain* 37°42N 6°30W **195** H4
Nervi *Italy* 44°23N 9°2E **198** D6
Neryungri *Russia* 57°38N 124°28E **215** D13
Nes *Iceland* 65°53N 17°24W **155** B9
Nes *Buskerud, Norway* 60°34N 9°59E **164** D6
Nesbyen *Norway* 60°34N 9°8E **164** D6
Nescopeck *U.S.A.* 41°3N 76°12W **313** E8
Nesebŭr *Bulgaria* 42°41N 27°46E **203** D11
Neset *Norway* 61°53N 10°7E **164** C7
Nesflaten *Norway* 59°38N 6°48E **164** E3
Nesjahverfi *Iceland* 64°20N 15°15W **155** C11
Neskantaga *Canada* 52°14N 87°53W **298** B2
Neskaupstaður *Iceland* 65°9N 13°42W **155** B13
Nesland *Norway* 59°31N 7°59E **164** E4
Neslandsvatn *Norway* 58°57N 9°10E **164** F6
Nesodden *Norway* 59°48N 10°41E **133** B3
Nesoddtangen *Norway* 59°48N 10°40E **133** A3
Nesøya *Norway* 59°52N 10°31E **133** A2
Ness, L. *U.K.* 57°15N 4°32W **167** D4
Ness City *U.S.A.* 38°27N 99°54W **308** F4
Nessebar = Nesebŭr *Bulgaria* 42°41N 27°46E **203** D11
Nesterov = Zhovkva *Ukraine* 50°4N 23°58E **177** C12
Nesterov *Russia* 54°38N 22°41E **184** D9
Nestorio *Greece* 40°24N 21°5E **202** F5
Nestos → *Europe* 40°54N 24°49E **203** F8
Nesttun *Norway* 60°19N 5°20E **164** D2
Nesvady *Slovak Rep.* 47°56N 18°7E **181** D11
Nesvizh = Nyasvizh *Belarus* 53°14N 26°38E **177** B14
Netaji Subhash Chandra Bose Int. ✈ (CCU) *India* 22°38N 88°26E **124** B2
Netanya *Israel* 32°20N 34°51E **251** F5
Netarhat *India* 23°29N 84°16E **243** H11
Nete → *Belgium* 51°7N 4°14E **170** C4
Netherdale *Australia* 21°10S 148°33E **280** b
Netherlands ■ *Europe* 52°0N 5°30E **170** C5
Netherlands Antilles = ABC Islands *W. Indies* 12°15N 69°0W **322** g
Netherlands East Indies = Indonesia ■ *Asia* 5°0S 115°0E **235** C4
Netherlands Guiana = Suriname ■ *S. Amer.* 4°0N 56°0W **329** C6
Neto → *Italy* 39°12N 17°9E **201** C10
Netrakona *Bangla.* 24°53N 90°47E **241** C3
Netrang *India* 21°39N 73°21E **242** J5
Nettancourt *France* 48°51N 4°57E **173** D11
Nettetal *Germany* 51°19N 6°12E **178** D2
Nettilling L. *Canada* 66°30N 71°0W **295** D17
Nettuno *Italy* 41°27N 12°39E **200** A5
Netzahualcóyotl, Presa *Mexico* 17°8N 93°35W **319** D6
Neu Aubing *Germany* 48°8N 11°25E **131** B1
Neu-Bentschen = Zbąszynek *Poland* 52°16N 15°51E **185** F2
Neu Buch *Germany* 52°37N 13°31E **115** A4
Neu Buchhorst *Germany* 52°24N 13°44E **115** B5
Neu Fahrland *Germany* 52°26N 13°3E **115** B1
Neu-Isenburg *Germany* 50°3N 8°42E **179** E4
Neu-Langenburg = Tukuyu *Tanzania* 9°17S 33°35E **269** D3
Neu Lindenberg *Germany* 52°36N 13°33E **115** A4
Neu-Mecklenberg = New Ireland *Papua N. G.* 3°20S 151°50E **286** B6
Neu Pommern = New Britain *Papua N. G.* 5°50S 150°20E **286** C6
Neu-Sandec = Nowy Sącz *Poland* 49°40N 20°41E **185** J7
Neu Sandez = Nowy Sącz *Poland* 49°40N 20°41E **185** J7
Neu-Ulm *Germany* 48°22N 10°0E **179** G6
Neubiberg *Germany* 48°4N 11°40E **131** B3
Neubrandenburg *Germany* 53°33N 13°15E **178** B9
Neubukow *Germany* 54°2N 11°39E **178** A7
Neuburg *Germany* 48°44N 11°11E **179** G7
Neuchâtel *Switz.* 47°0N 6°55E **179** J2
Neuchâtel □ *Switz.* 47°0N 6°55E **179** J2
Neuchâtel, Lac de *Switz.* 46°53N 6°50E **179** J2
Neudau *Austria* 47°11N 16°6E **180** D9
Neuenberg an der Elbe = Nymburk *Czech Rep.* 50°10N 15°1E **180** A8
Neuenhagen *Germany* 52°32N 13°38E **115** A4
Neuenhaus *Germany* 52°30N 6°58E **178** C2
Neuessling *Austria* 48°15N 16°32E **142** A3
Neuf-Brisach *France* 48°1N 7°30E **173** D14
Neufahrn *Bayern, Germany* 48°41N 12°11E **179** G8
Neufahrn *Bayern, Germany* 48°18N 11°40E **179** G7
Neufchâteau *Belgium* 49°50N 5°25E **170** E5
Neufchâteau *Vosges, France* 48°21N 5°40E **173** D12
Neufchâtel-en-Bray *France* 49°44N 1°26E **172** C8
Neufchâtel-sur-Aisne *France* 49°26N 4°1E **173** C11
Neuhaus = Jindřichův Hradec *Czech Rep.* 49°10N 15°2E **180** B8
Neuhaus *Germany* 53°17N 10°56E **178** B6
Neuhäusel = Nové Zámky *Slovak Rep.* 48°2N 18°8E **181** C11
Neuhausen *Germany* 48°9N 11°32E **131** B2
Neuherberg *Germany* 48°13N 11°35E **131** A2
Neuhönow *Germany* 52°34N 13°44E **115** A5
Neuillé-Pont-Pierre *France* 47°33N 0°33E **172** E7
Neuilly-Plaisance *France* 48°51N 2°30E **134** A4
Neuilly-St-Front *France* 49°10N 3°15E **173** C10
Neuilly-sur-Marne *France* 48°51N 2°31E **134** A4
Neuilly-sur-Seine *France* 48°53N 2°15E **134** A2
Neukagran *Austria* 48°14N 16°27E **142** A2
Neukalen *Germany* 53°49N 12°46E **178** B8
Neukettenhof *Austria* 48°7N 16°28E **142** B2
Neukölln *Germany* 52°28N 13°25E **115** B3
Neumarkt = Nowy Targ *Poland* 49°29N 20°2E **185** J7
Neumarkt = Środa Śląska *Poland* 51°10N 16°36E **185** G3
Neumarkt *Germany* 49°26N 11°27E **179** F7
Neumarktl = Tržič *Slovenia* 46°22N 14°18E **199** B11
Neumayer *Antarctica* 71°0S 68°30W **151** D17
Neumittelwalde = Międzybórz *Poland* 51°25N 17°34E **185** G4
Neumünster *Germany* 54°4N 9°58E **178** A5
Neung-sur-Beuvron *France* 47°30N 1°50E **173** E8
Neunkirchen *Austria* 47°43N 16°4E **180** D9
Neunkirchen *Saarland, Germany* 49°20N 7°9E **179** F3
Neuperlach *Germany* 48°6N 11°37E **131** B2
Neuquén *Argentina* 38°55S 68°0W **336** A3
Neuquén □ *Argentina* 38°0S 69°50W **334** D2
Neuquén → *Argentina* 38°59S 68°0W **336** A3
Neuried *Germany* 48°5N 11°27E **131** B1
Neuruppin *Germany* 52°55N 12°48E **178** C8
Neusalz an der Oder = Nowa Sól *Poland* 51°48N 15°44E **185** G2
Neusäss *Germany* 48°24N 10°50E **179** G6
Neusatz = Novi Sad *Serbia* 45°18N 19°52E **182** E4
Neuse → *U.S.A.* 35°6N 76°29W **315** D16
Neusiedl *Austria* 47°57N 16°50E **181** D9
Neusiedler See *Austria* 47°50N 16°47E **181** D9
Neusiedler See-Seewinkel △ *Austria* 47°50N 16°45E **181** D9
Neusohl = Banská Bystrica *Slovak Rep.* 48°46N 19°14E **181** C12
Neuss *Germany* 51°11N 6°42E **178** D2
Neussargues-Moissac *France* 45°9N 3°0E **174** C7
Neustadt = Lwówek *Poland* 52°28N 16°10E **185** F3
Neustadt = Prudnik *Poland* 50°20N 17°38E **185** H4
Neustadt = Wejherowo *Poland* 54°35N 18°12E **184** D5
Neustadt *Bayern, Germany* 49°44N 12°10E **179** F8
Neustadt *Bayern, Germany* 48°48N 11°46E **179** G7
Neustadt *Bayern, Germany* 49°34N 10°37E **179** F6
Neustadt *Bayern, Germany* 50°19N 11°7E **179** E7
Neustadt *Brandenburg, Germany* 52°50N 12°27E **178** C8
Neustadt *Hessen, Germany* 50°51N 9°9E **178** E5
Neustadt *Niedersachsen, Germany* 52°30N 9°30E **178** C5
Neustadt *Rhld-Pfz., Germany* 49°21N 8°10E **179** F4
Neustadt *Sachsen, Germany* 51°2N 14°12E **178** D10
Neustadt *Schleswig-Holstein, Germany* 54°6N 10°49E **178** A6
Neustadt *Thüringen, Germany* 50°45N 11°43E **178** E7
Neustädtel = Nowe Miasteczko *Poland* 51°42N 15°42E **185** G2
Neustädtl = Novo Mesto *Slovenia* 45°47N 15°12E **199** C12
Neustettin = Szczecinek *Poland* 53°43N 16°41E **184** E3
Neustift am Walde *Austria* 48°14N 16°17E **142** A1
Neustrelitz *Germany* 53°21N 13°4E **178** B9
Neusüssenbrunn *Austria* 48°16N 16°29E **142** A2
Neutitschein = Nový Jičín *Czech Rep.* 49°30N 18°2E **181** B11
Neuvic *France* 45°23N 2°16E **174** C6
Neuville-sur-Saône *France* 45°52N 4°51E **175** C8
Neuvy-le-Roi *France* 47°36N 0°36E **172** E7
Neuvy-St-Sépulchre *France* 46°35N 1°48E **173** F8
Neuvy-sur-Barangeon *France* 47°20N 2°15E **173** E9
Neuwaldegg *Austria* 48°14N 16°17E **142** A1
Neuwedell = Drawno *Poland* 53°13N 15°46E **185** E2
Neuwerk *Germany* 53°55N 8°30E **178** B4
Neuwied *Germany* 50°26N 7°29E **178** E3
Neva → *Russia* 59°56N 30°20E **188** C6
Nevada *Iowa, U.S.A.* 42°1N 93°27W **310** B3
Nevada *Mo., U.S.A.* 37°51N 94°22W **310** G2
Nevada □ *U.S.A.* 39°0N 117°0W **304** G5
Nevada City *U.S.A.* 39°16N 121°1W **306** F6
Nevado, Cerro *Argentina* 35°30S 68°32W **334** D2
Nevado de Colima = Volcán de Colima △ *Mexico* 19°30N 103°40W **318** D4
Nevado de Tres Cruces △ *Chile* 27°13S 69°5W **334** B2
Nevado del Huila △ *Colombia* 3°5N 75°58W **328** C2
Nevasa *India* 19°34N 75°0E **244** E2
Neve, Sa. da *Angola* 13°43S 13°10E **265** E2
Neve Ya'akov *West Bank* 31°50N 35°14E **123** A2
Nevel *Russia* 56°0N 29°55E **188** D5
Nevelsk *Russia* 46°40N 141°51E **215** E15
Nevers *France* 47°0N 3°9E **173** F10
Nevertire *Australia* 31°50S 147°44E **283** A7
Neves *Brazil* 22°51S 43°5W **135** B2
Nevesinje *Bos.-H.* 43°14N 18°6E **202** C2
Neville *Canada* 49°58N 107°39W **297** D7
Nevinnomyssk *Russia* 44°40N 42°0E **191** H6
Nevis *St. Kitts & Nevis* 17°0N 62°30W **322** d
Nevis Pk. *St. Kitts & Nevis* 17°9N 62°34W **322** d
Nevlunghavn *Norway* 58°58N 9°53E **164** F6
Nevoso, Mte. = Snežnik *Slovenia* 45°36N 14°35E **199** C11
Nevrokop = Gotse Delchev *Bulgaria* 41°36N 23°46E **202** E7
Nevşehir *Turkey* 38°33N 34°40E **212** C6
Nevşehir □ *Turkey* 38°50N 34°40E **212** C6
Nevskoye *Russia* 54°32N 22°39E **184** D9
Nevyansk *Russia* 57°30N 60°13E **186** C11
New → *Guyana* 3°20N 57°37W **329** C6
New → *W. Va., U.S.A.* 38°10N 81°12W **309** F13
New Aiyansh *Canada* 55°12N 129°4W **296** B3
New Albany *Ind., U.S.A.* 38°18N 85°49W **311** F11
New Albany *Miss., U.S.A.* 34°29N 89°0W **315** D10
New Albany *Pa., U.S.A.* 41°36N 76°27W **313** E8
New Amsterdam *Guyana* 6°15N 57°36W **329** B6
New Athens *U.S.A.* 38°19N 89°53W **310** F7
New Atlas = Akhali Atoni *Georgia* 43°7N 40°50E **191** J5
New Baghdād *Iraq* 33°18N 44°28E **113** B2
New Baltimore *U.S.A.* 42°41N 82°44W **312** D2
New Barakpur *India* 22°40N 88°26E **124** A2
New Barbadoes = Hackensack *U.S.A.* 40°52N 74°4W **132** A1
New Bedford *U.S.A.* 41°38N 70°56W **313** E14
New Berlin = North Canton *U.S.A.* 40°53N 81°24W **312** F3
New Berlin *Ill., U.S.A.* 39°44N 89°55W **310** E7
New Berlin *N.Y., U.S.A.* 42°37N 75°20W **313** D9
New Berlin *Pa., U.S.A.* 40°50N 76°57W **312** F8
New Berlin *Wis., U.S.A.* 42°59N 88°6W **311** B8
New Bern *U.S.A.* 35°7N 77°3W **315** D16
New Bethlehem *U.S.A.* 41°0N 79°20W **312** F5
New Bight *Bahamas* 24°19N 75°24W **321** B4
New Bloomfield *U.S.A.* 40°25N 77°11W **312** F7
New Boston *U.S.A.* 33°28N 94°25W **314** E7
New Braunfels *U.S.A.* 29°42N 98°8W **314** G5
New Brighton *N.Z.* 43°29S 172°43E **285** D7
New Brighton *N.Y., U.S.A.* 40°38N 74°5W **132** C1
New Brighton *Pa., U.S.A.* 40°42N 80°19W **312** F4
New Britain *Papua N. G.* 5°50S 150°20E **286** C6
New Britain *Conn., U.S.A.* 41°40N 72°47W **313** E12
New Britain Trench *Pac. Oc.* 6°0S 153°0E **276** J3
New Brockton *U.S.A.* 31°23N 85°56W **316** D4
New Brookland = West Columbia *U.S.A.* 33°59N 81°4W **316** B8
New Brunswick *U.S.A.* 40°30N 74°27W **313** F10
New Brunswick □ *Canada* 46°50N 66°30W **299** C6
New Buffalo *U.S.A.* 41°47N 86°45W **311** C10
New Bussa *Nigeria* 9°53N 4°31E **263** D5
New Caledonia ◪ *Pac. Oc.* 21°0S 165°0E **288** d
New Caledonia Trough *Pac. Oc.* 30°0S 165°0E **288** L8
New Canada *S. Africa* 26°12S 27°56E **123** B1
New Canada Dam *S. Africa* 26°12S 27°56E **123** B1
New Carlisle *Ind., U.S.A.* 41°45N 86°32W **311** C10
New Carlisle *Ohio, U.S.A.* 39°56N 84°2W **311** E12
New Castile = Castilla-La Mancha □ *Spain* 39°30N 3°30W **195** F7
New Castle *Ind., U.S.A.* 39°55N 85°22W **311** E11
New Castle *Ky., U.S.A.* 38°26N 85°10W **311** F11
New Castle *Pa., U.S.A.* 41°0N 80°21W **312** F4
New City *U.S.A.* 41°9N 73°59W **313** E11
New Concord *U.S.A.* 39°59N 81°54W **312** G3
New Cross *U.K.* 51°28N 0°1W **125** B3
New Cumberland *U.S.A.* 40°30N 80°36W **312** F4
New Cuyama *U.S.A.* 34°57N 119°38W **307** L7
New Delhi *India* 28°36N 77°11E **120** B2
New Denver *Canada* 50°0N 117°25W **296** D5
New Don Pedro Res. *U.S.A.* 37°43N 120°24W **306** H6
New Dorp *U.S.A.* 40°34N 74°7W **132** C1
New Dorp Beach *U.S.A.* 40°33N 74°6W **132** C1
New Ellenton *U.S.A.* 33°28N 81°41W **316** B8
New England *U.S.A.* 43°0N 71°0W **301** G25
New England *N. Dak., U.S.A.* 46°32N 102°52W **308** B2
New England △ *Australia* 30°25S 152°30E **283** A10
New England Aquarium *Boston, U.S.A.* **116** b3
New England Ra. *Australia* 30°20S 151°45E **281** E5
New England Seamounts *Atl. Oc.* 38°0N 63°0W **152** C5
New Forest △ *U.K.* 50°53N 1°34W **169** G6
New Franklin *U.S.A.* 39°1N 92°44W **310** E4

New Galloway *U.K.* 55°5N 4°9W **167** F4
New Georgia Is. *Solomon Is.* 8°15S 157°30E **287** M9
New Georgia Sound *Solomon Is.* 8°0S 158°20E **287** L9
New Glarus *U.S.A.* 42°49N 89°38W **310** B7
New Glasgow *Canada* 45°35N 62°36W **299** C7
New Grant *Trin. & Tob.* 10°17N 61°19W **323** t
New Guinea *Oceania* 4°0S 136°0E **276** B7
New Halfa = Halfa al Jadidah *Sudan* 15°20N 35°35E **266** A4
New Hamburg *Canada* 43°23N 80°42W **312** C4
New Hampshire □ *U.S.A.* 44°0N 71°30W **313** C13
New Hampton *U.S.A.* 43°3N 92°19W **310** A4
New Hanover *Papua N. G.* 2°30S 150°10E **286** B6
New Hanover *KwaZulu Natal, S. Africa* 29°22S 30°31E **271** C5
New Harmony *U.S.A.* 38°8N 87°56W **311** F9
New Hartford *U.S.A.* 43°4N 75°18W **313** C9
New Haven *Conn., U.S.A.* 41°18N 72°55W **313** E12
New Haven *Ill., U.S.A.* 37°55N 88°8W **311** G8
New Haven *Ind., U.S.A.* 41°4N 85°1W **311** C11
New Haven *Mich., U.S.A.* 42°44N 82°48W **312** D2
New Haven *Mo., U.S.A.* 38°37N 91°13W **310** F5
New Haven *N.Y., U.S.A.* 43°28N 76°18W **313** C8
New Hazelton *Canada* 55°20N 127°30W **296** B3
New Hebrides = Vanuatu ■ *Pac. Oc.* 15°0S 168°0E **287** E6
New Holland *U.S.A.* 40°6N 76°5W **313** F8
New Iberia *U.S.A.* 30°1N 91°49W **314** F9
New Ireland *Papua N. G.* 3°20S 151°50E **286** B6
New Ireland □ *Papua N. G.* 3°0S 151°30E **286** B6
New Jersey □ *U.S.A.* 40°0N 74°30W **309** F16
New Kensington *U.S.A.* 40°34N 79°46W **312** F5
New Lexington *U.S.A.* 39°43N 82°13W **309** F12
New Liskeard *Canada* 47°31N 79°41W **298** C4
New London *Conn., U.S.A.* 41°22N 72°6W **313** E12
New London *Iowa, U.S.A.* 40°55N 91°24W **310** D5
New London *Mo., U.S.A.* 39°35N 91°24W **310** E5
New London *Ohio, U.S.A.* 41°5N 82°24W **312** E2
New London *Wis., U.S.A.* 44°23N 88°45W **308** C9
New Madrid *U.S.A.* 36°36N 89°32W **308** G9
New Malden *U.K.* 51°24N 0°15W **125** B2
New Martinsville *U.S.A.* 39°39N 80°52W **309** F13
New Meadows *U.S.A.* 44°58N 116°18W **304** D5
New Melones L. *U.S.A.* 37°57N 120°31W **306** H6
New Mexico □ *U.S.A.* 34°30N 106°0W **305** J11
New Miami *U.S.A.* 39°26N 84°32W **311** E12
New Milford *Conn., U.S.A.* 41°35N 73°25W **313** E11
New Milford *N.Y., U.S.A.* 40°56N 74°0W **132** A1
New Milford *Pa., U.S.A.* 41°52N 75°44W **313** E9
New Mumbai = Navi Mumbai *India* 19°5N 73°0E **130** A2
New Norcia *Australia* 30°57S 116°13E **279** F2
New Norfolk *Australia* 42°46S 147°2E **281** G4
New Orleans *U.S.A.* 29°57N 90°4W **131** B2
New Orleans Int. ✈ **(MSY)** *U.S.A.* 30°0N 90°15W **131** B1
New Palestine *U.S.A.* 39°45N 85°52W **311** E11
New Paris *U.S.A.* 39°51N 84°48W **311** E12
New Pekin *U.S.A.* 38°30N 86°0W **311** F10
New Philadelphia *U.S.A.* 40°30N 81°27W **312** F3
New Plymouth *N.Z.* 39°4S 174°5E **284** F3
New Plymouth *Idaho, U.S.A.* 43°58N 116°49W **304** E5
New Pomerania = New Britain *Papua N. G.* 5°50S 150°20E **286** C6
New Port Richey *U.S.A.* 28°16N 82°43W **317** G7
New Providence *Bahamas* 25°25N 77°35W **153** b
New Quay *U.K.* 52°13N 4°21W **169** E3
New Radnor *U.K.* 52°15N 3°9W **169** E4
New Richmond *Qué., Canada* 48°15N 65°45W **299** C6
New Richmond *Ohio, U.S.A.* 38°57N 84°17W **311** F12
New Richmond *Wis., U.S.A.* 45°7N 92°32W **308** C7
New River → *U.S.A.* 26°6N 80°6W **129** B3
New River Gorge ⌓ *U.S.A.* 37°53N 81°5W **309** G13
New Roads *U.S.A.* 30°42N 91°26W **314** F9
New Rochelle *U.S.A.* 40°55N 73°46W **313** F11
New Rockford *U.S.A.* 47°41N 99°8W **308** B4
New Romney *U.K.* 50°59N 0°57E **169** G8
New Ross *Ireland* 52°23N 6°57W **166** D5
New Salem *U.S.A.* 46°51N 101°25W **308** B3
New Scone = Scone *U.K.* 56°25N 3°24W **167** E5
New Sharon *U.S.A.* 41°28N 92°39W **310** C4
New Siberian I. = Novaya Sibir, Ostrov *Russia* 75°10N 150°0E **215** B16
New Siberian Is. = Novosibirskiye Ostrova *Russia* 75°0N 142°0E **215** B15
New Smyrna Beach *U.S.A.* 29°1N 80°56W **317** F9
New South Wales □ *Australia* 33°0S 146°0E **283** B7
New Stuyahok *U.S.A.* 59°29N 157°20W **303** G8
New Tecumseth = Alliston *Canada* 44°9N 79°52W **312** B5
New Territories *China* 22°23N 114°10E **122** A1
New Toronto *Canada* 43°35N 79°30W **141** B1
New Town = Nowe Miasto *Warsaw, Poland* **143** a2
New Town *Edinburgh, U.K.* **121** a2
New Town *N. Dak., U.S.A.* 47°59N 102°30W **308** B2
New Tredegar *U.K.* 51°44N 3°16W **169** F4
New Ulm *U.S.A.* 44°19N 94°28W **308** C6
New Utrecht *U.S.A.* 40°36N 73°59W **132** C2
New Vienna *U.S.A.* 39°19N 83°42W **311** E13
New Washington *Phil.* 11°39N 122°26E **233** F4
New Waterford *Canada* 46°13N 60°4W **299** C7
New Westminster *Canada* 49°13N 122°55W **306** A4
New York *U.S.A.* 40°43N 74°0W **132** B2
New York □ *U.S.A.* 43°0N 75°0W **313** D9
New York Avenue *Washington, D.C., U.S.A.* **143** a2
New York J.F. Kennedy Int. ✈ **(JFK)** *U.S.A.* 40°38N 73°47W **313** F11
New York La Guardia ✈ **(LGA)** *U.S.A.* 40°46N 73°52W **132** B2
New York University *New York, U.S.A.* **132** d2
New Zealand ■ *Oceania* 40°0S 176°0E **284** G5
Newaj → *India* 24°24N 76°49E **242** G7
Newala *Tanzania* 10°58S 39°18E **269** E4
Newark *Del., U.S.A.* 39°41N 75°46W **309** F16
Newark *N.J., U.S.A.* 40°44N 74°10W **313** F10
Newark *N.Y., U.S.A.* 43°3N 77°6W **312** C7
Newark *Ohio, U.S.A.* 40°3N 82°24W **312** F2
Newark B. *U.S.A.* 40°40N 74°8W **132** B1
Newark Liberty Int. ✈ **(EWR)** *U.S.A.* 40°42N 74°10W **313** F10
Newark-on-Trent *U.K.* 53°5N 0°48W **168** D7
Newark Valley *U.S.A.* 42°14N 76°11W **313** D8
Newbattle *U.K.* 55°53N 3°4W **121** B3
Newberg *U.S.A.* 45°18N 122°58W **304** D2
Newberry *Fla., U.S.A.* 29°39N 82°37W **317** F7
Newberry *Mich., U.S.A.* 46°21N 85°30W **309** B11
Newberry *S.C., U.S.A.* 34°17N 81°37W **315** D14
Newberry Springs *U.S.A.* 34°50N 116°41W **307** L10
Newboro L. *Canada* 44°38N 76°20W **313** B8
Newbridge *Ireland* 53°11N 6°48W **166** C5
Newburg *U.S.A.* 37°55N 91°54W **310** G5
Newburgh *Ont., Canada* 44°19N 76°52W **312** B8
Newburgh *Ind., U.S.A.* 37°57N 87°24W **311** G9
Newburgh *N.Y., U.S.A.* 41°30N 74°1W **313** E10
Newbury *W. Berkshire, U.K.* 51°24N 1°20W **169** F6
Newbury *N.H., U.S.A.* 43°19N 72°3W **313** B12
Newbury *Vt., U.S.A.* 44°5N 72°4W **313** B12
Newbury Park *U.K.* 51°34N 0°5E **125** A4
Newburyport *U.S.A.* 42°49N 70°53W **313** D14
Newcastle *N.S.W., Australia* 33°0S 151°46E **283** B9
Newcastle *N.B., Canada* 47°1N 65°38W **299** C6
Newcastle *Ont., Canada* 43°55N 78°35W **298** D4
Newcastle *Limerick, Ireland* 52°27N 9°3W **166** D2
Newcastle *St. Kitts & Nevis* 17°14N 62°42W **322** d
Newcastle *KwaZulu Natal, S. Africa* 27°45S 29°58E **271** C4
Newcastle *Down, U.K.* 54°13N 5°54W **166** B6
Newcastle *Calif., U.S.A.* 38°53N 121°8W **306** G5
Newcastle *Wyo., U.S.A.* 43°50N 104°11W **304** E11
Newcastle Emlyn *U.K.* 52°2N 4°28W **169** E3
Newcastle Ra. *Australia* 15°45S 130°15E **278** C5
Newcastle-under-Lyme *U.K.* 53°1N 2°14W **168** D5
Newcastle-upon-Tyne *U.K.* 54°58N 1°36W **168** C6
Newcastle Waters *Australia* 17°30S 133°28E **280** B1
Newcomb *U.S.A.* 43°58N 74°10W **313** C10
Newcomerstown *U.S.A.* 40°16N 81°36W **312** F3
Newcraighall *U.K.* 55°56N 3°5W **121** B3
Newdegate *Australia* 33°6S 119°0E **279** F2
Newell *Queens., Australia* 16°20S 145°16E **280** B4
Newell *Iowa, U.S.A.* 42°36N 95°0W **310** B1
Newell *S. Dak., U.S.A.* 44°43N 103°25W **308** C2
Newenham, C. *U.S.A.* 58°39N 162°11W **303** G7
Newfane *U.S.A.* 43°17N 78°43W **312** C6
Newfield *U.S.A.* 42°18N 76°33W **313** D8
Newfound L. *U.S.A.* 43°40N 71°47W **313** C13
Newfoundland *Canada* 49°0N 55°0W **299** C8
Newfoundland *Pa., U.S.A.* 41°18N 75°19W **313** E9
Newfoundland & Labrador □ *Canada* 52°0N 58°0W **299** B8
Newhalen *U.S.A.* 59°43N 154°54W **303** G9
Newham □ *U.K.* 51°31N 0°3E **125** A4
Newhaven *E. Sussex, U.K.* 50°47N 0°3E **169** G8
Newhaven *Edinburgh, U.K.* 55°59N 3°11W **121** B2
Newington *Edinburgh, U.K.* 55°56N 3°10W **121** B2
Newington *London, U.K.* **125** c5
Newington *Ga., U.S.A.* 32°35N 81°30W **316** C8
Newkirk *U.S.A.* 36°53N 97°3W **314** C6
Newlands *S. Africa* 26°10S 27°57E **123** B1
Newlyn *U.K.* 50°6N 5°34W **169** G2
Newman *W. Austral., Australia* 23°18S 119°45E **278** D2
Newman *Calif., U.S.A.* 37°19N 121°1W **306** H5
Newman *Ill., U.S.A.* 39°48N 87°59W **311** E9
Newmarket *Ont., Canada* 44°3N 79°28W **312** B5
Newmarket *Cork, Ireland* 52°13N 9°0W **166** D2
Newmarket *Jamaica* 18°9N 77°55W **320** a
Newmarket *Suffolk, U.K.* 52°15N 0°25E **169** E8
Newmarket *N.H., U.S.A.* 43°5N 70°56W **313** C14
Newnan *U.S.A.* 33°23N 84°48W **316** B5
Newport = Nieuwpoort *Curaçao* 12°3N 68°49W **322** g
Newport *Vic., Australia* 37°50S 144°51E **128** B1
Newport *Mayo, Ireland* 53°53N 9°33W **166** C2
Newport *I. of W., U.K.* 50°42N 1°17W **169** G6
Newport *Newport, U.K.* 51°35N 3°0W **169** F5
Newport *Ark., U.S.A.* 35°37N 91°16W **314** D9
Newport *Fla., U.S.A.* 30°11N 84°10W **316** E5
Newport *Ind., U.S.A.* 39°53N 87°25W **311** E9
Newport *Ky., U.S.A.* 39°5N 84°29W **311** E12
Newport *N.H., U.S.A.* 43°22N 72°10W **313** C12
Newport *N.Y., U.S.A.* 43°11N 75°1W **313** C9
Newport *Oreg., U.S.A.* 44°39N 124°3W **304** D1
Newport *Pa., U.S.A.* 40°29N 77°8W **312** F7
Newport *R.I., U.S.A.* 41°29N 71°19W **313** E13
Newport *Tenn., U.S.A.* 35°58N 83°11W **315** D13
Newport *Vt., U.S.A.* 44°56N 72°13W **313** B12
Newport *Wash., U.S.A.* 48°11N 117°3W **304** B5
Newport □ *U.K.* 51°33N 3°1W **169** F4
Newport Beach *U.S.A.* 33°37N 117°56W **307** M9
Newport News *U.S.A.* 36°58N 76°25W **309** G15
Newport Pagnell *U.K.* 52°5N 0°43W **169** E7
Newquay *U.K.* 50°25N 5°6W **169** G2
Newry *U.K.* 54°11N 6°21W **166** B5
Newry Islands △ *Australia* 20°51S 148°56E **280** b
Newtok *U.S.A.* 60°56N 164°38W **303** F6
Newton *Ga., U.S.A.* 31°9N 84°20W **316** D5
Newton *Ill., U.S.A.* 38°59N 88°10W **311** F8
Newton *Iowa, U.S.A.* 41°42N 93°3W **310** C3
Newton *Kans., U.S.A.* 38°3N 97°21W **308** F5
Newton *Mass., U.S.A.* 42°21N 71°12W **116** B1
Newton *Miss., U.S.A.* 32°19N 89°10W **315** E10
Newton *N.C., U.S.A.* 35°40N 81°13W **315** D14
Newton *N.J., U.S.A.* 41°3N 74°45W **313** E10
Newton *Tex., U.S.A.* 30°51N 93°46W **314** F8
Newton Abbot *U.K.* 50°32N 3°37W **169** G4
Newton Aycliffe *U.K.* 54°37N 1°34W **168** C6
Newton Falls *N.Y., U.S.A.* 44°12N 74°59W **313** B10
Newton Falls *Ohio, U.S.A.* 41°11N 80°59W **312** E4
Newton L. *U.S.A.* 38°55N 88°15W **311** F8
Newton Stewart *U.K.* 54°57N 4°30W **167** G4
Newton Terrace *Barbados* 13°4N 59°32W **323** f
Newtonbrook *Canada* 43°47N 79°24W **141** A2
Newtongrange *U.K.* 55°53N 3°3W **121** B3
Newtonmore *U.K.* 57°4N 4°8W **167** D4
Newtontoppen *Svalbard* 79°0N 17°30E **154** B12
Newtonville *U.S.A.* 42°20N 71°11W **116** A1
Newtown *N.S.W., Australia* 33°54S 151°11E **139** B2
Newtown *Powys, U.K.* 52°31N 3°19W **169** E4
Newtown *Ind., U.S.A.* 40°13N 87°9W **311** D9
Newtown *Mo., U.S.A.* 40°22N 93°20W **310** D3
Newtownabbey *U.K.* 54°40N 5°56W **166** B6
Newtownards *U.K.* 54°36N 5°42W **166** B6
Newtownbarry = Bunclody *Ireland* 52°39N 6°40W **166** D5
Newtownstewart *U.K.* 54°43N 7°23W **166** B4
Newville *U.S.A.* 40°10N 77°24W **312** F7
Nexon *France* 45°41N 1°11E **174** C5
Neya *Russia* 58°21N 43°49E **190** A6
Neyrīz *Iran* 29°15N 54°19E **247** D7
Neyshābūr *Iran* 36°10N 58°50E **247** B8
Neyveli *India* 11°32N 79°29E **245** J4
Neyyattinkara *India* 8°26N 77°5E **245** K3
Nezametny = Aldan *Russia* 58°40N 125°30E **215** D13
Nezhin = Nizhyn *Ukraine* 51°5N 31°55E **189** G6
Nezperce *U.S.A.* 46°14N 116°14W **304** C5
Nezvysko *Ukraine* 48°46N 25°15E **183** B10
Nga, Laem *Thailand* 7°55N 98°27E **237** a
Ngaanyatjarra ☼ *Australia* 22°40S 127°0E **278** D4
Ngabang *Indonesia* 0°23N 109°55E **235** B3
Ngabe *Congo* 3°12S 16°12E **264** C3
Ngabordamlu, Tanjung *Indonesia* 6°56S 134°11E **231** F8
N'Gage *Angola* 7°46S 15°15E **265** D3
Ngaiphaipi *Burma* 22°14N 93°15E **241** D4
Ngala *Nigeria* 12°20N 14°11E **263** C7
Ngaliwurru Nungali ☼ *Australia* 15°42S 130°4E **278** C5
Ngalurrtju ☼ *Australia* 22°44S 132°5E **278** D5
Ngama *Chad* 11°45N 17°2E **259** F3
Ngambé *Centre, Cameroon* 5°48N 11°29E **263** D7
Ngambé *Littoral, Cameroon* 4°21N 10°40E **263** E7
Ngami Depression *Botswana* 20°30S 22°46E **270** B3
Ngamo *Zimbabwe* 19°3S 27°32E **269** F2
Ngamring *China* 29°14N 87°10E **218** F6
Nganbéto, L. de *Togo* 7°26N 1°25E **263** D5
Ngangala *South Sudan* 4°42N 31°55E **257** G3
Nganglong Kangri *China* 33°0N 81°0E **243** C9
Ngao *Thailand* 18°46N 99°59E **236** C2
Ngaoundéré *Cameroon* 7°15N 13°35E **264** A2
Ngapali *Burma* 18°26N 94°19E **241** F5
Ngapara *N.Z.* 44°57S 170°46E **285** E5
Ngape *Burma* 20°2N 94°28E **241** E5
Ngara *Tanzania* 2°29S 30°40E **268** C3
Ngardmau *Palau* 7°37N 134°34E **288** c
Ngardmau B. *Palau* 7°38N 134°34E **288** c
Ngardololok *Palau* 7°0N 134°14E **288** c
Ngaregur *Palau* 7°45N 134°37E **288** c
Ngarluma ☼ *Australia* 21°30S 118°30E **278** D2
Ngaruawahia *N.Z.* 37°42S 175°11E **284** D4
Ngaruroro → *N.Z.* 39°34S 176°55E **284** F5
Ngatangiia *Cook Is.* 21°14S 159°43W **289** h
Ngatapa *N.Z.* 38°32S 177°45E **284** E6
Ngathainggyaung *Burma* 17°24N 95°5E **241** G5
Ngau Chi Wan *China* 22°20N 114°12E **122** A2
Ngau Tau Kok *China* 22°19N 114°12E **122** B2
Ngauruhoe, Mt. *N.Z.* 39°13S 175°45E **284** F4
Ngawi *Indonesia* 7°24S 111°26E **235** D4
Ngcobo *S. Africa* 31°37S 28°0E **271** D4
Ngele *Dem. Rep. of the Congo* 0°30S 20°22E **264** C4
Ngelebok *Cameroon* 4°16N 14°3E **264** B2
Ngeregong *Palau* 7°6N 134°21E **288** c
Ngergoi *Palau* 7°5N 134°15E **288** c
Ngeru *Uganda* 0°27N 33°10E **268** B3
Ngesebus I. *Palau* 7°3N 134°15E **288** c
Nggatokae *Solomon Is.* 8°45S 158°15E **287** M10
Nggela Pile *Solomon Is.* 9°5S 160°20E **287** M11
Nggela Sule *Solomon Is.* 9°2S 160°12E **287** M11
Nghia Lo *Vietnam* 21°33N 104°28E **228** G5
Ngidinga *Dem. Rep. of the Congo* 5°37S 15°17E **265** D3
Ngo *Congo* 2°29S 15°45E **264** C3
Ngoap *Cameroon* 4°9N 12°51E **264** B2
Ngobasangel *Palau* 7°16N 134°19E **288** c
Ngoboli *South Sudan* 4°57N 32°37E **257** G3
Ngol = Raqaba ez Zarqa → *South Sudan* 9°14N 29°44E **257** F2
N'Gola *Angola* 14°10S 14°30E **265** E2
Ngoma *Malawi* 13°8S 33°45E **269** E3
Ngomahura *Zimbabwe* 20°26S 30°43E **269** G3
Ngomba *Tanzania* 8°20S 32°53E **269** D3
Ngomeni, Ras *Kenya* 2°59S 40°14E **268** C5
Ngong *Kenya* 1°22S 36°39E **268** C4
Ngong Shuen Chau *China* 22°19N 114°8E **122** B1
Ngongotaha *N.Z.* 38°5S 176°12E **284** E5
Ngonye Falls *Zambia* 16°40S 23°25E **265** F4
Ngop *South Sudan* 6°17N 30°9E **257** F3
Ngoring Hu *China* 34°55N 97°5E **218** E8
Ngorkou *Mali* 15°40N 3°41W **262** B4
Ngorongoro *Tanzania* 3°11S 35°32E **268** C4
Ngorongoro ⌓ *Tanzania* 2°40S 35°30E **268** C4
Ngoto *C.A.R.* 3°59N 17°19E **264** B3
Ngouo, Dj. *C.A.R.* 7°55N 24°38E **264** A4
Ngoura *Chad* 12°44N 16°21E **259** F3
Ngouri *Chad* 13°38N 15°22E **259** F3
Ngourti *Niger* 15°19N 13°12E **259** E2
Ngoussou *Gabon* 3°0S 11°7E **264** C2
Ngozi *Burundi* 2°54S 29°50E **268** C2
Ngua Kok Wan *China* 22°21N 114°5E **122** A1
Ngudu *Tanzania* 2°58S 33°25E **268** C3
Nguigmi *Niger* 14°20N 13°20E **259** F2
Nguila *Cameroon* 4°41N 11°43E **263** E7
Nguiu *Australia* 11°46S 130°38E **278** B5
Ngukurr *Australia* 14°44S 134°44E **280** A1
Ngum → *Laos* 18°31N 102°32E **236** C4
Nguna *Vanuatu* 17°26S 168°22E **287** G6
Ngundu *Zimbabwe* 18°11S 31°15E **269** F3
Ngunga *Tanzania* 3°37S 33°37E **268** C3
Nguru *Nigeria* 12°56N 10°29E **263** C7
Nguru Mts. *Tanzania* 6°0S 37°30E **268** D4
Ngusi *Malawi* 14°0S 34°50E **269** E3
Nguyen Binh *Vietnam* 22°39N 105°56E **228** F5
Ngwaketse □ *Botswana* 25°0S 25°0E **270** C3
Ngwedaung *Burma* 19°31N 97°9E **241** F6
Nha Bang *Vietnam* 10°37N 105°0E **237** G5
Nha Trang *Vietnam* 12°16N 109°10E **237** F7
Nhacoongo *Mozam.* 24°18S 35°14E **271** B6
Nhamaabué *Mozam.* 17°25S 35°5E **269** F4
Nhambiquara *Brazil* 12°50S 59°49W **331** C6
Nhamundá *Brazil* 2°14S 56°43W **329** D6
Nhamundá → *Brazil* 2°12S 56°41W **329** D6
Nhangulaze, L. *Mozam.* 24°0S 34°30E **271** B5
Nharêa *Angola* 11°38S 16°58E **265** E3
Nharnuwangga, Wajarri and Ngarlawangga ☼ *Australia* 24°50S 118°0E **279** D2
Nhava Sheva *India* 18°58N 72°55E **130** B2
Nhecolândia *Brazil* 19°17S 56°58W **331** D6
Nhill *Australia* 36°18S 141°40E **282** D4
Nho Quan *Vietnam* 20°18N 105°45E **228** G5
Nhulunbuy *Australia* 12°10S 137°20E **280** A2
Nhundo *Angola* 14°25S 21°23E **265** E4
Nia-nia *Dem. Rep. of the Congo* 1°30N 27°40E **268** B2
Niafounké *Mali* 16°0N 4°5W **262** B4
Niagara Falls *Ont., Canada* 43°7N 79°5W **312** C5
Niagara Falls *N.Y., U.S.A.* 43°5N 79°4W **312** C6
Niagara-on-the-Lake *Canada* 43°15N 79°4W **312** C5
Niah *Malaysia* 3°58N 113°46E **235** B4
Nialaha'u Pt. *Solomon Is.* 9°47S 161°34E **287** M11
Niamey *Niger* 13°27N 2°6E **263** C5
Niamtougou *Togo* 9°46N 1°6E **263** D5
Niandan-Koro *Guinea* 11°5N 9°15W **262** C3
Nianforando *Guinea* 9°37N 10°36W **262** D2
Niangara *Dem. Rep. of the Congo* 3°42N 27°50E **268** B2
Niangay, L. *Mali* 15°50N 3°0W **262** B4
Niangbo *Ivory C.* 8°49N 5°10W **262** D3
Niangoloko *Burkina Faso* 10°15N 4°55W **262** C4
Niangua → *U.S.A.* 38°58N 92°48W **310** G4
Niantic *U.S.A.* 41°20N 72°11W **313** E12
Niari *Congo* 4°9S 14°9E **264** C2
Niaro *Sudan* 10°38N 31°31E **257** E3
Nias *Indonesia* 1°0N 97°30E **234** B1
Niassa □ *Mozam.* 13°30S 36°0E **269** E4
Niassa ⌓ *Mozam.* 12°4S 36°57E **269** E4
Niāvarān *Iran* 35°47N 51°29E **141** A2
Nibāk *Si. Arabia* 24°25N 50°50E **247** E7
Nibe *Denmark* 56°59N 9°38E **163** H3
Nibra *India* 22°36N 88°15E **124** B1
Nicaragua ■ *Cent. Amer.* 11°40N 85°30W **320** D2
Nicaragua, L. de *Nic.* 12°0N 85°30W **320** D2
Nicastro *Italy* 38°59N 16°19E **201** D9
Nice *France* 43°42N 7°14E **175** E11
Nice-Côte-d'Azur ✈ **(NCE)** *France* 43°41N 7°12E **175** E11
Niceville *U.S.A.* 30°31N 86°30W **317** E3
Nichicun, L. *Canada* 53°5N 71°0W **299** B5
Nichinan *Japan* 31°38N 131°23E **222** F3
Nicholás, Canal *Caribbean* 23°30N 80°5W **320** B3
Nicholas Channel = Nicholás, Canal *Caribbean* 23°30N 80°5W **320** B3
Nicholasville *U.S.A.* 37°53N 84°34W **311** G12
Nicholls *U.S.A.* 31°31N 82°38W **316** D7
Nichols *U.S.A.* 42°1N 76°22W **313** D8
Nicholson *W. Austral., Australia* 18°2S 128°54E **278** C4
Nicholson *Pa., U.S.A.* 41°37N 75°47W **313** E9
Nicholson → *Australia* 17°31S 139°36E **280** B2
Nicholson L. *Canada* 62°40N 102°40W **297** A8
Nicholson Ra. *Australia* 27°15S 116°45E **279** E2
Nicholville *U.S.A.* 44°41N 74°39W **313** B10
Nickerie → *Suriname* 5°58N 57°0W **329** B6
Nico Pérez = José Batlle y Ordóñez *Uruguay* 33°20S 55°10W **335** C4
Nicobar Is. *Ind. Oc.* 8°0N 93°30E **245** L11
Nicola *Canada* 50°12N 120°40W **296** C4
Nicolls Town *Bahamas* 25°8N 78°0W **320** A4
Nicosia *Cyprus* 35°10N 33°25E **207** E9
Nicosia *Italy* 37°45N 14°24E **201** E7
Nicótera *Italy* 38°33N 15°56E **201** D8
Nicoya *Costa Rica* 10°9N 85°27W **320** D2
Nicoya, G. de *Costa Rica* 10°0N 85°0W **320** E3
Nicoya, Pen. de *Costa Rica* 9°45N 85°40W **320** E2
Nictheroy = Niterói *Brazil* 22°53S 43°7W **135** B2
Nida *Lithuania* 55°20N 21°4E **184** C8
Nidāl *Iraq* 33°19N 44°25E **113** B2
Nidaros = Trondheim *Norway* 63°36N 10°25E **164** A7
Nidd → *U.K.* 53°59N 1°23W **168** D6
Nidda *Germany* 50°23N 9°1E **179** E5
Nidda → *Germany* 50°17N 8°48E **179** E4
Niddrie *Vic., Australia* 37°44S 144°51E **128** A1
Niddrie *Edinburgh, U.K.* 55°56N 3°7W **121** B3
Nidri *Greece* 38°43N 20°42E **207** B2
Nidwalden □ *Switz.* 46°50N 8°25E **179** J4
Nidzica *Poland* 53°25N 20°28E **185** E7
Niebüll *Germany* 54°46N 8°48E **178** A4
Nied → *Germany* 49°23N 6°40E **173** C13
Nieder Neuendorf *Germany* 52°36N 13°12E **115** A2
Niederaula *Germany* 50°47N 9°36E **178** E5
Niederbayern □ *Germany* 48°40N 12°50E **179** G8
Niederbronn-les-Bains *France* 48°57N 7°39E **173** D14
Niedere Tauern *Austria* 47°20N 14°0E **180** D7
Niederlausitz *Germany* 51°42N 13°59E **178** D9
Niederösterreich □ *Austria* 48°25N 15°40E **180** C8
Niedersachsen □ *Germany* 52°50N 9°0E **178** C4
Niedersächsisches Wattenmeer △ *Germany* 53°45N 7°30E **178** B3
Niederschöneweide *Germany* 52°27N 13°30E **115** B3
Niederschönhausen *Germany* 52°35N 13°25E **115** A3
Niefang *Eq. Guin.* 1°50N 10°14E **264** B2
Niekerkshoop *S. Africa* 29°19S 22°51E **270** C3
Nielle *Ivory C.* 10°5N 5°38W **262** C3
Niellim *Chad* 9°42N 17°49E **259** G3
Niem *C.A.R.* 6°12N 15°14E **264** A3
Niemba *Dem. Rep. of the Congo* 5°58S 28°24E **268** D2
Niemen = Nemunas → *Lithuania* 55°25N 21°10E **184** C8
Niemeyer *Brazil* 22°59S 43°16W **135** B1
Niemodlin *Poland* 50°38N 17°38E **185** H4
Niemur *Australia* 35°17S 144°9E **282** C6
Nienburg *Germany* 52°39N 9°13E **178** C5
Niepolomice *Poland* 50°3N 20°13E **185** H7
Niers → *Germany* 51°43N 5°57E **178** D1
Niesky *Germany* 51°17N 14°49E **178** D10
Nieszawa *Poland* 52°52N 18°50E **185** F5
Nieu Bethesda *S. Africa* 31°51S 24°34E **270** D3
Nieuw Amsterdam *Suriname* 5°53N 55°5W **329** B6
Nieuw Nickerie *Suriname* 6°0N 56°59W **329** B6
Nieuwe Kerk *Amsterdam, Neths.* **112** a2
Nieuwendam *Neths.* 52°23N 4°57E **112** A2
Nieuwoudtville *S. Africa* 31°23S 19°7E **270** D2
Nieuwpoort *Belgium* 51°8N 2°45E **170** C2
Nieuwpoort *Curaçao* 12°3N 68°49W **322** g
Nieves, Pico de las *Canary Is.* 27°57N 15°35W **153** e1
Nièvre □ *France* 47°10N 3°40E **173** E10
Nif *Micronesia* 9°28N 138°4E **287** S16
Niga *Mali* 13°38N 5°27W **262** C3
Niğde *Turkey* 37°58N 34°40E **212** D6
Niğde □ *Turkey* 38°0N 34°30E **212** D6
Nigel *S. Africa* 26°27S 28°25E **271** C4
Niger □ *Nigeria* 10°0N 5°30E **263** D6
Niger ■ *W. Afr.* 17°30N 10°0E **259** E2
Niger → *W. Afr.* 5°33N 6°33E **263** D6
Niger Delta *Africa* 5°0N 6°0E **263** E6
Nigeria ■ *W. Afr.* 8°30N 8°0E **263** D6
Nighasin *India* 28°14N 80°52E **243** E9
Nightcaps *N.Z.* 45°57S 168°2E **285** F3
Nightmute *U.S.A.* 60°29N 164°44W **303** F6
Nigrita *Greece* 40°56N 23°29E **202** F7
Nihoa *U.S.A.* 23°6N 161°58W **302** G11
Nihon = Japan ■ *Asia* 36°0N 136°0E **221** G8
Nihonbashi *Tokyo, Japan* **140** b5
Nii-Jima *Japan* 34°20N 139°15E **223** C11
Niigata *Japan* 37°58N 139°0E **220** F9
Niigata □ *Japan* 37°15N 138°45E **221** F9
Niihama *Japan* 33°55N 133°16E **222** D5
Ni'ihau *U.S.A.* 21°54N 160°9W **302** B1
Niimi *Japan* 34°59N 133°28E **222** C5
Niipperi *Finland* 60°18N 24°45E **121** B1
Niislel Khureheh = Ulaanbaatar *Mongolia* 47°55N 106°53E **218** B10
Niitsu *Japan* 37°48N 139°7E **220** F9
Nij Laluk *India* 27°7N 93°56E **241** B4
Nijar *Spain* 36°53N 2°15W **197** J2
Nijil *Jordan* 30°32N 35°33E **251** H6
Nijkerk *Neths.* 52°13N 5°30E **170** B5
Nijmegen *Neths.* 51°50N 5°52E **170** C5
Nijverdal *Neths.* 52°22N 6°28E **170** B6
Nīk Pey *Iran* 36°50N 48°10E **213** D13
Nikao *Cook Is.* 21°12S 159°48W **289** h
Nikaweratiya *Sri Lanka* 7°45N 80°7E **245** L5
Nike *Nigeria* 6°26N 7°29E **263** D6
Nikea *Greece* 37°57N 23°38E **112** B1
Nikel *Russia* 69°24N 30°13E **160** B24
Nikiboko *Bonaire* 12°9N 68°16W **322** h
Nikiniki *Indonesia* 9°49S 124°30E **278** A3
Nikisiani *Greece* 40°57N 24°9E **203** F8
Nikiski *U.S.A.* 60°41N 151°18W **303** F10
Nikiti *Greece* 40°13N 23°43E **202** F7
Nikitinskiye promysly = Kirovskiy *Russia* 45°51N 48°11E **191** H9
Nikki *Benin* 9°58N 3°12E **263** D5
Nikkō *Japan* 36°45N 139°35E **223** A11
Nikkō △ *Japan* 36°56N 139°37E **221** F9
Nikolai *U.S.A.* 62°58N 154°10W **303** E9
Nikolainkaupunki = Vaasa *Finland* 63°6N 21°38E **160** E19
Nikolaistad = Vaasa *Finland* 63°6N 21°38E **160** E19
Nikolassee *Germany* 52°25N 13°12E **115** B2
Nikolayev = Mykolayiv *Ukraine* 46°58N 32°0E **189** J7
Nikolayevsk *Russia* 50°0N 45°35E **190** E7
Nikolayevsk-na-Amur *Russia* 53°8N 140°44E **215** D15
Nikolsburg = Mikulov *Czech Rep.* 48°48N 16°39E **181** D9
Nikolsk *Russia* 53°49N 46°4E **190** D8
Nikolsk-Ussuriysky = Ussuriysk *Russia* 43°48N 131°59E **220** C5
Nikolskaya Pestravka = Nikolsk *Russia* 53°49N 46°4E **190** D8
Nikolski *U.S.A.* 52°56N 168°52W **303** K5
Nikolskiy *Russia* 55°49N 37°29E **129** B1
Nikolskoye = Ussuriysk *Russia* 43°48N 131°59E **220** C5
Nikolskoye *Russia* 55°12N 166°0E **215** D17
Nikolsky Khutor = Sursk *Russia* 53°3N 45°40E **190** D7
Nikopol *Bulgaria* 43°43N 24°54E **203** C8
Nikopol *Ukraine* 47°35N 34°25E **189** J8
Nikopolis *Greece* 39°5N 20°43E **207** A2
Niksar *Turkey* 40°31N 37°2E **212** B7
Nīkshahr *Iran* 26°15N 60°10E **247** E9
Nikšić *Montenegro* 42°50N 18°57E **202** D2
Nikumaroro *Kiribati* 4°40S 174°32W **277** A16
Nikunau *Kiribati* 1°22S 176°28E **277** A14
Nîl, Nahr en → *Africa* 30°10N 31°6E **256** H7
Nîl el Abyad → *Sudan* 15°38N 32°31E **257** D3
Nîl el Azraq → *Sudan* 15°38N 32°31E **257** D3
Nila *Indonesia* 6°44S 129°31E **231** F7
Nilakkottai *India* 10°10N 77°52E **245** J3
Niland *U.S.A.* 33°14N 115°31W **307** M11
Nilanga *India* 18°6N 76°46E **244** E3
Nile = Nîl, Nahr en → *Africa* 30°10N 31°6E **256** H7
Nile Delta *Egypt* 31°40N 31°0E **256** H7
Niles *Ill., U.S.A.* 42°1N 87°48W **119** A2
Niles *Mich., U.S.A.* 41°50N 86°15W **311** C10
Niles *Ohio, U.S.A.* 41°11N 80°46W **312** E4
Niles Center = Skokie *U.S.A.* 42°2N 87°43W **119** A2
Nileshwar *India* 12°15N 75°6E **245** H2
Nilgiri Hills *India* 11°30N 76°30E **245** J3
Nilo Peçanha *Brazil* 13°37S 39°6W **333** D4
Nilsebu *Norway* 59°11N 6°39E **164** E3
Nilüfer → *Turkey* 40°18N 28°27E **203** F12
Nim Ka Thana *India* 27°44N 75°48E **242** F6
Nimach *India* 24°30N 74°56E **242** G6
Nimba, Mt. *Africa* 7°37N 8°25W **262** D3
Nimbahera *India* 24°37N 74°45E **242** G6
Nîmes *France* 43°50N 4°23E **175** E8
Nimfaíon, Ákra = Pines, Akra *Greece* 40°5N 24°20E **203** F8
Nimmitabel *Australia* 36°29S 149°15E **283** D8
Nīmrūz □ *Afghan.* 30°0N 62°0E **240** C1
Nimta *India* 22°40N 88°24E **124** A2
Nimule *South Sudan* 3°32N 32°3E **257** G3
Nimule △ *South Sudan* 3°38N 32°2E **257** G3
Nin *Croatia* 44°16N 15°12E **199** D12
Nīnawá *Iraq* 36°25N 43°10E **213** D10
Nīnawá □ *Iraq* 36°15N 43°0E **246** B4
Ninda *Angola* 14°47S 21°24E **265** E4
Nindigully *Australia* 28°21S 148°50E **281** D4
Nine Degree Channel *India* 9°0N 73°0E **245** K1
Ninepin Group *China* 22°16N 114°21E **219** a
Ninety Mile Beach *N.Z.* 34°48S 173°0E **284** A2
Ninety Mile Beach, The *Australia* 38°15S 147°24E **283** E7
Ninety Six *U.S.A.* 34°11N 82°1W **316** A7
Ninetyeast Ridge *Ind. Oc.* 1°0S 90°0E **273** E7
Nineveh = Nīnawá *Iraq* 36°25N 43°10E **213** D10
Ning Xian *China* 35°30N 107°58E **226** G4
Ningaloo Marine ⌓ *Australia* 22°23S 113°32E **278** D1
Ning'an *China* 44°22N 129°20E **227** B15
Ningbo *China* 29°51N 121°28E **229** C13
Ningcheng *China* 41°32N 119°53E **227** D10
Ningde *China* 26°38N 119°23E **229** D12
Ningdu *China* 26°25N 115°59E **229** D10
Ningerum *Papua N. G.* 5°41S 141°8E **286** C1
Ninggang *China* 26°42N 113°55E **229** D9
Ningguo *China* 30°35N 119°0E **229** B12
Ninghai *China* 29°15N 121°27E **229** C13
Ninghua *China* 26°14N 116°45E **229** D11
Ningi *Nigeria* 10°55N 9°30E **263** C6
Ningjin *China* 37°35N 114°57E **226** F8
Ningjing Shan *China* 31°0N 98°20E **228** C2
Ninglang *China* 27°20N 100°55E **228** D3
Ningling *China* 34°25N 115°22E **226** G8
Ningming *China* 22°8N 107°4E **228** F6
Ningnan *China* 27°5N 102°36E **228** D4
Ningpo = Ningbo *China* 29°51N 121°28E **229** C13
Ningqiang *China* 32°47N 106°15E **226** H4
Ningshan *China* 33°21N 108°21E **228** A7
Ningsia Hui A.R. = Ningxia Huizu Zizhiqu □ *China* 38°0N 106°0E **226** F4
Ningwu *China* 39°0N 112°18E **226** E7
Ningxia Huizu Zizhiqu □ *China* 38°0N 106°0E **226** F4
Ningxiang *China* 28°15N 112°30E **229** C9
Ningyang *China* 35°47N 116°45E **226** G9
Ningyuan *China* 25°37N 111°57E **229** E8
Ninh Binh *Vietnam* 20°15N 105°55E **228** G5
Ninh Giang *Vietnam* 20°44N 106°24E **236** B6
Ninh Hoa *Vietnam* 12°30N 109°7E **236** F7
Ninh Ma *Vietnam* 12°48N 109°21E **236** F7
Nini-Suhien △ *Ghana* 5°20N 2°34W **262** D4
Ninigo Group *Papua N. G.* 1°22S 144°17E **286** A3
Ninove *Belgium* 50°51N 4°2E **170** D4
Ninoy Aquino Int. ✈ **(MNL)** *Phil.* 14°31N 121°0E **127** B2
Nioaque *Brazil* 21°5S 55°50W **335** A4
Niobrara *U.S.A.* 42°45N 98°2W **308** D4
Niobrara → *U.S.A.* 42°46N 98°3W **308** D4
Nioki *Dem. Rep. of the Congo* 2°47S 17°40E **264** C3
Niokolo-Koba △ *Senegal* 13°3N 13°2W **262** C2
Niono *Mali* 14°15N 6°0W **262** C3
Nionsamoridougou *Guinea* 8°45N 8°50W **262** D3
Nioro du Rip *Senegal* 13°40N 15°50W **262** C1
Nioro du Sahel *Mali* 15°15N 9°30W **262** B3
Niort *France* 46°19N 0°29W **174** B3
Nioumachoua *Comoros Is.* 12°21S 43°42E **272** a
Nipa *Papua N. G.* 6°9S 143°29E **286** D2
Nipani *India* 16°20N 74°25E **245** F2
Nipawin *Canada* 53°20N 104°0W **297** C8
Nipfjället *Sweden* 61°59N 12°50E **162** C6
Nipigon *Canada* 49°0N 88°17W **298** C2
Nipigon, L. *Canada* 49°50N 88°30W **298** C2
Nipishish L. *Canada* 54°12N 60°45W **299** B7
Nipissing, L. *Canada* 46°20N 80°0W **298** C4
Nipomo *U.S.A.* 35°3N 120°29W **307** K6
Nippa *Japan* 35°31N 139°36E **140** B2
Nippon = Japan ■ *Asia* 36°0N 136°0E **221** G8
Nippori *Japan* 35°43N 139°45E **140** A3
Nipton *U.S.A.* 35°28N 115°16W **307** K11
Niquelândia *Brazil* 14°33S 48°23W **333** D2
Nīr *Iran* 38°2N 47°59E **213** C12
Nira → *India* 17°58N 75°8E **244** F2
Nirasaki *Japan* 35°42N 138°27E **223** B10
Nirayama = Izunokuni *Japan* 35°2N 138°55E **223** B10
Nirmal *India* 19°3N 78°20E **244** E4
Nirmali *India* 26°20N 86°35E **243** F12
Niš *Serbia* 43°19N 21°58E **202** C5
Nisa = Nysa → *Europe* 52°4N 14°46E **178** C10
Nisa *Portugal* 39°30N 7°41W **195** F3
Nisa *Turkmenistan* 37°59N 58°11E **247** B8
Nisāb *Si. Arabia* 29°11N 44°43E **246** D5
Nisāb *Yemen* 14°25N 46°29E **248** D4
Nišava → *Serbia* 43°20N 21°46E **202** C5
Niscemi *Italy* 37°9N 14°23E **201** E7
Nishi *Japan* 34°40N 135°28E **133** A1
Nishi-Sonogi-Hantō *Japan* 32°55N 129°45E **222** E1
Nishi-Tosa *Japan* 33°13N 132°46E **222** D4
Nishinari *Japan* 34°37N 135°28E **133** B1
Nishinomiya *Japan* 34°45N 135°20E **133** A1
Nishino'omote *Japan* 30°43N 130°59E **221** J5
Nishio *Japan* 34°52N 137°3E **223** C9
Nishiwaki *Japan* 34°59N 134°58E **222** C6
Nishiyodogawa *Japan* 34°41N 135°24E **133** A1
Nishtūn *Yemen* 15°49N 52°14E **249** D6
Nisibin = Nusaybin *Turkey* 37°3N 41°10E **213** D9
Niška Banja *Serbia* 43°18N 22°1E **202** C6
Niskibi → *Canada* 56°29N 88°9W **298** A2
Nisko *Poland* 50°35N 22°7E **185** H9
Nisporeni *Moldova* 47°4N 28°10E **183** C13
Nisqually → *U.S.A.* 47°7N 122°42W **306** C4
Nissaki *Greece* 39°43N 19°52E **206** B9
Nissan → *Sweden* 56°40N 12°51E **163** H6
Nissedal *Norway* 59°10N 8°30E **164** E5
Nisser *Norway* 59°7N 8°28E **164** E5
Nissiros *Greece* 36°35N 27°12E **205** E9
Nissum Bredning *Denmark* 56°40N 8°20E **163** H2
Nissum Fjord *Denmark* 56°20N 8°11E **163** H2
Nistru = Dnister → *Europe* 46°18N 30°17E **177** E16
Nisutlin → *Canada* 60°14N 132°34W **296** A2
Nitchequon *Canada* 53°10N 70°58W **299** B5
Niterói *Brazil* 22°53S 43°7W **135** B2
Nith → *Ont., Canada* 43°12N 80°23W **312** C4
Nith → *Dumf. & Gall., U.K.* 55°14N 3°33W **167** F5
Nitmiluk △ *Australia* 14°6S 132°15E **278** B5
Nitra *Slovak Rep.* 48°19N 18°4E **181** C11
Nitra → *Slovak Rep.* 47°46N 18°10E **181** D11
Nitriansky □ *Slovak Rep.* 48°10N 18°30E **181** C11
Nittenau *Germany* 49°12N 12°16E **179** F8
Niu Valley *U.S.A.* 21°19N 157°44W **302** K14
Niua Group *Tonga* 15°57S 173°45W **277** D16
Niuafo'ou *Tonga* 15°30S 175°58W **277** D15
Niuatoputapu *Tonga* 15°57S 173°45W **277** D16
Niue ⧄ *Pac. Oc.* 19°2S 169°54W **289** g
Niulakita *Pac. Oc.* 10°45S 179°30E **277** C14
Niulan Jiang → *China* 27°30N 103°5E **228** D4
Niulantsun *Taiwan* 25°1N 121°2E **225** A3
Niur *Indonesia* 0°26S 103°30E **234** C2
Niut *Indonesia* 0°55N 109°54E **235** B4
Niutao *Pac. Oc.* 6°7S 177°18E **277** B14
Niutou Shan *China* 29°5N 121°59E **229** C13
Niuzhuang *China* 40°58N 122°28E **224** B1
Nivala *Finland* 63°56N 24°57E **160** E21
Nivelles *Belgium* 50°35N 4°20E **170** D4
Nivernais *France* 47°15N 3°30E **173** E10
Niverville *Canada* 49°36N 97°3W **297** D9
Niwas *India* 23°3N 80°26E **243** H9
Nixa *U.S.A.* 37°3N 93°18W **308** G7
Nixon *U.S.A.* 29°16N 97°46W **314** G6
Nizam Sagar *India* 18°10N 77°58E **244** E3
Nizamabad *India* 18°45N 78°7E **244** E4
Nizamghat *India* 28°20N 95°45E **241** A5
Nizhne Kolymsk *Russia* 68°34N 160°55E **215** C17
Nizhne-Svirskiy ⌓ *Russia* 60°30N 32°55E **188** B7
Nizhnegorskiy = Nyzhnohirskyy *Ukraine* 45°27N 34°38E **189** K8
Nizhnekamsk *Russia* 55°38N 51°49E **190** C10
Nizhneudinsk *Russia* 54°54N 99°3E **215** D10
Nizhnevartovsk *Russia* 60°56N 76°38E **214** C8
Nizhniy Bestyakh *Russia* 61°57N 129°54E **215** C13
Nizhniy Chir *Russia* 48°22N 43°5E **191** F6
Nizhniy Lomov *Russia* 53°34N 43°38E **190** D6
Nizhniy Novgorod *Russia* 56°20N 44°0E **190** B7
Nizhniy Novgorod □ *Russia* 56°30N 44°30E **190** B7
Nizhniy Tagil *Russia* 57°55N 59°57E **186** C10
Nizhniye Kresty = Cherskiy *Russia* 68°45N 161°18E **215** C17
Nizhyn *Ukraine* 51°5N 31°55E **189** G6
Nizina Mazowiecka *Poland* 52°30N 21°0E **185** F8
Nizip *Turkey* 37°5N 37°50E **212** D7
Nizké Tatry *Slovak Rep.* 48°55N 19°30E **181** C12
Nizké Tatry △ *Slovak Rep.* 48°55N 19°37E **181** C12
Nízký Jeseník *Czech Rep.* 49°50N 17°30E **181** B10
Nizwá *Oman* 22°56N 57°32E **249** B7
Nizza Monferrato *Italy* 44°46N 8°21E **198** D5
Njakwa *Malawi* 11°1S 33°56E **269** E3
Njarðvíkur *Iceland* 63°59N 22°32W **155** D4
Njazidja = Grande Comore *Comoros Is.* 11°35S 43°20E **272** a
Njegoš *Montenegro* 42°53N 18°45E **202** D2
Njinjo *Tanzania* 8°48S 38°54E **269** D4
Njoko → *Zambia* 17°8S 24°4E **265** F4
Njombe *Tanzania* 9°20S 34°50E **269** D3
Njombe → *Tanzania* 6°56S 35°6E **268** D4
Njurundabommen *Sweden* 62°15N 17°25E **162** B11
Nkambe *Cameroon* 6°35N 10°40E **263** D7
Nkana *Zambia* 12°50S 28°8E **269** E2
Nkandla *S. Africa* 28°37S 31°5E **271** C5
Nkawkaw *Ghana* 6°36N 0°49W **263** D4
Nkayi *Congo* 4°9S 13°17E **264** C2
Nkayi *Zimbabwe* 19°41S 29°20E **269** F2
Nkhotakota *Malawi* 12°56S 34°15E **269** E3
Nkhotakota ⌓ *Malawi* 12°50S 34°0E **269** E3
Nkolabona *Gabon* 1°14N 11°43E **264** B2
Nkomi, Lagune *Gabon* 1°35S 9°17E **264** C1
Nkondwe *Tanzania* 5°51S 30°51E **268** D3
Nkone *Dem. Rep. of the Congo* 1°2S 22°20E **264** C4
Nkongsamba *Cameroon* 4°55N 9°55E **263** E6
Nkoteng *Cameroon* 4°31N 12°2E **264** B2
Nkunga *Dem. Rep. of the Congo* 4°41S 18°34E **265** C3
Nkurenkuru *Namibia* 17°42S 18°32E **270** A2
Nkwanta *Ghana* 6°10N 2°10W **262** D4
Nmai → *Burma* 25°30N 97°25E **228** F2
Noakhali *Bangla.* 22°48N 91°10E **241** D3
Noatak *U.S.A.* 67°34N 162°58W **303** C7
Noatak ⌓ *U.S.A.* 68°10N 160°0W **303** B8
Nob Hill *San Francisco, U.S.A.* **136** b1
Nobel *Canada* 45°25N 80°6W **312** A4
Nobeoka *Japan* 32°36N 131°41E **222** E3
Noble *U.S.A.* 38°42N 88°14W **311** F8
Noblejas *Spain* 39°58N 3°26W **194** F7
Noblesville *U.S.A.* 40°3N 86°1W **311** D11
Noboribetsu *Japan* 42°24N 141°6E **220** C10
Nocatee *U.S.A.* 27°10N 81°53W **317** H8
Noccundra *Australia* 27°50S 142°36E **281** D3
Noce → *Italy* 46°9N 11°4E **198** B8
Nocera Inferiore *Italy* 40°44N 14°38E **201** B7
Nocera Umbra *Italy* 43°5N 12°47E **199** E9
Noci *Italy* 40°48N 17°7E **201** B10
Nockeby *Sweden* 59°19N 17°56E **139** B1
Nocona *U.S.A.* 33°47N 97°44W **314** E6
Nocrich *Romania* 45°55N 24°26E **183** E9
Noda *Japan* 35°56N 139°52E **223** B11
Nodeland *Norway* 58°8N 7°51E **164** F4
Noel Kempff Mercado △ *Bolivia* 14°9S 60°49W **331** C5
Noel Park *U.K.* 51°35N 0°5W **125** A3
Nogal Valley = Nugaaleed, Dooxo *Somalia* 8°35N 48°35E **267** C6
Nogales *Sonora, Mexico* 31°19N 110°56W **318** A2
Nogales *Ariz., U.S.A.* 31°21N 110°56W **305** L8
Nogaro *France* 43°45N 0°2W **174** E3
Nogat → *Poland* 54°17N 19°17E **184** D6
Nōgata *Japan* 33°48N 130°44E **222** D2
Nogatino *Russia* 55°41N 37°41E **129** B3
Nogaysk = Prymorske *Ukraine* 46°48N 36°20E **189** J9
Nogent *France* 48°1N 5°20E **173** D12
Nogent-le-Rotrou *France* 48°20N 0°50E **172** D7
Nogent-sur-Marne *France* 48°50N 2°28E **134** A3

Nogent-sur-Seine France 48°30N 3°30E 173 D10
Noggara Ethiopia 13°54N 36°35E 257 E4
Noggerup Australia 33°32S 116°5E 279 F2
Noginsk Russia 64°30N 90°50E 215 C10
Nogliki Russia 51°50N 143°10E 215 D15
Nogoa → Australia 23°40S 147°55E 280 C4
Nogoyá Argentina 32°24S 59°48W 334 C4
Nógrád □ Hungary 48°0N 19°30E 182 C4
Noguera Pallaresa → Spain 41°55N 0°55E 196 D5
Noguera Ribagorçana → Spain 41°40N 0°43E 196 D5
Nohar India 29°11N 74°49E 242 E6
Nohfelden Germany 49°35N 7°7E 179 F3
Nohili Pt. U.S.A. 22°4N 159°47W 302 A2
Nohta India 23°40N 79°34E 243 H8
Nohwa S. Korea 34°10N 126°34E 224 E3
Nohwado S. Korea 34°12N 126°35E 224 E3
Noia Spain 42°48N 8°53W 194 C2
Noichi Japan 33°33N 133°42E 222 D5
Noida India 28°36N 77°19E 120 B2
Noipuos Papua N. G. 2°25S 150°7E 286 B6
Noire, Montagne France 43°28N 2°18E 174 E6
Noires, Mts. France 48°11N 3°40W 172 D3
Noirétable France 45°48N 3°46E 174 C7
Noirmoutier, Î. de France 46°58N 2°10W 172 F4
Noirmoutier-en-l'Île France 47°0N 2°14W 172 F4
Noiseau France 48°46N 2°32E 134 B4
Noisiel France 48°51N 2°37E 134 A4
Noisy-le-Grand France 48°50N 2°33E 134 B4
Noisy-le-Roi France 48°50N 2°3E 134 A1
Noisy-le-Sec France 48°53N 2°27E 134 A3
Nojane Botswana 23°15S 20°14E 270 B3
Nojima-Zaki Japan 34°54N 139°53E 223 C11
Nok Kundi Pakistan 28°50N 62°45E 240 C1
Nok Ta Phao, Ko Thailand 9°23N 99°40E 237 b
Nokaneng Botswana 19°40S 22°17E 270 A3
Nokia Finland 61°30N 23°30E 188 B2
Nokkala Finland 60°8N 24°45E 121 C1
Nokkeushi = Kitami Japan 43°48N 143°54E 220 C11
Nokomis Sask., Canada 51°35N 105°0W 297 C8
Nokomis Fla., U.S.A. 27°7N 82°27W 317 H7
Nokomis Ill., U.S.A. 39°18N 89°18W 310 E7
Nokomis L. Canada 57°0N 103°0W 297 B8
Nokou Chad 14°35N 14°47E 259 F2
Nokuku Vanuatu 14°54S 166°35E 287 D4
Nola C.A.R. 3°35N 16°4E 264 B3
Nola Italy 40°55N 14°33E 201 B7
Nolay France 46°58N 4°35E 173 F11
Noli, C. di Italy 44°12N 8°25E 198 D5
Nolinsk Russia 57°28N 49°57E 190 B9
Noma U.S.A. 30°59N 85°37W 316 E4
Noma Omuramba → Namibia 18°52S 20°53E 270 A3
Noma-Saki Japan 31°25N 130°7E 222 F2
Nomad Papua N. G. 6°19S 142°13E 286 D2
Nombre de Dios Panama 9°34N 79°28W 320 E4
Nome U.S.A. 64°30N 165°25W 303 D6
Nomentano Italy 41°55N 12°30E 136 B2
Nomgon Mongolia 42°50N 105°8E 226 C3
Nomi Japan 36°26N 136°25E 223 A8
Nomo-Zaki Japan 32°35N 129°44E 222 E1
Nomoneas Micronesia 7°24N 151°53E 287 T18
Nomuka Tonga 20°17S 174°48W 287 D13
Nomuka Group Tonga 20°20S 174°48W 287 D13
Nonacho L. Canada 61°42N 109°40W 297 A7
Nonakashinden Japan 35°44N 139°30E 140 A2
Nonancourt France 48°47N 1°11E 172 D8
Nonda Australia 20°40S 142°28E 280 C3
Nondalton U.S.A. 60°0N 154°51W 303 F9
None Italy 44°56N 7°32E 198 D4
Nong Chang Thailand 15°23N 99°51E 236 E2
Nong Han Res. Thailand 17°11N 104°9E 236 D5
Nong Het Laos 19°29N 103°59E 236 C4
Nong Khai Thailand 17°50N 102°46E 236 D4
Nong'an China 44°25N 125°5E 227 B13
Nongjrong India 25°29N 92°6E 241 C4
Nongminyundong Jiangxisuo China 23°7N 113°15E 121 B2
Nongoma S. Africa 27°58S 31°35E 271 C5
Nongpoh India 25°54N 91°53E 241 C3
Nongsa Indonesia 1°11N 104°8E 237 d
Nongstoin India 25°31N 91°16E 241 C3
Nonhyeon S. Korea 37°30N 127°1E 137 B2
Nono Ethiopia 8°32N 37°26E 266 C4
Nonoava Mexico 27°28N 106°44W 318 B3
Nonoc I. Phil. 9°51N 125°37E 233 G5
Nonoichi Japan 36°35N 136°35E 223 A8
Nonsan S. Korea 36°12N 127°5E 224 D3
Nonsuch B. Antigua & B. 17°3N 61°42W 322 b
Nonthaburi Thailand 13°50N 100°29E 113 A1
Nontron France 45°31N 0°40E 174 C4
Nonza France 42°47N 9°21E 175 F13
Noon Gun Cape Town, S. Africa 118 b1
Noonamah Australia 12°40S 131°4E 278 B5
Noondie, L. Australia 28°30S 119°30E 279 E2
Noonkanbah ✪ Australia 18°30S 124°50E 278 C3
Noord Aruba 12°34N 70°1W 322 f
Noord Brabant □ Neths. 51°40N 5°0E 170 C5
Noord Holland □ Neths. 52°30N 4°45E 170 B4
Noord Saliña Bonaire 12°11N 68°16W 322 h
Noordbeveland Neths. 51°35N 3°50E 170 C3
Noorderkerk Amsterdam, Neths. 112 a1
Noordgesig S. Africa 26°13S 27°56E 123 B1
Noordkaap Aruba 12°34N 70°1W 322 f
Noordoostpolder Neths. 52°45N 5°45E 170 B5
Noordpunt Bonaire 12°18N 68°23W 322 h
Noordpunt Curaçao 12°24N 69°10W 322 g
Noordwijk Neths. 52°14N 4°26E 170 B4
Noordzeekanaal Neths. 52°28N 4°47E 112 A1
Noorvik U.S.A. 66°50N 161°3W 303 C7
Noosa Heads Australia 26°25S 153°6E 281 D5
Nootka I. Canada 49°32N 126°42W 296 D3
Nopiming ⌂ Canada 50°30N 95°37W 297 C9
Nóqui Angola 5°55S 13°30E 265 D2
Nor-Bayzzet = Kamo Armenia 40°21N 45°7E 191 K7
Nora Eritrea 16°6N 40°4E 257 D5
Nora Sweden 59°32N 15°2E 162 E9
Nora Springs U.S.A. 43°9N 93°0W 310 A4
Noralea Phil. 6°32N 124°40E 233 H5
Noralee Canada 53°59N 126°26W 296 C3
Noranda = Rouyn-Noranda Canada 48°20N 79°0W 298 C4
Norberg Sweden 60°4N 15°56E 162 D9
Norborne U.S.A. 39°18N 93°40W 310 E3
Nórcia Italy 42°48N 13°5E 199 F10
Norco U.S.A. 33°56N 117°33W 307 M9
Norcross U.S.A. 33°56N 84°13W 316 B4
Nord □ Cameroon 8°30N 14°0E 263 D7
Nord □ France 50°15N 3°30E 173 B10
Nord, Gare du Paris, France 134 a4
Nord, Pt. Comoros Is. 11°22S 43°19E 272 a
Nord-Kivu □ Dem. Rep. of the Congo 1°0S 29°0E 268 C2
Nord-og-Østgrønland △ Greenland 75°0N 35°0W 154 C7
Nord-Ostsee-Kanal Germany 54°12N 9°32E 178 A5
Nord-Ouest □ Cameroon 6°20N 10°30E 263 D7
Nord-Pas-de-Calais □ France 50°30N 2°50E 173 B9
Nordagutu Norway 59°25N 9°20E 164 E6
Nordaustlandet Svalbard 79°14N 23°0E 150 B9
Nordberg Norway 61°54N 8°10E 164 C5
Nordborg Denmark 55°5N 9°50E 163 J3
Nordby Denmark 55°27N 8°24E 163 J2
Norddeich Germany 53°36N 7°9E 178 B3
Nordegg Canada 52°29N 116°5W 296 C5
Norden Germany 53°35N 7°12E 178 B3
Nordenham Germany 53°30N 8°28E 178 B4
Nordenskjöld Sea = Laptev Sea Russia 76°0N 125°0E 215 B13
Norderhov Norway 60°7N 10°17E 164 D7
Norderney Germany 53°42N 7°9E 178 B3
Norderstedt Germany 53°42N 10°1E 178 B6
Nordeste Azores 37°50N 25°10W 153 d3
Nordfjord Norway 61°55N 5°30E 164 C2
Nordfjordeid Norway 61°54N 6°0E 164 C2
Nordfriesische Inseln Germany 54°40N 8°20E 178 A4
Nordgrønland = Avannaarsua □ Greenland 80°0N 55°0W 154 B5
Nordhausen Germany 51°30N 10°47E 178 D6
Nordhorn Germany 52°26N 7°4E 178 C3
Norðoyar Færoe Is. 62°17N 6°35W 160 E9
Norðtunga Iceland 64°44N 21°24W 155 C5
Norður-múlasýsla Iceland 65°30N 15°0W 155 B11
Norðurbotn Iceland 65°36N 23°46W 155 B3
Norðurland Eystra □ Iceland 65°30N 17°0W 155 B9
Norðurland Vestra □ Iceland 65°30N 20°0W 155 B6
Nördinge-Nol Sweden 57°56N 12°5E 163 G6
Nordingrå Sweden 62°56N 18°17E 162 B12
Nordjylland □ Denmark 57°0N 9°30E 163 G3
Nordkapp Finnmark, Norway 71°10N 25°50E 160 A21
Nordkapp Svalbard 80°31N 20°0E 150 A9
Nordkinnhalvøya Norway 70°55N 27°40E 160 A22
Nördlicher Teutoburger Wald-Wiehengebirge ⌂ Germany 52°18N 8°10E 178 C4
Nördlingen Germany 48°48N 10°30E 179 G6
Nordmarka Norway 59°58N 10°41E 133 A3
Nordmøre Norway 63°6N 8°15E 164 B4
Nordostrundingen Greenland 81°22N 11°40W 154 A9
Nordøyane Norway 62°40N 6°0E 164 B3
Nordrand-Siedlung Austria 48°16N 16°26E 142 A2
Nordre Bergenhus = Sogn og Fjordane □ Norway 61°40N 6°45E 164 C3
Nördre Osa Norway 61°18N 11°45E 164 C8
Nordre Strømfjord Greenland 67°10N 53°35W 154 D5
Nordrhein-Westfalen □ Germany 51°45N 7°30E 178 D3
Nordsinni Norway 60°50N 9°57E 164 D6
Nordstedalsseter Norway 61°40N 7°48E 164 C4
Nordstrand Schleswig-Holstein, Germany 54°30N 8°52E 178 A4
Nordstrand Oslo, Norway 59°52N 10°48E 133 A3
Nordvik Russia 74°2N 111°32E 215 B12
Nore → Ireland 52°25N 6°58W 166 D4
Norefjell Norway 60°16N 9°29E 164 D6
Noreland Canada 44°43N 78°48W 312 B6
Noresund Norway 60°11N 9°37E 164 D6
Norfolk = Simcoe Canada 42°50N 80°23W 312 D4
Norfolk N.Y., U.S.A. 44°48N 74°59W 313 B10
Norfolk Nebr., U.S.A. 42°2N 97°25W 308 D5
Norfolk Va., U.S.A. 36°50N 76°17W 309 G15
Norfolk □ U.K. 52°39N 0°54E 169 E8
Norfolk Basin Pac. Oc. 32°0S 170°0E 277 G13
Norfolk Broads △ U.K. 52°45N 1°30E 169 E9
Norfolk I. Pac. Oc. 28°58S 168°3E 277 F12
Norfolk Ridge Pac. Oc. 29°0S 168°0E 288 K8
Norfork L. U.S.A. 36°15N 92°14W 314 C8
Norge = Norway ■ Europe 63°0N 11°0E 160 E14
Norheimsund Norway 60°23N 6°6E 164 D3
Norilsk Russia 69°20N 88°6E 215 C9
Norland U.S.A. 25°57N 80°12W 129 C2
Norma, Mt. Australia 20°55S 140°42E 280 C3
Normal U.S.A. 40°31N 88°59W 310 D8
Norman U.S.A. 35°13N 97°26W 314 D6
Norman → Australia 19°18S 141°51E 280 B3
Norman Manley Int. ✕ (KIN) Jamaica 17°56N 76°47W 320 a
Norman Park U.S.A. 31°16N 83°41W 316 D6
Norman Wells Canada 65°17N 126°51W 294 D6
Normanby N.Z. 39°32S 174°18E 284 F3
Normanby → Australia 14°23S 144°10E 280 A3
Normanby I. Papua N. G. 10°55S 151°5E 286 F6
Normandie France 48°45N 0°10E 171 B4
Normandie-Maine ⌂ France 48°30N 0°20W 172 D6
Normandin Canada 48°49N 72°31W 298 C5
Normandy = Normandie France 48°45N 0°10E 171 B4
Normanhurst, Mt. Australia 25°4S 122°30E 279 E3
Normanton Australia 17°40S 141°10E 280 B3
Normanville Australia 35°27S 138°18E 282 C3
Normétal Canada 49°0N 79°22W 298 C4
Norquay Canada 51°53N 102°5W 297 C8
Norquinco Argentina 41°51S 70°55W 336 B2
Norra Kvill △ Sweden 57°46N 15°35E 163 G9
Norra Ulvön Sweden 63°3N 18°40E 162 A12
Norrahammar Sweden 57°43N 14°7E 163 G8
Norrbottens län □ Sweden 66°50N 20°0E 160 C19
Norrdellen Sweden 61°53N 16°43E 162 C10
Nørre Åby Denmark 55°27N 9°52E 163 J3
Nørre Alslev Denmark 54°54N 11°52E 163 K5
Nørrebro Copenhagen, Denmark 118 a1
Norresundby Denmark 57°5N 9°52E 163 G3
Norrhult-Klavreström Sweden 57°7N 15°10E 163 G9
Norridge U.S.A. 41°57N 87°49W 119 B2
Norris City U.S.A. 37°59N 88°20W 311 G8
Norris Point Canada 49°31N 57°53W 299 C8
Norristown Ga., U.S.A. 32°30N 82°30W 316 C7
Norristown Pa., U.S.A. 40°7N 75°21W 313 F9
Norrköping Sweden 58°37N 16°11E 163 F10
Norrland Sweden 62°15N 15°45E 160 E16
Norrmalm Stockholm, Sweden 139 a1
Norrsundet Sweden 60°56N 17°8E 162 D11
Norrtälje Sweden 59°46N 18°42E 162 E12
Norseman Australia 32°8S 121°43E 279 F3
Norsewood N.Z. 40°3S 176°13E 284 G5
Norsjø Norway 59°18N 9°20E 164 E6
Norsk Russia 52°30N 130°5E 215 D14
Norsup Vanuatu 16°3S 167°24E 287 F5
Norte, C. Chile 27°3S 109°24W 330 b
Norte, Canal do → Brazil 0°40N 50°20W 329 C7
Norte, Pta. Argentina 42°5S 63°46W 336 B4
Norte, Pta. Chile 33°36S 78°54W 330 c
Norte, Pta. del Canary Is. 27°51N 17°57W 153 e1
Norte, Pta. do Azores 37°1N 25°4W 153 d4
Norte, Serra do Brazil 11°20S 59°0W 331 C6
Norte de Santander □ Colombia 8°0N 73°0W 328 B3
Norte Grande Azores 38°40N 28°4W 153 d1
Nortelândia Brazil 14°25S 56°48W 331 C6
North U.S.A. 33°37N 81°6W 316 B8
North, C. Canada 47°2N 60°20W 299 C7
North Adams U.S.A. 42°42N 73°7W 313 D11
North America 40°0N 100°0W 292 F10
North Andaman I. India 13°15N 92°55E 245 H11
North Arlington U.S.A. 40°47N 74°7W 132 B1
North Arm Canada 62°0N 114°30W 296 A5
North Atlanta U.S.A. 33°53N 84°19W 113 A3
North Augusta U.S.A. 33°30N 81°59W 316 B8
North Australian Basin Ind. Oc. 14°30S 116°30E 276 C2
North Ayrshire □ U.K. 55°45N 4°44W 167 F4
North Balabac Str. Phil. 8°8N 117°4E 233 G1
North Baltimore U.S.A. 41°11N 83°41W 311 C13
North Bass I. U.S.A. 41°40N 82°56W 312 E2
North Battleford Canada 52°50N 108°17W 297 C7
North Bay Canada 46°20N 79°30W 298 C4
North Bay Village U.S.A. 25°50N 80°9W 129 C3
North Beach San Francisco, U.S.A. 136 a2
North Belcher Is. Canada 56°50N 79°50W 298 A4
North Bend Oreg., U.S.A. 43°24N 124°14W 304 E1
North Bend Pa., U.S.A. 41°20N 77°42W 312 E7
North Bend Wash., U.S.A. 47°30N 121°47W 306 C5
North Bennington U.S.A. 42°56N 73°15W 313 D11
North Bergen U.S.A. 40°48N 74°0W 132 B1
North Berwick E. Loth., U.K. 56°4N 2°42W 167 E6
North Berwick Maine, U.S.A. 43°18N 70°44W 313 C14
North Borneo = Sabah □ Malaysia 6°0N 117°0E 235 A5
North Breakers Midway Is. 28°13N 177°24W 302 c
North Brother I. India 10°59N 92°40E 245 J11
North Bruce Canada 44°22N 81°26W 312 B3
North Bull I. Ireland 53°22N 6°9W 120 A3
North C. N.B., Canada 47°5N 64°0W 299 C7
North C. N.Z. 34°23S 173°4E 284 A2
North C. Papua N. G. 2°32S 150°50E 286 B6
North Canadian → U.S.A. 35°22N 95°37W 314 D7
North Canton U.S.A. 40°53N 81°24W 312 F3
North Cape = Nordkapp Norway 71°10N 25°50E 160 A21
North Caribou L. Canada 52°50N 90°40W 298 B1
North Carolina □ U.S.A. 35°30N 80°0W 315 D15
North Cascades △ U.S.A. 48°45N 121°10W 304 B3
North Cay Bahamas 25°6N 77°26W 153 b
North Channel Ont., Canada 46°0N 83°0W 298 C3
North Channel U.K. 55°13N 5°52W 167 F3
North Charleston U.S.A. 32°53N 79°58W 316 C10
North Cheam U.K. 51°22N 0°11W 125 B2
North Chicago U.S.A. 42°19N 87°51W 311 B9
North College Hill U.S.A. 39°13N 84°33W 311 E12
North Collins U.S.A. 42°35N 78°56W 312 D6
North Comino Channel Malta 36°1N 14°20E 206 E7
North Cotabato □ Phil. 7°10N 125°0E 233 H5
North Cray U.K. 51°25N 0°7E 125 B4
North Creek U.S.A. 43°42N 73°59W 313 C11
North Dakota □ U.S.A. 47°30N 100°15W 308 B3
North Decatur U.S.A. 33°48N 84°17W 113 B3
North Downs U.K. 51°19N 0°21E 169 F8
North Druid Hills U.S.A. 33°49N 84°17W 113 B3
North East U.S.A. 42°13N 79°50W 312 D5
North East □ Botswana 20°45S 27°30E 271 B4
North East B. Ascension I. 7°55S 14°21W 153 g
North East Frontier Agency = Arunachal Pradesh □ India 28°0N 95°0E 241 B5
North East Lincolnshire □ U.K. 53°34N 0°2W 168 D7
North Eastern □ Kenya 1°30N 40°0E 268 B5
North End Boston, U.S.A. 116 a3
North Esk → Angus, U.K. 56°46N 2°24W 167 E6
North Esk → Midloth., U.K. 55°54N 3°4W 121 B2
North European Plain Europe 55°0N 25°0E 158 E10
North Fabius → U.S.A. 39°54N 91°30W 310 E5
North Foreland U.K. 51°22N 1°28E 169 F9
North Fork U.S.A. 37°14N 119°21W 306 H7
North Fork, Salt → U.S.A. 39°26N 91°53W 310 E5
North Fork American → U.S.A. 38°57N 120°59W 306 G5
North Fork Edisto → U.S.A. 33°16N 80°54W 316 B9
North Fork Feather → U.S.A. 38°33N 121°30W 306 F5
North Fork Grand → U.S.A. 45°47N 102°16W 308 C2
North Fork Red → U.S.A. 34°24N 99°14W 314 D5
North Fort Myers U.S.A. 26°41N 81°53W 317 J8
North Frisian Is. = Nordfriesische Inseln Germany 54°40N 8°20E 178 A4
North Gower Canada 45°8N 75°43W 313 A9
North Greenfield = West Allis U.S.A. 43°1N 88°0W 311 B8
North Gyle U.K. 55°57N 3°19W 121 B2
North Hackensack U.S.A. 40°54N 74°2W 132 A1
North Harbor Phil. 14°37N 120°57E 127 B1
North Hd. N.S.W., Australia 33°49S 151°18E 139 A2
North Hd. W. Austral., Australia 30°14S 114°59E 279 F1
North Henik L. Canada 61°45N 97°40W 297 A9
North Highlands U.S.A. 38°40N 121°23W 306 G5
North Hollywood U.S.A. 34°9N 118°22W 126 B2
North Horr Kenya 3°20N 37°8E 268 B4
North I. India 10°8N 72°20E 245 J1
North I. Rift Valley, Kenya 4°5N 36°5E 268 B4
North I. N.Z. 38°0S 175°0E 284 E4
North I. Seychelles 4°25S 55°13E 272 c
North Judson U.S.A. 41°13N 86°46W 311 C10
North Kingsville U.S.A. 41°54N 80°42W 312 E4
North Kitui △ Kenya 0°15S 38°29E 268 C4
North Knife → Canada 58°53N 94°45W 297 B10
North Koel → India 24°45N 83°50E 243 G10
North Korea ■ Asia 40°0N 127°0E 224 C3
North L. Australia 32°30S 143°5E 282 B5
North Lakhimpur India 27°14N 94°7E 241 B5
North Lanarkshire □ U.K. 55°52N 3°56W 167 F5
North Las Vegas U.S.A. 36°11N 115°7W 124 A1
North Las Vegas ✕ (VGT) U.S.A. 36°12N 115°11W 124 A1
North Lexington U.S.A. 42°27N 71°14W 116 A1
North Liberty Ind., U.S.A. 41°32N 86°26W 311 C10
North Liberty Iowa, U.S.A. 41°46N 91°35W 310 C5
North Lincolnshire □ U.K. 53°36N 0°30W 168 D7
North Little Rock U.S.A. 34°45N 92°16W 314 D8
North Loup → U.S.A. 41°17N 98°24W 308 E4
North Luangwa △ Zambia 11°49S 32°9E 269 E3
North Magnetic Pole Arctic 82°18N 113°24W 150 A2
North Malé Atoll Maldives 4°25N 73°30E 272 d
North Malosmadulu Atoll Maldives 5°37N 72°55E 272 d
North Manchester U.S.A. 41°0N 85°46W 311 D11
North Mankato U.S.A. 44°10N 94°2W 308 C6
North Miami U.S.A. 25°53N 80°11W 129 C2
North Miami Beach U.S.A. 25°55N 80°9W 129 C2
North Minch U.K. 58°5N 5°55W 167 C3
North Moose L. Canada 54°4N 100°12W 297 C8
North Myrtle Beach U.S.A. 33°48N 78°42W 315 E15
North Nahanni → Canada 62°15N 123°20W 296 A4
North Naples U.S.A. 26°12N 81°48W 317 J8
North Nazimabad Pakistan 24°55N 67°3E 123 A2
North New River Canal U.S.A. 26°30N 80°30W 317 J9
North Nilandu Atoll Maldives 3°14N 72°56E 272 d
North Olmsted U.S.A. 41°25N 81°56W 312 E3
North Ossetia □ Russia 43°30N 44°30E 191 J7
North Pagai, I. = Pagai Utara, Pulau Indonesia 2°35S 100°0E 234 C2
North Palisade U.S.A. 37°6N 118°31W 306 H8
North Perry ✕ (HWO) U.S.A. 26°0N 80°14W 129 B2
North Platte U.S.A. 41°8N 100°46W 308 E3
North Platte → U.S.A. 41°7N 100°42W 308 E3
North Point U.S.A. 27°4N 82°10W 317 H7
North Point Park Boston, U.S.A. 116 a1
North Pole Arctic 90°0N 0°0 150 A
North Pole Alaska, U.S.A. 64°45N 147°21W 303 D11
North Portal Canada 49°0N 102°33W 297 D8
North Powder U.S.A. 45°2N 117°55W 304 D5
North Pt. Ascension I. 7°53S 14°23W 153 g
North Pt. Barbados 13°20N 59°37W 323 r
North Pt. Hong Kong, China 22°17N 114°12E 122 B2
North Pt. Mich., U.S.A. 45°2N 83°16W 312 A1
North Pt. Vanuatu 14°56S 168°6E 287 D6
North Queensferry U.K. 56°1N 3°24W 121 A1
North Quincy U.S.A. 42°16N 71°1W 116 B2
North Reef I. India 13°5N 92°43E 245 H11
North Res. U.S.A. 42°27N 71°6W 116 A2
North Rhine Westphalia = Nordrhein-Westfalen □ Germany 51°45N 7°30E 178 D3
North River Canada 53°49N 57°6W 299 B8
North Riverside U.S.A. 41°50N 87°48W 119 B2
North Ronaldsay U.K. 59°22N 2°26W 167 B6
North Salem U.S.A. 39°52N 86°39W 311 E10
North Saskatchewan → Canada 53°15N 105°5W 297 C7
North Saugus U.S.A. 42°29N 71°0W 116 A2
North Sea Europe 56°0N 4°0E 158 D6
North Seal → Canada 58°50N 98°7W 297 B9
North Sentinel I. India 11°33N 92°15E 245 J11
North Shields Australia 34°38S 135°52E 282 C1
North Shore U.S.A. 21°39N 158°30W 302 J13
North Shore Channel → U.S.A. 41°58N 87°42W 119 B2
North Slope U.S.A. 69°15N 152°0W 300 B9
North Solomons □ Papua N. G. 4°0S 155°0E 286 B8
North Somerset □ U.K. 51°24N 2°45W 169 F5
North Station Boston, U.S.A. 116 a2
North Sydney N.S.W., Australia 33°50S 151°13E 139 B2
North Sydney N.S., Canada 46°12N 60°15W 299 C7
North Syracuse U.S.A. 43°8N 76°7W 313 C8
North Taranaki Bight N.Z. 38°50S 174°15E 284 E3
North Thompson → Canada 50°40N 120°20W 296 C4
North Tonawanda U.S.A. 43°2N 78°53W 312 C6
North Troy U.S.A. 45°0N 72°24W 313 B12
North Twin I. Canada 53°20N 80°0W 298 B4
North Tyne → U.K. 55°0N 2°8W 168 B5
North Ubian I. Phil. 6°9N 120°27E 233 H3
North Uist U.K. 57°40N 7°15W 167 D1
North Union = Shaker Heights U.S.A. 41°28N 81°32W 312 E3
North Union St. Vincent 13°13N 61°8W 323 n
North Vancouver Canada 49°19N 123°4W 306 A3
North Vernon U.S.A. 39°0N 85°38W 311 F11
North Wabasca L. Canada 56°0N 113°55W 296 B6
North Walsham U.K. 52°50N 1°22E 168 E9
North Webster U.S.A. 41°25N 85°48W 311 C11
North West = Severo-Zapadnyy □ Russia 65°0N 40°0E 214 C4
North West □ Botswana 19°0S 22°30E 270 A3
North-West □ S. Africa 27°0S 25°0E 270 C4
North West Bluff Montserrat 16°49N 62°12W 323 p
North West C. Australia 21°45S 114°9E 278 D1
North West Frontier = Khyber Pakhtunkhwa □ Pakistan 34°0N 72°0E 242 C4
North West Highlands U.K. 57°33N 4°58W 167 D4
North West Pt. Jamaica 18°27N 78°13W 320 a
North West River Canada 53°30N 60°10W 299 B7
North Western □ Zambia 13°30S 25°30E 269 E2
North-Western Provinces and Oudh = Uttar Pradesh □ India 27°0N 80°0E 243 F9
North Wildwood U.S.A. 39°0N 74°48W 309 F16
North Woolwich U.K. 51°30N 0°3E 125 A4
North Yakima = Yakima U.S.A. 46°36N 120°31W 304 C3
North York Canada 43°45N 79°27W 141 A2
North York Moors U.K. 54°23N 0°53W 168 C7
North York Moors △ U.K. 54°27N 0°51W 168 C7
North Yorkshire □ U.K. 54°15N 1°25W 168 C6
Northallerton U.K. 54°20N 1°26W 168 C6
Northam W. Austral., Australia 31°35S 116°42E 279 F2
Northam Limpopo, S. Africa 24°56S 27°18E 270 B4
Northampton W. Austral., Australia 28°27S 114°33E 279 E1
Northampton Northants., U.K. 52°15N 0°53W 169 E7
Northampton Mass., U.S.A. 42°19N 72°38W 313 D12
Northampton Pa., U.S.A. 40°41N 75°30W 313 F9
Northamptonshire □ U.K. 52°16N 0°55W 169 E7
Northbridge N.S.W., Australia 33°49S 151°15E 139 A2
Northbridge Mass., U.S.A. 42°9N 71°39W 313 D13
Northbridge Park Australia 33°49S 151°15E 139 A2
Northbrook Ont., Canada 44°44N 77°9W 312 B7
Northbrook Ill., U.S.A. 42°7N 87°50W 119 A2
Northcliff S. Africa 26°8S 27°58E 123 A1
Northcliffe Australia 34°39S 116°7E 279 F2
Northcote Australia 37°46S 145°0E 128 A2
Northeast C. U.S.A. 63°18N 168°42W 303 E5
Northeast Pacific Basin Pac. Oc. 32°0N 145°0W 289 D13
Northeast Providence Channel W. Indies 26°0N 76°0W 320 A4
Northeastern Univ. U.S.A. 42°20N 71°4W 116 A2
Northeim Germany 51°42N 10°0E 178 D6
Northern = Limpopo □ S. Africa 24°5S 29°0E 271 B4
Northern □ Ghana 9°30N 1°0W 263 D4
Northern □ Malawi 11°0S 34°0E 269 E3
Northern □ Papua N. G. 9°0S 148°30E 286 E5
Northern □ S. Leone 9°15N 11°30W 262 D2
Northern □ Zambia 10°30S 31°0E 269 E3
Northern Aral Sea Kazakhstan 46°20N 60°30E 216 C6
Northern Areas = Gilgit-Baltistan □ Pakistan 36°30N 73°0E 243 A5
Northern Bahr el Ghazal □ South Sudan 8°0N 27°30E 257 F2
Northern Cape □ S. Africa 30°0S 20°0E 270 C3
Northern Circars India 17°30N 82°30E 244 F6
Northern Indian L. Canada 57°20N 97°20W 297 B9
Northern Ireland □ U.K. 54°45N 7°0W 166 B5
Northern Lau Group Fiji 17°30S 178°59W 287 A3
Northern Light L. Canada 48°15N 90°39W 298 C1
Northern Marianas ☒ Pac. Oc. 17°0N 145°0E 302 a
Northern Province □ S. Africa 24°0S 29°0E 271 B4
Northern Range Trin. & Tob. 10°46N 61°15W 323 t
Northern Rhodesia = Zambia ■ Africa 15°0S 28°0E 269 F2
Northern Samar □ Phil. 12°30N 124°40E 232 E5
Northern Sporades Greece 39°15N 23°30E 204 B5
Northern Territory □ Australia 20°0S 133°0E 278 D5
Northfield Ill., U.S.A. 42°5N 87°47W 119 A2
Northfield Minn., U.S.A. 44°27N 93°9W 308 C7
Northfield Vt., U.S.A. 44°9N 72°40W 313 B12
Northgate Canada 49°0N 102°16W 297 D8
Northland □ N.Z. 35°30S 173°30E 284 B2
Northmount Canada 43°46N 79°23W 141 A2
Northolt U.K. 51°32N 0°22W 125 A1
Northome U.S.A. 47°52N 94°17W 308 B6
Northport Ala., U.S.A. 33°14N 87°35W 315 E11
Northport Wash., U.S.A. 48°55N 117°48W 304 B5
Northumberland □ U.K. 55°12N 2°0W 168 B6
Northumberland, C. Australia 38°5S 140°40E 282 E4
Northumberland Heath U.K. 51°28N 0°10E 125 B5
Northumberland Is. Australia 21°30S 149°50E 280 C4
Northumberland Str. Canada 46°20N 64°0W 299 C7
Northville Ont., Canada 43°10N 81°56W 312 C3
Northville N.Y., U.S.A. 43°13N 74°11W 313 C10
Northway U.S.A. 62°58N 141°56W 303 E12
Northwest Atlantic Mid-Ocean Canyon Atl. Oc. 54°0N 48°0W 152 A7
Northwest Pacific Basin Pac. Oc. 32°0N 165°0E 288 D8
Northwest Providence Channel W. Indies 26°0N 78°0W 320 A4
Northwest Pt. Bahamas 25°4N 77°31W 153 b
Northwest Territories □ Canada 63°0N 118°0W 294 E8
Northwestern Hawaiian Is. Marine Nat. Monument = Papahānaumokuākea Marine Nat. Monument ⌂ U.S.A. 25°25N 170°35W 302 F9
Northwestern Station U.S.A. 41°52N 87°38W 119 B3
Northwestern Univ. U.S.A. 42°3N 87°40W 119 A2
Northwich U.K. 53°15N 2°31W 168 D5
Northwood London, U.K. 51°36N 0°25W 125 A1
Northwood Iowa, U.S.A. 43°27N 93°13W 308 D7
Northwood N. Dak., U.S.A. 47°44N 97°34W 308 B5
Northwood Park Canada 43°45N 79°30W 141 A1
Norton Kans., U.S.A. 39°50N 99°53W 308 F4
Norton Zimbabwe 17°52S 30°40E 269 F3
Norton B. U.S.A. 64°45N 161°15W 303 D7
Norton Sd. U.S.A. 63°50N 164°0W 303 E7
Norton Shores U.S.A. 43°10N 86°16W 311 A10
Nortorf Germany 54°10N 9°50E 178 A5
Norwalk Calif., U.S.A. 33°54N 118°4W 307 M8
Norwalk Conn., U.S.A. 41°7N 73°22W 313 E11
Norwalk Iowa, U.S.A. 41°29N 93°41W 310 C3
Norwalk Ohio, U.S.A. 41°15N 82°37W 312 E2
Norway Maine, U.S.A. 44°13N 70°32W 309 C18
Norway Mich., U.S.A. 45°47N 87°55W 308 C10
Norway ■ Europe 63°0N 11°0E 160 E14
Norway House Canada 53°59N 97°50W 297 C9
Norwegian B. Canada 77°30N 90°0W 295 B14
Norwegian Basin Atl. Oc. 68°0N 2°0W 150 C7
Norwegian Sea Atl. Oc. 66°0N 1°0E 158 B6
Norwich Ont., Canada 42°59N 80°36W 312 D4
Norwich Norfolk, U.K. 52°38N 1°18E 169 E9
Norwich Conn., U.S.A. 41°31N 72°5W 313 E12
Norwich N.Y., U.S.A. 42°32N 75°32W 313 D9
Norwood Ont., Canada 44°23N 77°59W 312 B7
Norwood Gauteng, S. Africa 26°9S 28°4E 123 A2
Norwood N.Y., U.S.A. 44°45N 75°0W 313 B10
Norwood Ohio, U.S.A. 39°9N 84°27W 311 E12
Norwood Park U.S.A. 41°59N 87°48W 119 B2
Noryangjin S. Korea 37°30N 126°56E 137 B1
Nosappu-Misaki Japan 45°26N 141°39E 220 C12
Noshaq Pakistan 36°24N 71°49E 240 A3
Noshiro Japan 40°12N 140°0E 220 D10
Nosivka Ukraine 50°50N 31°37E 189 G6
Nosovka = Nosivka Ukraine 50°50N 31°37E 189 G6
Nosratābād Iran 29°55N 60°0E 247 D8
Noss Hd. U.K. 58°28N 3°3W 167 C5
Nossa Senhora da Glória Brazil 10°14S 37°25W 332 D4
Nossa Senhora das Dores Brazil 10°29S 37°13W 332 D4
Nossa Senhora de Candelária Rio de J., Brazil 135 a2
Nossa Senhora do Livramento Brazil 15°48S 56°22W 331 D6
Nossa Senhora do Ó Brazil 23°30S 46°41W 137 B1
Nossa Senhora do Socorro Brazil 10°52S 37°7W 332 D4
Nossebro Sweden 58°12N 12°43E 163 F6
Nossegem Belgium 50°53N 4°30E 116 A3
Nossob → S. Africa 26°55S 20°45E 270 C3
Nossombougou Mali 13°5N 7°55W 262 C3
Nosy Varika Madag. 20°35S 48°32E 272 C2
Notasulga U.S.A. 32°34N 85°41W 316 C4
Noteć → Poland 52°44N 15°26E 185 F2
Notikewin → Canada 57°2N 117°38W 296 B5
Notio Aigaio □ Greece 36°52N 25°34E 205 E7
Notios Aiyaion = Notio Aigaio □ Greece 36°52N 25°34E 205 E7
Notios Evvoikos Kolpos Greece 38°20N 24°0E 204 C5
Noto Italy 36°53N 15°4E 201 F8
Noto, G. di Italy 36°50N 15°12E 201 F8
Noto, Val di Italy 37°14N 14°31E 201 E7
Noto-Hantō Japan 37°15N 136°40E 221 F8
Notodden Norway 59°35N 9°17E 164 E6
Notre-Dame Paris, France 134 c4
Notre-Dame, Basilique Montréal, Canada 130 c3
Notre-Dame, Bois France 48°45N 2°34E 134 B4
Notre Dame B. Canada 49°45N 55°30W 299 C8
Notre-Dame-de-Grace Canada 45°28N 73°38W 130 B2
Notre-Dame-de-Koartac = Quaqtaq Canada 60°55N 69°40W 295 E18
Notre-Dame-des-Bois Canada 45°24N 71°4W 313 A13
Notre-Dame-d'Ivugivic = Ivujivik Canada 62°24N 77°55W 295 E16
Notre-Dame-du-Nord Canada 47°36N 79°30W 298 C4
Notsé Togo 7°0N 1°17E 263 D5
Nottawasaga B. Canada 44°35N 80°15W 312 B4
Nottaway = Senneterre Canada 48°25N 77°15W 298 C4
Nottaway → Canada 51°22N 78°55W 298 B4
Notting Hill London, U.K. 125 b1
Nottingham U.K. 52°58N 1°10W 168 E6
Nottingham, City of □ U.K. 52°58N 1°10W 168 E6
Nottingham I. Canada 63°20N 77°55W 295 E16
Nottinghamshire □ U.K. 53°10N 1°3W 168 D6
Nottoway → U.S.A. 36°33N 76°55W 309 G15
Notwane → Botswana 23°35S 26°58E 270 B4
Nouâdhibou Mauritania 20°54N 17°0W 260 D1
Nouâdhibou, Dakhlet Mauritania 20°55N 16°52W 260 D1
Nouâdhibou, Râs Mauritania 20°50N 17°0W 260 D1
Nouakchott Mauritania 18°9N 15°58W 262 B1
Nouâmghâr Mauritania 19°20N 16°20W 262 B1
Nouméa N. Cal. 22°17S 166°30E 288 d
Nouna Burkina Faso 12°45N 3°52W 262 C4
Noupoort S. Africa 31°10S 24°57E 270 D3
Nouveau Comptoir = Wemindji Canada 53°0N 78°49W 298 B4
Nouvelle Amsterdam, Î. Ind. Oc. 38°30S 77°30E 273 H6
Nouvelle-Calédonie = New Caledonia ☒ Pac. Oc. 21°0S 165°0E 288 d
Nouvelle France Mauritius 20°22S 57°33E 272 e
Nouzonville France 49°48N 4°44E 173 C11
Nová Baňa Slovak Rep. 48°28N 18°39E 181 C11
Nová Bystřice Czech Rep. 49°2N 15°8E 180 B8
Nova Cruz Brazil 6°28S 35°25W 332 C4
Nova Era Brazil 19°45S 43°3W 333 E3
Nova Esperança Brazil 23°8S 52°24W 335 A5
Nova Fontesvila = Vila Machado Mozam. 19°15S 34°14E 269 F3
Nova-Freixo = Cuamba Mozam. 14°45S 36°22E 269 E4
Nova Friburgo Brazil 22°16S 42°30W 333 F3
Nova Gaia = Cambundi-Catembo Angola 10°10S 17°35E 265 E3
Nova Gorica Slovenia 45°57N 13°39E 199 C10
Nova Gradiška Croatia 45°17N 17°28E 182 E2
Nova Granada Brazil 20°30S 49°20W 333 F2
Nova Iguaçu Brazil 22°45S 43°28W 333 F3
Nova Iorque Brazil 7°0S 44°5W 332 C3
Nova Kakhovka Ukraine 46°42N 33°27E 189 J7
Nova Lamego Guinea-Biss. 12°19N 14°11W 262 C2
Nova Lisboa = Huambo Angola 12°42S 15°54E 265 E3
Nova Lusitânia Mozam. 19°50S 34°34E 269 F3
Nova Mambone Mozam. 21°0S 35°3E 271 B6
Nova Milanese Italy 45°35N 9°12E 128 A2
Nova Odesa Ukraine 47°19N 31°47E 189 J6
Nova Olinda do Norte Brazil 3°45S 59°3W 329 D6
Nová Paka Czech Rep. 50°29N 15°30E 180 A8
Nova Pavova Serbia 44°56N 20°14E 182 F5
Nova Ponte Brazil 19°8S 47°41W 333 E2
Nova Russas Brazil 4°42S 40°34W 332 B3
Nova Scotia □ Canada 45°10N 63°0W 299 C7
Nova Siri Italy 40°10N 16°35E 201 B9
Nova Sofala Mozam. 20°7S 34°42E 271 B5
Nova Ushytsya Ukraine 48°50N 27°17E 183 B12
Nova Varoš Serbia 43°29N 19°48E 202 C3
Nova Venécia Brazil 18°45S 40°24W 333 E3
Nova Vida Brazil 10°11S 62°47W 331 C5
Nova Zagora Bulgaria 42°32N 26°1E 203 D10
Novaci Macedonia 41°5N 21°29E 202 E5
Novaci Romania 45°10N 23°42E 183 E8
Novafeltria Italy 43°53N 12°17E 199 E9
Novannenskiy = Novoannenskiy Russia 50°32N 42°39E 190 E6
Novar Canada 45°27N 79°15W 312 A5
Novara Italy 45°28N 8°38E 198 C5
Novate Milanese Italy 45°30N 9°8E 128 A1
Novato U.S.A. 38°6N 122°35W 306 G4
Novaya Aleksandriya = Puławy Poland 51°23N 21°59E 185 G8
Novaya Bukhara = Kogon Uzbekistan 39°43N 64°33E 216 E6
Novaya Derevnya Russia 60°0N 30°19E 137 A1
Novaya Kakhovka = Nova Kakhovka Ukraine 46°42N 33°27E 189 J7
Novaya Kazanka = Zhangaqala Kazakhstan 48°56N 49°36E 191 F9
Novaya Ladoga Russia 60°7N 32°16E 188 B7
Novaya Lyalya Russia 59°4N 60°45E 186 C11
Novaya Pismyanka = Ridder Kazakhstan 50°20N 83°30E 217 B10
Novaya Sibir, Ostrov Russia 75°10N 150°0E 215 B16
Novaya Zemlya Russia 75°0N 56°0E 214 B6
Nové Město Praha, Czech Rep. 50°4N 14°25E 135 B2
Nové Město Slovak Rep. 48°45N 17°50E 181 C10
Nové Město na Moravě Czech Rep. 49°34N 16°5E 180 B9
Nové Město nad Metují Czech Rep. 50°20N 16°10E 181 A9
Nové Zámky Slovak Rep. 48°2N 18°8E 181 C11
Novelda Spain 38°24N 0°45W 197 G4
Novellara Italy 44°51N 10°44E 198 D7
Novelty U.S.A. 40°1N 92°12W 310 D4
Noventa Vicentina Italy 45°17N 11°32E 199 C8
Novgorod = Velikiy Novgorod Russia 58°30N 31°25E 188 C6
Novgorod □ Russia 58°30N 32°30E 188 C7
Novgorod-Severskiy = Novhorod-Siverskyy Ukraine 52°2N 33°10E 189 G7
Novgradets = Suvorovo Bulgaria 43°20N 27°35E 203 C11
Novhorod-Siverskyy Ukraine 52°2N 33°10E 189 G7
Novi Bečej Serbia 45°36N 20°10E 182 E5
Novi Iskar Bulgaria 42°48N 23°21E 202 D7
Novi Kneževac Serbia 46°4N 20°8E 182 D5
Novi Lígure Italy 44°46N 8°47E 198 D5
Novi Pazar Bulgaria 43°25N 27°15E 203 C11
Novi Pazar Serbia 43°12N 20°28E 202 C4
Novi Sad Serbia 45°18N 19°52E 182 E4
Novi Slankamen Serbia 45°8N 20°15E 182 E5
Novi Travnik Bos.-H. 44°10N 17°40E 182 F2
Novi Vinodolski Croatia 45°10N 14°48E 199 C11
Novigrad Istra, Croatia 45°19N 13°33E 199 C10
Novigrad Zadar, Croatia 44°10N 15°32E 199 D12
Novigradsko More Croatia 44°12N 15°33E 199 D12
Novinger U.S.A. 40°14N 92°43W 310 D4
Novo Acôrdo Brazil 10°10S 46°48W 332 D2
Novo Airão Brazil 2°40S 60°59W 329 D5
Novo Aripuanã Brazil 5°8S 60°22W 329 E5
Novo Cruzeiro Brazil 17°29S 41°53W 333 E3
Novo Hamburgo Brazil 29°37S 51°7W 335 B5
Novo Horizonte Brazil 21°25S 49°10W 333 F2
Novo Ivanivka Ukraine 45°55N 29°5E 183 E14
Novo-Mariinsk = Anadyr Russia 64°35N 177°20E 215 C18
Novo Mesto Slovenia 45°47N 15°12E 199 C12
Novo Miloševo Serbia 45°42N 20°20E 182 E5
Novo Nikolaevsk = Novosibirsk Russia 55°0N 83°5E 217 B10
Novo Paraíso Brazil 1°17N 60°28W 329 C5
Novo-Starobinsk = Salihorsk Belarus 52°51N 27°27E 177 B14

Novo Urgench = Urganch
Uzbekistan 41°40N 60°41E 216 D6
Novoaleksandrovsk = Zarasai
Lithuania 55°40N 26°20E 188 E4
Novoaleksandrovsk
Russia 45°29N 41°17E 191 H5
Novoaleksandrovskaya = Novoaleksandrovsk
Russia 45°29N 41°17E 191 H5
Novoaleksandrovskoye
Russia 59°50N 30°31E 137 B2
Novoaltaysk Russia 53°30N 84°0E 217 B10
Novoannenskiy Russia 50°32N 42°39E 190 E6
Novoazovsk Ukraine 47°15N 38°4E 189 J10
Novocheboksarsk Russia 56°5N 47°27E 190 B8
Novocherkassk Russia 47°27N 40°15E 191 G5
Novodevichy Convent
Russia 55°43N 37°34E 129 B2
Novodevichye Russia 53°37N 48°50E 190 D9
Novodvinsk Russia 64°25N 40°42E 186 B7
Novogireyevo Russia 55°45N 37°46E 129 B3
Novogrudok = Navahrudak
Belarus 53°40N 25°50E 177 B13
Novohrad-Volynskyy
Ukraine 50°34N 27°35E 177 C14
Novokachalinsk Russia 45°5N 132°0E 220 B5
Novokazalinsk = Zhangaqazaly
Kazakhstan 45°48N 62°6E 216 C6
Novokhopersk Russia 51°5N 41°39E 190 E5
Novokiyevskoye = Kraskino
Russia 42°44N 130°48E 220 C5
Novokuybyshevsk Russia 53°7N 49°58E 190 D9
Novokuznetsk Russia 53°45N 87°10E 217 B11
Novolazarevskaya
Antarctica 71°0S 12°0E 151 D3
Novolyalinsky = Novaya Lyalya
Russia 59°4N 60°45E 186 C11
Novomoskovsk Russia 54°5N 38°15E 188 E10
Novomoskovsk Ukraine 48°33N 35°17E 189 H8
Novomyrhorod Ukraine 48°45N 31°33E 189 H6
Novonikolayevka = Novoazovsk
Ukraine 47°15N 38°4E 189 J10
Novopolotsk = Navapolatsk
Belarus 55°32N 28°37E 188 E5
Novorossiysk Russia 44°43N 37°46E 189 K9
Novorybnoye Russia 72°50N 105°50E 215 B11
Novorzhev Russia 57°3N 29°25E 188 D5
Novosaratovka Russia 59°50N 30°32E 137 B3
Novosej Albania 41°56N 20°35E 202 E4
Novoselytsya Ukraine 48°14N 26°15E 183 B11
Novoshakhtinsk Russia 47°46N 39°58E 189 J10
Novosibirsk Russia 55°0N 83°5E 217 B10
Novosibirskiye Ostrova
Russia 75°0N 142°0E 215 B15
Novosibirskoye Vdkhr.
Russia 54°35N 82°35E 217 B10
Novosil Russia 52°59N 37°2E 189 F9
Novosokolniki Russia 56°20N 30°12E 188 D6
Novotitarovskaya Russia 45°17N 39°12E 191 H4
Novotroitsk Russia 51°10N 58°15E 186 D10
Novotroitskoye = Töle Bī
Kazakhstan 43°42N 73°46E 217 D8
Novoukrayinka Ukraine 48°25N 31°30E 189 H6
Novoulyanovsk Russia 54°8N 48°24E 190 C9
Novouzensk Russia 50°32N 48°17E 190 E9
Novovolynsk Ukraine 50°45N 24°4E 185 H11
Novovoronezhskiy
Russia 51°19N 39°13E 189 G10
Novoyavoriske Ukraine 49°53N 23°33E 185 J10
Novozybkov Russia 52°30N 32°0E 189 F6
Novska Croatia 45°19N 17°0E 199 C14
Nový Bor Czech Rep. 50°46N 14°35E 180 A7
Novy Bug = Novyy Buh
Ukraine 47°34N 32°29E 189 J7
Nový Bydžov Czech Rep. 50°14N 15°29E 180 A8
Novy Dvor Belarus 52°50N 24°21E 185 F11
Novy Dwór Mazowiecki
Poland 52°26N 20°44E 185 F7
Nový Jičín Czech Rep. 49°30N 18°2E 181 B11
Novy Margelan = Farghona
Uzbekistan 40°23N 71°19E 217 D8
Novyy Bor Russia 66°43N 52°19E 186 A9
Novyy Buh Ukraine 47°34N 32°29E 189 J7
Novyy Oskol Russia 50°44N 37°55E 189 G9
Novyy Port Russia 67°40N 72°30E 214 C8
Novyy Urengoy Russia 65°48N 76°52E 214 C8
Nowa Deba Poland 50°26N 21°41E 185 H8
Nowa Nowa Australia 37°44S 148°3E 283 D8
Nowa Ruda Poland 50°35N 16°30E 185 H3
Nowa Sarzyna Poland 50°21N 22°21E 185 H9
Nowa Sól Poland 51°48N 15°44E 185 G2
Nowata U.S.A. 36°42N 95°38W 314 C7
Nowbarān Iran 35°8N 49°42E 247 C6
Nowe Poland 53°41N 18°44E 184 E5
Nowe-Babice Poland 52°15N 20°51E 143 B1
Nowe Miasteczko Poland 51°42N 15°42E 185 G2
Nowe Miasto Mazowieckie,
Poland 51°38N 20°34E 185 G7
Nowe Miasto Warsaw, Poland 143 a2
Nowe Miasto Lubawskie
Poland 53°27N 19°33E 184 E6
Nowe Skalmierzyce Poland 51°43N 18°0E 185 G4
Nowe Warpno Poland 53°42N 14°18E 184 E1
Nowendoc Australia 31°32S 151°44E 283 A9
Nowendoc △ Australia 31°33S 151°45E 283 A9
Nowghāb Iran 33°53N 59°4E 247 C8
Nowgong = Nagaon India 26°20N 92°50E 242 D4
Nowgong India 25°4N 79°27E 243 G8
Nowitna Nat. Wildlife Refuge △
U.S.A. 64°40N 154°16W 303 D9
Nowogard Poland 53°41N 15°10E 184 E2
Nowogród Poland 53°14N 21°53E 185 E8
Nowogród Bobrzański
Poland 51°48N 15°15E 185 G2
Nowogrodziec Poland 51°12N 15°24E 185 G2
Noworadomsk = Radomsko
Poland 51°5N 19°28E 185 G6
Nowra Australia 34°53S 150°35E 283 C9
Nowrangapur India 19°14N 82°33E 244 E6
Nowshāk = Noshaq
Pakistan 36°24N 71°49E 240 A3
Nowshera Pakistan 34°0N 72°0E 240 B4
Nowy Dwór Gdański
Poland 54°13N 19°7E 184 D6
Nowy Sącz Poland 49°40N 20°41E 185 J7
Nowy Staw Poland 54°13N 19°2E 184 D6
Nowy Targ Poland 49°29N 20°2E 185 J7
Nowy Tomyśl Poland 52°19N 16°10E 185 F3
Nowy Wiśnicz Poland 49°55N 20°28E 185 J7
Noxen U.S.A. 41°25N 76°4W 313 E8
Noyabr'sk Russia 64°34N 76°21E 214 C8
Noyant France 47°30N 0°6E 172 E7
Noyers France 47°40N 4°0E 173 E10
Nöykkiö Finland 60°10N 24°42E 121 B1
Noyon Oise, France 49°34N 2°59E 173 C9
Noyon Mongolia 43°2N 102°4E 226 C2
Nozay France 47°34N 1°38W 172 E5
Nqutu S. Africa 28°13S 30°32E 271 C5
Nsa Congo 2°22S 15°19E 264 C3
Nsa, O. en → Algeria 32°28N 5°24E 261 B6
Nsa, Plateau de Congo 2°26S 15°20E 264 C3
Nsanje Malawi 16°55S 35°12E 269 F4
Nsawam Ghana 5°50N 0°24W 263 D4
Nseluka Zambia 9°58S 31°16E 269 D3
Nsok Eq. Guin. 1°10N 11°19E 264 B2
Nsomba Zambia 10°45S 29°51E 269 E2
Nsontin
Dem. Rep. of the Congo 3°7S 17°56E 264 C3
Nsopzup Burma 25°51N 97°30E 241 C6
Nsukka Nigeria 6°51N 7°29E 263 D6
Ntaria ☺ Australia 24°0S 132°41E 278 D5
Ntem → Cameroon 2°21N 9°49E 264 B2
Ntingui, Mt. Comoros Is. 12°12S 44°25E 272 a
Ntoum Gabon 0°22N 9°47E 264 B1
N'Tsama Congo 0°53S 14°44E 264 C2
Ntsaouéni Comoros Is. 11°27S 43°15E 272 a
Ntsoudjini Comoros Is. 11°39S 43°15E 272 a
Ntui Cameroon 4°27N 11°38E 263 E7
Ntungamo Uganda 0°56S 30°17E 268 C3
Nu Jiang → China 29°58N 97°25E 228 E2
Nu Shan China 26°0N 99°20E 228 E2
Nuakata I. Papua N. G. 10°17S 151°2E 286 F6
Nuba Mts. = Nubah, Jibalan
Sudan 12°0N 31°0E 257 E3
Nubah, Jibalan Sudan 12°0N 31°0E 257 E3
Nubia Africa 21°0N 32°0E 254 D7
Nubian Desert = Nûbîya, Es Sahrâ en
Sudan 21°30N 33°30E 256 C3
Nûbîya, Es Sahrâ en
Sudan 21°30N 33°30E 256 C3
Nubl Syria 36°22N 36°59E 250 B7
Nubledo Spain 43°31N 5°52W 194 B5
Nuboai Indonesia 2°10S 136°30E 231 E9
Nubra → India 34°35N 77°35E 243 B7
Nucet Romania 46°23N 22°35E 182 D7
Nueces → U.S.A. 27°51N 97°30W 314 H6
Nueltin L. Canada 60°30N 99°30W 297 A9
Nuestra Señora del Rosario de
Caá-Catí Argentina 27°45S 57°36W 334 B4
Nueva, I. Chile 55°13S 66°30W 336 E3
Nueva Antioquia Colombia 6°5N 69°26W 328 B4
Nueva Atzacoalco Mexico 19°29N 99°4W 128 B2
Nueva Carteya Spain 37°35N 4°28W 195 H6
Nueva Ciudad Guerrero
Mexico 26°34N 99°12W 319 B5
Nueva Ecija □ Phil. 15°35N 121°0E 232 D3
Nueva Esparta □ Venezuela 11°0N 64°0W 329 A5
Nueva Gerona Cuba 21°53N 82°49W 320 B3
Nueva Imperial Chile 38°45S 72°58W 336 A2
Nueva Loja = Lago Agrio
Ecuador 0°5N 76°52W 328 C2
Nueva Palmira Uruguay 33°52S 58°20W 334 C4
Nueva Pompeya
Argentina 34°40S 58°25W 117 C2
Nueva Rosita Mexico 27°57N 101°13W 318 B4
Nueva San Salvador
El Salv. 13°40N 89°18W 320 D2
Nueva Tabarca Spain 38°17N 0°30W 197 G4
Nueva Tenochtitlán
Mexico 19°27N 99°5W 128 B2
Nueva Vizcaya □ Phil. 16°20N 121°20E 232 C3
Nueve de Julio Argentina 35°0S 61°0W 334 D3
Nuevitas Cuba 21°30N 77°20W 320 B4
Nuevo, G. Argentina 43°0S 64°30W 336 B4
Nuevo Casas Grandes
Mexico 30°25N 107°55W 318 A3
Nuevo Laredo Mexico 27°30N 99°31W 319 B5
Nuevo León □ Mexico 25°20N 100°0W 318 C5
Nuevo Mundo, Cerro
Bolivia 21°55S 66°53W 330 E4
Nuevo Rocafuerte Ecuador 0°55S 75°27W 328 D2
Nugaal □ Somalia 8°10N 49°0E 267 C6
Nugaal → Somalia 8°0N 49°47E 267 C6
Nugaaleed, Dooxo Somalia 8°35N 48°35E 267 C6
Nugget Pt. N.Z. 46°27S 169°50E 285 G4
Nugrus, Gebel Egypt 24°47N 34°35E 256 C3
Nuguria Is. Papua N. G. 3°20S 154°45E 286 B8
Nuhaka N.Z. 39°3S 177°45E 284 F6
Nui Pac. Oc. 7°15S 177°10E 277 B14
Nuijala Finland 60°12N 24°46E 121 B1
Nuits-St-Georges France 47°10N 4°56E 173 E11
Nukey Bluff Australia 32°26S 135°29E 281 E2
Nukha = Şaki Azerbaijan 41°10N 47°5E 191 K8
Nukhayb Iraq 32°4N 42°3E 213 F10
Nukheila Sudan 19°1N 26°21E 256 D2
Nukiki Solomon Is. 6°46S 156°35E 287 L9
Nuku Papua N. G. 3°41S 142°28E 286 B2
Nuku Hiva French Polynesia 8°54S 140°6W 289 f
Nuku'alofa Tonga 21°10S 175°12W 287 Q13
Nukuhu Papua N. G. 5°34S 149°22E 286 C5
Nukulaelae Tuvalu 9°23S 179°52E 277 B14
Nukunonu Pac. Oc. 9°12S 171°54W 277 B16
Nukus Uzbekistan 42°27N 59°41E 216 D5
Nulato U.S.A. 64°43N 158°6W 303 D8
Nules Spain 39°51N 0°9W 196 F4
Nullagine Australia 21°53S 120°7E 278 D3
Nullagine → Australia 21°20S 120°20E 278 D3
Nullarbor Australia 31°28S 130°55E 279 F5
Nullarbor △ Australia 32°39S 130°0E 279 F2
Nullarbor Plain Australia 31°10S 129°0E 279 F4
Numabukuro Japan 35°43N 139°39E 140 A2
Numalla, L. Australia 28°43S 144°20E 281 D3
Numan Nigeria 9°29N 12°3E 263 D7
Numanuma Papua N. G. 9°41S 150°55E 286 E6
Numata Japan 36°45N 139°4E 223 A11
Numatinna → South Sudan 7°33N 27°20E 257 F2
Numaykoos Lake ⌓
Canada 57°52N 95°58W 297 B9
Numazu Japan 35°7N 138°51E 223 B10
Numbulwar Australia 14°15S 135°45E 280 A2
Numedal Norway 60°6N 9°6E 164 D6
Numfoor Indonesia 1°0S 134°50E 231 E8
Numurkah Australia 36°5S 145°26E 283 D6
Nunaksaluk I. Canada 55°49N 60°20W 299 A7
Nunap Isua Greenland 59°48N 43°55W 154 F6
Nunavik Greenland 71°50N 54°25W 154 C5
Nunavut □ Canada 66°0N 85°0W 295 D15
Nunda U.S.A. 42°35N 77°56W 312 D7
Nuneaton U.K. 52°32N 1°27W 169 E6
Nuñez Argentina 34°32S 58°27W 117 B2
Nungarin Australia 31°12S 118°6E 279 F2
Nungo Mozam. 13°23S 37°43E 269 E4
Nungwe Tanzania 2°48S 32°2E 268 C3
Nunhead U.K. 51°27N 0°3W 125 B3
Nunivak I. U.S.A. 60°10N 166°30W 303 F6
Nunkun India 33°57N 76°2E 243 C7
Ñuñoa Chile 33°27S 70°35W 137 B2
Nunukan Indonesia 4°4N 117°40E 235 B5
Nuoro Italy 40°20N 9°20E 200 B2
Nuozhadu Dam China 22°39N 100°25E 228 F3
Núpur Iceland 65°58N 23°36W 155 B3
Nuqayy, Jabal Libya 23°11N 19°30E 258 D3
Nuqūb Yemen 14°59N 45°48E 248 D4
Nuquí Colombia 5°42N 77°17W 328 B2
Nūr Iran 36°33N 52°1E 247 B7
Nur Dağı Turkey 36°54N 35°39E 250 B6
Nur Dağları Turkey 36°50N 36°23E 250 B7
Nura → Kazakhstan 50°30N 69°59E 216 B7
Nūrābād Hormozgān, Iran 27°47N 57°12E 247 E8
Nūrābād Lorestān, Iran 34°4N 47°58E 213 E12
Nurabad Uzbekistan 39°35N 66°17E 217 E7
Nure → Italy 45°3N 9°49E 198 C6
Nuremberg = Nürnberg
Germany 49°27N 11°3E 179 F7
Nuri Sonora, Mexico 28°5N 109°22W 318 B3
Nuri Sudan 18°29N 31°59E 256 D3
Nuriootpa Australia 34°27S 139°0E 282 C3
Nuristān □ Afghan. 35°20N 71°0E 240 B3
Nurlat Russia 54°29N 50°45E 190 C10
Nurmes Finland 63°33N 29°10E 160 E23
Nürnberg Germany 49°27N 11°3E 179 F7
Nurpur Pakistan 31°53N 71°54E 242 D4
Nurra, La Italy 40°45N 8°15E 200 B1
Nurran, L. = Terewah, L.
Australia 29°52S 147°35E 281 D4
Nurrari Lakes Australia 29°1S 130°5E 279 E5
Nurri Italy 39°43N 9°14E 200 C2
Nürtingen Germany 48°37N 9°19E 179 G5
Nurzec → Poland 52°37N 22°25E 185 F9
Nus Italy 45°45N 7°28E 198 C4
Nusa Dua Indonesia 8°48S 115°14E 231 K18
Nusa Tenggara Barat □
Indonesia 8°50S 117°30E 235 D5
Nusa Tenggara Timur □
Indonesia 9°30S 122°0E 231 F6
Nusaybin Turkey 37°3N 41°10E 213 D9
Nuşayrīyah, J. an Syria 35°20N 36°13E 250 C7
Nuşeirat Gaza Strip 31°27N 34°24E 251 G5
Nushki Pakistan 29°35N 66°0E 242 E2
Nusle Czech Rep. 50°3N 14°26E 135 B2
Nussdorf Austria 48°15N 16°21E 142 A2
Nuuk Greenland 64°10N 51°35W 154 E5
Nuupere, Pte. Moorea 17°36S 149°47W 289 e
Nuussauq Greenland 74°8N 57°3W 154 C5
Nu'uuli Amer. Samoa 14°19S 170°42W 302 f
Nuwakot Nepal 28°10N 83°55E 243 E10
Nuwara Eliya Sri Lanka 6°58N 80°48E 245 L5
Nuwayb'ī, W. an →
Si. Arabia 29°18N 34°57E 251 J5
Nuweiba' Egypt 28°59N 34°39E 251 K5
Nuwerus S. Africa 31°8S 18°24E 270 D2
Nuweveldberge S. Africa 32°10S 21°45E 270 D3
Nuyts, Pt. Australia 35°4S 116°38E 279 G2
Nuyts Arch. Australia 32°35S 133°20E 281 E1
N'Vinda Angola 13°8S 19°2E 265 E3
Nxai Pan △ Botswana 19°50S 24°46E 270 A3
Nxaunxau Botswana 18°57S 21°4E 270 A3
Nyaake Liberia 4°52N 7°37W 262 E3
Nyabessan Cameroon 2°28N 10°24E 264 B2
Nyabing Australia 33°33S 118°9E 279 F2
Nyack U.S.A. 41°5N 73°55W 313 E11
Nyagan Russia 62°30N 65°38E 214 C7
Nyah West Australia 35°16S 143°21E 282 C5
Nyahanga Tanzania 2°20S 33°37E 268 C3
Nyahua Tanzania 5°25S 33°23E 268 D3
Nyahururu Kenya 0°2N 36°27E 268 B4
Nyainqêntanglha Shan
China 30°0N 90°0E 218 F7
Nyakanazi Tanzania 3°2S 31°10E 268 C3
Nyakrom Ghana 5°40N 0°50W 263 D4
Nyâlâ Sudan 12°2N 24°58E 257 E1
Nyalam China 28°32N 86°4E 218 F6
Nyamandhlovu Zimbabwe 19°55S 28°16E 269 F2
Nyambiti Tanzania 2°48S 33°27E 268 C3
Nyamira Kenya 0°36S 34°52E 268 C3
Nyamlell South Sudan 9°7N 26°59E 257 F2
Nyamwaga Tanzania 1°27S 34°33E 268 C3
Nyandekwa Tanzania 3°57S 32°32E 268 C3
Nyanding → South Sudan 8°40N 32°41E 257 F3
Nyandoma Russia 61°40N 40°12E 188 B11
Nyanga Congo 2°52S 11°57E 264 C2
Nyanga Western Cape,
S. Africa 33°59S 18°35E 118 A2
Nyanga → Gabon 2°58S 10°15E 264 C2
Nyanga △ Zimbabwe 18°17S 32°46E 269 F3
Nyangana Namibia 18°0S 20°40E 270 A3
Nyanguge Tanzania 2°30S 33°12E 268 C3
Nyanji Zambia 14°25S 31°46E 269 E3
Nyankpala Ghana 9°21N 0°58W 263 D4
Nyanza Rwanda 2°20S 29°42E 268 C2
Nyanza □ Kenya 0°10S 34°15E 268 C3
Nyanza-Lac Burundi 4°21S 29°36E 268 C2
Nyaponges South Sudan 5°5N 33°45E 257 F3
Nyasa, L. = Malawi, L.
Africa 12°30S 34°30E 269 E3
Nyasaland = Malawi ■
Africa 11°55S 34°0E 269 E3
Nyasvizh Belarus 53°14N 26°38E 177 B14
Nyaungdon = Yandoon
Burma 17°0N 95°40E 241 G5
Nyaunglebin Burma 17°52N 96°42E 241 G6
Nyazepetrovsk Russia 56°3N 59°36E 186 C10
Nyazura Zimbabwe 18°40S 32°16E 269 F3
Nyazwidzi → Zimbabwe 20°0S 31°17E 269 G3
Nybergsund Norway 61°15N 12°19E 164 C9
Nyborg Denmark 55°18N 10°47E 163 J4
Nybro Sweden 56°44N 15°55E 163 H9
Nyda Russia 66°40N 72°58E 214 C8
Nyeboe Land Greenland 82°0N 57°0W 154 A5
Nyengo Swamp Zambia 14°51S 22°7E 265 E4
Nyeri Kenya 0°23S 36°56E 268 C4
Nyerol South Sudan 8°41N 32°1E 257 F3
Nyhammar Sweden 60°17N 14°58E 162 D8
Nyika △ Malawi 10°30S 33°53E 269 E3
Nyimba Zambia 14°33S 30°50E 269 E3
Nyinahin Ghana 6°43N 2°3W 262 D4
Nyingchi China 29°32N 94°25E 218 F7
Nyíradony Hungary 47°41N 21°55E 182 C6
Nyírbátor Hungary 47°49N 22°9E 182 C7
Nyíregyháza Hungary 47°58N 21°47E 182 C6
Nyiru, Mt. Kenya 2°8N 36°50E 268 B4
Nykarleby = Uusikaarlepyy
Finland 63°32N 22°31E 160 E20
Nykirke Norway 60°54N 10°19E 164 D7
Nykøbing Nordjylland,
Denmark 56°48N 8°51E 163 H2
Nykøbing Sjælland,
Denmark 54°56N 11°52E 163 K5
Nykøbing Sjælland,
Denmark 55°55N 11°40E 163 J5
Nyköping Sweden 58°45N 17°1E 163 F11
Nykroppa Sweden 59°37N 14°18E 162 E8
Nykvarn Sweden 59°11N 17°25E 162 E11
Nyland Sweden 63°1N 17°45E 162 A11
Nylstroom = Modimolle
S. Africa 24°42S 28°22E 271 B4
Nymagee Australia 32°7S 146°20E 283 B7
Nymboida △ Australia 29°38S 152°26E 281 D5
Nymburk Czech Rep. 50°10N 15°1E 180 A8
Nymphenburg Germany 48°9N 11°30E 131 B2
Nymphenburg, Schloss
Germany 48°9N 11°30E 131 B2
Nynäshamn Sweden 58°54N 17°57E 163 F11
Nyngan Australia 31°30S 147°8E 283 A7
Nyoma Rap India 33°10N 78°40E 243 C8
Nyoman = Nemunas →
Lithuania 55°25N 21°10E 184 C8
Nyon Switz. 46°23N 6°14E 179 J2
Nyong → Cameroon 3°17N 9°54E 263 E6
Nyons France 44°22N 5°10E 175 D9
Nyou Burkina Faso 12°42N 2°1W 263 C4
Nýrsko Czech Rep. 49°18N 13°9E 180 B6
Nysa Poland 50°30N 17°22E 185 H4
Nysa → Europe 52°4N 14°46E 178 C10
Nysa Kłodzka → Poland 50°49N 17°40E 185 H4
Nysætre Norway 62°2N 8°20E 164 B5
Nysäter Sweden 59°17N 12°47E 162 E6
Nyslott = Savonlinna
Finland 61°52N 28°53E 188 B5
Nyssa U.S.A. 43°53N 117°0W 304 E5
Nystad = Uusikaupunki
Finland 60°47N 21°25E 188 B1
Nysted Denmark 54°40N 11°44E 163 K5
Nyunzu
Dem. Rep. of the Congo 5°57S 27°58E 268 D2
Nyurba Russia 63°17N 118°28E 215 C12
Nyzhankovychi Ukraine 49°40N 22°49E 185 J9
Nyzhnohirskyy Ukraine 45°27N 34°38E 189 K8
Nyzhny Vorota Ukraine 48°46N 23°6E 182 B8
Nzébéla Guinea 8°9N 9°7W 262 D3
Nzega Tanzania 4°10S 33°12E 268 C3
Nzérékoré Guinea 7°49N 8°48W 262 D3
Nzeto Angola 7°10S 12°52E 265 D2
Nzilo, Chutes de
Dem. Rep. of the Congo 10°18S 25°27E 265 E5
Nzilo, L.
Dem. Rep. of the Congo 10°35S 25°30E 265 E5
N'zo → Ivory C. 6°15N 7°3W 262 D3
N'zo △ Ivory C. 6°15N 7°15W 262 D3
Nzubuka Tanzania 4°45S 32°50E 268 C3
Nzwani = Anjouan
Comoros Is. 12°15S 44°20E 272 a

O

O Barco Spain 42°23N 6°58W 194 C4
O Carballiño Spain 42°26N 8°5W 194 C2
O Corgo Spain 42°56N 7°25W 194 C3
O Le Pupū Pu'e △
Samoa 13°59S 171°43W 287 V20
O Pino Spain 42°56N 8°20W 194 C2
O Porriño Spain 42°10N 8°37W 194 C2
Ō-Shima Hokkaidō, Japan 41°30N 139°22E 220 D9
Ō-Shima Nagasaki, Japan 33°29N 129°33E 222 D1
Ō-Shima Shizuoka, Japan 34°44N 139°24E 223 C11
O.R. Tambo Int. ✈ (JNB)
S. Africa 27°7S 29°16E 123 A2
Oa, Mull of U.K. 55°35N 6°20W 167 F2
Oacoma U.S.A. 43°48N 99°24W 308 D4
Oahe, L. U.S.A. 44°27N 100°24W 308 C3
Oahe Dam U.S.A. 44°27N 100°24W 308 C3
O'ahu U.S.A. 21°28N 157°58W 302 K14
Oak Creek U.S.A. 42°52N 87°55W 311 B9
Oak Forest U.S.A. 41°37N 87°47W 119 D2
Oak Grove U.S.A. 33°50N 84°18W 113 A3
Oak Harbor U.S.A. 48°18N 122°39W 306 B4
Oak Hill Fla., U.S.A. 28°52N 80°51W 317 G9
Oak Hill Mass., U.S.A. 42°18N 71°10W 116 B1
Oak Hill W. Va., U.S.A. 37°59N 81°9W 309 G13
Oak Island U.S.A. 33°55N 78°10W 315 E15
Oak Lawn U.S.A. 41°42N 87°45W 119 C2
Oak Park Ga., U.S.A. 32°22N 82°19W 316 C7
Oak Park Ill., U.S.A. 41°52N 87°47W 119 B2
Oak Ridge U.S.A. 36°1N 84°16W 315 C12
Oak Street Beach U.S.A. 119 a2
Oak View Calif., U.S.A. 34°24N 119°18W 307 L7
Oak View Md., U.S.A. 39°1N 76°58W 143 A3
Oakan-Dake Japan 43°27N 144°10E 220 C12
Oakbank Australia 33°4S 140°33E 282 B4
Oakdale Calif., U.S.A. 37°46N 120°51W 306 H6
Oakdale Georgia, U.S.A. 33°51N 84°30W 113 A2
Oakdale La., U.S.A. 30°49N 92°40W 314 F8
Oakes U.S.A. 46°8N 98°6W 308 B4
Oakesdale U.S.A. 47°8N 117°15W 304 C5
Oakey Australia 27°25S 151°43E 281 D5
Oakfield Ga., U.S.A. 31°47N 83°58W 316 D6
Oakfield N.Y., U.S.A. 43°4N 78°16W 312 C6
Oakford U.S.A. 40°6N 89°58W 310 D7
Oakham U.K. 52°40N 0°43W 169 E7
Oakhurst U.S.A. 37°19N 119°40W 306 H7
Oakland Calif., U.S.A. 37°48N 122°18W 136 B3
Oakland Ill., U.S.A. 39°39N 88°2W 311 E8
Oakland Pa., U.S.A. 41°57N 75°36W 313 E9
Oakland City U.S.A. 38°20N 87°21W 311 F9
Oakland Park U.S.A. 26°10N 80°7W 129 A3
Oaklands Australia 35°34S 146°10E 283 C7
Oaklawn U.S.A. 38°46N 76°56W 143 C3
Oakleigh Australia 37°54S 145°5E 128 B2
Oakley Idaho, U.S.A. 42°15N 113°53W 304 E7
Oakley Kans., U.S.A. 39°8N 100°51W 308 F3
Oakover → Australia 21°0S 120°40E 278 D3
Oakridge U.S.A. 43°45N 122°28W 304 E2
Oaks, The Australia 34°3S 150°34E 283 C9
Oaktown U.S.A. 38°52N 87°27W 311 F9
Oakville Ont., Canada 43°27N 79°41W 312 C5
Oakville Wash., U.S.A. 46°51N 123°14W 306 D3
Oakwood U.S.A. 41°6N 84°23W 311 C12
Oakwood Beach U.S.A. 40°33N 74°7W 132 C1
Oamaru N.Z. 45°5S 170°59E 285 F5
Ōamishirasato Japan 35°31N 140°18E 223 B12
Oancea Romania 45°21N 27°42E 183 E12
Oarai Japan 36°21N 140°34E 223 A12
Oasi Faunistica di Vendicari △
Italy 36°49N 15°6E 201 F8
Oasis Calif., U.S.A. 37°29N 117°55W 306 H9
Oasis Calif., U.S.A. 33°28N 116°6W 307 M10
Oates Land Antarctica 69°0S 160°0E 151 C11
Oatley Australia 33°59S 151°4E 139 B1
Oatman U.S.A. 35°1N 114°19W 307 K12
Oaxaca Mexico 17°3N 96°43W 319 D5
Oaxaca □ Mexico 17°0N 96°30W 319 D5
Ob → Russia 66°45N 69°30E 214 C7
Oba Canada 49°4N 84°7W 298 C3
Obala Cameroon 4°9N 11°32E 263 E7
Obalende Nigeria 6°26N 3°25E 124 B2
Obama Fukui, Japan 35°30N 135°45E 223 B7
Obama Nagasaki, Japan 32°43N 130°13E 222 E2
Obama, Mt. Antigua & B. 17°2N 61°52W 322 b
Oban Nigeria 5°17N 8°33E 263 D6
Oban Argyll & Bute, U.K. 56°25N 5°29W 167 E3
Oba's Palace Nigeria 6°26N 3°22E 124 B2
Obbia = Hobyo Somalia 5°25N 48°30E 267 C6
Obdorsk = Salekhard
Russia 66°30N 66°35E 214 C7
Oberá Argentina 27°21S 55°2W 335 B4
Oberammergau Germany 47°36N 11°4E 179 H7
Oberasbach Germany 49°25N 10°57E 179 F6
Oberbayern □ Germany 48°5N 11°50E 179 G7
Oberburg = Gornji Grad
Slovenia 46°20N 14°52E 199 B11
Oberdonau = Oberösterreich □
Austria 48°10N 14°0E 180 C7
Oberdrauburg Austria 46°44N 12°58E 180 E5
Obere Donau △ Germany 48°5N 9°2E 179 G5
Oberer Bayerischer Wald △
Germany 49°15N 12°40E 179 F8
Oberföhring Germany 48°10N 11°37E 131 B2
Oberfranken □ Germany 50°10N 11°20E 179 E7
Oberglogau = Głogówek
Poland 50°21N 17°53E 185 H4
Oberhaching Germany 48°1N 11°35E 131 B2
Oberhausen Germany 51°28N 6°51E 178 D2
Oberkirch Germany 48°31N 8°4E 179 G4
Oberlaa Austria 48°8N 16°24E 142 B2
Oberlaibach = Vrhnika
Slovenia 45°58N 14°15E 199 C11
Oberlausitz Germany 51°16N 14°18E 178 D10
Oberlin Kans., U.S.A. 39°49N 100°32W 308 F3
Oberlin La., U.S.A. 30°37N 92°46W 314 F8
Oberlin Ohio, U.S.A. 41°18N 82°13W 312 E2
Oberlisse Austria 48°17N 16°26E 142 A2
Obermenzing Germany 48°10N 11°28E 131 B2
Obermoos Schwaige
Germany 48°14N 11°27E 131 A1
Obernai France 48°28N 7°30E 173 D14
Oberndorf Germany 48°17N 8°34E 179 G4
Obernigk = Oborniki Śląskie
Poland 51°17N 16°53E 185 G3
Oberon Australia 33°45S 149°52E 283 B8
Oberösterreich □ Austria 48°10N 14°0E 180 C7
Oberpfalz □ Germany 49°20N 12°10E 179 F8
Oberpfälzer Wald
Germany 49°30N 12°30E 179 F8
Oberpfälzer Wald △
Germany 49°40N 12°20E 179 F8
Oberschleissheim
Germany 48°15N 11°33E 131 A2
Oberschöneweide
Germany 52°27N 13°31E 115 B4
Oberstdorf Germany 47°24N 10°15E 179 H6
Oberting Gabon 0°22S 9°46E 264 C1
Obertyn Ukraine 48°42N 25°10E 183 B10
Oberursel Germany 50°11N 8°35E 179 E4
Oberwart Austria 47°17N 16°12E 181 D9
Obi, Kepulauan Indonesia 1°23S 127°45E 231 E7
Obiaruku Nigeria 5°51N 6°9E 263 D6
Óbidos Brazil 1°50S 55°30W 329 D6
Óbidos Portugal 39°19N 9°10W 195 F1
Obihiro Japan 42°56N 143°12E 220 C11
Obilatu Indonesia 1°25S 127°20E 231 E7
Obilnoye Russia 47°32N 44°30E 191 G7
Obing Germany 48°0N 12°24E 179 G8
Objat France 45°16N 1°24E 174 C5
Oblong U.S.A. 39°0N 87°55W 311 F9
Obluchye Russia 49°1N 131°4E 215 E14
Obninsk Russia 55°8N 36°37E 188 E9
Obo C.A.R. 5°20N 26°32E 264 A5
Obock Djibouti 12°0N 43°20E 257 E5
Obodivka Ukraine 48°24N 29°15E 183 B14
Oborniki Poland 52°39N 16°50E 185 F3
Oborniki Śląskie Poland 51°17N 16°53E 185 G3
Obouya Congo 0°56S 15°43E 264 C3
Oboyan Russia 51°15N 36°21E 189 G9
Obozerskaya = Obozerskiy
Russia 63°34N 40°21E 186 B7
Obozerskiy Russia 63°34N 40°21E 186 B7
Obrenovac Serbia 44°40N 20°11E 202 B4
O'Brien U.S.A. 30°2N 82°57W 316 E7
Obrovac Croatia 44°11N 15°41E 199 D12
Obruk Turkey 38°7N 33°12E 212 C5
Obrzycko Poland 52°42N 16°32E 185 F3
Observatory Sydney, Australia 139 a1
Observatory Gauteng,
S. Africa 26°10S 28°4E 123 B2
Observatory Inlet
Canada 55°10N 129°54W 296 B3
Obshchi Syrt Russia 52°0N 53°0E 158 E16
Obskaya Guba Russia 69°0N 73°0E 214 C8
Obu Japan 35°0N 136°58E 223 B8
Obuasi Ghana 6°17N 1°40W 263 D4
Obubra Nigeria 6°8N 8°20E 263 D6
Óbuda Hungary 47°33N 19°2E 117 A2
Obudu Nigeria 6°38N 9°5E 263 D6
Obukhovo Russia 59°53N 30°22E 137 B2
Obura Papua N. G. 6°25S 145°58E 286 D3
Obvodnyy Kanal Russia 59°54N 30°20E 137 B1
Obwalden □ Switz. 46°55N 8°15E 179 J4
Obzor Bulgaria 42°50N 27°52E 203 D11
Ocala U.S.A. 29°11N 82°8W 317 F7
Ocamo → Venezuela 2°48N 65°14W 329 C4
Ocampo Chihuahua,
Mexico 28°11N 108°23W 318 B3
Ocampo Tamaulipas,
Mexico 22°50N 99°20W 319 C5
Ocaña Colombia 8°15N 73°20W 328 B3
Ocaña Spain 39°55N 3°30W 194 F7
Occidental, Cordillera
Colombia 5°0N 76°0W 328 C2
Occidental, Cordillera Peru 14°0S 74°0W 330 C3
Occidental, Grand Erg
Algeria 30°20N 1°0E 261 B5
Ocean City Md., U.S.A. 38°20N 75°5W 309 F16
Ocean City N.J., U.S.A. 39°17N 74°35W 309 F16
Ocean City Wash., U.S.A. 47°4N 124°10W 306 C2
Ocean Falls Canada 52°18N 127°48W 296 C3
Ocean I. = Banaba
Kiribati 0°45S 169°50E 288 H8
Ocean Park Hong Kong,
China 22°13N 114°10E 122 B2
Ocean Park Wash.,
U.S.A. 46°30N 124°3W 306 D2
Oceano U.S.A. 35°6N 120°37W 307 K6
Oceanport U.S.A. 40°19N 74°3W 313 F10
Oceanside U.S.A. 33°12N 117°23W 307 M9
Ochagavia Spain 42°55N 1°5W 196 C3
Ochakiv Ukraine 46°37N 31°33E 189 J6
Ochamchire Georgia 42°46N 41°32E 191 J5
Ochi, Oros Greece 38°5N 24°25E 204 C6
Ochiai Japan 35°1N 133°45E 222 B5
Ochil Hills U.K. 56°14N 3°40W 167 E5
Ochlocknee U.S.A. 30°58N 84°3W 316 E5
Ochlockonee → U.S.A. 29°59N 84°26W 316 F5
Ocho Rios Jamaica 18°24N 77°6W 320 a
Ochopee U.S.A. 25°54N 81°18W 317 K8
Ochota Poland 52°13N 20°58E 143 B1
Ochsenfurt Germany 49°40N 10°4E 179 F6
Ochsenhausen Germany 48°4N 9°57E 179 G5
Ocilla U.S.A. 31°36N 83°15W 316 D6
Ockelbo Sweden 60°54N 16°45E 162 D10
Ocmulgee → U.S.A. 31°58N 82°33W 316 D7
Ocmulgee △ U.S.A. 32°49N 83°37W 316 C6
Ocna Mureş Romania 46°23N 23°55E 183 D8
Ocna Sibiului Romania 45°52N 24°2E 183 E9
Ocnele Mari Romania 45°8N 24°18E 183 E9
Ocniţa Moldova 48°25N 27°30E 183 B12
Ocoee U.S.A. 28°34N 81°32W 133 A1
Ocoña Peru 16°26S 73°8W 330 D3
Ocoña → Peru 16°28S 73°8W 330 D3
Oconee → U.S.A. 31°58N 82°33W 316 D7
Oconee, L. U.S.A. 33°28N 83°15W 316 B6
O'Connell Street Dublin, Ireland 120 b2
Oconomowoc U.S.A. 43°7N 88°30W 311 A8
Oconto U.S.A. 44°53N 87°52W 308 C10
Oconto Falls U.S.A. 44°52N 88°9W 308 C9
Ocosingo Mexico 16°53N 92°6W 319 D6
Ocotal Nic. 13°41N 86°31W 320 D2
Ocotlán Jalisco, Mexico 20°21N 102°46W 318 C4
Ocotlán Oaxaca, Mexico 16°48N 96°40W 319 D5
Ocreza → Portugal 39°32N 7°50W 195 F3
Öcsa Hungary 47°17N 19°15E 182 C4
Octeville France 49°38N 1°40W 172 C5
Ocumare del Tuy
Venezuela 10°7N 66°46W 328 A4
Ocurí Bolivia 18°45S 65°50W 331 D4
Oda Ghana 5°50N 0°51W 263 D4
Ōda Shimane, Japan 35°11N 132°30E 222 B4
Oda, J. Sudan 20°21N 36°39E 256 C4
Ódáðahraun Iceland 65°5N 17°0W 155 B9
Ŏdaejin N. Korea 41°34N 129°40E 224 B4
Odaesan △ S. Korea 37°40N 128°30E 224 D4
Odaiba Japan 35°38N 139°47E 140 B3
Ödåkra Sweden 56°7N 12°45E 163 H6
Ōdana Japan 35°33N 139°35E 140 B2
Odate Japan 40°16N 140°34E 220 D10
Odawara Japan 35°20N 139°6E 223 B11
Odda Norway 60°3N 6°35E 164 D3
Odder = Xuddur Somalia 4°11N 43°52E 267 D5
Odder Denmark 55°58N 10°10E 163 J4
Odei → Canada 56°6N 96°54W 297 B9
Odell U.S.A. 41°0N 88°31W 311 C8
Odemira Portugal 37°35N 8°40W 195 H2
Ödemiş Turkey 38°15N 28°0E 205 C9
Öden-Stockach Germany 48°5N 11°41E 131 B3
Ödenburg = Sopron
Hungary 47°45N 16°32E 182 C1
Odendaalsrus S. Africa 27°48S 26°45E 270 C4
Odensbacken Sweden 59°10N 15°32E 162 E9
Odense Denmark 55°22N 10°23E 163 J4
Odenwald = Neckartal-Odenwald △
Germany 49°30N 9°5E 179 F5
Odenwald Germany 49°35N 9°2E 179 F5
Oder → Europe 53°33N 14°38E 178 B10
Oder-Havel Kanal
Germany 52°52N 14°2E 178 C10
Oderzo Italy 45°47N 12°29E 199 C9
Odesa Ukraine 46°30N 30°45E 189 J6
Odesa □ Ukraine 47°20N 29°55E 189 J5
Ödeshög Sweden 58°14N 14°39E 163 F8
Odessa = Odesa Ukraine 46°30N 30°45E 189 J6
Odessa Ont., Canada 44°17N 76°43W 313 B8
Odessa Mo., U.S.A. 39°0N 93°57W 310 F3
Odessa Tex., U.S.A. 31°52N 102°23W 314 F3
Odessa Wash., U.S.A. 47°20N 118°41W 304 C4
Odiakwe Botswana 20°12S 25°17E 270 B4
Odiel → Spain 37°10N 6°55W 195 H4
Odienné Ivory C. 9°30N 7°34W 262 D3
Odilampi Finland 60°18N 24°45E 121 B1
Odimba Gabon 2°2S 9°33E 264 C2
Odintsovo Russia 55°40N 37°16E 188 E9
Odiongan Phil. 12°24N 121°59E 232 E3
Odisha □ India 20°0N 84°0E 244 E7
Odivelas Portugal 38°47N 9°10W 126 A1
Odobeşti Romania 45°43N 27°4E 183 E12
Odolanów Poland 51°34N 17°40E 185 G4
Odolany Poland 52°13N 20°55E 143 B1
O'Donnell U.S.A. 32°58N 101°50W 314 E4
O'Donnell Pt. Canada 45°5N 80°5W 312 A4
Odorheiu Secuiesc
Romania 46°21N 25°21E 183 D10
Odoyevo Russia 53°56N 36°42E 188 F9
Odra = Oder → Europe 53°33N 14°38E 178 B10
Odra → Spain 42°14N 4°17W 194 C6
Odum U.S.A. 31°40N 82°2W 316 D7
Odžaci Serbia 45°30N 19°17E 182 E4
Odžak Bos.-H. 45°3N 18°18E 182 E3
Odzala Congo 0°37N 14°57E 264 B2
Odzala △ Congo 0°55N 14°55E 264 B2
Odzi Zimbabwe 19°0S 32°20E 271 A5
Odzi → Zimbabwe 19°45S 32°23E 271 A5
Oebisfelde Germany 52°27N 10°57E 178 C6
Oecussi = Pante Macassar
E. Timor 9°30S 123°58E 231 F6
Oedong S. Korea 35°42N 129°14E 224 E4
Oeiras Brazil 7°0S 42°8W 332 C3
Oeiras Portugal 38°41N 9°18W 126 A1
Oeiras do Para Brazil 1°58S 49°51W 329 D8
Oelrichs U.S.A. 43°11N 103°14W 308 D2
Oels in Schlesien = Oleśnica
Poland 51°13N 17°22E 185 G4
Oelsnitz Germany 50°24N 12°10E 179 E8
Oelwein U.S.A. 42°41N 91°55W 310 B5
Oenarodo S. Korea 34°26N 127°30E 224 E3
Oeno I. Pac. Oc. 24°0S 131°0W 289 K14
Oenpelli = Gunbalanya
Australia 12°20S 133°4E 278 B5
Oetz Austria 47°13N 10°53E 180 D3
Of Turkey 40°59N 40°23E 213 B9
O'Fallon U.S.A. 38°49N 90°42W 310 F6
Ofanto → Italy 41°22N 16°13E 201 A9
Offa Nigeria 8°13N 4°42E 263 D5
Offaly □ Ireland 53°15N 7°30W 166 C4
Offenbach Germany 50°6N 8°44E 179 E4
Offenburg Germany 48°28N 7°56E 179 G3
Officer Cr. → Australia 27°46S 132°30E 279 E5
Offida Italy 42°56N 13°41E 199 F10
Offoué → Gabon 0°4S 11°44E 264 C2
Ofidousa Greece 36°33N 26°8E 205 E8
Ofin Nigeria 6°32N 3°30E 124 A3
Ofolanga Tonga 19°38S 174°27W 287 P13
Ofotfjorden Norway 68°27N 17°0E 160 B17
Ofte Norway 59°30N 8°12E 164 E5
Ofu Amer. Samoa 14°11S 169°41W 302 g
Ōfunato Japan 39°4N 141°43E 220 E10
Oga Japan 39°55N 139°50E 220 E9
Oga-Hantō Japan 39°58N 139°47E 220 E9
Ogaden Ethiopia 7°30N 45°30E 267 C6
Ōgaki Japan 35°21N 136°37E 223 B8
Ogallala U.S.A. 41°8N 101°43W 308 E3
Ogan → Indonesia 3°1S 104°44E 234 C2
Ogasawara Gunto Pac. Oc. 27°0N 142°0E 288 E6
Ogawa Japan 35°44N 139°28E 140 A1
Ogbomosho Nigeria 8°1N 4°11E 263 D5
Ogden Iowa, U.S.A. 42°2N 94°2W 310 B2
Ogden Utah, U.S.A. 41°13N 111°58W 304 F8
Ogden Park U.S.A. 41°46N 87°39W 119 C2
Ogden Slip U.S.A. 119 b3
Ogdensburg U.S.A. 44°42N 75°30W 313 B9
Ogea Driki Fiji 19°12S 178°27W 287 B3
Ogea Levu Fiji 19°8S 178°24W 287 B3
Ogeechee → U.S.A. 31°50N 81°3W 316 D8
Ogi Japan 33°20N 130°15E 222 D2
Ogikubo Japan 35°42N 139°37E 140 A2
Ogilby U.S.A. 32°49N 114°50W 307 N12
Oglat Beraber Algeria 30°15N 3°34W 260 B4
Oglat el Khnâchich Mali 21°51N 3°58W 260 D4
Oglesby U.S.A. 41°18N 89°4W 310 C7
Oglethorpe U.S.A. 32°18N 84°4W 316 C5
Óglio → Italy 45°2N 10°39E 198 C7
Óglio Nord △ Italy 45°22N 9°54E 198 C6
Óglio Sud △ Italy 45°7N 10°24E 198 C7
Ogmore Australia 22°37S 149°35E 280 C4
Ognon → France 47°16N 5°28E 173 E12
Ogo Nigeria 6°25N 3°24E 124 B2
Ogogoro Nigeria 6°25N 3°25E 124 B2
Ogoja Nigeria 6°38N 8°39E 263 D6
Ogoki Canada 51°38N 85°58W 298 B2
Ogoki → Canada 51°38N 85°57W 298 B2
Ogoki L. Canada 50°50N 87°10W 298 B2
Ogoki Res. Canada 50°45N 88°15W 298 B2
Ogooué → Gabon 1°0S 9°0E 264 C1
Ogōri Fukuoka, Japan 33°25N 130°30E 222 D2
Ogōri Yamaguchi, Japan 34°6N 131°24E 222 C3
Ogosta → Bulgaria 43°48N 23°55E 202 C7
Ogou → Togo 7°50N 1°29E 263 D5
Ogoueïleten Nmâdi
Mauritania 19°46N 11°1W 260 E2
Ogowe = Ogooué → Gabon 1°0S 9°0E 264 C1
Ogoyo Nigeria 6°25N 3°29E 124 B2
Ogr = Sharafa Sudan 11°59N 27°7E 257 E2
Ogražden Macedonia 41°30N 22°50E 202 E6
Ogre Latvia 56°49N 24°36E 188 D3
Ogrein Sudan 17°55N 34°50E 256 D3
Ogudu Nigeria 6°34N 3°24E 124 A2
Ogulin Croatia 45°16N 15°16E 199 C12
Ogun □ Nigeria 7°0N 3°0E 263 D5
Oguni Japan 33°11N 131°8E 222 D3
Ögur Iceland 66°2N 22°44W 155 A4
Ogurja Ada Turkmenistan 38°55N 53°2E 247 B7
Oguta Nigeria 5°44N 6°44E 263 D6
Oğuzeli Turkey 36°57N 37°30E 250 B8
Ogwashi-Uku Nigeria 6°15N 6°30E 263 D6
Ogwe Nigeria 5°0N 7°14E 263 E6
Ohai N.Z. 45°55S 168°0E 285 F3
Ohakune N.Z. 39°24S 175°24E 284 F4
Ohanet Algeria 28°44N 8°46E 261 C6
Ohangwena □ Namibia 17°30S 17°0E 270 A2
Ōhara Japan 35°15N 140°23E 223 B12
O'Hare Int., Chicago ✈ (ORD)
U.S.A. 41°59N 87°54W 311 C9
Ohata Japan 41°24N 141°10E 220 D10
Ohatchee U.S.A. 33°47N 86°0W 316 B4
Ohau, L. N.Z. 44°15S 169°53E 285 E4
Ohaupo N.Z. 37°56S 175°20E 284 D4
O'Higgins, C. Chile 27°5S 109°15W 330 b
O'Higgins, Pampa Chile 33°27S 70°40W 137 B2
O'Higgins, Pta. Chile 33°41S 79°0W 330 c
Ohio □ U.S.A. 40°15N 82°45W 312 F2
Ohio → U.S.A. 36°59N 89°8W 311 G8
Ohio City U.S.A. 40°46N 84°37W 311 D12
Ohiwa Harbour N.Z. 37°59S 177°10E 284 D6

Ohlau = Oława Poland 50°57N 17°20E 185 H4
Ohře → Czech Rep. 50°30N 14°10E 180 A7
Ohre → Sachsen-Anhalt, Germany 52°18N 11°46E 178 C7
Ohrid Macedonia 41°8N 20°52E 202 E4
Ohridsko Jezero Macedonia 41°8N 20°52E 202 E4
Ohrigstad S. Africa 24°39S 30°36E 271 B5
Öhringen Germany 49°12N 9°31E 179 F5
Ohura N.Z. 38°51S 174°59E 284 E3
Oi Qu → China 28°37N 98°16E 228 C2
Oiapoque Brazil 3°50N 51°50W 329 C7
Oiapoque → S. Amer. 4°8N 51°40W 329 C7
Oikou China 38°35N 117°42E 227 E9
Oil City U.S.A. 41°26N 79°42W 312 E5
Oil Springs Canada 42°47N 82°7W 312 D2
Oildale U.S.A. 35°25N 119°1W 307 K7
Ōimachi Japan 35°35N 139°43E 140 B3
Oinousa = Inousses Greece 38°33N 26°14E 205 C8
Oise □ France 49°28N 2°30E 173 C9
Oise → France 49°0N 2°4E 173 C9
Oistins Barbados 13°4N 59°33W 323 r
Ōita Japan 33°14N 131°36E 222 D3
Ōita □ Japan 33°15N 131°30E 222 D3
Ojai U.S.A. 34°27N 119°15W 307 L7
Ojcowski △ Poland 50°15N 19°50E 185 H6
Ojhar India 20°6N 73°56E 244 D1
Ojinaga Mexico 29°34N 104°25W 318 B4
Ojiya Japan 37°18N 138°48E 221 F9
Ojo Caliente Mexico 22°34N 102°15W 318 C4
Ojo de Liebre, L. Mexico 27°45N 114°15W 318 B2
Ojos del Salado, Cerro Argentina 27°0S 68°40W 334 B2
Ojota Nigeria 6°35N 3°23E 124 A2
Ojus U.S.A. 25°26N 80°9W 129 C3
Oka Nigeria 7°9N 3°38E 263 D5
Oka → Russia 56°20N 43°59E 190 B7
Okaba Indonesia 8°6S 139°42E 231 F9
Okahandja Namibia 22°0S 16°59E 270 B2
Okahukura N.Z. 38°48S 175°14E 284 E4
Okaihau N.Z. 35°19S 173°47E 284 B2
Okakarara Namibia 20°35S 17°27E 270 B2
Okalataka Congo 0°18S 14°54E 264 C2
Okanagan L. Canada 50°0N 119°30W 296 D5
Okandja Gabon 0°35S 13°45E 264 C2
Okano → Gabon 0°5S 10°57E 264 C2
Okanogan U.S.A. 48°22N 119°35W 304 B4
Okanogan → U.S.A. 48°6N 119°44W 304 B4
Okanogan Range N. Amer. 49°0N 119°55W 296 D5
Okány Hungary 46°52N 21°21E 182 D6
Okapa Papua N. G. 6°38S 145°39E 286 D3
Okapi ⌂ Dem. Rep. of the Congo 2°30N 27°20E 268 B2
Okaputa Namibia 20°5S 17°0E 270 B2
Okara Pakistan 30°50N 73°31E 242 D5
Okarito N.Z. 43°15S 170°9E 285 D5
Okato N.Z. 39°12S 173°53E 284 F2
Okau Micronesia 9°32N 138°6E 287 R16
Okaukuejo Namibia 19°10S 16°0E 270 A2
Okavango □ Namibia 18°0S 19°30E 270 A2
Okavango Delta Botswana 18°45S 22°45E 270 A3
Okavango Swamp = Okavango Delta Botswana 18°45S 22°45E 270 A3
Ōkawa Japan 33°9N 130°21E 222 D2
Okawville U.S.A. 38°26N 89°33W 310 F7
Okaya Japan 36°5N 138°10E 223 A10
Okayama Japan 34°40N 133°54E 222 C5
Okayama □ Japan 35°0N 133°50E 222 C5
Okazaki Japan 34°57N 137°10E 223 C9
Oke-Iho Nigeria 8°1N 3°18E 263 D5
Oke-Ira Nigeria 6°29N 3°22E 124 B2
Okęcie Poland 52°11N 20°56E 143 B1
Okęcie, Warszawa ✈ (WAW) Poland 52°9N 20°59E 143 B1
Okeechobee U.S.A. 27°15N 80°50W 317 H9
Okeechobee, L. U.S.A. 27°0N 80°50W 317 J9
Okefenokee ⌂ U.S.A. 30°45N 82°18W 316 E7
Okefenokee Swamp U.S.A. 30°40N 82°20W 316 E7
Okehampton U.K. 50°44N 4°0W 169 G4
Okemos U.S.A. 42°43N 84°26W 311 B12
Okene Nigeria 7°32N 6°11E 263 D6
Okeogbe Nigeria 6°24N 3°23E 124 B2
Oker → Germany 52°32N 10°22E 178 C6
Okha Gujarat, India 22°27N 69°4E 242 H3
Okha Russia 53°40N 143°0E 215 D15
Okhla India 28°33N 77°16E 120 B2
Okhotsk Russia 59°20N 143°10E 215 D15
Okhotsk, Sea of Asia 55°0N 145°0E 215 D15
Okhotskiy Perevoz Russia 61°52N 135°35E 215 C14
Okhta → Russia 59°56N 30°25E 137 B2
Okhtyrka Ukraine 50°25N 35°0E 189 G8
Oki-no-Shima Japan 32°44N 132°33E 222 E4
Oki-Shotō Japan 36°5N 133°15E 222 A5
Okiep S. Africa 29°39S 17°53E 270 C2
Okigwi Nigeria 5°52N 7°20E 263 D6
Okija Nigeria 5°54N 6°55E 263 D6
Okinawa Japan 26°19N 127°46E 288 a
Okinawa □ Japan 26°40N 128°0E 288 a
Okinawa-Guntō Japan 26°40N 128°0E 221 L4
Okinawa-Jima Japan 26°32N 128°0E 221 L4
Okino-erabu-Shima Japan 27°21N 128°33E 221 L4
Okitipupa Nigeria 6°31N 4°50E 263 D5
Okkervil → Russia 59°56N 30°30E 137 B2
Oklahoma □ U.S.A. 35°20N 97°30W 314 D6
Oklahoma City U.S.A. 35°30N 97°30W 314 D6
Oklawaha → U.S.A. 29°28N 81°41W 317 F8
Okmulgee U.S.A. 35°37N 95°58W 314 D7
Oknitsa = Ocniţa Moldova 48°25N 27°30E 183 B12
Oko, W. → Sudan 21°15N 35°56E 256 C4
Okolo Uganda 2°37N 31°8E 268 B3
Okolona Ky., U.S.A. 38°8N 85°41W 311 F11
Okolona Miss., U.S.A. 34°0N 88°45W 315 E10
Okombahe Namibia 21°23S 15°22E 270 B2
Okonek Poland 53°32N 16°51E 184 E3
Okotoks Canada 50°43N 113°58W 296 C6
Okoyo Congo 1°28S 15°0E 264 C3
Okrika Nigeria 4°40N 7°10E 263 E6
Okrzeszyn Poland 52°8N 21°8E 143 C2
Oksapmin Papua N. G. 5°17S 142°15E 286 C2
Øksendalsøra Norway 62°42N 8°27E 164 B5
Oksovskiy Russia 62°33N 39°57E 186 B6
Oksval Norway 59°51N 10°40E 133 A3
Oktwin Burma 18°49N 96°26E 241 F6
Oktyabrsk = Qandyaghash Kazakhstan 49°28N 57°25E 187 E10
Oktyabrsk Russia 53°11N 48°40E 190 D9
Oktyabrskiy = Aktsyabrski Belarus 52°38N 28°53E 177 B15
Oktyabrskiy Bashkortostan, Russia 54°28N 53°28E 186 D9
Oktyabrskiy Kamchatka, Russia 52°39N 156°14E 215 D16
Oktyabrskiy Moskva, Russia 55°41N 37°35E 129 B2
Oktyabrskiy Rostov, Russia 47°30N 40°4E 191 G5
Oktyabrskoy Revolyutsii, Ostrov Russia 79°30N 97°0E 215 B10
Oktyabrskoye = Zhovtneve Ukraine 46°54N 32°3E 189 J7
Ōkubo Tokyo, Japan 140 a2
Ōkuchi Japan 32°4N 130°37E 222 E2
Okulovka Russia 58°25N 33°19E 188 C7
Ōkura Japan 35°35N 139°27E 140 B1
Okuru N.Z. 43°55S 168°55E 285 D3
Okushiri-Tō Japan 42°15N 139°30E 220 C9
Okuta Nigeria 9°14N 3°12E 263 D5
Okwa → Botswana 22°30S 23°0E 270 B3
Ola Russia 59°35N 151°17E 215 D16
Ola Ark., U.S.A. 35°2N 93°13W 314 D8
Ólafsfjörður Iceland 66°4N 18°39W 155 A8
Ólafsvík Iceland 64°53N 23°43W 155 C3
Olaine Latvia 56°48N 23°59E 184 B10
Olancha U.S.A. 36°17N 118°1W 307 J8
Olancha Pk. U.S.A. 36°16N 118°7W 307 J8
Olanchito Honduras 15°30N 86°30W 320 C2
Öland Sweden 56°45N 16°38E 163 H10
Ölands norra udde Sweden 57°22N 17°5E 163 G11
Ölands södra udde Sweden 56°12N 16°23E 163 H10
Olanta U.S.A. 33°56N 79°56W 316 B10
Olar U.S.A. 33°11N 81°11W 316 B8
Olargues France 43°34N 2°53E 174 E6
Olari Finland 60°10N 24°44E 121 B1
Olaria Brazil 22°50S 43°16W 135 B1
Olary Australia 32°18S 140°19E 282 B4
Olascoaga Argentina 35°15S 60°39W 334 D3
Olathe U.S.A. 38°53N 94°49W 308 F6
Olavarría Argentina 36°55S 60°20W 334 D3
Oława Poland 50°57N 17°20E 185 H4
Olbernhau Germany 50°40N 13°19E 178 E9
Ólbia Italy 40°55N 9°31E 200 B2
Ólbia, G. di Italy 40°55N 9°39E 200 B2
Olching Germany 48°12N 11°21E 179 G7
Olcott U.S.A. 43°20N 78°42W 312 C6
Old Admiralty Russia 59°55N 30°20E 137 B1
Old Bahama Chan. = Bahama, Canal Viejo de W. Indies 22°10N 77°30W 320 B4
Old Baldy Pk. = San Antonio, Mt. U.S.A. 34°17N 117°38W 307 L9
Old Bar Australia 31°58S 152°35E 283 A10
Old Bridge U.S.A. 40°25N 74°22W 313 F10
Old Castile = Castilla y Leon □ Spain 42°0N 5°0W 194 D6
Old City Shanghai, China 31°13N 121°29E 138 B1
Old City Delhi, India 120 a3
Old City Jerusalem 123 b3
Old Crow Canada 67°30N 139°55W 294 D4
Old Dale U.S.A. 34°8N 115°47W 307 L11
Old Forge N.Y., U.S.A. 43°43N 74°58W 313 C10
Old Forge Pa., U.S.A. 41°22N 75°45W 313 E9
Old Fort = Purana Qila Delhi, India 120 c3
Old Fort B. Bahamas 25°3N 77°32W 153 b
Old Fort Pt. Montserrat 16°40N 62°11W 323 p
Old Fort York Canada 43°39N 79°24W 141 B2
Old Harbor Alaska, U.S.A. 57°12N 153°18W 303 H9
Old Harbor Mass., U.S.A. 42°19N 71°1W 116 B2
Old Harbour Jamaica 17°56N 77°7W 320 a
Old Harbour Bay Jamaica 17°54N 77°6W 320 a
Old Ironsides = U.S.S. Constitution Boston, U.S.A. 116 a3
Old Mapoon ◎ Australia 11°5S 142°22E 280 A3
Old Panamao Phil. 5°59N 121°13E 233 J3
Old Perlican Canada 48°5N 53°1W 299 C9
Old Road Bluff Antigua & B. 16°59N 61°50W 322 b
Old Road Town St. Kitts & Nevis 17°17N 62°47W 322 d
Old Roundhouse Toronto, Canada 141 c2
Old Shinyanga Tanzania 3°33S 33°27E 268 C3
Old Speck Mt. U.S.A. 44°34N 70°57W 313 B14
Old Town = Stare Miasto Warsaw, Poland 143 a2
Old Town Edinburgh, U.K. 121 b2
Old Town Fla., U.S.A. 29°36N 82°59W 317 F7
Old Town Ill., U.S.A. 41°54N 87°37W 119 B3
Old Town Maine, U.S.A. 44°56N 68°39W 309 C19
Old Town Hall = Altes Rathaus Munich, Germany 131 b3
Old Town Square Warsaw, Poland 143 a2
Old U.S. Mint New Orleans, U.S.A. 131 a3
Old Washington U.S.A. 40°2N 81°27W 312 F3
Old Wives L. Canada 50°5N 106°0W 297 C7
Oldbawn Ireland 53°17N 6°21W 120 B1
Oldbury U.K. 51°38N 2°33W 169 F5
Oldcastle Ireland 53°46N 7°10W 166 C4
Oldeani Tanzania 3°22S 35°35E 268 C4
Olden Norway 61°49N 6°49E 164 C3
Oldenburg Niedersachsen, Germany 53°9N 8°13E 178 B4
Oldenburg Schleswig-Holstein, Germany 54°17N 10°52E 178 A6
Oldenzaal Neths. 52°19N 6°53E 170 B6
Oldham U.K. 53°33N 2°7W 168 D5
Oldman → Canada 49°57N 111°42W 296 D6
Oldmeldrum U.K. 57°20N 2°19W 167 D6
Olds Canada 51°50N 114°10W 296 C6
Oldsmar U.S.A. 28°2N 82°39W 317 G7
Olduvai Gorge Tanzania 2°57S 35°23E 268 C4
Öldziyt Mongolia 44°40N 109°1E 226 B5
Ole Rømer Land Greenland 74°10N 24°30W 154 C8
Olean U.S.A. 42°5N 78°26W 312 D6
Oleby Sweden 60°8N 13°2E 162 D7
Olecko Poland 54°2N 22°31E 184 D9
Oléggio Italy 45°36N 8°38E 198 C5
Oleiros Portugal 39°56N 7°56W 194 F3
Oleiros Spain 43°20N 8°19W 194 B2
Olekma → Russia 60°22N 120°42E 215 C13
Olekminsk Russia 60°25N 120°30E 215 C13
Oleksandrivka Ukraine 48°55N 32°20E 189 H7
Oleksandriya Kirovohrad, Ukraine 48°42N 33°3E 189 H7
Oleksandriya Rivne, Ukraine 50°37N 26°19E 177 C14
Olema U.S.A. 38°3N 122°47W 306 G4
Ølen Norway 59°36N 5°48E 164 E2
Olenegorsk Russia 68°9N 33°18E 160 B25
Olenek Russia 68°28N 112°18E 215 C12
Olenek → Russia 73°0N 120°10E 215 B13
Olenino Russia 56°15N 33°30E 188 D7
Olenya = Olenegorsk Russia 68°9N 33°18E 160 B25
Oléron, Î. d' France 45°55N 1°15W 174 C2
Olesk Ukraine 51°6N 24°11E 185 G11
Oleśnica Poland 51°13N 17°22E 185 G4
Olesno Poland 50°51N 18°26E 185 H5
Oleta River State Rec. Area U.S.A. 25°55N 80°8W 129 C3
Olevsk Ukraine 51°12N 27°39E 177 C14
Olga, L. Canada 49°47N 77°15W 298 C4
Olgas, The = Kata Tjuta Australia 25°20S 130°50E 279 E5
Olgino Russia 60°0N 30°10E 137 B1
Ölgiy Mongolia 48°56N 89°57E 217 C11
Ølgod Denmark 55°49N 8°36E 163 J2
Olhão Portugal 37°3N 7°48W 195 H3
Olhopil Ukraine 48°12N 29°30E 183 B14
Olhovatka Russia 54°30N 22°18E 184 D9
Olib Croatia 44°23N 14°44E 199 D11
Oliena Italy 40°16N 9°24E 200 B2
Oliete Spain 41°1N 0°41W 196 D4
Olifants = Elefantes → Africa 24°10S 32°40E 271 B5
Olifants → Namibia 25°30S 19°30E 270 B2
Olifantshoek S. Africa 27°57S 22°42E 270 C3
Olimbos Greece 35°44N 27°11E 205 F9
Ólimbos, Óros = Olymbos Oros Greece 40°6N 22°23E 202 F6
Olímpia Brazil 20°44S 48°54W 335 A6
Olimpico, Estadio Mexico 19°20N 99°11W 128 C1
Olimpos-Beydaglari △ Turkey 36°36N 30°30E 205 E12
Olin U.S.A. 42°0N 91°9W 310 B5
Olinda Brazil 8°1S 34°51W 332 C5
Olite Spain 42°29N 1°40W 196 C3
Oliva Argentina 32°0S 63°38W 334 C3
Oliva Spain 38°58N 0°9W 197 G4
Oliva, Punta del Spain 43°37N 5°28W 194 B5
Oliva de la Frontera Spain 38°17N 6°54W 195 G4
Olivais Portugal 38°45N 9°7W 126 A2
Olivar de los Padres Mexico 19°21N 99°14W 128 B1
Olivar del Conde Mexico 19°22N 99°12W 128 B1
Olivares, Cerro los Argentina 30°18S 69°55W 334 C2
Olivares de Júcar Spain 39°46N 2°20W 196 F2
Olive Branch U.S.A. 34°57N 89°49W 315 D10
Olive Hill U.S.A. 38°18N 83°13W 311 F13
Olive Park U.S.A. 119 b3
Olivehurst U.S.A. 39°6N 121°34W 306 F5
Oliveira Brazil 20°39S 44°50W 333 F3
Oliveira de Azeméis Portugal 40°49N 8°29W 194 E2
Oliveira do Douro Portugal 41°5N 8°2W 194 D2
Oliveira dos Brejinhos Brazil 12°19S 42°54W 333 D3
Olivenza Spain 38°41N 7°9W 195 G3
Oliver Canada 49°13N 119°37W 296 D5
Oliver L. Canada 56°56N 103°22W 297 B8
Olives, Mt. of West Bank 31°46N 35°15E 123 B2
Olivet Loiret, France 47°51N 1°55E 173 E8
Olivet Mich., U.S.A. 42°27N 84°56W 311 B12
Olivia, L. U.S.A. 28°31N 81°31W 133 A1
Olivine Ra. N.Z. 44°15S 168°30E 285 E3
Olivos Argentina 34°30S 58°28W 117 B2
Olkhovka Russia 49°48N 44°32E 190 F7
Olkusz Poland 50°18N 19°33E 185 H6
Ollachea Peru 13°49S 70°29W 330 C3
Ollagüe Chile 21°15S 68°10W 334 A2
Ollombo Congo 1°18S 15°53E 264 C3
Olloua Congo 0°54S 14°34E 264 C2
Olmaliq Uzbekistan 40°50N 69°35E 217 D7
Olmedo Spain 41°20N 4°43W 194 D6
Olmeto France 41°43N 8°55E 175 G12
Olmos Peru 5°59S 79°46W 330 B2
Olmütz = Olomouc Czech Rep. 49°38N 17°12E 181 B10
Olney Ill., U.S.A. 38°44N 88°5W 311 F8
Olney Tex., U.S.A. 33°22N 98°45W 314 E5
Olofström Sweden 56°17N 14°32E 163 H8
Oloitokitok Kenya 2°56S 37°30E 268 C4
Ololi Congo 0°15S 14°36E 264 C2
Oloma Cameroon 3°29N 11°19E 263 E7
Olomane → Canada 50°14N 60°37W 299 B7
Olomouc Czech Rep. 49°38N 17°12E 181 B10
Olomoucký □ Czech Rep. 49°45N 17°5E 181 B10
Olona → Italy 45°29N 9°6E 128 B1
Olonets Russia 61°0N 32°54E 188 B7
Olongapo Phil. 14°50N 120°18E 232 D3
Olonne-sur-Mer France 46°32N 1°47W 174 B2
Oloron, Gave d' → France 43°33N 1°5W 174 E2
Oloron-Ste-Marie France 43°11N 0°38W 174 E3
Olosega Amer. Samoa 14°10S 169°37W 302 g
Olosenga = Swains I. Amer. Samoa 11°11S 171°4W 289 J11
Olot Spain 42°11N 2°30E 196 C7
Olovo Bos.-H. 44°8N 18°35E 182 F3
Olovyannaya Russia 50°58N 115°35E 215 D12
Oloy → Russia 66°29N 159°29E 215 C16
Olsberg Germany 51°21N 8°31E 178 D4
Olshammar Sweden 58°45N 14°48E 163 F8
Olshanka Ukraine 48°16N 30°58E 189 H6
Olshany Ukraine 50°3N 35°53E 189 G8
Olsztyn Poland 53°48N 20°29E 184 E7
Olsztynek Poland 53°34N 20°19E 184 E7
Olt □ Romania 44°20N 24°30E 183 F9
Olt → Romania 43°43N 24°51E 183 G9
Oltedal Norway 58°49N 6°2E 164 F3
Olten Switz. 47°21N 7°53E 179 H3
Olteniţa Romania 44°7N 26°42E 183 F11
Olton U.S.A. 34°11N 102°8W 314 D3
Oltu Turkey 40°35N 41°58E 213 B9
Oluan Pi Taiwan 21°53N 120°51E 225 E2
Oluanpi Taiwan 21°54N 120°51E 225 E2
Olula del Rio Spain 37°21N 2°18W 197 H2
Olur Turkey 40°49N 42°8E 213 B10
Olustee U.S.A. 30°12N 82°26W 316 E7
Olutanga Phil. 7°26N 122°54E 233 H4
Olutanga I. Phil. 7°22N 122°52E 233 H4
Olvega Spain 41°47N 2°0W 196 D2
Olvera Spain 36°55N 5°18W 195 J5
Olymbos Cyprus 35°21N 33°45E 207 E9
Olymbos Oros Greece 40°6N 22°23E 202 F6
Olympia Greece 37°39N 21°39E 204 D3
Olympia London, U.K. 125 c1
Olympia Wash., U.S.A. 47°3N 122°53W 306 D4
Olympia, L. U.S.A. 28°34N 81°31W 133 A1
Olympic △ U.S.A. 47°45N 123°43W 306 C3
Olympic Dam Australia 30°30S 136°55E 282 A2
Olympic Green China 39°59N 116°23E 114 B2
Olympic Mts. U.S.A. 47°55N 123°45W 306 C3
Olympic Park U.K. 51°33N 0°0 125 A3
Olympic Stadium = Turner Field U.S.A. 33°44N 84°23W 113 B2
Olympic Stadium Beijing, China 39°59N 116°23E 114 B2
Olympic Stadium Helsinki, Finland 60°11N 24°55E 121 B2
Olympique, Stade Canada 45°33N 73°33W 130 A2
Olympus Cyprus 34°56N 32°52E 207 F8
Olympus, Mt. = Olymbos Oros Greece 40°6N 22°23E 202 F6
Olympus, Mt. = Uludağ Turkey 40°4N 29°13E 203 F13
Olympus, Mt. U.S.A. 47°48N 123°43W 306 C3
Olyphant U.S.A. 41°27N 75°36W 313 E9
Olyutorskiy, Mys Russia 59°55N 170°27E 215 D18
Om → Russia 54°59N 73°22E 217 B8
Om Hajer Eritrea 14°20N 36°41E 257 E4
Om Koi Thailand 17°48N 98°22E 236 D2
Ōma Japan 41°45N 141°5E 220 D10
Ōmachi Japan 36°30N 137°50E 223 A9
Omae-Zaki Japan 34°36N 138°14E 223 C10
Ōmagari = Daisen Japan 39°27N 140°29E 220 E10
Omagh U.K. 54°36N 7°19W 166 B4
Omagh □ U.K. 54°35N 7°15W 166 B4
Omaha U.S.A. 41°17N 95°58W 308 E6
Omaheke □ Namibia 21°30S 19°0E 270 B2
Omak U.S.A. 48°25N 119°31W 304 B4
Omalos Greece 35°19N 23°55E 207 E4
Omalur India 11°44N 78°4E 245 J4
Oman ■ Asia 23°0N 58°0E 249 B7
Oman, G. of Asia 24°30N 58°30E 247 E8
Omapere N.Z. 35°37S 173°25E 284 B2
Omar Combon Somalia 3°10N 45°47E 267 D6
Omaruru Namibia 21°26S 16°0E 270 B2
Omaruru → Namibia 22°7S 14°15E 270 B1
Omate Peru 16°45S 71°0W 330 D3
Ombai, Selat Indonesia 8°30S 124°50E 231 F6
Omboué Gabon 1°35S 9°15E 264 C1
Ombrone → Italy 42°42N 11°5E 198 F8
Omchi Chad 21°22N 17°53E 259 D3
Omdurmân Sudan 15°40N 32°28E 257 D3
Ōme Japan 35°47N 139°15E 223 B11
Omega U.S.A. 31°21N 83°36W 316 D6
Omegna Italy 45°53N 8°24E 198 C5
Omemee Canada 44°18N 78°33W 312 B6
Omeo Australia 37°6S 147°36E 283 D7
Omeonga Dem. Rep. of the Congo 3°40S 24°22E 264 C4
Ometepe, I. de Nic. 11°32N 85°35W 320 D2
Ometepec Mexico 16°41N 98°25W 319 D5
Ōmi-Shima Ehime, Japan 34°15N 133°0E 222 C5
Ōmi-Shima Yamaguchi, Japan 34°25N 131°9E 222 C3
Omihachiman Japan 35°7N 136°3E 223 B8
Omin Micronesia 9°36N 138°9E 287 R16
Ominato Japan 41°17N 141°10E 220 D10
Omineca → Canada 56°3N 124°16W 296 B4
Omineca Mts. Canada 56°30N 125°30W 296 B3
Omiš Croatia 43°28N 16°40E 199 E13
Omišalj Croatia 45°13N 14°32E 199 C11
Omitara Namibia 22°16S 18°2E 270 B2
Ōmiya = Saitama Japan 35°54N 139°38E 223 B11
Ommaney, C. U.S.A. 56°10N 134°40W 303 H14
Omme Å → Denmark 55°56N 8°32E 163 J2
Ommen Neths. 52°31N 6°26E 170 B6
Ömnögovĭ □ Mongolia 43°15N 104°0E 226 C3
Omo → Ethiopia 6°25N 36°10E 257 F4
Omo △ Ethiopia 5°54N 35°55E 257 F4
Omo Valley Ethiopia 5°7N 36°0E 257 F4
Omodeo, L. Italy 40°8N 8°56E 200 B1
Omodhos Cyprus 34°51N 32°48E 207 F8
Omoï Congo 2°56S 13°13E 264 C2
Omoko Nigeria 5°19N 6°40E 263 D6
Omolon → Russia 68°42N 158°36E 215 C16
Omona Solomon Is. 7°30S 158°43E 287 L10
Omonia Square Athens, Greece 112 b1
Omono-Gawa → Japan 39°46N 140°3E 220 E10
Ōmori Japan 35°34N 139°43E 140 B3
Ompha Canada 45°0N 76°50W 313 B8
Omsk Russia 55°0N 73°12E 217 B8
Omsukchan Russia 62°32N 155°48E 215 C16
Ōmu Japan 44°34N 142°58E 220 B11
Omul, Vf. Romania 45°27N 25°29E 183 E10
Omulew → Poland 53°5N 21°33E 185 E8
Ōmura Japan 32°56N 129°57E 222 E1
Ōmura-Wan Japan 32°57N 129°52E 222 E1
Omuramba Omatako → Namibia 17°45S 20°25E 270 A2
Omuramba Ovambo → Namibia 18°45S 16°59E 270 A2
Omurtag Bulgaria 43°8N 26°26E 203 C10
Omusati □ Namibia 18°30S 15°0E 270 A1
Ōmuta Japan 33°5N 130°26E 222 D2
Omuthiya Namibia 17°43S 16°13E 270 A2
On-ma-thi Burma 22°17N 96°41E 241 D6
On-Take Japan 31°35N 130°39E 222 F2
Oña Spain 42°43N 3°25W 194 C7
Ona Fla., U.S.A. 27°29N 81°55W 317 H8
Ona Dikonde Dem. Rep. of the Congo 3°51S 24°11E 264 C4
Onaga U.S.A. 39°29N 96°10W 308 F5
Onalaska U.S.A. 43°53N 91°14W 308 D8
Onancock U.S.A. 37°43N 75°45W 309 G16
Onangue, L. Gabon 0°57S 10°4E 264 C1
Onaping L. Canada 47°3N 81°30W 298 C3
Onarga U.S.A. 40°43N 88°1W 311 D8
Oñati Spain 43°3N 2°25W 196 B2
Onavas Mexico 28°31N 109°35W 318 B3
Onawa U.S.A. 42°2N 96°6W 308 D5
Oncócua Angola 16°30S 13°25E 265 F2
Onda Spain 39°55N 0°17W 196 F4
Ondangwa Namibia 17°57S 16°4E 270 A2
Ondarroa Spain 43°19N 2°25W 196 B2
Ondas → Brazil 12°8S 44°55W 333 D3
Ondava → Slovak Rep. 48°27N 21°48E 181 C14
Ondjiva Angola 16°48S 15°50E 265 F3
Ondo Japan 34°11N 132°32E 222 C4
Ondo Nigeria 7°4N 4°47E 263 D5
Ondo □ Nigeria 6°45N 5°0E 263 D6
Öndörhaan Mongolia 47°19N 110°39E 219 B11
Öndverðarnes Iceland 64°52N 24°0W 155 C2
One and a Half Degree Channel Maldives 1°30N 73°20E 272 d
One Arm Point Australia 16°26S 123°3E 278 C3
One Arm Point ◎ Australia 16°31S 122°53E 278 C3
One Prudential Plaza U.S.A. 119 c2
One Tree Australia 34°11S 144°43E 281 E3
One World Trade Center U.S.A. 40°43N 74°1W 132 e1
Oneata Fiji 18°26S 178°25W 287 B3
Oneco U.S.A. 27°25N 82°31W 317 H7
Onega Russia 64°0N 38°10E 186 B6
Onega → Russia 63°58N 38°2E 186 B6
Onega, G. of = Onezhskaya Guba Russia 64°24N 36°38E 186 B6
Onega, L. = Onezhskoye Ozero Russia 61°44N 35°22E 188 B8
Onehunga N.Z. 36°55S 174°48E 284 C3
Oneida Ill., U.S.A. 41°4N 90°13W 310 C6
Oneida N.Y., U.S.A. 43°6N 75°39W 313 C9
Oneida L. U.S.A. 43°12N 75°54W 313 C9
O'Neill U.S.A. 42°27N 98°39W 308 D4
Onekotan, Ostrov Russia 49°25N 154°45E 215 E16
Onema Dem. Rep. of the Congo 4°35S 24°30E 265 C4
Oneonta U.S.A. 42°27N 75°4W 313 D9
Onerahi N.Z. 35°45S 174°22E 284 B3
Oneroa Cook Is. 21°15S 159°43W 289 h
Oneşti Romania 46°17N 26°47E 183 D11
Onezhskaya Guba Russia 64°24N 36°38E 186 B6
Onezhskoye Ozero Russia 61°44N 35°22E 188 B8
Ongarue N.Z. 38°42S 175°19E 284 E4
Ongea Levu = Ogea Levu Fiji 19°8S 178°24W 287 B3
Ongers → S. Africa 31°4S 23°13E 270 D3
Ongerup Australia 33°58S 118°28E 279 F2
Ongi Mongolia 45°27N 103°54E 226 B2
Ongjin N. Korea 37°56N 125°21E 224 D2
Ongkharak Thailand 14°8N 101°1E 236 E3
Ongniud Qi China 43°0N 118°38E 227 C10
Ongoka Dem. Rep. of the Congo 1°20S 26°0E 268 C2
Ongole India 15°33N 80°2E 245 G5
Ongon = Havirga Mongolia 45°41N 113°5E 226 B7
Ongouendjo Gabon 1°23S 9°5E 264 C1
Ongoujou Comoros Is. 12°18S 44°30E 272 a
Ongtüstik Qazaqstan □ Kazakhstan 43°0N 68°0E 217 D7
Ongwediva Namibia 17°47S 15°46E 270 A2
Oni Georgia 42°33N 43°26E 191 J6
Onida U.S.A. 44°42N 100°4W 308 C3
Onilahy → Madag. 23°34S 43°45E 272 C1
Onima Bonaire 12°15N 68°19W 322 h
Onisigun Nigeria 6°35N 3°24E 124 A2
Onitsha Nigeria 6°6N 6°42E 263 D6
Onna Japan 26°29N 127°51E 288 a
Ono Fiji 18°55S 178°29E 287 B2
Ono Fukui, Japan 35°59N 136°29E 223 B8
Ono Hyōgo, Japan 34°51N 134°56E 222 C6
Onoda Japan 33°59N 131°11E 222 C3
Onohara Japan 34°5N 133°40E 222 C5
Onoke, L. N.Z. 41°22S 175°8E 284 H4
Onomichi Japan 34°25N 133°12E 222 C5
Onotoa Kiribati 1°52S 175°34E 277 A14
Ons, I. de Spain 42°23N 8°55W 194 C2
Onsala Sweden 57°26N 12°0E 163 G6
Onslow Australia 21°40S 115°12E 278 D2
Onslow B. U.S.A. 34°20N 77°15W 315 D16
Ontake-San Japan 35°53N 137°29E 223 B9
Ontar Vanuatu 14°17S 167°27E 287 D5
Ontario Calif., U.S.A. 34°4N 117°39W 307 L9
Ontario Oreg., U.S.A. 44°2N 116°58W 304 D5
Ontario □ Canada 48°0N 83°0W 298 B2
Ontario, L. N. Amer. 43°20N 78°0W 312 C7
Ontario Science Centre Canada 43°43N 79°20W 141 A2
Ontinyent Spain 38°50N 0°35W 197 G4
Ontonagon U.S.A. 46°52N 89°19W 308 B9
Ontong Java Plateau Pac. Oc. 1°0N 157°0E 277 A10
Ontur Spain 38°38N 1°29W 197 G3
Onverwacht Suriname 5°35N 55°11W 329 B6
Onyx U.S.A. 35°41N 118°14W 307 K8
Oodaaq Greenland 83°40N 30°40W 154 A8
Oodnadatta Australia 27°33S 135°30E 281 D2
Oodweyne Somalia 9°25N 45°4E 267 C6
'Ō'ōkala U.S.A. 20°1N 155°17W 302 C6
Ōokayama Japan 35°36N 139°40E 140 B3
Ooku = Ōma Japan 41°45N 141°5E 220 D10
Ooldea Australia 30°27S 131°50E 279 F5
Oombulgurri Australia 15°15S 127°45E 278 C4
Oombulgurri ◎ Australia 15°10S 127°50E 278 C4
Oorindi Australia 20°40S 141°1E 280 C3
Oost-Vlaanderen □ Belgium 51°5N 3°50E 170 C3
Oostende Belgium 51°15N 2°54E 170 C2
Oosterhout Neths. 51°39N 4°47E 170 C4
Oosterschelde → Neths. 51°33N 4°0E 170 C4
Oosterwolde Neths. 53°0N 6°17E 170 B6
Oosteschelde △ Neths. 51°40N 3°40E 170 C3
Oostpunt Curaçao 12°2N 68°44W 322 g
Oostzaan Tuindorp Neths. 52°25N 4°54E 112 A2
Ootacamund = Udagamandalam India 11°30N 76°44E 245 J3
Ootha Australia 33°6S 147°29E 283 B7
Ootsa L. Canada 53°50N 126°2W 296 C3
Ooty = Udagamandalam India 11°30N 76°44E 245 J3
Op Luang △ Thailand 18°12N 98°32E 236 C2
Opa-Locka U.S.A. 25°54N 80°15W 129 C1
Opa-Locka ✈ (OPF) U.S.A. 25°54N 80°16W 129 C1
Opacz Poland 52°10N 20°53E 143 B1
Opaka Bulgaria 43°28N 26°10E 203 C10
Opala Dem. Rep. of the Congo 0°40S 24°20E 264 C4
Opalenica Poland 52°18N 16°24E 185 F3
Opan Bulgaria 42°13N 25°41E 203 D9
Opanake Sri Lanka 6°35N 80°40E 245 L5
Opapa N.Z. 39°47S 176°42E 284 F5
Opasatika Canada 49°30N 82°50W 298 C3
Opasquia ⌂ Canada 53°33N 93°5W 298 B1
Opatija Croatia 45°21N 14°17E 199 C11
Opatów Poland 50°50N 21°27E 185 H8
Opava Czech Rep. 49°57N 17°58E 181 B10
Opelika U.S.A. 32°39N 85°23W 316 C4
Opelousas U.S.A. 30°32N 92°5W 314 F8
Opémisca, L. Canada 49°56N 74°52W 298 C5
Opheim U.S.A. 48°51N 106°24W 304 B10
Ophir U.S.A. 63°10N 156°31W 303 E8
Ophirton S. Africa 26°13S 28°1E 123 B2
Ophthalmia Ra. Australia 23°15S 119°30E 278 D2
Opi Nigeria 6°36N 7°28E 263 D6
Opihikao U.S.A. 19°26N 154°53W 302 D7
Opinaca → Canada 52°15N 78°2W 298 B4
Opinaca, Rés. Canada 52°39N 76°20W 298 B4
Opinnagau → Canada 54°12N 82°25W 298 B3
Opiscotéo, L. Canada 53°10N 68°10W 299 B6
Opobo Nigeria 4°35N 7°34E 263 E6
Opochka Russia 56°42N 28°45E 188 D5
Opoczno Poland 51°22N 20°18E 185 G7
Opol Phil. 8°31N 124°34E 233 G5
Opole Poland 50°42N 17°58E 185 H4
Opole Lubelskie Poland 51°9N 21°58E 185 G8
Opolskie □ Poland 50°30N 18°0E 185 H5
Opon = Lapu-Lapu Phil. 10°20N 123°55E 233 F4
Oponono L. Namibia 18°8S 15°45E 270 A2
Opornyy = Borankul Kazakhstan 46°11N 54°25E 216 C4
Oporto = Porto Portugal 41°8N 8°40W 194 D2
Opotiki N.Z. 38°1S 177°19E 284 E6
Opp U.S.A. 31°17N 86°16W 316 D3
Oppdal Norway 62°35N 9°41E 164 B6
Oppegård Norway 59°45N 10°49E 133 B3
Oppeln = Opole Poland 50°42N 17°58E 185 H4
Oppem Belgium 50°56N 4°18E 116 A1
Óppido Mamertina Italy 38°16N 15°59E 201 D8
Oppland □ Norway 61°15N 9°40E 164 C6
Opportunity U.S.A. 47°39N 117°15W 304 C5
Oppsal Norway 59°53N 10°50E 133 A4
Oprişor Romania 44°17N 23°5E 182 F8
Oprtalj Croatia 45°23N 13°50E 199 C10
Opua N.Z. 35°19S 174°9E 284 B3
Opunake N.Z. 39°26S 173°52E 284 F2
Opuwo Namibia 18°3S 13°45E 270 A1
Opuzen Croatia 43°1N 17°34E 199 E14
Oquawka U.S.A. 40°56N 90°57W 310 D6
Or → Kazakhstan 51°11N 58°32E 216 B5
Ora Cyprus 34°51N 33°12E 207 F9
Ora Israel 31°45N 35°9E 123 B1
Oracabessa Jamaica 18°24N 76°57W 320 a
Oracle U.S.A. 32°37N 110°46W 305 K8
Oracuzar Peru 4°42S 78°6W 328 D2
Oradea Romania 47°2N 21°58E 182 C6
Oradell U.S.A. 40°57N 74°2W 132 A1
Oradell Res. U.S.A. 40°57N 74°1W 132 A1
Öræfajökull Iceland 64°2N 16°39W 155 C10
Orahovac = Rahovec Kosovo 42°24N 20°40E 202 D4
Orahovica Croatia 45°35N 17°52E 182 E2
Orai India 25°58N 79°30E 243 G8
Oraison France 43°55N 5°55E 175 E9
Oral = Zhayyq → Kazakhstan 47°0N 51°48E 187 E9
Oral Kazakhstan 51°20N 51°20E 190 E10
Oran Algeria 35°45N 0°39W 261 A4
Oran □ Algeria 35°0N 0°45W 261 B4
Orang △ India 26°37N 92°29E 241 B4
Orange N.S.W., Australia 33°15S 149°7E 283 B8
Orange Vaucluse, France 44°8N 4°47E 175 D8
Orange Calif., U.S.A. 33°47N 117°51W 307 M9
Orange Mass., U.S.A. 42°35N 72°19W 313 D12
Orange Tex., U.S.A. 30°6N 93°44W 314 F8
Orange Va., U.S.A. 38°15N 78°7W 309 F14
Orange → S. Africa 28°41S 16°28E 270 C2
Orange, C. Brazil 4°20N 51°30W 329 C7
Orange City U.S.A. 28°57N 81°18W 317 G8
Orange Cove U.S.A. 36°38N 119°19W 306 J7
Orange Free State = Free State □ S. Africa 28°30S 27°0E 270 C4
Orange Grove U.S.A. 27°58N 97°56W 314 H6
Orange Hill Barbados 13°12N 59°36W 323 r
Orange Hill Jamaica 18°16N 77°59W 320 a
Orange Hill St. Vincent 13°19N 61°7W 323 n
Orange L. U.S.A. 29°25N 82°13W 317 F7
Orange Park U.S.A. 30°10N 81°42W 316 E8
Orange River Colony = Free State □ S. Africa 28°30S 27°0E 270 C4
Orange Walk Belize 18°6N 88°33W 319 D7
Orangeburg U.S.A. 33°30N 80°52W 316 B9
Orangeville Ont., Canada 43°55N 80°5W 312 C4
Orangeville Ill., U.S.A. 42°28N 89°39W 310 B7
Orangi Pakistan 24°54N 67°0E 123 A2
Orango Guinea-Biss. 11°5N 16°0W 262 C1
Orani Phil. 14°49N 120°32E 232 D3
Oranienburg Germany 52°45N 13°14E 178 C9
Oranje = Orange → S. Africa 28°41S 16°28E 270 C2
Oranjemund Namibia 28°38S 16°29E 270 C2
Oranjerivier S. Africa 29°40S 24°12E 270 C3
Oranjestad Aruba 12°32N 70°2W 322 f
Oranjestad St. Eustatius 17°28N 62°59W 322 a
Orap Vanuatu 15°58S 167°20E 287 E5
Oras Phil. 12°9N 125°28E 232 E5
Orašje Bos.-H. 45°1N 18°42E 182 E3
Orăştie Romania 45°50N 23°10E 183 E8
Orava → Slovak Rep. 49°9N 19°8E 181 B12
Orava, Vodna nádriž Slovak Rep. 49°25N 19°35E 181 B12
Oraviţa Romania 45°2N 21°43E 182 E6
Orawia N.Z. 46°1S 167°50E 285 G2
Orb → France 43°15N 3°18E 174 E7
Orba → Italy 44°53N 8°37E 198 D5
Ørbæk Denmark 55°17N 10°39E 163 J4
Orbe Switz. 46°43N 6°32E 179 J2
Orbec France 49°1N 0°23E 172 C7
Orbetello Italy 42°27N 11°13E 199 F8
Órbigo → Spain 42°5N 5°42W 194 C5
Orbisonia U.S.A. 40°15N 77°54W 312 F7
Orbost Australia 37°40S 148°29E 283 D8
Örbyhus Sweden 60°15N 17°43E 162 D11
Orcadas Antarctica 60°44S 44°37W 151 C18
Orcas I. U.S.A. 48°42N 122°56W 306 B4
Orce Spain 37°44N 2°28W 197 H2
Orce → Spain 37°44N 2°28W 197 H2
Orchard City U.S.A. 38°50N 107°58W 304 G10
Orchard Homes U.S.A. 46°55N 114°4W 304 C6
Orchard Road Singapore 138 a1
Orchid I. = Lan Yü Taiwan 22°4N 121°25E 225 D3
Orchies France 50°28N 3°14E 173 B10
Orchila, I. Venezuela 11°48N 66°10W 321 D6
Orchilla, Pta. Canary Is. 27°42N 18°10W 153 e1
Órcia → Italy 42°58N 11°21E 199 F8
Orco → Italy 45°10N 7°52E 198 C4
Orcopampa Peru 15°20S 72°23W 330 D3
Orcutt U.S.A. 34°52N 120°27W 307 L6
Ord U.S.A. 41°36N 98°56W 308 E4
Ord → Australia 15°33S 128°15E 278 C4
Ord, Mt. Australia 17°20S 125°34E 278 C4
Ord Mts. U.S.A. 34°39N 116°45W 307 L10
Ordenes = Ordes Spain 43°5N 8°29W 194 B2
Orderville U.S.A. 37°17N 112°38W 305 H7
Ordes Spain 43°5N 8°29W 194 B2
Ordesa y Monte Perido △ Spain 42°40N 0°10W 196 C4
Ording = Sankt Peter-Ording Germany 54°20N 8°36E 178 A4
Ordos = Mu Us Shamo China 39°0N 109°0E 226 E5
Ordrup Denmark 55°45N 12°34E 118 A3
Ordu Turkey 40°55N 37°53E 212 B7
Ordu □ Turkey 41°0N 37°50E 212 B7
Ordubad Azerbaijan 38°54N 46°1E 213 C12
Orduña Álava, Spain 42°58N 2°58W 196 C2
Orduña Granada, Spain 37°20N 3°30W 195 H7
Ordway U.S.A. 38°13N 103°46W 304 G12
Ordzhonīkīdze = Denīsovka Kazakhstan 52°27N 61°39E 216 B6
Ordzhonīkīdze = Vladikavkaz Russia 43°0N 44°35E 191 J7
Ordzhonīkīdze = Yenakiyeve Ukraine 48°15N 38°15E 189 H10
Ordzhonīkīdze Ukraine 47°39N 34°3E 189 J8
Ore Dem. Rep. of the Congo 3°17N 29°30E 268 B2
Ore Mts. = Erzgebirge Germany 50°27N 12°55E 178 E8
Orealla Guyana 5°15N 57°23W 329 B6
Orebić Croatia 43°0N 17°11E 199 F14
Örebro Sweden 59°20N 15°18E 162 E9
Örebro län □ Sweden 59°27N 15°0E 162 E8
Orecchiella ⌂ Italy 44°16N 10°22E 198 D7
Ořech Czech Rep. 50°1N 14°17E 135 B1
Oregon Ill., U.S.A. 42°1N 89°20W 310 B7
Oregon Ohio, U.S.A. 41°38N 83°25W 311 C13
Oregon Wis., U.S.A. 42°56N 89°23W 310 B7
Oregon □ U.S.A. 44°0N 121°0W 304 E3
Oregon City U.S.A. 45°21N 122°36W 306 E4
Oregon Dunes ⌂ U.S.A. 43°40N 124°10W 304 E1
Öregrund Sweden 60°21N 18°30E 162 D12
Öregrundsgrepen Sweden 60°25N 18°15E 162 D12
Oregun Nigeria 6°35N 3°22E 124 A2
Orekhov = Orikhiv Ukraine 47°30N 35°48E 189 J8
Orekhovo-Zuyevo Russia 55°50N 38°55E 188 E10
Orel Russia 52°57N 36°3E 189 F9
Orel □ Russia 52°30N 36°40E 189 F9
Orellana □ Ecuador 0°45S 76°25W 328 D2
Orellana, Canal de Spain 39°2N 6°0W 195 F5
Orellana, Embalse de Spain 39°5N 5°10W 195 F5
Orellana la Vieja Spain 39°1N 5°32W 195 F5
Orem U.S.A. 40°19N 111°42W 304 F8
Ören Turkey 37°3N 27°57E 205 D9
Orenburg Russia 51°45N 55°6E 186 D10
Örencik Turkey 39°16N 29°33E 205 B11
Orense = Ourense Spain 42°19N 7°55W 194 C3
Orepuki N.Z. 46°19S 167°46E 285 G2
Ørestad Denmark 55°38N 12°35E 118 B3
Orestes Pereyra Mexico 26°30N 105°39W 318 B3
Orestiada Greece 41°30N 26°33E 203 E10
Øresund Europe 55°45N 12°40E 163 J6
Oretana, Cordillera = Toledo, Montes de Spain 39°33N 4°20W 195 F6
Oreti → N.Z. 46°28S 168°14E 285 G3
Orfanos Kolpos Greece 40°33N 24°0E 202 F7
Orford Ness U.K. 52°5N 1°35E 169 E9
Organ Pipe Cactus ⌂ U.S.A. 32°0N 112°52W 305 K7
Organos, Pta. de los Canary Is. 28°12N 17°17W 153 e1
Organyà Spain 42°13N 1°20E 196 C6
Orgaz Spain 39°39N 3°53W 195 F7
Ørgenvika Norway 60°17N 9°42E 164 D6
Orgeyev = Orhei Moldova 47°24N 28°50E 183 C13
Orgūn Afghan. 32°55N 69°12E 240 B3
Orhaneli Turkey 39°54N 28°59E 203 G12
Orhaneli → Turkey 39°50N 28°55E 203 G12
Orhangazi Turkey 40°29N 29°18E 203 F13
Orhei Moldova 47°24N 28°50E 183 C13
Orhon Gol → Mongolia 50°21N 106°0E 218 A10
Ória Italy 40°30N 17°38E 201 B10
Orida Niger 21°20N 12°15E 261 D7
Orient Heights U.S.A. 42°23N 70°59W 116 A3
Oriental □ Morocco 33°0N 2°0W 261 B4
Oriental, Cordillera Bolivia 17°0S 66°0W 331 D4
Oriental, Cordillera Colombia 6°0N 73°0W 328 B3
Oriental, Grand Erg Algeria 30°0N 6°30E 261 C6
Oriental Pearl Tower China 31°14N 121°30E 138 B2
Orientale □ Dem. Rep. of the Congo 2°20N 26°0E 268 B2
Oriente Argentina 38°44S 60°37W 334 D3
Orihuela Spain 38°7N 0°55W 197 G4
Orihuela del Tremedal Spain 40°33N 1°39W 196 E3
Orikhiv Ukraine 47°30N 35°48E 189 J8

Orikum *Albania* 40°20N 19°26E **202** F3
Oril → *Ukraine* 48°40N 34°39E **189** H8
Orillia *Canada* 44°40N 79°24W **312** B5
Orinduik *Guyana* 4°40N 60°3W **329** C5
Orinoco → *Venezuela* 9°15N 61°30W **329** B5
Orinoco, Delta del
Venezuela 9°0N 61°30W **329** B5
Orion *Canada* 49°27N 110°49W **297** D6
Orion *Ala., U.S.A.* 31°58N 86°0W **316** D4
Orion *Ill., U.S.A.* 41°21N 90°23W **310** C6
Oriskany *U.S.A.* 43°10N 75°20W **313** C9
Orissa = Odisha □ *India* 20°0N 84°0E **244** E7
Orissaare *Estonia* 58°34N 22°3E **188** C2
Oristano *Italy* 39°54N 8°36E **200** C1
Oristano, G. di *Italy* 39°50N 8°29E **200** C1
Orituco → *Venezuela* 8°45N 67°27W **328** B4
Oriximina *Brazil* 1°45S 55°52W **329** D6
Orizaba *Mexico* 18°58N 97°15W **319** D5
Orizaba, Pico de *Mexico* 18°51N 97°15W **319** D5
Orizare *Bulgaria* 42°44N 27°39E **203** D11
Orizona *Brazil* 17°3S 48°18W **333** E22
Ørje *Norway* 59°29N 11°39E **164** E8
Orjen *Bos.-H.* 42°35N 18°34E **202** D2
Orjiva *Spain* 36°53N 3°24W **195** J7
Orkanger *Norway* 63°18N 9°52E **164** A6
Örkelljunga *Sweden* 56°17N 13°17E **163** H7
Örken *Sweden* 57°6N 15°1E **163** G9
Örkény *Hungary* 47°9N 19°26E **182** C4
Orkhaniye = Botevgrad
Bulgaria 42°55N 23°47E **202** D7
Orkhon = Orhon Gol →
Mongolia 50°21N 106°0E **218** A10
Orkla → *Norway* 63°18N 9°51E **164** A6
Orkney *S. Africa* 26°58S 26°40E **270** C4
Orkney □ *U.K.* 59°2N 3°13W **167** B5
Orkney Is. *U.K.* 59°0N 3°0W **167** B6
Orland *Calif., U.S.A.* 39°45N 122°12W **306** F4
Orland *Ind., U.S.A.* 41°47N 85°12W **311** C11
Orland Park *U.S.A.* 41°38N 87°52W **119** D2
Orlando *U.S.A.* 28°32N 81°22W **133** A2
Orlando, C. d' *Italy* 38°10N 14°43E **201** D7
Orlando Dam *S. Africa* 26°15S 27°55E **123** B1
Orlando East *S. Africa* 26°14S 27°55E **123** B1
Orlando Executive ✈ (ORL)
U.S.A. 28°32N 81°20W **133** A2
Orlando Int. ✈ (MCO)
U.S.A. 28°26N 81°19W **133** B3
Orléanais *France* 48°0N 2°0E **173** E9
Orléans *Loiret, France* 47°54N 1°52E **173** E8
Orleans *Ind., U.S.A.* 38°40N 86°27W **311** F10
Orleans *Vt., U.S.A.* 44°49N 72°12W **313** E12
Orléans, Î. d' *Canada* 46°54N 70°58W **299** C5
Orléansville = Ech Chélif
Algeria 36°10N 1°20E **261** A5
Orlice → *Czech Rep.* 50°3N 15°50E **180** A8
Orlivka *Ukraine* 45°19N 28°27E **183** E13
Orlov = Khalturin *Russia* 58°40N 48°50E **186** C8
Orlov *Slovak Rep.* 49°17N 20°51E **181** B13
Orlov Gay *Russia* 50°56N 48°19E **190** D9
Orlová *Czech Rep.* 49°51N 18°26E **181** B11
Orlovat *Serbia* 45°14N 20°33E **182** E5
Orlovista *U.S.A.* 28°32N 81°27W **133** A2
Orly *France* 48°44N 2°23E **134** B3
Orly, Paris ✈ (ORY) *France* 48°44N 2°23E **134** B3
Ormara *Pakistan* 25°16N 64°33E **240** D2
Ormea *Italy* 44°9N 7°54E **198** D4
Ormesson-sur-Marne
France 48°47N 2°32E **134** B4
Ormília *Greece* 40°16N 23°39E **202** F7
Ormoc *Phil.* 11°0N 124°37E **233** F5
Ormond *Vic., Australia* 37°54S 145°1E **128** B2
Ormond *N.Z.* 38°33S 177°56E **284** E6
Ormond Beach *U.S.A.* 29°17N 81°3W **317** F8
Ormond-by-the-Sea
U.S.A. 29°21N 81°4W **317** F8
Ormondville *N.Z.* 40°5S 176°19E **284** G5
Ørmøya *Norway* 59°52N 10°43E **133** A4
Ormož *Slovenia* 46°25N 16°10E **199** B3
Ormskirk *U.K.* 53°35N 2°54W **168** D5
Ormstown *Canada* 45°8N 74°0W **313** A11
Ormtjernkampen △
Norway 61°12N 9°48E **164** C6
Ornans *France* 47°7N 6°10E **173** E13
Orne □ *France* 48°40N 0°5E **172** D7
Orne → *France* 49°18N 0°15W **172** C6
Orneta *Poland* 54°8N 20°9E **184** D7
Ornö *Sweden* 59°4N 18°24E **162** E12
Örnsköldsvik *Sweden* 63°17N 18°40E **162** A12
Oro *N. Korea* 40°1N 127°27E **224** B3
Oro → *Mexico* 25°35N 105°2W **318** B3
Oro Grande *U.S.A.* 34°36N 117°20W **307** L9
Oro Valley *U.S.A.* 32°26N 110°58W **305** K8
Orobie, Alpi *Italy* 46°7N 10°0E **198** B6
Orobie Bergamasche △
Italy 46°0N 9°45E **198** C6
Orobie Valtellinesi △ *Italy* 46°5N 9°45E **198** B6
Orocué *Colombia* 4°48N 71°20W **328** C3
Orodara *Burkina Faso* 11°0N 4°55W **262** C4
Orodo *Nigeria* 5°34N 7°4E **263** D6
Orofino *U.S.A.* 46°29N 116°15W **304** D5
Orohena, Mt. *Tahiti* 17°37S 149°28W **289** d
Orol Dengizi = Aral Sea
Asia 45°0N 58°20E **216** C5
Oromíya □ *Ethiopia* 7°0N 40°0E **257** F5
Oromocto *Canada* 45°54N 66°29W **299** C6
Oron *Nigeria* 4°48N 8°14E **263** E6
Orona *Kiribati* 4°31S 172°11W **287** H10
Orongo *Chile* 27°11S 109°27W **330** b
Orono *Ont., Canada* 43°59N 78°37W **312** C6
Orono *Maine, U.S.A.* 44°53N 68°40W **309** C19
Oronsay *U.K.* 56°1N 6°15W **167** E2
Oropesa *Spain* 39°57N 5°10W **194** F5
Oropuche → *Trin. & Tob.* 10°36N 61°5W **323** t
Oropuche Lagoon
Trin. & Tob. 10°14N 61°31W **323** t
Oroquieta *Phil.* 8°32N 123°44E **233** G4
Orós *Brazil* 6°15S 38°55W **332** C4
Orosei *Italy* 40°23N 9°42E **200** B2
Orosei, G. di *Italy* 40°15N 9°40E **200** B2
Orosháza *Hungary* 46°32N 20°42E **182** D5
Oroszlány *Hungary* 47°29N 18°19E **182** C4
Orote Pen. *Guam* 13°26N 144°38E **302** d
Orotukan *Russia* 62°16N 151°42E **215** C16
Oroville *Calif., U.S.A.* 39°31N 121°33W **306** F5
Oroville *Wash., U.S.A.* 48°56N 119°26W **304** B4
Oroville, L. *U.S.A.* 39°33N 121°29W **306** F5
Orpington *U.K.* 51°22N 0°6E **125** A4
Orrefors *Sweden* 56°50N 15°45E **163** H9
Orrick *U.S.A.* 39°13N 94°7W **302** B3
Orroroo *Australia* 32°43S 138°38E **282** B3
Orrviken *Sweden* 63°6N 14°26E **162** A8
Orsa *Sweden* 61°7N 14°37E **162** C8
Orsara di Púglia *Italy* 41°17N 15°16E **201** A8
Orsay *France* 48°42N 2°11E **134** C2
Orsay, Musée d' *Paris, France* **134** B3
Orsha *Belarus* 54°30N 30°25E **188** B6
Orsières *Switz.* 46°2N 7°9E **198** C4
Orsk *Russia* 51°12N 58°34E **186** E6
Orsova *Romania* 44°41N 22°25E **182** F7
Ørsted *Denmark* 56°30N 10°20E **163** H4
Ørsundsbro *Sweden* 59°44N 17°18E **162** E11
Orta, L. d' *Italy* 45°48N 8°21E **198** C5
Orta Nova *Italy* 41°19N 15°42E **201** A8

Ortaca *Turkey* 36°49N 28°45E **205** E10
Ortakent *Turkey* 37°5N 27°21E **205** D9
Ortaklar *Turkey* 37°53N 27°30E **205** D9
Ortaköy *Çorum, Turkey* 40°16N 35°15E **212** B6
Ortaköy *İstanbul, Turkey* 41°3N 29°1E **122** B2
Ortaköy *Niğde, Turkey* 38°44N 34°3E **212** C6
Orte *Italy* 42°27N 12°23E **199** F9
Ortegal, C. *Spain* 43°43N 7°52W **194** B3
Orteguaza → *Colombia* 0°43N 75°16W **328** C2
Ortelsburg = Szczytno
Poland 53°33N 21°0E **184** E7
Orthez *France* 43°29N 0°48W **174** E3
Ortica *Italy* 45°28N 9°16E **128** B2
Ortigueira *Spain* 43°40N 7°50W **194** B3
Orting *U.S.A.* 47°6N 122°12W **306** C4
Ortisei *Italy* 46°34N 11°40E **199** B8
Ortles *Italy* 46°31N 10°33E **198** B7
Ortnevik *Norway* 61°6N 6°7E **164** C3
Ortoire → *Trin. & Tob.* 10°20N 61°0W **323** t
Ortón → *Bolivia* 10°50S 67°0W **330** D4
Ortona *Italy* 42°21N 14°24E **199** F11
Ortonville *U.S.A.* 45°19N 96°27W **308** C5
Oruba *Nigeria* 6°34N 3°24E **124** A2
Orukuizui *Palau* 7°10N 134°15E **288** c
Orümïyeh *Iran* 37°40N 45°0E **213** D11
Orümïyeh, Daryācheh-ye
Iran 37°50N 45°30E **213** D11
Orune *Italy* 40°24N 9°22E **200** B2
Oruro *Bolivia* 18°0S 67°9W **330** D4
Oruro □ *Bolivia* 18°45S 67°30W **330** D4
Orust *Sweden* 58°11N 11°40E **163** F5
Oruzgān □ *Afghan.* 33°0N 66°0E **240** B2
Orvault *France* 47°17N 1°38W **172** E5
Orvieto *Italy* 42°43N 12°7E **199** F9
Orwell *N.Y., U.S.A.* 43°35N 75°50W **313** C9
Orwell *Ohio, U.S.A.* 41°32N 80°52W **312** E4
Orwell → *U.K.* 51°59N 1°18E **169** F9
Orwigsburg *U.S.A.* 40°38N 76°6W **313** F8
Oryakhovo *Bulgaria* 43°40N 23°57E **202** C7
Orynyn *Ukraine* 48°46N 26°24E **183** H11
Oryol = Orel *Russia* 52°57N 36°3E **189** F9
Orzinuovi *Italy* 45°24N 9°55E **198** C6
Orzyc → *Poland* 52°46N 21°14E **185** F8
Orzysz *Poland* 53°50N 21°58E **184** E8
Os *Norway* 62°30N 11°14E **164** B8
Osa *Russia* 57°17N 55°26E **186** C10
Osa → *Poland* 53°33N 18°46E **184** E5
Osa, Pen. de *Costa Rica* 8°0N 84°0W **320** E3
Osage *U.S.A.* 43°17N 92°49W **308** D7
Osage → *U.S.A.* 38°36N 91°57W **310** F5
Osage City *U.S.A.* 38°38N 95°50W **308** F6
Ōsaka □ *Japan* 34°42N 135°30E **133** B2
Ōsaka □ *Japan* 34°30N 135°30E **223** C7
Ōsaka Castle *Japan* 34°41N 135°30E **133** A2
Ōsaka Harbour *Japan* 34°38N 135°25E **133** A1
Ōsaka Itami Int. ✈ (ITM)
Japan 34°46N 135°26E **133** A1
Ōsaka Kansai Int. ✈ (KIX)
Japan 34°27N 135°12E **133** B2
Ōsaka-Wan *Japan* 34°30N 135°18E **223** C7
Osakarovka *Kazakhstan* 50°33N 72°34E **217** B8
Ōsaki *Kagoshima, Japan* 31°25N 131°2E **222** F3
Ōsaki *Miyagi, Japan* 38°34N 140°58E **220** E10
Ōsaki *Tōkyō, Japan* 35°36N 139°42E **140** B3
Osan *S. Korea* 37°11N 127°4E **224** C5
Osasco *Brazil* 23°31S 46°46W **137** B1
Osawatomie *U.S.A.* 38°31N 94°57W **308** F6
Osborn Plateau *Ind. Oc.* 14°45S 87°0E **273** F7
Osborne *U.S.A.* 39°26N 98°42W **308** F4
Osby *Sweden* 56°23N 13°59E **163** H7
Osceola *Ark., U.S.A.* 35°42N 89°58W **315** D10
Osceola *Iowa, U.S.A.* 41°2N 93°46W **310** C4
Osceola *Mo., U.S.A.* 38°3N 93°42W **310** F3
Oschatz *Germany* 51°17N 13°6E **178** D9
Oschersleben *Germany* 52°2N 11°14E **178** C7
Ōshiri *Japan* 40°43N 9°6E **200** B2
Oscoda *U.S.A.* 44°26N 83°20W **312** B1
Osdorf *Germany* 52°24N 13°20E **115** B3
Osdorp *Neths.* 52°22N 4°47E **112** A1
Ōse → *Japan* 42°23N 19°50E **200** B1
Osečina *Serbia* 44°23N 19°34E **182** E3
Ösel = Saaremaa *Estonia* 58°30N 22°30E **188** C2
Osery *Russia* 54°52N 38°28E **188** E10
Osgood *U.S.A.* 39°8N 85°18W **311** F11
Osgoode *Canada* 45°8N 75°36W **313** A9
Osgoode Hall *Toronto, Canada* **141** b2
Osh □ *Kyrgyzstan* 40°37N 72°49E **217** D8
Osh □ *Kyrgyzstan* 40°0N 73°0E **217** E8
Oshana □ *Namibia* 17°50S 15°40E **270** A2
Oshawa *Canada* 43°50N 78°50W **312** C6
Oshigambo *Namibia* 17°45S 16°5E **270** A2
Oshikoto □ *Namibia* 18°30S 17°0E **270** A2
Oshivelo *Namibia* 18°37S 17°10E **270** A2
Oshkosh *Nebr., U.S.A.* 41°24N 102°21W **308** E3
Oshkosh *Wis., U.S.A.* 44°1N 88°33W **308** D9
Oshmyany = Ashmyany
Belarus 54°26N 25°52E **177** A13
Oshnovïyeh *Iran* 37°2N 45°6E **213** D11
Oshodi □ *Nigeria* 6°33N 3°21E **124** A2
Oshogbo *Nigeria* 7°48N 4°37E **263** D5
Oshtorinān *Iran* 34°1N 48°38E **213** E13
Ōshū *Japan* 39°8N 141°8E **220** E10
Oshwe
Dem. Rep. of the Congo 3°25S 19°28E **264** C3
Osi *Nigeria* 8°8N 5°14E **263** D6
Osieczna *Poland* 51°55N 16°40E **185** G3
Osijek *Croatia* 45°34N 18°41E **182** E3
Ösimo *Italy* 40°45N 8°40E **200** B1
Ōsimo *Italy* 43°28N 13°30E **199** C10
Osintorf *Belarus* 54°40N 30°39E **188** B6
Osipenko = Berdyansk
Ukraine 46°45N 36°50E **189** J9
Osipovichi = Asipovichy
Belarus 53°19N 28°33E **177** B15
Osiyan *India* 26°43N 72°55E **242** F5
Osizweni *S. Africa* 27°49S 30°7E **271** C5
Oskaloosa *U.S.A.* 41°18N 92°39W **310** C8
Oskarshamn *Sweden* 57°15N 16°27E **163** G10
Oskarström *Sweden* 56°48N 12°58E **163** H6
Oskélanéo *Canada* 48°5N 75°15W **298** C4
Öskemen *Kazakhstan* 50°0N 82°36E **217** C10
Oskol → *Ukraine* 37°54N 46°8E **213** D12
Osku *Iran* 37°54N 46°8E **213** D12
Oslo *Norway* 59°54N 10°43E **133** A3
Oslo → *Norway* 59°54N 10°43E **164** D7
Oslo ✈ (OSL) *Norway* 60°11N 11°6E **133** A4
Oslob *Phil.* 9°31N 123°26E **233** G4
Oslofjorden *Norway* 59°20N 10°35E **164** E7
Osmanabad *India* 18°5N 76°10E **244** E3
Osmancık *Turkey* 40°58N 34°47E **212** B6
Osmaniye *Turkey* 41°35N 26°51E **203** D10
Osmannagar *India* 18°32N 79°20E **244** E4
Ōsmo *Sweden* 58°58N 17°55E **162** F11
Osnabrück *Germany* 52°17N 8°3E **178** C4
Ōsno Lubuskie *Poland* 52°28N 14°51E **185** F1
Osobłaha *Czech Rep.* 50°17N 17°44E **181** A10
Osogbo = Oshogbo *Nigeria* 7°48N 4°37E **263** D5
Osogovska Planina
Macedonia 42°10N 22°30E **202** D6
Ōsone *Japan* 35°31N 139°37E **140** B2
Ōsono *Italy* 44°42N 9°49E **198** D5
Osório *Brazil* 29°53S 50°17W **335** B5
Osório da Fonseca *Brazil* 3°52S 58°18W **329** D6
Osorno *Chile* 40°25N 73°0W **336** B2
Osorno *Spain* 42°24N 4°22W **194** C6

Osorno □ *Chile* 40°34S 73°9W **336** B2
Osorno, Vol. *Chile* 41°0S 72°30W **336** B2
Osorun *Nigeria* 6°33N 3°29E **124** A2
Osoyoos *Canada* 49°0N 119°30W **296** D5
Osoyro *Norway* 60°9N 5°30E **164** C2
Ōspakseyri *Iceland* 65°27N 21°26W **155** B5
Ospiate *Italy* 45°32N 9°6E **128** A1
Ospika → *Canada* 56°20N 124°0W **296** B4
Osprey *Australia* 27°12N 82°29W **317** H7
Osprey Reef *Australia* 13°55S 146°36E **280** A4
Oss *Neths.* 51°46N 5°32E **170** C5
Ossa, Mt. *Australia* 41°52S 146°3E **281** G4
Ossa, Oros *Greece* 39°47N 22°42E **204** B4
Ossa de Montiel *Spain* 38°58N 2°45W **197** G2
Ossabaw I. *U.S.A.* 31°50N 81°5W **316** D8
Ossabaw Sd. *U.S.A.* 31°50N 81°6W **316** D8
Osse → *Lot-et-Garonne,
France* 44°7N 0°17E **174** D4
Osse → *Nigeria* 6°10N 5°20E **263** D6
Ossersee = Zarasai
Lithuania 55°40N 26°20E **188** E4
Ossi *Italy* 40°40N 8°35E **200** B1
Ossining *U.S.A.* 41°10N 73°55W **313** E11
Ossipee *U.S.A.* 43°41N 71°7W **313** C13
Ossokmanuan L. *Canada* 53°25N 65°0W **299** B7
Ossora *Russia* 59°20N 163°13E **215** D17
Ostankino *Russia* 55°49N 37°37E **129** B2
Ostashkov *Russia* 57°4N 33°2E **188** D7
Østavall *Sweden* 62°26N 15°29E **162** B9
Østby *Norway* 61°15N 12°33E **164** C9
Oste → *Germany* 53°49N 9°2E **178** B5
Ostend = Oostende
Belgium 51°15N 2°54E **170** C2
Ostend *N.Z.* 36°48S 175°2E **284** B5
Oster *Ukraine* 50°57N 30°53E **177** C16
Ōra → *Norway* 58°9N 8°1E **164** F5
Otradnyy *Russia* 53°22N 51°21E **190** D10
Otranto *Italy* 40°9N 18°28E **201** B11
Otranto, C. d' *Italy* 40°7N 18°30E **201** B11
Otranto, Str. of *Italy* 40°15N 18°40E **201** B11
Otrobanda *Curaçao* 12°7N 68°57W **322** g
Otrokovice *Czech Rep.* 49°12N 17°32E **181** B10
Otse *S. Africa* 25°2S 25°45E **270** C4
Otsego *U.S.A.* 42°27N 85°42W **311** B11
Otsego L. *U.S.A.* 42°45N 74°53W **313** D10
Ōtsu *Japan* 35°0N 135°50E **223** C7
Otsuka *Japan* 35°43N 139°44E **140** A3
Otta *Norway* 61°46N 9°32E **164** C6
Otta → *Norway* 61°46N 9°31E **164** C6
Ottawa = Outaouais →
Canada 45°27N 74°8W **298** C5
Ottawa *Ont., Canada* 45°26N 75°42W **313** A9
Ottawa *Ill., U.S.A.* 41°21N 88°51W **311** C8
Ottawa *Kans., U.S.A.* 38°37N 95°16W **308** F6
Ottawa *Ohio, U.S.A.* 41°1N 84°3W **311** C12
Ottawa Is. *Canada* 59°35N 80°10W **295** F15
Ottélé *Cameroon* 3°38N 11°19E **263** E7
Ottensheim *Austria* 48°21N 14°12E **180** C7
Otter Cr. → *U.S.A.* 44°13N 73°17W **313** B11
Otter Creek *U.S.A.* 29°19N 82°46W **317** F7
Otter Lake *Canada* 45°17N 79°56W **312** A5
Otterbäcken *Sweden* - 58°57N 14°3E **163** F8
Otterbein *U.S.A.* 40°29N 87°6W **311** D9
Otterndorf *Germany* 53°48N 8°53E **178** B4
Otteroya *Norway* 62°45N 6°50E **164** B3
Otterup *Denmark* 55°30N 10°22E **163** J4
Otterville *Ont., Canada* 42°55N 80°36W **312** D4
Otterville *Mo., U.S.A.* 38°42N 92°55W **310** F4
Ottery *S. Africa* 34°1S 18°32E **118** B2
Ottery St. Mary *U.K.* 50°44N 3°17W **169** G4
Ottilien Reef *Papua N. G.* 4°33S 148°49E **286** D5
Ottumachau = Otmuchów
Poland 50°28N 17°10E **185** H4
Otto Beit Bridge *Zimbabwe* 15°59S 28°56E **269** F2
Ottobrunn *Germany* 48°3N 11°40E **131** B3
Ottosdal *S. Africa* 26°46S 25°59E **270** C4
Ottoville *U.S.A.* 40°57N 84°22W **311** D12
Ottumwa *U.S.A.* 41°1N 92°25W **310** C8
Otukpa *Nigeria* 7°9N 7°41E **263** D6
Otura □ *Bolivia* 19°45S 58°44W **331** D6
Oturkpo *Nigeria* 7°16N 8°8E **263** D6
Otvazhnoye = Zhiguleysk
Russia 53°28N 49°30E **190** D9
Otvazhny = Zhiguleysk
Russia 53°28N 49°30E **190** D9
Otway, B. *Chile* 53°30N 74°0W **336** D2
Otway, C. *Australia* 38°52S 143°30E **282** E5
Otway, Seno de *Chile* 53°0S 71°30W **336** D2
Otwock → *Poland* 52°5N 21°20E **185** F9
Otynya *Ukraine* 48°48N 24°51E **183** B9
Oú *Laos* 20°4N 102°13E **236** B4
Ou-Sammayaku *Japan* 39°20N 140°35E **220** E10
Ouachita □ *U.S.A.* 31°38N 91°49W **314** F9
Ouachita, L. *U.S.A.* 34°34N 93°12W **314** D8
Ouachita Mts. *U.S.A.* 34°30N 94°30W **314** D7
Ouadâne *Mauritania* 20°50N 11°40W **260** D2
Ouadda *C.A.R.* 8°15N 22°20E **264** A4
Ouaddaï □ *Chad* 13°0N 21°0E **259** F4
Ouagadougou
Burkina Faso 12°25N 1°30W **263** C4
Ouahigouya *Burkina Faso* 13°31N 2°25W **262** C4
Ouahran = Oran *Algeria* 35°45N 0°39W **261** A4
Ouallah *Comoros Is.* 12°19S 43°39E **272** a
Ouallam *Niger* 14°42N 2°2E **263** C5
Ouallene *Algeria* 24°41N 1°11E **261** D5
Ouanary *Fr. Guiana* 4°13N 51°40W **329** C7
Ouanda Djallé *C.A.R.* 8°55N 22°53E **264** A4
Ouandago *C.A.R.* 7°13N 18°50E **264** A3
Ouandja *C.A.R.* 8°28N 23°17E **264** A4
Ouandja, Bahr → *C.A.R.* 9°3N 21°43E **264** A4
Ouandja-Vakaga → *C.A.R.* 9°2N 22°18E **264** A4
Ouango *C.A.R.* 4°19N 22°30E **264** B4
Ouango *Comoros Is.* 12°9S 44°18E **272** a
Ouantou → *C.A.R.* 7°19N 15°18E **264** A3
Ouara → *C.A.R.* 5°3N 24°26E **264** A4
Ouarane *Mauritania* 21°0N 10°30W **260** D3
Ouargaye *Burkina Faso* 11°4N 0°19E **263** C5
Ouargla *Algeria* 31°59N 5°16E **261** B6
Ouargla □ *Algeria* 30°30N 6°10E **261** B6
Ouarkziz, Jebel *Algeria* 28°50N 8°0W **260** C3
Ouarra → *C.A.R.* 5°5N 24°26E **264** A4
Ouarzazate *Morocco* 30°55N 6°50W **260** B3
Ouassouas *Mali* 15°11N 0°43E **263** B5
Ouatagouna *Mali* 15°11N 0°43E **263** B5
Ouatere *C.A.R.* 5°30N 19°8E **264** A3
Oubangi →
Dem. Rep. of the Congo 0°30S 17°50E **264** C3
Oubarakai, O. → *Algeria* 27°20N 2°55E **261** C6
Oubari, O. *Algeria* 30°0N 9°0E **261** C7
Oudai *Spain* 37°14N 5°8W **195** H5
Oud Zuid *Amsterdam, Neths.* **112** c1
Oud[t]orp *Neths.* 51°50N 3°57E **170** C4
Oude Kerk *Amsterdam, Neths.* **112** a2
Oude Rijn → *Neths.* 52°12N 4°24E **170** B4
Oudega *Neths.* 53°8N 5°58E **170** A5
Oudenaarde *Belgium* 50°50N 3°37E **170** D3
Oudenbosch *Neths.* 51°35N 4°32E **170** C4
Ouderkerk *Neths.* 52°18N 4°55E **112** b2
Oudewater *Neths.* 52°2N 4°48E **170** B4
Oudon → *France* 47°41N 0°53W **172** E6

Ōtawara *Japan* 36°50N 140°5E **221** F10
Otchinjau *Angola* 16°30S 13°56E **265** F2
Otego *U.S.A.* 42°23N 75°10W **313** D9
Oteiza = Marítahog *Phil.* 8°48N 126°18E **233** G6
Otelec *Romania* 45°36N 20°50E **182** E5
Oteluk, L. *Canada* 56°9N 68°12W **299** A6
Otelu Roşu *Romania* 45°30N 22°22E **182** E7
Otero de Rey = Outeiro de Rei
Spain 43°7N 7°36W **194** B3
Othello *U.S.A.* 46°50N 119°10W **304** C4
Othoni *Greece* 39°52N 19°22E **206** B9
Othris, Oros *Greece* 39°2N 22°27E **204** B4
Oti → *Africa* 7°48N 0°8E **263** D5
Oti → *Togo* 10°40N 0°35E **263** D5
Otira *N.Z.* 42°49S 171°33E **285** D6
Otira Gorge *N.Z.* 42°53S 171°33E **285** D6
Otjenipene □ *Namibia* 21°8S 18°46E **270** B2
Otjiwarongo *Namibia* 20°30S 16°33E **270** B2
Otjozondjupa □ *Namibia* 21°0S 17°0E **270** B2
Oto Tolu Group *Tonga* 20°21S 174°32W **287** Q13
Otočac *Croatia* 44°53N 15°12E **199** D12
Otoineppu *Japan* 44°44N 142°16E **220** B11
Otok *Croatia* 43°42N 16°44E **199** E13
Otomari = Korsakov
Russia 46°36N 142°42E **215** E15
Oton *Phil.* 10°42N 122°29E **233** F4
Otopeni, Bucureşti ✈ (OTP)
Romania 44°30N 26°11E **183** F11
Otorohanga *N.Z.* 38°12S 175°14E **284** E4
Otoskwin → *Canada* 52°13N 88°6W **298** B2
Ōtoyo *Japan* 33°43N 133°45E **222** D5
Otpor = Zabaykalsk
Russia 49°40N 117°25E **215** E12

Oudtshoorn *S. Africa* 33°35S 22°14E **270** D3
Oued Zem *Morocco* 32°52N 6°34W **260** B3
Ouégoa □ *N. Cal.* 20°20S 164°26E **288** d
Oueita *Chad* 17°47N 20°39E **259** E4
Ouella *Niger* 14°48N 3°38E **263** C5
Ouellé *Ivory C.* 7°26N 4°1W **262** D4
Ouémé → *Benin* 6°30N 2°30E **263** D5
Ouenza *Algeria* 35°57N 8°4E **261** A6
Ouessa *Burkina Faso* 11°4N 2°47W **262** C4
Ouessant, Î. d' *France* 48°28N 5°6W **172** D1
Ouesso *Congo* 1°37N 16°5E **264** B3
Ouest, Pte. de l' *Canada* 49°52N 64°40W **299** C7
Ouezzane *Morocco* 34°51N 5°35W **260** B3
Ougarou *Burkina Faso* 12°10N 0°58E **263** C5
Oughter, L. *Ireland* 54°1N 7°28W **166** B4
Oughterard *Ireland* 53°26N 9°18W **166** C2
Ouham → *C.A.R.* 9°48N 21°32E **264** A4
Ouidah *Benin* 6°25N 2°0E **263** D5
Ouidi *Niger* 14°10N 13°0E **259** F2
Ouistreham *France* 49°17N 0°18W **172** C6
Oujda *Morocco* 34°41N 1°55W **261** B4
Oujeft *Mauritania* 20°2N 13°0W **260** D2
Oulad-Teïma *Morocco* 30°24N 9°12W **260** B3
Oulainen *Finland* 64°17N 24°47E **160** D21
Ould Yenjé *Mauritania* 15°38N 12°16W **262** B2
Ouled Djellal *Algeria* 34°28N 5°2E **261** B6
Ouled Naïl, Mts. des
Algeria 34°30N 3°30E **261** B6
Ouli *Cameroon* 5°12N 14°33E **264** B3
Oullins *France* 45°43N 4°49E **175** C8
Oulmès *Morocco* 33°17N 6°0W **260** B3
Oulu *Finland* 65°1N 25°29E **160** D21
Oulujärvi *Finland* 64°25N 27°15E **160** D22
Oulujoki → *Finland* 65°1N 25°30E **160** D21
Oulunkylä *Finland* 60°13N 24°58E **121** B2
Oulx *Italy* 45°2N 6°50E **198** D3
Oum Chalouba *Chad* 15°48N 20°46E **259** E4
Oum-el-Bouaghi *Algeria* 35°55N 7°6E **261** A6
Oum-el-Bouaghi □ *Algeria* 35°50N 7°5E **261** A6
Oum el Ksi *Algeria* 29°4N 6°59W **260** C3
Oum-er-Rbia, O. →
Morocco 33°19N 8°21W **260** B3
Oum Hadjer *Chad* 13°18N 19°41E **259** F3
Oum Hadjer, O. → *Chad* 16°38N 20°14E **259** E4
Oumé *Ivory C.* 6°21N 5°27W **262** D3
Oumm ed Droûs Guebli, Sebkhet
Mauritania 24°20N 11°45W **260** D2
Oumm ed Droûs Telli, Sebkhet
Mauritania 24°20N 11°30W **260** D2
Ounane, Dj. *Algeria* 25°4N 7°19E **261** C6
Ounasjoki → *Finland* 66°31N 25°40E **160** C21
Ounguati *Namibia* 22°0S 15°46E **270** B2
Ounianga Kébir *Chad* 19°4N 20°29E **259** E4
Ounianga Sérir *Chad* 18°54N 20°51E **259** E4
Ounissoui *Niger* 13°34N 12°13E **259** E2
Our → *Lux.* 49°55N 6°5E **176** E6
Oura, Akra *Greece* 38°10N 26°2E **205** C8
Oura-wan *Japan* 26°32N 128°4E **288** a
Ouranoupoli *Greece* 40°20N 23°57E **202** F7
Ouārène *Niger* 19°30N 7°10E **263** B6
Ourari, Tarso *Chad* 21°27N 17°27E **259** D3
Ouray *U.S.A.* 38°1N 107°40W **305** G10
Ourcq → *France* 49°1N 3°1E **173** C10
Ourcq, Canal de l' *France* 48°54N 2°28E **134** A4
Ourém *Brazil* 1°33S 47°6W **332** B2
Ourense *Spain* 42°19N 7°55W **194** C3
Ourense □ *Spain* 42°15N 7°51W **194** C3
Ouricuri *Brazil* 7°53S 40°5W **332** D3
Ourinhos *Brazil* 23°0S 49°54W **335** A6
Ourique *Portugal* 37°38N 8°16W **195** H2
Ouro Fino *Brazil* 22°16S 46°25W **335** A6
Ouro-Ndia *Mali* 15°17N 3°55W **262** C4
Ouro Prêto *Brazil* 20°20S 43°30W **333** F3
Ouro Prêto do Oeste
Brazil 10°40S 62°18W **331** C6
Ouro Sogui *Senegal* 15°36N 13°19W **262** B2
Ourthe → *Belgium* 50°29N 5°35E **170** D5
Ouse → *E. Sussex, U.K.* 50°47N 0°4E **169** G8
Ouse → *N. Yorks., U.K.* 53°44N 0°55W **168** E7
Oust *France* 42°52N 1°13E **174** F5
Oust → *France* 47°35N 2°6W **172** E4
Outamba-Kilimi △
S. Leone 9°50N 12°40W **262** D2
Outaouais → *Canada* 45°27N 74°8W **298** C5
Outapi *Namibia* 17°30S 15°0E **270** A2
Outardes → *Canada* 49°24N 69°30W **299** C6
Outat Oulad el Haj
Morocco 33°20N 3°42W **261** B4
Outeiro de Rei *Spain* 43°6N 7°36W **194** B3
Outer Hebrides *U.K.* 57°30N 7°15W **167** D1
Outer Mission *U.S.A.* 37°43N 122°26W **136** B2
Outes = A Serra de Outes
Spain 42°52N 8°55W **194** C2
Outjo *Namibia* 20°5S 16°7E **270** B2
Outlook *U.S.A.* 51°30N 107°0W **297** C7
Outokumpu *Finland* 62°43N 29°1E **160** E23
Outreau *France* 50°40N 1°36E **173** B8
Outremont *Canada* 45°31N 73°36W **130** A2
Ouvéa, Î. N. Cal. 43°59N 4°51E **175** E8
Ouvèze → *France* 43°59N 4°51E **175** E8
Ouyen *Australia* 35°1S 142°22E **282** C5
Ouzinkie *U.S.A.* 57°56N 152°30W **303** H9
Ouzouer-le-Marché *France* 47°54N 1°32E **173** E8
Ovacık *Turkey* 36°11N 33°40E **205** B9
Ovada *Italy* 44°38N 8°38E **198** D5
Ovahe *Chile* 27°5S 109°19W **330** b
Ovalau *Fiji* 17°40S 178°48E **287** a2
Ovalle *Chile* 30°33S 71°18W **334** C1
Ovamboland *Namibia* 18°30S 16°0E **270** A2
Ovan *Gabon* 0°19N 12°10E **264** B2
Ovanåker *Sweden* 61°9N 15°53E **162** C9
Ovar *Portugal* 40°51N 8°40W **194** E2
Ovau *Solomon Is.* 6°40S 156°8E **287** b2
Overath *Germany* 50°56N 7°17E **178** E3
Overflakkee *Neths.* 51°44N 4°10E **116** B3
Overijse *Belgium* 50°47N 4°32E **116** D2
Overijssel □ *Neths.* 52°25N 6°35E **170** B6
Overland *U.S.A.* 38°42N 90°21W **310** F7
Overland Park *U.S.A.* 38°58N 94°40W **308** F6
Overlander Roadhouse
Australia 26°19S 114°28E **281** E1
Overton *U.S.A.* 36°33N 114°27W **307** J12
Overtorneå *Sweden* 66°23N 23°38E **160** C20
Överum *Sweden* 57°59N 16°19E **163** F10
Ovid *Mich., U.S.A.* 43°1N 84°22W **311** A12
Ovid *Colo., U.S.A.* 40°58N 102°23W **308** E2
Ovidiopol *Ukraine* 46°15N 30°30E **183** E16
Ovidiu *Romania* 44°16N 28°27E **183** F13
Oviedo *Spain* 43°25N 5°50W **194** B5
Oviedo □ *Spain* 43°20N 6°0W **194** B5
Oviken *Sweden* 63°0N 14°23E **162** A7
Oviksfjällen *Sweden* 63°0N 13°49E **162** A7
Ovišrags *Latvia* 57°33N 21°44E **163** H11
Ovoot *Mongolia* 45°21N 113°45E **218** B9
Övör Hangay □ *Mongolia* 45°0N 102°30E **218** B9
Ovoro *Nigeria* 5°26N 7°16E **263** D6
Øvre Årdal *Norway* 61°19N 7°48E **164** C3
Øvre Fryken *Sweden* 60°0N 13°20E **163** E7
Øvre Rendal *Norway* 61°34N 11°1E **164** C8
Øvre Sirdal *Norway* 58°48N 6°43E **164** F3
Ovruch *Ukraine* 51°25N 28°45E **177** C15
Owaka *N.Z.* 46°27S 169°40E **285** G4

Oudzani *Namibia* 18°30S 16°0E **270** A2
Owando *Congo* 0°29S 15°55E **264** C3
Owariasahi *Japan* 35°10N 137°5E **223** B9
Owasco L. *U.S.A.* 42°50N 76°31W **313** D8
Owase *Japan* 34°7N 136°12E **223** C8
Owatonna *U.S.A.* 44°5N 93°14W **308** C7
Owbeh *Afghan.* 34°28N 63°10E **240** B1
Owego *U.S.A.* 42°6N 76°16W **313** D8
Owen *Australia* 34°15S 138°32E **282** B2
Owen, Mt. *N.Z.* 41°35S 172°33E **285** B7
Owen Falls Dam = Nalubaale Dam
Uganda 0°30N 33°5E **268** B3
Owen Sound *Canada* 44°35N 80°55W **312** B4
Owen Stanley Ra.
Papua N. G. 8°30S 147°0E **286** E4
Owendo *Gabon* 0°17N 9°30E **264** B1
Oweniny → *Ireland* 54°8N 9°34W **166** B2
Owens → *U.S.A.* 36°32N 117°59W **306** J9
Owens L. *U.S.A.* 36°26N 117°57W **307** J9
Owensboro *U.S.A.* 37°46N 87°7W **311** G9
Owensville *Ind., U.S.A.* 38°16N 87°41W **311** F9
Owensville *Mo., U.S.A.* 38°21N 91°30W **310** F5
Owenteik *Guyana* 4°27N 59°35W **329** C6
Owenton *U.S.A.* 38°32N 84°50W **311** F12
Owerri *Nigeria* 5°29N 7°0E **263** D6
Owhango *N.Z.* 39°0S 175°23E **284** F4
Owingsville *U.S.A.* 38°9N 83°46W **311** F13
Owl → *Canada* 57°51N 92°44W **297** B10
Owo *Nigeria* 7°10N 5°39E **263** D6
Owo → *Nigeria* 6°32N 3°24E **124** A2
Owosso *U.S.A.* 43°0N 84°10W **311** B12
Owyhee *U.S.A.* 41°57N 116°6W **304** F5
Owyhee → *U.S.A.* 43°49N 117°2W **304** E5
Owyhee, L. *U.S.A.* 43°38N 117°14W **304** E5
Ox Mts. = Slieve Gamph
Ireland 54°6N 9°0W **166** B3
Oxapampa *Peru* 10°33S 75°26W **330** C2
Öxarfjörður *Iceland* 66°15N 16°45W **155** A10
Oxbow *Canada* 49°14N 102°10W **297** D8
Oxelösund *Sweden* 58°43N 17°5E **163** F11
Oxford *N.Z.* 43°18S 172°11E **285** D7
Oxford *Oxon., U.K.* 51°46N 1°15W **169** F6
Oxford *Ala., U.S.A.* 33°36N 85°51W **316** B4
Oxford *Iowa, U.S.A.* 41°43N 91°47W **310** C9
Oxford *Mass., U.S.A.* 42°7N 71°52W **313** D13
Oxford *Mich., U.S.A.* 42°49N 83°16W **311** B13
Oxford *Miss., U.S.A.* 34°22N 89°31W **315** C10
Oxford *N.C., U.S.A.* 36°19N 78°35W **315** C15
Oxford *N.Y., U.S.A.* 42°27N 75°36W **313** D9
Oxford L. *Canada* 54°51N 95°37W **297** C9
Oxford Street *London, U.K.* **125** b3
Oxfordshire □ *U.K.* 51°48N 1°16W **169** F6
Oxgangs *U.K.* 55°54N 3°13W **121** B2
Oxia *Greece* 38°16N 21°5E **207** C3
Oxie *Sweden* 55°33N 13°5E **163** J7
Oxilithos *Greece* 38°35N 24°7E **204** C6
Oxley *Australia* 34°11S 144°6E **282** B2
Oxley Wild Rivers △
Australia 30°57S 152°12E **283** A10
Oxnard *U.S.A.* 34°12N 119°11W **307** L7
Oxon Hill *U.S.A.* 38°48N 76°59W **143** C3
Oxsjövålen *Sweden* 62°34N 13°57E **162** B7
Oxus = Amudarya →
Uzbekistan 43°58N 59°34E **216** C5
Oya *Malaysia* 2°55N 111°55E **235** B4
Oyabe *Japan* 36°47N 136°56E **223** A8
Oyama *Japan* 36°18N 139°48E **223** A11
Oyambre △ *Spain* 43°22N 4°21W **194** B6
Oyapock → *Fr. Guiana* 4°8N 51°40W **329** C7
Oyem *Gabon* 1°34N 11°31E **264** B2
Oyen *Canada* 51°22N 110°28W **297** C6
Øyer *Norway* 61°16N 10°22E **164** C7
Øyeren *Norway* 59°50N 11°15E **164** E8
Oykel → *U.K.* 57°56N 4°26W **167** D4
Oymyakon *Russia* 63°25N 142°44E **215** C15
Oyo *Congo* 0°0 15°51E **264** C3
Oyo *Nigeria* 7°46N 3°56E **263** D5
Oyo *Sudan* 21°58N 36°10E **256** C3
Oyo □ *Nigeria* 8°15N 3°30E **263** D5
Oyodo *Japan* 34°42N 135°29E **143** A5
Oyón *Peru* 10°37S 76°47W **330** C2
Oyonnax *France* 46°16N 5°40E **175** F12
Oyrot = Gorno-Altay □
Russia 51°0N 86°0E **217** B11
Oyrot-Tura = Gorno-Altaysk
Russia 51°50N 86°5E **217** D11
Øyslebø *Norway* 58°9N 7°34E **164** F4
Oyster Bay *U.S.A.* 40°52N 73°32W **313** F11
Oyster Harbour = Ladysmith
Canada 49°0N 123°49W **306** D6
Oyster Rock *India* 18°54N 72°49E **130** B1
Oyster Rocks *Pakistan* 24°48N 66°59E **123** B2
Øystese *Norway* 60°22N 6°9E **164** D3
Öyübari *Japan* 43°1N 142°5E **220** C11
Oyyl → *Kazakhstan* 49°4N 54°0E **216** C4
Özalp *Turkey* 38°39N 43°59E **213** C10
Ozamiz *Phil.* 8°15N 123°50E **233** G4
Ozar = Ojhar *India* 31°28N 85°59W **316** D4
Ozark *Ala., U.S.A.* 35°29N 93°50W **314** B8
Ozark *Ark., U.S.A.* 35°20N 93°50W **314** B8
Ozark Plateau *U.S.A.* 37°20N 91°40W **308** H8
Ozark Plateau *U.S.A.* 37°20N 91°40W **308** H8
Ozarks, L. of the *U.S.A.* 38°12N 92°38W **310** F4
Ozărów *Poland* 50°53N 21°40E **185** H8
Ózd *Hungary* 48°14N 20°15E **182** B5
Ozernovskiy *Russia* 51°30N 156°31E **215** D16
Ozernoye *Russia* 51°46N 57°16E **190** D6
Ozero Svityaz *Ukraine* 51°30N 23°50E **185** G10
Ozersk *Russia* 54°25N 22°0E **184** D8
Ozette, L. *U.S.A.* 48°6N 124°38W **306** B2
Ozieri *Italy* 40°35N 9°0E **200** B2
Ozimek *Poland* 50°41N 18°11E **185** H5
Ozinki *Russia* 51°12N 49°44E **190** D9
Ozior-la-Ferrière *France* 48°46N 2°40E **134** B4
Ozona *U.S.A.* 30°43N 101°12W **314** F4
Ozone Park *U.S.A.* 40°40N 73°50W **117** B2
Ozren *Bos.-H.* 44°8N 18°29E **182** E3
Özu *Ehime, Japan* 33°30N 132°33E **222** D4
Özu *Kumamoto, Japan* 32°52N 130°52E **222** D2
Ozuluama *Mexico* 21°40N 97°50W **319** C5
Ozurgeti *Georgia* 41°55N 42°0E **191** K5

P

Pa *Burkina Faso* 11°33N 3°19W **262** C4
Pa-an *Burma* 16°51N 97°40E **241** G6
Pa Mong Dam *Thailand* 18°0N 102°22E **236** D4
Pa Sak → *Thailand* 15°30N 101°0E **236** E3
Paama *Vanuatu* 16°28S 168°14E **287** F6
Paamiut *Greenland* 62°0N 49°43W **154** E6
Paar → *Germany* 48°46N 11°9E **179** G7
Paarl *S. Africa* 33°45S 18°56E **270** D2
Pa'auilo *U.S.A.* 20°2N 155°22W **302** D6
Pab Hills *Pakistan* 26°30N 66°45E **240** F2
Pabbay *U.K.* 57°46N 7°14W **167** D1
Pabbay = Bàghay *U.K.* 57°46N 7°14W **167** D1
Pabbi *Pakistan* 34°1N 71°48E **242** B4
Pabianice *Poland* 51°40N 19°20E **185** G6
Pabna *Bangla.* 24°1N 89°18E **241** G17
Pabo *Uganda* 3°1N 32°10E **268** B3

Pacaás Novos, Serra dos *Brazil* 10°45S 64°15W **331** C5
Pacaás Novos △ *Brazil* 11°0S 63°0W **331** C5
Pacaipampa *Peru* 5°35S 79°39W **330** B2
Pacaja → *Brazil* 1°56S 50°50W **332** B1
Pacajus *Brazil* 4°10S 38°31W **332** B4
Pacaraima, Sa. *S. Amer.* 4°0N 62°30W **329** C5
Pacarán *Peru* 12°50S 76°3W **330** C2
Pacaraos *Peru* 11°12S 76°42W **330** C2
Pacasmayo *Peru* 7°20S 79°35W **330** B2
Pace *U.S.A.* 30°36N 87°10W **317** E2
Paceco *Italy* 37°59N 12°33E **200** E5
Pachacamac *Peru* 12°14S 77°53W **330** C2
Pachang Hsi → *Taiwan* 23°20N 120°7E **225** C2
Pachao Yü *Taiwan* 23°22N 119°29E **225** C1
Pachia *Greece* 36°17N 25°50E **205** E7
Pachino *Italy* 36°43N 15°5E **201** F8
Pachitea → *Peru* 8°46S 74°33W **330** B3
Pachiza *Peru* 7°16S 76°46W **330** B2
Pachmarhi *India* 22°28N 78°26E **243** H8
Pachnai *India* 26°57N 92°19E **241** B4
Pachnes *Greece* 35°16N 24°4E **207** E5
Pacho *Colombia* 5°8N 74°10W **328** B3
Pachora *India* 20°38N 75°29E **244** D2
Pachpadra *India* 25°58N 72°10E **242** G5
Pachuca *Mexico* 20°7N 98°44W **319** C5
Pacific *U.S.A.* 38°29N 90°45W **310** F6
Pacific Antarctic Ridge *Pac. Oc.* 43°0S 115°0W **151** B13
Pacific City = Huntington Beach *U.S.A.* 33°40N 118°5W **307** M9
Pacific Grove *U.S.A.* 36°38N 121°56W **306** J5
Pacific Heights *U.S.A.* 37°47N 122°26W **136** B2
Pacific Manor *U.S.A.* 37°38N 122°27W **136** C2
Pacific Ocean 10°0N 140°0W **289** G14
Pacific Palisades *Calif., U.S.A.* 34°2N 118°32W **126** B1
Pacific Palisades *Hawai'i, U.S.A.* 21°25N 157°58W **302** K14
Pacific Rim △ *Canada* 48°40N 124°45W **306** B2
Pacifica *U.S.A.* 37°37N 122°27W **136** C2
Pacitan *Indonesia* 8°12S 111°7E **235** D4
Packsaddle *Australia* 30°36S 141°58E **282** A4
Packwood *U.S.A.* 46°36N 121°40W **306** D5
Paco *Phil.* 14°35N 120°59E **127** B1
Paco de Arcos *Portugal* 38°41N 9°17W **126** A1
Paço Imperial *Rio de J., Brazil* **135** a2
Pacov *Czech Rep.* 49°27N 15°0E **180** B8
Pacoval *Brazil* 2°40S 54°11W **329** D7
Pacuí → *Brazil* 16°46S 45°1W **333** E2
Pacy-sur-Eure *France* 49°1N 1°23E **172** C8
Padaido, Kepulauan *Indonesia* 1°15S 136°30E **231** E9
Padali = Amursk *Russia* 50°14N 136°54E **215** D14
Padampur *India* 20°59N 83°4E **244** D6
Padang *Kalimantan Barat, Indonesia* 1°39S 108°55E **235** C3
Padang *Riau, Indonesia* 1°30N 102°30E **237** M4
Padang *Sumatera Barat, Indonesia* 1°0S 100°20E **234** C2
Padang Endau *Malaysia* 2°40N 103°38E **237** L4
Padang Lawas *Indonesia* 1°40N 99°56E **234** B1
Padangpanjang *Indonesia* 0°40S 100°20E **234** C2
Padangsidempuan *Indonesia* 1°30N 99°15E **234** B1
Padangtikar *Indonesia* 0°44S 109°15E **235** C3
Padauari → *Brazil* 0°15S 64°5W **329** D5
Padaung *Burma* 18°43N 95°9E **241** F5
Padborg *Denmark* 54°49N 9°21E **163** K3
Padcaya *Bolivia* 21°52S 64°48W **331** E5
Paddington *N.S.W., Australia* 33°53S 151°14E **139** B2
Paddington *London, U.K.* **125** b2
Paddle Prairie *Canada* 57°57N 117°29W **296** B5
Paderborn *Germany* 51°42N 8°45E **178** D4
Paderno *Italy* 45°33N 9°9E **128** A1
Paderoo *India* 18°5N 82°40E **244** E6
Padeş, Vf. *Romania* 45°40N 22°22E **182** E7
Padilla *Bolivia* 19°19S 64°20W **331** D5
Padina *Romania* 44°50N 27°8E **183** F12
Padma *India* 24°12N 85°22E **243** G11
Padma → *Bangla.* 23°22N 90°32E **241** D3
Pádova *Italy* 45°25N 11°53E **199** C8
Padra *India* 22°15N 73°7E **242** H5
Padrão, Pta. *Angola* 6°5S 12°20E **265** D2
Padrauna *India* 26°54N 83°59E **243** F10
Padre I. *U.S.A.* 27°10N 97°25W **314** H6
Padre Island ⌓ *U.S.A.* 27°0N 97°25W **314** H6
Padrón *Spain* 42°41N 8°39W **194** C2
Padstow *U.K.* 50°33N 4°58W **169** G3
Padthaway *Australia* 36°36S 140°31E **282** D4
Padua = Pádova *Italy* 45°25N 11°53E **199** C8
Paducah *Ky., U.S.A.* 37°5N 88°37W **308** G9
Paducah *Tex., U.S.A.* 34°1N 100°18W **314** D4
Padukka *Sri Lanka* 6°50N 80°5E **245** L5
Padul *Spain* 37°1N 3°38W **195** H7
Padwa *India* 18°27N 82°47E **244** E6
Paea *Tahiti* 17°41S 149°35W **289** e
Paekakariki *N.Z.* 40°59S 174°58E **284** G3
Paektu-san *N. Korea* 41°59N 128°4E **224** B4
Paengaroa *N.Z.* 37°49S 176°29E **284** D5
Paeroa *N.Z.* 37°23S 175°41E **284** D4
Paesana *Italy* 44°41N 7°16E **198** D4
Paete *Phil.* 14°23N 121°29E **232** D3
Pafúri *Mozam.* 22°28S 31°17E **271** B5
Pag *Croatia* 44°25N 15°3E **199** D12
Paga *Gabon* 0°45S 10°21E **264** C2
Paga *Ghana* 11°1N 1°8W **263** C4
Pagadian *Phil.* 7°55N 123°30E **233** H4
Pagai Selatan, Pulau *Indonesia* 3°0S 100°15E **234** C2
Pagai Utara, Pulau *Indonesia* 2°35S 100°0E **234** C2
Pagalu = Annobón *Atl. Oc.* 1°25S 5°36E **255** G4
Pagalungan *Phil.* 7°4N 124°41E **233** H5
Pagan *Burma* 21°10N 94°52E **241** E5
Pagan *N. Marianas* 18°7N 145°46E **302** a
Pagara *India* 24°22N 80°1E **243** G9
Pagaralam *Indonesia* 4°1S 103°16E **234** C2
Pagastikos Kolpos *Greece* 39°15N 23°0E **204** B5
Pagatan *Indonesia* 3°33S 115°59E **235** C5
Page *U.S.A.* 36°57N 111°27W **305** H8
Pagėgiai *Lithuania* 55°9N 21°54E **184** C8
Pagei *Papua N. G.* 3°2S 141°10E **286** B1
Pageri *South Sudan* 4°0N 32°0E **257** G3
Paget, Mt. *S. Georgia* 54°26S 36°31W **326** H6
Paget I. *India* 13°26N 92°50E **245** H11
Pagewood *Australia* 33°56S 151°14E **139** B2
Pago B. *Guam* 13°25N 144°47E **302** d
Pago Pago *Amer. Samoa* 14°16S 170°43W **302** f
Pago Pago Harbor *Amer. Samoa* 14°17S 170°40W **302** f
Pagosa Springs *U.S.A.* 37°16N 107°1W **305** H10
Pagote *India* 18°53N 72°59E **130** B2
Pagri *China* 27°45N 89°10E **218** F6
Pagsanjan *Phil.* 14°16N 121°27E **232** D3
Pagua B. *Dominica* 15°32N 61°17W **323** k
Pagudpud *Phil.* 18°34N 120°47E **232** B3
Pagwa River *Canada* 50°2N 85°14W **298** B2
Pagwi *Papua N. G.* 4°4S 143°2E **286** C2
Pāhala *U.S.A.* 19°12N 155°29W **302** D6
Pahang □ *Malaysia* 3°30N 102°45E **237** L4
Pahang → *Malaysia* 3°30N 103°9E **237** L4
Paharpur *Bangla.* 24°51N 88°44E **241** C2
Pahia Pt. *N.Z.* 46°20S 167°41E **285** G2
Pahiatua *N.Z.* 40°27S 175°50E **284** G4
Pāhoa *U.S.A.* 19°30N 154°57W **302** D7
Pahokee *U.S.A.* 26°50N 80°40W **317** J9
Pahrump *U.S.A.* 36°12N 115°59W **307** J11
Pahute Mesa *U.S.A.* 37°20N 116°45W **306** H10
Pai *Thailand* 19°19N 98°27E **236** C2
Pai, I. do *Brazil* 22°59S 43°5W **135** B2
Paia *U.S.A.* 20°54N 156°22W **302** C5
Paichuan Liehtao *Taiwan* 25°58N 119°57E **225** b
Paicines *U.S.A.* 36°44N 121°17W **306** J5
Paide *Estonia* 58°53N 25°33E **188** C3
Paignton *U.K.* 50°26N 3°35W **169** G4
Paihia *N.Z.* 35°17S 174°6E **284** B3
Paiho *Taiwan* 23°21N 120°25E **225** C2
Paiján *Peru* 7°42S 79°20W **330** B2
Päijänne *Finland* 61°30N 25°30E **188** B3
Pailani *India* 25°45N 80°26E **243** G9
Pailin *Cambodia* 12°46N 102°36E **236** F4
Pailolo Channel *U.S.A.* 21°0N 156°40W **302** B5
Paimpol *France* 48°48N 3°4W **172** D3
Painan *Indonesia* 1°21S 100°34E **234** C2
Paine Grande, Cerro *Chile* 50°59S 73°4W **336** D2
Painesville *U.S.A.* 41°43N 81°15W **312** E3
Paint Hills = Wemindji *Canada* 53°0N 78°49W **298** B4
Paint L. *Canada* 55°28N 97°57W **297** B9
Painted Desert *U.S.A.* 36°0N 111°0W **305** H8
Paintsville *U.S.A.* 37°49N 82°48W **309** G12
País Vasco □ *Spain* 42°50N 2°45W **196** C2
Paisha *Taiwan* 23°40N 119°35E **225** C1
Paisley *Ont., Canada* 44°18N 81°16W **312** B3
Paisley *Renf., U.K.* 55°50N 4°25W **167** F4
Paisley *Oreg., U.S.A.* 42°42N 120°32W **304** E3
Païta *N. Cal.* 22°8S 166°22E **288** d
Paita *Peru* 5°11S 81°9W **330** B1
Paithan *India* 19°29N 75°23E **244** E2
Paiva → *Portugal* 41°4N 8°16W **194** D2
Paizhou *China* 30°12N 113°55E **229** B9
Paja, Cerro *Ecuador* 1°17S 90°26W **330** a
Pájara *Canary Is.* 28°21N 14°6W **153** e2
Pajares *Spain* 43°1N 5°46W **194** B5
Pajares, Puerto de *Spain* 42°58N 5°46W **194** C5
Pajarito *Colombia* 5°17N 72°43W **328** B3
Pajęczno *Poland* 51°10N 19°0E **185** G5
Paju *S. Korea* 37°45N 126°46E **224** D3
Pak Kok *China* 22°14N 114°7E **122** B1
Pak Kong *China* 22°22N 114°15E **122** A2
Pak Lay *Laos* 18°15N 101°27E **236** C3
Pak Ou *Laos* 20°3N 102°12E **236** B4
Pak Phanang *Thailand* 8°21N 100°12E **237** H3
Pak Sane *Laos* 18°22N 103°39E **236** C4
Pak Song *Laos* 15°11N 106°14E **236** E6
Pak Suang *Laos* 19°58N 102°15E **228** H4
Pak Tam Chung *China* 22°24N 114°19E **219** a
Pak Thong Chai *Thailand* 14°43N 102°1E **236** E4
Pakala *India* 13°29N 79°8E **245** H4
Pakaraima Mts. *Guyana* 5°15N 60°0W **329** B6
Pakaur *India* 24°38N 87°51E **243** G12
Pakch'ŏn *N. Korea* 39°44N 125°35E **224** C2
Pakenham *Vic., Australia* 38°6S 145°30E **283** E6
Pakenham *Ont., Canada* 45°18N 76°18W **313** A8
Pakhoi = Beihai *China* 21°28N 109°6E **228** G7
Pakhuis *S. Africa* 32°9S 19°5E **270** D2
Pakila *Finland* 60°15N 24°55E **121** B2
Pakistan ■ *Asia* 30°0N 70°0E **242** E4
Pakkading *Laos* 18°19N 103°59E **236** C4
Paklay = Sayaboury *Laos* 19°15N 101°45E **236** C3
Paklenica △ *Croatia* 44°20N 15°39E **199** D12
Pakokku *Burma* 21°20N 95°0E **241** E5
Pakość *Poland* 52°48N 18°6E **185** F5
Pakowki L. *Canada* 49°20N 111°0W **297** D6
Pakpattan *Pakistan* 30°25N 73°27E **242** D5
Pakrac *Croatia* 45°27N 17°12E **182** E2
Pakruojis *Lithuania* 55°58N 23°52E **184** C10
Paks *Hungary* 46°38N 18°55E **182** D3
Paktīā □ *Afghan.* 33°30N 69°15E **240** B3
Paktīkā □ *Afghan.* 32°30N 69°0E **240** B3
Paku, Tanjung *Indonesia* 3°6S 106°31E **234** C3
Pakwach *Uganda* 2°28N 31°27E **268** B3
Pakxe *Laos* 15°5N 105°52E **236** E5
Pal Lahara *India* 21°27N 85°11E **243** J11
Pala *Chad* 9°25N 15°5E **259** G3
Pala *Dem. Rep. of the Congo* 6°45S 29°30E **268** D2
Pala *Calif., U.S.A.* 33°22N 117°5W **307** M9
Palabek *Uganda* 3°22N 32°33E **268** B3
Palacio Real *Madrid, Spain* **127** b1
Palacios *U.S.A.* 28°42N 96°13W **314** G6
Palafrugell *Spain* 41°55N 3°10E **196** D8
Palagiano *Italy* 40°35N 17°2E **201** B10
Palagonía *Italy* 37°19N 14°45E **201** E7
Palagruža *Croatia* 42°24N 16°15E **199** F13
Palais Royal *Brussels, Belgium* **116** b3
Palaiseau *France* 48°42N 2°14E **134** B2
Palakkad *India* 10°46N 76°42E **245** J3
Palakol *India* 16°31N 81°46E **245** F5
Palalankwe *India* 10°52N 92°29E **245** J11
Palam *India* 19°0N 77°0E **244** E3
Palamas *Greece* 39°26N 22°4E **204** B4
Palamós *Spain* 41°50N 3°10E **196** D8
Palampur *India* 32°10N 76°30E **242** C7
Palamut *Turkey* 38°59N 27°41E **205** C9
Palana *Tas., Australia* 39°45S 147°55E **281** F4
Palana *Russia* 59°10N 159°59E **215** D16
Palanan *Phil.* 17°8N 122°29E **232** C4
Palanan B. *Phil.* 17°9N 122°27E **232** C4
Palanan Pt. *Phil.* 17°17N 122°30E **232** C4
Palandri *Pakistan* 33°42N 73°40E **243** C5
Palanga *Lithuania* 55°58N 21°3E **184** C8
Palanganene *Dem. Rep. of the Congo* 6°32S 18°52E **265** D3
Palangkaraya *Indonesia* 2°16S 113°56E **235** C4
Palani *India* 10°30N 77°30E **245** J3
Palani Hills *India* 10°14N 77°33E **245** J3
Palanpur *India* 24°10N 72°25E **242** G5
Palaoa Pt. *U.S.A.* 20°44N 156°58W **302** C5
Palapag *Phil.* 12°33N 125°7E **232** E5
Palapye *Botswana* 22°30S 27°7E **270** B4
Palar → *India* 12°27N 80°13E **245** H5
Palas *Pakistan* 35°4N 73°14E **243** B5
Palas de Rei *Spain* 42°52N 7°52W **194** C3
Palasan I. *Phil.* 14°51N 122°2E **232** D4
Palasponga *India* 21°47N 85°34E **243** J11
Palatine *U.S.A.* 42°7N 88°3W **311** B8
Palatka *Russia* 60°6N 150°54E **215** C16
Palatka *Fla., U.S.A.* 29°39N 81°38W **316** F8
Palau *Italy* 41°11N 9°23E **200** A2
Palau ■ *Palau* 7°30N 134°30E **288** c
Palaui I. *Phil.* 18°32N 122°8E **232** B4
Palauk *Burma* 13°10N 98°40E **236** F2
Palaw *Burma* 12°58N 98°39E **236** F2
Palawan *Phil.* 9°30N 118°30E **233** G2
Palawan □ *Phil.* 10°0N 119°0E **233** G2
Palawan Passage *Phil.* 10°0N 118°0E **233** G2
Palayan *Phil.* 15°36N 121°8E **232** D3
Palayankottai *India* 8°45N 77°45E **245** K3
Palazzo, Pte. *France* 42°28N 8°30E **175** F12
Palazzo San Gervásio *Italy* 40°56N 15°59E **201** B8
Palazzolo *Italy* 45°34N 9°9E **128** A1
Palazzolo Acréide *Italy* 37°4N 14°54E **201** E7
Palca *Chile* 19°7S 69°9W **330** D4
Paldiski *Estonia* 59°23N 24°9E **188** C3
Pale *Bos.-H.* 43°50N 18°38E **182** G3
Palekastro *Greece* 35°12N 26°15E **207** E7
Paleleh *Indonesia* 1°10N 121°50E **231** D6
Palembang *Indonesia* 3°0S 104°50E **234** C2
Palena → *Chile* 43°50S 73°50W **336** B2
Palena, L. *Chile* 43°55S 71°40W **336** B2
Palencia *Spain* 42°1N 4°34W **194** C6
Palencia □ *Spain* 42°31N 4°33W **194** C6
Paleng *Taiwan* 24°41N 121°23E **225** B3
Palenque *Mexico* 17°29N 92°1W **319** D6
Paleo Faliro *Greece* 37°53N 23°42E **112** B2
Paleochora *Greece* 35°16N 23°39E **207** E4
Paleokastritsa *Greece* 39°40N 19°41E **206** B9
Paleometokho *Cyprus* 35°7N 33°11E **207** E9
Paleopoli *Greece* 37°49N 24°50E **204** D6
Palermo *B. Aires, Argentina* 34°35S 58°24W **117** B2
Palermo *Colombia* 2°54N 75°26W **328** C2
Palermo *Italy* 38°7N 13°22E **200** D6
Palermo *Calif., U.S.A.* 39°26N 121°33W **306** F5
Palermo ✈ (PMO) *Italy* 38°11N 13°5E **200** D6
Paleros *Greece* 38°47N 20°53E **207** B2
Palestina = Jordânia *Brazil* 15°55S 40°11W **333** E3
Palestine *Asia* 32°0N 35°0E **251** G6
Palestine *Ill., U.S.A.* 39°0N 87°37W **311** F9
Palestine *Tex., U.S.A.* 31°46N 95°38W **314** F7
Palestrina *Italy* 41°50N 12°53E **199** G9
Paletwa *Burma* 21°10N 92°50E **241** E4
Palghat = Palakkad *India* 10°46N 76°42E **245** J3
Palgrave, Mt. *Australia* 23°22S 115°58E **278** D2
Palhais *Portugal* 38°37N 9°2W **126** B2
Pali *India* 25°50N 73°20E **242** G5
Pali *Taiwan* 25°8N 121°23E **225** A3
Pali-Aike △ *Chile* 52°6S 69°44W **336** D3
Palikea *U.S.A.* 21°26N 158°6W **302** K13
Palikir *Micronesia* 6°55N 158°9E **288** G7
Palimbang *Phil.* 6°12N 124°12E **233** H5
Palin, Mt. *Malaysia* 6°10N 117°10E **235** A5
Palinuro *Italy* 40°2N 15°17E **201** B8
Palinuro, C. *Italy* 40°2N 15°16E **201** B8
Paliouri, Akra *Greece* 39°57N 23°45E **202** G7
Palisades Park *U.S.A.* 40°50N 74°1W **132** A1
Palisades Res. *U.S.A.* 43°20N 111°12W **304** E8
Palisadoes, The *Jamaica* 17°57N 76°48W **320** a
Paliseul *Belgium* 49°54N 5°8E **170** E5
Palitana *India* 21°32N 71°49E **242** J4
Palizada *Mexico* 18°15N 92°5W **319** D6
Palk Bay *Asia* 9°30N 79°15E **245** K4
Palk Strait *Asia* 10°0N 79°45E **245** K4
Palkānah *Iraq* 35°49N 44°26E **246** C5
Palkonda *India* 18°36N 83°48E **244** E6
Palkonda Ra. *India* 13°50N 79°20E **245** H4
Palkot *India* 22°53N 84°39E **243** H11
Palla Road = Dinokwe *Botswana* 23°29S 26°37E **270** B4
Pallanza = Verbánia *Italy* 45°56N 8°33E **198** C5
Pallarenda *Australia* 19°12S 146°46E **280** B4
Pallasovka *Russia* 50°4N 47°0E **190** E8
Palleru → *India* 16°45N 80°2E **244** F5
Pallës, Bishti i *Albania* 41°24N 19°24E **202** E3
Pallinup → *Australia* 34°27S 118°50E **279** F2
Pallisa *Uganda* 1°12N 33°43E **268** B3
Palliser, C. *N.Z.* 41°37S 175°14E **284** H4
Palliser, Îs. *French Polynesia* 15°30S 146°30W **289** f
Palliser B. *N.Z.* 41°26S 175°5E **284** H4
Pallu *India* 28°59N 74°14E **242** E6
Palm Bay *U.S.A.* 28°2N 80°35W **317** G9
Palm Beach *Aruba* 12°34N 70°2W **322** f
Palm Beach *Fla., U.S.A.* 26°43N 80°2W **317** J9
Palm Coast *U.S.A.* 29°35N 81°12W **317** F8
Palm Deira, The *U.A.E.* 25°17N 55°15E **119** A2
Palm Desert *U.S.A.* 33°43N 116°22W **307** M10
Palm-Grove △ *Australia* 24°57S 149°21E **280** C4
Palm Harbor *U.S.A.* 28°5N 82°46W **317** G7
Palm Is. *Australia* 18°40S 146°35E **280** B4
Palm Jumeirah, The *U.A.E.* 25°11N 55°11E **119** B1
Palm Springs *U.S.A.* 33°50N 116°33W **307** M10
Palm Valley *U.S.A.* 30°11N 81°23W **316** E8
Palma = Paraná *Brazil* 12°30S 47°48W **333** D2
Palma *Mozam.* 10°46S 40°29E **269** E5
Palma → *Brazil* 12°33S 47°52W **333** D2
Palma, B. de *Spain* 39°30N 2°39E **206** B3
Palma de Mallorca *Spain* 39°35N 2°39E **206** B3
Palma de Mallorca ✈ (PMI) *Spain* 39°34N 2°43E **197** F7
Palma del Río *Spain* 37°43N 5°17W **195** H5
Palma di Montechiaro *Italy* 37°11N 13°46E **200** E6
Palma Nova = Palmanova *Spain* 39°32N 2°34E **206** B3
Palma Soriano *Cuba* 20°15N 76°0W **320** B4
Palmaner *India* 13°12N 78°45E **245** H4
Palmanova *Spain* 39°32N 2°34E **206** B3
Palmares *Brazil* 8°41S 35°28W **332** C4
Palmarito *Venezuela* 7°37N 70°10W **328** B3
Palmarola *Italy* 40°56N 12°51E **200** B5
Palmas *Paraná, Brazil* 26°29S 52°0W **335** B5
Palmas *Tocantins, Brazil* 10°13S 48°16W **332** D2
Palmas, C. *Liberia* 4°27N 7°46W **262** E3
Pálmas, G. di *Italy* 39°0N 8°30E **200** D1
Palmas de Monte Alto *Brazil* 14°16S 43°10W **333** D3
Palmdale *Calif., U.S.A.* 34°35N 118°7W **307** L8
Palmdale *Fla., U.S.A.* 26°57N 81°19W **317** J8
Palmeira *Brazil* 25°25S 50°0W **333** G2
Palmeira das Missões *Brazil* 27°55S 53°17W **335** B5
Palmeira dos Índios *Brazil* 9°25S 36°37W **332** C4
Palmeirais *Brazil* 6°0S 43°0W **332** C3
Palmeiras *Brazil* 12°31S 41°34W **333** D3
Palmeiras → *Brazil* 12°22S 47°8W **333** D2
Palmeirinhas, Pta. das *Angola* 9°2S 12°57E **265** D2
Palmela *Portugal* 38°32N 8°57W **195** G2
Palmelo *Brazil* 17°20S 48°27W **333** E2
Palmer *Antarctica* 64°35S 65°0W **151** C17
Palmer *Alaska, U.S.A.* 61°36N 149°7W **303** F10
Palmer → *Australia* 16°0S 142°26E **280** B3
Palmer Arch. *Antarctica* 64°15S 65°0W **151** C17
Palmer Lake *U.S.A.* 39°7N 104°55W **304** G11
Palmer Land *Antarctica* 73°0S 63°0W **151** D18
Palmerston = Darwin *Australia* 12°25S 130°51E **278** B5
Palmerston *N. Terr., Australia* 12°31S 130°59E **278** B5
Palmerston *Ont., Canada* 43°50N 80°51W **312** C4
Palmerston *Dublin, Ireland* 53°20N 6°22W **120** A1
Palmerston *N.Z.* 45°29S 170°43E **285** F5
Palmerston North *N.Z.* 40°21S 175°39E **284** G4
Palmerton *U.S.A.* 40°48N 75°37W **313** F9
Palmetto *Fla., U.S.A.* 27°31N 82°34W **317** H7
Palmetto *Ga., U.S.A.* 33°31N 84°40W **316** B5
Palmetto Pt. *Antigua & B.* 17°37N 61°51W **322** c
Palmetto Pt. *St. Kitts & Nevis* 17°18N 62°46W **322** d
Palmi *Italy* 38°21N 15°51E **201** D8
Palmira *Argentina* 32°59S 68°34W **334** C2
Palmira *Colombia* 3°32N 76°16W **328** C2
Palms *U.S.A.* 34°1N 118°24W **126** B2
Palmyra = Tudmur *Syria* 34°36N 38°15E **213** E8
Palmyra *Ill., U.S.A.* 39°26N 90°0W **310** E7
Palmyra *Mo., U.S.A.* 39°48N 91°32W **310** E5
Palmyra *N.J., U.S.A.* 40°0N 75°1W **313** F9
Palmyra *N.Y., U.S.A.* 43°5N 77°18W **312** C7
Palmyra *Pa., U.S.A.* 40°18N 76°36W **313** F8
Palmyra *Wis., U.S.A.* 42°52N 88°36W **311** B8
Palmyra Is. *Pac. Oc.* 5°52N 162°5W **289** G11
Palmyras = Santos Dumont *Brazil* 22°55S 43°10W **333** F3
Palmyras Pt. *India* 20°46N 87°1E **244** D8
Palo *Phil.* 11°10N 124°59E **233** F5
Palo Alto *U.S.A.* 37°27N 122°10W **306** H4
Palo Seco *Trin. & Tob.* 10°4N 61°36W **323** t
Palo Verde *U.S.A.* 33°26N 114°44W **307** M12
Palo Verde △ *Costa Rica* 10°21N 85°21W **320** D2
Paloh *Indonesia* 1°43N 109°18E **235** B3
Paloheinä *Finland* 60°15N 24°56E **121** B2
Paloich *South Sudan* 10°28N 32°32E **257** E3
Palomar Mt. *U.S.A.* 33°22N 116°50W **307** M10
Palomeras *Spain* 40°22N 3°39W **127** B2
Palompon *Phil.* 11°3N 124°23E **233** F5
Palopo *Indonesia* 3°0S 120°16E **231** E6
Palos, C. de *Spain* 37°38N 0°40W **197** H4
Palos de la Frontera *Spain* 37°14N 6°53W **195** H4
Palos Heights *U.S.A.* 41°39N 87°47W **119** D2
Palos Hills *U.S.A.* 41°42N 87°49W **119** C2
Palos Park *U.S.A.* 41°40N 87°50W **119** C1
Palos Verdes, Pt. *U.S.A.* 33°46N 118°25W **307** M8
Palos Verdes Estates *U.S.A.* 33°48N 118°23W **307** M8
Palpa *Peru* 14°30S 75°15W **330** C2
Palpara *India* 22°38N 88°22E **124** B2
Pålsboda *Sweden* 59°3N 15°22E **162** E9
Palu *Indonesia* 1°0S 119°52E **235** C5
Palu *Turkey* 38°45N 40°0E **213** C9
Paluan *Phil.* 13°26N 120°29E **232** E3
Paluke *Liberia* 5°2N 8°5W **262** D3
Paluma Ra. *Australia* 19°9S 146°22E **280** B4
Paluzza *Italy* 46°32N 13°1E **199** B10
Palwal *India* 28°8N 77°19E **242** E7
Pama *Burkina Faso* 11°19N 0°44E **263** C5
Pama → *C.A.R.* 4°23N 18°43E **264** B3
Pama ⌓ *Burkina Faso* 11°27N 0°40E **263** C5
Pamandzi *Mayotte* 12°47S 45°16E **272** b
Pamanukan *Indonesia* 6°16S 107°49E **235** D3
Pamban I. *India* 9°15N 79°20E **245** K4
Pamekasan *Indonesia* 7°10S 113°28E **235** D4
Pamenang *Indonesia* 8°24S 116°6E **231** J19
Pameungpeuk *Indonesia* 7°37S 107°43E **235** D3
Pamiers *France* 43°7N 1°39E **174** E5
Pamir *Tajikistan* 37°40N 73°0E **217** E8
Pamirsky Post = Murgap *Tajikistan* 38°10N 74°2E **217** E8
Pamlico → *U.S.A.* 35°20N 76°28W **315** D16
Pamlico Sd. *U.S.A.* 35°20N 76°0W **315** D17
Pampa *U.S.A.* 35°32N 100°58W **314** D4
Pampa de Agma *Argentina* 43°45S 69°40W **336** B3
Pampa de las Salinas *Argentina* 32°1S 66°58W **334** C2
Pampa Grande *Bolivia* 18°5S 64°6W **331** D5
Pampa Hermosa *Peru* 7°7S 75°4W **330** B2
Pampanga □ *Phil.* 15°4N 120°40E **232** D3
Pampanua *Indonesia* 4°16S 120°8E **231** E6
Pampas *Argentina* 35°0S 63°0W **334** D3
Pampas *Peru* 12°20S 74°50W **330** C3
Pampas → *Peru* 13°24S 73°12W **330** C3
Pampatar *Venezuela* 11°11N 63°48W **329** a
Pamphylia *Turkey* 37°0N 31°20E **250** B2
Pamplemousses *Mauritius* 20°6S 57°34E **272** e
Pamplona *Colombia* 7°23N 72°39W **328** B3
Pamplona *Phil.* 18°31N 121°20E **232** B3
Pamplona-Iruña *Spain* 42°48N 1°38W **196** C3
Pampoenpoort *S. Africa* 31°3S 22°40E **270** D3
Pamuk → *Turkey* 37°2N 34°49E **250** A5
Pamukçu *Turkey* 39°30N 27°54E **205** B9
Pamukkale *Turkey* 37°55N 29°8E **205** D11
Pan de Azúcar *Chile* 24°5S 68°10W **334** A2
Pan de Azúcar △ *Chile* 26°0S 70°40W **334** B1
Pan Xian *China* 25°46N 104°38E **228** E5
Pana *U.S.A.* 39°23N 89°5W **310** E7
Panabo *Phil.* 7°19N 125°42E **233** H5
Panaca *U.S.A.* 37°47N 114°23W **305** H6
Panacea *U.S.A.* 30°2N 84°23W **316** E5
Panadura *Sri Lanka* 6°47N 79°53E **245** L4
Panagyurishte *Bulgaria* 42°30N 24°15E **203** D8
Panaitan *Indonesia* 6°36S 105°12E **234** D3
Panajam *Indonesia* 1°15S 116°46E **235** C5
Panaji *India* 15°25N 73°50E **245** G1
Panamá *Panama* 9°0N 79°25W **320** c
Panama *Sri Lanka* 6°45N 81°48E **245** L5
Panama ■ *Cent. Amer.* 8°48N 79°55W **320** E4
Panamá, G. de *Panama* 8°4N 79°20W **320** E4
Panama, Isthmus of *Cent. Amer.* 9°0N 79°0W **292** J12
Panama Basin *Pac. Oc.* 5°0N 83°30W **289** G19
Panama Canal *Panama* 9°10N 79°37W **320** c
Panama City *U.S.A.* 30°10N 85°40W **316** E4
Panama City Beach *U.S.A.* 30°11N 85°48W **316** E4
Panamint Range *U.S.A.* 36°20N 117°20W **307** J9
Panamint Springs *U.S.A.* 36°20N 117°28W **307** J9
Panão *Peru* 9°55S 75°55W **330** B2
Panaon I. *Phil.* 9°50N 125°13E **233** G5
Panare *Thailand* 6°51N 101°30E **237** J3
Panarea *Italy* 38°38N 15°4E **201** D8
Panaro → *Italy* 44°55N 11°25E **199** D8
Panay *Phil.* 11°10N 122°30E **233** F4
Panay G. *Phil.* 11°0N 122°30E **233** F4
Pančevo *Serbia* 44°52N 20°41E **182** F5
Panch'iao *Taiwan* 25°1N 121°27E **225** A3
Panchur *India* 22°32N 88°16E **124** B1
Panciu *Romania* 45°54N 27°8E **183** E12
Pancol *Phil.* 10°52N 119°25E **233** F2
Pancorbo, Desfiladero *Spain* 42°32N 3°5W **194** C7
Pâncota *Romania* 46°20N 21°45E **182** D6
Panda *Mozam.* 24°2S 34°45E **271** B5
Pandacan *Phil.* 14°35N 121°0E **127** B2
Pandan *Malaysia* 1°32N 103°46E **237** d
Pandan *Antique, Phil.* 11°45N 122°10E **233** F4
Pandan *Catanduanes, Phil.* 14°3N 124°10E **232** D5
Pandan, Selat *Singapore* 1°15N 103°44E **138** B2
Pandan B. *Phil.* 11°43N 122°0E **233** F4
Pandan Res. *Singapore* 1°18N 103°44E **138** B2
Pandan Tampoi = Tampoi *Malaysia* 1°30N 103°39E **237** d
Pandanan I. *Phil.* 8°17N 117°13E **233** G1
Pandegelang *Indonesia* 6°25S 106°5E **234** D3
Pandhana *India* 21°42N 76°13E **242** J7
Pandharkawada *India* 20°1N 78°32E **244** D4
Pandharpur *India* 17°41N 75°20E **244** F2
Pandhurna *India* 21°36N 78°35E **244** D4
Pando *Uruguay* 34°44S 56°0W **335** C4
Pando □ *Bolivia* 11°20S 67°40W **330** C4
Pando, L. = Hope, L. *Australia* 28°24S 139°18E **281** D2
Pandokratoras *Greece* 39°45N 19°50E **206** B9
Pandora *Costa Rica* 9°43N 83°3W **320** E3
Pandrup *Denmark* 57°14N 9°40E **163** G3
Pandu *Dem. Rep. of the Congo* 4°59N 19°16E **264** B3
Panepistimio *Athens, Greece* **112** b2
Panevéggio-Pale di San Martino ⌓ *Italy* 46°14N 11°46E **199** B8
Panevėžys *Lithuania* 55°42N 24°25E **188** E3
Panfilov = Zharkent *Kazakhstan* 44°10N 80°0E **217** D10
Panfilovo *Russia* 50°25N 42°46E **190** E6
Pang Sida △ *Thailand* 14°5N 102°17E **236** E4
Panga *Dem. Rep. of the Congo* 1°52N 26°18E **268** B2
Pangaíon Óros *Greece* 40°50N 24°0E **203** F8
Pangala *Congo* 3°16S 14°34E **264** C2
Pangalanes, Canal des = Ampangalana, Lakandranon' *Madag.* 22°48S 47°50E **272** C2
Pangandaran *Indonesia* 7°40S 108°39E **235** D3
Pangandaran △ *Indonesia* 7°43S 108°42E **235** D3
Pangani *Tanzania* 5°25S 38°58E **268** D4
Pangani → *Tanzania* 5°26S 38°58E **268** D4
Pangantocan *Phil.* 7°50N 124°49E **233** H5
Pangar Djeréme ⌓ *Cameroon* 5°50N 13°10E **263** D7
Pangasinan □ *Phil.* 15°55N 120°20E **232** D3
Pangfou = Bengbu *China* 32°58N 117°20E **227** H9
Pangga, Tanjung *Indonesia* 8°54S 116°2E **231** K19
Panghsang = Bangkang *Burma* 22°4N 99°1E **228** F2
Pangil *Dem. Rep. of the Congo* 3°10S 26°35E **268** C2
Pangjiabu *China* 40°38N 115°26E **226** D8
Pangkah, Tanjung *Indonesia* 6°51S 112°33E **235** D4
Pangkai *Burma* 22°49N 98°39E **228** F2
Pangkajene *Indonesia* 4°46S 119°34E **235** C5
Pangkalanbrandan *Indonesia* 4°1N 98°20E **234** B1
Pangkalanbuun *Indonesia* 2°41S 111°37E **235** C4
Pangkalansusu *Indonesia* 4°2N 98°13E **234** B1
Pangkalpinang *Indonesia* 2°10S 106°10E **234** C3
Pangkoh *Indonesia* 3°5S 114°8E **235** C4
Pangkor, Pulau *Malaysia* 4°13N 100°34E **237** K3
Panglao *Phil.* 9°35N 123°45E **233** G4
Panglao I. *Phil.* 9°35N 123°48E **233** G4
Pangniqtuuq = Pangnirtung *Canada* 66°8N 65°43W **295** D18
Pangnirtung *Canada* 66°8N 65°43W **295** D18
Pango Alucuem *Angola* 8°43S 14°33E **265** D2
Pangody *Russia* 65°52N 74°27E **214** C8
Pangong Tso = Bangong Co *China* 33°45N 78°43E **243** C8
Pangrati *Greece* 37°56N 23°45E **112** B2
Pangsau Pass *Asia* 27°15N 96°10E **241** B6
Pangsua, Sungei → *Singapore* 1°25N 103°45E **138** A2
Pangtara *Burma* 20°57N 96°40E **241** E6
Panguipulli *Chile* 39°38S 72°20W **336** A2
Panguitch *U.S.A.* 37°50N 112°26W **305** H7
Panguna *Papua N. G.* 6°21S 155°25E **286** D8
Pangururan *Indonesia* 2°37N 98°42E **234** B1
Pangutaran *Phil.* 6°18N 120°35E **233** H3
Pangutaran Group *Phil.* 6°18N 120°34E **233** H3
Panhala *India* 16°49N 74°7E **244** F2
Panhandle *U.S.A.* 35°21N 101°23W **314** D4
Pani Mines *India* 22°29N 73°50E **242** H5
Pania-Mutombo *Dem. Rep. of the Congo* 5°11S 23°51E **265** D4
Pānī'au *U.S.A.* 21°56N 160°5W **302** B1
Panié, Mt. *N. Cal.* 20°36S 164°46E **288** d
Panihati *India* 22°41N 88°22E **124** A2
Panikota I. *India* 20°46N 71°21E **242** J4
Panipat *India* 29°25N 77°2E **242** E7
Paniqui *Phil.* 15°40N 120°34E **232** D3
Panitan *Phil.* 11°28N 122°46E **233** F4
Panj = Pyandzh → *Asia* 37°6N 68°20E **240** A2
Panjab *Afghan.* 34°23N 67°1E **240** B2
Panjakent *Tajikistan* 39°29N 67°37E **217** E7
Panjal Range = Pir Panjal Range *India* 32°30N 76°50E **242** C7
Panjang *Kepulauan Riau, Indonesia* 4°15N 108°12E **235** B3
Panjang *Lampung, Indonesia* 5°25S 105°20E **234** D3
Panjang, Bukit *Singapore* 1°22N 103°45E **138** A2
Panjgur *Pakistan* 27°0N 64°5E **240** D2
Panjhra → *India* 21°13N 74°57E **244** D2
Panjim = Panaji *India* 15°25N 73°50E **245** G1
Panjin *China* 41°3N 122°2E **227** D12
Panjnad → *Pakistan* 28°57N 70°30E **242** E4
Panjnad Barrage *Pakistan* 29°22N 71°15E **242** E4
Panjshīr □ *Afghan.* 35°50N 69°45E **240** B3
Panjwai *Afghan.* 31°26N 65°27E **242** D1
Panke → *Germany* 52°31N 13°22E **115** A3
Pankow *Germany* 52°34N 13°23E **115** A3
Pankshin *Nigeria* 9°16N 9°25E **263** D6
Panmunjŏm *N. Korea* 37°59N 126°38E **224** D3
Panna *India* 24°40N 80°15E **243** G9
Panna △ *India* 24°40N 80°0E **243** G8
Panna Hills *India* 24°40N 81°15E **243** G9
Pannawonica *Australia* 21°39S 116°19E **278** D2
Panngi *Vanuatu* 15°58S 168°12E **287** E6
Pano Akil *Pakistan* 27°51N 69°7E **242** F3
Pano Lefkara *Cyprus* 34°53N 33°20E **207** F9
Pano Panayia *Cyprus* 34°55N 32°38E **207** F8
Panopah *Indonesia* 1°55S 111°10E **235** C4
Panora *U.S.A.* 41°42N 94°22W **310** C2
Panorama *Brazil* 21°21S 51°51W **335** A5
Panormos *Greece* 35°25N 24°41E **207** E5
Panruti *India* 11°46N 79°35E **245** J4
Pansemal *India* 21°39N 74°42E **242** J6
Panshan = Panjin *China* 41°3N 122°2E **227** D12
Panshi *China* 42°58N 126°5E **227** C14
Pantabangan L. *Phil.* 15°50N 121°9E **232** D3
Pantanal Matogrossense △ *Brazil* 17°35S 57°27W **331** D6
Pantanaw *Burma* 16°59N 95°28E **241** G5
Pantanos de Centla ⌓ *Mexico* 18°25N 92°25W **319** D6
Pantar *Indonesia* 8°28S 124°10E **231** F6
Pante Macassar *E. Timor* 9°30S 123°58E **231** F6
Pantelleria *Italy* 36°50N 11°57E **200** F4
Panthéon *Paris, France* **134** c4
Pantheon *Rome, Italy* **136** b2
Panthersville *U.S.A.* 33°43N 84°16W **113** B3
Panti *Indonesia* 0°22N 100°3E **234** B2
Pantin *France* 48°53N 2°24E **134** A3
Pantin Sakan *Burma* 18°38N 97°33E **241** F6
Pantitlán *Mexico* 19°24N 99°4W **128** B2
Pantoja *Peru* 0°58S 75°10W **328** D2
Pantón *Spain* 42°31N 7°37W **194** C3
Pantukan *Phil.* 7°9N 125°54E **233** H5
Panu *Dem. Rep. of the Congo* 3°50S 19°10E **264** C3
Pánuco *Mexico* 22°3N 98°10W **319** C5
Panuitan I. *Phil.* 19°26N 121°30E **232** B3
Panukulan *Phil.* 14°56N 121°49E **232** D3
Panvel *India* 18°59N 73°4E **244** E1
Panyabungan *Indonesia* 0°51N 99°33E **234** B1
Panyam *Nigeria* 9°27N 9°8E **263** D6
Panyu = Guangzhou *China* 23°6N 113°13E **121** B2
Panyu *China* 23°1N 113°21E **121** B2
Panzhihua *China* 26°33N 101°44E **228** D3
Panzi *Dem. Rep. of the Congo* 7°17S 18°1E **265** D3
Pao → *Anzoátegui, Venezuela* 8°6N 64°17W **329** B5
Pao → *Apure, Venezuela* 8°33N 68°1W **328** B4
Paoay *Phil.* 18°3N 120°30E **232** B3
Paochi = Baoji *China* 34°20N 107°5E **226** G4
Paoki = Baoji *China* 34°20N 107°5E **226** G4
Páola *Italy* 39°21N 16°2E **201** C9
Paola *Malta* 35°52N 14°30E **206** F8
Paola *Kans., U.S.A.* 38°35N 94°53W **308** F6
Paoli *U.S.A.* 38°33N 86°28W **311** F10
Paonia *U.S.A.* 38°52N 107°36W **304** G10
Paopao *Moorea* 17°30S 149°49W **289** e
Paoting = Baoding *China* 38°50N 115°28E **226** E8
Paot'ou = Baotou *China* 40°32N 110°2E **226** D6
Paoua *C.A.R.* 7°9N 16°20E **264** A3
Pápa *Hungary* 47°22N 17°30E **182** C2
Päpä *Hawai'i, U.S.A.* 19°13N 155°52W **302** D6
Papa Stour *U.K.* 60°20N 1°42W **167** A7
Papa Westray *U.K.* 59°20N 2°55W **167** B6
Päpa'aloa *U.S.A.* 19°59N 155°13W **302** D6
Papadopoli, Palazzo *Venice, Italy* **142** b2
Papagayo → *Mexico* 16°46N 99°43W **319** D5
Papagayo, G. de *Costa Rica* 10°30N 85°50W **320** D2
Papagni → *India* 15°35N 77°45E **245** G3
Papahänaumokuäkea Marine Nat. Monument ⌓ *U.S.A.* 25°25N 170°35W **302** F9
Papaïchton *Fr. Guiana* 3°48N 54°10W **329** C7
Päpa'ikou *U.S.A.* 19°47N 155°6W **302** D6
Papakura *N.Z.* 37°4S 174°59E **284** D3
Papantla *Mexico* 20°27N 97°19W **319** C5
Papar *Malaysia* 5°45N 116°0E **235** A5
Papara *Tahiti* 17°43S 149°31W **289** e
Paparoa *N.Z.* 36°6S 174°16E **284** C3
Paparoa △ *N.Z.* 42°7S 171°26E **285** C6
Paparoa Ra. *N.Z.* 42°5S 171°35E **285** C6
Papas, Akra *Greece* 38°13N 21°20E **204** C3
Papatoetoe *N.Z.* 36°59S 174°51E **284** C3
Papatura *Solomon Is.* 7°32S 158°47E **287** L10
Papeete *Tahiti* 17°32S 149°34W **289** e
Papenburg *Germany* 53°5N 7°23E **178** B3
Papenoo *Tahiti* 17°30S 149°25W **289** e
Papenoo → *Tahiti* 17°30S 149°25W **289** e
Papetoai *Moorea* 17°29S 149°52W **289** e
Paphlagonia *Turkey* 41°30N 33°0E **212** B5
Paphos *Cyprus* 34°46N 32°25E **207** F8
Paphos ✈ (PFO) *Cyprus* 34°43N 32°30E **207** F8
Papien Chiang = Da → *Vietnam* 21°15N 105°20E **228** G5
Papikio Oros *Greece* 41°15N 25°13E **203** E9
Papiol *Spain* 41°25N 2°0E **114** A1
Paposo *Chile* 25°0S 70°30W **334** B1
Papoutsa *Cyprus* 34°54N 33°4E **207** F9
Papua □ *Indonesia* 4°0S 137°0E **231** E9
Papua, G. of *Papua N. G.* 9°0S 144°50E **286** E3
Papua New Guinea ■ *Oceania* 8°0S 145°0E **286** E3
Papudo *Chile* 32°29S 71°27W **334** C1
Papuk *Croatia* 45°30N 17°30E **182** E2
Papun *Burma* 18°2N 97°30E **241** F6
Papunya *Australia* 23°15S 131°54E **278** D5
Pará = Belém *Brazil* 1°20S 48°30W **332** B2
Pará □ *Brazil* 3°20S 52°0W **331** A7
Paraburdoo *Australia* 23°14S 117°32E **278** D2
Paracale *Phil.* 14°17N 122°48E **232** D4
Paracas, Pen. de *Peru* 13°53S 76°20W **330** C2
Paracatu *Brazil* 17°10S 46°50W **333** E2
Paracatu → *Brazil* 16°30S 45°4W **333** E2
Paracel Is. *S. China Sea* 15°50N 112°0E **230** A4
Parachilna *Australia* 31°10S 138°21E **282** A3
Parachinar *Pakistan* 33°55N 70°5E **242** C4
Paraćin *Serbia* 43°54N 21°27E **202** C5
Paracuru *Brazil* 3°24S 39°4W **332** B4
Parada, Punta *Peru* 15°22S 75°11W **330** D2
Paradas *Spain* 37°18N 5°29W **195** H5
Paradela *Spain* 42°44N 7°37W **194** C3
Paradera *Aruba* 12°32N 70°0W **322** f
Paradip *India* 20°15N 86°35E **244** D8
Paradise *Calif., U.S.A.* 39°46N 121°37W **306** F5
Paradise *Nev., U.S.A.* 36°5N 115°8W **124** B2
Paradise → *Canada* 53°27N 57°19W **299** B8
Paradise Hill *Canada* 53°32N 109°28W **297** C7
Paradise I. *Bahamas* 25°6N 77°19W **153** b
Paradise River *Canada* 53°27N 57°17W **299** B8
Paradise Valley *U.S.A.* 41°30N 117°32W **304** F5
Paradisi *Greece* 36°18N 28°7E **206** E12
Paragould *U.S.A.* 36°3N 90°29W **315** C9
Paragua = Palawan *Phil.* 9°30N 118°30E **233** G2
Paraguá → *Bolivia* 13°34S 61°53W **331** C5
Paragua → *Venezuela* 6°55N 62°55W **329** B5
Paraguaçu = Paraguaçu Paulista *Brazil* 22°22S 50°35W **335** A5
Paraguaçú → *Brazil* 12°45S 38°54W **333** D4
Paraguaçu Paulista *Brazil* 22°22S 50°35W **335** A5
Paraguaipoa *Venezuela* 11°21N 71°57W **328** A3
Paraguaná, Pen. de *Venezuela* 12°0N 70°0W **328** A4
Paraguarí *Paraguay* 25°36S 57°0W **334** B4
Paraguarí □ *Paraguay* 26°0S 57°10W **334** B4
Paraguay ■ *S. Amer.* 23°0S 57°0W **334** A4
Paraguay → *Paraguay* 27°18S 58°38W **334** B4
Paraíba = João Pessoa *Brazil* 7°10S 34°52W **332** C5
Paraíba □ *Brazil* 7°0S 36°0W **332** C4
Paraíba do Sul → *Brazil* 21°37S 41°3W **333** F3
Paraíso *Brazil* 19°3S 52°59W **331** D7
Paraíso *Tabasco, Mexico* 18°24N 93°14W **319** D6
Paraíso *Panama* 9°3N 79°38W **320** c
Parak *Iran* 27°38N 52°25E **247** E7
Parakhino Paddubye *Russia* 58°26N 33°10E **188** C7
Parakou *Benin* 9°25N 2°40E **263** D5
Parakylia *Australia* 30°24S 136°25E **282** A2
Paralimni *Cyprus* 35°2N 33°58E **207** E9
Paralio Astros *Greece* 37°25N 22°45E **204** D4
Paralkote *India* 19°47N 80°41E **244** E5
Param I. *Micronesia* 7°21N 151°47E **287** T18
Parama I. *Papua N. G.* 9°0S 143°25E **286** E2
Paramaribo *Suriname* 5°50N 55°10W **329** B6
Parambu *Brazil* 6°13S 40°43W **332** C3
Paramillo, Cerro *Colombia* 7°4N 75°55W **328** B2
Paramillo △ *Colombia* 7°37N 76°13W **328** B2
Paramirim *Brazil* 13°26S 42°15W **333** D3
Paramirim → *Brazil* 11°34S 43°18W **333** D3
Paramithia *Greece* 39°30N 20°35E **204** B2
Paramonga *Peru* 10°40S 77°50W **330** C2
Paramount Studios *U.S.A.* 34°5N 118°19W **126** B3
Paramus *U.S.A.* 40°56N 74°2W **132** A1
Paramushir, Ostrov *Russia* 50°24N 156°0E **215** D16
Paran → *Israel* 30°20N 35°10E **251** H6
Paraná *Argentina* 31°45S 60°30W **334** C3
Paraná *Brazil* 12°30S 47°48W **333** D2
Paraná □ *Brazil* 24°30S 51°0W **335** A5
Paraná → *Argentina* 33°43S 59°15W **334** C4
Paraná → *Brazil* 12°30S 48°14W **333** D2
Paranaguá *Brazil* 25°30S 48°30W **335** B6
Paranaíba *Brazil* 19°40S 51°11W **331** D7
Paranaíba → *Brazil* 20°6S 51°4W **333** F1
Paranapanema → *Brazil* 22°40S 53°9W **335** A5
Paranapiacaba, Serra do *Brazil* 24°31S 48°35W **335** A6
Paranaque *Phil.* 14°30N 120°59E **127** B1
Paranas *Phil.* 11°42N 125°2E **233** F5
Paranavaí *Brazil* 23°4S 52°56W **335** A5
Parang *Maguindanao, Phil.* 7°23N 124°16E **233** H5
Parang *Sulu, Phil.* 5°55N 120°54E **233** J3
Parangippettai *India* 11°30N 79°38E **245** J4
Parângul Mare, Vf. *Romania* 45°20N 23°37E **183** E8
Paranthan *Sri Lanka* 9°26N 80°24E **245** K5
Paraoa *French Polynesia* 19°9S 140°43W **289** f
Paraparaumu *N.Z.* 40°57S 175°3E **284** G4
Parapetí → *Bolivia* 18°58S 62°21W **331** D5
Paraspori, Akra *Greece* 35°55N 27°15E **205** F9
Parate Bueno *Venezuela* 10°59N 64°22W **329** a
Paratinga *Brazil* 12°40S 43°10W **333** D3
Paratoo *Australia* 32°42S 139°20E **282** B3
Paraúna *Brazil* 16°55S 50°26W **333** E1
Paray-le-Monial *France* 46°27N 4°7E **173** F11
Paray-Vieille-Poste *France* 48°42N 2°20E **134** B3
Parbati → *Mad. P., India* 25°50N 76°30E **242** G7

Parbati → Raj., India 26°54N 77°53E 242 F7
Parbatipur Bangla. 25°39N 88°55E 241 C2
Parbhani India 19°8N 76°52E 244 E3
Parchim Germany 53°26N 11°52E 178 B7
Parchwitz = Prochowice Poland 51°17N 16°20E 185 G3
Parco = Sinclair U.S.A. 41°47N 107°7W 304 F10
Parczew Poland 51°40N 22°52E 185 G9
Pardes Hanna-Karkur Israel 32°28N 34°57E 215 E3
Pardilla Spain 41°33N 3°43W 194 D7
Pardisān Nature Park Iran 35°44N 51°22E 141 A2
Pardo → Bahia, Brazil 15°40S 39°0W 333 E4
Pardo → Mato Grosso, Brazil 21°46S 52°9W 335 A5
Pardo → Minas Gerais, Brazil 15°48S 44°48W 333 E3
Pardo → São Paulo, Brazil 20°10S 48°38W 333 F2
Pardoo Roadhouse Australia 20°6S 119°3E 278 D2
Pardubice Czech Rep. 50°3N 15°45E 180 A8
Pardubický □ Czech Rep. 49°50N 16°0E 180 B8
Pardubitz = Pardubice Czech Rep. 50°3N 15°45E 180 A8
Pare Indonesia 7°43S 112°12E 231 G15
Pare Mts. Tanzania 4°0S 37°45E 268 C4
Parecis, Serra dos Brazil 13°0S 60°0W 331 C6
Paredes de Nava Spain 42°9N 4°42W 194 C6
Parel India 18°58N 72°49E 130 B1
Parelhas Brazil 6°41S 36°39W 332 C4
Paren Russia 62°30N 163°15E 215 C17
Parenda India 18°16N 75°28E 244 E2
Parengarenga Harbour N.Z. 34°31S 173°0E 284 A2
Parent Canada 47°55N 74°35W 298 C5
Parent, L. Canada 48°31N 77°1W 298 C4
Parentis-en-Born France 44°21N 1°4W 174 D2
Parepare Indonesia 4°0S 119°40E 235 C5
Parfino Russia 57°59N 31°34E 188 D6
Parga Greece 39°15N 20°29E 204 B2
Pargas = Länsi-Turunmaa Finland 60°18N 22°18E 188 B2
Pargi India 17°11N 77°53E 244 E3
Pargo, Pta. do Madeira 32°49N 17°17W 153 c
Parguera Puerto Rico 17°59N 67°3W 321 b
Parham Canada 44°39N 76°43W 313 B8
Pari Brazil 23°32S 46°36W 137 B2
Paria → U.S.A. 36°52N 111°36W 305 H8
Paria, G. de Venezuela 10°30N 61°40W 323 t
Paria, Pen. de Venezuela 10°50N 62°30W 329 A5
Pariaguán Venezuela 8°51N 64°34W 329 B5
Pariaman Indonesia 0°47S 100°11E 234 C2
Paricatuba Brazil 4°26S 61°53W 329 D5
Paricutín, Cerro Mexico 19°28N 102°15W 318 D4
Parigi Indonesia 0°50S 120°5E 231 E6
Parika Guyana 6°50N 58°20W 329 B6
Parikia Greece 37°6N 25°11E 205 D7
Parikkala Finland 61°33N 29°31E 188 B5
Parima, Serra Brazil 2°30N 64°0W 329 C5
Parinari Peru 4°35S 74°25W 330 A3
Pariñas, Pta. Peru 4°30S 82°0W 330 A1
Parincea Romania 46°27N 27°9E 183 D12
Paringa Australia 34°10S 140°46E 282 C4
Parintins Brazil 2°40S 56°50W 329 D6
Parioli Italy 41°55N 12°29E 136 B1
Pariparit Kyun Burma 14°52N 93°41E 245 G11
Paris Ont., Canada 43°12N 80°25W 312 C4
Paris Paris, France 48°53N 2°20E 134 A3
Paris Idaho, U.S.A. 42°14N 111°24W 304 E8
Paris Ill., U.S.A. 39°36N 87°42W 311 E9
Paris Ky., U.S.A. 38°13N 84°15W 311 F12
Paris Mo., U.S.A. 39°29N 92°0W 310 E5
Paris Tenn., U.S.A. 36°18N 88°19W 315 C10
Paris Tex., U.S.A. 33°40N 95°33W 314 E7
Paris, Ville de □ France 48°50N 2°20E 173 D9
Paris Charles de Gaulle ✈ (CDG) France 49°0N 2°32E 173 D9
Paris Orly ✈ (ORY) France 48°44N 2°23E 134 B3
Parish U.S.A. 43°25N 76°8W 313 C8
Parishville U.S.A. 44°38N 74°49W 313 B10
Pariti Indonesia 10°1S 123°45E 278 B3
Parje India 18°54N 72°57E 130 B2
Park U.S.A. 48°45N 122°18W 306 B4
Park City U.S.A. 37°48N 97°20W 308 G5
Pārk-e Āzādegān Iran 35°37N 51°28E 141 B2
Pārk-e Mellat Iran 35°47N 51°24E 141 A2
Park Falls U.S.A. 45°56N 90°27W 308 C8
Park Forest U.S.A. 41°29N 87°40W 311 C9
Park Head Canada 44°36N 81°9W 312 B3
Park Hills U.S.A. 37°51N 90°51W 310 G6
Park Range U.S.A. 40°41N 106°41W 304 F10
Park Rapids U.S.A. 46°55N 95°4W 308 B6
Park Ridge U.S.A. 42°2N 87°51W 119 A1
Park River U.S.A. 48°24N 97°45W 308 A5
Park Royal U.K. 51°31N 0°16W 125 A2
Park Rynie S. Africa 30°25S 30°45E 271 D5
Parkā Bandar Iran 25°55N 59°35E 247 E8
Parkal India 18°12N 79°43E 244 E4
Parkán = Štúrovo Slovak Rep. 47°48N 18°41E 181 D11
Parkano Finland 62°1N 23°0E 188 A2
Parkchester U.S.A. 40°49N 73°50W 132 B2
Parkdale Canada 43°38N 79°25W 141 B2
Parkent Uzbekistan 41°18N 69°40E 217 D7
Parker Ariz., U.S.A. 34°9N 114°17W 307 L12
Parker Pa., U.S.A. 41°5N 79°41W 312 E5
Parker Center Los Angeles, U.S.A. 127 b2
Parker Dam U.S.A. 34°18N 114°8W 307 L12
Parkersburg Iowa, U.S.A. 42°35N 92°47W 310 B4
Parkersburg W. Va., U.S.A. 39°16N 81°34W 309 F13
Parkes Australia 33°9S 148°11E 283 B8
Parkfield U.S.A. 35°54N 120°26W 306 K6
Parkhill Canada 43°15N 81°38W 312 C3
Parkhurst S. Africa 26°8S 28°1E 123 A2
Parkland U.S.A. 47°9N 122°26W 306 C4
Parklawn U.S.A. 38°50N 77°7W 143 B2
Parkmore S. Africa 26°5S 28°2E 123 A2
Parkside U.S.A. 37°44N 122°29W 136 B2
Parkston U.S.A. 43°24N 97°59W 308 D5
Parksville Canada 49°20N 124°21W 296 D4
Parktown S. Africa 26°10S 28°2E 123 B2
Parkview S. Africa 26°9S 28°1E 123 A2
Parkville U.S.A. 40°38N 73°57W 132 C2
Parkway U.S.A. 38°32N 121°26W 306 G5
Parkwood Gauteng, S. Africa 26°9S 28°2E 123 A2
Parkwood Western Cape, S. Africa 34°2S 18°30E 118 B1
Parla Spain 40°14N 3°46W 194 E7
Parlakimidi India 18°45N 84°5E 244 E7
Parlatuvier Trin. & Tob. 11°18N 60°39W 323 s
Parli India 18°50N 76°35E 244 E3
Parliament Budapest, Hungary 117 b2
Pârliţa Moldova 47°19N 27°52E 183 C12
Parma Italy 44°48N 10°20E 198 D7
Parma Idaho, U.S.A. 43°47N 116°57W 304 E5
Parma Ohio, U.S.A. 41°24N 81°43W 312 E3
Parma → Italy 44°56N 10°26E 198 D7
Parnaguá Brazil 10°10S 44°38W 332 D3
Parnaíba Brazil 2°54S 41°47W 332 B3
Parnaíba → Brazil 3°0S 41°50W 332 B3
Parnamirim Pernambuco, Brazil 8°5S 39°34W 332 C4
Parnamirim Rio Grande do N., Brazil 5°55S 35°15W 332 C4
Parnarama Brazil 5°31S 43°6W 332 C3
Parnassos Greece 38°35N 22°30E 204 C4
Parnassus N.Z. 42°42S 173°23E 285 C8
Parndana Australia 35°48S 137°12E 282 C2
Parner India 19°0N 74°26E 244 E2
Parnitha Greece 38°14N 23°45E 204 C5
Parnitha △ Greece 38°12N 23°44E 204 C5
Parnonas Oros Greece 37°15N 22°45E 204 D4
Pärnu Estonia 58°28N 24°33E 188 C3
Paro Dzong Bhutan 27°32N 89°53E 241 B2
Parola India 20°47N 75°7E 244 D2
Paroo → Australia 31°28S 143°32E 282 A5
Paros Greece 37°5N 25°12E 205 D7
Parow S. Africa 33°53S 18°37E 118 A2
Parowan U.S.A. 37°51N 112°50W 305 H7
Parpaillon France 44°30N 6°40E 175 D10
Parque Chacabuco Argentina 34°39S 58°26W 117 B2
Parque Patricios Argentina 34°38S 58°23W 117 B2
Parral Chile 36°10S 71°52W 334 D1
Parramatta Australia 33°48S 151°1E 283 B9
Parramatta → Australia 33°51S 151°3E 139 A1
Parras Mexico 25°25N 102°11W 318 B4
Parrett → U.K. 51°12N 3°1W 169 F4
Parris I. U.S.A. 32°20N 80°41W 316 C9
Parrish U.S.A. 27°35N 82°26W 317 H7
Parrott U.S.A. 31°54N 84°31W 316 D5
Parrsboro Canada 45°30N 64°25W 299 C7
Parry Channel Canada 74°15N 94°0W 295 C13
Parry I. Canada 45°18N 80°10W 312 A4
Parry Is. Canada 77°0N 110°0W 295 B10
Parry Sound Canada 45°20N 80°0W 312 A5
Parsābād Iran 39°39N 47°50E 213 C12
Parsaloi Kenya 1°16N 36°51E 268 B4
Parsberg Germany 49°10N 11°43E 179 F7
Parsęta → Poland 54°11N 15°34E 184 D2
Parsnip → Canada 55°10N 123°2W 296 B4
Parsons U.S.A. 37°20N 95°16W 308 G6
Parsons Ra. Australia 13°30S 135°15E 280 A2
Partabpur India 20°0N 80°42E 244 E5
Partanna Italy 37°43N 12°53E 200 E5
Partenio △ Italy 40°56N 14°38E 201 B7
Parthenay France 46°38N 0°16W 172 F6
Parthenon Athens, Greece 112 c2
Partinico Italy 38°3N 13°7E 200 D6
Partizansk Russia 43°8N 133°9E 215 E14
Partizánske Slovak Rep. 48°38N 18°23E 181 C11
Partridge I. Canada 55°59N 87°37W 298 A2
Partry Mts. Ireland 53°40N 9°28W 166 C2
Partur India 19°40N 76°14E 244 E3
Paru → Brazil 1°33S 52°38W 329 D7
Parú → Venezuela 4°20N 66°27W 328 C4
Paru de Oeste → Brazil 1°30N 56°0W 329 C6
Parucito → Venezuela 5°18N 65°59W 328 B4
Parur India 10°13N 76°14E 245 J3
Paruro Peru 13°45S 71°50W 330 C3
Parvān □ Afghan. 35°0N 69°0E 240 B3
Parvatipuram India 18°50N 83°25E 244 E6
Parvatsar India 26°52N 74°49E 242 F6
Pårydd Sweden 56°34N 15°55E 163 H9
Parys S. Africa 26°52S 27°29E 270 C4
Pas, Pta. des Spain 38°46N 1°26E 206 D1
Pas, The Canada 53°45N 101°15W 297 C8
Pas-de-Calais □ France 50°30N 2°10E 173 B9
Paşabahçe Turkey 41°6N 29°5E 122 B2
Pasada Spain 43°23N 5°40W 194 B5
Pasadena Nfld. & L., Canada 49°1N 57°36W 299 C8
Pasadena Calif., U.S.A. 34°9N 118°8W 126 B4
Pasadena Tex., U.S.A. 29°43N 95°13W 314 G7
Pasaje Ecuador 3°23S 79°50W 328 D2
Pasaje → Argentina 25°39S 63°56W 334 B3
Paşalimanı Turkey 40°29N 27°36E 203 F11
Pasar Indonesia 8°27S 114°54E 231 J17
Pasar Minggu Indonesia 6°16S 106°49E 122 B1
Pasargadae Iran 30°11N 53°10E 247 D7
Pasarkuok Indonesia 1°27S 100°36E 234 C2
Pasarsibuhuan Indonesia 1°3N 99°43E 234 B1
Pasay Phil. 14°32N 120°59E 127 B1
Pascagoula U.S.A. 30°21N 88°33W 315 F10
Pascagoula → U.S.A. 30°23N 88°37W 315 F10
Paşcani Romania 47°14N 26°45E 183 C11
Paschimbanga □ India 23°0N 88°0E 243 H13
Pasco U.S.A. 46°14N 119°6W 304 C4
Pasco □ Peru 10°40S 75°0W 330 C3
Pasco I. Australia 20°57S 115°20E 278 D2
Pascoag U.S.A. 41°57N 71°42W 313 E13
Pascoe Vale Australia 37°43S 144°55E 128 A1
Pascua, I. de Chile 27°7S 109°23W 330 b
Paseo de la Reforma Mexico City, Mexico 128 b2
Pasewalk Germany 53°30N 13°58E 178 B9
Pasfield L. Canada 58°24N 105°20W 297 B7
Pasha → Russia 60°29N 32°55E 188 B7
Pashmakli = Smolyan Bulgaria 41°35N 24°38E 203 E8
Pasig Phil. 14°33N 121°4E 127 B2
Pasig → Phil. 14°31N 121°6E 127 B2
Pasighat India 28°4N 95°21E 241 A5
Pasila Finland 60°12N 24°56E 121 B2
Pasing Germany 48°8N 11°28E 131 B1
Pasinler Turkey 39°59N 41°41E 213 C9
Pasir Mas Malaysia 6°2N 102°8E 237 J4
Pasir Panjang Singapore 1°18N 103°46E 138 B2
Pasir Putih Malaysia 5°50N 102°24E 237 K4
Pasir Ris Singapore 1°22N 103°56E 138 A3
Pasirian Indonesia 8°13S 113°8E 235 D4
Pasirkuning = Dabo Indonesia 0°30S 104°33E 234 C2
Pasirpengarayan Indonesia 0°51N 100°16E 234 B2
Påskallavik Sweden 57°10N 16°26E 163 G10
Paskūh Iran 27°34N 61°39E 247 E9
Pasłęk Poland 54°3N 19°41E 184 D6
Pasłęka → Poland 54°26N 19°46E 184 D6
Pasley, C. Australia 33°52S 123°35E 279 F3
Paşman Croatia 43°58N 15°20E 199 E12
Pasmore → Australia 31°5S 139°49E 282 A3
Pasni Pakistan 25°15N 63°27E 240 D1
Paso Bravo △ Paraguay 22°32S 57°5W 334 A4
Paso Cantinela Mexico 32°33N 115°47W 307 N11
Paso de Indios Argentina 43°55S 69°0W 336 B3
Paso de los Indios Argentina 38°32S 69°25W 336 A3
Paso de los Libres Argentina 29°44S 57°10W 334 B4
Paso de los Toros Uruguay 32°45S 56°30W 334 C4
Paso Flores Argentina 40°35S 70°38W 336 B2
Paso Robles U.S.A. 35°38N 120°41W 306 K6
Pasorapa Bolivia 18°16S 64°37W 331 D5
Paspébiac Canada 48°3N 65°17W 299 C6
Pasrur Pakistan 32°16N 74°43E 242 C6
Passage East Ireland 52°14N 7°0W 166 D5
Passage West Ireland 51°52N 8°21W 166 E3
Passaic U.S.A. 40°51N 74°7W 132 A1
Passaic → U.S.A. 40°42N 74°10W 132 B1
Passam Papua N. G. 3°41S 143°38E 286 B2
Passau Germany 48°34N 13°28E 179 G9
Passenheim = Pasym Poland 53°48N 20°49E 184 E7
Passero, C. Italy 36°41N 15°10E 201 F8
Passi Phil. 11°6N 122°38E 233 F4
Passirana Italy 45°32N 9°2E 128 A1
Passo Fundo Brazil 28°10S 52°20W 335 B5
Passos Brazil 20°45S 46°37W 333 F2
Passow Germany 53°8N 14°6E 178 B10
Passy France 45°55N 6°41E 175 C10
Pastavy Belarus 55°4N 26°50E 188 E4
Pastaza □ Ecuador 2°0S 77°0W 328 D2
Pastaza → Peru 4°50S 76°52W 328 D2
Pasto Colombia 1°13N 77°17W 328 C2
Pastol B. U.S.A. 63°7N 163°15W 303 E7
Pastos Bons Brazil 6°36S 44°5W 332 C3
Pastrana Spain 40°27N 2°53W 196 E2
Pasuquin Phil. 18°20N 120°37E 232 B3
Pasuruan Indonesia 7°40S 112°44E 235 D4
Pasym Poland 53°48N 20°49E 184 E7
Pásztó Hungary 47°52N 19°43E 182 C4
Pata Phil. 5°51N 121°10E 233 J3
Pata I. Phil. 5°49N 121°10E 233 J3
Patagonia Argentina 45°0S 69°0W 326 G3
Patagonia Ariz., U.S.A. 31°33N 110°45W 305 L8
Patambar Iran 29°45N 60°17E 247 D9
Patan = Lalitpur Nepal 27°40N 85°20E 243 F11
Patan = Somnath India 20°53N 70°22E 242 J4
Patan Gujarat, India 23°54N 72°14E 242 H5
Patan Maharashtra, India 17°22N 73°57E 244 F1
Patani Indonesia 0°20N 128°50E 231 D7
Pătârlagele Romania 45°19N 26°21E 183 E11
Pataudi India 28°18N 76°48E 242 E7
Patchewollock Australia 35°22S 142°12E 282 C5
Patchogue U.S.A. 40°46N 73°1W 313 F11
Pate Coast, Kenya 2°10S 41°0E 268 C5
Pate Taiwan 24°56N 121°17E 225 B3
Patea N.Z. 39°45S 174°30E 284 F3
Pategi Nigeria 8°50N 5°45E 263 D6
Patel Nagar India 28°39N 77°10E 120 B1
Patensie S. Africa 33°46S 24°49E 270 D3
Paterna Spain 39°30N 0°26W 197 F4
Paternion Austria 46°43N 13°38E 180 E6
Paternò Italy 37°34N 14°54E 201 E7
Pateros Manila, Phil. 14°32N 121°3E 127 B2
Pateros Wash., U.S.A. 48°3N 119°54W 304 B4
Paterson N.S.W., Australia 32°35S 151°36E 283 B9
Paterson N.J., U.S.A. 40°54N 74°9W 313 F10
Paterson Inlet N.Z. 46°56S 168°12E 285 G3
Paterson Ra. Australia 21°45S 122°10E 278 D3
Pathankot India 32°18N 75°45E 242 C6
Pathardi India 19°10N 75°11E 244 E2
Patharghata Bangla. 22°2N 89°58E 241 D2
Pathein = Bassein Burma 16°45N 94°30E 241 G5
Pathfinder Res. U.S.A. 42°28N 106°51W 304 E10
Pathiu Thailand 10°42N 99°19E 237 G2
Pathri India 19°15N 76°27E 244 E3
Pathum Thani Thailand 14°1N 100°32E 236 E3
Pathumwan Thailand 13°44N 100°31E 122 B2
Pati Indonesia 6°45S 111°1E 235 D4
Pati Pt. Guam 13°35N 144°57E 302 d
Patía Colombia 2°4N 77°4W 328 C2
Patía → Colombia 2°13N 78°40W 328 C2
Patiala Punjab, India 30°23N 76°26E 242 D7
Patiala Ut. P., India 27°43N 79°1E 243 F8
Patine Kouka Senegal 12°45N 13°45W 262 C2
Patipukur India 22°36N 88°24E 124 B2
Patisia Greece 38°2N 23°45E 112 A2
Patitiri Greece 39°8N 23°50E 204 B5
Patkai Bum India 27°0N 95°30E 241 B5
Patmos Greece 37°21N 26°36E 205 D8
Patna India 25°35N 85°12E 243 G11
Patnagarh India 20°43N 83°9E 244 D6
Patnanongan I. Phil. 14°48N 122°11E 232 D4
Patnongon Phil. 10°55N 122°0E 233 F4
Patnos Turkey 39°13N 42°51E 213 C10
Pato Branco Brazil 26°13S 52°40W 335 B5
Patoka L. U.S.A. 38°20N 86°40W 311 F10
Patong, Ao Thailand 7°54N 98°17E 237 a
Patonga Uganda 2°45N 33°15E 268 B3
Patos Albania 40°42N 19°38E 202 F3
Patos Brazil 6°55S 37°16W 332 C4
Patos, L. dos Brazil 31°20S 51°0W 335 C5
Patos, Río de los → Argentina 31°18S 69°25W 334 C2
Patos de Minas Brazil 18°35S 46°32W 333 E2
Patquía Argentina 30°2S 66°55W 334 C2
Patra Greece 38°14N 21°47E 204 C3
Patraikos Kolpos Greece 38°17N 21°30E 204 C3
Patras = Patra Greece 38°14N 21°47E 204 C3
Patreksfjörður Iceland 65°35N 24°0W 155 B2
Patriarsheye = Donskoy Russia 53°55N 38°15E 188 F10
Patricio Lynch, I. Chile 48°35S 75°30W 336 C1
Patriot Hills Antarctica 82°20S 81°25W 151 E16
Patrocínio Brazil 18°57S 47°0W 333 E2
Pattada Italy 40°35N 9°6E 200 B2
Pattadakal India 16°1N 75°42E 245 F2
Pattallassang Indonesia 5°26S 119°26E 235 D5
Pattani Thailand 6°48N 101°15E 237 J3
Pattaya Thailand 12°52N 100°55E 236 F3
Patten U.S.A. 46°0N 68°38W 309 B19
Patterson Calif., U.S.A. 37°28N 121°8W 306 H5
Patterson Ga., U.S.A. 31°23N 82°8W 316 D7
Patterson La., U.S.A. 29°42N 91°18W 314 G9
Patterson, Mt. U.S.A. 38°29N 119°20W 306 G7
Patteson, Passage Vanuatu 15°26S 168°12E 287 E6
Patti Punjab, India 31°17N 74°54E 242 D6
Patti Ut. P., India 25°55N 82°12E 243 G10
Patti Italy 38°8N 14°58E 201 D7
Pattoki Pakistan 31°5N 73°52E 242 D5
Patton = Monroeville U.S.A. 40°26N 79°45W 312 F5
Patton U.S.A. 40°38N 78°39W 312 F6
Pattonsburg U.S.A. 40°3N 94°8W 310 D2
Pattukkattai India 10°25N 79°20E 245 J4
Patu Brazil 6°6S 37°38W 332 C4
Patuakhali Bangla. 22°20N 90°25E 241 D3
Patuanak Canada 55°55N 107°43W 297 B7
Patuca → Honduras 15°50N 84°18W 320 C3
Patuca, Punta Honduras 15°49N 84°14W 320 C3
Patuca △ Honduras 14°30N 85°30W 320 D2
Pătulele Romania 44°21N 22°47E 182 F7
Patur India 20°27N 76°56E 244 D3
Patvinsuo △ Finland 63°7N 30°45E 160 E24
Pátzcuaro Mexico 19°31N 101°38W 318 D4
Pau France 43°19N 0°25W 174 E3
Pau, Gave de → France 43°33N 1°12W 174 E2
Pau d' Arco Brazil 7°30S 49°22W 332 C2
Pau dos Ferros Brazil 6°7S 38°10W 332 C4
Pauanui N.Z. 37°1S 175°52E 284 D4
Paucartambo Peru 13°19S 71°35W 330 C3
Paudash Canada 44°59N 77°58W 312 B7
Pauillac France 45°11N 0°46W 174 C3
Pauini Brazil 7°40S 66°58W 330 B4
Pauini → Brazil 1°42S 62°50W 329 D5
Pauk Burma 21°27N 94°30E 241 E5
Paukkaung Burma 18°54N 95°33E 241 F5
Pauktaw Burma 20°11N 93°4E 241 E4
Paul I. Canada 56°30N 61°20W 299 A7
Paul Isnard Fr. Guiana 4°47N 54°1W 329 C7
Paul Revere Park Boston, U.S.A. 116 a2
Paul Smiths U.S.A. 44°26N 74°15W 313 B10
Paulatuk Canada 69°25N 124°0W 294 D7
Paulding U.S.A. 41°8N 84°35W 311 C12
Paulding Bay S. Ocean 66°0S 118°0E 151 C8
Paulhan France 43°33N 3°28E 174 E7
Paulis = Isiro Dem. Rep. of the Congo 2°53N 27°40E 268 B2
Paulista = Paulistana Brazil 8°9S 41°9W 332 C3
Paulista Brazil 7°57S 34°53W 332 C5
Paulistana Brazil 8°9S 41°9W 332 C3
Paulström Sweden 57°28N 15°31E 163 G9
Paulo Afonso Brazil 9°21S 38°15W 332 C4
Paulo de Faria Brazil 20°2S 49°24W 333 F2
Paulo E. Virginia, Gruta Brazil 22°56S 43°16W 135 B1
Paulpietersburg S. Africa 27°23S 30°50E 271 C5
Pauls Valley U.S.A. 34°44N 97°13W 314 D6
Paulshof Germany 52°34N 13°42E 115 A5
Pauma Valley U.S.A. 33°16N 116°58W 307 M10
Paung Burma 16°37N 94°28E 241 G5
Paungde Burma 18°29N 95°30E 241 F5
Pauni India 20°48N 79°40E 244 D4
Pauri India 30°9N 78°47E 243 D8
Pausa Peru 15°16S 73°22W 330 D3
Pauto → Colombia 5°9N 70°55W 328 B3
Pavagada India 14°6N 77°16E 245 G3
Pāveh Iran 35°3N 46°22E 213 E12
Pavelets Russia 53°49N 39°14E 188 F10
Pavia Italy 45°7N 9°8E 198 C6
Pavilion U.S.A. 42°52N 78°1W 312 D6
Pavilly France 49°34N 0°57E 172 C7
Pāvilosta Latvia 56°53N 21°14E 184 B8
Pavlikeni Bulgaria 43°14N 25°20E 203 C9
Pavlodar Kazakhstan 52°33N 77°0E 217 B9
Pavlograd = Pavlohrad Ukraine 48°30N 35°52E 189 H8
Pavlohrad Ukraine 48°30N 35°52E 189 H8
Pavlovo Russia 55°58N 43°5E 190 C6
Pavlovsk Russia 50°26N 40°5E 190 E5
Pavlovskaya Russia 46°17N 39°47E 191 G4
Pavlovskiy-Posad Russia 55°47N 38°42E 188 E10
Pavo U.S.A. 30°58N 83°45W 316 E6
Pavullo nel Frignano Italy 44°20N 10°50E 198 D7
Pavuvu Solomon Is. 9°4S 159°8E 287 M10
Paw Paw Ill., U.S.A. 41°41N 88°59W 310 C8
Paw Paw Mich., U.S.A. 42°13N 85°53W 311 B11
Pawahku Burma 26°11N 98°40E 241 B7
Pawai, Pulau Singapore 1°11N 103°44E 237 d
Pawan → Indonesia 1°55S 110°0E 235 C4
Pawayan India 28°4N 80°6E 243 E9
Pawhuska U.S.A. 36°40N 96°20W 314 C6
Pawling U.S.A. 41°34N 73°36W 313 E11
Pawnee Ill., U.S.A. 39°36N 89°35W 310 E7
Pawnee Okla., U.S.A. 36°20N 96°48W 314 C6
Pawnee City U.S.A. 40°7N 96°9W 308 E5
Pawtucket U.S.A. 41°53N 71°23W 313 E13
Paxi Greece 39°14N 20°12E 206 C10
Paximadia Greece 35°0N 24°35E 207 F5
Paxson U.S.A. 63°2N 145°30W 303 E11
Paxton U.S.A. 40°27N 88°6W 311 D8
Paya Lebar Singapore 1°21N 103°52E 138 A3
Payagyi Burma 17°29N 96°32E 241 G6
Payakumbuh Indonesia 0°20S 100°35E 234 C2
Payapa = General Tinio Phil. 15°39N 121°10E 232 D3
Payas = Yakacık Turkey 36°46N 36°11E 250 B7
Payerne Switz. 46°49N 6°56E 179 J2
Payette U.S.A. 44°5N 116°56W 304 D5
Paymogo Spain 37°44N 7°21W 195 H3
Payne U.S.A. 41°5N 84°44W 311 C12
Payne Bay = Kangirsuk Canada 60°0N 70°0W 295 F18
Payne L. Canada 59°30N 74°30W 295 F17
Payne Pt. Ascension I. 7°57S 14°25W 153 g
Paynes Find Australia 29°15S 117°42E 279 E2
Paynesville Liberia 6°20N 10°45W 262 D2
Paynesville Minn., U.S.A. 45°23N 94°43W 308 C6
Payo Obispo = Chetumal Mexico 18°30N 88°20W 319 D7
Pays de la Loire □ France 47°45N 0°25W 172 E6
Paysandú Uruguay 32°19S 58°8W 334 C4
Payson Ariz., U.S.A. 34°14N 111°20W 305 J8
Payson Utah, U.S.A. 40°3N 111°44W 304 F8
Paz → Guatemala 13°44N 90°10W 320 D1
Paz, B. de la Mexico 24°9N 110°25W 318 C2
Pāzanān Iran 30°35N 49°59E 247 D6
Pazar Turkey 41°10N 40°50E 213 B9
Pazarcık Turkey 37°30N 37°17E 212 D7
Pazardzhik Bulgaria 42°12N 24°20E 203 D8
Pazardzhik □ Bulgaria 42°12N 24°20E 203 D8
Pazarköy Turkey 39°51N 27°24E 205 B9
Pazarlar Turkey 39°0N 29°7E 205 C11
Pazaryeri Turkey 40°0N 29°56E 205 B11
Pazaryolu Turkey 40°21N 40°47E 213 B9
Pazin Croatia 45°14N 13°56E 199 C10
Pazña Bolivia 18°36S 66°55W 330 D4
Pčinja → Macedonia 41°50N 21°45E 202 E5
Pe Ell U.S.A. 46°34N 123°18W 306 D3
Pea → U.S.A. 31°1N 85°51W 316 D4
Peabody U.S.A. 42°31N 70°56W 313 D14
Peace → Alta., Canada 59°0N 111°25W 296 B6
Peace → Fla., U.S.A. 26°56N 82°6W 317 J7
Peace Point Canada 59°7N 112°27W 296 B6
Peace River Canada 56°15N 117°18W 296 B5
Peach Springs U.S.A. 35°32N 113°25W 305 J7
Peachland Canada 49°47N 119°45W 296 D5
Peachtree City U.S.A. 33°25N 84°35W 316 B5
Peacock Pt. Wake I. 19°16N 166°37E 302 b
Peak, The = Kinder Scout U.K. 53°24N 1°52W 168 D6
Peak, The Ascension I. 7°57S 14°20W 153 g
Peak Charles △ Australia 32°42S 121°10E 279 F3
Peak District △ U.K. 53°24N 1°46W 168 D6
Peak Hill Australia 32°47S 148°11E 283 B8
Peak Ra. Australia 22°50S 148°20E 280 C4
Peake Australia 35°25S 139°55E 282 C3
Peake Cr. → Australia 28°2S 136°7E 281 D2
Peakhurst Australia 33°57S 151°3E 139 B1
Peal de Becerro Spain 37°55N 3°7W 195 H7
Peale, Mt. U.S.A. 38°26N 109°14W 305 G9
Peale I. Wake I. 19°18N 166°37E 302 b
Peania Greece 37°56N 23°50E 112 B3
Pearblossom U.S.A. 34°30N 117°55W 307 L9
Pearl U.S.A. 39°28N 90°38W 310 E6
Pearl → U.S.A. 30°11N 89°32W 315 F10
Pearl and Hermes Reef U.S.A. 27°55N 175°45W 302 F8
Pearl Banks Sri Lanka 8°45N 79°45E 245 K4
Pearl City U.S.A. 21°24N 157°59W 302 K14
Pearl Harbor U.S.A. 21°21N 157°57W 302 K14
Pearl Harbor Nat. Wildlife Refuge △ U.S.A. 21°23N 157°59W 302 K14
Pearl River = Zhu Jiang → China 22°45N 113°37E 229 F9
Pearl River U.S.A. 41°4N 74°2W 313 E10
Pearl River Bridge China 22°15N 113°48E 219 a
Pearls Grenada 12°9N 61°37W 323 q
Pearls Rock Grenada 12°9N 61°36W 323 q
Pearsall U.S.A. 28°54N 99°6W 314 G5
Pearson U.S.A. 31°18N 82°51W 316 D7
Pearson Int. Toronto ✈ (YYZ) Canada 43°46N 79°35W 141 A1
Peary Land Greenland 82°40N 33°0W 154 A7
Pease → U.S.A. 34°12N 99°2W 314 D5
Peawanuck Canada 55°15N 85°12W 298 A2
Pebane Mozam. 17°10S 38°8E 269 F4
Pebas Peru 3°10S 71°46W 328 D3
Pebble, I. Falk. Is. 51°20S 59°40W 153 f
Pebble Beach U.S.A. 36°34N 121°57W 306 J5
Peć = Pejë Kosovo 42°40N 20°17E 202 D4
Peçanha Brazil 18°33S 42°34W 333 E3
Pecatonica U.S.A. 42°19N 89°22W 310 B7
Pecatonica → U.S.A. 42°26N 89°12W 310 B7
Péccioli Italy 43°33N 10°43E 198 E7
Pechea Romania 45°36N 27°49E 183 E12
Pechenga Russia 69°29N 31°4E 160 B24
Pechenizhyn Ukraine 48°30N 24°48E 183 B9
Pechiguera, Pta. Canary Is. 28°51N 13°53W 153 e2
Pechnezhskoye Vdkhr. Ukraine 50°5N 36°54E 189 G9
Pechora Russia 65°10N 57°11E 186 A10
Pechora → Russia 68°13N 54°15E 186 A9
Pechorskaya Guba Russia 68°40N 54°0E 186 A9
Pechory Russia 57°48N 27°40E 188 D4
Pecica Romania 46°10N 21°3E 182 D6
Pecka Serbia 44°18N 19°33E 202 B3
Peckham U.K. 51°28N 0°3W 125 B3
Pécora, C. Italy 39°27N 8°23E 200 C1
Pecos N. Mex., U.S.A. 35°35N 105°41W 305 J11
Pecos Tex., U.S.A. 31°26N 103°30W 314 F3
Pecos → U.S.A. 29°42N 101°22W 314 G4
Pécs Hungary 46°5N 18°15E 182 D3
Pedasí Panama 7°32N 80°2W 320 E3
Pedda Bellala India 19°4N 78°49E 244 E4
Peddapalli India 18°40N 79°24E 244 E4
Peddapuram India 17°6N 82°8E 244 F6
Pedder, L. Australia 42°55S 146°10E 281 G4
Peddie S. Africa 33°14S 27°7E 271 D4
Pedernales Dom. Rep. 18°2N 71°44W 321 C5
Pedernales Ecuador 0°5N 80°3W 328 C1
Pederstrup Denmark 55°44N 12°20E 118 A2
Pedieos → Cyprus 35°10N 33°54E 207 E9
Pedirka Desert Australia 26°47S 134°11E 281 A1
Pedra Azul Brazil 16°2S 41°17W 333 E3
Pedra Branca Brazil 0°51N 51°58W 329 C7
Pedra Grande, Recifes de Brazil 17°45S 38°58W 333 E4
Pedra Lume C. Verde Is. 16°40N 22°52W 153 j
Pedralbes Spain 41°23N 2°7E 114 A1
Pedras Negras Brazil 12°51S 62°54W 331 C5
Pedras Tinhosas, I. São Tomé & Príncipe 1°22N 7°17E 265 a
Pedregal de San Angel, Jardines del Mexico 19°19N 99°12W 128 C1
Pedreguer Spain 38°48N 0°3E 197 G5
Pedreiras Brazil 4°32S 44°40W 332 B3
Pedro Afonso Brazil 9°0S 48°10W 332 C2
Pedro Bank Caribbean 17°5N 78°20W 320 C4
Pedro Bay U.S.A. 59°47N 154°7W 303 G9
Pedro Cays Jamaica 17°5N 77°48W 320 C4
Pedro Chico Colombia 1°4N 70°25W 328 C3
Pedro de Valdivia Chile 22°55S 69°38W 334 A2
Pedro Dorado Colombia 1°0N 70°14W 328 C3
Pedro González Venezuela 11°7N 63°56W 329 a
Pedro Juan Caballero Paraguay 22°30S 55°40W 335 A4
Pedro Miguel Locks Panama 9°1N 79°36W 320 c
Pedro Muñoz Spain 39°25N 2°56W 195 F8
Pedro Pt. = North West Pt. Jamaica 18°27N 78°13W 320 a
Pedrógão Grande Portugal 39°55N 8°9W 194 F2
Pee Dee = Great Pee Dee → U.S.A. 33°21N 79°10W 315 E15
Peebinga Australia 34°52S 140°57E 282 C4
Peebles Borders, U.K. 55°40N 3°11W 167 F5
Peebles Ohio, U.S.A. 38°57N 83°24W 311 F13
Peekskill U.S.A. 41°17N 73°55W 313 E11
Peel I. of Man 54°13N 4°40W 168 C3
Peel → N.S.W., Australia 30°50S 150°29E 283 A9
Peel → N.W.T., Canada 67°0N 135°0W 294 D5
Peel Sd. Canada 73°0N 96°0W 294 C12
Peene → Germany 54°9N 13°46E 178 A9
Peera Peera Poolanna L. Australia 26°30S 138°0E 281 D2
Peerless Lake Canada 56°37N 114°40W 296 B6
Peers Canada 53°40N 116°0W 296 C5
Peery L. Australia 30°45S 143°35E 282 A5
Pegasus Bay N.Z. 43°20S 173°10E 285 D8
Peggau Austria 47°12N 15°21E 180 D8
Peggy Guggenheim, Collezione Venice, Italy 142 b2
Pegnitz Germany 49°44N 11°31E 179 F7
Pegnitz → Germany 49°30N 10°59E 179 F6
Pego Spain 38°51N 0°8W 197 G4
Pegu Burma 17°20N 96°29E 241 G6
Pegu □ Burma 17°30N 96°30E 241 G6
Pegu Yoma Burma 19°0N 96°0E 241 F6
Peguera Spain 39°32N 2°26E 206 B3
Pehčevo Macedonia 41°41N 22°55E 202 E6
Pehlivanköy Turkey 41°20N 26°55E 203 E10
Pehuajó Argentina 35°45S 62°0W 334 D3
Pei Xian China 34°44N 116°55E 226 G9
Peian = Bei'an China 48°10N 126°20E 219 B14
Peihai = Beihai China 21°28N 109°6E 228 G7
Peikang Taiwan 23°34N 120°18E 225 C2
Peikang Hsi → Taiwan 24°2N 120°50E 225 B2
Peikant'ang Taiwan 26°13N 120°0E 225 b
Peimen Taiwan 23°16N 120°7E 225 C2
Peinan Taiwan 22°47N 121°7E 225 D3
Peinan Hsi → Taiwan 22°46N 121°10E 225 D3
Peinanchu Shan Taiwan 23°3N 120°52E 225 C2
Peine Chile 23°45S 68°8W 334 A2
Peine Niedersachsen, Germany 52°19N 10°14E 178 C6
Pei'ping = Beijing China 39°53N 116°21E 114 B1
Peipu Taiwan 24°2N 121°36E 225 B3
Peipus, L. = Chudskoye, Ozero Russia 58°13N 27°30E 188 C4
Peissenberg Germany 47°48N 11°4E 179 H7
Peitawu Shan Taiwan 22°38N 120°46E 225 D2
Peitou Changhua, Taiwan 23°52N 120°30E 225 C2
Peitou T'aipei, Taiwan 25°11N 121°27E 225 A3
Peitun Taiwan 24°10N 120°41E 225 B2
Peitz Germany 51°51N 14°24E 178 D10
Peixe Brazil 12°0S 48°40W 333 D2
Peixe → Brazil 21°31S 51°58W 333 F1
Peixoto de Azeredo → Brazil 10°6S 55°31W 331 C6
Pejantan, Pulau Indonesia 0°7N 107°13E 234 B3
Pejë Kosovo 42°40N 20°17E 202 D4
Pek → Serbia 44°45N 21°29E 202 B5
Pekalongan Indonesia 6°53S 109°40E 235 D3
Pekan Malaysia 3°30N 103°25E 237 L4
Pekan Nenas Malaysia 1°31N 103°31E 237 d
Pekanbaru Indonesia 0°30N 101°15E 234 B2
Pekin U.S.A. 40°35N 89°40W 310 D7
Peking = Beijing China 39°53N 116°21E 114 B1
Pekutatan Indonesia 8°25S 114°49E 231 J17
Pela Greece 40°46N 22°23E 202 F6
Pelabuhan Ratu, Teluk Indonesia 7°5S 106°30E 234 D3
Pelabuhanratu Indonesia 7°0S 106°32E 234 D3
Pélagos = Kira Panagia Greece 39°17N 24°4E 204 B6
Pelaihari Indonesia 3°55S 114°45E 235 C4
Pelat, Mt. France 44°16N 6°42E 175 D10
Pelcowizna Poland 52°17N 21°0E 143 B2
Pelczyce Poland 53°3N 15°16E 185 E2
Peleaga, Vf. Romania 45°22N 22°55E 182 E7
Pelechuco Bolivia 14°48S 69°4W 330 C4
Pelée, Mt. Martinique 14°48N 61°10W 322 j
Pelee, Pt. Canada 41°54N 82°31W 298 D3
Pelee I. Canada 41°47N 82°40W 312 E2
Pelejo Peru 6°10S 75°49W 330 B2
Pelekech Kenya 3°52N 35°8E 268 B4
Peleliu I. Palau 7°1N 134°15E 288 c
Peleng Indonesia 1°20S 123°30E 231 E6
Pelenge Dem. Rep. of the Congo 2°44S 22°39E 264 C4
Pelentong Malaysia 1°32N 103°49E 237 d
Pélézi Ivory C. 7°17N 6°54W 262 D3
Pelham U.S.A. 31°8N 84°9W 316 D5
Pelhřimov Czech Rep. 49°24N 15°12E 180 B8
Pelican U.S.A. 57°58N 136°14W 296 B1
Pelican L. Canada 52°28N 100°20W 297 C8
Pelican Narrows Canada 55°10N 102°56W 297 B8
Pelion U.S.A. 33°46N 81°15W 316 B8
Pelister △ Macedonia 41°0N 21°10E 202 F5
Pelješac Croatia 42°55N 17°25E 199 F14
Pelkosenniemi Finland 67°6N 27°28E 160 C22
Pell City U.S.A. 33°35N 86°17W 316 B3
Pella Northern Cape, S. Africa 29°1S 19°6E 270 C2
Pella Iowa, U.S.A. 41°25N 92°55W 310 C4
Pella □ Greece 40°52N 22°0E 202 F6
Pello Finland 66°47N 23°59E 160 C20
Pellworm Germany 54°31N 8°39E 178 A4
Pelly → Canada 62°47N 137°19W 296 A1
Pelly Bay Canada 68°38N 89°50W 295 D14
Peloponnesos □ Greece 37°10N 22°0E 204 D4
Peloponnisos Station Athens, Greece 112 a1
Peloritani, Monti Italy 38°3N 15°20E 201 D8
Pelorus → N.Z. 41°16S 173°45E 285 B8
Pelorus Sd. N.Z. 40°59S 173°59E 285 A8
Pelotas Brazil 31°42S 52°23W 335 C5
Pelotas → Brazil 27°28S 51°55W 335 B5
Pelovo Bulgaria 43°26N 24°17E 203 C8
Pelplin Poland 53°55N 18°42E 184 E5
Pelvoux, Massif du France 44°52N 6°20E 175 D10
Pemalang Indonesia 6°53S 109°23E 235 D3
Pemanggil, Pulau Malaysia 2°37N 104°21E 237 L5
Pematangsiantar Indonesia 2°57N 99°5E 234 B1
Pemba Mozam. 12°58S 40°30E 269 E5
Pemba Zambia 16°30S 27°28E 269 F2
Pemba Channel Tanzania 5°0S 39°37E 268 D4
Pemba I. Tanzania 5°0S 39°45E 268 D4
Pemberton W. Austral., Australia 34°30S 116°0E 279 F2
Pemberton B.C., Canada 50°25N 122°50W 296 C4
Pembina → Canada 54°45N 114°17W 296 C6
Pembroke Ont., Canada 45°50N 77°7W 298 C4
Pembroke Trin. & Tob. 11°13N 60°37W 323 s
Pembroke Pembs., U.K. 51°41N 4°55W 169 F3
Pembroke Ga., U.S.A. 32°8N 81°37W 316 C8
Pembroke Park U.S.A. 25°59N 80°10W 129 C2
Pembroke Pines U.S.A. 26°0N 80°13W 129 B1
Pembrokeshire □ U.K. 51°52N 4°56W 169 F3
Pembrokeshire Coast △ U.K. 51°50N 5°2W 169 F2
Pembuang → Indonesia 3°24S 112°33E 235 C4
Pen India 18°45N 73°5E 244 E1
Pen-y-bont ar Ogwr = Bridgend U.K. 51°30N 3°34W 169 F4
Pen-y-Ghent U.K. 54°10N 2°14W 168 C5
Peña, Sierra de la Spain 42°32N 0°45W 196 C4
Peña de Francia, Sierra de la Spain 40°32N 6°10W 194 E4
Peñafiel Portugal 41°12N 8°17W 194 D2
Peñafiel Spain 41°35N 4°7W 194 D6
Peñaflor Spain 37°43N 5°21W 195 H5
Penal Trin. & Tob. 10°9N 61°29W 323 t
Peñalara Spain 40°51N 3°57W 194 E7
Peñalolén Chile 33°28S 70°32W 137 B2
Penalva Brazil 3°18S 45°10W 332 B2
Penal/Debe □ Trin. & Tob. 10°14N 61°27W 323 t
Penamacôr Portugal 40°10N 7°10W 194 E3
Penang = Pinang Malaysia 5°25N 100°15E 237 c
Penápolis Brazil 21°30S 50°0W 335 A6
Peñaranda de Bracamonte Spain 40°53N 5°13W 194 E5
Peñarroya Spain 40°25N 0°40W 196 E4
Peñarroya-Pueblonuevo Spain 38°19N 5°16W 195 G5
Penarth U.K. 51°26N 3°11W 169 F4
Peñas, C. de Spain 43°42N 5°52W 194 B5
Peñas, G. de Chile 47°0S 75°0W 336 C2
Peñas, Pta. Venezuela 11°17N 62°0W 329 A5
Peñas de San Pedro Spain 38°44N 2°0W 197 G3
Peñas del Chache Canary Is. 29°6N 13°33W 153 e2
Peñausende Spain 41°17N 5°52W 194 D5
Pench → India 21°17N 79°10E 244 D4
Pench △ India 21°45N 79°20E 243 J8
Pench'i = Benxi China 41°20N 123°48E 224 B1
Pend Oreille → U.S.A. 49°4N 117°37W 304 B5
Pend Oreille, L. U.S.A. 48°10N 116°21W 304 B5
Pendalofos Greece 40°14N 21°12E 202 F5
Pendé → C.A.R. 7°55N 16°36E 264 A3
Pendembu Eastern, S. Leone 8°10N 10°42W 262 D2
Pendembu Northern, S. Leone 9°7N 11°14W 262 D2
Pendências Brazil 5°15S 36°43W 332 C4
Pender B. Australia 16°45S 122°42E 278 C3
Pendik Turkey 40°53N 29°13E 203 F13
Pendjari → Benin 10°55N 0°50E 263 C5
Pendjari △ Benin 11°15N 1°32E 263 C5
Pendleton Ind., U.S.A. 40°0N 85°45W 311 E11
Pendleton Oreg., U.S.A. 45°40N 118°47W 304 D4
Pendopo Indonesia 3°16S 103°52E 234 C2
Pendra India 22°46N 81°57E 243 H9
Pendzhikent = Panjakent Tajikistan 39°29N 67°37E 217 E7
Penebangan Indonesia 1°13S 109°15E 235 C3
Peneda-Gerês △ Portugal 41°57N 8°15W 194 D2
Penedo Brazil 10°15S 36°36W 332 D4
Penelokan Indonesia 8°17S 115°22E 231 J18
Penetanguishene Canada 44°50N 79°55W 312 B5
Penfield U.S.A. 41°13N 78°35W 312 E6
Penfro = Pembroke U.K. 51°41N 4°55W 169 F3
Peng Chau China 22°17N 114°2E 219 a
Peng Siang → Singapore 1°24N 103°43E 138 A2
Peng'an China 31°2N 106°22E 228 B6
Penganga → India 19°53N 79°9E 244 E4
Penge Kasai-Or., Dem. Rep. of the Congo 5°30S 24°33E 265 D4
Penge Sud-Kivu, Dem. Rep. of the Congo 4°27S 28°25E 268 C2
Penge London, U.K. 51°24N 0°3W 125 B3
P'enghu □ Taiwan 23°30N 119°30E 225 C1
P'enghu Ch'üntou Taiwan 23°34N 119°30E 225 C1
P'enghu Tao Taiwan 23°34N 119°37E 225 C1
Penglai China 37°48N 120°42E 227 F11
Pengshan China 30°14N 103°58E 228 B4
Pengshui China 29°17N 108°12E 228 C7
Penguin Australia 41°8S 146°6E 281 G4
Pengxi China 30°44N 105°45E 228 B5
Pengze China 29°52N 116°32E 229 C11
Pengzhou China 31°4N 103°32E 228 B4
Penha Brazil 22°49S 43°17W 135 A1
Penhalonga Zimbabwe 18°52S 32°40E 269 F3
Peniche Portugal 39°19N 9°22W 195 F1
Penicuik U.K. 55°50N 3°13W 121 B2
Penida, Nusa Indonesia 8°45S 115°30E 231 K18
Peninnes, Alpes = Pennine, Alpi Alps 46°4N 7°30E 179 J3
Peninsular Malaysia □ Malaysia 4°0N 102°0E 237 L4
Peñíscola Spain 40°22N 0°24E 196 E5
Penitente, Serra do Brazil 8°45S 46°20W 332 C2
Penjaringan Indonesia 6°7S 106°48E 122 A1
Pēnjwīn Iraq 35°37N 45°56E 213 E11
Penki = Benxi China 41°20N 123°48E 224 B1
Penkridge U.K. 52°44N 2°6W 168 E5
Penmarch France 47°49N 4°21W 172 E2
Penmarch, Pte. de France 47°48N 4°22W 172 E2
Penn = Penn Hills U.S.A. 40°28N 79°52W 312 F5

Penn Hills *U.S.A.* 40°28N 79°52W **312** F5
Penn Station *New York, U.S.A.* **132** c2
Penn Yan *U.S.A.* 42°40N 77°3W **312** D7
Penna, Punta della *Italy* 42°10N 14°43E **199** F11
Pennant *Canada* 50°32N 108°14W **297** C7
Penne *Italy* 42°27N 13°55E **199** F10
Penner → *India* 14°35N 80°10E **245** G5
Penneshaw *Australia* 35°44S 137°56E **282** C2
Pennine, Alpi *Alps* 46°4N 7°30E **179** J3
Pennines *U.K.* 54°45N 2°27W **168** C5
Pennington *U.S.A.* 39°15N 121°47W **306** F5
Pennington → *Nigeria* 4°45N 5°35E **263** E6
Pennino, Mte. *Italy* 43°6N 12°53E **199** E9
Pennsburg *U.S.A.* 40°23N 75°29W **313** F9
Pennsylvania □ *U.S.A.* 40°45N 77°30W **309** E15
Pennsylvania Avenue
Washington, D.C., U.S.A. **143** b2
Penville *U.S.A.* 40°30N 85°9W **311** D11
Penny *Canada* 53°51N 121°20W **296** C4
Peno *Russia* 57°2N 32°49E **188** D7
Penobscot → *U.S.A.* 44°30N 68°48W **309** C19
Penobscot B. *U.S.A.* 44°35N 68°50W **309** C19
Penola *Australia* 37°25S 140°48E **282** D4
Penong *Australia* 31°56S 133°1E **279** F5
Penonomé *Panama* 8°31N 80°21W **320** E3
Penot, Mt. *Vanuatu* 16°20S 167°31E **287** E5
Penrhyn *Cook Is.* 9°0S 158°0W **289** H12
Penrith *N.S.W., Australia* 33°43S 150°38E **283** B9
Penrith *Cumb., U.K.* 54°40N 2°45W **168** C5
Penryn *U.K.* 50°9N 5°7W **169** G2
Pensacola *U.S.A.* 30°25N 87°13W **317** E2
Pensacola B. *U.S.A.* 30°25N 87°5W **317** E2
Pensacola Mts. *Antarctica* 84°0S 40°0W **151** E1
Pense *Canada* 50°25N 104°59W **297** C8
Penshurst *Australia* 37°49S 142°20E **282** D5
Pensiangan *Malaysia* 4°33N 116°19E **235** B5
Pentadaktylos *Cyprus* 35°20N 33°20E **207** E9
Pentagon *U.S.A.* 38°53N 77°3W **143** B2
Pentecost = Pentecôte
Vanuatu 15°42S 168°10E **287** E6
Pentecostes *Brazil* 3°48S 39°17W **332** B4
Pentecôte *Vanuatu* 15°42S 168°10E **287** E6
Penticton *Canada* 49°30N 119°38W **296** D5
Pentland *Australia* 20°32S 145°25E **280** C4
Pentland Firth *U.K.* 58°43N 3°10W **167** C5
Pentland Hills *U.K.* 55°48N 3°25W **167** F5
Penukonda *India* 14°5N 77°38E **245** G3
Penza *Russia* 53°15N 45°5E **190** D7
Penza □ *Russia* 52°50N 44°50E **190** D7
Penzance *U.K.* 50°7N 5°33W **169** G2
Penzberg *Germany* 47°45N 11°22E **179** H7
Penzhino *Russia* 63°30N 167°55E **215** C17
Penzhinskaya Guba
Russia 61°30N 163°0E **215** C17
Penzing *Austria* 48°11N 16°18E **142** A1
Penzlin *Germany* 53°30N 13°5E **178** B9
People's Park *China* 31°13N 121°28E **138** B1
People's Square *China* 31°13N 121°28E **138** B1
Peoria *Ariz., U.S.A.* 33°43N 112°14W **305** K7
Peoria *Ill., U.S.A.* 40°42N 89°36W **310** D7
Peoria Heights *U.S.A.* 40°45N 89°35W **310** D7
Peotone *U.S.A.* 41°20N 87°48W **311** C9
Pepacton Res. *U.S.A.* 42°5N 74°58W **313** D10
Pepani → *S. Africa* 25°49S 22°47E **270** C3
Pepeekeo *U.S.A.* 19°51N 155°6W **302** D6
Pepel *S. Leone* 8°40N 13°5W **262** D2
Peqin *Albania* 41°3N 19°44E **202** E3
Pera Hd. *Australia* 12°55S 141°37E **280** A3
Perabumulih *Indonesia* 3°27S 104°15E **234** C2
Perachora *Greece* 38°2N 22°56E **204** C4
Perachori *Greece* 38°21N 20°43E **207** C2
Perak □ *Malaysia* 5°0N 101°0E **237** K3
Perak → *Malaysia* 4°0N 100°50E **237** K3
Perales del Alfambra *Spain* 40°38N 1°0W **196** E4
Perales del Puerto *Spain* 40°10N 6°40W **194** E4
Perales del Río *Spain* 40°18N 3°38W **127** C2
Perama *Kerkyra, Greece* 39°34N 19°54E **206** B9
Perama *Kriti, Greece* 35°20N 24°40E **207** E11
Perancak *Indonesia* 8°24S 114°37E **231** J17
Peräpohjola *Finland* 66°16N 26°10E **160** C22
Perast *Montenegro* 42°31N 18°47E **202** D2
Peratia *Greece* 38°49N 20°45E **207** B2
Peravillo *Mexico City, Mexico* **128** a3
Percé *Canada* 48°31N 64°13W **299** C7
Perche *France* 48°31N 1°1E **172** D8
Perche, Collines du *France* 48°30N 0°40E **171** B4
Perche □ *France* 48°24N 0°46E **172** D7
Perchtoldsdorf *Austria* 48°7N 16°17E **142** B1
Percival Lakes *Australia* 21°25S 125°0E **278** D4
Percy *Manche, France* 48°55N 1°11W **172** D5
Percy *Ill., U.S.A.* 38°5N 89°41W **310** F7
Percy Is. *Australia* 21°39S 150°16E **280** C5
Perdido → *Argentina* 42°55S 67°0W **336** B3
Perdido, Mte. *Spain* 42°40N 0°5E **196** C5
Perdizes *Brazil* 23°32S 46°39W **137** B2
Perdu, Mt. = Perdido, Mte.
Spain 42°40N 0°5E **196** C5
Perechyn *Ukraine* 48°44N 22°28E **182** B7
Perehinske *Ukraine* 48°49N 24°11E **183** B9
Pereira *Colombia* 4°49N 75°43W **328** C2
Perelazovskiy *Russia* 49°8N 42°35E **191** F6
Peremul Par *India* 11°10N 72°4E **245** J1
Peremyshl = Przemyśl
Poland 49°50N 22°45E **185** J9
Perené → *Peru* 11°9S 74°14W **330** C3
Perenjori *Australia* 29°26S 116°16E **279** E2
Peresecina *Moldova* 47°16N 28°46E **183** C13
Pereslavl-Zalesskiy
Russia 56°45N 38°50E **188** D10
Peretu *Romania* 44°3N 25°5E **183** F10
Pereyaslav-Khmelnytskyy
Ukraine 50°3N 31°28E **189** G6
Pereyma *Ukraine* 48°4N 29°30E **183** B14
Pérez, I. *Mexico* 22°24N 89°42W **319** C7
Perg *Austria* 48°15N 14°38E **180** C7
Pergamino *Argentina* 33°52S 60°30W **334** C3
Pergamon Museum *Berlin, Germany* **115** a4
Pergau → *Malaysia* 5°23N 102°2E **237** K3
Perge *Turkey* 37°3N 30°56E **250** A1
Pergine Valsugana *Italy* 46°4N 11°14E **199** B8
Pérgola *Italy* 43°34N 12°50E **199** E9
Perham *U.S.A.* 46°36N 95°34W **308** B6
Perhentian, Kepulauan
Malaysia 5°54N 102°42E **237** K4
Peri → *Turkey* 38°53N 39°52E **213** C8
Periam *Romania* 46°2N 20°52E **182** D5
Péribonka → *Canada* 48°45N 72°5W **299** C5
Péribonka, L. *Canada* 50°1N 71°10W **299** B5
Péribonka, La Centrale de
Canada 49°30N 71°10W **299** C5
Perico *Argentina* 24°20S 65°5W **334** A2
Pericos *Mexico* 25°3N 107°42W **318** B3
Périers *France* 49°11N 1°25W **172** C5
Périgord *France* 45°0N 0°40E **174** D4
Périgord-Limousin ⌂
France 45°40N 0°50E **174** C4
Périgueux *France* 45°10N 0°42E **174** C4
Perijá, Sierra de *Colombia* 9°30N 73°3W **328** B3
Perijá △ *Venezuela* 9°30N 72°55W **328** B3
Peringat *Malaysia* 6°2N 102°17E **237** J4
Perisher Valley *Australia* 36°27S 148°25E **283** D8
Peristera *Greece* 39°15N 23°58E **204** B5
Peristeri *Greece* 38°1N 23°42E **112** A2
Peristerona → *Cyprus* 35°8N 33°5E **207** E9
Perito Moreno *Argentina* 46°36S 70°56W **336** C2
Perito Moreno △
Argentina 47°49S 72°17W **336** C2
Peritoró *Brazil* 4°20S 44°18W **332** B3
Perivale *U.K.* 51°31N 0°18W **125** A2
Perivol = Dragovishtitsa
Bulgaria 42°22N 22°39E **202** D6
Periyakulam *India* 10°5N 77°30E **245** J3
Periyar → *India* 10°15N 76°10E **245** J3
Periyar, L. *India* 9°25N 77°10E **245** K3
Periyar △ *India* 9°25N 77°10E **245** K3
Perk *Belgium* 50°56N 4°30E **116** A2
Perkasie *U.S.A.* 40°22N 75°18W **313** F9
Perković *Croatia* 43°41N 16°10E **199** E13
Perlach *Germany* 48°5N 11°35E **131** B2
Perlacher Forst *Germany* 48°4N 11°32E **131** B2
Perlas, Arch. de las *Panama* 8°41N 79°7W **320** E4
Perlas, Punta de *Nic.* 12°30N 83°30W **320** D3
Perleberg *Germany* 53°5N 11°52E **178** B7
Perlez *Serbia* 45°11N 20°22E **182** E5
Perlis □ *Malaysia* 6°30N 100°15E **237** J2
Perm *Russia* 58°0N 56°10E **186** C10
Përmet *Albania* 40°15N 20°21E **202** F4
Permskoye = Komsomolsk-na-
Amur *Russia* 50°30N 137°0E **219** A16
Pernambuco = Recife *Brazil* 8°0S 35°0W **332** C5
Pernambuco □ *Brazil* 8°0S 37°0W **332** C4
Pernambuco Abyssal Plain
Atl. Oc. 5°0S 24°0W **152** G9
Pernatty Lagoon
Australia 31°30S 137°12E **282** A2
Pernik *Bulgaria* 42°35N 23°2E **202** D7
Pernik □ *Bulgaria* 42°35N 23°2E **202** D7
Pernov = Pärnu *Estonia* 58°28N 24°33E **188** C3
Pero *Italy* 45°30N 9°5E **128** A1
Peron Is. *Australia* 13°9S 130°4E **278** B5
Peron Pen. *Australia* 26°0S 113°10E **279** E1
Péronne *France* 49°55N 2°57E **173** C9
Peropak, Bukit *Singapore* 1°19N 103°42E **138** B2
Perosa Argentina *Italy* 44°58N 7°10E **198** D4
Perovo *Russia* 55°44N 37°45E **129** B3
Perovsk = Qyzylorda
Kazakhstan 44°48N 65°28E **217** D7
Perow *Canada* 54°35N 126°10W **296** C3
Perparim = Pogradec
Albania 40°54N 20°37E **202** F4
Perpignan *France* 42°42N 2°53E **174** F6
Perrégaux = Mohammadia
Algeria 35°33N 0°3E **261** A5
Perrine *U.S.A.* 25°36N 80°21W **317** K9
Perris *U.S.A.* 33°47N 117°14W **307** M9
Perros-Guirec *France* 48°49N 3°28W **172** D3
Perry *Fla., U.S.A.* 30°7N 83°35W **316** E6
Perry *Ga., U.S.A.* 32°28N 83°44W **316** C6
Perry *Iowa, U.S.A.* 41°51N 94°6W **310** C2
Perry *Mich., U.S.A.* 42°50N 84°13W **311** B12
Perry *Mo., U.S.A.* 39°26N 91°40W **310** E5
Perry *N.Y., U.S.A.* 42°42N 78°0W **312** D7
Perry *Okla., U.S.A.* 36°17N 97°14W **314** C6
Perrysburg *U.S.A.* 41°34N 83°38W **311** C13
Perryton *U.S.A.* 36°24N 100°48W **314** C4
Perryville *Alaska, U.S.A.* 55°55N 159°9W **303** J8
Perryville *Mo., U.S.A.* 37°43N 89°52W **310** G7
Persan *France* 49°9N 2°16E **173** C9
Persberg *Sweden* 59°47N 14°15E **162** E8
Perşembe *Turkey* 41°5N 37°46E **212** B7
Persepolis *Iran* 29°55N 52°50E **247** D7
Perseverancia *Bolivia* 14°44S 62°48W **331** C5
Pershing Square *Los Angeles, U.S.A.* **127** c1
Pershotravensk *Ukraine* 50°13N 27°40E **177** C14
Pershotravnevoye =
Pershotravensk
Ukraine 50°13N 27°40E **177** C14
Persia = Iran ■ *Asia* 33°0N 53°0E **247** C7
Persian Gulf *Asia* 27°0N 50°0E **247** E6
Perstorp *Sweden* 56°10N 13°25E **163** H7
Pertek *Turkey* 38°51N 39°19E **213** C8
Perth *W. Austral.,*
Australia 31°57S 115°52E **279** F2
Perth *Ont., Canada* 44°55N 76°15W **313** B8
Perth *Perth & Kinr., U.K.* 56°24N 3°26W **167** E5
Perth & Kinross □ *U.K.* 56°45N 3°55W **167** E5
Perth Amboy *U.S.A.* 40°30N 74°15W **313** F10
Perth-Andover *Canada* 46°44N 67°42W **299** C6
Pertuis *France* 43°42N 5°30E **175** E9
Pertusato, C. *France* 41°21N 9°11E **175** G13
Pertusella *Italy* 45°35N 9°3E **128** A1
Peru *Ill., U.S.A.* 41°20N 89°8W **310** C7
Peru *Ind., U.S.A.* 40°45N 86°4W **311** D10
Peru *N.Y., U.S.A.* 44°35N 73°32W **313** B11
Peru ■ *S. Amer.* 4°0S 75°0W **328** D3
Peru Basin *Pac. Oc.* 20°0S 95°0W **289** J18
Peru-Chile Trench *Pac. Oc.* 20°0S 72°0W **326** E3
Perúgia *Italy* 43°7N 12°23E **199** E9
Perušić *Croatia* 44°40N 15°22E **199** D12
Peruvian Vale *St. Vincent* 13°11N 61°12W **323** n
Pervomaysk *Russia* 54°56N 43°58E **190** C6
Pervomaysk *Ukraine* 48°10N 30°46E **189** H6
Pervomayskiy *Kazakhstan* 50°16N 82°0E **217** B10
Pervouralsk *Russia* 56°59N 59°59E **186** C10
Pervouralsky = Pervouralsk
Russia 56°59N 59°59E **186** C10
Pesada *Greece* 38°7N 20°35E **207** C2
Pesagot *West Bank* 31°54N 35°13E **123** A2
Pesanggrahag, Kali →
Indonesia 6°10S 106°44E **122** B1
Pésaro *Italy* 43°54N 12°55E **199** E9
Pescadores = P'enghu Ch'üntou
Taiwan 23°34N 119°30E **225** C1
Pescara *Italy* 42°28N 14°13E **199** F11
Pescara → *Italy* 42°28N 14°13E **199** F11
Peschanokopskoye *Russia* 46°14N 41°4E **191** G5
Peschanoye = Yashkul
Russia 46°11N 45°21E **191** G7
Peschiera Borromeo *Italy* 45°26N 9°19E **128** B2
Péscia *Italy* 43°54N 10°41E **198** E7
Pescina *Italy* 42°2N 13°39E **199** F10
Pesek, Pulau *Singapore* 1°17N 103°41E **138** C2
Peshawar *Pakistan* 34°2N 71°37E **242** B4
Peshkopi *Albania* 41°41N 20°25E **202** E4
Peshtera *Bulgaria* 42°2N 24°18E **203** D8
Peshtigo *U.S.A.* 45°3N 87°45W **308** C10
Peski *Russia* 51°14N 42°29E **190** E6
Peski *Turkmenistan* 38°11N 62°59E **216** E6
Pêso da Régua *Portugal* 41°10N 7°47W **194** D3
Pesochnya = Kirov *Russia* 54°3N 34°20E **188** E8
Pesqueira *Brazil* 8°20S 36°42W **332** C4
Pessac *France* 44°48N 0°37W **174** D3
Pest *Hungary* 47°29N 19°4E **117** B2
Pest □ *Hungary* 47°29N 19°5E **182** C4
Pesterzsébet *Hungary* 47°26N 19°6E **117** B2
Pesthidegkút *Hungary* 47°33N 18°57E **117** A1
Pestimre *Hungary* 47°24N 19°11E **117** B3
Pestlőrinc *Hungary* 47°26N 19°11E **117** B3
Pestovo = Zavolzhye
Russia 56°37N 43°26E **190** B6
Pestovo *Russia* 58°33N 35°42E **188** C8
Pestravka *Russia* 52°28N 49°57E **190** D9
Pestújhely *Hungary* 47°32N 19°7E **117** A2
Petah Tiqwa *Israel* 32°6N 34°53E **251** C3
Petalas *Greece* 38°25N 21°5E **207** C3
Petalidi *Greece* 36°57N 21°55E **204** E3
Petaling Jaya *Malaysia* 3°4N 101°42E **237** L3
Petaloudes *Greece* 36°18N 28°5E **206** E12
Petaluma *U.S.A.* 38°14N 122°39W **306** G4
Pétange *Lux.* 49°33N 5°55E **170** E5
Petare *Venezuela* 10°29N 66°49W **321** D6
Petaro *Pakistan* 25°31N 68°18E **242** G3
Petas *Helsinki, Finland* 60°15N 24°50E **121** B2
Petas *Greece* 39°10N 21°2E **204** B3
Petatlán *Mexico* 17°31N 101°16W **318** D4
Petauke *Zambia* 14°14S 31°20E **269** E3
Petawawa *Canada* 45°54N 77°17W **298** C4
Petén Itzá, L. *Guatemala* 16°58N 89°50W **320** C2
Peter I. *Br. Virgin Is.* 18°22N 64°35W **321** b
Peter I. Øy *Antarctica* 69°0S 91°0W **151** C16
Peter Pond L. *Canada* 55°55N 108°44W **297** B7
Peterbell *Canada* 48°36N 83°21W **298** C3
Peterborough *S. Austral.,*
Australia 32°58S 138°51E **282** B3
Peterborough *Ont.,*
Canada 44°20N 78°20W **312** B6
Peterborough *Peterborough,*
U.K. 52°35N 0°15W **169** E7
Peterborough *N.H.,*
U.S.A. 42°53N 71°57W **313** D13
Peterborough □ *U.K.* 52°35N 0°15W **169** E7
Peterculter *U.K.* 57°6N 2°16W **167** D6
Peterhead *U.K.* 57°31N 1°48W **167** D7
Peterhof = Petrodvorets
Russia 59°52N 29°54E **188** C5
Peterlee *U.K.* 54°47N 1°20W **168** C6
Petermann ⊙ *Australia* 24°58S 130°0E **279** E4
Petermann Bjerg
Greenland 73°7N 28°25W **154** C8
Petermann Gletscher
Greenland 80°30N 60°0W **154** A4
Petermann Ranges
Australia 26°0S 130°30E **279** E5
Peter's Mine *Guyana* 6°14N 59°20W **329** B6
Petersburg = Peterborough
Australia 32°58S 138°51E **282** B3
Petersburg *Alaska,*
U.S.A. 56°48N 132°58W **303** H14
Petersburg *Ill., U.S.A.* 40°1N 89°51W **310** D7
Petersburg *Ind., U.S.A.* 38°30N 87°17W **311** F9
Petersburg *Mich., U.S.A.* 41°54N 83°43W **311** C13
Petersburg *Pa., U.S.A.* 40°34N 78°3W **312** F6
Petersburg *Va., U.S.A.* 37°14N 77°24W **309** G15
Petersburg *W. Va., U.S.A.* 39°1N 79°5W **309** F14
Petersfield *U.K.* 51°1N 0°56W **169** F7
Petershagen *Germany* 52°23N 8°58E **178** C4
Petilia Policastro *Italy* 39°7N 16°48E **201** C9
Petit Batanga *Cameroon* 3°15N 9°54E **264** B1
Petit-Bourg *Guadeloupe* 16°11N 61°37W **322** e
Petit-Canal *Guadeloupe* 16°25N 61°31W **322** e
Petit Cul-de-Sac Marin
Guadeloupe 16°12N 61°33W **322** e
Petit Dominique *Grenada* 12°30N 61°24W **323** q
Petit-Goâve *Haiti* 18°27N 72°51W **321** C5
Petit Lac Manicouagan
Canada 51°25N 67°40W **299** B6
Petit Loango ⌂ *Gabon* 2°20S 9°40E **264** C1
Petit-Mécatina →
Canada 50°40N 59°30W **299** B8
Petit-Mécatina, Î. du
Canada 50°30N 59°25W **299** B8
Petit Piton *St. Lucia* 13°51N 61°5W **323** m
Petit Raffray *Mauritius* 20°0S 57°36E **272** e
Petit-Saguenay *Canada* 48°15N 70°4W **299** C5
Petit Saint Bernard, Col du
Italy 45°40N 6°52E **175** C10
Petit Saut, Barrage de
Fr. Guiana 5°0N 53°10W **329** C7
Petit Soufrière B. *Dominica* 15°23N 61°15W **323** k
Petitcodiac *Canada* 45°57N 65°11W **299** C6
Petite Anse *Martinique* 14°28N 61°4W **322** j
Petite-Île *Réunion* 21°20S 55°35E **272** f
Petite Martinique *Grenada* 12°31N 61°23W **323** q
Petite Rivière *Mauritius* 20°11S 57°26E **272** e
Petite Savane *Dominica* 15°15N 61°17W **323** k
Petite Terre = Pamandzi
Mayotte 12°47S 45°16E **272** b
Petite Terre, Îles de la
Guadeloupe 16°13N 61°9W **322** e
Petites-Anses *Guadeloupe* 15°51N 61°38W **322** e
Petitjean = Sidi Kacem
Morocco 34°12N 5°42W **260** B3
Petitot → *Canada* 60°14N 123°29W **296** A4
Petitsikapau L. *Canada* 54°37N 66°25W **299** B6
Petlad *India* 22°30N 72°45E **242** H5
Peto *Mexico* 20°8N 88°55W **319** C7
Petone *N.Z.* 41°13S 174°53E **284** H3
Petorca *Chile* 32°15S 70°56W **334** C1
Petoskey *U.S.A.* 45°22N 84°57W **309** C11
Petra *Jordan* 30°20N 35°22E **251** H6
Petra *Spain* 39°37N 3°6E **206** B4
Petra, Ostrov *Russia* 76°15N 118°30E **215** B12
Petra Velikogo, Zaliv
Russia 42°40N 132°0E **220** C6
Petre, Pt. *Canada* 43°50N 77°9W **312** C7
Petrel = Petrer *Spain* 38°30N 0°46W **197** G4
Petrella, Monte *Italy* 41°18N 13°40E **200** A6
Petrer *Spain* 38°30N 0°46W **197** G4
Petreto-Bicchisano *France* 41°47N 8°58E **175** G12
Petrich *Bulgaria* 41°24N 23°13E **202** E7
Petrified Forest △ *U.S.A.* 35°0N 109°30W **305** J9
Petrijanec *Croatia* 46°23N 16°17E **199** B13
Petrikov = Pyetrikaw
Belarus 52°11N 28°29E **177** B15
Petrila *Romania* 45°29N 23°29E **183** E8
Petrillo Music Shell *U.S.A.* **119** c2
Petrinja *Croatia* 45°28N 16°18E **199** C13
Petrodvorets *Russia* 59°52N 29°54E **188** C5
Petrograd = Sankt-Peterburg
Russia 59°55N 30°20E **137** B1
Petrogradskaya Storona
Russia 59°56N 30°20E **137** B2
Petrolândia *Brazil* 9°5S 38°20W **332** C4
Petrolia *Canada* 42°54N 82°9W **312** D2
Petrolina *Brazil* 9°24S 40°30W **332** C3
Petromaryevka = Pervomaysk
Ukraine 48°10N 30°46E **189** H6
Petropavl *Kazakhstan* 54°53N 69°13E **217** B7
Petropavlovsk = Petropavl
Kazakhstan 54°53N 69°13E **217** B7
Petropavlovsk-Kamchatskiy
Russia 53°3N 158°43E **215** D16
Petropavlovskiy = Akhtubinsk
Russia 48°13N 46°7E **191** F8
Petropavlovsky = Severouralsk
Russia 60°9N 59°57E **186** B10
Petrópolis *Brazil* 22°33S 43°9W **333** F3
Petroşani *Romania* 45°28N 23°20E **183** E8
Petroupoli *Greece* 38°3N 23°40E **112** A2
Petrova Gora *Croatia* 45°15N 15°45E **199** C12
Petrovac *Montenegro* 42°13N 18°57E **202** D2
Petrovac *Serbia* 44°22N 21°26E **202** B5
Petrovaradin *Serbia* 45°16N 19°55E **182** E4
Petrovgrad = Zrenjanin
Serbia 45°22N 20°23E **182** E5
Petrovice *Czech Rep.* 50°2N 14°33E **135** B3
Petrovsk *Russia* 52°22N 45°19E **190** D7
Petrovsk-Port = Makhachkala
Russia 43°0N 47°30E **191** J8
Petrovsk-Zabaykalskiy
Russia 51°20N 108°55E **215** D11
Petrovskaya *Russia* 45°25N 37°58E **189** K9
Petrovskiy Park *Russia* 55°47N 37°34E **129** B2
Petrovsko-Razumovskoye
Russia 55°49N 37°34E **129** B2
Petrovskoye = Svetlograd
Russia 45°25N 42°58E **191** H6
Petrovsky Zavod = Petrovsk-
Zabaykalskiy *Russia* 51°20N 108°55E **215** D11
Petrozavodsk *Russia* 61°41N 34°20E **188** B8
Petrus Steyn *S. Africa* 27°38S 28°8E **271** C4
Petrusburg *S. Africa* 29°4S 25°26E **270** C4
Petsamo = Pechenga
Russia 69°29N 31°4E **160** B24
Pettycur *U.K.* 56°4N 3°10W **121** A2
Petukhovo *Russia* 55°6N 67°58E **217** A7
Petuna = Fuyu *China* 45°12N 124°43E **227** B13
Petzeck *Austria* 46°57N 12°48E **180** E5
Peumo *Chile* 34°21S 71°12W **334** C1
Peureulak *Indonesia* 4°48N 97°45E **234** B1
Peusangan → *Indonesia* 5°16N 96°51E **234** A1
Peutie *Belgium* 50°56N 4°27E **116** A2
Pevek *Russia* 69°41N 171°19E **215** C18
Pevely *U.S.A.* 38°17N 90°24W **310** F6
Peveragno *Italy* 44°20N 7°37E **198** D4
Peyrehorade *France* 43°34N 1°7W **174** E2
Peyruis *France* 44°1N 5°56E **175** D9
Pézenas *France* 43°28N 3°24E **174** E7
Pezinok *Slovak Rep.* 48°17N 17°17E **181** C10
Pfaffenhofen *Germany* 48°31N 11°31E **179** G7
Pfälzerwald ⌂ *Germany* 49°18N 9°55E **179** F5
Pfarrkirchen *Germany* 48°25N 12°56E **179** G8
Pfaueninsel *Germany* 52°26N 13°7E **115** B1
Pfeffenhausen *Germany* 48°39N 11°58E **179** G7
Pforzheim *Germany* 48°52N 8°41E **179** G4
Pfullendorf *Germany* 47°55N 9°15E **179** H5
Pfungstadt *Germany* 49°48N 8°35E **179** F4
Pha Taem △ *Thailand* 15°32N 105°30E **236** E5
Phaestos *Greece* 35°2N 24°50E **207** E6
Phagwara *India* 31°10N 75°40E **242** D6
Phala *Botswana* 23°45S 26°50E **270** B4
Phalaborwa *S. Africa* 23°57S 31°7E **271** B5
Phalera = Phulera *India* 26°52N 75°16E **242** F6
Phalodi *India* 27°12N 72°24E **242** F5
Phalsbourg *France* 48°46N 7°15E **173** D14
Phaltan *India* 17°59N 74°26E **244** F2
Phaluai, Ko *Thailand* 9°32N 99°41E **237** b
Phan *Thailand* 19°28N 99°43E **236** C2
Phan Rang-Thap Cham
Vietnam 11°34N 109°0E **237** G7
Phan Ri Cua *Vietnam* 11°16N 108°40E **237** G7
Phan Si Pan *Vietnam* 22°18N 103°46E **236** A4
Phan Thiet *Vietnam* 11°1N 108°9E **237** G7
Phan Thiet, Vinh *Vietnam* 10°53N 108°5E **237** G7
Phan Wa, Laem *Thailand* 7°47N 98°25E **237** a
Phanae *Greece* 38°8N 25°57E **205** C7
Phanat Nikhom *Thailand* 13°27N 101°11E **236** F3
Phangan, Ko *Thailand* 9°45N 100°0E **237** H3
Phangnga *Thailand* 8°28N 98°30E **237** H2
Phangnga, Ao *Thailand* 8°16N 98°33E **237** a
Phanom Sarakham
Thailand 13°45N 101°21E **236** F3
Phaphund *India* 26°36N 79°28E **243** F8
Pharenda *India* 27°5N 83°17E **243** F10
Pharr *U.S.A.* 26°12N 98°11W **314** H5
Phatthalung *Thailand* 7°39N 100°6E **237** J3
Phawngpui Blue Mountain △
India 22°45N 93°5E **241** D4
Phaya Thai *Thailand* 13°45N 100°37E **113** B2
Phayam, Ko *Thailand* 9°44N 98°25E **237** H2
Phayao *Thailand* 19°11N 99°55E **236** C2
Phelps *U.S.A.* 42°58N 77°3W **312** D7
Phelps L. *Canada* 59°15N 103°15W **297** B8
Phenix City *U.S.A.* 32°28N 85°1W **316** C4
Phet Buri = Phetchaburi
Thailand 13°1N 99°55E **236** F2
Phetchabun *Thailand* 16°25N 101°8E **236** D3
Phetchabun, Thiu Khao
Thailand 16°0N 101°20E **236** E3
Phetchaburi *Thailand* 13°1N 99°55E **236** F2
Phi Phi, Ko *Thailand* 7°45N 98°46E **237** J2
Phiafay *Laos* 14°48N 106°0E **236** E6
Phibun Mangsahan
Thailand 15°14N 105°14E **236** E5
Phichai *Thailand* 17°22N 100°10E **236** D3
Phichit *Thailand* 16°26N 100°22E **236** D3
Phihai *Pakistan* 24°50N 67°8E **123** A2
Philadelphia *Miss., U.S.A.* 32°46N 89°7W **315** E10
Philadelphia *N.Y., U.S.A.* 44°9N 75°43W **313** B9
Philadelphia *Pa., U.S.A.* 39°57N 75°9W **313** G9
Philip *U.S.A.* 44°2N 101°40W **308** C3
Philip Smith Mts. *U.S.A.* 68°0N 148°0W **303** C10
Philipi *Greece* 41°1N 24°16E **203** E8
Philippeville = Skikda
Algeria 36°50N 6°58E **261** A6
Philippeville *Belgium* 50°12N 4°33E **170** D4
Philippi *U.S.A.* 39°9N 80°3W **309** F13
Philippi L. *Australia* 24°20S 138°55E **280** C2
Philippine Basin *Pac. Oc.* 17°0N 132°0E **288** F5
Philippine Sea *Pac. Oc.* 18°0N 125°0E **288** F4
Philippine Trench = Mindanao
Trench *Pac. Oc.* 12°0N 126°6E **232** C5
Philippines ■ *Asia* 12°0N 123°0E **232** E4
Philippolis *S. Africa* 30°15S 25°16E **270** D4
Philippopolis = Plovdiv
Bulgaria 42°8N 24°44E **203** D8
Philipsburg *Qué., Canada* 45°2N 73°5W **313** A11
Philipsburg *St.-Maarten* 18°3N 63°5W **322** a
Philipsburg *Mont.,*
U.S.A. 46°20N 113°18W **304** C7
Philipsburg *Pa., U.S.A.* 40°54N 78°13W **312** F6
Philipstown = Daingean
Ireland 53°18N 7°17W **166** C4
Philipstown *S. Africa* 30°28S 24°30E **270** D3
Phillip B. *Australia* 33°58S 151°14E **139** B2
Phillip I. *Australia* 38°30S 145°12E **283** E6
Phillips *U.S.A.* 45°42N 90°24W **308** C8
Phillipsburg *Ga., U.S.A.* 31°25N 83°30W **316** D6
Phillipsburg *Kans., U.S.A.* 39°45N 99°19W **308** F4
Phillipsburg *N.J., U.S.A.* 40°42N 75°12W **313** F9
Philmont *U.S.A.* 42°15N 73°39W **313** D11
Philomath *Ga., U.S.A.* 33°44N 82°59W **316** B7
Philomath *Oreg., U.S.A.* 44°32N 123°22W **304** D2
Phimai *Thailand* 15°13N 102°30E **236** E4
Phitsanulok *Thailand* 16°50N 100°12E **236** D3
Phnom Kulen △
Cambodia 13°38N 104°15E **236** F5
Phnom Penh *Cambodia* 11°33N 104°55E **237** G5
Phnum Penh = Phnom Penh
Cambodia 11°33N 104°55E **237** G5
Pho, Laem *Thailand* 6°55N 101°19E **237** J3
Phoenicia *U.S.A.* 42°5N 74°14W **313** D10
Phoenix *Mauritius* 20°17S 57°30E **272** e
Phoenix *Ariz., U.S.A.* 33°26N 112°4W **305** K7
Phoenix *Ill., U.S.A.* 41°36N 87°37W **119** D3
Phoenix *N.Y., U.S.A.* 43°14N 76°18W **313** C8
Phoenix Is. *Kiribati* 3°30S 172°0W **277** A16
Phoenix Park *Ireland* 53°21N 6°20W **120** A2
Phoenixville *U.S.A.* 40°8N 75°31W **313** F9
Phon *Thailand* 15°49N 102°36E **236** E4
Phong → *Thailand* 16°23N 102°56E **236** D4
Phong Nha -Ke Bang △
Vietnam 17°30N 106°10E **236** D6
Phong Saly *Laos* 21°42N 102°9E **228** G4
Phong Tho *Vietnam* 22°32N 103°21E **236** A4
Phonhong *Laos* 18°30N 102°25E **236** C4
Phonsavan *Laos* 19°27N 103°10E **236** C4
Phonum *Thailand* 8°49N 98°48E **237** H2
Phosphate Hill *Australia* 21°53S 139°58E **280** C2
Photharam *Thailand* 13°41N 99°51E **236** F2
Phra Kaeo *Bangkok, Thailand* **113** B2
Phra Khanong *Thailand* 13°40N 100°36E **113** B2
Phra Nakhon *Thailand* 13°45N 100°30E **113** B2
Phra Nakhon Si Ayutthaya
Thailand 14°25N 100°30E **236** E3
Phra Pradaeng *Thailand* 13°39N 100°33E **113** C2
Phra Thong, Ko *Thailand* 9°5N 98°17E **237** H2
Phrae *Thailand* 18°7N 100°9E **236** C3
Phranakhon *Thailand* 13°44N 100°29E **113** B1
Phrom Phiram *Thailand* 17°2N 100°12E **236** D3
Phrom Thep, Laem *Thailand* 7°45N 98°19E **237** a
Phrygia *Turkey* 38°40N 30°0E **212** C4
Phu Bia *Laos* 19°10N 103°0E **236** C4
Phu Chong -Na Yoi △
Thailand 14°25N 105°30E **236** E5
Phu Hin Rong Kla △
Thailand 17°0N 100°59E **236** D3
Phu Kao -Phu Phan Kham △
Thailand 16°53N 102°31E **236** D4
Phu Kradung △ *Thailand* 17°2N 101°44E **236** D3
Phu Loi *Laos* 20°14N 103°14E **236** B4
Phu Luang △ *Thailand* 17°15N 101°29E **236** D3
Phu Ly *Vietnam* 20°35N 105°50E **228** G5
Phu My *Vietnam* 14°15N 109°5E **236** E7
Phu Pha Man △ *Thailand* 16°44N 101°50E **236** D3
Phu Phan △ *Thailand* 17°0N 103°56E **236** D4
Phu Quoc, Dao *Vietnam* 10°20N 104°0E **237** G4
Phu Sa Dok Bua △
Thailand 16°11N 104°45E **236** D5
Phu Sang △ *Thailand* 19°35N 100°19E **236** C3
Phu Tho *Vietnam* 21°24N 105°13E **228** G5
Phu Wiang △ *Thailand* 16°39N 102°23E **236** D4
Phuc Yen *Vietnam* 21°16N 105°45E **228** G5
Phuket *Thailand* 7°53N 98°24E **237** a
Phuket, Ko *Thailand* 8°0N 98°22E **237** a
Phul *India* 30°19N 75°14E **242** D6
Phulad *India* 25°38N 73°49E **242** G5
Phulbani *India* 20°28N 84°14E **244** D7
Phulbari *India* 25°55N 90°2E **243** G14
Phulchari *Bangla.* 25°11N 89°37E **241** C2
Phulera *India* 26°52N 75°16E **242** F6
Phulpur *India* 25°31N 82°49E **243** G10
Phunphin *Thailand* 9°7N 99°12E **237** H2
Phuntsholing *Bhutan* 26°51N 89°23E **243** F13
Phuphrabat *Thailand* 17°40N 102°45E **236** D4
Phuthaditjhaba *S. Africa* 28°29S 28°48E **271** C4
Phyu = Pyu *Burma* 18°30N 96°28E **241** F6
Pia ⊙ *Australia* 27°7S 116°23E **279** E2
Piaçabuçu *Brazil* 10°24S 36°25W **332** D4
Piacenza *Italy* 45°1N 9°40E **198** C6
Piai, Tanjung *Malaysia* 1°17N 103°30E **237** d
Piako → *N.Z.* 37°12S 175°30E **284** D4
Pian Cr. → *Australia* 30°2S 148°12E **281** E4
Pian-Upe ⌂ *Uganda* 1°44N 34°20E **268** B3
Piana *France* 42°15N 8°34E **175** F12
Pianella *Italy* 42°24N 14°2E **199** F11
Piangil *Australia* 35°5S 143°20E **282** C5
Pianosa *Puglia, Italy* 42°12N 15°44E **199** F12
Pianosa *Toscana, Italy* 42°35N 10°5E **198** F7
Piao'ertun *China* 41°50N 123°47E **227** D12
Piapot *Canada* 49°59N 109°8W **297** D7
Piarco *Trin. & Tob.* 10°35N 61°20W **323** t
Piarco Int. ✈ (POS)
Trin. & Tob. 10°36N 61°20W **323** t
Pias *Portugal* 38°1N 7°29W **195** G3
Piaseczno *Poland* 52°5N 21°2E **185** F8
Piaski *Poland* 51°8N 22°52E **185** G9
Piastów *Poland* 52°12N 20°48E **185** F7
Piatã *Brazil* 13°9S 41°48W **333** D3
Piatra *Romania* 43°51N 25°9E **183** G10
Piatra Craiului △
Romania 45°30N 25°12E **183** E10
Piatra Neamţ *Romania* 46°56N 26°21E **183** D11
Piatra Olt *Romania* 44°22N 24°16E **183** F9
Piauí □ *Brazil* 7°0S 43°0W **332** C3
Piauí → *Brazil* 6°38S 42°42W **332** C3
Piave → *Italy* 45°32N 12°44E **199** C9
Piazza Ármerina *Italy* 37°21N 14°20E **201** E7
Pibor → *South Sudan* 7°35N 33°0E **257** F3
Pibor Post *South Sudan* 6°47N 33°3E **257** F3
Pica *Chile* 20°35S 69°25W **330** E4
Picardie □ *France* 49°50N 3°0E **173** C10
Picardie, Plaine de *France* 50°0N 2°0E **173** C9
Picardy = Picardie □
France 49°50N 3°0E **173** C10
Picasso, Museu *Barcelona, Spain* **114** c2
Picayune *U.S.A.* 30°32N 89°41W **315** F10
Piccadilly *London, U.K.* **125** b3
Picerno *Italy* 40°38N 15°38E **201** B8
Pichhor *India* 25°58N 78°20E **243** G8
Pichilemu *Chile* 34°22S 72°0W **334** C1
Pichincha, □ *Ecuador* 0°10S 78°40W **328** D2
Pichor *India* 25°11N 78°11E **242** G8
Pickerel L. *Canada* 48°40N 91°25W **298** C1
Pickering *U.K.* 54°15N 0°46W **168** C7
Pickering, Vale of *U.K.* 54°14N 0°45W **168** C7
Pickle Lake *Canada* 51°30N 90°12W **298** B1
Pickwick L. *U.S.A.* 35°4N 88°15W **315** D10
Pico *Azores* 38°28N 28°20W **153** d1
Pico, Ponta do *Azores* 38°28N 28°25W **153** d1
Pico Bonito △ *Honduras* 15°34N 86°48W **320** C2
Pico da Neblina △ *Brazil* 0°19N 66°28W **328** C4
Pico Rivera *U.S.A.* 33°59N 118°5W **126** C4
Pico Truncado *Argentina* 46°40S 68°0W **336** C3
Picos = Colinas *Brazil* 6°0S 44°10W **332** C3
Picos *Brazil* 7°5S 41°28W **332** C3
Picos de Europa △ *Spain* 43°14N 4°59W **194** B6
Picota *Peru* 6°54S 76°24W **330** B2
Picton *N.S.W., Australia* 34°12S 150°34E **283** C9
Picton *Ont., Canada* 44°1N 77°9W **312** B7
Picton *N.Z.* 41°18S 174°3E **285** B9
Picton, I. *Chile* 55°2S 66°57W **336** E3
Pictou *Canada* 45°41N 62°42W **299** C7
Picture Butte *Canada* 49°55N 112°45W **296** D6
Pictured Rocks ⌂
U.S.A. 46°30N 86°30W **308** B10
Picuí *Brazil* 6°31S 36°21W **332** C4
Picún Leufú *Argentina* 39°30S 69°5W **336** A3
Pidbuzh *Ukraine* 49°19N 23°14E **185** J10
Pidurutalagala *Sri Lanka* 7°10N 80°50E **245** L5
Piechowice *Poland* 50°51N 15°36E **185** H2
Piedade *Rio de J., Brazil* 22°52S 43°18W **135** B1
Piedade *Lisboa, Portugal* 38°49N 9°16W **126** A1
Piedade, Cova da *Portugal* 38°40N 9°8W **126** A2
Piedecuesta *Colombia* 6°59N 73°3W **328** B3
Piedimonte Matese *Italy* 41°22N 14°22E **201** A7
Piedmont = Piemonte □
Italy 45°0N 8°0E **198** D5
Piedmont *Ala., U.S.A.* 33°55N 85°37W **316** B4
Piedmont *S.C., U.S.A.* 34°42N 82°28W **292** F11
Piedmont Park *U.S.A.* 33°47N 84°22W **113** B2
Piedra → *Spain* 41°18N 1°47W **196** D3
Piedra del Águila *Argentina* 40°2S 70°4W **336** B2
Piedra del Águila, Embalse
Argentina 40°15S 70°4W **336** B2
Piedra Lais *Venezuela* 3°10N 65°50W **328** C4
Piedrabuena *Spain* 39°0N 4°10W **195** G6
Piedrahita *Spain* 40°28N 5°23W **194** E5
Piedralaves *Spain* 40°19N 4°42W **194** E6
Piedras, R. de las → *Peru* 12°30S 69°15W **330** C4
Piedras Blancas *Spain* 43°33N 5°58W **194** B5
Piedras Negras *Mexico* 28°42N 100°31W **318** B4
Piedras Pt. *Phil.* 10°11N 118°48E **233** F2
Piekar = Piekary Śląskie
Poland 50°24N 18°57E **185** H5
Piekary Śląskie *Poland* 50°24N 18°57E **185** H5
Pieksämäki *Finland* 62°18N 27°10E **188** A4
Pielinen *Finland* 63°15N 29°40E **160** E23
Piemonte □ *Italy* 45°0N 8°0E **198** D5
Pienaarsrivier *S. Africa* 25°15S 28°18E **271** C4
Pieniężno *Poland* 54°14N 20°8E **184** D7
Pieninský △ *Europe* 49°25N 20°28E **181** B13
Pieńsk *Poland* 51°16N 15°2E **185** G2
Pienza *Italy* 43°4N 11°40E **199** E8
Piercefield *U.S.A.* 44°13N 74°35W **313** B10
Pierceland *Canada* 54°20N 109°46W **297** C7
Pieria □ *Greece* 40°13N 22°25E **202** F6
Pierpont *U.S.A.* 41°45N 80°34W **312** E4
Pierre *U.S.A.* 44°22N 100°21W **308** C3
Pierre-Buffière *France* 45°41N 1°22E **174** C5
Pierre-de-Bresse *France* 46°54N 5°13E **173** F12
Pierre Elliott Trudeau ✈ (YUL)
Canada 45°28N 73°44W **130** B1
Pierrefonds *Canada* 45°29N 73°51W **313** A11
Pierrefontaine-les-Varans
France 47°14N 6°32E **173** E13
Pierrefort *France* 44°55N 2°50E **174** D6
Pierrelatte *France* 44°23N 4°43E **175** D8
Pierson *U.S.A.* 29°14N 81°28W **317** F8
Piešťany *Slovak Rep.* 48°38N 17°55E **181** C10
Piesting → *Austria* 48°6N 16°40E **181** C9
Pieszyce *Poland* 50°43N 16°33E **185** H3
Piet Retief *S. Africa* 27°1S 30°50E **271** C5
Pietarsaari *Finland* 63°40N 22°43E **160** E20
Pieter Both *Mauritius* 20°11S 57°32E **272** e
Pietermaritzburg *S. Africa* 29°35S 30°25E **271** C5
Pietersburg = Polokwane
S. Africa 23°54S 29°25E **271** B4
Pietragalla *Italy* 40°45N 15°53E **201** B8
Pietralata *Italy* 41°55N 12°33E **136** B2
Pietrasanta *Italy* 43°57N 10°14E **198** E7
Pietroşiţa *Romania* 45°11N 25°26E **183** E10
Pietrosul, Vf. *Maramureş,*
Romania 47°35N 24°43E **183** C9
Pietrosul, Vf. *Suceava,*
Romania 47°12N 25°18E **183** C10
Pieve di Cadore *Italy* 46°26N 12°22E **199** B9
Pieve di Teco *Italy* 44°3N 7°56E **198** D4
Pievepélago *Italy* 44°12N 10°37E **198** D7
Pigaditsa *Greece* 39°59N 21°23E **202** G5
Pigeon *Guadeloupe* 16°9N 61°46W **322** e
Pigeon I. *India* 14°2N 74°20E **245** G2
Pigeon I. *St. Lucia* 14°5N 60°58W **323** m
Pigeon L. *Canada* 44°27N 78°30W **312** B6
Piges *Greece* 39°17N 21°25E **204** B3
Piggott *U.S.A.* 36°23N 90°11W **315** C9
Pigna *Italy* 43°56N 7°40E **198** E4
Pigüe *Argentina* 37°36S 62°25W **334** D3
Piha *N.Z.* 36°57S 174°28E **284** C3
Pihani *India* 27°36N 80°15E **243** F9
Pihlajamäki *Finland* 60°14N 24°56E **121** B2
Pihlajasaari *Finland* 60°8N 24°55E **121** C2
Pihlajavesi *Finland* 61°45N 28°45E **188** B5
Pijijiapan *Mexico* 15°42N 93°14W **319** D6
Pikalevo *Russia* 59°37N 34°9E **188** C8
Pikangikum *Canada* 51°49N 94°0W **297** C10
Pikes Peak *U.S.A.* 38°50N 105°3W **304** G11
Piketberg *S. Africa* 32°55S 18°40E **270** D2
Pikeville *U.S.A.* 37°29N 82°31W **309** G12
Pikit *Phil.* 7°4N 124°41E **233** H5
Pikou *China* 39°18N 122°22E **227** E12
Pikounda *Congo* 0°30N 16°44E **264** B3
Pikwitonei *Canada* 55°35N 97°9W **297** B9
Piła *Poland* 53°10N 16°48E **185** E3
Pila *Spain* 38°16N 1°11W **197** G3
Pilanesberg △ *S. Africa* 25°15S 27°4E **270** C4
Pilani *India* 28°22N 75°33E **242** E6
Pilar *Brazil* 9°36S 35°56W **332** C4
Pilar *Paraguay* 26°50S 58°20W **334** B4
Pilar *Capiz, Phil.* 11°29N 123°0E **233** F4
Pilar *Sorsogon, Phil.* 12°56N 123°40E **232** E4
Pilar de la Horadada *Spain* 37°52N 0°47W **197** H4
Pilares *Brazil* 22°52S 43°18W **135** B1
Pilas Group *Phil.* 6°45N 121°35E **233** H3
Pilat ⌂ *France* 45°20N 4°30E **175** C8
Pilawa *Poland* 51°57N 21°32E **185** G8
Pilaya → *Bolivia* 20°55S 64°4W **331** E5
Pilbara *Australia* 21°15S 118°16E **278** D2
Pilcomaya → *Paraguay* 25°21S 57°42W **334** B4
Pilea *Greece* 40°32N 22°59E **202** F6
Pilgrim's Rest *S. Africa* 24°55S 30°44E **271** B5
Pilgrimstad *Sweden* 62°57N 15°2E **162** B9
Pili *Greece* 36°50N 27°15E **205** E9
Pili *Phil.* 13°33N 123°19E **232** E4
Pilibhit *India* 28°40N 79°50E **243** E8
Pilica → *Poland* 51°52N 21°17E **185** G8
Pilio, Oros *Greece* 39°27N 23°3E **204** B5
Pilipinas = Philippines ■
Asia 12°0N 123°0E **232** E4
Pilis *Hungary* 47°17N 19°35E **182** C4
Pilisvörösvár *Hungary* 47°38N 18°56E **182** C3
Pilkhawa *India* 28°43N 77°42E **242** E7
Pillar B. *Ascension I.* 7°59S 14°21W **153** g
Pillaro *Ecuador* 1°10S 78°32W **328** D2
Pillau = Baltiysk *Russia* 54°41N 19°58E **184** D6
Pilliga *Australia* 30°21S 148°54E **281** E4
Pilos *Greece* 36°55N 21°42E **204** E3
Pilot Grove *U.S.A.* 38°53N 92°55W **310** F4
Pilot Mound *Canada* 49°15N 98°54W **297** D9
Pilot Point *Alaska, U.S.A.* 57°34N 157°35W **303** H8
Pilot Point *Tex., U.S.A.* 33°24N 96°58W **314** E6
Pilot Rock *U.S.A.* 45°29N 118°50W **304** D4
Pilot Station *U.S.A.* 61°56N 162°53W **303** F7
Pilote → *Martinique* 14°28N 60°55W **322** j
Pilsen = Plzeň *Czech Rep.* 49°45N 13°22E **180** B6
Pilsen = Pilzno *Poland* 49°58N 21°16E **185** J8
Pilštanj *Slovenia* 46°8N 15°39E **199** B12
Piltene *Latvia* 57°13N 21°40E **184** A8
Pilton *U.K.* 55°58N 3°13W **121** B2
Pilzno *Poland* 49°58N 21°16E **185** J8
Pima *U.S.A.* 32°54N 109°50W **305** K9
Pimba *Australia* 31°18S 136°46E **282** A2
Pimenta Bueno *Brazil* 11°35S 61°10W **331** C5
Pimenteiras *Brazil* 13°40S 60°58W **331** C5
Pimentel *Peru* 6°45S 79°55W **330** B2
Pimlico *London, U.K.* **125** c3
Pimpri Chinchwad *India* 18°37N 73°47E **244** E1
Pimu *Dem. Rep. of the Congo* 1°42N 20°58E **264** B4
Pin Valley △ *India* 31°50N 77°50E **242** D7
Pina de Ebro *Spain* 41°29N 0°33W **196** D4
Pinamalayan *Phil.* 13°2N 121°29E **232** E3
Pinang *Malaysia* 5°25N 100°15E **237** c
Pinang □ *Malaysia* 5°20N 100°20E **237** K3
Pinar, C. des *Spain* 39°53N 3°12E **206** B4
Pinar del Río *Cuba* 22°26N 83°40W **320** B3
Pınarbaşı *Çanakkale,*
Turkey 39°53N 26°15E **205** B8
Pınarbaşı *Kayseri, Turkey* 38°43N 36°23E **212** C7
Pınarhisar *Turkey* 41°37N 27°30E **203** E11
Pinatubo, Mt. *Phil.* 15°8N 120°21E **232** D3
Pinawa *Canada* 50°9N 95°50W **297** C9
Pincehely *Hungary* 46°41N 18°27E **182** D3
Pinchang *China* 31°36N 107°3E **228** B6
Pincher Creek *Canada* 49°30N 113°57W **296** D6
Pinchi L. *Canada* 54°38N 124°30W **296** C4
Pinckard *U.S.A.* 31°19N 85°33W **316** D4
Pinckneyville *U.S.A.* 38°5N 89°23W **310** F7
Pińczów *Poland* 50°32N 20°32E **185** H7
Pind Dadan Khan *Pakistan* 32°36N 73°7E **242** C5
Pindar *Australia* 28°30S 115°47E **279** E2
Pindaré → *Brazil* 3°17S 44°47W **332** B3
Pindaré-Mirim *Brazil* 3°37S 45°21W **332** B2
Pindera Downs ⊙
Australia 29°24S 142°37E **281** A3
Pindi Gheb *Pakistan* 33°14N 72°21E **242** C5
Pindiga *Nigeria* 9°58N 10°53E **263** D7
Pindobal *Brazil* 3°16S 48°25W **332** B2

Pindos △ Greece 39°52N 21°11E 204 B3
Pindos Oros Greece 40°0N 21°0E 204 B3
Pindus Mts. = Pindos Oros Greece 40°0N 21°0E 204 B3
Pine → B.C., Canada 56°8N 120°43W 296 B4
Pine → Sask., Canada 58°50N 105°38W 297 B7
Pine Bluff U.S.A. 34°13N 92°1W 314 D8
Pine Bluffs U.S.A. 41°11N 104°4W 304 F11
Pine Castle U.S.A. 28°28N 81°22W 133 B2
Pine City U.S.A. 45°50N 92°59W 308 C7
Pine Cr. → U.S.A. 41°10N 77°16W 312 E7
Pine Creek Australia 13°50S 131°50E 278 B5
Pine Falls Canada 50°34N 96°11W 297 C9
Pine Flat L. U.S.A. 36°50N 119°20W 306 J7
Pine Grove Ont., Canada 43°47N 79°34W 141 A1
Pine Grove Pa., U.S.A. 40°33N 76°23W 313 F8
Pine Hill Australia 23°38S 146°57E 280 C4
Pine Hills U.S.A. 28°33N 81°27W 133 A2
Pine I. U.S.A. 26°36N 82°7W 317 J7
Pine Island U.S.A. 26°5N 80°16W 129 B1
Pine Island Glacier Antarctica 76°0S 100°0W 151 D15
Pine Level U.S.A. 32°4N 86°4W 316 C3
Pine Mountain U.S.A. 32°49N 84°51W 316 C5
Pine Pass Canada 55°25N 122°42W 296 B4
Pine Point Canada 60°50N 114°28W 296 A6
Pine Ridge N.S.W., Australia 31°30S 150°28E 283 A9
Pine Ridge S. Dak., U.S.A. 43°2N 102°33W 308 D2
Pine River Man., Canada 51°45N 100°30W 297 C8
Pine River Minn., U.S.A. 46°43N 94°24W 308 B6
Pine Valley U.S.A. 32°50N 116°32W 307 N10
Pinecrest Calif., U.S.A. 38°12N 120°1W 306 G6
Pinecrest Fla., U.S.A. 25°40N 80°18W 129 D1
Pineda de Mar Spain 41°37N 2°42E 196 D7
Pinedale Calif., U.S.A. 36°50N 119°48W 306 J7
Pinedale Wyo., U.S.A. 42°52N 109°52W 304 E9
Pinega → Russia 64°30N 44°19E 186 B8
Pinehouse L. Canada 55°32N 106°35W 297 B7
Pineimuta → Canada 52°8N 88°33W 298 B1
Pinellas Park U.S.A. 27°50N 82°41W 317 H7
Pinerolo Italy 44°53N 7°21E 198 D4
Pines, Akra Greece 40°5N 24°20E 203 F8
Pineto Italy 42°36N 14°4E 199 F11
Pinetop-Lakeside U.S.A. 34°9N 109°58W 305 J9
Pinetown S. Africa 29°48S 30°54E 271 C5
Pinetta U.S.A. 30°36N 83°21W 316 E6
Pineview U.S.A. 32°7N 83°30W 316 C6
Pineville La., U.S.A. 31°19N 92°26W 314 F8
Pineville S.C., U.S.A. 33°26N 80°1W 316 B9
Pinewood U.S.A. 33°44N 80°27W 316 B9
Pinewood Park U.S.A. 25°52N 80°13W 129 C2
Piney France 48°22N 4°21E 173 D11
Ping → Thailand 15°42N 100°9E 236 E3
Pingaring Australia 32°40S 118°32E 279 F2
Pingba China 26°23N 106°12E 228 D6
Pingbian China 23°0N 103°45E 228 F4
Pingchuan China 27°35N 101°55E 228 D3
Pingding China 37°47N 113°38E 226 F7
Pingdingshan China 33°43N 113°27E 226 H7
Pingdu China 36°42N 119°59E 227 F10
Pingelly Australia 32°32S 117°5E 279 F2
Pingguo China 23°19N 107°36E 228 F6
Pinghe China 24°17N 117°21E 229 E11
Pinghu China 30°40N 121°2E 229 B13
Pingjiang China 28°45N 113°36E 229 C9
Pingle China 24°40N 110°40E 229 E8
Pingli China 32°27N 109°22E 228 A7
Pingliang China 35°35N 106°31E 226 G4
Pinglin Taiwan 24°56N 121°42E 225 B3
Pinglu China 39°31N 112°30E 226 E7
Pingluo China 38°52N 106°30E 226 E4
Pingnan Fujian, China 26°55N 119°0E 229 D12
Pingnan Guangxi Zhuangzu, China 23°33N 110°22E 229 F8
Pingo Gabon 1°19S 10°55E 264 C2
Pingquan China 41°1N 118°37E 227 D10
Pingrup Australia 33°32S 118°29E 279 F2
Pingshan China 28°39N 104°3E 228 C5
Pingtan China 25°31N 119°47E 229 E12
Pingtang China 25°49N 107°17E 228 E6
P'ingtung Taiwan 22°38N 120°30E 225 D2
P'ingtung □ Taiwan 22°30N 120°40E 225 D2
Pingwu China 32°25N 104°30E 226 H3
Pingxiang Guangxi Zhuangzu, China 22°6N 106°46E 228 F6
Pingxiang Jiangxi, China 27°43N 113°48E 229 D9
Pingyao China 37°12N 112°10E 226 F7
Pingyi China 35°30N 117°35E 227 G9
Pingyin China 36°20N 116°25E 226 F9
Pingyuan Guangdong, China 24°37N 115°57E 229 E10
Pingyuan Shandong, China 37°10N 116°22E 226 F9
Pingyuanjie China 23°45N 103°48E 228 F4
Pingzhou China 23°1N 113°11E 221 B2
Pinhal Novo Portugal 38°38N 8°55W 195 G2
Pinheiro = Icoraci Brazil 1°18S 48°28W 332 B2
Pinheiro Brazil 2°31S 45°5W 332 B2
Pinheiro Machado Brazil 31°34S 53°23W 335 C5
Pinheiros → Brazil 23°37S 46°44W 137 B1
Pinhel Portugal 40°50N 7°1W 194 E3
Pinhuá → Brazil 6°21S 65°0W 331 B5
Pini Indonesia 0°10N 98°40E 234 B1
Pinios → Ilia, Greece 37°48N 21°20E 204 D3
Pinios → Trikala, Greece 39°55N 22°41E 204 B4
Pinjarra Australia 32°37S 115°52E 279 F2
Pinjrapur Pakistan 24°53N 67°4E 123 A2
Pink Beach Bonaire 12°5N 68°17W 322 h
Pink Mountain Canada 57°3N 122°52W 296 B4
Pinkafeld Austria 47°22N 16°9E 181 D9
Pinlaung Burma 20°8N 96°47E 241 E6
Pinlebu Burma 24°5N 95°22E 241 C5
Pinnacle Is. = Senkaku-Shotō E. China Sea 25°45N 123°30E 221 M1
Pinnacles ⌂ U.S.A. 36°25N 121°12W 306 J5
Pinnaroo Australia 35°17S 140°53E 282 C4
Pinneberg Germany 53°40N 9°48E 178 B5
Pinner U.K. 51°35N 0°22W 125 A1
Pinner Green U.K. 51°35N 0°23W 125 A1
Pino Hachado, Paso S. Amer. 38°39S 70°54W 336 A2
Pinon Hills U.S.A. 34°26N 117°39W 307 L9
Pinos Mexico 22°18N 101°34W 318 C4
Pinos, Mt. U.S.A. 34°49N 119°8W 307 L7
Pinos Pt. U.S.A. 36°38N 121°57W 305 H3
Pinos Puente Spain 37°15N 3°45W 195 H7
Pinrang Indonesia 3°46S 119°41E 235 C5
Pins, Î. des N. Cal. 22°37S 167°30E 288 d
Pins, Pte. aux Canada 42°15N 81°51W 312 D3
Pinsk Belarus 52°10N 26°1E 177 B14
Pinta, Canal de Ecuador 0°27N 90°38W 330 a
Pinta, I. Ecuador 0°35N 90°44W 330 a
Pintados Chile 20°35S 69°40W 330 E4
Pinturas → Argentina 46°30S 70°20W 336 C2
Pintuyan Phil. 9°57N 125°15E 233 G5
Pinukpuk Phil. 17°35N 121°22E 232 C3
Pinyang China 27°42N 120°31E 229 D13
Pinyug Russia 60°5N 48°0E 186 B8
Pio Duran Phil. 13°2N 123°25E 232 E4
Pio V. Corpuz Phil. 11°55N 124°2E 233 F5
Pio XII Brazil 3°53S 45°17W 332 B2
Pioche U.S.A. 37°56N 114°27W 305 H6
Pioltello Italy 45°30N 9°19E 128 A2
Piombino Italy 42°55N 10°32E 198 F7
Piombino, Canale di Italy 42°53N 10°30E 198 F7
Pioner, Ostrov Russia 79°50N 92°0E 215 B10
Pionerskiy Russia 54°56N 20°14E 184 D7
Pionki Poland 51°29N 21°28E 185 G8
Piopiotaki = Milford Sd. N.Z. 44°41S 167°47E 285 E2
Piorini → Brazil 3°23S 63°30W 329 D5
Piorini, L. Brazil 3°15S 62°35W 329 D5
Piotrków Trybunalski Poland 51°23N 19°43E 185 G6
Piove di Sacco Italy 45°18N 12°2E 199 C9
Pīp Iran 26°45N 60°10E 247 E9
Pipar India 26°25N 73°31E 242 F5
Pipar Road India 26°27N 73°27E 242 F5
Piparia Mad. P., India 22°45N 78°23E 242 H8
Piparia Mad. P., India 21°49N 77°37E 242 J7
Piparo Trin. & Tob. 10°20N 61°20W 323 t
Pipas Angola 14°57S 12°11E 265 E2
Piperi Greece 39°20N 24°19E 204 B6
Piperno = Priverno Italy 41°28N 13°11E 200 A6
Pipestone U.S.A. 44°0N 96°19W 308 D5
Pipestone → Canada 52°53N 89°23W 298 B2
Pipestone Cr. → Canada 49°38N 100°15W 297 D8
Pipiriki N.Z. 39°26S 175°5E 284 F4
Piplan Pakistan 32°17N 71°21E 242 C4
Piploda India 23°37N 74°56E 242 H6
Pipmuacan, Rés. Canada 49°45N 70°30W 299 C5
Pippingarra Australia 20°27S 118°42E 278 D2
Pipriac France 47°59N 1°58W 172 E5
Piqua U.S.A. 40°9N 84°15W 311 D12
Piquet Carneiro Brazil 5°48S 39°25W 332 C4
Piquiri → Brazil 24°3S 54°14W 335 A5
Pir Panjal Range India 32°30N 76°50E 242 C7
Pīr Sohrāb Iran 25°44N 60°54E 247 E9
Pira Benin 8°28N 1°48E 263 D5
Piracanjuba Brazil 17°18S 49°1W 333 E2
Piracicaba Brazil 22°45S 47°40W 335 A6
Piracuruca Brazil 3°50S 41°50W 332 B3
Pirae Tahiti 17°31S 149°32W 289 e
Piræus = Pireas Greece 37°57N 23°42E 112 B1
Piraiévs = Pireas Greece 37°57N 23°42E 112 B1
Pirajuçara → Brazil 23°33S 46°42W 137 B1
Pirajuí Brazil 21°59S 49°29W 335 A6
Piram I. India 21°36N 72°21E 242 J5
Piran Slovenia 45°31N 13°33E 199 C10
Pirané Argentina 25°42S 59°6W 334 B4
Piranhas Brazil 9°27S 37°46W 332 C4
Pirano = Piran Slovenia 45°31N 13°33E 199 C10
Pīrānshahr Iran 36°41N 45°8E 213 D11
Pirapemas Brazil 3°43S 44°14W 332 B3
Pirapora Brazil 17°20S 44°56W 333 E3
Pirara Guyana 3°37N 59°40W 329 C6
Pirawa India 24°10N 76°2E 242 G7
Piray → Bolivia 16°32S 63°45W 331 D5
Pirdop Bulgaria 42°40N 24°10E 203 D8
Pireas Greece 37°57N 23°42E 112 B1
Pires do Rio Brazil 17°18S 48°17W 333 E2
Pirganj Bangla. 25°51N 88°24E 241 C2
Pirgi Greece 38°13N 25°59E 205 C7
Pirgos Ilia, Greece 37°40N 21°27E 204 D3
Pirgos Kriti, Greece 35°0N 25°9E 207 E6
Pirgovo Bulgaria 43°44N 25°43E 203 C9
Piribebuy Paraguay 25°26S 57°2W 334 B4
Pirimapun Indonesia 6°20S 138°24E 231 F9
Pirin △ Bulgaria 41°48N 23°22E 202 E7
Pirin Planina Bulgaria 41°40N 23°30E 202 E7
Pirinçi Turkey 41°10N 28°52E 122 B1
Pirineos = Pyrénées Europe 42°45N 0°18E 174 F4
Piripiri Brazil 4°15S 41°46W 332 B3
Piritu Venezuela 9°23N 69°12W 328 B4
Pirituba Brazil 23°29S 46°44W 137 A1
Pirkkola Finland 60°14N 24°55E 121 B2
Pirlangimpi Australia 11°24S 130°26E 278 B5
Pirmasens Germany 49°12N 7°36E 179 F3
Pirna Germany 50°57N 13°56E 178 E9
Pirojpur Bangla. 22°35N 90°1E 241 D3
Pirot Serbia 43°9N 22°33E 202 C6
Piru Indonesia 3°4S 128°12E 231 E7
Piru Calif., U.S.A. 34°25N 118°48W 307 L8
Piryatin = Pyryatyn Ukraine 50°15N 32°25E 189 G7
Pisa Italy 43°43N 10°23E 198 E7
Pisa → Poland 53°14N 21°52E 185 E8
Pisa, Firenze ✕ (PSA) Italy 43°40N 10°22E 198 E7
Pisa Ra. N.Z. 44°52S 169°12E 285 E4
Pisac Peru 13°25S 71°50W 330 C3
Pisagne Italy 45°45N 10°10E 198 C7
Pisagua Chile 19°40S 70°15W 330 D3
Pisarovina Croatia 45°35N 15°50E 199 C12
Pisau, Tanjong Malaysia 6°4N 117°59E 235 A5
Pisba △ Colombia 10°39N 74°30W 328 A3
Pisco Peru 13°50S 76°12W 330 C2
Piscu Romania 45°30N 27°43E 183 E12
Pisek Czech Rep. 49°19N 14°10E 180 B7
Pisgat O'mer West Bank 31°49N 35°14E 123 B2
Pisgat Ze'ev West Bank 31°49N 35°14E 123 B2
Pishan China 37°30N 78°33E 217 E9
Pishcha Ukraine 51°35N 23°50E 185 G10
Pishchanka Ukraine 48°12N 28°54E 183 B13
Pīshīn Iran 26°6N 61°47E 247 E9
Pishin Pakistan 30°35N 67°0E 242 D2
Pishin Lora → Pakistan 29°9N 64°5E 242 E1
Pishpek = Bishkek Kyrgyzstan 42°54N 74°46E 217 D8
Pisidia Turkey 37°30N 31°40E 212 D4
Pising Indonesia 5°8S 121°53E 231 F6
Pisiou, Pte. Guadeloupe 15°59N 61°13W 322 e
Pismo Beach U.S.A. 35°9N 120°38W 307 K6
Pisnice Czech Rep. 49°59N 14°28E 135 C2
Piso, L. Liberia 6°50N 11°15W 262 D2
Pissila Burkina Faso 13°7N 0°50W 263 C4
Pissis, Cerro Argentina 27°45S 68°48W 334 B2
Pissos France 44°19N 0°49W 174 D3
Pissouri Cyprus 34°40N 32°42E 207 F8
Pisticci Italy 40°23N 16°33E 201 B9
Pistóia Italy 43°55N 10°54E 198 E7
Pistol B. Canada 62°25N 92°37W 297 A10
Pisuerga → Spain 41°33N 4°52W 194 D6
Pisz Poland 53°38N 21°49E 184 E8
Pit → U.S.A. 40°47N 122°6W 304 F2
Pita Guinea 11°5N 12°15W 262 C2
Pitalito Colombia 1°51N 76°2W 328 C2
Pitampura India 28°41N 77°7E 120 A1
Pitanga Brazil 24°46S 51°44W 333 F1
Pitangui Brazil 19°40S 44°54W 333 E3
Pitarpunga L. Australia 34°24S 143°30E 282 C5
Pitcairn I. Pac. Oc. 25°5S 130°5W 289 K14
Pitch Pt. Trin. & Tob. 10°15N 61°37W 323 t
Piteå Sweden 65°20N 21°25E 160 D19
Piteälven → Sweden 65°20N 21°25E 160 D19
Piterka Russia 50°41N 47°29E 190 E8
Pitești Romania 44°52N 24°54E 183 F9
Pithapuram India 17°10N 82°15E 244 F6
Pithara Australia 30°20S 116°35E 279 F2
Pithio Greece 41°24N 26°40E 203 E10
Pithiviers France 48°10N 2°13E 173 D9
Pithora India 21°16N 82°31E 244 D6
Pithoragarh India 29°35N 80°13E 243 E9
Pithoro Pakistan 25°31N 69°23E 242 G3
Piti Guam 13°28N 144°41E 302 d
Pitigliano Italy 42°38N 11°40E 199 F8
Pitkäjärvi Finland 60°15N 24°45E 121 B1
Pitkyaranta Russia 61°34N 31°37E 188 B6
Pitlochry U.K. 56°42N 3°44W 167 E5
Pitnak = Drujba Uzbekistan 41°13N 61°18E 216 D6
Pitoa Cameroon 9°23N 13°32E 264 A2
Pitogo Phil. 13°47N 122°5E 232 E4
Piton, Pte. du Guadeloupe 16°30N 61°26W 322 e
Piton de la Petite Rivière Noire Mauritius 20°24S 57°23E 272 e
Pitons, Anses des St. Lucia 13°49N 61°4W 323 m
Pitou Taiwan 23°53N 120°27E 225 C2
Pitou Chiao Taiwan 25°8N 121°55E 225 A3
Pitrufquén Chile 38°59S 72°39W 336 A2
Pitschen = Byczyna Poland 51°7N 18°12E 185 G5
Pitsilia Cyprus 34°55N 33°0E 207 F9
Pitt, Pta. Ecuador 0°43S 89°14W 330 a
Pitt I. B.C., Canada 53°30N 129°50W 296 C3
Pitt I. N.Z. 44°15S 176°15W 285 a
Pitti I. India 10°50N 72°38E 245 J1
Pittsburg Calif., U.S.A. 38°2N 121°53W 306 G5
Pittsburg Kans., U.S.A. 37°25N 94°42W 308 G6
Pittsburg Tex., U.S.A. 33°0N 94°59W 314 E7
Pittsburgh U.S.A. 40°26N 79°58W 312 F5
Pittsfield Ill., U.S.A. 39°36N 90°49W 310 E6
Pittsfield Maine, U.S.A. 44°47N 69°23W 309 C19
Pittsfield Mass., U.S.A. 42°27N 73°15W 313 D11
Pittsfield N.H., U.S.A. 43°18N 71°20W 313 C13
Pittston U.S.A. 41°19N 75°47W 313 E9
Pittsview U.S.A. 32°11N 85°10W 316 C4
Pittsworth Australia 27°41S 151°37E 281 D5
Pituri → Australia 22°35S 138°30E 280 C2
Pium Brazil 10°27S 49°11W 332 D2
Piumafua Mt. Amer. Samoa 14°11S 169°37W 302 f
Piumhi Brazil 20°28S 45°58W 333 F2
Piura Peru 5°15S 80°38W 330 B1
Piura □ Peru 5°10S 80°0W 330 B2
Piuthan Nepal 28°7N 82°56E 243 E10
Piva → Montenegro 43°20N 18°50E 202 C2
Pivijay Colombia 10°28N 74°37W 328 A3
Piwniczna Poland 49°27N 20°42E 185 J7
Pixian China 30°48N 103°52E 228 B4
Pixley U.S.A. 35°58N 119°18W 306 K7
Pizarra Spain 36°36N 4°42W 195 J6
Pizarro Colombia 4°58N 77°22W 328 C2
Pizhou = Pei Xian China 34°44N 116°55E 226 G9
Pizhou China 34°18N 117°57E 227 G9
Pizzo Italy 38°44N 16°10E 201 D9
Placentia Canada 47°20N 54°0W 299 C9
Placentia B. Canada 47°0N 54°40W 299 C9
Placer Masbate, Phil. 11°52N 123°55E 233 F4
Placer Surigao N., Phil. 9°36N 125°38E 233 G5
Placerville U.S.A. 38°44N 120°48W 306 G6
Placetas Cuba 22°15N 79°44W 320 B4
Plácido de Castro Brazil 10°20S 67°11W 330 C4
Plačkovica Macedonia 41°45N 22°30E 202 E6
Plaine des Jarres Laos 19°27N 103°10E 236 C4
Plaine Magnien Mauritius 20°25S 57°39E 272 e
Plaines des Papayes Mauritius 20°3S 57°34E 272 e
Plainfield Ill., U.S.A. 41°37N 88°12W 311 C8
Plainfield Ind., U.S.A. 39°42N 86°24W 311 E10
Plainfield N.J., U.S.A. 40°37N 74°25W 313 F10
Plainfield Ohio, U.S.A. 40°13N 81°43W 312 F3
Plainfield Vt., U.S.A. 44°17N 72°26W 313 B12
Plains Ga., U.S.A. 32°2N 84°24W 316 C5
Plains Mont., U.S.A. 47°28N 114°53W 304 C6
Plains Tex., U.S.A. 33°11N 102°50W 314 E3
Plainview Nebr., U.S.A. 42°21N 97°47W 308 D5
Plainview Tex., U.S.A. 34°11N 101°43W 314 D4
Plainwell U.S.A. 42°27N 85°38W 311 B11
Plaisance France 43°36N 0°3E 174 E4
Plaistow U.S.A. 42°50N 71°6W 313 D13
Plaju Indonesia 2°58S 104°49E 234 C2
Plaka Greece 40°0N 25°24E 205 B7
Plaka, Akra Greece 35°11N 26°19E 207 E7
Plakenska Planina Macedonia 41°14N 21°2E 202 E5
Plampang Indonesia 8°47S 117°46E 235 D5
Planá Czech Rep. 49°50N 12°44E 180 B5
Plana Cays Bahamas 22°38N 73°30W 321 B5
Planada U.S.A. 37°16N 120°19W 306 H6
Planchón Peru 12°14S 69°11W 330 C4
Plancoët France 48°32N 2°13W 172 D4
Plandište Serbia 45°16N 21°10E 182 E6
Planegg Germany 48°6N 11°25E 131 B1
Planeta Rica Colombia 8°25N 75°36W 328 B2
Plano Ill., U.S.A. 41°40N 88°32W 311 C8
Plano Tex., U.S.A. 33°1N 96°42W 314 E6
Plant City U.S.A. 28°1N 82°7W 317 G7
Plantation U.S.A. 26°7N 80°14W 129 B2
Plantation Isles U.S.A. 26°6N 80°14W 129 B2
Plaquemine U.S.A. 30°17N 91°14W 314 F9
Plaridel Phil. 8°37N 123°42E 233 G4
Plasencia Spain 40°3N 6°8W 194 E4
Plaški Croatia 45°4N 15°22E 199 C12
Plassen Norway 61°9N 12°30E 164 C9
Plast Russia 54°22N 60°50E 216 B6
Plaster City U.S.A. 32°47N 115°51W 307 N11
Plaster Rock Canada 46°53N 67°22W 299 C6
Plastun Russia 44°45N 136°19E 220 B8
Plasy Czech Rep. 49°56N 13°24E 180 B6
Plata, Río de la → S. Amer. 34°45S 57°30W 334 C4
Plátani → Italy 37°23N 13°16E 200 E6
Platanos Greece 35°28N 23°33E 207 E4
Plataria Greece 39°27N 20°16E 206 C10
Plateau □ Nigeria 8°30N 9°0E 263 D6
Plateau d'Ipassa △ Gabon 0°26N 12°40E 264 B2
Plathe = Ploty Poland 53°48N 15°18E 184 E2
Platinum U.S.A. 59°1N 161°49W 303 G7
Plato Colombia 9°47N 74°47W 328 B3
Platte U.S.A. 43°23N 98°51W 308 D4
Platte → Mo., U.S.A. 39°16N 94°50W 310 E2
Platte → Nebr., U.S.A. 41°4N 95°53W 308 E6
Platte City U.S.A. 39°22N 94°47W 310 E2
Platteville U.S.A. 42°44N 90°29W 310 B6
Plattling Germany 48°46N 12°53E 179 G8
Plattsburg U.S.A. 39°34N 94°27W 310 E2
Plattsburgh U.S.A. 44°42N 73°28W 313 B11
Plattsmouth U.S.A. 41°1N 95°53W 308 E6
Plau Germany 53°27N 12°15E 178 B8
Plauen Germany 50°30N 12°8E 178 E8
Plauer See Germany 53°28N 12°17E 178 B8
Plav Montenegro 42°38N 19°57E 202 D3
Plavinas Latvia 56°35N 25°46E 188 D3
Plavnica Montenegro 42°20N 19°13E 202 D3
Plavno Croatia 44°9N 16°10E 199 D13
Plavsk Russia 53°40N 37°18E 188 F9
Playa Blanca Canary Is. 28°51N 13°50W 152 F6
Playa de las Americas Canary Is. 28°5N 16°43W 153 e1
Playa de Mogán Canary Is. 27°48N 15°47W 153 e1
Playa del Carmen Mexico 20°37N 87°4W 319 C7
Playa del Inglés Canary Is. 27°45N 15°33W 153 e1
Playa Esmerelda Canary Is. 28°8N 14°16W 153 e2
Playas Ecuador 2°38S 80°23W 328 D1
Playgreen L. Canada 54°0N 98°15W 297 C9
Plaza Mayor Madrid, Spain 127 b2
Pleasant Bay Canada 46°51N 60°48W 299 C7
Pleasant Hill Calif., U.S.A. 37°57N 122°4W 306 H4
Pleasant Hill Ill., U.S.A. 39°27N 90°52W 310 E6
Pleasant Hill Mo., U.S.A. 38°47N 94°16W 310 F2
Pleasant Mount U.S.A. 41°44N 75°26W 313 E9
Pleasant Point N.Z. 44°16S 171°9E 285 E6
Pleasant Prairie U.S.A. 42°33N 87°56W 311 B9
Pleasanton Calif., U.S.A. 37°39N 121°52W 306 H5
Pleasanton Tex., U.S.A. 28°58N 98°29W 314 G5
Pleasantville Iowa, U.S.A. 41°23N 93°18W 310 C3
Pleasantville N.J., U.S.A. 39°24N 74°32W 309 F16
Pleasantville Pa., U.S.A. 41°35N 79°34W 312 E5
Pleasure Island U.S.A. 28°21N 81°31W 133 B1
Pleasure Ridge Park U.S.A. 38°9N 85°50W 311 F11
Pléaux France 45°8N 2°13E 174 C6
Plei Ku Vietnam 13°57N 108°0E 236 F7
Plélan-le-Grand France 48°0N 2°7W 172 D4
Pléneuf-Val-André France 48°35N 2°32W 172 D4
Plenița Romania 44°14N 23°10E 183 F8
Plenty → Australia 23°25S 136°31E 280 C2
Plenty, B. of N.Z. 37°45S 177°0E 284 D6
Plentywood U.S.A. 48°47N 104°34W 304 B11
Plérin France 48°32N 2°46W 172 D4
Plesetsk Russia 62°43N 40°20E 186 B7
Pleskau = Pskov Russia 57°50N 28°25E 188 D5
Plessisville Canada 46°14N 71°47W 299 C5
Plestin-les-Grèves France 48°40N 3°39W 172 D3
Pleszew Poland 51°53N 17°47E 185 G4
Pleternica Croatia 45°17N 17°48E 182 E2
Plétipi, L. Canada 51°44N 70°6W 299 B5
Pleven Bulgaria 43°26N 24°37E 203 C8
Pleven □ Bulgaria 43°26N 24°37E 203 C8
Plevna Canada 44°58N 76°59W 312 B8
Plitvice Lakes = Plitvička Jezera △ Croatia 44°54N 15°35E 199 D12
Plitvička Jezera △ Croatia 44°54N 15°35E 199 D12
Plješevica Croatia 44°45N 15°45E 199 D12
Pljevlja Montenegro 43°21N 19°21E 202 C3
Ploaghe Italy 40°40N 8°45E 200 B1
Ploče Croatia 43°4N 17°26E 199 E14
Plock Poland 52°32N 19°40E 185 F6
Plöckenpass Italy 46°37N 12°57E 199 B9
Plöckenstein Germany 48°46N 13°51E 179 G9
Ploemeur France 47°44N 3°26W 172 E3
Ploërmel France 47°55N 2°26W 172 E4
Plöhnen = Płońsk Poland 52°37N 20°21E 185 F7
Ploiești Romania 44°57N 26°5E 183 F11
Plomari Greece 38°59N 26°22E 205 C8
Plombières-les-Bains France 47°58N 6°27E 173 E13
Plomin Croatia 45°8N 14°10E 199 C11
Plön Germany 54°9N 10°24E 178 A6
Plonge, Lac la Canada 55°8N 107°20W 297 B7
Płońsk Poland 52°37N 20°21E 185 F7
Plopeni Romania 45°4N 25°59E 183 E10
Plopișului, Munții Romania 47°5N 22°30E 182 C7
Plotsk = Plock Poland 52°32N 19°40E 185 F6
Ploty Poland 53°48N 15°18E 184 E2
Plouaret France 48°37N 3°28W 172 D3
Plouay France 47°55N 3°21W 172 E3
Ploučnice → Czech Rep. 50°46N 14°13E 180 A7
Ploudalmézeau France 48°34N 4°41W 172 D2
Plouescat France 48°39N 4°10W 172 D2
Plougasnou France 48°42N 3°49W 172 D3
Plougastel-Daoulas France 48°22N 4°17W 172 D2
Plouguerneau France 48°36N 4°30W 172 D2
Plouha France 48°41N 2°57W 172 D4
Plouhinec France 48°0N 4°29W 172 E2
Plovdiv Bulgaria 42°8N 24°44E 203 D8
Plovdiv □ Bulgaria 42°15N 24°30E 203 D8
Plover Cove Res. China 22°28N 114°15E 219 a
Pluies, R. des → Réunion 20°52S 55°31E 272 f
Plum U.S.A. 40°29N 79°47W 312 F5
Plum I. U.S.A. 41°11N 72°12W 313 E12
Plumas U.S.A. 39°45N 120°4W 306 F6
Plummer U.S.A. 47°20N 116°53W 304 C5
Plumridge Lakes Australia 29°26S 125°16E 279 E4
Plumstead Western Cape, S. Africa 34°1S 18°28E 118 B1
Plumstead London, U.K. 51°29N 0°5E 125 B4
Plumtree Zimbabwe 20°27S 27°55E 269 G2
Plungė Lithuania 55°53N 21°59E 184 C8
Pluvigner France 47°46N 3°1W 172 E3
Plužine Montenegro 43°8N 18°51E 202 C2
Plymouth Montserrat 16°42N 62°13W 323 p
Plymouth Trin. & Tob. 11°14N 60°48W 323 s
Plymouth Plymouth, U.K. 50°22N 4°10W 169 G3
Plymouth Calif., U.S.A. 38°29N 120°51W 306 G6
Plymouth Ill., U.S.A. 40°18N 90°58W 310 D6
Plymouth Ind., U.S.A. 41°21N 86°19W 311 C10
Plymouth Mass., U.S.A. 41°57N 70°40W 313 E14
Plymouth N.C., U.S.A. 35°52N 76°43W 315 D16
Plymouth N.H., U.S.A. 43°46N 71°41W 313 C13
Plymouth Pa., U.S.A. 41°14N 75°57W 313 E9
Plymouth Wis., U.S.A. 43°45N 87°59W 308 D10
Plympton-Wyoming = Wyoming Canada 42°57N 82°7W 312 D2
Plynlimon = Pumlumon Fawr U.K. 52°28N 3°46W 169 E4
Plyussa Russia 58°28N 29°27E 188 C5
Plyussa → Russia 59°4N 28°6E 188 C5
Plyushchevo Russia 55°44N 37°45E 129 B3
Plzeň Czech Rep. 49°45N 13°22E 180 B6
Plzeňský □ Czech Rep. 49°35N 13°0E 180 B6
Pmere Nyente ☺ Australia 24°15S 136°10E 280 C2
Pniewy Poland 52°31N 16°16E 185 F3
Pnika Athens, Greece 112 c1
Pô Burkina Faso 11°14N 1°5W 263 C4
Po → Italy 44°57N 12°4E 199 D9
Po, Foci del Italy 44°55N 12°30E 199 D9
Pô △ Burkina Faso 11°25N 1°5W 263 C4
Po Hai = Bo Hai China 39°0N 119°0E 227 E10
Po Toi China 22°10N 114°16E 122 B2
Po Toi O China 22°16N 114°17E 122 B2
Poasco Italy 45°24N 9°16E 128 B2
Pobé Benin 7°0N 2°56E 263 D5
Pobé Burkina Faso 13°53N 1°42W 263 C4
Pobeda Russia 65°12N 146°12E 215 C15
Pobedy, Pik Kyrgyzstan 42°0N 79°58E 217 D9
Pobiedziska Poland 52°29N 17°11E 185 F4
Pobladura del Valle Spain 42°6N 5°44W 194 C5
Poblet, Monestir de Spain 41°22N 1°4E 196 D6
Pobra de Trives Spain 42°20N 7°10W 194 C3
Pocahontas Ark., U.S.A. 36°16N 90°58W 315 C9
Pocahontas Ill., U.S.A. 38°50N 89°33W 310 F7
Pocahontas Iowa, U.S.A. 42°44N 94°40W 310 B2
Pocatello U.S.A. 42°52N 112°27W 304 E7
Počátky Czech Rep. 49°15N 15°14E 180 B8
Pocheon S. Korea 37°53N 127°13E 224 D3
Pochep Russia 52°58N 33°29E 189 F7
Pochinki Russia 54°41N 44°59E 190 C7
Pochinok Russia 54°28N 32°29E 188 E7
Pöchlarn Austria 48°12N 15°12E 180 C8
Poci Venezuela 5°57N 61°29W 329 B5
Pocinhos Brazil 7°4S 36°3W 332 C4
Pocking Germany 48°23N 13°19E 179 G9
Pocklington Reef Papua N. G. 10°51S 155°44E 286 F8
Poções Brazil 14°31S 40°21W 333 D3
Pocomoke City U.S.A. 38°5N 75°34W 309 F16
Poconé Brazil 16°15S 56°37W 331 D6
Poços de Caldas Brazil 21°50S 46°33W 335 A6
Podbaba Czech Rep. 50°7N 14°22E 135 B2
Podbořany Czech Rep. 50°14N 13°25E 180 A6
Poddębice Poland 51°54N 18°58E 185 G5
Poděbrady Czech Rep. 50°9N 15°8E 180 A8
Podensac France 44°40N 0°22W 174 D3
Podenzano Italy 44°57N 9°41E 198 D6
Podgorač Croatia 45°27N 18°13E 182 E3
Podgorica Montenegro 42°30N 19°19E 202 D3
Podgorie Albania 40°49N 20°48E 202 F4
Podile India 15°37N 79°37E 245 G4
Podilska Vysochyna Ukraine 49°0N 28°0E 183 B13
Podkarpackie □ Poland 50°0N 22°10E 185 H9
Podkova Bulgaria 41°24N 25°24E 203 E9
Podlapača Croatia 44°37N 15°47E 199 D12
Podlaskie □ Poland 53°10N 23°0E 185 E10
Podocarpus △ Ecuador 4°13S 79°2W 328 D2
Podoleni Romania 46°46N 26°39E 183 D11
Podoli Czech Rep. 50°2N 14°25E 135 B2
Podolínec Slovak Rep. 49°16N 20°31E 181 B13
Podolsk Russia 55°25N 37°30E 188 E9
Podor Senegal 16°40N 15°2W 262 B1
Podporozhye Russia 60°55N 34°2E 188 B8
Podu Iloaiei Romania 47°13N 27°16E 183 C12
Podu Turcului Romania 46°11N 27°25E 183 D12
Podujevo = Besianë Kosovo 42°54N 21°10E 202 D5
Podyji △ Czech Rep. 48°51N 15°57E 180 C8
Poechos Peru 4°41S 80°34W 328 D1
Poel Germany 54°0N 11°25E 178 B6
Pofadder S. Africa 29°10S 19°22E 270 C2
Poggiardo Italy 40°3N 18°23E 201 B11
Poggibonsi Italy 43°28N 11°9E 198 E8
Pòggio Mirteto Italy 42°16N 12°41E 199 F9
Pogoanele Romania 44°55N 27°0E 183 F12
Pogorzela Poland 51°50N 17°12E 185 G4
Pogoso Dem. Rep. of the Congo 6°46S 17°12E 265 D3
Pogradec Albania 40°54N 20°37E 202 F4
Pogranichnyy Russia 44°25N 131°24E 220 B5
Poh Indonesia 0°46S 122°51E 231 E6
Pohang S. Korea 36°1N 129°23E 224 D4
Pohjanmaa □ Finland 62°58N 22°50E 160 E20
Pohjois-Pirkkala = Nokia Finland 61°30N 23°30E 188 B2
Pohnpei Micronesia 6°55N 158°10E 288 G7
Pohorelá Slovak Rep. 48°50N 20°2E 181 C13
Pohořelice Czech Rep. 48°59N 16°31E 181 C9
Pohorje Slovenia 46°30N 15°20E 199 B12
Pohri India 25°32N 77°22E 242 G6
Pōhue B. U.S.A. 19°0N 155°48W 302 E6
Poi Solomon Is. 10°9S 161°42E 287 N11
Poiana Mare Romania 43°57N 23°5E 182 G8
Poiana Ruscăi, Munții Romania 45°45N 22°25E 182 E7
Poiana Stampei Romania 47°19N 25°8E 183 C10
Poie Dem. Rep. of the Congo 2°50S 23°14E 264 C4
Poike, Península Chile 27°6S 109°15W 330 b
Poindimié N. Cal. 20°56S 165°20E 288 d
Poinsett, C. Antarctica 65°42S 113°18E 151 C8
Point Arena U.S.A. 38°55N 123°41W 306 G3
Point Baker U.S.A. 56°21N 133°37W 296 B2
Point Calimere India 10°17N 79°49E 245 J4
Point Fortin Trin. & Tob. 10°10N 61°42W 323 t
Point Hope U.S.A. 68°21N 166°47W 303 B6
Point L. Canada 65°15N 113°4W 294 D9
Point Lay U.S.A. 69°46N 163°3W 303 B7
Point Lisas Trin. & Tob. 10°24N 61°29W 323 t
Point Pedro Sri Lanka 9°50N 80°15E 245 K5
Point Pelee △ Canada 41°57N 82°31W 312 E2
Point Pleasant N.J., U.S.A. 40°5N 74°4W 313 F10
Point Pleasant W. Va., U.S.A. 38°51N 82°8W 309 F12
Point Reyes ⌂ U.S.A. 38°10N 122°55W 306 G2
Point Salines Int. ✕ (GND) Grenada 12°0N 61°46W 323 q
Pointe-à-Pierre Trin. & Tob. 10°19N 61°28W 323 t
Pointe-à-Pitre Guadeloupe 16°15N 61°32W 322 e
Pointe-au-Pic = La Malbaie Canada 47°40N 70°10W 299 C5
Pointe-Aux-Trembles Canada 45°38N 73°30W 130 A2
Pointe-Claire Canada 45°26N 73°50W 313 A11
Pointe-Gatineau Canada 45°27N 75°41W 313 A9
Pointe Michel Dominica 15°15N 61°23W 323 k
Pointe-Noire Congo 4°48S 11°53E 265 C2
Pointe-Noire Guadeloupe 16°14N 61°47W 322 e
Poio Spain 42°28N 8°41W 194 C2
Poipet Cambodia 13°39N 102°33E 236 F4
Poirino Italy 44°56N 7°48E 198 D4
Poisonbush Ra. Australia 22°30S 121°30E 278 D3
Poissonnier Pt. Australia 19°57S 119°10E 278 C2
Poissy France 48°55N 2°2E 134 A1
Poitiers France 46°35N 0°20E 172 F7
Poitou France 46°40N 0°10W 174 B3
Poitou-Charentes □ France 46°10N 0°15E 174 B4
Poix-de-Picardie France 49°47N 1°58E 173 C8
Poix-Terron France 49°38N 4°38E 173 C11
Pojoaque U.S.A. 35°54N 106°1W 305 J10
Pok Fu Lam China 22°16N 114°7E 122 B1
Pōka'ī B. U.S.A. 21°27N 158°12W 302 K13
Pokaran India 27°0N 71°50E 242 F4
Pokataroo Australia 29°30S 148°36E 281 D4
Pokcheon S. Korea 37°28N 127°8E 137 C2
Pokhara Nepal 28°14N 83°58E 243 E10
Pokhvistnevo Russia 53°36N 52°0E 190 D11
Pokigron Suriname 4°30N 55°22W 329 C6
Poko Dem. Rep. of the Congo 3°7N 26°52E 268 B2
Poko South Sudan 5°41N 31°55E 257 F3
Pokrov Russia 55°55N 39°7E 188 E10
Pokrovka = Kyzyl-Suu Kyrgyzstan 42°20N 78°0E 217 D9
Pokrovsk = Engels Russia 51°28N 46°6E 190 E8
Pokrovsk Russia 61°29N 129°0E 215 C13
Pokrovskoy = Priazovskoye Ukraine 46°44N 35°40E 189 J8
Pokrovskoye Russia 47°25N 38°54E 189 J10
Pol-e Dokhtar Iran 33°9N 47°42E 213 F12
Pol-e Khomri Afghan. 35°56N 68°42E 240 B3
Pol-e Zahāb Iran 34°27N 45°51E 213 E11
Pola = Istra Croatia 45°10N 14°0E 199 C10
Pola = Pula Croatia 44°54N 13°57E 199 D10
Pola Russia 57°55N 32°0E 188 D7
Pola de Allande Spain 43°16N 6°37W 194 B4
Pola de Lena Spain 43°10N 5°49W 194 B5
Pola de Siero Spain 43°24N 5°39W 194 B5
Pola de Somiedo Spain 43°5N 6°15W 194 B4
Pola I. Amer. Samoa 14°14S 170°40W 302 f
Polacca U.S.A. 35°50N 110°23W 305 J8
Polan Iran 25°30N 61°10E 247 E9
Pol'ana Slovak Rep. 48°38N 19°29E 181 C12
Poland U.S.A. 43°13N 75°3W 313 C9
Poland ■ Europe 52°0N 20°0E 185 G3
Polanica-Zdrój Poland 50°24N 16°32E 185 H3
Polaniec Poland 50°26N 21°17E 185 H8
Polanów Poland 54°7N 16°41E 184 D3
Polar Bear ⌂ Canada 55°0N 83°45W 298 A2
Polatlı Turkey 39°36N 32°9E 212 C5
Polatsk Belarus 55°30N 28°50E 188 E5
Polavaram India 17°15N 81°38E 244 F5
Polcura Chile 37°17S 71°43W 334 D1
Połczyn-Zdrój Poland 53°47N 16°5E 184 E3
Poldasht Iran 39°20N 45°4E 213 C11
Polesk △ Poland 51°29N 23°5E 185 G10
Polessk Russia 54°50N 21°8E 184 D8
Polesye = Pripet Marshes Europe 52°10N 27°10E 177 B15
Polevskoy Russia 56°26N 60°11E 186 C11
Polewali Indonesia 3°25S 119°20E 235 C5
Polgar Hungary 47°54N 21°6E 182 C6
Poli Cameroon 8°34N 13°15E 263 D7
Policastro, G. di Italy 40°0N 15°35E 201 C8
Police Poland 53°33N 14°33E 184 E1
Police, Pte. Seychelles 4°51S 55°32E 272 c
Polichnitos Greece 39°6N 26°10E 205 B8
Polička Czech Rep. 49°43N 16°15E 181 B9
Policoro Italy 40°13N 16°41E 201 B9
Poliegos Greece 36°45N 24°38E 204 E6
Poligiros Greece 40°23N 23°25E 202 F7
Polignano a Mare Italy 41°0N 17°13E 201 A9
Poligny France 46°50N 5°42E 173 F12
Polillo Phil. 14°43N 121°56E 232 D3
Polillo Is. Phil. 14°56N 122°0E 232 D4
Polillo Str. Phil. 14°44N 121°51E 232 D3
Polis Cyprus 35°2N 32°26E 207 E8
Polistena Italy 38°24N 16°4E 201 D9
Pölitz = Police Poland 53°33N 14°33E 184 E1
Polk U.S.A. 41°22N 79°56W 312 E5
Polkowice Poland 51°29N 16°3E 185 G3
Polkwitz = Polkowice Poland 51°29N 16°3E 185 G3
Polla Italy 40°31N 15°29E 201 B8
Pollachi India 10°35N 77°0E 245 J3
Pollença Spain 39°54N 3°1E 206 B4
Pollença, B. de Spain 39°53N 3°8E 206 B4
Pollfoss Norway 61°58N 7°54E 164 C4
Póllica Italy 40°11N 15°3E 201 B8
Pollino, Mte. Italy 39°55N 16°11E 201 C9
Pollino △ Italy 40°0N 16°12E 201 C9
Polna Russia 58°31N 28°5E 188 C5
Polnovat Russia 63°50N 65°54E 214 C7
Polo Ill., U.S.A. 41°59N 89°35W 310 C7
Polo Mo., U.S.A. 39°33N 94°3W 310 E2
Pology Ukraine 47°29N 36°15E 189 J9
Polokwane S. Africa 23°54S 29°25E 271 B4
Polokwane → S. Africa 22°25S 30°5E 271 B5
Polomolok Phil. 6°13N 125°3E 233 H5
Polonnaruwa Sri Lanka 7°56N 81°0E 245 L5
Polonne Ukraine 50°6N 27°30E 177 C14
Polonnoye = Polonne Ukraine 50°6N 27°30E 177 C14
Polski Trŭmbesh Bulgaria 43°20N 25°38E 203 C9
Polsko Kosovo Bulgaria 43°23N 25°38E 203 C9
Polson U.S.A. 47°41N 114°9W 304 C6
Poltár Slovak Rep. 48°26N 19°48E 181 C12
Poltava Ukraine 49°35N 34°35E 189 H8
Poltava □ Ukraine 50°15N 33°15E 189 G7
Polton U.K. 55°52N 3°7W 121 B3
Poltoratsk = Ashgabat Turkmenistan 37°58N 58°24E 247 B8
Põltsamaa Estonia 58°39N 25°58E 188 C3
Polunochnoye Russia 60°52N 60°25E 214 C7
Polur India 12°32N 79°11E 245 H4
Põlva Estonia 58°3N 27°3E 188 C4
Polvoranca, Parque de Spain 40°19N 3°48W 127 C1
Polyana Ukraine 48°38N 22°58E 182 B7
Polyarny Russia 69°8N 33°20E 160 B25
Polyarnyye Zori Russia 67°22N 32°30E 160 C25
Polynesia Pac. Oc. 10°0S 162°0W 289 F11
Polynesian Cultural Center U.S.A. 21°38N 157°55W 302 J14
Polynésie française = French Polynesia ☑ Pac. Oc. 20°0S 145°0W 289 f
Polyustrovo Russia 59°57N 30°25E 137 B2
Pomabamba = Azurduy Bolivia 19°59S 64°29W 331 D5
Pomabamba Peru 8°50S 77°28W 330 B2
Pomarance Italy 43°18N 10°52E 198 E7
Pombal Brazil 6°45S 37°50W 332 C4
Pombal Portugal 39°55N 8°40W 194 F2
Pombia Greece 35°0N 24°51E 207 F5
Pombos, B. dos Angola 11°40S 13°47E 265 E2
Pomene Mozam. 22°53S 35°33E 271 B6
Pomeroy Ohio, U.S.A. 39°2N 82°2W 309 F12
Pomeroy Wash., U.S.A. 46°28N 117°36W 304 C5
Pomézia Italy 41°40N 12°30E 200 A5
Pomichna Ukraine 48°13N 31°36E 189 H6
Pomio Papua N. G. 5°32S 151°33E 286 C6
Pomme de Terre L. U.S.A. 37°54N 93°19W 310 G3
Pomme Rose Grenada 12°3N 61°39W 323 q
Pomona Queens., Australia 26°22S 152°52E 281 D5
Pomona Calif., U.S.A. 34°4N 117°45W 307 L9
Pomona Park U.S.A. 29°30N 81°36W 317 F8
Pomorie Bulgaria 42°32N 27°41E 203 D11
Pomorskie □ Poland 54°30N 18°0E 184 D5
Pomorskie, Pojezierze Poland 53°40N 16°37E 184 E3
Pomos Cyprus 35°9N 32°33E 207 E8
Pomos, C. Cyprus 35°10N 32°33E 207 E8
Pompano Beach U.S.A. 26°14N 80°7W 129 A3
Pompei Italy 40°45N 14°30E 201 B7
Pompey France 48°46N 6°6E 173 D13
Pompeys Pillar U.S.A. 45°59N 107°57W 304 D10
Pompeys Pillar ⌂ U.S.A. 46°0N 108°0W 304 D10
Pompidou, Centre Paris, France 134 b4
Pomprap Thailand 13°44N 100°30E 113 B2
Pompton Lakes U.S.A. 41°0N 74°17W 313 F10
Ponape = Pohnpei Micronesia 6°55N 158°10E 288 G7
Ponask L. Canada 54°0N 92°41W 298 B1
Ponca U.S.A. 42°34N 96°43W 308 D5
Ponca City U.S.A. 36°42N 97°5W 314 C6
Ponce Puerto Rico 18°1N 66°37W 321 C6
Ponce de Leon U.S.A. 30°44N 85°56W 316 E4
Ponce de Leon B. U.S.A. 25°15N 81°10W 317 K8
Ponchatoula U.S.A. 30°26N 90°26W 315 F9
Poncheville, L. Canada 50°10N 76°55W 298 B4
Pond U.S.A. 35°43N 119°20W 307 K7
Pond Inlet Canada 72°40N 77°0W 295 C16
Pondicherry = Puducherry India 11°59N 79°50E 245 J4
Pondo Papua N. G. 4°33S 151°38E 286 C6
Pondok Gede Indonesia 6°17S 106°55E 122 A2
Pondok Indah Indonesia 6°16S 106°46E 122 B1
Ponds, I. of Canada 53°27N 55°52W 299 B8
Ponérihouen N. Cal. 21°5S 165°24E 288 d
Ponferrada Spain 42°32N 6°35W 194 C4
Pongo, Wadi → South Sudan 8°42N 27°40E 257 F2
Poniatowa Poland 51°11N 22°3E 185 G9
Poniec Poland 51°48N 16°50E 185 G3
Ponikva Slovenia 46°16N 15°26E 199 B12
Ponizovkino = Krasnyy Profintern Russia 57°45N 40°27E 188 D11
Ponnaiyar → India 11°50N 79°45E 245 J4
Ponnani India 10°45N 75°59E 245 J2
Ponneri India 13°20N 80°15E 245 H5
Ponnuru India 16°5N 80°34E 245 F5
Ponoka Canada 52°42N 113°40W 296 C6
Ponorogo Indonesia 7°52S 111°27E 235 D4
Ponot Phil. 8°25N 123°0E 233 G4
Ponoy Russia 67°0N 41°13E 186 A7
Ponoy → Russia 66°59N 41°17E 186 A7
Pons = Ponts Spain 41°55N 1°12E 196 D6
Pons France 45°35N 0°34W 174 C3
Ponsul → Portugal 39°40N 7°31W 194 F3
Pont-à-Mousson France 48°54N 6°1E 173 D13
Pont-Audemer France 49°21N 0°30E 172 C7
Pont-Aven France 47°51N 3°47W 172 E3
Pont Canavese Italy 45°25N 7°36E 198 C4
Pont Casse Dominica 15°22N 61°21W 323 k
Pont-d'Ain France 46°3N 5°21E 173 F12
Pont-de-Roide France 47°23N 6°45E 173 E13
Pont-de-Salars France 44°18N 2°44E 174 D6
Pont-de-Vaux France 46°26N 4°56E 173 F11
Pont-de-Veyle France 46°17N 4°53E 173 F11
Pont-du-Château France 45°47N 3°15E 173 G10
Pont du Gard France 43°56N 4°32E 175 E8

Pont-l'Abbé *France* 47°52N 4°15W **172** E2
Pont-l'Évêque *France* 49°18N 0°11E **172** C7
Pont-St-Esprit *France* 44°16N 4°40E **175** D8
Pont-St-Martin *Italy* 45°36N 7°48E **198** C4
Pont-Ste-Maxence *France* 49°18N 2°36E **172** C9
Pont-sur-Yonne *France* 48°18N 3°10E **173** D10
Pont-Viau *Canada* 45°35N 73°41W **130** A1
Ponta de Pedras *Brazil* 1°23S 48°52W **332** B2
Ponta Delgada *Flores, Azores* 39°31N 31°13W **153** d2
Ponta Delgada *São Miguel, Azores* 37°44N 25°40W **153** d3
Ponta Delgada ✕ (PDL) *Azores* 37°44N 25°41W **153** d3
Ponta do Sol *Madeira* 32°42N 17°7W **153** c
Ponta Grossa *Brazil* 25°7S 50°10W **335** B5
Ponta Porã *Brazil* 22°20S 55°35W **335** A4
Pontacq *France* 43°11N 0°8W **174** E3
Pontailler-sur-Saône *France* 47°13N 5°25E **173** E12
Pontal → *Brazil* 9°8S 40°12W **332** C3
Pontalina *Brazil* 17°31S 49°27W **333** E2
Pontarlier *France* 46°54N 6°20E **173** F13
Pontassieve *Italy* 43°46N 11°26E **199** E8
Pontault-Combault *France* 48°47N 2°36E **134** B4
Pontaumur *France* 45°52N 2°40E **174** C6
Pontcharra *France* 45°26N 6°1E **175** C10
Pontchartrain, L. *U.S.A.* 30°5N 90°5W **315** F9
Pontchâteau *France* 47°25N 2°5W **172** E4
Ponte Alta, Serra do *Brazil* 19°42S 47°40W **333** E2
Ponte Alta do Norte *Brazil* 10°45S 47°34W **332** D2
Ponte Branca *Brazil* 16°27S 52°40W **331** D7
Ponte da Barca *Portugal* 41°48N 8°25W **194** D2
Ponte de Sor *Portugal* 39°17N 8°1W **195** F2
Ponte dell'Ólio *Italy* 44°52N 9°39E **198** D6
Ponte di Legno *Italy* 46°16N 10°31E **198** B7
Ponte do Lima *Portugal* 41°46N 8°35W **194** D2
Ponte do Pungué *Mozam.* 19°30S 34°33E **269** F3
Ponte-Leccia *France* 42°28N 9°13E **175** F13
Ponte nelle Alpi *Italy* 46°11N 12°16E **199** B9
Ponte Nova *Brazil* 20°25S 42°54W **333** F3
Ponte Vedra Beach *U.S.A.* 30°15N 81°23W **316** E8
Ponteareas *Spain* 42°10N 8°28W **194** C2
Pontebba *Italy* 46°30N 13°18E **199** B10
Ponteceso *Spain* 43°15N 8°54W **194** B2
Pontecorvo *Italy* 41°27N 13°40E **200** A6
Pontedeume *Spain* 43°24N 8°10W **194** B2
Ponteix *Canada* 49°46N 107°29W **297** D7
Pontes e Lacerda *Brazil* 15°12S 59°22W **331** D6
Pontevedra *Capiz, Phil.* 11°29N 122°50E **233** F4
Pontevedra *Neg. Occ., Phil.* 10°22N 122°52E **233** F4
Pontevedra *Spain* 42°26N 8°40W **194** C2
Pontevedra □ *Spain* 42°25N 8°39W **194** C2
Pontevedra, R. de → *Spain* 42°22N 8°45W **194** C2
Pontevico *Italy* 45°16N 10°5E **198** C7
Pontiac *Ill., U.S.A.* 40°53N 88°38W **311** D8
Pontiac *Mich., U.S.A.* 42°38N 83°18W **311** B13
Pontian Kechil *Malaysia* 1°29N 103°23E **237** d
Pontianak *Indonesia* 0°3S 109°15E **235** C3
Pontine Is. = Ponziane, Ísole *Italy* 40°55N 12°57E **200** B5
Pontine Mts. = Kuzey Anadolu Dağları *Turkey* 41°0N 36°45E **212** B7
Pontinha *Portugal* 38°45N 9°11W **126** A1
Pontinia *Italy* 41°25N 13°2E **200** A6
Pontivy *France* 48°5N 2°58W **172** D4
Pontoise *France* 49°3N 2°5E **173** C9
Ponton → *Canada* 58°27N 116°11W **296** B5
Pontorson *France* 48°34N 1°30W **172** D5
Pontrémoli *Italy* 44°22N 9°53E **198** D6
Pontrieux *France* 48°42N 3°10W **172** D3
Ponts *Spain* 41°55N 1°12E **196** D6
Pontypool *Ont., Canada* 44°6N 78°38W **312** B6
Pontypool *Torf., U.K.* 51°42N 3°2W **169** F4
Ponza *Italy* 40°54N 12°58E **200** B5
Ponziane, Ísole *Italy* 40°55N 12°57E **200** B5
Poochera *Australia* 32°43S 134°51E **281** E1
Poole *Trin. & Tob.* 10°17N 61°14W **323** t
Poole *Poole, U.K.* 50°43N 1°59W **169** G6
Poole □ *U.K.* 50°43N 1°59W **169** G6
Poole → *Trin. & Tob.* 10°15N 61°5W **323** t
Pooler *U.S.A.* 32°7N 81°15W **316** C8
Poona = Pune *India* 18°29N 73°57E **244** E1
Poonamallee *India* 13°3N 80°10E **245** H5
Pooncarie *Australia* 33°22S 142°31E **282** B5
Poopelloe L. *Australia* 31°40S 144°0E **282** A6
Poopó *Bolivia* 18°23S 66°59W **330** D4
Poopó, L. de *Bolivia* 18°30S 67°35W **330** D4
Poor Knights Is. *N.Z.* 35°29S 174°43E **284** B3
Poorman *U.S.A.* 64°5N 155°33W **303** D9
Popa *Gabon* 1°35S 12°32E **264** C2
Popa, Mt. *Burma* 20°55N 95°15E **241** E5
Popayán *Colombia* 2°27N 76°36W **328** C2
Poperinge *Belgium* 50°51N 2°42E **170** D2
Popiltah L. *Australia* 33°10S 141°42E **282** B4
Popina *Bulgaria* 44°7N 26°57E **203** B10
Popio L. *Australia* 33°10S 141°52E **282** B4
Poplar *London, U.K.* 51°30N 0°0 **125** A3
Poplar *Mont., U.S.A.* 48°7N 105°12W **304** B11
Poplar → *Canada* 53°0N 97°19W **297** C9
Poplar Bluff *U.S.A.* 36°46N 90°24W **308** G8
Poplar Head = Dothan *U.S.A.* 31°13N 85°24W **316** D4
Poplarville *U.S.A.* 30°51N 89°32W **315** F10
Popocatépetl, Volcán *Mexico* 19°2N 98°38W **319** D5
Popokabaka *Dem. Rep. of the Congo* 5°41S 16°40E **265** D3
Pópoli *Italy* 42°10N 13°50E **199** F10
Popolo *Dem. Rep. of the Congo* 2°22N 21°8E **264** B4
Popolo, Porta del *Rome, Italy* **136** a2
Popomanaseu, Mt. *Solomon Is.* 9°40S 160°1E **287** M11
Popondetta *Papua N. G.* 8°48S 148°17E **286** E5
Popovača *Croatia* 45°30N 16°41E **199** C13
Popovo *Bulgaria* 43°21N 26°18E **203** C10
Poppberg *Germany* 49°26N 11°37E **179** F7
Poppi *Italy* 43°43N 11°46E **199** E8
Poppintree *Ireland* 53°23N 6°17W **120** A2
Poprad *Slovak Rep.* 49°3N 20°18E **181** B13
Poprad → *Slovak Rep.* 49°38N 20°42E **181** B13
Poradaha *Bangla.* 23°51N 89°1E **241** D2
Porali → *Pakistan* 25°58N 66°26E **242** G2
Porangaba *Brazil* 8°48S 70°36W **330** B3
Porangahau *N.Z.* 40°17S 176°37E **284** G6
Porangatu *Brazil* 13°26S 49°10W **333** D2
Porbandar *India* 21°44N 69°43E **242** J3
Porce → *Colombia* 7°28N 74°53W **328** B3
Porcher I. *Canada* 53°50N 130°30W **296** C2
Porco *Bolivia* 19°50S 65°59W **331** D4
Porcos → *Brazil* 12°42S 45°7W **333** D2
Porcuna *Spain* 37°52N 4°11W **195** H6
Porcupine → *Sask., Canada* 59°11N 104°46W **297** B8
Porcupine → *Alaska, U.S.A.* 66°34N 145°19W **303** C11
Porcupine Abyssal Plain *Atl. Oc.* 48°0N 8°0W **152** B10
Porcupine Gorge △ *Australia* 20°22S 144°26E **280** C3
Pordenone *Italy* 45°57N 12°39E **199** C9
Pordim *Bulgaria* 43°23N 24°51E **203** C8
Pore *Colombia* 5°43N 72°0W **328** B3
Poreč *Croatia* 45°14N 13°36E **199** C10
Porecatu *Brazil* 22°43S 51°24W **333** F1
Porechye = Demidov *Russia* 55°16N 31°30E **188** E6
Poretskoye *Russia* 55°9N 46°21E **190** C8
Porgera *Papua N. G.* 5°28S 143°12E **286** C2
Pori *Finland* 61°29N 21°48E **188** B1
Pori *Greece* 35°58N 23°13E **204** F5
Porkhov *Russia* 57°45N 29°38E **188** D5
Porlamar *Venezuela* 10°57N 63°51W **329** a
Porlezza *Italy* 46°2N 9°7E **198** B6
Porma → *Spain* 42°49N 5°28W **194** C5
Pormpuraaw *Australia* 14°59S 141°26E **280** A3
Pormpuraaw ◎ *Australia* 14°55S 141°47E **280** A3
Pornic *France* 47°7N 2°5W **172** E4
Poronaysk *Russia* 49°13N 143°0E **219** B17
Poros *Attiki, Greece* 37°30N 23°30E **204** D5
Poros *Kefalonia, Greece* 38°9N 20°47E **207** C2
Poros *Lefkada, Greece* 38°38N 20°43E **207** B2
Poroshiri-Dake *Japan* 42°41N 142°52E **220** C11
Poroszló *Hungary* 47°39N 20°40E **182** C5
Poroto Mts. *Tanzania* 9°0S 33°30E **269** D3
Porpoise B. *Antarctica* 66°0S 127°0E **151** C9
Porpoise Pt. *Ascension I.* 7°54S 14°21W **153** g
Porquerolles, Î. de *France* 43°0N 6°13E **175** F10
Porrentruy *Switz.* 47°25N 7°6E **179** H3
Porreres *Spain* 39°31N 3°2E **206** B4
Porsangerfjorden *Norway* 70°40N 25°40E **160** A21
Porsgrunn *Norway* 59°10N 9°40E **164** E6
Port Adelaide *Australia* 34°50S 138°30E **282** C3
Port Alberni *Canada* 49°14N 124°50W **296** D4
Port Albert *Australia* 38°42S 146°42E **283** E7
Port Alexander *U.S.A.* 56°15N 134°38W **303** H14
Port Alfred *S. Africa* 33°36S 26°55E **270** D4
Port Alice *Canada* 50°20N 127°25W **296** C3
Port Allegany *U.S.A.* 41°48N 78°17W **312** E6
Port Allen *U.S.A.* 30°27N 91°12W **314** F9
Port Alma *Queens., Australia* 23°38S 150°53E **280** C5
Port Alma *Ont., Canada* 42°10N 82°14W **312** D2
Port Angeles *U.S.A.* 48°7N 123°27W **306** B3
Port Antonio *Jamaica* 18°10N 76°26W **320** a
Port Aransas *U.S.A.* 27°50N 97°4W **314** H6
Port Arthur *Tas., Australia* 43°7S 147°50E **281** G4
Port Arthur *Tex., U.S.A.* 29°54N 93°56W **314** G8
Port au Choix *Canada* 50°43N 57°22W **299** B8
Port au Port B. *Canada* 48°40N 58°50W **299** C8
Port-au-Prince *Haiti* 18°40N 72°20W **321** C5
Port Augusta *Australia* 32°30S 137°50E **282** B2
Port Austin *U.S.A.* 44°3N 83°1W **312** B2
Port Authority Bus Terminal *New York, U.S.A.* **132** c2
Port-aux-Français *Kerguelen* 49°21S 70°13E **273** J6
Port Bergé Vaovao *Madag.* 15°33S 47°40E **272** B2
Port Blair *India* 11°40N 92°45E **245** J11
Port Blandford *Canada* 48°20N 54°10W **299** C9
Port Botany *Australia* 33°58S 151°13E **139** B2
Port-Bouët *Ivory C.* 5°16N 3°57W **262** D4
Port Bradshaw *Australia* 12°30S 137°20E **280** A2
Port Broughton *Australia* 33°37S 137°56E **282** B2
Port Bruce *Canada* 42°39N 81°0W **312** D4
Port Burwell *Canada* 42°40N 80°48W **312** D4
Port Byron *U.S.A.* 41°36N 90°20W **310** C6
Port Campbell *Vic., Australia* 38°37S 143°1E **282** E5
Port Campbell *India* 11°56N 92°37E **245** J11
Port Campbell △ *Australia* 38°8S 143°6E **282** E5
Port Canning *India* 22°23N 88°40E **243** H13
Port Carling *Canada* 45°7N 79°35W **312** A5
Port-Cartier *Canada* 50°2N 66°50W **299** B6
Port Chalmers *N.Z.* 45°49S 170°30E **285** F5
Port Charles *N.Z.* 36°33S 175°30E **284** C4
Port Charlotte *U.S.A.* 26°59N 82°6W **317** J7
Port Chester *U.S.A.* 41°0N 73°40W **313** F11
Port Clements *Canada* 53°40N 132°10W **296** C2
Port Clinton *U.S.A.* 41°31N 82°56W **311** C14
Port Colborne *Canada* 42°50N 79°10W **312** D5
Port Coquitlam *Canada* 49°15N 122°45W **306** A4
Port Cornwallis *India* 13°17N 93°5E **245** H11
Port Credit *Canada* 43°33N 79°35W **312** C5
Port-Cros △ *France* 43°0N 6°24E **175** F10
Port Curtis *Australia* 23°57S 151°20E **280** C5
Port d'Alcúdia *Spain* 39°50N 3°7E **206** B4
Port Dalhousie *Canada* 43°13N 79°16W **312** C5
Port d'Andratx *Spain* 39°32N 2°23E **206** B3
Port Darwin *N. Terr., Australia* 12°24S 130°45E **278** B5
Port Darwin *Falk. Is.* 51°50S 59°0W **153** f
Port Davey *Australia* 43°16S 145°55E **281** G4
Port-de-Bouc *France* 43°24N 4°59E **175** E8
Port-de-Paix *Haiti* 19°50N 72°50W **321** C5
Port de Pollença *Spain* 39°54N 3°4E **206** B4
Port de Sóller *Spain* 39°48N 2°42E **206** B3
Port Dickson *Malaysia* 2°30N 101°49E **237** L3
Port Douglas *Australia* 16°30S 145°30E **280** B4
Port Dover *Canada* 42°47N 80°12W **312** D4
Port Edward *Canada* 54°12N 130°10W **296** C2
Port Elgin *Canada* 44°25N 81°25W **312** B3
Port Elizabeth *S. Africa* 33°58S 25°40E **270** D4
Port Ellen *U.K.* 55°38N 6°11W **167** F2
Port Elliot *Australia* 35°32S 138°41E **282** C3
Port-en-Bessin-Huppain *France* 49°21N 0°45W **172** C6
Port Erin *I. of Man* 54°5N 4°45W **168** C3
Port Essington *Australia* 11°15S 132°10E **278** B5
Port Etienne = Nouâdhibou *Mauritania* 20°54N 17°0W **260** D1
Port Ewen *U.S.A.* 41°54N 73°59W **313** E11
Port Fairy *Australia* 38°22S 142°12E **282** E5
Port Fitzroy *N.Z.* 36°8S 175°20E **284** C4
Port Florence = Kisumu *Kenya* 0°3S 34°45E **268** C3
Port Fouâd = Bûr Fuad *Egypt* 31°15N 32°20E **256** H8
Port Francqui = Ilebo *Dem. Rep. of the Congo* 4°17S 20°55E **265** C4
Port Gamble *U.S.A.* 47°51N 122°34W **306** C4
Port-Gentil *Gabon* 0°40S 8°50E **264** C1
Port Germein *Australia* 33°1S 138°1E **281** E2
Port Ghalib *Egypt* 25°20N 34°50E **246** E2
Port Gibson *U.S.A.* 31°58N 90°59W **314** F9
Port Glasgow *U.K.* 55°56N 4°41W **167** F4
Port-Gueydon = Azeffoun *Algeria* 36°51N 4°26E **261** A5
Port Harcourt *Nigeria* 4°40N 7°10E **263** E6
Port Hardy *Canada* 50°41N 127°30W **296** C3
Port Harrison = Inukjuak *Canada* 58°25N 78°15W **295** F16
Port Hawkesbury *Canada* 45°36N 61°22W **299** C7
Port Hedland *Australia* 20°25S 118°35E **278** D2
Port Heiden *U.S.A.* 56°55N 158°41W **303** H8
Port Henry *U.S.A.* 44°3N 73°28W **313** B11
Port Herald = Nsanje *Malawi* 16°55S 35°12E **269** F4
Port Hood *Canada* 46°0N 61°32W **299** C7
Port Hope *Ont., Canada* 43°56N 78°20W **312** C6
Port Hope *Mich., U.S.A.* 43°57N 82°43W **312** C2
Port Hope Simpson *Canada* 52°33N 56°18W **299** B8
Port Hueneme *U.S.A.* 34°7N 119°12W **307** L7
Port Huron *U.S.A.* 42°58N 82°26W **312** D2
Port Iliç *Azerbaijan* 38°53N 48°47E **213** C13
Port Jefferson *U.S.A.* 40°57N 73°3W **313** F11
Port Jervis *U.S.A.* 41°22N 74°41W **313** E10
Port-Joinville *France* 46°45N 2°23W **172** F4
Port Katon *Russia* 46°52N 38°46E **189** J10
Port Kembla *Australia* 34°52S 150°49E **283** C9
Port Kenny *Australia* 33°10S 134°41E **281** E1
Port-la-Nouvelle *France* 43°1N 3°3E **174** E7
Port Láirge = Waterford *Ireland* 52°15N 7°8W **166** D4
Port Lavaca *U.S.A.* 28°37N 96°38W **314** G6
Port Leyden *U.S.A.* 43°35N 75°21W **313** C9
Port Lincoln *Australia* 34°42S 135°52E **282** C1
Port Lions *U.S.A.* 57°52N 152°53W **303** H9
Port Loko *S. Leone* 8°48N 12°46W **262** D2
Port Louis *Morbihan, France* 47°42N 3°22W **172** E3
Port-Louis *Guadeloupe* 16°28N 61°32W **322** e
Port Louis *Mauritius* 20°10S 57°30E **272** e
Port Lyautey = Kenitra *Morocco* 34°15N 6°40W **260** B3
Port MacDonnell *Australia* 38°5S 140°48E **282** E4
Port McNeill *Canada* 50°35N 127°6W **296** C3
Port Macquarie *Australia* 31°25S 152°25E **283** A10
Port Maria *Jamaica* 18°22N 76°54W **320** a
Port Mathurin *Rodrigues* 19°41S 63°25E **273** F5
Port Matilda *U.S.A.* 40°48N 78°3W **312** F6
Port Mayaca *U.S.A.* 26°59N 80°36W **317** J9
Port McNicoll *Canada* 44°44N 79°48W **312** B5
Port Mearnóg = Portmarnock *Ireland* 53°26N 6°8W **120** A3
Port Melbourne *Australia* 37°50S 144°54E **128** B1
Port Mellon *Canada* 49°32N 123°31W **296** D4
Port-Menier *Canada* 49°51N 64°15W **299** C7
Port Moller *U.S.A.* 55°59N 160°34W **303** J7
Port Moody *Canada* 49°17N 122°51W **306** A4
Port Morant *Jamaica* 17°54N 76°19W **320** a
Port Moresby *Papua N. G.* 9°24S 147°8E **286** E4
Port Mourant *Guyana* 6°15N 57°20W **329** B6
Port Musgrave *Australia* 11°55S 141°50E **280** A3
Port Narevin *Vanuatu* 18°45S 169°10E **287** H7
Port-Navalo *France* 47°34N 2°54W **172** E4
Port Neches *U.S.A.* 30°0N 93°59W **314** G8
Port Nicholson *N.Z.* 41°20S 174°52E **284** H3
Port Nolloth *S. Africa* 29°17S 16°52E **270** C2
Port Nouveau-Québec = Kangiqsualujjuaq *Canada* 58°30N 65°59W **295** F18
Port of Climax *Canada* 49°10N 108°20W **297** D7
Port of Coronach *Canada* 49°7N 105°31W **297** D7
Port of Spain *Trin. & Tob.* 10°40N 61°31W **323** t
Port Olry *Vanuatu* 15°1S 167°4E **287** E5
Port Orange *U.S.A.* 29°9N 80°59W **317** F9
Port Orchard *U.S.A.* 47°32N 122°38W **306** C4
Port Orford *U.S.A.* 42°45N 124°30W **304** E1
Port Pegasus *N.Z.* 47°12S 167°41E **285** H2
Port Perry *Canada* 44°6N 78°56W **312** B6
Port Phillip B. *Australia* 38°10S 144°50E **283** E6
Port Pirie *Australia* 33°10S 138°1E **282** B3
Port Rashid *U.A.E.* 25°16N 55°17E **119** A2
Port Renfrew *Canada* 48°30N 124°20W **306** B2
Port Richmond *U.S.A.* 40°38N 74°7W **132** C1
Port Roper *Australia* 14°45S 135°25E **280** A2
Port Rowan *Canada* 42°40N 80°30W **312** D4
Port Royal *Jamaica* 17°56N 76°51W **320** a
Port Royal Sd. *U.S.A.* 32°15N 80°40W **316** C9
Port Saeed *U.A.E.* 25°15N 55°20E **119** B2
Port Safaga = Bûr Safâga *Egypt* 26°43N 33°57E **246** E2
Port Said = Bûr Sa'îd *Egypt* 31°16N 32°18E **256** H8
Port St. Joe *U.S.A.* 29°49N 85°18W **316** F4
Port St. Johns *U.S.A.* 28°29N 80°47W **317** G9
Port St. Johns = Umzimvubu *S. Africa* 31°38S 29°33E **271** D4
Port-St-Louis-du-Rhône *France* 43°23N 4°49E **175** E8
Port St. Lucie *U.S.A.* 27°18N 80°21W **317** H9
Port-Ste-Marie *France* 44°15N 0°25E **174** D4
Port Salerno *U.S.A.* 27°9N 80°12W **317** H9
Port Sanilac *U.S.A.* 43°26N 82°33W **312** C2
Port Severn *Canada* 44°48N 79°43W **312** B5
Port Shelter *China* 22°20N 114°17E **122** A2
Port Shepstone *S. Africa* 30°44S 30°28E **271** D5
Port Simpson *Canada* 54°30N 130°20W **296** C2
Port Stanley = Stanley *Falk. Is.* 51°40S 59°51W **153** f
Port Stanley *Canada* 42°40N 81°10W **312** D3
Port Sudan = Bûr Sûdân *Sudan* 19°32N 37°9E **256** D4
Port Sulphur *U.S.A.* 29°29N 89°42W **315** G10
Port-sur-Saône *France* 47°42N 6°2E **173** E13
Port Talbot *U.K.* 51°35N 3°47W **169** F4
Port Taufiq = Bûr Taufiq *Egypt* 29°54N 32°32E **256** J8
Port Townsend *U.S.A.* 48°7N 122°45W **306** B4
Port Union *Canada* 43°47N 79°7W **141** A4
Port-Vato *Vanuatu* 16°20S 168°1E **287** F6
Port-Vendres *France* 42°32N 3°8E **174** F7
Port Victoria *Australia* 34°30S 137°29E **282** C2
Port Vila *Vanuatu* 17°45S 168°18E **287** G6
Port Vladimir *Russia* 69°25N 33°6E **160** B25
Port Wakefield *Australia* 34°12S 138°10E **282** C3
Port Washington *U.S.A.* 43°23N 87°53W **308** D10
Port Weld = Kuala Sepetang *Malaysia* 4°49N 100°28E **237** K3
Port Wentworth *U.S.A.* 32°9N 81°10W **316** C8
Porta Orientalis *Romania* 45°6N 22°18E **177** F12
Portachuelo *Bolivia* 17°10S 63°20W **331** D5
Portacloy *Ireland* 54°20N 9°46W **166** B2
Portadown *U.K.* 54°25N 6°27W **166** B5
Portaferry *U.K.* 54°23N 5°33W **166** B6
Portage *Ind., U.S.A.* 41°34N 87°11W **311** C10
Portage *Mich., U.S.A.* 42°12N 85°35W **311** B11
Portage *Pa., U.S.A.* 40°23N 78°41W **312** F6
Portage *Wis., U.S.A.* 43°33N 89°28W **308** D9
Portage → *U.S.A.* 41°31N 83°5W **311** C14
Portage la Prairie *Canada* 49°58N 98°18W **297** D9
Portage Park *U.S.A.* 41°56N 87°45W **119** B2
Portageville *U.S.A.* 36°26N 89°42W **308** G9
Portal *U.S.A.* 32°33N 81°56W **316** C8
Portal de la Pau, Plaza *Barcelona, Spain* **114** c2
Portalegre *Portugal* 39°19N 7°25W **195** F3
Portalegre □ *Portugal* 39°20N 7°40W **195** F3
Portales *U.S.A.* 34°11N 103°20W **305** J12
Portarlington *Ireland* 53°9N 7°14W **166** C4
Portbou *Spain* 42°25N 3°9E **196** C8
Porteira *Brazil* 1°5S 57°4W **329** D6
Porteirinha *Brazil* 15°44S 43°2W **333** E3
Portel *Brazil* 1°57S 50°49W **332** B1
Portel *Portugal* 38°19N 7°41W **195** G3
Portela, Lisboa ✕ (LIS) *Portugal* 38°46N 9°8W **126** A2
Porter *U.S.A.* 41°36N 87°4W **311** C9
Porter, L. *U.S.A.* 28°30N 81°19W **133** A3
Porter L. *N.W.T., Canada* 61°41N 108°5W **297** A7
Porter L. *Sask., Canada* 56°20N 107°20W **297** B7
Porterville *Western Cape, S. Africa* 33°0S 19°0E **270** D2
Porterville *Calif., U.S.A.* 36°4N 119°1W **306** J8
Portes-lès-Valence *France* 44°52N 4°54E **175** D8
Porth Tywyn = Burry Port *U.K.* 51°41N 4°15W **169** F3
Porthcawl *U.K.* 51°29N 3°42W **169** F4
Porthill *U.S.A.* 48°59N 116°30W **304** B5
Porthmadog *U.K.* 52°55N 4°8W **168** E3
Portile de Fier *Europe* 44°44N 22°30E **182** F7
Portimão *Portugal* 37°8N 8°32W **195** H2
Portishead *U.K.* 51°29N 2°46W **169** F5
Portiţei, Gura *Romania* 44°40N 29°0E **183** F14
Portknockie *U.K.* 57°42N 2°51W **167** D6
Portland *N.S.W., Australia* 33°20S 150°0E **283** B9
Portland *Vic., Australia* 38°20S 141°35E **282** E4
Portland *Ont., Canada* 44°42N 76°12W **313** B8
Portland *Conn., U.S.A.* 41°34N 72°38W **313** E12
Portland *Fla., U.S.A.* 30°31N 86°12W **316** E3
Portland *Ind., U.S.A.* 40°26N 84°59W **311** D12
Portland *Maine, U.S.A.* 43°39N 70°16W **309** D18
Portland *Mich., U.S.A.* 42°52N 84°54W **311** B12
Portland *Oreg., U.S.A.* 45°32N 122°37W **306** E4
Portland *Pa., U.S.A.* 40°55N 75°6W **313** F9
Portland *Tex., U.S.A.* 27°53N 97°20W **314** H6
Portland, I. of *U.K.* 50°33N 2°26W **169** G5
Portland, Récif *French Polynesia* 23°42S 134°30W **289** f
Portland B. *Australia* 38°15S 141°45E **282** E4
Portland Bight *Jamaica* 17°52N 77°5W **320** a
Portland Bill *U.K.* 50°31N 2°28W **169** G5
Portland Canal *U.S.A.* 55°56N 130°0W **296** B2
Portland I. *N.Z.* 39°20S 177°51E **284** F6
Portland Int. ✕ (PDX) *U.S.A.* 45°35N 122°36W **306** E4
Portland Pt. *Ascension I.* 7°59S 14°25W **153** g
Portland Pt. *Jamaica* 17°42N 77°11W **320** a
Portlaoise *Ireland* 53°2N 7°18W **166** C4
Portmadoc = Porthmadog *U.K.* 52°55N 4°8W **168** E3
Portmarnock *Ireland* 53°26N 6°8W **120** A3
Portmore *Jamaica* 17°53N 76°53W **320** a
Porto *Brazil* 3°54S 42°42W **332** B3
Porto *Corse-du-Sud, France* 42°16N 8°42E **175** F12
Porto *Portugal* 41°8N 8°40W **194** D2
Porto □ *Portugal* 41°8N 8°20W **194** D2
Porto, G. de *France* 42°17N 8°34E **175** F12
Porto Acre *Brazil* 9°34S 67°31W **330** B4
Pôrto Alegre = Luzilândia *Brazil* 3°28S 42°22W **332** B3
Pôrto Alegre *Pará, Brazil* 4°22S 52°44W **329** D7
Pôrto Alegre *Rio Grande do S., Brazil* 30°5S 51°10W **335** C5
Porto Alegre *São Tomé & Principe* 0°2N 6°32E **265** a
Porto Amboim = Gunza *Angola* 10°50S 13°50E **265** E2
Porto Amélia = Pemba *Mozam.* 12°58S 40°30E **269** E5
Porto Azzurro *Italy* 42°46N 10°24E **198** F7
Porto Brandão *Portugal* 38°40N 9°12W **126** A1
Porto Cajueiro *Brazil* 11°3S 55°53W **331** C6
Porto Colom *Spain* 39°26N 3°15E **206** B4
Porto Cristo *Spain* 39°33N 3°20E **206** B4
Pôrto da Fôlha *Brazil* 9°55S 37°17W **332** C4
Porto de Moz *Brazil* 1°41S 52°13W **329** D7
Porto de Pedras *Brazil* 9°10S 35°17W **332** C4
Pôrto des Meinacos *Brazil* 12°33S 53°7W **331** C7
Pôrto dos Gaúchos *Brazil* 11°32S 57°16W **331** C6
Porto Empédocle *Italy* 37°17N 13°32E **200** E6
Porto Esperança *Brazil* 19°37S 57°29W **331** D6
Porto Espirídão *Brazil* 15°51S 58°28W **331** D6
Porto Formoso *Azores* 37°49N 25°25W **153** d3
Porto Franco *Brazil* 6°20S 47°24W **332** C2
Porto Grande *Brazil* 0°42N 51°24W **329** C7
Porto Inglês *C. Verde Is.* 15°21N 23°10W **153** j
Porto Jofre *Brazil* 17°20S 56°48W **331** D6
Porto Lengone = Porto Azzurro *Italy* 42°46N 10°24E **198** F7
Porto Maurizio = Impéria *Italy* 43°53N 8°3E **198** E5
Porto Mendes *Brazil* 24°30S 54°15W **335** A5
Porto Moniz *Madeira* 32°52N 17°11W **153** c
Porto Murtinho *Brazil* 21°45S 57°55W **331** E6
Porto Nacional *Brazil* 10°40S 48°30W **332** D2
Porto-Novo *Benin* 6°23N 2°42E **263** D5
Pôrto Novo *Rio de J., Brazil* 22°50S 43°7W **135** A2
Porto Novo Cr. → *Nigeria* 6°25N 3°22E **124** B2
Porto Primavera, Represa *Brazil* 22°10S 52°45W **335** A5
Porto San Giòrgio *Italy* 43°11N 13°48E **199** E10
Porto Sant' Elpidio *Italy* 43°15N 13°43E **199** E10
Porto Santana *Brazil* 0°3S 51°11W **329** D7
Porto Santo, I. de *Madeira* 33°45N 16°25W **260** B1
Porto Santo Stéfano *Italy* 42°26N 11°7E **198** F8
Porto São José *Brazil* 22°43S 53°10W **335** A5
Porto Seguro = Guadalupe *Brazil* 6°44S 43°47W **332** C3
Porto Seguro *Brazil* 16°26S 39°5W **333** E4
Porto Tolle *Italy* 44°56N 12°22E **199** D9
Porto Tórres *Italy* 40°50N 8°24E **200** B1
Porto União *Brazil* 26°10S 51°10W **335** B5
Porto-Vecchio *France* 41°35N 9°16E **175** G13
Porto Velho *Brazil* 8°46S 63°54W **331** B5
Porto Walter *Brazil* 8°15S 72°40W **330** B3
Portobello *U.K.* 55°57N 3°7W **121** B3
Portobelo *Panama* 9°35N 79°42W **320** E4
Portoferráio *Italy* 42°48N 10°20E **198** F7
Portofino *Italy* 44°18N 9°12E **198** D6
Portogruaro *Italy* 45°47N 12°50E **199** C9
Portola *U.S.A.* 39°49N 120°28W **306** F6
Portomaggiore *Italy* 44°42N 11°48E **199** D8
Portopetro *Spain* 39°22N 3°13E **206** B4
Portør *Norway* 58°48N 9°28E **164** F6
Portoscuso *Italy* 39°12N 8°24E **200** C1
Portovénere *Italy* 44°3N 9°51E **198** D6
Portoviejo *Ecuador* 1°7S 80°28W **328** D1
Portpatrick *U.K.* 54°51N 5°7W **167** G3
Portree *U.K.* 57°25N 6°12W **167** D2
Portrero *U.S.A.* 37°46N 122°25W **136** B3
Portrush *U.K.* 55°12N 6°40W **166** A5
Portsmouth *Dominica* 15°34N 61°27W **323** k
Portsmouth *Portsmouth, U.K.* 50°48N 1°6W **169** G6
Portsmouth *N.H., U.S.A.* 43°5N 70°45W **313** C14
Portsmouth *Ohio, U.S.A.* 38°44N 82°57W **309** F12
Portsmouth *R.I., U.S.A.* 41°36N 71°15W **313** E13
Portsmouth *Va., U.S.A.* 36°58N 76°23W **309** G15
Portsmouth □ *U.K.* 50°48N 1°6W **169** G6
Portsoy *U.K.* 57°41N 2°41W **167** D6
Portstewart *U.K.* 55°11N 6°43W **166** A5
Porttipahdan tekojärvi *Finland* 68°5N 26°40E **160** B22
Portugal ■ *Europe* 40°0N 8°0W **194** F3
Portugalete *Spain* 43°19N 3°4W **196** B1
Portuguesa □ *Venezuela* 9°10N 69°15W **328** B4
Portuguese East Africa = Mozambique ■ *Africa* 19°0S 35°0E **269** F4
Portuguese Guinea = Guinea-Bissau ■ *Africa* 12°0N 15°0W **262** C2
Portuguese Timor = East Timor ■ *Asia* 8°50S 126°0E **231** F7
Portuguese West Africa = Angola ■ *Africa* 12°0S 18°0E **265** E3
Portumna *Ireland* 53°6N 8°14W **166** C3
Portville *U.S.A.* 42°3N 78°20W **312** D6
Poruma *Australia* 10°2S 143°4E **280** a
Porus *Jamaica* 18°2N 77°25W **320** a
Porvenir *Bolivia* 11°10S 68°50W **330** C4
Porvenir *Chile* 53°10S 70°16W **336** G2
Porvoo *Finland* 60°24N 25°40E **188** B3
Porzuna *Spain* 39°9N 4°9W **195** F6
Pos Chiquito *Aruba* 12°27N 69°57W **322** f
Posada *Italy* 40°38N 9°43E **200** B2
Posada → *Italy* 40°39N 9°45E **200** B2
Posadas *Argentina* 27°30S 55°50W **335** B4
Posadas *Spain* 37°47N 5°11W **195** H5
Poschiavo *Switz.* 46°19N 10°4E **179** J6
Posen = Poznań *Poland* 52°25N 16°55E **185** F3
Posen *U.S.A.* 41°38N 87°42W **119** D2
Posets *Spain* 42°39N 0°25E **196** C5
Poseyville *U.S.A.* 38°10N 87°47W **311** F9
Poshan = Boshan *China* 36°28N 117°49E **227** F9
Posht-e Badam *Iran* 33°2N 55°23E **247** C7
Posidium *Greece* 35°30N 27°10E **205** F9
Poso *Indonesia* 1°20S 120°55E **231** E6
Poso, Danau *Indonesia* 1°52S 120°35E **231** E6
Posoegroenoe *Suriname* 4°23N 55°43W **329** C6
Posof *Turkey* 41°30N 42°43E **213** B10
Pospelikha *Russia* 51°57N 81°46E **217** B10
Posse *Brazil* 14°4S 46°18W **333** D2
Possedimenti Italiani dell'Egeo = Dodecanese *Greece* 36°35N 27°0E **205** E8
Possel *C.A.R.* 5°5N 19°10E **264** A3
Possession I. *Antarctica* 72°4S 172°0E **151** D11
Pössneck *Germany* 50°42N 11°35E **178** E7
Possum Kingdom L. *U.S.A.* 32°52N 98°26W **314** E5
Post *U.S.A.* 33°12N 101°23W **314** E4
Post Falls *U.S.A.* 47°43N 116°57W **304** C5
Postavy = Pastavy *Belarus* 55°4N 26°50E **188** E4
Poste, R. du *Mauritius* 20°29S 57°36E **272** e
Poste de Flacq *Mauritius* 20°9S 57°43E **272** e
Poste de Flacq → *Mauritius* 20°9S 57°44E **272** e
Poste-de-la-Baleine = Kuujjuarapik *Canada* 55°20N 77°35W **298** A4
Postmasburg *S. Africa* 28°18S 23°5E **270** C3
Postojna *Slovenia* 45°46N 14°12E **199** C11
Poston *U.S.A.* 34°0N 114°24W **307** M12
Postumia = Postojna *Slovenia* 45°46N 14°12E **199** C11
Postville *Nfld. & L., Canada* 54°54N 59°47W **299** B8
Postville *Iowa, U.S.A.* 43°5N 91°34W **310** A5
Posyet *Russia* 42°39N 130°48E **220** C5
Potamos *Antikythira, Greece* 35°52N 23°15E **204** F5
Potamos *Kythira, Greece* 36°15N 22°58E **204** E4
Potchefstroom *S. Africa* 26°41S 27°7E **270** C4
Potcoava *Romania* 44°30N 24°39E **183** F9
Poté *Brazil* 17°49S 41°49W **333** E3
Poteau *U.S.A.* 35°3N 94°37W **314** D7
Poteet *U.S.A.* 29°2N 98°35W **314** G5
Potenza *Italy* 40°38N 15°48E **201** B8
Potenza → *Italy* 43°25N 13°40E **199** E10
Potenza Picena *Italy* 43°22N 13°37E **199** E10
Poteriteri, L. *N.Z.* 46°5S 167°10E **285** G2
Potgietersrus = Mokopane *S. Africa* 24°10S 28°55E **271** B4
Poti *Georgia* 42°10N 41°38E **191** J5
Potiraguá *Brazil* 15°36S 39°53W **333** E4
Potiskum *Nigeria* 11°39N 11°2E **263** C7
Potlogi *Romania* 44°34N 25°34E **183** F10
Potomac → *U.S.A.* 38°0N 76°23W **309** F14
Potomac Overlook Reg. Park ⌂ *U.S.A.* 38°55N 77°6W **143** B2
Potomac Park *Washington, D.C., U.S.A.* **143** c1
Potosí *Bolivia* 19°38S 65°50W **331** D4
Potosi *Mo., U.S.A.* 37°56N 90°47W **310** G6
Potosí □ *Bolivia* 20°31S 67°0W **330** E4
Potosi Mt. *U.S.A.* 35°57N 115°29W **307** K11
Pototan *Phil.* 10°54N 122°38E **233** F4
Potrerillos *Chile* 26°30S 69°30W **334** B2
Potrero Pt. *U.S.A.* 37°45N 122°22W **136** B2
Potsdam *Brandenburg, Germany* 52°23N 13°3E **115** B1
Potsdam *N.Y., U.S.A.* 44°40N 74°59W **313** B10
Potsdamer Platz *Berlin, Germany* **115** b3
Pottangi *India* 18°34N 82°58E **244** E6
Pottenstein *Germany* 49°46N 11°24E **179** F7
Potters Village *Antigua & B.* 17°5N 61°49W **322** b
Pottersville *U.S.A.* 43°43N 73°50W **313** C11
Pottery Hill = Abû Ballas *Egypt* 24°26N 27°36E **256** C2
Pottstown *U.S.A.* 40°15N 75°39W **313** F9
Pottsville *U.S.A.* 40°41N 76°12W **313** F8
Pottuvil *Sri Lanka* 6°55N 81°50E **245** L5
Potzham *Germany* 48°1N 11°36E **131** B2
Pötzleinsdorf *Austria* 48°14N 16°17E **142** A1
P'otzu *Taiwan* 23°28N 120°15E **225** C2
Pouancé *France* 47°44N 1°10W **172** E5
Pouce Coupé *Canada* 55°40N 120°10W **296** B4
Pouébo *N. Cal.* 20°24S 164°36E **288** d
Poughkeepsie *U.S.A.* 41°42N 73°56W **313** E11
Pouilly-sur-Loire *France* 47°17N 2°57E **173** E9
Poulan *U.S.A.* 31°31N 83°47W **316** D6
Poulaphouca Res. *Ireland* 53°8N 6°30W **166** C5
Poulsbo *U.S.A.* 47°44N 122°38W **306** C4
Poultney *U.S.A.* 43°31N 73°14W **313** C11
Poulton-le-Fylde *U.K.* 53°51N 2°58W **168** D5
Poum *N. Cal.* 20°14S 164°2E **288** d
Pounga-Nganda *Gabon* 2°58S 10°51E **264** C2
Pouso Alegre *Mato Grosso, Brazil* 11°46S 57°16W **331** C6
Pouso Alegre *Minas Gerais, Brazil* 22°14S 45°57W **335** A6
Pouso Alto = Piracanjuba *Brazil* 17°18S 49°1W **333** E2
Pout *Senegal* 14°45N 17°0W **262** C1
Pouthisat *Cambodia* 12°34N 103°50E **236** F4
Pouytenga *Burkina Faso* 12°15N 0°25W **263** C4
Pouzauges *France* 46°47N 0°50W **172** F6
Pova de Santa Iria *Portugal* 38°51N 9°4W **195** G1
Považská Bystrica *Slovak Rep.* 49°8N 18°27E **181** B11
Povenets *Russia* 62°50N 34°50E **186** B5
Poverty B. *N.Z.* 38°43S 178°2E **284** E7
Povlen *Serbia* 44°9N 19°44E **202** B3
Póvoa de Lanhosa *Portugal* 41°33N 8°15W **194** D2
Póvoa de Santo Adriao *Portugal* 38°47N 9°9W **126** A2
Póvoa de Varzim *Portugal* 41°25N 8°46W **194** D2
Povoação *Azores* 37°45N 25°15W **153** d3
Povorino *Russia* 51°12N 42°5E **190** E6
Povorotnyy, Mys *Russia* 42°40N 133°2E **220** C6
Povungnituk = Puvirnituq *Canada* 60°2N 77°10W **295** E16
Powassan *Canada* 46°5N 79°25W **298** C4
Poway *U.S.A.* 32°58N 117°2W **307** N9
Powązki *Poland* 52°15N 20°58E **143** B1
Powder → *U.S.A.* 46°45N 105°26W **304** C11
Powder River *U.S.A.* 43°2N 106°59W **304** E10
Powder Springs *U.S.A.* 33°52N 84°41W **316** B5
Powell *U.S.A.* 44°45N 108°46W **304** D9
Powell, L. *U.S.A.* 36°57N 111°29W **305** H8
Powell River *Canada* 49°50N 124°35W **296** D4
Powelton *U.S.A.* 33°26N 82°52W **316** B7
Power House = Drayton Valley *Canada* 53°12N 114°58W **296** C6
Powers *U.S.A.* 45°41N 87°32W **308** C10
Powiśle *Poland* 52°14N 21°1E **143** B2
Pownal *U.S.A.* 42°45N 73°14W **313** D11
Powsin *Poland* 52°8N 21°6E **143** C2
Powsinek *Poland* 52°9N 21°6E **143** C2
Powys □ *U.K.* 52°20N 3°20W **169** E4
Poxoréo *Brazil* 15°50S 54°23W **331** D7
Poya *N. Cal.* 21°19S 165°7E **288** d
Poyan Res. *Singapore* 1°22N 103°40E **138** A2
Poyang Hu *China* 29°5N 116°20E **229** C11
Poyarkovo *Russia* 49°36N 128°41E **215** E13
Poysdorf *Austria* 48°40N 16°37E **181** C9
Poza de la Sal *Spain* 42°35N 3°31W **194** C7
Poza Rica *Mexico* 20°33N 97°27W **319** C5
Pozantı *Turkey* 37°25N 34°50E **212** D6
Požarevac *Serbia* 44°35N 21°18E **202** B5
Pozazal, Puerto *Spain* 42°56N 4°10W **194** C6
Požega *Croatia* 45°20N 17°40E **182** E2
Požega *Serbia* 43°53N 20°2E **202** C4
Poznań *Poland* 52°25N 16°55E **185** F3
Poznań ✕ (POZ) *Poland* 52°26N 16°45E **185** F3
Pozo *U.S.A.* 35°20N 120°24W **307** K6
Pozo Alcón *Spain* 37°42N 2°56W **195** H8
Pozo Almonte *Chile* 20°10S 69°50W **330** E4
Pozo Colorado *Paraguay* 23°30S 58°45W **334** A4
Pozoblanco *Spain* 38°23N 4°51W **195** G6
Pozorrubio *Phil.* 16°7N 120°33E **232** C3
Pozuelo de Alarcón *Spain* 40°24N 3°49W **127** B1
Pozuzo *Peru* 10°5S 75°35W **330** C2
Pozzallo *Italy* 36°43N 14°51E **201** F7
Pozzomaggiore *Italy* 40°24N 8°39E **200** B1
Pozzuoli *Italy* 40°49N 14°7E **201** B7
Pra → *Ghana* 5°1N 1°37W **263** D4
Prabuty *Poland* 53°47N 19°15E **184** E6
Prača *Bos.-H.* 43°47N 18°43E **182** G3
Prachatice *Czech Rep.* 49°1N 14°0E **180** B6
Prachin Buri *Thailand* 14°0N 101°25E **236** F3
Prachuap Khirikhan *Thailand* 11°49N 99°48E **237** G2
Pradelles *France* 44°46N 3°52E **174** D7
Pradera *Colombia* 3°25N 76°15W **328** C2
Prades *France* 42°38N 2°23E **174** F6
Prado *Brazil* 17°20S 39°13W **333** E4
Prado, Museo del *Madrid, Spain* **127** b3
Prado Churubusco *Mexico* 19°20N 99°8W **128** B2
Prado del Rey *Spain* 36°48N 5°33W **195** J5
Præstø *Denmark* 55°8N 12°2E **163** J6
Praga *Poland* 52°15N 21°2E **143** B2
Pragersko *Slovenia* 46°27N 15°42E **199** B12
Prague = Praha *Czech Rep.* 50°4N 14°25E **135** B2
Praha *Czech Rep.* 50°4N 14°25E **135** B2
Praha ✕ (PRG) *Czech Rep.* 50°6N 14°16E **135** B1
Prahecq *France* 46°19N 0°26W **174** B3
Prahita → *India* 19°0N 79°55E **244** E4
Prahova □ *Romania* 45°10N 26°0E **183** E10
Prahova → *Romania* 44°50N 25°50E **183** F10
Prahovo *Serbia* 44°18N 22°39E **202** B6
Praia *Azores* 39°3N 27°58W **153** d1
Praia *C. Verde Is.* 15°2N 23°34W **153** j
Praia a Mare *Italy* 39°50N 15°45E **201** C8
Praia da Vitória *Azores* 38°44N 27°4W **153** d1
Praia do Norte *Azores* 38°36N 28°46W **153** d1
Praia Grande *Brazil* 24°0S 46°24W **333** F2
Praid *Romania* 46°32N 25°10E **183** D10
Prainha *Azores* 38°27N 28°12W **153** d1
Prainha *Pará, Brazil* 1°45S 53°30W **329** D7
Prainha Nova *Brazil* 7°10S 60°30W **331** B5
Praires, R. des → *Canada* 45°38N 73°36W **130** A2
Prairie *Australia* 20°50S 144°35E **280** C3
Prairie City *U.S.A.* 44°28N 118°43W **304** D4
Prairie Dog Town Fork Red → *U.S.A.* 34°34N 99°58W **314** D5
Prairie du Chien *U.S.A.* 43°3N 91°9W **310** A5
Prairie du Rocher *U.S.A.* 38°5N 90°6W **310** F6
Prairie Village *U.S.A.* 38°58N 94°38W **310** F2
Prairies, L. of the *Canada* 51°16N 101°32W **297** C8
Pramanda *Greece* 39°32N 21°8E **204** B3
Prambanan *Indonesia* 7°45S 110°29E **235** D4
Prambanan △ *Indonesia* 7°45S 110°28E **231** G14
Prampram *Ghana* 5°43N 0°8E **263** D5
Pran Buri *Thailand* 12°23N 99°55E **236** F2
Prándarjökull *Iceland* 64°40N 14°55W **155** C12
Prang *Ghana* 8°1N 0°56W **263** D4
Prapat *Indonesia* 2°41N 98°58E **234** B1
Praslin *St. Lucia* 13°52N 60°54W **323** m
Praslin *Seychelles* 4°18S 55°45E **272** c
Prasonisi, Akra *Greece* 35°42N 27°46E **206** F11
Prassberg = Mozirje *Slovenia* 46°22N 14°58E **199** B11
Praszka *Poland* 51°5N 18°31E **185** G5
Prata *Brazil* 19°25S 48°54W **333** E2
Pratabpur *India* 23°28N 83°15E **243** H10
Pratapgarh *Raj., India* 24°2N 74°40E **242** G6
Pratapgarh *Ut. P., India* 25°56N 81°59E **243** G9
Pratas I. = Dongsha Dao *S. China Sea* 20°45N 116°43E **229** G11
Prater *Austria* 48°12N 16°25E **142** A2
Prato *Italy* 43°53N 11°6E **198** E8
Prátola Peligna *Italy* 42°6N 13°52E **199** F10
Prats-de-Mollo-la-Preste *France* 42°25N 2°27E **174** F6
Pratt *U.S.A.* 37°39N 98°44W **308** G4
Prattville *U.S.A.* 32°28N 86°29W **315** E11
Praust = Pruszcz Gdański *Poland* 54°17N 18°40E **184** D5
Pravara → *India* 19°35N 74°45E **244** E2
Pravdinsk *Kaliningrad, Russia* 54°27N 21°1E **184** D8
Pravdinsk *Nizhniy Novgorod, Russia* 56°29N 43°28E **190** B6
Pravets *Bulgaria* 42°53N 23°55E **202** D7
Pravia *Spain* 43°30N 6°12W **194** B4
Praya *Indonesia* 8°39S 116°17E **235** D5
Prayag = Allahabad *India* 25°25N 81°58E **243** G9
Pré-en-Pail *France* 48°28N 0°12W **172** D6
Preah Vihear *Cambodia* 14°23N 104°41E **236** E5
Preau *Trin. & Tob.* 10°12N 61°19W **323** t
Preble *U.S.A.* 42°44N 76°8W **313** D8
Prêcheur *Martinique* 14°48N 61°13W **322** j
Precipice △ *Australia* 25°18S 150°5E **281** D5
Precordillera *Argentina* 30°0S 69°1W **334** C2
Precotto *Italy* 45°30N 9°13E **128** A2
Predáppio *Italy* 44°6N 11°59E **199** D8
Predazzo *Italy* 46°19N 11°36E **199** B8
Predeal *Romania* 45°30N 25°34E **183** E10
Predejane *Serbia* 42°51N 22°9E **202** D6
Preeceville *Canada* 51°57N 102°40W **297** C8
Preetz *Germany* 54°14N 10°18E **178** A6
Pregolya → *Russia* 54°41N 20°22E **184** D7
Pregrada *Croatia* 46°11N 15°45E **199** B12
Preiļi *Latvia* 56°18N 26°43E **188** D4
Preko *Croatia* 44°7N 15°10E **199** D12
Prelog *Croatia* 46°18N 16°32E **199** B13
Premer *Australia* 31°29S 149°56E **283** A8
Prémery *France* 47°10N 3°18E **173** E10
Premià de Mar *Spain* 41°29N 2°22E **196** D7
Premont *U.S.A.* 27°22N 98°7W **314** H5
Premuda *Croatia* 44°20N 14°36E **199** D11
Prenestino Labicano *Italy* 41°53N 12°33E **136** B2
Prentice *U.S.A.* 45°33N 90°17W **308** C8
Prenzlau *Germany* 53°19N 13°50E **178** B9
Prenzlauerberg *Germany* 52°32N 13°24E **115** A3
Preobrazheniye *Russia* 42°54N 133°54E **220** C6
Preparis I. = Pariparit Kyun *Burma* 14°52N 93°41E **245** G11
Preparis North Channel *Ind. Oc.* 15°27N 94°5E **245** G11
Preparis South Channel *Ind. Oc.* 14°33N 93°30E **245** G11
Přerov *Czech Rep.* 49°28N 17°27E **181** B10
Prescott *Ont., Canada* 44°45N 75°30W **313** B9
Prescott *Ariz., U.S.A.* 34°33N 112°28W **305** J7
Prescott *Ark., U.S.A.* 33°48N 93°23W **314** E8
Prescott Valley *U.S.A.* 34°40N 112°18W **305** J7
Preservation Inlet *N.Z.* 46°8S 166°35E **285** G1
Preševo *Serbia* 42°19N 21°39E **202** D5

Presho U.S.A. 43°54N 100°3W 308 D3
Presicce Italy 39°54N 18°16E 201 C11
Presidencia de la Plaza Argentina 27°0S 59°50W 334 B4
Presidencia Roque Saenz Peña Argentina 26°45S 60°30W 334 B3
Président-Thiers, Récif French Polynesia 24°30S 146°0W 289 f
Presidente Dutra Brazil 5°15S 44°30W 332 C3
Presidente Epitácio Brazil 21°56S 52°6W 333 F1
Presidente Figueiredo Brazil 1°57S 60°2W 329 D5
Presidente Hayes □ Paraguay 24°0S 59°0W 334 A4
Presidente Juán Perón = Chaco □ Argentina 26°30S 61°0W 334 B3
Presidente Médici Brazil 11°17S 61°55W 331 C5
Presidente Prudente Brazil 22°5S 51°25W 335 A5
Presidente Vargas = Nova Era Brazil 19°45S 43°3W 333 E3
Presidio U.S.A. 29°34N 104°22W 314 G2
Preslav Bulgaria 43°10N 26°52E 203 C10
Preslavska Planina Bulgaria 43°10N 26°45E 203 C10
Prešov Slovak Rep. 49°0N 21°15E 181 B14
Prešovský □ Slovak Rep. 49°10N 21°0E 181 B13
Prespa Bulgaria 41°44N 24°55E 203 E8
Prespa, L. = Prespansko Jezero Macedonia 40°55N 21°0E 202 F5
Prespa △ Greece 40°48N 21°4E 202 F5
Prespansko Jezero Macedonia 40°55N 21°0E 202 F5
Presque I. U.S.A. 42°10N 80°6W 312 D4
Presque Isle U.S.A. 46°41N 68°1W 309 B19
Pressburg = Bratislava Slovak Rep. 48°10N 17°7E 181 C10
Prestatyn U.K. 53°20N 3°24W 168 D4
Prestea Ghana 5°22N 2°7W 262 D4
Presteigne U.K. 52°17N 3°0W 169 E5
Přeštice Czech Rep. 49°34N 13°20E 180 B6
Presto Bolivia 18°55S 64°56W 331 D5
Preston Vic., Australia 37°44S 145°0E 128 A1
Preston Ont., Canada 43°23N 80°21W 312 C4
Preston Lancs., U.K. 53°46N 2°42W 168 D5
Preston Ga., U.S.A. 32°4N 84°32W 316 C5
Preston Idaho, U.S.A. 42°6N 111°53W 304 E8
Preston Iowa, U.S.A. 42°3N 90°24W 310 B6
Preston Minn., U.S.A. 43°40N 92°5W 308 D7
Preston Mo., U.S.A. 37°56N 93°13W 310 G3
Preston, C. Australia 20°51S 116°12E 278 D2
Prestonsburg U.S.A. 37°40N 82°47W 309 G12
Prestranda Norway 59°6N 9°4E 162 E3
Prestwick U.K. 55°29N 4°37W 167 F4
Prêto → Amazonas, Brazil 0°8S 64°6W 329 D5
Prêto → Bahia, Brazil 11°21S 43°52W 332 D3
Prêto do Igapó-Açu → Brazil 4°26S 59°48W 329 D6
Pretoria S. Africa 25°44S 28°12E 271 C4
Pretos Forros, Sa. dos Brazil 22°54S 43°17W 135 B1
Preuilly-sur-Claise France 46°51N 0°56E 172 F7
Preussisch-Eylau = Bagrationovsk Russia 54°23N 20°39E 184 D7
Preussisch Friedland = Debrzno Poland 53°31N 17°14E 184 E4
Preussisch Holland = Pasłęk Poland 54°3N 19°41E 184 D6
Preussisch-Stargard = Starogard Gdański Poland 53°59N 18°30E 184 E5
Preveza Greece 38°57N 20°45E 207 B2
Preveza □ Greece 39°10N 20°40E 204 B2
Preveza-Lefkada ✈ (PVK) Greece 38°57N 20°45E 207 B2
Préville Canada 45°28N 73°29W 130 B3
Prey Veng Cambodia 11°35N 105°29E 237 G5
Přezletice Czech Rep. 50°9N 14°34E 135 B3
Priazovskoye Ukraine 46°44N 35°40E 189 J8
Pribalkhash = Balqash Kazakhstan 46°50N 74°50E 214 E8
Pribilof Is. U.S.A. 57°0N 170°0W 303 H5
Priboj Serbia 43°35N 19°32E 202 C3
Příbram Czech Rep. 49°41N 14°2E 180 B7
Price U.S.A. 39°36N 110°49W 304 G8
Price, C. India 13°34N 93°3E 245 H11
Price I. Canada 52°23N 128°41W 296 C3
Prichard U.S.A. 30°44N 88°5W 315 F10
Prickly Pear Cays Anguilla 18°16N 63°11W 322 a
Prickly Pt. Grenada 11°59N 61°45W 323 q
Priego Spain 40°26N 2°21W 196 E2
Priego de Córdoba Spain 37°27N 4°12W 195 H6
Priekule Latvia 56°26N 21°35E 184 B8
Priekule Lithuania 55°33N 21°19E 184 C8
Prien Germany 47°51N 12°20E 179 H8
Prienai Lithuania 54°38N 23°57E 184 D10
Prieska S. Africa 29°40S 22°42E 270 C3
Priest L. U.S.A. 48°35N 116°52W 304 B5
Priest River U.S.A. 48°11N 116°55W 304 B5
Priest Valley U.S.A. 36°10N 120°39W 306 J6
Prieto Diaz Phil. 13°2N 124°12E 232 E5
Prievidza Slovak Rep. 48°46N 18°36E 181 C11
Prignitz Germany 53°6N 11°45E 178 B7
Prijedor Bos.-H. 44°58N 16°41E 199 D13
Prijepolje Serbia 43°27N 19°40E 202 C3
Prikaspiyskaya Nizmennost = Caspian Depression Eurasia 47°0N 48°0E 191 G9
Prikro Ivory C. 7°40N 3°59W 262 D4
Prikubanskaya Nizmennost Russia 45°39N 38°33E 191 H4
Prilep Macedonia 41°21N 21°32E 202 E5
Priluki = Pryluky Ukraine 50°30N 32°24E 189 G7
Prima Porta Italy 42°0N 12°30E 136 B1
Primavalle Italy 41°55N 12°25E 136 B1
Prime Seal I. Australia 40°3S 147°43E 281 G4
Primeira Cruz Brazil 2°30S 43°26W 332 B3
Primkenau = Przemków Poland 51°31N 15°48E 185 G2
Primo Tapia Mexico 32°16N 116°54W 307 N10
Primorsk Kaliningrad, Russia 54°44N 20°0E 184 D6
Primorsk St. Petersburg, Russia 60°22N 28°37E 188 B5
Primorskiy Kray □ Russia 45°0N 135°0E 220 B7
Primorsko Bulgaria 42°15N 27°44E 203 D11
Primorsko-Akhtarsk Russia 46°2N 38°10E 189 J10
Primrose S. Africa 26°11S 28°9E 123 B2
Primrose L. Canada 54°55N 109°45W 297 C7
Prince Albert Sask., Canada 53°15N 105°50W 297 C7
Prince Albert Western Cape, S. Africa 33°12S 22°2E 270 D3
Prince Albert △ Canada 54°0N 106°25W 297 C7
Prince Albert Mts. Antarctica 76°0S 161°30E 151 D11
Prince Albert Pen. Canada 72°30N 116°0W 294 C8
Prince Albert Sd. Canada 70°25N 115°0W 294 C9
Prince Alfred, C. Canada 74°20N 124°40W 150 B1
Prince Charles I. Canada 67°47N 76°12W 295 D16
Prince Charles Mts. Antarctica 72°0S 67°0E 151 D6
Prince Edward Fracture Zone Ind. Oc. 46°0S 35°0E 151 A4
Prince Edward I. □ Canada 46°20N 63°20W 299 C7
Prince Edward Is. Ind. Oc. 46°35S 38°0E 273 J2
Prince George Canada 53°55N 122°50W 296 C4
Prince of Wales, C. U.S.A. 65°36N 168°5W 303 D5
Prince of Wales I. Queens., Australia 10°40S 142°10E 286 F2
Prince of Wales I. Nunavut, Canada 73°0N 99°0W 294 C12
Prince of Wales I. Alaska, U.S.A. 55°47N 132°50W 303 J14
Prince of Wales Icefield Canada 78°15N 79°0W 295 B16
Prince of Wales Str. Canada 73°0N 117°0W 294 C8
Prince Patrick I. Canada 77°0N 120°0W 295 B8
Prince Regent Inlet Canada 73°0N 90°0W 295 C14
Prince Rupert Canada 54°20N 130°20W 296 C2
Prince Rupert B. Dominica 15°34N 61°29W 323 k
Prince Rupert Bluff Pt. Dominica 15°35N 61°29W 323 k
Prince William Sd. U.S.A. 60°40N 147°0W 303 F11
Princes Street Edinburgh, U.K. 121 b2
Princes Town Trin. & Tob. 10°16N 61°23W 323 t
Princesa Isabel Brazil 7°44S 38°0W 332 C4
Princess Charlotte B. Australia 14°25S 144°0E 280 A3
Princess Elizabeth Trough S. Ocean 64°10S 83°0E 151 C7
Princess May Ranges Australia 15°30S 125°30E 278 C4
Princess Royal I. Canada 53°0N 128°40W 296 C3
Princeton B.C., Canada 49°27N 120°30W 296 D4
Princeton Calif., U.S.A. 39°24N 122°1W 306 F4
Princeton Ill., U.S.A. 41°23N 89°28W 310 C7
Princeton Ind., U.S.A. 38°21N 87°34W 311 F9
Princeton Ky., U.S.A. 37°7N 87°53W 308 G10
Princeton Mo., U.S.A. 40°24N 93°35W 310 D3
Princeton N.J., U.S.A. 40°21N 74°39W 313 F10
Princeton W. Va., U.S.A. 37°22N 81°6W 309 G13
Princeville Hawai'i, U.S.A. 22°13N 159°29W 302 A2
Princeville Ill., U.S.A. 40°56N 89°46W 310 D7
Príncipe São Tomé & Príncipe 1°37N 7°25E 265 a
Principe da Beira Brazil 12°20S 64°30W 331 C5
Prineville U.S.A. 44°18N 120°51W 304 D3
Pringles Bay Dominica 15°21N 61°25W 323 k
Pringsewu Indonesia 5°24S 104°55E 234 D2
Prins Christian Sund Greenland 60°4N 43°10W 154 E6
Prins Harald Kyst Antarctica 70°0S 35°1E 151 D4
Prins Karls Forland Svalbard 78°30N 11°0E 154 B12
Prinsesse Astrid Kyst Antarctica 70°45S 12°30E 151 D3
Prinsesse Ragnhild Kyst Antarctica 70°15S 27°30E 151 D4
Printer's Row U.S.A. 119 d2
Prinzapolca Nic. 13°20N 83°35W 320 D3
Prior, C. Spain 43°34N 8°17W 194 B2
Priozersk Russia 61°2N 30°7E 188 B6
Pripet = Prypyat → Europe 51°20N 30°15E 177 C16
Pripet Marshes Europe 52°10N 27°10E 177 B15
Pripyat Marshes = Pripet Marshes Europe 52°10N 27°10E 177 B15
Pripyats = Prypyat → Europe 51°20N 30°15E 177 C16
Prishib = Leninsk Russia 48°40N 45°15E 191 F7
Prishtinë Kosovo 42°40N 21°13E 202 D5
Prislop, Pasul Romania 47°37N 24°48E 183 C9
Pristen Russia 51°15N 36°44E 189 G9
Priština = Prishtinë Kosovo 42°40N 21°13E 202 D5
Pritzwalk Germany 53°9N 12°10E 178 B8
Privas France 44°45N 4°37E 175 D8
Priverno Italy 41°28N 13°11E 200 A6
Privolzhsk Russia 57°23N 41°16E 190 B5
Privolzhskaya Vozvyshennost Russia 51°0N 46°0E 190 E7
Privolzhskiy Russia 51°25N 46°3E 190 E8
Privolzhskiy □ Russia 56°0N 50°0E 214 D6
Privolzhye Russia 52°52N 48°33E 190 D9
Priyutnoye Russia 46°12N 43°40E 191 G6
Prizren Kosovo 42°13N 20°45E 202 D4
Prizzi Italy 37°43N 13°26E 200 E6
Prnjavor Bos.-H. 44°52N 17°43E 182 F2
Probolinggo Indonesia 7°46S 113°13E 235 D4
Prochowice Poland 51°17N 16°20E 185 G3
Proctor U.S.A. 43°40N 73°2W 313 C11
Proddatur India 14°45N 78°30E 245 G4
Prodhromos Cyprus 34°57N 32°50E 207 F8
Proença-a-Nova Portugal 39°45N 7°54W 194 F3
Profilia Greece 36°5N 27°51E 206 E11
Profondeville Belgium 50°23N 4°52E 170 D4
Progreso Coahuila, Mexico 27°28N 100°59W 318 B4
Progreso Yucatán, Mexico 21°20N 89°40W 319 C7
Progreso Nacional Mexico 19°30N 99°9W 128 A2
Progress Antarctica 66°22S 76°22E 151 C12
Progress Russia 49°45N 129°37E 215 E13
Prokhladnyy Russia 43°50N 44°2E 191 J7
Prokletije Albania 42°30N 19°45E 202 D3
Prokopyevsk Russia 54°0N 86°45E 217 B11
Prokuplje Serbia 43°16N 21°36E 202 C5
Proletarsk Russia 46°42N 41°50E 191 G5
Proletarskaya = Proletarsk Russia 46°42N 41°50E 191 G5
Prome Burma 18°49N 95°13E 241 F5
Promise City U.S.A. 40°45N 93°9W 310 D3
Promzino = Surskoye Russia 54°30N 46°44E 190 C8
Prophet → Canada 58°48N 122°40W 296 B4
Prophet River Canada 58°6N 122°43W 296 B4
Prophetstown U.S.A. 41°40N 89°56W 310 C7
Propriá Brazil 10°13S 36°51W 332 D4
Propriano France 41°41N 8°52E 175 G12
Prosek Czech Rep. 50°7N 14°30E 135 B3
Proserpine Australia 20°21S 148°36E 280 b
Proskurov = Khmelnytskyy Ukraine 49°23N 27°0E 177 D14
Prosna → Poland 52°6N 17°44E 185 F4
Prospect N.Y., U.S.A. 43°18N 75°9W 313 C9
Prospect Ohio, U.S.A. 40°27N 83°11W 311 D13
Prospect Hill Park U.S.A. 42°23N 71°13W 116 A1
Prosperidad Phil. 8°34N 125°52E 233 G5
Prosperity U.S.A. 30°51N 85°56W 316 E4
Prosperous B. St. Helena 15°56S 5°39W 153 h
Prosser U.S.A. 46°12N 119°46W 304 C4
Prossnitz = Prostějov Czech Rep. 49°30N 17°9E 181 B10
Prostějov Czech Rep. 49°30N 17°9E 181 B10
Prostki Poland 53°42N 22°25E 184 E9
Proston Australia 26°8S 151°32E 281 D5
Proszowice Poland 50°13N 20°16E 185 H7
Proti Greece 37°5N 21°32E 204 D3
Provadiya Bulgaria 43°12N 27°30E 203 C11
Provence France 43°40N 5°46E 175 E9
Provence-Alpes-Côte d'Azur □ France 44°0N 6°15E 175 D10
Providence Seychelles 9°14S 51°2E 273 E4
Providence Ky., U.S.A. 37°24N 87°46W 308 G10
Providence R.I., U.S.A. 41°49N 71°24W 313 E13
Providence, C. N.Z. 45°59S 166°29E 285 F1
Providence Bay Canada 45°41N 82°15W 298 C3
Providence Mts. U.S.A. 35°10N 115°15W 307 K11
Providencia Chile 33°25S 70°36W 137 B2
Providencia, I. de Colombia 13°25N 81°26W 320 D3
Provideniya Russia 64°23N 173°18W 215 C19
Provincetown U.S.A. 42°3N 70°11W 309 D18
Provins France 48°33N 3°15E 173 D10
Provo U.S.A. 40°14N 111°39W 304 F8
Provost Canada 52°25N 110°20W 297 C6
Prozor Bos.-H. 43°50N 17°34E 182 G2
Prrenjas Albania 41°4N 20°32E 202 E4
Prudentópolis Brazil 25°12S 50°57W 333 G1
Prudhoe Bay U.S.A. 70°18N 148°22W 303 A10
Prudhoe I. Australia 21°19S 149°41E 280 C4
Prud'homme Canada 52°20N 105°54W 297 C7
Prudnik Poland 50°20N 17°38E 185 H4
Průhonice Czech Rep. 50°0N 14°33E 135 C3
Prüm Germany 50°12N 6°25E 179 E2
Prundu Romania 44°6N 26°14E 183 F11
Prundu Bârgăului Romania 47°13N 24°46E 183 C9
Pruszcz Gdański Poland 54°17N 18°40E 184 D5
Pruszków Poland 52°9N 20°49E 185 F7
Prut → Romania 45°28N 28°10E 183 E13
Pruzhany Belarus 52°33N 24°28E 177 B13
Prvič Croatia 44°55N 14°47E 199 D11
Prydz B. Antarctica 69°0S 74°0E 151 C6
Pryluky Ukraine 50°30N 32°24E 189 G7
Prymorske Ukraine 46°48N 36°20E 189 J9
Pryor U.S.A. 36°19N 95°19W 314 C7
Prypyat → Europe 51°20N 30°15E 177 C16
Przasnysz Poland 53°2N 20°54E 185 E7
Przedbórz Poland 51°6N 19°53E 185 G6
Przedecz Poland 52°20N 18°53E 185 F5
Przemków Poland 51°31N 15°48E 185 G2
Przemyśl Poland 49°50N 22°45E 185 J9
Przeworsk Poland 50°6N 22°32E 185 H9
Przewóz Poland 51°28N 14°57E 185 G1
Przhevalsk = Karakol Kyrgyzstan 42°30N 78°20E 217 D9
Przysucha Poland 51°22N 20°38E 185 G7
Psachna Greece 38°34N 23°35E 204 C5
Psara Greece 38°37N 25°38E 205 C7
Psathoura Greece 39°30N 24°12E 204 B6
Pserimos Greece 36°56N 27°8E 205 E9
Psichiko Greece 38°1N 23°46E 112 A2
Psiloritis, Oros Greece 35°15N 24°45E 207 E5
Psira Greece 35°12N 25°52E 207 E6
Pskov Russia 57°50N 28°25E 188 D5
Pskov □ Russia 57°20N 29°0E 188 D5
Pskovskoye, Ozero Russia 58°0N 27°58E 188 D5
Psol → Ukraine 49°10N 33°37E 189 H7
Psunj Croatia 45°25N 17°19E 182 E2
Pteleos Greece 39°3N 22°57E 204 B4
Ptich = Ptsich → Belarus 52°9N 28°52E 177 B15
Ptichia = Vidos Greece 39°38N 19°55E 206 B9
Ptolemaida Greece 40°30N 21°43E 202 F5
Ptsich → Belarus 52°9N 28°52E 177 B15
Ptuj Slovenia 46°28N 15°50E 199 B12
Ptujska Gora Slovenia 46°23N 15°47E 199 B12
Pu Xian China 36°24N 111°6E 226 F6
Pua Thailand 19°11N 100°55E 236 C3
Pua'ena Pt. U.S.A. 21°36N 158°6W 302 J13
Puán Argentina 37°30S 62°45W 334 D3
Pu'an Guizhou, China 25°46N 104°57E 228 E5
Pu'apu'a Samoa 13°34S 172°9W 287 V19
Pubei China 22°16N 109°31E 228 F7
Pucacuro → Peru 3°20S 74°58W 328 D3
Pucallpa Peru 8°25S 74°30W 330 B3
Pucará Bolivia 18°43S 64°11W 331 D5
Pucará Cajamarca, Peru 6°0S 79°7W 330 B2
Pucará Puno, Peru 15°5S 70°24W 330 D3
Pucarani Bolivia 16°23S 68°30W 330 D4
Pucheng China 27°59N 118°31E 229 D12
Pucheni Romania 45°12N 25°17E 183 E10
Puchheim Germany 48°9N 11°21E 179 G7
Puch'on = Bucheon S. Korea 37°28N 126°45E 224 D3
Púchov Slovak Rep. 49°8N 18°20E 181 B11
Pucio Pt. Phil. 11°46N 121°51E 233 F3
Pucioasa Romania 45°5N 25°25E 183 E10
Pučišća Croatia 43°22N 16°43E 199 E13
Puck Poland 54°45N 18°23E 184 D5
Pucka, Zatoka Poland 54°30N 18°40E 184 D5
Puçol Spain 39°37N 0°18W 197 F4
Pudasjärvi Finland 65°23N 26°53E 160 D22
Puding China 26°18N 105°44E 228 D5
Pudong New Area China 31°13N 121°30E 138 B2
Pudozh Russia 61°48N 36°32E 188 B9
Pudu = Suizhou China 31°42N 113°24E 229 B9
Puducherry India 11°59N 79°50E 245 J4
Pudukkottai India 10°28N 78°47E 245 J4
Pue Cook Is. 21°12S 159°45W 289 h
Puebla Mexico 19°3N 98°12W 319 D5
Puebla □ Mexico 18°50N 98°0W 319 D5
Puebla de Alcocer Spain 38°59N 5°14W 195 G5
Puebla de Don Fadrique Spain 37°58N 2°25W 197 H2
Puebla de Don Rodrigo Spain 39°5N 4°37W 195 F6
Puebla de Guzmán Spain 37°37N 7°15W 195 H3
Puebla de la Calzada Spain 38°54N 6°37W 195 G4
Puebla de Sanabria Spain 42°4N 6°38W 194 C4
Puebla de Trives = Pobra de Trives Spain 42°20N 7°10W 194 C3
Pueblo U.S.A. 38°16N 104°37W 304 G11
Pueblo Libre Peru 12°5S 77°4W 124 B2
Pueblo Nuevo = El Pobleneu Spain 41°23N 2°11E 114 A2
Pueblo Nuevo Spain 40°25N 3°37W 127 B2
Puelches Argentina 38°5S 65°51W 334 D2
Puelén Argentina 37°32S 67°38W 334 D2
Puente Alto Chile 33°32S 70°35W 334 C1
Puente-Genil Spain 37°22N 4°47W 195 H6
Puente la Reina Spain 42°40N 1°49W 196 C3
Puente San Miguel Spain 43°21N 4°5W 194 B6
Puenteareas = Ponteareas Spain 42°10N 8°28W 194 C2
Puentedeume = Pontedeume Spain 43°24N 8°10W 194 B2
Puentes de Garcia Rodriguez = As Pontes de García Rodríguez Spain 43°27N 7°50W 194 B3
Pu'er China 23°0N 101°15E 228 F3
Puerca, Pta. Puerto Rico 18°13N 65°36W 321 b
Puerco → U.S.A. 34°22N 107°50W 305 J10
Puerta del Sol, Plaza Madrid, Spain 127 b2
Puerto Acosta Bolivia 15°32S 69°15W 330 D4
Puerto Aisén Chile 45°27S 73°0W 336 C2
Puerto Ángel Mexico 15°40N 96°29W 319 D5
Puerto Arista Mexico 15°56N 93°48W 319 D6
Puerto Armuelles Panama 8°20N 82°51W 320 E3
Puerto Asis Colombia 0°30N 76°30W 328 C2
Puerto Ayacucho Venezuela 5°40N 67°35W 328 B4
Puerto Ayora Ecuador 0°45S 90°19W 330 a
Puerto Baquerizo Moreno Ecuador 0°54S 89°36W 330 a
Puerto Barrios Guatemala 15°40N 88°32W 320 C2
Puerto Bermejo Argentina 26°55S 58°34W 334 B4
Puerto Bermúdez Peru 10°20S 74°58W 330 C3
Puerto Bolívar Ecuador 3°19S 79°55W 328 D2
Puerto Cabello Venezuela 10°28N 68°1W 328 A4
Puerto Cabezas Nic. 14°0N 83°30W 320 D3
Puerto Cabo Gracias á Dios Nic. 15°0N 83°10W 320 D3
Puerto Capaz = El Jebha Morocco 35°11N 4°43W 260 A4
Puerto Carreño Colombia 6°12N 67°22W 328 B4
Puerto Castilla Honduras 16°0N 86°0W 320 C2
Puerto Chicama Peru 7°45S 79°20W 330 B2
Puerto Cisnes Chile 44°45S 72°42W 336 B2
Puerto Coig Argentina 50°54S 69°15W 336 D3
Puerto Cortés Honduras 15°51N 88°0W 320 C2
Puerto Cumarebo Venezuela 11°29N 69°30W 328 A4
Puerto de Alcudia = Port d'Alcúdia Spain 39°50N 3°7E 206 B4
Puerto de Cabras = Puerto del Rosario Canary Is. 28°30N 13°52W 153 e2
Puerto de Cabrera Spain 39°8N 2°56E 206 B3
Puerto de Gran Tarajal Canary Is. 28°13N 14°1W 153 e2
Puerto de la Cruz Canary Is. 28°24N 16°32W 153 e1
Puerto de los Angeles ⌓ Mexico 23°39N 105°45W 318 C3
Puerto de Mazarrón Spain 37°34N 1°15W 197 H3
Puerto de Pozo Negro Canary Is. 28°19N 13°55W 153 e2
Puerto de Sóller = Port de Sóller Spain 39°48N 2°42E 206 B3
Puerto de Somosierra Spain 41°9N 3°35W 194 D7
Puerto del Carmen Canary Is. 28°55N 13°38W 153 e2
Puerto del Rosario Canary Is. 28°30N 13°52W 153 e2
Puerto Deseado Argentina 47°55S 66°0W 336 C3
Puerto Escondido Mexico 15°50N 97°3W 319 D5
Puerto Gaitán Colombia 4°19N 72°4W 328 C3
Puerto Galera Phil. 13°30N 120°57E 232 E3
Puerto Guaraní Paraguay 21°18S 57°55W 331 E6
Puerto Heath Bolivia 12°34S 68°39W 330 C4
Puerto Huitoto Colombia 0°18N 74°3W 328 C3
Puerto Inca Peru 9°22S 74°54W 330 B3
Puerto Inírida Colombia 3°53N 67°52W 328 C4
Puerto Juárez Mexico 21°11N 86°49W 319 C7
Puerto La Cruz Venezuela 10°13N 64°38W 329 A5
Puerto Leguízamo Colombia 0°12S 74°46W 328 D3
Puerto Lempira Honduras 15°16N 83°46W 320 C3
Puerto Libertad Mexico 29°55N 112°43W 318 B2
Puerto Limón Colombia 3°23N 73°30W 328 C3
Puerto Lobos Argentina 42°0S 65°3W 336 B3
Puerto López Colombia 4°5N 72°58W 328 C3
Puerto Lumbreras Spain 37°34N 1°48W 197 H3
Puerto Madero Argentina 34°37S 58°21W 117 B2
Puerto Madryn Argentina 42°48S 65°4W 336 B3
Puerto Maldonado Peru 12°30S 69°10W 330 C4
Puerto Manatí Cuba 21°22N 76°50W 320 B4
Puerto Mariti Colombia 1°10S 69°59W 328 D4
Puerto Mercedes Colombia 1°11N 72°53W 328 C3
Puerto Mexico = Coatzacoalcos Mexico 18°7N 94°25W 319 D6
Puerto Miraña Colombia 1°20S 70°19W 328 D3
Puerto Montt Chile 41°28S 73°0W 336 B2
Puerto Morazán Nic. 12°51N 87°11W 320 D2
Puerto Morelos Mexico 20°50N 86°52W 319 C7
Puerto Nariño Colombia 4°56N 67°48W 328 C4
Puerto Natales Chile 51°45S 72°15W 336 D2
Puerto Nuevo Colombia 5°53N 69°56W 328 B4
Puerto Ordaz Venezuela 8°16N 62°44W 329 B5
Puerto Oscuro Chile 31°24S 71°35W 334 C1
Puerto Padre Cuba 21°13N 76°35W 320 B4
Puerto Páez Venezuela 6°13N 67°28W 328 B4
Puerto Peñasco Mexico 31°20N 113°33W 318 A2
Puerto Pinasco Paraguay 22°36S 57°50W 334 A4
Puerto Pirámides Argentina 42°35S 64°20W 336 B4
Puerto Piritu Venezuela 10°4N 65°3W 329 A4
Puerto Plata Dom. Rep. 19°48N 70°45W 321 C5
Puerto Pollensa = Port de Pollença Spain 39°54N 3°4E 206 B4
Puerto Portillo Peru 9°45S 72°42W 330 B3
Puerto Princesa Phil. 9°46N 118°45E 233 G2
Puerto Princesa Subterranean River △ Phil. 10°10N 118°55E 233 F2
Puerto Quepos Costa Rica 9°29N 84°6W 320 E3
Puerto Real Spain 36°33N 6°12W 195 J4
Puerto Rico Bolivia 11°5S 67°38W 330 C4
Puerto Rico Canary Is. 27°47N 15°42W 153 e1
Puerto Rico ⊠ W. Indies 18°15N 66°45W 321 C6
Puerto Rico Trench Atl. Oc. 19°50N 66°0W 321 C6
Puerto Rondón Colombia 6°17N 71°6W 328 B3
Puerto Saavedra Chile 38°47S 73°24W 336 A2
Puerto San Julián Argentina 49°15S 67°45W 336 C3
Puerto Santa Cruz Argentina 50°0S 68°32W 336 D3
Puerto Sastre Paraguay 22°2S 57°55W 334 A4
Puerto Serrano Spain 36°56N 5°33W 195 J5
Puerto Siles Bolivia 12°48S 65°5W 331 C4
Puerto Suárez Bolivia 18°58S 57°52W 331 D6
Puerto Supe Peru 11°0S 77°30W 330 C2
Puerto Tejada Colombia 3°14N 76°24W 328 C2
Puerto Umbría Colombia 0°52N 76°33W 328 C2
Puerto Vallarta Mexico 20°37N 105°15W 318 C3
Puerto Varas Chile 41°19S 72°59W 336 B2
Puerto Velasco Ibarra Ecuador 1°17S 90°29W 330 a
Puerto Villamil Ecuador 0°56S 91°1W 330 a
Puerto Villazón Bolivia 13°32S 61°57W 331 C5
Puerto Wilches Colombia 7°21N 73°54W 328 B3
Puerto Williams Chile 54°56S 67°37W 336 D3
Puertollano Spain 38°43N 4°7W 195 G6
Puesto Cunambo Peru 2°10S 76°0W 328 D2
Pueu Tahiti 17°44S 149°13W 289 e
Pueyrredón, L. Argentina 47°20S 72°0W 336 C2
Púez Odle ⌓ Italy 46°37N 11°48E 199 B8
Puffin I. Ireland 51°50N 10°24W 166 E1
Pugachev Russia 52°0N 48°49E 190 D9
Pugal India 28°30N 72°48E 242 E5
Puge Sichuan, China 27°20N 102°31E 228 D4
Puge Tanzania 4°45S 33°11E 268 C3
Puget Sound U.S.A. 47°50N 122°30W 306 C4
Puget-Théniers France 43°58N 6°53E 175 E10
Púglia □ Italy 41°15N 16°15E 201 A9
Pugŏdong N. Korea 42°5N 130°0E 224 A5
Pugu Tanzania 6°55S 39°4E 268 D4
Pūgūnzī Iran 25°49N 59°10E 247 E8
Puha N.Z. 38°30S 177°50E 284 E6
Puhuangyu China 39°50N 116°22E 114 B2
Pui Romania 45°30N 23°4E 182 E8
Puica Peru 15°0S 72°33W 330 D3
Puieşti Romania 46°25N 27°33E 183 D12
Puig Major Spain 39°48N 2°47E 206 B3
Puigcerdà Spain 42°24N 1°50E 196 C6
Puigmal Spain 42°23N 2°7E 196 C7
Puigpunyent Spain 39°38N 2°32E 206 B3
Puijiang China 30°14N 103°30E 228 B4
Puisaye, Collines de la France 47°37N 3°20E 173 E10
Puiseaux France 48°11N 2°30E 173 D9
Puistola Finland 60°16N 25°2E 121 B3
Pujehun S. Leone 7°23N 11°45W 262 D2
Pujiang China 29°29N 119°54E 229 C12
Pujilí Ecuador 0°57S 78°41W 328 D2
Pujols France 44°48N 0°2W 174 D3
Pujon Indonesia 1°19S 114°19E 235 C4
Pujon-ho N. Korea 40°35N 127°35E 224 B3
Puka Puka French Polynesia 14°49S 138°48W 289 f
Puka Ruha French Polynesia 18°20S 137°2W 289 f
Pukaki, L. N.Z. 44°4S 170°1E 285 E5
Pukalani U.S.A. 20°51N 156°20W 302 C5
Pukapuka Cook Is. 10°53S 165°49W 289 J11
Pukaskwa △ Canada 48°20N 86°0W 298 C2
Pukatawagan Canada 55°45N 101°20W 297 B8
Pukchin N. Korea 40°12N 125°45E 224 B2
Pukch'ŏng N. Korea 40°14N 128°10E 224 B4
Pukë Albania 42°2N 19°53E 202 D3
Pukearuhe N.Z. 38°55S 174°31E 284 E3
Pukekohe N.Z. 37°12S 174°55E 284 D3
Puketeraki Ra. N.Z. 42°58S 172°13E 285 C7
Puketoi Ra. N.Z. 40°30S 176°5E 284 G5
Pukeuri N.Z. 45°4S 171°2E 285 F6
Pukhrayan India 26°14N 79°51E 243 F8
Pukinmäki Finland 60°15N 24°57E 121 B2
Puksubaek-san N. Korea 40°42N 127°45E 224 B3
Pula Croatia 44°54N 13°57E 199 D10
Pula Italy 39°1N 9°0E 200 C1
Pulacayo Bolivia 20°25S 66°41W 330 E4
Pulandian China 39°25N 121°58E 227 E11
Pulanduta Pt. Phil. 11°54N 123°9E 233 F4
Pulangpisau Indonesia 2°46S 114°13E 235 C4
Pulaski N.Y., U.S.A. 43°34N 76°8W 313 C8
Pulaski Tenn., U.S.A. 35°12N 87°2W 315 D11
Pulaski Va., U.S.A. 37°3N 80°47W 309 G13
Pulau → Indonesia 5°50S 138°15E 231 F9
Pulau Gili Indonesia 8°21S 116°1E 231 J19
Pulau Miangas Indonesia 5°35N 126°34E 233 J6
Puławy Poland 51°23N 21°59E 185 G8
Pulga U.S.A. 39°48N 121°29W 306 F5
Pulgaon India 20°44N 78°21E 244 D4
Puli Taiwan 23°58N 120°57E 225 C2
Pulicat India 13°25N 80°19E 245 H5
Pulicat L. India 13°40N 80°15E 245 H5
Pulivendla India 14°25N 78°14E 245 G4
Puliyangudi India 9°11N 77°24E 245 K3
Pulkovo Int. ✈ (LED) Russia 59°48N 30°18E 137 C1
Pullach Germany 48°3N 11°31E 131 B1
Pullman U.S.A. 46°44N 117°10W 304 C5
Pullman Historic District U.S.A. 41°41N 87°36W 119 C3
Pulo Gadung Indonesia 6°11S 106°54E 122 B2
Pulog, Mt. Phil. 16°40N 120°50E 232 C3
Pułtusk Poland 52°43N 21°6E 185 F8
Pülümür Turkey 39°30N 39°51E 213 C8
Pumlumon Fawr U.K. 52°28N 3°46W 169 E4
Puna Bolivia 19°45S 65°28W 331 D4
Puná, I. Ecuador 2°55S 80°5W 328 D1
Punaauia Tahiti 17°37S 149°34W 289 e
Pūnak Iran 35°46N 51°20E 141 A2
Punakha Dzong Bhutan 27°42N 89°52E 241 B2
Punalur India 9°0N 76°56E 245 K3
Punalu'u U.S.A. 21°35N 157°53W 302 J14
Punasar India 27°6N 73°6E 242 F5
Punata Bolivia 17°32S 65°50W 331 D4
Punch India 33°48N 74°4E 243 C6
Punch → Pakistan 33°12N 73°40E 242 C5
Punchbowl Australia 33°55S 151°3E 139 B1
Punda Curaçao 12°6N 68°55W 322 g
Punda Maria S. Africa 22°40S 31°5E 271 B5
Punde India 18°53N 72°57E 130 B2
Pune India 18°29N 73°57E 244 E1
Punggol Singapore 1°23N 103°54E 138 A3
Punggol, Sungei → Singapore 1°24N 103°54E 138 A3
Punggol Pt. Singapore 1°24N 103°54E 138 A3
Pungo Andongo Angola 9°44S 15°35E 265 D3
P'ungsan N. Korea 40°50N 128°9E 224 B4
Pungsan S. Korea 36°34N 128°34E 224 D4
Pungue, Ponte de Mozam. 19°0S 34°0E 269 F3
Puning China 23°20N 116°12E 229 F11
Punjab □ India 31°0N 76°0E 242 D7
Punjab □ Pakistan 32°0N 72°30E 242 E6
Punjabi Bagh India 28°40N 77°6E 120 A1
Puno Peru 15°55S 70°3W 330 D3
Puno □ Peru 15°0S 70°0W 330 C3
Punpun → India 25°31N 85°18E 243 G11
Punta, Cerro de Puerto Rico 18°10N 66°37W 321 b
Punta Alta Argentina 38°53S 62°4W 336 A4
Punta Arenas Chile 53°10S 71°0W 336 D2
Punta Cana ✈ (PUJ) Dom. Rep. 18°34N 68°21W 321 C6
Punta Cardón Venezuela 11°38N 70°14W 328 A3
Punta Coles Peru 17°43S 71°23W 330 D3
Punta de Bombón Peru 17°10S 71°48W 330 D3
Punta de Piedras Venezuela 10°54N 64°5W 329 a
Punta del Díaz Chile 28°0S 70°45W 334 B1
Punta del Hidalgo Canary Is. 28°33N 16°19W 153 e1
Punta Delgado Argentina 42°43S 63°38W 336 B4
Punta Gorda Belize 16°10N 88°45W 320 C2
Punta Gorda Fla., U.S.A. 26°56N 82°3W 317 J7
Punta Prieta Mexico 28°58N 114°17W 318 B2
Punta Prima Spain 39°48N 4°16E 206 B5
Punta Umbría Spain 37°10N 6°56W 195 H4
Puntarenas Costa Rica 10°0N 84°50W 320 E3
Puntland Somalia 9°0N 50°0E 267 C6
Punto Fijo Venezuela 11°50N 70°13W 328 A3
Punxsutawney U.S.A. 40°57N 78°59W 312 F6
Punyu = Guangzhou China 23°6N 113°13E 121 B2
Puotila Finland 60°13N 25°6E 121 B3
Pupuan Indonesia 8°19S 115°0E 231 J18
Pūpūkea U.S.A. 21°40N 158°3W 302 J13
Puqi China 29°40N 113°50E 229 C9
Puquio Peru 14°45S 74°10W 330 C3
Pur → Russia 67°31N 77°55E 214 C8
Puracé, Vol. Colombia 2°21N 76°23W 328 C2
Puracé △ Colombia 2°10N 76°21W 328 C2
Puračić Bos.-H. 44°33N 18°28E 182 F3
Puralia = Puruliya India 23°17N 86°24E 243 H12
Purana Qila Delhi, India 120 c3
Puranpur India 28°31N 80°9E 243 E9
Purari → Papua N. G. 7°49S 145°0E 286 D3
Purbalingga Indonesia 7°23S 109°21E 235 D3
Purbeck, Isle of U.K. 50°39N 1°59W 169 G5
Purcell U.S.A. 35°1N 97°22W 314 D6
Purcell Mts. Canada 49°55N 116°15W 296 D5
Purdy Canada 45°19N 77°44W 312 A7
Puri India 19°50N 85°58E 244 E7
Purificación Colombia 3°51N 74°55W 328 C3
Purmerend Neths. 52°32N 4°58E 170 B4
Purna → India 19°6N 77°2E 244 E3
Purnia India 25°45N 87°31E 243 G12
Purnululu △ Australia 17°20S 128°20E 278 C4
Pursat = Pouthisat Cambodia 12°34N 103°50E 236 F4
Purukcahu Indonesia 0°35S 114°35E 235 C4
Puruliya India 23°17N 86°24E 243 H12
Purus → Brazil 3°42S 61°28W 329 D5
Purutu I. Papua N. G. 8°24S 143°27E 286 E2
Puruvesi Finland 61°50N 29°30E 188 B5
Purvis U.S.A. 31°9N 89°25W 315 F10
Pŭrvomay Bulgaria 42°8N 25°17E 203 D9
Purwa India 26°28N 80°47E 243 F9
Purwakarta Indonesia 6°35S 107°29E 235 D3
Purwo, Tanjung Indonesia 8°44S 114°21E 231 K18
Purwodadi Indonesia 7°7S 110°55E 235 D4
Purwokerto Indonesia 7°25S 109°14E 235 D3
Purworejo Indonesia 7°43S 110°2E 235 D4
Puryŏng N. Korea 42°5N 129°43E 224 A4
Pus → India 19°55N 77°55E 244 E3
Pusa India 25°59N 85°41E 243 G11
Pusad India 19°56N 77°36E 244 E3
Pusan = Busan S. Korea 35°5N 129°0E 224 E4
Pushkin Russia 59°45N 30°25E 188 C6
Pushkino Moskva, Russia 56°2N 37°49E 188 D9
Pushkino Saratov, Russia 51°16N 47°0E 190 E8
Püspökladány Hungary 47°19N 21°6E 182 C6
Pustoshka Russia 56°20N 29°30E 188 D5
Puszczykowo Poland 52°18N 16°49E 185 F3
Put-in-Bay U.S.A. 41°39N 82°49W 312 E2
Putahow L. Canada 59°54N 100°40W 297 B8
Putai Taiwan 23°23N 120°9E 225 C2
Putao Burma 27°28N 97°30E 241 B6
Putaruru N.Z. 38°2S 175°50E 284 E4
Putatan Malaysia 5°53N 116°3E 235 A5
Putbus Germany 54°22N 13°28E 178 A9
Puteaux France 48°53N 2°14E 134 A2
Puteran Indonesia 7°5S 114°0E 235 D4
Putian China 25°23N 119°0E 229 E12
Putignano Italy 40°51N 17°7E 201 B10
Putina Peru 14°55S 69°55W 330 C4
Puting, Tanjung Indonesia 3°31S 111°46E 235 C4
Putlitz Germany 53°15N 12°2E 178 B8
Putna Romania 47°50N 25°33E 183 C10
Putna → Romania 45°42N 27°26E 183 E12
Putnam U.S.A. 41°55N 71°55W 313 E13
Putney London, U.K. 51°27N 0°13W 125 B2
Putney Ga., U.S.A. 31°29N 84°8W 316 D5
Putnok Hungary 48°18N 20°26E 182 B5
Putorana, Gory Russia 69°0N 95°0E 215 C10
Putorino N.Z. 39°4S 176°58E 284 F5
Putrajaya Malaysia 2°55N 101°40E 237 L3
Putre Chile 18°12S 69°35W 330 D4
Puttalam Sri Lanka 8°1N 79°55E 245 K5
Puttalam Lagoon Sri Lanka 8°15N 79°45E 245 K4
Puttegga Norway 62°13N 7°42E 164 B4
Puttgarden Germany 54°30N 11°10E 178 A7
Püttlingen Germany 49°17N 6°53E 179 F2
Puttur Andhra Pradesh, India 13°27N 79°33E 245 H4
Puttur Karnataka, India 12°46N 75°12E 245 H2
Putty Australia 32°57S 150°42E 283 B9
Putumayo → S. Amer. 3°7S 67°58W 328 D4
Putuo Shanghai, China 31°15N 121°24E 138 B1
Putuo Zhejiang, China 29°56N 122°20E 229 C14
Putussibau Indonesia 0°50N 112°56E 235 B4
Pututahi N.Z. 38°39S 177°53E 284 E6
Putxet Spain 41°24N 2°8E 114 A1
Putyla Ukraine 48°0N 25°5E 183 B10
Pu'uanahulu U.S.A. 19°49N 155°51W 302 D6
Pu'uhonua o Hōnaunau ⌓ U.S.A. 19°25N 155°54W 302 D6
Pu'uka'aumakua U.S.A. 21°30N 157°54W 302 J14
Pu'ukeahiakahoe U.S.A. 21°23N 157°49W 302 K14
Pu'ukoholā Heiau ⌓ U.S.A. 20°1N 155°49W 302 C6
P'u'ula'ula U.S.A. 20°42N 156°15W 302 C5
Pu'u'oke'oke'o U.S.A. 19°13N 155°44W 302 D6
Pu'uwai U.S.A. 21°54N 160°12W 302 B1
Puvirnituq Canada 60°2N 77°10W 295 E16
Puxi China 31°12N 121°30E 138 B1
Puy-de-Dôme France 45°46N 2°57E 174 C6
Puy-de-Dôme □ France 45°40N 3°5E 174 C7
Puy-l'Évêque France 44°31N 1°9E 174 D5
Puyallup U.S.A. 47°12N 122°18W 306 C4
Puyang China 35°40N 115°1E 226 G8
Puyehue Chile 40°40S 72°37W 336 B2
Puyehue △ Chile 40°27S 72°6W 336 B2
Puylaurens France 43°35N 2°0E 174 E6
Puyo Ecuador 1°28S 77°59W 328 D2
Puysegur Pt. N.Z. 46°9S 166°37E 285 G1
Pūzeh Rīg Iran 27°20N 58°40E 247 E8
Puzhaykove Ukraine 48°7N 29°50E 183 B14
Pwani □ Tanzania 7°0S 39°0E 268 D4
Pweto Dem. Rep. of the Congo 8°25S 28°51E 269 D2
Pwinbyu Burma 20°23N 94°40E 241 E5
Pwllheli U.K. 52°53N 4°25W 168 E3
Pyana → Russia 55°43N 46°1E 190 C8
Pyandzh → Asia 37°6N 68°20E 240 A2
Pyaozero, Ozero Russia 66°5N 30°58E 160 C24
Pyapon Burma 16°20N 95°40E 241 G5
Pyasina → Russia 73°30N 87°0E 215 B9
Pyatigorsk Russia 44°2N 43°6E 191 H6
Pyatykhatky Ukraine 48°28N 33°38E 189 H7
Pyawbwe Burma 20°35N 96°4E 241 E6
Pyay = Prome Burma 18°49N 95°13E 241 F5
Pyaye Burma 19°12N 95°10E 241 F5
Pydhuni Mumbai, India 130 b2
Pydna Greece 40°20N 22°34E 202 F6
Pye = Prome Burma 18°49N 95°13E 241 F5
Pyeonghae S. Korea 36°43N 129°26E 224 D4
Pyeongtaek S. Korea 37°1N 127°4E 224 D3
Pyetrikaw Belarus 52°11N 28°29E 177 B15
Pyhäjoki → Finland 64°28N 24°14E 160 D21
Pyin-Oo-Lwin = Maymyo Burma 22°2N 96°28E 236 A1
Pyinbauk Burma 19°10N 95°12E 241 F5
Pyingaing Burma 23°9N 94°50E 241 D5
Pyinkayaing Burma 15°58N 94°24E 241 H5
Pyinmana Burma 19°45N 96°12E 241 F6
Pyinyaung Burma 20°49N 96°25E 241 E6
Pyla Cyprus 35°1N 33°41E 250 C4
Pyla, C. Cyprus 34°56N 33°51E 207 F9
Pymatuning Res. U.S.A. 41°30N 80°28W 312 E4
Pyŏktong N. Korea 40°50N 125°50E 224 B2
P'yŏnganbuk-do □ N. Korea 40°0N 125°15E 224 C2
P'yŏngannam-do □ N. Korea 39°30N 126°24E 224 C3
Pyŏnggang N. Korea 38°24N 127°17E 224 C3
P'yŏngsong N. Korea 39°14N 125°52E 224 C2
P'yŏngyang N. Korea 39°0N 125°30E 224 C2
P'yŏngyang □ N. Korea 39°4N 125°50E 224 C2
Pyote U.S.A. 31°32N 103°8W 314 F3
Pyramid L. U.S.A. 40°1N 119°35W 304 F4
Pyramid Pk. U.S.A. 36°25N 116°37W 307 J10
Pyramid Pt. Ascension I. 7°55S 14°24W 153 g
Pyramids Egypt 29°58N 31°9E 117 B1
Pyrénées Europe 42°45N 0°18E 174 F4
Pyrénées △ France 42°52N 0°10W 174 F3
Pyrénées-Atlantiques □ France 43°10N 0°50W 174 E3
Pyrénées-Orientales □ France 42°35N 2°26E 174 F6
Pyry Poland 52°8N 21°0E 143 C1
Pyryatyn Ukraine 50°15N 32°25E 189 G7
Pyrzyce Poland 53°10N 14°55E 185 E1
Pyskowice Poland 50°24N 18°38E 185 H5
Pytalovo Russia 57°5N 27°55E 188 D4
Pyttegga = Puttegga Norway 62°13N 7°42E 164 B4
Pyu Burma 18°30N 96°28E 241 F6
Pyzdry Poland 52°11N 17°42E 185 F4

Q

Qaanaaq Greenland 77°30N 69°10W 154 B4
Qäbälä Azerbaijan 40°58N 47°47E 191 K8
Qabanbay Kazakhstan 45°50N 80°37E 217 C10
Qabirri → Azerbaijan 41°3N 46°17E 191 K8
Qabr Hūd Yemen 16°9N 49°34E 249 C5
Qachasnek S. Africa 30°6S 28°42E 271 D4

Qādisiyah, Buhayrat al *Iraq* 34°20N 42°12E **213** E10
Qādub *Yemen* 12°37N 53°57E **249** D6
Qa'el Jafr *Jordan* 30°20N 36°25E **251** H7
Qa'emābād *Iran* 31°44N 60°2E **247** D9
Qā'emshahr *Iran* 36°30N 52°53E **247** B7
Qagan Nur *Jilin, China* 45°15N 124°18E **227** B13
Qagan Nur *Nei Monggol Zizhiqu, China* 43°30N 114°55E **226** C8
Qahar Youyi Zhongqi *China* 41°12N 112°40E **226** D7
Qahremānshahr = Kermānshāh *Iran* 34°23N 47°0E **213** E12
Qaidam Pendi *China* 37°0N 95°0E **218** D8
Qaiyara *Iraq* 35°48N 43°17E **213** E10
Qajarīyeh *Iran* 31°1N 48°22E **247** D6
Qala *Malta* 36°2N 14°19E **206** E7
Qala, Ras il *Malta* 36°2N 14°20E **206** E7
Qala-i-Jadid = Spīn Būldak *Afghan.* 31°1N 66°25E **242** D2
Qala Point = Qala, Ras il *Malta* 36°2N 14°20E **206** E7
Qala Viala *Pakistan* 30°49N 67°17E **242** D2
Qala Yangi *Afghan.* 34°20N 66°30E **242** B2
Qalācheh *Afghan.* 35°30N 67°43E **240** B2
Qalaikhum = Kalaikhum *Tajikistan* 38°28N 70°46E **217** E8
Qalandiya *West Bank* 31°52N 35°12E **123** A2
Qalansīyah *Yemen* 12°41N 53°29E **249** D6
Qal'at al Akhḑar *Si. Arabia* 28°4N 37°9E **251** K8
Qal'at al Bīshah *Si. Arabia* 20°0N 42°36E **248** C3
Qal'at Dīzah *Iraq* 36°11N 45°7E **213** D11
Qalāt-i-Ghilzai *Afghan.* 32°15N 66°58E **240** B2
Qal'at Salah el Din *Syria* 34°46N 36°15E **250** D7
Qal'at Şāliḩ *Iraq* 31°31N 47°16E **246** D5
Qal'at Sukkar *Iraq* 31°51N 46°5E **213** G12
Qal'eh Morghī *Iran* 35°38N 51°22E **141** B2
Qal'eh-ye Bost *Afghan.* 31°30N 64°21E **240** C2
Qal'eh-ye Now *Afghan.* 35°0N 63°5E **240** B1
Qal'eh-ye Panjeh *Afghan.* 37°0N 72°35E **240** A4
Qal'eh-ye Sarkari *Afghan.* 35°54N 67°17E **240** B2
Qal'eh-ye Valī *Afghan.* 35°46N 63°45E **240** B1
Qalyûb *Egypt* 30°12N 31°11E **251** H2
Qalyûbîya □ *Egypt* 30°18N 31°18E **251** H2
Qamani'tuaq = Baker Lake *Canada* 64°20N 96°3W **294** E12
Qamar, Ghubbat al *Yemen* 16°20N 52°30E **249** C6
Qamar, Jabal al *Oman* 16°48N 53°15E **249** C6
Qamdo *China* 31°15N 97°6E **228** B1
Qamea *Fiji* 16°45S 179°45W **287** A3
Qamīnis *Libya* 31°40N 20°1E **258** B4
Qammieh Point *Malta* 35°58N 14°19E **206** F7
Qamruddin Karez *Pakistan* 31°45N 68°20E **242** D3
Qandahār = Kandahār *Afghan.* 31°32N 65°43E **240** C2
Qandahār = Kandahār □ *Afghan.* 31°0N 65°0E **240** C2
Qandala *Somalia* 11°30N 49°58E **267** B6
Qandyaghash *Kazakhstan* 49°28N 57°25E **187** E10
Qapān *Iran* 37°40N 55°47E **247** B7
Qapqal *China* 43°48N 81°5E **217** D10
Qapshaghay *Kazakhstan* 43°51N 77°14E **217** D9
Qapshaghay Bögeni *Kazakhstan* 43°45N 77°50E **217** D9
Qaqortoq *Greenland* 60°43N 46°0W **154** E6
Qâra *Egypt* 29°38N 26°30E **256** B2
Qarā', Jabal al *Oman* 17°15N 54°15E **249** C6
Qara Dāgh *Iraq* 35°18N 45°18E **213** E11
Qara Qash → *China* 35°0N 78°30E **243** B8
Qarabalyq *Kazakhstan* 53°45N 62°2E **216** B6
Qarabutaq *Kazakhstan* 50°0N 60°14E **216** C6
Qaraçala *Azerbaijan* 39°45N 48°53E **191** L9
Qaraçuxar *Azerbaijan* 40°25N 50°1E **191** K10
Qaraghandy *Kazakhstan* 49°50N 73°10E **217** C8
Qaraghayly *Kazakhstan* 49°26N 76°0E **214** E8
Qārah *Si. Arabia* 29°55N 40°3E **246** D4
Qarah Āghāj *Iran* 37°8N 46°58E **213** D12
Qarakol *Uzbekistan* 39°32N 63°50E **216** E6
Qaraoba *Kazakhstan* 47°6N 56°15E **216** C5
Qaraqīya Oyysy *Kazakhstan* 43°27N 51°45E **216** D4
Qaraqosh *Iraq* 36°16N 43°22E **213** D10
Qarataū *Ongtüstik Qazaqstan, Kazakhstan* 43°30N 69°30E **217** D7
Qarataū *Zhambyl, Kazakhstan* 43°10N 70°28E **217** D8
Qarāvol *Afghan.* 37°14N 68°46E **240** A3
Qarazhal *Kazakhstan* 48°2N 70°49E **214** E8
Qarchak *Iran* 35°25N 51°34E **247** C6
Qardho *Somalia* 9°30N 49°6E **267** C6
Qardud *Sudan* 10°20N 29°56E **257** E2
Qareh → *Iran* 39°25N 47°22E **213** C12
Qareh Tekān *Iran* 36°38N 49°29E **247** B6
Qarnein *U.A.E.* 24°56N 52°52E **247** E7
Qarokŭl = Karakul, Ozero *Tajikistan* 39°5N 73°25E **217** E8
Qarqan He → *China* 39°30N 88°30E **217** E11
Qarqaraly *Kazakhstan* 49°26N 75°30E **217** C9
Qarqin *Afghan.* 37°24N 66°4E **240** A2
Qarrasa *Sudan* 14°38N 32°5E **257** E3
Qarshi *Uzbekistan* 38°53N 65°48E **217** E7
Qartabā *Lebanon* 34°4N 35°50E **250** D6
Qārūh *Kuwait* 28°49N 48°46E **247** D6
Qaryat al Gharab *Iraq* 31°27N 44°48E **246** D5
Qaryat al 'Ulyā *Si. Arabia* 27°33N 47°42E **246** E5
Qarynzharyq Oyysy *Kazakhstan* 42°55N 54°25E **216** D4
Qaşbah, Râs al *Si. Arabia* 28°2N 34°38E **251** K5
Qāsemābād *Iran* 35°46N 51°30E **141** A3
Qashqadaryo □ *Uzbekistan* 38°35N 66°0E **217** E7
Qasigiannguit *Greenland* 68°50N 51°18W **154** D5
Qasr 'Amra *Jordan* 31°48N 36°35E **246** D3
Qaşr Bū Hadi *Libya* 31°1N 16°45E **258** B3
Qaşr-e Fīrūzeh *Iran* 35°29N 51°31E **141** B3
Qaşr-e Qand *Iran* 26°15N 60°45E **247** E9
Qaşr-e Shīrīn *Iran* 34°31N 45°35E **213** E11
Qasr Farâfra *Egypt* 27°0N 28°1E **256** B2
Qaşr Larocu *Libya* 26°32N 13°19E **258** C2
Qasuittuq = Resolute *Canada* 74°42N 94°54W **295** C13
Qa'ţabah *Yemen* 13°51N 44°42E **248** D4
Qatanā *Syria* 33°26N 36°4E **250** E7
Qaţānan, Ra's *Yemen* 12°21N 53°33E **249** D6
Qatane *West Bank* 31°50N 35°6E **123** B1
Qatar ■ *Asia* 25°30N 51°15E **247** E6
Qatlīsh *Iran* 37°50N 57°19E **247** B8
Qattâra *Egypt* 30°12N 27°3E **256** A2
Qattâra, Munkhafed el *Egypt* 29°30N 27°30E **256** B2
Qattâra Depression = Qattâra, Munkhafed el *Egypt* 29°30N 27°30E **256** B2
Qawām al Ḩamzah = Al Ḩamzah *Iraq* 31°43N 44°58E **246** D5
Qawra Point *Malta* 35°58N 14°26E **206** F7
Qāyen *Iran* 33°40N 59°10E **247** C8
Qaynar *Kazakhstan* 49°12N 77°22E **217** C9
Qazaly *Kazakhstan* 45°45N 62°6E **216** C6
Qazaqstan = Kazakhstan ■ *Asia* 50°0N 70°0E **217** C8
Qazaqtyng Usaqshogylyghy *Kazakhstan* 50°0N 72°0E **217** C8
Qazax *Azerbaijan* 41°5N 45°21E **191** K7
Qazımämmäd *Azerbaijan* 40°3N 49°0E **191** K9
Qazvīn *Iran* 36°15N 50°0E **247** B6
Qazvīn □ *Iran* 36°20N 50°0E **247** B6
Qazyghurt *Kazakhstan* 41°45N 69°23E **217** D7
Qeisari = Caesarea *Israel* 32°30N 34°53E **251** F5
Qeissan *Sudan* 11°4N 34°40E **257** E3
Qena *Egypt* 26°10N 32°43E **256** B3
Qena, W. → *Egypt* 26°12N 32°44E **256** B3
Qeqertarsuaq *Greenland* 69°45N 53°30W **154** D5
Qeqertarsuaq *Greenland* 69°15N 53°38W **154** D5
Qeqertarsuatsiaat *Greenland* 63°5N 50°45W **154** E5
Qeshlāq *Iran* 34°55N 46°28E **213** E12
Qeshm *Iran* 26°55N 56°10E **247** E8
Qeydār *Iran* 36°6N 48°35E **213** D13
Qeys *Iran* 26°32N 53°58E **249** A6
Qezel Owzen → *Iran* 36°45N 49°22E **247** B6
Qezi'ot *Israel* 30°52N 34°26E **251** H5
Qi Xian *China* 34°40N 114°48E **226** G8
Qian Gorlos *China* 45°5N 124°42E **227** B13
Qian Hai *China* 22°32N 113°54E **219** a
Qian Xian *China* 34°31N 108°15E **226** G5
Qian'an *China* 40°0N 118°41E **227** E10
Qiancheng *China* 27°12N 109°50E **228** D7
Qianjiang *Guangxi Zhuangzu, China* 23°38N 108°58E **228** F7
Qianjiang *Hubei, China* 30°24N 112°55E **229** B9
Qianjiang *Sichuan, China* 29°33N 108°47E **228** C7
Qianjin *China* 47°34N 133°4E **219** B15
Qianmen *China* 39°51N 116°21E **114** B2
Qianshan *Anhui, China* 30°37N 116°35E **229** B11
Qianshan *Guangdong, China* 22°15N 113°31E **219** a
Qianwei *China* 29°13N 103°56E **228** C4
Qianxi *China* 27°3N 106°3E **228** D6
Qianyang *Hunan, China* 27°18N 110°10E **229** D8
Qianyang *Shaanxi, China* 34°40N 107°8E **226** G4
Qianyang *Zhejiang, China* 30°11N 119°25E **229** B12
Qi'ao *China* 22°25N 113°39E **219** a
Qi'ao Dao *China* 22°25N 113°38E **219** a
Qiaocun *China* 39°56N 112°55E **226** E7
Qiaojia *China* 26°56N 102°58E **228** D4
Qichun *China* 30°18N 115°25E **229** B10
Qidong *Hunan, China* 26°49N 112°7E **229** D9
Qidong *Jiangsu, China* 31°48N 121°38E **229** B13
Qiemo *China* 38°8N 85°32E **217** E11
Qijiang *China* 28°57N 106°35E **228** C6
Qijiaojing *China* 43°28N 91°36E **217** D12
Qikiqtarjuaq *Canada* 67°33N 63°0W **295** D19
Qila Saifullāh *Pakistan* 30°45N 68°17E **242** D3
Qilian Shan *China* 38°30N 96°0E **218** D8
Qimen *China* 29°50N 117°42E **229** C11
Qin He → *China* 35°1N 113°22E **226** G7
Qin Jiang → *Guangxi Zhuangzu, China* 21°53N 108°35E **228** F7
Qin Jiang → *Jiangxi, China* 26°15N 115°55E **229** D10
Qin Ling = Qinling Shandi *China* 33°50N 108°10E **226** H5
Qināb, W. → *Yemen* 17°55N 49°59E **249** C5
Qin'an *China* 34°48N 105°40E **226** G3
Qing Xian *China* 38°35N 116°45E **226** E9
Qingcheng *China* 37°15N 117°40E **227** F9
Qingcheng Shan *China* 30°58N 103°31E **228** B4
Qingchuan *China* 32°36N 105°9E **226** H3
Qingdao *China* 36°5N 120°20E **227** F11
Qingfeng *China* 35°52N 115°8E **226** G8
Qinghai □ *China* 36°0N 98°0E **218** D8
Qinghai Hu *China* 36°40N 100°10E **218** D9
Qinghe *China* 46°37N 90°25E **217** C12
Qinghecheng *China* 41°28N 124°15E **224** B2
Qinghemen *China* 41°48N 121°25E **227** D11
Qinghuayuan *China* 39°59N 116°19E **114** B1
Qingjian *China* 37°8N 110°8E **226** F6
Qingjiang = Huaiyin *China* 33°30N 119°2E **227** H10
Qingliu *China* 26°11N 116°48E **229** D11
Qinglong *China* 25°49N 105°12E **228** E5
Qingningsi *China* 31°16N 121°33E **138** B2
Qingping *China* 26°39N 107°47E **228** D6
Qingshui *China* 34°48N 106°8E **226** G4
Qingshuihe *China* 39°55N 111°35E **226** E6
Qingtian *China* 28°12N 120°15E **229** C13
Qingtongxia *China* 38°2N 106°3E **226** E4
Qingtongxia Shuiku *China* 37°50N 105°58E **226** F3
Qingxi *China* 27°8N 108°43E **228** D7
Qingxu *China* 37°34N 112°22E **226** F7
Qingyang *Anhui, China* 30°38N 117°50E **229** B11
Qingyang *Gansu, China* 36°2N 107°55E **226** F4
Qingyi Jiang → *China* 29°32N 103°44E **228** C4
Qingyuan *Guangdong, China* 23°40N 112°59E **229** F9
Qingyuan *Liaoning, China* 42°10N 124°55E **224** A2
Qingyuan *Zhejiang, China* 27°36N 119°3E **229** D12
Qingyun *China* 37°45N 117°20E **227** F9
Qingzhen *China* 26°31N 106°25E **228** D6
Qinhuangdao *China* 39°56N 119°30E **227** E10
Qinling Shandi *China* 33°50N 108°10E **226** H5
Qinshui *China* 35°40N 112°8E **226** G7
Qinyang = Jiyuan *China* 35°7N 112°57E **226** G7
Qinyang *China* 35°5N 112°56E **226** G7
Qinyuan *China* 36°29N 112°20E **226** F7
Qinzhou *China* 21°58N 108°38E **228** G7
Qionghai *China* 19°15N 110°26E **236** C8
Qionglai *China* 30°25N 103°31E **228** B4
Qionglai Shan *China* 31°0N 102°30E **228** B4
Qiongshan *China* 19°51N 110°26E **236** C8
Qiongzhou Haixia *China* 20°10N 110°15E **236** B8
Qiqihar *China* 47°26N 124°0E **219** B13
Qira *China* 37°0N 80°48E **217** E10
Qirâiya, W. → *Egypt* 30°27N 34°0E **251** H5
Qiryat Ata *Israel* 32°47N 35°6E **250** F6
Qiryat Gat *Israel* 31°32N 34°46E **251** G5
Qiryat Mal'akhi *Israel* 31°44N 34°44E **251** G5
Qiryat Shemona *Israel* 33°13N 35°35E **250** E6
Qiryat Yam *Israel* 32°51N 35°4E **250** F6
Qirzah, W. → *Libya* 30°56N 14°31E **258** B2
Qishan *China* 34°25N 107°38E **226** G4
Qishn *Yemen* 15°26N 51°40E **249** D5
Qitai *China* 44°2N 89°35E **217** D11
Qitaihe *China* 45°48N 130°51E **220** B5
Qītbīt, W. → *Oman* 19°15N 54°23E **249** C6
Qiubei *China* 24°2N 104°12E **228** E5
Qixia *China* 37°17N 120°52E **227** F11
Qiyang *China* 26°35N 111°50E **229** D8
Qızılağac Körfäzi *Azerbaijan* 39°9N 49°0E **213** C13
Qobda *Kazakhstan* 50°55N 54°31E **216** B4
Qods *Iran* 35°45N 51°15E **247** C6
Qojūr *Iran* 36°12N 47°55E **246** B5
Qolhak *Iran* 35°45N 51°26E **247** C6
Qom *Iran* 34°40N 51°0E **247** C6
Qom □ *Iran* 34°40N 51°0E **247** C6
Qomolangma Feng = Everest, Mt. *Nepal* 28°5N 86°58E **243** E12
Qomsheh *Iran* 32°0N 51°55E **247** D6
Qong Muztag *China* 35°42N 82°22E **217** E10
Qoqek = Tacheng *China* 46°40N 82°58E **217** C10
Qoqon = Qŭqon *Uzbekistan* 40°31N 70°56E **217** D8
Qoraqalpoghistan □ *Uzbekistan* 43°0N 58°0E **216** D5
Qorghalzhyn *Kazakhstan* 50°25N 69°11E **217** B7
Qormi *Malta* 35°53N 14°28E **206** F7
Qorveh *Iran* 35°10N 47°48E **213** E12
Qosshaghyl *Kazakhstan* 46°40N 54°0E **187** E9
Qostanay *Kazakhstan* 53°10N 63°35E **216** B6
Qotanqaraghay *Kazakhstan* 49°10N 85°36E **217** C11
Qoţūr *Iran* 38°28N 44°25E **213** C11
Qoz Salsilgo *C.A.R.* 10°45N 22°54E **264** A4
Qrejten Point *Malta* 35°57N 14°27E **206** F7
Qu Jiang → *China* 30°1N 106°24E **228** B6
Qu Xian *China* 30°48N 106°58E **228** B6
Quabbin Res. *U.S.A.* 42°20N 72°20W **313** D12
Quadraro *Italy* 41°51N 12°33E **136** B2
Quaid-i-Azam *Pakistan* 24°50N 66°59E **123** A1
Quairading *Australia* 32°0S 117°21E **279** F2
Quakenbrück *Germany* 52°41N 7°57E **178** C3
Quakertown *U.S.A.* 40°26N 75°21W **313** F9
Qualicum Beach *Canada* 49°22N 124°26W **296** D4
Quambatook *Australia* 35°49S 143°34E **282** C5
Quambone *Australia* 30°57S 147°53E **283** A7
Quamby *Australia* 20°22S 140°17E **280** C3
Quan Long = Ca Mau *Vietnam* 9°7N 105°8E **237** H5
Quanah *U.S.A.* 34°18N 99°44W **314** D5
Quandialla *Australia* 34°1S 147°47E **283** C7
Quang Ngai *Vietnam* 15°13N 108°58E **236** E7
Quang Tri *Vietnam* 16°45N 107°13E **236** D6
Quang Yen *Vietnam* 20°56N 106°52E **228** G6
Quannan *China* 24°45N 114°33E **229** E10
Quantock Hills *U.K.* 51°8N 3°10W **169** F4
Quanyang *China* 42°21N 127°32E **227** C14
Quanzhou *Fujian, China* 24°55N 118°34E **229** E12
Quanzhou *Guangxi Zhuangzu, China* 25°57N 111°5E **229** E8
Qu'Appelle → *Canada* 50°33N 103°53W **297** C8
Quaqtaq *Canada* 60°55N 69°40W **295** E18
Quaraí *Brazil* 30°15S 56°20W **334** C4
Quarré-les-Tombes *France* 47°21N 4°0E **173** E11
Quarteira *Portugal* 37°4N 8°6W **195** H2
Quarter, The *Anguilla* 18°13N 63°3W **322** a
Quarter D'Orléans *St.-Martin* 18°5N 63°2W **322** a
Quartier Militaire *Mauritius* 20°14S 57°35E **272** e
Quartiere Zingone *Italy* 45°25N 9°3E **128** B1
Quartu Sant'Elena *Italy* 39°15N 9°10E **200** C2
Quartzsite *U.S.A.* 33°40N 114°13W **307** M12
Quatre, I. à *St. Vincent* 12°59N 61°15W **323** n
Quatre Bornes *Mauritius* 20°15S 57°28E **272** e
Quatsino Sd. *Canada* 50°25N 127°58W **296** C3
Quba *Azerbaijan* 41°21N 48°32E **191** K9
Qubeiba *West Bank* 31°50N 35°8E **123** A1
Qūchān *Iran* 37°10N 58°27E **247** B8
Quds *Iraq* 33°23N 44°24E **113** A2
Queanbeyan *Australia* 35°17S 149°14E **283** C8
Québec *Canada* 46°52N 71°13W **299** C5
Québec □ *Canada* 48°0N 74°0W **299** B6
Quebo *Guinea-Biss.* 11°20N 14°56W **262** C2
Quebrada del Condorito △ *Argentina* 31°49S 64°40W **334** C3
Quebradillas *Puerto Rico* 18°29N 66°56W **321** b
Quedlinburg *Germany* 51°47N 11°8E **178** D7
Queen Alexandra Ra. *Antarctica* 85°0S 170°0E **151** E11
Queen Charlotte B. *Falk. Is.* 51°50S 60°40W **153** f
Queen Charlotte City *Canada* 53°15N 132°2W **296** C2
Queen Charlotte Is. = Haida Gwaii *Canada* 53°20N 132°10W **296** C2
Queen Charlotte Sd. *B.C., Canada* 51°0N 128°0W **296** C3
Queen Charlotte Sd. *N.Z.* 41°10S 174°15E **285** B9
Queen Charlotte Strait *Canada* 50°45N 127°10W **296** C3
Queen City *U.S.A.* 40°25N 92°34W **310** D4
Queen Elizabeth △ *Uganda* 0°0 30°0E **268** C3
Queen Elizabeth Is. *Canada* 76°0N 95°0W **295** B13
Queen Elizabeth Nat. Park = Ruwenzori △ *Uganda* 0°20N 30°0E **268** B2
Queen Mary Land *Antarctica* 70°0S 95°0E **151** D7
Queen Mary Res. *U.K.* 51°24N 0°27W **125** B1
Queen Maud G. *Canada* 68°15N 102°30W **294** D11
Queen Maud Land = Dronning Maud Land *Antarctica* 72°30S 12°0E **151** D3
Queen Maud Mts. *Antarctica* 86°0S 160°0W **151** E12
Queen Street *Edinburgh, U.K.* **121** a1
Queen Victoria Market *Australia* 37°47S 144°57W **128** A1
Queens Channel *Australia* 15°0S 129°30E **278** C4
Queens-Midtown Tunnel *New York, U.S.A.* **132** d2
Queen's Quay Terminal *Toronto, Canada* **141** c2
Queensboro Bridge *New York, U.S.A.* **132** c3
Queensbury *U.K.* 51°35N 0°16W **125** A2
Queenscliff *Australia* 38°16S 144°39E **282** E6
Queenscliffe *Australia* 33°47S 151°17E **139** A2
Queensferry *U.K.* 55°59N 3°23W **121** B1
Queensland *U.S.A.* 31°46N 83°14W **316** D6
Queensland □ *Australia* 22°0S 142°0E **280** C3
Queensland Plateau *Pac. Oc.* 17°0S 150°0E **276** D8
Queenstown = Cobh *Ireland* 51°51N 8°17W **166** E3
Queenstown *Tas., Australia* 42°4S 145°35E **281** G4
Queenstown *N.Z.* 45°1S 168°40E **285** F3
Queenstown *Singapore* 1°18N 103°48E **138** B2
Queenstown *Eastern Cape, S. Africa* 31°52S 26°52E **270** D4
Queets *U.S.A.* 47°32N 124°19W **306** C2
Queguay Grande → *Uruguay* 32°9S 58°9W **334** C4
Queimada, Pta. da *Azores* 38°23N 28°14W **153** d1
Queimadas *Brazil* 11°0S 39°38W **332** D4
Queiros, C. *Vanuatu* 14°55S 167°1E **287** D5
Quela *Angola* 9°10S 16°56E **265** D3
Quelimane *Mozam.* 17°53S 36°58E **269** F4
Quellerina *S. Africa* 26°9S 27°56E **123** A1
Quellón *Chile* 43°7S 73°37W **336** B2
Quelo *Angola* 6°29S 12°36E **265** D2
Quelpart = Jeju-do *S. Korea* 33°29N 126°34E **224** a
Queluz *Portugal* 38°45N 9°14W **126** A1
Quemado *N. Mex., U.S.A.* 34°20N 108°30W **305** J9
Quemado *Tex., U.S.A.* 28°56N 100°37W **314** G4
Quemoy = Chinmen *Taiwan* 24°26N 118°19E **225** a
Quemú-Quemú *Argentina* 36°3S 63°36W **334** D3
Quepem *India* 15°13N 74°3E **245** G2
Quequén *Argentina* 38°30S 58°30W **334** D4
Querco *Peru* 13°50S 74°52W **330** C3
Querétaro *Mexico* 20°36N 100°23W **318** C4
Querétaro □ *Mexico* 21°0N 99°55W **318** C5
Querfurt *Germany* 51°23N 11°35E **178** D7
Quérigut *France* 42°42N 2°6E **174** F6
Querqueville *France* 49°40N 1°42W **172** C5
Quesada *Spain* 37°51N 3°4W **195** H7
Queshan *China* 32°55N 114°2E **229** A10
Quesnel *Canada* 53°0N 122°30W **296** C4
Quesnel → *Canada* 52°58N 122°29W **296** C4
Quesnel L. *Canada* 52°30N 121°20W **296** C4
Questa *U.S.A.* 36°42N 105°36W **305** H11
Questembert *France* 47°40N 2°28W **172** E4
Quetena *Bolivia* 22°10S 67°25W **330** E4
Quetico △ *Canada* 48°30N 91°45W **298** C1
Quetrequile *Argentina* 41°33S 69°22W **336** B3
Quetta *Pakistan* 30°15N 66°55E **242** D2
Quetzaltenango *Guatemala* 14°50N 91°30W **320** D1
Queulat △ *Chile* 44°29S 72°24W **336** B2
Quevedo *Ecuador* 1°2S 79°29W **328** D2
Queyras △ *France* 44°45N 6°50E **175** D10
Quezon *Phil.* 9°15N 117°59E **233** G1
Quezon □ *Phil.* 14°40N 121°30E **232** D3
Quezon △ *Phil.* 14°0N 121°55E **232** D3
Quezon City *Phil.* 14°37N 121°2E **127** B2
Qufār *Si. Arabia* 27°26N 41°37E **246** E4
Qufu *China* 35°36N 116°58E **226** G9
Qui Nhon *Vietnam* 13°40N 109°13E **236** F7
Quibala *Angola* 10°46S 14°59E **265** E2
Quibaxe *Angola* 8°24S 14°27E **265** D2
Quibdó *Colombia* 5°42N 76°40W **328** B2
Quiberon *France* 47°29N 3°9W **172** E3
Quiberon, Presqu'île de *France* 47°30N 3°8W **172** E3
Quiçama △ *Angola* 9°41S 13°35E **265** D2
Quickborn *Germany* 53°42N 9°52E **178** B5
Quiet L. *Canada* 61°5N 133°5W **296** A2
Quiindy *Paraguay* 25°58S 57°14W **334** B4
Quilá *Mexico* 24°23N 107°13W **318** C3
Quilán, C. *Chile* 43°15S 74°30W **336** B2
Quilcene *U.S.A.* 47°49N 122°53W **306** C4
Quilenda *Angola* 10°39S 14°20E **265** E2
Quilengues *Angola* 14°12S 14°12E **265** E2
Quilicura *Chile* 33°22S 70°43W **137** B1
Quilimarí *Chile* 32°5S 71°30W **334** C1
Quilino *Argentina* 30°14S 64°29W **334** C3
Quill, The *St. Eustatius* 17°28N 62°57W **322** a
Quillabamba *Peru* 12°50S 72°50W **330** C3
Quillacollo *Bolivia* 17°26S 66°17W **330** D4
Quillagua *Chile* 21°40S 69°40W **334** A2
Quillan *France* 42°53N 2°10E **174** F6
Quillota *Chile* 32°54S 71°16W **334** C1
Quilmes *Argentina* 34°43S 58°15W **334** C4
Quilon = Kollam *India* 8°50N 76°38E **245** K3
Quilpie *Australia* 26°35S 144°11E **281** D3
Quilpué *Chile* 33°5S 71°33W **334** C1
Quilua *Mozam.* 16°17S 39°54E **269** F4
Quimbele *Angola* 6°17S 16°41E **265** D3
Quimbo *Angola* 14°4S 16°11E **265** E3
Quimbonge *Angola* 8°36S 18°30E **265** D3
Quime *Bolivia* 17°2S 67°15W **330** D4
Quimilí *Argentina* 27°40S 62°30W **334** B3
Quimper *France* 48°0N 4°9W **172** E2
Quimperlé *France* 47°53N 3°33W **172** E3
Quinam B. *Trin. & Tob.* 10°4N 61°30W **323** t
Quinault → *U.S.A.* 47°21N 124°18W **306** C2
Quince Mil *Peru* 13°15S 70°40W **330** C3
Quincy *Calif., U.S.A.* 39°56N 120°57W **306** F6
Quincy *Fla., U.S.A.* 30°35N 84°34W **316** E5
Quincy *Ill., U.S.A.* 39°56N 91°23W **310** E5
Quincy *Mass., U.S.A.* 42°14N 71°0W **116** B2
Quincy *Mich., U.S.A.* 41°57N 84°53W **311** C12
Quincy *Wash., U.S.A.* 47°14N 119°51W **304** C4
Quincy B. *U.S.A.* 42°16N 70°59W **116** B3
Quines *Argentina* 32°13S 65°48W **334** C2
Quinga *Mozam.* 15°49S 40°15E **269** F5
Quingey *France* 47°7N 5°52E **173** E12
Quingombe *Angola* 6°38S 13°1E **265** D2
Quinhagak *U.S.A.* 59°45N 161°54W **303** G7
Quinhámel *Guinea-Biss.* 11°53N 15°51W **262** C1
Quiniluban Group *Phil.* 11°27N 120°48E **233** F3
Quinta Normal *Chile* 33°26S 70°42W **137** B1
Quintana de la Serena *Spain* 38°45N 5°40W **195** G5
Quintana Roo □ *Mexico* 19°40N 88°30W **319** D7
Quintanar de la Orden *Spain* 39°36N 3°5W **195** F7
Quintanar de la Sierra *Spain* 41°57N 2°55W **196** D2
Quintanar del Rey *Spain* 39°21N 1°56W **197** F3
Quintero *Chile* 32°45S 71°30W **334** C1
Quintin *France* 48°26N 2°56W **172** D4
Quinto *Spain* 41°25N 0°32W **196** D4
Quinto de Stampi *Italy* 45°24N 9°10E **128** B2
Quinto Romano *Italy* 45°28N 9°7E **128** B1
Quinzáu *Angola* 6°51S 12°44E **265** D2
Quipar → *Spain* 38°15N 1°40W **197** G3
Quipeio *Angola* 12°27S 15°20E **265** E3
Quirihue *Chile* 36°15S 72°35W **334** D1
Quirima *Angola* 10°47S 18°6E **265** E3
Quirimbas △ *Mozam.* 12°30S 40°15E **269** E5
Quirimbo *Angola* 10°36S 14°12E **265** E2
Quirinale *Italy* 41°53N 12°29E **136** B1
Quirinale, Palazzo dei *Rome, Italy* **136** b3
Quirindi *Australia* 31°28S 150°40E **283** A9
Quirino □ *Phil.* 16°15N 121°40E **232** C3
Quirinópolis *Brazil* 18°32S 50°30W **333** E1
Quiroga *Spain* 42°28N 7°18W **194** C3
Quiruvilca *Peru* 8°1S 78°19W **330** B2
Quissac *France* 43°55N 4°0E **175** E8
Quissanga *Mozam.* 12°24S 40°28E **269** E5
Quissico *Mozam.* 24°42S 34°44E **271** B5
Quissongo *Angola* 10°2S 15°5E **265** E3
Quitapa *Angola* 10°20S 18°19E **265** E3
Quitilipi *Argentina* 26°50S 60°13W **334** B3
Quitman *U.S.A.* 30°47N 83°34W **316** E6
Quito *Ecuador* 0°15S 78°35W **328** D2
Quitralco △ *Chile* 45°43S 73°25W **336** C2
Quixadá *Brazil* 4°55S 39°0W **332** B4
Quixaxe *Mozam.* 15°17S 40°4E **269** F5
Quixeramobim *Brazil* 5°12S 39°17W **332** C4
Quixico *Angola* 7°59S 14°25E **265** D2
Quixinge *Angola* 9°52S 14°23E **265** D2
Quizenga *Angola* 9°21S 15°28E **265** D3
Qujing *China* 25°32N 103°41E **228** E4
Qulan *Kazakhstan* 42°55N 72°43E **214** E8
Qul'ân, Jazâ'ir *Egypt* 24°22N 35°31E **246** E2
Qulsary *Kazakhstan* 46°59N 54°1E **187** E9
Qumbu *S. Africa* 31°10S 28°48E **271** D4
Qunayyin, Sabkhat al *Libya* 30°10N 21°0E **258** B4
Quneitra = Al Qunayţirah *Syria* 33°5N 35°45E **250** E6
Qŭnghirot *Uzbekistan* 43°2N 58°50E **216** D5
Qu'nyido *China* 31°15N 98°6E **228** B2
Quoin I. *Australia* 14°54S 129°32E **278** B4
Quoin Pt. *S. Africa* 34°46S 19°37E **270** D2
Quorn *Australia* 32°25S 138°5E **282** B3
Qŭqon *Uzbekistan* 40°31N 70°56E **217** D8
Qurein *Sudan* 13°30N 34°50E **257** E3
Qŭrghonteppa *Tajikistan* 37°50N 68°47E **217** E7
Qurimbas △ *Mozam.* 12°20S 40°10E **269** E5
Qurnat as Sawdā' *Lebanon* 34°18N 36°6E **250** D7
Quryq *Kazakhstan* 43°12N 51°39E **216** D4
Qûs *Egypt* 25°55N 32°50E **256** B3
Qusar *Azerbaijan* 41°25N 48°26E **191** K9
Quşaybā' *Si. Arabia* 26°53N 43°35E **246** E4
Qusaybah *Iraq* 34°24N 40°59E **213** E9
Quşay'ir *Yemen* 14°55N 50°20E **249** D5
Quseir *Egypt* 26°7N 34°16E **246** E2
Quseir Amra = Qasr 'Amra *Jordan* 31°48N 36°35E **246** D3
Qūshchī *Iran* 37°59N 45°3E **213** D11
Qusmuryn *Kazakhstan* 52°27N 64°36E **216** B6
Qusmuryn Köli *Kazakhstan* 52°41N 64°48E **216** B6
Qutang Gorge = Qutang Xia *China* 31°0N 109°40E **228** B7
Qutang Xia *China* 31°0N 109°40E **228** B7
Qutb Minar *India* 28°31N 77°11E **120** B2
Quthing *Lesotho* 30°25S 27°36E **271** D4
Qūţīābād *Iran* 35°47N 48°30E **213** E13
Quttinirpaaq △ *Canada* 82°13N 72°13W **295** A17
Quwayq → *Syria* 36°20N 37°10E **250** B8
Quweisna *Egypt* 30°34N 31°9E **251** H2
Quwo *China* 35°38N 111°25E **226** G6
Quyang *China* 38°35N 114°40E **226** E8
Quynh Nhai *Vietnam* 21°49N 103°33E **236** B4
Quyon *Canada* 45°31N 76°14W **313** A8
Quzhou *China* 28°57N 118°54E **229** C12
Quzi *China* 36°20N 107°20E **226** F4
Qvareli *Georgia* 41°57N 45°47E **191** K7
Qytet Stalin = Kuçovë *Albania* 40°47N 19°57E **202** F3
Qyzylorda *Kazakhstan* 44°48N 65°28E **217** D7
Qyzylorda □ *Kazakhstan* 45°0N 65°0E **216** D6
Qyzylzhar *Kazakhstan* 48°17N 69°38E **217** C7

R

R.F.K. Memorial Stadium *U.S.A.* 38°52N 76°58W **143** B3
Ra, Ko *Thailand* 9°13N 98°16E **237** H2
Raab *Austria* 48°21N 13°39E **180** C6
Raahe *Finland* 64°40N 24°28E **160** D21
Raalte *Neths.* 52°23N 6°16E **170** B6
Ra'ananna *Israel* 32°10N 34°52E **251** F5
Raas *Indonesia* 7°8S 114°33E **235** D4
Raasay *U.K.* 57°25N 6°4W **167** D2
Raasay, Sd. of *U.K.* 57°30N 6°8W **167** D2
Raasdorf *Austria* 48°14N 16°33E **142** A3
Raasepori *Finland* 60°0N 23°26E **188** B2
Rab *Croatia* 44°45N 14°45E **199** D11
Raba *Indonesia* 8°36S 118°55E **235** D5
Rába → *Hungary* 47°38N 17°38E **182** C2
Raba → *Poland* 50°8N 20°30E **185** H7
Rabaçal → *Portugal* 41°30N 7°12W **194** D3
Rabah *Nigeria* 13°5N 5°30E **263** C6
Rabai *Kenya* 3°50S 39°31E **268** C4
Rabak *Sudan* 13°9N 32°44E **257** E3
Rabaraba *Papua N. G.* 9°58S 149°49E **286** E5
Rabastens *France* 43°50N 1°43E **174** E5
Rabastens-de-Bigorre *France* 43°23N 0°9E **174** E4
Rabat = Victoria *Malta* 36°3N 14°14E **206** E6
Rabat *Malta* 35°53N 14°24E **206** F7
Rabat *Morocco* 34°2N 6°48W **260** B3
Rabat □ *Morocco* 34°10N 6°45W **260** B3
Rabaul *Papua N. G.* 4°24S 152°18E **286** C7
Rabbit Flat *Australia* 20°11S 130°1E **278** D5
Rabbit Lake Mine *Canada* 58°4N 104°5W **297** B8
Rabi *Fiji* 16°30S 179°59W **287** A3
Rābigh *Si. Arabia* 22°50N 39°5E **248** B2
Rabka *Poland* 49°37N 19°59E **185** J6
Râbniţa *Moldova* 47°45N 29°0E **183** C14
Rābor *Iran* 29°17N 56°55E **247** D8
Rabwah = Chenab Nagar *Pakistan* 31°45N 72°55E **242** D5
Rača *Serbia* 44°14N 21°0E **202** B4
Răcăciuni *Romania* 46°20N 26°59E **183** D11
Răcăşdia *Romania* 44°59N 21°36E **182** F6
Racconigi *Italy* 44°46N 7°46E **198** D4
Raccoon → *U.S.A.* 41°35N 93°37W **310** C3
Raccoon Cr. → *U.S.A.* 39°47N 87°23W **311** E9
Race, C. *Canada* 46°40N 53°5W **299** C9
Race Course *Jamaica* 17°51N 77°20W **320** a
Race Pond *U.S.A.* 31°1N 82°8W **316** D7
Rach Gia *Vietnam* 10°5N 105°5E **237** G5
Rach Soi *Vietnam* 9°57N 105°7E **237** H5
Racha Noi, Ko *Thailand* 7°30N 98°19E **237** J2
Racha Yai, Ko *Thailand* 7°36N 98°21E **237** J2
Rachid *Mauritania* 18°45N 11°35W **262** B2
Raciąż *Poland* 52°46N 20°10E **185** F7
Racibórz *Poland* 50°7N 18°18E **185** H5
Racichy *Belarus* 53°44N 23°42E **184** E10
Racine *U.S.A.* 42°44N 87°47W **311** B9
Račişdorf = Rača *Serbia* 44°14N 21°0E **202** B4
Rackerby *U.S.A.* 39°26N 121°22W **306** F5
Råda *Sweden* 60°0N 13°36E **162** E7
Radama, Nosy *Madag.* 14°0S 47°47E **272** A2
Radama, Saikanosy *Madag.* 14°16S 47°53E **272** A2
Radan *Serbia* 42°59N 21°29E **202** D5
Rădăuţi *Romania* 47°50N 25°59E **183** C10
Rădăuţi-Prut *Romania* 48°14N 26°48E **183** B11
Radbuza → *Czech Rep.* 49°45N 13°22E **180** B6
Radcliff *U.S.A.* 37°51N 85°57W **311** G11
Radcliffe College *U.S.A.* 42°22N 71°7W **116** A2
Radeberg *Germany* 51°7N 13°53E **178** D9
Radebeul *Germany* 51°6N 13°39E **178** D9
Radeče *Slovenia* 46°5N 15°14E **199** B12
Radekhiv *Ukraine* 50°25N 24°32E **177** C13
Radekhov = Radekhiv *Ukraine* 50°25N 24°32E **177** C13
Radenthein *Austria* 46°48N 13°43E **180** E6
Radew → *Poland* 54°2N 15°52E **184** D2
Radford *U.S.A.* 37°8N 80°34W **309** G13
Radhanpur *India* 23°50N 71°38E **242** H4
Rådhus *Oslo, Norway* **133** b1
Radhwa, Jabal *Si. Arabia* 24°34N 38°18E **246** E3
Radika → *Macedonia* 41°38N 20°37E **202** E4
Radisson *Qué., Canada* 53°47N 77°37W **298** B4
Radisson *Sask., Canada* 52°30N 107°20W **297** C7
Radium Hot Springs *Canada* 50°35N 116°2W **296** C5
Radlice *Czech Rep.* 50°3N 14°23E **135** B2
Radlje ob Dravi *Slovenia* 46°38N 15°13E **199** B12
Radmannsdorf = Radovljica *Slovenia* 46°22N 14°12E **199** B11
Radnevo *Bulgaria* 42°17N 25°58E **203** D9
Radnice *Czech Rep.* 49°51N 13°35E **180** B6
Radnor Forest *U.K.* 52°17N 3°10W **169** E4
Radolfzell *Germany* 47°39N 8°59E **179** H4
Radom *Poland* 51°23N 21°12E **185** G8
Radom △ *Sudan* 9°20N 23°50E **264** A4
Radomir *Bulgaria* 42°37N 22°59E **202** D6
Radomka → *Poland* 51°43N 21°28E **185** G8
Radomsko *Poland* 51°5N 19°28E **185** G6
Radomyshl *Ukraine* 50°30N 29°12E **177** C15
Radomyśl Wielki *Poland* 50°14N 21°15E **185** H8
Radość *Poland* 52°11N 21°11E **143** B3
Radoszyce *Poland* 51°4N 20°15E **185** G7
Radotín *Czech Rep.* 49°59N 14°21E **135** C2
Radoviš *Macedonia* 41°38N 22°28E **202** E6
Radovljica *Slovenia* 46°22N 14°12E **199** B11
Radstadt *Austria* 47°24N 13°28E **180** D6
Radstock, C. *Australia* 33°12S 134°20E **281** E1
Răducăneni *Romania* 46°58N 27°54E **183** D12
Raduša *Macedonia* 42°7N 21°15E **202** D5
Raduzhnyy *Russia* 62°5N 77°28E **214** C8
Radvanichy *Belarus* 52°1N 24°0E **185** F11
Radviliškis *Lithuania* 55°49N 23°33E **184** C10
Radville *Canada* 49°30N 104°15W **297** D8
Radwā, J. *Si. Arabia* 24°34N 38°18E **256** C4
Radymno *Poland* 49°59N 22°52E **185** J9
Radzanów *Poland* 52°56N 20°8E **185** F7
Radziejów *Poland* 52°40N 18°30E **185** F5
Radzyń Chełmiński *Poland* 53°23N 18°55E **184** E5
Radzyń Podlaski *Poland* 51°47N 22°37E **185** G9
Rae *Canada* 62°50N 116°3W **296** A5
Rae Bareli *India* 26°18N 81°20E **243** F9
Rae Isthmus *Canada* 66°40N 87°30W **295** D14
Raeren *Belgium* 50°41N 6°7E **170** D6
Raeside, L. *Australia* 29°20S 122°0E **279** E3
Raetihi *N.Z.* 39°25S 175°17E **284** F4
Rafaela *Argentina* 31°10S 61°30W **334** C3
Rafah *Gaza Strip* 31°18N 34°14E **251** G5
Rafai *C.A.R.* 4°59N 23°58E **264** B4
Rafat *West Bank* 31°52N 35°11E **123** A2
Raffadali *Italy* 37°24N 13°32E **200** E6
Raffili *South Sudan* 6°50N 28°0E **257** F2
Raffles Hotel *Singapore* **138** b3
Raffles Park *Singapore* 1°19N 103°48E **138** B2
Rafḩā *Si. Arabia* 29°35N 43°35E **246** D4
Rafina *Greece* 38°2N 24°0E **204** C6
Rafsanjān *Iran* 30°30N 56°5E **247** D8
Raft Pt. *Australia* 16°4S 124°26E **278** C3
Râgâ *South Sudan* 8°28N 25°41E **257** F2
Râgâ → *South Sudan* 8°41N 25°52E **257** F2
Ragachow *Belarus* 53°8N 30°5E **177** B16
Ragag *Sudan* 10°59N 24°40E **257** E2
Ragang, Mt. *Phil.* 7°43N 124°32E **233** H5
Ragay *Phil.* 13°49N 122°47E **232** E4
Ragay G. *Phil.* 13°30N 122°45E **232** E4
Ragged, Mt. *Australia* 33°27S 123°25E **279** F3
Rāgh *Afghan.* 37°32N 70°27E **240** A3
Raghunathpalli *India* 22°14N 84°48E **243** H11
Raghunathpur *India* 23°33N 86°40E **243** H12
Raglan *N.Z.* 37°55S 174°55E **284** D3
Raglan Harbour *N.Z.* 37°47S 174°50E **284** D3
Ragland *U.S.A.* 33°45N 86°9W **316** B3
Ragnit = Neman *Russia* 55°2N 22°2E **184** C9
Raguda, Ghubbet *Somalia* 10°43N 46°22E **267** B6
Ragusa = Dubrovnik *Croatia* 42°39N 18°6E **202** D2
Ragusa *Italy* 36°55N 14°44E **201** F7
Raha *Indonesia* 4°55S 123°0E **231** E6
Rahad, Nahr ed → *Sudan* 14°28N 33°31E **257** E3
Rahad al Bardī *Sudan* 11°20N 23°40E **259** F4
Rahaeng = Tak *Thailand* 16°52N 99°8E **236** D2
Rahat *Israel* 31°24N 34°45E **251** G5
Rahat, Ḩarrat *Si. Arabia* 23°0N 40°5E **256** C5
Rahatgarh *India* 23°47N 78°22E **243** H8
Rahden *Germany* 52°26N 8°36E **178** C4
Raheb, Ras ir- *Malta* 35°54N 14°20E **206** F7
Raheita *Eritrea* 12°46N 43°4E **257** E5
Raheng = Tak *Thailand* 16°52N 99°8E **236** D2
Raheny *Ireland* 53°22N 6°10W **120** A3
Rahimyar Khan *Pakistan* 28°30N 70°25E **242** E4
Rāhjerd *Iran* 34°22N 50°22E **247** C6
Rahnsdorf *Germany* 52°25N 13°41E **115** B5
Rahole △ *Kenya* 0°5N 38°57E **268** B4
Råholt *Norway* 60°16N 11°11E **164** D8
Rahon *India* 31°3N 76°7E **242** D7
Rahotu *N.Z.* 39°20S 173°49E **284** F2
Rahovec *Kosovo* 42°24N 20°40E **202** D4
Rahuri *India* 19°23N 74°39E **244** E2
Rai, Hon *Vietnam* 9°48N 104°38E **237** H5
Raiatéa, Î. *French Polynesia* 16°50S 151°25W **289** f
Raichur *India* 16°10N 77°20E **245** F3
Raiford *U.S.A.* 30°4N 82°14W **316** E7
Raiganj *India* 25°37N 88°10E **243** G13
Raigarh *India* 21°56N 83°25E **244** D6
Raighar *India* 19°51N 82°6E **244** E6
Raijua *Indonesia* 10°37S 121°36E **231** F6
Raikot *India* 30°41N 75°42E **242** D6
Railton *Australia* 41°25S 146°28E **281** G4
Rainbow Bridge △ *U.S.A.* 37°5N 110°58W **305** H8
Rainbow City *U.S.A.* 33°57N 86°5W **316** B3
Rainbow Lake *Canada* 58°30N 119°23W **296** B5
Rainier *U.S.A.* 46°53N 122°41W **306** D4
Rainier, Mt. *U.S.A.* 46°52N 121°46W **306** D5
Rainy L. *Canada* 48°42N 93°10W **297** D10
Rainy River *Canada* 48°43N 94°29W **297** D10
Raippaluoto *Finland* 63°13N 21°14E **160** E19
Raipur *India* 21°17N 81°45E **244** D5
Rairakhol *India* 21°4N 84°21E **244** D7
Ra'is *Si. Arabia* 23°33N 38°43E **256** C4
Raisen *India* 23°20N 77°48E **242** H8
Raisio *Finland* 60°28N 22°11E **188** B2
Raivavae *French Polynesia* 23°52S 147°40W **289** f
Raj Ghat *Delhi, India* **120** b3
Raj Nandgaon *India* 21°5N 81°5E **244** D5
Raj Nilgiri *India* 21°28N 86°46E **243** J12
Raja, Ujung *Indonesia* 3°40N 96°25E **234** B1
Raja Ampat, Kepulauan *Indonesia* 0°30S 130°0E **231** E8
Rajah Sikatuna △ *Phil.* 9°40N 124°20E **233** G5
Rajahmundry *India* 17°1N 81°48E **244** F5
Rajaji △ *India* 30°10N 78°20E **242** D8
Rajakylä *Finland* 60°15N 25°25E **121** B3
Rajampet *India* 14°11N 79°10E **245** G4
Rajang → *Malaysia* 2°30N 112°0E **235** B4
Rajang Mangroves △ *Malaysia* 2°6N 111°16E **235** B4
Rajanpur *Pakistan* 29°6N 70°19E **242** E4
Rajapalaiyam *India* 9°25N 77°35E **245** K3
Rajapur *India* 16°40N 73°31E **244** F1
Rajasthan □ *India* 26°45N 73°30E **242** F5
Rajasthan Canal = Indira Gandhi Canal *India* 28°0N 72°0E **242** F5
Rajauri *India* 33°25N 74°21E **243** C6
Rajbari *Bangla.* 23°47N 89°41E **241** D2
Rajendranagar *India* 17°18N 78°27E **244** F4
Rajgarh *Mad. P., India* 24°2N 76°45E **242** G7
Rajgarh *Raj., India* 27°14N 76°38E **242** F7
Rajgarh *Raj., India* 28°40N 75°25E **242** E6
Rajghat Dam *India* 24°45N 78°20E **244** B4
Rajgir *India* 25°2N 85°25E **243** G11
Rajgród *Poland* 53°42N 22°42E **184** E9
Rajim *India* 20°58N 81°53E **244** D5
Rajkot *India* 22°15N 70°56E **242** H4
Rajmahal Hills *India* 24°30N 87°30E **243** G12
Rajpath *Delhi, India* **120** c2
Rajpipla *India* 21°50N 73°30E **244** D1
Rajpur *India* 22°18N 74°21E **242** H6
Rajpura *Delhi, India* 28°41N 77°12E **120** A2
Rajpura *Punjab, India* 30°25N 76°32E **242** D7
Rajputana = Rajasthan □ *India* 26°45N 73°30E **242** F5
Rajsamand = Kankroli *India* 25°4N 73°53E **242** G5
Rajshahi *Bangla.* 24°22N 88°39E **241** C2
Rajshahi □ *Bangla.* 25°0N 89°0E **241** C2
Rājū *Syria* 36°40N 36°40E **250** B7
Rajula *India* 21°3N 71°26E **242** J4
Rajur *India* 20°7N 78°55E **244** D4
Rajura *India* 19°47N 79°22E **244** E4
Rakaia *N.Z.* 43°45S 172°1E **285** D7
Rakaia → *N.Z.* 43°36S 172°15E **285** D7
Rakan, Ra's *Qatar* 26°10N 51°20E **247** E6
Rakaposhi *Pakistan* 36°10N 74°25E **243** A6
Rakata, Pulau *Indonesia* 6°10S 105°20E **234** D3
Rakbah, Sahl *Si. Arabia* 22°15N 41°0E **256** C5
Rakhine □ *Burma* 19°0N 94°15E **241** F5
Rakhiv *Ukraine* 48°3N 24°12E **183** B9
Rakhni *Pakistan* 30°4N 69°56E **242** D3
Rakhni → *Pakistan* 29°31N 69°36E **242** E3
Rakhny-Lisovi *Ukraine* 48°47N 28°29E **183** B13
Rakhyūt *Oman* 16°44N 53°20E **249** C6
Rakiraki *Fiji* 17°22S 178°11E **287** A2
Rakitnoye *Russia* 45°36N 134°17E **220** B7
Rakitovo *Bulgaria* 41°59N 24°5E **203** E8
Rakiura = Stewart I. *N.Z.* 46°58S 167°54E **285** G2
Rakkestad *Norway* 59°25N 11°21E **164** E8
Rakoniewice *Poland* 52°10N 16°16E **185** F3
Rakops *Botswana* 21°1S 24°28E **270** B3
Rákos-patak → *Hungary* 47°29N 19°12E **117** B3
Rákoshegy *Hungary* 47°27N 19°14E **117** B3
Rákoskeresztúr *Hungary* 47°29N 19°15E **117** B3

Råkoskert Hungary 47°27N 19°18E 117 B3
Rákosliget Hungary 47°29N 19°16E 117 B3
Rákospalota Hungary 47°34N 19°7E 117 A2
Rákosszentmihály
Hungary 47°31N 19°8E 117 A2
Rakovica Croatia 44°59N 15°38E 199 D12
Rakovník Czech Rep. 50°6N 13°42E 180 A6
Rakovski Bulgaria 42°21N 24°57E 203 D8
Raków Poland 52°11N 20°56E 143 B1
Rakshan → Pakistan 27°10N 63°25E 240 D1
Rakvere Estonia 59°20N 26°25E 188 C4
Raleigh Fla., U.S.A. 29°25N 82°32W 317 F7
Raleigh N.C., U.S.A. 35°47N 78°39W 315 D15
Ralik Chain Pac. Oc. 8°0N 168°0E 288 G8
Ralja Serbia 44°33N 20°34E 202 B4
Rälla Sweden 56°40N 16°30E 163 H10
Ralls U.S.A. 33°41N 101°24W 314 E4
Ralston U.S.A. 41°30N 76°57W 312 E8
Ram West Bank 31°51N 35°14E 123 A2
Ram → Canada 62°1N 123°41W 296 A4
Rām Allāh West Bank 31°55N 35°10E 123 A2
Rama Nic. 12°9N 84°15W 320 D3
Ramacca Italy 37°23N 14°42E 201 E7
Ramachandrapuram India 16°50N 82°4E 244 F6
Ramadān Iraq 33°19N 44°20E 113 B2
Ramagiri Udayagiri India 19°5N 84°18E 244 E7
Ramagundam India 18°55N 79°15E 244 E4
Ramakona India 21°43N 78°50E 243 J8
Ramakrishna Puram
India 28°32N 77°10E 120 B1
Ramales de la Victoria
Spain 43°15N 3°28W 194 B7
Ramalho, Serra do Brazil 13°45S 44°0W 333 D3
Rāmallāh = Rām Allāh
West Bank 31°55N 35°10E 123 A2
Raman Thailand 6°29N 101°18E 237 J3
Ramanathapuram India 9°25N 78°55E 245 K4
Ramanathpur India 22°41N 88°14E 124 A1
Ramanujganj India 23°48N 83°42E 243 H10
Ramas C. India 15°5N 73°55E 245 G1
Ramat Allon West Bank 31°49N 35°12E 123 B2
Ramat Eshkol West Bank 31°48N 35°13E 123 B2
Ramat Gan Israel 32°4N 34°48E 251 F5
Ramat Razi'el Israel 31°46N 35°4E 123 B1
Ramat Shafet West Bank 31°48N 35°12E 123 B2
Ramatlhabama S. Africa 25°37S 25°33E 270 C4
Ramban India 33°14N 75°12E 243 C6
Rambervillers France 48°20N 6°38E 173 D13
Rambi = Rabi Fiji 16°30S 179°59W 287 A3
Rambipuji Indonesia 8°12S 113°37E 235 D4
Rambler Channel China 22°21N 114°6E 122 A1
Rambouillet France 48°39N 1°50E 173 D8
Rambrai India 25°40N 91°19E 241 C3
Rambutyo I. Papua N. G. 2°18S 147°49E 286 B4
Ramdurg India 15°58N 75°22E 245 G2
Rame Hd. Australia 37°47S 149°30E 283 D8
Ramechhap Nepal 27°25N 86°10E 243 F12
Ramenki Russia 55°41N 37°28E 129 B1
Ramenskoye Russia 55°32N 38°15E 188 E10
Ramer U.S.A. 32°3N 86°13W 316 C3
Ramersdorf Germany 48°6N 11°35E 131 B2
Rameses Station Egypt 30°3N 31°15E 117 A2
Rameswaram India 9°17N 79°18E 245 K4
Ramganga → India 27°5N 79°58E 243 F8
Ramgarh Bangla. 22°59N 91°44E 241 D3
Ramgarh Jharkhand, India 23°40N 85°35E 243 H11
Ramgarh Raj., India 27°16N 75°14E 242 F6
Ramgarh Raj., India 27°30N 70°36E 242 F4
Rāmhormoz Iran 31°15N 49°35E 247 D6
Ramiān Iran 37°3N 55°16E 247 B7
Ramiers Haiti 19°34N 72°14W 321 C5
Ramingining Australia 12°19S 135°3E 280 A2
Ramla Israel 31°55N 34°52E 251 G5
Ramlat Zalţan Libya 28°30N 19°30E 258 C3
Ramlu Eritrea 13°32N 41°40E 257 E5
Ramm = Rum Jordan 29°39N 35°26E 251 J6
Râmna → Romania 45°36N 27°3E 183 E12
Ramnad = Ramanathapuram
India 9°25N 78°55E 245 K4
Ramnagar Jammu & Kashmir,
India 32°47N 75°18E 243 C6
Ramnagar Uttarakhand,
India 29°24N 79°7E 243 E8
Ramnäs Sweden 59°46N 16°12E 162 E10
Râmnicu Sărat Romania 45°26N 27°3E 183 E12
Râmnicu Vâlcea Romania 45°9N 24°21E 183 E9
Ramnous Greece 38°12N 24°3E 204 C6
Ramon Isabela, Phil. 16°50N 121°31E 232 C3
Ramon Russia 51°55N 39°21E 189 G10
Ramona U.S.A. 33°2N 116°52W 307 M10
Ramonville-St-Agne
France 43°33N 1°28E 174 E5
Ramore Canada 48°30N 80°25W 298 C3
Ramos Brazil 22°50S 43°14W 135 B1
Ramos → Nigeria 5°8N 5°22E 263 D6
Ramos I. Phil. 8°6N 117°1E 233 G1
Ramos Mejía Argentina 34°39S 58°33W 117 B1
Ramot West Bank 31°48N 35°13E 123 B2
Ramotswa Botswana 24°50S 25°52E 270 B4
Rampanalgas Trin. & Tob. 10°44N 60°59W 323 t
Rampart U.S.A. 65°30N 150°10W 303 D10
Rampur H.P., India 31°26N 77°43E 242 D7
Rampur Mad. P., India 23°25N 73°53E 242 H5
Rampur Odisha, India 21°48N 83°58E 244 D6
Rampur Ut. P., India 28°44N 77°18E 120 A2
Rampur Ut. P., India 28°50N 79°5E 243 E8
Rampur Hat India 24°10N 87°50E 243 G12
Rampura India 24°30N 75°27E 242 G6
Ramrama Tola India 21°52N 79°55E 243 J8
Ramree I. Burma 19°0N 93°40E 241 F5
Ramsagar △ Bangla. 25°33N 88°37E 241 C2
Rāmsar Iran 36°53N 50°41E 247 B6
Ramsey I. of Man 54°20N 4°22W 168 C3
Ramsey Ill., U.S.A. 39°8N 89°7W 310 E7
Ramsey N.J., U.S.A. 41°4N 74°9W 313 E10
Ramsey L. Canada 47°13N 82°15W 298 C3
Ramsgate N.S.W.,
Australia 33°58S 151°8E 139 B1
Ramsgate Kent, U.K. 51°20N 1°25E 169 F9
Ramshai India 26°44N 88°51E 241 B2
Ramsjö Sweden 62°11N 15°37E 162 B9
Ramstein Germany 49°27N 7°32E 179 F3
Ramtek India 21°20N 79°15E 244 D4
Ramu Kenya 3°55N 41°10E 268 B5
Ramu → Papua N. G. 4°0S 144°41E 286 C3
Ramvik Sweden 62°49N 17°51E 162 B11
Ramville, Î. = Chancel, Î.
Martinique 14°41N 60°53W 322 j
Rana Pratap Sagar Dam
India 24°58N 75°38E 242 G6
Ranaghat India 23°15N 88°35E 243 H13
Ranahu Pakistan 25°55N 69°45E 242 G3
Ranai Indonesia 3°55N 108°22E 235 B3
Ranau Malaysia 6°2N 116°40E 235 A5
Ranau, Danau Indonesia 4°49S 103°55E 234 C2
Rancagua Chile 34°10S 70°50W 334 C1
Rance → France 48°34N 1°59W 172 D5
Rancharia Brazil 22°15S 50°55W 333 F1
Rancheria → Canada 60°13N 129°7W 296 A3
Ranchester U.S.A. 44°54N 107°10W 304 D10
Ranchi India 23°19N 85°27E 243 H11
Rancho Cordova U.S.A. 38°36N 121°18W 306 G5
Rancho Cucamonga
U.S.A. 34°10N 117°30W 307 L9
Rancho Park U.S.A. 34°3N 118°26W 126 B2
Ranco, L. Chile 40°15S 72°25W 336 B2
Rand Australia 35°33S 146°32E 283 C7
Rand ✕ (QRA) S. Africa 26°14S 28°8E 123 B2
Randaberg Norway 59°1N 5°36E 164 E2
Randabygda Norway 61°51N 6°20E 164 C3
Randalls I. U.S.A. 40°47N 73°55W 132 B2
Randalstown U.K. 54°45N 6°19W 166 B5
Randan France 46°2N 3°21E 173 F10
Randazzo Italy 37°53N 14°57E 201 E7
Randburg S. Africa 26°5S 27°57E 123 A1
Rander India 21°14N 72°47E 244 D1
Randers Denmark 56°29N 10°1E 163 H4
Randers Fjord Denmark 56°37N 10°20E 163 H4
Randfontein S. Africa 26°8S 27°45E 271 C4
Randhart S. Africa 26°6S 28°7E 123 B2
Randle U.S.A. 46°32N 121°57W 306 D5
Randolph Mass., U.S.A. 42°10N 71°2W 313 D13
Randolph N.Y., U.S.A. 42°10N 78°59W 312 D6
Randolph Utah, U.S.A. 41°40N 111°11W 304 F8
Randolph Vt., U.S.A. 43°55N 72°40W 313 C12
Randpark Ridge S. Africa 26°6S 27°58E 123 A1
Randsburg U.S.A. 35°22N 117°39W 307 K9
Randsfjorden Norway 60°25N 10°24E 164 D7
Randsverk Norway 61°44N 9°3E 164 C6
Randwick Australia 33°54S 151°14E 139 B2
Råneälven → Sweden 65°50N 22°20E 160 D20
Ranelagh Ireland 53°20N 6°15W 120 A2
Ranenburg = Chaplygin
Russia 53°15N 40°0E 188 F11
Ranfurly N.Z. 45°7S 170°6E 285 F5
Rangae Thailand 6°19N 101°44E 237 J4
Rangamati Bangla. 22°38N 92°12E 241 D4
Rangapara India 26°49N 92°39E 241 B4
Rangárvallasýsla Iceland 63°55N 20°0W 155 D7
Rangataua N.Z. 39°26S 175°28E 284 F4
Rangaunu B. N.Z. 34°51S 173°15E 284 A2
Range, The Zimbabwe 19°2S 31°2E 269 F3
Rangeley U.S.A. 44°58N 70°39W 313 B14
Rangeley L. U.S.A. 44°55N 70°43W 313 B14
Rangely U.S.A. 40°5N 108°48W 304 F9
Ranger U.S.A. 32°28N 98°41W 314 E5
Ranggia India 26°28N 91°38E 241 B3
Rangiora N.Z. 43°19S 172°36E 285 D7
Rangiroa French Polynesia 15°10S 147°35W 289 f
Rangitaiki N.Z. 38°52S 176°24E 284 E5
Rangitaiki → N.Z. 37°54S 176°49E 284 D5
Rangitata → N.Z. 43°45S 171°15E 285 D6
Rangitikei → N.Z. 40°17S 175°15E 284 G4
Rangitoto ke te tonga = D'Urville I.
N.Z. 40°50S 173°55E 285 A8
Rangitoto Ra. N.Z. 38°25S 175°35E 284 E4
Rangkasbitung Indonesia 6°21S 106°15E 234 D3
Rangoon Burma 16°45N 96°20E 241 G6
Rangoon ☐ Burma 17°0N 96°10E 241 G6
Rangoon → Burma 16°28N 96°40E 241 G6
Rangpur Bangla. 25°42N 89°22E 241 C2
Rangpuri India 28°32N 77°8E 120 B1
Rangsang Indonesia 1°20N 103°5E 237 M4
Rangwe Kenya 0°36S 34°35E 266 E3
Ranibennur India 14°35N 75°30E 245 G2
Raniganj India 27°3N 82°13E 243 F9
Ranikhet India 29°39N 79°25E 243 E8
Ranippettai India 12°56N 79°23E 245 H4
Raniwara India 24°50N 72°10E 242 G5
Rāniyah Iraq 36°15N 44°53E 213 D11
Ranka India 23°59N 83°47E 243 H10
Ranken → Australia 20°31S 137°36E 280 C2
Rankin Ill., U.S.A. 40°28N 87°54W 311 D9
Rankin Tex., U.S.A. 31°13N 101°56W 314 F4
Rankin Inlet Canada 62°30N 93°0W 294 E13
Rankins Springs
Australia 33°49S 146°14E 283 B7
Rankovicevo = Kraljevo
Serbia 43°44N 20°41E 202 C4
Rankweil Austria 47°17N 9°39E 180 D2
Rannersdorf Austria 48°7N 16°27E 142 B2
Rannoch, L. U.K. 56°41N 4°20W 167 E4
Rannoch Moor U.K. 56°38N 4°48W 167 E4
Rano Kau Chile 27°11S 109°26W 330 b
Rano Raraku, Volcán
Chile 27°7S 109°17W 330 b
Ranobe → Madag. 17°10S 44°8E 272 B1
Ranobe, Helodranon' i
Madag. 23°3S 43°33E 272 C1
Ranohira Madag. 22°29S 45°24E 272 C2
Ranomafana Toamasina,
Madag. 18°57S 48°50E 272 B2
Ranomafana Toliara,
Madag. 24°34S 47°0E 272 C2
Ranomafana △ Madag. 21°16S 47°25E 272 C2
Ranomena Madag. 23°25S 47°17E 272 C2
Ranon Vanuatu 16°8S 168°7E 287 F6
Ranong Thailand 9°56N 98°40E 237 H2
Ranongga Solomon Is. 8°5S 156°35E 287 M9
Ranotsara Nord Madag. 22°48S 46°36E 272 C2
Ranpur India 20°5N 85°20E 244 D7
Rānsa Iran 33°39N 48°18E 247 C6
Ransbèche Belgium 50°56N 4°27E 116 B2
Ransdorp Neths. 52°24N 5°0E 112 A2
Ransiki Indonesia 1°30S 134°10E 231 E8
Ransom U.S.A. 41°9N 88°39W 311 C8
Rantabe Madag. 15°42S 49°39E 272 B2
Rantau Indonesia 2°56S 115°9E 235 C5
Rantau Abang Malaysia 4°52N 103°24E 237 K4
Rantauparjang Kalimantan Tengah,
Indonesia 1°22S 112°4E 235 C4
Rantauparjang Kalimantan Timur,
Indonesia 2°9N 117°25E 235 B5
Rantauprapat Indonesia 2°15N 99°50E 234 B1
Rantaupulut Indonesia 1°55S 112°12E 235 C4
Rantemario Indonesia 3°15S 119°57E 231 E5
Ranthambore △ India 26°10N 76°30E 242 F7
Rantoul U.S.A. 40°19N 88°9W 311 D8
Ranum Denmark 56°54N 9°14E 163 H3
Ranvad India 18°53N 72°55E 130 B2
Ranyah, W. → Si. Arabia 21°18N 43°20E 248 B3
Raohe China 46°47N 134°0E 220 A7
Raon l'Étape France 48°24N 6°50E 173 D13
Raoping China 23°42N 117°1E 229 F11
Raoui, Erg er Algeria 29°0N 2°0W 261 C4
Raoul I. Pac. Oc. 29°16S 177°54W 277 F15
Raoyang China 38°15N 115°45E 226 E8
Rap, Ko Thailand 9°19N 99°58E 237 b
Rapa French Polynesia 27°35S 144°20W 289 f
Rapa Nui = Pascua, I. de
Chile 27°7S 109°23W 330 b
Rapallo Italy 44°21N 9°14E 198 D6
Rapar India 23°34N 70°38E 242 H4
Rāpch Iran 25°40N 59°15E 247 E8
Rapel, Lago Chile 34°20S 71°14W 334 C1
Raper, C. Canada 69°44N 67°6W 295 D18
Rapid City U.S.A. 44°5N 103°14W 308 C2
Rapid River U.S.A. 45°55N 86°58W 308 C10
Rapla Estonia 59°1N 24°52E 188 C3
Raposo Portugal 38°40N 9°11W 126 A1
Rapperswil Switz. 47°14N 8°45E 176 A4
Rapti → India 26°18N 83°41E 243 F10
Rapu Rapu I. Phil. 13°12N 124°9E 232 E5
Raqaba ez Zarqa →
South Sudan 9°14N 29°44E 257 F2
Rāqūbah Libya 28°58N 19°2E 258 C3
Raquette → U.S.A. 45°0N 74°42W 313 B10
Raquette Lake U.S.A. 43°49N 74°40W 313 C10
Rara △ Nepal 29°30N 82°10E 243 E10
Raraka French Polynesia 16°10S 144°54W 289 f
Raroia French Polynesia 16°1S 142°27W 289 f
Rarotonga Cook Is. 21°30S 160°0W 289 h
Ra's al 'Ayn Syria 36°45N 40°12E 213 D9
Ras al Hadd Oman 22°30N 59°50E 249 B7
Ra's al Khaymah U.A.E. 25°50N 55°59E 247 E7
Ra's aţ Tib Tunisia 37°1N 11°2E 258 A2
Râs el Ma Algeria 34°26N 0°50W 261 B4
Râs el Mâ Mali 16°35N 4°30W 262 B4
Râs el Oued Algeria 35°57N 5°2E 261 A6
Râs Ghârib Egypt 28°6N 33°18E 256 B3
Ras Köh Pakistan 28°43N 64°55E 240 C2
Ra's Lānūf Libya 30°46N 18°11E 258 B3
Râs Muhammad △ Egypt 27°45N 34°16E 256 B3
Ra's Shamrah Syria 35°35N 35°45E 250 C6
Ras Sudr Egypt 29°40N 32°42E 256 B3
Rasa, Pta. Argentina 36°20S 56°41W 334 D4
Rasa, Punta Argentina 40°50S 62°15W 336 B4
Rasa I. Phil. 9°13N 118°26E 233 G2
Rasca, Pta. de la
Canary Is. 27°59N 16°41W 153 e1
Raşcani Moldova 47°58N 27°33E 183 C12
Rasdhoo Maldives 4°17N 72°58E 272 d
Rasdu Atoll Maldives 4°18N 72°58E 272 d
Raseiniai Lithuania 55°25N 23°5E 184 C10
Rashad Sudan 11°55N 31°0E 257 E3
Rashîd Egypt 31°21N 30°22E 256 H7
Rashîd, Masabb Egypt 31°22N 30°17E 256 H7
Rashin = Najin N. Korea 42°12N 130°15E 224 A5
Rashmi India 25°4N 74°22E 242 G6
Rasht Iran 37°20N 49°40E 213 D13
Rashtrapati Bhawan Delhi, India 120 c1
Rasi Salai Thailand 15°20N 104°9E 236 E5
Rasipuram India 11°30N 78°15E 245 J4
Raška Serbia 43°19N 20°39E 202 C4
Raskot Nepal 29°14N 81°39E 243 E9
Râşnov Romania 45°35N 25°27E 183 E10
Rasŏn ☐ N. Korea 42°21N 130°23E 224 A5
Rason L. Australia 28°45S 124°25E 279 E3
Raşova Romania 44°15N 27°55E 183 F12
Rasovo Bulgaria 43°42N 23°17E 202 C7
Rasra India 25°50N 83°50E 243 G10
Rasskazovo Russia 52°35N 41°50E 190 D5
Rast Romania 43°53N 23°16E 183 G8
Rastaala Finland 60°15N 24°47E 121 B1
Rastatt Germany 48°50N 8°11E 179 G4
Rastede Germany 53°15N 8°12E 178 B4
Rastenburg = Kętrzyn
Poland 54°7N 21°22E 184 D8
Rastila Finland 60°12N 25°7E 121 B3
Răstolița Romania 46°59N 24°58E 183 D9
Rastyapino = Dzerzhinsk
Russia 56°14N 43°30E 190 B6
Rasua Garhi Nepal 28°17N 85°23E 243 E11
Rasul Pakistan 32°42N 73°34E 242 C5
Raszków Poland 51°43N 17°40E 185 G4
Raszyn Poland 52°9N 20°54E 143 C1
Rat → Canada 49°35N 97°10W 297 D9
Rat Buri = Ratchaburi
Thailand 13°30N 99°54E 236 F2
Rat I. St. Lucia 14°2N 60°58W 323 m
Rat I. Alaska, U.S.A. 51°48N 178°15E 303 L2
Rat Islands U.S.A. 52°0N 178°0E 303 L2
Rat L. Canada 56°10N 99°40W 297 B9
Ratak Chain Pac. Oc. 1°0N 170°0E 288 G8
Rätan Sweden 62°29N 14°33E 162 B8
Ratangarh India 28°5N 74°35E 242 E6
Ratāwī Iraq 30°38N 47°13E 246 D5
Ratcatchers L. Australia 32°38S 143°12E 282 B5
Ratchaburi Thailand 13°30N 99°54E 236 F2
Rath India 25°36N 79°37E 243 G8
Rath Luirc = Charleville
Ireland 52°21N 8°40W 166 D3
Rathangan Ireland 53°14N 7°0W 166 C4
Rathbun L. U.S.A. 40°54N 93°5W 310 D4
Rathdrum Ireland 52°56N 6°14W 166 D5
Rathedaung Burma 20°29N 92°45E 241 E4
Rathenow Germany 52°37N 12°19E 178 C8
Rathfarnham Ireland 53°18N 6°16W 120 B2
Rathkeale Ireland 52°32N 8°56W 166 D3
Rathlin I. U.K. 55°18N 6°14W 166 A5
Rathmelton Ireland 55°2N 7°39W 166 A4
Ratho U.K. 55°55N 3°23W 121 B1
Ratho Station U.K. 55°56N 3°23W 121 B1
Ratibor = Racibórz Poland 50°7N 18°18E 185 H5
Rätikon Austria 47°0N 9°55E 180 D2
Ratingen Germany 51°18N 6°52E 178 D2
Ratlam India 23°20N 75°0E 242 H6
Ratmanova Ostrov
Russia 65°46N 169°6W 300 B6
Ratnagiri India 16°57N 73°18E 244 F1
Ratnapura Sri Lanka 6°40N 80°20E 245 L5
Rato Portugal 38°43N 9°8W 126 A2
Ratodero Pakistan 27°48N 68°18E 242 F3
Raton U.S.A. 36°54N 104°24W 305 H11
Ratschach = Radeče
Slovenia 46°5N 15°14E 199 B12
Rattaphum Thailand 7°8N 100°16E 237 J3
Ratten Austria 47°28N 15°44E 180 D8
Rattray Hd. U.K. 57°38N 1°50W 167 D7
Rättvik Sweden 60°52N 15°7E 162 D9
Ratz, Mt. Canada 57°23N 132°12W 296 B2
Ratzebuhr = Okonek
Poland 53°32N 16°51E 184 E3
Ratzeburg Germany 53°40N 10°46E 178 B6
Rau Indonesia 0°34N 100°1E 234 B2
Raub Malaysia 3°47N 101°52E 237 L3
Rauch Argentina 36°45S 59°5W 334 D4
Raudales Mexico 17°27N 93°39W 319 D6
Raudeberg Norway 61°59N 5°7E 164 C2
Raufarhöfn Iceland 66°27N 15°57W 155 A11
Raufoss Norway 60°44N 10°37E 164 D7
Rauhellern Norway 60°15N 7°50E 164 D4
Raukumara N.Z. 38°5S 177°55E 284 E6
Raukumara Ra. N.Z. 38°5S 177°55E 284 E6
Raul Soares Brazil 20°5S 42°22W 333 F3
Rauma Finland 61°10N 21°30E 188 B1
Rauma → Norway 62°34N 7°43E 164 B4
Raumo = Rauma Finland 61°10N 21°30E 188 B1
Raung, Gunung Indonesia 8°8S 114°3E 231 J17
Raurkela India 22°14N 84°50E 243 H11
Rausu-Dake Japan 44°4N 145°7E 220 B12
Răut → Moldova 47°15N 29°9E 183 C14
Rava-Ruska Ukraine 50°15N 23°42E 185 H10
Rava Russkaya = Rava-Ruska
Ukraine 50°15N 23°42E 185 H10
Ravahere French Polynesia 18°14S 142°9W 289 f
Ravalli U.S.A. 47°17N 114°11W 304 C6
Ravänsar Iran 34°43N 46°40E 213 E12
Ravanusa Italy 37°16N 13°58E 200 E6
Rāvar Iran 31°20N 56°51E 247 D8
Ravelston U.K. 55°57N 3°14W 121 B2
Ravena U.S.A. 42°28N 73°49W 313 D11
Ravenel U.S.A. 32°46N 80°15W 316 C9
Ravenna Italy 44°25N 12°12E 199 D9
Ravenna Nebr., U.S.A. 41°1N 98°55W 308 E4
Ravenna Ohio, U.S.A. 41°9N 81°15W 312 E3
Ravensburg Germany 47°46N 9°36E 179 H5
Ravenshoe Australia 17°37S 145°29E 280 B4
Ravensthorpe Australia 33°35S 120°2E 279 F3
Ravenswood Queens.,
Australia 20°6S 146°54E 280 C4
Ravenswood W. Va.,
U.S.A. 38°57N 81°46W 309 F13
Ravensworth Australia 32°26S 151°4E 283 B9
Ravenwood U.S.A. 40°22N 94°41W 310 D2
Raver India 21°15N 76°2E 244 D3
Ravi → Pakistan 30°35N 71°49E 242 D4
Ravine Chaude Guadeloupe 16°14N 61°40W 322 e
Ravna Gora Croatia 45°24N 14°50E 199 C11
Ravna Reka Serbia 44°1N 21°35E 202 B5
Ravne na Koroškem
Slovenia 46°36N 14°59E 199 B11
Rawa Mazowiecka
Poland 51°46N 20°12E 185 G7
Rawaki Kiribati 3°43S 170°43W 277 A16
Rawalpindi Pakistan 33°38N 73°8E 242 C5
Rawamangun Indonesia 6°11S 106°52E 122 B2
Rawang Malaysia 3°20N 101°35E 237 L3
Rawene N.Z. 35°25S 173°32E 284 B2
Rawi, Ko Thailand 6°33N 99°14E 237 J2
Rawicz Poland 51°36N 16°52E 185 G3
Rawitsch = Rawicz
Poland 51°36N 16°52E 185 G3
Rawka → Poland 52°9N 20°8E 185 F7
Rawlinna Australia 30°58S 125°28E 279 F4
Rawlins U.S.A. 41°47N 107°14W 304 F10
Rawlinson Ra. Australia 24°40S 128°30E 279 D4
Rawson Argentina 43°15S 65°5W 336 B3
Raxaul India 26°59N 84°51E 243 F11
Ray U.S.A. 48°21N 103°10W 308 A2
Ray, C. Canada 47°33N 59°15W 299 C8
Ray City U.S.A. 31°5N 83°11W 316 D6
Ray Mts. U.S.A. 66°0N 152°0W 303 D10
Raya Ring, Ko Thailand 8°18N 98°29E 237 a
Rayachoti India 14°4N 78°50E 245 G4
Rayadurg India 14°40N 76°50E 245 G3
Rayagada India 19°15N 83°20E 244 E6
Raychikhinsk Russia 49°46N 129°25E 215 E13
Räyen Iran 29°34N 57°26E 247 D8
Rayle U.S.A. 33°48N 82°54W 316 B7
Rayleigh U.K. 51°36N 0°37E 169 F8
Raymond Alta., Canada 49°30N 112°35W 296 D6
Raymond Calif., U.S.A. 37°13N 119°54W 306 H7
Raymond Ill., U.S.A. 39°19N 89°34W 310 E7
Raymond N.H., U.S.A. 43°2N 71°11W 313 C13
Raymond Wash., U.S.A. 46°41N 123°44W 306 D3
Raymond Terrace
Australia 32°45S 151°44E 283 B9
Raymondville U.S.A. 26°29N 97°47W 314 H6
Raymore Canada 51°25N 104°31W 297 C8
Rayners Lane U.K. 51°34N 0°23W 125 A1
Raynes Park U.K. 51°24N 0°12W 125 B2
Rayón Mexico 29°43N 110°35W 318 B2
Rayong Thailand 12°40N 101°20E 236 F3
Raypur India 22°28N 88°22E 124 C2
Raystown L. U.S.A. 40°25N 78°5W 312 F6
Raytown U.S.A. 39°1N 94°28W 310 E2
Rayville U.S.A. 32°29N 91°46W 314 E9
Raz, Pte. du France 48°2N 4°47W 172 D2
Razan Iran 35°23N 49°2E 213 E13
Ražana Serbia 44°6N 19°55E 202 B3
Ražanj Serbia 43°40N 21°31E 202 C5
Razāzah, Buḩayrat ar
Iraq 32°40N 43°35E 213 F10
Razazah, L. = Razāzah, Buḩayrat ar
Iraq 32°40N 43°35E 213 F10
Razdelna Bulgaria 43°13N 27°41E 203 C11
Razdel'naya = Rozdilna
Ukraine 46°50N 30°2E 183 D15
Razdolnoye Russia 43°30N 131°52E 220 C5
Razdolnoye Ukraine 45°46N 33°29E 189 K7
Razeh Iran 32°47N 48°9E 247 C6
Razgrad Bulgaria 43°33N 26°34E 203 C10
Razgrad ☐ Bulgaria 43°33N 26°30E 203 C10
Razim, Lacul Romania 44°50N 29°0E 183 F14
Razlog Bulgaria 41°53N 23°28E 202 E7
Razmak Pakistan 32°45N 69°50E 242 C3
Re, Cu Lao Vietnam 15°22N 109°8E 236 E7
Ré, Î. de France 46°12N 1°30W 174 B2
Reach Falls Jamaica 18°2N 76°18W 320 a
Reading Reading, U.K. 51°27N 0°58W 169 F7
Reading Mich., U.S.A. 41°50N 84°45W 311 C12
Reading Ohio, U.S.A. 39°13N 84°26W 311 E12
Reading Pa., U.S.A. 40°20N 75°56W 313 F9
Reading ☐ U.K. 51°27N 0°58W 169 F7
Real, Cordillera Bolivia 17°0S 67°10W 330 D4
Real Felipe, Fuerte Peru 12°4S 77°9W 124 B2
Realejo Alto Canary Is. 28°22N 16°34W 153 e1
Realicó Argentina 35°0S 64°15W 334 D3
Réalmont France 43°48N 2°10E 174 E6
Ream Cambodia 10°34N 103°39E 237 G4
Ream △ Cambodia 10°30N 103°45E 237 G4
Reams, L. U.S.A. 28°26N 81°34W 133 B1
Réao French Polynesia 18°31S 136°23W 289 f
Reay Forest U.K. 58°22N 4°55W 167 C4
Rebais France 48°50N 3°10E 173 D10
Rebecca, L. Australia 30°0S 122°15E 279 F3
Rebi Indonesia 6°23S 134°7E 231 F8
Rebiana Libya 24°12N 22°10E 258 D4
Rebiana, Sahrâ' Libya 24°30N 21°0E 258 D3
Reboly Russia 63°49N 30°47E 160 E24
Rebun-Tō Japan 45°23N 141°2E 220 B10
Recanati Italy 43°24N 13°32E 199 E10
Recaş Romania 45°46N 21°30E 182 E6
Recco Italy 44°22N 9°9E 198 D6
Recherche, Arch. of the
Australia 34°15S 122°50E 279 F3
Rechna Doab Pakistan 31°35N 73°30E 242 D5
Rechytsa Belarus 52°21N 30°24E 177 B16
Recife Brazil 8°0S 35°0W 332 B5
Recife Seychelles 4°36S 55°42E 272 c
Recklinghausen Germany 51°37N 7°12E 178 D3
Reckong Peo India 31°32N 78°16E 242 D8
Reclining Buddha = Wat Pho
Bangkok, Thailand 113 b1
Recoleta B. Aires,
Argentina 34°36S 58°24W 117 B2
Recoleta Santiago, Chile 33°25S 70°40W 137 B2
Reconquista Argentina 29°10S 59°45W 334 B4
Recreio Brazil 8°0S 58°25W 331 B6
Recreo Argentina 29°25S 65°10W 334 B2
Recuay Peru 9°43S 77°28W 330 B2
Recz Poland 53°16N 15°31E 185 E2
Red = Hong → Vietnam 20°16N 106°34E 236 B5
Red → U.S.A. 31°1N 91°45W 314 F9
Red Bank U.S.A. 40°21N 74°5W 313 F10
Red Bay Canada 51°44N 56°25W 299 B8
Red Bluff U.S.A. 40°11N 122°15W 304 F2
Red Bluff Res. U.S.A. 31°54N 103°55W 305 L12
Red Bud U.S.A. 38°13N 89°59W 310 F7
Red Cliffs Australia 34°19S 142°11E 282 C5
Red Cloud U.S.A. 40°5N 98°32W 308 E4
Red Creek U.S.A. 43°14N 76°45W 313 C8
Red Deer Canada 52°20N 113°50W 296 C6
Red Deer → Alta., Canada 50°58N 110°0W 297 C7
Red Deer → Man.,
Canada 52°53N 101°1W 297 C8
Red Deer L. Canada 52°55N 101°20W 297 C8
Red Devil U.S.A. 61°46N 157°19W 303 F8
Red Fort = Lal Qila Delhi, India 120 a3
Red Hook U.S.A. 41°55N 73°53W 313 E11
Red Indian L. Canada 48°35N 57°0W 299 C8
Red L. Canada 51°3N 93°49W 297 C10
Red Lake Canada 51°3N 93°49W 297 C10
Red Lake Falls U.S.A. 47°53N 96°16W 308 B5
Red Lake Road Canada 49°59N 93°25W 297 C10
Red Lodge U.S.A. 45°11N 109°15W 304 D9
Red Mountain U.S.A. 35°37N 117°38W 307 K9
Red Oak U.S.A. 41°1N 95°14W 308 E6
Red River of the North →
N. Amer. 49°0N 97°15W 308 A5
Red Rock Canada 48°55N 88°15W 298 C2
Red Rock, L. U.S.A. 41°22N 92°59W 310 C3
Red Rocks Pt. Australia 32°13S 127°32E 279 F4
Red Sea Asia 25°0N 36°0E 238 E3
Red Slate Mt. U.S.A. 37°31N 118°52W 306 H8
Red Square Moscow, Russia 129 b2
Red Sucker L. Canada 54°9N 93°40W 298 B1
Red Tower Pass = Turnu Roşu, P.
Romania 45°33N 24°17E 183 E9
Red Volta → Africa 10°34N 0°30W 263 C4
Red Wing U.S.A. 44°34N 92°31W 308 C7
Reda Poland 54°40N 18°19E 184 D5
Redang, Pulau Malaysia 5°49N 103°2E 237 K4
Redange Lux. 49°46N 5°52E 170 E5
Redbridge ☐ U.K. 51°35N 0°7E 125 A4
Redcar U.K. 54°37N 1°4W 168 C6
Redcar & Cleveland ☐ U.K. 54°29N 1°0W 168 C7
Redcliff Canada 50°10N 110°50W 304 A8
Redcliffe Australia 27°12S 153°6E 281 D5
Redcliffe, Mt. Australia 28°30S 121°30E 279 E3
Reddersburg S. Africa 29°41S 26°10E 270 C4
Reddick Fla., U.S.A. 29°22N 82°12W 317 F7
Reddick Ill., U.S.A. 41°6N 88°15W 311 C8
Redding Calif., U.S.A. 40°35N 122°24W 304 F2
Redding Iowa, U.S.A. 40°36N 94°23W 310 D2
Redditch U.K. 52°18N 1°55W 169 E6
Redenção Brazil 4°13S 38°43W 332 B4
Redentore, Chiesa del Venice, Italy 142 c2
Redfern Australia 33°54S 151°12E 139 B2
Redfield U.S.A. 44°53N 98°31W 308 C4
Redford U.S.A. 44°38N 73°48W 313 B11
Redhead Trin. & Tob. 10°44N 60°58W 323 t
Redkey U.S.A. 40°21N 85°9W 311 D11
Redkino Russia 56°39N 36°16E 188 D9
Redlands U.S.A. 34°4N 117°11W 307 M9
Redmond Oreg., U.S.A. 44°17N 121°11W 304 D3
Redmond Wash., U.S.A. 47°40N 122°7W 306 C4
Redon France 47°40N 2°6W 172 E4
Redonda Antigua & B. 16°58N 62°19W 321 C7
Redonda, Pta. Chile 27°10S 109°22W 330 b
Redondela Spain 42°15N 8°38W 194 C2
Redondo Portugal 38°39N 7°37W 195 G3
Redondo Beach U.S.A. 33°50N 118°23W 307 M8
Redoubt Volcano U.S.A. 60°29N 152°45W 303 F9
Redpath Sugar Museum
Toronto, Canada 141 c3
Redruth U.K. 50°14N 5°14W 169 G2
Redvers Canada 49°35N 101°40W 297 D8
Redwater Canada 53°55N 113°6W 296 C6
Redwood U.S.A. 44°18N 75°48W 313 B9
Redwood △ U.S.A. 41°40N 124°5W 304 F1
Redwood City U.S.A. 37°30N 122°15W 306 H4
Redwood Falls U.S.A. 44°32N 95°7W 308 C6
Ree, L. Ireland 53°35N 8°0W 166 C3
Reed City U.S.A. 43°53N 85°31W 309 D11
Reed L. Canada 54°38N 100°30W 297 C8
Reedley U.S.A. 36°36N 119°27W 306 J7
Reedsburg U.S.A. 43°32N 90°0W 308 D8
Reedsport U.S.A. 43°42N 124°6W 304 E1
Reedsville U.S.A. 40°39N 77°35W 312 F7
Reedy Creek Australia 36°58S 140°2E 282 D4
Reef Is. Pac. Oc. 10°15S 166°10E 277 C12
Reefton N.Z. 42°6S 171°51E 285 C6
Rees Germany 51°46N 6°24E 178 D2
Reese → U.S.A. 40°48N 117°4W 304 F5
Reetz = Recz Poland 53°16N 15°31E 185 E2
Refahiye Turkey 39°54N 38°47E 213 C8
Reflecting Pool Washington, D.C., U.S.A. 143 b1
Refshaleøen Denmark 55°41N 12°36E 118 A3
Reftele Sweden 57°11N 13°35E 163 G7
Refugio U.S.A. 28°18N 97°17W 314 G6
Rega → Poland 54°10N 15°18E 184 D2
Regalbuto Italy 37°39N 14°38E 201 E7
Regana, C. de Spain 39°25N 2°43E 206 B3
Regar = Tursunzoda
Tajikistan 38°30N 68°14E 217 E7
Regen Germany 48°58N 13°8E 179 G9
Regen → Germany 49°1N 12°6E 179 F8
Regeneração Brazil 6°15S 42°41W 332 C3
Regensburg Germany 49°1N 12°6E 179 F8
Regenstauf Germany 49°7N 12°8E 179 F8
Regents Park Gauteng,
S. Africa 26°14S 28°3E 123 B2
Regent's Park London, U.K. 125 a2
Regenwalde = Resko
Poland 53°47N 15°25E 184 E2
Reggâne = Zaouiet Reggâne
Algeria 26°32N 0°3E 261 C5
Reggello Italy 43°41N 11°32E 199 E8
Réggio di Calàbria Italy 38°6N 15°39E 201 D8
Réggio nell'Emília Italy 44°43N 10°36E 198 D7
Reghin Romania 46°46N 24°42E 183 D9
Regina Sask., Canada 50°27N 104°35W 297 C8
Régina Fr. Guiana 4°19N 52°8W 329 C7
Regina Beach Canada 50°47N 105°0W 297 C8
Register U.S.A. 32°22N 81°53W 316 C8
Registro Brazil 24°29S 47°49W 335 A6
Rego Park U.S.A. 40°43N 73°51W 132 B2
Reguengos de Monsaraz
Portugal 38°25N 7°32W 195 G3
Rehar → India 23°55N 82°40E 243 H10
Rehli India 23°38N 79°5E 243 H8
Rehoboth Namibia 23°15S 17°4E 270 B2
Rehovot Israel 31°54N 34°48E 251 G5
Reibell = Ksar Chellala
Algeria 35°13N 2°19E 261 A5
Reichenau = Rychnov nad Kněžnou
Czech Rep. 50°10N 16°17E 181 A9
Reichenbach = Dzierżoniów
Poland 50°45N 16°39E 185 H3
Reichenbach Germany 50°37N 12°17E 178 E8
Reichenberg = Liberec
Czech Rep. 50°47N 15°7E 180 A8
Reichshof = Rzeszów
Poland 50°5N 21°58E 185 H8
Reichstag Berlin, Germany 115 a3
Reid Australia 30°49S 128°26E 279 F4
Reidsville Ga., U.S.A. 32°6N 82°7W 316 C7
Reidsville N.C., U.S.A. 36°21N 79°40W 315 C15
Reifnig = Ribnica
Slovenia 45°45N 14°45E 199 C11
Reigate U.K. 51°14N 0°12W 169 F7
Reillo Spain 39°54N 1°53W 196 F3
Reims France 49°15N 4°1E 173 C11
Reina Adelaida, Arch.
Chile 52°20S 74°0W 336 D2
Reina Beatrix Int. ✕ (AUA)
Aruba 12°30N 70°1W 322 f
Reina Sofía, Centro de Arte
Madrid, Spain 127 c3
Reina Sofia, Tenerife ✕ (TFS)
Canary Is. 28°3N 16°33W 153 e1
Reinbeck U.S.A. 42°19N 92°36W 310 B4
Reinbek Germany 53°30N 10°16E 178 B6
Reindeer → Canada 55°36N 103°11W 297 B8
Reindeer I. Canada 52°30N 98°0W 297 C9
Reindeer L. Canada 57°15N 102°15W 297 B8
Reinga, C. N.Z. 34°25S 172°43E 284 A1
Reinheimen △ Norway 62°10N 7°45E 164 B4
Reinickendorf Germany 52°34N 13°22E 115 A3
Reinosa Spain 43°2N 4°15W 194 B6
Reinsvoll Norway 60°40N 10°38E 164 D7
Reitan Norway 62°49N 11°22E 164 B8
Reitz S. Africa 27°48S 28°29E 271 C4
Reivilo S. Africa 27°36S 24°8E 270 C3
Rejaf South Sudan 4°45N 31°35E 257 G3
Rejmyre Sweden 58°50N 15°55E 163 F9
Rejowiec Fabryczny
Poland 51°5N 23°17E 185 G10
Reka → Slovenia 45°40N 14°0E 199 C11
Rekohu = Chatham I.
N.Z. 43°50S 176°20W 285 a
Rekola Finland 60°19N 25°4E 121 B3
Rekovac Serbia 43°51N 21°3E 202 C5
Relámpago, Pta. Venezuela 11°3N 64°23W 329 a
Reliance Canada 63°0N 109°20W 297 A7
Relizane Algeria 35°44N 0°31E 261 A5
Relizane ☐ Algeria 35°45N 0°55E 261 A5
Remad, Oued → Algeria 33°28N 1°20W 261 B4
Rémalard France 48°26N 0°47E 172 D7
Remanso Brazil 9°41S 42°4W 332 C3
Remarkable, Mt.
Australia 32°48S 138°10E 282 B3
Remarkables, The N.Z. 45°10S 168°50E 285 F3
Rembang Indonesia 6°42S 111°21E 235 D4
Rembau Malaysia 2°35N 102°6E 234 B2
Rembert U.S.A. 34°6N 80°32W 316 A9
Rembertów Poland 52°15N 21°9E 143 B2
Rembrandthuis Amsterdam, Neths. 112 b3
Rembrandtpark Neths. 52°22N 4°51E 112 A2
Rembrandtplein Amsterdam, Neths. 112 b2
Remchi Algeria 35°2N 1°26W 261 A4
Remedios Colombia 7°2N 74°41W 328 B3
Remedios Panama 8°15N 81°50W 320 E3
Remedios de Escalada
Argentina 34°43S 58°24W 117 C2
Remeshk Iran 26°55N 58°50E 247 E8
Remetea Romania 46°45N 25°29E 183 D10
Remich Lux. 49°32N 6°22E 170 E6
Remington U.S.A. 40°46N 87°9W 311 D9
Rémire Fr. Guiana 4°53N 52°17W 329 C7
Remiremont France 48°2N 6°36E 173 D13
Remo Ethiopia 6°48N 41°20E 257 F5
Rémola, Estany del Spain 41°16N 2°4E 114 B1
Remontnoye Russia 46°34N 43°37E 191 G6
Remoulins France 43°55N 4°35E 175 E8
Rempang Indonesia 0°51N 104°10E 234 B2
Rempart → Mauritius 20°19S 57°22E 272 e
Remparts → Réunion 21°22S 55°37E 272 f
Remscheid Germany 51°11N 7°12E 178 D3
Ren Xian China 37°8N 114°40E 226 F8
Rena Norway 61°8N 11°20E 164 C8
Rena → Norway 61°8N 11°23E 164 C8
Renascença Brazil 3°50S 66°21W 328 D4
Renca Chile 33°24S 70°42W 137 B1
Rend Lake U.S.A. 38°2N 88°58W 310 F8
Rendang Indonesia 8°26S 115°25E 231 J18
Rende Italy 39°20N 16°11E 201 C9
Rendezvous Barbados 13°4N 59°35W 323 r
Rendina Greece 39°4N 21°58E 204 B3
Rendova Solomon Is. 8°33S 157°17E 287 M9
Rendsburg Germany 54°17N 9°39E 178 A5
Renfrew Canada 45°30N 76°40W 313 A8
Renfrewshire ☐ U.K. 55°49N 4°38W 167 F4
Renfroe U.S.A. 32°14N 84°43W 316 C5
Rengat Indonesia 0°30S 102°45E 234 C2
Rengo Chile 34°24S 70°50W 334 C1
Renhua China 25°5N 113°40E 229 E9
Renhuai China 27°48N 106°24E 228 D6
Reni = Taranagar India 28°43N 74°50E 242 E6
Reni Ukraine 45°28N 28°15E 183 E13
Renigunta India 13°38N 79°30E 245 H4
Renk South Sudan 11°50N 32°50E 257 E3
Renland Greenland 71°10N 26°30W 154 C8
Renmark Australia 34°11S 140°43E 282 C4
Rennebu Norway 62°52N 9°49E 164 B6
Rennell Solomon Is. 11°40S 160°10E 287 N11
Rennell Sd. Canada 53°23N 132°35W 296 C2
Rennemoulin France 48°50N 2°2E 134 A1
Renner Springs Australia 18°20S 133°47E 280 B1
Rennes France 48°7N 1°41W 172 D5
Rennick Glacier
Antarctica 70°30S 161°45E 151 D11
Rennie L. Canada 61°32N 105°35W 297 A7
Reno U.S.A. 39°31N 119°48W 306 F7
Reno → Italy 44°38N 12°16E 199 D9
Renovo U.S.A. 41°20N 77°45W 312 E7
Renqiu China 38°43N 116°5E 226 E9
Rens Denmark 54°54N 9°5E 163 K3
Renshou China 29°59N 104°9E 228 C5
Rensselaer Ind., U.S.A. 40°57N 87°9W 311 D9
Rensselaer N.Y., U.S.A. 42°38N 73°45W 313 D11
Renton U.S.A. 47°28N 122°12W 306 C4
Renukoot India 24°12N 83°2E 243 G10
Renwick N.Z. 41°30S 173°51E 285 B8
Renwick Gallery
Washington, D.C., U.S.A. 143 a1
Réo Burkina Faso 12°28N 2°35W 262 C4
Reocín = Puente San Miguel
Spain 43°21N 4°5W 194 B6
Reotipur India 25°33N 83°45E 243 G10
Repalle India 16°2N 80°45E 245 F5
Répcelak Hungary 47°24N 17°1E 182 C2
Řeporyje Czech Rep. 50°1N 14°18E 135 B1
Reppen = Rzepin Poland 52°20N 14°49E 185 F1
Republic Mo., U.S.A. 37°7N 93°29W 308 G7
Republic Wash., U.S.A. 48°39N 118°44W 304 B4
Republican → U.S.A. 39°4N 96°48W 308 F5
Republiek Suriname 5°30N 55°13W 329 B6
Republika Srpska ☐
Bos.-H. 44°56N 17°11E 199 D14
République, Place de la Paris, France 134 b5
Repulse B. Australia 20°35S 148°46E 280 b
Repulse Bay Nunavut,
Canada 66°30N 86°30W 295 D14
Repulse Bay Hong Kong,
China 22°13N 114°10E 122 B2
Repy Czech Rep. 50°4N 14°17E 135 B1
Requena Peru 5°5S 73°52W 330 B3
Requena Spain 39°30N 1°4W 197 F3
Requin Bay Grenada 12°2N 61°39W 323 q
Réquista France 44°1N 2°32E 174 D6
Reşadiye Muğla, Turkey 36°45N 27°39E 205 E9
Reşadiye Tokat, Turkey 40°23N 37°20E 212 B7
Reşadiye Yarımadası
Turkey 36°40N 27°45E 205 E9
Resavica Serbia 44°4N 21°31E 202 B5
Resen Macedonia 41°5N 21°0E 202 E5
Reserve U.S.A. 33°43N 108°45W 305 K9
Resht = Rasht Iran 37°20N 49°40E 213 D13
Residenz Germany 48°8N 11°34E 131 B2
Residenzmuseum Munich, Germany 131 b3
Resistencia Argentina 27°30S 59°0W 334 B4
Reşiţa Romania 45°18N 21°53E 182 E6
Resko Poland 53°47N 15°25E 184 E2
Reso = Raisio Finland 60°28N 22°11E 188 B2
Resolute Canada 74°42N 94°54W 295 C13
Resolution I. Nunavut,
Canada 61°30N 65°0W 295 E19
Resolution I. N.Z. 45°40S 166°40E 285 F1
Resplandes Brazil 6°17S 45°13W 332 C2
Resplendor Brazil 19°20S 41°15W 333 E3
Ressano Garcia Mozam. 25°25S 32°0E 271 C5
Restinga, L. de la Venezuela 10°59N 64°8W 329 a
Restinga de Jurubatiba △
Brazil 22°5S 41°20W 333 F3
Reston Canada 49°33N 101°6W 297 D8
Resulayn = Ceylanpınar
Turkey 36°50N 40°2E 213 D9
Reszel Poland 54°4N 21°10E 184 D8
Retalhuleu Guatemala 14°33N 91°46W 320 D1
Retenue, L. de
Dem. Rep. of the Congo 11°0S 27°0E 269 E2
Retezat, Munţii Romania 45°25N 23°0E 182 E8
Retezat △ Romania 45°23N 22°56E 182 E7
Retford U.K. 53°19N 0°56W 168 D7

Rodopi □ *Greece* 41°5N 25°30E **203** E9
Rodopos *Greece* 35°34N 23°45E **207** E4
Rodovre *Denmark* 55°40N 12°26E **118** A2
Rodrigo de Freitas, L.
Brazil 22°58S 43°12W **135** B1
Rodrigues *Ind. Oc.* 19°45S 63°20E **273** F5
Roe → *U.K.* 55°6N 6°59W **166** A5
Roebling *U.S.A.* 40°7N 74°47W **313** F10
Roebourne *Australia* 20°44S 117°9E **278** D2
Roebuck B. *Australia* 18°5S 122°20E **278** C3
Roebuck Roadhouse
Australia 17°59S 122°36E **278** C3
Roermond *Neths.* 51°12N 6°0E **170** C6
Roes Welcome Sd. *Canada* 65°0N 87°0W **295** E14
Roeselare *Belgium* 50°57N 3°7E **170** D3

Rogachev = Ragachow
Belarus 53°8N 30°5E **177** B16
Rogačica *Serbia* 44°4N 19°40E **202** B3
Rogagua, L. *Bolivia* 13°43S 66°50W **330** C4
Rogaland □ *Norway* 59°12N 6°20E **164** E3
Rogaška Slatina *Slovenia* 46°15N 15°42E **199** B12
Rogatec *Slovenia* 46°15N 15°46E **199** B12
Rogatica *Bos.-H.* 43°47N 19°0E **182** G4
Rogatyn *Ukraine* 49°24N 24°36E **177** D13
Rogen *Sweden* 62°20N 12°20E **164** E6
Rogers *U.S.A.* 36°20N 94°7W **314** C7
Rogers Centre *Toronto, Canada* **141** c1
Rogers City *U.S.A.* 45°25N 83°49W **309** C12
Rogers Park *U.S.A.* 42°0N 87°40W **319** A3
Rogersville *Canada* 46°44N 65°26W **299** C6
Roggan → *Canada* 54°24N 79°25W **298** B4
Roggan L. *Canada* 54°8N 77°50W **298** B4
Roggeveen Basin
Pac. Oc. 31°30S 95°30W **289** L18
Roggeveldberge *S. Africa* 32°10S 20°10E **270** D3
Roggiano Gravina *Italy* 39°37N 16°9E **201** C9
Rogliano *Haute-Corse,*
France 42°57N 9°30E **175** F13
Rogliano *Italy* 39°11N 16°19E **201** C9
Rogoaguado, L. *Bolivia* 13°0S 65°30W **331** C4
Rogojampi *Indonesia* 8°19S 114°17E **231** J17
Rogožno *Poland* 52°45N 16°59E **185** F3
Rogue → *U.S.A.* 42°26N 124°26W **304** E1
Roha *India* 18°26N 73°7E **244** E1
Rohan *France* 48°4N 2°45W **172** D4
Rohnert Park *U.S.A.* 38°16N 122°40W **306** G4
Rohri *Pakistan* 27°45N 68°51E **242** F3
Rohri Canal *Pakistan* 26°15N 68°27E **242** F3
Rohtak *India* 28°55N 76°43E **242** E7
Rohtisch-Sauerbrunn = Rogaška
Slatina *Slovenia* 46°15N 15°42E **199** B12
Roi Et *Thailand* 16°4N 103°40E **236** D4
Roi-Georges, Îs. du
French Polynesia 14°32S 145°8W **289** f
Roihuvuori *Finland* 60°11N 25°2E **121** B3
Roing *India* 28°9N 95°51E **241** A5
Roissy-en-Brie *France* 48°48N 2°39E **134** B4
Roja *Latvia* 57°29N 22°43E **184** A9
Rojas *Argentina* 34°10S 60°45W **334** C3
Rojiste *Romania* 44°4N 23°56E **183** F8
Rojo, C. *Mexico* 21°33N 97°20W **319** C5
Rokan → *Indonesia* 2°0N 100°50E **234** B2
Rokel → *S. Leone* 8°30N 12°48W **262** D2
Rokin *Amsterdam, Neths.* **112** b2
Rokiškis *Lithuania* 55°55N 25°35E **188** E3
Rokitno *Russia* 50°57N 35°56E **189** G8
Rokycany *Czech Rep.* 49°43N 13°35E **180** B6
Rokytka → *Czech Rep.* **116** B1
Rolândia *Brazil* 23°18S 51°23W **335** A5
Røldal *Norway* 59°47N 6°50E **164** F3
Rolfe *U.S.A.* 42°49N 94°31W **310** B2
Rolla *Mo., U.S.A.* 37°57N 91°46W **310** G5
Rolla *N. Dak., U.S.A.* 48°52N 99°37W **308** A4
Rolleston *Queens.,*
Australia 24°28S 148°35E **280** C4
Rolleston *N.Z.* 43°35S 172°24E **285** F7
Rolling Fork → *U.S.A.* 37°55N 85°50W **311** G11
Rollingstone *Australia* 19°2S 146°24E **280** B4
Rom *Vest-Agder, Norway* 58°8N 7°7E **164** F4
Rom *South Sudan* 9°54N 32°16E **257** F3
Roma *Queens., Australia* 26°32S 148°49E **281** D4
Roma *Italy* 41°54N 12°28E **136** B1
Roma *Sweden* 57°32N 18°26E **163** G12
Roma Fiumicino ✈ (FCO)
Italy 41°48N 12°15E **199** G9
Roma-Los Saenz *U.S.A.* 26°24N 99°1W **314** H5
Roma Urbe ✈ *Italy* 41°57N 12°30E **136** B2
Római-Fürdő *Hungary* 47°34N 19°4E **117** A2
Romain, C. *U.S.A.* 33°0N 79°22W **315** E15
Romaine → *Canada* 50°18N 63°47W **299** B7
Romainville *France* 48°52N 2°26E **134** A3
Roman *Bulgaria* 43°8N 23°57E **202** C7
Roman *Romania* 46°57N 26°55E **183** D11
Roman Forum = Foro Romano
Rome, Italy **136** c3
Roman-Kosh, Gora
Ukraine 44°37N 34°15E **189** K8
Romanche → *France* 45°5N 5°43E **175** C9
Romang *Indonesia* 7°30S 127°20E **237** F7
Români *Egypt* 30°59N 32°38E **251** H3
Romania ■ *Europe* 46°0N 25°0E **183** D10
Romanija *Bos.-H.* 43°50N 18°45E **182** G3
Romano, C. *U.S.A.* 25°51N 81°41W **317** H13
Romano, Cayo *Cuba* 22°0N 77°30W **320** B4
Romano Banco *Italy* 45°26N 9°7E **154** d1
Romanov-Borisoglebsk = Tutayev
Russia 57°53N 39°32E **188** D10
Romanovka = Basarabeasca
Moldova 46°21N 28°58E **183** D13
Romanovna-Murmane =
Murmansk *Russia* 68°57N 33°10E **160** B25
Romanovsk = Kropotkin
Russia 45°28N 40°28E **191** H5
Romanovskiy Khutor = Kropotkin
Russia 45°28N 40°28E **191** H5
Romans-sur-Isère *France* 45°3N 5°3E **175** C9
Romanshorn *Switz.* 47°33N 9°22E **179** H5
Romanzof C. *U.S.A.* 61°49N 166°6W **303** F6
Rombari *South Sudan* 4°33N 31°0E **257** G3
Romblon *Phil.* 12°33N 122°17E **232** E4
Romblon □ *Phil.* 12°30N 122°15E **232** E4
Romblon Pass. *Phil.* 12°27N 122°12E **232** E4
Rome = Roma *Italy* 41°54N 12°28E **136** B1
Rome *Ga., U.S.A.* 34°15N 85°10W **315** D12
Rome *N.Y., U.S.A.* 43°13N 75°27E **313** D9
Romema *Israel* 31°48N 35°12E **232** B4
Romeoville *U.S.A.* 41°39N 88°3W **311** C8
Rometta *Italy* 38°10N 15°25E **201** D8
Romilly-sur-Seine *France* 48°31N 3°44E **173** D10
Romiton *Uzbekistan* 39°56N 64°22E **216** E6
Rommani *Morocco* 33°31N 6°40W **260** B4
Romney *U.S.A.* 39°21N 78°45W **309** F14
Romney Marsh *U.K.* 51°2N 0°54E **169** F8
Romny *Ukraine* 50°48N 33°28E **189** G7
Rømø *Denmark* 55°10N 8°30E **163** J5
Romodanovo *Russia* 49°55N 33°15E **189** G7
Romont *Switz.* 46°42N 6°54E **179** J2
Romorantin-Lanthenay
France 47°21N 1°45E **173** E8
Rompin → *Malaysia* 2°49N 103°29E **237** L4
Romsdalen *Norway* 62°25N 7°52E **164** B4

Romsdalsfjorden *Norway* 62°38N 7°20E **164** B4
Romsey *U.K.* 51°0N 1°29W **169** G6
Ron *India* 15°40N 75°44E **245** G2
Ron *Vietnam* 17°53N 106°27E **236** D6
Rona *U.K.* 57°34N 5°59W **167** D3
Ronald Reagan Nat. Washington ✈
(DCA) *U.S.A.* 38°51N 77°2W **143** B2
Ronan *U.S.A.* 47°32N 114°6W **304** C6
Roncador, Cayos *Colombia* 13°32N 80°4W **320** D3
Roncador, Serra do
Brazil 12°30S 52°30W **333** D1
Ronciglione *Italy* 42°17N 12°13E **199** F9
Ronco → *Italy* 44°24N 12°12E **199** D9
Ronda *Spain* 36°46N 5°12W **195** J5
Ronda, Serranía de *Spain* 36°44N 5°3W **195** J5
Rondane *Norway* 61°57N 9°50E **164** C6
Rondane △ *Norway* 61°55N 9°44E **164** C6
Ronde, Pt. *Dominica* 15°33N 61°29W **323** k
Ronde I. *Grenada* 12°29N 61°36W **323** q
Rondebosch *S. Africa* 33°58S 18°28E **118** A1
Rondón *Colombia* 6°17N 71°6W **328** B3
Rondônia *Brazil* 10°52S 61°57W **331** C5
Rondônia □ *Brazil* 11°0S 63°0W **331** C5
Rondonópolis *Brazil* 16°28S 54°38W **331** D7
Rondslottet *Norway* 61°55N 9°45E **164** C6
Rondu *Pakistan* 35°32N 75°10E **243** B6
Rong, Koh *Cambodia* 10°45N 103°15E **237** G4
Rong Jiang → *China* 24°35N 109°20E **228** E7
Rong Xian *China* 22°50N 110°31E **229** F8
Rong'an *China* 25°14N 109°22E **228** E7
Rongcheng *China* 29°20N 105°32E **228** C5
Rongcheng *China* 37°9N 122°23E **227** F12
Ronge, L. la *Canada* 55°6N 105°17W **297** B7
Rongjiang *China* 25°57N 108°28E **228** E7
Rongotea *N.Z.* 40°19S 175°25E **284** G4
Rongshui *China* 25°6N 109°12E **228** E7
Rongxian *China* 29°23N 104°22E **228** C5
Rønne *Denmark* 55°6N 14°43E **163** J8
Rønne Ice Shelf
Antarctica 77°30S 60°0W **151** D18
Ronneby *Sweden* 56° 2N 15°17E **163** H9
Ronnebyån → *Sweden* 56° 11N 15°17E **163** H9
Rönnöfors *Sweden* 58°56N 15°2E **163** F9
Ronsard, C. *Australia* 24°46S 113°10E **279** D1
Ronse *Belgium* 50°45N 3°35E **170** D3
Ronuro → *Brazil* 11°56S 53°33W **333** C8
Roodepoort *S. Africa* 26°11S 27°54E **271** C4
Roodhouse *U.S.A.* 39°29N 90°24W **310** E6
Roof Butte *U.S.A.* 36°28N 109°5W **305** H9
Rooiboklaagte → *Namibia* 20°50S 21°0E **270** B3
Rooiwaal *Venezuela* 55°11N 3°11W **166** C3
Rooniu, Mt. *Tahiti* 17°49S 149°12W **289** e
Roopville *U.S.A.* 33°27N 85°8W **316** B4
Roorkee *India* 29°52N 77°59E **242** E7
Roosendaal *Neths.* 51°32N 4°29E **170** C4
Roosevelt *U.S.A.* 40°18N 109°59W **304** F9
Roosevelt → *Brazil* 7°55S 60°20W **331** B5
Roosevelt, Mt. *Canada* 58°26N 125°20W **296** B3
Roosevelt I. *Antarctica* 79°30S 162°0W **151** D12
Roosevelt I. *New York, U.S.A.* **132** c3
Ropczyce *Poland* 50°4N 21°38E **185** H8
Roper → *Australia* 14°43S 135°27E **280** A2
Roper Bar *Australia* 14°44S 134°44E **280** A1
Roper River = St. Vidgeon's ◦
Australia 14°47S 134°53E **280** A1
Roppongi *Tokyo, Japan* **140** c3
Roque Pérez *Argentina* 35°25S 59°24W **334** D4
Roquefort *France* 4°2N 0°20W **172** D3
Roquemaure *France* 44°3N 4°48E **175** D8
Roquetas de Mar *Spain* 36°46N 2°36W **197** J2
Roquetes *Spain* 4C°50N 0°30E **196** C5
Roquevaire *France* 4.3°20N 5°36E **175** E9
Roraima □ *Brazil* 2°0N 61°30W **329** C5
Roraima, Mt. *Venezuela* 5°10N 60°40W **329** B5
Røros *Norway* 62°35N 11°23E **164** B8
Rorschach *Switz.* 47°28N 9°28E **179** H5
Ros Comáin = Roscommon
Ireland 53°38N 8°11W **166** C3
Ros Mhic Thriúin = New Ross
Ireland 52°23N 6°57W **166** D5
Rosa *Zambia* 9°33S 31°15E **269** D3
Rosa, C. *Algeria* 37°0N 8°16E **261** A6
Rosa, C. *Galápagos Is., Ecuador* 1°4S 91°10W **330** a
Rosa, Monte *Europe* 45°57N 7°53E **198** C4
Rosais, Pta. dos *Azores* 38°45N 28°19W **153** d1
Rosal de la Frontera *Spain* 37°59N 7°13W **195** H3
Rosales *Phil.* 15°54N 120°38E **232** D3
Rosalia *U.S.A.* 47°14N 117°22W **304** C5
Rosalie *Dominica* 15°22N 61°16W **323** k
Rosalie → *Dominica* 15°22N 61°15W **323** k
Rosalind Bank *Caribbean* 16°30N 80°30W **320** D3
Rosamond *U.S.A.* 34°52N 118°10W **307** L8
Rosans *France* 4c°24N 5°29E **175** D9
Rosario *Argentina* 33°0S 60°40W **334** C3
Rosário *Maranhão, Brazil* 3°0S 44°15W **332** B3
Rosario *Sinaloa, Mexico* 22°58N 105°53W **318** C3
Rosario *Paraguay* 24°30S 57°35W **334** A4
Rosario *Agusan del S., Phil.* 8°2'.4N 125°58E **233** G7
Rosario *Batangas, Phil.* 13°50N 121°12E **232** E3
Rosario, Villa del
Venezuela 10°19N 72°19W **328** A3
Rosario de la Frontera
Argentina 25°50S 65°0W **334** B3
Rosario de Lerma
Argentina 24°59S 65°35W **334** A2
Rosario del Tala
Argentina 32°20S 59°10W **334** C4
Rosário do Sul *Brazil* 30°15S 54°55W **335** C5
Rosário Oeste *Brazil* 14°50S 56°25W **331** D6
Rosarito *Baja Calif.,*
Mexico 32°20N 117°2W **307** N9
Rosarito *Baja Calif.,*
Mexico 28°38N 114°1W **318** B2
Rosarno *Italy* 38°29N 15°58E **201** D8
Rosas = Roses *Spain* 42°19N 3°10E **196** C8
Roscoe *Mo., U.S.A.* 37°58N 93°48W **310** G3
Roscoe *N.Y., U.S.A.* 41°56N 74°55W **313** E10
Roscoff *France* 4°6'44N 3°58W **172** D3
Roscommon *Ireland* 53°38N 8°11W **166** C3
Roscommon □ *Ireland* 53°49N 8°23E **166** C3
Roscrea *Ireland* 52°57N 7°49W **166** D4
Rose → *Australia* 14°16S 135°45E **280** A2
Rose, L. *Bahamas* 21°0N 73°30W **321** B5
Rose, L., Fla., U.S.A.* 28°32N 81°30W **133** A1
Rose Belle *Mauritius* 20°24S 57°36E **272** e
Rose Blanche *Canada* 47°38N 58°45W **299** C8
Rose Bowl *U.S.A.* 34°9N 118°10W **126** B4
Rose Hall Great House
Jamaica 18°31N 77°49W **320** a
Rose Hill = Port Mourant
Guyana 6°15N 57°20W **329** B6
Rose Hill *Va., U.S.A.* 38°47N 77°6W **143** C2
Rose Pt. *Canada* 54° 11N 131°39W **296** C2
Rose Rock *Grenada* 12°24N 61°28W **323** q
Rose Valley *Canada* 52°19N 103°49W **297** C8
Roseau *Dominica* 15°17N 61°24W **323** k
Roseau *Minn., U.S.A.* 48°51N 95°46W **308** A6
Rosebank *Gauteng, S. Africa* 26°8S 28°2E **123** A2
Rosebery *N.S.W.,*
Australia 33°52S 151°12E **139** B2
Rosebery *Tas., Australia* 41°46S 145°33E **281** G4
Rosebud *Vic., Australia* 38°21S 144°54E **282** E6
Rosebud *S. Dak., U.S.A.* 43°14N 100°51W **308** D3
Rosebud *Tex., U.S.A.* 31°4N 96°59W **314** F6
Roseburg *U.S.A.* 43°13N 123°20W **304** E2

Rosedal La Candelaria
Mexico 19°20N 99°10W **128** B2
Rosedale *U.S.A.* 33°51N 91°2W **315** E9
Rosehearty *U.K.* 57°42N 2°7W **167** D6
Roseires Res. *Sudan* 11°51N 34°23E **266** B3
Roseland *Calif., U.S.A.* 38°25N 122°43W **306** G4
Roseland *Ill., U.S.A.* 41°42N 87°37W **319** C3
Rosemary *Canada* 50°46N 112°5W **296** C6
Rosemead *U.S.A.* 34°4N 118°4W **126** B4
Rosemont *Qué., Canada* 45°34N 73°33W **130** A2
Rosemont *Ill., U.S.A.* 41°59N 87°53W **119** B1
Rosenberg = Olesno
Poland 50°51N 18°26E **185** H5
Rosenberg = Susz *Poland* 53°44N 19°20E **184** E6
Rosenberg *U.S.A.* 29°34N 95°49W **314** G7
Rosenborg Slot *Copenhagen, Denmark* **118** b2
Rosendaël *France* 51°3N 2°24E **173** A9
Rosendal *Norway* 59°59N 6°0E **164** E3
Rosendale *U.S.A.* 40°4N 94°51W **310** D2
Rosenheim *Germany* 47°51N 12°7E **179** H8
Rosenthal *Germany* 52°35N 13°22E **115** A3
Roses *Spain* 42°19N 3°10E **196** C8
Roses, G. de *Spain* 42°10N 3°15E **196** C8
Roseto degli Abruzzi *Italy* 42°41N 14°1E **199** F11
Rosetown *U.S.A.* 51°35N 107°59W **297** C7
Rosetta = Rashid *Egypt* 31°21N 30°22E **266** B3
Rosettenville *S. Africa* 26°15S 28°3E **123** B2
Roseville *Calif., U.S.A.* 38°45N 121°17W **306** G5
Roseville *Ill., U.S.A.* 40°44N 90°40W **310** D6
Roseville *Mich., U.S.A.* 42°30N 82°56W **119** C13
Roseville *Pa., U.S.A.* 41°51N 76°57W **313** E8
Rosewell *U.K.* 55°51N 3°8W **121** B3
Rosewood *Australia* 27°38S 152°36E **281** D5
Rosherville Dam *S. Africa* 26°13S 28°6E **123** B2
Roshkhvār *Iran* 34°58N 59°37E **247** C8
Rosières-en-Santerre
France 49°49N 2°42E **173** C9
Rosignano Marittimo
Italy 43°24N 10°28E **198** E7
Rosignol *Guyana* 6°15N 57°30W **329** B6
Roşiori de Vede *Romania* 44°9N 25°0E **183** F10
Rositsa *Bulgaria* 43°57N 27°57E **203** C11
Rositsa → *Bulgaria* 43°10N 25°30E **203** C9
Rösjön *Sweden* 59°26N 18°0E **134** a2
Roskilde *Denmark* 55°38N 12°3E **163** J6
Roskovec *Albania* 40°44N 19°43E **202** F3
Roslags-Näsby *Sweden* 59°25N 18°3E **134** a2
Roslavl *Russia* 53°57N 32°55E **188** F7
Roslin *U.K.* 55°51N 3°11W **121** B3
Roslindale *U.S.A.* 42°17N 71°7W **116** B2
Rosmaninhal *Portugal* 39°44N 7°5W **194** F3
Rosmead *S. Africa* 31°29S 25°8E **270** D4
Røsnæs *Denmark* 55°44N 10°55E **163** J4
Rosny-sous-Bois *France* 48°52N 2°30E **134** A4
Rosolini *Italy* 36°49N 14°57E **201** F7
Rosporden *France* 47°57N 3°50W **172** E3
Ross *Tas., Australia* 42°2S 147°30E **281** G4
Ross *N.Z.* 42°53S 170°49E **285** C5
Ross Béthio *Mauritania* 16°15N 16°9W **262** B1
Ross Dependency
Antarctica 76°0S 170°0W **151** D12
Ross I. *Antarctica* 77°30S 168°0E **151** D11
Ross Ice Shelf *Antarctica* 80°0S 180°0E **151** E12
Ross L. *U.S.A.* 48°44N 121°4W **304** B3
Ross-on-Wye *U.K.* 51°54N 2°34W **169** F5
Ross River *N. Terr.,*
Australia 23°44S 134°30E **280** C1
Ross River *Yukon,*
Canada 62°30N 131°30W **296** A2
Ross Sea *Antarctica* 74°0S 178°0E **151** D11
Rossall Pt. *U.K.* 53°55N 3°3W **168** D4
Rossan Pt. *Ireland* 54°42N 8°47W **166** B3
Rossano *Italy* 39°36N 16°39E **201** C9
Rossburn *Canada* 50°40N 100°49W **297** C8
Rosseau *Canada* 45°16N 79°39W **312** A5
Rosseau, L. *Canada* 45°10N 79°35W **312** A5
Rössel = Reszel *Poland* 54°4N 21°10E **184** D8
Rossel I. *Papua N.G.* 11°21S 154°9E **286** B8
Rosses, The *Ireland* 55°2N 8°20W **166** A3
Rossford *U.S.A.* 41°36N 83°34W **311** E13
Rossignol L. *Canada* 52°43N 73°40W **298** B5
Rossignol L. *Canada* 44°12N 65°10W **299** D6
Rossiya = Russia ■
Eurasia 62°0N 105°0E **215** C11
Rosskreppfjorden *Norway* 59°4N 7°10E **164** E4
Rossland *Canada* 49°6N 117°50W **296** D5
Rosslare *Ireland* 52°15N 6°20W **166** D5
Rosslare Europort = Rosslare
Harbour *Ireland* 52°15N 6°20W **166** D5
Rosslare Harbour *Ireland* 52°15N 6°20W **166** D5
Rosslau *Germany* 51°52N 12°15E **178** D8
Rosslyn *U.S.A.* 38°53N 77°4W **143** B2
Rossmore *Canada* 44°8N 77°23W **312** B7
Rosso *Mauritania* 16°40N 15°45W **262** B1
Rosso, C. *France* 42°13N 8°32E **175** F12
Rossosh *Russia* 50°15N 39°28E **189** G10
Rossvatnet *Norway* 65°45N 14°5E **160** D6
Rossville *Ill., U.S.A.* 40°23N 87°40W **311** D9
Rossville *Ind., U.S.A.* 40°25N 86°36W **311** D10
Røst *Norway* 67°32N 12°10E **160** C15
Rostaq = Ar Rustãq *Oman* 23°23N 57°26E **249** B7
Rostãq *Afghan.* 37°79N 69°48W **240** A3
Rosthern *Canada* 52°40N 106°20W **297** C7
Rostock *Germany* 54°5N 12°8E **178** A8
Rostov *Don, Russia* 47°15N 39°45E **189** G12
Rostov *Yaroslavl, Russia* 57°14N 39°25E **188** D10
Rostov □ *Russia* 48°50N 41°10E **191** F5
Rostrenen *France* 48°14N 3°21W **172** D3
Roswell *Ga., U.S.A.* 34°2N 84°22W **316** A5
Roswell *N. Mex., U.S.A.* 33°24N 104°32W **305** K11
Rosyth *U.K.* 56°2N 3°25W **121** A1
Rot-Front = Dobropole
Ukraine 48°25N 37°2E **189** H9
Rota *N. Marianas* 14°9N 145°12E **302** a
Rota *Spain* 36°37N 6°20W **195** J4
Rotan *U.S.A.* 32°51N 100°28W **314** E4
Rote *Indonesia* 10°50S 123°0E **231** F6
Rotenburg *Hessen, Germany* 50°59N 9°44E **178** E5
Rotenburg *Niedersachsen,*
Germany 53°6N 9°25E **178** B5
Roth *Germany* 49°15N 11°5E **179** F7
Rothaargebirge *Germany* 51°6N 8°13E **178** D4
Rothenburg ob der Tauber
Germany 49°23N 10°11E **179** F6
Rother → *U.K.* 50°59N 0°45E **169** G8
Rothera *Antarctica* 67°34S 68°8W **151** C17
Rotherham *U.K.* 53°26N 1°20W **168** D6
Rotherhithe *U.K.* 51°29N 0°2W **125** B3
Rothes *U.K.* 57°32N 3°13W **167** D5
Rothesay *N.B., Canada* 45°23N 66°0W **299** D6
Rothesay *Argyll & Bute, U.K.* 55°50N 5°3W **167** F3
Rothiesholm *Australia* 36°22S 146°5E **283** D7
Rothschmaige *Germany* 48°14N 11°27E **131** A1
Roti *Indonesia* 10°50S 123°0E **231** F6
Rotja, Pta. *Spain* 38°38N 1°35E **206** D2
Rotnes *Norway* 60°1N 10°51E **134** d3
Rotondo, Mte. *France* 42°14N 9°8E **175** F13
Rotoiti, L. *Bay of Plenty,*
N.Z. 38°2S 176°28E **284** B5
Rotoiti, L. *West Coast, N.Z.* 41°51S 172°49E **285** D5
Rotoma, L. *N.Z.* 38°2S 176°35E **284** B5
Rotondo, Mte. *France* 42°14N 9°8E **175** F13
Rotoroa, L. *N.Z.* 41°55S 172°39E **285** B7

Rotorua *N.Z.* 38°9S 176°16E **284** E5
Rotorua, L. *N.Z.* 38°5S 176°18E **284** E5
Rott → *Germany* 48°27N 13°25E **179** G9
Rottenburg *Germany* 48°28N 8°55E **179** G4
Rottenmann *Austria* 47°31N 14°22E **180** D7
Rotterdam *Neths.* 51°55N 4°30E **170** C4
Rotterdam *N.Y., U.S.A.* 42°48N 74°1W **313** D10
Rottne *Sweden* 57°1N 14°54E **163** H8
Rottnest I. *Australia* 32°0S 115°27E **279** F2
Rottumeroog *Neths.* 53°33N 6°34E **170** A6
Rottweil *Germany* 48°9N 8°37E **179** G4
Rotuma *Fiji* 12°25S 177°5E **277** C14
Roubaix *France* 50°40N 3°10E **173** B10
Rouche Island *St. Lucia* 13°57N 60°52W **323** m
Roudnice nad Labem
Czech Rep. 50°25N 14°15E **180** A7
Rouen *France* 49°27N 1°4E **172** C8
Rouergue *France* 44°15N 2°0E **174** D5
Rouge Hill *Canada* 43°48N 79°6W **141** A4
Rough Ridge *N.Z.* 45°10S 169°55E **285** F3
Rouillac *France* 45°47N 0°4W **174** C3
Rouissat *Algeria* 31°55N 5°20E **261** B6
Rouleau *Canada* 50°10N 104°56W **297** C8
Roulers = Roeselare
Belgium 50°57N 3°7E **170** D3
Round Hill *Jamaica* 18°20N 78°12W **320** a
Round Hill *St. Kitts & Nevis* 17°11N 62°36W **322** d
Round I. *China* 22°13N 114°11E **122** B2
Round Mountain *Australia* 38°43N 117°4W **304** G5
Round Mt. *Australia* 30°26S 152°16E **281** E5
Round Rock *U.S.A.* 30°31N 97°41W **314** F6
Roundhouse Park *Toronto, Canada* **141** c2
Roundup *U.S.A.* 46°27N 108°33W **304** C9
Roura *Fr. Guiana* 4°44N 52°20W **329** C7
Rousay *U.K.* 59°10N 3°2W **167** B5
Rouses Point *U.S.A.* 44°59N 73°22W **313** B11
Rouseville *U.S.A.* 41°28N 79°42W **312** E5
Roussillon *Isère, France* 45°24N 4°49E **175** C8
Roussillon *Pyrénées-Or.,*
France 42°30N 2°35E **174** F6
Rouxville *S. Africa* 30°25S 26°50E **270** D4
Rouyn-Noranda *Canada* 48°20N 79°0W **298** C4
Rovaniemi *Finland* 66°29N 25°41E **160** C21
Rovato *Italy* 45°34N 10°0E **198** D7
Rovenki *Ukraine* 48°5N 39°21E **189** H10
Roverbella *Italy* 45°3N 11°3E **198** D8
Rovereto *Italy* 45°53N 11°3E **198** C8
Roverud *Norway* 60°15N 12°3E **164** D9
Rovigno = Rovinj *Croatia* 45°5N 13°40E **199** C10
Rovigo *Italy* 45°4N 11°47E **199** C8
Rovinj *Croatia* 45°5N 13°40E **199** C10
Rovira *Colombia* 4°15N 75°20W **328** C2
Rovno = Rivne *Ukraine* 50°40N 26°10E **177** C14
Rovnoye *Russia* 50°52N 46°3E **190** E8
Rovuma = Ruvuma →
Tanzania 10°29S 40°28E **269** E5
Row'ãn *Iran* 35°8N 48°51E **247** C6
Rowena *Australia* 29°48S 148°55E **281** D4
Rowley I. *Canada* 69°6N 77°52W **295** D16
Rowley Shoals *Australia* 17°30S 119°0E **278** C2
Roxa *Guinea-Biss.* 11°15N 15°45W **262** C1
Roxas *Capiz, Phil.* 11°36N 122°49E **233** F4
Roxas *Isabela, Phil.* 17°8N 121°36E **232** C3
Roxas *Mind. Or., Phil.* 12°35N 121°31E **232** E3
Roxas *Palawan, Phil.* 10°20N 119°21E **233** F2
Roxboro *U.S.A.* 36°24N 78°59W **315** C15
Roxborough *Trin. & Tob.* 11°16N 60°35W **323** s
Roxburgh *N.Z.* 45°33S 169°19E **285** F3
Roxbury *Mass., U.S.A.* 42°18N 71°5W **116** B2
Roxbury *N.Y., U.S.A.* 42°17N 74°33W **313** D10
Roxbury *Pa., U.S.A.* 40°6N 77°39W **312** F7
Roxby Downs *Australia* 30°43S 136°46E **281** E2
Roxen *Sweden* 58°30N 15°40E **163** F9
Roxeth *U.K.* 51°33N 0°20W **125** A1
Roy *Mont., U.S.A.* 47°20N 108°58W **304** C9
Roy *N. Mex., U.S.A.* 35°57N 104°12W **305** J11
Roy *U.S.A.* 41°10N 112°2W **304** F7
Roy Thomson Hall *Toronto, Canada* **141** b2
Royal △ *Australia* 34°5S 151°5E **283** C9
Royal Bardia △ *Nepal* 28°20N 81°20E **243** E9
Royal Botanic Gardens
Sydney, Australia **139** B2
Royal Botanic Gardens *Edinburgh,*
U.K. 55°58N 3°12W **121** B2
Royal Canal *Ireland* 53°30N 7°13W **166** C4
Royal Center *U.S.A.* 40°52N 86°30W **311** D10
Royal Chitawan △ *Nepal* 26°30N 84°30E **243** F11
Royal Exhibition Building
Australia 37°48S 144°58E **128** B2
Royal Geographical Society Is.
Canada 68°56N 100°15W **294** D11
Royal Leamington Spa
U.K. 52°18N 1°31W **169** E6
Royal Manas △ *Bhutan* 26°45N 90°50E **241** B3
Royal Natal △ *S. Africa* 28°43S 28°51E **271** C4
Royal Oak *U.S.A.* 42°30N 83°9W **311** B13
Royal Observatory *U.K.* 51°29N 0°0W **121** B2
Royal Palace = Koninklijk Paleis
Amsterdam, Neths. **112** a2
Royal Palace = Kungliga Slottet
Stockholm, Sweden **139** b2
Royal Palace = Palacio Real
Madrid, Spain **127** b1
Royal Palace = Palais Royal
Brussels, Belgium **116** b3
Royal Palace = Slottet *Oslo, Norway* **133** a1
Royal Palm Beach *U.S.A.* 26°42N 80°14W **317** J9
Royal Tunbridge Wells *U.K.* 51°7N 0°16E **169** F8
Royal Turf Club *Bangkok, Thailand* **113** b2
Royale, Isle *U.S.A.* 48°0N 88°54W **308** B9
Royalla *Australia* 35°30S 149°9E **283** C8
Royan *France* 45°37N 1°2W **174** C2
Rumãh *Si. Arabia* 25°29N 47°10E **246** E5
Rumah Kulit *Malaysia* 2°9N 114°14E **235** B4
Rumania = Romania ■
Europe 46°0N 25°0E **183** D10
Rumaylah *Iraq* 30°47N 47°37E **246** D5
Rumaylah, 'Urūq ar
Si. Arabia 21°20N 48°30E **249** B5
Rumbalara *Australia* 25°20S 134°29E **281** D1
Rumbek *South Sudan* 6°54N 29°37E **257** F2
Rumburk *Czech Rep.* 50°58N 14°33E **180** A7
Rumelihisari *Turkey* 41°4N 29°2E **122** B2
Rumford *U.S.A.* 44°33N 70°33W **313** B14
Rumia *Poland* 54°37N 18°25E **184** A5
Rumilly *France* 45°53N 5°56E **175** C10
Rummelsburg = Miastko
Poland 54°0N 16°58E **184** A3
Rummã → *China* 21°3N 85°5E **244** E7

Rungis *France* 48°44N 2°20E **134** B3
Rungwa *Tanzania* 6°55S 33°32E **268** D3
Rungwa → *Tanzania* 7°36S 31°50E **268** D3
Rungwa △ *Tanzania* 6°53S 34°2E **268** D3
Rungwe *Tanzania* 9°11S 33°32E **269** D3
Rungwe, Mt. *Tanzania* 9°8S 33°40E **269** D3
Runka *Nigeria* 12°28N 7°20E **263** C6
Runn *Sweden* 60°30N 15°40E **162** D9
Runton Ra. *Australia* 23°31S 123°6E **278** D3
Ruo Shui → *China* 41°0N 100°16E **218** C9
Ruokolahti *Finland* 61°17N 28°50E **188** B5
Ruoqiang *China* 38°55N 88°10E **217** E11
Rupa *India* 27°15N 92°21E **241** B4
Rupar *India* 31°2N 76°38E **242** D7
Rupat *Indonesia* 1°45N 101°40E **234** B2
Rupea *Romania* 46°2N 25°13E **183** D10
Rupen → *India* 23°28N 71°31E **242** H4
Rupert *U.S.A.* 42°37N 113°41W **304** E6
Rupert → *Canada* 51°29N 78°45W **298** B4
Rupert B. *Canada* 51°35N 79°0W **298** B4
Rupert House = Waskaganish
Canada 51°30N 78°40W **298** B4
Rupsa *India* 21°37N 87°1E **243** J12
Rupununi → *Guyana* 4°3N 58°35W **329** C6
Rur → *Germany* 51°11N 5°59E **178** D1
Rurópolis *Brazil* 4°3S 54°59W **329** D7
Rurrenabaque *Bolivia* 14°30S 67°32W **330** C4
Rururu *French Polynesia* 22°26S 151°20W **289** f
Rus → *Spain* 39°30N 2°30W **197** F2
Rusãfa *Iraq* 33°21N 44°23E **113** A2
Rusambo *Zimbabwe* 16°30S 32°4E **269** F3
Rusape *Zimbabwe* 18°35S 32°8E **269** F3
Ruschuk = Ruse *Bulgaria* 43°48N 25°59E **203** C9
Ruse *Bulgaria* 43°48N 25°59E **203** C9
Ruse □ *Bulgaria* 43°35N 25°40E **203** C9
Ruseţu *Romania* 44°57N 27°14E **183** F12
Rush *Ireland* 53°31N 6°6W **166** C5
Rush Green *U.K.* 51°33N 0°10E **125** A5
Rushan *China* 36°56N 121°30E **227** F11
Rushden *U.K.* 52°18N 0°35W **169** E7
Rushikulya → *India* 19°23N 85°5E **244** F7
Rushmore, Mt. *U.S.A.* 43°53N 103°28W **308** D2
Rushville *Ill., U.S.A.* 40°7N 90°34W **310** D6
Rushville *Ind., U.S.A.* 39°37N 85°27W **311** F11
Rushville *Nebr., U.S.A.* 42°43N 102°28W **308** D3
Rushworth *Australia* 36°32S 145°1E **283** D6
Ruskin *U.S.A.* 27°43N 82°26W **317** H7
Russa *India* 22°29N 88°21E **124** C2
Russas *Brazil* 4°55S 37°50W **332** B4
Russell *Man., Canada* 50°50N 101°20W **297** C8
Russell *N.Z.* 35°16S 174°10E **284** B5
Russell *Fla., U.S.A.* 30°3N 81°45W **316** E6
Russell *Kans., U.S.A.* 38°54N 98°52W **308** F4
Russell *N.Y., U.S.A.* 44°27N 75°9W **313** B9
Russell *Pa., U.S.A.* 41°56N 79°8W **312** E5
Russell Cave △ *U.S.A.* 34°59N 85°49W **315** D12
Russell Is. *Solomon Is.* 9°4S 159°12E **287** M10
Russell L. *Man., Canada* 56°15N 101°30W **297** B8
Russell L. *N.W.T., Canada* 63°5N 115°44W **296** A5
Russellkonda *India* 19°57N 84°42E **244** F7
Russells Point *U.S.A.* 40°28N 83°54W **311** D13
Russellville *Ala., U.S.A.* 34°30N 87°44W **315** D11
Russellville *Ark., U.S.A.* 35°17N 93°8W **314** D8
Russellville *Ky., U.S.A.* 36°51N 86°53W **308** G10
Rüsselsheim *Germany* 49°59N 8°25E **179** F4
Russi *Italy* 44°22N 12°2E **199** D9
Russia ■ *Eurasia* 62°0N 105°0E **215** C11
Russian → *U.S.A.* 38°27N 123°8W **306** G3
Russian Hill *San Francisco, U.S.A.* **136** a1
Russian Mission *U.S.A.* 61°47N 161°19W **303** F7
Russiaville *U.S.A.* 40°25N 86°16W **311** D10
Rust *Austria* 47°49N 16°42E **181** D9
Rustam Shahr *Pakistan* 26°58N 66°6E **242** F2
Rustavi *Georgia* 41°30N 45°0E **191** F7
Rustenburg *S. Africa* 25°41S 27°14E **270** C4
Ruston *U.S.A.* 32°32N 92°38W **314** E8
Rutana *Burundi* 3°55S 30°0E **268** C3
Rute *Spain* 37°19N 4°23W **195** H6
Ruteng *Indonesia* 8°35S 120°30E **231** F6
Rutenga *Zimbabwe* 21°15S 30°44E **269** G3
Ruth *U.S.A.* 43°42N 82°45W **312** C2
Rutherford *Calif., U.S.A.* 38°26N 122°24W **306** G4
Rutherford *N.J., U.S.A.* 40°49N 74°6W **132** B1
Rutherglen *Australia* 36°5S 146°29E **283** D7
Rutherglen *U.K.* 43°37N 72°58W **313** C12
Rutland □ *U.K.* 52°38N 0°40W **169** E7
Rutland I. *India* 11°25N 92°10E **245** J11
Rutland Water *U.K.* 52°39N 0°38W **169** E7
Rutledge → *Canada* 61°4N 112°0W **296** A6
Rutledge L. *Canada* 61°33N 110°47W **297** A6
Rutqa, W. → *Syria* 33°27N 79°42E **217** F9

Rydzyna Poland 51°47N 16°39E 185 G3
Rye U.K. 50°57N 0°45E 169 G8
Rye → U.K. 54°11N 0°44W 168 C7
Rye Bay U.K. 50°52N 0°49E 169 G8
Rye Patch Res. U.S.A. 40°28N 118°19W 304 F4
Ryegate U.S.A. 46°18N 109°15W 304 C9
Ryerson University Toronto, Canada 141 a3
Ryfylke Norway 59°25N 6°25E 164 E3
Rykene Norway 58°24N 8°37E 164 F5
Ryki Poland 51°38N 21°56E 185 G8
Rykovo = Yenakiyeve Ukraine 48°15N 38°15E 189 H10
Ryley Canada 53°17N 112°26W 296 C6
Rylsk Russia 51°36N 34°43E 189 G8
Rylstone Australia 32°46S 149°58E 283 B8
Rymanów Poland 49°35N 21°51E 185 J8
Ryn Poland 53°57N 21°34E 184 E8
Ryn Peski = Naryn Qum Kazakhstan 47°30N 49°0E 191 G9
Ryogoku Japan 35°40N 139°48E 140 A3
Ryōhaku-Sanchi Japan 36°9N 136°49E 223 A8
Ryojun = Lüshun China 38°45N 121°15E 227 E11
Ryōtsu Japan 38°5N 138°26E 220 E9
Rypin Poland 53°3N 19°25E 185 E6
Ryssby Sweden 56°52N 14°10E 163 H8
Rysy Europe 49°10N 20°4E 181 B13
Ryūgasaki Japan 35°54N 140°11E 223 B12
Ryukyu Is. = Ryūkyū-Rettō Japan 26°0N 126°0E 221 M3
Ryūkyū-Rettō Japan 26°0N 126°0E 221 M3
Ryūō = Kai Japan 35°42N 138°30E 223 B10
Rzepin Poland 52°20N 14°49E 185 F1
Rzeszów Poland 50°5N 21°58E 185 H8
Rzhev Russia 56°20N 34°20E 188 D8
Rzhevka Russia 59°59N 30°31E 137 B3

S

Sa Cabaneta Spain 39°37N 2°45E 206 B3
Sa Canal Spain 38°51N 1°23E 206 D1
Sa Conillera Spain 38°59N 1°13E 206 D1
Sa Dec Vietnam 10°20N 105°46E 237 G5
Sa Dragonera Spain 39°35N 2°19E 206 B3
Sa Kaeo Thailand 13°49N 102°4E 236 F4
Sa-koi Burma 19°54N 97°3E 241 F6
Sa Mesquida Spain 39°55N 4°16E 206 B5
Sa Pa Vietnam 22°20N 103°47E 236 A4
Sa Pobla Spain 39°46N 3°1E 206 B4
Sa Savina Spain 38°44N 1°25E 206 D1
Sa'a Solomon Is. 9°43S 161°35E 287 M11
Sa'ādat Shahr Iran 30°10N 53°5E 247 D7
Sa'ādatābād Hormozgān, Iran 28°3N 55°53E 247 D7
Sa'ādatābād Kermān, Iran 29°40N 55°51E 247 D7
Sa'ādatābād Tehrān, Iran 35°47N 51°22E 141 A2
Saadūn Iraq 33°19N 44°25E 113 B2
Saale → Germany 51°56N 11°54E 178 D7
Saaler Bodden Germany 54°20N 12°27E 178 A8
Saalfeld Germany 50°38N 11°21E 178 E7
Saalfelden Austria 47°25N 12°51E 180 D5
Saane → Switz. 47°8N 7°10E 179 H3
Saanich Canada 48°29N 123°26W 306 B3
Saar → Europe 49°41N 6°32E 170 E6
Saar-Hunsrück △ Germany 49°30N 6°50E 179 F2
Saar in Mähren = Žďár nad Sázavou Czech Rep. 49°34N 15°57E 180 B8
Saarbrücken Germany 49°14N 6°59E 179 F2
Saarburg Germany 49°36N 6°32E 179 F2
Saaremaa Estonia 58°30N 22°30E 188 C2
Saarijärvi Finland 62°43N 25°16E 160 E21
Saarland □ Germany 49°20N 7°0E 179 F2
Saarlautern = Saarlouis Germany 49°18N 6°45E 179 F2
Saarlouis Germany 49°18N 6°45E 179 F2
Saatlı Azerbaijan 39°55N 48°22E 213 C13
Saavedra Argentina 34°33S 58°29W 117 B2
Saaz = Žatec Czech Rep. 50°20N 13°32E 180 A6
Sab 'Ābar Syria 33°46N 37°41E 212 F7
Saba W. Indies 17°38N 63°14W 322 a
Šabac Serbia 44°48N 19°42E 202 B3
Sabadell Spain 41°28N 2°7E 196 D7
Sabae Japan 35°57N 136°11E 223 B8
Sabah □ Malaysia 6°0N 117°0E 235 A5
Şabāḩ, Wadi → Si. Arabia 23°50N 48°30E 249 B5
Sabak Bernam Malaysia 3°46N 100°58E 237 L3
Sabalān, Kūhhā-ye Iran 38°15N 47°45E 213 C12
Sabalana, Kepulauan Indonesia 6°45S 118°50E 231 F5
Sabalana, Kepuluauan Indonesia 6°45S 118°49E 235 D5
Sabana, Arch. de Cuba 23°0N 80°0W 320 B3
Sabana de la Mar Dom. Rep. 19°7N 69°24W 321 C6
Sabana Grande Puerto Rico 18°5N 66°58W 321 b
Sabana Westpunt = Westpunt Curaçao 12°22N 69°10W 322 g
Sábanalarga Colombia 10°38N 74°55W 328 A3
Sabaneta Pt. N. Marianas 15°17N 145°49E 302 e
Sabang Indonesia 5°50N 95°15E 234 A1
Şabanözü Turkey 40°28N 33°16E 212 B5
Săbăoani Romania 47°1N 26°51E 183 C11
Sabari → India 17°35N 81°16E 244 F5
Sabarmati → India 22°18N 72°22E 242 H5
Sab'atayn, Ramlat as Yemen 15°30N 46°10E 248 D4
Sabattis U.S.A. 44°6N 74°40W 313 B10
Sabáudia Italy 41°18N 13°1E 200 A6
Sabaya Bolivia 19°1S 68°23W 330 D4
Şabāyā, Jaza'ir Si. Arabia 18°35N 41°3E 248 C3
Saberania Indonesia 2°5S 138°18E 231 E9
Sabhā Libya 27°9N 14°29E 258 C2
Sabhar Bangla. 23°50N 90°15E 241 D3
Sabi → India 28°29N 76°44E 242 E7
Sabi Game Reserve = Kruger △ S. Africa 24°50S 26°10E 271 B4
Sabidana, J. Sudan 18°4N 36°50E 256 D4
Sabie S. Africa 25°10S 30°48E 271 C5
Sabina U.S.A. 39°29N 83°38W 311 E13
Sabinal U.S.A. 29°19N 99°28W 314 G5
Sabiñánigo Spain 42°31N 0°22W 196 C4
Sabinar, Punta del Spain 36°43N 2°44W 197 J2
Sabinas Mexico 27°51N 101°7W 318 B4
Sabinas → Mexico 27°37N 100°42W 318 B4
Sabinas Hidalgo Mexico 26°30N 100°10W 318 B4
Sabine → U.S.A. 29°59N 93°47W 314 G8
Sabine L. U.S.A. 29°53N 93°51W 314 G8
Sabine Pass U.S.A. 29°44N 93°54W 314 G8
Sabinópolis Brazil 18°40S 43°6W 333 E3
Sabinov Slovak Rep. 49°6N 21°5E 181 B14
Sabirabad Azerbaijan 40°5N 48°30E 191 K9
Sabka Chad 19°15N 16°35E 259 E3
Sablayan Phil. 12°50N 120°50E 232 E3
Sable Canada 55°30N 68°21W 299 A6
Sable, C. N.S., Canada 43°29N 65°38W 299 D6
Sable, C. Fla., U.S.A. 25°9N 81°8W 317 K8
Sable I. N.S., Canada 44°0N 60°0W 299 D8
Sable I. Papua N. G. 3°38S 154°42E 286 B8
Sablé-sur-Sarthe France 47°50N 0°20W 172 E6
Saboeiro Brazil 6°32S 39°54W 332 C4
Saboli India 28°42N 77°18E 120 A2
Sabonkafi Niger 14°40N 8°45E 259 F1
Sabor → Portugal 41°10N 7°7W 194 D3
Sabou Burkina Faso 12°1N 2°15W 262 C4
Sabres France 44°9N 0°43W 174 D3
Sabrina Coast Antarctica 68°0S 120°0E 151 C9
Sabtang I. Phil. 20°19N 121°52E 232 A3
Sabugal Portugal 40°20N 7°5W 194 E3
Sabugo Portugal 38°49N 9°17W 126 A1
Sabula U.S.A. 42°4N 90°10W 310 B6
Sabulubek Indonesia 1°36S 98°40E 234 C1
Sabuncu Turkey 39°33N 30°12E 205 B12
Şabyā Si. Arabia 17°9N 42°37E 248 C3
Sabzevār Iran 36°15N 57°40E 247 B8
Sabzi Mand India 28°40N 77°12E 120 A2
Sabzvārān = Jiroft Iran 28°45N 57°50E 247 D8
Sac City U.S.A. 42°25N 95°0W 310 B2
Sacaolo Angola 12°58S 22°28E 265 E4
Sacatengo Angola 13°16S 21°20E 265 E4
Sacavém Portugal 38°47N 9°5W 126 A2
Sacca Fisola Venice, Italy 142 c1
Sacca San Biágio Venice, Italy 142 c1
Sacedón Spain 40°29N 2°41W 196 E2
Săcele Romania 45°37N 25°41E 183 E10
Sacheon S. Korea 35°0N 128°6E 224 E4
Sachigo → Canada 55°6N 88°58W 298 A2
Sachigo, L. Canada 53°50N 92°12W 298 B1
Sachimbo Angola 9°14S 20°16E 265 D4
Sachin India 21°5N 72°53E 244 D1
Sachkhere Georgia 42°25N 43°28E 191 J6
Sachsen □ Germany 50°55N 13°10E 178 E9
Sachsen-Anhalt □ Germany 52°0N 12°0E 178 D7
Sächsische Schweiz △ Germany 50°55N 14°10E 178 E10
Sacile Italy 45°57N 12°30E 199 C9
Sackets Harbor U.S.A. 43°57N 76°7W 313 C8
Sackville Canada 45°54N 64°22W 299 C7
Saclay France 48°43N 2°10E 134 B2
Saclay, Étang de France 48°44N 2°9E 134 B1
Saco Maine, U.S.A. 43°30N 70°27W 313 C14
Saco Mont., U.S.A. 48°28N 107°21W 304 B10
Sacol I. Phil. 6°58N 122°13E 233 H4
Sacomã Brazil 23°36S 46°35W 137 B2
Sacramento = Itatupã Brazil 0°37S 51°12W 329 D7
Sacramento Brazil 19°53S 47°27W 333 E2
Sacramento Calif., U.S.A. 38°35N 121°29W 306 G5
Sacramento → U.S.A. 38°3N 121°56W 306 G5
Sacramento Mts. U.S.A. 32°30N 105°30W 305 K11
Sacramento Valley U.S.A. 39°30N 122°0W 306 G5
Sacratif, C. Spain 36°42N 3°28W 195 J7
Sacré Cœur Paris, France 134 a4
Sacrow Germany 52°25N 13°6E 115 B1
Sacrower See Germany 52°26N 13°6E 115 B1
Săcueni Romania 47°20N 22°5E 182 C7
Sada Mayotte 12°51S 45°6E 272 b
Sada Spain 43°22N 8°15W 194 B2
Sada-Misaki Japan 33°20N 132°5E 222 D4
Sada-Misaki-Hantō Japan 33°22N 132°1E 222 D4
Sădaba Spain 42°19N 1°12W 196 C3
Sadabad India 27°27N 78°3E 242 F8
Şa'dah Yemen 16°15N 43°37E 248 D3
Şa'dah □ Yemen 16°15N 43°37E 248 C3
Sadang S. Korea 37°29N 126°58E 137 C1
Sadani Tanzania 5°58S 38°35E 268 D4
Sadani △ Tanzania 6°3S 38°47E 268 D4
Sadao Thailand 6°38N 100°26E 237 J3
Sadar Bazar Delhi, India 120 a1
Sadaseopet India 17°38N 77°59E 244 F3
Sadd el Aali Egypt 23°54N 32°54E 256 C3
Saddle → U.S.A. 40°51N 74°6W 132 A1
Saddle Brook U.S.A. 40°53N 74°5W 132 A1
Saddle Hill St. Kitts & Nevis 17°7N 62°33W 322 d
Saddle Mt. U.S.A. 45°58N 123°41W 306 E3
Saddle Pk. India 13°9N 93°1E 245 H11
Saddle Pt. St. Helena 15°57S 5°38W 153 h
Sade Nigeria 11°22N 10°45E 263 C7
Şadh Oman 17°3N 55°4E 249 D6
Sadhoowa Trin. & Tob. 10°8N 61°27W 323 t
Sadimi Dem. Rep. of the Congo 9°25S 23°32E 265 D4
Sadiola Mali 13°50N 11°40W 262 C2
Sadiya India 27°50N 95°40E 241 B5
Sadīyah, Hawr as Iraq 32°15N 46°30E 213 F12
Sadlers St. Kitts & Nevis 17°24N 62°47W 322 d
Sado Japan 38°0N 138°25E 220 F9
Sado → Portugal 38°29N 8°55W 195 G2
Sadon Russia 42°52N 43°58E 191 J6
Sadovoye Russia 47°47N 44°31E 191 G7
Sadowara Japan 32°2N 131°26E 222 E3
Sadr Pakistan 24°51N 67°2E 123 A2
Sadr City Iraq 33°23N 44°27E 113 A2
Sadra India 23°21N 72°43E 242 H5
Sadrazamköy = Liveras Cyprus 35°23N 32°57E 207 E8
Sadri India 25°11N 73°26E 242 G5
Sadyba Poland 52°11N 21°3E 143 B2
Sæbøvik Norway 59°47N 5°40E 164 E2
Sæby Denmark 57°21N 10°30E 163 G4
Saegertown U.S.A. 41°43N 80°9W 312 E4
Saelices Spain 39°55N 2°49W 196 F2
Sætre Norway 59°41N 10°33E 164 E7
Sævareid Norway 60°11N 5°46E 164 D2
Safaalan Turkey 41°26N 28°6E 203 E12
Şafājah Si. Arabia 26°25N 39°0E 246 E3
Šafárikovo = Tornal'a Slovak Rep. 48°25N 20°20E 181 C13
Safata B. Samoa 14°0S 171°50W 287 W20
Safdar Jang's Tomb India 28°35N 77°12E 120 B2
Safed Koh Afghan. 34°0N 70°0E 240 B3
Säffle Sweden 59°8N 12°55E 162 E6
Safford U.S.A. 32°50N 109°43W 305 K9
Saffron Walden U.K. 52°1N 0°16E 169 E8
Safi Morocco 32°18N 9°20W 260 B3
Safia Papua N. G. 9°35S 148°38E 286 E5
Safia, Hamada Mali 23°10N 4°15W 260 D4
Şafīābād Iran 36°45N 57°58E 247 B8
Safid Dasht Iran 33°27N 48°11E 247 C6
Safid Kūh Afghan. 34°45N 63°0E 240 B1
Safid Rūd → Iran 37°23N 50°11E 247 B6
Safipur India 26°44N 80°21E 243 F9
Şāfitā Syria 34°48N 36°7E 250 D7
Safonovo Russia 55°4N 33°16E 188 E7
Safranbolu Turkey 41°15N 32°41E 212 B5
Saft el Laban Egypt 30°1N 31°10E 117 A2
Saft Rashîn Egypt 28°58N 30°55E 256 J7
Safune Samoa 13°25S 172°21W 287 V19
Şafwān Iraq 30°7N 47°43E 246 D5
Sag Harbor U.S.A. 41°0N 72°18W 313 F12
Sag Sag Papua N. G. 5°32S 148°23E 286 C5
Saga Kōchi, Japan 33°5N 133°6E 222 D5
Saga Saga, Japan 33°15N 130°16E 222 D2
Saga □ Japan 33°15N 130°20E 222 D2
Sagae Japan 38°22N 140°17E 220 E10
Sagaing Burma 21°52N 95°59E 241 E5
Sagaing □ Burma 23°55N 95°56E 241 D5
Sagala Mali 14°9N 6°38W 262 C3
Sagami-Nada Japan 34°58N 139°30E 223 C11
Sagami-Wan Japan 35°15N 139°25E 223 B11
Sagamihara Japan 35°33N 139°25E 223 B11
Sagamore U.S.A. 40°46N 79°14W 312 F5
Sagan = Żagań Poland 51°39N 15°22E 185 G2
Saganaga L. Canada 48°14N 90°52W 308 A8
Saganoseki Japan 33°15N 131°53E 222 D3
Saganthit Kyun Burma 11°56N 98°29E 237 G2
Sagar Karnataka, India 14°14N 75°6E 245 G2
Sagar Mad. P., India 23°50N 78°44E 243 H8
Sagara Japan 34°41N 138°12E 223 C10
Sagara, L. Tanzania 5°20S 31°0E 268 D3
Sagarejo Georgia 41°44N 45°19E 191 K7
Sagarmatha = Everest, Mt. Nepal 28°5N 86°58E 243 E12
Sagarmatha △ Nepal 27°55N 86°45E 243 F12
Sagavanirktok → U.S.A. 70°19N 147°53W 303 A11
Sagay Phil. 10°57N 123°25E 233 F4
Sagene Norway 59°55N 10°46E 133 A3
Saghîr, El Bahr el → Egypt 31°8N 31°54E 256 H7
Sagiada Greece 39°38N 20°12E 206 B10
Saginaw U.S.A. 43°26N 83°56W 309 D12
Saginaw B. U.S.A. 43°50N 83°40W 309 D12
Sagleipie Liberia 7°0N 8°52W 262 D3
Saglouc = Salluit Canada 62°14N 75°38W 295 E16
Sagone France 42°7N 8°42E 175 F12
Sagone, G. de France 42°4N 8°40E 175 F12
Sagrada Familia, Templo de Barcelona, Spain 114 a2
Sagres Portugal 37°0N 8°58W 195 J2
Sagu Burma 20°13N 94°46E 241 E5
Sagua la Grande Cuba 22°50N 80°10W 320 B3
Saguache U.S.A. 38°5N 106°8W 304 G10
Saguaro △ U.S.A. 32°12N 110°38W 305 K8
Saguenay → Canada 48°22N 71°0W 299 C5
Saguia el Hamra → W. Sahara 27°24N 13°43W 260 C2
Sagunt Spain 39°42N 0°18W 196 F4
Sagunto = Sagunt Spain 39°42N 0°18W 196 F4
Sagvåg Norway 59°46N 5°25E 164 E2
Sagwara India 23°41N 74°1E 242 H6
Sahaba Sudan 18°57N 30°25E 256 D3
Sahagún Colombia 8°57N 75°27W 328 B2
Sahagún Spain 42°18N 5°2W 194 C5
Saḩam al Jawlān Syria 32°45N 35°55E 250 F6
Sahamandrevo Madag. 23°15S 45°35E 272 C2
Sahand, Kūh-e Iran 37°44N 46°27E 213 D12
Sahar, Mumbai ✈ (BOM) India 19°5N 72°51E 130 A2
Sahara Africa 23°0N 5°0E 254 D4
Saḩara, G. Egypt 28°2N 34°26E 251 K5
Saharan Atlas = Saharien, Atlas Algeria 33°30N 1°0E 261 B5
Saharan Seamounts Atl. Oc. 25°30N 19°50W 152 D10
Saharanpur India 29°58N 77°33E 242 E7
Saharien, Atlas Algeria 33°30N 1°0E 261 B5
Saharsa India 25°53N 86°36E 243 G12
Sahasinaka Madag. 21°49S 47°49E 272 C2
Sahaswan India 28°5N 78°45E 243 E8
Saheira, W. el → Egypt 30°5N 33°25E 251 H4
Sahel Africa 16°0N 5°0E 254 E3
Sahel, Canal du Mali 14°20N 6°0W 262 C3
Sahibganj India 25°12N 87°40E 243 G12
Sāḩilīyah Iraq 33°43N 42°42E 213 F10
Sahiwal Pakistan 30°45N 73°8E 242 D5
Şahneh Iran 34°29N 47°41E 213 E12
Sahrawi = Western Sahara ■ Africa 25°0N 13°0W 260 D2
Sahuaripa Mexico 29°3N 109°14W 318 B3
Sahuarita U.S.A. 31°57N 110°58W 305 L8
Sahuayo de Diaz Mexico 20°4N 102°43W 318 C4
Šahy Slovak Rep. 48°4N 18°55E 181 C11
Sai → India 25°39N 82°47E 243 G10
Sai Buri Thailand 6°43N 101°45E 237 J3
Sai-Cinza Brazil 6°17S 57°42W 331 B6
Sai Kung China 22°23N 114°16E 122 A2
Sai Thong △ Thailand 15°56N 101°10E 236 E3
Sai Wan Ho China 22°17N 114°12E 122 B2
Sai Ying Pun China 22°17N 114°8E 122 B1
Sai Yok △ Thailand 14°25N 98°40E 236 E2
Saibai I. Australia 9°25S 142°40E 280 a
Sa'id Bundâs South Sudan 8°24N 24°48E 259 G4
Saïda Algeria 34°50N 0°11E 261 B5
Saïda □ Algeria 34°40N 0°20E 261 B5
Sa'īdābād = Sīrjān Iran 29°30N 55°45E 247 D7
Sa'īdābād Iran 36°8N 54°11E 247 B7
Saidaiji Japan 34°39N 134°2E 222 C6
Saïdia Morocco 35°5N 2°14W 261 A4
Saidor Papua N. G. 5°40S 146°29E 286 C4
Saidpur Bangla. 25°48N 89°0E 241 C2
Saidpur India 25°33N 83°11E 243 G10
Saidu Sharif Pakistan 34°43N 72°24E 243 B5
Saignes France 45°20N 2°31E 174 C6
Saigō Japan 36°12N 133°20E 222 A5
Saigon = Thanh Pho Ho Chi Minh Vietnam 10°58N 106°40E 237 G6
Saiha India 22°29N 92°58E 241 D4
Saijō Japan 33°55N 133°11E 222 D5
Saikai △ Japan 33°12N 129°36E 222 D1
Saikhoa Ghat India 27°50N 95°40E 241 B5
Saiki Japan 32°58N 131°51E 222 E3
Sailana India 23°28N 74°55E 242 H6
Saillans France 44°42N 5°12E 175 D9
Sailolof Indonesia 1°15S 130°46E 231 E8
Sailu India 19°28N 76°28E 244 E3
Saimaa Finland 61°15N 28°15E 188 B5
Saimbeyli Turkey 37°59N 36°6E 212 D7
Saimen = Saimaa Finland 61°15N 28°15E 188 B5
Şa'in Dezh Iran 36°40N 46°25E 213 D12
St. Abb's Head U.K. 55°55N 2°8W 167 F6
St-Affrique France 43°57N 2°53E 174 E6
St-Agrève France 45°0N 4°23E 175 C8
St-Aignan France 47°16N 1°22E 172 E8
St. Alban's Nfld. & L., Canada 47°51N 55°50W 299 C8
St. Albans Herts., U.K. 51°45N 0°19W 169 F7
St. Albans Vt., U.S.A. 44°49N 73°5W 313 B11
St. Albans W. Va., U.S.A. 38°23N 81°50W 309 F13
St. Alban's Head U.K. 50°34N 2°4W 169 G5
St. Albert Canada 53°37N 113°32W 296 C6
St-Amand-en-Puisaye France 47°32N 3°5E 173 E10
St-Amand-les-Eaux France 50°27N 3°25E 173 B10
St-Amand-Montrond France 46°43N 2°30E 173 F9
St-Amarin France 47°54N 7°2E 173 E14
St-Amour France 46°26N 5°21E 173 F12
St-André Montréal, Canada 130 c1
St-André Réunion 20°57S 55°39E 272 f
St-André-de-Cubzac France 44°59N 0°26W 174 D3
St-André-les-Alpes France 43°58N 6°30E 175 E10
St. Andrew Sd. U.S.A. 30°58N 81°25W 316 E8
St. Andrew's Nfld. & L., Canada 47°45N 59°15W 299 C8
St. Andrews N.Z. 44°33S 171°10E 285 E6
St. Andrews Fife, U.K. 56°20N 2°47W 167 E6
St. Andrews S.C., U.S.A. 32°47N 80°0W 316 C9
St-Anicet Canada 45°8N 74°22W 313 A10
St. Anne U.S.A. 41°1N 87°43W 311 C9
St. Annes Canada 49°40N 96°39W 297 D9
St. Anns B. Canada 46°22N 60°25W 299 C7
St. Ann's Bay Jamaica 18°26N 77°12W 320 a
St. Anthony Nfld. & L., Canada 51°22N 55°35W 299 B8
St. Anthony Idaho, U.S.A. 43°58N 111°41W 304 E8
St-Antoine Canada 46°22N 64°45W 299 C7
St-Antonin-Noble-Val France 44°10N 1°45E 174 D5
St-Arnaud = El Eulma Algeria 36°9N 5°42E 261 A6
St. Arnaud Australia 36°40S 143°16E 282 D5
St. Arnaud Ra. N.Z. 42°1S 172°53E 285 C7
St-Astier France 45°8N 0°31E 174 C4
St-Aubin France 48°44N 2°8E 134 B1
St-Aubin-du-Cormier France 48°15N 1°26W 172 D5
St-Augustin Canada 51°13N 58°38W 299 B8
St-Augustin → Canada 51°16N 58°40W 299 B8
St. Augustine U.S.A. 29°54N 81°19W 316 F8
St. Augustine Beach U.S.A. 29°51N 81°16W 316 F8
St-Aulaye France 45°12N 0°9E 174 C4
St. Austell U.K. 50°20N 4°47W 169 G3
St-Avold France 49°6N 6°43E 173 C13
St. Barbe Canada 51°12N 56°46W 299 B8
St-Barthélemy ☑ W. Indies 17°50N 62°50W 322 a
St-Barthélemy Channel St.-Martin 18°0N 63°0W 322 a
St. Barts = St-Barthélemy ☑ W. Indies 17°50N 62°50W 322 a
St. Basil's Cathedral Moscow, Russia 129 b3
St. Bathans N.Z. 44°53S 169°50E 285 E4
St. Bathan's, Mt. N.Z. 44°45S 169°45E 285 E4
St-Béat France 42°55N 0°41E 174 F4
St. Bees Hd. U.K. 54°31N 3°38W 168 C4
St. Bees I. Australia 20°56S 149°26E 280 b
St-Benoît Réunion 21°2S 55°43E 272 f
St-Benoît-du-Sault France 46°26N 1°24E 174 B5
St-Bonnet-en-Champsaur France 44°40N 6°5E 175 D10
St-Brevin-les-Pins France 47°14N 2°10W 172 E4
St-Brice-en-Coglès France 48°25N 1°22W 172 D5
St. Bride's Canada 46°56N 54°10W 299 C9
St. Brides B. U.K. 51°49N 5°9W 169 F2
St-Brieuc France 48°30N 2°46W 172 D4
St-Calais France 47°55N 0°45E 172 E7
St-Cast-le-Guildo France 48°37N 2°18W 172 D4
St. Catharines Canada 43°10N 79°15W 312 C5
St. Catherine, Mt. Grenada 12°10N 61°40W 323 q
St. Catherine Pt. Bermuda 32°23N 64°40W 153 a
St. Catherines I. U.S.A. 31°40N 81°10W 316 D8
St. Catherine's Monastery Egypt 28°34N 33°58E 251 K4
St. Catherine's Pt. U.K. 50°34N 1°18W 169 G6
St-Céré France 44°51N 1°54E 174 D5
St-Cergue Switz. 46°27N 6°10E 179 J2
St-Cernin France 45°5N 2°25E 174 C6
St-Chamond France 45°28N 4°31E 175 C8
St. Charles Ill., U.S.A. 41°54N 88°19W 311 C8
St. Charles Md., U.S.A. 38°36N 76°56W 309 F15
St. Charles Mo., U.S.A. 38°47N 90°29W 310 F6
St. Charles Va., U.S.A. 36°48N 83°4W 309 G12
St-Chély-d'Apcher France 44°48N 3°17E 174 D7
St-Chinian France 43°25N 2°56E 174 E6
St. Christopher = St. Kitts W. Indies 17°20N 62°40W 322 d
St. Christopher-Nevis = St. Kitts & Nevis ■ W. Indies 17°20N 62°40W 322 d
St-Ciers-sur-Gironde France 45°17N 0°37W 174 C3
St. Clair Ga., U.S.A. 33°9N 82°13W 316 B7
St. Clair Mich., U.S.A. 42°50N 82°30W 312 D2
St. Clair Mo., U.S.A. 38°21N 90°59W 310 F6
St. Clair Pa., U.S.A. 40°43N 76°12W 313 F8
St. Clair → U.S.A. 42°38N 82°31W 312 D2
St. Clair, L. S. Austral., Australia 37°20S 139°55E 282 D3
St. Clair, L. N. Amer. 42°27N 82°39W 312 D2
St. Clair Shores U.S.A. 42°30N 82°53W 311 B14
St. Clairsville U.S.A. 40°5N 80°54W 312 F4
St-Claud France 45°54N 0°28E 174 C4
St. Claude Canada 49°40N 98°20W 297 D9
St-Claude Jura, France 46°22N 5°52E 173 F12
St-Claude Guadeloupe 16°3N 61°42W 322 e
St. Clears U.K. 51°49N 4°31W 169 F3
St-Clet Canada 45°21N 74°13W 313 A10
St. Cloud France 48°50N 2°12E 134 A2
St. Cloud Fla., U.S.A. 28°15N 81°17W 317 G8
St. Cloud Minn., U.S.A. 45°34N 94°10W 308 C6
St. Cricq, C. Australia 25°17S 113°6E 279 E1
St. Croix U.S. Virgin Is. 17°45N 64°45W 321 C7
St. Croix → U.S.A. 44°45N 92°48W 308 C7
St. Croix Falls U.S.A. 45°24N 92°38W 308 C7
St-Cyprien France 42°37N 3°2E 174 F7
St-Cyr-l'École France 48°47N 2°4E 134 B1
St-Cyr-l'École ✈ France 48°48N 2°4E 134 B1
St-Cyr-sur-Mer France 43°11N 5°43E 175 E9
St. David U.S.A. 40°30N 90°3W 310 D6
St. David's Nfld. & L., Canada 48°12N 58°52W 299 C8
St. David's Grenada 12°2N 61°40W 323 q
St. David's Pembs., U.K. 51°53N 5°16W 169 F2
St. David's Head U.K. 51°54N 5°19W 169 F2
St. David's I. Bermuda 32°21N 64°39W 153 a
St-Denis = Sig Algeria 35°32N 0°12W 261 A4
St-Denis Seine-St-Denis, France 48°56N 2°20E 134 A3
St-Denis Réunion 20°52S 55°27E 272 f
St-Denis → Réunion 20°55S 55°27E 272 f
St-Denis ✈ (RUN) Réunion 20°53S 55°32E 272 f
St-Dié France 48°17N 6°56E 173 D13
St-Dizier France 48°38N 4°56E 173 D11
St-Égrève France 45°14N 5°41E 175 C9
St. Elias, Mt. U.S.A. 60°18N 140°56W 303 F12
St. Elias Mts. N. Amer. 60°33N 139°28W 296 A1
St-Élie Fr. Guiana 4°49N 53°17W 329 C7
St. Elmo U.S.A. 39°2N 88°51W 311 E8
St-Eloy-les-Mines France 46°10N 2°51E 173 F9
St-Émilion France 44°53N 0°9W 174 D3
St-Étienne France 45°27N 4°22E 175 C8
St-Étienne → Réunion 21°17S 55°25E 272 f
St-Étienne-de-Tinée France 44°16N 6°56E 175 D10
St-Étienne-du-Rouvray France 49°23N 1°6E 172 C8
St. Eugène Canada 45°30N 74°28W 313 A10
St. Eustatius W. Indies 17°20N 63°0W 322 a
St-Exupery, Lyon ✈ (LYS) France 45°44N 5°2E 175 C9
St-Fargeau France 47°39N 3°4E 173 E10
St-Félicien Canada 48°40N 72°25W 298 C5
St. Ferdinand = Florissant U.S.A. 38°47N 90°19W 310 F6
St-Florent France 42°41N 9°18E 175 F13
St-Florent, G. de France 42°47N 9°12E 175 F13
St-Florent-sur-Cher France 46°59N 2°15E 173 F9
St-Florentin France 48°0N 3°45E 173 E10
St-Flour France 45°2N 3°6E 174 C7
St. Francis U.S.A. 39°47N 101°48W 308 F3
St. Francis → U.S.A. 34°38N 90°36W 315 D9
St. Francis, C. S. Africa 34°14S 24°49E 270 D3
St. Francisville Ill., U.S.A. 38°36N 87°39W 311 F9
St. Francisville La., U.S.A. 30°47N 91°23W 314 F9
St-François Guadeloupe 16°16N 61°18W 322 e
St-François, L. Canada 45°10N 74°22W 313 A10
St-Fulgent France 46°50N 1°10W 172 F5
St-Gabriel Canada 46°17N 73°24W 298 C5
St. Gallen = Sankt Gallen Switz. 47°26N 9°22E 179 H5
St-Galmier France 45°35N 4°19E 173 G11
St-Gaudens France 43°6N 0°44E 174 E4
St-Gaultier France 46°39N 1°26E 172 F8
St-Gengoux-le-National France 46°37N 4°40E 173 F11
St-Geniez-d'Olt France 44°27N 2°58E 174 D6
St. George Queens., Australia 28°1S 148°30E 281 D4
St. George Bermuda 32°22N 64°40W 153 a
St. George N.B., Canada 45°11N 66°50W 299 C6
St. George Ont., Canada 43°15N 80°15W 312 C4
St. George Ga., U.S.A. 30°31N 82°2W 316 E7
St. George S.C., U.S.A. 33°11N 80°35W 316 B9
St. George Utah, U.S.A. 37°6N 113°35W 305 H7
St. George, C. Nfld. & L., Canada 48°30N 59°16W 299 C8
St. George, C. Papua N. G. 4°49S 152°53E 286 C7
St. George, C. Fla., U.S.A. 29°40N 85°5W 316 F4
St. George I. Alaska, U.S.A. 56°35N 169°35W 303 H5
St. George I. Fla., U.S.A. 29°35N 84°55W 316 F5
St. George Ra. Australia 18°40S 125°0E 278 C4
St-George's Canada 48°26N 58°31W 299 C8
St-Georges Qué., Canada 46°8N 70°40W 299 C5
St-Georges Fr. Guiana 3°53N 51°50W 329 C7
St. George's Grenada 12°5N 61°43W 323 q
St. George's B. Canada 48°24N 58°53W 299 C8
St. Georges Basin N.S.W., Australia 35°7S 150°36E 283 C9
St. Georges Basin W. Austral., Australia 15°23S 125°2E 278 C4
St. George's Channel Europe 52°0N 6°0W 166 E6
St. George's Channel India 7°15N 93°43E 245 L11
St. George's Channel Papua N. G. 4°10S 152°20E 286 C7
St. Georges Harbour Bermuda 32°33N 64°42W 153 a
St. Georges Hd. Australia 35°12S 150°42E 283 C9
St. Georges I. Bermuda 32°23N 64°40W 153 a
St-Georges-lès-Baillargeaux France 46°41N 0°22E 174 B4
St-Germain, Forêt de France 48°57N 2°5E 134 A1
St-Germain-de-Calberte France 44°13N 3°48E 174 D7
St-Germain-en-Laye France 48°53N 2°4E 134 A1
St-Germain-Lembron France 45°27N 3°14E 174 C7
St-Gervais-d'Auvergne France 46°4N 2°50E 173 F9
St-Gervais-les-Bains France 45°53N 6°42E 175 C10
St-Gildas, Pte. de France 47°8N 2°14W 172 E4
St. Giles Cathedral Edinburgh, U.K. 121 b2
St-Gilles Brussels, Belgium 50°49N 4°20E 116 B2
St-Gilles Gard, France 43°40N 4°26E 175 E8
St-Gilles-les-Bains Réunion 21°2S 55°14E 272 f
St-Gilles-les-Hauts Réunion 21°2S 55°15E 272 f
St-Girons Ariège, France 42°59N 1°8E 174 F5
St-Girons Landes, France 43°56N 1°18W 174 E2
St. Gotthard P. = San Gottardo, P. del Switz. 46°33N 8°33E 179 J4
St. Helena Atl. Oc. 15°58S 5°42W 153 h
St. Helena Calif., U.S.A. 38°30N 122°28W 306 G4
St. Helena, Mt. U.S.A. 38°40N 122°36W 306 G4
St. Helena B. S. Africa 32°40S 18°10E 270 D2
St. Helena Sd. U.S.A. 32°15N 80°25W 316 C9
St. Helens Tas., Australia 41°20S 148°15E 281 G4
St. Helens Mersey., U.K. 53°27N 2°44W 168 D5
St. Helens Oreg., U.S.A. 45°52N 122°48W 306 E4
St. Helens, Mt. U.S.A. 46°12N 122°12W 306 D4
St. Helier Chan. Is., U.K. 49°10N 2°7W 169 H5
St. Helier London, U.K. 51°23N 0°11W 125 B2
St-Herblain France 47°13N 1°40W 172 E5
St-Hilaire-du-Harcouët France 48°35N 1°5W 172 D5
St-Hippolyte France 47°19N 6°50E 173 E13
St-Hippolyte-du-Fort France 43°58N 3°52E 174 E7
St-Honoré-les-Bains France 46°54N 3°50E 173 F10
St-Hubert Canada 45°29N 73°25W 130 B3
St-Hubert, Galeries Royales Brussels, Belgium 116 b2
St-Hyacinthe Canada 45°40N 72°58W 298 C5
St. Ignace U.S.A. 45°52N 84°44W 309 C11
St. Ignace I. Canada 48°45N 88°0W 298 C2
St. Ignatius U.S.A. 47°19N 114°6W 304 C6
St-Imier Switz. 47°9N 6°58E 179 H2
St. Isaac's Cathedral Russia 59°55N 30°19E 137 B1
St. Ives Cambs., U.K. 52°20N 0°4W 169 E7
St. Ives Corn., U.K. 50°12N 5°30W 169 G2
St-Jacques Montréal, Canada 130 a2
St-Jacques → Canada 45°26N 73°29W 130 B3
St-James France 48°31N 1°20W 172 D5
St. James Minn., U.S.A. 43°59N 94°38W 308 D6
St. James Mo., U.S.A. 38°0N 91°37W 310 G5
St. James Cathedral Toronto, Canada 141 b3
St. James's London, U.K. 125 b3
St-Jean St. Barts 17°53N 62°50W 322 a
St-Jean → Canada 50°17N 64°20W 299 B7
St-Jean, L. Canada 48°40N 72°0W 299 C5
St-Jean Baptiste Montréal, Canada 130 a1
St-Jean-d'Angély France 45°57N 0°31W 174 C3
St-Jean-de-Braye France 47°53N 1°58E 173 E8
St-Jean-de-Luz France 43°23N 1°39W 174 E2
St-Jean-de-Maurienne France 45°16N 6°21E 175 C10
St-Jean-de-Monts France 46°47N 2°4W 172 F4
St-Jean-du-Gard France 44°7N 3°52E 174 D7
St-Jean-en-Royans France 45°1N 5°18E 175 C9
St-Jean-Pied-de-Port France 43°10N 1°14W 174 E2
St-Jean-Port-Joli Canada 47°15N 70°13W 299 C5
St-Jean-sur-Richelieu Canada 45°20N 73°20W 313 A11
St-Jérôme Canada 45°47N 74°0W 298 C5
St. Joe U.S.A. 41°19N 84°54W 311 C12
St. John N.B., Canada 45°20N 66°8W 299 C6
St. John Kans., U.S.A. 38°0N 98°46W 308 F4
St. John → Liberia 6°40N 9°10W 262 D2
St. John → N. Amer. 45°12N 66°5W 309 C20
St. John, C. Canada 50°0N 55°32W 299 C8
St. John I. U.S. Virgin Is. 18°20N 64°42W 321 b
St. John's Antigua & B. 17°6N 61°51W 322 b
St. John's Nfld. & L., Canada 47°35N 52°40W 299 C9
St. Johns Montserrat 16°46N 62°11W 323 p
St. Johns Ariz., U.S.A. 34°30N 109°22W 305 J9
St. Johns Mich., U.S.A. 43°0N 84°33W 311 B12
St. Johns → U.S.A. 30°24N 81°24W 316 E8
St. John's Cathedral Hong Kong, China 122 c1
St. John's Pt. Ireland 54°34N 8°27W 166 B3
St. Johnsbury U.S.A. 44°25N 72°1W 313 B12
St. Johnston Village Antigua & B. 17°7N 61°50W 322 b
St. Johnsville U.S.A. 43°0N 74°43W 313 C10
St-Joost-Ten-Node Belgium 50°51N 4°21E 116 A2
St. Joseph Ont., Canada 43°24N 81°42W 312 C3
St. Joseph Dominica 15°24N 61°26W 323 n
St-Joseph Martinique 14°39N 61°4W 322 j
St-Joseph Réunion 21°22S 55°37E 272 f
St. Joseph Mayaro, Trin. & Tob. 10°18N 60°59W 323 t
St. Joseph Tunapuna, Trin. & Tob. 10°40N 61°25W 323 t
St. Joseph Ill., U.S.A. 40°7N 88°2W 311 D8
St. Joseph La., U.S.A. 31°55N 91°14W 314 F9
St. Joseph Mich., U.S.A. 42°6N 86°29W 311 B10
St. Joseph Mo., U.S.A. 39°46N 94°50W 310 E2
St. Joseph → U.S.A. 42°7N 86°29W 311 B10
St. Joseph, I. Canada 46°12N 83°58W 298 C3
St. Joseph, L. Canada 51°10N 90°35W 298 B1
St. Joseph Pt. U.S.A. 29°52N 85°24W 316 F4
St-Juéry France 43°57N 2°12E 174 E6
St. Julian's Malta 35°55N 14°29E 206 F7
St-Julien-Chapteuil France 45°2N 4°4E 175 C8
St-Julien-de-Vouvantes France 47°38N 1°13W 172 E5
St-Julien-en-Genevois France 46°9N 6°5E 173 F13
St-Junien France 45°53N 0°55E 174 C4
St-Just-en-Chaussée France 49°30N 2°25E 173 C9
St-Just-en-Chevalet France 45°55N 3°50E 174 C7
St. Kilda Vic., Australia 37°51S 144°58E 128 B1
St. Kilda N.Z. 45°53S 170°31E 285 F5
St. Kilda W. Isles, U.K. 57°49N 8°34W 165 C2
St. Kitts W. Indies 17°20N 62°40W 322 d
St. Kitts & Nevis ■ W. Indies 17°20N 62°40W 322 d
St-Lambert Qué., Canada 45°30N 73°29W 130 A3
St-Lambert Yvelines, France 48°43N 2°1E 134 B1
St. Laurent Canada 50°25N 97°58W 297 C9
St-Laurent Canada 45°30N 73°43W 130 A1
St-Laurent-de-la-Salanque France 42°46N 2°59E 174 F6
St-Laurent du Maroni Fr. Guiana 5°29N 54°3W 329 B7
St-Laurent-du-Pont France 45°23N 5°45E 175 C9
St-Laurent-en-Grandvaux France 46°35N 5°58E 173 F12
St-Laurent-Médoc France 45°8N 0°49W 174 C3
St. Lawrence Queens., Australia 22°16S 149°31E 280 C4
St. Lawrence Nfld. & L., Canada 46°54N 55°23W 299 C8
St. Lawrence → Canada 49°30N 66°0W 299 C6
St. Lawrence, Gulf of Canada 48°25N 62°0W 299 C7
St. Lawrence I. U.S.A. 63°30N 170°30W 303 E5
St. Lawrence Islands △ Canada 44°27N 75°52W 313 B9
St. Lawrence Market Toronto, Canada 141 b3
St-Lazare, Gare Paris, France 134 a3
St. Léonard Canada 47°12N 67°58W 299 C6
St-Léonard Canada 45°35N 73°34W 130 A2
St-Léonard-de-Noblat France 45°49N 1°29E 174 C5
St-Leu Réunion 21°9S 55°18E 272 f
St. Lewis → Canada 52°26N 56°11W 299 B8
St-Lô France 49°7N 1°5W 172 C5
St-Louis Montréal, Canada 130 b2
St-Louis Haut-Rhin, France 47°30N 7°34E 173 E14
St-Louis Guadeloupe 15°56N 61°19W 322 e
St-Louis Réunion 21°16S 55°25E 272 f
St-Louis Senegal 16°8N 16°27W 262 B1
St. Louis U.S.A. 38°37N 90°11W 310 F6
St-Louis □ Senegal 16°20N 15°0W 262 B2
St. Louis → U.S.A. 46°44N 92°9W 308 B7
St. Louis Lambert Int. ✈ (STL) U.S.A. 38°45N 90°22W 310 F6
St-Loup-sur-Semouse France 47°53N 6°16E 173 E13
St-Luc Canada 45°22N 73°18W 313 A11
St. Lucia ■ W. Indies 14°0N 60°57W 323 m
St. Lucia, L. S. Africa 28°5S 32°30E 271 C5
St. Lucia △ S. Africa 28°6S 32°27E 271 C5
St. Lucia Channel W. Indies 14°15N 61°0W 321 D7
St. Lucie U.S.A. 27°29N 80°20W 317 H9
St. Lucie Canal U.S.A. 27°10N 80°18W 317 H9
St. Maarten ☑ W. Indies 18°2N 63°5W 322 a
St. Magnus B. U.K. 60°25N 1°35W 167 A7
St-Maixent-l'École France 46°24N 0°12W 174 B3
St-Malo France 48°39N 2°1W 172 D4
St-Malo, G. de France 48°50N 2°30W 172 D4
St-Mandé France 48°50N 2°24E 134 A3
St-Mandrier-sur-Mer France 43°4N 5°57E 175 E9
St-Marc Haiti 19°10N 72°41W 321 C5
St-Marcellin France 45°9N 5°20E 175 C9
St-Marcouf, Îs. France 49°30N 1°10W 172 C5
St. Margaret's Ireland 53°25N 6°18W 120 A2
St. Maries U.S.A. 47°19N 116°35W 304 C5
St. Mark B. Grenada 12°11N 61°42W 323 q
St. Marks U.S.A. 30°9N 84°12W 316 E5
St. Mark's Square = San Marco, Piazza Venice, Italy 142 b3
St-Martin ☑ W. Indies 18°5N 63°5W 322 a
St-Martin, Bois France 48°48N 2°35E 134 B4
St-Martin, C. Martinique 14°52N 61°14W 322 j
St. Martin, L. Canada 51°40N 98°30W 297 C9
St-Martin-de-Crau France 43°38N 4°48E 175 E8
St-Martin-de-Ré France 46°12N 1°21W 174 B2
St-Martin-d'Hères France 45°9N 5°45E 175 C9
St-Martin-Vésubie France 44°4N 7°15E 175 D11
St. Martin's I. Bangla. 20°36N 92°20E 241 E4
St-Martory France 43°9N 0°56E 174 E4
St. Mary U.S.A. 37°53N 89°57W 310 G7
St. Mary, Mt. Papua N. G. 8°8S 147°2E 286 E4
St. Mary Cray U.K. 51°23N 0°7E 125 B4
St. Mary Is. India 13°20N 74°35E 245 H2
St. Mary Pk. Australia 31°32S 138°34E 282 A3
St. Marys Tas., Australia 41°35S 148°11E 281 G4
St. Marys Ont., Canada 43°20N 81°10W 312 C3
St. Mary's Trin. & Tob. 10°14N 61°33W 323 t
St. Mary's Corn., U.K. 49°55N 6°18W 169 H1
St. Mary's Orkney, U.K. 58°54N 2°54W 167 C6
St. Marys Alaska, U.S.A. 62°4N 163°10W 303 E7
St. Marys Ga., U.S.A. 30°44N 81°33W 316 E8
St. Marys Ohio, U.S.A. 40°33N 84°24W 311 D12
St. Marys Pa., U.S.A. 41°26N 78°34W 312 E6
St. Marys → U.S.A. 30°43N 81°27W 316 E8
St. Mary's, C. Canada 46°50N 54°12W 299 C9
St. Mary's B. Canada 46°50N 53°50W 299 C9
St. Mary's Bay Canada 44°25N 66°10W 299 D6
St. Mary's Cathedral San Francisco, U.S.A. 136 c1
St-Mathieu, Pte. France 48°20N 4°45W 172 D2
St. Matthew I. U.S.A. 60°24N 172°42W 303 F4
St. Matthews Ky., U.S.A. 38°15N 85°39W 311 F11
St. Matthews S.C., U.S.A. 33°40N 80°46W 316 B9
St. Matthews, I. = Zadetkyi Kyun Burma 10°0N 98°25E 237 G2
St. Matthias Group Papua N. G. 1°30S 150°0E 286 A6
St-Maur-des-Fossés France 48°48N 2°29E 134 B3
St-Maurice France 48°49N 2°24E 134 B3
St-Maurice → Canada 46°21N 72°31W 298 C5
St. Mawes U.K. 50°10N 5°2W 169 G2
St-Maximin-la-Ste-Baume France 43°27N 5°52E 175 E9
St-Médard-en-Jalles France 44°53N 0°43W 174 D3
St-Méen-le-Grand France 48°11N 2°12W 172 D4
St. Meinrad U.S.A. 38°10N 86°49W 311 F10
St. Michael U.S.A. 63°29N 162°2W 303 E7
St. Michael's Cathedral Toronto, Canada 141 a3
St-Michel Canada 45°34N 73°37W 130 A2
St-Mihiel France 48°54N 5°32E 173 D12
St-Nazaire France 47°17N 2°12W 172 E4
St. Neots U.K. 52°14N 0°15W 169 E7
St-Nicolas-de-Port France 48°38N 6°18E 173 D13
St-Omer France 50°45N 2°15E 173 B9
St-Ouen France 48°56N 2°20E 134 A3
St-Palais-sur-Mer France 45°38N 1°5W 174 C2
St. Pamphile Canada 46°58N 69°48W 299 C6
St. Pancras International London, U.K. 125 a4
St-Pardoux-la-Rivière France 45°29N 0°45E 174 C4
St. Paris U.S.A. 40°8N 83°58W 311 D13
St-Pascal Canada 47°32N 69°48W 299 C6

St. Patricks Barbados 13°6N 59°30W 323 r
St. Patrick's Cathedral Dublin, Ireland 120 c1
St. Patrick's Cathedral New York, U.S.A. 132 c2
St. Patrick's Church Toronto, Canada 141 a1
St. Paul Canada 54°0N 111°17W 296 C6
St-Paul Alpes-de-Haute-Provence, France 44°31N 6°45E 175 D10
St-Paul Réunion 20°59S 55°17E 272 f
St. Paul Alaska, U.S.A. 57°7N 170°17W 303 H5
St. Paul Ind., U.S.A. 39°26N 85°38W 311 E11
St. Paul Minn., U.S.A. 44°56N 93°5W 308 C7
St. Paul Nebr., U.S.A. 41°13N 98°27W 308 E4
St-Paul → Canada 51°27N 57°42W 299 B8
St. Paul → Liberia 6°25N 10°48W 262 D2
St. Paul, Î. Ind. Oc. 38°55S 77°34E 273 H6
St-Paul-de-Fenouillet France 42°48N 2°30E 174 F6
St. Paul I. N.S., Canada 47°12N 60°9W 299 C7
St. Paul I. Alaska, U.S.A. 57°10N 170°15W 303 H5
St-Paul-lès-Dax France 43°44N 1°3W 174 E2
St. Paul's Bay Malta 35°57N 14°24E 206 F7
St. Paul's Cathedral London, U.K. 125 b4
St. Paul's Cray U.K. 51°23N 0°6E 125 B4
St-Péray France 44°57N 4°50E 175 D8
St. Pete Beach U.S.A. 27°43N 82°44W 317 H7
St. Peter U.S.A. 44°20N 93°57W 308 C7
St. Peter & St. Paul San Francisco, U.S.A. 136 a2
St. Peter Port U.K. 49°26N 2°33W 169 H5
St. Peters N.S.W., Australia 33°55S 151°11E 139 B2
St. Peters N.S., Canada 45°40N 60°53W 299 C7
St. Peters P.E.I., Canada 46°25N 62°35W 299 C7
St. Peters Montserrat 16°43N 62°13W 323 p
St. Peters Mo., U.S.A. 38°48N 90°37W 310 F6
St. Peter's Square = San Pietro, Piazza Rome, Italy 136 b1
St. Petersburg = Sankt-Peterburg Russia 59°55N 30°20E 137 B1
St. Petersburg U.S.A. 27°46N 82°40W 317 H7
St. Petersburg Pulkovo Int. ✈ (LED) Russia 59°48N 30°18E 137 C1
St-Philbert-de-Grand-Lieu France 47°2N 1°39W 172 E5
St-Phillippe Réunion 21°21S 55°44E 272 f
St-Pie Canada 45°30N 72°54W 313 A12
St-Pierre Qué., Canada 45°27N 73°38W 130 B2
St-Pierre Martinique 14°45N 61°10W 322 j
St. Pierre Mauritius 20°13S 57°31E 272 e
St-Pierre Réunion 21°19S 55°28E 272 f
St-Pierre St-P. & M. 46°46N 56°12W 299 C8
St. Pierre Seychelles 9°20S 46°0E 273 E3
St-Pierre, L. Canada 46°12N 72°52W 298 C5
St-Pierre, Rade de Martinique 14°44N 61°11W 322 j
St-Pierre-de-la-Pointe-aux-Esquimaux = Havre-St.-Pierre Canada 50°18N 63°33W 299 B7
St-Pierre-d'Oléron France 45°57N 1°19W 174 C2
St-Pierre-en-Port France 49°48N 0°30E 172 C7
St-Pierre-et-Miquelon ☐ N. Amer. 46°55N 56°10W 299 C8
St-Pierre-le-Moûtier France 46°47N 3°7E 173 F10
St-Pierre-sur-Dives France 49°2N 0°1W 172 C6
St-Pieters Leew Belgium 50°47N 4°16E 116 B1
St-Pol-de-Léon France 48°41N 4°0W 172 D3
St-Pol-sur-Mer France 51°1N 2°20E 173 A9
St-Pol-sur-Ternoise France 50°23N 2°20E 173 B9
St-Pons France 43°30N 2°45E 174 E6
St-Pourçain-sur-Sioule France 46°18N 3°18E 173 F10
St-Priest France 45°42N 4°57E 175 C8
St-Quay-Portrieux France 48°39N 2°51W 172 D4
St-Quentin N.B., Canada 47°30N 67°23W 299 C6
St-Quentin Aisne, France 49°50N 3°16E 173 C10
St-Quentin, Étang de France 48°47N 2°0E 134 B1
St-Rambert-d'Albon France 45°17N 4°49E 175 C8
St-Raphaël France 43°25N 6°46E 175 E10
St. Regis U.S.A. 47°18N 115°6W 304 C6
St. Regis Falls U.S.A. 44°40N 74°32W 313 B10
St-Renan France 48°26N 4°37W 172 D2
St. Robert U.S.A. 37°50N 92°11W 310 G4
St-Saëns France 49°41N 1°16E 172 C8
St-Savin France 46°34N 0°53E 174 B4
St-Savinien France 45°53N 0°42W 174 C3
St. Sebastien, Tanjon' i Madag. 12°26S 48°44E 272 A2
St-Seine-l'Abbaye France 47°26N 4°47E 173 E11
St-Sernin-sur-Rance France 43°54N 2°35E 174 E6
St-Sever France 43°45N 0°35W 174 E3
St-Siméon Canada 47°51N 69°54W 299 C6
St. Simons I. U.S.A. 31°12N 81°15W 316 D8
St. Simons Island U.S.A. 31°9N 81°22W 316 D8
St. Stephen N.B., Canada 45°16N 67°17W 299 C6
St. Stephen S.C., U.S.A. 33°24N 79°55W 316 B10
St. Stephen's Basilica Budapest, Hungary 117 b2
St. Stephen's Cathedral = Stephansdom Vienna, Austria 142 b2
St. Stephen's Green Dublin, Ireland 120 c3
St-Stevens-Woluwe Belgium 50°52N 4°26E 116 A2
St-Sulpice France 43°46N 1°41E 174 E5
St-Sulpice-Laurière France 46°3N 1°29E 174 B5
St-Sulpice-les-Feuilles France 46°19N 1°21E 174 B5
St-Syprien = St-Cyprien France 42°37N 3°2E 174 F7
St. Teresa U.S.A. 29°55N 84°27W 316 F5
St-Thégonnec France 48°31N 3°57W 172 D3
St. Thomas = Charlotte Amalie U.S. Virgin Is. 18°21N 64°56W 321 C7
St. Thomas Canada 42°45N 81°10W 312 D3
St. Thomas Bay Malta 35°51N 14°34E 206 F8
St. Thomas I. U.S. Virgin Is. 18°20N 64°55W 321 C7
St-Tite Canada 46°45N 72°34W 298 C5
St-Trond = Sint-Truiden Belgium 50°48N 5°10E 170 D5
St-Tropez France 43°17N 6°38E 175 E10
St-Vaast-la-Hougue France 49°35N 1°17W 172 C5
St-Valery-en-Caux France 49°52N 0°43E 172 C7
St-Valéry-sur-Somme France 50°11N 1°38E 173 B8
St-Vallier France 46°38N 4°22E 173 F11
St-Vallier-de-Thiey France 43°42N 6°51E 175 E10
St-Varent France 46°53N 0°13W 172 F6
St-Vaury France 46°12N 1°46E 174 B5
St. Vidgeon's ☺ Australia 14°47S 134°53E 280 A1
St. Vincent = São Vicente C. Verde Is. 17°0N 25°0W 153 j
St. Vincent Italy 45°45N 7°39E 198 C4
St. Vincent W. Indies 13°15N 61°10W 323 n
St. Vincent, G. Australia 35°0S 138°0E 282 C3
St. Vincent & the Grenadines ■ W. Indies 13°0N 61°10W 323 n
St-Vincent-de-Paul Canada 45°36N 73°39W 130 A2
St-Vincent-de-Tyrosse France 43°39N 1°19W 174 E2
St. Vincent I. U.S.A. 29°42N 85°3W 317 F4
St. Vincent Passage W. Indies 13°30N 61°0W 321 D7
St-Vith Belgium 50°17N 6°9E 170 D6
St-Vivien-de-Médoc France 45°25N 1°2W 174 C2
St. Walburg Canada 53°39N 109°12W 297 C7
St. Xavier Univ. U.S.A. 41°42N 87°42W 119 C2
St-Yrieix-la-Perche France 45°31N 1°12E 174 C5
Saintala India 20°26N 83°20E 244 D6
Ste-Adresse France 49°31N 0°5E 172 C7
Ste-Agathe-des-Monts Canada 46°3N 74°17W 298 C5
Ste-Anne Guadeloupe 16°13N 61°24W 322 e
Ste-Anne Martinique 14°25N 60°54W 322 j
Ste-Anne Réunion 21°4S 55°45E 272 f
Ste-Anne Seychelles 4°36S 55°31E 272 c
Ste-Anne, L. Canada 50°0N 67°42W 299 B6
Ste-Anne-des-Monts Canada 49°8N 66°30W 299 C6
Ste-Catherine Canada 45°24N 73°34W 130 B2
Ste-Croix Switz. 46°49N 6°34E 179 J2
Ste-Enimie France 44°22N 3°26E 174 D7
Ste-Foy-la-Grande France 44°50N 0°13E 174 D4
Ste. Genevieve U.S.A. 37°59N 90°2W 310 G6
Ste-Hélène, Î. Canada 45°31N 73°32W 130 A2
Ste-Hermine France 46°32N 1°4W 174 B2
Ste-Livrade-sur-Lot France 44°24N 0°36E 174 D4
Ste-Luce Martinique 14°28N 60°55W 322 j
Ste. Madeleine Trin. & Tob. 10°16N 61°26W 323 t
Ste-Marguerite Guadeloupe 16°23N 61°24W 322 e
Ste-Marguerite → Canada 50°9N 66°36W 299 B6
Ste-Marie Canada 46°26N 71°0W 299 C5
Ste. Marie Gabon 3°48S 11°1E 264 C2
Ste-Marie Guadeloupe 16°6N 61°33W 322 e
Ste-Marie Martinique 14°48N 61°1W 322 j
Ste-Marie Réunion 20°53S 55°33E 272 f
Ste-Marie, Ile = Boraha, Nosy Madag. 16°50S 49°55E 272 B2
Ste-Marie-aux-Mines France 48°15N 7°12E 173 D14
Ste-Marthe Guadeloupe 16°15N 61°15W 322 e
Ste-Maure-de-Touraine France 47°7N 0°37E 172 E7
Ste-Maxime France 43°19N 6°39E 175 E10
Ste-Menehould France 49°5N 4°54E 173 C11
Ste-Mère-Église France 49°24N 1°19W 172 C5
Ste-Rose Guadeloupe 16°20N 61°45W 322 e
Ste-Rose Réunion 21°8S 55°45E 272 f
Ste. Rose du Lac Canada 51°4N 99°30W 297 C9
Ste-Savine France 48°18N 4°3E 173 D11
Ste-Sigolène France 45°15N 4°14E 175 C8
Ste-Suzanne Réunion 20°54S 55°36E 272 f
Saintes France 45°45N 0°37W 174 C3
Saintes, Canal des Guadeloupe 15°55N 61°40W 322 e
Saintes, Îs. des Guadeloupe 15°50N 61°35W 322 e
Stes-Maries-de-la-Mer France 43°26N 4°26E 175 E8
Saintfield U.K. 54°28N 5°49W 166 B6
Saintonge France 45°40N 0°50W 174 C3
Saipal Nepal 29°50N 81°40E 243 E9
Saipan N. Marianas 15°12N 145°45E 302 e
Saipan Channel N. Marianas 15°5N 145°41E 302 e
Sairang India 23°50N 92°45E 241 D4
Sairecábur, Cerro Bolivia 22°43S 67°54W 334 A2
Saitama Japan 35°54N 139°38E 223 B11
Saitama ☐ Japan 36°25N 139°30E 223 A11
Saiteli = Kadınhanı Turkey 38°14N 32°13E 212 C5
Saiţi Moldova 46°33N 29°24E 183 D14
Saito Japan 32°3N 131°24E 222 E3
Saiwai Japan 35°32N 139°41E 140 B3
Saiyid Pakistan 33°7N 73°2E 242 C5
Saja-Besaya ⌂ Spain 43°10N 4°9W 194 B6
Sajama Bolivia 18°7S 69°0W 330 D4
Sajama, Nevado Bolivia 18°6S 68°54W 330 D4
Sajan Serbia 45°50N 20°20E 182 E5
Sajó → Hungary 47°56N 21°7E 182 C6
Sajókazinc = Kazincbarcika Hungary 48°17N 20°36E 182 B5
Sajószentpéter Hungary 48°12N 20°44E 182 B5
Sajum India 33°20N 79°0E 243 C8
Sak → S. Africa 30°52S 20°25E 270 D3
Saka Kenya 0°9S 39°20E 268 B4
Saka Kalat Pakistan 27°3N 65°3E 240 D2
Sakaba Nigeria 11°4N 5°35E 263 C6
Sakai Fukui, Japan 36°9N 136°16E 223 A8
Sakai Ōsaka, Japan 34°34N 135°27E 133 B1
Sakai Harbour Japan 34°36N 135°26E 133 B1
Sakaide Japan 34°19N 133°50E 222 C5
Sakaiminato Japan 35°38N 133°11E 222 B5
Sakākah Si. Arabia 30°0N 40°8E 246 D4
Sakakawea, L. U.S.A. 47°30N 101°25W 308 B3
Sakami → Canada 53°40N 76°40W 298 B4
Sakami, L. Canada 53°15N 77°0W 298 B4
Sâkâne, 'Erg i-n Mali 20°30N 1°30W 260 D4
Sakania Dem. Rep. of the Congo 12°43S 28°30E 269 E2
Sakar I. Papua N. G. 5°25S 148°6E 286 C5
Sakaraha Madag. 22°55S 44°32E 272 C1
Sakartvelo = Georgia ■ Asia 42°0N 43°0E 191 J6
Sakarya Turkey 40°48N 30°25E 212 B4
Sakarya ☐ Turkey 40°45N 30°25E 212 B4
Sakarya → Turkey 41°7N 30°39E 212 B4
Sakashima-Guntō Japan 24°46N 124°0E 221 M2
Sakassou Ivory C. 7°29N 5°19W 262 D3
Sakata Japan 38°55N 139°50E 220 E9
Sakawa Japan 33°28N 133°11E 222 D5
Sakchu N. Korea 40°23N 125°2E 224 B2
Sakeny → Madag. 20°0S 45°25E 272 C2
Sakété Benin 6°40N 2°45E 263 D5
Sakha ☐ Russia 66°0N 130°0E 215 C14
Sakhalin Russia 51°0N 143°0E 215 D15
Sakhalinskiy Zaliv Russia 54°0N 141°0E 215 D15
Sakhi Gopal India 19°58N 85°50E 244 E7
Şaki Azerbaijan 41°10N 47°5E 191 K8
Šakiai Lithuania 54°59N 23°2E 184 D10
Sakiz-Adasi = Chios Greece 38°27N 26°9E 205 C8
Sakmara → Russia 51°46N 55°1E 216 B5
Sakoli India 21°5N 79°59E 244 D4
Sakon Nakhon Thailand 17°10N 104°9E 236 D5
Sakra, Pulau Singapore 1°15N 103°41E 138 B2
Sakrand Pakistan 26°10N 68°15E 242 F3
Sakri Maharashtra, India 21°2N 74°20E 244 D2
Sakri Maharashtra, India 26°13N 86°5E 243 F12
Sakrivier S. Africa 30°54S 20°28E 270 D3
Sakskøbing Denmark 54°49N 11°39E 163 K5
Sakti India 22°2N 82°58E 243 H10
Saku Japan 36°17N 138°31E 223 A10
Sakuma Japan 35°3N 137°49E 223 B9
Sakura Japan 35°43N 140°14E 223 B12
Sakurai Japan 34°30N 135°51E 223 C7
Sakurajima = On-Take Japan 31°35N 130°39E 222 F2
Saky Ukraine 45°9N 33°34E 189 K7
Säkylä Finland 61°4N 22°20E 162 F9
Sal C. Verde Is. 16°45N 22°55W 153 j
Sal → Russia 47°31N 40°45E 191 G5
Sal Rei C. Verde Is. 16°11N 22°53W 153 j
Sala Eritrea 16°53N 37°36E 257 D4
Šal'a Slovak Rep. 48°10N 17°50E 181 C10
Sala Sweden 59°58N 16°35E 162 E10
Sala → Eritrea 16°53N 37°36E 257 D4
Sala, O. → Chad 17°0N 20°53E 259 E4
Sala Consilina Italy 40°23N 15°36E 201 B8
Sala-y-Gómez Pac. Oc. 26°29S 105°28W 289 K17
Sala y Gómez Ridge Pac. Oc. 25°0S 98°0W 289 K18
Salaberry-de-Valleyfield Canada 45°15N 74°8W 313 A10
Salacgrīva Latvia 57°45N 24°21E 184 A11
Salada, L. Mexico 32°20N 115°40W 305 K6
Saladas Argentina 28°15S 58°40W 334 B4
Saladillo Argentina 35°40S 59°55W 334 D4
Saladin's Castle = Qal'at Salah el Din Syria 34°46N 36°15E 250 D7
Salado → B. Aires, Argentina 35°44S 57°22W 334 D4
Salado → La Pampa, Argentina 37°30S 67°0W 336 A3
Salado → Río Negro, Argentina 41°34S 65°3W 336 B3
Salado → Santa Fe, Argentina 31°40S 60°41W 334 C3
Salado → Tamaulipas, Mexico 26°52N 99°19W 314 H5
Salaga Ghana 8°31N 0°31W 263 D4
Şalāh Syria 32°40N 36°45E 250 F7
Şalāḩ ad Dīn ☐ Iraq 34°35N 43°35E 246 C4
Salahin Somalia 2°57N 46°26E 267 D6
Sălaj ☐ Romania 47°15N 23°0E 182 C8
Salakos Greece 36°17N 27°57E 206 E11
Salal Chad 14°48N 17°12E 259 F3
Salala Liberia 6°42N 10°7W 262 D2
Salala Sudan 21°17N 36°16E 256 C4
Şalālah Oman 16°56N 53°59E 249 C6
Salam Iraq 33°20N 44°20E 113 A2
Salamanca Chile 31°46S 70°59W 334 C1
Salamanca Madrid, Spain 40°25N 3°41W 127 B1
Salamanca Salamanca, Spain 40°58N 5°39W 194 E5
Salamanca N.Y., U.S.A. 42°10N 78°43W 312 D6
Salamanca ☐ Spain 40°57N 5°40W 194 E5
Salamat ☐ Chad 11°0N 20°30E 259 F4
Salamat, Bahr → Chad 9°20N 18°0E 259 G3
Salāmatābād Iran 35°39N 47°50E 246 C5
Salamina Colombia 5°25N 75°29W 328 B2
Salamina Greece 37°56N 23°30E 204 D5
Salamis Cyprus 35°11N 33°54E 207 E9
Salamonie L. U.S.A. 40°46N 85°37W 311 D11
Salar de Atacama Chile 23°30S 68°25W 334 A2
Salar de Uyuni Bolivia 20°30S 67°45W 330 E4
Sălard Romania 47°12N 22°3E 182 C7
Salas Spain 43°25N 6°15W 194 B4
Salas de los Infantes Spain 42°2N 3°17W 194 C7
Salatiga Indonesia 7°19S 110°30E 235 D4
Salavat Russia 53°21N 55°55E 186 D10
Salaverry Peru 8°15S 79°0W 330 B2
Salawati Indonesia 1°7S 130°52E 231 E8
Salawin △ Thailand 18°18N 97°40E 236 C1
Salay Phil. 8°52N 124°47E 233 G5
Salaya India 22°19N 69°35E 242 H3
Salayar Indonesia 6°7S 120°30E 231 F6
Salazar → Spain 42°40N 1°20W 196 C3
Salazie Réunion 21°2S 55°32E 272 f
Salazie, Cirque de Réunion 21°3S 55°30E 272 f
Salbris France 47°25N 2°3E 173 E9
S'Albufera Spain 39°47N 3°7E 206 B4
S'albufera d'es Grau Spain 39°56N 4°16E 206 B5
Salcantay, Nevado Peru 13°19S 72°33W 330 C3
Salcedo Phil. 11°9N 125°40E 233 F5
Sălciua Romania 46°24N 23°26E 183 D8
Salcombe U.K. 50°14N 3°47W 169 G4
Saldaña Spain 42°32N 4°48W 194 C6
Saldanha S. Africa 33°0S 17°58E 270 D2
Saldanha B. S. Africa 33°6S 18°0E 270 D2
Saldus Latvia 56°38N 22°30E 184 B9
Saldus ☐ Latvia 56°35N 22°30E 184 B9
Sale Vic., Australia 38°6S 147°6E 283 E7
Sale Burma 20°50N 94°45E 241 E5
Sale Italy 44°59N 8°48E 198 D5
Salé Morocco 34°3N 6°48W 260 B3
Sale Gt. Man., U.K. 53°26N 2°19W 168 D5
Sale City U.S.A. 31°16N 84°1W 316 D5
Salée, Rivière Guadeloupe 16°17N 61°33W 322 e
Salegard = Salekhard Russia 66°30N 66°35E 214 C7
Saleh, Teluk Indonesia 8°34S 117°52E 235 D5
Salekhard Russia 66°30N 66°35E 214 C7
Salelologa Samoa 13°41S 172°11W 287 V19
Salem India 11°40N 78°11E 245 J4
Salem Montserrat 16°45N 62°13W 323 p
Salem Fla., U.S.A. 29°53N 83°25W 316 F6
Salem Ill., U.S.A. 38°38N 88°57W 310 F8
Salem Ind., U.S.A. 38°36N 86°6W 311 F10
Salem Mass., U.S.A. 42°31N 70°53W 313 D14
Salem Mo., U.S.A. 37°39N 91°32W 308 G8
Salem N.H., U.S.A. 42°45N 71°12W 313 D13
Salem N.J., U.S.A. 39°34N 75°28W 309 F16
Salem N.Y., U.S.A. 43°10N 73°20W 313 C11
Salem Ohio, U.S.A. 40°54N 80°52W 312 F4
Salem Oreg., U.S.A. 44°56N 123°2W 304 D2
Salem S. Dak., U.S.A. 43°44N 97°23W 308 D5
Salem Va., U.S.A. 37°18N 80°3W 309 G13
Salemi Italy 37°49N 12°48E 200 E5
Sälen Sweden 61°20N 13°10E 162 C7
Salernes France 43°34N 6°15E 175 E10
Salerno Italy 40°41N 14°47E 201 B7
Salerno, G. di Italy 40°32N 14°42E 201 B7
Sales Brazil 4°2S 63°40W 329 D5
Salford U.K. 53°30N 2°18W 168 D5
Salgótarján Hungary 48°5N 19°47E 182 B4
Salgueiro Brazil 8°4S 39°6W 332 C3
Salher India 20°40N 73°55E 244 D1
Salhus Norway 60°30N 5°15E 162 D4
Salhyr → Ukraine 45°38N 35°1E 189 K8
Salibabu Indonesia 3°51N 126°40E 231 D7
Salibea = Salybia Trin. & Tob. 10°43N 61°2W 323 t
Salibia Dominica 15°30N 61°16W 323 k
Salida U.S.A. 38°32N 106°0W 304 G11
Salies-de-Béarn France 43°28N 0°56W 174 E3
Salihli Turkey 38°28N 28°8E 212 C3
Salihorsk Belarus 52°51N 27°27E 177 B14
Salin Burma 20°35N 94°40E 241 E5
Salina Italy 38°34N 14°50E 201 D7
Salina Kans., U.S.A. 38°50N 97°37W 308 F5
Salina Utah, U.S.A. 38°58N 111°51W 304 G8
Salina Cruz Mexico 16°10N 95°12W 319 D5
Salina di Margherita di Savoia ⌂ Italy 41°23N 16°4E 201 A9
Salinas = Salinópolis Brazil 0°40S 47°20W 332 B2
Salinas Brazil 16°10S 42°10W 333 E3
Salinas Ecuador 2°10S 80°58W 328 D1
Salinas Calif., U.S.A. 36°40N 121°39W 306 J5
Salinas → Guatemala 16°28N 90°31W 319 D6
Salinas → Calif., U.S.A. 36°45N 121°48W 306 J5
Salinas, B. das Angola 14°11S 12°21E 265 E2
Salinas, B. de Nic. 11°4N 85°45W 320 D2
Salinas, Pampa de las Argentina 31°58S 66°42W 334 C2
Salinas Ambargasta Argentina 29°0S 65°0W 334 B3
Salinas de Hidalgo Mexico 22°38N 101°43W 318 C4
Salinas Grandes Argentina 30°0S 65°0W 334 C3
Salinas Pueblo Missions ⌂ U.S.A. 34°6N 106°4W 305 J10
Salinas Valley U.S.A. 36°15N 121°15W 306 J5
Saline U.S.A. 42°10N 83°47W 311 B13
Saline → Ark., U.S.A. 33°10N 92°8W 314 E8
Saline → Kans., U.S.A. 38°52N 97°30W 308 F5
Saline B. Trin. & Tob. 10°42N 61°2W 323 t
Saline di Trapani e Paceco ⌂ Italy 37°59N 12°28E 200 E5
Saline I. Grenada 12°26N 61°28W 323 q
Salines, C. de ses Spain 39°16N 3°4E 206 B4
Salines, Étang des Martinique 14°24N 60°52W 322 j
Salines, Pt. Grenada 12°0N 61°48W 323 q
Salines, Pte. de Martinique 14°23N 60°53W 322 j
Salinópolis Brazil 0°40S 47°20W 332 B2
Salins-les-Bains France 46°58N 5°52E 173 F12
Salir Portugal 37°14N 8°2W 195 H2
Salisbury = Harare Zimbabwe 17°43S 31°2E 269 F3
Salisbury S. Austral., Australia 34°46S 138°38E 282 C3
Salisbury Dominica 15°26N 61°27W 323 k
Salisbury Wilts., U.K. 51°4N 1°47W 169 F6
Salisbury Md., U.S.A. 38°22N 75°36W 309 F16
Salisbury Mo., U.S.A. 39°25N 92°48W 310 E4
Salisbury N.C., U.S.A. 35°40N 80°29W 315 D14
Salisbury I. Canada 63°30N 77°0W 295 E16
Salisbury Plain U.K. 51°14N 1°55W 169 F6
Sălişte Romania 45°45N 23°56E 183 E8
Salitre → Brazil 9°29S 40°39W 332 C3
Salkehatchie → U.S.A. 32°37N 80°53W 316 C9
Şalkhad Syria 32°29N 36°43E 251 F7
Salkove Ukraine 48°15N 29°59E 183 B14
Salla Finland 66°50N 28°49E 160 C23
Sallanches France 45°55N 6°38E 175 C10
Sallent Spain 41°49N 1°54E 196 D6
Salles France 44°33N 0°52W 174 D3
Salles-Curan France 44°11N 2°48E 174 D6
Salling Denmark 56°40N 8°55E 163 H2
Salliq = Coral Harbour Canada 64°8N 83°10W 295 E15
Sallisaw U.S.A. 35°28N 94°47W 314 D7
Sallom Sudan 19°17N 37°6E 256 D4
Salluit Canada 62°14N 75°38W 295 E16
Sallyana Nepal 28°22N 82°10E 243 E10
Sallynoggin Ireland 53°17N 6°8W 120 B3
Salmān Pak Iraq 33°6N 44°34E 213 G11
Salmannsdorf Austria 48°14N 16°14E 142 A1
Salmās Iran 38°11N 44°47E 213 C11
Salmedina Spain 40°18N 3°35W 127 C2
Salmerón Spain 40°33N 2°29W 196 E2
Salmo Canada 49°10N 117°20W 296 D5
Salmon U.S.A. 45°11N 113°54W 304 D7
Salmon → B.C., Canada 54°3N 122°40W 296 C4
Salmon → Idaho, U.S.A. 45°51N 116°47W 304 D5
Salmon Arm Canada 50°40N 119°15W 296 C5
Salmon Gums Australia 32°59S 121°38E 279 F3
Salmon Pt. Canada 43°52N 77°15W 312 C7
Salmon River Mts. U.S.A. 44°50N 115°30W 304 D6
Salmon River Res. U.S.A. 43°32N 75°55W 313 C9
Salo C.A.R. 3°10N 16°8E 264 B3
Salo Finland 60°22N 23°10E 188 B2
Salò Italy 45°36N 10°31E 198 C7
Salobreña Spain 36°44N 3°35W 195 J7
Salome U.S.A. 33°47N 113°37W 307 M13
Salomea Poland 52°11N 20°55E 143 B1
Salomon, C. Martinique 14°30N 61°6W 322 j
Salon India 26°2N 81°27E 243 F9
Salon-de-Provence France 43°39N 5°6E 175 E9
Salonga → Dem. Rep. of the Congo 0°10S 19°50E 264 C4
Salonga-Nord △ Dem. Rep. of the Congo 1°55S 21°45E 264 C4
Salonga-Sud △ Dem. Rep. of the Congo 2°25S 21°0E 264 C4
Salonica = Thessaloniki Greece 40°38N 22°58E 202 F6
Salonta Romania 46°49N 21°42E 182 D6
Salop = Shropshire ☐ U.K. 52°36N 2°45W 169 E5
Salor → Spain 39°39N 7°3W 195 F3
Salou Spain 41°4N 1°8E 196 D6
Salou, C. de Spain 41°3N 1°10E 196 D6
Saloum → Senegal 13°50N 16°45W 262 C1
Salpausselkä Finland 61°3N 26°15E 188 B4
Salsacate Argentina 31°20S 65°5W 334 C2
Salses France 42°50N 2°55E 174 F6
Salsette I. India 19°2N 72°53E 130 A2
Salsk Russia 46°28N 41°30E 191 G5
Salso → Italy 37°6N 13°57E 200 E6
Salsomaggiore Terme Italy 44°49N 9°59E 198 D6
Salt Spain 41°59N 2°47E 196 D7
Salt → Alta., Canada 60°0N 112°25W 296 B6
Salt → Ariz., U.S.A. 33°23N 112°19W 305 K7
Salt → Mo., U.S.A. 39°28N 91°4W 310 E5
Salt Cay Bahamas 25°6N 77°18W 153 b
Salt Flats = Witte Pan Bonaire 12°3N 68°17W 322 h
Salt Fork Red → U.S.A. 34°27N 99°21W 314 D5
Salt L. N.S.W., Australia 30°6S 142°8E 281 E3
Salt L. Hawai'i, U.S.A. 21°21N 157°55W 302 K14
Salt Lake City = Bidhan Nagar India 22°35N 88°25E 124 B2
Salt Lake City U.S.A. 40°45N 111°53W 304 F8
Salt Range Pakistan 32°30N 72°25E 242 C5
Salt River S. Africa 34°6S 18°28E 118 A1
Salt Springs U.S.A. 29°21N 81°44W 317 F8
Salt Water L. India 22°33N 88°26E 124 B2
Salta Argentina 24°57S 65°25W 334 A2
Salta ☐ Argentina 24°48S 65°30W 334 A2
Saltara Italy 43°45N 12°50E 199 E9
Saltash U.K. 50°24N 4°14W 169 G3
Saltburn by the Sea U.K. 54°35N 0°58W 168 C7
Saltcoats U.K. 55°38N 4°47W 167 F4
Saltee Is. Ireland 52°7N 6°37W 166 D5
Salters U.S.A. 33°36N 79°51W 316 B10
Saltfjellet Norway 66°40N 15°15E 160 C16
Saltfjorden Norway 67°15N 14°10E 160 C16
Saltholm Denmark 55°38N 12°43E 163 J6
Salthólmavík Iceland 65°24N 21°57W 155 B5
Saltillo Mexico 25°25N 101°0W 318 B4
Salto Argentina 34°20S 60°15W 334 C3
Salto Uruguay 31°27S 57°50W 334 C4
Salto da Divisa Brazil 16°0S 39°57W 333 E4
Salto del Guaira Paraguay 24°3S 54°17W 335 A5
Salton City U.S.A. 33°18N 115°57W 307 M11
Salton Sea U.S.A. 33°15N 115°45W 307 M11
Saltpond Ghana 5°15N 1°3W 263 D4
Saltrod Norway 58°30N 8°49E 164 F5
Saltsburg U.S.A. 40°29N 79°27W 312 F5
Saltsjö-Duvnäs Sweden 59°18N 18°12E 139 B3
Saltsjöbaden Sweden 59°15N 18°20E 162 E12
Saluda U.S.A. 34°0N 81°46W 316 A8
Saluda → U.S.A. 34°1N 81°4W 316 A8
Salug Phil. 8°7N 122°47E 233 G4
Salûm Egypt 31°31N 25°7E 256 A2
Salûm, Khâlig el Egypt 31°35N 25°24E 256 A2
Salur India 18°27N 83°18E 244 E6
Salut, Is. du Fr. Guiana 5°15N 52°35W 329 B7
Saluzzo Italy 44°39N 7°29E 198 D4
Salvación, B. Chile 50°50S 75°10W 336 D1
Salvador Brazil 13°0S 38°30W 333 D4
Salvador Sask., Canada 52°10N 109°32W 297 C7
Salvador, El ■ Cent. Amer. 13°50N 89°0W 320 D2
Salvador, L. U.S.A. 29°43N 90°15W 315 G9
Salvaterra Brazil 0°46S 48°31W 332 B2
Salvaterra de Magos Portugal 39°1N 8°47W 195 F2
Salvisa U.S.A. 37°54N 84°51W 311 G12
Sálvora, I. de Spain 42°30N 8°58W 194 C2
Salween → Burma 16°31N 97°37E 241 G6
Salyan Azerbaijan 39°33N 48°59E 213 C13
Salybia Trin. & Tob. 10°43N 61°2W 323 t
Salza → Austria 47°40N 14°43E 180 D7
Salzach → Austria 48°12N 12°56E 180 C5
Salzburg Austria 47°48N 13°2E 180 D6
Salzburg ☐ Austria 47°15N 13°0E 180 D6
Salzburgen = Château-Salins France 48°50N 6°30E 173 D13
Salzgitter Germany 52°9N 10°19E 178 C6
Salzkotten Germany 51°40N 8°37E 178 D4
Salzwedel Germany 52°52N 11°10E 178 C7
Sam Gabon 0°58N 11°16E 264 B2
Sam India 26°50N 70°31E 242 F4
Sam Neua Laos 20°29N 104°5E 228 G5
Sam Ngao Thailand 17°18N 99°0E 236 D2
Sam Rayburn Res. U.S.A. 31°4N 94°5W 314 F7
Sam Rong, Laem Thailand 9°35N 100°4E 237 b
Sam Son Vietnam 19°44N 105°54E 236 C5
Sama de Langreo = Langreo Spain 43°18N 5°40W 194 B5
Samacimbo Angola 13°33S 16°59E 265 E3
Şamad Oman 22°48N 58°9E 249 B7
Samagaltay Russia 50°36N 95°3E 217 B13
Samā'il Oman 23°40N 57°50E 249 B7
Samaipata Bolivia 18°9S 63°52W 331 D5
Samal Phil. 7°5N 125°42E 233 H5
Samal I. Phil. 7°3N 125°44E 233 H5
Samales Group Phil. 6°0N 122°0E 233 J3
Samalkot India 17°3N 82°13E 244 F6
Samâlût Egypt 28°20N 30°42E 256 B3
Samana India 30°10N 76°13E 242 D7
Samana Cays Bahamas 23°3N 73°45W 321 B5
Samandağ Turkey 36°5N 35°59E 250 B6
Samandıra Turkey 40°59N 29°13E 203 F13
Samanga Tanzania 8°20S 39°13E 269 D4
Samangān ☐ Afghan. 36°15N 68°3E 240 A3
Samangwa Dem. Rep. of the Congo 4°23S 24°10E 265 C4
Samani Japan 42°7N 142°56E 220 C11
Samanli Dağları Turkey 40°32N 29°10E 203 F13
Samannûd Egypt 30°57N 31°14E 251 H2
Samar Phil. 12°0N 125°0E 233 F5
Samar ☐ Phil. 11°50N 125°0E 233 F5
Samar Sea Phil. 12°0N 124°15E 232 E5
Samara Russia 53°8N 50°6E 190 D10
Samara → Russia 53°10N 50°4E 190 D10
Samara → Ukraine 48°28N 35°7E 189 H8
Samarai Papua N. G. 10°39S 150°41E 286 F6
Samaria = Shōmrōn West Bank 32°15N 35°13E 251 F6
Samaria West Bank 32°17N 35°12E 251 F6
Samaria △ Greece 35°17N 23°58E 207 E4
Samariapo Venezuela 5°15N 67°48W 328 B4
Samarinda Indonesia 0°30S 117°9E 235 C5
Samarkand = Samarqand Uzbekistan 39°40N 66°55E 217 E7
Samarkandskiy = Temirtau Kazakhstan 50°5N 72°56E 217 B8
Samarqand Uzbekistan 39°40N 66°55E 217 E7
Samarqand ☐ Uzbekistan 39°35N 66°35E 217 E7
Sāmarrā' Iraq 34°12N 43°52E 213 E10
Samastipur India 25°50N 85°50E 243 G11
Samatya Turkey 40°59N 28°55E 122 C1
Samaúma Brazil 7°50S 60°2W 331 B5
Şamaxi Azerbaijan 40°38N 48°37E 191 K9
Samba Equateur, Dem. Rep. of the Congo 0°13N 21°25E 264 B4
Samba Maniema, Dem. Rep. of the Congo 4°38S 26°22E 265 C5
Samba Jammu & Kashmir, India 32°32N 75°10E 243 C6
Samba Caju Angola 8°46S 15°24E 265 D3
Sambaíba Brazil 7°8S 45°21W 332 C2
Sambalpur India 21°28N 84°4E 244 D7
Sambar, Tanjung Indonesia 2°59S 110°19E 235 C4
Sambas Indonesia 1°20N 109°20E 235 B3
Sambava Madag. 14°16S 50°10E 272 A3
Sambawizi Zimbabwe 18°24S 26°13E 269 F2
Sambhajinagar = Aurangabad India 19°50N 75°23E 244 E2
Sambhal India 28°35N 78°37E 243 E8
Sambhar India 26°52N 75°6E 242 F6
Sambhar L. India 26°55N 75°12E 242 F6
Sambiase Italy 38°58N 16°17E 201 D9
Sambir Ukraine 49°30N 23°10E 185 J10
Sambo Angola 13°3S 16°8E 265 E3
Sambo Indonesia 3°22S 118°52E 235 C5
Samboja Indonesia 1°1S 117°1E 235 C5
Sambor Cambodia 12°46N 106°0E 236 F6
Sambor Prei Kuk Cambodia 12°46N 105°58E 236 F5
Samborombón, B. Argentina 36°5S 57°20W 334 D4
Sambuca di Sicilia Italy 37°39N 13°7E 200 E6
Samburu ⌂ Kenya 0°37N 37°31E 268 B4
Samcheok S. Korea 37°30N 129°10E 224 D4
Same Tanzania 4°2S 37°38E 268 C4
Samer France 50°38N 1°44E 173 B8
Samet, Ko Thailand 12°34N 101°27E 236 F3
Samfya Zambia 11°22S 29°31E 269 E2
Samḩah Yemen 12°15N 53°5E 249 D6
Samḩān, Jabal Oman 17°12N 54°55E 249 C6
Sami Greece 38°15N 20°39E 207 C2
Samka Burma 20°9N 96°57E 241 E6
Şämkir Azerbaijan 40°50N 46°0E 191 K8
Şamlı Turkey 39°48N 27°51E 205 B9
Sammanturai Sri Lanka 7°36N 81°39E 245 L5
Samnah Si. Arabia 25°10N 37°15E 246 E3
Samnū Libya 27°15N 14°55E 258 C2
Samo Alto Chile 30°22S 71°0W 334 C1
Samoa ■ Pac. Oc. 14°0S 172°0W 287 V20
Samoan Is. Pac. Oc. 14°0S 171°0W 287 V20
Samobor Croatia 45°47N 15°44E 199 C12
Samoëns France 46°5N 6°45E 173 F13
Samokov Bulgaria 42°18N 23°35E 202 D7
Šamorín Slovak Rep. 48°2N 17°19E 181 C10
Samorogouan Burkina Faso 11°21N 4°57W 262 C4
Samos Greece 37°45N 26°50E 205 D8
Samoš Serbia 45°13N 20°46E 182 E5
Samos Spain 42°44N 7°20W 194 C3
Samos ☐ Greece 37°45N 26°50E 205 D8
Samoset U.S.A. 27°28N 82°33W 317 H7
Samosir Indonesia 2°55N 98°50E 234 B1
Samothráki = Mathraki Greece 39°48N 19°31E 206 B9
Samothraki Greece 40°28N 25°28E 203 F9
Samoylovka Russia 51°12N 43°43E 190 E6
Sampa Angola 10°38S 18°56E 265 E3
Sampa Ghana 8°0N 2°36W 262 D4
Sampacho Argentina 33°20S 64°50W 334 C3
Sampalan Indonesia 8°41S 115°34E 231 K18
Sampaloc Phil. 14°36N 120°59E 127 B1
Sampang Indonesia 7°11S 113°13E 235 D4
Samper de Calanda Spain 41°11N 0°28W 196 D4
Sampéyre Italy 44°34N 7°11E 198 D4
Samphan Thawong Thailand 13°44N 100°31E 113 B2
Sampit Indonesia 2°34S 113°0E 235 C4
Sampit → Indonesia 2°44S 112°54E 235 C4
Sampit, Teluk Indonesia 3°5S 113°3E 235 C4
Sampun Papua N. G. 5°21S 152°8E 286 C7
Samrong Cambodia 14°15N 103°30E 236 E4
Samseon S. Korea 37°34N 127°0E 137 B2
Samsø Denmark 55°50N 10°35E 163 J4
Samsø Bælt Denmark 55°45N 10°45E 163 J4
Samson U.S.A. 31°7N 86°3W 316 D3
Samsun Turkey 41°15N 36°22E 212 B7
Samsun ☐ Turkey 41°10N 36°10E 212 B7
Samtah Si. Arabia 16°36N 42°56E 248 C3
Samtredia Georgia 42°7N 42°24E 191 J6
Samuel Smith Park Canada 43°35N 79°30W 141 B1
Samui, Ko Thailand 9°30N 100°0E 237 b
Samur → Russia 41°53N 48°32E 191 K9
Samurskiy Khrebet Russia 41°55N 47°11E 191 K8
Samusole Dem. Rep. of the Congo 10°2S 24°0E 265 E4
Samut Prakan Thailand 13°40N 100°36E 113 B2
Samut Sakhon Thailand 13°32N 100°17E 236 F3
Samut Songkhram Thailand 13°24N 100°1E 236 F3
Samwari Pakistan 28°30N 66°46E 242 E2
San Mali 13°15N 4°57W 262 C4
San → Cambodia 13°32N 105°57E 236 F5
San → Poland 50°45N 21°51E 185 H8
San Adrián Spain 42°20N 1°56W 196 C3
San Adrián, C. de Spain 43°21N 8°50W 194 B2
San Agustin Colombia 1°53N 76°16W 328 C2
San Agustin Romblon, Phil. 12°34N 122°6E 232 E4
San Agustin, C. Phil. 6°20N 126°13E 233 H6
San Agustín de Valle Fértil Argentina 30°35S 67°30W 334 C2
San Ambrosio Pac. Oc. 26°28S 79°53W 326 F3
San Andreas U.S.A. 38°12N 120°41W 306 G6
San Andres Catanduanes, Phil. 13°36N 124°6E 232 E5
San Andres Romblon, Phil. 13°19N 122°41E 232 E4
San Andres Romblon, Phil. 12°31N 122°2E 232 E4
San Andrés Barcelona, Spain 41°26N 2°11E 114 A2
San Andrés, I. de Caribbean 12°42N 81°46W 320 D3
San Andrés del Rabanedo Spain 42°37N 5°36W 194 C5
San Andres Mts. U.S.A. 33°0N 106°30W 305 K10
San Andres Pt. Phil. 13°34N 121°52E 232 E3
San Andrés Tuxtla Mexico 18°27N 95°13W 319 D5
San Angel Mexico 19°20N 99°11W 128 B1
San Angelo U.S.A. 31°28N 100°26W 314 F4
San Angelo Raffaele Venice, Italy 142 b2
San Anselmo U.S.A. 37°59N 122°34W 306 H4
San Antonio Belize 16°15N 89°2W 320 C2
San Antonio Chile 33°40S 71°40W 334 C1
San Antonio Phil. 14°57N 120°5E 232 D3
San Antonio N. Mex., U.S.A. 33°55N 106°52W 305 K10
San Antonio Tex., U.S.A. 29°25N 98°29W 314 G5
San Antonio Amazonas, Venezuela 3°30N 66°44W 328 C4
San Antonio Nueva Esparta, Venezuela 10°57N 63°54W 329 a
San Antonio → U.S.A. 28°30N 96°54W 314 G6
San Antonio, C. Argentina 36°15S 56°40W 334 D4
San Antonio, C. de Cuba 21°50N 84°57W 320 B3
San Antonio, C. de Spain 38°48N 0°12E 197 G5
San Antonio, Mt. U.S.A. 34°17N 117°38W 307 L9
San Antonio B. Phil. 8°38N 117°35E 233 G1
San Antonio de los Baños Cuba 22°54N 82°31W 320 B3
San Antonio de los Cobres Argentina 24°10S 66°17W 334 A2
San Antonio Oeste Argentina 40°40S 65°0W 336 B4
San Arcángelo Italy 40°14N 16°14E 201 B9
San Ardo U.S.A. 36°1N 120°54W 306 J6
San Augustín Canary Is. 27°47N 15°32W 153 e1
San Augustine U.S.A. 31°32N 94°7W 314 F7
San Bartolomé Canary Is. 28°59N 13°37W 153 e2
San Bartolomé de Tirajana Canary Is. 27°54N 15°34W 153 e1
San Bartolomeo in Galdo Italy 41°24N 15°1E 201 A8
San Basilio Italy 41°56N 12°35E 136 B2
San Benedetto del Tronto Italy 42°57N 13°53E 199 F10
San Benedetto Po Italy 45°2N 10°55E 198 C7
San Benedicto, I. Mexico 19°18N 110°49W 318 D2
San Benito U.S.A. 26°8N 97°38W 314 H6
San Benito → U.S.A. 36°53N 121°34W 306 J5
San Benito Mt. U.S.A. 36°22N 120°37W 306 J6
San Bernardino U.S.A. 34°7N 117°19W 307 L9
San Bernardino Mts. U.S.A. 34°10N 116°45W 307 L10
San Bernardino Str. Phil. 12°30N 124°10E 232 E5
San Bernardo Chile 33°40S 70°50W 334 C1
San Bernardo, I. de Colombia 9°45N 75°50W 328 B2
San-Beyse = Choybalsan Mongolia 48°4N 114°30E 219 B11
San Biagio Venice, Italy 142 b4
San Blas Mexico 26°5N 108°46W 318 B3
San Blas, Arch. de Panama 9°50N 78°31W 320 E4
San Blas, C. U.S.A. 29°40N 85°21W 316 F4
San Bonifacio Italy 45°24N 11°16E 199 C8
San Borja Bolivia 14°50S 66°52W 330 C4
San Borja Lima, Peru 12°6S 76°59W 124 B3
San Bòvio Italy 45°27N 9°18E 128 B2
San Bruno, Pt. U.S.A. 37°39N 122°22W 136 C2
San Bruno Mountain State Park ⌂ U.S.A. 37°41N 122°26W 136 B2
San Buenaventura = Ventura U.S.A. 34°17N 119°18W 307 L7
San Buenaventura Bolivia 14°28S 67°35W 330 C4
San Buenaventura Coahuila, Mexico 27°5N 101°32W 318 B4
San Carlos = Butuku-Luba Eq. Guin. 3°29N 8°33E 263 E6
San Carlos = Sant Carles Spain 39°3N 1°34E 206 C2
San Carlos Argentina 33°50S 69°0W 334 C2
San Carlos Bolivia 17°24S 63°45W 331 D5
San Carlos Chile 36°10S 72°0W 334 D1
San Carlos Baja Calif. S., Mexico 24°47N 112°7W 318 C2
San Carlos Coahuila, Mexico 29°1N 100°51W 318 B4
San Carlos Nic. 11°12N 84°50W 320 D3
San Carlos Neg. Occ., Phil. 10°29N 123°25E 233 F4
San Carlos Pangasinan, Phil. 15°55N 120°20E 232 D3
San Carlos Uruguay 34°46S 54°58W 335 C5
San Carlos Ariz., U.S.A. 33°21N 110°27W 305 K8
San Carlos Amazonas, Venezuela 1°55N 67°4W 328 C4
San Carlos Cojedes, Venezuela 9°40N 68°36W 328 B4
San Carlos de Bariloche Argentina 41°10S 71°25W 336 B2
San Carlos de Bolívar Argentina 36°15S 61°6W 334 D3
San Carlos de la Rápita = Sant Carles de la Ràpita Spain 40°37N 0°35E 196 E5
San Carlos de Rio Negro Venezuela 1°55N 67°4W 328 C4
San Carlos del Zulia Venezuela 9°1N 71°55W 328 B3
San Carlos L. U.S.A. 33°11N 110°32W 305 K8
San Carlos Park U.S.A. 26°28N 81°49W 317 J8

San Cataldo Italy 37°29N 13°59E 200 E6
San Celoni = Sant Celoni
Spain 41°42N 2°30E 196 D7
San Clemente Chile 35°30S 71°29W 334 D1
San Clemente Spain 39°24N 2°25W 197 F2
San Clemente Calif., U.S.A. 33°26N 117°37W 307 M9
San Clemente I. U.S.A. 32°53N 118°29W 307 N8
San Cristóbal = Es Migjorn Gran
Spain 39°57N 4°3E 206 B5
San Cristóbal B. Aires, Argentina 34°38S 58°23W 117 B2
San Cristóbal Santa Fe, Argentina 30°20S 61°10W 334 C3
San Cristóbal Colombia 2°18S 73°2W 328 D3
San Cristóbal Dom. Rep. 18°25N 70°6W 321 C5
San Cristóbal Solomon Is. 10°30S 161°0E 287 N11
San Cristobal Madrid, Spain 40°25N 3°35W 127 B2
San Cristóbal Venezuela 7°46N 72°14W 328 B3
San Cristóbal, Cerro Chile 33°25S 70°38W 137 B2
San Cristóbal, I. Ecuador 0°50S 89°26W 330 a
San Cristóbal, Virgen del
Chile 33°25S 70°38W 137 B2
San Cristóbal de La Laguna = La Laguna Canary Is. 28°28N 16°18W 153 e1
San Cristóbal de las Casas
Mexico 16°45N 92°38W 319 D6
San Cristoforo Italy 45°26N 9°9E 128 B1
San Damiano d'Asti Italy 44°50N 8°4E 198 D5
San Daniele del Friuli Italy 46°9N 13°1E 199 B10
San Diego Calif., U.S.A. 32°42N 117°9W 307 N9
San Diego Tex., U.S.A. 27°46N 98°14W 314 H5
San Diego, C. Argentina 54°40S 65°10W 336 D3
San Diego de la Unión
Mexico 21°28N 100°52W 318 C4
San Diego Int. ✈ (SAN)
U.S.A. 32°44N 117°11W 307 N9
San Dimitri, Ras Malta 36°4N 14°11E 206 E6
San Dimitri Point = San Dimitri, Ras Malta 36°4N 14°11E 206 E6
San Donà di Piave Italy 45°38N 12°34E 199 C9
San Donato Milanese Italy 45°24N 9°16E 128 B2
Sân el Hagar Egypt 30°58N 31°52E 251 H2
San Estanislao Paraguay 24°39S 56°26W 334 A4
San Esteban △ Venezuela 10°24N 67°58W 328 A4
San Esteban de Gormaz
Spain 41°34N 3°13W 196 D1
San Eugenio = Artigas
Uruguay 30°20S 56°30W 334 C4
San Felice Circeo Italy 41°14N 13°5E 200 A6
San Felice sul Panaro Italy 44°50N 11°8E 199 D8
San Felipe Chile 32°43S 70°42W 334 C1
San Felipe Colombia 1°55N 67°6W 328 C4
San Felipe Baja Calif., Mexico 31°1N 114°52W 318 A2
San Felipe Phil. 15°4N 120°4E 232 D3
San Felipe Venezuela 10°20N 68°44W 328 A4
San Felipe ➔ U.S.A. 33°10N 115°49W 307 M11
San Félix Chile 28°56S 70°28W 334 B1
San Félix Pac. Oc. 26°23S 80°0W 326 F2
San Fernando = Sant Ferran
Spain 38°42N 1°28E 206 D1
San Fernando Chile 34°30S 71°0W 334 C1
San Fernando Tamaulipas, Mexico 24°51N 98°10W 319 C5
San Fernando Cebu, Phil. 10°10N 123°42E 233 F4
San Fernando La Union, Phil. 16°40N 120°23E 232 C3
San Fernando Pampanga, Phil. 15°5N 120°37E 232 D3
San Fernando Romblon, Phil. 12°18N 122°36E 232 E4
San Fernando Cádiz, Spain 36°28N 6°17W 195 J4
San Fernando Trin. & Tob. 10°16N 61°28W 323 t
San Fernando Calif., U.S.A. 34°17N 118°26W 307 L8
San Fernando de Apure
Venezuela 7°54N 67°15W 328 B4
San Fernando de Atabapo
Venezuela 4°3N 67°42W 328 C4
San Fernando di Púglia
Italy 41°18N 16°5E 201 A9
San Francesco di Paola Venice, Italy 142 b4
San Francique = Erin
Trin. & Tob. 10°5N 61°39W 323 t
San Francisco Córdoba, Argentina 31°30S 62°5W 334 C3
San Francisco Bolivia 15°16S 65°31W 331 D4
San Francisco Peru 12°36S 73°49W 330 C3
San Francisco Agusan del S., Phil. 8°30N 125°56E 233 G5
San Francisco Cebu, Phil. 10°39N 124°23E 233 F5
San Francisco Quezon, Phil. 13°21N 122°31E 232 E4
San Francisco S. Leyte, Phil. 10°4N 125°9E 233 F5
San Francisco Calif., U.S.A. 37°46N 122°23W 136 B2
San Francisco ➔ U.S.A. 32°59N 109°22W 305 K9
San Francisco, C. de
Colombia 6°18N 77°29W 328 B2
San Francisco, Paso de
S. Amer. 27°0S 68°0W 334 B2
San Francisco B. U.S.A. 37°39N 122°14W 136 B3
San Francisco Culhuacán
Mexico 19°19N 99°8W 128 C2
San Francisco de Macanao
Venezuela 11°1N 64°17W 329 a
San Francisco de Macorís
Dom. Rep. 19°19N 70°15W 321 C5
San Francisco del Monte de Oro
Argentina 32°36S 66°8W 334 C2
San Francisco del Oro
Mexico 26°52N 105°51W 318 B3
San Francisco della Vigna Venice, Italy 142 b3
San Francisco Int. ✈ (SFO)
U.S.A. 37°37N 122°22W 306 H4
San Francisco Javier = Sant Francesc de Formentera
Spain 38°42N 1°26E 206 D1
San Fratello Italy 38°1N 14°36E 201 D7
San Fruttuoso Italy 45°34N 9°14E 128 A2
San Gabriel Chile 33°47S 70°15W 334 C1
San Gabriel Ecuador 0°36N 77°49W 328 C2
San Gabriel Calif., U.S.A. 34°5N 118°5W 126 B4
San Gabriel ➔ U.S.A. 33°58N 118°5W 126 C4
San Gabriel Chilac
Mexico 18°19N 97°21W 319 D5
San Gabriel Mts. U.S.A. 34°17N 117°38W 307 L9
San Gavino Monreale Italy 39°33N 8°47E 200 C1
San Gerardo Venice, Italy 142 c1
San Geremia Venice, Italy 142 a2
San German Puerto Rico 18°4N 67°4W 321 b
San Giacomo dall'Orio Venice, Italy 142 b2
San Gil Colombia 6°33N 73°8W 328 B3
San Giljan = St. Julian's
Malta 35°55N 14°29E 206 F7
San Gimignano Italy 43°28N 11°2E 198 E8
San Giobbe Venice, Italy 142 a2
San Giorgio degli Schiavoni, Scuola di Venice, Italy 142 b3
San Giórgio di Nogaro
Italy 45°50N 13°13E 199 C10
San Giórgio Iónico Italy 40°27N 17°23E 201 B10
San Giorgio Maggiore Venice, Italy 142 c3
San Giorgio Maggiore, Isola di Venice, Italy 142 c3
San Giovani e Paolo Venice, Italy 142 b3
San Giovanni Bianco Italy 45°52N 9°39E 198 C6
San Giovanni in Bragora Venice, Italy 142 b3
San Giovanni in Fiore
Italy 39°15N 16°42E 201 C9
San Giovanni in Persiceto
Italy 44°38N 11°11E 199 D8
San Giovanni Rotondo
Italy 41°42N 15°44E 199 G12
San Giovanni Valdarno
Italy 43°34N 11°32E 199 E8
San Giuliano Milanese
Italy 45°24N 9°17E 128 B2
San Giuliano Terme Italy 43°46N 10°26E 198 E7
San Gorgonio Mt.
U.S.A. 34°6N 116°50W 307 L10
San Gottardo, P. del Switz. 46°33N 8°33E 179 J4
San Gregorio Uruguay 32°37S 55°40W 335 C4
San Gregorio Calif., U.S.A. 37°20N 122°23W 306 H4
San Guillermo △
Argentina 27°50S 69°45W 334 B2
San Guiseppe Jato Italy 37°57N 13°11E 200 E6
San Ignacio Belize 17°10N 89°5W 320 C2
San Ignacio Beni, Bolivia 14°53S 65°36W 331 C4
San Ignacio Santa Cruz, Bolivia 16°20S 60°55W 331 D5
San Ignacio Baja Calif. S., Mexico 27°27N 112°51W 318 B2
San Ignacio Paraguay 26°52S 57°3W 334 B4
San Ignacio Peru 5°8S 78°59W 330 B2
San Ignacio, L. Mexico 26°54N 113°13W 318 B2
San Ildefonso Phil. 15°4N 120°56E 232 D3
San Ildefonso, C. Phil. 16°0N 122°1E 232 C4
San Ildefonso Pen. Phil. 16°9N 122°5E 232 C4
San Isidro Argentina 34°29S 58°31W 334 C4
San Isidro Lima, Peru 12°5S 77°2W 124 B2
San Isidro Phil. 6°50N 126°5E 233 H6
San Isidro de Potot = Burgos
Phil. 16°4N 119°52E 232 C2
San Jacinto Colombia 9°50N 75°8W 328 B2
San Jacinto Phil. 12°34N 123°44E 232 E4
San Jacinto Calif., U.S.A. 33°47N 116°57W 307 M10
San Jaime = Sant Jaume
Spain 39°54N 4°4E 206 B5
San Javier Misiones, Argentina 27°55S 55°5W 335 B4
San Javier Santa Fe, Argentina 30°40S 59°55W 334 C4
San Javier Beni, Bolivia 14°34S 64°42W 331 C5
San Javier Santa Cruz, Bolivia 16°18S 62°30W 331 D5
San Javier Chile 35°40S 71°45W 334 D1
San Javier Spain 37°49N 0°50W 197 H4
San Jerónimo Lidice
Mexico 19°19N 99°14W 128 C1
San Jerónimo Taviche
Mexico 16°44N 96°35W 319 D5
San Joaquín Bolivia 13°4S 64°49W 331 C5
San Joaquín Santiago, Chile 33°29S 70°35W 137 B2
San Joaquin Phil. 10°35N 122°8E 233 F4
San Joaquin Calif., U.S.A. 36°36N 120°11W 306 J6
San Joaquín ➔ Bolivia 13°8S 63°41W 331 C5
San Joaquin ➔ Calif., U.S.A. 38°4N 121°51W 306 G5
San Joaquín, Cerro Ecuador 0°53S 89°30W 330 a
San Joaquin Valley
U.S.A. 37°20N 121°0W 306 J6
San Jon U.S.A. 35°6N 103°20W 305 J12
San Jordi = Sant Jordi
Spain 39°33N 2°46E 206 B3
San Jorge Argentina 31°54S 61°50W 334 C3
San Jorge Solomon Is. 8°28S 159°38E 287 M10
San Jorge, B. Mexico 31°20N 113°20W 318 A2
San Jorge, G. Argentina 46°0S 66°0W 336 C3
San José = San Josep Spain 38°55N 1°18E 206 D1
San José Argentina 32°12S 58°15W 334 C4
San José Costa Rica 9°55N 84°2W 320 E3
San José Guatemala 14°0N 90°50W 320 D1
San Jose N. Marianas 14°58N 145°37E 302 e
San José Mind. Occ., Phil. 12°27N 121°4E 232 E3
San Jose Nueva Ecija, Phil. 15°45N 120°55E 232 D3
San Jose Calif., U.S.A. 37°20N 121°53W 306 H5
San Jose Ill., U.S.A. 40°18N 89°36W 310 D7
San Jose ➔ U.S.A. 34°25N 106°45W 305 J10
San José, Golfo Argentina 42°20S 64°18W 336 B4
San José, I. Mexico 25°0N 110°38W 318 C2
San José de Buenavista
Phil. 10°45N 121°56E 233 F3
San José de Chiquitos
Bolivia 17°53S 60°50W 331 D5
San José de Feliciano
Argentina 30°26S 58°46W 334 C4
San José de Guanipa
Venezuela 8°53N 64°9W 329 B5
San José de Jáchal
Argentina 30°15S 68°46W 334 C2
San José de Mayo
Uruguay 34°27S 56°40W 334 C4
San José de Ocuné
Colombia 4°15N 70°20W 328 C3
San José de Uchapiamonas
Bolivia 14°13S 68°5W 330 C4
San José del Cabo Mexico 23°3N 109°41W 318 C3
San José del Guaviare
Colombia 2°35N 72°38W 328 C3
San José del Monte Phil. 14°49N 121°3E 232 D3
San José do Anauá Brazil 0°58N 61°22W 329 C5
San José Río Hondo
Mexico 19°26N 99°14W 128 B1
San Josep Spain 38°55N 1°18E 206 D1
San Juan Argentina 31°30S 68°30W 334 C2
San Juan Antioquia, Colombia 8°46N 76°32W 328 B2
San Juan Curaçao 12°15N 69°6W 322 g
San Juan Ica, Peru 15°22S 75°7W 330 D2
San Juan Batangas, Phil. 13°50N 121°24E 232 E3
San Juan S. Leyte, Phil. 10°16N 125°10E 233 F5
San Juan Puerto Rico 18°28N 66°7W 321 C6
San Juan Trin. & Tob. 10°39N 61°29W 323 t
San Juan □ Argentina 31°9S 69°0W 334 C2
San Juan ➔ Argentina 32°20S 67°25W 334 C2
San Juan ➔ Bolivia 21°2S 65°19W 331 E4
San Juan ➔ Colombia 4°3N 77°27W 328 C2
San Juan ➔ Nic. 10°56N 83°42W 320 D3
San Juan ➔ Manila, Phil. 14°35N 121°0E 127 B2
San Juan ➔ Utah, U.S.A. 37°16N 110°26W 305 H8
San Juan ➔ Nueva Esparta, Venezuela 10°56N 63°57W 329 a
San Juan ➔ Sucre, Venezuela 10°14N 62°38W 329 A5
San Juan, C. Argentina 54°44S 63°44W 336 D4
San Juan, C. Eq. Guin. 1°5N 9°20E 264 B1
San Juan Bautista = Sant Joan de Labritja Spain 39°5N 1°31E 206 C2
San Juan Bautista = Villahermosa
Mexico 17°59N 92°55W 319 D6
San Juan Bautista Chile 33°37S 78°50W 330 c
San Juan Bautista
Paraguay 26°37S 57°6W 334 B4
San Juan Bautista Calif., U.S.A. 36°51N 121°32W 306 J5
San Juan Bautista Venezuela 11°1N 63°56W 329 a
San Juan Capistrano
U.S.A. 33°30N 117°40W 307 M9
San Juan Cr. ➔ U.S.A. 35°40N 120°22W 306 J5
San Juan de Aragón
Mexico 19°28N 99°4W 128 B2
San Juan de Aragón, Parque
Mexico 19°27N 99°4W 128 B2
San Juan de Guadelupe
Mexico 24°38N 102°44W 318 C4
San Juan de Guía, Cabo de
Colombia 11°21N 73°59W 328 A3
San Juan de la Costa
Mexico 24°20N 110°41W 318 C2
San Juan de los Lagos
Mexico 21°15N 102°18W 318 C4
San Juan de los Morros
Venezuela 9°55N 67°21W 328 B4
San Juan de Lurigancho
Peru 11°59S 77°0W 124 A2
San Juan de Manapiare
Venezuela 5°15N 66°5W 328 B4
San Juan de Villa Hermosa = Villahermosa Mexico 17°59N 92°55W 319 D6
San Juan del César
Colombia 10°46N 73°1W 328 A3
San Juan del Monte Phil. 14°36N 121°1E 127 B2
San Juan del Norte Nic. 10°58N 83°40W 320 D3
San Juan del Norte, B. de
Nic. 11°0N 83°40W 320 D3
San Juan del Río Mexico 20°23N 100°0W 319 C5
San Juan del Sur Nic. 11°20N 85°51W 320 D2
San Juan I. U.S.A. 48°32N 123°5W 306 B3
San Juan Island △ U.S.A. 48°35N 123°8W 306 B4
San Juan Ixtacala Mexico 19°31N 99°10W 128 A1
San Juan Mts. U.S.A. 37°30N 107°0W 305 H10
San Julian Phil. 11°45N 125°27E 233 F5
San Just, Sierra de Spain 40°45N 0°49W 196 E4
San Just Desvern Spain 41°22N 2°4E 114 A1
San Justo B. Aires, Argentina 34°40S 58°33W 117 C1
San Justo Santa Fe, Argentina 30°47S 60°30W 334 C3
San Kamphaeng Thailand 18°45N 99°8E 236 C2
San Lázaro, C. Mexico 24°50N 112°18W 318 C2
San Leandro U.S.A. 37°42N 122°9W 306 H4
San Leonardo de Yagüe
Spain 41°51N 3°5W 196 D1
San Lorenzo = Sant Llorenç des Cardassar Spain 39°37N 3°17E 206 B4
San Lorenzo Argentina 32°45S 60°45W 334 C3
San Lorenzo Beni, Bolivia 15°22S 65°48W 331 D4
San Lorenzo Tarija, Bolivia 21°26S 64°47W 331 E5
San Lorenzo Ecuador 1°15N 78°50W 328 C2
San Lorenzo Venice, Italy 142 b3
San Lorenzo Paraguay 25°20S 57°32W 334 B4
San Lorenzo ➔ Mexico 24°15N 107°24W 318 C3
San Lorenzo, I. Baja Calif., Mexico 28°38N 112°51W 318 B2
San Lorenzo, I. Peru 12°7S 77°15W 330 C2
San Lorenzo, Mte.
Argentina 47°40S 72°20W 336 C2
San Lorenzo de la Parrilla
Spain 39°51N 2°22W 196 F2
San Lorenzo de Morunys = Sant Llorenç de Morunys
Spain 42°8N 1°35E 196 C6
San Lorenzo Tezonco
Mexico 19°19N 99°3W 128 C2
San Lucas = Cabo San Lucas
Mexico 22°53N 109°54W 318 C3
San Lucas Bolivia 20°5S 65°7W 331 E4
San Lucas Baja Calif. S., Mexico 27°10N 112°14W 318 B2
San Lucas Calif., U.S.A. 36°8N 121°1W 306 J5
San Lucas, C. Mexico 22°52N 109°53W 318 C3
San Lúcido Italy 39°18N 16°3E 201 C9
San Luis = Entre Ríos
Bolivia 21°30S 64°25W 334 A3
San Luis = Sevilla
Colombia 4°16N 75°57W 328 C2
San Luis Argentina 33°20S 66°20W 334 C2
San Luis Pinar del Río, Cuba 22°17N 83°46W 320 B3
San Luis Guatemala 16°14N 89°27W 320 C2
San Luis Lima, Peru 12°4S 77°0W 124 B2
San Luis Ariz., U.S.A. 32°29N 114°47W 305 K6
San Luis Colo., U.S.A. 37°12N 105°25W 305 H11
San Luis □ Argentina 34°0S 66°0W 334 C2
San Luis, I. Mexico 29°58N 114°26W 318 B2
San Luis, L. de Bolivia 13°45S 64°0W 331 C5
San Luis, Sierra de
Argentina 32°30S 66°10W 334 C2
San Luis de la Paz
Mexico 21°18N 100°31W 318 C4
San Luis Obispo U.S.A. 35°17N 120°40W 307 K6
San Luis Potosí Mexico 22°9N 100°59W 318 C4
San Luis Potosí □ Mexico 23°0N 101°0W 318 C4
San Luis Res. U.S.A. 37°4N 121°5W 306 H5
San Luis Río Colorado
Mexico 32°29N 114°58W 318 A2
San Manuel Phil. 16°4N 120°40E 232 C3
San Manuel Ariz., U.S.A. 32°36N 110°38W 305 K8
San Marco Venice, Italy 142 b3
San Marco, C. Italy 39°51N 8°26E 200 C1
San Marco, Canale di Venice, Italy 142 b3
San Marco, Piazza Venice, Italy 142 b3
San Marco Argentano
Italy 39°33N 16°7E 201 C9
San Marco in Lámis
Italy 41°43N 15°38E 199 G12
San Marcos Colombia 8°39N 75°8W 328 B2
San Marcos Guatemala 14°59N 91°52W 320 D1
San Marcos Calif., U.S.A. 33°9N 117°10W 307 M9
San Marcos Tex., U.S.A. 29°53N 97°56W 314 G6
San Marcos, I. Mexico 27°13N 112°6W 318 B2
San Mariano Phil. 17°0N 122°2E 232 C4
San Marino San Marino 43°55N 12°30E 199 E9
San Marino Calif., U.S.A. 34°7N 118°5W 126 B4
San Marino ■ Europe 43°56N 12°25E 199 E9
San Martín = Tarapoto
Peru 6°30S 76°20W 330 B2
San Martín Antarctica 68°11S 67°0W 151 C17
San Martín Argentina 33°5S 68°28W 334 C2
San Martín Colombia 3°42N 73°42W 328 C3
San Martín Barcelona, Spain 41°24N 2°11E 114 A2
San Martín □ Peru 7°0S 76°50W 330 B2
San Martín ➔ Bolivia 13°8S 63°43W 331 C5
San Martín, L. Argentina 48°50S 72°50W 336 C2
San Martín de la Vega
Spain 40°13N 3°34W 194 E7
San Martín de los Andes
Argentina 40°10S 71°20W 336 B2
San Martín de Porras Peru 12°1S 77°5W 124 B2
San Martín de Valdeiglesias
Spain 40°21N 4°24W 194 E6
San Mateo = Sant Mateu Baleares, Spain 39°3N 1°23E 206 C1
San Mateo = Sant Mateu Valencia, Spain 40°28N 0°10E 196 E5
San Mateo Isabela, Phil. 16°54N 121°33E 232 C3
San Mateo Calif., U.S.A. 37°34N 122°19W 306 H4
San Mateo Tlaltenango
Mexico 19°20N 99°16W 128 B1
San Matías Bolivia 16°25S 58°20W 331 D6
San Matías, G. Argentina 41°30S 64°0W 336 B4
San Michele, Isola di Venice, Italy 142 a3
San Miguel = Linapacan
Phil. 11°30N 119°52E 233 F2
San Miguel = Sant Miquel
Spain 39°3N 1°26E 206 C1
San Miguel = Sarrat Phil. 18°9N 120°39E 232 B3
San Miguel Bolivia 16°42S 61°1W 331 C5
San Miguel Santiago, Chile 33°29S 70°39W 137 B2
San Miguel El Salv. 13°30N 88°12W 320 D2
San Miguel Panama 8°27N 78°55W 320 E4
San Miguel Lima, Peru 12°5S 77°6W 124 B2
San Miguel Bulacan, Phil. 15°9N 120°59E 232 D3
San Miguel Palawan, Phil. 11°30N 119°51E 233 F2
San Miguel Surigao S., Phil. 9°3N 125°59E 233 G5
San Miguel Calif., U.S.A. 35°45N 120°42W 306 K6
San Miguel ➔ Bolivia 13°52S 63°56W 331 C5
San Miguel ➔ Ecuador 0°25N 76°30W 328 C2
San Miguel, Golfo de
Panama 8°22N 78°17W 328 B2
San Miguel B. Phil. 13°51N 123°11E 232 E4
San Miguel de Huachi
Bolivia 15°40S 67°15W 330 D4
San Miguel de Tucumán
Argentina 26°50S 65°20W 334 B2
San Miguel del Monte
Argentina 35°23S 58°50W 334 D4
San Miguel I. U.S.A. 34°2N 120°23W 307 L6
San Miguel Is. Phil. 7°45N 118°28E 233 H2
San Miguelito Panama 9°2N 79°30W 320 c
San Millán de la Cogolla
Spain 42°19N 2°51W 196 C2
San Miniato Italy 43°41N 10°51E 198 E7
San Narciso Phil. 15°34N 122°34E 232 E4
San Nicolas = Sint Nicolaas
Curaçao 12°17N 69°8W 322 g
San Nicolás B. Aires, Argentina 34°36S 58°22W 117 B2
San Nicolás Canary Is. 27°58N 15°47W 153 e1
San Nicolas Phil. 18°10N 120°36E 232 B3
San Nicolás de los Arroyos
Argentina 33°25S 60°10W 334 C3
San Nicolas I. U.S.A. 33°15N 119°30W 307 M7
San Nicolo dei Mendicoli Venice, Italy 142 b1
San Onofre Colombia 9°44N 75°32W 328 B2
San Onofre Calif., U.S.A. 33°22N 117°34W 307 M9
San Onófrio Italy 38°42N 16°8E 201 D9
San Pablo Bolivia 21°43S 66°38W 334 A2
San Pablo Isabela, Phil. 17°27N 121°48E 232 C3
San Pablo Laguna, Phil. 14°11N 121°31E 232 D3
San Pablo Calif., U.S.A. 37°58N 122°21W 306 H4
San Pablo de Manta = Manta
Ecuador 1°0S 80°40W 328 D1
San Pantalon Venice, Italy 142 b2
San Pãolo di Civitate
Italy 41°44N 15°15E 199 G12
San Pascual Phil. 13°8N 122°59E 232 E4
San Pedro B. Aires, Argentina 33°40S 59°40W 334 C4
San Pedro Misiones, Argentina 26°30S 54°10W 335 B5
San Pedro Chile 33°54S 71°28W 334 C1
San Pedro Colombia 4°56N 71°53W 328 C3
San Pedro Ivory C. 4°50N 6°33W 262 E3
San Pedro Baja Calif. S., Mexico 23°55N 110°17W 318 C2
San Pedro Peru 14°49S 74°5W 330 C3
San Pedro □ Paraguay 24°0S 57°0W 334 A4
San Pedro ➔ Chihuahua, Mexico 28°21N 105°25W 318 B3
San Pedro ➔ Nayarit, Mexico 21°45N 105°30W 318 C3
San Pedro ➔ Ariz., U.S.A. 32°59N 110°47W 305 K8
San Pedro, Pta. Chile 25°30S 70°38W 334 B1
San Pedro, Sierra de Spain 39°18N 6°40W 195 F4
San Pedro B. Phil. 11°10N 125°6E 233 F5
San Pedro Channel
U.S.A. 33°30N 118°25W 307 M8
San Pedro de Arimena
Colombia 4°37N 71°42W 328 C3
San Pedro de Atacama
Chile 22°55S 68°15W 334 A2
San Pedro de Coche
Venezuela 10°47N 64°0W 329 a
San Pedro de Jujuy
Argentina 24°12S 64°55W 334 A3
San Pedro de las Colonias
Mexico 25°45N 102°59W 318 B4
San Pedro de Lloc Peru 7°15S 79°28W 330 B2
San Pedro de Macorís
Dom. Rep. 18°30N 69°18W 321 C6
San Pedro del Norte Nic. 13°4N 84°33W 320 D3
San Pedro del Paraná
Paraguay 26°43S 56°13W 334 B4
San Pedro del Pinatar
Spain 37°50N 0°50W 197 H4
San Pedro Mártir Spain 41°23N 2°6E 114 A1
San Pedro Mártir, Sa. de
Mexico 30°45N 115°13W 318 A1
San Pedro Ocampo = Melchor Ocampo Mexico 24°51N 101°39W 318 C4
San Pedro Pochutla
Mexico 15°44N 96°28W 319 D5
San Pedro Sula Honduras 15°30N 88°0W 320 C2
San Pedro Tututepec
Mexico 16°9N 97°38W 319 D5
San Pedro Zacatenco
Mexico 19°30N 99°6W 128 A2
San Pietro Italy 39°8N 8°17E 200 C1
San Pietro, Isola di Venice, Italy 142 b4
San Pietro, Piazza Rome, Italy 136 b1
San Pietro di Castello Venice, Italy 142 b4
San Pietro Vernótico Italy 40°29N 18°0E 201 B11
San Po Kong China 22°20N 114°11E 122 A2
San Polo Venice, Italy 142 b2
San Rafael Argentina 34°40S 68°21W 334 C2
San Rafael Bolivia 16°45S 60°34W 331 D5
San Rafael Trin. & Tob. 10°34N 61°16W 323 t
San Rafael Calif., U.S.A. 37°58N 122°32W 306 H4
San Rafael N. Mex., U.S.A. 35°7N 107°53W 305 J10
San Rafael Venezuela 10°58N 71°46W 328 A3
San Rafael Chamapa
Mexico 19°27N 99°15W 128 B1
San Rafael Hills U.S.A. 34°10N 118°12W 126 A3
San Rafael Mt. U.S.A. 34°41N 119°52W 307 L7
San Rafael Mts. U.S.A. 34°40N 119°50W 307 L7
San Ramón Bolivia 13°17S 64°43W 331 C5
San Ramón de la Nueva Orán
Argentina 23°10S 64°20W 334 A3
San Remo Italy 43°49N 7°46E 198 E4
San Román, C. Venezuela 12°12N 70°0W 328 A4
San Roque Argentina 28°25S 58°45W 334 B4
San Roque Manila, Phil. 14°37N 121°5E 127 B2
San Roque N. Samar, Phil. 12°37N 124°52E 232 E5
San Roque Spain 36°17N 5°21W 195 J5
San Rosendo Chile 37°16S 72°43W 334 D1
San Saba U.S.A. 31°12N 98°43W 314 F5
San Salvador El Salv. 13°40N 89°10W 320 D2
San Salvador Venice, Italy 142 b3
San Salvador, Canal de
Ecuador 0°25S 90°30W 330 a
San Salvador, I. Ecuador 0°16S 90°42W 330 a
San Salvador de Jujuy
Argentina 24°10S 64°48W 334 A3
San Salvador I. Bahamas 24°0N 74°30W 321 B5
San Salvo Italy 42°3N 14°36E 199 F11
San Sebastián = Donostia-San Sebastián Spain 43°17N 1°58W 196 B3
San Sebastián Argentina 53°10S 68°30W 336 D3
San Sebastián Puerto Rico 18°20N 66°59W 321 b
San Sebastián de la Gomera
Canary Is. 28°5N 17°7W 153 e1
San Sebastiano Venice, Italy 142 b2
San Serra = Son Serra
Spain 39°43N 3°13E 206 B4
San Serverino Marche
Italy 43°13N 13°10E 199 E10
San Severo Italy 41°41N 15°23E 199 G12
San Simeon U.S.A. 35°39N 121°11W 306 K5
San Simeon Grande Venice, Italy 142 b2
San Simon U.S.A. 32°16N 109°14W 305 K9
San Siro Italy 45°28N 9°7E 128 B1
San Souci Australia 33°59S 151°8E 139 B1
San Stefano Venice, Italy 142 b2
San Stéfano di Cadore
Italy 46°34N 12°33E 199 B9
San Stino di Livenza Italy 45°44N 12°41E 199 C9
San Telmo = Sant Elm
Spain 39°35N 2°21E 206 B3
San Telmo B. Aires, Argentina 34°37S 58°23W 117 B2
San Telmo Baja Calif., Mexico 30°58N 116°6W 318 A1
San Teodoro Phil. 13°26N 121°1E 232 E3
San Tiburcio Mexico 24°8N 101°32W 318 C4
San Trovaso Venice, Italy 142 c2
San Valentin, Mte. Chile 46°30S 73°30W 336 C2
San Vicenç dels Horts Spain 41°23N 2°0E 114 A1
San Vicente de Alcántara
Spain 39°22N 7°8W 195 F3
San Vicente de Cañete
Peru 13°8S 76°30W 330 C2
San Vicente de la Barquera
Spain 43°23N 4°29W 194 B6
San Vicente del Caguán
Colombia 2°7N 74°46W 328 C3
San Vincenzo Italy 43°6N 10°32E 198 E7
San Vito Costa Rica 8°50N 82°58W 320 E3
San Vito Italy 39°26N 9°32E 200 C2
San Vito, C. Italy 38°11N 12°41E 200 D5
San Vito al Tagliamento
Italy 45°54N 12°52E 199 C9
San Vito Chietino Italy 42°18N 14°27E 199 F11
San Vito dei Normanni
Italy 40°39N 17°42E 201 B10
San Yanaro Colombia 2°47N 69°42W 328 C4
San Zaccaria Venice, Italy 142 b3
Sana' = Şan'ā' Yemen 15°27N 44°12E 248 D4
Saña Peru 6°54S 79°36W 330 B2
Şan'ā' Yemen 15°27N 44°12E 248 D4
Şan'ā' □ Yemen 15°27N 44°12E 248 D4
Sana ➔ Bos.-H. 45°3N 16°23E 199 C13
Sanaa = Şan'ā' Yemen 15°27N 44°12E 248 D4
Sanaag □ Somalia 10°30N 48°0E 267 B6
Sanaba Burkina Faso 12°25N 3°47W 262 C4
Sanae IV Antarctica 70°20S 9°0W 151 D2
Şanāfīr Si. Arabia 27°56N 34°42E 251 L5
Sanaga ➔ Cameroon 3°35N 9°38E 263 E6
Sanak I. U.S.A. 54°25N 162°40W 303 J7
Sanalona, Presa Mexico 24°49N 107°7W 318 C3
Sanām Si. Arabia 23°40N 44°45E 248 B4
Sanana Indonesia 2°4S 125°58E 231 E7
Sanand India 22°59N 72°25E 242 H5
Sanandaj Iran 35°18N 47°1E 213 E12
Sanandita Bolivia 21°40S 63°45W 334 A3
Sanaroa I. Papua N. G. 9°37S 151°0E 286 E6
Sanary-sur-Mer France 43°7N 5°49E 175 E9
Sanāw Yemen 17°50N 51°5E 249 C5
Sanawad India 22°11N 76°5E 242 H7
Sanbancho Tokyo, Japan 140 a3
Sanbe-San Japan 35°6N 132°38E 222 B4
Sancellas = Sencelles Spain 39°39N 2°54E 206 B3
Sancergues France 47°10N 2°54E 173 E9
Sancerre France 47°20N 2°50E 173 E9
Sancerrois, Collines du
France 47°20N 2°40E 173 E9
Sancha He ➔ China 26°48N 106°7E 228 D6
Sanchahe China 44°50N 126°2E 227 B14
Sánchez Dom. Rep. 19°15N 69°36W 321 C6
Sanchez Mira Phil. 18°34N 121°14E 232 B3
Sanchi India 23°28N 77°44E 242 H7
Sanchih Taiwan 25°15N 121°30E 225 A3
Sanchor India 24°45N 71°55E 242 G4
Sanch'ung Taiwan 25°4N 121°30E 225 A3
Sanco Pt. Phil. 8°15N 126°27E 233 G6
Sancoins France 46°47N 2°55E 173 F9
Sancti Spíritus Cuba 21°52N 79°33W 320 B4
Sancy, Puy de France 45°32N 2°50E 174 C6
Sand = Polokwane ➔
S. Africa 22°25S 30°5E 271 B5
Sand Norway 59°29N 6°16E 164 E3
Sand Bank B.
St. Kitts & Nevis 17°15N 62°38W 322 d
Sand Cr. ➔ U.S.A. 39°3N 85°51W 311 E11
Sand Hills Guyana 6°27N 58°19W 329 B6
Sand Hills Nebr., U.S.A. 42°10N 101°30W 308 D3
Sand I. Midway Is. 28°12N 177°22W 302 e
Sand I. Hawai'i, U.S.A. 21°19N 157°53W 302 K14
Sand Islet Midway Is. 28°16N 177°22W 302 e
Sand Lakes △ Canada 57°51N 98°32W 297 B9
Sand Point U.S.A. 55°20N 160°30W 303 J7
Sand Springs U.S.A. 36°9N 96°7W 314 C6
Sanda Japan 34°53N 135°14E 223 C7
Sandai Indonesia 1°15S 110°31E 235 C4
Sandakan Malaysia 5°53N 118°4E 235 A5
Sandalwood Australia 34°55S 140°9E 282 C4
Sandan = Sambor
Cambodia 12°46N 106°0E 236 F6
Sandane Norway 61°46N 6°13E 164 C3
Sandanski Bulgaria 41°35N 23°16E 202 E7
Sandaré Mali 14°40N 10°15W 262 C2
Sandared Sweden 57°43N 12°47E 163 G6
Sandarne Sweden 61°16N 17°9E 162 C11
Sanday U.K. 59°16N 2°31W 167 B6
Sande Møre og Romsdal, Norway 62°15N 5°27E 164 B2
Sande Sogn og Fjordane, Norway 61°20N 5°47E 164 C2
Sande Vestfold, Norway 59°36N 10°12E 162 E4
Sandefjord Norway 59°10N 10°15E 164 E7
Sandeid Norway 59°33N 5°52E 164 E2
Sanders Ariz., U.S.A. 35°13N 109°20W 305 J9
Sanders Ky., U.S.A. 38°40N 84°56W 311 F12
Sanderson Fla., U.S.A. 30°15N 82°16W 316 E7
Sanderson Tex., U.S.A. 30°9N 102°24W 314 F3
Sandersville U.S.A. 32°59N 82°48W 316 C7
Sandfire Roadhouse
Australia 19°45S 121°15E 278 C3
Sandfloeggа Norway 59°58N 7°10E 164 E4
Sandfly L. Canada 55°43N 106°6W 297 B7
Sandfontein Namibia 23°48S 19°1E 270 B2
Sandhammaren Sweden 55°23N 14°14E 163 J8
Sandheads, The India 21°10N 88°20E 241 E2
Sandgerði Iceland 64°3N 22°42W 161 C3
Sandia Peru 14°10S 69°30W 330 C4
Sandıklı Turkey 38°28N 30°17E 205 C12
Sandila India 27°5N 80°31E 243 F9
Sandilands Bahamas 25°3N 77°19W 153 b
Sanding Indonesia 3°28S 100°40E 234 C2
Sanding, Selat Indonesia 3°24S 100°34E 234 C2
Sandnes Aust-Agder, Norway 58°53N 7°45E 164 F4
Sandnes Rogaland, Norway 58°50N 5°45E 164 F2
Sandnessjøen Norway 66°2N 12°38E 160 C15
Sandoa Dem. Rep. of the Congo 9°41S 23°0E 265 D4
Sandomierz Poland 50°40N 21°43E 185 H8
Săndominic Romania 46°35N 25°47E 183 D10
Sandona Colombia 1°17N 77°28W 328 C2
Sandongo Angola 15°30S 21°28E 265 F4
Sandoval U.S.A. 38°37N 89°7W 310 F7
Sandover ➔ Australia 21°43S 136°32E 280 C2
Sandoway = Thandwe
Burma 18°20N 94°30E 241 F5
Sandown S. Africa 26°5S 28°4E 123 A2
Sandown Park Races U.K. 51°22N 0°21W 125 B1
Sandoy Færoe Is. 61°52N 6°46W 160 F9
Sandpoint U.S.A. 48°17N 116°33W 304 B5
Sandray U.K. 56°53N 7°31W 167 E1
Sandringham U.K. 52°51N 0°31E 168 E8
Sandstone Australia 27°59S 119°16E 279 E2
Sandton S. Africa 26°5S 28°4E 123 A2
Sandu China 26°0N 107°52E 228 E6
Sandumba Angola 13°45S 17°34E 265 E3
Sandur India 15°6N 76°33E 245 F3
Sandusky Mich., U.S.A. 43°25N 82°50W 312 C2
Sandusky Ohio, U.S.A. 41°27N 82°42W 312 E2
Sandusky ➔ U.S.A. 41°27N 83°0W 311 C14
Sandveld Namibia 21°25S 20°0E 270 B3
Sandvig Denmark 55°18N 14°47E 163 J8
Sandvika Norway 59°54N 10°31E 133 A2
Sandviken Sweden 60°38N 16°46E 162 D10
Sandwich U.S.A. 41°39N 88°37W 311 C8
Sandwich, C. Australia 18°14S 146°18E 280 B4
Sandwich B. Nfld. & L., Canada 53°40N 57°15W 299 B8
Sandwich B. Namibia 23°25S 14°20E 270 B1
Sandwip I. Bangla. 22°30N 91°25E 241 D3
Sandy Oreg., U.S.A. 45°24N 122°16W 306 E4
Sandy Pa., U.S.A. 41°6N 78°46W 312 E6
Sandy Utah, U.S.A. 40°32N 111°50W 304 F8
Sandy B. St. Helena 16°0S 5°43W 153 h
Sandy Bay Canada 55°31N 102°19W 297 B8
Sandy Bight Australia 33°50S 123°20E 279 F3
Sandy C. Queens., Australia 24°42S 153°15E 280 C5
Sandy C. Tas., Australia 41°25S 144°45E 281 G3
Sandy Cay Bahamas 23°13N 75°18W 321 B4
Sandy Cr. ➔ N.S.W., Australia 31°54S 145°18E 281 B4
Sandy Cr. ➔ Wyo., U.S.A. 41°51N 109°47W 304 F9
Sandy Creek U.S.A. 43°38N 76°5W 313 C8
Sandy Ground Village
Anguilla 18°12N 63°6W 322 a
Sandy Hill B. Anguilla 18°13N 63°1W 322 a
Sandy I. Anguilla 18°13N 63°7W 322 a
Sandy I. Grenada 12°29N 61°29W 323 q
Sandy I. Grenada 12°13N 61°35W 323 q
Sandy L. Canada 53°2N 93°0W 298 B1
Sandy Lake Canada 53°0N 93°15W 298 B1
Sandy Point India 10°32N 92°22E 245 J11
Sandy Point Town
St. Kitts & Nevis 17°22N 62°51W 322 d
Sandy Springs U.S.A. 33°56N 84°23W 316 B5
Sandy Valley U.S.A. 35°49N 115°38W 307 K11
Sandyford Ireland 53°17N 6°13W 120 B2
Sandymount Ireland 53°20N 6°13W 120 B2
Sånfjället △ Sweden 62°17N 13°35E 162 B7
Sanford Fla., U.S.A. 28°48N 81°16W 317 G8
Sanford Maine, U.S.A. 43°27N 70°47W 313 C14
Sanford N.C., U.S.A. 35°29N 79°10W 315 D15
Sanford ➔ Australia 27°22S 115°53E 279 E2
Sanford, Mt. U.S.A. 62°13N 144°8W 303 E11
Sang-i-Masha Afghan. 33°8N 67°27E 242 C2
Sanga Angola 11°9S 15°21E 265 E3
Sanga Mozam. 12°22S 35°21E 269 E4
Sanga ➔ Congo 1°5S 17°0E 264 C3
Sangaie
Dem. Rep. of the Congo 6°48S 22°46E 265 D4
Sangamner India 19°37N 74°15E 244 E2
Sangamon ➔ U.S.A. 40°1N 90°26W 310 D6
Sangān Iran 34°23N 60°15E 247 C9
Sanganeb Atoll △ Sudan 19°33N 37°11E 256 D4
Sangar Afghan. 32°56N 65°30E 242 C1
Sangar Russia 64°2N 127°31E 215 C13
Sangar Sarai Afghan. 34°27N 70°35E 242 B4
Sangareddi India 17°38N 78°7E 244 F4
Sangaredi Guinea 11°7N 13°52W 262 C2
Sangarh ➔ Pakistan 30°43N 70°44E 242 D4
Sangasanga Indonesia 0°36S 117°13E 235 C5
Sangasso Mali 12°5N 5°35W 262 C3
Sangatte France 50°56N 1°44E 173 B8
Sangāw Iraq 35°17N 45°10E 213 E11
Sangay Ecuador 2°0S 78°20W 328 D2
Sangay △ Ecuador 2°15S 78°26W 328 D2
Sangbé Cameroon 6°3N 12°28E 264 A2
Sangchris L. U.S.A. 39°39N 89°29W 310 E7
Sangdong S. Korea 37°7N 128°49E 224 D4
Sange Dem. Rep. of the Congo 6°58S 28°21E 268 D2
Sangeang Indonesia 8°12S 119°6E 235 D5
Sangenjaya Japan 35°37N 139°39E 140 B2
Sângeorz-Băi Romania 47°22N 24°41E 183 C9
Sanger U.S.A. 36°42N 119°33W 306 J7
Sângera Moldova 46°55N 28°58E 183 D13
Sangerhausen Germany 51°28N 11°18E 178 D7
Sanggan He ➔ China 38°12N 117°15E 226 E9
Sanggau Kalimantan Barat, Indonesia 0°5N 110°30E 235 B4
Sanggau Kalimantan Barat, Indonesia 1°7N 109°36E 235 B3
Sanggye S. Korea 37°38N 127°3E 137 B2
Sanghar Pakistan 26°2N 68°57E 242 F3
Sangihe, Kepulauan
Indonesia 3°0N 125°30E 231 D7
Sangihe, Pulau Indonesia 3°35N 125°30E 231 D7
Sangin Afghan. 32°4N 64°50E 240 B2
Sangiran Indonesia 7°25S 110°55E 234 F4
Sangiran △ Indonesia 7°27S 110°50E 231 G14
Sangju S. Korea 36°25N 128°10E 224 D4
Sangkapura Indonesia 5°52S 112°40E 235 D4
Sangkha Thailand 14°37N 103°52E 236 E4
Sangkhla Buri Thailand 14°57N 98°28E 236 E2
Sangkulirang Indonesia 0°59N 117°58E 235 B5
Sangla Pakistan 31°43N 73°23E 242 D5
Sangley Pt. Phil. 14°29N 120°54E 127 C1
Sangli India 16°55N 74°33E 244 F2
Sangmélima Cameroon 2°57N 12°1E 263 E7
Sango Angola 9°51S 15°44E 265 D2
Sango Zimbabwe 18°44S 31°44E 269 F3
Sangod India 24°55N 76°17E 242 G7
Sangole India 17°26N 75°12E 244 F2
Sangorodok = Ust-Vorkuta
Russia 67°24N 64°0E 186 A11
Sangpang Bum Burma 26°30N 95°50E 241 B5
Sangre de Cristo Mts.
U.S.A. 37°30N 105°20W 305 H11
Sangre Grande Trin. & Tob. 10°35N 61°8W 323 t
Sangro ➔ Italy 42°14N 14°32E 199 F11
Sangrur India 30°14N 75°50E 242 D6
Sangudo Canada 53°50N 114°54W 296 C6
Sangue ➔ Brazil 11°1S 58°39W 331 C6
Sangüesa Spain 42°37N 1°17W 196 C3
Sanguinaires, Îs. France 41°51N 8°36E 175 G12
Sangzhi China 29°25N 110°12E 229 C8
Sanhala Ivory C. 10°3N 6°51W 262 C3
Sanhsia Taiwan 24°56N 121°22E 225 B3
Sanhsien Hualien, Taiwan 23°8N 121°25E 225 C3
Sanhsien T'aitung, Taiwan 23°24N 121°19E 225 C3

Sanhsing Taiwan 24°40N 121°36E 225 B3
Sani Taiwan 24°24N 120°46E 225 B2
Sanibel U.S.A. 26°27N 82°1W 317 J7
Sanibel I. U.S.A. 26°26N 82°6W 317 J7
Sanikluaq Canada 56°32N 79°14W 298 A4
Sanin-Kaigan △ Japan 35°39N 134°37E 222 B6
Sanirajak = Hall Beach
Canada 68°46N 81°12W 295 D15
Sanjawi Pakistan 30°17N 68°21E 242 D3
Sanje Uganda 0°49S 31°30E 268 C3
Sanjiang China 25°48N 109°37E 228 E7
Sanjo Japan 37°37N 138°57E 220 F9
Sankarankovil India 9°10N 77°35E 245 K3
Sankeshwar India 16°23N 74°32E 245 F2
Sankh → India 22°15N 84°48E 243 H11
Sankosh → India 26°24N 89°47E 241 B2
Sankrail India 22°33N 88°13E 124 B1
Sankt Andrä Austria 46°46N 14°50E 180 E7
Sankt Anton Austria 47°8N 10°16E 179 H6
Sankt Augustin Germany 50°45N 7°10E 178 E3
Sankt Blasien Germany 47°47N 8°7E 179 H4
Sankt Gallen Switz. 47°26N 9°22E 179 H5
Sankt Gallen □ Switz. 47°25N 9°22E 179 H5
Sankt Goar Germany 50°12N 7°43E 179 E3
Sankt Ingbert Germany 49°16N 7°6E 179 F3
Sankt Johann im Pongau
Austria 47°22N 13°12E 180 D6
Sankt Johann in Tirol
Austria 47°30N 12°25E 180 D5
Sankt Marein = Smarje
Slovenia 46°15N 15°34E 199 B12
Sankt Michel = Mikkeli
Finland 61°43N 27°15E 188 B4
Sankt Moritz Switz. 46°30N 9°51E 179 J5
Sankt Peter-Ording
Germany 54°20N 8°36E 178 A4
Sankt-Peterburg Russia 59°55N 30°20E 137 B1
Sankt Pölten Austria 48°12N 15°38E 180 C8
Sankt Ulrich = Ortisei
Italy 46°34N 11°40E 199 B8
Sankt Valentin Austria 48°11N 14°33E 180 C7
Sankt Veit Austria 48°11N 16°16E 142 A1
Sankt Veit an der Glan
Austria 46°47N 14°22E 180 E7
Sankt Wendel Germany 49°27N 7°9E 179 F3
Sankt Wolfgang Austria 47°43N 13°27E 180 D6
Sankuru →
Dem. Rep. of the Congo 4°17S 20°25E 265 C4
Sanlihe China 39°53N 116°18E 114 B1
Sanlin China 31°9N 121°29E 138 C1
Sanlintang China 31°9N 121°29E 138 C1
Sanliurfa Turkey 37°12N 38°50E 213 D8
Sanliurfa □ Turkey 37°0N 39°0E 213 D8
Sanlúcar de Barrameda
Spain 36°46N 6°21W 195 J4
Sanluri Italy 39°34N 8°54E 200 C1
Sânmartin Romania 46°19N 25°58E 183 D10
Sanmen China 29°5N 121°35E 229 C13
Sanmenxia China 34°47N 111°12E 226 G6
Sanming China 26°15N 117°40E 229 D11
Sanmu Kantō, Japan 34°11N 134°37E 222 C6
Sanmu Shikoku, Japan 35°36N 140°25E 223 B12
Sannan Japan 35°2N 135°1E 223 B7
Sannat Malta 36°1N 14°15E 206 E6
Sanndraigh = Sandray
U.K. 56°53N 7°31W 167 E1
Sannicandro Garganico
Italy 41°50N 15°34E 199 G12
Sânnicolau Mare Romania 46°5N 20°39E 182 D5
Sannieshof S. Africa 26°30S 25°47E 270 C4
Sannīn, J. Lebanon 33°57N 35°52E 250 E6
Sanniquellie Liberia 7°19N 8°38W 262 D3
Sannûr Egypt 28°58N 31°3E 251 K2
Sannûr, W. → Egypt 28°59N 31°3E 251 K2
Sano Japan 36°19N 139°35E 223 A11
Sanok Poland 49°35N 22°10E 185 J9
Sanqingshan △ China 28°54N 118°3E 229 C12
Sanquhar U.K. 55°22N 3°54W 167 F5
Sanquianga △ Colombia 2°33N 78°14W 328 C2
Sans Spain 41°22N 2°7E 114 A1
Sans Souci St. Vincent 13°13N 61°7W 323 n
Sans Souci Trin. & Tob. 10°50N 61°0W 323 t
Sansanding Mali 13°48N 6°0W 262 C3
Sansané Niger 13°50N 1°36E 263 C5
Sansepolcro Italy 43°34N 12°8E 199 E9
Sansha China 26°58N 120°12E 229 D13
Sanshui China 23°10N 112°56E 229 F9
Sanski Most Bos.-H. 44°46N 16°40E 199 D13
Sanssouci Germany 52°23N 13°2E 115 B1
Sansui China 26°58N 108°39E 228 D7
Sant Agusti Barcelona, Spain 114 c2
Sant Ambrogio, Basilica di
Italy 45°27N 9°10E 128 B2
Sant' Andrea Venice, Italy 142 b1
Sant Antoni de Portmany
Spain 38°59N 1°19E 206 D1
Sant Boi de Llobregat Spain 41°20N 2°2E 114 A1
Sant Carles Spain 39°3N 1°34E 206 C2
Sant Carles de la Ràpita
Spain 40°37N 0°35E 196 E5
Sant Celoni Spain 41°42N 2°30E 196 D7
Sant Cugat Spain 41°28N 2°5E 114 A1
Sant' Elena Venice, Italy 142 c4
Sant' Elena, Darsena di Venice, Italy 142 c4
Sant' Elena, Isola di Venice, Italy 142 c4
Sant Elm Spain 39°35N 2°21E 206 B3
Sant Feliu de Guíxols Spain 41°45N 3°1E 196 D8
Sant Feliu de Llobregat
Spain 41°22N 2°2E 114 A1
Sant Ferran Spain 38°42N 1°28E 206 D1
Sant Francesc de Formentera
Spain 38°42N 1°26E 206 D1
Sant Jaume Spain 39°54N 4°4E 206 B5
Sant Joan Spain 39°36N 3°4E 206 B4
Sant Joan d'Alacant Spain 38°24N 0°26W 197 G4
Sant Joan de Labritja Spain 39°5N 1°31E 206 C2
Sant Joan Despi Spain 41°22N 2°2E 114 A1
Sant Jordi Ibiza, Spain 38°53N 1°24E 206 D1
Sant Jordi Mallorca, Spain 39°33N 2°46E 206 B3
Sant Jordi, G. de Spain 40°53N 1°2E 196 E6
Sant Llorenç de Morunys
Spain 42°8N 1°35E 196 C6
Sant Llorenç del Munt y l'Obac △
Spain 41°39N 1°55W 196 D3
Sant Llorenç des Cardassar
Spain 39°37N 3°17E 206 B4
Sant Maria del Mar Barcelona, Spain 114 b3
Sant Mateu Baleares, Spain 39°3N 1°23E 206 C1
Sant Mateu Valencia, Spain 40°28N 0°10E 196 E5
Sant Miquel Spain 39°3N 1°26E 206 C1
Sant Pau del Camp Barcelona, Spain 114 c2
Sant Salvador Spain 39°27N 3°11E 206 B4
Sant Vicent del Raspeig
Spain 38°24N 0°31W 197 G4
Santa Peru 8°59S 78°40W 330 B2
Sant' Ágata Militello Italy 38°2N 14°8E 201 D7
Santa Agnès Spain 39°3N 1°21E 206 C1
Santa Ana Beni, Bolivia 13°50S 65°40W 331 C4
Santa Ana La Paz, Bolivia 15°31S 67°30W 330 D4
Santa Ana Santa Cruz,
Bolivia 18°43S 58°44W 331 D6
Santa Ana Santa Cruz,
Bolivia 16°37S 60°43W 331 D5
Santa Ana Ecuador 1°16S 80°20W 328 D1
Santa Ana El Salv. 14°0N 89°31W 320 D2
Santa Ana Guam 13°32N 145°46E 302 d
Santa Ana Sonora, Mexico 30°33N 111°7W 318 A2
Santa Ana Cagayan, Phil. 18°28N 122°20E 232 B4
Santa Ana Manila, Phil. 14°34N 121°0E 127 B2
Santa Ana Solomon Is. 10°50S 162°30E 287 N12
Santa Ana Calif., U.S.A. 33°46N 117°52W 307 M9
Santa Ana → Venezuela 9°30N 71°57W 328 B3
Santa Ana de los Rios de Cuenca =
Cuenca Ecuador 2°50S 79°9W 328 D2
Sant' Ángelo Lodigiano
Italy 45°14N 9°25E 198 C6
Santa Anita Park U.S.A. 34°8N 118°5W 126 B4
Sant' Antíoco Italy 39°4N 8°27E 200 C1
Santa Bárbara Santa Maria,
Azores 36°59N 25°4W 153 d4
Santa Bárbara Terciera,
Azores 38°41N 27°20W 153 d1
Santa Bárbara Chile 37°40S 72°1W 334 D1
Santa Bárbara Colombia 5°53N 75°35W 328 B2
Santa Bárbara Curaçao 12°5N 68°51W 322 g
Santa Bárbara Honduras 14°53N 88°14W 320 D2
Santa Bárbara Chihuahua,
Mexico 26°48N 105°49W 318 B3
Santa Barbara Phil. 10°50N 122°32E 233 F4
Santa Bárbara Spain 40°42N 0°29E 196 E5
Santa Barbara Calif.,
U.S.A. 34°25N 119°42W 307 L7
Santa Bárbara Amazonas,
Venezuela 3°57N 67°6W 328 C4
Santa Bárbara Barinas,
Venezuela 7°47N 71°10W 328 B3
Santa Bárbara, Mt. Spain 37°23N 2°50W 197 H2
Santa Bárbara, Serra de
Azores 38°44N 27°19W 153 d1
Santa Barbara Channel
U.S.A. 34°15N 120°0W 307 L7
Santa Barbara I. U.S.A. 33°29N 119°2W 307 M7
Santa Catalina Colombia 10°36N 75°17W 328 A2
Santa Catalina Neg. Or.
Phil. 9°20N 122°52E 233 G4
Santa Catalina
Solomon Is. 10°53S 162°29E 287 N12
Santa Catalina, Gulf of
U.S.A. 33°10N 117°50W 307 N9
Santa Catalina, I.
Mexico 25°40N 110°47W 318 B2
Santa Catalina I. U.S.A. 33°23N 118°25W 307 M8
Santa Catarina □ Brazil 27°25S 48°30W 335 B6
Santa Catarina, I. de
Brazil 27°30S 48°40W 335 B6
Santa Caterina Venice, Italy 142 a3
Santa Caterina di Pittinuri
Italy 40°6N 8°27E 200 B1
Santa Caterina Villarmosa
Italy 37°35N 14°2E 201 E7
Santa Cecília Brazil 26°56S 50°18W 335 B5
Santa Clara Cuba 22°20N 80°0W 320 B4
Santa Clara Calif., U.S.A. 37°21N 121°57W 306 H5
Santa Clara N.Y., U.S.A. 44°38N 74°27W 313 B10
Santa Clara Utah, U.S.A. 37°8N 113°39W 305 H7
Santa Clara → Mexico 29°51N 107°6W 318 A3
Santa Clara, I. Chile 33°42S 79°0W 330 c
Santa Clara de Olimar
Uruguay 32°50S 54°54W 335 C5
Santa Clara Valley
U.S.A. 36°50N 121°30W 306 J5
Santa Clarita U.S.A. 34°24N 118°33W 307 L8
Santa Clotilde Peru 2°33S 73°45W 328 D3
Santa Coloma de Farners
Spain 41°50N 2°39E 196 D7
Santa Coloma de Gramenet
Spain 41°27N 2°13E 114 A2
Santa Comba Spain 43°2N 8°49W 194 B2
Santa Croce Venice, Italy 142 b2
Santa Croce Camerina
Italy 36°50N 14°31E 201 F7
Santa Croce di Magliano
Italy 41°42N 14°59E 199 G11
Santa Cruz Aruba 12°30N 69°59W 322 f
Santa Cruz Bolivia 17°43S 63°10W 331 D5
Santa Cruz Brazil 6°13S 36°1W 332 C4
Santa Cruz Chile 34°38S 71°27W 334 C1
Santa Cruz Costa Rica 10°15N 85°35W 320 D2
Santa Cruz Curaçao 12°18N 69°7W 322 g
Santa Cruz Maharashtra,
India 19°4N 72°51E 130 A1
Santa Cruz Jamaica 18°3N 77°43W 320 a
Santa Cruz Madeira 32°42N 16°46W 153 c
Santa Cruz Peru 5°40S 75°56W 330 B2
Santa Cruz Davao del S.,
Phil. 6°50N 125°25E 233 H5
Santa Cruz Laguna, Phil. 14°20N 121°24E 232 D3
Santa Cruz Manila, Phil. 14°36N 120°58E 127 B1
Santa Cruz Marinduque,
Phil. 13°28N 122°2E 232 E4
Santa Cruz Mind. Occ.,
Phil. 13°4N 120°43E 232 E3
Santa Cruz Zambales,
Phil. 15°46N 119°55E 232 D2
Santa Cruz Calif., U.S.A. 36°58N 122°1W 306 J4
Santa Cruz Venezuela 8°3N 64°27W 329 B5
Santa Cruz → Argentina 50°10S 68°20W 336 D3
Santa Cruz □ Argentina 49°0S 70°0W 336 C3
Santa Cruz □ Bolivia 17°43S 63°10W 331 D5
Santa Cruz, B. Curaçao 12°18N 69°10W 322 g
Santa Cruz, I. Ecuador 0°38S 90°23W 330 a
Santa Cruz, I. de Brazil 22°51S 43°7W 135 B2
Santa Cruz Cabrália Brazil 16°17S 39°2W 333 E4
Santa Cruz da Graciosa
Azores 39°5N 28°1W 153 d1
Santa Cruz das Flores
Azores 39°27N 31°7W 153 d2
Santa Cruz de Bravo = Felipe
Carrillo Puerto Mexico 19°38N 88°3W 319 D7
Santa Cruz de la Palma
Canary Is. 28°41N 17°46W 153 e1
Santa Cruz de la Palma ✕ (SPC)
Canary Is. 28°40N 17°45W 153 e1
Santa Cruz de Mompox = Mompós
Colombia 9°14N 74°26W 328 B3
Santa Cruz de Mudela
Spain 38°39N 3°28W 195 G7
Santa Cruz de Olorde Spain 41°25N 2°3E 114 A1
Santa Cruz de Tenerife
Canary Is. 28°28N 16°15W 153 e1
Santa Cruz del Norte Cuba 23°9N 81°55W 320 B3
Santa Cruz del Retamar
Spain 40°8N 4°14W 194 E6
Santa Cruz del Sur Cuba 20°44N 78°0W 320 B4
Santa Cruz do Rio Pardo
Brazil 22°54S 49°37W 335 A6
Santa Cruz do Sul Brazil 29°42S 52°25W 335 B5
Santa Cruz I. U.S.A. 34°1N 119°43W 307 M7
Santa Cruz Is. Solomon Is. 10°30S 166°0E 277 C12
Santa Cruz la Vieja △
Bolivia 17°55S 60°50W 331 D5
Santa Cruz Mts. Jamaica 17°58N 77°43W 320 a
Santa Domingo, Cay
Bahamas 21°25N 75°45W 320 B4
Sant' Egidio alla Vibrata
Italy 42°49N 13°42E 199 F10
Santa Elena Argentina 30°58S 59°47W 334 C4
Santa Elena Ecuador 2°16S 80°52W 328 D1
Santa Elena Camarines N.,
Phil. 14°12N 122°24E 232 D4
Santa Elena Manila, Phil. 14°38N 121°5E 127 B2
Santa Elena, C. Costa Rica 10°54N 85°56W 320 D2
Santa Elena del Gomero
Chile 43°28S 70°45W 137 B1
Sant' Eufémia, G. di Italy 38°51N 16°4E 201 D9
Santa Eulalia Spain 41°25N 2°10E 114 A2
Santa Eulària des Riu
Spain 38°59N 1°32E 206 D2
Santa Fé Argentina 31°35S 60°41W 334 C3
Santa Fe Nueva Vizcaya,
Phil. 16°10N 120°57E 232 C3
Santa Fe Romblon, Phil. 12°10N 122°0E 232 E4
Santa Fé Spain 37°11N 3°43W 195 H7
Santa Fe N. Mex., U.S.A. 35°41N 105°57W 305 J11
Santa Fé □ Argentina 31°50S 60°55W 334 C3
Santa Fé, Canal de Ecuador 0°48S 89°55W 330 a
Santa Fé, I. Ecuador 0°49S 90°5W 330 a
Santa Fé do Sul Brazil 20°13S 50°56W 333 F1
Santa Fe Springs U.S.A. 33°56N 118°3W 126 C4
Santa Filomena Brazil 9°6S 45°50W 332 C2
Santa Fiora Italy 42°50N 11°35E 199 F8
Santa Gertrudis Spain 39°0N 1°26E 206 C1
Santa Giustina Italy 46°10N 12°5E 199 B9
Santa Helena Brazil 2°14S 45°18W 332 B2
Santa Helena de Goiás
Brazil 17°53S 50°35W 333 E1
Santa Inês Bahia, Brazil 13°17S 39°48W 333 D4
Santa Inês Maranhão,
Brazil 3°39S 45°20W 332 B2
Santa Inés Extremadura,
Spain 38°32N 5°37W 195 G5
Santa Inés, I. Chile 54°0S 73°0W 336 D2
Santa Iria da Azóia Portugal 38°49N 9°5W 126 A2
Santa Isabel = Rey Malabo
Eq. Guin. 3°45N 8°50E 263 E6
Santa Isabel Argentina 36°10S 66°54W 334 D2
Santa Isabel Puerto Rico 17°58N 66°24W 321 b
Santa Isabel Solomon Is. 8°0S 159°0E 287 M10
Santa Isabel do Araguaia
Brazil 6°7S 48°19W 332 C2
Santa Isabel do Morro
Brazil 11°34S 50°40W 333 D1
Santa Isabel do Rio Negro
Brazil 0°24S 65°2W 329 D4
Santa Julia Chile 33°30S 70°35W 137 C2
Santa Lucía Corrientes,
Argentina 28°58S 59°5W 334 B4
Santa Lucía San Juan,
Argentina 31°30S 68°30W 334 C2
Santa Lucía Canary Is. 27°55N 5°32W 153 e1
Santa Lucia Phil. 17°7N 120°27E 232 C3
Santa Lucía Spain 37°35N 0°58W 197 H4
Santa Lucía Uruguay 34°27S 56°24W 334 C4
Santa Lucia, Stazione Venice, Italy 142 a2
Santa Lucia Range
U.S.A. 36°0N 121°20W 306 K5
Santa Luzia = Luziânia
Brazil 16°20S 48°0W 333 E2
Santa Luzia Brazil 19°47S 43°52W 333 E3
Santa Luzia C. Verde Is. 16°50N 24°35W 153 j
Santa Margalida Spain 39°42N 3°6E 206 B4
Santa Margarita
Argentina 38°28S 61°35W 334 D3
Santa Margarita Calif.,
U.S.A. 35°23N 120°37W 306 K6
Santa Margarita →
U.S.A. 33°13N 117°23W 307 M9
Santa Margarita, I.
Mexico 24°27N 111°50W 318 C2
Santa Margherita Italy 38°58N 8°58E 200 D1
Santa Margherita Ligure
Italy 44°20N 9°11E 198 D6
Santa Maria Argentina 26°40S 66°0W 334 B2
Santa Maria Azores 36°58N 25°6W 153 d4
Santa Maria Brazil 29°40S 53°48W 335 B5
Santa Maria C. Verde Is. 16°31N 22°53W 153 j
Santa María Mexico City, Mexico 128 a1
Santa Maria Ilocos S.,
Phil. 17°22N 120°29E 232 C3
Santa Maria Isabela, Phil. 17°28N 121°45E 232 C3
Santa Maria Calif.,
U.S.A. 34°57N 120°26W 307 L6
Santa María → Mexico 31°0N 107°14W 318 A3
Santa María, B. de Mexico 25°4N 108°6W 318 B3
Santa Maria, C. de
Portugal 36°58N 7°53W 195 J3
Santa María, I. Ecuador 1°17S 90°26W 330 a
Santa Maria Cápua Vétere
Italy 41°5N 14°15E 201 A7
Santa Maria da Feira
Portugal 40°55N 8°35W 194 E2
Santa Maria da Vitória
Brazil 13°24S 44°12W 333 D3
Santa María de Guadalupe =
Guadalupe Spain 39°27N 5°17W 195 F5
Santa María de Ipire
Venezuela 8°49N 65°19W 329 B4
Santa Maria dei Frari Venice, Italy 142 b2
Santa Maria dei Miracoli Venice, Italy 142 b3
Santa Maria del Camí
Spain 39°38N 2°47E 206 B3
Santa Maria della Misericórdia
Venice, Italy 142 a3
Santa Maria della Pianto Venice, Italy 142 b3
Santa Maria della Salute Venice, Italy 142 c2
Santa Maria della Visitazione
Venice, Italy 142 b3
Santa Maria delle Penitenti
Venice, Italy 142 a2
Santa Maria di Léuca, C.
Italy 39°47N 18°22E 201 C11
Santa Maria do Boiaçu
Brazil 0°25S 61°48W 329 D5
Santa Maria do Suaçuí
Brazil 18°12S 42°25W 333 E3
Santa Maria dos Marmelos
Brazil 6°7S 61°51W 331 B5
Santa Maria Formosa Venice, Italy 142 b3
Santa Maria la Real de Nieva
Spain 41°4N 4°24W 194 D6
Santa Maria Maggiore, Ex Chiesa di
Venice, Italy 142 b1
Santa Marinella Italy 42°2N 11°52E 199 F8
Santa Marta Colombia 11°15N 74°13W 328 A3
Santa Marta, Sierra Nevada de
Colombia 10°55N 73°50W 328 A3
Santa Marta de Tormes
Spain 40°57N 5°38W 194 E5
Santa Marta Grande, C.
Brazil 28°43S 48°50W 335 B6
Santa Marta Ortigueira, Ría de
Spain 43°44N 7°45W 194 B3
Santa Martabaai = Sint Marthabaai
Curaçao 12°17N 69°8W 322 g
Santa Maura = Lefkada
Greece 38°40N 20°43E 207 B2
Santa Monica U.S.A. 34°1N 118°29W 126 B2
Santa Monica Mts.
U.S.A. 34°6N 118°29W 126 B2
Santa Monica Mts. ⌂
U.S.A. 34°4N 118°44W 307 L8
Santa Olalla Spain 40°2N 4°25W 194 E6
Santa Olalla del Cala
Spain 37°54N 6°14W 195 H4
Santa Paula U.S.A. 34°21N 119°4W 307 L7
Santa Pola Spain 38°13N 0°35W 197 G4
Santa Ponça Spain 39°30N 2°28E 206 B3
Santa Quitéria Brazil 4°20S 40°10W 332 B3
Santa Rita = Itumbiara
Brazil 18°20S 49°10W 333 E2
Santa Rita Amazonas,
Brazil 3°29S 69°19W 328 D4
Santa Rita Paraíba, Brazil 7°8S 34°58W 332 C5
Santa Rita Colombia 4°53N 68°24W 328 C4
Santa Rita Guam 13°23N 144°40E 302 d
Santa Rita Samar, Phil. 11°27N 124°56E 233 F5
Santa Rita Zulia, Venezuela 10°32N 71°32W 328 A3
Santa Rita de Cássia Brazil 11°0S 44°32W 332 D3
Santa Rita do Araguaia =
Guiratinga Brazil 16°21S 53°45W 331 D7
Santa Rita do Araguaia
Brazil 17°20S 53°12W 331 D7
Santa Rosa = Bella Unión
Uruguay 30°15S 57°40W 334 C4
Santa Rosa La Pampa,
Argentina 36°40S 64°17W 334 D3
Santa Rosa San Luis,
Argentina 32°21S 65°10W 334 C2
Santa Rosa Beni, Bolivia 14°10S 66°53W 330 C4
Santa Rosa Pando, Bolivia 10°36S 67°20W 330 C4
Santa Rosa Santa Cruz,
Bolivia 17°7S 63°35W 331 D5
Santa Rosa Brazil 27°52S 54°29W 335 B5
Santa Rosa Colombia 3°32N 69°48W 328 C4
Santa Rosa Curaçao 12°7N 68°53W 322 g
Santa Rosa El Oro, Ecuador 3°27S 79°58W 328 D2
Santa Rosa Galápagos Is.,
Ecuador 0°40S 90°25W 330 a
Santa Rosa Puno, Peru 14°30S 70°50W 330 C3
Santa Rosa San Martín,
Peru 6°41S 76°37W 330 B2
Santa Rosa Phil. 15°25N 120°57E 232 D3
Santa Rosa Calif., U.S.A. 38°26N 122°43W 306 G4
Santa Rosa N. Mex.,
U.S.A. 34°57N 104°41W 305 J11
Santa Rosa Amazonas,
Venezuela 1°29N 66°55W 328 C4
Santa Rosa, Mt. Guam 13°32N 144°55E 302 d
Santa Rosa and San Jacinto Mts. ⌂
U.S.A. 33°28N 116°20W 307 M10
Santa Rosa Beach U.S.A. 30°22N 86°14W 316 E3
Santa Rosa de Amanadona
Venezuela 1°29N 66°55W 328 C4
Santa Rosa de Cabal
Colombia 4°52N 75°38W 328 C2
Santa Rosa de Copán
Honduras 14°47N 88°46W 320 D2
Santa Rosa de la Roca
Bolivia 16°3S 61°34W 331 D5
Santa Rosa de Locobe
Chile 33°25S 70°33W 137 B2
Santa Rosa de Osos
Colombia 6°39N 75°28W 328 B2
Santa Rosa de Río Primero
Argentina 31°8S 63°20W 334 C3
Santa Rosa de Viterbo
Colombia 5°53N 72°59W 328 B3
Santa Rosa del Palmar
Bolivia 16°54S 62°24W 331 D5
Santa Rosa I. Calif.,
U.S.A. 33°58N 120°6W 307 M6
Santa Rosa I. Fla., U.S.A. 30°20N 86°50W 317 E3
Santa Rosa Range
U.S.A. 41°45N 117°40W 304 F5
Santa Rosalía Mexico 27°19N 112°17W 318 B2
Santa Stae Venice, Italy 142 b2
Santa Sylvina Argentina 27°50S 61°10W 334 B3
Santa Tecla = Nueva San Salvador
El Salv. 13°40N 89°18W 320 D2
Santa Teresa Argentina 33°25S 60°47W 334 C3
Santa Teresa N. Terr.,
Australia 24°8S 134°22E 280 C1
Santa Teresa Brazil 19°55S 40°36W 333 E3
Santa Teresa Tamaulipas,
Mexico 25°17N 97°51W 319 B5
Santa Teresa Venezuela 4°43N 61°4W 329 C5
Santa Teresa △ Uruguay 33°57S 53°31W 335 C5
Santa Teresa de la Ovalle
Chile 33°22S 70°44W 137 B1
Santa Teresa di Riva Italy 37°57N 15°22E 201 E8
Santa Teresa Gallura Italy 41°14N 9°11E 200 A2
Santa Teresinha Brazil 10°28S 50°31W 332 D1
Santa Teresita Argentina 36°32S 56°41W 334 D4
Santa Uxía de Ribeira
Spain 42°36N 8°58W 194 C2
Santa Vitória Brazil 18°50S 50°8W 333 E1
Santa Vitória do Palmar
Brazil 33°32S 53°25W 335 C5
Santa Ynez → U.S.A. 34°41N 120°36W 307 L6
Santa Ynez Mts. U.S.A. 34°30N 120°0W 307 L6
Santa Ysabel U.S.A. 33°7N 116°40W 307 M10
Santadi Italy 39°5N 8°43E 200 C1
Santaella Spain 37°34N 4°51W 195 H6
Santahamina Finland 60°8N 25°2E 121 C3
Santahar Bangla. 24°48N 88°59E 241 C2
Santai China 31°5N 104°58E 228 B5
Santaluz Brazil 11°15S 39°22W 332 D4
Santan Indonesia 0°3S 117°28E 235 C5
Santana = Uruaçu Brazil 14°30S 49°10W 333 D2
Santana Bahia, Brazil 13°2S 44°5W 333 D3
Santana São Paulo, Brazil 23°29S 46°36W 137 A2
Santana Madeira 32°48N 16°52W 153 c
Sântana Romania 46°20N 21°30E 182 D6
Santana, Coxilha de
Brazil 30°50S 55°35W 335 C4
Santana do Ipanema
Brazil 9°22S 37°14W 332 C4
Santana do Livramento
Brazil 30°55S 55°30W 335 C4
Santana do Paranaíba = Paranaíba
Brazil 19°40S 51°11W 331 D7
Santander Colombia 3°1N 76°28W 328 C2
Santander Phil. 9°25N 123°20E 233 G4
Santander Spain 43°27N 3°51W 194 B7
Santander □ Colombia 7°0N 73°15W 328 B3
Santander Jiménez
Mexico 24°13N 98°28W 319 C5
Sant'Angelo, Castel Rome, Italy 136 b1
Santanilla, Is. Honduras 17°22N 83°57W 320 C3
Santanyí Spain 39°20N 3°5E 206 B4
Santaquin U.S.A. 39°59N 111°47W 304 G8
Santarcángelo di Romagna
Italy 44°4N 12°26E 199 D9
Santarém Brazil 2°25S 54°42W 329 D7
Santarém Portugal 39°12N 8°42W 195 F2
Santarém □ Portugal 39°10N 8°40W 195 F2
Santaren Channel
W. Indies 24°0N 79°30W 320 B4
Santee U.S.A. 32°50N 116°58W 307 N10
Santee → U.S.A. 33°7N 79°17W 315 E15
Santeny France 48°43N 2°34E 114 B3
Santéramo in Colle Italy 40°49N 16°45E 201 B9
Santerno → Italy 44°34N 11°58E 199 D8
Santhià Italy 45°22N 8°10E 198 C5
Santi Taiwan 22°43N 120°39E 225 D2
Santi-Quaranta = Sarandë
Albania 39°52N 19°55E 206 B9
Santiago = Río Grande de
Santiago → Mexico 21°36N 105°26W 318 C3
Santiago = São Tiago
C. Verde Is. 15°0N 23°40W 153 j
Santiago Brazil 29°11S 54°52W 335 B5
Santiago Canary Is. 28°2N 17°12W 153 e1
Santiago Chile 33°26S 70°40W 137 B2
Santiago Panama 8°0N 81°0W 320 E3
Santiago Peru 14°11S 75°43W 330 C2
Santiago Ilocos S., Phil. 17°18N 120°27E 232 C3
Santiago Isabela, Phil. 16°41N 121°33E 232 C3
Santiago → Peru 4°27S 77°38W 328 D2
Santiago, C. Chile 50°46S 75°27W 336 D1
Santiago, I. = San Salvador, I.
Ecuador 0°16S 90°42W 330 a
Santiago, Punta de Eq. Guin. 3°12N 8°40E 263 E6
Santiago, Sierra de
Bolivia 18°25S 59°25W 331 D6
Santiago Benítez ✕ (SCL)
Chile 33°33S 70°42W 137 B1
Santiago de Chiquitos
Bolivia 18°19S 59°34W 331 D6
Santiago de Chuco Peru 8°9S 78°11W 330 B2
Santiago de Compostela
Spain 42°52N 8°37W 194 C2
Santiago de Cuba Cuba 20°0N 75°49W 320 C4
Santiago de los Caballeros
Dom. Rep. 19°30N 70°40W 321 C5
Santiago de Surco Peru 12°9S 77°0W 124 B2
Santiago del Estero
Argentina 27°50S 64°15W 334 B3
Santiago del Estero □
Argentina 27°40S 63°15W 334 B3
Santiago del Teide
Canary Is. 28°17N 16°48W 153 e1
Santiago do Boqueirão = Santiago
Brazil 29°11S 54°52W 335 B5
Santiago do Cacém
Portugal 38°1N 8°42W 195 G2
Santiago I. Phil. 16°23N 119°56E 232 C2
Santiago Ixcuintla
Mexico 21°49N 105°13W 318 C3
Santiago Jamiltepec
Mexico 16°17N 97°49W 319 D5
Santiago Papasquiaro
Mexico 25°3N 105°25W 318 C3
Santiago Pinotepa Nacional
Mexico 16°19N 98°1W 319 D5
Santiaguillo, L. de
Mexico 24°48N 104°48W 318 C4
Santialing Taiwan 25°5N 121°51E 225 A3
Santiao Chiao Taiwan 25°1N 122°0E 225 A3
Santiaolun Taiwan 23°39N 120°9E 225 C2
Santiguila Mali 12°42N 7°25W 262 C3
Santillana del Mar Spain 43°24N 4°6W 194 B6
Santisteban del Puerto
Spain 38°17N 3°15W 195 G7
Santo → Peru 8°56S 78°37W 330 B2
Santo Amaro Bahia,
Brazil 12°30S 38°43W 333 D4
Santo Amaro São Paulo,
Brazil 23°39S 46°42W 137 B1
Santo Amaro Lisboa,
Portugal 38°42N 9°11W 126 A1
Santo Anastácio Brazil 21°58S 51°39W 335 A5
Santo André Brazil 23°39S 46°29W 335 A6
Santo André Lisboa,
Portugal 38°38N 9°3W 126 B2
Santo Ângelo Brazil 28°15S 54°15W 335 B5
Santo Antão C. Verde Is. 16°52N 25°10W 153 j
Santo Antão do Tojal
Portugal 38°49N 9°9W 126 A2
Santo Antônia
São Tomé & Príncipe 1°37N 7°27E 265 a
Santo Antônio Brazil 2°24S 60°58W 329 D5
Santo Antônio, Qta. de
Portugal 38°39N 9°15W 126 B1
Santo Antônio da Cachoeira =
Itaguatins Brazil 5°47S 47°29W 332 C2
Santo Antônio de Jesus
Brazil 12°58S 39°16W 333 D4
Santo Antônio do Abaixo = Santo
Antônio do Leverger
Brazil 15°52S 56°5W 331 D6
Santo Antônio do Içá Brazil 3°5S 67°57W 328 D4
Santo Antônio do Leverger
Brazil 15°52S 56°5W 331 D6
Santo Corazón Bolivia 18°0S 58°45W 331 D6
Santo Cosimo e Damiano, Ex Chiesa
di Venice, Italy 142 c2
Santo Domingo
Dom. Rep. 18°30N 69°59W 321 C6
Santo Domingo Baja Calif. S.,
Mexico 25°29N 111°55W 318 B2
Santo Domingo Nic. 12°14N 84°59W 320 D3
Santo Domingo de la Calzada
Spain 42°26N 2°57W 196 C2
Santo Domingo de los Colorados
Ecuador 0°15S 79°9W 328 D2
Santo Domingo Pueblo
U.S.A. 35°31N 106°22W 305 J10
Santo Domingo Tehuantepec =
Tehuantepec Mexico 16°21N 95°13W 319 D5
Santo Nino I. Phil. 11°54N 124°26E 233 F5
Santo Stéfano di Camastro
Italy 38°1N 14°22E 201 D7
Santo Tirso Portugal 41°21N 8°28W 194 D2
Santo Tomás Galápagos Is.,
Ecuador 0°51S 91°2W 330 a
Santo Tomás Baja Calif.,
Mexico 31°33N 116°24W 318 A1
Santo Tomás Peru 14°26S 72°8W 330 C3
Santo Tomas Phil. 7°32N 125°37E 233 H5
Santo Tomas, Univ. of
Phil. 14°36N 120°59E 127 B1
Santo Tomás, Volcán
Ecuador 0°48S 91°7W 330 a
Santo Tomé Argentina 28°40S 56°5W 335 B4
Santo Tomé de Guayana = Ciudad
Guayana Venezuela 8°0N 62°30W 329 B5
Santomera Spain 38°4N 1°3W 197 G3
Santoña Spain 43°29N 3°27W 194 B7
Santorini Greece 36°23N 25°27E 205 E7
Santos Brazil 24°0S 46°20W 335 A6
Santos, Sierra de los Spain 38°7N 5°12W 195 G5
Santos Dumont Brazil 22°55S 43°10W 333 F3
Santos Dumont ✕ (SDU)
Brazil 22°54S 43°9W 135 B2
Santoshpur India 22°31N 88°16E 124 B1
Santragachi India 22°35N 88°17E 124 B1
Santry Ireland 53°24N 6°15W 120 A2
Santuario de Aves Laguna
Colorada △ Bolivia 22°10S 67°45W 334 A2
Sanuki Japan 34°19N 134°10E 222 C6
Sanur Indonesia 8°41S 115°15E 231 K18
Sanwan Taiwan 24°39N 120°57E 225 B2
Sanwer India 22°59N 75°50E 242 H6
Sanxenxo Spain 42°24N 8°49W 194 C2
Sanxia Shuiku China 30°3N 107°58E 228 B6
Sanxiang China 22°21N 113°25E 219 a
Sanya China 18°14N 109°29E 236 C7
San'yō Japan 34°2N 131°5E 222 C3
Sanyuan China 34°35N 108°58E 226 G5
Sanyuanli China 23°9N 113°14E 121 B2
Sanyuki-Sammyaku Japan 34°5N 134°0E 222 C6
Sanza Pombo Angola 7°18S 15°56E 265 D3
São Bartolomeu de Messines
Portugal 37°15N 8°17W 195 H2
São Benedito = Beneditinos
Brazil 5°27S 42°22W 332 C3
São Benedito Brazil 4°3S 40°53W 332 B3
São Benedito → Brazil 9°11S 57°2W 331 B6
São Bento Brazil 2°42S 44°50W 332 B3
São Bento do Norte Brazil 5°4S 36°2W 332 C4
São Bernardo do Campo
Brazil 23°45S 46°34W 333 F2
São Borja Brazil 28°39S 56°0W 335 B4
São Brás de Alportel
Portugal 37°8N 7°37W 195 H3
São Braz, C. de Angola 9°58S 13°19E 265 D2
São Caetano do Sul Brazil 23°37S 46°34W 137 B2
São Caitano Brazil 8°21S 36°6W 332 C4
São Carlos Brazil 22°0S 47°50W 335 A6
São Conrado Brazil 23°0S 43°17W 135 B1
São Cristóvão Rio de J.,
Brazil 22°53S 43°13W 135 B1
São Cristóvão Sergipe,
Brazil 11°1S 37°15W 332 D4
São Domingo do Capim
Brazil 1°41S 47°47W 332 B2
São Domingos Brazil 13°25S 46°19W 333 D2
São Domingos
Guinea-Biss. 12°19N 16°13W 262 C1
São Domingos da Boa Vista = São
Domingo do Capim
Brazil 1°41S 47°47W 332 B2
São Domingos do Maranhão
Brazil 5°42S 44°22W 332 C3
São Felipe = Eirunepé
Brazil 6°35S 69°53W 330 B4
São Felipe = Içana Brazil 0°21N 67°19W 328 C4
São Félix Brazil 11°36S 50°39W 333 D1
São Félix do Xingu Brazil 6°38S 51°59W 331 B7
São Filipe C. Verde Is. 15°2N 24°30W 153 j
São Francisco = Itapagé
Brazil 3°41S 39°34W 332 B4
São Francisco Brazil 16°0S 44°50W 333 E3
São Francisco → Brazil 10°30S 36°24W 332 D4
São Francisco do Maranhão
Brazil 6°15S 42°52W 332 C3
São Francisco do Sul
Brazil 26°15S 48°36W 335 B6
São Francisco Penitência
Rio de J., Brazil 135 b1
São Gabriel Brazil 30°20S 54°20W 335 C5
São Gabriel da Cachoeira
Brazil 0°8S 67°5W 328 D4
São Gabriel da Palha
Brazil 18°47S 40°39W 333 E3
São Gonçalo = Araripina
Brazil 7°33S 40°34W 332 C3
São Gonçalo Brazil 22°48S 43°5W 333 F3
São Gotardo Brazil 19°19S 46°3W 333 E2
Sao Hill Tanzania 8°20S 35°12E 269 D4
São João Guinea-Biss. 11°32N 15°25W 262 C1
São João da Baliza Brazil 0°52N 59°52W 329 C6
São João da Barra Brazil 21°38S 41°3W 333 F3
São João da Boa Vista
Brazil 22°0S 46°52W 335 A6
São João da Madeira
Portugal 40°54N 8°30W 194 E2
São João da Pesqueira
Portugal 41°8N 7°24W 194 D3
São João da Ponte Brazil 15°56S 44°1W 333 E3
São João de Meriti Brazil 22°48S 43°21W 333 F3
São João de Montenegro =
Montenegro Brazil 29°39S 51°29W 335 B5
São João del Rei Brazil 21°8S 44°15W 333 F3
São João do Araguaia
Brazil 5°23S 48°46W 332 C2
São João do Paraíso Brazil 15°19S 42°1W 333 E3
São João do Piauí Brazil 8°21S 42°15W 332 C3
São João do Sul Angola 15°46S 12°0E 265 F2
São João dos Patos Brazil 6°30S 43°42W 332 C3
São Joaquim Amazonas,
Brazil 0°1S 67°16W 328 D4
São Joaquim Sta. Catarina,
Brazil 28°18S 49°56W 335 B6
São Joaquim △ Brazil 28°12S 49°37W 335 B6
São Joaquim da Barra
Brazil 20°35S 47°53W 333 F2
São Jorge Azores 38°38N 28°3W 153 d1
São Jorge, Canal de Azores 38°30N 28°0W 153 d1
São Jorge, Castelo de
Portugal 38°42N 9°8W 126 A2
São Jorge, Pta. de Azores 38°42N 27°3W 153 d1
São Jorge, Pta. de Madeira 32°50N 16°53W 153 c
São José Brazil 27°38S 48°39W 335 B6
São José, B. de Brazil 2°38S 44°4W 332 B3
São José da Lagoa = Nova Era
Brazil 19°45S 43°3W 333 E3
São José da Laje Brazil 9°1S 36°3W 332 C4
São José de Mipibu Brazil 6°5S 35°15W 332 C4
São José de Ribamar Brazil 2°33S 44°3W 332 B3
São José de Tocantins = Niquelândia
Brazil 14°33S 48°23W 333 D2
São José do Norte Brazil 32°1S 52°3W 335 C5
São José do Peixe Brazil 7°24S 42°34W 332 C3
São José do Rio Preto
Brazil 20°50S 49°20W 335 A6
São José dos Campos
Brazil 23°7S 45°52W 335 A6
São José dos Cocais = Nossa
Senhora do Livramento
Brazil 15°48S 56°22W 331 D6
São José dos Matões = Parnarama
Brazil 5°31S 43°6W 332 C3
São Juliao do Tojal Portugal 38°49N 9°8W 126 A2
São Leopoldo Brazil 29°50S 51°10W 335 B5
São Lourenço Brazil 22°7S 45°3W 333 F2
São Lourenço → Brazil 17°53S 57°27W 331 D6
São Lourenço, Pantanal do
Brazil 17°30S 56°20W 331 D6
São Lourenço, Pta. de
Madeira 32°44N 16°39W 153 c
São Lourenço do Sul
Brazil 31°22S 51°58W 335 C5
São Luís Brazil 2°39S 44°15W 332 B3
São Luís do Curu Brazil 3°40S 39°14W 332 B4
São Luís do Tapajós Brazil 4°25S 56°12W 329 D6
São Luís Gonzaga = Ipixuna
Brazil 7°0S 71°40W 330 B3
São Luís Gonzaga Brazil 28°25S 55°0W 335 B5
São Marcos → Brazil 18°15S 47°37W 333 E2
São Marcos, B. de Brazil 2°0S 44°0W 332 B3
São Martinho da Cortiça
Portugal 40°18N 8°8W 194 E2
São Mateus Azores 38°26N 28°27W 153 d1
São Mateus Brazil 18°44S 39°50W 333 E4
São Mateus → Brazil 18°35S 39°44W 333 E4
São Mateus do Sul Brazil 25°52S 50°23W 335 B5
São Miguel Azores 37°47N 25°30W 153 d3
São Miguel do Araguaia
Brazil 13°19S 50°13W 333 D1
São Miguel do Guamá
Brazil 1°37S 47°29W 332 B2
São Miguel do Oeste
Brazil 26°45S 53°34W 335 B5
São Miguel dos Campos
Brazil 9°47S 36°5W 332 C4
São Nicolau C. Verde Is. 16°20N 24°20W 153 j
São Nicolau → Angola 14°16S 12°22E 265 E2
São Nicolau → Brazil 5°45S 42°2W 332 C3
São Paulo Atl. Oc. 0°56N 29°22W 152 F9
São Paulo Brazil 23°32S 46°38W 137 B2
São Paulo □ Brazil 22°0S 49°0W 335 A6
São Paulo Congonhas ✕ (CGH)
Brazil 23°38S 46°39W 137 B2
São Paulo de Olivença
Brazil 3°27S 68°48W 328 D4

São Pedro Atl. Oc. 0°56N 29°22W 152 F9
São Pedro do Sul Portugal 40°46N 8°4W 194 E2
São Rafael Brazil 5°47S 36°55W 332 C4
São Raimundo das Mangabeiras Brazil 7°1S 45°29W 332 C2
São Raimundo Nonato Brazil 9°1S 42°42W 332 C3
São Romão Brazil 16°22S 45°4W 333 E2
São Roque Madeira 32°46N 16°48W 153 c
São Roque, C. de Brazil 5°30S 35°16W 332 C4
São Roque do Pico Azores 38°31N 28°19W 153 d1
São Salvador do Congo = Mbanza Congo Angola 6°18S 14°16E 265 D2
São Sebastião Azores 38°39N 27°6W 153 d1
São Sebastião, I. de Brazil 23°50S 45°18W 335 A6
São Sebastião do Paraíso Brazil 20°54S 46°59W 335 A6
São Simão Brazil 18°56S 50°30W 333 E1
São Teotónio Portugal 37°30N 8°42W 195 H2
São Tiago C. Verde Is. 15°0N 23°40W 153 j
São Tomé Brazil 5°58S 36°4W 332 C4
São Tomé São Tomé & Príncipe 0°10N 6°39E 265 a
São Tomé, C. de Brazil 22°0S 40°59W 333 F3
São Tomé, Pico de São Tomé & Príncipe 0°16N 6°33E 265 a
São Tomé & Príncipe ■ Africa 0°12N 6°39E 265 a
São Vicente = Araguatins Brazil 5°38S 48°7W 332 C2
São Vicente Brazil 23°57S 46°23W 335 A6
São Vicente C. Verde Is. 17°0N 25°0W 153 j
São Vicente Madeira 32°48N 17°3W 153 c
São Vicente, C. de Portugal 37°0N 9°0W 195 H1
Saona, I. Dom. Rep. 18°10N 68°40W 321 C6
Saône → France 45°44N 4°50E 173 G11
Saône-et-Loire □ France 46°30N 4°50E 173 F11
Saonek Indonesia 0°22S 130°55E 231 E8
Saoura, O. → Algeria 29°0N 0°55W 261 C4
Sapa India 22°30N 88°15E 124 B1
Sapam, Ao Thailand 8°0N 98°26E 237 a
Sapanca Turkey 40°41N 30°16E 212 B4
Sapanjang Indonesia 7°10S 115°50E 235 D5
Sapão → Brazil 11°1S 45°32W 332 D2
Saparua Indonesia 3°33S 128°40E 231 E7
Sapateiro, Cor. do → Brazil 23°35S 46°41W 137 B1
Sapé Brazil 7°6S 35°13W 332 C4
Sape Indonesia 8°34S 118°59E 235 D5
Sape, Teluk Indonesia 8°32S 119°4E 235 D5
Sapele Nigeria 5°50N 5°40E 263 D6
Sapelo I. U.S.A. 31°25N 81°12W 316 D8
Sapelo Sound U.S.A. 31°30N 81°10W 316 D8
Sapes Greece 41°2N 25°43E 203 E9
Şaphane Turkey 39°1N 29°13E 205 B11
Sapi ⌂ Zimbabwe 15°48S 29°42E 269 F2
Sapienza Greece 36°45N 21°43E 204 E3
Sapindji Dem. Rep. of the Congo 9°39S 23°12E 265 D4
Sapo △ Liberia 5°15N 8°30W 262 D3
Sapone Burkina Faso 12°3N 1°35W 263 C4
Saposoa Peru 6°55S 76°45W 330 B2
Sapotskina Belarus 53°49N 23°40E 184 E10
Sapouy Burkina Faso 11°34N 1°44W 263 C4
Sapozhok Russia 53°59N 40°41E 190 D5
Sapphire Australia 23°28S 147°43E 280 C4
Sappho U.S.A. 48°4N 124°16W 306 B2
Sapporo Japan 43°0N 141°21E 220 C10
Sapri Italy 40°4N 15°38E 201 B8
Sapt Kosi → Nepal 26°32N 86°56E 243 F12
Sapu Angola 12°28S 19°26E 265 E3
Sapudi Indonesia 7°6S 114°20E 235 D4
Sapulpa U.S.A. 35°59N 96°5W 314 D6
Sapulut Malaysia 4°42N 116°28E 235 B5
Saqqez Iran 36°15N 46°20E 213 D12
Sar Dasht Āzarbāyjān-e Gharbī, Iran 36°9N 45°28E 213 D11
Sar Dasht Khuzestān, Iran 32°32N 48°52E 247 C6
Sar-e Pol Afghan. 36°10N 66°0E 240 A2
Sar-e Pol □ Afghan. 36°20N 65°50E 240 A2
Sar Gachīneh = Yāsūj Iran 30°31N 51°31E 247 D6
Sar Passage Palau 7°12N 134°22E 288 c
Sar Planina Macedonia 42°0N 21°0E 202 E4
Sara Burkina Faso 11°40N 3°53W 262 C4
Sara Niger 20°46N 12°35E 259 D2
Sara Phil. 11°16N 123°1E 233 F4
Šara △ Serbia 42°12N 21°0E 202 D5
Sara Buri = Saraburi Thailand 14°30N 100°55E 236 E3
Sarāb Iran 37°55N 47°40E 213 D12
Sarābādī Iraq 33°1N 44°48E 246 C5
Sarabît el Khâdim Egypt 29°2N 33°25E 251 J4
Sarābleh Iran 33°44N 46°34E 213 F12
Saraburi Thailand 14°30N 100°55E 236 E3
Saradiya India 21°34N 70°2E 242 J4
Saraféré Mali 15°50N 3°40W 262 B4
Saragossa = Zaragoza Spain 41°39N 0°53W 196 D4
Saraguro Ecuador 3°35S 79°16W 328 D2
Sarahs Turkmenistan 36°32N 61°13E 247 B9
Sarai Naurang Pakistan 32°50N 70°47E 242 C4
Saraikela India 22°42N 85°56E 243 H11
Saraipali India 21°20N 82°59E 244 D6
Saraiu Romania 44°43N 28°10E 183 F13
Sarajevo Bos.-H. 43°52N 18°26E 182 G3
Sarakhs = Sarahs Turkmenistan 36°32N 61°13E 247 B9
Sarakhs Iran 36°32N 61°9E 216 E6
Saramacca → Suriname 5°50N 55°55W 329 B6
Saramati Burma 25°44N 95°2E 241 C5
Saran, Gunung Indonesia 0°30S 111°25E 235 C4
Saranac U.S.A. 42°56N 85°13W 311 B11
Saranac Lake U.S.A. 44°20N 74°10W 313 B10
Saranac Lakes U.S.A. 44°20N 74°28W 313 B10
Saranda Tanzania 5°45S 34°59E 268 D3
Sarandë Albania 39°52N 19°55E 206 B9
Sarandí Argentina 34°40S 58°20W 117 C2
Sarandí del Yí Uruguay 33°18S 55°38W 335 C4
Sarandí Grande Uruguay 33°44S 56°20W 334 C4
Sarangani □ Phil. 5°45N 125°20E 233 J5
Sarangani B. Phil. 6°0N 125°13E 233 J5
Sarangani I. Phil. 5°26N 125°28E 233 J5
Sarangani Is. Phil. 5°25N 125°25E 233 J5
Sarangarh India 21°30N 83°5E 244 D6
Saranovo = Septemvri Bulgaria 42°13N 24°6E 203 D8
Saransk Russia 54°10N 45°10E 190 C7
Sarapul Russia 56°28N 53°48E 186 C9
Sarāqib Syria 35°52N 36°47E 250 C7
Sarar Plain = Bannaanka Saraar Somalia 9°25N 46°17E 267 C6
Sarasota U.S.A. 27°20N 82°32W 317 H7
Saraswati → India 22°46N 88°15E 124 A1
Sarata Ukraine 46°1N 29°40E 183 D14
Sarata → Ukraine 45°51N 29°41E 183 E14
Saratoga Calif., U.S.A. 37°16N 122°2W 306 H4
Saratoga Wyo., U.S.A. 41°27N 106°49W 304 F10
Saratoga ⌂ U.S.A. 43°0N 73°38W 313 D11
Saratoga L. U.S.A. 43°1N 73°44W 313 C11
Saratoga Springs U.S.A. 43°5N 73°47W 313 C11
Saratok Malaysia 1°55N 111°17E 235 B4
Saratov Russia 51°30N 46°2E 190 E7
Saratov □ Russia 51°50N 46°20E 190 E8
Sarāvān Iran 27°25N 62°15E 247 E9
Saravane Laos 15°43N 106°25E 236 E6
Sarawak □ Malaysia 2°0N 113°0E 235 B4
Saray Tekirdağ, Turkey 41°26N 27°55E 203 E11
Saray Van, Turkey 38°38N 44°9E 213 C11
Saraya Senegal 12°50N 11°45W 262 C2
Saraycık Turkey 39°1N 29°49E 205 B11
Sarayköy Turkey 37°55N 28°54E 205 D10
Saraylar Turkey 40°39N 27°40E 203 F11
Sarayönü Turkey 38°16N 32°24E 212 C5
Sarbāz Iran 26°38N 61°19E 247 E9
Sarbīsheh Iran 32°30N 59°40E 247 C8
Sárbogárd Hungary 46°50N 18°40E 182 D3
Sarca → Italy 45°52N 10°52E 198 C7
Sarcelles France 49°1N 2°23E 173 D9
Sarda → India 27°21N 81°23E 243 F9
Sardalas Libya 25°50N 10°34E 258 C2
Sardar Sarovar Dam India 21°50N 73°50E 244 D1
Sardarshahr India 28°30N 74°29E 242 E6
Sardegna □ Italy 40°0N 9°0E 200 B1
Sardhana India 29°9N 77°39E 242 E7
Sardina, Pta. Canary Is. 28°9N 15°44W 153 e1
Sardinata Colombia 8°5N 72°48W 328 B3
Sardinia = Sardegna □ Italy 40°0N 9°0E 200 B1
Sardinia U.S.A. 39°0N 83°49W 311 F13
Sardis Turkey 38°28N 27°58E 205 C10
Sardis Ga., U.S.A. 32°58N 81°46W 316 C8
Sārdūīyeh = Dar Mazār Iran 29°14N 57°20E 247 D8
Sarecky potok → Czech Rep. 50°7N 14°23E 135 B2
Saren Indonesia 8°26S 115°34E 231 J18
S'Arenal Spain 39°30N 2°45E 206 B3
Sarentino Italy 46°38N 11°21E 199 B8
Saréyamou Mali 16°7N 3°10W 262 B4
Sargasso Sea Atl. Oc. 27°0N 72°0W 292 G13
Sargent U.S.A. 33°26N 84°52W 316 B5
Sargodha Pakistan 32°10N 72°40E 242 C5
Sarh Chad 9°5N 18°23E 259 G3
Sarhala Ivory C. 8°22N 6°8W 262 D3
Sarhro, Jebel Morocco 31°6N 5°0W 260 B4
Sārī Iran 36°30N 53°4E 247 B7
Sari d'Orcino France 42°3N 8°49E 175 F12
Saria Greece 35°54N 27°17E 205 F9
Saria India 21°38N 83°22E 243 J10
Sariab Pakistan 30°6N 66°59E 242 D2
Sarıbeyler Turkey 39°24N 27°35E 205 B9
Saricumbe Angola 12°12S 19°46E 265 E3
Sarigan N. Marianas 16°43N 145°47E 302 a
Sarıgöl Turkey 38°14N 28°41E 212 C3
Sarıkamış Turkey 40°22N 42°35E 213 B10
Sarıkaya Turkey 39°29N 35°22E 212 C6
Sarikei Malaysia 2°8N 111°30E 235 B4
Sarıköy Turkey 40°12N 27°37E 203 F11
Sarila India 25°46N 79°41E 243 G8
Sarimbun Singapore 1°24N 103°40E 138 A2
Sarimbun Res. Singapore 1°25N 103°41E 138 A2
Sarina Australia 21°22S 149°13E 280 C4
Sariñena Spain 41°47N 0°10W 196 D4
Sarinleey Somalia 2°22N 42°17E 267 D5
Sarıoğlan Turkey 39°5N 35°59E 212 C6
Sariri Papua N. G. 9°11S 148°35E 286 E5
Sarita U.S.A. 27°13N 97°47W 314 H6
Sarıveliler Turkey 36°41N 32°37E 250 B3
Sariwŏn N. Korea 38°31N 125°46E 224 C2
Sarıyar Barajı Turkey 40°2N 31°33E 212 B4
Sarıyer Turkey 41°10N 29°3E 122 A2
Sarız Turkey 38°28N 36°30E 212 C7
Sarju → India 27°21N 81°23E 243 F9
Sark U.K. 49°25N 2°22W 169 H5
Sarkad Hungary 46°47N 21°23E 182 D6
Sarkari Tala India 27°39N 70°52E 242 F4
Şarkışla Turkey 39°21N 36°25E 212 C7
Şarköy Turkey 40°36N 27°6E 203 F11
Sarlat-la-Canéda France 44°54N 1°13E 174 D5
Şărmăşag Romania 47°21N 22°50E 182 C7
Sărmaşu Romania 46°45N 24°13E 183 D9
Sarmi Indonesia 1°49S 138°44E 231 E9
Sarmiento Argentina 45°35S 69°5W 336 C3
Sarmizegetusa Romania 45°31N 22°47E 182 E7
Särna Sweden 61°41N 13°8E 162 C7
Sarnano Italy 43°2N 13°18E 199 E10
Sarnen Switz. 46°53N 8°13E 179 J4
Sarnia Canada 42°58N 82°23W 312 D2
Sarno Italy 40°49N 14°37E 201 B7
Sarnthein = Sarentino Italy 46°38N 11°21E 199 B8
Särö Sweden 57°31N 11°57E 163 G5
Sarolangun Indonesia 2°19S 102°42E 234 C2
Saronikos Kolpos Greece 37°45N 23°45E 204 D5
Saronno Italy 45°38N 9°2E 198 C6
Saros Körfezi Turkey 40°30N 26°15E 203 F10
Sárospatak Hungary 48°18N 21°33E 182 B6
Sarowbī Afghan. 34°36N 69°44E 240 B3
Sarpsborg Norway 59°16N 11°7E 164 E8
Sarqan Kazakhstan 45°24N 79°55E 217 C9
Sarracín Spain 42°15N 3°45W 194 C7
Sarralbe France 49°0N 7°1E 173 D14
Sarrat Phil. 18°9N 120°39E 232 B3
Sarre = Saar → Europe 49°41N 6°32E 170 E6
Sarre Italy 45°40N 7°15E 198 C4
Sarre-Union France 48°57N 7°4E 173 D14
Sarrebourg France 48°43N 7°3E 173 D14
Sarreguemines France 49°5N 7°4E 173 C14
Sarriá Barcelona, Spain 41°22N 2°8E 114 A1
Sarria Galicia, Spain 42°49N 7°29W 194 C3
Sarrión Spain 40°9N 0°49W 196 E4
Sarro Mali 13°40N 5°15W 262 C3
Sarsing Iraq 37°2N 43°20E 213 D10
Sarstedt Germany 52°14N 9°52E 178 C5
Sarsuna India 22°28N 88°17E 124 C1
Sartell U.S.A. 45°37N 94°12W 308 C6
Sartène France 41°38N 8°58E 175 G12
Sarthe □ France 47°58N 0°10E 172 E7
Sarthe → France 47°33N 0°31W 172 E6
Sartilly France 48°45N 1°28W 172 D5
Sartrouville France 48°56N 2°10E 134 A2
Saruhanlı Turkey 38°44N 27°36E 205 C9
Sărulești Romania 44°25N 26°39E 183 F11
Saruna → Pakistan 26°31N 67°7E 242 F2
Sarupeta India 26°30N 91°5E 241 B3
Sarur Azerbaijan 39°22N 45°5E 213 C11
Saruwaged Ra. Papua N. G. 6°13S 146°45E 286 D4
Sárvár Hungary 47°15N 16°56E 182 C1
Sarvar India 26°4N 75°0E 242 F6
Sarvestān Iran 29°20N 53°10E 247 D7
Särvfjället Sweden 62°42N 13°30E 162 B7
Sárvíz → Hungary 46°24N 18°41E 182 D3
Sary-Tash Kyrgyzstan 39°44N 73°15E 217 E8
Sarych, Mys Ukraine 44°25N 33°45E 189 K7
Saryesik-Atyraū Qumy Kazakhstan 45°30N 76°0E 217 C9
Sarykamyshskoye, Ozero = Saryqamysh Köli Turkmenistan 41°56N 57°25E 216 D5
Sarykemer Kazakhstan 43°0N 71°30E 217 D8
Sarykenggir → Kazakhstan 48°22N 67°59E 217 C7
Sarykōl Kazakhstan 53°20N 65°12E 216 B7
Sarykolskiy Khrebet Tajikistan 38°30N 74°30E 217 E8
Saryözek Kazakhstan 44°22N 77°59E 217 D9
Saryqamysh Köli Turkmenistan 41°56N 57°25E 216 D5
Saryshaghan Kazakhstan 46°12N 73°38E 217 C8
Sarysu → Kazakhstan 45°12N 66°36E 217 C7
Sarzana Italy 44°7N 9°58E 198 D6
Sarzeau France 47°31N 2°48W 172 E4
Sasabeneh Ethiopia 7°59N 44°43E 267 C5
Sasad Hungary 47°28N 19°0E 117 B2
Sasamungga Solomon Is. 7°0S 156°50E 287 L9
Sasan Gir India 21°10N 70°36E 242 J4
Sasaram India 24°57N 84°5E 243 G11
Sasari, Mt. Solomon Is. 8°10S 159°30E 287 M10
Sasayama Japan 35°4N 135°13E 223 B7
Sasebo Japan 33°10N 129°43E 222 D1
Saser Kangri India 34°50N 77°50E 243 B7
Sashalom Hungary 47°30N 19°10E 117 A3
Saska Poland 52°14N 21°3E 143 B2
Saskatchewan □ Canada 54°40N 106°0W 297 C7
Saskatchewan → Canada 53°37N 100°40W 297 C8
Saskatoon Canada 52°10N 106°38W 297 C7
Saskylakh Russia 71°55N 114°1E 215 B12
Sasolburg S. Africa 26°46S 27°49E 271 C4
Sason Turkey 38°19N 41°24E 213 C9
Sasovo Russia 54°25N 41°55E 190 C5
Sassandra Ivory C. 4°55N 6°8W 262 E3
Sassandra → Ivory C. 4°58N 6°5W 262 E3
Sássari Italy 40°43N 8°34E 200 B1
Sassie Australia 10°2S 142°51E 280 a
Sassnitz Germany 54°29N 13°39E 178 A9
Sasso Marconi Italy 44°24N 11°15E 199 D8
Sassocorvaro Italy 43°47N 12°30E 199 E9
Sassoferrato Italy 43°26N 12°51E 199 E9
Sassuolo Italy 44°33N 10°47E 198 D7
Sástago Spain 41°19N 0°21W 196 D4
Sastamala Finland 61°20N 22°54E 188 B2
Sastown Liberia 4°45N 8°27W 262 E3
Sasvad India 18°20N 74°2E 244 E2
Sasyk, Ozero Ukraine 45°45N 29°40E 183 E14
Sasyqköl Kazakhstan 46°35N 81°0E 217 C10
Sata-Misaki Japan 31°0N 130°40E 222 F2
Satadougou Mali 12°25N 11°25W 262 C2
Satakunta □ Finland 61°45N 23°0E 160 F20
Satalice Czech Rep. 50°7N 14°34E 135 B3
Satama-Soukoura Ivory C. 7°55N 4°27W 262 D4
Satara India 17°44N 73°58E 244 F1
Satara S. Africa 24°29S 31°47E 271 B5
Sätbaev Kazakhstan 48°10N 67°31E 217 C7
Satbarwa India 23°55N 84°16E 243 H11
Satellite Beach U.S.A. 28°10N 80°36W 317 G9
Säter Sweden 60°21N 15°45E 162 D9
Satevó Mexico 27°57N 106°7W 318 B3
Satgachi India 22°37N 88°25E 124 B2
Satilla → U.S.A. 30°59N 81°29W 316 E8
Satipo Peru 11°15S 74°25W 330 C3
Satka Russia 55°3N 59°1E 186 C10
Satkania Bangla. 22°4N 92°3E 241 D4
Satkhira Bangla. 22°43N 89°8E 241 D2
Satmala Hills Andhra Pradesh, India 19°45N 78°45E 244 E4
Satmala Hills Maharashtra, India 20°15N 74°40E 244 D2
Satna India 24°35N 80°50E 243 G9
Šator Bos.-H. 44°11N 16°37E 199 D13
Sátoraljaújhely Hungary 48°25N 21°41E 182 B6
Satpura △ India 22°40N 78°15E 242 H8
Satpura Ra. India 21°25N 76°10E 244 D3
Sätra Sweden 59°17N 17°54E 139 B1
Satrup Germany 54°41N 9°36E 178 A5
Satsuma-Hantō Japan 31°25N 130°25E 222 F2
Satsuma-Sendai Japan 31°50N 130°20E 222 F2
Satsuma-Shotō Japan 30°0N 130°0E 221 K5
Sattahip Thailand 12°41N 100°54E 236 F3
Sattenapalle India 16°25N 80°6E 245 F5
Sattru Phai Bangkok, Thailand 113 b2
Satu Mare Romania 47°46N 22°55E 182 C7
Satu Mare □ Romania 47°45N 23°0E 182 C8
Satui Indonesia 3°50S 115°27E 235 C5
Satun Thailand 6°43N 100°2E 237 J3
Satupa'itea Samoa 13°45S 172°18W 287 V19
Saturnina → Brazil 12°15S 58°10W 331 C6
Sauce = Juan L. Lacaze Uruguay 34°26S 57°25W 334 C4
Sauce Argentina 30°5S 58°46W 334 C4
Sauceda Mexico 25°46N 101°19W 318 B4
Saucillo Mexico 28°1N 105°17W 318 B3
Sauda Norway 59°40N 6°20E 164 E3
Saudasjøen Norway 59°38N 6°17E 164 E3
Saúde Bahia, Brazil 10°56S 40°24W 332 D3
Saúde São Paulo, Brazil 23°36S 46°37W 137 B2
Sauðárkrókur Iceland 65°45N 19°40W 155 B7
Saudi Arabia ■ Asia 26°0N 44°0E 246 B3
Sauerland Germany 51°12N 7°59E 176 C4
Saugatuck U.S.A. 42°40N 86°12W 311 B10
Saugeen → Canada 44°30N 81°22W 312 B3
Saugerties U.S.A. 42°5N 73°57W 313 D11
Saugues France 44°58N 3°32E 174 D7
Saugus Calif., U.S.A. 34°25N 118°32W 307 L8
Saugus Mass., U.S.A. 42°28N 71°0W 116 A2
Saugus → U.S.A. 42°27N 70°58W 116 A2
Saujbulagh = Mahābād Iran 36°50N 45°45E 213 D11
Saujon France 45°41N 0°55W 174 C3
Sauk Centre U.S.A. 45°44N 94°57W 308 C6
Sauk City U.S.A. 43°17N 89°43W 310 A7
Sauk Rapids U.S.A. 45°35N 94°10W 308 C6
Saül Fr. Guiana 3°37N 53°12W 329 C7
Sauland Norway 59°37N 8°56E 164 E5
Saulgau Germany 48°1N 9°29E 179 G5
Saulieu France 47°17N 4°14E 173 E11
Sault France 44°6N 5°24E 175 D9
Sault-au-Récollet Canada 45°35N 73°39W 130 A2
Sault Ste. Marie Ont., Canada 46°30N 84°20W 298 C3
Sault Ste. Marie Mich., U.S.A. 46°30N 84°21W 309 B11
Saumalkol Kazakhstan 53°17N 68°6E 217 B7
Saumlaki Indonesia 7°55S 131°20E 231 F8
Saumur France 47°15N 0°5W 172 E6
Saundatti India 15°47N 75°7E 245 G2
Saunders, C. N.Z. 45°53S 170°45E 285 F5
Saunders I. Antarctica 57°48S 26°28W 151 B1
Saunders Pt. Australia 27°52S 125°38E 279 E4
Saunemin U.S.A. 40°54N 88°24W 311 D8
Saupite Angola 13°54S 17°43E 265 E3
Saurbær Norðurland Eystra, Iceland 65°27N 18°13W 155 B8
Saurbær Vesturland, Iceland 64°24N 21°35W 155 C5
Sauri Nigeria 11°42N 6°44E 263 C6
Saurimo Angola 9°40S 20°12E 265 D4
Sausalito U.S.A. 37°51N 122°29W 136 A2
Sautatá Colombia 7°50N 77°4W 328 B2
Sauteurs Grenada 12°14N 61°38W 323 q
Sauveterre-de-Béarn France 43°24N 0°57W 174 E3
Sauzé-Vaussais France 46°8N 0°8E 174 B4
Savá Honduras 15°32N 86°15W 320 C2
Sava Italy 40°24N 17°33E 201 B10
Sava → Serbia 44°50N 20°26E 182 F5
Savage U.S.A. 47°27N 104°21W 304 C11
Savage I. = Niue ☑ Pac. Oc. 19°2S 169°54W 289 g
Savage River Australia 41°31S 145°14E 282 G4
Savai'i Samoa 13°28S 172°24W 287 V19
Savalou Benin 7°57N 1°58E 263 D5
Savane Mozam. 19°37S 35°8E 269 F4
Savaneta Aruba 12°27N 69°56W 322 f
Savanna U.S.A. 42°5N 90°8W 310 B6
Savanna-la-Mar Jamaica 18°10N 78°10W 320 a
Savannah Ga., U.S.A. 32°5N 81°6W 316 C8
Savannah Mo., U.S.A. 39°56N 94°50W 310 E2
Savannah Tenn., U.S.A. 35°14N 88°15W 315 D10
Savannah → U.S.A. 32°2N 80°53W 316 C9
Savannah Beach = Tybee Island U.S.A. 32°1N 80°51W 316 C9
Savannakhet Laos 16°30N 104°49E 236 D5
Savanne, Piton Mauritius 20°26S 57°29E 272 e
Savannes B. St. Lucia 13°45N 60°56W 323 m
Savant L. Canada 50°16N 90°44W 298 B1
Savant Lake Canada 50°14N 90°40W 298 B1
Savantvadi India 15°55N 73°54E 245 G1
Savanur India 14°59N 75°21E 245 G2
Savarkundla = Kundla India 21°21N 71°25E 242 J4
Săvârşin Romania 46°1N 22°14E 182 D7
Savaştepe Turkey 39°22N 27°42E 205 B9
Savda India 21°9N 75°56E 244 D2
Savé Benin 8°2N 2°29E 263 D5
Save → Haute-Garonne, France 43°47N 1°17E 174 E5
Save → Mozam. 21°16S 34°0E 271 B5
Sāveh Iran 35°2N 50°20E 247 C6
Savelugu Ghana 9°38N 0°54W 263 D4
Savenay France 47°20N 1°55W 172 E5
Săveni Romania 47°57N 26°52E 183 C11
Saverdun France 43°14N 1°34E 174 E5
Saverne France 48°43N 7°20E 173 D14
Savigliano Italy 44°38N 7°40E 198 D4
Savigny-sur-Braye France 47°53N 0°49E 172 E7
Sávio → Italy 44°19N 12°20E 199 D9
Šavnik Montenegro 42°59N 19°10E 202 D3
Savo Finland 62°45N 27°30E 160 E22
Savo Solomon Is. 9°8S 159°48E 287 M10
Savoie □ France 45°26N 6°25E 175 C10
Savolax = Savo Finland 62°45N 27°30E 160 E22
Savona Italy 44°17N 8°30E 198 D5
Savona N.Y., U.S.A. 42°17N 77°13W 312 D7
Savonet Curaçao 12°21N 69°7W 322 g
Savonlinna Finland 61°52N 28°53E 188 B5
Savoonga U.S.A. 63°42N 170°29W 303 E5
Savoy = Savoie □ France 45°26N 6°25E 175 C10
Şavşat Turkey 41°15N 42°20E 213 B10
Sävsjö Sweden 57°20N 14°40E 163 G8
Savur Turkey 37°34N 40°53E 246 B4
Savusavu Fiji 16°34S 179°15E 287 A2
Savusavu B. Fiji 16°45S 179°15E 287 A2
Sawah Besar Indonesia 6°8S 106°49E 122 A1
Sawahlunto Indonesia 0°40S 100°52E 234 C2
Sawai Indonesia 3°0S 129°5E 231 E7
Sawai Madhopur India 26°0N 76°25E 242 G7
Sawaleke Fiji 17°59S 179°18E 287 A2
Sawang Daen Din Thailand 17°28N 103°28E 236 D4
Sawankhalok Thailand 17°19N 99°50E 236 D2
Sawara Japan 35°55N 140°30E 223 B12
Sawatch Range U.S.A. 39°0N 106°30W 304 G10
Sawdā', Jabal as Libya 28°51N 15°12E 258 C3
Sawel Mt. U.K. 54°50N 7°2W 166 B4
Sawfajjin, W. → Libya 31°41N 14°44E 258 B2
Sawi Thailand 10°14N 99°5E 237 G2
Sawla Ghana 9°17N 2°25W 262 D4
Sawmills Zimbabwe 19°30S 28°2E 269 F2
Şawqirah Oman 18°7N 56°32E 249 C7
Şawqirah, Ghubbat Oman 18°35N 57°0E 249 C7
Sawtell Australia 30°19S 153°6E 283 A10
Sawtelle U.S.A. 34°2N 118°27W 126 B2
Sawtooth ⌂ U.S.A. 44°0N 114°50W 304 D6
Sawtooth Range U.S.A. 44°3N 114°58W 304 D6
Sawu Indonesia 10°35S 121°50E 231 F6
Sawu Sea Indonesia 9°30S 121°50E 231 F6
Sawyers → Australia 18°25S 140°53E 280 B3
Saxmundham U.K. 52°13N 1°30E 169 E9
Saxony = Sachsen □ Germany 50°55N 13°10E 178 E9
Saxony, Lower = Niedersachsen □ Germany 52°50N 9°0E 178 C4
Saxton U.S.A. 40°13N 78°15W 312 F6
Say Mali 13°50N 4°57W 262 C4
Say Niger 13°8N 2°22E 263 C5
Saya Nigeria 9°30N 3°18E 263 D5
Sayabec Canada 48°35N 67°41W 299 C6
Sayaboury Laos 19°15N 101°45E 236 C3
Sayán Peru 11°8S 77°12W 330 C2
Sayan, Vostochnyy Russia 54°0N 96°0E 215 D10
Sayan, Zapadnyy Russia 52°30N 94°0E 217 B12
Sayanogorsk Russia 53°5N 91°23E 215 D10
Saydā Lebanon 33°35N 35°25E 250 E6
Sayghān Afghan. 35°10N 67°55E 240 B2
Sayhandulaan = Öldziyt Mongolia 44°40N 109°1E 226 B5
Sayhūt Yemen 15°12N 51°10E 249 D5
Saykhin Kazakhstan 48°50N 46°47E 191 F8
Saylac Somalia 11°21N 43°30E 267 B5
Saylorville L. U.S.A. 41°48N 93°46W 310 C3
Saynshand = Buyant-Uhaa Mongolia 44°55N 110°11E 226 B6
Sayō Japan 34°59N 134°22E 222 C6
Sayre Okla., U.S.A. 35°18N 99°38W 314 D5
Sayre Pa., U.S.A. 41°59N 76°32W 313 E8
Sayreville U.S.A. 40°28N 74°22W 313 F10
Sayula Mexico 19°52N 103°36W 318 D4
Say'ūn Yemen 15°56N 48°47E 249 D5
Sayward Canada 50°21N 125°55W 296 C3
Saza Japan 33°14N 129°39E 222 D1
Sazanit Albania 40°30N 19°20E 202 F3
Sázava → Czech Rep. 49°53N 14°24E 180 B7
Sazin Pakistan 35°35N 73°30E 243 B5
Sazlika → Bulgaria 41°59N 25°50E 203 E9
Sbeïtla Tunisia 35°12N 9°7E 258 A1
Scaër France 48°2N 3°42W 172 D3
Scafell Pike U.K. 54°27N 3°14W 168 C4
Scalea Italy 39°49N 15°47E 201 C8
Scalloway U.K. 60°9N 1°17W 167 A7
Scalpay U.K. 57°18N 6°0W 167 D3
Scalzi, Ponte degli Venice, Italy 142 b1
Scammon Bay U.S.A. 61°51N 165°35W 303 F6
Scandia Canada 50°20N 112°2W 296 C6
Scandiano Italy 44°36N 10°43E 198 D7
Scandicci Italy 43°45N 11°11E 199 E8
Scandinavia Europe 64°0N 12°0E 160 E15
Scansano Italy 42°41N 11°20E 199 F8
Scapa Flow U.K. 58°53N 3°3W 167 C5
Scappoose U.S.A. 45°45N 122°53W 306 E4
Scarámia, Capo Italy 36°47N 14°29E 201 F7
Scarba U.K. 56°11N 5°43W 167 E3
Scarborough Ont., Canada 43°44N 79°14W 141 A3
Scarborough Trin. & Tob. 11°11N 60°42W 323 s
Scarborough N. Yorks., U.K. 54°17N 0°24W 168 C7
Scarborough Bluffs Canada 43°42N 79°14W 141 A3
Scarborough Shoal S. China Sea 15°0N 117°50E 232 D1
Scargill N.Z. 42°56S 172°58E 285 C7
Scariff I. Ireland 51°44N 10°15W 166 E1
Scarp U.K. 58°1N 7°8W 167 C1
Scarpanto = Karpathos Greece 35°37N 27°10E 205 F9
Scarpe-Escaut ⌂ France 50°26N 3°23E 173 B10
Scarsdale Australia 37°41S 143°39E 282 D5
Sceaux France 48°46N 2°17E 134 B2
Scebeli = Shabeelle → Somalia 2°0N 44°0E 267 D5
Šćedro Croatia 43°6N 16°43E 199 E13
Scenery, Mt. Saba 17°38N 63°14W 322 a
Schaalsee ⌂ Germany 53°36N 10°55E 178 B6
Schaarbeek Belgium 50°52N 4°22E 116 A2
Schaffhausen Switz. 47°42N 8°39E 179 H4
Schagen Neths. 52°49N 4°48E 170 B4
Schaghticoke U.S.A. 42°54N 73°35W 313 D11
Schärding Austria 48°27N 13°27E 180 C6
Scharfenberg Germany 52°35N 13°15E 115 A2
Scharfenwiese = Ostrołęka Poland 53°4N 21°32E 185 E8
Scharhörn Germany 53°57N 8°24E 178 B4
Schässburg = Sighişoara Romania 46°12N 24°50E 183 D9
Scheessel Germany 53°10N 9°29E 178 B5
Schefferville Canada 54°48N 66°50W 299 B6
Scheibbs Austria 48°1N 15°9E 180 C8
Scheldt = Schelde → Belgium 51°15N 4°16E 170 C4
Schelde → Belgium 51°15N 4°16E 170 C4
Schell City U.S.A. 38°1N 94°7W 310 F2
Schell Creek Ra. U.S.A. 39°25N 114°40W 304 G6
Schellsburg U.S.A. 40°3N 78°39W 312 F6
Schemnitz = Banská Štiavnica Slovak Rep. 48°25N 18°55E 181 C11
Schenectady U.S.A. 42°49N 73°57W 313 D11
Schenevus U.S.A. 42°33N 74°50W 313 D10
Scherfede Germany 51°32N 9°2E 178 D5
Schesslitz Germany 49°58N 11°1E 179 F7
Schiavoni, Riva degli Venice, Italy 142 b3
Schiedam Neths. 51°55N 4°25E 170 C4
Schieratz = Sieradz Poland 51°37N 18°41E 185 G5
Schiermonnikoog Neths. 53°30N 6°15E 170 A6
Schiermonnikoog △ Neths. 53°30N 6°15E 170 A6
Schiller Woods U.S.A. 41°57N 87°51W 119 B1
Schiltigheim France 48°35N 7°45E 173 D14
Schinousa Greece 36°53N 25°31E 205 E7
Schio Italy 45°43N 11°21E 199 C8
Schiphol, Amsterdam ✕ (AMS) Neths. 52°18N 4°45E 112 B1
Schippenbeil = Sępopol Poland 54°16N 21°2E 184 D8
Schivelbein = Świdwin Poland 53°47N 15°49E 184 E2
Schlachtensee Germany 52°26N 13°13E 115 B2
Schladming Austria 47°23N 13°41E 180 D6
Schlanders = Silandro Italy 46°38N 10°46E 198 B7
Schlawa = Sława Poland 51°52N 16°2E 185 G3
Schlei → Germany 54°40N 10°0E 178 A5
Schleiden Germany 50°31N 6°28E 178 E2
Schleinitz Ra. Papua N. G. 3°0S 151°30E 286 B6
Schleiz Germany 50°35N 11°49E 178 E7
Schlesiersee = Sława Poland 51°52N 16°2E 185 G3
Schleswig Germany 54°31N 9°34E 178 A5
Schleswig-Holstein □ Germany 54°30N 9°30E 178 A5
Schlettstadt = Sélestat France 48°16N 7°26E 173 D14
Schlichtingsheim = Szlichtyngowa Poland 51°42N 16°15E 185 G3
Schlochau = Człuchów Poland 53°41N 17°22E 184 E4
Schloppe = Człopa Poland 53°6N 16°6E 185 E3
Schlossgarten Germany 52°31N 13°18E 115 A2
Schlüchtern Germany 50°20N 9°32E 179 E5
Schmalkalden Germany 50°44N 10°26E 178 E6
Schmargendorf Germany 52°28N 13°17E 115 B2
Schmölln Germany 50°54N 12°19E 178 E8
Schneeberg Austria 47°47N 15°48E 180 D8
Schneeberg Sachsen, Germany 50°35N 12°38E 178 E8
Schneidemühl = Piła Poland 53°10N 16°48E 185 E3
Schneider U.S.A. 41°13N 87°28W 311 C9
Schneverdingen Germany 53°7N 9°48E 178 B5
Schœlcher Martinique 14°36N 61°7W 322 j
Schofield Barracks U.S.A. 21°29N 158°7W 302 K13
Schoharie U.S.A. 42°40N 74°19W 313 D10
Schoharie Cr. → U.S.A. 42°57N 74°18W 313 D10
Schokland Neths. 52°38N 5°46E 170 B5
Scholls U.S.A. 45°24N 122°56W 306 E4
Schönau = Swierzawa Poland 51°1N 15°54E 185 G2
Schönberg Mecklenburg-Vorpommern, Germany 53°52N 10°56E 178 B6
Schönberg Schleswig-Holstein, Germany 54°23N 10°21E 178 A6
Schönblick Germany 52°27N 13°43E 115 B5
Schönbrunn Austria 48°10N 16°19E 142 A1
Schönbuch ⌂ Germany 48°35N 9°2E 179 G5
Schönebeck Germany 52°2N 11°44E 178 C7
Schöneberg Germany 52°28N 13°20E 115 B3
Schönefeld Germany 52°22N 13°33E 115 B4
Schöneiche Germany 52°28N 13°41E 115 B5
Schöngau Germany 47°47N 10°53E 179 H6
Schöningen Germany 52°8N 10°56E 178 C6
Schönlanke = Trzcianka Poland 53°3N 16°25E 185 E3
Schönstein = Šoštanj Slovenia 46°23N 15°4E 199 B12
Schönwalde Germany 52°37N 13°7E 115 A1
Schoolcraft U.S.A. 42°7N 85°38W 311 B11
Schopfheim Germany 47°38N 7°50E 179 H3
Schorndorf Germany 48°47N 9°32E 179 G5
Schortens Germany 53°31N 7°56E 178 B3
Schotscheklof Cape Town, S. Africa 118 b1
Schottegat Curaçao 12°7N 68°55W 322 g
Schouten I. Australia 42°20S 148°20E 281 G4
Schouten Is. = Supiori Indonesia 1°0S 136°0E 231 E9
Schouten Is. Papua N. G. 3°30S 144°30E 286 B3
Schouwen Neths. 51°43N 3°45E 170 C3
Schramberg Germany 48°13N 8°22E 179 G4
Schrankogel Austria 47°3N 11°7E 180 D4
Schreiber Canada 48°45N 87°20W 298 C2
Schrems Austria 48°47N 15°4E 180 C8
Schrobenhausen Germany 48°34N 11°16E 179 G7
Schroffenstein Namibia 27°11S 18°42E 270 C2
Schroon Lake U.S.A. 43°50N 73°46W 313 C11
Schröttersburg = Płock Poland 52°32N 19°40E 185 F6
Schruns Austria 47°5N 9°56E 180 D2
Schuchye = Shchūchīnsk Kazakhstan 52°56N 70°12E 217 B8
Schuler Canada 50°20N 110°6W 297 C6
Schulzendorf Germany 52°36N 13°16E 115 A2
Schumacher Canada 48°30N 81°16W 298 C3
Schurz U.S.A. 38°57N 118°49W 304 G4
Schuyler U.S.A. 41°27N 97°4W 308 E5
Schuylerville U.S.A. 43°6N 73°35W 313 C11
Schuylkill → U.S.A. 39°53N 75°12W 313 G9
Schuylkill Haven U.S.A. 40°37N 76°11W 313 F8
Schwabach Germany 49°19N 11°2E 179 F7
Schwaben □ Germany 48°15N 10°30E 179 G6
Schwabing Germany 48°9N 11°35E 131 B2
Schwäbisch-Fränkischer Wald ⌂ Germany 49°0N 9°30E 179 G5
Schwäbisch Gmünd Germany 48°48N 9°47E 179 G5
Schwäbisch Hall Germany 49°6N 9°44E 179 F5
Schwäbische Alb Germany 48°20N 9°30E 179 G5
Schwabmünchen Germany 48°10N 10°46E 179 G6
Schwalmstadt Germany 50°55N 9°10E 178 E5
Schwandorf Germany 49°20N 12°7E 179 F8
Schwanebeck Germany 52°37N 13°32E 115 A4
Schwanenwerder Germany 52°26N 13°10E 115 B2
Schwaner, Pegunungan Indonesia 1°0S 112°30E 235 C4
Schwanewede Germany 53°14N 8°35E 178 B4
Schwarmstedt Germany 52°39N 9°38E 178 C5
Schwarze Elster → Germany 51°48N 12°50E 178 D8
Schwarzenberg Germany 50°32N 12°47E 178 E8
Schwarzlackenau Austria 48°16N 16°23E 142 A2
Schwarzrand Namibia 25°37S 16°50E 270 C2
Schwarzwald Germany 48°30N 8°20E 179 G4
Schwatka Mts. U.S.A. 67°20N 156°30W 303 C8
Schwaz Austria 47°20N 11°44E 180 D4
Schwechat Austria 48°8N 16°28E 142 B2
Schwechat, Wien ✕ (VIE) Austria 48°7N 16°35E 142 B3
Schwedt Germany 53°3N 14°16E 178 B10
Schweidnitz = Świdnica Poland 50°50N 16°30E 185 H3
Schweinfurt Germany 50°3N 10°14E 179 E6
Schweiz = Switzerland ■ Europe 46°30N 8°0E 179 J4
Schweizer-Reneke S. Africa 27°11S 25°18E 270 C4
Schwenningen = Villingen-Schwenningen Germany 48°3N 8°26E 179 G4
Schwerin = Skwierzyna Poland 52°33N 15°30E 185 F2
Schwerin Germany 53°36N 11°22E 178 B7
Schweriner See Germany 53°43N 11°28E 178 B7
Schwetzingen Germany 49°23N 8°35E 179 F4
Schwiebus = Świebodzin Poland 52°15N 15°31E 185 F2
Schwyz Switz. 47°2N 8°39E 179 H4
Schwyz □ Switz. 47°2N 8°39E 179 H4
Sciacca Italy 37°31N 13°3E 200 E6
Scicli Italy 36°47N 14°42E 201 F7
Science and Industry, Museum of U.S.A. 41°47N 87°34W 119 C3
Sciliar ⌂ Italy 46°28N 11°35E 199 B8
Scilla Italy 38°15N 15°43E 201 D8
Scilly, Isles of U.K. 49°56N 6°22W 169 H1
Ścinawa Poland 51°25N 16°26E 185 G3
Scione Greece 39°57N 23°36E 202 G7
Scioto → U.S.A. 38°44N 83°1W 311 D13
Scituate U.S.A. 42°12N 70°44W 313 D14
Scobey U.S.A. 48°47N 105°25W 304 B11
Scomenzera, Canale Venice, Italy 142 b1
Scone N.S.W., Australia 32°5S 150°52E 283 B9
Scone Perth & Kin., U.K. 56°25N 3°24W 167 E5
Scopus, Mt. West Bank 31°48N 35°14E 123 B2
Scordia Italy 37°18N 14°51E 201 E7
Scoresby Sund Greenland 70°28N 21°46W 154 C8
Scoresbysund = Ittoqqortoormiit Greenland 70°20N 23°0W 154 C8
Scorniceşti Romania 44°34N 24°33E 183 F9
Scotia Calif., U.S.A. 40°29N 124°6W 304 F1
Scotia N.Y., U.S.A. 42°50N 73°58W 313 D11
Scotia Sea Antarctica 56°5S 56°0W 151 B18
Scotland Canada 43°1N 80°22W 312 C4
Scotland □ U.K. 57°0N 4°0W 167 E5
Scott Antarctica 77°50S 166°45E 151 D11
Scott, C. Australia 13°30S 129°49E 278 B4
Scott Circle Washington, D.C., U.S.A. 143 a1
Scott City U.S.A. 38°29N 100°54W 308 F3
Scott Glacier Antarctica 66°15S 100°5E 151 C8
Scott I. Antarctica 67°0S 179°0E 151 C11
Scott Is. Canada 50°48N 128°40W 296 C3
Scott L. Canada 59°55N 106°18W 297 B7
Scott Monument Edinburgh, U.K. 121 b2
Scott Reef Australia 14°0S 121°50E 278 B3
Scottburgh S. Africa 30°15S 30°47E 271 D5
Scottdale Georgia, U.S.A. 33°47N 84°16W 113 B3
Scottdale Pa., U.S.A. 40°6N 79°35W 312 F5
Scottish Borders □ U.K. 55°35N 2°50W 167 F6
Scotts Head N.S.W., Australia 30°45S 153°0E 283 A10
Scotts Head Dominica 15°13N 61°23W 323 k
Scotts Head Village Dominica 15°12N 61°22W 323 k
Scotts Valley U.S.A. 37°3N 122°1W 306 H4
Scottsbluff U.S.A. 41°52N 103°40W 308 E2
Scottsboro U.S.A. 34°40N 86°2W 315 D11
Scottsburg U.S.A. 38°41N 85°47W 311 F11
Scottsdale Tas., Australia 41°9S 147°31E 281 G4
Scottsdale Ariz., U.S.A. 33°40N 111°53W 305 K8
Scottsville Ky., U.S.A. 36°45N 86°11W 308 G10
Scottsville N.Y., U.S.A. 43°2N 77°47W 312 C7
Scottville U.S.A. 43°58N 86°17W 308 D10
Scranton U.S.A. 41°25N 75°40W 313 E9
Screven U.S.A. 31°29N 82°1W 316 D7
Scrub I. Anguilla 18°19N 62°55W 322 a
Scugog, L. Canada 44°10N 78°55W 312 B6
Sculeni Moldova 47°20N 27°37E 183 C12
Scunthorpe U.K. 53°36N 0°39W 168 D7
Scuol Schuls Switz. 46°48N 10°17E 179 J6
Scutari = Shkodër Albania 42°4N 19°32E 202 D3
Scutari = Üsküdar Turkey 41°1N 29°0E 122 B2
Sea Is. U.S.A. 31°30N 81°7W 316 D9
Sea Lake Australia 35°28S 142°55E 282 C5
Sea Point S. Africa 34°5S 18°23E 118 A1
Seabra = Tarauacá Brazil 8°6S 70°48W 330 B3
Seabra Brazil 12°25S 41°46W 333 D3
Seabrook, L. Australia 30°55S 119°40E 279 F2
Seacliff U.S.A. 37°47N 122°28W 136 B2
Seaford E. Sussex, U.K. 50°47N 0°7E 169 G8
Seaford Del., U.S.A. 38°39N 75°37W 309 F16
Seaforth N.S.W., Australia 33°48S 151°15E 139 A2
Seaforth Queens., Australia 20°55S 148°57E 280 b
Seaforth Ont., Canada 43°35N 81°25W 312 C3
Seaforth, L. U.K. 57°52N 6°36W 167 D2
Seagate U.S.A. 40°34N 74°0W 132 C1
Seagraves U.S.A. 32°57N 102°34W 314 E3
Seaham U.K. 54°50N 1°20W 168 C6
Seal → Canada 59°4N 94°48W 297 B10
Seal I. Anguilla 18°16N 63°9W 322 a
Seal L. Canada 54°20N 61°30W 299 B7
Seale U.S.A. 32°18N 85°10W 316 C4
Sealy U.S.A. 29°47N 96°9W 314 G6
Seaman U.S.A. 38°57N 83°34W 311 F13
Searchlight U.S.A. 35°28N 114°55W 307 K12
Searcy U.S.A. 35°15N 91°44W 314 D9
Searles L. U.S.A. 35°44N 117°21W 307 K9
Sears Tower = Willis Tower U.S.A. 119 c1
Seascale U.K. 54°24N 3°29W 168 C4
Seaside Calif., U.S.A. 36°37N 121°50W 306 J5
Seaside Oreg., U.S.A. 46°0N 123°56W 306 D3
Seaspray Australia 38°25S 147°15E 283 E7
Seattle U.S.A. 47°36N 122°19W 306 C4
Seattle-Tacoma Int. ✕ (SEA) U.S.A. 47°27N 122°18W 306 C4
Seaward Kaikoura Ra. N.Z. 42°10S 173°44E 285 C8
SeaWorld U.S.A. 28°24N 81°28W 133 B2
Seba Indonesia 10°29S 121°50E 231 F6
Sebago L. U.S.A. 43°52N 70°34W 313 C14
Sebago Lake U.S.A. 43°51N 70°34W 313 C14
Sebakung Indonesia 1°37S 116°25E 235 C5
Sebangau △ Indonesia 2°34S 113°58E 235 C4
Sebangka Indonesia 0°7N 104°36E 234 B2
Sebastian U.S.A. 27°49N 80°28W 317 H9
Sebastián Vizcaíno, B. Mexico 28°0N 114°30W 318 B2

Sebastopol = Sevastopol Ukraine 44°35N 33°30E 189 K7
Sebastopol U.S.A. 38°24N 122°49W 306 G4
Sebatik Asia 4°10N 117°45E 235 B5
Sebba Burkina Faso 13°35N 0°32E 263 C5
Sebderat Eritrea 15°26N 36°42E 257 D4
Sebdou Algeria 34°38N 1°19W 261 B4
Sébé ~ Gabon 1°2S 13°6E 264 C2
Sébékoro Mali 12°58N 9°0W 262 C3
Seben Turkey 40°24N 31°34E 212 D4
Šeberov Czech Rep. 50°0N 14°30E 135 B3
Sebeş Romania 45°58N 23°34E 183 E8
Sebeşului, Munţii Romania 45°36N 23°40E 183 E8
Sebezh Russia 56°14N 28°22E 188 D5
Sebha = Sabhā Libya 27°9N 14°29E 258 C2
Sébi Mali 15°50N 4°12W 262 B4
Şebinkarahisar Turkey 40°22N 38°28E 213 B8
Sebiş Romania 46°23N 22°13E 182 D7
Seblat Indonesia 3°14S 101°38E 234 C2
Sebnitz Germany 50°58N 14°15E 178 E10
Sebou, Oued ~ Morocco 34°16N 6°40W 260 B3
Sebring Fla., U.S.A. 27°30N 81°27W 317 H8
Sebring Ohio, U.S.A. 40°55N 81°2W 312 F3
Sebringville Canada 43°24N 81°4W 312 C3
Sebta = Ceuta N. Afr. 35°52N 5°18W 260 A3
Sebuku Indonesia 3°30S 116°25E 235 C5
Sebuku, Teluk Indonesia 4°0N 118°10E 235 B5
Sečanj Serbia 45°25N 20°47E 182 E5
Secaucus U.S.A. 40°47N 74°3W 132 B1
Secchia ~ Italy 45°4N 11°0E 198 C8
Sechelt Canada 49°25N 123°42W 296 D4
Sechura Peru 5°35S 80°50W 330 B1
Sechura, Desierto de Peru 6°0S 80°30W 330 B1
Seclin France 50°33N 3°2E 173 B10
Second World War Memorial Washington, D.C., U.S.A. 143 b1
Secondigny France 46°37N 0°26W 172 F6
Sečovce Slovak Rep. 48°42N 21°40E 181 C14
Secretary I., N.Z. 45°15S 166°56E 285 F1
Secunderabad India 17°28N 78°30E 244 F4
Sécure ~ Bolivia 15°10S 64°52W 331 D5
Security U.S.A. 38°45N 104°45W 304 C11
Sedalia U.S.A. 38°42N 93°14W 314 F8
Sedam India 17°11N 77°17E 244 F3
Sedan S. Austral., Australia 34°34S 139°19E 282 C3
Sedan Ardennes, France 49°43N 4°57E 173 C11
Sedan Kans., U.S.A. 37°8N 96°11W 308 G5
Sedano Spain 42°43N 3°49W 194 C7
Sedaw Burma 22°19N 96°19E 241 D6
Sedbergh U.K. 54°20N 2°31W 168 C5
Seddon N.Z. 41°40S 174°7E 285 B9
Seddonville N.Z. 41°33S 172°1E 285 B7
Sédé Bogér Israel 30°52N 34°47E 251 H5
Sedeh Fārs, Iran 30°45N 52°11E 247 D7
Sedeh Khorāsān, Iran 33°20N 59°14E 247 C8
Séderon France 44°12N 5°32E 175 D9
Sederot Israel 31°32N 34°37E 251 G5
Sédhiou Senegal 12°44N 15°30W 262 C1
Sedico Italy 46°8N 12°6E 199 B9
Sedláany Czech Rep. 49°40N 14°25E 180 B7
Sedley Canada 50°10N 104°0W 297 C8
Sedom Israel 31°5N 35°20E 251 G6
Sedona U.S.A. 34°52N 111°46W 305 J8
Sedova, Pik Russia 73°29N 54°58E 214 B6
Sedrata Algeria 36°7N 7°31E 261 A6
Sedro-Woolley U.S.A. 48°30N 122°14W 306 B4
Šeduva Lithuania 55°45N 23°45E 184 C10
Sędziszów Poland 50°35N 20°4E 185 H7
Sędziszów Małopolski Poland 50°5N 21°45E 185 H8
Seebad Ahlbeck Germany 53°56N 14°10E 178 B10
Seeburg = Jeziorany Poland 53°58N 20°46E 184 E7
Seeburg Germany 52°30N 13°7E 115 A1
Seefeld Germany 52°37N 13°40E 115 A5
Seefeld in Tirol Austria 47°19N 11°13E 180 D4
Seegefeld Germany 52°33N 13°8E 115 A1
Seehausen Germany 52°54N 11°45E 178 C7
Seeheim Namibia 26°50S 17°45E 270 C2
Seeheim-Jugenheim Germany 49°49N 8°40E 179 F4
Seehof Germany 52°24N 13°17E 115 B2
Seeis Namibia 22°29S 17°39E 270 B2
Seekoei ~ S. Africa 30°18S 25°1E 270 D4
Seeley's Bay Canada 44°29N 76°14W 313 B8
Seelow Germany 52°32N 14°23E 178 C10
Sées France 48°38N 0°10E 172 D7
Seesen Germany 51°54N 10°10E 178 D6
Seevetal Germany 53°26N 10°1E 178 B6
Seewinkel = Neusiedler See-Seewinkel 47°50N 16°45E 181 D9
Şefaatli Turkey 39°30N 34°45E 212 C6
Seferihisar Turkey 38°10N 26°50E 205 C8
Séféto Mali 14°8N 9°49W 262 C3
Sefophe Botswana 22°11S 27°58E 271 B4
Sefrou Morocco 33°52N 4°52W 260 B4
Sefton N.Z. 43°15S 172°41E 285 D7
Sefuri-San Japan 33°28N 130°18E 222 D2
Sefwi Bekwai Ghana 6°10N 2°25W 262 D4
Seg-ozero Russia 63°20N 33°46E 186 B5
Segag Ethiopia 7°39N 42°50E 267 C5
Segamat Malaysia 2°30N 102°50E 237 L4
Ségbana Benin 10°55N 3°42E 263 C5
Segbwema S. Leone 8°0N 11°0W 262 D2
Segeltorp Sweden 59°16N 17°56E 139 B1
Segesta Italy 37°56N 12°50E 200 E5
Seget Indonesia 1°24S 130°58E 231 E8
Segewold = Sigulda Latvia 57°10N 24°55E 188 D3
Segezha Russia 63°44N 34°19E 186 B5
Seggueur, O. ~ Algeria 32°14N 1°48E 261 B5
Seghe Solomon Is. 8°32S 157°54E 287 M9
Segmon Sweden 59°17N 13°3E 162 E7
Segonzac France 45°36N 0°14W 174 C3
Segorbe Spain 39°50N 0°30W 196 F4
Ségou Mali 13°30N 6°16W 262 C3
Ségou □ Mali 14°0N 6°0W 262 C3
Segovia = Coco ~ Cent. Amer. 15°0N 83°8W 320 D3
Segovia Colombia 7°7N 74°42W 328 B3
Segovia Spain 40°57N 4°10W 194 E6
Segovia □ Spain 40°55N 4°10W 194 E6
Segra Italy 45°29N 9°17E 128 B2
Segré France 47°40N 0°43E 196 D5
Segre ~ Spain 41°40N 0°43E 196 D5
Seguam I. U.S.A. 52°19N 172°30W 303 K4
Seguam Pass U.S.A. 52°0N 172°30W 303 K4
Séguédine Niger 20°9N 12°55E 259 D2
Séguéla Ivory C. 7°55N 6°40W 262 D3
Seguin U.S.A. 29°34N 97°58W 314 G6
Segundo ~ Argentina 30°53S 62°44W 334 C3
Segura ~ Spain 38°3N 0°44W 197 G4
Segura, Sierra de Spain 38°5N 2°45W 197 G2
Seguro Italy 45°28N 9°3E 128 B2
Seh Konj, Kūh-e Iran 30°0N 57°30E 247 D8
Seh Qal'eh Iran 33°40N 58°24E 247 C8
Sehitwa Botswana 20°30S 22°30E 270 B3

Sehlabathebe △ Lesotho 29°53S 29°7E 271 C4
Sehore India 23°10N 77°5E 242 H7
Sehulea Papua N. G. 9°58S 151°10E 286 E6
Sehwan Pakistan 26°28N 67°53E 242 F2
Şeica Mare Romania 46°1N 24°7E 183 D9
Seikan Tunnel Japan 41°28N 140°10E 220 D10
Seikpyu Burma 20°54N 94°48E 241 E5
Seil U.K. 56°18N 5°38W 167 E3
Seiland Norway 70°25N 23°15E 160 A20
Seilhac France 45°22N 1°43E 174 C5
Seiling U.S.A. 36°6N 98°56W 314 C5
Şeinăjoki Finland 62°40N 22°51E 160 E20
Seine ~ France 49°26N 0°26E 172 C7
Seine, B. de la France 49°40N 0°40W 172 C6
Seine-et-Marne □ France 48°45N 3°0E 173 D10
Seine-Inférieure = Seine-Maritime □ France 49°40N 1°0E 172 C7
Seine-Maritime □ France 49°40N 1°0E 172 C7
Seine-St-Denis □ France 48°58N 2°24E 173 D9
Seini Romania 47°44N 23°21E 183 C8
Seirijai Lithuania 54°14N 23°49E 184 D10
Seis de Septiembre = Moron Argentina 34°39S 58°37W 334 C4
Seistan = Sīstān Asia 30°50N 61°0E 247 D9
Seistan, Daryācheh-ye = Sīstān, Daryācheh-ye Iran 31°0N 61°0E 247 D9
Seitler = Nyzhnohirskyy Ukraine 45°27N 34°38E 189 K8
Seixal Portugal 38°38N 9°6W 195 G1
Sejerø Denmark 55°54N 11°9E 163 J5
Sejerø Bugt Denmark 55°53N 11°15E 163 J5
Sejny Poland 54°6N 23°21E 184 D10
Seka Ethiopia 8°10N 36°52E 257 F4
Sekadau Indonesia 0°1N 110°54E 235 C4
Sekayu Indonesia 2°51S 103°51E 234 C2
Seke Tanzania 3°20S 33°31E 268 C3
Seke-Banza Dem. Rep. of the Congo 5°20S 13°16E 265 D2
Sekenke Tanzania 4°18S 34°11E 268 C3
Sekhira Tunisia 34°20N 10°5E 258 B2
Seki Japan 35°29N 136°55E 223 B8
Seki Turkey 36°48N 29°33E 205 E11
Sekigahara Japan 35°22N 136°28E 223 B8
Sekondi-Takoradi Ghana 4°58N 1°45W 262 E4
Sekota Ethiopia 12°40N 39°2E 257 E4
Sekseüil Kazakhstan 47°5N 61°9E 216 C6
Sekudai Malaysia 1°32N 103°39E 237 d
Sekuma Botswana 24°36S 23°50E 270 C3
Selah U.S.A. 46°39N 120°32W 304 C3
Selama Malaysia 5°12N 100°42E 237 K3
Selangor □ Malaysia 3°10N 101°30E 237 L3
Selárgius Italy 39°16N 9°10E 200 C2
Selaru Indonesia 8°9S 131°0E 231 F8
Selatan, Selat Malaysia 5°15N 100°20E 237 c
Selatpanjang Indonesia 1°0N 102°43E 234 B2
Selawik U.S.A. 66°36N 160°0W 303 C8
Selawik L. U.S.A. 66°30N 160°45W 303 C7
Selawik Nat. Wildlife Refuge △ U.S.A. 66°35N 159°10W 303 C8
Selb Germany 50°10N 12°7E 179 E8
Selbusjøen Norway 63°15N 10°50E 164 A7
Selby Gauteng, S. Africa 26°12S 28°2E 123 B2
Selby N. Yorks., U.K. 53°47N 1°5W 168 D6
Selby S. Dak., U.S.A. 45°31N 100°2W 308 C3
Selca Croatia 43°20N 16°50E 199 E13
Selçuk Turkey 37°56N 27°22E 205 D9
Selden U.S.A. 39°33N 100°34W 308 F3
Seldovia U.S.A. 59°26N 151°43W 303 G10
Sele ~ Italy 40°29N 14°56E 201 B7
Selebi-Phikwe Botswana 21°58S 27°48E 271 B4
Selemdzha ~ Russia 51°42N 128°53E 215 D13
Selendi Manisa, Turkey 38°43N 28°50E 205 C10
Selendi Manisa, Turkey 38°46N 27°53E 205 C9
Selenga = Selenge Mörön ~ Asia 52°16N 106°16E 218 A10
Selenge Dem. Rep. of the Congo 1°8S 18°11E 264 C3
Selenge Mörön ~ Asia 52°16N 106°16E 218 A10
Selenicë Albania 40°33N 19°39E 202 F3
Selenter See Germany 54°18N 10°26E 178 A6
Sélestat France 48°16N 7°26E 173 D14
Seletan, Tanjung Indonesia 4°10S 114°40E 235 C4
Seletar Singapore 1°22N 103°53E 138 A3
Seletar, Pulau Singapore 1°26N 103°51E 138 A3
Seletar Hills Singapore 1°25N 103°52E 138 A3
Seletar Res. Singapore 1°24N 103°48E 138 A2
Selevac Serbia 44°28N 20°52E 182 E4
Selfoss Iceland 63°56N 21°0W 155 D6
Selhurst U.K. 51°23N 0°5W 125 B3
Sélibabi Mauritania 15°10N 12°15W 262 B2
Seliger, Ozero Russia 57°15N 33°0E 188 D7
Seligman U.S.A. 35°20N 112°53W 305 J7
Şelim Turkey 40°30N 42°46E 213 B10
Selima Sudan 21°22N 29°19E 256 D2
Selimiye Turkey 37°24N 27°40E 205 D9
Selinda Spillway ~ Botswana 18°35S 23°10E 270 A3
Sélingué, L. de Mali 11°37N 8°14W 262 C3
Selinsgrove U.S.A. 40°48N 76°52W 312 F8
Selizharovo Russia 56°51N 33°27E 188 D7
Selje Norway 62°3N 5°22E 164 B2
Seljord Norway 59°30N 8°40E 164 E5
Selkirk Man., Canada 50°10N 96°55W 297 C9
Selkirk Ont., Canada 42°49N 79°56W 312 D5
Selkirk U.K. 55°33N 2°50W 167 F6
Selkirk I. = Horse I. Canada 53°20N 99°6W 297 C9
Selkirk Mts. Canada 51°15N 117°40W 294 G8
Sellafield U.K. 54°25N 3°29W 168 C4
Sellama Sudan 12°51N 29°46E 257 E2
Sellia Greece 35°12N 24°23E 203 D6
Sellières France 46°50N 5°32E 173 F12
Sells U.S.A. 31°55N 111°53W 305 L8
Sellye Hungary 45°52N 17°51E 182 E2
Selma Ala., U.S.A. 32°25N 87°1W 315 E11
Selma Calif., U.S.A. 36°34N 119°37W 306 J7
Selma N.C., U.S.A. 35°32N 78°17W 315 D15
Selmer U.S.A. 35°10N 88°36W 315 D10
Selong Indonesia 8°39S 116°32E 235 D5
Selongey France 47°36N 5°11E 173 E12
Selouane Morocco 35°7N 2°57W 261 A4
Selous ~ Tanzania 8°37S 37°42E 268 D4
Selowandoma Falls Zimbabwe 21°15S 31°50E 269 G3
Selpele Indonesia 0°1S 130°5E 231 E8
Selsey Bill U.K. 50°43N 0°47W 169 G7
Seltso Russia 53°22N 34°4E 188 F8
Şelu Indonesia 7°32S 130°55E 231 F8
Sélune ~ France 48°38N 1°22W 172 D5
Selva = La Selva del Camp Spain 41°13N 1°9E 196 D6
Selva Argentina 29°50S 62°0W 334 B3
Selva Mallorca, Spain 39°46N 2°54E 195 B9
Selva Lancandona = Montes Azules △ Mexico 16°21N 91°3W 319 D6
Selvas Brazil 6°30S 67°0W 330 B4
Selwyn L. Canada 60°0N 104°30W 297 B8
Selwyn Mts. Canada 63°0N 130°0W 294 C6

Selwyn Passage Vanuatu 16°3S 168°12E 287 F6
Selwyn Ra. Australia 21°10S 140°0E 280 C3
Selyatyn Ukraine 47°50N 25°12E 183 C10
Sem Norway 59°14N 10°17E 164 E7
Sem Kolodezy = Lenine Ukraine 45°17N 35°46E 189 K8
Semadrek = Samothraki Greece 40°28N 25°28E 203 F9
Seman ~ Albania 40°47N 19°30E 202 F3
Semangka, Teluk Indonesia 5°36S 104°42E 234 D2
Semarang Indonesia 7°0S 110°26E 235 D4
Semarapura = Klungkung Indonesia 8°32S 115°24E 231 K18
Sematan Malaysia 1°48N 109°46E 235 B3
Semayang, Danau Indonesia 0°14S 116°28E 235 C5
Sembabule Uganda 0°4S 31°25E 268 C3
Sembawang Singapore 1°27N 103°50E 138 A2
Sembé Congo 1°39N 14°36E 264 B2
Sembilang △ Indonesia 1°59S 104°34E 234 C2
Sembilan, Pulau Indonesia 8°28S 115°11E 231 J18
Şemdinli Turkey 37°18N 44°35E 213 D11
Sémé Senegal 15°4N 13°41W 262 B2
Semeih Sudan 12°43N 30°53E 257 E3
Semendua Dem. Rep. of the Congo 3°10S 18°6E 264 C3
Semenivka Chernihiv, Ukraine 52°8N 32°36E 189 F7
Semenivka Kremenchuk, Ukraine 49°37N 33°10E 189 H7
Semenov Russia 56°43N 44°30E 190 B7
Semeru Indonesia 8°4S 112°55E 235 D4
Semey Kazakhstan 50°30N 80°10E 217 B10
Semichi Is. U.S.A. 52°42N 174°0E 303 K1
Semikarakorskiy Russia 47°25N 40°48E 191 G5
Semiluki Russia 51°41N 39°2E 189 H10
Seminoe Res. U.S.A. 42°9N 106°55W 304 E10
Seminole Fla., U.S.A. 27°50N 82°47W 317 M4
Seminole Okla., U.S.A. 35°14N 96°41W 314 D6
Seminole Tex., U.S.A. 32°43N 102°39W 314 E3
Seminole, L. U.S.A. 30°43N 84°52W 316 E5
Seminole Draw ~ U.S.A. 32°27N 102°20W 314 E3
Semipalatinsk = Semey Kazakhstan 50°30N 80°10E 217 B10
Semirara I. Phil. 12°4N 121°23E 232 E3
Semirara Is. Phil. 12°0N 121°20E 233 F3
Semisopochnoi I. U.S.A. 51°55N 179°36E 303 L2
Semitau Indonesia 0°29N 111°57E 235 B4
Semliki ~ Uganda 0°49N 30°4E 268 B3
Semlin = Zemun Serbia 44°51N 20°25E 202 B4
Semmelweis Museum Budapest, Hungary 117 c2
Semmering P. Austria 47°41N 15°45E 180 D8
Semnān Iran 35°40N 53°23E 247 C7
Semnān □ Iran 36°0N 54°0E 247 C7
Sempang Mengayou, Tanjong Malaysia 7°0N 116°40E 235 A5
Semporna Malaysia 4°30N 118°33E 235 B5
Sempu, Pulau Indonesia 2°51S 112°58E 235 C4
Semur-en-Auxois France 47°30N 4°20E 173 E11
Semyonovka = Arsenev Russia 44°10N 133°15E 220 B6
Semyonovskoye = Bereznik Russia 62°51N 42°40E 186 B7
Sen ~ Cambodia 12°32N 104°28E 236 F5
Sena Bolivia 11°32S 67°11W 330 C4
Sena Iran 28°27N 51°36E 247 D6
Sena Mozam. 17°25S 35°0E 269 F4
Sena ~ Bolivia 11°31S 67°11W 330 C4
Sena Madureira Brazil 9°5S 68°45W 330 B4
Senachwine L. U.S.A. 41°10N 89°18W 310 C7
Senador José Porfirio Brazil 2°35S 51°55W 329 D7
Senador Pompeu Brazil 5°40S 39°20W 332 C4
Senago Italy 45°34N 9°7E 128 B3
Senaja Malaysia 6°45N 117°3E 235 A5
Senaki Georgia 42°15N 42°1E 191 F7
Senang, Pulau Singapore 1°11N 103°52E 237 d
Senanga Zambia 16°7S 23°16E 265 F4
Senatobia U.S.A. 34°37N 89°58W 315 D10
Sencelles Spain 39°39N 2°54E 206 B3
Senda = Satsuma-Sendai Japan 31°50N 130°20E 222 F2
Sendafa Ethiopia 9°11N 39°3E 257 F4
Sendai Kagoshima, Japan 31°50N 130°20E 222 F2
Sendai-Wan Japan 38°15N 141°0E 220 E10
Senden Bayern, Germany 48°19N 10°4E 179 G6
Senden Nordrhein-Westfalen, Germany 51°52N 7°22E 178 D3
Sendhwa India 21°41N 75°6E 242 J6
Sendling Tor Platz Munich, Germany 131 c1
Sendurjana India 21°32N 78°17E 244 D4
Sene ~ Ghana 7°30N 0°33W 263 D4
Senec Slovak Rep. 48°12N 17°23E 181 C10
Seneca Ill., U.S.A. 41°19N 88°37W 311 C8
Seneca S.C., U.S.A. 34°41N 82°57W 315 D13
Seneca Falls U.S.A. 42°55N 76°48W 312 D8
Seneca L. U.S.A. 42°40N 76°54W 312 D8
Senecaville L. U.S.A. 39°55N 81°25W 312 G3
Senegal ■ W. Afr. 14°30N 14°30W 262 C2
Sénégal ~ W. Afr. 15°48N 16°32W 262 B1
Senegambia Africa 12°45N 12°0W 254 E2
Senegambia & Niger = Mali ■ Africa 17°0N 3°0W 262 B4
Senekal S. Africa 28°20S 27°36E 271 C4
Senftenberg Germany 51°32N 14°0E 178 D10
Senga Hill Zambia 9°19S 31°11E 269 D3
Senge Khambab = Indus ~ Pakistan 24°20N 67°47E 242 G2
Sengerema Tanzania 2°42S 32°35E 268 C3
Sengeti Indonesia 1°28S 103°31E 234 C2
Senggigi Indonesia 8°29S 116°2E 231 J17
Sengiley Russia 53°58N 48°46E 190 D9
Sengua ~ Zimbabwe 17°7S 28°5E 269 F2
Senguerr ~ Argentina 45°35S 68°56W 333 F3
Senhor-do-Bonfim Brazil 10°30S 40°10W 332 D3
Senica Slovak Rep. 48°41N 17°25E 181 C10
Senigállia Italy 43°43N 13°13E 199 E10
Senio ~ Italy 44°35N 12°15E 199 D9
Senirkent Turkey 38°6N 30°33E 205 C12
Senise Italy 40°9N 16°17E 201 B9
Senj Croatia 45°0N 14°58E 198 D11
Senja Norway 69°25N 17°30E 160 B17
Senju Japan 35°44N 139°48E 140 A3
Senkaku-Shotō E. China Sea 25°45N 123°30E 221 M1
Senkang Singapore 1°23N 103°53E 138 A3
Senlis France 49°13N 2°35E 173 C9
Senmonorom Cambodia 12°27N 107°12E 236 F6
Senmut Sudan 13°30N 33°35E 257 E3
Sennār □ Sudan 13°30N 33°35E 257 E3
Sennen U.K. 50°4N 5°42W 169 G2
Senneterre Canada 48°25N 77°15W 298 C4
Sennori Italy 40°47N 8°36E 200 B2
Senonches France 48°34N 1°2E 172 D8
Senorbì Italy 39°32N 9°8E 200 C2
Senožeče Slovenia 45°43N 14°3E 199 C11
Senqu = Orange ~ S. Africa 28°41S 16°28E 270 C2
Senriyama Japan 34°47N 135°30E 133 A7

Sens France 48°11N 3°15E 173 D10
Senta Serbia 45°55N 20°3E 182 E5
Sentani, Danau Indonesia 0°51N 112°6E 235 B4
Sentery = Lubao Dem. Rep. of the Congo 5°17S 25°42E 265 D5
Sentinel U.S.A. 32°52N 113°13W 305 K7
Šentjernej Slovenia 46°1N 15°24E 199 B12
Šentjur Slovenia 46°13N 15°24E 199 B12
Sentosa Singapore 1°16N 103°50E 138 B2
Sentry Hill St.-Maarten 18°2N 63°4W 322 a
Senwabarana S. Africa 23°17S 29°7E 271 B4
Senya Beraku Ghana 5°28N 0°31W 263 D4
Seo de Urgel = La Seu d'Urgell Spain 42°22N 1°23E 196 C6
Seobinggo S. Korea 37°31N 126°58E 137 B1
Seocho S. Korea 37°28N 127°0E 137 C1
Seodaemun S. Korea 37°34N 126°55E 137 B1
Seogwipo S. Korea 33°13N 126°34E 224 a
Seohara India 29°15N 78°33E 243 E8
Seokgwan Grotto S. Korea 35°46N 129°20E 224 E4
Seokkwan S. Korea 37°35N 127°2E 137 B2
Seonath ~ India 21°44N 82°28E 243 J10
Seongbuk S. Korea 37°35N 127°0E 137 B1
Seongdong S. Korea 37°33N 127°1E 137 B2
Seongmodo S. Korea 37°41N 126°19E 137 B2
Seongnam S. Korea 37°26N 127°8E 137 C2
Seongsu S. Korea 37°32N 127°2E 137 B2
Seoni India 22°5N 79°30E 243 H8
Seoni Malwa India 22°27N 77°28E 242 H8
Seonsan S. Korea 36°14N 128°17E 224 E4
Seonyudo S. Korea 35°49N 126°24E 224 E3
Seoraksan S. Korea 38°7N 128°27E 224 D4
Seoriuarayan India 21°45N 82°34E 244 D6
Seosan S. Korea 36°47N 126°27E 224 D3
Seoul = Sŏul S. Korea 37°31N 126°58E 137 B1
Seoul Nat. Univ. S. Korea 37°28N 126°57E 137 C1
Seoul Tower S. Korea 37°33N 126°59E 137 B1
Separation Pt. N.Z. 40°47S 172°59E 285 A7
Sepasu Indonesia 0°43N 117°34E 235 B5
Sepatini ~ Brazil 7°36S 65°24W 330 B4
Sepik ~ Papua N. G. 3°49S 144°30E 286 B3
Sepo-ri N. Korea 38°57N 127°25E 224 D3
Sepólia Greece 38°1N 23°42E 112 A2
Spólno Krajeńskie Poland 53°26N 17°30E 184 E4
Sepone Laos 16°45N 106°13E 236 D6
Sepopol Poland 54°16N 21°2E 184 D8
Seppa India 27°16N 92°54E 241 F19
Sept-Îles Canada 50°13N 66°22W 299 B6
Septemvri Bulgaria 42°13N 24°6E 203 D8
Sepúlveda Spain 41°18N 3°45W 194 D7
Sepúlveda Dam Rec. Area △ U.S.A. 34°10N 118°28W 126 A2
Sequeros Spain 40°31N 6°2W 194 E4
Sequim U.S.A. 48°5N 123°6W 306 B3
Sequoia △ U.S.A. 36°30N 118°30W 306 J8
Serafimovich Russia 49°36N 42°43E 190 F6
Seraing Belgium 50°35N 5°32E 170 D5
Serakhis ~ Cyprus 35°13N 32°55E 207 D11
Seram Indonesia 3°10S 129°0E 231 E7
Seram Sea Indonesia 2°30S 128°30E 231 E7
Serampore = Shrirampur India 22°44N 88°21E 243 H13
Seranantsara Madag. 18°30S 49°5E 272 B2
Serang Indonesia 6°8S 106°10E 234 D3
Serangoon Singapore 1°23N 103°54E 138 A3
Serangoon, Pulau Singapore 1°23N 103°56E 138 A3
Serangoon Harbour Singapore 1°23N 103°57E 138 A3
Serasan Indonesia 2°29N 109°4E 235 B3
Serasan, Selat Indonesia 2°20N 109°0E 235 B3
Seravezza Italy 43°59N 10°13E 198 E7
Seraya Indonesia 1°16N 103°43E 138 A2
Şerbal, G. Egypt 28°40N 33°39E 251 K4
Şerbettar Turkey 41°27N 26°46E 203 E10
Sercaia Romania 45°49N 25°9E 183 E10
Serchhip India 23°18N 92°51E 241 D4
Serdar Turkmenistan 39°4N 56°23E 247 B8
Serdo Ethiopia 11°56N 41°14E 257 E5
Serdobol = Sortavala Russia 61°42N 30°41E 188 B5
Serdobsk Russia 52°28N 44°10E 190 D7
Serdnye Ukraine 48°32N 22°30E 182 B7
Şereflikoçhisar Turkey 38°56N 33°32E 212 C5
Seregno Italy 45°39N 9°12E 198 C6
Seremban Malaysia 2°43N 101°53E 237 L3
Serengeti Plain Tanzania 2°40S 35°0E 268 C4
Serenje Zambia 13°14S 30°15E 269 E3
Seret ~ Ukraine 49°20N 25°5E 183 D9
Sereth = Siret ~ Romania 45°24N 28°1E 183 E12
Sergach Russia 55°30N 45°30E 190 C7
Sergeevka Kazakhstan 53°52N 67°24E 217 B7
Sergen Turkey 41°41N 27°42E 203 E11
Sergeya Kirova, Ostrova Russia 77°30N 89°0E 215 B10
Sergino Russia 62°25N 65°12E 214 C7
Sergipe □ Brazil 10°30S 37°30W 332 D4
Sergiyev Posad Russia 56°20N 38°10E 188 D10
Sergo = Stakhanov Ukraine 48°35N 38°40E 189 H10
Serhetabat Turkmenistan 35°20N 62°18E 247 D9
Seria Brunei 4°37N 114°23E 235 B4
Serian Malaysia 1°10N 110°31E 235 B4
Seriate Italy 45°41N 9°43E 198 C6
Seribu □ Indonesia 5°32S 106°33E 234 D3
Seribudolok Indonesia 2°55N 98°37E 234 B1
Sericho Kenya 1°5N 39°5E 268 B5
Sérifontaine France 49°20N 1°45E 173 C8
Sérifos Greece 37°9N 24°30E 204 D6
Sérigny ~ Canada 56°47N 66°0W 299 A6
Sérina Italy 45°52N 9°39E 128 A4
Seringapatam Reef Australia 13°38S 122°5E 274 B3
Sevastopol Ukraine 38°53N 79°9W 143 E7
Seririt Indonesia 8°12S 114°56E 231 J18
Sérkout Algeria 23°56N 6°47E 261 D6
Sermaize-les-Bains France 48°47N 4°54E 173 D11
Sermata Indonesia 8°15S 128°50E 231 F7
Sermersuaq Greenland 79°30N 62°0W 154 B4
Sérmide Italy 45°0N 11°18E 199 D8
Sernovodsk Russia 53°58N 51°16E 190 D10
Sernur Russia 56°49N 49°2E 190 B9
Serock Poland 52°31N 21°4E 185 F8
Seroe Colorado Aruba 12°25N 69°52W 322 d
Serón Spain 37°20N 2°29W 197 H2
Seròs Spain 41°22N 0°24E 196 D5

Severo-Yeniseyskiy Russia 60°22N 93°1E 215 C10
Severo-Zapadnyy □ Russia 65°0N 40°0E 214 C4
Severobaykalsk Russia 55°39N 109°19E 215 D11
Severočeský □ Czech Rep. 50°30N 14°0E 180 A7
Severodonetsk = Syeverodonetsk Ukraine 48°58N 38°35E 189 H10
Severodvinsk Russia 64°27N 39°58E 186 B6
Severomoravský □ Czech Rep. 49°38N 17°40E 181 B10
Severomorsk Russia 69°5N 33°27E 160 B25
Severouralsk Russia 60°9N 59°57E 186 B10
Seversk Russia 56°38N 84°49E 214 D9
Sévesco ~ Italy 45°35N 9°9E 128 A3
Sevier ~ U.S.A. 39°4N 113°6W 304 G7
Sevier Desert U.S.A. 39°40N 112°45W 304 G7
Sevier L. U.S.A. 38°54N 113°9W 304 G6
Sevilla Colombia 4°16N 75°57W 328 C2
Sevilla Spain 37°23N 5°58W 195 H5
Sevilla □ Spain 37°25N 5°58W 195 H5
Seville = Sevilla Spain 37°23N 5°58W 195 H5
Seville Fla., U.S.A. 29°19N 81°30W 317 F8
Seville Ohio, U.S.A. 41°1N 81°52W 312 F3
Sevlievo Bulgaria 43°2N 25°6E 203 C9
Sevnica Slovenia 46°2N 15°19E 199 B12
Sevran France 48°56N 2°31E 134 A4
Sèvre-Nantaise ~ France 47°12N 1°33W 172 E5
Sèvre-Niortaise ~ France 46°28N 0°50W 174 B3
Sevsk Russia 52°10N 34°30E 189 F8
Sewa ~ S. Leone 7°20N 12°10W 262 D2
Sewani India 28°58N 75°39E 242 E6
Seward Alaska, U.S.A. 60°7N 149°27W 303 F10
Seward Nebr., U.S.A. 40°55N 97°6W 308 E6
Seward Pa., U.S.A. 40°25N 79°1W 312 F5
Seward Peninsula U.S.A. 65°0N 164°0W 303 C7
Sewell Chile 34°10S 70°23W 334 C1
Sewer Indonesia 5°53S 134°40E 231 F8
Sewickley U.S.A. 40°32N 80°12W 312 F4
Sewri India 18°59N 72°50E 138 D8
Sexsmith Canada 55°21N 118°47W 296 B5
Seychelles ■ Ind. Oc. 5°0S 56°0E 272 c
Seyðisfjörður Iceland 65°16N 13°57W 155 B13
Seydişehir Turkey 37°25N 31°51E 212 D4
Seydvān Iran 38°34N 45°2E 213 C11
Seyhan ~ Turkey 36°43N 34°53E 250 B5
Seyhan Baraji Turkey 37°2N 35°18E 212 D6
Seyitgazi Turkey 39°27N 30°43E 205 B12
Seyitömer Turkey 39°34N 29°52E 205 B11
Seym ~ Ukraine 51°27N 32°34E 189 G7
Seymen Turkey 41°6N 27°57E 203 E11
Seymour Vic., Australia 37°2S 145°10E 283 D6
Seymour Eastern Cape, S. Africa 32°33S 26°46E 271 D4
Seymour Conn., U.S.A. 41°24N 73°4W 313 E11
Seymour Ind., U.S.A. 38°58N 85°53W 311 F11
Seymour Tex., U.S.A. 33°35N 99°16W 314 E5
Seyne France 44°21N 6°22E 175 D10
Seyssel France 45°57N 5°50E 175 C9
Sežana Slovenia 45°43N 13°41E 199 C10
Sézanne France 48°40N 3°40E 173 D10
Sezze Italy 41°30N 13°3E 200 A6
Sfântu Gheorghe Covasna, Romania 45°52N 25°48E 183 E10
Sfântu Gheorghe Tulcea, Romania 44°53N 29°36E 183 F14
Sfântu Gheorghe, Brațul ~ Romania 44°51N 29°36E 183 F14
Sfax Tunisia 34°49N 10°48E 258 B2
Sfax □ Tunisia 34°40N 10°20E 261 B7
Sforzesco, Castello Italy 45°28N 9°10E 128 B2
Sha Kok Mei China 22°23N 114°16E 122 A2
Sha Tau Kok China 22°33N 114°13E 219 a
Sha Tin China 22°23N 114°12E 122 A2
Sha Xi ~ China 26°35N 118°0E 229 D12
Sha Xian China 26°23N 117°45E 229 D11
Shaanxi □ China 35°0N 109°0E 226 G5
Sha'ar Binyamin West Bank 31°52N 35°16E 123 A2
Shaba = Katanga □ Dem. Rep. of the Congo 8°0S 25°0E 268 D2
Shaba ~ Kenya 0°38N 37°48E 268 B4
Shabeellaha Dhexe □ Somalia 3°0N 46°0E 267 D6
Shabeellaha Hoose □ Somalia 1°0N 44°0E 267 E5
Shabeelle ~ Somalia 2°0N 44°0E 267 D5
Shabestar Iran 38°11N 45°41E 213 C11
Shabla Bulgaria 43°31N 28°32E 203 C12
Shabogamo L. Canada 53°15N 66°30W 299 B6
Shabrâmant Egypt 29°56N 31°11E 117 B2
Shabunda Dem. Rep. of the Congo 2°40S 27°16E 268 C2
Shabwah Yemen 15°22N 47°1E 248 D4
Shabwah □ Yemen 15°22N 47°1E 248 D4
Shache China 38°20N 77°10E 217 F9
Shackleton Fracture Zone S. Ocean 60°0S 60°0W 151 B18
Shackleton Ice Shelf Antarctica 66°0S 100°0E 150 C8
Shackleton Inlet Antarctica 83°0S 160°0E 151 E11
Shādegān Iran 30°40N 48°38E 247 D6
Shadi Jiangxi, China 26°7N 114°47E 229 D10
Shadi Jammu & Kashmir, India 33°24N 77°14E 243 C7
Shadrinsk Russia 56°5N 63°32E 214 D7
Shady Dale U.S.A. 33°24N 83°36W 316 B6
Shady Grove U.S.A. 30°17N 83°38W 316 E6
Shadyside U.S.A. 39°58N 80°45W 312 G4
Shafer, L. U.S.A. 40°46N 86°46W 311 D10
Shaffa Nigeria 10°30N 12°6E 263 C7
Shafter U.S.A. 35°30N 119°16W 307 K7
Shaftesbury U.K. 51°0N 2°11W 169 F5
Shaftsbury U.S.A. 43°0N 73°11W 313 D11
Shag Pt., N.Z. 45°29S 170°52E 285 F4
Shag Rocks Atl. Oc. 53°0S 41°0W 152 M7
Shagamu Nigeria 6°51N 3°39E 263 D5
Shageluk U.S.A. 62°41N 159°34W 303 E8
Shagram Pakistan 36°24N 72°20E 243 A5
Shah Alam Malaysia 3°5N 101°32E 237 L3
Shah Alizai Pakistan 29°25N 68°0E 242 E3
Shah Bunder Pakistan 24°13N 67°56E 242 G2
Shāh Jūy Afghan. 32°31N 67°25E 242 C2
Shah Mosque Iran 35°41N 51°25E 141 A2
Shahabad Punjab, India 30°10N 76°55E 242 D7
Shahabad Raj., India 27°36N 79°56E 243 F8
Shahabad Ut. P., India 27°36N 79°56E 243 F8
Shahadpur Pakistan 25°55N 68°35E 242 G3
Shahapur India 15°50N 74°34E 245 G2
Shahba Syria 32°52N 36°38E 250 D7
Shahbazpur I. Bangla. 22°30N 90°45E 241 D3
Shahdad Iran 30°30N 57°40E 247 D8
Shahdad, Namakzār-e Iran 30°20N 58°20E 247 D8
Shahdadpur Pakistan 25°55N 68°35E 242 G3
Shahdara India 28°40N 77°18E 120 A2
Shahdol India 23°19N 81°26E 243 H9
Shahe China 37°0N 114°30E 226 F8
Shahganj India 26°3N 82°44E 243 F10
Shahgarh India 27°15N 69°50E 242 F3
Shahhāt Libya 32°48N 21°54E 258 B3
Shahīdān Afghan. 34°42N 67°45E 240 A2
Shahin Shahr Iran 32°49N 51°32E 247 C6

Shahjahanpur India 27°54N 79°57E 243 F8
Shahpur = Salmās Iran 38°11N 44°47E 213 C11
Shahpur Karnataka, India 16°40N 76°48E 244 F3
Shahpur Mad. P., India 22°12N 77°58E 242 H7
Shahpur Baluchistan, Pakistan 28°46N 68°27E 242 E3
Shahpur Punjab, Pakistan 32°17N 72°26E 242 C5
Shahpur Chakar Pakistan 26°9N 68°39E 242 F3
Shahpura Mad. P., India 23°10N 80°45E 243 H9
Shahpura Raj., India 25°38N 74°56E 242 G6
Shahr-e Bābak Iran 30°7N 55°9E 247 D7
Shahr-e Kord Iran 32°15N 50°55E 247 C6
Shahr-e Rey Iran 35°36N 51°25E 141 B2
Shahrak-e Golshahr Iran 35°37N 51°18E 141 B1
Shahrak-e Qods Iran 35°47N 51°22E 141 A2
Shāhrakht Iran 33°38N 60°16E 247 C9
Shāhrezā = Qomsheh Iran 32°0N 51°55E 247 D6
Shahrig Pakistan 30°15N 67°40E 242 D2
Shahrisabz Uzbekistan 39°3N 66°50E 217 E7
Shāhrud = Emāmrūd Iran 36°30N 55°0E 247 B7
Shahukou China 40°20N 112°18E 226 D7
Shaikh Aomar Iraq 33°20N 44°23E 113 A2
Shaikhabad Afghan. 34°2N 68°45E 242 B3
Shajapur India 23°27N 76°21E 242 H7
Shajing China 22°44N 113°48E 219 a
Shajuwan Taiwan 23°13N 121°23E 225 C3
Shakargarh Pakistan 32°17N 75°10E 242 C6
Shakawe Botswana 18°28S 21°49E 270 A3
Shakenge Dem. Rep. of the Congo 6°14S 18°41E 265 D3
Shaker Heights U.S.A. 41°28N 81°32W 312 E3
Shakhrisyabz = Shahrisabz Uzbekistan 39°3N 66°50E 217 E7
Shakhtersk Russia 49°10N 142°8E 215 E15
Shakhtīnsk Kazakhstan 49°42N 72°35E 217 C8
Shakhty Russia 47°40N 40°16E 191 G5
Shakhtyorskoye = Pershotravensk Ukraine 50°13N 27°40E 177 C14
Shakhunya Russia 57°40N 46°46E 190 B8
Shaki Nigeria 8°41N 3°21E 263 D5
Shākir Egypt 27°30N 33°59E 256 B3
Shakotan-Hantō Japan 43°10N 140°30E 220 C10
Shaksam Valley Asia 36°0N 76°20E 243 A7
Shaktoolik U.S.A. 64°20N 161°9W 303 D7
Shakurbasti India 28°41N 77°6E 120 A1
Shala, L. Ethiopia 7°30N 38°30E 257 F4
Shali Russia 43°9N 45°55E 191 J7
Shalim Oman 18°7N 55°38E 249 C6
Shalkar Köli Kazakhstan 50°35N 51°47E 190 E10
Shalkiya India 22°36N 88°21E 124 B2
Shallow Lake Canada 44°36N 81°5W 312 B3
Shalqar Kazakhstan 47°48N 59°39E 216 C5
Shalqar Köli Kazakhstan 50°33N 51°40E 216 B4
Shalskiy Russia 61°48N 35°58E 188 B8
Shalu Taiwan 24°14N 120°34E 225 B2
Shaluli Shan China 30°40N 99°55E 228 B2
Shām Iran 26°39N 57°21E 247 E8
Shām, Bādiyat ash Asia 32°0N 40°0E 246 C3
Shām, J. ash Oman 23°14N 57°16E 249 B7
Sham Shui Po China 22°19N 114°9E 122 B1
Shamâl Bahr el Ghazal = Northern Bahr el Ghazal □ South Sudan 8°0N 27°30E 257 F2
Shamâl Dârfûr □ Sudan 15°0N 25°0E 257 E2
Shamâl Kordofân □ Sudan 15°0N 30°0E 257 E3
Shamâl Sînî □ Egypt 30°30N 33°30E 251 H4
Shamapur India 28°44N 77°8E 120 A1
Shamattawa Canada 55°51N 92°5W 298 A1
Shamattawa → Canada 55°1N 85°23W 298 A2
Shambe South Sudan 7°8N 30°46E 257 F3
Shambe △ South Sudan 6°57N 30°50E 257 F3
Shambu Ethiopia 9°32N 37°3E 257 F4
Shamgong Dzong Bhutan 27°13N 90°35E 241 B3
Shamian China 23°6N 113°13E 121 B2
Shamīl Iran 27°30N 56°55E 247 E8
Shamkhor = Şämkir Azerbaijan 40°50N 46°0E 191 K8
Shāmkūh Iran 35°47N 57°50E 247 C8
Shamli India 29°32N 77°18E 242 E7
Shammar, Jabal Si. Arabia 27°40N 41°0E 246 E4
Shamo = Gobi Asia 44°0N 110°0E 226 C6
Shamo, L. Ethiopia 5°45N 37°30E 257 F4
Shamokin U.S.A. 40°47N 76°34W 313 F8
Shamrock Ont., Canada 45°23N 76°50W 313 A8
Shamrock Tex., U.S.A. 35°13N 100°15W 314 D4
Shamva Zimbabwe 17°20S 31°32E 269 F3
Shan □ Burma 21°30N 98°30E 241 E7
Shan Mei China 22°24N 114°10E 122 A2
Shan Xian China 34°50N 116°5E 226 G9
Shana = Kurilsk Russia 45°14N 147°53E 215 E15
Shanan → Ethiopia 8°0N 40°20E 257 F5
Shanchengzhen China 42°20N 125°20E 224 A2
Shāndak Iran 28°28N 60°27E 247 D9
Shandan China 38°45N 101°15E 218 D9
Shandon U.S.A. 35°39N 120°23W 306 K6
Shandong □ China 36°0N 118°0E 227 G10
Shandong Bandao China 37°0N 121°0E 227 F11
Shandur Pass Pakistan 36°4N 72°31E 243 A5
Shang Xian = Shangzhou China 33°50N 109°58E 226 H5
Shangalowe Dem. Rep. of the Congo 10°50S 26°30E 269 E2
Shangani Zimbabwe 19°41S 29°20E 271 A4
Shangani → Zimbabwe 18°41S 27°10E 269 F2
Shangbancheng China 40°50N 118°1E 227 D10
Shangcheng China 31°47N 115°26E 229 B10
Shangchuan Dao China 21°40N 112°50E 229 G9
Shangdu China 41°30N 113°30E 226 D7
Shanggao China 28°17N 114°55E 229 C10
Shanghai China 31°15N 121°26E 138 B2
Shanghai Hongqiao Int. ✈ (SHA) China 31°12N 121°20E 138 B1
Shanghai Pudong Int. ✈ (PVG) China 31°9N 121°47E 138 B2
Shanghai Shi □ China 31°0N 121°30E 229 B13
Shanghang China 25°2N 116°23E 229 E11
Shanghe China 37°20N 117°10E 227 F9
Shangjao = Shangrao China 28°25N 117°59E 229 C11
Shanglin China 23°27N 108°33E 228 F7
Shangnan China 33°32N 110°50E 226 H6
Shangqiu China 34°26N 115°36E 226 G8
Shangrao China 28°25N 117°59E 229 C11
Shangri-La = Zhongdian China 27°48N 99°42E 228 D2
Shangshui China 33°32N 114°35E 226 H8
Shangsi China 22°8N 107°58E 228 F6
Shangyi China 41°4N 113°57E 226 D7
Shangyou China 25°48N 114°32E 229 E10
Shangyu China 30°3N 120°52E 229 B13
Shangzhi China 45°22N 127°56E 227 B14
Shangzhou China 33°50N 109°58E 226 H5
Shanhetun China 44°33N 127°15E 227 B14
Shanhu Tan Taiwan 23°12N 120°23E 225 C2
Shanhua Taiwan 23°8N 120°17E 225 C2
Shani Nigeria 10°14N 12°2E 263 C7
Shānidar Iraq 36°48N 44°14E 213 D11
Shankill Ireland 53°14N 6°7W 120 B3
Shanklin U.K. 50°38N 1°11W 169 G6
Shanlin Taiwan 23°0N 120°32E 225 C2
Shannon N.Z. 40°33S 175°25E 284 G4
Shannon → Ireland 52°35N 9°30W 166 D2
Shannon ✈ (SNN) Ireland 52°42N 8°57W 166 D3
Shannon, Mouth of the Ireland 52°30N 9°55W 166 D2
Shannon △ Australia 34°35S 116°25E 279 F2
Shannon Ø Greenland 75°10N 18°30W 154 B9
Shannonbridge Ireland 53°17N 8°3W 166 C3
Shannontown U.S.A. 33°53N 80°21W 316 B9
Shanshan China 42°52N 90°10E 217 D12
Shanshang Taiwan 23°6N 120°21E 225 C2
Shansi = Shanxi □ China 37°0N 112°0E 226 F7
Shantar, Ostrov Bolshoy Russia 55°9N 137°40E 215 D14
Shantipur India 23°17N 88°25E 243 H13
Shantou China 23°18N 116°40E 229 F11
Shantung = Shandong □ China 36°0N 118°0E 227 G10
Shanwei China 22°48N 115°22E 229 F10
Shanxi □ China 37°0N 112°0E 226 F7
Shanyang China 33°31N 109°55E 226 H5
Shanyin China 39°25N 112°56E 226 E7
Shaodong China 27°15N 111°43E 229 D8
Shaoguan China 24°48N 113°35E 229 E9
Shaohing = Shaoxing China 30°0N 120°35E 229 C13
Shaoshan China 27°55N 112°33E 229 D9
Shaowu China 27°22N 117°28E 229 D11
Shaoxing China 30°0N 120°35E 229 C13
Shaoyang Hunan, China 26°59N 111°20E 229 D8
Shaoyang Hunan, China 27°14N 111°25E 229 D8
Shap U.K. 54°32N 2°40W 168 C5
Shapinsay U.K. 59°3N 2°51W 167 B6
Shaqlāwah Iraq 36°23N 44°20E 213 D11
Shaqq el Gi'eifer → Sudan 15°16N 26°0E 257 D2
Shaqra' Si. Arabia 25°15N 45°16E 246 E5
Shar Kazakhstan 49°35N 81°2E 217 C10
Sharafa Sudan 11°59N 27°7E 257 E2
Sharafkhāneh Iran 38°11N 45°29E 213 C11
Sharashova Belarus 52°34N 24°12E 185 F11
Sharavati → India 14°20N 74°25E 245 G2
Sharbaqty Kazakhstan 51°23N 78°17E 217 B9
Sharbithāt, Ra's ash Oman 17°56N 56°21E 249 C7
Sharbot Lake Canada 44°46N 76°41W 313 B8
Shard Building London, U.K. 125 b5
Shardara, Step Kazakhstan 42°20N 68°0E 217 D7
Sharhorod Ukraine 48°45N 28°5E 183 B13
Shari Japan 43°55N 144°40E 220 C12
Shariff Aguak = Maganoy Phil. 6°51N 124°31E 233 H5
Shariff Kabunsuan □ Phil. 7°5N 124°5E 233 H5
Sharjah = Ash Shāriqah U.A.E. 25°23N 55°26E 247 E7
Shark B. Australia 25°30S 113°32E 279 E1
Shark Bay △ Australia 25°30S 113°30E 279 E1
Sharm el Sheikh Egypt 27°53N 34°18E 251 L5
Sharon Ont., Canada 44°6N 79°26W 312 B5
Sharon Mass., U.S.A. 42°7N 71°11W 313 D13
Sharon Pa., U.S.A. 41°14N 80°31W 312 E4
Sharon Wis., U.S.A. 42°30N 88°44W 311 B8
Sharon Springs Kans., U.S.A. 38°54N 101°45W 308 F3
Sharon Springs N.Y., U.S.A. 42°48N 74°37W 313 D10
Sharonville U.S.A. 39°16N 84°25W 311 E12
Sharp I. China 22°21N 114°17E 122 A2
Sharp Pk. Phil. 5°58N 125°31E 233 J5
Sharp Pt. Australia 10°58S 142°43E 286 F2
Sharpe L. Canada 54°24N 93°40W 298 B1
Sharpes U.S.A. 28°26N 80°46W 317 G9
Sharpsville U.S.A. 41°15N 80°29W 312 E4
Sharq el Istiwa'iya = Eastern Equatoria □ South Sudan 5°0N 33°0E 257 G3
Sharqi, Al Jabal ash Lebanon 33°40N 36°10E 250 E7
Sharqīya □ Egypt 30°48N 31°48E 251 H2
Sharr Kosovo 42°5N 20°41E 202 D4
Sharya Russia 58°22N 45°20E 190 A7
Shasha Ethiopia 6°29N 35°59E 257 F4
Shashemene Ethiopia 7°13N 38°33E 257 F4
Shashi Botswana 21°15S 27°27E 271 B4
Shashi → Africa 21°14S 29°20E 269 G2
Shasta, Mt. U.S.A. 41°25N 122°12W 304 F2
Shasta L. U.S.A. 40°43N 122°25W 304 F2
Shastrinagar India 28°40N 77°10E 120 A2
Shatawi Sudan 14°39N 32°9E 257 E3
Shāṭi', Wādī ash → Libya 27°30N 15°0E 258 C3
Shatilki = Svyetlahorsk Belarus 52°38N 29°46E 177 B15
Shatsk Russia 54°5N 41°45E 190 C5
Shatsk Ukraine 51°29N 23°55E 185 G10
Shatsky Rise Pac. Oc. 34°0N 157°0E 288 D7
Shatskyi △ Ukraine 51°30N 23°52E 185 G10
Shatt al Arab Asia 29°57N 48°34E 247 D6
Shatura Russia 55°33N 39°21E 188 E10
Shaturtof = Shatura Russia 55°33N 39°21E 188 E10
Shau Kei Wan China 22°16N 114°13E 122 B2
Shaumyani = Shulaveri Georgia 41°22N 44°45E 191 K7
Shaunavon Canada 49°35N 108°25W 297 D7
Shaver L. U.S.A. 37°9N 119°18W 306 H7
Shavgar = Türkistan Kazakhstan 43°17N 68°16E 217 D7
Shavli = Šiauliai Lithuania 55°56N 23°15E 184 C10
Shaw → Australia 20°21S 119°17E 278 D2
Shaw I. Australia 20°30S 149°2E 280 b
Shawanaga Canada 45°31N 80°17W 312 A4
Shawangunk Mts. U.S.A. 41°35N 74°30W 313 E10
Shawano U.S.A. 44°47N 88°36W 308 C9
Shawinigan Canada 46°35N 72°50W 298 C5
Shawmari, J. ash Jordan 30°35N 36°35E 251 H7
Shawnee Ga., U.S.A. 32°29N 81°25W 316 C8
Shawnee Kans., U.S.A. 39°1N 94°43W 310 E2
Shawnee Okla., U.S.A. 35°20N 96°55W 314 D6
Shawocun China 39°53N 116°13E 114 B1
Shay Gap Australia 20°30S 120°10E 278 D3
Shayang China 30°42N 112°29E 229 B9
Shaybārā Si. Arabia 25°26N 36°47E 246 E3
Shayib el Banat, Gebel Egypt 26°59N 33°29E 256 B3
Shaykh, J. ash Lebanon 33°25N 35°50E 250 E6
Shaykh Miskīn Syria 32°49N 36°9E 250 F7
Shaykh Sa'd Iraq 32°34N 46°17E 213 F12
Shaykh 'Uthmān Yemen 12°52N 44°59E 248 D4
Shaytansky Zavod = Pervouralsk Russia 56°59N 59°59E 186 C10
Shayuan China 23°5N 113°15E 121 B2
Shāzand Iran 33°56N 49°24E 247 C6
Shazud Tajikistan 37°45N 72°25E 217 E8
Shcheglovo = Kemerovo Russia 55°20N 86°5E 214 D9
Shchekino Russia 54°1N 37°34E 188 E9
Shcherbakov = Rybinsk Russia 58°5N 38°50E 188 C10
Shchigry Russia 51°55N 36°58E 189 G9
Shchors Ukraine 51°48N 31°56E 189 G6
Shchūchīnsk Kazakhstan 52°56N 70°12E 217 B8
She Xian Anhui, China 29°50N 118°25E 229 C12
She Xian Hebei, China 36°30N 113°40E 226 F7
Shea Guyana 2°48N 59°4W 329 C6
Shebekino Russia 50°28N 36°54E 189 G9
Shebela → Ethiopia 7°32N 45°43E 267 C6
Shebele = Shabeelle → Somalia 2°0N 44°0E 267 D5
Shebele Ethiopia 8°8N 42°40E 267 C5
Sheberghān Afghan. 36°40N 65°45E 240 A2
Sheboygan U.S.A. 43°46N 87°45W 308 D10
Shebshi Mts. Nigeria 8°30N 12°0E 263 D7
Shediac Canada 46°14N 64°32W 299 C7
Sheelin, L. Ireland 53°48N 7°20W 166 C4
Sheen, L. U.S.A. 28°25N 81°31W 133 B1
Sheenjek → U.S.A. 66°45N 144°33W 303 C11
Sheep Haven Ireland 55°11N 7°52W 166 A4
Sheep Range U.S.A. 36°35N 115°15W 307 J11
Sheepshead Bay U.S.A. 40°35N 73°55W 132 C2
Sheerness U.K. 51°26N 0°47E 169 F8
Sheet Harbour Canada 44°56N 62°31W 299 D7
Sheffield N.Z. 43°23S 172°1E 285 D7
Sheffield S. Yorks., U.K. 53°23N 1°28W 168 D6
Sheffield Ala., U.S.A. 34°46N 87°41W 315 D11
Sheffield Ill., U.S.A. 41°21N 89°44W 310 C7
Sheffield Iowa, U.S.A. 42°54N 93°13W 310 B3
Sheffield Mass., U.S.A. 42°5N 73°21W 313 D11
Sheffield Pa., U.S.A. 41°42N 79°3W 312 E5
Shegaon India 20°48N 76°47E 244 D3
Shehojele Ethiopia 10°40N 35°9E 257 E4
Shehong China 30°54N 105°18E 228 B5
Shehuen → Argentina 49°35S 69°34W 336 C3
Shei-Pa △ Taiwan 24°36N 121°22E 225 B3
Shei Shan Taiwan 24°22N 121°15E 225 B3
Sheikh, W. el → Egypt 28°41N 33°41E 251 K4
Sheikh Zayed Canal Egypt 23°30N 30°15E 256 C3
Sheikh Zayed Road U.A.E. 25°11N 55°15E 119 B2
Sheikhpura India 25°9N 85°53E 243 G11
Shek Hasan Ethiopia 12°5N 35°58E 257 E4
Shek O China 22°13N 114°15E 122 B2
Shekhupura Pakistan 31°42N 73°58E 242 D5
Sheki = Şaki Azerbaijan 41°10N 47°5E 191 K8
Shekki = Zhongshan China 22°26N 113°20E 229 F9
Shekou China 22°30N 113°55E 219 a
Shelbina U.S.A. 39°47N 92°2W 310 E4
Shelburn U.S.A. 39°11N 87°24W 311 E9
Shelburne N.S., Canada 43°47N 65°20W 299 D6
Shelburne Ont., Canada 44°4N 80°15W 312 B4
Shelburne Vt., U.S.A. 44°23N 73°14W 313 B11
Shelburne B. Australia 11°50S 142°50E 286 F2
Shelburne Falls U.S.A. 42°36N 72°45W 313 D12
Shelby Mich., U.S.A. 43°37N 86°22W 308 D10
Shelby Miss., U.S.A. 33°57N 90°46W 315 E9
Shelby Mont., U.S.A. 48°30N 111°51W 304 B8
Shelby N.C., U.S.A. 35°17N 81°32W 315 D14
Shelby Ohio, U.S.A. 40°53N 82°40W 312 F2
Shelbyville Ill., U.S.A. 39°24N 88°48W 311 E8
Shelbyville Ind., U.S.A. 39°31N 85°47W 311 E11
Shelbyville Ky., U.S.A. 38°13N 85°14W 311 F11
Shelbyville Mo., U.S.A. 39°48N 92°2W 310 E4
Shelbyville Tenn., U.S.A. 35°29N 86°28W 315 D11
Shelbyville, L. U.S.A. 39°26N 88°46W 311 E8
Sheldon Ill., U.S.A. 40°46N 87°34W 311 D9
Sheldon Iowa, U.S.A. 43°11N 95°51W 308 D6
Sheldon Mo., U.S.A. 37°40N 94°18W 310 G2
Sheldon S.C., U.S.A. 32°36N 80°48W 316 C9
Sheldon Point U.S.A. 62°32N 164°52W 303 E6
Sheldrake Canada 50°20N 64°51W 299 B7
Shelek Kazakhstan 43°33N 78°17E 217 D9
Shelengo, Khawr → Sudan 10°33N 28°40E 257 E2
Shelikhova, Zaliv Russia 59°30N 157°0E 215 D16
Shelikof Strait U.S.A. 57°30N 155°0W 303 H9
Shell Beach = Huntington Beach U.S.A. 33°40N 118°5W 307 M9
Shell Lakes Australia 29°20S 127°30E 279 E4
Shellbrook Canada 53°13N 106°24W 297 C7
Shellharbour Australia 34°31S 150°51E 283 C9
Shellman U.S.A. 31°46N 84°37W 316 D5
Shellsburg U.S.A. 42°6N 91°52W 310 B5
Shelon → Russia 58°13N 30°47E 188 C6
Shelter Bay = Port-Cartier Canada 50°2N 66°50W 299 B6
Shelter I. Hong Kong, China 22°19N 114°17E 122 B2
Shelter I. N.Y., U.S.A. 41°4N 72°20W 313 E12
Shelton Conn., U.S.A. 41°19N 73°5W 313 E11
Shelton Wash., U.S.A. 47°13N 123°6W 306 C3
Shemakha = Şamaxı Azerbaijan 40°38N 48°37E 191 K9
Shemonaïkha Kazakhstan 50°37N 81°54E 217 B10
Shëmri Albania 42°7N 20°13E 202 D4
Shemsi Sudan 19°2N 29°57E 256 D2
Shen Xian China 36°15N 115°40E 226 F8
Shenandoah Iowa, U.S.A. 40°46N 95°22W 308 E6
Shenandoah Pa., U.S.A. 40°49N 76°12W 313 F8
Shenandoah Va., U.S.A. 38°29N 78°37W 309 F14
Shenandoah → U.S.A. 39°19N 77°44W 309 F15
Shenandoah △ U.S.A. 38°35N 78°22W 309 F14
Shenchi China 39°8N 112°10E 226 E7
Shencottah India 8°59N 77°18E 245 K3
Shendam Nigeria 8°49N 9°30E 263 D6
Shendī Sudan 16°46N 33°22E 257 D3
Shendurni India 20°39N 75°36E 244 D2
Shenge S. Leone 7°54N 12°55W 262 D2
Shengfang China 39°3N 116°42E 226 E9
Shëngjergj Albania 41°17N 20°10E 202 E4
Shëngjin Albania 41°50N 19°35E 202 E3
Shengzhou China 29°35N 120°50E 229 C13
Shenjingzi China 44°40N 124°30E 227 B13
Shenkang Taiwan 24°9N 120°39E 225 B2
Shenmu China 38°50N 110°29E 226 E6
Shennongjia China 31°43N 110°44E 229 B8
Shenqiu China 33°25N 115°5E 226 H8
Shensi = Shaanxi □ China 35°0N 109°0E 226 G5
Shenyang China 41°48N 123°27E 224 B1
Shenzhen China 22°32N 114°5E 229 F10
Shenzhen Bao'an Int. ✈ (SZX) China 22°41N 113°49E 219 a
Shenzhen Shuiku China 22°34N 114°8E 219 a
Shenzhen Wan China 22°27N 113°55E 219 a
Sheo India 26°11N 71°15E 242 F4
Sheopur Kalan India 25°40N 76°40E 242 G7
Shepetivka Ukraine 50°10N 27°10E 177 C14
Shepherd Is. Vanuatu 16°55S 168°36E 287 F6
Shepherds Bush U.K. 51°30N 0°13W 125 A2
Shepherdsville U.S.A. 37°59N 85°43W 311 G11
Shepparton Australia 36°23S 145°26E 283 D6
Shepperton U.K. 51°23N 0°26W 125 B1
Sheppey, I. of U.K. 51°25N 0°48E 169 F8
Shepton Mallet U.K. 51°11N 2°33W 169 F5
Sheqi China 33°12N 112°57E 226 H7
Sher Khan Qala Afghan. 29°53N 66°13E 240 C2
Sher Qila Pakistan 36°7N 74°2E 243 A6
Sherab Sudan 10°44N 24°41E 257 E1
Sherabad Uzbekistan 37°40N 67°1E 217 E7
Sherborne U.K. 50°57N 2°31W 169 G5
Sherbro → S. Leone 7°45N 12°55W 262 D2
Sherbro I. S. Leone 7°30N 12°40W 262 D2
Sherbrooke N.S., Canada 45°8N 61°59W 299 C7
Sherbrooke Qué., Canada 45°28N 71°57W 313 A13
Sherburne U.S.A. 42°41N 75°30W 313 D9
Sherburne Reef Papua N. G. 3°20S 148°0E 286 B5
Sherda Chad 20°7N 16°46E 259 D3
Shereik Sudan 18°44N 33°47E 256 D3
Sheremetyevo ✈ (SVO) Russia 55°58N 37°25E 129 A1
Shergaon India 27°7N 92°16E 241 B4
Shergarh India 26°20N 72°18E 242 F5
Sherghati India 24°34N 84°47E 243 G11
Sheridan Ark., U.S.A. 34°19N 92°24W 314 D8
Sheridan Ill., U.S.A. 41°32N 88°41W 311 C8
Sheridan Ind., U.S.A. 40°8N 86°13W 311 D10
Sheridan Wyo., U.S.A. 44°48N 106°58W 304 D10
Sheringham U.K. 52°56N 1°13E 168 E9
Sherkin I. Ireland 51°28N 9°26W 166 E2
Sherkot India 29°22N 78°35E 243 E8
Sherlovaya Gora Russia 50°34N 116°15E 215 D12
Sherman N.Y., U.S.A. 42°9N 79°35W 312 D5
Sherman Tex., U.S.A. 33°38N 96°36W 314 E6
Sherman Oaks U.S.A. 34°8N 118°29W 126 B2
Sherman Park U.S.A. 41°47N 87°39W 119 C2
Sherpur Bangla. 25°0N 90°0E 241 C3
Sherpur India 25°34N 83°47E 243 G10
Sherridon Canada 55°8N 101°5W 297 B8
Sherriffs St. Kitts & Nevis 17°10N 62°32W 322 d
Shertallai = Cherthala India 9°42N 76°20E 245 K3
Sherwood U.S.A. 41°17N 84°33W 311 C12
Sherwood, L. U.S.A. 28°33N 81°29W 133 A2
Sherwood Forest U.K. 53°6N 1°7W 168 D6
Sherwood Park Canada 53°31N 113°19W 296 C6
Sheslay → Canada 58°48N 132°5W 296 B2
Shet Bandar India 18°57N 72°55E 130 B2
Shethanei L. Canada 58°48N 97°50W 297 B9
Shetland □ U.K. 60°30N 1°30W 167 A7
Shetland Is. U.K. 60°30N 1°30W 167 A7
Shetou Taiwan 23°53N 120°35E 225 C2
Shetpe Kazakhstan 44°10N 52°7E 216 D4
Shetrunji → India 21°19N 72°7E 242 J5
Sheung Fa Shan China 22°23N 114°5E 122 A1
Sheung Lau Wan China 22°16N 114°16E 122 B2
Sheung Shui China 22°31N 114°7E 219 a
Sheung Wan China 22°16N 114°9E 122 B1
Sheva India 18°56N 72°57E 130 B2
Sheva Nhava India 18°57N 72°57E 130 B2
Shevaroy Hills India 11°58N 78°12E 245 J4
Shevchenkovo = Dolynska Ukraine 48°6N 32°46E 189 H7
Shevchenkove Ukraine 45°33N 29°20E 183 E14
Shevgaon India 19°21N 75°14E 244 E2
Shevisheh Iran 35°21N 46°40E 213 E12
Shewa Ethiopia 9°33N 38°10E 257 F4
Shewa Gimira Ethiopia 7°4N 35°51E 257 F4
Shey-Phoksundo △ Nepal 29°30N 82°45E 243 E10
Sheyang China 33°48N 120°29E 227 H11
Sheyenne → U.S.A. 47°2N 96°50W 308 B5
Shiashkotan, Ostrov Russia 48°49N 154°6E 215 E16
Shiba Tokyo, Japan 140 c4
Shibām Yemen 15°59N 48°36E 249 D5
Shibata Japan 37°57N 139°20E 220 F9
Shibecha Japan 43°17N 144°36E 220 C12
Shibetsu Hokkaidō, Japan 43°30N 145°10E 220 C12
Shibetsu Hokkaidō, Japan 44°10N 142°23E 220 B11
Shibîn el Kôm Egypt 30°31N 30°55E 256 H7
Shibîn el Qanâtir Egypt 30°19N 31°19E 256 H7
Shibing China 27°2N 108°7E 228 D7
Shibogama L. Canada 53°35N 88°15W 298 B2
Shibpur India 22°34N 88°19E 124 B1
Shibukawa Japan 36°29N 139°0E 223 A11
Shibushi Japan 31°25N 131°8E 222 F3
Shibushi-Wan Japan 31°24N 131°8E 222 F3
Shibuya Tokyo, Japan 140 c1
Shicheng China 26°22N 116°20E 229 D11
Shicheng Dao China 39°31N 122°59E 224 C1
Shickshinny U.S.A. 41°9N 76°9W 313 E8
Shickshock Mts. = Chic-Chocs, Mts. Canada 48°55N 66°0W 299 C6
Shidād Si. Arabia 21°19N 40°3E 248 B3
Shidao China 36°50N 122°25E 227 F12
Shiderti → Kazakhstan 52°32N 74°50E 217 B8
Shidian China 24°40N 99°5E 228 E2
Shido = Sanuki Japan 34°19N 134°10E 222 C6
Shiel, L. U.K. 56°48N 5°34W 167 E3
Shield, C. Australia 13°20S 136°20E 280 A2
Shieli Kazakhstan 44°20N 66°15E 217 D7
Shifang China 31°8N 104°10E 228 B5
Shiga □ Japan 35°20N 136°0E 223 B8
Shigaib Sudan 15°5N 23°35E 259 E4
Shigu China 26°51N 99°56E 228 D2
Shiguaigou China 40°52N 110°15E 226 D6
Shihan Yemen 17°42N 52°27E 249 C6
Shihan, W. → Yemen 17°24N 51°26E 249 C5
Shihchiachuangi = Shijiazhuang China 38°2N 114°28E 226 E8
Shihezi China 44°15N 86°2E 217 D11
Shihiu Taiwan 24°38N 121°10E 225 B3
Shihkangkeng Taiwan 24°1N 120°57E 225 B2
Shihmen Taiwan 25°17N 121°33E 225 A3
Shihmen Shuiku Taiwan 24°49N 121°21E 225 B3
Shihtan Taiwan 24°32N 120°55E 225 B2
Shiiba Japan 32°29N 131°4E 222 E3
Shiikh Somalia 9°56N 45°13E 267 C6
Shijak Albania 41°21N 19°33E 202 E3
Shijiazhuang China 38°2N 114°28E 226 E8
Shijiu Hu China 31°25N 118°50E 229 B12
Shikarpur India 28°17N 78°7E 242 E8
Shikarpur Pakistan 27°57N 68°39E 242 F3
Shikhrany = Kanash Russia 55°30N 47°32E 190 C8
Shikine-Jima Japan 34°19N 139°13E 223 C11
Shikohabad India 27°6N 78°36E 243 F8
Shikokochūō Japan 34°1N 133°34E 222 C5
Shikoku Japan 33°30N 133°30E 222 D5
Shikoku □ Japan 33°30N 133°30E 222 D5
Shikoku-Sanchi Japan 33°30N 133°30E 222 D5
Shikotan, Ostrov Asia 43°47N 146°44E 215 E15
Shikotsu-Ko Japan 42°45N 141°25E 220 C10
Shikotsu-Tōya △ Japan 44°4N 145°8E 220 C10
Shikuka = Poronaysk Russia 49°13N 143°0E 219 B17
Shilabo Ethiopia 6°5N 44°46E 267 C5
Shiliguri India 26°45N 88°25E 241 B2
Shilihe China 39°50N 116°25E 114 B2
Shiliu = Changjiang China 19°20N 108°55E 236 C7
Shilka Russia 52°0N 115°55E 215 D12
Shilka → Russia 53°20N 121°26E 215 D13
Shillelagh Ireland 52°45N 6°32W 166 D5
Shillington U.S.A. 40°18N 75°58W 313 F9
Shillong India 25°35N 91°53E 241 C3
Shilo West Bank 32°4N 35°18E 251 F6
Shilong China 23°5N 113°52E 229 F9
Shilou China 37°0N 110°48E 226 F6
Shilovo Russia 54°25N 40°57E 190 C5
Shima-Hantō Japan 34°22N 136°45E 223 C8
Shimabara Japan 32°48N 130°20E 222 E2
Shimada Japan 34°49N 138°10E 223 C10
Shimane □ Japan 35°0N 132°30E 222 C4
Shimane-Hantō Japan 35°30N 133°0E 222 B5
Shimanovsk Russia 52°15N 127°30E 215 D13
Shimanto Kōchi, Japan 33°12N 133°8E 222 D5
Shimanto Kōchi, Japan 32°59N 132°56E 222 E4
Shimba Hills ⌂ Kenya 4°14S 39°25E 268 C4
Shimbiris Somalia 10°44N 47°14E 267 B6
Shimen China 29°35N 111°20E 229 C8
Shimenjie China 29°29N 116°48E 229 C11
Shimian China 29°17N 102°23E 228 C4
Shimizu Japan 35°0N 138°30E 223 C10
Shimla India 31°2N 77°9E 242 D7
Shimo-Jima Japan 32°15N 130°7E 222 E2
Shimo-Koshiki-Jima Japan 31°40N 129°43E 222 F1
Shimoda Japan 34°40N 138°57E 223 C10
Shimodate Japan 36°20N 139°55E 223 A11
Shimoga India 13°57N 75°32E 245 H2
Shimogawara Japan 35°39N 139°27E 140 B1
Shimokita-Hantō Japan 41°20N 141°0E 220 D10
Shimoni Kenya 4°38S 39°20E 268 C4
Shimonita Japan 36°13N 138°47E 223 A10
Shimonoseki Japan 33°58N 130°55E 222 D2
Shimosalo Japan 35°45N 139°31E 140 A2
Shimoshakujii Japan 35°43N 139°35E 140 A2
Shimotsuma Japan 36°11N 139°58E 223 A11
Shimpuru Rapids Namibia 17°45S 19°55E 265 F3
Shimsha → India 13°15N 77°10E 245 H3
Shimsk Russia 58°15N 30°50E 188 C6
Shin, L. U.K. 58°5N 4°30W 167 C4
Shin-Nan'yō Japan 34°3N 131°49E 222 C3
Shin-Tone-Gawa → Japan 35°44N 140°51E 223 B12
Shinagawa Japan 35°36N 139°44E 140 B3
Shinan China 22°44N 109°53E 228 F7
Shinano-Gawa → Japan 36°50N 138°30E 221 F9
Shinās Oman 24°46N 56°28E 247 E8
Shīndand Afghan. 33°12N 62°8E 240 B1
Shing Mun Res. China 22°23N 114°8E 122 A1
Shingbwiyang Burma 26°41N 96°13E 241 B6
Shinglehouse U.S.A. 41°58N 78°12W 312 E6
Shingū Japan 33°40N 135°55E 223 D7
Shingwidzi S. Africa 23°5S 31°25E 271 B5
Shinji Japan 35°24N 132°54E 222 B4
Shinji-Ko Japan 35°26N 132°57E 222 B4
Shinjō Japan 38°46N 140°18E 220 E10
Shinjuku Tokyo, Japan 140 a1
Shinjuku Nat. Garden Tokyo, Japan 140 a2
Shinkafe Nigeria 13°8N 6°29E 263 C6
Shinkoiwa Japan 35°43N 139°51E 140 A4
Shinminato = Imizu Japan 36°47N 137°4E 223 A9
Shinnakano Japan 35°41N 139°40E 140 A3
Shinshār Syria 34°36N 36°43E 250 D7
Shinshiro Japan 34°54N 137°30E 223 C9
Shintuya Peru 12°41S 71°15W 330 C3
Shinyanga Tanzania 3°45S 33°27E 268 C3
Shinyanga □ Tanzania 3°50S 34°0E 268 C3
Shio-no-Misaki Japan 33°25N 135°45E 223 D7
Shiogama Japan 38°19N 141°1E 220 E10
Shiojiri Japan 36°6N 137°58E 223 A9
Shipai China 23°8N 113°20E 121 B3
Shipchenski Prokhod Bulgaria 42°45N 25°15E 203 D9
Shiphoirt, L. = Seaforth, L. U.K. 57°52N 6°36W 167 D2
Shiping China 23°45N 102°23E 228 F4
Shippagan Canada 47°45N 64°45W 299 C7
Shippensburg U.S.A. 40°3N 77°31W 312 F7
Shippenville U.S.A. 41°15N 79°28W 312 E5
Shiprock U.S.A. 36°47N 108°41W 305 H9
Shiqian China 27°32N 108°13E 228 D7
Shiqma, N. → Israel 31°37N 34°30E 251 G5
Shiquan China 33°5N 108°15E 228 A7
Shiquan He = Indus → Pakistan 24°20N 67°47E 242 G2
Shīr Khān Afghan. 37°11N 68°36E 240 A3
Shīr Kūh Iran 31°39N 54°3E 247 D7
Shirabad = Sherabad Uzbekistan 37°40N 67°1E 217 E7
Shiragami-Misaki Japan 41°24N 140°12E 220 D10
Shirahama Japan 33°41N 135°20E 223 D7
Shirakawa Fukushima, Japan 37°7N 140°13E 221 F10
Shirakawa Gifu, Japan 36°17N 136°56E 223 A8
Shirane-San Gumma, Japan 36°48N 139°22E 223 A11
Shirane-San Yamanashi, Japan 35°42N 138°9E 223 B10
Shiraoi Japan 42°33N 141°21E 220 C10
Shirati Tanzania 1°8S 33°59E 266 E3
Shīrāz Iran 29°42N 52°30E 247 D7
Shirbīn Egypt 31°11N 31°32E 256 H7
Shire → Africa 17°42S 35°19E 269 F4
Shiren China 41°57N 126°34E 227 D14
Shiretoko △ Japan 44°15N 145°15E 220 B12
Shiretoko-Misaki Japan 44°21N 145°20E 220 B12
Shirinab → Pakistan 30°15N 66°28E 242 D2
Shirinashi → Japan 34°38N 135°27E 133 B1
Shiriya-Zaki Japan 41°25N 141°30E 220 D10
Shirley U.S.A. 39°53N 85°35W 311 E11
Shirogane Japan 35°37N 139°44E 140 B3
Shiroishi Japan 38°0N 140°37E 220 F10
Shirol India 16°47N 74°41E 244 F2
Shiroro Res. Nigeria 9°56N 6°54E 263 D6
Shirpur India 21°21N 74°57E 244 D2
Shirshov Ridge Pac. Oc. 58°0N 170°0E 288 B8
Shīrvān Iran 37°30N 57°50E 247 B8
Shirwa, L. = Chilwa, L. Malawi 15°15S 35°40E 269 F4
Shishaldin Volcano U.S.A. 54°45N 163°58W 303 J7
Shishi China 24°44N 118°37E 229 E12
Shishmaref U.S.A. 66°15N 166°4W 303 C6
Shishou China 29°38N 112°22E 229 C9
Shisur Oman 18°15N 53°39E 249 C6
Shitai China 30°12N 117°25E 229 B11
Shitata South Sudan 4°30N 30°10E 257 G3
Shitennoji Temple Japan 34°39N 135°31E 133 B2
Shithāthah Iraq 32°34N 43°28E 213 G10
Shivamogga = Shimoga India 13°57N 75°32E 245 H2
Shively U.S.A. 38°12N 85°49W 311 F11
Shivpuri India 25°26N 77°42E 242 G7
Shiweitang China 23°6N 113°12E 121 B2
Shixian China 43°5N 129°50E 227 C15
Shixing China 24°46N 114°5E 229 E10
Shiyan Guangdong, China 22°42N 113°56E 219 a
Shiyan Hubei, China 32°35N 110°45E 229 A8
Shiyan Shuiku China 22°42N 113°54E 219 a
Shiyata Egypt 29°25N 25°7E 256 B2
Shizhu China 29°58N 108°7E 228 C7
Shizong China 24°50N 104°0E 228 E5
Shizuishan China 39°15N 106°50E 226 E4
Shizuoka Japan 34°57N 138°24E 223 C10
Shizuoka □ Japan 35°15N 138°40E 223 B10
Shkhara Georgia 43°0N 43°8E 213 A10
Shklov = Shklow Belarus 54°16N 30°15E 177 A16
Shklow Belarus 54°16N 30°15E 177 A16
Shkodër Albania 42°4N 19°32E 202 D3
Shkodra = Shkodër Albania 42°4N 19°32E 202 D3
Shkumbini → Albania 41°2N 19°31E 202 E3
Shmidta, Ostrov Russia 81°0N 91°0E 215 A10
Shō-Gawa → Japan 36°47N 137°4E 223 A9
Shoal Cr. → U.S.A. 39°44N 93°32W 310 E3
Shoal L. Canada 49°33N 95°1W 297 D9
Shoal Lake Canada 50°30N 100°35W 297 C8
Shoalhaven → Australia 34°54S 150°42E 283 C9
Shoals U.S.A. 38°40N 86°47W 311 F10
Shōbara Japan 34°51N 133°1E 222 C5
Shōdo-Shima Japan 34°30N 134°15E 222 C6
Shogunle Nigeria 6°34N 3°20E 124 A2
Sholapur = Solapur India 17°43N 75°56E 244 F2
Shomolu Nigeria 6°32N 3°22E 124 A2
Shōmrōn West Bank 32°15N 35°13E 251 F6
Shonian Harb. Palau 7°10N 134°23E 288 c
Shonzhy Kazakhstan 43°32N 79°28E 217 D9
Shooters Hill U.K. 51°28N 0°4E 125 B4
Shoranur India 10°46N 76°19E 245 J3
Shorapur India 16°31N 76°48E 245 F3
Shoreditch London, U.K. 125 a5
Shoreham U.S.A. 43°53N 73°18W 313 C11
Shoreham by Sea U.K. 50°50N 0°16W 169 G7
Shorewood U.S.A. 43°5N 87°53W 311 A9
Shori → Pakistan 28°29N 69°44E 242 E3
Shorkot Pakistan 30°50N 72°0E 242 D4
Shorkot Road Pakistan 30°47N 72°15E 242 D5
Shorter U.S.A. 32°24N 85°57W 316 C4
Shorterville U.S.A. 31°34N 85°6W 316 D4
Shortland I. Solomon Is. 7°0S 155°45E 287 L8
Shortland Is. Solomon Is. 7°0S 156°0E 287 L8
Shortlands U.K. 51°23N 0°0 125 B4
Shortt's I. India 20°47N 87°4E 244 D8
Shoshone Calif., U.S.A. 35°58N 116°16W 307 K10
Shoshone Idaho, U.S.A. 42°56N 114°25W 304 E6
Shoshone L. U.S.A. 44°22N 110°43W 304 D8
Shoshone Mts. U.S.A. 39°20N 117°25W 304 G5
Shoshong Botswana 22°56S 26°31E 270 B4
Shoshoni U.S.A. 43°14N 108°7W 304 E9
Shostka Ukraine 51°57N 33°32E 189 G7
Shot Iran 39°12N 44°49E 213 C11
Shotor Khūn Afghan. 34°19N 64°56E 240 B2
Shotover → N.Z. 44°59S 168°41E 285 E3
Shou Xian China 32°37N 116°42E 229 A11
Shouchang China 29°18N 119°12E 229 C12
Shouchia Taiwan 22°14N 120°51E 225 D2
Shoufeng Taiwan 23°52N 121°30E 225 C3
Shouguang China 37°52N 118°45E 227 F10
Shouning China 27°27N 119°31E 229 D12
Shouyang China 37°54N 113°8E 226 F7
Show Low U.S.A. 34°15N 110°2W 305 J8
Showa Japan 35°36N 138°29E 223 B10
Showak Sudan 14°23N 35°52E 257 E4
Shpola Ukraine 49°1N 31°30E 189 H6
Shpykiv Ukraine 48°47N 28°34E 183 B13
Shqipëria = Albania ■ Europe 41°0N 20°0E 202 E4
Shreveport U.S.A. 32°31N 93°45W 314 E8
Shrewsbury U.K. 52°43N 2°45W 169 E5
Shri Mohangarh India 27°17N 71°18E 242 F4
Shrigonda India 18°37N 74°41E 244 E2
Shrirampur India 22°44N 88°21E 243 H13
Shropshire □ U.K. 52°36N 2°45W 169 E5
Shtërpcë Kosovo 42°14N 21°1E 202 D5
Shū Kazakhstan 43°36N 73°42E 217 D8
Shū → Kazakhstan 45°0N 67°44E 217 D7
Shu'afat West Bank 31°49N 35°14E 123 B2
Shuangbai China 24°42N 101°38E 228 E3
Shuangcheng China 45°20N 126°15E 227 B14
Shuangfeng China 27°29N 112°11E 229 D9
Shuanggou China 34°2N 117°30E 227 G9
Shuangjiang China 23°26N 99°58E 228 F2
Shuangliao China 43°29N 123°30E 227 C12
Shuangshanzi China 40°20N 119°8E 227 D10
Shuangyang China 43°28N 125°40E 227 C13
Shuangyashan China 46°28N 131°5E 219 B15
Shu'b, Ra's Yemen 12°30N 53°25E 249 D6
Shubarqudyq Kazakhstan 49°13N 56°34E 216 C5
Shubarshī Kazakhstan 48°39N 57°11E 216 C5
Shubrâ Egypt 30°5N 31°14E 117 A2
Shubrâ el Kheima Egypt 30°4N 31°14E 117 A2
Shubrâ Khit Egypt 31°2N 30°42E 256 H7
Shucheng China 31°28N 116°57E 229 B11
Shugozero Russia 59°54N 34°10E 188 C8
Shuguri Falls Tanzania 8°33S 37°22E 269 D4
Shuḩayr Yemen 14°41N 49°23E 249 D5
Shuiding = Huocheng China 44°0N 80°48E 217 D10
Shuiji China 27°13N 118°20E 229 D12
Shuikou China 23°10N 113°10E 121 A2
Shuili Taiwan 23°49N 120°51E 225 C2
Shuilien Taiwan 23°47N 121°34E 225 C3
Shuishang Taiwan 23°25N 120°23E 225 C2
Shuitiliao Taiwan 22°23N 120°35E 225 D2
Shujalpur India 23°18N 76°46E 242 H7
Shukpa Kunzang India 34°22N 78°22E 243 B8
Shulan China 44°28N 127°0E 227 B14
Shulaveri Georgia 41°22N 44°45E 191 K7
Shule China 39°25N 76°3E 217 E9
Shule He → China 40°20N 92°50E 218 C7
Shullsburg U.S.A. 42°35N 90°13W 310 B6
Shumagin Is. U.S.A. 55°7N 160°30W 303 J7
Shumanay Uzbekistan 42°38N 58°55E 216 D5
Shumen Bulgaria 43°18N 26°55E 203 C10
Shumerlya Russia 55°30N 46°25E 190 C8
Shumikha Russia 55°10N 63°15E 214 D7
Shûna, W. el → Egypt 30°38N 32°6E 251 J3
Shunān Japan 34°3N 131°50E 222 C3
Shunchang China 26°54N 117°48E 229 D11
Shunde China 22°42N 113°14E 229 F9
Shungay Kazakhstan 48°30N 46°45E 191 F8
Shungnak U.S.A. 66°52N 157°9W 303 C8
Shuo Xian = Shuozhou China 39°20N 112°33E 226 E7
Shuozhou China 39°20N 112°33E 226 E7
Shuqrā' Yemen 13°22N 45°44E 248 D4
Shūr → Fārs, Iran 28°30N 55°0E 247 D7
Shūr → Kermān, Iran 30°52N 57°37E 247 D8
Shūr → Yazd, Iran 31°45N 55°15E 247 D7
Shūr Āb Iran 34°23N 51°11E 247 C6
Shūr Gaz Iran 29°10N 59°20E 247 D8
Shūrāb Iran 33°43N 56°29E 247 C8
Shuri Japan 26°13N 127°43E 288 a
Shūrjestān Iran 31°24N 52°25E 247 D7
Shurkhua Burma 22°15N 93°38E 241 D4
Shurugwi Zimbabwe 19°40S 30°0E 269 F3
Shūsf Iran 31°50N 60°5E 247 D9
Shūsh Iran 32°11N 48°15E 213 F13
Shusha Azerbaijan 39°46N 46°45E 213 C12
Shushenskoye Russia 53°19N 91°56E 217 B12
Shūshtar Iran 32°0N 48°50E 247 D6
Shuswap L. Canada 50°55N 119°3W 296 C5
Shute Harbour △ Australia 20°17S 148°47E 280 b
Shuya Russia 56°50N 41°28E 190 B5
Shuyak I. U.S.A. 58°31N 152°30W 303 G9
Shuyang China 34°10N 118°42E 227 G10
Shuzenji = Izu Japan 34°58N 138°56E 223 C10
Shūzū Iran 29°52N 54°30E 247 D7
Shwangliao = Liaoyuan China 42°58N 125°2E 227 C13
Shwebo Burma 22°30N 95°45E 241 D5
Shwegu Burma 24°15N 96°26E 241 C6
Shwegun Burma 17°9N 97°39E 241 G6
Shwegyin Burma 17°55N 96°59E 241 G6
Shweli → Burma 23°45N 96°45E 241 D6
Shwenyaung Burma 20°46N 96°57E 241 E6
Shyamnagar India 13°21N 92°57E 245 H11
Shyghanaq Kazakhstan 45°6N 73°59E 217 C8
Shyghys Qazaqstan □ Kazakhstan 48°30N 82°0E 217 D10
Shymkent Kazakhstan 42°18N 69°36E 217 D7
Shyok India 34°13N 78°12E 243 B8
Shyok → Pakistan 35°13N 75°53E 243 B6
Shyroke Odesa, Ukraine 45°59N 30°5E 183 E15
Shyroke Ternopil, Ukraine 48°13N 23°6E 182 B8
Si Kiang = Xi Jiang → China 22°5N 113°20E 229 F9
Si Lanna △ Thailand 19°17N 99°12E 236 C2
Si Nakarin Res. Thailand 14°35N 99°0E 236 E2
Si-ngan = Xi'an China 34°15N 109°0E 226 G5
Si Phangnga Thailand 9°8N 98°29E 237 H2
Si Prachan Thailand 14°37N 100°9E 236 E3
Si Racha Thailand 13°10N 100°48E 236 F3
Si Sa Ket Thailand 15°8N 104°23E 236 E5
Siachen Glacier Asia 35°20N 77°30E 243 B7
Sīah Chashmeh Iran 39°3N 44°25E 213 C11
Siahaf → Pakistan 29°3N 68°57E 242 E3
Siahan Range Pakistan 27°30N 64°40E 240 D2
Siak → Indonesia 1°13N 102°9E 234 B2
Siak Sri Indrapura Indonesia 0°51N 102°0E 234 B2

Sialkot Pakistan 32°32N 74°30E 242 C6
Sialum Papua N. G. 6°5S 147°36E 286 D4
Siam = Thailand ■ Asia 16°0N 102°0E 236 E4
Sian = Xi'an China 34°15N 109°0E 226 G5
Sian Ka'an ⌂ Mexico 19°35N 87°40W 319 D7
Siangtan = Xiangtan China 27°51N 112°54E 229 D9
Sianów Poland 54°13N 16°18E 184 D3
Siantan Indonesia 3°10N 106°15E 234 B3
Siàpo → Venezuela 2°7N 66°28W 328 C4
Sīāreh Iran 28°5N 60°14E 247 D9
Siargao I. Phil. 9°52N 126°3E 233 G6
Siasi Phil. 5°34N 120°50E 233 J3
Siasi I. Phil. 5°33N 120°51E 233 J3
Siassi Papua N. G. 5°40S 147°51E 286 C4
Siatista Greece 40°15N 21°33E 202 F5
Siaton Phil. 9°4N 123°2E 233 G4
Siau Indonesia 2°50N 125°25E 231 D7
Šiauliai Lithuania 55°56N 23°15E 184 C10
Šiauliai □ Lithuania 55°56N 23°19E 184 C10
Siavonga Zambia 16°33S 28°42E 271 A4
Siazan = Siyäzän Azerbaijan 41°3N 49°10E 191 K9
Sibâi, Gebel el Egypt 25°45N 34°10E 246 E2
Sibang Gabon 0°25N 9°31E 264 B1
Sibang Bali, Indonesia 8°34S 115°13E 231 K18
Sibay Russia 52°42N 58°39E 186 D10
Sibay I. Phil. 11°51N 121°29E 233 F3
Sibayi, L. S. Africa 27°20S 32°45E 271 C5
Sibdu Sudan 10°57N 26°17E 257 E2
Šibenik Croatia 43°48N 15°54E 199 E12
Siberia = Sibirskiy □ Russia 58°0N 90°0E 215 D10
Siberia Russia 60°0N 100°0E 210 B12
Siberië Curaçao 12°14N 69°3W 322 g
Siberut Indonesia 1°30S 99°0E 234 C1
Siberut, Selat Indonesia 0°42S 98°35E 234 C1
Siberut △ Indonesia 1°17S 98°45E 234 C1
Sibi Pakistan 29°30N 67°54E 242 E2
Sibigo Indonesia 2°50N 95°54E 234 B1
Sibiloi △ Kenya 4°0N 36°20E 268 B4
Sibirskiy □ Russia 58°0N 90°0E 215 D10
Sibirtsevo Russia 44°12N 132°26E 220 B5
Sibiti Congo 3°38S 13°19E 264 C2
Sibiu Romania 45°45N 24°9E 183 E9
Sibiu □ Romania 45°50N 24°15E 183 E9
Sibium Mts. Papua N. G. 9°19S 148°25E 286 E5
Sibley Ill., U.S.A. 40°35N 88°23W 311 D8
Sibley Iowa, U.S.A. 43°24N 95°45W 308 D6
Sibo Sweden 61°13N 16°37E 162 C10
Sibolga Indonesia 1°42N 98°45E 234 B1
Siborongborong Indonesia 2°13N 98°58E 237 L2
Sibsagar India 27°0N 94°36E 241 B5
Sibu Malaysia 2°18N 111°49E 235 B4
Sibuco Phil. 7°20N 122°10E 233 H4
Sibuguey B. Phil. 7°50N 122°45E 233 H4
Sibut C.A.R. 5°46N 19°10E 264 A3
Sibutu Phil. 4°45N 119°30E 235 B5
Sibutu Group Phil. 4°45N 119°20E 233 J2
Sibutu I. Phil. 4°47N 119°29E 233 J2
Sibutu Passage E. Indies 4°50N 120°0E 233 J3
Sibuyan I. Phil. 12°25N 122°40E 232 E4
Sibuyan Sea Phil. 12°30N 122°20E 232 E4
Sic Romania 46°56N 23°53E 183 D8
Sicamous Canada 50°49N 119°0W 296 C5
Sicapoo, Mt. Phil. 18°1N 120°56E 232 B3
Sicasica Bolivia 17°22S 67°45W 330 D4
Siccus → Australia 31°55S 139°17E 282 A3
Sichelberg = Sierpc Poland 52°55N 19°43E 185 F6
Sichon Thailand 9°0N 99°54E 237 H2
Sichuan □ China 30°30N 103°0E 228 B5
Sichuan Pendi China 31°0N 105°0E 228 B5
Sicilia Italy 37°30N 14°30E 201 E7
Sicily = Sicilia Italy 37°30N 14°30E 201 E7
Sicily, Str. of Medit. S. 37°35N 11°56E 200 E4
Sico → Honduras 15°58N 84°58W 320 C3
Sicuani Peru 14°21S 71°10W 330 C3
Šid Serbia 45°8N 19°14E 182 E4
Sidamo Ethiopia 5°0N 37°50E 257 G4
Sidaouet Niger 18°34N 8°3E 259 E1
Sidari Greece 39°47N 19°41E 206 B9
Sidcup U.K. 51°25N 0°6E 125 B4
Siddapur India 14°20N 74°53E 245 G2
Siddhapur India 23°56N 72°25E 242 H5
Siddipet India 18°5N 78°51E 244 E4
Side Turkey 36°45N 31°23E 250 B2
Sidensjö Sweden 63°18N 18°17E 162 A12
Sidéradougou Burkina Faso 10°42N 4°12W 262 C4
Siderno Italy 38°16N 16°18E 201 D9
Sideros, Akra Greece 35°19N 26°19E 207 E7
Sidhauli India 27°17N 80°50E 243 F9
Sidhi India 24°25N 81°53E 243 G9
Sîdi Abd el Rahmân Egypt 30°55N 29°44E 256 A2
Sîdi Barrâni Egypt 31°38N 25°58E 256 A2
Sidi-bel-Abbès Algeria 35°13N 0°39W 261 A4
Sidi-bel-Abbès □ Algeria 34°50N 0°30W 261 B4
Sidi Bennour Morocco 32°40N 8°25W 260 B3
Sidi Bou Zid Tunisia 35°1N 9°16E 258 B1
Sidi Bou Zid □ Tunisia 35°0N 9°30E 258 B1
Sidi Boubekeur Algeria 35°1N 0°4E 261 A5
Sîdi Haneish Egypt 31°10N 27°35E 256 A2
Sidi Ifni Morocco 29°29N 10°12W 260 C2
Sidi Kacem Morocco 34°12N 5°42W 260 B3
Sîdi Omar Egypt 31°24N 24°57E 256 A1
Sidi Slimane Morocco 34°16N 5°56W 260 B3
Sidi Smaïl Morocco 32°50N 8°31W 260 B3
Sīdī 'Uzayz Libya 31°41N 24°55E 258 B4
Sidikalang Indonesia 2°45N 98°19E 237 L2
Sidimo Somalia 2°27N 41°58E 267 D5
Siding No 14 = Ponoka Canada 52°42N 113°40W 296 C6
Sidirokastro Greece 41°13N 23°24E 202 E7
Sidlaw Hills U.K. 56°32N 3°2W 167 E5
Sidley, Mt. Antarctica 77°2S 126°2W 151 D14
Sidmouth U.K. 50°40N 3°15W 169 G4
Sidmouth, C. Australia 13°25S 143°36E 280 A3
Sidney B.C., Canada 48°39N 123°24W 306 B3
Sidney Mont., U.S.A. 47°43N 104°9W 304 C11
Sidney N.Y., U.S.A. 42°19N 75°24W 313 D9
Sidney Nebr., U.S.A. 41°8N 102°59W 308 E2
Sidney Ohio, U.S.A. 40°17N 84°9W 311 D12
Sidney Lanier, L. U.S.A. 34°10N 84°4W 316 A5
Sido Mali 11°37N 7°29W 262 C3
Sidoarjo Indonesia 7°27S 112°43E 235 D4
Sidoktaya Burma 20°27N 94°15E 241 E5
Sidon = Saydā Lebanon 33°35N 35°25E 250 E6
Sidra = Surt Libya 31°11N 16°39E 258 B3
Sidra, G. of = Surt, Khalīj Libya 31°40N 18°30E 258 B3
Sidrolândia Brazil 20°55S 54°58W 331 E7
Siebenhirten Austria 48°8N 16°17E 142 B1
Siedlce Poland 52°10N 22°20E 185 F9
Siedlung Germany 52°35N 13°7E 115 A1
Sieg → Germany 50°46N 7°6E 178 E3
Siegburg Germany 50°47N 7°12E 178 E3
Siegen Germany 50°51N 8°0E 178 E4
Siekierki Poland 52°12N 21°4E 143 B2
Sielce Poland 52°12N 21°2E 143 B2
Siem Pang Cambodia 14°7N 106°23E 236 E6
Siem Reap = Siemreab Cambodia 13°20N 103°52E 236 F4
Siemensstadt Germany 52°32N 13°16E 115 A2
Siemiatycze Poland 52°27N 22°53E 185 F9
Siemreab Cambodia 13°20N 103°52E 236 F4
Siena Italy 43°19N 11°21E 199 E8
Sieniawa Poland 50°11N 22°38E 185 H9
Sienyang = Xianyang China 34°20N 108°40E 226 G5
Sieradz Poland 51°37N 18°41E 185 G5
Sieraków Poland 52°39N 16°2E 185 F3
Sierck-les-Bains France 49°26N 6°20E 173 C13
Sierning Austria 48°2N 14°18E 180 C7
Sierpc Poland 52°55N 19°43E 185 F6
Sierpe, Bocas de la Venezuela 10°0N 61°30W 329 G9
Sierra Blanca U.S.A. 31°11N 105°22W 314 F2
Sierra Blanca Peak U.S.A. 33°23N 105°49W 305 K11
Sierra City U.S.A. 39°34N 120°38W 306 F6
Sierra Colorada Argentina 40°35S 67°50W 336 B3
Sierra de Agalta △ Honduras 15°1N 85°48W 320 C2
Sierra de Aracena y Picas de Aroche ⌂ Spain 37°53N 6°41W 195 H4
Sierra de Bahoruco △ Dom. Rep. 18°10N 71°25W 321 C5
Sierra de Baza ⌂ Spain 37°20N 2°48W 197 H2
Sierra de Castril ⌂ Spain 37°54N 2°50W 197 H2
Sierra de Espuña ⌂ Spain 37°50N 1°31W 197 H3
Sierra de Grazalema ⌂ Spain 36°31N 5°28W 195 J5
Sierra de Gredos ⌂ Spain 40°17N 5°17W 194 E5
Sierra de Hornachuelos ⌂ Spain 37°56N 5°14W 195 H5
Sierra de Huétor ⌂ Spain 37°14N 3°30W 195 H7
Sierra de la Culata △ Venezuela 8°48N 70°56W 328 B3
Sierra de la Macarena △ Colombia 11°19N 74°1W 328 A3
Sierra de las Nieves ⌂ Spain 36°42N 5°0W 195 J6
Sierra de las Quijadas △ Argentina 32°29S 67°5W 334 C2
Sierra de María-Los Vélez ⌂ Spain 37°41N 2°10W 197 H2
Sierra de San Luis △ Venezuela 11°11N 69°33W 328 A4
Sierra de San Pedro Mártir △ Mexico 31°10N 115°30W 318 A1
Sierra de Yeguas Spain 37°7N 4°52W 195 H6
Sierra del São Mamede ⌂ Portugal 39°17N 7°18W 195 F3
Sierra Gorda Chile 22°50S 69°15W 334 A2
Sierra Grande Argentina 41°36S 65°22W 336 B3
Sierra Leone ■ W. Afr. 9°0N 12°0W 262 D2
Sierra Leone Basin Atl. Oc. 5°0N 17°0W 152 F10
Sierra Leone Rise Atl. Oc. 7°0N 22°0W 152 F9
Sierra Madre Mexico 16°0N 93°0W 319 D6
Sierra Madre Calif., U.S.A. 34°9N 118°3W 126 B4
Sierra Madre Occidental Mexico 27°0N 107°0W 318 B3
Sierra Madre Oriental Mexico 25°0N 100°0W 318 C5
Sierra Mágina ⌂ Spain 37°44N 3°28W 195 H7
Sierra Mojada Mexico 27°18N 103°41W 318 B4
Sierra Nevada Spain 37°3N 3°15W 195 H7
Sierra Nevada Calif., U.S.A. 39°0N 120°30W 306 H8
Sierra Nevada ⌂ Spain 37°4N 3°7W 195 H7
Sierra Norte de Sevilla ⌂ Spain 37°55N 5°46W 195 H5
Sierra Subbéticas ⌂ Spain 37°26N 4°18W 195 H6
Sierra Vista U.S.A. 31°33N 110°18W 305 L8
Sierras de Cardeña y Montoro ⌂ Spain 38°13N 4°15W 195 G6
Sierras de Cazorla, Segura y las Villas ⌂ Spain 37°0N 2°45W 197 J2
Sierraville U.S.A. 39°36N 120°22W 306 F6
Sierre Switz. 46°17N 7°31E 179 J3
Sievering Austria 48°15N 16°20E 142 A2
Sīf Yemen 15°19N 48°20E 249 D5
Sifani Ethiopia 12°18N 40°19E 257 E5
Sifié Ivory C. 8°0N 7°5W 262 D3
Sifnos Greece 37°0N 24°45E 204 E6
Sifton Canada 51°21N 100°8W 297 C8
Sifton Pass Canada 57°52N 126°15W 296 B3
Sig Algeria 35°32N 0°12W 261 A4
Sigaboy = Governor Generoso Phil. 6°39N 126°5E 233 H6
Sigatoka Fiji 18°8S 177°32E 287 B1
Sigdal Norway 60°3N 9°38E 164 D6
Sigean France 43°2N 2°58E 174 E6
Siggiewi Malta 35°51N 14°26E 206 F7
Sighetu-Marmaţiei Romania 47°57N 23°52E 183 C8
Sighişoara Romania 46°12N 24°50E 183 D9
Sighthill U.K. 55°56N 3°17W 121 B2
Sigiriya Sri Lanka 7°57N 80°45E 245 L5
Sigli Indonesia 5°25N 96°0E 234 A1
Siglufjörður Iceland 66°12N 18°55W 155 A8
Siglunes Iceland 66°12N 18°50W 155 A8
Sigmaringen Germany 48°5N 9°12E 179 G5
Signa Italy 43°45N 11°10E 198 E8
Signakhi = Tsnori Georgia 41°40N 45°57E 191 K7
Signal de Botrang Belgium 50°29N 6°4E 170 D6
Signal Hill S. Africa 34°5S 18°24E 118 A1
Signal Pk. U.S.A. 33°20N 114°2W 307 M12
Signy I. Antarctica 60°43S 45°36W 151 C18
Signy-l'Abbaye France 49°40N 4°25E 173 C11
Sigourney U.S.A. 41°20N 92°12W 310 C4
Sigsbee U.S.A. 31°16N 83°52W 316 D6
Sigsbee Deep Caribbean 25°0N 92°0W 152 D1
Sígsig Ecuador 3°0S 78°50W 328 D2
Sigtuna Sweden 59°36N 17°44E 162 E11
Sigüenza Spain 41°3N 2°40W 196 D2
Siguiri Guinea 11°31N 9°10W 262 C3
Sigulda Latvia 57°10N 24°55E 188 D3
Siguniangshan China 31°15N 103°10E 228 B4
Sihanoukville = Kampong Saom Cambodia 10°38N 103°30E 237 G4
Sihawa India 20°19N 81°55E 244 D5
Siheung Gyeonggi-do, S. Korea 37°25N 126°47E 224 D3
Siheung Seoul, S. Korea 37°28N 126°54E 137 C1
Sihong China 33°27N 118°16E 227 H10
Sihora India 23°29N 80°6E 243 H9
Sihuas Peru 8°40S 77°40W 330 B2
Sihui China 23°20N 112°40E 229 F9
Siikajoki → Finland 64°50N 24°43E 160 D21
Siilinjärvi Finland 63°4N 27°39E 160 E22
Siirt Turkey 37°57N 41°55E 213 D9
Siirt □ Turkey 37°55N 41°55E 213 D9
Sijarira Ra. = Chizarira Zimbabwe 17°36S 27°45E 269 F2
Sijungjung Indonesia 0°42S 100°58E 234 C2
Sika India 22°26N 69°47E 242 H3
Sikanni Chief → Canada 57°47N 122°15W 296 B4
Sikao Thailand 7°34N 99°21E 237 J2
Sikar India 27°33N 75°10E 242 F6
Sikasso Mali 11°18N 5°35W 262 C3
Sikasso □ Mali 10°55N 7°0W 262 C3
Sikátorpuszta Hungary 47°34N 19°10E 117 A3
Sikelenge Zambia 14°53S 24°14E 265 E4
Sikeston U.S.A. 36°53N 89°35W 308 G9
Sikhote Alin, Khrebet Russia 45°0N 136°0E 220 B8
Sikhote Alin Ra. = Sikhote Alin, Khrebet Russia 45°0N 136°0E 220 B8
Sikia Greece 40°2N 23°56E 202 F7
Sikinos Greece 36°40N 25°8E 205 E7
Sikkim □ India 27°50N 88°30E 241 B2
Siklós Hungary 45°50N 18°19E 182 E3
Sil → Spain 42°27N 7°43W 194 C3
Silacayoapan Mexico 17°30N 98°9W 319 D5
Šilalė Lithuania 55°28N 22°12E 184 C9
Silampur India 28°39N 77°16E 120 B2
Silandro Italy 46°38N 10°46E 198 B7
Silang Phil. 14°14N 120°58E 232 D3
Silawad India 21°54N 74°54E 242 J6
Silay Phil. 10°47N 122°58E 233 F4
Silba Croatia 44°24N 14°41E 199 D11
Silchar India 24°49N 92°48E 241 C4
Sildegapet Norway 62°5N 5°0E 164 B2
Şile Turkey 41°10N 29°37E 203 E13
Silent Valley △ India 11°10N 76°20E 245 J3
Siler City U.S.A. 35°44N 79°28W 315 D15
Sileru → India 17°49N 81°24E 244 F5
Silesia = Śląsk Poland 51°0N 16°30E 176 C9
Silet Algeria 22°44N 4°37E 261 D5
Siletitengiz Köli Kazakhstan 53°20N 73°10E 217 B8
Silgarhi Doti Nepal 29°15N 81°0E 243 E9
Silghat India 26°35N 93°0E 241 B4
Silhouette Seychelles 4°29S 55°12E 272 c
Sili Burkina Faso 11°37N 2°30W 262 C4
Siliana Tunisia 36°5N 9°22E 261 A6
Siliana □ Tunisia 36°0N 9°20E 261 A6
Silifke Turkey 36°22N 33°58E 250 B4
Siliguri = Shiliguri India 26°45N 88°25E 241 B2
Silil Somalia 11°0N 43°26E 267 B5
Siling Co China 31°50N 89°20E 218 E6
Silistea Nouă Romania 44°23N 25°1E 183 F10
Silistra Bulgaria 44°6N 27°19E 203 B11
Silistra □ Bulgaria 44°6N 27°19E 203 B11
Silivri Turkey 41°4N 28°14E 203 E12
Siljan Telemark, Norway 59°18N 9°42E 164 E6
Siljan Sweden 60°55N 14°45E 162 D8
Siljansnäs Sweden 60°47N 14°52E 162 D8
Silkeborg Denmark 56°10N 9°32E 163 H3
Silkwood Australia 17°45S 146°2E 280 B4
Silla Spain 39°22N 0°25W 197 F4
Sillajhuay, Cordillera Chile 19°46S 68°40W 330 D4
Sillamäe Estonia 59°24N 27°45E 188 C4
Sillé-le-Guillaume France 48°10N 0°8W 172 D6
Silleda Spain 42°42N 8°14W 194 C2
Sillein = Žilina Slovak Rep. 49°12N 18°42E 181 B11
Sillim S. Korea 37°28N 126°56E 137 C1
Sillod India 20°18N 75°39E 244 D2
Silloth U.K. 54°52N 3°23W 168 C4
Sillustani Peru 15°50S 70°7W 330 D3
Silo Greece 41°10N 25°53E 203 E9
Siloam Springs U.S.A. 36°11N 94°32W 314 C7
Silopi Turkey 37°15N 42°27E 213 D10
Siltou Chad 16°46N 15°33E 259 E3
Siluko Nigeria 6°35N 5°10E 263 D6
Šilutė Lithuania 55°21N 21°33E 184 C8
Silva Porto = Kuito Angola 12°22S 16°55E 265 E3
Silvan Turkey 38°7N 41°2E 213 C9
Silvani India 23°18N 78°25E 243 H8
Silvassa India 20°16N 73°1E 244 D1
Silver, L. U.S.A. 28°35N 81°23W 133 A2
Silver Bank W. Indies 20°30N 69°45W 321 B6
Silver Bank Passage W. Indies 20°0N 70°0W 321 B5
Silver City U.S.A. 32°46N 108°17W 305 K9
Silver Cr. → U.S.A. 43°16N 119°13W 304 E4
Silver Creek U.S.A. 42°33N 79°10W 312 D5
Silver Grove U.S.A. 39°2N 84°23W 311 E12
Silver Hill Montserrat 16°49N 62°11W 323 p
Silver Hill Md., U.S.A. 38°49N 76°55W 143 B3
Silver L. U.S.A. 38°39N 120°6W 306 G6
Silver Lake Calif., U.S.A. 34°5N 118°15W 126 B3
Silver Lake Calif., U.S.A. 35°21N 116°7W 307 K10
Silver Lake Ind., U.S.A. 41°4N 85°53W 311 C11
Silver Lake Oreg., U.S.A. 43°8N 121°3W 304 E3
Silver Lake Wis., U.S.A. 42°33N 88°13W 311 B8
Silver Spring U.S.A. 38°59N 77°2W 143 A2
Silver Springs U.S.A. 29°13N 82°3W 317 F7
Silverdalen Sweden 57°32N 15°45E 163 G9
Silvermine Mts. Ireland 52°47N 8°15W 166 D3
Silvermine Nature Reserve S. Africa 34°6S 18°27E 118 B1
Silverton N.S.W., Australia 31°52S 141°10E 282 A4
Silverton Colo., U.S.A. 37°49N 107°40W 305 H10
Silverton Tex., U.S.A. 34°28N 101°19W 314 D4
Silves Brazil 2°54S 58°27W 329 D6
Silves Portugal 37°11N 8°26W 195 H2
Silvi Marina Italy 42°34N 14°5E 199 F11
Silvia Colombia 2°37N 76°21W 328 C2
Silvies → U.S.A. 43°34N 119°2W 304 E4
Silvolantekojärvi Finland 60°17N 24°54E 121 B2
Silvrettahorn Switz. 46°50N 10°6E 198 B7
Silwa Bahari Egypt 24°45N 32°55E 256 C3
Silz Austria 47°16N 10°56E 180 D3
Sim, C. Morocco 31°26N 9°51W 260 B3
Simakumba Zambia 14°12S 23°16E 265 E4
Simaltala India 24°43N 86°33E 243 G12
Simaluguri India 26°55N 94°46E 241 B5
Sim'ān, J. Syria 36°25N 36°53E 250 B7
Simanggang = Bandar Sri Aman Malaysia 1°15N 111°32E 235 B4
Simao China 22°47N 101°5E 228 F3
Simão Dias Brazil 10°44S 37°49W 332 D4
Simara I. Phil. 12°48N 122°3E 232 E4
Simard, L. Canada 47°40N 78°40W 298 C4
Şīmareh → Iran 33°9N 47°41E 213 F12
Simav Turkey 39°4N 28°58E 205 B10
Simav → Turkey 40°23N 28°31E 203 F12
Simav Dağları Turkey 39°10N 28°30E 205 B10
Simba Dem. Rep. of the Congo 0°38N 22°59E 264 B4
Simba Tanzania 2°10S 37°36E 268 C4
Simbach Germany 48°16N 13°2E 179 G9
Simberi I. Papua N. G. 2°38S 152°0E 286 B7
Simbirsk = Ulyanovsk Russia 54°20N 48°25E 190 C9
Simbo Solomon Is. 8°16S 156°33E 287 M9
Simbo Tanzania 4°51S 29°41E 268 C2
Simcoe Canada 42°50N 80°23W 312 D4
Simcoe, L. Canada 44°25N 79°20W 312 B5
Simdega India 22°37N 84°31E 243 H11
Simei Singapore 1°20N 103°47E 138 A3
Simeonovgrad Bulgaria 42°1N 25°50E 203 D9
Simeria Romania 45°51N 23°1E 182 E8
Simeto → Italy 37°24N 15°6E 201 E8
Simeulue Indonesia 2°45N 95°45E 234 B1
Simferopol Ukraine 44°55N 34°3E 189 K8
Simi Greece 36°35N 27°50E 205 E9
Simi Valley U.S.A. 34°16N 118°47W 307 L8
Simien △ Ethiopia 13°19N 38°0E 257 E4
Simikot Nepal 30°0N 81°50E 243 E9
Similajau △ Malaysia 3°27N 113°15E 235 B4
Simineh → Iran 36°59N 45°54E 213 D11
Simití Colombia 7°58N 73°57W 328 B3
Simitli Bulgaria 41°52N 23°7E 202 E7
Simla = Shimla India 31°2N 77°9E 242 D7
Simla India 22°35N 88°22E 124 B2
Simlångsdalen Sweden 56°43N 13°6E 163 H7
Şimleu-Silvaniei Romania 47°17N 22°50E 182 C7
Simlipal △ India 21°45N 86°30E 243 J12
Simmering Austria 48°10N 16°24E 142 A2
Simmering Heide Austria 48°10N 16°26E 142 A2
Simmern Germany 49°58N 7°30E 179 F3
Simmie Canada 49°56N 108°6W 297 D7
Simmler U.S.A. 35°21N 119°59W 307 K7
Simnas Lithuania 54°24N 23°39E 184 D10
Simo älv = Simojoki → Finland 65°35N 25°1E 160 D21
Simões Brazil 7°36S 40°49W 332 C3
Simojoki → Finland 65°35N 25°1E 160 D21
Simojovel Mexico 17°12N 92°38W 319 D6
Simonette → Canada 55°9N 118°15W 296 B5
Simonière, Plaine de la Guadeloupe 16°16N 61°19W 322 e
Simonkylä Finland 60°18N 25°1E 121 B3
Šimonovany = Partizánske Slovak Rep. 48°38N 18°23E 181 C11
Simonstown S. Africa 34°14S 18°26E 270 D2
Simontornya Hungary 46°45N 18°33E 182 D3
Simpang Indonesia 1°16S 104°4E 234 C2
Simpang Empat Malaysia 5°27N 100°29E 237 c
Simpangkiri → Indonesia 2°50N 97°40E 234 B1
Simplício Mendes Brazil 7°51S 41°54W 332 C3
Simplonpass Switz. 46°15N 8°3E 179 J4
Simplontunnel Switz. 46°15N 8°7E 179 J4
Simpson, Mt. Papua N. G. 10°2S 149°34E 286 F5
Simpson Bay Lagoon St.-Martin 18°3N 63°6W 322 a
Simpson Desert Australia 25°0S 137°0E 280 D2
Simpson Desert △ Australia 24°59S 138°21E 280 C2
Simpson Pen. Canada 68°34N 88°45W 295 D14
Simrishamn Sweden 55°33N 14°22E 163 J8
Simsbury U.S.A. 41°53N 72°48W 313 E12
Simsonbaai St.-Maarten 18°2N 63°7W 322 a
Simuk Indonesia 0°4S 97°52E 234 C1
Simunjan Malaysia 1°25N 110°45E 235 B4
Simunul Phil. 4°54N 119°51E 233 J2
Simushir, Ostrov Russia 46°50N 152°30E 215 E16
Sin Cowe I. S. China Sea 9°53N 114°19E 230 C4
Sin-do N. Korea 39°52N 124°14E 224 C2
Sina → India 17°30N 75°55E 244 F2
Sina Dhago Somalia 5°50N 47°0E 267 C6
Sinabang Indonesia 2°30N 96°24E 234 B1
Sinabung Indonesia 3°10N 98°23E 234 B1
Sinai = Es Sînâ' Egypt 29°0N 34°0E 246 D2
Sinai, Mt. = Mûsa, Gebel Egypt 28°33N 33°59E 251 K4
Sinai, Mt. Grenada 12°4N 61°42W 323 q
Sinai Peninsula Egypt 29°30N 34°0E 251 J5
Sinaia Romania 45°21N 25°38E 183 E10
Sinait Phil. 17°52N 120°27E 232 C3
Sinako, Mt. Phil. 7°30N 125°17E 233 H5
Sinaloa □ Mexico 25°0N 107°30W 318 C3
Sinaloa de Leyva Mexico 25°50N 108°14W 318 B3
Sinalunga Italy 43°12N 11°44E 199 E8
Sinan China 27°56N 108°13E 228 D7
Sînandrei Romania 45°52N 21°13E 182 E6
Sinarades Greece 39°34N 19°51E 206 B9
Sīnāwan Libya 31°0N 10°37E 258 B2
Sinbaungwe Burma 19°43N 95°10E 241 F5
Sinbo Burma 24°46N 97°3E 241 C6
Sincan Turkey 40°0N 32°36E 212 B5
Sincanlı Turkey 38°45N 30°15E 205 C12
Sincé Colombia 9°15N 75°9W 328 B2
Sincelejo Colombia 9°18N 75°24W 328 B2
Sinch'ang N. Korea 40°7N 128°28E 224 B4
Sincheorwon S. Korea 38°8N 127°18E 224 C3
Sinch'ŏn N. Korea 38°17N 125°21E 224 C2
Sinchon Seoul, S. Korea 37°34N 126°57E 137 B1
Sinclair U.S.A. 41°47N 107°7W 304 F10
Sinclair, L. U.S.A. 33°8N 83°12W 316 B6
Sinclair Mills Canada 54°5N 121°40W 296 C4
Sinclair's B. U.K. 58°31N 3°5W 167 C5
Sinclairville U.S.A. 42°16N 79°16W 312 D5
Sind = Sindh □ Pakistan 26°0N 69°0E 242 G3
Sind → Jammu & Kashmir, India 34°18N 74°45E 243 B6
Sind → Mad. P., India 26°26N 79°13E 243 F8
Sind Sagar Doab Pakistan 32°0N 71°30E 242 D4
Sindal Denmark 57°28N 10°10E 163 G4
Sindang S. Korea 37°35N 127°2E 137 B2
Sindangan Phil. 8°10N 123°5E 233 G4
Sindangan B. Phil. 8°11N 122°50E 233 G4
Sindangbarang Indonesia 7°27S 107°1E 234 D3
Sindara Gabon 1°7S 10°41E 264 C2
Sinde Zambia 17°28S 25°51E 269 F2
Sindelfingen Germany 48°42N 9°0E 179 G4
Sindewahi India 20°17N 79°39E 244 D4
Sindgi India 16°55N 76°14E 244 F3
Sindh = Indus → Pakistan 24°20N 67°47E 242 G2
Sindh □ Pakistan 26°0N 69°0E 242 G3
Sindhnur India 15°47N 76°46E 245 F3
Sindhuli Garhi Nepal 27°16N 85°58E 243 F11
Sindi India 20°48N 78°52E 244 D4
Sındırgı Turkey 39°13N 28°10E 205 B10
Sindou Burkina Faso 10°35N 5°4W 262 C3
Sindri India 23°45N 86°42E 243 H12
Sine → Senegal 14°10N 16°28W 262 C1
Sinegorskiy Russia 47°55N 40°52E 191 G5
Sinekli Turkey 41°14N 28°12E 203 E12
Sinelnikovo = Synelnykove Ukraine 48°25N 35°30E 189 H8
Sinendé Benin 10°20N 2°22E 263 C5
Sines Portugal 37°56N 8°51W 195 H2
Sines, C. de Portugal 37°58N 8°53W 195 H2
Sineu Spain 39°38N 3°1E 206 B4
Sinewit, Mt. Papua N. G. 4°44S 152°2E 286 C7
Sinfra Ivory C. 6°35N 5°56W 262 D3
Sing Buri Thailand 14°53N 100°25E 236 E3
Sing Sing = Ossining U.S.A. 41°10N 73°55W 313 E11
Singa Sudan 13°10N 33°57E 257 E3
Singako Chad 9°50N 19°24E 259 G3
Singalila △ India 27°10N 88°5E 241 B2
Singanallur India 11°2N 77°1E 245 J3
Singapore ■ Asia 1°17N 103°51E 138 B3
Singapore, Straits of Asia 1°15N 104°0E 237 d
Singapore Changi ✕ (SIN) Singapore 1°23N 103°59E 138 A3
Singaraja Indonesia 8°7S 115°6E 231 J18
Singatoka = Sigatoka Fiji 18°8S 177°32E 287 B1
Singen Germany 47°45N 8°50E 179 H4
Singida Tanzania 4°49S 34°48E 268 C3
Singida □ Tanzania 6°0S 34°30E 268 D3
Singkang Indonesia 4°8S 120°1E 231 E6
Singkarak, Danau Indonesia 0°36S 100°32E 234 C2
Singkawang Indonesia 1°0N 108°57E 235 B3
Singkep Indonesia 0°30S 104°25E 234 C2
Singkil Indonesia 2°17N 97°49E 237 L1
Singkuang Indonesia 1°3N 98°55E 237 L2
Singleton Australia 32°33S 151°10E 283 B9
Singleton, Mt. N. Terr., Australia 22°0S 130°46E 278 D5
Singleton, Mt. W. Austral., Australia 29°27S 117°15E 279 E2
Singö Sweden 60°12N 18°45E 162 D12
Singoli India 25°0N 75°22E 242 G6
Singora = Songkhla Thailand 7°13N 100°37E 237 J3
Singrauli India 24°7N 82°23E 243 G10
Singri India 26°36N 92°29E 241 B4
Singsås Norway 62°56N 10°37E 164 B7
Singu Burma 22°33N 96°0E 241 D6
Sinharaja Sri Lanka 6°25N 80°30E 245 L5
Sinhgarh India 18°22N 73°45E 244 E1
Sinhŭng Hamgyŏngnam-do, N. Korea 40°11N 127°34E 224 B3
Sinhŭng Hamgyŏngnam-do, N. Korea 41°8N 127°31E 224 B3
Siniloan Phil. 14°25N 121°27E 232 D3
Sining = Xining China 36°34N 101°40E 218 D9
Siniscóla Italy 40°34N 9°41E 200 B2
Sinj Croatia 43°42N 16°39E 199 E13
Sinjai Indonesia 5°7S 120°20E 231 F6
Sinjajevina Montenegro 42°57N 19°22E 202 D3
Sinjār Iraq 36°19N 41°52E 213 D9
Sinjār Syria 35°35N 37°0E 250 C8
Sinjār, Jabal Iraq 36°23N 41°47E 213 D9
Sinkat Sudan 18°55N 36°49E 256 D4
Sinki, Selat Singapore 1°15N 103°42E 138 B2
Sinkiang = Xinjiang Uygur Zizhiqu □ China 42°0N 86°0E 217 D11
Sinko Guinea 8°53N 8°16W 262 D3
Sinlumkaba Burma 24°16N 97°31E 241 C6
Sinmak N. Korea 38°25N 126°14E 224 C3
Sinmi-do N. Korea 39°33N 124°53E 224 C2
Sínnai Italy 39°18N 9°13E 200 C2
Sinnar India 19°48N 74°0E 244 E2
Sinni → Italy 40°8N 16°41E 201 B9
Sinnuris Egypt 29°26N 30°31E 256 J7
Sinoie, Lacul Romania 44°35N 28°50E 183 F13
Sinop Turkey 42°1N 35°11E 212 A6
Sinop □ Turkey 42°0N 35°0E 212 B6
Sinor India 21°55N 73°20E 242 J5
Sinp'o N. Korea 40°0N 128°13E 224 C4
Sinsa S. Korea 37°31N 127°0E 137 B2
Sinsang N. Korea 39°38N 127°24E 224 C3
Sinsheim Germany 49°15N 8°52E 179 F4
Sinsiang = Xinxiang China 35°18N 113°50E 226 G7
Sinsk Russia 61°8N 126°48E 215 C13
Sint Annabaai Curaçao 12°6N 68°55W 322 g
Sint Christoffelberg Curaçao 12°20N 69°8W 322 g
Sint-Genesius-Rode Belgium 50°45N 4°22E 116 B2
Sint-Hubert Belgium 50°2N 5°23E 170 D5
Sint Jorisbaai Curaçao 12°7N 68°48W 322 g
Sint Marie, K. Curaçao 12°11N 69°3W 322 g
Sint Marthabaai Curaçao 12°17N 69°8W 322 g
Sint Michiel Curaçao 12°8N 69°0W 322 g
Sint Nicolaas Aruba 12°27N 69°54W 322 f
Sint Nicolaas Curaçao 12°17N 69°8W 322 g
Sint-Niklaas Belgium 51°10N 4°8E 170 C4
Sint-Truiden Belgium 50°48N 5°10E 170 D5
Sint Willibrordus Curaçao 12°12N 69°4W 322 g
Sintang Indonesia 0°5N 111°35E 235 B4
Sinton U.S.A. 28°2N 97°31W 314 G6
Sintra Portugal 38°47N 9°25W 195 G1
Sintra-Cascais ⌂ Portugal 38°50N 9°25W 195 G1
Sinŭiju N. Korea 40°5N 124°24E 224 B2
Sinujif Somalia 8°33N 48°59E 267 C6
Sinyukha → Ukraine 48°3N 30°51E 189 H6
Sinzig Germany 50°32N 7°14E 178 E3
Sio → Hungary 46°20N 18°53E 182 D3
Siocon Phil. 7°40N 122°10E 233 H4
Siófok Hungary 46°54N 18°3E 182 D3
Sioma Zambia 16°40S 23°32E 265 F4
Sioma Ngwezi △ Zambia 17°14S 23°26E 265 F4
Sion Maharashtra, India 19°3N 72°52E 130 A2
Sion Switz. 46°14N 7°20E 179 J3
Sion Mills U.K. 54°48N 7°29W 166 B4
tSionainn, An = Shannon → Ireland 52°35N 9°30W 166 D2
Sioux Center U.S.A. 43°5N 96°11W 308 D5
Sioux City U.S.A. 42°30N 96°24W 308 D5
Sioux Falls U.S.A. 43°33N 96°44W 308 D5
Sioux Lookout Canada 50°10N 91°50W 298 B1
Sioux Narrows Canada 49°25N 94°10W 297 D10
Sipadan Malaysia 4°6N 118°38E 235 B5
Sipalay Phil. 9°45N 122°24E 233 G4
Šipan Croatia 42°45N 17°52E 202 D1
Sipang, Tanjong Malaysia 1°48N 110°20E 235 B4
Siparia Trin. & Tob. 10°8N 61°31W 323 t
Siparia □ Trin. & Tob. 10°9N 61°28W 323 t
Sipil Dağı △ Turkey 38°35N 27°30E 205 C9
Siping China 43°8N 124°21E 227 C13
Sipitang Malaysia 5°5N 115°33E 235 A5
Sipiwesk L. Canada 55°5N 97°35W 297 B9
Siple I. Antarctica 73°40S 125°10W 151 D14
Sipocot Phil. 13°46N 122°58E 232 E4
Šipovo Bos.-H. 44°16N 17°6E 182 F2
Sipra → India 23°55N 75°28E 242 H6
Sipson U.K. 51°29N 0°26W 125 B1
Sipsongpanna = Xishuangbanna China 22°5N 101°1E 228 F3
Sipur India 21°11N 85°9E 244 D7
Sipura Indonesia 2°18S 99°40E 234 C1
Sipura, Selat Indonesia 2°27S 99°54E 234 C1
Siqeil Egypt 30°7N 31°10E 117 A1
Siqirah Yemen 12°37N 54°20E 249 D6
Siqueira Campos Brazil 23°42S 49°50W 333 F2
Siquia → Nic. 12°10N 84°20W 320 D3
Siquijor Phil. 9°12N 123°35E 233 G4
Siquijor □ Phil. 9°11N 123°35E 233 G4
Siquirres Costa Rica 10°6N 83°30W 320 D3
Siquisique Venezuela 10°34N 69°42W 328 A4
Şīr Abu Nu'ayr U.A.E. 25°20N 54°20E 247 E7
Şīr Banī Yās U.A.E. 24°19N 52°37E 247 E7
Sir Edward Pellew Group Australia 15°40S 137°10E 280 B2
Sir Graham Moore Is. Australia 13°53S 126°34E 278 B4
Sir James MacBrien, Mt. Canada 62°7N 127°41W 294 E6
Sira India 13°41N 76°49E 245 H3
Sira Vest-Agder, Norway 58°24N 6°40E 164 F3
Sira → Norway 58°23N 6°34E 164 F3
Siracusa Italy 37°4N 15°17E 201 E8
Sirajganj Bangla. 24°25N 89°47E 241 C2
Sirakoro Mali 12°41N 9°14W 262 C3
Şiran Turkey 40°11N 39°7E 213 B8
Sirasso Ivory C. 9°16N 6°6W 262 D3
Sirathu India 25°39N 81°19E 243 G9
Siraway Phil. 7°34N 122°8E 233 H4
Sirdalsvatnet Norway 58°34N 6°43E 164 F3
Sīrdān Iran 36°39N 49°12E 213 D13
Sirdaryo □ Uzbekistan 40°30N 68°45E 217 D7
Sire Ethiopia 6°55N 35°36E 257 F4
Siren U.S.A. 45°47N 92°24W 308 C7
Sirente-Velino ⌂ Italy 42°10N 13°32E 199 F10
Sirer Spain 38°56N 1°22E 206 D1
Siret Romania 47°55N 26°5E 183 C11
Siret → Romania 45°24N 28°1E 183 E12
Sirevåg Norway 58°30N 5°48E 164 F2
Sirghāyā Syria 33°51N 36°8E 250 E7
Şiria Romania 46°16N 21°38E 182 D6
Sirik, Tanjong Malaysia 2°47N 111°15E 235 B4
Sirikit Res. Thailand 17°45N 100°34E 236 C3
Sirinat △ Thailand 8°6N 98°17E 237 a
Sirino, Mte. Italy 40°7N 15°50E 201 B8
Sīrjān Iran 29°30N 55°45E 247 D7
Sirkali = Sirkazhi India 11°15N 79°41E 245 J4
Sirkazhi India 11°15N 79°41E 245 J4
Sirmans U.S.A. 30°21N 83°39W 316 E6
Sirmaur India 24°51N 81°23E 243 G9
Sirmilik △ Canada 72°50N 80°35W 295 C15
Sirna Greece 36°22N 26°42E 205 E8
Şirnak Turkey 37°32N 42°28E 213 D10
Sirohi India 24°52N 72°53E 242 G5
Sirombu Indonesia 0°57N 97°25E 234 B1
Sironj India 24°5N 77°39E 242 G7
Síros = Ermoupoli Greece 37°28N 24°57E 204 D6
Siroz = Serres Greece 41°5N 23°31E 202 E7
Sirpur India 19°29N 79°36E 244 E4
Sirr, Nafud as Si. Arabia 25°33N 44°35E 246 E5
Sirrayn Si. Arabia 19°38N 40°36E 248 C3
Sirretta Pk. U.S.A. 35°56N 118°19W 307 K8
Sīrrī Iran 25°55N 54°32E 247 E7
Sirsa India 29°33N 75°4E 242 E6
Sirsa → India 26°51N 79°4E 243 F8
Sirsi India 14°40N 74°49E 245 G2
Sirsilla India 18°23N 78°50E 244 E4
Sirte = Surt Libya 31°11N 16°39E 258 B3
Siruela Spain 38°58N 5°3W 195 G5
Siruguppa India 15°38N 76°54E 245 F3
Sirur India 18°50N 74°23E 244 E2
Şirvan Azerbaijan 39°59N 48°52E 191 L9
Sirvān → Iran 35°4N 46°50E 213 E12
Sisak Croatia 45°30N 16°21E 199 C13
Sisante Spain 39°25N 2°12W 197 F2
Sisargas, Is. Spain 43°21N 8°50W 194 B2
Sishen S. Africa 27°47S 22°59E 270 C3
Sishui China 35°42N 117°18E 227 G9
Sisian Armenia 39°31N 46°1E 213 C12
Sisiga Solomon Is. 7°54S 159°10E 287 L10
Sisimiut Greenland 66°40N 53°30W 154 D5
Sisipuk L. Canada 55°45N 101°50W 297 B8
Şişli Turkey 41°3N 28°58E 122 B1
Sisophon Cambodia 13°38N 102°59E 236 F4
Sissano Papua N. G. 3°0S 142°3E 286 B2
Sisseton U.S.A. 45°40N 97°3W 308 C5
Sisson = Mount Shasta U.S.A. 41°19N 122°19W 304 F2
Sissonne France 49°34N 3°51E 173 C10
Sīstān Asia 30°50N 61°0E 247 D9
Sīstan, Daryācheh-ye Iran 31°0N 61°0E 247 D9
Sīstān va Balūchestān □ Iran 27°0N 62°0E 247 E9
Sisteron France 44°12N 5°57E 175 D9
Sisters U.S.A. 44°18N 121°33W 304 D3
Sisters, The Grenada 12°18N 61°36W 323 q
Sisters, The Seychelles 4°16S 55°52E 272 c
Sisters Pk. Ascension I. 7°56S 14°22W 153 g
Sisters Rocks Trin. & Tob. 11°20N 60°39W 323 s
Siswa Bazar India 27°9N 83°46E 243 F10
Sitakili Mali 13°7N 11°14W 262 C2
Sitakunda Bangla. 22°37N 91°39E 241 D3
Sitamarhi India 26°37N 85°30E 243 F11
Sitampiky Madag. 16°41S 46°6E 272 B2
Sitangkai Phil. 4°40N 119°24E 233 J2
Sitapur India 27°38N 80°45E 243 F9
Siteki Swaziland 26°32S 31°58E 271 C5
Sitges Spain 41°17N 1°47E 196 D6
Sithonia Greece 40°0N 23°45E 202 F7
Sitia Greece 35°13N 26°6E 207 E7
Sitia ✕ (JSH) Greece 35°15N 26°5E 207 E7
Sítio da Abadia Brazil 14°48S 46°16W 333 D2
Sitito-Ozima Ridge Pac. Oc. 23°0N 143°0E 288 E6
Sitka U.S.A. 57°3N 135°20W 296 B1
Sitka ⌂ U.S.A. 57°3N 135°19W 303 H14
Sitkaing = Sagaing Burma 21°52N 95°59E 241 E5
Sitkinak I. U.S.A. 56°33N 154°10W 303 H9
Sitoti Botswana 23°15S 23°40E 270 B3
Sitra Egypt 28°40N 26°53E 256 B2
Sittang Myit → Burma 17°20N 96°45E 241 G6
Sittard Neths. 51°0N 5°52E 170 C5
Sittaung Burma 24°10N 94°35E 241 C5
Sittensen Germany 53°17N 9°32E 178 B5
Sittingbourne U.K. 51°21N 0°45E 169 F8
Sittona Eritrea 14°25N 37°23E 257 E4
Sittoung = Sittang Myit → Burma 17°20N 96°45E 241 G6
Sittwe Burma 20°18N 92°45E 241 E4
Situbondo Indonesia 7°42S 113°56E 235 D4
Siufaalete Pt. Amer. Samoa 14°17S 169°29W 302 f
Siulagi Pt. Amer. Samoa 14°13S 169°30W 302 g
Si'umu Samoa 14°1S 171°48W 287 W20
Siuna Nic. 13°37N 84°45W 320 D3
Siuri India 23°50N 87°34E 243 H12
Siutghiol, Lacul Romania 44°15N 28°35E 183 F13
Sivaganga India 9°50N 78°28E 245 K4
Sivagiri India 9°16N 77°26E 245 K3
Sivakasi India 9°24N 77°47E 245 K3
Sīvand Iran 30°5N 52°55E 247 D7
Sivas Turkey 39°43N 36°58E 212 C7
Sivas □ Turkey 39°45N 37°0E 212 C7
Sivasamudram India 12°16N 77°10E 245 H3
Sivaslı Turkey 38°31N 29°42E 205 C11
Siverek Turkey 37°50N 39°19E 213 D8
Sivomaskinskiy Russia 66°40N 62°35E 186 A11
Sivota Greece 39°24N 20°13E 206 C10
Sivrihisar Turkey 39°30N 31°35E 212 C4
Sivros Greece 38°40N 20°39E 207 B2
Sîwa Egypt 29°11N 25°31E 256 B2
Sîwa, El Wâhât es Egypt 29°10N 25°30E 256 B2
Siwa Oasis = Sîwa, El Wâhât es Egypt 29°10N 25°30E 256 B2
Siwalik Range Nepal 28°0N 83°0E 243 F10
Siwan India 26°13N 84°21E 243 F11
Siwana India 25°38N 72°25E 242 G5
Six Cross Roads Barbados 13°7N 59°28W 323 r
Sixian China 33°30N 117°50E 227 H9
Sixmilebridge Ireland 52°44N 8°46W 166 D3
Sixth Cataract Sudan 16°20N 32°42E 257 D3
Siyabuswa S. Africa 25°7S 29°3E 271 C4
Siyah Kuh, Kavīr-e Iran 32°55N 53°55E 247 C7
Siyâl, Jazâ'ir Egypt 22°49N 36°12E 256 C4
Siyang China 33°42N 118°40E 227 H10
Siyäzän Azerbaijan 41°3N 49°10E 191 K9
Siziwang Qi China 41°25N 111°40E 226 D6
Sjælland Denmark 55°30N 11°30E 163 J5
Sjælland □ Denmark 55°30N 11°30E 163 J5
Sjællands Odde Denmark 55°58N 11°24E 163 J5
Sjenica Serbia 43°16N 20°0E 202 C3
Sjoa Norway 61°41N 9°33E 164 C6
Sjöbo Sweden 55°37N 13°45E 163 J7
Sjøholt Norway 62°27N 6°52E 164 B3
Sjølisand Norway 61°29N 11°18E 164 C8
Sjötofta Sweden 57°22N 13°17E 163 G7
Sjötorp Sweden 58°50N 14°0E 163 F8
Sjumen = Shumen Bulgaria 43°18N 26°55E 203 C10
Sjuntorp Sweden 58°12N 12°13E 163 F6
Skåbu Norway 61°32N 9°24E 164 C6
Skadarsko Jezero Europe 42°10N 19°20E 202 D3
Skadarsko Jezero △ Montenegro 42°10N 19°20E 202 D3
Skadovsk Ukraine 46°17N 32°52E 189 J7
Skælskør Denmark 55°15N 11°18E 163 J5
Skærbæk Denmark 55°9N 8°45E 163 J2
Skaftafell Iceland 64°1N 17°0W 155 C9
Skaftafell △ Iceland 64°9N 16°50W 155 C9
Skagafjarðarsýsla Iceland 65°30N 19°0W 155 B7
Skagafjörður Iceland 65°54N 19°35W 155 B7
Skagastølstindane Norway 61°28N 7°52E 164 C4
Skagaströnd Iceland 65°50N 20°19W 155 B6
Skagatá Iceland 66°7N 20°6W 155 A6
Skagen Denmark 57°43N 10°35E 163 G4
Skagern Sweden 59°0N 14°20E 162 E8
Skagerrak Denmark 57°30N 9°0E 163 G2
Skagit → U.S.A. 48°23N 122°22W 306 B4
Skagway U.S.A. 59°28N 135°19W 303 G14
Skala Greece 38°5N 20°47E 207 C2
Skala nad Zbruczem = Skala-Podilska Ukraine 48°50N 26°15E 183 B11
Skala-Podilska Ukraine 48°50N 26°15E 183 B11
Skalat Ukraine 49°23N 25°55E 177 D13
Skálavík Iceland 66°11N 23°29W 155 A3
Skalbmierz Poland 50°20N 20°25E 185 H7
Skälderviken Sweden 56°22N 12°30E 163 H6

Skålevik Norway 58°5N 8°1E **164** F5
Skalica Slovak Rep. 48°50N 17°15E **181** C10
Skallingen Denmark 55°32N 8°13E **163** J2
Skalni Dol = Kamenyak
 Bulgaria 43°24N 26°57E **203** C10
Skanderborg Denmark 56°2N 9°55E **163** H3
Skåne Sweden 55°59N 13°30E **163** J7
Skåne län □ Sweden 55°54N 14°0E **163** H7
Skaneateles U.S.A. 42°57N 76°26W **313** D8
Skaneateles L. U.S.A. 42°51N 76°22W **313** D8
Skånninge Sweden 58°24N 15°5E **163** F9
Skånevik Norway 59°43N 5°53E **164** E2
Skänninge Sweden 58°24N 15°5E **163** F9
Skanör med Falsterbo
 Sweden 55°24N 12°50E **163** J6
Skansen Sweden 59°19N 18°7E **139** B2
Skantzoura Greece 39°5N 24°6E **204** B6
Skara Sweden 58°25N 13°30E **163** F7
Skärblacka Sweden 58°35N 15°54E **163** F9
Skarð Iceland 65°17N 22°19W **155** B4
Skardu Pakistan 35°20N 75°44E **243** B6
Skare Hordaland, Norway 59°55N 6°36E **164** E3
Skåre Sweden 59°26N 13°26E **162** E7
Skärhamn Sweden 57°59N 11°34E **163** G5
Skärholmen Sweden 59°16N 17°53E **139** B1
Skarnes Norway 60°15N 11°41E **164** D8
Skarpäng Sweden 59°26N 18°0E **139** A2
Skarpnäck Sweden 59°16N 18°7E **139** B2
Skarszewy Poland 54°4N 18°25E **184** D5
Skaryszew Poland 51°19N 21°15E **185** G8
Skaryszewski, Park Poland 52°15N 21°3E **143** B2
Skarżysko-Kamienna
 Poland 51°7N 20°52E **185** G7
Skattkärr Sweden 59°24N 13°40E **162** E7
Skattungbyn Sweden 61°10N 14°56E **162** C8
Skawina Poland 49°59N 19°48E **185** J6
Skee Sweden 59°58N 18°36E **162** E12
Skeena → Canada 54°9N 130°5W **296** C2
Skeena Mts. Canada 56°56N 11°19E **163** F5
Skei Norway 61°34N 6°28E **164** C3
Skeiðarársandur Iceland 63°54N 17°14W **155** D9
Skeiðflötur Iceland 63°26N 19°11W **155** D7
Skeleton Coast ∆ Namibia 20°0S 13°20E **270** B1
Skellefteå Sweden 64°45N 20°50E **160** D19
Skellefteälven → Sweden 64°45N 21°10E **160** D19
Skelleftehamn Sweden 64°40N 21°9E **160** D19
Skellig Michael = Great Skellig
 Ireland 51°47N 10°33W **166** E1
Skender Vakuf Bos.-H. 44°29N 17°22E **182** F7
Skënderaj Kosovo 42°45N 20°47E **202** D4
Skeppsholmen Stockholm, Sweden **139** c3
Skerries The U.K. 53°35N 6°8W **166** C5
Skerries, The U.K. 53°25N 4°36W **168** D3
Skhidnytsya Ukraine 49°13N 23°20E **185** J10
Skhiza Greece 36°41N 21°40E **204** E3
Ski Norway 59°43N 10°52E **164** E7
Skiathos Greece 39°12N 23°30E **204** B5
Skibbereen Ireland 51°33N 9°16E **166** E2
Skiddaw U.K. 54°39N 3°9W **168** C4
Skidegate Canada 53°15N 132°1W **296** C2
Skidra Greece 40°46N 22°1E **202** F6
Skien Norway 59°12N 9°35E **164** E6
Skierniewice Poland 51°58N 20°10E **185** G7
Skihist, Mt. Canada 50°12N 121°54W **296** C4
Skikda Algeria 36°50N 6°58E **261** A6
Skikda □ Algeria 36°45N 6°50E **261** A6
Skillet Fork → U.S.A. 38°5N 88°5W **311** F8
Skillingaryd Sweden 57°27N 14°5E **163** G8
Skillinge Sweden 55°30N 14°16E **163** J8
Skilloura Cyprus 35°14N 33°10E **207** D2
Skinari, Akra Greece 37°56N 20°42E **207** D2
Skinnastaður Iceland 66°4N 16°27W **155** A10
Skinnskatteberg Sweden 59°50N 15°42E **162** E9
Skipton Vic., Australia 37°39S 143°40E **282** D5
Skipton N. Yorks., U.K. 53°58N 2°3W **168** D5
Skiptvet Norway 59°28N 11°11E **164** E8
Skiring, C. Senegal 12°26N 16°46W **262** C1
Skirmish Pt. Australia 11°59S 134°17E **280** A1
Skiropoula Greece 38°50N 24°21E **204** C6
Skiros Greece 38°55N 24°34E **204** C6
Skivarp Sweden 55°26N 13°34E **163** J7
Skive Denmark 56°33N 9°2E **163** H3
Skjærhalden Norway 59°2N 11°2E **164** E8
Skjálfandafljót → Iceland 65°59N 17°25W **155** B9
Skjálfandi Iceland 66°5N 17°30W **155** A9
Skjeberg Norway 59°12N 11°12E **164** E8
Skjern Denmark 55°57N 8°30E **163** J2
Skjern Å → Denmark 55°50N 8°30E **163** J2
Skjold Norway 59°31N 5°34E **164** E2
Skjolden Norway 61°29N 7°36E **164** C4
Skjöldólfsstaðir Iceland 65°5N 15°5E **155** B11
Skjønhaug Norway 59°40N 11°15E **164** E8
Skobelev = Farghona
 Uzbekistan 40°23N 71°19E **217** D10
Škocjanske Jame Slovenia 45°40N 14°0E **199** C10
Skoczów Poland 49°49N 18°45E **185** J5
Skodje Norway 62°30N 6°43E **164** B3
Škofja Loka Slovenia 46°9N 14°19E **199** B11
Skógar Iceland 63°32N 19°28W **155** D7
Skógarnes Iceland 64°46N 22°34W **155** C3
Skoghall Sweden 59°20N 13°30E **162** E7
Skogskyrkogården Sweden 59°16N 18°5E **139** B2
Skogstorp Sweden 59°19N 16°29E **162** E10
Skoki Poland 52°40N 17°11E **185** F4
Skokie U.S.A. 42°2N 87°45W **119** A2
Skokie → U.S.A. 42°3N 87°43W **119** A2
Skokie Heritage Museum
 U.S.A. 42°2N 87°44W **119** A2
Skoklefall Norway 59°50N 10°40E **133** A3
Skole Ukraine 49°3N 23°30E **177** D12
Skollenborg Norway 59°38N 9°43E **164** E6
Sköndal Sweden 59°15N 18°6E **139** B2
Skopelos Greece 39°9N 23°47E **204** B5
Skopi Greece 35°11N 26°2E **207** E13
Skopin Russia 53°55N 39°32E **188** F10
Skopje Macedonia 42°1N 21°26E **202** D5
Skopje ✕ (SKP) Macedonia 41°59N 21°29E **202** E5
Skoppum Norway 59°25N 10°27E **164** E7
Skórcz Poland 53°47N 18°30E **184** E5
Skørping Denmark 56°50N 9°53E **163** H3
Skotfoss Norway 59°12N 9°30E **164** E6
Skotterud Norway 60°0N 12°7E **164** E8
Skövde Sweden 58°24N 13°50E **163** F7
Skovlunde Denmark 55°42N 12°25E **163** J6
Skovorodino Russia 54°0N 124°0E **215** D13
Skowshoved Denmark 55°46N 12°36E **163** J6
Skowhegan U.S.A. 44°46N 69°43W **309** C13
Skradin Croatia 43°52N 15°53E **199** D11
Skrea Sweden 56°53N 12°34E **163** H6
Skreia Norway 60°39N 10°56E **164** D7
Skrim Norway 59°31N 9°38E **164** E6
Skrunda Latvia 56°41N 22°1E **180** C4
Skrwa → Poland 52°35N 19°32E **185** F6
Skudeneshavn Norway 59°10N 5°10E **164** E2
Skuleskogen △ Sweden 63°5N 18°30E **162** A12
Skull Ireland 51°32N 9°34E **166** E2
Skultorp Sweden 58°24N 13°51E **163** F7
Skultuna Sweden 59°43N 16°25E **162** E10
Skunk → U.S.A. 40°42N 91°7W **310** E8
Skuodas Lithuania 56°16N 21°33E **139** E13
Skuru Sweden 59°18N 18°12E **139** B2
Skurup Sweden 55°28N 13°30E **163** J7
Skutskär Sweden 60°37N 17°25E **162** D11
Skútustaðir Iceland 65°34N 17°2W **155** B9
Skvyra Ukraine 49°44N 29°40E **177** D15

Skwierzyna Poland 52°33N 15°30E **185** F2
Sky Dome = Rogers Centre
 Toronto, Canada **141** c1
Sky Lake U.S.A. 28°27N 81°23W **133** B2
Skye U.K. 57°15N 6°10W **167** D2
Skykomish U.S.A. 47°42N 121°22W **304** C3
Skyring, Seno Chile 52°35S 72°0W **336** D3
Skyros = Skiros Greece 38°55N 24°34E **204** C6
Skyttorp Sweden 60°5N 17°44E **162** D11
Slade Green U.K. 51°27N 0°11E **125** B5
Slade Point Australia 21°4S 149°13E **280** b
Slade Pt. Australia 21°4S 149°13E **280** b
Slættaratindur Færoe Is. 62°18N 7°1W **160** E9
Slagelse Denmark 55°23N 11°19E **163** J5
Slamet Indonesia 7°16S 109°8E **235** D3
Slaney → Ireland 52°26N 6°33W **166** D5
Slaney Ireland 53°42N 6°33W **166** C5
Slănic Romania 45°14N 25°58E **183** E10
Slano Croatia 42°48N 17°53E **202** D1
Slantsy Russia 59°7N 28°5E **188** C5
Slaný Czech Rep. 50°13N 14°6E **180** A7
Sląsk Poland 51°0N 16°30E **176** C9
Śląskie □ Poland 50°30N 19°0E **185** H6
Slåtbaken Sweden 58°25N 16°45E **163** F10
Slate Is. Canada 48°40N 87°0W **298** C2
Slater U.S.A. 39°13N 93°4W **310** E3
Slatina Croatia 45°42N 17°45E **182** E2
Slatina Romania 44°28N 24°22E **183** F9
Slatina Timiş Romania 45°15N 22°17E **182** E7
Slatington U.S.A. 40°45N 75°37W **313** F9
Slaton U.S.A. 33°26N 101°39W **314** E4
Slave → Canada 61°18N 113°39W **296** A6
Slave Coast W. Afr. 6°0N 2°30E **263** D5
Slave Lake Canada 55°17N 114°43W **296** B6
Slave Pt. Canada 61°11N 115°56W **296** A5
Slavgorod Russia 53°1N 78°37E **217** B9
Slavinja Serbia 43°9N 22°50E **202** C6
Slavkov u Brna Czech Rep. 49°10N 16°52E **181** B9
Slavkovský Les =
 Czech Rep. 50°5N 12°44E **180** A5
Slavonija Europe 45°11N 18°1E **182** E3
Slavonski Brod Croatia 45°11N 18°1E **182** E3
Slavsk Russia 55°3N 21°41E **184** C8
Slavsk Ukraine 48°51N 23°27E **183** B8
Slavskoye Russia 54°30N 20°27E **184** C6
Slavuta Ukraine 50°15N 27°2E **177** C14
Slavyanka Russia 42°53N 131°21E **220** C5
Slavyanovo Bulgaria 43°28N 24°52E **203** C8
Slavyansk = Slovyansk
 Ukraine 48°55N 37°36E **189** H9
Slavyansk-na-Kubani
 Russia 45°15N 38°11E **189** K10
Sława Poland 51°52N 16°2E **185** G3
Sławharad Belarus 53°27N 31°0E **177** B16
Sławno Poland 54°20N 16°41E **184** D3
Sławoborze Poland 53°55N 15°42E **184** E2
Slea Hd. Ireland 52°6N 10°27W **166** D1
Sleaford U.K. 53°0N 0°24W **168** D7
Sleaford B. Australia 34°55S 135°45E **281** E2
Sleat, Sd. of U.K. 57°5N 5°47W **167** D3
Sleðbrjótur Iceland 65°34N 14°30W **155** B12
Sleeper Is. Canada 58°30N 81°0W **298** C5
Sleeping Bear Dunes △
 U.S.A. 44°50N 86°5W **308** C10
Sleepy Eye U.S.A. 44°18N 94°43W **308** C6
Sleetmute U.S.A. 61°42N 157°10W **303** F8
Slemon L. Canada 63°13N 116°4W **296** A5
Slepende Norway 59°52N 10°30E **133** A2
Ślesin Poland 52°22N 18°14E **185** F5
Slide Mt. U.S.A. 42°0N 74°25W **315** F10
Slidre Norway 61°5N 8°58E **164** C5
Sliema Malta 35°55N 14°30E **206** F8
Slieve Aughty Ireland 53°4N 8°30E **166** C3
Slieve Bloom Ireland 53°4N 7°40E **166** C4
Slieve Donard U.K. 54°11N 5°55W **166** B6
Slieve Gamph Ireland 54°6N 9°0W **166** B3
Slieve Gullion U.K. 54°7N 6°26W **166** B5
Slieve League Ireland 54°40N 8°42W **166** B3
Slieve Mish Ireland 52°12N 9°50W **166** D2
Slievenamon Ireland 52°25N 7°34W **166** D4
Sligachan = Sligo Ireland 54°16N 8°28W **166** B3
Sligo Sligo, Ireland 54°16N 8°28W **166** B3
Sligo Pa., U.S.A. 41°6N 79°29W **312** E5
Sligo □ Ireland 54°8N 8°42W **166** B3
Sligo B. Ireland 54°18N 8°40W **166** B3
Slipi Indonesia 6°11S 106°47E **122** B1
Slippery Rock U.S.A. 41°4N 80°3W **312** E4
Slite Sweden 57°42N 18°48E **163** G12
Śliteres △ Latvia 57°41N 22°21E **184** B9
Sliven Bulgaria 42°42N 26°19E **203** D10
Slivnitsa Bulgaria 42°50N 23°2E **202** D7
Slivnec Czech Rep. 50°1N 14°21E **135** B2
Slivnitsa Bulgaria 42°50N 23°2E **202** D7
Sloan U.S.A. 35°57N 115°13W **307** K11
Sloansville U.S.A. 42°45N 74°22W **313** D10
Slobidka Ukraine 47°54N 29°21E **183** C14
Slobodskoy Russia 58°40N 50°6E **186** C9
Slobozia Moldova 46°45N 29°42E **183** D14
Slobozia Argeş, Romania 44°30N 25°14E **183** F10
Slobozia Ialomița,
 Romania 44°34N 27°23E **183** F12
Slocan Canada 49°48N 117°28W **296** D5
Slocomb U.S.A. 31°7N 85°36W **316** D4
Slomikhino = Zhalpaqtal
 Kazakhstan 49°42N 49°25E **190** F9
Slomniki Poland 50°16N 20°4E **185** H7
Slonim Belarus 53°4N 25°19E **177** B13
Slot, The = New Georgia Sound
 Solomon Is. 8°0S 158°0E **287** L9
Sloten Neths. 52°21N 4°48E **112** A1
Sloterdijk Neths. 52°23N 4°51E **112** A1
Sloterpark Neths. 52°22N 4°49E **112** A1
Slottet Oslo, Norway **133** a1
Slough U.K. 51°30N 0°36W **169** F7
Slough □ U.K. 51°30N 0°36W **169** F7
Sloughhouse U.S.A. 38°26N 121°12W **306** G5
Slovak Rep. ■ Europe 48°30N 20°0E **181** C13
Slovakia = Slovak Rep. ■
 Europe 48°30N 20°0E **181** C13
Slovakian Ore Mts. = Slovenské
 Rudohorie Slovak Rep. 48°45N 20°0E **181** C13
Slovenia ■ Europe 45°58N 14°30E **199** C11
Slovenija = Slovenia ■
 Europe 45°58N 14°30E **199** C11
Slovenj Gradec Slovenia 46°31N 15°5E **199** B12
Slovenská = Slovak Rep. ■
 Europe 48°30N 20°0E **181** C13
Slovenská Bistrica
 Slovenia 46°24N 15°35E **199** B12
Slovenské Konjice
 Slovenia 46°20N 15°28E **199** B12
Slovenské Rudohorie
 Slovak Rep. 48°45N 20°0E **181** C13
Slovenský Raj △
 Slovak Rep. 48°53N 20°25E **181** C13
Słowiński △ Poland 54°43N 17°6E **184** D4
Słubice Poland 52°22N 14°35E **185** F1
Sluch → Ukraine 51°37N 26°38E **177** C14
Sluis Neths. 51°18N 3°23E **170** C3
Slunj Croatia 45°6N 15°33E **199** C12
Slunchev Bryag Bulgaria 42°40N 27°41E **203** D11

Słupca Poland 52°15N 17°52E **185** F4
Słupia → Poland 54°35N 16°51E **184** D3
Słupsk Poland 54°30N 17°3E **184** D4
Slurry S. Africa 25°49S 25°42E **270** D4
Slutsk = Pavlovsk Russia 50°26N 40°5E **190** E5
Slutsk Belarus 53°2N 27°31E **177** B14
Służew Poland 52°10N 21°1E **143** B2
Słuzewiec Poland 52°10N 21°0E **143** B2
Slyne Hd. Ireland 53°25N 10°10W **166** C1
Slyudyanka Russia 51°40N 103°40E **215** D11
Smaalenene = Østfold □
 Norway 59°25N 11°2E **164** E8
Småland Sweden 57°15N 15°25E **163** G9
Smålandsfarvandet
 Denmark 55°10N 11°20E **163** J5
Smålandsstenar Sweden 57°10N 13°25E **163** G7
Smaldeel = Theunissen
 S. Africa 28°26S 26°43E **270** C4
Smalltree L. Canada 61°0N 105°0W **297** A8
Smallwood Res. Canada 54°20N 87°24W **314** A7
Smara W. Sahara 26°48N 11°41W **260** C2
Smarhon Belarus 54°20N 26°24E **177** A14
Smarje Slovenia 46°15N 15°34E **199** B12
Smartt Syndicate Dam
 S. Africa 30°45S 23°10E **270** D3
Smartville U.S.A. 39°13N 121°18W **306** F5
Smeaton Canada 53°30N 104°49W **297** C8
Smedby Sweden 56°41N 16°13E **163** H10
Smederevo Serbia 44°40N 20°57E **202** B4
Smederevska Palanka
 Serbia 44°22N 20°58E **202** B4
Smedjebacken Sweden 60°8N 15°25E **162** D9
Smela = Smila Ukraine 49°15N 31°58E **189** H6
Smerwick Harbour
 Ireland 52°12N 10°23W **166** D1
Smethport U.S.A. 41°49N 78°27W **312** E6
Smichov Czech Rep. 50°4N 14°23E **135** B2
Smidovich Russia 48°36N 133°49E **215** E14
Śmigiel Poland 52°1N 16°32E **185** F3
Smila Ukraine 49°15N 31°58E **189** H6
Smith Canada 55°10N 114°0W **296** B6
Smith B. U.S.A. 70°30N 154°20W **303** A9
Smith Center U.S.A. 39°47N 98°47W **308** F4
Smith Forest Preserve
 U.S.A. 41°59N 87°45W **119** B2
Smith I. Nunavut, Canada 60°45N 78°25W **295** E16
Smith I. India 13°20N 93°4E **245** H11
Smith Islands △ Australia 20°40S 149°9E **280** b
Smith River △ U.S.A. 41°55N 124°0W **304** F2
Smith Sd. N. Amer. 78°25N 74°0W **154** B3
Smithburne → Australia 17°3S 140°57E **280** B3
Smithers Canada 54°45N 127°10W **296** C3
Smithfield Free State,
 S. Africa 30°9S 26°30E **271** D4
Smithfield N.C., U.S.A. 35°31N 78°21W **315** D15
Smithfield Utah, U.S.A. 41°50N 111°50W **304** F8
Smiths U.S.A. 32°32N 85°6W **316** C4
Smiths Falls Canada 44°55N 76°0W **313** B9
Smithsonian Institution
 Washington, D.C., U.S.A. **143** b2
Smithton Australia 40°53S 145°6E **282** D4
Smithville Ont., Canada 43°6N 79°33W **312** C5
Smithville Ga., U.S.A. 31°54N 84°15W **316** D5
Smithville Mo., U.S.A. 39°23N 94°34W **310** E2
Smithville Tex., U.S.A. 30°1N 97°10W **314** F6
Smoke Creek Desert
 U.S.A. 40°30N 119°40W **304** F4
Smoky → Canada 56°10N 117°21W **296** B5
Smoky Bay Australia 32°22S 134°13E **281** E1
Smoky Hill → U.S.A. 39°4N 96°48W **308** F5
Smoky Hills U.S.A. 39°15N 99°30W **308** F4
Smoky Lake Canada 54°10N 112°30W **296** C6
Smøla Norway 63°23N 8°3E **164** A5
Smolensk Russia 54°45N 32°5E **188** E7
Smolensk □ Russia 55°20N 33°0E **188** E7
Smolikas, Oros Greece 40°9N 20°58E **202** F4
Smolnik Slovak Rep. 48°43N 20°44E **181** C13
Smolny Russia 59°56N 30°24E **137** B2
Smolny Cathedral Russia 59°56N 30°24E **137** B2
Smolyan Bulgaria 41°36N 24°38E **203** E8
Smolyan □ Bulgaria 41°36N 24°38E **203** E8
Smooth Rock Falls
 Canada 49°17N 81°37W **298** C3
Smoothstone L. Canada 54°40N 106°50W **297** C7
Smorgon = Smarhon
 Belarus 54°20N 26°24E **177** A14
Smotrych Ukraine 48°57N 26°33E **183** B11
Smotrych → 45°57N 27°44E **183** E12
Smyadovo Bulgaria 43°2N 27°1E **203** C11
Smygehamn Sweden 55°21N 13°22E **163** J7
Smyghuk Sweden 55°21N 13°23E **163** J7
Smyley I. Antarctica 72°55S 78°0W **151** D17
Smyrna = İzmir Turkey 38°25N 27°8E **205** C9
Smyrna Del., U.S.A. 39°18N 75°36W **309** F16
Smyrna Ga., U.S.A. 33°53N 84°31W **316** B3
Smyrna Tenn., U.S.A. 35°59N 86°31W **315** D11
Snæfell Iceland 64°48N 15°34W **155** C11
Snaefell I. of Man 54°16N 4°27W **168** C3
Snæfellsjökull Iceland 64°49N 23°46W **155** C3
Snæfellsnessýsla Iceland 65°0N 23°0W **155** C3
Snake → U.S.A. 46°12N 119°2W **304** C4
Snake Creek Canal
 U.S.A. 25°57N 80°19W **129** C2
Snake I. Australia 38°47S 146°33E **283** E7
Snake Pt. Anguilla 18°17N 62°58W **322** a
Snake Range U.S.A. 39°0N 114°20W **304** G6
Snake River Plain U.S.A. 42°50N 114°0W **304** E7
Snarøya Norway 59°52N 10°33E **133** A2
Snasahögarna Sweden 63°13N 12°21E **162** A6
Snåsavatnet Norway 64°12N 12°0E **160** D15
Snättringe Sweden 59°15N 17°58E **139** B1
Snedsted Denmark 56°55N 8°32E **163** H2
Sneek Neths. 53°2N 5°40E **170** A5
Sneem Ireland 51°50N 9°54W **166** E2
Sneeuberge S. Africa 31°46S 24°20E **270** D3
Snegurovka = Tetiyev
 Ukraine 49°22N 29°38E **177** D15
Snejbjerg Denmark 56°8N 8°54E **163** H2
Snelling Calif., U.S.A. 37°31N 120°26W **306** H6
Snelling S.C., U.S.A. 33°15N 81°27W **316** C6
Snells Beach N.Z. 36°25S 174°44E **284** C3
Snezhnoye Ukraine 48°0N 38°58W **189** J10
Sněžka Europe 50°41N 15°50E **185** H3
Sněžnik Slovenia 45°36N 14°35E **199** C11
Śniadowo Poland 53°0N 22°0E **185** E8
Śniardwy, Jezioro Poland 53°48N 21°50E **184** E8
Snizort, L. U.K. 57°33N 6°28W **167** D2
Snøhetta Norway 62°19N 9°16E **164** B6
Snohomish U.S.A. 47°55N 122°6W **304** C3
Snønuten Norway 59°31N 6°37E **164** E3
Snoqualmie U.S.A. 47°31N 121°49W **306** C5
Snoqualmie Pass U.S.A. 47°25N 121°25W **304** C4
Snoul Cambodia 12°4N 106°26E **237** F6
Snover U.S.A. 43°27N 82°58W **312** C2
Snovsk = Shchors
 Ukraine 51°48N 31°56E **189** G6
Snow Hill U.S.A. 38°11N 75°24W **309** F16
Snow Lake Canada 54°52N 100°3W **297** C8
Snow Mt. Calif., U.S.A. 39°23N 122°45W **306** F4

Snow Mt. Maine, U.S.A. 45°18N 70°48W **313** A14
Snow Shoe U.S.A. 41°2N 77°57W **312** E7
Snowbird L. Canada 60°45N 103°0W **297** A8
Snowdon U.K. 53°4N 4°5W **168** D3
Snowdonia △ U.K. 53°7N 3°59W **168** D4
Snowdoun U.S.A. 32°15N 86°18W **316** C3
Snowdrift = Łutsel K'e
 Canada 62°24N 110°44W **297** A6
Snowdrift → Canada 62°24N 110°44W **297** A6
Snowflake U.S.A. 34°30N 110°5W **305** J8
Snowshoe Pk. U.S.A. 48°13N 115°41W **304** B6
Snowtown Australia 33°46S 138°14E **282** B3
Snowville U.S.A. 41°58N 112°43W **304** F7
Snowy → Australia 37°46S 148°30E **283** D8
Snowy Mt. U.S.A. 43°42N 74°23W **313** C10
Snowy Mts. Australia 36°30S 148°20E **283** D8
Snowy River △ Australia 37°15S 147°29E **283** D7
Snug Corner Bahamas 22°33N 73°52W **321** B5
Snug Harbour Canada 45°22N 80°17W **312** A4
Snyatyn Ukraine 48°27N 25°38E **183** B10
Snyder Okla., U.S.A. 34°40N 98°57W **314** D5
Snyder Tex., U.S.A. 32°44N 100°55W **314** E4
Soacha Colombia 4°35N 74°13W **328** C3
Soahanina Madag. 18°42S 44°13E **272** B7
Soalala Madag. 16°6S 45°20E **272** B7
Soaloka Madag. 18°32S 45°15E **272** B7
Soamanonga Madag. 23°52S 44°47E **272** C7
Soan → Pakistan 33°1N 71°44E **242** C4
Soanierana-Ivongo
 Madag. 16°55S 49°35E **272** B8
Soanindraniny Madag. 19°54S 47°14E **272** B8
Soar → Ukraine 45°56N 24°55E **183** E9
Soavina Romania 20°23S 46°56E **272** C2
Soavinandriana Madag. 19°9S 46°45E **272** B2
Soba Nigeria 10°58N 8°4E **263** C6
Sobaeksan △ S. Korea 36°55N 128°31E **224** G7
Sobat, Nahr → South Sudan 9°22N 31°33E **257** F13
Soběslav Czech Rep. 49°16N 14°45E **180** B8
Sobhapur India 22°47N 78°17E **242** H8
Sobinka Russia 56°0N 40°0E **188** E11
Sobо-Yama Japan 32°51N 131°22E **222** E3
Søborg Denmark 55°43N 12°29E **118** A2
Sobótka Poland 50°54N 16°44E **185** H3
Sobradinho, Represa de
 Brazil 9°30S 42°0W **332** C3
Sobral Brazil 3°50S 40°20W **332** B3
Sobrance Slovak Rep. 48°45N 22°11E **181** C15
Sobreda Portugal 38°39N 9°11E **196** C1
Sobreira Formosa Portugal 39°46N 7°51W **194** F3
Soc Giang Vietnam 22°54N 106°1E **228** F6
Soc Trang Vietnam 9°37N 105°50E **237** H5
Soča → Europe 46°20N 13°40E **180** G6
Socastee U.S.A. 33°41N 78°59W **315** E15
Soccskargen □ Phil. 6°30N 125°0E **233** J5
Sochaczew Poland 52°15N 20°13E **185** F7
Soch'e = Shache China 38°20N 77°16E **217** E9
Sochi Russia 43°35N 39°40E **191** J4
Sochos Greece 40°48N 23°22E **202** F7
Social Circle U.S.A. 33°39N 83°43W **316** B3
Société, Îs. de la
 French Polynesia 17°0S 151°0W **289** f
Society Hill U.S.A. 34°30N 79°27W **315** D14
Society Is. = Société, Îs. de la
 French Polynesia 17°0S 151°0W **289** f
Socompa, Portezuelo de
 Chile 24°27S 68°18W **334** A2
Socorro → Fronteiras Brazil 7°5S 40°37W **332** C3
Socorro Colombia 6°29N 73°16W **328** B3
Socorro Phil. 9°37N 125°58E **233** G5
Socorro N. Mex., U.S.A. 34°4N 106°54W **305** J10
Socorro Tex., U.S.A. 31°39N 106°18W **314** F11
Socorro, I. Mexico 18°45N 110°58W **318** D2
Socotra Yemen 12°30N 54°0E **249** D6
Socovos Spain 38°20N 1°58W **197** G3
Socuéllamos Spain 39°16N 2°47W **197** F2
Soda L. U.S.A. 35°10N 116°4W **307** K10
Soda Plains India 35°30N 79°0E **243** B8
Soda Springs U.S.A. 42°39N 111°36W **304** E8
Sodankylä Finland 67°29N 26°40E **160** C22
Soddy-Daisy U.S.A. 35°17N 85°10W **315** D12
Söderala Sweden 61°17N 16°55E **162** C11
Söderåsen △ Sweden 56°5N 13°13E **163** H7
Söderbärke Sweden 60°5N 15°33E **162** D9
Söderby Sweden 60°23N 17°25E **162** D11
Söderhamn Sweden 61°18N 17°10E **162** C11
Söderköping Sweden 58°31N 16°20E **163** F10
Södermalm Sweden 59°18N 18°4E **139** B2
Södermanland Sweden 58°56N 16°55E **161** G17
Södermanlands län □
 Sweden 59°10N 16°30E **162** E10
Södertälje Sweden 59°12N 17°39E **162** E11
Sodiri Sudan 14°27N 29°0E **257** E12
Sodo Ethiopia 7°0N 37°41E **257** F14
Sodpur India 22°42N 88°24E **245** H13
Sodwana Bay △ S. Africa 27°35S 32°43E **271** C6
Soe Indonesia 9°52S 124°17E **235** D3
Soekmekaar = Morebeng
 S. Africa 23°30S 29°55E **271** B4

Sohm Abyssal Plain Atl. Oc. 36°0N 55°0W **152** C6
Sombo Angola 8°42S 20°59E **266** F4
Sombor Serbia 45°46N 19°9E **182** E4
Sombra Canada 42°43N 82°29W **312** D2
Sombrerete Mexico 23°38N 103°39W **318** C4
Sombrero Anguilla 18°37N 63°30W **322** C2
Sombrero Channel India 7°41N 93°35E **245** L11
Somcuta Mare Romania 47°31N 23°28E **183** C8
Somdari India 25°47N 72°38E **242** G5
Someido □ Spain 43°5N 6°11W **194** B4
Somers U.S.A. 48°5N 114°13W **304** B6
Somerset Bermuda 32°17N 64°52W **153** a
Somerset Ky., U.S.A. 37°5N 84°36W **309** G11
Somerset Mass., U.S.A. 41°47N 71°8W **313** E13
Somerset Md., U.S.A. 38°57N 77°5W **143** B2
Somerset □ U.K. 51°9N 3°0W **169** F5
Somerset East S. Africa 32°42S 25°35E **270** D4
Somerset I. Bermuda 32°17N 64°52W **153** a
Somerset I. Nunavut,
 Canada 73°30N 93°0W **294** C13
Somerset West S. Africa 34°8S 18°50E **270** E2
Somersworth U.S.A. 43°16N 70°52W **313** C14
Somerton U.S.A. 32°36N 114°43W **305** K6
Somerville Mass., U.S.A. 42°22N 71°5W **116** A2
Somerville N.J., U.S.A. 40°35N 74°38W **313** F10
Somes → Romania 47°49N 22°43E **182** C7
Someşul Mare → Romania 47°18N 24°52E **182** C7
Somme □ France 49°57N 2°20E **173** C9
Somme → France 50°11N 1°38E **172** B8
Somme, B. de la France 50°14N 1°33E **172** B8
Sommen, Östergötland, Sweden 58°12N 15°18E **163** F8
Sommen Östergötland,
 Sweden 58°0N 15°15E **163** F9
Sommepy-Tahure France 49°15N 4°31E **173** C11
Sömmerda Germany 51°9N 11°7E **178** D7
Sommesous France 48°44N 4°12E **173** D11
Sommières France 43°47N 4°6E **175** E8
Somnath India 20°53N 70°22E **242** J4
Somogy □ Hungary 46°19N 17°30E **182** D2
Somogyszob Hungary 46°18N 17°20E **182** D2
Somosomo Fiji 16°47S 179°58W **287** K13
Somosomo Str. Fiji 16°0S 180°0E **287** K13
Somoto Nic. 13°28N 86°37W **320** D2
Sompolno Poland 52°26N 18°30E **185** F5
Somport, Túnel de Spain 42°48N 0°31W **196** C4
Somuncurá, Meseta de
 Argentina 41°30S 67°0W **336** B3
Sonamarg India 12°36N 75°52E **245** H2
Sonamukhi India 23°29N 91°15E **241** D3
Sonar → India 24°24N 79°56E **243** G8
Sonar → India 18°54N 72°59E **130** B2
Sönch'ŏn N. Korea 39°48N 124°55E **224** C2
Sondags → S. Africa 33°44S 25°51E **270** D4
Sóndalo Italy 46°20N 10°19E **181** A11
Sønderborg Denmark 54°55N 9°49E **163** K3
Sønderho Denmark 55°27N 8°34E **163** J1
Sønder Felding Denmark 55°57N 8°47E **163** J2
Sønder Omme Denmark 55°50N 8°54E **163** J2
Sønderborg Denmark 54°55N 9°49E **163** K3
Sondershausen Germany 51°22N 10°52E **178** D6
Søndersø Germany 55°46N 12°21E **118** A2
Søndre Bergenhus = Hordaland □
 Norway 60°25N 6°15E **164** D3
Søndre Strømfjord = Kangerlussuaq
 Greenland 66°59N 50°40W **154** C5
Søndre Trondhjem =
 Sør-Trøndelag □ Norway 63°0N 11°0E **164** A7
Sóndrio Italy 46°10N 9°52E **180** A9
Sondur → India 20°40N 82°1E **244** D6
Sone Mozam. 17°23S 34°55E **268** F6
Sonepat India 29°0N 77°5E **242** E7
Sonepur India 20°55N 83°50E **244** D6
Sonfim Brazil 6°0S 67°52W **330** B4
Song Nigeria 9°49N 12°39E **263** C7
Song Thailand 18°28N 100°11E **236** C3
Song Cau Vietnam 13°27N 109°18E **236** F7
Song-Köl Kyrgyzstan 41°50N 75°12E **217** D9
Song Ma Vietnam 20°56N 103°53E **228** F4
Song Qingling, Former Residence of
 Beijing, China **114** a2
Song Xian China 34°12N 112°8E **222** G7
Songadh India 21°9N 73°33E **244** D1
Songan Indonesia 8°13S 115°24E **231** J18
Songavatnet Norway 59°52N 7°32E **164** E4
Songea Tanzania 10°40S 35°40E **269** E4
Songeons France 49°32N 1°50E **172** C8
Sönggan N. Korea 40°47N 126°34E **224** C2
Songgang China 22°46N 113°50E **219** G3
Songhua Hu China 43°35N 126°50E **224** D7
Songhua Jiang →
 China 47°45N 132°30E **219** B15
Songimvelo △ S. Africa 25°50S 31°2E **271** C5
Songjiang Jilin, China 42°34N 128°20E **224** A4
Songjiang Shanghai,
 China 31°1N 121°12E **228** B13
Songjianghe China 42°11N 127°29E **224** C3
Söngjin = Kimch'aek
 N. Korea 40°40N 129°10E **224** C5
Songkan China 28°35N 106°52E **228** D6
Songkhla Thailand 7°13N 100°37E **237** J3
Songming China 25°18N 103°2E **234** E4
Songnim N. Korea 38°45N 125°39E **224** E2
Songnisan △ S. Korea 36°34N 127°52E **224** G6
Songo Angola 7°22S 14°51E **265** D2
Songo Mozam. 15°34N 32°38E **271** A5
Songololo = Mbanza Ngungu
 Dem. Rep. of the Congo 5°12S 14°53E **265** D2
Songololo
 Dem. Rep. of the Congo 5°42S 14°2E **265** D2
Songpa S. Korea 37°30N 127°7E **137** D2
Songpan China 32°40N 103°30E **234** B5
Songtao China 28°11N 109°10E **228** C7
Songwe
 Dem. Rep. of the Congo 3°20S 26°16E **268** C2
Songwe → Africa 9°33S 33°58E **269** D3
Songxi China 27°31N 118°44E **229** D12
Songxian China 30°12N 111°45E **228** C8
Sonhat India 23°29N 82°31E **243** H10
Sonid Youqi China 42°45N 112°48E **222** C6
Sonid Zuoqi China 43°50N 113°42E **222** C6
Sonipat India 29°0N 77°5E **242** E7
Sonkach India 22°59N 76°21E **242** H7
Sonkovo Russia 57°50N 37°5E **188** D9
Sonmiani Pakistan 25°25N 66°40E **242** G2
Sonmiani B. Pakistan 25°15N 66°30E **242** G2
Sonnino Italy 41°25N 13°14E **200** A6
Sono → Minas Gerais,
 Brazil 17°2S 45°32W **333** E2
Sono → Tocantins, Brazil 9°58S 48°11W **332** C2
Sonobe = Nantan Japan 35°6N 135°28E **227** G7

Sonoma *U.S.A.* 38°18N 122°28W **306** G4
Sonora *Calif., U.S.A.* 37°59N 120°23W **306** H6
Sonora *Tex., U.S.A.* 30°34N 100°39W **314** F4
Sonora → *Mexico* 29°20N 110°40W **318** B2
Sonora → *Mexico* 29°5N 112°50N 0W **318** A2
Sonoran Desert *U.S.A.* 33°40N 113°30W **307** L12
Sonqor *Iran* 34°47N 47°36E **213** E12
Sonseca *Spain* 39°42N 3°57W **195** F7
Sonsón *Colombia* 5°43N 75°18W **328** B2
Sonsonate *El Salv.* 13°43N 89°44W **320** D2
Sonstorp *Sweden* 58°44N 15°38E **163** F9
Sonthofen *Germany* 47°30N 10°16E **179** H6
Sony Picture Studio
U.S.A. 34°1N 118°4W **126** B2
Soo *Japan* 31°40N 131°5E **222** F3
Soochow = Suzhou
China 31°19N 120°38E **229** B13
Sooke *Canada* 48°13N 123°43W **306** B3
Sool → *Somalia* 8°40N 47°30E **267** C6
Soomaaliya = Somalia ■
Africa 7°0N 47°0E **267** C6
Sop Hao *Laos* 20°33N 104°27E **228** G5
Sop Prap *Thailand* 17°53N 99°20E **236** D2
Sopachuy *Bolivia* 19°29S 64°31W **331** D5
Sopchoppy *U.S.A.* 30°4N 84°29W **316** E5
Sopelana *Spain* 43°23N 2°58W **196** B2
Soperton *U.S.A.* 32°23N 82°35W **316** C7
Sopi *Indonesia* 2°34N 128°28E **231** D7
Sopo, Nahr → *South Sudan* 8°40N 26°30E **257** F2
Sopot *Bulgaria* 42°39N 24°45E **203** D8
Sopot *Poland* 54°27N 18°31E **184** D5
Sopot *Serbia* 44°29N 20°36E **202** B4
Sopotnica *Macedonia* 41°18N 21°13E **202** E5
Sopron *Hungary* 47°45N 16°32E **182** C1
Sopur *India* 34°18N 74°27E **243** B6
Šor-Rondane *Antarctica* 72°0S 25°0E **151** D4
Šor-Trondelag □ *Norway* 63°0N 11°0E **164** A7
Sora *Italy* 41°43N 13°37E **199** G10
Sorab *India* 14°23N 75°6E **245** G2
Sorada *India* 19°45N 84°26E **244** E7
Sorah *Pakistan* 27°13N 68°56E **242** F3
Söräker *Sweden* 62°30N 17°32E **162** B11
Sorang *Kazakhstan* 49°46N 72°51E **217** C8
Sorano *Italy* 42°41N 11°43E **199** F8
Soraon *India* 25°37N 81°51E **243** G9
Sorata *Bolivia* 15°50S 68°40W **330** D4
Sorbas *Spain* 37°6N 2°7W **197** H2
Sörbygden *Sweden* 62°48N 16°12E **162** B10
Sord = Swords *Ireland* 53°28N 6°13W **120** A2
Sordellen *Sweden* 61°48N 16°43E **162** C10
Sore *France* 44°18N 0°35W **174** D3
Sore Osa → *Norway* 61°18N 11°46E **164** C8
Sorel-Tracy *Canada* 46°0N 73°10W **298** C5
Soresina *Italy* 45°17N 9°51E **198** B6
Sörforsa *Sweden* 61°43N 16°58E **162** C10
Sörgona *Italy* 40°1N 9°6E **200** B2
Sorgues *France* 44°1N 4°53E **175** D8
Sorgun *Turkey* 39°46N 35°11E **212** C6
Sorgun → *Turkey* 36°36N 34°20E **250** B5
Sori *Papua N. G.* 1°58S 146°42E **286** A4
Soria *Spain* 41°43N 2°32W **196** D2
Soria □ *Spain* 41°46N 2°28W **196** D2
Soriano *Uruguay* 33°24S 58°19W **334** C4
Soriano nel Cimino *Italy* 42°25N 12°14E **199** F9
Sorkh, Kuh-e *Iran* 35°40N 58°30E **247** C8
Soro *Denmark* 55°26N 11°32E **163** J5
Soro *Guinea* 10°9N 9°48W **262** C3
Soroca *Moldova* 48°8N 28°12E **183** B13
Sorocaba *Brazil* 23°31S 47°27W **335** A6
Sorochinsk *Russia* 52°26N 53°10E **186** D9
Soroka = Belomorsk
Russia 64°35N 34°54E **186** B5
Soroki = Soroca *Moldova* 48°8N 28°12E **183** B13
Sorokino = Krasnodon
Ukraine 48°17N 39°44E **189** H10
Soroksár *Hungary* 47°24N 19°7E **117** B2
Soroksári Duna →
Hungary 47°25N 19°5E **117** B2
Sorong *Indonesia* 0°55S 131°15E **231** E8
Soroti *Uganda* 1°43N 33°35E **268** B3
Söröya *Norway* 70°40N 22°30E **160** A20
Söröyane *Norway* 62°25N 5°32E **164** B2
Söröysundet *Norway* 70°25N 23°0E **160** A20
Sorraia → *Portugal* 38°55N 8°53W **195** G2
Sorrell *Australia* 42°47S 147°34E **281** G4
Sorrento *Italy* 40°37N 14°22E **201** B7
Sorsele *Sweden* 65°31N 17°30E **160** D17
Sörsjön *Sweden* 61°24N 13°5E **162** C7
Sorso *Italy* 40°48N 8°34E **200** B1
Sorsogon *Phil.* 13°0N 124°0E **232** E5
Sorsogon □ *Phil.* 12°50N 123°55E **232** E4
Sortavala *Russia* 61°42N 30°41E **188** B6
Sortino *Italy* 37°9N 15°2E **201** E8
Sortland *Norway* 68°42N 15°25E **160** B16
Sortot *Sudan* 19°3N 30°28E **256** D3
Sorum *Norway* 60°30N 10°17E **164** D7
Sorvizhi *Russia* 57°52N 48°32E **190** B9
Sos del Rey Católico *Spain* 42°30N 1°13W **196** C3
Soscumica, L. *Canada* 50°15N 77°27W **298** B4
Sösdala *Sweden* 56°2N 13°41E **163** H7
Sosenka → *Russia* 55°46N 37°43E **129** B3
Sosna → *Russia* 52°42N 38°55E **189** F10
Sosnogorsk *Russia* 63°37N 53°51E **186** B9
Sosnovka *Kirov, Russia* 56°17N 51°17E **190** B10
Sosnovka *St. Petersburg,
Russia* 60°0N 30°22E **137** B2
Sosnovka *Tambov, Russia* 53°13N 41°24E **190** D5
Sosnovyy Bor *Russia* 59°55N 29°6E **188** C5
Sosnowiec *Poland* 50°20N 19°10E **185** H6
Sosnowiec = Sosnowiec
Poland 50°20N 19°10E **185** H6
Soso *C.A.R.* 3°55N 15°30E **264** B3
Sospel *France* 43°52N 7°27E **175** E11
Sospiri, Ponte dei *Venice, Italy* **142** b3
Sossus Vlei *Namibia* 24°40S 15°23E **270** B2
Šoštanj *Slovenia* 46°23N 15°4E **199** B12
Sôsura *N. Korea* 42°16N 130°36E **224** A5
Sot → *India* 27°27N 79°37E **243** F8
Sotasæter *Norway* 61°49N 7°43E **164** C4
Sotavento *C. Verde Is.* 15°0N 24°0W **158** j
Sotik *Kenya* 0°41S 35°7E **268** C4
Sotkamo *Finland* 64°8N 28°23E **160** D23
Soto del Barco *Spain* 43°32N 6°4W **194** B4
Soto la Marina *Mexico* 23°46N 98°13W **319** C5
Soto la Marina →
Mexico 23°45N 97°45W **319** C5
Sotouboua *Togo* 8°59N 0°59E **263** C6
Sotrondio *Spain* 43°17N 5°36W **194** B5
Souf, Adrar W. *Sahara* 21°42N 11°0W **260** D3
Sotuta *Mexico* 20°36N 89°1W **319** C7
Souanké *Congo* 2°10N 14°3E **264** B2
Soubré *Ivory C.* 5°50N 6°35W **262** D3
Souda *Greece* 35°29N 24°4E **207** E5
Soufkamo *Finland* 64°8N 28°23E **160** D23
Soufli *Greece* 12°16N 69°6W **322** g
Soto → *Curaçao* 43°32N 6°4W **194** B4
Soto del Barco *Spain*
Souderton *U.S.A.* 40°19N 75°19W **313** B9
Soufrière *Dominica* 15°13N 61°22W **323** k
Soufrière *Guadeloupe* 16°5N 61°40W **322** b
Soufrière *St. Lucia* 13°51N 61°3W **323** m
Soufrière Bay *Dominica* 15°43N 61°22W **323** k

Soufrière Bay *St. Lucia* 13°51N 61°4W **323** m
Soufrière Hills Volcano
Montserrat 16°43N 62°10W **323** p
Souillac *Lot, France* 44°53N 1°29E **174** D5
Souillac *Mauritius* 20°31S 57°31E **272** e
Souilly *France* 49°3N 5°17E **173** C12
Souk-Ahras *Algeria* 36°23N 7°57E **261** A6
Souk-Ahras □ *Algeria* 36° 0N 7°55E **261** A6
Souk el Arba du Rharb
Morocco 34°33N 5°59W **260** B3
Soukhouma *Laos* 14°38N 105°48E **236** E5
Soûl = Seoul *S. Korea* 37°31N 126°58E **137** B2
Soulac-sur-Mer *France* 45°30N 1°7W **174** C2
Soulougou *Burkina Faso* 11°3N 0°25E **263** C5
Soultz-sous-Forêts *France* 48°57N 7°52E **173** D14
Sound, The = Øresund
Europe 55°45N 12°40E **163** J6
Sound, The *U.K.* 50°20N 4°10W **169** G3
Sound I. *India* 12°58N 92°59E **245** H11
Soundview *U.S.A.* 40°49N 73°53W **132** E7
Sounio, Akra *Greece* 37°37N 24°1E **204** D6
Sour el Ghozlane *Algeria* 36°1'0N 3°45E **261** A5
Sources, Mt. aux *Lesotho* 28°45S 28°50E **271** C4
Soure *Brazil* 0°35S 48°30W **332** B2
Soure *Portugal* 40°4N 8°38W **194** E2
Souris *Man., Canada* 49°40N 100°20W **297** D8
Souris *P.E.I., Canada* 46°21N 62°15W **299** C7
Souris → *N. Amer.* 49°40N 99°34W **308** A4
Sourou → *Africa* 12°43N 3°25W **262** C4
Sourpi *Greece* 39°6N 22°54E **204** B4
Sous, O. → *Morocco* 30°27N 9°31W **260** B3
Sous le Vent, Is.
French Polynesia 16°30S 155°30W **289** f
Sous le Vent, Région
Réunion 21°12S 55°20E **272** f
Sous-Massa △ *Morocco* 31°2N 9°35W **260** B3
Sous-Massa-Drâa □
Morocco 30°43N 8°30W **260** B3
Sousa *Brazil* 6°45S 38°10W **332** C4
Sousel *Portugal* 38°57N 7°40W **195** G3
Sousse *Tunisia* 35°50N 10°38E **258** A2
Sousse □ *Tunisia* 35°40N 10°30E **261** A7
Soustons *France* 43°45N 1°19W **174** E2
Sout → *S. Africa* 31°35S 18°24E **270** D2
South Africa ■ *Africa* 32°0S 23°0E **270** D3
South America 10°0S 60°0W **326** E5
South Andaman *India* 11°45N 92°10E **245** J11
South Aulatsivik I.
Canada 56°45N 61°30W **299** A7
South Australia □
Australia 32°0S 139°0E **282** B3
South Australian Basin
Ind. Oc. 38°0S 126°0E **288** L4
South Ayrshire □ *U.K.* 55°18N 4°41W **167** F4
South Baldy Pk. *U.S.A.* 34°6N 107°11W **305** J10
South Bass I. *U.S.A.* 41°39N 82°49E **312** E2
South Bay *U.S.A.* 26°40N 80°43W **317** J9
South Beach *Bahamas* 25°1N 77°20W **153** b
South Beach *Fla., U.S.A.* 25°46N 80°7W **129** D3
South Beach *N.Y., U.S.A.* 40°35N 74°4W **132** C1
South Beach Harbor
San Francisco, U.S.A. **136** c3
South Beloit *U.S.A.* 42°29N 89°2W **310** B7
South Bend *Ind., U.S.A.* 41°41N 86°15W **311** C10
South Bend *Wash.,
U.S.A.* 46°40N 123°48W **306** B3
South Bend Park *U.S.A.* 33°42N 84°23W **113** B2
South Boston *Mass., U.S.A.* 42°20N 71°2W **116** A2
South Boston *Va., U.S.A.* 36°42N 78°54W **309** G14
South Branch *Canada* 47°55N 59°2W **299** C8
South Branch Chicago River → *U.S.A.* **119** d1
South Brook *Canada* 49°25N 56°5W **299** C8
South Brother I. *India* 10°56N 92°37E **245** J11
South Bruny I. *Australia* 43°20S 147°15E **281** A4
South C. = Kalae *U.S.A.* 18°55N 155°41W **302** E6
South Carolina □ *U.S.A.* 34°0N 81°0W **315** E14
South Channel *Phil.* 14°18N 120°37E **232** D3
South Charleston *U.S.A.* 38°22N 81°44W **309** F13
South China Sea *Asia* 10°0N 113°0E **230** C4
South Comino Channel
Malta 36°0N 14°20E **206** F7
South Congaree *U.S.A.* 33°53N 81°9W **316** B5
South Cotabato □ *Phil.* 6°0N 125°0E **233** J5
South Cumberland Is. □
Australia 20°42S 149°11E **280** b
South Dakota □ *U.S.A.* 44°15N 100°0W **308** C4
South Dayton *U.S.A.* 42°21N 79°3W **312** D5
South Daytona *U.S.A.* 29°10N 81°0W **317** F8
South Decatur *U.S.A.* 33°44N 84°16W **113** B3
South Deerfield *U.S.A.* 42°29N 72°37W **313** D12
South Deering *U.S.A.* 41°42N 87°33W **119** C3
South Downs *U.K.* 50°52N 0°25W **169** G7
South Downs △ *U.K.* 50°50N 0°50W **169** G7
South East □ *Botswana* 25°0S 25°40E **270** C4
South East B. *Ascension I.* 7°57S 14°18W **153** g
South East C. *Australia* 43°40S 146°50E **281** A4
South East Forest △
Australia 37°0S 149°30E **283** D8
South East Is. *Australia* 34°17S 123°30E **279** F3
South El Monte *U.S.A.* 34°3N 118°2W **126** B4
South Elgin *U.S.A.* 41°59N 88°18W **311** C8
South Esk → *U.K.* 56°43N 2°31W **167** E6
South Fiji Basin *Pac. Oc.* 26°0S 175°0E **288** K9
South Fork American →
U.S.A. 38°57N 120°59W **306** G5
South Fork Edisto →
U.S.A. 33°1N 80°54W **316** D6
South Fork Feather →
U.S.A. 39°17N 121°36W **306** F5
South Fork Grand →
U.S.A. 45°43N 102°17W **308** C2
South Fork Licking →
U.S.A. 38°40N 84°18W **311** F12
South Fork Milk →
U.S.A. 48°4N 106°19W **304** B10
South Fork Republican →
U.S.A. 40°3N 101°33W **308** E3
South Gate *U.S.A.* 33°56N 118°12W **126** C3
South Georgia *Antarctica* 54°30S 37°0W **151** B1
South Gloucestershire □
U.K. 51°32N 2°28W **169** F5
South Hadley *U.S.A.* 42°16N 72°35W **313** D12
South Harbor *Phil.* 14°34N 120°58E **127** B1
South Harrow *U.K.* 51°33N 0°21W **125** A1
South Haven *U.S.A.* 42°24N 86°16W **311** D10
South Hd. *Australia* 33°50S 151°16E **139** B2
South Henik L. *Canada* 61°30N 97°30W **297** A9
South Hill Village *Anguilla* 18°11N 63°5W **322** a
South Hills △ *U.S.A.* 26°14S 28°5E **122** B2
South Holland *U.S.A.* 41°36N 87°36W **119** D3
South Horr *Kenya* 2°12N 36°56E **268** B4
South I. *India* 10°3N 72°17E **245** J1
South I. *N.Z.* 44°0S 170°0E **285** E5
South Indian Lake
Canada 56°47N 98°56W **297** B9
South Invercargill *N.Z.* 46°26S 168°23E **285** B3
South Island □ *Kenya* 2°39N 36°35E **268** B4
South Kensington *London, U.K.* **125** c2
South Kitui △ *Kenya* 1°48S 38°46E **268** C4
South Knife → *Canada* 58°55N 94°37W **297** B10
South Koel → *India* 22°32N 85°14E **243** H11
South Korea ■ *Asia* 36°0N 128°0E **224** D4

South Lake Tahoe
U.S.A. 38°57N 119°59W **306** G6
South Lanarkshire □ *U.K.* 55°37N 3°53W **167** F5
South Lawn *U.S.A.* 38°47N 77°0W **143** C2
South Loup → *U.S.A.* 41°4N 98°39W **308** E4
South Luangwa △ *Zambia* 13°0S 31°20E **269** E3
South Lyon *U.S.A.* 42°28N 83°39W **311** B13
South Magnetic Pole
Antarctica 64°8S 138°8E **151** C9
South Malé Atoll *Maldives* 4°0N 73°25E **272** d
South Malosmadulu Atoll
Maldives 5°12N 73°0E **272** d
South Miami *U.S.A.* 25°42N 80°17W **129** D1
South Milwaukee *U.S.A.* 42°55N 87°52W **311** B9
South Molton *U.K.* 51°1N 3°51W **169** F4
South Monroe *U.S.A.* 41°54N 83°26W **311** C13
South Moose L. *Canada* 53°49N 100°1W **297** C8
South Nahanni →
Canada 61°3N 123°21W **296** A4
South Nation → *Canada* 45°34N 75°6W **313** A9
South Natuna Is. = Natuna Selatan,
Kepulauan *Indonesia* 2°45N 109°0E **235** B3
South Negril Pt. *Jamaica* 18°16N 78°22W **320** a
South New Hebrides Trench
Pac. Oc. 22°30S 170°0E **277** E13
South Newport *U.S.A.* 31°38N 81°24W **316** D8
South Nilandu Atoll
Maldives 2°52N 72°57E **272** d
South Norwood *U.K.* 51°23N 0°3W **125** B3
South of Market *San Francisco, U.S.A.* **136** c2
South Orkney Is.
Antarctica 63°0S 45°0W **151** C18
South Ossetia □ *Georgia* 42°21N 44°2E **191** J7
South Otselic *U.S.A.* 42°38N 75°46W **313** D9
South Ozone Park *U.S.A.* 40°41N 73°49W **132** B3
South Pagai, I. = Pagai Selatan,
Pulau *Indonesia* 3°0S 100°15E **234** C2
South Paris *U.S.A.* 44°14N 70°31W **313** B14
South Pasadena *U.S.A.* 34°7N 118°9W **126** B4
South Pekin *U.S.A.* 40°30N 89°39W **310** D7
South Pittsburg *U.S.A.* 35°1N 85°42W **315** D12
South Platte → *U.S.A.* 41°7N 100°42W **308** E3
South Pole *Antarctica* 90°0S 0°0 **151** E
South Ponte Vedra Beach
U.S.A. 30°3N 81°20W **316** E8
South Porcupine *Canada* 48°30N 81°12W **298** C3
South Portland *U.S.A.* 43°38N 70°15W **309** D18
South Pt. *Ascension I.* 8°0S 14°24W **153** g
South Pt. *Barbados* 13°2N 59°32W **323** r
South Pt. *Mich., U.S.A.* 44°52N 83°19W **312** B1
South Pt. = Kalae *U.S.A.* 18°55N 155°41W **302** E6
South Res. *U.S.A.* 42°26N 71°6W **116** A2
South River *Ont., Canada* 45°52N 79°23W **298** C4
South River *N.J., U.S.A.* 40°27N 74°23W **313** F10
South Ronaldsay *U.K.* 58°48N 2°58W **167** C6
South Ruislip *U.K.* 51°33N 0°24W **125** A1
South Rukuru *Malawi* 10°44S 34°14E **269** E3
South San Francisco
U.S.A. 37°38N 122°26W **136** C2
South San Gabriel *U.S.A.* 34°3N 118°6W **126** B4
South Sandwich Is.
Antarctica 57°0S 27°0W **151** B1
South Sandwich Trench
Atl. Oc. 56°0S 24°0W **151** B1
South Saskatchewan →
Canada 53°15N 105°5W **297** C7
South Seal → *Canada* 58°48N 98°8W **297** B9
South Sentinel I. *India* 10°59N 92°14E **245** J11
South Shetland Is.
Antarctica 62°0S 59°0W **151** C18
South Shields *U.K.* 55°0N 1°25W **168** C6
South Shore *U.S.A.* 41°45N 87°34W **119** C3
South Sioux City *U.S.A.* 42°28N 96°24W **308** D6
South Sister *U.S.A.* 44°4N 121°51W **304** D3
South Solomon Trench
Pac. Oc. 11°0S 164°30E **277** C11
South Soufrière Hills
Montserrat 16°41N 62°10W **323** p
South Street *Boston, U.S.A.* **116** c2
South Sudan ■ *Africa* 8°0N 30°0E **257** F3
South Taranaki Bight
N.Z. 39°40S 174°5E **284** F3
South Tasman Rise
S. Ocean 48°0S 146°0E **151** A10
South Thompson →
Canada 50°40N 120°20W **296** C4
South Twin I. *Canada* 53°7N 79°52W **298** B4
South Tyne → *U.K.* 54°59N 2°8W **168** C5
South Ubian *Phil.* 5°11N 120°30E **233** J3
South Uist *U.K.* 57°20N 7°15W **167** D1
South Valley *U.S.A.* 35°1N 106°41W **305** J10
South Venice *U.S.A.* 27°3N 82°25W **317** H7
South Verde I. *Phil.* 10°4N 119°13E **233** F2
South Wayne *U.S.A.* 42°34N 89°53W **310** B7
South Wellesley Is.
Australia 16°58S 139°17E **280** B2
South West Africa = Namibia ■
Africa 22°0S 18°9E **270** B2
South West B. *Ascension I.* 7°58S 14°25W **153** g
South West B. *Bahamas* 25°0N 77°33W **153** b
South West C. *Tas.,
Australia* 43°34S 146°3E **281** A4
South West C. *N.Z.* 47°17S 167°28E **285** H2
South West Pt.
Papua N. G. 2°14S 146°34E **286** B4
South West Pt. *St. Helena* 15°59S 5°48W **153** h
South West Rocks
Australia 30°52S 153°3E **283** A10
South Whitley *U.S.A.* 41°5N 85°38W **311** C11
South Williamsport *U.S.A.* 41°13N 77°0W **312** E8
South Yemen = Yemen ■
Asia 15°0N 44°0E **248** D4
South Yorkshire □ *U.K.* 53°27N 1°36W **168** D6
Southall *U.K.* 51°30N 0°22W **125** A1
Southampton *Ont.,
Canada* 44°30N 81°25W **312** B2
Southampton
*Southampton,
U.K.* 50°54N 1°23W **169** G6
Southampton *N.Y.,
U.S.A.* 40°53N 72°23W **313** F12
Southampton I. *Canada* 64°30N 84°0W **298** A2
Southaven *U.S.A.* 34°59N 90°0W **313** C4
Southbank *Canada* 54°2N 125°46W **296** C3
Southborough *U.K.* 51°23N 0°13E **125** D4
Southbridge *N.Z.* 43°48S 172°16E **285** E4
Southbridge *Mass., U.S.A.* 42°5N 72°2W **313** D12
Southeast C. *U.S.A.* 62°56N 169°39W **303** E5
Southeast Indian Ridge
Ind. Oc. 43°0S 80°0E **273** J10
Southend *Sask., Canada* 56°19N 103°22W **297** B8
Southend *London, U.K.* 51°25N 0°0 **125** B3
Southend-on-Sea *U.K.* 51°32N 0°44E **169** F8
Southend-on-Sea □ *U.K.* 51°32N 0°44E **169** F8
Southern = Yedebub Biheroch
Bihereshoch na Hizboch □
Ethiopia 6°0N 36°0E **257** F4
Southern = Yuzhnyy □
Russia 44°0N 40°0E **214** E5
Southern □ *Malawi* 15°0S 35°0E **269** F4
Southern □ *S. Leone* 8°0N 12°30W **262** D2
Southern □ *Zambia* 16°20S 26°20E **269** F2
Southern □ *S. Sudan* 6°0N 28°0E **257** F2
Southern Alps *N.Z.* 43°41S 170°11E **285** E3
Southern California, Univ. of
U.S.A. 34°1N 118°17W **126** B3
Southern Cross *Australia* 31°12S 119°15E **279** F2

Southern Highlands □
Papua N. G. 6°15S 143°25E **286** D2
Southern Indian L.
Canada 57°10N 98°30W **297** B9
Southern Lau Group
Fiji 18°40S 178°40W **287** B3
Southern Leyte □ *Phil.* 10°30N 125°10E **233** F5
Southern Ocean 62°0S 60°0E **151** C6
Southern Pines *U.S.A.* 35°11N 79°24W **315** D15
Southern Uplands *U.K.* 55°28N 3°52W **167** F5
Southern Rhodesia = Zimbabwe ■
Africa 19°0S 30°0E **269** F3
Southfield *U.S.A.* 42°28N 83°15W **311** B13
Southfields *U.K.* 51°26N 0°11W **125** B2
Southington *U.S.A.* 41°36N 72°53W **313** E12
Southland □ *N.Z.* 45°30S 168°0E **285** F3
Southold *U.S.A.* 41°4N 72°26W **313** E12
Southport *Queens.,
Australia* 27°58S 153°25E **281** D5
Southport *Mersey., U.K.* 53°39N 3°0W **168** D4
Southport *Fla., U.S.A.* 30°17N 85°38W **316** E4
Southport *La., U.S.A.* 29°57N 90°8W **131** B2
Southport *N.Y., U.S.A.* 42°3N 76°49W **312** D8
Southwest *Australia* 51°29N 0°6W **125** B3
Southwest △ *Australia* 43°8S 146°5E **281** G4
Southwest Museum
U.S.A. 34°6N 118°13W **126** B3
Southwest Pacific Basin
Pac. Oc. 40°0S 140°0W **277** G17
Southwest Pt.
U.S. Virgin Is. 17°40N 64°55W **321** b
Southwold *U.K.* 52°20N 1°41E **169** E9
Southwood △ *Australia* 27°48S 150°8E **281** D5
Soutpansberg *S. Africa* 23°0S 29°30E **271** B4
Souvigny *France* 46°33N 3°10E **173** F10
Sovang *Denmark* 55°34N 12°37E **118** B3
Sovata *Romania* 46°35N 25°3E **183** D10
Soverato *Italy* 38°41N 16°33E **201** D9
Sovetsk *Kaliningrad, Russia* 55°6N 21°50E **184** C8
Sovetsk *Kirov, Russia* 57°38N 48°53E **190** B9
Sovetskaya Gavan
Russia 48°58N 140°18E **215** E15
Sovetskoye = Zelenokumsk
Russia 44°24N 44°0E **191** H6
Soviciille *Italy* 43°17N 11°13E **199** E8
Sovik *Norway* 62°33N 6°17E **164** B3
Soweto *S. Africa* 26°14S 27°52E **135** B3
Sowhānak *Iran* 35°48N 51°31E **141** A3
Sowma'eh Sarā *Iran* 37°17N 49°18E **213** D13
Soya *Japan* 45°28N 141°56E **140** A4
Sōya-Kaikyō = La Perouse Str.
Asia 45°40N 142°0E **220** B11
Sōya-Misaki *Japan* 45°30N 141°55E **222** A8
Soyangho *S. Korea* 37°57N 127°54E **224** D3
Soyaux *France* 45°39N 0°12E **174** C4
Soyland *Norway* 58°41N 5°36E **164** F2
Soyo *Angola* 6°13S 12°20E **265** D2
Sozaq *Kazakhstan* 44°8N 68°28E **217** D7
Sozh → *Belarus* 51°57N 30°48E **177** B16
Sozopol *Bulgaria* 42°23N 27°42E **203** D11
Spa *Belgium* 50°29N 5°53E **170** D5
Spaans Lagoen *Aruba* 12°28N 69°58E **322** f
Spaanse Water *Curaçao* 12°4N 68°51E **322** g
Spaatz I. *Antarctica* 73°10S 75°0W **151** D17
Spaccaforno = Íspica *Italy* 36°47N 14°55E **201** F7
Spain ■ *Europe* 39°0N 4°0W **192** D3
Spalato = Split *Croatia* 43°31N 16°26E **199** E13
Spalding *S. Austral.,
Australia* 33°30S 138°37E **282** B3
Spalding *Lincs., U.K.* 52°48N 0°9W **168** E7
Spanaway *U.S.A.* 47°6N 122°26W **306** C4
Spandau *Germany* 52°33N 13°9E **115** A1
Spânga *Sweden* 59°23N 17°53E **139** A1
Spangler *U.S.A.* 40°39N 78°48W **312** F6
Spanische Reitschule *Vienna, Austria* **142** b1
Spanish *Canada* 46°12N 82°20W **298** C3
Spanish Fork *U.S.A.* 40°7N 111°39W **304** F8
Spanish Pt. *Antigua & B.* 17°33N 61°44W **322** c
Spanish Pt. *Bermuda* 32°18N 64°49W **153** a
Spanish Riding School = Spanische
Reitschule *Vienna, Austria* **142** b1
Spanish Town
Br. Virgin Is. 18°26N 64°26W **321** b
Spanish Town *Jamaica* 18°0N 76°57W **320** a
Sparks *Ga., U.S.A.* 31°11N 83°26W **316** D6
Sparks *Nev., U.S.A.* 39°32N 119°45W **306** F7
Sparrenhem *Sweden* 59°4N 16°49E **162** E10
Sparrow Bay *Grenada* 12°30N 61°27W **323** q
Sparta = Sparti *Greece* 37°5N 22°25E **204** D4
Sparta *Ill., U.S.A.* 38°8N 89°42W **310** F7
Sparta *Mich., U.S.A.* 43°10N 85°42W **311** A11
Sparta *N.J., U.S.A.* 41°2N 74°38W **313** D10
Sparta *Wis., U.S.A.* 43°56N 90°49W **308** D8
Spartanburg *U.S.A.* 34°56N 81°57W **315** D14
Spartel, C. *Morocco* 35°47N 5°56W **260** A3
Sparti *Greece* 37°5N 22°25E **204** D4
Spartivento, C. *Calabria,
Italy* 37°55N 16°4E **201** D9
Spartivento, C. *Sard., Italy* 38°53N 8°50E **200** D1
Spartochori *Greece* 38°40N 20°46E **204** C2
Sparwood *Canada* 49°44N 114°53W **296** D6
Spas-Demensk *Russia* 54°20N 34°0E **188** E17
Spas-Klepiki *Russia* 55°10N 40°10E **188** E11
Spassk Dalniy *Russia* 44°40N 132°48E **220** B6
Spassk-Ryazanskiy
Russia 54°24N 40°25E **188** E11
Spatha, Akra *Greece* 35°42N 23°43E **207** E4
Spatsizi → *Canada* 57°42N 128°7W **296** B3
Spatsizi Plateau Wilderness △
Canada 57°40N 128°0W **296** B3
Spean → *U.K.* 56°55N 4°59W **167** E4
Spearfish *U.S.A.* 44°30N 103°52W **308** C2
Spearman *U.S.A.* 36°12N 101°12W **314** C4
Spectacle I. *U.S.A.* 42°19N 70°59W **116** B3
Speculator *U.S.A.* 43°30N 74°22W **313** C10
Speed *Australia* 35°21S 142°27E **282** C5
Speedway *U.S.A.* 39°48N 86°16W **311** F10
Speery I. *St. Helena* 16°1S 5°46W **153** h
Speia *Moldova* 46°59N 29°19E **183** D14
Speicher-See *Germany* 48°12N 11°42E **131** A3
Speightstown *Barbados* 13°15N 59°39W **323** r
Speising *Austria* 48°10N 16°17E **142** B1
Speke Gulf *Tanzania* 2°20S 32°50E **268** C3
Spello *Italy* 42°59N 12°40E **199** F9
Spence Bay = Taloyoak
Canada 69°30N 93°32W **294** D13
Spencer *Idaho, U.S.A.* 44°22N 112°11W **304** D7
Spencer *Ind., U.S.A.* 39°17N 86°46W **311** E10
Spencer *Iowa, U.S.A.* 43°9N 95°9W **308** D6
Spencer *N.Y., U.S.A.* 42°13N 76°30W **313** D8
Spencer *Nebr., U.S.A.* 42°53N 98°42W **308** D4
Spencer *C. Australia* 35°20S 136°53E **282** C2
Spencer *B. Namibia* 25°30S 14°47E **270** C1
Spencer G. *Australia* 34°0S 137°20E **282** C2
Spencerville *Ont., U.S.A.* 40°43N 84°21W **311** D12
Spences Bridge *Canada* 50°25N 121°20W **296** C4
Spennymoor *U.K.* 54°42N 1°36W **168** C6
Spenser Mts. *N.Z.* 42°15S 172°45E **285** E4
Spentrup *Denmark* 56°33N 10°3E **163** H4
Sperchios → *Greece* 38°57N 22°3E **204** C4
Sperillen *Norway* 60°28N 10°13E **164** D7
Sperrin Mts. *U.K.* 54°50N 7°0W **166** C8
Sre Ambel *Cambodia* 11°8N 103°46E **237** G4

Sre Khtum *Cambodia* 12°10N 106°52E **237** F6
Sre Umbell = Sre Ambel
Cambodia 11°8N 103°46E **237** G4
Srebarna *Bulgaria* 44°6N 27°4E **203** B11
Srebrenica *Bos.-H.* 44°6N 19°18E **182** F4
Sredinnyy Khrebet *Russia* 57°0N 160°0E **215** D17
Sredinnyy Ra. = Sredinnyy Khrebet
Russia 57°0N 160°0E **215** D17
Središče *Slovenia* 46°24N 16°17E **199** B13
Sredna Gora *Bulgaria* 42°40N 24°20E **203** D8
Srednaya Bugaria *Russia* 59°49N 30°22E **137** C2
Srednekolymsk *Russia* 67°27N 153°40E **215** C16
Sredni Rodopi *Bulgaria* 41°40N 24°45E **203** E8
Srednogorie *Bulgaria* 42°43N 24°10E **203** D8
Šrem *Poland* 52°6N 17°2E **185** F4
Sremska Mitrovica *Serbia* 44°59N 19°38E **182** F4
Sremski Karlovci *Serbia* 45°12N 19°56E **182** E4
Srepok → *Cambodia* 13°33N 106°16E **236** F6
Sretensk *Russia* 52°10N 117°40E **215** D12
Sri Aman = Bandar Sri Aman
Malaysia 1°15N 111°32E **235** B4
Sri Kalahasti *India* 13°45N 79°44E **245** H4
Sri Lanka ■ *Asia* 7°30N 80°50E **245** L5
Sri Pada = Adam's Peak
Sri Lanka 6°48N 80°30E **245** L5
Sriharikota I. *India* 13°40N 80°20E **245** H5
Srikakulam *India* 18°14N 83°58E **244** E6
Srinagar *India* 34°5N 74°50E **243** B6
Sripur *Bangla.* 24°14N 90°30E **241** G17
Srivardhan *India* 18°4N 73°3E **244** E1
Srivilliputtur *India* 9°31N 77°40E **245** K3
Środa Śląska *Poland* 51°10N 16°36E **185** G3
Środa Wielkopolski
Poland 52°15N 17°19E **185** F4
Sródmieście *Poland* 52°13N 21°0E **143** B2
Srono *Indonesia* 8°24S 114°16E **231** J17
Srpska Crnja *Serbia* 45°38N 20°44E **182** E5
Srpski Itebej *Serbia* 45°35N 20°44E **182** E5
Srungavarapukota *India* 18°7N 83°10E **244** E6
Ssese Is. = Sese Is. *Uganda* 0°20S 32°20E **268** C3
Ssuhu *Taiwan* 23°38N 120°13E **225** C2
Staaken *Germany* 52°31N 13°8E **115** A1
Staaten → *Australia* 16°24S 141°17E **280** B3
Staaten River △ *Australia* 16°15S 142°40E **280** B3
Stabekk *Norway* 59°54N 10°36E **133** A2
Staberhuk *Germany* 54°23N 11°18E **178** A7
Stade *Germany* 53°35N 9°29E **178** B5
Staðarfell *Iceland* 65°7N 22°12W **155** B4
Staðarhólskirkja *Iceland* 65°23N 21°58W **155** B4
Staðastaður *Iceland* 64°49N 23°1W **155** C3
Stadhavet *Norway* 62°13N 5°0E **164** B2
Stadhiou *Athens, Greece* **112** c3
Stadhuis *Amsterdam, Neths.* **112** b3
Staður *Norðurland Vestra
Iceland* 65°9N 21°3W **155** B5
Staður *Vestfirðir Iceland* 66°15N 22°50W **155** A4
Stadtlandet *Norway* 62°10N 5°10E **164** B2
Stadlau *Austria* 48°13N 16°27E **142** A2
Stadshuset *Stockholm, Sweden* **139** b1
Stadskanaal *Neths.* 53°4N 6°55E **170** A6
Stadsschouwburg *Amsterdam, Neths.* **112** c1
Stadtallendorf *Germany* 50°48N 9°1E **178** E5
Stadthagen *Germany* 52°19N 9°13E **178** C5
Stadtlohn *Germany* 51°59N 6°55E **178** D2
Stadtroda *Germany* 50°52N 11°44E **178** E7
Stafafell *Iceland* 64°25N 14°52W **155** C12
Staffa *U.K.* 56°27N 6°21W **167** E2
Staffanstorp *Sweden* 55°39N 13°13E **163** J7
Stafford *Staffs., U.K.* 52°49N 2°7W **168** E5
Stafford *Kans., U.S.A.* 37°58N 98°36W **308** E4
Stafford, L. *U.S.A.* 29°20N 82°29W **317** F7
Stafford Springs *U.S.A.* 41°57N 72°18W **313** E12
Staffordshire □ *U.K.* 52°53N 2°10W **168** E5
Stagnone *Italy* 37°53N 12°26E **200** E5
Stagnone di Marsala △
Italy 37°52N 12°26E **200** E5
Staines *U.K.* 51°26N 0°29W **169** F7
Stains *France* 48°57N 2°22E **134** A3
Stainz *Austria* 46°53N 15°17E **142** D1
Stakhanov *Ukraine* 48°35N 38°40E **189** H10
Stalać *Serbia* 43°43N 21°28E **202** C5
Stalden *Switz.* 46°14N 7°52E **198** C4
Stalin = Kuçovë *Albania* 40°47N 19°57E **202** F3
Stalin = Varna *Bulgaria* 43°13N 27°56E **203** C11
Stalin Pk. = Gerlachovský štít
Slovak Rep. 49°10N 20°7E **181** B13
Stalin Pk. = imeni Ismail Samani,
Pik *Tajikistan* 39°0N 72°2E **217** E8
Stalin Pk. = Musala
Bulgaria 42°13N 23°37E **202** D7
Stalinabad = Dushanbe
Tajikistan 38°33N 68°48E **217** E7
Stalingrad = Volgograd
Russia 48°40N 44°25E **191** F7
Staliniri = Tskhinvali
Georgia 42°14N 44°1E **191** J7
Stalinogorsk = Novomoskovsk
Russia 54°5N 38°15E **188** E9
Stalinogród = Katowice
Poland 50°17N 19°5E **185** H6
Stalinsk = Novokuznetsk
Russia 53°45N 87°10E **217** B11
Stalinstadt = Eisenhüttenstadt
Germany 52°9N 14°38E **178** C10
Stallarholmen *Sweden* 59°22N 17°12E **162** E10
Ställdalen *Sweden* 59°56N 14°56E **162** E8
Stalowa Wola *Poland* 50°34N 22°3E **185** H9
Stalybridge *U.K.* 53°28N 2°3W **168** D5
Stamford *Queens.,
Australia* 21°15S 143°46E **280** C3
Stamford *Lincs., U.K.* 52°39N 0°29W **169** E7
Stamford *Conn., U.S.A.* 41°3N 73°32W **313** E11
Stamford *Tex., U.S.A.* 32°57N 99°48W **314** E5
Stamford Hill *U.K.* 51°34N 0°4W **125** A3
Stammersdorf *Austria* 48°18N 16°24E **142** A2
Stamnes *Norway* 60°40N 5°45E **164** D2
Stamping Ground
U.S.A. 38°16N 84°41W **311** F12
Stampriet *Namibia* 24°20S 18°28E **270** B2
Stamps *U.S.A.* 33°22N 93°30W **314** E8
Stanberry *U.S.A.* 40°13N 94°35W **310** D2
Stančevo = Kalipetrovo
Bulgaria 44°5N 27°14E **203** B11
Standish *U.S.A.* 43°59N 83°57W **309** D12
Standerton *S. Africa* 26°55S 29°7E **271** C4
Standish *U.S.A.* 43°59N 83°57W **309** D12
Stanford *S. Africa* 34°26S 19°29E **270** E2
Stanford *Mont., U.S.A.* 47°9N 110°13W **304** C8
Stånga *Sweden* 57°17N 18°29E **163** G12
Stanger *S. Africa* 29°27S 31°14E **271** C5
Stangtsäben = Salpausselkä
Finland 61°3N 26°15E **188** B4
Stanhope *Vic., Australia* 36°27S 144°59E **283** C6
Stanhope *Iowa, U.S.A.* 42°17N 93°48W **310** D3
Stanimaka = Asenovgrad
Bulgaria 42°1N 24°51E **203** D8
Stanišić *Serbia* 45°56N 19°10E **182** E3
Stanislaus → *U.S.A.* 37°40N 121°14W **306** H5
Stanislav = Ivano-Frankivsk
Ukraine 48°40N 24°40E **183** B8
Stanisław = Ivano-Frankivsk
Ukraine 48°40N 24°40E **183** B8
Stanley *Tas., Australia* 40°46S 145°19E **281** G4
Stanley *Hong Kong, China* 22°13N 114°12E **122** B2

Stanley Falk. Is. 51°40S 59°51W 153 f
Stanley Durham, U.K. 54°53N 1°41W 168 C6
Stanley Idaho, U.S.A. 44°13N 114°56W 304 D6
Stanley N. Dak., U.S.A. 48°19N 102°23W 308 A2
Stanley N.Y., U.S.A. 42°48N 77°6W 312 D7
Stanley Falls = Boyoma, Chutes
  Dem. Rep. of the Congo 0°35N 25°23E 264 B5
Stanley Mission Canada 55°25N 104°33W 297 B8
Stanley Pen. China 22°12N 114°12E 122 B2
Stanley Pool = Malebo, Pool
  Africa 4°17S 15°20E 265 C3
Stanley Res. India 11°50N 77°40E 245 J3
Stanleyville = Kisangani
  Dem. Rep. of the Congo 0°35N 25°15E 268 B2
Stanmore U.K. 51°37N 0°18W 125 A2
Stannards U.S.A. 42°5N 77°55W 312 D7
Stanovoy Khrebet Russia 55°0N 130°0E 215 D14
Stanovoy Ra. = Stanovoy Khrebet
  Russia 55°0N 130°0E 215 D14
Stansmore Ra. Australia 21°23S 128°33E 278 D4
Stansted, London ✈ (STN)
  U.K. 51°54N 0°14E 169 F8
Stanthorpe Australia 28°36S 151°59E 281 D5
Stanton Ky., U.S.A. 37°54N 83°52W 311 G13
Stanton Tex., U.S.A. 32°8N 101°48W 314 E4
Stantsiya Regar = Tursunzoda
  Tajikistan 38°30N 68°14E 217 E7
Stanwood U.S.A. 41°50N 122°23W 306 B4
Staples Ont., Canada 42°10N 82°35W 312 D2
Staples Minn., U.S.A. 46°21N 94°48W 308 B6
Stapleton N.Y., U.S.A. 40°36N 74°5W 132 C1
Stapleton Nebr., U.S.A. 41°29N 100°31W 308 E3
Stąporków Poland 51°9N 20°31E 185 G7
Star City Canada 52°50N 104°20W 297 C8
Star Ferry Hong Kong, China 122 a2
Star Harbour
  Solomon Is. 10°47S 162°19E 287 N12
Star Lake U.S.A. 44°10N 75°2W 313 B9
Stará Ďala = Hurbanovo
  Slovak Rep. 47°51N 18°11E 181 D11
Stará Ľubovňa
  Slovak Rep. 49°18N 20°42E 181 B13
Stara Moravica Serbia 45°50N 19°30E 182 E4
Stara Pazova Serbia 44°58N 20°10E 182 F5
Stara Planina Bulgaria 43°15N 23°0E 202 C7
Stara Sil Ukraine 49°29N 22°58E 185 J9
Stará Turá Slovak Rep. 48°47N 17°42E 181 C10
Stara Ushytsya Ukraine 48°35N 27°8E 183 B12
Stara Zagora Bulgaria 42°26N 25°39E 203 D9
Stara Zagora □ Bulgaria 42°26N 25°39E 203 D9
Starachowice Poland 51°3N 21°2E 185 G8
Staraya Derevnya Russia 59°58N 30°15E 137 B1
Staraya Russa Russia 57°58N 31°23E 188 D6
Starbuck I. Kiribati 5°37S 155°55W 289 H12
Starchiojd Romania 45°19N 26°11E 183 C11
Starcke △ Australia 14°56S 145°2E 280 A4
Staré Město Czech Rep. 50°5N 14°25E 135 B2
Stare Miasto Warsaw, Poland 143 a2
Stargard in Pommern = Stargard
  Szczeciński Poland 53°20N 15°0E 184 E2
Stargard Szczeciński
  Poland 53°20N 15°0E 184 E2
Stårheim Norway 61°56N 5°40E 164 C2
Stari Bar Montenegro 42°7N 19°10E 202 D2
Stari Bečej = Bečej Serbia 45°36N 20°3E 182 E5
Stari Grad Croatia 43°10N 16°38E 199 E13
Stari Trg Slovenia 45°29N 15°7E 199 C12
Staritsa Russia 56°33N 34°55E 188 D8
Starke U.S.A. 29°57N 82°7W 316 F7
Starke, L. U.S.A. 28°34N 81°32W 133 A1
Starkville U.S.A. 33°28N 88°49W 315 E10
Starnberg Germany 48°0N 11°19E 179 H7
Starnberger See Germany 47°54N 11°19E 179 H7
Starobilsk Ukraine 49°16N 39°0E 189 H10
Starodub Russia 52°30N 32°50E 188 F7
Starogard Gdański Poland 53°59N 18°30E 184 E5
Starokonstantinov =
  Starokonstyantyniv
  Ukraine 49°48N 27°10E 177 D14
Starokonstyantyniv
  Ukraine 49°48N 27°10E 177 D14
Starokozache Ukraine 46°20N 29°59E 183 D14
Starominskaya Russia 46°33N 39°0E 191 G4
Staroshcherbinovskaya
  Russia 46°40N 38°53E 191 G4
Starrs Mill U.S.A. 33°19N 84°31W 316 B5
Start Pt. U.K. 50°13N 3°39W 169 G4
Stary Sącz Poland 49°33N 20°35E 185 J7
Staryy Biryuzyak Russia 44°46N 46°50E 191 H8
Staryy Chartoriysk
  Ukraine 51°15N 25°54E 177 C13
Staryy Krym Ukraine 45°3N 35°8E 189 K8
Staryy Margilan = Marghilon
  Uzbekistan 40°27N 71°42E 217 D8
Staryy Oskol Russia 51°19N 37°55E 189 G9
Staryy Sambir Ukraine 49°27N 22°59E 185 J9
Stassfurt Germany 51°51N 11°35E 178 D7
Staszów Poland 50°33N 21°10E 185 H8
State Center U.S.A. 42°1N 93°10W 310 B3
State College U.S.A. 40°48N 77°52W 312 F7
State Street U.S.A. 119 c2
Stateline U.S.A. 38°57N 119°56W 306 G7
Staten, I. = Estados, I. de Los
  Argentina 54°40S 64°30W 336 D4
Staten I. U.S.A. 40°35N 74°9W 313 F10
Staten Island Zoo U.S.A. 40°38N 74°6W 132 C1
Staten Islands Ferry Terminal
  U.S.A. 40°38N 74°4W 132 C1
Statenice Czech Rep. 50°9N 14°19E 135 B1
Statenville U.S.A. 30°42N 83°2W 316 E6
Statesboro U.S.A. 32°27N 81°47W 316 D8
Statesville U.S.A. 35°47N 80°53W 315 D14
Statham U.S.A. 33°58N 83°35W 316 B6
Stathelle Norway 59°3N 9°41E 164 E6
Statia = St. Eustatius
  W. Indies 17°20N 63°0W 322 a
Statue Square Hong Kong, China 122 c1
Stauffer U.S.A. 34°45N 119°3W 307 L7
Staunton Ill., U.S.A. 39°1N 89°47W 310 F7
Staunton Va., U.S.A. 38°9N 79°4W 309 F14
Stavanger = Rogaland □
  Norway 59°12N 6°20E 164 E3
Stavanger Norway 58°57N 5°40E 164 F2
Stavelot Belgium 50°23N 5°55E 170 D5
Stavern Norway 59°0N 10°1E 164 F7
Staveren Neths. 52°53N 5°22E 170 B5
Stavropol Russia 45°5N 42°0E 191 H6
Stavropol' Russia 47°20N 42°0E 191 G6
Stavros Cyprus 35°1N 32°38E 207 E11
Stavros Ithaki, Greece 38°27N 20°35E 207 C2
Stavros Kriti, Greece 35°12N 24°45E 207 E5
Stavros, Akra Greece 35°26N 24°58E 207 D5
Stavroupoli Greece 41°12N 24°45E 203 D8
Stawell Australia 37°5S 142°47E 282 D5
Stawell → Australia 20°20S 142°55E 280 C3
Stawiski Poland 53°22N 22°9E 184 E9
Stawiszyn Poland 51°56N 18°4E 185 G5
Stayner Canada 44°25N 80°5W 312 B4
Stayton U.S.A. 44°48N 122°48W 306 D2
Stazione Marittima, Basino della
  Venice, Italy 142 b1
Steamboat Springs
  U.S.A. 40°29N 106°50W 304 F10
Stean Norway 59°16N 8°33E 164 E5
Stebbins U.S.A. 63°31N 162°17W 303 E7

Steblevë Albania 41°23N 20°33E 202 E4
Stedelijk Museum Neths. 52°21N 4°52E 112 A2
Steele Ala., U.S.A. 33°56N 86°12W 316 B3
Steele N. Dak., U.S.A. 46°51N 99°55W 308 B4
Steele Creek Australia 37°44S 144°52E 128 A1
Steelton U.S.A. 40°14N 76°50W 312 F8
Steelville U.S.A. 37°58N 91°22W 310 G5
Steen River Canada 59°40N 117°12W 296 B5
Steenkool = Bintuni
  Indonesia 2°7S 133°32E 231 E8
Steenokkerzeel Belgium 50°55N 4°31E 116 A2
Steens Mt. U.S.A. 42°35N 118°40W 304 E4
Steenstrup Gletscher
  Greenland 75°15N 57°0W 154 B5
Steenwijk Neths. 52°47N 6°7E 170 B6
Steep Pt. Australia 26°8S 113°8E 279 E1
Steep Rock Canada 51°30N 98°48W 297 C9
Steer, L. U.S.A. 28°31N 81°30W 133 A2
Ştefan Vodă Moldova 46°27N 29°42E 183 D14
Ştefăneşti Romania 47°44N 27°15E 183 C12
Stefanie = Chew Bahir
  Ethiopia 4°40N 36°50E 257 G4
Stefanie L. = Chew Bahir
  Ethiopia 4°40N 36°50E 257 G4
Stefansson Bay Antarctica 67°20S 59°8E 151 C11
Stefansson I. Canada 73°20N 105°45W 295 C10
Stege Denmark 54°59N 12°18E 163 K6
Stegi = Siteki Swaziland 26°32S 31°58E 271 C5
Steglitz Germany 52°27N 13°19E 115 B2
Stegman = Artesia
  U.S.A. 32°51N 104°24W 305 K11
Ştei Romania 46°32N 22°27E 182 D6
Steiermark □ Austria 47°26N 15°0E 180 D8
Steigerwald Germany 49°44N 10°26E 179 F6
Steigerwald △ Germany 49°50N 10°30E 179 F6
Steilacoom U.S.A. 47°10N 122°36W 306 C4
Steilrandberge Namibia 17°45S 13°20E 270 A1
Stein = Kamnik Slovenia 46°14N 14°37E 199 B11
Steinbach Canada 49°32N 96°40W 297 D9
Steinfurt Germany 52°9N 7°20E 178 C3
Steinhatchee U.S.A. 29°40N 83°23W 316 F6
Steinhausen Namibia 21°49S 18°20E 270 B2
Steinheim Germany 51°51N 9°5E 178 D5
Steinhuder Meer Germany 52°29N 9°21E 178 C5
Steinhuder Meer △
  Germany 52°30N 9°16E 178 C5
Steinkjer Norway 64°1N 11°31E 160 D14
Steinkopf S. Africa 29°18S 17°43E 270 C2
Steinshamn Norway 62°47N 6°28E 164 B3
Stellarton Canada 45°32N 62°30W 299 C7
Stellenbosch S. Africa 33°58S 18°50E 270 D2
Stelvio, Paso dello Italy 46°32N 10°27E 198 B7
Stenay France 49°29N 5°12E 173 C12
Stendal Germany 52°36N 11°53E 178 C7
Stende Latvia 57°11N 22°33E 166 B4
Stenen Koraal Curaçao 12°10N 68°56W 322 g
Stenhamra Sweden 59°20N 17°41E 162 E11
Stenhuvud △ Sweden 55°39N 14°15E 163 J8
Stenstorp Sweden 58°16N 13°45E 163 F7
Stenungsund Sweden 58°6N 11°50E 163 F5
Steornabhaigh = Stornoway
  U.K. 58°13N 6°23W 167 C2
Stepanakert = Xankändi
  Azerbaijan 39°52N 46°49E 213 C12
Stepanavan Armenia 41°1N 44°23E 191 K7
Stepaside Ireland 53°15N 6°12W 120 B2
Stephansdom Vienna, Austria 142 b2
Stephens, C. N.Z. 40°42S 173°57E 285 A8
Stephens Creek Australia 31°50S 141°30E 282 A4
Stephens I. B.C., Canada 54°10N 130°45W 296 C2
Stephens I. N.Z. 40°40S 174°1E 285 A9
Stephens L. Canada 56°32N 95°0W 297 B9
Stephenville Nfld. & L.,
  Canada 48°31N 58°35W 299 C8
Stephenville Tex., U.S.A. 32°13N 98°12W 314 E5
Stepnica Poland 53°38N 14°36E 184 E1
Stepnogorsk Kazakhstan 52°21N 71°53E 217 D8
Stepnoi = Elista Russia 46°16N 44°14E 191 G7
Steppe Asia 50°0N 50°0E 210 C7
Steps Pt. Amer. Samoa 14°23S 170°45W 302 f
Sterea Ellas □ Greece 38°50N 23°0E 204 C4
Sterkstroom S. Africa 31°32S 26°32E 270 D4
Sterling Alaska, U.S.A. 60°32N 150°46W 303 F10
Sterling Colo., U.S.A. 40°37N 103°13W 304 F12
Sterling Ill., U.S.A. 41°48N 89°42W 310 C7
Sterling Kans., U.S.A. 38°13N 98°12W 308 F4
Sterling City U.S.A. 31°51N 101°0W 314 F4
Sterling Heights U.S.A. 42°35N 83°2W 311 B13
Sterling Park U.S.A. 37°41N 122°27W 136 B2
Sterling Run U.S.A. 41°25N 78°12W 312 E6
Sterlitamak Russia 53°40N 56°0E 186 D10
Sternberg Germany 53°42N 11°50E 178 B7
Šternberk Czech Rep. 49°45N 17°15E 181 B10
Sternes Greece 35°30N 24°9E 207 E5
Sterzing = Vipiteno Italy 46°54N 11°26E 198 B8
Stettin = Szczecin Poland 53°27N 14°27E 184 E1
Stettiner Haff Germany 53°47N 14°15E 178 B10
Stettler Canada 52°19N 112°40W 296 C6
Steubenville U.S.A. 40°22N 80°37W 312 F4
Stevenage U.K. 51°55N 0°13W 169 F7
Stevens Point U.S.A. 44°31N 89°34W 308 C9
Stevens Pottery U.S.A. 32°57N 83°17W 316 C6
Stevens Village U.S.A. 66°1N 149°6W 303 C10
Stevenson → Australia 27°6S 135°33E 280 A1
Stevenson L. Canada 53°55N 96°0W 297 C9
Stevensville U.S.A. 46°30N 114°5W 304 C6
Stevns Klint Denmark 55°17N 12°28E 163 J6
Steward U.S.A. 41°51N 89°1W 310 C7
Stewardson U.S.A. 39°16N 88°38W 311 E8
Stewart B.C., Canada 55°56N 129°57W 296 B3
Stewart Nev., U.S.A. 39°5N 119°46W 306 F7
Stewart → Canada 63°19N 139°26W 294 E4
Stewart, C. Australia 11°57S 134°56E 280 A1
Stewart, I. Chile 54°50S 71°15W 336 D2
Stewart I. N.Z. 46°58S 167°54E 285 J2
Stewart Point U.S.A. 38°39N 123°24W 306 G3
Stewartville U.S.A. 43°51N 92°29W 310 D8
Stewiacke Canada 45°9N 63°22W 299 C7
Steynsburg S. Africa 31°15S 25°49E 270 D4
Steyr Austria 48°3N 14°25E 180 C7
Steyr → Austria 48°3N 14°25E 180 C7
Steytlerville S. Africa 33°17S 24°19E 270 D3
Stia Italy 43°48N 11°42E 199 E8
Stickleigh udde Sweden 59°23N 18°6E 139 a2
Stickney U.S.A. 41°49N 87°46W 119 C2
Stigler U.S.A. 35°15N 95°8W 311 H2
Stigliano Italy 40°24N 16°14E 201 B9
Stigtomta Sweden 58°47N 16°48E 163 F10
Stikine → Canada 56°40N 132°30W 296 B2
Stilfontein S. Africa 26°51S 26°50E 270 D4
Stilida Greece 38°55N 22°47E 204 C4
Stillorgan Ireland 53°17N 6°11W 120 B2
Stillwater N.Z. 42°36S 171°22E 285 B5
Stillwater N.Y., U.S.A. 42°55N 73°41W 313 C11
Stillwater Okla., U.S.A. 36°7N 97°4W 314 C6
Stillwater Range U.S.A. 39°50N 118°5W 304 G4
Stillwater Res. U.S.A. 43°54N 75°3W 313 C9
Štilo, Pta. Italy 38°26N 16°35E 201 D9

Štip Macedonia 41°42N 22°10E 202 E6
Štira Greece 38°9N 24°14E 204 C6
Stirling Ont., Canada 44°18N 77°33W 312 B7
Stirling N.Z. 46°14S 169°49E 285 G4
Stirling Stirling, U.K. 56°8N 3°57W 167 E5
Stirling □ U.K. 56°12N 4°18W 167 E4
Stirling Ra. Australia 34°23S 118°0E 279 F2
Stirling Range △
  Australia 34°26S 118°20E 279 F2
Stittsville Canada 45°15N 75°55W 313 A9
Stjernoya Norway 70°20N 22°40E 160 A20
Stjordalshalsen Norway 63°29N 10°51E 164 A7
Stock Island U.S.A. 24°32N 81°34W 317 L8
Stocka Sweden 61°53N 17°20E 162 C11
Stockaryd Sweden 57°19N 14°36E 163 G8
Stockbridge U.S.A. 42°27N 84°11W 311 B12
Stockbridge Mich.,
  U.S.A. 42°27N 84°11W 311 B12
Stockerau Austria 48°24N 16°12E 181 C9
Stockholm Sweden 59°19N 18°4E 162 E12
Stockholm Arlanda ✈ (ARN)
  Sweden 59°41N 17°56E 139 A1
Stockholms län □
  Sweden 59°30N 18°20E 162 E12
Stockport U.K. 53°25N 2°9W 168 D5
Stocksbridge U.K. 53°29N 1°35W 168 D6
Stocksund Sweden 59°23N 18°3E 139 A2
Stockton Calif., U.S.A. 37°58N 121°17W 306 H5
Stockton Ill., U.S.A. 42°21N 90°1W 310 B6
Stockton Kans., U.S.A. 39°26N 99°16W 308 F4
Stockton Mo., U.S.A. 37°42N 93°48W 310 G3
Stockton-on-Tees U.K. 54°35N 1°19W 168 C6
Stockton-on-Tees □ U.K. 54°35N 1°19W 168 C6
Stockton Plateau U.S.A. 30°50N 102°30W 314 F3
Stoczek Łukowski Poland 51°58N 21°58E 185 G8
Stöde Sweden 62°28N 16°35E 162 B10
Stöðvarfjörður Iceland 64°49N 13°52W 155 C13
Stodůlky Czech Rep. 50°3N 14°19E 135 B1
Stoeng Treng Cambodia 13°31N 105°58E 236 F5
Stoer, Pt. of U.K. 58°16N 5°23W 167 C3
Stogovo Macedonia 41°31N 20°38E 202 E4
Stoholm Denmark 56°30N 9°8E 163 H3
Stoke U.K. 41°10S 173°14E 285 B8
Stoke Newington U.K. 51°33N 0°4W 125 A3
Stoke-on-Trent U.K. 53°1N 2°11W 168 D5
Stoke-on-Trent □ U.K. 53°1N 2°11W 168 D5
Stokes □ U.S.A. 36°18N 81°28W 312 B3
Stokes Bay Canada 45°0N 81°28W 312 B3
Stokes Pt. Australia 40°10S 143°56E 281 G3
Stokes Ra. Australia 15°50S 130°50E 278 C5
Stokksnes Iceland 64°14N 14°58E 155 D13
Stokkseyri Iceland 64°14N 14°54E 160 B16
Stokmarknes Norway 68°34N 14°54E 160 B16
Stolac Bos.-H. 43°5N 17°59E 202 C1
Stolbovoy, Ostrov
  Russia 74°44N 135°14E 215 B14
Stolbtsy = Stowbtsy
  Belarus 53°30N 26°43E 177 B14
Stolin Belarus 51°53N 26°50E 177 C14
Stöllet Sweden 60°26N 13°16E 162 D7
Stolnici Romania 44°31N 24°48E 183 F9
Stolp = Słupsk Poland 54°30N 17°3E 184 D4
Stolpmünde = Ustka
  Poland 54°35N 16°55E 184 D3
Stomio Greece 35°21N 23°32E 207 E4
Ston Croatia 42°51N 17°43E 199 F14
Stone Canyon Res.
  U.S.A. 34°6N 118°27W 126 B2
Stone Mountain U.S.A. 33°49N 84°10W 316 B5
Stone Zoo U.S.A. 42°28N 71°6W 116 A2
Stoneboro U.S.A. 41°20N 80°7W 312 E4
Stonebridge U.K. 51°32N 0°16W 125 A2
Stoneham U.S.A. 42°29N 71°5W 116 A2
Stonehaven U.K. 56°59N 2°12W 167 E6
Stonehenge Queens.,
  Australia 24°22S 143°17E 280 C3
Stonehenge Wilts., U.S.A. 51°9N 1°45W 169 F6
Stonewall Canada 50°10N 97°19W 297 C9
Stoneyfjorden Norway 61°26N 5°10E 164 C2
Stonington U.S.A. 39°44N 89°12W 310 E7
Stony Brook Res. U.S.A. 42°15N 71°8W 116 B3
Stony Creek U.S.A. 41°38N 71°41W 119 C2
Stony Hill Jamaica 18°5N 76°48W 320 a
Stony I. U.S.A. 43°53N 76°19W 313 C8
Stony L., Man., Canada 58°51N 98°40W 297 B9
Stony L. Ont., Canada 44°30N 78°5W 312 B6
Stony Point U.S.A. 41°14N 73°59W 313 E11
Stony Pt. U.S.A. 43°50N 76°18W 313 C8
Stony Rapids Canada 59°16N 105°50W 297 B7
Stony River U.S.A. 61°47N 156°35W 303 F8
Stony Tunguska = Tunguska,
  Podkamennaya →
  Russia 61°50N 90°13E 215 C10
Stonyford U.S.A. 39°23N 122°33W 306 F4
Stopnica Poland 50°27N 20°57E 185 H7
Storå Sweden 59°42N 15°6E 162 E9
Storå → Denmark 56°20N 8°19E 163 H2
Stora Gla Sweden 59°30N 12°30E 162 E6
Stora Le Sweden 59°5N 11°55E 162 E5
Stora Lulevatten Sweden 67°10N 19°30E 160 C18
Stora Värtan Sweden 59°25N 18°7E 139 A2
Stóra-Vatnshorn Iceland 65°4N 21°33E 155 D4
Storavan Sweden 65°45N 18°10E 160 D18
Stord Norway 59°52N 5°23E 164 E2
Stordalen Norway 62°23N 7°0E 164 B4
Store Bælt Denmark 55°20N 11°0E 163 J4
Store Hareskov Denmark 55°46N 12°23E 118 A2
Store Heddinge Denmark 55°18N 12°23E 163 J6
Store Jukleggi = Høgeloft
  Norway 61°33N 8°12E 164 C5
Store Koldewey Greenland 76°30N 19°0W 154 B9
Store Magleby Denmark 55°35N 12°35E 118 B3
Store Mosse △ Sweden 57°18N 13°55E 163 G7
Store Sotra Norway 60°18N 5°4E 164 D1
Storebro Sweden 57°35N 15°52E 163 G9
Støren Norway 63°3N 10°18E 164 A7
Storerikvollen Norway 63°7N 11°58E 164 A8
Storfjellsætra Norway 61°40N 10°0E 164 C7
Storfjorden Norway 62°25N 6°35E 164 B3
Storforshei Norway 66°23N 14°17E 162 G8
Storholmen Sweden 59°23N 18°8E 139 A2
Storico Navale, Museo Venice, Italy 142 b3
Storidalur Iceland 63°38N 19°57W 155 C6
Storinupur Iceland 64°3N 20°10W 155 C6
Storkerson Pen.
  Canada 72°30N 106°30W 294 C10
Storm B. Australia 43°10S 147°30E 281 G4
Storm Lake U.S.A. 42°39N 95°13W 310 B2
Stormberge S. Africa 31°16S 26°17E 270 D4
Stormsrivier S. Africa 33°59S 23°52E 270 D3
Stornoway U.K. 58°13N 6°23W 167 C2
Storo Italy 45°51N 10°35E 198 C7
Storozhinets = Storozhynets
  Ukraine 48°14N 25°45E 183 B10
Storozhynets Ukraine 48°14N 25°45E 183 B10
Storr, The U.K. 57°30N 6°13W 167 D2
Storrs U.S.A. 41°49N 72°15E 169 F5
Storsjøen Hedmark,
  Norway 60°20N 11°40E 164 C8
Storsjøen Hedmark,
  Norway 61°30N 11°14E 164 C8

Storsjön Gävleborg,
  Sweden 60°35N 16°45E 162 D10
Storsjön Jämtland, Sweden 63°9N 14°30E 162 A8
Storsjön Jämtland, Sweden 63°9N 14°30E 162 A8
Storsolnkletten Norway 61°59N 10°16E 164 C7
Storstrømmen Greenland 76°17N 22°25W 154 B8
Storuman Sweden 65°13N 16°50E 160 D17
Storuman, L. Sweden 65°13N 16°50E 160 D17
Storuvellir Iceland 65°30N 17°29W 155 B9
Storvätteshågna Sweden 62°6N 12°30E 162 B6
Storviglen Norway 62°32N 12°2E 164 B9
Storvik Sweden 60°35N 16°33E 162 D10
Storvreta Sweden 59°58N 17°44E 162 E11
Story City U.S.A. 42°11N 93°36W 310 B3
Stouffville Canada 43°58N 79°15W 312 C5
Stoughton Sask., Canada 49°40N 103°0W 297 D8
Stoughton Wis., U.S.A. 42°55N 89°13W 310 B8
Stour → Dorset, U.K. 50°43N 1°47W 169 G6
Stour → Kent, U.K. 51°18N 1°22E 169 F9
Stour → Suffolk, U.K. 51°57N 1°4E 169 F9
Stout L. Canada 52°0N 94°40W 297 C10
Stove Pipe Wells Village
  U.S.A. 36°35N 117°11W 307 J9
Støvring Denmark 56°54N 9°50E 163 H3
Stow U.S.A. 41°10N 81°27W 312 E3
Stowbtsy Belarus 53°30N 26°43E 177 B14
Stowmarket U.K. 52°12N 1°0E 169 E9
Stoyka Russia 59°57N 30°25E 137 B2
Strabane U.K. 54°50N 7°27W 166 B4
Stracin Macedonia 42°13N 22°2E 202 D6
Stradella Italy 45°5N 9°18E 198 C6
Strahan Australia 42°9S 145°20E 281 G4
Straiton U.K. 55°33N 3°9W 167 E5
Strajitsa Bulgaria 43°14N 25°58E 203 C9
Strakonice Czech Rep. 49°15N 13°53E 180 B5
Straldzha Bulgaria 42°35N 26°40E 203 D10
Stralsund Germany 54°18N 13°4E 178 A9
Strand Western Cape,
  S. Africa 34°9S 18°48E 270 D2
Strand London, U.K. 125 b4
Stranda Møre og Romsdal,
  Norway 62°19N 6°58E 164 B3
Stranda Nord-Trøndelag,
  Norway 63°33N 10°14E 160 E14
Strandasýsla Iceland 65°45N 21°45W 155 B5
Strandby Denmark 57°30N 10°29E 163 G4
Strandfontein S. Africa 34°4S 18°34E 116 B2
Strangford S. Africa 30°25S 27°37W 166 B6
Strängnäs Sweden 59°23N 17°2E 162 E11
Stranorlar Ireland 54°48N 7°46W 166 B4
Stranraer U.K. 54°54N 5°1W 167 G3
Strasbourg Sask., Canada 51°4N 104°55W 297 C8
Strasbourg Bas-Rhin,
  France 48°35N 7°42E 173 C14
Strasburg Germany 53°30N 13°43E 178 B9
Strășeni Moldova 47°8N 28°36E 183 C13
Strasnice Czech Rep. 50°5N 14°28E 135 B2
Stråssa Sweden 59°44N 15°12E 162 E9
Strassburg = Aiud
  Romania 46°19N 23°44E 183 D8
Strasstrassbinding Germany 48°6N 11°41E 113 A3
Stratford N.S.W., Australia 32°7S 151°55E 283 B9
Stratford Vic., Australia 37°59S 147°7E 283 D7
Stratford Ont., Canada 43°23N 81°0W 312 C4
Stratford N.Z. 39°20S 174°19E 284 F3
Stratford Calif., U.S.A. 36°11N 119°49W 306 J7
Stratford Conn., U.S.A. 41°12N 73°8W 313 E11
Stratford Tex., U.S.A. 36°20N 102°4W 314 C3
Stratford-upon-Avon U.K. 52°12N 1°42W 169 E6
Strath Spey U.K. 57°9N 3°49W 167 D5
Strathalbyn Australia 35°13S 138°53E 282 C3
Strathaven U.K. 55°40N 4°5W 167 F4
Strathcona △ Canada 49°38N 125°40W 296 D3
Strathfield Australia 33°52S 151°5E 139 B1
Strathmore Alta., Canada 51°5N 113°18W 296 C6
Strathmore Angus, U.K. 56°37N 3°7W 167 E5
Strathmore Calif., U.S.A. 36°9N 119°4W 306 J7
Strathnaver Canada 53°20N 122°33W 296 C4
Strathpeffer U.K. 57°35N 4°32W 167 D4
Strathroy Canada 42°58N 81°38W 312 D3
Strathy Pt. U.K. 58°36N 4°1W 167 C4
Strattanville U.S.A. 41°12N 79°19W 312 E5
Stratton U.S.A. 45°8N 70°26W 313 A14
Stratton Mt. U.S.A. 43°4N 72°55W 313 C12
Straubing Germany 48°52N 12°34E 179 G8
Straumnes Iceland 66°26N 23°8W 155 A3
Strausberg Germany 52°35N 13°54E 178 C9
Strawberry → U.S.A. 40°10N 110°24W 304 F8
Strawberry Point U.S.A. 42°41N 91°32W 310 B5
Strážnice Czech Rep. 48°54N 17°19E 181 C10
Streaky B. Australia 32°48S 134°13E 281 E1
Streaky Bay Australia 32°51S 134°18E 281 E1
Streatham U.K. 51°25N 0°7W 125 B3
Streatham Vale U.K. 51°24N 0°8W 125 B3
Streator U.S.A. 41°8N 88°50W 311 D8
Středočeský □ Czech Rep. 49°55N 14°30E 180 B7
Streetsboro U.S.A. 41°14N 81°21W 312 E3
Streetsville Canada 43°35N 79°42W 312 C5
Strehaia Romania 44°37N 23°10E 183 F8
Strehlen = Strzelin Poland 50°46N 17°2E 185 H4
Strelcha Bulgaria 42°30N 24°19E 203 D8
Streng → Cambodia 13°12N 103°37E 236 F4
Stresa Italy 45°52N 8°28E 198 C5
Střešovice Czech Rep. 50°5N 14°23E 135 B2
Streymoy Faroe Is. 62°8N 7°5W 160 E9
Strezhevoy Russia 60°42N 77°34E 214 C8
Stříbro Czech Rep. 49°44N 13°0E 180 B4
Strickland → Papua N. G. 7°35S 141°36E 286 D1
Striegau = Strzegom
  Poland 50°58N 16°20E 185 H3
Strilky Ukraine 49°25N 23°3E 185 J9
Strimonas → Greece 40°46N 23°51E 202 F7
Strip, The U.S.A. 36°7N 115°10W 124 B2
Střížkov Czech Rep. 50°8N 14°28E 135 B2
Stroeder Argentina 40°12S 62°37W 336 F4
Strofades Greece 37°15N 21°0E 204 D3
Strokestown Ireland 53°47N 8°5W 166 C3
Stroma Ethiopia 58°41N 3°7W 167 C5
Strombe-Bever Belgium 50°54N 4°21E 116 A2
Stromberg-Heuchelberg △
  Germany 49°8N 8°50E 179 F4
Stromboli Italy 38°47N 15°13E 201 D8
Stromeferry U.K. 57°21N 5°33W 167 D3
Stromness U.K. 58°58N 3°17W 167 C5
Stromsbruk Sweden 61°52N 17°18E 162 C11
Strömsnäsbruk Sweden 56°35N 13°45E 163 H6
Strömstad Sweden 58°56N 11°10E 163 F5
Strömsund Sweden 63°51N 15°33E 160 E17
Stronghurst U.S.A. 40°45N 90°55W 310 D6
Stronsay U.K. 59°7N 2°38W 167 B6
Strongili Greece 35°13N 26°40E 207 E8
Strongoli Italy 39°16N 17°3E 201 C10
Stronie Śląskie Poland 50°18N 16°50E 185 H3
Stronsay U.K. 59°7N 2°38W 167 B6
Strood U.K. 51°23N 0°28E 169 F8
Stroud Road Australia 32°18S 151°57E 283 B9
Stroud U.K. 51°45N 2°13W 169 F5
Stroudsburg U.S.A. 40°59N 75°12W 313 F9
Stroumbi Cyprus 34°53N 32°29E 207 F8

Sucuriú → Brazil 20°47S 51°38W 331 E7
Sucy-en-Brie France 48°46N 2°31E 134 B4
Sud □ Cameroon 2°30N 11°45E 263 D7
Sud, Pte. Comoros Is. 11°53S 43°29E 272 a
Sud, Pte. du Canada 49°3N 62°14W 299 C7
Sud-Kivu □
  Dem. Rep. of the Congo 3°0S 28°30E 268 C2
Sud-Ouest □ Cameroon 5°25N 9°20E 263 D6
Sud Ouest, Pte. Mauritius 20°28S 57°18E 272 e
Suda → Russia 59°0N 37°40E 188 C9
Sudak Ukraine 44°51N 34°57E 189 K8
Sudan ■ Africa 15°0N 30°0E 257 E3
Sudan U.S.A. 34°4N 102°31W 314 D3
Sudan ■ Africa 15°0N 30°0E 257 E3
Sudbury Ont., Canada 46°30N 81°0W 298 C3
Sudbury U.K. 52°2N 0°45E 169 E8
Sudd South Sudan 8°20N 30°0E 257 G3
Suddie Guyana 7°8N 58°29W 329 B6
Sudeifel =
  Deutsch-Luxemburgischer △
  Germany 49°58N 6°12E 179 F2
Süderbrarup Germany 54°38N 9°45E 178 A5
Süderlügum Germany 54°52N 8°54E 178 A4
Süderoogsand Germany 54°27N 8°28E 178 A4
Sudeten Mts. = Sudety
  Europe 50°20N 16°45E 181 A9
Sudety Europe 50°20N 16°45E 181 A9
Súðavík Iceland 66°2N 23°0W 155 A3
Súðheide △ Germany 52°46N 10°10E 178 C6
Suður-múlasýsla Iceland 65°0N 14°30W 155 C12
Suður-þingeyjarsýsla
  Iceland 65°30N 17°0W 155 B8
Suðureyri Iceland 66°7N 23°32W 155 A3
Suðurland □ Iceland 63°50N 19°30W 155 C7
Suðurnes □ Iceland 63°55N 22°30W 155 D3
Suðuroy Færoe Is. 61°32N 6°50W 160 F9
Sudi Tanzania 10°11S 39°57E 269 E4
Sudirman, Pegunungan
  Indonesia 4°30S 137°0E 231 E9
Sudiți Romania 44°35N 27°38E 183 F12
Sudogda Russia 55°55N 40°50E 188 C12
Sudong, Pulau Singapore 1°13N 103°44E 237 d
Sudostroy = Severodvinsk
  Russia 64°27N 39°58E 186 B6
Sudova Vyshnya Ukraine 49°46N 23°22E 185 J10
Sudzha Russia 51°14N 35°17E 189 G8
Sue → South Sudan 7°41N 28°3E 257 G2
Sue, L. U.S.A. 28°34N 81°21W 133 A2
Sueca Spain 39°12N 0°21W 191 C5
Suedinenie Bulgaria 42°16N 24°33E 203 D8
Suemez I. U.S.A. 55°15N 133°20W 296 D2
Sueyoshi = Soo Japan 31°40N 131°5E 222 F3
Suez, G. of = Suweis, Khalig el
  Egypt 28°40N 33°0E 256 J8
Suez Canal = Suweis, Qanâ es
  Egypt 31°0N 32°20E 256 H8
Suffield Canada 50°12N 111°10W 296 C6
Suffolk U.S.A. 36°44N 76°35W 309 G15
Suffolk □ U.K. 52°16N 1°0E 169 E9
Şufian Iran 38°16N 45°58E 213 C11
Suga-no-Sen Japan 35°25N 134°25E 222 B6
Sugag Romania 45°47N 23°37E 183 E8
Sugaing = Sagaing Burma 21°52N 95°59E 241 E5
Sugamo Japan 35°44N 139°43E 146 C3
Sugar → U.S.A. 42°26N 89°12W 310 B7
Sugar Cr. → Ill., U.S.A. 40°9N 89°36E 310 E7
Sugar Cr. → Ind., U.S.A. 39°51N 87°21W 311 E9
Sugar Grove U.S.A. 41°59N 79°20W 312 E5
Sugar Hill U.S.A. 34°6N 84°2W 316 A5
Sugar Loaf Mt. = Açúcar, Pão de
  Brazil 22°56S 43°9W 328 H6
Sugar Loaf Pt. St. Helena 15°54S 5°42W 153 h
Sugarcreek U.S.A. 41°25N 79°52W 312 E5
Sugarive → India 26°16N 86°24E 243 F12
Sugbai Passage Phil. 5°22N 120°33E 233 c
Suge Japan 35°37N 139°32E 146 D2
Sughd □ Tajikistan 40°0N 69°0E 217 E7
Sugihwaras Indonesia 4°1S 103°46E 234 C2
Suginami Japan 35°42N 139°37E 146 C3
Suğla Gölü Turkey 37°20N 32°0E 212 D5
Sugluk = Salluit Canada 62°14N 75°38W 295 E16
Sugō Japan 34°30N 139°33E 146 E2
Sugun China 39°22N 76°47E 217 F2
Suha Reke = Therandë
  Kosovo 42°21N 20°50E 202 D5
Suhaia, Lacul Romania 43°45N 25°15E 183 G10
Şuḩār Oman 24°20N 56°40E 247 E8
Suhbaatar Mongolia 50°17N 106°10E 218 A10
Sühbaatar □ Mongolia 46°30N 113°35E 218 B9
Suheli Par India 10°5N 72°17E 245 J1
Suhl Germany 50°36N 10°42E 179 E6
Şuhut Turkey 38°31N 30°32E 205 C12
Sui Pakistan 28°37N 69°19E 244 F3
Sui Xian = Suizhou China 31°42N 113°50E 226 B6
Suiá Missu → Brazil 11°13S 53°15W 331 C7
Šuica Bos.-H. 43°52N 17°11E 182 G2
Suichang China 28°29N 119°15E 229 C12
Suichuan China 26°20N 114°32E 229 D10
Suide China 37°30N 110°12E 226 F6
Suifenhe China 44°25N 131°10E 227 B16
Suihua China 46°32N 126°55E 227 B14
Suijiang China 28°37N 103°59E 228 C4
Suining Hunan, China 26°35N 110°10E 229 D8
Suining Jiangsu, China 33°56N 117°58E 227 H9
Suining Sichuan, China 30°26N 105°35E 228 B5
Suippes France 49°8N 4°32E 173 C11
Suir → Ireland 52°16N 7°9W 166 D4
Suisse = Switzerland ■
  Europe 46°30N 8°0E 179 J4
Suisun City U.S.A. 38°15N 122°2W 306 G4
Suita Japan 34°45N 135°32E 223 G7
Suitland U.S.A. 38°50N 76°55W 143 B3
Suixi China 21°19N 110°18E 228 G6
Suiyang Guizhou, China 27°58N 107°18E 228 D6
Suiyang Heilongjiang,
  China 44°30N 130°56E 227 B16
Suizhong China 40°21N 120°20E 227 D11
Suizhou China 31°42N 113°50E 226 B6
Sujangarh India 27°42N 74°31E 242 F6
Sujiatun China 41°39N 123°20E 227 D12
Sujica Bos.-H. 43°52N 17°11E 182 G2
Sukabumi Indonesia 6°56S 106°50E 234 D4
Sukadana Kalimantan Barat,
  Indonesia 1°10S 110°0E 235 C4
Sukadana Lampung,
  Indonesia 5°5S 105°33E 235 D4
Sukagawa Japan 37°17N 140°23E 221 F10
Sukaraja Indonesia 8°30S 113°23E 234 C2
Sukarnapura = Jayapura
  Indonesia 2°28S 140°38E 231 E10
Sukarno, Puntjak = Jaya, Puncak
  Indonesia 3°57S 137°17E 231 E9
Sukawati Indonesia 8°35S 115°17E 231 K18
Sukch'ŏn N. Korea 39°22N 125°35E 224 C2
Sukhindol Bulgaria 43°11N 25°10E 203 C9

Tabubil Papua N. G. 5°20S 141°15E 286 C1
Tabuenca Spain 41°42N 1°33W 196 D3
Tabuk Phil. 17°24N 121°25E 232 C3
Tabūk Si. Arabia 28°23N 36°36E 251 K7
Tabūk □ Si. Arabia 27°40N 36°50E 246 E3
Tabunifi Micronesia 9°28N 138°4E 287 S16
Taburno-Camposauro ⌂ Italy 41°8N 14°37E 201 A7
Tabwemasana, Mt. Vanuatu 15°20S 166°44E 287 E4
Täby Sweden 59°26N 18°2E 139 A2
Tacámbaro de Codallos Mexico 19°14N 101°28W 318 D4
Tacarigua Trin. & Tob. 10°38N 61°22W 323 t
Tacarigua Venezuela 11°3N 63°54W 329 a
Tacariqua, Laguna de Venezuela 10°15N 65°50W 328 A4
Tacheng Xinjiang Uygur, China 46°40N 82°58E 217 C10
Tacheng Taiwan 23°51N 120°19E 225 C2
Tach'i Taiwan 24°53N 121°17E 225 B3
Tachia Taiwan 24°25N 120°28E 225 B2
Tachia Hsi → Taiwan 24°20N 120°33E 225 B3
Tachibana-Wan Japan 32°45N 130°7E 222 E2
Tachikawa Japan 35°42N 139°25E 223 B11
Tachilek Burma 20°26N 99°52E 236 B2
Tach'ing Shan = Daqing Shan China 40°40N 111°0E 226 D6
Táchira □ Venezuela 8°7N 72°15W 328 B3
Tachiumet Libya 26°19N 10°3E 258 C2
Tachoshui Taiwan 24°20N 121°44E 225 B3
Tachov Czech Rep. 49°47N 12°39E 180 B5
Tácina → Italy 38°57N 16°55E 201 D9
Tacloban Phil. 11°15N 124°58E 233 F5
Tacna Peru 18°0S 70°20W 330 D3
Tacna □ Peru 17°40S 70°20W 330 D3
Tacoma U.S.A. 47°14N 122°26W 306 C4
Tacopaya = Zudañez Bolivia 19°6S 64°44W 331 D5
Tacuarembó Uruguay 31°45S 56°0W 335 C4
Tacuba Mexico 19°26N 99°11W 128 B1
Tacubaya Mexico 19°24N 99°10W 128 B1
Tacurong Phil. 6°40N 124°41E 233 H5
Tacutu = Takutu → Guyana 3°30N 60°29W 329 C5
Tada-u Burma 21°49N 95°58E 241 E5
Tadahadi Solomon Is. 10°18S 161°35E 287 N11
Tademaït, Plateau du Algeria 28°30N 2°30E 261 C5
Tādepallegudem India 16°50N 81°30E 244 F5
Tadéra Niger 20°29N 8°18E 261 D6
Tadine N. Cal. 21°33S 167°52E 288 d
Tadio, L. Ivory C. 5°10N 5°15W 262 D3
Tadjerdjeri, O. → Algeria 26°0N 8°0E 261 C6
Tadjerouna Algeria 33°31N 2°3E 261 B5
Tadjettaret, O. → Algeria 21°20N 7°22E 261 D6
Tadjmout Laghouat, Algeria 33°52N 2°30E 261 B5
Tadjmout Saoura, Algeria 25°37N 3°48E 261 C5
Tadjoura Djibouti 11°50N 42°55E 257 E5
Tadjoura, Golfe de Djibouti 11°50N 43°0E 257 E5
Tadla-Azilal □ Morocco 32°0N 6°30W 260 B3
Tadmor N.Z. 41°27S 172°45E 285 B7
Tadoba △ India 20°30N 78°20E 244 D4
Tadotsu Japan 34°16N 133°45E 222 C5
Tadoule L. Canada 58°36N 98°20W 297 B9
Tadoussac Canada 48°11N 69°42W 299 C6
Tadpatri India 14°55N 78°1E 245 G4
Tadrés ⌂ Niger 16°0N 7°10E 263 B6
Tadzhikistan = Tajikistan ■ Asia 38°30N 70°0E 217 E8
Tae-an S. Korea 36°45N 126°17E 224 D3
Tae-an △ S. Korea 36°40N 126°0E 224 D3
Taebaek S. Korea 37°10N 128°59E 224 D4
Taebaeksan S. Korea 37°5N 128°54E 224 D4
T'aebaeksanmaek S. Korea 37°40N 128°50E 224 D4
Taedong-gang → N. Korea 38°41N 125°15E 224 C2
Taedong-man N. Korea 38°4N 125°7E 224 C2
Taegu = Daegu S. Korea 35°50N 128°37E 224 E4
Taegwan N. Korea 40°13N 125°12E 224 B2
Taehung N. Korea 40°5N 126°56E 224 B3
Taehwa-do N. Korea 39°26N 124°36E 224 C2
Taejŏn = Daejeon S. Korea 36°20N 127°28E 224 D3
Tælavåg Norway 60°15N 4°58E 164 D1
Taen, Ko Thailand 9°22N 99°57E 237 b
Tafalla Spain 42°30N 1°41W 196 C3
Tafar South Sudan 6°52N 28°15E 257 F2
Tafassasset, O. → Algeria 22°0N 9°57E 261 D6
Tafelbaai = Table B. S. Africa 33°35S 18°25E 118 A1
Tafelberg Curaçao 12°4N 68°50W 322 g
Tafelney, C. Morocco 31°3N 9°51W 260 B3
Tafermaar Indonesia 6°47S 134°10E 231 F8
Taffermit Morocco 29°37N 9°15W 260 C3
Tafi Viejo Argentina 26°43S 65°17W 334 B2
Tafīhān Iran 29°25N 52°39E 247 D7
Tafilalet Morocco 31°20N 4°45W 260 B4
Tafiré Ivory C. 9°4N 5°4W 262 D3
Tafjord Norway 62°14N 7°24E 164 B4
Tafnidilt Morocco 28°47N 10°58W 260 C2
Tafo Ghana 6°15N 0°20W 263 D4
Tafraoute Morocco 29°50N 8°58W 260 C3
Tafresh Iran 34°45N 49°57E 247 C6
Taft Iran 31°45N 54°14E 247 D7
Taft Phil. 11°57N 125°30E 233 F5
Taft Calif., U.S.A. 35°8N 119°28W 307 K7
Taft Fla., U.S.A. 28°25N 81°21W 133 B2
Taftan Pakistan 29°0N 61°30E 240 C1
Taftān, Kūh-e Iran 28°40N 61°0E 247 D9
Tafu Taiwan 23°37N 121°23E 225 C3
Tafwap India 7°23N 93°43E 245 L11
Taga Samoa 13°46S 172°28W 287 V19
Taga Dzong Bhutan 27°5N 89°55E 241 B2
Tagana-an Phil. 9°42N 125°35E 233 G5
Taganrog Russia 47°12N 38°50E 189 J10
Taganrogskiy Zaliv Russia 47°0N 38°30E 189 J10
Tagânt □ Mauritania 19°0N 10°0W 260 E3
Tagap Ga Burma 26°56N 96°13E 241 B6
Tagauayan I. Phil. 10°58N 121°13E 233 F3
Tagaung Burma 23°30N 96°2E 241 D6
Tagawa Japan 33°38N 130°51E 222 D2
Tagaytay Phil. 14°6N 120°56E 232 D3
Tagbilaran Phil. 9°39N 123°51E 233 G4
Tagdempt = Tiaret Algeria 35°20N 1°21E 261 A5
Tage Papua N. G. 6°19S 143°20E 286 D2
Tageren Canal Micronesia 9°33N 138°8E 287 R16
Tággia Italy 43°52N 7°51E 198 E4
Taghit Algeria 30°58N 2°0W 261 B4
Tagig → Phil. 14°31N 121°5E 127 B2
Tagish Canada 60°19N 134°16W 296 A2
Tagish L. Canada 60°10N 134°20W 296 A2
Tagkawayan Phil. 13°58N 122°32E 232 E4
Tagliacozzo Italy 42°4N 13°14E 199 F10
Tagliamento → Italy 45°38N 13°6E 199 C10
Táglio di Po Italy 45°0N 12°12E 199 D9
Tagna Colombia 2°24S 70°37W 328 D3
Tago Phil. 9°2N 126°13E 233 G6
Tago, Mt. Phil. 8°23N 125°5E 233 G5
Tagomago Spain 39°2N 1°39E 206 C2
Tagourāret Mauritania 17°45N 7°45W 262 B3
Tagpochau, Mt. N. Marianas 15°11N 145°44E 302 e
Taguatinga Distrito Federal, Brazil 16°12S 44°35W 333 E2
Taguatinga Tocantins, Brazil 12°27S 46°22W 333 D2
Tagudin Phil. 16°56N 120°27E 232 C3
Taguenout Chagguerret Mali 21°14N 0°48W 261 D4
Taguig Phil. 14°31N 121°4E 127 B2
Tagula Papua N. G. 11°22S 153°15E 286 F7
Tagula I. Papua N. G. 11°30S 153°30E 286 F7
Tagum Phil. 7°33N 125°53E 233 H5
Tagus = Tejo → Europe 38°40N 9°24W 195 F2
Tahakopa N.Z. 46°30S 169°23E 285 G4
Tahala Morocco 34°0N 4°28W 260 B4
Tahan, Gunung Malaysia 4°34N 102°17E 237 K4
Tahānah-ye sūr Gol Afghan. 31°43N 67°53E 240 C2
Tahara Japan 34°40N 137°16E 223 C9
Tahat Algeria 23°18N 5°33E 261 D6
Tāherī Iran 27°43N 52°20E 247 E7
Tahgong Pt. N. Marianas 15°6N 145°39E 302 e
Tahifet Algeria 22°58N 6°0E 261 D6
Tahiti French Polynesia 17°37S 149°27W 289 e
Tahlab → Pakistan 28°9N 62°45E 240 C1
Tahlequah U.S.A. 35°55N 94°58W 314 D7
Tahoe, L. U.S.A. 39°6N 120°2W 306 G6
Tahoe City U.S.A. 39°10N 120°9W 306 F6
Tahoka U.S.A. 33°10N 101°48W 314 E4
Taholah U.S.A. 47°21N 124°17W 306 C2
Tahora N.Z. 39°2S 174°49E 284 F3
Tahoua Niger 14°57N 5°16E 263 C6
Tahrir Square Egypt 30°2N 31°14E 117 A2
Tahrūd Iran 29°26N 57°49E 247 D8
Tahsis Canada 49°55N 126°40W 296 D3
Tahta Egypt 26°44N 31°32E 256 B3
Tahtaköprü Turkey 39°57N 29°39E 203 G13
Tahtalı Dağları Turkey 38°20N 36°0E 212 C7
Tahu Taiwan 24°26N 120°52E 225 B2
Tahuamanú → Bolivia 11°6S 67°36W 330 C4
Tahuata, I. French Polynesia 9°57S 139°5W 289 f
Tahulandang Indonesia 2°27N 125°23E 231 D7
Tahuna Indonesia 3°38N 125°30E 231 D7
Taï Ivory C. 5°55N 7°30W 262 D3
Taï △ Ivory C. 5°25N 7°5W 262 D3
Tai Hu China 31°5N 120°10E 229 B12
Tai Lo Shan China 22°21N 114°13E 122 A2
Tai Mo Shan China 22°25N 114°7E 219 a
Tai O China 22°15N 113°52E 219 a
Tai Pang Wan China 22°33N 114°24E 219 a
Tai Po China 22°27N 114°10E 219 a
Tai Po Tsai China 22°20N 114°15E 122 A2
Tai Rom Yen △ Thailand 8°45N 99°30E 237 H2
Tai Seng Singapore 1°20N 103°53E 138 A3
Tai Shui Hang China 22°24N 114°13E 122 A2
Tai Tam B. China 22°12N 114°13E 122 B2
Tai Tam Tuk Res. China 22°14N 114°13E 122 B2
Tai Wai China 22°22N 114°10E 122 A2
Tai Wan Tau China 22°17N 114°17E 122 B2
Tai Wo Hau China 22°21N 114°7E 122 A1
Tai Yue Shan = Lantau I. China 22°15N 113°56E 219 a
Tai'an China 36°12N 117°8E 227 F9
Taiarapu, Presqu'île de Tahiti 17°47S 149°14W 289 e
Taibai Shan China 33°57N 107°45E 226 H4
Taibei = T'aipei Taiwan 25°4N 121°29E 225 A3
Taibique Canary Is. 27°42N 17°58W 153 e1
Taibus Qi China 41°54N 115°22E 226 D8
Taicang China 31°30N 121°5E 229 B13
Taichow = Taizhou China 32°28N 119°55E 229 A12
T'aichung Taiwan 24°9N 120°37E 225 B2
Taieri → N.Z. 46°3S 170°12E 285 G5
Taigu China 37°28N 112°30E 226 F7
Taihang Shan China 36°0N 113°30E 226 G7
Taihape N.Z. 39°41S 175°48E 284 F4
Taihe Anhui, China 33°20N 115°42E 226 H8
Taihe Jiangxi, China 26°47N 114°52E 229 D10
Taihoku = T'aipei Taiwan 25°4N 121°29E 225 A3
Taihsi Taiwan 23°51N 120°16E 225 C2
Taihu China 30°22N 116°20E 229 B11
Taijiang China 26°39N 108°21E 228 D7
Taikang China 34°5N 114°50E 226 G8
Taikkyi Burma 17°20N 96°0E 241 G6
Tailem Bend Australia 35°12S 139°29E 282 C3
Tailfingen Germany 48°15N 9°1E 179 G5
T'ailuko Taiwan 24°9N 121°37E 225 B3
T'aimali Taiwan 22°36N 121°0E 225 D2
Taimyr Peninsula = Taymyr, Poluostrov Russia 75°0N 100°0E 215 B11
Tain U.K. 57°49N 4°4W 167 D4
Tainaka Japan 34°36N 135°35E 133 B2
T'ainan Taiwan 23°0N 120°10E 225 D2
T'ainan □ Taiwan 23°15N 120°20E 225 C2
Tainggyo Burma 17°49N 94°29E 241 G5
Taining China 26°54N 117°9E 229 D11
Taiobeiras Brazil 15°49S 42°14W 333 E3
Taipa China 22°10N 113°35E 219 a
T'aipei Taiwan 25°4N 121°29E 225 A3
T'aipei □ Taiwan 24°50N 121°35E 225 B3
Taiping Anhui, China 30°15N 118°6E 229 B12
Taiping Malaysia 4°51N 100°44E 237 K3
Taipingchuan China 44°23N 123°11E 227 B12
Taipingzhen China 33°35N 111°42E 226 H6
Taipu Brazil 5°37S 35°36W 332 C4
Tairenpokpi India 24°39N 93°40E 241 C4
Tairua N.Z. 37°0S 175°51E 284 D4
Tais Indonesia 4°6S 102°34E 234 C2
Taisha Japan 35°24N 132°40E 222 B4
Taishan Guangdong, China 22°14N 112°41E 229 F9
Taishan Shandong, China 36°25N 117°20E 227 F9
Taishō Japan 34°38N 135°27E 133 B1
Taishun China 27°30N 119°42E 229 D12
Taita Hills Kenya 3°25S 38°15E 268 C4
Taitao, C. Chile 45°53S 75°5W 336 C1
Taitao, Pen. de Chile 46°30S 75°0W 336 C2
T'aitung Taiwan 22°43N 121°4E 225 D3
T'aitung □ Taiwan 23°0N 121°0E 225 D3
Taivalkoski Finland 65°33N 28°12E 160 D23
Taiwan ■ Asia 23°30N 121°0E 225 C3
Taiwan Strait Asia 24°40N 120°0E 229 E12
Taixing China 32°11N 120°0E 229 A13
Taiyara Sudan 13°12N 30°47E 257 E3
Taiyiba Israel 32°36N 35°27E 250 F6
Taiyuan China 37°52N 112°33E 226 F7
Taizhong = T'aichung Taiwan 24°9N 120°37E 225 B2
Taizhou Jiangsu, China 32°28N 119°55E 229 A12
Taizhou Zhejiang, China 28°40N 121°24E 229 C13
Taizhou Liedao China 28°30N 121°55E 229 C13
Ta'izz Yemen 13°35N 44°2E 248 D4
Ta'izz □ Yemen 13°35N 44°2E 248 D4
Taj Mahal India 27°10N 78°2E 242 F8
Tājābād Iran 30°2N 54°24E 247 D7
Tajapuru, Furo do Brazil 1°50S 50°25W 332 B1
Tajarḥī Libya 24°21N 14°28E 258 D2
Tajen Taiwan 22°17N 120°53E 225 D2
Tajikistan ■ Asia 38°30N 70°0E 217 E8
Tajima = Minamiaizu Japan 37°12N 139°46E 221 F9
Tajimi Japan 35°19N 137°8E 223 B9
Tajo = Tejo → Europe 38°40N 9°24W 195 F2
Tajrīsh Iran 35°48N 51°25E 141 A2
Tajumulco, Vol. Guatemala 15°2N 91°55W 320 C1
Tājūrā Libya 32°51N 13°21E 258 B2
Tak Thailand 16°52N 99°8E 236 D2
Takāb Iran 36°24N 47°7E 213 D12
Takabanare-shima Japan 26°22N 127°59E 288 a
Takabba Kenya 3°21N 40°13E 267 D5
Takachiho Japan 32°42N 131°18E 222 E3
Takachu Botswana 22°37S 21°58E 270 B3
Takada Japan 37°7N 138°15E 221 F9
Takahagi Japan 36°43N 140°45E 221 F10
Takahashi Japan 34°51N 133°39E 222 C5
Takaido Japan 35°40N 139°37E 140 A2
Takaishi Japan 35°36N 139°31E 140 B2
Takaka N.Z. 40°51S 172°50E 285 A7
Takaki = Yamato Japan 35°27N 139°25E 223 B11
Takalar Indonesia 5°28S 119°24E 235 D5
Takalous, O. → Algeria 22°36N 7°21E 261 D6
Takamaka Seychelles 4°50S 55°30E 272 c
Takamatsu Japan 34°20N 134°5E 222 C6
Takanabe Japan 32°8N 131°30E 222 E3
Takangkou Taiwan 23°28N 121°29E 225 C3
Takaoka Japan 36°47N 137°0E 223 A9
Takapau N.Z. 40°2S 176°21E 284 G5
Takapuna N.Z. 36°47S 174°47E 284 C3
Takarazuka Japan 34°47N 135°20E 133 A1
Takaroa French Polynesia 14°28S 144°58W 289 f
Takasago Japan 35°44N 134°52E 140 A4
Takasaki Japan 36°20N 139°0E 223 A11
Takashima Japan 35°24N 136°2E 223 B8
Takatsu Japan 35°36N 139°37E 140 B2
Takatsuki Japan 34°51N 135°37E 223 C7
Takaungu Kenya 3°38S 39°52E 268 C4
Takayama Japan 36°18N 137°11E 223 A9
Takayama-Bonchi Japan 36°0N 137°18E 223 B9
Take-Shima Japan 30°49N 130°26E 221 J5
Takefu = Echizen Japan 35°50N 136°10E 223 B8
Takehara Japan 34°21N 132°55E 222 C4
Takengon Indonesia 4°45N 96°50E 234 B1
Takeo Cambodia 10°59N 104°47E 237 G5
Takeo Japan 33°12N 130°1E 222 D2
Tåkern Sweden 58°22N 14°45E 163 F8
Takeshima = Liancourt Rocks Asia 37°15N 131°52E 221 F5
Takeshita Japan 35°33N 139°32E 140 B2
Tākestān Iran 36°0N 49°40E 247 C6
Taketa Japan 32°58N 131°24E 222 E3
Takh India 33°6N 77°32E 243 C7
Takhār □ Afghan. 36°40N 70°0E 240 A3
Takhiatash Uzbekistan 42°20N 59°33E 216 D5
Takhmau Cambodia 11°29N 104°57E 237 G5
Takht-e Soleyman Iran 36°36N 47°14E 213 D12
Takht-Sulaiman Pakistan 31°40N 69°58E 242 D3
Taki Papua N. G. 6°29S 155°52E 286 D8
Takiéta Niger 13°41N 8°32E 263 C6
Takikawa Japan 43°33N 141°54E 220 C10
Takinegawa Japan 35°45N 139°44E 140 A3
Takla L. Canada 55°15N 125°45W 296 B3
Takla Landing Canada 55°30N 125°50W 296 B3
Taklamakan China 38°0N 83°0E 217 E10
Taklamakan Shamo = Taklamakan China 38°0N 83°0E 217 E10
Takoma Park U.S.A. 38°58N 77°0W 143 B2
Takotna U.S.A. 62°59N 156°4W 303 E8
Taksim Turkey 41°2N 28°58E 122 B1
Taksimo Russia 56°20N 114°52E 215 D12
Taku Japan 33°18N 130°3E 222 D2
Taku → Canada 58°30N 133°50W 296 B2
Takua Thung Thailand 8°24N 98°27E 237 a
Takum India 27°47N 93°37E 241 B4
Takum Nigeria 7°18N 9°36E 263 D6
Takume French Polynesia 15°49S 142°12W 289 f
Takundi Dem. Rep. of the Congo 4°45S 16°34E 265 C3
Takutu → Guyana 3°30N 60°29W 329 C5
Tal Halāl Iran 28°54N 55°1E 247 D7
Tala Uruguay 34°21S 55°46W 335 C4
Talachyn Belarus 54°25N 29°42E 188 E5
Talacogon Phil. 8°32N 125°39E 233 G5
Talagang Pakistan 32°55N 72°25E 242 C5
Talagante Chile 33°40S 70°50W 334 C1
Talahouhait Algeria 24°52N 1°5E 261 D5
Talaide Portugal 38°44N 9°18W 126 A1
Talaimannar Sri Lanka 9°6N 79°43E 245 K4
Talaïnt Morocco 29°41N 9°40W 260 C3
Talak Niger 18°0N 5°0E 263 B6
Talakag Phil. 8°16N 124°37E 233 G5
Talamanca, Cordillera de Cent. Amer. 9°20N 83°20W 320 E3
Talampaya △ Argentina 29°43S 67°42W 334 B2
Talangbetutu Indonesia 2°53S 104°41E 234 C2
Talant France 47°19N 4°58E 173 E11
Talara Peru 4°38S 81°18W 330 A1
Talas Kyrgyzstan 42°30N 72°13E 217 D8
Talas Turkey 38°41N 35°33E 212 C6
Talas □ Kyrgyzstan 42°20N 72°0E 217 D8
Talas → Kazakhstan 44°0N 70°20E 217 D8
Talas Ala Too Kyrgyzstan 42°15N 72°0E 217 D8
Talasea Papua N. G. 5°20S 150°2E 286 C6
Talasskiy Alatau = Talas Ala Too Kyrgyzstan 42°15N 72°0E 217 D8
Talâta Egypt 30°36N 32°20E 251 H3
Talata Mafara Nigeria 12°38N 6°4E 263 C6
Talaud, Kepulauan Indonesia 4°30N 126°50E 231 D7
Talaud Is. = Talaud, Kepulauan Indonesia 4°30N 126°50E 231 D7
Talavera de la Reina Spain 39°55N 4°46W 194 F6
Talavera la Real Spain 38°53N 6°46W 195 G4
Talawgyi Burma 25°4N 97°19E 241 C6
Talayan Phil. 6°52N 124°24E 233 H5
Talayuela Spain 39°59N 5°36W 194 F5
Talbandh India 22°3N 86°20E 243 H12
Talbert, Sillon de France 48°53N 3°5W 172 D3
Talbot Australia 37°10S 143°44E 282 D5
Talbot, C. Australia 13°48S 126°43E 278 B4
Talbotton U.S.A. 32°41N 84°32W 316 C5
Talbragar → Australia 32°12S 148°37E 283 B8
Talca Chile 35°28S 71°40W 334 D1
Talcahuano Chile 36°40S 73°10W 334 D1
Talcher India 21°0N 85°18E 244 D7
Talcho Niger 14°44N 3°28E 263 C5
Taldy Kurgan = Taldyqorghan Kazakhstan 45°10N 78°45E 217 C9
Taldyqorghan Kazakhstan 45°10N 78°45E 217 C9
Tālesh Iran 37°58N 48°58E 213 D13
Tālesh, Kūhhā-ye Iran 37°42N 48°55E 213 D13
Talgar = Talghar Kazakhstan 43°19N 77°15E 217 D9
Talghar Kazakhstan 43°19N 77°15E 217 D9
Talguharai Sudan 18°19N 35°56E 256 D4
Talguppa India 14°13N 74°56E 245 G2
Tali Post South Sudan 5°55N 30°44E 257 F3
Taliabu Indonesia 1°50S 125°0E 231 E6
Taliao Taiwan 22°36N 120°23E 225 D2
Talibon Phil. 10°9N 124°20E 233 F5
Talichien Taiwan 24°58N 121°55E 225 B3
Taliganga India 22°30N 88°22E 124 B2
Talihina U.S.A. 34°45N 95°3W 314 D7
Talikota India 16°29N 76°17E 245 F3
Talikud I. Phil. 6°56N 125°41E 233 H5
Talin Taiwan 23°36N 120°27E 225 C2
Talipapa Phil. 14°41N 121°1E 127 A2
Talipaw Phil. 5°59N 121°7E 233 J3
Talipparamba India 12°3N 75°21E 245 H2
Talisay Phil. 10°44N 122°58E 233 F4
Talisayan Phil. 9°0N 124°55E 233 G5
Taliwang Indonesia 8°50S 116°55E 235 D5
Talkeetna U.S.A. 62°20N 150°6W 303 E10
Talkha Egypt 31°3N 31°22E 251 G2
Tálknafjörður Iceland 65°34N 24°0W 155 B2
Talkot Nepal 29°37N 81°19E 243 E9
Tall 'Afar Iraq 36°22N 42°27E 213 D10
Tall Kalakh Syria 34°41N 36°15E 250 D7
Tall Kayf Iraq 36°29N 43°7E 213 D10
Talla Egypt 28°5N 30°43E 256 B3
Talladega U.S.A. 33°26N 86°6W 316 B3
Tallaganda △ Australia 35°29S 149°37E 283 C8
Tallaght Ireland 53°17N 6°22W 120 B1
Tallahassee U.S.A. 30°27N 84°17W 316 E5
Tallangatta Australia 36°15S 147°19E 283 D7
Tallapoosa U.S.A. 33°45N 85°17W 316 B4
Tallapoosa → U.S.A. 32°30N 86°16W 316 C3
Tallard France 44°28N 6°3E 175 D10
Tallarook Australia 37°5S 145°6E 283 D6
Tallassee U.S.A. 32°32N 85°54W 316 C4
Tällberg Sweden 60°51N 15°2E 162 D9
Tallering Pk. Australia 28°6S 115°37E 279 E2
Talli Pakistan 29°32N 68°8E 242 E3
Tallinn Estonia 59°22N 24°48E 188 C3
Tallkrogen Sweden 59°16N 18°4E 139 B2
Tallmadge U.S.A. 41°6N 81°27W 312 E3
Tallulah U.S.A. 32°25N 91°11W 314 E9
Tălmaciu Romania 45°38N 24°19E 183 E9
Talmest Morocco 31°48N 9°21W 260 B3
Talmont-St-Hilaire France 46°27N 1°37W 174 B2
Talnakh Russia 69°29N 88°22E 215 C9
Talne Ukraine 48°50N 30°44E 189 H6
Talnoye = Talne Ukraine 48°50N 30°44E 189 H6
Taloda India 21°34N 74°11E 244 D2
Talodi Sudan 10°35N 30°22E 257 E3
Talofofo Guam 13°21N 144°45E 302 d
Tālogān Afghan. 36°44N 69°33E 240 A3
Talovaya Russia 51°6N 40°45E 190 E5
Taloyoak Canada 69°32N 93°32W 294 D13
Talpa de Allende Mexico 20°23N 104°51W 318 C4
Talparo Trin. & Tob. 10°30N 61°17W 323 t
Talparo → Trin. & Tob. 10°34N 61°17W 323 t
Talquin, L. U.S.A. 30°23N 84°39W 316 E5
Talsi Latvia 57°10N 22°30E 184 A9
Talsi □ Latvia 57°20N 22°40E 184 A9
Talsinnt Morocco 32°33N 3°27W 261 B4
Taltal Chile 25°23S 70°33W 334 B1
Taltson → Canada 61°24N 112°46W 296 A6
Talu Indonesia 0°13N 99°58E 234 B1
Taluk Indonesia 0°31S 101°34E 234 C2
Talwood Australia 28°29S 149°29E 281 D4
Talyawalka Cr. → Australia 32°28S 142°22E 282 B5
Tam Dao △ Vietnam 21°45N 105°45E 236 B5
Tam Ky Vietnam 15°34N 108°29E 236 E7
Tam Quan Vietnam 14°35N 109°3E 236 E7
Tama Tōkyō, Japan 35°38N 139°26E 140 B1
Tama Iowa, U.S.A. 41°58N 92°35W 310 C4
Tama → Japan 35°32N 139°39E 140 B2
Tama ⌂ Ethiopia 5°55N 36°5E 257 F4
Tama Abu, Banjaran Malaysia 3°50N 115°5E 235 B5
Tama Kyūryō Japan 35°34N 139°30E 140 B2
Tamada Algeria 21°34N 3°20E 261 D5
Tamaden Japan 35°39N 139°38E 140 B2
Tamagawa-josui → Japan 35°41N 139°47E 140 A1
Tamakautoga Cook Is. 19°5S 169°55W 289 g
Tamalameque Colombia 8°52N 73°49W 328 B3
Tamale Ghana 9°22N 0°50W 263 D4
Taman Russia 45°14N 36°41E 189 K9
Taman Negara △ Malaysia 4°38N 102°26E 237 K4
Taman Sari Indonesia 6°8S 106°48E 122 A1
T'aman Shan Taiwan 24°42N 121°27E 225 B3
Tamana Japan 32°58N 130°32E 222 E2
Tamana Kiribati 2°30S 175°59E 277 A14
Tamana, Mt. Trin. & Tob. 10°28N 61°12W 323 t
Tamanar Morocco 31°1N 9°46W 260 B3
Tamanduateí → Brazil 23°37S 46°38W 137 B2
Tamanhint Libya 27°13N 14°37E 258 C2
Tamani Mali 13°20N 6°50W 262 C3
Tamano Japan 34°29N 133°59E 222 C5
Tamanrasset Algeria 22°50N 5°30E 261 D6
Tamanrasset □ Algeria 23°45N 4°40E 261 D5
Tamanrasset, O. → Algeria 22°0N 2°0E 261 D5
Tamanthi Burma 25°19N 95°17E 241 C5
Tamaqua U.S.A. 40°48N 75°58W 313 F9
Tamar → U.K. 50°27N 4°15W 169 G3
Támara Colombia 5°50N 72°10W 328 B3
Tamarac U.S.A. 26°12N 80°15W 129 A1
Tamarin Mauritius 20°19S 57°20E 272 e
Tamarinda Spain 39°55N 3°49E 206 B4
Tamarite de Litera Spain 41°52N 0°25E 196 D5
Tamaroa U.S.A. 38°8N 89°14W 310 F7
Tamashima Japan 34°32N 133°40E 221 G6
Tamási Hungary 46°40N 18°18E 182 D3
Tamaské Niger 14°49N 5°43E 263 C6
Tamatave = Toamasina Madag. 18°10S 49°25E 272 B2
Tamaulipas □ Mexico 24°0N 98°45W 319 C5
Tamaulipas, Sierra de Mexico 23°30N 98°20W 319 C5
Tamazula Mexico 24°57N 106°57W 318 C3
Tamazunchale Mexico 21°16N 98°47W 319 C5
Tamba-Dabatou Guinea 11°50N 10°40W 262 C2
Tambach Kenya 0°36N 35°31E 268 B4
Tambacounda Senegal 13°45N 13°40W 262 C2
Tambacounda □ Senegal 14°0N 13°0W 262 C2
Tambaram India 12°55N 80°7E 245 H5
Tambea Solomon Is. 9°16S 159°41E 287 M10
Tambelan, Kepulauan Indonesia 1°0N 107°30E 235 B3
Tambellup Australia 34°4S 117°37E 279 F2
Tambo Queens., Australia 24°54S 146°14E 280 C4
Tambo Peru 12°57S 74°1W 330 C3
Tambo → Peru 10°42S 73°47W 330 C3
Tambo de Mora Peru 13°30S 76°8W 330 C2
Tambobamba Peru 13°54S 72°8W 330 C3
Tamboerskloof S. Africa 33°56S 18°25E 118 A1
Tambohorano Madag. 17°30S 43°58E 272 B1
Tambopata → Peru 13°21S 69°36W 330 C4
Tambora Jakarta, Indonesia 6°8S 106°47E 122 A1
Tambora Nusa Tenggara Barat, Indonesia 8°12S 118°5E 235 D5
Tamboritha, Mt. Australia 37°31S 146°40E 283 D7
Tamboura C.A.R. 5°10N 25°12E 264 A5
Tambov Russia 52°45N 41°28E 190 D5
Tambov □ Russia 52°50N 41°20E 190 D5
Tambre → Spain 42°49N 8°53W 194 C2
Tambuku Indonesia 7°8S 113°40E 235 D4
Tambul Papua N. G. 5°54S 143°54E 286 C2
Tambunar Malaysia 5°43N 116°24E 235 A5
Tamburâ South Sudan 5°40N 27°25E 257 F2
Tambuyukan, Gunong Malaysia 6°13N 116°39E 235 A5
Tâmchekket Mauritania 17°25N 10°40W 262 B2
Tame Colombia 6°28N 71°44W 328 B3
Tâmega → Portugal 41°5N 8°21W 194 D2
Tamegroute Morocco 30°15N 5°39W 260 B3
Tamelelt Morocco 31°50N 7°32W 260 B3
Tamenglong India 25°0N 93°35E 241 C4
Tamerza Tunisia 34°23N 7°58E 258 B1
Tamgak, Adrar Niger 19°12N 8°35E 259 E1
Tamgué, Massif du Guinea 12°0N 12°18W 262 C2
Tami Is. Papua N. G. 6°46S 147°55E 286 D4
Tamiahua, L. de Mexico 21°35N 97°35W 319 C5
Tamiami Canal U.S.A. 25°50N 81°0W 317 K8
Tamianglayang Indonesia 2°7S 115°10E 235 C5
Tamil Nadu □ India 11°0N 77°0E 245 J3
Tamis → Serbia 44°51N 20°39E 182 F5
Tamiya Egypt 29°29N 30°58E 256 J7
Tamlelt, Plaine de Morocco 32°30N 2°20W 261 B4
Tamluk India 22°18N 87°58E 243 H12
Tammerfors = Tampere Finland 61°30N 23°50E 188 B2
Tammisalo Finland 60°11N 25°5E 121 B3
Tammûh Egypt 29°55N 31°15E 117 B2
Tämnaren Sweden 60°10N 17°25E 162 D11
Tampa Angola 15°30S 13°27E 265 F2
Tampa Fla., U.S.A. 27°56N 82°27W 317 H7
Tampa, Tanjung Indonesia 8°55S 116°12E 231 K19
Tampa B. U.S.A. 27°50N 82°30W 317 H7
Tampa Int. ✈ (TPA) U.S.A. 27°59N 82°32W 317 H7
Tamparan Phil. 7°53N 124°20E 233 H5
Tampere Finland 61°30N 23°50E 188 B2
Tampico Tamaulipas, Mexico 22°13N 97°51W 319 C5
Tampico Ill., U.S.A. 41°38N 89°47W 310 C7
Tampin Malaysia 2°28N 102°13E 237 L4
Tampines Singapore 1°21N 103°56E 138 A3
Tampoi Malaysia 1°30N 103°39E 237 d
Tamrah Si. Arabia 20°24N 45°25E 248 B4
Tamri Morocco 30°49N 9°50W 260 B3
Tamrida = Qādub Yemen 12°37N 53°57E 249 D6
Tamsagbulag Mongolia 47°14N 117°21E 219 B12
Tamsweg Austria 47°7N 13°49E 180 D6
Tamu Burma 24°13N 94°12E 241 C5
Tamuja → Spain 39°38N 6°29W 195 F4
Tamuning Guam 13°29N 144°47E 302 d
Tamworth N.S.W., Australia 31°7S 150°58E 283 A9
Tamworth Ont., Canada 44°29N 77°0W 312 B8
Tamworth Staffs., U.K. 52°39N 1°41W 169 E6
Tan An Vietnam 10°32N 106°25E 237 G6
Tan Chau Vietnam 10°48N 105°12E 237 G5
T'an-do N. Korea 39°30N 124°41E 224 C2
Tan Hiep Vietnam 10°27N 106°21E 237 G6
Tan Iddah Algeria 26°33N 9°42E 261 C6
Tan-Tan Morocco 28°29N 11°1W 260 C2
Tan Yen Vietnam 22°4N 105°3E 236 A5
Tana → Coast, Kenya 2°32S 40°31E 268 C5
Tana → Finnmark, Norway 70°30N 28°14E 160 A23
Tana, L. Ethiopia 13°5N 37°30E 257 E4
Tana River Primate ⌂ Kenya 1°55S 40°7E 268 C5
Tanabe Japan 33°44N 135°22E 223 D7
Tanabi Brazil 20°37S 49°37W 333 F2
Tanacross U.S.A. 63°23N 143°21W 303 E12
Tanafjorden Norway 70°45N 28°25E 160 A23
Tanaga I. U.S.A. 51°48N 177°53W 303 L3
Tanaga Volcano U.S.A. 51°53N 178°8W 303 L3
Tanah Abang Indonesia 6°12S 106°48E 122 B1
Tanah Kusir Indonesia 6°15S 106°46E 122 B1
Tanah Merah Malaysia 5°48N 102°9E 237 K4
Tanahbala Indonesia 0°30S 98°30E 234 C1
Tanahgrogot Indonesia 1°55S 116°15E 235 C5
Tanahjampea Indonesia 7°10S 120°35E 231 F6
Tanahmasa Indonesia 0°12S 98°39E 234 C1
Tanahmerah Indonesia 6°5S 140°16E 231 F10
Tanahputih Indonesia 1°40N 101°3E 234 B2
Tanakpur India 29°5N 80°7E 243 E9
Tanamalwila Sri Lanka 6°26N 81°8E 245 L5
Tanami Desert Australia 18°50S 132°0E 278 C5
Tanana U.S.A. 65°10N 152°4W 303 D9
Tanana → U.S.A. 65°10N 151°58W 303 D10
Tananarive = Antananarivo Madag. 18°55S 47°31E 272 B2
Tananger Norway 58°57N 5°37E 164 F2
Tanannt Morocco 31°54N 6°56W 260 B3
Tanapag N. Marianas 15°14N 145°45E 302 e
Tánaro → Italy 44°55N 8°40E 198 D5
Tanauan Phil. 14°5N 121°10E 232 D3
Tanay Phil. 14°30N 121°17E 232 D3
Tanba-Sanchi Japan 35°7N 135°48E 223 B7
Tancheng China 34°25N 118°20E 227 G10
Tanch'ŏn N. Korea 40°27N 128°54E 224 B4
Tanda Ut. P., India 26°33N 82°35E 243 F10
Tanda Ut. P., India 28°57N 78°56E 243 E8
Tanda Ivory C. 7°48N 3°10W 262 D4
Tandag Phil. 9°4N 126°9E 233 G6
Tandaia Tanzania 9°25S 34°15E 269 D3
Tăndărei Romania 44°39N 27°40E 183 F12
Tandaué Angola 16°58S 18°5E 265 F3
Tandil Argentina 37°15S 59°6W 334 D4
Tandil, Sa. del Argentina 37°30S 59°0W 334 D4
Tandin Burma 19°33N 93°58E 241 F4
Tandjilé □ Chad 9°30N 16°30E 259 G3
Tandjilé → Chad 9°45N 15°50E 259 G3
Tandlianwala Pakistan 31°3N 73°9E 242 D5
Tando Adam Pakistan 25°45N 68°40E 242 G3
Tando Allahyar Pakistan 25°28N 68°43E 242 G3
Tando Bago Pakistan 24°47N 68°58E 242 G3
Tando Mohommed Khan Pakistan 25°8N 68°32E 242 G3
Tando-Zinze Angola 5°22S 12°30E 265 D2
Tandou-Bengou Congo 3°50S 11°44E 264 C2
Tandou L. Australia 32°40S 142°5E 282 B5
Tandoureh △ Iran 37°50N 59°0E 247 B8
Tandragee U.K. 54°21N 6°24W 166 B5
Tandsjöborg Sweden 61°42N 14°43E 162 C8
Tandubas Phil. 5°8N 120°20E 233 J3
Tandula → India 21°6N 81°14E 244 D5
Tandula Tank India 20°40N 81°12E 244 D5
Tandur Andhra Pradesh, India 19°11N 79°30E 244 E4
Tandur Andhra Pradesh, India 17°14N 77°35E 244 F3
Tane-ga-Shima Japan 30°30N 131°0E 221 J5
Taneatua N.Z. 38°4S 177°1E 284 E6
Tanen Tong Dan = Dawna Ra. Burma 16°30N 98°30E 236 D2
Tanew → Poland 50°29N 22°16E 185 H9
Tanezrouft Algeria 23°9N 0°11E 261 D5
Tanezzuft, W. → Libya 25°51N 10°19E 258 C2
Tang, Koh Cambodia 10°16N 103°7E 237 G4
Tang, Ra's-e Iran 25°21N 59°52E 247 E8
Tang Krasang Cambodia 12°34N 105°3E 236 F5
Tanga Tanzania 5°5S 39°2E 268 D4
Tanga □ Tanzania 5°20S 38°0E 268 D4
Tanga Is. Papua N. G. 3°20S 153°15E 286 B7
Tanga Langua Grenada 12°14N 61°39W 323 q
Tangail Bangla. 24°15N 89°55E 241 C2
Tangalla Sri Lanka 6°1N 80°48E 245 L5
Tanganyika = Tanzania ■ Africa 6°0S 34°0E 268 D3
Tanganyika, L. Africa 6°40S 30°0E 268 D3
Tangará da Serra Brazil 14°50S 57°47W 331 C6
Tangarare Solomon Is. 9°36S 159°41E 287 M10
Tangasseri India 8°53N 76°35E 245 K3
Tangaza Nigeria 13°19N 4°55E 263 C5
Tangelo Park U.S.A. 28°27N 81°26W 133 B2
Tangen Norway 60°37N 11°15E 164 D8
Tanger Morocco 35°50N 5°49W 260 A3
Tanger-Med Morocco 35°53N 5°30W 195 K5
Tanger-Tétouan □ Morocco 35°50N 5°50W 260 A3
Tangerang Indonesia 6°11S 106°37E 234 D3
Tangerhütte Germany 52°26N 11°48E 178 C7
Tangermünde Germany 52°33N 11°58E 178 C7
Tanggu China 39°2N 117°40E 227 E9
Tanggula Shan China 32°40N 92°10E 218 E7
Tanggula Shankou China 32°42N 92°27E 218 E7
Tanghe China 32°47N 112°50E 226 H7
Tanghla Range = Tanggula Shan China 32°40N 92°10E 218 E7
Tangi India 19°56N 85°24E 244 E7
Tangier = Tanger Morocco 35°50N 5°49W 260 A3
Tangjia China 22°22N 113°35E 219 a
Tangjia Wan China 22°21N 113°36E 219 a
Tango-Hantō Japan 35°45N 135°10E 223 B7
Tangorin Australia 21°47S 144°12E 280 C3
Tangorombohitr'i Makay Madag. 21°0S 45°15E 272 C2
Tangra Yumco China 31°0N 86°38E 218 E6
Tangshan China 39°38N 118°10E 227 E10
Tangtou China 35°28N 118°30E 227 G10
Tangub Phil. 8°3N 123°44E 233 G4
Tanguen-Dassouri Burkina Faso 12°16N 1°42W 263 C4
Tanguiéta Benin 10°35N 1°21E 263 C5
Tangxi China 29°3N 119°25E 229 C12
Tangyan He → China 28°54N 108°19E 228 C7
Tangyin China 35°54N 114°21E 226 G8
Taniantaweng Shan China 31°20N 98°0E 228 B2
Taniao Taiwan 22°23N 120°53E 225 D2
Tanimbar, Kepulauan Indonesia 7°30S 131°30E 231 F8
Tanimbar Is. = Tanimbar, Kepulauan Indonesia 7°30S 131°30E 231 F8
Tanintharyi = Tenasserim Burma 12°6N 99°3E 237 F2
Tanis Egypt 31°0N 31°54E 251 H2
Tanjay Phil. 9°30N 123°5E 233 G4
Tanjong Pelepas Malaysia 1°21N 103°33E 237 d
Tanjong Po Malaysia 1°45N 110°30E 235 B4
Tanjore = Thanjavur India 10°48N 79°12E 245 J4
Tanjung Kalimantan Selatan, Indonesia 2°10S 115°25E 235 C5
Tanjung Nusa Tenggara Barat, Indonesia 8°21S 116°9E 231 J19
Tanjung Datu △ Malaysia 2°13N 109°3E 235 B3
Tanjung Duren Indonesia 6°10S 106°46E 122 B1
Tanjung Malim Malaysia 3°42N 101°31E 237 L3
Tanjung Priok Indonesia 6°6S 106°52E 122 A2
Tanjung Putung △ Indonesia 2°54S 111°59E 235 C4
Tanjung Tokong Malaysia 5°28N 100°18E 237 c
Tanjungbalai Kepulauan Riau, Indonesia 1°0N 103°25E 234 B2
Tanjungbalai Sumatera Utara, Indonesia 2°55N 99°44E 234 B1
Tanjungbatu Kalimantan Selatan, Indonesia 3°0S 116°13E 235 C5
Tanjungbatu Kalimantan Timur, Indonesia 2°23N 118°3E 235 B5
Tanjungbatu Kepulauan Riau, Indonesia 0°37N 103°25E 234 B2
Tanjungisui Indonesia 0°30S 116°8E 235 C5
Tanjungkarang Telukbetung = Bandar Lampung Indonesia 5°20S 105°10E 234 D3
Tanjungpandan Indonesia 2°43S 107°38E 235 C3
Tanjungpinang Indonesia 1°5N 104°30E 234 B2
Tanjungpriok Indonesia 6°8S 106°55E 234 D3
Tanjungraja Indonesia 3°21S 104°46E 234 C2
Tanjungredeb Indonesia 2°9N 117°29E 235 B5
Tanjungselor Indonesia 2°55N 117°25E 235 B5
Tank Pakistan 32°14N 70°25E 242 C4
Tankhala India 21°58N 73°47E 242 J5
Tankwa-Karoo △ S. Africa 32°14S 19°50E 270 D2
Tanlu Taiwan 22°12N 120°44E 225 D2
Tanna Vanuatu 19°30S 169°20E 287 J7
Tännäs Sweden 62°26N 12°42E 162 B6
Tannersville U.S.A. 41°3N 75°18W 313 E9
Tannis Bugt Denmark 57°40N 10°15E 163 G4
Tannu Ola Asia 51°0N 94°0E 217 B12
Tannum Sands Australia 23°57S 151°22E 280 C5
Tano → Ghana 5°7N 2°56W 262 D4
Tanombella Algeria 25°30N 5°49E 261 C6
Tanon Str. Phil. 10°20N 123°30E 233 F4
Tanout Niger 14°50N 8°55E 259 F1
Tanquinho Brazil 11°58S 39°6W 333 D4
Tanshui Taiwan 25°10N 121°28E 225 A3
Tanshui Kang → Taiwan 25°10N 121°25E 225 A3
Tansilla Burkina Faso 12°25N 4°23W 262 C4
Tansing Nepal 27°52N 83°33E 243 F10
Tanta Egypt 30°45N 30°57E 256 H7
Tantabin Burma 17°1N 95°59E 241 G5
Tantoyuca Mexico 21°21N 98°14W 319 C5
Tantung = Dandong China 40°10N 124°20E 224 B2
T'antzu Taiwan 24°13N 120°42E 225 B2
Tanuku India 16°45N 81°44E 244 F5
Tanum Norway 59°53N 10°28E 133 A1
Tanūmah Si. Arabia 18°58N 42°10E 248 C3
Tanumshede Sweden 58°42N 11°20E 163 F5
Tanunda Australia 34°30S 139°0E 282 C3
Tanur India 11°1N 75°52E 245 J2
Tanus France 44°8N 2°19E 174 D6
Tanzania ■ Africa 6°0S 34°0E 268 D3
Tanzawa-Sanchi Japan 35°27N 139°0E 223 B11
Tanzhou China 22°16N 113°28E 219 a
Tanzilla → Canada 58°8N 130°43W 296 B2
Tao, Ko Thailand 10°5N 99°52E 237 G2
Tao'an = Taonan China 45°22N 122°40E 227 B12
Tao'er He → China 45°45N 124°5E 227 B13
Taohua Dao China 29°50N 122°20E 229 C14
Taolanaro Madag. 25°2S 47°0E 272 D2
Taole China 38°48N 106°40E 226 E4
Taonan China 45°22N 122°40E 227 B12
Taora Solomon Is. 7°21S 157°30E 287 L9
Taormina Italy 37°51N 15°17E 201 E8
Taos U.S.A. 36°24N 105°35W 305 H11
Taoudenni Mali 22°40N 3°55W 260 D4
Taoudrart, Adrar Algeria 24°25N 2°24E 261 D5
Taounate Morocco 34°25N 4°41W 260 B4
Taourirt Algeria 26°37N 0°20E 261 C5
Taourirt Morocco 34°25N 2°53W 261 B4
Taouz Morocco 30°53N 4°0W 260 B4
Taoyuan Hunan, China 28°55N 111°16E 229 C8
T'aoyüan Kaohsung, Taiwan 23°9N 120°46E 225 C2
T'aoyüan Yünlin, Taiwan 25°0N 121°4E 225 B3
T'aoyüan □ Taiwan 24°55N 121°15E 225 B3
Tapa Estonia 59°15N 25°50E 161 G21
Tapa Shan = Daba Shan China 32°0N 109°0E 228 B7
Tapachula Mexico 14°54N 92°17W 319 E6
Tapada Portugal 38°49N 9°16W 126 A1
Tapah Malaysia 4°12N 101°15E 237 K3
Tapajós → Brazil 2°24S 54°41W 329 D7
Tapaktuan Indonesia 3°15N 97°10E 234 B1
Tapanahoni → Suriname 4°20N 54°25W 329 C7
Tapanila Finland 60°15N 25°2E 121 B3
Tapanui N.Z. 45°56S 169°18E 285 F4
Taparo Pt. Trin. & Tob. 10°3N 61°38W 323 t
Tapauá Brazil 5°40S 64°20W 331 B5
Tapauá → Brazil 5°40S 64°21W 331 B5
Tapaz Phil. 11°16N 122°32E 233 F4
Tapes Brazil 30°40S 51°23W 335 C5
Tapeta Liberia 6°29N 8°52W 262 D3
Taphan Hin Thailand 16°13N 100°26E 236 D3
Tapia de Casariego Spain 43°34N 6°56W 194 B4
Tapiales Argentina 34°42S 58°30W 117 C1
Tapiantana Channel Phil. 6°22N 122°1E 233 H4
Tapiantana Group Phil. 6°20N 122°0E 233 H4

Tapiau = Gvardeysk Russia 54°39N 21°5E 184 D8
Tapilon = Daanbantayan Phil. 11°17N 124°2E 233 F5
Taping Taiwan 24°6N 120°53E 225 B2
Tapini Papua N. G. 8°19S 147°0E 286 E4
Tapiola Finland 60°10N 24°48E 121 B1
Tapiraí Brazil 19°52S 46°1W 333 E2
Tapirapé → Brazil 10°41S 50°38W 332 D1
Tapirapecó, Serra Venezuela 1°10N 65°0W 329 C5
Taplan Australia 34°33S 140°52E 282 C4
Taplejung Nepal 27°1N 86°16E 243 F12
Tapo-Capara △ Venezuela 7°55N 71°15W 328 B3
Tapoeripa Suriname 5°22N 56°34W 329 B6
Tapolca Hungary 46°53N 17°29E 182 D2
Tapsia India 22°32N 88°23E 124 B2
Tapti → India 21°8N 72°41E 244 D1
Tapu Taiwan 23°18N 120°35E 225 C2
Tapuae-o-Uenuku N.Z. 42°0S 173°39E 285 C8
Tapul Phil. 5°42N 120°55E 233 J3
Tapul Group Phil. 5°35N 120°50E 233 J3
Tapul I. Phil. 5°43N 120°55E 233 J3
Tapun India 27°35N 96°22E 241 B6
Tapurucuará Brazil 0°24S 65°2W 329 D4
Taputapu, C. Amer. Samoa 14°20S 170°51W 302 f
Taputimu Amer. Samoa 14°21S 170°46W 302 f
Ţaqţaq Iraq 35°53N 44°35E 213 E11
Taquara Brazil 29°36S 50°46W 335 B5
Taquari → Brazil 19°15S 57°17W 331 D6
Taquaritinga Brazil 21°24S 48°30W 333 F2
Tara Queens., Australia 27°17S 150°31E 281 D5
Tara Ont., Canada 44°28N 81°9W 312 B3
Tara Maharashtra, India 19°5N 72°49E 130 A1
Tara Japan 33°2N 130°11E 222 D2
Tara Russia 56°55N 74°24E 214 D8
Tara Zambia 16°58S 26°45E 269 F2
Tara → Montenegro 43°21N 18°51E 202 C2
Tara △ Serbia 43°55N 19°30E 202 C3
Tara-Dake Japan 32°58N 130°6E 222 E2
Taraba □ Nigeria 8°0N 10°30E 263 D7
Taraba → Nigeria 8°30N 10°15E 263 D7
Tarabuco Bolivia 19°10S 64°57W 331 D5
Tarābulus Lebanon 34°31N 35°50E 250 D6
Tarābulus Libya 32°49N 13°7E 258 B2
Tarābulus Libya 31°0N 13°0E 258 B2
Tarabya Turkey 41°8N 29°3E 122 B2
Taraclia Taraclia, Moldova 45°54N 28°40E 183 E13
Taraclia Tighina, Moldova 46°34N 29°7E 183 D14
Taradale N.Z. 39°33S 176°53E 284 F5
Taradehi India 23°18N 79°21E 243 H8
Tarāghīn Libya 26°0N 14°30E 258 C2
Taragi Japan 32°16N 130°56E 222 E2
Tarahouahout Algeria 22°41N 5°59E 261 D6
Tarajalejo Canary Is. 28°12N 14°7W 153 e2
Tarakan Indonesia 3°20N 117°35E 235 B5
Tarakit, Mt. Kenya 2°2N 35°10E 268 B4
Taralga Australia 34°26S 149°52E 283 C8
Tarama-Jima Japan 24°39N 124°42E 221 M2
Taramakau → N.Z. 42°34S 171°8E 285 C6
Taran, Mys Russia 54°56N 19°59E 184 D6
Taranagar India 28°43N 74°50E 242 E6
Taranaki □ N.Z. 39°25S 174°30E 284 F3
Taranaki, Mt. N.Z. 39°17S 174°5E 284 F3
Tarancón Spain 40°1N 3°1W 196 E1
Tarangire △ Tanzania 4°21S 36°7E 268 C4
Taransay U.K. 57°54N 7°0W 167 D1
Táranto Italy 40°28N 17°14E 201 B10
Táranto, G. di Italy 40°8N 17°20E 201 B10
Tarapacá Colombia 2°56S 69°46W 328 D4
Tarapacá □ Chile 20°45S 69°30W 334 A2
Tarapoto Peru 6°30S 76°20W 330 B2
Taraquá Brazil 0°6N 68°28W 328 C4
Tarare France 45°54N 4°26E 175 C8
Tararua Ra. N.Z. 40°45S 175°25E 284 G4
Tarasag Vanuatu 14°12S 167°36E 287 D5
Tarasaigh = Taransay U.K. 57°54N 7°0W 167 D1
Tarascon France 43°48N 4°39E 175 E8
Tarascon-sur-Ariège France 42°50N 1°36E 174 F5
Tarashcha Ukraine 49°30N 30°31E 177 D16
Tarata Peru 17°27S 70°2W 330 D3
Tarauacá Brazil 8°6S 70°48W 330 B3
Tarauacá → Brazil 6°42S 69°48W 330 B4
Taravao Tahiti 17°43S 149°18W 289 e
Taravao, Isthme de Tahiti 17°43S 149°19W 289 e
Taravo → France 41°42N 8°49E 175 G12
Tarawa Kiribati 1°30N 173°0E 288 G9
Tarawai I. Papua N. G. 3°13S 143°15E 286 B2
Tarawera N.Z. 39°2S 176°36E 284 F5
Tarawera, L. N.Z. 38°13S 176°27E 284 E5
Tarawera, Mt. N.Z. 38°14S 176°32E 284 E5
Taraz Kazakhstan 42°54N 71°22E 217 D8
Tarazona Spain 41°55N 1°43W 196 D3
Tarazona de la Mancha Spain 39°16N 1°55W 197 F3
Tårbæk Denmark 55°46N 12°35E 118 A3
Tarbagatay, Khrebet Kazakhstan 48°0N 83°0E 217 C10
Tarbaj Kenya 2°12N 40°8E 267 D5
Tarbat Ness U.K. 57°52N 3°47W 167 D5
Tarbela Dam Pakistan 34°8N 72°52E 242 B5
Tarbert Kerry, Ireland 52°34N 9°22W 166 D2
Tarbert Argyll & Bute, U.K. 55°52N 5°25W 167 F3
Tarbert W. Isles, U.K. 57°54N 6°49W 167 D2
Tarbes France 43°15N 0°3E 174 E4
Tarboro U.S.A. 35°54N 77°32W 315 D16
Tărcău, Munţii Romania 46°39N 26°7E 183 D11
Tarcento Italy 46°13N 13°13E 199 B10
Tarchomin Poland 52°19N 20°58E 143 B1
Tarcoola Australia 30°44S 134°36E 281 E1
Tarcoon Australia 30°15S 146°43E 281 E4
Tarcutta Australia 35°16S 147°44E 283 C7
Tardeo India 18°57N 72°48E 130 B1
Tardets-Sorholus France 43°8N 0°52W 174 E3
Tardoire → France 45°52N 0°14E 174 C4
Taredjerdja Algeria 25°12N 2°32E 261 C5
Taree Australia 31°50S 152°30E 283 A10
Tarella Australia 31°2S 143°2E 282 A5
Tarf, Ras Morocco 35°40N 5°11W 260 A3
Ţarfā, Ra's aţ Si. Arabia 17°2N 42°22E 248 C3
Tarfa, W. el → Egypt 28°25N 30°50E 256 B3
Tarfaya Morocco 27°55N 12°55W 260 C2
Târgovişte Romania 44°55N 25°27E 183 F10
Targówek Poland 52°16N 21°3E 143 B2
Târgu Bujor Romania 45°52N 27°54E 183 E12
Târgu Cărbuneşti Romania 44°57N 23°31E 183 F8
Târgu Frumos Romania 47°12N 27°2E 183 C12
Târgu Jiu Romania 45°5N 23°19E 183 E8
Târgu Lăpuş Romania 47°27N 23°52E 183 C8
Târgu Mureş Romania 46°31N 24°38E 183 D9
Târgu Neamţ Romania 47°12N 26°25E 183 C11
Târgu Ocna Romania 46°16N 26°39E 183 D11
Târgu Secuiesc Romania 46°0N 26°10E 183 E11
Targuist Morocco 34°59N 4°14W 260 B4
Târguşor Romania 44°27N 28°25E 183 F13
Tărhăus, Vf. Romania 46°40N 26°8E 183 D11
Tarhbalt Morocco 30°39N 5°20W 260 B3
Tarhūnah Libya 32°27N 13°36E 258 B2
Tari Papua N. G. 5°54S 142°59E 286 C2
Táriba Venezuela 7°49N 72°13W 328 B3
Ţarif U.A.E. 24°3N 53°46E 247 E7
Tarifa Spain 36°1N 5°36W 195 J5
Tarigtig Pt. Phil. 16°25N 122°14E 232 C4
Tarija Bolivia 21°30S 64°40W 334 A3
Tarija □ Bolivia 21°30S 63°30W 334 A3
Tarik I. Micronesia 7°20N 151°46E 287 T18
Tariku → Indonesia 2°55S 138°26E 231 E9
Tarīm Yemen 16°3N 49°0E 249 C5
Tarim Basin = Tarim Pendi China 40°0N 84°0E 217 E10
Tarim He → China 39°30N 88°30E 217 E11
Tarim Pendi China 40°0N 84°0E 217 E10
Tarime Tanzania 1°21S 34°22E 266 E3
Taritatu → Indonesia 2°54S 138°27E 231 E9
Tarka → S. Africa 32°10S 26°0E 270 D4
Tarka La Bhutan 27°12N 89°44E 243 F13
Tarkastad S. Africa 32°0S 26°16E 270 D4
Tarkhankut, Mys Ukraine 45°25N 32°30E 189 K7
Tarko Sale Russia 64°55N 77°50E 214 C8
Tarkwa Ghana 5°20N 2°0W 262 D4
Tarlac Phil. 15°29N 120°35E 232 D3
Tarlac □ Phil. 15°30N 120°30E 232 D3
Tarm Denmark 55°56N 8°31E 163 J2
Tarma Peru 11°25S 75°45W 330 C2
Tarmiya Iraq 33°40N 44°23E 213 G11
Tarn □ France 43°49N 2°8E 174 E6
Tarn → France 44°5N 1°6E 174 D5
Tarn-et-Garonne □ France 44°8N 1°20E 174 D5
Tarna → Hungary 47°31N 19°59E 182 C4
Târnava Mare → Romania 46°10N 23°43E 183 D8
Târnava Mică → Romania 46°9N 23°55E 183 D8
Târnăveni Romania 46°19N 24°13E 183 D9
Tårnby Denmark 55°37N 12°35E 118 B3
Tarnica Poland 49°4N 22°44E 185 J9
Tarnobrzeg Poland 50°35N 21°41E 185 H8
Tarnogród Poland 50°22N 22°45E 185 H9
Tarnopol = Ternopil Ukraine 49°30N 25°40E 177 D13
Tarnos France 43°32N 1°28W 174 E2
Târnova Moldova 48°10N 27°40E 183 B12
Târnova Romania 45°23N 21°59E 182 E6
Tarnów Poland 50°3N 21°0E 185 H8
Tarnowitz = Tarnowskie Góry Poland 50°27N 18°54E 185 H5
Tarnowskie Góry Poland 50°27N 18°54E 185 H5
Tärnsjö Sweden 60°9N 16°56E 162 D10
Táro → Italy 45°2N 10°15E 198 C7
Taroko △ Taiwan 24°10N 121°33E 225 B3
Ţārom Iran 28°11N 55°46E 247 D7
Taroom Australia 25°36S 149°48E 281 D4
Taroudannt Morocco 30°30N 8°52W 260 B3
Taroume Cook Is. 21°15S 159°45W 289 h
Tarp Germany 54°39N 9°24E 178 A5
Tarpeena Australia 37°37S 140°47E 282 D4
Tarpon Springs U.S.A. 28°9N 82°45W 317 G7
Tarqua Bay Nigeria 6°24N 3°23E 124 B2
Tarquínia Italy 42°15N 11°45E 199 F8
Tarra Bulga △ Australia 38°27S 146°31E 283 E7
Tarrafal C. Verde Is. 15°18N 23°39W 153 j
Tarragona Spain 41°5N 1°17E 196 D6
Tarragona □ Spain 41°5N 1°0E 196 D6
Tarraleah Australia 42°17S 146°26E 281 G4
Tarrasa = Terrassa Spain 41°34N 2°1E 196 D7
Tàrrega Spain 41°39N 1°9E 196 D6
Tarrytown Ga., U.S.A. 32°19N 82°34W 316 C7
Tarrytown N.Y., U.S.A. 41°4N 73°52W 313 E11
Tårs Denmark 57°23N 10°7E 163 G4
Tarsus Turkey 36°58N 34°55E 250 B5
Tarsus → Turkey 36°46N 34°52E 250 B5
Tartagal Argentina 22°30S 63°50W 334 A3
Tartane Martinique 14°45N 60°55W 322 j
Tärtär Azerbaijan 40°20N 46°58E 191 K8
Tärtär → Azerbaijan 40°26N 47°20E 191 K8
Tartas France 43°50N 0°49W 174 E3
Tartu Estonia 58°20N 26°44E 188 C4
Ţarţūs Syria 34°55N 35°55E 250 D6
Ţarţūs □ Syria 35°0N 36°0E 250 D7
Tarumirim Brazil 19°16S 41°59W 333 E3
Tarumizu Japan 31°29N 130°42E 222 F2
Tarussa Russia 54°44N 37°10E 188 E9
Tarutao = Ko Tarutao △ Thailand 6°31N 99°26E 237 J2
Tarutao, Ko Thailand 6°33N 99°40E 237 J2
Tarutung Indonesia 2°0N 98°54E 234 B1
Tarutyne Ukraine 46°12N 29°9E 183 D14
Tarvísio Italy 46°30N 13°35E 199 B10
Tarxien Malta 35°52N 14°31E 206 F8
Taşağıl Turkey 36°55N 31°14E 250 B2
Tasahku Burma 27°33N 97°52E 241 B6
Tasaret, O. → Algeria 26°25N 1°59E 261 C5
Tasāwah Libya 26°0N 13°30E 258 C2
Tasböget Kazakhstan 44°46N 65°33E 217 D7
Tasek Merimbun △ Brunei 4°31N 114°41E 235 B4
Taseko → Canada 52°8N 123°45W 296 C4
Tasgaon India 17°2N 74°39E 244 F2
Tash-Kömür Kyrgyzstan 41°40N 72°10E 217 D8
Tashauz = Daşoguz Turkmenistan 41°49N 59°58E 216 D5
Tashi Chho Dzong = Thimphu Bhutan 27°31N 89°45E 241 B2
Tashino = Pervomaysk Russia 54°56N 43°58E 190 C6
Ţashk, Daryācheh-ye Iran 29°45N 53°35E 247 D7
Tashkent = Toshkent Uzbekistan 41°20N 69°10E 217 D7
Tashtagol Russia 52°47N 87°53E 217 B11
Tashu Taiwan 22°41N 120°25E 225 D2
Tasiilaq Greenland 65°40N 37°20W 154 D7
Tasik Bera Malaysia 3°5N 102°38E 234 B2
Tasik Kenyir Malaysia 5°5N 102°45E 234 A2
Tasikmalaya Indonesia 7°18S 108°12E 235 D3
Tåsinge Denmark 55°0N 10°35E 163 J4
Tåsjön Sweden 64°15N 15°40E 160 D16
Task Niger 14°56N 10°46E 259 F2
Taskan Russia 62°59N 150°20E 215 C16
Taşkent Turkey 36°55N 32°29E 250 B3
Taşköprü Turkey 41°30N 34°15E 212 B6
Taskul Papua N. G. 2°32S 150°27E 286 B6
Taşlâc Moldova 47°4N 29°24E 183 C14
Taşliçay Turkey 39°38N 43°22E 213 C10
Tasman □ N.Z. 41°30S 172°40E 285 B7
Tasman → N.Z. 43°48S 170°8E 285 D5
Tasman, Mt. N.Z. 43°34S 170°12E 285 D5
Tasman Abyssal Plain Pac. Oc. 34°30S 153°15E 276 G9
Tasman B. N.Z. 40°59S 173°25E 285 A8
Tasman Basin Pac. Oc. 46°0S 158°0E 288 M7
Tasman Glacier N.Z. 43°37S 170°12E 285 D5
Tasman Mts. N.Z. 41°3S 172°25E 285 B7
Tasman Pen. Australia 43°10S 148°0E 281 G4
Tasman Sea Pac. Oc. 36°0S 160°0E 277 H10
Tasmania □ Australia 42°0S 146°30E 281 G4
Tasmanian Wilderness World Heritage Area △ Australia 43°0S 146°0E 281 G4
Tăşnad Romania 47°30N 22°33E 182 C7
Taşova Turkey 40°45N 36°19E 212 B7
Tassili n'Ajjer Algeria 25°47N 8°1E 261 C6
Tassili n'Ajjer △ Algeria 26°5N 6°0E 258 C1
Tassili-Oua-n-Ahaggar Algeria 20°41N 5°30E 261 D6
Tassili Tin-Rerhoh Algeria 20°5N 3°55E 261 D5
Taşucu Turkey 36°19N 33°52E 250 B4
Taşucu Körfezi Turkey 36°16N 33°56E 250 B4
Tasuj Iran 38°18N 45°23E 213 C11
Tat Ton △ Thailand 15°57N 102°2E 236 E4
Tata Hungary 47°37N 18°19E 182 C3
Tata Morocco 29°46N 7°56W 260 C3
Tatabánya Hungary 47°32N 18°25E 182 C3
Tatakoto French Polynesia 17°20S 138°23W 289 f
Tatamá △ Colombia 5°5N 76°9W 328 B2
Tatamba Solomon Is. 8°21S 159°51E 287 M10
Tataouine Tunisia 32°57N 10°29E 258 B2
Tataouine □ Tunisia 32°0N 10°0E 261 B7
Tatar-Pazardzhik = Pazardzhik Bulgaria 42°12N 24°20E 203 D8
Tatar Republic = Tatarstan □ Russia 55°30N 51°30E 190 C10
Tatarbunary Ukraine 45°50N 29°39E 183 E14
Tatarsk Russia 55°14N 76°0E 217 A9
Tatarskiy Proliv Russia 50°0N 141°0E 215 E15
Tatarstan □ Russia 55°30N 51°30E 190 C10
Tatatóváros = Tata Hungary 47°37N 18°19E 182 C3
Tatatua, Pte. Tahiti 17°44S 149°8W 289 e
Tatau Malaysia 2°53N 112°51E 235 B4
Tatau I. Papua N. G. 2°48S 151°57E 286 B6
Tatebayashi Japan 36°15N 139°32E 223 A11
Tateshina-Yama Japan 36°8N 138°11E 223 A10
Tateyama Chiba, Japan 35°0N 139°50E 223 C11
Tateyama Toyama, Japan 36°40N 137°35E 223 A9
Tathlina L. Canada 60°33N 117°39W 296 A5
Tathlīth Si. Arabia 19°32N 43°30E 248 C3
Tathlīth, W. → Si. Arabia 20°35N 44°20E 248 B4
Tathong Channel China 22°15N 114°16E 122 B2
Tathong Pt. China 22°14N 114°17E 122 B2
Tathra Australia 36°44S 149°59E 283 D8
Tatinnai L. Canada 60°55N 97°40W 297 A9
Tatitlek U.S.A. 60°52N 146°41W 303 F11
Tatkon Burma 20°7N 96°13E 241 E6
Tatla Lake Canada 52°0N 124°20W 296 C4
Tatlısu = Akanthou Cyprus 35°22N 33°45E 207 E9
Tatlısu Turkey 40°24N 27°55E 203 F11
Tatnam, C. Canada 57°16N 91°0W 297 B10
Tatra = Tatry Slovak Rep. 49°20N 20°0E 181 B13
Tatranský △ Slovak Rep. 49°10N 20°0E 181 B13
Tatry Slovak Rep. 49°20N 20°0E 181 B13
Tatshenshini → Canada 59°28N 137°45W 296 B1
Tatshenshini-Alsek ⌓ Canada 59°55N 137°45W 296 B1
Tatsuno Hyōgo, Japan 34°52N 134°33E 222 C6
Tatsuno Nagano, Japan 35°58N 138°0E 223 B10
Tatta = Thatta Pakistan 24°42N 67°55E 242 G2
Tatuapé Brazil 23°31S 46°33W 137 B2
Tatuī Brazil 23°25S 47°53W 335 A6
Tatum U.S.A. 33°16N 103°19W 305 K12
Tat'ung = Datong China 40°6N 113°18E 226 D7
Tatura Australia 36°29S 145°16E 283 D6
Tatvan Turkey 38°31N 42°15E 213 C10
Ta'ū Amer. Samoa 14°15S 169°30W 302 g
Tau Rogaland, Norway 59°3N 5°55E 164 E2
Tauá Brazil 6°1S 40°26W 332 C3
Taubaté Brazil 23°0S 45°36W 335 A6
Tauberbischofsheim Germany 49°37N 9°39E 179 F5
Taucha Germany 51°23N 12°29E 178 D8
Tauern Austria 47°15N 12°40E 176 E7
Tauern-tunnel Austria 47°0N 13°12E 180 D6
Taufikia South Sudan 9°24N 31°37E 257 F3
Taufkirchen Germany 48°2N 11°36E 131 B2
Taulé France 48°37N 3°55W 172 D3
Taumarunui N.Z. 38°53S 175°15E 284 E4
Taumaturgo Brazil 8°54S 72°51W 330 B3
Taung S. Africa 27°33S 24°47E 270 C3
Taungdwingyi Burma 20°1N 95°40E 241 E5
Taunggyi Burma 20°50N 97°0E 241 E6
Taungoo = Tounggoo Burma 19°0N 96°30E 241 F6
Taungtha Burma 21°12N 95°25E 241 E5
Taungup Burma 18°51N 94°14E 241 F5
Taungup Pass Burma 18°40N 94°45E 241 F5
Taunsa Pakistan 30°42N 70°39E 242 D4
Taunsa Barrage Pakistan 30°42N 70°50E 242 D4
Taunton Somst., U.K. 51°1N 3°5W 169 F4
Taunton Mass., U.S.A. 41°54N 71°6W 313 E13
Taunus Germany 50°13N 8°34E 179 E4
Taupo N.Z. 38°41S 176°7E 284 E5
Taupo, L. N.Z. 38°46S 175°55E 284 E4
Tauragė Lithuania 55°14N 22°16E 184 C9
Tauragė □ Lithuania 55°15N 22°17E 184 C9
Tauranga N.Z. 37°42S 176°11E 284 D5
Tauranga Harb. N.Z. 37°30S 176°5E 284 D5
Taureau, Rés. Canada 46°46N 73°50W 298 C5
Tauri → Papua N. G. 8°8S 146°8E 286 E4
Taurianova Italy 38°21N 16°1E 201 D9
Tauroa Pt. N.Z. 35°10S 173°4E 284 B2
Taurus Mts. = Toros Dağları Turkey 37°0N 32°30E 250 B3
Taus = Domažlice Czech Rep. 49°28N 12°58E 180 B5
Tauste Spain 41°58N 1°18W 196 D3
Tautira Tahiti 17°44S 149°9W 289 e
Tauyskaya Guba Russia 59°20N 150°20E 215 D16
Tauz = Tovuz Azerbaijan 41°0N 45°40E 191 K7
Tavan Bogd Uul Mongolia 49°10N 87°49E 217 C11
Tavares U.S.A. 28°48N 81°44W 317 G8
Tavares, I. dos Brazil 22°49S 43°6W 135 A2
Tavas Turkey 37°34N 29°4E 205 D11
Tavastehus = Hämeenlinna Finland 61°0N 24°28E 188 B3
Tavda Russia 58°7N 65°8E 214 D7
Tavda → Russia 57°47N 67°18E 214 D7
Taverner B. Canada 67°12N 72°25W 295 D17
Tavernes de la Valldigna Spain 39°5N 0°13W 197 F4
Tavernier U.S.A. 25°1N 80°31W 317 K9
Taveta Kenya 3°23S 37°37E 268 C4
Taveuni Fiji 16°51S 179°58W 287 A3
Taviano Italy 39°59N 18°5E 201 C11
Tavignano → France 42°7N 9°33E 175 F13
Tavira Portugal 37°8N 7°40W 195 H3
Tavistock Ont., Canada 43°19N 80°50W 312 C4
Tavistock Devon, U.K. 50°33N 4°9W 169 G3
Tavolara Italy 40°54N 9°42E 200 B2
Távora → Portugal 41°8N 7°35W 194 D3
Tavoy Burma 14°2N 98°12E 236 E2
Tavoy Pt. Burma 13°32N 98°10E 236 F2
Tavrichanka Russia 43°18N 131°59E 220 C5
Tavropos → Greece 39°10N 21°45E 204 B3
Tavros Greece 37°57N 23°43E 112 B2
Tavşanlı Turkey 39°32N 29°30E 205 B11
Tavua Fiji 17°37S 177°5E 287 A1
Tavuki Fiji 19°7S 178°8E 287 B2
Taw → U.K. 51°4N 4°4W 169 F3
Tawa → India 22°48N 77°48E 242 H8
Tawa Res. India 22°35N 78°5E 244 C4
Tawa Tawa Mal Reef Papua N. G. 11°3S 152°55E 286 F7
Tawai India 27°48N 96°47E 241 B6
Tawang India 27°35N 91°52E 241 B3
Tawas City U.S.A. 44°16N 83°31W 309 C12
Tawau Malaysia 4°20N 117°55E 235 B5
Tawau Hills △ Malaysia 4°20N 117°54E 235 B5
Taweisha Sudan 12°19N 26°40E 257 E2
Tawi-tawi □ Phil. 5°0N 120°0E 233 J3
Tawi-tawi I. Phil. 5°10N 120°15E 233 J3
Tawngche Burma 26°34N 95°38E 241 B5
Tawu Taiwan 22°22N 120°54E 225 D2
Ţāwūq Iraq 35°8N 44°26E 213 E11
Tāwurghā' Libya 32°1N 15°2E 258 B3
Tāwurghā', Sabkhat Libya 31°51N 15°15E 258 B3
Taxco Mexico 18°33N 99°36W 319 D5
Taxila Pakistan 33°42N 72°52E 242 C5
Taxkorgan Tajik Zizhixian China 37°49N 75°14E 217 E9
Tay → U.K. 56°37N 3°38W 167 E5
Tay, Firth of U.K. 56°25N 3°8W 167 E5
Tay, L. W. Austral., Australia 32°55S 120°48E 279 F3
Tay, L. Perth & Kinr., U.K. 56°32N 4°8W 167 E4
Tay ⌓ U.K. 56°43N 3°59W 167 E5
Tay Ninh Vietnam 11°20N 106°5E 237 G6
Tayabamba Peru 8°15S 77°16W 330 B2
Tayabas = Quezon Phil. 9°15N 117°59E 233 G1
Tayabas Phil. 14°1N 121°35E 232 D3
Tayabas B. Phil. 13°45N 121°45E 232 E3
Tayan Indonesia 0°1S 110°7E 235 C4
Taygetos Oros Greece 37°0N 22°23E 204 D4
Taylakova Russia 59°13N 74°0E 214 D8
Taylor B.C., Canada 56°13N 120°40W 296 B4
Taylor Fla., U.S.A. 30°26N 82°18W 316 E7
Taylor Mich., U.S.A. 42°14N 83°16W 311 B13
Taylor Nebr., U.S.A. 41°46N 99°23W 308 E4
Taylor Pa., U.S.A. 41°23N 75°43W 313 E9
Taylor Tex., U.S.A. 30°34N 97°25W 314 F6
Taylor, Mt. N.Z. 43°30S 171°20E 285 D6
Taylor, Mt. N. Mex., U.S.A. 35°14N 107°37W 305 J10
Taylorsville U.S.A. 38°2N 85°21W 311 F11
Taylorsville L. U.S.A. 38°0N 85°15W 311 G11
Taylorville U.S.A. 39°33N 89°18W 310 E7
Taymā Si. Arabia 27°35N 38°45E 246 E3
Taymyr, Oz. Russia 74°20N 102°0E 215 B11
Taymyr, Poluostrov Russia 75°0N 100°0E 215 B11
Taypaq Kazakhstan 49°0N 51°47E 187 E9
Tayport U.K. 56°27N 2°52W 167 E6
Tayrona △ Colombia 11°20N 74°2W 328 A3
Tayshet Russia 55°58N 98°1E 215 D10
Taytay Phil. 10°45N 119°30E 233 F2
Taytay B. Phil. 10°55N 119°35E 233 F2
Tayuan Taiwan 25°3N 121°11E 225 A3
Tayug Phil. 16°2N 120°45E 232 C3
Tayüling Taiwan 24°11N 121°18E 225 B3
Tāyyebād Iran 34°45N 60°45E 247 C9
Tāyyebād □ Iran 34°44N 60°44E 247 C9
Tayynsha Kazakhstan 53°50N 69°45E 217 B7
Taz → Russia 67°32N 78°40E 214 C8
Taza Morocco 34°16N 4°6W 260 B4
Taza-Al Hoceïma-Taounate □ Morocco 34°15N 3°20W 261 B4
Tāza Khurmātū Iraq 35°18N 44°20E 213 E11
Taza-Taou □ Morocco 34°15N 4°10W 260 B4
Tazawa-Ko Japan 39°43N 140°40E 220 E10
Taze Burma 22°57N 95°24E 241 D5
Tazenakht Morocco 30°35N 7°12W 260 B3
Tazerbo Libya 25°45N 21°0E 258 C4
Tazin → Canada 59°48N 109°55W 297 B7
Tazin L. Canada 59°44N 108°42W 297 B7
Tazlina U.S.A. 62°4N 146°27W 303 E11
Tazouikert Mali 21°27N 1°16W 261 D4
Tazoult Algeria 35°29N 6°11E 261 A6
Tazovskiy Russia 67°30N 78°44E 214 C8
Tazrouk Algeria 23°24N 6°15E 261 D6
Tbilisi Georgia 41°43N 44°50E 191 K7
Tchad = Chad ■ Africa 15°0N 17°15E 259 F3
Tchad, L. Chad 13°30N 14°30E 259 F2
Tchaourou Benin 8°58N 2°40E 263 D5
Tch'eng-tou = Chengdu China 30°38N 104°2E 228 B5
Tchentlo L. Canada 55°15N 125°0W 296 B4
Tchetti Benin 7°50N 1°40E 263 D5
Tchibanga Gabon 2°45S 11°0E 264 C2
Tchien Liberia 5°59N 8°15W 262 D3
Tchin Tabaraden Niger 15°58N 5°56E 263 B6
Tchogha Zanbil = Choghā Zanbīl Iran 32°1N 48°32E 247 C6
Tchollíré Cameroon 8°24N 14°10E 264 A2
Tch'ong-k'ing = Chongqing China 29°35N 106°25E 228 C6
Tchoupitoulas Street New Orleans, U.S.A. 131 b2
Tczew Poland 54°8N 18°50E 184 D5
TD Garden Boston, U.S.A. 116 a2
Te Anau N.Z. 45°25S 167°43E 285 F2
Te Anau, L. N.Z. 45°15S 167°45E 285 F2
Te Araroa N.Z. 37°39S 178°25E 284 D7
Te Aroha N.Z. 37°32S 175°44E 284 D4
Te Awamutu N.Z. 38°1S 175°20E 284 E4
Te Ika a Maui = North I. N.Z. 38°0S 175°0E 284 E4
Te Kaha N.Z. 37°44S 177°52E 284 D6
Te Karaka N.Z. 38°26S 177°53E 284 E6
Te Kauwhata N.Z. 37°25S 175°9E 284 D4
Te Kopuru N.Z. 36°2S 173°56E 284 C2
Te Kou Cook Is. 21°14S 159°46W 289 h
Te Kuiti N.Z. 38°20S 175°11E 284 E4
Te Manga Cook Is. 21°14S 159°45W 289 h
Te-n-Dghâmcha, Sebkhet Mauritania 18°30N 15°55W 262 B1
Te Nggano, L. Solomon Is. 11°40S 160°19E 287 N11
Te Puke N.Z. 37°46S 176°22E 284 D5
Te Teko N.Z. 38°2S 176°48E 284 E5
Te Waewae B. N.Z. 46°13S 167°33E 285 G2
Te Wai Pounamu = South I. N.Z. 44°0S 170°0E 285 E5
Tea → Brazil 0°30S 65°9W 328 D4
Teaca Romania 46°55N 24°30E 183 D9
Teague U.S.A. 31°38N 96°17W 314 F6
Teahupoo Tahiti 17°50S 149°16W 289 e
Teaneck U.S.A. 40°53N 74°1W 132 A1
Teano Italy 41°15N 14°4E 201 A7
Teapa Mexico 17°33N 92°57W 319 D6
Teba Spain 36°59N 4°55W 195 J6
Tebakang Malaysia 1°6N 110°30E 235 B4
Tébarat Niger 14°49N 4°27E 263 C5
Teberau → Malaysia 1°30N 103°42E 237 d
Teberda Russia 43°30N 41°46E 191 J5
Tébessa Algeria 35°22N 8°8E 261 A6
Tébessa □ Algeria 35°0N 7°50E 261 B6
Tebet Indonesia 6°14S 106°50E 122 B2
Tebicuary → Paraguay 26°36S 58°16W 334 B4
Tebingtinggi Riau, Indonesia 1°0N 102°45E 234 B2
Tebingtinggi Sumatera Selatan, Indonesia 3°36S 103°4E 234 C2
Tebingtinggi Sumatera Utara, Indonesia 3°20N 99°9E 234 B1
Tébourba Tunisia 36°49N 9°51E 258 A1
Téboursouk Tunisia 36°29N 9°10E 258 A1
Tebulos Georgia 42°36N 45°17E 191 J7
Tecamachalco Mexico 19°25N 99°14W 128 B1
Tecate Mexico 32°34N 116°38W 307 N10
Tecer Dağları Turkey 39°27N 37°27E 212 C7
Tech → France 42°36N 3°3E 174 F7
Techiman Ghana 7°35N 1°58W 262 D4
Techirghiol Romania 44°4N 28°32E 183 F13
Techou = Dezhou China 37°26N 116°18E 226 F9
Tecka Argentina 43°29S 70°48W 336 B2
Tecomán Mexico 18°55N 103°53W 318 D4
Tecopa U.S.A. 35°51N 116°13W 307 K10
Tecoripa Mexico 28°37N 109°57W 318 B3
Tecuala Mexico 22°23N 105°27W 318 C3
Tecuci Romania 45°51N 27°27E 183 E12
Tecumseh Ont., Canada 42°19N 82°54W 312 D2
Tecumseh Mich., U.S.A. 42°0N 83°57W 311 B13
Tecumseh Okla., U.S.A. 35°15N 96°56W 314 D6
Ted Somalia 4°24N 43°55E 267 D5
Ted Williams Tunnel U.S.A. 42°21N 71°1W 116 A2
Teddington U.K. 51°25N 0°20W 125 B1
Tedjert Algeria 21°23N 6°25E 261 D6
Tedzhen = Tejen Turkmenistan 37°23N 60°31E 216 E6
Tees → U.K. 54°37N 1°10W 168 C6
Tees B. U.K. 54°40N 1°9W 168 C6
Teeswater Canada 43°59N 81°17W 312 C3
Tefé Brazil 3°25S 64°50W 329 D5
Tefé → Brazil 3°35S 64°47W 329 D5
Tefenni Turkey 37°18N 29°45E 205 D11
Tegal Indonesia 6°52S 109°8E 235 D3
Tegallalang Indonesia 8°27S 115°17E 231 J18
Tegalsari Indonesia 8°25S 114°8E 231 J17
Tegano, L. = Te Nggano, L. Solomon Is. 11°40S 160°19E 287 N11
Tegel Germany 52°34N 13°16E 115 A2
Tegeler See Germany 52°34N 13°15E 115 A2
Tegelort Germany 52°34N 13°13E 115 A2
Tegernsee Germany 47°43N 11°46E 179 H7
Teggiano Italy 40°23N 15°32E 201 B8
Tegid, L. = Bala, L. U.K. 52°53N 3°37W 168 E4
Tegina Nigeria 10°5N 6°11E 263 C6
Tegua Vanuatu 13°15S 166°37E 287 C4
Tegucigalpa Honduras 14°5N 87°14W 320 D2
Teguidda i-n-Tessoum Niger 17°25N 6°37E 263 B6
Teguise Canary Is. 29°3N 13°33W 153 e2
Tehachapi U.S.A. 35°8N 118°27W 307 K8
Tehachapi Mts. U.S.A. 35°0N 118°30W 307 L8
Tehamiyam Sudan 18°20N 36°32E 256 D4
Teheran = Tehrān Iran 35°41N 51°25E 141 A2
Tehilla Sudan 17°42N 36°6E 256 D4
Téhini Ivory C. 9°39N 3°40W 262 D4
Tehoru Indonesia 3°23S 129°30E 231 E7
Tehrān Iran 35°41N 51°25E 141 A2
Tehrān □ Iran 35°30N 51°30E 247 C6
Tehrān Mehrābād ✈ (THR) Iran 35°41N 51°18E 141 A1
Tehrān Pārs Iran 35°44N 51°32E 141 A3
Tehri India 30°23N 78°29E 243 D8
Tehuacán Mexico 18°27N 97°23W 319 D5
Tehuantepec Mexico 16°21N 95°13W 319 D5
Tehuantepec, G. de Mexico 15°50N 95°12W 319 D5
Tehuantepec, Istmo de Mexico 17°15N 94°30W 319 D6
Tehuantepec Fracture Zone Pac. Oc. 13°0N 97°0W 289 F18
Tei Tong Tsui China 22°16N 114°17E 122 B2
Teide, Pico de Canary Is. 28°15N 16°38W 153 e1
Teifi → U.K. 52°5N 4°41W 169 E3
Teigebyen Norway 60°12N 11°0E 162 D5
Teign → U.K. 50°32N 3°32W 169 G4
Teignmouth U.K. 50°33N 3°31W 169 G4
Teiuş Romania 46°12N 23°40E 183 D8
Teixeira Brazil 7°13S 37°15W 332 C4
Teixeira Pinto Guinea-Biss. 12°3N 16°0W 262 C1
Tejakula Indonesia 8°8S 115°20E 231 J18
Tejen Turkmenistan 37°23N 60°31E 216 E6
Tejen → Turkmenistan 37°24N 60°38E 247 B9
Tejo → Europe 38°40N 9°24W 195 F2
Tejo, Rio → Portugal 38°45N 9°3W 126 A2
Tejon Pass U.S.A. 34°49N 118°53W 307 L8
Tekamah U.S.A. 41°47N 96°13W 308 E5
Tekapo → N.Z. 44°13S 170°21E 285 E5
Tekapo, L. N.Z. 43°53S 170°33E 285 D5
Tekax Mexico 20°12N 89°17W 319 C7
Teke Turkey 41°4N 29°39E 203 E13
Tekeli Kazakhstan 44°50N 79°0E 217 D9
Tekeze → Ethiopia 14°20N 35°50E 257 E4
Tekeze Dam Ethiopia 13°10N 38°45E 257 E4
Tekija Serbia 44°42N 22°26E 202 B6
Tekirdağ Turkey 40°58N 27°30E 203 F11
Tekirdağ □ Turkey 41°0N 27°0E 203 E11
Tekirova Turkey 36°30N 30°32E 205 E12
Tekkali India 18°37N 84°15E 244 E7
Tekke Turkey 40°42N 36°12E 212 B7
Tekman Turkey 39°38N 41°29E 213 C9
Teknaf Bangla. 20°52N 92°18E 241 E4
Tekoa U.S.A. 47°14N 117°4W 304 C5
Tekokota French Polynesia 17°18S 142°34W 289 f
Tekong Besar, Pulau Singapore 1°25N 104°3E 237 d
Tekouiât, O. → Algeria 22°25N 2°35E 261 D5
Tékro Chad 19°32N 20°56E 259 E4
Tekstilyshchik Russia 55°42N 37°41E 129 B3
Tel → India 20°50N 83°54E 244 D6
Tel Aviv-Yafo Israel 32°4N 34°48E 251 F5
Tel Lakhish Israel 31°34N 34°51E 251 G5
Tel Megiddo Israel 32°35N 35°11E 250 F6
Tela Honduras 15°40N 87°28W 320 C2
Télagh Algeria 34°51N 0°32W 261 B4
Telanaipura = Jambi Indonesia 1°38S 103°30E 234 C2
Telangana India 17°30N 78°30E 244 F4
Telašćica ⌓ Croatia 43°55N 15°10E 199 E12
Telavi Georgia 42°0N 45°30E 191 J7
Telč Czech Rep. 49°11N 15°28E 180 B8
Telciu Romania 47°25N 24°24E 183 C9
Telde Canary Is. 27°59N 15°25W 153 e1
Tele → Dem. Rep. of the Congo 2°48N 23°54E 264 B4
Telefomin Papua N. G. 5°10S 141°31E 286 C1
Telegraph Creek Canada 58°0N 131°10W 296 B2
Telegraph Hill San Francisco, U.S.A. 136 a2
Telekhany = Tsyelyakhany Belarus 52°30N 25°46E 177 B13
Telemark Norway 59°15N 7°40E 161 G12
Telemark □ Norway 59°25N 8°30E 164 E5
Télemsès Niger 15°37N 4°44E 263 B5
Telén Argentina 36°15S 65°31W 334 D2
Telen → Indonesia 0°10S 117°20E 235 C5
Teleneşti Moldova 47°30N 28°22E 183 C13
Teleng Iran 25°47N 61°3E 247 E9
Teleño Spain 42°23N 6°22W 194 C4
Teleorman □ Romania 44°0N 25°0E 183 G10
Teleorman → Romania 43°52N 25°26E 183 G10
Telerhteba, Djebel Algeria 24°10N 6°51E 261 D6
Teles Pires → Brazil 7°21S 58°3W 331 B6
Telescope Pk. U.S.A. 36°10N 117°5W 307 J9
Telescope Pt. Grenada 12°7N 61°36W 323 q
Teletaye Mali 16°31N 1°30E 263 B5
Teletskoye, Oz. Russia 51°40N 87°30E 217 B11
Telford U.K. 52°40N 2°27W 169 E5
Telford and Wrekin □ U.K. 52°45N 2°27W 168 E5
Telfs Austria 47°19N 11°4E 180 D4
Telhal Portugal 38°48N 9°18W 126 A1
Telida U.S.A. 63°23N 153°16W 303 E9
Télimélé Guinea 10°54N 13°2W 262 C2
Teljo, J. Sudan 14°42N 25°26E 257 E2
Telkwa Canada 54°41N 127°5W 296 C3
Tell City U.S.A. 37°57N 86°46W 311 G10
Teller U.S.A. 65°16N 166°22W 303 D6
Tellicherry = Thalassery India 11°45N 75°30E 245 J2
Telluride U.S.A. 37°56N 107°49W 305 H10
Telok Blangah Singapore 1°17N 103°49E 138 B2
Teloloapán Mexico 18°21N 99°51W 319 D5
Telpos Iz Russia 63°16N 59°13E 186 B10
Telsen Argentina 42°30S 66°50W 336 B3
Telšiai Lithuania 55°59N 22°14E 184 C9
Telšiai □ Lithuania 55°59N 22°15E 184 C9
Teltow Germany 52°23N 13°17E 115 B2
Teltow kanal Germany 52°26N 13°29E 115 B3
Teluk Anson = Teluk Intan Malaysia 4°3N 101°0E 237 K3
Teluk Bahang Malaysia 5°28N 100°13E 237 c
Teluk Betung = Bandar Lampung Indonesia 5°20S 105°10E 234 D3
Teluk Intan Malaysia 4°3N 101°0E 237 K3
Teluk Kumbar Malaysia 5°18N 100°14E 237 c
Telukbatang Indonesia 1°10S 109°46E 235 C3
Telukbayur Kalimantan Timur, Indonesia 2°9N 117°24E 235 B5
Telukbayur Sumatera Barat, Indonesia 0°59S 100°23E 234 C2
Telukbutun Indonesia 4°13N 108°12E 235 B3
Telukdalam Indonesia 0°33N 97°50E 234 B1
Tema Ghana 5°41N 0°0 263 D5
Temagami, L. Canada 47°0N 80°10W 298 C3
Temasint Algeria 23°18N 7°40E 261 D6
Tematangi French Polynesia 21°41S 140°40W 289 f
Temax Mexico 21°9N 88°56W 319 C7
Temba S. Africa 25°20S 28°17E 271 C4
Tembagapura Indonesia 4°20S 137°0E 231 E9
Tembe Dem. Rep. of the Congo 0°16S 28°14E 268 C2
Tembe ⌓ S. Africa 26°51S 32°24E 271 C5
Tembesi → Indonesia 1°43S 103°6E 234 C2
Tembilahan Indonesia 0°19S 103°9E 234 C2
Temblador Venezuela 8°59N 62°44W 329 B5
Tembleque Spain 39°41N 3°30W 194 F7
Temblor Range U.S.A. 35°20N 119°50W 307 K7
Tembo Aluma Angola 7°42S 17°17E 265 D3
Teme → U.K. 52°11N 2°13W 169 E5
Temecula U.S.A. 33°30N 117°9W 307 M9
Temengor, Tasik Malaysia 5°24N 101°18E 237 K3
Temerloh Malaysia 3°27N 102°25E 237 L4
Temiang Indonesia 0°19N 104°23E 234 B2
Teminabuan Indonesia 1°26S 132°1E 231 E8
Temir Kazakhstan 49°1N 57°14E 187 E10
Temir-Khan-Shura = Buynaksk Russia 42°48N 47°7E 191 J8
Temirtau Kazakhstan 50°5N 72°56E 217 B8
Temirtau Russia 53°10N 87°30E 217 B11
Témiscamie → Canada 50°59N 73°5W 299 B5
Témiscaming Canada 46°44N 79°5W 298 C4
Témiscamingue, L. Canada 47°10N 79°25W 298 C4
Temnikov Russia 54°40N 43°11E 190 C6
Temo → Italy 40°17N 8°28E 200 B1
Temora Australia 34°30S 147°30E 283 C7
Temosachic Mexico 28°57N 107°51W 318 B3
Tempe U.S.A. 33°24N 111°54W 305 K8
Tempelburg = Czaplinek Poland 53°34N 16°14E 184 E3
Tempelhof Germany 52°27N 13°23E 115 B3
Temperance U.S.A. 41°47N 83°34W 311 C13
Tempino Indonesia 1°46S 103°30E 234 C2
Témpio Pausánia Italy 40°54N 9°6E 200 B2
Tempiute U.S.A. 37°39N 115°38W 306 H11
Templar Bank S. China Sea 9°0N 117°30E 233 F1
Temple U.S.A. 31°6N 97°21W 314 F6
Temple B. Australia 12°15S 143°3E 286 G2
Temple City U.S.A. 34°6N 118°3W 126 B4
Temple Hills U.S.A. 38°48N 76°56W 143 C3
Temple Mount Jerusalem 123 b3
Temple of Heaven China 39°52N 116°23E 114 B2
Temple of the Dawn = Arun Bangkok, Thailand 113 b1
Temple Terrace U.S.A. 28°2N 82°23W 317 G7
Templemore Ireland 52°47N 7°51W 166 D4
Templeogue Ireland 53°18N 6°18W 120 B2
Templeton U.S.A. 35°33N 120°42W 306 K6
Templeton → Australia 21°0S 138°40E 280 C2
Templin Germany 53°7N 13°28E 178 B9
Templo Mayor Mexico City, Mexico 128 b3
Tempoal de Sánchez Mexico 21°31N 98°23W 319 C5
Temppeliaukio Church Finland 60°10N 24°56E 121 B2
Tempué Angola 13°27S 18°49E 265 E3
Temryuk Russia 45°15N 37°24E 189 K9
Temska → Serbia 43°17N 22°33E 202 C6
Temuco Chile 38°45S 72°40W 336 A2
Temuka N.Z. 44°14S 171°17E 285 E6
Ten Degree Channel India 10°0N 92°30E 245 K11
Ten Thousand Is. U.S.A. 25°55N 81°45W 317 K8
Tena Ecuador 0°59S 77°49W 328 D2
Tenabo Mexico 20°3N 90°14W 319 C6
Tenafly U.S.A. 40°54N 73°58W 132 A2
Tenaha U.S.A. 31°57N 94°15W 314 F7
Tenakee Springs U.S.A. 57°47N 135°13W 296 B1
Tenali India 16°15N 80°35E 245 F5
Tenancingo Mexico 18°58N 99°38W 319 D5
Tenango del Valle Mexico 19°7N 99°33W 319 D5
Tenaro, Akra Greece 36°22N 22°27E 204 E4
Tenasserim Burma 12°6N 99°3E 237 F2
Tenasserim □ Burma 14°0N 98°30E 236 F2
Tenasserim → Burma 12°24N 98°37E 236 F2
Tenayuca, Piramide de Mexico 19°31N 99°10W 128 A1
Tenby U.K. 51°40N 4°42W 169 F3
Tenda, Colle di France 44°7N 7°36E 175 D11
Tendaho Ethiopia 11°48N 40°54E 257 E5
Tende France 44°5N 7°35E 175 D11
Tendelti Sudan 13°1N 31°55E 257 E3
Tendjedi, Adrar Algeria 23°41N 7°32E 261 D6
Tendō Japan 38°20N 140°30E 220 E10
Tendrara Morocco 33°3N 1°58W 261 B4
Tendrovskaya Kosa Ukraine 46°16N 31°35E 189 J6
Tendukhera India 23°24N 79°33E 243 H8
Teneguía, Volcanes de Canary Is. 28°28N 17°51W 153 e1
Teneida Egypt 25°30N 29°19E 256 B2
Tenenkou Mali 14°28N 4°55W 262 C4
Tenente Marques → Brazil 11°10S 59°56W 331 C6
Ténéré Niger 19°0N 10°30E 259 E2
Ténéré, Erg du Niger 17°35N 10°55E 259 E2
Tenerife Canary Is. 28°15N 16°35W 153 e1
Tenerife, Pico Canary Is. 27°43N 18°1W 153 e1
Tenerife Norte ✈ (TFN) Canary Is. 28°28N 16°17W 153 e1
Tenerife Sur ✈ (TFS) Canary Is. 28°3N 16°33W 153 e1
Ténès Algeria 36°31N 1°14E 261 A5
Teng Xian Guangxi Zhuangzu, China 23°21N 110°56E 229 F8
Teng Xian Shandong, China 35°5N 117°10E 227 G9
Tengah → Singapore 1°23N 103°43E 138 A2
Tengah, Kepulauan Indonesia 7°5S 118°15E 235 D5
Tengchong China 25°0N 98°28E 228 E2
Tengchowfu = Penglai China 37°48N 120°42E 227 F11
Tenggarong Indonesia 0°24S 116°58E 235 C5
Tengger Feng China 43°12N 86°48E 217 D11
Tengger Shamo China 38°0N 104°10E 226 F3
Tenggol, Pulau Malaysia 4°48N 103°41E 237 K4
Tengiz Köli Kazakhstan 50°30N 69°0E 217 B7
Tengzhou China 35°4N 117°9E 227 G9
Tenhult Sweden 57°41N 14°20E 163 G8
Teniente Enciso △ Paraguay 21°5S 61°8W 334 A3
Tenille U.S.A. 29°46N 83°19W 316 F6
Tenino U.S.A. 46°51N 122°51W 306 D4

Tenkasi India 8°55N 77°20E 245 K3
Tenke Katanga, Dem. Rep. of the Congo 11°22S 26°40E 269 E2
Tenke Katanga, Dem. Rep. of the Congo 10°32S 26°7E 269 E2
Tenkodogo Burkina Faso 11°54N 0°19W 263 C4
Tenna ➜ Italy 43°14N 13°47E 199 E10
Tennant Creek Australia 19°30S 134°15E 280 B1
Tennessee □ U.S.A. 36°0N 86°30W 315 D11
Tennessee ➜ U.S.A. 37°4N 88°34W 315 C10
Tennille U.S.A. 32°56N 82°48W 316 C7
Tennoji Japan 34°39N 135°30E 133 B2
Teno, Pta. de Canary Is. 28°21N 16°55W 153 e1
Tenojoki = Tana ➜ Norway 70°30N 28°14E 160 A23
Tenom Malaysia 5°4N 115°57E 235 A5
Tenosique Mexico 17°29N 91°26W 319 D6
Tenri Japan 34°39N 135°49E 223 C7
Tenryū Japan 34°52N 137°49E 223 C9
Tenryū-Gawa ➜ Japan 35°39N 137°48E 223 B9
Tensift, Oued ➜ Morocco 32°3N 9°28W 260 B3
Tente Indonesia 8°35S 118°41E 235 D5
Tenterden U.K. 51°4N 0°42E 169 F8
Tenterfield Australia 29°0S 152°0E 281 D5
Tenuaiur, Uad ➜ W. Sahara 21°36N 16°0W 260 D1
Teo = A Ramallosa Spain 42°45N 8°30W 194 C2
Teófilo Otoni Brazil 17°50S 41°30W 333 E3
Tepa Indonesia 7°52S 129°31E 231 F7
Tepa Pt. Cook Is. 19°6S 169°55W 289 g
Tepalcatepec ➜ Mexico 18°35N 101°59W 318 D4
Tepalcates Mexico 19°23N 99°3W 128 B2
Tepecik Bursa, Turkey 40°7N 28°25E 203 F12
Tepecik Kütahya, Turkey 39°32N 29°28E 205 B11
Tepehuanes Mexico 25°21N 105°44W 318 B3
Tepelenë Albania 40°17N 20°2E 202 F4
Tepequem, Serra Brazil 3°45N 61°45W 329 C5
Tepetongo Mexico 22°28N 103°9W 318 C4
Tepeyac △ Mexico 19°30N 99°7W 128 B2
Tepic = Nayarit □ Mexico 22°0N 105°0W 318 C4
Tepic Mexico 21°30N 104°54W 318 C4
Teplá Czech Rep. 49°59N 12°52E 180 B5
Teplice Czech Rep. 50°40N 13°48E 180 A6
Teplitz = Teplice Czech Rep. 50°40N 13°48E 180 A6
Teplyk Ukraine 48°40N 29°44E 183 B14
Tequila Mexico 20°54N 103°47W 318 C4
Ter ➜ Spain 42°2N 3°12E 196 C8
Ter Apel Neths. 52°53N 7°5E 170 B7
Téra Niger 14°0N 0°45E 263 C5
Tera ➜ Spain 41°54N 5°44W 194 D5
Tera Kora Bonaire 12°11N 68°16W 322 h
Teraina Kiribati 4°43N 160°25W 289 G12
Terakeka South Sudan 5°26N 31°45E 257 F3
Téramo Italy 42°39N 13°42E 199 F10
Terang Australia 38°15S 142°55E 282 E5
Terang, Teluk Indonesia 8°44S 116°0E 231 K19
Terawhiti, C. N.Z. 41°16S 174°38E 284 H3
Terazit, Massif de Niger 20°2N 8°30E 259 D1
Tercan Turkey 39°47N 40°23E 213 C9
Terceira Azores 38°43N 27°13W 153 d1
Tercero ➜ Argentina 32°58S 61°47W 334 C3
Terdal India 16°33N 75°3E 244 F2
Terebovlya Ukraine 49°18N 25°44E 177 D13
Teregova Romania 45°10N 22°16E 182 E7
Tereida Sudan 10°35N 31°17E 257 E3
Terek ➜ Russia 44°0N 47°30E 191 J8
Terengganu □ Malaysia 4°55N 103°0E 237 K4
Terenos Brazil 20°26S 54°50W 331 E7
Terepaima △ Venezuela 9°58N 69°17W 328 B4
Tereshka ➜ Russia 51°48N 46°26E 190 E8
Teresina Brazil 5°9S 42°45W 332 C3
Teresinha Brazil 0°58N 52°2W 329 C7
Terespol Poland 52°5N 23°37E 185 F10
Teressa India 8°15N 93°10E 245 K11
Teresva Ukraine 48°0N 23°42E 183 B8
Terewah, L. Australia 29°52S 147°35E 281 D4
Terges ➜ Portugal 37°49N 7°41W 195 H3
Tergnier France 49°40N 3°17E 173 C10
Terhazza Mali 23°38N 5°22W 260 D3
Teridgerie Cr. ➜ Australia 30°25S 148°50E 283 A8
Terijoki = Zelenogorsk Russia 60°12N 29°43E 188 B5
Terlizzi Italy 41°8N 16°32E 201 A9
Termas de Río Hondo Argentina 27°29S 64°52W 334 B3
Terme Turkey 41°11N 37°0E 212 B7
Términi Imerese Italy 37°59N 13°42E 200 E6
Términos, L. de Mexico 18°37N 91°33W 319 D6
Termit, Massif de Niger 16°2N 11°20E 259 E2
Termiz Uzbekistan 37°15N 67°15E 217 E7
Térmoli Italy 42°0N 15°0E 199 F12
Ternate Indonesia 0°45N 127°25E 231 D7
Terneuzen Neths. 51°20N 3°50E 170 C3
Terney Russia 45°3N 136°37E 220 B8
Terni Italy 42°34N 12°37E 199 F9
Ternitz Austria 47°43N 16°2E 180 D9
Ternivka Ukraine 48°32N 29°58E 183 B14
Ternopil Ukraine 49°30N 25°40E 177 D13
Ternopil □ Ukraine 48°10N 25°10E 177 D13
Ternopol = Ternopil Ukraine 49°30N 25°40E 177 D13
Terowie Australia 33°8S 138°55E 282 B3
Terpni Greece 40°55N 23°26E 202 F7
Terra Bella U.S.A. 35°58N 119°3W 307 K7
Terra Nova △ Canada 48°33N 53°55W 299 C9
Terrace Canada 54°30N 128°35W 296 C3
Terrace Bay Canada 48°47N 87°5W 298 C2
Terracina Italy 41°17N 13°15E 200 A6
Terralba Italy 39°43N 8°39E 200 C1
Terranova di Sicilia = Gela Italy 37°4N 14°15E 201 E7
Terranova Pausania = Ólbia Italy 40°55N 9°31E 200 B2
Terrasini Italy 38°10N 13°4E 200 D6
Terrassa Spain 41°34N 2°1E 196 D7
Terrasson-la-Villedieu France 45°8N 1°18E 174 C5
Terrazzano Italy 45°32N 9°4E 128 A1
Terre-de-Bas Guadeloupe 15°51N 61°38W 322 e
Terre-de-Bas Guadeloupe 16°10N 61°7W 322 e
Terre-de-Haut Guadeloupe 15°52N 61°34W 322 e
Terre des Hommes Canada 45°31N 73°32W 130 A2
Terre Haute U.S.A. 39°28N 87°25W 311 E9
Terre Rouge Mauritius 20°7S 57°31E 272 e
Terrebonne B. U.S.A. 29°5N 90°35W 315 G9
Terrecht Mali 19°35N 0°22E 261 D4
Terrell U.S.A. 32°44N 96°17W 314 E6
Terrenceville Canada 47°40N 54°44W 299 C9
Terrick Terrick △ Australia 36°8S 144°13E 282 D6
Terrugem Portugal 38°41N 9°17W 126 A1
Terry U.S.A. 46°47N 105°19W 304 C11
Terrytown U.S.A. 29°54N 90°1W 131 B2
Terryville U.S.A. 41°41N 73°3W 313 E11
Terschelling Neths. 53°25N 5°20E 170 A5
Tersko-Kumskiy Kanal Russia 44°32N 44°38E 191 H7
Tertenia Italy 39°42N 9°34E 200 C2
Terter = Tärtär ➜ Azerbaijan 40°26N 47°20E 191 K8
Teruel Spain 40°22N 1°8W 196 E3
Teruel □ Spain 40°48N 1°0W 196 E4
Tervel Bulgaria 43°45N 27°28E 203 C11
Tervola Finland 66°6N 24°49E 160 C21
Tervuren Belgium 50°49N 4°31E 116 B3
Tervuren, Park van Belgium 50°49N 4°31E 116 B3
Teryaweynya L. Australia 32°18S 143°22E 282 B5
Tešanj Bos.-H. 44°38N 18°1E 182 F3
Teschen = Cieszyn Poland 49°45N 18°35E 185 J5
Teseney Eritrea 15°5N 36°42E 257 D4
Tesha ➜ Russia 55°38N 42°9E 190 C6
Teshekpuk L. U.S.A. 70°35N 153°26W 303 A9
Teshio Japan 44°53N 141°44E 220 B10
Teshio-Gawa ➜ Japan 44°53N 141°45E 220 B10
Tešica Serbia 43°27N 21°45E 202 C5
Tesiyn Gol ➜ Mongolia 50°40N 93°20E 218 A7
Teslić Bos.-H. 44°37N 17°54E 182 F2
Teslin Canada 60°10N 132°43W 296 A2
Teslin ➜ Canada 61°34N 134°35W 296 A2
Teslin L. Canada 60°15N 132°57W 296 A2
Tesouro Brazil 16°4S 53°34W 331 D7
Tessalit Mali 20°12N 1°0E 261 D5
Tessaoua Niger 13°47N 7°56E 259 F1
Tessin Germany 54°2N 12°26E 178 A8
Tessit Mali 15°13N 0°18E 263 B5
Tessounfat Mali 22°53N 0°32E 261 D5
Test ➜ U.K. 50°56N 1°29W 169 G6
Testa del Gargano Italy 41°50N 16°10E 199 G13
Testigos, Is. Los Venezuela 11°23N 63°7W 321 D7
Tét Hungary 47°30N 17°33E 182 C2
Têt ➜ France 42°44N 3°2E 174 F7
Tetachuck L. Canada 53°18N 125°55W 296 C3
Tetas, Pta. Chile 23°31S 70°38W 334 A1
Tete Mozam. 16°13S 33°33E 269 F3
Tete □ Mozam. 15°15S 32°40E 269 F3
Tetenga, Caleta Chile 27°9S 109°19W 330 b
Tetepare Solomon Is. 8°45S 157°35E 287 M9
Teterev ➜ Ukraine 51°1N 30°5E 177 C16
Teterow Germany 53°46N 12°34E 178 B8
Teteven Bulgaria 42°58N 24°17E 203 D8
Tethul ➜ Canada 60°35N 112°12W 296 A6
Tetiyev Ukraine 49°22N 29°38E 177 D15
Tetlin U.S.A. 63°8N 142°31W 303 E12
Tetlin Junction U.S.A. 63°19N 142°36W 303 E12
Tetlin Nat. Wildlife Refuge ⌂ U.S.A. 62°40N 141°50W 303 E12
Tetlit Zheh = Fort McPherson Canada 67°30N 134°55W 294 D5
Teton ➜ U.S.A. 47°56N 110°31W 304 C8
Tétouan Morocco 35°35N 5°21W 260 A3
Tetovo Macedonia 42°1N 20°59E 202 D4
Tetschen = Děčín Czech Rep. 50°47N 14°12E 180 A7
Tetuán Spain 40°27N 3°42W 127 B1
Tetufera, Mt. Tahiti 17°40S 149°26W 289 e
Tetyukhe = Dalnegorsk Russia 44°32N 135°33E 220 B7
Tetyushi Russia 54°55N 48°49E 190 C9
Teuco ➜ Argentina 25°35S 60°11W 334 B3
Teufelsberg Germany 52°29N 13°14E 115 B2
Teulada Italy 38°58N 8°46E 200 D1
Teulon Canada 50°23N 97°16W 297 C9
Teun Indonesia 6°59S 129°8E 231 F7
Teuri-Tō Japan 44°26N 141°19E 220 B10
Teutoburger Wald Germany 52°5N 8°22E 178 C4
Teutopolis U.S.A. 39°8N 88°29W 311 E8
Tevere ➜ Italy 41°44N 12°14E 199 G9
Tevere ⌂ Italy 42°46N 12°14E 199 F9
Teverya Israel 32°47N 35°32E 250 F6
Teviot ➜ U.K. 55°29N 2°38W 167 F6
Tewantin Australia 26°27S 153°3E 281 D5
Teweh ➜ Indonesia 0°58N 114°54E 235 C5
Tewkesbury U.K. 51°59N 2°9W 169 F5
Texada I. Canada 49°40N 124°25W 296 D4
Texarkana Ark., U.S.A. 33°26N 94°2W 314 E7
Texarkana Tex., U.S.A. 33°26N 94°3W 314 E7
Texas Australia 28°49S 151°9E 281 D5
Texas □ U.S.A. 31°40N 98°30W 314 F5
Texas City U.S.A. 29°24N 94°54W 314 G7
Texel Neths. 53°5N 4°50E 170 A4
Texline U.S.A. 36°23N 103°2W 314 C3
Texoma, L. U.S.A. 33°50N 96°34W 314 E6
Teykovo Russia 56°55N 40°30E 188 D11
Teyvareh Afghan. 33°30N 64°24E 240 B2
Teza ➜ Russia 56°32N 41°53E 190 B5
Tezin Afghan. 34°24N 69°30E 242 B3
Teziutlán Mexico 19°49N 97°21W 319 D5
Tezpur India 26°40N 92°45E 241 B4
Tezu India 27°55N 96°10E 241 B6
Tezzeron L. Canada 54°43N 124°30W 296 C4
Tha-anne ➜ Canada 60°31N 94°37W 297 A10
Tha Deua Laos 17°57N 102°53E 236 D4
Tha Deua Laos 19°26N 101°50E 236 C3
Tha Li Thailand 17°37N 101°25E 236 D3
Tha Pla Thailand 17°48N 100°32E 236 D3
Tha Rua Thailand 14°34N 100°44E 236 E3
Tha Sala Thailand 8°40N 99°56E 237 H2
Tha Song Yang Thailand 17°34N 97°55E 236 D1
Thaba Putsoa Lesotho 29°45S 28°0E 271 D4
Thaba-Tseka Lesotho 29°32S 28°36E 271 C4
Thabana Ntlenyana Lesotho 29°30S 29°16E 271 C4
Thabaung Burma 17°2N 94°48E 241 G5
Thabazimbi S. Africa 24°40S 27°21E 271 B4
Thabeikkyin Burma 22°53N 95°59E 241 D5
Thabt, G. el Egypt 28°17N 34°1E 251 K5
Thādiq Si. Arabia 25°18N 45°52E 246 E5
Thai Binh Vietnam 20°35N 106°1E 228 G6
Thai Muang Thailand 8°24N 98°16E 237 H2
Thai Nguyen Vietnam 21°35N 105°55E 228 G5
Thailand ■ Asia 16°0N 102°0E 236 E4
Thailand, G. of Asia 11°30N 101°0E 237 G3
Thakhek Laos 17°25N 104°45E 236 D5
Thakurgaon Bangla. 26°2N 88°34E 241 B2
Thal Pakistan 33°28N 70°33E 242 C4
Thal Desert Pakistan 31°10N 71°30E 242 D4
Thala Tunisia 35°35N 8°40E 258 A1
Thala La = Hkakabo Razi Burma 28°25N 97°23E 228 C1
Thalabarivat Cambodia 13°33N 105°57E 236 F5
Thalang = Amphoe Thalang Thailand 8°1N 98°20E 237 a
Thalang Thailand 8°2N 98°20E 237 a
Thalara Nepal 29°29N 80°59E 243 E9
Thalassery India 11°45N 75°30E 245 J2
Thale Sap Songkhla Thailand 7°12N 100°28E 237 J3
Thalkirchen Germany 48°6N 11°32E 131 B2
Thallon Australia 28°39S 148°49E 281 D4
Thalu, Ko Thailand 9°26N 99°54E 237 b
Thalwil Switz. 47°17N 8°35E 179 H4
Tham Lot Thailand 19°34N 98°16E 236 C2
Thamarīt Oman 17°39N 54°2E 249 D6
Thame ➜ U.K. 51°39N 1°9W 169 F6
Thames N.Z. 37°7S 175°34E 284 D4
Thames ➜ Ont., Canada 42°20N 82°25W 312 D2
Thames ➜ U.K. 51°29N 0°34E 169 F8
Thames ➜ Conn., U.S.A. 41°18N 72°5W 313 E12
Thames, Firth of N.Z. 37°0S 175°25E 284 D4
Thames Ditton U.K. 51°23N 0°20W 125 B1
Thames Estuary U.K. 51°29N 0°52E 169 F8
Thamesford Canada 43°4N 81°0W 312 C4
Thamesmead U.K. 51°30N 0°7E 125 A4
Thamesville Canada 42°33N 81°59W 312 D3
Thāmit, W. ➜ Libya 31°11N 16°8E 258 B3
Thamūd Yemen 17°18N 49°55E 249 C5
Than India 22°34N 71°11E 242 H4
Than Kyun Burma 9°49N 98°4E 237 H1
Than Uyen Vietnam 22°0N 103°54E 236 B4
Thana Cr. ➜ India 19°4N 72°54E 130 A2
Thana Gazi India 27°25N 76°19E 242 F7
Thanbyuzayat Burma 15°58N 97°44E 241 G6
Thandaung Burma 19°4N 96°41E 241 F6
Thandla India 23°0N 74°34E 242 H6
Thandwe Burma 18°20N 94°30E 241 F5
Thane India 19°12N 72°59E 244 E1
Thanesar India 30°1N 76°52E 242 D7
Thanet, I. of U.K. 51°21N 1°20E 169 F9
Thangool Australia 24°38S 150°42E 280 C5
Thanh Hoa Vietnam 19°48N 105°46E 236 C5
Thanh Hung Vietnam 9°55N 105°43E 237 H5
Thanh Pho Ho Chi Minh Vietnam 10°58N 106°40E 237 G6
Thanh Thuy Vietnam 22°55N 104°51E 236 A5
Thanjavur India 10°48N 79°12E 245 J4
Thanlwin = Salween ➜ Burma 16°31N 97°37E 241 G6
Thanlyin = Syriam Burma 16°44N 96°19E 241 G6
Thann France 47°48N 7°5E 173 E14
Thano Bula Khan Pakistan 25°22N 67°50E 242 G2
Thanya Buri Thailand 14°1N 100°45E 236 E3
Thaoge ➜ Botswana 20°27S 22°36E 270 B3
Thaolintoa L. Canada 61°30N 96°25W 297 A9
Thaon-les-Vosges France 48°15N 6°24E 173 D13
Thap Lan △ Thailand 14°15N 102°16E 236 E4
Thap Sakae Thailand 11°30N 99°37E 237 G2
Thap Than Thailand 15°27N 99°54E 236 E2
Thar Desert India 28°0N 72°0E 242 F5
Tharad India 24°30N 71°44E 242 G4
Thargomindah Australia 27°58S 143°46E 281 D3
Tharp Fracture Zone S. Ocean 54°0S 135°0W 151 B14
Tharrawaddy Burma 17°38N 95°48E 241 G5
Tharrawaw Burma 17°41N 95°28E 241 G5
Tharthār, Buḩayrat ath Iraq 34°0N 43°15E 213 E10
Tharthar, L. = Tharthār, Buḩayrat ath Iraq 34°0N 43°15E 213 E10
Tharthār, W. ath ➜ Iraq 34°32N 43°4E 213 E10
Thasopoula Greece 40°49N 24°45E 203 F8
Thasos Greece 40°40N 24°40E 203 F8
That Khe Vietnam 22°16N 106°28E 228 F6
Thatcher Ariz., U.S.A. 32°51N 109°46W 305 K9
Thatcher Colo., U.S.A. 37°33N 104°7W 305 H11
Thaton Burma 16°55N 97°22E 241 G6
Thatta Pakistan 24°42N 67°55E 242 G2
Thau, Bassin de France 43°23N 3°36E 174 E7
Thaungdut Burma 24°30N 94°40E 241 C5
Thawatti Burma 19°32N 96°16E 241 F6
Thayawthadangy Kyun Burma 12°19N 98°0E 236 F1
Thayer U.S.A. 36°31N 91°33W 308 G8
Thayetmyo Burma 19°20N 95°10E 241 F5
Thazi Magwe, Burma 19°59N 95°3E 241 F5
Thazi Mandalay, Burma 21°0N 96°5E 241 E6
Thbeng Meanchey Cambodia 13°49N 104°58E 236 F5
The Broads U.K. 52°45N 1°30E 168 E9
The Everglades U.S.A. 25°50N 81°0W 317 K9
The Gulf = Persian Gulf Asia 27°0N 50°0E 247 E6
The Hague = 's-Gravenhage Neths. 52°7N 4°17E 170 B4
The Pas Canada 53°45N 101°15W 297 C8
The Wash U.K. 52°58N 0°20E 168 E8
The Weald U.K. 51°4N 0°20E 169 F8
Thebes = Thiva Greece 38°19N 23°19E 204 C5
Thebes Egypt 25°40N 32°35E 256 B3
Thedford U.S.A. 41°59N 100°35W 308 E3
Theebine Australia 25°57S 152°34E 281 D5
Thègon Burma 18°39N 95°25E 241 F5
Thekulthili L. Canada 61°3N 110°0W 297 A7
Thelon ➜ Canada 64°16N 96°4W 297 A8
Thénezay France 46°44N 0°2W 172 F6
Thenon France 45°9N 1°4E 174 C5
Theodore Queens., Australia 24°55S 150°3E 280 C5
Theodore Sask., Canada 51°26N 102°55W 297 C8
Theodore Ala., U.S.A. 30°33N 88°10W 315 F10
Theodore Roosevelt △ U.S.A. 47°0N 103°25W 308 B2
Theodore Roosevelt L. U.S.A. 33°40N 111°10W 305 K8
Thepha Thailand 6°52N 100°58E 237 J3
Thérain ➜ France 49°15N 2°27E 173 C9
Therandë Kosovo 42°21N 20°50E 202 D4
Theresa U.S.A. 44°13N 75°48W 313 B9
Theressa U.S.A. 29°50N 82°4W 316 F7
Therma = Eagle Nest U.S.A. 36°33N 105°16W 305 H11
Thermopolis U.S.A. 43°39N 108°13W 304 E9
Thermopylæ Greece 38°48N 22°35E 204 C4
Thesprotia □ Greece 39°27N 20°22E 204 B2
Thessalon Canada 46°20N 83°30W 298 C3
Thessalonica, Gulf of = Thessaloniki Kolpos Greece 40°15N 22°45E 202 F6
Thessaloniki Greece 40°38N 22°58E 202 F6
Thessaloniki □ Greece 40°45N 23°0E 202 F7
Thessaloniki ✕ (SKG) Greece 40°30N 23°0E 202 F7
Thessaloniki Kolpos Greece 40°15N 22°45E 202 F6
Thessaly □ Greece 39°25N 22°0E 204 B4
Thetford U.K. 52°25N 0°45E 169 E8
Thetford Mines Canada 46°8N 71°18W 299 C5
Theun ➜ Laos 18°19N 104°0E 236 C5
Theunissen S. Africa 28°26S 26°43E 270 C4
Thevenard Australia 32°9S 133°38E 281 E1
Thiais France 48°46N 2°23E 134 B3
Thiamis ➜ Greece 39°15N 20°6E 204 B2
Thibaud Dominica 15°36N 61°24W 323 k
Thiberville France 49°8N 0°27E 172 C7
Thibodaux U.S.A. 29°48N 90°49W 315 G9
Thicket Portage Canada 55°19N 97°42W 297 B9
Thief River Falls U.S.A. 48°7N 96°10W 308 A5
Thiel Mts. Antarctica 85°15S 91°0W 151 E16
Thiene Italy 45°42N 11°29E 199 C8
Thiérache France 49°51N 3°45E 173 C10
Thiers France 45°52N 3°33E 174 C7
Thiès Senegal 14°50N 16°51W 262 C1
Thiès □ Senegal 14°45N 16°50W 262 C1
Thiesi Italy 40°31N 8°43E 200 B1
Thika Kenya 1°1S 37°5E 268 C4
Thille-Boubacar Senegal 16°31N 15°5W 262 B1
Thimân, W. ➜ Egypt 28°4N 33°45E 251 K4
Thimphu Bhutan 27°31N 89°45E 241 B2
Thina ➜ S. Africa 31°18S 29°13E 271 D4
Thinadhoo Maldives 0°32N 72°56E 272 d
Thingangyun Burma 16°49N 96°12E 241 G6
Þingeyjarsýsla Iceland 65°40N 16°30W 155 B10
Þingeyri Iceland 65°52N 23°30W 155 B2
Þingmúli Iceland 65°21N 14°37W 155 B12
Þingvallavatn Iceland 64°11N 21°9W 155 C5
Þingvellir Iceland 64°15N 21°7W 155 C5
Þingvellir △ Iceland 64°16N 21°5W 155 C5
Thio N. Cal. 21°37S 166°14E 288 d
Thionville France 49°20N 6°10E 173 C13
Thira = Santorini Greece 36°23N 25°27E 205 E7
Thirasia Greece 36°26N 25°21E 205 E7
Third Cataract Sudan 19°42N 30°20E 256 D3
Thirsk U.K. 54°14N 1°19W 168 C6
Thiruvananthapuram India 8°41N 77°0E 245 K3
Thiruvarur India 10°46N 79°38E 245 J4
Thisio Athens, Greece 112 c1
Thisted Denmark 56°58N 8°40E 163 H2
Þistilfjörður Iceland 66°18N 15°24W 155 A11
Thistle I. Australia 35°0S 136°8E 282 C2
Thistletown Canada 43°44N 79°34W 141 A1
Thitgy Burma 18°15N 96°13E 241 F6
Thithia = Cicia Fiji 17°45S 179°18W 287 A3
Thitpokpin Burma 19°24N 95°58E 241 F5
Thiva Greece 38°19N 23°19E 204 C5
Thiviers France 45°25N 0°54E 174 C4
Thizy France 46°2N 4°18E 173 F11
Þjórsá ➜ Iceland 63°47N 20°48W 155 D6
Thlewiaza ➜ Canada 60°29N 94°40W 297 A10
Thmar Puok Cambodia 13°57N 103°4E 236 F4
Tho Chu, Dao Vietnam 9°20N 103°28E 237 H4
Tho Vinh Vietnam 19°16N 105°42E 236 C5
Thoa ➜ Canada 60°31N 109°47W 297 A7
Thoen Thailand 17°43N 99°12E 236 D2
Thoeng Thailand 19°41N 100°12E 236 C3
Thomas U.S.A. 35°45N 98°45W 314 D5
Thomas, L. Australia 26°4S 137°58E 281 D2
Thomas Circle Washington, D.C., U.S.A. 143 a1
Thomas Hill Res. U.S.A. 39°34N 92°39W 310 E4
Thomas Hubbard, C. Canada 82°0N 94°25W 295 A13
Thomaston U.S.A. 32°53N 84°20W 316 C5
Thomastown Australia 37°40S 145°2E 128 A2
Thomasville Ala., U.S.A. 31°55N 87°44W 315 F11
Thomasville Ga., U.S.A. 30°50N 83°59W 316 E6
Thomasville N.C., U.S.A. 35°53N 80°5W 315 D14
Thompson Man., Canada 55°45N 97°52W 297 B9
Thompson Pa., U.S.A. 41°52N 75°31W 313 E9
Thompson ➜ B.C., Canada 50°15N 121°24W 296 C4
Thompson ➜ Mo., U.S.A. 39°46N 93°37W 310 E3
Thompson Falls U.S.A. 47°36N 115°21W 304 C6
Thompson I. U.S.A. 42°19N 70°59W 116 B3
Thompson Pk. U.S.A. 41°0N 123°2W 304 F2
Thompson Sd. N.Z. 45°8S 166°46E 285 F1
Thompson Springs U.S.A. 38°58N 109°43W 304 G9
Thompsontown U.S.A. 40°33N 77°14W 312 F7
Thomson Ga., U.S.A. 33°28N 82°30W 316 B7
Thomson Ill., U.S.A. 41°58N 90°6W 310 C6
Thomson ➜ Australia 25°11S 142°53E 280 C3
Thomson's Falls = Nyahururu Kenya 0°2N 36°27E 268 B4
Thon Buri Thailand 13°45N 100°29E 113 B1
Thônes France 45°54N 6°18E 175 C10
Thong Yang Thailand 9°28N 99°56E 237 b
Thongwa Burma 16°45N 96°33E 241 G6
Thonon-les-Bains France 46°22N 6°29E 173 F13
Thonze Burma 17°38N 95°47E 241 G5
Thoothukudi = Tuticorin India 8°50N 78°12E 245 K4
Thorez Ukraine 48°4N 38°34E 189 H10
Þórisjökull Iceland 64°32N 20°43W 155 C6
Þórisvatn Iceland 64°20N 18°55W 155 C8
Þorkötlustaðir Iceland 63°50N 22°24W 155 D4
Þorlákshöfn Iceland 63°51N 21°22W 155 D5
Thorn = Toruń Poland 53°2N 18°39E 185 E5
Thornaby on Tees U.K. 54°33N 1°18W 168 C6
Thornbury Vic., Australia 37°44S 145°1E 128 A2
Thornbury Ont., Canada 44°34N 80°26W 312 B4
Thornbury N.Z. 46°17S 168°9E 285 G3
Thorncliffe Canada 43°42N 79°20W 141 A2
Thorne U.K. 53°37N 0°57W 168 D7
Thornhill Canada 43°48N 79°25W 141 A2
Thornton Ont., Canada 44°16N 79°43W 312 B5
Thornton Western Cape, S. Africa 33°55S 18°32E 118 A2
Thornton Colo., U.S.A. 39°52N 104°58W 304 G11
Thornton Iowa, U.S.A. 42°57N 93°23W 310 B3
Thornton Heath U.K. 51°23N 0°6W 125 B3
Thorntown U.S.A. 40°8N 86°36W 311 D10
Thorold Canada 43°7N 79°12W 312 C5
Thorpes Barbados 13°9N 59°37W 323 r
Þórshöfn Iceland 66°12N 15°20W 155 A11
Thouarcé France 47°17N 0°30W 172 E6
Thouars France 47°0N 0°15W 172 F6
Thoubal India 24°38N 94°1E 241 C5
Thouet ➜ France 47°17N 0°6W 172 E6
Thouin, C. Australia 20°20S 118°10E 278 D2
Thousand Islands U.S.A. 44°20N 76°0W 313 B9
Thousand Oaks U.S.A. 34°10N 118°50W 307 L8
Thrace Turkey 41°0N 27°0E 203 F10
Thrace, Sea of Greece 40°30N 25°0E 203 F8
Thredbo Australia 36°31S 148°20E 283 D8
Three Forks U.S.A. 45°54N 111°33W 304 D8
Three Gorges Dam China 30°45N 111°15E 229 B8
Three Gorges Res. = Sanxia Shuiku China 30°3N 107°58E 228 B6
Three Hills Canada 51°43N 113°15W 296 C6
Three Hummock I. Australia 40°25S 144°55E 281 G3
Three Oaks U.S.A. 41°48N 86°36W 311 C10
Three Pagodas Pass Asia 15°20N 98°30E 236 E2
Three Points, C. Ghana 4°42N 2°6W 262 E4
Three Rivers Calif., U.S.A. 36°26N 118°54W 306 J8
Three Rivers Mich., U.S.A. 41°57N 85°38W 311 C11
Three Rivers Tex., U.S.A. 28°28N 98°11W 314 G5
Three Sisters Is. Solomon Is. 10°10S 161°57E 287 N11
Three Springs Australia 29°32S 115°45E 279 E2
Threipmuir Res. U.K. 55°51N 3°19W 121 B2
Thrissur India 10°30N 76°18E 245 J3
Throg's Neck U.S.A. 40°48N 73°49W 132 B3
Throssell, L. Australia 27°33S 124°10E 279 E3
Throssell Ra. Australia 22°3S 121°43E 278 D3
Thrumshing △ Bhutan 27°25N 90°50E 241 B3
Thrushton △ Australia 27°47S 147°40E 281 D4
Thu Dau Mot Vietnam 10°58N 106°39E 237 G6
Thua ➜ Kenya 1°31S 39°30E 268 C4
Thuamal Rampur India 19°23N 82°56E 244 E6
Thuan Hoa Vietnam 8°58N 105°30E 237 H5
Thubun Lakes Canada 61°30N 112°0W 297 A6
Thueyts France 44°41N 4°9E 175 D8
Thugga = Dougga Tunisia 36°25N 9°13E 258 A1
Thuin Belgium 50°20N 4°17E 170 D4
Thuir France 42°38N 2°45E 174 F6
Thule = Qaanaaq Greenland 77°30N 69°10W 154 B4
Thule Air Base = Uummannaq Greenland 77°33N 68°52W 154 B4
Thun Switz. 46°45N 7°38E 179 J3
Thunder B. U.S.A. 45°0N 83°20W 312 B1
Thunder Bay Canada 48°20N 89°15W 298 C2
Thunderbolt U.S.A. 32°3N 81°4W 316 C8
Thunersee Switz. 46°43N 7°39E 179 J3
Thung Salaeng Luang △ Thailand 16°43N 100°50E 236 D3
Thung Song Thailand 8°10N 99°40E 237 H2
Thungyai △ Thailand 15°20N 98°55E 236 E2
Thunkar Bhutan 27°55N 91°0E 241 B3
Thuong Tra Vietnam 16°2N 107°42E 236 D6
Thur ➜ Switz. 47°32N 9°10E 179 H5
Thurgau □ Switz. 47°34N 9°10E 179 H5
Thüringen □ Germany 51°0N 11°0E 178 D6
Thüringer Wald Germany 50°35N 11°0E 178 E6
Thuringowa △ Australia 19°18S 146°43E 280 B4
Thurles Ireland 52°41N 7°49W 166 D4
Thurn P. Austria 47°20N 12°25E 180 D5
Thurrock □ U.K. 51°31N 0°23E 169 F8
Thursday I. Australia 10°30S 142°3E 286 F2
Thurso Qué., Canada 45°36N 75°15W 298 C4
Thurso Highl., U.K. 58°36N 3°32W 167 C5
Thurso ➜ U.K. 58°36N 3°32W 167 C5
Thurston I. Antarctica 72°0S 100°0W 151 D16
Thury-Harcourt France 48°59N 0°30W 172 D6
Thutade L. Canada 57°0N 126°55W 296 B3
Thy Denmark 56°52N 8°25E 163 H2
Thy △ Denmark 56°55N 8°25E 163 H2
Thyborøn Denmark 56°42N 8°12E 163 H2
Þykkvabæjarklaustur Iceland 63°30N 18°22W 155 D8
Þykkvibær Iceland 63°45N 20°37W 155 D6
Thyolo Malawi 16°7S 35°5E 269 F4
Thyssen-Bornemisza, Museo Madrid, Spain 127 b3
Ti-n-Amzi ➜ Niger 18°20N 4°32E 263 B5
Ti-n-Barraouene, O. ➜ Africa 18°40N 4°5E 261 E5
Ti-n-Rerhoh Algeria 20°44N 4°2E 261 D5
Ti-n-Tanetfirt Algeria 24°49N 3°48E 261 D5
Ti-n-Tarabine, O. ➜ Algeria 21°16N 7°25E 261 D6
Ti-n-Toumma Niger 16°4N 12°40E 259 E2
Ti-n-Zaouatene Algeria 19°55N 2°55E 261 E5
Ti-Tree Australia 22°5S 133°22E 280 C1
Tiadiaye Senegal 14°25N 16°40W 262 C1
Tiahuanaco Bolivia 16°33S 68°42W 330 D4
Tian Shan Asia 40°30N 76°0E 217 D9
Tian'anmen Square Beijing, China 114 c2
Tianchang China 32°40N 119°0E 229 A12
Tiancun China 39°54N 116°12E 114 B1
Tiandeng China 23°6N 107°7E 228 F6
Tiandong China 23°36N 107°8E 228 F6
Tian'e China 25°1N 107°9E 228 E6
Tianguá Brazil 3°44S 40°59W 332 B3
Tianhe Guangdong, China 23°7N 113°21E 121 B3
Tianhe Guangxi Zhuangzu, China 24°48N 108°40E 228 E7
Tianjin China 39°7N 117°12E 227 E9
Tianjin Shi □ China 39°8N 117°12E 227 E9
Tianjun China 38°0N 98°30E 218 D8
Tiankoura Burkina Faso 10°47N 3°17W 262 C4
Tianlin China 24°21N 106°12E 228 E6
Tianmen China 30°39N 113°9E 229 B9
Tianquan China 30°7N 102°43E 228 B4
Tianshifu China 41°17N 124°22E 224 B2
Tianshui China 34°32N 105°40E 226 G3
Tiantai China 29°10N 121°2E 229 C13
Tiantan Park Beijing, China 114 c3
Tianya China 18°18N 109°20E 236 C7
Tianyang China 23°42N 106°53E 228 F6
Tianyar Indonesia 8°12S 115°30E 231 J18
Tianzhen China 40°24N 114°5E 226 D8
Tianzhu China 26°54N 109°11E 228 D7
Tianzhuangtai China 40°43N 122°5E 227 D12
Tiarei Tahiti 17°32S 149°20W 289 e
Tiaret Algeria 35°20N 1°21E 261 A5
Tiaret □ Algeria 34°30N 1°30E 261 B5
Tias Canary Is. 28°57N 13°39W 153 e2
Tiassalé Ivory C. 5°58N 4°57W 262 D4
Tibagi Brazil 24°30S 50°24W 335 A5
Tibagi ➜ Brazil 22°47S 51°1W 335 A5
Tibastī, Sarīr Libya 22°50N 18°30E 258 D3
Tibati Cameroon 6°22N 12°30E 263 D7
Tibe Ethiopia 9°2N 37°12E 257 F4
Tiber = Tevere ➜ Italy 41°44N 12°14E 199 G9
Tiber Res. U.S.A. 48°19N 111°6W 304 B8
Tiberias = Teverya Israel 32°47N 35°32E 250 F6
Tiberias, L. = Yam Kinneret Israel 32°45N 35°35E 250 F6
Tibesti Chad 21°0N 17°30E 259 D3
Tibet = Xizang Zizhiqu □ China 32°0N 88°0E 218 E6
Tibet, L. U.S.A. 28°27N 81°31W 133 B1
Tibet, Plateau of Asia 32°0N 86°0E 210 E10
Tibiao Phil. 11°17N 122°2E 233 F4
Tibidabo Spain 41°25N 2°6E 114 A1
Tibiri Niger 13°34N 7°4E 263 C6
Țibleș, Vf. Romania 47°32N 24°15E 183 C9
Țibleșului, Munții Romania 47°38N 24°5E 183 C9
Tibnī Syria 35°36N 39°50E 213 E8
Tibooburra Australia 29°26S 142°1E 281 D3
Tibradden Mt. Ireland 53°15N 6°16W 120 B2
Tibrikot Nepal 29°3N 82°48E 243 E10
Tibro Sweden 58°28N 14°10E 163 F8
Tiburon U.S.A. 37°52N 122°27W 136 A2
Tiburón, I. Mexico 29°0N 112°25W 318 B2
Tiburtino Italy 41°53N 12°30E 136 B2
Ticao I. Phil. 12°31N 123°42E 232 E4
Tice U.S.A. 26°40N 81°49W 317 J8
Tichît Mauritania 18°21N 9°29W 262 B3
Tichla Mauritania 21°36N 14°58W 260 D2
Ticho Ethiopia 7°50N 39°32E 257 F4
Ticino □ Switz. 46°20N 8°45E 179 J4
Ticino ➜ Italy 45°9N 9°14E 198 C6
Ticleni Romania 44°53N 23°24E 183 F8
Ticomán Mexico 19°31N 99°8W 128 A2
Ticonderoga U.S.A. 43°51N 73°26W 313 C11
Ticul Mexico 20°24N 89°32W 319 C7
Tidaholm Sweden 58°12N 13°58E 163 F7
Tidal Basin Washington, D.C., U.S.A. 143 c1
Tidan Sweden 58°34N 14°1E 163 F8
Tiddim Burma 23°28N 93°45E 241 D4
Tiden India 7°15N 93°33E 245 L11
Tideridjaouine, Adrar Algeria 23°0N 2°15E 261 D5
Tidikelt Algeria 26°58N 1°30E 261 C5
Tidioute U.S.A. 41°41N 79°24W 312 E5
Tidjikja Mauritania 18°29N 11°35W 262 B2
Tidmore = Seminole U.S.A. 35°14N 96°41W 314 D6
Tidore Indonesia 0°40N 127°25E 231 D7
Tiébissou Ivory C. 7°9N 5°10W 262 D3
Tiéboro Chad 21°20N 17°7E 259 D3
Tiefa China 42°28N 123°26E 224 A1
Tiefersee Germany 52°24N 13°5E 115 B1
Tiegang Shuiku China 22°37N 113°53E 219 a
Tiel Neths. 51°53N 5°26E 170 C5
Tiel Senegal 14°55N 15°5W 262 C1
Tieli China 46°57N 128°3E 219 B14
Tieling China 42°20N 123°55E 224 A1
Tielt Belgium 51°0N 3°20E 170 C3
Tien Shan = Tian Shan Asia 40°30N 76°0E 217 D9
Tien-tsin = Tianjin China 39°7N 117°12E 227 E9
Tien Yen Vietnam 21°20N 107°24E 236 B6
T'ienching = Tianjin China 39°7N 117°12E 227 E9
T'ienchung Taiwan 23°52N 120°35E 225 C2
Tienen Belgium 50°48N 4°57E 170 D4
Tiénigbé Ivory C. 8°11N 5°43W 262 D3
Tientsin = Tianjin China 39°7N 117°12E 227 E9
Tiergarten Germany 52°31N 13°20E 115 A3
Tieri Australia 23°2S 148°21E 280 C4
Tieroko, Tarso Chad 20°45N 17°52E 259 D3
Tierp Sweden 60°20N 17°30E 162 D11
Tierra Amarilla Chile 27°28S 70°18W 334 B1
Tierra Amarilla N. Mex., U.S.A. 36°42N 106°33W 305 H10
Tierra Colorada Mexico 17°11N 99°32W 319 D5
Tierra de Barros Spain 38°40N 6°30W 195 G4
Tierra de Campos Spain 42°10N 4°50W 194 C6
Tierra del Fuego □ Argentina 54°0S 67°45W 336 D3
Tierra del Fuego, I. Grande de Argentina 54°0S 69°0W 336 D3
Tierra del Fuego △ Argentina 54°50S 68°23W 336 D3
Tierradentro Colombia 2°35N 76°22W 328 C2
Tierralta Colombia 8°11N 76°4W 328 B2
Tiétar ➜ Spain 39°50N 6°1W 194 F4
Tieté ➜ Brazil 20°40S 51°35W 335 A5
Tifarati W. Sahara 26°9N 10°33W 260 C2
Tiffin U.S.A. 41°7N 83°11W 311 C13
Tiffin ➜ U.S.A. 41°17N 84°23W 311 C12
Tiflèt Morocco 33°54N 6°20W 260 B3
Tiflis = Tbilisi Georgia 41°43N 44°50E 191 K7
Tifton U.S.A. 31°27N 83°31W 316 D6
Tifu Indonesia 3°39S 126°24E 231 E7
Tiga, Î. N. Cal. 21°7S 167°49E 288 d
Tiga Res. Nigeria 11°35N 8°30E 263 C6
Tigalda I. U.S.A. 54°6N 165°5W 303 J6
Tigaon Phil. 13°38N 123°30E 232 E4
Tigbauan Phil. 10°41N 122°27E 233 F4
Tiger Leaping Gorge = Hutiao Xia China 27°13N 100°9E 228 D3
Tighina Moldova 46°50N 29°30E 183 D14
Tigil Russia 57°49N 158°40E 215 D16
Tigiria India 20°29N 85°31E 244 D7
Tignall U.S.A. 33°52N 82°44W 316 B7
Tignish Canada 46°58N 64°2W 299 C7
Tigray □ Ethiopia 13°35N 39°15E 257 E4
Tigre ➜ Peru 4°30S 74°10W 328 D3
Tigre ➜ Venezuela 9°20N 62°30W 329 B5
Tigre, Pta. de Venezuela 11°5N 64°11W 329 a
Tigris = Dijlah, Nahr ➜ Asia 31°0N 47°25E 246 D5
Tiguentourine Algeria 27°52N 9°8E 261 C6
Tigveni Romania 45°10N 24°31E 183 E9
Tigyaing Burma 23°45N 96°10E 241 D6
Tigzerte, O. ➜ Morocco 28°10N 9°37W 260 C3
Tîh, Gebel el Egypt 29°32N 33°26E 256 B3
Tihodaine, Erg de Algeria 25°15N 7°15E 261 C6
Tihwa = Ürümqi China 43°45N 87°45E 217 D11
Tijara India 27°56N 76°31E 242 F7
Tijerhof S. Africa 33°53S 18°30E 118 A2
Tiji Libya 32°0N 11°18E 258 B2
Tijuana Mexico 32°32N 117°1W 307 N9
Tijuca Brazil 22°56S 43°13W 135 B1
Tijuca, Pico da Brazil 22°56S 43°15W 135 B1
Tijuca △ Brazil 22°56S 43°14W 135 B1
Tikahau French Polynesia 15°0S 148°10W 289 f
Tikal Guatemala 17°13N 89°24W 320 C2
Tikamgarh India 24°44N 78°50E 243 G8
Tikaré Burkina Faso 13°15N 1°43W 263 C4
Tikchik Lakes U.S.A. 60°0N 159°0W 303 G8
Tikéi French Polynesia 14°58S 144°32W 289 f
Tikhonkaya = Birobidzhan Russia 48°50N 132°50E 219 B15
Tikhoretsk Russia 45°56N 40°5E 191 H5
Tikhvin Russia 59°35N 33°30E 188 C7
Tikirarjuaq = Whale Cove Canada 62°10N 92°34W 297 A10
Tikkadouine, Adrar Algeria 24°28N 1°30E 261 D5
Tikkurila Finland 60°17N 25°2E 121 B3
Tīkmehdāsh Iran 37°16N 46°54E 213 D12
Tiko Cameroon 4°4N 9°20E 263 E6
Tikopia Pac. Oc. 12°19S 168°49E 277 C12
Tikrīt Iraq 34°35N 43°37E 213 E10
Tiksi Russia 71°40N 128°45E 215 B13
Tilā' al 'Alī Jordan 32°0N 35°52E 251 G6
Tiladummati Atoll Maldives 7°0N 73°20E 272 d
Tilak Nagar India 28°38N 77°5E 120 B1
Tilamuta Indonesia 0°32N 122°23E 231 D6
Tilanqiao China 31°15N 121°29E 138 B1
Tilburg Neths. 51°31N 5°6E 170 C5
Tilbury Ont., Canada 42°17N 82°23W 312 D2
Tilbury Essex, U.K. 51°27N 0°22E 169 F8
Tilcara Argentina 23°36S 65°23W 334 A2
Tilden U.S.A. 42°3N 97°50W 308 D5
Tilemsi, Vallée du Mali 17°42N 0°15E 263 B5
Tilhar India 28°0N 79°45E 243 F8
Tilia, O. ➜ Algeria 27°32N 0°55E 261 C5
Tilichiki Russia 60°27N 166°5E 215 C17
Tililane Algeria 27°49N 0°6W 261 C4
Tilin Burma 21°41N 94°6E 241 E5
Tilissos Greece 35°20N 25°1E 207 E6
Till ➜ U.K. 55°41N 2°13W 168 B5
Tillabéri Niger 14°28N 1°28E 263 C5
Tillamook U.S.A. 45°27N 123°51W 304 D2
Tillanchong I. India 8°30N 93°37E 245 K11
Tillberga Sweden 59°40N 16°39E 162 E10
Tillia Niger 16°8N 4°47E 263 B5
Tillman U.S.A. 32°28N 81°6W 316 C8
Tillsonburg Canada 42°53N 80°44W 312 D4
Tillyeria Cyprus 35°6N 32°40E 207 E8
Tilogne Senegal 16°0N 13°40W 262 B2
Tilos Greece 36°27N 27°27E 205 E9
Tilpa Australia 30°57S 144°24E 282 A6
Tilrhemt Algeria 33°9N 3°22E 261 B5
Tilsit = Sovetsk Russia 55°6N 21°50E 184 C8
Tilt ➜ U.K. 56°46N 3°51W 167 E5
Tilton U.S.A. 43°27N 71°36W 313 C13
Tiltonsville U.S.A. 40°10N 80°41W 312 F4
Tim Denmark 56°12N 8°19E 163 H2
Tima Egypt 26°54N 31°25E 256 B3
Timah, Bukit Singapore 1°21N 103°46E 138 A2
Timanah Asia 19°0N 41°0E 248 C3
Timanfaya △ Canary Is. 29°0N 13°46W 153 e2
Timanskiy Kryazh Russia 65°58N 50°5E 186 A9
Timaru N.Z. 44°23S 171°14E 285 E6
Timashevo Russia 53°22N 51°9E 190 D10
Timashevsk Russia 45°35N 39°0E 191 H4
Timau Kenya 0°4N 37°15E 268 B4
Timbaki Greece 35°4N 24°45E 207 E5
Timbaúba Brazil 7°31S 35°19W 332 C4
Timbedgha Mauritania 16°17N 8°16W 262 B3
Timber Creek Australia 15°40S 130°29E 278 C5
Timber Lake U.S.A. 45°26N 101°5W 308 C3
Timber Mt. U.S.A. 37°6N 116°28W 306 H10
Timbío Colombia 2°20N 76°40W 328 C2
Timbiquí Colombia 2°46N 77°42W 328 C2
Timbo Guinea 10°35N 11°50W 262 C2
Timbo Liberia 5°35N 9°45W 262 D3
Timboon Australia 38°30S 142°58E 282 E5
Timbué, Ponta Mozam. 18°47S 36°22E 269 F4
Timbuktu = Tombouctou Mali 16°50N 3°0W 262 B4
Timdjaouine Algeria 21°37N 4°30E 261 D5
Timeïaouine Algeria 20°27N 1°50E 261 D5
Timellouline Algeria 29°22N 8°55E 261 C6
Times Square New York, U.S.A. 132 c2
Timétrine Mali 19°19N 0°34W 263 B4
Timétrine, Mts. Mali 19°25N 1°0W 263 B4
Timfi Oros Greece 39°59N 20°45E 204 B2
Timfristos, Oros Greece 38°57N 21°50E 204 C3
Timgad Algeria 35°29N 6°28E 261 A6
Timhadit Morocco 33°15N 5°4W 260 B3
Timi Cyprus 34°44N 32°31E 207 F8
Timia Niger 18°4N 8°40E 259 E1
Timika Indonesia 4°47S 136°32E 231 E9
Timimoun Algeria 29°14N 0°16E 261 C5
Timimoun, Sebkha de Algeria 28°50N 0°46E 261 C5
Timiris, Râs Mauritania 19°21N 16°30W 262 B1
Timiryazev Park Russia 55°49N 37°33E 129 B2
Timiș = Tamis ➜ Serbia 44°51N 20°39E 182 F5
Timiș □ Romania 45°40N 21°30E 182 E6
Timiskaming, L. = Témiscamingue, L. Canada 47°10N 79°25W 298 C4
Timișoara Romania 45°43N 21°15E 182 E6

Timmersdala Sweden 58°32N 13°46E 163 F7
Timmins Canada 48°28N 81°25W 298 C3
Timmonsville U.S.A. 34°8N 79°57W 316 A10
Timok → Serbia 44°10N 22°40E 202 B6
Timoleague Ireland 51°39N 8°46W 166 E3
Timon Brazil 5°8S 42°52W 332 C3
Timor Asia 9°0S 125°0E 231 F7
Timor Leste = East Timor ■ Asia 8°50S 126°0E 231 F7
Timor Sea Ind. Oc. 12°0S 127°0E 278 B4
Timrå Sweden 62°29N 17°18E 162 B11
Timucuan ⌂ U.S.A. 30°28N 81°27W 316 E8
Tīn, Ra's at Libya 32°37N 23°8E 258 B4
Tin Alkoum Algeria 24°42N 10°17E 261 D7
Tin Amzi, O. → Algeria 18°20N 4°32E 261 D6
Tin Atanai Algeria 25°52N 1°37E 261 C5
Tin Can Bay Australia 25°56S 153°0E 281 D5
Tin Can I. Nigeria 6°26N 3°21E 124 B2
Tin Ethisane Mali 19°3N 0°52W 263 B4
Tin Gornai Mali 16°38N 0°38W 263 B4
Tin Mt. U.S.A. 36°50N 117°10W 306 J9
Tin Shui Wai China 22°28N 114°0E 219 a
Tina = Thina → S. Africa 31°18S 29°13E 271 D4
Tîna, Khalîg el Egypt 31°10N 32°40E 251 G3
Tinaca Pt. Phil. 5°30N 125°25E 233 J5
Tinaco Venezuela 9°42N 68°26W 328 B4
Tinajo Canary Is. 29°4N 13°42W 153 e2
Tinca Romania 46°46N 21°58E 182 D6
Tindal Australia 14°31S 132°22E 278 B5
Tindivanam India 12°15N 79°44E 245 H4
Tindouf Algeria 27°42N 8°10W 260 C3
Tindouf □ Algeria 27°25N 5°50W 260 C3
Tinée → France 43°55N 7°11E 175 E11
Tineo Spain 43°21N 6°27W 194 B4
Tinerhir Morocco 31°29N 5°31W 260 B3
Tinfouchi Algeria 28°52N 5°49W 260 C3
Tinfunque △ Paraguay 23°55S 60°17W 334 A3
Ting Jiang → China 24°45N 116°35E 229 E11
Ting Kau China 22°22N 114°4E 122 A1
Tinggi, Pulau Malaysia 2°18N 104°7E 237 L5
Tinghert, Ḥamādat Libya 29°0N 11°0E 258 C2
Tingi Mts. S. Leone 8°55N 10°47W 262 D2
Tingkan Taiwan 23°48N 120°52E 225 C2
Tingkawk Sakan Burma 26°4N 96°44E 241 B6
Tinglayan Phil. 17°15N 121°9E 232 C3
Tinglev Denmark 54°57N 9°13E 163 K3
Tingmerkpuk Mt. U.S.A. 68°34N 162°28W 303 B7
Tingo Maria Peru 9°10S 75°54W 330 B2
Tingrela Ivory C. 10°27N 6°25W 262 C3
Tingri China 28°34N 86°38E 218 F6
Tingsryd Sweden 56°31N 15°0E 163 H9
Tingstäde Sweden 57°44N 18°37E 163 G12
Tingvoll Norway 62°55N 8°12E 164 B5
Tingwon Group Papua N. G. 2°37S 149°42E 286 B5
Tinh Bien Vietnam 10°36N 104°57E 237 G5
Tinharé, I. de Brazil 13°30S 38°58W 333 D4
Tinian N. Marianas 15°0N 145°38E 302 e
Tinian Channel N. Marianas 14°54N 145°36E 302 e
Tinigua △ Colombia 2°30N 74°8W 328 C3
Tiniguiban Phil. 11°22N 119°30E 233 F2
Tinjar → Malaysia 4°4N 114°18E 235 B4
Tinkisso → Guinea 11°21N 9°10W 262 C3
Tinn = Atrå Norway 59°59N 8°45E 164 E5
Tinnevelly = Tirunelveli India 8°45N 77°45E 245 K3
Tinnoset Norway 59°43N 9°3E 164 E6
Tinnsjå Norway 59°55N 8°54E 164 E5
Tinogasta Argentina 28°5S 67°32W 334 B2
Tinos Greece 37°33N 25°8E 205 D7
Tiñoso, C. Spain 37°32N 1°6W 197 H3
Tinpahar India 24°59N 87°44E 243 G12
Tinputz Papua N. G. 5°33S 155°0E 286 C8
Tinrhert, Plateau du Algeria 29°30N 9°0E 258 C1
Tinsukia India 27°29N 95°20E 241 B5
Tinta Peru 14°3S 71°20W 330 C3
Tintamarre, Île St.-Martin 18°7N 63°2W 322 a
Tintâne Mauritania 16°18N 10°10W 262 B2
Tintina Argentina 27°2S 62°45W 334 B3
Tintinara Australia 35°48S 140°2E 282 C4
Tintioulé Guinea 10°13N 9°12W 262 C3
Tinto → Spain 37°12N 6°55W 195 H4
Tinui N.Z. 40°52S 176°5E 284 G5
Tinwald N.Z. 43°55S 171°43E 285 D6
Tiobraid Árann = Tipperary Ireland 52°28N 8°10W 166 D3
Tioga N. Dak., U.S.A. 48°24N 102°56W 308 A2
Tioga Pa., U.S.A. 41°55N 77°8W 312 E7
Tioman, Pulau Malaysia 2°50N 104°10E 237 L5
Tione di Trento Italy 46°2N 10°43E 198 B7
Tionesta U.S.A. 41°30N 79°28W 312 E5
Tior South Sudan 6°26N 31°11E 257 F3
Tiouliline Algeria 27°1N 0°2W 261 C4
Tipaza Algeria 36°35N 2°26E 261 A5
Tipaza □ Algeria 36°35N 2°25E 261 A5
Tipitapa Nic. 12°12N 86°5W 320 D2
Tipp City U.S.A. 39°58N 84°11W 311 E12
Tippecanoe → U.S.A. 40°30N 86°45W 311 D10
Tipperary Ireland 52°28N 8°10W 166 D3
Tipperary □ Ireland 52°37N 7°55W 166 D4
Tipton Calif., U.S.A. 36°4N 119°19W 306 J7
Tipton Ind., U.S.A. 40°17N 86°2W 311 D10
Tipton Iowa, U.S.A. 41°46N 91°8W 310 C5
Tipton Mo., U.S.A. 38°39N 92°47W 310 F4
Tipton Mt. U.S.A. 35°32N 114°12W 307 K12
Tiptonville U.S.A. 36°23N 89°29W 315 C10
Tiptur India 13°15N 76°26E 245 H3
Tiquié → Brazil 0°5N 68°25W 328 C4
Tiquina Bolivia 16°13S 68°50W 330 D4
Tira West Bank 31°52N 35°7E 123 A1
Tiracambu, Serra do Brazil 3°15S 46°30W 332 B2
Tirad Pass △ Phil. 17°3N 120°38E 232 C3
Tirahart, O. → Algeria 23°45N 3°10E 261 D5
Tīrān Iran 32°45N 51°8E 247 C6
Tīrān Si. Arabia 27°57N 34°32E 251 L5
Tiranë Albania 41°18N 19°49E 202 E3
Tiranë ✈ (TIA) Albania 41°57N 19°42E 202 E3
Tirano Italy 46°13N 10°10E 198 B7
Tirari Desert Australia 28°22S 138°7E 281 D2
Tiraspol Moldova 46°55N 29°35E 183 D14
Tiratimine Algeria 25°56N 3°37E 261 C5
Tirau N.Z. 37°58S 175°46E 284 D4
Tirdout Mali 16°7N 1°5W 263 B4
Tire Turkey 38°5N 27°45E 205 C9
Tirebolu Turkey 40°58N 38°45E 213 B8
Tiree U.K. 56°31N 6°55W 167 E2
Tiree, Passage of U.K. 56°30N 6°30W 167 E2
Tirgovişte = Târgovişte Romania 44°55N 25°27E 183 F10
Tîrgu Jiu = Târgu Jiu Romania 45°5N 23°19E 183 E8
Tîrgu Mureş = Târgu Mureş Romania 46°31N 24°38E 183 D9
Tirgua △ Venezuela 10°5N 68°48W 328 A4
Tirich Mir Pakistan 36°15N 71°55E 240 A3
Tiriolo Italy 38°57N 16°30E 201 D9
Tiririca, Serra da Brazil 17°6S 47°6W 333 E2
Tiriro Guinea 10°27N 8°40W 262 C3
Tiris Zemmour □ Mauritania 24°0N 9°0W 260 D3
Tiritiri o te Moana = Southern Alps N.Z. 43°41S 170°11E 285 D5
Tirna → India 18°4N 76°57E 244 E3
Tirnavos Greece 39°45N 22°18E 204 B4
Tirodi India 21°40N 79°44E 244 D4
Tirol □ Austria 47°3N 10°43E 180 D3
Tiros Brazil 19°0S 45°58W 333 E2
Tirrukkovil Sri Lanka 7°7N 81°51E 245 L5
Tirsa Egypt 29°57N 31°12E 117 B2
Tirschenreuth Germany 49°53N 12°19E 179 F8
Tirschtiegel = Trzciel Poland 52°23N 15°50E 185 F2
Tirso → Italy 39°53N 8°32E 200 C1
Tirstrup Denmark 56°18N 10°42E 163 H4
Tirtagangga Indonesia 8°24S 115°35E 231 J18
Tirthahalli India 13°42N 75°14E 245 H2
Tirua Pt. N.Z. 38°25S 174°40E 284 E3
Tiruchchendur India 8°30N 78°11E 245 K4
Tiruchchirappalli India 10°45N 78°45E 245 J4
Tirukkoyilur India 11°57N 79°12E 245 J4
Tirumangalam India 9°49N 77°58E 245 K3
Tirumayam India 10°14N 78°45E 245 J4
Tirunelveli India 8°45N 77°45E 245 K3
Tirupati India 13°39N 79°25E 245 H4
Tiruppattur Tamil Nadu, India 10°8N 78°37E 245 J4
Tiruppattur Tamil Nadu, India 12°30N 78°30E 245 H4
Tiruppur India 11°5N 77°22E 245 J3
Tirur India 10°54N 75°55E 245 J2
Tiruttani India 13°11N 79°58E 245 H4
Tiruvadaimarudur India 11°2N 79°27E 245 J4
Tiruvalla India 9°23N 76°34E 245 K3
Tiruvallar India 13°9N 79°57E 245 H4
Tiruvannamalai India 12°15N 79°5E 245 H4
Tiruvottipuram India 12°39N 79°33E 245 H4
Tiruvottiyur India 13°10N 80°22E 245 H5
Tis Issat Ethiopia 11°25N 37°45E 257 E4
Tisa India 32°50N 76°9E 242 C7
Tisa → Serbia 45°15N 20°17E 182 E5
Tisdale Canada 52°50N 104°0W 297 C8
Tishomingo U.S.A. 34°14N 96°41W 314 D6
Tishrīyaa Iraq 33°18N 44°24E 113 B2
Tisjön Sweden 60°56N 13°0E 162 D7
Tisnaren Sweden 58°58N 15°56E 163 F9
Tišnov Czech Rep. 49°21N 16°25E 181 B9
Tisovec Slovak Rep. 48°41N 19°56E 181 C12
Tissamaharama Sri Lanka 6°17N 81°17E 245 L5
Tissemsilt Algeria 35°35N 1°50E 261 A5
Tissemsilt □ Algeria 35°45N 1°45E 261 A5
Tissint Morocco 29°57N 7°16W 260 C3
Tista → India 25°23N 89°43E 241 C2
Tistedal Norway 59°8N 11°27E 164 E8
Tisza = Tisa → Serbia 45°15N 20°17E 182 E5
Tiszaföldvár Hungary 46°58N 20°14E 182 D5
Tiszafüred Hungary 47°38N 20°50E 182 C5
Tiszalök Hungary 48°1N 21°20E 182 B6
Tiszavasvári Hungary 47°58N 21°18E 182 C6
Tit Ahaggar, Algeria 23°0N 5°10E 261 D6
Tit Tademait, Algeria 27°0N 1°29E 261 C5
Tit-Ary Russia 71°55N 127°2E 215 B13
Titabar India 26°36N 94°12E 241 B5
Titaguas Spain 39°53N 1°6W 196 F3
Titao Burkina Faso 13°45N 2°5W 263 C4
Titel Serbia 45°10N 20°18E 182 E5
Tithwal Pakistan 34°21N 73°50E 243 B5
Titicaca, L. S. Amer. 15°30S 69°30W 330 D4
Titikaveka Cook Is. 21°16S 159°45W 289 h
Titisee Germany 47°54N 8°10E 179 H4
Tititira Hd. N.Z. 43°36S 169°25E 285 D4
Titiut Burma 18°54N 95°16E 241 F5
Titiwa Nigeria 12°14N 12°53E 263 C7
Titlagarh India 20°15N 83°11E 244 D6
Tito Italy 40°35N 15°40E 201 B8
Titograd = Podgorica Montenegro 42°30N 19°19E 202 D3
Titova Korenica Croatia 44°45N 15°41E 199 D12
Titu Romania 44°39N 25°32E 183 F10
Titule Dem. Rep. of the Congo 3°15N 25°31E 268 B2
Titusville Fla., U.S.A. 28°37N 80°49W 317 G9
Titusville Pa., U.S.A. 41°38N 79°41W 312 E5
Tiu Keng Leng China 22°18N 114°15E 122 B2
Tivaouane Senegal 14°56N 16°45W 262 C1
Tivat Montenegro 42°28N 18°43E 202 D2
Tivedens △ Sweden 58°45N 14°35E 163 F8
Tiverton Ont., Canada 44°16N 81°32W 312 B3
Tiverton Devon, U.K. 50°54N 3°29W 169 G4
Tivoli Grenada 12°10N 61°37W 323 q
Tivoli Italy 41°58N 12°45E 199 G9
Tiwanaku = Tiahuanaco Bolivia 16°33S 68°42W 330 D4
Tiwī Oman 22°45N 59°12E 249 B7
Tiwi ✪ Australia 11°33S 130°42E 278 B5
Tiyo Eritrea 14°41N 40°15E 257 E5
Tizapán Mexico 19°19N 99°13W 128 C1
Tizga Morocco 32°1N 5°9W 260 B3
Ti'zi N'Isli Morocco 32°28N 5°47W 260 B3
Tizi-Ouzou Algeria 36°42N 4°3E 261 A5
Tizi-Ouzou □ Algeria 36°35N 4°5E 261 A5
Tizimín Mexico 21°9N 88°9W 319 C7
Tiznados → Venezuela 8°16N 67°47W 328 B4
Tiznap He → China 38°21N 77°26E 217 E9
Tiznit Morocco 29°48N 9°45W 260 C3
Tjæreborg Denmark 55°28N 8°36E 163 J2
Tjällmo Sweden 58°43N 15°21E 163 F9
Tjeggelvas Sweden 66°37N 17°45E 160 C17
Tjieggelvas = Tjeggelvas Sweden 66°37N 17°45E 160 C17
Tjirebon = Cirebon Indonesia 6°45S 108°32E 235 D3
Tjirrkarli ✪ Australia 26°0S 125°28E 279 E4
Tjluring Indonesia 8°25S 114°13E 231 J17
Tjøme Norway 59°8N 10°26E 164 E7
Tjörn Sweden 58°0N 11°35E 163 F5
Tjukayirla Roadhouse Australia 27°9S 124°34E 279 E3
Tjurabalan ✪ Australia 19°50S 128°0E 278 C4
Tkibuli = Tqibuli Georgia 42°26N 43°0E 191 J6
Tkvarcheli = Tqvarcheli Georgia 42°47N 41°42E 191 J5
Tlacotalpan Mexico 18°37N 95°40W 319 D5
Tlahualilo de Zaragoza Mexico 26°7N 103°27W 318 B4
Tlalnepantla → Mexico 19°30N 99°18W 128 A1
Tlalpan Mexico 19°18N 99°10W 128 C2
Tlaquepaque Mexico 20°39N 103°19W 318 C4
Tlaxcala Mexico 19°19N 98°14W 319 D5
Tlaxcala □ Mexico 19°25N 98°10W 319 D5
Tlaxiaco Mexico 17°25N 97°35W 319 D5
Tlemcen Algeria 34°52N 1°21W 261 B4
Tlemcen □ Algeria 34°38N 1°30W 261 B4
Tleta Sidi Bouguedra Morocco 32°16N 9°59W 260 B3
Tlokweng Botswana 24°40S 25°58E 270 B4
Tlumach Ukraine 48°51N 25°0E 183 B10
Tłuszcz Poland 52°25N 21°25E 185 F8
Tlyarata Russia 42°9N 46°26E 191 J8
Tmassah Libya 26°19N 15°51E 258 C3
To Bong Vietnam 12°45N 109°16E 236 F7
To Kwai Wan China 22°18N 114°11E 122 B2
To-Shima Japan 34°31N 139°17E 223 C11
Toa Payoh Singapore 1°20N 103°51E 138 A3
Toad → Canada 59°25N 124°57W 296 B4
Toad River Canada 58°51N 125°14W 296 B3
Toamasina Madag. 18°10S 49°25E 272 B2
Toamasina □ Madag. 18°0S 49°0E 272 B2
Toay Argentina 36°43S 64°38W 334 D3
Toba China 31°19N 97°42E 228 B1
Toba Japan 34°30N 136°51E 223 C8
Toba, Danau Indonesia 2°30N 98°30E 234 B1
Toba Kakar Pakistan 31°30N 69°0E 242 D3
Toba Tek Singh Pakistan 30°55N 72°25E 242 D5
Tobago Trin. & Tob. 11°10N 60°30W 323 s
Tobarra Spain 38°37N 1°44W 197 G3
Tobelo Indonesia 1°45N 127°56E 231 D7
Tobercurry Ireland 54°3N 8°44W 166 B3
Tobermory Ont., Canada 45°12N 81°40W 312 A3
Tobermory Argyll & Bute, U.K. 56°38N 6°5W 167 E2
Tobi Palau 2°40N 131°10E 231 D8
Tobi-Shima Japan 41°12N 139°34E 220 D9
Tobias Fornier = Dao Phil. 10°30N 121°57E 233 F3
Tobiishi Hana Iwo Jima 24°45N 141°17E 288 b
Tobin, L. Australia 21°45S 125°49E 278 D4
Tobin L. Canada 53°35N 103°30W 297 C8
Toblach = Dobbiaco Italy 46°44N 12°14E 199 B9
Toboali Indonesia 3°0S 106°25E 234 C3
Tobol → Russia 58°10N 68°12E 214 D7
Toboli Indonesia 0°38S 120°5E 231 E6
Tobolsk Russia 58°15N 68°10E 214 D7
Tobor Senegal 12°40N 16°15W 262 C1
Toboso Phil. 10°43N 123°31E 233 F4
Tobruk = Tubruq Libya 32°7N 23°55E 258 B4
Tobyhanna U.S.A. 41°11N 75°25W 313 E9
Tobyl = Tobol → Russia 58°10N 68°12E 214 D7
Tobyl Kazakhstan 52°41N 62°34E 216 B6
Tocache Nuevo Peru 8°9S 76°26W 330 B2
Tocantinia Brazil 9°33S 48°22W 332 C2
Tocantinópolis Brazil 6°20S 47°25W 332 C2
Tocantins □ Brazil 10°0S 48°0W 332 D2
Tocantins → Brazil 1°45S 49°10W 332 B2
Toccoa U.S.A. 34°35N 83°19W 315 D13
Toce → Italy 45°56N 8°29E 198 C5
Tochi → Pakistan 32°49N 70°41E 242 C4
Tochigi Japan 36°25N 139°45E 223 A11
Tochigi □ Japan 36°45N 139°45E 223 A11
Tocina Spain 37°37N 5°44W 195 H5
Töcksfors Sweden 59°31N 11°52E 162 E5
Točná Czech Rep. 49°58N 14°25E 135 C2
Toco Chile 22°5S 69°35W 330 E4
Toco Trin. & Tob. 10°49N 60°57W 323 t
Toco Hills U.S.A. 33°49N 84°20W 113 B2
Toconao Chile 23°11S 68°1W 334 A2
Tocopilla Chile 22°5S 70°10W 334 A1
Tocqueville = Râs el Oued Algeria 35°57N 5°2E 261 A6
Tocumwal Australia 35°51S 145°31E 283 C6
Tocuyo → Venezuela 11°3N 68°23W 328 A4
Tocuyo de la Costa Venezuela 11°2N 68°23W 328 A4
Todalen Norway 62°49N 8°44E 164 B5
Todd → Australia 24°52S 135°48E 280 C2
Todds Road Trin. & Tob. 10°28N 61°20W 323 t
Toddu Atoll Maldives 4°25N 72°57E 272 d
Todeli Indonesia 1°40S 124°29E 231 E6
Todenyang Kenya 4°35N 35°56E 268 B4
Todgarh India 25°42N 73°58E 242 G5
Todi Italy 42°47N 12°24E 199 F9
Todos os Santos, B. de Brazil 12°48S 38°38W 333 D4
Todos Santos Mexico 23°26N 110°13W 318 C2
Todt Hill U.S.A. 40°36N 74°6W 132 C1
Todtnau Germany 47°49N 7°56E 179 H3
Toe Hd. U.K. 57°50N 7°8W 167 D1
Toecé Burkina Faso 11°50N 1°16W 263 C4
Toekomstig Stuwmeer Suriname 4°45N 57°30W 329 C6
Toetoes B. N.Z. 46°42S 168°41E 285 G3
Tofield Canada 53°25N 112°40W 296 C6
Tofino Canada 49°11N 125°55W 296 D3
Töfsingdalen △ Sweden 62°10N 12°28E 162 B6
Tofte Norway 59°33N 10°34E 164 E7
Tofua Tonga 19°45S 175°5W 287 P13
Toga Vanuatu 13°26S 166°42E 287 C4
Tōgane Japan 35°33N 140°22E 223 B12
Togba Mauritania 17°26N 10°12W 262 B2
Togbo C.A.R. 6°0N 17°27E 264 A3
Togdheer □ Somalia 9°20N 45°25E 267 C6
Togdheer → Somalia 6°26N 48°39E 267 C6
Togiak U.S.A. 59°4N 160°24W 303 G7
Togiak Nat. Wildlife Refuge ⌂ U.S.A. 59°20N 160°15W 303 G7
Togian, Kepulauan Indonesia 0°20S 121°50E 231 E6
Togliatti Russia 53°32N 49°24E 190 D9
Togo ■ W. Afr. 8°30N 1°35E 263 D5
Togo Wichale Somalia 9°22N 43°40E 267 C5
Tögrög Mongolia 47°25N 92°13E 217 C12
Togtoh China 40°15N 111°10E 226 D6
Tohiea, Mt. Moorea 17°33S 149°49W 289 e
Tohma → Turkey 38°29N 38°23E 212 C8
Tōhoku □ Japan 39°50N 141°45E 220 E10
Töhöm Mongolia 44°27N 108°2E 226 B5
Tohopekaliga, East L. U.S.A. 28°18N 81°15W 317 G8
Tohopekaliga, L. U.S.A. 28°12N 81°24W 317 G8
Toi Cook Is. 18°57S 169°51W 289 g
Toi Japan 34°54N 138°47E 223 C10
Toibalewe India 10°32N 92°30E 245 J11
Toiny St.-Martin 17°53N 62°47W 322 a
Toinya South Sudan 6°17N 29°46E 257 F2
Toiyabe Range U.S.A. 39°30N 117°0W 304 G5
Tojikiston = Tajikistan ■ Asia 38°30N 70°0E 217 E8
Tōjō Japan 34°53N 133°16E 222 C5
Tok U.S.A. 63°20N 142°59W 303 E12
Toka Guyana 3°58N 59°17W 329 C6
Tokaanu N.Z. 38°58S 175°46E 284 E4
Tokachi-Dake Japan 43°17N 142°5E 220 C11
Tokachi-Gawa → Japan 42°44N 143°42E 220 C11
Tōkagi Japan 35°42N 139°55E 140 A4
Tokai Japan 35°2N 136°55E 223 B8
Tokai Plantation S. Africa 34°3S 18°24E 118 B1
Tokaichiba Japan 35°31N 139°30E 140 B2
Tokaj Hungary 48°8N 21°27E 182 B6
Tokala Indonesia 1°30S 121°40E 231 E6
Tōkamachi Japan 37°8N 138°43E 221 F9
Tokanui N.Z. 46°34S 168°56E 285 G3
Tokar Sudan 18°27N 37°56E 256 D4
Tokara-Rettō Japan 29°37N 129°43E 221 K4
Tokarahi N.Z. 44°56S 170°39E 285 E5
Tokashiki-Shima Japan 26°11N 127°21E 221 L3
Tokat Turkey 40°22N 36°35E 212 B7
Tokat □ Turkey 40°15N 36°30E 212 B7
Tŏkch'ŏn N. Korea 39°45N 126°18E 224 C3
Tokdo = Liancourt Rocks Asia 37°15N 131°52E 221 F5
Tokeland U.S.A. 46°42N 123°59W 306 D3
Tokelau Is. □ Pac. Oc. 9°0S 171°45W 277 B16
Toki Japan 35°18N 137°8E 223 B9
Toki Pt. Wake I. 19°19N 166°35E 302 b
Tokmak Kyrgyzstan 42°49N 75°15E 217 D9
Tokmak Ukraine 47°16N 35°42E 189 J8
Toko Ra. Australia 23°5S 138°20E 280 C2
Tokomaru Bay N.Z. 38°8S 178°22E 284 E7
Tokoname Japan 34°53N 136°51E 223 C8
Tokoro-Gawa → Japan 44°7N 144°5E 220 B12
Tokoroa N.Z. 38°13S 175°50E 284 E4
Tokorozawa Japan 35°47N 139°28E 223 B11
Toksook Bay U.S.A. 60°32N 165°0W 303 F6
Toksun China 42°47N 88°38E 217 D11
Toktogul Kyrgyzstan 41°50N 72°50E 217 D8
Toku Tonga 18°10S 174°11W 287 P13
Tokuji Japan 34°11N 131°42E 222 C3
Tokuno-Shima Japan 27°56N 128°55E 221 L4
Tokushima Japan 34°4N 134°34E 222 C6
Tokushima □ Japan 33°55N 134°0E 222 D6
Tokuyama = Shūnan Japan 34°3N 131°50E 222 C3
Tōkyō Japan 35°43N 139°45E 140 B3
Tōkyō □ Japan 35°40N 139°30E 223 B11
Tōkyō B. = Tōkyō-Wan Japan 35°25N 139°50E 140 B4
Tōkyō Disneyland Japan 35°37N 139°53E 140 B4
Tōkyō Haneda ✈ (HND) Japan 35°33N 139°46E 140 B3
Tōkyō Harbour Japan 35°38N 139°46E 140 B3
Tōkyō Narita ✈ (NRT) Japan 35°45N 140°25E 223 B12
Tōkyō Sky Tree Japan 35°42N 139°49E 140 A3
Tōkyō-Wan Japan 35°25N 139°50E 140 B4
Tokzār Afghan. 35°52N 66°26E 240 B2
Tol I. Micronesia 7°20N 151°37E 287 U17
Tolaga Bay N.Z. 38°21S 178°20E 284 E7
Tolageak U.S.A. 70°3N 162°27W 303 A7
Tolbo Mongolia 48°25N 90°17E 217 C12
Tolbukhin = Dobrich Bulgaria 43°37N 27°49E 203 C11
Tolé C.A.R. 6°34N 16°1E 264 A3
Töle Bī Kazakhstan 43°42N 73°46E 217 D8
Toledo Brazil 24°44S 53°45W 335 A5
Toledo Phil. 10°23N 123°38E 233 F4
Toledo Spain 39°50N 4°2W 194 F6
Toledo Ill., U.S.A. 39°16N 88°15W 311 E8
Toledo Iowa, U.S.A. 42°0N 92°35W 310 C4
Toledo Ohio, U.S.A. 41°39N 83°33W 311 C13
Toledo Oreg., U.S.A. 44°37N 123°56W 304 D2
Toledo Wash., U.S.A. 46°26N 122°51W 306 D4
Toledo, Montes de Spain 39°33N 4°20W 195 F6
Toledo Bend Res. U.S.A. 31°11N 93°34W 314 F8
Tolentino Italy 43°12N 13°17E 199 E10
Tolfa Italy 42°9N 11°56E 199 F8
Tolga Algeria 34°40N 5°22E 261 B6
Tolga Queens., Australia 17°15S 145°29E 280 B4
Tolga Hedmark, Norway 62°26N 11°1E 164 B8
Tolhuaca △ Chile 38°15S 71°50W 336 A2
Toli China 45°57N 83°37E 217 C10
Toliara Madag. 23°21S 43°40E 272 C1
Toliara □ Madag. 21°0S 45°0E 272 C2
Tolima Colombia 4°40N 75°19W 328 C2
Tolima □ Colombia 3°45N 75°15W 328 C2
Tolitoli Indonesia 1°5N 120°50E 231 D6
Tolka → Ireland 53°21N 6°14W 120 A1
Tolkmicko Poland 54°19N 19°31E 184 D6
Tollarp Sweden 55°55N 13°58E 163 J7
Tollensesee Germany 53°30N 13°13E 178 B9
Tollhouse U.S.A. 37°1N 119°24W 306 H7
Tollygunge = Taliganga India 22°30N 88°22E 124 B2
Tolmachevo Russia 58°56N 29°51E 188 C5
Tolmezzo Italy 46°24N 13°1E 199 B10
Tolmin Slovenia 46°11N 13°45E 199 B10
Tolna Hungary 46°25N 18°48E 182 D3
Tolna □ Hungary 46°30N 18°30E 182 D3
Tolo Dem. Rep. of the Congo 2°55S 18°34E 264 C3
Tolo, Teluk Indonesia 2°20S 122°10E 231 E6
Tolo Harbour China 22°27N 114°12E 219 a
Tolochin = Talachyn Belarus 54°25N 29°42E 188 E5
Tolokiwa I. Papua N. G. 5°19S 147°37E 286 C4
Tolong B. Phil. 9°20N 122°49E 233 G4
Tolono U.S.A. 39°59N 88°16W 311 E8
Tolosa Spain 43°8N 2°5W 196 B2
Tolox Spain 36°41N 4°54W 195 J6
Toltén Chile 39°13S 74°14W 336 A2
Toluca México, Mexico 19°17N 99°40W 319 D5
Toluca Ill., U.S.A. 41°0N 89°8W 310 C7
Tolworth U.K. 51°22N 0°17W 125 B2
Tolyatti = Togliatti Russia 53°32N 49°24E 190 D9
Tom Burke S. Africa 23°5S 28°0E 271 B4
Tom Price Australia 22°40S 117°48E 278 D2
Toma Burkina Faso 12°45N 2°53W 262 C4
Tomah U.S.A. 43°59N 90°30W 308 D8
Tomahawk U.S.A. 45°28N 89°44W 308 C9
Tomai Moldova 46°34N 28°19E 183 D13
Tomakomai Japan 42°38N 141°36E 220 C10
Tomales U.S.A. 38°15N 122°53W 306 G4
Tomales B. U.S.A. 38°15N 123°58W 306 G3
Tomanivi Fiji 17°37S 178°1E 287 A2
Tomar Portugal 39°36N 8°25W 195 F2
Tomarza Turkey 38°27N 35°48E 212 C6
Tomás Barrón Bolivia 17°35S 67°31W 330 D4
Tomashevka Belarus 51°33N 23°36E 185 G10
Tomashpil Ukraine 48°32N 28°31E 183 B13
Tomaszów Lubelski Poland 50°27N 23°25E 185 H10
Tomaszów Mazowiecki Poland 51°30N 20°2E 185 G7
Tomatlán Mexico 19°56N 105°15W 318 D3
Tomb of the Kings Jerusalem 123 a2
Tomba di Nerone Italy 41°58N 12°26E 136 B1
Tombadonkéa Guinea 11°0N 14°25W 262 C2
Tombador, Serra do Brazil 12°0S 58°0W 331 C6
Tombe South Sudan 5°53N 31°40E 257 F3
Tombeau Bay Mauritius 20°6S 57°30E 272 e
Tombel Cameroon 4°45N 9°40E 264 B1
Tombigbee → U.S.A. 31°8N 87°57W 315 F11
Tomboco Angola 6°48S 13°18E 265 D2
Tombouctou Mali 16°50N 3°0W 262 B4
Tombouctou □ Mali 20°0N 3°0W 262 B4
Tombstone U.S.A. 31°43N 110°4W 305 L8
Tombua Angola 15°55S 11°55E 265 F2
Tomé Chile 36°36S 72°57W 334 D1
Tome Japan 38°40N 141°20E 220 E10
Tomé-Açu Brazil 2°25S 48°9W 332 B2
Tomelilla Sweden 55°33N 13°58E 163 J7
Tomelloso Spain 39°10N 3°2W 195 F7
Tomil Micronesia 9°31N 138°9E 287 R16
Tomil Harbor Pac. Oc. 9°30N 138°10E 287 R16
Tomingley Australia 32°26S 148°16E 283 B8
Tomini Indonesia 0°30N 120°30E 231 D6
Tomini, Teluk Indonesia 0°10S 121°0E 231 E6
Tominian Mali 13°17N 4°35W 262 C4
Tomiño Spain 41°59N 8°46W 194 D2
Tomintoul U.K. 57°15N 3°23W 167 D5
Tomioka Japan 36°15N 138°54E 223 A10
Tomislavgrad Bos.-H. 43°42N 17°13E 182 G2
Tomkinson Ranges Australia 26°11S 129°5E 279 E4
Tommot Russia 59°4N 126°20E 215 D13
Tommy Thompson Park Canada 43°38N 79°20W 141 B3
Tomnop Ta Suos Cambodia 11°20N 104°15E 237 G5
Tomo Colombia 2°38N 67°32W 328 C4
Tomo → Colombia 5°20N 67°48W 328 B4
Tomobe Japan 36°20N 140°20E 223 A12
Tomra Norway 62°34N 6°56E 164 B3
Toms Place U.S.A. 37°34N 118°41W 306 H8
Toms River U.S.A. 39°58N 74°12W 313 G10
Tomsk Russia 56°30N 85°5E 214 D9
Tomtabacken Sweden 57°30N 14°30E 163 G8
Tömük Turkey 36°42N 34°23E 250 B5
Tona Spain 41°51N 2°14E 196 D7
Tonalá Chiapas, Mexico 16°4N 93°45W 319 D6
Tonalá Jalisco, Mexico 20°37N 103°14W 318 C4
Tonale, Passo del Italy 46°16N 10°35E 198 B7
Tonami Japan 36°40N 136°58E 223 A8
Tonantins Brazil 2°45S 67°45W 328 D4
Tonasket U.S.A. 48°42N 119°26W 304 B4
Tonate Fr. Guiana 5°0N 52°28W 329 C7
Tonawanda U.S.A. 43°1N 78°53W 312 D6
Tonb Iran 26°15N 55°15E 247 E7
Tonbo Burma 18°31N 95°5E 241 F5
Tonbridge U.K. 51°11N 0°17E 169 F8
Tonda Papua N. G. 8°55S 141°34E 286 E1
Tondabayashi Japan 34°30N 135°36E 223 C7
Tondano Indonesia 1°35N 124°54E 231 D6
Tondela Portugal 40°31N 8°5W 194 E2
Tønder Denmark 54°58N 8°50E 163 K2
Tondern = Tønder Denmark 54°58N 8°50E 163 K2
Tondi India 9°45N 79°4E 245 K4
Tondi Kiwindi Niger 14°28N 2°2E 263 C5
Tondibi Mali 16°39N 0°14W 263 B4
Tondo Phil. 14°36N 120°57E 127 B1
Tondoro Namibia 17°45S 18°50E 270 A2
Tone → Australia 34°25S 116°25E 279 F2
Tone-Gawa → Japan 35°44N 140°51E 223 B12
Tonekābon Iran 36°45N 51°12E 247 B6
Tong I. Papua N. G. 2°2S 147°47E 286 B4
Tong Xian China 39°55N 116°35E 226 E9
Tong-yeong S. Korea 34°50N 128°20E 224 E4
Tonga Cameroon 4°58N 10°42E 264 B2
Tonga South Sudan 9°28N 31°3E 257 F3
Tonga ■ Pac. Oc. 19°50S 174°30W 287 P13
Tonga Trench Pac. Oc. 18°0S 173°0W 277 D16
Tongaat S. Africa 29°33S 31°9E 271 C5
Tongala Australia 36°14S 144°56E 283 D6
Tong'an China 24°37N 118°8E 229 E12
Tongareva = Penrhyn Cook Is. 9°0S 158°0W 289 H12
Tongariro, Mt. N.Z. 39°8S 175°38E 284 F4
Tongariro △ N.Z. 39°8S 175°33E 284 F4
Tongass Nat. Forest U.S.A. 54°45N 133°0W 303 J14
Tongatapu Tonga 21°10S 175°10W 287 Q13
Tongatapu Group Tonga 21°0S 175°0W 287 Q13
Tongbai China 32°20N 113°23E 229 A9
Tongbinggo S. Korea 37°31N 126°58E 137 B1
Tongcheng Anhui, China 31°4N 116°56E 229 B11
Tongcheng Hubei, China 29°15N 113°50E 229 C9
Tongchuan China 35°6N 109°3E 226 G5
Tongdao China 26°10N 109°42E 228 D7
Tongeren Belgium 50°47N 5°28E 170 D5
Tonggu China 28°31N 114°20E 229 C10
Tonggu Jiao China 22°22N 113°37E 219 a
Tongguan China 34°40N 110°25E 226 G6
Tonghai China 24°10N 102°53E 228 E4
Tonghua China 41°42N 125°58E 224 B2
Tongi = Tungi Bangla. 23°53N 90°24E 241 D3
Tongjiang Heilongjiang, China 47°40N 132°27E 219 B15
Tongjiang Sichuan, China 31°58N 107°11E 228 B6
Tongjosŏn Man N. Korea 39°30N 128°0E 224 C4
Tongking, G. of = Tonkin, G. of Asia 20°0N 108°0E 236 C7
Tongliang China 29°50N 106°3E 228 C6
Tongliao China 43°38N 122°18E 227 C12
Tongling China 30°55N 117°48E 229 B11
Tonglu China 29°45N 119°37E 229 C12
Tongnan = Anyue China 30°9N 105°50E 228 B5
Tongoa Vanuatu 16°54S 168°34E 287 F6
Tongobory Madag. 23°32S 44°20E 272 C1
Tongoy Chile 30°16S 71°31W 334 C1
Tongqiao China 31°21N 121°22E 138 A1
Tongquil I. Phil. 6°2N 121°51E 233 H3
Tongren Guizhou, China 27°43N 109°11E 228 D7
Tongren Qinghai, China 35°25N 102°5E 218 D9
Tongres = Tongeren Belgium 50°47N 5°28E 170 D5
Tongsa Dzong Bhutan 27°31N 90°31E 241 B3
Tongsha Tao Taiwan 26°12N 128°28E 225 b
Tongshi China 18°30N 109°20E 236 C7
Tongue U.K. 58°29N 4°25W 167 C4
Tongue → U.S.A. 46°25N 105°52W 304 C11
Tongwei China 35°0N 105°5E 226 G3
Tongxiang China 30°39N 120°34E 229 B13
Tongxin China 36°59N 105°58E 226 F3
Tongyang N. Korea 39°9N 126°53E 224 C3
Tongyu China 44°45N 123°4E 227 B12
Tongzhou China 32°12N 121°2E 229 A13
Tongzi China 28°9N 106°49E 228 C6
Tonica U.S.A. 41°13N 89°4W 310 C7
Tonj South Sudan 7°20N 28°44E 257 F2
Tonj → South Sudan 7°31N 28°55E 257 F2
Tonk India 26°6N 75°54E 242 F6
Tonkawa U.S.A. 36°41N 97°18W 314 C6
Tonkin = Bac Phan Vietnam 22°0N 105°0E 228 G5
Tonkin, G. of Asia 20°0N 108°0E 236 C7
Tonlé Sap Cambodia 13°0N 104°0E 236 F5
Tonnay-Charente France 45°56N 0°55W 174 C3
Tonneins France 44°23N 0°19E 174 D4
Tonnerre France 47°51N 3°59E 173 E10
Tönning Germany 54°19N 8°56E 178 A4
Tono Japan 39°19N 141°32E 220 E10
Tonoas I. Micronesia 7°22N 151°52E 287 T18
Tonopah U.S.A. 38°4N 117°14W 305 G5
Tonoshō Japan 34°29N 134°11E 222 C6
Tonosí Panama 7°20N 80°20W 320 E3
Tons → Haryana, India 30°30N 77°39E 242 D7
Tons → Ut. P., India 26°1N 83°33E 243 F10
Tønsberg Norway 59°19N 10°25E 164 E7
Tonsina U.S.A. 61°39N 145°11W 303 F11
Tonstad Norway 58°40N 6°45E 164 F3
Tonto △ U.S.A. 33°39N 111°7W 305 K8
Tonumea Tonga 20°30S 174°30W 287 Q13
Tonya Turkey 40°53N 39°16E 213 B8
Tonzang Burma 23°36N 93°42E 241 D4
Tonzi Burma 24°39N 94°57E 241 C5
Toobanna Australia 18°42S 146°9E 280 B4
Toodyay Australia 31°34S 116°28E 279 F2
Tooele U.S.A. 40°32N 112°18W 304 F7
Toompine Australia 27°15S 144°19E 281 D3
Toomsboro U.S.A. 32°50N 83°5W 316 C6
Toora Australia 38°39S 146°23E 283 E7
Toora-Khem Russia 52°28N 96°17E 217 B13
Toorak Australia 37°50S 145°1E 128 B2
Tootias Somalia 3°57N 43°57E 267 D5
Toowoomba Australia 27°32S 151°56E 281 D5
Top Springs Australia 16°37S 131°51E 278 C5
Topalu Romania 44°31N 28°3E 183 F13
Topanga State Park ⌂ U.S.A. 34°7N 118°31W 126 B1
Topaz U.S.A. 38°41N 119°30W 306 G7
Topeka U.S.A. 39°3N 95°40W 308 F6
Topkapı Turkey 41°1N 28°55E 122 B1
Topkapı Palaca Turkey 41°1N 28°59E 122 B1
Topl'a → Slovak Rep. 48°45N 21°45E 181 C14
Topley Canada 54°49N 126°18W 296 C3
Toplica → Serbia 43°15N 21°49E 202 C5
Toplița Romania 46°55N 25°20E 183 D10
Topo Azores 38°33N 27°46W 153 d1
Topo, Pta. do Azores 38°33N 27°46W 153 d1
Topocalma, Pta. Chile 34°10S 72°2W 334 C1
Topock U.S.A. 34°46N 114°29W 307 L12
Topola Serbia 44°17N 20°41E 202 B4
Topolčani Macedonia 41°14N 21°25E 202 E5
Topol'čany Slovak Rep. 48°35N 18°12E 181 C11
Topolnitsa → Bulgaria 42°11N 24°18E 203 D8
Topolobampo Mexico 25°36N 109°3W 318 B3
Topoloveni Romania 44°49N 25°5E 183 F10
Topolovgrad Bulgaria 42°5N 26°20E 203 D10
Topolvățu Mare Romania 45°46N 21°41E 182 E6
Topozero, Ozero Russia 65°35N 32°0E 160 D25
Toppenish U.S.A. 46°23N 120°19W 304 C3
Topraisar Romania 44°1N 28°27E 183 F13
Toprakkale Turkey 37°5N 36°8E 250 A7
Topusko Croatia 45°18N 15°59E 199 C12
Toquepala Peru 17°24S 70°25W 330 D3
Toqyraūyn → Kazakhstan 46°48N 75°24E 217 C9
Tor di Quinto Italy 41°56N 12°27E 136 B1
Tor Pignattara Italy 41°53N 12°31E 136 B2
Tor Sapienza Italy 41°53N 12°35E 136 B2
Torà Spain 41°49N 1°25E 196 D6
Tora Kit South Sudan 11°2N 32°36E 257 E3
Toranomon Tokyo, Japan 140 c3
Torata Peru 17°23S 70°1W 330 D3
Torbalı Turkey 38°10N 27°21E 205 C9
Torbat-e Heydārīyeh Iran 35°15N 59°12E 247 C8
Torbat-e Jām Iran 35°16N 60°35E 247 C9
Torbay Canada 47°40N 52°42W 299 C9
Torbay □ U.K. 50°26N 3°31W 169 G4
Tørberget Norway 61°8N 12°7E 164 C9
Torbjörntorp Sweden 58°12N 13°36E 163 F7
Torcy France 48°51N 2°39E 134 A4
Tordesillas Spain 41°30N 5°0W 194 D6
Töreboda Sweden 58°41N 14°7E 163 F8
Torekov Sweden 56°26N 12°37E 163 H6
Torellò Spain 42°3N 2°16E 196 C7
Toreno Spain 42°42N 6°30W 194 C4
Torfaen □ U.K. 51°43N 3°3W 169 F4
Torfajökull Iceland 63°54N 19°0W 155 D7
Torgau Germany 51°34N 13°0E 178 D8
Torgelow Germany 53°37N 14°1E 178 B10
Torghay Kazakhstan 49°38N 63°29E 216 C6
Torghay → Kazakhstan 48°1N 62°45E 216 C6
Torghay Ustirti Asia 51°0N 63°0E 216 B6
Torghay Zhylghasy Kazakhstan 52°0N 64°30E 216 B6
Torgovaya = Salsk Russia 46°28N 41°30E 191 G5
Torhamn Sweden 56°6N 15°50E 163 H9
Torhout Belgium 51°5N 3°7E 170 C3
Torhovytsya Ukraine 48°36N 25°26E 183 B10
Tori Ethiopia 7°53N 33°35E 257 F3
Tori-Shima Japan 30°29N 140°19E 221 J10
Torigni-sur-Vire France 49°3N 0°58W 172 C6
Torija Spain 40°44N 3°2W 196 E1
Torilla Pen. Australia 22°29S 150°5E 280 C5
Torino Italy 45°3N 7°40E 198 C4
Torit South Sudan 4°27N 32°31E 257 G3
Torkamān Iran 37°35N 47°23E 213 D12
Torkovichi Russia 58°51N 30°21E 188 C6
Tormac Romania 45°30N 21°30E 182 E6
Tormes → Spain 41°18N 6°29W 194 D4
Tornado Mt. Canada 49°55N 114°40W 296 D6
Tornal'a Slovak Rep. 48°25N 20°20E 181 C13
Torneå = Tornio Finland 65°50N 24°12E 160 D21
Torneälven → Europe 65°50N 24°12E 160 D21
Torneträsk Sweden 68°24N 19°15E 160 B18
Torngat Mountains Nat. Park △ Canada 59°0N 63°40W 295 F19
Torngat Mts. Canada 59°0N 63°40W 295 F19
Tornio Finland 65°50N 24°12E 160 D21
Tornionjoki = Torneälven → Europe 65°50N 24°12E 160 D21
Tornquist Argentina 38°8S 62°15W 334 D3
Toro Baleares, Spain 39°59N 4°8E 206 B5
Toro Zamora, Spain 41°35N 5°24W 194 D5
Torö Sweden 58°48N 17°50E 163 F11
Toro, Cerro del Chile 29°10S 69°50W 334 B2
Toro ⌂ Uganda 1°5N 30°22E 268 B3
Toro Pk. U.S.A. 33°34N 116°24W 307 M10
Torodi Niger 13°7N 1°47E 263 C5
Torokina Papua N. G. 6°14S 155°3E 286 D8
Törökszentmiklós Hungary 47°11N 20°27E 182 C5
Toronto N.S.W., Australia 33°0S 151°30E 283 B9
Toronto Ont., Canada 43°39N 79°20W 141 B2
Toronto Ohio, U.S.A. 40°28N 80°36W 312 F4
Toronto, Univ. of Canada 43°39N 79°23W 141 B2
Toronto City Centre ✈ (YTZ) Canada 43°38N 79°24W 141 B2
Toronto Harbour Canada 43°38N 79°21W 141 B2
Toronto I. Canada 43°37N 79°23W 141 B2
Toronto Lester B. Pearson Int. ✈ (YYZ) Canada 43°46N 79°35W 141 A1
Toropets Russia 56°30N 31°40E 188 D6
Tororo Uganda 0°45N 34°12E 268 B3
Toros Dağları Turkey 37°0N 32°30E 250 B3
Toros Monumental, Templo de Barcelona, Spain 114 a3
Torotoro Bolivia 18°7S 65°46W 331 D4
Torotoro △ Bolivia 18°5S 65°46W 331 D4
Torpa India 22°57N 85°6E 243 H11
Torpo Norway 60°40N 8°43E 164 D5
Torquay Vic., Australia 38°20S 144°19E 282 E6
Torquay Torbay, U.K. 50°27N 3°32W 169 G4
Torquemada Spain 42°2N 4°19W 194 C6
Torrais, Pta. Azores 39°43N 31°7W 153 a2
Torrance U.S.A. 33°50N 118°20W 307 M8
Torrão Portugal 38°16N 8°11W 195 G2
Torre Annunziata Italy 40°45N 14°27E 201 B7
Torre de Moncorvo Portugal 41°12N 7°8W 194 D3
Torre del Campo Spain 37°46N 3°53W 195 H7
Torre del Greco Italy 40°47N 14°22E 201 B7
Torre del Mar Spain 36°44N 4°6W 195 J6
Torre Latino-Americana Mexico City, Mexico 128 b2
Torre Lupara Italy 41°59N 12°39E 136 B2
Torre Nova Italy 41°51N 12°36E 136 B2
Torre-Pacheco Spain 37°44N 0°57W 197 H4
Torre Péllice Italy 44°49N 7°13E 198 D4
Torreblanca Spain 40°14N 0°12E 196 E5
Torrecampo Spain 38°29N 4°41W 195 G6
Torrecilla en Cameros Spain 42°15N 2°38W 196 C2
Torredembarra Spain 41°9N 1°24E 196 D6
Torredonjimeno Spain 37°46N 3°57W 195 H7
Torrejón de Ardoz Spain 40°27N 3°29W 194 E7
Torrejoncillo Spain 39°54N 6°28W 194 F4
Torrelaguna Spain 40°50N 3°38W 194 E7
Torrelavega Spain 43°20N 4°5W 194 B6
Torrellas → Spain 41°23N 2°11E 114 A1
Torremaggiore Italy 41°41N 15°17E 199 G12
Torremolinos Spain 36°38N 4°30W 195 J6
Torrens, L. Australia 31°0S 137°50E 282 A2
Torrens Cr. → Australia 22°23S 145°9E 280 C4
Torrens Creek Australia 20°48S 145°3E 280 C4
Torrent Spain 39°27N 0°28W 197 F4
Torrenueva Spain 38°38N 3°22W 195 G7
Torreón Mexico 25°33N 103°26W 318 B4
Torreperogil Spain 38°2N 3°17W 195 G7
Torres Brazil 29°21S 49°44W 335 B5
Torres Mexico 28°46N 110°47W 318 B2
Torres, Is. Vanuatu 13°15S 166°37E 287 C4
Torres del Paine △ Chile 51°3S 72°58W 336 D2
Torres Novas Portugal 39°27N 8°33W 195 F2
Torres Strait Australia 9°50S 142°20E 280 a
Torres Vedras Portugal 39°5N 9°15W 195 F1
Torrevécchia Italy 41°55N 12°25E 136 B1
Torrevieja Spain 37°59N 0°42W 197 H4
Torrey U.S.A. 38°18N 111°25W 304 G8
Torricelli Mts. Papua N. G. 3°23S 142°15E 286 B2
Torridge → U.K. 51°0N 4°13W 169 G3
Torridon, L. U.K. 57°35N 5°50W 167 D3
Torrijos Phil. 13°19N 122°5E 232 E4
Torrijos Spain 39°59N 4°18W 194 F6

Tubau Malaysia 3°10N 113°40E 235 B4
Tubbataha Reefs ⌂ Phil. 8°53N 119°53E 233 G2
Tubigon Phil. 9°57N 123°58E 233 G4
Tübingen Germany 48°31N 9°4E 179 G5
Tubod Phil. 8°3N 123°48E 233 G4
Tubou Fiji 18°13S 178°48W 287 B3
Tubruq Libya 32°7N 23°55E 258 B4
Tubuaï French Polynesia 23°18S 149°30W 289 f
Tubuaï, Îs. French Polynesia 25°0S 150°0W 289 f
Tuburan Basilan, Phil. 6°39N 122°16E 233 H4
Tuburan Cebu, Phil. 10°44N 123°49E 233 F4
Tuc Trung Vietnam 11°1N 107°12E 237 G6
Tucacas Venezuela 10°48N 68°19W 328 A4
Tucano Brazil 10°58S 38°48W 332 D4
T'uch'ang Taiwan 24°35N 121°29E 225 B3
Tuchitua Canada 60°55N 129°13W 296 A3
Tuchodi → Canada 58°17N 123°42W 296 B4
Tuchola Poland 53°33N 17°52E 184 E4
Tuchoměřice Czech Rep. 50°7N 14°16E 135 B1
Tuchów Poland 49°54N 21°1E 185 J8
Tuckahoe U.S.A. 40°56N 73°49W 132 A3
Tuckanarra Australia 27°7S 118°5E 279 E2
Tucker U.S.A. 33°51N 84°13W 316 B5
Tuckers Town Bermuda 32°20N 64°42W 153 a
Tucson U.S.A. 32°13N 110°58W 305 K8
Tucumán ☐ Argentina 26°48S 66°2W 334 B2
Tucumcari U.S.A. 35°10N 103°44W 305 J12
Tucunaré Brazil 5°18S 55°51W 331 B6
Tucupido Venezuela 9°17N 65°47W 328 B4
Tucupita Venezuela 9°2N 62°3W 329 B5
Tucuruí Brazil 3°42S 49°44W 332 B2
Tucuruí, Represa de Brazil 4°0S 49°30W 332 B2
Tucuruvi Brazil 23°28S 46°35W 137 A2
Tuczno Poland 53°13N 16°10E 185 E3
Tuddal Norway 59°46N 8°49E 164 E5
Tudela Spain 42°4N 1°39W 196 C3
Tudmur Syria 34°36N 38°15E 213 E8
Tudor, L. Canada 55°50N 65°25W 299 A6
Tudora Romania 47°31N 26°45E 183 C11
Tuella → Portugal 41°30N 7°12W 194 D3
Tuen Mun China 22°24N 113°59E 219 a
Tuensang India 26°17N 94°50E 241 B5
Tueré → Brazil 2°48S 50°59W 332 B1
Tufanbeyli Turkey 38°15N 36°13E 212 C7
Tufello Italy 41°56N 12°32E 136 B2
Tüffer = Laško Slovenia 46°10N 15°16E 199 B12
Tufi Papua N. G. 9°8S 149°19E 286 E5
Tufnell Park U.K. 51°33N 0°8W 125 A3
Tufsingdal Norway 62°18N 11°44E 164 B8
Tufts Abyssal Plain Pac. Oc. 47°0N 140°0W 289 C14
Tufts Univ. U.S.A. 42°24N 71°7W 116 A2
Tufu Pt. Amer. Samoa 14°13S 169°30W 302 g
Tug Hill Plateau U.S.A. 43°45N 75°50W 313 C9
Tugaya Phil. 7°53N 124°10E 233 H5
Tugela → S. Africa 29°14S 31°30E 271 C5
Tugela Falls S. Africa 28°42S 29°51E 271 C4
Tughlakabad India 28°30N 77°16E 120 B2
Tugidak I. U.S.A. 56°30N 154°40W 303 H9
Tuguegarao Phil. 17°35N 121°42E 232 C3
Tugur Russia 53°44N 136°45E 215 D14
Tui Spain 42°3N 8°39W 194 C2
Tuileries, Jardin des Paris, France 134 b3
Tuineje Canary Is. 28°19N 14°3W 153 e2
Tukangbesi, Kepulauan Indonesia 6°0S 124°0E 231 F6
Tukarak I. Canada 56°15N 78°45W 298 A4
Tukayyid Iraq 29°47N 45°36E 246 D5
Tûkh Egypt 30°21N 31°12E 256 H7
Tukhlya Ukraine 48°55N 23°28E 183 B8
Tukituki → N.Z. 39°36S 176°56E 284 F5
Tukobo Ghana 5°1N 2°47W 262 D4
Tūkrah Libya 32°30N 20°37E 258 B4
Tuktoyaktuk Canada 69°27N 133°2W 294 D5
Tuktuk Indonesia 2°37N 98°54E 234 B1
Tuktut Nogait △ Canada 69°15N 122°0W 294 D7
Tuku Taiwan 23°41N 120°23E 225 C2
Tukums Latvia 56°58N 23°10E 184 B10
Tukums ☐ Latvia 56°55N 23°0E 184 B10
Tukuran Phil. 7°51N 123°34E 233 H4
Tukuyu Tanzania 9°17S 33°35E 269 D3
Tula Amer. Samoa 14°15S 170°34W 302 f
Tula Hidalgo, Mexico 20°3N 99°21W 319 C5
Tula Tamaulipas, Mexico 23°0N 99°43W 319 C5
Tula Nigeria 9°51N 11°27E 263 D7
Tula Russia 54°13N 37°38E 188 E9
Tula ☐ Russia 53°45N 37°30E 188 F9
Tulach Mhór = Tullamore Ireland 53°16N 7°31W 166 C4
Tulagi Solomon Is. 9°5S 160°10E 287 M11
Tūlak Afghan. 33°55N 63°40E 240 B1
Tulan Taiwan 22°53N 121°13E 225 D3
Tulancingo Mexico 20°5N 98°22W 319 C5
Tulangbawang → Indonesia 4°24S 105°52E 234 C3
Tulare Serbia 42°48N 21°28E 202 D5
Tulare Calif., U.S.A. 36°13N 119°21W 306 J7
Tulare Lake Bed U.S.A. 36°0N 119°48W 306 K7
Tularosa U.S.A. 33°5N 106°1W 305 K10
Tulbagh S. Africa 33°16S 19°6E 270 D2
Tulcán Ecuador 0°48N 77°43W 328 C2
Tulcea Romania 45°13N 28°46E 183 E13
Tulcea ☐ Romania 45°0N 28°30E 183 E13
Tulchyn Ukraine 48°41N 28°49E 183 B13
Tüledi Araldary Kazakhstan 45°2N 50°16E 191 H10
Tūleh Iran 34°35N 52°33E 247 C7
Tulemalu L. Canada 62°58N 99°25W 297 A9
Tulgheş Romania 46°58N 25°45E 183 D10
Tuli Zimbabwe 21°58S 29°13E 269 G2
Tulia U.S.A. 34°32N 101°46W 314 D4
Tuliszków Poland 52°5N 18°18E 185 F5
Tulita Canada 64°57N 125°30W 294 E6
Ţūlkarm West Bank 32°19N 35°2E 251 F6
Tulla Ireland 52°53N 8°46W 166 D3
Tullahoma U.S.A. 35°22N 86°13W 315 D11
Tullamarine Australia 37°41S 144°50E 128 A1
Tullamore N.S.W., Australia 32°39S 147°36E 283 B7
Tullamore Offaly, Ireland 53°16N 7°31W 166 C4
Tulle France 45°16N 1°46E 174 C5
Tulln Austria 48°20N 16°4E 180 C9
Tullow Ireland 52°49N 6°45W 166 D5
Tullus Sudan 11°7N 24°31E 257 E1
Tully Queens., Australia 17°56S 145°55E 280 B4
Tully N.Y., U.S.A. 42°48N 76°7W 313 D8
Ţulmaythah Libya 32°40N 20°55E 258 B4
Tulnici Romania 45°51N 26°38E 183 E11
Tulovo Bulgaria 42°33N 25°32E 203 D9
Tulsa U.S.A. 36°10N 95°55W 314 C7
Tulse Hill U.K. 51°26N 0°6W 125 B3
Tulsequah Canada 58°39N 133°35W 296 B2
Tulu Milki Ethiopia 9°55N 38°20E 257 F4
Tulu Welel Ethiopia 8°56N 34°47E 257 F3
Tuluá Colombia 4°6N 76°11W 328 C2
Tuluceşti Romania 45°34N 28°2E 183 E13
Tuluksak U.S.A. 61°6N 160°58W 303 F7
Tulum Mexico 20°13N 87°28W 319 C7
Tulun Russia 54°32N 100°35E 215 D11
Tulungagung Indonesia 8°5S 111°54E 235 D4
Tuluran I. Phil. 10°58N 119°16E 233 F2
Tuma Russia 55°10N 40°30E 188 E11
Tuma → Nic. 13°6N 84°35W 320 D3
Tumacacori ⌂ U.S.A. 31°35N 111°6W 305 L8
Tumaco Colombia 1°50N 78°45W 328 C2
Tumaco, Ensenada Colombia 1°55N 78°45W 328 C2
Tumakuru = Tumkur India 13°18N 77°6E 245 H3
Tumatumari Guyana 5°20N 58°55W 329 B6
Tumauini Phil. 17°17N 121°49E 232 C3
Tumba Dem. Rep. of the Congo 3°10S 23°36E 264 C4
Tumba Sweden 59°12N 17°48E 162 E11
Tumba, L. Dem. Rep. of the Congo 0°50S 18°0E 264 C3
Tumbangsamba Indonesia 1°27S 113°7E 235 C4
Tumbarumba Australia 35°44S 148°0E 283 C8
Tumbaya Argentina 23°50S 65°26W 334 A2
Tumbes Peru 3°37S 80°27W 330 A1
Tumbes ☐ Peru 3°50S 80°30W 330 A1
Tumbler Ridge Canada 55°8N 121°0W 296 B4
Tumbur South Sudan 4°20N 31°34E 257 G3
Tumbwe Dem. Rep. of the Congo 11°25S 27°15E 269 E2
Tumby Bay Australia 34°21S 136°8E 282 C2
Tumd Youqi China 40°30N 110°30E 226 D6
Tumen China 43°0N 129°50E 224 A4
Tumen Jiang → China 42°20N 130°35E 224 A5
Tumeremo Venezuela 7°18N 61°30W 329 B5
Tumindao I. Phil. 4°41N 119°24E 233 J2
Tumiritinga Brazil 18°58S 41°38W 333 E3
Tumkur India 13°18N 77°6E 245 H3
Tumon B. Guam 13°31N 144°48E 302 d
Tump Pakistan 26°7N 62°16E 240 D1
Tumpat Malaysia 6°11N 102°10E 237 J4
Tumsar India 21°26N 79°45E 244 D4
Tumu Ghana 10°56N 1°56W 262 C4
Tumucumaque, Serra Brazil 2°0N 55°0W 329 C7
Tumupasa Bolivia 14°9S 67°55W 330 C4
Tumut Australia 35°16S 148°13E 283 C8
Tumwater U.S.A. 47°1N 122°54W 306 C4
Tun Sweden 58°26N 12°43E 163 F6
Tuna India 22°59N 70°5E 242 H4
Tunapuna Trin. & Tob. 10°38N 61°24W 323 t
Tunas de Zaza Cuba 21°39N 79°34W 320 B4
Tunbridge Wells = Royal Tunbridge Wells U.K. 51°7N 0°16E 169 F8
Tunçbilek Turkey 39°37N 29°29E 205 B11
Tunceli Turkey 39°6N 39°31E 213 C8
Tunceli ☐ Turkey 39°5N 39°35E 213 C8
Tunchang China 19°21N 110°5E 236 C8
Tuncurry Australia 32°17S 152°29E 283 B10
Tundla India 27°12N 78°17E 242 F8
Tundubai Sudan 18°36N 28°35E 256 D2
Tunduru Tanzania 11°8S 37°25E 269 E4
Tundzha → Bulgaria 41°40N 26°35E 203 E10
Tung Chung China 22°17N 113°57E 219 a
Tung Lung Chau China 22°15N 114°17E 122 B2
Tung O China 22°11N 114°8E 122 B1
Tunga → India 15°0N 75°50E 245 G2
Tunga Pass Asia 29°0N 94°14E 241 A5
Tungabhadra → India 15°57N 78°15E 245 G4
Tungabhadra Dam India 15°0N 75°50E 245 G2
Tungao Taiwan 24°31N 121°50E 225 B3
Tungaru Sudan 10°9N 30°52E 257 E3
Tungawan Phil. 7°30N 122°20E 233 H4
Tungchi Yü Taiwan 23°15N 119°40E 225 C1
Tungch'uan = Dongchuan China 26°8N 103°1E 228 D4
Tungho Taiwan 22°58N 121°18E 225 D3
T'unghsiao Taiwan 24°29N 120°40E 225 B2
Tunghwa = Tonghua China 41°42N 125°58E 224 B2
Tungi Bangla. 23°53N 90°24E 241 D3
Tungkang Taiwan 22°27N 120°26E 225 D2
Tungku Malaysia 5°1N 118°53E 235 A5
Tungla Nic. 13°24N 84°21W 320 D3
T'unglo Taiwan 24°30N 120°47E 225 B2
Tungnafellsjökull Iceland 64°45N 17°55W 155 C9
Tungsha Tao = Dongsha Dao S. China Sea 20°45N 116°43E 229 G11
Tungshan Taiwan 24°38N 121°47E 225 B3
Tungshih Changhua, Taiwan 24°12N 120°43E 225 B2
Tungshih Chiai, Taiwan 23°27N 120°8E 225 C2
Tungsten Canada 61°57N 128°16W 296 A3
Tungufell Iceland 64°17N 20°10W 155 C6
Tungurahua ☐ Ecuador 1°15S 78°35W 328 D2
Tunguska, Nizhnyaya → Russia 65°48N 88°4E 215 C9
Tunguska, Podkamennaya → Russia 61°50N 90°13E 215 C10
Tungyin Tao Taiwan 26°22N 128°29E 225 b
Tuni India 17°22N 82°36E 244 F6
Tunia Colombia 2°41N 76°31W 328 C2
Tunica U.S.A. 34°41N 90°23W 315 D9
Tunis Baghdād, Iraq 33°23N 44°21E 113 A2
Tunis Tunisia 36°50N 10°11E 258 A2
Tunis ☐ Tunisia 36°46N 10°10E 261 A7
Tunis ✈ (TUN) Tunisia 36°52N 10°14E 200 F3
Tunis, Golfe de Tunisia 37°0N 10°30E 258 A2
Tunisia ■ Africa 33°30N 9°10E 258 B1
Tunja Colombia 5°33N 73°25W 328 B3
Tunkhannock U.S.A. 41°32N 75°57W 313 E9
Tunliu China 36°13N 112°52E 226 F7
Tunnel Creek △ Australia 17°41S 125°18E 278 C4
Tunnsjøen Norway 64°45N 13°25E 160 D15
Tunø Denmark 55°57N 10°27E 163 J4
Tuntutuliak U.S.A. 60°22N 162°38W 303 F7
Tunu ☐ Greenland 75°0N 30°0W 154 C7
Tununak U.S.A. 60°37N 165°15W 303 F6
Tunungayualok I. Canada 56°0N 61°0W 299 A7
Tunuyán Argentina 33°35S 69°0W 334 C2
Tunuyán → Argentina 33°33S 67°30W 334 C2
Tunxi = Huangshan China 30°8N 118°9E 229 B12
Tuo Jiang → China 28°50N 105°35E 228 C5
Tuolumne U.S.A. 37°58N 120°15W 306 H6
Tuolumne → U.S.A. 37°36N 121°13W 306 H5
Tuomarila Finland 60°11N 24°41E 121 B1
Tüp Kyrgyzstan 42°45N 78°20E 217 D9
Tūp Āghāj Iran 36°3N 47°50E 213 D12
Tupã Brazil 21°57S 50°28W 335 A5
Tupaciguara Brazil 18°35S 48°42W 333 E2
Tupelo U.S.A. 34°16N 88°43W 315 D10
Tupik Russia 55°42N 33°22E 188 E7
Tupinambarana, I. Brazil 3°0S 58°0W 329 D6
Tupirama Brazil 8°58S 48°12W 332 C2
Tupiratins Brazil 8°23S 48°8W 332 C2
Tupiza Bolivia 21°30S 65°40W 334 A2
Tupižnica Serbia 43°43N 22°10E 202 C6
Tupman U.S.A. 35°18N 119°21W 307 K7
Tupper Canada 55°32N 120°1W 296 B4
Tupper L. U.S.A. 44°10N 74°32W 313 B10
Tupper Lake U.S.A. 44°14N 74°28W 313 B10
Tüpqarghan Muyis Kazakhstan 44°40N 50°19E 191 H10
Tupungato, Cerro S. Amer. 33°15S 69°50W 334 C2
Tuquan China 45°18N 121°38E 227 B11
Túquerres Colombia 1°5N 77°37W 328 C2
Tura India 25°30N 90°16E 241 C3
Tura Russia 64°20N 100°17E 215 C11
Turabah Ḥā'il, Si. Arabia 28°20N 43°15E 246 D4
Turabah Makkah, Si. Arabia 21°15N 41°34E 248 B3
Turagua, Serranía Venezuela 7°20N 64°35W 329 B5
Turakina N.Z. 40°3S 175°16E 284 G4
Turakina → N.Z. 40°5S 175°8E 284 G4
Turakirae Hd. N.Z. 41°26S 174°56E 284 H3
Turama → Papua N. G. 7°40S 143°50E 286 D2
Tūrān Iran 35°39N 56°42E 247 C8
Turan Russia 51°55N 94°0E 217 B12
Tūrān △ Iran 35°45N 56°30E 247 C8
Turan Lowland Asia 43°30N 62°0E 216 D6
Turangi N.Z. 38°59S 175°48E 284 E4
Ţurayf Si. Arabia 31°41N 38°39E 246 D3
Turbaco Colombia 10°21N 75°25W 328 A2
Turbacz Poland 49°30N 20°8E 185 J7
Turbat Pakistan 25°59N 63°4E 240 D1
Turbe Bos.-H. 44°15N 17°35E 182 F2
Turbeville U.S.A. 33°54N 80°1W 316 B9
Turbo Colombia 8°6N 76°43W 328 B2
Turčianske Teplice Slovak Rep. 48°52N 18°52E 181 C11
Turco Bolivia 18°10S 68°11W 330 D4
Turcoaia Romania 45°7N 28°11E 183 E13
Turda Romania 46°34N 23°47E 183 D8
Tureberg Sweden 59°25N 17°55E 139 A1
Turéia French Polynesia 20°50S 138°32W 289 f
Turek Poland 52°3N 18°30E 185 F5
Turfan = Turpan China 43°58N 89°10E 217 D11
Turfan Basin = Turpan Pendi China 42°40N 89°25E 217 D11
Turfan Depression = Turpan Pendi China 42°40N 89°25E 217 D11
Turffontein S. Africa 26°14S 28°2E 123 B2
Turgayskaya Stolovaya Strana = Torghay Ustirti Asia 51°0N 63°0E 216 B6
Turgeon → Canada 50°0N 78°56W 298 C4
Tŭrgovishte Bulgaria 43°17N 26°38E 203 C10
Tŭrgovishte ☐ Bulgaria 43°17N 26°38E 203 C10
Turgut Turkey 37°22N 28°4E 205 D10
Turgutlu Turkey 38°30N 27°43E 205 C9
Turgwe → Zimbabwe 21°31S 32°15E 271 B5
Turhal Turkey 40°24N 36°5E 212 B7
Turia → Spain 39°27N 0°19W 197 F4
Turiaçu Brazil 1°40S 45°19W 332 B2
Turiaçu → Brazil 1°36S 45°19W 332 B2
Turiec → Slovak Rep. 49°7N 18°55E 181 B11
Turin = Torino Italy 45°3N 7°40E 198 C4
Turinskaya Kultbaza = Tura Russia 64°20N 100°17E 215 C11
Turka Ukraine 49°10N 23°2E 185 J10
Turkana, L. Africa 3°30N 36°5E 268 B4
Turkayel Ethiopia 8°7N 45°21E 267 C6
Türkeli Turkey 40°30N 27°30E 203 F11
Turkestan = Türkistan Kazakhstan 43°17N 68°16E 217 D7
Turkestan Range Asia 39°35N 69°0E 217 E7
Túrkeve Hungary 47°6N 20°44E 182 C5
Turkey ■ Eurasia 39°0N 36°0E 212 C7
Turkey → U.S.A. 42°43N 91°2W 310 B5
Turkey Creek = Warmun Australia 17°2S 128°12E 278 C4
Turkey L. U.S.A. 28°30N 81°28W 133 A2
Turkey Lake Park U.S.A. 28°30N 81°28W 133 A2
Turki Russia 52°0N 43°15E 190 D6
Türkistan Kazakhstan 43°17N 68°16E 217 D7
Türkmenabat Turkmenistan 39°6N 63°34E 247 B9
Türkmenbashi Turkmenistan 40°5N 53°5E 247 A7
Turkmenistan ■ Asia 39°0N 59°0E 216 E5
Türkmenli Turkey 39°45N 26°30E 205 B8
Türkoğlu Turkey 37°23N 36°50E 212 D7
Turks & Caicos Is. ☑ W. Indies 21°20N 71°20W 321 B5
Turks Island Passage Turks & Caicos 21°25N 71°19W 321 B5
Turku Finland 60°30N 22°19E 188 B2
Turkwel → Kenya 3°6N 36°6E 268 B4
Turlock U.S.A. 37°30N 120°51W 306 H6
Turnagain Australia 9°34S 142°17E 280 a
Turnagain → Canada 59°12N 127°35W 296 B3
Turnagain, C. N.Z. 40°28S 176°38E 284 G5
Turneffe Is. Belize 17°20N 87°50W 320 C2
Turner U.S.A. 48°51N 108°24W 304 B9
Turner Field U.S.A. 33°44N 84°23W 113 B2
Turner Pt. Australia 11°47S 133°32E 280 A1
Turner Valley Canada 50°40N 114°17W 296 C6
Turners Falls U.S.A. 42°36N 72°33W 313 D12
Turner's Pen. S. Leone 7°22N 12°24W 262 D2
Turnham Green U.K. 51°29N 0°16W 125 B2
Turnhouse U.K. 55°57N 3°20W 121 B1
Turnhout Belgium 51°19N 4°57E 170 C4
Türnitz Austria 47°55N 15°29E 180 D8
Turnor L. Canada 56°35N 108°35W 297 B7
Turnov Czech Rep. 50°34N 15°10E 180 A8
Tŭrnovo = Veliko Tŭrnovo Bulgaria 43°5N 25°41E 203 C9
Turnu Măgurele Romania 43°46N 24°56E 183 G9
Turnu Roşu, P. Romania 45°33N 24°17E 183 E9
Turobin Poland 50°50N 22°44E 185 H9
Tuross Head Australia 36°3S 150°8E 283 D9
Turpan China 43°58N 89°10E 217 D11
Turpan Pendi China 42°40N 89°25E 217 D11
Turrawan Australia 30°28S 149°53E 283 A8
Turrës, Kala e Albania 41°10N 19°28E 202 E3
Turriff U.K. 57°32N 2°27W 167 D6
Tursāq Iraq 33°27N 45°47E 213 F11
Tursi Italy 40°15N 16°28E 201 B9
Tursunzoda Tajikistan 38°30N 68°14E 217 E7
Turtle Head I. Australia 10°56S 142°37E 286 F2
Turtle Is. Phil. 6°7N 118°14E 233 H2
Turtle Is. S. Leone 7°40N 13°0W 262 D2
Turtle Islands Phil. 6°13N 118°6E 235 A5
Turtle L. Canada 53°36N 108°38W 297 C7
Turtle Lake U.S.A. 47°31N 100°53W 308 B3
Turtleford Canada 53°23N 108°57W 297 C7
Turtucaia = Tutrakan Bulgaria 44°2N 26°40E 203 B10
Turua N.Z. 37°14S 175°35E 284 D4
Turukhansk Russia 65°21N 88°5E 215 C9
Turyinskiye Rudniki = Krasnoturinsk Russia 59°46N 60°12E 186 C11
Turzovka Slovak Rep. 49°25N 18°35E 181 B11
Tuscaloosa U.S.A. 33°12N 87°34W 315 E11
Tuscánia Italy 42°25N 11°52E 199 F8
Tuscany = Toscana ☐ Italy 43°25N 11°0E 198 E8
Tuscarawas → U.S.A. 40°24N 81°25W 312 F3
Tuscarora Mt. U.S.A. 40°55N 77°55W 312 F7
Tuscola Ill., U.S.A. 39°48N 88°17W 311 E8
Tuscola Tex., U.S.A. 32°12N 99°48W 314 E5
Tuscolana, Via Italy 41°52N 12°31E 136 B2
Tuscumbia Ala., U.S.A. 34°44N 87°42W 315 D11
Tuscumbia Mo., U.S.A. 38°14N 92°28W 310 F4
Tuskegee U.S.A. 32°25N 85°42W 316 C4
Tusket Wedge = Wedgeport Canada 43°44N 65°59W 299 D6
Tustna Norway 63°10N 8°5E 164 A5
Tuszyn Poland 51°36N 19°33E 185 G6
Tutak Turkey 39°31N 42°46E 213 C10
Tutayev Russia 57°53N 39°32E 188 D10
Tuticorin India 8°50N 78°12E 245 K4
Tutin Serbia 42°58N 20°20E 202 D4
Tutóia Brazil 2°45S 42°20W 332 B3
Tutong Brunei 4°47N 114°40E 235 B4
Tutova → Romania 46°7N 27°30E 183 D12
Tutrakan Bulgaria 44°2N 26°40E 203 B10
Tuttle Creek L. U.S.A. 39°15N 96°36W 308 F5
Tuttlingen Germany 47°58N 8°48E 179 H4
Tutuala E. Timor 8°25S 127°15E 231 F7
Tutuba Vanuatu 15°33S 167°16E 287 E5
Tutubeia Papua N. G. 9°34S 150°40E 286 E6
Tutuila Amer. Samoa 14°19S 170°50W 302 f
Tutuko, Mt. N.Z. 44°35S 168°1E 285 E3
Tutun Egypt 29°9N 30°46E 256 J7
Tütz = Tuczno Poland 53°13N 16°10E 185 E3
Tuul Gol → Mongolia 48°30N 104°25E 218 B9
Tuva ☐ Russia 51°30N 95°0E 217 B12
Tuvalu ■ Pac. Oc. 8°0S 178°0E 277 B14
Tuvuca Fiji 17°40S 178°48W 287 A3
Tūwal Si. Arabia 22°17N 39°6E 248 B2
Tuxer Alpen Austria 47°10N 11°45E 180 D4
Tuxpan Mexico 20°57N 97°24W 319 C5
Tuxtla Gutiérrez Mexico 16°45N 93°7W 319 D6
Tuy = Tui Spain 42°3N 8°39W 194 C2
Tuy Duc Vietnam 12°15N 107°27E 237 F6
Tuy Phong Vietnam 11°14N 108°43E 237 G7
Tuya L. Canada 59°7N 130°35W 296 B2
Tuyen Hoa Vietnam 17°50N 106°10E 236 D6
Tuyen Quang Vietnam 21°50N 105°10E 228 G5
Tuymazy Russia 54°36N 53°42E 216 B4
Tūysarkān Iran 34°33N 48°27E 213 E13
Tuyün = Duyun China 26°18N 107°29E 228 D6
Tuz Gölü Turkey 38°42N 33°18E 212 C5
Ţūz Khurmātū Iraq 34°56N 44°38E 213 E11
Tuzi Montenegro 42°22N 19°20E 202 D3
Tuzigoot △ U.S.A. 34°46N 112°2W 305 J7
Tuzla Bos.-H. 44°34N 18°41E 182 F3
Tuzla Turkey 36°42N 35°6E 250 B6
Tuzlov → Russia 47°17N 39°57E 189 J10
Tuzluca Turkey 40°3N 43°39E 213 B10
Tuzly Ukraine 45°54N 30°6E 183 E15
Tvååker Sweden 57°4N 12°25E 163 G6
Tvardiţa Moldova 46°9N 28°58E 183 D13
Tvedestrand Norway 58°38N 8°58E 164 F5
Tver Russia 56°55N 35°59E 188 D8
Tver ☐ Russia 56°50N 35°0E 188 D8
Tvrdošin Slovak Rep. 49°21N 19°35E 181 B12
Tvrdošovce Slovak Rep. 48°6N 18°4E 181 C11
Tvŭrditsa Bulgaria 42°42N 25°53E 203 D9
Twain U.S.A. 40°1N 121°3W 306 E5
Twain Harte U.S.A. 38°2N 120°14W 306 G6
Twardogóra Poland 51°23N 17°28E 185 G4
Twee River Namibia 25°27S 19°27E 270 C2
Tweed Canada 44°29N 77°19W 312 B7
Tweed → U.K. 55°45N 2°0W 167 F6
Tweed Heads Australia 28°10S 153°31E 281 D5
Tweedsmuir ⌂ Canada 53°0N 126°20W 296 C3
Twelve Apostles S. Africa 33°58S 18°23E 118 A1
Twentieth Century Fox Studios U.S.A. 34°4N 118°25W 126 B2
Twentynine Palms U.S.A. 34°8N 116°3W 307 L10
Tweya Dem. Rep. of the Congo 0°54S 18°58E 264 C3
Twickenham U.K. 51°26N 0°20W 125 B1
Twickenham Rugby Ground U.K. 51°27N 0°20W 125 B1
Twillingate Canada 49°42N 54°45W 299 C9
Twin Bridges U.S.A. 45°33N 112°20W 304 D7
Twin City U.S.A. 32°35N 82°10W 316 C7
Twin Falls Canada 53°30N 64°32W 299 B7
Twin Falls Idaho, U.S.A. 42°34N 114°28W 304 E6
Twin Hills U.S.A. 59°23N 159°58W 303 G8
Twin Lakes U.S.A. 30°43N 83°13W 316 E6
Twin Peaks U.S.A. 37°45N 122°26W 136 B2
Twin Valley U.S.A. 47°16N 96°16W 308 B5
Twinnge Burma 23°10N 96°2E 241 D6
Twinsburg U.S.A. 41°19N 81°26W 312 E3
Twistringen Germany 52°48N 8°37E 178 C4
Twitchell Res. U.S.A. 34°59N 120°19W 307 L6
Two Boats Village Ascension I. 7°56S 14°22W 153 g
Two Harbors U.S.A. 47°2N 91°40W 308 B8
Two Hills Canada 53°43N 111°52W 296 C6
Two Rivers U.S.A. 44°9N 87°34W 308 C10
Two Rock Mt. Ireland 53°15N 6°14W 120 B2
Two Rocks Australia 31°30S 115°35E 279 F2
Two Thumb Ra. N.Z. 43°45S 170°44E 285 D5
Twofold B. Australia 37°8S 149°59E 283 D8
Twyfelfontein Namibia 20°34S 14°22E 270 B1
Ty Ty U.S.A. 31°28N 83°39W 316 D6
Tyachiv Ukraine 48°1N 23°35E 177 D12
Tybee Island U.S.A. 32°1N 80°51W 316 C9
Tychy Poland 50°9N 18°59E 185 H5
Tyczyn Poland 49°58N 22°2E 185 J9
Tydal Norway 63°4N 11°34E 164 A8
Tyin Norway 61°18N 8°15E 164 C5
Tykocin Poland 53°13N 22°46E 185 E9
Tyler Minn., U.S.A. 44°17N 96°8W 308 C5
Tyler Tex., U.S.A. 32°21N 95°18W 314 E7
Tyligul → Ukraine 47°4N 30°57E 189 J6
Tylldal Norway 62°8N 10°48E 164 B7
Tymanivka Ukraine 48°34N 28°50E 183 B13
Tymon North Ireland 53°18N 6°20W 120 B1
Týn nad Vltavou Czech Rep. 49°13N 14°26E 180 B7
Tynda Russia 55°10N 124°43E 215 D13
Tyndall U.S.A. 43°0N 97°50W 308 D5
Tyndinsky = Tynda Russia 55°10N 124°43E 215 D13
Tyne → U.K. 54°59N 1°32W 168 C6
Tyne & Wear ☐ U.K. 55°6N 1°17W 168 B6
Týnec nad Sázavou Czech Rep. 49°50N 14°36E 180 B7
Tynemouth U.K. 55°1N 1°26W 168 B6
Tynset Norway 62°17N 10°47E 164 B7
Tyonek U.S.A. 61°4N 151°8W 303 F10
Tyre = Sūr Lebanon 33°19N 35°16E 250 E6
Tyresta △ Sweden 59°12N 18°14E 162 E12
Tyrifjorden Norway 60°2N 10°8E 164 D7
Tyringe Sweden 56°9N 13°35E 163 H7
Tyristrand Norway 60°4N 10°6E 164 D7
Tyrnyauz Russia 43°21N 42°45E 191 J6
Tyrol = Tirol ☐ Austria 47°3N 10°43E 180 D3
Tyrone U.S.A. 40°40N 78°14W 312 F6
Tyrone ☐ U.K. 54°38N 7°11W 166 B4
Tyrrel Bay Grenada 12°27N 61°28W 323 q
Tyrrell → Australia 35°26S 142°51E 282 C5
Tyrrell, L. Australia 35°20S 142°50E 282 C5
Tyrrell L. Canada 63°7N 105°27W 297 A7
Tyrrhenian Sea Medit. S. 40°0N 12°30E 192 D6
Tysfjorden Norway 68°7N 16°25E 160 B17
Tysmenytsya Ukraine 48°54N 24°51E 183 B9
Tysnes Norway 60°1N 5°30E 164 D2
Tysnesøya Norway 60°0N 5°35E 164 D2
Tysse Norway 60°23N 5°47E 164 D2
Tyssedal Norway 60°7N 6°35E 164 D3
Tystberga Sweden 58°51N 17°15E 163 F11
Tytuvėnai Lithuania 55°36N 23°12E 184 C10
Tyub Karagan, Mys = Tüpqarghan Muyis Kazakhstan 44°40N 50°19E 191 H10
Tyuleni, Ostrova = Tüledi Araldary Kazakhstan 45°2N 50°16E 191 H10
Tyuleniy Russia 44°28N 47°30E 191 H8
Tyuleniy, Mys Azerbaijan 40°12N 50°22E 191 K10
Tyulgan Russia 52°22N 56°12E 186 D10
Tyumen Russia 57°11N 65°29E 214 D7
Tyup = Tüp Kyrgyzstan 42°45N 78°20E 217 D9
Tywi → U.K. 51°48N 4°21W 169 F3
Tywyn U.K. 52°35N 4°5W 169 E3
Tzaneen S. Africa 23°47S 30°9E 271 B5
Tzermiado Greece 35°12N 25°29E 207 E6
Tzia = Kea Greece 37°35N 24°22E 204 D6
Tzoumérka, Óros = Athamanon Oros Greece 39°30N 21°26E 204 B3
Tzukong = Zigong China 29°15N 104°48E 228 C5
Tzukuan Taiwan 22°46N 120°16E 225 D2
Tzupo = Boshan China 36°28N 117°49E 227 F9
Tzutung Taiwan 23°45N 120°30E 225 C2

U

U.S.A. = United States of America ■ N. Amer. 37°0N 96°0W 301 H20
U.S. Capitol Washington, D.C., U.S.A. 143 b3
U.S. Cellular Field U.S.A. 41°50N 87°37W 119 C3
U.S.S. Arizona ⌂ U.S.A. 21°22N 157°57W 302 K14
U.S.S. Constitution Boston, U.S.A. 116 a3
U.S. Virgin Is. ☑ W. Indies 18°20N 65°0W 321 C7
Ua Huka French Polynesia 8°55S 139°32W 289 f
Ua Pu French Polynesia 9°25S 140°0W 289 f
Uachadi, Sierra = Uasadi-jidi Venezuela 4°54N 65°18W 329 C4
Uad Atui → W. Sahara 20°4N 15°59W 260 D2
Uad el Jat → W. Sahara 26°47N 13°3W 260 C2
Uaimh, An = Navan Ireland 53°39N 6°41W 166 C5
Uainambi Colombia 1°43N 69°51W 328 C4
Uamba Angola 7°21S 16°10E 265 D3
Uanle Uen = Wanleweyne Somalia 2°37N 44°54E 267 D5
Uasadi-jidi Venezuela 4°54N 65°18W 329 C4
Uati-Paraná → Brazil 1°51S 65°37W 328 D4
Uatumã → Brazil 2°26S 57°37W 329 D6
Uauá Brazil 9°50S 39°28W 332 C4
Uaupés Brazil 0°8S 67°5W 328 D4
Uaupés → Brazil 0°2N 67°16W 328 C4
Uaxactún Guatemala 17°25N 89°29W 320 C2
Ub Serbia 44°28N 20°6E 202 B4
Ubá Brazil 21°8S 43°0W 333 F3
Uba Nigeria 10°29N 13°13E 263 C7
Ubai Papua N. G. 5°39S 150°38E 286 C6
Ubaitaba Brazil 14°18S 39°20W 333 D4
Ubajara △ Brazil 3°55S 40°50W 332 B3
Ubangi = Oubangi → Dem. Rep. of the Congo 0°30S 17°50E 264 C3
Ubaté Colombia 5°19N 73°49W 328 B3
Ubauro Pakistan 28°15N 69°45E 242 E3
Ubay Phil. 10°3N 124°28E 233 F5
Ubaye → France 44°28N 6°18E 175 D10
Ubayyiḍ, W. al → Iraq 32°34N 43°48E 213 F10
Ube Japan 33°56N 131°15E 222 D3
Úbeda Spain 38°3N 3°23W 195 G7
Ubeidiya West Bank 31°43N 35°17E 123 B2
Uberaba Brazil 19°50S 47°55W 333 E2
Uberaba → Brazil 23°35S 46°41W 137 B2
Uberaba, L. Brazil 17°30S 57°50W 331 D6
Uberlândia Minas Gerais, Brazil 19°0S 48°20W 333 E2
Uberlândia Roraïma, Brazil 0°48N 59°20W 329 C6
Überlingen Germany 47°46N 9°10E 179 H5
Ubiaja Nigeria 6°41N 6°22E 263 D6
Ubin, Pulau Singapore 1°24N 103°57E 138 A3
Ubly U.S.A. 43°42N 82°55W 312 C2
Ubolratna Res. Thailand 16°45N 102°30E 236 D4
Ubombo S. Africa 27°31S 32°4E 271 C5
Ubon Ratchathani Thailand 15°15N 104°50E 236 E5
Ubondo Dem. Rep. of the Congo 0°55S 25°42E 268 C2
Ubort → Belarus 52°6N 28°30E 177 B15
Ubrique Spain 36°41N 5°27W 195 J5
Ubud Indonesia 8°30S 115°16E 231 J18
Ubuna Solomon Is. 10°11S 161°24E 287 N11
Ubundu Dem. Rep. of the Congo 0°22S 25°30E 264 C5
Ucar Azerbaijan 40°31N 47°39E 191 K8
Ucayali → Peru 4°30S 73°30W 328 D3
Uccle Belgium 50°48N 4°22E 116 B2
Uchab Namibia 19°47S 17°42E 270 A2
Uchiko Japan 33°33N 132°39E 222 D4
Uchiura-Wan Japan 42°25N 140°40E 220 C10
Uchiza Peru 8°25S 76°20W 330 B2
Uchquduq Uzbekistan 41°50N 62°50E 216 D6
Uchte Germany 52°30N 8°54E 178 C4
Uchur → Russia 58°48N 130°35E 215 D14
Uckermark Germany 53°5N 13°30E 178 B9
Ucluelet Canada 48°57N 125°32W 296 D3
Úcua Angola 8°43S 14°8E 265 D2
Uda → Russia 54°42N 135°14E 215 D14
Uda Walawe △ Sri Lanka 6°20N 81°0E 245 L5
Udachnyy Russia 66°25N 112°24E 215 C12
Udagamandalam India 11°30N 76°44E 245 J3
Udainagar India 22°33N 76°13E 242 H7
Udaipur Raj., India 24°36N 73°44E 242 G5
Udaipur Tripura, India 23°32N 91°30E 241 D3
Udaipur Garhi Nepal 27°0N 86°35E 243 F12
Udala India 21°35N 86°34E 243 J12
Udalguri India 26°46N 92°8E 241 B4
Udayagiri Andhra Pradesh, India 14°52N 79°19E 245 G4
Udayagiri Odisha, India 20°8N 84°23E 244 D7
Udbina Croatia 44°31N 15°47E 199 D12
Uddeholm Sweden 60°1N 13°38E 162 D7
Uddevalla Sweden 58°21N 11°55E 163 F5
Uddheden Sweden 59°57N 12°54E 162 E6
Uddjaure Sweden 65°56N 17°49E 160 D17
Udelnaya Russia 60°0N 30°21E 137 A2
Udelnoe Russia 59°58N 30°20E 137 B1
Uden Neths. 51°40N 5°37E 170 C5
Udgir India 18°25N 77°5E 244 E3
Udhampur India 33°0N 75°5E 243 C6
Udi Nigeria 6°17N 7°21E 263 D6
Údine Italy 46°3N 13°14E 199 B10
Udintsev Fracture Zone S. Ocean 57°0S 145°0W 151 B13
Udlding Germany 48°15N 11°25E 131 A1
Udmurtia ☐ Russia 57°30N 52°30E 186 C9
Udon Thani Thailand 17°29N 102°46E 236 D4
Udong Cambodia 11°48N 104°45E 237 G5
Udot I. Micronesia 7°22N 151°42E 287 T17
Udskaya Guba Russia 54°50N 135°45E 215 D14
Udu Pt. Fiji 16°9S 179°57W 287 A3
Udumalaippettai India 10°35N 77°15E 245 J3
Udupi India 13°25N 74°42E 245 H2
Udva India 20°5N 73°0E 244 D1
Udvoy Balkan Bulgaria 42°50N 26°50E 203 D10
Udzungwa △ Tanzania 7°52S 36°35E 268 D4
Udzungwa Range Tanzania 9°30S 35°10E 269 D4
Ueckermünde Germany 53°44N 14°1E 178 B10
Ueda Japan 36°24N 138°16E 223 A10
Uedineniya, Os. Russia 78°0N 85°0E 150 B12
Uele → Dem. Rep. of the Congo 3°45N 24°45E 264 B4
Uelen Russia 66°10N 170°0W 215 C19
Uelzen Germany 52°57N 10°32E 178 C6
Ueno Mie, Japan 34°45N 136°8E 223 C8
Ueno Tōkyō, Japan 35°42N 139°46E 140 A3
Uetersen Germany 53°40N 9°40E 178 B5
Uetze Germany 52°28N 10°11E 178 C6
Ufa Russia 54°45N 55°55E 186 D10
Ufa → Russia 54°40N 56°0E 186 D10
Uffenheim Germany 49°33N 10°14E 179 F6
Ugab → Namibia 20°55S 13°30E 270 B1
Ugalla → Tanzania 5°8S 30°42E 268 D3
Ugalla River ⌂ Tanzania 5°50S 31°54E 268 D3
Uganda ■ Africa 2°0N 32°0E 268 B3
Ugento Italy 39°56N 18°10E 201 C11
Ugep Nigeria 5°53N 8°2E 263 D6
Ughelli Nigeria 5°33N 6°0E 263 D6
Ugie S. Africa 31°10S 28°13E 271 D4
Ugíjar Spain 36°58N 3°7W 195 J7
Ugine France 45°45N 6°25E 175 C10
Uglegorsk Russia 49°5N 142°2E 215 E15
Uglich Russia 57°33N 38°20E 188 D10
Ugljan Croatia 44°12N 15°10E 199 D12
Ugljane Croatia 43°35N 16°46E 199 E13
Ugolny = Beringovskiy Russia 63°3N 179°19E 215 C18
Ugolny = Karpinsk Russia 59°45N 60°1E 186 C11
Ugolnye Kopi = Kopeysk Russia 55°7N 61°37E 216 A6
Ugolnye Kopi Russia 64°44N 177°42E 215 C18
Ugoofaaru Maldives 5°40N 73°0E 272 d
Ugra → Russia 54°30N 36°7E 188 E9
Ugŭrchin Bulgaria 43°6N 24°26E 203 C8
Uh → Slovak Rep. 48°37N 22°0E 181 C15
Uherské Hradiště Czech Rep. 49°4N 17°30E 181 B10
Uherský Brod Czech Rep. 49°1N 17°40E 181 B10
Úhlava → Czech Rep. 49°45N 13°24E 180 B6
Uhlenhorst Namibia 23°45S 17°55E 270 B2
Uhniv Ukraine 50°22N 23°45E 185 H10
Üholičky Czech Rep. 50°9N 14°19E 135 B1
Uhrichsville U.S.A. 40°24N 81°21W 312 F3
Uhřiněves Czech Rep. 50°2N 14°35E 135 B3
Uibhist a Deas = South Uist U.K. 57°20N 7°15W 167 D1
Uibhist a Tuath = North Uist U.K. 57°40N 7°15W 167 D1
Uiche Angola 12°2S 20°51E 265 E4
Uido S. Korea 34°36N 125°50E 224 E2
Uig U.K. 57°35N 6°21W 167 D2
Uíge Angola 7°30S 14°40E 265 D2
Uíge ☐ Angola 7°0S 16°0E 265 D3
Uiha Tonga 19°54S 174°25W 287 P13
Uijeongbu S. Korea 37°44N 127°2E 224 D3
Ŭiju N. Korea 40°15N 124°35E 224 B2
Uinta Mts. U.S.A. 40°45N 110°30W 304 F8
Uiryeong S. Korea 35°19N 128°15E 224 E4
Uis Namibia 21°8S 14°49E 270 B1
Uiseong S. Korea 36°21N 128°45E 224 D4
Uitenhage S. Africa 33°40S 25°28E 270 D4
Uithoorn Neths. 52°14N 4°50E 112 B1
Uithuizen Neths. 53°24N 6°41E 170 A6
Ujazd Poland 50°23N 18°21E 185 H5
Ujazdów Poland 52°13N 21°1E 143 B2
Ujazdowski Castle Warsaw, Poland 143 c3
Újfehértó Hungary 47°49N 21°41E 182 C6
Ujh → India 32°10N 75°18E 242 C6
Ujhani India 28°0N 79°6E 243 F8
Uji Japan 34°53N 135°48E 223 C7
Uji-guntō Japan 31°15N 129°25E 221 J4
Ujiyamada = Ise Japan 34°25N 136°45E 223 C8
Ujjain India 23°9N 75°43E 242 H6
Újpalota Hungary 47°32N 19°8E 117 A2
Újpest Hungary 47°35N 19°4E 117 A2
Ujście Poland 53°3N 16°45E 185 E3
Újszász Hungary 47°19N 20°7E 182 C5
Ujung Kulon △ Indonesia 6°46S 105°19E 234 D3
Ujung Pandang = Makassar Indonesia 5°10S 119°20E 235 D5
Uka Russia 57°50N 162°0E 215 D17
Ukai Sagar India 21°20N 73°43E 244 D1
Ukara I. Tanzania 1°50S 33°0E 268 C3
Uke-Shima Japan 28°2N 129°14E 221 K4
Ukerewe I. Tanzania 2°0S 33°0E 268 C3
uKhahlamba Drakensberg ⌂ S. Africa 29°27S 29°30E 271 C4
Ukholovo Russia 53°47N 40°30E 190 D5
Ukhrul India 25°10N 94°25E 241 C5
Ukhta Russia 63°34N 53°41E 186 B9
Uki Ni Masi Solomon Is. 10°15S 161°47E 287 N11
Ukiah U.S.A. 39°9N 123°13W 306 F3
Ukita Japan 35°40N 139°51E 140 A4
Ukmergė Lithuania 55°15N 24°45E 188 E3
Ukraine ■ Europe 49°0N 32°0E 189 H7
Uku Angola 11°24S 14°22E 265 E2
Ukwi Botswana 23°29S 20°30E 270 B3
Ula Turkey 37°6N 28°25E 212 D3
Ulaan Nuur Mongolia 44°30N 103°40E 226 B2
Ulaan-Uul Mongolia 46°4N 100°49E 226 B6
Ulaanbaatar Mongolia 47°55N 106°53E 218 B10
Ulaangom Mongolia 50°5N 92°10E 217 B12
Ulaanjirem Mongolia 45°5N 105°30E 226 B3
Ulak I. U.S.A. 51°22N 178°57W 303 L3
Ulala = Gorno-Altaysk Russia 51°50N 86°5E 217 B11
Ulalu I. Micronesia 7°23N 151°41E 287 T17
Ulamambri Australia 31°19S 149°23E 283 A8
Ulamba Dem. Rep. of the Congo 9°3S 23°38E 265 D4
Ulamona Papua N. G. 5°0S 151°15E 286 C6
Ulan Bator = Ulaanbaatar Mongolia 47°55N 106°53E 218 B10
Ulan Erge Russia 46°19N 44°53E 191 G7
Ulan Khol Russia 45°18N 47°4E 191 H8
Ulan Ude Russia 51°45N 107°40E 219 A10
Ulanhad = Chifeng China 42°18N 118°58E 227 C10
Ulanhot = Horqin Youyi Qianqi China 46°5N 122°3E 227 A12
Ulanów Poland 50°30N 22°16E 185 H9
Ulansuhai Nur China 40°53N 108°51E 226 D5
Ulaş Sivas, Turkey 39°26N 37°2E 212 C7
Ulaş Tekirdağ, Turkey 41°14N 27°42E 203 E11
Ulawa Solomon Is. 9°46S 161°57E 287 M11
Ulaya Morogoro, Tanzania 7°3S 36°55E 268 D4
Ulaya Tabora, Tanzania 4°25S 33°30E 268 C3
Ulcinj Montenegro 41°58N 19°10E 202 E3
Ulco S. Africa 28°21S 24°15E 270 C3
Ule älv = Oulujoki → Finland 65°1N 25°30E 160 D21
Ule träsk = Oulujärvi Finland 64°25N 27°15E 160 D22
Uleåborg = Oulu Finland 65°1N 25°29E 160 D21
Ulefoss Norway 59°17N 9°16E 164 E6
Uleta U.S.A. 25°27N 80°10W 129 C2
Ulëz Albania 41°46N 19°54E 202 E3
Ulfborg Denmark 56°16N 8°20E 163 H2
Ulhasnagar India 19°15N 73°10E 244 E1
Uliastay Mongolia 47°56N 97°28E 218 B8
Uljin S. Korea 36°59N 129°24E 224 D4
Uljma Serbia 45°2N 21°10E 182 E6
Ülken Kazakhstan 45°12N 73°58E 217 C8
Ülken Borsyq Qumy Kazakhstan 47°0N 59°11E 216 C5
Ulla → Spain 42°39N 8°44W 194 C2
Ulladulla Australia 35°21S 150°29E 283 C9
Ullal India 12°48N 74°51E 245 H2
Ullapool U.K. 57°54N 5°9W 167 D3
Ullared Sweden 57°8N 12°42E 163 G6
Ulldecona Spain 40°36N 0°20E 196 E5
Ullerup Denmark 55°34N 12°36E 118 B3
Ulleungdo S. Korea 37°30N 130°30E 224 D5
Ullevål Norway 59°56N 10°46E 133 A3
Ullswater Ont., Canada 45°12N 79°29W 312 A5
Ullswater Cumb., U.K. 54°34N 2°52W 168 C5
Ulm Germany 48°23N 9°58E 179 G5
Ulmarra Australia 29°37S 153°4E 281 D5
Ulmeni Buzău, Romania 45°4N 26°40E 183 E11
Ulmeni Maramureş, Romania 47°28N 23°18E 183 C8
Ulonguè Mozam. 14°37S 34°19E 269 E3
Ulricehamn Sweden 57°46N 13°26E 163 G7
Ulrika Sweden 58°5N 15°23E 163 F9
Ulriksdal Sweden 59°23N 17°59E 139 A1
Ulsan S. Korea 35°20N 129°15E 224 E4
Ulsberg Norway 62°45N 10°0E 164 B6

440 Ulsta
INDEX

Ulsta U.K. 60°30N 1°9W 167 A7
Ulsteinvik Norway 62°21N 5°53E 164 B2
Ulster □ U.K. 54°35N 6°30W 166 B5
Ulstrem Bulgaria 42°1N 26°27E 203 D10
Ultima Australia 35°30S 143°18E 282 C5
Ulu Temburong △ Brunei 4°27N 115°15E 235 B5
Ulubat Gölü Turkey 40°9N 28°35E 203 F12
Ulubey Turkey 38°25N 29°18E 205 C11
Uluborlu Turkey 38°4N 30°28E 205 C12
Uluçinar Turkey 36°24N 35°53E 250 B6
Uludağ Turkey 40°4N 29°13E 203 F13
Uludağ △ Turkey 40°5N 29°12E 203 F13
Uludere Turkey 37°28N 42°42E 213 D10
Ulugqat China 39°48N 74°15E 217 E8
Uluguru Mts. Tanzania 7°15S 37°40E 268 D4
Ulukışla = Marathóvounos
Cyprus 35°13N 33°37E 207 E9
Ulukışla Turkey 37°33N 34°28E 212 D6
Ulundi S. Africa 28°20S 31°25E 271 C5
Ulungur He ➔ China 47°1N 87°24E 217 C11
Ulungur Hu China 47°20N 87°10E 217 C11
Ulupalakua U.S.A. 20°39N 156°24W 302 C5
Uluru Australia 25°23S 131°5E 279 E5
Uluru-Kata Tjuta △
Australia 25°19S 131°1E 279 E5
Ulutau Kazakhstan 48°39N 67°1E 217 C7
Uluwatu Indonesia 8°50S 115°5E 231 K18
Ulva U.K. 56°29N 6°13W 167 E2
Ulverston U.K. 54°13N 3°5W 168 C4
Ulverstone Australia 41°11S 146°11E 281 G4
Ulvik Norway 60°35N 6°54E 164 D3
Ulya Russia 59°10N 142°0E 215 D15
Ulyanka Russia 59°50N 30°14E 137 B1
Ulyanovo Russia 54°50N 22°6E 184 D9
Ulyanovsk Russia 54°20N 48°25E 190 C9
Ulyanovsk □ Russia 54°5N 48°5E 190 C9
Ulyasutay = Uliastay
Mongolia 47°56N 97°28E 218 B8
Ulysses Kans., U.S.A. 37°35N 101°22W 308 G3
Ulysses Pa., U.S.A. 41°54N 77°46W 312 E7
Ulysses, Mt. Canada 57°20N 124°5W 296 B4
Ulysses S. Grant Nat. Historic Site ⌂
U.S.A. 38°33N 90°28W 310 F6
Ulyzhylanshyq ➔
Kazakhstan 48°51N 63°46E 216 C6
Um Al Khanazir I. Iraq 33°17N 44°22E 113 B2
Umag Croatia 45°26N 13°31E 199 C10
Umala Bolivia 17°25S 68°5W 330 D4
'Umān = Oman ■ Asia 23°0N 58°0E 249 B7
Uman Ukraine 48°40N 30°12E 177 D16
Uman I. Micronesia 7°17N 151°52E 287 U18
Umaria India 23°35N 80°50E 243 H9
Umarkhed India 19°37N 77°46E 244 E3
Umarkot Pakistan 25°15N 69°40E 242 G3
Umarpada India 21°27N 73°30E 242 J5
Umatac Guam 13°18N 144°39E 302 d
Umatilla U.S.A. 45°55N 119°21W 304 D4
Umba Russia 66°42N 34°11E 186 A5
Umbagog L. U.S.A. 44°46N 71°3W 313 B13
Umbakumba Australia 13°47S 136°50E 280 A2
Umbértide Italy 43°18N 12°20E 199 E9
Umboi I. Papua N. G. 5°40S 148°0E 286 C5
Umbrella Mts. N.Z. 45°35S 169°5E 285 F4
Umbria □ Italy 42°53N 12°30E 199 F9
Umeå Sweden 63°45N 20°20E 160 E19
Umeälven ➔ Sweden 63°45N 20°20E 160 E19
Umeda Japan 34°41N 135°29E 113 A1
Umera Indonesia 0°12S 129°37E 231 E7
Umerkhadi Mumbai, India 130 b2
Umfuli ➔ Zimbabwe 17°30S 29°23E 269 F2
Umfurudzi ⌂ Zimbabwe 17°6S 31°40E 269 F3
Umgusa Zimbabwe 19°29S 27°52E 269 F2
Umgwenya ➔ Mozam. 25°14S 32°18E 271 C5
Umiat U.S.A. 69°22N 152°8W 303 B9
Umiray Phil. 15°13N 121°25E 232 D3
Umiujaq Canada 56°33N 76°33W 298 A4
Umka Serbia 44°40N 20°19E 202 B4
Umkomaas S. Africa 30°13S 30°48E 271 D5
Umm ad Daraj, J. Jordan 32°18N 35°48E 251 F6
Umm al Arānib Libya 26°10N 14°43E 258 C2
Umm al Khashab
Si. Arabia 17°23N 42°32E 256 D5
Umm al Qaywayn U.A.E. 25°30N 55°35E 247 E7
Umm al Qittayn Jordan 32°18N 36°40E 251 F7
Umm al Rasas Jordan 31°30N 35°55E 251 G6
Umm al Sheif U.A.E. 25°9N 55°13E 119 B1
Umm al' Abīd Libya 27°31N 15°2E 258 C3
Umm Arda Sudan 15°17N 32°31E 257 D3
Umm Bāb Qatar 25°12N 50°48E 247 E6
Umm Badr Sudan 14°13N 27°58E 257 E2
Umm Bel Sudan 13°35N 28°0E 257 E2
Umm Birkah Si. Arabia 27°44N 36°31E 256 B4
Umm Boim Sudan 11°43N 25°27E 257 E2
Umm Dam Sudan 13°45N 30°59E 257 E3
Umm Debi Sudan 14°37N 30°23E 257 E3
Umm Dubban Sudan 15°23N 32°52E 257 D3
Umm Durman = Omdurmān
Sudan 15°40N 32°28E 257 D3
Umm el Fahm Israel 32°31N 35°9E 251 F6
Umm Gafala Sudan 13°22N 27°15E 257 E2
Umm Gimala Sudan 11°52N 28°12E 257 E2
Umm Inderaba Sudan 17°30N 33°13E 256 D3
Umm Isheirât, G. Egypt 28°21N 34°18E 251 K5
Umm Keddada Sudan 13°33N 26°35E 257 E2
Umm Koweika Sudan 13°10N 32°16E 257 E3
Umm Lajj Si. Arabia 25°0N 37°23E 246 E3
Umm Merwa Sudan 18°4N 32°30E 256 D3
Umm Qantur Sudan 14°17N 31°22E 257 E3
Umm Qasr Iraq 30°1N 47°58E 246 D5
Umm Qurein Sudan 9°58N 28°55E 257 F2
Umm Ruwaba Sudan 12°50N 31°20E 257 E3
Umm Saiyala Sudan 14°25N 31°10E 257 E3
Umm Shanqa Sudan 13°14N 27°14E 257 E2
Umm Shugeira Sudan 13°39N 29°37E 266 B2
Umm Shutur South Sudan 7°17N 33°14E 257 F3
Umm Sidr Sudan 14°29N 25°10E 257 E2
Umm Suqeim U.A.E. 25°11N 55°14E 119 B1
Umm Tais ⌂ Qatar 26°7N 51°15E 247 E6
Umm Urūmah Si. Arabia 25°43N 36°35E 256 B4
Umm Zehetir Egypt 28°48N 32°31E 256 J8
Umnak I. U.S.A. 53°15N 168°20W 303 K5
Umniati ➔ Zimbabwe 16°49S 28°45E 269 F2
Umpqua ➔ U.S.A. 43°40N 124°12W 304 E1
Umpulo Angola 12°38S 17°42E 265 E3
Ümraniye Turkey 41°1N 29°4E 122 B2
Umred India 20°51N 79°18E 244 D4
Umreth India 22°41N 73°4E 242 H5
Umri India 19°2N 77°39E 244 E3
Umtata = Mthatha
S. Africa 31°36S 28°49E 271 D4
Umuahia Nigeria 5°31N 7°26E 263 D6
Umuarama Brazil 23°45S 53°20W 335 A5
Umuda I. Papua N. G. 8°29S 143°46E 284 C2
Umurbey Turkey 40°13N 26°36E 203 F10
Umvukwe Ra. Zimbabwe 16°45S 30°45E 269 F3
Umzimvubu S. Africa 31°38S 29°33E 271 D4
Umzingwane ➔
Zimbabwe 22°12S 29°56E 269 G2
Umzinto = eMuziwezinto
S. Africa 30°15S 30°45E 271 D5
Una India 20°46N 71°8E 242 J4
Una ➔ Bos.-H. 45°0N 16°20E 199 D13
Unac ➔ Bos.-H. 44°30N 16°9E 199 D13
Unaðsdalur Iceland 66°7N 22°36W 155 A4
Unadilla Ga., U.S.A. 32°16N 83°44W 316 C6
Unadilla N.Y., U.S.A. 42°20N 75°19W 313 D9
Unai Brazil 16°23S 46°53W 333 E2
Unalakleet U.S.A. 63°52N 160°47W 303 E7
Unalaska U.S.A. 53°53N 166°32W 303 K6
Unalaska I. U.S.A. 53°35N 166°50W 303 K6
'Unayzah Si. Arabia 26°6N 43°58E 246 E4
'Unayzah, J. Asia 32°12N 39°18E 213 F8
Uncastillo Spain 42°21N 1°8W 196 C3
Uncia Bolivia 18°25S 66°40W 330 D4
Uncompahgre Peak
U.S.A. 38°4N 107°28W 304 G10
Uncompahgre Plateau
U.S.A. 38°20N 108°15W 304 G9
Undara Volcanic △
Australia 18°14S 144°41E 280 B3
Unden Sweden 58°45N 14°25E 163 F8
Underbool Australia 35°10S 141°51E 282 C4
Underground Atlanta
U.S.A. 33°45N 84°24W 113 B2
Underhill, L. U.S.A. 28°32N 81°20W 133 A3
Undersaker Sweden 63°19N 13°21E 162 A7
Underwood Canada 44°18N 81°29W 312 B3
Undredal Norway 60°57N 7°6E 164 D4
Unea I. Papua N. G. 4°53S 149°9E 286 C5
Unecha Russia 52°50N 32°37E 189 F7
Unieuxi ➔ Brazil 0°37S 65°34W 328 D4
Unětický potok ➔
Czech Rep. 50°9N 14°24E 135 B2
Unga I. U.S.A. 55°15N 160°40W 303 J7
Ungarie Australia 33°38S 146°56E 283 B7
Ungarisch-Hradisch = Uherské
Hradiště Czech Rep. 49°4N 17°30E 181 B10
Ungarisch-Ostra = Uherský Brod
Czech Rep. 49°1N 17°40E 181 B10
Ungarra Australia 34°12S 136°2E 282 C2
Ungat Papua N. G. 2°40S 150°15E 286 B6
Ungava, Pén. d' Canada 60°0N 74°0W 295 F17
Ungava B. Canada 59°30N 67°30W 295 F18
Ungeny = Ungheni
Moldova 47°11N 27°51E 183 C12
Unggi N. Korea 42°16N 130°28E 224 A5
Ungheni Moldova 47°11N 27°51E 183 C12
Unguala ➔ Ethiopia 8°6N 41°9E 257 F5
Unguz = Uzhhorod
Ukraine 48°36N 22°18E 182 B7
Ungwana B. Kenya 2°45S 40°20E 268 C5
Ungwatiri Sudan 16°52N 36°10E 257 D4
Unhos Portugal 38°49N 9°7W 126 A2
Uni Russia 57°46N 51°31E 190 B10
União Brazil 4°35S 42°52W 332 B3
União da Vitória Brazil 26°13S 51°5W 335 B5
União dos Palmares Brazil 9°10S 36°2W 332 C4
Uničov Czech Rep. 49°46N 17°8E 181 B10
Unidad Santa Fe Mexico 19°23N 99°13W 128 B1
Uniejów Poland 51°59N 18°46E 185 G5
Unije Croatia 44°40N 14°15E 199 D11
Unimak I. U.S.A. 54°45N 164°0W 303 J7
Unimak Pass. U.S.A. 54°15N 164°30W 303 J6
Unini ➔ Brazil 1°41S 61°31W 329 D5
Union Miss., U.S.A. 32°34N 89°7W 315 E10
Union Mo., U.S.A. 38°27N 91°0W 310 F6
Union Ohio, U.S.A. 39°55N 84°12W 311 E12
Union S.C., U.S.A. 34°43N 81°37W 315 D14
Union City Calif., U.S.A. 37°36N 122°1W 306 H4
Union City Ga., U.S.A. 33°35N 84°33W 316 B5
Union City New York, U.S.A. 132 b1
Union City Ohio, U.S.A. 40°12N 84°48W 311 D12
Union City Pa., U.S.A. 41°54N 79°51W 312 E5
Union City Tenn., U.S.A. 36°26N 89°3W 315 C10
Union Dale U.S.A. 41°43N 75°29W 313 E9
Union Gap U.S.A. 46°33N 120°28W 304 C3
Union Grove U.S.A. 42°41N 88°3W 311 B8
Union I. St. Vincent 12°36N 61°26W 323 n
Union Park U.S.A. 28°34N 81°17W 317 G8
Union Passenger Terminal
New Orleans, U.S.A. 131 b1
Union Point U.S.A. 33°37N 83°4W 316 B6
Union Port U.S.A. 40°48N 73°51W 132 B2
Union Springs Ala., U.S.A. 32°9N 85°43W 316 C4
Union Springs N.Y.,
U.S.A. 42°50N 76°41W 313 D8
Union Square Hong Kong,
China 22°19N 114°9E 122 B1
Union Square San Francisco, U.S.A. 136 b2
Union Star U.S.A. 39°59N 94°36W 310 E2
Union Station Toronto, Canada 141 c2
Union Station Washington, D.C., U.S.A. 143 b3
Union Station Ill., U.S.A. 119 c1
Union Station Los Angeles, U.S.A. 127 b3
Union Station Plaza
Washington, D.C., U.S.A. 143 b3
Uniondale S. Africa 33°39S 23°7E 270 D3
Uniontown Ky., U.S.A. 37°47N 87°56W 311 G9
Uniontown Pa., U.S.A. 39°54N 79°44W 309 F14
Unionville Ga., U.S.A. 31°26N 83°30W 316 D6
Unionville Mo., U.S.A. 40°29N 93°1W 310 D3
Unirea Romania 44°15N 27°35E 183 F12
United Arab Emirates ■
Asia 23°50N 54°0E 247 F7
United Arab Republic = Egypt ■
Africa 28°0N 31°0E 256 B3
United Center U.S.A. 41°53N 87°41W 119 B2
United Kingdom ■ Europe 53°0N 2°0W 165 E6
United Nations Headquarters
New York, U.S.A. 132 c3
United Provinces = Uttar Pradesh □
India 27°0N 80°0E 243 F9
United States of America ■
N. Amer. 37°0N 96°0W 301 H20
Unity Canada 52°30N 109°5W 297 C7
Unity □ South Sudan 8°30N 30°0E 257 F3
Universal Studios Calif.,
U.S.A. 34°9N 118°21W 126 B2
Universal Studios Fla.,
U.S.A. 28°29N 81°29W 133 B2
Universales, Mtes. Spain 40°18N 1°33W 196 E3
Universidad Spain 40°27N 3°44W 127 B1
University City U.S.A. 38°39N 90°18W 310 F6
University Park Md.,
U.S.A. 38°58N 76°56W 143 B3
University Park N. Mex.,
U.S.A. 32°17N 106°45W 305 K10
University Place U.S.A. 47°14N 122°33W 306 C4
Unjha India 23°46N 72°24E 242 H5
Unmet Vanuatu 16°8S 167°15E 287 F5
Unna Germany 51°32N 7°42E 178 D3
Unnao India 26°35N 80°30E 243 F9
Uno, Ilha Guinea-Biss. 11°15N 16°13W 262 C1
Unpongkor Vanuatu 18°50S 168°59E 287 H6
Unruhstadt = Kargowa
Poland 52°5N 15°51E 185 F2
Unsan N. Korea 40°6N 125°54E 224 B2
Unsengedsi ➔ Zimbabwe 15°43S 31°14E 269 F3
Unst U.K. 60°44N 0°53W 167 A8
Unstrut ➔ Germany 51°10N 11°48E 178 D7
Unter den Linden Berlin, Germany 115 a4
Unterbiberg Germany 48°6N 11°38E 131 B2
Unterdrauburg = Dravograd
Slovenia 46°36N 15°5E 199 B12
Unterföhring Germany 48°11N 11°38E 131 A3
Unterfranken □ Germany 50°0N 10°0E 179 F5
Unterhaching Germany 48°3N 11°37E 131 B2
Unterlaa Austria 48°6N 16°24E 142 B2
Untermenzing Germany 48°10N 11°28E 131 A1
Unterschleissheim
Germany 48°17N 11°34E 179 G7
Unuk ➔ Canada 56°5N 131°3W 296 B2
Ünye Turkey 41°5N 37°15E 212 B7
Unzen-Amakusa △
Japan 32°15N 130°10E 222 E2
Unzen-Dake Japan 32°45N 130°17E 222 E2
Unzha Russia 58°0N 44°0E 190 A7
Unzha ➔ Russia 57°49N 43°47E 190 B6
Ong Bi Vietnam 21°2N 106°47E 236 B6
Uotsuri-Shima
E. China Sea 25°45N 123°29E 221 M1
Uozu Japan 36°48N 137°24E 223 A9
Upata Venezuela 8°1N 62°24W 329 B5
Upatoi Cr. ➔ U.S.A. 32°22N 84°58W 316 C5
Upemba, L.
Dem. Rep. of the Congo 8°30S 26°20E 269 D2
Upemba △
Dem. Rep. of the Congo 9°0S 26°35E 269 D2
Upernavik Greenland 72°49N 56°20W 154 C5
Upington S. Africa 28°25S 21°15E 270 C3
Upleta India 21°46N 70°16E 242 J4
'Upolu Samoa 13°58S 172°0W 287 V20
Upolu Pt. U.S.A. 20°16N 155°52W 302 C6
Upper □ Ghana 10°30N 1°30W 263 C4
Upper Alkali L. U.S.A. 41°47N 120°8W 304 F3
Upper Arlington U.S.A. 40°0N 83°4W 311 E13
Upper Arrow L. Canada 50°30N 117°50W 296 C5
Upper Austria = Oberösterreich □
Austria 48°10N 14°0E 180 C7
Upper B. U.S.A. 40°40N 74°3W 132 C1
Upper Daly ◎ Australia 14°26S 131°3E 278 B5
Upper Darby U.S.A. 39°55N 75°16W 309 F16
Upper East Side New York, U.S.A. 132 b3
Upper Elmers End U.K. 51°23N 0°1W 125 B3
Upper Foster L. Canada 56°47N 105°20W 297 B7
Upper Hutt N.Z. 41°8S 175°5E 284 H4
Upper Klamath L.
U.S.A. 42°25N 121°55W 304 E3
Upper Lake U.S.A. 39°10N 122°54W 306 F4
Upper Liard Canada 60°3N 128°54W 296 A3
Upper Manilla Australia 30°38S 150°40E 283 A9
Upper Manzanilla
Trin. & Tob. 10°31N 61°4W 323 t
Upper Missouri Breaks ⌂
U.S.A. 47°50N 109°55W 304 C9
Upper Musquodoboit
Canada 45°10N 62°58W 299 C7
Upper New York B. = Upper B.
U.S.A. 40°40N 74°3W 132 C1
Upper Nile □ South Sudan 9°30N 33°0E 257 F3
Upper Norwood U.K. 51°24N 0°6W 125 B3
Upper Peirce Res.
Singapore 1°22N 103°47E 138 A2
Upper Red L. U.S.A. 48°8N 94°45W 308 A6
Upper Sandusky U.S.A. 40°50N 83°17W 311 D13
Upper Senegal & Niger = Mali ■
Africa 17°0N 3°0W 262 B4
Upper Sydenham U.K. 51°26N 0°4W 125 B3
Upper Tooting U.K. 51°25N 0°9W 125 B3
Upper Volta = Burkina Faso ■
Africa 12°0N 1°0W 262 C4
Upper West Side New York, U.S.A. 132 a2
Upphärad Sweden 58°9N 12°19E 163 F6
Uppland Sweden 59°59N 17°48E 162 D12
Upplands-Väsby Sweden 59°31N 17°54E 162 E11
Uppsala Sweden 59°53N 17°38E 162 E11
Uppsala län □ Sweden 60°0N 17°30E 162 D11
Upshi India 33°48N 77°52E 243 C7
Upton London, U.K. 51°32N 0°1E 125 A4
Upton Wyo., U.S.A. 44°6N 104°38W 304 D11
Uptown U.S.A. 41°58N 87°40W 119 B2
Uqsuqtuuq = Gjoa Haven
Canada 68°38N 95°53W 294 D12
Ur Iraq 30°55N 46°25E 246 D5
Ur Kut Somalia 3°31N 42°47E 267 D5
Ura-Tyube = Istaravshān
Tajikistan 39°55N 69°1E 217 E7
Urabá, G. de Colombia 8°25N 76°53W 328 B2
Urad Qianqi China 40°40N 108°30E 226 D5
Uraga-Suidō Japan 35°13N 139°45E 223 B11
Urahoro Japan 42°50N 143°40E 220 C11
Urakawa Japan 42°9N 142°47E 220 C11
Ural = Uralskiy □ Russia 64°0N 70°0E 214 C7
Ural = Zhayyq ➔
Kazakhstan 47°0N 51°48E 187 E9
Ural Australia 33°21S 146°12E 283 B7
Ural Mts. = Uralskie Gory
Eurasia 60°0N 59°0E 186 C10
Uralla Australia 30°37S 151°29E 283 A9
Uralmedstroy = Krasnouralsk
Russia 58°21N 60°3E 186 C11
Uralsk = Oral Kazakhstan 51°20N 51°20E 190 E10
Uralskie Gory Eurasia 60°0N 59°0E 186 C10
Uralskiy □ Russia 64°0N 70°0E 214 C7
Urambo Tanzania 5°4S 32°0E 268 D3
Uran India 18°53N 72°56E 130 B2
Urana Australia 35°15S 146°21E 283 C7
Urana, L. Australia 35°16S 146°10E 283 C7
Urandangi Australia 21°32S 138°14E 280 C2
Uranga Australia 30°31S 153°1E 283 A10
Uranium City Canada 59°34N 108°37W 297 B7
Urapuntja = Utopia
Australia 22°14S 134°33E 280 C1
Uraricaá ➔ Brazil 3°20N 61°56W 329 C5
Uraricoera Brazil 3°27N 60°59W 329 C5
Uraricoera ➔ Brazil 3°2N 60°30W 329 C5
Urasoe Japan 26°15N 127°43E 288 a
Uravakonda India 14°57N 77°12E 245 G3
Urawa = Saitama Japan 35°54N 139°38E 223 B11
Uray Russia 60°5N 65°15E 214 C7
Urayasu Japan 35°39N 139°53E 140 B4
'Uray'irah Si. Arabia 25°57N 48°53E 247 E6
Urbakh = Pushkino Russia 51°16N 47°0E 190 E8
Urbana Ill., U.S.A. 40°7N 88°12W 311 D8
Urbana Ohio, U.S.A. 40°7N 83°45W 311 D13
Urbandale U.S.A. 41°38N 93°43W 310 C3
Urbánia Italy 43°40N 12°31E 199 E9
Urbano Santos Brazil 3°12S 43°23W 332 B3
Urbe ✕ Italy 41°57N 12°30E 136 B2
Urbel ➔ Spain 42°21N 3°40W 194 C7
Urbino Italy 43°43N 12°38E 199 E9
Urbión, Picos de Spain 42°1N 2°52W 196 C2
Urca Brazil 22°56S 43°9W 135 B2
Urcos Peru 13°40S 71°38W 330 C3
Urdaneta Phil. 15°59N 120°34E 232 D3
Urdinarrain Argentina 32°37S 58°52W 334 C4
Urdos France 42°51N 0°35W 174 F3
Ure ➔ U.K. 54°5N 1°20W 168 C6
Uren Russia 57°35N 45°55E 190 B7
Urengoy Russia 65°58N 78°22E 214 C8
Ureparapara Vanuatu 13°32S 167°20E 287 D5
Ures Mexico 29°26N 110°24W 318 B2
Ureshino Japan 33°6N 129°59E 222 D1
Urewera △ N.Z. 38°29S 177°7E 284 E6
Urfa = Sanliurfa Turkey 37°12N 38°50E 213 D8
Urga = Ulaanbaatar
Mongolia 47°55N 106°53E 218 B10
Urganch Uzbekistan 41°40N 60°41E 216 D6
Urgench = Urganch
Uzbekistan 41°40N 60°41E 216 D6
Ürgüp Turkey 38°38N 34°56E 212 C6
Uri India 34°8N 74°2E 243 B6
Uri □ Switz. 46°43N 8°35E 179 J4
Uribante ➔ Venezuela 7°25N 71°50W 328 B3
Uribe Colombia 3°13N 74°24W 328 C3
Uribia Colombia 11°43N 72°16W 328 A3
Uricani Romania 45°20N 23°9E 182 E8
Urimba Angola 10°56S 16°32E 265 E3
Uriondo Bolivia 21°41S 64°41W 334 A3
Urique Mexico 27°13N 107°55W 318 B3
Urique ➔ Mexico 26°29N 107°58W 318 B3
Uritsk Russia 59°49N 30°10E 137 C1
Urk Neths. 52°39N 5°36E 170 B5
Urkiola ⌂ Spain 43°6N 1°2W 196 B3
Urla Turkey 38°20N 26°47E 205 C8
Urlați Romania 44°59N 26°15E 183 F11
Urmia = Orūmīyeh Iran 37°40N 45°0E 213 D11
Urmia, L. = Orūmīyeh,
Daryācheh-ye Iran 37°50N 45°30E 213 D11
Ürom Hungary 47°35N 19°1E 117 A2
Uromi Nigeria 6°42N 6°20E 263 D6
Uroševac = Ferizaj Kosovo 42°23N 21°10E 202 D5
Ŭroteppa = Istaravshān
Tajikistan 39°55N 69°1E 217 E7
Uroyan, Montanas de
Puerto Rico 18°12N 66°50W 321 b
Urrampinyi Iltjiltarri ◎
Australia 24°20S 132°10E 278 D5
Urrao Colombia 6°20N 76°11W 328 B2
Urshult Sweden 56°31N 14°50E 163 H8
Ursus Poland 52°11N 20°52E 143 B1
Ursvik Sweden 59°23N 17°57E 139 A1
Uru Uru, L. Bolivia 18°6S 67°8W 330 D4
Uruaçu Brazil 14°30S 49°10W 333 D2
Uruanã Brazil 15°30S 49°41W 333 E2
Uruapan Mexico 19°24N 102°3W 318 D4
Uruará Brazil 3°42S 53°51W 329 D7
Uruará ➔ Brazil 2°6S 53°38W 329 D7
Urubamba Peru 13°20S 72°10W 330 C3
Urubamba ➔ Peru 10°43S 73°48W 330 C3
Urubaxi ➔ Brazil 0°31S 64°50W 329 D5
Urubu ➔ Brazil 2°55S 58°25W 329 D6
Urucará Brazil 2°32S 57°45W 329 D6
Uruçuí Brazil 7°20S 44°28W 332 C3
Uruçuí, Serra do Brazil 9°0S 44°45W 332 C3
Uruçuí Prêto ➔ Brazil 7°20S 44°38W 332 C3
Urucuia ➔ Brazil 16°8S 45°5W 333 E2
Uruguai ➔ Brazil 26°0S 53°30W 335 B5
Uruguaiana Brazil 29°50S 57°0W 334 B4
Uruguay ■ S. Amer. 32°30S 56°30W 334 C4
Uruguay ➔ S. Amer. 34°12S 58°18W 334 C4
Urukthapel I. Palau 7°17N 134°25E 288 c
Uruma Japan 26°21N 127°52E 288 a
Urumchi = Ürümqi
China 43°45N 87°45E 217 D11
Ürümqi China 43°45N 87°45E 217 D11
Uruna ◎ Australia 24°3S 133°1E 278 D5
Urundi = Burundi ■ Africa 3°15S 30°0E 268 C3
Urup ➔ Russia 45°0N 41°10E 191 H5
Urup, Ostrov Russia 46°0N 151°0E 215 E16
Urutai Brazil 17°28S 48°12W 333 E2
Uryupinsk Russia 50°45N 41°58E 190 E5
Ürzhar Kazakhstan 47°5N 81°38E 217 C10
Urzhum Russia 57°10N 49°56E 190 B9
Urziceni Romania 44°40N 26°42E 183 F11
Usa Japan 33°31N 131°21E 222 D3
Usa ➔ Russia 66°16N 59°49E 186 A10
Uşak Turkey 38°43N 29°28E 205 C11
Uşak □ Turkey 38°30N 29°0E 205 C11
Usakos Namibia 21°54S 15°31E 270 B2
Usborne, Mt. Falk. Is. 51°40S 59°55W 153 F4
Ušće Serbia 43°30N 20°39E 202 C4
Usedom Germany 53°55N 14°2E 178 B10
Usedom ⌂ Germany 53°55N 14°0E 178 B10
Useless Loop Australia 26°8S 113°23E 279 E1
Usera Spain 40°22N 3°42W 127 B1
'Usfān Si. Arabia 21°58N 39°27E 248 B2
Ushakova, Ostrov Russia 82°0N 80°0E 215 A8
Ushakovo Russia 54°37N 20°16E 184 D7
Ushant = Ouessant, Î. d'
France 48°28N 5°6W 172 D1
Üsharal Kazakhstan 46°10N 80°56E 217 C10
Ushashi Tanzania 1°59S 33°57E 268 C3
Ushat South Sudan 7°59N 29°28E 257 F2
'Ushayrah Ar Riyāḑ,
Si. Arabia 25°35N 45°47E 246 E5
'Ushayrah Makkah,
Si. Arabia 21°46N 40°42E 256 C5
Ushibuka Japan 32°11N 130°1E 222 E2
Ushigome Japan 35°42N 139°44E 140 A3
Üshtöbe Kazakhstan 45°16N 78°0E 217 C9
Ushuaia Argentina 54°50S 68°23W 336 D3
Ushumun Russia 52°47N 126°32E 215 D13
Ushytsya ➔ Ukraine 48°35N 27°8E 183 B12
Usina Brazil 22°57S 43°17W 135 B1
Usino Papua N. G. 5°32S 145°23E 286 C3
Usinsk Russia 65°57N 57°27E 186 A10
Usk Canada 54°38N 128°26W 296 C3
Usk ➔ U.K. 51°33N 2°58W 169 F5
Uska India 27°12N 83°7E 243 F10
Uskedalen Norway 59°56N 5°53E 164 E2
Üsküb = Skopje Macedonia 42°1N 21°26E 202 D5
Üsküdar Turkey 41°1N 29°0E 122 B2
Uslar Germany 51°39N 9°38E 178 D5
Usman Russia 52°5N 39°48E 189 F10
Usoke Tanzania 5°8S 32°24E 268 D3
Usolye-Sibirskoye
Russia 52°48N 103°40E 215 D11
Usolye-Solikamskoye = Berezniki
Russia 59°24N 56°46E 186 C10
Usoro Nigeria 5°33N 6°11E 263 D6
Uspallata, P. de Argentina 32°37S 69°22W 334 C2
Uspenka = Kirovskiy
Russia 45°7N 133°30E 220 B6
Ussel France 45°32N 2°18E 174 C6
Usson-du-Poitou France 46°16N 0°31E 174 B4
Ussuriysk Russia 43°48N 131°59E 220 C5
Ussurka Russia 45°12N 133°31E 220 B6
Ust-Aldan = Batamay
Russia 63°30N 129°15E 215 C13
Ust-Amginskoye = Khandyga
Russia 62°42N 135°35E 215 C14
Ust-Buzulukskaya Russia 50°8N 42°11E 190 E6
Ust-Chaun Russia 68°47N 170°30E 215 C18
Ust-Chorna Ukraine 48°19N 23°56E 183 B8
Ust-Donetskiy Russia 47°35N 40°55E 191 G5
Ust-Ilimpeya = Yukta
Russia 63°26N 105°42E 215 C11
Ust-Ilimsk Russia 58°3N 102°39E 215 D11
Ust-Ishim Russia 57°45N 71°10E 214 D8
Ust-Kamchatsk Russia 56°10N 162°28E 215 D17
Ust-Kamenogorsk = Öskemen
Kazakhstan 50°0N 82°36E 217 C10
Ust-Khayryuzovo
Russia 57°15N 156°45E 215 D16
Ust-Kut Russia 56°50N 105°42E 215 D11
Ust-Kuyga Russia 70°1N 135°43E 215 B14
Ust-Labinsk Russia 45°15N 39°41E 191 H4
Ust-Luga Russia 59°35N 28°20E 188 C5
Ust-Maya Russia 60°30N 134°28E 215 C14
Ust-Medveditskaya = Serafimovich
Russia 49°36N 42°43E 190 F6
Ust-Mil Russia 59°40N 133°11E 215 D14
Ust-Nera Russia 64°35N 143°15E 215 C15
Ust-Nyukzha Russia 56°34N 121°37E 215 D13
Ust-Olenek Russia 73°0N 120°5E 215 B12
Ust-Omchug Russia 61°9N 149°38E 215 C15
Ust-Port Russia 69°40N 84°26E 214 C9
Ust-Slavyanka Russia 59°51N 30°32E 137 C3
Ust-Sysolsk = Syktyvkar
Russia 61°45N 50°40E 186 B9
Ust-Tsilma Russia 65°28N 52°11E 186 A9
Ust-Urt = Ustyurt Plateau
Asia 44°0N 55°0E 216 D5
Ust-Usa Russia 66°2N 56°57E 186 A10
Ust-Vorkuta Russia 67°24N 64°0E 186 A11
Ust-Zhuya = Chara
Russia 56°54N 118°20E 215 D12
Ustaoset Norway 60°30N 8°2E 164 D5
Ustaritz France 43°24N 1°27W 174 E2
Ústecký □ Czech Rep. 50°30N 14°0E 180 A7
Uster Switz. 47°22N 8°43E 179 H4
Ústí nad Labem Czech Rep. 50°41N 14°3E 180 A7
Ústí nad Orlicí Czech Rep. 49°58N 16°24E 181 B9
Ustica Italy 38°42N 13°11E 200 D6
Ustinov = Izhevsk Russia 56°51N 53°14E 186 C9
Ustka Poland 54°35N 16°55E 184 D3
Ustroń Poland 49°43N 18°48E 185 J5
Ustrzyki Dolne Poland 49°27N 22°40E 185 J9
Ustupo Panama 9°27N 78°34W 328 B2
Ustyluh Ukraine 50°51N 24°10E 185 H11
Ustyurt Plateau Asia 44°0N 55°0E 216 D5
Ustyuzhna Russia 58°50N 36°32E 188 C9
Usu China 44°27N 84°40E 217 D10
Usuki Japan 33°8N 131°49E 222 D3
Usulután El Salv. 13°25N 88°28W 320 D2
Usumacinta ➔ Mexico 18°24N 92°38W 319 D6
Usumbura = Bujumbura
Burundi 3°16S 29°18E 268 C2
Usure Tanzania 4°40S 34°22E 268 C3
Usutuo ➔ Mozam. 26°48S 32°7E 271 C5
Uta Indonesia 4°33S 136°0E 231 E9
Utah □ U.S.A. 39°20N 111°30W 304 G8
Utah L. U.S.A. 40°12N 111°48W 304 F8
Utansjö Sweden 62°46N 17°55E 162 B11
Utara, Selat Malaysia 5°28N 100°20E 237 c
Utarni India 26°5N 71°58E 242 F4
Utatlan Guatemala 15°2N 91°11W 320 C1
Ute Creek ➔ U.S.A. 35°21N 103°50W 305 J12
Utebo Spain 41°43N 1°0W 196 D3
Utegi Tanzania 1°19S 34°13E 266 E3
Uteke Sweden 59°24N 18°15E 139 A3
Utena Lithuania 55°27N 25°40E 188 E3
Utete Tanzania 8°0S 38°45E 268 D4
Uthai Thani Thailand 15°22N 100°3E 236 E3
Uthal Pakistan 25°44N 66°40E 242 G2
Utiariti Brazil 13°0S 58°10W 331 C6
Utica N.Y., U.S.A. 43°6N 75°14W 313 C9
Utica Ohio, U.S.A. 40°14N 82°27W 312 F2
Utiel Spain 39°37N 1°11W 197 F3
Utikuma L. Canada 55°50N 115°30W 296 B5
Utila Honduras 16°6N 86°56W 320 C2
Utinga Brazil 12°6S 41°5W 333 D3
Utkela India 20°6N 83°10E 244 D6
Utlängen Sweden 56°2N 15°48E 163 H9
Utne Norway 60°25N 6°37E 164 D3
Utnur India 19°22N 78°46E 244 E4
Uto Japan 32°41N 130°40E 222 E2
Utö Sweden 58°56N 18°16E 162 F12
Utopia Australia 22°14S 134°33E 280 C1
Utrata Poland 52°15N 21°4E 143 B2
Utraula India 27°19N 82°25E 243 F10
Utrecht Neths. 52°5N 5°8E 170 B5
Utrecht KwaZulu Natal,
S. Africa 27°38S 30°20E 271 C5
Utrecht □ Neths. 52°6N 5°7E 170 B5
Utrera Spain 37°12N 5°48W 195 H5
Utría △ Colombia 5°57N 77°21W 328 B2
Utsira Norway 59°19N 4°53E 164 E1
Utsjoki ➔ Finland 69°51N 26°59E 160 B22
Utsunomiya Japan 36°30N 139°50E 223 A11
Uttar Pradesh □ India 27°0N 80°0E 243 F9
Uttaradit Thailand 17°36N 100°5E 236 D3
Uttarakhand □ India 30°0N 79°30E 243 D8
Uttaranchal = Uttarakhand □
India 30°0N 79°30E 243 D8
Uttarpara India 22°39N 88°21E 124 B1
Utterslev Mose Denmark 55°42N 12°29E 118 A2
Utterson Canada 45°12N 79°19W 312 A5
Uttoxeter U.K. 52°54N 1°52W 168 E6
Utuado Puerto Rico 18°16N 66°42W 321 b
Uummannaq Avannaarsua,
Greenland 77°33N 68°52W 154 B4
Uummannaq Kitaa,
Greenland 70°58N 52°17W 150 B5
Uummannarsuaq = Nunap Isua
Greenland 59°48N 43°55W 154 F6
Uunartoq Qeqertoq
Greenland 71°33N 21°47W 154 C8
Uusikaarlepyy Finland 63°32N 22°31E 160 E20
Uusikaupunki Finland 60°47N 21°25E 188 B1
Uva Russia 56°59N 52°13E 190 B11
Uvá ➔ Colombia 3°41N 70°3W 328 C3
Uvac ➔ Serbia 43°35N 19°30E 202 C3
Uvalda U.S.A. 32°2N 82°31W 316 C7
Uvalde U.S.A. 29°13N 99°47W 314 G5
Uvarovo Russia 51°59N 42°14E 190 E6
Uvat Russia 59°5N 68°50E 214 D7
Uvdal Norway 60°17N 8°48E 164 D5
Uvéa, I. Wall. & F. Is. 13°18S 176°10W 277 C15
Uvinza Tanzania 5°5S 30°24E 268 D3
Uvira Dem. Rep. of the Congo 3°22S 29°3E 268 C2
Uvs □ Mongolia 49°38N 93°0E 217 C12
Uvs Nuur Mongolia 50°20N 92°30E 217 B12
Uwa Japan 33°22N 132°31E 222 D4
'Uwairidh, Ḩarrat al
Si. Arabia 26°50N 38°0E 246 E3
Uwajima Japan 33°10N 132°35E 222 D4
Uwanda △ Tanzania 7°46S 32°0E 268 D3
Uweinat, Jebel Sudan 21°54N 24°58E 256 C1
Uxbridge Canada 44°6N 79°7W 312 B5
Uxin Qi China 38°50N 109°5E 226 E5
Uxmal Mexico 20°22N 89°46W 319 C7
Uyak U.S.A. 57°38N 154°0W 303 H9
Üydzin Mongolia 44°9N 107°0E 226 B4
Uyo Nigeria 5°1N 7°53E 263 D6
Uyu ➔ Burma 24°51N 94°57E 241 C5
Üyüklü Tepe Turkey 37°5N 27°21E 205 D9
Uyûn Mûsa Egypt 29°53N 32°40E 251 J3
Uyuni Bolivia 20°28S 66°47W 330 E4
Uzbekistan ■ Asia 41°30N 65°0E 217 D7
Uzboy ➔ Turkmenistan 39°30N 55°0E 247 B7
Uzen, Mal ➔ Kazakhstan 49°4N 49°44E 191 F9
Uzerche France 45°25N 1°34E 174 C5
Uzès France 44°1N 4°26E 175 D8
Uzh ➔ Ukraine 51°15N 30°12E 177 C16
Uzhgorod = Uzhhorod
Ukraine 48°36N 22°18E 182 B7
Uzhhorod Ukraine 48°36N 22°18E 182 B7
Uzhok Ukraine 48°59N 22°52E 182 B7
Užice Serbia 43°55N 19°50E 202 C3
Uzlovaya Russia 54°0N 38°5E 188 F10
Üzümlü Turkey 36°44N 29°14E 205 E11
Uzunceburç Turkey 36°35N 33°57E 250 B4
Uzunköprü Turkey 41°16N 26°43E 203 E10
Uzunkuyu Turkey 38°17N 26°33E 205 C8

V

V.C. Bird Int. ✕ (ANU)
Antigua & B. 17°8N 61°47W 322 b
Vaal ➔ S. Africa 29°4S 23°38E 270 C3
Vaal Dam S. Africa 27°0S 28°14E 271 C4
Vaalwater S. Africa 24°15S 28°8E 271 B4
Vaasa Finland 63°6N 21°38E 160 E19
Vabre France 43°42N 2°24E 174 E6
Vác Hungary 47°49N 19°10E 182 C4
Vacaos, Mare aux
Mauritius 20°22S 57°30E 272 e
Vacaria Brazil 28°31S 50°52W 335 B5
Vacasa Fiji 17°15S 179°31W 287 A3
Vacaville U.S.A. 38°21N 121°59W 306 G5
Vaccarès, Étang de France 43°32N 4°34E 175 E8
Vach = Vakh ➔ Russia 60°45N 76°45E 214 C8
Vache, Î. à Haiti 18°2N 73°35W 321 C5
Väckelsång Sweden 56°37N 14°58E 163 H8
Vaclavské náměstí Prague, Czech Rep. 135 b2
Vacoas Mauritius 20°18S 57°29E 272 e
Vada India 19°39N 73°8E 244 E1
Vadakara India 11°35N 75°40E 245 J2
Vadaul India 19°2N 72°52E 130 A2
Väddö Sweden 60°0N 18°50E 162 D12
Vadehavet △ Denmark 55°20N 8°30E 163 J2
Väderstad Sweden 58°19N 14°55E 163 F8
Vadheim Norway 61°13N 5°49E 164 C2
Vadnagar India 23°47N 72°40E 242 H5
Vado Ligure Italy 44°17N 8°26E 198 D5
Vadodara India 22°20N 73°10E 242 H5
Vadsø Norway 70°3N 29°50E 160 A23
Vadstena Sweden 58°28N 14°54E 163 F8
Vaduj India 17°36N 74°27E 244 F2
Vaduz Liech. 47°8N 9°31E 179 H5
Værlandet Norway 61°18N 4°44E 164 C1
Værøy Norway 67°40N 12°40E 160 C15
Vagalat Albania 39°44N 20°8E 206 B10
Vågåmo Norway 61°52N 9°6E 164 C6
Vágar Færoe Is. 62°5N 7°15W 160 E9
Vaggeryd Sweden 57°30N 14°10E 163 G8
Vagharshapat = Ejmiatsin
Armenia 40°12N 44°19E 191 K7
Vaghena Solomon Is. 7°25S 157°45E 287 L9
Vaghia Greece 38°19N 23°11E 204 C5
Vagia, Akra Greece 36°15N 28°11E 206 E12
Vagney France 48°1N 6°43E 173 D13
Vagnhärad Sweden 58°57N 17°33E 163 F11
Vagos Portugal 40°33N 8°42W 194 E2
Vågsfjorden Norway 68°50N 16°50E 160 B17
Váh ➔ Slovak Rep. 47°43N 18°7E 181 D11
Vahitahi French Polynesia 18°44S 138°52W 289 f
Vahsel B. Antarctica 75°0S 35°0W 151 D1
Váhtjer = Gällivare
Sweden 67°9N 20°40E 160 C19
Vai Greece 35°15N 26°18E 207 E7
Vaiea Cook Is. 19°6S 169°54W 289 g
Vaigai ➔ India 9°15N 79°10E 245 K4
Vaiges France 48°2N 0°30W 172 D6
Vaihingen Germany 48°54N 8°57E 179 G4
Vaihiria, L. Tahiti 17°40S 149°25W 289 e
Vaijapur India 19°58N 74°45E 244 E2
Vaikam India 9°45N 76°25E 245 K3
Vail U.S.A. 39°40N 106°20W 304 G10
Vailala ➔ Papua N. G. 7°57S 145°25E 286 D3
Vailhau, Récif Comoros Is. 11°48S 43°4E 272 a
Vailly-sur-Aisne France 49°24N 3°31E 173 C10
Vailoatai Amer. Samoa 14°21S 170°46W 302 f
Vaippar ➔ India 9°0N 78°25E 245 K4
Vairaatea French Polynesia 19°19S 139°20W 289 f
Vairao Tahiti 17°47S 149°17W 289 e
Vaires-sur-Marne France 48°52N 2°38E 134 A4
Vaisali ➔ India 26°28N 78°53E 243 F8
Vaison-la-Romaine France 44°14N 5°4E 175 D9
Vaitogi Amer. Samoa 14°24S 170°44W 302 f
Vaitupu Pac. Oc. 7°28S 178°41E 277 B14
Vajpur India 21°24N 73°17E 244 D1
Vakaga ➔ C.A.R. 9°48N 21°32E 264 A4
Vakarai Sri Lanka 8°8N 81°26E 245 K5
Vakarel Bulgaria 42°35N 23°40E 202 D7
Vakfıkebir Turkey 41°2N 39°17E 213 B8
Vakh ➔ Russia 60°45N 76°45E 214 C8
Vakhtan Russia 57°53N 46°47E 190 B8
Vaksdal Norway 60°29N 5°45E 164 D2
Vakuta I. Papua N. G. 8°51S 151°10E 286 E6
Vál Hungary 47°22N 18°40E 182 C3
Val Camónica Italy 45°57N 10°17E 198 C7
Val-de-Marne □ France 48°45N 2°28E 173 D9
Val-d'Isère France 45°27N 6°59E 175 C10
Val-d'Oise □ France 49°5N 2°10E 173 C9
Val-d'Or Canada 48°7N 77°47W 298 C4
Val Grande △ Italy 46°3N 8°25E 198 B5
Val Marie Canada 49°15N 107°45W 297 D7
Val Thorens France 45°20N 6°33E 175 C10
Valaam Russia 61°22N 30°57E 188 B6
Valadares Portugal 41°5N 8°38W 194 D2
Valahia Romania 44°35N 25°0E 183 F9
Valaichenai Sri Lanka 7°54N 81°32E 245 L5
Valais □ Switz. 46°12N 7°45E 179 J3
Valais, Alpes du Switz. 46°5N 7°35E 179 J3
Valandovo Macedonia 41°19N 22°34E 202 E6
Valašské Meziříčí
Czech Rep. 49°29N 17°59E 181 B10
Valatie U.S.A. 42°24N 73°40W 313 D11
Valaxa Greece 38°50N 24°29E 204 C6
Vålberg Sweden 59°23N 13°11E 162 E7
Valbo Sweden 60°40N 17°0E 162 D10
Valbondione Italy 46°2N 10°1E 198 B7
Valby Denmark 55°39N 12°29E 118 B2
Valcamonica = Val Camónica
Italy 45°57N 10°17E 198 C7
Vâlcani Romania 46°0N 20°26E 182 D5
Valcannuta Italy 41°52N 12°25E 136 B1
Vâlcea □ Romania 45°0N 24°10E 183 F9
Valcheta Argentina 40°40S 66°8W 336 B3
Valdagno Italy 45°39N 11°18E 199 C8
Valdahon France 47°8N 6°21E 173 E13
Valdai Hills = Valdayskaya
Vozvyshennost Russia 57°0N 33°30E 188 D7
Valday Russia 57°58N 33°9E 188 D7
Valdayskaya Vozvyshennost
Russia 57°0N 33°30E 188 D7
Valdeazogues ➔ Spain 38°45N 4°55W 195 G6
Valdecañas, Embalse de
Spain 39°45N 5°25W 194 F5
Valdelatas Spain 40°31N 3°42W 127 A1
Valdemarsvik Sweden 58°14N 16°40E 163 F10
Valdemoro Spain 40°12N 3°40W 194 E7
Valdepeñas Spain 38°43N 3°25W 195 G7
Valderaduey ➔ Spain 41°31N 5°42W 194 D5
Valdérice Italy 38°4N 12°37E 200 D5
Valderrobres Spain 40°53N 0°9E 196 E5
Valdés, Pen. Argentina 42°30S 63°45W 336 B4
Valdez Ecuador 1°15N 79°0W 328 C2
Valdez Alaska, U.S.A. 61°7N 146°16W 303 F11
Valdgeym = Dobropole
Ukraine 48°25N 37°2E 189 H9
Valdivia Chile 39°50S 73°14W 336 A2
Valdivia Colombia 7°11N 75°27W 328 B2
Valdivia Abyssal Plain
S. Ocean 62°30S 70°0E 151 C6
Valdobbiàdene Italy 45°54N 12°0E 199 C8
Valdosta U.S.A. 30°50N 83°17W 316 E6
Valdoviño Spain 43°36N 8°8W 194 B2
Valdres Norway 61°5N 9°5E 164 C6
Vale Georgia 41°30N 42°58E 191 K6
Vale Oreg., U.S.A. 43°59N 117°15W 304 E5
Vale of Glamorgan □ U.K. 51°28N 3°25W 169 F4
Valea lui Mihai Romania 47°32N 22°11E 182 C7
Valea Mărului Romania 45°49N 27°42E 183 E12
Valemount Canada 52°50N 119°15W 296 C5
Valença = Valença do Piauí
Brazil 6°20S 41°45W 332 C3
Valença Brazil 13°20S 39°5W 333 D4
Valença Portugal 42°1N 8°34W 194 C2
Valença do Piauí Brazil 6°20S 41°45W 332 C3
Valençay France 47°9N 1°34E 173 E8
Valence France 44°57N 4°54E 175 D8

Valence d'Agen *France* 44°6N 0°53E **174** D4
Valencia *Phil.* 7°57N 125°3E **233** H5
Valencia *Spain* 39°27N 0°23W **197** F4
Valencia *Trin. & Tob.* 10°39N 61°11W **323** t
Valencia *N. Mex.,*
 U.S.A. 34°48N 106°43W **309** J10
Valencia *Venezuela* 10°11N 68°0W **328** A4
Valencia □ *Spain* 39°20N 0°40W **197** F4
Valencia ✈ (VLC) *Spain* 39°29N 0°26W **197** F4
Valencia, G. de *Spain* 39°30N 0°20E **195** F5
Valencia de Alcántara
 Spain 39°25N 7°14W **195** F3
Valencia de Don Juan
 Spain 42°17N 5°31W **194** C5
Valenciennes *France* 50°20N 3°34E **173** B10
Văleni *Romania* 44°15N 24°45E **183** F9
Văleni de Munte *Romania* 45°11N 26°2E **183** E11
Valensole *France* 43°50N 5°59E **175** E9
Valentigney *France* 47°27N 6°51E **173** E13
Valentín *Russia* 43°8N 134°17E **220** C7
Valentine *Nebr., U.S.A.* 42°52N 100°33W **308** D3
Valentine *Tex., U.S.A.* 30°35N 104°30W **314** F2
Valenza *Italy* 45°1N 8°38E **198** C5
Vâler *Hedmark, Norway* 60°41N 11°50E **164** D8
Vâler *Østfold, Norway* 59°23N 10°51E **164** E7
Valera *Piemonte, Italy* 45°33N 9°3E **128** A1
Valera *Venezuela* 9°19N 70°37W **328** B3
Valesdir *Vanuatu* 16°47S 168°10E **287** F6
Valestrand *Norway* 59°40N 5°26E **164** E2
Valga *Estonia* 57°47N 26°2E **188** D4
Valguarnera Caropepe
 Italy 37°30N 14°23E **201** E7
Valier *U.S.A.* 48°18N 112°16W **304** B7
Valinco, G. de *France* 41°40N 8°52E **175** G12
Valjevo *Serbia* 44°18N 19°53E **202** B3
Valka *Latvia* 57°46N 26°3E **188** D3
Valkeakoski *Finland* 61°16N 24°2E **182** B4
Valkenswaard *Neths.* 51°21N 5°29E **170** C5
Vall de Uxó = La Vall d'Uixó
 Spain 39°49N 0°15W **196** F4
Valla *Sweden* 59°2N 16°20E **162** E10
Valladolid *Yucatán,*
 Mexico 20°41N 88°12W **319** C7
Valladolid *Spain* 41°38N 4°43W **194** D6
Valladolid □ *Spain* 41°38N 4°43W **194** D6
Vallata *Italy* 41°2N 15°15E **201** A8
Vallcarca *Spain* 41°25N 2°9E **114** A1
Valldemossa *Spain* 39°43N 2°37E **206** B3
Valldoreix *Spain* 41°27N 2°3E **114** A1
Valle *Norway* 59°13N 7°33E **164** E4
Valle d'Aosta □ *Italy* 45°45N 7°15E **198** C4
Valle de Aran *Spain* 42°50N 0°55E **196** C5
Valle de la Pascua
 Venezuela 9°13N 66°0W **328** B4
Valle de las Palmas
 Mexico 32°20N 116°43W **307** N10
Valle de Santiago
 Mexico 20°23N 101°12W **318** C4
Valle de Zaragoza
 Mexico 27°25N 105°50W **318** B3
Valle del Cauca □
 Colombia 3°45N 76°30W **328** C2
Valle del Ticino △ *Italy* 45°22N 9°0E **198** C6
Valle Fértil, Sierra del
 Argentina 30°20S 68°0W **334** C2
Valle Gran Rey *Canary Is.* 28°5N 17°20W **153** t
Valle Hermoso *Mexico* 25°39N 97°40W **319** B5
Valle Nacional *Mexico* 17°47N 96°18W **319** D5
Vallecas *Spain* 40°22N 3°37W **127** B2
Vallecas, Cumbres de
 Spain 40°20N 3°33W **127** B2
Valledupar *Colombia* 10°29N 73°15W **328** A3
Vallée de Mai △ *Seychelles* 4°19S 55°44E **272** c
Vallegrande *Bolivia* 18°30S 64°10W **331** D5
Vallehermoso *Canary Is.* 28°10N 17°15W **153** e1
Vallejo *U.S.A.* 38°7N 122°14W **306** G4
Vallenar *Chile* 28°30S 70°50W **330** B2
Vallensbæk *Denmark* 55°38N 12°21E **118** B2
Vallensbæk Strand
 Denmark 55°36N 12°22E **118** B2
Vallentuna *Sweden* 59°32N 18°5E **162** E12
Vallentunasjön *Sweden* 59°27N 18°1E **139** A2
Valleranello *Italy* 41°46N 12°29E **136** C1
Valleraugue *France* 44°6N 3°39E **174** D7
Vallet *France* 47°10N 1°15W **172** E5
Valletta *Malta* 35°54N 14°31E **206** F8
Valley, The *Anguilla* 18°13N 63°4W **322** a
Valley Center *U.S.A.* 33°13N 117°2W **307** M9
Valley City *U.S.A.* 46°55N 98°0W **308** B5
Valley Falls *Oreg., U.S.A.* 42°29N 120°17W **304** E3
Valley Falls *R.I., U.S.A.* 41°54N 71°24W **313** E13
Valley Junction = West Des Moines
 U.S.A. 41°35N 93°43W **310** C3
Valley of Flowers △ *India* 30°50N 79°40E **243** D8
Valley of the Kings *Egypt* 25°31N 32°34E **256** B3
Valley Springs *U.S.A.* 38°12N 120°50W **306** G6
Valley Station *U.S.A.* 38°6N 85°52W **311** F11
Valley View *U.S.A.* 40°39N 76°33W **313** F8
Valley Wells *U.S.A.* 35°27N 115°46W **307** K11
Valleyview *Canada* 55°5N 117°17W **296** B5
Valli di Comácchio *Italy* 44°40N 12°15E **199** D9
Vallimanca, Arroyo
 Argentina 35°40S 59°10W **334** D4
Vallisaari *Finland* 60°7N 25°0E **121** C3
Vallo della Lucánia *Italy* 40°14N 15°16E **201** B8
Vallon-Pont-d'Arc *France* 44°24N 4°24E **175** D8
Vallorbe *Switz.* 46°42N 6°20E **179** J2
Valls *Spain* 41°18N 1°15E **196** D6
Vallvidrera *Spain* 41°24N 2°6E **114** A1
Vallvik *Sweden* 61°11N 17°10E **162** C11
Valmaseda = Balmaseda
 Spain 43°11N 3°12W **196** B1
Valmeyer *U.S.A.* 38°18N 90°19W **310** F6
Valmiera *Latvia* 57°37N 25°29E **188** D3
Valnera *Spain* 43°9N 3°40W **194** B7
Valognes *France* 49°30N 1°28W **172** C5
Valona = Vlorë *Albania* 40°32N 19°28E **202** F3
Valongo *Portugal* 41°8N 8°30W **194** D2
Valozhyn *Belarus* 54°3N 26°30E **177** A14
Valpaços *Portugal* 41°36N 7°17W **194** D3
Valparaíso *India* 10°22N 76°58E **245** J3
Valparaíso *Chile* 33°2S 71°40W **334** C1
Valparaíso *Zacatecas,*
 Mexico 22°46N 103°34W **318** C4
Valparaíso *Fla., U.S.A.* 30°31N 86°30W **317** E3
Valparaíso *Ind., U.S.A.* 41°28N 87°4W **310** E2
Valparaíso □ *Chile* 33°2S 71°40W **334** C1
Valpovo *India* 15°32N 74°8E **245** G2
Valréas *France* 44°24N 5°0E **175** D9
Vals → *S. Africa* 27°23S 26°30E **270** D4
Vals, Tanjung *Indonesia* 8°26S 137°25E **231** F9
Vals-les-Bains *France* 44°42N 4°24E **175** D8
Valsad *India* 20°40N 72°58E **244** D1
Valsamata *Greece* 38°11N 20°36E **207** C2
Valtimbjóðstaður *Iceland* 65°11N 14°59W **155** D6
Valti *Greece* 38°27N 21°7E **207** C3
Valuyki *Russia* 50°10N 38°5E **189** G10
Valverde *Canary Is.* 27°48N 17°55W **153** e1
Valverde del Camino
 Spain 37°35N 6°47W **195** H4

Valverde del Fresno *Spain* 40°15N 6°51W **194** E3
Valverde → *Spain* 40°15N 6°51W **114** A1
Vama *Romania* 47°34N 25°42E **183** C10
Vámbori *India* 19°17N 74°44E **244** E2
Vamdrup *Denmark* 55°25N 9°17E **163** J3
Vámhus *Sweden* 61°7N 14°29E **162** C8
Vamizi, I. *Mozam.* 11°25 40°40E **269** E5
Vammala = Sastamala
 Finland 61°20N 22°54E **188** B2
Vamos *Greece* 35°24N 24°13E **207** E6
Vamsadhara → *India* 18°21N 84°8E **244** E7
Van *Turkey* 38°30N 43°20E **213** C10
Van □ *Turkey* 38°30N 43°20E **213** C10
Van, L. = Van Gölü
 Turkey 38°30N 43°0E **213** C10
Van Alstyne *U.S.A.* 33°25N 96°35W **314** E6
Van Blommestein Meer
 Suriname 4°45N 55°5W **329** C6
Van Buren = Kettering
 U.S.A. 39°41N 84°10W **311** E12
Van Buren *N.B., Canada* 47°10N 67°55W **299** C6
Van Buren *Ark., U.S.A.* 35°26N 94°21W **314** D7
Van Buren *Maine, U.S.A.* 47°10N 67°58W **299** B20
Van Buren *Mo., U.S.A.* 37°0N 91°1W **308** G8
Van Canh *Vietnam* 13°37N 109°0E **236** F7
Van Diemen, C. *N. Terr.,*
 Australia 11°9S 130°24E **278** B5
Van Diemen, C. *Queens.,*
 Australia 16°30S 139°46E **280** B2
Van Gölü *Turkey* 38°30N 43°0E **213** C10
Van Horn *U.S.A.* 31°3N 104°50W **314** F2
Van Horne *U.S.A.* 42°1N 92°5W **310** B4
Van Meter *U.S.A.* 41°32N 93°57W **310** C3
Van Ninh *Vietnam* 12°42N 109°14E **236** F7
Van Rees, Pegunungan
 Indonesia 2°35S 138°15E **231** E9
Van Tivu *India* 8°51N 78°15E **245** K4
Van Wert *U.S.A.* 40°52N 84°35W **311** D12
Van Yen *Vietnam* 21°4N 104°42E **228** G5
Van Zylsrus *S. Africa* 26°52S 22°4E **270** C3
Vanadzor *Armenia* 40°48N 44°30E **191** K7
Vanak *Iran* 35°45N 51°23E **141** A2
Vanavara *Russia* 60°22N 102°16E **215** C11
Vanceburg *U.S.A.* 38°36N 83°19W **311** F13
Vancouver, C., *Canada* 49°15N 123°7W **306** A3
Vancouver *Wash., U.S.A.* 45°38N 122°40W **306** E4
Vancouver, C. *Australia* 35°2S 118°11E **279** G2
Vancouver, Mt. *U.S.A.* 60°20N 139°41W **303** F13
Vancouver I. *Canada* 49°50N 126°0W **306** B2
Vancouver Int. ✈ (YVR)
 Canada 49°12N 123°10W **306** A3
Vanda = Vantaa *Finland* 60°18N 24°56E **121** B2
Vandalia *Ill., U.S.A.* 38°58N 89°6W **310** F7
Vandalia *Mo., U.S.A.* 39°19N 91°29W **310** E5
Vandalia *Ohio, U.S.A.* 39°54N 84°12W **311** E12
Vandavasi *India* 12°30N 79°30E **245** H4
Vandeloos B. *Sri Lanka* 8°0N 81°45E **245** L5
Vandenberg Village
 U.S.A. 34°43N 120°28W **307** L6
Vandergrift *U.S.A.* 40°36N 79°34W **312** F5
Vanderhoof *Canada* 54°0N 124°0W **296** C4
Vanderkloof Dam *S. Africa* 30°4S 24°40E **270** D3
Vanderlin I. *Australia* 15°44S 137°2E **280** B2
Vänern *Sweden* 58°47N 13°30E **163** F7
Vänersborg *Sweden* 58°26N 12°19E **163** F6
Vang *Norway* 61°8N 8°34E **164** D5
Vang Vieng *Laos* 18°58N 102°32E **236** C4
Vanga *Kenya* 4°35S 39°12E **268** C4
Vangaindrano *Madag.* 23°21S 47°36E **272** C2
Vänge *Sweden* 59°50N 17°20E **162** E11
Vanged *Denmark* 55°45N 12°30E **118** A3
Vangsnes *Norway* 61°9N 6°39E **164** D3
Vanguard *Canada* 49°55N 107°20W **297** D7
Vangunu *Solomon Is.* 8°40S 158°5E **287** M10
Vanikoro *Pac. Oc.* 11°39S 166°54E **277** C12
Vaników *Turkey* 41°3N 29°3E **122** B2
Vanimo *Papua N. G.* 2°42S 141°21E **286** B1
Vanino *Russia* 48°50N 140°5E **215** E15
Vanivilasa Sagara *India* 13°45N 76°30E **245** H3
Vaniyambadi *India* 12°46N 78°44E **245** H4
Vânju Mare *Romania* 44°25N 22°52E **182** F7
Vankleek Hill *Canada* 45°32N 74°40W **313** A10
Vanlose *Denmark* 55°41N 12°28E **118** B3
Vännäs *Sweden* 63°58N 19°48E **160** E18
Vannes *France* 47°40N 2°47W **172** E4
Vannøya *Norway* 70°6N 19°50E **160** A18
Vanoise, Massif de la
 France 45°25N 6°40E **175** C10
Vanrhynsdorp *S. Africa* 31°36S 18°44E **270** E2
Vansada *India* 20°47N 73°25E **244** D1
Vansbro *Sweden* 60°32N 14°15E **162** D8
Vanse *Norway* 58°6N 6°41E **164** F3
Vansittart B. *Australia* 14°3S 126°17E **278** B4
Vansittart I. *Canada* 65°50N 84°0W **299** D15
Vantaa *Finland* 60°18N 24°56E **121** B2
Vantaanjoki → *Finland* 60°18N 24°55E **121** B2
Vantaanpuisto *Finland* 60°18N 24°55E **121** B2
Vanua Balavu *Fiji* 17°12S 178°50W **287** A3
Vanua Lava *Vanuatu* 13°50S 167°30E **287** C5
Vanua Mbalavu = Vanua Balavu
 Fiji 16°33S 179°15W **287** A3
Vanua Vatu *Fiji* 18°22S 179°15W **287** B3
Vanuatu ■ *Pac. Oc.* 15°0S 168°0E **287** E6
Vanves *France* 48°49N 2°17E **134** B2
Vanwyksvlei *S. Africa* 30°18S 21°49E **270** D3
Vao *N. Cal.* 22°39S 167°32E **288** d
Vapi *India* 20°22N 72°54E **244** D1
Vapnyarka *Ukraine* 48°32N 28°45E **183** B13
Var □ *France* 43°27N 6°18E **175** E10
Var → *France* 43°39N 7°12E **175** E11
Vara *Sweden* 58°16N 12°55E **163** F6
Vara, Pico da *Azores* 37°46N 25°13W **153** d3
Varada → *India* 15°0N 75°40E **245** G2
Varades *France* 47°25N 1°1W **172** E5
Varáita → *Italy* 44°9N 7°53E **198** D4
Varaldsøy *Norway* 60°6N 5°59E **164** D2
Varale *Ivory C.* 9°40N 3°17W **262** D4
Varallo *Italy* 45°49N 8°15E **198** C5
Varāmīn *Iran* 35°20N 51°39E **247** C6
Varāmīn □ *Iran* 35°18N 51°35E **247** B6
Varanasi *India* 25°22N 83°0E **243** G10
Varangerfjorden *Norway* 70°3N 29°25E **160** A23
Varangerhalvøya
 Norway 70°25N 29°30E **160** A23
Varano, Lago di *Italy* 41°53N 15°45E **199** G12
Varaždin *Croatia* 46°20N 16°20E **199** B13
Varazze *Italy* 44°22N 8°34E **198** D5
Varberg *Sweden* 57°6N 12°20E **163** G6
Varcar Vakuf = Mrkonjić Grad
 Bos.-H. 44°26N 17°4E **182** F2
Vardak □ *Afghan.* 34°0N 68°0E **240** B3
Varde *Denmark* 55°38N 8°29E **163** J2
Varde Å → *Denmark* 55°35N 8°19E **163** J2
Varden *Armenia* 40°10N 45°43E **191** K7
Vardø *Norway* 70°23N 31°15E **160** A24
Varel *Germany* 53°23N 8°8E **178** B4
Varella, Mui = Nay, Mui
 Vietnam 12°54N 109°26E **236** F7
Vārena *Lithuania* 54°12N 24°30E **188** E3
Varennes-sur-Allier
 France 46°19N 3°24E **173** F10
Varennes-Vauzelles *France* 47°3N 3°9E **173** E10

Vareš *Bos.-H.* 44°12N 18°23E **182** F3
Varese *Italy* 45°48N 8°50E **198** C5
Vârfurile *Romania* 46°19N 22°31E **182** D7
Vârgârda *Sweden* 57°59N 12°48E **244** E2
Vargem Bonita *Brazil* 20°20S 46°22W **333** F2
Vargem Grande *Brazil* 3°33S 43°56W **332** B3
Varginha *Brazil* 21°33S 45°25W **335** A6
Vârgön *Sweden* 58°22N 12°20E **163** F6
Varhaug *Norway* 58°37N 5°41E **164** F2
Vari *Greece* 38°24N 20°35E **207** C2
Varillas *Chile* 24°0S 70°10W **334** A1
Varkaus *Finland* 62°19N 27°50E **188** B4
Varkiza *Greece* 37°50N 23°49E **112** C2
Vârmdölandet *Sweden* 59°20N 18°33E **162** E12
Vârmeln *Sweden* 59°35N 12°54E **162** E6
Vârmlands län □ *Sweden* 60°0N 13°20E **162** E7
Vârmlandsbro *Sweden* 59°11N 13°0E **162** E7
Varna *Bulgaria* 43°13N 27°56E **203** C11
Varna □ *Bulgaria* 43°20N 27°30E **203** C11
Varna → *India* 16°48N 74°32E **244** E2
Vârnamo *Sweden* 57°10N 14°3E **163** G8
Várnjárga = Varangerhalvøya
 Norway 70°25N 29°30E **160** A23
Varnsdorf *Czech Rep.* 50°55N 14°35E **180** A7
Varnville *U.S.A.* 32°51N 81°5W **316** C8
Várpalota *Hungary* 47°12N 18°8E **182** D2
Vars *Ont., Canada* 45°21N 75°21W **313** A9
Vars *Hautes-Alpes, France* 44°37N 6°42E **175** D10
Vartdal *Norway* 62°20N 6°8E **164** B3
Vartíokylä *Finland* 60°13N 25°5E **121** B3
Vartíosaari *Finland* 60°11N 25°5E **121** B3
Varto *Turkey* 39°10N 41°27E **213** C9
Varvarin *Serbia* 43°43N 21°20E **202** C5
Varysburg *U.S.A.* 42°46N 78°19W **312** D6
Varzaneh *Iran* 32°25N 52°40E **247** C7
Varzaqān *Iran* 38°29N 46°42E **213** B11
Várzea Alegre *Brazil* 6°47S 39°17W **332** C4
Várzea da Palma *Brazil* 17°54S 44°44W **333** E3
Várzea Grande *Brazil* 15°39S 56°8W **331** D6
Varzi *Italy* 44°49N 9°12E **198** D6
Varzo *Italy* 46°12N 8°15E **198** B5
Varzy *France* 47°22N 3°20E **173** E10
Vasa = Vaasa *Finland* 63°6N 21°38E **160** E19
Vasa Barris → *Brazil* 11°10S 37°10W **332** D4
Vasai-Virar *India* 19°28N 72°48E **244** E1
Vasilevichi *Belarus* 52°15N 29°50E **177** B16
Vasiliko = Michurin
 Bulgaria 42°9N 27°51E **203** D11
Vasilikón *Greece* 38°37N 23°36E **207** B2
Vasilikós *Greece* 37°43N 20°59E **207** D2
Vasilkov = Vasylkiv
 Ukraine 50°7N 30°15E **177** C16
Vasilyevskiy, Ostrov
 Russia 59°55N 30°16E **137** B1
Vasilyova Sloboda = Chkolovsk
 Russia
Vasilyovo = Chkolovsk
 Russia 56°50N 43°10E **190** B6
Väskinde *Sweden* 57°40N 18°20E **163** G10
Vaslui *Romania* 46°38N 27°42E **183** D12
Vaslui □ *Romania* 46°30N 27°45E **183** D12
Väsman *Sweden* 60°9N 15°5E **162** D9
Vassar *Man., Canada* 49°10N 95°55W **297** D9
Vassar *Mich., U.S.A.* 43°22N 83°35W **309** D12
Vassfaret *Norway* 60°38N 9°28E **164** D6
Västerås *Sweden* 59°37N 16°38E **162** E10
Västerbotten *Sweden* 64°36N 20°4E **160** D19
Västerdalälven → *Sweden* 60°30N 13°10E **163** F7
Västergötland *Sweden* 58°0N 13°10E **163** F7
Västerhaninge *Sweden* 59°7N 18°6E **162** E12
Västervik *Sweden* 57°43N 16°33E **163** G10
Västmanland *Sweden* 59°45N 16°0E **161** G17
Västmanlands län □
 Sweden 59°45N 16°20E **162** E10
Vasto *Italy* 42°8N 14°40E **199** F11
Västra Götalands Län □
 Sweden 58°30N 13°0E **163** F6
Vasvár *Hungary* 47°3N 16°47E **182** C1
Vasylivka *Ukraine* 47°33N 35°2E **189** E8
Vasylkiv *Ukraine* 50°7N 30°15E **177** C16
Vat Phou *Laos* 14°51N 105°49E **236** E5
Vatan *France* 47°4N 1°50E **173** E8
Vaté = Efate, I. *Vanuatu* 17°40S 168°25E **287** G6
Vatersay *U.K.* 56°55N 7°32W **167** E1
Vathi *Greece* 38°41N 20°47E **207** B2
Vathía *Greece* 36°29N 22°29E **204** E4
Vatia *Amer. Samoa* 14°15S 170°40W **302** t
Vatican City ■ *Europe* 41°54N 12°27E **136** B1
Vaticano, C. *Italy* 38°37N 15°50E **201** D8
Vatili *Cyprus* 35°6N 33°40E **207** E9
Vatin *Serbia* 45°12N 21°20E **182** E6
Vatiu = Atiu *Cook Is.* 20°0S 158°10W **289** J12
Vatnajökull *Iceland* 64°30N 16°48W **155** C10
Vatnajökull △ *Iceland* 64°24N 16°48W **155** C10
Vatnás *Norway* 59°58N 9°37E **164** E6
Vatnsfjörður *Iceland* 65°56N 22°30W **155** B4
Vatoa *Tonga* 59°50N 19°0E **162** E12
Vatolakkos *Greece* 35°27N 23°53E **207** E4
Vatoloha *Madag.* 17°52S 47°48E **272** B2
Vatomandry *Madag.* 19°20S 48°59E **272** B2
Vatra-Dornei *Romania* 47°22N 25°22E **183** C10
Vatrak → *India* 23°9N 73°2E **242** H5
Vattaru Atoll *Maldives* 3°16N 73°25E **272** d
Vättern *Sweden* 58°25N 14°30E **163** F8
Vatulele *Fiji* 18°33S 177°37E **287** B1
Vatu Vara *Fiji* 17°26S 179°31W **287** A3
Vaucluse □ *France* 44°3N 5°10E **175** E9
Vaucluse *France* 43°51N 5°7E **136** A1
Vauclin, Pte. du *Martinique* 14°34N 60°53W **322** j
Vaucluse House *Australia* 33°51S 151°15E **139** B4
Vaucouleurs *France* 48°36N 5°40E **173** D12
Vaughn *Mont., U.S.A.* 47°33N 111°33W **304** C8
Vaughn *N. Mex., U.S.A.* 34°36N 105°13W **305** J11
Vaujours *France* 48°56N 2°34E **134** A4
Vaujours L. *Canada* 55°27N 74°15W **298** A5
Vaupés □ = Uaupés → *Brazil* 0°2N 67°16W **328** D4
Vaupés □ *Colombia* 1°0N 71°0W **328** C3
Vauxhall *Canada* 50°5N 112°9W **296** C6
Vauxhall *London, U.K.* 51°29N 0°7W **125** c4
Vav *India* 24°22N 71°31E **242** G4
Vavatenina *Madag.* 17°28S 49°12E **272** B2
Vava'u *Tonga* 18°36S 174°0W **287** P14
Vava'u Group *Tonga* 18°40S 174°0W **287** P14
Vavoua *Ivory C.* 7°23N 6°29W **262** D3

Vavuniya *Sri Lanka* 8°45N 80°30E **245** K5
Vawkavysk *Belarus* 53°9N 24°30E **177** B13
Vaxholm *Sweden* 59°25N 18°20E **162** E12
Växjö *Sweden* 56°52N 14°50E **163** H8
Vaxtorp *Sweden* 56°25N 13°8E **163** H7
Vayalpad *India* 13°39N 78°38E **245** H4
Vayenga = Severomorsk
 Russia 69°5N 33°27E **160** B25
Vaygach, Ostrov *Russia* 70°0N 60°0E **214** C7
Veadeiros *Brazil* 14°7S 47°31W **333** D2
Veaikevárri = Svappavaara
 Sweden 67°40N 21°3E **160** C19
Vechelde *Germany* 52°16N 10°22E **178** C6
Vechta *Germany* 52°44N 8°17E **178** C4
Vechte → *Neths.* 52°34N 6°6E **170** B6
Vecsés *Hungary* 47°26N 19°19E **117** B3
Vedaranniyam *India* 10°25N 79°50E **245** J4
Veddige *Sweden* 57°17N 12°20E **163** G6
Vedea → *Romania* 43°42N 25°41E **183** G10
Vedia *Argentina* 34°30S 61°31W **334** C3
Vedi *Armenia* 39°54N 44°43E **213** C11
Vega *Norway* 65°40N 11°55E **160** D14
Vedum *Sweden* 58°11N 13°0E **163** F7
Veendersburg *U.S.A.* 40°7N 87°16W **311** D9
Veendam *Neths.* 53°5N 6°52E **170** A6
Veenendaal *Neths.* 52°2N 5°34E **170** B5
Vefsna → *Norway* 65°48N 13°10E **160** D15
Vega *Nordland, Norway* 65°40N 11°55E **160** D14
Vega *Tex., U.S.A.* 35°15N 102°26W **314** D3
Vega Baja *Puerto Rico* 18°25N 66°20W **321** b
Vega de Ribadeo = Vegadeo
 Spain 43°27N 7°4W **194** B3
Vegadeo *Spain* 43°27N 7°4W **194** B3
Vegárshei *Norway* 58°44N 8°51E **164** F5
Vegas Verde = North Las Vegas
 U.S.A. 36°11N 115°7W **124** A1
Veggli *Norway* 60°3N 9°9E **164** D6
Veglia = Krk *Croatia* 45°8N 14°40E **199** C11
Vegoritida, L. *Greece* 40°45N 21°45E **202** F5
Vegreville *U.S.A.* 53°30N 112°5W **296** C6
Veiholmen *Norway* 63°30N 8°0E **164** B3
Veimandu Channel *Maldives* 2°10N 73°20E **272** d
Veinge *Sweden* 56°33N 13°4E **163** H7
Veisiejai *Lithuania* 54°6N 23°42E **184** D9
Vejbystrand *Sweden* 56°19N 12°45E **163** H6
Vejen *Denmark* 55°30N 9°9E **163** J3
Vejer de la Frontera *Spain* 36°15N 5°59W **195** J5
Vejle *Denmark* 55°43N 9°30E **163** J3
Vejle Fjord *Denmark* 55°40N 9°50E **163** J3
Vela Luka *Croatia* 42°59N 16°44E **199** F13
Velachha *India* 21°26N 73°1E **244** D1
Velanai I. *Sri Lanka* 9°45N 79°45E **245** K4
Velas *Azores* 38°41N 28°13W **153** e1
Velas, C. *Costa Rica* 10°21N 85°52W **320** D2
Velasco, Sierra de
 Argentina 29°20S 67°10W **334** B2
Velay, Mts. du *France* 45°0N 3°40E **174** D7
Velbert *Germany* 51°20N 7°3E **178** D3
Velddrif *S. Africa* 32°42S 18°11E **270** D2
Velebit △ *Croatia* 44°30N 15°15E **199** D12
Velebit Planina *Croatia* 44°50N 15°20E **199** D12
Velebitski Kanal *Croatia* 44°45N 14°55E **199** D11
Veleka → *Bulgaria* 42°4N 27°58E **203** D11
Veleň *Czech Rep.* 50°10N 14°33E **135** A3
Velence-tó *Hungary* 47°13N 18°36E **182** C3
Velenje *Slovenia* 46°23N 15°8E **199** B12
Veles *Macedonia* 41°46N 21°47E **202** E5
Veleshtica *Czech Rep.* 50°5N 14°21E **135** A3
Velestíno *Greece* 39°23N 22°43E **204** D4
Vélez *Colombia* 6°1N 73°41W **328** B3
Vélez-Málaga *Spain* 36°48N 4°5W **195** J6
Vélez Rubio *Spain* 37°41N 2°5W **197** H2
Velhas → *Brazil* 17°13S 44°49W **333** E3
Velika *Croatia* 45°27N 17°40E **182** E2
Velika Gorica *Croatia* 45°44N 16°5E **199** C13
Velika Kapela *Croatia* 45°10N 15°5E **199** C12
Velika Kikinda = Kikinda
 Serbia 45°50N 20°30E **182** E5
Velika Kladuša *Bos.-H.* 45°11N 15°48E **199** C12
Velika Kruša = Krushë e Madhe
 Kosovo 42°20N 20°36E **202** D4
Velika Morava → *Serbia* 44°43N 21°3E **202** B5
Velika Plana *Serbia* 44°20N 21°4E **202** B5
Velikaya → *Russia* 57°48N 28°10E **188** D5
Velikaya Kema *Russia* 45°30N 137°12E **220** B8
Velikaya Lepetikha
 Ukraine 47°2N 33°58E **189** J7
Velike Lašče *Slovenia* 45°49N 14°45E **199** C11
Veliki Jastrebac *Serbia* 43°25N 21°30E **202** C5
Veliki Kanal *Serbia* 45°45N 19°15E **182** E4
Veliki Popović *Serbia* 44°8N 21°18E **202** B5
Velikiy Ustyug *Russia* 60°47N 46°20E **186** B8
Velikiye Luki *Russia* 56°25N 30°32E **188** D6
Velikonda Range *India* 14°45N 79°10E **245** G4
Veliko Tŭrnovo *Bulgaria* 43°5N 25°41E **203** C9
Veliko Tŭrnovo □ *Bulgaria* 43°0N 25°30E **203** C9
Vélingara *Kolda, Senegal* 13°12N 14°5W **262** C2
Vélingara *Louga, Senegal* 15°0N 14°40W **262** B2
Velingrad *Bulgaria* 42°4N 23°58E **202** D7
Velino, Mte. *Italy* 42°9N 13°23E **199** F10
Vélizy-Villacoublay *France* 48°47N 2°11E **134** B2
Velka-Chuchle *Czech Rep.* 50°1N 14°23E **135** B2
Veľ·ké Kapušany
 Slovak Rep. 48°34N 22°5E **181** C15
Velké Karlovice
 Czech Rep. 49°20N 18°17E **181** B11
Velké Meziříčí *Czech Rep.* 49°21N 16°1E **180** B9
Velké Přílepy *Czech Rep.* 50°9N 14°19E **135** B1
Veľ·ký Javorník
 Slovak Rep. 49°19N 18°22E **181** B11
Veľ·ký Krtíš *Slovak Rep.* 48°13N 19°21E **181** C12
Veľ·ký Meder *Slovak Rep.* 47°52N 17°46E **181** C10
Veľ·ký Tribeč *Slovak Rep.* 48°28N 18°15E **181** C11
Vella, G. *Solomon Is.* 8°0S 156°0E **287** M9
Vella Lavella *Solomon Is.* 7°45S 156°40E **287** L9
Vellar → *India* 11°30N 79°36E **245** J4
Velletri *Italy* 41°41N 12°47E **200** A5
Vellinge *Sweden* 55°29N 13°2E **163** J6
Vellmar *Germany* 51°22N 9°28E **178** D5
Vellore *India* 12°57N 79°10E **245** H4
Velopoula *Greece* 36°55N 23°27E **204** E5
Velsk *Russia* 61°10N 42°5E **188** B15
Velten *Germany* 52°42N 13°10E **178** C9
Veluwezoom △ *Neths.* 52°5N 6°0E **170** B6
Velva *U.S.A.* 48°4N 100°56W **308** A3
Velvendos *Greece* 40°15N 22°6E **202** F6
Velykyi Mykhaylivka
 Ukraine 47°4N 29°52E **183** C14
Velyki Luchky *Ukraine* 48°27N 22°44E **181** C14
Velykyy Berezhny *Ukraine* 48°50N 22°34E **181** A14
Velykyy Bychkiv *Ukraine* 47°58N 24°1E **183** B9
Vemb *Denmark* 56°21N 8°21E **163** H1
Vembanad L. *India* 9°36N 76°15E **245** K3
Vemdalen *Sweden* 62°27N 13°51E **162** B7
Ven *Sweden* 55°55N 12°45E **163** J6
Venado *Mexico* 22°56N 101°10W **318** C4
Venado Tuerto *Argentina* 33°50S 62°0W **334** C3
Venafro *Italy* 41°28N 14°3E **201** A7
Venarey-les-Laumes
 France 47°32N 4°26E **173** E11
Vavouá *Ivory C.* 7°23N 6°29W **262** D3

Venaria *Italy* 45°8N 7°38E **198** C4
Venčane *Serbia* 44°24N 20°28E **202** B4
Vence *France* 43°43N 7°6E **175** E11
Venda Seca *Portugal* 38°46N 9°15W **126** A1
Vendas Novas *Portugal* 38°39N 8°27W **195** G2
Vendée □ *France* 46°50N 1°35W **172** F5
Vendée → *France* 46°20N 1°10W **172** F5
Vendéen, Bocage *France* 46°40N 1°20W **174** B2
Vendeuvre-sur-Barse
 France 48°14N 4°28E **173** D11
Vendôme *France* 47°47N 1°3E **172** E8
Vendramin Calergi, Palazzo
 Venice, Italy **142** a2
Vendrell = El Vendrell
 Spain 41°10N 1°30E **196** D6
Vendsyssel *Denmark* 57°22N 10°0E **163** G4
Vendychany *Ukraine* 48°50N 27°14E **183** B13
Venelles *France* 43°35N 5°28E **175** E9
Véneta, L. *Venice, Italy* **142** a4
Venetian Islands *U.S.A.* 25°47N 80°9W **129** D3
Venetie *U.S.A.* 67°1N 146°25W **303** C11
Véneto □ *Italy* 45°30N 12°0E **199** C9
Venev *Russia* 54°22N 38°17E **188** E10
Venézia, G. di *Italy* 45°15N 13°0E **199** C10
Venézia, Palazzo *Rome, Italy* **136** c2
Venézia *Venice, Italy* **142** b3
Venézia Tridentina = Trentino-Alto
 Adige □ *Italy* 46°30N 11°0E **199** B8
Venezuela ■ *S. Amer.* 8°0N 66°0W **328** B4
Venezuela, G. de *Venezuela* 11°30N 71°0W **328** A3
Venezuelan Basin
 Cent. Amer. 14°0N 68°0W **321** C6
Vengurla *India* 15°53N 73°45E **245** G1
Vengurla Rocks *India* 15°55N 73°22E **245** G1
Venice = Venézia *Venice, Italy* **142** b3
Venice *Fla., U.S.A.* 27°6N 82°27W **317** H7
Vénissieux *France* 45°42N 4°53E **175** C8
Venjan *Sweden* 60°57N 13°55E **162** D7
Venjansjön *Sweden* 60°54N 14°0E **162** D8
Venkatagiri *India* 14°0N 79°35E **245** H4
Venkatapuram *India* 18°20N 80°30E **245** E5
Venlo *Neths.* 51°22N 6°11E **170** C6
Vennachar Junction
 Canada 45°5N 77°14W **312** A7
Vennesla *Norway* 58°15N 7°59E **164** F4
Venosa *Italy* 40°58N 15°49E **201** B8
Venraij *Neths.* 51°31N 6°0E **170** C6
Vent, Îs. du
 French Polynesia 17°30S 149°30W **289** f
Venta *Lithuania* 56°12N 22°42E **184** B9
Venta → *Latvia* 57°24N 21°33E **184** A8
Venta de Baños *Spain* 41°55N 4°31W **194** D6
Venta de Cardeña = Cardeña
 Spain 38°16N 4°20W **195** G6
Ventana, Sa. de la
 Argentina 38°0S 62°30W **334** D3
Ventas *Spain* 40°26N 3°40W **127** B2
Ventersburg *S. Africa* 28°7S 27°9E **270** D4
Ventersdorp *S. Africa* 26°19S 26°48E **270** D4
Venterstad *S. Africa* 30°47S 25°48E **270** D4
Ventimíglia *Italy* 43°47N 7°36E **198** E4
Ventnor *U.K.* 50°36N 1°12W **169** G6
Ventoro del Cano *Spain* 40°23N 3°49W **127** B1
Ventotène *Italy* 40°47N 13°25E **200** B6
Ventoux, Mt. *France* 44°10N 5°17E **175** D9
Ventspils *Latvia* 57°25N 21°32E **184** A8
Ventspils □ *Latvia* 57°20N 21°50E **184** A8
Ventuari → *Venezuela* 3°58N 67°2W **328** C5
Ventucopa *U.S.A.* 34°50N 119°29W **307** L7
Ventura *U.S.A.* 34°17N 119°18W **307** L7
Venus B. *Australia* 38°40S 145°42E **283** E6
Venustiano Carranza *Baja Calif.,*
 Mexico 30°25N 115°53W **318** A1
Venustiano Carranza *Distrito Federal,*
 Mexico 19°25N 99°5W **128** B2
Venustiano Carranza, Presa
 Mexico 27°30N 100°37W **318** B4
Vera *Argentina* 29°30S 60°20W **334** B3
Vera *Spain* 37°15N 1°51W **197** H3
Veracruz *Mexico* 19°11N 96°8W **319** D5
Veracruz □ *Mexico* 19°0N 96°15W **319** D5
Veraval *India* 20°53N 70°27E **242** J4
Verbánia *Italy* 45°56N 8°33E **198** C5
Verbicaro *Italy* 39°46N 15°55E **201** C8
Vercelli *Italy* 45°19N 8°25E **198** C5
Verchovchevo *Ukraine* 48°32N 34°10E **189** H8
Vercors △ *France* 44°57N 5°25E **175** D9
Verdalsøra *Norway* 63°48N 11°30E **160** E14
Verde → *Argentina* 41°56S 65°5W **336** B3
Verde → *Goiás, Brazil* 19°11S 50°44W **333** E1
Verde → *Goiás, Brazil* 18°1S 49°21W **333** D1
Verde → *Mato Grosso,*
 Brazil 11°54S 55°48W **331** C6
Verde → *Mato Grosso do Sul,*
 Brazil 21°25S 52°20W **331** E7
Verde → *São Paulo, Brazil* 23°29S 46°27W **137** A1
Verde → *Chihuahua,*
 Mexico 26°39N 107°11W **318** B3
Verde → *Jalisco, Mexico* 21°42N 103°14W **318** C4
Verde → *Oaxaca, Mexico* 15°59N 97°50W **319** D5
Verde → *Paraguay* 23°9S 57°37W **334** A4
Verde → *Ariz., U.S.A.* 33°33N 111°40W **305** K8
Verde, Cay *Bahamas* 23°0N 75°5W **321** B4
Verde Grande → *Brazil* 16°13S 43°49W **333** E3
Verde I. □ *Italy* 11°54S 49°48W **331** D2
Verde Island Pass. *Phil.* 13°34N 120°51E **232** E3
Verde Pequeno → *Brazil* 14°48S 43°31W **333** D3
Verden *Germany* 52°55N 9°14E **178** C5
Verdi *Athina, Greece* 37°58N 23°40E **112** A2
Verdi *Nev., U.S.A.* 39°31N 119°59W **306** F7
Verdikoussa *Greece* 39°47N 21°59E **204** B3
Verdon → *France* 43°43N 5°46E **175** E9
Verdon, Gorges du *France* 43°50N 6°20E **175** E10
Verdun *Meuse, France* 49°9N 5°24E **173** C12
Verdun-sur-le-Doubs
 France 46°54N 5°1E **173** F12
Vereeniging *S. Africa* 26°38S 27°57E **271** C4
Verga, C. *Guinea* 10°30N 14°10W **262** C2
Vergara *Uruguay* 32°56S 53°57W **334** C5
Vergato *Italy* 44°17N 11°7E **198** D8
Vérgina = Aigai *Greece* 40°28N 22°19E **202** F6
Vergt *France* 45°2N 0°43E **174** D4
Verhalom *Hungary* 47°31N 19°1E **117** A2
Verín *Spain* 41°57N 7°27W **194** D3
Vi Thanh *Vietnam* 9°42N 105°26E **237** H5
Viacha *Bolivia* 16°39S 68°18W **330** D4
Viadana *Italy* 44°55N 10°30E **198** D7
Viamão *Brazil* 30°5S 51°0W **335** D5
Viana *Brazil* 3°13S 44°55W **332** B3
Viana *Spain* 42°31N 2°22W **196** C2
Viana do Alentejo *Portugal* 38°17N 7°59W **195** G3
Viana do Bolo *Spain* 42°11N 7°6W **194** C3
Viana do Castelo *Portugal* 41°42N 8°50W **194** C2
Viana do Castelo □
 Portugal 41°50N 8°30W **194** D2

Vianden Lux. 49°56N 6°12E 170 E6
Viangchan = Vientiane
Laos 17°58N 102°36E 236 D4
Vianópolis Brazil 16°40S 48°35W 333 E2
Vianos Greece 35°2N 25°21E 207 E6
Viar → Spain 37°36N 5°50W 195 H5
Viaréggio Italy 43°52N 10°14E 198 E7
Viaur → France 44°8N 1°58E 174 D5
Vibble Sweden 57°37N 18°16E 163 G12
Vibo Valéntia Italy 38°40N 16°6E 201 D9
Viborg Denmark 56°27N 9°23E 163 H3
Vibraye France 48°3N 0°44E 172 D7
Vic Spain 41°58N 2°19E 196 D7
Vic, Étang de France 43°29N 3°50E 174 E7
Vic-en-Bigorre France 43°24N 0°3E 174 E4
Vic-Fezensac France 43°47N 0°19E 174 E4
Vic-le-Comte France 45°39N 3°14E 173 G10
Vic-sur-Cère France 44°59N 2°38E 174 D6
Vicálvaro Spain 40°24N 3°36W 127 B2
Vicar Spain 36°50N 2°38W 197 J2
Vicente Lopez Argentina 34°31S 58°30W 117 B2
Vicente Pérez Rosales △
Chile 41°11S 72°12W 336 B2
Vicenza Italy 45°33N 11°33E 199 C8
Vich = Vic Spain 41°58N 2°19E 196 D7
Vichada □ Colombia 5°0N 69°30W 328 C4
Vichada → Colombia 4°55N 67°50W 328 C4
Vichuga Russia 57°12N 41°55E 190 B5
Vichy France 46°9N 3°26E 173 F10
Vickan Sweden 57°25N 6°10E 164 G3
Vicksburg Ariz., U.S.A. 33°45N 113°45W 307 M13
Vicksburg Mich., U.S.A. 42°7N 85°32W 311 B11
Vicksburg Miss., U.S.A. 32°21N 90°53W 315 E9
Vico France 42°10N 8°49E 175 F12
Vico, L. di Italy 42°19N 12°10E 199 F9
Vico del Gargano Italy 41°54N 15°57E 199 G12
Viçosa Brazil 9°28S 36°14W 332 C4
Viçosa do Ceará Brazil 3°34S 41°5W 332 B3
Vicovu de Sus Romania 47°56N 25°41E 183 C10
Victor India 21°0N 71°30E 242 J4
Victor Emanuel Ra.
Papua N. G. 5°20S 142°15E 286 C2
Victor Harbor Australia 35°30S 138°37E 282 C3
Victor Hugo = Hamadia
Algeria 35°28N 1°57E 261 A5
Victoria = Bandar Labuan
Malaysia 5°20N 115°14E 235 A5
Victoria Argentina 32°40S 60°10W 334 C3
Victoria B.C., Canada 48°30N 123°25W 306 B3
Victoria Chile 38°13S 72°20W 336 A2
Victoria Hong Kong, China 22°17N 114°9E 122 B2
Victoria Grenada 12°12N 61°42W 323 q
Victoria Guinea 10°50N 14°32W 262 C2
Victoria Gozo, Malta 36°3N 14°14E 206 E6
Victoria Mind. Or., Phil. 13°12N 121°12E 232 E3
Victoria Tarlac, Phil. 15°35N 120°41E 232 D3
Victoria Romania 45°44N 24°41E 183 E9
Victoria Seychelles 4°38S 55°28E 272 c
Victoria London, U.K. 125 c3
Victoria Kans., U.S.A. 38°52N 99°9W 308 F4
Victoria Tex., U.S.A. 28°48N 97°0W 314 G6
Victoria □ Australia 37°0S 144°0E 282 D6
Victoria → Australia 15°10S 129°40E 278 C4
Victoria, Grand L. Canada 47°31N 77°30W 298 C4
Victoria, L. Africa 1°0S 33°0E 268 C3
Victoria, L. N.S.W.,
Australia 33°57S 141°15E 282 B4
Victoria, Mt. = Tomanivi
Fiji 17°37S 178°1E 287 a1
Victoria, Mt. Burma 21°14N 93°55E 241 E4
Victoria, Mt. Papua N. G. 8°55S 147°32E 286 E4
Victoria, Pont Canada 45°29N 73°32W 130 B2
Victoria and Alfred Waterfront
Cape Town, S. Africa 118 a1
Victoria Beach Canada 50°40N 96°35W 297 C9
Victoria de Durango = Durango
Mexico 24°3N 104°39W 318 C4
Victoria de las Tunas = Las Tunas
Cuba 20°58N 76°59W 324 B4
Victoria Falls Zimbabwe 17°58S 25°52E 269 F2
Victoria Fjord Greenland 82°10N 46°0W 154 A6
Victoria Gardens India 18°58N 72°50E 130 B2
Victoria Harbour Ont.,
Canada 44°45N 79°45W 312 B5
Victoria Harbour Hong Kong,
China 22°17N 114°10E 122 B1
Victoria I. Canada 71°0N 111°0W 294 C9
Victoria Island Nigeria 6°25N 3°25E 124 B2
Victoria L. Nfld. & L.,
Canada 48°20N 57°27W 299 C8
Victoria L. Gauteng, S. Africa 26°13S 28°9E 123 B2
Victoria Lawn Tennis Courts
Australia 37°50S 145°1E 128 B2
Victoria Ld. Antarctica 75°0S 160°0E 151 D11
Victoria Nile → Uganda 2°14N 31°26E 268 B3
Victoria Park Singapore 1°19N 103°49E 138 B2
Victoria Peak China 22°16N 114°8E 122 B1
Victoria Peaks Phil. 9°22N 118°20E 233 G2
Victoria Pk. Belize 16°48N 88°37W 319 D7
Victoria Ra. N.Z. 42°12S 172°7E 285 C7
Victoria River Australia 16°25S 131°0E 278 C5
Victoria Str. Canada 69°31N 100°30W 294 D11
Victoria Terminus = Chhatrapati
Shivaji Terminus India 18°56N 72°50E 130 B2
Victoria West S. Africa 31°25S 23°4E 270 D3
Victoria Wharf Cape Town, S. Africa 118 a2
Victorias Phil. 10°54N 123°5E 233 F4
Victoriaville Canada 46°4N 71°56W 299 C5
Victorica Argentina 36°20S 65°30W 334 D2
Victorville U.S.A. 34°32N 117°18W 307 L9
Vicuña Chile 30°0S 70°50W 334 C1
Vicuña Mackenna
Argentina 33°53S 64°25W 334 C3
Vidal U.S.A. 34°7N 114°31W 307 L12
Vidalia U.S.A. 32°13N 82°25W 316 C7
Vidamlya Belarus 52°19N 23°47E 185 F10
Vidauban France 43°25N 6°27E 175 E10
Viddolatno = Vindelälven →
Sweden 63°55N 19°50E 160 E18
Videbæk Denmark 56°6N 8°38E 163 H2
Videle Romania 44°17N 25°31E 183 F10
Videsæter Norway 61°57N 7°14E 164 C4
Vidette U.S.A. 33°2N 82°15W 316 B7
Vidigueira Portugal 38°12N 7°48W 195 G3
Vidin Bulgaria 43°59N 22°50E 202 C6
Vidin □ Bulgaria 43°59N 22°50E 202 C6
Vidio, C. Spain 43°35N 6°14W 194 B4
Vidisha India 23°28N 77°53E 242 H7
Vidos Greece 39°38N 19°55E 206 B9
Vidra Romania 45°56N 26°55E 183 E11
Viduša Bos.-H. 42°55N 18°21E 202 D2
Vidzy Belarus 55°23N 26°37E 188 E4
Viechtach Germany 49°4N 12°53E 179 F8
Viedma Argentina 40°50S 63°0W 336 B4
Viedma, L. Argentina 49°30S 72°30W 336 C2
Vieille Case Dominica 15°36N 61°24W 323 k
Vieira do Minho Portugal 41°38N 8°8W 194 D2
Vielha Spain 42°43N 0°44E 196 C5
Viella = Vielha Spain 42°43N 0°44E 196 C5
Vielsalm Belgium 50°17N 5°54E 170 D5
Vienenburg Germany 51°57N 10°34E 178 D6
Vieng Pou Kha Laos 20°41N 101°4E 228 G3
Vienna = Wien Austria 48°12N 16°22E 142 A2
Vienna Ont., Canada 42°41N 80°48W 312 D4
Vienna Ga., U.S.A. 32°6N 83°47W 316 C6
Vienna Ill., U.S.A. 37°25N 88°54W 308 G9
Vienna Mo., U.S.A. 38°11N 91°57W 310 F5
Vienne France 45°31N 4°53E 175 C8
Vienne □ France 46°30N 0°42E 174 B4
Vienne → France 47°13N 0°5E 172 E7
Vientiane Laos 17°58N 102°36E 236 D4
Vientos, Paso de los
Caribbean 20°0N 74°0W 321 C5
Vieques Puerto Rico 18°8N 65°25W 321 b
Vierge Pt. St. Lucia 13°49N 60°53W 323 m
Vierkant Pt. Bonaire 12°7N 68°17W 322 h
Viernheim Germany 49°31N 8°35E 179 F4
Viersen Germany 51°15N 6°23E 178 D2
Vierwaldstättersee Switz. 47°0N 8°30E 179 J4
Vierzon France 47°13N 2°5E 173 E9
Vieste Italy 41°53N 16°10E 199 G13
Viet Quang Vietnam 22°30N 104°48E 228 F5
Viet Tri Vietnam 21°18N 105°25E 236 B5
Vietnam ■ Asia 19°0N 106°0E 236 C6
Vietnam Veterans Memorial
U.S.A. 38°53N 77°2W 143 B2
Vietnam War Museum
U.S.A. 41°58N 87°39W 119 B3
Vietz = Witnica Poland 52°40N 14°54E 185 F1
Vieux-Boucau-les-Bains
France 43°48N 1°23W 174 E2
Vieux Bourg Guadeloupe 16°20N 61°36W 322 e
Vieux Carré = French Quarter
New Orleans, U.S.A. 131 a2
Vieux Fort Guadeloupe 15°57N 61°41W 322 e
Vieux Fort Marie-Galante,
Guadeloupe 15°59N 61°15W 322 e
Vieux Fort St. Lucia 13°46N 60°58W 323 m
Vieux Fort, Pte. du
Guadeloupe 15°57N 61°42W 322 e
Vieux Fort, R. du →
Guadeloupe 15°59N 61°17W 322 e
Vieux Grand Port Mauritius 20°22S 57°42E 272 e
Vieux-Habitants Guadeloupe 16°4N 61°46W 322 e
Vieux-Habitants, Rivière des →
Guadeloupe 16°3N 61°46W 322 e
Vieux-Montréal Montreal, Canada 130 b3
View Park U.S.A. 34°0N 118°20W 126 B3
Vif France 45°5N 5°41E 175 C9
Viga Phil. 13°52N 124°18E 232 E5
Vigan Phil. 17°35N 120°28E 232 C3
Vigário Geral Brazil 22°48S 43°18W 135 A1
Vigeland Norway 58°5N 7°18E 164 F4
Vigentino Italy 45°26N 9°13E 128 B2
Vigévano Italy 45°19N 8°51E 198 C5
Viggbyholm Sweden 59°26N 18°7E 139 A2
Vighignolo Italy 45°29N 9°2E 128 B1
Vigia = Almenara Brazil 16°11S 40°42W 333 E3
Vigia Brazil 0°50S 48°5W 332 B2
Vigla Greece 39°7N 20°50E 207 A2
Viglas, Akra Greece 35°54N 27°51E 206 F11
Vignemale France 42°47N 0°10W 174 F3
Vigneulles-lès-Hattonchâtel
France 48°59N 5°43E 173 D12
Vignola Italy 44°29N 11°1E 198 D8
Vigo Spain 42°12N 8°41W 194 C2
Vigo, Ría de Spain 42°15N 8°45W 194 C2
Vigrestad Norway 58°34N 5°42E 164 F2
Vigsø Bugt Denmark 57°8N 8°47E 163 G2
Vihiers France 47°10N 0°30W 172 E6
Vihowa Pakistan 31°8N 70°30E 242 D4
Vihowa → Pakistan 31°8N 70°41E 242 D4
Viikki Finland 60°13N 25°1E 121 B3
Viipuri = Vyborg Russia 60°43N 28°47E 188 B5
Vijayadurg India 16°30N 73°25E 244 F1
Vijayawada India 16°31N 80°39E 244 F5
Vijosë → Albania 40°37N 19°24E 202 F3
Vik Iceland 63°25N 19°1W 155 D7
Vik Sogn og Fjordane, Norway 61°21N 6°6E 164 C3
Vika Sweden 60°57N 14°28E 162 D8
Vikarabad India 17°20N 77°54E 244 F3
Vikarbyn Sweden 60°55N 15°1E 162 D9
Vike Norway 60°42N 5°35E 164 D2
Vikedal Norway 59°30N 5°55E 164 E2
Vikeke = Viqueque
E. Timor 8°52S 126°23E 231 F7
Vikeland = Vigeland
Norway 58°5N 7°18E 164 F4
Viken Skåne, Sweden 56°9N 12°34E 163 H6
Viken Västra Götaland,
Sweden 58°39N 14°20E 163 F8
Vikersund Norway 59°58N 9°59E 164 E6
Vikesá Norway 58°38N 6°3E 164 F3
Vikevåg Norway 59°5N 5°41E 164 E2
Vikhammer Norway 63°26N 10°37E 164 A7
Vikhroli India 19°6N 72°55E 130 A2
Viking Canada 53°7N 111°50W 296 C6
Vikmanshyttan Sweden 60°18N 15°50E 162 D9
Vikna Norway 64°55N 10°58E 160 D14
Vikos-Aoos △ Greece 40°0N 20°45E 204 B2
Vikøyri Norway 61°4N 6°34E 164 C3
Vila Alferes Chamusca = Guijá
Mozam. 24°27S 33°0E 271 B5
Vila António Enes = Angoche
Mozam. 16°8S 39°55E 269 F4
Vila Baleira Madeira 33°4N 16°20W 260 B1
Vila Bela da Santissima Trindade
Brazil 15°0S 59°57W 331 C6
Vila Cabral = Lichinga
Mozam. 13°13S 35°11E 269 E4
Vila Cabral = Niassa □
Mozam. 13°30S 36°0E 269 E4
Vila da Maganja Mozam. 17°18S 37°30E 269 F4
Vila da Ribeira Brava
C. Verde Is. 16°32N 24°25W 153 j
Vila de Rei Portugal 39°41N 8°9W 194 F2
Vila do Bispo Portugal 37°5N 8°53W 195 H2
Vila do Conde Portugal 41°21N 8°45W 194 D2
Vila do Porto Azores 36°56N 25°9W 153 d4
Vila Franca de Xira
Portugal 38°57N 8°59W 195 G2
Vila Franca do Campo
Azores 37°43N 25°26W 153 d3
Vila Gamito Mozam. 14°12S 33°0E 269 E3
Vila Gomes da Costa
Mozam. 24°20S 33°37E 271 B5
Vila Guilherme Brazil 23°30S 46°38W 137 B2
Vila Isabel Brazil 22°55S 43°15W 135 B1
Vila Jaguára Brazil 23°30S 46°45W 137 B1
Vila Machado Mozam. 19°15S 34°14E 269 F3
Vila Madalena Brazil 23°32S 46°41W 137 B1
Vila Maria Brazil 23°31S 46°36W 137 B2
Vila Mariana Brazil 23°34S 46°38W 137 B2
Vila Mouzinho Mozam. 14°48S 34°25E 269 E3
Vila Nova de Famalicão
Portugal 41°25N 8°32W 194 D2
Vila Nova de Fos Côa
Portugal 41°5N 7°9W 194 D3
Vila Nova de Gaia Portugal 41°8N 8°37W 194 D2
Vila Nova de Gaza = Xai-Xai
Mozam. 25°6S 33°31E 271 C5
Vila Nova de Ourém
Portugal 39°40N 8°35W 194 F2
Vila Nova do Corvo Azores 39°40N 31°8W 153 d2
Vila Pereira de Eça = Ondjiva
Angola 16°48S 15°50E 265 F3
Vila Pery = Manica
Mozam. 18°58S 32°59E 271 A5
Vila Pouca de Aguiar
Portugal 41°30N 7°38W 194 D3
Vila Prudente Brazil 23°35S 46°33W 137 B2
Vila Real Portugal 41°17N 7°48W 194 D3
Vila-Real Spain 39°55N 0°3W 196 F4
Vila Real □ Portugal 41°36N 7°35W 194 D3
Vila Real de Santo António
Portugal 37°10N 7°28W 195 H3
Vila-seca Spain 41°7N 1°9E 196 D6
Vila Texeira da Silva = Luau
Angola 10°40S 22°10E 265 E4
Vila Vasco da Gama
Mozam. 14°54S 32°14E 269 E3
Vila Velha Amapá, Brazil 3°13N 51°13W 329 C7
Vila Velha Espírito Santo,
Brazil 20°20S 40°17W 333 F3
Vila Velha Sergipe, Brazil 11°20S 38°9W 332 D4
Vila Viçosa Portugal 38°45N 7°27W 195 G3
Viladecans Spain 41°18N 2°1E 114 B1
Vilafranca del Maestrat
Spain 40°26N 0°16W 196 E4
Vilafranca del Penedès
Spain 41°21N 1°40E 196 D6
Vilagarcía de Arousa
Spain 42°34N 8°46W 194 C2
Vilaine → France 47°30N 2°27W 172 E4
Vilakalaka Vanuatu 15°25S 167°42E 287 E5
Vilanandro, Tanjona
Madag. 16°11S 44°27E 272 B1
Vilanculos Mozam. 22°1S 35°17E 271 B6
Vilanova i la Geltrú Spain 41°13N 1°40E 196 D6
Vilar Formoso Portugal 40°38N 6°45W 194 E4
Vilaseca-Salou = Vila-seca
Spain 41°7N 1°9E 196 D6
Vilbjerg Denmark 56°12N 8°46E 163 H2
Vilcabamba, Cordillera
Peru 13°0S 73°0W 330 C3
Vilcanchos Peru 13°40S 74°25W 330 C3
Vilcheka, Ostrov Russia 80°0N 58°31E 214 B6
Vilcheka, Zemlya Russia 80°30N 60°30E 150 A11
Vilches Spain 38°12N 3°30W 195 G7
Vile Parle India 19°6N 72°51E 130 A2
Vileyka Belarus 54°30N 26°53E 177 A14
Vilhelmina Sweden 64°35N 16°39E 160 D17
Vilhena Brazil 12°40S 60°5W 331 C5
Viliya = Neris → Lithuania 55°8N 24°16E 188 E3
Viljandi Estonia 58°28N 25°30E 188 C3
Viljoensdorp = Newcastle
S. Africa 27°45S 29°58E 271 C4
Vilkaviškis Lithuania 54°39N 23°2E 184 D10
Vilkija Lithuania 55°3N 23°35E 184 C10
Vil'kitskogo, Proliv Russia 78°0N 103°0E 215 B11
Vilkomir = Ukmergė
Lithuania 55°15N 24°45E 188 E3
Vilkovo = Vylkove
Ukraine 45°28N 29°32E 183 E14
Villa Abecia Bolivia 21°0S 68°18W 334 A2
Villa Adelina Argentina 34°31S 58°33W 117 B1
Villa Ana Argentina 28°28S 59°40W 334 B4
Villa Angela Argentina 27°34S 60°45W 334 B3
Villa Ballester Argentina 34°33S 58°33W 117 B1
Villa Barilari Argentina 34°42S 58°20W 117 C2
Villa Bella = Serra Talhada
Brazil 7°59S 38°18W 332 C4
Villa Bella Bolivia 10°25S 65°22W 331 C4
Villa Borghese Rome, Italy 136 a3
Villa Bosch Argentina 34°35S 58°33W 117 B1
Villa Bruzual Venezuela 9°20N 69°6W 328 C4
Villa C. Colon Argentina 34°41S 58°21W 117 C2
Villa Cañás Argentina 34°0S 61°35W 334 C3
Villa Cecilia = Ciudad Madero
Mexico 22°19N 97°50W 319 C5
Villa Cisneros = Dakhla
W. Sahara 23°50N 15°53W 260 D1
Villa Ciudadela Argentina 34°38S 58°33W 117 B1
Villa Constitución
Argentina 33°15S 60°20W 334 C3
Villa de Arriaga Mexico 21°56N 101°20W 318 C4
Villa de Cura Venezuela 10°2N 67°29W 328 A4
Villa de Guadalupe Mexico 19°29N 99°6W 128 B2
Villa de María Argentina 29°55S 63°43W 334 B3
Villa de Méndez Mexico 25°7N 98°34W 319 B5
Villa del Nevoso = Ilirska-Bistrica
Slovenia 45°34N 14°14E 199 C11
Villa del Rio Spain 37°59N 4°17W 195 H6
Villa del Rosario
Venezuela 10°19N 72°19W 328 A3
Villa Devoto Argentina 34°36S 58°31W 117 B1
Villa Diamante Argentina 34°41S 58°25W 117 C2
Villa Dolores Argentina 31°58S 65°15W 334 C2
Villa Dominico Argentina 34°41S 58°19W 117 C3
Villa Gesell Argentina 37°15S 56°55W 334 D4
Villa Grove U.S.A. 39°52N 88°10W 311 E8
Villa Guillermina
Argentina 28°15S 59°29W 334 B4
Villa Hayes Paraguay 25°5S 57°20W 334 B4
Villa Hidalgo Mexico 24°15N 99°26W 319 C5
Villa Iris Argentina 38°12S 63°12W 334 D3
Villa Lugano Argentina 34°41S 58°27W 117 C2
Villa Lynch Argentina 34°35S 58°31W 117 B1
Villa Madero Argentina 34°41S 58°30W 117 C1
Villa María Argentina 32°20S 63°10W 334 C3
Villa Mazán Argentina 28°40S 66°30W 334 B2
Villa Minozzo Italy 44°22N 10°28E 198 D7
Villa Montes Bolivia 21°10S 63°30W 334 A3
Villa Ocampo Argentina 28°30S 59°20W 334 B4
Villa Ocampo Durango,
Mexico 26°27N 105°31W 318 B3
Villa Ojo de Agua
Argentina 29°30S 63°44W 334 B3
Villa Regina Argentina 39°6S 67°4W 336 A3
Villa Rica U.S.A. 33°44N 84°55W 316 B5
Villa Sáenz Peña
Argentina 34°37S 58°32W 117 B1
Villa San Giovanni Italy 38°13N 15°38E 201 D8
Villa San Martín Argentina 28°15S 64°9W 334 B3
Villa Sanjurjo = Al Hoceïma
Morocco 35°8N 3°58W 261 A4
Villa Santina Italy 46°24N 12°55E 199 B9
Villa Unión Mexico 23°12N 106°14W 318 C3
Villa Urquiza Argentina 34°34S 58°28W 117 B2
Villaba Phil. 11°13N 124°24E 233 F5
Villablino Spain 42°57N 6°19W 194 C4
Villacarlos Spain 39°53N 4°17E 206 B5
Villacarriedo Spain 43°14N 3°48W 194 B7
Villacarrillo Spain 38°7N 3°3W 195 G7
Villacastín Spain 40°46N 4°25W 194 E6
Villach Austria 46°37N 13°51E 180 E6
Villacidro Italy 39°27N 8°44E 200 C1
Villada Spain 42°15N 4°59W 194 C6
Villadiego Spain 42°31N 4°1W 194 C6
Villadóssola Italy 46°4N 8°16E 198 B5
Villafeliche Spain 41°10N 1°30W 196 D3
Villafranca Spain 42°17N 1°46W 196 C3
Villafranca de los Barros
Spain 38°35N 6°18W 195 G4
Villafranca de los Caballeros
Spain 39°26N 3°21W 195 F7
Villafranca del Cid = Vilafranca del
Maestrat Spain 40°26N 0°16W 196 E4
Villafranca del Panadés =
Vilafranca del Penedès
Spain 41°21N 1°40E 196 D6
Villafranca di Verona
Italy 45°21N 10°50E 198 C7
Villafranca Tirrena Italy 38°20N 15°25E 201 D8
Villagio Mussolini = Arboréa
Italy 39°46N 8°35E 200 C1
Villagrán Mexico 24°29N 99°29W 319 C5
Villaguay Argentina 32°0S 59°0W 334 C4
Villaharta Spain 38°9N 4°54W 195 G6
Villahermosa Tabasco,
Mexico 17°59N 92°55W 319 D6
Villahermosa Spain 38°46N 2°52W 197 G2
Villaines-la-Juhel France 48°21N 0°20W 172 D6
Villajoyosa Spain 38°30N 0°12W 197 G4
Villalba Puerto Rico 18°8N 66°30W 321 b
Villalba Spain 43°26N 7°40W 194 B3
Villalba de Guardo Spain 42°42N 4°49W 194 C6
Villalón de Campos Spain 42°5N 5°4W 194 C5
Villalpando Spain 41°51N 5°25W 194 D5
Villaluenga de la Sagra
Spain 40°2N 3°54W 194 E7
Villamanán Spain 42°19N 5°35W 194 C5
Villamartín Spain 36°52N 5°38W 195 J5
Villamayor de Santiago
Spain 39°50N 2°59W 196 F2
Villamblard France 45°2N 0°32E 174 C4
Villanova Monteleone
Italy 40°30N 8°28E 200 B1
Villanueva Colombia 10°37N 72°59W 328 A3
Villanueva N. Mex.,
U.S.A. 35°16N 105°22W 305 J11
Villanueva de Castellón
Spain 39°5N 0°31W 197 F4
Villanueva de Córdoba
Spain 38°20N 4°38W 195 G6
Villanueva de la Fuente
Spain 38°42N 2°42W 197 G2
Villanueva de la Serena
Spain 38°59N 5°50W 195 G5
Villanueva de la Sierra
Spain 40°12N 6°24W 194 E4
Villanueva de los Castillejos
Spain 37°30N 7°15W 195 H3
Villanueva de los Infantes
Spain 38°43N 3°1W 195 G7
Villanueva del Arzobispo
Spain 38°10N 3°0W 197 G2
Villanueva del Fresno
Spain 38°23N 7°10W 195 G3
Villanueva y Geltrú = Vilanova i la
Geltrú Spain 41°13N 1°40E 196 D6
Villaputzu Italy 39°26N 9°34E 200 C2
Villaquilambre Spain 42°39N 5°33W 194 C5
Villar del Arzobispo Spain 39°44N 0°50W 196 F4
Villar del Rey Spain 39°7N 6°50W 195 F4
Villard-de-Lans France 45°3N 5°33E 175 C9
Villarramiel Spain 42°2N 4°55W 194 C6
Villarreal = Vila-Real Spain 39°55N 0°3W 196 F4
Villarrica Chile 39°15S 72°15W 336 A2
Villarrica Paraguay 25°40S 56°30W 334 B4
Villarrica △ Chile 39°24S 71°46W 336 A2
Villarrobledo Spain 39°18N 2°36W 197 F2
Villarroya de la Sierra
Spain 41°27N 1°46W 196 D3
Villarrubia de los Ojos
Spain 39°14N 3°36W 195 F7
Villars-les-Dombes France 46°0N 5°3E 173 F12
Villasayas Spain 41°24N 2°39W 196 D2
Villaseco de los Gamitos
Spain 41°2N 6°7W 194 D4
Villasimius Italy 39°8N 9°31E 200 C2
Villastar Spain 40°17N 1°9W 196 E3
Villatobas Spain 39°54N 3°20W 194 F7
Villaverde Spain 40°21N 3°42W 127 B1
Villaverde Bajo Spain 40°20N 3°40W 127 B1
Villavicencio Argentina 32°28S 69°0W 334 C2
Villavicencio Colombia 4°9N 73°37W 328 C3
Villaviciosa Spain 43°32N 5°27W 194 B5
Villazón Bolivia 22°0S 65°35W 334 A2
Ville-d'Avray France 48°49N 2°11E 134 B2
Ville-Marie Canada 47°20N 79°30W 298 C4
Ville Platte U.S.A. 30°41N 92°17W 314 F8
Villecresnes France 48°43N 2°31E 134 B4
Villedieu-les-Poêles France 48°50N 1°13W 172 D5
Villefort France 44°28N 3°56E 174 D7
Villefranche-de-Lauragais
France 43°25N 1°44E 174 E5
Villefranche-de-Rouergue
France 44°21N 2°2E 174 D6
Villefranche-du-Périgord
France 44°38N 1°5E 174 D5
Villefranche-sur-Saône
France 45°59N 4°43E 175 C8
Villejuif France 48°47N 2°21E 134 B3
Villel Spain 40°14N 1°12W 196 E3
Villemomble France 48°52N 2°30E 134 A4
Villemur-sur-Tarn France 43°51N 1°31E 174 E5
Villena Spain 38°39N 0°52W 197 G4
Villenauxe-la-Grande
France 48°35N 3°33E 173 D10
Villenave-d'Ornon France 44°46N 0°33W 174 D3
Villeneuve-d'Ascq France 50°38N 3°9E 173 B10
Villeneuve-la-Garenne
France 48°56N 2°19E 134 A2
Villeneuve-l'Archevêque
France 48°14N 3°32E 173 D10
Villeneuve-le-Roi France 48°43N 2°24E 134 B3
Villeneuve-lès-Avignon
France 43°58N 4°49E 175 E8
Villeneuve-St-Georges
France 48°43N 2°27E 134 B3
Villeneuve-sur-Allier
France 46°40N 3°13E 173 F10
Villeneuve-sur-Lot France 44°24N 0°42E 174 D4
Villeneuve-sur-Yonne
France 48°5N 3°18E 173 D10
Villeparisis France 48°56N 2°36E 134 A5
Villeréal France 44°38N 0°45E 174 D4
Villers-Bocage France 49°3N 0°40W 172 C6
Villers-Cotterêts France 49°15N 3°4E 173 C10
Villers-sur-Mer France 49°21N 0°2W 172 C6
Villersexel France 47°33N 6°26E 173 E13
Villerupt France 49°28N 5°55E 173 C12
Villeurbanne France 45°46N 4°55E 175 C8
Villevaudé France 48°55N 2°39E 134 A5
Villiers S. Africa 27°2S 28°36E 271 C4
Villiers-le-Bâcle France 48°44N 2°8E 134 B1
Villiers-sur-Marne France 48°49N 2°32E 134 B4
Villingen-Schwenningen
Germany 48°3N 8°26E 179 G4
Villinki Finland 60°9N 25°6E 121 C3
Villisca U.S.A. 40°56N 94°59W 310 D2
Villmanstrand = Lappeenranta
Finland 61°3N 28°12E 188 B5
Villoresi, Canale Italy 45°33N 9°9E 128 A1
Villupuram India 11°59N 79°31E 245 J4
Vilna = Vilnius Lithuania 54°38N 25°19E 188 E3
Vilna Canada 54°7N 111°55W 296 C6
Vilnius Lithuania 54°38N 25°19E 188 E3
Vils Austria 47°33N 10°38E 180 D3
Vils → Bayern, Germany 48°38N 13°11E 179 G9
Vils → Bayern, Germany 49°10N 11°57E 179 F7
Vilsbiburg Germany 48°26N 12°22E 179 G8
Vilshofen Germany 48°37N 13°11E 179 G9
Vilusi Montenegro 42°44N 18°34E 202 D2
Vilvoorde Belgium 50°56N 4°26E 116 A2
Vilyuchinsk Russia 52°55N 158°24E 215 D16
Vilyuy → Russia 64°24N 126°26E 215 C13
Vilyuysk Russia 63°40N 121°35E 215 C13
Vilyuyskoye Vdkhr.
Russia 63°0N 112°0E 215 C12
Vimianzo Spain 43°7N 9°2W 194 B1
Vimioso Portugal 41°35N 6°31W 194 D4
Vimmerby Sweden 57°40N 15°55E 163 G9
Vimodrone Italy 45°30N 9°16E 128 A2
Vimont Canada 45°36N 73°43W 130 A1
Vimoutiers France 48°57N 0°10E 172 D7
Vimperk Czech Rep. 49°3N 13°46E 180 B6
Vina → Cameroon 7°45N 15°36E 264 A3
Viña del Mar Chile 33°0S 71°30W 334 C1
Vinanmek Mansion Bangkok, Thailand 113 a2
Vinarós Spain 40°30N 0°27E 196 E5
Vincendo Réunion 21°21S 55°41E 272 f
Vincennes Val-de-Marne,
France 48°51N 2°26E 134 A3
Vincennes Ind., U.S.A. 38°41N 87°32W 311 F9
Vincennes, Bois de France 48°49N 2°26E 134 B3
Vincennes Bay S. Ocean 66°0S 109°0E 151 C8
Vincent U.S.A. 34°33N 118°11W 307 L8
Vinces Ecuador 1°32S 79°45W 328 D2
Vinchina Argentina 28°45S 68°15W 334 B2
Vindava = Ventspils
Latvia 57°25N 21°32E 184 A8
Vindelälven → Sweden 63°55N 19°50E 160 E18
Vindeln Sweden 64°12N 19°43E 160 D18
Vinderup Denmark 56°29N 8°45E 163 H2
Vindhya Ra. India 22°50N 77°0E 242 H7
Vine Grove U.S.A. 37°49N 85°59W 311 G11
Vineland Fla., U.S.A. 28°23N 81°30W 133 B1
Vineland N.J., U.S.A. 39°29N 75°2W 309 F16
Vineuil France 47°35N 1°22E 172 E8
Vinga Romania 46°1N 21°14E 182 D6
Vingåker Sweden 59°2N 15°52E 162 E9
Vingelen Norway 62°25N 10°52E 164 B7
Vingnes Norway 61°7N 10°26E 164 C7
Vinh Vietnam 18°45N 105°38E 236 C5
Vinh Loi = Bac Lieu
Vietnam 9°17N 105°43E 237 H5
Vinh Long Vietnam 10°16N 105°57E 237 G5
Vinh Moc Vietnam 21°18N 105°1E 236 B5
Vinh Yen Vietnam 21°21N 105°35E 228 G5
Vinhais Portugal 41°50N 7°5W 194 D3
Vinica Croatia 46°20N 16°9E 199 B13
Vinica Macedonia 41°53N 22°30E 202 E6
Vinica Slovenia 45°28N 15°16E 199 C12
Vinings U.S.A. 33°53N 84°29W 113 A2
Vinita U.S.A. 36°39N 95°9W 314 C7
Vinje Sør-Trøndelag, Norway 63°12N 9°0E 164 A5
Vinje Telemark, Norway 59°37N 7°51E 164 E4
Vinjo Norway 60°48N 6°30E 164 D3
Vinkovci Croatia 45°19N 18°48E 182 E3
Vinnitsa = Vinnytsya
Ukraine 49°15N 28°30E 177 D15
Vinnytsya Ukraine 49°15N 28°30E 177 D15
Vinnytsya □ Ukraine 49°20N 28°15E 177 D15
Vinodelnoye = Ipatovo
Russia 45°45N 42°50E 191 H6
Vinohrady Prague, Czech Rep. 135 c3
Vinoř Czech Rep. 50°8N 14°34E 135 B3
Vinslöv Sweden 56°7N 13°55E 163 H7
Vinson Massif Antarctica 78°35S 85°25W 151 D16
Vinstra Norway 61°37N 9°44E 164 C6
Vinstra → Norway 61°37N 9°44E 164 C6
Vintar Phil. 18°14N 120°39E 232 B3
Vintjärn Sweden 60°50N 16°4E 162 D10
Vinton Calif., U.S.A. 39°48N 120°10W 306 F6
Vinton Iowa, U.S.A. 42°10N 92°1W 310 B4
Vinton La., U.S.A. 30°11N 93°35W 314 F8
Vinţu de Jos Romania 46°0N 23°30E 183 D8
Vinukonda India 16°4N 79°45E 245 F4
Viöl Germany 54°34N 9°11E 178 A5
Viola U.S.A. 41°12N 90°35W 310 C6
Violet Hill China 22°15N 114°11E 122 B2
Violet Town Australia 36°38S 145°42E 283 D6
Violet Valley ✪ Australia 17°10S 127°55E 278 C4
Vioolsdrif S. Africa 28°46S 17°39E 270 C2
Viotia □ Greece 38°20N 23°0E 204 C5
Vipacco = Vipava
Slovenia 45°51N 13°58E 199 C10
Vipava Slovenia 45°51N 13°58E 199 C10
Vipiteno Italy 46°54N 11°26E 199 B8
Viqueque E. Timor 8°52S 126°23E 231 F7
Vir Croatia 44°17N 15°3E 199 D12
Virac Phil. 13°30N 124°20E 232 E5
Virachey Cambodia 13°59N 106°49E 236 F6
Virachey △ Cambodia 14°14N 106°55E 236 E6
Virago Sd. Canada 54°0N 132°30W 296 C2
Virajpet = Virarajendrapet
India 12°10N 75°50E 245 H2
Viramgam India 23°5N 72°0E 242 H5
Viranşehir Turkey 37°13N 39°45E 213 D8
Virányos Hungary 47°31N 18°59E 117 A1
Virarajendrapet India 12°10N 75°50E 245 H2
Virawah Pakistan 24°31N 70°46E 242 G4
Virbalis Lithuania 54°39N 22°49E 184 D9
Virden Man., Canada 49°50N 100°56W 297 D8
Virden Ill., U.S.A. 39°30N 89°46W 310 E7
Vire France 48°50N 0°53W 172 D6
Vire → France 49°20N 1°7W 172 C5
Virei Angola 15°43S 12°52E 265 F2
Virgem da Lapa Brazil 16°49S 42°21W 333 E3
Virgenes, C. Argentina 52°19S 68°21W 336 D3
Virgin → U.S.A. 36°28N 114°21W 305 H6
Virgin Gorda Br. Virgin Is. 18°30N 64°26W 321 C7
Virgin Is. (British) ☑
W. Indies 18°30N 64°30W 321 C7
Virgin Is. (U.S.) ☑
W. Indies 18°20N 65°0W 321 C7
Virgin Islands △
U.S. Virgin Is. 18°21N 64°43W 321 b
Virginia Free State, S. Africa 28°8S 26°55E 270 C4
Virginia Ill., U.S.A. 39°57N 90°13W 310 E6
Virginia Minn., U.S.A. 47°31N 92°32W 308 B7
Virginia □ U.S.A. 37°30N 78°45W 309 G14
Virginia, L. U.S.A. 28°35N 81°20W 133 A2
Virginia Beach U.S.A. 36°49N 76°9W 309 F16
Virginia City Mont.,
U.S.A. 45°18N 111°56W 304 D8
Virginia City Nev., U.S.A. 39°19N 119°39W 306 F7
Virginia Falls Canada 61°38N 125°42W 296 A3
Virginia Gardens U.S.A. 25°48N 80°18W 129 D1
Virginia Key U.S.A. 25°44N 80°8W 129 D3
Virginiatown Canada 48°9N 79°36W 298 C4
Virje Croatia 46°4N 16°59E 199 B13
Viroflay France 48°48N 2°10E 134 B2
Vironas Greece 37°55N 23°46E 112 B2
Viroqua U.S.A. 43°34N 90°53W 308 D8
Virovitica Croatia 45°51N 17°21E 182 E2
Virpazar Montenegro 42°14N 19°6E 202 D3
Virpur India 21°51N 70°42E 242 J4
Virsbo Sweden 59°52N 16°2E 162 E10
Virserum Sweden 57°20N 15°35E 163 G9
Virton Belgium 49°35N 5°32E 170 E5
Virú Peru 8°25S 78°45W 330 B2
Virudunagar India 9°30N 77°58E 245 K3
Virum Denmark 55°47N 12°27E 118 A2
Virunga △
Dem. Rep. of the Congo 0°5N 29°38E 268 B2
Vis Croatia 43°4N 16°10E 199 E13
Visalia U.S.A. 36°20N 119°18W 306 J7
Visayan Sea Phil. 11°30N 123°30E 233 F4
Visayas □ Phil. 9°30N 122°45E 233 G4
Visby Sweden 57°37N 18°18E 163 G12
Viscount Melville Sd.
Canada 74°10N 108°0W 295 C10
Visé Belgium 50°44N 5°41E 170 D5
Vise, Ostrov Russia 79°33N 76°50E 214 B8
Višegrad Bos.-H. 43°47N 19°17E 182 G4
Viseu Brazil 1°10S 46°5W 332 B2
Viseu Portugal 40°40N 7°55W 194 E3
Viseu □ Portugal 40°40N 7°55W 194 E3
Vişeu de Sus Romania 47°45N 24°25E 183 C9
Vishakhapatnam India 17°45N 83°20E 244 F6
Vişina Romania 43°52N 24°27E 183 G9
Vişineşti Moldova 46°20N 28°27E 183 D13
Visingsö Sweden 58°2N 14°20E 163 F8
Visitacion Valley U.S.A. 37°42N 122°23W 136 B2
Viskafors Sweden 57°37N 12°50E 163 G6
Viskan → Sweden 57°14N 12°12E 163 G6
Viški Kanal Croatia 43°4N 16°5E 199 E13
Vislanda Sweden 56°46N 14°30E 163 H8
Visnagar India 23°45N 72°32E 242 H5
Višnja Gora Slovenia 45°58N 14°45E 199 C11
Viso, Mte. Italy 44°38N 7°5E 198 D4
Viso del Marqués Spain 38°32N 3°34W 195 G7
Visoko Bos.-H. 43°58N 18°10E 182 G3
Visokoi I. Antarctica 56°43S 27°15W 151 B1
Visp Switz. 46°17N 7°52E 179 J3
Vissefjärda Sweden 56°32N 15°35E 163 H9
Visselhövede Germany 52°59N 9°34E 178 C5
Vissenbjerg Denmark 55°23N 10°7E 163 J4
Vista U.S.A. 33°12N 117°14W 307 M9
Vista Alegre Santiago,
Chile 33°30S 70°43W 137 C1
Vista Alegre Lima, Peru 12°9S 76°59W 124 B3
Vista Grove U.S.A. 33°51N 84°16W 113 A3
Vistabella Trin. & Tob. 10°17N 61°27W 323 t
Vistonida, L. Greece 41°0N 25°7E 203 E9
Vistonikos, Ormos = Vistonida, L.
Greece 41°0N 25°25E 203 E9
Vistula = Wisła → Poland 54°22N 18°55E 184 D5
Vistula Lagoon = Zalew Wiślany
Poland 54°20N 19°50E 184 D6
Vit → Bulgaria 43°30N 24°30E 203 C8
Vita India 17°17N 74°33E 244 F2
Vitacura Chile 33°23S 70°35W 137 B2
Vitanje Slovenia 46°25N 15°18E 199 B12
Vitebsk = Vitsyebsk
Belarus 55°10N 30°15E 188 E6
Viterbo Italy 42°25N 12°6E 199 F9
Vitez Bos.-H. 44°10N 17°48E 182 F2
Viti Levu Fiji 17°30S 177°30E 287 A1
Vitiaz Str. Papua N. G. 5°40S 147°10E 286 C4
Vitiaz Trench Pac. Oc. 10°0S 170°0E 277 C13
Vitigudino Spain 41°1N 6°26W 194 D4
Vitim Russia 59°28N 112°35E 215 D12
Vitim → Russia 59°26N 112°34E 215 D12
Vitina Bos.-H. 43°17N 17°29E 199 E14
Vitina Greece 37°40N 22°10E 204 D4
Vitínia Italy 41°47N 12°24E 136 C1
Vitkov Czech Rep. 49°46N 17°45E 181 B10
Vitória = Vitória de Santo Antão
Brazil 8°10S 35°20W 332 C4
Vitória Espírito Santo,
Brazil 20°20S 40°22W 333 F3
Vitória Pará, Brazil 2°54S 52°1W 329 D7
Vitória da Conquista
Brazil 14°51S 40°51W 333 D3
Vitória de Santo Antão
Brazil 8°10S 35°20W 332 C4
Vitoria-Gasteiz Spain 42°50N 2°41W 196 C2
Vitória Seamount Atl. Oc. 20°0S 44°0W 152 J8
Vitorino Freire Brazil 4°4S 45°10W 332 B2
Vitosha △ Bulgaria 42°36N 23°18E 202 D7
Vitré France 48°8N 1°12W 172 D5
Vitry-le-François France 48°43N 4°33E 173 D11
Vitry-sur-Seine France 48°47N 2°23E 134 B3
Vitsand Sweden 60°20N 13°0E 162 D7
Vitsi, Oros Greece 40°40N 21°25E 202 F5
Vitsyebsk Belarus 55°10N 30°15E 188 E6
Vitsyebsk □ Belarus 55°10N 28°50E 188 E5
Vittaryd Sweden 56°58N 13°57E 163 H7
Vitteaux France 47°24N 4°30E 173 E11
Vittel France 48°12N 5°57E 173 D12
Vittória Italy 36°57N 14°32E 201 F7
Vittório = Vittório Véneto
Italy 45°59N 12°18E 199 C9
Vittório Véneto Italy 45°59N 12°18E 199 C9
Vittoriosa Malta 35°54N 14°31E 206 F8
Vittsjö Sweden 56°20N 13°40E 163 H7
Viveiro Spain 43°39N 7°38W 194 B3
Vivian U.S.A. 32°53N 93°59W 314 E8
Viviers France 44°30N 4°40E 175 D8
Vivonne S. Austral.,
Australia 35°59S 137°9E 282 C2
Vivonne Vienne, France 46°25N 0°15E 174 B4
Vivonne B. Australia 35°59S 137°9E 282 C2
Viwa Fiji 17°10S 177°58E 287 A1
Vizagapatam = Vishakhapatnam
India 17°45N 83°20E 244 F6
Vizandino, Moussio Athens, Greece 112 b3
Vizcaíno, Desierto de
Mexico 27°30N 113°45W 318 B2
Vizcaíno, Sierra Mexico 27°30N 114°0W 318 B2
Vizcaya □ Spain 43°15N 2°45W 196 B2
Vize Turkey 41°34N 27°45E 203 E11
Vizianagaram India 18°6N 83°30E 244 E6
Vizille France 45°5N 5°46E 175 C9
Viziñada Croatia 45°20N 13°46E 199 C10
Viziru Romania 45°0N 27°43E 183 E12
Vizlinsky Zaliv = Zalew Wiślany
Poland 54°20N 19°50E 184 D6
Vizzini Italy 37°10N 14°45E 201 E7
Vlaardingen Neths. 51°55N 4°21E 170 C4
Vlachiotis Greece 36°52N 22°42E 204 E4
Vlădeasa, Vf. Romania 46°47N 22°50E 182 D7
Vladičin Han Serbia 42°42N 22°1E 202 D6
Vladikavkaz Russia 43°0N 44°35E 191 J7
Vladimir Russia 56°15N 40°30E 188 D11
Vladimir □ Russia 56°5N 40°10E 190 B5
Vladimir Volynskiy = Volodymyr-
Volynskyy Ukraine 50°50N 24°18E 177 C13
Vladimirci Serbia 44°36N 19°50E 202 B3
Vladimirovac Serbia 45°1N 20°53E 182 E5
Vladimirovka = Yuzhno-
Sakhalinsk Russia 46°58N 142°45E 219 B17
Vladimirovka Russia 48°27N 46°10E 191 F8
Vladimirovo Bulgaria 43°32N 23°22E 202 C7
Vladislavovka Ukraine 45°15N 35°29E 189 K8
Vladivostok Russia 43°10N 131°53E 220 C5
Vladykino Russia 55°51N 37°35E 129 A2
Vlăhiţa Romania 46°21N 25°31E 183 D10
Vlasenica Bos.-H. 44°11N 18°59E 182 F3
Vlašić Bos.-H. 44°19N 17°37E 182 F2
Vlašim Czech Rep. 49°40N 14°53E 180 B7
Vlasinsko Jezero Serbia 42°44N 22°22E 202 D6
Vlasotince Serbia 42°59N 22°7E 202 D6
Vlieland Neths. 53°16N 4°55E 170 A4
Vlissingen Neths. 51°26N 3°34E 170 C3
Vlkolínec Slovak Rep. 49°1N 19°16E 181 B12
Vlorë Albania 40°32N 19°28E 202 F3
Vlorës, Gjiri i Albania 40°29N 19°27E 202 F3
Vltava → Czech Rep. 50°21N 14°30E 180 A7
Vo Dat Vietnam 11°9N 107°31E 237 G6
Vobarno Italy 45°39N 10°30E 198 C7
Voćin Croatia 45°37N 17°33E 182 E2
Vöcklabruck Austria 48°1N 13°39E 180 C6
Vodice Croatia 43°47N 15°47E 199 E12
Vodňany Czech Rep. 49°9N 14°11E 180 B7
Vodnjan Croatia 44°59N 13°52E 199 D10
Vodopyanovo = Donskoy
Russia 53°55N 38°15E 188 F10
Voe U.K. 60°21N 1°16W 167 A7
Vogan Togo 6°23N 1°30E 263 D5
Vogar Iceland 63°58N 22°22W 155 D4
Vogel Pk. Nigeria 8°24N 11°47E 263 D7

Vogelkop = Doberai, Jazirah
  Indonesia 1°25S 133°0E **231** E8
Vogelsberg *Germany* 50°31N 9°12E **178** E5
Voghera *Italy* 44°59N 9°1E **198** D6
Voh *N. Cal.* 20°58S 164°42E **288** d
Vohibinany *Madag.* 18°49S 49°4E **272** B2
Vohilava *Madag.* 21°4S 48°0E **272** C2
Vohimarina = Iharana
  Madag. 13°25S 50°0E **272** A3
Vohimena, Tanjon' i
  Madag. 25°36S 45°8E **272** D2
Vohipeno *Madag.* 22°22S 47°51E **272** C2
Voi *Kenya* 3°25S 38°32E **268** C4
Void-Vacon *France* 48°40N 5°36E **173** D12
Voinești *Iași, Romania* 47°5N 27°27E **183** C12
Voinești *Prahova, Romania* 45°14N 25°14E **183** D10
Voinjama *Liberia* 8°25N 9°44W **262** D3
Voiron *France* 45°22N 5°35E **175** C9
Voisey B. *Canada* 56°15N 61°50W **299** A7
Voitsberg *Austria* 47°3N 15°9E **180** D8
Vojens *Denmark* 55°16N 9°18E **163** J3
Vojmsjön *Sweden* 65°0N 16°24E **160** D17
Vojnić *Croatia* 45°19N 15°43E **199** C12
Vojnik *Italy* 46°18N 15°19E **199** B12
Vojvodina □ *Serbia* 45°20N 20°0E **182** E5
Vokeo I. *Papua N. G.* 3°14S 144°2E **286** B3
Vokhtoga *Russia* 58°46N 41°8E **188** C11
Vokovice *Czech Rep.* 50°5N 14°21E **135** B2
Volary *Czech Rep.* 48°54N 13°52E **180** C6
Volborg *U.S.A.* 45°51N 105°41W **304** D11
Volcán de Colima △
  Mexico 19°30N 103°40W **318** D4
Volcano *U.S.A.* 19°26N 155°14W **302** D6
Volcano Is. = Kazan-Rettō
  Pac. Oc. 25°0N 141°0E **288** E6
Volcans □ *Rwanda* 1°30S 29°26E **268** C2
Volcans d'Auvergne △
  France 45°20N 2°40E **174** C6
Volchansk = Vovchansk
  Ukraine 50°17N 36°58E **189** G9
Volchikha *Russia* 52°2N 80°23E **217** B10
Volchya → *Ukraine* 48°32N 36°0E **189** H8
Volda *Norway* 62°9N 6°5E **164** B3
Volga = Privolzhskiy □
  Russia 56°0N 50°0E **214** C6
Volga *Russia* 57°58N 38°16E **188** C10
Volga → *Russia* 46°0N 48°30E **191** G9
Volga Hts. = Privolzhskaya
  Vozvyshennost *Russia* 51°0N 46°0E **190** E7
Volgelsdorf *Germany* 52°30N 13°44E **115** B5
Volgo-Baltiyskiy Kanal
  Russia 60°0N 38°0E **188** B9
Volgo-Donskoy Kanal
  Russia 49°40N 43°37E **191** F7
Volgodonsk *Russia* 47°33N 42°5E **191** G6
Volgograd *Russia* 48°40N 44°25E **191** F7
Volgograd □ *Russia* 49°40N 44°0E **190** F7
Volgogradskoye Vdkhr.
  Russia 50°0N 45°20E **190** E8
Volgorechensk *Russia* 57°28N 41°14E **190** D5
Volimes *Greece* 37°52N 23°39E **207** D2
Volintiri *Moldova* 46°26N 29°37E **183** D14
Volissos *Greece* 38°29N 25°54E **205** C7
Volkach *Germany* 49°52N 10°14E **179** F6
Völkermarkt *Austria* 46°39N 14°39E **180** E7
Volkhonka-Zil *Russia* 55°39N 37°37E **129** C2
Volkhov *Russia* 59°55N 32°15E **188** C7
Volkhov → *Russia* 60°8N 32°20E **188** B7
Volkhovstroy = Volkhov
  Russia 59°55N 32°15E **188** C7
Völklingen *Germany* 49°15N 6°50E **179** F2
Volkovysk = Vawkavysk
  Belarus 53°9N 24°30E **177** B13
Volksrust *S. Africa* 27°24S 29°53E **271** C4
Voll *Norway* 62°31N 7°27E **164** B4
Vollen *Norway* 59°48N 13°27E **133** B1
Volochanka *Russia* 71°0N 94°28E **215** B10
Volodarsk *Russia* 56°12N 43°15E **190** B6
Volodarskoye *Russia* 59°54N 33°23E **137** B2
Volodymyr-Volynskyy
  Ukraine 50°50N 24°18E **177** C13
Vologda *Russia* 59°10N 39°45E **188** C10
Vologda □ *Russia* 60°15N 39°0E **188** B10
Volokolamsk *Russia* 56°5N 35°57E **188** D8
Volokonovka *Russia* 50°33N 37°52E **189** G9
Volos *Greece* 39°24N 22°59E **206** B4
Vološinovo = Novi Bečej
  Serbia 45°36N 23°10E **182** E5
Volosovo *Russia* 59°27N 29°32E **188** C5
Volovets *Ukraine* 48°43N 23°11E **183** B8
Volovo *Russia* 53°35N 39°1E **188** F10
Volozhin = Valozhyn
  Belarus 54°3N 26°30E **177** A14
Volsk *Russia* 52°5N 47°22E **190** D8
Volta □ *Ghana* 7°0N 0°30E **263** D5
Volta → *Ghana* 5°46N 0°41E **263** D5
Volta, L. *Ghana* 7°30N 0°0 **263** D5
Volta Blanche = White Volta →
  Ghana 9°10N 1°15W **263** D4
Volta Redonda *Brazil* 22°31S 44°5W **333** F3
Voltaire, C. *Australia* 14°16S 125°35E **278** B4
Volterra *Italy* 43°24N 10°51E **198** E7
Voltri *Italy* 44°26N 8°45E **198** D5
Volturno → *Italy* 41°1N 13°55E **200** A6
Volubilis *Morocco* 34°2N 5°33W **264** B3
Volvi, L. *Greece* 40°40N 23°34E **202** F7
Volyn □ *Ukraine* 51°15N 24°30E **177** C13
Volyně *Czech Rep.* 49°10N 13°53E **180** B6
Volynkina-Derevnya
  Russia 59°53N 30°18E **137** B1
Volžsk *Russia* 55°57N 48°23E **190** C9
Volžhskiy *Russia* 17°30S 177°15E **287** A11
Vomo *Fiji* 17°30S 177°15E **287** A11
Vonavona *Solomon Is.* 8°15S 157°5E **287** M9
Vondelpark *Neths.* 52°21N 4°52E **112** A2
Vondrozo *Madag.* 22°49S 47°20E **272** C2
Vonitsa *Greece* 38°55N 20°52E **207** B2
Vopnafjörður *Iceland* 65°45N 14°50W **155** B12
Vorarlberg □ *Austria* 47°20N 10°0E **180** D2
Voras Oros *Greece* 55°39N 9°6E **163** J3
Vorbasse *Denmark* 55°39N 9°6E **163** J3
Vorchdorf *Austria* 48°0N 13°55E **180** D6
Vorderrhein → *Switz.* 46°49N 9°25E **179** J5
Vordingborg *Denmark* 55°0N 11°54E **163** J6
Vorë *Albania* 41°23N 19°40E **202** E3
Voreppe *France* 45°18N 5°39E **175** C9
Vori *Greece* 34°48N 24°27E **205** E7
Vorios Evvoikos Kolpos
  Greece 38°45N 23°15E **204** C5
Vorkuta *Russia* 67°48N 64°20E **186** A11
Vorma → *Norway* 60°9N 11°27E **164** D8
Vormsi *Estonia* 59°1N 23°13E **188** C2
Vorona → *Russia* 51°40N 41°30E **190** E6
Voronezh *Russia* 51°40N 39°10E **190** G10
Voronezh □ *Russia* 51°47N 39°28E **189** G7
Voronezh *Ukraine* 51°30N 39°30E **190** E4
Voronezh → *Russia* 51°40N 39°10E **190** G10
Vorontsovo-Aleksandrovskoye =
  Zelenokumsk *Russia* 44°24N 44°0E **191** H6
Voroshilov = Ussuriysk
  Russia 43°48N 131°59E **220** C5
Voroshilovgrad = Luhansk
  Ukraine 48°38N 39°15E **189** H10
Voroshilovsk = Alchevsk
  Ukraine 48°30N 38°45E **189** H10

Voroshilovsk = Stavropol
  Russia 45°5N 42°0E **191** H6
Vorpommersche
  Boddenlandschaft △
  Germany 54°25N 12°32E **178** A8
Vorskla → *Ukraine* 48°50N 34°10E **189** H8
Võrts järv *Estonia* 58°16N 26°3E **188** C4
Võru *Estonia* 57°48N 26°54E **188** D4
Vösendorf *Austria* 48°7N 16°20E **142** B2
Vosges *France* 48°20N 7°10E **173** D13
Vosges □ *France* 48°12N 6°20E **173** D13
Vosges du Nord △ *France* 49°0N 7°30E **173** D14
Voskopojë *Albania* 40°38N 20°33E **202** F4
Voskresensk *Russia* 55°19N 38°43E **188** D10
Voskresenskoye *Russia* 56°51N 45°30E **190** B7
Voss *Norway* 60°38N 6°26E **164** D3
Vostok = Neftegorsk
  Russia 44°25N 39°45E **191** H4
Vostok *Antarctica* 78°0S 106°50E **151** D8
Vostok I. *Kiribati* 10°5S 152°23W **289** J12
Votice *Czech Rep.* 49°38N 14°39E **180** B7
Votkinsk *Russia* 57°0N 53°55E **186** C9
Votkinskoye Vdkhr.
  Russia 57°22N 55°12E **186** C10
Votuporanga *Brazil* 20°24S 49°59W **333** F2
Vouga → *Portugal* 40°41N 8°40W **194** E2
Vouillé *France* 46°38N 0°10E **172** F7
Voula *Greece* 37°49N 23°45E **112** C2
Vouliagmeni *Greece* 37°50N 23°46E **112** C2
Voulkaria, L. *Greece* 38°52N 20°50E **207** B2
Voulou *C.A.R.* 8°33N 22°36E **264** A4
Vouxa, Akra *Greece* 35°37N 23°32E **204** D6
Vouzela *Portugal* 4°43N 8°7W **194** E2
Vouziers *France* 49°22N 4°40E **173** C11
Vovchansk *Ukraine* 50°17N 36°58E **189** G9
Vovodo → *C.A.R.* 5°40N 24°21E **264** A4
Vowchyn *Belarus* 52°18N 23°18E **185** F10
Voyageurs □ *U.S.A.* 48°32N 93°0W **308** A7
Voynitsa *Russia* 65°10N 30°20E **160** D24
Voyvozh *Russia* 62°56N 54°56E **214** C6
Vozhe, Ozero *Russia* 60°45N 39°0E **188** B10
Vozhega *Russia* 60°29N 40°12E **188** B11
Voznesensk *Ukraine* 47°35N 31°21E **189** J6
Voznesenye *Russia* 61°0N 35°28E **188** B8
Vrå *Denmark* 57°21N 9°56E **163** G3
Vráble *Slovak Rep.* 48°15N 18°16E **181** C11
Vračevšnica *Serbia* 44°2N 20°34E **202** B4
Vrachneika *Greece* 38°10N 21°40E **204** C3
Vrådal *Norway* 59°20N 8°25E **164** E5
Vranča □ *Romania* 45°50N 26°45E **183** E11
Vrancei, Munții *Romania* 46°0N 26°30E **183** E11
Vrangel *Russia* 42°43N 133°5E **220** C6
Vrangelya, Ostrov *Russia* 71°0N 180°0E **215** B18
Vranica *Bos.-H.* 43°55N 17°50E **182** G2
Vranje *Serbia* 42°34N 21°54E **202** D5
Vranjska Banja *Serbia* 42°34N 22°1E **202** D6
Vranov nad Topľou
  Slovak Rep. 48°53N 21°40E **181** C14
Vransko *Slovenia* 46°17N 14°58E **199** B11
Vransko Jezero *Croatia* 43°53N 15°34E **199** E12
Vrapčiště *Macedonia* 41°50N 20°53E **202** E4
Vratsa *Bulgaria* 43°15N 23°30E **202** C7
Vratsa □ *Bulgaria* 43°15N 23°30E **202** C7
Vråvatn *Norway* 59°20N 8°8E **164** E5
Vrbas *Serbia* 45°40N 19°40E **182** E4
Vrbas → *Bos.-H.* 45°8N 17°29E **182** E2
Vrbnik *Croatia* 45°4N 14°40E **199** C11
Vrbovec *Croatia* 45°53N 16°28E **199** C13
Vrbovsko *Croatia* 45°24N 15°5E **199** C12
Vrchlabí *Czech Rep.* 50°38N 15°37E **180** A8
Vrede *S. Africa* 27°24S 29°6E **271** C4
Vredefort *S. Africa* 27°0S 27°22E **270** C4
Vredehoek *S. Africa* 33°57S 18°25E **118** A1
Vreden *Germany* 52°2N 6°50E **178** C2
Vredenburg *S. Africa* 32°56S 18°0E **270** D2
Vredendal *S. Africa* 31°41S 18°35E **270** D2
Vretstorp *Sweden* 59°1N 14°53E **162** E8
Vrgorac *Croatia* 43°12N 17°20E **199** E14
Vrhnika *Slovenia* 45°58N 14°15E **199** C11
Vriddhachalam *India* 11°30N 79°20E **245** J4
Vridi *Ivory C.* 5°15N 4°3W **262** D4
Vrigstad *Sweden* 57°21N 14°28E **163** G8
Vrindavan *India* 27°37N 77°40E **242** F7
Vrisses *Greece* 35°23N 24°13E **205** D6
Vrnograč *Bos.-H.* 45°10N 15°57E **199** C12
Vrondados *Greece* 38°25N 26°7E **205** C8
Vrpolje *Croatia* 45°13N 18°24E **182** E3
Vršac *Serbia* 45°8N 21°20E **182** E6
Vrsacki Kanal *Serbia* 45°15N 21°0E **182** E5
Vršovice *Czech Rep.* 50°4N 14°28E **135** B2
Vrútky *Slovak Rep.* 49°8N 18°55E **181** B11
Vryburg *S. Africa* 26°55S 24°45E **270** C3
Vryheid *S. Africa* 27°45S 30°47E **271** C5
Vsetín *Czech Rep.* 49°20N 18°0E **181** B11
Vu Liet *Vietnam* 18°43N 105°23E **236** C5
Vúcha → *Bulgaria* 42°0N 24°26E **203** D8
Vučitrn = Vushtrri
  Kosovo 42°49N 20°59E **202** D4
Vuga *South Sudan* 5°21N 29°40E **257** F2
Vukovar *Croatia* 45°21N 18°59E **182** E4
Vuktyl *Russia* 63°52N 57°20E **214** C6
Vulcan *Alta., Canada* 50°25N 113°15W **296** C6
Vulcan *Romania* 45°23N 23°17E **183** E8
Vulcano *Italy* 38°24N 14°58E **201** D7
Vălchedruma *Bulgaria* 43°42N 23°27E **202** C7
Vulkaneshty = Vulcanești
  Moldova 45°41N 28°18E **183** E13
Vunduzi → *Mozam.* 18°56S 34°1E **269** F3
Vung Tau *Vietnam* 10°21N 107°4E **237** G6
Vunidawa *Fiji* 17°50S 178°21E **287** A2
Vunisea *Fiji* 19°3S 178°10E **287** B2
Vuranggo *Solomon Is.* 6°39S 156°38E **287** L9
Vărbitsa *Bulgaria* 42°59N 26°40E **203** D10
Vurshets *Bulgaria* 43°12N 23°16E **202** C7
Vushtrri *Kosovo* 42°49N 20°59E **202** D4
Vutcani *Romania* 46°26N 27°59E **183** D12
Vuzlove *Ukraine* 48°22N 22°24E **182** B7
Vwaza △ *Malawi* 10°58S 33°25E **269** E3
Vyara *India* 21°8N 73°28E **244** D1
Vyartsilya *Russia* 62°8N 30°45E **188** A6
Vyatka = Kirov *Russia* 58°35N 49°40E **186** C8
Vyatka → *Russia* 55°37N 51°28E **190** C10
Vyatskiye Polyany *Russia* 56°14N 51°15E **190** C10
Vyazemskiy *Russia* 47°32N 134°45E **215** E14
Vyazma *Russia* 55°10N 34°15E **188** D8
Vyazniki *Russia* 56°10N 42°10E **190** B6
Vyborg *Russia* 60°43N 28°47E **188** B5
Vyborgskaya Storona
  Russia 59°57N 30°22E **137** B2
Vychegda → *Russia* 61°18N 46°36E **186** B8
Východné Beskydy
  Europe 49°20N 22°0E **181** B15
Vyerkhnyadzvinsk
  Belarus 55°45N 27°58E **188** E4
Vyg-ozero *Russia* 63°47N 34°29E **188** B9
Vyhoda *Ukraine* 48°19N 23°55E **183** B8
Vykhino *Russia* 55°42N 37°50E **129** C3
Vyksa *Russia* 55°19N 42°11E **190** C6
Vylkove *Ukraine* 45°28N 29°32E **183** F14
Vylok *Ukraine* 48°6N 22°52E **183** B7
Vynohradiv *Ukraine* 48°9N 23°2E **183** B7
Vypin *India* 10°10N 76°15E **245** J3
Vyrnwy, L. *U.K.* 52°48N 3°31W **169** E4
Vyšehrad *Czech Rep.* 50°4N 14°25E **135** B2
Vyshkiv *Ukraine* 48°44N 23°39E **183** B8

Vyshkove *Ukraine* 48°3N 23°25E **183** B8
Vyshniy Volochek *Russia* 57°30N 34°30E **188** D8
'Vyshzha = imeni 26 Bakinskikh
  Komissarov
  Turkmenistan 39°22N 54°10E **247** B7
Vyškov *Czech Rep.* 49°17N 17°0E **181** B9
Vysokaye *Belarus* 52°22N 23°29E **185** F10
Vysoké Mýto *Czech Rep.* 49°58N 16°10E **181** B9
Vysokovsk *Russia* 56°22N 36°30E **188** D9
Vyšší Brod *Czech Rep.* 48°37N 14°19E **180** C7
Vytegra *Russia* 61°0N 36°27E **188** B9
Vyzhnytsya *Ukraine* 48°15N 25°11E **183** B10
Vyzhnytsya △ *Ukraine* 48°7N 25°15E **183** B10

W

W du Benin △ *Benin* 11°57N 2°43E **263** C5
W du Burkina Faso △
  Burkina Faso 11°52N 2°50E **263** C5
W du Niger △ *Niger* 13°31N 2°28E **263** C5
W.A.C. Bennett Dam
  Canada 56°2N 122°6W **296** B4
Wa *Ghana* 10°7N 2°25W **262** C4
Waag = Váh → *Slovak Rep.* 47°43N 18°7E **181** C9
Waal → *Neths.* 51°37N 5°0E **170** C5
Waalwijk *Neths.* 51°42N 5°4E **170** C5
Waanyi-Garawa ◎
  Australia 18°2S 137°33E **280** B2
Waat *South Sudan* 8°10N 32°7E **257** F3
Wabag *Papua N. G.* 5°32S 143°40E **286** C2
Wabakimi △ *Canada* 50°43N 89°29W **298** B2
Wabana *Canada* 47°40N 53°0W **299** C9
Wabasca → *Canada* 58°22N 115°20W **296** B5
Wabasca-Desmarais
  Canada 55°57N 113°56W **296** B6
Wabash *U.S.A.* 40°48N 85°49W **311** D11
Wabash → *U.S.A.* 37°48N 88°2W **311** G8
Wabasso *U.S.A.* 27°45N 80°26W **317** M5
Wabawng *Burma* 26°20N 97°25E **241** B6
Wabi → *Ethiopia* 7°45N 40°50E **257** F5
Wabigoon L. *Canada* 49°44N 92°44W **297** D10
Wabowden *Canada* 54°55N 98°38W **297** C9
Wąbrzeźno *Poland* 53°16N 18°57E **185** G5
Wabu Hu *China* 32°20N 116°50E **229** A11
Wabuda I. *Papua N. G.* 8°23S 143°37E **286** E2
Wabuk Pt. *Canada* 55°20N 85°5W **298** A2
Wabush *Canada* 52°55N 66°52W **299** B6
Waccasassa B. *U.S.A.* 29°10N 82°50W **317** F7
Wachau *Austria* 48°21N 15°26E **180** C8
Wąchock *Poland* 51°4N 21°1E **185** H8
Wachtersbach *Germany* 50°14N 9°17E **179** E5
Wacissa *U.S.A.* 30°22N 83°59W **316** E6
Waco *U.S.A.* 31°33N 97°9W **314** F6
Waconichi, L. *Canada* 50°8N 74°0W **298** B5
Wad Banda *Sudan* 13°10N 27°56E **257** E11
Wad al Haddad *Sudan* 13°50N 33°30E **257** E3
Wad en Nau *Sudan* 14°10N 33°34E **257** E3
Wad Hamid *Sudan* 16°30N 32°45E **257** D3
Wad Medani *Sudan* 14°28N 33°30E **257** E3
Wad Thana *Pakistan* 27°22N 66°23E **242** F2
Wadai = Ouaddaï □ *Chad* 13°0N 21°0E **259** F4
Wadala *India* 19°1N 72°51E **130** A2
Wadayama *Japan* 35°19N 134°52E **222** B6
Wadbilliga △ *Australia* 36°25S 149°35E **283** C8
Waddān *Libya* 29°9N 16°10E **258** C3
Waddeneilanden *Neths.* 53°25N 5°10E **170** A5
Waddenzee *Neths.* 53°6N 5°10E **170** A5
Waddingham *U.S.A.* 44°52N 75°12W **313** B9
Waddington, Mt.
  Canada 51°23N 125°15W **296** C3
Waddy Pt. *Australia* 24°58S 153°21E **281** C5
Wadebridge *U.K.* 50°31N 4°51W **169** G3
Wadena *Sask., Canada* 51°57N 103°47W **297** C8
Wadena *Minn., U.S.A.* 46°26N 95°8W **308** B6
Wädenswil *Switz.* 47°14N 8°40E **179** F4
Wadern *Germany* 49°32N 6°53E **179** F2
Wadeye *Australia* 14°28S 129°52E **278** B4
Wadgaon *India* 18°44N 73°39E **244** E1
Wadhams *Canada* 51°30N 127°30W **296** C3
Wadhwan *India* 22°42N 71°41E **242** H4
Wadi *India* 17°4N 76°59E **244** F3
Wadi, Chappal *Nigeria* 7°2N 11°43E **263** D7
Wadi al-Arayis *West Bank* 31°43N 35°15E **123** B2
Wādī al Ḥayāt □ *Libya* 26°26N 12°30E **258** C2
Wādī as Sīr *Jordan* 31°56N 35°49E **251** G6
Wadi ash Shāṭi □ *Libya* 27°42N 13°37E **258** C2
Wādī Feirân *Egypt* 28°42N 33°19E **251** K4
Wādī Fira □ *Chad* 15°0N 21°0E **259** F4
Wad Fukin *West Bank* 31°42N 35°7E **123** B1
Wādī Gemāl, I. *Egypt* 24°39N 35°8E **256** C3
Wadi Halfa *Sudan* 21°53N 31°19E **256** C3
Wādī Mūsā *Jordan* 30°19N 35°29E **251** H6
Wādī Rum △ *Jordan* 29°30N 35°20E **251** J6
Wadian *China* 32°42N 112°29E **229** A9
Wadlew *Poland* 51°31N 19°23E **185** G6
Wadley *Ala., U.S.A.* 33°7N 85°34W **316** B4
Wadley *Ga., U.S.A.* 32°52N 82°24W **316** C7
Wadowice *Poland* 49°52N 19°30E **185** A6
Wadsworth *Nev., U.S.A.* 39°38N 119°17W **304** A4
Wadsworth *Ohio, U.S.A.* 41°1N 81°44W **312** E3
Waduk Pluit *Indonesia* 6°6S 106°46E **122** A1
Waegwan *S. Korea* 35°59N 128°23E **224** E4
Wafangdian *China* 39°38N 121°58E **227** E11
Wafania
  Dem. Rep. of the Congo 1°23S 20°22E **264** C4
Wafrah *Kuwait* 28°33N 47°56E **246** D5
Wagadugu = Ouagadougou
  Burkina Faso 12°25N 1°30W **263** C4
Wagait △ *Australia* 13°1S 130°5E **278** B5
Wageima = Wakema
  Burma 16°30N 95°11E **241** G5
Wagener *U.S.A.* 33°39N 81°22W **316** B8
Wageningen *Neths.* 51°58N 5°40E **170** C5
Wageningen *Suriname* 5°50N 56°50W **329** B6
Wager B. *Canada* 65°26N 88°40W **295** C14
Wagga Wagga *Australia* 35°7S 147°24E **283** C7
Waggaman *U.S.A.* 29°55N 90°12W **131** B1
Waghai *India* 20°46N 73°29E **244** D1
Waghete *Indonesia* 4°10S 135°50E **231** E9
Wagin *Australia* 33°17S 117°25E **279** F2
Wagner *U.S.A.* 43°5N 98°18W **308** D4
Wagon Mound *U.S.A.* 36°1N 104°42W **305** H11
Wagowiec *Poland* 52°48N 17°11E **185** F4
Wah *Pakistan* 33°45N 72°40E **242** C5
Wah Fu *China* 22°15N 114°8E **122** B1
Wahai *Indonesia* 2°48S 129°35E **231** E7
Waharoa *N.Z.* 37°46S 175°45E **284** D4
Wahda = Unity □
  South Sudan 8°30N 30°0E **257** F3
Wahda *Iraq* 33°18N 44°28E **251** C5
Wahiawā *U.S.A.* 21°30N 158°2W **302** K13
Wahiawā District
  U.S.A. 21°31N 157°58W **302** J14
Wahiawā Res. *U.S.A.* 21°30N 158°3W **302** K13
Wahībah, Ramlat al
  Oman 21°15N 58°45E **249** E1
Wābid *Egypt* 30°48N 32°21E **251** H3
Wahni *Ethiopia* 12°40N 36°31E **257** E4
Wahoo *U.S.A.* 41°13N 96°37W **308** E6
Wahpeton *U.S.A.* 46°16N 96°36W **308** B5
Währing *Austria* 48°14N 16°20E **142** A2

Wahx, Ras il- *Malta* 35°56N 14°20E **206** F7
Wai *India* 17°56N 73°57E **244** F1
Wai'ale'ale *U.S.A.* 22°4N 159°30W **302** A2
Waki = *Mima Japan* 34°4N 134°9E **222** C6
Wakkanai *Japan* 45°28N 141°35E **220** B10
Wakkerstroom *S. Africa* 27°24S 30°10E **271** C5
Wakool *Australia* 35°5S 143°33E **282** C5
Wakool → *Australia* 35°5S 143°33E **282** C5
Wakre *Indonesia* 0°19S 131°5E **231** E8
Waku *Papua N. G.* 6°5S 149°9E **286** C6
Wakuach, L. *Canada* 55°34N 67°32W **299** A6
Wakulla *U.S.A.* 30°14N 84°14W **316** E5
Wakunai *Papua N. G.* 5°52S 155°13E **286** C6
Wakurawang *Australia* 33°0N 118°34E **283** B9
Walagunya ◎ *Australia* 23°10S 120°50E **278** D3
Walalmba *Zambia* 13°30S 28°42E **269** E2
Walbury Hill *U.K.* 51°21N 1°28W **169** F6
Walcha *Australia* 30°55S 151°31E **283** B8
Walcheren *Neths.* 51°30N 3°35E **170** C3
Walcott *U.S.A.* 41°46N 106°51W **304** F10
Walcz *Poland* 53°17N 16°27E **185** E3
Waldbröl *Germany* 50°52N 7°37E **178** E3
Waldburg Ra. *Australia* 24°40S 117°35E **278** D2
Waldeck *Germany* 51°12N 9°4E **178** D5
Walden *Colo., U.S.A.* 40°44N 106°17W **304** F10
Walden *N.Y., U.S.A.* 41°34N 74°11W **313** E10
Waldenburg = Wałbrzych
  Poland 50°45N 16°18E **185** H3
Waldesruh *Germany* 52°28N 13°37E **115** B4
Waldkirch *Germany* 48°5N 7°58E **179** G3
Waldkirchen *Germany* 48°44N 13°37E **179** G9
Waldkraiburg *Germany* 48°11N 12°24E **179** G8
Waldo *U.S.A.* 29°48N 82°10W **316** F7
Waldperlach *Germany* 48°4N 11°40E **131** B3
Waldport *U.S.A.* 44°26N 124°4W **304** D1
Waldron *U.S.A.* 34°54N 94°5W **314** D7
Waldtrudering *Germany* 48°6N 11°42E **131** B3
Waldviertel *Austria* 48°30N 15°0E **180** C8
Walebing *Australia* 30°41S 116°13E **279** F2
Walembele *Ghana* 10°30N 1°58W **262** C4
Walensee *Switz.* 47°7N 9°13E **179** F4
Wales □ *U.K.* 52°19N 4°43W **169** E3
Wales *U.S.A.* 52°19N 4°43W **169** E3
Wales I. *Canada* 68°1N 86°40W **295** D14
Walewale *Ghana* 10°21N 0°52W **262** C4
Walgett *Australia* 30°0S 148°5E **281** E4
Walgreen Coast
  Antarctica 75°15S 105°0W **151** D15
Walhalla *Australia* 37°56S 146°29E **283** C7
Walis I. *Papua N. G.* 3°14S 143°18E **286** B2
Walker *S. Africa* 42°58S 85°46W **311** B11
Walker *Minn., U.S.A.* 47°6N 94°35W **308** B6
Walker, L. *Canada* 50°20N 67°11W **299** B6
Walker L. *Man., Canada* 54°42N 95°57W **297** C9
Walker L. *Nev., U.S.A.* 38°42N 118°43W **304** G7
Walkerston *Australia* 21°11S 149°8E **280** b
Walkerton *Canada* 44°10N 81°10W **312** B3
Walkerton *Ind., U.S.A.* 41°28N 86°29W **311** C10
Walkinshaw *Ireland* 53°19N 6°20W **120** B1
Wall *U.S.A.* 44°0N 102°8W **308** C2
Wall Street *New York, U.S.A.* **132** f1
Walla Walla *N.S.W.,
  Australia* 35°45S 146°54E **283** C7
Walla Walla *Wash.,
  U.S.A.* 46°4N 118°20W **304** D4
Wallabout Bay *New York, U.S.A.* **132** f2
Wallace *Idaho, U.S.A.* 47°28N 115°56W **304** C6
Wallace *N.C., U.S.A.* 34°44N 77°59W **315** D16
Wallaceburg *Canada* 42°34N 82°23E **312** D2
Wallacetown *N.Z.* 46°21S 168°19E **285** G2
Wallachia = Valahia
  Romania 44°35N 25°0E **183** F9
Wallal *Australia* 26°32S 146°7E **281** D3
Wallam Cr. → *Australia* 28°40S 147°20E **281** D4
Wallambin, L. *Australia* 30°57S 117°35E **279** F2
Wallan *Australia* 37°26S 144°59E **283** C6
Wallangarra *Australia* 28°56S 151°58E **281** D5
Wallaroo *Australia* 33°56S 137°39E **282** B2
Walldürn *Germany* 49°34N 9°22E **179** F5
Wallenhorst *Germany* 52°21N 8°1E **178** C4
Wallerawang *Australia* 33°25S 150°4E **283** B9
Wallingat △ *Australia* 32°14S 152°25E **283** B10
Wallingford *Conn.,
  U.S.A.* 41°27N 72°50W **313** E12
Wallingford *Vt., U.S.A.* 43°28N 72°58W **313** C12
Wallis & Futuna, Îs. ☐
  Pac. Oc. 13°18S 176°10W **277** E15
Wallowa *U.S.A.* 45°34N 117°32W **304** D5
Wallowa Mts. *U.S.A.* 45°20N 117°30W **304** D5
Walls *U.K.* 60°14N 1°33W **167** A7
Walls of Jerusalem △
  Australia 41°56S 146°15E **281** G4
Wallsend *Australia* 32°55S 151°40E **283** B9
Wallula *U.S.A.* 46°5N 118°54W **304** D4
Wallumbilla *Australia* 26°33S 149°9E **281** D4
Walmsley L. *Canada* 63°25N 108°36W **297** A7
Walney, I. of *U.K.* 54°6N 3°15W **169** C4
Walnut *U.S.A.* 41°33N 89°36W **310** C7
Walnut Canyon △
  U.S.A. 35°15N 111°20W **305** J8
Walnut Creek *U.S.A.* 37°54N 122°4W **306** H4
Walnut Grove *U.S.A.* 34°4N 86°18W **316** A4
Walnut Hill *U.S.A.* 41°23S 174°7E **305** D13
Walnut Ridge *U.S.A.* 36°4N 90°57W **315** C9
Walpeup *Australia* 35°7S 142°2E **282** C5
Walpole *W. Austral.,
  Australia* 34°58S 116°44E **279** F2
Walpole *Mass., U.S.A.* 42°9N 71°15W **313** D13
Walpole-Nornalup △
  Australia 35°0S 116°45E **279** G2
Wals *Austria* 47°47N 12°58E **180** D6
Walsall *U.K.* 52°35N 1°58W **169** E6
Walsenburg *U.S.A.* 37°38N 104°47W **305** H11
Walsh → *Australia* 16°31S 143°42E **280** B3
Walsingham *Canada* 42°40N 80°31W **312** D4
Walsrode *Germany* 52°51N 9°37E **178** C5
Walt Disney Concert Hall
  Los Angeles, U.S.A. **127** b1
Walt Disney World
  U.S.A. 28°22N 81°33W **133** A2
Waltair = Vāc *Hungary* 47°49N 19°10E **181** C10
Waltham *U.S.A.* 17°44N 83°23E **244** F6
Walterboro *U.S.A.* 32°55N 80°40W **316** C9
Walters *U.S.A.* 34°22N 98°19W **314** D5
Walthall *U.S.A.* 33°36N 89°17W **315** J10
Waltershausen *Germany* 50°54N 10°33E **178** E6
Waltershausen Gletscher
  Greenland 73°54N 24°25W **154** C13
Waltham *U.S.A.* 42°23N 71°14W **116** A1
Waltham Forest □ *U.K.* 51°35N 0°0 **125** C3
Walthamstow *U.K.* 51°34N 0°1W **125** C3
Waltman *U.S.A.* 43°4N 107°12W **304** E10
Walton *U.S.A.* 42°10N 75°8W **313** D9
Walton N.Y., U.S.A.* 42°10N 75°8W **313** D9
Walton-on-Thames *U.K.* 51°23N 0°25W **125** D2
Walton-on-the-Naze *U.K.* 51°51N 1°17E **169** F9
Walu *Burma* 22°20N 93°37E **241** H18
Walu *Fiji* 35°59N 147°44E **283** C7
Walvis Bay *Namibia* 23°0S 14°28E **270** A1
Walvisbaai = Walvis Bay
  Namibia 23°0S 14°28E **270** A1
Walwa *Australia* 35°59N 147°44E **283** C7

Wamba *Équateur,
  Dem. Rep. of the Congo* 1°37S 22°30E **264** C4
Wamba *Orientale,
  Dem. Rep. of the Congo* 2°10N 27°57E **268** B2
Wamba *Rift Valley, Kenya* 0°58N 37°19E **268** B4
Wamba *Nigeria* 8°57N 8°42E **263** D6
Wamba →
  Dem. Rep. of the Congo 3°56S 17°12E **265** C3
Wambardi ◎ *Australia* 16°2S 130°55E **278** C5
Wambeek *Belgium* 50°55N 4°3E **116** A3
Wamego *U.S.A.* 39°12N 96°18W **308** F5
Wamena *Indonesia* 4°4S 138°57E **231** E9
Wampana Karlantijpa ◎
  Australia 17°45S 132°10E **278** C5
Wampaya ◎ *Australia* 17°20S 135°0E **280** B2
Wampsville *U.S.A.* 43°4N 75°42W **313** C9
Wamsutter *U.S.A.* 41°40N 107°58W **304** F10
Wamulan *Indonesia* 3°27S 126°7E **231** E7
Wan Chai *China* 22°16N 114°10E **122** B2
Wan Chai Lanes *Hong Kong, China* **122** c2
Wan Hat *Burma* 20°14N 97°53E **241** E6
Wan Kinghao *Burma* 21°34N 98°17E **241** F7
Wan Lai-kam *Burma* 21°21N 98°22E **241** F7
Wan Tup *Burma* 21°13N 98°42E **228** G2
Wan Xian *China* 38°47N 115°7E **226** E8
Wana *Pakistan* 32°20N 69°32E **242** C3
Wanaaring *Australia* 29°38S 144°9E **281** D3
Wanaka *N.Z.* 44°42S 169°9E **285** E4
Wanaka, L. *N.Z.* 44°33S 169°7E **285** E4
Wan'an *China* 26°26N 114°49E **229** D10
Wanapiri *Indonesia* 4°5S 135°50E **231** E9
Wanapitei L. *Canada* 46°45N 80°40W **298** C3
Wanbi *Australia* 34°46S 140°17E **282** B4
Wandai = McKinley Sea
  Arctic 82°0N 0°0 **154** A11
Wanderáma *Ivory C.* 8°37N 4°25W **262** D4
Wandhari *Pakistan* 27°42N 66°48E **242** F2
Wanding *China* 24°5N 98°4E **228** E2
Wandle → *U.K.* 51°27N 0°12W **125** B2
Wandoan *Australia* 26°5S 149°55E **281** D4
Wandsworth □ *U.K.* 51°27N 0°11W **125** B2
Wandur Marine △ *India* 11°30N 92°30E **245** J11
Wanfu *China* 40°8N 122°38E **224** B1
Wang → *Thailand* 17°8N 99°2E **236** D2
Wang Kai *South Sudan* 9°3N 29°23E **257** F2
Wang Noi *Thailand* 14°13N 100°44E **236** E3
Wang Saphung *Thailand* 17°18N 101°46E **236** D3
Wang Thong *Thailand* 16°50N 100°26E **236** D3
Wanga
  Dem. Rep. of the Congo 2°58N 29°12E **268** B2
Wanga *Taiwan* 23°21N 119°29E **225** C1
Wanganella *Australia* 35°6S 144°49E **283** C6
Wanganui *N.Z.* 39°56S 175°3E **284** F4
Wanganui → *N. Coast,
  N.Z.* 43°3S 170°26E **285** D5
Wanganui → *Wanganui-Manawatu,
  N.Z.* 39°55S 175°3E **284** F4
Wangaratta *Australia* 36°21S 146°19E **283** C7
Wangary *Australia* 34°35S 135°29E **281** E2
Wangcang *China* 32°18N 106°20E **228** A6
Wangcheng *China* 28°22N 112°49E **229** D9
Wangcun *China* 36°41N 117°41E **227** F9
Wangdu *China* 38°40N 115°7E **226** E8
Wangdu Phodrang
  Bhutan 27°28N 89°54E **241** B2
Wangen *Germany* 47°41N 9°50E **179** H5
Wangerin = Węgorzyno
  Poland 53°32N 15°33E **184** E2
Wangerooge *Germany* 53°47N 7°54E **178** B3
Wangiwangi *Indonesia* 5°22S 123°37E **231** F6
Wangjiang *China* 30°10N 116°42E **229** B11
Wangjing *China* 40°0N 116°28E **114** B2
Wangkung *Taiwan* 23°57N 120°20E **225** C2
Wangmo *China* 25°1N 106°5E **228** E6
Wangolodougou *Ivory C.* 9°55N 5°10W **262** D3
Wangqing *China* 43°12N 129°42E **227** C15
Wani *India* 20°5N 78°55E **244** D4
Wanigela *Papua N. G.* 9°2S 149°9E **286** E5
Wanimiyn ◎ *Australia* 15°55S 130°49E **278** C5
Wanjina Wunggurr Wilinggin ◎
  Australia 16°0S 127°0E **278** C4
Wanjina *Taiwan* 23°43N 121°25E **225** C2
Wankaner *India* 22°35N 71°0E **242** H4
Wankhede Stadium *Mumbai, India* **130** c2
Wanless *Canada* 54°11N 101°21W **297** C8
Wanleweyne *Somalia* 2°37N 44°54E **267** G3
Wanli *Taiwan* 25°10N 121°41E **225** A3
Wanluan *Taiwan* 22°34N 120°32E **225** D2
Wannian *China* 28°42N 117°4E **229** D11
Wannian *Taiwan* 18°48N 110°22E **236** C8
Wannoo Billabong Roadhouse
  Australia 27°25S 115°49E **279** E2
Wannsee *Germany* 52°25S 13°9E **115** B3
Wanon Niwat *Thailand* 17°38N 103°46E **236** D4
Wanqinsha *China* 22°43N 113°33E **219** a
Wanrong *China* 35°25N 110°50E **226** G6
Wanroij *Neths.* 51°38N 5°52E **111** C5
Wansen = Wiązów
  Poland 50°50N 17°10E **185** H4
Wanshan *China* 27°30N 109°12E **229** D7
Wanshan Qundao *China* 21°57N 113°45E **219** a
Wansheng *China* 28°57N 106°53E **228** C6
Wanstead *N.Z.* 40°8S 176°30E **284** G5
Wanstead *London, U.K.* 51°34N 0°1E **125** C4
Wantage *U.K.* 51°35N 1°25W **169** F6
Wantan *Taiwan* 22°35N 120°29E **225** D2
Wantoulia *Taiwan* 24°1N 120°41E **225** B2
Wanxian *China* 30°42N 108°20E **228** B7
Wanyuan *China* 32°4N 108°3E **228** A7
Wanzai *Guangdong, China* 22°12N 113°33E **219** a
Wanzai *Jiangxi, China* 28°7N 114°30E **229** C10
Wanzai *Jiangxi, China* 40°34N 124°12E **219** C3
Wapakoneta *U.S.A.* 40°34N 84°12W **312** E2
Wapawekka L. *Canada* 54°55N 104°40W **297** C8
Wapato *U.S.A.* 46°27N 120°25W **304** C3
Wapawekka L. *Canada* 54°55N 104°40W **297** C8
Wapikopa L. *Canada* 52°56N 87°53W **298** B2
Wapinda
  Dem. Rep. of the Congo 3°41N 22°48E **264** B4
Wapiti → *Canada* 55°5N 118°18W **296** B5
Wapping *U.K.* 51°30N 0°3W **125** C3
Wappingers Falls *U.S.A.* 41°36N 73°55W **313** E11
Wapsipinicon → *U.S.A.* 41°44N 90°19W **310** C8
Wapusk △ *Canada* 57°46N 93°22W **297** B10
War Galoh *Somalia* 6°17N 47°31E **267** G6
War in the Pacific Nat. Hist. Park ◎
  Guam 13°24N 144°39E **302** d
Warab *South Sudan* 8°8N 28°37E **257** F2
Warabi *Japan* 35°49N 139°41E **232** B3
Waraseoni *India* 21°56S 80°3E **244** D4
Waratah *Australia* 41°30S 145°30E **281** G4
Waratah B. *Australia* 38°54S 146°5E **283** D6
Warba *Germany* 51°26N 9°9E **178** D5
Warburton *Vic., Australia* 37°47S 145°42E **283** D6
Warburton *W. Austral.,
  Australia* 26°8S 126°35E **279** E4
Warburton → *Australia* 28°4S 137°28E **281** D2

Warburton Groove *Australia* 28°18S 137°8E **281** A2
Warburton Ra. *Australia* 25°55S 126°28E **279** E4
Ward *N.Z.* 41°49S 174°11E **285** B9
Ward → *Australia* 26°28S 146°6E **281** D4
Ward Hunt, C. *Papua N. G.* 8°2S 148°10E **286** E6
Ward Hunt Str. *Papua N. G.* 9°30S 150°0E **286** E6
Ward Mt. *U.S.A.* 37°12N 118°54W **306** H8
Wardang I. *Australia* 34°30S 137°20E **282** C2
Warden *S. Africa* 27°50S 29°0E **271** C4
Wardha *India* 20°45N 78°39E **244** D4
Wardha → *India* 19°57N 79°11E **244** E4
Wardija Point *Malta* 36°2N 14°11E **206** E6
Wards I. *U.S.A.* 40°47N 73°55W **132** B2
Wardsville *Canada* 42°39N 81°45W **312** D3
Ware *Herts., U.K.* 51°49N 0°0 **169** F8
Ware *Mass., U.S.A.* 42°16N 72°14W **313** D12
Waregem *Belgium* 50°53N 3°27E **170** D3
Wareham *U.S.A.* 41°46N 70°43W **313** E14
Waremme *Belgium* 50°43N 5°15E **170** D5
Waren *Germany* 53°31N 12°40E **178** B8
Warendorf *Germany* 51°57N 8°1E **178** D4
Waresboro *U.S.A.* 31°15N 82°29W **316** D7
Waria → *Papua N. G.* 7°49S 147°41E **286** D4
Warialda *Australia* 29°29S 150°33E **281** D5
Warin Chamrap *Thailand* 15°12N 104°53E **236** E5
Warka *Poland* 51°47N 21°12E **185** G8
Warkopi *Indonesia* 1°12S 134°9E **231** E8
Warkworth *N.Z.* 36°24S 174°41E **284** C3
Warm Baths = Bela Bela *S. Africa* 24°51S 28°19E **271** B4
Warm Springs *Ga., U.S.A.* 32°53N 84°41W **316** C5
Warm Springs *Nev., U.S.A.* 38°10N 116°20W **305** G5
Warman *Canada* 52°19N 106°30W **297** C7
Warmbad = Bela Bela *S. Africa* 24°51S 28°19E **271** B4
Warmbad *Namibia* 28°25S 18°42E **270** C2
Warming I. = Uunartoq Qeqertoq *Greenland* 71°33N 21°47W **154** C8
Warmińsko-Mazurskie □ *Poland* 54°0N 21°0E **184** D8
Warminster *Wilts., U.K.* 51°12N 2°10W **169** F5
Warminster *Pa., U.S.A.* 40°12N 75°6W **313** F9
Warmun *Australia* 17°2S 128°12E **278** C4
Warnberg *Germany* 48°4N 11°31E **131** B2
Warnemünde *Germany* 54°10N 12°4E **178** A8
Warner Brothers Studios *U.S.A.* 34°9N 118°20W **126** B2
Warner Mts. *U.S.A.* 41°40N 120°15W **304** F3
Warner Robins *U.S.A.* 32°37N 83°36W **316** C6
Warnes *Bolivia* 17°30S 63°10W **331** D5
Warnow → *Germany* 54°6N 12°9E **178** A8
Waroona *Australia* 32°50S 115°58E **279** F2
Warora *India* 20°14N 79°1E **244** D4
Warrabah △ *Australia* 30°31S 150°56E **283** A10
Warrabri ◎ *Australia* 21°1S 134°19E **280** C1
Warracknabeal *Australia* 36°9S 142°26E **282** D5
Warragul *Australia* 38°10S 145°58E **283** E6
Warrâq el 'Arab *Egypt* 30°4N 31°11E **117** A2
Warrego → *Australia* 30°24S 145°21E **281** E4
Warrego Ra. *Australia* 24°58S 146°0E **280** C4
Warren *N.S.W., Australia* 31°42S 147°51E **283** A7
Warren *Ark., U.S.A.* 33°37N 92°4W **314** E8
Warren *Ill., U.S.A.* 42°29N 90°0W **310** B7
Warren *Ind., U.S.A.* 40°41N 85°26W **311** D11
Warren *Mich., U.S.A.* 42°28N 83°1W **311** B13
Warren *Minn., U.S.A.* 48°12N 96°46W **308** A5
Warren *Ohio, U.S.A.* 41°14N 80°49W **312** E4
Warren *Pa., U.S.A.* 41°51N 79°9W **312** E5
Warrenpoint *U.K.* 54°6N 6°15W **166** B5
Warrensburg *Ill., U.S.A.* 39°56N 89°4W **310** E7
Warrensburg *Mo., U.S.A.* 38°46N 93°44W **310** F3
Warrensburg *N.Y., U.S.A.* 43°29N 73°46W **313** C11
Warrenton *Northern Cape, S. Africa* 28°9S 24°47E **270** C3
Warrenton *Ga., U.S.A.* 33°24N 82°40W **316** B7
Warrenton *Mo., U.S.A.* 38°49N 91°9W **310** F5
Warrenton *Oreg., U.S.A.* 46°10N 123°56W **306** D3
Warrenville *U.S.A.* 33°33N 81°48W **316** B8
Warri *Nigeria* 5°30N 5°41E **263** D6
Warringal Park *Australia* 37°45S 145°4E **128** A2
Warrington *N.Z.* 45°43S 170°35E **285** F5
Warrington *Warrington, U.K.* 53°24N 2°35W **168** D5
Warrington *Fla., U.S.A.* 30°23N 87°17W **317** E2
Warrington □ *U.K.* 53°24N 2°35W **168** D5
Warriston *U.K.* 55°58N 3°11W **121** B2
Warrnambool *Australia* 38°25S 142°30E **282** E5
Warroad *U.S.A.* 48°54N 95°19W **308** A6
Warrumbungle △ *Australia* 31°18S 149°1E **283** A8
Warruwi *Australia* 11°36S 133°20E **280** A1
Warsak Dam *Pakistan* 34°11N 71°19E **242** B4
Warsaw = Warszawa *Poland* 52°14N 21°0E **143** B2
Warsaw *Ill., U.S.A.* 40°22N 91°26W **310** D5
Warsaw *Ind., U.S.A.* 41°14N 85°51W **311** C11
Warsaw *Ky., U.S.A.* 38°47N 84°54W **311** F12
Warsaw *Mo., U.S.A.* 38°15N 93°23W **310** F3
Warsaw *N.Y., U.S.A.* 42°45N 78°8W **312** D6
Warsaw *Ohio, U.S.A.* 40°20N 82°0W **312** F3
Warshiikh *Somalia* 2°28N 45°55E **267** D6
Warstein *Germany* 51°26N 8°22E **178** D4
Warszawa *Poland* 52°14N 21°0E **143** B2
Warszawa ✕ **(WAW)** *Poland* 52°9N 20°59E **143** B1
Warta *Poland* 51°43N 18°38E **185** G5
Warta → *Poland* 52°35N 14°39E **185** F1
Wartenberg *Germany* 52°34N 13°31E **115** A4
Wartenburg = Barczewo *Poland* 53°50N 20°42E **184** E7
Warthbrücken = Koło *Poland* 52°14N 18°40E **185** F5
Warthe = Warta → *Poland* 52°35N 14°39E **185** F1
Warthen *U.S.A.* 33°6N 82°48W **316** B7
Warthenau = Zawiercie *Poland* 50°30N 19°24E **185** H6
Waru *Indonesia* 3°30S 130°36E **231** E8
Warud *India* 21°30N 78°16E **244** D4
Warumungu ◎ *Australia* 19°15S 134°44E **280** B1
Warwick *Queens., Australia* 28°10S 152°1E **281** D5
Warwick *Warks., U.K.* 52°18N 1°35W **169** E6
Warwick *Ga., U.S.A.* 31°50N 83°57W **316** D6
Warwick *N.Y., U.S.A.* 41°16N 74°22W **313** E10
Warwick *R.I., U.S.A.* 41°42N 71°28W **313** E13
Warwickshire □ *U.K.* 52°14N 1°38W **169** E6
Wasaga Beach *Canada* 44°31N 80°1W **312** B4
Wasagaming *Canada* 50°39N 99°58W **297** C9
Wasatch Ra. *U.S.A.* 40°0N 111°30W **304** F8
Wasbank *S. Africa* 28°15S 30°9E **271** C5
Wasco *Calif., U.S.A.* 35°36N 119°20W **307** K7
Wasco *Oreg., U.S.A.* 45°36N 120°42W **304** D3
Wase *Nigeria* 9°4N 9°54E **263** D6
Waseca *U.S.A.* 44°5N 93°30W **308** C7
Wasekamio L. *Canada* 56°45N 108°45W **297** B7
Wasgomuwa △ *Sri Lanka* 7°45N 81°0E **245** L5
Wash, The *U.K.* 52°58N 0°20E **168** E8
Washago *Canada* 44°45N 79°20W **312** B5
Washburn *Ill., U.S.A.* 40°55N 89°17W **310** D7
Washburn *N. Dak., U.S.A.* 47°17N 101°2W **308** B3
Washburn *Wis., U.S.A.* 46°40N 90°54W **308** B8
Washim *India* 20°3N 77°0E **244** D3
Washington *Bonaire* 12°17N 68°23W **322** h
Washington *Tyne & W., U.K.* 54°55N 1°30W **168** C6
Washington *D.C., U.S.A.* 38°53N 77°2W **143** B2
Washington *Ga., U.S.A.* 33°44N 82°44W **316** B7
Washington *Ill., U.S.A.* 40°42N 89°24W **310** D7
Washington *Ind., U.S.A.* 38°40N 87°10W **311** F9
Washington *Iowa, U.S.A.* 41°18N 91°42W **310** C5
Washington *Mo., U.S.A.* 38°33N 91°1W **310** F5
Washington *N.C., U.S.A.* 35°33N 77°3W **315** D16
Washington *N.J., U.S.A.* 40°46N 74°59W **313** F10
Washington *Pa., U.S.A.* 40°10N 80°15W **312** F4
Washington *Utah, U.S.A.* 37°8N 113°31W **305** H7
Washington □ *U.S.A.* 47°30N 120°30W **304** C3
Washington, Mt. *U.S.A.* 44°16N 71°18W **313** B13
Washington Court House *U.S.A.* 39°32N 83°26W **311** E13
Washington Heights *U.S.A.* 40°51N 73°56W **132** A2
Washington I. *U.S.A.* 45°23N 86°54W **308** C10
Washington Land *Greenland* 80°30N 66°0W **154** A4
Washington Monument *Washington, D.C., U.S.A.* **143** b1
Washington Park *U.S.A.* 41°47N 87°36W **119** C3
Washington Ronald Reagan Nat. ✕ **(DCA)** *U.S.A.* 38°51N 77°2W **143** B2
Washington Slagbaai △ *Bonaire* 12°16N 68°23W **322** h
Washougal *U.S.A.* 45°35N 122°21W **306** E4
Washpool △ *Australia* 29°22S 152°20E **281** D5
Washuk *Pakistan* 27°42N 64°45E **240** D2
Wasian *Indonesia* 1°47S 133°19E **231** E8
Wasilków *Poland* 53°12N 23°13E **185** E10
Wasilla *U.S.A.* 61°35N 149°26W **303** F10
Wasini Marine ⌂ *Kenya* 4°33S 39°14E **268** C4
Wasior *Indonesia* 2°43S 134°30E **231** E8
Wasiri *Indonesia* 7°30S 126°30E **231** F7
Wāsiţ □ *Iraq* 32°50N 45°50E **213** F11
Wasjabo *Suriname* 5°13N 57°11W **329** B6
Waskaganish *Canada* 51°30N 78°40W **298** B4
Waskaiowaka L. *Canada* 56°33N 96°23W **297** B9
Waskesiu Lake *Canada* 53°55N 106°5W **297** C7
Wassaw I. *U.S.A.* 31°53N 80°58W **316** D9
Wassaw Sd. *U.S.A.* 31°55N 80°55W **316** D9
Wasserburg *Germany* 48°3N 12°14E **179** G8
Wasserkuppe *Germany* 50°29N 9°55E **178** E5
Wassy *France* 48°30N 4°58E **173** D11
Wasu *Papua N. G.* 5°58S 147°12E **286** C4
Wasua *Papua N. G.* 8°18S 142°52E **286** E2
Waswanipi *Canada* 49°40N 76°29W **298** C4
Waswanipi, L. *Canada* 49°35N 76°40W **298** C4
Wat Pho *Bangkok, Thailand* **113** b1
Watagans △ *Australia* 33°0S 151°28E **283** B9
Watam *Papua N. G.* 3°55S 144°33E **286** B3
Watampone *Indonesia* 4°29S 120°25E **231** E6
Watamu *Kenya* 3°23S 40°0E **268** C5
Watansoppeng *Indonesia* 4°10S 119°56E **235** C5
Watarrka △ *Australia* 24°20S 131°30E **278** D5
Watee *Solomon Is.* 10°30S 162°2E **287** N12
Watenstadt-Salzgitter = Salzgitter *Germany* 52°9N 10°19E **178** C6
Water of Leith → *U.K.* 55°59N 3°10W **121** B1
Water Park Pt. *Australia* 22°56S 150°47E **280** C5
Water Tower Place *U.S.A.* **119** a2
Water Valley *U.S.A.* 34°10N 89°38W **315** D10
Waterberg Plateau ⌂ *Namibia* 20°25S 17°18E **270** B2
Waterberge *S. Africa* 24°10S 28°0E **271** B4
Waterbury *Conn., U.S.A.* 41°33N 73°3W **313** E11
Waterbury *Vt., U.S.A.* 44°20N 72°46W **313** B12
Waterbury L. *Canada* 58°10N 104°22W **297** B8
Waterdown *Canada* 43°20N 79°53W **312** C5
Wateree → *U.S.A.* 33°45N 80°37W **316** B9
Waterford *Ont., Canada* 42°56N 80°17W **312** D4
Waterford *Waterford, Ireland* 52°15N 7°8W **166** D4
Waterford *Calif., U.S.A.* 37°38N 120°46W **306** H6
Waterford *Mich., U.S.A.* 42°45N 83°32W **311** B13
Waterford *Pa., U.S.A.* 41°57N 79°59W **312** E5
Waterford *Wis., U.S.A.* 42°46N 88°13W **311** B8
Waterford □ *Ireland* 52°10N 7°40W **166** D4
Waterford Harbour *Ireland* 52°8N 6°58W **166** D5
Watergraafsmeer *Neths.* 52°21N 4°56E **112** A2
Waterhen L. *Canada* 52°10N 99°40W **297** C9
Waterland *Neths.* 52°26N 4°58E **112** A2
Waterloo *Belgium* 50°43N 4°25E **116** B2
Waterloo *Ont., Canada* 43°30N 80°32W **312** C4
Waterloo *Qué., Canada* 45°22N 72°32W **313** A12
Waterloo *S. Leone* 8°26N 13°8W **262** D2
Waterloo *Trin. & Tob.* 10°28N 61°28W **323** t
Waterloo *London, U.K.* **125** b4
Waterloo *Ill., U.S.A.* 38°20N 90°9W **310** F6
Waterloo *Ind., U.S.A.* 41°26N 85°1W **311** C11
Waterloo *Iowa, U.S.A.* 42°30N 92°21W **310** B4
Waterloo *N.Y., U.S.A.* 42°54N 76°52W **312** D8
Waterloo *Wis., U.S.A.* 43°11N 88°59W **310** A8
Waterman *U.S.A.* 41°46N 88°47W **311** C8
Watermeal-Boitsfort *Belgium* 50°48N 4°25E **116** B2
Watersmeet *U.S.A.* 46°16N 89°11W **308** B9
Waterton Lakes △ *Canada* 48°45N 115°0W **296** D6
Watertown *Conn., U.S.A.* 41°36N 73°7W **313** E11
Watertown *Fla., U.S.A.* 30°11N 82°36W **316** E7
Watertown *Mass., U.S.A.* 42°22N 71°10W **116** A1
Watertown *N.Y., U.S.A.* 43°59N 75°55W **313** C9
Watertown *S. Dak., U.S.A.* 44°54N 97°7W **308** C5
Watertown *Wis., U.S.A.* 43°12N 88°43W **311** A8
Waterval-Boven = Emgwenya *S. Africa* 25°40S 30°18E **271** C5
Waterville *Qué., Canada* 45°16N 71°54W **313** A13
Waterville *Maine, U.S.A.* 44°33N 69°38W **309** C19
Waterville *N.Y., U.S.A.* 42°56N 75°23W **313** D9
Waterville *Pa., U.S.A.* 41°19N 77°21W **312** E7
Waterville *Wash., U.S.A.* 47°39N 120°4W **304** C3
Watervliet *Mich., U.S.A.* 42°11N 86°18W **311** B10
Watervliet *N.Y., U.S.A.* 42°44N 73°42W **313** D11
Wates *Indonesia* 7°51S 110°10E **235** D4
Watford *Ont., Canada* 42°57N 81°53W **312** D3
Watford *Herts., U.K.* 51°40N 0°24W **169** F7
Watford City *U.S.A.* 47°48N 103°17W **308** B2
Wathaman → *Canada* 57°16N 102°59W **297** B8
Wathaman L. *Canada* 56°58N 103°44W **297** B8
Watheroo *Australia* 30°15S 116°5E **279** F2
Watheroo △ *Australia* 30°19S 115°48E **279** F2
Wating *China* 35°40N 106°38E **226** G4
Watîr, W. → *Egypt* 29°0N 34°40E **251** K5
Watkins Glen *U.S.A.* 42°23N 76°52W **312** D8
Watkinsville *U.S.A.* 33°52N 83°25W **316** B6
Watling I. = San Salvador I. *Bahamas* 24°0N 74°30W **321** B5
Watom I. *Papua N. G.* 4°7S 152°4E **286** C7
Watonga *U.S.A.* 35°51N 98°25W **314** D5
Watrous *Canada* 51°40N 105°25W **297** C7
Watrous *N. Mex., U.S.A.* 35°48N 104°59W **305** J11
Watsa *Dem. Rep. of the Congo* 3°4N 29°30E **268** B2
Watseka *U.S.A.* 40°47N 87°44W **310** D9
Watsi Kenga *Dem. Rep. of the Congo* 0°49S 20°34E **264** C4
Watson *Canada* 52°10N 104°30W **297** C8
Watson Lake *Canada* 60°6N 128°49W **296** A3
Watsonia *Australia* 37°43S 145°6E **128** A2
Watsontown *U.S.A.* 41°5N 76°52W **312** E8
Watsonville *U.S.A.* 36°55N 121°45W **306** J5
Watt Mt. *Dominica* 15°19N 61°19W **323** k
Wattiwarriganna Cr. → *Australia* 28°57S 136°10E **281** D2
Watts *U.S.A.* 33°56N 118°15W **126** C3
Wattwil *Switz.* 47°18N 9°6E **179** H5
Watu *Dem. Rep. of the Congo* 3°18S 20°3E **264** C4
Watuata = Batuata *Indonesia* 6°12S 122°42E **231** F6
Watubela, Kepulauan *Indonesia* 4°28S 131°35E **231** E8
Watubela Is. = Watubela, Kepulauan *Indonesia* 4°28S 131°35E **231** E8
Wau *Papua N. G.* 7°21S 146°47E **286** D4
Wau *South Sudan* 7°45N 28°1E **257** F2
Waubamik *Canada* 45°27N 80°1W **312** A4
Waubay *U.S.A.* 45°20N 97°18W **308** C5
Waubra *Australia* 37°21S 143°39E **282** D5
Wauchope *N.S.W., Australia* 31°28S 152°45E **283** A10
Wauchope *N. Terr., Australia* 20°36S 134°15E **280** C1
Wauchula *U.S.A.* 27°33N 81°49W **317** H8
Waukarlycarly, L. *Australia* 21°18S 121°56E **278** D3
Waukeenah *U.S.A.* 30°25N 83°57W **316** E6
Waukegan *U.S.A.* 42°22N 87°50W **311** B9
Waukesha *U.S.A.* 43°1N 88°14W **311** B8
Waukon *U.S.A.* 43°16N 91°29W **308** D8
Waunakee *U.S.A.* 43°11N 89°27W **310** A7
Waupaca *U.S.A.* 44°21N 89°5W **308** C9
Waupun *U.S.A.* 43°38N 88°44W **308** D9
Waurika *U.S.A.* 34°10N 98°0W **314** D6
Wausau *Fla., U.S.A.* 30°38N 85°35W **316** E4
Wausau *Wis., U.S.A.* 44°58N 89°38W **308** C9
Wauseon *U.S.A.* 41°33N 84°8W **311** C12
Wautoma *U.S.A.* 44°4N 89°18W **308** C9
Wauwatosa *U.S.A.* 43°2N 88°0W **311** A9
Wave Hill = Kalkarindji *Australia* 17°30S 130°47E **278** C5
Wave Rock ⌂ *Australia* 32°26S 118°53E **279** F2
Waveland *U.S.A.* 39°53N 87°3W **311** E9
Waveney → *U.K.* 52°35N 1°39E **169** E9
Waverley *N.S.W., Australia* 33°53S 151°15E **139** B2
Waverley *N.Z.* 39°46S 174°37E **284** F3
Waverley *Gauteng, S. Africa* 26°7S 28°4E **123** A2
Waverley *Mass., U.S.A.* 42°23N 71°10W **116** A1
Waverley Station *Edinburgh, U.K.* **121** b3
Waverly *Ala., U.S.A.* 32°44N 85°35W **316** C4
Waverly *Fla., U.S.A.* 27°59N 81°37W **317** H8
Waverly *Ga., U.S.A.* 31°6N 81°43W **316** D8
Waverly *Ill., U.S.A.* 39°36N 89°57W **310** E7
Waverly *Iowa, U.S.A.* 42°44N 92°29W **310** B4
Waverly *Mo., U.S.A.* 39°13N 93°31W **310** E3
Waverly *N.Y., U.S.A.* 42°1N 76°32W **313** E8
Waverly Hall *U.S.A.* 32°41N 84°44W **316** C5
Wavre *Belgium* 50°43N 4°38E **170** D4
Wâw = Wau *South Sudan* 7°45N 28°1E **257** F2
Waw *Burma* 17°28N 96°41E **241** G6
Wāw al Kabīr *Libya* 25°20N 16°43E **258** C3
Wāw an Nāmūs *Libya* 24°55N 17°46E **258** D3
Wawa *Ont., Canada* 47°59N 84°47W **298** C3
Wawa *Nigeria* 9°54N 4°27E **263** D5
Wawa *Sudan* 20°30N 30°22E **256** C3
Wawanesa *Canada* 49°36N 99°40W **297** D9
Wawasee, L. *U.S.A.* 41°24N 85°42W **311** C11
Wawer *Poland* 52°13N 21°8E **143** B2
Wawoi → *Papua N. G.* 7°48S 143°16E **286** D2
Wawona *U.S.A.* 37°32N 119°39W **306** H7
Wawrzyszew *Poland* 52°17N 20°53E **143** B1
Waxahachie *U.S.A.* 32°24N 96°51W **314** E6
Waxxari *China* 38°42N 87°19E **217** E11
Way, L. *Australia* 26°45S 120°16E **279** E3
Way Kambas △ *Indonesia* 4°54S 105°43E **234** C3
Waya *Fiji* 17°19S 177°10E **287** A1
Waycross *U.S.A.* 31°13N 82°21W **316** D7
Wayi *South Sudan* 5°8N 30°10E **257** F3
Wayland *Mich., U.S.A.* 42°40N 85°39W **311** B11
Wayland *N.Y., U.S.A.* 42°34N 77°35W **312** D7
Wayne *Nebr., U.S.A.* 42°14N 97°1W **308** D5
Wayne *W. Va., U.S.A.* 38°13N 82°27W **309** F12
Wayne City *U.S.A.* 38°21N 88°35W **311** F8
Wayne County, Detroit ✕ **(DTW)** *U.S.A.* 42°13N 83°21W **311** B13
Wayne Lakes *U.S.A.* 40°1N 84°40W **311** D12
Waynesboro *Ga., U.S.A.* 33°6N 82°1W **316** B7
Waynesboro *Miss., U.S.A.* 31°40N 88°39W **315** F10
Waynesboro *Pa., U.S.A.* 39°45N 77°35W **309** F15
Waynesboro *Va., U.S.A.* 38°4N 78°53W **309** F14
Waynesburg *U.S.A.* 39°54N 80°11W **309** F13
Waynesville *Ga., U.S.A.* 31°15N 81°50W **316** D8
Waynesville *Mo., U.S.A.* 37°50N 92°12W **310** G4
Waynesville *N.C., U.S.A.* 35°28N 82°58W **315** D13
Waynesville *Ohio, U.S.A.* 39°32N 84°5W **311** E12
Waynoka *U.S.A.* 36°35N 98°53W **314** C5
Wayside *U.S.A.* 33°43N 83°57W **316** B6
Waza *Afghan.* 33°22N 69°26E **240** B3
Waza △ *Cameroon* 11°15N 14°38E **259** F2
Wazikhwah *Afghan.* 32°11N 68°21E **240** B3
Wāzin *Libya* 31°58N 10°40E **258** B2
Wazirabad *Delhi, India* 28°43N 77°13E **120** A2
Wazirabad *Pakistan* 32°30N 74°8E **242** C6
Waziristan *Pakistan* 33°0N 70°0E **242** C4
Wazīrīya *Iraq* 33°22N 44°23E **113** A2
Wazirpur *India* 28°41N 77°10E **120** A2
Wda → *Poland* 53°25N 18°29E **184** E5
We *Indonesia* 5°51N 95°18E **234** A1
Wé *N. Cal.* 20°55S 167°16E **288** d
Weald, The *U.K.* 51°4N 0°20E **169** F8
Wealdstone *U.K.* 51°35N 0°17W **125** A1
Weam *Papua N. G.* 8°37S 141°8E **286** E1
Wear → *U.K.* 54°55N 1°23W **168** C6
Weatherford *Okla., U.S.A.* 35°32N 98°43W **314** D5
Weatherford *Tex., U.S.A.* 32°46N 97°48W **314** E6
Weaubleau *U.S.A.* 37°54N 93°32W **310** G3
Weaverville *U.S.A.* 40°44N 122°56W **304** F2
Webb City *U.S.A.* 37°9N 94°28W **308** G6
Webequie *Canada* 52°59N 87°21W **298** B2
Weber *N.Z.* 40°24S 176°20E **284** G5
Weber Basin *Indonesia* 6°0S 131°0E **276** B5
Webo = Nyaake *Liberia* 4°52N 7°37W **262** E3
Webster *Mass., U.S.A.* 42°3N 71°53W **313** D13
Webster *N.Y., U.S.A.* 43°13N 77°26W **312** C7
Webster *S. Dak., U.S.A.* 45°20N 97°31W **308** C5
Webster City *U.S.A.* 42°28N 93°49W **310** B3
Webster Springs *U.S.A.* 38°29N 80°25W **309** F13
Webuye *Kenya* 0°37N 34°46E **268** B3
Weda *Indonesia* 0°21N 127°50E **231** D7
Weda, Teluk *Indonesia* 0°20N 128°0E **231** D7
Weddell Abyssal Plain *S. Ocean* 65°0S 20°0W **151** C2
Weddell I. *Falk. Is.* 51°50S 61°0W **153** f
Weddell Sea *Antarctica* 72°30S 40°0W **151** D1
Wedderburn *Australia* 36°26S 143°33E **282** D5
Weddin Mts. △ *Australia* 33°59S 148°0E **283** C8
Wedding *Germany* 52°32N 13°21E **115** A3
Wedel *Germany* 53°34N 9°42E **178** B5
Wedemark *Germany* 52°32N 9°43E **178** C5
Wedgeport *Canada* 43°44N 65°59W **299** D6
Wednesday I. *Australia* 10°31S 142°16E **286** F2
Wedowee *U.S.A.* 33°19N 85°29W **316** B4
Wedza *Zimbabwe* 18°40S 31°33E **269** F3
Wee Waa *Australia* 30°11S 149°26E **281** E4
Weed *U.S.A.* 41°25N 122°23W **304** F2
Weed Heights *U.S.A.* 38°59N 119°13W **306** G7
Weedsport *U.S.A.* 43°2N 76°33W **313** C8
Weedville *U.S.A.* 41°17N 78°30W **312** E6
Weehawken *New York, U.S.A.* **132** b1
Weeki Wachee *U.S.A.* 28°32N 82°35W **317** G7
Weel Shimbirro *Somalia* 2°23N 44°14E **267** D5
Weenen *S. Africa* 28°48S 30°7E **271** C5
Weener *Germany* 53°9N 7°20E **178** B3
Weerribben △ *Neths.* 52°47N 5°58E **170** B5
Weert *Neths.* 51°15N 5°43E **170** C5
Weesp *Neths.* 52°18N 5°2E **112** B3
Wegierska-Górka *Poland* 49°36N 19°7E **185** J6
Wegliniec *Poland* 51°18N 15°10E **185** G2
Węgorzewo *Poland* 54°13N 21°43E **184** D8
Węgorzyno *Poland* 53°32N 15°33E **184** E2
Węgrów *Poland* 52°24N 22°0E **185** F9
Wei He → *Hebei, China* 36°10N 115°45E **226** F8
Wei He → *Shaanxi, China* 34°38N 110°15E **226** G6
Weichang *China* 41°58N 117°49E **227** D9
Weichuan *China* 34°20N 113°59E **226** G7
Weida *Germany* 50°46N 12°2E **178** E8
Weiden *Germany* 49°41N 12°10E **179** F8
Weidling *Austria* 48°17N 16°18E **142** A1
Weidlingbach *Austria* 48°16N 16°15E **142** A1
Weifang *China* 36°44N 119°7E **227** F10
Weihai *China* 37°30N 122°6E **227** F12
Weihui *China* 35°25N 114°3E **226** G8
Weil *Germany* 47°35N 7°37E **179** H3
Weilburg *Germany* 50°28N 8°17E **178** E4
Weilheim *Germany* 47°50N 11°9E **179** H7
Weimar *Germany* 50°58N 11°19E **178** E7
Weinan *China* 34°31N 109°29E **226** G5
Weingarten *Germany* 49°3N 8°31E **179** F4
Weinheim *Germany* 49°32N 8°39E **179** F4
Weining *China* 26°50N 104°17E **228** D5
Weipa *Australia* 12°40S 141°50E **280** A3
Weir → *Queens., Australia* 28°20S 149°50E **281** D4
Weir → *Man., Canada* 56°54N 93°21W **297** B10
Weir, L. *U.S.A.* 29°0N 81°57W **317** F8
Weir River *Canada* 56°49N 94°6W **297** B10
Weirsdale *U.S.A.* 28°59N 81°55W **317** G8
Weirton *U.S.A.* 40°24N 80°35W **312** F4
Weiser *U.S.A.* 44°15N 116°58W **304** D5
Weishan *Shandong, China* 34°47N 117°5E **227** G9
Weishan *Yunnan, China* 25°12N 100°20E **228** E3
Weishan Hu *China* 34°35N 117°14E **227** G9
Weissenburg *Germany* 49°2N 10°58E **179** F6
Weissenfels *Germany* 51°11N 12°0E **178** D7
Weissensee *Germany* 52°33N 13°27E **115** A3
Weisskirchen = Hranice *Czech Rep.* 49°34N 17°45E **181** B10
Weisswasser *Germany* 51°30N 14°36E **178** D10
Weistritz = Bystrzyca → *Dolnośląskie, Poland* 51°12N 16°55E **185** G3
Weistritz = Bystrzyca → *Lubelskie, Poland* 51°21N 22°46E **185** G9
Weitra *Austria* 48°41N 14°54E **180** C7
Weixi *China* 27°10N 99°10E **228** D2
Weixin *China* 27°48N 105°3E **228** D5
Weiyuan *Gansu, China* 35°7N 104°10E **226** G3
Weiyuan *Sichuan, China* 29°35N 104°36E **228** C5
Weiz *Austria* 47°13N 15°39E **180** D8
Weizhou Dao *China* 21°0N 109°5E **228** G7
Wejherowo *Poland* 54°35N 18°12E **184** D5
Wekoewa Pt. *Bonaire* 12°13N 68°24W **322** h
Wekusko L. *Canada* 54°40N 99°50W **297** C9
Welch *U.S.A.* 37°26N 81°35W **309** G13
Welchman Hall *Barbados* 13°11N 59°34W **323** r
Weldya *Ethiopia* 11°50N 39°34E **257** E4
Welega *Ethiopia* 9°25N 34°20E **257** F3
Welford △ *Australia* 25°5S 143°16E **280** D3
Weligama *Sri Lanka* 5°58N 80°25E **245** M5
Welkite *Ethiopia* 8°15N 37°42E **257** F4
Welkom *S. Africa* 28°0S 26°46E **270** C4
Welland *Canada* 43°0N 79°15W **312** D5
Welland → *U.K.* 52°51N 0°5W **169** E7
Wellawaya *Sri Lanka* 6°44N 81°6E **245** L5
Welles Harbor *Midway Is.* 28°13N 177°25W **302** c
Wellesley Hills *U.S.A.* 42°18N 71°16W **116** B1
Wellesley Is. *Australia* 16°42S 139°30E **280** B2
Wellesley Islands ◎ *Australia* 16°32S 139°23E **280** B2
Welling *U.K.* 51°27N 0°6E **125** B4
Wellingborough *U.K.* 52°19N 0°41W **169** E7
Wellington *N.S.W., Australia* 32°35S 148°59E **283** B8
Wellington *Ont., Canada* 43°57N 77°20W **312** C7
Wellington *N.Z.* 41°19S 174°46E **284** H3
Wellington *Western Cape, S. Africa* 33°38S 19°1E **270** D2
Wellington *Somst., U.K.* 50°58N 3°13W **169** G4
Wellington *Telford & Wrekin, U.K.* 52°42N 2°30W **169** E5
Wellington *Colo., U.S.A.* 40°42N 105°0W **304** F11
Wellington *Fla., U.S.A.* 26°39N 80°15W **317** J9
Wellington *Kans., U.S.A.* 37°16N 97°24W **308** G5
Wellington *Mass., U.S.A.* 42°24N 71°5W **116** A2
Wellington *Mo., U.S.A.* 39°8N 93°59W **310** E3
Wellington *Nev., U.S.A.* 38°45N 119°23W **306** G7
Wellington *Ohio, U.S.A.* 41°10N 82°13W **312** E2
Wellington *Tex., U.S.A.* 34°51N 100°13W **314** D4
Wellington □ *N.Z.* 41°0S 175°30E **284** G4
Wellington, I. *Chile* 49°30S 75°0W **336** C2
Wellington, L. *Australia* 38°6S 147°20E **283** E7
Wellington Chan. *Canada* 75°0N 93°0W **295** C13
Wellman *U.S.A.* 41°28N 91°50W **310** C5
Wells *Somst., U.K.* 51°13N 2°39W **169** F5
Wells *Maine, U.S.A.* 43°20N 70°35W **313** C14
Wells *N.Y., U.S.A.* 43°24N 74°17W **313** C10
Wells *Nev., U.S.A.* 41°7N 114°58W **304** F6
Wells, L. *Australia* 26°44S 123°15E **279** E3
Wells, Mt. *Australia* 17°25S 127°8E **278** C4
Wells Fargo Center *Los Angeles, U.S.A.* **127** b1
Wells Gray ⌂ *Canada* 52°30N 120°15W **296** C4
Wells-next-the-Sea *U.K.* 52°57N 0°51E **168** E8
Wells River *U.S.A.* 44°9N 72°4W **313** B12
Wellsboro *U.S.A.* 41°45N 77°18W **312** E7
Wellsburg *U.S.A.* 40°16N 80°37W **312** F4
Wellsford *N.Z.* 36°16S 174°32E **284** C3
Wellston = Warner Robins *U.S.A.* 32°37N 83°36W **316** C6
Wellsville *Mo., U.S.A.* 39°4N 91°34W **310** E5
Wellsville *N.Y., U.S.A.* 42°7N 77°57W **312** D7
Wellsville *Ohio, U.S.A.* 40°36N 80°39W **312** F4
Wellsville *Utah, U.S.A.* 41°38N 111°56W **304** F8
Wellton *U.S.A.* 32°40N 114°8W **305** K6
Welmel, Wabi → *Ethiopia* 5°38N 40°47E **257** F5
Welo *Ethiopia* 11°50N 39°48E **257** E4
Welo *Somalia* 9°25N 48°55E **267** C6
Wels *Austria* 48°9N 14°1E **180** C7
Welshpool *Vic., Australia* 38°42S 146°26E **283** E7
Welshpool *Powys, U.K.* 52°39N 3°8W **169** E4
Weltevreden Park *S. Africa* 26°7S 27°56E **123** A1
Welungen = Wieluń *Poland* 51°15N 18°34E **185** G5
Welwitschia = Khorixas *Namibia* 20°16S 14°59E **270** B1
Welwyn Garden City *U.K.* 51°48N 0°12W **169** F7
Wem *U.K.* 52°52N 2°44W **168** E5
Wembere → *Tanzania* 4°10S 34°15E **268** C3
Wembley *U.K.* 51°33N 0°17W **125** A2
Wemindji *Canada* 53°0N 78°49W **298** B4
Wemmel *Belgium* 50°55N 4°18E **116** A1
Wemmer Pan *S. Africa* 26°13S 28°3E **123** B2
Wemyss *Canada* 44°52N 76°23W **313** B8
Wen Xian *Gansu, China* 32°43N 104°36E **226** H3
Wen Xian *Henan, China* 34°55N 113°5E **226** G7
Wenatchee *U.S.A.* 47°25N 120°19W **304** C3
Wenceslas Square = Vaclavské náměstí *Prague, Czech Rep.* **135** b2
Wenchang *China* 19°38N 110°42E **236** C8
Wencheng *China* 27°46N 120°4E **229** D13
Wenchi *Ghana* 7°46N 2°8W **262** D4
Wenchow = Wenzhou *China* 28°0N 120°38E **229** D13
Wenchuan *China* 31°22N 103°35E **228** B4
Wenden *U.S.A.* 33°49N 113°33W **307** M13
Wendeng *China* 37°15N 122°5E **227** F12
Wendenschloss *Germany* 52°24N 13°35E **115** B4
Wendesi *Indonesia* 2°30S 134°17E **231** E8
Wendo *Ethiopia* 6°40N 38°27E **257** F4
Wendover *U.S.A.* 40°44N 114°2W **304** F6
Weng'an *China* 27°5N 107°25E **228** D6
Wengcheng *China* 24°22N 113°50E **229** E9
Wengen *Switz.* 46°37N 7°55E **173** F14
Wengyuan *China* 24°20N 114°9E **229** E10
Wenling *China* 28°21N 121°20E **229** C13
Wenlock → *Australia* 12°2S 141°55E **286** G1
Wennington *U.K.* 51°30N 0°12E **125** A5
Weno *Pac. Oc.* 7°27N 151°52E **287** T18
Wenona *U.S.A.* 41°3N 89°3W **310** C7
Wenshan *China* 23°20N 104°18E **228** F5
Wenshang *China* 35°45N 116°30E **226** G9
Wenshui *China* 37°26N 112°1E **226** F7
Wensleydale *U.K.* 54°17N 2°0W **168** C6
Wensu *China* 41°15N 80°10E **217** D10
Wensum → *U.K.* 52°40N 1°15E **168** E8
Wentworth *Australia* 34°2S 141°54E **282** C4
Wentzel L. *Canada* 59°2N 114°28W **296** B6
Wentzville *U.S.A.* 38°49N 90°51W **310** F6
Wenut *Indonesia* 3°11S 133°19E **231** E8
Wenxi *China* 35°20N 111°10E **226** G6
Wenzhou *China* 28°0N 120°38E **229** D13
Weott *U.S.A.* 40°20N 123°55W **304** F2
Wepener *S. Africa* 29°42S 27°3E **270** C4
Werda *Botswana* 25°24S 23°15E **270** C3
Werdau *Germany* 50°44N 12°22E **178** E8
Werder *Ethiopia* 6°58N 45°1E **267** C6
Werder *Brandenburg, Germany* 52°23N 12°55E **178** C8
Werdohl *Germany* 51°15N 7°46E **178** D3
Wereilu *Ethiopia* 10°40N 39°28E **257** E4
Weri *Indonesia* 3°10S 132°38E **231** E8
Werneck *Germany* 49°58N 10°5E **179** F6
Werneuchen *Germany* 52°38N 13°44E **115** A5
Wernigerode *Germany* 51°50N 10°47E **178** D6
Werra → *Germany* 51°24N 9°39E **178** D5
Werribee *Australia* 37°54S 144°40E **283** E6
Werrikimbe △ *Australia* 31°11S 152°15E **283** A10
Werrimull *Australia* 34°25S 141°38E **282** C4
Werris Creek *Australia* 31°18S 150°38E **283** A9
Werschetz = Vršac *Serbia* 45°8N 21°20E **182** E6
Wertach → *Germany* 48°22N 10°54E **179** G6
Wertheim *Germany* 49°45N 9°32E **179** F5
Wertingen *Germany* 48°33N 10°41E **179** G6
Wesel *Germany* 51°39N 6°37E **178** D2
Weser → *Germany* 53°36N 8°28E **178** B4
Weser-Ems □ *Germany* 53°0N 7°30E **178** C3
Weserbergland *Germany* 52°12N 9°7E **178** C5
Weserbergland Schaumburg Hameln ⌂ *Germany* 52°8N 9°20E **178** C5
Wesermünde = Bremerhaven *Germany* 53°33N 8°36E **178** B4
Weslaco *U.S.A.* 26°10N 97°58W **314** H6
Weslemkoon L. *Canada* 45°2N 77°25W **312** A7
Wesley *Dominica* 15°33N 61°18W **323** k
Wesleyville *Nfld. & L., Canada* 49°9N 53°33W **299** C9
Wesleyville *Pa., U.S.A.* 42°9N 80°1W **312** D4
Wessel, C. *Australia* 10°59S 136°46E **280** A2
Wessel Is. *Australia* 11°10S 136°45E **280** A2
Wesselburen *Germany* 54°13N 8°54E **178** A4
Wessex *U.K.* 51°0N 2°0W **169** F5
Wessington Springs *U.S.A.* 44°5N 98°34W **308** C4
West *U.S.A.* 31°48N 97°6W **314** F6
West → *U.S.A.* 42°52N 72°33W **313** D12
West Allis *U.S.A.* 43°1N 88°0W **311** B8
West Antarctica *Antarctica* 80°0S 90°0W **151** D15
West Baines → *Australia* 15°38S 129°59E **278** C4
West Bank ■ *Asia* 32°6N 35°13E **251** F6
West Bend *U.S.A.* 43°25N 88°11W **308** D9
West Bengal = Paschimbanga □ *India* 23°0N 88°0E **243** H13
West Berkshire □ *U.K.* 51°25N 1°17W **169** F6
West Beskids = Západné Beskydy *Europe* 49°30N 19°0E **181** B12
West Branch *U.S.A.* 44°17N 84°14W **309** C11
West Branch Susquehanna → *U.S.A.* 40°53N 76°48W **313** F8
West Bromwich *U.K.* 52°32N 1°59W **169** E6
West Burra *U.K.* 60°5N 1°21W **167** A7
West Canada Cr. → *U.S.A.* 43°1N 74°58W **313** C10
West Caroline Basin *Pac. Oc.* 4°0N 138°0E **288** G5
West Carrollton *U.S.A.* 39°40N 84°17W **311** E12
West Chazy *U.S.A.* 44°49N 73°28W **313** B11
West Chester *U.S.A.* 39°58N 75°36W **313** G9
West Chicago *U.S.A.* 41°53N 88°12W **311** C8
West Coast □ *N.Z.* 43°15S 170°10E **285** D5
West Coast ⌂ *Namibia* 21°53S 14°14E **270** B1
West Coast △ *S. Africa* 33°13S 18°0E **270** D2
West Columbia *S.C., U.S.A.* 33°59N 81°4W **316** B8
West Columbia *Tex., U.S.A.* 29°9N 95°39W **314** G7
West Covina *U.S.A.* 34°4N 117°54W **307** L9
West Des Moines *U.S.A.* 41°35N 93°43W **310** C3
West Don → *Canada* 43°44N 79°24W **141** A2
West Drayton *U.K.* 51°30N 0°28W **125** A1
West Dunbartonshire □ *U.K.* 55°59N 4°30W **167** F4
West End *Bahamas* 26°41N 78°58W **320** A4
West End *Boston, U.S.A.* **116** b1
West End Village *Anguilla* 18°10N 63°10W **322** a
West Falkland *Falk. Is.* 51°40S 60°0W **153** f
West Fargo *U.S.A.* 46°52N 96°54W **308** B5
West Fiji Basin *Pac. Oc.* 17°0S 173°0E **288** J9
West Fjord = Vestfjorden *Norway* 67°55N 14°0E **160** C16
West Fork Trinity → *U.S.A.* 32°48N 96°54W **314** E6
West Frankfort *U.S.A.* 37°54N 88°55W **310** G8
West Grand L. *U.S.A.* 45°14N 67°51W **309** C20
West Green *U.S.A.* 31°37N 82°44W **316** D7
West Ham *U.K.* 51°31N 0°1E **125** A4
West Harrow *U.K.* 51°34N 0°21W **125** A1
West Hartford *U.S.A.* 41°45N 72°44W **313** E12
West Haven *U.S.A.* 41°17N 72°57W **313** E12
West Hazleton *U.S.A.* 40°58N 76°0W **313** F9
West Heath *U.K.* 51°29N 0°7E **125** B4
West Hill *Canada* 43°46N 79°10W **141** A3
West Hollywood *U.S.A.* 34°5N 118°21W **126** B2
West Hurley *U.S.A.* 41°59N 74°7W **313** E10
West I. *India* 13°35N 92°54E **245** H11
West Ice Shelf *Antarctica* 67°0S 85°0E **151** C7
West Indies *Cent. Amer.* 15°0N 65°0W **321** D7
West Jefferson *U.S.A.* 39°57N 83°17W **311** E13
West Jordan *U.S.A.* 40°36N 111°56W **304** F8
West Kensington *London, U.K.* **125** c1
West Kilburn *London, U.K.* **125** a1
West Lafayette *U.S.A.* 40°27N 86°55W **311** D10
West Lamma Channel *China* 22°14N 114°4E **122** B1
West Liberty *Iowa, U.S.A.* 41°34N 91°16W **310** C5
West Liberty *Ky., U.S.A.* 37°55N 83°16W **311** G13
West Liberty *Ohio, U.S.A.* 40°15N 83°45W **311** D13
West Linn *U.S.A.* 45°21N 122°36W **306** E4
West Lorne *Canada* 42°36N 81°36W **312** D3
West Los Angeles, Univ. of *U.S.A.* 34°7N 118°23W **126** C2
West Lothian □ *U.K.* 55°54N 3°36W **167** F5
West Lunga → *Zambia* 13°6S 24°39E **265** E4
West Lunga △ *Zambia* 12°49S 24°47E **265** E4
West MacDonnell △ *Australia* 23°38S 132°59E **278** D5
West Mariana Basin *Pac. Oc.* 15°0N 137°0E **288** F5
West Medford *U.S.A.* 42°25N 71°7W **116** A2
West Memphis *U.S.A.* 35°8N 90°10W **315** D9
West Miami *U.S.A.* 25°45N 80°17W **129** D1
West Midlands □ *U.K.* 52°26N 2°0W **169** E6
West Mifflin *U.S.A.* 40°21N 79°52W **312** F5
West Milford *U.S.A.* 41°8N 74°22W **313** E10
West Milton *Ohio, U.S.A.* 39°58N 84°20W **311** E12
West Milton *Pa., U.S.A.* 41°1N 76°50W **312** E8
West Molesey *U.K.* 51°24N 0°22W **125** B1
West Monroe *U.S.A.* 32°31N 92°9W **314** E8
West New Britain □ *Papua N. G.* 5°0S 149°30E **286** C5
West New York *New York, U.S.A.* **132** a1
West Newton *U.S.A.* 40°14N 79°46W **312** F5
West Nicholson *Zimbabwe* 21°2S 29°20E **269** G2
West Odessa *U.S.A.* 31°50N 102°30W **314** F3
West of Twin Peaks *U.S.A.* 37°43N 122°27W **136** B2
West Palm Beach *U.S.A.* 26°43N 80°3W **317** J9
West Palm Beach Canal *U.S.A.* 26°40N 80°15W **317** J9
West Park *Gauteng, S. Africa* 26°9S 27°59E **123** A1
West Park *Fla., U.S.A.* 25°59N 80°12W **129** C2
West Pensacola *U.S.A.* 30°25N 87°16W **317** E2
West Plains *U.S.A.* 36°44N 91°51W **308** G8
West Point *Ga., U.S.A.* 32°53N 85°11W **316** C4
West Point *Iowa, U.S.A.* 40°43N 91°27W **310** D5
West Point *Ky., U.S.A.* 37°59N 85°57W **311** G11
West Point *Miss., U.S.A.* 33°36N 88°39W **315** E10
West Point *N.Y., U.S.A.* 41°24N 73°58W **313** E11
West Point *Nebr., U.S.A.* 41°51N 96°43W **308** E5
West Point *Va., U.S.A.* 37°32N 76°48W **309** G15
West Point L. *U.S.A.* 33°8N 85°0W **316** B4
West Pt. = Ouest, Pte. de l' *Canada* 49°52N 64°40W **299** C7
West Pt. *Australia* 35°1S 135°56E **282** C1
West Ra. *Papua N. G.* 4°15S 141°30E **286** C1
West Road → *Canada* 53°18N 122°53W **296** C4
West Rouge *Canada* 43°48N 79°7W **141** A4
West Roxbury *U.S.A.* 42°16N 71°9W **116** B2
West Rutland *U.S.A.* 43°36N 73°3W **313** C11
West Salem *U.S.A.* 38°31N 88°1W **310** F8
West Schelde = Westerschelde → *Neths.* 51°25N 3°25E **170** C3
West Seneca *U.S.A.* 42°51N 78°48W **312** D6
West Sepik □ *Papua N. G.* 3°30S 142°0E **286** B2
West Siberian Plain *Russia* 62°0N 75°0E **210** B9
West Sussex □ *U.K.* 50°55N 0°30W **169** G7
West Terre Haute *U.S.A.* 39°28N 87°27W **311** E9
West-Terschelling *Neths.* 53°22N 5°13E **170** A5
West Town *U.S.A.* 41°53N 87°42W **119** B2
West Union *Iowa, U.S.A.* 42°57N 91°49W **310** B5
West Union *Ohio, U.S.A.* 38°48N 83°33W **311** F13
West Unity *U.S.A.* 41°35N 84°26W **311** C12
West Valley City *U.S.A.* 40°42N 111°58W **304** F8
West Virginia □ *U.S.A.* 38°45N 80°30W **309** F13
West-Vlaanderen □ *Belgium* 51°0N 3°0E **170** D2
West Walker → *U.S.A.* 38°54N 119°9W **306** G7
West Wharf *Pakistan* 24°49N 66°58E **123** B1
West Wyalong *Australia* 33°56S 147°10E **283** B7
West Yellowstone *U.S.A.* 44°40N 111°6W **304** D8
West Yorkshire □ *U.K.* 53°45N 1°40W **168** D6
Westall, Pt. *Australia* 32°55S 134°4E **281** E1
Westbay *U.S.A.* 30°18N 85°52W **316** E4
Westbourne Green *London, U.K.* **125** a1
Westbrook *U.S.A.* 43°41N 70°22W **309** D18
Westbury *Australia* 41°30S 146°51E **281** G4
Westby *U.S.A.* 48°52N 104°3W **304** B11
Westchester *Calif., U.S.A.* 33°57N 118°23W **126** C2
Westchester *N.Y., U.S.A.* 40°51N 73°51W **132** A2
Westcliff *S. Africa* 26°10S 28°1E **123** B2
Westdene *S. Africa* 26°10S 27°59E **123** B1
Westend *Helsinki, Finland* 60°9N 24°48E **121** C1
Westend *Calif., U.S.A.* 35°42N 117°24W **307** K9
Wester Hailes *U.K.* 55°55N 3°16W **121** B2
Westerham *Germany* 48°3N 11°36E **131** B2
Westerland *Germany* 54°54N 8°17E **178** A4
Westerly *U.S.A.* 41°22N 71°50W **313** E13
Western □ *Ghana* 5°30N 2°30W **262** D4
Western □ *Kenya* 0°30N 34°30E **268** B3
Western □ *Papua N. G.* 7°30S 142°0E **286** D2
Western □ *S. Leone* 8°30N 13°20W **262** D2
Western □ *Zambia* 15°0S 24°4E **265** F4
Western Addition *U.S.A.* 37°47N 122°25W **136** B2
Western Australia □ *Australia* 25°0S 118°0E **279** E2
Western Bahr el Ghazâl □ *South Sudan* 7°30N 25°30E **257** F2
Western Cape □ *S. Africa* 34°0S 20°0E **270** D3
Western Dvina = Daugava → *Latvia* 57°4N 24°3E **188** D3
Western Equatoria □ *South Sudan* 5°0N 30°0E **257** G3
Western Ghats *India* 14°0N 75°0E **245** H2
Western Highlands □ *Papua N. G.* 5°45S 144°30E **286** C3
Western Isles = Eilean Siar □ *U.K.* 57°30N 7°10W **167** D1
Western Sahara ■ *Africa* 25°0N 13°0W **260** D2
Western Samoa = Samoa ■ *Pac. Oc.* 14°0S 172°0W **287** V20
Western Sierra Madre = Madre Occidental, Sierra *Mexico* 27°0N 107°0W **318** B3
Western Wall *Jerusalem* **123** b3
Westernport *U.S.A.* 39°29N 79°3W **309** F14
Westerschelde → *Neths.* 51°25N 3°25E **170** C3
Westerstede *Germany* 53°15N 7°55E **178** B3
Westerwald *Germany* 50°38N 7°56E **178** E3
Westfield *Ill., U.S.A.* 39°27N 88°0W **311** E8
Westfield *Ind., U.S.A.* 40°2N 86°8W **311** D10
Westfield *Mass., U.S.A.* 42°7N 72°45W **313** D12
Westfield *N.Y., U.S.A.* 42°20N 79°35W **312** D5
Westfield *Pa., U.S.A.* 41°55N 77°32W **312** E7
Westgate *La., U.S.A.* 30°0N 90°13W **131** A1
Westgate *Md., U.S.A.* 38°57N 77°6W **143** B2
Westhill *U.K.* 57°9N 2°19W **167** D6
Westhope *U.S.A.* 48°55N 101°1W **308** A3
Westlake *Western Cape, S. Africa* 34°4S 18°26E **118** B1
Westlake *Calif., U.S.A.* 34°4N 118°15W **126** B3
Westlake *Calif., U.S.A.* 37°42N 122°29W **136** B2
Westland *U.S.A.* 42°15N 83°20W **311** B13
Westland △ *N.Z.* 43°16S 170°16E **285** D5
Westland Bight *N.Z.* 42°55S 170°5E **285** C5
Westlock *Canada* 54°9N 113°55W **296** C6
Westmar *Australia* 27°55S 149°44E **281** D4
Westmeath □ *Ireland* 53°33N 7°34W **166** C4
Westminster *London, U.K.* 51°30N 0°7W **125** A3

Westminster Calif., U.S.A. 33°45N 118°0W 307 M8
Westminster Colo., U.S.A. 39°50N 105°2W 304 G11
Westminster Md., U.S.A. 39°34N 76°59W 309 F15
Westmont U.S.A. 40°19N 78°58W 312 F6
Westmorland U.S.A. 33°2N 115°37W 307 M11
Westmount Canada 45°29N 73°35W 130 B2
Weston Ont., Canada 43°42N 79°30W 141 A1
Weston Ohio, U.S.A. 41°21N 83°47W 311 C13
Weston Oreg., U.S.A. 45°49N 118°26W 304 D4
Weston W. Va., U.S.A. 39°2N 80°28W 309 F13
Weston I. Canada 52°33N 79°36W 298 B4
Weston-super-Mare U.K. 51°21N 2°58W 169 F5
Westover U.S.A. 40°45N 78°40W 312 F6
Westphalia U.S.A. 38°26N 92°0W 310 F5
Westport Ont., Canada 44°40N 76°25W 313 B8
Westport Mayo, Ireland 53°48N 9°31W 166 C2
Westport N.Z. 41°46S 171°37E 285 B6
Westport Ind., U.S.A. 39°11N 85°34W 311 E11
Westport N.Y., U.S.A. 44°11N 73°26W 313 B11
Westport Oreg., U.S.A. 46°8N 123°23W 306 D3
Westport Wash., U.S.A. 46°53N 124°6W 306 D2
Westpunt Curaçao 12°22N 69°10W 322 g
Westray Man., Canada 53°36N 101°24W 297 C8
Westray Orkney, U.K. 59°18N 3°0W 167 B5
Westree Canada 47°26N 81°34W 298 C3
Westville Calif., U.S.A. 39°8N 120°42W 306 F6
Westville Fla., U.S.A. 30°46N 85°51W 316 E4
Westville Ill., U.S.A. 40°2N 87°38W 311 D9
Westville Ind., U.S.A. 41°32N 86°54W 311 C10
Westwego U.S.A. 29°54N 90°8W 131 B2
Westwood U.S.A. 40°18N 121°0W 304 F3
Westwood Lake U.S.A. 25°44N 80°23W 317 K9
Westwood Village U.S.A. 34°3N 118°26W 126 B2
Westzaan Neths. 52°28N 4°46E 112 A1
Wetar Indonesia 7°48S 126°30E 231 F7
Wetaskiwin Canada 52°55N 113°24W 296 C6
Wetherby U.K. 53°56N 1°23W 168 D6
Wethersfield U.S.A. 41°42N 72°40W 313 E12
Wetlet Burma 22°20N 95°53E 241 D5
Wetteren Belgium 51°0N 3°53E 170 D3
Wetton S. Africa 34°0S 18°31E 118 B2
Wetumpka U.S.A. 32°32N 86°13W 316 C3
Wetzlar Germany 50°32N 8°31E 178 E4
Wevok U.S.A. 68°53N 166°13W 303 B6
Wewahitchka U.S.A. 30°7N 85°12W 316 E4
Wewak Papua N. G. 3°38S 143°41E 286 B2
Wewoka U.S.A. 35°9N 96°30W 314 D6
Wexford Ont., Canada 43°45N 79°18W 141 A3
Wexford Wexford, Ireland 52°20N 6°28W 166 D5
Wexford □ Ireland 52°20N 6°25W 166 D5
Wexford Harbour Ireland 52°20N 6°25W 166 D5
Weybridge U.K. 51°22N 0°27W 125 B1
Weyburn Canada 49°40N 103°50W 297 D8
Weyer Markt Austria 47°51N 14°40E 180 D7
Weyhe Germany 52°58N 8°49E 178 C4
Weyib → Ethiopia 7°15N 40°15E 257 F5
Weymouth N.S., Canada 44°30N 66°1W 299 D6
Weymouth Dorset, U.K. 50°37N 2°28W 169 G5
Weymouth Mass., U.S.A. 42°13N 70°58W 313 D14
Weymouth, C. Australia 12°37S 143°27E 280 A3
Wezembeek-Oppem Belgium 50°51N 4°29E 116 A2
Wha Ti Canada 63°8N 117°16W 294 E8
Whakaari N.Z. 37°30S 177°13E 284 D6
Whakamaru N.Z. 38°23S 175°50E 284 E4
Whakatane N.Z. 37°57S 177°1E 284 D6
Whakatane → N.Z. 37°57S 177°1E 284 D6
Whale = Baleine → Canada 58°15N 67°40W 299 A6
Whale B. Burma 11°37N 98°38E 237 G2
Whale Cove Canada 62°10N 92°34W 297 A10
Whale Pt. Ascension I. 7°57S 14°18W 153 g
Whale Valley = Hitan, W. el Egypt 29°19N 30°10E 256 J7
Whales, B. of Antarctica 78°0S 160°0W 151 D12
Whalsay U.K. 60°22N 0°59W 167 A8
Whangaehu → N.Z. 40°3S 175°6E 284 G4
Whangamata N.Z. 37°12S 175°53E 284 D4
Whangamomona N.Z. 39°8S 174°44E 284 F3
Whanganui △ N.Z. 39°17S 174°53E 284 F3
Whangaparaoa Pen. N.Z. 36°40S 174°45E 284 C4
Whangarei N.Z. 35°43S 174°21E 284 B3
Whangarei Harb. N.Z. 35°45S 174°28E 284 B3
Whangaroa Harb. N.Z. 35°4S 173°46E 284 B2
Whangaruru Harb. N.Z. 35°24S 174°23E 284 B3
Wharanui N.Z. 41°55S 174°6E 285 B9
Wharekauri = Chatham Is. Pac. Oc. 44°0S 176°40W 285 a
Wharfe → U.K. 53°51N 1°9W 168 D6
Wharfedale U.K. 54°6N 2°1W 168 C5
Wharton N.J., U.S.A. 40°54N 74°35W 313 F10
Wharton Pa., U.S.A. 41°31N 78°1W 312 E6
Wharton Tex., U.S.A. 29°19N 96°6W 314 G6
Wharton Basin Ind. Oc. 22°0S 92°0E 273 F8
Whataroa N.Z. 43°18S 170°24E 285 D5
Whataroa → N.Z. 43°7S 170°16E 285 D5
Whatcom = Bellingham U.S.A. 48°46N 122°29W 306 B4
Wheatfield U.S.A. 41°13N 87°4W 311 C9
Wheatland Calif., U.S.A. 39°1N 121°25W 306 F5
Wheatland Ind., U.S.A. 38°40N 87°19W 311 F9
Wheatland Wyo., U.S.A. 42°3N 104°58W 304 E11
Wheatley Canada 42°6N 82°27W 312 D2
Wheaton Ill., U.S.A. 41°52N 88°6W 311 C8
Wheaton Md., U.S.A. 39°3N 77°3W 309 F15
Wheaton Minn., U.S.A. 45°48N 96°30W 308 C5
Wheelbarrow Pk. U.S.A. 37°26N 116°5W 306 H10
Wheeler Oreg., U.S.A. 45°41N 123°53W 304 D2
Wheeler Tex., U.S.A. 35°27N 100°16W 314 D4
Wheeler → Canada 57°2N 67°13W 299 A6
Wheeler L. U.S.A. 34°48N 87°23W 315 D11
Wheeler Pk. N. Mex., U.S.A. 36°34N 105°25W 305 H11
Wheeler Pk. Nev., U.S.A. 38°57N 114°15W 304 G6
Wheeler Ridge U.S.A. 35°0N 118°57W 307 L8
Wheelersburg U.S.A. 38°44N 82°51W 309 F12
Wheeling U.S.A. 40°4N 80°43W 312 F4
Whernside U.K. 54°14N 2°24W 168 C5
Whiddy I. Ireland 51°41N 9°31W 166 E2
Whim Creek Australia 20°50S 117°49E 278 D2
Whirlwind Reef Papua N. G. 4°42S 148°16E 286 C5
Whiskey Jack L. Canada 58°23N 101°55W 297 B8
Whiskeytown-Shasta-Trinity ⌂ U.S.A. 40°45N 122°15W 304 F2
Whistleduck Cr. → Australia 20°15S 135°18E 280 C2
Whistler Canada 50°7N 122°58W 296 C4
Whitby Ont., Canada 43°52N 78°56W 312 C6
Whitby N. Yorks., U.K. 54°29N 0°37W 168 C7
Whitcombe Pass N.Z. 43°13S 170°55E 285 D5
White → Ark., U.S.A. 33°57N 91°5W 314 E9
White → Ind., U.S.A. 38°25N 87°45W 311 F9
White → S. Dak., U.S.A. 43°42N 99°27W 308 D4
White → Tex., U.S.A. 33°14N 100°56W 314 E4
White → Utah, U.S.A. 40°4N 109°41W 304 F9
White → Vt., U.S.A. 43°37N 72°20W 313 C12
White → Wash., U.S.A. 47°12N 122°15W 306 C4
White, L. Australia 21°9S 128°56E 278 D4
White B. Canada 50°0N 56°35W 299 C8
White Bird U.S.A. 45°46N 116°18W 304 D5
White Butte U.S.A. 46°23N 103°18W 308 B2
White City Fla., U.S.A. 29°53N 85°13W 316 F4
White City Oreg., U.S.A. 42°26N 122°51W 304 E2
White Cliffs Australia 30°50S 143°10E 282 A5
White Cloud Hill = Baiyun Mountain Scenic Area China 23°11N 113°17E 121 A2
White Desert = Es Sahrâ al Beida Egypt 27°50N 28°45E 256 B2
White Hall U.S.A. 39°26N 90°24W 310 E6
White Haven U.S.A. 41°4N 75°47W 313 E9
White Horse, Vale of U.K. 51°37N 1°30W 169 F6
White House, The Washington, D.C., U.S.A. 143 b1
White I. = Whakaari N.Z. 37°30S 177°13E 284 D6
White I. Grenada 12°26N 61°28W 323 q
White L. Ont., Canada 45°18N 76°31W 313 A8
White L. La., U.S.A. 29°44N 92°30W 314 G8
White Lake Canada 45°21N 76°29W 313 A8
White Mountain U.S.A. 64°41N 163°24W 303 D7
White Mountain Peak U.S.A. 37°38N 118°15W 307 H8
White Mountains Nat. Recr. Area ⌂ U.S.A. 65°30N 147°40W 303 D11
White Mts. Alaska, U.S.A. 65°30N 146°30W 303 D11
White Mts. Calif., U.S.A. 37°30N 118°15W 306 H8
White Mts. N.H., U.S.A. 44°15N 71°15W 313 B13
White Mts. △ Australia 20°43S 145°12E 280 C4
White Nile = Nîl el Abyad → Sudan 15°38N 32°31E 257 D3
White Nile Dam = Khazzān Jabal al Awliyā Sudan 15°24N 32°20E 257 D3
White Oak U.S.A. 31°2N 81°43W 316 D8
White Otter L. Canada 49°5N 91°55W 298 C1
White Pass U.S.A. 46°38N 121°24W 306 D5
White Pigeon U.S.A. 41°48N 85°39W 311 C11
White Plains Ga., U.S.A. 33°28N 83°1W 316 B6
White Plains N.Y., U.S.A. 41°2N 73°46W 313 E11
White River Ont., Canada 48°35N 85°20W 298 C2
White River S. Dak., U.S.A. 43°34N 100°45W 308 D3
White Rock B.C., Canada 49°2N 122°48W 306 A4
White Rock N. Mex., U.S.A. 35°50N 106°12W 305 J10
White Russia = Belarus ■ Europe 53°30N 27°0E 177 B14
White Sands ⌂ U.S.A. 32°46N 106°20W 305 K10
White Sea = Beloye More Russia 66°30N 38°0E 186 A6
White Springs U.S.A. 30°20N 82°45W 316 E7
White Sulphur Springs Mont., U.S.A. 46°33N 110°54W 304 C8
White Sulphur Springs W. Va., U.S.A. 37°48N 80°18W 309 G13
White Swan U.S.A. 46°23N 120°44W 306 D6
White Volta → Ghana 9°10N 1°15W 263 D4
Whitechapel U.K. 51°31N 0°3W 125 A3
Whitecliffs N.Z. 43°26S 171°55E 285 D6
Whitecourt Canada 54°10N 115°45W 296 C5
Whiteface Mt. U.S.A. 44°22N 73°54W 313 B11
Whitefield U.S.A. 44°23N 71°37W 313 B13
Whitefish U.S.A. 48°25N 114°20W 304 B6
Whitefish B. U.S.A. 46°40N 84°55W 298 C3
Whitefish Bay U.S.A. 43°6N 87°54W 311 A9
Whitefish L. Canada 62°41N 106°48W 297 A7
Whitefish Pt. U.S.A. 46°45N 84°59W 309 B11
Whitegull, L. = Goélands, L. aux Canada 55°27N 64°17W 299 A7
Whitehall Dublin, Ireland 53°22N 6°16W 120 A2
Whitehall London, U.K. 125 b3
Whitehall Mich., U.S.A. 43°24N 86°21W 308 D10
Whitehall Mont., U.S.A. 45°52N 112°6W 304 D7
Whitehall N.Y., U.S.A. 43°33N 73°24W 313 C11
Whitehall Wis., U.S.A. 44°22N 91°19W 308 C8
Whitehaven U.K. 54°33N 3°35W 168 C4
Whitehorse Canada 60°43N 135°3W 296 A1
Whiteman Ra. Papua N. G. 5°55S 150°0E 286 C6
Whitemark Australia 40°7S 148°3E 281 G4
Whiteplains Liberia 6°28N 10°40W 262 D2
Whiteriver U.S.A. 33°50N 109°58W 305 K9
Whitesand → Canada 60°9N 115°45W 296 A5
Whitesands S. Africa 34°23S 20°50E 270 D3
Whitesboro N.Y., U.S.A. 43°7N 75°18W 313 C9
Whitesboro Tex., U.S.A. 33°39N 96°54W 314 E6
Whiteshell ⌂ Canada 50°0N 95°40W 297 D9
Whiteside, Canal Chile 53°55S 70°15W 336 D2
Whiteville U.S.A. 34°20N 78°42W 315 D15
Whitewater U.S.A. 42°50N 88°44W 311 B8
Whitewater B. U.S.A. 25°15N 81°0W 317 K9
Whitewater Baldy U.S.A. 33°20N 108°39W 305 K9
Whitewater L. Canada 50°50N 89°10W 298 B2
Whitewood Queens., Australia 21°28S 143°30E 280 C3
Whitewood Sask., Canada 50°20N 102°20W 297 C8
Whitfield Australia 36°42S 146°24E 283 D7
Whithorn U.K. 54°44N 4°26W 167 G4
Whitianga N.Z. 36°47S 175°41E 284 C4
Whiting U.S.A. 41°41N 87°30W 311 C9
Whitman U.S.A. 42°5N 70°56W 313 D14
Whitmore Mts. Antarctica 82°35S 104°30W 151 E15
Whitmore Village U.S.A. 21°31N 158°1W 302 J13
Whitney Ont., Canada 45°31N 78°14W 312 A6
Whitney Nev., U.S.A. 36°4N 115°5W 124 B2
Whitney, Mt. U.S.A. 36°35N 118°18W 306 J8
Whitney Point U.S.A. 42°20N 75°58W 313 D9
Whitstable U.K. 51°21N 1°3E 169 F9
Whitsunday I. Australia 20°15S 149°4E 280 b
Whitsunday Islands △ Australia 20°15S 149°0E 280 b
Whittemore U.S.A. 43°4N 94°26W 310 A2
Whittier Alaska, U.S.A. 60°47N 148°41W 303 F10
Whittier Calif., U.S.A. 33°58N 118°2W 126 C4
Whittier Narrows Recreation Area ⌂ U.S.A. 34°2N 118°4W 126 B4
Whittlesea Australia 37°27S 145°9E 283 D6
Whitton U.K. 51°27N 0°21W 125 B1
Wholdaia L. Canada 60°43N 104°20W 297 A8
Whyalla Australia 33°2S 137°30E 282 B2
Wiang Kosai △ Thailand 17°54N 99°29E 236 D2
Wiang Sa Thailand 18°34N 100°45E 236 C3
Wiarton Canada 44°40N 81°10W 312 B3
Wiawso Ghana 6°10N 2°25W 262 D4
Wiay U.K. 57°24N 7°13W 167 D1
Wiązów Poland 50°50N 17°10E 185 H4
Wibaux U.S.A. 46°59N 104°11W 304 C11
Wichabai Guyana 2°57N 59°35W 329 C6
Wichian Buri Thailand 15°39N 101°7E 236 E3
Wichita U.S.A. 37°42N 97°20W 308 G5
Wichita Falls U.S.A. 33°54N 98°30W 314 E5
Wick U.K. 58°26N 3°5W 167 C5
Wickenburg U.S.A. 33°58N 112°44W 305 K7
Wickepin Australia 32°50S 117°30E 279 F2
Wickham Australia 20°42S 117°11E 278 D2
Wickham, C. Australia 39°35S 143°57E 281 F3
Wickliffe U.S.A. 41°36N 81°28W 312 E3
Wicklow Ireland 52°59N 6°3W 166 D5
Wicklow □ Ireland 52°57N 6°25W 166 D5
Wicklow Hd. Ireland 52°58N 6°0W 166 D6
Wicklow Mts. Ireland 52°58N 6°26W 166 C5
Wicklow Mts. △ Ireland 53°6N 6°21W 166 C5
Widawa Poland 51°27N 18°51E 185 G5
Widawka → Poland 51°27N 18°52E 185 G5
Wide B. Papua N. G. 5°5S 152°5E 286 C7
Widgeegoara Cr. → Australia 28°51S 146°34E 281 D4
Widgiemooltha Australia 31°30S 121°34E 279 F3
Widnes U.K. 53°23N 2°45W 168 D5
Wido S. Korea 35°35N 126°17E 224 E3
Więcbork Poland 53°21N 17°30E 185 E4
Wieden Austria 48°11N 16°22E 142 A2
Wiehengebirge = Nördlicher Teutoburger Wald-Wiehengebirge ⌂ Germany 52°18N 8°10E 178 C4
Wiehl Germany 50°56N 7°34E 178 E3
Wiek Germany 54°37N 13°17E 178 A9
Wielbark Poland 53°24N 20°55E 184 E7
Wieleń Poland 52°53N 16°9E 185 F3
Wielichowo Poland 52°7N 16°22E 185 F3
Wieliczka Poland 50°0N 20°5E 185 J7
Wielkopolski △ Poland 52°18N 16°45E 185 F3
Wielkopolskie □ Poland 52°10N 17°30E 185 F4
Wieluń Poland 51°15N 18°34E 185 G5
Wien Austria 48°12N 16°22E 142 A2
Wien-Schwechat ✈ (VIE) Austria 48°7N 16°35E 142 B3
Wiener Neustadt Austria 47°49N 16°16E 181 D9
Wienerberg Austria 48°9N 16°21E 142 B2
Wieprz → Poland 51°34N 21°49E 185 G8
Wieprza → Poland 54°26N 16°25E 184 D3
Wieruszów Poland 51°19N 18°9E 185 G5
Wierzbno Poland 52°11N 21°1E 143 B2
Wiesbaden Germany 50°4N 8°14E 179 E4
Wiesental Germany 49°13N 8°31E 179 F4
Wiesloch Germany 49°18N 8°41E 179 F4
Wiesmoor Germany 53°24N 7°47E 178 B3
Wieżyca Poland 54°14N 18°8E 184 D5
Wigan U.K. 53°33N 2°38W 168 D5
Wiggins Colo., U.S.A. 40°14N 104°4W 304 F11
Wiggins Miss., U.S.A. 30°51N 89°8W 315 F10
Wight, I. of U.K. 50°41N 1°17W 169 G6
Wigierski △ Poland 54°5N 23°5E 184 D10
Wigry, Jezioro Poland 54°2N 23°8E 184 D10
Wigston U.K. 52°35N 1°6W 169 E6
Wigton U.K. 54°50N 3°10W 168 C4
Wigtown U.K. 54°53N 4°27W 167 G4
Wigtown B. U.K. 54°46N 4°15W 167 G4
Wijde Wormer Neths. 52°28N 4°52E 112 A2
Wik and Wikway People ◎ Australia 13°55S 142°28E 280 A3
Wil Switz. 47°28N 9°3E 179 H5
Wilamowice Poland 49°55N 19°9E 185 J6
Wilanów Poland 52°10N 21°4E 143 B2
Wilanówka → Poland 52°13N 21°6E 143 C2
Wilber U.S.A. 40°29N 96°58W 308 E5
Wilberforce Canada 45°2N 78°13W 312 A6
Wilberforce, C. Australia 11°54S 136°35E 280 A2
Wilburton U.S.A. 34°55N 95°19W 314 D7
Wilcannia Australia 31°30S 143°26E 282 A5
Wilcox U.S.A. 41°35N 78°41W 312 E6
Wildbad Germany 48°44N 8°33E 179 G4
Wildcat Cr. → U.S.A. 40°28N 86°52W 311 D10
Wildenschwert = Ústí nad Orlicí Czech Rep. 49°58N 16°24E 181 B9
Wildeshausen Germany 52°54N 8°27E 178 C4
Wildeshauser Geest ⌂ Germany 52°54N 8°30E 178 C4
Wildomar U.S.A. 33°36N 117°16W 307 M9
Wildon Austria 46°52N 15°31E 180 E8
Wildrose U.S.A. 36°14N 117°11W 307 J9
Wilds, The S. Africa 26°10S 28°2E 123 B2
Wildspitze Austria 46°53N 10°53E 180 E3
Wildwood U.S.A. 28°52N 82°2W 317 G7
Wilga → Poland 51°52N 21°18E 185 G8
Wilge → S. Africa 27°3S 28°20E 271 C4
Wilhelm, Mt. Papua N. G. 5°50S 145°1E 286 C3
Wilhelm II Coast Antarctica 68°0S 90°0E 151 C7
Wilhelmina Geb. Suriname 3°50N 56°30W 329 C6
Wilhelmina Top = Trikora, Puncak Indonesia 4°15S 138°45E 231 E9
Wilhelmsburg Austria 48°6N 15°36E 180 C8
Wilhelmshagen Germany 52°26N 13°42E 115 B5
Wilhelmshaven Germany 53°31N 8°7E 178 B4
Wilhelmstal Namibia 21°58S 16°21E 270 B2
Wilis Indonesia 7°51S 111°48E 235 D4
Wilkes-Barre U.S.A. 41°15N 75°53W 313 E9
Wilkes I. Wake I. 19°18N 166°34E 302 b
Wilkes Land Antarctica 69°0S 120°0E 151 D9
Wilket Creek Park Canada 43°43N 79°21W 141 A2
Wilkie Canada 52°27N 108°42W 297 C7
Wilkieston U.K. 55°54N 3°24W 121 B1
Wilkins Ice Shelf Antarctica 70°30S 72°0W 151 C17
Wilkinsburg U.S.A. 40°26N 79°52W 312 F5
Wilkinson Lakes Australia 29°40S 132°39E 279 E5
Will Rogers State Historical Park ⌂ U.S.A. 34°2N 118°30W 126 B1
Willacoochee U.S.A. 31°20N 83°3W 316 D6
Willandra △ Australia 33°12S 145°0E 283 B6
Willandra Creek → Australia 33°22S 145°52E 282 B6
Willapa B. U.S.A. 46°40N 124°0W 306 D3
Willapa Hills U.S.A. 46°35N 123°25W 306 D3
Willard U.S.A. 41°3N 82°44W 312 E2
Willare Bridge Roadhouse Australia 17°43S 123°38E 278 C3
Willaumez Pen. Papua N. G. 5°15S 150°2E 286 C6
Willbriggie Australia 34°28S 146°2E 283 C7
Willbrook Ireland 53°17N 6°16W 120 B2
Willcox U.S.A. 32°15N 109°50W 305 K9
Willemstad Curaçao 12°5N 68°55W 322 g
Willenberg = Wielbark Poland 53°24N 20°55E 184 E7
Willesden U.K. 51°32N 0°15W 125 A2
Willesden Green U.K. 51°32N 0°13W 125 A2
Willi Willi △ Australia 30°57S 152°27E 283 A10
William → Canada 59°8N 109°19W 297 B7
William, Mt. Australia 37°17S 142°35E 282 D5
William 'Bill' Dannelly Res. U.S.A. 32°6N 87°24W 315 E11
William Creek Australia 28°58S 136°22E 281 D2
Williamnagar India 25°31N 90°37E 241 C3
Williams W. Austral., Australia 33°2S 116°52E 279 F2
Williams Ariz., U.S.A. 35°15N 112°11W 305 J7
Williams Calif., U.S.A. 39°9N 122°9W 306 F4
Williams Harbour Canada 52°33N 55°47W 299 B8
Williams Lake Canada 52°10N 122°10W 296 C4
Williamsbridge U.S.A. 40°52N 73°51W 132 A2
Williamsburg Fla., U.S.A. 28°24N 81°26W 133 B2
Williamsburg Iowa, U.S.A. 41°40N 92°1W 310 C4
Williamsburg Ky., U.S.A. 36°44N 84°10W 309 G11
Williamsburg New York, U.S.A. 132 f3
Williamsburg Pa., U.S.A. 40°28N 78°12W 312 F6
Williamsburg Va., U.S.A. 37°16N 76°43W 309 G15
Williamsburg Bridge New York, U.S.A. 132 e2
Williamsfield U.S.A. 40°55N 90°1W 310 D6
Williamson N.Y., U.S.A. 43°14N 77°11W 312 C7
Williamson W. Va., U.S.A. 37°41N 82°17W 309 G12
Williamsport Ind., U.S.A. 40°17N 87°17W 311 D9
Williamsport Pa., U.S.A. 41°15N 77°1W 312 E7
Williamston Mich., U.S.A. 42°41N 84°17W 311 B12
Williamston N.C., U.S.A. 35°51N 77°4W 315 D16
Williamstown Vic., Australia 37°51S 144°52E 128 B1
Williamstown Ky., U.S.A. 38°38N 84°34W 311 F12
Williamstown Mass., U.S.A. 42°43N 73°12W 313 D11
Williamstown N.Y., U.S.A. 43°26N 75°53W 313 C9
Williamsville U.S.A. 39°57N 89°33W 310 E7
Willikies Antigua & B. 17°3N 61°42W 322 b
Willimantic U.S.A. 41°43N 72°13W 313 E12
Willingboro U.S.A. 40°3N 74°54W 309 E16
Willis, L. U.S.A. 28°23N 81°28W 133 B2
Willis Tower U.S.A. 119 c1
Willisburg U.S.A. 37°49N 85°8W 311 G11
Williston Northern Cape, S. Africa 31°20S 20°53E 270 D3
Williston Fla., U.S.A. 29°23N 82°27W 317 F7
Williston N. Dak., U.S.A. 48°9N 103°37W 308 A2
Williston S.C., U.S.A. 33°24N 81°25W 316 B8
Williston L. Canada 56°0N 124°0W 296 B4
Willits U.S.A. 39°25N 123°21W 304 G2
Willmar U.S.A. 45°7N 95°3W 308 C6
Willmore Wilderness ⌂ Canada 53°45N 119°30W 296 C5
Willoughby N.S.W., Australia 33°48S 151°12E 139 A2
Willoughby Ohio, U.S.A. 41°39N 81°24W 312 E3
Willoughby B. Antigua & B. 17°2N 61°44W 322 b
Willow U.S.A. 61°45N 150°3W 303 F10
Willow Bunch Canada 49°20N 105°35W 297 D7
Willow L. Canada 62°10N 119°8W 296 A5
Willow Tree Australia 31°40S 150°45E 283 A9
Willow Wall, The China 42°10N 122°0E 227 C12
Willowdale Ont., Canada 43°46N 79°25W 141 A2
Willowdale La., U.S.A. 30°0N 90°12W 131 A1
Willowick U.S.A. 41°38N 81°28W 312 E3
Willowlake → Canada 62°42N 123°8W 296 A4
Willowmore S. Africa 33°15S 23°30E 270 D3
Willows U.S.A. 39°31N 122°12W 306 F4
Willowvale = Gatyana S. Africa 32°16S 28°31E 271 D4
Wills, L. Australia 21°25S 128°51E 278 D4
Wills Cr. → Australia 22°43S 140°2E 280 C3
Willsboro U.S.A. 44°21N 73°24W 313 B11
Willunga Australia 35°15S 138°30E 282 C3
Wilma U.S.A. 30°9N 84°58W 316 E5
Wilmersdorf Berlin, Germany 115 c1
Wilmette U.S.A. 42°4N 87°42W 119 A2
Wilmington S. Austral., Australia 32°39S 138°7E 282 B3
Wilmington Kent, U.K. 51°25N 0°12E 125 B5
Wilmington Del., U.S.A. 39°45N 75°33W 309 F16
Wilmington Ill., U.S.A. 41°18N 88°9W 311 C8
Wilmington N.C., U.S.A. 34°14N 77°55W 315 D16
Wilmington Ohio, U.S.A. 39°27N 83°50W 311 E13
Wilmington Vt., U.S.A. 42°52N 72°52W 313 D12
Wilmslow U.K. 53°19N 2°13W 168 D5
Wilna = Vilnius Lithuania 54°38N 25°19E 188 E3
Wilpattu △ Sri Lanka 8°20N 79°50E 245 K4
Wilpena Australia 31°31S 138°37E 282 A3
Wilpena Cr. → Australia 31°25S 139°29E 282 A3
Wilsall U.S.A. 45°59N 110°38W 304 D8
Wilson N.C., U.S.A. 35°44N 77°55W 315 D16
Wilson N.Y., U.S.A. 43°19N 78°50W 312 C6
Wilson Pa., U.S.A. 40°41N 75°15W 313 F9
Wilson → Australia 16°48S 128°16E 278 C4
Wilson Bluff Australia 31°41S 129°0E 279 F4
Wilson Inlet Australia 35°0S 117°22E 279 G2
Wilson Str. Solomon Is. 8°0S 156°39E 287 M9
Wilsons Promontory Australia 38°59S 146°23E 283 E7
Wilsons Promontory △ Australia 38°59S 146°23E 283 D7
Wilster Germany 53°55N 9°23E 178 B5
Wilton Iowa, U.S.A. 41°35N 91°1W 310 C5
Wilton N. Dak., U.S.A. 47°10N 100°47W 308 B3
Wilton → Australia 14°45S 134°33E 280 A1
Wilton Manors U.S.A. 26°9N 80°8W 129 B3
Wiltshire □ U.K. 51°18N 1°53W 169 F6
Wiltz Lux. 49°57N 5°55E 170 E5
Wiluna Australia 26°36S 120°14E 279 E3
Wimbledon U.K. 51°25N 0°13W 125 B2
Wimbledon Common U.K. 51°26N 0°14W 125 B2
Wimbledon Park U.K. 51°25N 0°11W 125 B2
Wimbledon Tennis Ground U.K. 51°25N 0°12W 125 B2
Wimborne Minster U.K. 50°48N 1°59W 169 G6
Wimereux France 50°45N 1°37E 173 B8
Wimmera → Australia 36°8S 141°56E 282 D4
Winam G. Kenya 0°20S 34°15E 268 C3
Winamac U.S.A. 41°3N 86°36W 311 C10
Winburg S. Africa 28°30S 27°2E 270 C4
Winchelsea Australia 38°10S 144°1E 282 E6
Winchendon U.S.A. 42°41N 72°3W 313 D12
Winchester N.Z. 44°11S 171°17E 285 E6
Winchester Hants., U.K. 51°4N 1°18W 169 F6
Winchester Conn., U.S.A. 41°53N 73°9W 313 E11
Winchester Idaho, U.S.A. 46°14N 116°38W 304 C5
Winchester Ill., U.S.A. 39°38N 90°27W 310 E6
Winchester Ind., U.S.A. 40°10N 84°59W 311 D12
Winchester Ky., U.S.A. 37°59N 84°11W 311 G12
Winchester Mass., U.S.A. 42°26N 71°8W 116 A2
Winchester N.H., U.S.A. 42°46N 72°23W 313 D12
Winchester Nev., U.S.A. 36°7N 115°7W 124 B2
Winchester Ohio, U.S.A. 38°56N 83°39W 311 F13
Winchester Tenn., U.S.A. 35°11N 86°7W 315 D11
Winchester Va., U.S.A. 39°11N 78°10W 309 F14
Wind → U.S.A. 43°12N 108°12W 304 E9
Wind Cave △ U.S.A. 43°32N 103°17W 308 D2
Wind Point U.S.A. 42°47N 87°46W 311 B9
Wind River Range U.S.A. 43°0N 109°30W 304 E9
Windamere, L. Australia 32°48S 149°51E 283 B8
Windau = Ventspils Latvia 57°25N 21°32E 184 A8
Windber U.S.A. 40°14N 78°50W 312 F6
Winder U.S.A. 34°0N 83°45W 316 A6
Windermere Western Cape, S. Africa 33°55S 18°30E 118 A2
Windermere Cumb., U.K. 54°23N 2°55W 168 C5
Windermere Fla., U.S.A. 28°29N 81°32W 133 B1
Windfall U.S.A. 40°22N 85°57W 311 D11
Windhoek Namibia 22°35S 17°4E 270 B2
Windidda ◎ Australia 26°23S 122°12E 279 E3
Windisch-Feistritz = Slovenska Bistrica Slovenia 46°24N 15°35E 199 B12
Windischgarsten Austria 47°42N 14°21E 180 D7
Windischgratz = Slovenj Gradec Slovenia 46°31N 15°5E 199 B12
Windjana Gorge △ Australia 17°51S 125°0E 278 C3
Windom U.S.A. 43°52N 95°7W 308 D6
Windorah Australia 25°24S 142°36E 280 D3
Window Rock U.S.A. 35°41N 109°3W 305 J9
Windrush → U.K. 51°43N 1°24W 169 F6
Windsor N.S.W., Australia 33°37S 150°50E 283 B9
Windsor N.S., Canada 44°59N 64°5W 299 D7
Windsor Ont., Canada 42°18N 83°0W 312 D2
Windsor N.Z. 44°59S 170°49E 285 E5
Windsor Gauteng, S. Africa 26°7S 27°59E 123 A1
Windsor Windsor & Maidenhead, U.K. 51°29N 0°36W 169 F7
Windsor Calif., U.S.A. 38°33N 122°49W 306 G4
Windsor Colo., U.S.A. 40°29N 104°54W 304 F11
Windsor Conn., U.S.A. 41°50N 72°39W 313 E12
Windsor Ill., U.S.A. 39°26N 88°36W 311 E8
Windsor Mo., U.S.A. 38°32N 93°31W 310 F3
Windsor N.Y., U.S.A. 42°5N 75°37W 313 D9
Windsor Vt., U.S.A. 43°29N 72°24W 313 C12
Windsor, Gare Montréal, Canada 130 c2
Windsor & Maidenhead □ U.K. 51°29N 0°40W 169 F7
Windsor Caves Jamaica 18°21N 77°39W 320 a
Windsor Hills U.S.A. 33°59N 118°22W 126 C2
Windsorton S. Africa 28°16S 24°44E 270 C3
Windward Grenada 12°31N 61°26W 323 q
Windward Is. W. Indies 13°0N 61°0W 321 D7
Windward Passage = Vientos, Paso de los Caribbean 20°0N 74°0W 321 C5
Windward Side Saba 17°38N 63°14W 322 a
Windy Arbour Ireland 53°18N 6°14W 120 B2
Winefred L. Canada 55°30N 110°30W 297 B6
Winejok South Sudan 9°1N 27°30E 257 F2
Winfield Iowa, U.S.A. 41°7N 91°26W 310 C5
Winfield Kans., U.S.A. 37°15N 96°59W 308 G5
Winfield Mo., U.S.A. 39°0N 90°44W 310 F6
Wingate Mts. Australia 14°25S 130°40E 278 B5
Wingellina = Irrunytju Australia 26°3S 128°56E 279 E4
Wingham N.S.W., Australia 31°48S 152°22E 283 A10
Wingham Ont., Canada 43°55N 81°20W 312 C3
Winisk → Canada 55°17N 85°5W 298 A2
Winisk L. Canada 52°55N 87°22W 298 B2
Wink U.S.A. 31°45N 103°9W 314 F3
Winkler Canada 49°10N 97°56W 297 D9
Winklern Austria 46°52N 12°52E 180 E5
Winlock U.S.A. 46°30N 122°56W 306 D4
Winneba Ghana 5°25N 0°36W 263 D4
Winnebago U.S.A. 42°16N 89°15W 310 B7
Winnebago, L. U.S.A. 44°0N 88°26W 308 D9
Winnecke Cr. → Australia 18°35S 131°34E 278 C5
Winnemucca U.S.A. 40°58N 117°44W 304 F5
Winnemucca L. U.S.A. 40°7N 119°21W 304 F4
Winner U.S.A. 43°22N 99°52W 308 D4
Winnetka U.S.A. 42°6N 87°45W 119 A2
Winnett U.S.A. 47°0N 108°21W 304 C9
Winnfield U.S.A. 31°56N 92°38W 314 F8
Winnibigoshish, L. U.S.A. 47°27N 94°13W 308 B6
Winning Germany 48°2N 11°37E 131 B2
Winnipeg Canada 49°54N 97°9W 297 D9
Winnipeg → Canada 50°38N 96°19W 297 C9
Winnipeg, L. Canada 52°0N 97°0W 297 C9
Winnipeg Beach Canada 50°30N 96°58W 297 C9
Winnipegosis Canada 51°39N 99°55W 297 C9
Winnipegosis L. Canada 52°30N 100°0W 297 C9
Winnipesaukee, L. U.S.A. 43°38N 71°21W 313 C13
Winnisquam L. U.S.A. 43°33N 71°31W 313 C13
Winnsboro La., U.S.A. 32°10N 91°43W 314 E9
Winnsboro S.C., U.S.A. 34°23N 81°5W 315 D14
Winnsboro Tex., U.S.A. 32°58N 95°17W 314 E7
Winokapau, L. Canada 53°15N 62°50W 299 B7
Winona Minn., U.S.A. 44°3N 91°39W 308 C8
Winona Miss., U.S.A. 33°29N 89°44W 315 E10
Winooski U.S.A. 44°29N 73°11W 313 B11
Winooski → U.S.A. 44°32N 73°17W 313 B11
Winschoten Neths. 53°9N 7°3E 170 A7
Winsen Germany 53°22N 10°13E 178 B6
Winsford U.K. 53°12N 2°31W 168 D5
Winslow = Bainbridge Island U.S.A. 47°38N 122°32W 306 C4
Winslow Ariz., U.S.A. 35°2N 110°42W 305 J8
Winslow Ind., U.S.A. 38°23N 87°13W 311 F9
Winslow Reef Kiribati 1°36S 174°57W 277 A16
Winsted U.S.A. 41°55N 73°4W 313 E11
Winston-Salem U.S.A. 36°6N 80°15W 315 C14
Winter Garden U.S.A. 28°34N 81°35W 317 G8
Winter Haven U.S.A. 28°1N 81°44W 317 G8
Winter Park U.S.A. 28°36N 81°20W 317 G8
Winterberg Germany 51°11N 8°33E 178 D4
Winterhaven U.S.A. 32°44N 114°38W 307 N12
Winters U.S.A. 38°32N 121°58W 306 G5
Winterset U.S.A. 41°20N 94°1W 310 C3
Wintersville U.S.A. 40°23N 80°42W 312 F4
Winterswijk Neths. 51°58N 6°43E 170 C6
Winterthur Switz. 47°30N 8°44E 179 H4
Winthrop U.S.A. 48°28N 120°10W 304 B3
Winton Queens., Australia 22°24S 143°3E 280 C3
Winton N.Z. 46°8S 168°20E 285 G3
Wintua Vanuatu 16°30S 167°26E 287 F5
Wipper → Germany 51°16N 11°12E 178 D7
Wirlyajarrayi ◎ Australia 21°45S 132°35E 278 D5
Wirraminna Australia 31°12S 136°13E 282 A2
Wirrulla Australia 32°24S 134°31E 281 E1
Wisbech U.K. 52°41N 0°9E 169 E8
Wisconsin □ U.S.A. 44°45N 89°30W 310 B7
Wisconsin → U.S.A. 43°0N 91°15W 310 A5
Wisconsin Rapids U.S.A. 44°23N 89°49W 308 C9
Wisdom U.S.A. 45°37N 113°27W 304 D7
Wiseman U.S.A. 67°25N 150°6W 303 C10
Wishaw U.K. 55°46N 3°54W 167 F5
Wishek U.S.A. 46°16N 99°33W 308 B4
Wisła Poland 49°38N 18°53E 185 J5
Wisła → Poland 54°22N 18°55E 184 D5
Wisłok → Poland 50°13N 22°32E 185 H9
Wisłoka → Poland 50°27N 21°23E 185 H8
Wismar Mecklenburg-Vorpommern, Germany 53°54N 11°29E 178 B7
Wismar Guyana 5°59N 58°18W 329 B6
Wisner U.S.A. 41°59N 96°55W 308 E5
Wissant France 50°52N 1°40E 173 B8
Wissembourg France 49°2N 7°57E 173 C14
Wissous France 48°44N 2°19E 134 B2
Wisznice Poland 51°48N 23°13E 185 G10
Witbank = eMalahleni S. Africa 25°51S 29°14E 271 C4
Witches Gorge = Wu Xia China 31°2N 110°10E 229 B8
Witdraai S. Africa 26°58S 20°48E 270 C3
Witham U.K. 51°48N 0°40E 169 F8
Witham → U.K. 52°59N 0°2W 168 E7
Withernsea U.K. 53°44N 0°1E 168 D8
Withlacoochee → Fla., U.S.A. 30°24N 83°10W 316 E6
Withlacoochee → Fla., U.S.A. 29°0N 82°45W 317 G7
Witjira △ Australia 26°22S 135°37E 281 D2
Witkowo Poland 52°26N 17°45E 185 F4
Witless Bay Canada 47°17N 52°50W 299 C9
Witney U.K. 51°48N 1°28W 169 F6
Witnica Poland 52°40N 14°54E 185 F1
Witnossob → Namibia 23°55S 18°45E 270 C3
Witriver S. Africa 25°20S 31°0E 271 C5
Wittdün Germany 54°38N 8°23E 178 A4
Witte Pan Bonaire 12°3N 68°17W 322 h
Witten Germany 51°26N 7°20E 178 D3
Wittenau Germany 52°35N 13°19E 115 A2
Wittenberge Germany 53°0N 11°45E 178 B7
Wittenburg Germany 53°31N 11°4E 178 B7
Wittenheim France 47°44N 7°20E 173 E14
Wittenoom Australia 22°15S 118°20E 278 D2
Witti, Banjaran Malaysia 5°11N 116°29E 235 A5
Wittingau = Třeboň Czech Rep. 49°1N 14°48E 180 B7
Wittingen Germany 52°44N 10°44E 178 C6
Wittlich Germany 49°59N 6°53E 179 F2
Wittmund Germany 53°34N 7°46E 178 B3
Wittow Germany 54°38N 13°20E 178 A9
Wittstock Germany 53°10N 12°28E 178 B8
Witu Kenya 2°23S 40°26E 268 C5
Witu Is. Papua N. G. 4°50S 149°25E 286 C5
Witvlei Namibia 22°23S 18°32E 270 B2
Witwatersrand, Univ. of S. Africa 26°11S 28°1E 123 B2
Witzenhausen Germany 51°20N 9°51E 178 D5
Wiwon N. Korea 40°54N 126°3E 224 B3
Wixom U.S.A. 42°32N 83°32W 311 B13
Wkra → Poland 52°27N 20°44E 185 F7
Władysławowo Poland 54°48N 18°25E 184 D5
Wleń Poland 51°2N 15°39E 185 G2
Wlingi Indonesia 8°5S 112°25E 235 D4
Włochy Poland 52°12N 20°54E 143 B1
Włocławek Poland 52°40N 19°3E 185 F6
Włodawa Poland 51°33N 23°31E 185 G10
Włoszczowa Poland 50°50N 19°55E 185 H6
Wo Mei China 22°21N 114°15E 122 A2
Wo Yi Hop China 22°23N 114°8E 122 A1
Woburn Ont., Canada 43°46N 79°12W 141 A3
Woburn Mass., U.S.A. 42°29N 71°9W 116 A2
Wodian China 32°50N 112°35E 226 H7
Wodonga Australia 36°5S 146°50E 283 D7
Wodzisław Śląski Poland 50°1N 18°26E 185 H5
Wœrth France 48°57N 7°45E 173 D14
Wohlau = Wołów Poland 51°20N 16°38E 185 G3
Woinbogoin China 32°51N 98°39E 228 A2
Woippy France 49°10N 6°8E 173 C13
Woitape Papua N. G. 8°33S 147°15E 286 E4
Wojcieszow Poland 50°58N 15°55E 185 H2
Wokam Indonesia 5°45S 134°28E 231 F8
Wokha India 26°6N 94°16E 241 B5
Woking U.K. 51°19N 0°34W 169 F7
Wokingham U.K. 51°24N 0°49W 169 F7
Wokingham □ U.K. 51°25N 0°51W 169 F7
Woko △ Australia 31°46S 151°49E 283 A9
Wola Poland 52°14N 20°57E 143 B1
Wolbrom Poland 50°24N 19°45E 185 H6
Wolcottville U.S.A. 41°32N 85°22W 311 C11
Wołczyn Poland 51°1N 18°3E 185 G5
Woldegk Germany 53°27N 13°34E 178 B9
Woldenberg = Dobiegniew Poland 52°59N 15°45E 185 F2
Woldenberg Park New Orleans, U.S.A. 131 b3
Wolf → Canada 60°17N 132°33W 296 A2
Wolf, Volcán Ecuador 0°2N 91°20W 330 a
Wolf Creek U.S.A. 47°0N 112°4W 304 C7
Wolf L. Canada 60°24N 131°40W 296 A2
Wolf Point U.S.A. 48°5N 105°39W 304 B11
Wolfe Creek Crater △ Australia 19°10S 127°47E 278 C4
Wolfe I. Canada 44°7N 76°20W 313 B8
Wolfeboro U.S.A. 43°35N 71°13W 313 C13
Wolfen Germany 51°39N 12°15E 178 D8
Wolfenbüttel Germany 52°10N 10°33E 178 C6
Wolfratshausen Germany 47°54N 11°24E 179 H7
Wolfsberg Austria 46°50N 14°52E 180 E7
Wolfsburg Germany 52°25N 10°48E 178 C6
Wolgast Germany 54°3N 13°44E 178 A9
Wolgok S. Korea 37°35N 127°1E 137 B2
Wolhusen Switz. 47°4N 8°4E 179 H4
Wolica Poland 52°7N 20°51E 143 C1
Wolin Poland 53°50N 14°37E 184 E1
Woliński △ Poland 53°57N 14°28E 184 E1
Wollaston U.S.A. 42°15N 71°2W 116 B2
Wollaston, Is. Chile 55°40S 67°30W 336 E3
Wollaston Forland Greenland 74°25N 19°40W 154 C9
Wollaston L. Canada 58°7N 103°10W 297 B8
Wollaston Lake Canada 58°3N 103°33W 297 B8
Wollaston Pen. Canada 69°30N 115°0W 294 D9
Wollemi △ Australia 33°0S 150°30E 283 B9
Wollongong Australia 34°25S 150°54E 283 C9
Wolmar = Valmiera Latvia 57°37N 25°29E 188 D3
Wolmaransstad S. Africa 27°12S 25°59E 270 C4
Wolmirstedt Germany 52°14N 11°37E 178 C7
Wołomin Poland 52°19N 21°15E 185 F8
Wołów Poland 51°20N 16°38E 185 G3
Wolseley S. Austral., Australia 36°23S 140°54E 282 D4
Wolseley Western Cape, S. Africa 33°26S 19°7E 270 D2
Wolsey U.S.A. 44°25N 98°28W 308 C4
Wolstenholme, C. Canada 62°35N 77°30W 292 C12
Wolsztyn Poland 52°8N 16°5E 185 F3
Woltersdorf Germany 52°27N 13°44E 115 B5
Woluwe-St-Lambert Belgium 50°50N 4°24E 116 A2
Woluwe-St-Pierre Belgium 50°50N 4°25E 116 A2
Wolvega Neths. 52°52N 6°0E 170 B6
Wolverhampton U.K. 52°35N 2°7W 169 E5
Wondai Australia 26°20S 151°49E 281 D5
Wonenara Papua N. G. 6°48S 145°53E 286 D3
Wong Chuk Hang China 22°15N 114°10E 122 B2
Wong Chuk Wan China 22°23N 114°17E 122 A2
Wong Chuk Yeung China 22°24N 114°15E 122 A2
Wonga Wongué △ Gabon 0°29S 9°25E 264 C1
Wongalarroo L. Australia 31°32S 144°0E 282 A6
Wongan Hills Australia 30°51S 116°37E 279 F2
Wonju S. Korea 37°22N 127°58E 224 D3
Wonosari Indonesia 7°58S 110°36E 231 G14
Wonosobo Indonesia 7°22S 109°54E 235 D3
Wonowon Canada 56°44N 121°48W 296 B4
Wŏnsan N. Korea 39°11N 127°27E 224 C3
Wonthaggi Australia 38°37S 145°37E 283 E6
Wood Buffalo △ Canada 59°0N 113°41W 296 B6
Wood Green U.K. 51°36N 0°6W 125 A3
Wood Is. Australia 16°24S 123°19E 278 C3
Wood L. Canada 55°17N 103°17W 297 B8
Wood Ridge U.S.A. 40°50N 74°4W 132 A1
Wood River U.S.A. 38°52N 90°5W 310 F6
Wood-Tikchik State Park ⌂ U.S.A. 59°30N 158°30W 303 G8
Woodah, I. Australia 13°27S 136°10E 280 A2
Woodbine U.S.A. 30°58N 81°44W 316 E8
Woodbine Race Track Canada 43°43N 79°36W 141 A1
Woodbourne U.S.A. 41°46N 74°36W 313 E10
Woodbridge Ont., Canada 43°47N 79°36W 141 A1
Woodbridge Suffolk, U.K. 52°6N 1°20E 169 E9
Woodbridge B. Dominica 15°19N 61°25W 323 k
Woodburn N.S.W., Australia 29°6S 153°23E 281 A5
Woodburn Oreg., U.S.A. 45°9N 122°51W 304 D2
Woodbury U.S.A. 32°59N 84°35W 316 C5
Woodenbong Australia 28°24S 152°39E 281 D5
Woodend Australia 37°20S 144°33E 282 D6
Woodford Queens., Australia 26°58S 152°47E 281 D5
Woodford London, U.K. 51°36N 0°1E 125 A4
Woodford Bridge U.K. 51°36N 0°3E 125 A4
Woodford Green U.K. 51°36N 0°1E 125 A4
Woodfords U.S.A. 38°47N 119°50W 306 G7
Woodhaven U.S.A. 40°41N 73°51W 132 B2
Woodhouselee U.K. 55°52N 3°13W 121 B2
Woodlake U.S.A. 36°25N 119°6W 306 J7
Woodland Calif., U.S.A. 38°41N 121°46W 306 G5
Woodland Maine, U.S.A. 45°9N 67°25W 309 C20
Woodland Pa., U.S.A. 41°0N 78°21W 312 F6
Woodland Wash., U.S.A. 45°54N 122°45W 306 E4

446 Woodland Caribou INDEX

Woodland Caribou ⌂ Canada 51°0N 94°45W **297** C10
Woodlands Singapore 1°26N 103°46E **138** A2
Woodlands, The U.S.A. 30°9N 95°29W **314** F7
Woodlark I. Papua N. G. 9°10S 152°50E **286** E7
Woodmont U.S.A. 38°59N 77°5W **143** B2
Woodonga Australia 36°10S 146°50E **281** F4
Woodridge Canada 49°20N 96°9W **297** D9
Woodroffe, Mt. Australia 26°20S 131°45E **279** E5
Woods, L. Australia 17°50S 133°30E **280** B1
Woods, L. of the N. Amer. 49°15N 94°45W **297** D10
Woods Bay Canada 45°8N 79°59W **312** A5
Woodside S. Austral., Australia 34°58S 138°52E **282** C3
Woodside Vic., Australia 38°31S 146°52E **283** E7
Woodside London, U.K. 51°23N 0°4W **125** B3
Woodside N.Y., U.S.A. 40°44N 73°54W **132** B2
Woodson U.S.A. 39°37N 90°14W **310** E6
Woodstock N.S.W., Australia 33°45S 148°53E **283** B8
Woodstock Queens., Australia 19°35S 146°50E **280** B4
Woodstock N.B., Canada 46°11N 67°37W **299** C6
Woodstock Ont., Canada 43°10N 80°45W **312** C4
Woodstock Western Cape, S. Africa 33°55S 18°27E **118** A1
Woodstock Oxon., U.K. 51°51N 1°20W **169** F6
Woodstock Ill., U.S.A. 42°19N 88°27W **311** B8
Woodstock N.Y., U.S.A. 42°2N 74°7W **313** D10
Woodstock Vt., U.S.A. 43°37N 72°31W **313** C12
Woodsville U.S.A. 44°9N 72°2W **313** B13
Woodview Canada 44°35N 78°8W **312** B6
Woodville N.Z. 40°20S 175°53E **284** G4
Woodville Fla., U.S.A. 30°19N 84°15W **316** E5
Woodville Ga., U.S.A. 33°40N 83°7W **316** B6
Woodville Miss., U.S.A. 31°6N 91°18W **314** F9
Woodville Ohio, U.S.A. 41°27N 83°22W **311** C13
Woodville Tex., U.S.A. 30°47N 94°25W **314** F7
Woodward U.S.A. 36°26N 99°24W **314** C5
Woody U.S.A. 35°42N 118°50W **307** K8
Woody → Canada 52°31N 100°51W **297** C8
Woolacombe U.K. 51°10N 4°13W **169** F3
Woolamai, C. Australia 38°30S 145°23E **283** E6
Woolbrook Australia 30°56S 151°25E **283** A9
Wooler U.K. 55°33N 2°1W **168** B5
Woolgoolga Australia 30°6S 153°11E **281** E5
Woollahra Australia 33°53S 151°15E **139** B2
Woolloomooloo Sydney, Australia **139** b2
Woolooware B. Australia 34°1S 151°8E **139** C1
Woolwich U.K. 51°29N 0°4E **125** B4
Woolworth Building New York, U.S.A. **132** e1
Woomargama △ Australia 35°50S 147°15E **283** C7
Woomera Australia 31°5S 136°50E **282** A2
Woonsocket R.I., U.S.A. 42°0N 71°31W **313** E13
Woonsocket S. Dak., U.S.A. 44°3N 98°17W **308** C4
Wooramel → Australia 25°47S 114°10E **279** E1
Wooramel Roadhouse Australia 25°45S 114°17E **279** E1
Wooroonooran △ Australia 16°25S 146°1E **280** B4
Wooster U.S.A. 40°48N 81°56W **312** F3
Woqooyi Galbeed □ Somalia 10°0N 44°30E **267** C5
Woraksan △ S. Korea 36°50N 128°5E **224** D4
Worcester Western Cape, S. Africa 33°39S 19°27E **270** D2
Worcester Worcs., U.K. 52°11N 2°12W **169** E5
Worcester Mass., U.S.A. 42°16N 71°48W **313** D13
Worcester N.Y., U.S.A. 42°36N 74°45W **313** D10
Worcestershire □ U.K. 52°13N 2°10W **169** E5
Worden U.S.A. 38°56N 89°50W **310** F7
Wörgl Austria 47°29N 12°3E **180** D5
Worker's Stadium China 39°55N 116°25E **114** B2
Workington U.K. 54°39N 3°33W **168** C4
Worksop U.K. 53°18N 1°7W **168** D6
Workum Neths. 52°59N 5°26E **170** B5
Worland U.S.A. 44°1N 107°57W **304** D10
World Bank Washington, D.C., U.S.A. **143** b1
World Financial Center New York, U.S.A. **132** e1
World Financial Centre Shanghai, China 31°14N 121°30E **138** B2
World Trade Center, Site of former = National September 11 Memorial and Museum New York, U.S.A. **132** e1
World War Two Memorial Washington, D.C., U.S.A. **143** b1
Worli India 19°1N 72°49E **130** A1
Wormhout France 50°52N 2°28E **173** B9
Worms Germany 49°37N 8°21E **179** F4
Worsley Canada 56°31N 119°8W **296** B5
Wörth Bayern, Germany 49°1N 12°24E **179** F8
Worth Ill., U.S.A. 41°41N 87°47W **119** C2
Wortham U.S.A. 31°47N 96°28W **314** F6
Wörther See Austria 46°37N 14°10E **180** E7
Worthing U.K. 50°49N 0°21W **169** G7
Worthington Ind., U.S.A. 39°7N 86°59W **311** E10
Worthington Minn., U.S.A. 43°37N 95°36W **308** D6
Worthington Ohio, U.S.A. 40°5N 83°1W **311** D13
Worthington Pa., U.S.A. 40°50N 79°38W **312** F5
Wosi Indonesia 0°15S 128°0E **231** E7
Wote Kenya 1°47S 37°38E **268** C4
Wotjalum ✪ Australia 16°30S 123°45E **278** C3
Wotjobaluk ✪ Australia 37°0S 142°0E **281** C3
Wou-han = Wuhan China 30°31N 114°18E **229** B10
Wour Chad 21°14N 16°0E **259** D3
Wousi = Wuxi China 31°33N 120°18E **229** B13
Wowoni Indonesia 4°5S 123°5E **231** E6
Woy Woy Australia 33°30S 151°19E **283** B9
Wrangel I. = Vrangelya, Ostrov Russia 71°0N 180°0E **215** B18
Wrangell U.S.A. 56°28N 132°23W **296** B2
Wrangell Mts. U.S.A. 61°30N 142°0W **303** F12
Wrangell-St. Elias △ U.S.A. 61°0N 142°0W **303** F12
Wrath, C. U.K. 58°38N 5°1W **167** C3
Wray U.S.A. 40°5N 102°13W **304** F12
Wrekin, The U.K. 52°41N 2°32W **169** E5
Wrens U.S.A. 33°12N 82°23W **316** B7
Wren's Nest U.S.A. 33°44N 84°25W **113** B2
Wrexham U.K. 53°3N 3°0W **168** D4
Wrexham □ U.K. 53°1N 2°58W **168** D5
Wriezen Germany 52°42N 14°7E **178** C10
Wright = Paranas Phil. 11°42N 125°2E **233** F5
Wright Fla., U.S.A. 30°27N 86°38W **317** E3
Wright Wyo., U.S.A. 43°45N 105°28W **304** E11
Wright Pt. Canada 43°48N 81°44W **312** C3
Wrightmyo India 11°47N 92°43E **245** J11
Wrightson, Mt. U.S.A. 31°42N 110°51W **305** L8
Wrightsville U.S.A. 32°44N 82°43W **316** C7
Wrightwood U.S.A. 34°22N 117°38W **307** L9
Wrigley Canada 63°16N 123°37W **294** E7
Wrigley Building U.S.A. **119** b2
Wrigley Field U.S.A. 41°56N 87°39W **119** B3
Wrocław Poland 51°5N 17°5E **185** G4
Wronki Poland 52°41N 16°21E **185** F3
Września Poland 52°21N 17°36E **185** F4
Wschowa Poland 51°48N 16°20E **185** G3
Wu Hsi → Taiwan 24°9N 120°31E **225** B2
Wu Jiang → China 29°40N 107°20E **228** C6
Wu Kau Tang China 22°30N 114°14E **219** a
Wu Xia China 31°2N 110°10E **229** B8
Wu'an China 36°40N 114°15E **226** F8
Wubalawun ✪ Australia 15°28S 133°1E **278** C5
Wubin Australia 30°6S 116°37E **279** F2
Wubu China 37°28N 110°42E **226** F6
Wuchang China 44°55N 127°5E **227** B14
Wucheng China 37°12N 116°20E **226** F9
Wuch'i Taiwan 24°16N 120°31E **225** B2
Wuchieh Taiwan 24°41N 121°47E **225** B3
Wuchow = Wuzhou China 23°30N 111°18E **229** F8
Wuchuan Guangdong, China 21°33N 110°43E **229** G8
Wuchuan Guizhou, China 28°25N 108°3E **228** C7
Wuchuan Nei Monggol Zizhiqu, China 41°5N 111°28E **226** D6
Wuda China 39°29N 106°42E **226** E4
Wudang Shan China 32°23N 111°2E **229** A8
Wuday'ah Si. Arabia 17°2N 47°7E **248** C4
Wudi China 37°40N 117°35E **227** F9
Wuding China 25°24N 102°21E **228** E4
Wuding He → China 37°2N 110°23E **226** F6
Wudinna Australia 33°0S 135°22E **281** E2
Wudongde Dam China 26°20N 102°15E **228** D4
Wudu China 33°22N 104°54E **226** H3
Wufeng Henan, China 30°12N 110°42E **229** B8
Wufeng Taiwan 24°4N 120°42E **225** B2
Wugang China 26°44N 110°35E **229** D8
Wugong Shan China 27°30N 114°0E **229** D9
Wuguishan China 22°25N 113°25E **219** a
Wugullar = Beswick Australia 14°34S 132°53E **278** B5
Wuhai China 39°39N 106°48E **226** E4
Wuhan China 30°31N 114°18E **229** B10
Wuhe China 33°10N 117°50E **227** H9
Wuhlgarten Germany 52°31N 13°34E **115** A4
Wuhsi = Wuxi China 31°33N 120°18E **229** B13
Wuhu China 31°22N 118°21E **229** B12
Wujiang China 31°10N 120°38E **229** B13
Wujiaochang China 31°18N 121°31E **138** B2
Wujih Taiwan 24°6N 120°38E **225** B2
Wukari Nigeria 7°51N 9°42E **263** D6
Wulai Taiwan 24°52N 121°33E **225** B3
Wulajie China 44°6N 126°33E **227** B14
Wulanbulang China 41°5N 110°55E **226** D6
Wular L. India 34°20N 74°30E **243** B6
Wulehe Ghana 8°39N 0°0 **263** D5
Wulff Land Greenland 82°0N 49°0W **154** A6
Wulian China 35°40N 119°12E **227** G10
Wulian Feng China 27°48N 103°36E **228** D4
Wuliang Shan China 24°30N 100°40E **228** E3
Wuliaru Indonesia 7°27S 131°0E **231** F8
Wulicheng Taiwan 23°47N 121°0E **225** C3
Wuling Shan China 30°0N 110°0E **228** C7
Wulingyuan ⌂ China 29°20N 110°30E **229** C8
Wulong China 29°22N 107°43E **228** C6
Wulong △ China 31°8N 103°5E **228** B4
Wulu Taiwan 23°10N 121°2E **225** C3
Wulumuchi = Ürümqi China 43°45N 87°45E **217** D11
Wum Cameroon 6°24N 10°2E **263** D7
Wumeng Shan China 26°48N 104°0E **228** D5
Wuming China 23°12N 108°18E **228** F7
Wun Rog South Sudan 9°0N 28°20E **257** F2
Wundanyi Kenya 3°24S 38°22E **268** C4
Wundwin Burma 21°5N 96°4E **241** E6
Wuning China 29°17N 115°5E **229** C10
Wunna → India 20°18N 78°48E **244** D4
Wunnummin L. Canada 52°55N 89°10W **298** B2
Wunsiedel Germany 50°2N 12°0E **179** E8
Wunstorf Germany 52°25N 9°26E **178** C5
Wuntho Burma 23°55N 95°45E **241** D5
Wupatki ⌂ U.S.A. 35°35N 111°20W **305** J8
Wuping China 25°5N 116°5E **229** E11
Wuppertal Nordrhein-Westfalen, Germany 51°16N 7°12E **178** D3
Wuppertal Western Cape, S. Africa 32°13S 19°12E **270** D2
Wuqia China 39°40N 75°7E **217** E9
Wuqing China 39°23N 117°4E **227** E9
Würm → Germany 48°8N 11°27E **131** B1
Würm-kanal Germany 48°13N 11°29E **131** A1
Wurralibi ✪ Australia 15°43S 137°1E **280** B2
Wurtsboro U.S.A. 41°35N 74°29W **313** E10
Würzburg Germany 49°46N 9°55E **179** F5
Wurzen Germany 51°22N 12°44E **178** D8
Wushan China 34°43N 104°53E **226** G3
Wushi China 41°9N 79°13E **217** D9
Wushishi Nigeria 9°46N 6°7E **263** D6
Wusi Vanuatu 15°21S 166°40E **287** E4
Wusih = Wuxi China 31°33N 120°18E **229** B13
Wusong China 31°22N 121°29E **138** A1
Wutach → Germany 47°37N 8°15E **179** H4
Wutai China 38°40N 113°12E **226** E7
Wutai Shan China 39°3N 113°32E **226** E7
Wuting = Huimin China 37°27N 117°28E **227** F9
Wutong China 25°24N 110°4E **229** E8
Wutonghaolai China 42°50N 120°5E **227** C11
Wutongqiao China 29°22N 103°50E **228** C4
Wutung Papua N. G. 2°37S 141°1E **286** B1
Wuwei Anhui, China 31°18N 117°54E **229** B11
Wuwei Gansu, China 37°57N 102°34E **218** D9
Wuxi Jiangsu, China 31°33N 120°18E **229** B13
Wuxi Sichuan, China 31°23N 109°35E **228** B7
Wuxiang China 36°49N 112°50E **226** F7
Wuxuan China 23°34N 109°38E **228** F7
Wuxue China 29°52N 115°30E **229** C10
Wuyang China 33°25N 113°35E **226** H7
Wuyi Hebei, China 37°46N 115°56E **226** F8
Wuyi Zhejiang, China 28°52N 119°50E **229** C12
Wuyi Shan China 27°0N 117°0E **229** D11
Wuyishan China 27°45N 118°0E **229** D12
Wuyishan △ China 27°55N 117°54E **229** D11
Wuyo Nigeria 10°23N 11°50E **263** C7
Wuyuan Jiangxi, China 29°15N 117°50E **229** C11
Wuyuan Nei Monggol Zizhiqu, China 41°2N 108°20E **226** D5
Wuzhai China 38°54N 111°48E **226** E6
Wuzhi Shan China 18°45N 109°45E **236** C7
Wuzhong China 38°2N 106°12E **226** E4
Wuzhou China 23°30N 111°18E **229** F8
Wuzishan = Tongshi China 18°30N 109°20E **236** C7
Wyaaba Cr. → Australia 16°27S 141°35E **280** B3
Wyalkatchem Australia 31°8S 117°22E **279** F2
Wyalusing U.S.A. 41°40N 76°16W **313** E8
Wyandotte U.S.A. 42°12N 83°9W **311** B13
Wyandra Australia 27°12S 145°56E **281** D4
Wyangala, L. Australia 33°54S 149°0E **283** B8
Wyara, L. Australia 28°42S 144°14E **281** D3
Wycheproof Australia 36°5S 143°17E **282** D5
Wycliffe Well Australia 20°48S 134°14E **280** C1
Wyczółki Poland 52°9N 20°59E **143** C1
Wye → U.K. 51°38N 2°40W **169** F5
Wyemandoo Australia 28°28S 118°29E **279** E2
Wygoda Poland 52°7N 21°5E **143** C1
Wyk Germany 54°41N 8°33E **178** A4
Wymondham U.K. 52°35N 1°7E **169** E9
Wymore U.S.A. 40°7N 96°40W **308** E5
Wynberg S. Africa 34°2S 18°28E **118** B1
Wyndham W. Austral., Australia 15°33S 128°3E **278** C4
Wyndham N.Z. 46°20S 168°51E **285** G3
Wynne U.S.A. 35°14N 90°47W **315** D9
Wynyard Tas., Australia 41°5S 145°44E **281** G4
Wynyard Sask., Canada 51°45N 104°10W **297** C8
Wyola L. Australia 29°8S 130°17E **279** E5
Wyoming Ont., Canada 42°57N 82°7W **312** D2
Wyoming Ill., U.S.A. 41°4N 89°47W **310** C7
Wyoming Iowa, U.S.A. 42°4N 91°0W **310** B6
Wyoming Mich., U.S.A. 42°54N 85°42W **311** B11
Wyoming □ U.S.A. 43°0N 107°30W **304** E10
Wyomissing U.S.A. 40°20N 75°59W **313** F9
Wyong Australia 33°14S 151°24E **283** B9
Wyperfeld △ Australia 35°35S 141°42E **282** C4
Wyrzysk Poland 53°10N 17°17E **185** E4
Wyśmierzyce Poland 51°37N 20°50E **185** G7
Wysoka Poland 53°13N 17°2E **185** E4
Wysokie Poland 50°55N 22°40E **185** H9
Wysokie Mazowieckie Poland 52°55N 22°30E **185** F9
Wyszków Poland 52°36N 21°25E **185** F8
Wyszogród Poland 52°23N 20°9E **185** F7
Wytheville U.S.A. 36°57N 81°5W **309** G13
Wyżyna Małopolska Poland 50°45N 20°0E **185** H7

X

Xa-Cassau Angola 9°5S 20°15E **265** D4
Xa-Muteba Angola 9°34S 17°50E **265** D3
Xaafuun Somalia 10°25N 51°16E **267** B7
Xaafuun, Ras Somalia 10°27N 51°24E **267** B7
Xabregas Portugal 38°43N 9°6W **126** A2
Xaçmaz Azerbaijan 41°31N 48°42E **191** K9
Xaghra Malta 36°3N 14°16E **206** E7
Xai-Xai Mozam. 25°6S 33°31E **271** C5
Xaidulla China 36°28N 77°59E **217** E9
Xaignabouri = Sayaboury Laos 19°15N 101°45E **236** C3
Xainza China 30°58N 88°35E **218** E6
Xalapa Mexico 19°32N 96°55W **319** D5
Xalin Somalia 9°6N 48°37E **267** C6
Xallas → Spain 42°54N 9°8W **194** C1
Xambioá Brazil 6°25S 48°40W **332** C2
Xangongo Angola 16°45S 15°5E **265** F3
Xankändi Azerbaijan 39°52N 46°49E **213** C12
Xanlar = Goygöl Azerbaijan 40°37N 46°12E **191** K8
Xanten Germany 51°39N 6°26E **178** D2
Xanthi Greece 41°10N 24°58E **203** E8
Xanthi □ Greece 41°10N 24°58E **203** E8
Xanthos Turkey 36°19N 29°18E **205** E11
Xanxerê Brazil 26°53S 52°23W **335** B5
Xapuri Brazil 10°35S 68°35W **330** C4
Xar Moron He → China 43°25N 120°35E **227** C11
Xarardheere Somalia 4°33N 47°38E **267** D6
Xarrë Albania 39°44N 20°3E **206** B10
Xátiva Spain 38°59N 0°32W **197** G4
Xau, L. Botswana 21°15S 24°44E **270** B3
Xavantina Brazil 21°15S 52°48W **335** A5
Xayar China 41°13N 82°48E **217** D10
Xebert China 44°2N 122°0E **227** B12
Xenia U.S.A. 39°41N 83°56W **311** E13
Xeropotamos → Cyprus 34°42N 32°33E **207** F8
Xertigny France 48°3N 6°24E **173** D13
Xewkija Malta 36°2N 14°15E **206** E7
Xhora S. Africa 31°55S 28°38E **271** D4
Xhumo Botswana 21°7S 24°35E **270** B3
Xi Jiang → China 22°5N 113°20E **229** F9
Xi Ujimqin Qi China 44°32N 117°40E **227** B9
Xi Xian Henan, China 32°20N 114°43E **229** A10
Xi Xian Shanxi, China 36°41N 110°58E **226** F6
Xia Xian China 35°8N 111°12E **226** G6
Xiachengzi China 44°40N 130°18E **227** B16
Xiachuan Dao China 21°40N 112°40E **229** G9
Xiaguan China 25°32N 100°16E **218** F9
Xiajiang China 27°30N 115°10E **229** D10
Xiajin China 36°56N 116°0E **226** F9
Xiamen China 24°25N 118°4E **229** E12
Xi'an China 34°15N 109°0E **226** G5
Xian Xian China 38°12N 116°6E **226** E9
Xianfeng China 29°40N 109°8E **228** C7
Xiang Jiang → China 28°55N 112°50E **229** C9
Xiang Khouang Laos 19°17N 103°25E **236** C4
Xiangcheng Henan, China 33°50N 113°27E **226** H7
Xiangcheng Sichuan, China 28°53N 99°47E **228** C2
Xiangdu China 23°13N 106°58E **228** F6
Xiangfan China 32°2N 112°8E **229** A9
Xianggang = Hong Kong □ China 22°11N 114°14E **219** a
Xianghuang Qi China 42°2N 113°50E **226** C7
Xiangjiaba Dam China 28°37N 104°17E **228** C5
Xiangning China 35°58N 110°50E **226** G6
Xiangquan China 36°30N 113°1E **226** F7
Xiangquan He = Sutlej → Pakistan 29°23N 71°3E **242** E4
Xiangshan China 29°29N 121°51E **229** C13
Xiangshui China 34°12N 119°33E **227** G10
Xiangtan China 27°51N 112°54E **229** D9
Xiangxiang China 27°43N 112°28E **229** D9
Xiangyin China 28°38N 112°54E **229** C9
Xiangyun China 25°34N 100°35E **228** E3
Xiangzhou China 23°58N 109°40E **228** F7
Xianju China 28°51N 120°44E **229** C13
Xianning China 29°51N 114°16E **229** C10
Xianshui He → China 30°10N 100°59E **228** B3
Xiantao China 30°25N 113°25E **229** B9
Xianyang China 34°20N 108°40E **226** G5
Xianyou China 25°22N 118°38E **229** E12
Xiao Hinggan Ling China 49°0N 127°0E **219** B14
Xiao Xian China 34°15N 116°55E **226** G9
Xiaofeng China 30°35N 119°32E **229** B12
Xiaogan China 30°52N 113°55E **229** B9
Xiaogang Park China 23°6N 113°16E **121** B2
Xiaojin China 30°59N 102°21E **228** B4
Xiaolan China 22°38N 113°13E **229** F9
Xiaoping China 23°12N 113°13E **121** A2
Xiaoshan China 30°12N 120°18E **229** B13
Xiaowan Dam China 24°42N 100°5E **228** E3
Xiaowutai Shan China 39°51N 114°59E **226** E8
Xiaoyi China 37°8N 111°48E **226** F6
Xiapu China 26°54N 119°59E **229** D12
Xiashachong China 23°8N 113°9E **121** B1
Xiashan = Zhanjiang China 21°15N 110°20E **229** G8
Xiawa China 42°35N 120°38E **227** C11
Xiayi China 34°15N 116°10E **226** G9
Xichang Guangdong, China 23°9N 113°13E **121** B2
Xichang Sichuan, China 27°51N 102°19E **228** D4
Xicheng Beijing, China **114** b1
Xichong China 30°57N 105°54E **228** B5
Xichou China 23°25N 104°42E **228** F5
Xichuan China 33°0N 111°30E **226** H6
Xidan China 39°52N 116°20E **114** B2
Xide China 28°8N 102°19E **228** C4
Xiemahe China 31°38N 111°12E **229** B8
Xifei He → China 32°45N 116°40E **226** H9
Xifeng Gansu, China 35°40N 107°40E **226** G4
Xifeng Guizhou, China 27°7N 106°42E **228** D6
Xifeng Liaoning, China 42°42N 124°45E **227** C13
Xifengzhen = Xifeng China 35°40N 107°40E **226** G4
Xigazê China 29°5N 88°45E **218** F6
Xihe China 34°2N 105°20E **226** G3
Xihua China 33°45N 114°30E **226** H8
Xilagani Greece 40°58N 25°28E **203** F9
Xili Shuiku China 22°36N 113°57E **219** a
Xiliao He → China 43°32N 123°35E **227** C12
Xilin China 24°30N 105°6E **228** E5
Xiling Gorge = Xiling Xia China 30°54N 110°48E **229** B8
Xiling Xia China 30°54N 110°48E **229** B8
Xilinhot China 43°52N 116°2E **226** C9
Xilokastro Greece 38°5N 22°38E **204** C4
Xiluodu Dam China 28°12N 103°34E **228** C4
Ximana Mozam. 19°24S 33°58E **269** F3
Xime Guinea-Biss. 11°59N 14°57W **262** C2
Ximeng China 22°50N 99°27E **228** F2
Ximiao China 40°59N 100°12E **218** C9
Xin Jiang → China 28°45N 116°35E **229** C11
Xin Xian = Xinzhou China 38°22N 112°46E **226** E7
Xin'anjiang Shuiku China 29°33N 118°56E **229** C12
Xinavane Mozam. 25°2S 32°47E **271** C5
Xinbin China 41°40N 125°2E **224** B2
Xincai China 32°43N 114°58E **229** A10
Xinchang China 29°28N 120°52E **229** C13
Xincheng Guangxi Zhuangzu, China 24°5N 108°39E **228** E7
Xincheng Jiangxi, China 26°48N 114°6E **229** D10
Xinchengzi China 42°2N 123°30E **224** A1
Xinfeng Guangdong, China 24°5N 114°16E **229** E10
Xinfeng Jiangxi, China 27°7N 116°11E **229** D11
Xinfeng Jiangxi, China 25°27N 114°58E **229** E10
Xinfengjiang Shuiku China 23°52N 114°30E **229** F10
Xing Xian China 38°27N 111°7E **226** E6
Xing'an Guangxi Zhuangzu, China 25°38N 110°40E **229** E8
Xingan Jiangxi, China 27°46N 115°20E **229** D10
Xingcheng China 40°40N 120°45E **227** D11
Xingguo China 26°21N 115°21E **229** D10
Xinghe China 40°55N 113°55E **226** D7
Xinghua China 32°58N 119°48E **227** H10
Xinghua Wan China 25°15N 119°20E **229** E12
Xinglong China 40°25N 117°30E **227** D9
Xingning China 24°3N 115°42E **229** E10
Xingping China 34°20N 108°28E **226** G5
Xingren China 25°24N 105°11E **228** E5
Xingshan China 31°15N 110°45E **229** B8
Xingtai China 37°3N 114°32E **226** F8
Xingu → Brazil 1°30S 51°53W **329** D7
Xingwen China 28°22N 104°50E **228** C5
Xingxingxia China 41°47N 95°0E **218** C7
Xingyang China 34°45N 112°52E **226** G7
Xingyi China 25°3N 104°59E **228** E5
Xinhe China 37°30N 115°15E **226** F8
Xinhe Xinjiang Uygur, China 41°33N 82°37E **217** D10
Xinhua China 27°42N 111°13E **229** D8
Xinhuang China 27°21N 109°12E **228** D7
Xinhui China 22°25N 113°0E **229** F9
Xining China 36°34N 101°40E **218** D9
Xinji China 37°55N 115°13E **226** E8
Xinjian China 28°37N 115°46E **229** C10
Xinjiang China 35°34N 111°11E **226** G6
Xinjiang Uygur Zizhiqu □ China 42°0N 86°0E **217** D11
Xinjin = Pulandian China 39°25N 121°58E **227** E11
Xinjin China 30°24N 103°47E **228** B4
Xinkai He → China 43°32N 123°35E **227** C12
Xinken China 22°39N 113°36E **219** a
Xinle China 38°25N 114°40E **226** E8
Xinlitun China 42°0N 122°8E **227** D12
Xinlong China 30°57N 100°12E **228** B3
Xinmi China 34°30N 113°25E **226** G7
Xinmin China 41°59N 122°50E **224** B1
Xinning China 26°28N 110°50E **229** D8
Xinping China 24°5N 101°59E **228** E3
Xinshao China 27°21N 111°26E **229** D8
Xintai China 35°55N 117°45E **227** G9
Xintian China 25°55N 112°13E **229** E9
Xinwan China 22°47N 113°40E **219** a
Xinxiang China 35°18N 113°50E **226** G7
Xinxing China 22°35N 112°15E **229** F9
Xinyang China 32°6N 114°3E **229** A10
Xinye China 32°30N 112°21E **229** A9
Xinyi Guangdong, China 22°25N 111°0E **229** F8
Xinyi Nei Monggol Zizhiqu, China 34°23N 118°21E **227** G10
Xinyu China 27°49N 114°58E **229** D10
Xinzhan China 43°50N 127°18E **227** C14
Xinzheng China 34°20N 113°45E **226** G7
Xinzhou Hainan, China 19°43N 109°17E **236** C7
Xinzhou Hubei, China 30°50N 114°48E **229** B10
Xinzhou Shanxi, China 38°22N 112°46E **226** E7
Xinzo de Limia Spain 42°3N 7°47W **194** C3
Xiongyuecheng China 40°12N 122°5E **227** D12
Xiping Henan, China 33°22N 114°5E **226** H8
Xiping Henan, China 33°25N 111°8E **226** H6
Xiping Zhejiang, China 28°16N 119°29E **229** C12
Xique-Xique Brazil 10°50S 42°40W **332** D3
Xiruá → Brazil 6°3S 67°50W **330** B4
Xisha Qundao = Paracel Is. S. China Sea 15°50N 112°0E **230** A4
Xishuangbanna China 22°5N 101°1E **228** F3
Xishui Guizhou, China 28°19N 106°9E **228** C6
Xishui Hubei, China 30°30N 115°15E **229** B10
Xitole Guinea-Biss. 11°43N 14°50W **262** C2
Xiu Shui → China 29°13N 116°0E **229** C11
Xiuning China 29°45N 118°10E **229** C12
Xiuren China 24°27N 110°12E **229** E8
Xiushan China 28°25N 108°57E **228** C7
Xiushui China 29°2N 114°33E **229** C10
Xiuwen China 26°49N 106°32E **228** D6
Xiuyan China 40°18N 123°11E **227** D12
Xiva Uzbekistan 41°30N 60°18E **216** D6
Xixabangma Feng China 28°20N 85°40E **243** E11
Xixia China 33°25N 111°29E **226** H6
Xixiang Guangdong, China 22°34N 113°52E **219** a
Xixiang Shaanxi, China 33°0N 107°44E **226** H4
Xixón = Gijón Spain 43°32N 5°42W **194** B5
Xiyang China 37°38N 113°38E **226** F7
Xizang Zizhiqu □ China 32°0N 88°0E **218** E6
Xizhimen China 39°55N 116°19E **114** B1
Xlendi Malta 36°1N 14°12E **206** E6
Xochimilco, Parque Ecológico Mexico 19°18N 99°5W **128** C2
Xochob Mexico 19°21N 89°48W **319** D7
Xo'jayli Uzbekistan 42°29N 59°31E **216** D5
Xorazm □ Uzbekistan 43°0N 60°0E **216** D6
Xu Beihong Memorial Hall Beijing, China **114** a2
Xu Jiang → China 28°0N 116°25E **229** D11
Xuan Loc Vietnam 10°56N 107°14E **237** G6
Xuan'en China 30°0N 109°30E **228** C7
Xuanhan China 31°18N 107°38E **228** B6
Xuanhua China 40°40N 115°2E **226** D8
Xuanwei China 26°15N 103°59E **228** D5
Xuanwu Beijing, China **114** c1
Xuanzhou China 30°56N 118°43E **229** B12
Xuchang China 34°2N 113°48E **226** G7
Xudat Azerbaijan 41°38N 48°41E **191** K9
Xuddur Somalia 4°11N 43°52E **267** D5
Xuefeng Shan China 27°5N 110°35E **229** D8
Xuejiaping China 31°39N 110°16E **229** B8
Xuhui China 31°11N 121°26E **138** B1
Xujiahui China 31°11N 121°25E **138** B1
Xun Jiang → China 23°35N 111°30E **229** F8
Xun Xian China 35°42N 114°33E **226** G8
Xundian China 25°36N 103°15E **228** E4
Xunwu China 24°54N 115°37E **229** E10
Xunyang China 32°48N 109°22E **226** H5
Xunyi China 35°8N 108°20E **226** G5
Xupu China 27°53N 110°32E **229** D8
Xúquer → Spain 39°5N 0°10W **197** F4
Xushui China 39°2N 115°40E **226** E8
Xuwen China 20°20N 110°10E **229** G8
Xuyi China 32°55N 118°32E **229** A12
Xuyong China 28°10N 105°22E **228** C5
Xuzhou China 34°18N 117°10E **227** G9
Xylophagou Cyprus 34°54N 33°51E **207** F9

Y

Y Drenewydd = Newtown U.K. 52°31N 3°19W **169** E4
Y Fenni = Abergavenny U.K. 51°49N 3°1W **169** F4
Y Gelli Gandryll = Hay-on-Wye U.K. 52°5N 3°8W **169** E4
Y Trallwng = Welshpool U.K. 52°39N 3°8W **169** E4
Y.S. Falls Jamaica 18°9N 77°49W **320** a
Ya Xian = Sanya China 18°14N 109°29E **236** C7
Yaamba Australia 23°8S 150°22E **280** C5
Ya'an China 29°58N 103°5E **228** C4
Yaapeet Australia 35°45S 142°3E **282** C5
Yaba Nigeria 6°30N 3°22E **124** A2
Yabassi Cameroon 4°30N 9°57E **263** E6
Yabayo Ivory C. 5°56N 6°36W **262** D3
Yabelo Ethiopia 4°50N 38°8E **257** G4
Yabelo △ Ethiopia 6°0N 37°50E **257** F4
Yablanitsa Bulgaria 43°2N 24°5E **203** C8
Yablonovyy Khrebet Russia 53°0N 114°0E **215** D12
Yablonovyy Ra. = Yablonovyy Khrebet Russia 53°0N 114°0E **215** D12
Yabluniv Ukraine 48°24N 24°57E **183** B9
Yablunytsya Ukraine 48°19N 24°29E **183** B9
Yabrai Shan China 39°40N 103°0E **226** E2
Yabrūd Syria 33°58N 36°39E **250** E7
Yabucoa Puerto Rico 18°3N 65°53W **321** b
Yacambú △ Venezuela 9°42N 69°27W **328** B4
Yacheng China 18°22N 109°6E **236** C7
Yackandandah Australia 36°18S 146°52E **283** D7
Yacuiba Bolivia 22°0S 63°43W **334** A3
Yacuma → Bolivia 13°38S 65°23W **331** C4
Yadgir India 16°45N 77°5E **244** F3
Yadkin → U.S.A. 35°23N 80°4W **315** D14
Yadong China 27°26N 88°56E **241** B2
Yadrin Russia 55°57N 46°12E **190** C8
Yadua Fiji 16°49S 178°18E **287** A2
Yaeyama-Rettō Japan 24°30N 123°40E **221** M1
Yafran Libya 32°4N 12°31E **258** B2
Yaftābād Iran 35°37N 51°17E **141** B1
Yagaba Ghana 10°14N 1°20W **263** C4
Yagaji-shima Japan 26°39N 128°0E **288** a
Yagasa Cluster Fiji 18°57S 178°28W **287** B3
Yağcılar Turkey 39°25N 28°23E **205** B10
Yagodnoye Russia 62°33N 149°40E **215** C15
Yagoua Cameroon 10°20N 15°13E **259** F3
Yaguas → Peru 2°45S 70°10W **328** D3
Yahara Japan 35°44N 139°37E **140** A2
Yahila Orientale, Dem. Rep. of the Congo 0°13N 24°28E **264** B4
Yahila Orientale, Dem. Rep. of the Congo 1°48N 23°37E **264** B4
Yahk Canada 49°6N 116°10W **296** D5
Yaho Japan 35°40N 139°26E **140** A1
Yahotyn Ukraine 50°17N 31°46E **189** G6
Yahuma Dem. Rep. of the Congo 1°0N 23°10E **264** B4
Yahyalı Turkey 38°5N 35°2E **212** C6
Yaita Japan 36°48N 139°56E **221** F9
Yaiza Canary Is. 28°57N 13°46W **153** e2
Yaizu Japan 34°52N 138°20E **223** C10
Yajiang China 30°2N 100°57E **228** B3
Yajua Nigeria 11°27N 12°49E **263** C7
Yakacık Turkey 36°46N 36°11E **250** B7
Yakage Japan 34°37N 133°35E **222** C5
Yakamba Dem. Rep. of the Congo 2°42N 19°38E **264** B3
Yakapınar Turkey 36°57N 35°36E **250** B6
Yakeshi China 49°17N 120°44E **219** B13
Yakima U.S.A. 46°36N 120°31W **304** C3
Yakima → U.S.A. 46°15N 119°14W **304** C4
Yakire Japan 35°45N 139°54E **140** A4
Yakishiri-Jima Japan 44°26N 141°25E **220** B10
Yako Burkina Faso 12°59N 2°15W **262** C4
Yakobi I. U.S.A. 58°0N 136°30W **296** B1
Yakoma Dem. Rep. of the Congo 4°5N 22°27E **264** B4
Yakoruda Bulgaria 42°1N 23°39E **202** D7
Yakossi C.A.R. 5°37N 23°19E **264** A4
Yakovlevka Russia 44°26N 133°28E **220** B6
Yakovlevskoye = Privolzhsk Russia 57°23N 41°16E **190** B5
Yaksu S. Korea 37°34N 127°1E **137** B2
Yaku-Shima Japan 30°20N 130°30E **221** J5
Yakumo Japan 42°15N 140°16E **220** C10
Yakutat U.S.A. 59°33N 139°44W **303** G13
Yakutat B. U.S.A. 59°45N 140°45W **303** G12
Yakutia = Sakha □ Russia 66°0N 130°0E **215** C14
Yakutsk Russia 62°5N 129°50E **215** C13
Yakymivka Ukraine 46°44N 35°0E **189** J8
Yala Thailand 6°33N 101°18E **237** J3
Yala △ Sri Lanka 6°20N 81°30E **245** L5
Yalata Australia 31°59S 132°26E **279** F5
Yalata ✪ Australia 31°35S 132°7E **279** F5
Yalboroo Australia 20°50S 148°40E **280** b
Yale U.S.A. 43°8N 82°48W **312** C2
Yalgorup △ Australia 32°39S 115°38E **279** F2
Yali Dem. Rep. of the Congo 0°4N 21°3E **264** B4
Yaligimba Dem. Rep. of the Congo 2°13N 22°56E **264** B4
Yalikanda Dem. Rep. of the Congo 0°23N 24°47E **264** B4
Yalinga C.A.R. 6°33N 23°10E **264** A4
Yalkabul, Pta. Mexico 21°32N 88°37W **319** C7
Yallahs Jamaica 17°53N 76°35W **320** a
Yallahs Hill Jamaica 17°54N 76°30W **320** a
Yalleroi Australia 24°3S 145°42E **280** C4
Yalobusha → U.S.A. 33°33N 90°10W **315** E9
Yaloké C.A.R. 5°19N 17°5E **264** A3
Yalong China 18°12N 109°42E **236** C7
Yalong Jiang → China 26°40N 101°55E **228** D3
Yalova Turkey 40°41N 29°15E **203** F13
Yalpirakinu ✪ Australia 22°24S 132°15E **278** D5
Yalpuh, Ozero Ukraine 45°30N 28°41E **183** E13
Yalta Ukraine 44°30N 34°10E **189** K8
Yalu Jiang → China 39°55N 124°19E **224** C2
Yalvaç Turkey 38°17N 31°10E **212** C4
Yam Australia 9°54S 142°46E **280** a
Yam Ha Melaḥ = Dead Sea Asia 31°30N 35°30E **251** G6
Yam Kinneret Israel 32°45N 35°35E **250** F6
Yamada = Kama Japan 35°33N 130°49E **222** D2
Yamada Kanagawa, Japan 35°33N 139°37E **140** B2
Yamada Ōsaka, Japan 34°47N 135°32E **133** A2
Yamaga Japan 33°1N 130°41E **222** D2
Yamagata Japan 38°15N 140°15E **220** E10
Yamagata □ Japan 38°30N 140°0E **220** E10
Yamagawa Japan 31°12N 130°39E **222** F2
Yamaguchi Japan 34°10N 131°32E **222** C3
Yamaguchi □ Japan 34°20N 131°40E **222** C3
Yamal, Poluostrov Russia 71°0N 70°0E **214** B8
Yamal Pen. = Yamal, Poluostrov Russia 71°0N 70°0E **214** B8
Yamanaka Japan 36°15N 136°22E **223** A8
Yamanashi Japan 35°41N 138°42E **223** B10
Yamanashi □ Japan 35°40N 138°40E **223** B10
Yamantau, Gora Russia 54°15N 58°6E **186** D10
Yamasaki Japan 35°0N 134°32E **222** C6
Yamato Japan 35°27N 139°25E **223** B11
Yamato → Japan 34°36N 135°26E **133** B1
Yamato Ridge Sea of Japan 39°20N 135°0E **220** E7
Yamatotakada Japan 34°31N 135°45E **223** C7
Yamba Australia 29°26S 153°23E **281** D5
Yambarran Ra. Australia 15°10S 130°25E **278** C5
Yambata Dem. Rep. of the Congo 2°26N 21°58E **264** B4
Yambéring Guinea 11°50N 12°18W **262** C2
Yâmbiô South Sudan 4°35N 28°16E **257** G2
Yambol Bulgaria 42°30N 26°30E **203** D10
Yambol □ Bulgaria 42°30N 26°30E **203** D10
Yamboyo Dem. Rep. of the Congo 0°40N 22°18E **264** B4
Yamburg Russia 68°21N 77°8E **214** C8
Yambuya Dem. Rep. of the Congo 1°17N 24°34E **264** B4
Yamdena Indonesia 7°45S 131°20E **231** F8
Yame Japan 33°13N 130°35E **222** D2
Yamethin Burma 20°29N 96°18E **241** E6
Y'Ami I. Phil. 21°6N 121°57E **232** A3
Yamma Yamma, L. Australia 26°16S 141°20E **281** D3
Yamoussoukro Ivory C. 6°49N 5°17W **262** D3
Yampa → U.S.A. 40°32N 108°59W **304** F9
Yampi Sd. Australia 16°8S 123°38E **278** C3
Yampil Moldova 48°15N 28°15E **177** D15
Yampol = Yampil Moldova 48°15N 28°15E **177** D15
Yamrat Nigeria 10°11N 9°55E **263** C6
Yamrukchal = Botev Bulgaria 42°44N 24°52E **203** D8
Yamu, Laem Thailand 7°59N 98°26E **237** a
Yamuna → India 25°30N 81°53E **243** G9
Yamunanagar India 30°7N 77°17E **242** D7
Yamzho Yumco China 28°48N 90°35E **218** F7
Yan Nigeria 10°5N 12°11E **263** C7
Yan Kit Singapore 1°21N 103°58E **138** A3
Yan Oya → Sri Lanka 9°0N 81°10E **245** K5
Yana → Russia 71°30N 136°0E **215** B14
Yanagawa Japan 33°10N 130°24E **222** D2
Yanahara Japan 34°58N 134°2E **222** C6
Yanai Japan 33°58N 132°7E **222** D4
Yan'an China 36°35N 109°26E **226** F5
Yanaul Russia 56°25N 55°0E **186** C10
Yanbian China 26°47N 101°31E **228** D3
Yanbu China 23°5N 113°9E **121** B1
Yanbu 'al Baḥr Si. Arabia 24°0N 38°5E **246** F3
Yanchang China 36°43N 110°1E **226** F6
Yancheng Henan, China 33°35N 114°0E **226** H8
Yancheng Jiangsu, China 33°23N 120°8E **227** H11
Yanchep Australia 31°33S 115°37E **279** F2
Yanchi China 37°48N 107°20E **226** F4
Yanchuan China 36°51N 110°10E **226** F6
Yanco Australia 34°38S 146°27E **283** C7
Yanco Cr. → Australia 35°14S 145°35E **283** C6
Yandang Shan China 28°0N 120°25E **229** D13
Yandeyarra ✪ Australia 21°17S 118°24E **278** D2
Yandicoogina Australia 22°49S 119°12E **278** D2
Yandina Solomon Is. 9°7S 159°13E **287** M10
Yandja Dem. Rep. of the Congo 1°41S 17°43E **264** C3
Yandongi Dem. Rep. of the Congo 2°51N 22°16E **264** B4
Yandoon Burma 17°0N 95°40E **241** G5
Yanfeng China 25°52N 101°8E **228** E3
Yanfolila Mali 11°11N 8°9W **262** C3
Yang Xian China 33°15N 107°30E **228** A6
Yang-yang S. Korea 38°4N 128°38E **224** C4
Yang-Yang Senegal 15°30N 15°20W **262** B1
Yangambi Dem. Rep. of the Congo 0°47N 24°24E **264** B4
Yangbi China 25°41N 99°58E **228** E2
Yangcheng China 35°28N 112°22E **226** G7
Yangcheon S. Korea 37°30N 126°51E **137** B1
Yangchow = Yangzhou China 32°21N 119°26E **229** A12
Yangch'ü = Taiyuan China 37°52N 112°33E **226** F7
Yangchüan = Yangquan China 37°58N 113°31E **226** F7
Yangchun China 22°11N 111°48E **229** F8
Yangdok N. Korea 39°13N 126°38E **224** C3
Yanggang-do □ N. Korea 41°15N 128°0E **224** B4
Yanggao China 40°21N 113°55E **226** D7
Yanggu China 36°8N 115°43E **226** F8
Yanghuayuan China 39°49N 116°18E **114** C1
Yangiyul Uzbekistan 41°0N 69°3E **217** D7
Yangjae S. Korea 37°29N 127°2E **137** C2
Yangjiang China 21°50N 111°59E **229** G8
Yangjiazhuang China 31°22N 121°25E **138** A1
Yangjing China 31°15N 121°32E **138** B2
Yangju S. Korea 37°47N 127°7E **224** D3
Yangliuqing China 39°2N 117°5E **227** E9
Yangmei Taiwan 24°55N 121°8E **225** B3
Yangmingshan △ Taiwan 25°9N 121°32E **225** A3
Yangon = Rangoon Burma 16°45N 96°20E **241** G6
Yangonde Dem. Rep. of the Congo 0°3N 22°43E **264** B4
Yangping China 31°12N 111°25E **229** B8
Yangpingguan China 32°58N 106°5E **228** A6
Yangpu China 31°16N 121°32E **138** B2
Yangpu Park China 31°17N 121°31E **138** B2
Yangquan China 37°58N 113°31E **226** F7
Yangsan S. Korea 35°20N 129°2E **224** E4
Yangshan China 24°30N 112°40E **229** E9
Yangshuo China 24°48N 110°29E **229** E8
Yangtse = Chang Jiang → China 31°48N 121°10E **229** B13
Yangtze Kiang = Chang Jiang → China 31°48N 121°10E **229** B13
Yangudi Rassa △ Ethiopia 10°50N 40°42E **257** E5
Yangxin China 29°50N 115°12E **229** C10
Yangyuan China 40°1N 114°10E **226** D8
Yangzhong China 32°22N 119°22E **229** A12
Yangzhou China 32°21N 119°26E **229** A12
Yanhe China 28°31N 108°29E **228** C7
Yanji China 42°59N 129°30E **227** C15
Yanjin China 28°5N 104°18E **228** C5
Yanjing China 29°7N 98°33E **228** C2
Yankari △ Nigeria 9°50N 10°28E **259** G2
Yankton U.S.A. 42°53N 97°23W **308** D5
Yankunytjatjara-Antakirinja ✪ Australia 27°20S 134°30E **281** A1
Yannawa Thailand 13°43N 100°32E **113** B2
Yanonge Dem. Rep. of the Congo 0°35N 24°38E **264** B4
Yanov = Ivanava Belarus 52°7N 25°29E **177** B13
Yanqi China 42°5N 86°35E **217** D11
Yanqing China 40°30N 115°58E **226** D8
Yanshan Hebei, China 38°4N 117°22E **227** E9
Yanshan Jiangxi, China 28°15N 117°41E **229** C11
Yanshan Yunnan, China 23°35N 104°20E **228** F5
Yanshou China 45°28N 128°22E **227** B15
Yantabulla Australia 29°21S 145°0E **281** D4
Yantai China 37°34N 121°22E **227** F11
Yantarnyy Russia 54°52N 19°57E **184** D6
Yantian China 22°35N 114°16E **219** a

Yanting China 31°11N 105°24E 228 B5
Yantongshan China 43°17N 126°0E 227 C14
Yantra → Bulgaria 43°40N 25°37E 203 C9
Yanuca Fiji 18°24S 178°0E 287 B1
Yanununbeyan △ Australia 35°29S 149°24E 283 C8
Yanwa China 27°35N 98°55E 228 D2
Yanyuan China 27°25N 101°30E 228 D3
Yanzhou China 35°35N 116°49E 226 G9
Yao Chad 12°56N 17°33E 259 F3
Yao Japan 34°37N 135°36E 223 C7
Yao Xian China 34°55N 108°59E 226 G5
Yao Yai, Ko Thailand 8°7N 98°37E 237 a
Yao'an China 25°31N 101°18E 228 E3
Yaoundé Cameroon 3°50N 11°35E 263 E7
Yaowan China 34°15N 118°3E 227 G10
Yap Pac. Oc. 9°30N 138°10E 287 R16
Yapacana △ Venezuela 3°49N 66°44W 328 C4
Yapehe Dem. Rep. of the Congo 0°13S 24°28E 264 C4
Yapei Ghana 9°10N 1°10W 263 D4
Yapen Indonesia 1°50S 136°0E 231 E9
Yapen, Selat Indonesia 1°20S 136°10E 231 E9
Yapero Indonesia 4°59S 137°11E 231 E9
Yappar → Australia 18°22S 141°16E 280 B3
Yapuparra ☼ Australia 27°15S 126°20E 279 E4
Yaqaga Fiji 16°35S 178°36E 287 A2
Yaqui → Mexico 27°37N 110°39W 318 B2
Yar-Sale Russia 66°50N 70°50E 214 C8
Yaracuy □ Venezuela 10°20N 68°45W 328 A4
Yaracuy → Venezuela 10°33N 68°15W 328 A4
Yaraka Australia 24°53S 144°3E 280 C3
Yaransk Russia 57°22N 47°49E 190 B8
Yarbasan Turkey 38°59N 28°49E 205 C10
Yardımcı Burnu Turkey 36°13N 30°25E 205 E12
Yare → U.K. 52°35N 1°38E 169 E9
Yaremcha Ukraine 48°27N 24°33E 183 B9
Yaren Nauru 0°33S 166°55E 288 H8
Yarensk Russia 62°11N 49°15E 186 B8
Yarfa Si. Arabia 24°37N 38°35E 256 C4
Yarí → Colombia 0°20S 72°20W 328 D3
Yarīm Yemen 14°20N 44°22E 248 D4
Yaritagua Venezuela 10°5N 69°8W 328 A4
Yarkand = Shache China 38°20N 77°10E 217 E9
Yarkant He → China 40°26N 80°59E 217 D10
Yarker Canada 44°23N 76°46W 313 B8
Yarkhun → Pakistan 36°17N 72°30E 243 A5
Yarlung Ziangbo Jiang = Brahmaputra → Asia 23°40N 90°35E 241 D3
Yarmouth Canada 43°50N 66°7W 299 D6
Yarmūk Iraq 33°18N 44°19E 113 B1
Yarmūk → Syria 32°42N 35°40E 250 F6
Yaroslavl Russia 57°35N 39°55E 188 D10
Yaroslavl □ Russia 59°20N 38°30E 188 C10
Yarra → Trin. & Tob. 10°48N 61°21W 323 t
Yarra Bend Park Australia 37°47S 145°0E 128 A2
Yarra Ranges △ Australia 37°40S 145°3E 283 D7
Yarra Yarra Lakes Australia 29°40S 115°45E 279 E2
Yarram Australia 38°29S 146°39E 283 E7
Yarraman Australia 26°50S 152°0E 281 D5
Yarras Australia 31°25S 152°20E 283 A10
Yarraville Australia 37°48S 144°53E 128 A1
Yarrawonga Australia 36°0S 146°0E 283 D7
Yarrie Australia 20°40S 120°12E 278 D3
Yartsevo Sib., Russia 60°20N 90°0E 215 C10
Yartsevo Smolensk, Russia 55°6N 32°43E 188 E7
Yarumal Colombia 6°58N 75°24W 328 B2
Yasa Dem. Rep. of the Congo 3°50S 21°25E 264 C4
Yasawa Fiji 16°47S 177°31E 287 A1
Yasawa Group Fiji 17°0S 177°23E 287 A1
Yaselda Belarus 52°7N 26°28E 177 B14
Yasen Ukraine 48°45N 24°10E 183 B9
Yashbum Yemen 14°19N 46°56E 248 D4
Yashi Nigeria 12°23N 7°54E 263 C6
Yashikera Nigeria 9°44N 3°29E 263 D5
Yashiro-Jima Japan 33°55N 132°15E 222 D4
Yashkul Russia 46°11N 45°21E 191 G7
Yasi = Türkistan Kazakhstan 43°17N 68°16E 217 D7
Yasin Pakistan 36°24N 73°23E 243 A5
Yasinovataya Ukraine 48°7N 37°57E 189 H9
Yasinski, L. Canada 53°16N 77°35W 298 B4
Yasinya Ukraine 48°16N 24°21E 183 B9
Yasnyy Russia 51°1N 59°58E 216 B5
Yasothon Thailand 15°50N 104°10E 236 E5
Yass Australia 34°49S 148°54E 283 C8
Yasugi Japan 35°26N 133°15E 222 B5
Yāsūj Iran 30°31N 51°31E 247 D6
Yasuní △ Ecuador 1°19S 76°3W 328 D2
Yat Niger 20°28N 13°27E 259 D2
Yata → Bolivia 10°29S 65°26W 331 C4
Yata → C.A.R. 10°23N 22°45E 264 A4
Yata-Ngaya ⌂ C.A.R. 9°15N 23°25E 264 A4
Yatağan Turkey 37°20N 28°10E 205 D10
Yatakala Niger 14°50N 0°22E 263 C5
Yaté N. Cal. 22°9S 166°57E 288 d
Yates Center U.S.A. 37°53N 95°44W 308 G6
Yates Pt. N.Z. 44°29S 167°49E 285 E2
Yathkyed L. Canada 62°40N 98°0W 297 A9
Yathong Australia 32°37S 145°33E 283 B6
Yatolemu Dem. Rep. of the Congo 0°25N 24°35E 264 B4
Yatsuo Japan 36°34N 137°8E 223 A9
Yatsushiro Japan 32°30N 130°40E 222 E2
Yatsushiro-Kai Japan 32°30N 130°25E 222 E2
Yatta Plateau Kenya 2°0S 38°0E 268 C4
Yatua → Venezuela 1°30N 66°30W 328 C4
Yauca Peru 15°39S 74°35W 330 D3
Yauco Puerto Rico 18°2N 66°51W 321 b
Yauri Peru 14°47S 71°25W 330 C3
Yauya Peru 8°59S 77°17W 330 B2
Yauyos Peru 12°19S 75°50W 330 C2
Yauza → Russia 55°54N 37°43E 129 B4
Yaval India 21°10N 75°42E 244 D2
Yavarí → Peru 4°21S 70°2W 330 A3
Yávaros Mexico 26°42N 109°31W 318 B3
Yavatmal India 20°20N 78°15E 244 D4
Yavero → Peru 12°6S 72°57W 330 C3
Yavne Israel 31°52N 34°45E 251 G5
Yavoriv Ukraine 49°55N 23°20E 177 D12
Yavorov = Yavoriv Ukraine 49°55N 23°20E 177 D12
Yavuzeli Turkey 37°18N 37°24E 212 D7
Yawatahama Japan 33°27N 132°24E 222 D4
Yawnghwe Burma 20°39N 96°56E 241 E6
Yawri B. S. Leone 8°22N 13°0W 262 D2
Yaxi China 27°33N 106°41E 228 D6
Yaxian = Sanya China 18°14N 109°29E 236 C7
Yayama Dem. Rep. of the Congo 1°16S 23°7E 264 C4
Yayladağı Turkey 35°54N 36°3E 250 C7
Yazd Iran 31°55N 54°27E 247 D7
Yazd □ Iran 32°0N 55°0E 247 D7
Yazd-e Khvāst Iran 31°31N 52°7E 247 D7
Yazdān Iran 33°30N 60°50E 240 B1
Yazıköy Turkey 36°40N 27°20E 205 E9
Yazman Pakistan 29°8N 71°45E 242 E4
Yazoo → U.S.A. 32°22N 90°54W 315 E9
Yazoo City U.S.A. 32°51N 90°25W 315 E9
Ybbs Austria 48°12N 15°4E 180 C8
Ybycuí △ Paraguay 26°5S 56°46W 334 B4
Ybytyruzú △ Paraguay 25°51S 56°11W 335 B4
Ye Burma 15°15N 97°15E 236 E1
Ye-ngan Burma 21°9N 96°27E 241 E6
Ye-u Burma 22°46N 95°26E 241 D5
Ye Xian = Laizhou China 37°8N 119°57E 227 F10
Ye Xian China 33°35N 113°25E 226 H7
Yea Australia 37°14S 145°26E 283 D6
Yeading U.K. 51°31N 0°23W 125 A1
Yebawmi Burma 25°15N 95°45E 241 C5
Yebbi-Souma Chad 21°7N 17°54E 259 D3
Yebyu Burma 14°15N 98°13E 236 E2
Yecheng China 37°54N 77°26E 217 E9
Yecheon S. Korea 36°39N 128°27E 224 D4
Yecla Spain 38°35N 1°5W 197 G3
Yécora Mexico 28°20N 108°58W 318 B3
Yedashe Burma 19°10N 96°20E 241 F6
Yedebub Biheroch Bihereseboch na Hizboch □ Ethiopia 12°0N 36°0E 257 F4
Yedigöller △ Turkey 40°55N 31°55E 212 B4
Yedikule Turkey 40°59N 28°55E 122 C1
Yedintsy = Edineţ Moldova 48°9N 27°18E 183 B12
Yedri Chad 22°25N 17°30E 259 D3
Yedseram → Nigeria 12°30N 14°5E 263 C7
Yeed Somalia 4°33N 43°2E 267 D5
Yefremov Russia 53°8N 38°3E 188 F10
Yegguéba Niger 19°59N 12°52E 259 E2
Yeghegnadzor Armenia 39°44N 45°19E 213 C11
Yegorlyk → Russia 46°35N 41°57E 191 G5
Yegorlykskaya Russia 46°35N 40°35E 191 G5
Yegoryevsk Russia 55°27N 38°55E 188 E10
Yegri-Dere = Ardino Bulgaria 41°34N 25°9E 203 E9
Yegros Paraguay 26°20S 56°25W 334 B4
Yehbuah Indonesia 8°23S 114°45E 231 J17
Yehuda, Midbar Israel 31°35N 35°15E 251 G6
Yei South Sudan 4°9N 30°40E 257 G3
Yei, Nahr → South Sudan 6°15N 30°13E 257 F3
Yeji Ghana 8°13N 0°39W 263 D4
Yejmiadzin = Ejmiatsin Armenia 40°12N 44°19E 191 K7
Yekaterinburg Russia 56°50N 60°30E 214 D7
Yekaterinenshtadt = Marks Russia 51°45N 46°50E 190 E8
Yekaterinodar = Krasnodar Russia 45°5N 39°0E 191 H4
Yekumbe Dem. Rep. of the Congo 1°2S 23°27E 264 C4
Yelan Russia 50°55N 43°43E 190 E6
Yelandur India 12°6N 77°0E 245 H3
Yelarbon Australia 28°33S 150°38E 281 D5
Yelatma Russia 55°0N 41°45E 190 C5
Yelcho, L. Chile 43°18S 72°18W 336 B2
Yelenovka = Sevan Armenia 40°33N 44°56E 191 K7
Yelenovskiye Karyery = Dokuchayevsk Ukraine 47°44N 37°40E 189 J9
Yelets Russia 52°40N 38°30E 189 F10
Yélimané Mali 15°9N 10°34W 262 B2
Yelin = Lingshui China 18°27N 110°0E 236 C8
Yelizavetgrad = Kirovohrad Ukraine 48°35N 32°20E 189 H7
Yelizovo Russia 53°11N 158°23E 215 D16
Yell U.K. 60°35N 1°5W 167 A7
Yell Sd. U.K. 60°33N 1°15W 167 A7
Yellamanchilli = Elamanchili India 17°33N 82°50E 244 F6
Yellandu India 17°39N 80°23E 244 F5
Yellapur India 14°58N 74°43E 245 G2
Yellareddi India 18°12N 78°2E 244 E4
Yellow = Huang He → China 37°55N 118°50E 227 F10
Yellow → U.S.A. 30°30N 87°0W 317 E3
Yellow Sea China 35°0N 123°0E 227 G12
Yellowhead Pass Canada 52°53N 118°25W 296 C5
Yellowknife Canada 62°27N 114°29W 296 A6
Yellowknife → Canada 62°31N 114°19W 296 A6
Yellowstone → U.S.A. 47°59N 103°59W 304 C12
Yellowstone △ U.S.A. 44°40N 110°30W 304 D8
Yellowstone L. U.S.A. 44°27N 110°22W 304 D8
Yelnya Russia 54°35N 33°15E 188 E7
Yelsk Belarus 51°50N 29°10E 177 C15
Yelwa Nigeria 10°49N 4°41E 263 C5
Yemanzhelinsk Russia 54°58N 61°18E 216 B6
Yemassee U.S.A. 32°41N 80°51W 316 C9
Yembongo Dem. Rep. of the Congo 3°12N 19°2E 264 B3
Yemen ■ Asia 15°0N 44°0E 248 D4
Yemin Moshe Jerusalem 123 b2
Yemmiganur India 15°44N 77°29E 245 G3
Yen Bai Vietnam 21°42N 104°52E 228 G5
Yenagoa Nigeria 4°58N 6°16E 263 E6
Yenakiyeve Ukraine 48°15N 38°15E 189 H10
Yenakiyevo = Yenakiyeve Ukraine 48°15N 38°15E 189 H10
Yenangyat Burma 21°6N 94°48E 241 E5
Yenangyaung Burma 20°30N 95°0E 241 E5
Yenanma Burma 19°46N 94°49E 241 F5
Yenbo = Yanbu 'al Baḩr Si. Arabia 24°0N 38°5E 246 F3
Yenchao Taiwan 22°46N 120°21E 225 D2
Yenda Australia 34°13S 146°14E 283 C7
Yende Millimou Guinea 8°55N 10°10W 262 D2
Yendéré Burkina Faso 10°12N 4°59W 262 C4
Yendi Ghana 9°29N 0°1W 263 D4
Yengisar China 38°56N 76°9E 217 E9
Yengo Congo 0°22N 15°29E 264 B3
Yengo △ Australia 33°0S 150°55E 283 B9
Yéni Niger 13°30N 3°1E 263 C5
Yenı Erenköy = Yialousa Cyprus 35°32N 34°10E 207 E10
Yeni-Pazar = Novi Pazar Serbia 43°12N 20°28E 202 C4
Yenıbogaziçi = Áyios Seryios Cyprus 35°12N 33°53E 207 E9
Yenice Ankara, Turkey 39°14N 32°42E 212 C5
Yenice Aydın, Turkey 37°49N 28°35E 205 D10
Yenice Çanakkale, Turkey 39°55N 27°17E 205 B9
Yenice Edirne, Turkey 40°42N 26°9E 203 F10
Yenice Kahramanmaraş, Turkey 37°0N 35°4E 250 B6
Yenice → Turkey 37°37N 35°33E 212 D6
Yenifoça Turkey 38°44N 26°51E 205 C8
Yenihisar = Didim Turkey 37°22N 27°16E 205 D9
Yenikapı Turkey 41°0N 28°56E 122 B1
Yeniköy Bursa, Turkey 40°31N 29°22E 203 F13
Yeniköy Çanakkale, Turkey 39°55N 26°10E 205 B8
Yeniköy İstanbul, Turkey 41°6N 29°3E 122 B2
Yeniköy Kütahya, Turkey 38°52N 29°17E 205 C11
Yenipazar Turkey 37°49N 28°11E 205 D10
Yenişehir Turkey 40°16N 29°38E 203 F13
Yenisey → Russia 71°50N 82°40E 214 B9
Yeniseysk Russia 58°27N 92°13E 215 D10
Yeniseyskiy Zaliv Russia 72°20N 81°0E 214 B9
Yenki = Yanji China 42°59N 129°30E 227 C15
Yenne France 45°43N 5°44E 175 C9
Yenotayevka Russia 47°15N 47°0E 191 G8
Yenpu Taiwan 22°45N 120°35E 225 D2
Yenshui Taiwan 23°19N 120°16E 225 C2
Yenyuka Russia 57°57N 121°15E 215 D13
Yeo → U.K. 51°2N 2°49W 169 G5
Yeo, L. Australia 28°0S 124°30E 279 E3
Yeo I. Canada 45°24N 81°48W 312 A3
Yeoju S. Korea 37°20N 127°35E 224 D3
Yeola India 20°2N 74°30E 244 D2
Yeon-gi S. Korea 36°35N 127°15E 224 D3
Yeoncheon S. Korea 38°5N 127°4E 224 C3
Yeong-am S. Korea 34°47N 126°42E 224 E3
Yeong-ilman S. Korea 36°4N 129°28E 224 D4
Yeong-wol S. Korea 37°11N 128°28E 224 D4
Yeong-yang S. Korea 36°39N 129°7E 224 D4
Yeongcheon S. Korea 35°58N 128°56E 224 E4
Yeongdeok S. Korea 36°24N 129°22E 224 D4
Yeongdeungpo S. Korea 37°31N 126°54E 137 B1
Yeongdong Chungcheongbuk-do, S. Korea 36°10N 127°46E 224 D3
Yeongdong Seoul, S. Korea 37°30N 127°1E 137 B2
Yeonggwang S. Korea 35°16N 126°30E 224 E3
Yeongheungdo S. Korea 37°15N 126°27E 224 D3
Yeongju S. Korea 36°50N 128°40E 224 D4
Yeongju △ S. Korea 35°45N 129°20E 224 D4
Yeonpyeongdo S. Korea 37°40N 125°45E 224 D2
Yeosu S. Korea 34°47N 127°45E 224 E3
Yeotmal = Yavatmal India 20°20N 78°15E 244 D4
Yeouido S. Korea 37°31N 126°55E 137 B1
Yeovil U.K. 50°57N 2°38W 169 G5
Yepes Spain 39°55N 3°39W 194 F7
Yeppoon Australia 23°5S 150°47E 280 C5
Yerba Buena I. U.S.A. 37°48N 122°21W 136 B2
Yerbent Turkmenistan 39°19N 58°36E 247 B8
Yerbogachen Russia 61°16N 108°0E 215 C11
Yerevan Armenia 40°10N 44°31E 191 K7
Yerington U.S.A. 38°59N 119°10W 304 G4
Yerkesik Turkey 37°7N 28°19E 205 D10
Yerköy Turkey 39°38N 34°28E 212 C6
Yerla → India 16°50N 74°30E 244 F2
Yermo U.S.A. 34°54N 116°50W 307 L10
Yerolakkos Cyprus 35°11N 33°15E 207 E9
Yeropol Russia 65°15N 168°40E 215 C17
Yeroskipos Cyprus 34°46N 32°28E 207 F8
Yerres France 48°43N 2°30E 134 B4
Yershov Russia 51°23N 48°27E 190 E9
Yerupajá, Cerro Peru 10°16S 76°55W 330 C2
Yerushalayim = Jerusalem Israel/West Bank 31°47N 35°10E 123 B2
Yerville France 49°40N 0°53E 172 C7
Yes Tor U.K. 50°41N 4°0W 169 G4
Yesagyo Burma 21°38N 95°14E 241 E5
Yesan S. Korea 36°41N 126°51E 224 D3
Yeshin Burma 23°43N 95°6E 241 D5
Yeşikent = Erzin Turkey 36°57N 36°11E 250 B7
Yeşil → Turkey 37°20N 33°16E 250 A4
Yeşildere Turkey 37°9N 33°31E 250 A4
Yeşilhisar Turkey 38°20N 35°5E 212 C6
Yeşilırmak → Turkey 41°22N 36°37E 212 B7
Yeşilkent Turkey 36°57N 36°12E 212 D7
Yeşilköy Turkey 40°57N 28°49E 203 F12
Yeşilova Turkey 37°31N 29°46E 205 D11
Yeşilyurt Manisa, Turkey 38°22N 28°40E 205 C10
Yeşilyurt Muğla, Turkey 37°10N 28°20E 205 D10
Yeski Dzhumaya = Târgovişte Romania 44°55N 25°27E 183 F10
Yesnogorsk Russia 54°32N 37°38E 188 E9
Yeso U.S.A. 34°26N 104°37W 305 J11
Yessentuki Russia 44°5N 42°53E 191 H6
Yessey Russia 68°29N 102°10E 215 C11
Yeste Spain 38°22N 2°19W 197 G2
Yetman Australia 28°56S 150°48E 281 D5
Yetti Mauritania 26°10N 7°50W 260 C3
Yeu, Î. d' France 46°42N 2°20W 172 F4
Yevdokimovskoye = Krasnogvardeyskoye Russia 45°52N 41°33E 191 H5
Yevlakh = Yevlax Azerbaijan 40°39N 47°7E 191 K8
Yevlax Azerbaijan 40°39N 47°7E 191 K8
Yevpatoriya Ukraine 45°15N 33°20E 189 K7
Yeya → Russia 46°40N 38°40E 191 G4
Yeysk Russia 46°40N 38°12E 189 J10
Yezd = Yazd Iran 31°55N 54°27E 247 D7
Yezerishche Belarus 55°50N 30°0E 188 E5
Ygatimi Paraguay 24°5S 55°40W 335 A4
Yhati Paraguay 25°45S 56°35W 334 B4
Yhú Paraguay 25°0S 56°0W 335 B4
Yí → Uruguay 33°7S 57°8W 334 C4
Yi 'Allaq, G. Egypt 30°21N 33°31E 251 H4
Yi He → China 34°10N 118°8E 227 G10
Yi Xian Anhui, China 29°55N 117°57E 229 C11
Yi Xian Hebei, China 39°20N 115°30E 226 E8
Yi Xian Liaoning, China 41°30N 121°22E 227 D11
Yialiás → Cyprus 35°9N 33°44E 207 E9
Yialousa Cyprus 35°32N 34°10E 207 E10
Yibin China 28°45N 104°32E 228 C5
Yichang China 30°40N 111°20E 229 B8
Yicheng Henan, China 31°41N 112°12E 229 B9
Yicheng Shanxi, China 35°42N 111°40E 226 G6
Yichuan China 36°2N 110°10E 226 F6
Yichun Heilongjiang, China 47°44N 128°52E 219 B14
Yichun Jiangxi, China 27°48N 114°22E 229 D10
Yidu China 36°43N 118°28E 227 F10
Yidun China 30°22N 99°21E 228 B2
Yifag Ethiopia 12°4N 37°46E 257 E4
Yifeng China 28°22N 114°45E 229 C10
Yigo Guam 13°32N 144°53E 302 d
Yiheyuan China 39°59N 116°15E 114 B1
Yihuang China 27°30N 116°12E 229 D11
Yijun China 35°28N 109°8E 226 G5
Yılanlıkale Turkey 36°59N 35°47E 250 B6
Yıldız Dağları Turkey 41°48N 27°36E 203 E11
Yıldız Park Turkey 41°2N 29°1E 122 B2
Yıldızeli Turkey 39°51N 36°36E 212 C7
Yilehuli Shan China 51°20N 124°20E 219 A13
Yiliang Yunnan, China 27°38N 104°2E 228 D5
Yiliang Yunnan, China 24°56N 103°11E 228 E4
Yılmazköy = Skilloura Cyprus 35°14N 33°10E 207 E9
Yilong China 31°34N 106°23E 228 B6
Yima China 34°44N 111°53E 226 G6
Yimen China 24°40N 102°10E 228 E4
Yimianpo China 45°7N 128°2E 227 B15
Yin Xu China 36°7N 114°18E 226 F8
Yi'nan China 35°31N 118°24E 227 G10
Yinchuan China 38°30N 106°15E 226 E4
Yindaik Burma 23°35N 95°22E 241 D5
Yindarlgooda, L. Australia 30°40S 121°52E 279 F3
Yindjibarndi ☼ Australia 22°0S 118°35E 278 D2
Ying He → China 32°30N 116°30E 226 H9
Ying Xian China 39°32N 113°10E 226 E7
Yingcheng China 30°56N 113°35E 229 B9
Yingde China 24°10N 113°25E 229 E9
Yingjiang China 24°41N 97°55E 228 E1
Yingjing China 29°41N 102°52E 228 C4
Yingkiong India 28°37N 95°3E 241 A5
Yingkou China 40°37N 122°18E 224 B1
Yingkow = Yingkou China 40°37N 122°18E 224 B1
Yingpanshui China 37°26N 104°18E 226 F3
Yingshan Hubei, China 30°41N 115°32E 229 B10
Yingshan Sichuan, China 31°4N 106°35E 228 B6
Yingshang China 32°38N 116°12E 229 A11
Yingtan China 28°12N 117°0E 229 C11
Yingualyalya ☼ Australia 18°49S 129°12E 278 C4
Yinhangzhen China 31°20N 121°31E 138 A2
Yining China 43°58N 81°10E 217 D10
Yiningarra ☼ Australia 20°53S 129°27E 278 D4
Yinjiang China 28°1N 108°21E 228 C7
Yinmabin Burma 22°10N 94°55E 241 D5
Yioúra = Giaros Greece 37°32N 24°40E 204 D6
Yipinglang China 25°10N 101°52E 228 E3
Yirba Muda Ethiopia 6°12N 38°42E 257 F4
Yirga Alem Ethiopia 6°48N 38°22E 257 F4
Yirol South Sudan 6°33N 30°30E 257 F3
Yirrkala Australia 12°14S 136°56E 280 A2
Yishan China 24°28N 108°38E 228 E7
Yishui China 35°47N 118°30E 227 G10
Yishun Singapore 1°26N 103°51E 138 A3
Yitong China 43°13N 125°20E 227 C13
Yiwu China 29°20N 120°3E 229 C13
Yixing China 31°21N 119°48E 229 B12
Yiyang Henan, China 34°27N 112°10E 226 G7
Yiyang Hunan, China 28°35N 112°18E 229 C9
Yiyang Jiangxi, China 28°22N 117°20E 229 C11
Yizhang China 25°27N 112°57E 229 E9
Yizheng China 32°18N 119°10E 229 A12
Ylästö Finland 60°17N 24°54E 121 B2
Yli-Kitka Finland 66°8N 28°30E 160 C23
Yliki, L. Greece 38°24N 23°15E 204 C5
Ylitornio Finland 66°19N 23°39E 160 C20
Ylivieska Finland 64°4N 24°28E 160 D21
Ymer Ø Greenland 73°9N 24°20W 154 C8
Yngaren Sweden 58°50N 16°35E 163 F10
Yoakum U.S.A. 29°17N 97°9W 314 G6
Yob ⌂ Eritrea 17°15N 37°50E 257 D4
Yobe □ Nigeria 12°0N 11°30E 263 C7
Yoboki Djibouti 11°30N 42°6E 267 B5
Yobuko Japan 33°32N 129°54E 222 D1
Yodo → Japan 34°45N 135°35E 133 A2
Yog Pt. Phil. 14°6N 124°12E 232 D5
Yoğuntaş Turkey 41°50N 27°4E 203 E11
Yogyakarta Indonesia 7°49S 110°22E 235 D4
Yogyakarta □ Indonesia 7°48S 110°22E 235 D4
Yoho △ Canada 51°25N 116°30W 296 C5
Yojoa, L. de Honduras 14°53N 88°0W 320 D2
Yok Don △ Vietnam 12°50N 107°40E 236 F6
Yokadouma Cameroon 3°26N 14°55E 264 B2
Yōkaichi Japan 35°6N 136°12E 223 B8
Yōkaichiba Japan 35°42N 140°33E 223 B12
Yokkaichi Japan 34°55N 136°38E 223 C8
Yoko Cameroon 5°32N 12°20E 263 D7
Yokohama Japan 35°27N 139°28E 223 B11
Yokosuka Japan 35°20N 139°40E 223 B11
Yokote Japan 39°20N 140°30E 220 E10
Yola Nigeria 9°10N 12°29E 263 D7
Yolaina, Cordillera de Nic. 11°30N 84°0W 320 D3
Yolombo Dem. Rep. of the Congo 1°36S 23°12E 264 C4
Ýolöten Turkmenistan 37°18N 62°21E 247 B9
Yom → Thailand 15°35N 100°1E 236 E3
Yombi Gabon 1°26S 10°37E 264 C2
Yona Guam 13°25N 144°46E 302 d
Yonago Japan 35°25N 133°19E 222 B5
Yonaguni-Jima Japan 24°27N 123°0E 221 M1
Yonaha-Dake Japan 26°43N 128°13E 288 a
Yŏnan N. Korea 37°55N 126°11E 224 D3
Yonezawa Japan 37°57N 140°4E 220 F10
Yong-in S. Korea 37°14N 127°12E 224 D3
Yong Peng Malaysia 2°0N 103°3E 237 M4
Yong Sata Thailand 7°8N 99°41E 237 J2
Yongama Dem. Rep. of the Congo 0°2N 24°35E 264 B4
Yongamp'o N. Korea 39°56N 124°23E 224 C2
Yong'an China 25°59N 117°25E 229 E11
Yongchang China 38°17N 102°7E 218 D9
Yongcheng China 33°55N 116°20E 226 H9
Yongchuan China 29°17N 105°55E 228 C5
Yongchun China 25°16N 118°20E 229 E12
Yongde China 24°5N 99°25E 228 E2
Yongdeng China 36°38N 103°25E 226 F2
Yongding China 24°43N 116°45E 229 E11
Yongdingman China 39°50N 116°20E 114 B2
Yonge Street Toronto, Canada 141 b3
Yongfeng China 27°20N 115°22E 229 D10
Yongfu China 24°59N 109°59E 228 E7
Yongfucun China 23°8N 113°17E 121 B2
Yonggyap Pass Asia 29°17N 95°37E 241 A5
Yonghe China 36°46N 110°38E 226 F6
Yonghong India 26°28N 94°58E 241 B5
Yŏnghŭng N. Korea 39°31N 127°18E 224 C3
Yŏnghŭng-man N. Korea 39°14N 127°30E 224 C3
Yongji Jilin, China 43°33N 126°13E 227 C14
Yongji Shanxi, China 34°52N 110°28E 226 G6
Yongjia China 28°10N 120°45E 229 C13
Yongkang Yunnan, China 24°9N 99°20E 228 E2
Yongkang Zhejiang, China 28°55N 120°2E 229 C13
Yongnian China 36°47N 114°29E 226 F8
Yongning Guangxi Zhuangzu, China 22°44N 108°28E 228 F7
Yongning Ningxia Huizu, China 38°15N 106°14E 226 E4
Yongping China 25°27N 99°38E 228 E2
Yongren China 26°4N 101°40E 228 D3
Yongsan S. Korea 37°32N 126°58E 137 B1
Yongshan China 28°11N 103°35E 228 C4
Yongsheng China 26°38N 100°46E 228 D3
Yongshun China 29°2N 109°51E 228 C7
Yongtai China 25°49N 118°58E 229 E12
Yongxin = Jinggangshan China 26°58N 114°15E 229 D10
Yongxing China 26°9N 113°8E 229 D9
Yongxiu China 29°2N 115°42E 229 C10
Yongzhou China 26°17N 111°37E 229 D8
Yonibana S. Leone 8°30N 12°19W 262 D2
Yonkers U.S.A. 40°56N 73°52W 132 A2
Yonne □ France 47°50N 3°40E 173 E10
Yonne → France 48°23N 2°58E 173 D9
Yopal Colombia 5°21N 72°23W 328 B3
York W. Austral., Australia 31°52S 116°47E 279 F2
York Ont., Canada 43°40N 79°26W 141 A2
York York, U.K. 53°58N 1°6W 168 D6
York Ala., U.S.A. 32°29N 88°18W 315 E10
York Nebr., U.S.A. 40°52N 97°36W 308 E5
York Pa., U.S.A. 39°58N 76°44W 309 F15
York, C. Australia 10°42S 142°31E 286 F2
York, City of □ U.K. 53°58N 1°6W 168 D6
York, Kap Greenland 75°55N 66°25W 154 B4
York, Vale of U.K. 54°15N 1°25W 168 C6
York I. Antigua & B. 17°2N 61°40W 322 b
York Mills Canada 43°45N 79°22W 141 A2
York Sd. Australia 15°0S 125°5E 278 C4
York Univ. Canada 43°43N 79°22W 141 A1
Yorke Pen. Australia 34°50S 137°40E 282 C2
Yorketown Australia 35°2S 137°33E 282 C2
Yorkshire Dales △ U.K. 54°12N 2°10W 168 C5
Yorkshire Wolds U.K. 54°8N 0°31W 168 C7
Yorkton Canada 51°11N 102°28W 297 C8
Yorkville Calif., U.S.A. 38°52N 123°13W 306 G3
Yorkville Ga., U.S.A. 33°55N 84°58W 316 B5
Yorkville Ill., U.S.A. 41°38N 88°27W 311 C8
Yoro Honduras 15°9N 87°7W 320 C2
Yoron-Jima Japan 27°2N 128°26E 221 L4
Yorosso Mali 12°17N 4°55W 262 C4
Yos Sudarso, Pulau = Dolak, Pulau Indonesia 8°0S 138°30E 231 F9
Yosemite △ U.S.A. 37°45N 119°40W 306 H7
Yosemite Village U.S.A. 37°45N 119°35W 306 H7
Yoshida Japan 34°40N 132°42E 222 C4
Yoshimatsu Japan 32°0N 130°47E 222 F2
Yoshino-Kumano △ Japan 34°12N 135°55E 223 C7
Yoshinogawa Japan 34°4N 134°21E 222 C6
Yoshkar Ola Russia 56°38N 47°55E 190 B8
Yotala Bolivia 19°10S 65°17W 331 D4
Yotsuya Tokyo, Japan 140 a2
Yotvata Israel 29°55N 35°2E 251 J6
You Jiang → China 22°50N 108°6E 228 F6
You Xian China 27°1N 113°17E 229 D9
You'anmen China 39°51N 116°19E 114 B1
Youbou Canada 48°53N 124°13W 306 B2
Youghal Ireland 51°56N 7°52W 166 E4
Youghal B. Ireland 51°55N 7°49W 166 E4
Youkounkoun Guinea 12°35N 13°11W 262 C2
Young N.S.W., Australia 34°19S 148°18E 283 C8
Young Sask., Canada 51°47N 105°45W 297 C7
Young Uruguay 32°44S 57°36W 334 C4
Young I. Antarctica 66°25S 162°24E 151 C11
Young Ra. N.Z. 44°10S 169°30E 285 E4
Younghusband, L. Australia 30°50S 136°5E 282 A2
Younghusband Pen. Australia 36°0S 139°25E 282 D3
Youngsfield S. Africa 34°0S 18°30E 118 B1
Youngstown Alta., Canada 51°35N 111°10W 297 C6
Youngstown Fla., U.S.A. 30°22N 85°26W 316 E4
Youngstown N.Y., U.S.A. 43°15N 79°3W 312 C5
Youngstown Ohio, U.S.A. 41°6N 80°39W 312 E4
Youngsville U.S.A. 41°51N 79°19W 312 E5
Youngwood U.S.A. 40°14N 79°34W 312 F5
Youssoufia Morocco 32°16N 8°31W 260 B3
Youxi China 26°10N 118°13E 229 D12
Youyang China 28°47N 108°42E 228 C7
Youyu China 40°10N 112°20E 226 D7
Yozgat Turkey 39°51N 34°47E 212 C6
Yozgat □ Turkey 39°30N 35°0E 212 C6
Ypacaraí △ Paraguay 25°18S 57°19W 334 B4
Ypané → Paraguay 23°29S 57°19W 334 A4
Yport France 49°45N 0°15E 172 C7
Ypres = Ieper Belgium 50°51N 2°53E 170 D2
Ypsilanti U.S.A. 42°14N 83°37W 311 B13
Yr Wyddgrug = Mold U.K. 53°9N 3°8W 168 D4
Yreka U.S.A. 41°44N 122°38W 304 F2
Yrghyz Kazakhstan 48°37N 61°16E 216 C6
Yrghyz → Kazakhstan 48°6N 62°30E 216 C6
Ysabel Chan. Papua N. G. 2°0S 150°0E 286 B6
Yssingeaux France 45°9N 4°8E 175 C8
Ystabøhamn Norway 59°3N 5°23E 164 E2
Ystad Sweden 55°26N 13°50E 163 J7
Ysyk-Köl = Balykchy Kyrgyzstan 42°26N 76°12E 217 D9
Ysyk-Köl Kyrgyzstan 42°25N 77°15E 217 D9
Ysyk-Köl □ Kyrgyzstan 42°0N 78°0E 217 D9
Ythan → U.K. 57°19N 1°59W 167 D7
Ytre Arna Norway 60°27N 5°25E 164 D2
Ytre Enebakk Norway 59°44N 11°0E 164 E8
Ytre Rendal Norway 61°46N 11°8E 164 C8
Ytteran Sweden 63°16N 14°7E 162 A8
Ytterhogdal Sweden 62°12N 14°56E 162 B8
Yttermalung Sweden 60°35N 13°51E 162 D7
Ytyk-Kyuyel Russia 62°30N 133°45E 215 C14
Yu Jiang → China 23°22N 110°3E 228 F7
Yü Shan Taiwan 23°25N 120°52E 225 C2
Yü Shan △ Taiwan 24°45N 121°12E 225 C3
Yu Xian = Yuzhou China 34°10N 113°28E 226 G7
Yu Xian Hebei, China 39°50N 114°35E 226 E8
Yu Xian Shanxi, China 38°5N 113°20E 226 E7
Yuan Jiang → Hunan, China 28°55N 111°50E 229 C8
Yuan Jiang → Yunnan, China 22°20N 103°59E 228 F4
Yuan'an China 31°3N 111°34E 229 B8
Yüanch'ang Taiwan 23°39N 120°18E 225 C2
Yuanjiang Hunan, China 28°47N 112°21E 229 C9
Yuanjiang Yunnan, China 23°32N 102°0E 228 F4
Yüanli Taiwan 24°27N 120°39E 225 B2
Yüanlin Taiwan 23°58N 120°30E 225 C2
Yuanling China 28°29N 110°22E 229 C8
Yuanmingyuan Park China 40°0N 116°17E 114 A1
Yuanmou China 25°42N 101°53E 228 E3
Yuanping China 38°42N 112°46E 226 E7
Yuanqu China 35°18N 111°40E 226 G6
Yuanshan Taiwan 24°45N 121°43E 225 B3
Yuanxiatian China 23°12N 113°17E 121 A2
Yuanyang Henan, China 35°3N 113°58E 226 G7
Yuanyang Yunnan, China 23°10N 102°43E 228 F4
Yuat → Papua N. G. 4°10S 143°52E 286 C2
Yuba → U.S.A. 39°8N 121°36W 306 F5
Yuba City U.S.A. 39°8N 121°37W 306 F5
Yūbari Japan 43°4N 141°59E 220 C10
Yubdo Ethiopia 8°58N 35°24E 257 F4
Yūbetsu Japan 44°13N 143°50E 220 B11
Yucatán □ Mexico 20°50N 89°0W 319 C7
Yucatán, Canal de Caribbean 22°0N 86°30W 320 B2
Yucatán, Península de Mexico 19°30N 89°0W 292 H11
Yucatan Basin Cent. Amer. 19°0N 86°0W 320 C3
Yucatan Channel = Yucatán, Canal de Caribbean 22°0N 86°30W 320 B2
Yucca U.S.A. 34°52N 114°9W 307 L12
Yucca Valley U.S.A. 34°8N 116°27W 307 L10
Yucheng China 36°55N 116°32E 226 F9
Yüch'ih Taiwan 23°54N 120°56E 225 C2
Yuching Taiwan 23°7N 120°27E 225 C2
Yuci = Jinzhong China 37°42N 112°46E 226 F7
Yudu China 25°59N 115°30E 229 E10
Yuechi China 30°34N 106°25E 228 B6
Yuen Long China 22°26N 114°2E 219 a
Yuendumu Australia 22°16S 131°49E 278 D5
Yuendumu ☼ Australia 22°21S 131°40E 278 D5
Yueqing China 28°9N 120°59E 229 C13
Yueqing Wan China 28°5N 121°20E 229 D13
Yuexi Anhui, China 30°50N 116°20E 229 B11
Yuexi Sichuan, China 28°37N 102°26E 228 C4
Yuexiu China 23°8N 113°16E 121 B2
Yuexiu Park China 23°8N 113°16E 121 B2
Yueyang China 29°21N 113°5E 229 C9
Yufu-Dake Japan 33°17N 131°33E 222 D3
Yugan China 28°43N 116°37E 229 C11
Yuğluk Dağı Turkey 36°59N 33°50E 250 B4
Yugo-Zarad Russia 55°40N 37°30E 129 B2
Yugorenok Russia 59°47N 137°40E 215 D14
Yuhuan China 28°9N 121°12E 229 C13
Yühuan Dao China 28°5N 121°15E 229 C13
Yujiang China 28°10N 116°43E 229 C11
Yukhnov Russia 54°44N 35°15E 188 E8
Yūki Japan 36°18N 139°53E 223 A11
Yukon U.S.A. 35°31N 97°45W 314 D6
Yukon → U.S.A. 62°32N 163°54W 303 E7
Yukon-Charley Rivers ⌂ U.S.A. 65°15N 144°0W 303 D12
Yukon Delta Nat. Wildlife Refuge ⌂ U.S.A. 61°0N 163°0W 303 F7
Yukon Flats U.S.A. 66°40N 145°45W 303 C11
Yukon Territory □ Canada 63°0N 135°0W 294 E5
Yüksekova Turkey 37°34N 44°16E 213 D11
Yukta Russia 63°26N 105°42E 215 C11
Yukuhashi Japan 33°44N 130°59E 222 D2
Yulara Australia 25°10S 130°55E 279 E5
Yule → Australia 20°41S 118°17E 278 D2
Yuleba Australia 26°37S 149°24E 281 D4
Yulee U.S.A. 30°38N 81°36W 316 E8
Yuli China 41°19N 86°15E 217 D11
Yuli Nigeria 9°44N 10°12E 263 D7
Yüli Taiwan 23°20N 121°18E 225 C3
Yulin Guangxi Zhuangzu, China 22°40N 110°8E 229 F8
Yulin Hainan, China 18°10N 109°31E 236 C7
Yulin Shaanxi, China 38°20N 109°30E 226 E5
Yulong Xueshan China 27°6N 100°10E 228 D3
Yuma Ariz., U.S.A. 32°43N 114°37W 307 N12
Yuma Colo., U.S.A. 40°8N 102°43W 304 F12
Yuma, B. de Dom. Rep. 18°20N 68°35W 321 C6
Yumali Australia 35°32S 139°45E 282 C3
Yumbe Uganda 3°28N 31°15E 268 B3
Yumbi Équateur, Dem. Rep. of the Congo 1°53S 16°34E 264 C3
Yumbi Maniema, Dem. Rep. of the Congo 1°12S 26°15E 268 C2
Yumbo Colombia 3°35N 76°28W 328 C2
Yumen China 39°50N 97°30E 218 D8
Yumurtalık Turkey 36°45N 35°48E 250 B6
Yun Gui Gaoyuan China 26°0N 104°0E 228 E3
Yun Ling Shan China 27°0N 99°20E 228 D2
Yun Xian Hubei, China 32°50N 110°46E 226 H6
Yun Xian Yunnan, China 24°27N 100°8E 228 E3
Yuna Australia 28°20S 115°0E 279 E2
Yunak Turkey 38°49N 31°43E 212 C4
Yunan China 23°12N 111°30E 229 F8
Yunaska I. U.S.A. 52°38N 170°40W 303 K5
Yuncheng Henan, China 35°36N 115°57E 226 G8
Yuncheng Shanxi, China 35°2N 111°0E 226 G6
Yunfu China 22°50N 112°5E 229 F9
Yung Shue Wan China 22°13N 114°6E 122 B1
Yungan Taiwan 22°49N 120°12E 225 D2
Yungang Shiku China 40°6N 113°7E 226 D7
Yungas Bolivia 17°0S 66°0W 331 D4
Yungay Chile 37°10S 72°5W 334 D1
Yungay Peru 9°2S 77°45W 330 B2
Yungk'ang Taiwan 23°2N 120°15E 225 C2
Yungki = Jilin China 43°44N 126°30E 227 C14
Yungning = Nanning China 22°48N 108°20E 228 F7
Yunhe China 28°8N 119°33E 229 C12
Yunkai Dashan China 22°30N 111°0E 229 F8
Yunkanjini ☼ Australia 22°33S 131°6E 278 D5
Yünlin □ Taiwan 23°40N 120°20E 225 C2
Yunling Shan China 28°30N 98°50E 218 F8
Yunlong China 25°57N 99°13E 228 E2
Yunmeng China 31°2N 113°43E 229 B9
Yunnan □ China 25°0N 102°0E 228 E4
Yunotsu Japan 35°5N 132°21E 222 B4
Yunquera de Henares Spain 40°47N 3°11W 196 E1
Yunshui Taiwan 23°23N 120°31E 225 C2
Yunt Dağı Turkey 38°56N 27°13E 205 C9
Yunta Australia 32°34S 139°36E 281 E2
Yunxi China 33°0N 110°22E 226 H6
Yunxiao China 23°59N 117°18E 229 F11
Yunyang Chongqing, China 31°2N 108°51E 228 B7
Yunyang Henan, China 33°26N 112°42E 229 A9
Yupanqui Basin Pac. Oc. 19°0S 101°0W 289 J17
Yuping China 27°13N 108°56E 228 D7
Yupukarri Guyana 3°45N 59°20W 329 C6
Yuqing China 27°13N 107°53E 228 D6
Yuraygir △ Australia 29°45S 153°15E 281 D5
Yurga Russia 55°42N 84°51E 214 D9
Yurihonjō Japan 39°23N 140°3E 220 E10
Yurimaguas Peru 5°55S 76°7W 330 B2
Yurkiyka Ukraine 48°42N 28°35E 183 B13
Yurungkax He → China 38°5N 80°34E 217 E10
Yuryev = Tartu Estonia 58°20N 26°44E 188 C4
Yuryev-Polskiy Russia 56°30N 39°40E 188 D10
Yuryevets Russia 57°25N 43°2E 190 B6
Yuscarán Honduras 13°58N 86°45W 320 D2
Yûsef, Bahr → Egypt 28°25N 30°35E 256 B3
Yushan China 28°42N 118°10E 229 C12
Yushanzhen China 29°28N 108°22E 228 C7
Yushe China 37°4N 112°58E 226 F7
Yushu Jilin, China 44°43N 126°38E 227 B14
Yushu Qinghai, China 33°5N 96°55E 218 E8
Yūsofābād Iran 35°43N 51°24E 141 A2
Yusufeli Turkey 40°50N 41°33E 213 B9
Yutai China 35°0N 116°45E 226 G9
Yutian Hebei, China 39°53N 117°45E 227 E9
Yutian Sinkiang-Uigur, China 36°52N 81°42E 217 E10
Yütze = Jinzhong China 37°42N 112°46E 226 F7
Yüweng Tao Taiwan 23°36N 119°30E 225 C1
Yuxarı Qarabağ = Nagorno-Karabakh □ Azerbaijan 39°55N 46°45E 213 C12
Yuxi China 24°30N 102°35E 228 E4
Yuyao China 30°3N 121°10E 229 B13
Yuzawa Japan 39°10N 140°30E 220 E10
Yuzha Russia 56°34N 42°1E 190 B6
Yuzhno-Kurilsk Russia 44°1N 145°51E 215 E15
Yuzhno-Sakhalinsk Russia 46°58N 142°45E 219 B17
Yuzhno-Sukhokumsk Russia 44°40N 45°35E 191 H7
Yuzhnouralsk Russia 54°26N 61°15E 216 B6
Yuzhnyy □ Russia 44°0N 40°0E 214 E5
Yuzhou China 34°10N 113°28E 226 G7
Yuzovka = Donetsk Ukraine 48°0N 37°45E 189 J9
Yvelines □ France 48°40N 1°45E 173 D8
Yverdon-les-Bains Switz. 46°47N 6°39E 179 J2
Yvetot France 49°37N 0°44E 172 C7
Yzeure France 46°33N 3°22E 173 F10

Z

Za'abeel U.A.E. 25°13N 55°19E 119 B2
Zaandam Neths. 52°26N 4°49E 112 A1
Zaandijk Neths. 52°28N 4°49E 112 A1
Zaanstad Neths. 52°27N 4°50E 112 A1
Zab, Monts du Algeria 34°55N 5°0E 261 B6
Zāb al Kabīr → Iraq 36°1N 43°24E 213 D10
Zāb aş Şaghīr → Iraq 35°17N 43°29E 213 E10
Žabalj Serbia 45°21N 20°5E 182 E5
Žabari Serbia 44°22N 21°15E 202 B5
Zabarjad Egypt 23°40N 36°12E 256 C4
Zabaykalsk Russia 49°40N 117°25E 215 E12
Zabbar Malta 35°53N 14°32E 206 F8
Záběhlice Czech Rep. 50°3N 14°29E 135 B2
Zabīd Yemen 14°0N 43°10E 248 D3
Zabīd, W. → Yemen 14°7N 43°6E 248 D3
Zabki Poland 52°17N 21°6E 143 B2
Ząbkowice Śląskie Poland 50°35N 16°50E 185 H3
Žabljak Montenegro 43°18N 19°5E 202 C3
Zabłudów Poland 53°0N 23°19E 185 F9
Żabno Poland 50°9N 20°53E 185 H7
Zabol Iran 31°0N 61°32E 247 D9
Zābol □ Afghan. 32°0N 67°0E 240 C2
Zābolī Iran 27°10N 61°35E 247 E9
Zabolotiv Ukraine 48°28N 25°18E 183 B10
Zabolottya Ukraine 51°38N 24°16E 185 G11
Zabré Burkina Faso 11°12N 0°36W 263 C4
Zábřeh Czech Rep. 49°53N 16°52E 181 B9
Zabrze Poland 50°18N 18°50E 185 H5
Zabuzhzhya Ukraine 51°21N 23°42E 185 G10
Zabzuga Ghana 9°20N 0°30E 263 D5
Zacapa Guatemala 14°59N 89°31W 320 D2
Zacapu Mexico 19°50N 101°43W 318 D4
Zacatecas Mexico 22°47N 102°35W 318 C4
Zacatecas □ Mexico 23°0N 103°0W 318 C4
Zacatecoluca El Salv. 13°29N 88°51W 320 D2
Zacharo Greece 37°30N 21°39E 204 D3
Zachary U.S.A. 30°39N 91°9W 314 F9
Zachodnio-Pomorskie □ Poland 53°40N 15°50E 184 E2
Żacisze Poland 52°17N 21°4E 143 B2
Zacoalco de Torres Mexico 20°14N 103°35W 318 C4
Zacualtipán Mexico 20°39N 98°36W 319 C5
Zadar Croatia 44°8N 15°14E 199 D12
Zadawa Nigeria 11°33N 10°19E 263 C7
Zadetkyi Kyun Burma 10°0N 98°25E 237 G2

Zadonsk Russia 52°25N 38°56E 189 F10
Zafarqand Iran 33°11N 52°29E 247 C7
Zafra Spain 38°26N 6°30W 195 G4
Żagań Poland 51°39N 15°22E 185 G2
Zagaoua Chad 16°0N 21°10E 259 E4
Žagarė Lithuania 56°21N 23°15E 184 B10
Zagazig Egypt 30°40N 31°30E 256 H7
Zāgheh Iran 33°30N 48°42E 247 C6
Zaghouan Tunisia 36°23N 10°10E 258 A2
Zaghouan □ Tunisia 36°20N 10°0E 261 A7
Zaglou Algeria 27°17N 0°3W 261 C4
Zagnanado Benin 7°18N 2°28E 263 D5
Zagora Greece 39°27N 23°6E 204 B5
Zagora Morocco 30°22N 5°51W 260 B3
Zagorje Slovenia 46°8N 15°0E 199 B11
Zagórów Poland 52°10N 17°54E 185 F4
Zagorsk = Sergiyev Posad Russia 56°20N 38°10E 188 D10
Zagorsky = Krasnozavodsk Russia 56°27N 38°25E 188 D10
Zagórz Poland 49°30N 22°14E 185 J9
Zagreb Croatia 45°50N 15°58E 199 C12
Zagreb ✕ (ZAG) Croatia 45°45N 16°4E 199 C13
Zāgros, Kūhhā-ye Iran 33°45N 48°5E 247 C6
Zagros Mts. = Zāgros, Kūhhā-ye Iran 33°45N 48°5E 247 C6
Žagubica Serbia 44°15N 21°47E 202 B5
Zaguinaso Ivory C. 10°1N 6°14W 262 C3
Zagyva → Hungary 47°5N 20°4E 182 C5
Zahamena △ Madag. 17°37S 48°49E 272 B2
Zāhedān Fārs, Iran 28°46N 53°52E 247 D7
Zāhedān Sīstān va Balūchestān, Iran 29°30N 60°50E 247 D9
Zahirabad India 17°43N 77°37E 244 F3
Zahlah Lebanon 33°52N 35°50E 250 E6
Zahna Germany 51°55N 12°49E 178 D8
Záhony Hungary 48°25N 22°11E 182 B7
Zahrā Iraq 33°22N 44°19E 113 A1
Ẓahrān Si. Arabia 17°40N 43°30E 248 C3
Zainsk Russia 55°18N 52°4E 190 C11
Zaïre = Congo → Africa 6°4S 12°24E 265 D2
Zaïre = Congo, Dem. Rep. of the ■ Africa 3°0S 23°0E 265 C4
Zaïre □ Angola 7°0S 14°0E 265 D2
Zaječar Serbia 43°53N 22°18E 202 C6
Zaka Zimbabwe 20°20S 31°29E 271 B5
Zakamensk Russia 50°23N 103°17E 215 D11
Zakani Dem. Rep. of the Congo 2°33N 23°16E 264 B4
Zakarpattya □ Ukraine 48°20N 23°20E 183 B8
Zakataly = Zaqatala Azerbaijan 41°38N 46°35E 191 K8
Zakbayemé Cameroon 4°2N 10°34E 264 B2
Zakhodnaya Dzvina = Daugava → Latvia 57°4N 24°3E 188 D3
Zākhū Iraq 37°10N 42°50E 213 D10
Zakinthos = Zakynthos Greece 37°47N 20°54E 207 D2
Zakinthos, Diavlos Greece 37°50N 21°0E 207 D2
Zakopane Poland 49°18N 19°57E 185 J6
Zakouma Chad 10°54N 19°49E 259 F3
Zakouma △ Chad 10°52N 19°45E 259 F3
Zakroczym Poland 52°26N 20°38E 185 F7
Zakros Greece 35°6N 26°10E 207 E7
Zakynthos Greece 37°47N 20°54E 207 D2
Zakynthos □ Greece 37°47N 20°57E 204 D2
Zakynthos ✕ (ZTH) Greece 37°45N 20°50E 207 D2
Zala Angola 7°52S 13°42E 265 D2
Zala Ethiopia 6°28N 37°13E 257 F4
Zala □ Hungary 46°42N 16°50E 182 D1
Zala → Hungary 46°43N 17°16E 182 D2
Zalaegerszeg Hungary 46°53N 16°47E 182 D1
Zalakomár Hungary 46°33N 17°10E 182 D2
Zalalövő Hungary 46°51N 16°35E 182 D1
Zalamea de la Serena Spain 38°40N 5°38W 195 G5
Zalamea la Real Spain 37°41N 6°38W 195 H4
Zalantun China 48°0N 122°43E 219 B13
Zalari Russia 53°33N 102°30E 215 D11
Zalău Romania 47°12N 23°3E 182 C8
Žalec Slovenia 46°16N 15°10E 199 B12
Zaleshchiki = Zalishchyky Ukraine 48°45N 25°45E 183 B10
Zalesye Russia 54°50N 21°31E 184 D8
Zalew Wiślany Poland 54°20N 19°50E 184 D6
Zalewo Poland 53°50N 19°41E 184 E6
Ẓalīm Si. Arabia 22°43N 42°10E 248 B3
Zalingei Sudan 12°51N 23°29E 259 F4
Zalishchyky Ukraine 48°45N 25°45E 183 B10
Zalmah, J. az Libya 25°30N 24°40E 258 C4
Žalov Czech Rep. 50°10N 14°22E 135 A2
Zalṭan Al Wāḥāt, Libya 28°51N 19°52E 258 C3
Zalṭan An Nuqāṭ al Khams, Libya 32°57N 11°52E 258 B2
Zalun Burma 17°29N 95°34E 241 G5
Załuski Poland 52°9N 20°55E 143 C1
Zama L. Canada 58°45N 119°5W 296 B5
Zambales □ Phil. 15°20N 120°10E 232 D3
Zambales Mts. Phil. 15°45N 120°5E 232 D3
Zambeke Dem. Rep. of the Congo 2°8N 25°17E 268 B2
Zambeze → Africa 18°35S 36°20E 269 F4
Zambezi = Zambeze → Africa 18°35S 36°20E 269 F4
Zambezi Zambia 13°30S 23°15E 265 E4
Zambezi △ Zimbabwe 17°54S 25°41E 269 F2
Zambezia □ Mozam. 16°15S 37°30E 269 F4
Zambia ■ Africa 15°0S 28°0E 269 F2
Zamboanga Phil. 6°59N 122°3E 233 H4
Zamboanga del Norte □ Phil. 8°0N 123°0E 233 G4
Zamboanga del Sur □ Phil. 7°40N 123°0E 233 H4
Zamboanga Pen. Phil. 7°32N 122°16E 233 H4
Zamboanguita Phil. 9°6N 123°11E 233 G4
Zambrano Colombia 9°45N 74°49W 328 B3
Zambrów Poland 52°59N 22°14E 185 F9
Zamdorf Germany 48°8N 11°35E 131 B2
Zametchino Russia 53°30N 42°30E 190 D6
Zamfara □ Nigeria 12°10N 6°0E 263 C6
Zamfara → Nigeria 12°5N 4°2E 263 C5
Zamora Ecuador 4°4S 78°58W 328 D2
Zamora Michoacan, Mexico 19°59N 102°16W 318 D4
Zamora Spain 41°30N 5°45W 194 D5
Zamora □ Spain 41°30N 5°46W 194 D5
Zamora → Ecuador 2°59S 78°15W 328 D2
Zamora-Chinchipe □ Ecuador 4°15S 78°50W 328 D2
Zamość Poland 50°43N 23°15E 185 H10
Zamtang China 32°26N 101°6E 228 A3
Zamuro, Sierra del Venezuela 4°0N 62°30W 329 C5
Zamzam, W. → Libya 30°58N 14°48E 258 B2
Zan Ghana 9°26N 0°17W 263 D4
Zanaga Congo 2°48S 13°48E 264 C2
Záncara → Spain 39°18N 3°18W 197 F1
Zanda China 31°32N 79°50E 218 E4
Zanderij Suriname 5°50N 55°16W 329 B6
Zandu Dem. Rep. of the Congo 5°11S 18°16E 265 D3
Zandvoort Neths. 52°22N 4°32E 170 B4
Zanesville U.S.A. 39°56N 82°1W 312 G2
Zanevka Russia 59°55N 30°31E 137 B3
Zangābād Iran 38°26N 46°44E 246 B5
Zangliveri Greece 40°36N 23°15E 202 F7
Zangoza = Sangüesa Spain 42°37N 1°17W 196 C3
Zangue → Mozam. 17°50S 35°21E 269 F4
Zanjān Iran 36°40N 48°35E 213 D13
Zanjān □ Iran 37°20N 49°30E 247 B6
Zanjān → Iran 37°8N 47°47E 247 B6
Zannone Italy 40°58N 13°3E 200 B6
Zanow = Sianów Poland 54°13N 16°18E 184 D3
Zante = Zakynthos Greece 37°47N 20°54E 207 D2
Zanthus Australia 31°2S 123°34E 279 F3
Zanzibar Tanzania 6°12S 39°12E 268 D4
Zanzūr Libya 32°55N 13°1E 258 B2
Zaouatallaz Algeria 24°52N 8°26E 261 D6
Zaouiet El-Kala = Bordj Omar Driss Algeria 28°10N 6°40E 261 C6
Zaouiet Reggâne Algeria 26°32N 0°3E 261 C5
Zaoyang China 32°10N 112°45E 229 A9
Zaozernyy Kazakhstan 53°6N 71°9E 217 B8
Zaozhuang China 34°50N 117°35E 227 G9
Zap Suyu = Zāb al Kabīr → Iraq 36°1N 43°24E 213 D10
Zapadna Morava → Serbia 43°38N 21°30E 202 C5
Zapadnaya Dvina = Daugava → Latvia 57°4N 24°3E 188 D3
Zapadnaya Dvina Russia 56°15N 32°3E 188 D7
Západné Beskydy Europe 49°30N 19°0E 181 B12
Zapadni Rodopi Bulgaria 41°50N 24°0E 202 E7
Západočeský □ Czech Rep. 49°35N 13°0E 180 B6
Zapala Argentina 39°0S 70°5W 336 A2
Zapaleri, Cerro Bolivia 22°49S 67°11W 334 A2
Zapata U.S.A. 26°55N 99°16W 314 H5
Zapatón → Spain 39°0N 6°49W 195 F4
Zapiga Chile 19°40S 69°55W 330 D4
Zapolyarnyy Russia 69°26N 30°51E 160 B24
Zapopán Mexico 20°43N 103°24W 318 C4
Zaporizhzhya Ukraine 47°50N 35°10E 189 J8
Zaporizhzhya □ Ukraine 46°55N 35°50E 189 J8
Zaporozhye = Zaporizhzhya Ukraine 47°50N 35°10E 189 J8
Zapote Phil. 14°27N 120°56E 127 C1
Zappeion Athens, Greece 112 c2
Zaqatala Azerbaijan 41°38N 46°35E 191 K8
Zara Turkey 39°58N 37°43E 212 C7
Zarafshon Uzbekistan 41°34N 64°12E 216 D6
Zaragoza Colombia 7°30N 74°52W 328 B3
Zaragoza Coahuila, Mexico 28°29N 100°55W 318 B4
Zaragoza Nuevo León, Mexico 23°58N 99°46W 319 C5
Zaragoza Spain 41°39N 0°53W 196 D4
Zaragoza □ Spain 41°35N 1°0W 196 D4
Zarand Kermān, Iran 30°46N 56°34E 247 D8
Zarand Markazī, Iran 35°18N 50°25E 247 C6
Zărandului, Munții Romania 46°14N 22°7E 182 D7
Zaranj Afghan. 30°55N 61°55E 240 C1
Zarasai Lithuania 55°40N 26°20E 188 E4
Zárate Argentina 34°7S 59°0W 334 C4
Zarautz Spain 43°17N 2°10W 196 B2
Zaraysk Russia 54°48N 38°53E 188 E10
Zaraza Venezuela 9°21N 65°19W 329 B4
Zard, Kūh-e Iran 32°22N 50°4E 247 C6
Zāreh Iran 35°7N 49°9E 247 C6
Zari Nigeria 13°4N 12°45E 263 C7
Zaria Nigeria 11°0N 7°40E 263 C6
Zarineh → Iran 36°17N 46°26E 213 D12
Zarinsk Russia 53°43N 84°55E 217 B10
Żarki Poland 50°38N 19°23E 185 H6
Zarko Greece 39°38N 22°6E 204 B4
Zarneh Iran 33°55N 46°10E 246 C5
Zărnești Romania 45°33N 25°18E 183 E10
Zaros Greece 35°8N 24°54E 207 E5
Żarów Poland 50°56N 16°29E 185 H3
Zarqā', Nahr az → Jordan 32°10N 35°37E 251 F6
Zarrīn Iran 32°46N 54°37E 247 C7
Zarrīnābād Iran 36°25N 48°17E 213 D13
Zaruma Ecuador 3°40S 79°38W 328 D2
Żary Poland 51°37N 15°10E 185 G2
Zarza de Granadilla Spain 40°14N 6°3W 194 E4
Zarzaïtine Algeria 28°15N 9°34E 261 C6
Zarzal Colombia 4°24N 76°4W 328 C2
Zarzis Tunisia 33°31N 11°2E 258 B2
Zas Spain 43°4N 8°53W 194 B2
Zashaghan Kazakhstan 51°11N 51°20E 216 D4
Zaskar → India 34°13N 77°20E 243 B7
Zaskar Mts. India 33°15N 77°30E 243 C7
Zastavna Ukraine 48°31N 25°51E 183 B10
Zastron S. Africa 30°18S 27°7E 270 D4
Žatec Czech Rep. 50°20N 13°32E 180 A6
Zaterechnyy Russia 44°48N 45°11E 191 H7
Zatishye = Elektrostal Russia 55°41N 38°32E 188 E10
Zator Poland 49°59N 19°28E 185 J6
Zatyshshya Ukraine 47°20N 29°51E 183 C14
Zavala Bos.-H. 42°50N 17°59E 202 D1
Zavāreh Iran 33°29N 52°28E 247 C7
Zave Zimbabwe 17°6S 30°1E 271 A5
Zaventem Belgium 50°53N 4°28E 116 A2
Zavetnoye Russia 47°13N 43°50E 191 G6
Zavidovići Bos.-H. 44°27N 18°10E 182 F3
Zavitaya = Zavitinsk Russia 50°10N 129°20E 215 D13
Zavitinsk Russia 50°10N 129°20E 215 D13
Zavodovski I. Antarctica 56°0S 27°45W 151 B1
Zavodskoy = Komsomolskiy Russia 54°27N 45°33E 190 C7
Zavolzhsk Russia 57°30N 42°0E 190 B6
Zavolzhye = Zavolzhsk Russia 57°30N 42°3E 190 B6
Zavolzhye Russia 56°37N 43°26E 190 B6
Zawady Poland 52°10N 21°6E 143 B2
Zawadzkie Poland 50°37N 18°28E 185 H5
Zawichost Poland 50°48N 21°51E 185 H8
Zawidów Poland 51°1N 15°1E 185 G2
Zawiercie Poland 50°30N 19°24E 185 H6
Zāwīyah, J. az Syria 35°45N 36°35E 250 C7
Zāwiyat al Bayḍā = Al Bayḍā Libya 32°50N 21°44E 258 B4
Zāwiyat Masūs Libya 31°35N 21°1E 258 B4
Zāwiyet Abû Musallam Egypt 29°56N 31°9E 117 B1
Zawrā' Park Iraq 33°18N 44°23E 113 B2
Zâwyet Shammas Egypt 31°30N 26°37E 256 A2
Zâwyet Um el Rakham Egypt 31°18N 27°1E 256 A2
Zâwyet Ungeîla Egypt 31°23N 26°42E 256 A2
Zāyā Iraq 33°33N 44°13E 246 C5
Zāyandeh → Iran 32°35N 52°0E 247 C7
Ẓaymah Si. Arabia 21°37N 40°6E 248 C2
Zaysan Kazakhstan 47°28N 84°52E 217 C10
Zaysan Köli Kazakhstan 48°0N 83°0E 217 C10
Zayü China 28°48N 97°27E 218 F8
Zazafotsy Madag. 21°11S 46°21E 272 C2
Zāzamt, W. → Libya 30°29N 14°30E 258 B2
Zázir, O. → Algeria 22°0N 5°40E 261 D6
Zázrivá Slovak Rep. 49°16N 19°7E 181 B12
Zbarazh Ukraine 49°43N 25°44E 183 B10
Zbąszyń Poland 52°14N 15°56E 185 F2
Zbąszynek Poland 52°16N 15°51E 185 F2
Zblewo Poland 53°56N 18°19E 184 E5
Zbraslav Czech Rep. 49°58N 14°23E 135 C2
Zbruch → Ukraine 48°32N 26°27E 183 B11
Žďár nad Sázavou Czech Rep. 49°34N 15°57E 180 B8
Zdiby Czech Rep. 50°9N 14°27E 135 B2
Zdolbuniv Ukraine 50°30N 26°15E 177 C14
Ždrelo Serbia 44°16N 21°28E 202 B5
Zduńska Wola Poland 51°37N 18°59E 185 G5
Zduny Poland 51°39N 17°21E 185 G4
Zearing U.S.A. 42°10N 93°18W 310 B3
Zeballos Canada 49°59N 126°50W 296 D3
Zebbug Malta 35°52N 14°26E 206 F7
Zebbug Gozo, Malta 36°4N 14°14E 206 E6
Zebediela S. Africa 24°20S 29°17E 271 B4
Zebila Ghana 10°55N 0°30W 263 C4
Zebulon U.S.A. 33°6N 84°21W 316 B5
Zeebrugge Belgium 51°19N 3°12E 170 C3
Zeehan Australia 41°52S 145°25E 281 G4
Zeekoevlei S. Africa 34°4S 18°31E 118 B2
Zeeland U.S.A. 42°49N 86°1W 311 B10
Zeeland □ Neths. 51°30N 3°50E 170 C3
Zeelandia St. Eustatius 17°30N 62°59W 322 a
Zeerust S. Africa 25°31S 26°4E 270 C4
Ẓefat Israel 32°58N 35°29E 250 F6
Zegdou Algeria 29°51N 4°45W 260 C4
Zege Ethiopia 11°43N 37°18E 257 E4
Zeggerene, Iracher Mali 16°49N 2°16E 263 B5
Zégoua Mali 10°32N 5°35W 262 C3
Zehak Iran 30°53N 61°42E 247 D9
Zehden = Cedynia Poland 52°53N 14°12E 185 F1
Zehdenick Germany 52°58N 13°20E 178 C9
Zehlendorf Germany 52°26N 13°16E 115 B2
Zeigler U.S.A. 37°54N 89°3W 310 G7
Zeil, Mt. Australia 23°30S 132°23E 278 D5
Zeila = Saylac Somalia 11°21N 43°30E 267 B5
Zeist Neths. 52°5N 5°15E 170 B5
Zeitz Germany 51°2N 12°7E 178 D8
Zejtun Malta 35°51N 14°32E 206 F8
Żelechów Poland 51°49N 21°54E 185 G8
Zelena Ukraine 48°3N 24°45E 183 B9
Zelená Hora Czech Rep. 49°34N 15°56E 180 B8
Zelengora Bos.-H. 43°22N 18°30E 202 C2
Zelenodolsk Russia 55°55N 48°30E 190 C9
Zelenogorsk Russia 60°12N 29°43E 188 B5
Zelenograd Russia 56°1N 37°12E 188 D9
Zelenogradsk Russia 54°53N 20°29E 184 D7
Zelenokumsk Russia 44°24N 44°0E 191 H6
Zeleqa, W. → Egypt 29°7N 34°31E 251 J5
Železná Ruda Czech Rep. 49°8N 13°15E 180 B6
Železnik Serbia 44°43N 20°23E 202 B4
Zelfana Algeria 32°27N 4°15E 261 B5
Zelienople U.S.A. 40°48N 80°8W 312 F4
Želiezovce Slovak Rep. 48°3N 18°40E 181 C11
Zelina Croatia 45°57N 16°16E 199 C13
Zell Baden-W., Germany 47°42N 7°52E 179 H3
Zell Rhld-Pfz., Germany 50°1N 7°10E 179 E3
Zell am See Austria 47°19N 12°47E 180 D5
Zella-Mehlis Germany 50°39N 10°40E 178 E6
Zelmen = Rovnoye Russia 50°52N 46°3E 190 E8
Zelów Poland 51°28N 19°14E 185 G6
Zeltweg Austria 47°11N 14°45E 180 D7
Zelyony Dol = Zelenodolsk Russia 55°55N 48°30E 190 C9
Žemaitijos △ Lithuania 56°2N 21°55E 184 B8
Zembra, I. Tunisia 37°5N 10°56E 258 A2
Zemgale = Jelgava Latvia 56°41N 23°49E 184 B10
Zémio C.A.R. 5°2N 25°5E 264 A5
Zemlya Imperatora Nikolaya II = Severnaya Zemlya Russia 79°0N 100°0E 215 B11
Zemmora Algeria 35°44N 0°51E 261 A5
Zemmur W. Sahara 25°5N 12°0W 260 C2
Zemongo △ C.A.R. 6°45N 25°5E 264 A5
Zemoul, O. → Algeria 29°15N 7°0W 260 C3
Zempelburg = Sępólno Krajeńskie Poland 53°26N 17°30E 184 E4
Zempléni-hegység Hungary 48°25N 21°25E 182 B6
Zemplínska šírava Slovak Rep. 48°48N 22°0E 181 C15
Zempoala Mexico 19°27N 96°23W 319 D5
Zemun Serbia 44°51N 20°25E 202 B4
Zendeh Jān Afghan. 34°21N 61°45E 240 B1
Zengbé Cameroon 5°46N 13°4E 263 D7
Zengcheng China 23°13N 113°52E 229 F9
Zenica Bos.-H. 44°10N 17°57E 182 F2
Zenne → Belgium 51°4N 4°26E 116 A2
Zentsūji Japan 34°14N 133°47E 222 C5
Zenza → Angola 8°45S 13°24E 265 D2
Zenza do Itombe Angola 9°16S 14°13E 265 D2
Žepče Bos.-H. 44°28N 18°2E 182 F3
Zephyr Field U.S.A. 29°58N 90°12W 131 B1
Zephyrhills U.S.A. 28°14N 82°11W 317 G7
Zepu China 38°11N 77°16E 217 E9
Zeraf, Bahr ez → South Sudan 9°42N 30°52E 257 F3
Żerań Poland 52°18N 20°58E 143 B1
Zerbst Germany 51°58N 12°5E 178 D8
Zerhamra Algeria 29°58N 2°30W 261 C4
Żerków Poland 52°4N 17°32E 185 F4
Zermatt Switz. 46°2N 7°46E 179 J3
Zernez Switz. 46°42N 10°7E 179 J6
Zernograd Russia 46°52N 40°19E 191 G5
Zernovoy = Zernograd Russia 46°52N 40°19E 191 G5
Zero Milestone Washington, D.C., U.S.A. 143 b1
Zergan Albania 41°27N 20°20E 202 E4
Zerzeń Poland 52°12N 21°7E 143 B2
Zestaponi Georgia 42°6N 43°0E 191 J6
Zetel Germany 53°25N 7°58E 178 B3
Zetland = Shetland □ U.K. 60°30N 1°30W 167 A7
Zeulenroda Germany 50°39N 11°59E 178 E7
Zévallos Guadeloupe 16°18N 61°17W 322 e
Zeven Germany 53°17N 9°16E 178 B5
Zevenaar Neths. 51°56N 6°5E 170 C6
Zévio Italy 45°22N 11°8E 198 C8
Zeya Russia 53°48N 127°14E 215 D13
Zeya → Russia 51°42N 128°53E 215 D13
Zeyne Turkey 36°25N 33°31E 250 B4
Zeyskoye Vdkhr. Russia 54°30N 127°30E 215 D13
Zeytinbağı Turkey 40°24N 28°47E 203 F12
Zeytinburnu Turkey 40°58N 28°53E 122 C1
Zeytindağ Turkey 38°58N 27°4E 205 C9
Zghartā Lebanon 34°21N 35°53E 250 D6
Zgierz Poland 51°50N 19°27E 185 G6
Zgorzelec Poland 51°10N 15°0E 185 G2
Zguriṭa Moldova 48°8N 28°1E 183 B13
Zhabei China 31°16N 121°26E 138 B1
Zhabinka Belarus 52°13N 24°2E 185 F11
Zhabokrych Ukraine 48°23N 28°59E 183 B13
Zhalaghash Kazakhstan 45°5N 64°40E 216 C6
Zhalpaqtal Kazakhstan 49°42N 49°25E 190 F9
Zhaltyr Kazakhstan 51°37N 69°49E 217 B7
Zhambyl = Taraz Kazakhstan 42°54N 71°22E 217 D8
Zhambyl □ Kazakhstan 44°0N 72°0E 217 D8
Zhanatas Kazakhstan 43°35N 69°35E 217 D7
Zhangaly Kazakhstan 47°1N 50°37E 191 G10
Zhangaözen Kazakhstan 43°18N 52°48E 187 F9
Zhangaqala Kazakhstan 48°56N 49°36E 191 F9
Zhangaqazaly Kazakhstan 45°48N 62°6E 216 C6
Zhangatas = Zhanatas Kazakhstan 43°35N 69°35E 217 D7
Zhangbei China 41°10N 114°45E 226 D8
Zhangguangcai Ling China 45°0N 129°0E 227 B15
Zhangjiabian China 22°33N 113°28E 219 a
Zhangjiagang China 31°55N 120°30E 229 B13
Zhangjiakou China 40°48N 114°55E 226 D8
Zhangping China 25°17N 117°23E 229 E11
Zhangpu China 24°8N 117°35E 229 E11
Zhangshu China 28°4N 115°29E 229 C10
Zhangye China 38°50N 100°23E 218 D9
Zhangzhou China 24°30N 117°35E 229 E11
Zhanhua China 37°40N 118°8E 227 F10
Zhänibek Kazakhstan 49°25N 46°50E 190 F8
Zhanjiang China 21°15N 110°20E 229 G8
Zhannetty, Ostrov Russia 76°43N 158°0E 215 B16
Zhanyi China 25°38N 103°48E 228 E4
Zhanyu China 44°30N 122°30E 227 B12
Zhao Xian China 37°43N 114°45E 226 F8
Zhao'an China 23°41N 117°10E 229 F11
Zhaocheng China 36°22N 111°38E 226 F6
Zhaodong China 46°4N 125°59E 219 B13
Zhaojue China 28°1N 102°49E 228 C4
Zhaoping China 24°11N 110°48E 229 E8
Zhaoqing China 23°0N 112°20E 229 F9
Zhaotong China 27°20N 103°44E 228 D4
Zhaoyang Hu China 35°4N 116°47E 226 G9
Zhaoyuan Heilongjiang, China 45°27N 125°0E 227 B13
Zhaoyuan Shandong, China 37°20N 120°23E 227 F11
Zhar, Mali Kosovo 42°20N 21°0E 202 D5
Zhari Namco China 31°6N 85°36E 218 E6
Zharkent Kazakhstan 44°10N 80°0E 217 D10
Zharkovskiy Russia 55°56N 32°19E 188 E7
Zhashkiv Ukraine 49°15N 30°5E 177 D16
Zhashui China 33°40N 109°8E 226 H5
Zhaslyk Uzbekistan 43°58N 57°10E 216 D5
Zhayrang Kazakhstan 48°20N 70°10E 217 C8
Zhayylma Kazakhstan 51°37N 61°33E 216 B6
Zhayyq → Kazakhstan 47°0N 51°48E 187 E9
Zhdanov = Mariupol Ukraine 47°5N 37°31E 189 J9
Zhdanov Russia 55°44N 37°41E 129 B3
Zhecheng China 34°7N 115°20E 226 G8
Zhegao China 31°46N 117°45E 229 B11
Zhejiang □ China 29°0N 120°0E 229 C13
Zheleznodorozhnyy = Qŭnghirot Uzbekistan 43°2N 58°50E 216 D5
Zheleznodorozhnyy Kaliningrad, Russia 54°22N 21°19E 184 D8
Zheleznodorozhnyy Komi, Russia 62°35N 50°55E 186 B9
Zheleznogorsk Russia 52°22N 35°23E 189 F8
Zheleznogorsk-Ilimskiy Russia 56°34N 104°8E 215 D11
Zheltyye Vody = Zhovti Vody Ukraine 48°21N 33°31E 189 H7
Zhen'an China 33°27N 109°9E 228 A7
Zhenba China 32°34N 107°58E 228 A6
Zhenfeng China 25°22N 105°40E 228 E5
Zheng'an China 28°32N 107°27E 228 C6
Zhengding China 38°8N 114°32E 226 E8
Zhenghe China 27°20N 118°50E 229 D12
Zhengyang China 32°37N 114°22E 229 A10
Zhengyangguan China 32°30N 116°29E 229 A11
Zhengzhou China 34°45N 113°34E 226 G7
Zhenhai China 29°59N 121°42E 229 C13
Zhenjiang China 32°11N 119°26E 229 A12
Zhenkang China 23°58N 99°0E 228 F2
Zhenlai China 45°50N 123°5E 227 B12
Zhenning China 26°4N 105°45E 228 D5
Zhenping Henan, China 33°10N 112°16E 226 H7
Zhenping Shaanxi, China 31°59N 109°31E 228 B7
Zhenru China 31°16N 121°22E 138 B1
Zhenxiong China 27°27N 104°50E 228 D5
Zhenyuan Gansu, China 35°35N 107°30E 226 G4
Zhenyuan Guizhou, China 27°4N 108°21E 228 D7
Zhenyuan Yunnan, China 23°51N 100°59E 228 F3
Zherdevka Russia 51°56N 41°29E 190 E5
Zherebkove Ukraine 47°50N 29°52E 183 C14
Zhernovka Russia 59°56N 30°30E 137 B2
Zherong China 27°15N 119°52E 229 D12
Zhetiqara Kazakhstan 52°11N 61°12E 216 B6
Zhezdi Kazakhstan 48°3N 67°3E 217 C7
Zhezqazghan Kazakhstan 47°44N 67°40E 217 C7
Zhicheng China 30°25N 111°27E 229 B8
Zhicun China 23°0N 113°12E 121 B2
Zhidan China 36°48N 108°48E 226 F5
Zhigansk Russia 66°48N 123°27E 215 C13
Zhigulevsk Russia 53°28N 49°30E 190 D9
Zhijiang Hubei, China 30°28N 111°45E 229 B8
Zhijiang Hunan, China 27°27N 109°42E 228 D7
Zhijin China 26°37N 105°45E 228 D5
Zhilinda Russia 70°0N 114°20E 215 C12
Zhilino Russia 54°54N 21°54E 184 D8
Zhirnovsk Russia 50°57N 44°49E 190 E7
Zhirnovsky = Zhirnovsk Russia 50°57N 44°49E 190 E7
Zhirnoye = Zhirnovsk Russia 50°57N 44°49E 190 E7
Zhitomir = Zhytomyr Ukraine 50°20N 28°40E 177 C15
Zhizdra Russia 53°45N 34°40E 188 F8
Zhlobin Belarus 52°55N 30°0E 177 B16
Zhmerynka Ukraine 49°2N 28°2E 177 D15
Zhob Pakistan 31°20N 69°31E 242 D3
Zhob → Pakistan 32°4N 69°50E 242 C3
Zhodzina Belarus 54°5N 28°17E 177 A15
Zhokhova, Ostrov Russia 76°4N 152°40E 215 B16
Zholkev = Zhovkva Ukraine 50°4N 23°58E 177 C12
Zholkva = Zhovkva Ukraine 50°4N 23°58E 177 C12
Zhongba China 29°39N 84°10E 218 F5
Zhongdian China 27°48N 99°42E 228 D2
Zhongdong China 22°48N 107°47E 228 F6
Zhongdu China 24°40N 109°40E 228 E7
Zhongguancun China 39°59N 116°18E 114 B1
Zhongjiang China 30°53N 104°46E 228 B5
Zhongning China 37°29N 105°40E 226 F3
Zhongshan Antarctica 69°0S 39°50E 151 C6
Zhongshan Guangdong, China 22°26N 113°20E 229 F9
Zhongshan Guangxi Zhuangzu, China 24°29N 111°18E 229 E8
Zhongshan Park Beijing, China 114 c3
Zhongshan Park Shanghai, China 31°13N 121°24E 138 B1
Zhongshankong China 22°35N 113°29E 219 a
Zhongtiao Shan China 35°0N 111°10E 226 G6
Zhongwei China 37°30N 105°12E 226 F3
Zhongxian China 30°10N 107°58E 228 B6
Zhongxiang China 31°12N 112°34E 229 B9
Zhongyang China 37°20N 111°11E 226 F6
Zhorany Ukraine 51°19N 23°58E 185 G10
Zhosaly Kazakhstan 45°29N 64°4E 216 C6
Zhoucun Guangdong, China 23°11N 113°11E 121 A2
Zhoucun Shandong, China 36°47N 117°48E 227 F9
Zhoujiadu China 31°11N 121°29E 138 B1
Zhoujiazhen China 31°16N 121°33E 138 B2
Zhoukou China 33°38N 114°38E 226 H8
Zhoukoudian China 39°41N 115°56E 226 E8
Zhouning China 27°12N 119°20E 229 D12
Zhoushan China 30°1N 122°6E 229 B14
Zhoushan Dao China 30°5N 122°10E 229 C14
Zhouzhi China 34°10N 108°12E 226 G5
Zhouzhuangzi China 39°51N 116°16E 114 B1
Zhovkva Ukraine 50°4N 23°58E 177 C12
Zhovti Vody Ukraine 48°21N 33°31E 189 H7
Zhovtneve Lubelskie, Ukraine 50°42N 24°12E 185 H11
Zhovtneve Mykolayiv, Ukraine 46°54N 32°3E 189 J7
Zhu Jiang → China 22°45N 113°37E 229 F9
Zhuanghe China 39°40N 123°0E 224 C1
Zhucheng China 36°0N 119°27E 227 G10
Zhugqu China 33°40N 104°30E 226 H3
Zhuhai China 22°17N 113°34E 229 F9
Zhuji China 29°40N 120°10E 229 C13
Zhujiang Kou China 22°20N 113°45E 219 a
Zhukovka Russia 53°35N 33°50E 188 F7
Zhulebino Russia 55°42N 37°50E 129 B4
Zhumadian China 32°59N 114°2E 229 A10
Zhuo Xian = Zhuozhou China 39°28N 115°58E 226 E8
Zhuolu China 40°20N 115°12E 226 D8
Zhuozhou China 39°28N 115°58E 226 E8
Zhuozi China 41°0N 112°25E 226 D7
Zhur Kosovo 42°13N 20°34E 202 D4
Zhushadi China 23°11N 113°22E 121 A3
Zhushan China 32°15N 110°13E 229 A8
Zhuxi China 32°25N 109°40E 228 A7
Zhuzhou China 27°49N 113°12E 229 D9
Zhvanets Ukraine 48°33N 26°30E 183 B11
Zhympīty Kazakhstan 50°16N 52°35E 216 B4
Zhytomyr Ukraine 50°20N 28°40E 177 C15
Zhytomyr □ Ukraine 50°50N 28°10E 177 C14
Zi Shui → China 28°40N 112°40E 229 C9
Žiar nad Hronom Slovak Rep. 48°35N 18°53E 181 C11
Ziarat Pakistan 30°25N 67°49E 242 D2
Zibo China 36°47N 118°3E 227 F10
Zichang China 37°18N 109°40E 226 F5
Zidarovo Bulgaria 42°20N 27°24E 203 D11
Zidi = Wandhari Pakistan 27°42N 66°48E 242 F2
Ziębice Poland 50°37N 17°2E 185 H4
Ziebingen = Cybinka Poland 52°12N 14°46E 185 F1
Ziegenhals = Głuchołazy Poland 50°19N 17°24E 185 H4
Zielenzig = Sulęcin Poland 52°26N 15°10E 185 F2
Zielona Poland 52°14N 21°11E 143 B3
Zielona Góra Poland 51°57N 15°31E 185 G2
Zielonka Poland 52°18N 21°9E 143 B2
Zierikzee Neths. 51°40N 3°55E 170 C3
Ziesar Germany 52°16N 12°17E 178 C8
Zifta Egypt 30°43N 31°14E 256 H7
Zighan Libya 25°29N 22°8E 258 C4
Zigon Burma 18°20N 95°37E 241 F5
Zigong China 29°15N 104°48E 228 C5
Ziguéy Chad 14°43N 15°50E 259 F3
Ziguinchor Senegal 12°35N 16°20W 262 C1
Ziguinchor □ Senegal 12°45N 16°20W 262 C1
Zihuatanejo Mexico 17°39N 101°33W 318 D4
Zijin China 23°33N 115°8E 229 F10
Zile Turkey 40°15N 35°52E 212 B6
Žilina Slovak Rep. 49°12N 18°42E 181 B11
Žilinský □ Slovak Rep. 49°10N 19°0E 181 B12
Zillah Libya 28°30N 17°33E 258 C3
Zillertaler Alpen Austria 47°6N 11°45E 180 D4
Zima Russia 54°0N 102°5E 215 D11
Zimapán Mexico 20°45N 99°21W 319 C5
Zimba Zambia 17°20S 26°11E 269 F2
Zimbabwe Zimbabwe 20°16S 30°54E 269 G3
Zimbabwe ■ Africa 19°0S 30°0E 269 F3
Zimmi S. Leone 7°20N 11°20W 262 D2
Zimnicea Romania 43°40N 25°22E 183 G10
Zimovniki Russia 47°10N 42°25E 191 G6
Zina Cameroon 11°19N 14°59E 259 F2
Zinave △ Mozam. 21°35S 33°40E 271 B5
Zinder Niger 13°48N 9°0E 259 F1
Zinder □ Niger 15°0N 10°30E 263 C7
Zinga C.A.R. 3°49N 18°34E 264 B3
Zinga Tanzania 9°16S 38°49E 269 D4
Zingaro △ Italy 38°6N 12°53E 200 D5
Zingst Germany 54°26N 12°39E 178 A8
Ziniaré Burkina Faso 12°35N 1°18W 263 C4
Zinjibār Yemen 13°5N 45°23E 248 D4
Zinnowitz Germany 54°4N 13°54E 178 A9
Zinovyevsk = Kirovohrad Ukraine 48°35N 32°20E 189 H7
Zion St. Kitts & Nevis 17°8N 62°33W 322 d
Zion Ill., U.S.A. 42°27N 87°50W 311 B9
Zion △ U.S.A. 37°15N 113°5W 305 H7
Zionsville U.S.A. 39°57N 86°16W 311 E10
Zipaquirá Colombia 5°0N 74°0W 328 C3
Zirbitzkogel Austria 47°4N 14°34E 180 D7
Zirc Hungary 47°17N 17°52E 182 C2
Žiri Slovenia 46°5N 14°5E 199 B11
Žirje Croatia 43°39N 15°42E 199 E12
Zirke = Sieraków Poland 52°39N 16°2E 185 F3
Zirl Austria 47°17N 11°14E 180 D4
Zirndorf Germany 49°27N 10°57E 179 F6
Ziro India 27°37N 93°44E 241 B5
Ziros Greece 35°5N 26°8E 207 E7
Zirreh, Gowd-e Afghan. 29°45N 62°0E 240 C1
Zisterdorf Austria 48°33N 16°45E 181 C9
Zitácuaro Mexico 19°24N 100°22W 318 D4
Žitava → Slovak Rep. 48°14N 18°21E 181 C11
Zitelle, Chiesa delle Venice, Italy 142 c3
Žitište Serbia 45°30N 20°32E 182 E5
Zitong China 31°37N 105°10E 228 B5
Zitsa Greece 39°47N 20°40E 204 B2
Zittau Germany 50°53N 14°48E 178 E10
Zitundo Mozam. 26°48S 32°47E 271 C5
Živinice Bos.-H. 44°27N 18°36E 182 F3
Ziwa Maghariba = Kagera □ Tanzania 2°0S 31°30E 268 C3
Ziway Ethiopia 7°56N 38°43E 266 C4
Ziway, L. Ethiopia 8°0N 38°50E 257 F4
Zixi China 27°45N 117°4E 229 D11
Zixing China 25°59N 113°21E 229 E9
Ziyamet = Leonárisso Cyprus 35°28N 34°8E 207 E10
Ziyang Shaanxi, China 32°32N 108°31E 226 H5
Ziyang Sichuan, China 30°6N 104°40E 228 B5
Ziyuan China 26°2N 110°40E 229 D8
Ziyun China 25°45N 106°5E 228 E6
Ziz, Oued → Morocco 31°40N 4°15W 260 B4
Zizhong China 29°48N 104°47E 228 C5
Zizhuyuan Park China 39°54N 116°18E 114 B1
Žižkov Czech Rep. 50°5N 14°28E 135 B2
Zizur Mayor Spain 42°47N 1°41W 196 C3
Zlarin Croatia 43°42N 15°49E 199 E12
Zlatar Croatia 46°5N 16°3E 199 B13
Zlatar Serbia 43°25N 19°47E 202 C3
Zlataritsa Bulgaria 43°2N 25°55E 203 C9
Zlaté Moravce Slovak Rep. 48°23N 18°24E 181 C11
Zlatibor Serbia 43°45N 19°43E 202 C3
Zlatitsa Bulgaria 42°41N 24°7E 203 D8
Zlatna Romania 46°8N 23°11E 183 D8
Zlatna Panega Bulgaria 43°5N 24°9E 203 C8
Zlatni Pyasŭtsi Bulgaria 43°17N 28°3E 203 C12
Zlatograd Bulgaria 41°22N 25°7E 203 E9
Zlatoust Russia 55°10N 59°40E 186 C10
Zletovo Macedonia 41°59N 22°17E 202 E6
Zličín Czech Rep. 50°3N 14°17E 135 B1
Zlin Czech Rep. 49°14N 17°40E 181 B10
Zlínský □ Czech Rep. 49°20N 17°40E 181 B10
Zlītan Libya 32°32N 14°35E 258 B2
Złocieniec Poland 53°30N 16°1E 184 E3
Złoczew Poland 51°24N 18°35E 185 G5
Zlot Serbia 44°1N 21°58E 202 B5
Złotoryja Poland 51°8N 15°55E 185 G2
Złotów Poland 53°22N 17°2E 184 E4
Zmeinogorsk Kazakhstan 51°10N 82°13E 217 B10
Żmigród Poland 51°28N 16°53E 185 G3
Zmiyev Ukraine 49°39N 36°27E 189 H9
Znamenka = Znamyanka Ukraine 48°45N 32°30E 189 H7
Znamensk Russia 54°36N 21°13E 184 D8
Znamyanka Ukraine 48°45N 32°30E 189 H7
Żnin Poland 52°51N 17°44E 185 F4
Znojmo Czech Rep. 48°50N 16°2E 180 C9
Zobeyrī Iran 34°10N 46°40E 246 C5
Zobia Dem. Rep. of the Congo 3°0N 25°59E 268 B2
Zobten = Sobótka Poland 50°54N 16°44E 185 H3
Zócalo Mexico City, Mexico 128 b3
Zoetermeer Neths. 52°3N 4°30E 170 B4
Zogang China 29°55N 97°42E 228 C1
Zogno Italy 45°48N 9°40E 198 C6
Zografou Greece 37°58N 23°47E 112 B2
Zohreh → Iran 30°16N 51°15E 247 D6
Zolfo Springs U.S.A. 27°30N 81°48W 317 H8
Żoliborz Poland 52°16N 20°57E 143 B1
Zolochiv Ukraine 49°45N 24°51E 177 D13
Zolotonosha Ukraine 49°39N 32°5E 189 H7
Zolotyy Potik Ukraine 48°54N 25°20E 183 B10
Zomba Malawi 15°22S 35°19E 269 F4
Zongo Dem. Rep. of the Congo 4°20N 18°35E 264 B3
Zonguldak Turkey 41°28N 31°50E 212 B4
Zonguldak □ Turkey 41°20N 31°45E 212 B4
Zongyang China 30°42N 117°12E 229 B11
Zonnebloem S. Africa 33°56S 18°26E 118 A1
Zonqor Pt. Malta 35°52N 14°34E 206 F8
Zonza France 41°45N 9°11E 175 G13
Zoo Baba Niger 18°13N 13°2E 259 E2
Zorgo Burkina Faso 12°15N 0°35W 263 C4
Zorita Spain 39°17N 5°39W 195 F5
Zorleni Romania 46°14N 27°44E 183 D12
Zornitsa Bulgaria 42°23N 26°58E 203 D10
Zorritos Peru 3°43S 80°40W 330 A1
Żory Poland 50°3N 18°44E 185 H5
Zorzor Liberia 7°46N 9°28W 262 D3
Zossen Germany 52°13N 13°27E 178 C9
Zou Xiang China 35°30N 116°58E 226 G9
Zouan-Hounien Ivory C. 6°55N 8°15W 262 D3
Zouar Chad 20°30N 16°32E 259 D3
Zouérate = Zouîrât Mauritania 22°44N 12°21W 260 D2
Zouîrât Mauritania 22°44N 12°21W 260 D2
Zouri Gabon 1°1S 8°53E 264 C1
Zourika Niger 19°16N 7°52E 259 E1
Zourma Burkina Faso 11°20N 0°50W 263 C4
Zousfana, O. → Algeria 31°28N 2°17W 261 B4
Zoutkamp Neths. 53°20N 6°18E 170 A6
Zrenjanin Serbia 45°22N 20°23E 182 E5
Zuarungu Ghana 10°49N 0°46W 263 C4
Zuatá → Venezuela 7°52N 65°22W 329 B4
Zuba Nigeria 9°11N 7°12E 263 D6
Zubayr Yemen 15°3N 42°10E 248 D3
Zubin Potok Kosovo 42°54N 20°41E 202 D4
Zubtsov Russia 56°10N 34°34E 188 D8
Zudañez Bolivia 19°6S 64°44W 331 D5
Zuénoula Ivory C. 7°34N 6°3W 262 D3
Zuera Spain 41°52N 0°49W 196 D4
Zuetina = Az Zuwaytīnah Libya 30°58N 20°7E 258 B4
Ẓufār Oman 17°40N 54°0E 249 C6
Ẓufār □ Oman 18°0N 54°0E 249 C6
Zug Switz. 47°10N 8°31E 179 H4
Zug W. Sahara 21°36N 14°9W 260 D2
Zugdidi Georgia 42°30N 41°55E 191 J5
Zugersee Switz. 47°7N 8°35E 179 H4
Zugliget Hungary 47°30N 18°59E 117 B1
Zugló Hungary 47°31N 19°8E 117 A2
Zugspitze Germany 47°25N 10°59E 179 H6
Zuhd, J. az Si. Arabia 28°20N 35°17E 251 K6
Zuid-Holland □ Neths. 52°0N 4°35E 170 C4
Zuidbeveland Neths. 51°30N 3°50E 170 C3
Zuiderwoude Neths. 52°26N 5°2E 112 A3
Zuidhorn Neths. 53°15N 6°23E 170 A6
Zújar Spain 37°34N 2°50W 195 H8
Zújar → Spain 39°1N 5°47W 195 G5
Żukowo Poland 54°21N 18°22E 184 D5
Zula Eritrea 15°17N 39°40E 257 D4
Zulia □ Venezuela 10°0N 72°10W 328 B3
Züllichau = Sulechów Poland 52°5N 15°40E 185 F2
Zülpich Germany 50°41N 6°39E 178 E2
Zülz = Biała Poland 50°24N 17°40E 185 H4
Zumaia Spain 43°19N 2°15W 196 B2
Zumárraga Spain 43°5N 2°19W 196 B2
Zumbi Brazil 22°49S 43°10W 135 A1
Zumbo Mozam. 15°35S 30°26E 269 F3
Zummo Nigeria 9°51N 12°59E 263 D7
Zumpango Mexico 19°48N 99°6W 319 D5
Zunderdorp Neths. 52°24N 4°58E 112 A2
Zundi Angola 10°28S 16°48E 265 E3
Zungeru Nigeria 9°48N 6°8E 263 D6
Zunheboto India 25°58N 94°31E 241 C5
Zunhua China 40°18N 117°58E 227 D9
Zuni Pueblo U.S.A. 35°4N 108°51W 305 J9
Zunyi China 27°42N 106°53E 228 D6
Zuo Jiang → China 22°50N 108°6E 228 F6
Zuoquan China 37°1N 113°27E 226 F7
Zuozhou China 22°42N 107°27E 228 F6
Županja Croatia 45°4N 18°43E 182 E3
Zurbāṭīyah Iraq 33°9N 46°3E 213 F12
Zürich Switz. 47°22N 8°32E 179 H4
Zürich □ Switz. 47°26N 8°40E 179 H4
Zürichsee Switz. 47°18N 8°40E 179 H4
Żuromin Poland 53°4N 19°51E 185 E6
Zurrieq Malta 35°50N 14°28E 206 F7
Žut Croatia 43°52N 15°17E 199 E12
Zutphen Neths. 52°9N 6°12E 170 B6
Zuurberg △ S. Africa 33°12S 25°32E 270 D4
Zuvuvu → Brazil 23°40S 46°42W 137 C1
Zuwārah Libya 32°58N 12°1E 258 B2
Zūzan Iran 34°22N 59°53E 247 C8
Žužemberk Slovenia 45°52N 14°56E 199 C11
Zvanka = Volkhov Russia 59°55N 32°15E 188 C7
Zvečan Kosovo 42°54N 20°50E 202 D4
Zvenigorodka = Svenyhorodka Ukraine 49°4N 30°56E 189 H6
Zvezdets Bulgaria 42°6N 27°26E 203 D11
Zvishavane Zimbabwe 20°17S 30°2E 269 G3
Zvolen Slovak Rep. 48°33N 19°10E 181 C12
Zvonce Serbia 42°57N 22°34E 202 D6
Zvornik Bos.-H. 44°26N 19°5E 182 F4
Zwanenburg Neths. 52°23N 4°45E 112 A1
Zwedru = Tchien Liberia 5°59N 8°15W 262 D3
Zweibrücken Germany 49°15N 7°21E 179 F3
Zwenkau Germany 51°13N 12°20E 178 D8
Zwettl Austria 48°35N 15°9E 180 C8
Zwickau Germany 50°44N 12°30E 178 E8
Zwierzyniec Poland 50°36N 22°58E 185 H9
Zwiesel Germany 49°1N 13°13E 179 F9
Zwittau = Svitavy Czech Rep. 49°47N 16°28E 181 B9
Zwoleń Poland 51°21N 21°36E 185 G8
Zwölfaxing Austria 48°6N 16°28E 142 B2
Zwolle Neths. 52°31N 6°6E 170 B6
Zwolle La., U.S.A. 31°38N 93°39W 314 F8
Żychlin Poland 52°15N 19°37E 185 F6
Żyrardów Poland 52°3N 20°28E 185 F7
Zyryan Kazakhstan 49°43N 84°20E 217 C10
Zyryanka Russia 65°45N 150°51E 215 C16
Zyryanovsk = Zyryan Kazakhstan 49°43N 84°20E 217 C10
Żywiec Poland 49°42N 19°10E 185 J6

KEY TO EUROPEAN MAP PAGES

155 ICELAND

WORLD COUNTRY INDEX

Afghanistan	240	**G**ermany	178–179	**O**man	249
Albania	202	Ghana	262–263		
Algeria	260–261	Greece	202–205	**P**akistan	240
Angola	265	Greenland	154	Panama	320
Argentina	334, 336	Guadeloupe	322	Papua New Guinea	286
Armenia	213	Guatemala	320	Paraguay	334–335
Australia	278–283	Guinea	262	Peru	328, 330
Austria	180–181	Guinea-Bissau	262	Philippines	232–233
Azerbaijan	213	Guyana	329	Poland	184–185
Azores	153			Portugal	194–195
		Haiti	321	Puerto Rico	321
Bahamas	320–321	Honduras	320		
Bahrain	249	Hungary	182	**Q**atar	249
Bangladesh	241				
Barbados	322	**I**celand	155	**R**éunion	272
Belarus	188–189	India	241, 242–245	Romania	182–183
Belgium	170	Indonesia	230–231, 234–235	Russia	186–191, 214–215
Belize	320	Iran	246–247	Rwanda	268
Benin	263	Iraq	246–247		
Bhutan	241	Irish Republic	166	**S**amoa	287
Bolivia	330–331	Israel	250–251	Saudi Arabia	246–249
Bosnia-Herzegovina	198, 202	Italy	198–201	Scotland	167
Botswana	270	Ivory Coast	262	Senegal	262
Brazil	328–335			Serbia	182, 202
Brunei	235	**J**amaica	320	Seychelles	272
Bulgaria	202–203	Japan	220–223	Sierra Leone	262
Burkina Faso	262–263	Jordan	251	Singapore	237
Burma (Myanmar)	236–237, 241			Slovak Republic	181
Burundi	268	**K**azakhstan	216–217	Slovenia	199
		Kenya	268	Solomon Is.	287
Cambodia	236–237	Korea, North	224	Somali Republic	267
Canary Is.	153	Korea, South	224	South Africa	270–271
Cameroon	259, 264	Kosovo	202	Spain	194–197
Canada	294–299	Kuwait	246–247	Sri Lanka	245
Cape Verde Is.	153	Kyrgyzstan	217	Sudan	256–257
Central African Republic	264			Sudan, South	257
Chad	259	**L**aos	236	Suriname	329
Chile	330, 334, 336	Latvia	188	Swaziland	271
China	218–219, 226–229	Lebanon	250	Sweden	160–163
Colombia	328	Lesotho	271	Switzerland	179
Comoros	272	Liberia	262	Syria	212–213
Congo	264–265	Libya	258		
Congo, Dem. Rep.		Lithuania	188	**T**aiwan	225
of the	264–265, 268–269	Luxembourg	170	Tajikistan	217
Costa Rica	320			Tanzania	268–269
Croatia	182, 199	**M**acedonia	202	Thailand	236–237
Cuba	320–321	Madagascar	272	Togo	263
Cyprus	207	Malawi	269	Tonga	287
Czech Republic	180–181	Malaysia	234–235	Trinidad and Tobago	323
		Mali	260–263	Tunisia	261
Denmark	163	Malta	206	Turkey	212–213
Djibouti	267	Martinique	322	Turkmenistan	216–217
Dominican Republic	321	Mauritania	260, 262		
		Mauritius	272	**U**ganda	268
Ecuador	328	Mexico	318–319	Ukraine	189
Egypt	256	Moldova	183	United Arab Emirates	249
El Salvador	320	Mongolia	218–219	United Kingdom	166–169
England	168–169	Montenegro	202	USA	300–317
Equatorial Guinea	264	Morocco	260–261	Uruguay	334–335
Eritrea	266–267	Mozambique	269, 271	Uzbekistan	216–217
Estonia	188				
Ethiopia	266–267	**N**amibia	270	**V**anuatu	287
		Nepal	243	Venezuela	328–329
Fiji	287	Netherlands	170	Vietnam	236–237
Finland	160–161	New Zealand	284–285		
France	172–175	Nicaragua	320	**W**ales	168–169
French Guiana	329	Niger	259, 263		
		Nigeria	263	**Y**emen	248–249
Gabon	264	Northern Ireland	166		
Gambia	262	Norway	160–161, 164	**Z**ambia	265, 269
Georgia	213			Zimbabwe	269

Arctic Circle

160 Faeroe Is.

165

167 Shetland Is.

167 Orkney Is.

168 Edinburgh p121

166

176

170

UNITED KINGDOM

Dublin p120

IRELAND

London p125

192

171

172

174 FRAN

194

196

ANDORRA

Barcelona p114

PORTUGAL

SPAIN

Madrid p127

206

Lisbon p126

Bai

MOROCCO

A